2024
Harris Directory of
Delaware
Businesses

Published April 2024 next update April 2025

WARNING: Purchasers and users of this directory may not use this directory to compile mailing lists, other marketing aids and other types of data, which are sold or otherwise provided to third parties. Such use is wrongful, illegal and a violation of the federal copyright laws.

CAUTION: Because of the many thousands of establishment listings contained in this directory and the possibilities of both human and mechanical error in processing this information, Mergent Inc. cannot assume liability for the correctness of the listings or information on which they are based. Hence, no information contained in this work should be relied upon in any instance where there is a possibility of any loss or damage as a consequence of any error or omission in this volume.

Publisher

Mergent Inc.
444 Madison Ave
New York, NY 10022

©Mergent Inc All Rights Reserved
2024 Mergent Business Press
ISSN 1080-2614
ISBN 979-8-89251-070-7

TABLE OF CONTENTS

Summary of Contents & Explanatory Notes 4
User's Guide to Listings 6

Geographic Section
County/City Cross-Reference Index 9
Establishments Listed by City 11

Standard Industrial Classification (SIC) Section
SIC Alphabetical Index 733
SIC Numerical Index 737
Establishments Listed by SIC 743

Alphabetic Section
Establishments Listed by Establishment Name 983

Products & Services Section
Products & Services Index 1305
Establishments Listed by Product or Service Category 1315

SUMMARY OF CONTENTS

Number of Companies 20,995
Number of Decision Makers 21,090
Minimum Number of Employees (Services) 5
Minimum Number of Employees (Manufacturers) 2

EXPLANATORY NOTES

How to Cross-Reference in This Directory

Sequential Entry Numbers. Each establishment in the Geographic Section is numbered sequentially (G-0000). The number assigned to each establishment is referred to as its "entry number." To make cross-referencing easier, each listing in the Geographic, SIC, Alphabetic and Product Sections includes the establishment's entry number. To facilitate locating an entry in the Geographic Section, the entry numbers for the first listing on the left page and the last listing on the right page are printed at the top of the page next to the city name.

Source Suggestions Welcome

Although all known sources were used to compile this directory, it is possible that companies were inadvertently omitted. Your assistance in calling attention to such omissions would be greatly appreciated. A special form on the facing page will help you in the reporting process.

Analysis

Every effort has been made to contact all firms to verify their information. The one exception to this rule is the annual sales figure, which is considered by many companies to be confidential information. Therefore, estimated sales have been calculated by multiplying the nationwide average sales per employee for the firm's major SIC/NAICS code by the firm's number of employees. Nationwide averages for sales per employee by SIC/NAICS codes are provided by the U.S. Department of Commerce and are updated annually. All sales—sales (est)—have been estimated by this method. The exceptions are parent companies (PA), division headquarters (DH) and headquarter locations (HQ) which may include an actual corporate sales figure—sales (corporate-wide) if available.

Types of Companies

Descriptive and statistical data are included for companies in the entire state. These comprise manufacturers, machine shops, fabricators, assemblers and printers. Also identified are corporate offices in the state.

Employment Data

The employment figure shown in the Products & Services Section includes male and female employees and embraces all levels of the company. This directory includes manufacturing companies with 2 or more employees and service companies with 5 or more employees. This figure is for the facility listed and does not include other plants or offices. It should be recognized that these figures represent an approximate year-round average. These employment figures are broken into codes A through F and used in the Alphabetic and Geographic Sections to further help you in qualifying a company. Be sure to check the footnotes at the bottom of the page for the code breakdowns.

Standard Industrial Classification (SIC)

The Standard Industrial Classification (SIC) system used in this directory was developed by the federal government for use in classifying establishments by the type of activity they are engaged in. The SIC classifications used in this directory are from the 1987 edition published by the U.S. Government's Office of Management and Budget. The SIC system separates all activities into broad industrial divisions (e.g., manufacturing, mining, retail trade). It further subdivides each division. The range of manufacturing industry classes extends from two-digit codes (major industry group) to four-digit codes (product).

For example:

Industry Breakdown	Code	Industry, Product, etc.
*Major industry group	20	Food and kindred products
Industry group	203	Canned and frozen foods
*Industry	2033	Fruits and vegetables, etc.

*Classifications used in this directory

Only two-digit and four-digit codes are used in this directory.

Arrangement

1. The **Geographic Section** contains complete in-depth corporate data. This section is sorted by cities listed in alphabetical order and companies listed alphabetically within each city. A County/City Index for referencing cities within counties precedes this section.

> IMPORTANT NOTICE: It is a violation of both federal and state law to transmit an unsolicited advertisement to a facsimile machine. Any user of this product that violates such laws may be subject to civil and criminal penalties, which may exceed $500 for each transmission of an unsolicited facsimile. Mergent Inc. provides fax numbers for lawful purposes only and expressly forbids the use of these numbers in any unlawful manner.

2. The **Standard Industrial Classification (SIC) Section** lists companies under approximately 500 four-digit SIC codes. An alphabetical and a numerical index precedes this section. A company can be listed under several codes. The codes are in numerical order with companies listed alphabetically under each code.

3. The **Alphabetic Section** lists all companies with their full physical or mailing addresses and telephone number.

4. The **Product & Services Section** lists companies under unique Harris categories. An index precedes this section. Companies can be listed under several categories.

USER'S GUIDE TO LISTINGS

GEOGRAPHIC SECTION

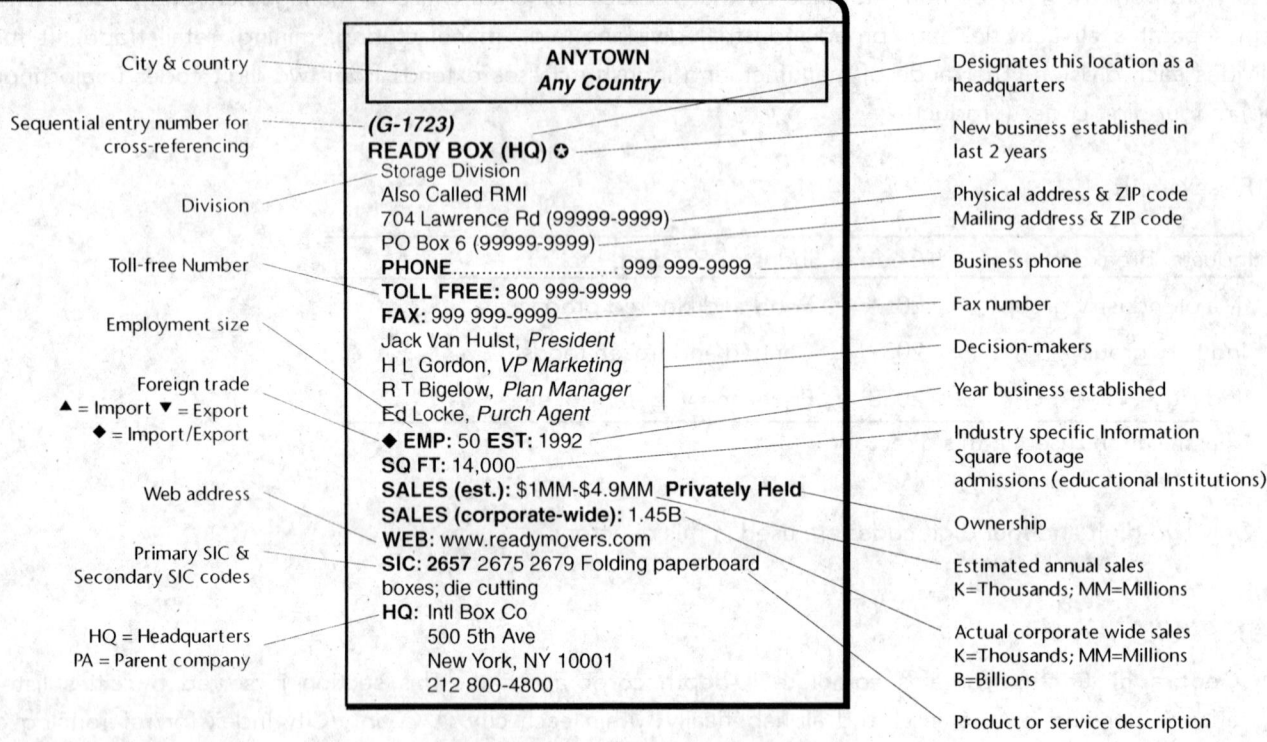

SIC SECTION

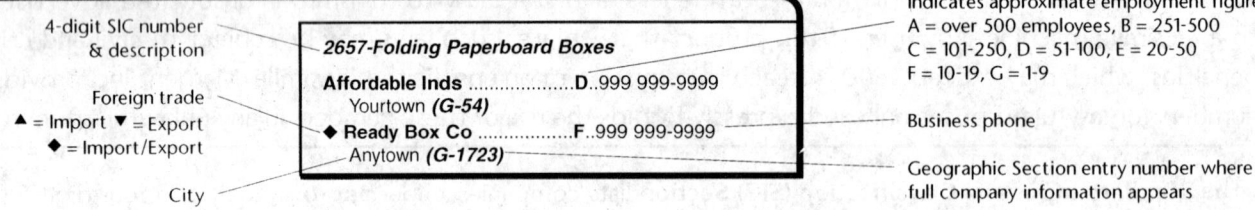

ALPHABETIC SECTION

PRODUCTS & SERVICES SECTION

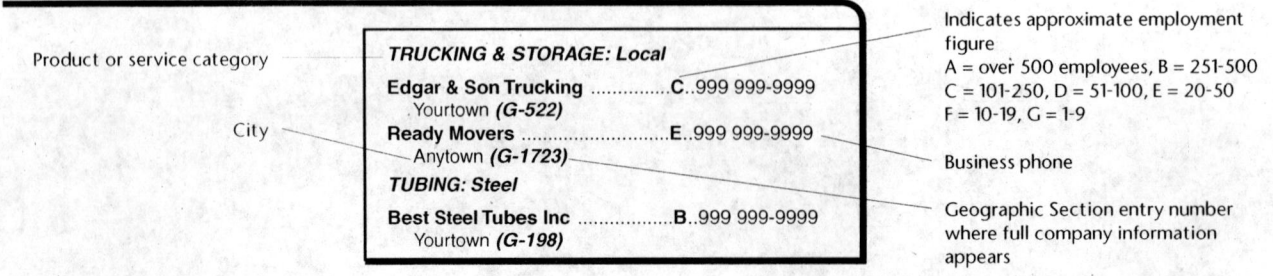

GEOGRAPHIC SECTION
Companies sorted by city in alphabetical order
In-depth company data listed

STANDARD INDUSTRIAL CLASSIFICATIONS
Alphabetical index of classification descriptions
Numerical index of classification descriptions
Companies sorted by SIC product groupings

ALPHABETIC SECTION
Company listings in alphabetical order

PRODUCTS AND SERVICES INDEX
Products and Services categories listed in alphabetical order

PRODUCTS & SERVICES SECTION
Companies sorted by product & service classifications

COUNTY/CITY CROSS-REFERENCE INDEX

Kent

City	Entry #
Camden	(G-786)
Camden Wyoming	(G-902)
Cheswold	(G-988)
Clayton	(G-1347)
Dover	(G-1677)
Felton	(G-3937)
Frederica	(G-4163)
Harrington	(G-4720)
Hartly	(G-4853)
Houston	(G-5434)
Kenton	(G-5452)
Leipsic	(G-5629)
Magnolia	(G-6712)
Marydel	(G-6795)
Smyrna	(G-13623)
Viola	(G-14092)
Woodside	(G-20974)
Wyoming	(G-20979)

New Castle

City	Entry #
Bear	(G-1)
Christiana	(G-990)
Claymont	(G-1012)
Delaware City	(G-1527)
Elsmere	(G-3930)
Greenville	(G-4583)
Historic New Castle	(G-4914)
Hockessin	(G-5107)
Hst Newcastle	(G-5451)
Middletown	(G-6813)
Montchanin	(G-8735)
New Castle	(G-8742)
Newark	(G-9702)
Newport	(G-12439)
Odessa	(G-12581)
Port Penn	(G-12588)
Rockland	(G-13028)
Saint Georges	(G-13032)
Talleyville	(G-13944)
Townsend	(G-13948)
Wilmington	(G-14099)
Winterthur	(G-20972)
Yorklyn	(G-20991)

Sussex

City	Entry #
Bethany Beach	(G-573)
Bethel	(G-653)
Bridgeville	(G-655)
Dagsboro	(G-1409)
Delmar	(G-1560)
Dewey Beach	(G-1661)
Ellendale	(G-3910)
Farmington	(G-3932)
Fenwick Island	(G-4039)
Frankford	(G-4059)
Georgetown	(G-4188)
Greenwood	(G-4585)
Harbeson	(G-4679)
Laurel	(G-5457)
Lewes	(G-5634)
Lincoln	(G-6653)
Milford	(G-7753)
Millsboro	(G-8157)
Millville	(G-8512)
Milton	(G-8552)
Nassau	(G-8740)
Ocean View	(G-12457)
Rehoboth Beach	(G-12589)
Seaford	(G-13041)
Selbyville	(G-13457)

GEOGRAPHIC SECTION

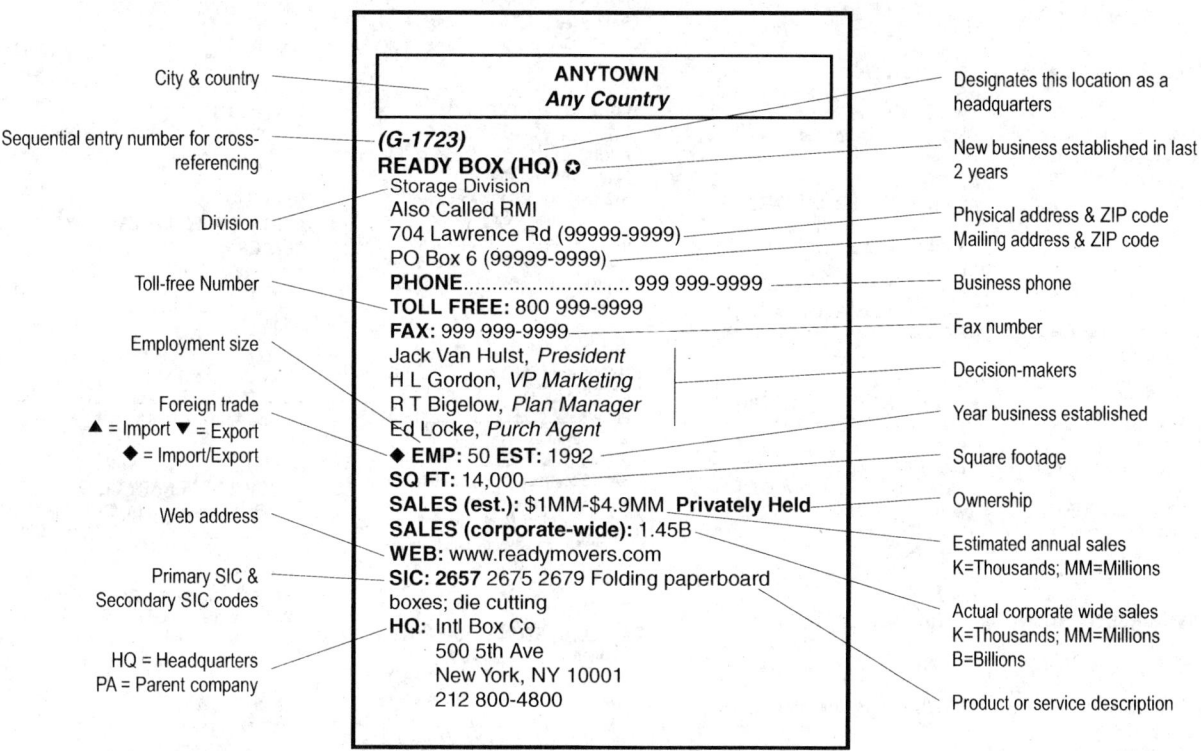

See footnotes for symbols and codes identification.
- This section is in alphabetical order by city.
- Companies are sorted alphabetically under their respective cities.
- To locate cities within a county refer to the County/City Cross Reference Index.

IMPORTANT NOTICE: It is a violation of both federal and state law to transmit an unsolicited advertisement to a facsimile machine. Any user of this product that violates such laws may be subject to civil and criminal penalties which may exceed $500 for each transmission of an unsolicited facsimile. Harris InfoSource provides fax numbers for lawful purposes only and expressly forbids the use of these numbers in any unlawful manner.

Bear
New Castle County

(G-1)
302 ELITE ATHLETES
213 Hazel Dr (19701-1960)
PHONE............................302 834-7991
Jalputnia Trader, *Asst Sec*
EMP: 5 **EST:** 2018
SALES (est): 109.37K **Privately Held**
SIC: 7941 Sports clubs, managers, and promoters

(G-2)
3B BRAES BROWN BAGS
950 Rue Madora (19701-2575)
PHONE............................302 544-0779
Christy Mannering, *Prin*
EMP: 5 **EST:** 2014
SALES (est): 77.16K **Privately Held**
Web: www.braesbrownbags.org
SIC: 8641 Civic and social associations

(G-3)
431 CORPORATION
4185 Kirkwood St Georges Rd (19701-2272)
P.O. Box 1187 (19701-7187)
PHONE............................352 385-1427
Greg Harrison, *Dir*
EMP: 12
SIC: 8732 Market analysis or research
PA: 431 Corporation
   28334 Churchill Smith Ln
   Mount Dora FL 32757

(G-4)
5LINX
729 Ellen Dr (19701-5801)
P.O. Box 1533 (19701-7533)
PHONE............................302 981-2529
Delphine Fombi Ndifor, *Prin*
EMP: 5 **EST:** 2018
SALES (est): 67.75K **Privately Held**
Web: www.myepiccompany.com
SIC: 8748 Business consulting, nec

(G-5)
7 JEWEL LOGISTICS LLC
2 N Sherman Dr (19701-3087)
PHONE............................409 350-9759
EMP: 5 **EST:** 2021
SALES (est): 260.43K **Privately Held**
SIC: 4789 Transportation services, nec

(G-6)
A & C UNLIMITED
107 Bell Ct (19701-1097)
PHONE............................302 379-7112
EMP: 6 **EST:** 2012
SALES (est): 69.13K **Privately Held**
SIC: 1711 Plumbing, heating, air-conditioning

(G-7)
A AND H NURSING ADMINISTRA
94 Dasher Ave (19701-1174)
PHONE............................302 544-4474
Holly A Mcconomy, *Prin*
EMP: 10 **EST:** 2008
SALES (est): 114.01K **Privately Held**
SIC: 8059 Nursing and personal care, nec

(G-8)
A CHILDS WORLD LLC
300 Bear Christiana Rd (19701-1040)
PHONE............................302 322-9386
Stephanie Fagles, *Dir*
EMP: 16 **EST:** 2006
SALES (est): 236.85K **Privately Held**
Web: www.achildsworld.org
SIC: 8351 Preschool center

(G-9)
A COLLINS TRUCKING INC
314 Turnberry Ct (19701-4720)
PHONE............................302 438-8334
Aubrey Collins Senior, *CEO*
Bryan J Collins, *VP*
EMP: 5 **EST:** 2002
SALES (est): 257.72K **Privately Held**
SIC: 4212 Local trucking, without storage

(G-10)
A HAIR HUB LLC
119 Banff St (19701-4705)
PHONE............................267 206-0569
Amanda Hubbard, *Managing Member*
EMP: 6 **EST:** 2017
SALES (est): 47K **Privately Held**
Web: www.ahairhubllc.com
SIC: 7231 7389 Beauty shops; Business services, nec

(G-11)
AC ENGINEERING
135 Emerald Ridge Dr (19701-2280)
PHONE............................215 873-6482
Victor Changlee, *Pt*
EMP: 2 **EST:** 2012
SALES (est): 129.59K **Privately Held**

Bear - New Castle County (G-12)   GEOGRAPHIC SECTION

SIC: 3621 Armatures, industrial

(G-12)
ACCESSCARE INC
502 Beechwood Ct (19701-5307)
PHONE..................302 836-9314
Abdul Conteh, *Prin*
EMP: 8 EST: 2010
SALES (est): 100.8K **Privately Held**
Web: www.ncaccesscare.org
SIC: 8621 Nursing association

(G-13)
ACCURATE & HEATING
17 Riva Ridge Ln (19701-3355)
PHONE..................302 561-5749
EMP: 5 EST: 2017
SALES (est): 243.56K **Privately Held**
SIC: 1711 Plumbing contractors

(G-14)
ADDALLI LANDSCAPING
2546 Red Lion Rd (19701-2429)
PHONE..................302 836-2002
EMP: 5 EST: 1994
SALES (est): 263.05K **Privately Held**
Web: www.addallilandscaping.com
SIC: 0781 Landscape services

(G-15)
ADEPT CLEANING & RESTORATION
503 E Pompeii Dr (19701-2529)
PHONE..................302 385-6653
EMP: 5 EST: 2019
SALES (est): 67.5K **Privately Held**
Web: www.adeptrestoration.com
SIC: 7699 Cleaning services

(G-16)
ADKESS TRANSPORT SERVICES LLC
14 Winchester Ct (19701-2232)
PHONE..................978 235-3924
Godwin Adansi, *Prin*
EMP: 5 EST: 2015
SALES (est): 307.12K **Privately Held**
SIC: 4789 Transportation services, nec

(G-17)
ADVANCED PLUMBING & MAINT LLC
20 Valerie Dr (19701-1749)
PHONE..................302 584-4001
Andi Stansky, *Prin*
EMP: 5 EST: 2015
SALES (est): 22.81K **Privately Held**
Web: www.advancedplumbingandmaintenance.com
SIC: 7349 Building maintenance services, nec

(G-18)
ADVANTAGE DELAWARE
134 Antlers Ln (19701-3710)
PHONE..................302 365-5398
Nancy J Wolf, *Prin*
EMP: 8 EST: 2009
SIC: 6712 Bank holding companies

(G-19)
AFFINITY WOMENS HEALTH LLC
121 Becks Woods Dr Ste 100 (19701-3851)
PHONE..................302 468-4320
Stanley Wiercinski, *Prin*
EMP: 9 EST: 2013
SALES (est): 142.74K **Privately Held**
Web: www.affinitywomens.com
SIC: 8011 Gynecologist

(G-20)
AFFORDABLE INSUR NETWRK DEL
1218 Pulaski Hwy Ste 490 (19701-4300)
PHONE..................800 681-7261
Sam Peppelman, *Prin*
EMP: 5 EST: 2003
SALES (est): 405.65K **Privately Held**
Web: www.ainofde.com
SIC: 6411 Insurance agents, nec

(G-21)
AIDEN AUTO REPAIR CENTER
804 Pulaski Hwy (19701-1226)
PHONE..................302 898-5777
Eddie White, *Prin*
EMP: 6 EST: 2015
SALES (est): 62.89K **Privately Held**
SIC: 7538 General automotive repair shops

(G-22)
AIT ADVANCED INFOTECH INC
467 Carson Dr (19701-1314)
PHONE..................302 454-8620
EMP: 9 EST: 1991
SALES (est): 655.16K **Privately Held**
Web: www.aitus.org
SIC: 7379 Computer related consulting services

(G-23)
AKSHAR MEDICAL SERVICE
417 Oregano Ct (19701-6019)
PHONE..................302 369-3533
EMP: 6 EST: 2017
SALES (est): 149.01K **Privately Held**
SIC: 8099 Health and allied services, nec

(G-24)
ALEX EVANS ASPHALT PAVING LLC
827 Sparrow Ln (19701-1109)
PHONE..................302 363-3796
EMP: 7 EST: 2009
SALES (est): 237.09K **Privately Held**
SIC: 1611 Surfacing and paving

(G-25)
ALL AMERICAN TREE EXPERTS
107 Mahon Ln (19701-3817)
PHONE..................302 419-4876
Steven Hendricks, *Owner*
EMP: 5 EST: 2015
SALES (est): 70.22K **Privately Held**
Web: www.allamericantreeexperts.com
SIC: 0783 Planting, pruning, and trimming services

(G-26)
ALL ROCK & MULCH LLC
1570 Red Lion Rd (19701-1870)
PHONE..................302 838-7625
EMP: 2 EST: 2014
SALES (est): 161.08K **Privately Held**
SIC: 3271 5083 Blocks, concrete: landscape or retaining wall; Landscaping equipment

(G-27)
ALL WEATHER ROOFING CO
200 Suffolk Blvd (19701-2234)
PHONE..................302 836-6400
EMP: 6 EST: 1983
SALES (est): 450.86K **Privately Held**
Web: www.allweatherroofingcompanyde.com
SIC: 1761 Roofing contractor

(G-28)
ALLISONS AUTO CYCLE KSTOMZ LLC
Also Called: Allison's Auto
700 Julian Ln (19701-2432)
PHONE..................302 836-4222
Charles Allison, *Managing Member*
EMP: 5 EST: 2016
SALES (est): 267.08K **Privately Held**
SIC: 7538 General automotive repair shops

(G-29)
ALPHA COMM LLC
717 Javelin Way (19701-3131)
PHONE..................302 784-0645
EMP: 11 EST: 2018
SALES (est): 25K **Privately Held**
Web: www.alphacomm.com
SIC: 7374 7373 7389 Data processing and preparation; Computer-aided system services; Personal service agents, brokers, and bureaus

(G-30)
AMERICAN MARTIAL ARTS INST
402 Eden Cir (19701-4304)
PHONE..................302 834-4060
Ron Sutcarotte, *Pr*
▼ EMP: 11 EST: 2005
SALES (est): 267.77K **Privately Held**
Web: www.dewushu.com
SIC: 7999 7991 Martial arts school, nec; Physical fitness clubs with training equipment

(G-31)
AMERICAN STONE CRAFTERS INC
7 Hawkins Ct (19701-1622)
PHONE..................302 834-8891
EMP: 5 EST: 2007
SALES (est): 90.32K **Privately Held**
SIC: 1741 1742 1771 Masonry and other stonework; Plastering, plain or ornamental; Stucco, gunite, and grouting contractors

(G-32)
AMERICAN SURGERY CENTER
161 Becks Woods Dr (19701-3833)
PHONE..................302 266-9166
Susan Andersen, *COO*
EMP: 15 EST: 2015
SALES (est): 463.03K **Privately Held**
Web: www.americansurgery.org
SIC: 8011 Surgeon

(G-33)
AMERICAN TREE CO LLC
915 Sugar Pine Dr (19701-2166)
PHONE..................302 836-1664
Pat Poore, *Prin*
EMP: 5 EST: 2005
SALES (est): 235.01K **Privately Held**
Web: www.americantreeco-de.com
SIC: 0783 Tree trimming services for public utility lines

(G-34)
AMERICAS GOT FUNDING
1148 Pulaski Hwy Ste 404 (19701-1305)
PHONE..................866 975-8363
EMP: 5 EST: 2011
SALES (est): 130.64K **Privately Held**
Web: www.americasgotfunding.com
SIC: 6153 Working capital financing

(G-35)
AMERIHEALTH CARITAS DELAWARE
1142 Pulaski Hwy (19701-1305)
PHONE..................844 211-0966
EMP: 16 EST: 2019
SALES (est): 277.31K **Privately Held**
Web: www.amerihealthcaritasde.com
SIC: 8099 Health and allied services, nec

(G-36)
ANGELS MESSIAHS FOUNDATION
360 Foxhunt Dr (19701-2537)
P.O. Box 1151 (19701-7151)
PHONE..................302 365-5516
Michael Higgin, *Admn*
Michael Higgin, *Dir*
EMP: 10 EST: 2014
SALES (est): 622.13K **Privately Held**
SIC: 8322 Adult day care center

(G-37)
ANIMAL HAVEN VETERINARY CENTER
757 Pulaski Hwy Ste 6 (19701-5215)
PHONE..................302 326-1400
Charlotte Fagraeus, *Prin*
EMP: 6 EST: 2005
SALES (est): 278.3K **Privately Held**
Web: www.animalhavenvet.com
SIC: 0742 Animal hospital services, pets and other animal specialties

(G-38)
ANIMAL VETERINARY CENTER LLC
160 Bear Christiana Rd (19701-1042)
PHONE..................302 322-6488
Jim Berg D.v.m. D.v.m., *Prin*
EMP: 9 EST: 2001
SALES (est): 402.93K **Privately Held**
Web: www.heartandpaw.com
SIC: 0742 Animal hospital services, pets and other animal specialties

(G-39)
ANYTIME FITNESS
235 Governors Pl (19701-3026)
PHONE..................302 834-2348
EMP: 9 EST: 2011
SALES (est): 91.91K **Privately Held**
Web: www.anytimefitness.com
SIC: 7991 Physical fitness clubs with training equipment

(G-40)
APEX CONTRACTORS LLC
1148 Pulaski Hwy (19701-1305)
PHONE..................302 670-7799
EMP: 6 EST: 2009
SALES (est): 116.44K **Privately Held**
SIC: 1799 Special trade contractors, nec

(G-41)
AQUAFLOW PUMP & SUPPLY COMPANY (PA)
1561 Pulaski Hwy (19701-1303)
P.O. Box 98 (19701-0098)
PHONE..................302 834-1311
Henry King Junior, *Pr*
Henry King Iii, *VP*
Edward King, *Treas*
EMP: 15 EST: 1972
SQ FT: 14,000
SALES (est): 12.84MM
SALES (corp-wide): 12.84MM **Privately Held**
Web: www.aquaflowusa.com
SIC: 5084 Pumps and pumping equipment, nec

(G-42)
AQUILA OF DELAWARE INC (PA)
4185 Kirkwood St Georges Rd (19701-2272)
PHONE..................302 999-1106
Joan Chatterton, *Pr*
EMP: 15 EST: 1990
SALES (est): 5.13MM **Privately Held**
Web: www.aquilaofde.com

2024 Harris Directory of Delaware Businesses

▲ = Import ▼ = Export
◆ = Import/Export

GEOGRAPHIC SECTION
Bear - New Castle County (G-71)

SIC: 8748   Business consulting, nec

(G-43)
ARIHANT ENTERPRISE LLC
140 Foxhunt Dr (19701-2535)
PHONE..............................302 353-4400
Deepal Shah, *Managing Member*
EMP: 3
SALES (est): 248.62K **Privately Held**
SIC: 3555   Printing presses

(G-44)
ARLON LLC (HQ)
Also Called: Arlon Mtl Tech Microwave Mtls
1100 Governor Lea Rd (19701-1927)
PHONE..............................302 834-2100
Bob Carini, *Pr*
Pat Dillon, *
▲ EMP: 140 EST: 1988
SQ FT: 7,500
SALES (est): 48.17MM
SALES (corp-wide): 971.17MM **Publicly Held**
Web: www.arlonecp.com
SIC: 2822   Silicone rubbers
PA: Rogers Corporation
2225 W Chandler Blvd
Chandler AZ 85224
480 917-6000

(G-45)
ARLON MED INTERNATIONAL LLC
1100 Governor Lea Rd (19701-1927)
PHONE..............................302 834-2100
Carlos Feliciano, *Prin*
EMP: 14 EST: 2012
SALES (est): 911.37K
SALES (corp-wide): 971.17MM **Publicly Held**
SIC: 5085   Abrasives
PA: Rogers Corporation
2225 W Chandler Blvd
Chandler AZ 85224
480 917-6000

(G-46)
ARLON PARTNERS INC
1100 Governor Lea Rd (19701-1927)
PHONE..............................302 595-1234
EMP: 5 EST: 2013
SALES (est): 173K **Privately Held**
Web: www.rogerscorp.com
SIC: 5085   Abrasives

(G-47)
ARROW LEASING CORP
Also Called: Arrow Sanitary Service
1772 Pulaski Hwy (19701-1712)
PHONE..............................302 834-4546
TOLL FREE: 800
Albert T Sammons Junior, *Pr*
EMP: 10 EST: 1957
SQ FT: 5,200
SALES (est): 887.01K **Privately Held**
Web: www.arrowsanitary.com
SIC: 7359 7699   Equipment rental and leasing, nec; Septic tank cleaning service

(G-48)
ART FITNESS
109 Faraday Ct (19701-3021)
PHONE..............................302 373-5148
Alisa Adams, *Mgr*
EMP: 5 EST: 2018
SALES (est): 29.54K **Privately Held**
SIC: 7991   Physical fitness facilities

(G-49)
ARTHUR COPPEDGE
Also Called: Arty's Trucking
7 Paynter St (19701-3078)
PHONE..............................302 229-7581
Arthur Coppedge, *Owner*
EMP: 5 EST: 2011
SALES (est): 68.96K **Privately Held**
SIC: 3537   Trucks: freight, baggage, etc.: industrial, except mining

(G-50)
ARTISANS BANK INC
1124 Pulaski Hwy (19701-1305)
PHONE..............................302 834-8800
Alice Candeloro, *Mgr*
EMP: 8
SALES (corp-wide): 25.62MM **Privately Held**
Web: www.artisansbank.com
SIC: 6036 6029   State savings banks, not federally chartered; Commercial banks, nec
PA: Artisans Bank Inc
2961 Centerville Rd # 101
Wilmington DE 19808
302 658-6881

(G-51)
ASSETBOOK
125 Rickey Blvd Unit 453 (19701-8620)
P.O. Box 453 (19701-0453)
PHONE..............................301 387-3238
EMP: 17 EST: 2006
SQ FT: 1,800
SALES (est): 1.12MM **Privately Held**
Web: www.assetbook.com
SIC: 7372   Business oriented computer software

(G-52)
ATI HOLDINGS LLC
Also Called: ATI Physical Therapy
1015 E Songsmith Dr (19701-1194)
PHONE..............................302 836-5670
Kathleen Iffland, *Brnch Mgr*
EMP: 7
SALES (corp-wide): 635.67MM **Publicly Held**
Web: www.atipt.com
SIC: 8049   Physical therapist
HQ: Ati Holdings, Llc
790 Remington Blvd
Bolingbrook IL 60440

(G-53)
ATI HOLDINGS LLC
Also Called: ATI Physical Therapy
100 Becks Woods Dr (19701-3835)
PHONE..............................302 392-3400
EMP: 10
SALES (corp-wide): 635.67MM **Publicly Held**
Web: www.atipt.com
SIC: 8049   Physical therapist
HQ: Ati Holdings, Llc
790 Remington Blvd
Bolingbrook IL 60440

(G-54)
ATKINS HOME HEALTH AID AGENCY
18 Calvarese Dr (19701-6006)
PHONE..............................302 832-0315
Paulette Atkins, *Prin*
EMP: 8 EST: 2011
SALES (est): 80.78K **Privately Held**
SIC: 8082   Home health care services

(G-55)
BAKER SAFETY EQUIPMENT INC
107 Delilah Dr (19701-4833)
PHONE..............................302 376-9302
Dawn Nutter, *Pr*
Mark D Baker, *VP*
Ralph T Baker, *CEO*
EMP: 6 EST: 1983
SQ FT: 600,000
SALES (est): 600K **Privately Held**
Web: www.lifechute.com
SIC: 5047 2221   Industrial safety devices: first aid kits and masks; Nylon broadwoven fabrics

(G-56)
BARBARA KWAKYE-SAFO
113 Faraday Ct (19701-3064)
PHONE..............................302 559-1955
Barbara Kwakye-safo, *Mgr*
EMP: 6 EST: 2017
SALES (est): 22.18K **Privately Held**
SIC: 8049   Offices of health practitioner

(G-57)
BARTECH AGENCY INC
1148 Pulaski Hwy Ste 107 (19701-1305)
PHONE..............................302 317-2399
Peter Palli, *Pr*
EMP: 12 EST: 2002
SALES (est): 121.86K **Privately Held**
SIC: 7371   Computer software development and applications

(G-58)
BAVARIAN CLLISION NEW GRDN INC
119 Pigeon Run Dr (19701-1513)
PHONE..............................610 268-3966
Thomas Laughlin, *Sec*
EMP: 6 EST: 2017
SALES (est): 75.36K **Privately Held**
SIC: 7538   General automotive repair shops

(G-59)
BE BLESSED DESIGN GROUP LLC
Also Called: Bbdg
808 Lowell Dr (19701-4948)
PHONE..............................302 561-3793
EMP: 3 EST: 2016
SALES (est): 94.65K **Privately Held**
SIC: 2396 5699 7389 2299   Apparel and other linings, except millinery; Customized clothing and apparel; Apparel designers, commercial; Apparel filling: cotton waste, kapok, and related material

(G-60)
BEACON TECHNOLOGIES LLC
336 Brandywine Dr (19701-3202)
PHONE..............................302 438-9728
EMP: 14 EST: 2013
SALES (est): 92.73K **Privately Held**
Web: www.beacontechnologies.com
SIC: 8742   Marketing consulting services

(G-61)
BEAR CHIROPRACTIC CENTER DC
811 Governors Pl (19701-3046)
PHONE..............................302 836-8361
Alexander Bohatiuk, *Owner*
Alexander N Bohativk D.c., *Owner*
EMP: 5 EST: 1990
SALES (est): 219.9K **Privately Held**
Web: www.bearchiro.com
SIC: 8041   Offices and clinics of chiropractors

(G-62)
BEAR DE
258 E Scotland Dr (19701-1738)
P.O. Box 130 (19701-0130)
PHONE..............................302 836-6050
EMP: 5 EST: 2011
SALES (est): 156.95K **Privately Held**
Web: www.bearcf.com
SIC: 6531   Real estate brokers and agents

(G-63)
BEAR FORGE AND MACHINE CO INC
Also Called: Stafford Precision
147 School Bell Rd (19701-1191)
PHONE..............................302 322-5199
William Stafford, *Pr*
EMP: 2 EST: 1974
SQ FT: 7,000
SALES (est): 239.25K **Privately Held**
Web: www.staffordprecision.com
SIC: 3469 7692   Machine parts, stamped or pressed metal; Welding repair

(G-64)
BEAR HOSPITALITY INC
Also Called: Best Western Plus
875 Pulaski Hwy (19701-1252)
PHONE..............................302 326-2500
Ann Watkins, *Pr*
EMP: 7 EST: 1995
SALES (est): 696.64K **Privately Held**
Web: www.bestwestern.com
SIC: 7011   Hotels and motels

(G-65)
BEAR INT MED PEDS
26 Dunleary Dr (19701-6355)
PHONE..............................302 595-2146
EMP: 5 EST: 2017
SALES (est): 106.44K **Privately Held**
SIC: 8099   Health and allied services, nec

(G-66)
BEAR-GLASGOW DENTAL LLC
1106 Pulaski Hwy (19701-1332)
PHONE..............................302 836-9330
Neil Woloshin, *Prin*
EMP: 10 EST: 2018
SALES (est): 73.67K **Privately Held**
Web: www.bearglasgowdental.com
SIC: 8021   Dentists' office

(G-67)
BELLA TILE AND STONE LLC
802 Archer Pl (19701-2712)
PHONE..............................302 275-4550
Ryan Bordas, *Prin*
EMP: 5 EST: 2015
SALES (est): 54.48K **Privately Held**
SIC: 1743   Tile installation, ceramic

(G-68)
BELLALINE DESIGN LLC
106 Loretta Ln (19701-1694)
PHONE..............................302 293-5676
EMP: 5 EST: 2018
SALES (est): 82.72K **Privately Held**
SIC: 1521   Single-family housing construction

(G-69)
BENNY BENNETT CONTRACTING
637 S Huckleberry Ave (19701-1339)
PHONE..............................302 290-1613
Benjamin Bennett, *Prin*
EMP: 6 EST: 2018
SALES (est): 240.8K **Privately Held**
SIC: 1799   Special trade contractors, nec

(G-70)
BETTER LIFE ENERPRISE
187 Willamette Dr (19701-4803)
PHONE..............................302 312-9156
EMP: 5 EST: 2017
SALES (est): 188.19K **Privately Held**
SIC: 6311   Life insurance

(G-71)
BIG BOX USA LLC
459 Carson Dr (19701-1314)
PHONE..............................302 595-3324

Bear - New Castle County (G-72) — **GEOGRAPHIC SECTION**

EMP: 7 EST: 2017
SALES (est): 114.57K Privately Held
Web: www.bigboxusa.com
SIC: 4789 Transportation services, nec

(G-72)
BISHOP CLEANING AND MAINT LLC
1023 King James Ct (19701-4738)
PHONE..................302 277-8815
Dwight Bishop Ii, CEO
EMP: 5 EST: 2021
SALES (est): 75K Privately Held
SIC: 1542 Commercial and office building contractors

(G-73)
BLACK MAGIC SEALCOATING
214 Edgewood Dr (19701-2013)
PHONE..................302 832-7906
Jeffrey Darrah, Owner
EMP: 5 EST: 2004
SALES (est): 248.88K Privately Held
Web: www.blackmagicsealcoating.net
SIC: 1611 Surfacing and paving

(G-74)
BLACKWELL SOLUTION
128 Emerald Ridge Dr (19701-2281)
PHONE..................302 660-2054
Richard F Blackwell, CEO
EMP: 5 EST: 2010
SALES (est): 148.88K Privately Held
Web: www.theblackwellsolutionllc.com
SIC: 7371 Computer software development

(G-75)
BLESSED BEGINNINGS LRNG CTR
117 Portside Ct (19701-2287)
PHONE..................302 838-9112
Randee Briggs, Prin
EMP: 12 EST: 2010
SALES (est): 110.92K Privately Held
SIC: 8351 Child day care services

(G-76)
BLUE HERON ENT INC
Also Called: Blue Heron Discount Cards
600 Garron Point Pass (19701-1992)
PHONE..................302 834-1521
Samantha Young, Prin
EMP: 4 EST: 2008
SALES (est): 84.45K Privately Held
Web: www.blueheroncards.com
SIC: 2754 Business form and card printing, gravure

(G-77)
BOBCAT OF NEW CASTLE LLC (PA)
1872 Pulaski Hwy (19701-1710)
PHONE..................732 780-6880
Robert Woods, Pr
EMP: 23 EST: 2015
SALES (est): 4.59MM
SALES (corp-wide): 4.59MM Privately Held
Web: bobcatnewcastle.morbarkdealers.com
SIC: 1794 Excavation work

(G-78)
BODY BRAIN SYNC INC
17 Perth St (19701-4761)
PHONE..................302 498-9234
Gladys Smith, Prin
EMP: 8 EST: 2018
SALES (est): 197.89K Privately Held
SIC: 8011 Offices and clinics of medical doctors

(G-79)
BRADLEY & SONS DESIGNER CON
1 Tammie Dr (19701-1758)
PHONE..................302 836-8031
Bob Bradley, Owner
Robin Bradley, Off Mgr
EMP: 5 EST: 1975
SALES (est): 260K Privately Held
SIC: 1771 Concrete work

(G-80)
BRANDYWINE ELECTRONICS CORP
Also Called: Brandywine Elec Ltd Belcom
611 Carson Dr (19701-1450)
PHONE..................302 324-9992
Joseph Dombroski, Pr
Ronald Casalvera, VP
EMP: 12 EST: 1974
SQ FT: 10,084
SALES (est): 2.54MM Privately Held
Web: www.bel.com
SIC: 1731 5064 3651 7359 Sound equipment specialization; Video camera-audio recorders (camcorders); Household audio and video equipment; Audio-visual equipment and supply rental

(G-81)
BRENDA ANNS HAIR SALON
1745 Bear Corbitt Rd (19701-1528)
PHONE..................302 312-7658
Brenda Spencer, Owner
EMP: 5 EST: 2016
SALES (est): 44.02K Privately Held
SIC: 7231 Hairdressers

(G-82)
BRIE D BOLGER
4 Emerald Ridge Dr (19701-2252)
PHONE..................302 668-8268
Brie Bolger, Mgr
EMP: 6 EST: 2017
SALES (est): 24.08K Privately Held
SIC: 8049 Offices of health practitioner

(G-83)
BRODIE CONSULTING MICK GROUP
4 Chilmark Ct (19701-3815)
PHONE..................302 468-6425
Mick Brodie, Mgr
EMP: 6 EST: 2015
SALES (est): 276.49K Privately Held
Web: www.mickbrodie.com
SIC: 8748 Safety training service

(G-84)
BULLS HOME SERVICES CO
Also Called: Five Star Painting of Newark
317 Manubay Ct (19701-1613)
PHONE..................302 540-1381
Curtis Bull, Prin
EMP: 8 EST: 2016
SALES (est): 389.18K Privately Held
SIC: 1721 Painting and paper hanging

(G-85)
BURNSIES PLUMBING LLC
20 Pear Dr (19701-4136)
PHONE..................215 275-0723
EMP: 6 EST: 2016
SALES (est): 293.33K Privately Held
SIC: 1711 Plumbing contractors

(G-86)
BYERS INDUSTRIAL SERVICES LLC
1501 Porter Rd (19701-2111)
PHONE..................302 836-4790
Tom Moore, Mgr
EMP: 165
Web: www.byersindustrial.com
SIC: 1731 General electrical contractor
PA: Byers Industrial Services, Llc.
1100 Grant Ave
Franklinville NJ 08322

(G-87)
C & K BUILDERS LLC
Also Called: Kokoszka Ent
334 Bear Christiana Rd (19701-1040)
PHONE..................302 324-9811
Jospeh Kokoszka, Managing Member
EMP: 6 EST: 1994
SALES (est): 657.6K Privately Held
Web: www.ckbuilderscustomhomes.com
SIC: 1521 General remodeling, single-family houses

(G-88)
CALIBER BODYWORKS TEXAS INC
Also Called: Caliber Collision Centers
731 Rue Madora (19701-2543)
PHONE..................302 832-1660
EMP: 34
SALES (corp-wide): 1.54MM Privately Held
Web: www.caliber.com
SIC: 7532 Body shop, automotive
PA: Caliber Bodyworks Of Texas Llc
2941 Lake Vista Dr
Lewisville TX 75067
469 794-5653

(G-89)
CARDENTI ELECTRIC
109 E Scotland Dr (19701-1756)
PHONE..................302 834-1278
Maria Cardenti, Sec
Lori Cardenti, Mgr
EMP: 10 EST: 1979
SQ FT: 2,500
SALES (est): 801.32K Privately Held
Web: www.cardentielectric.com
SIC: 1731 Electrical work

(G-90)
CAREER RADY EDUCATN FOUNDATION
2595 Mccoy Rd (19701-1913)
PHONE..................302 540-2733
Eva Foxwell, Pr
EMP: 5 EST: 2018
SALES (est): 70.11K Privately Held
Web: www.crteaching.com
SIC: 8699 Charitable organization

(G-91)
CARROLL GROUP INC
1271 Quintilio Dr (19701-6005)
PHONE..................302 836-6180
Debra Carroll, Prin
EMP: 5 EST: 2020
SALES (est): 119.02K Privately Held
SIC: 6531 Real estate agent, residential

(G-92)
CATCH-A-WEB CLEANING INC
2099 Red Lion Rd (19701-1853)
PHONE..................302 836-1970
EMP: 5 EST: 2011
SALES (est): 62.77K Privately Held
SIC: 7349 Janitorial service, contract basis

(G-93)
CEDARBROOK CAMP IN PA
822 Percheron Dr (19701-2202)
PHONE..................302 463-0137
Paula Worden, Ofcr
EMP: 5 EST: 2019
SALES (est): 74.07K Privately Held
Web: www.cedarbrookcamps.com
SIC: 7032 Sporting and recreational camps

(G-94)
CFT AMBULANCE SERVICE INC
33 Pear Dr (19701-4135)
PHONE..................302 984-2255
Denette Lawson, Pr
EMP: 8 EST: 2001
SQ FT: 2,000
SALES (est): 230.81K Privately Held
Web: www.hi5s.com
SIC: 4119 Ambulance service

(G-95)
CHAMBERLAIN AND CO CSTM PNTG
142 Willow Oak Blvd (19701-4877)
PHONE..................610 633-2011
EMP: 5 EST: 2017
SALES (est): 42.66K Privately Held
Web: www.chamberlainpaint.com
SIC: 1721 Painting and paper hanging

(G-96)
CHAMBERS BROS LOGISTICS LLC
4 Kerry Ct (19701-6346)
PHONE..................302 307-3668
EMP: 7 EST: 2020
SALES (est): 537.25K Privately Held
SIC: 5088 Transportation equipment and supplies

(G-97)
CHARITY CROSSING INC
2 Pear Dr (19701-4134)
PHONE..................302 983-2271
Jay Muthukamatch, CEO
EMP: 10 EST: 2016
SALES (est): 456.55K Privately Held
Web: www.charitycrossing.org
SIC: 8699 Charitable organization

(G-98)
CHESHIRE ENTERPRISE LLC
100 E Scotland Dr (19701-1756)
PHONE..................302 365-6225
EMP: 5 EST: 2015
SALES (est): 312.23K Privately Held
Web: www.cheshirenterprise.com
SIC: 5084 Industrial machinery and equipment

(G-99)
CHRIS CURRY DR
3 Dogwood Ct (19701-4132)
PHONE..................302 365-5457
Chris Curry, Prin
EMP: 8 EST: 2009
SALES (est): 70.62K Privately Held
SIC: 8011 Offices and clinics of medical doctors

(G-100)
CHRISTIANA FIRE COMPANY
1714 Porter Rd (19701-2110)
PHONE..................302 834-2433
Jeff Tillinghast, Chief
EMP: 8
SALES (corp-wide): 5.15MM Privately Held
Web: www.christianafc.org
SIC: 9224 4119 Fire protection, Local government; Ambulance service
PA: Christiana Fire Company
2 E Main St
Christiana DE 19702
302 737-2433

(G-101)
CHRISTIANA INN
875 Pulaski Hwy (19701-1252)

GEOGRAPHIC SECTION
Bear - New Castle County (G-130)

PHONE..................302 276-1659
Robert Allen, *Pr*
EMP: 13 **EST:** 2012
SALES (est): 72.89K **Privately Held**
SIC: 7011 Inns

(G-102)
CHRISTIANA MEADOWS LLC
Also Called: Christiana Meadows Apartments
265 Bear Christiana Rd (19701-1047)
PHONE..................302 322-6161
Brock Vinton, *Pr*
Carmen Facciolo, *VP*
EMP: 12 **EST:** 1989
SALES (est): 956.3K **Privately Held**
Web: www.christiana-meadows.com
SIC: 6513 Apartment hotel operation

(G-103)
CHRISTINA NEWTON
925 Bear Corbitt Rd (19701-1323)
PHONE..................302 454-2400
Christina Newton, *Prin*
EMP: 6 **EST:** 2017
SALES (est): 86.83K **Privately Held**
Web: www.christinak12.org
SIC: 8049 Offices of health practitioner

(G-104)
CIRCLE D ENTERPRISES INC
Also Called: Even Flow Irrigation
201 Silver Birch Ln (19701-2385)
PHONE..................302 544-2654
Don Timlin, *Owner*
EMP: 5 **EST:** 2011
SALES (est): 209.67K **Privately Held**
Web: www.evenflowirrigation.com
SIC: 4971 Irrigation systems

(G-105)
CITIFINANCIAL CREDIT COMPANY
Also Called: Citifinancial
619 Governors Pl (19701-3034)
P.O. Box 598 (19701-0598)
PHONE..................302 834-6677
John Barkley, *Mgr*
EMP: 6
SALES (corp-wide): 101.08B **Publicly Held**
SIC: 6153 6141 Short-term business credit institutions, except agricultural; Personal credit institutions
HQ: Citifinancial Credit Company
300 Saint Paul Pl Fl 3
Baltimore MD 21202
410 332-3000

(G-106)
CITIZENS BANK NATIONAL ASSN
Also Called: Citizens Bank
146 Foxhunt Dr (19701-2535)
PHONE..................302 834-2611
Eric Quinones, *Brnch Mgr*
EMP: 10
SALES (corp-wide): 9.07B **Publicly Held**
Web: www.govplus.com
SIC: 6022 State commercial banks
HQ: Citizens Bank, National Association
1 Citizens Plz
Providence RI 02903

(G-107)
CITYLINE RENTAL
146 Countryside Ln (19701-2008)
PHONE..................302 834-3142
Frank Woodruff, *Owner*
EMP: 5 **EST:** 2011
SALES (est): 221.87K **Privately Held**
SIC: 7359 Party supplies rental services

(G-108)
CLARK CONSTRUCTION INC
4542 Kirkwood St Georges Rd (19701-2069)
PHONE..................302 832-1288
EMP: 6 **EST:** 2011
SALES (est): 209.27K **Privately Held**
SIC: 1521 Single-family housing construction

(G-109)
CLARK SERVICES INC DELAWARE
900 Julian Ln (19701-2277)
PHONE..................302 834-0556
Mark Clark, *Pr*
Kathleen Clark, *VP*
EMP: 5 **EST:** 1997
SQ FT: 5,000
SALES (est): 711.83K **Privately Held**
Web: www.clarkhvacservices.com
SIC: 1711 5983 Warm air heating and air conditioning contractor; Fuel oil dealers

(G-110)
CLICK FOR SAVINGS LLC
5104 Christiana Mdws (19701-1156)
PHONE..................302 300-0202
Adam Cotter, *Prin*
EMP: 6 **EST:** 2016
SALES (est): 226.66K **Privately Held**
SIC: 8399 Advocacy group

(G-111)
CLUB 6 BARBERSHOP
112 Mario Dr (19701-6002)
PHONE..................302 276-1624
James Pressley, *Pr*
EMP: 3 **EST:** 2021
SALES (est): 83.91K **Privately Held**
SIC: 3999 5087 Barber and beauty shop equipment; Beauty salon and barber shop equipment and supplies

(G-112)
CLUB BRENNAN
1 Primrose Dr (19701-6393)
PHONE..................302 838-9530
Jack Hilman, *Pr*
EMP: 9 **EST:** 1998
SALES (est): 97.67K **Privately Held**
Web: www.clubbrennan.net
SIC: 7997 Swimming club, membership

(G-113)
COLONIAL HOME IMPROVEMENTS
807 Seymour Rd (19701-1121)
PHONE..................302 275-8247
EMP: 6 **EST:** 2017
SALES (est): 91.48K **Privately Held**
SIC: 1521 Single-family housing construction

(G-114)
COMMUNITY PWERED FEDERAL CR UN (PA)
1758 Pulaski Hwy (19701-1712)
PHONE..................302 368-2396
Anthony Hinds, *CEO*
EMP: 9 **EST:** 1962
SALES (est): 5.19MM
SALES (corp-wide): 5.19MM **Privately Held**
Web: www.cpwrfcu.org
SIC: 6061 Federal credit unions

(G-115)
COMPREHENSIVE ACCIDENT INJURY
131 Becks Woods Dr (19701-3833)
PHONE..................302 563-7442
EMP: 9 **EST:** 2018
SALES (est): 362.07K **Privately Held**
Web: www.comprehensiveaccidentandinjury.com
SIC: 8041 Offices and clinics of chiropractors

(G-116)
COMPUTER JOCKS
726 Pulaski Hwy (19701-5210)
PHONE..................302 544-6448
Richard Veid, *Prin*
EMP: 5 **EST:** 2008
SALES (est): 279.01K **Privately Held**
Web: www.webeatthegeeks.com
SIC: 7378 Computer maintenance and repair

(G-117)
CONCRETE WALLS INC
3415 Wrangle Hill Rd Ste 2 (19701-4812)
P.O. Box 4434 (19807-0434)
PHONE..................302 293-7061
EMP: 7
SALES (est): 751.91K **Privately Held**
Web: www.concretewallsde.com
SIC: 1611 Concrete construction: roads, highways, sidewalks, etc.

(G-118)
CONSTRUCTION UNLIMITED INC
705 Elizabeth Ln (19701-2603)
PHONE..................302 836-3140
Jim Cammock, *Pr*
Debbie Cammock, *VP*
Cathie Filipkowski, *Sec*
EMP: 7 **EST:** 1980
SALES (est): 1.29MM **Privately Held**
Web: www.constructionunlimited.com
SIC: 1542 1751 Commercial and office building contractors; Carpentry work

(G-119)
CONTINENTAL HEALTH CARE SVCS
113 Newton Dr (19701-3022)
PHONE..................240 461-8569
Lucas N Fon, *Prin*
EMP: 7 **EST:** 2012
SALES (est): 76.64K **Privately Held**
SIC: 8099 Health and allied services, nec

(G-120)
COOPER LEVENSON PA
30 Foxhunt Dr U 30 (19701-2534)
PHONE..................302 838-2600
EMP: 8
SALES (corp-wide): 22.83MM **Privately Held**
Web: www.cooperlevenson.com
SIC: 8111 General practice attorney, lawyer
PA: Cooper Levenson, P.A.
1125 Atlantic Ave Fl 3
Atlantic City NJ
609 344-3161

(G-121)
COPPAGE PAVING INC
1378 Porter Rd (19701-1707)
PHONE..................443 309-9796
EMP: 5 **EST:** 2018
SALES (est): 204.25K **Privately Held**
SIC: 1611 Surfacing and paving

(G-122)
COUNSELING SERVICES CORP
29 E Savannah Dr (19701-1663)
PHONE..................302 898-5184
Brigida Rodriguez, *Owner*
EMP: 7 **EST:** 2014
SALES (est): 32.92K **Privately Held**
SIC: 8322 General counseling services

(G-123)
CRAFTSMAN REVISIONS
70 Bristle Cone Dr (19701-2160)
PHONE..................302 834-9252
Richard Emerson, *Prin*
EMP: 6 **EST:** 2018
SALES (est): 223.1K **Privately Held**
Web: www.craftsmanrevisions.com
SIC: 1751 Carpentry work

(G-124)
CREATIVE EDUCATION INC
Also Called: Creative Education
128 Pisces Dr (19701-6833)
PHONE..................610 268-2770
Joanna Collins, *CEO*
Lisa Voicheck, *Sec*
EMP: 12 **EST:** 1999
SALES (est): 215.59K **Privately Held**
SIC: 8351 Preschool center

(G-125)
CREATIVE PLAY DAY SCHOOL
128 Pisces Dr (19701-6833)
PHONE..................610 268-2770
Joana Collin, *Dir*
EMP: 12 **EST:** 2008
SALES (est): 238.34K **Privately Held**
Web: www.cpds.biz
SIC: 8351 Preschool center

(G-126)
CRESCENT DENTAL ASSOCIATES
100 Becks Woods Dr (19701-3835)
PHONE..................302 836-6968
EMP: 10 **EST:** 2011
SALES (est): 244.26K **Privately Held**
Web: www.crescentdentalde.com
SIC: 8021 Dentists' office

(G-127)
CROSSFIT BEAR
2611 Del Laws Rd (19701-1706)
PHONE..................302 540-4394
EMP: 5 **EST:** 2013
SALES (est): 93.32K **Privately Held**
Web: www.bearcf.com
SIC: 7991 Health club

(G-128)
CRUISE SHOPPE INC
26 Valerie Dr (19701-1749)
PHONE..................302 737-7220
EMP: 7 **EST:** 1989
SQ FT: 750
SALES (est): 840.46K **Privately Held**
Web: www.cruiseshoppe.com
SIC: 4724 Travel agencies

(G-129)
D & S WAREHOUSING INC
300 D And S Ln (19701-1317)
PHONE..................302 731-7440
EMP: 6 **EST:** 1970
SALES (est): 67.81K **Privately Held**
SIC: 4225 General warehousing

(G-130)
DANA E HERBERT
Also Called: Desserts By Dana
22 Peterson Pl (19701-3082)
PHONE..................302 721-5798
Dana E Herbert, *Prin*
EMP: 7 **EST:** 2010
SALES (est): 164.55K **Privately Held**
SIC: 2024 Ice cream and frozen deserts

Bear - New Castle County (G-131) GEOGRAPHIC SECTION

(G-131)
DAVID BRIDGE
245 Benjamin Blvd (19701-1693)
PHONE.....................302 429-3317
David Bridge, *Owner*
EMP: 5 **EST:** 2015
SALES (est): 104.09K **Privately Held**
SIC: 1623 Water, sewer, and utility lines

(G-132)
DAVID JENKINS
Also Called: Diamond Glo Cleaning Solutions
522 Liam Pl (19701-2442)
PHONE.....................302 304-5568
David Jenkins, *Owner*
EMP: 6 **EST:** 2014
SALES (est): 175.69K **Privately Held**
Web: www.diamondglosolutions.com
SIC: 7699 Cleaning services

(G-133)
DAVID M SARTIN SR
1984 Porter Rd (19701-2189)
PHONE.....................302 838-1074
David Sartin, *Prin*
EMP: 5 **EST:** 2004
SALES (est): 625.75K **Privately Held**
Web: www.sartinspaving.com
SIC: 1611 Highway and street paving contractor

(G-134)
DAVID M WAGNER
Also Called: Daves Lawn Care & Landscaping
812 Archer Pl (19701-2712)
PHONE.....................302 832-8336
David M Wagner, *Owner*
EMP: 5 **EST:** 2004
SALES (est): 229.67K **Privately Held**
SIC: 0782 Lawn care services

(G-135)
DAVIN MANAGEMENT GROUP LLC
808 Jeffrey Pine Dr (19701-2162)
PHONE.....................302 367-6563
Craig Holmes, *Pr*
EMP: 15 **EST:** 2018
SALES (est): 420.98K **Privately Held**
SIC: 8741 7389 Management services; Business Activities at Non-Commercial Site

(G-136)
DAWN MC KENZIE DVM
3052 Wrangle Hill Rd (19701-1714)
PHONE.....................302 521-8206
Dawn Mckenzie, *Prin*
EMP: 5 **EST:** 2009
SALES (est): 78.7K **Privately Held**
SIC: 0742 Animal hospital services, pets and other animal specialties

(G-137)
DBW TAX SERVICES
222 Guilford St (19701-4702)
PHONE.....................302 276-0428
Dorothy Williams, *Prin*
EMP: 5 **EST:** 2017
SALES (est): 39.77K **Privately Held**
Web: www.dbwtax.com
SIC: 7291 Tax return preparation services

(G-138)
DEAFINITIONS & INTERPRETING
1148 Pulaski Hwy Ste 236 (19701-1305)
PHONE.....................302 563-7714
Andrea Mattie, *Coordtr*
EMP: 11 **EST:** 2007
SALES (est): 181.51K **Privately Held**
Web: www.deafinterpreting.com

SIC: 7389 Translation services

(G-139)
DEBALLI DISTINCTIVE PROPERTIES
1126 Pulaski Hwy (19701-1306)
PHONE.....................302 376-1113
Debbie Gawel, *Prin*
EMP: 5 **EST:** 2016
SALES (est): 177.66K **Privately Held**
Web: www.deballirealestate.com
SIC: 6531 Real estate agent, residential

(G-140)
DEDO VENTURES & HEALTH INC
26 Forsythia Ln (19701-6304)
PHONE.....................302 838-1445
Kehinde Adedoyin, *Owner*
EMP: 7 **EST:** 2009
SALES (est): 60.61K **Privately Held**
SIC: 8099 Health and allied services, nec

(G-141)
DELAWARE ARTS CONSERVATORY
723 Rue Madora Ste 4 (19701-2597)
PHONE.....................302 595-4160
Tracy Friswell Jacobs, *Pt*
Laura Russo, *Pt*
Bryan Russo, *Pt*
Scott Jacobs, *Pt*
EMP: 8 **EST:** 2009
SALES (est): 133.43K **Privately Held**
Web: www.delarts.com
SIC: 8999 7911 Artist's studio; Dance studio and school

(G-142)
DELAWARE BEER WORKS INC
Also Called: Stewart's Brewing Company
219 Governors Pl (19701-3026)
PHONE.....................302 836-2739
EMP: 26 **EST:** 1995
SQ FT: 5,600
SALES (est): 456.78K **Privately Held**
Web: www.stewartsbrewingcompany.com
SIC: 5812 2082 American restaurant; Beer (alcoholic beverage)

(G-143)
DELAWARE COBRAS INC
122 Honora Dr (19701-2042)
PHONE.....................302 983-3500
Richard Edwards, *Prin*
EMP: 6 **EST:** 2015
SALES (est): 181.48K **Privately Held**
Web: test.delawarecobras.com
SIC: 7997 Baseball club, except professional and semi-professional

(G-144)
DELAWARE CURATIVE
609 Governors Pl (19701-3034)
PHONE.....................302 836-5670
EMP: 5 **EST:** 2000
SALES (est): 72.19K **Privately Held**
SIC: 8049 Physical therapist

(G-145)
DELAWARE DENTAL SOLUTIONS LLC
131 Becks Woods Dr (19701-3833)
PHONE.....................302 409-3050
EMP: 16 **EST:** 2020
SALES (est): 663.89K **Privately Held**
Web: www.dedentalsolutions.com
SIC: 8021 Dentists' office

(G-146)
DELAWARE DEPARTMENT TRNSP
Also Called: North District Engrg Cnstr

250 Bear Christiana Rd (19701-1041)
PHONE.....................302 326-8950
Mark Alexander, *Brnch Mgr*
EMP: 41
SALES (corp-wide): 11.27B **Privately Held**
Web: www.deldot.gov
SIC: 1611 9621 Highway and street construction; Regulation, administration of transportation
HQ: Delaware Department Of Transportation
800 S Bay Rd Ste 1
Dover DE 19901

(G-147)
DELAWARE ELITE TRACK CLUB
46 Owls Nest Cir (19701-2733)
PHONE.....................302 521-2243
Suyen Estelow, *Prin*
EMP: 7 **EST:** 2015
SALES (est): 61.97K **Privately Held**
Web: www.delawareelitetrackclub.com
SIC: 7997 Membership sports and recreation clubs

(G-148)
DELAWARE FURY INC
114 Greenbrier Dr (19701-2097)
PHONE.....................302 838-3120
Thomas Boyd, *Prin*
EMP: 5 **EST:** 2019
SALES (est): 117.26K **Privately Held**
Web: www.delawarefurytravel.com
SIC: 7997 Membership sports and recreation clubs

(G-149)
DELAWARE HEATING & AC
Also Called: Honeywell Authorized Dealer
713 Millcreek Ln (19701-3011)
PHONE.....................302 738-4669
Frank J Bartuski, *Pr*
EMP: 11 **EST:** 1993
SALES (est): 374.37K **Privately Held**
Web: www.delawareheatandair.com
SIC: 1711 Warm air heating and air conditioning contractor

(G-150)
DELAWARE LAWN & TREE SERVICE
1756 Bear Corbitt Rd (19701-1538)
PHONE.....................302 834-7406
Edward R Vickers, *Pr*
Edward R Vicker Junior, *VP*
EMP: 10 **EST:** 1964
SQ FT: 3,500
SALES (est): 627.36K **Privately Held**
Web: www.midcountygarden.com
SIC: 0781 5261 Landscape architects; Nursery stock, seeds and bulbs

(G-151)
DELAWARE MOVING & STORAGE INC
214 Bear Christiana Rd (19701-1041)
PHONE.....................302 322-0311
James D Hopkins, *Pr*
Andrew Hopkins, *
David Hopkins, *
EMP: 51 **EST:** 1984
SQ FT: 8,700
SALES (est): 4.56MM **Privately Held**
Web: www.delawaremovingandstorage.com
SIC: 4214 4225 4213 Household goods moving and storage, local; General warehousing and storage; Trucking, except local

(G-152)
DELAWARE POWER WASH PLUS LLC
36 Orchid Dr (19701-6322)
PHONE.....................302 415-1066
EMP: 6 **EST:** 2018
SALES (est): 86.07K **Privately Held**
SIC: 1799 Exterior cleaning, including sandblasting

(G-153)
DELAWARE REAL ESTATE SEARCH
1126 Pulaski Hwy (19701-1305)
PHONE.....................302 437-6516
EMP: 5 **EST:** 2008
SALES (est): 167.24K **Privately Held**
Web: www.deballirealestate.com
SIC: 6531 Real estate agent, residential

(G-154)
DELAWARE ROCK GYM INC
520 Carson Dr (19701-1318)
PHONE.....................302 838-5850
Matt Mccorquodal, *Prin*
EMP: 6 **EST:** 2006
SALES (est): 112.86K **Privately Held**
Web: www.derockgym.com
SIC: 7991 Health club

(G-155)
DELAWARE SECRETARY OF STATE
Also Called: State Del Veterans Mem Cmtry
2465 Chesapeake City Rd (19701-2344)
PHONE.....................302 834-8046
EMP: 7
SALES (corp-wide): 11.27B **Privately Held**
Web: vets.delaware.gov
SIC: 0782 9199 9451 Cemetery upkeep services; General government administration; Administration of veterans' affairs
HQ: Delaware Secretary Of State
401 Federal St Ste 3
Dover DE 19901
302 739-4111

(G-156)
DELAWARE SIDING CO INC
3310 Wrangle Hill Rd Ste 113 (19701-1874)
PHONE.....................302 778-4771
Jason Whittaker, *Prin*
EMP: 5 **EST:** 2016
SALES (est): 81K **Privately Held**
SIC: 1761 Roofing contractor

(G-157)
DELAWARE SIDING COMPANY INC
723 Rue Madora Ste 8 (19701-2597)
PHONE.....................302 836-6971
Jason Whitaker, *Pr*
EMP: 6 **EST:** 1996
SALES (est): 945.99K **Privately Held**
SIC: 1761 Siding contractor

(G-158)
DELAWARE SPINE REHABILITATION
131 Becks Woods Dr (19701-3833)
PHONE.....................302 273-0064
EMP: 5 **EST:** 2018
SALES (est): 102.91K **Privately Held**
SIC: 8049 Physical therapist

(G-159)
DELAWARE VETERANS INC
Also Called: POST 2
2465 Chesapeake City Rd (19701-2344)
P.O. Box 417 (19903-0417)
PHONE.....................302 674-9956
Paul Giery, *Pr*
John Knotts, *Sec*

Paul Eacino, *Treas*
EMP: 10 **EST:** 1940
SALES (est): 137.78K **Privately Held**
Web: vets.delaware.gov
SIC: 8641   Veterans' organization

(G-160)
DELAWARE VETERINARY MED ASSN
3052 Wrangle Hill Rd (19701-1714)
PHONE..............................302 242-7014
Peter Veith, *Ofcr*
EMP: 5 **EST:** 2015
SALES (est): 122.05K **Privately Held**
Web: www.devma.org
SIC: 0742   Veterinary services, specialties

(G-161)
DELAWARE WOMENS BOWLING ASSN
9 Winchester Ct (19701-2232)
PHONE..............................302 834-7002
Barbara Bardsley, *Pr*
Carolyn Powell, *VP*
Ruth-ann Sydnor, *Sec*
EMP: 6 **EST:** 1969
SALES (est): 198.6K **Privately Held**
SIC: 7933   Ten pin center

(G-162)
DELDEN INSTALLATIONS
3125 Chipmunk Ct (19701-2757)
PHONE..............................302 423-1279
David Deneau, *Prin*
EMP: 5 **EST:** 2017
SALES (est): 58.37K **Privately Held**
SIC: 1799   Special trade contractors, nec

(G-163)
DELISLE K-9 OFFCER SFETY FNDTI
413 Brandywine Dr (19701-1271)
PHONE..............................302 893-7324
Valerie Delisle, *Prin*
EMP: 5 **EST:** 2016
SALES (est): 61.9K **Privately Held**
SIC: 8641   Civic and social associations

(G-164)
DEREK LAWSON
235 Rice Dr (19701-1896)
PHONE..............................302 588-3618
Derek Lawson, *Pr*
EMP: 6 **EST:** 2017
SALES (est): 24.4K **Privately Held**
SIC: 8049   Offices of health practitioner

(G-165)
DEWITT HEATING & AC
1 Joanne Ct (19701-1884)
PHONE..............................267 228-7355
Stanley Wiley, *Pr*
EMP: 8 **EST:** 2012
SALES (est): 827.46K **Privately Held**
Web: www.dewitthvac.com
SIC: 1711 7389   Warm air heating and air conditioning contractor; Business Activities at Non-Commercial Site

(G-166)
DEWITT HVAC
1 Joanne Ct (19701-1884)
PHONE..............................267 228-7355
EMP: 8 **EST:** 2017
SALES (est): 256.09K **Privately Held**
Web: www.dewitthvac.com
SIC: 1711   Warm air heating and air conditioning contractor

(G-167)
DIAMOND STATE PROPS
463 Granger Dr (19701-2175)
PHONE..............................302 528-7146
Joe Winnington, *Prin*
EMP: 4 **EST:** 2016
SALES (est): 192K **Privately Held**
SIC: 3369   Nonferrous foundries, nec

(G-168)
DIAMOND STATE TIRE INC
3482 Wrangle Hill Rd (19701-1845)
PHONE..............................302 836-1919
Ed Long, *Pr*
Steve Bailey, *VP*
EMP: 10 **EST:** 1989
SQ FT: 12,000
SALES (est): 1.97MM **Privately Held**
Web: www.diamondstatetire.com
SIC: 5531 7534   Automotive tires; Tire retreading and repair shops

(G-169)
DIMPLE CONSTRUCTION INC
3310 Wrangle Hill Rd Ste 112 (19701-1874)
P.O. Box 1250 (19701-7250)
PHONE..............................302 559-7535
Amrinder Singh, *CEO*
EMP: 5 **EST:** 2008
SALES (est): 278.14K **Privately Held**
SIC: 1521   New construction, single-family houses

(G-170)
DIONNE MICHELLES LUXURY HAIR
6 Ritchie Dr (19701-1119)
PHONE..............................484 362-9242
Dionne Gibbs-baynard, *Prin*
EMP: 5 **EST:** 2017
SALES (est): 49.95K **Privately Held**
Web: www.dionnemichellesbeautique.com
SIC: 7231   Hairdressers

(G-171)
DIVINITY PRESS
1203 Hurlock Ct (19701-4960)
PHONE..............................267 981-4002
EMP: 5 **EST:** 2012
SALES (est): 62.93K **Privately Held**
Web: www.divinitypress.com
SIC: 2741   Miscellaneous publishing

(G-172)
DM KTURE LLC
15 Wisteria Way (19701-6376)
PHONE..............................201 892-3028
EMP: 2 **EST:** 2021
SALES (est): 62.38K **Privately Held**
SIC: 2051 7389   Bakery: wholesale or wholesale/retail combined; Business services, nec

(G-173)
DMS SOLUTION
26 Foxhunt Dr (19701-2534)
PHONE..............................302 753-0040
Roy Finkelman, *Prin*
EMP: 6 **EST:** 2010
SALES (est): 210.82K **Privately Held**
SIC: 8621   Accounting association

(G-174)
DMS SOLUTION
2104 Christiana Mdws (19701-2840)
PHONE..............................302 689-6558
EMP: 6 **EST:** 2018
SALES (est): 108.62K **Privately Held**
Web: www.dmssolutioncpa.com
SIC: 6512   Commercial and industrial building operation

(G-175)
DOCS MEDICAL LLC
25 Dynasty Dr (19701-4011)
PHONE..............................301 401-1489
Marvin Nune, *Prin*
Sandra Anderson, *Prin*
Jesse Longoria, *Prin*
EMP: 3 **EST:** 2019
SALES (est): 164.94K **Privately Held**
SIC: 3841 2676 3827 5021   Surgical and medical instruments; Sanitary paper products; Optical instruments and lenses; Furniture

(G-176)
DOROSHOW PSQALE KRWITZ SGEL BH
1701 Pulaski Hwy (19701-1711)
PHONE..............................302 832-3200
Kristine Wallace, *Brnch Mgr*
EMP: 7
SALES (corp-wide): 9.95MM **Privately Held**
Web: www.dplaw.com
SIC: 8111   General practice attorney, lawyer
PA: Doroshow Pasquale Krawitz Siegel Bhaya
1202 Kirkwood Hwy
Wilmington DE 19805
302 998-2397

(G-177)
DOT FOODS INC
301 American Blvd (19701-4932)
PHONE..............................302 300-4239
Joe Little, *Genl Mgr*
EMP: 100
SALES (corp-wide): 1.09B **Privately Held**
Web: www.dotfoods.com
SIC: 4225 5142   General warehousing and storage; Packaged frozen goods
PA: Dot Foods, Inc.
1 Dot Way
Mount Sterling IL 62353
217 773-4411

(G-178)
DOUBLE S DEVELOPERS INC
Also Called: Double S Co
1919 Red Lion Rd (19701-1855)
PHONE..............................302 838-8880
EMP: 7 **EST:** 1990
SQ FT: 2,100
SALES (est): 234.35K **Privately Held**
SIC: 1521   Single-family housing construction

(G-179)
DOW ADVANCED MATERIALS
200 D And S Ln (19701-1316)
PHONE..............................302 607-3061
EMP: 5 **EST:** 2010
SALES (est): 151.27K **Privately Held**
SIC: 7389   Music and broadcasting services

(G-180)
DOYLE TIMOTHY F M DO
1721 Pulaski Hwy (19701-1711)
PHONE..............................302 836-5410
Timothy Doyle, *Mgr*
EMP: 7 **EST:** 2014
SALES (est): 147.84K **Privately Held**
SIC: 8011   Opthalmologist

(G-181)
DR WEIDONG YANG DENTAL OFFICE
131 Becks Woods Dr (19701-3833)
PHONE..............................302 409-3050
EMP: 7 **EST:** 2019
SALES (est): 61.51K **Privately Held**
Web: www.dedentalsolutions.com
SIC: 8021   Dentists' office

(G-182)
DSD PHOTOGRAPHY INC
43 Wicklow Rd (19701-6349)
PHONE..............................678 622-5910
EMP: 5 **EST:** 2018
SALES (est): 119.41K **Privately Held**
SIC: 7221   Photographer, still or video

(G-183)
DUNCAN S CONCRETE
324 N Red Lion Ter (19701-1029)
PHONE..............................302 395-1552
EMP: 5 **EST:** 2010
SALES (est): 242.48K **Privately Held**
SIC: 1771   Concrete work

(G-184)
DYNASTY STYLING STUDIOS LLC
1661 Pulaski Hwy (19701-1453)
PHONE..............................302 595-3042
EMP: 5 **EST:** 2018
SALES (est): 418.1K **Privately Held**
Web: www.dynastystylingstudios.com
SIC: 7231   Hairdressers

(G-185)
EAGLE ERECTORS INC
3500 Wrangle Hill Rd (19701-1843)
PHONE..............................302 832-9586
Al Klerlein, *Pr*
John Klerlein, *VP*
EMP: 19 **EST:** 1993
SQ FT: 30,000
SALES (est): 2.87MM **Privately Held**
Web: www.eagleerectors.com
SIC: 3441 3312   Fabricated structural metal; Blast furnaces and steel mills

(G-186)
EAK CONSTRUCTION INC
2806 Christiana Mdws (19701-2854)
PHONE..............................302 893-8497
EMP: 5 **EST:** 2011
SALES (est): 451.32K **Privately Held**
SIC: 1521   Single-family housing construction

(G-187)
EALING MEDIA & TECH (US) LTD
139 Rickey Blvd (19701-2540)
PHONE..............................909 576-4828
Dingjian Zhang, *Prin*
EMP: 5 **EST:** 2018
SALES (est): 284.68K **Privately Held**
SIC: 5092   Toys and games

(G-188)
EARTHSHIP LLC
465 Carson Dr (19701-1314)
PHONE..............................239 850-8682
EMP: 6 **EST:** 2017
SALES (est): 67.93K **Privately Held**
Web: www.earthship.com
SIC: 8741   Construction management

(G-189)
EAST COAST GAMES INC
24 Eaton Pl (19701-2370)
PHONE..............................302 838-0669
James Servia, *Pr*
EMP: 10 **EST:** 2003
SALES (est): 735.16K **Privately Held**
SIC: 3577   Computer peripheral equipment, nec

Bear - New Castle County (G-190)   GEOGRAPHIC SECTION

(G-190)
EAST WEST ENGINEERING INC
130 Wynnefield Rd (19701-4854)
P.O. Box 32 (19701-0032)
PHONE..................302 528-0652
William W Li, *Pr*
EMP: 7 **EST:** 2008
SALES (est): 405.88K **Privately Held**
Web: www.eastwestengineer.com
SIC: 8711 Consulting engineer

(G-191)
EASTERN MAIL TRANSPORT INC
900 Julian Ln (19701-2277)
PHONE..................302 838-0500
Byron D Williams, *Pr*
Marjorie Williams, *VP*
EMP: 15 **EST:** 1980
SALES (est): 565.38K **Privately Held**
SIC: 4213 4212 Trucking, except local; Mail carriers, contract

(G-192)
ECONOTRANSFER COMPANY INC
451 Carson Dr (19701-1314)
PHONE..................302 365-6664
EMP: 7 **EST:** 2017
SALES (est): 917.62K **Privately Held**
Web: www.econotransfer.com
SIC: 5099 Durable goods, nec

(G-193)
EDDIE SIMPSON STANLEY CONTG
104 Northwind Rd (19701-1280)
PHONE..................302 276-0569
Eddie Simpson Stanley, *Owner*
EMP: 6 **EST:** 2016
SALES (est): 89.62K **Privately Held**
Web: www.estanleycontracting.com
SIC: 1799 Special trade contractors, nec

(G-194)
EDGAR SILVESTRE PAINTING SVC
230 Landau Way (19701-1144)
PHONE..................302 670-7702
Edgar Silbestre, *Prin*
EMP: 5 **EST:** 2014
SALES (est): 65.62K **Privately Held**
SIC: 1721 Painting and paper hanging

(G-195)
EDLYNCARE LLC
Also Called: Home Healthcare Agency
821 Seymour Rd (19701-1121)
PHONE..................267 474-0486
Linda Agyapong, *Ex Dir*
EMP: 70 **EST:** 2011
SALES (est): 4.82MM **Privately Held**
Web: www.edlyncare.com
SIC: 8059 Personal care home, with health care

(G-196)
EDWARD PAPIRO
4 Heagy Ct (19701-2041)
PHONE..................302 757-9813
Edward Papiro, *Prin*
EMP: 5 **EST:** 2016
SALES (est): 167.26K **Privately Held**
SIC: 0781 Landscape services

(G-197)
EDYTHE L PRIDGEN
450 S Hyde Pl (19701-1070)
PHONE..................302 652-8887
EMP: 4 **EST:** 2016
SALES (est): 92.3K **Privately Held**
SIC: 2752 Commercial printing, lithographic

(G-198)
EIDP INC
Also Called: Dupont
407 Cheer Ct (19701-3366)
PHONE..................302 695-7141
Ellen Kullman, *Brnch Mgr*
EMP: 6
SALES (corp-wide): 17.23B **Publicly Held**
Web: www.dupont.com
SIC: 2879 Agricultural chemicals, nec
HQ: Eidp, Inc.
9330 Zionsville Rd
Indianapolis IN 46268
833 267-8382

(G-199)
ELANCO INC
723 Rue Madora Ste 6 (19701-2597)
PHONE..................302 731-8500
Anthony Gonzon, *Prin*
EMP: 5 **EST:** 2008
SALES (est): 785.31K **Privately Held**
Web: www.elancoheatexchangers.com
SIC: 3443 Fabricated plate work (boiler shop)

(G-200)
ELKTON BEAR DENTAL
34 Waterton Dr (19701-4916)
PHONE..................302 836-1670
Jessica Baker, *Prin*
EMP: 6 **EST:** 2018
SALES (est): 171.19K **Privately Held**
Web: www.elktonbeardental.com
SIC: 8021 Dentists' office

(G-201)
EMITT LLC
121 Hadrian Close (19701-8308)
PHONE..................302 757-2353
EMP: 10 **EST:** 2021
SALES (est): 59.21K **Privately Held**
SIC: 7999 7389 Physical fitness instruction; Business Activities at Non-Commercial Site

(G-202)
ENCHANTED CHILD CARE INTL INC
Also Called: Celebree Learning Centers
1205 Quintilio Dr (19701-6005)
PHONE..................302 834-0436
Lisa Henkel, *Brnch Mgr*
EMP: 5
Web: www.celebree.com
SIC: 8351 Group day care center
PA: Celebree Holding, Inc.
1306 Bellona Ave Ste A
Lutherville Timonium MD 21093

(G-203)
ENVIROTECH LLC
13 Bryan Cir (19701-6359)
P.O. Box 1276 (19701-7276)
PHONE..................302 834-5011
Benjamin Smith, *Prin*
EMP: 8 **EST:** 2010
SALES (est): 999.12K
SALES (corp-wide): 3.28B **Publicly Held**
Web: www.envirotech.com
SIC: 3625 Control equipment, electric
HQ: Itt Llc
1133 Westchester Ave N-100
White Plains NY 10604
914 641-2000

(G-204)
ENVISION IT PUBLICATIONS LLC
Also Called: Stylish Stylus, The
1148 Pulaski Hwy (19701-1306)
PHONE..................800 329-9411
Candice Huddy, *Pr*
Thomas Kenny, *VP*
EMP: 2 **EST:** 2009
SALES (est): 99.57K **Privately Held**
SIC: 2721 8999 7389 8732 Periodicals, publishing and printing; Commercial and literary writings; Apparel designers, commercial; Survey service: marketing, location, etc.

(G-205)
EQUITY LIFESTYLE
205 Joan Dr (19701-1300)
PHONE..................302 595-2833
EMP: 5 **EST:** 2017
SALES (est): 113.48K **Privately Held**
SIC: 6512 Nonresidential building operators

(G-206)
EROSION CONTROL SERVICES DE
1432 Elk Way (19701-3707)
PHONE..................302 218-8913
Robert Mcgowan, *Pr*
EMP: 10 **EST:** 2008
SALES (est): 315.06K **Privately Held**
SIC: 1731 Environmental system control installation

(G-207)
EUGENE CUMMINGS PC
27 Craig Rd (19701-1125)
PHONE..................312 984-0144
Eugene Cummings, *Owner*
EMP: 7 **EST:** 1996
SALES (est): 493.46K **Privately Held**
SIC: 8111 General practice law office

(G-208)
EVAN W SMITH FUNERAL SERVICES
219 Niobrara Ln (19701-4805)
PHONE..................302 494-1847
Laura Smith, *Prin*
EMP: 5 **EST:** 2018
SALES (est): 64.04K **Privately Held**
Web: www.evanwsmithfuneralservices.com
SIC: 7261 Funeral home

(G-209)
EVANS CHARLES CONTRACTING
509 Southwind Rd (19701-1286)
PHONE..................701 340-9530
Charles Evans, *Owner*
EMP: 5 **EST:** 2009
SALES (est): 228.07K **Privately Held**
SIC: 5082 General construction machinery and equipment

(G-210)
EVANS PAVING LLC
828 Sparrow Ln (19701-1110)
PHONE..................302 322-6863
EMP: 5 **EST:** 2019
SALES (est): 490.23K **Privately Held**
Web: www.evanspavingllc.com
SIC: 1611 Surfacing and paving

(G-211)
EVCO AUTO INC DBA A TO Z AUTO
469 County Rd (19701-1811)
PHONE..................302 595-3078
EMP: 5 **EST:** 2017
SALES (est): 66.94K **Privately Held**
SIC: 7538 General automotive repair shops

(G-212)
EVERLAST INTERACTIVE LLC
515 Equinox Dr (19701-6819)
PHONE..................347 992-3783
John Curtis, *Prin*
EMP: 5 **EST:** 2016
SALES (est): 73.8K **Privately Held**
Web: www.everlastin.com
SIC: 7374 Computer graphics service

(G-213)
EWS FUNERAL HOME
219 Niobrara Ln (19701-4805)
PHONE..................302 494-1847
Evan Smith, *Prin*
EMP: 5 **EST:** 2017
SALES (est): 64.49K **Privately Held**
SIC: 7261 Funeral home

(G-214)
EXCEL EDUCATION DAY CARE LLC
234 Rickey Blvd (19701-2541)
PHONE..................302 832-1833
Tammy Nichols, *Owner*
EMP: 8 **EST:** 2017
SALES (est): 37.57K **Privately Held**
SIC: 7032 Sporting and recreational camps

(G-215)
EXPEDIA CRUISESHIPCENTERS
126 Foxhunt Dr (19701-2535)
PHONE..................302 444-8447
EMP: 6 **EST:** 2014
SALES (est): 260.52K **Privately Held**
SIC: 4724 Travel agencies

(G-216)
EXPERIENCE SAIL LLC
168 Willamette Dr (19701-4802)
PHONE..................302 545-8149
EMP: 5 **EST:** 2015
SALES (est): 76.88K **Privately Held**
Web: www.experiencesail.com
SIC: 7999 Fishing boats, party: operation

(G-217)
F & S BOAT WORKS
353 Summit Pointe Cir (19701-2604)
PHONE..................302 838-5500
James Floyd, *Owner*
EMP: 12 **EST:** 1999
SALES (est): 637.63K **Privately Held**
Web: www.fsyachts.com
SIC: 3732 Boats, fiberglass: building and repairing

(G-218)
FACTORS ETC INC
1218 Pulaski Hwy Ste 484 (19701-4300)
PHONE..................302 834-1625
Harry Lee Geissler Junior, *Pr*
EMP: 8 **EST:** 1973
SALES (est): 133.28K **Privately Held**
SIC: 2752 2759 Transfers, decalcomania or dry: lithographed; Screen printing

(G-219)
FAIR INSURANCE AGENCY INC
881 Pulaski Hwy (19701-1252)
P.O. Box 655 (19701-0655)
PHONE..................302 395-0740
Latannia Fair, *Prin*
EMP: 6 **EST:** 2004
SALES (est): 271.08K **Privately Held**
Web: www.savers-rooter.com
SIC: 6411 Insurance agents, nec

(G-220)
FAIRWINDS BAPTIST CHURCH INC
Also Called: Fairwinds Christian School
801 Seymour Rd (19701-1121)
PHONE..................302 322-1029
Pastor Carlo Destefano, *Prin*
EMP: 7 **EST:** 1953
SALES (est): 990.91K **Privately Held**
Web: www.fairwindsbaptist.com

GEOGRAPHIC SECTION
Bear - New Castle County (G-249)

SIC: 8661 8699 Baptist Church; Charitable organization

(G-221)
FAVHOMETHEATER
11 Monferrato Ct (19701-2530)
PHONE.................................302 897-7168
EMP: 6 EST: 2014
SALES (est): 95.79K Privately Held
SIC: 1731 Fiber optic cable installation

(G-222)
FAZE II INC
881 Pulaski Hwy (19701-1252)
PHONE.................................302 328-7891
Kanu Kingsley, CEO
EMP: 5 EST: 2015
SALES (est): 193.54K Privately Held
SIC: 6531 Real estate agents and managers

(G-223)
FEENEY CHROPRACTIC CARE CTR PA
Also Called: Feeney Chrprctic Care Cntre PA
835 Pulaski Hwy (19701-1240)
PHONE.................................302 328-0200
John Feeney, Owner
EMP: 7 EST: 1995
SQ FT: 5,000
SALES (est): 265.7K Privately Held
Web: www.feeneychiropractic.com
SIC: 8041 Offices and clinics of chiropractors

(G-224)
FIRST CHOICE HEALTH CARE INC
12 Foxhunt Dr (19701-2534)
PHONE.................................302 836-6150
Ronald Saggese, Pr
EMP: 7 EST: 1991
SQ FT: 1,400
SALES (est): 361.15K Privately Held
SIC: 8041 Offices and clinics of chiropractors

(G-225)
FIRST MONTGOMERY PROPERTIES
Also Called: Fox Run Apartments
900 Woodchuck Pl (19701-2775)
PHONE.................................302 834-8272
Kelly Crowley, Mgr
EMP: 20
SALES (corp-wide): 21.54MM Privately Held
Web: www.morgan-properties.com
SIC: 6531 6513 Real estate leasing and rentals; Apartment building operators
PA: First Montgomery Properties, Ltd.
160 Clubhouse Rd
King Of Prussia PA 19406
610 265-2800

(G-226)
FIRST STATE ENDOCRINOLOGY
1404 Olmsted Dr (19701-4957)
PHONE.................................302 836-6969
EMP: 6 EST: 2017
SALES (est): 62.67K Privately Held
SIC: 8011 Endocrinologist

(G-227)
FIRST STATE ENT ASSOCIATION
1011 Powell Ct (19701-4949)
PHONE.................................302 836-8961
Jagdeep Hundal, Prin
EMP: 10 EST: 2015
SALES (est): 96.36K Privately Held
SIC: 8011 Ears, nose, and throat specialist; physician/surgeon

(G-228)
FIRST STATE LANDSCAPING
214 Springwood Dr (19701-3602)
P.O. Box 1369 (19701-7369)
PHONE.................................302 420-8604
EMP: 6 EST: 2010
SALES (est): 201.72K Privately Held
Web: www.firststatelandscaping.com
SIC: 0781 Landscape services

(G-229)
FIRST STATE PHYSICIANS INC (PA)
12 Foxhunt Dr (19701-2534)
PHONE.................................302 836-6150
Kevin Mcdermott, Pr
EMP: 6 EST: 2001
SALES (est): 369.17K
SALES (corp-wide): 369.17K Privately Held
Web: www.firststatephysicians.com
SIC: 8041 Offices and clinics of chiropractors

(G-230)
FLADGER & ASSOCIATES INC
204 Stewards Ct (19701-2296)
PHONE.................................302 836-3100
Michael Fladger, CEO
Michael Fladger, Pr
EMP: 14 EST: 1992
SQ FT: 2,500
SALES (est): 2.36MM Privately Held
Web: www.fladgerassociates.net
SIC: 7361 Executive placement

(G-231)
FLASH TRAINING CENTER
1390 Red Lion Rd (19701-1819)
PHONE.................................302 943-4668
Dwayne Thomas, Prin
EMP: 7 EST: 2011
SALES (est): 80.12K Privately Held
Web: www.flashtrainingde.com
SIC: 7991 Health club

(G-232)
FLOWRITE INC
Also Called: Flowrite Plumbing
102 Country Woods Dr (19701-1436)
PHONE.................................302 547-5657
Bill Ebert, Prin
EMP: 9 EST: 1998
SALES (est): 974.04K Privately Held
Web: www.flowritedelaware.com
SIC: 1711 Plumbing contractors

(G-233)
FOUNDING PRINCIPALS LLC
936 King James Ct (19701-4737)
PHONE.................................917 693-7533
Alana Williams, Managing Member
EMP: 5
SALES (est): 71.79K Privately Held
SIC: 8742 7389 Business planning and organizing services; Business Activities at Non-Commercial Site

(G-234)
FOX RUN AUTOMOTIVE INC
610 Connor Blvd (19701-1745)
PHONE.................................302 834-1200
EMP: 17 EST: 1994
SQ FT: 7,000
SALES (est): 2.1MM Privately Held
Web: www.foxrunauto.com
SIC: 7538 General automotive repair shops

(G-235)
FRANK AUSTIN
250 Mariners Way (19701-2292)
PHONE.................................302 832-9167
Frank Austin, Owner
EMP: 6 EST: 2018
SALES (est): 68.49K Privately Held
SIC: 8049 Offices of health practitioner

(G-236)
FRANK FALCO MD
Also Called: Comprhnsive Spine Spt Medicine
100 Becks Woods Dr Ste 102 (19701-3835)
PHONE.................................302 392-6501
EMP: 10 EST: 1997
SALES (est): 280.01K Privately Held
SIC: 8011 Physicians' office, including specialists

(G-237)
FREDS STORES TENNESSEE INC (PA)
Also Called: Fred's
27 Crimson King Dr (19701-2392)
P.O. Box 2153 (35287-0002)
PHONE.................................800 746-7287
Michael J Hayes, CEO
▲ EMP: 600 EST: 2018
SALES (est): 228.38MM
SALES (corp-wide): 228.38MM Privately Held
SIC: 5331 4731 Variety stores; Freight transportation arrangement

(G-238)
FREEDOM DRAIN CLG PIPE SVCS LL
6 S Muirfield Ln (19701-4754)
PHONE.................................484 480-1368
Isael Martinez, Managing Member
EMP: 6 EST: 2021
SALES (est): 491.49K Privately Held
SIC: 1711 Plumbing contractors

(G-239)
FULL SUPPORT TECHNOLOGIES LLC
930 Mather Dr (19701-4942)
PHONE.................................302 832-2307
Reverend Ayoolu Odumosu, Prin
EMP: 5 EST: 2019
SALES (est): 106.92K Privately Held
SIC: 8399 Advocacy group

(G-240)
FULL-TILT SECURITY
238 Cornwell Dr (19701-3128)
PHONE.................................302 722-0275
Khimula Taylor, Prin
EMP: 5 EST: 2019
SALES (est): 40.76K Privately Held
SIC: 7993 Video game arcade

(G-241)
FURNITURE WHL CONNECTION INC
Also Called: Furniture Solution
1890 Pulaski Hwy (19701-1710)
PHONE.................................302 836-6000
EMP: 18 EST: 1994
SQ FT: 8,000
SALES (est): 1.72MM Privately Held
Web: www.furnituresolution.com
SIC: 5712 5021 Mattresses; Furniture

(G-242)
FUTURE PROMISES FOUNDATION
1745 Bear Corbitt Rd (19701-1528)
P.O. Box 843 (19701-0843)
PHONE.................................302 365-5735
EMP: 5 EST: 2018
SALES (est): 38.73K Privately Held
Web: www.futurepromises.org
SIC: 8641 Civic and social associations

(G-243)
G PARKER CONTRACTING
225 Shorewind Rd (19701-1288)
PHONE.................................302 304-2940
Gene Parker, Prin
EMP: 5 EST: 2017
SALES (est): 95.27K Privately Held
SIC: 1799 Special trade contractors, nec

(G-244)
G2 GROUP INC
Also Called: G2 Lab Group
88 Loblolly Ln (19701-2167)
PHONE.................................302 836-4202
Gerald V Holmes, Pr
John K Holmes, VP
Susan D Holmes, Sec
EMP: 7 EST: 2007
SALES (est): 466.44K Privately Held
Web: www.g2grouplab.com
SIC: 5712 1751 Customized furniture and cabinets; Cabinet building and installation

(G-245)
GAMMA THETA LMBDA EDCATN FNDTI
2 N Sherman Dr (19701-3087)
P.O. Box 25209 (19899-5209)
PHONE.................................302 983-9429
Michael Yancey, Pr
Charles Baylor Junior, Prin
Kevin Mcallister, Prin
Reginald Hughes, Prin
El Cid Jones, Prin
EMP: 6 EST: 2014
SALES (est): 147.01K Privately Held
Web: www.gtledf.org
SIC: 4832 Educational

(G-246)
GATEWAY INTERNATIONAL 360 LLC
159 Meridian Blvd (19701-6841)
PHONE.................................302 250-4990
EMP: 10 EST: 2015
SALES (est): 1.01MM Privately Held
Web: www.gatewayintl360.com
SIC: 8742 Management consulting services

(G-247)
GENESIS AUTOMOBILE ACQUIRERS
138 Banff St (19701-4708)
PHONE.................................757 717-1673
Herbert Okine, Owner
EMP: 5 EST: 2017
SALES (est): 28.25K Privately Held
SIC: 7538 General automotive repair shops

(G-248)
GL ROBINS CO INC
Also Called: Supercuts
1233 Quintilio Dr (19701-6005)
PHONE.................................302 834-1272
Stacey Noble, Brnch Mgr
EMP: 8
SALES (corp-wide): 4.5MM Privately Held
Web: www.supercuts.com
SIC: 7231 Unisex hair salons
PA: Gl Robins Co Inc
4919 Township Line Rd # 250
Drexel Hill PA 19026
610 399-4400

(G-249)
GLASGOW SHOPPING CENTER CORP
2750 Wrangle Hill Rd (19701-1732)
PHONE.................................302 836-1503
W Thomas Peoples, VP
Robert C Peoples Junior, VP
Harrison B Peoples, VP

Bear - New Castle County (G-250) — GEOGRAPHIC SECTION

EMP: 5 EST: 1983
SQ FT: 2,000
SALES (est): 520K **Privately Held**
SIC: 6512 Commercial and industrial building operation

(G-250)
GODDESS SCENT CANDLES LLC
3 Berwick Ln (19701-4767)
PHONE..................................973 885-0606
EMP: 6
SALES (est): 86.31K **Privately Held**
SIC: 5199 7389 Candles; Business services, nec

(G-251)
GOLDMINE ENTERPRISES INC
930 Woods Rd (19701-2106)
PHONE..................................302 834-4314
▲ EMP: 2 EST: 1981
SALES (est): 107.6K **Privately Held**
SIC: 3961 Jewelry apparel, non-precious metals

(G-252)
GOTSHADEONLINE INC
Also Called: Formula One Tinting Graphics
1700 Firedancer Ln (19701-5216)
PHONE..................................302 832-8468
Sylvia Gourley, *Pr*
EMP: 6 EST: 2008
SALES (est): 548.21K **Privately Held**
Web: www.gotshadeonline.com
SIC: 1799 3993 7319 Glass tinting, architectural or automotive; Signs and advertising specialties; Transit advertising services

(G-253)
GOTTI BOYZ ENTERTAINMENT
1314 Elk Way (19701-2747)
PHONE..................................302 409-2901
Naiseem Butts, *CEO*
EMP: 5 EST: 2021
SALES (est): 244.68K **Privately Held**
SIC: 2741 Music book and sheet music publishing

(G-254)
GREAT MINDS
54 Lochview Dr (19701-1353)
PHONE..................................302 834-4906
Jennifer Harry, *Owner*
EMP: 8 EST: 2015
SALES (est): 72.52K **Privately Held**
SIC: 8351 Preschool center

(G-255)
GREAT NEW BGNNNGS ST ANDREWS I
Also Called: Early Education
14 Saint Andrews Dr (19701-4762)
PHONE..................................302 838-1000
Linda Clark, *Pr*
EMP: 35 EST: 2005
SALES (est): 1.96MM **Privately Held**
Web: www.gnbkids.com
SIC: 8351 Preschool center

(G-256)
GREEN DOT CAPITAL LLC
203 Cornwell Dr (19701-3103)
PHONE..................................302 395-0500
Ernest Green, *Prin*
EMP: 5 EST: 2017
SALES (est): 245.06K **Privately Held**
SIC: 6799 Investors, nec

(G-257)
H & C AUTO CARE
1280 Porter Rd (19701-1311)
PHONE..................................302 494-8989
Hernandez Nelson, *Prin*
EMP: 6 EST: 2017
SALES (est): 28.25K **Privately Held**
SIC: 7538 General automotive repair shops

(G-258)
H & M ACOUSTICAL SERVICES INC
777 White Rock Rd (19701-1058)
PHONE..................................302 218-7783
Jason Henderson, *Owner*
EMP: 9 EST: 2006
SALES (est): 22.28K **Privately Held**
Web: www.handmacoustical.com
SIC: 1742 Drywall

(G-259)
H & R BLOCK INC
Also Called: H & R Block
54 Foxhunt Dr (19701-2534)
PHONE..................................302 836-2700
EMP: 5
SALES (corp-wide): 3.47B **Publicly Held**
Web: www.hrblock.com
SIC: 7291 Tax return preparation services
PA: H & R Block, Inc.
    1 H And R Block Way
    Kansas City MO 64105
    816 854-3000

(G-260)
H WELLS PAVING & SEALCOATING
712 Cardinal Ave (19701-1104)
PHONE..................................302 857-9243
Henry Wells, *Prin*
EMP: 7 EST: 2014
SALES (est): 214.26K **Privately Held**
Web: www.hwellspavingandsealcoating.com
SIC: 1611 Surfacing and paving

(G-261)
H WELLS PAVING & SEALCOATING
149 Hadrian Close (19701-8308)
PHONE..................................302 838-2727
EMP: 5 EST: 2018
SALES (est): 108.95K **Privately Held**
SIC: 1611 Surfacing and paving

(G-262)
HAGE TOOL AND MACHINE INC
3415 Wrangle Hill Rd Ste 7 (19701-4812)
PHONE..................................302 836-4850
George Kennedy Junior, *Owner*
EMP: 5 EST: 2007
SALES (est): 488.62K **Privately Held**
Web: www.hagetool.com
SIC: 3599 Machine shop, jobbing and repair

(G-263)
HALPERN EYE ASSOCIATES INC
1237 Quintilio Dr (19701-6005)
PHONE..................................302 838-0800
Dana Hobbs, *Brnch Mgr*
EMP: 8
SALES (corp-wide): 9.06MM **Privately Held**
Web: www.myeyedr.com
SIC: 8042 Specialized optometrists
PA: Halpern Eye Associates, Inc.
    885 S Governors Ave
    Dover DE 19904
    302 734-5861

(G-264)
HAND STONE MASSAGE FACIAL SPA
213 Governors Pl (19701-3026)
PHONE..................................302 261-9716
Brittany Negreann, *Mgr*
EMP: 6 EST: 2016
SALES (est): 44.93K **Privately Held**
Web: www.handandstone.com
SIC: 7299 Massage parlor

(G-265)
HARVARD ENVIRONMENTAL INC
760 Pulaski Hwy (19701-5200)
PHONE..................................302 326-2333
Wesley Morrison, *Pr*
EMP: 15 EST: 1993
SQ FT: 2,500
SALES (est): 976.67K **Privately Held**
Web: www.harvardenvironmental.com
SIC: 8748 Environmental consultant

(G-266)
HEALING ADULTS & ADOLESCENTS
Also Called: Haart Program
3560 Wrangle Hill Rd (19701-1843)
PHONE..................................302 836-4000
EMP: 10 EST: 2015
SALES (est): 267.76K **Privately Held**
Web: www.haartprogram.org
SIC: 8049 Offices of health practitioner

(G-267)
HEALTHCARE OPRTONS MGT ENTERPR
221 Mariners Way (19701-2293)
PHONE..................................302 832-9572
Joseph Richichi, *Prin*
EMP: 6 EST: 2019
SALES (est): 97.54K **Privately Held**
SIC: 8099 Health and allied services, nec

(G-268)
HEIDIS ACADEMY OF PRFRMG ARTS
1218 Pulaski Hwy (19701-4318)
PHONE..................................302 293-7868
Heidi Yancey, *Ex Dir*
Joanne Irby, *Admn*
EMP: 10 EST: 2007
SALES (est): 283.92K **Privately Held**
SIC: 7922 Performing arts center production

(G-269)
HERBERT MRS SHERYL A
135 Emerald Ridge Dr (19701-2280)
PHONE..................................215 668-1849
Sheryl A Herbert Ma, *Prin*
EMP: 7 EST: 2019
SALES (est): 120.11K **Privately Held**
SIC: 8011 Offices and clinics of medical doctors

(G-270)
HERTIAGE BUILDERS & IMPROVEMEN
9 Linn Ct (19701-1351)
PHONE..................................302 275-8675
Tom Miller, *Owner*
EMP: 5 EST: 1999
SALES (est): 195.63K **Privately Held**
SIC: 1799 Special trade contractors, nec

(G-271)
HERTRCHS FMLY AUTO DEALERSHIPS
100 Buckley Blvd (19701-1257)
PHONE..................................302 276-2554
EMP: 7 EST: 2019
SALES (est): 28.25K **Privately Held**
Web: www.hertrchs.com
SIC: 7538 General automotive repair shops

(G-272)
HIGHDEF TRANSPORTATION LLC
8 Dover Ct (19701-1618)
PHONE..................................610 212-8596
Samuel Sanders, *CEO*
EMP: 7 EST: 2019
SALES (est): 246.1K **Privately Held**
SIC: 8748 Business consulting, nec

(G-273)
HIGHFIELD ELECTRIC LLC
304 Genoa Dr (19701-2522)
PHONE..................................302 836-4300
EMP: 6 EST: 2019
SALES (est): 486.29K **Privately Held**
Web: www.highfieldelectric.com
SIC: 7539 Electrical services

(G-274)
HIGHLAND CONSTRUCTION LLC
3415 Wrangle Hill Rd Ste 10 (19701-4812)
PHONE..................................302 286-6990
EMP: 17 EST: 2001
SQ FT: 4,800
SALES (est): 3.77MM **Privately Held**
Web: www.highlandconstructionllc.com
SIC: 1611 1771 4212 Concrete construction: roads, highways, sidewalks, etc.; Blacktop (asphalt) work; Local trucking, without storage

(G-275)
HILLARY J WHITE SOHO SLON SPA
1582 Red Lion Rd (19701-1816)
P.O. Box 516 (19701-0516)
PHONE..................................302 838-2110
Hillary J White, *Prin*
EMP: 5 EST: 2013
SALES (est): 52.05K **Privately Held**
Web: www.hjwsalonspa.com
SIC: 7231 Cosmetology and personal hygiene salons

(G-276)
HNS PLUMBING SERVICES LLC
418 Pencader Ln (19701-2304)
PHONE..................................302 650-9010
EMP: 14 EST: 2016
SALES (est): 866.4K **Privately Held**
SIC: 1711 Plumbing contractors

(G-277)
HOLISTIC ELEVATION LLC
2220 Porter Rd (19701-2022)
PHONE..................................302 278-0026
EMP: 5 EST: 2017
SALES (est): 245.59K **Privately Held**
Web: www.holisticelevation.org
SIC: 8748 8093 Educational consultant; Mental health clinic, outpatient

(G-278)
HOME BASE ARMS
2126 Old Kirkwood Rd (19701-2249)
PHONE..................................302 983-6816
William Tucker, *Prin*
EMP: 5 EST: 2016
SALES (est): 60.83K **Privately Held**
SIC: 7699 Gun services

(G-279)
HOUSE OF HARMONY HAIR SALON
35 Killane St (19701-4703)
PHONE..................................302 420-4565
Kimberly Harmon, *Prin*
EMP: 5 EST: 2016
SALES (est): 45.31K **Privately Held**
SIC: 7231 Hairdressers

GEOGRAPHIC SECTION

Bear - New Castle County (G-310)

(G-280)
I AM CONSULTING GROUP INC
12 Dunleary Dr (19701-6355)
P.O. Box 884 (19701-0884)
PHONE..............................302 521-4999
Valerie Brown Baul, *Pr*
EMP: 10 **EST:** 2010
SALES (est): 427.31K **Privately Held**
SIC: 8748 Business consulting, nec

(G-281)
IDEASPACE OPEN MNDS FOUNDATION
106 Bernice Dr (19701-2000)
PHONE..............................808 444-4578
EMP: 6 **EST:** 2018
SALES (est): 98.96K **Privately Held**
SIC: 8641 Civic and social associations

(G-282)
IJN HEALTH SYSTEMS LLC
603 Parkman Ct (19701-4940)
PHONE..............................855 202-5993
EMP: 11 **EST:** 2019
SALES (est): 517.45K **Privately Held**
Web: www.ijnhealthsystems.com
SIC: 8082 Home health care services

(G-283)
IKARUS NEST INC
192 Bear Christiana Rd (19701-1196)
PHONE..............................415 727-2401
Ishan Kumar, *CEO*
EMP: 10
SALES (est): 348.32K **Privately Held**
SIC: 7371 Custom computer programming services

(G-284)
INKA AND EZRA FOUNDATION INC ✪
719 Lexington Dr (19701-2582)
PHONE..............................301 535-1000
Annick S Fonkoua, *Pr*
EMP: 5 **EST:** 2022
SALES (est): 219.98K **Privately Held**
Web: www.inkaandezrafoundation.org
SIC: 6732 7389 Trusts: educational, religious, etc.; Business services, nec

(G-285)
INNPROS INC
Also Called: AmericInn Lodge & Suites
875 Pulaski Hwy (19701-1252)
PHONE..............................302 326-2500
Ann Watkins, *CEO*
Ginny Wilkins, *Genl Mgr*
EMP: 10 **EST:** 2002
SALES (est): 437.66K **Privately Held**
SIC: 7041 Membership-basis organization hotels

(G-286)
INTERNTIONAL MKT SUPPLIERS INC
Also Called: IMS
400 Carson Dr (19701-1314)
PHONE..............................302 392-1840
Bruce Hugelmeyer, *CEO*
Francis Nuzzi, *Pr*
EMP: 12 **EST:** 1997
SQ FT: 21,000
SALES (est): 4.95MM **Privately Held**
Web: www.registrar-transfers.com
SIC: 5169 Chemicals and allied products, nec

(G-287)
INUMSOFT INC
2500 Wrangle Hill Rd Ste 222 (19701-3836)
PHONE..............................302 533-5403
Pbvs Lakshmi Meka, *Pr*
EMP: 6 **EST:** 2007
SALES (est): 460K **Privately Held**
SIC: 7371 7379 Computer software development; Computer related consulting services

(G-288)
IODPARTS TECHNOLOGIES INC
512 Liam Pl (19701-2442)
PHONE..............................732 369-9939
EMP: 8 **EST:** 2018
SALES (est): 896.69K **Privately Held**
Web: www.iodparts.com
SIC: 5065 Electronic parts

(G-289)
IRENE C SZETO MD LLC
121 Becks Woods Dr Ste 100 (19701-3851)
PHONE..............................302 832-1560
Irene C Szeto Md, *Owner*
EMP: 5 **EST:** 2000
SALES (est): 427.6K **Privately Held**
SIC: 8011 Internal medicine, physician/surgeon

(G-290)
ISAAC F DAVIS
40 Blue Spruce Dr (19701-4128)
PHONE..............................302 656-2050
Isaac F Davis, *Pr*
EMP: 5 **EST:** 2010
SALES (est): 190.81K **Privately Held**
SIC: 7389 Business Activities at Non-Commercial Site

(G-291)
ITS R JOY LLC
11 Shawn Ln (19701-6334)
PHONE..............................215 315-8300
EMP: 30 **EST:** 2019
SALES (est): 772.04K **Privately Held**
Web: www.itsrjoy.com
SIC: 7389 7342 Business Activities at Non-Commercial Site; Disinfecting services

(G-292)
J & K AUTO REPAIR INC
Also Called: J&K Fleet Service
3310 Wrangle Hill Rd Ste 109 (19701-1874)
PHONE..............................302 834-8025
EMP: 7 **EST:** 1989
SALES (est): 422.85K **Privately Held**
SIC: 7538 7539 General automotive repair shops; Brake services

(G-293)
J N HOOKER INC
Also Called: All About Kidz
1799 Pulaski Hwy (19701-1711)
PHONE..............................302 838-5650
Jahara Hooker, *Pr*
EMP: 24 **EST:** 2010
SQ FT: 9,000
SALES (est): 489.18K **Privately Held**
SIC: 8351 Child day care services

(G-294)
J N N FOUNDATION
175 Portside Ct (19701-2287)
PHONE..............................800 493-1069
EMP: 6 **EST:** 2018
SALES (est): 76.08K **Privately Held**
Web: www.jnnfoundation.org
SIC: 8641 Civic and social associations

(G-295)
JAED CORPORATION (PA)
Also Called: Studio Jaed
2500 Wrangle Hill Rd Ste 110 (19701-3840)
PHONE..............................302 832-1652
James A Hutchison Iii, *CEO*
Beatrice Cook, *CFO*
Edward Lupineck, *Sr VP*
Philip Conte, *Prin*
Joseph Skinner, *Prin*
EMP: 16 **EST:** 1978
SQ FT: 5,500
SALES (est): 2.87MM
SALES (corp-wide): 2.87MM **Privately Held**
Web: www.studiojaed.com
SIC: 8712 8711 Architectural engineering; Engineering services

(G-296)
JAIRUS ENTERPRISES INC
1218 Pulaski Hwy Ste 484 (19701-4300)
PHONE..............................302 834-1625
Richard Thomas, *Pr*
EMP: 5 **EST:** 1997
SQ FT: 6,000
SALES (est): 308.94K **Privately Held**
Web: www.jairussportswear.com
SIC: 2396 Screen printing on fabric articles

(G-297)
JAMES BOYLAND
1237 Quintilio Dr (19701-6005)
PHONE..............................302 838-0800
James Boyland, *Prin*
EMP: 8 **EST:** 2018
SALES (est): 180.9K **Privately Held**
SIC: 8011 Offices and clinics of medical doctors

(G-298)
JAMES PARKER CONTRACTING
1706 Bear Corbitt Rd (19701-1538)
PHONE..............................302 507-6200
EMP: 5 **EST:** 2017
SALES (est): 98.63K **Privately Held**
SIC: 1799 Special trade contractors, nec

(G-299)
JAYANT H SHUKLA DR
22 Kimmie Ct (19701-1746)
PHONE..............................302 834-0222
Jayant Shukla, *Prin*
EMP: 9 **EST:** 2004
SALES (est): 82.49K **Privately Held**
SIC: 8011 Offices and clinics of medical doctors

(G-300)
JAZZERCISE
Also Called: Jazzercise
345 School Bell Rd (19701-1135)
PHONE..............................302 690-3447
EMP: 7 **EST:** 2018
SALES (est): 99.08K **Privately Held**
Web: www.jazzercise.com
SIC: 7991 Aerobic dance and exercise classes

(G-301)
JBA ENTERPRISES LLC
109 Peace Ct W (19701-3372)
PHONE..............................302 834-6685
Charles Jones, *Managing Member*
EMP: 5 **EST:** 2019
SALES (est): 150K **Privately Held**
SIC: 7349 7389 Janitorial service, contract basis; Business Activities at Non-Commercial Site

(G-302)
JEFFERY BRANNAN
118 Countryside Ln (19701-2008)
PHONE..............................302 547-1659
Jeffery Brannan, *Prin*
EMP: 5 **EST:** 2018
SALES (est): 378.3K **Privately Held**
Web: www.brannanconstruction.com
SIC: 1521 General remodeling, single-family houses

(G-303)
JERRY O THOMPSON PRNTNG
4 Ogden Ct (19701-2056)
PHONE..............................302 832-1309
Jerry Thompson, *Prin*
EMP: 5 **EST:** 2010
SALES (est): 65.8K **Privately Held**
SIC: 2752 Commercial printing, lithographic

(G-304)
JESSICA L DESROSIERS
105 Nashua Ct (19701-3324)
PHONE..............................443 617-5152
Jessica Desrosiers, *Mgr*
EMP: 6 **EST:** 2017
SALES (est): 22.18K **Privately Held**
SIC: 8049 Offices of health practitioner

(G-305)
JJID INC
100 Julian Ln (19701-2274)
PHONE..............................302 836-0414
EMP: 50 **EST:** 1995
SALES (est): 28.7MM **Privately Held**
Web: www.jjid.com
SIC: 1611 1629 General contractor, highway and street construction; Waste water and sewage treatment plant construction

(G-306)
JMT INTER LLC
415 Aldwych Dr (19701-2586)
PHONE..............................302 312-5177
▲ **EMP:** 4 **EST:** 2009
SALES (est): 491.37K **Privately Held**
Web: www.jmtinter.com
SIC: 3411 Food and beverage containers

(G-307)
JOHN WASNIEWSKI III DMD
262 Foxhunt Dr (19701-2536)
PHONE..............................302 832-1371
EMP: 8 **EST:** 2018
SALES (est): 195.73K **Privately Held**
Web: www.drwasniewski.com
SIC: 8021 Dentists' office

(G-308)
JOHNS AUTO PARTS INC
10 Nick Ct (19701-1120)
PHONE..............................302 322-3273
John Elasic, *Pr*
Deborah Elasic, *VP*
EMP: 11 **EST:** 1984
SALES (est): 425.63K **Privately Held**
Web: www.lkqcorp.com
SIC: 5013 Automotive supplies and parts

(G-309)
JOHNSON SHAWANDA
Also Called: Jj's Lrng Exprnce Chldcare Ctr
114 Stoneridge Pl (19701-1952)
PHONE..............................302 722-1715
Shawanda Johnson, *Owner*
Keith Johnson, *Prin*
EMP: 6 **EST:** 2016
SALES (est): 29.69K **Privately Held**
SIC: 8351 Child day care services

(G-310)
JOSHI MEDICAL PA
417 Oregano Ct (19701-6019)

Bear - New Castle County (G-311)   GEOGRAPHIC SECTION

PHONE..........................302 838-8858
EMP: 6 EST: 2015
SALES (est): 161.18K **Privately Held**
SIC: **8099** Health and allied services, nec

(G-311)
JP MCFARLANE LLC
718 Seymour Rd (19701-1164)
PHONE..........................302 709-1515
EMP: 4 EST: 2012
SALES (est): 172.59K **Privately Held**
SIC: **3489** Ordnance and accessories, nec

(G-312)
JPMORGAN CHASE & CO
501 Bear Christiana Rd (19701-1050)
PHONE..........................800 935-9935
EMP: 5
SALES (corp-wide): 154.79B **Publicly Held**
Web: www.jpmorganchase.com
SIC: **6021** 6211 6162 6141 National commercial banks; Security brokers and dealers; Mortgage bankers and loan correspondents; Automobile loans, including insurance
PA: Jpmorgan Chase & Co.
383 Madison Ave
New York NY 10179
212 270-6000

(G-313)
JR ROBERT M THOMPSON DVM
3052 Wrangle Hill Rd (19701-1714)
PHONE..........................302 261-2683
Robert Thompson, *Owner*
EMP: 5 EST: 2018
SALES (est): 56.48K **Privately Held**
Web: www.lumspondanimalhospital.com
SIC: **0742** Animal hospital services, pets and other animal specialties

(G-314)
JSM TRANSPORT & HAULAGE LLC
33 Wellspring Dr (19701-1360)
P.O. Box 388 (19701-0388)
PHONE..........................302 836-8057
Jean M Milfort, *Prin*
EMP: 5 EST: 2016
SALES (est): 169.49K **Privately Held**
SIC: **4212** Light haulage and cartage, local

(G-315)
JT HOOVER CONCRETE INC
3415 Wrangle Hill Rd Ste 1 (19701-4812)
PHONE..........................302 832-2139
John T Hoover, *Pr*
EMP: 45 EST: 1986
SALES (est): 5.69MM **Privately Held**
Web: www.jthoover.com
SIC: **1771** Concrete work

(G-316)
JTH EXCAVATING INC
3415 Wrangle Hill Rd # 2 (19701-4812)
PHONE..........................302 832-7699
John T Hoover, *Pr*
EMP: 6 EST: 2015
SALES (est): 98.08K **Privately Held**
SIC: **1794** Excavation work

(G-317)
JUST ONE EMBROIDERER
17 Decidedly Ln (19701-3347)
PHONE..........................302 832-9655
Joe Loughlin, *Prin*
EMP: 4 EST: 2017
SALES (est): 100.28K **Privately Held**
SIC: **2395** Embroidery and art needlework

(G-318)
JV S CLEANING SERVICES
1148 Pulaski Hwy Ste 151 (19701-1305)
PHONE..........................302 345-7679
Joan Virgil, *Prin*
EMP: 5 EST: 2003
SALES (est): 70.86K **Privately Held**
SIC: **7349** Cleaning service, industrial or commercial

(G-319)
JW STRIPING
153 N Gabriel Dr (19701-4829)
PHONE..........................302 832-7762
John Whitcombe, *Prin*
EMP: 5 EST: 2012
SALES (est): 42.92K **Privately Held**
SIC: **7532** Lettering and painting services

(G-320)
JWR 1 LLC
11 Biltmore Ct (19701-4005)
PHONE..........................302 379-9951
Erin Rautio, *Owner*
EMP: 5 EST: 2015
SALES (est): 71.17K **Privately Held**
SIC: **7218** Industrial launderers

(G-321)
KAREN E STARR CPA
306 Carya Ct (19701-1755)
PHONE..........................302 834-1718
Karen Starr, *Prin*
EMP: 5 EST: 2007
SALES (est): 65.32K **Privately Held**
SIC: **8721** Certified public accountant

(G-322)
KATE G SHUMAKER
2500 Wrangle Hill Rd (19701-3836)
PHONE..........................302 327-1100
Kate Shumaker, *Prin*
EMP: 5 EST: 2007
SALES (est): 114.07K **Privately Held**
SIC: **8111** General practice attorney, lawyer

(G-323)
KATLYN CO CERAMICS
9 Moores Dr (19701-1402)
PHONE..........................302 528-1322
EMP: 3 EST: 2015
SALES (est): 105.92K **Privately Held**
SIC: **3269** Pottery products, nec

(G-324)
KELLY WALKER DDS
1991 Pulaski Hwy (19701-1708)
PHONE..........................302 832-2200
Kelly Walker, *Owner*
EMP: 5 EST: 2011
SALES (est): 488.12K **Privately Held**
Web: www.kellywalkerdds.com
SIC: **8021** Dentists' office

(G-325)
KENKAY INC
40 Decidedly Ln (19701-3354)
PHONE..........................302 838-7797
Kurt Lane, *Prin*
EMP: 5 EST: 2019
SALES (est): 201.92K **Privately Held**
SIC: **4215** Courier services, except by air

(G-326)
KEVIN GARBER
Also Called: Carpentry Unlimited
148 Carlotta Dr (19701-2104)
PHONE..........................302 834-0639
Kevin Garber, *Owner*
EMP: 8 EST: 1989
SALES (est): 514.54K **Privately Held**
Web: www.carpentryunlimiteddE.com
SIC: **1751** Carpentry work

(G-327)
KIDZ CHOICE LLC
1230 Pulaski Hwy (19701-1305)
PHONE..........................302 365-6787
EMP: 13 EST: 2019
SALES (est): 285.68K **Privately Held**
SIC: **8351** Child day care services

(G-328)
KIDZ INK
345 School Bell Rd (19701-1135)
PHONE..........................302 327-0686
EMP: 5
SALES (corp-wide): 4.11MM **Privately Held**
Web: www.kidzearlylearning.com
SIC: **8351** Child day care services
PA: Kidz Ink
1703 Porter Rd
Bear DE 19701
302 838-1500

(G-329)
KIDZ INK
14 Saint Andrews Dr (19701-4762)
PHONE..........................302 838-1000
EMP: 6
SALES (corp-wide): 4.11MM **Privately Held**
Web: www.kidzearlylearning.com
SIC: **8351** Child day care services
PA: Kidz Ink
1703 Porter Rd
Bear DE 19701
302 838-1500

(G-330)
KIDZ INK (PA)
1703 Porter Rd (19701-2119)
PHONE..........................302 838-1500
Linda Clark, *Pr*
EMP: 11 EST: 1998
SQ FT: 7,800
SALES (est): 4.11MM
SALES (corp-wide): 4.11MM **Privately Held**
Web: www.kidzearlylearning.com
SIC: **8351** Preschool center

(G-331)
KIRKLEY CONSTRUCTION LLC
109 Michael Ln (19701-2054)
PHONE..........................302 276-9795
Vincent Kirkley, *Prin*
EMP: 5 EST: 2017
SALES (est): 154.59K **Privately Held**
SIC: **1521** Single-family housing construction

(G-332)
KNIGHTS CLMBUS DEL STATE CNCIL
1 Wales Cir (19701-3101)
PHONE..........................302 836-8235
EMP: 5 EST: 2011
SALES (est): 58.97K **Privately Held**
Web: www.kofc.org
SIC: **8641** Fraternal associations

(G-333)
KORTECH CONSULTING INC
13 Primrose Dr (19701-6317)
PHONE..........................302 559-4612
Alioune Tounkara, *CEO*
EMP: 10 EST: 2015
SALES (est): 518.49K **Privately Held**
SIC: **7379** 7371 8742 8243 Computer related consulting services; Computer software development; Management consulting services; Software training, computer

(G-334)
KREATIVE SERVICES
3835 Wrangle Hill Rd (19701-1919)
PHONE..........................302 545-5030
Jamie Williams, *Prin*
EMP: 7 EST: 2010
SALES (est): 404.06K **Privately Held**
SIC: **1799** Fence construction

(G-335)
KW SOLAR SOLUTIONS INC
2444 Denny Rd (19701-2314)
PHONE..........................302 838-8400
Dale Wolf, *Pr*
EMP: 8 EST: 2004
SALES (est): 971.64K **Privately Held**
Web: www.kwsolar.net
SIC: **1711** Solar energy contractor

(G-336)
KW SOLAR SOLUTIONS INC
2444 Denny Rd (19701-2314)
PHONE..........................302 838-8400
Dale Wolf, *Pr*
EMP: 8 EST: 2012
SALES (est): 403.91K **Privately Held**
Web: www.kwsolar.net
SIC: **1711** Solar energy contractor

(G-337)
L & K REAL ESTATE LLC
4 Dornoch Ln (19701-4764)
PHONE..........................484 410-4898
EMP: 10 EST: 2021
SALES (est): 420.06K **Privately Held**
SIC: **8748** 7389 Business consulting, nec; Business Activities at Non-Commercial Site

(G-338)
LASER IMAGES OF DELAWARE INC
100 E Scotland Dr (19701-1756)
PHONE..........................302 836-8610
Ed Bell, *Pr*
Nancy Bell, *VP*
EMP: 7 EST: 1989
SQ FT: 5,000
SALES (est): 599.39K **Privately Held**
SIC: **7378** 5734 Computer and data processing equipment repair/maintenance; Computer software and accessories

(G-339)
LAWRENCE BOONE SELECTIONS LLC
Also Called: Boone Selections
434 Brandywine Dr (19701-1271)
PHONE..........................757 602-5173
Lawrence Boone, *Pt*
EMP: 5 EST: 2014
SALES (est): 109.6K **Privately Held**
SIC: **5182** Wine

(G-340)
LAZYBONES INC
11 Brighton Way (19701-2279)
PHONE..........................302 530-7114
Rob Johnson, *Mgr*
EMP: 6 EST: 2013
SALES (est): 244.55K **Privately Held**
Web: www.mylazybones.com
SIC: **7215** Laundry, coin-operated

GEOGRAPHIC SECTION

Bear - New Castle County (G-372)

(G-341)
LCB CONSULTING INC
204 Somerton Ct (19701-4868)
PHONE..................................302 836-1396
Bradley Lamonte, *Prin*
EMP: 5 **EST:** 2008
SALES (est): 82.45K **Privately Held**
SIC: 8748 Business consulting, nec

(G-342)
LEARNING CIRCLE CHILD CARE
765 Old Porter Rd (19701-1841)
PHONE..................................302 834-1473
Diane Callaway, *Owner*
EMP: 5 **EST:** 1998
SALES (est): 172.87K **Privately Held**
SIC: 8351 Child day care services

(G-343)
LEGEND ENTERPRISES LLC
1857 Pulaski Hwy (19701-1731)
PHONE..................................267 278-9892
EMP: 5 **EST:** 2016
SQ FT: 1,500
SALES (est): 223.96K **Privately Held**
SIC: 7389 Personal service agents, brokers, and bureaus

(G-344)
LEKUCHE AUTOS & GENERAL MERCH
717a Pulaski Hwy (19701-1236)
PHONE..................................302 887-6748
Lekuche Badmus, *Prin*
EMP: 6 **EST:** 2015
SALES (est): 342.36K **Privately Held**
SIC: 7538 General automotive repair shops

(G-345)
LENZINIFORDELAWARE
517 Equinox Dr (19701-6819)
PHONE..................................302 836-6287
EMP: 5 **EST:** 2014
SALES (est): 60.89K **Privately Held**
SIC: 7335 Commercial photography

(G-346)
LEOUNES KIRSTEN
1016 Brandywine Dr (19701-3208)
PHONE..................................302 229-5029
Kirsten H Leounes Lmt, *Owner*
EMP: 5 **EST:** 2018
SALES (est): 61.19K **Privately Held**
SIC: 8322 Individual and family services

(G-347)
LIFE BEHAVIORAL HLTH CONSULTA
709 Ellen Dr (19701-1128)
PHONE..................................302 312-6104
EMP: 6 **EST:** 2014
SALES (est): 95.74K **Privately Held**
SIC: 8099 Health and allied services, nec

(G-348)
LILY B LLC
127 George Ct (19701-1882)
PHONE..................................302 290-5223
EMP: 13 **EST:** 2011
SALES (est): 460.06K **Privately Held**
SIC: 7389 Business Activities at Non-Commercial Site

(G-349)
LIMESTONE OPEN MRI LLC
Also Called: Bear Mri & Imaging Center
101 Becks Woods Ste 103 (19701-3854)
PHONE..................................302 246-2001
EMP: 6
SALES (corp-wide): 1.51MM **Privately Held**

Web: www.bearmri.com
SIC: 8011 Radiologist
PA: Limestone Open Mri, Llc
      2060 Limestone Rd
      Wilmington DE 19808
      302 246-2001

(G-350)
LINDA PUTNAM DAY CARE
525 Deer Run (19701-2716)
PHONE..................................302 836-1033
Linda Putnam, *Prin*
EMP: 5 **EST:** 2005
SALES (est): 121.22K **Privately Held**
SIC: 8351 Child day care services

(G-351)
LNC CLEANING COMPANY LLC
1 Walnut Ct (19701-4130)
PHONE..................................302 437-6547
Lakeesha Smith, *Prin*
EMP: 5 **EST:** 2015
SALES (est): 51.96K **Privately Held**
SIC: 7699 Cleaning services

(G-352)
LOCAL LIFE MARKETING GROUP LLC
125 Rickey Blvd Unit 1253 (19701-8653)
PHONE..................................877 514-4052
Robert Greenawalt, *CEO*
Robert Greenawalt, *Managing Member*
EMP: 7 **EST:** 2020
SALES (est): 276.06K **Privately Held**
SIC: 8742 7389 Marketing consulting services; Business services, nec

(G-353)
LUCYS HOUSEKEPPERS
14 Meridian Blvd (19701-6805)
PHONE..................................302 893-9946
Lucy Navas, *Prin*
EMP: 5 **EST:** 2018
SALES (est): 56.97K **Privately Held**
SIC: 7699 Cleaning services

(G-354)
LUMS POND ANIMAL HOSPITAL INC
3052 Wrangle Hill Rd (19701-1714)
PHONE..................................302 836-5585
EMP: 50 **EST:** 1993
SALES (est): 1.84MM **Privately Held**
Web: www.lumspondanimalhospital.com
SIC: 0742 Animal hospital services, pets and other animal specialties

(G-355)
LUX SPA & NAILS
122 Foxhunt Dr (19701-2535)
PHONE..................................302 834-4899
EMP: 6 **EST:** 2018
SALES (est): 65.23K **Privately Held**
Web: www.luxspaandnails.com
SIC: 7231 Manicurist, pedicurist

(G-356)
M J BILECKI CONTRACTING
2 Constance Ct (19701-1680)
PHONE..................................302 357-7455
Michael John Bilecki, *Prin*
EMP: 5 **EST:** 2015
SALES (est): 75.55K **Privately Held**
SIC: 1799 Special trade contractors, nec

(G-357)
M&S AUTO GROUP INC
104 Loretta Ln (19701-1694)
PHONE..................................302 834-7905
Suleiman Zomut, *Owner*
EMP: 5 **EST:** 2018

SALES (est): 28.25K **Privately Held**
SIC: 7538 General automotive repair shops

(G-358)
MAACO COLLISION REPAIR
105 Emerald Ridge Dr (19701-2280)
PHONE..................................302 753-8721
Daniel Frost, *Prin*
EMP: 5 **EST:** 2018
SALES (est): 27.23K **Privately Held**
SIC: 7532 Paint shop, automotive

(G-359)
MALARKEY TATTOO LLC
730 Pulaski Hwy (19701-5210)
PHONE..................................302 304-5382
Shon W Willis, *Prin*
EMP: 5 **EST:** 2019
SALES (est): 174.92K **Privately Held**
Web: www.malarkeytattoo.com
SIC: 7299 Tattoo parlor

(G-360)
MANOR EXXON INC
131 W Savannah Dr (19701-1638)
PHONE..................................302 834-6691
Cliff Galvin, *Pr*
EMP: 8 **EST:** 1983
SQ FT: 20,000
SALES (est): 1.04MM **Privately Held**
SIC: 5541 7538 Filling stations, gasoline; General automotive repair shops

(G-361)
MANSION HOUSE FARM PAINTBALL
557 Mansion House Rd (19701-2027)
PHONE..................................302 650-3141
Donald Campbell, *Prin*
EMP: 5 **EST:** 2017
SALES (est): 50.62K **Privately Held**
Web: www.mhfpaintball.com
SIC: 7999 Amusement and recreation, nec

(G-362)
MANUFACTURERS & TRADERS TR CO
Also Called: M&T
10 Foxhunt Dr (19701-2534)
PHONE..................................302 651-8828
Nancy Choma, *Mgr*
EMP: 5
SALES (corp-wide): 8.6B **Publicly Held**
Web: ir.mtb.com
SIC: 6022 State commercial banks
HQ: Manufacturers And Traders Trust Company
      1 M&T Plz Fl 3
      Buffalo NY 14203
      716 842-4200

(G-363)
MARJANO LLC
Also Called: Sign-A-Rama
14 Orchid Dr (19701-6330)
PHONE..................................302 454-7446
EMP: 3 **EST:** 2010
SALES (est): 79.39K **Privately Held**
Web: www.signarama.com
SIC: 3993 Signs and advertising specialties

(G-364)
MARK WIECZOREK DMD PC
Also Called: Newtown Family Dentistry
494 Bear Christiana Rd (19701-1039)
PHONE..................................302 838-3384
Mark Wieczorek, *Prin*
Wanda Ayala, *Prin*
EMP: 10 **EST:** 2008
SALES (est): 493.76K **Privately Held**
Web: www.newtownfamilydentist.com

SIC: 8021 Dentists' office

(G-365)
MASTER TECH INC
Also Called: Master Tech Pnt Collision Ctr
743 Rue Madora (19701-2543)
PHONE..................................302 832-1660
Jim Hill, *Pr*
Enoch Anderson, *VP*
EMP: 11 **EST:** 1992
SQ FT: 9,000
SALES (est): 440.47K **Privately Held**
SIC: 7532 Body shop, automotive

(G-366)
MATTHEW AND RICHARD ENTP LLC
36 E Moyer Dr (19701-4116)
PHONE..................................267 767-0290
Brian Spencer, *Mgr*
EMP: 5 **EST:** 2003
SALES (est): 51.43K **Privately Held**
SIC: 7929 Entertainers and entertainment groups

(G-367)
MAVEN SECURITY CONSULTING INC
512 Portrush Pass (19701-1986)
P.O. Box 243 (20146-0243)
PHONE..................................302 365-6862
David Rhoades, *Pr*
EMP: 6 **EST:** 2001
SALES (est): 476.26K **Privately Held**
Web: www.mavensecurity.com
SIC: 7379 Online services technology consultants

(G-368)
MAX ONE PRINTING
310 Chattahoochee Dr (19701-4808)
PHONE..................................302 897-9050
David Dale, *Owner*
EMP: 2 **EST:** 1999
SALES (est): 77.73K **Privately Held**
SIC: 2759 Commercial printing, nec

(G-369)
MEDICAL ASSOCIATES BEAR INC
121 Becks Woods Dr Ste 100 (19701-3851)
PHONE..................................302 832-6768
Rene Padillo Md, *Pr*
EMP: 7 **EST:** 2006
SALES (est): 498.93K **Privately Held**
SIC: 8011 Surgeon

(G-370)
MENARK TECHNOLOGIES INC
101 Rachel Dr (19701-4847)
PHONE..................................302 379-2185
EMP: 6 **EST:** 2019
SALES (est): 114.1K **Privately Held**
Web: www.menark.com
SIC: 7379 Computer related consulting services

(G-371)
MHYHWH LLC
937 Woods Rd (19701-2128)
PHONE..................................302 518-0992
EMP: 5 **EST:** 2020
SALES (est): 68.89K **Privately Held**
SIC: 7389 Business Activities at Non-Commercial Site

(G-372)
MICAN TECHNOLOGIES INC (PA)
2500 Wrangle Hill Rd Ste 224
  (19701-3836)
PHONE..................................302 703-0708
Satya S Kusampudi, *Pr*
Siva Kanumuri, *VP*

(PA)=Parent Co (HQ)=Headquarters
✪ = New Business established in last 2 years

2024 Harris Directory of Delaware Businesses

EMP: 113 EST: 2007
SQ FT: 1,100
SALES (est): 5.34MM
SALES (corp-wide): 5.34MM Privately Held
Web: www.micantech.net
SIC: 7371 Computer software development and applications

(G-373)
MICHAEL A PEYTON LCSW
120 Brittany Way (19701-2096)
PHONE..................302 836-5311
Michael A Peyton, Prin
EMP: 6 EST: 2020
SALES (est): 121.95K Privately Held
SIC: 8322 Individual and family services

(G-374)
MICHAEL A SINCLAIR INC
705 Connell Dr (19701-2241)
PHONE..................302 834-8144
EMP: 5 EST: 1990
SALES (est): 490.78K Privately Held
Web: www.naapd.org
SIC: 4212 0781 Truck rental with drivers; Landscape services

(G-375)
MICHAEL GALLAGHER JEWELERS
102 Foxhunt Dr (Fox Run Shopping Center) (19701-2535)
PHONE..................302 836-2925
Michael E Gallagher, Pr
Kathleen M Gallagher, VP
EMP: 5 EST: 1975
SQ FT: 1,400
SALES (est): 782.83K Privately Held
Web: www.michaelgallagherjewelers.com
SIC: 5944 7631 Jewelry, precious stones and precious metals; Jewelry repair services

(G-376)
MOHAMMED M ALI M D
703 Varsity Ln (19701-3909)
PHONE..................302 328-2895
Mohammed Ali, Pr
EMP: 8 EST: 2017
SALES (est): 59.55K Privately Held
SIC: 8011 Offices and clinics of medical doctors

(G-377)
MOLECULAR IMAGING SERVICES INC
Also Called: Moleclar Imging Svcs Intl Chst
10 Whitaker Ct (19701-2383)
PHONE..................302 450-4505
Frank Digregorio, Pr
EMP: 5 EST: 2001
SALES (est): 1.39MM Privately Held
Web: www.mismedical.com
SIC: 8071 X-ray laboratory, including dental

(G-378)
MONTGOMERY ELECTRIC
224 Cheyenne Dr (19701-2179)
PHONE..................302 832-0945
Tobi Montgomery, Prin
EMP: 5 EST: 2010
SALES (est): 130.37K Privately Held
SIC: 1731 General electrical contractor

(G-379)
MOORE STAFFING AGENCY LLC
112 Grove Mansion Way (19701-1435)
PHONE..................215 300-2770
Lisa Moore, CEO
EMP: 5 EST: 2000
SALES (est): 5.42MM Privately Held
SIC: 7361 8741 8744 Employment agencies; Administrative management; Facilities support services

(G-380)
MORE ABOUT YOU INC
25 Forsythia Ln (19701-6301)
PHONE..................302 229-4414
Ema Ndi, Prin
EMP: 7 EST: 2019
SALES (est): 62.05K Privately Held
Web: www.moreaboutyouinc.com
SIC: 8093 Mental health clinic, outpatient

(G-381)
MRT LLC
2420 Porter Rd (19701-2020)
PHONE..................856 685-1602
Mike Mcgavisk, Prin
EMP: 6 EST: 2010
SALES (est): 134.25K Privately Held
SIC: 6531 Real estate brokers and agents

(G-382)
MS GOVERNORS SQUARE SHOPPING C
1229 Quintilio Dr (19701-6005)
PHONE..................302 838-3384
Tim Marrisey, Prin
EMP: 14 EST: 2009
SALES (est): 202.85K Privately Held
SIC: 8021 Dentists' office

(G-383)
MY EYE DR OPTOMETRISTS LLC
Also Called: Myeyedr
1237 Quintilio Dr (19701-6005)
PHONE..................302 838-0800
EMP: 6
SALES (corp-wide): 100.43MM Privately Held
Web: www.myeyedr.com
SIC: 8042 Offices and clinics of optometrists
PA: My Eye Dr. Optometrists, Llc
8614 Wstwd Ctr Dr Ste 900
Vienna VA 22182
703 847-8899

(G-384)
MY MEDICARE ADVISOR LLC
429 Leo Ln (19701-6811)
PHONE..................302 602-9426
EMP: 5 EST: 2018
SALES (est): 89.71K Privately Held
Web: www.insuranceyoukeep.com
SIC: 8099 Health and allied services, nec

(G-385)
MYSTIC ENERGY GUIDES INC
126 Brittany Way (19701-2096)
PHONE..................302 518-2068
Jane Bradd, Prin
EMP: 5 EST: 2017
SALES (est): 44.07K Privately Held
SIC: 7999 Tour and guide services

(G-386)
N U FRIENDSHIP OUTREACH INC
20 Waterton Dr (19701-4914)
P.O. Box 2172 (19899-2172)
PHONE..................302 836-0404
EMP: 5 EST: 2010
SALES (est): 128.44K Privately Held
Web: www.nufoutreach.org
SIC: 8322 Outreach program

(G-387)
N&D NAIL SALON
14 Foxhunt Dr (19701-2534)
PHONE..................302 834-4899
EMP: 5 EST: 1995
SALES (est): 75.2K Privately Held
SIC: 7231 Manicurist, pedicurist

(G-388)
NANCY COTUGNA DR
11 Andrew Ln (19701-1542)
PHONE..................302 261-6255
Nancy Cotugna, Prin
EMP: 9 EST: 2009
SALES (est): 68.84K Privately Held
SIC: 8011 General and family practice, physician/surgeon

(G-389)
NATIONAL BARBERZ ASSOCIATION
402 Connor Blvd (19701-1743)
PHONE..................302 365-6169
EMP: 5 EST: 2013
SALES (est): 75.99K Privately Held
SIC: 8611 Business associations

(G-390)
NEIGHBOR CARE HOME CARE & FMLY
3 Zinnia Ct (19701-6305)
PHONE..................302 290-0341
EMP: 6 EST: 2017
SALES (est): 107.55K Privately Held
Web: www.neighborcare-hcfs.com
SIC: 8082 Home health care services

(G-391)
NEW CASTLE 100 ARCHERS CLUB
2 Kenley Ct (19701-1623)
PHONE..................302 722-7997
John Henry, Prin
EMP: 5 EST: 2019
SALES (est): 90.79K Privately Held
Web: www.nc100archers.com
SIC: 7997 Membership sports and recreation clubs

(G-392)
NEW CASTLE DANCE ACADEMY
Also Called: New Castle Dance & Mus Academy
460 Eden Cir (19701-4304)
PHONE..................302 836-2060
Valerie Gooding, Owner
EMP: 10 EST: 1978
SALES (est): 229.96K Privately Held
SIC: 7911 Dance studio and school

(G-393)
NEW LIFE FNDATION RECOVERY INC
1541 Church Rd (19701-1826)
PHONE..................302 317-2212
Morgan Ikonne, Ex Dir
Jennifer Ikonne, Pr
Barbara Mack, Sec
Yvette Chase, Treas
Benjamin Godwins, Bd of Dir
EMP: 5 EST: 2018
SALES (est): 276.03K Privately Held
Web: www.newlifefoundationrecovery.com
SIC: 8093 Specialty outpatient clinics, nec

(G-394)
NEWARK GLASS & MIRROR INC
151 Rickey Blvd (19701-2540)
P.O. Box 1462 (19701-7462)
PHONE..................302 834-1158
Martha Joseph, Pr
Walter E Joseph, VP
EMP: 8 EST: 1981
SALES (est): 368.16K Privately Held
Web: www.newarkglassmirror.com
SIC: 5231 1793 Glass; Glass and glazing work

(G-395)
NEWARK KNIGHTS FTBLL AND
625 Corsica Ave (19701-2548)
P.O. Box 494 (19701-0494)
PHONE..................302 846-7776
EMP: 10 EST: 2016
SALES (est): 32.59K Privately Held
Web: knights-copier-service-de.hub.biz
SIC: 7011 Hotels and motels

(G-396)
NEWCOSMOS LLC
52 Blue Spruce Dr (19701-4128)
PHONE..................302 838-1935
Xiang Yu, Pt
EMP: 2 EST: 2003
SALES (est): 120.82K Privately Held
SIC: 3663 Satellites, communications

(G-397)
NHANCE
500 Connor Blvd (19701-1744)
PHONE..................866 944-9663
EMP: 7 EST: 2018
SALES (est): 380.24K Privately Held
Web: www.nhance.com
SIC: 1752 Floor laying and floor work, nec

(G-398)
NKITA ENTERPRISES LLC
23 Lotus Cir S (19701-6315)
PHONE..................302 295-2363
Natalie Kita, Prin
EMP: 6 EST: 2016
SALES (est): 170.6K Privately Held
SIC: 7221 Photographer, still or video

(G-399)
NOVA INDUSTRIES LLC
47 Courtland Cir (19701-1205)
PHONE..................302 218-4837
EMP: 4 EST: 2008
SALES (est): 106.66K Privately Held
SIC: 3999 Atomizers, toiletry

(G-400)
NOVACARE REHABILITATION
256 Foxhunt Dr (19701-2536)
PHONE..................302 597-9256
EMP: 23 EST: 2017
SALES (est): 74.84K Privately Held
Web: www.novacare.com
SIC: 8049 Physical therapist

(G-401)
NOW CARE PAIN RELIEF CENTER
757 Pulaski Hwy (19701-5214)
PHONE..................302 276-1951
EMP: 7 EST: 2017
SALES (est): 189.35K Privately Held
Web: www.nowcarepainrelief.com
SIC: 8099 Health and allied services, nec

(G-402)
NX LEVEL MARKETING LLC
105 Gambel Ct (19701-4913)
PHONE..................215 880-4749
EMP: 5 EST: 2015
SALES (est): 269.2K Privately Held
SIC: 8742 Management consulting services

GEOGRAPHIC SECTION

Bear - New Castle County (G-433)

(G-403)
O MORALES STUCCO PLASTER INC
7 Hawkins Ct (19701-1622)
PHONE.................................302 834-8891
Orlando Morales, *Pr*
EMP: 6 **EST:** 2006
SALES (est): 373.24K **Privately Held**
SIC: 1771 1742 Exterior concrete stucco contractor; Plastering, plain or ornamental

(G-404)
OCEANSTAR TECHNOLOGIES INC
203 Mariners Way (19701-2291)
PHONE.................................302 542-1900
Fred Eisele, *Pr*
Mary Eisele, *VP*
EMP: 5 **EST:** 2000
SALES (est): 265.77K **Privately Held**
SIC: 8742 Business management consultant

(G-405)
OLACOLE FOUNDATION
931 Rue Madora (19701-2545)
PHONE.................................215 279-4742
Remy Cole, *Prin*
EMP: 5 **EST:** 2016
SALES (est): 40.1K **Privately Held**
SIC: 8641 Civic and social associations

(G-406)
OLDCASTLE INC
1250 Porter Rd (19701-1311)
PHONE.................................302 836-6492
EMP: 7 **EST:** 2019
SALES (est): 45.78K **Privately Held**
Web: www.oldcastleinfrastructure.com
SIC: 3272 Concrete products, nec

(G-407)
ON THE SPOT MASSAGE
2871 Red Lion Rd (19701-2425)
PHONE.................................302 545-5200
Patricia Ann Reilly, *Prin*
EMP: 7 **EST:** 2019
SALES (est): 88.1K **Privately Held**
SIC: 8093 Rehabilitation center, outpatient treatment

(G-408)
ONE TUCH PRPERTY SOLUTIONS LLC
100 Gambel Ct (19701-4913)
PHONE.................................302 765-8519
Tracy Wilson, *Managing Member*
EMP: 5 **EST:** 2020
SALES (est): 210.92K **Privately Held**
Web: www.onetouchpropertysolutions.com
SIC: 3589 Commercial cleaning equipment

(G-409)
OPUS MARKETING GROUP
178 Lake Arrowhead Cir (19701-3811)
PHONE.................................302 275-2336
EMP: 6 **EST:** 2017
SALES (est): 88.32K **Privately Held**
Web: www.opusmarketinggroup.com
SIC: 8742 Marketing consulting services

(G-410)
OUR CHILDRENS LEARNING CTR
313 Sun Blvd (19701-6807)
PHONE.................................302 565-1272
EMP: 9 **EST:** 2010
SALES (est): 52.68K **Privately Held**
SIC: 8351 Child day care services

(G-411)
PACE ELEC & GENERATOR SVCS
105 Carson Dr (19701-1319)
PHONE.................................302 328-2600
EMP: 45 **EST:** 2011
SALES (est): 3.88MM **Privately Held**
Web: www.pacegenerators.com
SIC: 1731 General electrical contractor

(G-412)
PALMER & ASSOCIATES INC
14 Lauren Dr (19701-1805)
PHONE.................................302 834-9329
Thomas Palmer, *Pr*
Barbara Palmer, *Sec*
EMP: 9 **EST:** 1979
SQ FT: 3,200
SALES (est): 1.21MM **Privately Held**
SIC: 1611 1794 Highway and street paving contractor; Excavation and grading, building construction

(G-413)
PALMER & SONS ELECTRIC IN
226 Cheyenne Dr (19701-2179)
PHONE.................................302 290-4899
Buster Stewart, *Prin*
EMP: 6 **EST:** 2006
SALES (est): 170K **Privately Held**
SIC: 1731 General electrical contractor

(G-414)
PANDA EARLY EDUCATION CTR INC (PA)
105 Emerald Ridge Dr (19701-2280)
PHONE.................................302 832-1891
EMP: 9 **EST:** 1995
SALES (est): 972.48K **Privately Held**
SIC: 8351 Preschool center

(G-415)
PASCAL NGALIM
Also Called: Sylvan Friendly Movers
35 Pear Dr (19701-4135)
PHONE.................................302 983-2322
Pascal Ngalim, *Owner*
EMP: 5 **EST:** 2020
SALES (est): 103.15K **Privately Held**
SIC: 4789 Cargo loading and unloading services

(G-416)
PASSION CARE SERVICES INC
3727 Wrangle Hill Rd (19701-1918)
P.O. Box 1307 (19701-7307)
PHONE.................................302 832-2622
Lola Mayo, *Pr*
EMP: 17 **EST:** 2000
SALES (est): 644.39K **Privately Held**
Web: www.passioncareacademy.com
SIC: 8351 Preschool center

(G-417)
PATHWAYS2HEALING
59 Paisley St (19701-4719)
PHONE.................................302 540-4632
EMP: 5 **EST:** 2011
SALES (est): 61.66K **Privately Held**
SIC: 8049 Offices of health practitioner

(G-418)
PATRICIA MCKAY
Also Called: Patty Cakes Childcare
337 Starboard Dr (19701-2299)
P.O. Box 12 (19701-0012)
PHONE.................................302 563-5334
Patricia Mckay, *Prin*
EMP: 5 **EST:** 2011
SALES (est): 61.78K **Privately Held**

SIC: 8351 Preschool center

(G-419)
PATTERSON-SCHWARTZ
40 Treelane Dr (19701-3024)
P.O. Box 481 (19701-0481)
PHONE.................................215 805-8238
Ray Dudkewitz, *Prin*
EMP: 6 **EST:** 2016
SALES (est): 111.2K **Privately Held**
Web: www.pattersonschwartz.com
SIC: 6531 Real estate agent, residential

(G-420)
PAULS INC
Also Called: Paul's Machine Shop
61 Cypress Bridge Pl (19701-1013)
PHONE.................................302 328-0191
Paul Longacre, *Pr*
Patricia Longacre, *VP*
EMP: 5 **EST:** 1926
SQ FT: 3,200
SALES (est): 356.79K **Privately Held**
SIC: 3599 7692 Machine shop, jobbing and repair; Welding repair

(G-421)
PENCADER MECHANICAL CONTRS
75 Lark Ave (19701-1162)
PHONE.................................302 368-9144
Rick Adams, *Mgr*
EMP: 6 **EST:** 1961
SALES (est): 728.37K **Privately Held**
Web: www.penmech.com
SIC: 1711 Mechanical contractor

(G-422)
PERFECT FINISH LLC
3415 Wrangle Hill Rd (19701-4812)
PHONE.................................302 480-3167
Finish Perfect, *Prin*
EMP: 7 **EST:** 2014
SALES (est): 75.73K **Privately Held**
Web: www.perfectfinishcleaningllc.com
SIC: 7699 Cleaning services

(G-423)
PHYLLIS M GREEN
Also Called: Hannahs Christian HM Day Care
329 N Red Lion Ter (19701-1028)
PHONE.................................302 354-6986
Phyllis M Green, *Prin*
EMP: 8 **EST:** 2011
SALES (est): 237.95K **Privately Held**
SIC: 8082 Home health care services

(G-424)
PHYSICIANS PLUS SPINE & REHAB
1701 Pulaski Hwy (19701-1711)
PHONE.................................302 261-6221
Michelle Feeney, *Mgr*
EMP: 6 **EST:** 2013
SALES (est): 228.52K **Privately Held**
Web: www.spineandrehabcenter.com
SIC: 8041 Offices and clinics of chiropractors

(G-425)
PILOTS4RENT INC
1148 Pulaski Hwy (19701-1306)
PHONE.................................561 704-2885
Susan Anderson, *Prin*
EMP: 5 **EST:** 2016
SALES (est): 162.05K **Privately Held**
SIC: 7363 Pilot service, aviation

(G-426)
PIRANHA SPORTS LLC
230 Mariners Way (19701-2292)
PHONE.................................302 893-1997
Roy Weiss, *Prin*

EMP: 7 **EST:** 2012
SALES (est): 96.7K **Privately Held**
SIC: 7032 Sporting camps

(G-427)
PLUCK HVAC
105 Ponder Ct (19701-3392)
PHONE.................................302 836-8596
Kathleen Pluck, *Pr*
EMP: 5 **EST:** 2008
SALES (est): 77.39K **Privately Held**
SIC: 1711 Heating and air conditioning contractors

(G-428)
PNC BANK NATIONAL ASSOCIATION
Also Called: PNC
250 Foxhunt Dr (19701-2536)
PHONE.................................302 832-8750
Laura Mestro, *Mgr*
EMP: 5
SALES (corp-wide): 23.54B **Publicly Held**
Web: www.pncbank.com
SIC: 6021 National trust companies with deposits, commercial
HQ: Pnc Bank, National Association
300 5th Ave
Pittsburgh PA 15222
877 762-2000

(G-429)
POST SHIPPER LLC
601 Carson Dr (19701-1450)
PHONE.................................302 444-8144
Mahmuoud Alshoushan, *Pr*
EMP: 10 **EST:** 2015
SALES (est): 1.13MM **Privately Held**
Web: www.postshipper.com
SIC: 4731 Agents, shipping

(G-430)
POWER HOUSE GLOBAL ENTPS INC
362 Macdonald Close (19701-8303)
PHONE.................................215 660-0071
David Hopkins, *Pr*
EMP: 88 **EST:** 2016
SALES (est): 255.93K **Privately Held**
SIC: 7922 Entertainment promotion

(G-431)
POWER TRANS INC
706 Carson Dr (19701-1454)
PHONE.................................302 918-7674
Justin Bailey, *Mgr*
EMP: 7 **EST:** 2016
SALES (est): 196.92K **Privately Held**
Web: www.powertrans.org
SIC: 4111 Local and suburban transit

(G-432)
PPMI INC
200 Canonero Dr (19701-3334)
P.O. Box 378 (19732-0378)
PHONE.................................302 584-1972
EMP: 14 **EST:** 2015
SALES (est): 227.35K **Privately Held**
SIC: 8741 Business management

(G-433)
PRAIZE FITNESS
38 Saint George Ter (19701-1091)
PHONE.................................302 312-7416
Ebony Winn, *Prin*
EMP: 5 **EST:** 2017
SALES (est): 50.31K **Privately Held**
SIC: 7991 Physical fitness facilities

(G-434)
PRECISION BUILDERS INC
1148 Pulaski Hwy # 107 (19701-1305)
PHONE.................................302 420-1391
Thomas Paul Wright, *Owner*
EMP: 7 **EST:** 2005
SALES (est): 386.56K **Privately Held**
Web: www.precisionbuildersremodeling.com
SIC: 1521 New construction, single-family houses

(G-435)
PREFERRED SECURITY INC
1570 Red Lion Rd (19701-1870)
P.O. Box 127 (19701-0127)
PHONE.................................302 834-7800
EMP: 6 **EST:** 1993
SQ FT: 4,500
SALES (est): 597.98K **Privately Held**
Web: www.preferredsecurityinc.com
SIC: 1731 1799 Fire detection and burglar alarm systems specialization; Central vacuum cleaning system installation

(G-436)
PREFERRED TRNSP SYSTEMS LLC
Also Called: Preferred Transportation
101 E Beaver Ct (19701-1082)
P.O. Box 867 (19701-0867)
PHONE.................................302 323-0828
Gary Arters, *Managing Member*
EMP: 6 **EST:** 1994
SALES (est): 600K **Privately Held**
SIC: 4119 4111 Vanpool operation; Airport limousine, scheduled service

(G-437)
PREMIER HEALTH SERVICE LLC
131 Becks Woods Dr (19701-3833)
PHONE.................................302 597-6810
Hassan Hayat, *Mgr*
EMP: 13 **EST:** 2018
SALES (est): 138.79K **Privately Held**
SIC: 8099 Health and allied services, nec

(G-438)
PRIME TIME PROPERTIES LLC
167 Willamette Dr (19701-4803)
PHONE.................................302 763-6050
EMP: 5 **EST:** 2007
SALES (est): 282.95K **Privately Held**
SIC: 6512 8742 6799 Nonresidential building operators; Real estate consultant; Real estate investors, except property operators

(G-439)
PROFESSIONSALE INC
1148 Pulaski Hwy Ste 134 (19701-1305)
PHONE.................................646 262-9101
EMP: 5 **EST:** 2009
SALES (est): 57.72K **Privately Held**
SIC: 7374 Computer graphics service

(G-440)
PROMAX PAINTERS
205 Christiana Mdws (19701-2802)
P.O. Box 429 (19701-0429)
PHONE.................................302 312-8415
Joseph Chambers, *Prin*
EMP: 5 **EST:** 2017
SALES (est): 70.71K **Privately Held**
SIC: 1721 Painting and paper hanging

(G-441)
PROMO BUILDER LLC
602 Carson Dr (19701-1450)
PHONE.................................773 502-5796
Mukhabat Usmanova, *Managing Member*
EMP: 15 **EST:** 2019
SALES (est): 581.23K **Privately Held**
SIC: 3581 Automatic vending machines

(G-442)
PURUSHAS PICKS INC
Also Called: My Baby's Heartbeat Bear
3310 Wrangle Hill Rd Ste 107 (19701-1874)
PHONE.................................302 918-7663
Purusha Rivera, *Pr*
Sheldon Thomas, *VP*
EMP: 6 **EST:** 2011
SALES (est): 922.88K **Privately Held**
Web: www.mybabysheartbeatbear.com
SIC: 5047 5999 Medical equipment and supplies; Medical apparatus and supplies

(G-443)
R AND JC ONSTRUCTION INC
331 Corbitt Cir (19701-1543)
PHONE.................................302 419-7393
EMP: 6 **EST:** 2018
SALES (est): 276.55K **Privately Held**
Web: www.rjconstructioninc.com
SIC: 1521 General remodeling, single-family houses

(G-444)
R D COLLINS & SONS
19 Shellbark Dr (19701-2141)
PHONE.................................302 834-3409
Doug Collins, *Owner*
EMP: 10 **EST:** 1987
SQ FT: 1,500
SALES (est): 406.39K **Privately Held**
SIC: 0782 0781 Lawn services; Landscape services

(G-445)
R&R ASPHALT PAVING
734 Pulaski Hwy Lot 1 (19701-5201)
PHONE.................................302 312-8355
Richard Smith, *Prin*
EMP: 5 **EST:** 2018
SALES (est): 98.19K **Privately Held**
SIC: 1771 Blacktop (asphalt) work

(G-446)
RAYMOND SHEPHARD
3815 Wrangle Hill Rd (19701-1919)
PHONE.................................302 834-8405
Raymond Shephard, *Prin*
EMP: 5 **EST:** 2011
SALES (est): 181.21K **Privately Held**
SIC: 1522 Residential construction, nec

(G-447)
RE/MAX PREMIER PROPERTIES
Also Called: Re/Max
309 Corbitt Cir (19701-1543)
PHONE.................................302 883-9202
Tess Adams, *Prin*
EMP: 5 **EST:** 2017
SALES (est): 82.65K **Privately Held**
Web: www.premierpropertiesde.com
SIC: 6531 Real estate agent, residential

(G-448)
RECYCLERS OF DELAWARE LLC
1148 Pulaski Hwy Ste 107-313 (19701-1305)
PHONE.................................856 466-9067
Thomas Toy, *Prin*
EMP: 5 **EST:** 2011
SALES (est): 107.78K **Privately Held**
SIC: 4953 Recycling, waste materials

(G-449)
RED BIRD EGG FARM INC (PA)
1701 Red Lion Rd (19701-1813)
PHONE.................................302 834-2571
Kenneth Steele, *Pr*
Shirley Steele, *
EMP: 38 **EST:** 1938
SQ FT: 2,000
SALES (est): 1.92MM
SALES (corp-wide): 1.92MM **Privately Held**
SIC: 0252 Chicken eggs

(G-450)
REGIS CORPORATION
Also Called: Holiday Hair 238
420 Eden Cir (19701-4304)
PHONE.................................302 834-9916
EMP: 10
SALES (corp-wide): 233.33MM **Publicly Held**
Web: www.signaturestyle.com
SIC: 7231 Unisex hair salons
PA: Regis Corporation
3701 Wayzata Blvd Ste 500
Minneapolis MN 55416
952 947-7777

(G-451)
REIS ENTERPRISES LLC
504 Connor Blvd (19701-1744)
PHONE.................................302 740-8382
Soner Kece, *Pr*
EMP: 5 **EST:** 2016
SALES (est): 465.81K **Privately Held**
Web: www.paintbyreis.com
SIC: 1721 Residential painting

(G-452)
RELIANCE HEALTHCARE LLC
1993 Pulaski Hwy (19701-1708)
PHONE.................................302 838-3100
Nazar Qayum, *Asst Sec*
EMP: 8 **EST:** 2017
SALES (est): 501.18K **Privately Held**
Web: www.reliancehealthllc.com
SIC: 8099 Health and allied services, nec

(G-453)
RETRO FITNESS
835 Pulaski Hwy (19701-1240)
PHONE.................................302 276-0828
Ryan Sykes, *Genl Mgr*
EMP: 13 **EST:** 2013
SALES (est): 393.16K **Privately Held**
Web: www.retrofitness.com
SIC: 7991 Physical fitness facilities

(G-454)
REYBOLD
50 Turnberry Ct (19701-4700)
PHONE.................................302 584-7975
EMP: 10 **EST:** 2019
SALES (est): 111.37K **Privately Held**
Web: www.reybold.com
SIC: 6513 Apartment building operators

(G-455)
REYBOLD CONSTRUCTION CORP
116 E Scotland Dr (19701-1766)
PHONE.................................302 832-7100
Jerome Heisler Junior, *Pr*
Jerome S Heisler Junior, *Pr*
James Grygiel, *
Jerome Heisler Senior, *Ch*
EMP: 45 **EST:** 1986
SQ FT: 12,000
SALES (est): 8.72MM **Privately Held**
Web: www.reybold.com
SIC: 6552 1542 1541 Land subdividers and developers, residential; Commercial and office building, new construction; Warehouse construction

(G-456)
REYBOLD CONSTRUCTION GROUP LLC
116 E Scotland Dr (19701-1766)
PHONE.................................302 832-7100
EMP: 15 **EST:** 2021
SALES (est): 606.4K **Privately Held**
Web: www.reybold.com
SIC: 1794 Excavation work

(G-457)
REYBOLD GROUP
701 Observatory Dr (19701-6835)
PHONE.................................302 834-1740
EMP: 7 **EST:** 2018
SALES (est): 222.31K **Privately Held**
Web: www.reybold.com
SIC: 5085 Industrial supplies

(G-458)
REYBOLD GROUP OF COMPANIES INC (PA)
116 E Scotland Dr (19701-1766)
PHONE.................................302 832-7100
Jerome S Heisler Junior, *Pr*
James R Grygiel, *
Jerome S Heisler Senior, *Stockholder*
EMP: 48 **EST:** 1987
SQ FT: 6,450
SALES (est): 10.3MM
SALES (corp-wide): 10.3MM **Privately Held**
Web: www.reybold.com
SIC: 6531 Real estate managers

(G-459)
REYBOLD GROUP OF COMPANIES INC
Also Called: Hunters Run Associates
114 E Scotland Dr (19701-1756)
PHONE.................................302 834-2544
EMP: 8
SALES (corp-wide): 10.3MM **Privately Held**
Web: www.reybold.com
SIC: 6515 Mobile home site operators
PA: The Reybold Group Of Companies Inc
116 E Scotland Dr
Bear DE 19701
302 832-7100

(G-460)
RIALE SYSTEM SERVICES
301 Dasher Cir (19701-1170)
PHONE.................................302 328-3848
Ronald J Riale Junior, *Prin*
EMP: 5 **EST:** 2003
SALES (est): 100.24K **Privately Held**
SIC: 1521 Single-family housing construction

(G-461)
RIDGE IT SOLUTIONS INC
152 Hammersmith Way (19701-2320)
PHONE.................................302 455-8566
Sairamakrishna Edara, *CEO*
EMP: 5 **EST:** 2017
SALES (est): 770.43K **Privately Held**
Web: www.ridgeitsolutionsinc.com
SIC: 7371 Computer software systems analysis and design, custom

(G-462)
RIGHT COAST PRO
116 Michael Ln (19701-2053)
PHONE.................................302 832-1517
John Johnston, *Prin*
EMP: 5 **EST:** 2014
SALES (est): 59.17K **Privately Held**
Web: www.rightcoastpro.com

GEOGRAPHIC SECTION

Bear - New Castle County (G-492)

SIC: 7997 Membership sports and recreation clubs

(G-463)
ROBERT C PEOPLES INC
Also Called: Peoples, R C
2750 Wrangle Hill Rd (19701-1732)
PHONE..............................302 834-5268
Dorothy M Peoples, *Pr*
Harrison B Peoples, *
W Thomas Peoples, *
Robert C Peoples Junior, *VP*
Carol Manubay, *
EMP: 55 **EST:** 1956
SQ FT: 4,000
SALES (est): 7.92MM **Privately Held**
Web: www.peoplesplaza.com
SIC: 1521 1542 New construction, single-family houses; Commercial and office building, new construction

(G-464)
ROBERT F MULLEN INSURANCE AGCY
Also Called: State Farm Insurance
887 Pulaski Hwy (19701-1252)
PHONE..............................302 322-5331
Robert F Mullen, *Owner*
EMP: 6 **EST:** 1983
SALES (est): 487.87K **Privately Held**
Web: www.safewithmullen.com
SIC: 6411 Insurance agents and brokers

(G-465)
ROBIN DRIVE AUTO LLC
804 Pulaski Hwy (19701-1226)
PHONE..............................302 326-2437
EMP: 7 **EST:** 2010
SALES (est): 370.92K **Privately Held**
Web: www.robindriveauto.com
SIC: 7538 General automotive repair shops

(G-466)
ROCKY LAC LLC
1012 San Remo Ct Ste A (19701-2519)
PHONE..............................302 440-5561
EMP: 10 **EST:** 2017
SALES (est): 472.53K **Privately Held**
SIC: 6531 Real estate agents and managers

(G-467)
ROGERS CORPORATION
Also Called: Rogers
1100 Governor Lea Rd (19701-1927)
PHONE..............................302 834-2100
Tom Magnani, *Brnch Mgr*
EMP: 101
SALES (corp-wide): 971.17MM **Publicly Held**
Web: www.rogerscorp.com
SIC: 2822 3672 Synthetic rubber; Printed circuit boards
PA: Rogers Corporation
2225 W Chandler Blvd
Chandler AZ 85224
480 917-6000

(G-468)
ROHANS BUS SERVICE INC
7 Whirlaway Dr (19701-3310)
PHONE..............................302 332-8498
Rohan Miller, *Prin*
EMP: 5 **EST:** 2018
SALES (est): 253.91K **Privately Held**
SIC: 4141 Local bus charter service

(G-469)
RON G WILLIAMS M D
341 Starboard Dr (19701-2299)
P.O. Box 667 (19701-0667)
PHONE..............................302 838-2238
Ron Williams, *Owner*
EMP: 5 **EST:** 2018
SALES (est): 54.13K **Privately Held**
SIC: 8011 Offices and clinics of medical doctors

(G-470)
ROSELLE D ALBERT PT
22 E Savannah Dr (19701-1662)
PHONE..............................302 373-5753
Roselle Albert, *Prin*
EMP: 6 **EST:** 2011
SALES (est): 64.97K **Privately Held**
SIC: 8049 Physical therapist

(G-471)
ROSY CLEANING SERVICES
1602 Christiana Mdws (19701-2830)
PHONE..............................302 723-7610
Rosalba Cruz, *Prin*
EMP: 5 **EST:** 2017
SALES (est): 23.7K **Privately Held**
SIC: 7699 Cleaning services

(G-472)
ROYAL BROADCASTING INC
18 Monticello Dr (19701-2076)
PHONE..............................302 838-4543
Andrew L Shearer, *Prin*
EMP: 5 **EST:** 2009
SALES (est): 86.23K **Privately Held**
SIC: 4832 Radio broadcasting stations

(G-473)
ROYALE GROUP INC
400 Carson Dr (19701-1314)
PHONE..............................201 845-4666
EMP: 6 **EST:** 2014
SALES (est): 200.2K **Privately Held**
Web: www.royalepigments-chem.com
SIC: 5169 Chemicals and allied products, nec

(G-474)
ROYALE PIGMENTS & CHEM INC
Also Called: Awsm Industries
400 Carson Dr (19701-1314)
PHONE..............................201 845-4666
John Logue, *CEO*
Lisa Lindis, *
Megan Logue, *
▲ **EMP:** 30 **EST:** 1985
SALES (est): 4.69MM **Privately Held**
Web: www.royalepigments-chem.com
SIC: 5169 2869 Chemicals, industrial and heavy; Industrial organic chemicals, nec

(G-475)
ROYALE PIGMENTS AND CHEM LLC
400 Carson Dr (19701-1314)
PHONE..............................201 845-4666
Lindsay A Logue, *Managing Member*
▲ **EMP:** 5 **EST:** 1986
SALES (est): 1.08MM **Privately Held**
Web: www.royalepigments-chem.com
SIC: 5169 Chemicals, industrial and heavy

(G-476)
RRR REALTY GROUP LLC
102 Cornwell Dr (19701-3102)
PHONE..............................302 836-9836
Jasmine Wiley, *Asst Sec*
EMP: 5 **EST:** 2018
SALES (est): 158.61K **Privately Held**
SIC: 6531 Real estate brokers and agents

(G-477)
S T PROGRESSIVE STRIDES
718 Thyme Dr (19701-6018)
PHONE..............................410 775-8103
Jackie Smith, *CEO*
EMP: 7 **EST:** 2017
SALES (est): 77.28K **Privately Held**
SIC: 8093 Rehabilitation center, outpatient treatment

(G-478)
SACCO LAWN CARE
225 Forrestal Dr (19701-1642)
P.O. Box 1411 (19701-7411)
PHONE..............................302 545-3803
EMP: 5 **EST:** 2015
SALES (est): 243.35K **Privately Held**
SIC: 0782 Lawn care services

(G-479)
SARA CLEANING SERVICE
230 Landau Way (19701-1144)
PHONE..............................856 498-3244
Sara Silvestre, *Prin*
EMP: 6 **EST:** 2014
SALES (est): 54.36K **Privately Held**
SIC: 7699 Cleaning services

(G-480)
SCHOOL BELL APARTMENTS LP
2000 Varsity Ln (19701-3900)
PHONE..............................302 328-9500
Yvonne Ryder, *Mgr*
EMP: 6 **EST:** 2001
SALES (est): 893.26K **Privately Held**
Web: www.schoolbellapartments.com
SIC: 6513 Apartment building operators

(G-481)
SCHOOLTOOLSTV
10 S Sherman Dr (19701-3088)
PHONE..............................415 948-0668
EMP: 5 **EST:** 2017
SALES (est): 44.19K **Privately Held**
SIC: 8641 Civic and social associations

(G-482)
SCHWERMAN TRUCKING CO
3340 Wrangle Hill Rd (19701-1846)
PHONE..............................302 832-3103
Paul Womax, *Brnch Mgr*
EMP: 31
SALES (corp-wide): 140.73MM **Privately Held**
Web: www.tankstar.com
SIC: 4213 Contract haulers
HQ: Schwerman Trucking Co.
611 S 28th St
Milwaukee WI 53215
414 671-1600

(G-483)
SEQUOIA PROPERTIES INC
27 Craig Rd (19701-1125)
PHONE..............................847 599-9099
Jean Cumming, *Pr*
EMP: 7 **EST:** 1998
SALES (est): 603.42K **Privately Held**
SIC: 7331 Mailing service

(G-484)
SERVPRO BEAR-NEW CASTLE INC
301 Carson Dr (19701-1374)
PHONE..............................302 392-6000
Richard Massey, *Prin*
EMP: 18 **EST:** 2009
SALES (est): 890.91K **Privately Held**
Web: www.servprobearnewcastle.com
SIC: 7349 Building maintenance services, nec

(G-485)
SERVPRO OF UPPER DARBY
Also Called: SERVPRO
301 Carson Dr (19701-1374)
P.O. Box 715 (19701-0715)
PHONE..............................302 392-6000
EMP: 8 **EST:** 2019
SALES (est): 44.48K **Privately Held**
Web: www.servproupperdarby.com
SIC: 7349 Building maintenance services, nec

(G-486)
SHACKLEFORD LDSCP GRP LLC
605 Green Tree Ln (19701-1074)
P.O. Box 1244 (19701-7244)
PHONE..............................302 883-9602
Kevin Shackleford Junior, *Pr*
EMP: 5 **EST:** 2018
SALES (est): 74.52K **Privately Held**
SIC: 0781 Landscape services

(G-487)
SHAVERS CONSWALLA U MD
207 Hazel Dr (19701-1970)
PHONE..............................267 975-9571
Conswalla Shavers Md, *Owner*
EMP: 7 **EST:** 2018
SALES (est): 79K **Privately Held**
SIC: 8011 Internal medicine, physician/surgeon

(G-488)
SHEET METAL CONTRACTING CO
3445 Wrangle Hill Rd (19701-1831)
P.O. Box 307 (19701-0307)
PHONE..............................302 834-3727
Jeffrey Bupp, *Pr*
Thomas R Douglas, *Treas*
EMP: 20 **EST:** 1910
SQ FT: 24,000
SALES (est): 3.34MM **Privately Held**
Web: www.sheetmetalcontracting.com
SIC: 3444 3599 Sheet metal specialties, not stamped; Machine shop, jobbing and repair

(G-489)
SHINE THROUGH WINDOW CLG LLC
410 Pheasant Cir (19701-2723)
PHONE..............................302 261-6459
Jameel Milburn, *Prin*
EMP: 5 **EST:** 2014
SALES (est): 29.22K **Privately Held**
SIC: 7349 Window cleaning

(G-490)
SHORE CHEM LLC
400 Carson Dr (19701-1314)
PHONE..............................201 845-4666
John Logue, *Managing Member*
▲ **EMP:** 10 **EST:** 2004
SALES (est): 1.53MM **Privately Held**
SIC: 5169 2899 Industrial chemicals; Chemical preparations, nec

(G-491)
SIEMENS AG
217 Benjamin Blvd (19701-1692)
PHONE..............................302 836-2933
EMP: 6 **EST:** 2018
SALES (est): 86.69K **Privately Held**
SIC: 3661 Telephones and telephone apparatus

(G-492)
SIGN CRAFTERS
48 Castle Run Dr (19701-1416)
PHONE..............................302 832-8300
Joel Wild, *Owner*
EMP: 6 **EST:** 2008

Bear - New Castle County (G-493)

GEOGRAPHIC SECTION

SALES (est): 65.87K **Privately Held**
Web: www.signcrafters-inc.com
SIC: 3993 Signs, not made in custom sign painting shops

(G-493)
SIMON EYE ASSOCIATES PA
116 Foxhunt Dr Ste 116 (19701-2535)
PHONE................302 834-4305
Simon Charles, *Brnch Mgr*
EMP: 14
Web: www.simoneye.com
SIC: 8042 Offices and clinics of optometrists
PA: Simon Eye Associates, P.A.
5301 Limestone Rd Ste 128
Wilmington DE 19808

(G-494)
SIVAD PPE LLC
703 Carson Dr (19701-1454)
PHONE................302 208-2233
Lenzie Davis, *Managing Member*
EMP: 40 EST: 2020
SALES (est): 16MM **Privately Held**
Web: www.sivadppe.com
SIC: 5047 Medical equipment and supplies

(G-495)
SK SERVICES LLC
204 Benjamin Blvd (19701-1689)
PHONE................302 834-9133
Stephen Kuhls, *Prin*
EMP: 5 EST: 2017
SALES (est): 98.33K **Privately Held**
SIC: 7361 Employment agencies

(G-496)
SLATER NURSING SERVICE
1148 Pulaski Hwy (19701-1305)
PHONE................302 419-6237
Khaliel Slater, *Owner*
EMP: 6 EST: 2016
SALES (est): 93.72K **Privately Held**
SIC: 8049 Nurses and other medical assistants

(G-497)
SMALL WONDER FITNESS
2611 Del Laws Rd (19701-1706)
PHONE................302 838-0865
Quinn Megargel, *Prin*
EMP: 6 EST: 2012
SALES (est): 150K **Privately Held**
SIC: 7991 Physical fitness facilities

(G-498)
SMARTY PANTS EARLY EDUCATION
146 Willamette Dr (19701-4802)
PHONE................302 985-3770
EMP: 6 EST: 2017
SALES (est): 57.91K **Privately Held**
SIC: 8351 Preschool center

(G-499)
SONNYS AUTO SERVICES INC
111 Emerald Ridge Dr (19701-2280)
PHONE................302 287-7677
EMP: 6 EST: 2015
SALES (est): 49.34K **Privately Held**
SIC: 7538 General automotive repair shops

(G-500)
SOPHISTICUTS INC
3 Rice Dr (19701-1890)
PHONE................302 834-7427
Theresa Williams, *Pr*
EMP: 6 EST: 1988
SALES (est): 77.41K **Privately Held**
SIC: 7231 Unisex hair salons

(G-501)
SOUTH JERSEY PAVING
518 Turnberry Ct (19701-4729)
PHONE................856 498-8647
Rochelle Reilly, *Prin*
EMP: 6 EST: 2009
SALES (est): 247.92K **Privately Held**
SIC: 1611 Highway and street paving contractor

(G-502)
SOUTHSIDE CONSTRUCTION LLC
3310 Wrangle Hill Rd Ste 8 (19701-1874)
PHONE................302 500-9268
Alexander Leiva, *Managing Member*
EMP: 3
SALES (est): 135.7K **Privately Held**
SIC: 2493 Insulation and roofing material, reconstituted wood

(G-503)
SPARKLEAN LAUNDROMAT
1126 Pulaski Hwy (19701-1305)
PHONE................302 365-6665
EMP: 7 EST: 2015
SALES (est): 253.74K **Privately Held**
SIC: 7215 Laundry, coin-operated

(G-504)
SPEC PROCESSING GROUP INC
Also Called: Spg
2266 Porter Rd (19701-2022)
PHONE................302 295-2197
James Mentz, *Pr*
EMP: 6 EST: 2006
SALES (est): 426.1K **Privately Held**
SIC: 0711 Soil preparation services

(G-505)
SPRING RAIN IRRIGATION INC
29 Pegasus Pl (19701-2378)
PHONE................302 838-9610
EMP: 5 EST: 2009
SALES (est): 63K **Privately Held**
SIC: 1711 Irrigation sprinkler system installation

(G-506)
SRHK ENTERPRISES LLC
110 Gambel Ct (19701-4913)
PHONE................302 834-2345
EMP: 5 EST: 2018
SALES (est): 121.09K **Privately Held**
SIC: 7389 Business services, nec

(G-507)
SSC PARKING LLC SAM STANFORD
615 Parkman Ct (19701-4940)
PHONE................302 561-0088
EMP: 5 EST: 2016
SALES (est): 131.86K **Privately Held**
SIC: 7521 Automobile parking

(G-508)
ST ANDREWS APARTMENTS
50 Turnberry Ct (19701-4700)
PHONE................302 834-8600
Jerry Heisler, *Owner*
EMP: 5 EST: 2001
SALES (est): 233.43K **Privately Held**
Web: www.reybold.com
SIC: 6513 Apartment building operators

(G-509)
ST ANDREWS MAINTENANCE
104 E Scotland Dr (19701-1756)
PHONE................302 832-2675
Rechel Riley, *Prin*
EMP: 5 EST: 2009
SALES (est): 154.78K **Privately Held**
SIC: 7349 Building maintenance services, nec

(G-510)
STAR ART INC
1272 Porter Rd (19701-1311)
P.O. Box 828 (19701-0828)
PHONE................302 261-6732
EMP: 4 EST: 2019
SALES (est): 92.3K **Privately Held**
Web: www.colorprintingbystarart.com
SIC: 2752 Commercial printing, lithographic

(G-511)
STATE FARM INSURANCE
Also Called: State Farm Insurance
2500 Wrangle Hill Rd Ste 125 (19701-3836)
PHONE................302 834-5467
EMP: 42 EST: 2018
SALES (est): 282.22K **Privately Held**
Web: www.statefarm.com
SIC: 6411 Insurance agents and brokers

(G-512)
STAY TRUE PLUMBING
693 Old Porter Rd (19701-1864)
PHONE................302 464-1198
EMP: 8 EST: 2014
SALES (est): 955.19K **Privately Held**
Web: staytrueplumbing-com.stackstaging.com
SIC: 1711 Plumbing contractors

(G-513)
STREAK FREE CLG BY PTTICOM LLC
130 Bernice Dr (19701-2016)
PHONE................302 261-6933
James Lee, *Prin*
EMP: 5 EST: 2016
SALES (est): 58.62K **Privately Held**
SIC: 7699 Cleaning services

(G-514)
STUDIO 923
724 Pulaski Hwy (19701-5210)
PHONE................302 276-1413
Cassandra Walley, *Prin*
EMP: 5 EST: 2016
SALES (est): 51.11K **Privately Held**
SIC: 7299 Miscellaneous personal service

(G-515)
SUMMIT BRIDGE VET HOSP LLC
3930 Red Lion Rd (19701-2426)
PHONE................302 834-7387
Jessica Berkeridge, *Pr*
EMP: 5 EST: 2020
SALES (est): 327.92K **Privately Held**
Web: www.summit-vet.com
SIC: 0742 Animal hospital services, pets and other animal specialties

(G-516)
SUMMIT MECHANICAL INC
304 Carson Dr (19701-1374)
P.O. Box 1398 (19701-7398)
PHONE................302 836-8814
Edward M Mendez, *Pr*
EMP: 35 EST: 2007
SQ FT: 13,000
SALES (est): 5.19MM **Privately Held**
Web: www.summitmechanical.org
SIC: 1711 Mechanical contractor

(G-517)
SUMMIT NORTH MARINA
3000 Summit Harbour Pl (19701-2609)
PHONE................302 836-1800
Henry Heiman, *Pr*
Darrell Baker, *VP*
William Freas, *Sec*
Ed Falkowski, *Stockholder*
Albert Forwood, *Stockholder*
EMP: 16 EST: 1989
SQ FT: 1,800
SALES (est): 970.03K **Privately Held**
Web: www.summitnorthmarina.com
SIC: 5941 4493 Sporting goods and bicycle shops; Marinas

(G-518)
SUMMIT NORTH MARINA LLC
Also Called: Summit North Marina
3000 Summit Harbour Pl (19701-2609)
PHONE................302 836-1800
Darrell Baker, *Pr*
William Freas, *VP*
EMP: 11 EST: 2010
SALES (est): 270.34K **Privately Held**
SIC: 4493 Marinas

(G-519)
SUNSHINE KIDS ACADEMY
25 Paynter St (19701-3079)
PHONE................302 444-4270
Gladys Nuahma, *Owner*
EMP: 6 EST: 2009
SALES (est): 87.37K **Privately Held**
Web: www.sunshinekidsacademy.org
SIC: 8351 Group day care center

(G-520)
SUPERIOR SEALING SERVICES D
613 Pulaski Hwy (19701-1235)
P.O. Box 3539 (19807-0539)
PHONE................610 717-6237
Mark Mitchell, *Pr*
EMP: 10 EST: 2015
SALES (est): 973.89K **Privately Held**
Web: www.superiorsealingservices.com
SIC: 1771 Concrete work

(G-521)
SURF N SUDS LAUNDRIES
20 Foxhunt Dr (19701-2534)
PHONE................302 836-9120
Scot Sauer, *Prin*
EMP: 6 EST: 2018
SALES (est): 29.9K **Privately Held**
Web: www.surfnsuds.us
SIC: 7215 Laundry, coin-operated

(G-522)
T&T CUSTOM EMBROIDERY INC
51 Rawlings Dr (19701-1519)
PHONE................302 420-9454
Terrance Wiggins, *Pr*
Monique Springer, *Sec*
EMP: 2 EST: 2007
SALES (est): 127K **Privately Held**
Web: www.tntcustomembroidery.com
SIC: 2395 Embroidery products, except Schiffli machine

(G-523)
TA MANAGEMENT & CONSULTING
309 Corbitt Cir (19701-1543)
PHONE................302 317-1538
Tess Adams, *Prin*
EMP: 5 EST: 2017
SQ FT: 2,200
SALES (est): 186.25K **Privately Held**
Web: www.tamanagementandconsulting.com
SIC: 8748 Business consulting, nec

GEOGRAPHIC SECTION
Bear - New Castle County (G-554)

(G-524)
TAEKWONDO FITNESS CTR OF DEL
Also Called: Doctor Laubers Karate Plus
1230 Pulaski Hwy (19701-1305)
PHONE.................................302 836-8264
Harold Lauber Ph.d., *Pr*
EMP: 6
SALES (corp-wide): 243.03K **Privately Held**
SIC: 7999 Martial arts school, nec
PA: Taekwondo Fitness Center Of Delaware, Inc
515 E Basin Rd
New Castle DE
302 328-5755

(G-525)
TASK FORCE SECURITY SVCS LLC
1148 Pulaski Hwy (19701-1305)
PHONE.................................302 476-4064
EMP: 5 **EST:** 2020
SALES (est): 125K **Privately Held**
SIC: 6411 Inspection and investigation services, insurance

(G-526)
TAT TRUCKING INC
3482 Wrangle Hill Rd (19701-1845)
PHONE.................................302 832-2667
Mike Atack, *Pr*
EMP: 14 **EST:** 1989
SALES (est): 896.02K **Privately Held**
SIC: 7513 Truck rental and leasing, no drivers

(G-527)
TEEPEE FANTASYS LLC
105 Grand Canyon Ct (19701-1784)
PHONE.................................267 334-1270
Jessica Murray, *Managing Member*
EMP: 5 **EST:** 2020
SALES (est): 53.55K **Privately Held**
SIC: 7389 Decoration service for special events

(G-528)
THAT CLEANING SOLUTIONS LLC
47 Paisley St (19701-4719)
PHONE.................................302 442-8148
EMP: 5 **EST:** 2019
SALES (est): 222.57K **Privately Held**
SIC: 7699 Cleaning services

(G-529)
THERAPY CONCIERGE LLC
516 Daniels Ct (19701-1178)
PHONE.................................302 319-3040
EMP: 7 **EST:** 2017
SALES (est): 79.58K **Privately Held**
SIC: 8093 Rehabilitation center, outpatient treatment

(G-530)
THIRST 2 LEARN
891 Pulaski Hwy (19701-1252)
PHONE.................................302 293-2304
Pierre Smythe, *Dir*
EMP: 10 **EST:** 2011
SALES (est): 217.67K **Privately Held**
SIC: 8351 Child day care services

(G-531)
THOMAS SCOTT GILLESPIE
66 Grand Teton Dr (19701-1791)
PHONE.................................302 750-0813
EMP: 5 **EST:** 2009
SALES (est): 137.43K **Privately Held**
SIC: 1799 Special trade contractors, nec

(G-532)
TINY TOTS AND TODDLERS LLC
Also Called: Tiny Tots and Toddlers
505 Eldridge Ct (19701-4862)
PHONE.................................302 838-8787
EMP: 9 **EST:** 2011
SALES (est): 60.44K **Privately Held**
SIC: 8351 Child day care services

(G-533)
TLALOC BUILDING SERVICES INC
738 Pulaski Hwy Trlr 29b (19701-1248)
PHONE.................................302 559-6459
Ecequier Kyon, *Pr*
EMP: 5 **EST:** 2012
SALES (est): 53K **Privately Held**
SIC: 7349 Building cleaning service

(G-534)
TLALOC LANDSCAPE LLC
234 Landau Way (19701-1144)
PHONE.................................302 562-9087
Martin Villacana, *Pr*
EMP: 6 **EST:** 2010
SALES (est): 245.41K **Privately Held**
SIC: 0781 Landscape services

(G-535)
TMS NRHLTH CTRS TYSONS CRNR LL
121 Becks Woods Dr Ste 202 (19701-3851)
PHONE.................................302 994-4010
EMP: 3
SALES (corp-wide): 29.8MM **Privately Held**
Web: www.greenbrooktms.com
SIC: 3312 Blast furnaces and steel mills
PA: Tms Neurohealth Centers Tysons Corner, Llc
8405 Greensboro Dr # 120
Mc Lean VA 22102
703 356-1568

(G-536)
TODD E WATSON DC
12 Foxhunt Dr (19701-2534)
PHONE.................................615 500-6825
Todd Watson, *Ofcr*
EMP: 7 **EST:** 2017
SALES (est): 37.19K **Privately Held**
SIC: 8041 Offices and clinics of chiropractors

(G-537)
TOP NOTCH BEAUTY
120 Mario Dr (19701-6002)
PHONE.................................302 501-5442
EMP: 6 **EST:** 2019
SALES (est): 241.18K **Privately Held**
Web: topnotch.skincaretherapy.net
SIC: 7231 Hairdressers

(G-538)
TOWN AND COUNTRY TRUST
Also Called: Brandywine Wods Aprtmnts Sites
270 Brandywine Dr (19701-3201)
PHONE.................................302 328-8700
Jennifer Tyre, *Mgr*
EMP: 29
SALES (corp-wide): 49.91MM **Privately Held**
Web: www.brandywinewoods.com
SIC: 6513 Apartment building operators
PA: The Town And Country Trust
75 2nd Ave Ste 200
Needham MA 02494
781 449-6650

(G-539)
TRASH FOR CASH
208 Timber Knoll Dr (19701-1438)
PHONE.................................302 540-1513
Lauren Jones, *Prin*
EMP: 5 **EST:** 2010
SALES (est): 64.22K **Privately Held**
SIC: 8399 Advocacy group

(G-540)
TRI-STATE UNDERGROUND INC
2141 Old Kirkwood Rd (19701-2248)
PHONE.................................302 293-9352
Richard Hess, *Pr*
EMP: 6 **EST:** 2009
SQ FT: 1,100
SALES (est): 981.87K **Privately Held**
Web: www.tristateug.com
SIC: 1623 Underground utilities contractor

(G-541)
TRINITY 3 ENTERPRISES INC
38 Ayrshire St (19701-4710)
PHONE.................................267 973-2666
Sandy Brown, *Pr*
Harry Brown, *VP*
EMP: 5 **EST:** 2004
SALES (est): 250.9K **Privately Held**
SIC: 4213 Trucking, except local

(G-542)
TROY FARMER
16 Catherine Ct (19701-2298)
PHONE.................................888 711-0094
Troy Farmer, *Prin*
EMP: 7 **EST:** 2017
SALES (est): 68.27K **Privately Held**
SIC: 8322 Individual and family services

(G-543)
TWIN ANGELS SERVICE
1373 Kit Cir (19701-3112)
PHONE.................................302 545-6749
George Deangelis, *Prin*
EMP: 5 **EST:** 2011
SALES (est): 44.17K **Privately Held**
Web: www.twinangelshandymanservice.com
SIC: 7299 Handyman service

(G-544)
TYNE SUNDERLAND LLC
Also Called: Liberty Tax
413 Eden Cir (19701-4304)
PHONE.................................302 526-1608
EMP: 5 **EST:** 2021
SALES (est): 68.89K **Privately Held**
Web: www.libertytax.com
SIC: 7389 Tax collection agency

(G-545)
U HAUL NEIGHBORHOOD DEALER
214 Bear Christiana Rd (19701-1041)
PHONE.................................302 613-0207
J D Hopkins, *Owner*
EMP: 7 **EST:** 2014
SALES (est): 122.39K **Privately Held**
Web: www.uhaul.com
SIC: 7513 Truck rental and leasing, no drivers

(G-546)
U HAUL NEIGHBORHOOD DEALER
1590 Red Lion Rd (19701-1816)
PHONE.................................302 832-1433
Alan Pavlic, *Owner*
EMP: 8 **EST:** 2015
SALES (est): 153.07K **Privately Held**
Web: www.uhaul.com
SIC: 7513 Truck rental and leasing, no drivers

(G-547)
UDAAN INC
5 Brittany Ln (19701-6384)
PHONE.................................267 408-3001
Kalol Ray, *Dir*
Sandhitsu Das, *Treas*
EMP: 5 **EST:** 2015
SALES (est): 18.75K **Privately Held**
SIC: 6732 Trusts: educational, religious, etc.

(G-548)
UNIQUE BUSINESS SOLUTIONS
26 Airdrie Dr (19701-2359)
PHONE.................................302 750-0930
EMP: 5 **EST:** 2014
SALES (est): 82.98K **Privately Held**
Web: www.uniquebizsol.com
SIC: 8741 Business management

(G-549)
UNIQUE FINISHES INC
Also Called: Mr Sandless
1838 Red Lion Rd (19701-1833)
PHONE.................................302 419-8557
Anthony Chambers, *CEO*
EMP: 9 **EST:** 2003
SALES (est): 230.71K **Privately Held**
Web: www.mrsandless.com
SIC: 1752 Wood floor installation and refinishing

(G-550)
UNITED MEDICAL CLINIC LLC
161 Becks Woods Dr (19701-3833)
PHONE.................................302 451-5610
EMP: 9 **EST:** 2019
SALES (est): 445.38K **Privately Held**
Web: www.umclinic.net
SIC: 8011 General and family practice, physician/surgeon

(G-551)
UNITED MEDICAL CLINICS OF DE
121 Becks Woods Dr Ste 100 (19701-3851)
PHONE.................................302 451-5607
EMP: 19 **EST:** 2012
SALES (est): 5.39MM **Privately Held**
Web: www.umclinic.net
SIC: 8099 Health and allied services, nec

(G-552)
UNITED MEDICAL LLC
161 Becks Woods Dr (19701-3833)
PHONE.................................302 266-9166
Kemal Erkan, *Owner*
EMP: 84 **EST:** 2005
SALES (est): 10.37MM **Privately Held**
Web: www.umusa.net
SIC: 8011 Offices and clinics of medical doctors

(G-553)
UPBOUND GROUP INC
Also Called: Rent-A-Center
38 Foxhunt Dr # 40 (19701-2534)
PHONE.................................302 838-7333
J R Mallon, *Mgr*
EMP: 5
Web: www.rentacenter.com
SIC: 7359 Appliance rental
PA: Upbound Group, Inc.
5501 Headquarters Dr
Plano TX 75024

(G-554)
UPS AUTHORIZED RETAILER
Also Called: UPS

Bear - New Castle County (G-555)

GEOGRAPHIC SECTION

1148 Pulaski Hwy (19701-1305)
PHONE..................................302 834-1600
EMP: 11 EST: 2011
SALES (est): 436.56K **Privately Held**
Web: www.theupsstore.com
SIC: **7389** Mailbox rental and related service

(G-555)
USW LOCAL 4-898
1520 Porter Rd (19701-2112)
PHONE..................................302 836-6689
EMP: 8 EST: 2010
SALES (est): 91.87K **Privately Held**
SIC: **8631** Labor union

(G-556)
V & A PAINTING LLC
232 Landau Way (19701-1144)
PHONE..................................443 466-2344
Henry Llerena, *Prin*
EMP: 5 EST: 2016
SALES (est): 88.07K **Privately Held**
SIC: **1721** Painting and paper hanging

(G-557)
VSG BUSINESS SOLUTIONS LLC
221 Cornwell Dr (19701-3103)
PHONE..................................302 261-3209
EMP: 50 EST: 2014
SALES (est): 1.26MM **Privately Held**
Web: www.vsgbusinesssolutions.com
SIC: **7379** Online services technology consultants

(G-558)
WALLEYS TRUCKING INC
29 Emerald Ridge Dr (19701-2233)
P.O. Box 11624 (19850-1624)
PHONE..................................302 893-8652
Lyn Walters, *Pr*
Marcia Walters, *VP*
EMP: 9 EST: 2005
SALES (est): 491.18K **Privately Held**
SIC: **4212** Dump truck haulage

(G-559)
WAYNE I TUCKER
100 Becks Woods Dr Ste 202 (19701-3835)
PHONE..................................302 838-1100
Cheryl Tucker, *Prin*
EMP: 6 EST: 2002
SALES (est): 486.65K **Privately Held**
SIC: **8011** General and family practice, physician/surgeon

(G-560)
WB PAVING LLC
1387 Red Lion Rd (19701-1818)
PHONE..................................302 838-1886
Charlott Baker, *Prin*
EMP: 5 EST: 2007
SALES (est): 597.2K **Privately Held**
Web: www.wbpaving.com
SIC: **1611** Highway and street paving contractor

(G-561)
WELCOME HOME GETAWAYS LLC
1148 Pulaski Hwy Ste 197 (19701-1305)
PHONE..................................724 426-5534
Pamela Andrews, *CEO*
EMP: 5 EST: 2016
SALES (est): 56.39K **Privately Held**
Web: www.welcomehomegetawaysllc.com
SIC: **7261** 7389 6531 Funeral home; Business services, nec; Real estate listing services

(G-562)
WELLS FARGO BANK NATIONAL ASSN
1601 Governors Pl (19701-3054)
PHONE..................................302 832-6104
Meg Thomas, *Brnch Mgr*
EMP: 5
SALES (corp-wide): 82.86B **Publicly Held**
Web: www.wellsfargo.com
SIC: **6021** National commercial banks
HQ: Wells Fargo Bank, National Association
420 Montgomery St San
San Francisco CA 94104
605 575-6900

(G-563)
WESTSIDE FAMILY HEALTHCARE INC
404 Foxhunt Dr (19701-2538)
PHONE..................................302 836-2864
EMP: 35
Web: www.westsidehealth.org
SIC: **8011** 8021 General and family practice, physician/surgeon; Offices and clinics of dentists
PA: Westside Family Healthcare, Inc.
300 Water St Ste 200
Wilmington DE 19801

(G-564)
WICKED WITCH STUDIO
267 W Red Lion Dr (19701-5905)
PHONE..................................302 838-2011
Katherine Casale, *Prin*
EMP: 5 EST: 2010
SALES (est): 63.42K **Privately Held**
SIC: **7299** Miscellaneous personal service

(G-565)
WILSON PUBLICATIONS LLC
331 N Red Lion Ter (19701-1028)
PHONE..................................215 237-2344
EMP: 4 EST: 2016
SALES (est): 44.88K **Privately Held**
Web: www.wilsonpublicationsllc.com
SIC: **2741** Miscellaneous publishing

(G-566)
WORKING EVERY SHIFT TRNSPRTING
735 Roger Chaffee Sq Mx (19701-6855)
PHONE..................................267 262-3453
EMP: 30 EST: 2020
SALES (est): 250K **Privately Held**
SIC: **4789** Freight car loading and unloading

(G-567)
WORLD HOSPITAL INC
102 Sweethollow Dr (19701-3376)
PHONE..................................609 254-3391
EMP: 9 EST: 2011
SALES (est): 138.88K **Privately Held**
SIC: **8062** General medical and surgical hospitals

(G-568)
WRECK MASTERS DEMO DERBY
221 Kline St (19701-2218)
PHONE..................................302 368-5544
Joe Fields, *Owner*
EMP: 10 EST: 2000
SALES (est): 611.13K **Privately Held**
SIC: **5531** 7514 Auto and home supply stores ; Rent-a-car service

(G-569)
XAVIER ENTERTAINMENT INC
1031 Roger Chaffee Sq (19701-6852)
PHONE..................................215 356-8314
Tyrone Martin, *Pr*
EMP: 5 EST: 1999
SALES (est): 480.45K **Privately Held**
SIC: **4213** 4212 4214 Trucking, except local; Local trucking, without storage; Local trucking with storage

(G-570)
YOGA FOR YOU
201 Lake Ozarks Dr (19701-3800)
PHONE..................................302 832-0675
Melissa Stanley, *Prin*
EMP: 5 EST: 2018
SALES (est): 20.78K **Privately Held**
SIC: **7999** Yoga instruction

(G-571)
ZACH PHILIPPE SATE FARM INS
2500 Wrangle Hill Rd Ste 125 (19701-3836)
PHONE..................................302 327-0120
Zach Philippe, *Admn*
EMP: 6 EST: 2018
SALES (est): 264.99K **Privately Held**
SIC: **6411** Insurance agents and brokers

(G-572)
ZANES SIDING AND TRIM
2327 Chesapeake City Rd (19701-2332)
PHONE..................................302 377-5394
EMP: 5 EST: 2017
SALES (est): 196.36K **Privately Held**
SIC: **1761** Siding contractor

Bethany Beach
Sussex County

(G-573)
ALLMOND & EASTBURN
Also Called: Allmond, Charles M III
34952 Belle Rd (19930-2824)
PHONE..................................302 764-2193
Thomas Eastburn, *Pt*
EMP: 5 EST: 1990
SALES (est): 454.54K **Privately Held**
SIC: **8111** General practice attorney, lawyer

(G-574)
AON CONSTRUCTION SERVICES LLC
961b Hawksbill St (19930-9647)
PHONE..................................302 858-6178
Frank Costango, *Prin*
EMP: 5 EST: 2015
SALES (est): 76.8K **Privately Held**
SIC: **1521** Single-family housing construction

(G-575)
AXION FINANCIAL GROUP LLC
33258 Kent Ave (19930-3787)
PHONE..................................267 261-4177
EMP: 5 EST: 2016
SALES (est): 156.35K **Privately Held**
Web: www.axionfinancial.com
SIC: **6282** Investment advice

(G-576)
BEACH BREAK & BAKRIE
123 Garfield Pkwy (19930-7747)
PHONE..................................302 537-3800
Beth Webb, *Owner*
EMP: 7 EST: 2011
SALES (est): 813.14K **Privately Held**
SIC: **5149** Bakery products

(G-577)
BEACH HOUSE RESOURCES
29l Atlantic Ave # 199 (19930-7737)
PHONE..................................703 980-3336
Paul Denault, *Prin*
EMP: 14 EST: 2007
SALES (est): 249.86K **Privately Held**
Web: www.beach-house-resources.com
SIC: **7011** Bed and breakfast inn

(G-578)
BETHANY AREA REALTY
778 Garfield Pkwy (19930-9219)
P.O. Box 1322 (19930-1322)
PHONE..................................302 539-7500
Ann Raskauskas, *Pr*
EMP: 6 EST: 2017
SALES (est): 224.76K **Privately Held**
Web: www.bethanyarearealty.com
SIC: **6531** Real estate agent, residential

(G-579)
BETHANY BCH OCEAN STES RSDNCE
99 Hollywood St (19930-7749)
PHONE..................................302 539-3201
Patrick Staib, *Genl Mgr*
EMP: 23 EST: 2015
SALES (est): 470.96K **Privately Held**
Web: www.bboceansuites.com
SIC: **7011** Resort hotel

(G-580)
BETHANY BEACH BED & BREAKFAST
33391 Ocean Pines Ln (19930-3735)
PHONE..................................301 651-2278
EMP: 8 EST: 2015
SALES (est): 55.44K **Privately Held**
Web: www.bethanybeachbedandbreakfast.com
SIC: **7011** Motel, franchised

(G-581)
BETHANY BEACH GOODS & RENTALS
163 Scannell Blvd (19930-9210)
P.O. Box 1587 (19930-1587)
PHONE..................................207 266-1682
Kirstie Dubois, *Prin*
EMP: 5 EST: 2016
SALES (est): 226.02K **Privately Held**
SIC: **7359** Equipment rental and leasing, nec

(G-582)
BETHANY BEACH VACATION RENTALS
39682 Sunrise Ct (19930-3469)
PHONE..................................302 539-9400
Patrick Davis, *Prin*
EMP: 6 EST: 2016
SALES (est): 82.65K **Privately Held**
Web: www.lfvacations.com
SIC: **6531** Real estate agent, residential

(G-583)
BETHANY BEACH VLNTR FIRE CO (PA)
215 Hollywood St (19930)
P.O. Box 950 (19930-0950)
PHONE..................................302 539-7700
EMP: 42 EST: 1948
SALES (est): 315.38K **Privately Held**
Web: www.bethanybeachfire.com
SIC: **7389** 8699 Fire protection service other than forestry or public; Charitable organization

(G-584)
BETHANY CYCLE & FITNESS INC (PA)
Also Called: Bethany Cycle and Fitness
792b Garfield Pkwy (19930-9723)
PHONE..................................302 537-9982

Alton Jones, *Pr*
Mona Jones, *Sec*
EMP: 5 **EST**: 1992
SQ FT: 1,600
SALES (est): 794.58K **Privately Held**
Web: www.bethanycycle.com
SIC: 5941 7699 Bicycle and bicycle parts; Recreational sporting equipment repair services

(G-585)
BETHANY RESORT FURNISHINGS
939 N Pennsylvania Ave (19930-3467)
P.O. Box 397 (19930-0397)
PHONE..................................302 539-4000
Kimmerly Messick, *Owner*
EMP: 6 **EST**: 2015
SALES (est): 45K **Privately Held**
Web: www.bethanyresortfurnishings.com
SIC: 1799 Home/office interiors finishing, furnishing and remodeling

(G-586)
BETHANY SEA-CREST INC
99 Atlantic Garfield Pkwy (19930-7737)
P.O. Box 370 (19930-0370)
PHONE..................................302 539-7621
Elizabeth Hammond, *Pr*
Asher E Hammond Junior, *VP*
EMP: 5 **EST**: 1976
SQ FT: 3,000
SALES (est): 795.89K **Privately Held**
Web: www.bethanyseacrest.com
SIC: 5947 5632 7011 Gift shop; Costume jewelry; Motels

(G-587)
BLUE SHORE INC
601 Holly Ct (19930-9638)
PHONE..................................301 890-9797
EMP: 6 **EST**: 2018
SALES (est): 57.16K **Privately Held**
Web: www.blueshoreinc.com
SIC: 7699 Cleaning services

(G-588)
BONIE L BURNQUIST M D P A
433 Canal Way W (19930-9007)
PHONE..................................302 537-6110
EMP: 6 **EST**: 2018
SALES (est): 89.4K **Privately Held**
SIC: 8011 General and family practice, physician/surgeon

(G-589)
CARL M FREEMAN ASSOCIATES INC
Also Called: Sea Colony
  Rte 1 & Pennsylvania Ave (19930)
  P.O. Box 480 (19930-0480)
PHONE..................................302 539-6961
Patrick Davis, *Genl Mgr*
EMP: 85
SALES (corp-wide): 42.66MM **Privately Held**
Web: www.freemancompanies.com
SIC: 1531 6531 6519 6513 Condominium developers; Real estate agents and managers; Real property lessors, nec; Apartment building operators
PA: Carl M. Freeman Associates, Inc.
  909 Rose Ave Ste 1000
  Rockville MD 20852
  240 453-3000

(G-590)
CHESTER MARINA LLC
33309 Kent Ave (19930-3730)
PHONE..................................302 829-8218
EMP: 5 **EST**: 2016
SALES (est): 113.35K **Privately Held**
SIC: 4493 Marinas

(G-591)
COLDWELL BANKER
39682 Sunrise Ct (19930-3469)
P.O. Box 640 (19930-0640)
PHONE..................................302 539-4086
EMP: 19 **EST**: 1964
SALES (est): 785.77K **Privately Held**
Web: www.coldwellbanker.com
SIC: 6531 Real estate agent, residential

(G-592)
D M F ASSOCIATES INC
Also Called: Bennett Realty
  Rte 1 Evergreen St (19930)
PHONE..................................302 539-0606
EMP: 5 **EST**: 1970
SALES (est): 496.31K **Privately Held**
Web: www.bennett-realty.com
SIC: 6531 Real estate agent, residential

(G-593)
DAISY HORA
39682 Sunrise Ct (19930-3469)
PHONE..................................302 727-6299
Daisy Hora, *Prin*
EMP: 5 **EST**: 2016
SALES (est): 73.93K **Privately Held**
Web: www.daisyhorarealtor.com
SIC: 6531 Escrow agent, real estate

(G-594)
DEBORAH L WAYLAND
Also Called: Eastern Shore Wedding & Events
603 Sussex Ct (19930-9697)
PHONE..................................443 669-3106
Deborah L Wayland, *Prin*
EMP: 5 **EST**: 2012
SALES (est): 67.86K **Privately Held**
Web: www.familylifecampaign.org
SIC: 7299 Wedding consultant

(G-595)
DELAWARE BOTANIC GARDENS INC
201 Ashwood St (19930)
P.O. Box 360 (19930-0360)
PHONE..................................202 262-9501
Raymond Sander, *Prin*
Sheryl Swed, *Prin*
EMP: 6 **EST**: 2017
SALES (est): 88.11K **Privately Held**
Web: www.delawaregardens.org
SIC: 8422 Botanical garden

(G-596)
DELAWARE DIGITAL MEDIA LLC
Also Called: Florida Digital Media LLC
32895 Coastal Hwy Unit 201b (19930-3784)
PHONE..................................302 278-8080
Kerri Fox, *Prin*
EMP: 5 **EST**: 2018
SALES (est): 224.56K **Privately Held**
Web: www.delawaredigitalmedia.com
SIC: 4899 Communication services, nec

(G-597)
DIESTE MARK DESIGN BUILD LLC
32895 Coastal Hwy Unit 201 (19930-3784)
PHONE..................................301 921-9050
EMP: 10 **EST**: 2002
SALES (est): 992.78K **Privately Held**
Web: www.markdiestedesignbuild.com
SIC: 1522 Remodeling, multi-family dwellings

(G-598)
DR RAJSHEKAR NARASIMAIAH MD
33188 Coastal Hwy Unit 4 (19930-3779)
PHONE..................................302 537-1100
EMP: 6 **EST**: 2018
SALES (est): 47.09K **Privately Held**
SIC: 8011 Offices and clinics of medical doctors

(G-599)
ELLEN RICE GALLERY
98 Garfield Pkwy Unit 109 (19930-7755)
PHONE..................................302 539-3405
Ellen Rice, *Owner*
EMP: 7 **EST**: 2016
SALES (est): 204.72K **Privately Held**
Web: www.ellenrice.gallery
SIC: 8412 Art gallery

(G-600)
EVENTIDE HOSPITALITY LLC ✿
Also Called: Addy Sea, The
  99 Ocean View Pkwy (19930-9262)
PHONE..................................202 725-6357
EMP: 15 **EST**: 2022
SALES (est): 456.21K **Privately Held**
SIC: 7011 Bed and breakfast inn

(G-601)
FELLS POINTS SURF
114 Garfield Pkwy (19930-7705)
PHONE..................................302 537-7873
EMP: 4 **EST**: 2018
SALES (est): 138.09K **Privately Held**
Web: www.fellspointsurf.com
SIC: 3949 Surfboards

(G-602)
FRONTGATE LLC
Also Called: Julesk
33258 Kent Ave (19930-3787)
PHONE..................................302 245-6654
Nick Kypreos, *Managing Member*
Julie Kypreos, *Managing Member*
EMP: 2 **EST**: 2011
SALES (est): 64.88K **Privately Held**
SIC: 3171 Women's handbags and purses

(G-603)
GALLO REALTY INC
33292 Coastal Hwy Unit 1 (19930-3703)
PHONE..................................888 624-6794
Elizabeth D Gallo, *Brnch Mgr*
EMP: 6
SALES (corp-wide): 1.72MM **Privately Held**
Web: beachrentals.penfedrealty.com
SIC: 6531 Real estate agent, residential
PA: Gallo Realty Inc
  37230 Rehoboth Avenue Ext
  Rehoboth Beach DE 19971
  302 945-7368

(G-604)
GOODBITE USA INC
56140 Pine Cone Ln (19930)
PHONE..................................516 761-4386
David Hraska, *Prin*
EMP: 3
SALES (est): 135.7K **Privately Held**
SIC: 2051 Bakery: wholesale or wholesale/retail combined

(G-605)
GREGG WHITE CONTRACTING
300 Hollywood St (19930-9164)
PHONE..................................302 542-9552
Gregg White, *Owner*
EMP: 5 **EST**: 2018
SALES (est): 246.11K **Privately Held**
SIC: 1521 Single-family housing construction

(G-606)
GW SOLUTIONS LLC
237 Oyster Shell Cv (19930-9001)
PHONE..................................240 578-5981
EMP: 5 **EST**: 1996
SQ FT: 3,570
SALES (est): 283.26K **Privately Held**
SIC: 7371 Computer software development

(G-607)
HIGHLAND CONSULTING GROUP INC
Also Called: Dignan Group
505 Fairway Dr (19930-9611)
PHONE..................................301 408-0600
David Dignan, *Pr*
EMP: 6
SALES (corp-wide): 2.06MM **Privately Held**
SIC: 7311 Advertising agencies
PA: Highland Consulting Group Inc
  933 S Talbot St Ste 15
  Saint Michaels MD 21663
  410 745-3036

(G-608)
HUGH H HICKMAN & SONS INC
300 Ocean View Pkwy (19930-9211)
P.O. Box 1000 (19930-1000)
PHONE..................................302 539-9741
Tim Tribbitt, *Pr*
EMP: 14 **EST**: 1957
SQ FT: 703
SALES (est): 663.11K **Privately Held**
Web: www.hughhickman.com
SIC: 1521 New construction, single-family houses

(G-609)
INTOUCH BODY THERAPY LLC
33012 Coastal Hwy Unit 4 (19930-3777)
PHONE..................................302 537-0510
Dianna Moesce, *Prin*
EMP: 8 **EST**: 2012
SALES (est): 108.32K **Privately Held**
SIC: 8093 Rehabilitation center, outpatient treatment

(G-610)
ISLAND BOY ENTERPRISE LLC
35 Inlet View Ct (19930-9251)
PHONE..................................904 347-4563
Joe Cole, *Managing Member*
EMP: 2 **EST**: 2018
SALES (est): 100K **Privately Held**
SIC: 7372 Application computer software

(G-611)
JACK HICKMAN REAL ESTATE
Also Called: White's Creek Manor
33188 Coastal Hwy Unit 2 (19930-3779)
P.O. Box 1 (19930-0001)
PHONE..................................302 539-8000
Jack Hickman, *Pr*
Chad Hickman, *VP*
EMP: 10 **EST**: 1973
SALES (est): 971.56K **Privately Held**
Web: www.jackhickmanrealestate.com
SIC: 6552 1521 4493 Land subdividers and developers, residential; New construction, single-family houses; Marinas

(G-612)
JOE MAGGIO REALTY
8 N Pennsylvania Ave (19930-9746)
PHONE..................................302 539-9300
EMP: 6
SALES (corp-wide): 478.96K **Privately Held**
Web: www.rehobothleweshomes.com

Bethany Beach - Sussex County (G-613)

SIC: 6531 Real estate agent, residential
PA: Joe Maggio Realty
37169 Rehobth Ave Ext
Rehoboth Beach DE 19971
302 251-8792

(G-613)
KNIGHTS OF COLUMBUS
Also Called: Knights of Columbus
967a Tortoise St (19930-9648)
P.O. Box 654 (19930-0654)
PHONE...................703 615-3372
Richard Morin, Prin
EMP: 5 EST: 2017
SALES (est): 56.05K Privately Held
Web: www.kofc.org
SIC: 8641 Fraternal associations

(G-614)
LEGUM & NORMAN MID-WEST LLC
44 Edgewater House Rd (19930)
PHONE...................302 537-9499
Craig Clarke, Brnch Mgr
EMP: 7
SALES (corp-wide): 22.03MM Privately Held
Web: www.legumnorman.com
SIC: 6531 Condominium manager
PA: Legum & Norman Mid-West, Llc
3130 Frview Pk Dr Ste 200
Falls Church VA 22042
703 600-6000

(G-615)
LESLIE KOPP INC
33298 Coastal Hwy (19930-3781)
P.O. Box 1301 (19930-1301)
PHONE...................302 541-5207
Leslie Kopp, Owner
EMP: 10 EST: 2013
SALES (est): 671.57K Privately Held
Web: www.bestofbethany.com
SIC: 6531 Real estate agent, residential

(G-616)
LIGHTHOUSE REALTY GROUP I
782 Garfield Pkwy Ste 202 (19930-9224)
PHONE...................302 541-4440
EMP: 5 EST: 2016
SALES (est): 90.91K Privately Held
Web: www.lighthousehome.net
SIC: 6531 Real estate agent, residential

(G-617)
MARK B BROWN DDS
32895 Coastal Hwy Unit 102 (19930-3782)
PHONE...................302 537-1200
Mark Brown, Off Mgr
EMP: 9 EST: 2017
SALES (est): 67.67K Privately Held
SIC: 8021 Dentists' office

(G-618)
MARNIE CUSTOM HOMES
33298 Coastal Hwy Unit 3 (19930-3781)
PHONE...................302 616-2664
EMP: 6 EST: 2019
SALES (est): 279.65K Privately Held
Web: www.marniehomes.com
SIC: 1521 New construction, single-family houses

(G-619)
MARNIE PROPERTIES
P.O. Box 176 (19930-0176)
PHONE...................302 462-5312
Marnie Oursler, Prin
EMP: 9 EST: 2008
SALES (est): 920.22K Privately Held
Web: www.marniehomes.com

SIC: 6512 Nonresidential building operators

(G-620)
MERIS GARDENS BED & BREAKFAST
33309 Kent Ave (19930-3730)
PHONE...................302 752-4962
EMP: 11 EST: 2015
SALES (est): 303.05K Privately Held
Web: www.merisgardensbethany.com
SIC: 7011 Bed and breakfast inn

(G-621)
MERIS PROPERTY LLC
26 N Pennsylvania Ave (19930-9263)
PHONE...................301 928-6519
Michael S Daniels, Prin
EMP: 5 EST: 2011
SALES (est): 195.31K Privately Held
SIC: 6512 Nonresidential building operators

(G-622)
NAGORKA
303 Wellington Pkwy (19930-9543)
PHONE...................302 537-2392
Diane S Nagorka, Prin
EMP: 5 EST: 2008
SALES (est): 58.36K Privately Held
SIC: 2389 Clergymen's vestments

(G-623)
NINETY ONE HOLDING INC
56140 Pine Cone Ln (19930-4133)
PHONE...................212 203-7900
Bleron Baraliu, CEO
Eleonora Gashi, Pr
EMP: 21 EST: 2018
SALES (est): 458.75K Privately Held
SIC: 7371 Custom computer programming services

(G-624)
OCEAN ATLANTIC SOTHEBYS INTL
26 N Pennsylvania Ave (19930-9263)
PHONE...................302 539-1033
William Lucks, Mgr
EMP: 15 EST: 2011
SALES (est): 459.71K Privately Held
Web: www.oceanatlantic.net
SIC: 6531 Real estate brokers and agents

(G-625)
PATERSON SCHWARTZ REAL ESTATE
26 N Pennsylvania Ave (19930-9263)
PHONE...................302 537-1300
Jason Giles, Pr
EMP: 12 EST: 2016
SALES (est): 163.47K Privately Held
Web: www.pattersonschwartz.com
SIC: 6531 Real estate agent, residential

(G-626)
PAUL AMOS
Also Called: Holiday Inn
39642 Jefferson Bridge Rd (19930-3723)
PHONE...................302 541-9200
Brad Clark, Mgr
EMP: 41 EST: 2001
SALES (est): 380.44K Privately Held
Web: www.holidayinn.com
SIC: 7011 Hotels and motels

(G-627)
PIVOTAL MEDICAL
413 Salt Pond Rd (19930-9595)
PHONE...................302 299-5795
Charles Pann, Prin
EMP: 5 EST: 2017
SALES (est): 76K Privately Held

SIC: 8099 Health and allied services, nec

(G-628)
PRIVACY POLICY/UNITED CUSTOM C
33012 Coastal Hwy Unit 5 (19930-3777)
PHONE...................302 537-1717
Robin Salisbury, Pr
EMP: 6 EST: 2017
SALES (est): 147.71K Privately Held
Web: www.unitedcustomcontractors.com
SIC: 1799 Special trade contractors, nec

(G-629)
PROPERTY IMPROVEMENTS LLC
144 Brandywine Dr (19930-9738)
PHONE...................610 692-5343
Stephan Walker, Prin
EMP: 8 EST: 2008
SALES (est): 395.85K Privately Held
Web: www.propertyimprovementsllc.com
SIC: 6512 Nonresidential building operators

(G-630)
RASKAUKAS JOSEPH C ATY LAW
33176 Coastal Hwy (19930-3758)
P.O. Box 1509 (19930-1509)
PHONE...................302 537-2000
J C Raskauskas, Owner
Joseph C Raskauskas, Owner
EMP: 6 EST: 1996
SALES (est): 470.61K Privately Held
SIC: 8111 General practice attorney, lawyer

(G-631)
RE/MAX
Also Called: Re/Max
300 Ocean View Pkwy (19930-9211)
PHONE...................302 381-2540
EMP: 5 EST: 2018
SALES (est): 218.33K Privately Held
Web: www.remax.com
SIC: 6531 Real estate agent, residential

(G-632)
REMAX BY SEA
Also Called: Re/Max
R 1 5th D St (19930)
P.O. Box 1499 (19930-1499)
PHONE...................302 541-5000
Frank Serio, Pt
EMP: 5 EST: 2000
SALES (est): 209.72K Privately Held
Web: www.remax.com
SIC: 6531 Real estate agent, residential

(G-633)
RESIDENCE INN BY MARIOTT
Also Called: Residence Inn By Marriott
99 Hollywood St (19930-7749)
PHONE...................302 539-3200
EMP: 13 EST: 2018
SALES (est): 163.94K Privately Held
Web: residence-inn.marriott.com
SIC: 7011 Hotels and motels

(G-634)
RESORTQUEST DELAWARE RE LLC (DH)
Also Called: Resort Quest Delaware Beaches
33546 Market Pl (19930-4269)
P.O. Box 480 (19930-0480)
PHONE...................302 541-8999
Patrick Davis, Genl Mgr
EMP: 5 EST: 1997
SALES (est): 9.37MM Publicly Held
Web: www.vacasa.com
SIC: 6531 6519 Real estate leasing and rentals; Real property lessors, nec
HQ: Wyndham Exchange And Rentals, Inc.
7 Sylvan Way

Parsippany NJ 07054

(G-635)
RESORTQUEST SERVICE CENTER
33260 Coastal Hwy Unit 1 (19930-3780)
PHONE...................302 541-5977
EMP: 5 EST: 2018
SALES (est): 100.7K Privately Held
Web: www.vacasa.com
SIC: 6512 Commercial and industrial building operation

(G-636)
RHONDA FRICK
33298 Coastal Hwy (19930-3781)
PHONE...................302 236-1456
Rhonda Frick, Prin
EMP: 6 EST: 2010
SALES (est): 105.43K Privately Held
Web: www.rhondafrick.com
SIC: 6531 Real estate agent, residential

(G-637)
ROBERTS PROPERTY MGT LLC
107 Canal Rd (19930-9507)
PHONE...................302 537-5371
Dennis Roberts, Prin
EMP: 5 EST: 2010
SALES (est): 246.32K Privately Held
Web: www.robertspropertymgmt.com
SIC: 8741 Management services

(G-638)
SALT POND ASSOCIATES
Also Called: Salt Pond Golf Club
400 Bethany Loop (19930-9020)
PHONE...................302 539-2750
Rupert Smith, Pt
Ken Simpler, Mng Pt
Nancy Smith, Pt
Karen Simpler, Pt
Raymond Marchetti, Pt
EMP: 21 EST: 1988
SALES (est): 2.05MM Privately Held
Web: www.saltpondgolf.com
SIC: 6552 7997 Land subdividers and developers, residential; Golf club, membership

(G-639)
SCHIFF GROUP LLC
606 Pond View Dr (19930-9727)
PHONE...................301 325-1359
David Schiff, Pr
EMP: 8 EST: 2009
SQ FT: 1,000
SALES (est): 718.96K Privately Held
Web: www.theschiffgroup.com
SIC: 7812 8999 8748 Motion picture and video production; Communication services; Business consulting, nec

(G-640)
SEA COLONY LLC
Also Called: Sea Colony
2 Edgewater House Rd (19930-8091)
PHONE...................302 537-8888
EMP: 14 EST: 2019
SALES (est): 59.3K Privately Held
SIC: 7011 Resort hotel

(G-641)
SEA STUDIO ARCHITECTS
658 Tingle Ave (19930-9711)
PHONE...................302 364-0821
EMP: 8 EST: 2017
SALES (est): 45.65K Privately Held
Web: www.seagreenstudio.com
SIC: 8712 Architectural engineering

GEOGRAPHIC SECTION
Bridgeville - Sussex County (G-669)

(G-642)
SHIRLEY PRICE SELLS
33298 Coastal Hwy (19930-3781)
PHONE......................302 236-7046
EMP: 5 **EST:** 2018
SALES (est): 82.65K **Privately Held**
Web: www.shirleypricesells.com
SIC: 6531 Real estate agent, residential

(G-643)
SUSSEX SHORES BEACH ASSN
P.O. Box 309 (19930-0309)
PHONE......................302 539-7511
EMP: 14 **EST:** 2009
SALES (est): 298.21K **Privately Held**
Web: www.wilgusassociates.com
SIC: 8699 Membership organizations, nec

(G-644)
SUSSEX SHORES WATER CO CORP
39602 Water Works Ct (19930-3516)
P.O. Box 170 (19930-0170)
PHONE......................302 539-7611
Christine Mason, *Pr*
Pamela Short, *Ch Bd*
Richard Russo, *Ch Bd*
EMP: 7 **EST:** 1955
SALES (est): 1.11MM **Privately Held**
Web: www.sussexshoreswater.com
SIC: 4941 Water supply

(G-645)
T K O DESIGNS INC
Also Called: T K O
100 Garfield Pkwy (19930-7705)
P.O. Box 146 (19930-0146)
PHONE......................302 539-6992
Alice Klein, *Pr*
Bryant Poark, *VP*
EMP: 3 **EST:** 1980
SALES (est): 233.6K **Privately Held**
SIC: 3961 5944 Costume jewelry; Jewelry stores

(G-646)
TAGGART PROFESSIONAL CENTER
32895 Coastal Hwy Unit 203b (19930-3782)
PHONE......................410 491-7311
John Taggart, *Prin*
EMP: 5 **EST:** 2012
SALES (est): 27.65K **Privately Held**
SIC: 7299 Massage parlor

(G-647)
WARD & TAYLOR LLC
33548 Market Pl Unit 3 (19930-3719)
PHONE......................302 539-3537
EMP: 5
Web: www.wardtaylor.com
SIC: 8111 Real estate law
PA: Ward & Taylor, Llc
  2710 Centerville Rd # 210
  Wilmington DE 19808

(G-648)
WARNER TANSEY INC
Pennsylvania Ave (19930)
P.O. Box 337 (19930-0337)
PHONE......................302 539-3001
Deborha Conneen, *Pr*
EMP: 7 **EST:** 1975
SALES (est): 844.07K **Privately Held**
Web: www.tanseywarner.com
SIC: 6531 Real estate brokers and agents

(G-649)
WATERMARK AT NORTH BETHANY
36903 S Silver Sands Dr (19930-9539)
PHONE......................302 539-3223
EMP: 6 **EST:** 2017
SALES (est): 121.11K **Privately Held**
Web: www.sellingdelawarehomes.com
SIC: 6531 Real estate agent, residential

(G-650)
WILGUS ASSOCIATES INC (PA)
32904 Coastal Hwy (19930-3707)
PHONE......................302 539-7511
Michael W Wilgus, *Pr*
David Wilgus, *Sec*
EMP: 23 **EST:** 1947
SQ FT: 8,000
SALES (est): 8.51MM
SALES (corp-wide): 8.51MM **Privately Held**
Web: www.wilgusassociates.com
SIC: 6411 6531 Insurance brokers, nec; Real estate brokers and agents

(G-651)
WOMENS CIVIC CLUB BETHANY BCH
332 Sandpiper Dr (19930-9086)
P.O. Box 935 (19930-0935)
PHONE......................302 539-7515
Cheryl Dorfman, *Prin*
EMP: 7 **EST:** 2011
SALES (est): 105.6K **Privately Held**
Web: www.bethanybeachchristianchurch.org
SIC: 7997 Membership sports and recreation clubs

(G-652)
WYNDHAM VACATION RENTALS
33176 Coastal Hwy (19930-3758)
P.O. Box 480 (19930-0480)
PHONE......................877 893-2487
Patrick Davis, *Mgr*
EMP: 7 **EST:** 2017
SALES (est): 114.15K **Privately Held**
Web: www.lfvacations.com
SIC: 7359 Equipment rental and leasing, nec

Bethel
Sussex County

(G-653)
CALLOWAY FARMS
6445 Baileys Landing Dr (19931-3113)
PHONE......................302 875-0476
Gary Calloway, *Prin*
EMP: 8 **EST:** 2011
SALES (est): 494.96K **Privately Held**
SIC: 0191 General farms, primarily crop

(G-654)
GREENLAND SOD FARM LLC
8268 Snake Rd (19931-3106)
PHONE......................302 258-7543
EMP: 5 **EST:** 2006
SALES (est): 92.64K **Privately Held**
SIC: 0181 Sod farms

Bridgeville
Sussex County

(G-655)
1EVANS ENVIRONMENTAL SERV
14844 Deer Forest Rd (19933-4455)
PHONE......................410 635-8304
Duane R Evans, *Prin*
EMP: 5 **EST:** 2010
SALES (est): 142.59K **Privately Held**
SIC: 8999 Earth science services

(G-656)
1ST CHOICE PAINTING LLC
10795 Rifle Range Rd (19933-4036)
PHONE......................302 278-2684
Marco Sanchez, *Prin*
EMP: 8 **EST:** 2018
SALES (est): 231.05K **Privately Held**
SIC: 1721 Painting and paper hanging

(G-657)
36 BUILDERS INC
16255 Sussex Hwy (19933-2968)
PHONE......................302 349-9480
EMP: 20 **EST:** 2008
SALES (est): 3MM **Privately Held**
Web: www.itsjustabetterhouse.com
SIC: 1521 New construction, single-family houses

(G-658)
4TROY FOUNDATION
12453 Redden Rd (19933-4180)
PHONE......................302 448-9203
Christina Haynes, *Prin*
Troy Haynes, *Prin*
Mary Ross, *Prin*
Lefeisha Cannon, *Prin*
EMP: 13 **EST:** 2020
SALES (est): 132.63K **Privately Held**
SIC: 8641 Civic and social associations

(G-659)
A C SCHULTES OF DELAWARE INC (HQ)
16289 Sussex Hwy (19933-2968)
P.O. Box 188 (19933-0188)
PHONE......................302 337-0700
R Michael Collison, *Pr*
EMP: 11 **EST:** 1921
SQ FT: 1,500
SALES (est): 2.7MM **Privately Held**
Web: www.acschultes.com
SIC: 1781 Servicing, water wells
PA: A.C.S. & Sons, Inc.
  664 S Evergreen Ave
  Woodbury Heights NJ 08097

(G-660)
A-TEAM CLEANING LLC
7019 Seashore Hwy (19933-3109)
PHONE......................302 858-8709
Kristin Todd, *Prin*
EMP: 5 **EST:** 2016
SALES (est): 55.7K **Privately Held**
SIC: 7699 Cleaning services

(G-661)
ACORN SITE FURNISHINGS
5218 Federalsburg Rd (19933-3552)
PHONE......................302 249-4979
Anthony Corum, *Sls Mgr*
EMP: 2 **EST:** 2013
SALES (est): 121.38K **Privately Held**
SIC: 2531 7389 Picnic tables or benches, park; Business Activities at Non-Commercial Site

(G-662)
ALL-SPAN INC (PA)
9347 Allspan Dr (19933-2982)
PHONE......................302 349-9460
David Miller, *Pr*
Herb Troyer, *
Jj Carter, *
Charlotte Torbert, *MNG**
Matt Brennan, *
▼ **EMP:** 37 **EST:** 1999
SQ FT: 34,000
SALES (est): 9.65MM **Privately Held**
Web: www.allspaninc.com

SIC: 3448 Trusses and framing, prefabricated metal

(G-663)
AMANDA LYNN FERENC LPN
6755 Cannon Rd (19933-3549)
PHONE......................302 841-2498
Amanda Lynn Ferenc, *Prin*
EMP: 9 **EST:** 2012
SALES (est): 80.08K **Privately Held**
SIC: 8011 Offices and clinics of medical doctors

(G-664)
AMH ENTERPRISES LLC
8805 Newton Rd (19933-2946)
PHONE......................302 337-0300
Austin Hubbard, *Managing Member*
Traci Creighton, *
EMP: 21 **EST:** 2010
SALES (est): 1.25MM **Privately Held**
Web: www.amhbulk.com
SIC: 4213 Trucking, except local

(G-665)
AMP ELECTRIC LLC
302 Earlee Ave (19933-1304)
PHONE......................302 337-8050
Steve Mccarron, *Prin*
Phillip Andrew, *Prin*
EMP: 9 **EST:** 2016
SALES (est): 723.18K **Privately Held**
SIC: 1731 Electrical work

(G-666)
ARCTEC AIR HEATING & COOLING
21965 Palomino Way (19933-4575)
PHONE......................302 629-7129
Jeremy Booros, *Owner*
EMP: 6 **EST:** 2005
SALES (est): 512.6K **Privately Held**
Web: www.arctecair.com
SIC: 1711 Warm air heating and air conditioning contractor

(G-667)
ARDEX LABORATORIES INC
5027 Dublin Hill Rd (19933-3030)
PHONE......................302 363-1005
EMP: 5 **EST:** 2018
SALES (est): 70.48K **Privately Held**
Web: www.ardex.com
SIC: 8734 Testing laboratories

(G-668)
ASI TRANSPORT LLC
9347 Allspan Dr (19933-2982)
PHONE......................302 349-9460
David Miller, *Pr*
James Carter, *VP*
EMP: 6 **EST:** 2002
SQ FT: 5,000
SALES (est): 712.11K **Privately Held**
SIC: 4212 4213 Local trucking, without storage; Trucking, except local
PA: All-Span, Inc.
  9347 Allspan Dr
  Bridgeville DE 19933

(G-669)
AUGUSTO & SONS LANDSCAPING LLC
17490 Cedar Corners Rd (19933-4291)
PHONE......................302 278-9196
EMP: 5 **EST:** 2016
SALES (est): 242.01K **Privately Held**
Web: www.landscapinggeorgetown.net
SIC: 0781 Landscape services

Bridgeville - Sussex County (G-670)   GEOGRAPHIC SECTION

(G-670)
AUTOMATION AIR INC
16782 Oak Rd (19933-3910)
PHONE..................................973 875-6676
William Schnabel, *Pr*
EMP: 7 EST: 1980
SALES (est): 792.64K **Privately Held**
Web: www.automationair.com
SIC: 5084 Drilling equipment, excluding bits

(G-671)
BALDWIN SAYRE INC
17882 Potato Ln (19933-3154)
PHONE..................................302 337-0309
Daniel Baldwin, *Pr*
Diane Baldwin, *VP*
EMP: 5 EST: 1948
SQ FT: 20,000
SALES (est): 796.38K **Privately Held**
SIC: 0161 5153 Corn farm, sweet; Corn

(G-672)
BG WELDING LLC
14047 Redden Rd (19933-4175)
PHONE..................................302 228-7260
Jose Angel Campos Junior, *Prin*
EMP: 5 EST: 2019
SALES (est): 88.73K **Privately Held**
SIC: 7692 Welding repair

(G-673)
BLUE COLLAR UTILITIES LLC ◆
7003 Seashore Hwy (19933-3109)
PHONE..................................410 422-0886
Stephanie Jarmon, *Prin*
EMP: 5 EST: 2022
SALES (est): 68.89K **Privately Held**
SIC: 7389 Business Activities at Non-Commercial Site

(G-674)
BRAVOS CONSTRUCTION LLC
20871 Sanfilippo Rd (19933-4549)
PHONE..................................302 249-0039
Israel Bravo Lopez, *Prin*
EMP: 8 EST: 2010
SALES (est): 484.56K **Privately Held**
SIC: 1521 Single-family housing construction

(G-675)
BRIDGEVILLE AUTO CENTER INC
Rte 13 S (19933)
P.O. Box 185 (19933-0185)
PHONE..................................302 337-3100
Joseph Johnson, *Pr*
Toni Johnson, *VP*
EMP: 6 EST: 1985
SQ FT: 20,000
SALES (est): 502.04K **Privately Held**
Web: www.lkqparts.net
SIC: 5015 Motor vehicle parts, used

(G-676)
BRIDGEVILLE HISTORICAL SOCIETY
102 Willin Ave (19933-1318)
PHONE..................................302 337-7600
EMP: 7 EST: 1992
SALES (est): 31.41K **Privately Held**
Web: www.bridgevillehistoricalsocietyde.org
SIC: 8412 Historical society

(G-677)
BRIDGEVILLE LIONS CLUB INC
P.O. Box 414 (19933-0414)
PHONE..................................302 629-9543
Willis Dewey, *Pr*
Richard Tull, *Treas*
EMP: 7 EST: 2007
SQ FT: 4,000
SALES (est): 25K **Privately Held**
Web: www.applescrapple.com
SIC: 7997 Membership sports and recreation clubs

(G-678)
BRIDGEVILLE SENIOR CENTER
414 Market St (19933-1133)
PHONE..................................302 337-8771
EMP: 5 EST: 1975
SALES (est): 200.47K **Privately Held**
SIC: 8322 Senior citizens' center or association

(G-679)
C+M FARMS LLC
11433 Michael Ave (19933-4088)
PHONE..................................302 841-1847
Christopher Short, *Pr*
Matthew Short, *Prin*
EMP: 6 EST: 2016
SALES (est): 146.62K **Privately Held**
SIC: 0161 Watermelon farm

(G-680)
CANNON COLD STORAGE LLC
Also Called: Cannon Cold Storage
8141 Seashore Hwy (19933-3117)
PHONE..................................302 337-5500
Bob Huntsberger, *Managing Member*
EMP: 30 EST: 1995
SALES (est): 2.02MM **Privately Held**
Web: www.simmonsanimalnutrition.com
SIC: 4225 8748 General warehousing and storage; Business consulting, nec

(G-681)
CENTAUR TRAINING LLC
22000 Heritage Farm Rd (19933-4503)
PHONE..................................302 629-8783
Dean Roles, *Prin*
EMP: 7 EST: 2010
SALES (est): 69.62K **Privately Held**
SIC: 7948 Racehorse training

(G-682)
CHRISS CAR CARE ROAD
473 Seaford (19933)
PHONE..................................302 628-4695
Christopher Joseph, *Prin*
EMP: 5 EST: 2007
SALES (est): 75.85K **Privately Held**
SIC: 7538 General automotive repair shops

(G-683)
CJ S AUTOS
20354 Sussex Hwy (19933-4608)
PHONE..................................302 500-0822
Charles Jordan, *Prin*
EMP: 6 EST: 2018
SALES (est): 96.72K **Privately Held**
Web: www.bridgevillemechanic.com
SIC: 7538 General automotive repair shops

(G-684)
CJS AUTOS LLC
20354 Sussex Hwy (19933-4608)
PHONE..................................302 337-8880
Charles F Jordan, *Prin*
EMP: 6 EST: 2019
SALES (est): 259.28K **Privately Held**
Web: www.bridgevillemechanic.com
SIC: 7538 General automotive repair shops

(G-685)
COMPADRE CONCRETE
100b John St (19933-1121)
PHONE..................................302 228-0763
EMP: 5 EST: 2018
SALES (est): 96.58K **Privately Held**
SIC: 1771 Concrete work

(G-686)
CORNERSTONE COMMUNITY CTR LLC
55 Church St (19933-1031)
PHONE..................................302 258-6459
EMP: 5 EST: 2021
SALES (est): 32.92K **Privately Held**
SIC: 8322 Community center

(G-687)
COVERDALE COMMUNITY COUNCIL
11575 Fisher Cir (19933-4389)
P.O. Box 646 (19933-0646)
PHONE..................................302 337-7179
Evelyn Wilson, *Pr*
EMP: 6 EST: 1990
SALES (est): 137.91K **Privately Held**
SIC: 8399 Community development groups

(G-688)
CREATIVE ASSEMBLIES INC
17053 Tatman Farm Rd (19933-4193)
PHONE..................................302 956-6194
Raymond Hance, *Pr*
EMP: 10 EST: 1982
SQ FT: 9,000
SALES (est): 935.27K **Privately Held**
Web: www.creativeassemblies.com
SIC: 3443 3585 Cooling towers, metal plate; Dehumidifiers electric, except portable

(G-689)
DATA GUARD RECYCLING INC
9174 Redden Rd (19933-4723)
PHONE..................................302 337-8870
Clint Phillips, *Managing Member*
EMP: 5 EST: 2003
SALES (est): 867.83K **Privately Held**
SIC: 4953 Recycling, waste materials

(G-690)
DAVID PRICE
14655 Russell Rd (19933-4267)
PHONE..................................410 708-7133
EMP: 5 EST: 2017
SALES (est): 71.22K **Privately Held**
SIC: 7999 Outfitters, recreation

(G-691)
DELAWARE DEPT HLTH SOCIAL SVCS
Also Called: Bridgeville State Services
400 Mill St (19933-1114)
PHONE..................................302 337-8261
Ruthie Adams Hunter, *Dir*
EMP: 8
SALES (corp-wide): 11.27B **Privately Held**
Web: www.delaware.gov
SIC: 8322 9441 Individual and family services; Administration of social and manpower programs
HQ: Delaware Dept Of Health And Social Services
1901 N Dupont Hwy
New Castle DE 19720

(G-692)
DELMARVA BUILDERS INC
20846 Camp Rd (19933-4626)
PHONE..................................302 629-9123
John A Mc Farland, *Pr*
EMP: 8 EST: 1981
SALES (est): 671.13K **Privately Held**
SIC: 1521 1542 1781 New construction, single-family houses; Commercial and office building, new construction; Water well drilling

(G-693)
DELMARVA RUBBER & GASKET CO
16356 Sussex Hwy (19933-3056)
P.O. Box 249 (19933-0249)
PHONE..................................302 424-8300
Richard Phillips, *Pr*
EMP: 8 EST: 1985
SALES (est): 1.96MM **Privately Held**
Web: www.delmarvarubber.com
SIC: 5085 Rubber goods, mechanical

(G-694)
DELMARVA TEEN CHALLENGE
10968 Leadership Way (19933-3988)
PHONE..................................302 337-9100
EMP: 7 EST: 2018
SALES (est): 102.41K **Privately Held**
Web: www.delmarvateenchallenge.org
SIC: 8322 Individual and family services

(G-695)
DOWN UNDER BOXING CLUB
19124 Wesley Church Rd (19933-3764)
P.O. Box 605 (19933-0605)
PHONE..................................302 745-4392
Bruce Hibbs Senior, *Owner*
EMP: 6 EST: 2010
SALES (est): 45.59K **Privately Held**
SIC: 7997 Membership sports and recreation clubs

(G-696)
DRIVEWAY MINT PVNG/SLCTING LLC
7031 Cannon Rd (19933-3722)
PHONE..................................302 228-2644
EMP: 2 EST: 2008
SALES (est): 178.4K **Privately Held**
SIC: 2951 Asphalt paving mixtures and blocks

(G-697)
EAST BAY AGGREGATES LLC
8805 Newton Rd (19933-2946)
PHONE..................................302 337-0311
EMP: 7 EST: 2019
SALES (est): 1.07MM **Privately Held**
Web: www.eastbayag.com
SIC: 5032 Aggregate

(G-698)
ER LAWN CARE LLC
14008 Deer Forest Rd (19933-4213)
PHONE..................................302 519-3173
Erik Peterson, *Prin*
EMP: 5 EST: 2017
SALES (est): 23.96K **Privately Held**
SIC: 0782 Lawn care services

(G-699)
EVANS FARMS LLC
9843 Seashore Hwy (19933-4620)
PHONE..................................302 337-8130
Kevin Evans, *Managing Member*
EMP: 6 EST: 1943
SALES (est): 998.03K **Privately Held**
Web: www.evansfarmsproduce.com
SIC: 0161 7389 Vegetables and melons; Business Activities at Non-Commercial Site

(G-700)
EXPERT REFRIGERATIONSERVICE LL
2932 Mcdowell Rd (19933-3259)
PHONE..................................302 745-4181
EMP: 5 EST: 2019
SALES (est): 239.88K **Privately Held**
SIC: 1711 Refrigeration contractor

GEOGRAPHIC SECTION
Bridgeville - Sussex County (G-730)

(G-701)
FOUR PAWS ANIMAL HOSPITAL PA
21804 Eskridge Rd (19933-4509)
PHONE.................................302 629-7297
Michael Metzler D.v.m., *Pr*
EMP: 12 **EST:** 1992
SALES (est): 461.84K **Privately Held**
SIC: 0742 Animal hospital services, pets and other animal specialties

(G-702)
FROZEN FARMER LLC
9843 Seashore Hwy (19933-4620)
PHONE.................................302 337-8444
Evans Katey, *Prin*
EMP: 9 **EST:** 2015
SALES (est): 598.63K **Privately Held**
Web: www.thefrozenfarmer.com
SIC: 0191 General farms, primarily crop

(G-703)
GENES LIMOUSINE SERVICE INC
501 Market St (19933-1156)
PHONE.................................410 479-8470
Howard Mullins, *Pr*
EMP: 9 **EST:** 1999
SALES (est): 434.7K **Privately Held**
SIC: 4119 Limousine rental, with driver

(G-704)
GOODSCENTS INC
5270 Baker Rd (19933-3514)
PHONE.................................302 628-8042
EMP: 5 **EST:** 2011
SALES (est): 153.14K **Privately Held**
SIC: 5122 Perfumes

(G-705)
GREENWOOD PALLET CO
16849 Road Runner Dr (19933-2996)
PHONE.................................302 337-8181
T Tennefos, *Prin*
EMP: 4 **EST:** 2007
SALES (est): 247.34K **Privately Held**
SIC: 2448 5031 Pallets, wood; Pallets, wood

(G-706)
H C DAVIS INC
Also Called: Shore Pride Foods
Pine Alley (19933)
P.O. Box 346 (19933-0346)
PHONE.................................302 337-7001
Harry C Davis Iii, *Pr*
Matt Davis, *VP*
Jenny Davis, *Treas*
Wanda S Davis, *Sec*
EMP: 8 **EST:** 1919
SQ FT: 5,000
SALES (est): 1.88MM **Privately Held**
Web: www.hcdavis.com
SIC: 5143 5142 5147 Dairy products, except dried or canned; Packaged frozen goods; Meats, fresh

(G-707)
HAB NAB TRUCKING INC
8805 Newton Rd (19933-2946)
PHONE.................................302 245-6900
Michael J Hubbard, *Pr*
Janet Hubbard, *
EMP: 9 **EST:** 1979
SQ FT: 10,700
SALES (est): 492.42K **Privately Held**
SIC: 4213 4212 Contract haulers; Local trucking, without storage

(G-708)
HARRISON FAMILY PRACTICE INC
18119 Sussex Hwy Unit 1 (19933-4095)
PHONE.................................302 956-6986
Valerie Harrison, *Asst Sec*
EMP: 9 **EST:** 2018
SALES (est): 366.16K **Privately Held**
SIC: 8011 General and family practice, physician/surgeon

(G-709)
HARRY A LEHMAN III MD PA
38 Snowy Egret Ct (19933-2404)
PHONE.................................302 629-5050
EMP: 10 **EST:** 1995
SALES (est): 246.77K **Privately Held**
SIC: 8011 Pediatrician

(G-710)
HELENA AGRI-ENTERPRISES LLC
16635 Adams Rd (19933-2906)
PHONE.................................302 337-3881
Rick Adams, *Brnch Mgr*
EMP: 6
Web: www.helenaagri.com
SIC: 5191 Chemicals, agricultural
HQ: Helena Agri-Enterprises, Llc
225 Schilling Blvd
Collierville TN 38017
901 761-0050

(G-711)
HOBDAY GROUP LTD
7222 Seashore Hwy (19933-3112)
PHONE.................................302 337-9567
David Hobday, *Prin*
EMP: 5 **EST:** 2009
SALES (est): 177.93K **Privately Held**
Web: www.thehobdaygroup.com
SIC: 8748 Business consulting, nec

(G-712)
HOPKINS CONSTRUCTION INC
18904 Maranatha Way Unit 1 (19933-4057)
PHONE.................................302 337-3366
Joann Hopkins, *Pr*
R Keller Hopkins, *Resident Chief Executive Officer*
Joanne Hopkins, *Sec*
EMP: 13 **EST:** 1988
SQ FT: 12,000
SALES (est): 2.79MM **Privately Held**
SIC: 1623 Sewer line construction

(G-713)
HORNEY INDUSTRIAL ELEC INC (PA)
Also Called: Hie
114 N Main St (19933-1146)
P.O. Box 700 (19933-0700)
PHONE.................................302 337-3600
EMP: 3 **EST:** 1990
SALES (est): 999.05K **Privately Held**
Web: www.horneyonline.com
SIC: 3829 Measuring and controlling devices, nec

(G-714)
HRC INC
203 S Main St (19933-1239)
P.O. Box 376 (19933-0376)
PHONE.................................302 604-3782
EMP: 6 **EST:** 2015
SALES (est): 300.67K **Privately Held**
SIC: 1751 Carpentry work

(G-715)
HYDROSEEDING CO LLC
22021 Eskridge Rd (19933-4515)
PHONE.................................302 858-8171
EMP: 5 **EST:** 2016
SALES (est): 41.2K **Privately Held**
SIC: 5084 Industrial machinery and equipment

(G-716)
INTERNAL MEDICINE BRIDGEVILLE
Also Called: Smith, Kenneth MD
8991 Redden Rd (19933-4746)
PHONE.................................302 337-3300
Kenneth Smith Md, *Owner*
EMP: 6 **EST:** 1993
SALES (est): 486.05K **Privately Held**
SIC: 8011 Internal medicine, physician/surgeon

(G-717)
JASON LEWIS PUSEY
4379 Federalsburg Rd (19933-3330)
PHONE.................................302 245-6545
Jason Pusey, *Prin*
EMP: 5 **EST:** 2011
SALES (est): 182.47K **Privately Held**
SIC: 7389 Business Activities at Non-Commercial Site

(G-718)
JERSEY CLIPPERS LLC
Also Called: Great Clips
134 Widgeon Way (19933-2421)
PHONE.................................302 956-0138
EMP: 8 **EST:** 2002
SALES (est): 79.48K **Privately Held**
Web: www.greatclips.com
SIC: 7231 Unisex hair salons

(G-719)
JL MECHANICAL INC
Also Called: Honeywell Authorized Dealer
5460 Hartzell Rd (19933-3458)
PHONE.................................302 337-7855
EMP: 9 **EST:** 2009
SALES (est): 324.95K **Privately Held**
Web: www.honeywell.com
SIC: 7389 Design services

(G-720)
JOEYS TOWING LLC
4450 Dublin Hill Rd (19933-2733)
PHONE.................................610 342-7417
EMP: 5 **EST:** 2015
SALES (est): 244.64K **Privately Held**
SIC: 7549 Towing services

(G-721)
JOHN T ELLIOTT
10456 Seashore Hwy (19933-4661)
PHONE.................................302 337-7075
John T Elliott, *Prin*
EMP: 5 **EST:** 2012
SALES (est): 218.82K **Privately Held**
SIC: 1521 Single-family housing construction

(G-722)
KENNY BROTHERS PRODUCE LLC
16440 Adams Rd (19933-2910)
P.O. Box 728 (19933-0728)
PHONE.................................302 337-3007
Michael Kenny, *Managing Member*
EMP: 5 **EST:** 2002
SQ FT: 1,500
SALES (est): 557.34K **Privately Held**
SIC: 2035 Cucumbers, pickles and pickle salting

(G-723)
KROEGERS SALVAGE INC
15896 White Pine Ln (19933-4184)
PHONE.................................302 381-7082
Joel H Kroeger, *Pr*
Joel Kroeger, *Pr*
EMP: 17 **EST:** 1987
SALES (est): 3.04MM **Privately Held**
SIC: 4953 Recycling, waste materials

(G-724)
LARRYS BUILDING
11404 Abbys Way (19933-4498)
PHONE.................................302 670-8803
Larry Chapman, *Prin*
EMP: 5 **EST:** 2018
SALES (est): 63.73K **Privately Held**
SIC: 1522 Residential construction, nec

(G-725)
LEMS APPLIANCE REPAIR LLC
109 S Main St (19933-1124)
PHONE.................................302 539-2200
Lemuel Rodan, *Managing Member*
EMP: 7 **EST:** 2019
SALES (est): 100K **Privately Held**
Web: www.lemsappliancerepair.com
SIC: 7699 Household appliance repair services

(G-726)
LR CONSTRUCTION LLC
11304 3rd St (19933-4443)
PHONE.................................302 249-4507
Marco Lopez, *Owner*
EMP: 5 **EST:** 2010
SALES (est): 170.3K **Privately Held**
Web: www.lrconstructionde.com
SIC: 1521 Single-family housing construction

(G-727)
M L MORRIS INC
Also Called: Automotive/Construction
17044 N Main St Ste 5 (19933-2992)
PHONE.................................302 956-0678
Marvin Morris Junior, *CEO*
EMP: 5 **EST:** 2009
SALES (est): 479.14K **Privately Held**
SIC: 1521 5521 Single-family housing construction; Used car dealers

(G-728)
MARLETTE R LOFLAND
Also Called: Colorful World Daycare
20255 Wilson Farm Rd (19933-3742)
PHONE.................................302 628-1521
Arthur Lofland, *Prin*
EMP: 5 **EST:** 2012
SALES (est): 108.98K **Privately Held**
SIC: 8351 Group day care center

(G-729)
MCCREA EQUIPMENT COMPANY INC
16855 Sussex Hwy (19933-4012)
PHONE.................................302 337-8249
EMP: 27
SALES (corp-wide): 44.06MM **Privately Held**
Web: www.mccreaway.com
SIC: 1711 Warm air heating and air conditioning contractor
PA: Mccrea Equipment Company, Inc.
4463 Beech Rd
Temple Hills MD 20748
301 423-6623

(G-730)
MEHERRIN AG & CHEM CO
18441 Wesley Church Rd (19933-3702)
PHONE.................................302 337-0330
Chris Griffith, *Mgr*
EMP: 6
SALES (corp-wide): 1.13B **Privately Held**
Web: www.meherrinag.com
SIC: 2879 4226 Agricultural chemicals, nec; Special warehousing and storage, nec
PA: Meherrin Agricultural & Chemical Co
413 Main St
Severn NC 27877
252 585-1744

Bridgeville - Sussex County (G-731) GEOGRAPHIC SECTION

(G-731)
MESSICK & GRAY CNSTR INC (PA)
Also Called: Bridgeville Machining
9003 Fawn Rd (19933-2941)
PHONE.................................302 337-8777
Alan Messick, *Pr*
Thomas Messick, *VP*
Shirley Messick, *Sec*
EMP: 49 **EST:** 1963
SQ FT: 7,000
SALES (est): 22.9MM
SALES (corp-wide): 22.9MM **Privately Held**
Web: www.messickandgray.com
SIC: 5084 5083 7699 3441 Industrial machinery and equipment; Agricultural machinery, nec; Industrial machinery and equipment repair; Fabricated structural metal

(G-732)
METRO EQP & SHEETMETAL PDTS
16855 Sussex Hwy (19933-4012)
PHONE.................................302 337-8249
EMP: 5 **EST:** 2019
SALES (est): 127.48K **Privately Held**
SIC: 3444 Sheet metalwork

(G-733)
MID-SHORE ENVMTL SVCS INC
7481 Federalsburg Rd (19933-3656)
PHONE.................................302 736-5504
Paul M Pearson, *Ex VP*
Paul Pearson, *VP*
Michael Stang, *Pr*
EMP: 8 **EST:** 1999
SALES (est): 225.11K **Privately Held**
SIC: 4953 Recycling, waste materials

(G-734)
MILLER METAL FABRICATION INC
16356 Sussex Hwy Unit 4 (19933-3056)
P.O. Box 249 (19933-0249)
PHONE.................................302 337-2291
Martin W Miller Junior, *Pr*
Dave Morris, *
Michael Elwani, *
▲ **EMP:** 100 **EST:** 1982
SQ FT: 50,000
SALES (est): 17.16MM **Privately Held**
Web: www.millermetal.com
SIC: 3441 3053 5051 3542 Fabricated structural metal; Gaskets, all materials; Sheets, metal; Mechanical (pneumatic or hydraulic) metal forming machines

(G-735)
MONKEYS IN TREES LLC
4528 Saddle Up Cir (19933-2862)
PHONE.................................302 519-4551
EMP: 5 **EST:** 2018
SALES (est): 252.05K **Privately Held**
Web: www.monkeysintreesllc.com
SIC: 0782 Lawn care services

(G-736)
NANTICOKE EZ LAB
9111 Antique Aly Unit 1 (19933-4682)
PHONE.................................302 337-8571
EMP: 6 **EST:** 2019
SALES (est): 89.63K **Privately Held**
Web: www.tidalhealth.org
SIC: 8734 Testing laboratories

(G-737)
NATIONAL TRUCKING LLC
10887 Rifle Range Rd (19933-4035)
PHONE.................................302 465-3692
Rosanna Mena, *Prin*
EMP: 5 **EST:** 2015

SALES (est): 285.94K **Privately Held**
SIC: 4213 Trucking, except local

(G-738)
NEWS PRINT SHOP
16694 Emma Jane Ln (19933-2904)
P.O. Box 127 (19933-0127)
PHONE.................................302 337-8283
Sandy Rementer, *Pr*
EMP: 7 **EST:** 1951
SQ FT: 1,000
SALES (est): 467.26K **Privately Held**
Web: www.mybabydolltravel2.com
SIC: 2752 Offset printing

(G-739)
O A NEWTON & SON CO
16356 Sussex Hwy (19933-3056)
P.O. Box 397 (19933-0397)
PHONE.................................302 337-8211
EMP: 35 **EST:** 2010
SALES (est): 3.29MM **Privately Held**
Web: www.oanewton.com
SIC: 0191 General farms, primarily crop

(G-740)
O A NEWTON & SON COMPANY
16356 Sussex Hwy Unit 1 (19933-3056)
P.O. Box 397 (19933-0397)
PHONE.................................302 337-3782
Robert F Rider Junior, *Pr*
Susan Rider, *
▲ **EMP:** 32 **EST:** 1916
SQ FT: 100,000
SALES (est): 8.06MM **Privately Held**
Web: www.oanewton.com
SIC: 5083 3599 5084 Irrigation equipment; Machine shop, jobbing and repair; Materials handling machinery

(G-741)
OLD DOMINION FREIGHT LINE INC
1664 Emma Jane Ln (19933)
PHONE.................................302 337-8793
Rich Molnar, *Mgr*
EMP: 5
SALES (corp-wide): 6.26B **Publicly Held**
Web: www.odfl.com
SIC: 4213 Contract haulers
PA: Old Dominion Freight Line Inc
500 Old Dominion Way
Thomasville NC 27360
336 889-5000

(G-742)
OMS MECHANICAL INC
17974 Meadow Dr (19933-3960)
PHONE.................................302 745-7424
Turunz Paesachov, *Prin*
EMP: 6 **EST:** 2005
SALES (est): 80.02K **Privately Held**
Web: www.omsmechanical.com
SIC: 1711 Mechanical contractor

(G-743)
ORCURTO ENTERPRISES
48 Ruddy Duck Ln (19933-2423)
PHONE.................................302 604-7039
Dale Orcurto, *Prin*
EMP: 5 **EST:** 2010
SALES (est): 106.79K **Privately Held**
SIC: 1522 Residential construction, nec

(G-744)
PARKER GROUP
5649 Ray Rd (19933-3124)
PHONE.................................302 217-6692
Renee Parker, *Prin*
EMP: 11 **EST:** 2019
SALES (est): 121.42K **Privately Held**

Web: www.theparkergroup.com
SIC: 6531 Real estate brokers and agents

(G-745)
PASSWATERS LANDSCAPING
18956 Sussex Hwy (19933-4604)
PHONE.................................302 542-8077
EMP: 12 **EST:** 2015
SALES (est): 544.85K **Privately Held**
Web: www.passwaterslandscaping.com
SIC: 0781 Landscape services

(G-746)
PERDUE FARMS INC
Also Called: Perdue Farms
16447 Adams Rd (19933-2911)
PHONE.................................302 337-2210
Charles Broderick, *Mgr*
EMP: 116
SALES (corp-wide): 1.24B **Privately Held**
Web: www.perdue.com
SIC: 2015 Poultry slaughtering and processing
PA: Perdue Farms Incorporated
31149 Old Ocean City Rd
Salisbury MD 21804
800 473-7383

(G-747)
PERFECTIONAL CLEANING
25 Laverty Ln (19933-1335)
PHONE.................................302 864-7112
Gary Bell, *Prin*
EMP: 5 **EST:** 2018
SALES (est): 52K **Privately Held**
SIC: 7699 Cleaning services

(G-748)
PET POULTRY PRODUCTS LLC
7494 Federalsburg Rd (19933-3662)
PHONE.................................302 337-8223
Robert Hunsberger, *Pr*
Mark Hunsberger, *
Wanda Stewart, *
▼ **EMP:** 38 **EST:** 1967
SQ FT: 145,000
SALES (est): 8.05MM
SALES (corp-wide): 1.94B **Privately Held**
Web: www.simmonsanimalnutrition.com
SIC: 5144 5113 Poultry products, nec; Boxes and containers
HQ: Simmons Animal Nutrition, Inc.
601 N Hico St
Siloam Springs AR 72761

(G-749)
PICTSWEET COMPANY
18215 Wesley Church Rd (19933)
P.O. Box 398 (19933-0398)
PHONE.................................302 337-8206
Edward Carey, *Mgr*
EMP: 55
SALES (corp-wide): 403.32MM **Privately Held**
Web: www.pictsweetfarms.com
SIC: 2038 Ethnic foods, nec, frozen
PA: The Pictsweet Company
10 Pictsweet Dr
Bells TN 38006
731 663-7600

(G-750)
PINE BREEZE FARMS INC
3583 Buck Fever Rd (19933-2517)
PHONE.................................302 337-7717
Richard Carlisrle, *Pr*
Katheerine Carlisrle, *VP*
EMP: 7 **EST:** 1968
SALES (est): 948.95K **Privately Held**
SIC: 0161 Vegetables and melons

(G-751)
PINNACLE HOME IMPROVEMENT LLC
17780 Meadow Dr (19933-3922)
PHONE.................................302 569-5311
Robert Horseman, *Prin*
EMP: 5 **EST:** 2017
SALES (est): 122.12K **Privately Held**
SIC: 1521 Single-family housing construction

(G-752)
PNC BANK NATIONAL ASSOCIATION
Also Called: PNC
100 S Laws St (19933-1108)
PHONE.................................302 337-3500
Denise Taylor, *Mgr*
EMP: 9
SALES (corp-wide): 23.54B **Publicly Held**
Web: www.pnc.com
SIC: 6021 National trust companies with deposits, commercial
HQ: Pnc Bank, National Association
300 5th Ave
Pittsburgh PA 15222
877 762-2000

(G-753)
POWER TRANS INC
9029 Fawn Rd (19933-2941)
PHONE.................................302 337-3016
Alan Messick, *Pr*
Steven Small, *Sec*
Thomas Messick, *Stockholder*
EMP: 17 **EST:** 1967
SQ FT: 12,000
SALES (est): 5.02MM **Privately Held**
Web: www.powertrans.org
SIC: 5084 5999 Industrial machine parts; Electronic parts and equipment

(G-754)
PRICES LANDSCAPING & HARDSCAP
14490 Deer Forest Rd (19933-4217)
PHONE.................................302 280-3072
David Wayne Price Junior, *Prin*
EMP: 6 **EST:** 2011
SALES (est): 235.94K **Privately Held**
Web: www.priceslandscape.com
SIC: 0781 Landscape services

(G-755)
PROLINE BUILDERS LLC
11225 Tyler Dr (19933-4080)
PHONE.................................302 956-0426
Bryan Carey, *Prin*
EMP: 5 **EST:** 2015
SALES (est): 86.09K **Privately Held**
SIC: 1521 New construction, single-family houses

(G-756)
PROVIDENCE AT HERITAGE SH
21 White Pelican Ct (19933-2403)
PHONE.................................302 337-1040
Dorothy Harper, *Prin*
EMP: 6 **EST:** 2006
SALES (est): 253.49K **Privately Held**
Web: www.heritageshores.com
SIC: 8741 Construction management

(G-757)
PYRAMID TRANSPORT INC
18119 Sussex Hwy Unit 2 (19933-4095)
P.O. Box 187 (19933-0187)
PHONE.................................302 337-9340
Jim Hitchens, *Pr*
EMP: 50 **EST:** 1993
SQ FT: 10,000

GEOGRAPHIC SECTION
Bridgeville - Sussex County (G-784)

SALES (est): 10.31MM **Privately Held**
Web: www.pyramidtransport.com
SIC: **4213** Trucking, except local

(G-758)
QUALITY CONSTRUCTION CLEANING
8902 Cannon Rd (19933-4639)
PHONE..................302 956-0752
Roxana Flores, *Owner*
EMP: 9 EST: 2013
SALES (est): 496.27K **Privately Held**
SIC: **1521** Single-family housing construction

(G-759)
R & S FABRICATION INC
7159 Seashore Hwy (19933-3111)
P.O. Box 903 (19973-0903)
PHONE..................302 629-0377
Larry Rust, *Pr*
Richard Ray, *VP*
EMP: 11 EST: 1989
SQ FT: 80,000
SALES (est): 498.7K **Privately Held**
SIC: **1796** Machinery installation

(G-760)
RALPH AND PAUL ADAMS INC
Also Called: Rapa Scrapple
103 Railroad Ave (19933-1153)
PHONE..................800 338-4727
Donna Seefried, *Genl Mgr*
Phillip Jones, *
EMP: 350 EST: 1958
SALES (est): 39.87MM
SALES (corp-wide): 158.03MM **Privately Held**
Web: www.rapascrapple.com
SIC: **2013** 5147 Scrapple, from purchased meat; Meats, fresh
PA: Jones Dairy Farm
    800 Jones Ave
    Fort Atkinson WI 53538
    920 563-2432

(G-761)
RENTOKIL NORTH AMERICA INC
Also Called: Ehlrlich, J C Pest Control
18904 Maranatha Way (19933-4057)
PHONE..................302 337-8100
EMP: 60
SALES (corp-wide): 4.47B **Privately Held**
SIC: **7342** Pest control in structures
HQ: Rentokil North America, Inc.
    1125 Berkshire Blvd # 15
    Wyomissing PA 19610
    470 643-3300

(G-762)
ROBERT DAVISON
110 Widgeon Way (19933-2421)
PHONE..................301 518-0516
Robert Davison, *Pr*
EMP: 8 EST: 2017
SALES (est): 89.91K **Privately Held**
SIC: **8011** Offices and clinics of medical doctors

(G-763)
RRP MECHANICAL WELDING LLC
16750 Oak Rd (19933-3910)
PHONE..................302 448-1051
Renato Reyna-pastrana, *Asst Sec*
EMP: 5 EST: 2018
SALES (est): 43.94K **Privately Held**
SIC: **7692** Welding repair

(G-764)
SHARKS SERVICE CENTER LLC
7451 Federalsburg Rd (19933-3656)
PHONE..................302 337-8233
EMP: 9 EST: 1988
SQ FT: 7,000
SALES (est): 743.16K **Privately Held**
Web: www.sharksservicecenter.com
SIC: **7699** 7538 Industrial machinery and equipment repair; General truck repair

(G-765)
SHARP TECH SYSTEMS LLC
7019 Seashore Hwy (19933-3109)
P.O. Box 698 (19933-0698)
PHONE..................302 956-9525
Anthony Sharp, *Prin*
EMP: 5 EST: 2018
SALES (est): 219.06K **Privately Held**
Web: www.sharptech.us
SIC: **7379** Computer related consulting services

(G-766)
SIMMONS ANIMAL NUTRITION INC
Also Called: Simmons Feed Ingrdnts Cnon Col
7494 Federalsburg Rd (19933-3662)
P.O. Box 128 (19933-0128)
PHONE..................302 337-8223
EMP: 11
SALES (corp-wide): 1.94B **Privately Held**
Web: www.simmonsfoods.com
SIC: **2048** Prepared feeds, nec
HQ: Simmons Animal Nutrition, Inc.
    601 N Hico St
    Siloam Springs AR 72761

(G-767)
SIMMONS ANIMAL NUTRITION INC
Also Called: Simmons Feed Ingrdnts Brdgvlle
8141 Seashore Hwy (19933-3117)
PHONE..................302 337-5500
EMP: 69
SALES (corp-wide): 1.94B **Privately Held**
Web: www.simmonsfoods.com
SIC: **2048** 4225 Prepared feeds, nec; General warehousing and storage
HQ: Simmons Animal Nutrition, Inc.
    601 N Hico St
    Siloam Springs AR 72761

(G-768)
SP AUTO PARTS INC
Also Called: Sp Auto Parts
7514 Federalsburg Rd (19933-3660)
PHONE..................302 337-8897
EMP: 5
SALES (corp-wide): 9.68MM **Privately Held**
Web: www.spautoparts.com
SIC: **5013** Automotive supplies and parts
PA: Sp Auto Parts, Inc.
    201 Executive Dr
    Moorestown NJ 08057
    856 273-9252

(G-769)
STARK TRUSS COMPANY INC
16632 Nates Way (19933-2994)
PHONE..................302 337-9470
Doug Warren, *Brnch Mgr*
EMP: 3
SALES (corp-wide): 144.79MM **Privately Held**
Web: www.starktruss.com
SIC: **2439** Trusses, wooden roof
PA: Stark Truss Company, Inc.
    109 Miles Ave Sw
    Canton OH 44710
    330 478-2100

(G-770)
SUPERIOR OUTDOOR LLC
14456 Redden Rd (19933-4159)
PHONE..................302 841-9827
EMP: 6 EST: 2010
SALES (est): 82.46K **Privately Held**
Web: www.superioroutdoors.com
SIC: **8611** Contractors' association

(G-771)
SUSAN J HOWLETT
32 Canvasback Cir (19933-2428)
PHONE..................302 670-1055
Susan J Howlett, *Prin*
EMP: 7 EST: 2012
SALES (est): 63.38K **Privately Held**
SIC: **8049** Offices of health practitioner

(G-772)
SUSSEX TREE INC
20350 Nelson Dr (19933-4557)
PHONE..................302 629-9899
Jeff Meredith, *Pr*
EMP: 8 EST: 1987
SALES (est): 1.01MM **Privately Held**
Web: www.sussextreeinc.com
SIC: **0783** Planting, pruning, and trimming services

(G-773)
SWEEP DREAM CLEANING SERVICES
11378 2nd St (19933-4447)
PHONE..................302 569-5519
Esmeralda Velasquez, *Prin*
EMP: 5 EST: 2015
SALES (est): 49.56K **Privately Held**
SIC: **7699** Cleaning services

(G-774)
T S SMITH & SONS INC
8899 Redden Rd (19933-4749)
P.O. Box 275 (19933-0275)
PHONE..................302 337-8271
Matthew W Smith, *Pr*
Thomass S Smith, *Sec*
EMP: 16 EST: 1910
SALES (est): 445.33K **Privately Held**
Web: domains.squadhelp.com
SIC: **0175** 0251 0116 0111 Apple orchard; Broiler, fryer, and roaster chickens; Soybeans; Wheat

(G-775)
TOMS CABINET SHOP INC
20983 Sanfilippo Rd (19933-4548)
PHONE..................302 258-6285
Thomas Lee, *Owner*
EMP: 3 EST: 2007
SALES (est): 238.77K **Privately Held**
Web: www.tomscabinetshop.com
SIC: **2434** Wood kitchen cabinets

(G-776)
U-HAUL NEIGHBORHOOD DEALER
Also Called: U-Haul
9588 Bridgeville Ctr (19933-4678)
PHONE..................302 721-6064
Richard Smith, *Mgr*
EMP: 7 EST: 2016
SALES (est): 70.4K **Privately Held**
Web: www.uhaul.com
SIC: **7513** Truck rental and leasing, no drivers

(G-777)
URYS TRANSPORTATION LLC
11429 Liden St (19933-4006)
PHONE..................302 841-9464
Urys Matos, *Asst Sec*
EMP: 5 EST: 2018
SALES (est): 227.1K **Privately Held**
SIC: **4789** Transportation services, nec

(G-778)
UTILITY LINES CNSTR SVCS LLC
18109 Sussex Hwy (19933-4010)
PHONE..................302 337-9980
Tim Jahnigen, *Brnch Mgr*
EMP: 6
SALES (corp-wide): 1.16B **Privately Held**
Web: www.ulcs-llc.com
SIC: **1623** Underground utilities contractor
HQ: Utility Lines Construction Services, Llc
    708 Blair Mill Rd
    Willow Grove PA 19090
    215 784-4463

(G-779)
UTILITY/STERN SHORE TRLR SLS I
9126 Redden Rd (19933-4723)
P.O. Box 159 (19933-0159)
PHONE..................302 337-7400
Kenneth Abbott, *Pr*
EMP: 9 EST: 2014
SALES (est): 367.5K **Privately Held**
SIC: **5599** 3715 5012 5013 Utility trailers; Truck trailers; Trailers for trucks, new and used; Trailer parts and accessories

(G-780)
VINTAGE CANDLE COMPANY
16734 Oak Rd (19933-3910)
PHONE..................302 643-9343
Michelle Clouser, *Prin*
EMP: 4 EST: 2013
SALES (est): 85.85K **Privately Held**
Web: www.vintagecandlecompany.com
SIC: **3999** Candles

(G-781)
WELLERS TIRE SERVICE INC
Also Called: Weller's Utility Trailers
16889 N Main St (19933-2976)
PHONE..................302 337-8228
James J Weller Junior, *Pr*
EMP: 10 EST: 1975
SQ FT: 3,600
SALES (est): 1.65MM **Privately Held**
Web: www.wellers.com
SIC: **5531** 5014 5511 Automotive tires; Automobile tires and tubes; Trucks, tractors, and trailers: new and used

(G-782)
WESTERN SUSSEX ANIMAL HOSP INC
16487 Sussex Hwy (19933-2991)
PHONE..................302 337-7387
Craig Metzner, *Prin*
EMP: 6 EST: 2012
SALES (est): 477.36K **Privately Held**
Web: www.westernsussexvet.com
SIC: **0742** Animal hospital services, pets and other animal specialties

(G-783)
WESTMOR INDUSTRIES
16941 Sussex Hwy (19933-4011)
P.O. Box 219 (19933-0219)
PHONE..................302 956-0243
EMP: 4 EST: 2017
SALES (est): 194.33K **Privately Held**
SIC: **3999** Manufacturing industries, nec

(G-784)
WHEATLEY FARMS INC
19115 Freeland Ln (19933-4072)
PHONE..................302 337-7286
E Dale Wheatley, *Pr*

Bridgeville - Sussex County (G-785) GEOGRAPHIC SECTION

Jeffrey Wheatley, *VP*
Gail Wheatley, *Sec*
EMP: 9 **EST:** 1940
SALES (est): 983.44K **Privately Held**
Web: www.wheatleyfarms.com
SIC: 0191 General farms, primarily crop

(G-785)
ZONE CONTROL HVAC INC
6422 Ray Rd (19933-3127)
PHONE............................302 752-6697
Damion Tallent, *Mgr*
EMP: 5 **EST:** 2019
SALES (est): 222.01K **Privately Held**
SIC: 1711 Warm air heating and air conditioning contractor

Camden
Kent County

(G-786)
ABSOLUTE HEALTH LLC
301 E Camden Wyoming Ave (19934-1210)
PHONE............................302 535-8236
Joseph C Vincent, *Prin*
EMP: 9 **EST:** 2011
SALES (est): 393.31K **Privately Held**
Web: www.absolutehealthclinic.org
SIC: 8041 Offices and clinics of chiropractors

(G-787)
AGAINST ALL ODDS LLC
27 Spring Ridge Way (19934-4431)
PHONE............................302 943-7321
Amy Nelson, *Prin*
EMP: 5 **EST:** 2018
SALES (est): 97.15K **Privately Held**
SIC: 8399 Advocacy group

(G-788)
ALL ABOUT LAWNS IRRIGATION
34 Deer Jump Cir (19934-4223)
PHONE............................302 242-6861
Steven Miller, *Prin*
EMP: 5 **EST:** 2017
SALES (est): 186.32K **Privately Held**
Web: www.allaboutlawnsirrigation.com
SIC: 4971 Irrigation systems

(G-789)
ALL UNITED PRPTS SOLUTIONS LLC
4034 Willow Grove Rd (19934-3148)
PHONE............................310 853-2223
Michael Mcpherson Junior, *Managing Member*
EMP: 13 **EST:** 2019
SALES (est): 570.11K **Privately Held**
SIC: 6798 Real estate investment trusts

(G-790)
ALPHA PHI DELTA FRATERNITY
257 E Camden Wyoming Ave Ste A (19934-1298)
PHONE............................302 531-7854
Joseph Piras, *Prin*
EMP: 17 **EST:** 2012
SALES (est): 249.87K **Privately Held**
Web: www.apd.org
SIC: 8641 University club

(G-791)
ALVIS D BURRIS
199 South St (19934-1300)
PHONE............................302 697-3125
Alvis Burris, *Prin*
EMP: 12 **EST:** 2014
SALES (est): 541.64K **Privately Held**
Web: www.burriscosmeticandfamilydentistry.com
SIC: 8021 Dentists' office

(G-792)
BARCLAY FARMS
1 Paynters Way (19934-4556)
PHONE............................302 697-6939
Sam Sobel, *Pr*
EMP: 7 **EST:** 2001
SALES (est): 567.41K **Privately Held**
Web: www.hometownamerica.com
SIC: 6552 Land subdividers and developers, residential

(G-793)
BLUEOCEAN COMMUNICATIONS LLC
2140 S Dupont Hwy (19934-1249)
PHONE............................617 586-6633
EMP: 5 **EST:** 2018
SALES (est): 470.63K **Privately Held**
SIC: 1623 Underground utilities contractor

(G-794)
BOLDY FOODS LLC ✪
2140 S Dupont Hwy (19934-1249)
PHONE............................415 616-2965
Amanda Bhavani, *Managing Member*
EMP: 4 **EST:** 2023
SALES (est): 180.26K **Privately Held**
SIC: 2092 Fresh or frozen fish or seafood chowders, soups, and stews

(G-795)
BUOY HYDRATION INC
2140 S Dupont Hwy (19934-1249)
PHONE............................314 230-5106
Daniel Schindler, *CEO*
Cole Puchi, *COO*
Eddie Zelenak, *CMO*
EMP: 5 **EST:** 2017
SALES (est): 640K **Privately Held**
SIC: 2023 Dietary supplements, dairy and non-dairy based

(G-796)
BURKHAN INTERNATIONAL DEV CORP
Also Called: Bidc
2140 S Dupont Hwy (19934-1249)
PHONE............................202 790-8050
Shahal Khan, *CEO*
EMP: 40 **EST:** 2021
SALES (est): 942.69K **Privately Held**
SIC: 7389 Business services, nec

(G-797)
BURRIS COSMTC & FMLY DENTISTRY
199 South St (19934-1300)
PHONE............................302 697-3125
Alvis Burris, *Prin*
EMP: 11 **EST:** 2018
SALES (est): 318K **Privately Held**
Web: www.burriscosmeticandfamilydentistry.com
SIC: 8021 Dentists' office

(G-798)
C L BURCHENAL OIL CO INC
109 S Main St (19934-1320)
PHONE............................302 697-1517
Terry Burchenal, *Pr*
Paullinia Burchenal, *Sec*
EMP: 6 **EST:** 1945
SQ FT: 2,000
SALES (est): 494.65K **Privately Held**
SIC: 5983 5172 Fuel oil dealers; Fuel oil

(G-799)
CAMDEN - WYOMING LIONS CLUB
220 Weeks Dr (19934-1246)
PHONE............................302 697-6565
EMP: 5 **EST:** 2010
SALES (est): 35.32K **Privately Held**
SIC: 8641 Civic associations

(G-800)
CAMDEN COUNSELING LLC
258 E Camden Wyoming Ave (19934-1303)
PHONE............................302 698-9109
EMP: 5 **EST:** 2019
SALES (est): 113.3K **Privately Held**
SIC: 8322 General counseling services

(G-801)
CAMDENWYOMING SEWER & WTR AUTH
16 Sw St (19934-1324)
P.O. Box 405 (19934-0405)
PHONE............................302 697-6372
Harold Scott, *Superintnt*
EMP: 18 **EST:** 1986
SALES (est): 2.32MM **Privately Held**
Web: www.cwswa.com
SIC: 4952 4941 Sewerage systems; Water supply

(G-802)
CARING MATTERS HOME CARE
283 Orchard Grove Dr (19934-4908)
PHONE............................302 993-1121
Stacy Mullin, *Pr*
EMP: 14 **EST:** 2013
SALES (est): 200.17K **Privately Held**
Web: www.caringmattershomecare.com
SIC: 8082 Home health care services

(G-803)
CARL KING TIRE CO INC (PA)
109 S Main St (19934-1320)
P.O. Box 1004 (19934-0504)
PHONE............................302 697-9506
Bruce King, *Pr*
Carl King, *
Richard Hawes, *
EMP: 45 **EST:** 1976
SQ FT: 20,000
SALES (est): 8.39MM
SALES (corp-wide): 8.39MM **Privately Held**
SIC: 5014 5013 5531 Automobile tires and tubes; Automotive batteries; Automotive tires

(G-804)
CARVERS CONSTRUCTION LLC
209 Eagle View Ln (19934-2009)
PHONE............................302 505-0260
EMP: 4 **EST:** 2021
SALES (est): 110.83K **Privately Held**
SIC: 1389 7389 Construction, repair, and dismantling services; Business services, nec

(G-805)
CENSYS INC
3500 S Dupont Hwy (19934)
PHONE............................248 629-0125
EMP: 5 **EST:** 2017
SALES (est): 105.83K **Privately Held**
Web: www.censys.com
SIC: 8741 Business management

(G-806)
CHRISTANA CARE HM HLTH CMNTY S
Also Called: Christiana Care Dover
2116 S Dupont Hwy Ste 2 (19934-1259)
PHONE............................302 698-4300
EMP: 207
SALES (corp-wide): 666.58K **Privately Held**
Web: www.christianacare.org
SIC: 8082 7361 Visiting nurse service; Nurses' registry
HQ: Christiana Care Home Health And Community Services Inc
1 Reads Way Ste 100
New Castle DE 19720
302 327-5583

(G-807)
CONDOR TECHNOLOGIES INC
110 N Main St Ste H (19934-1232)
PHONE............................302 698-4444
Andrew Nowak, *CEO*
Jennifer Nowak, *VP*
EMP: 7 **EST:** 1976
SQ FT: 1,000
SALES (est): 2.42MM **Privately Held**
Web: www.condortechnologies.com
SIC: 5074 Water softeners

(G-808)
CONTRACTORS FLOORING DEL LLC
91 Brenda Ln Ste C (19934-2290)
PHONE............................302 698-4221
EMP: 5 **EST:** 2018
SALES (est): 96.58K **Privately Held**
Web: www.contractorsflooringde.com
SIC: 1771 Flooring contractor

(G-809)
CREATIVE PROMOTIONS
38 South St (19934-1337)
PHONE............................302 697-7896
EMP: 3 **EST:** 1987
SALES (est): 194.54K **Privately Held**
SIC: 2759 5199 5943 Commercial printing, nec; Advertising specialties; Office forms and supplies

(G-810)
CROSSOVER SPORTS ENTRMT LLC ✪
Also Called: Crossover Grid
2140 S Dupont Hwy (19934-1249)
P.O. Box 917 (11803-0917)
PHONE............................516 728-5360
Jared Wolff, *CEO*
Cheryl Pritzker, *CFO*
EMP: 2 **EST:** 2023
SALES (est): 92.41K **Privately Held**
SIC: 2741 Internet publishing and broadcasting

(G-811)
CURVES INTERNATIONAL INC
Also Called: Curves
103 South St # 2 (19934-1338)
PHONE............................302 698-1481
Christina Grellch, *Pr*
EMP: 6 **EST:** 2005
SALES (est): 93.13K **Privately Held**
Web: www.curves.com
SIC: 7991 Exercise salon

(G-812)
CYCLOPS NET INC
2140 S Dupont Hwy (19934-1249)
PHONE............................844 979-0222
Reilly Blake Johnson, *CEO*
EMP: 8 **EST:** 2019
SALES (est): 294.17K **Privately Held**
SIC: 8748 7319 7389 Business consulting, nec; Display advertising service; Inspection and testing services

GEOGRAPHIC SECTION
Camden - Kent County (G-840)

(G-813)
DAL CONSTRUCTION
8331 Willow Grove Rd (19934-2538)
PHONE..................302 538-5310
Dan Irwin, Pt
EMP: 6 **EST:** 2014
SALES (est): 225.62K Privately Held
SIC: 1542 Commercial and office building, new construction

(G-814)
DAWSON BUS SERVICE INC (PA)
405 E Camden Wyoming Ave (19934-1211)
PHONE..................302 697-9501
TOLL FREE: 800
Willaim A Dawson, Pr
Willaim A Dawson, Pr
William R Dawson, *
John Thomas Dawson, *
Lisa Dawson, *
EMP: 87 **EST:** 1941
SQ FT: 5,000
SALES (est): 2.85MM
SALES (corp-wide): 2.85MM Privately Held
Web: www.dawsonbusservice.com
SIC: 4142 4151 Bus charter service, except local; School buses

(G-815)
DE SLEEP DISORDER CENTERS LLC
2116 S Dupont Hwy Ste 3 (19934-1259)
PHONE..................302 697-2749
EMP: 6 **EST:** 2019
SALES (est): 151.31K Privately Held
Web: www.delsleep.com
SIC: 8093 Rehabilitation center, outpatient treatment

(G-816)
DELAWARE ADOLESCENT PROGRAM INC
Also Called: Tot's Turf Child Care Center
185 South St (19934-1300)
PHONE..................302 531-0257
EMP: 25
SALES (corp-wide): 1.52MM Privately Held
Web: www.totsturfelc.org
SIC: 8322 Social service center
PA: Delaware Adolescent Program Incorporated
1901 S College Ave
Newark DE 19702
302 268-7218

(G-817)
DELAWARE STATE FARM BUREAU INC
Also Called: DELAWARE FARM BUREAU
3457 S Dupont Hwy (19934-1371)
PHONE..................302 697-3183
Gary Warren, Pr
Pamela Bakerain, Ex Dir
Laura Faircloth, Prin
EMP: 5 **EST:** 1936
SQ FT: 6,000
SALES (est): 803.39K Privately Held
Web: www.defb.org
SIC: 8611 Business associations

(G-818)
DIANES NAIL AND SPA
3469 S Dupont Hwy (19934-1371)
PHONE..................302 538-7185
EMP: 6 **EST:** 2014
SALES (est): 79.81K Privately Held
SIC: 7231 Manicurist, pedicurist

(G-819)
DILLS ELECTRIC
11924 Willow Grove Rd (19934-2267)
PHONE..................302 674-3444
Charles Dill, Owner
EMP: 2 **EST:** 1975
SALES (est): 70.15K Privately Held
SIC: 7694 Electric motor repair

(G-820)
DINING SOFTWARE GROUP INC
2140 S Dupont Hwy (19934-1249)
P.O. Box 271148 (80027-5021)
PHONE..................720 236-9572
Jaspal Singh, Pr
EMP: 9 **EST:** 2016
SALES (est): 605.48K Privately Held
Web: www.diningtek.com
SIC: 7371 Computer software development and applications

(G-821)
DIXON HUGHES GOODMAN LLP
1 S Main St (19934-1318)
PHONE..................336 714-8100
EMP: 6 **EST:** 2018
SALES (est): 26.39K Privately Held
SIC: 8721 Certified public accountant

(G-822)
DOVER FAMILY CHIROPRACTIC
120 Old Camden Rd Ste C (19934-5501)
PHONE..................302 531-1900
Brian Errico, Owner
EMP: 5 **EST:** 1992
SALES (est): 180K Privately Held
Web: www.doverfamilychiro.com
SIC: 8041 Offices and clinics of chiropractors

(G-823)
DOVER KENT COUNTY MPO
1783 Friends Way (19934-1377)
PHONE..................302 387-6030
Stephen Kingsberry, Prin
EMP: 9 **EST:** 2011
SALES (est): 477.59K Privately Held
Web: doverkentmpo.delaware.gov
SIC: 1611 General contractor, highway and street construction

(G-824)
EASTERN SHORE ENERGY INC
11550 Willow Grove Rd (19934-2297)
P.O. Box 158 (19934-0158)
PHONE..................302 697-9230
Fred Ellingsworth, Pr
Leslie Betts, *
EMP: 26 **EST:** 1981
SQ FT: 5,000
SALES (est): 2.36MM Privately Held
SIC: 1711 Warm air heating and air conditioning contractor

(G-825)
EASTERN SHORE EQUIPMENT CO
Also Called: Eseco
12244 Willow Grove Rd (19934-2281)
P.O. Box 1001 (19934-0501)
PHONE..................302 697-3300
Robert Bole, Pr
Theodore Bole, Pr
Alma Bole, Treas
Thomas Bole, VP
Elizabeth Boaman, Sec
EMP: 5 **EST:** 1961
SQ FT: 3,500
SALES (est): 998.74K Privately Held
SIC: 5085 Industrial supplies

(G-826)
EASTERN SPECIALTY FINANCE INC
Also Called: Check 'n Go 2907
374 Walmart Dr Ste 3 (19934-1372)
PHONE..................302 697-4290
Nicole Cammen, Brnch Mgr
EMP: 10
SALES (corp-wide): 696.24MM Privately Held
Web: locations.checkngo.com
SIC: 6141 Personal credit institutions
HQ: Eastern Specialty Finance, Inc.
7755 Montgomery Rd # 400
Cincinnati OH

(G-827)
EHELP HEALTH CORPORATION (PA) ✪
2140 S Dupont Hwy (19934-1249)
PHONE..................404 964-0906
Kenyotta Hannah, CEO
EMP: 5 **EST:** 2022
SALES (est): 206.48K
SALES (corp-wide): 206.48K Privately Held
SIC: 7371 Software programming applications

(G-828)
ELEGANT IMAGES LLP
10 S West St (19934-1324)
PHONE..................302 698-5250
Carol Smith, Pt
Brian Smith, Pt
EMP: 9 **EST:** 1999
SALES (est): 226K Privately Held
SIC: 7231 Beauty shops

(G-829)
ELGOOD SOLUTIONS INC
2140 S Dupont Hwy (19934-1249)
PHONE..................610 420-7207
Eli Sved, CEO
Rahul Alreja, Pr
EMP: 2 **EST:** 2020
SALES (est): 129.11K Privately Held
SIC: 3842 5047 5999 Personal safety equipment; Medical equipment and supplies; Medical apparatus and supplies

(G-830)
EMPIRE MEDICAL LLC
379 Walmart Dr (19934-1365)
PHONE..................443 553-0057
EMP: 8 **EST:** 2017
SALES (est): 143.11K Privately Held
SIC: 8099 Health and allied services, nec

(G-831)
EMPOWER HEALTHCARE ASSETS INC
2140 S Dupont Hwy (19934-1249)
PHONE..................604 789-2146
Steven Mcauley, CEO
EMP: 5 **EST:** 2019
SIC: 6719 Holding companies, nec

(G-832)
EVEREST HOTEL GROUP LLC (PA)
2140 S Dupont Hwy (19934-1249)
PHONE..................213 272-0088
Marshall Young, CEO
Li Hui Lo, COO
EMP: 15 **EST:** 2017
SQ FT: 5,000
SALES (est): 6.23MM
SALES (corp-wide): 6.23MM Privately Held
SIC: 7011 8741 Hotels; Hotel or motel management

(G-833)
FAMLEE FERTILITY INC
Also Called: Famlee
2140 S Dupont Hwy (19934-1249)
PHONE..................503 388-6915
Shelley Bailey Koranda, CEO
EMP: 9 **EST:** 2020
SALES (est): 163.94K Privately Held
Web: www.famlee.com
SIC: 8011 Fertility specialist, physician

(G-834)
FANTASY NFT LLC
2140 S Dupont Hwy (19934-1249)
PHONE..................423 313-3436
Richard Ryan, Prin
EMP: 5
SALES (est): 199.4K Privately Held
SIC: 7371 Computer software development and applications

(G-835)
FIRST NATIONAL BNK OF WYOMING
Also Called: First National Bank
4566 S Dupont Hwy (19934-1363)
PHONE..................302 697-2666
Joseph E Chippie, Pr
Mary E Benham, *
EMP: 22 **EST:** 1909
SALES (est): 2.5MM Privately Held
Web: www.fnbwyomingde.com
SIC: 6021 National commercial banks

(G-836)
FIRST STATE ANIMAL CENTER
32 Shelter Cir (19934-2293)
PHONE..................302 943-6032
EMP: 13 **EST:** 2017
SALES (est): 1.24MM Privately Held
Web: www.fsac-spca.org
SIC: 8699 Animal humane society

(G-837)
FIRST STATE PICKLEBALL CLB INC
32 Cox Ln (19934-4558)
PHONE..................302 387-1030
EMP: 6 **EST:** 2015
SALES (est): 88K Privately Held
Web: www.firststatepickleball.org
SIC: 7997 Membership sports and recreation clubs

(G-838)
FUTURE BRIGHT PEDIATRICS LLC (PA)
Also Called: Bright Future Pediatrics
120 Old Camden Rd Ste B (19934-5501)
PHONE..................302 538-6258
Elsayed Abdelsalam, Managing Member
EMP: 7 **EST:** 2011
SALES (est): 2.47MM
SALES (corp-wide): 2.47MM Privately Held
Web: www.brightfuturepediatrics.com
SIC: 8011 Pediatrician

(G-839)
GOD SAID I LOVE YOU LTD
401 Eagle Nest Dr (19934-2917)
PHONE..................302 697-0647
James Neyhart, Prin
EMP: 5 **EST:** 2017
SALES (est): 56.49K Privately Held
SIC: 4832 Religious

(G-840)
GRAVATT PAINTING
217 Willow Ave (19934-1356)
PHONE..................302 632-2835
Kevin Gravatt, Prin

Camden - Kent County (G-841)   GEOGRAPHIC SECTION

EMP: 5 **EST:** 2018
SALES (est): 98.83K **Privately Held**
SIC: 1721 Painting and paper hanging

(G-841)
GREET 26 INC
2140 S Dupont Hwy (19934-1249)
PHONE..................................310 601-2648
Alon Abady, *Pr*
EMP: 5 **EST:** 2020
SALES (est): 46.16K **Privately Held**
SIC: 7371 Software programming applications

(G-842)
GYMSTARZ GYMNASTICS ACADEMY
23 Cochran Ln (19934-2287)
PHONE..................................302 697-1221
EMP: 5 **EST:** 2011
SALES (est): 132.42K **Privately Held**
Web: www.gymstarzgymnastics.com
SIC: 7999 Gymnastic instruction, non-membership

(G-843)
HANDY & HARMAN
Handy & Harman Tube Co
12244 Willow Grove Rd (19934-2281)
PHONE..................................302 697-9521
John Coates, *Brnch Mgr*
EMP: 15
SALES (corp-wide): 1.7B **Publicly Held**
Web: www.handytube.com
SIC: 3317 Steel pipe and tubes
HQ: Handy & Harman
C/O Steel Partners
New York NY 10022
212 520-2300

(G-844)
HANDYTUBE CORPORATION (DH)
Also Called: Handy & Harman
12244 Willow Grove Rd (19934-2281)
PHONE..................................302 697-9521
John Coates, *Pr*
▲ **EMP:** 155 **EST:** 1980
SALES (est): 43.79MM
SALES (corp-wide): 1.7B **Publicly Held**
Web: www.handytube.com
SIC: 3317 Steel pipe and tubes
HQ: Handy & Harman
C/O Steel Partners
New York NY 10022
212 520-2300

(G-845)
HANDYTUBE CORPORATION
Also Called: Camden Metals
124 Vepco Blvd (19934-2286)
PHONE..................................302 697-9521
Tim Karly, *Mgr*
EMP: 70
SALES (corp-wide): 1.7B **Publicly Held**
Web: www.handytube.com
SIC: 5051 Steel
HQ: Handytube Corporation
12244 Willow Grove Rd
Camden DE 19934

(G-846)
HEALING GARDEN AT FNDG AVALON
102 S Main St (19934-1321)
PHONE..................................302 535-7883
Jacquelyn R Edwards-rowe, *Owner*
EMP: 5 **EST:** 2016
SALES (est): 32.37K **Privately Held**
Web: www.findingavalon.org
SIC: 8049 Offices of health practitioner

(G-847)
HEARX USA INC
Also Called: Hearxgroup
2140 S Dupont Hwy (19934-1249)
PHONE..................................415 212-5500
Nj Klopper, *Pr*
EMP: 60 **EST:** 2018
SALES (est): 8.63MM **Privately Held**
Web: www.hearxgroup.com
SIC: 3845 Audiological equipment, electromedical

(G-848)
HENRY EASHUM & SON INC
20 S Dupont Hwy (19934-1309)
PHONE..................................302 697-6164
Mildred Eashum, *Pr*
EMP: 10 **EST:** 1949
SALES (est): 800K **Privately Held**
Web: www.eashumplumbing.com
SIC: 1711 Warm air heating and air conditioning contractor

(G-849)
HI NEO INC
2140 S Dupont Hwy (19934-1249)
PHONE..................................917 514-9010
Tanya Tohill-farber, *CEO*
EMP: 6 **EST:** 2020
SALES (est): 56.54K **Privately Held**
Web: www.hineo.com
SIC: 7372 Application computer software

(G-850)
HIGH TIDE LAB
23 Cochran Ln (19934-2287)
PHONE..................................302 538-7041
EMP: 5 **EST:** 2019
SALES (est): 235.46K **Privately Held**
SIC: 8734 Testing laboratories

(G-851)
HIGH VUE LOGGING INC
12090 Willow Grove Rd (19934-2269)
PHONE..................................302 697-3606
Charles Harvey, *Pt*
Herbert Harvey, *Pt*
EMP: 2 **EST:** 1999
SALES (est): 130.21K **Privately Held**
SIC: 2411 Logging camps and contractors

(G-852)
HILTON BUS SERVICE
168 Vepco Blvd (19934-2286)
P.O. Box 394 (19934-0394)
PHONE..................................302 697-7676
EMP: 7 **EST:** 1997
SALES (est): 396.73K **Privately Held**
Web: www.hiltonbus.com
SIC: 4131 Intercity and rural bus transportation

(G-853)
HOWARD INDUSTRIES LLC (PA)
Also Called: Loot Kit Studios
2140 S Dupont Hwy (19934-1249)
PHONE..................................217 836-4476
EMP: 5 **EST:** 2015
SALES (est): 404.32K
SALES (corp-wide): 404.32K **Privately Held**
SIC: 7371 Computer software development and applications

(G-854)
ICE CREMEE CREATIONS
42 Doe Hill Ct (19934-1771)
P.O. Box 71 (11510-0071)
PHONE..................................516 450-2144
Cyancy Mccargo, *Managing Member*

EMP: 3
SALES (est): 135.7K **Privately Held**
SIC: 3999 7389 Manufacturing industries, nec; Business services, nec

(G-855)
IDRCH3 MINISTRIES
49 Brenda Ln (19934-2282)
PHONE..................................302 344-6957
EMP: 7
SALES (est): 101.65K **Privately Held**
SIC: 8322 Individual and family services

(G-856)
ITEXUS LLC
4034 Willow Grove Rd (19934-3148)
PHONE..................................917 618-9804
EMP: 8 **EST:** 2016
SALES (est): 46.16K **Privately Held**
Web: www.itexus.com
SIC: 7371 Computer software development

(G-857)
J I BEILER HOMES LLC
Also Called: John I Beiler Developers
106 Orchard Grove Way (19934-9610)
PHONE..................................302 697-1553
EMP: 5 **EST:** 1996
SALES (est): 517.33K **Privately Held**
Web: www.beilerhomes.com
SIC: 1521 New construction, single-family houses

(G-858)
JAMES L WEBB PAVING CO INC
11804 Willow Grove Rd (19934-2266)
PHONE..................................302 697-2000
James L Webb, *Pr*
Henrietta Webb, *Sec*
EMP: 6 **EST:** 1968
SQ FT: 300
SALES (est): 577.58K **Privately Held**
SIC: 1771 1611 Concrete work; Surfacing and paving

(G-859)
JAREL INDUSTRIES LLC
3411 S Dupont Hwy (19934-1371)
PHONE..................................336 782-0697
EMP: 5 **EST:** 2010
SALES (est): 232.11K **Privately Held**
SIC: 3842 3199 7389 Personal safety equipment; Harness or harness parts; Business services, nec

(G-860)
JOEL CRISSMAN
3407 Westville Rd (19934-1441)
PHONE..................................302 492-1757
Joel Crissman, *Prin*
EMP: 5 **EST:** 2008
SALES (est): 203.25K **Privately Held**
SIC: 1521 General remodeling, single-family houses

(G-861)
JORGE & EVONNES AUTO BODY LLC
8506 Willow Grove Rd (19934-2431)
PHONE..................................302 382-1460
Evonne Marker, *Prin*
EMP: 5 **EST:** 2016
SALES (est): 59.16K **Privately Held**
SIC: 7532 Body shop, automotive

(G-862)
JULIETH AI TECHNOLOGIES INC
2140 S Dupont Hwy (19934-1249)
PHONE..................................512 680-1855
Scotland Butler, *CEO*

EMP: 12
SALES (est): 406.37K **Privately Held**
SIC: 7371 Computer software development

(G-863)
KARVE BUILDERS LLC ✪
2140 S Dupont Hwy (19934-1249)
PHONE..................................403 471-2285
Aaron Joyes, *Dir*
EMP: 6 **EST:** 2023
SALES (est): 59.87K **Privately Held**
SIC: 1521 New construction, single-family houses

(G-864)
KATIE BENNETT
Also Called: State Farm Insurance
2150 S Dupont Hwy (19934-1249)
PHONE..................................302 697-2650
Katie Bennett, *Owner*
Paula Bowmen, *Mgr*
EMP: 9 **EST:** 1975
SALES (est): 593.4K **Privately Held**
Web: www.katiebennett.net
SIC: 6411 Insurance agents and brokers

(G-865)
KEEP IT - MOVING & LABOR LLC
11361 Willow Grove Rd (19934-2251)
PHONE..................................302 469-1161
Kenneth Sanders, *Managing Member*
EMP: 15 **EST:** 2010
SALES (est): 501.09K **Privately Held**
Web: www.keepitmovingandlabor.com
SIC: 4212 Moving services

(G-866)
KENT CNTY SOC FOR THE PRVNTION
Also Called: KENT COUNTY SPCA
32 Shelter Cir (19934-2293)
PHONE..................................302 698-3006
Alex Moore, *Pr*
Frank Newon, *
EMP: 19 **EST:** 1962
SQ FT: 10,000
SALES (est): 1.76MM **Privately Held**
Web: www.kentcountyspca.com
SIC: 8699 Animal humane society

(G-867)
KENT LANDSCAPING CO LLC
109 S Main St (19934-1320)
P.O. Box 300 (19934-0300)
PHONE..................................302 535-4296
Justin King, *Prin*
EMP: 10 **EST:** 2009
SALES (est): 711.84K **Privately Held**
SIC: 0781 Landscape services

(G-868)
LIVING PIXELS STUDIO LLC
4034 Willow Grove Rd (19934-3148)
PHONE..................................650 464-6899
Nimro D Santo, *Pr*
EMP: 5 **EST:** 2020
SALES (est): 117.25K **Privately Held**
SIC: 7372 Application computer software

(G-869)
LOGICALLY AI INC
2140 S Dupont Hwy (19934-1249)
PHONE..................................202 768-9876
Brian Murphy, *VP*
EMP: 17
SALES (est): 481.45K **Privately Held**
SIC: 7374 Data processing and preparation

GEOGRAPHIC SECTION Camden - Kent County (G-898)

(G-870)
LOWES HOME CENTERS LLC
Also Called: Lowe's
516 Walmart Dr (19934-1360)
PHONE..................................302 697-0700
Mike Snowden, *Mgr*
EMP: 121
SALES (corp-wide): 97.06B **Publicly Held**
Web: www.lowes.com
SIC: **5211** 5031 5722 5064 Home centers; Building materials, exterior; Household appliance stores; Electrical appliances, television and radio
HQ: Lowe's Home Centers, Llc
 1000 Lowes Blvd
 Mooresville NC 28117
 336 658-4000

(G-871)
MARIE E DYE
239 Old North Rd (19934-1241)
PHONE..................................302 698-4280
Marie E Dye, *Prin*
EMP: 8 EST: 2012
SALES (est): 42.83K **Privately Held**
SIC: **8049** Offices of health practitioner

(G-872)
MAST HOMES LLC
2397 Sandy Bend Rd (19934-1415)
PHONE..................................302 632-7735
Matthew Mast, *Prin*
EMP: 6 EST: 2018
SALES (est): 432.06K **Privately Held**
SIC: **1522** Residential construction, nec

(G-873)
MATTHEW W SPENCE INC
329 E Camden Wyoming Ave (19934-1210)
PHONE..................................302 697-3284
Matthew Spence, *Owner*
EMP: 8 EST: 1995
SALES (est): 76.93K **Privately Held**
Web: www.mwspence.com
SIC: **1794** Excavation work

(G-874)
MECHANICAL SOLUTIONS LLC
6944 Westville Rd (19934-3913)
PHONE..................................302 900-1950
Chris Naylor, *Prin*
EMP: 6 EST: 2018
SALES (est): 86.05K **Privately Held**
Web: www.mechsolutions1.com
SIC: **1711** Mechanical contractor

(G-875)
MILLENNIAL INFORMATICS LLC
2140 S Dupont Hwy (19934-1249)
PHONE..................................302 446-3800
Emmanuel Egbo, *Managing Member*
EMP: 9 EST: 2019
SALES (est): 326.49K **Privately Held**
SIC: **8742** Management information systems consultant

(G-876)
MILLER JOHN H PLUMBING & HTG
Also Called: John H Miller Sons Plbg Htg AC
220 Old North Rd (19934-1242)
PHONE..................................302 697-1012
John H Miller Iii, *Pr*
John H Miller Iv, *VP*
David Miller, *Treas*
Joanie L Miller, *Sec*
EMP: 10 EST: 1971
SALES (est): 625K **Privately Held**
SIC: **1711** Plumbing contractors

(G-877)
MINOR FIGURES INC
2140 S Dupont Hwy (19934-1249)
PHONE..................................714 875-3449
Stuart Forsyth, *CEO*
Toby Kill, *Sls Dir*
EMP: 9 EST: 2019
SALES (est): 1.64MM
SALES (corp-wide): 36.75MM **Privately Held**
Web: us.minorfigures.com
SIC: **2086** Soft drinks: packaged in cans, bottles, etc.
PA: Minor Figures Limited
 Unit 12a
 London E17 5
 207 148-4565

(G-878)
MOTIVERSE LABS INC ✪
2140 S Dupont Hwy (19934-1249)
PHONE..................................206 391-7995
Alexander Simpson, *CEO*
EMP: 4 EST: 2023
SALES (est): 171.34K **Privately Held**
SIC: **7372** Educational computer software

(G-879)
MURRAY PHILLIPS PA
257 E Camden Wyoming Ave (19934-1298)
PHONE..................................302 697-2499
EMP: 5 EST: 2017
SALES (est): 57.87K **Privately Held**
Web: www.murrayphillipslaw.com
SIC: **8111** General practice law office

(G-880)
NORTHEASTERN SUPPLY INC
Also Called: Northeastern Supply
100 S Dupont Hwy (19934-1311)
PHONE..................................302 698-1414
Dave Deason, *Mgr*
EMP: 5
SALES (corp-wide): 195.02MM **Privately Held**
Web: www.northeastern.com
SIC: **5074** Plumbing fittings and supplies
PA: Northeastern Supply, Inc.
 8323 Pulaski Hwy
 Baltimore MD 21237
 410 574-0010

(G-881)
ONECLICK CLEANERS
121 N Main St (19934-1247)
PHONE..................................302 697-8000
Ben Abiona, *Pr*
EMP: 6 EST: 2015
SALES (est): 31.55K **Privately Held**
Web: www.oneclickcleaners.com
SIC: **7216** Drycleaning plants, except rugs

(G-882)
ONFIDO INC
2140 S Dupont Hwy (19934-1249)
PHONE..................................415 855-7113
EMP: 5 EST: 2015
SALES (est): 65.78K **Privately Held**
SIC: **8742** Marketing consulting services

(G-883)
OTC TRADE LLC
2140 S Dupont Hwy (19934-1249)
PHONE..................................603 820-5820
EMP: 5 EST: 2019
SALES (est): 103.69K **Privately Held**
Web: www.otctrade.com
SIC: **7371** 7389 Computer software development and applications; Financial services

(G-884)
PENCO CORPORATION
2000 S Dupont Hwy (19934-1375)
PHONE..................................302 698-3108
David Blades, *Brnch Mgr*
EMP: 6
SALES (corp-wide): 24.24MM **Privately Held**
Web: www.pencocorp.com
SIC: **5074** Plumbing fittings and supplies
PA: Penco Corporation
 1503 W Stein Hwy
 Seaford DE 19973
 302 629-7911

(G-885)
POSITIVE OTLOOK GDNCE SVCS INC
110 Thomas Harmon Dr (19934-4720)
P.O. Box 471016 (20753-1016)
PHONE..................................240 761-3460
William Allen Iii, *Pr*
EMP: 9 EST: 2009
SALES (est): 115.96K **Privately Held**
Web: www.positiveoutlookgs.org
SIC: **8699** Charitable organization

(G-886)
PROPER-TEES LLC
2140 S Dupont Hwy (19934-1249)
PHONE..................................323 981-9809
EMP: 3 EST: 2018
SALES (est): 80.37K **Privately Held**
SIC: **2759** Screen printing

(G-887)
QUALITY BUILDERS INC
213 Willow Ave (19934-1356)
PHONE..................................302 697-0664
Mary Ressler, *Pr*
EMP: 5 EST: 1994
SALES (est): 568.37K **Privately Held**
SIC: **1521** General remodeling, single-family houses

(G-888)
RAPTA INC
2140 S Dupont Hwy (19934-1249)
PHONE..................................408 627-2556
Aaron Brown, *CEO*
Matthew Thornton, *CMO*
EMP: 4
SALES (est): 180.26K **Privately Held**
SIC: **3829** Measuring and controlling devices, nec

(G-889)
REGIS CORPORATION
263 Walmart Dr (19934-1308)
PHONE..................................302 697-6220
Alicia Lopez, *Brnch Mgr*
EMP: 8
SALES (corp-wide): 233.33MM **Publicly Held**
Web: www.regiscorp.com
SIC: **7231** Unisex hair salons
PA: Regis Corporation
 3701 Wayzata Blvd Ste 500
 Minneapolis MN 55416
 952 947-7777

(G-890)
ROSAS DINER LLC
221 Hillcrest Ct (19934-1281)
P.O. Box 541 (19934-0541)
PHONE..................................302 336-8243
EMP: 4 EST: 2020
SALES (est): 20K **Privately Held**
SIC: **2099** Seasonings and spices

(G-891)
S AND J CONTRACTING LLC
1331 Hollering Hill Rd (19934-3040)
PHONE..................................302 382-0769
Steve Montsch, *Prin*
EMP: 5 EST: 2017
SALES (est): 62.18K **Privately Held**
SIC: **1799** Special trade contractors, nec

(G-892)
SHELLS EARLY LRNG CTR CAMDEN
2116 S Dupont Hwy (19934-1259)
PHONE..................................302 698-1556
Melissa Barrett, *Owner*
EMP: 11 EST: 2015
SALES (est): 90.8K **Privately Held**
Web: www.shellschildcare.com
SIC: **8351** Group day care center

(G-893)
SHOWBIZ TRUCKING LLC
1850 Henry Cowgill Rd (19934-2616)
P.O. Box 528 (08101-0528)
PHONE..................................302 526-6337
Tabius Wilson Senior, *Prin*
EMP: 5 EST: 2019
SALES (est): 264.5K **Privately Held**
SIC: **4213** 7389 Refrigerated products transport; Business Activities at Non-Commercial Site

(G-894)
SUPERCUTS
Also Called: Supercuts
374 Walmart Dr (19934-1372)
PHONE..................................302 698-1988
Heather Greenlee, *Mgr*
EMP: 6 EST: 2010
SALES (est): 32.8K **Privately Held**
Web: www.supercuts.com
SIC: **7231** Unisex hair salons

(G-895)
SYSTEMS ORCHESTRATION LLC
288 Cambridge Rd (19934-1204)
PHONE..................................302 363-5168
David Harman, *Pr*
EMP: 5 EST: 2014
SALES (est): 75.97K **Privately Held**
SIC: **7929** Orchestras or bands, nec

(G-896)
THREESIXTYTRADE LLC
2140 S Dupont Hwy (19934-1249)
PHONE..................................214 810-2922
EMP: 6
SALES (est): 303.5K **Privately Held**
SIC: **5045** Computers, peripherals, and software

(G-897)
TK BLIER INCORPORATED
2140 S Dupont Hwy (19934-1249)
PHONE..................................207 760-7076
Troy Blier, *Managing Member*
Troy Blier, *Ex Dir*
EMP: 32 EST: 2016
SALES (est): 1.31MM **Privately Held**
SIC: **8742** Industry specialist consultants

(G-898)
TURNING PT COUNSELING CTR LLC
1 N Main St (19934-1227)
PHONE..................................214 883-5148
EMP: 6 EST: 2017
SALES (est): 64.06K **Privately Held**
SIC: **8059** Personal care home, with health care

(PA)=Parent Co (HQ)=Headquarters
✪ = New Business established in last 2 years

Camden - Kent County (G-899)
GEOGRAPHIC SECTION

(G-899)
WYOMING MILLWORK CO (PA)
140 Vepco Blvd (19934-2286)
PHONE..................................302 697-8650
David Failing, *Pr*
Craig Failing, *VP*
EMP: 40 **EST:** 1994
SALES (est): 64.58MM **Privately Held**
Web: www.wyomingmillwork.com
SIC: 2431 Millwork

(G-900)
YOUNG SOLES INC
2140 S Dupont Hwy (19934-1249)
PHONE..................................516 643-0445
Stuart Anderson, *Pr*
EMP: 5 **EST:** 2020
SALES (est): 50K **Privately Held**
SIC: 5139 Footwear

(G-901)
YOUNIQUE
106 Stevens St (19934-1358)
PHONE..................................302 632-3060
Christina Jackson, *Prin*
EMP: 5 **EST:** 2016
SALES (est): 60.25K **Privately Held**
Web: www.youniqueproducts.com
SIC: 7991 Physical fitness facilities

Camden Wyoming
Kent County

(G-902)
4 POINTS TWING RADSIDE SVC LLC
5425 Willow Grove Rd (19934-2826)
PHONE..................................302 538-8935
Janet Kope, *Owner*
EMP: 8 **EST:** 2017
SALES (est): 589.43K **Privately Held**
Web: www.4pointstowing.com
SIC: 7549 Towing service, automotive

(G-903)
A + FLOOR STORE INC
Also Called: A Plus Floor Store
166 Roundabout Trl (19934-9672)
PHONE..................................302 698-2166
Robert S Dashiell, *Pr*
EMP: 7 **EST:** 1993
SQ FT: 5,000
SALES (est): 291.92K **Privately Held**
SIC: 5713 5023 Floor covering stores; Floor coverings

(G-904)
AAA PORTABLE RESTROOM CO INC
108 Gardengate Rd (19934-9648)
PHONE..................................909 981-0090
Samuel B Roth, *Pr*
Leslie Roth, *VP*
EMP: 9 **EST:** 1998
SALES (est): 774.56K **Privately Held**
SIC: 7359 Portable toilet rental

(G-905)
ACCESS QUALITY HEALTHCARE
608 Raven Cir (19934-4021)
PHONE..................................302 698-2150
Aaron Green, *Prin*
EMP: 6 **EST:** 2018
SALES (est): 192.16K **Privately Held**
SIC: 8099 Health and allied services, nec

(G-906)
ADVANCE CONSTRUCTION CO DEL
280 Banning Rd (19934-1758)
PHONE..................................302 697-9444
Robert C Sylvester, *Pr*
Judith Ann Sylvester, *Sec*
Robert T Sylvester, *VP*
EMP: 10 **EST:** 1965
SQ FT: 4,500
SALES (est): 1.03MM **Privately Held**
SIC: 1521 1542 1541 General remodeling, single-family houses; Commercial and office building, new construction; Prefabricated building erection, industrial

(G-907)
ALFRED B LAUDER DDS
508 Eagle Nest Dr (19934-2024)
PHONE..................................302 697-7188
Alfred Lauder, *Prin*
EMP: 10 **EST:** 2009
SALES (est): 103.85K **Privately Held**
SIC: 8021 Dentists' office

(G-908)
ALFRED LAUDER DDS
508 Eagle Nest Dr (19934-2024)
PHONE..................................302 678-9742
Alfred Lauder D.d.s., *Owner*
EMP: 5 **EST:** 1998
SALES (est): 245.07K **Privately Held**
Web: www.dentistdover-de.com
SIC: 8021 Dentists' office

(G-909)
ALL RESTORED INC
137 Sarah Cir (19934-2360)
PHONE..................................302 697-7810
EMP: 7 **EST:** 2020
SALES (est): 567.31K **Privately Held**
Web: www.allrestoredinc.com
SIC: 1521 General remodeling, single-family houses

(G-910)
ALL RESTORED INC
1638 Thicket Rd (19934-2350)
PHONE..................................302 222-3537
Dallas Glass, *Prin*
EMP: 8 **EST:** 2010
SALES (est): 426.59K **Privately Held**
Web: www.allrestoredinc.com
SIC: 1799 Special trade contractors, nec

(G-911)
ALLENS TERMITE & PEST MGMT
5991 Mud Mill Rd (19934-3420)
PHONE..................................302 698-1496
Ernest Shell, *Owner*
EMP: 5 **EST:** 2009
SALES (est): 106.97K **Privately Held**
SIC: 8741 Management services

(G-912)
ALUMINUM BUILDING COMPANY
10957 Willow Grove Rd (19934-2256)
PHONE..................................302 423-8829
Chad Collins, *Prin*
EMP: 6 **EST:** 2008
SALES (est): 209.71K **Privately Held**
SIC: 1799 Special trade contractors, nec

(G-913)
APPLIED TECHNOLOGIES INC
169 Roundabout Trl (19934-9673)
PHONE..................................302 670-4601
Brian T Valeski, *Pr*
EMP: 6 **EST:** 2002
SALES (est): 365.68K **Privately Held**
Web: www.ceoappliedtechnologiesinc.com
SIC: 7379 Online services technology consultants

(G-914)
B & T CONTRACTING
4158 Westville Rd (19934-1427)
PHONE..................................302 492-8415
Allen Troyer, *Pt*
EMP: 7 **EST:** 1986
SQ FT: 3,262
SALES (est): 142.34K **Privately Held**
SIC: 1799 Special trade contractors, nec

(G-915)
B DIAMOND FEED COMPANY
2140 Jebb Rd (19934-3630)
PHONE..................................302 697-7576
Sam Berry, *Owner*
EMP: 2 **EST:** 1973
SALES (est): 103.64K **Privately Held**
SIC: 2048 5191 Livestock feeds; Animal feeds

(G-916)
BAYSIDE SEALCOATING SUPPLY
6453 Mud Mill Rd (19934-3415)
PHONE..................................302 697-6441
EMP: 5
Web: www.baysidesealcoating.net
SIC: 1611 Surfacing and paving
PA: Bayside Sealcoating Supply
540 S Bedford St
Georgetown DE

(G-917)
BOYDS TRAILOR HITCHES
Also Called: Boyds Crane
3178 S State St (19934-1830)
PHONE..................................302 697-9000
Ken Boyd, *Pr*
EMP: 6 **EST:** 2004
SALES (est): 620.64K **Privately Held**
Web: www.boydswelding.com
SIC: 5051 7692 1799 5531 Steel; Welding repair; Special trade contractors, nec; Trailer hitches, automotive

(G-918)
BOYDS WELDING INC
3178 S State St (19934-1830)
PHONE..................................302 697-9000
M Kenneth Boyd, *Pr*
Janet Boyd, *Sec*
EMP: 7 **EST:** 1973
SQ FT: 5,000
SALES (est): 801.11K **Privately Held**
Web: www.boydswelding.com
SIC: 7692 Welding repair

(G-919)
BRAUN ENGINEERING & SURVEYING
863 Allabands Mill Rd (19934-2132)
PHONE..................................302 698-0701
David Braun, *Pr*
Patricia Braun, *VP*
Janette Lafashia, *Off Mgr*
EMP: 6 **EST:** 1976
SQ FT: 4,000
SALES (est): 162.59K **Privately Held**
Web: www.braunengineering.net
SIC: 8713 7334 Surveying services; Photocopying and duplicating services

(G-920)
BRUTE PERFORMANCE INC ◆
303 Chanticleer Cir (19934-5419)
PHONE..................................757 477-7136
Timothy Leahey, *CEO*
EMP: 5 **EST:** 2022
SALES (est): 313.14K **Privately Held**
SIC: 7389 Business Activities at Non-Commercial Site

(G-921)
CAMDEN-WYOMING ROTARY CLUB
6 Bob White Pl (19934-9522)
P.O. Box 223 (19934-0223)
PHONE..................................302 697-2724
EMP: 6 **EST:** 2011
SALES (est): 53.77K **Privately Held**
Web: www.cwrotary.org
SIC: 7997 Membership sports and recreation clubs

(G-922)
CAPRIOTTIS OF MILFORD
457 Banning Rd (19934-1765)
PHONE..................................302 424-3309
Ray Rodriguez, *Owner*
EMP: 6 **EST:** 2001
SALES (est): 506.26K **Privately Held**
SIC: 2841 Soap and other detergents

(G-923)
CHARLES E CARLSON
Also Called: Blue Hen Courier
3670 Willow Grove Rd (19934-3144)
PHONE..................................302 284-3184
Charles E Carlson, *Prin*
EMP: 5 **EST:** 2009
SALES (est): 242.76K **Privately Held**
SIC: 4215 Courier services, except by air

(G-924)
CLYDE V BUSH SR
Also Called: Clyde V Bush Sr Arms
95 Goshawk Ln (19934-2300)
PHONE..................................302 697-1723
EMP: 5 **EST:** 2009
SALES (est): 46.08K **Privately Held**
SIC: 7699 Gun services

(G-925)
COASTAL LANDSCAPING LLC
1 Clubhouse Dr (19934-9501)
PHONE..................................302 222-0098
EMP: 5 **EST:** 2016
SALES (est): 79.14K **Privately Held**
SIC: 0781 Landscape counseling and planning

(G-926)
COMPLETE PROPERTIES SERVICES
116 Sarah Cir Ste D (19934-2203)
PHONE..................................302 242-8666
John Fuchs, *Pr*
Buddy Snyder, *Mgr*
EMP: 8 **EST:** 2005
SALES (est): 200.72K **Privately Held**
SIC: 0781 Landscape services

(G-927)
COMPUTOOLS LLC
341 Raven Cir (19934-4033)
PHONE..................................617 861-0016
Sergii Tymchuk, *CEO*
EMP: 13 **EST:** 2016
SALES (est): 381.14K **Privately Held**
Web: www.computools.com
SIC: 7371 Computer software development

(G-928)
CONTRUCTION JONES AND LDSCPG
5169 Mud Mill Rd (19934-2913)
PHONE..................................302 423-6456
Chris Jones, *Prin*
EMP: 5 **EST:** 2011
SALES (est): 148.08K **Privately Held**
SIC: 0781 Landscape services

GEOGRAPHIC SECTION — Camden Wyoming - Kent County (G-959)

(G-929)
COUNTRY COMFORTS
Also Called: Flashback Farms
6309 Mud Mill Rd (19934-3416)
PHONE..................302 242-8527
EMP: 5
SALES (est): 100K **Privately Held**
SIC: 0272 Horses and other equines

(G-930)
CRUISE ONE
159 Orchard Grove Ct (19934-4901)
PHONE..................302 698-6468
Elaine Nolan, *Mgr*
EMP: 5 EST: 2008
SALES (est): 373.65K **Privately Held**
Web: www.cruiseone.com
SIC: 4724 4481 Travel agencies; Deep sea passenger transportation, except ferry

(G-931)
CURRENT SOLUTIONS INC
1100 Apple Grove School Rd (19934-4112)
PHONE..................302 736-5210
Christina Wolf, *Pr*
Gary Wolf, *Sec*
EMP: 7 EST: 1996
SALES (est): 453.03K **Privately Held**
Web: www.currentsolutionspc.com
SIC: 1731 General electrical contractor

(G-932)
DIAMOND MINDS LLC
4470 Mud Mill Rd (19934-3008)
PHONE..................302 359-5069
Jeanine M Pennington, *Prin*
EMP: 6 EST: 2012
SALES (est): 70.78K **Privately Held**
Web: www.diamondmindsllc.org
SIC: 4899 Communication services, nec

(G-933)
DIAMOND STATE PEST CONTROL CO
244 Morgans Choice Rd (19934-3517)
P.O. Box 401 (19934-0401)
PHONE..................302 250-3403
Deeann Mccauley, *Prin*
EMP: 6 EST: 2018
SALES (est): 189K **Privately Held**
Web: www.diamondstatepestcontrol.com
SIC: 7342 Pest control in structures

(G-934)
DIRECT & CORRECT INC
6236 Mud Mill Rd (19934-3406)
PHONE..................302 697-7117
Karen Pollard, *Pr*
Jake Pollard, *VP*
Angel Jones, *Off Mgr*
Mandy Pollard Sign, *Shop Manager*
EMP: 7 EST: 2011
SALES (est): 251.68K **Privately Held**
Web: www.directandcorrect.com
SIC: 7389 Flagging service (traffic control)

(G-935)
DOMINOS BODY SHOP
467 Moose Lodge Rd (19934-2234)
PHONE..................302 697-3801
Frank Domino, *Owner*
EMP: 5 EST: 1966
SQ FT: 4,600
SALES (est): 334.47K **Privately Held**
SIC: 7532 Body shop, automotive

(G-936)
DRY BULK TRANSPORTATION LLC
303 Chanticleer Cir (19934-5419)
PHONE..................561 409-7818
Piero M Ferri, *Pr*
EMP: 8 EST: 2014
SALES (est): 365.73K **Privately Held**
SIC: 4789 Transportation services, nec

(G-937)
DUNAMS-HMES DVINE INTRVNTION I
1328 Rising Sun Rd Ste 1 (19934-1914)
P.O. Box 37 (19960-0037)
PHONE..................302 393-5778
Vanessa Brinkley, *Prin*
Vanessa Johnson Brinkley, *Pr*
EMP: 5 EST: 2016
SALES (est): 174.14K **Privately Held**
SIC: 8361 8322 Residential care; Emergency shelters

(G-938)
DURHAM TRANSPORT LLC
135 Goshawk Ln (19934-2368)
PHONE..................302 270-2178
EMP: 5 EST: 2019
SALES (est): 204.64K **Privately Held**
SIC: 4789 Transportation services, nec

(G-939)
ELECTRIC MOTOR WHOLESALE INC
2575 Morgans Choice Rd (19934-3655)
PHONE..................302 653-1844
Wendy Frye, *Pr*
Edward Frye, *VP*
EMP: 17 EST: 2018
SALES (est): 3.14MM **Privately Held**
SIC: 5063 5085 Motor controls, starters and relays: electric; Power transmission equipment and apparatus

(G-940)
ELECTRIC MOTOR WHOLESALE INC
2575 Morgans Choice Rd (19934-3655)
PHONE..................302 653-1844
Wendy Frye, *Pr*
Wendy L Frye, *Pr*
Edward Frye, *VP*
EMP: 19 EST: 2002
SQ FT: 4,000
SALES (est): 7.63MM **Privately Held**
Web: www.electricmotorwholesale.com
SIC: 5063 5085 Motor controls, starters and relays: electric; Power transmission equipment and apparatus

(G-941)
ERVIN H YODER
5338 Mud Mill Rd (19934-2905)
PHONE..................302 492-1835
Ervin H Yoder, *Prin*
EMP: 5 EST: 2009
SALES (est): 120.35K **Privately Held**
SIC: 1521 Single-family housing construction

(G-942)
ESTESTWINS TRUCKING LLC
5269 Mud Mill Rd (19934-2912)
PHONE..................267 773-2991
Craig Estes, *Managing Member*
EMP: 5 EST: 2016
SALES (est): 170K **Privately Held**
SIC: 4212 7389 Dump truck haulage; Business Activities at Non-Commercial Site

(G-943)
FALASCO MASONRY INC
3152 S State St (19934-1809)
PHONE..................302 697-8971
Joseph Falasco, *Pr*
Trish Alexander, *Sec*
EMP: 6 EST: 1990
SQ FT: 3,500
SALES (est): 439.1K **Privately Held**
Web: www.stonegateassociates.net
SIC: 1741 Masonry and other stonework

(G-944)
FIFER ORCHARDS INC
1919 Allabands Mill Rd (19934-2121)
PHONE..................302 697-2141
Carlton C Fifer, *Pr*
Mary Fennemore,
▼ EMP: 125 EST: 1919
SQ FT: 150,000
SALES (est): 11.52MM **Privately Held**
Web: www.fiferorchards.com
SIC: 0161 0175 Asparagus farm; Apple orchard

(G-945)
FIRST STATE STRINGS INC
140 Metz Dr (19934-1702)
PHONE..................302 331-7362
Steve Gaston, *Prin*
EMP: 5 EST: 2008
SALES (est): 80.51K **Privately Held**
SIC: 7929 Orchestras or bands, nec

(G-946)
FLY HIGH CHEER AND TUMBLE LLC
149 Estates Dr (19934-4601)
PHONE..................585 317-1442
EMP: 7 EST: 2019
SALES (est): 193.75K **Privately Held**
Web: www.flyhighcheerandtumble.com
SIC: 7999 Gymnastic instruction, non-membership

(G-947)
FORWARD DISCOVERY INC
27 Milbourn Manor Dr (19934-3638)
PHONE..................703 647-6364
Art Ehuan, *Pr*
EMP: 6 EST: 2007
SALES (est): 278.07K **Privately Held**
SIC: 7379 Online services technology consultants

(G-948)
GARCIA MOISES LLC
507 Rising Sun Rd (19934-1927)
PHONE..................302 698-1930
Moises Garcia, *Owner*
EMP: 6 EST: 2010
SALES (est): 99.89K **Privately Held**
SIC: 1751 Carpentry work

(G-949)
GOLDSBORO SAND AND GRAVEL
2904 Willow Grove Rd (19934-3211)
PHONE..................410 310-0402
Arlene Seaman, *Prin*
EMP: 5 EST: 2017
SALES (est): 120.04K **Privately Held**
SIC: 1442 Construction sand and gravel

(G-950)
GOLSONEL GLOBAL LLC
33 Quigley Ct (19934-4751)
PHONE..................267 461-8400
EMP: 2 EST: 2021
SALES (est): 95.58K **Privately Held**
SIC: 3537 7389 Trucks, tractors, loaders, carriers, and similar equipment; Business Activities at Non-Commercial Site

(G-951)
GREEN OPPORTUNITIES CORP
3051 Willow Grove Rd (19934-3220)
PHONE..................302 535-2235
Brittanie A Davidson, *Prin*
EMP: 11 EST: 2010
SALES (est): 700.85K **Privately Held**
Web: www.greenopportunities.org
SIC: 4953 Recycling, waste materials

(G-952)
HANDY HUSBAND LLC
8771 Willow Grove Rd (19934-2472)
PHONE..................302 697-7552
Dorothea Handy, *Prin*
EMP: 5 EST: 2010
SALES (est): 57.16K **Privately Held**
SIC: 7299 Handyman service

(G-953)
HIGHWAY TRAFFIC CONTROLLERS
6236 Mud Mill Rd (19934-3406)
PHONE..................302 697-7117
Karen Pollard, *Pr*
Sue Snyder, *Sec*
EMP: 7 EST: 1995
SALES (est): 117.52K **Privately Held**
SIC: 7389 Flagging service (traffic control)

(G-954)
IMAGINEYU DESIGNS LLC
49 Filbert Dr (19934-2206)
PHONE..................302 387-1230
EMP: 5 EST: 2012
SALES (est): 264.81K **Privately Held**
SIC: 7389 Interior design services

(G-955)
ITS ALL GOOD IN DELAWARE INC
P.O. Box 493 (19934-0493)
PHONE..................302 698-1232
EMP: 5 EST: 2011
SALES (est): 90.19K **Privately Held**
Web: www.itsallgoodindelaware.com
SIC: 8699 Charitable organization

(G-956)
JIMMY SMALLS LANDSCAPING LLC
91 Brenda Ln Ste A (19934-2290)
PHONE..................302 730-0150
Bobbie Pearson, *Prin*
EMP: 10 EST: 2011
SALES (est): 511.95K **Privately Held**
SIC: 0781 Landscape services

(G-957)
JOHN HIOTT REFRIGERATION & AC
9166 Willow Grove Rd (19934-2437)
PHONE..................302 697-3050
John Hiott, *Pr*
Brenda Hiott, *Treas*
Debbie Hiott, *Sec*
EMP: 10 EST: 1972
SALES (est): 997.69K **Privately Held**
SIC: 1711 Refrigeration contractor

(G-958)
JOHN T PEARSON
1508 Darling Farm Rd (19934-3734)
PHONE..................302 653-2322
John Pearson, *Owner*
EMP: 8 EST: 2017
SALES (est): 23.6K **Privately Held**
SIC: 8049 Offices of health practitioner

(G-959)
KEVIN ELZIE
Also Called: K & J and Company
301 Westhill Dr (19934-2385)
PHONE..................302 697-6273
Kevin Elzie, *Prin*
EMP: 6 EST: 2011
SALES (est): 118.41K **Privately Held**
SIC: 1522 Hotel/motel and multi-family home construction

Camden Wyoming - Kent County (G-960)

(G-960)
MARK E HANDLEY
156 Henry Cowgill Rd (19934-2758)
PHONE..................302 284-9550
Mark E Handley, *Prin*
EMP: 5 EST: 2011
SALES (est): 73.98K **Privately Held**
SIC: 7291 Tax return preparation services

(G-961)
MATRIX NETWORK SOLUTIONS LLC
18 Bandcroft Dr (19934-4328)
PHONE..................302 331-7330
EMP: 5 EST: 2011
SALES (est): 23.46K **Privately Held**
SIC: 7379 Computer related consulting services

(G-962)
MILFORD EARLY LEARNING CENTER
592 Ashland Ave (19934-2481)
PHONE..................302 331-6612
Esther Graham, *Prin*
EMP: 10 EST: 2010
SALES (est): 122.65K **Privately Held**
SIC: 8351 Preschool center

(G-963)
MILLMAR CONTRACTING LLC
2353 Honeysuckle Rd (19934-3760)
PHONE..................302 697-6581
Melvin E Millen, *Prin*
EMP: 5 EST: 2016
SALES (est): 56.76K **Privately Held**
SIC: 1799 Special trade contractors, nec

(G-964)
MY SALON SUITE
160 Humphreys Dr (19934-1967)
PHONE..................302 233-6947
EMP: 6 EST: 2018
SALES (est): 55.21K **Privately Held**
Web: www.mysalonsuite.com
SIC: 7231 Beauty shops

(G-965)
PIESHALAAMANDA
1201 Pony Track Rd (19934-3128)
PHONE..................302 492-3227
Richard Pieshala, *Owner*
EMP: 5 EST: 2015
SALES (est): 65.86K **Privately Held**
SIC: 1799 Special trade contractors, nec

(G-966)
QUAIL ASSOCIATES INC
Also Called: Wild Quail Golf & Country Club
1 Clubhouse Dr (19934-9501)
PHONE..................302 697-4660
Ric Mccall, *Genl Mgr*
EMP: 45 EST: 1986
SQ FT: 20,000
SALES (est): 1.93MM **Privately Held**
Web: www.wildquail.com
SIC: 7997 7299 Golf club, membership; Banquet hall facilities

(G-967)
QUALITY LAWN CARE HOME RE
4 Turtle Dr (19934-1801)
PHONE..................302 331-5892
EMP: 8 EST: 2009
SALES (est): 73.31K **Privately Held**
SIC: 8059 Nursing and personal care, nec

(G-968)
RAFAEL ZARAGOZA DR
6 Pintail Pl (19934-9533)
PHONE..................302 697-2336
Rafael Zaragoza, *Prin*
EMP: 9 EST: 2004
SALES (est): 99.91K **Privately Held**
SIC: 8011 Offices and clinics of medical doctors

(G-969)
RIGHT WAY FLAGGING AND SIGN CO
173 Brenda Ln Ste C (19934-2292)
P.O. Box 1013 (19934-0513)
PHONE..................302 698-5229
Roger E Satterfield, *Pr*
Ann M Satterfield, *
Melissa B Button, *
EMP: 12 EST: 2004
SQ FT: 32,000
SALES (est): 470.88K **Privately Held**
SIC: 7389 7359 Flagging service (traffic control); Equipment rental and leasing, nec

(G-970)
RIVER ROCK CONTRACTING LLC
2942 S State St (19934-1807)
PHONE..................302 538-7169
EMP: 6 EST: 2020
SALES (est): 450.87K **Privately Held**
SIC: 1799 Special trade contractors, nec

(G-971)
ROBERT LARIMORE
328 Moose Lodge Rd (19934-2216)
PHONE..................302 730-8682
Robert Larimore, *Owner*
EMP: 6 EST: 1977
SALES (est): 280K **Privately Held**
SIC: 8713 Surveying services

(G-972)
RWM PLUMBING
10785 Willow Grove Rd (19934-2258)
PHONE..................302 697-1705
R Wayne Mabrey, *Prin*
EMP: 5 EST: 2008
SALES (est): 63.5K **Privately Held**
SIC: 1711 Plumbing contractors

(G-973)
SALT AIR HOMES
223 Wynsome Blvd (19934-5331)
PHONE..................302 698-4146
EMP: 5 EST: 2016
SALES (est): 222.59K **Privately Held**
Web: www.saltairhomes.com
SIC: 6531 Real estate agents and managers

(G-974)
SEW HAPPY QUILTS LLC
1095 Hollering Hill Rd (19934-3043)
PHONE..................302 382-5565
Barbara Durham, *Prin*
EMP: 5 EST: 2018
SALES (est): 18.95K **Privately Held**
SIC: 7299 Quilting for individuals

(G-975)
SHADDAI I EL
280 Banning Rd (19934-1758)
PHONE..................302 632-7535
EMP: 5 EST: 2011
SALES (est): 47.69K **Privately Held**
SIC: 7999 Fishing boats, party: operation

(G-976)
SHELDE CONSTRUCTION
355 Allabands Mill Rd (19934-2137)
PHONE..................561 723-5314
Curtis Derricks, *Prin*
EMP: 5 EST: 2014
SALES (est): 106.46K **Privately Held**
SIC: 1521 Single-family housing construction

(G-977)
SINGLE SOURCE INC
91 Brenda Ln Ste D (19934-2290)
PHONE..................302 697-6156
EMP: 5 EST: 2017
SALES (est): 210.98K **Privately Held**
SIC: 5013 Body repair or paint shop supplies, automotive

(G-978)
SISSYS CLOSET INC
73 Pear Blossom Ln (19934-4911)
PHONE..................302 698-1327
Grizel Muniz, *Owner*
EMP: 6 EST: 2015
SALES (est): 84.72K **Privately Held**
SIC: 7212 Garment pressing and cleaners' agents

(G-979)
SJM SALES INC
500 Eagle Nest Dr (19934-2024)
PHONE..................302 697-6748
Tony Marano, *Pr*
Deborah Marano, *VP*
EMP: 2 EST: 1992
SALES (est): 153.22K **Privately Held**
SIC: 3949 Sporting and athletic goods, nec

(G-980)
SMUCKER COMPANY LLC
116 Sarah Cir (19934-2203)
PHONE..................302 322-9285
Linda Crumley, *Prin*
EMP: 37 EST: 2019
SALES (est): 243.74K **Privately Held**
Web: www.smuckercompany.com
SIC: 1742 Drywall

(G-981)
STEVEN T MILLER
1856 Honeysuckle Rd (19934-3702)
PHONE..................302 697-3541
Steven T Miller, *Prin*
EMP: 6 EST: 2012
SALES (est): 146.44K **Privately Held**
SIC: 1741 Stone masonry

(G-982)
TIDEMARK LLC
57 Castle Pines Ct (19934-4622)
PHONE..................302 359-4646
EMP: 5 EST: 2010
SALES (est): 92.63K **Privately Held**
Web: www.tidemarkde.com
SIC: 6531 Real estate brokers and agents

(G-983)
TINMAN ENTERPRISES LLC
630 Raven Cir (19934-4021)
PHONE..................302 698-1630
John Tinsley, *Owner*
EMP: 5 EST: 2012
SALES (est): 233.55K **Privately Held**
Web: www.tin-man.net
SIC: 8748 Business consulting, nec

(G-984)
TOTAL PEST SOLUTIONS
309 Quail Run (19934-9518)
PHONE..................302 275-7159
Joel Mick, *Prin*
EMP: 9 EST: 2010
SALES (est): 196.04K **Privately Held**
Web: www.jempestsolutions.com
SIC: 7342 Pest control in structures

(G-985)
WARNER M SCHLAUPITZ
4624 Westville Rd (19934-1503)
PHONE..................302 492-3451
Warner M Schlaupitz, *Prin*
EMP: 5 EST: 2006
SQ FT: 1,848
SALES (est): 79.16K **Privately Held**
SIC: 0191 General farms, primarily crop

(G-986)
WEBB & FAMILY LLC
816 Thicket Rd (19934-3609)
PHONE..................302 697-7108
Bryce Webb, *Prin*
EMP: 5 EST: 2017
SALES (est): 76.98K **Privately Held**
SIC: 7389 Business services, nec

(G-987)
ZIMMER US INC
82 Brookwood Dr (19934-3677)
PHONE..................617 272-0062
EMP: 11 EST: 2018
SALES (est): 474.1K
SALES (corp-wide): 6.94B **Publicly Held**
Web: www.zimmerbiomet.com
SIC: 3842 Orthopedic appliances
PA: Zimmer Biomet Holdings, Inc.
    345 E Main St
    Warsaw IN 46580
    574 267-6131

Cheswold
Kent County

(G-988)
GREAT CLIPS FOR HAIR
Also Called: Great Clips
137 Jerome Dr (19936)
PHONE..................302 677-1838
EMP: 5 EST: 2018
SALES (est): 47.66K **Privately Held**
Web: www.greatclips.com
SIC: 7231 Unisex hair salons

(G-989)
ROYS ELECTRICAL SERVICE INC
543 Main St (19936)
P.O. Box 178 (19936-0178)
PHONE..................302 674-3199
James Roy Junior, *Pr*
Nancy P Roy, *Sec*
EMP: 7 EST: 1947
SQ FT: 1,840
SALES (est): 532.29K **Privately Held**
Web: www.royselectricalservice.com
SIC: 7629 7694 5999 Generator repair; Motor repair services; Alcoholic beverage making equipment and supplies

Christiana
New Castle County

(G-990)
ACRE MORTGAGE & FINANCIAL
56 W Main St Ste 107 (19702-1539)
PHONE..................302 737-5853
Sandy Cline, *Mgr*
EMP: 5 EST: 2009
SALES (est): 484.18K **Privately Held**
Web: www.acremortgage.com
SIC: 6162 Mortgage bankers and loan correspondents

GEOGRAPHIC SECTION　　　　　　　　　　　　　　　　　　　　　　　　　　　Claymont - New Castle County (G-1020)

(G-991)
ADIRONDACK BHVRAL HLTHCARE LLC
Also Called: Allied Behavioral Health
1400 Peoples Plz Ste 204 (19702-5708)
PHONE..................................302 832-1282
EMP: 5 **EST:** 1996
SALES (est): 438.88K **Privately Held**
Web: www.alliedbehavioralhealthde.com
SIC: 8049 Clinical psychologist

(G-992)
AVEANNA HEALTHCARE AS LLC
56 W Main St Ste 211 (19702-1500)
PHONE..................................302 504-4101
EMP: 11 **EST:** 2018
SALES (est): 283.52K **Privately Held**
Web: www.aveanna.com
SIC: 8082 Home health care services

(G-993)
BOGO PUBLICATIONS LLC
6 Donegal Ct (19702-2053)
PHONE..................................877 514-4052
Robert Greenawalt, CEO
EMP: 4 **EST:** 2021
SALES (est): 61.45K **Privately Held**
SIC: 2741 7389 Miscellaneous publishing; Business services, nec

(G-994)
EIDP INC
Also Called: Dupont
600 Eagle Run Rd (19702-1607)
PHONE..................................302 733-9200
Roger Sharp, Brnch Mgr
EMP: 50
SALES (corp-wide): 17.23B **Publicly Held**
Web: www.dupont.com
SIC: 3555 3844 3699 Printing trades machinery; X-ray apparatus and tubes; Electrical equipment and supplies, nec
HQ: Eidp, Inc.
　9330 Zionsville Rd
　Indianapolis IN 46268
　833 267-8382

(G-995)
EMPLOYERS BENCH INC
40 W Main St Ste 855 (19702)
PHONE..................................973 757-1912
Sushil Kumar, Serv Delivery
EMP: 10 **EST:** 2016
SALES (est): 348.77K **Privately Held**
SIC: 7363 Labor resource services

(G-996)
FUN ADVENTURES LLC
Also Called: Urban Air Adventure Park
531 W Main St (19702-1647)
PHONE..................................302 223-5182
EMP: 6 **EST:** 2018
SALES (est): 54.79K **Privately Held**
SIC: 7996 Theme park, amusement

(G-997)
GSF MORTGAGE CORPORATION
Also Called: Go Mortgage
56 W Main St Ste 204 (19702-1500)
PHONE..................................302 373-5853
Sandy Cline, Brnch Mgr
EMP: 60
Web: www.gomortgage.com
SIC: 6162 Mortgage bankers
PA: Gsf Mortgage Corporation
　15430 W Capitol Dr # 100
　Brookfield WI 53045

(G-998)
GSM PLANET INCORP
19 Peddlers Row (19702-1525)
PHONE..................................302 455-1111
EMP: 5 **EST:** 2015
SALES (est): 94.78K **Privately Held**
SIC: 4812 Cellular telephone services

(G-999)
GT WORLD MACHINERIES USA INC
40 W Main St (19702-1501)
PHONE..................................800 242-4935
Majid Tahmassbi, CEO
EMP: 5 **EST:** 2015
SQ FT: 4,500
SALES (est): 100.21K **Privately Held**
SIC: 5064 Air conditioning appliances

(G-1000)
JR WALTER J KAMINSKI DDS
100 Christiana Vlg Prof Ctr (19702-1510)
PHONE..................................302 738-3666
Walter J Kaminski Junior D.d.s ., Owner
Walter J Kaminski Junior, Owner
EMP: 7 **EST:** 1978
SALES (est): 216.05K **Privately Held**
SIC: 8021 Specialized dental practitioners

(G-1001)
KIMMEL CRTER RMAN PLTZ ONILL P (PA)
Also Called: KIMMEL, CARTER, ROMAN, PELTZ &
56 W Main St Ste 400 (19702-1505)
P.O. Box 8149 (19714-8149)
PHONE..................................302 565-6100
Morton Richard Kimmel, Pr
EMP: 19 **EST:** 1973
SQ FT: 2,500
SALES (est): 2.36K
SALES (corp-wide): 2.36K **Privately Held**
Web: www.kimmelcarter.com
SIC: 8111 General practice law office

(G-1002)
KIRK & ASSOCIATES LLC
56 W Main St Ste 305 (19702-1503)
PHONE..................................302 444-4733
Maryann Kirk, Ex Dir
EMP: 10 **EST:** 2013
SALES (est): 602.14K **Privately Held**
Web: www.kirkassoc.com
SIC: 8742 Management consulting services

(G-1003)
LITTLE PEOPLE CHILD DEV
122 E Main St (19702-3100)
PHONE..................................302 328-1481
EMP: 10 **EST:** 2016
SALES (est): 59.91K **Privately Held**
SIC: 8351 Preschool center

(G-1004)
LUKERATIVE SOLUTIONS INC
56 W Main St (19702-1505)
PHONE..................................302 294-6468
Shane Lukenda, Owner
EMP: 5 **EST:** 2016
SALES (est): 130.66K **Privately Held**
SIC: 8742 Marketing consulting services

(G-1005)
MERRY MAIDS
Also Called: Merry Maids
56 W Main St Ste 107 (19702-1539)
PHONE..................................302 223-9259
EMP: 5 **EST:** 2018
SALES (est): 20.74K **Privately Held**
Web: www.merrymaids.com

SIC: 7349 Maid services, contract or fee basis

(G-1006)
PANDA EARLY EDUCATION CTR INC
122 E Main St (19702-3100)
PHONE..................................302 832-1891
Collen Corkey, Dir
EMP: 10
SIC: 8351 Preschool center
PA: Early Panda Education Center Inc
　105 Emerald Ridge Dr
　Bear DE 19701

(G-1007)
PLASTI PALLETS CORP
6 Albe Dr (19702-1322)
PHONE..................................302 737-1977
Carmen Micucio, VP
Melvin Messinger, Pr
EMP: 6 **EST:** 1992
SALES (est): 300K **Privately Held**
SIC: 3089 Pallets, plastics

(G-1008)
SARDO & SONS WAREHOUSING INC (PA)
56 W Main St Ste 208 (19702-1500)
PHONE..................................302 369-2100
Angelo Sardo, Pr
Laurie Pietruczenia, Acctg Mgr
▲ **EMP:** 5 **EST:** 1952
SALES (est): 18.85MM
SALES (corp-wide): 18.85MM **Privately Held**
Web: www.sswi.com
SIC: 4225 4212 General warehousing; Local trucking, without storage

(G-1009)
SOUTHEASTERN HOME HEALTH SVCS
56 W Main St Ste 211 (19702-1500)
PHONE..................................214 466-1351
EMP: 7 **EST:** 2013
SALES (est): 106.46K **Privately Held**
SIC: 8099 Health and allied services, nec

(G-1010)
STEINEBACH ROBERT AND ASSOC
Also Called: Nationwide
20 Peddlers Row (19702-1525)
P.O. Box 1713 (19701-7713)
PHONE..................................302 328-1212
EMP: 6
SALES (est): 1.06MM **Privately Held**
SIC: 6411 Insurance agents, brokers, and service

(G-1011)
SYNERGY DIRECT MORTGAGE
9 Peddlers Row (19702-1525)
PHONE..................................302 283-0833
Don Scioli, Pr
EMP: 6 **EST:** 2000
SALES (est): 396.87K **Privately Held**
SIC: 6163 Mortgage brokers arranging for loans, using money of others

Claymont
New Castle County

(G-1012)
4BOA LLC ✪
2803 Philadelphia Pike Ste 4027 (19703-2506)
PHONE..................................323 747-7771
EMP: 20 **EST:** 2022
SALES (est): 588.11K **Privately Held**

SIC: 7371 Software programming applications

(G-1013)
5 STAR HVACR LLC
2803 Philadelphia Pike Ste 1254 (19703-2506)
PHONE..................................610 508-6464
EMP: 6
SALES (est): 322.03K **Privately Held**
SIC: 1711 Plumbing, heating, air-conditioning

(G-1014)
52ND & FOREVER MEDIA LLC
302 Chapel Ave (19703-3210)
PHONE..................................302 463-0014
EMP: 5 **EST:** 2017
SALES (est): 40.12K **Privately Held**
SIC: 4899 Communication services, nec

(G-1015)
9ROUND FITNESS
3533 Philadelphia Pike (19703)
PHONE..................................302 504-4787
EMP: 6 **EST:** 2018
SALES (est): 29.54K **Privately Held**
Web: www.9round.com
SIC: 7991 Physical fitness facilities

(G-1016)
A PLACE TO GROW FMLY CHLD CARE
3067 W Court Ave (19703-2020)
PHONE..................................302 897-8944
EMP: 8 **EST:** 2014
SALES (est): 60.36K **Privately Held**
SIC: 8351 Child day care services

(G-1017)
ACCURETIX LLC
2803b Philadelphia Pike # 4177 (19703-2525)
PHONE..................................646 434-6917
Ahmed Jaafar, Managing Member
EMP: 7
SALES (est): 264.9K **Privately Held**
SIC: 7371 Computer software development

(G-1018)
ACE YOUR PARTY
904 Peachtree Rd Apt L (19703-2251)
PHONE..................................302 415-1670
Edwin Weightman, Prin
EMP: 9 **EST:** 2017
SALES (est): 50.24K **Privately Held**
SIC: 4119 Limousine rental, with driver

(G-1019)
ACKRELL SPAC PARTNERS I CO
2093 Philadelphia Pike # 1968 (19703-2424)
PHONE..................................650 560-4753
Jason M Roth, CEO
Michael K Ackrell, Ch Bd
Shannon Soqui, Non-Executive Vice Chairman of the Board
Stephen N Cannon, Pr
Long Long, CFO
EMP: 5 **EST:** 2018
SALES (est): **Privately Held**
SIC: 6799 Investors, nec

(G-1020)
ADAPTY INC
2093 Philadelphia Pike Ste 9181 (19703-2424)
PHONE..................................415 800-3343
EMP: 6 **EST:** 2019
SALES (est): 163.27K **Privately Held**
Web: www.adapty.io

Claymont - New Castle County (G-1021)

SIC: 7373 Computer system selling services

(G-1021)
ADVANCED FUEL POLSG SVC INC
950 Ridge Rd Ste A6 (19703-3526)
PHONE.................................302 477-1040
EMP: 2
SALES (corp-wide): 238.66K Privately Held
Web: www.advancedfuelpolishing.com
SIC: 1389 Bailing, cleaning, swabbing, and treating of wells
PA: Advanced Fuel Polishing Service Inc.
1125 Grinnell Rd
Wilmington DE 19803
610 459-3092

(G-1022)
ADVANCED POWER GENERATION
950 Ridge Rd Ste A6 (19703-3526)
PHONE.................................302 375-6145
Donald Depew, *Prin*
EMP: 9 EST: 2014
SALES (est): 460.02K Privately Held
Web: www.advancedpowergeneration.com
SIC: 1731 General electrical contractor

(G-1023)
ADVANCED TREATMENT SYSTEMS
2999 Philadelphia Pike (19703-2507)
PHONE.................................302 792-0700
Nicole Moore, *Dir*
EMP: 9 EST: 2002
SALES (est): 196.98K Privately Held
SIC: 8093 Substance abuse clinics (outpatient)

(G-1024)
ADYN INC
2093 Philadelphia Pike (19703-2424)
PHONE.................................206 451-7105
EMP: 6 EST: 2019
SALES (est): 73.33K Privately Held
Web: www.adyn.com
SIC: 8093 Birth control clinic

(G-1025)
AFLAC DISTRICT OFFCIE
1102 Society Dr (19703-1780)
PHONE.................................302 375-6885
Leia Rappaport, *Prin*
EMP: 6 EST: 2016
SALES (est): 105K Privately Held
Web: www.aflac.com
SIC: 6411 Insurance agents, brokers, and service

(G-1026)
AGAVE TECH INC
2093 Philadelphia Pike (19703-2424)
PHONE.................................805 394-3112
Tom Reno, *CEO*
EMP: 6
SALES (est): 252.85K Privately Held
SIC: 7372 Prepackaged software

(G-1027)
AIR MEDICS HVAC LLC
950 Ridge Rd Ste C15 (19703-3536)
PHONE.................................302 439-4254
EMP: 5 EST: 2021
SALES (est): 76K Privately Held
Web: www.airmedicshvac.info
SIC: 8099 Health and allied services, nec

(G-1028)
AKIMBO INC
2093 Philadelphia Pike # 3022 (19703-2424)
PHONE.................................302 204-5299
Alex Peck, *Pr*
EMP: 5 EST: 2020
SALES (est): 134.18K Privately Held
SIC: 2741 Internet publishing and broadcasting

(G-1029)
ALL MIGHTY CLEAN COMPANY
55 Denham Ave (19703-2709)
PHONE.................................302 798-1013
Sandra Munden, *Prin*
EMP: 5 EST: 2008
SALES (est): 48.09K Privately Held
SIC: 7699 Cleaning services

(G-1030)
ALLPOWER GENERATOR SALES & SVC
100 Naamans Rd Ste 1h (19703-2735)
PHONE.................................302 793-1690
Don Depew, *Prin*
EMP: 5 EST: 2004
SALES (est): 521.25K Privately Held
Web: www.allpowergenerator.com
SIC: 5063 Generators

(G-1031)
AMC - COMMERCIAL INC
316 Governor Printz Blvd (19703-2911)
PHONE.................................302 229-0051
Charles Lee, *Pr*
EMP: 7 EST: 2010
SALES (est): 219.32K Privately Held
SIC: 8741 Management services

(G-1032)
AMEKEN NETWORK GROUP INC
405 Maple Ln (19703-1824)
PHONE.................................302 545-3472
Samuel Mwangi, *Pr*
EMP: 10 EST: 2007
SALES (est): 325.81K Privately Held
SIC: 8741 Management services

(G-1033)
AMERIBULK TRANSPORT LLC (PA)
6300 Philadelphia Pike (19703-2712)
PHONE.................................302 792-1190
Kevin Loughery, *Pr*
EMP: 18 EST: 2020
SALES (est): 2.44MM
SALES (corp-wide): 2.44MM Privately Held
Web: www.ameribulktransport.com
SIC: 4213 Trucking, except local

(G-1034)
AMERICAN WOOD DESIGN
100 Naamans Rd Ste 4b (19703-2737)
PHONE.................................302 792-2100
EMP: 8 EST: 2019
SALES (est): 53.36K Privately Held
Web: www.americanwooddesign.com
SIC: 1751 Carpentry work

(G-1035)
AMSCHEL CAPITAL LLC
2093 Philadelphia Pike Ste 2711 (19703-2424)
PHONE.................................302 298-1199
Arik Shalom, *Managing Member*
EMP: 10 EST: 2021
SALES (est): 445.48K Privately Held
SIC: 8741 Management services

(G-1036)
AMSCHEL CAPITAL LLC
2093 Philadelphia Pike (19703-2424)
PHONE.................................302 298-1199

EMP: 10
SALES (est): 5MM Privately Held
Web: www.mbxcapital.com
SIC: 8741 Management services

(G-1037)
AN EVENT 2 REMEMBER
9 Colin Ct (19703-1102)
PHONE.................................215 783-9744
Jocelyn Thorpe, *Prin*
EMP: 5 EST: 2009
SALES (est): 80.19K Privately Held
SIC: 7231 Beauty shops

(G-1038)
ANDREW W VIOHL
Also Called: A W Viohl General Contracting
2405 Mckinley Ave (19703-1831)
PHONE.................................302 388-7721
Andrew W Viohl, *Prin*
EMP: 6 EST: 2010
SALES (est): 110K Privately Held
Web: www.viohlcontracting.com
SIC: 1799 Special trade contractors, nec

(G-1039)
APARTMENT COMMUNITIES INC
Also Called: Harbor House Apts
31 Harbor Dr Apt 2 (19703-2946)
PHONE.................................302 798-9100
Beth Mc Hugh, *Mgr*
EMP: 10 EST: 1979
SALES (est): 662.56K Privately Held
Web: www.liveatharborhouse.com
SIC: 6513 Apartment building operators

(G-1040)
APG INC
100 Naamans Rd (19703-2737)
PHONE.................................302 746-7167
EMP: 6 EST: 2013
SALES (est): 137.75K Privately Held
SIC: 1731 General electrical contractor

(G-1041)
APPLY CO
2093 Philadelphia Pike Ste 3581 (19703-2424)
PHONE.................................775 343-5307
James Schlauch, *CEO*
EMP: 6
SALES (est): 68.89K Privately Held
SIC: 7371 Computer software writing services

(G-1042)
ARKSHELL CORPORATION
2093a Philadelphia Pike Ste 279 (19703-2424)
PHONE.................................917 985-8529
Nash B, *VP*
EMP: 10 EST: 2021
SALES (est): 964.88K Privately Held
Web: www.arkshellgroup.com
SIC: 2092 Fresh or frozen packaged fish

(G-1043)
ARRAY CORPORATION
2093 Philadelphia Pike # 5334 (19703-2424)
PHONE.................................650 241-1382
Fouad Elnaggar, *CEO*
Andrew Rankin, *Dir*
EMP: 10 EST: 2020
SALES (est): 1.06MM Privately Held
SIC: 7361 Employment agencies

(G-1044)
ASHISH ANAND MD
7403 Society Dr (19703-1772)

PHONE.................................617 953-5914
EMP: 7 EST: 2012
SALES (est): 87.53K Privately Held
SIC: 8011 Orthopedic physician

(G-1045)
ATIBA MUSIC SERVICES
41 2nd Ave (19703-2001)
PHONE.................................302 981-7157
Colvin Fields, *Prin*
EMP: 5 EST: 2018
SALES (est): 51.74K Privately Held
SIC: 7379 Computer related consulting services

(G-1046)
AURISTA TECHNOLOGIES INC
Also Called: Aurista
100 Naamans Rd Ste 3c (19703-2737)
PHONE.................................302 792-4900
Ronald D Graf, *Pr*
Ronald Graf, *Pr*
EMP: 15 EST: 1987
SQ FT: 3,500
SALES (est): 1.51MM Privately Held
Web: www.coin-jewelry.com
SIC: 5094 3471 3873 Clocks, watches, and parts; Plating and polishing; Watches and parts, except crystals and jewels

(G-1047)
AW VIOHL CONTRACTING LLC
950 Ridge Rd (19703-3523)
PHONE.................................302 375-6166
EMP: 6 EST: 2018
SALES (est): 456.21K Privately Held
Web: www.viohlcontracting.com
SIC: 1799 Special trade contractors, nec

(G-1048)
AZZOTA CORPORATION
Also Called: Labshops
100 Naamans Rd Ste 5i (19703-2700)
PHONE.................................877 649-2746
Xiaoli He, *CEO*
EMP: 2 EST: 2007
SALES (est): 250.75K Privately Held
Web: www.labshops.com
SIC: 3821 Laboratory equipment: fume hoods, distillation racks, etc.

(G-1049)
B2B LISTS LLC
2093 Philadelphia Pike # 5376 (19703-2424)
PHONE.................................302 601-7207
EMP: 51 EST: 2019
SALES (est): 1.31MM Privately Held
Web: www.b2b-lists.com
SIC: 7331 Mailing list management

(G-1050)
BABY APRON LLC
2093 Philadelphia Pike Ste 8950 (19703-2424)
PHONE.................................800 796-4406
EMP: 8 EST: 2016
SALES (est): 638.43K Privately Held
SIC: 2037 2038 5963 Frozen fruits and vegetables; Frozen specialties, nec; Direct selling establishments

(G-1051)
BASEMENT CIRCUIT TRAINING
100 Naamans Rd Ste 5g (19703-2700)
PHONE.................................302 824-8078
Greg Cephas, *Owner*
EMP: 6 EST: 2013
SALES (est): 61.01K Privately Held

GEOGRAPHIC SECTION   Claymont - New Castle County (G-1080)

SIC: 7991   Physical fitness facilities

(G-1052)
BASIGO INC
2803 Philadelphia Pike Ste B (19703-2506)
PHONE.................................510 735-6240
Abhijit Bhattacharya, *CEO*
EMP: 61
SIC: 6719   Holding companies, nec

(G-1053)
BATTLEBOOST INC
2093 Philadelphia Pike Ste 4343
(19703-2424)
PHONE.................................302 499-2000
Ahmed Alghalaini, *CEO*
EMP: 5 **EST:** 2019
SALES (est): 100K **Privately Held**
SIC: 7999   Games, instruction

(G-1054)
BC HOME HEALTH CARE SERVICES
Also Called: Home Helpers
3301 Green St (19703-2052)
PHONE.................................302 746-7844
Joseph Munis, *Pr*
EMP: 27 **EST:** 2014
SALES (est): 1.81MM **Privately Held**
Web: www.homehelpershomecare.com
SIC: 8082   Home health care services

(G-1055)
BEETRONICS INC
2093 Philadelphia Pike # 4945
(19703-2424)
PHONE.................................302 455-2070
Thomas Dekker, *CEO*
EMP: 5 **EST:** 2020
SALES (est): 223.51K **Privately Held**
Web: www.beetronics.com
SIC: 3651   Household audio and video equipment

(G-1056)
BENCHMARK TRANSMISSION INC
2610 Philadelphia Pike Ste 1a
(19703-2574)
PHONE.................................302 792-2300
Michael Neubauer, *CEO*
EMP: 5 **EST:** 1988
SALES (est): 450.32K **Privately Held**
Web: www.benchmarkonline.biz
SIC: 7539 7537   Automotive repair shops, nec ; Automotiv e transmission repair shops

(G-1057)
BENEPASS INC
2093 Philadelphia Pike (19703-2424)
PHONE.................................917 540-2391
Jaclyn Chen, *Pr*
EMP: 6 **EST:** 2019
SALES (est): 504.82K **Privately Held**
Web: www.getbenepass.com
SIC: 8742   Human resource consulting services

(G-1058)
BENGA INC
2093 Philadelphia Pike Ste 3620
(19703-2424)
PHONE.................................617 579-8636
Tomer Biger, *CEO*
EMP: 10 **EST:** 2021
SALES (est): 454.77K **Privately Held**
Web: www.getbenga.com
SIC: 7372   Application computer software

(G-1059)
BERRODIN CO
Also Called: Berrodin Parts Warehouse
100 Naamans Rd Ste 4d (19703-2737)
PHONE.................................302 395-1100
EMP: 8
SALES (corp-wide): 9.59MM **Privately Held**
Web: www.berrodin.com
SIC: 5013   Automotive supplies and parts
PA: Berrodin Co.
     790 Burmont Rd
     Drexel Hill PA 19026
     610 259-8700

(G-1060)
BETTER BUSINESS RE INC ✪
2803 Philadelphia Pike # 4036
(19703-2506)
PHONE.................................609 746-9833
Daryl G Norton, *CEO*
EMP: 3 **EST:** 2022
SALES (est): 122.08K **Privately Held**
SIC: 3589   Commercial cleaning equipment

(G-1061)
BEYOND EXPECTED LLC
391 Harbor Dr Apt 5 (19703-2660)
PHONE.................................302 384-1205
EMP: 20
SALES (est): 612.9K **Privately Held**
SIC: 8742   Management consulting services

(G-1062)
BNAI BRITH CLAYMONT LP
8000 Society Dr (19703-1702)
PHONE.................................302 798-6846
EMP: 9 **EST:** 2015
SALES (est): 264.87K **Privately Held**
SIC: 1521   Single-family housing construction

(G-1063)
BNAI BRITH SNIOR CTZENS HSING
Also Called: B'Nai B'Rith House
8000 Society Dr (19703-1702)
PHONE.................................302 798-6846
David Schlaker, *Pr*
Jack Levine, *VP*
EMP: 8 **EST:** 1979
SQ FT: 150,000
SALES (est): 955.84K **Privately Held**
Web: www.bnaibrithhouse.org
SIC: 6513   Retirement hotel operation

(G-1064)
BOYS & GIRLS CLUBS DEL INC
Also Called: Claymont Boys and Girls Club
500 Darley Rd Unit 2 (19703-2261)
PHONE.................................302 792-3780
Rebecca Wilczynski, *Dir*
EMP: 15
SALES (corp-wide): 33.26MM **Privately Held**
Web: www.bgclubs.org
SIC: 8641   Youth organizations
PA: Boys & Girls Clubs Of Delaware, Inc.
     669 S Union St
     Wilmington DE 19805
     302 658-1870

(G-1065)
BRANDY WINE SENIOR CENTER
3301 Green St (19703-2052)
PHONE.................................302 798-5562
Phyllis Hicks, *Dir*
Beverly Henry, *Sec*
EMP: 9 **EST:** 1977
SALES (est): 337.07K **Privately Held**
Web: www.claymontcenter.org
SIC: 8322   Senior citizens' center or association

(G-1066)
BRANDYWINE CLUB INC
135 Princeton Ave (19703-2608)
PHONE.................................302 798-9891
John Raughley, *Pr*
Lloyd Godshalk, *VP*
EMP: 6 **EST:** 1948
SQ FT: 6,500
SALES (est): 243.88K **Privately Held**
SIC: 8641   Fraternal associations

(G-1067)
BRANDYWINE EDUCATION ASSN
1000 Pennsylvania Ave (19703-1200)
P.O. Box 731 (19703-0731)
PHONE.................................302 793-5048
EMP: 8 **EST:** 2019
SALES (est): 38.73K **Privately Held**
Web: www.brandywineea.org
SIC: 8641   Civic and social associations

(G-1068)
BUSIBUD INC
2093a Philadelphia Pike Ste 422
(19703-2424)
PHONE.................................626 228-1855
Maxim Gorky Saini, *Pr*
EMP: 100 **EST:** 2012
SALES (est): 2.58MM **Privately Held**
SIC: 7371   Custom computer programming services

(G-1069)
CABINETS TO GO LLC
203 Naamans Rd Ste 1 (19703-2795)
PHONE.................................302 439-4989
Charles Rifon, *Brnch Mgr*
EMP: 2
SALES (corp-wide): 99.82MM **Privately Held**
Web: www.cabinetstogo.com
SIC: 2434   Wood kitchen cabinets
PA: Cabinets To Go, Llc
     2350 Wo Smith Dr
     Lawrenceburg TN 38464
     909 646-5900

(G-1070)
CAL AGENTS REALTY INC
2093 Philadelphia Pike Ste 2828n
(19703-2424)
PHONE.................................408 219-1728
EMP: 7 **EST:** 2016
SALES (est): 417.92K **Privately Held**
Web: www.thecalagents.com
SIC: 6531   Real estate brokers and agents

(G-1071)
CAMERON JONES
Also Called: Time Is Money Courier Pros
371 Harbor Dr Apt 9 (19703-2657)
PHONE.................................610 880-7700
Cameron Jones, *Owner*
EMP: 15 **EST:** 2021
SALES (est): 265.66K **Privately Held**
SIC: 7389   Business Activities at Non-Commercial Site

(G-1072)
CANDLE PARLOUR
12 Commonwealth Ave (19703-2012)
PHONE.................................302 408-0890
EMP: 4 **EST:** 2018
SALES (est): 131.9K **Privately Held**
SIC: 3999   Candles

(G-1073)
CAPSULA INC
2093 Philadelphia Pike (19703-2424)
PHONE.................................562 466-0155
Anton Vasilev, *CEO*
EMP: 5
SIC: 6719   Holding companies, nec

(G-1074)
CARMEN R BENITEZ
3047 Greenshire Ave (19703-2000)
PHONE.................................302 793-2061
Carmen R Benitez, *Prin*
EMP: 5 **EST:** 2010
SALES (est): 96.64K **Privately Held**
SIC: 8351   Preschool center

(G-1075)
CAS PRPERTY PRESERVATION LLC
7509 Governor Printz Blvd (19703-2414)
PHONE.................................302 416-2377
Joseph A Rice, *Prin*
EMP: 5 **EST:** 2011
SALES (est): 134.8K **Privately Held**
Web: www.coreassetservices.com
SIC: 6512   Nonresidential building operators

(G-1076)
CATALYST HANDLING RESOURCES
950 Ridge Rd Ste E3 (19703-3520)
PHONE.................................302 798-2200
John Wooten, *Owner*
EMP: 13 **EST:** 1997
SALES (est): 491.22K **Privately Held**
Web: www.catalysthandling.com
SIC: 5084   Materials handling machinery

(G-1077)
CD DIAGNOSTICS INC (HQ)
650 Naamans Rd Ste 100 (19703-2301)
PHONE.................................302 367-7770
Richard Birkmeyer, *Pr*
Carl Deirmengian, *CMO*
EMP: 50 **EST:** 2008
SALES (est): 10.57MM
SALES (corp-wide): 6.94B **Publicly Held**
Web: www.cddiagnostics.com
SIC: 8071   Medical laboratories
PA: Zimmer Biomet Holdings, Inc.
     345 E Main St
     Warsaw IN 46580
     574 267-6131

(G-1078)
CDS GLOBAL LLC
2093 Philadelphia Pike # 5 (19703-2424)
PHONE.................................302 307-6831
Emir Kiamilev, *CEO*
Fouad Kiamilev, *Engr*
Hamzah Ahemed, *COO*
Rodney Mcgee, *Pr*
EMP: 23 **EST:** 2021
SALES (est): 1.07MM **Privately Held**
SIC: 3489   Projectors: depth charge, grenade, rocket, etc.

(G-1079)
CENTRIQ TECHNOLOGIES INC
2093 Philadelphia Pike Ste 4321
(19703-2424)
PHONE.................................651 353-0691
Edwin Veelo, *COO*
EMP: 7
SALES (est): 254.53K **Privately Held**
SIC: 7371   Computer software development and applications

(G-1080)
CENTRITO LLC ✪
2093 Philadelphia Pike # 1434
(19703-2424)
PHONE.................................919 728-9401
EMP: 20 **EST:** 2022
SALES (est): 588.11K **Privately Held**

Claymont - New Castle County (G-1081)

SIC: 7371 Computer software development

(G-1081)
CEREBRAL MED GROUP A PROF CORP
2093 Philadelphia Pike # 9898 (19703-2424)
PHONE.....................415 403-2156
Sajad Zalzala, *CEO*
Michael Brandis, *Sec*
EMP: 53 EST: 2019
SALES (est): 3.96MM **Privately Held**
SIC: 8011 Medical centers

(G-1082)
CHANGING MY DIRECTION LLC
2803 Philadelphia Pike Ste B (19703-2506)
PHONE.....................302 510-9873
Cordaro Rhodes, *Managing Member*
EMP: 5 EST: 2016
SALES (est): 347.8K **Privately Held**
SIC: 4789 Cargo loading and unloading services

(G-1083)
CHARLES MOON PLUMBING & HTG (PA)
2505 Philadelphia Pike Ste C (19703-2511)
PHONE.....................302 798-6666
EMP: 7 EST: 1993
SQ FT: 3,800
SALES (est): 986.87K **Privately Held**
Web: www.charlesmoonplumbing.com
SIC: 1711 Plumbing contractors

(G-1084)
CHART EXCHANGE
3001 Philadelphia Pike (19703-2580)
PHONE.....................850 376-6435
EMP: 6 EST: 2017
SALES (est): 43.5K **Privately Held**
Web: www.chart-markets.com
SIC: 7372 Prepackaged software

(G-1085)
CHOCOLATE EDITIONS INC
2614 Philadelphia Pike (19703-2504)
PHONE.....................302 479-8400
Edward Przelomski, *CEO*
Cher L Przelomski, *Pr*
EMP: 3 EST: 1993
SQ FT: 1,200
SALES (est): 491.41K **Privately Held**
SIC: 2066 Chocolate

(G-1086)
CIGNA GLOBAL HOLDINGS INC (DH)
Also Called: Cigna
590 Naamans Rd (19703-2308)
PHONE.....................302 797-3469
Joanne Dorak, *Pr*
Paul B Lukens, *Ch Bd*
EMP: 11 EST: 2003
SALES (est): 113.87MM
SALES (corp-wide): 180.52B **Publicly Held**
SIC: 6311 6512 6411 Life insurance; Nonresidential building operators; Property and casualty insurance agent
HQ: Cigna Holdings, Inc.
590 Naamans Rd
Claymont DE 19703
215 761-1000

(G-1087)
CIGNA HOLDINGS INC (DH)
Also Called: Cigna
590 Naamans Rd (19703-2308)
PHONE.....................215 761-1000
Paul B Lukens, *Ch Bd*
William C Hartman, *Pr*
Maureen H Ryan, *VP*
Samuel E Larosa, *VP*
Andrew Kielty, *Dir*
EMP: 11 EST: 1982
SALES (est): 14.71B
SALES (corp-wide): 180.52B **Publicly Held**
Web: www.cigna.com
SIC: 6311 6321 6331 6512 Life insurance; Health insurance carriers; Fire, marine, and casualty insurance; Commercial and industrial building operation
HQ: Cigna Holding Company
900 Cottage Grove Rd
Bloomfield CT 06002
860 226-6000

(G-1088)
CITY WIDE TRANSPORTATION INC
6705 Governor Printz Blvd (19703)
PHONE.....................302 792-1225
Vitor Thomas, *Pr*
Victor Thomas, *Owner*
EMP: 5 EST: 1992
SALES (est): 226.59K **Privately Held**
Web: www.cwlimo.com
SIC: 4119 Limousine rental, with driver

(G-1089)
CLAROS FARM INC ◊
2093a Philadelphia Pike Ste 410 (19703-2424)
PHONE.....................415 347-1321
EMP: 6 EST: 2023
SALES (est): 128.34K **Privately Held**
SIC: 0762 Farm management services

(G-1090)
CLAYMONT CHIROPRACTIC OFFICE
2100 Philadelphia Pike (19703-2427)
PHONE.....................302 798-1587
Joseph Irwin, *Owner*
EMP: 6 EST: 2018
SALES (est): 104.17K **Privately Held**
Web: claymont-chiropractic-office.business.site
SIC: 8041 Offices and clinics of chiropractors

(G-1091)
CLAYMONT CMPRHNSIVE TRTMNT CTR
2999 Philadelphia Pike (19703-2507)
PHONE.....................302 792-0700
EMP: 7 EST: 2020
SALES (est): 359.63K **Privately Held**
Web: www.ctcprograms.com
SIC: 8093 Substance abuse clinics (outpatient)

(G-1092)
CLAYMONT COMMUNITY CENTER INC
Also Called: BRANDYWINE COM RSRC CNCL
3301 Green St (19703-2062)
PHONE.....................302 792-2757
James Thornton, *Ex Dir*
EMP: 24 EST: 1975
SALES (est): 1.4MM **Privately Held**
Web: www.claymontcenter.org
SIC: 8322 Community center

(G-1093)
CLAYMONT NAILS
2081 Philadelphia Pike (19703-2424)
PHONE.....................302 798-8220
Tommy Nguyen, *Owner*
EMP: 5 EST: 2017
SALES (est): 20.99K **Privately Held**
Web: claymont-laundromat-laundromat.business.site
SIC: 7231 Manicurist, pedicurist

(G-1094)
CLAYMONT NUTRITION
8 Commonwealth Ave (19703-2012)
PHONE.....................302 792-7818
EMP: 5 EST: 2019
SALES (est): 41.61K **Privately Held**
SIC: 8099 Nutrition services

(G-1095)
CLOOTRACK SOFTWARE LABS INC ◊
2093 Philadelphia Pike (19703-2424)
PHONE.....................302 204-1872
Shameel Abdulla, *CEO*
EMP: 5 EST: 2022
SALES (est): 267K **Privately Held**
SIC: 7371 Custom computer programming services

(G-1096)
CLUTTERBOT INC
2093 Philadelphia Pike Ste 1348 (19703-2424)
PHONE.....................425 679-1348
Justin Hamilton, *CEO*
EMP: 5 EST: 2020
SALES (est): 238.85K **Privately Held**
SIC: 7371 Computer software development and applications

(G-1097)
COIT CLG RSTORATION WILMINGTON
950 Ridge Rd Ste C2 (19703-3510)
PHONE.....................302 322-1099
EMP: 8 EST: 2019
SALES (est): 27.18K **Privately Held**
Web: www.coit.com
SIC: 7217 Carpet and upholstery cleaning

(G-1098)
CONEXIO CARE INC
590 Naamans Rd (19703-2308)
PHONE.....................302 442-6622
Lynn Kovich, *CEO*
EMP: 26 EST: 2021
SALES (est): 2.58MM **Privately Held**
Web: www.conexiocare.org
SIC: 8051 8361 Skilled nursing care facilities; Residential care

(G-1099)
CONNECTONS CMNTY SPPORT PRGRAM (PA)
Also Called: Connections
590 Naamans Rd (19703-2308)
PHONE.....................302 984-2302
Catherine D Mckay, *CEO*
EMP: 70 EST: 1985
SALES (est): 124.57MM **Privately Held**
Web: coras.flywheelsites.com
SIC: 8322 8361 8049 Rehabilitation services; Mentally handicapped home; Psychiatric social worker

(G-1100)
CONTINENTAL WARRANTY CORP
99 Wiltshire Rd (19703-3307)
P.O. Box 207 (19703-0207)
PHONE.....................302 375-0401
Mario Volpe, *Pr*
Dorothy A Volpe, *
EMP: 38 EST: 1999
SQ FT: 6,550
SALES (est): 1.89MM **Privately Held**
Web: www.continentalwarranty.org
SIC: 7549 Automotive customizing services, nonfactory basis

(G-1101)
COSLS LLC
2093 Philadelphia Pike Ste 3093 (19703-2424)
PHONE.....................877 900-7373
Sohaib Khan, *Managing Member*
EMP: 10
SALES (est): 348.32K **Privately Held**
SIC: 7371 Custom computer programming services

(G-1102)
CRESCENT COMMUNITIES LLC
321 Harbor Dr (19703-2646)
PHONE.....................302 798-8400
Debra Mcelwee, *Prin*
EMP: 5 EST: 2016
SALES (est): 126.27K **Privately Held**
Web: www.crescentcommunities.com
SIC: 6513 Apartment building operators

(G-1103)
CRESSONA ASSOCIATES LLC
1308 Society Dr (19703-1743)
PHONE.....................302 792-2737
EMP: 9 EST: 1994
SALES (est): 206.88K **Privately Held**
SIC: 6531 Real estate managers

(G-1104)
CROSS OVER CAMO LLC
7205 Governor Printz Blvd (19703-2470)
PHONE.....................302 798-1898
EMP: 5 EST: 2009
SALES (est): 86.19K **Privately Held**
SIC: 2311 Military uniforms, men's and youths': purchased materials

(G-1105)
CTO LAB INC
2093 Philadelphia Pike Ste 5021 (19703-2424)
PHONE.....................415 702-5014
Mesut Boydas, *CEO*
EMP: 8
SALES (est): 306.16K **Privately Held**
SIC: 7371 Computer software development and applications

(G-1106)
CYPH INC
Also Called: Cyph
2093a Philadelphia Pike Ste 152 (19703-2424)
P.O. Box 3402 (22103-3402)
PHONE.....................931 297-4462
Ryan Lester, *CEO*
Joshua Boehm, *COO*
EMP: 2 EST: 2014
SALES (est): 234.24K **Privately Held**
SIC: 7372 Prepackaged software

(G-1107)
DACK REALTY CORP (PA)
Also Called: Donald Jaffey Enterprises
1308 Society Dr (19703-1743)
PHONE.....................302 792-2737
Donald Jaffey, *Pr*
EMP: 8 EST: 1954
SQ FT: 2,000
SALES (est): 812.7K
SALES (corp-wide): 812.7K **Privately Held**
Web: dack1realty.wixsite.com
SIC: 6531 6512 6513 Real estate managers; Shopping center, property operation only; Apartment building operators

GEOGRAPHIC SECTION
Claymont - New Castle County (G-1137)

(G-1108)
DANE WATERS
1 Hillside Rd (19703-2602)
PHONE..................302 377-9999
Dane Waters, *Pt*
EMP: 7 **EST:** 2000
SALES (est): 391.21K **Privately Held**
SIC: 3629 Static elimination equipment, industrial

(G-1109)
DAVES SERVICE CENTER
950 Ridge Rd Ste A6 (19703-3526)
PHONE..................302 798-1776
Anthony Mattera, *Prin*
EMP: 8 **EST:** 2008
SALES (est): 328.75K **Privately Held**
SIC: 7539 7538 Automotive repair shops, nec ; General automotive repair shops

(G-1110)
DAVIS SERVICES
3 N Avon Dr (19703-1501)
PHONE..................302 792-1754
EMP: 7 **EST:** 2016
SALES (est): 68.82K **Privately Held**
Web: www.davisservicesinc.com
SIC: 1711 Warm air heating and air conditioning contractor

(G-1111)
DD INC DE LLC
907 Providence Ave (19703-1862)
PHONE..................302 669-9269
Renee Kreske, *Prin*
EMP: 5 **EST:** 2014
SALES (est): 282.53K **Privately Held**
SIC: 5012 Automobiles and other motor vehicles

(G-1112)
DE NOVO FOODS INC (PA)
2093 Philadelphia Pike # 9 (19703-2424)
PHONE..................302 613-1351
Jean Louwrens, *CEO*
Richard Grieves, *COO*
EMP: 6 **EST:** 2021
SALES (est): 72.34K
SALES (corp-wide): 72.34K **Privately Held**
SIC: 8731 Biological research

(G-1113)
DELAWARE HOTEL ASSOCIATES LP
Also Called: Crowne Plaza Wilmington North
630 Naamans Rd (19703-2310)
PHONE..................302 792-2700
Tim Zezulka, *Genl Mgr*
Kevin Cushing, *
EMP: 80 **EST:** 2012
SALES (est): 3.53MM **Privately Held**
Web: www.cpwilmingtonnorth.com
SIC: 7011 Hotels

(G-1114)
DELAWARE PRIDE INC
10 Hickman Rd (19703-3514)
P.O. Box 9834 (19714-4934)
PHONE..................302 265-3020
EMP: 6 **EST:** 1998
SALES (est): 65.1K **Privately Held**
Web: www.delawarepride.org
SIC: 8322 7371 Outreach program; Computer software development and applications

(G-1115)
DELAWARE STATE DENTAL SOCIETY
2803 Philadelphia Pike (19703-2506)
PHONE..................302 368-7634
Beetty Dencler, *Ex Dir*
EMP: 9 **EST:** 1850
SALES (est): 417.8K **Privately Held**
Web: www.delawarestatedentalsociety.org
SIC: 8621 Dental association

(G-1116)
DELDEO BUILDERS INC
100 Naamans Rd Ste 3f (19703-2737)
PHONE..................302 791-0243
Louis M Deldeo, *Pr*
Marc T Wolfe, *Sec*
Marion E Deldeo, *VP*
EMP: 10 **EST:** 1962
SQ FT: 1,200
SALES (est): 1.94MM **Privately Held**
Web: deldeo-builders.claymont.delawareb.com
SIC: 1542 1522 Commercial and office building, new construction; Residential construction, nec

(G-1117)
DENDI INC
2093 Philadelphia Pike # 1420 (19703-2424)
PHONE..................919 448-5511
EMP: 19 **EST:** 2018
SALES (est): 565.63K **Privately Held**
SIC: 7371 Custom computer programming services

(G-1118)
DIANE LACASH INC
8 Denham Ave (19703-2710)
PHONE..................302 608-2477
Otto Gibbs, *Prin*
EMP: 3 **EST:** 2020
SALES (est): 250K **Privately Held**
SIC: 2051 Bakery: wholesale or wholesale/retail combined

(G-1119)
DIVERSIO INC (PA)
2093a Philadelphia Pike Ste 384 (19703-2424)
PHONE..................855 647-4155
Laura Mcgee, *Pr*
EMP: 28 **EST:** 2021
SALES (est): 1.27MM
SALES (corp-wide): 1.27MM **Privately Held**
SIC: 5045 Computer software

(G-1120)
DOOR & GATE CO LLC
130 Hickman Rd Ste 26 (19703-3552)
PHONE..................888 505-6962
Frank Burger, *Prin*
EMP: 10 **EST:** 2010
SALES (est): 2.15MM **Privately Held**
Web: www.doorandgateusa.com
SIC: 5039 Prefabricated structures

(G-1121)
DR DAVID DEFRIES CHIROPRACTOR
2 Drexel Rd (19703-2456)
PHONE..................610 494-0412
David Defries, *Prin*
EMP: 5 **EST:** 2016
SALES (est): 85.17K **Privately Held**
Web: www.mybackcracker.com
SIC: 8041 Offices and clinics of chiropractors

(G-1122)
DRAGONS LAIR PRINTING LLC
Also Called: D L Printing
130 Hickman Rd Ste 24 (19703-3552)
PHONE..................302 798-4465
Bob Chavis, *Prin*
EMP: 4 **EST:** 2003
SALES (est): 342.88K **Privately Held**
Web: www.dlprintingllc.com
SIC: 2759 Screen printing

(G-1123)
DREAMSCAPE LANDSCAPING
60 Colby Ave (19703-2708)
P.O. Box 730 (19703-0730)
PHONE..................302 354-5247
EMP: 5 **EST:** 2010
SALES (est): 195.95K **Privately Held**
Web: www.dreamscapelandscapingllc.com
SIC: 0781 Landscape services

(G-1124)
DRONE CONSULTING PROS INC
Also Called: Pooolipript
2093 Philadelphia Pike (19703-2424)
PHONE..................561 766-5176
EMP: 5 **EST:** 2019
SALES (est): 200.26K **Privately Held**
SIC: 8748 Business consulting, nec

(G-1125)
E ELECTRIC
311 Delaware Ave (19703-1972)
PHONE..................302 547-3151
EMP: 5 **EST:** 2014
SALES (est): 57.13K **Privately Held**
SIC: 1731 Electrical work

(G-1126)
EAGLE ONE FEDERAL CREDIT UNION
3301 Philadelphia Pike (19703-3102)
P.O. Box 543 (19703-0543)
PHONE..................302 798-7749
Jerry Piper, *Prin*
EMP: 6
SALES (corp-wide): 4.14MM **Privately Held**
Web: www.eagleonefcu.org
SIC: 6061 Federal credit unions
PA: Eagle One Federal Credit Union
7500 Lindbergh Blvd
Philadelphia PA 19176
267 298-1480

(G-1127)
EARL CARTER
98 Harvey Rd (19703-1973)
PHONE..................302 375-0354
Earl Carter, *Prin*
EMP: 7 **EST:** 2017
SALES (est): 58.78K **Privately Held**
SIC: 8322 Individual and family services

(G-1128)
EDWARD J HENNESSY
Also Called: Edward Hennessy Tile
17 Franklin Ave (19703-2033)
PHONE..................302 798-8019
Edward J Hennessy, *Prin*
EMP: 5 **EST:** 2009
SALES (est): 75.13K **Privately Held**
SIC: 1743 Tile installation, ceramic

(G-1129)
ELITE USA FASHION LLC
650 Naamans Rd Ste 204 (19703-2318)
PHONE..................810 410-5403
EMP: 5 **EST:** 2019
SALES (est): 192.34K **Privately Held**
Web: www.elite-usa.com
SIC: 7389 Design services

(G-1130)
ELITE WORLDWIDE INC ✪
2093 Philadelphia Pike (19703-2424)
PHONE..................833 200-5185
Ernest Gilley, *CEO*
EMP: 6 **EST:** 2022
SALES (est): 544.18K **Privately Held**
SIC: 5112 Business forms

(G-1131)
EMISSION FREE GENERATORS INC
2093 Philadelphia Pike Ste 2099 (19703-2424)
PHONE..................440 503-7405
Mark Collins, *Managing Member*
EMP: 5
SALES (est): 376.42K **Privately Held**
SIC: 3621 Generators and sets, electric

(G-1132)
EMPIRE GROUP INTERNATIONAL
3506 Philadelphia Pike (19703-3109)
PHONE..................302 791-1100
David Donaldson, *Pr*
EMP: 5 **EST:** 2016
SALES (est): 115.03K **Privately Held**
Web: www.empiregroupde.com
SIC: 6531 Real estate agents and managers

(G-1133)
EPIC TIDES LLC
2093a Philadelphia Pike Ste 246 (19703-2424)
PHONE..................646 535-6523
EMP: 5 **EST:** 2020
SALES (est): 152.29K **Privately Held**
SIC: 7379 Online services technology consultants

(G-1134)
ESPINOZA ORLANDO
Also Called: Orlandos Sealcoating
7 Virginia Ave (19703-3516)
PHONE..................302 442-5007
Orlando Espinoza, *Prin*
EMP: 6 **EST:** 2010
SALES (est): 209.66K **Privately Held**
SIC: 1611 Surfacing and paving

(G-1135)
ESTABLISHING BLACK MEN LLC
P.O. Box 182 (19703-0182)
PHONE..................215 432-7469
EMP: 8 **EST:** 2017
SALES (est): 108.6K **Privately Held**
SIC: 8611 Community affairs and services

(G-1136)
ESTIA HOSPITALITY GROUP INC (PA)
Also Called: Claymont Foods
3526 Philadelphia Pike (19703-3109)
PHONE..................302 798-5319
Spiro Demetratos, *Pt*
Bob Hionis, *Pt*
EMP: 8 **EST:** 1969
SQ FT: 1,600
SALES (est): 1.1MM
SALES (corp-wide): 1.1MM **Privately Held**
Web: www.claymontsteakshop.com
SIC: 5812 5147 5148 Sandwiches and submarines shop; Meats and meat products ; Fresh fruits and vegetables

(G-1137)
EVAN HURST PROPERTY MANAGEMENT
Also Called: Evan Hurst Lawn & Landscaping
100 Naamans Rd (19703-2737)
PHONE..................302 375-0398
Chris Evans, *Pr*
EMP: 8 **EST:** 2004
SALES (est): 214.91K **Privately Held**

Claymont - New Castle County (G-1138)

GEOGRAPHIC SECTION

SIC: 0782 Lawn services

(G-1138)
EVEN & ODD MINDS LLC
3430 Philadelphia Pike Unit 55
(19703-7300)
PHONE..................949 246-4789
EMP: 10
SALES (corp-wide): 2.44MM **Privately Held**
Web: www.eominds.com
SIC: 8742 Human resource consulting services
PA: Even & Odd Minds Llc
   1521 Concord Pike Ste 301
   Wilmington DE 19803
   619 663-7284

(G-1139)
EVERYTALE INC
2093 Philadelphia Pike # 221 (19703-2424)
PHONE..................650 989-9807
EMP: 23 EST: 2019
SALES (est): 144.61K **Privately Held**
SIC: 7371 Computer software development and applications

(G-1140)
EVRAZ CLAYMONT STEEL HOLDINGS INC
Also Called: Evraz
4001 Philadelphia Pike (19703-2727)
PHONE..................302 792-5400
◆ EMP: 400
SIC: 3312 Plate, steel

(G-1141)
EVRAZ CLAYMONT STEEL INC
4001 Philadelphia Pike (19703-2727)
PHONE..................302 792-5400
EMP: 359
SIC: 3312 3494 Plate, steel; Valves and pipe fittings, nec

(G-1142)
EXEC-PRO RECRUITING
5 Dustin Dr (19703-1107)
PHONE..................302 379-7553
John Grandizio, *Prin*
EMP: 6 EST: 2010
SALES (est): 101.6K **Privately Held**
SIC: 7361 Employment agencies

(G-1143)
EXIM ROUTES INC
2803 Philadelphia Pike B (19703-2506)
PHONE..................302 551-6829
EMP: 6 EST: 2021
SALES (est): 87.5K **Privately Held**
SIC: 5093 Scrap and waste materials

(G-1144)
FAIRVILLE MANAGEMENT CO LLC
Also Called: Overlook Colony
3207 E Brandywine Ave (19703-2007)
PHONE..................302 798-1736
EMP: 7
SALES (corp-wide): 2.12MM **Privately Held**
Web: www.fairvillemanagement.com
SIC: 6513 Apartment building operators
PA: Fairville Management Company. Llc
   726 Yorklyn Rd Ste 200
   Hockessin DE 19707
   302 489-2000

(G-1145)
FAITH VICTORY CHRISTN ACADEMY
301 Commonwealth Ave (19703-2063)
PHONE..................302 333-0855
EMP: 10 EST: 2010
SALES (est): 157.22K **Privately Held**
SIC: 8351 Child day care services

(G-1146)
FAMILY UNIT FITNESS
2309 Wilson Ave (19703-1842)
PHONE..................267 403-6695
Brea Young, *Prin*
EMP: 5 EST: 2017
SALES (est): 29.54K **Privately Held**
SIC: 7991 Physical fitness facilities

(G-1147)
FANHOUSE INC
2093a Philadelphia Pike (19703-2424)
PHONE..................415 598-7628
Jerry Meng, *Ch Bd*
EMP: 10 EST: 2020
SALES (est): 469.32K **Privately Held**
SIC: 7371 Computer software development and applications

(G-1148)
FAQX INC
2093 Philadelphia Pike (19703-2424)
PHONE..................646 437-6797
Marco Bianco, *CEO*
EMP: 6 EST: 2021
SALES (est): 135.94K **Privately Held**
SIC: 7299 Information services, consumer

(G-1149)
FAST CARE MEDICAL AID UNIT LLC
Also Called: Gotadoc
2722 Philadelphia Pike (19703-2568)
P.O. Box 428 (21922-0428)
PHONE..................302 793-7506
Zahid Aslam, *Managing Member*
EMP: 5 EST: 2012
SALES (est): 198.14K **Privately Held**
Web: www.fastcaremedical.com
SIC: 8099 Medical services organization

(G-1150)
FLYING LOCKSMITHS LLC
1002 Society Dr (19703-1782)
PHONE..................302 607-7999
EMP: 7 EST: 2020
SALES (est): 47.61K **Privately Held**
Web: www.flyinglocksmiths.com
SIC: 7699 Locksmith shop

(G-1151)
FOX POINT PROGRAMS INC
3001 Philadelphia Pike (19703-2580)
PHONE..................800 499-7242
Glenn W Clark, *Pr*
EMP: 14 EST: 2005
SALES (est): 1.09MM **Privately Held**
Web: www.foxpointprg.com
SIC: 6411 Insurance agents, nec

(G-1152)
FRASCELLA ENTERPRISES INC
Also Called: Cashtoday Financial Centers
650 Naamans Rd Ste 300 (19703-2300)
PHONE..................267 467-4496
David Frascella, *Pr*
EMP: 6 EST: 2000
SQ FT: 4,500
SALES (est): 407.13K **Privately Held**
SIC: 6159 Small business investment companies

(G-1153)
FUROBINC LLC ✪
2803 Philadelphia Pike (19703-2506)
PHONE..................302 202-4551
EMP: 5 EST: 2022
SALES (est): 87.5K **Privately Held**
SIC: 5092 Toys and games

(G-1154)
G4S SECURE SOLUTIONS USA INC
650 Naamans Rd Ste 200 (19703-2318)
PHONE..................215 957-7603
Matthew Schwartz, *Brnch Mgr*
EMP: 13
SALES (corp-wide): 2.67MM **Privately Held**
Web: www.g4s.com
SIC: 7381 Security guard service
HQ: G4s Secure Solutions (Usa) Inc.
   1395 University Blvd
   Jupiter FL 33458
   561 622-5656

(G-1155)
GB SHADES LLC (PA)
Also Called: Goodwin Brothers Shading & Spc
100 Naamans Rd Ste 5f (19703-2700)
PHONE..................302 798-3028
John Goodwin, *Managing Member*
Jj Purpura, *General Member*
EMP: 9 EST: 2005
SQ FT: 4,800
SALES (est): 31.2MM **Privately Held**
Web: www.gbshades.com
SIC: 5023 Window furnishings

(G-1156)
GEBHART FUNERAL HOME INC
3401 Philadelphia Pike (19703-3105)
PHONE..................302 798-7726
Chandler Gebhart Iii, *Pr*
Chandler Gebhart Iv, *VP*
EMP: 6 EST: 1972
SALES (est): 232.93K **Privately Held**
Web: www.gebhartfuneralhomes.com
SIC: 7261 Funeral home

(G-1157)
GENCO
2803 B Philly Pike Ste 112 (19703)
PHONE..................302 588-5872
Cesar Estrada, *Owner*
EMP: 2 EST: 2015
SQ FT: 600
SALES (est): 57K **Privately Held**
SIC: 2099 Food preparations, nec

(G-1158)
GENERATION CLEANING SVC LLC
605 New York Ave (19703-1957)
PHONE..................302 492-2772
EMP: 5
SALES (est): 70.36K **Privately Held**
SIC: 7349 7389 Building and office cleaning services; Business Activities at Non-Commercial Site

(G-1159)
GENESEC INC
62 Lake Forest Blvd (19703)
PHONE..................917 656-5742
John Entwistle, *Pr*
EMP: 5 EST: 2015
SALES (est): 191.46K **Privately Held**
SIC: 7379 Computer hardware requirements analysis

(G-1160)
GENUINE PARTS COMPANY
Also Called: NAPA Auto Parts
319 Ridge Rd (19703-3508)
PHONE..................610 494-6355
Stanley Wielosik, *Genl Mgr*
EMP: 5
SALES (corp-wide): 22.1B **Publicly Held**
Web: www.genpt.com
SIC: 5531 5013 Automotive parts; Automotive supplies and parts
PA: Genuine Parts Company
   2999 Wildwood Pkwy
   Atlanta GA 30339
   678 934-5000

(G-1161)
GIAN-CO
Also Called: Brandywine Vending
2 Stockdale Ave (19703-2917)
PHONE..................302 798-7100
Charles Gianakis, *Pr*
Cynthia Contis, *Sec*
EMP: 12 EST: 1981
SQ FT: 5,400
SALES (est): 195.29K **Privately Held**
SIC: 7359 Vending machine rental

(G-1162)
GITDUCK INC
2093 Philadelphia Pike (19703-2424)
PHONE..................415 969-3825
Thiago Montero, *CEO*
EMP: 5
SALES (est): 199.4K **Privately Held**
Web: www.nimblo.com
SIC: 7371 Computer software development and applications

(G-1163)
GLOBAL COMM INNOVATIONS LLC
2093 Philadelphia Pike (19703-2424)
PHONE..................302 546-5010
EMP: 6 EST: 2020
SALES (est): 1.2MM **Privately Held**
SIC: 7374 Computer processing services

(G-1164)
GLOBAL SHIPPING CENTER LLC
2803 Philadelphia Pike Ste B (19703-2506)
PHONE..................302 798-4321
Rona Mendosia, *Owner*
EMP: 10 EST: 2013
SALES (est): 344.44K **Privately Held**
Web: www.globalexpress-shippingcenter.com
SIC: 7389 Mailbox rental and related service

(G-1165)
GLOBBING LLC
950 Ridge Rd (19703-3523)
PHONE..................408 903-4209
EMP: 20 EST: 2015
SQ FT: 1,440
SALES (est): 2.2MM **Privately Held**
Web: www.globbing.com
SIC: 4225 4226 4783 General warehousing and storage; Special warehousing and storage, nec; Packing and crating

(G-1166)
GO MOZAIC LLC
3042 Greenshire Ave (19703-2058)
P.O. Box 11 (19703-0011)
PHONE..................302 438-4141
EMP: 3 EST: 2011
SALES (est): 152.22K **Privately Held**
Web: www.gomozaic.com
SIC: 2761 Manifold business forms

(G-1167)
GOLDEN RECURSION INC
Also Called: Golden
2093a Philadelphia Pike Ste 206 (19703-2424)
PHONE..................415 779-4053
Jude Gomila, *CEO*
EMP: 16 EST: 2016

SQ FT: 400
SALES (est): 2.41MM Privately Held
SIC: 5045 7372 Computer software; Business oriented computer software

(G-1168)
GOLDEN STAR ENTERPRISES LTD
2803 Philadelphia Pike Ste B (19703-2506)
PHONE..................888 680-8033
EMP: 3 EST: 1993
SALES (est): 45.08K Privately Held
SIC: 7372 Prepackaged software

(G-1169)
GOVSIMPLIFIED LLC
Also Called: Ein Taxid Registration
2093 Philadelphia Pike # 3338 (19703-2424)
PHONE..................888 629-8008
Guillaume Lellouche, CEO
EMP: 8 EST: 2014
SALES (est): 234.47K Privately Held
Web: www.govsimplified.com
SIC: 7381 7371 Guard services; Computer software development and applications

(G-1170)
GREEN CANDY SOLUTIONS INC ✪
2093a Philadelphia Pike Ste 486 (19703-2424)
PHONE..................302 599-7944
Denys Koblia, Pr
EMP: 20 EST: 2023
SALES (est): 588.11K Privately Held
SIC: 7371 Computer software development and applications

(G-1171)
GREY MOUNTAIN EQUITIES LLC ✪
2803 Philadelphia Pike B-260 (19703-2506)
PHONE..................623 387-0744
Michael Montano, Managing Member
EMP: 6 EST: 2023
SALES (est): 65.64K Privately Held
SIC: 7011 Tourist camps, cabins, cottages, and courts

(G-1172)
GRIECO
3401 Philadelphia Pike (19703-3105)
PHONE..................302 792-1293
Matt Grieco, Owner
EMP: 6 EST: 2011
SALES (est): 96K Privately Held
SIC: 7261 Funeral home

(G-1173)
GTECH CLEANING SERVICES LLC
950 Ridge Rd Ste B5 (19703-3527)
P.O. Box 33 (19703-0033)
PHONE..................302 494-2102
Tyreese Green, Managing Member
EMP: 50 EST: 2001
SALES (est): 836.68K Privately Held
Web: www.gtechcleaning.com
SIC: 7699 Cleaning services

(G-1174)
HALOALI TEETH WHITENING LLC
409 Fillmore Ct (19703-2254)
PHONE..................302 300-4042
Aliha Walker, Managing Member
EMP: 5
SALES (est): 213.35K Privately Held
Web: www.haloali.com
SIC: 5999 7389 Toiletries, cosmetics, and perfumes; Business Activities at Non-Commercial Site

(G-1175)
HEAL ROOM INC
2093 Philadelphia Pike # 1313 (19703-2424)
PHONE..................770 597-3366
Santiago De Bedout, CEO
EMP: 5 EST: 2020
SALES (est): 46.16K Privately Held
SIC: 7371 Computer software development and applications

(G-1176)
HEALING TOUCH MASSAGE
613 Delancey Pl (19703-1928)
PHONE..................302 791-0235
Robin Stump, Prin
EMP: 6 EST: 2017
SALES (est): 74.28K Privately Held
SIC: 8049 Offices of health practitioner

(G-1177)
HEALTH CARE SOLUTIONS OF
131 Woodgreen Rd (19703-1315)
PHONE..................484 234-2427
EMP: 6 EST: 2018
SALES (est): 154.57K Privately Held
SIC: 8099 Health and allied services, nec

(G-1178)
HELLOGURU INC
2093 Philadelphia Pike # 4072 (19703-2424)
PHONE..................754 303-3278
Felipe Abello, CEO
EMP: 5
SALES (est): 46.16K Privately Held
Web: www.helloguru.io
SIC: 7371 Computer software development

(G-1179)
HIDDEN LAKE GAMES LLC
2093 Philadelphia Pike # 8830 (19703-2424)
PHONE..................302 305-1070
Timur Karbaya, CEO
EMP: 5
SALES (est): 230.82K Privately Held
SIC: 7371 Computer software development and applications

(G-1180)
HOLIDAY INN SELECT
Also Called: Holiday Inn
630 Naamans Rd (19703-2310)
PHONE..................302 792-2700
Joe Podolinsky, Owner
EMP: 17 EST: 2001
SALES (est): 200.5K Privately Held
Web: www.holidayinn.com
SIC: 7011 Hotels and motels

(G-1181)
HONEYWELL INTERNATIONAL INC
Also Called: Honeywell
6100 Philadelphia Pike (19703-2716)
PHONE..................302 791-6700
Amado Vidin, Brnch Mgr
EMP: 26
SALES (corp-wide): 35.47B Publicly Held
Web: www.honeywell.com
SIC: 2819 2911 2899 2869 Boron compounds, nec, not from mines; Petroleum refining; Chemical preparations, nec; Industrial organic chemicals, nec
PA: Honeywell International Inc.
855 S Mint St
Charlotte NC 28202
704 627-6200

(G-1182)
HOWARTH GRANITE HOLDINGS LLC
Also Called: Elegantly Set In Stone
2703 Philadelphia Pike Ste D (19703-2571)
PHONE..................302 543-6739
Susanne Howarth, Managing Member
EMP: 8 EST: 2014
SALES (est): 423.28K Privately Held
Web: www.elegantlysetinstone.com
SIC: 1743 Terrazzo, tile, marble and mosaic work

(G-1183)
ICONICO LLC
2093 Philadelphia Pike 2248 (19703-2424)
PHONE..................650 681-9211
EMP: 5 EST: 2020
SALES (est): 199.4K Privately Held
Web: www.iconico.us
SIC: 7371 Software programming applications

(G-1184)
INDEPENDENT ELEC SVCS LLC
Also Called: Independent Electrical Svcs
26 Rolling Rd (19703-2464)
PHONE..................302 383-2761
Dave Smagala, Pr
Dave Smagala, Prin
EMP: 53 EST: 2011
SALES (est): 3.54MM Privately Held
SIC: 1731 7539 3699 General electrical contractor; Electrical services; Electrical equipment and supplies, nec

(G-1185)
INOVA BUSINESS SOLUTIONS LLC
2093a Philadelphia Pike Ste 223 (19703-2424)
PHONE..................251 316-0180
Abdelrahman Mousa, VP
EMP: 9 EST: 2021
SALES (est): 368.75K Privately Held
SIC: 7371 Computer software development and applications

(G-1186)
INSTAPANEL INC
2093 Philadelphia Pike Pmb 4330 (19703-2424)
PHONE..................415 727-7279
Daavid Kahn, CEO
EMP: 9 EST: 2015
SALES (est): 458.37K Privately Held
Web: www.instapanel.com
SIC: 8732 Sociological research

(G-1187)
INTELLGENT SLTIONS ALIANCE LLC
905 Providence Ave (19703-1862)
PHONE..................754 300-0051
EMP: 23 EST: 2021
SALES (est): 709.32K Privately Held
SIC: 8742 Management consulting services

(G-1188)
INTERSTATE HOTELS RESORTS INC
Also Called: Holiday Inn
630 Naamans Rd (19703-2310)
PHONE..................302 792-2700
Walter Conner, Brnch Mgr
EMP: 10
Web: www.holidayinn.com
SIC: 7011 Hotels
HQ: Interstate Hotels & Resorts, Inc.
5301 Headquarters Dr
Plano TX 75024
703 387-3100

(G-1189)
ISTORAGE
100 Hickman Rd (19703-3503)
PHONE..................302 798-6661
EMP: 6 EST: 2017
SALES (est): 77.98K Privately Held
Web: www.istorage.com
SIC: 4225 General warehousing and storage

(G-1190)
ITGLOBALCOM CORP
2093 Philadelphia Pike 2345 (19703-2424)
PHONE..................302 498-8359
Vitaliy Gritsay, CEO
EMP: 6 EST: 2019
SALES (est): 74.93K Privately Held
Web: www.itglobal.com
SIC: 4813 Internet host services

(G-1191)
ITS MY ART LLC
7423 Society Dr (19703-1776)
PHONE..................302 750-1380
Shonte Young, Asst Sec
EMP: 5 EST: 2015
SALES (est): 34.26K Privately Held
SIC: 7999 Art gallery, commercial

(G-1192)
J LOTTER MANAGEMENT
1002 Society Dr (19703-1782)
PHONE..................302 308-3939
EMP: 5 EST: 2017
SALES (est): 215.19K Privately Held
SIC: 8741 Management services

(G-1193)
JACKSUN INC
Also Called: Jacksun
2093 Philadelphia Pike Ste 1182 (19703-2424)
PHONE..................800 861-7050
Kevious Douglas, Ch Bd
EMP: 33 EST: 2020
Web: www.jacksunholdings.com
SIC: 6719 Investment holding companies, except banks

(G-1194)
JAMES MACHINE SHOP INC
3102 W Brandywine Ave (19703-2010)
PHONE..................302 798-5679
Frank James, Pr
Thomas James, Stockholder
Frank James, VP
Harry James, Treas
EMP: 3 EST: 1926
SQ FT: 5,341
SALES (est): 203.09K Privately Held
SIC: 3599 Machine shop, jobbing and repair

(G-1195)
JAMMY INSTRUMENTS US CORP
2093 Philadelphia Pike (19703-2424)
PHONE..................209 813-4052
Oleg Domansky, CEO
EMP: 12 EST: 2019
SALES (est): 797.2K Privately Held
SIC: 3931 Musical instruments, electric and electronic, nec

(G-1196)
JBCOMPANY LLC
Philadelphia Pike Ste B #507 (19703)
PHONE..................406 623-8593
Bjorn Faber, Managing Member
EMP: 6
SALES (est): 85.84K Privately Held
SIC: 5084 Industrial machinery and equipment

Claymont - New Castle County (G-1197)

(G-1197)
JC INDUSTRIAL SOLUTIONS INC
950 Ridge Rd Ste C13 (19703-3538)
P.O. Box 937 (19357-0937)
PHONE..................484 720-8381
Joseph Coursey, *Prin*
EMP: 2 EST: 2012
SALES (est): 204.51K **Privately Held**
Web: www.jcisinc.net
SIC: **3492** 7389 Hose and tube fittings and assemblies, hydraulic/pneumatic; Business Activities at Non-Commercial Site

(G-1198)
JEANFREAU CARPENTRY SERVICES
130 Hickman Rd Ste 8 (19703-3519)
PHONE..................302 563-6449
Robert Jeanfreau, *Prin*
EMP: 6 EST: 2013
SALES (est): 77.65K **Privately Held**
SIC: **1751** Carpentry work

(G-1199)
JOHNS WASHER REPAIR
Also Called: Johns Maytag
3309 Philadelphia Pike (19703-3102)
PHONE..................302 792-2333
John Passero, *Owner*
EMP: 9 EST: 1972
SALES (est): 298.95K **Privately Held**
Web: www.johnshomeappliancecenter.com
SIC: **7629** 5722 Electrical household appliance repair; Household appliance stores

(G-1200)
JORDAN CABINETRY & WD TURNING
84 S Avon Dr (19703-1405)
PHONE..................302 792-1009
Timothy R Jordan, *Owner*
EMP: 2 EST: 1997
SALES (est): 67.58K **Privately Held**
SIC: **2517** Home entertainment unit cabinets, wood

(G-1201)
JOURNEYS
8103 Governor Printz Blvd (19703-2912)
PHONE..................443 945-0615
Rebecca D Trent, *Owner*
EMP: 9 EST: 2017
SALES (est): 114.43K **Privately Held**
SIC: **8011** Offices and clinics of medical doctors

(G-1202)
JRP INDUSTRIAL SERVICES LLC
100 Naamans Rd Ste 2g (19703-2736)
PHONE..................302 439-4092
Herby Smith, *Pr*
EMP: 9 EST: 2014
SALES (est): 472.44K **Privately Held**
SIC: **0781** Landscape services

(G-1203)
JUSTITSELECTRIC
950 Ridge Rd (19703-3523)
PHONE..................215 715-7314
EMP: 7 EST: 2019
SALES (est): 242.12K **Privately Held**
Web: www.justitselectric.com
SIC: **1731** General electrical contractor

(G-1204)
KAMINSKI SERVICE CENTER
3506 Philadelphia Pike (19703-3109)
PHONE..................302 375-6379
EMP: 5 EST: 2017
SALES (est): 28.25K **Privately Held**
SIC: **7538** General automotive repair shops

(G-1205)
KATE W BERNSTEIN
8103 Governor Printz Blvd (19703-2912)
PHONE..................302 597-9911
EMP: 7 EST: 2018
SALES (est): 71.47K **Privately Held**
SIC: **8011** Offices and clinics of medical doctors

(G-1206)
KIDMORE END DEVELOPERS LLC
2900 Society Dr (19703-1739)
PHONE..................302 562-5110
Victoria Spiro, *Prin*
EMP: 5 EST: 2016
SALES (est): 177.04K **Privately Held**
SIC: **6552** Subdividers and developers, nec

(G-1207)
KING
732 Peachtree Rd Apt E (19703-2238)
PHONE..................302 930-0139
Nakia Hart, *Prin*
EMP: 6 EST: 2017
SALES (est): 102.16K **Privately Held**
Web: www.crashchampions.com
SIC: **7532** Body shop, automotive

(G-1208)
KNIGHTS INN
Also Called: Knights Inn
7811 Governor Printz Blvd (19703-2615)
PHONE..................302 798-9914
Sam Patel, *Prin*
EMP: 11 EST: 2018
SALES (est): 35.85K **Privately Held**
Web: www.redlion.com
SIC: **7011** Hotels and motels

(G-1209)
KUMAR PROPERTIES LLC
2093 Philadelphia Pike (19703-2424)
PHONE..................337 284-5975
Jay Kumar, *Managing Member*
EMP: 6 EST: 2017
SALES (est): 600K **Privately Held**
SIC: **6531** Real estate managers

(G-1210)
L C K MANAGMENT INC
8 Ruby Dr (19703-1413)
PHONE..................609 820-2980
Orlando Cedres, *Dir*
EMP: 9 EST: 2018
SALES (est): 250.26K **Privately Held**
SIC: **8741** Business management

(G-1211)
LAN-TECH INC
Also Called: Lantech-lt
2093 Philadelphia Pike Ste 2001 (19703-2424)
PHONE..................877 311-1030
EMP: 6 EST: 1992
SALES (est): 99.02K **Privately Held**
SIC: **7374** Data processing and preparation

(G-1212)
LC DISTRIBUTORS INC
950 Ridge Rd Ste E1 (19703-3520)
PHONE..................484 326-9805
William F Crockett, *Pr*
EMP: 5 EST: 1995
SALES (est): 156.46K **Privately Held**
SIC: **5199** Advertising specialties

(G-1213)
LC MANAGEMENT
590 Naamans Rd (19703-2308)
PHONE..................302 439-3523
EMP: 10 EST: 2019
SALES (est): 192.47K **Privately Held**
Web: www.capanomanagement.com
SIC: **8741** Management services

(G-1214)
LEGENDS OF VENARI INC
2803 Philadelphia Pike (19703-2506)
PHONE..................226 338-6622
EMP: 7
SALES (est): 277.92K **Privately Held**
SIC: **7372** Prepackaged software

(G-1215)
LEON N WEINER & ASSOCIATES INC
Also Called: Stoneybrook Apts
1114 Andrea Ct (19703-2242)
PHONE..................302 798-3446
EMP: 6
SALES (corp-wide): 73.09K **Privately Held**
Web: www.lnwa.com
SIC: **6513** Apartment building operators
PA: Leon N. Weiner & Associates, Inc.
1 Fox Pt Ctr 4 Denny Rd
Wilmington DE 19809
302 656-1354

(G-1216)
LETTERHEAD INC
2093 Philadelphia Pike Ste 3050 (19703-2424)
PHONE..................305 988-0808
Christopher Sopher, *CEO*
EMP: 7 EST: 2021
SALES (est): 581.36K **Privately Held**
SIC: **7371** Software programming applications

(G-1217)
LIBERTY TAX SERVICE
2618 Philadelphia Pike (19703-2504)
PHONE..................302 762-1010
Felix Strater, *Prin*
EMP: 7 EST: 2010
SALES (est): 127.7K **Privately Held**
Web: www.libertytax.com
SIC: **7291** Tax return preparation services

(G-1218)
LIFTOFF AGENT INC
Also Called: Liftoff Agent
2093 Philadelphia Pike # 3 (19703-2424)
PHONE..................925 462-5001
Norman L Kinsey Iii, *CEO*
EMP: 8 EST: 2017
SALES (est): 500K **Privately Held**
SIC: **7371** Computer software systems analysis and design, custom

(G-1219)
LITTLE BLESSINGS CHILDCARE
26 Glenrock Dr (19703-1225)
PHONE..................215 510-4514
Samantha Silkovich, *Prin*
EMP: 8 EST: 2017
SALES (est): 49.88K **Privately Held**
SIC: **8351** Child day care services

(G-1220)
LITTLE LEARNER INC
41 N Avon Dr (19703-1503)
PHONE..................302 798-5570
Sandra V Desmond, *Pr*
EMP: 9 EST: 1988
SALES (est): 70.96K **Privately Held**
SIC: **8351** Preschool center

(G-1221)
LIVEWARE INC
1506 Society Dr (19703-1740)
PHONE..................302 791-9446
EMP: 10 EST: 1990
SQ FT: 3,000
SALES (est): 743.79K **Privately Held**
Web: www.workbigger.com
SIC: **7379** 2731 Computer related consulting services; Books, publishing only

(G-1222)
LOAN TILL PAYDAY LLC
2604 Philadelphia Pike (19703-2504)
PHONE..................302 792-5001
EMP: 16
Web: www.loantillpaydaydelaware.com
SIC: **6163** Loan agents
PA: Loan Till Payday Llc
1901 W 4th St &Lincln
Wilmington DE

(G-1223)
LOCAL PLUMBING
2095 Philadelphia Pike (19703-2424)
PHONE..................302 746-3101
EMP: 5 EST: 2016
SALES (est): 87.54K **Privately Held**
SIC: **1711** Plumbing contractors

(G-1224)
LOCKHART CONSTRUCTION LLC
809 Parkside Blvd Bldg 1 (19703-1038)
PHONE..................302 753-5461
James Lockhart, *Owner*
EMP: 8 EST: 2017
SALES (est): 436.51K **Privately Held**
Web: www.lockhartconstructionllc.com
SIC: **1521** New construction, single-family houses

(G-1225)
LOGICLEAN LLC
6300 Philadelphia Pike (19703-2712)
PHONE..................302 298-0054
EMP: 6
SALES (est): 182.31K **Privately Held**
Web: www.logicleanllc.com
SIC: **7349** Chemical cleaning services

(G-1226)
LOUIS DOLENTE & SONS LLC
3759 Green St (19703-2071)
PHONE..................610 874-2100
EMP: 20 EST: 1916
SALES (est): 2.07MM **Privately Held**
SIC: **1771** 1611 1794 Concrete work; Surfacing and paving; Excavation work

(G-1227)
M L PARKER CONSTRUCTION INC
950 Ridge Rd Ste C6 (19703-3528)
PHONE..................302 798-8530
Michael L Parker, *Pr*
EMP: 10 EST: 1992
SQ FT: 10,000
SALES (est): 454.35K **Privately Held**
Web: www.mlparkerconst.com
SIC: **1521** 1542 New construction, single-family houses; Commercial and office building, new construction

(G-1228)
MADISON ADOPTION ASSOCIATES (PA)
1102 Society Dr (19703-1780)
PHONE..................302 475-8977
Aleda Madison, *Pr*

GEOGRAPHIC SECTION
Claymont - New Castle County (G-1257)

Diana Madison, *Dir*
EMP: 5 **EST:** 1981
SALES (est): 1.86MM **Privately Held**
Web: www.madisonadoption.org
SIC: 8322 Adoption services

(G-1229)
MANAGEMENT SYSTEMS IMPROVEMENT
61 Balfour Ave (19703-2705)
PHONE..............................860 478-7496
EMP: 6 **EST:** 2016
SALES (est): 226.71K **Privately Held**
Web: www.msi-aqr.com
SIC: 8742 Business management consultant

(G-1230)
MANUFACTURERS & TRADERS TR CO
Also Called: M&T
3503 Philadelphia Pike (19703-3106)
PHONE..............................302 472-3262
Anthony Watts, *Brnch Mgr*
EMP: 5
SALES (corp-wide): 8.6B **Publicly Held**
Web: ir.mtb.com
SIC: 6022 State commercial banks
HQ: Manufacturers And Traders Trust Company
1 M&T Plz Fl 3
Buffalo NY 14203
716 842-4200

(G-1231)
MARK JONES PAVING
123 Hilldale Ct (19703-1306)
PHONE..............................302 355-0695
Mark Jones, *Prin*
EMP: 8 **EST:** 2015
SALES (est): 297.11K **Privately Held**
SIC: 1611 Surfacing and paving

(G-1232)
MEINEKE CAR CARE CENTER 671
Also Called: Meineke Discount Mufflers
3005 Philadelphia Pike (19703-2524)
PHONE..............................302 746-2026
EMP: 10 **EST:** 2017
SALES (est): 223.04K **Privately Held**
Web: www.meineke.com
SIC: 7538 General automotive repair shops

(G-1233)
MERATALK LLC
2093 Philadelphia Pike Ste 1748 (19703-2424)
PHONE..............................914 241-5226
EMP: 6 **EST:** 2019
SALES (est): 68.89K **Privately Held**
Web: www.meratalk.com
SIC: 8748 Telecommunications consultant

(G-1234)
MESSER LLC
6000 Philadelphia Pike (19703-2717)
P.O. Box 590 (19703-0590)
PHONE..............................302 798-9342
Todd Quintard, *Brnch Mgr*
EMP: 58
SALES (corp-wide): 1.63B **Privately Held**
Web: www.messeramericas.com
SIC: 2813 Nitrogen
HQ: Messer Llc
200 Smrst Corp Blvd # 7000
Bridgewater NJ 08807
800 755-9277

(G-1235)
METICULOUS HOME INC ✪
Also Called: Meticulous
2093 Philadelphia Pike # 7717 (19703-2424)
PHONE..............................302 878-7879
Juan Carlos Lopez Pendas, *CEO*
EMP: 15 **EST:** 2022
SALES (est): 581.23K **Privately Held**
SIC: 3639 Household appliances, nec

(G-1236)
MILL CREEK METALS INC
3 1/2 Yale Ave (19703-2975)
P.O. Box 7493 (19803-0493)
PHONE..............................302 529-7020
Mark Gillan, *Pr*
Tina Gillan, *Sec*
EMP: 10 **EST:** 1998
SQ FT: 4,500
SALES (est): 949.63K **Privately Held**
SIC: 5033 1761 Roofing and siding materials ; Roofing, siding, and sheetmetal work

(G-1237)
MIND & MATTER
8103 Governor Printz Blvd (19703-2912)
PHONE..............................302 345-0575
EMP: 5 **EST:** 2015
SALES (est): 102K **Privately Held**
SIC: 8049 Offices of health practitioner

(G-1238)
MINDSPACEWEB LLC
2803 Philadelphia Pike B (19703-2506)
PHONE..............................302 360-8744
Subham Mahapatra, *Managing Member*
EMP: 5 **EST:** 2020
SALES (est): 40K **Privately Held**
SIC: 7371 Software programming applications

(G-1239)
MINUTE LOAN CENTER
3603a Philadelphia Pike (19703-3111)
PHONE..............................302 791-9557
EMP: 6 **EST:** 2018
SALES (est): 162K **Privately Held**
Web: www.minuteloancenter.com
SIC: 6141 Personal credit institutions

(G-1240)
MITHRIL CABLE NETWORK INC
Also Called: Mithril Cable Network
2093 Philadelphia Pike Rm 19-62 (19703-2424)
PHONE..............................213 373-4381
Jun Li, *Prin*
EMP: 11 **EST:** 2019
SALES (est): 423.69K **Privately Held**
SIC: 7371 Computer software development and applications

(G-1241)
MITTELMAN DENTAL LAB
108 Delaware Ave (19703-1904)
PHONE..............................302 798-7440
Larry Mittelman, *Owner*
EMP: 9 **EST:** 1983
SQ FT: 800
SALES (est): 261.3K **Privately Held**
SIC: 8072 Crown and bridge production

(G-1242)
MMM TV MOUNTING & ENTRMT LLC
2803 Philadelphia Pike B (19703-2506)
PHONE..............................267 310-5925
EMP: 2 **EST:** 2020
SALES (est): 88.38K **Privately Held**
SIC: 3651 Home entertainment equipment, electronic, nec

(G-1243)
MOCHA TECHNOLOGIES INC
2093 Philadelphia Pike # 1395 (19703-2424)
PHONE..............................408 556-9930
EMP: 15 **EST:** 2020
SALES (est): 209.5K **Privately Held**
SIC: 7371 Computer software development and applications

(G-1244)
MOVING AS ONE LLC
2803 Philadelphia Pike Ste B1045 (19703-2506)
PHONE..............................301 701-0434
Angel Forte, *Managing Member*
EMP: 12
SALES (est): 181.3K **Privately Held**
SIC: 7299 Handyman service

(G-1245)
MR WINDOW WASHER
126 Glenrock Dr (19703-1321)
PHONE..............................302 588-3624
Blase Maitland, *Prin*
EMP: 5 **EST:** 2011
SALES (est): 66.39K **Privately Held**
SIC: 3452 Washers

(G-1246)
MULTIPLES ADAMS SERVICE LLC
42 2nd Ave (19703-2002)
PHONE..............................302 792-0710
Khalif Adams, *CEO*
EMP: 10 **EST:** 2021
SALES (est): 240.76K **Privately Held**
SIC: 7389 Business services, nec

(G-1247)
MUNTERS CORPORATION
100 Naamans Rd Ste 5l (19703-2731)
PHONE..............................302 798-2455
Larry Waltmenire, *Mgr*
EMP: 10
SALES (corp-wide): 990.05MM **Privately Held**
Web: www.munters.us
SIC: 3585 Refrigeration and heating equipment
HQ: Munters Corporation
79 Monroe St
Amesbury MA 01913

(G-1248)
NEGATIVE EMISSIONS MTLS INC
2093 Philadelphia Pike (19703-2424)
PHONE..............................929 388-3352
Jeremy Ley, *CEO*
Kevin Tidwell, *Dir*
Sarah Sclerisa, *Dir*
David Dreizinger, *Dir*
EMP: 7 **EST:** 2021
SALES (est): 615.54K **Privately Held**
SIC: 3341 Nickel smelting and refining (secondary)

(G-1249)
NESMITH & COMPANY INC
Academy Electrical Contractors
100 Naamans Rd Ste 2d (19703-2736)
PHONE..............................215 755-4570
William J Galbraith Junior, *Brnch Mgr*
EMP: 30
SALES (corp-wide): 3.17MM **Privately Held**
SIC: 1731 General electrical contractor
PA: Nesmith & Company, Inc.
419 Titan St
Philadelphia PA 19147
215 755-4570

(G-1250)
NEURO OPHTHALMOLOGIC ASSO
1201 Society Dr (19703-1777)
PHONE..............................302 792-1616
EMP: 8 **EST:** 2010
SALES (est): 113.01K **Privately Held**
SIC: 8011 Neurologist

(G-1251)
NEXT LEVEL HOME IMPROVEMENTS ✪
25 Cameo Rd (19703-1506)
PHONE..............................484 469-1767
Kyle Winkfield, *CEO*
Kyle Winkfield, *Prin*
EMP: 2 **EST:** 2022
SALES (est): 66.21K **Privately Held**
SIC: 1389 7389 Construction, repair, and dismantling services; Business Activities at Non-Commercial Site

(G-1252)
NGROW INC
2093 Philadelphia Pike (19703-2424)
PHONE..............................603 764-7274
Aleksandr Sergeev, *CEO*
EMP: 14 **EST:** 2021
SALES (est): 544.32K **Privately Held**
SIC: 7371 Software programming applications

(G-1253)
NINJASALARY INC
2093 Philadelphia Pike (19703-2424)
PHONE..............................888 201-1107
Akshay Sanghai, *CEO*
EMP: 9
SALES (est): 313.29K **Privately Held**
SIC: 7371 Computer software development and applications

(G-1254)
NINO FINANCE INC
Also Called: Cointracker
2093 Philadelphia Pike (19703-2424)
PHONE..............................415 236-7591
EMP: 6 **EST:** 2017
SALES (est): 64.47K **Privately Held**
SIC: 7374 Data processing and preparation

(G-1255)
NORTHEAST EARLY LRNG CTR LLC
Also Called: Thirst 2 Learn Child Dev Ctr
2400 Philadelphia Pike (19703-2431)
PHONE..............................302 475-7080
Linda Benson-fleming, *Managing Member*
EMP: 9 **EST:** 2011
SALES (est): 247.44K **Privately Held**
SIC: 8299 8351 Arts and crafts schools; Child day care services

(G-1256)
OCEANPORT LLC
6200 Philadelphia Pike (19703-2715)
PHONE..............................302 792-2212
William Creighton, *Managing Member*
▲ **EMP:** 15 **EST:** 2006
SALES (est): 1.91MM **Privately Held**
Web: www.oceanportllc.com
SIC: 1479 Rock salt mining

(G-1257)
OLD SCHOOL HEATING & COOLING
2 Woodsedge (19703-2964)
PHONE..............................302 383-7036
EMP: 8 **EST:** 2017
SALES (est): 249.91K **Privately Held**
SIC: 1711 Heating and air conditioning contractors

Claymont - New Castle County (G-1258)

(G-1258)
OPENEDUCAT INC
2803 Philadelphia Pike Ste B # 1117 (19703-2506)
PHONE.................................302 261-5133
EMP: 5 EST: 2020
SALES (est): 106.45K Privately Held
Web: www.openeducat.org
SIC: 7371 Computer software development

(G-1259)
OUTERHAVEN PRODUCTIONS
12 Glenrock Dr (19703-1231)
PHONE.................................302 792-9169
EMP: 6 EST: 2014
SALES (est): 54.5K Privately Held
Web: www.theouterhaven.net
SIC: 7822 Motion picture and tape distribution

(G-1260)
PARKER CONSTRUCTION INC
950 Ridge Rd Ste C6 (19703-3528)
PHONE.................................302 798-8530
Michael Parker, Pr
EMP: 5 EST: 2005
SQ FT: 1,914
SALES (est): 502.03K Privately Held
Web: www.mlparkerconst.com
SIC: 1799 Athletic and recreation facilities construction

(G-1261)
PEN ENTERPRISES LLC
2811 Philadelphia Pike Ste 2 (19703-2506)
PHONE.................................302 798-0268
Eliot Swane Junior, Managing Member
EMP: 10 EST: 2005
SALES (est): 304.59K Privately Held
SIC: 7389 Business services, nec

(G-1262)
PENSKE TRUCK RENTAL
601 Naamans Rd (19703-2309)
PHONE.................................302 746-3020
EMP: 11 EST: 2018
SALES (est): 50.83K Privately Held
Web: www.pensketruckrental.com
SIC: 7513 Truck rental and leasing, no drivers

(G-1263)
PIXXY SOLUTIONS LLC
2093 Philadelphia Pike # 4 (19703-2424)
PHONE.................................631 609-6686
David Miller, CEO
EMP: 40 EST: 2019
SALES (est): 974.43K Privately Held
Web: www.pixxysolutions.com
SIC: 7336 Graphic arts and related design

(G-1264)
PLENTEOUS CONSULTING LLC
Also Called: Televon
2093 Philadelphia Pike (19703-2424)
PHONE.................................724 325-1660
Michael Breier, Pr
EMP: 7 EST: 2017
SALES (est): 585.73K Privately Held
Web: www.televon.com
SIC: 8748 Business consulting, nec

(G-1265)
POLAR SIGNALS INC (PA)
2093 Philadelphia Pike (19703-2424)
PHONE.................................765 679-9318
Frederic Branczyk, CEO
EMP: 7 EST: 2020
SALES (est): 179.21K
SALES (corp-wide): 179.21K Privately Held
Web: www.polarsignals.com
SIC: 7371 Computer software development and applications

(G-1266)
PREMIERE STUDIO LLC
42 Colby Ave (19703-2708)
PHONE.................................347 336-0791
EMP: 10
SALES (est): 355.79K Privately Held
SIC: 7336 Commercial art and illustration

(G-1267)
PRISCILLA LANCASTER
302 Harvey Rd (19703-1942)
PHONE.................................302 792-8305
Priscilla Lancaster, Prin
EMP: 7 EST: 2010
SALES (est): 98.09K Privately Held
SIC: 3315 Wire and fabricated wire products

(G-1268)
PRODUCTIVE CO INC
2093 Philadelphia Pike (19703-2424)
PHONE.................................415 304-6782
EMP: 5
SALES (est): 68.89K Privately Held
Web: www.productive.io
SIC: 7371 Computer software development and applications

(G-1269)
PTA DELAWARE CONGRESS
Also Called: Darley Road Pta
3401 Green St (19703-2065)
PHONE.................................302 792-3916
Jamie Setley, Prin
EMP: 9 EST: 2012
SALES (est): 105.41K Privately Held
Web: www.pto.org
SIC: 8641 Parent-teachers' association

(G-1270)
PULSE TECHNOLOGIES INC ◆
2093 Philadelphia Pike # 2180 (19703-2424)
PHONE.................................785 258-6423
Evgeni Virnik, Prin
EMP: 5 EST: 2022
SALES (est): 106.69K Privately Held
Web: www.pulsetechnologies.com
SIC: 3841 Surgical and medical instruments

(G-1271)
QBEAN INTERNATIONAL LLC
2803 Philadelphia Pike Ste B # 429 (19703-2506)
PHONE.................................917 781-6274
EMP: 5 EST: 2020
SALES (est): 100K Privately Held
Web: www.globalexpress-shippingcenter.com
SIC: 6282 Investment advice

(G-1272)
QREPUBLIK INC
2093 Philadelphia Pike # 2012 (19703-2424)
PHONE.................................559 475-8262
Sergey Vishchipnov, CEO
EMP: 2 EST: 2019
SALES (est): 70.98K Privately Held
SIC: 7372 Prepackaged software

(G-1273)
QUICK COPIES
2605 Philadelphia Pike (19703-2503)
PHONE.................................302 374-0798
EMP: 4 EST: 2019
SALES (est): 90.56K Privately Held
SIC: 2752 Offset printing

(G-1274)
RAWR IMPORTS GROUP LLC
779 Montclair Dr Apt 3 (19703-3615)
P.O. Box 11301 (19850-1301)
PHONE.................................609 271-3455
Kizito Chayee, CEO
EMP: 5 EST: 2019
SALES (est): 100K Privately Held
SIC: 5088 1389 5999 Transportation equipment and supplies; Construction, repair, and dismantling services; Miscellaneous retail stores, nec

(G-1275)
RED SPARK LP
Also Called: 50onred
2093 Philadelphia Pike Ste 1072 (19703-2424)
PHONE.................................215 695-5002
Stephen Gill, Pt
EMP: 42 EST: 2009
SALES (est): 2.93MM Privately Held
Web: www.red-spark.com
SIC: 7371 Computer software development and applications

(G-1276)
REDCIRCLE TECHNOLOGIES INC
2093 Philadelphia Pike (19703-2424)
PHONE.................................844 404-2525
Michael Kadin, CEO
EMP: 12 EST: 2018
SALES (est): 656.08K Privately Held
Web: www.getredcircle.com
SIC: 7371 Computer software development

(G-1277)
RENTDROP INC
2093 Philadelphia Pike Ste 8419 (19703-2424)
PHONE.................................302 250-2525
Remen Okoruwa, CEO
Benjamin Keller, COO
EMP: 8 EST: 2020
SALES (est): 306.16K Privately Held
SIC: 7371 Computer software development and applications

(G-1278)
RESERVE AT DARLEY GREEN
700 Darley Green Dr (19703-3120)
PHONE.................................302 525-8450
EMP: 5 EST: 2019
SALES (est): 85.38K Privately Held
Web: www.livedarley.com
SIC: 6513 Apartment building operators

(G-1279)
RETROLIO GAMES LLC
2093 Philadelphia Pike (19703-2424)
PHONE.................................423 873-8768
EMP: 14
SALES (est): 1.06MM Privately Held
SIC: 5092 Video games

(G-1280)
RMDC INC
698 Naamans Rd (19703-2310)
PHONE.................................302 798-8800
EMP: 5 EST: 2017
SALES (est): 310.1K Privately Held
SIC: 7389 Business services, nec

(G-1281)
ROBO WUNDERKIND INC ◆
2093 Philadelphia Pike Pmb 2664 (19703-2424)
PHONE.................................857 353-8899
Anna Iarotska, CEO
EMP: 10 EST: 2022
SALES (est): 250K Privately Held
SIC: 5087 Service establishment equipment

(G-1282)
ROCKWOOD PROGRAMS INC (PA)
3001 Philadelphia Pike Ste 1 (19703-2580)
PHONE.................................302 765-6000
Glenn Clark, Pr
Frank Huver, *
Darryl Mccallin, VP
EMP: 35 EST: 1996
SQ FT: 5,000
SALES (est): 7.42MM
SALES (corp-wide): 7.42MM Privately Held
Web: www.rockwoodinsurance.com
SIC: 6411 Insurance brokers, nec

(G-1283)
ROMANTIC AI INC
2093 Philadelphia Pike (19703-2424)
PHONE.................................415 404-9188
Pavel Khegai, CEO
EMP: 10
SALES (est): 348.32K Privately Held
SIC: 7371 Computer software development and applications

(G-1284)
RUABIT LLC ◆
2093a Philadelphia Pike Ste 450 (19703-2424)
PHONE.................................765 772-0806
Mingyu Tan, Managing Member
EMP: 4 EST: 2023
SALES (est): 261.29K Privately Held
SIC: 7372 Prepackaged software

(G-1285)
SATORI CI LLC
2093 Philadelphia Pike Apt 2772 (19703-2424)
PHONE.................................302 526-0557
Fernando Arnaboldi, Managing Member
EMP: 5
SALES (est): 199.4K Privately Held
SIC: 7371 Custom computer programming services

(G-1286)
SEAGER INSIGHT
2803 Philadelphia Pike B (19703-2506)
PHONE.................................302 526-0597
EMP: 6 EST: 2018
SALES (est): 172.43K Privately Held
SIC: 8011 Offices and clinics of medical doctors

(G-1287)
SEAN OHAGAN LLC
1302 Society Dr (19703-1743)
PHONE.................................302 798-7572
Sean O'Hagan, Pr
EMP: 5 EST: 2015
SALES (est): 133.13K Privately Held
Web: www.seanohaganinsurance.com
SIC: 6411 Insurance agents and brokers

(G-1288)
SELECT AUTO INC
507 Darley Rd (19703-2208)
PHONE.................................215 423-6522
Bernard O'neill, Prin
EMP: 5 EST: 2011
SALES (est): 75.14K Privately Held
Web: www.select-part.com
SIC: 7538 General automotive repair shops

GEOGRAPHIC SECTION
Claymont - New Castle County (G-1318)

(G-1289)
SHE BASH LLC
2093a Philadelphia Pike Ste 184 (19703-2424)
PHONE..................................302 204-6700
EMP: 7 **EST:** 2018
SALES (est): 402.72K **Privately Held**
Web: www.shebash.io
SIC: 7371 7373 Computer software systems analysis and design, custom; Systems software development services

(G-1290)
SID HARVEY INDUSTRIES INC
130 Hickman Rd Ste 32 (19703-3552)
PHONE..................................302 746-7760
John Dobies, *Brnch Mgr*
EMP: 6
SALES (corp-wide): 426.73MM **Privately Held**
Web: www.sidharvey.com
SIC: 5074 Heating equipment (hydronic)
PA: Sid Harvey Industries, Inc.
605 Locust St Ste A
Garden City NY 11530
516 745-9200

(G-1291)
SIMPLECAR LLC
2803 Philadelphia Pike (19703-2506)
PHONE..................................857 380-7275
EMP: 50 **EST:** 2021
SALES (est): 832.01K **Privately Held**
SIC: 7299 Valet parking

(G-1292)
SMJS CO
2093 Philadelphia Pike Ste 7143de (19703-2424)
PHONE..................................415 326-4441
Mohith Julapaloi, *CEO*
Steven Syverud, *Pr*
EMP: 5 **EST:** 2021
SALES (est): 46.16K **Privately Held**
SIC: 7371 Computer software development and applications

(G-1293)
SOCIAL FINANCE INC
650 Naamans Rd Ste 300 (19703-2300)
PHONE..................................707 473-3000
EMP: 6 **EST:** 2018
SALES (est): 204.08K **Privately Held**
Web: www.socialfinance.org
SIC: 7389 Financial services

(G-1294)
SOKOWATCH INC
2093 Philadelphia Pike (19703-2424)
PHONE..................................805 479-5544
EMP: 20 **EST:** 2013
SALES (est): 1.08MM **Privately Held**
SIC: 7379 Online services technology consultants

(G-1295)
SOMAR GENERAL CONTRACTING LLC
804 Peachtree Rd Apt I (19703-2286)
PHONE..................................302 561-3360
Jimmy Ramos, *Prin*
EMP: 5 **EST:** 2017
SALES (est): 56.76K **Privately Held**
SIC: 1799 Special trade contractors, nec

(G-1296)
SOPHISTOR INC
2093 Philadelphia Pike Ste 1028 (19703-2424)
PHONE..................................415 800-1028
Victor Gonzalez, *CEO*
EMP: 5
SALES (est): 199.4K **Privately Held**
SIC: 7371 Computer software writing services

(G-1297)
SPACE SOFT INC
2803 Philadelphia Pike Ste B597 (19703-2506)
PHONE..................................413 337-7223
Zeeshan Sheikh, *Prin*
EMP: 5
SALES (est): 46.16K **Privately Held**
SIC: 7371 Computer software development and applications

(G-1298)
SPECTRUM MILL INC ✪
2093a Philadelphia Pike Ste 323 (19703-2424)
PHONE..................................941 815-9454
Abdulla Albastaki, *Prin*
EMP: 10 **EST:** 2022
SALES (est): 215.45K **Privately Held**
SIC: 8049 Offices of health practitioner

(G-1299)
STACLAR INC
2093 Philadelphia Pike (19703-2424)
PHONE..................................628 213-1140
Joel Carvalho, *CEO*
Matthias Merkel, *Ex VP*
EMP: 7 **EST:** 2019
SALES (est): 2.5MM **Privately Held**
SIC: 7389 Music distribution systems

(G-1300)
STAIRCASE INC
2093 Philadelphia Pike # 2024 (19703-2424)
PHONE..................................215 693-5686
Adam Kalamchi, *CEO*
EMP: 25 **EST:** 2019
SALES (est): 1.26MM **Privately Held**
SIC: 7373 Systems integration services

(G-1301)
STARLITERS DANCE STUDIO INC
14 Brookview Ave (19703-2902)
PHONE..................................302 798-6330
Brian Wiells, *Owner*
EMP: 8 **EST:** 1994
SALES (est): 60.57K **Privately Held**
Web: www.starlitersdance.com
SIC: 8641 Civic and social associations

(G-1302)
STEAGLE CONSULTING GROUP LLC
950 Ridge Rd (19703-3523)
PHONE..................................302 439-4301
Kevin Runge, *Prin*
EMP: 5 **EST:** 2016
SALES (est): 79.42K **Privately Held**
SIC: 8999 Scientific consulting

(G-1303)
STEPHEN HANNIG
2601 Washington Ave (19703-2453)
PHONE..................................302 792-1342
EMP: 5 **EST:** 2011
SALES (est): 63.83K **Privately Held**
SIC: 0782 Lawn care services

(G-1304)
STM CONSULTING INC
2093a Philadelphia Pike Ste 133 (19703-2424)
PHONE..................................408 341-6900
Vidur Gupta, *Dir*
Madhu Nairr, *VP*
EMP: 10 **EST:** 2020
SALES (est): 1.07MM **Privately Held**
Web: www.consultstm.com
SIC: 5045 7361 7363 7371 Computers, peripherals, and software; Employment agencies; Help supply services; Custom computer programming services

(G-1305)
STOLTZ REALTY CO
Also Called: Society Hill Apts
7120 Society Dr (19703-1773)
PHONE..................................302 798-8500
Sue Carson, *Mgr*
EMP: 10
SALES (corp-wide): 2.49MM **Privately Held**
Web: www.galmangroup.com
SIC: 6531 6513 Real estate brokers and agents; Apartment building operators
PA: Stoltz Realty Co
3704 Kennett Pike Ste 200
Wilmington DE 19807
302 656-2852

(G-1306)
STONEYBROOK PRSRVTION ASSOC LL
Also Called: Stoneybrook Apartments
1117 Cedartree Ct (19703-2244)
PHONE..................................302 764-9430
EMP: 10 **EST:** 2013
SALES (est): 406.87K **Privately Held**
SIC: 6513 Apartment building operators

(G-1307)
SUBSCRIPT INC
2093 Philadelphia Pike Ste 5554 (19703-2424)
PHONE..................................302 470-8144
EMP: 6 **EST:** 2021
SALES (est): 46.16K **Privately Held**
Web: www.subscript.com
SIC: 7371 Computer software development and applications

(G-1308)
SUPEROPS INC
Also Called: Superops
2093 Philadelphia Pike # 2105 (19703-2424)
PHONE..................................510 330-2676
Arvind Parthiban, *Pr*
EMP: 5 **EST:** 2019
SALES (est): 256.9K **Privately Held**
SIC: 7371 Computer software development

(G-1309)
TERNARY INC
2093 Philadelphia Pike Ste 5312 (19703-2424)
PHONE..................................650 759-5277
Aleksandr Kipervarg, *CEO*
EMP: 30 **EST:** 2020
SALES (est): 4MM **Privately Held**
Web: www.ternary.app
SIC: 7371 Software programming applications

(G-1310)
TERRA SYSTEMS INC
130 Hickman Rd Ste 1 (19703-3519)
PHONE..................................302 798-9553
Richard L Raymond Junior, *Pr*
Michael Lee, *VP*
EMP: 24 **EST:** 1992
SQ FT: 1,500
SALES (est): 4.98MM **Privately Held**
Web: www.terrasystems.net
SIC: 8748 4959 Environmental consultant; Environmental cleanup services

(G-1311)
TERRA SYSTEMS OF DELAWARE LLC
130 Hickman Rd Ste 1 (19703-3519)
PHONE..................................302 798-9553
EMP: 7
SALES (est): 298.62K **Privately Held**
SIC: 2899 Oils and essential oils

(G-1312)
THOMAS E CAMERON
Also Called: AAA Tree & Shrub of Delaware
833 Causez Ave (19703-1033)
PHONE..................................302 345-6708
Thomas E Cameron, *Prin*
EMP: 5 **EST:** 2010
SALES (est): 72.8K **Privately Held**
SIC: 0783 Planting, pruning, and trimming services

(G-1313)
THRIVE AGRITECH
2093 Philadelphia Pike # 9047 (19703-2424)
PHONE..................................800 205-7216
Brian Bennett, *CEO*
EMP: 10 **EST:** 2015
SALES (est): 206.98K **Privately Held**
Web: www.thriveagritech.com
SIC: 8748 Business consulting, nec

(G-1314)
TOMAROS CHANGE
357 Lenape Way (19703-3323)
PHONE..................................856 542-8861
Ferdinand Pilgrim, *Prin*
EMP: 6 **EST:** 2016
SALES (est): 78.59K **Privately Held**
Web: www.tomaros-change.org
SIC: 8322 General counseling services

(G-1315)
TOMAROS CHANGE
1261 Parish Ave (19703-3338)
PHONE..................................844 222-8500
EMP: 5 **EST:** 2019
SALES (est): 167.5K **Privately Held**
Web: www.tomaros-change.org
SIC: 8322 General counseling services

(G-1316)
TRANSFORMIFY INC
2093 Philadelphia Pike (19703-2424)
PHONE..................................302 205-0685
EMP: 5
SALES (est): 70.36K **Privately Held**
SIC: 7373 Computer integrated systems design

(G-1317)
TRINITY ENTERPRISES LLC
3230 Philadelphia Pike (19703-3103)
PHONE..................................302 449-1301
EMP: 5 **EST:** 2008
SALES (est): 397.55K **Privately Held**
SIC: 8748 Business consulting, nec

(G-1318)
TRIPROBOTICS INC
Also Called: Triprobotics
2093 Philadelphia Pike # 2 (19703-2424)
PHONE..................................646 798-7137
Vladimir Melnic, *CEO*
Serghei Culicovschi, *CEO*
EMP: 11 **EST:** 2021
SALES (est): 521.63K **Privately Held**

Claymont - New Castle County (G-1319)

SIC: 7371 Computer software development and applications

(G-1319)
TRIUMPH LABS INC
2093 Philadelphia Pike Ste 4204 (19703-2424)
PHONE..................561 886-7121
Jared Geller, *CEO*
Jacob Brooks, *Pr*
EMP: 5 EST: 2020
SALES (est): 46.16K **Privately Held**
SIC: 7371 Computer software development and applications

(G-1320)
TUKEL INC
2093 Philadelphia Pike Ste 2108 (19703-2424)
PHONE..................302 520-2380
Cenk Tukel, *CEO*
EMP: 10 EST: 2018
SALES (est): 356.58K **Privately Held**
SIC: 8721 Accounting, auditing, and bookkeeping

(G-1321)
ULTIMATE MATERIAL SPRAYING LLC
617 Delancey Pl (19703-1928)
PHONE..................302 723-2356
EMP: 6 EST: 2019
SALES (est): 400K **Privately Held**
SIC: 8711 Building construction consultant

(G-1322)
UNITED CHECK CASHING
Also Called: Gdf Financial
95 Naamans Rd Ste 37a (19703)
PHONE..................302 792-2545
EMP: 5 EST: 1995
SQ FT: 1,600
SALES (est): 684.17K **Privately Held**
Web: www.unitedcheckcashing.com
SIC: 6099 Check cashing agencies

(G-1323)
UNLIMITED RESTORATION INC
130 Hickman Rd (19703-3552)
PHONE..................302 439-4213
EMP: 8 EST: 2017
SALES (est): 32.92K **Privately Held**
Web: www.urinow.com
SIC: 8322 Alcoholism counseling, nontreatment

(G-1324)
UPBOUND GROUP INC
Also Called: Rent-A-Center
333 Naamans Rd Ste 21 (19703-2808)
PHONE..................302 798-0663
EMP: 5
Web: www.rentacenter.com
SIC: 7359 Appliance rental
PA: Upbound Group, Inc.
5501 Headquarters Dr
Plano TX 75024

(G-1325)
URSPAYCE INC
2093 Philadelphia Pike (19703-2424)
PHONE..................302 440-2880
Priyank Jain, *CEO*
EMP: 8
SALES (est): 312.73K **Privately Held**
SIC: 7373 Systems software development services

(G-1326)
VARIDA-TECH INC
2093 Philadelphia Pike (19703-2424)
PHONE..................781 819-0259
Ram Majhi, *Dir*
EMP: 15
SALES (est): 505.06K **Privately Held**
Web: www.varida-tech.com
SIC: 7361 Employment agencies

(G-1327)
VEHO TECH INC
2093 Philadelphia Pike Ste 8346 (19703-2424)
PHONE..................720 466-3788
Itamar Zur, *CEO*
EMP: 28 EST: 2017
SALES (est): 13.91MM **Privately Held**
Web: www.shipveho.com
SIC: 7372 Prepackaged software

(G-1328)
VIRASOFT CORPORATION
2093 Philadelphia Pike # 2627te (19703-2424)
PHONE..................281 851-9080
EMP: 5 EST: 2021
SALES (est): 72.91K **Privately Held**
SIC: 8742 Management consulting services

(G-1329)
VISION LIMOUSINE
21 Benning Rd (19703-1205)
PHONE..................302 584-0622
Darryl Bryant, *Pt*
EMP: 6
SALES (est): 130K **Privately Held**
SIC: 4111 Airport limousine, scheduled service

(G-1330)
VISUAL COMMUNICATIONS INC
Also Called: Vci
3724 Philadelphia Pike (19703-3412)
PHONE..................302 792-9500
Robert S Burt, *Pr*
EMP: 7 EST: 1990
SQ FT: 1,800
SALES (est): 684.5K **Privately Held**
Web: www.electronicsigns.com
SIC: 7629 5999 Business machine repair, electric; Communication equipment

(G-1331)
VIVKY OF DELAWARE INC
7811 Governor Printz Blvd (19703-2615)
PHONE..................302 798-9914
Sam Patel, *Genl Mgr*
EMP: 17 EST: 2007
SALES (est): 95.03K **Privately Held**
SIC: 7011 Hotel, franchised

(G-1332)
VOXPOPIN INC
Also Called: Vqxpopin
2803 Philadelphia Pike (19703-2506)
P.O. Box 574 (19703-0574)
PHONE..................202 567-7483
Lauren Solomon, *CEO*
EMP: 2 EST: 2021
SALES (est): 87.4K **Privately Held**
SIC: 7372 Application computer software

(G-1333)
WAVETEC NORTH AMERICA INC ◎
2093 Philadelphia Pike (19703-2424)
PHONE..................323 284-5084
Tobias Bessone, *CEO*
EMP: 50 EST: 2022
SALES (est): 1.17MM **Privately Held**
SIC: 7379 Online services technology consultants

(G-1334)
WE GOT CARS 4 CASH INC ◎
Also Called: Connected Capital LLC
1507 Historical Way Unit 7 (19703-3342)
PHONE..................215 399-6978
David Ware, *CEO*
EMP: 5 EST: 2022
SALES (est): 245.73K **Privately Held**
SIC: 4741 7389 Rental of railroad cars; Business Activities at Non-Commercial Site

(G-1335)
WEELWORK INC
619 New York Ave (19703-1957)
PHONE..................800 546-8607
EMP: 5 EST: 2019
SALES (est): 209.45K **Privately Held**
Web: www.weelwork.pro
SIC: 8742 Human resource consulting services

(G-1336)
WHEREBYUS ENTERPRISES INC
2093 Philadelphia Pike (19703-2424)
PHONE..................305 988-0808
Christopher Sopher, *CEO*
Christopher Sopher, *Pr*
EMP: 15 EST: 2014
SALES (est): 939.57K **Privately Held**
Web: www.whereby.us
SIC: 2741 5734 Internet publishing and broadcasting; Software, business and non-game

(G-1337)
WILMINGTON SAVINGS FUND SOC
Also Called: Wsfs Bank
2105 Philadelphia Pike (19703-2426)
PHONE..................302 792-6435
EMP: 5
SALES (corp-wide): 641.85MM **Publicly Held**
SIC: 6022 State commercial banks
HQ: Wilmington Savings Fund Society
500 Delaware Ave
Wilmington DE 19801
302 792-6000

(G-1338)
WILSON TRAVEL AND GETAWAY
206 Woodgreen Ct (19703-1318)
PHONE..................302 559-3412
Lola Wilson, *Prin*
EMP: 9 EST: 2010
SALES (est): 80.19K **Privately Held**
SIC: 4724 Tourist agency arranging transport, lodging and car rental

(G-1339)
WOODACRES ASSOCIATES LP
Also Called: Woodacres Apts
915 Cedartree Ln (19703-1687)
PHONE..................302 792-0243
Cheri Prather, *Pt*
EMP: 10 EST: 1960
SQ FT: 30,000
SALES (est): 578.87K **Privately Held**
SIC: 6513 Apartment building operators

(G-1340)
WRIGHT CHOICE CHILD CARE
3031 W Court Ave (19703-2020)
PHONE..................302 798-0758
Carmen Wright, *Prin*
EMP: 5 EST: 2011
SALES (est): 199.59K **Privately Held**
SIC: 8351 Child day care services

(G-1341)
XEROICTECH INC
2803 Philadelphia Pike Ste B (19703-2506)
PHONE..................302 252-1617
Ripan Bhattacharjee, *CEO*
EMP: 15
SALES (est): 505.06K **Privately Held**
SIC: 7373 Systems software development services

(G-1342)
YANIMED LLC
2093a Philadelphia Pike Ste 286 (19703-2424)
PHONE..................929 556-6522
EMP: 15 EST: 2021
SALES (est): 1.05MM **Privately Held**
Web: www.yanimed.com
SIC: 5047 Medical equipment and supplies

(G-1343)
YES HARDSOFT SOLUTIONS INC
351 Lenape Way (19703-3323)
PHONE..................609 632-0397
EMP: 5
SALES (corp-wide): 1.44MM **Privately Held**
Web: www.yesgroups.net
SIC: 7379 Computer related consulting services
PA: Yes Hardsoft Solutions, Inc
3626 Silverside Rd
Wilmington DE 19810
609 632-0397

(G-1344)
ZARLA INC
2093 Philadelphia Pike Ste 2555 (19703-2424)
PHONE..................833 469-2752
Adam Seabrook, *CEO*
EMP: 5
SALES (est): 199.4K **Privately Held**
Web: www.zarla.com
SIC: 7371 Computer software development and applications

(G-1345)
ZENBANX HOLDING LTD (DH)
650 Naamans Rd Ste 300 (19703-2300)
PHONE..................310 749-3101
Arkadi Kuhlmann, *CEO*
Arkadi Kuhlman, *CEO*
EMP: 6 EST: 2012
SALES (est): 2.05MM
SALES (corp-wide): 1.76B **Publicly Held**
SIC: 7371 Computer software development
HQ: Social Finance, Inc.
234 1st St
San Francisco CA 94105
415 930-4467

(G-1346)
ZENKODERS LLC ◎
2803 Philadelphia Pike Ste B429 (19703-2506)
PHONE..................302 261-2627
EMP: 6 EST: 2022
SALES (est): 68.89K **Privately Held**
SIC: 7371 Computer software development and applications

Clayton
Kent County

(G-1347)
ABRAHAMS SEED LLC
246 Coldwater Dr (19938-3902)
P.O. Box 374 (19938-0374)

PHONE..................302 588-1913
EMP: 6 **EST:** 2009
SALES (est): 123.81K **Privately Held**
SIC: 7349 Building maintenance services, nec

(G-1348)
ALLIANCE BUS DEV CONCEPTS LLC
1480 Alley Corner Rd (19938-2630)
PHONE..................803 814-4004
EMP: 10
SALES (est): 316.2K **Privately Held**
SIC: 8742 8748 7389 Construction project management consultant; Telecommunications consultant

(G-1349)
ANGLIN ASSOCIATES LLC
Also Called: Anglin Aircraft Recovery Svc
4901 Holletts Corner Rd (19938-3156)
PHONE..................302 653-3500
EMP: 10 **EST:** 2003
Web: www.anglinair.com
SIC: 6719 Personal holding companies, except banks

(G-1350)
ARB HEAVENLY HOMES LLC
41 Andover Branch Rd (19938-3947)
PHONE..................215 919-8272
EMP: 5 **EST:** 2019
SALES (est): 119.02K **Privately Held**
SIC: 6531 Real estate leasing and rentals

(G-1351)
ATLANTIC TRACTOR LLC
Also Called: John Deere Authorized Dealer
315 Main St (19938-7702)
P.O. Box 1125 (19938-1125)
PHONE..................302 653-8536
Mike Kern, *Mgr*
EMP: 22
SALES (corp-wide): 51.66MM **Privately Held**
Web: www.deere.com
SIC: 5083 Agricultural machinery and equipment
PA: Atlantic Tractor Llc
720 Wheeler School Rd
Whiteford MD 21160
410 457-3696

(G-1352)
BALLARD BUILDERS LLC
101 S Bassett St (19938-7714)
PHONE..................302 363-1677
EMP: 11 **EST:** 2002
SQ FT: 1,500
SALES (est): 1.4MM **Privately Held**
SIC: 1542 Commercial and office buildings, prefabricated erection

(G-1353)
BARIATRIC BEAUTIFUL BARBII LLC
148 Parma Dr (19938-4203)
PHONE..................302 279-6938
EMP: 10 **EST:** 2015
SALES (est): 160K **Privately Held**
SIC: 8049 Nurses and other medical assistants

(G-1354)
BEYOND DETAILS
117 Cool Breeze Dr (19938-3503)
PHONE..................302 223-6156
David Strong, *Prin*
EMP: 5 **EST:** 2014
SALES (est): 38.83K **Privately Held**
SIC: 7542 Washing and polishing, automotive

(G-1355)
BLAKGOLD INNOVATIVE INC
96 Penrose Branch Rd (19938-3981)
PHONE..................302 220-0530
Ryan Hamilton, *Owner*
EMP: 5 **EST:** 2002
SALES (est): 40.57K **Privately Held**
Web: www.dnbar.com
SIC: 2741 Miscellaneous publishing

(G-1356)
CLAYTON FIRE COMPANY PRPTS LLC
300 East St (19938-7707)
P.O. Box 1050 (19938-1050)
PHONE..................302 653-7317
EMP: 9 **EST:** 2015
SALES (est): 431.04K **Privately Held**
Web: www.clayton45.com
SIC: 7389 Fire protection service other than forestry or public

(G-1357)
COUNTRY ROADS VETERINARY SVC
2681 Shaws Corner Rd (19938-3222)
PHONE..................302 514-9087
EMP: 6 **EST:** 2012
SALES (est): 313.31K **Privately Held**
Web: www.myroadvet.com
SIC: 0742 Animal hospital services, pets and other animal specialties

(G-1358)
D J BYLER
5290 Judith Rd (19938-2820)
PHONE..................302 653-4602
Danny Byler, *Prin*
EMP: 6 **EST:** 2005
SALES (est): 105.14K **Privately Held**
SIC: 1751 Carpentry work

(G-1359)
DEL FAB CONSTRUCTION LLC
2373 Harvey Straughn Rd (19938-9729)
P.O. Box 645 (19938-0645)
PHONE..................302 943-9131
Jaclyn Czachorowski, *Pr*
EMP: 5 **EST:** 2010
SALES (est): 256.44K **Privately Held**
Web: www.delfabconstruction.com
SIC: 1521 Single-family housing construction

(G-1360)
DULIN BROTHERS
938 Blackiston Church Rd (19938-2301)
PHONE..................302 653-5365
Lee Dulin Junior, *Pt*
Donald Dulin, *Pt*
Norman Dulin, *Pt*
Donald Dulin Junior, *Pt*
William Dulin, *Pt*
EMP: 6 **EST:** 1929
SALES (est): 898.93K **Privately Held**
SIC: 0241 0119 Dairy farms; Feeder grains

(G-1361)
EAGLE BUILDING AND GROUNDS
2817 Shaws Corner Rd (19938-3220)
PHONE..................302 508-5403
Ken Duphily, *Prin*
EMP: 5 **EST:** 2017
SALES (est): 148.27K **Privately Held**
SIC: 0782 Lawn and garden services

(G-1362)
EAGLE IRRIGATION INC
837 Daisey Rd (19938-2976)
PHONE..................302 223-1176
James Kreck, *Pr*
EMP: 6 **EST:** 2005
SALES (est): 200.42K **Privately Held**
SIC: 4971 Irrigation systems

(G-1363)
EAGLE MHC COMPANY
Also Called: Eagle Group
100 Industrial Blvd (19938-8900)
PHONE..................302 653-3000
Larry Mcallister, *Pr*
▲ **EMP:** 380 **EST:** 1998
SALES (est): 109.85MM
SALES (corp-wide): 109.85MM **Privately Held**
Web: www.eaglegrp.com
SIC: 3589 8099 Commercial cooking and foodwarming equipment; Blood related health services
PA: Metal Masters Foodservice Equipment Co., Inc.
100 Industrial Blvd
Clayton DE 19938
302 653-3000

(G-1364)
EAST COAST AVIATION LLC
1505 Clayton Delaney Rd (19938-9781)
PHONE..................302 650-9889
Sean Waterland, *Prin*
EMP: 6 **EST:** 2016
SALES (est): 252.09K **Privately Held**
SIC: 4581 Airports, flying fields, and services

(G-1365)
EASTERN SHORE LITE INDUSTRIES
5908 Judith Rd (19938-2827)
PHONE..................302 653-8687
Michael A Briggs, *Prin*
EMP: 2 **EST:** 2000
SALES (est): 92.83K **Privately Held**
SIC: 3999 Manufacturing industries, nec

(G-1366)
EZ MANUFACTURING COMPANY LLC
500 N Bassett St (19938-7782)
P.O. Box 63 (19977-0063)
PHONE..................302 653-6567
Eugene Fox, *Managing Member*
EMP: 5 **EST:** 2007
SALES (est): 718.88K **Privately Held**
Web: www.formationcables.com
SIC: 5014 Tire and tube repair materials

(G-1367)
FOREST VIEW NURSERY
1313 Blackbird Forest Rd (19938-9747)
PHONE..................302 653-7757
John Ellingsworth Iii, *Pr*
Irene Ellingsworth, *Sec*
EMP: 8 **EST:** 1951
SQ FT: 5,800
SALES (est): 715.77K **Privately Held**
Web: www.forestviewnursery.com
SIC: 0181 Nursery stock, growing of

(G-1368)
GATEWAY CONSTRUCTION INC
498 Sudlersville Rd (19938-2772)
P.O. Box 308 (19953-0308)
PHONE..................302 653-4400
Mark Kohout, *Pr*
Cynthia Swyka, *VP*
EMP: 7 **EST:** 2001
SQ FT: 1,500
SALES (est): 1.05MM **Privately Held**
Web: www.gatewayconstructionofdelaware.com
SIC: 1799 Building site preparation

(G-1369)
GEORGE SWIRE SR
790 Daisey Rd (19938-2971)
PHONE..................302 690-6995
EMP: 4 **EST:** 2016
SALES (est): 25.09K **Privately Held**
Web: www.georgesplasmacuttershop.com
SIC: 7692 Welding repair

(G-1370)
HEROES SELF DEFENSE FOUNDATION
579 Coldwater Dr (19938-3913)
PHONE..................609 335-2391
Ryan Quackenbush, *Prin*
EMP: 6 **EST:** 2018
SALES (est): 21.8K **Privately Held**
SIC: 8641 Civic and social associations

(G-1371)
IMPACT INSURANCE AGENCY
Also Called: Nationwide
312 Main St (19938-7701)
P.O. Box 145 (19938-0145)
PHONE..................302 363-7785
Cory Thomas, *Prin*
EMP: 5 **EST:** 2017
SALES (est): 450.87K **Privately Held**
Web: www.impactmyinsurance.com
SIC: 6411 Insurance agents, nec

(G-1372)
INTEGRITY CLEANING SVCS LLC
331 Coldwater Dr (19938-3916)
P.O. Box 1431 (19701-7431)
PHONE..................302 353-9315
EMP: 6 **EST:** 2009
SALES (est): 119.33K **Privately Held**
SIC: 7699 Cleaning services

(G-1373)
INTEGRITY MGT SOLUTION INC
312 Seeneytown Rd (19938-3248)
PHONE..................302 270-8976
Henry Mast, *Prin*
EMP: 5 **EST:** 2014
SALES (est): 483.18K **Privately Held**
SIC: 1521 Single-family housing construction

(G-1374)
ITS ALL ABOUT YOU MSSGE&BDYWRK
77 E Radison Run (19938-3831)
PHONE..................302 563-3443
Karyn Malloch-bailey, *Prin*
EMP: 6 **EST:** 2011
SALES (est): 120.63K **Privately Held**
SIC: 7299 Massage parlor

(G-1375)
JEFF HOPKINS LLC
572 Delaney Maryland Rd (19938-9541)
PHONE..................302 653-6413
Jeff Hopkins, *Prin*
EMP: 6 **EST:** 2004
SALES (est): 100K **Privately Held**
Web: www.perfectdomain.com
SIC: 0191 General farms, primarily crop

(G-1376)
JILL L ALFREE
2308 Downs Chapel Rd (19938-2012)
PHONE..................302 653-9107
Jill Alfree, *Prin*
EMP: 5 **EST:** 2013
SALES (est): 214.1K **Privately Held**
SIC: 7389 Design services

Clayton - Kent County (G-1377) — GEOGRAPHIC SECTION

(G-1377)
JUNES TOUCH
59 Gravelly Run Branch Rd (19938-3934)
PHONE................................631 603-9293
Jaz Williams, *Prin*
EMP: 5 EST: 2017
SALES (est): 46.99K **Privately Held**
SIC: 7699 Cleaning services

(G-1378)
KAIROS LANDSCAPING
5644 Millington Rd (19938-2515)
PHONE................................302 399-4724
EMP: 5 EST: 2013
SALES (est): 221.81K **Privately Held**
SIC: 0781 Landscape services

(G-1379)
KATHLEENS CREATIONS
137 Downs Chapel Rd (19938-2729)
PHONE................................302 492-8749
Kathleen Fairchild, *Prin*
EMP: 5 EST: 2015
SALES (est): 48.67K **Privately Held**
SIC: 7231 Beauty shops

(G-1380)
KEES COOKIES & CUPCAKES LLC
308 Main St (19938-7701)
PHONE................................302 223-6784
Niya Boldne, *Prin*
EMP: 7 EST: 2017
SQ FT: 450
SALES (est): 949.37K **Privately Held**
Web: www.keesbakeshop.com
SIC: 5149 Cookies

(G-1381)
KENTON CHAIR SHOP
291 Blackiston Rd (19938-2266)
PHONE................................302 653-2411
Fred Zimmerman, *Pt*
EMP: 10 EST: 1984
SALES (est): 936.18K **Privately Held**
SIC: 2511 5712 Chairs, household, except upholstered: wood; Furniture stores

(G-1382)
KRM STABLES
1225 Clyton Grenspring Rd (19938-9731)
PHONE................................302 653-3838
EMP: 5 EST: 2008
SALES (est): 97.47K **Privately Held**
SIC: 0752 Training services, horses (except racing horses)

(G-1383)
LARKINS BUS SERVICE LLC
512 S Bassett St (19938-7736)
PHONE................................302 653-5855
EMP: 6 EST: 2007
SALES (est): 138.63K **Privately Held**
SIC: 4151 School buses

(G-1384)
MARY E MAHONEY
44 Christiana River Dr (19938-3921)
PHONE................................302 757-9656
Mary Mahoney, *Mgr*
EMP: 5 EST: 2017
SALES (est): 166.23K **Privately Held**
SIC: 8049 Offices of health practitioner

(G-1385)
METAL MSTERS FDSERVICE EQP INC (PA)
Also Called: Eagle Foodservice
100 Industrial Blvd (19938-8900)
PHONE................................302 653-3000
Larry N Mcallister, *Pr*
Betty Mcallister, *VP*
Darko Orsic, *
Michele Poperechny, *
◆ EMP: 186 EST: 1978
SQ FT: 475,000
SALES (est): 109.85MM
SALES (corp-wide): 109.85MM **Privately Held**
Web: www.eaglemhc.com
SIC: 3589 3556 Commercial cooking and foodwarming equipment; Food products machinery

(G-1386)
MGL SCREEN PRINTING
47 S Longwood Ln (19938-1934)
PHONE................................302 450-6250
EMP: 3 EST: 2014
SALES (est): 54.92K **Privately Held**
SIC: 2752 Commercial printing, lithographic

(G-1387)
MONROE MECHANICAL CONTRACTING
370 Christiana River Dr (19938-3925)
PHONE................................302 223-6020
Jay R Beers, *Pr*
EMP: 5 EST: 1987
SALES (est): 393.6K **Privately Held**
SIC: 1711 Warm air heating and air conditioning contractor

(G-1388)
MORGAN LOUISE FNDTN LLC
148 Parma Ln (19938-4203)
PHONE................................302 670-5792
EMP: 10 EST: 2017
SALES (est): 150K **Privately Held**
Web: www.morganlouisefoundation.org
SIC: 8051 7389 Skilled nursing care facilities ; Business services, nec

(G-1389)
MRT ENTERPRISES INC (PA)
286 Whitetail Run (19938-4108)
PHONE................................302 593-3070
Mark Edward Thompson, *Prin*
EMP: 5 EST: 2013
SALES (est): 233.53K
SALES (corp-wide): 233.53K **Privately Held**
Web: www.fastfix.com
SIC: 8748 Business consulting, nec

(G-1390)
NATHAN DAVID FRETZ
Also Called: B C Builders
2362 Clayton Delaney Rd (19938-9512)
PHONE................................302 218-3338
EMP: 5 EST: 2009
SALES (est): 67.31K **Privately Held**
SIC: 1521 New construction, single-family houses

(G-1391)
NEXSIGNS LLC
711 Coldwater Dr (19938-3911)
PHONE................................302 508-2615
EMP: 4 EST: 2016
SALES (est): 82.1K **Privately Held**
SIC: 2752 Commercial printing, lithographic

(G-1392)
NORTH EAST HIGH SCHL FOOTBALL
201 Stirrup Rd (19938-4672)
PHONE................................330 338-2993
Christopher Schleich, *Prin*
EMP: 5 EST: 2017
SALES (est): 41.89K **Privately Held**
SIC: 7941 Football club

(G-1393)
NU - VISION AUTO GLASS LLC
622 Hopewell Dr (19938-2229)
PHONE................................302 389-8700
Anthony Campagnini, *Asst Sec*
EMP: 5 EST: 2018
SALES (est): 31.07K **Privately Held**
Web: www.nvautoglass.com
SIC: 7538 General automotive repair shops

(G-1394)
PCA PTO
273 W Duck Creek Rd (19938-7719)
PHONE................................302 250-8377
Colleen Owens, *Prin*
EMP: 8 EST: 2018
SALES (est): 86.24K **Privately Held**
Web: www.pcapto.org
SIC: 8641 Parent-teachers' association

(G-1395)
PERFECTLY OK PRODUCTIONS
846 Underwoods Corner Rd (19938-2244)
PHONE................................302 233-3208
EMP: 5 EST: 2017
SALES (est): 56.22K **Privately Held**
SIC: 7822 Motion picture and tape distribution

(G-1396)
PERSON 2 PERSON TRNSP LLC
129 Spelt Dr (19938-7780)
PHONE................................302 900-1061
EMP: 7
SALES (est): 313.65K **Privately Held**
SIC: 4789 Transportation services, nec

(G-1397)
PIERCE PT INC
80 Thomas Davis Dr (19938-2570)
PHONE................................302 659-0821
EMP: 5 EST: 2010
SALES (est): 50.11K **Privately Held**
SIC: 8049 Offices of health practitioner

(G-1398)
POWER ELECTRONICS INC
310 S Bassett St (19938-7711)
P.O. Box 537 (19938-0537)
PHONE................................302 653-4822
John Hubbard, *VP*
Karen Taylor, *
EMP: 24 EST: 1988
SQ FT: 20,000
SALES (est): 935.62K **Privately Held**
SIC: 3444 3613 Sheet metal specialties, not stamped; Control panels, electric

(G-1399)
PREFERRED ENVIROMENTAL
2300 W Fourth St Ste E104 (19938)
PHONE................................610 364-1106
EMP: 8 EST: 2011
SALES (est): 389.88K **Privately Held**
SIC: 4959 Environmental cleanup services

(G-1400)
RAYMOND M SMITH JR
2752 Downs Chapel Rd (19938-2016)
PHONE................................302 670-3801
Raymond M Smith Junior, *Prin*
EMP: 5 EST: 2010
SALES (est): 163.61K **Privately Held**
SIC: 1522 Residential construction, nec

(G-1401)
RISA MALONE MA CCC-SLP
192 Riverdale Ln (19938-3823)
PHONE................................352 536-9187
EMP: 5 EST: 2011
SALES (est): 59.65K **Privately Held**
SIC: 8049 Speech pathologist

(G-1402)
RUSSELL D EARNEST & ASSOC
P.O. Box 1132 (19938-1132)
PHONE................................302 659-0730
Russell Earnest, *Prin*
EMP: 5 EST: 1997
SALES (est): 70.11K **Privately Held**
SIC: 2741 Miscellaneous publishing

(G-1403)
S&S PAINTING LLC
58 Sammon Dr (19938-3298)
PHONE................................302 766-2476
James Sayers, *Prin*
EMP: 5 EST: 2015
SALES (est): 95.33K **Privately Held**
Web: www.sspaintingdelaware.com
SIC: 1721 Painting and paper hanging

(G-1404)
SCOTTONS SANITATION LLC
643 Deer Antler Rd (19938-2536)
PHONE................................302 382-5743
Donald Scotton, *Prin*
EMP: 5 EST: 2014
SALES (est): 37.76K **Privately Held**
SIC: 4953 Rubbish collection and disposal

(G-1405)
SELECT STAINLESS PRODUCTS LLC
100 Industrial Blvd (19938-8900)
P.O. Box 1129 (19938-1129)
PHONE................................302 653-3062
Jason Keller Managing, *Prin*
EMP: 7 EST: 2014
SALES (est): 404.58K **Privately Held**
SIC: 3914 Silverware and plated ware

(G-1406)
STAN T LEPKOWSKI
94 Downs Chapel Rd (19938-2701)
PHONE................................302 393-9093
Stan T Lepkowski, *Prin*
EMP: 5 EST: 2009
SALES (est): 93.5K **Privately Held**
SIC: 7389 Business Activities at Non-Commercial Site

(G-1407)
SUMMERFIELD ELEC SOLUTIONS LLC
1633 Clayton Delaney Rd (19938-9710)
PHONE................................302 824-3045
Eric M Summerfield, *Prin*
EMP: 7 EST: 2019
SALES (est): 939.87K **Privately Held**
SIC: 4911 Electric services

(G-1408)
WILSON SEALCOATING
1597 Holletts Corner Rd (19938-2925)
PHONE................................302 653-0201
Linda K Wilson, *Prin*
EMP: 6 EST: 2016
SALES (est): 107.97K **Privately Held**
SIC: 1611 Surfacing and paving

Dagsboro
Sussex County

(G-1409)
A G CONCRETE WORKS LLC
Also Called: AG Concrete Works
31883 New St (19939-3832)

GEOGRAPHIC SECTION
Dagsboro - Sussex County (G-1437)

PHONE..................302 841-2227
EMP: 5 **EST:** 2009
SALES (est): 382.42K **Privately Held**
SIC: 1771 Concrete work

(G-1410)
ALANA ROSE FOUNDATION INC
35017 Hoot Owl Ln (19939-3403)
PHONE..................302 519-5973
EMP: 5 **EST:** 2016
SALES (est): 38.73K **Privately Held**
SIC: 8641 Civic and social associations

(G-1411)
ALLEN HARIM FOODS LLC
26867 Nine Foot Rd (19939-4429)
PHONE..................302 732-9511
Frank Wills, *Mgr*
EMP: 252
SALES (corp-wide): 345.31MM **Privately Held**
Web: www.allenharimllc.com
SIC: 0254 Poultry hatcheries
HQ: Allen Harim Foods, Llc
  29984 Pinnacle Way
  Millsboro DE 19966
  302 629-9136

(G-1412)
ARCTIC HEATING AND AC
28896 Hudson Rd (19939-3845)
PHONE..................302 537-6988
Russell Queen, *Owner*
EMP: 7 **EST:** 2015
SALES (est): 208.69K **Privately Held**
Web: www.arcticheatandair.com
SIC: 1711 Warm air heating and air conditioning contractor

(G-1413)
ARMY NATIONAL GUARD DELAWARE
Also Called: O M S 5
Rd 2 (19939)
P.O. Box 214c (19939-0214)
PHONE..................302 855-7456
Paul Baker, *Brnch Mgr*
EMP: 6
SALES (corp-wide): 11.27B **Privately Held**
SIC: 7538 9711 General automotive repair shops; National Guard
HQ: National Guard, Delaware
  1 Vavala Way
  New Castle DE 19720

(G-1414)
ATLANTIC ELEVATORS
Also Called: De Atlantic Elevator
27515 Hodges Ln (19939-5404)
PHONE..................302 537-8304
EMP: 7 **EST:** 1989
SALES (est): 1.11MM **Privately Held**
Web: www.deatlanticelevator.com
SIC: 5084 3534 Elevators; Elevators and moving stairways

(G-1415)
ATLANTIC RADON SYSTEMS INC
30829 W Lagoon Rd (19939-4032)
PHONE..................610 869-9066
Peter D Weber, *Prin*
EMP: 6 **EST:** 2007
SALES (est): 134.11K **Privately Held**
Web: www.atlanticradon.com
SIC: 8734 Testing laboratories

(G-1416)
B&O CLEANING SERVICE
30328 Bunting Rd (19939-3905)
PHONE..................302 604-0108
Bianey Cordoba, *Prin*
EMP: 6 **EST:** 2017
SALES (est): 221.15K **Privately Held**
SIC: 7699 Cleaning services

(G-1417)
BANKS FARMS LLC
30190 Whites Neck Rd (19939-3468)
PHONE..................302 542-4100
David Banks, *Managing Member*
EMP: 5 **EST:** 2012
SALES (est): 467.87K **Privately Held**
SIC: 0191 4213 General farms, primarily crop ; Heavy hauling, nec

(G-1418)
BLADES H V A C SERVICES
Also Called: Honeywell Authorized Dealer
32798 Swamp Rd (19939-4425)
PHONE..................302 539-4436
Brandon Blades, *Owner*
EMP: 5 **EST:** 2008
SALES (est): 491.28K **Privately Held**
Web: www.bladesvac.com
SIC: 1711 Heating and air conditioning contractors

(G-1419)
BRAFMAN FAMILY DENTISTRY PC
31381 Dogwood Acres Dr Unit 2 (19939-4076)
PHONE..................302 732-3852
Wendy Brafman D.m.d., *Pr*
Kevin Brafman D.m.d., *VP*
EMP: 15 **EST:** 2002
SALES (est): 556.43K **Privately Held**
Web: www.brafdentistry.com
SIC: 8021 Dentists' office

(G-1420)
BREWINGTON ELECTRIC
Rural Rt 26 (19939)
P.O. Box 93 (19939-0093)
PHONE..................302 732-3570
George Brewington, *Owner*
EMP: 6 **EST:** 2004
SALES (est): 251.62K **Privately Held**
Web: www.brewingtonelectricllc.com
SIC: 1731 General electrical contractor

(G-1421)
BUNTINGS GARAGE INC
28506 Carebear Ln (19939-3943)
PHONE..................302 732-9021
Ellison Bunting, *Pr*
Keith Bunting, *VP*
Sara Bunting, *Treas*
EMP: 11 **EST:** 1972
SALES (est): 423.18K **Privately Held**
Web: www.buntingsgarage.com
SIC: 4492 7539 4214 Towing and tugboat service; Automotive repair shops, nec; Local trucking with storage

(G-1422)
CAREY JR JAMES E INC (PA)
30618 Dupont Blvd Unit 1 (19939-5402)
P.O. Box 1500 (19966-5500)
PHONE..................302 934-8383
James E Carey Junior, *Pr*
EMP: 9 **EST:** 1973
SQ FT: 1,200
SALES (est): 2MM
SALES (corp-wide): 2MM **Privately Held**
SIC: 6411 Insurance agents, nec

(G-1423)
CECO INC
27515 Hodges Ln Unit N1 (19939-5404)
PHONE..................302 732-3919
Dell Morsberger, *Mgr*
EMP: 40
SALES (corp-wide): 3.68MM **Privately Held**
SIC: 4225 General warehousing and storage
PA: Ceco, Inc.
  6770 Oak Hall Ln Ste 117
  Columbia MD 21045
  410 995-6270

(G-1424)
CEDAR NECK DECOR LLC
30980 Country Gdns Q1 (19939-5441)
PHONE..................918 497-7179
EMP: 4 **EST:** 2018
SALES (est): 83.52K **Privately Held**
SIC: 2499 Decorative wood and woodwork

(G-1425)
CHARLES MOON PLUMBING
33214 Main St (19939-3809)
P.O. Box 221 (19939-0221)
PHONE..................302 732-3555
EMP: 6 **EST:** 2020
SALES (est): 248.75K **Privately Held**
Web: www.delawareplumbing.com
SIC: 1711 Plumbing contractors

(G-1426)
CHARLES MOON PLUMBING
32980 Dupont Blvd (19939-4464)
PHONE..................302 732-3555
Charles Moon, *Prin*
EMP: 7 **EST:** 2016
SALES (est): 229.01K **Privately Held**
Web: www.charlesmoonplumbing.com
SIC: 1711 Plumbing contractors

(G-1427)
CHRISTINE E FOX DDS
31059 Dupont Blvd (19939-4439)
PHONE..................302 732-9850
Christine Fox, *Prin*
EMP: 9 **EST:** 2014
SALES (est): 89.7K **Privately Held**
Web: www.dagsborodentist.com
SIC: 8021 Dentists' office

(G-1428)
COASTAL RESTORATIONS INC
104 Riverview Dr (19939-4304)
P.O. Box 1248 (19970-1248)
PHONE..................443 859-4505
Glenn Cave, *Pr*
EMP: 8 **EST:** 2018
SALES (est): 225.62K **Privately Held**
Web: www.decoastalrestoration.com
SIC: 1799 Special trade contractors, nec

(G-1429)
COMMUNICATIONS & WIRING CO
Also Called: 1 Smart Home
34423 Sylvan Vue Dr (19939-4106)
PHONE..................302 539-0809
Lew Reeves, *Owner*
EMP: 6 **EST:** 1999
SQ FT: 2,500
SALES (est): 412.69K **Privately Held**
Web: www.communicationswiring.com
SIC: 1731 Telephone and telephone equipment installation

(G-1430)
CONCIERGE BEACH SERVICE
30728 Irons Ln (19939-3451)
PHONE..................302 541-0303
EMP: 5 **EST:** 2014
SALES (est): 44.52K **Privately Held**
SIC: 7299 Miscellaneous personal service

(G-1431)
CONSOLIDATED CONTRACTING LLC
30237 Whites Neck Rd (19939-3470)
PHONE..................302 727-9795
Ralph Whitley, *Pr*
EMP: 6 **EST:** 2017
SALES (est): 56.76K **Privately Held**
Web: www.consolidatedcontracting.com
SIC: 1542 Commercial and office building, new construction

(G-1432)
CONTINNTAL SEARCH OUTPLACEMENT
30022 Judson Ln (19939-3381)
PHONE..................302 927-0200
Daniel Simmons, *Pr*
EMP: 9 **EST:** 2014
SALES (est): 230.19K **Privately Held**
Web: www.continentalsearch.com
SIC: 7361 Executive placement

(G-1433)
CRIPPLE CREEK GOLF & CNTRY CLB
29494 Cripple Creek Dr (19939-3423)
PHONE..................302 539-1446
Don Pharr, *Pr*
William Clarke, *
Marry Alice Senneman, *
EMP: 29 **EST:** 1983
SQ FT: 8,800
SALES (est): 4.03MM **Privately Held**
Web: www.cripplecreekgolf.com
SIC: 7997 Country club, membership

(G-1434)
DELAWARE LRNG INST CSMTLOGY IN
32448 Royal Blvd Unit A (19939-3899)
PHONE..................302 732-6704
Cindy Dunham, *Dir*
John Cook, *Dir*
Melody Morgan, *Prin*
EMP: 16 **EST:** 1999
SALES (est): 534.85K **Privately Held**
Web: www.delawarecosmetology.com
SIC: 7231 7999 Cosmetology school; Massage instruction

(G-1435)
DELAWARE MOBILE SURFISHERMEN
P.O. Box 105 (19951-0105)
PHONE..................302 945-1320
EMP: 5 **EST:** 2008
SALES (est): 109.03K **Privately Held**
SIC: 8641 Civic and social associations

(G-1436)
DELAWARE SEASHORE PRESERVATION
200 Summer Ct (19939)
PHONE..................302 227-0478
EMP: 6 **EST:** 2011
SALES (est): 66.28K **Privately Held**
Web: www.dspf.net
SIC: 8641 Civic and social associations

(G-1437)
DELAWARE SIDING COMPANY INC
27515 Hodges Ln (19939-5404)
PHONE..................302 732-1440
EMP: 5 **EST:** 2013
SALES (est): 61.92K **Privately Held**
SIC: 1761 Skylight installation

Dagsboro - Sussex County (G-1438)

(G-1438)
DELMARVA ARBORISTS LLC
32712 Swamp Rd (19939-5425)
PHONE....................302 581-9494
Mauricio Soares, *Managing Member*
EMP: 8 **EST:** 2017
SALES (est): 502.39K **Privately Held**
SIC: 0783 0851 Ornamental shrub and tree services; Forestry services

(G-1439)
DELMARVALOUS
30748 Long Leaf Rd (19939-4025)
PHONE....................302 200-2001
EMP: 4 **EST:** 2018
SALES (est): 156.05K **Privately Held**
Web: www.delmarvalousllc.com
SIC: 3442 Metal doors, sash, and trim

(G-1440)
DISCOVERY ISLAND PRESCHOOL
32532 Smith Dr (19939)
PHONE....................302 732-7529
Kerry Clark, *Owner*
EMP: 10 **EST:** 1998
SALES (est): 161.24K **Privately Held**
SIC: 8351 Preschool center

(G-1441)
DJH ENTERPRISES VII LLC
Also Called: Merry Maids 462 1052
32442 Royal Blvd Unit 2 (19939-5427)
PHONE....................410 749-0100
John Hynes Junior, *Prin*
Darlene Schott, *
EMP: 5 **EST:** 2016
SALES (est): 186.36K **Privately Held**
SIC: 4581 Aircraft cleaning and janitorial service

(G-1442)
DOWNTOEARTHLAWN&LANDSCAPE LLC
406 Walnut Ct (19939-9732)
PHONE....................302 381-5051
EMP: 5 **EST:** 2010
SALES (est): 211.56K **Privately Held**
SIC: 0781 Landscape services

(G-1443)
EDWARD J STEEN
700 Cherry Dr (19939-9762)
PHONE....................302 732-6963
Edward Steen, *Prin*
EMP: 9 **EST:** 2004
SALES (est): 489.46K **Privately Held**
SIC: 0119 0139 Cash grains, nec; Feeder crops

(G-1444)
ELAINE CNROY MORE CHRTBLFNDTIO
29582 Vines Creek Rd (19939-3815)
PHONE....................302 296-6580
Elaine Moore, *Prin*
EMP: 6 **EST:** 2015
SALES (est): 47.53K **Privately Held**
SIC: 8699 Charitable organization

(G-1445)
ENTERPRISE LSG PHLADELPHIA LLC
Also Called: Enterprise Rent-A-Car
27424 Auto Works Ave (19939-5426)
PHONE....................302 732-3534
Nicole Delmastro, *Brnch Mgr*
EMP: 6
SALES (corp-wide): 7.04B **Privately Held**
Web: www.enterprise.com
SIC: 7514 Rent-a-car service
HQ: Enterprise Leasing Company Of Philadelphia, Llc
2434 W Main St 2436
Norristown PA 19403

(G-1446)
FAIRWAY VILLAS CONDO ASSN
1 Cripple Creek Dr (19939-9200)
PHONE....................302 539-0414
William Collins, *Pr*
EMP: 5 **EST:** 2008
SALES (est): 110.95K **Privately Held**
SIC: 8641 Condominium association

(G-1447)
FIRST STATE UNDERGROUND INC
32353 Smith Dr (19939-3890)
PHONE....................302 381-5601
Kristina Gardner, *Brnch Mgr*
EMP: 36
SALES (corp-wide): 247.63K **Privately Held**
SIC: 1623 Water, sewer, and utility lines
PA: First State Underground, Inc.
29799 Iron Branch Rd
Millsboro DE 19966
302 381-5601

(G-1448)
FLOLEFT LLC
29585 Carnoustie Ct Unit 802 (19939-3437)
PHONE....................302 648-2088
EMP: 6 **EST:** 2011
SALES (est): 240.54K **Privately Held**
Web: www.floleft.com
SIC: 1623 Transmitting tower (telecommunication) construction

(G-1449)
FLUOR CORP
29416 Power Plant Rd (19939-4906)
PHONE....................302 934-7742
EMP: 5 **EST:** 2019
SALES (est): 36.24K **Privately Held**
Web: www.fluor.com
SIC: 8711 Engineering services

(G-1450)
FLW WOOD PRODUCTS INC
Also Called: FLW WOOD PRODUCTS INC.
33290 Bayberry Ct (19939-4923)
PHONE....................410 259-4674
EMP: 9
SALES (corp-wide): 100MM **Privately Held**
Web: www.flwinternational.com
SIC: 5099 Wood and wood by-products
PA: F.L.W. Wood Products, Inc.
100 Prnctn S Corpt Ctr # 270
Ewing NJ 08628
609 520-8333

(G-1451)
FORTRESS HOME MAINTENANCE SERV
31275 Gray Rd (19939-4213)
PHONE....................302 539-3446
Patty Mullikin, *Managing Member*
EMP: 5 **EST:** 2007
SALES (est): 174.25K **Privately Held**
Web: www.fortressprowatch.com
SIC: 7349 Building maintenance services, nec

(G-1452)
GEORGES TREES PLUS LLC
209 Woodland Ct (19939-9232)
PHONE....................302 539-0660
Valorie Frinder, *Prin*
EMP: 5 **EST:** 2014
SALES (est): 194.69K **Privately Held**
SIC: 5149 Cookies

(G-1453)
GOLD STANDARD INSPTN CO LLC
30838 Vines Creek Rd (19939-4385)
PHONE....................302 381-0590
Todd Williams, *Prin*
EMP: 5 **EST:** 2017
SALES (est): 258.9K **Privately Held**
Web: www.goldstandardinspections.com
SIC: 7389 Building inspection service

(G-1454)
GULLS WAY CAMPGROUND
30738 Gulls Way Dr (19939-4393)
PHONE....................302 732-6383
EMP: 7 **EST:** 2018
SALES (est): 100.96K **Privately Held**
Web: www.gullsway.com
SIC: 7033 Campgrounds

(G-1455)
GULLS WAY CAMPGROUND
Rte 26 (19939)
PHONE....................302 732-6383
Lina Cropper, *Pr*
Wayne Cropper, *Pr*
Dawn Cropper, *VP*
EMP: 6 **EST:** 1986
SALES (est): 273.98K **Privately Held**
Web: www.gullsway.com
SIC: 7033 Campgrounds

(G-1456)
GULLS WAY INC
Also Called: Gull's Way Campground
Rural Route 2 Box 45 (19939)
PHONE....................302 732-9629
Lina Cropper, *Pr*
Wayne Cropper, *VP*
Dawn Farmer, *Sec*
EMP: 6 **EST:** 1985
SALES (est): 256.82K **Privately Held**
Web: www.gullsway.com
SIC: 7033 Campgrounds

(G-1457)
H&K GROUP INC
Dagsboro Material
30548 Thorogoods Rd (19939)
PHONE....................302 934-7635
Steve Nelson, *Off Mgr*
EMP: 6
SALES (corp-wide): 132.8MM **Privately Held**
Web: www.hkgroup.com
SIC: 3281 Stone, quarrying and processing of own stone products
PA: H&K Group, Inc.
2052 Lucon Rd
Skippack PA 19474
610 584-8500

(G-1458)
HALL OF FAME LLC
30003 Pawley Island Ct (19939-3378)
PHONE....................443 373-4046
Michael P Hall, *Prin*
EMP: 5 **EST:** 2015
SALES (est): 134.19K **Privately Held**
SIC: 0752 Training services, horses (except racing horses)

(G-1459)
HAMILTON HOME SERVICES LLC
32889 Vines Creek Rd (19939-4020)
PHONE....................302 430-6505
Ryan Hamilton, *Prin*
EMP: 5 **EST:** 2015
SALES (est): 67.46K **Privately Held**
SIC: 7261 Funeral home

(G-1460)
HARVEST CONSUMER PRODUCTS LLC
350 Clayton St (19939)
PHONE....................302 732-6624
Joe Kollock Iii, *Pr*
EMP: 62
SALES (corp-wide): 10.9MM **Privately Held**
SIC: 2499 5191 5193 2875 Mulch, wood and bark; Hay; Flowers and florists supplies; Fertilizers, mixing only
PA: Harvest Consumer Products, Llc
1432 Main St Ste 1
Waltham MA 02451
980 444-2000

(G-1461)
HEAL WELL LLC
29967 Sawmill Dr (19939-3353)
PHONE....................302 542-7095
Jennifer Rodgers, *Prin*
EMP: 6 **EST:** 2017
SALES (est): 53.41K **Privately Held**
SIC: 8322 Individual and family services

(G-1462)
HEATHERS HOME WORKS LLC
29475 Vines Creek Rd (19939-3839)
PHONE....................302 927-0016
EMP: 6 **EST:** 2017
SALES (est): 22.81K **Privately Held**
Web: www.heathershomeworks.com
SIC: 7699 Cleaning services

(G-1463)
HICKORY HILL BUILDERS INC
25714 Timmons Ln (19939-4472)
PHONE....................302 934-6109
Todd Timmons, *Pr*
Ralph Timmons Junior, *VP*
Pauline Timmons, *Sec*
EMP: 5 **EST:** 2007
SALES (est): 705.3K **Privately Held**
Web: www.hickoryhillbuildersinc.com
SIC: 1521 New construction, single-family houses

(G-1464)
HILLTOP HOSTEL
34508 Quail Ln (19939-3342)
PHONE....................202 291-9591
Ronald Watson, *Prin*
EMP: 16 **EST:** 2010
SALES (est): 92.6K **Privately Held**
SIC: 7011 Hotels

(G-1465)
HOME IMPROVEMENTS
34816 Stream Ct (19939-3332)
PHONE....................302 537-1102
John Blaa, *Prin*
EMP: 5 **EST:** 2010
SALES (est): 158.6K **Privately Held**
SIC: 1521 Single-family housing construction

(G-1466)
INDIAN RIVER POWER LLC
29416 Power Plant Rd (19939-4906)
PHONE....................302 934-3527
EMP: 8 **EST:** 2015
SALES (est): 3.68MM **Publicly Held**
SIC: 4931 Electric and other services combined
PA: Nrg Energy, Inc.

GEOGRAPHIC SECTION
Dagsboro - Sussex County (G-1496)

910 Louisiana St Ste B200
Houston TX 77002

(G-1467)
INSIGHT HOMES
33288 Bayberry Ct (19939-4923)
PHONE.................................302 927-0235
Rob Lisle, *Owner*
EMP: 7 **EST:** 2013
SALES (est): 124.17K **Privately Held**
Web: www.itsjustabetterhouse.com
SIC: 6531 Real estate agent, residential

(G-1468)
ISLAND OF MISFITS LLC
32448 Royal Blvd Ste A (19939-3899)
PHONE.................................302 732-6704
John Cook, *Prin*
EMP: 9 **EST:** 2017
SALES (est): 249.55K **Privately Held**
SIC: 7231 Cosmetology school

(G-1469)
JAMES WILLEY MASONRY LLC
201 Chapel Of Ease St (19939-1807)
P.O. Box 92 (19939-0092)
PHONE.................................302 258-6242
EMP: 5 **EST:** 2009
SALES (est): 116.98K **Privately Held**
SIC: 1741 Masonry and other stonework

(G-1470)
JERRY S MEIKLEJOHN
30622 Sandy Landing Rd (19939-4219)
PHONE.................................302 745-2632
EMP: 7 **EST:** 2012
SALES (est): 415.77K **Privately Held**
SIC: 1522 Residential construction, nec

(G-1471)
JUSTIN OAKLEY
30598 Holts Landing Rd (19939-3444)
PHONE.................................302 752-8277
Justin Oakley, *Pr*
EMP: 7 **EST:** 2017
SALES (est): 108.09K **Privately Held**
SIC: 8049 Offices of health practitioner

(G-1472)
KAREN HEALING HANDS
32277 Falling Point Rd R (19939-4068)
PHONE.................................302 841-8933
EMP: 6 **EST:** 2010
SALES (est): 63.07K **Privately Held**
SIC: 8049 Massage Therapist

(G-1473)
KIDZ AKADEMY CORP
32442 Royal Blvd (19939-5427)
PHONE.................................302 732-6077
EMP: 6 **EST:** 2009
SALES (est): 245.08K **Privately Held**
Web: www.kidzakademyabc.com
SIC: 8351 Group day care center

(G-1474)
LBG HOMES LLC
33334 Main St (19939-3812)
PHONE.................................302 360-0300
Robert Horsey, *Pt*
EMP: 5 **EST:** 2017
SALES (est): 107.13K **Privately Held**
Web: www.lbghomes.com
SIC: 6531 Real estate brokers and agents

(G-1475)
LONG & FOSTER
34071 Moccasin Way (19939-4117)
P.O. Box 127 (19939-0127)
PHONE.................................302 569-0012
Elizabeth Kapp, *Prin*
EMP: 5 **EST:** 2018
SALES (est): 114.81K **Privately Held**
Web: www.longandfoster.com
SIC: 6531 Real estate brokers and agents

(G-1476)
M B CUES
30700 Shell Rd (19939-4371)
PHONE.................................443 309-3495
EMP: 3 **EST:** 2018
SALES (est): 78.91K **Privately Held**
SIC: 3949 Sporting and athletic goods, nec

(G-1477)
M N K MAINTENANCE AND REM
32034 Helm St (19939-3817)
PHONE.................................302 841-5884
EMP: 5 **EST:** 2009
SALES (est): 66.94K **Privately Held**
SIC: 7349 Building maintenance services, nec

(G-1478)
MAIN OFFICE INC
32096 Sussex St (19939-3861)
PHONE.................................302 732-3460
Lisa Blanchette, *Pr*
EMP: 2 **EST:** 2005
SALES (est): 243.84K **Privately Held**
SIC: 3694 Distributors, motor vehicle engine

(G-1479)
MARVEL PORTABLE WELDING INC
32887 Dupont Blvd (19939-4466)
P.O. Box 27 (19939-0027)
PHONE.................................302 732-9480
Kendall R Marvel, *Pr*
Linda M Marvel, *VP*
EMP: 9 **EST:** 1978
SQ FT: 3,300
SALES (est): 888.8K **Privately Held**
Web: www.marvelswelding.com
SIC: 7692 Welding repair

(G-1480)
MCCOMRICK INSURANCE SERVICES
3394 N Main St (19939)
P.O. Box 8 (19939-0008)
PHONE.................................302 732-6655
Calvin Mccomrick, *Pr*
Jane Mccomrick, *VP*
EMP: 8 **EST:** 1982
SALES (est): 644.4K **Privately Held**
Web: www.minsuranceservices.com
SIC: 6411 Insurance agents, nec

(G-1481)
MEDIACOM LLC
Also Called: MEDIACOM LLC
32441 Royal Blvd (19939-3860)
PHONE.................................302 732-9332
David Kane, *Mgr*
EMP: 10
SALES (corp-wide): 2.13B **Privately Held**
Web: www.mediacomcable.com
SIC: 4841 Cable television services
HQ: Mediacom, Llc
1 Mediacom Way
Mediacom Park NY 10918

(G-1482)
MICHAEL BUTTERWORTH DR
31059 Dupont Blvd (19939-4439)
PHONE.................................302 732-9850
Amy R Hall, *Prin*
EMP: 15 **EST:** 2007
SALES (est): 859.5K **Privately Held**
Web: www.dagsborodentist.com
SIC: 8011 8021 Physicians' office, including specialists; Offices and clinics of dentists

(G-1483)
MORNING STAR CONSTRUCTION LLC
103 Wood Duck Ct (19939-2005)
PHONE.................................302 539-0791
EMP: 8 **EST:** 2002
SALES (est): 2.05MM **Privately Held**
Web: www.mscbuilders.com
SIC: 1521 New construction, single-family houses

(G-1484)
MORRIS E JUSTICE INC
33897 Em Calhoun Ln (19939-4171)
PHONE.................................302 539-7731
Morris Justice, *Pr*
Sara Justice, *Prin*
EMP: 5 **EST:** 1968
SALES (est): 329.38K **Privately Held**
SIC: 4212 Dump truck haulage

(G-1485)
MORSE HOME IMPROVEMENT LLC
Also Called: Morse Home Improvement
33334 Main St (19939-3812)
PHONE.................................302 663-0042
Thomas Morse, *Owner*
EMP: 21 **EST:** 2017
SALES (est): 2.39MM **Privately Held**
Web: www.morsehomeimprovement.com
SIC: 1521 1761 General remodeling, single-family houses; Roofing contractor

(G-1486)
N V R MORTGAGE
32442 Royal Blvd Unit 3 (19939-5427)
PHONE.................................302 732-1570
Todd Hickman, *Mgr*
EMP: 6 **EST:** 2017
SALES (est): 157.85K **Privately Held**
Web: www.nvrmortgage.com
SIC: 6162 Mortgage bankers and loan correspondents

(G-1487)
NATIONWIDE INSRNCE CREY INSUR
Also Called: Nationwide
30618 Dupont Blvd Unit 1 (19939-5402)
PHONE.................................302 934-8383
EMP: 12 **EST:** 2019
SALES (est): 462.95K **Privately Held**
Web: www.careinsurancegroup.net
SIC: 6411 Insurance agents, nec

(G-1488)
NEW YORK BLOOD CENTER INC
32445 Royal Blvd Unit B (19939-3860)
PHONE.................................302 737-8405
EMP: 8
SALES (corp-wide): 29.61MM **Privately Held**
Web: www.delmarvablood.org
SIC: 8099 Blood bank
PA: New York Blood Center, Inc.
100 Hygeia Dr
Newark DE 19713
302 737-8405

(G-1489)
NORMAN LAW FIRM
30838 Vines Creek Rd Unit 3 (19939-4385)
PHONE.................................302 537-3788
Norman Donald, *Prin*
EMP: 10 **EST:** 2013
SALES (est): 430.48K **Privately Held**
Web: www.thenormanlawfirm.com

SIC: 8111 General practice law office

(G-1490)
NORTH STAR HEATING & AIR INC
Also Called: Honeywell Authorized Dealer
30968 Vines Creek Rd (19939-4357)
PHONE.................................302 732-3967
Harry Jarvis, *Pr*
Tina Jarvis, *
EMP: 25 **EST:** 1998
SQ FT: 10,000
SALES (est): 2.41MM **Privately Held**
Web: www.northstar-hvac.com
SIC: 1711 Warm air heating and air conditioning contractor

(G-1491)
NV HOMES
32448 Royal Blvd Unit 2 (19939-3899)
PHONE.................................302 732-9900
Dana Andrews, *Mgr*
EMP: 8 **EST:** 2012
SALES (est): 233.01K **Privately Held**
Web: www.nvhomes.com
SIC: 1531 Speculative builder, single-family houses

(G-1492)
NVR INC
Also Called: Ryan Homes
32448 Royal Blvd Ste B (19939-3899)
PHONE.................................302 732-9900
Todd Hickman, *Mgr*
EMP: 9
Web: www.nvrinc.com
SIC: 1521 New construction, single-family houses
PA: Nvr, Inc.
11700 Plaza America Dr # 500
Reston VA 20190

(G-1493)
OCEAN VIEW PLUMBING INC
Also Called: Ocean View Plumbing & Heating
R R 4 Box 21 A (19939)
PHONE.................................302 732-9117
Richard Shaubach, *Pr*
Eric Ankrom, *VP*
Mariann Shaubach, *Treas*
EMP: 31 **EST:** 1982
SQ FT: 9,999
SALES (est): 2.41MM **Privately Held**
Web: www.oceanviewplumbing.com
SIC: 1711 Plumbing contractors

(G-1494)
OSULLIVAN INSURANCE AGENCY
32177 Dupont Blvd (19939-5424)
PHONE.................................302 927-0927
Eugene O'sullivan, *Pr*
EMP: 5 **EST:** 2016
SALES (est): 102.64K **Privately Held**
SIC: 6411 Insurance agents and brokers

(G-1495)
OX POND INDUSTRIES
29489 Colony Dr (19939-3319)
PHONE.................................703 608-7769
Bill Mcgrail, *Prin*
EMP: 4 **EST:** 2016
SALES (est): 83.87K **Privately Held**
SIC: 3544 Special dies, tools, jigs, and fixtures

(G-1496)
PIERSON CULVER LLC
27517 Hodges Ln (19939-5401)
PHONE.................................302 732-1145
Dean Pierson, *Prin*
EMP: 6 **EST:** 2007

Dagsboro - Sussex County (G-1497)

SALES (est): 587.07K **Privately Held**
SIC: **1521** 4213 Mobile home repair, on site; Mobile homes transport

(G-1497)
RENOVE MED SPA
21 Bethany Forest Dr (19939-9212)
PHONE..................................302 584-3216
Michelle Parsons, *Prin*
EMP: 5 EST: 2010
SALES (est): 89.85K **Privately Held**
Web: www.renovemedspa.org
SIC: **7991** Spas

(G-1498)
RESTARANT ACTN MD-TLANTIC WHSE
33334 Main St (19939-3812)
PHONE..................................302 462-6678
EMP: 6 EST: 2018
SALES (est): 20.78K **Privately Held**
SIC: **7999** Recreation services

(G-1499)
RICKARDS AUTO BODY
30450 Marina Rd (19939-3981)
PHONE..................................302 934-9600
EMP: 7 EST: 2015
SALES (est): 222.28K **Privately Held**
Web: www.rickardsautobody.com
SIC: **7532** Paint shop, automotive

(G-1500)
RIVER ASPHALT LLC
30548 Thorogoods Rd (19939-4528)
PHONE..................................302 934-0881
Steve Green, *Prin*
EMP: 5 EST: 2004
SALES (est): 529.74K **Privately Held**
Web: www.geolyn.com
SIC: **1611** Highway and street paving contractor

(G-1501)
RUDY MARINE INC
Also Called: Rudy's Outboard Service
32606 Dupont Blvd (19939-4462)
PHONE..................................302 999-8735
Thomas Rudloff, *Pr*
EMP: 12 EST: 1987
SALES (est): 2.09MM **Privately Held**
Web: www.rudymarine.com
SIC: **5551** 7699 Motor boat dealers; Marine engine repair

(G-1502)
RUPPERT LANDSCAPE LLC
28091 Nine Foot Rd (19939-4432)
PHONE..................................302 537-2771
EMP: 55
Web: www.ruppertlandscape.com
SIC: **0781** Landscape services
PA: Ruppert Landscape, Llc
23601 Laytonsville Rd
Laytonsville MD 20882

(G-1503)
SAMS PAINTING
204 Sandy Beach Dr (19939-9735)
PHONE..................................302 430-1241
Sam Grijalva, *Mgr*
EMP: 5 EST: 2017
SALES (est): 100.51K **Privately Held**
SIC: **1721** Painting and paper hanging

(G-1504)
SHIPWRECKED
28293 Clayton St (19939-3854)
P.O. Box 438 (19939-0438)
PHONE..................................410 271-9563

Vicki Ober, *Prin*
EMP: 10 EST: 2017
SALES (est): 109.84K **Privately Held**
SIC: **6512** Nonresidential building operators

(G-1505)
SMITH AND SON LAWN SERVICE
Also Called: Smith & Son Lawn Service
30037 Lewis Ln (19939-4555)
PHONE..................................302 934-1778
Roger Smith, *Prin*
EMP: 5 EST: 2010
SALES (est): 62.69K **Privately Held**
SIC: **0782** Lawn care services

(G-1506)
SOUTH NEWPORT CO INC
Also Called: Clayton Theatre
33246 Main St (19939-3827)
P.O. Box 351 (19939-0351)
PHONE..................................302 732-9606
Joanne Howe, *Pr*
EMP: 10 EST: 2000
SALES (est): 266.61K **Privately Held**
Web: www.theclaytontheatre.com
SIC: **7832** Motion picture theaters, except drive-in

(G-1507)
SOUTHERN STATES COOP INC
Also Called: Dagsboro Serv-Dagsboro BR
302 Clayton St (19939)
P.O. Box 278 (19939-0278)
PHONE..................................302 732-6651
Brian Schilling, *Brnch Mgr*
EMP: 48
SALES (corp-wide): 1.71B **Privately Held**
Web: www.southernstates.com
SIC: **2048** 2875 Prepared feeds, nec; Fertilizers, mixing only
PA: Southern States Cooperative, Incorporated
6606 W Broad St Ste B
Richmond VA 23230
804 281-1000

(G-1508)
SPN TITLE SERVICES
30838 Vines Creek Rd Unit 8 (19939-4385)
PHONE..................................302 537-1540
Stephen P Norman, *Prin*
EMP: 6 EST: 2011
SALES (est): 124.9K **Privately Held**
Web: www.spntitle.com
SIC: **6541** Title and trust companies

(G-1509)
STATE FARM
Also Called: State Farm Insurance
30170 Irons Ln (19939-3476)
PHONE..................................302 258-9989
William Reese, *Prin*
EMP: 7 EST: 2018
SALES (est): 222.79K **Privately Held**
Web: www.statefarm.com
SIC: **6411** Insurance agents and brokers

(G-1510)
SUCK IT UP INC
30310 Adams Rd (19939-3948)
PHONE..................................410 258-8023
EMP: 5 EST: 2019
SALES (est): 226.99K **Privately Held**
SIC: **7699** Cleaning services

(G-1511)
SUPERIOR DRYWALL INC
30996 Country Gdns Ste R1 (19939-5429)
P.O. Box 730 (19966-0730)
PHONE..................................302 732-9800

Michael Myers, *Pr*
EMP: 10 EST: 1979
SQ FT: 1,600
SALES (est): 989.65K **Privately Held**
Web: www.superdrywall.com
SIC: **1742** 1721 Drywall; Exterior residential painting contractor

(G-1512)
SUSSEX VETERINARY HOSPITAL
30053 Vine St Rd (19939)
PHONE..................................302 732-9433
EMP: 5 EST: 1974
SALES (est): 277.88K **Privately Held**
SIC: **0742** Animal hospital services, pets and other animal specialties

(G-1513)
SYSTEMS TECH & SCIENCE LLC
34394 Indian River Dr (19939-3304)
PHONE..................................703 757-2010
William Evers, *Pr*
EMP: 6 EST: 1998
SALES (est): 380.56K **Privately Held**
SIC: **8748** Business consulting, nec

(G-1514)
TENNIS STRING KING
29348 Turnberry Dr (19939-3412)
PHONE..................................215 280-2783
EMP: 5 EST: 2011
SALES (est): 104.91K **Privately Held**
SIC: **7997** Tennis club, membership

(G-1515)
THIS N THAT FITNESS
30954 Holts Landing Rd (19939-4189)
PHONE..................................302 542-7115
Erin Brenan, *Prin*
EMP: 5 EST: 2018
SALES (est): 107.84K **Privately Held**
Web: www.thisnthatfitde.com
SIC: **7991** Physical fitness facilities

(G-1516)
THORO-GOODS CONCRETE CO INC (PA)
30548 Thorogoods Rd (19939-4528)
P.O. Box 407 (19966-0407)
PHONE..................................302 934-8102
Frank W Thoroughgood, *Pr*
Glenn B Thoroughgood, *
Shirley Wilson, *
EMP: 21 EST: 1958
SALES (est): 2.81MM
SALES (corp-wide): 2.81MM **Privately Held**
SIC: **3273** Ready-mixed concrete

(G-1517)
TIDALHLTH PNNSULA REGIONAL INC
Also Called: Dagsboro Family Practice Rts 113 & 26th (19939)
PHONE..................................302 732-8400
EMP: 10
SALES (corp-wide): 1.18MM **Privately Held**
Web: www.tidalhealth.org
SIC: **8062** 8011 General medical and surgical hospitals; General and family practice, physician/surgeon
HQ: Tidalhealth Peninsula Regional, Inc.
100 E Carroll St
Salisbury MD 21801
410 546-6400

(G-1518)
TONY MILAM - STATE FARM INS AG
32442 Royal Blvd Unit 3 (19939-5427)

PHONE..................................302 732-3220
Anthony W Milam, *Owner*
EMP: 7 EST: 2018
SALES (est): 179.57K **Privately Held**
Web: www.tonymilam.com
SIC: **6411** Insurance agents and brokers

(G-1519)
TOP NOTCH PLUMBING LLC
29498 Piney Neck Rd (19939-3917)
PHONE..................................302 381-9096
John T Handy Iv, *Prin*
EMP: 5 EST: 2017
SALES (est): 113.83K **Privately Held**
SIC: **1711** Plumbing contractors

(G-1520)
TUCKAHOE ACRES CAMPING RESORT
36031 Tuckahoe Trl (19939-2003)
P.O. Box 7 (19939-0007)
PHONE..................................302 539-1841
Mark Browne, *Pr*
Van Browne, *Chief Business Officer*
EMP: 9 EST: 1966
SALES (est): 462.13K **Privately Held**
Web: www.tuckahoeacres.com
SIC: **7033** Trailer park

(G-1521)
ULTIMATE TAN MILLSBORO INC
25714 Timmons Ln (19939-4472)
PHONE..................................302 934-1400
Pauline Timons, *Prin*
EMP: 5 EST: 2004
SALES (est): 180.4K **Privately Held**
SIC: **7231** Facial salons

(G-1522)
UNITED ELECTRIC SUPPLY CO INC
27519 Hodges Ln Bldg P (19939-5401)
PHONE..................................302 732-1291
Nick O'lone, *Mgr*
EMP: 7
SALES (corp-wide): 244.47MM **Privately Held**
Web: www.unitedelectric.com
SIC: **5063** Electrical supplies, nec
PA: United Electric Supply Company, Inc.
10 Bellecor Dr
New Castle DE 19720
800 322-3374

(G-1523)
VICKERS BALLOONING LLC
28091 Nine Foot Rd (19939-4432)
PHONE..................................302 462-1830
EMP: 5 EST: 2011
SALES (est): 52.6K **Privately Held**
SIC: **7999** Hot air balloon rides

(G-1524)
VILLAGE DEVELOPERS INC
31003 Country Gdns Unit 1 (19939-5403)
P.O. Box 1680 (19966-5680)
PHONE..................................302 732-3400
EMP: 6 EST: 1990
SQ FT: 1,000
SALES (est): 895.4K **Privately Held**
Web: www.villagedevelop.com
SIC: **1521** New construction, single-family houses

(G-1525)
WATER SYSTEM SERVICES INC
32464 Beechwood Ln (19939-4392)
PHONE..................................302 732-1490
Mark Mills, *Pr*
EMP: 6 EST: 2006
SALES (est): 86.22K **Privately Held**

GEOGRAPHIC SECTION   Delaware City - New Castle County (G-1551)

Web: www.waterfrontproperty.ca
SIC: 1781 Water well drilling

(G-1526)
WEST THIRD ENTERPRISES LLC
Also Called: Natural Lawn Care of America
30996 Country Gdns (19939-5429)
PHONE..................302 732-3133
EMP: 7 EST: 2010
SALES (est): 235.26K Privately Held
SIC: 0782 Lawn care services

Delaware City
New Castle County

(G-1527)
ABSOLUTE EQUITY
501 Clinton St (19706-7713)
PHONE..................302 983-2591
Paul Zugehoer, Pt
Linda Zugehoer, Pt
EMP: 7 EST: 2006
SQ FT: 1,000
SALES (est): 98.19K Privately Held
SIC: 1542 Commercial and office building contractors

(G-1528)
AIR PRODUCTS AND CHEMICALS INC
Also Called: Air Products
4550 Wrangle Hill Rd (19706)
PHONE..................302 834-6033
EMP: 5
SALES (corp-wide): 12.6B Publicly Held
Web: www.airproducts.com
SIC: 2911 5541 Petroleum refining; Gasoline service stations
PA: Air Products And Chemicals, Inc.
1940 Air Products Blvd
Allentown PA 18106
610 481-4911

(G-1529)
AIRGAS USA LLC
4442 Wrangle Rd (19706)
P.O. Box 272 (19706-0272)
PHONE..................302 834-7404
Ted Salazar, Mgr
EMP: 16
SALES (corp-wide): 101.26MM Privately Held
Web: www.airgas.com
SIC: 5169 2813 Carbon dioxide; Industrial gases
HQ: Airgas Usa, Llc
259 N Radnor Chester Rd
Radnor PA 19087
216 642-6600

(G-1530)
AMAKOR INC
72 Clinton St (19706-7702)
P.O. Box 636 (19706-0636)
PHONE..................302 834-8664
Steve Serbu, VP
Barbara Serbu, Sec
Ryan Jackson, Pr
EMP: 10 EST: 1988
SQ FT: 3,500
SALES (est): 2.13MM Privately Held
Web: www.amakor.com
SIC: 1542 Commercial and office building, new construction

(G-1531)
AMERICAN BIRDING ASSN INC (PA)
93 Clinton St Ste Aba (19706-7701)
P.O. Box 184 (78065-0184)
PHONE..................302 838-3660
Lou Morrell, Ch
EMP: 5 EST: 1984
SALES (est): 1.64MM
SALES (corp-wide): 1.64MM Privately Held
Web: www.aba.org
SIC: 8621 Scientific membership association

(G-1532)
CAKE SISTERS ✪
88 Clinton St (19706-7702)
PHONE..................302 838-1958
EMP: 3 EST: 2022
SALES (est): 66.57K Privately Held
Web: www.thecakesisters.com
SIC: 2051 Cakes, pies, and pastries

(G-1533)
CD CREAM
Also Called: Crabby Dick's Creamery
32 Clinton St (19706-7700)
PHONE..................302 832-5425
EMP: 5 EST: 2015
SALES (est): 159.08K Privately Held
SIC: 2021 Creamery butter

(G-1534)
CONNECTONS CMNTY SPPORT PRGRAM
Also Called: Meadows, The
New Castle Ave (19706)
PHONE..................302 834-8400
EMP: 21
Web: coras.flywheelsites.com
SIC: 8322 8361 Rehabilitation services; Residential care
PA: Connections Community Support Programs, Inc.
590 Naamans Rd
Claymont DE 19703

(G-1535)
CUTTING EDGE
511 5th St (19706-7729)
P.O. Box 104 (19706-0104)
PHONE..................302 834-8723
Sean Johnson, Pt
Steve Divirgilio, Pt
EMP: 18 EST: 1998
SALES (est): 4.92MM Privately Held
Web: www.thecuttingedgeofde.com
SIC: 0781 Landscape services

(G-1536)
DELAWARE CITY FIRE CO NO 1
815 5th St (19706-7723)
P.O. Box 251 (19706-0251)
PHONE..................302 834-9336
Paul H Johnson Senior, Pr
EMP: 9 EST: 2015
SALES (est): 2.34MM Privately Held
Web: www.dcfc15.com
SIC: 5099 Fire extinguishers

(G-1537)
DELAWARE CITY RECREATION CLUB
5th And Wahington (19706)
P.O. Box 538 (19706-0538)
PHONE..................302 834-9900
Shawn Wagner, Pr
Lillard Brown, VP
Sandra Rynolds, Sec
Nancy Hettich, Treas
Charles Hall, Pr
EMP: 7 EST: 1970
SALES (est): 184.44K Privately Held
Web: www.delawarecity.com

SIC: 8641 Bars and restaurants, members only

(G-1538)
DELAWARE CY VLNTR FIRE CO NO 1
815 5th St (19706-7723)
P.O. Box 251 (19706-0251)
PHONE..................302 834-9336
Wally Poppe, Pr
James D Rosseel, *
EMP: 35 EST: 1987
SQ FT: 27,000
SALES (est): 1.96MM Privately Held
Web: www.dcfc15.com
SIC: 4119 0851 Ambulance service; Fire prevention services, forest

(G-1539)
EIDP INC
Also Called: Dupont Red Lion
755 Govonor Lea Rd (19706)
PHONE..................302 834-5901
Steve Birkel, Brnch Mgr
EMP: 51
SALES (corp-wide): 17.23B Publicly Held
Web: www.dupont.com
SIC: 2819 Elements
HQ: Eidp, Inc.
9330 Zionsville Rd
Indianapolis IN 46268
833 267-8382

(G-1540)
ELITE PROPERTY MAINTENANCE
201 5th St (19706-7735)
PHONE..................302 836-1865
Paul H Johnson, Prin
EMP: 5 EST: 2010
SALES (est): 44.37K Privately Held
SIC: 7349 Building maintenance services, nec

(G-1541)
FORAKER OIL INC
5th & Clinton St (19706)
P.O. Box 4013 (19706-4013)
PHONE..................302 834-7595
Warner T Foraker Junior, Pr
Lynn Foraker, VP
EMP: 8 EST: 1961
SQ FT: 2,000
SALES (est): 768.32K Privately Held
Web: www.forakeroil.com
SIC: 5983 4212 Fuel oil dealers; Local trucking, without storage

(G-1542)
FORGED CREATIONS
124 Clinton St (19706-7706)
PHONE..................302 832-1631
EMP: 5 EST: 2008
SALES (est): 70.69K Privately Held
Web: www.forgedcreations.com
SIC: 8999 Artist

(G-1543)
FORT DELAWARE SOCIETY
33 Staff Ln (19706-7809)
P.O. Box 553 (19706-0553)
PHONE..................302 834-1630
William Robelen, Pr
Edith Mahoney, VP
Thomas Smith, Sec
Kay Keenan, Treas
EMP: 5 EST: 1950
SALES (est): 43.62K Privately Held
Web: www.fortdelaware.org
SIC: 8412 Museum

(G-1544)
FRIENDS OF THE AFRICAN UNION
407 Clinton St (19706-7711)
P.O. Box 4159 (19706-4159)
PHONE..................302 834-7525
Wes Jones, Finance
EMP: 7 EST: 1998
SQ FT: 500
SALES (est): 96.54K Privately Held
Web: www.africanunioncemetery.org
SIC: 8641 Civic and social associations

(G-1545)
FT DUPONT REDEVELOPMENT A
260 Old Elm Ave (19706-4300)
PHONE..................302 838-7374
EMP: 5 EST: 2019
SALES (est): 222.18K Privately Held
Web: www.fortdupont.org
SIC: 2879 Agricultural chemicals, nec

(G-1546)
GAUDENZIA INC
171 New Castle Ave (19706-7807)
PHONE..................302 836-8260
Michael Coyle, Prin
EMP: 15 EST: 2018
SALES (est): 54.13K Privately Held
Web: www.gaudenzia.org
SIC: 8361 Rehabilitation center, residential: health care incidental

(G-1547)
HELENE DAY CARE PRE-SCHOOL
311 Monroe St (19706-7743)
PHONE..................302 834-9060
EMP: 8 EST: 2015
SALES (est): 24.6K Privately Held
SIC: 8351 Preschool center

(G-1548)
MALGIERO HELEN A DAY CARE
311 Monroe St (19706-7743)
P.O. Box 4118 (19706-4118)
PHONE..................302 834-9060
H Malgiero, Prin
EMP: 5 EST: 2005
SALES (est): 56.18K Privately Held
SIC: 8351 Child day care services

(G-1549)
NICKLE INSURANCE AGENCY INC
Also Called: Nationwide
119 Washington St (19706-7783)
P.O. Box 4080 (19706-4080)
PHONE..................302 834-9700
Henry Nickle, Pr
EMP: 7 EST: 1931
SQ FT: 1,500
SALES (est): 746.74K Privately Held
Web: www.nationwide.com
SIC: 6411 6531 Insurance brokers, nec; Real estate brokers and agents

(G-1550)
P S C CONTRACTING INC
704 5th St (19706-7810)
P.O. Box 319 (19706-0319)
PHONE..................302 838-2998
EMP: 10 EST: 1988
SALES (est): 709.81K Privately Held
Web: www.psccontracting.com
SIC: 1731 Electrical work

(G-1551)
P S C ELECTRIC CONTRACTOR INC
704 5th St (19706-7810)
P.O. Box 319 (19706-0319)
PHONE..................302 838-2998
Preston Carden, CEO

Delaware City - New Castle County (G-1552)

EMP: 14 EST: 1988
SALES (est): 510.38K **Privately Held**
Web: www.psccontracting.com
SIC: **1731** General electrical contractor

(G-1552)
POLICE ATHLETIC LEAGUE
250 5th St (19706-7722)
PHONE.................................302 834-8460
EMP: 6 EST: 2012
SALES (est): 99.33K **Privately Held**
Web: www.palde.org
SIC: **8699** Athletic organizations

(G-1553)
PRO CLEAN WILMINGTON INC
Also Called: Pro Clean Company
210 Clinton St (19706-7708)
P.O. Box 638 (19706-0638)
PHONE.................................302 836-8080
EMP: 5 EST: 1996
SALES (est): 519.49K **Privately Held**
SIC: **1522** Residential construction, nec

(G-1554)
PROCLEAN INC
P.O. Box 638 (19706-0638)
PHONE.................................302 656-8080
William G Baker Senior, *Pr*
EMP: 20 EST: 1987
SQ FT: 8,000
SALES (est): 1MM **Privately Held**
SIC: **1799** 7217 7216 5713 Cleaning building exteriors, nec; Carpet and furniture cleaning on location; Drapery, curtain drycleaning; Carpets

(G-1555)
PSC PROPERTIES LLC
704 5th St (19706-7810)
P.O. Box 319 (19706-0319)
PHONE.................................302 832-2076
EMP: 5 EST: 2011
SALES (est): 507.73K **Privately Held**
Web: www.pscproperties.net
SIC: **6512** Nonresidential building operators

(G-1556)
RALPH BURDICK DO
900 5th St (19706-7736)
P.O. Box 300 (19706-0300)
PHONE.................................302 834-3600
Ralph Burdick D.o.s., *Owner*
Ralph Burdick, *Owner*
EMP: 5 EST: 1987
SALES (est): 299.94K **Privately Held**
SIC: **8031** Offices and clinics of osteopathic physicians

(G-1557)
SEAWAY SERVICE INC
34 Clinton St (19706-7700)
PHONE.................................302 834-7101
Philip Cruchley, *Pr*
Robert Janiszewski, *Sec*
EMP: 10 EST: 1972
SQ FT: 500
SALES (est): 197.36K **Privately Held**
SIC: **4959** Oil spill cleanup

(G-1558)
SLICE OF WOOD LLC
70 Clinton St (19706-7702)
PHONE.................................315 335-0917
Steve Redmond, *Owner*
EMP: 5 EST: 2017
SALES (est): 83.07K **Privately Held**
SIC: **2511** Wood household furniture

(G-1559)
TIRUPATI INC
600 5th St (19706-7730)
PHONE.................................302 836-8335
EMP: 5 EST: 2013
SALES (est): 277.94K **Privately Held**
SIC: **7389** Business Activities at Non-Commercial Site

Delmar
Sussex County

(G-1560)
ADKINS CUSTOM CONTRACTING LLC
18575 Line Church Rd (19940-4008)
PHONE.................................302 841-3885
William Adkins, *Prin*
EMP: 6 EST: 2018
SALES (est): 246.05K **Privately Held**
SIC: **1799** Special trade contractors, nec

(G-1561)
AFFORDABLE PLUMBING & ELC INC
36842 Red Berry Rd (19940-2347)
P.O. Box 246 (19940-0246)
PHONE.................................443 235-9222
John Middleton, *Owner*
EMP: 8 EST: 2017
SALES (est): 433.74K **Privately Held**
SIC: **1711** Plumbing contractors

(G-1562)
ALL TECH SEALCOATING LLC
36834 Red Berry Rd (19940-2347)
PHONE.................................302 907-0311
Nicole Condon, *Prin*
EMP: 7 EST: 2017
SALES (est): 171.6K **Privately Held**
SIC: **1611** Surfacing and paving

(G-1563)
AMBIENT CARE EXPRESS
31010 Thornton Blvd Unit 2 (19940-3599)
PHONE.................................302 629-3099
EMP: 6 EST: 2016
SALES (est): 109.08K **Privately Held**
SIC: **8011** Primary care medical clinic

(G-1564)
AMERICAN LGION POST 15 GLEN RY
Also Called: American Legion
104 N 2nd St (19940-1143)
PHONE.................................410 726-4580
EMP: 7 EST: 2011
SALES (est): 59.7K **Privately Held**
Web: www.legion.org
SIC: **8641** Veterans' organization

(G-1565)
AMICK FARMS LLC
10392 Allens Mill Rd (19940-3517)
P.O. Box 269 (19940-0269)
PHONE.................................302 846-9511
Scott Lee, *Mgr*
EMP: 246
Web: www.amickfarms.com
SIC: **0191** General farms, primarily crop
HQ: Amick Farms, Llc
  7155 Batesburg Hwy
  Batesburg SC 29006
  803 532-1400

(G-1566)
APPLIANCES ZONE
34936 Sussex Hwy (19940-3351)
PHONE.................................302 280-6073
Jose Correa, *Owner*
EMP: 6 EST: 2010
SALES (est): 353.11K **Privately Held**
Web: www.appliancezonedelmar.com
SIC: **5064** Electrical appliances, major

(G-1567)
ARABIAN LIGHTS DANCE CO INC
38052 Old Stage Rd (19940-3551)
PHONE.................................410 543-4538
Lisa Henry, *Ofcr*
EMP: 5 EST: 2012
SALES (est): 56.43K **Privately Held**
Web: www.arabianlightsdanceco.com
SIC: **7922** Theatrical producers and services

(G-1568)
BOWDEN CONSTRUCTION LLC
14147 Line Rd (19940-4160)
PHONE.................................302 907-0430
Peggy E Bowden, *Prin*
EMP: 5 EST: 2016
SALES (est): 193.07K **Privately Held**
Web: bowden-construction-llc.business.site
SIC: **1521** Single-family housing construction

(G-1569)
BRYAN & BRITTINGHAM INC
38148 Bi State Blvd (19940-3435)
P.O. Box 156 (19940-0156)
PHONE.................................302 846-9500
Robert Messick, *Pr*
Margaret Messick, *VP*
EMP: 10 EST: 1952
SQ FT: 22,500
SALES (est): 1.89MM **Privately Held**
Web: www.bryanandbrittingham.com
SIC: **5191** 5999 5251 Feed; Feed and farm supply; Hardware stores

(G-1570)
BURKE EQUIPMENT COMPANY
Also Called: Kubota Authorized Dealer
11196 E Snake Rd (19940-3452)
PHONE.................................302 248-7070
Mark Timmons, *Brnch Mgr*
EMP: 45
SALES (corp-wide): 8.93MM **Privately Held**
Web: www.burkeequipment.com
SIC: **5046** 5083 Commercial equipment, nec ; Farm and garden machinery
PA: Burke Equipment Company
  54 Andrews Lake Rd
  Felton DE 19943
  302 697-3200

(G-1571)
BV TEAGARDEN & SON CNSTR LLC
36421 Saint George Rd (19940-3497)
PHONE.................................410 330-1733
EMP: 5 EST: 2016
SALES (est): 232.15K **Privately Held**
SIC: **1521** Single-family housing construction

(G-1572)
CAR DOC
9534 Shadow Point Ln (19940-3281)
PHONE.................................301 302-3362
Larry Martin, *Prin*
EMP: 6 EST: 2018
SALES (est): 232.36K **Privately Held**
Web: www.cardocdelmar.com
SIC: **7538** General automotive repair shops

(G-1573)
CARR COURIER SERVICE INC
12294 Coachmen Ln (19940-2432)
PHONE.................................302 846-9826
Norman Carr, *Prin*
EMP: 5 EST: 2009
SALES (est): 177.36K **Privately Held**
SIC: **4215** Courier services, except by air

(G-1574)
CASH ADVANCE PLUS
38650 Sussex Hwy Unit 8 (19940-3527)
PHONE.................................302 846-3900
Ed Wilgus, *Owner*
EMP: 5
SALES (corp-wide): 3.12MM **Privately Held**
Web: www.moneygram.com
SIC: **6141** Personal credit institutions
PA: Cash Advance Plus
  N607 N 607 N Dual Hwy Rr
  Seaford DE 19973
  302 629-6266

(G-1575)
CAT WELDING LLC
37544 Horsey Church Rd (19940-3279)
PHONE.................................302 846-3509
Chad Avery Timmons, *Prin*
EMP: 5 EST: 2016
SALES (est): 65.38K **Privately Held**
SIC: **7692** Welding repair

(G-1576)
CHANCELLOR CARE CTR OF DELMAR
Also Called: Chancellor Care Center Delmar
101 Delaware Ave (19940-1110)
PHONE.................................302 846-3077
Michel Augsburger, *Pr*
EMP: 21 EST: 1992
SQ FT: 30,000
SALES (est): 378.28K **Privately Held**
SIC: **8051** 8052 Skilled nursing care facilities ; Intermediate care facilities

(G-1577)
CHESLANTIC OVERHEAD DOOR
23 Shannon St (19940-1176)
PHONE.................................443 880-0378
Philip L Donoway Junior, *Prin*
EMP: 3 EST: 2004
SALES (est): 146.15K **Privately Held**
SIC: **3442** Garage doors, overhead: metal

(G-1578)
CHEWS UNLIMITED LLC
38113 Brittingham Rd (19940-4169)
PHONE.................................302 280-6137
Brandon Chew, *Prin*
EMP: 6 EST: 2012
SALES (est): 432.25K **Privately Held**
SIC: **1522** Residential construction, nec

(G-1579)
CLARK BENSON CONTRACTING
37034 Saint George Rd (19940-3326)
PHONE.................................302 846-9119
Clark Benson, *Prin*
EMP: 5 EST: 2008
SALES (est): 109.43K **Privately Held**
SIC: **1799** Special trade contractors, nec

(G-1580)
CLASSIC CANVAS LLC
3505 May Twilley Rd (19940-3077)
PHONE.................................443 359-0150
Joshua Littleton, *Prin*
EMP: 6 EST: 2017
SALES (est): 229.6K **Privately Held**
SIC: **2211** Canvas

GEOGRAPHIC SECTION
Delmar - Sussex County (G-1607)

(G-1581)
COASTAL BATH LLC
106 N Pennsylvania Ave (19940-1133)
PHONE..................302 742-9128
EMP: 6 **EST:** 2021
SALES (est): 267.31K **Privately Held**
Web: www.coastalbaths.com
SIC: 1799 Kitchen and bathroom remodeling

(G-1582)
COLUMBIA VENDING SERVICE INC
10000 Old Racetrack Rd (19940-3495)
P.O. Box 449 (19940-0449)
PHONE..................302 856-7000
Mike Tyler, *Mgr*
EMP: 10
SQ FT: 1,000
SALES (corp-wide): 2.11MM **Privately Held**
Web: www.columbiamg.com
SIC: 5962 7699 Sandwich and hot food vending machines; Vending machine repair
PA: Columbia Vending Service, Inc.
  6424 Frankford Ave 26
  Baltimore MD 21206
  410 485-3700

(G-1583)
CONCRETE BLDG SYSTEMS DEL INC
Also Called: CBS
9283 Old Racetrack Rd (19940-3398)
P.O. Box 48 (19940-0048)
PHONE..................302 846-3645
Todd Stephens, *Pr*
Renae Stephens, *
EMP: 25 **EST:** 1981
SQ FT: 2,000
SALES (est): 2.36MM **Privately Held**
Web: www.ernestmaier.com
SIC: 1771 Concrete work

(G-1584)
CRYSTAL STEEL FABRICATORS INC
N 2nd (19940)
PHONE..................302 846-0277
Micheal Smith, *Mgr*
EMP: 18
Web: www.crystalsteel.com
SIC: 3441 Fabricated structural metal
PA: Crystal Steel Fabricators Inc
  9317 Old Racetrack Rd
  Delmar DE 19940

(G-1585)
CRYSTAL STEEL FABRICATORS INC (PA)
Also Called: Crystal Metalworks Inc Fairfax
9317 Old Racetrack Rd (19940-3065)
PHONE..................302 846-0613
William Lo, *Pr*
Jeff Lo, *
EMP: 84 **EST:** 1992
SQ FT: 50,000
SALES (est): 45.35MM **Privately Held**
Web: www.crystalsteel.com
SIC: 3441 Building components, structural steel

(G-1586)
D&C LOGGING
16075 Russell Rd (19940-4137)
PHONE..................302 846-3982
David Carptner, *Owner*
EMP: 4 **EST:** 1996
SALES (est): 273.2K **Privately Held**
SIC: 2411 Logging camps and contractors

(G-1587)
DELMARVA PERFORMANCE AND REPR
502 N Bi State Blvd (19940-1101)
PHONE..................302 858-3546
EMP: 8 **EST:** 2016
SALES (est): 460.79K **Privately Held**
Web: www.delmarvaperformanceandrepair.com
SIC: 7699 Repair services, nec

(G-1588)
DELMARVA REFRIGERATION INC
504 N Pennsylvania Ave (19940-1137)
P.O. Box 38 (19940-0038)
PHONE..................302 846-2727
Lou Alberti, *Pr*
Cathy Alberti, *VP*
EMP: 9 **EST:** 1983
SQ FT: 3,000
SALES (est): 350.56K **Privately Held**
SIC: 7623 1711 5078 5074 Refrigeration repair service; Warm air heating and air conditioning contractor; Commercial refrigeration equipment; Heating equipment (hydronic)

(G-1589)
DICKERSON FENCE CO INC
36947 Saint George Rd (19940-3324)
PHONE..................302 846-2227
Scott Dickerson, *Pr*
Ronald Dickerson, *VP*
EMP: 7 **EST:** 1980
SALES (est): 630.33K **Privately Held**
Web: www.dickersonfence.com
SIC: 1799 Fence construction

(G-1590)
DONNA BRITTINGHAM MS
38076 Brittingham Rd (19940-4113)
PHONE..................302 846-3661
Donna Brittingham, *Owner*
EMP: 5 **EST:** 2008
SALES (est): 221.93K **Privately Held**
SIC: 0119 0139 Cash grains, nec; Feeder crops

(G-1591)
DUANE EDWARD RUARK
6988 Beagle Dr (19940-3171)
PHONE..................302 846-2332
Ketteh Ruark, *Pr*
EMP: 3 **EST:** 2004
SALES (est): 168.72K **Privately Held**
SIC: 3531 Bulldozers (construction machinery)

(G-1592)
E Z CASH OF DELAWARE INC (PA)
300 N Bi State Blvd Ste 1 (19940-1235)
PHONE..................302 846-2920
Marion Adkins, *Pr*
EMP: 6 **EST:** 1998
SALES (est): 3.02MM
SALES (corp-wide): 3.02MM **Privately Held**
Web: www.ezcashde.com
SIC: 6141 Personal credit institutions

(G-1593)
ELLIOTT JOHN
36411 August Rd (19940-2343)
PHONE..................302 846-2487
EMP: 5 **EST:** 1945
SALES (est): 132.11K **Privately Held**
Web: www.elliottfrantz.com
SIC: 0111 0115 0116 Wheat; Corn; Soybeans

(G-1594)
ENVIROTROLS GROUP INC
105 E State St (19940-1155)
P.O. Box 467 (19940-0467)
PHONE..................302 846-9103
Laura Vernon, *Pr*
Jeffrey Vernon, *VP*
EMP: 8 **EST:** 1994
SALES (est): 800K **Privately Held**
Web: www.envirotrolsgroup.com
SIC: 1731 Energy management controls

(G-1595)
EURSHALL MILLERS AUTOBODY
36371 Sussex Hwy (19940-3500)
PHONE..................410 742-7329
EMP: 5 **EST:** 2019
SALES (est): 151.81K **Privately Held**
Web: www.emillersautobody.com
SIC: 7532 Body shop, automotive

(G-1596)
FIREMENS HSTRCAL FNDTION DLMAR
601 Delaware Ave (19940-1321)
PHONE..................302 846-3014
EMP: 5 **EST:** 2011
SALES (est): 62.02K **Privately Held**
SIC: 8641 Civic and social associations

(G-1597)
FUNFULL INC
Also Called: Technology
31236 Meadowview Sq (19940-3475)
PHONE..................888 386-3855
Vishal Patel, *CEO*
EMP: 11 **EST:** 2020
SALES (est): 394.61K **Privately Held**
Web: www.funfull.com
SIC: 7922 7371 7929 Entertainment promotion; Software programming applications; Entertainment service

(G-1598)
GENERAL REFRIGERATION COMPANY (PA)
34971 Sussex Hwy (19940-3399)
P.O. Box 140 (19940-0140)
PHONE..................302 846-3073
Frank Nechay, *Pr*
Rudolph Nechay, *
David Hartig, *
Eva M Nechay, *
EMP: 41 **EST:** 1971
SQ FT: 18,000
SALES (est): 14.19MM
SALES (corp-wide): 14.19MM **Privately Held**
Web: www.generalrefrig.com
SIC: 1711 3585 Refrigeration contractor; Air conditioning condensers and condensing units

(G-1599)
GREAT GAINES LLC (PA)
Also Called: All Pro Security
4574 White Deer Rd (19940-3049)
PHONE..................443 248-3952
Tashawna Gaines, *Managing Member*
EMP: 6 **EST:** 2020
SALES (est): 72.19K
SALES (corp-wide): 72.19K **Privately Held**
SIC: 7381 Security guard service

(G-1600)
HARVEST MINISTRIES INC
305 N Bi State Blvd (19940-1212)
P.O. Box 506 (19940-0506)
PHONE..................302 846-3001
Mark Frazier, *Pr*
EMP: 6 **EST:** 1996
SALES (est): 55.02K **Privately Held**
SIC: 8699 Food co-operative

(G-1601)
HOPKINS TAX & ACCOUNTING LLC
36885 Columbia Rd (19940-3065)
PHONE..................302 846-2303
Roy Hopkins, *Prin*
EMP: 7 **EST:** 2012
SALES (est): 58.44K **Privately Held**
Web: www.hopkinstaxaccounting.com
SIC: 7291 Tax return preparation services

(G-1602)
ILLUMINATION TECHNOLOGY INC
38024 N Spring Hill Rd (19940-3113)
PHONE..................410 430-5349
EMP: 4 **EST:** 2018
SALES (est): 88.38K **Privately Held**
Web: www.illuminationtechnology.com
SIC: 3646 Commercial lighting fixtures

(G-1603)
J & A OVERHEAD DOOR INC
Also Called: Overhead Doors
16937 Whitesville Rd (19940-4032)
PHONE..................302 846-9915
Jason A Yoder Junior, *Sec*
Jason A Yoder Junior, *Pr*
Amy J Yoder, *Sec*
Jason A Yoder Junior, *Owner*
EMP: 5 **EST:** 2003
SQ FT: 2,400
SALES (est): 855K **Privately Held**
Web: www.jnaohd.com
SIC: 1751 Garage door, installation or erection

(G-1604)
J WILLIAM GORDY FUEL CO (PA)
Also Called: Exxon Food Mart
106 N Pennsylvania Ave (19940-1133)
P.O. Box 7366 (34101-7366)
PHONE..................302 846-3425
J William Gordy, *Pr*
Ee Gordy, *Sec*
Karen Gordy, *VP*
EMP: 8 **EST:** 1950
SQ FT: 3,000
SALES (est): 2.6MM
SALES (corp-wide): 2.6MM **Privately Held**
Web: www.exxon.com
SIC: 5411 5172 5541 Convenience stores; Gasoline; Gasoline service stations

(G-1605)
JERRY A FLETCHER
Also Called: Jerry A Fletcher Catering
34301 Rider Rd (19940-3001)
PHONE..................302 875-9057
Jerry A Fletcher, *Prin*
EMP: 5 **EST:** 2011
SALES (est): 166.66K **Privately Held**
SIC: 4899 Communication services, nec

(G-1606)
JIN PEN FEET MASSAGE
38660 Sussex Hwy Unit 3 (19940-3529)
PHONE..................302 228-2846
Raymond Dukes, *Prin*
EMP: 6 **EST:** 2017
SALES (est): 70.75K **Privately Held**
SIC: 8049 Massage Therapist

(G-1607)
JOB PRINTING
36729 Bi State Blvd (19940-3427)
PHONE..................302 907-0416
Jeffrey F Walbert, *Prin*

Delmar - Sussex County (G-1608)

GEOGRAPHIC SECTION

EMP: 5 EST: 2010
SALES (est): 62.73K **Privately Held**
SIC: 2752 Offset printing

(G-1608)
JOHNSON CONTROLS INC
Also Called: Johnson Controls
34898 Sussex Hwy (19940-3395)
PHONE..................302 715-5208
EMP: 19
Web: www.johnsoncontrols.com
SIC: 2531 Seats, automobile
HQ: Johnson Controls, Inc.
5757 N Green Bay Ave
Milwaukee WI 53209
920 245-6409

(G-1609)
K AND B HVAC SVCS LLC
Also Called: Honeywell Authorized Dealer
18228 Whitesville Rd (19940-4024)
PHONE..................302 846-3111
Brett Elkington, *Managing Member*
EMP: 7 EST: 2012
SALES (est): 708.99K **Privately Held**
Web: www.kbhvacdelaware.com
SIC: 1711 Warm air heating and air conditioning contractor

(G-1610)
KENCO TROPHY SALES
301 Lincoln Ave (19940-1237)
PHONE..................302 846-3339
Kenneth W Birch Senior, *Owner*
EMP: 2 EST: 1977
SALES (est): 83.39K **Privately Held**
SIC: 2499 Trophy bases, wood

(G-1611)
KNEPPS CONSTRUCTION
38120 Brittingham Rd (19940-4114)
PHONE..................302 846-3360
EMP: 5 EST: 2009
SALES (est): 237.39K **Privately Held**
SIC: 1521 Single-family housing construction

(G-1612)
LADYBUG PEST MANAGEMENT INC
15307 Britt Ln (19940-4167)
PHONE..................302 846-2295
Sandra Honess, *Prin*
EMP: 8 EST: 2009
SALES (est): 235.43K **Privately Held**
Web: www.ladybugpm.com
SIC: 7342 Pest control in structures

(G-1613)
LARRY HILL FARMS INC
Rt 1 Box 518 (19940)
PHONE..................302 875-0886
Larry Hill, *Pr*
Bonnie Hill, *Treas*
Alex Hill, *VP*
Wade Hill, *Sec*
EMP: 8 EST: 1986
SALES (est): 469.71K **Privately Held**
SIC: 1542 Farm building construction

(G-1614)
LARRY HILL FARMS LLC
36292 Old Stage Rd (19940-2411)
PHONE..................302 245-6657
EMP: 10 EST: 2015
SALES (est): 175.69K **Privately Held**
SIC: 0251 Broiling chickens, raising of

(G-1615)
LIL RED HEN NURSERY SCHL INC
400 N Bi State Blvd (19940-1205)
PHONE..................302 846-2777
Ann Atkinson, *Pr*
Tom Atkinson, *Prin*
EMP: 21 EST: 1985
SALES (est): 452.26K **Privately Held**
Web: www.lilredhen.com
SIC: 8351 Preschool center

(G-1616)
MANUFACTURERS & TRADERS TR CO
Also Called: M&T
38716 Sussex Hwy (19940-3516)
PHONE..................302 855-2297
Keith Atkins, *Brnch Mgr*
EMP: 5
SALES (corp-wide): 8.6B **Publicly Held**
Web: ir.mtb.com
SIC: 6022 State commercial banks
HQ: Manufacturers And Traders Trust Company
1 M&T Plz Fl 3
Buffalo NY 14203
716 842-4200

(G-1617)
MARLEN D SCHLABACH
36170 Smith Mill Ch Rd (19940-4252)
PHONE..................302 236-5394
Marlen Schlabach, *Prin*
EMP: 5 EST: 2009
SALES (est): 82.66K **Privately Held**
SIC: 8748 Safety training service

(G-1618)
MAYR ENTERPRISES LLC
7175 W Line Rd (19940-3164)
PHONE..................302 846-2999
Edward Mayr, *Prin*
EMP: 5 EST: 2015
SALES (est): 200.92K **Privately Held**
SIC: 8748 Business consulting, nec

(G-1619)
MEADOWBROOK FARMS INC
14702 Baker Rd (19940-4144)
PHONE..................443 735-6244
EMP: 5 EST: 2019
SALES (est): 239.57K **Privately Held**
SIC: 0191 General farms, primarily crop

(G-1620)
METAL SHOP LLC
10690 Allens Mill Rd (19940-3532)
PHONE..................302 846-2988
Sherry Disharoon, *Owner*
EMP: 12 EST: 2007
SALES (est): 958.88K **Privately Held**
Web: www.themetalshopmotorsports.com
SIC: 7699 7389 Welding equipment repair; Metal cutting services

(G-1621)
MIRWORTH ENTERPRISE INC
Also Called: Children's Theater of Delmarva
404 Lincoln Ave (19940-1240)
P.O. Box 531 (19940-0531)
PHONE..................302 846-0218
Carlos Mir, *Pr*
EMP: 7 EST: 1996
SALES (est): 80.08K **Privately Held**
Web: www.theaterofdelmarva.org
SIC: 7922 Legitimate live theater producers

(G-1622)
MISSION FITNESS STUDIO LLC
6 N Pennsylvania Ave (19940-1132)
PHONE..................302 535-1129
EMP: 9
SALES (est): 138.12K **Privately Held**
Web: www.missionfitnessstudio.com
SIC: 7991 Physical fitness facilities

(G-1623)
MONRO INC
Also Called: Mr Tire 1210
5 Gerald Ct (19940-3566)
PHONE..................302 846-2732
William Hamm, *Brnch Mgr*
EMP: 6
SALES (corp-wide): 1.33B **Publicly Held**
Web: locations.mrtire.com
SIC: 5531 7549 7538 Automotive tires; Automotive maintenance services; General automotive repair shops
PA: Monro, Inc.
200 Holleder Pkwy
Rochester NY 14615
585 647-6400

(G-1624)
MORRIS MASONRY
14175 Line Rd (19940-4160)
PHONE..................410 726-6277
Roland Morris, *Owner*
EMP: 5 EST: 1993
SALES (est): 248.95K **Privately Held**
SIC: 1741 Masonry and other stonework

(G-1625)
MOTION INDUSTRIES INC
38541 Sussex Hwy (19940-3512)
PHONE..................302 462-3130
Kelly Larger, *Mgr*
EMP: 22
SQ FT: 24,750
SALES (corp-wide): 22.1B **Publicly Held**
Web: www.motionindustries.com
SIC: 5085 Industrial supplies
HQ: Motion Industries, Inc.
1605 Alton Rd
Birmingham AL 35210
205 956-1122

(G-1626)
NEW IMAGE PROPERTY MAINTENANCE
10191 Old Crow Rd (19940-3414)
PHONE..................302 396-0451
Nathan Andrade, *Prin*
EMP: 5 EST: 2018
SALES (est): 20.74K **Privately Held**
SIC: 7349 Building maintenance services, nec

(G-1627)
OM GANESH TWO LLC
Also Called: Wireless Nation
31010 Thornton Blvd Unit 3 (19940-3599)
PHONE..................410 720-9374
Ash Thakur, *Managing Member*
EMP: 6 EST: 2016
SALES (est): 109.89K **Privately Held**
SIC: 7389 Business Activities at Non-Commercial Site

(G-1628)
PENINSULA ANMAL HOSP ORTHPDICS
38375 Old Stage Rd (19940-3569)
PHONE..................302 846-9011
Frances Haberstroh Ms, *Prin*
EMP: 9 EST: 2014
SALES (est): 504.34K **Privately Held**
Web: www.penanimal.com
SIC: 0742 Animal hospital services, pets and other animal specialties

(G-1629)
PENINSULA TECHNICAL SERVICES I
38224 Old Stage Rd (19940-3547)
P.O. Box 149 (19940-0149)
PHONE..................302 907-0554
Mark A Frazier, *Prin*
EMP: 3 EST: 2008
SALES (est): 165.86K **Privately Held**
Web: www.peninsulatechnical.com
SIC: 7692 Welding repair

(G-1630)
PET MEDICAL CENTER
Rte 13 (19940)
PHONE..................302 846-2869
Richard Long, *Owner*
EMP: 7 EST: 1997
SALES (est): 302.87K **Privately Held**
SIC: 0742 Animal hospital services, pets and other animal specialties

(G-1631)
RE/MAX COAST COUNTRY
Also Called: Re/Max
38613 Benro Dr Unit 5 (19940-3571)
PHONE..................302 846-0200
Pamela Price, *Prin*
EMP: 5 EST: 2018
SALES (est): 196.66K **Privately Held**
Web: www.remax.com
SIC: 6531 Real estate agent, residential

(G-1632)
ROSS ELECTRICAL SERVICES LLC
14292 Pepperbox Rd (19940-4151)
PHONE..................443 614-7294
Brian Ross, *Prin*
EMP: 5 EST: 2019
SALES (est): 186.13K **Privately Held**
SIC: 4911 Electric services

(G-1633)
RUSSELL SMART HOME IMPRVS LLC
37787 Eagles Run (19940-4178)
PHONE..................302 846-2404
EMP: 5 EST: 2019
SALES (est): 482.79K **Privately Held**
Web: www.smartimprovements.net
SIC: 1521 General remodeling, single-family houses

(G-1634)
SAMUEL PRETTYMAN
36603 Bi State Blvd (19940-3424)
PHONE..................302 858-8886
Samuel Prettyman, *Prin*
EMP: 5 EST: 2012
SALES (est): 248.05K **Privately Held**
SIC: 0782 Lawn care services

(G-1635)
SHORE RV RENTALS
38373 Sussex Hwy (19940-3509)
PHONE..................443 235-2183
Rick Anderson, *Prin*
EMP: 5 EST: 2005
SALES (est): 86.05K **Privately Held**
Web: www.miamirv2rent.com
SIC: 7359 Equipment rental and leasing, nec

(G-1636)
SHORT FUNERAL HOME INC (PA)
13 E Grove St (19940-1114)
P.O. Box 204 (19940-0204)
PHONE..................302 846-9814
Amy Short, *Pr*
Tom Jewel, *VP*
EMP: 6 EST: 1865
SQ FT: 5,800

GEOGRAPHIC SECTION — Dewey Beach - Sussex County (G-1663)

SALES (est): 522.04K
SALES (corp-wide): 522.04K **Privately Held**
Web: www.shortfh.com
SIC: **7261** 5999 Funeral home; Vaults and safes

(G-1637)
SHUBERT ENTERPRISES INC
Also Called: Scott & Sons Landscaping
11077 Iron Hill Rd (19940-3523)
PHONE.................302 846-3122
Scott Shubert, *Pr*
Monica Shubert, *
Janie Shubert, *
EMP: 13 EST: 1997
SALES (est): 521.56K **Privately Held**
SIC: **0782** Landscape contractors

(G-1638)
SUNBELT RENTALS INC
36412 Sussex Hwy (19940-3501)
PHONE.................302 907-1921
Joseph Bussard, *Brnch Mgr*
EMP: 9
SALES (corp-wide): 9.67B **Privately Held**
Web: www.sunbeltrentals.com
SIC: **7353** Heavy construction equipment rental
HQ: Sunbelt Rentals, Inc.
1799 Innovation Pt
Fort Mill SC 29715
803 578-5811

(G-1639)
TELCO ENVIROTROLS INC
105 E State St (19940-1155)
P.O. Box 467 (19940-0467)
PHONE.................302 846-9103
EMP: 10 EST: 2017
SALES (est): 896.18K **Privately Held**
Web: www.telcoenvirotrols.com
SIC: **4813** Local and long distance telephone communications

(G-1640)
TERRA FIRMA OF DELMARVA INC
38156 Brittingham Rd (19940-4114)
P.O. Box 478 (19940-0478)
PHONE.................302 846-3350
Vicki Pusey, *Pr*
Chris Pusey, *Prin*
Vicki Pusey, *Prin*
Phillip W Pusey, *Prin*
EMP: 22 EST: 2006
SALES (est): 2.38MM **Privately Held**
Web: www.terrafirmacorp.com
SIC: **1771** 1611 Parking lot construction; Surfacing and paving

(G-1641)
THERMO KING CORPORATION
Also Called: Thermo King Chesapeake
36550 Sussex Hwy (19940-3503)
PHONE.................302 907-0345
Donald Hall, *Brnch Mgr*
EMP: 6
Web: www.thermoking.com
SIC: **5078** Refrigeration equipment and supplies
HQ: Thermo King Llc
314 W 90th St
Bloomington MN 55420
952 887-2200

(G-1642)
THERMO KING LLC
Also Called: Thermo King of Delaware
36550 Sussex Hwy (19940-3503)
P.O. Box 1642 (19973-8942)
PHONE.................302 907-0345
Donald Hall, *Mgr*
EMP: 5
Web: www.thermoking.com
SIC: **5078** Refrigeration equipment and supplies
HQ: Thermo King Llc
314 W 90th St
Bloomington MN 55420
952 887-2200

(G-1643)
TRIGLIA EXPRESS INC
38001 Bi State Blvd (19940-3433)
PHONE.................302 846-2248
EMP: 8 EST: 1990
SQ FT: 100,000
SALES (est): 637.25K **Privately Held**
SIC: **4731** Freight forwarding

(G-1644)
TRIGLIA TRANS CO
Bystate Blvd (19940)
P.O. Box 218 (19940-0218)
PHONE.................302 846-3795
Rosemary Lynch, *Pr*
Toney Triglia, *VP*
Carrie Williams, *Mgr*
EMP: 8 EST: 1948
SALES (est): 159.95K **Privately Held**
SIC: **7363** Truck driver services

(G-1645)
TRIGLIAS TRANSPORTATION CO
Rte 13 A (19940)
P.O. Box 187 (19940-0187)
PHONE.................302 846-2141
Rosemary Lynch, *Pr*
Anthony Triglia, *VP*
Justin Lych, *Treas*
George Lynch, *Sec*
EMP: 20 EST: 1940
SQ FT: 7,200
SALES (est): 836.51K **Privately Held**
SIC: **4212** 4213 Delivery service, vehicular; Contract haulers

(G-1646)
TRINITY MEDICAL CENTER PA
8 E Grove St (19940-1115)
PHONE.................302 846-0618
Khalil Gorgui, *Prin*
EMP: 5 EST: 2008
SALES (est): 169.91K **Privately Held**
SIC: **8031** 8011 Offices and clinics of osteopathic physicians; Medical centers

(G-1647)
TRIPLE TZZ HVAC LLC
17114 Whitesville Rd (19940-4029)
PHONE.................302 846-3220
Terry Oliphant, *Prin*
EMP: 6 EST: 2017
SALES (est): 194.58K **Privately Held**
SIC: **1711** Heating and air conditioning contractors

(G-1648)
U S 13 DRAGWAY INC (PA)
Also Called: Delaware Intl Speedway
36952 Sussex Hwy (19940-3507)
PHONE.................302 875-1911
EMP: 66 EST: 1967
SQ FT: 8,000
SALES (est): 2.37MM **Privately Held**
Web: www.delawareracing.com
SIC: **7948** Auto race track operation

(G-1649)
UNITED RENTALS NORTH AMER INC
Also Called: United Rentals
38190 Old Stage Rd # A (19940-3550)
PHONE.................302 907-0292
Kenny Midgett, *Mgr*
EMP: 5
SALES (corp-wide): 14.33B **Publicly Held**
Web: www.unitedrentals.com
SIC: **7359** Equipment rental and leasing, nec
HQ: United Rentals (North America), Inc.
100 Frst Stmford Pl Ste 7
Stamford CT 06902
203 622-3131

(G-1650)
UNITED RENTALS NORTH AMER INC
Also Called: United Rentals
38352 Sussex Hwy (19940-3508)
PHONE.................302 846-0955
Bruce Austin, *Mgr*
EMP: 10
SALES (corp-wide): 14.33B **Publicly Held**
Web: www.unitedrentals.com
SIC: **7359** Rental store, general
HQ: United Rentals (North America), Inc.
100 Frst Stmford Pl Ste 7
Stamford CT 06902
203 622-3131

(G-1651)
UPS STORE
38660 Sussex Hwy Unit 10 (19940-3529)
PHONE.................302 907-0455
EMP: 6 EST: 2019
SALES (est): 241.26K **Privately Held**
Web: www.theupsstore.com
SIC: **7389** Mailbox rental and related service

(G-1652)
US 13 SPEEDWAY
36952 Sussex Hwy (19940-3507)
PHONE.................302 846-3911
Charles Cathell, *Mgr*
EMP: 6 EST: 2014
SALES (est): 63.65K **Privately Held**
SIC: **7948** Auto race track operation

(G-1653)
VALLEJO VZQUEZ SONS HRVSTG LLC
15705 Gathering Garden Ln (19940-4267)
PHONE.................616 902-5851
EMP: 5 EST: 2021
SALES (est): 79.72K **Privately Held**
SIC: **4731** Freight transportation arrangement

(G-1654)
WELDING BY JACKSON
10178 Jackson St (19940-3301)
P.O. Box 39 (19940-0039)
PHONE.................302 846-3090
Helen Jackson, *Prin*
EMP: 2 EST: 2008
SALES (est): 151.06K **Privately Held**
SIC: **7692** Welding repair

(G-1655)
WHITE DEER AUTO
6234 White Deer Rd (19940-3145)
PHONE.................302 846-0547
Stephen Mollock, *Prin*
EMP: 5 EST: 2017
SALES (est): 28.25K **Privately Held**
SIC: **7538** General automotive repair shops

(G-1656)
WHITETAIL COUNTRY LOG & HLG
Also Called: Whitetail Country Log & Hlg
16075 Russell Rd (19940-4137)
PHONE.................302 846-3982
EMP: 4 EST: 1996
SALES (est): 458.32K **Privately Held**
SIC: **2411** 0811 4212 Logging camps and contractors; Timber tracts; Local trucking, without storage

(G-1657)
WIDGEON ENTERPRISES INC
38204 Old Stage Rd (19940-3547)
P.O. Box 468 (19940-0468)
PHONE.................302 846-9763
David P Widgeon, *Pr*
Larry Widgeon, *VP*
Faye Widgeon, *Sec*
EMP: 6 EST: 1972
SALES (est): 412.21K **Privately Held**
Web: www.widgeonenterprises.com
SIC: **7699** 5046 Scale repair service; Scales, except laboratory

(G-1658)
WILKINS WILDLIFE & BEDBUG 911
36627 Bi State Blvd (19940-3424)
PHONE.................302 236-3533
EMP: 5 EST: 2017
SALES (est): 59.24K **Privately Held**
Web: www.wilkinswildlifebedbug911.com
SIC: **7342** Pest control in structures

(G-1659)
WINDOW MAN
38001 Bi State Blvd (19940-3433)
PHONE.................302 381-4888
Joseph S Triglia, *Prin*
EMP: 5 EST: 2009
SALES (est): 196.29K **Privately Held**
SIC: **5031** Windows

(G-1660)
YODER OVERHEAD DOOR COMPANY
Also Called: Yoder Overhead Door Co.
36318 Sussex Hwy (19940-3573)
PHONE.................302 875-0663
Nolan Brunk, *Genl Mgr*
EMP: 6 EST: 1988
SQ FT: 3,300
SALES (est): 736.65K **Privately Held**
Web: www.yoderdoors.com
SIC: **1751** 7699 Garage door, installation or erection; Door and window repair

Dewey Beach
Sussex County

(G-1661)
ADAMS OCEANFRONT RESORT
Also Called: Adams Oceanfront Villas
4 Read Ave (19971-2311)
PHONE.................302 227-3030
Harold E Dukes Junior, *Owner*
EMP: 12 EST: 1976
SQ FT: 14,000
SALES (est): 244.11K **Privately Held**
Web: www.adamsoceanfront.com
SIC: **7011** Motels

(G-1662)
ATLANTIC VIEW MOTEL
2 Clayton St (19971-2307)
PHONE.................302 227-3878
Kenneth Simpler, *Owner*
EMP: 10 EST: 1984
SALES (est): 121.39K **Privately Held**
Web: www.atlanticview.com
SIC: **7011** Motels

(G-1663)
BAY RESORT
1607 Bayard Ave (19971-3342)
PHONE.................302 227-1598

Dan Fosnocht, *Mgr*
EMP: 13 **EST:** 2007
SALES (est): 237.37K **Privately Held**
Web: www.bayresort.com
SIC: 7011 Resort hotel

(G-1664)
BEACH BREAK
2104 Highway One (19971-2317)
PHONE.................................302 226-3450
Robert Bishop, *Owner*
EMP: 6 **EST:** 2006
SALES (est): 390.67K **Privately Held**
SIC: 6099 Automated teller machine (ATM) network

(G-1665)
BELL BUOY MOTEL
Also Called: Bellbuoy Inn
21 Vandyke St (19971-2510)
PHONE.................................302 227-6000
Tim Mahoney, *Pt*
EMP: 5 **EST:** 1996
SALES (est): 153.74K **Privately Held**
Web: www.surfshantymotel.com
SIC: 7011 Motels

(G-1666)
DEWEY BEACH HOUSE
Also Called: Beach House Dewey Hotel
1710 Coastal Hwy (19971-2333)
PHONE.................................302 227-4000
EMP: 15 **EST:** 2013
SALES (est): 359.44K **Privately Held**
Web: www.blockpartyhotels.com
SIC: 7011 Motels

(G-1667)
DEWEY BEACH YOGA LLC
119 Jersey St (19971-3415)
PHONE.................................443 250-6770
Carole Seibel, *Prin*
EMP: 5 **EST:** 2017
SALES (est): 38.56K **Privately Held**
SIC: 7999 Yoga instruction

(G-1668)
DEWEY BEER & FOOD COMPANY LLC
Also Called: Dewey Beer Company
2100 Coastal Hwy (19971-2317)
PHONE.................................302 227-1182
Brandon Smith, *Prin*
Mike Reilly, *Prin*
Scot Kaufman, *Prin*
EMP: 16 **EST:** 2016
SALES (est): 1.64MM **Privately Held**
Web: www.deweybeerco.com
SIC: 2082 5813 Beer (alcoholic beverage); Beer garden (drinking places)

(G-1669)
FELLS POINT SURF CO LLC
23 Bellevue St (19971-2301)
PHONE.................................302 212-2005
EMP: 6 **EST:** 2012
SALES (est): 115.12K **Privately Held**
Web: www.fellspointsurf.com
SIC: 3949 Surfboards

(G-1670)
HUDSON SCHOLASTIC
109a Clayton St (19971-3336)
PHONE.................................302 463-0840
Amy Hudson, *Owner*
EMP: 5 **EST:** 2013
SALES (est): 91.81K **Privately Held**
SIC: 1611 Highway and street construction

(G-1671)
HYATT PLACE
1301 Coastal Hwy (19971-2416)
PHONE.................................302 864-9100
EMP: 27 **EST:** 2013
SALES (est): 1.85MM **Privately Held**
Web: www.hpdeweybeach.com
SIC: 7011 Hotels and motels

(G-1672)
JUNGLE JIMS TOTAL PET CARE
1705 Coastal Hwy (19971-2323)
PHONE.................................302 212-5055
James Caperelli, *Prin*
EMP: 6 **EST:** 2018
SALES (est): 203.47K **Privately Held**
Web: www.junglejimstotalpetcare.com
SIC: 0752 Grooming services, pet and animal specialties

(G-1673)
LOUDOUN MODERN LLC
10 Vandyke St B (19971-2510)
PHONE.................................703 447-6688
Alison M Naden, *Admn*
EMP: 5 **EST:** 2007
SALES (est): 74.05K **Privately Held**
SIC: 7389 Business services, nec

(G-1674)
MOORE PARTNERSHIP
Also Called: Bay Resort Motel
126 Bellevue St (19971-3202)
P.O. Box 461 (19971-0461)
PHONE.................................302 227-5253
Robert H Moore, *Pt*
Ronald T Moore, *Pt*
EMP: 15 **EST:** 1983
SQ FT: 20,700
SALES (est): 650.84K **Privately Held**
Web: www.bayresort.com
SIC: 7011 Motels

(G-1675)
SURF CLUB
1 Read Ave (19971-2311)
PHONE.................................302 227-7059
EMP: 6 **EST:** 1993
SALES (est): 383.71K **Privately Held**
Web: www.surfclubhotel.com
SIC: 7011 Resort hotel

(G-1676)
VENUS ON HALFSHELL
136 Dagsworthy Ave (19971)
PHONE.................................302 227-9292
Bill Galbraith, *Prin*
EMP: 7 **EST:** 2004
SALES (est): 197.66K **Privately Held**
SIC: 5812 5146 Seafood restaurants; Fish and seafoods

Dover
Kent County

(G-1677)
1080 SLVER LK BLVD OPRTONS LLC
Also Called: Silver Lake Center
1080 Silver Lake Blvd (19904-2410)
PHONE.................................610 444-6350
EMP: 19 **EST:** 2007
SALES (est): 1.22MM **Privately Held**
SIC: 8051 Convalescent home with continuous nursing care

(G-1678)
111 MEDCO LLC
8 The Grn Ste 8178 (19901-3618)
PHONE.................................888 711-7090
EMP: 5 **EST:** 2018
SALES (est): 58.72K **Privately Held**
SIC: 2841 Soap and other detergents

(G-1679)
1203 WALKER RD OPERATIONS LLC
Also Called: Heritage At Dover
1203 Walker Rd (19904-6541)
PHONE.................................302 735-8800
EMP: 511
SALES (est): 41.47MM **Privately Held**
SIC: 8051 Skilled nursing care facilities
HQ: Genesis Healthcare Llc
101 E State St
Kennett Square PA 19348

(G-1680)
1ST STATE POWER CLEAN LLC
1609 Forrest Ave (19904-9725)
PHONE.................................302 735-7974
EMP: 5 **EST:** 2006
SALES (est): 169.18K **Privately Held**
Web: www.1ststatepowercleanllc.com
SIC: 7699 Cleaning services

(G-1681)
22 SOLUTIONS LLC
8 The Grn (19901-3618)
PHONE.................................901 672-0006
EMP: 10 **EST:** 2020
SALES (est): 500K **Privately Held**
Web: www.22solutions.com
SIC: 7379 Online services technology consultants

(G-1682)
247 DIGIMEDIA INC
8 The Grn (19901-3618)
PHONE.................................302 401-6369
Fakhra Khan, *CEO*
EMP: 20 **EST:** 2018
SALES (est): 250K **Privately Held**
Web: www.247digimedia.com
SIC: 8742 Marketing consulting services

(G-1683)
280 GROUP LLC
1151 Walker Rd (19904-6600)
PHONE.................................408 834-7518
Rina Alexin, *CEO*
Brian Lawley, *Managing Member**
EMP: 30 **EST:** 2012
SALES (est): 2.64MM **Privately Held**
Web: www.280group.com
SIC: 8748 8742 Business consulting, nec; Training and development consultant

(G-1684)
2YUM INC (PA)
8 The Grn Ste A (19901-3618)
PHONE.................................626 420-4851
Yu Yang, *Pr*
EMP: 7 **EST:** 2018
SALES (est): 239.2K
SALES (corp-wide): 239.2K **Privately Held**
SIC: 4213 5961 7371 7389 Automobiles, transport and delivery; Food, mail order; Computer software development and applications; Business services, nec

(G-1685)
302 CONTRACTING LLC
2428 W Denneys Rd (19904-4707)
PHONE.................................302 677-1912
Matt Rycewicz, *Prin*
EMP: 5 **EST:** 2017
SALES (est): 56.76K **Privately Held**
SIC: 1799 Special trade contractors, nec

(G-1686)
4 ELEMENTS ES LLC
1061 S Little Creek Rd Trlr 230 (19901-5000)
PHONE.................................302 670-5575
Enrique Lujan Flores, *Prin*
EMP: 6 **EST:** 2018
SALES (est): 327.22K **Privately Held**
SIC: 4911 Electric services

(G-1687)
436 AERIAL PORT SQUADRON
150 Patriot Way (19902)
PHONE.................................302 677-3169
Christina Mcmillen, *Prin*
EMP: 6 **EST:** 2012
SALES (est): 138.16K **Privately Held**
SIC: 8641 Condominium association

(G-1688)
44 AASHA HOSPITALITY ASSOC LLC
Also Called: Hilton
1706 N Dupont Hwy (19901-2219)
PHONE.................................302 674-3784
EMP: 21 **EST:** 2008
SALES (est): 145.93K **Privately Held**
Web: www.hiltongrandvacations.com
SIC: 7011 Resort hotel

(G-1689)
6-4-3 FITNESS CORP
9 E Loockerman St Ste 3a (19901-7316)
PHONE.................................347 441-9690
Manuel Tavarez, *CEO*
Manuel Tavarez, *Pr*
EMP: 7 **EST:** 2016
SALES (est): 150K **Privately Held**
SIC: 7991 Physical fitness facilities

(G-1690)
70 INC
8 The Grn Ste B (19901-3618)
PHONE.................................310 529-1526
Jacob Lewin, *CEO*
EMP: 7
SALES (est): 78.16K **Privately Held**
SIC: 2759 Commercial printing, nec

(G-1691)
9222 ENTERPRISES LLC
8 The Grn (19901-3618)
PHONE.................................888 551-1393
EMP: 5
SALES (est): 199.4K **Privately Held**
SIC: 8748 Business consulting, nec

(G-1692)
9ZEST INC
8 The Grn Ste 5910 (19901-3618)
PHONE.................................703 666-8122
Manoj Agarwala, *Pr*
Archana Agarwala, *Ofcr*
EMP: 10 **EST:** 2015
SALES (est): 80.92K **Privately Held**
Web: www.9zest.com
SIC: 7991 Physical fitness facilities

(G-1693)
A CENTER FOR MNTAL WLLNESS CMN ✪
121 W Loockerman St (19904-7325)
PHONE.................................302 674-1397
EMP: 27 **EST:** 2022
SALES (est): 552.55K **Privately Held**
SIC: 8093 Mental health clinic, outpatient

(G-1694)
A CENTER FOR MNTAL WLLNESS INC

GEOGRAPHIC SECTION
Dover - Kent County (G-1722)

121 W Loockerman St (19904-7325)
PHONE................302 674-1397
Lauren E Tinsley, Pr
Leticia Thomas, Off Mgr
EMP: 50 EST: 2008
SALES (est): 2.09MM Privately Held
Web: www.acfmw.com
SIC: 8322 General counseling services

(G-1695)
A PEACFUL PL INTGRTED CARE LLC
1001 S Bradford St Ste 7 (19904-4153)
PHONE................302 264-3692
Ericka Daniel, CEO
EMP: 13 EST: 2020
SALES (est): 292.05K Privately Held
Web: www.apeacefulplaceintegratedcare.com
SIC: 7389 Business services, nec

(G-1696)
A REGISTERED AGENT INC
8 The Grn Ste 1 (19901-3618)
PHONE................302 288-0670
Steve Workheimer, Pr
EMP: 5 EST: 2016
SALES (est): 609.23K Privately Held
Web: www.delawareregisteredagent.com
SIC: 6282 Investment advice

(G-1697)
A&M TRANSPORTATION INC
120 N St Ate St (19901)
PHONE................781 227-1357
Aram Davtyan, Pr
EMP: 9 EST: 2017
SALES (est): 66.89K Privately Held
SIC: 7537 Automotive transmission repair shops

(G-1698)
A+ CLEANING SOLUTIONS INC
3500 S Dupont Hwy (19901-6041)
PHONE................423 693-7554
Andrew Foster, CEO
EMP: 5
SALES (est): 47.02K Privately Held
Web: www.thecleaningauthority.com
SIC: 7349 Cleaning service, industrial or commercial

(G-1699)
A-TO-Z MANAGEMENT LLC
8 The Grn Ste 14696 (19901-3618)
PHONE................302 500-5230
Arielle Ziemba, Managing Member
EMP: 6
SALES (est): 307.28K Privately Held
SIC: 7389 8742 Business Activities at Non-Commercial Site; Management consulting services

(G-1700)
AAA CLUB ALLIANCE INC
Also Called: AAA Dover
124 Greentree Dr (19904-7648)
PHONE................302 674-8020
Donna Jackson, Genl Mgr
EMP: 78
SALES (corp-wide): 485.77MM Privately Held
Web: cluballiance.aaa.com
SIC: 8699 4724 6331 Automobile owners' association; Travel agencies; Fire, marine, and casualty insurance
PA: Aaa Club Alliance Inc.
  1 River Pl
  Wilmington DE 19801
  302 299-4700

(G-1701)
ABANDON INC
8 The Grn (19901-3618)
PHONE................858 863-7190
Ya Ding, CEO
EMP: 5
SALES (est): 199.4K Privately Held
SIC: 7371 Computer software development

(G-1702)
ABC VIRGINIA WIRELESS
1616 S Governors Ave (19904-7004)
PHONE................302 744-8473
EMP: 5 EST: 2016
SALES (est): 35.32K Privately Held
SIC: 4812 Cellular telephone services

(G-1703)
ABRA AUTO BODY & GLASS
Also Called: ABRA Autobody & Glass
5825 W Denneys Rd (19904-1360)
PHONE................302 674-4525
Carl M Cimino, Pr
EMP: 6 EST: 2017
SALES (est): 29.95K Privately Held
Web: www.abraauto.com
SIC: 7532 Body shop, automotive

(G-1704)
ACCELCARE WUND PRFSSNALS DEL P
73 Greentree Dr (19904-7646)
PHONE................800 261-0048
Arti Masturzo, Prin
EMP: 9 EST: 2016
SALES (est): 145.17K Privately Held
SIC: 8011 Offices and clinics of medical doctors

(G-1705)
ACCELSIORS LLC
3500 S Dupont Hwy Ste G101 (19901-6041)
PHONE................302 450-1883
Mihaly Juhasz, CEO
EMP: 8 EST: 2012
SALES (est): 113.92K Privately Held
Web: www.accelsiors.com
SIC: 7389 Business services, nec

(G-1706)
ACCESS DENTAL LLC
446 S New St A (19904-6725)
PHONE................302 674-3303
EMP: 8 EST: 2006
SALES (est): 509.47K Privately Held
Web: www.accessdentalllc.com
SIC: 8021 Dental clinic

(G-1707)
ACCESS LABOR SERVICE INC
1102 S State St (19901-4124)
PHONE................302 741-2575
Butch Brooks, Brnch Mgr
EMP: 31
SALES (corp-wide): 4.74MM Privately Held
Web: www.accesslaborservice.com
SIC: 7363 Temporary help service
PA: Access Labor Service Inc
  2203 N Dupont Hwy
  New Castle DE 19720
  302 326-2575

(G-1708)
ACCURATE INSULATION LLC
143 Hatchery Rd (19901-1502)
PHONE................302 336-8401
EMP: 20 EST: 2017
SALES (est): 483.64K
SALES (corp-wide): 2.67B Publicly Held
Web: www.accurateinsulationdelaware.com
SIC: 1742 Insulation, buildings
PA: Installed Building Products, Inc.
  495 S High St Ste 50
  Columbus OH 43215
  614 221-3399

(G-1709)
ACCUTAX
408 Martin St (19901-4530)
PHONE................302 735-9747
Debbie Clough, Owner
EMP: 5 EST: 1985
SALES (est): 89.92K Privately Held
SIC: 7291 Tax return preparation services

(G-1710)
ACE HANDYMAN SERVICES
371 W North St (19904-6713)
PHONE................302 899-7300
EMP: 5
SALES (est): 66.03K Privately Held
Web: www.acehandymanservices.com
SIC: 7299 Handyman service

(G-1711)
ACM CORP
Also Called: American Consumer Marketing
218 Canal St (19904-5729)
PHONE................302 736-3864
Peter Robinson, Pr
Lynn Robinson, Sec
EMP: 5 EST: 1985
SQ FT: 4,000
SALES (est): 171.02K Privately Held
SIC: 5141 Food brokers

(G-1712)
ACQUISITION INTL HOLDINGS INC
8 The Grn Ste 8382 (19901-3618)
PHONE................302 603-7795
Carey Vann Chisolm, Pr
EMP: 5 EST: 2020
SALES (est): 285.88K Privately Held
SIC: 6153 Working capital financing

(G-1713)
ACS AERO 2 GAMMA US LLC
850 New Burton Rd Ste 201 (19904-5786)
PHONE................800 483-1140
EMP: 6 EST: 2021
SALES (est): 168.46K Privately Held
SIC: 7359 Equipment rental and leasing, nec

(G-1714)
ACTORS ATTIC
Also Called: Bewitched
525 Otis Dr (19901-4645)
PHONE................302 734-8214
Susan Betts, Owner
EMP: 2 EST: 1989
SALES (est): 179.38K Privately Held
Web: www.actorsattic.com
SIC: 5999 7359 2395 Theatrical equipment and supplies; Equipment rental and leasing, nec; Embroidery and art needlework

(G-1715)
ADA L GONZALEZ M D
156 S State St (19901-7314)
PHONE................302 724-4567
EMP: 10 EST: 2017
SALES (est): 310.64K Privately Held
Web: www.alphatitlellc.com
SIC: 8011 Offices and clinics of medical doctors

(G-1716)
ADD MARKETING GROUP LLC ✪
611 S Dupont Hwy Ste 102 (19901-4507)
PHONE................347 668-0992
Danielle Pignatello, Pr
EMP: 5 EST: 2023
SALES (est): 71.79K Privately Held
SIC: 8742 7389 8743 Marketing consulting services; Artists' agents and brokers; Promotion service

(G-1717)
ADEX CORPORATION
8 The Grn (19901-3618)
PHONE................703 618-9670
Hank Eng, CEO
EMP: 5 EST: 2020
SALES (est): 255.26K Privately Held
Web: www.adextelecom.com
SIC: 8742 Human resource consulting services

(G-1718)
ADMIRAL TIRE
Also Called: Edge Water Tire
280 Cowgill St (19901-4500)
P.O. Box 699 (21037-0699)
PHONE................302 734-5911
Bob Wilson, Pr
EMP: 9 EST: 1979
SQ FT: 6,400
SALES (est): 627.8K Privately Held
Web: www.admiraltire.com
SIC: 7538 5531 5014 General automotive repair shops; Automotive tires; Automobile tires and tubes

(G-1719)
ADROIT LOGISTICS LLC
8 The Grn (19901-3618)
PHONE................385 381-0007
Ashwini Sharma, Pr
Eshwini Sharma, Managing Member
EMP: 8 EST: 2021
SALES (est): 961.37K Privately Held
SIC: 4731 Freight forwarding

(G-1720)
ADT LLC
263 N Dupont Hwy (19901-7509)
PHONE................313 778-1493
EMP: 71
SALES (corp-wide): 6.4B Publicly Held
Web: www.adt.com
SIC: 7382 Burglar alarm maintenance and monitoring
HQ: Adt Llc
  1501 W Yamato Rd
  Boca Raton FL 33431
  561 988-3600

(G-1721)
ADTELLIGENT INC
8 The Green Ste R (19901-3618)
PHONE................833 222-2102
EMP: 85
SALES (corp-wide): 1.25MM Privately Held
Web: www.adtelligent.com
SIC: 7311 Advertising agencies
PA: Adtelligent Inc.
  500 Fashion Ave Fl 8
  New York NY 10018
  833 222-2102

(G-1722)
ADVANCE TRUCKING SOLUTIONS LLC ✪
1151 Walker Rd (19904-6600)
PHONE................302 281-4191

Dover - Kent County (G-1723)   **GEOGRAPHIC SECTION**

Tony Xu, *Prin*
EMP: 5 EST: 2022
SALES (est): 77.34K Privately Held
SIC: 4212 Local trucking, without storage

(G-1723)
ADVANCED BIOMEDICAL INC
9 E Loockerman St Ste 3a (19901-7316)
PHONE..................302 730-1880
EMP: 7 EST: 2016
SALES (est): 141.23K Privately Held
SIC: 8011 Offices and clinics of medical doctors

(G-1724)
ADVANCED ENDOSCOPY CENTER LLC
742 S Governors Ave Ste 2 (19904-4111)
PHONE..................302 678-0725
Natwarlal V Ramani Md, *Mgr*
EMP: 6 EST: 2001
SALES (est): 475.08K Privately Held
SIC: 8011 Endocrinologist

(G-1725)
ADVANCED MECHANICAL INC
Also Called: R & D Mechanical
509 Hatchery Rd Ste B (19901-1603)
P.O. Box 653 (19903-0653)
PHONE..................302 734-5583
Robin Thompson, *Pr*
EMP: 18 EST: 1997
SALES (est): 1.3MM Privately Held
SIC: 1711 Heating and air conditioning contractors

(G-1726)
ADVANTECH INC
151 Garrison Oak Dr (19901-3364)
PHONE..................302 674-8405
Eric Schaeffer, *Pr*
Melville Warren, *Sec*
EMP: 40 EST: 1990
SQ FT: 4,500
SALES (est): 10.25MM
SALES (corp-wide): 490.06MM Privately Held
Web: www.advantechsecurity.net
SIC: 7382 Security systems services
HQ: A3 Communications, Inc.
1038 Kinley Rd Bldg B
Irmo SC 29063

(G-1727)
AEGIS-CC LLC
8 The Grn Ste A (19901-3618)
PHONE..................814 661-5844
EMP: 2 EST: 2021
SALES (est): 87.4K Privately Held
Web: www.aegisconsent.com
SIC: 7372 Educational computer software

(G-1728)
AEJ LTD LIABILITY COMPANY ◇
611 S Dupont Hwy Ste 102 (19901-4507)
PHONE..................847 274-1084
Benjamin Aspero, *Managing Member*
EMP: 3 EST: 2023
SALES (est): 128.34K Privately Held
SIC: 7372 Prepackaged software

(G-1729)
AERONEX LLC
1111b S Governors Ave Ste 6573 (19904-6903)
PHONE..................206 809-0009
Ravi Gokulgandhi, *Managing Member*
EMP: 5
SALES (est): 199.4K Privately Held

SIC: 7371 Computer software development and applications

(G-1730)
AEROSMITH LLC
Also Called: Petspy
8 The Grn A (19901-3618)
PHONE..................302 546-5465
EMP: 7 EST: 2021
SALES (est): 85.25K Privately Held
SIC: 3545 Collars (machine tool accessories)

(G-1731)
AESIMMONS LLC (PA) ◇
Also Called: Ae Simmons
1221 College Park Dr # 116 (19904-8726)
PHONE..................347 864-6294
EMP: 22 EST: 2022
SALES (est): 1.05MM
SALES (corp-wide): 1.05MM Privately Held
SIC: 6733 Personal investment trust management

(G-1732)
AETHING INC ◇
1111b S Governors Ave # 6113 (19904-6903)
PHONE..................917 640-2582
Ihar Kul, *CEO*
EMP: 5 EST: 2022
SALES (est): 203.68K Privately Held
SIC: 7373 Computer integrated systems design

(G-1733)
AETHO LLC
Also Called: Aetho
8 The Grn Ste A (19901-3618)
PHONE..................215 821-7290
Harrison Lee, *CEO*
Ian Nott, *Engr*
EMP: 10 EST: 2014
SALES (est): 417.03K Privately Held
Web: www.beame.me
SIC: 7371 8999 Software programming applications; Communication services

(G-1734)
AFFINITY HOMECARE SERVICES
1040 S State St (19901-6925)
P.O. Box 535 (19903-0535)
PHONE..................302 264-9363
EMP: 7 EST: 2018
SALES (est): 242.34K Privately Held
SIC: 8082 Home health care services

(G-1735)
AFFORDABLE ROOFING LLC
70 Humpsman Dr (19904-1445)
PHONE..................302 363-8429
Robert Gras, *Prin*
EMP: 5 EST: 2011
SALES (est): 99K Privately Held
SIC: 1761 Roofing contractor

(G-1736)
AFTERMATH SERVICES LLC
160 Greentree Dr Ste 101 (19904-7620)
PHONE..................302 357-3780
Amanda Ellison, *Owner*
EMP: 35
SALES (corp-wide): 26.06MM Privately Held
Web: www.aftermath.com
SIC: 6512 Commercial and industrial building operation
HQ: Aftermath Services Llc
75 Executive Dr Ste 200
Aurora IL 60504
630 551-0735

(G-1737)
AG INDUSTRIAL INC
36 Victory Chapel Rd (19904-5127)
PHONE..................888 289-1779
EMP: 6 EST: 2019
SALES (est): 272.17K Privately Held
Web: www.agindustrial.com
SIC: 5083 Agricultural machinery and equipment

(G-1738)
AGENT STAFFING SERVICES LLC
200 Nob Hill Rd (19901-8846)
PHONE..................302 244-2676
Kia Peterson, *Prin*
EMP: 5 EST: 2019
SALES (est): 75.28K Privately Held
Web: www.agentstaffingservices.com
SIC: 7361 Employment agencies

(G-1739)
AGFIRST FARM CREDIT BANK
1410 S State St (19901-4948)
P.O. Box 418 (19903-0418)
PHONE..................302 734-7534
Martin Desmond, *Mgr*
EMP: 8
SALES (corp-wide): 493.46MM Privately Held
Web: www.agfirst.com
SIC: 6111 Federal and federally sponsored credit agencies
PA: Agfirst Farm Credit Bank
1901 Main St
Columbia SC 29201
803 799-5000

(G-1740)
AGILE COCKPIT LLC
160 Greentree Dr (19904-7620)
PHONE..................646 220-3377
EMP: 5 EST: 2017
SALES (est): 112.8K Privately Held
Web: www.agilecockpit.nl
SIC: 5045 Computer software

(G-1741)
AGILE COLIVING SYSTEMS LLC
8 The Grn Ste R (19901-3618)
PHONE..................310 980-0644
EMP: 15 EST: 2020
SALES (est): 538.26K Privately Held
SIC: 2426 Furniture stock and parts, hardwood

(G-1742)
AGILE DCNTMINATION SYSTEMS LLC
8 The Grn Ste R (19901-3618)
PHONE..................310 980-0644
EMP: 15 EST: 2020
SALES (est): 300K Privately Held
SIC: 5087 Cleaning and maintenance equipment and supplies

(G-1743)
AGILE IP LLC
8 The Grn Ste R (19901-3618)
PHONE..................310 980-0644
EMP: 15 EST: 2020
SALES (est): 1.15MM Privately Held
SIC: 5122 Proprietary (patent) medicines, nec

(G-1744)
AGILE MEDICAL SYSTEMS LLC
8 The Grn Ste R (19901-3618)
PHONE..................310 980-0644
EMP: 10 EST: 2020
SALES (est): 697.87K Privately Held

SIC: 5047 Medical equipment and supplies

(G-1745)
AGILE SHELTER SYSTEMS LLC
8 The Grn Ste R (19901-3618)
PHONE..................310 980-0644
EMP: 15 EST: 2020
SALES (est): 300K Privately Held
SIC: 8322 Emergency shelters

(G-1746)
AGLIDE INC (PA) ◇
1111b S Governors Ave Ste 6311 (19904-6903)
PHONE..................302 213-0357
EMP: 8 EST: 2023
SALES (est): 68.89K
SALES (corp-wide): 68.89K Privately Held
SIC: 7371 Computer software development and applications

(G-1747)
AGRICULTURE UNITED STATES DEPT
Also Called: AGRICULTURE, UNITED STATES DEPARTMENT OF
800 S Bay Rd Ste 2 (19901-4685)
PHONE..................302 741-2600
Edwin Alexander, *Brnch Mgr*
EMP: 8
Web: www.usda.gov
SIC: 8999 Artists and artists' studios
HQ: U S Department Of Agriculture
1400 Independence Ave Sw
Washington DC 20250
202 720-3631

(G-1748)
AGS ROYALTY MANAGEMENT LLC
8 The Grn (19901-3618)
PHONE..................888 292-6995
EMP: 5
SALES (est): 212.45K Privately Held
SIC: 8741 7389 Business management; Business Activities at Non-Commercial Site

(G-1749)
AGTS LLC
8 The Grn Ste 10746 (19901-3618)
PHONE..................800 496-3379
EMP: 5 EST: 2020
SALES (est): 129.73K Privately Held
SIC: 7373 Systems engineering, computer related

(G-1750)
AHL ORTHODONTICS
1004 S State St (19901-6901)
PHONE..................302 678-3000
Jamie Ahl, *Owner*
EMP: 12 EST: 2013
SALES (est): 880.74K Privately Held
Web: www.aoortho.com
SIC: 8021 Orthodontist

(G-1751)
AHM TV PROD INC ◇
548 Roberta Ave (19901-4646)
PHONE..................929 332-0350
Horace Williams, *CEO*
EMP: 14 EST: 2022
SALES (est): 491.36K Privately Held
SIC: 7311 Advertising agencies

(G-1752)
AID IN DOVER INC
801 W Division St (19904-2735)
PHONE..................302 734-7610
Beverly C Williams, *Dir*
Margaret Iorii, *Ofcr*

GEOGRAPHIC SECTION
Dover - Kent County (G-1782)

Gerald Buckworth, *Treas*
I Kenneth Richter, *Pr*
John Leone, *VP*
EMP: 6 **EST:** 1974
SALES (est): 201.16K **Privately Held**
Web: www.aidindover.org
SIC: 8322 Youth center

(G-1753)
AILINK TECHNOLOGY CORPORATION
8 The Grn Ste A (19901-3618)
PHONE.................858 568-2137
Yilun Zhu, *Pr*
EMP: 2 **EST:** 2020
SALES (est): 103.92K **Privately Held**
SIC: 7372 Application computer software

(G-1754)
AIR APPS INC
Also Called: Air Apps
8 The Grn (19901-3618)
PHONE.................302 339-3843
Filipe Ferreira, *CEO*
EMP: 56 **EST:** 2021
SALES (est): 1.18MM **Privately Held**
SIC: 7371 Custom computer programming services

(G-1755)
AIR CONDITIONING PRODUCTS LLC
850 New Burton Rd Ste 201 (19904-5786)
PHONE.................800 483-1140
EMP: 9 **EST:** 2021
SALES (est): 71.79K **Privately Held**
Web: www.acpshutters.com
SIC: 8742 Marketing consulting services

(G-1756)
AIR FORCE US DEPT OF
Also Called: Dover Air Force Base
262 Chad St (19902-5012)
PHONE.................302 674-0942
EMP: 21
Web: www.af.mil
SIC: 8322 9711 Individual and family services ; Air Force
HQ: The United States Department Of Air Force
10690 Air Force Pentagon
Washington DC 20330

(G-1757)
AIRESPA WORLDWIDE WHL LLC
8 The Grn (19901-3618)
PHONE.................908 227-4441
EMP: 2 **EST:** 2018
SALES (est): 153.89K **Privately Held**
SIC: 3599 Air intake filters, internal combustion engine, except auto

(G-1758)
AJUSTA TU CORONA INC (PA) ✪
8 The Grn Ste A (19901-3618)
PHONE.................203 434-0356
Lillian Maldonado, *CEO*
EMP: 10 **EST:** 2023
SALES (est): 340.31K
SALES (corp-wide): 340.31K **Privately Held**
SIC: 8999 7389 Services, nec; Business Activities at Non-Commercial Site

(G-1759)
AKBELL GLOBAL COMMODITIES LLC
221 College Pk Dr Ste 116 (19904)
PHONE.................347 615-5014
EMP: 3 **EST:** 2020
SALES (est): 104.39K **Privately Held**

SIC: 1311 Crude petroleum and natural gas production

(G-1760)
ALCHEME BIO INC
8 The Grn Ste 13081 (19901-3618)
PHONE.................858 291-9708
Vanessa Small, *CEO*
EMP: 2
SALES (est): 92.41K **Privately Held**
SIC: 2835 Diagnostic substances

(G-1761)
ALEX PROPERTY MANAGEMENT LLC
8 The Grn Ste 8678 (19901-3618)
PHONE.................302 384-9845
Vast Mandros, *Managing Member*
EMP: 850 **EST:** 2020
SALES (est): 6.9MM **Privately Held**
Web: www.alexpropertymgmt.com
SIC: 6531 7389 Real estate managers; Business Activities at Non-Commercial Site

(G-1762)
ALIUM CONSULTANCY LLC
8 The Grn Ste A (19901-3618)
PHONE.................347 414-8851
Anald Vilhete, *Managing Member*
EMP: 27 **EST:** 2020
SALES (est): 1.06MM **Privately Held**
SIC: 7361 Employment agencies

(G-1763)
ALL LIVES MATTER LLC
8 The Grn Ste A (19901-3618)
PHONE.................252 767-9291
Nilin Patel, *Prin*
EMP: 3 **EST:** 2016
SALES (est): 71.13K **Privately Held**
SIC: 7372 7389 Application computer software; Business Activities at Non-Commercial Site

(G-1764)
ALL SEASONS LANDSCAPING INC
154 S Fairfield Dr (19901-5725)
PHONE.................302 423-8001
EMP: 7 **EST:** 2017
SALES (est): 108.04K **Privately Held**
Web: www.aslcustom.com
SIC: 0781 Landscape services

(G-1765)
ALL SMILES FAMILY & COSME
95 Wolf Creek Blvd Ste 3 (19901-4965)
PHONE.................302 734-5303
Neena Mukkamala, *Prin*
EMP: 5 **EST:** 2006
SALES (est): 499.65K **Privately Held**
Web: www.allsmilesdelaware.com
SIC: 8021 Dentists' office

(G-1766)
ALL THINGS INSPIRING WELLNESS
531 Pear St (19904-2928)
PHONE.................302 943-5503
Theresia Stubblefield, *Prin*
EMP: 6 **EST:** 2016
SALES (est): 71.78K **Privately Held**
Web: allthingsinspiringwellness.abmp.com
SIC: 8099 Health and allied services, nec

(G-1767)
ALL TUNE & LUBE
Also Called: All Tune & Lube
4200 N Dupont Hwy Ste 5 (19901-2400)
PHONE.................302 744-9081
EMP: 5 **EST:** 2019

SALES (est): 36.18K **Privately Held**
Web: www.alltuneandlube.com
SIC: 7538 General automotive repair shops

(G-1768)
ALLAN B STANLEY
2571 Kenton Rd (19904-1342)
PHONE.................302 678-4774
Allan B Stanley, *Prin*
EMP: 5 **EST:** 2009
SALES (est): 62.78K **Privately Held**
SIC: 3949 Game calls

(G-1769)
ALLAN MYERS MD INC
440 Twin Oak Dr (19904-1908)
PHONE.................302 883-3501
Bobby Shade, *Mgr*
EMP: 231
SALES (corp-wide): 1.24B **Privately Held**
Web: www.allanmyers.com
SIC: 1611 General contractor, highway and street construction
HQ: Allan Myers Md, Inc.
2011 Bel Air Rd
Fallston MD 21047
410 776-2000

(G-1770)
ALLEN ESTATES LLC
8 The Grn Ste F (19901-3618)
PHONE.................302 496-7250
EMP: 5 **EST:** 2020
SALES (est): 105K **Privately Held**
SIC: 6799 Real estate investors, except property operators

(G-1771)
ALLIED ANESTHESIA ASSOC LLC
75 Old Mill Rd (19901-6290)
PHONE.................302 547-3620
Steven Shields, *Prin*
EMP: 5 **EST:** 2009
SALES (est): 191.13K **Privately Held**
SIC: 8011 Anesthesiologist

(G-1772)
ALLKARE INC
8 The Grn Ste 12777 (19901-3618)
PHONE.................302 212-0917
EMP: 5 **EST:** 2018
SALES (est): 94.19K **Privately Held**
Web: www.allkareinc.com
SIC: 8748 Business consulting, nec

(G-1773)
ALOE & CARR PA
Also Called: Cammarato & Aloe PA
850 S State St Ste 2 (19901-4113)
PHONE.................302 736-6631
EMP: 6 **EST:** 1994
SALES (est): 522.86K **Privately Held**
Web: www.aloeandcarr.com
SIC: 8021 Endodontist

(G-1774)
ALPHA PHI DELTA
236 N Governors Ave (19904-3116)
PHONE.................302 377-5789
Jim Lentini, *Prin*
EMP: 8 **EST:** 2011
SALES (est): 66.79K **Privately Held**
Web: www.apd.org
SIC: 8641 University club

(G-1775)
ALPINE CONTRACTORS LLC
200 Weston Dr (19904-2786)
PHONE.................302 343-9954
Henry Mast, *Pr*

EMP: 12 **EST:** 2016
SALES (est): 1.41MM **Privately Held**
Web: www.alpine-contractors.com
SIC: 5082 General construction machinery and equipment

(G-1776)
ALTEA RESOURCES LLC
3500 S Dupont Hwy (19901-6041)
PHONE.................713 242-1460
EMP: 12 **EST:** 2009
SQ FT: 764
SALES (est): 254.9K **Privately Held**
Web: www.altea-energy.com
SIC: 7361 8742 Employment agencies; Business planning and organizing services

(G-1777)
ALTR SOLUTIONS LLC
8 The Grn Ste A (19901-3618)
PHONE.................888 757-2587
EMP: 10 **EST:** 2016
SALES (est): 973.59K **Privately Held**
Web: www.altr.com
SIC: 7372 5734 Business oriented computer software; Software, business and non-game

(G-1778)
ALVISSAI INC
8 The Grn (19901-3618)
PHONE.................470 202-3431
Pavel Overtchouk, *CEO*
EMP: 5
SALES (est): 70.36K **Privately Held**
SIC: 7379 Online services technology consultants

(G-1779)
AMAA MANAGEMENT CORPORATION
Also Called: Comfort Inn
764 Dover Leipsic Rd (19901-2055)
PHONE.................302 677-0505
Shalin Patel, *Pr*
Nilesh Patel, *VP*
EMP: 34 **EST:** 2007
SALES (est): 342.16K **Privately Held**
Web: www.choicehotels.com
SIC: 7011 Hotels and motels

(G-1780)
AMANDA C SZYMCZAK
103 Mont Blanc Blvd (19904-7615)
PHONE.................302 678-3020
EMP: 8 **EST:** 2018
SALES (est): 112.2K **Privately Held**
SIC: 8011 Offices and clinics of medical doctors

(G-1781)
AMAZED APPS LLC
8 The Grn (19901-3618)
PHONE.................916 934-9210
EMP: 5
SALES (est): 68.89K **Privately Held**
SIC: 7371 7389 Computer software development and applications; Business Activities at Non-Commercial Site

(G-1782)
AMC MUSEUM FOUNDATION
1301 Heritage Rd (19902)
P.O. Box 2050 (19902-2050)
PHONE.................302 677-5938
Mike Leister, *Dir*
Michael Quarnaccio, *Ch*
EMP: 8 **EST:** 1986
SALES (est): 86.52K **Privately Held**
Web: www.amcmuseum.org

SIC: 5399 7997 8412 Army-Navy goods stores; Aviation club, membership; Museum

(G-1783)
AME LIFE LLC
Also Called: AME-Life
8 The Grn Ste 7302 (19901-3618)
PHONE.....................305 517-7707
Ezequiel Crivolotti, Managing Member
EMP: 9 EST: 2007
SALES (est): 897.3K Privately Held
SIC: 5099 Lifesaving and survival equipment (non-medical)

(G-1784)
AMERICAN CHIROPRACTIC CENTER
230 Beiser Blvd Ste 101 (19904-7791)
P.O. Box 727 (19950-0727)
PHONE.....................302 450-3153
Michael Sharkey, Prin
EMP: 6 EST: 2017
SALES (est): 85.21K Privately Held
SIC: 8041 Offices and clinics of chiropractors

(G-1785)
AMERICAN FDRTION STATE CNTY MN
177 Candlewick Dr (19901-5708)
PHONE.....................302 698-5034
Richard J Schlauch Junior, Prin
EMP: 5 EST: 2012
SALES (est): 66.69K Privately Held
SIC: 8631 Labor union

(G-1786)
AMERICAN RENAL
107 Mont Blanc Blvd (19904-7624)
PHONE.....................302 672-7901
EMP: 5 EST: 2019
SALES (est): 90.45K Privately Held
Web: www.innovativerenal.com
SIC: 8092 Kidney dialysis centers

(G-1787)
AMINO-CHEM (US) LLC
160 Greentree Dr Ste 101 (19904-7620)
PHONE.....................281 305-8668
EMP: 9 EST: 2020
SALES (est): 2.13MM Privately Held
Web: www.amino-chem.com
SIC: 2899 Chemical preparations, nec
PA: Zhejiang Longsheng Group Co., Ltd. No.1, Longsheng Avenue, Daoxu Sub-District, Shangyu District Shaoxing ZJ 31236

(G-1788)
AMREC HOLDINGS INC
Also Called: Amrec
8 The Grn Ste 4257 (19901-3618)
PHONE.....................302 273-0000
Andrew Vilenchik, Pr
Richard Storholm, *
EMP: 75 EST: 2018
Web: www.amrec.com
SIC: 6719 3621 1796 Holding companies, nec; Power generators; Power generating equipment installation

(G-1789)
ANALYTICA LLC
800 N State St Ste 402 (19901-3925)
PHONE.....................214 223-2055
Daniel Held, Prin
Kevin Johnson, Prin
EMP: 10 EST: 2014
SALES (est): 100K Privately Held
Web: www.analytica.net
SIC: 7371 Computer software development

(G-1790)
ANAMO INC
28 Old Rudnick Ln (19901-4912)
PHONE.....................702 852-2992
Jonathan Goetsch, Sec
Alex Pododbas, Dir
Harry Mcnab, Dir
EMP: 3 EST: 2018
SALES (est): 71.13K Privately Held
SIC: 7372 Prepackaged software

(G-1791)
ANATROPE INC
3500 S Dupont Hwy (19901-6041)
PHONE.....................202 507-9441
Tiffany Rad, CEO
EMP: 2
SALES (est): 130.18K Privately Held
SIC: 3571 Electronic computers

(G-1792)
ANDREA M D ARELLANO
811 S Governors Ave (19904-4158)
PHONE.....................302 678-0510
EMP: 8 EST: 2017
SALES (est): 54.13K Privately Held
SIC: 8011 Offices and clinics of medical doctors

(G-1793)
ANDREAS RAUER MD PA
16 Old Rudnick Ln (19901-4912)
PHONE.....................302 734-1760
Andreas Rauer Md, Owner
EMP: 9 EST: 1979
SALES (est): 433.52K Privately Held
Web: www.unitedenergycorp.com
SIC: 8011 General and family practice, physician/surgeon

(G-1794)
ANGELA DAYCAR NANA LIL
117 Hitching Post Dr (19904-6520)
PHONE.....................302 672-9167
EMP: 7 EST: 2011
SALES (est): 66.2K Privately Held
SIC: 8351 Child day care services

(G-1795)
ANGLE PLANNING CONCEPTS
Also Called: Nationwide
31 Saulsbury Rd # B (19904-3444)
PHONE.....................302 735-7526
John Rowley, Pr
EMP: 9 EST: 2010
SALES (est): 811.52K Privately Held
Web: www.anglefinancialservices.com
SIC: 6411 Insurance agents, brokers, and service

(G-1796)
ANIMAL INN INC
2308 Seeneytown Rd (19904-1650)
PHONE.....................302 653-5560
Gail Warren, Pr
Debbie Eckels, VP
EMP: 6 EST: 1988
SALES (est): 154.96K Privately Held
SIC: 0752 Boarding services, kennels

(G-1797)
ANNALISE-AI INC
8 The Grn Ste R (19901-3618)
PHONE.....................440 281-5115
Lakshmi Gudapakkam, CEO
Emilio Bosa, Mgr
EMP: 7 EST: 2021
SALES (est): 264.9K Privately Held
SIC: 7371 Computer software development and applications

(G-1798)
ANYMONEY LLC
8 The Grn (19901-3618)
PHONE.....................818 431-5251
EMP: 10
SALES (est): 348.32K Privately Held
SIC: 7389 Financial services

(G-1799)
ANYTIME FITNESS
880 S Governors Ave (19904-4152)
PHONE.....................302 229-1716
Jennifer Boyd, Prin
EMP: 9 EST: 2016
SALES (est): 54.08K Privately Held
Web: www.anytimefitness.sg
SIC: 7991 Physical fitness clubs with training equipment

(G-1800)
AOP HOLDING COMPANY LLC (PA) ◆
8 The Grn Ste R (19901-3618)
PHONE.....................346 561-4123
Paul Choi, Managing Member
EMP: 8 EST: 2023
SALES (est): 359.55K
SALES (corp-wide): 359.55K Privately Held
SIC: 4931 7389 Cogeneration of electric power; Business services, nec

(G-1801)
APARTA HOSPITALITY TECH ◆
8 The Grn Ste A (19901-3618)
PHONE.....................617 383-3239
Vitaly Likhachev, Pr
EMP: 5 EST: 2023
SALES (est): 219.88K Privately Held
SIC: 6531 7389 Real estate brokers and agents; Business Activities at Non-Commercial Site

(G-1802)
APEX BUILDERS LLC
152 Old Forge Dr (19904-6528)
PHONE.....................302 242-1059
EMP: 5 EST: 2013
SALES (est): 121.54K Privately Held
SIC: 1521 New construction, single-family houses

(G-1803)
APEX LAWN & HOME
42 E Inner Cir (19904-6075)
PHONE.....................302 670-4363
Joseph Konrad, Prin
EMP: 5 EST: 2011
SALES (est): 23.96K Privately Held
SIC: 0782 Lawn care services

(G-1804)
APPA INC
8 The Grn Ste 7868 (19901-3618)
PHONE.....................302 440-1448
Luisa Manyoma, COO
EMP: 8 EST: 2018
SALES (est): 495.48K Privately Held
Web: www.appamia.com
SIC: 4812 Cellular telephone services

(G-1805)
APPIC STARS LLC
8 The Grn Ste 4524 (19901-3618)
PHONE.....................903 224-6469
EMP: 5 EST: 2018
SALES (est): 189.57K Privately Held
SIC: 7371 Computer software development and applications

(G-1806)
APPLIED BIOFEEDBACK SOLUTIONS
1485 S Governors Ave (19904-7017)
PHONE.....................302 674-3225
Robert A Gorkin, Prin
EMP: 7 EST: 2010
SALES (est): 148.66K Privately Held
Web: www.appliedbiofeedbacksolutions.com
SIC: 8093 Mental health clinic, outpatient

(G-1807)
APPOINTED PARTNERS PUBG INC
8 The Grn Ste 11910 (19901-3618)
PHONE.....................302 446-3675
Schrieka Clifford, Pr
EMP: 3 EST: 2021
SALES (est): 81.11K Privately Held
SIC: 2731 Book publishing

(G-1808)
APPRICOT INC
8 The Grn (19901-3618)
PHONE.....................484 291-8922
David Blbulian, CEO
EMP: 9 EST: 2021
SALES (est): 313.29K Privately Held
SIC: 7371 Computer software development and applications

(G-1809)
APPS BY CS LLC
1041 N Dupont Hwy (19901-2006)
PHONE.....................866 235-9752
Christopher Sturgill, Managing Member
EMP: 4
SALES (est): 56.54K Privately Held
SIC: 7372 Application computer software

(G-1810)
ARCADIA PROPERTIES LLC
561 N Dupont Hwy (19901-3960)
PHONE.....................302 747-5050
EMP: 16 EST: 1999
SALES (est): 1.16MM Privately Held
Web: www.arcadiaproperties.net
SIC: 6512 Nonresidential building operators

(G-1811)
ARDEXO INC
Also Called: Ardexo Housing Solutions
8 The Grn Ste 4810 (19901-3618)
PHONE.....................855 617-7500
Robert Caskey, CEO
EMP: 6 EST: 2016
SQ FT: 500
SALES (est): 214.86K Privately Held
SIC: 7371 7373 8741 7372 Computer software systems analysis and design, custom; Office computer automation systems integration; Business management ; Prepackaged software

(G-1812)
ARGO AI CORPORATION ◆
8 The Grn Ste D (19901-3618)
PHONE.....................516 602-9295
Marc Sylvestre, Prin
EMP: 6 EST: 2023
SALES (est): 70.36K Privately Held
SIC: 7374 Data processing and preparation

(G-1813)
ARION LLC
9 E Loockerman St Ste 311 (19901-8305)
PHONE.....................215 531-1673
Alberto Chamorro, Prin
EMP: 6
SALES (est): 246.16K Privately Held

GEOGRAPHIC SECTION   Dover - Kent County (G-1842)

SIC: 7389 Business Activities at Non-Commercial Site

(G-1814)
ARKLIGHT ARSENAL LLC
8 The Grn Ste 8692 (19901-3618)
PHONE..................................844 722-3766
Ikaika Enos, *CEO*
EMP: 5 **EST:** 2021
SALES (est): 203.26K **Privately Held**
SIC: 7389 5961 Business Activities at Non-Commercial Site; Electronic shopping

(G-1815)
ARMA TEL LLC
8 The Grn Ste A (19901-3618)
PHONE..................................302 480-9394
Kate Portnaya, *CEO*
EMP: 21 **EST:** 2018
SALES (est): 1.24MM **Privately Held**
SIC: 4813 Telephone communication, except radio

(G-1816)
ARMED FORCES MED EXAMINER SYS
115 Purple Heart Ave (19902-5051)
PHONE..................................302 346-8653
Lanelle Chisolm, *
EMP: 39 **EST:** 2012
SQ FT: 117,000
SALES (est): 2.66MM **Privately Held**
SIC: 8071 9711 Pathological laboratory; Army

(G-1817)
ARMY & AIR FORCE EXCHANGE SVC
Also Called: Dover Afb Child Care Center
260 Chad St (19902-5012)
PHONE..................................302 677-3716
Patty Porter, *Dir*
EMP: 11
Web: www.shopmyexchange.com
SIC: 8351 9711 Group day care center; Air Force
HQ: Army & Air Force Exchange Service
3911 S Walton Walker Blvd
Dallas TX 75236
214 312-2011

(G-1818)
AROVO US INC ✪
8 The Grn Ste 14569 (19901-3618)
PHONE..................................952 290-0799
Nathalie Vandeghinste, *CEO*
Matt Britton, *
EMP: 50 **EST:** 2023
SALES (est): 5.26MM
SALES (corp-wide): 576.07K **Privately Held**
Web: www.arovo.com
SIC: 3421 2844 3631 3469 Cutlery; Perfumes, cosmetics and other toilet preparations; Household cooking equipment ; Household cooking and kitchen utensils, metal
HQ: Arovo B.V.
Doblijn 26
Amsterdam NH 1046
852738886

(G-1819)
ARSENEAU CPA LLC (PA) ✪
65 N Dupont Hwy (19901-4265)
PHONE..................................302 854-0133
EMP: 6 **EST:** 2022
SALES (est): 340.83K
SALES (corp-wide): 340.83K **Privately Held**

SIC: 8721 Accounting services, except auditing

(G-1820)
ART TURE
47 Rodney Rd (19901-3828)
PHONE..................................302 893-0156
Arden Bardol, *Prin*
EMP: 5 **EST:** 2009
SALES (est): 60.38K **Privately Held**
SIC: 8999 Artist's studio

(G-1821)
ARTFUL BARBER
301 W Loockerman St (19904-3249)
PHONE..................................302 672-0818
Jihad Muhammad, *Prin*
EMP: 5 **EST:** 2015
SALES (est): 50.31K **Privately Held**
SIC: 7241 Barber shops

(G-1822)
ARTHUR W HENRY DDS INC
748 S New St (19904-3573)
PHONE..................................302 734-8101
Arthur W Henry D.d.s., *Pr*
EMP: 6 **EST:** 1964
SALES (est): 259.83K **Privately Held**
SIC: 8021 Dentists' office

(G-1823)
ARTID LLC (PA)
8 The Grn Ste E (19901-3618)
PHONE..................................302 898-6307
EMP: 6 **EST:** 2020
SALES (est): 89.81K
SALES (corp-wide): 89.81K **Privately Held**
SIC: 7371 Computer software development

(G-1824)
ARTIMUS LLC
8 The Grn Ste A (19901-3618)
PHONE..................................302 546-5350
EMP: 10 **EST:** 2021
SALES (est): 348.32K **Privately Held**
SIC: 7389 Purchasing service

(G-1825)
ARTISANS BANK INC
1555 S Governors Ave (19904-7019)
PHONE..................................302 674-3214
Kathleen Cooper, *Mgr*
EMP: 8
SALES (corp-wide): 25.62MM **Privately Held**
Web: www.artisansbank.com
SIC: 6036 6035 State savings banks, not federally chartered; Federal savings institutions
PA: Artisans Bank Inc
2961 Centerville Rd # 101
Wilmington DE 19808
302 658-6881

(G-1826)
ARUA INC
8 The Grn Ste 300 (19901-3618)
PHONE..................................302 396-9868
Artem Artemiuk, *CEO*
EMP: 5
SALES (est): 216.69K **Privately Held**
SIC: 7371 Computer software development and applications

(G-1827)
ARYVVE TECHNOLOGIES LLC
1675 S State St Ste B (19901-5140)
PHONE..................................678 977-1250
Ray Lee, *Managing Member*
EMP: 5 **EST:** 2018

SALES (est): 86.84K **Privately Held**
SIC: 4121 Taxicabs

(G-1828)
ASCENT RESEARCH LLC
8 The Grn Ste 10331 (19901-3618)
PHONE..................................703 801-1490
EMP: 2 **EST:** 2020
SALES (est): 86.67K **Privately Held**
SIC: 3842 Surgical appliances and supplies

(G-1829)
ASD TRUCKING INC
2505 White Oak Rd (19901-3345)
PHONE..................................302 744-9832
Amrinder Singh, *Prin*
EMP: 5 **EST:** 2013
SALES (est): 109.5K **Privately Held**
SIC: 4212 Local trucking, without storage

(G-1830)
ASHELY B MORRISON
1001 S Bradford St Ste 9 (19904-4153)
PHONE..................................302 526-1959
Ashely Morrison, *Prin*
EMP: 6 **EST:** 2017
SALES (est): 22.18K **Privately Held**
SIC: 8049 Offices of health practitioner

(G-1831)
ASHTRAY MANAGEMENT LLC
8 The Grn Ste A (19901-3618)
PHONE..................................424 258-9228
EMP: 5 **EST:** 2020
SALES (est): 500K **Privately Held**
SIC: 7929 Entertainment service

(G-1832)
ASHWEB INC ✪
611 S Dupont Hwy Ste 102 (19901-4507)
PHONE..................................844 493-6249
Yoonho Jeon, *CEO*
EMP: 5 **EST:** 2022
SALES (est): 63.4K **Privately Held**
SIC: 7371 Computer software development and applications

(G-1833)
ASPLUNDH TREE EXPERT LLC
100 Carlsons Way Ste 14 (19901-2365)
PHONE..................................302 678-4702
Steve Miller, *VP*
EMP: 7
SALES (corp-wide): 1.16B **Privately Held**
Web: www.asplundh.com
SIC: 1629 1623 Railroad and subway construction; Water, sewer, and utility lines
PA: Asplundh Tree Expert, Llc
708 Blair Mill Rd
Willow Grove PA 19090
215 784-4200

(G-1834)
ASSET ASSISTANCE LLC
72 Representative Ln (19904-2491)
PHONE..................................302 364-3362
EMP: 5 **EST:** 2015
SALES (est): 500K **Privately Held**
SIC: 1522 Residential construction, nec

(G-1835)
ASSISTED LIVING CONCEPTS LLC
Also Called: Dover Place
1203 Walker Rd (19904-6541)
PHONE..................................302 735-8800
Beth Kelly, *Brnch Mgr*
EMP: 15
SALES (corp-wide): 571.18MM **Privately Held**

SIC: 8361 Residential care
HQ: Assisted Living Concepts, Llc
141 W Jackson Blvd # 2650
Chicago IL 60604

(G-1836)
ASSOCIATED SVC SPECIALIST INC
Also Called: Psycho Therapeutic Services
630 W Division St Ste E (19904-2760)
PHONE..................................302 672-7159
Sharon Stevens, *Branch Manager*
Sharon Stephenson, *Executive Director*
EMP: 10
SIC: 8361 Children's home
PA: Associated Service Specialist, Inc.
870 High St Ste 2
Chestertown MD 21620

(G-1837)
ASSOCIATES CONTRACTING INC
Also Called: Honeywell Authorized Dealer
1661 S Dupont Hwy (19901-5129)
P.O. Box 1070 (19975-1070)
PHONE..................................302 734-4311
James Morris, *Pr*
George Brown, *Sec*
Wayne Reed, *Treas*
EMP: 18 **EST:** 1986
SQ FT: 6,000
SALES (est): 434.58K **Privately Held**
Web: www.associatescontractinginc.com
SIC: 1711 1731 Plumbing contractors; General electrical contractor

(G-1838)
ASSURED AFFLUENCE LLC ✪
8 The Grn Ste 8374 (19901-3618)
PHONE..................................609 468-0250
Robert Jefferson, *Managing Member*
EMP: 2 **EST:** 2022
SALES (est): 92.41K **Privately Held**
SIC: 3531 7389 Log splitters; Business Activities at Non-Commercial Site

(G-1839)
ASTRO-LYFE LLC
1041 N Dupont Hwy (19901-2006)
PHONE..................................240 410-9665
EMP: 15
SALES (est): 217.43K **Privately Held**
SIC: 8999 Services, nec

(G-1840)
AT CONTRACTING LLC
391 Rose Valley School Rd (19904-5527)
PHONE..................................302 678-4898
Alfred R Troyer, *Asst Sec*
EMP: 5 **EST:** 2018
SALES (est): 56.76K **Privately Held**
SIC: 1799 Special trade contractors, nec

(G-1841)
AT HOME CARE AGENCY
57 Saulsbury Rd (19904-3479)
PHONE..................................302 883-2059
EMP: 6 **EST:** 2019
SALES (est): 417.33K **Privately Held**
SIC: 8082 Home health care services

(G-1842)
AT HOME INFUCARE LLC
373 W North St Ste A (19904-6748)
PHONE..................................302 883-2059
George Aboagye, *Prin*
EMP: 8 **EST:** 2012
SALES (est): 130.44K **Privately Held**
SIC: 8082 Home health care services

Dover - Kent County (G-1843)   **GEOGRAPHIC SECTION**

(G-1843)
AT&T MOBILITY LLC
Also Called: Cingular Wireless
275 N Dupont Hwy (19901-7509)
PHONE...............................302 674-4888
EMP: 10
SALES (corp-wide): 120.74B **Publicly Held**
Web: www.att.com
SIC: **4812** Cellular telephone services
HQ: At&t Mobility Llc
    1025 Lenox Park Blvd Ne
    Brookhaven GA 30319
    800 331-0500

(G-1844)
ATHARI INC
278 Jordan Dr (19904-2005)
PHONE...............................312 358-4933
Oluwapelumi Adeleke, *Prin*
EMP: 10 EST: 2018
SALES (est): 77.06K **Privately Held**
SIC: **8699** Charitable organization

(G-1845)
ATI HOLDINGS LLC
Also Called: ATI Physical Therapy
1288 S Governors Ave (19904-4802)
PHONE...............................302 677-0100
Jamie Smoot, *Brnch Mgr*
EMP: 16
SALES (corp-wide): 635.67MM **Publicly Held**
Web: www.atipt.com
SIC: **8049** Physical therapist
HQ: Ati Holdings, Llc
    790 Remington Blvd
    Bolingbrook IL 60440

(G-1846)
ATI HOLDINGS LLC
200 Banning St Ste 230 (19904-3487)
PHONE...............................302 747-5280
EMP: 7
SALES (corp-wide): 635.67MM **Publicly Held**
Web: www.atipt.com
SIC: **8049** Physical therapist
HQ: Ati Holdings, Llc
    790 Remington Blvd
    Bolingbrook IL 60440

(G-1847)
ATLANTIC FINANCE
71 Greentree Dr (19904-7646)
PHONE...............................302 730-1988
Daniel Gardner, *Owner*
EMP: 7 EST: 2014
SALES (est): 157.31K **Privately Held**
Web: www.atlanticfinanceandpawn.com
SIC: **6141** Personal credit institutions

(G-1848)
ATLANTIC HOME LOANS INC
1198 S Governors Ave (19904-6930)
PHONE...............................302 363-3950
Ed Buchser, *CEO*
EMP: 6 EST: 2012
SALES (est): 384.92K **Privately Held**
SIC: **6162** Mortgage bankers

(G-1849)
ATLAS AWAITS LLC ◆
8 The Grn (19901-3618)
PHONE...............................724 715-3774
Zachary Meyers, *Managing Member*
EMP: 5 EST: 2022
SALES (est): 76.34K **Privately Held**
SIC: **6531** Real estate managers

(G-1850)
ATLAS BEAUTY LLC
8 The Grn Ste B (19901-3618)
PHONE...............................904 382-3487
EMP: 8
SALES (est): 306.16K **Privately Held**
SIC: **7389** 5961 Business Activities at Non-Commercial Site; Electronic shopping

(G-1851)
ATOMIC DEVELOPMENT INC
850 New Burton Rd (19904-5785)
PHONE...............................424 354-9865
Pradeep Nalluri, *CEO*
EMP: 5
SALES (est): 199.4K **Privately Held**
SIC: **7371** Computer software development

(G-1852)
ATTENTIS CONSULTING INC
8 The Grn Ste 7066 (19901-3618)
PHONE...............................570 575-7283
Patrick Spillane, *Pr*
Heather Spillane, *Sec*
EMP: 11 EST: 2019
SALES (est): 654.06K **Privately Held**
Web: www.attentisconsulting.com
SIC: **7379** Computer related consulting services

(G-1853)
AU-NATUREL SERVICES LLC ◆
Also Called: Au-Naturel Services
8 The Grn Ste R (19901-3618)
PHONE...............................775 484-5210
Oscar Lemus, *Managing Member*
EMP: 8 EST: 2022
SALES (est): 414.38K **Privately Held**
SIC: **7361** 7389 Employment agencies; Business services, nec

(G-1854)
AURUM CAPITAL VENTURES INC
3500 S Dupont Hwy (19901-6041)
PHONE...............................877 467-7780
John Paul Baric, *Prin*
EMP: 5 EST: 2018
SALES (est): 317.69K **Privately Held**
SIC: **6799** Venture capital companies

(G-1855)
AUTO PLUS AUTO PARTS
120 S Governors Ave (19904-3223)
PHONE...............................302 678-8400
EMP: 5 EST: 2019
SALES (est): 28.25K **Privately Held**
Web: autoplus1.cypresstg.com
SIC: **7538** General automotive repair shops

(G-1856)
AVANTA INC
8 The Grn Ste R (19901-3618)
PHONE...............................925 818-4760
Mark Fedin, *CEO*
EMP: 46
SALES (corp-wide): 446.9K **Privately Held**
Web: www.avanta.co
SIC: **7371** Computer software development
HQ: Avanta, Inc.
    1470 Civic Ct Ste 309
    Concord CA 94520
    925 818-4760

(G-1857)
AVOMD INC
32 W Loockerman St Ste 107 (19904-7352)
PHONE...............................631 786-3867
EMP: 15 EST: 2020
SALES (est): 46.16K **Privately Held**
Web: www.avomd.io

SIC: **7371** Computer software development

(G-1858)
AXIA MANAGEMENT
222 S Dupont Hwy Frnt (19901-3778)
PHONE...............................302 674-2200
Tom Kramedas, *Pt*
Greg Kramedas, *Pt*
Tina Kramedas, *Pt*
EMP: 10 EST: 2000
SALES (est): 444.55K **Privately Held**
Web: www.axiahotelgroup.com
SIC: **8741** Hotel or motel management

(G-1859)
AXIOM RESOURCES LLC
160 Greentree Dr Ste 101 (19904-7620)
PHONE...............................410 756-0440
Brandon Kaissi, *Genl Mgr*
EMP: 10 EST: 2016
SALES (est): 449.06K **Privately Held**
SIC: **7379** Online services technology consultants

(G-1860)
AXIS CAPITAL USA LLC
1675 S State St Ste B (19901-5140)
PHONE...............................855 205-5577
EMP: 19 EST: 2017
SALES (est): 17.11MM **Privately Held**
Web: www.axiscapital.com
SIC: **6081** Agencies of foreign banks
PA: Axis Bank Limited
    Axis House, C-2, Wadia International Centre
    Mumbai MH 40002

(G-1861)
AXTRA3D INC ◆
8 The Grn Ste A (19901-3618)
PHONE...............................302 288-0670
Gianni Zitelli, *CEO*
EMP: 20 EST: 2022
SALES (est): 1.38MM **Privately Held**
SIC: **3571** Electronic computers

(G-1862)
B JAMES ROGGE DDS
838 Walker Rd Ste 21-1 (19904-2751)
PHONE...............................302 736-1423
B James Rogge D.d.s., *Owner*
EMP: 6 EST: 1990
SALES (est): 273.18K **Privately Held**
Web: www.walkersquaredental.com
SIC: **8021** Oral pathologist

(G-1863)
B MERIT CO
8 The Grn Ste A (19901-3618)
PHONE...............................888 263-7481
Kristin Pringle, *Pr*
EMP: 12 EST: 2021
SALES (est): 606.14K **Privately Held**
SIC: **8742** 5999 Retail trade consultant; Miscellaneous retail stores, nec

(G-1864)
B P SERVICES
Also Called: BP
547 N Bradford St (19904-7205)
PHONE...............................302 399-4132
Joseph Mesick, *Asstg*
EMP: 6 EST: 2010
SALES (est): 157.93K **Privately Held**
SIC: **8999** Personal services

(G-1865)
B SAFE INC
Also Called: Delaware Electric Signal
1490 E Lebanon Rd (19901-5833)

PHONE...............................302 422-3916
EMP: 25
SALES (corp-wide): 9.72MM **Privately Held**
Web: www.bsafealarms.com
SIC: **1731** 7382 Fire detection and burglar alarm systems specialization; Burglar alarm maintenance and monitoring
PA: B Safe, Inc.
    109 Baltimore Ave
    Wilmington DE 19805
    302 633-1833

(G-1866)
BABA SALI LLC
9 E Loockerman St Ste 311 (19901-8305)
PHONE...............................917 647-0561
EMP: 5 EST: 2020
SALES (est): 100K **Privately Held**
SIC: **7379** Online services technology consultants

(G-1867)
BAGGAGE HUB INC
3500 S Dupont Hwy (19901-6041)
PHONE...............................628 666-0150
EMP: 5 EST: 2017
SALES (est): 152.47K **Privately Held**
SIC: **4212** Baggage transfer

(G-1868)
BAIRD MANDALAS BROCKSTEDT LLC (PA)
6 S State St (19901-7363)
PHONE...............................302 677-0061
Kevin Baird, *Prin*
EMP: 11 EST: 2009
SALES (est): 11.1MM
SALES (corp-wide): 11.1MM **Privately Held**
Web: www.bmbde.com
SIC: **8111** General practice attorney, lawyer

(G-1869)
BALATROON GAMES INC ◆
8 The Grn Ste A (19901-3618)
PHONE...............................647 986-9268
Mark Turetski, *CEO*
EMP: 7 EST: 2023
SALES (est): 355.22K **Privately Held**
SIC: **5092** Video games

(G-1870)
BANCROFT CONSTRUCTION COMPANY
479 Chevron St (19902-5062)
PHONE...............................302 655-3434
Stephen Mockbee, *Prin*
EMP: 13
SALES (corp-wide): 125.83MM **Privately Held**
Web: www.bancroftconstruction.com
SIC: **1521** Single-family housing construction
PA: Bancroft Construction Company
    1300 N Grant Ave Ste 101
    Wilmington DE 19806
    302 655-3434

(G-1871)
BANDAI NAMCO AMUS AMER INC
Also Called: Jolly Time
1365 N Dupont Hwy Ste 4004 (19901-8710)
PHONE...............................302 734-3623
Dana Nichols, *Brnch Mgr*
EMP: 5
Web: www.bandainamco-am.com
SIC: **7993** Video game arcade

HQ: Bandai Namco Amusement America Inc.
1550 Glenlake Ave
Itasca IL 60143
847 264-5612

(G-1872)
BANDS CA INC ✪
Also Called: Bands
8 The Grn Ste 6772 (19901-3618)
PHONE.................................206 396-7035
Rameen Satar, *CEO*
EMP: 6 **EST:** 2023
SALES (est): 237.56K **Privately Held**
SIC: 7371 Custom computer programming services

(G-1873)
BANKERS LIFE
Also Called: Bankers Life
99 Wolf Creek Blvd Ste 1b (19901-4968)
PHONE.................................302 232-5006
EMP: 5 **EST:** 2018
SALES (est): 243.58K **Privately Held**
Web: branches.bankerslife.com
SIC: 6411 Insurance agents, brokers, and service

(G-1874)
BARREL FUEL TECHNOLOGIES INC
3500 S Dupont Hwy (19901-6041)
PHONE.................................832 405-4806
Marc Chairello, *CEO*
Paul Martinez, *COO*
Emilio Lopez, *CAO*
EMP: 3 **EST:** 2021
SALES (est): 263.49K **Privately Held**
SIC: 3728 Aircraft parts and equipment, nec

(G-1875)
BARRETT BUSINESS SERVICES INC
Also Called: Bbsi
116 E Water St (19901-3614)
PHONE.................................302 674-2206
Larry Lewis, *Mgr*
EMP: 5
SQ FT: 1,375
SALES (corp-wide): 1.05B **Publicly Held**
Web: www.bbsi.com
SIC: 7361 7363 Employment agencies; Temporary help service
PA: Barrett Business Services Inc
8100 Ne Parkway Dr # 200
Vancouver WA 98662
360 828-0700

(G-1876)
BARROS MC NMARA MLKWICZ TYLOR
2 W Loockerman St (19904-7324)
P.O. Box 1298 (19903-1298)
PHONE.................................302 734-8400
Edward Mcnamara, *Pr*
Michael Malkiewicz, *VP*
EMP: 16 **EST:** 1964
SALES (est): 1.92MM **Privately Held**
Web: www.firststatelawyers.com
SIC: 8111 General practice attorney, lawyer

(G-1877)
BARRY GOLDSTEIN MD
1325 S State St Ste 204 (19901-4945)
PHONE.................................302 734-4130
Barry Goldstein, *Owner*
EMP: 5 **EST:** 1990
SALES (est): 53.3K **Privately Held**
Web: www.barrygoldsteinmd.com
SIC: 8011 Psychiatrist

(G-1878)
BASEDASH INC
8 The Grn Ste 5775 (19901-3618)
PHONE.................................302 244-0916
Max Musing, *CEO*
EMP: 5
SALES (est): 223.79K **Privately Held**
SIC: 7371 Computer software development and applications

(G-1879)
BASEMARK INC (PA)
3500 S Dupont Hwy (19901-6041)
PHONE.................................832 483-7093
Tero Sarkkinen, *CEO*
Eric Zapalac, *VP*
EMP: 4 **EST:** 2018
SALES (est): 334.06K
SALES (corp-wide): 334.06K **Privately Held**
Web: www.basemark.com
SIC: 7372 Application computer software

(G-1880)
BASETWO ARTFCAL INTLLGNCE USA ✪
Also Called: Basetwo
838 Walker Rd Ste 21-2 (19904-2751)
PHONE.................................519 400-8770
Thouheed Abdul Gaffoor, *CEO*
EMP: 6 **EST:** 2022
SALES (est): 237.56K **Privately Held**
Web: www.basetwo.ai
SIC: 7371 Computer software systems analysis and design, custom

(G-1881)
BATTLE PROVEN FOUNDATION
368 Artis Dr (19904-5643)
P.O. Box 710672 (20171-0672)
PHONE.................................703 216-1986
Terrence Hill, *otb*
Stephen Fails, *Ex Dir*
EMP: 7 **EST:** 2012
SALES (est): 75.97K **Privately Held**
Web: www.battleprovenfoundation.org
SIC: 8641 Veterans' organization

(G-1882)
BAWA INC
45 Old Mill Rd (19901-6290)
PHONE.................................302 698-3200
Melissa Wagner, *CFO*
Lucienne Babbitt, *VP*
Mark Babbitt, *Pr*
EMP: 6 **EST:** 2014
SALES (est): 247.73K **Privately Held**
SIC: 7359 5251 Lawn and garden equipment rental; Builders' hardware

(G-1883)
BAY ANESTHESIA ASSOCIATES LLC
640 S State St (19901-3530)
PHONE.................................302 598-9139
Steven Shields, *Mgr*
EMP: 14 **EST:** 2016
SALES (est): 4.47MM **Privately Held**
SIC: 8011 Anesthesiologist

(G-1884)
BAY DEVELOPERS INC
Also Called: Stoltzfus Mast
200 Weston Dr (19904-2786)
PHONE.................................302 736-0924
Henry S Mast, *Pr*
EMP: 15 **EST:** 1988
SALES (est): 3.77MM **Privately Held**
Web: www.hmastgroup.com
SIC: 1542 1521 Commercial and office building, new construction; New construction, single-family houses

(G-1885)
BAYADA
655 S Bay Rd Ste 1g (19901-4694)
PHONE.................................302 213-5024
Jennifer Joana, *Dir*
EMP: 16 **EST:** 2017
SALES (est): 213.75K **Privately Held**
Web: www.bayada.com
SIC: 8082 Home health care services

(G-1886)
BAYADA HOME HEALTH CARE INC
655 S Bay Rd Ste 1g (19901-4694)
PHONE.................................302 736-6001
EMP: 64
SALES (corp-wide): 694.21MM **Privately Held**
Web: www.bayada.com
SIC: 8082 Visiting nurse service
PA: Bayada Home Health Care, Inc.
1 W Main St
Moorestown NJ 08057
856 231-1000

(G-1887)
BAYADA HOME HEALTH CARE INC
Also Called: Central Delaware Nursing
655 S Bay Rd Ste 1g (19901-4694)
PHONE.................................302 213-5040
EMP: 59
SALES (corp-wide): 694.21MM **Privately Held**
Web: www.bayada.com
SIC: 8082 Visiting nurse service
PA: Bayada Home Health Care, Inc.
1 W Main St
Moorestown NJ 08057
856 231-1000

(G-1888)
BAYHEALTH ENT OF DOVER
826 S Governors Ave (19904-4107)
PHONE.................................302 674-3752
Catherine Wright Md, *Prin*
EMP: 16 **EST:** 2016
SALES (est): 382.53K **Privately Held**
Web: www.bayhealth.org
SIC: 8099 Health and allied services, nec

(G-1889)
BAYHEALTH MED CTR INC-OCC HLTH
Also Called: Healthworks
1275 S State St (19901-6927)
PHONE.................................302 678-1303
Dennis E Klima, *Ch*
John T Fifer, *Vice Chairman*
Gerald L White, *CFO*
EMP: 41 **EST:** 1985
SALES (est): 690.15K **Privately Held**
Web: www.bayhealth.org
SIC: 8062 General medical and surgical hospitals

(G-1890)
BAYHEALTH MEDICAL CENTER INC (PA)
640 S State St (19901-3530)
PHONE.................................302 674-4700
Terry Murphy, *Pr*
EMP: 167 **EST:** 1925
SALES (est): 919.75MM **Privately Held**
Web: www.bayhealth.org
SIC: 8062 General medical and surgical hospitals

(G-1891)
BAYHEALTH PRIMARY CARE DOVER W
720 S Queen St (19904-3567)
PHONE.................................302 734-7834
EMP: 9 **EST:** 2020
SALES (est): 276.17K **Privately Held**
Web: www.bayhealth.org
SIC: 8062 General medical and surgical hospitals

(G-1892)
BB BUILDER LLC
1452 W Denneys Rd (19904-4936)
PHONE.................................302 670-1972
Bennie Beachy, *Prin*
EMP: 5 **EST:** 2018
SALES (est): 201.96K **Privately Held**
SIC: 1521 New construction, single-family houses

(G-1893)
BE BOLD
421 Ridgely Blvd (19904-4010)
PHONE.................................302 415-5242
Tamika Lee, *Prin*
EMP: 5 **EST:** 2015
SALES (est): 107.5K **Privately Held**
SIC: 8641 Civic and social associations

(G-1894)
BE HUMANE CO ✪
Also Called: Be Human E
8 The Grn (19901-3618)
PHONE.................................720 419-5362
Sara Filipcic, *CEO*
EMP: 5 **EST:** 2022
SALES (est): 199.4K **Privately Held**
SIC: 7371 7389 Computer software development and applications; Business services, nec

(G-1895)
BE WELL MASSAGE AND SKIN CARE
554 Garton Ln (19904-4887)
PHONE.................................302 883-3066
EMP: 6 **EST:** 2018
SALES (est): 42.83K **Privately Held**
Web: www.bewellde.com
SIC: 8049 Massage Therapist

(G-1896)
BEACH ASSOCIATES INC
Also Called: R.R. Beach Associates
9 E Loockerman St Ste 2a (19901-7343)
PHONE.................................866 744-9911
Jay Schukoske, *Pr*
Jennifer Truesdale, *Sec*
Shelby Truesdale, *VP*
EMP: 11 **EST:** 2000
SQ FT: 2,000
SALES (est): 595.5K **Privately Held**
Web: www.beachassoc.com
SIC: 7322 Collection agency, except real estate

(G-1897)
BEACON INTERACTIVE INC ✪
8 The Grn Ste A (19901-3618)
PHONE.................................414 306-5978
Jingyu Xiao, *CEO*
EMP: 12 **EST:** 2023
SALES (est): 406.37K **Privately Held**
SIC: 7371 Custom computer programming services

Dover - Kent County (G-1898) — GEOGRAPHIC SECTION

(G-1898)
BEAR ASSOCIATES LLC
209 Massey Dr (19904-5882)
PHONE..................302 735-5558
EMP: 5 EST: 2005
SQ FT: 2,201
SALES (est): 246.86K Privately Held
Web: www.bearassoc.com
SIC: 7336 Graphic arts and related design

(G-1899)
BEAR FINANCIAL GROUP LLC
Also Called: Key Advisors Group
846 Walker Rd Ste 31-2 (19904-2756)
PHONE..................302 735-9909
Doug Ferris, Owner
EMP: 7 EST: 1999
SALES (est): 172.75K Privately Held
SIC: 8742 Financial consultant

(G-1900)
BEAUTY MAX INC
1634 S Governors Ave (19904-7004)
PHONE..................302 735-1705
Sung Kim, Pr
EMP: 2 EST: 1997
SALES (est): 198.83K Privately Held
SIC: 2842 7231 Polishes and sanitation goods; Beauty shops

(G-1901)
BECAUSE LOVE ALLOWS COMPASSION
270 Beechwood Ave (19901-5233)
PHONE..................302 674-2496
Anne Coleman, Owner
Shakira Hameen, Sec
EMP: 7 EST: 1994
SALES (est): 44.66K Privately Held
SIC: 8699 Charitable organization

(G-1902)
BECKER MORGAN GROUP INC
309 S Governors Ave (19904-6705)
PHONE..................302 734-7950
Gregory Z Moore, Brnch Mgr
EMP: 26
SALES (corp-wide): 13.27MM Privately Held
Web: www.beckermorgan.com
SIC: 8711 8712 Civil engineering; Architectural services
PA: Becker Morgan Group Inc
312 W Main St Ste 3fl
Salisbury MD 21801
410 546-9100

(G-1903)
BEEZ DRIVERS INC ◇
838 Walker Rd Ste 21-2 (19904-2751)
PHONE..................917 392-9111
Rex Huang, CEO
EMP: 2 EST: 2023
SALES (est): 87.4K Privately Held
SIC: 7372 Prepackaged software

(G-1904)
BEGINNINGS & BEYOND NURERY SCH
710 Buckson Dr (19901-3922)
PHONE..................302 678-0445
Danielle Harrison, Dir
EMP: 15 EST: 2019
SALES (est): 24.63K Privately Held
Web: www.beginnings-beyond.com
SIC: 8351 Preschool center

(G-1905)
BEGINNINGS AND BEYOND INC
402 Cowgill St (19901-4512)
PHONE..................302 734-2464
Danielle Harrison, Pr
EMP: 23 EST: 2010
SALES (est): 214.01K Privately Held
Web: www.beginnings-beyond.com
SIC: 8351 Preschool center

(G-1906)
BELKINS INC
8 The Grn Ste 4331 (19901-3618)
PHONE..................302 261-5393
EMP: 67 EST: 2021
SALES (est): 1.15MM Privately Held
Web: www.belkins.io
SIC: 4141 Local bus charter service

(G-1907)
BELLA MEDISPA INC
435 S Dupont Hwy (19901-4513)
PHONE..................302 736-6334
Troy Windham, Pr
EMP: 6 EST: 2021
SALES (est): 582.24K Privately Held
SIC: 7991 Spas

(G-1908)
BELLE ENERGIE LLC
37 Richard Lee Ct (19904-1760)
PHONE..................302 690-3188
EMP: 5 EST: 2020
SALES (est): 42.95K Privately Held
SIC: 8999 Personal services

(G-1909)
BENCH ACCOUNTING INC
874 Walker Rd (19904-2778)
PHONE..................888 760-1940
EMP: 6 EST: 2018
SALES (est): 272.62K Privately Held
Web: www.bench.co
SIC: 8721 Accounting, auditing, and bookkeeping

(G-1910)
BENEVLENT PRTECTIVE ORDER ELKS
Also Called: ELKS LODGE 1903
200 Saulsbury Rd (19904-2721)
PHONE..................302 736-1903
Richard Woodhall, Pr
EMP: 8 EST: 1954
SQ FT: 4,000
SALES (est): 350.89K Privately Held
SIC: 8641 Fraternal associations

(G-1911)
BENJAMIN WOLF GROUP LLC
8 The Grn Ste 11166 (19901-3618)
PHONE..................302 487-1827
EMP: 7 EST: 2020
SALES (est): 239.5K Privately Held
Web: www.benjaminwolfgroup.com
SIC: 8721 Certified public accountant

(G-1912)
BENNETT DET PRTECTIVE AGCY INC (PA)
Also Called: Bennett Security Service
335 Martin St (19901-4527)
P.O. Box 344 (19903-0344)
PHONE..................302 734-2480
Edward J Bennett, CEO
Judy L Bennett, Sec
EMP: 6 EST: 1960
SQ FT: 2,200
SALES (est): 8.3MM
SALES (corp-wide): 8.3MM Privately Held
SIC: 7381 Security guard service

(G-1913)
BENNIE SMITH FUNERAL HOME INC (PA)
717 W Division St (19904-2731)
P.O. Box 691 (19903-0691)
PHONE..................302 678-8747
Bennie Smith, Pr
EMP: 9 EST: 1994
SALES (est): 1.16MM Privately Held
Web: www.benniesmithfuneralhome.com
SIC: 7261 Funeral home

(G-1914)
BERNARD LIMPERT
Also Called: Stage One
1465 S Governors Ave (19904-7017)
PHONE..................302 674-8280
Bernard Limpert, Owner
Billy J Smith, Pr
EMP: 5 EST: 2000
SALES (est): 324.8K Privately Held
SIC: 7538 7539 7533 General automotive repair shops; Brake services; Muffler shop, sale or repair and installation

(G-1915)
BERRY INTERNATIONAL INC
606 Pear St Unit 1 (19904-2832)
PHONE..................302 674-1300
EMP: 9 EST: 1990
SQ FT: 105,000
SALES (est): 916.87K Privately Held
SIC: 4212 Moving services
PA: Diamond State Corporation
602 Pear St
Dover DE 19904

(G-1916)
BEST PERIODT LLC
8 The Grn Ste 12587 (19901-3618)
PHONE..................302 291-2275
J Dean Jones, CFO
EMP: 4 EST: 2021
SALES (est): 197.1K Privately Held
Web: www.bestperiodt.com
SIC: 2676 Feminine hygiene paper products

(G-1917)
BEST ROOFING AND SIDING CO
5091 N Dupont Hwy (19901-2346)
PHONE..................302 678-5700
John Gearhart, Owner
EMP: 8 EST: 1971
SALES (est): 785.16K Privately Held
SIC: 1761 Roofing contractor

(G-1918)
BESTEMPS
Also Called: Bestemps of Dover
385 W North St (19904-6748)
PHONE..................302 674-4357
Patsy Ware, Pr
Kari Jenkins, Sec
EMP: 5 EST: 2007
SALES (est): 494.57K Privately Held
Web: www.bestemps.com
SIC: 7361 Employment agencies

(G-1919)
BETH A CANALICHIO LCSW LTD
884 Walker Rd Ste C (19904-2758)
PHONE..................302 734-7760
Beth Canalichio, Prin
EMP: 42
SIC: 8322 Social worker
PA: Beth A. Canalichio Lcsw, Ltd.
863 Buttner Pl
Dover DE 19904

(G-1920)
BETH A CANALICHIO LCSW LTD (PA)
863 Buttner Pl (19904-2406)
PHONE..................302 734-7760
EMP: 5 EST: 2000
SALES (est): 123.92K Privately Held
SIC: 8322 Social worker

(G-1921)
BETSSON US CORP
1675 S State St Ste B (19901-5140)
PHONE..................800 316-6660
Pontus Lindvall, VP
EMP: 7 EST: 2020
SALES (est): 109.25K Privately Held
SIC: 8748 Business consulting, nec

(G-1922)
BETTER EARTH LLC
160 Greentree Dr Ste 101 (19904-7620)
PHONE..................302 242-3644
EMP: 7 EST: 2014
SALES (est): 45.24K Privately Held
Web: www.becompostable.com
SIC: 4813 Internet host services

(G-1923)
BETTER HOME SERVICES
1183 Rose Dale Ln (19904-1613)
PHONE..................302 250-9860
EMP: 5 EST: 2016
SALES (est): 34.76K Privately Held
SIC: 7349 Building maintenance services, nec

(G-1924)
BETTER LIFE CHIROPRACTIC
1111 S Governors Ave (19904-6903)
PHONE..................302 535-9204
EMP: 5 EST: 2019
SALES (est): 37.19K Privately Held
SIC: 8041 Offices and clinics of chiropractors

(G-1925)
BEY HOLLYWOOD LLC
8 The Grn Ste R (19901-3618)
PHONE..................209 789-5132
EMP: 4 EST: 2020
SALES (est): 77.45K Privately Held
SIC: 3161 Clothing and apparel carrying cases

(G-1926)
BEYOND LEDGER LLC
8 The Grn Ste A (19901-3618)
PHONE..................313 471-0462
EMP: 5 EST: 2017
SALES (est): 202.73K Privately Held
Web: www.beyondtheledger.net
SIC: 8721 Accounting, auditing, and bookkeeping

(G-1927)
BFPE INTERNATIONAL INC
155 Commerce Way (19904-8306)
PHONE..................302 346-4800
EMP: 6
SALES (corp-wide): 120.1MM Privately Held
Web: www.bfpe.com
SIC: 1731 Fire detection and burglar alarm systems specialization
PA: Bfpe International, Inc.
7512 Connelley Dr
Hanover MD 21076
410 768-2200

GEOGRAPHIC SECTION   Dover - Kent County (G-1958)

(G-1928)
BG LABORATORY
383 Mockingbird Ave (19904-4840)
PHONE.................302 535-3954
EMP: 7 **EST:** 2018
SALES (est): 47.44K **Privately Held**
SIC: 8071 Medical laboratories

(G-1929)
BGM COMPLIANCE LLC
8 The Grn Ste 7485 (19901-3618)
PHONE.................302 450-1149
Carolyn Moore, *Managing Member*
EMP: 10 **EST:** 2017
SALES (est): 274.4K **Privately Held**
SIC: 7361 Employment agencies

(G-1930)
BHAKTI CONSULTING LLC
614 N Dupont Hwy Ste 200 (19901-3900)
PHONE.................302 742-1964
Glenda Hallett, *Admn*
EMP: 5 **EST:** 2014
SALES (est): 288.16K **Privately Held**
SIC: 8742 Marketing consulting services

(G-1931)
BHAOO INC
8 The Grn (19901-3618)
PHONE.................832 888-3694
Faisal Qadeer, *CEO*
EMP: 20 **EST:** 2021
SALES (est): 600.73K **Privately Held**
Web: www.bhaooinc.com
SIC: 7336 7371 8742 Graphic arts and related design; Computer software writing services; Marketing consulting services

(G-1932)
BIG BRTHERS BIG SISTERS OF DEL
1001 S Bradford St Ste 1 (19904-4153)
PHONE.................302 998-3577
Mary Fox, *Pr*
Mary Fox, *Ex Dir*
EMP: 21 **EST:** 2006
SALES (est): 1.34MM **Privately Held**
Web: www.bbbsde.org
SIC: 8322 Youth center

(G-1933)
BIG DATA ELEMENTS LLC (PA)
8 The Grn Ste A (19901-3618)
PHONE.................917 620-2337
EMP: 7 **EST:** 2018
SALES (est): 100K
SALES (corp-wide): 100K **Privately Held**
SIC: 7371 Computer software development and applications

(G-1934)
BIG DAY TRUCKING LLC ✪
8 The Grn Ste 14688 (19901-3618)
PHONE.................302 900-1190
Jermaine Bradley, *Managing Member*
EMP: 5 **EST:** 2023
SALES (est): 296.01K **Privately Held**
Web: www.bigdaytrucking.com
SIC: 4213 7389 Trucking, except local; Business Activities at Non-Commercial Site

(G-1935)
BIG ELD LLC
8 The Grn (19901-3618)
PHONE.................302 549-0333
EMP: 5
SALES (est): 199.4K **Privately Held**
SIC: 7371 Computer software development and applications

(G-1936)
BIG SOFA TECHNOLOGIES INC
874 Walker Rd Ste C (19904-2778)
PHONE.................630 839-9332
EMP: 4 **EST:** 2019
SALES (est): 185.08K **Privately Held**
SIC: 7372 Prepackaged software

(G-1937)
BIGINSIGHTS LLC
8 The Grn Ste A (19901-3618)
PHONE.................618 819-0902
EMP: 10
SALES (est): 355.79K **Privately Held**
SIC: 7379 Computer related consulting services

(G-1938)
BILLS HOME CARE SERVICE LLC
160 Beech Dr (19904-9439)
PHONE.................302 526-2071
Mark Wojtkiewicz, *Prin*
EMP: 8 **EST:** 2018
SALES (est): 231.45K **Privately Held**
SIC: 8082 Home health care services

(G-1939)
BINARY TECHNOLOGY LLC
8 The Grn Ste R (19901-3618)
PHONE.................302 455-7400
EMP: 10 **EST:** 2020
SALES (est): 457.67K **Privately Held**
Web: binary.llc
SIC: 7379 Online services technology consultants

(G-1940)
BIOTECH MENTOR LLC
8 The Grn (19901-3618)
PHONE.................617 460-4983
EMP: 25
SALES (est): 641.67K **Privately Held**
SIC: 8748 7389 Business consulting, nec; Business services, nec

(G-1941)
BIRDIE SSOT LLC
Also Called: Birdie
3500 S Dupont Hwy (19901-6041)
PHONE.................857 361-6883
EMP: 8 **EST:** 2018
SALES (est): 345.87K **Privately Held**
SIC: 7371 Computer software development and applications

(G-1942)
BITS & BYTES INC
2953 Dyke Branch Rd (19901)
P.O. Box 751 (19903-0751)
PHONE.................302 674-2999
Henry Forester, *Pr*
Debbie Caffo, *Sec*
Michelle Rae Condon, *Treas*
EMP: 7 **EST:** 1990
SQ FT: 1,000
SALES (est): 977.3K **Privately Held**
Web: www.bitbyteinc.net
SIC: 5045 5734 8243 7371 Computers, peripherals, and software; Computer and software stores; Software training, computer ; Computer software systems analysis and design, custom

(G-1943)
BLACK GODS AND GODDESS LLC (PA) ✪
8 The Grn Ste A (19901-3618)
PHONE.................708 665-0949
EMP: 7 **EST:** 2022
SALES (est): 253.99K

SALES (corp-wide): 253.99K **Privately Held**
Web: www.blackgodsandgoddess.com
SIC: 5932 7389 Clothing, secondhand; Business Activities at Non-Commercial Site

(G-1944)
BLACK LOTUS VENTURES LLC
8 The Grn Ste R (19901-3618)
PHONE.................650 260-4684
Malik Mbaye, *Managing Member*
EMP: 15 **EST:** 2021
SALES (est): 515.3K **Privately Held**
Web: www.blacklotus.co
SIC: 8742 Business management consultant

(G-1945)
BLACK MATH LABS INC
8 The Grn Ste A (19901-3618)
PHONE.................858 349-9446
Mohammad Kurabi, *Dir*
EMP: 5
SALES (est): 210.3K **Privately Held**
SIC: 7371 Software programming applications

(G-1946)
BLAZE COIN LLC
Also Called: Information Technology
8 The Grn Ste B (19901-3618)
PHONE.................509 768-2249
Ankush Sood, *Prin*
Shamik Kundu, *Prin*
EMP: 7 **EST:** 2019
SALES (est): 291.93K **Privately Held**
SIC: 7389 Business Activities at Non-Commercial Site

(G-1947)
BLEND NETWORK INC
8 The Grn (19901-3618)
PHONE.................267 521-8845
Jeff Tepel, *CEO*
EMP: 5
SALES (est): 101.79K **Privately Held**
SIC: 8621 Professional organizations

(G-1948)
BLENHEIM HOSPITALITY LLC
655 N Dupont Hwy (19901-3936)
PHONE.................302 677-0900
Lisa Venzon, *Prin*
EMP: 16 **EST:** 2010
SALES (est): 91.44K **Privately Held**
Web: www.blenheimhospitality.com
SIC: 7011 Hotels and motels

(G-1949)
BLJ&D FLAGGING LLC
820 Carvel Dr Apt J12 (19901-6666)
P.O. Box 13 (19903-0013)
PHONE.................302 272-0574
Corlet Demby, *Owner*
EMP: 15 **EST:** 2017
SALES (est): 476.88K **Privately Held**
Web: bljdflaggingllc.weebly.com
SIC: 7389 Metal cutting services

(G-1950)
BLOCKWARE SOLUTIONS LLC
8 The Grn (19901-3618)
PHONE.................512 905-5209
EMP: 15 **EST:** 2021
SALES (est): 1.01MM **Privately Held**
Web: www.blockwaresolutions.com
SIC: 7379 7389 Online services technology consultants; Business services, nec

(G-1951)
BLOG - CARE FIRST DENTAL TEAM
1250 S Governors Ave (19904-4802)
PHONE.................302 741-2044
EMP: 9 **EST:** 2017
SALES (est): 211.87K **Privately Held**
Web: www.carefirstdentalteam.com
SIC: 8021 Dentists' office

(G-1952)
BLUE MARLIN ICE LLC
273 Walnut Shade Rd (19904-6474)
PHONE.................302 697-7800
Jon Nichols Junior, *CEO*
EMP: 4 **EST:** 2014
SQ FT: 4,800
SALES (est): 497.02K **Privately Held**
Web: www.bluemarlinice.com
SIC: 4222 2097 Warehousing, cold storage or refrigerated; Block ice

(G-1953)
BLUE RIDGE CONSULTANTS LLC (PA) ✪
8 The Grn Ste B (19901-3618)
PHONE.................248 345-2294
Justin Kuta, *Managing Member*
EMP: 5 **EST:** 2022
SALES (est): 209.21K
SALES (corp-wide): 209.21K **Privately Held**
SIC: 7372 Application computer software

(G-1954)
BLUE RIDGE HOME CARE INC
9 E Loockerman St Ste 210 (19901-7347)
PHONE.................302 397-8211
EMP: 5 **EST:** 2017
SALES (est): 67.24K **Privately Held**
Web: www.blueridgedelaware.com
SIC: 8082 Home health care services

(G-1955)
BNL CONSULTING LLC
100 Campus Dr (19904-1383)
PHONE.................302 857-1057
EMP: 6 **EST:** 2018
SALES (est): 300K **Privately Held**
SIC: 8742 Restaurant and food services consultants

(G-1956)
BOA FINANCIAL LLC
Also Called: Hildr Group
8 The Grn Ste 1 (19901-3618)
PHONE.................888 444-5371
Steven Hackney, *CEO*
EMP: 7 **EST:** 2018
SALES (est): 842.6K **Privately Held**
SIC: 2311 3829 3821 2211 Men's and boys' uniforms; Thermometers, including digital: clinical; Incubators, laboratory; Surgical fabrics, cotton

(G-1957)
BOB SIMMONS AGENCY
Also Called: State Farm Insurance
1460 E Lebanon Rd (19901-5833)
PHONE.................302 698-1970
EMP: 5 **EST:** 1995
SALES (est): 371.3K **Privately Held**
Web: www.statefarm.com
SIC: 6411 Insurance agents and brokers

(G-1958)
BODY INTERACT INC
614 N Dupont Hwy Ste 210 (19901-3900)
PHONE.................512 910-8350
Pedro Pinto, *CEO*
EMP: 11 **EST:** 2018

SALES (est): 472.17K **Privately Held**
Web: www.bodyinteract.com
SIC: 7299 7379 Miscellaneous personal service; Computer related services, nec
PA: Take The Wind, S.A.
Quinta Da Portela, Lote V2.2
Coimbra 3030-

(G-1959)
BOEING COMPANY
Also Called: Boeing
639 Evreux St (19902-5139)
P.O. Box 2047 (19902-2047)
PHONE..............................302 735-2922
EMP: 2
SALES (corp-wide): 77.79B **Publicly Held**
Web: www.boeing.com
SIC: 3721 Airplanes, fixed or rotary wing
PA: The Boeing Company
929 Long Bridge Dr
Arlington VA 22202
703 414-6338

(G-1960)
BOLDLATINA DIGITAL GROUP PBC
8 The Grn (19901-3618)
PHONE..............................415 754-0143
Michelle Olvera, *CEO*
EMP: 2 **EST**: 2020
SALES (est): 92.41K **Privately Held**
Web: www.boldlatina.com
SIC: 2721 Magazines: publishing only, not printed on site

(G-1961)
BONNIE RELOCATION LLC
40 Ridgely St (19904-2710)
PHONE..............................302 538-0673
EMP: 9 **EST**: 2016
SALES (est): 471.71K **Privately Held**
SIC: 4214 Furniture moving and storage, local

(G-1962)
BOOKITNGO CORP
8 The Grn (19901-3618)
PHONE..............................949 899-7684
Aman Mohindra, *Pr*
EMP: 5 **EST**: 2021
SALES (est): 107.01K **Privately Held**
SIC: 7371 7389 Computer software development and applications; Business services, nec

(G-1963)
BOONOOB INC
8 The Grn Ste 12218 (19901-3618)
PHONE..............................302 288-0670
Hesam Jafari, *CEO*
EMP: 6 **EST**: 2021
SALES (est): 275.71K **Privately Held**
Web: www.boonoob.com
SIC: 7371 Computer software development and applications

(G-1964)
BOSCO INSURANCE AGENCY
625 S Dupont Hwy Ste 101 (19901-4504)
PHONE..............................302 678-0647
Jim Watkins, *VP*
James A Watkins, *Pt*
EMP: 6 **EST**: 1976
SALES (est): 420.96K **Privately Held**
SIC: 6411 Insurance agents, brokers, and service

(G-1965)
BOSPHORUS TEXTILE LLC
Also Called: WHOleseller& Retailer
8 The Grn (19901-3618)
PHONE..............................202 629-6563
Celal Varol, *Pr*
Celal Varol, *CEO*
EMP: 11 **EST**: 2010
SALES (est): 524.42K **Privately Held**
SIC: 7389 Textile and apparel services

(G-1966)
BOTTLE OF SMOKE PRESS
902 Wilson Dr (19904-2437)
P.O. Box 66 (12589-0066)
PHONE..............................302 399-1856
Bill Roberts, *Prin*
EMP: 5 **EST**: 2010
SALES (est): 58.57K **Privately Held**
Web: www.bospress.net
SIC: 2741 Miscellaneous publishing

(G-1967)
BOYS & GIRLS CLUB OF DE
864 Center Rd (19901-5908)
PHONE..............................302 677-6376
Roxanne Lee, *Mgr*
EMP: 15 **EST**: 2014
SALES (est): 95.47K **Privately Held**
Web: www.bgclubs.org
SIC: 8641 Youth organizations

(G-1968)
BOYS & GIRLS CLUBS DEL INC
Also Called: Boys & Girls Club of Dover
375 Simon Cir (19904-3437)
PHONE..............................302 678-5182
Renata Stewart, *Dir*
EMP: 5
SALES (corp-wide): 33.26MM **Privately Held**
Web: www.bgclubs.org
SIC: 8641 Youth organizations
PA: Boys & Girls Clubs Of Delaware, Inc.
669 S Union St
Wilmington DE 19805
302 658-1870

(G-1969)
BRADFORD FAMILY PHYSICIANS LLC
1055 S Bradford St (19904-4141)
PHONE..............................302 730-3750
EMP: 9 **EST**: 2016
SALES (est): 226.53K **Privately Held**
SIC: 8011 Offices and clinics of medical doctors

(G-1970)
BRAIN INJURY ASSOCIATION DEL
Also Called: Biad
840 Walker Rd Ste A (19904-2727)
P.O. Box 1897 (19903-1897)
PHONE..............................302 346-2083
Jim Mills, *Pr*
Sharon Lyons, *VP*
EMP: 8 **EST**: 1987
SALES (est): 44.36K **Privately Held**
Web: www.biade.org
SIC: 8699 Charitable organization

(G-1971)
BRAND EVANGELISTS FOR BUTY INC
8 The Grn Ste R (19901-3618)
PHONE..............................973 970-0812
Stephanie Davis, *CEO*
EMP: 7
SALES (est): 78.16K **Privately Held**
SIC: 2844 Face creams or lotions

(G-1972)
BRANTIMUS LOGISTICS LLC ◆
8 The Grn Ste 8643 (19901-3618)
PHONE..............................302 990-4110
EMP: 25 **EST**: 2022
SALES (est): 1.08MM **Privately Held**
Web: www.brantimus.com
SIC: 4731 Freight transportation arrangement

(G-1973)
BRASWELL ENTERPRISES LLC ◆
8 The Grn Ste A (19901-3618)
PHONE..............................470 588-2087
Bayek Braswell, *Managing Member*
EMP: 13 **EST**: 2023
SIC: 6719 Holding companies, nec

(G-1974)
BRAVATICS LLC
8 The Grn Ste B (19901-3618)
PHONE..............................703 966-0516
Senakpon Gebedo, *Managing Member*
EMP: 5 **EST**: 2020
SALES (est): 50K **Privately Held**
SIC: 7379 Computer related consulting services

(G-1975)
BRAVIN PUBLISHING LLC
1041 N Dupont Hwy (19901-2006)
PHONE..............................347 921-0443
Keith Belvin, *CEO*
EMP: 2 **EST**: 2010
SALES (est): 240K **Privately Held**
Web: www.bravinpublishing.com
SIC: 2741 Miscellaneous publishing

(G-1976)
BRENFORD ANIMAL HOSPITAL P A (PA)
Also Called: Hammer, Greg S
4118 N Dupont Hwy (19901-1523)
PHONE..............................302 678-9418
Craig Stonesifer, *Pt*
Greg Hammer, *Pt*
EMP: 22 **EST**: 1974
SQ FT: 3,875
SALES (est): 2.49MM
SALES (corp-wide): 2.49MM **Privately Held**
Web: www.brenfordanimalhospital.com
SIC: 0742 0752 Animal hospital services, pets and other animal specialties; Animal boarding services

(G-1977)
BRIAN K MUMMERT
526 Rose Dale Ln (19904-1606)
PHONE..............................302 678-2260
Brian K Mummert, *Prin*
EMP: 7 **EST**: 2010
SALES (est): 296.99K **Privately Held**
SIC: 1522 Residential construction, nec

(G-1978)
BRICK DOCTOR INC (PA)
130 Kruser Blvd (19901-3265)
PHONE..............................302 678-3380
Jason Goodnight, *Pr*
Ellen Capitan, *VP*
EMP: 10 **EST**: 1984
SQ FT: 1,600
SALES (est): 1.5MM
SALES (corp-wide): 1.5MM **Privately Held**
Web: www.thebrickdoctor.com
SIC: 1741 1611 1771 Unit paver installation; Sidewalk construction; Sidewalk contractor

(G-1979)
BRIDGESTONE RET OPERATIONS LLC
Also Called: Firestone
625 S Bay Rd (19901-4601)
PHONE..............................302 734-4522
Joseph Litz, *Mgr*
EMP: 8
Web: www.bridgestoneamericas.com
SIC: 5531 7534 Automotive tires; Rebuilding and retreading tires
HQ: Bridgestone Retail Operations, Llc
333 E Lake St Ste 300
Bloomingdale IL 60108
630 259-9000

(G-1980)
BRIGHT SIDE EXTERIORS
615 Otis Dr (19901-4644)
P.O. Box 931 (19903-0931)
PHONE..............................302 674-4642
EMP: 7 **EST**: 2018
SALES (est): 450.85K **Privately Held**
Web: www.trustbrightside.com
SIC: 0782 Lawn and garden services

(G-1981)
BRISYN PROS CLEANING SERVICE
55 Saint Bernadino Cir (19904-7652)
PHONE..............................302 399-7366
Kevin B Hughes, *Prin*
EMP: 5 **EST**: 2015
SALES (est): 43.31K **Privately Held**
SIC: 7699 Cleaning services

(G-1982)
BRITTNEY ANN FISCHBECK LLC
8 The Grn Ste 14852 (19901-3618)
PHONE..............................302 219-6491
Brittney Fischbeck, *Managing Member*
EMP: 6
SALES (est): 68.89K **Privately Held**
SIC: 7389 Business services, nec

(G-1983)
BROOKDALE DOVER
150 Saulsbury Rd (19904-2776)
PHONE..............................302 674-4407
EMP: 13 **EST**: 2018
SALES (est): 1.14MM **Privately Held**
Web: www.brookdale.com
SIC: 8051 Skilled nursing care facilities

(G-1984)
BROOKS MACHINE INC (PA)
Also Called: Brooks Metal Saws Repair
716 S West St (19904-3513)
PHONE..............................302 674-5900
Linda Brooks, *Pr*
Paul A Brooks Ii, *VP*
John W Brooks, *Stockholder*
EMP: 7 **EST**: 1982
SQ FT: 4,800
SALES (est): 692.59K
SALES (corp-wide): 692.59K **Privately Held**
Web: www.brooks-saws.com
SIC: 7699 5084 Industrial machinery and equipment repair; Metalworking machinery

(G-1985)
BROWN SHIELS & OBRIEN
108 E Water St (19901-3614)
P.O. Box F (19903-1556)
PHONE..............................302 734-4766
Roy Shiels, *Pt*
Herman Cubbiage Brown, *Pt*
John E O'brien, *Pt*
EMP: 8 **EST**: 1965
SALES (est): 489.24K **Privately Held**
SIC: 8111 General practice attorney, lawyer

(G-1986)
BROWN SHELS BAUREGARD LLC
148 S Bradford St (19904-7318)

P.O. Box 1556 (19903-1556)
PHONE..................................302 226-2270
Andre M Beauregard, *Pr*
EMP: 8 **EST:** 2010
SALES (est): 451.22K **Privately Held**
SIC: 8111 General practice attorney, lawyer

(G-1987)
BRUNSWICK DOVERAMA
1600 S Governors Ave (19904-7004)
PHONE..................................302 734-7501
Carmine Alessandro, *Mgr*
EMP: 8 **EST:** 2015
SALES (est): 226.32K **Privately Held**
SIC: 7933 Ten pin center

(G-1988)
BSR TRADE LLC
8 The Grn Ste 6258 (19901-3618)
PHONE..................................646 250-4409
EMP: 5 **EST:** 2017
SALES (est): 164.36K **Privately Held**
SIC: 6799 Commodity contract trading companies

(G-1989)
BUILDERS & REMODELERS ASSOC DE
109 E Division St (19901-7303)
PHONE..................................302 678-1520
Verity Watson, *Ex VP*
EMP: 5 **EST:** 2017
SALES (est): 101.48K **Privately Held**
Web: www.brad-de.org
SIC: 8611 Trade associations

(G-1990)
BUILDING BLOCKS FOR LEARNI
88 Beech Dr (19904-9428)
PHONE..................................302 677-0248
Patricia C Slentz, *Prin*
EMP: 9 **EST:** 2008
SALES (est): 76.42K **Privately Held**
SIC: 8351 Child day care services

(G-1991)
BULLENT INVESTMENT LLC
Also Called: Azap Finance
8 The Grn Ste A (19901-3618)
PHONE..................................877 214-7707
EMP: 8 **EST:** 2021
SALES (est): 306.16K **Privately Held**
SIC: 7389 Financial services

(G-1992)
BULLSEYE ENTERTAINMENT TECH CO
Also Called: Be-Tech Group Company
8 The Grn Ste 8136 (19901-3618)
PHONE..................................302 924-5034
Cesar Espitia, *Ch Bd*
EMP: 25 **EST:** 2018
SALES (est): 864.01K **Privately Held**
SIC: 7373 7371 8748 Systems engineering, computer related; Computer software development; Business consulting, nec

(G-1993)
BURKE DERMATOLOGY (PA)
95 Wolf Creek Blvd Ste 1 (19901-4965)
PHONE..................................302 734-3376
Thomas Burke, *Prin*
EMP: 5 **EST:** 2010
SALES (est): 708.4K
SALES (corp-wide): 708.4K **Privately Held**
Web: www.burkedermatology.com
SIC: 8011 Dermatologist

(G-1994)
BURKES SEAL COATING
22 Howell St (19901-5517)
PHONE..................................302 697-7635
Aaron Burke, *Prin*
EMP: 6 **EST:** 2012
SALES (est): 62.88K **Privately Held**
SIC: 1799 Coating, caulking, and weather, water, and fireproofing

(G-1995)
BURRIS LOGISTICS
309 Concord Rd (19904-9100)
PHONE..................................302 839-5129
EMP: 9
SALES (corp-wide): 1.24B **Privately Held**
Web: www.burrislogistics.com
SIC: 4789 Freight car loading and unloading
PA: Burris Logistics
    501 Se 5th St
    Milford DE 19963
    302 839-4531

(G-1996)
BURROUGHS EXPRESS LLC
59 Stoney Dr (19904-9735)
PHONE..................................410 476-1764
Christopher Burroughs, *CEO*
EMP: 5 **EST:** 2020
SALES (est): 255.15K **Privately Held**
SIC: 4213 7389 Trucking, except local; Business Activities at Non-Commercial Site

(G-1997)
BUSINESS INTERFACE MD LLC
1203 College Park Dr Ste 101 (19904-8703)
PHONE..................................302 735-7739
Ira Roach, *Managing Member*
EMP: 8 **EST:** 2013
SALES (est): 118.41K **Privately Held**
SIC: 8011 Physicians' office, including specialists

(G-1998)
BUYCRYPT INC
8 The Grn Ste A (19901-3618)
PHONE..................................309 733-4157
EMP: 5 **EST:** 2020
SALES (est): 104.73K **Privately Held**
Web: www.buycrypt.com
SIC: 7389 Brokers' services

(G-1999)
BUZE MOBILE INC ✪
8 The Grn Ste 16808 (19901-3618)
PHONE..................................630 331-0553
Michael Conlee, *CEO*
Ibrahim Ahmed, *Treas*
EMP: 5 **EST:** 2023
SALES (est): 199.4K **Privately Held**
SIC: 7371 Custom computer programming services

(G-2000)
BVI GROUP LLC
8 The Grn Ste 6006 (19901-3618)
PHONE..................................954 604-9363
EMP: 5 **EST:** 2018
SALES (est): 161.03K **Privately Held**
SIC: 4812 Radiotelephone communication

(G-2001)
BYDARKMATTER LLC
1111b S Governors Ave Ste 6502 (19904-6903)
PHONE..................................850 801-2732
EMP: 5
SALES (est): 199.4K **Privately Held**
SIC: 7371 Computer software development and applications

(G-2002)
BYLER SAWMILL
2846 Yoder Dr (19904-5845)
PHONE..................................302 730-4208
Crist Byler, *Owner*
EMP: 3 **EST:** 2004
SALES (est): 103.02K **Privately Held**
SIC: 2421 Sawmills and planing mills, general

(G-2003)
BYLERWILLIAMR
502 W Denneys Rd (19904-4925)
PHONE..................................302 653-3727
William Byler, *Prin*
EMP: 6 **EST:** 2010
SALES (est): 132.12K **Privately Held**
SIC: 1799 Special trade contractors, nec

(G-2004)
C & L CLEANERS INC
266 Galaxy St Bldg Afb (19902-5056)
PHONE..................................302 736-5171
Shunli Lou, *Prin*
EMP: 5 **EST:** 2018
SALES (est): 77.06K **Privately Held**
SIC: 7216 Cleaning and dyeing, except rugs

(G-2005)
C & N SERVICES LLC
Also Called: Plumbing and Mechanical Contr
126 Thornhill Ct (19904-1055)
PHONE..................................302 883-1046
Carl Rifino, *Managing Member*
EMP: 5 **EST:** 2020
SALES (est): 439.9K **Privately Held**
Web: www.cnservicesllc.org
SIC: 1711 Plumbing contractors

(G-2006)
C AND C DRYWALL CONTRACTORS N
730 Horsepond Rd (19901-7240)
PHONE..................................302 242-3305
EMP: 14 **EST:** 2019
SALES (est): 892.98K **Privately Held**
SIC: 1799 Special trade contractors, nec

(G-2007)
C EDGAR WOOD INC (PA)
Also Called: L&W Insurance Agency
1154 S Governors Ave (19904-6904)
P.O. Box 918 (19903-0918)
PHONE..................................302 674-3500
Davis H Wood, *Pr*
Andy Cousins, *
EMP: 34 **EST:** 1974
SALES (est): 4.06MM
SALES (corp-wide): 4.06MM **Privately Held**
Web: www.lwinsurance.com
SIC: 6411 Insurance agents, nec

(G-2008)
C-SCHELL SPINE SPECLST-C SCHEL
1169 Walker Rd (19904-6539)
PHONE..................................302 736-1223
Chris Schellinger, *Prin*
EMP: 7 **EST:** 2011
SALES (est): 247.53K **Privately Held**
Web: www.purewellchiro.com
SIC: 8041 Offices and clinics of chiropractors

(G-2009)
C4-NVIS USA LLC
8 The Grn Ste 6794 (19901-3618)
PHONE..................................213 465-5089
EMP: 2 **EST:** 2017
SALES (est): 33.14K **Privately Held**
SIC: 4813 3663 8748 7389 Long distance telephone communications; Radio broadcasting and communications equipment; Telecommunications consultant; Business Activities at Non-Commercial Site

(G-2010)
CADIA REHABILITATION
1225 Walker Rd (19904-6541)
PHONE..................................302 734-1199
EMP: 22 **EST:** 2018
SALES (est): 687.15K **Privately Held**
Web: www.cadiahealthcare.com
SIC: 8322 Rehabilitation services

(G-2011)
CAESAR RODNEY SCHOOL DISTRICT
Also Called: W B Simpson Elementary School
950 Center (19901-5998)
PHONE..................................302 697-3207
Michael Kijowski, *Prin*
EMP: 56
SALES (corp-wide): 97.62MM **Privately Held**
Web: www.crk12.org
SIC: 8211 8351 Public elementary school; Child day care services
PA: Caesar Rodney School District
    7 Front St
    Wyoming DE 19934
    302 698-4800

(G-2012)
CALIBER CLUB SHOOTING SPT INC
Also Called: Xcal Shooting Sports & Fitnes
8 The Grn (19901-3618)
PHONE..................................703 283-3533
Ghattas Hajjo, *Prin*
EMP: 5 **EST:** 2017
SALES (est): 85.55K **Privately Held**
SIC: 7389 Business services, nec

(G-2013)
CALIBER COLLISION
5825 W Denneys Rd (19904-1360)
PHONE..................................302 674-4525
EMP: 6 **EST:** 2020
SALES (est): 222.91K **Privately Held**
Web: www.caliber.com
SIC: 7536 7532 Automotive glass replacement shops; Top and body repair and paint shops

(G-2014)
CALL RINGS LLC
8 The Grn Ste 13074 (19901-3618)
PHONE..................................302 250-4030
Alan Argaman, *Managing Member*
EMP: 35 **EST:** 2021
SALES (est): 1.03MM **Privately Held**
Web: www.callrings.com
SIC: 7379 Online services technology consultants

(G-2015)
CAMDEN CIGARS
4004 S Dupont Hwy (19901-6077)
PHONE..................................302 698-1000
Barret Munoz, *Owner*
EMP: 5 **EST:** 2014
SALES (est): 175.72K **Privately Held**
SIC: 5194 Cigars

(G-2016)
CAMDEN PRIMARY CARE
4601 S Dupont Hwy Ste 2 (19901-6405)
PHONE..................................302 698-1100

EMP: 8 EST: 2019
SALES (est): 619.47K Privately Held
Web: www.camdenwalkin.com
SIC: 8011 General and family practice, physician/surgeon

(G-2017)
CAMDEN WALK-IN LLC
4601 S Dupont Hwy (19901-6405)
PHONE..................................302 698-1100
Ronnie N Diem, Owner
EMP: 11 EST: 2015
SALES (est): 531.34K Privately Held
Web: www.camdenwalkin.com
SIC: 8011 Clinic, operated by physicians

(G-2018)
CAMIO LLC ○
8 The Grn (19901-3618)
PHONE..................................585 851-8550
Mustapha Boussaid, Managing Member
EMP: 11 EST: 2023
SALES (est): 397.02K Privately Held
SIC: 7371 Custom computer programming services

(G-2019)
CANCER CARE CTRS AT BAY HLTH
Also Called: Costleigh, Brian J MD
793 S Queen St (19904-3568)
PHONE..................................302 674-4401
Sean Mace, Mgr
William Holden, Prin
Luther Brady Md, Pr
Dennis Klima, Sec
EMP: 13 EST: 1987
SQ FT: 7,000
SALES (est): 5.73MM
SALES (corp-wide): 5.73MM Privately Held
Web: www.bayhealth.org
SIC: 8062 General medical and surgical hospitals
PA: Bay Health Development Inc
640 S State St
Dover DE 19901
302 744-7994

(G-2020)
CANEKAST INC (PA)
1111 S Governors Ave (19904-6903)
PHONE..................................952 448-2801
Reg Zeller, CEO
Seth Cutler, Pr
EMP: 4 EST: 2021
SALES (est): 5.54MM
SALES (corp-wide): 5.54MM Privately Held
Web: www.canekast.com
SIC: 3559 Foundry, smelting, refining, and similar machinery

(G-2021)
CAPITAL SCHOOL DISTRICT
Also Called: Dover Mntessori Cntry Day Schl
126 Mourning Dove Ln (19901-9319)
PHONE..................................302 678-8394
Margaret Kling, Dir
EMP: 5
SALES (corp-wide): 98.83MM Privately Held
Web: www.capital.k12.de.us
SIC: 8211 8351 Public elementary school; Montessori child development center
PA: Capital School District
198 Commerce Way
Dover DE 19904
302 672-1500

(G-2022)
CAPITOL CLEANERS & LDRERS INC (PA)
Also Called: Capitol Uniform & Linen Svc
195 Commerce Way (19904-8224)
PHONE..................................302 674-1511
E Stuart Outten Junior, Pr
EMP: 68 EST: 1933
SQ FT: 28,000
SALES (est): 2.64MM
SALES (corp-wide): 2.64MM Privately Held
Web: www.capitollinen.com
SIC: 7212 7213 Laundry and drycleaner agents; Linen supply

(G-2023)
CAPITOL NRSING RHBLTTION CTR L
Also Called: Capital Hlthcare Svcs Nrsing R
1225 Walker Rd (19904-6541)
PHONE..................................302 734-1199
EMP: 47 EST: 1994
SALES (est): 7.07MM Privately Held
Web: www.cadiahealthcare.com
SIC: 8059 8093 8051 Nursing home, except skilled and intermediate care facility; Rehabilitation center, outpatient treatment; Skilled nursing care facilities

(G-2024)
CAPITOLS OF JCS LLC
73 Greentree Dr Ste 401 (19904-7646)
PHONE..................................302 918-5599
EMP: 6 EST: 2021
SALES (est): 203.91K Privately Held
SIC: 6531 Real estate leasing and rentals

(G-2025)
CAPRINI SUITES LLC
8 The Grn Ste 12426 (19901-3618)
PHONE..................................302 200-8904
EMP: 10 EST: 2021
SALES (est): 384.08K Privately Held
SIC: 6531 7389 Real estate leasing and rentals; Business Activities at Non-Commercial Site

(G-2026)
CAPSA SOLUTIONS LLC
160 Greentree Dr (19904-7620)
PHONE..................................800 437-6633
Andrew Sherrill, Pr
Drew Kniese, CFO
Eric Webb, COO
EMP: 9 EST: 2010
SALES (est): 109.92K Privately Held
Web: www.capsahealthcare.com
SIC: 7371 Software programming applications

(G-2027)
CARBON DIRECT INC (PA)
850 New Burton Rd Ste 201 (19904-5786)
PHONE..................................212 742-3719
Jonathan Goldberg, CEO
Jessica Isaacs, VP
EMP: 16 EST: 2020
SALES (est): 11MM
SALES (corp-wide): 11MM Privately Held
SIC: 8731 Commercial physical research

(G-2028)
CARDA HEALTH INC
8 The Grn (19901-3618)
PHONE..................................415 497-8417
Harry Difrancesco, CEO
Andrew West, Prin
EMP: 15 EST: 2020
SALES (est): 1.03MM Privately Held
Web: www.cardahealth.com

SIC: 7371 Computer software development and applications

(G-2029)
CAREER ASSOCIATES INC
Also Called: Bestemps Career Asso Resume Sv
385 W North St Ste A (19904-6748)
PHONE..................................302 674-4357
EMP: 5
SIC: 7363 Temporary help service
PA: Career Associates Inc
100 Clemwood St
Salisbury MD

(G-2030)
CAREERONESTOP DOVER ONE STOP
655 S Bay Rd (19901-4615)
PHONE..................................302 739-5473
EMP: 8 EST: 2016
SALES (est): 129.51K Privately Held
SIC: 8331 7361 Manpower training; Employment agencies

(G-2031)
CARPEDIEM HEALTH LLC
8 The Grn Ste 240 (19901-3618)
PHONE..................................347 467-4444
EMP: 2 EST: 2017
SALES (est): 79.36K Privately Held
SIC: 2339 2329 Women's and misses' athletic clothing and sportswear; Men's and boys' sportswear and athletic clothing

(G-2032)
CARSON CITY IC LLC
3500 S Dupont Hwy (19901-6041)
PHONE..................................520 261-8094
Jacob H Stephens, Managing Member
EMP: 5 EST: 2021
SALES (est): 90.16K Privately Held
SIC: 1711 Solar energy contractor

(G-2033)
CARZATY INC
874 Walker Rd Ste C (19904-2778)
P.O. Box 729 (01740-0729)
PHONE..................................650 396-0144
Hassan Jaffar, CEO
EMP: 14 EST: 2017
SALES (est): 540.89K Privately Held
SIC: 5961 7371 Electronic shopping; Computer software development and applications

(G-2034)
CASH ADVANCE
71 Greentree Dr (19904-7646)
PHONE..................................302 730-1988
Greg Johnson, Prin
EMP: 5 EST: 2010
SALES (est): 162.89K Privately Held
Web: www.opencashadvance.com
SIC: 6141 Personal credit institutions

(G-2035)
CASH PLUS 231
429 S New St (19904-6715)
P.O. Box 80 (19903-0080)
PHONE..................................302 526-2386
EMP: 7 EST: 2014
SALES (est): 94.43K Privately Held
Web: www.cashplusinc.com
SIC: 6099 Check cashing agencies

(G-2036)
CASHION MEDIA MANAGEMENT
300 Stonewater Way (19904-1554)
PHONE..................................302 674-8321

Caitlin N Cashion, Prin
EMP: 5 EST: 2017
SALES (est): 94.44K Privately Held
SIC: 8741 Management services

(G-2037)
CATHERINE KOTALIS
540 S Governors Ave (19904-3530)
PHONE..................................302 526-1470
Catherine Kotalis, Prin
EMP: 7 EST: 2017
SALES (est): 103.76K Privately Held
SIC: 8049 Offices of health practitioner

(G-2038)
CATHOLIC CHARITIES INC
Also Called: Energy Assistance Program
2099 S Dupont Hwy (19901-5568)
PHONE..................................302 674-1600
Katrina A Furlong, Div/Sub He
EMP: 5
SALES (corp-wide): 8.08MM Privately Held
Web: www.catholiccharitiesusa.org
SIC: 8322 Social service center
PA: Catholic Charities Inc
2601 W 4th St
Wilmington DE 19805
302 655-9624

(G-2039)
CATHOLIC CHARITIES INC
Also Called: Delaware Day Treatment
1155 Walker Rd (19904-6539)
PHONE..................................302 674-1600
Vallerie Roach, Pt
EMP: 6
SALES (corp-wide): 8.08MM Privately Held
Web: www.catholiccharitiesusa.org
SIC: 8322 8351 Social service center; Group day care center
PA: Catholic Charities Inc
2601 W 4th St
Wilmington DE 19805
302 655-9624

(G-2040)
CATOVERA CORP
8 The Grn Ste 300 (19901-3618)
PHONE..................................804 814-0301
EMP: 8
SALES (est): 306.16K Privately Held
SIC: 7371 Computer software development and applications

(G-2041)
CE BUYS LLC
9 E Loockerman St Ste 205 (19901-7347)
PHONE..................................650 245-6238
Nicholas Pang, Prin
EMP: 5 EST: 2010
SALES (est): 97.29K Privately Held
SIC: 8742 Marketing consulting services

(G-2042)
CEDCOMM LLC
8 The Grn (19901-3618)
PHONE..................................646 653-0233
EMP: 5 EST: 2018
SALES (est): 500K Privately Held
SIC: 8748 Telecommunications consultant

(G-2043)
CELAVIE BIOSCIENCES LLC
615 S Dupont Hwy (19901-4517)
PHONE..................................516 593-5633
EMP: 7 EST: 2010
SALES (est): 425.6K Privately Held
Web: www.celavie.com

GEOGRAPHIC SECTION
Dover - Kent County (G-2069)

SIC: **8731** Biotechnical research, commercial

(G-2044)
CELESSTIA HEALTH LLC
8 The Grn Unit 6121 (19901-3618)
PHONE................................302 241-0601
Peter Mankowski, *CEO*
EMP: 5 **EST:** 2017
SALES (est): 60.56K **Privately Held**
Web: www.celesstia.com
SIC: **8099** Health and allied services, nec

(G-2045)
CELL SURGEON
4004 S Dupont Hwy (19901-6077)
PHONE................................302 423-4441
EMP: 6 **EST:** 2019
SALES (est): 197.06K **Privately Held**
Web: www.cell-surgeon.com
SIC: **7699** Repair services, nec

(G-2046)
CENTER AT EDEN HILL
300 Banning St (19904-3457)
PHONE................................302 677-7100
EMP: 14 **EST:** 2019
SALES (est): 7.19MM **Privately Held**
Web: www.centeratedenhill.com
SIC: **8051** Skilled nursing care facilities

(G-2047)
CENTRAL DEL CHMBER OF COMMERCE
Also Called: CHAMBER OF COMMERCE OF CENTRAL
435 N Dupont Hwy (19901-3907)
PHONE................................302 734-7513
Judy Diogo, *Pr*
Jennette Wessel, *Ex VP*
EMP: 5 **EST:** 1919
SALES (est): 591.79K **Privately Held**
Web: www.cdcc.net
SIC: **8611** Chamber of Commerce

(G-2048)
CENTRAL DEL FMLY FOOT CARE
1326 S Governors Ave Ste B (19904-4800)
PHONE................................302 678-3338
Robert J Gemignani, *Prin*
EMP: 8 **EST:** 2009
SALES (est): 167.47K **Privately Held**
SIC: **8043** Offices and clinics of podiatrists

(G-2049)
CENTRAL DEL HBTAT FOR HMNITY I
Also Called: HABITAT FOR HUMANITY
2311 S Dupont Hwy (19901-5514)
PHONE................................302 526-2366
Tammy Ordway, *Pr*
EMP: 15 **EST:** 2011
SALES (est): 2.24MM **Privately Held**
Web: www.centraldelawarehabitat.org
SIC: **8399** Community development groups

(G-2050)
CENTRAL DELAWARE FMLY MEDICINE
95 Wolf Creek Blvd Ste 2 (19901-4965)
PHONE................................302 735-1616
Doctor Theresa Little, *Owner*
Theresa Little, *Owner*
EMP: 15 **EST:** 1998
SALES (est): 805.4K **Privately Held**
SIC: **8011** General and family practice, physician/surgeon

(G-2051)
CENTRAL DELAWARE SPEECH
541 S Red Haven Ln (19901-6483)
PHONE................................302 538-5696
Kathleen Anderson, *Dir*
EMP: 12 **EST:** 2014
SALES (est): 223.43K **Privately Held**
Web: www.centraldelawareslp.com
SIC: **8049** Speech pathologist

(G-2052)
CENTRIEN CONSULTING SVCS LLC ✪
8 The Grn Ste 10333 (19901-3618)
PHONE................................844 741-0000
Padmini Bhowmik, *Pr*
Bhavin Patel, *
EMP: 50 **EST:** 2022
SALES (est): 2.35MM
SALES (corp-wide): 2.35MM **Privately Held**
SIC: **7379** Computer related consulting services
PA: Centrien Consulting Group Llc
  1309 Coffeen Ave Ste 4580
  Sheridan WY 82801
  844 741-0000

(G-2053)
CENTURY ENGINEERING INC
550 S Bay Rd (19901-4603)
PHONE................................302 734-9188
Scott L Rathfon, *Brnch Mgr*
EMP: 21
SALES (corp-wide): 458.93MM **Privately Held**
Web: www.centuryeng.com
SIC: **8711** Consulting engineer
HQ: Century Engineering, Inc.
  10710 Gilroy Rd
  Hunt Valley MD 21031
  443 589-2400

(G-2054)
CHAINGPT LLC ✪
8 The Grn Ste A (19901-3618)
PHONE................................302 382-7528
Ilan Rakhmanov, *Managing Member*
EMP: 6 **EST:** 2023
SALES (est): 311.93K **Privately Held**
SIC: **5045** Computer software

(G-2055)
CHANDLERS CON PLCMENT GROUP LL
4604 N Dupont Hwy (19901-1564)
PHONE................................302 377-0017
EMP: 6 **EST:** 2018
SALES (est): 115.27K **Privately Held**
SIC: **1771** Concrete work

(G-2056)
CHARA TEA LLC (PA) ✪
8 The Grn (19901-3618)
PHONE................................856 250-7180
John Herman, *Managing Member*
EMP: 9 **EST:** 2022
SALES (est): 237K
SALES (corp-wide): 237K **Privately Held**
Web: www.charatea.com
SIC: **5149** **7389** Coffee and tea; Business services, nec

(G-2057)
CHARLES DEMPSEY FARMS
Also Called: Dempsey Farms
1708 Fast Landing Rd (19901-2718)
PHONE................................302 734-4937
Alice May Dempsey, *Pt*
Greg Dempsey, *Pt*
Bruce Dempsey, *Pt*
EMP: 9 **EST:** 1915
SALES (est): 563.37K **Privately Held**
SIC: **0119** **0241** Feeder grains; Milk production

(G-2058)
CHESAPEAKE SERVICE COMPANY (HQ)
500 Energy Ln Ste 400 (19901-4989)
PHONE................................302 734-6799
Ralph J Adkins, *Ch*
EMP: 9 **EST:** 1993
SALES (est): 2.46MM
SALES (corp-wide): 680.7MM **Publicly Held**
Web: www.chpk.com
SIC: **4924** Natural gas distribution
PA: Chesapeake Utilities Corporation
  500 Energy Ln
  Dover DE 19901
  302 734-6799

(G-2059)
CHESAPEAKE UTILITIES CORP (PA)
Also Called: Chesapeake Utilities
500 Energy Ln (19901-4988)
P.O. Box 615 (19903-0615)
PHONE................................302 734-6799
Jeffry M Householder, *Pr*
John R Schimkaitis, *
Beth W Cooper, *Ex VP*
James F Moriarty, *Corporate Secretary*
Jeffrey S Sylvester, *Sr VP*
EMP: 101 **EST:** 1859
SALES (est): 680.7MM
SALES (corp-wide): 680.7MM **Publicly Held**
Web: www.chpk.com
SIC: **4923** **4911** Gas transmission and distribution; Distribution, electric power

(G-2060)
CHILDREN FIRST LRNG CTR INC
760 Townsend Blvd (19901-2515)
PHONE................................302 674-5227
Quiana Nieves, *Pr*
EMP: 9 **EST:** 2003
SALES (est): 346.11K **Privately Held**
Web: www.childrenfirstlearningcenter.com
SIC: **8351** Group day care center

(G-2061)
CHILDREN FMILIES FIRST DEL INC
Also Called: Children & Families First
91 Wolf Creek Blvd (19901-4914)
PHONE................................302 674-8384
Alais Erickson, *Mgr*
EMP: 5
SALES (corp-wide): 17.22MM **Privately Held**
Web: www.cffde.org
SIC: **8322** **8399** Social service center; Council for social agency
PA: Children & Families First Delaware Inc.
  809 N Washington St
  Wilmington DE 19801
  302 658-5177

(G-2062)
CHILDREN S SECRET GARDEN
717 Hatchery Rd (19901-1509)
PHONE................................302 730-1717
Pamela Harper, *Owner*
EMP: 7 **EST:** 2000
SALES (est): 58.81K **Privately Held**
SIC: **8351** Group day care center

(G-2063)
CHILDRENS ADVOCACY CTR OF DEL (PA)
611 S Dupont Hwy Ste 201 (19901-4507)
PHONE................................302 741-2123
Randall Williams, *CEO*
EMP: 7 **EST:** 2005
SALES (est): 1.75MM
SALES (corp-wide): 1.75MM **Privately Held**
Web: www.cacofde.org
SIC: **8322** Child related social services

(G-2064)
CHILDRENS HOSP NNTAL CNSRTIUM
8 The Grn Ste 10426 (19901-3618)
PHONE................................215 873-9492
EMP: 8 **EST:** 2018
SALES (est): 2.86MM **Privately Held**
Web: www.thechnc.org
SIC: **8731** Commercial physical research

(G-2065)
CHIMES INC
Also Called: Chimes Metro
165 Commerce Way (19904-8224)
PHONE................................302 730-0747
Amy Salzman, *Brnch Mgr*
EMP: 27
Web: www.chimes.org
SIC: **8322** Social service center
HQ: The Chimes Inc
  4815 Seton Dr
  Baltimore MD 21215
  410 358-6400

(G-2066)
CHIMES INC
3499 Cypress St (19901-7928)
PHONE................................302 678-3270
Calvin Mackey, *Prin*
EMP: 26
Web: www.chimes.org
SIC: **8361** Mentally handicapped home
HQ: The Chimes Inc
  4815 Seton Dr
  Baltimore MD 21215
  410 358-6400

(G-2067)
CHOICES 1ST LLC
1326 S Governors Ave (19904-4800)
PHONE................................302 674-4204
William Gale, *Prin*
EMP: 8 **EST:** 2013
SALES (est): 129K **Privately Held**
SIC: **8322** General counseling services

(G-2068)
CHOPRA HLCO LLC ✪
838 Walker Rd Ste 21-2 (19904-2751)
PHONE................................631 413-4249
Simon Belsham, *Pr*
EMP: 11 **EST:** 2023
SALES (est): 716.38K **Publicly Held**
SIC: **8093** Detoxification center, outpatient
PA: The Healing Company Inc
  135 W 50th St Fl 2
  New York NY 10020

(G-2069)
CHORES R US INC
Also Called: Chorerelief
8 The Grn Ste A (19901-3618)
PHONE................................844 442-4673
Tarik Khribech, *Pr*
EMP: 12 **EST:** 2017
SALES (est): 554.16K **Privately Held**
SIC: **7371** **7389** Computer software development and applications; Business Activities at Non-Commercial Site

Dover - Kent County (G-2070) — GEOGRAPHIC SECTION

(G-2070)
CHOUDHARY CHITRA MD
1058 S Governors Ave (19904-6920)
PHONE..................302 401-1500
Chitra Choudhary Md, *Owner*
EMP: 8 **EST:** 2017
SALES (est): 54.13K **Privately Held**
SIC: 8011 Offices and clinics of medical doctors

(G-2071)
CHRIS COCKER
Also Called: Coker Concrete
300 Artis Dr (19904-5643)
PHONE..................302 744-9184
EMP: 12
SALES (est): 610.43K **Privately Held**
SIC: 1771 Concrete work

(G-2072)
CHURCH OF GOD IN CHRIST
Also Called: Drop A Tot Pre-School Day Care
120a S Governors Ave (19904-3223)
P.O. Box 174 (19903-0174)
PHONE..................302 678-1949
Kemuel Butler, *Dir*
EMP: 15 **EST:** 1982
SALES (est): 108.48K **Privately Held**
Web: www.msicogic.org
SIC: 8351 8661 Child day care services; Churches, temples, and shrines

(G-2073)
CINDERELLAS CLEANING LLC
512 N Dupont Hwy (19901-3961)
PHONE..................302 632-6036
Angela Dimondi, *Prin*
EMP: 5 **EST:** 2014
SALES (est): 69.07K **Privately Held**
Web: www.cinderellascleaningde.com
SIC: 7699 Cleaning services

(G-2074)
CINENSO INC
8 The Grn Ste R (19901-3618)
PHONE..................424 245-5799
EMP: 5
SALES (est): 46.16K **Privately Held**
SIC: 7371 Computer software development and applications

(G-2075)
CINNAMON TECHNOLOGIES INC
8 The Grn Ste B (19901-3618)
PHONE..................530 413-5533
EMP: 5 **EST:** 2020
SALES (est): 211.33K **Privately Held**
SIC: 7371 Computer software development and applications

(G-2076)
CIRCLE GROUP INC
735 Holly Dr (19904-4331)
PHONE..................302 241-0018
EMP: 9 **EST:** 2017
SALES (est): 52.6K **Privately Held**
SIC: 1742 Drywall

(G-2077)
CIRKLA INC (PA) ◆
8 The Grn Ste R (19901-3618)
PHONE..................415 851-4635
Bhav Goel, *CEO*
EMP: 25 **EST:** 2022
SALES (est): 755.89K
SALES (corp-wide): 755.89K **Privately Held**
SIC: 4783 Packing and crating

(G-2078)
CITIZENS BANK NATIONAL ASSN
Also Called: Citizens Bank
779 N Dupont Hwy (19901-3938)
PHONE..................302 734-0200
Vicky Antoniou, *Mgr*
EMP: 37
SALES (corp-wide): 9.07B **Publicly Held**
Web: www.govplus.com
SIC: 6022 State commercial banks
HQ: Citizens Bank, National Association
1 Citizens Plz
Providence RI 02903

(G-2079)
CITY CAB OF DELAWARE INC (PA)
1203 State College Rd (19904)
PHONE..................302 734-5968
Tom Antionio, *Pr*
Vicki Antiono, *VP*
EMP: 9 **EST:** 1943
SALES (est): 481.92K **Privately Held**
Web: www.citycabde.com
SIC: 4121 Taxicabs

(G-2080)
CITY ELECTRIC SUPPLY DOVER
401 Cassidy Dr Ste A (19901-4975)
PHONE..................302 672-3100
EMP: 5 **EST:** 2019
SALES (est): 302.97K **Privately Held**
SIC: 5099 Durable goods, nec

(G-2081)
CITY OF DOVER
Also Called: Electric Department
860 Buttner Pl (19904-2405)
P.O. Box 475 (19903-0475)
PHONE..................302 736-7070
EMP: 30
SALES (corp-wide): 32.9MM **Privately Held**
Web: www.cityofdover.com
SIC: 4911 9611 Distribution, electric power; Energy development and conservation agency, government
PA: Dover, City Of (Inc)
15 Loockerman Plz
Dover DE 19901
302 736-7004

(G-2082)
CITY OF DOVER
Also Called: Finance Department
5 E Reed St (19901-7334)
PHONE..................302 736-7018
Donna Mitchell, *Contrlr*
EMP: 8
SALES (corp-wide): 32.9MM **Privately Held**
Web: www.cityofdover.com
SIC: 8721 Payroll accounting service
PA: Dover, City Of (Inc)
15 Loockerman Plz
Dover DE 19901
302 736-7004

(G-2083)
CITY OF DOVER
Also Called: Customer Services Department
5 E Reed St Ste 100 (19901-7334)
PHONE..................302 736-7035
Kirby Hudson, *Assistant City Manager*
EMP: 12
SALES (corp-wide): 32.9MM **Privately Held**
Web: www.cityofdover.com
SIC: 7389 9199 Financial services; General government administration, Local government
PA: Dover, City Of (Inc)
15 Loockerman Plz
Dover DE 19901
302 736-7004

(G-2084)
CITY OF DOVER
Also Called: Information Technology Dept
15 Loockerman Plz (19901-7327)
PHONE..................302 736-5071
Andrew Siegel, *Dir*
EMP: 19
SALES (corp-wide): 32.9MM **Privately Held**
Web: www.cityofdover.com
SIC: 7373 9199 Office computer automation systems integration; General government administration
PA: Dover, City Of (Inc)
15 Loockerman Plz
Dover DE 19901
302 736-7004

(G-2085)
CITY WIDE MAINTENANCE CO INC
Also Called: City Wide Facility Solutions
755 Walker Rd Ste A (19904-2801)
PHONE..................302 526-2833
EMP: 130
SALES (corp-wide): 48.81MM **Privately Held**
Web: www.gocitywide.com
SIC: 7349 Janitorial service, contract basis
HQ: City Wide Maintenance Co., Inc.
15230 W 105th Ter
Lenexa KS 66219
913 888-5700

(G-2086)
CLAIMMYBADGE LLC ◆
Also Called: Technology
8 The Grn Ste B (19901-3618)
PHONE..................347 236-8109
Kent Moy, *Managing Member*
EMP: 2 **EST:** 2023
SALES (est): 87.4K **Privately Held**
SIC: 7372 Prepackaged software

(G-2087)
CLEAN CARS INC
805 Forest St (19904-3417)
PHONE..................302 734-8234
Victor Diangrant, *Prin*
EMP: 6 **EST:** 2008
SALES (est): 90.6K **Privately Held**
SIC: 7699 Cleaning services

(G-2088)
CLEAN DELAWARE
3799 N Dupont Hwy (19901-1574)
PHONE..................302 462-1451
Michael Steiner, *Prin*
EMP: 7 **EST:** 2016
SALES (est): 168.99K **Privately Held**
Web: www.cleandelaware.com
SIC: 7699 Cleaning services

(G-2089)
CLEAN GENIE
201 Charring Cross Dr (19904-9783)
PHONE..................302 241-4708
Jenay Friend, *Prin*
EMP: 5 **EST:** 2015
SALES (est): 34.7K **Privately Held**
SIC: 7699 Cleaning services

(G-2090)
CLEAN ME OUT CLEANING SVCS LLC
1008 Hayes Cir (19904-3474)
PHONE..................302 480-4788
EMP: 5
SALES (est): 108.41K **Privately Held**
SIC: 7699 Cleaning services

(G-2091)
CLEANER BRANDS WORLDWIDE LLC
8 The Grn Ste R (19901-3618)
PHONE..................646 867-8328
EMP: 5 **EST:** 2021
SALES (est): 210.11K **Privately Held**
SIC: 2842 Disinfectants, household or industrial plant

(G-2092)
CLICK2BUY LLC (PA) ◆
8 The Grn Ste B (19901-3618)
PHONE..................347 698-7660
M A Zabala Martinez, *Managing Member*
Miguel A Zabala Martinez, *Managing Member*
EMP: 6 **EST:** 2023
SALES (est): 76.37K
SALES (corp-wide): 76.37K **Privately Held**
SIC: 5961 7389 General merchandise, mail order; Business services, nec

(G-2093)
CLIFTON LEASING CO INC (PA)
Also Called: Delmarva Kenworth Trucks
613 Clara St (19904-3011)
P.O. Box 603 (19903-0603)
PHONE..................302 674-2300
Richard Weyandt, *Pr*
Matt Weyandt, *VP*
Lynne Bergold, *Treas*
Pam Weyandt, *Sec*
EMP: 21 **EST:** 1964
SQ FT: 5,000
SALES (est): 8.5MM
SALES (corp-wide): 8.5MM **Privately Held**
Web: www.paccar.com
SIC: 5511 7513 7699 Trucks, tractors, and trailers: new and used; Truck leasing, without drivers; Marine engine repair

(G-2094)
CLINGS BLINGS & THINGS
913 Schoolhouse Ln (19904-2417)
PHONE..................302 734-9103
Grant Jones, *Prin*
EMP: 6 **EST:** 2014
SALES (est): 93.1K **Privately Held**
Web: www.clingsblingsandthings.com
SIC: 7379 Computer related services, nec

(G-2095)
CLOTHES AND CRYSTALS LLC
245 Charring Cross Dr (19904-9702)
PHONE..................302 316-3405
EMP: 5 **EST:** 2020
SALES (est): 104.73K **Privately Held**
SIC: 7389 Business Activities at Non-Commercial Site

(G-2096)
CLOUDSTAFF USA LLC
1221 College Park Dr Ste 116 (19904-8726)
PHONE..................800 730-8615
EMP: 9 **EST:** 2021
SALES (est): 374.08K **Privately Held**
SIC: 7389 Business services, nec
HQ: Cloudstaff Hk Limited
8/F Shun On Comm Bldg
Central District HK

(G-2097)
CLOUDXPERTS LLC
8 The Grn Ste 5210 (19901-3618)

GEOGRAPHIC SECTION
Dover - Kent County (G-2126)

PHONE..............................302 257-5686
Salman Khan, *CEO*
Muzzamil Mubeen, *Prin*
EMP: 5 **EST:** 2015
SALES (est): 240.35K **Privately Held**
SIC: 7373 Computer systems analysis and design

(G-2098)
CNC DRYWALL NORTH
730 Horsepond Rd (19901-7240)
PHONE..............................302 307-6400
EMP: 7 **EST:** 2017
SALES (est): 237.43K **Privately Held**
SIC: 1742 Drywall

(G-2099)
CNTRL DE GSTROENTEROLGYASSOC I
644 S Queen St Ste 106 (19904-3543)
PHONE..............................302 678-9002
Wendy Silicato, *Off Mgr*
EMP: 10 **EST:** 2013
SALES (est): 222.29K **Privately Held**
SIC: 8011 Pediatrician

(G-2100)
CNU FIT LLC
1404 Forrest Ave Ste 9 (19904-3478)
PHONE..............................302 744-9037
Evans Armantrading, *Managing Member*
EMP: 8 **EST:** 2013
SQ FT: 1,500
SALES (est): 483.77K **Privately Held**
Web: www.cnufit.com
SIC: 7991 7299 Exercise salon; Massage parlor

(G-2101)
CNWYNN PUBLICATIONS
1102 Dwight Ct (19904-2690)
P.O. Box 328 (19936-0328)
PHONE..............................484 753-1568
Chistian Wynn, *Prin*
EMP: 5 **EST:** 2017
SALES (est): 62.36K **Privately Held**
SIC: 2741 Miscellaneous publishing

(G-2102)
CO-OP KITCHEN LLC ✿
8 The Grn Ste A (19901-3618)
PHONE..............................407 342-2295
Ryan Feldman, *Managing Member*
EMP: 3 **EST:** 2023
SALES (est): 78.16K **Privately Held**
SIC: 3944 Electronic games and toys

(G-2103)
COACH TRANSPORT LLC
29 S Turnberry Dr (19904-2348)
PHONE..............................302 983-7339
Milton Collins, *Prin*
EMP: 5 **EST:** 2017
SALES (est): 355.9K **Privately Held**
SIC: 4789 Transportation services, nec

(G-2104)
COAST 2 COAST LOGISTICS LLC
611 S Dupont Hwy Ste 102 (19901-4507)
PHONE..............................857 212-9832
Ralph Simon, *Managing Member*
EMP: 5
SALES (est): 220.71K **Privately Held**
SIC: 4213 Trucking, except local

(G-2105)
COASTAL CAR WASH LLC
1117 S Dupont Hwy (19901-4423)
PHONE..............................302 883-3554
Scott Becker, *
EMP: 30 **EST:** 2019
SALES (est): 1.03MM **Privately Held**
Web: www.coastal-carwash.com
SIC: 7542 Washing and polishing, automotive

(G-2106)
COASTAL LANDSCAPING LLC
30 The Grn (19901-3612)
PHONE..............................302 678-0983
Peter Malmberg, *Prin*
EMP: 6 **EST:** 2019
SALES (est): 376.33K **Privately Held**
SIC: 0781 Landscape services

(G-2107)
COASTLINE REALTY LLC
830 Walker Rd Ste 11-1 (19904-2748)
PHONE..............................302 735-7526
John Rowley, *Asst Sec*
EMP: 5 **EST:** 2018
SALES (est): 234.42K **Privately Held**
SIC: 7389 Financial services

(G-2108)
CODE509COM INC
8 The Grn Ste A (19901-3618)
PHONE..............................941 263-3509
EMP: 4 **EST:** 2019
SALES (est): 74.42K **Privately Held**
SIC: 2844 Perfumes, cosmetics and other toilet preparations

(G-2109)
CODONRX LLC
8 The Grn (19901-3618)
PHONE..............................773 612-5828
Kevin White, *Managing Member*
EMP: 6
SALES (est): 237.56K **Privately Held**
SIC: 7389 2023 Business Activities at Non-Commercial Site; Dietary supplements, dairy and non-dairy based

(G-2110)
COGENCY GLOBAL INC
850 New Burton Rd Ste 201 (19904-5786)
PHONE..............................800 483-1140
Bruce Jacobi, *CEO*
EMP: 25
SALES (corp-wide): 45.9MM **Privately Held**
Web: www.cogencyglobal.com
SIC: 8111 Legal services
PA: Cogency Global Inc.
    122 E 42nd St Fl 18
    New York NY 10168
    212 947-7200

(G-2111)
COGNICOR TECHNOLOGIES INC
8 The Grn (19901-3618)
PHONE..............................650 444-2076
Sindhu Joseph, *CEO*
EMP: 8 **EST:** 2019
SALES (est): 406.71K **Privately Held**
Web: www.cognicor.com
SIC: 7371 Computer software development

(G-2112)
COLMORGEN
640 S State St (19901-3530)
PHONE..............................302 744-6220
EMP: 11 **EST:** 2010
SALES (est): 192.38K **Privately Held**
Web: www.bayhealth.org
SIC: 8011 Physical medicine, physician/surgeon

(G-2113)
COLONIAL INV MANAGMENT CO
Also Called: Dover Garden Court Apartments
9 E Loockerman St Ste C (19901-8306)
PHONE..............................302 736-0674
Adelle Welzel, *Mgr*
EMP: 6 **EST:** 1951
SALES (est): 608.18K **Privately Held**
Web: www.colonialinvestment.com
SIC: 6513 Apartment building operators

(G-2114)
COMCAST CBLE CMMUNICATIONS LLC
Also Called: Comcast
5729 W Denneys Rd (19904-1365)
PHONE..............................410 497-4600
Brian Lynch, *Brnch Mgr*
EMP: 10
SALES (corp-wide): 121.57B **Publicly Held**
Web: www.cmcsa.com
SIC: 4841 Cable television services
HQ: Comcast Cable Communications, Llc
    1701 John F Kennedy Blvd
    Philadelphia PA 19103

(G-2115)
COMCAST CORPORATION
Also Called: Xfinity Store By Comcast
1580 N Dupont Hwy (19901-2215)
PHONE..............................800 266-2278
EMP: 5
SALES (corp-wide): 121.57B **Publicly Held**
Web: corporate.comcast.com
SIC: 4841 Cable television services
PA: Comcast Corporation
    1 Comcast Ctr
    Philadelphia PA 19103
    215 286-1700

(G-2116)
COMCAST OF DELMARVA LLC
Also Called: Comcast
5729 W Denneys Rd (19904-1365)
PHONE..............................215 286-3345
EMP: 25 **EST:** 2011
SALES (est): 1.83MM
SALES (corp-wide): 121.57B **Publicly Held**
SIC: 4841 Cable television services
PA: Comcast Corporation
    1 Comcast Ctr
    Philadelphia PA 19103
    215 286-1700

(G-2117)
COMMITTEE TO ELECT BRAD EABY
233 Pebble Valley Dr (19904-9467)
PHONE..............................302 670-4806
Bradley Eaby, *Prin*
EMP: 5 **EST:** 2011
SALES (est): 181.22K **Privately Held**
SIC: 5072 Brads

(G-2118)
COMMONSPIRIT HEALTH LLC
838 Walker Rd Ste 21-2 (19904-2751)
PHONE..............................302 336-8212
EMP: 17 **EST:** 2018
SALES (est): 2.59MM **Privately Held**
Web: www.commonspirit.org
SIC: 8062 General medical and surgical hospitals

(G-2119)
COMMUNITY LEGAL AID SOCIETY
Also Called: Disabilities Law Program
840 Walker Rd (19904-2727)
PHONE..............................302 674-8503
Christopher White, *Dir*
EMP: 8
SALES (corp-wide): 5.71MM **Privately Held**
Web: www.declasi.org
SIC: 8111 Legal aid service
PA: Community Legal Aid Society Inc
    100 W 10th St Ste 801
    Wilmington DE 19801
    302 757-7001

(G-2120)
COMMUNITYLIVING INC
145 Kings Hwy (19901-8307)
PHONE..............................302 735-4534
Simon Akama, *Mgr*
EMP: 8 **EST:** 2016
SALES (est): 62.82K **Privately Held**
SIC: 8322 Public welfare center

(G-2121)
COMPASSNATE SOC OF CHRST ST ST
126 Cresthaven Ln (19901-6454)
PHONE..............................914 482-2562
Peter Joseph Avitabile, *Pr*
EMP: 5 **EST:** 2020
SALES (est): 45.1K **Privately Held**
SIC: 8699 Charitable organization

(G-2122)
COMPLETE CARE AT SILVER LK LLC
1080 Silver Lake Blvd (19904-2410)
PHONE..............................302 734-5990
EMP: 23 **EST:** 2021
SALES (est): 6.17MM **Privately Held**
Web: www.ccsilverlake.com
SIC: 8051 Convalescent home with continuous nursing care

(G-2123)
COMPLETE RSRVTION SLUTIONS LLC
Also Called: Royal Island Cruise Line
8 The Grn Ste 5863 (19901-3618)
PHONE..............................800 672-8522
Sean Engler, *Managing Member*
EMP: 14 **EST:** 2017
SALES (est): 437.13K **Privately Held**
SIC: 7519 Travel, camping or recreational trailer rental

(G-2124)
COMPLIANCE ENVIRONMENTAL INC
150 S Bradford St (19904-7318)
PHONE..............................302 674-4427
EMP: 5 **EST:** 1993
SALES (est): 696.77K **Privately Held**
Web: www.compliancecanhelp.com
SIC: 8748 Environmental consultant

(G-2125)
COMPREHENSIVE CHIROPRACTIC
850 New Burton Rd (19904-5786)
PHONE..............................302 346-4744
Michael Gondolfo, *Owner*
EMP: 5 **EST:** 2018
SALES (est): 166.12K **Privately Held**
Web: www.comp-chiro.com
SIC: 8041 Offices and clinics of chiropractors

(G-2126)
COMPRISE IT SOLUTIONS LLC
8th The Green Ste 14916 (19901-3618)
PHONE..............................302 337-4036
Manish Bhalla, *Managing Member*
EMP: 22
SALES (est): 652.3K **Privately Held**

Dover - Kent County (G-2127) GEOGRAPHIC SECTION

SIC: 7361 7371 Labor contractors (employment agency); Custom computer programming services

(G-2127)
COMPUTER SERVICES OF DELAWARE
Also Called: Payroll Services of Delaware
1991 S State St Ste B (19901-5811)
PHONE.................................302 697-8644
EMP: 6 EST: 1984
SALES (est): 344.22K **Privately Held**
Web: www.delaware.gov
SIC: 7374 Data processing service

(G-2128)
CONCRETE SERVICES INC
794 Rose Valley School Rd (19904-5508)
PHONE.................................302 883-2883
Brian Lilly, *Pr*
Mark Lily, *VP*
Barbara Lily, *Sec*
EMP: 7 EST: 1986
SALES (est): 493.28K **Privately Held**
SIC: 1771 Concrete work

(G-2129)
CONEY STEAM AND CLEAN
Also Called: Hbg Finest Carpet Cleaning
621 William St (19904-2969)
PHONE.................................302 670-0183
Latisha T Coney, *Prin*
EMP: 5 EST: 2011
SALES (est): 67.35K **Privately Held**
Web: www.coneysteamteam.com
SIC: 7699 Cleaning services

(G-2130)
CONFABULOUS INC
3500 S Dupont Hwy (19901-6041)
PHONE.................................917 727-5919
Peter Cashmore, *CEO*
Colin Cashmore, *CFO*
EMP: 2 EST: 2020
SALES (est): 105.52K **Privately Held**
SIC: 7372 Application computer software

(G-2131)
CONFERATU INC
850 New Burton Rd Ste 201 (19904-5786)
PHONE.................................415 599-6407
Sonali Maitra, *CEO*
EMP: 2 EST: 2021
SALES (est): 56.54K **Privately Held**
SIC: 7372 Application computer software

(G-2132)
CONNECTED INC ◊
Also Called: Connected
8 The Grn Ste B (19901-3618)
PHONE.................................858 833-8768
Daria Kroshkina, *Prin*
EMP: 5 EST: 2023
SALES (est): 349.63K **Privately Held**
SIC: 7372 Prepackaged software

(G-2133)
CONSOL USA INC
8 The Grn Ste 8212 (19901-3618)
PHONE.................................302 401-6537
Robert Tibbs, *Prin*
Malcolm Goodwin, *Pr*
EMP: 7
SALES (est): 905.12K **Privately Held**
Web: www.consol-usa.com
SIC: 7379 Computer related services, nec

(G-2134)
COORDLE INC ◊
8 The Grn Ste B (19901-3618)
PHONE.................................419 618-0949
Jennifer Fry, *Prin*
EMP: 6 EST: 2022
SALES (est): 307.72K **Privately Held**
SIC: 5112 Stationery and office supplies

(G-2135)
COPIA POWER OPCO LLC (PA) ◊
850 New Burton Rd (19904-5785)
PHONE.................................612 961-5783
EMP: 11 EST: 2022
SALES (est): 11.5MM
SALES (corp-wide): 11.5MM **Privately Held**
SIC: 4911 Generation, electric power

(G-2136)
COR3 CAPITAL LLC
1675 S State St Ste B (19901-5140)
PHONE.................................941 402-8101
Ian Russ, *Managing Member*
EMP: 5 EST: 2021
SALES (est): 247.95K **Privately Held**
Web: www.cor3.com
SIC: 6531 Real estate brokers and agents

(G-2137)
CORE PHYSICAL THERAPY
71 Mcbry Dr (19901-4407)
PHONE.................................302 423-0236
Glenn Brown, *Prin*
EMP: 10 EST: 2014
SALES (est): 238.06K **Privately Held**
Web: www.coredelaware.com
SIC: 8049 Physical therapist

(G-2138)
COREMOND LLC
8 The Grn (19901-3618)
PHONE.................................267 797-7090
EMP: 5
SALES (est): 68.89K **Privately Held**
SIC: 7371 7389 Software programming applications; Business Activities at Non-Commercial Site

(G-2139)
CORNELL PROPERTY MGT CORP
14 Rockford Xing (19901-4074)
PHONE.................................302 674-1460
EMP: 6 EST: 2021
SALES (est): 259.66K **Privately Held**
SIC: 6513 Apartment building operators

(G-2140)
CORP1 INC
614 N Dupont Hwy Ste 210 (19901-3900)
PHONE.................................302 736-3466
Kelly Manchester, *Pr*
Kelly A Mckown, *Pr*
Glenda K Hallett, *VP*
EMP: 17 EST: 1989
SALES (est): 1.12MM **Privately Held**
Web: www.corp1.com
SIC: 8111 Legal services

(G-2141)
CORPORATE KIDS LRNG CTR INC
605 S Bay Rd (19901-4601)
PHONE.................................302 678-0688
EMP: 17 EST: 1996
SQ FT: 1,800
SALES (est): 687.46K **Privately Held**
SIC: 8351 Preschool center

(G-2142)
COSMOPROF
261 N Dupont Hwy (19901-7540)
PHONE.................................302 674-5360
EMP: 5 EST: 2014
SALES (est): 92.36K **Privately Held**
Web: stores.cosmoprofbeauty.com
SIC: 5087 Beauty parlor equipment and supplies

(G-2143)
COTE CUSTOM WORKS LLC
2457 Pearsons Corner Rd (19904-5171)
PHONE.................................302 359-2596
Allen Cote, *Asst Sec*
EMP: 5 EST: 2017
SALES (est): 55.35K **Privately Held**
SIC: 1522 Residential construction, nec

(G-2144)
COUNTRY BUILDERS INC
818 Nault Rd (19904-5809)
PHONE.................................302 735-5530
Dawn Barrett, *Prin*
EMP: 5 EST: 2010
SALES (est): 222.24K **Privately Held**
Web: www.countrybuildersincorporated.com
SIC: 1521 New construction, single-family houses

(G-2145)
COUNTRY VILLAGE APARTMENTS
480 Country Dr (19901-5612)
PHONE.................................302 674-0991
Joanne Kelly, *Mgr*
Jim Hall, *Mgr*
EMP: 8 EST: 1980
SALES (est): 610.11K **Privately Held**
SIC: 6513 Apartment building operators

(G-2146)
COUNTY SEAT APARTMENTS LL
200 Weston Dr (19904-2786)
PHONE.................................302 856-7577
EMP: 6 EST: 2019
SALES (est): 519.18K **Privately Held**
SIC: 6513 Apartment building operators

(G-2147)
COUPERT SCIENCE LLC
8 The Grn (19901-3618)
PHONE.................................206 445-0706
Jimmy Zhao, *CEO*
EMP: 20
SALES (est): 588.11K **Privately Held**
SIC: 7371 Computer software development and applications

(G-2148)
COURTLAND MANOR INC
889 S Little Creek Rd (19901-4721)
PHONE.................................302 674-0566
Irma C Schurman, *Pr*
Sandy Schurman, *
Richard Schurman, *
EMP: 31 EST: 1967
SQ FT: 4,200
SALES (est): 6.83MM **Privately Held**
Web: www.courtlandmanor.com
SIC: 8059 8051 Convalescent home; Skilled nursing care facilities

(G-2149)
COWRIES & CALABASH LLC ◊
8 The Grn Ste A (19901-3618)
PHONE.................................917 727-8940
Lauren Solomon, *Managing Member*
EMP: 5 EST: 2022
SALES (est): 20.78K **Privately Held**

SIC: 7999 7389 Physical fitness instruction; Business services, nec

(G-2150)
CR NEWLIN TRUCKING INC
2199 Fast Landing Rd (19901-2725)
PHONE.................................302 678-9124
Christopher Newlin, *Pr*
Renee Newlin, *VP*
EMP: 5 EST: 1998
SALES (est): 252.98K **Privately Held**
SIC: 4212 Local trucking, without storage

(G-2151)
CRATA INC ◊
8 The Grn Ste A (19901-3618)
PHONE.................................214 606-1731
Sun Afolabi, *Prin*
EMP: 10 EST: 2023
SALES (est): 303.07K **Privately Held**
SIC: 7389 3571 Business Activities at Non-Commercial Site; Computers, digital, analog or hybrid

(G-2152)
CRATIS SOLUTIONS INC
8 The Grn Ste 5910 (19901-3618)
PHONE.................................515 423-7259
Stanley Wilson, *Pr*
EMP: 5
SALES (est): 179.75K **Privately Held**
SIC: 7371 Custom computer programming services

(G-2153)
CRAWLR INNOVATIONS INC
8 The Grn Ste B (19901-3618)
PHONE.................................912 515-9087
Jacqueline Zantow, *CEO*
EMP: 2 EST: 2021
SALES (est): 56.54K **Privately Held**
SIC: 7372 Application computer software

(G-2154)
CRAZY MAPLE INTERACTIVE INC
8 The Grn (19901-3618)
PHONE.................................408 603-7526
Yi Jia, *CEO*
EMP: 10 EST: 2021
SALES (est): 46.54K **Privately Held**
SIC: 7929 7389 Entertainment group; Business Activities at Non-Commercial Site

(G-2155)
CREATOPY INC ◊
Also Called: Creatopy
8 The Grn Ste R (19901-3618)
PHONE.................................339 217-6684
Dan Oros, *CEO*
Andrei Tudoran, *CFO*
EMP: 80 EST: 2023
SALES (est): 5.29MM **Privately Held**
Web: www.creatopy.com
SIC: 8742 Marketing consulting services

(G-2156)
CREDIBLOCKCOM LLC
8 The Grn Ste 8364 (19901-3618)
PHONE.................................803 619-9458
EMP: 5
SALES (est): 46.16K **Privately Held**
Web: www.crediblock.net
SIC: 7371 Computer software development

(G-2157)
CREDIT INSIDER LLC
8 The Grn Ste 10494 (19901-3618)
PHONE.................................302 232-5644
EMP: 5 EST: 2020
SALES (est): 65K **Privately Held**

GEOGRAPHIC SECTION
Dover - Kent County (G-2188)

SIC: 6111 Commodity Credit Corporation

(G-2158)
CREST CENTRAL
300 W Water St (19904-6743)
PHONE.................................302 736-0576
Theresa Evans Carter, *Dir*
Samantha Hurd, *Dir*
EMP: 14 **EST:** 2003
SALES (est): 157.07K **Privately Held**
Web: www.crestcentral.com
SIC: 8069 Drug addiction rehabilitation hospital

(G-2159)
CRIMSON STRATEGY GROUP LLP
8 The Grn Ste 10235 (19901-3618)
PHONE.................................302 503-5698
Greg Brown, *Pt*
EMP: 5 **EST:** 2019
SALES (est): 252.29K **Privately Held**
SIC: 8742 Management consulting services

(G-2160)
CROSSRATE TECHNOLOGIES LLC
8 The Grn (19901-3618)
PHONE.................................323 643-5178
EMP: 5
SALES (est): 73.93K **Privately Held**
SIC: 7372 7389 Prepackaged software; Business services, nec

(G-2161)
CROSSROADS OF DELAWARE
2 Forest St (19904-3211)
PHONE.................................302 744-9999
Mike Barbier, *Owner*
EMP: 5 **EST:** 2012
SALES (est): 76.58K **Privately Held**
Web: www.delaware.gov
SIC: 8322 Family (marriage) counseling

(G-2162)
CRUDE GOLD RESEARCH LLC
8 The Grn Ste A (19901-3618)
PHONE.................................646 681-7317
Ramnarayan Sharma, *Managing Member*
EMP: 14 **EST:** 2016
SQ FT: 850
SALES (est): 970.85K **Privately Held**
Web: www.goldcruderesearch.com
SIC: 6282 Investment advice

(G-2163)
CRUISE A LIFETIME USA INC
505 Brookfield Dr (19901-6534)
PHONE.................................302 697-2139
EMP: 5 **EST:** 2016
SALES (est): 32.06K **Privately Held**
SIC: 6311 Life insurance

(G-2164)
CRUZ PUBLISHING GROUP
64 Representative Ln (19904-2491)
PHONE.................................302 287-2938
Laura Cruz, *Prin*
EMP: 4 **EST:** 2018
SALES (est): 65.65K **Privately Held**
SIC: 2741 Miscellaneous publishing

(G-2165)
CRYPTO WORLD JOURNAL INC
8 The Grn # A (19901-3618)
PHONE.................................302 213-8136
Andrew Vilenchik, *Pr*
Rich Storholm, *Sec*
EMP: 15 **EST:** 2018
SALES (est): 495.39K **Privately Held**
Web: www.cryptoworldjournal.com

SIC: 7371 8299 Computer software development and applications; Educational services

(G-2166)
CRYPTOFI INC ✪
8 The Grn (19901-3618)
PHONE.................................312 813-7188
EMP: 20 **EST:** 2022
SALES (est): 1.03MM **Privately Held**
Web: www.cryptofi.tech
SIC: 7371 7389 Software programming applications; Business Activities at Non-Commercial Site

(G-2167)
CT INNOVATIONS LLC ✪
8 The Grn Ste A (19901-3618)
PHONE.................................209 559-3595
EMP: 8 **EST:** 2022
SALES (est): 357.82K **Privately Held**
SIC: 3999 7389 Manufacturing industries, nec; Business services, nec

(G-2168)
CTB INTL LLC
The Grn Ste 8325 (19901)
PHONE.................................217 415-4843
Christina Taylor, *Managing Member*
EMP: 5
SALES (est): 86.31K **Privately Held**
SIC: 5122 Cosmetics

(G-2169)
CULTURETECH SOLUTIONS LLC (PA) ✪
8 The Grn Ste A (19901-3618)
PHONE.................................415 936-5799
EMP: 7 **EST:** 2022
SALES (est): 289.61K
SALES (corp-wide): 289.61K **Privately Held**
SIC: 7379 7389 Computer related services, nec; Business services, nec

(G-2170)
CURLEY & BENTON LLC
Also Called: Curley and Funk
250 Beiser Blvd Ste 202 (19904-7795)
PHONE.................................302 674-3333
Edward Curley, *Owner*
EMP: 6 **EST:** 2005
SALES (est): 809.34K **Privately Held**
Web: www.delawaretoday.com
SIC: 8111 General practice attorney, lawyer

(G-2171)
CURRENT SOLUTIONS
1160 Rose Valley School Rd (19904-5513)
PHONE.................................302 724-5243
EMP: 7 **EST:** 2016
SALES (est): 263.93K **Privately Held**
SIC: 1623 Pipeline construction, nsk

(G-2172)
CUSHMAN FOUNDRY LLC
1111 S Governors Ave (19904-6903)
PHONE.................................513 984-5570
John Beyersdorfer, *Managing Member*
John C Beyersdorfer, *Managing Member*
EMP: 24 **EST:** 1911
SALES (est): 3.06MM **Privately Held**
Web: www.cushmanfoundry.com
SIC: 3365 Aluminum and aluminum-based alloy castings

(G-2173)
CUSTOM CON RESTORATION LLC
131 Cantwell Dr (19904-1584)
PHONE.................................302 670-9525

John Zucchero, *Prin*
EMP: 5 **EST:** 2018
SALES (est): 113.6K **Privately Held**
SIC: 1771 Concrete work

(G-2174)
CUSTOM DECOR INC
1585 Mckee Rd # 1 (19904-1380)
P.O. Box 336 (19936-0336)
PHONE.................................302 735-7600
William Scotton, *Pr*
Lesterlee Scotton, *VP*
♦ **EMP:** 17 **EST:** 1973
SALES (est): 1.17MM **Privately Held**
Web: www.customdecornet.com
SIC: 2399 Emblems, badges, and insignia

(G-2175)
CYCHET LLC
8 The Grn (19901-3618)
PHONE.................................929 265-8351
EMP: 10 **EST:** 2018
SALES (est): 487.1K **Privately Held**
Web: www.cychet.com
SIC: 8748 Environmental consultant

(G-2176)
CYNTHIA P MANGUBAT M D
819 S Governors Ave (19904-4158)
PHONE.................................302 883-3677
Cynthia P Mangubat, *Prin*
EMP: 9 **EST:** 2018
SALES (est): 203.1K **Privately Held**
SIC: 8011 Gynecologist

(G-2177)
CYNTHIA S DEVINE
240 Beiser Blvd Ste 101 (19904-8208)
PHONE.................................302 678-8447
Cynthia Devine Np-c, *Owner*
EMP: 6 **EST:** 2017
SALES (est): 79.03K **Privately Held**
SIC: 8049 Offices of health practitioner

(G-2178)
D & J WELDING LLC
8 The Grn (19901-3618)
PHONE.................................347 706-5561
EMP: 10
SALES (est): 216.36K **Privately Held**
SIC: 1389 7389 Construction, repair, and dismantling services; Business services, nec

(G-2179)
D 4 BROWN LLC
8 The Grn Ste 4000 (19901-3618)
PHONE.................................518 986-6809
Deron Brown, *Managing Member*
EMP: 6
SALES (est): 76.63K **Privately Held**
SIC: 4213 Trucking, except local

(G-2180)
D BY D PRINTING LLC
5083 N Dupont Hwy (19901-2346)
PHONE.................................302 659-3373
Dennis Connell, *Managing Member*
EMP: 3 **EST:** 2008
SQ FT: 2,500
SALES (est): 242.99K **Privately Held**
Web: www.delawaresignshop.com
SIC: 2261 3993 Screen printing of cotton broadwoven fabrics; Signs and advertising specialties

(G-2181)
D LAVERNE BEILER
220 Beiser Blvd (19904-7790)
PHONE.................................302 378-4644

D Laverne Beiler, *Prin*
EMP: 5 **EST:** 2010
SALES (est): 96.27K **Privately Held**
SIC: 8721 Certified public accountant

(G-2182)
D-STAFFING CONSULTING SVCS LLC
8 The Grn Ste 6060 (19901-3618)
PHONE.................................302 402-5678
EMP: 75 **EST:** 2017
SALES (est): 1.44MM **Privately Held**
Web: www.d-staff.com
SIC: 7361 Employment agencies

(G-2183)
D1 EXPRESS INC
15 Maggies Way Ste 1 (19901-4892)
PHONE.................................302 883-9572
Anton Rybantsev, *CEO*
Konstantin Tsoklan, *Pr*
EMP: 5 **EST:** 2016
SALES (est): 83.41K **Privately Held**
SIC: 4731 Freight forwarding

(G-2184)
DAHCOR LLC
8 The Grn Ste A (19901-3618)
PHONE.................................302 257-2803
EMP: 5 **EST:** 2020
SALES (est): 47.08K **Privately Held**
SIC: 3949 7389 Racket sports equipment; Business services, nec

(G-2185)
DAILY BYTE LLC
8 The Grn Ste A (19901-3618)
PHONE.................................516 236-9638
EMP: 5 **EST:** 2020
SALES (est): 46.16K **Privately Held**
SIC: 7371 Computer software development and applications

(G-2186)
DAKK HOLDINGS LLC
Also Called: Ecommerence
8 The Grn (19901-3618)
P.O. Box 563 (22555-0563)
PHONE.................................571 335-7844
Derek Greene, *CEO*
EMP: 6 **EST:** 2012
SALES (est): 308.6K **Privately Held**
SIC: 7389 5961 Business Activities at Non-Commercial Site; Electronic shopping

(G-2187)
DALE MAPLE COUNTRY CLUB INC
180 Mapledale Cir (19904-7118)
PHONE.................................302 674-2505
Larry Mc Allister, *Pr*
EMP: 49 **EST:** 1925
SQ FT: 8,750
SALES (est): 2.04MM **Privately Held**
Web: www.mapledalecc.com
SIC: 7997 Country club, membership

(G-2188)
DAMON BACA
Also Called: Cross Border It
8 The Grn Ste 8 (19901-3618)
PHONE.................................858 837-0800
Damon Baca, *Owner*
EMP: 6 **EST:** 2019
SQ FT: 15,000
SALES (est): 259.44K **Privately Held**
SIC: 7372 7389 Prepackaged software; Drawback service, customs

(G-2189)
DANCE CONSERVATORY
Also Called: Ballet Theatre of Dover
522 Otis Dr (19901-4630)
P.O. Box 493 (19903-0493)
PHONE.................................302 734-9717
Teresa Emmons, *Owner*
EMP: 9 **EST:** 1984
SALES (est): 231.8K **Privately Held**
Web: www.dancebtd.com
SIC: 7911 Dance studio and school

(G-2190)
DANELLA LINE SERVICES CO INC
874 Walker Rd (19904-2778)
PHONE.................................302 893-1253
Daniel L Stockdale, *Admn*
EMP: 89
SALES (corp-wide): 545.12MM **Privately Held**
Web: www.danella.com
SIC: 8741 Construction management
HQ: Danella Line Services Company, Inc.
  2290 Butler Pike
  Plymouth Meeting PA 19462

(G-2191)
DANIEL A YODER
2956 Yoder Dr (19904-5846)
PHONE.................................302 730-4076
Daniel Yoder, *Prin*
EMP: 6 **EST:** 2014
SALES (est): 145.83K **Privately Held**
SIC: 2431 Millwork

(G-2192)
DANIEL J FAY DMD PA ✪
748 S New St Ste C (19904-3573)
PHONE.................................302 734-8101
EMP: 5 **EST:** 2022
SALES (est): 242.31K **Privately Held**
Web: www.drdanielfay.com
SIC: 8021 Dentists' office

(G-2193)
DANIEL MARELLI
540 S Governors Ave (19904-3530)
PHONE.................................302 744-7980
Daniel Marelli, *Pr*
EMP: 10 **EST:** 2017
SALES (est): 244.37K **Privately Held**
SIC: 8011 Offices and clinics of medical doctors

(G-2194)
DANIELLE HILL TRAINING CENTER
2075 Sharon Hill Rd (19904-5354)
PHONE.................................302 363-1484
EMP: 5 **EST:** 2016
SALES (est): 59.52K **Privately Held**
Web: www.daniellehilltrainingcenter.com
SIC: 0272 Horse farm

(G-2195)
DANIELLE WIGGINS
121 W Loockerman St (19904-7325)
PHONE.................................302 494-3397
Danielle Wiggins, *Owner*
EMP: 5 **EST:** 2018
SALES (est): 68.17K **Privately Held**
SIC: 8322 Individual and family services

(G-2196)
DARWELL INC
874 Walker Rd (19904-2778)
PHONE.................................302 204-0939
Nicolay Trzhascal, *CEO*
EMP: 7
SALES (est): 264.9K **Privately Held**
SIC: 7371 Computer software development and applications

(G-2197)
DATASEA INC
8 The Grn Ste R (19901-3618)
PHONE.................................267 752-9029
Zhixin Liu, *Ch Bd*
Zhixin Liu, *Ch Bd*
Mingzhou Sun, *CFO*
EMP: 123 **EST:** 2014
SALES (est): 17.08MM **Privately Held**
SIC: 7372 Prepackaged software

(G-2198)
DAVAIT INC
8 The Grn Ste B (19901-3618)
PHONE.................................302 930-0095
Eugenio Grytsenko, *CEO*
EMP: 7
SALES (est): 264.9K **Privately Held**
SIC: 7389 7371 Business Activities at Non-Commercial Site; Computer software development

(G-2199)
DAVES DISC MFFLERS OF DVER DE
Also Called: Meineke Discount Mufflers
1312 S Dupont Hwy (19901-4404)
PHONE.................................302 678-8803
David Kaplan, *Pr*
EMP: 6 **EST:** 1985
SQ FT: 3,200
SALES (est): 444.37K **Privately Held**
Web: www.meineke.com
SIC: 7533 Muffler shop, sale or repair and installation

(G-2200)
DAYS INN DOVER DOWNTOWN
Also Called: Days Inn
272 N Dupont Hwy (19901-7510)
PHONE.................................302 674-8002
Hatal Christian, *Owner*
EMP: 48 **EST:** 1988
SALES (est): 240.48K **Privately Held**
Web: www.wyndhamhotels.com
SIC: 7011 Hotels and motels

(G-2201)
DAYSHAPE CORP (PA) ✪
874 Walker Rd Ste C (19904-2778)
PHONE.................................929 512-5582
Andrew Bone, *CEO*
EMP: 6 **EST:** 2022
SALES (est): 270.03K
SALES (corp-wide): 270.03K **Privately Held**
SIC: 7371 Computer software development

(G-2202)
DBAZA INC
Also Called: Za Health
614 N Dupont Hwy Ste 210 (19901-3900)
P.O. Box 3513 (19807-0513)
PHONE.................................302 467-3081
Sergey Sirotinin, *CEO*
EMP: 5 **EST:** 1997
SALES (est): 879.22K **Privately Held**
Web: www.dbaza.com
SIC: 7372 7371 Educational computer software; Computer software systems analysis and design, custom

(G-2203)
DE COLORES FAMILY CHILD CARE
917 Monroe Ter (19904-4119)
PHONE.................................302 883-3298
Sarita Medero, *Prin*
EMP: 10 **EST:** 2010
SALES (est): 57.5K **Privately Held**
SIC: 8351 Child day care services

(G-2204)
DEALL LLC
8 The Grn (19901-3618)
PHONE.................................305 790-0109
EMP: 15
SALES (est): 490.69K **Privately Held**
SIC: 7389 Financial services

(G-2205)
DECENNIUM MANAGEMENT GROUP
8 The Grn Ste 4738 (19901-3618)
P.O. Box 702 (07203-0702)
PHONE.................................302 600-3644
Regina Robinson-har, *Pr*
Regina Robinson, *Prin*
EMP: 4 **EST:** 2017
SALES (est): 234K **Privately Held**
SIC: 8742 8748 1389 Programmed instruction service; Business consulting, nec ; Construction, repair, and dismantling services

(G-2206)
DECISIONRX INC
8 The Grn Ste A (19901-3618)
PHONE.................................800 957-3606
Jim Wallace, *CEO*
EMP: 13
SALES (est): 254.39K **Privately Held**
SIC: 8099 Health and allied services, nec

(G-2207)
DEE & DOREENS TEAM
1671 S State St (19901-5148)
PHONE.................................302 677-0030
Dee Demolen, *Owner*
EMP: 6 **EST:** 2004
SALES (est): 202.09K **Privately Held**
SIC: 6531 Real estate brokers and agents

(G-2208)
DEHUI SOLAR POWER INC
9 E Loockerman St Ste 311 (19901-8305)
PHONE.................................864 326-7936
EMP: 6 **EST:** 2018
SALES (est): 495.61K **Privately Held**
SIC: 8742 Business management consultant

(G-2209)
DEL DOT CANAL DIST
800 S Bay Rd Ste 1 (19901-4677)
PHONE.................................410 742-9361
EMP: 7 **EST:** 2018
SALES (est): 113.98K **Privately Held**
SIC: 8611 Business associations

(G-2210)
DEL HOMES INC
1567 Mckee Rd (19904-1380)
PHONE.................................302 730-1479
EMP: 18
SALES (corp-wide): 3.42MM **Privately Held**
SIC: 1521 New construction, single-family houses
PA: Del Homes Inc
  1309 Ponderosa Dr
  Magnolia DE 19962
  302 697-8204

(G-2211)
DEL-MAR APPLIANCE OF DELAWARE (PA)
Also Called: Del-Mar Appliance
230 S Governors Ave (19904-6704)
PHONE.................................302 674-2414
Jo Ann Mandarano, *Pr*
Bruce Nygard, *VP*
EMP: 8 **EST:** 1968
SQ FT: 12,000
SALES (est): 602.09K
SALES (corp-wide): 602.09K **Privately Held**
SIC: 7629 5722 Electrical household appliance repair; Electric household appliances

(G-2212)
DEL-MR-VA CNCIL INC BOY SCUTS (PA)
Also Called: BOY SCOUTS OF AMERICA
1910 Baden Powell Way (19904-6473)
PHONE.................................302 622-3300
Patrick Sterrett, *Ex Dir*
EMP: 16 **EST:** 1916
SALES (est): 4.36MM
SALES (corp-wide): 4.36MM **Privately Held**
SIC: 8641 Boy Scout organization

(G-2213)
DEL-ONE FEDERAL CREDIT UNION
150 E Water St Ste 1 (19901-3619)
PHONE.................................302 739-2390
Sharee Coleman, *VP*
EMP: 9
Web: www.del-one.org
SIC: 6061 Federal credit unions
PA: Del-One Federal Credit Union
  270 Beiser Blvd
  Dover DE 19904

(G-2214)
DEL-ONE FEDERAL CREDIT UNION (PA)
270 Beiser Blvd (19904-7790)
PHONE.................................302 734-4496
EMP: 45 **EST:** 1960
SALES (est): 22.25MM **Privately Held**
Web: www.del-one.org
SIC: 6061 6163 Federal credit unions; Loan brokers

(G-2215)
DELAVE DENIM CO LLC (PA)
Also Called: D Lav Denim Co
8 The Grn Ste 4000 (19901-3618)
PHONE.................................302 308-5161
EMP: 6 **EST:** 2020
SALES (est): 212.75K
SALES (corp-wide): 212.75K **Privately Held**
SIC: 5651 7389 Unisex clothing stores; Business services, nec

(G-2216)
DELAWARE AG MUSEUM ASSN
866 N Dupont Hwy (19901-2003)
PHONE.................................302 734-1618
Carolyn Claypoole, *Ex Dir*
Grier Stayton, *Bd of Dir*
EMP: 9 **EST:** 1974
SQ FT: 300,000
SALES (est): 503.14K **Privately Held**
Web: www.agriculturalmuseum.org
SIC: 8412 7299 Museum; Facility rental and party planning services

(G-2217)
DELAWARE BAIL BONDS
414 Denison St (19901)
PHONE.................................302 734-9881
Berry Udoff, *Mgr*
EMP: 8 **EST:** 1997
SALES (est): 330.46K **Privately Held**
Web: www.lyonsbailbonds.com
SIC: 7389 Bail bonding

GEOGRAPHIC SECTION
Dover - Kent County (G-2242)

(G-2218)
DELAWARE BREAST CANCER COALIT
Also Called: Delaware Brast Cncer Coalition
165 Commerce Way Ste 2 (19904-8224)
PHONE.................................302 672-6435
Lois Wilkinson, *Brnch Mgr*
EMP: 5
Web: www.debreastcancer.org
SIC: 8322 Individual and family services
PA: Delaware Breast Cancer Coalition, Inc.
100 W 10th St Ste 209
Wilmington DE 19801

(G-2219)
DELAWARE BRICK COMPANY
492 Webbs Ln (19904-5440)
PHONE.................................302 883-2807
Jim Pelaclathan, *Mgr*
EMP: 6
SALES (corp-wide): 10.59MM **Privately Held**
Web: www.delawarebrick.com
SIC: 5032 5082 Brick, stone, and related material; Masonry equipment and supplies
PA: Delaware Brick Company
1114 Centerville Rd
Wilmington DE 19804
302 994-0948

(G-2220)
DELAWARE CHARMS
206 Richard Bassett Rd (19904-5429)
PHONE.................................302 480-4951
India Scott, *Prin*
EMP: 5 **EST:** 2018
SALES (est): 55.84K **Privately Held**
SIC: 8322 Individual and family services

(G-2221)
DELAWARE CNNBIS ADVCACY NTWRK
438 S State St (19901-6724)
PHONE.................................302 404-4208
Adam Windett, *Prin*
EMP: 8 **EST:** 2017
SALES (est): 3.72K **Privately Held**
Web: www.delawarecannabis.org
SIC: 8611 Business associations

(G-2222)
DELAWARE COASTAL ANESTHESIA LL
100 Scull Ter (19901-3577)
PHONE.................................302 275-5777
Roderick Relova, *Prin*
EMP: 9 **EST:** 2008
SALES (est): 248.37K **Privately Held**
SIC: 8011 Anesthesiologist

(G-2223)
DELAWARE COMPANY HOUSE LLC
8 The Grn Ste R (19901-3618)
PHONE.................................302 526-4784
EMP: 12 **EST:** 2017
SALES (est): 366.25K **Privately Held**
Web: www.delaware.gov
SIC: 7389 Business services, nec

(G-2224)
DELAWARE CRDOVASCULAR ASSOC PA
1113 S State St Ste 100 (19901-4112)
PHONE.................................302 734-7676
Teri Flores, *Mgr*
EMP: 16
Web: www.decardio.com
SIC: 8011 Cardiologist and cardio-vascular specialist

PA: Delaware Cardiovascular Associates, P.A.
1403 Foulk Rd Ste 101a
Wilmington DE 19803

(G-2225)
DELAWARE DEADLY WEAPONS
861 Silver Lake Blvd Ste 203 (19904-2467)
PHONE.................................302 736-5159
Nancy Fields, *Mgr*
EMP: 7 **EST:** 2017
SALES (est): 293.6K **Privately Held**
Web: www.baytobaynews.com
SIC: 6411 Insurance agents, brokers, and service

(G-2226)
DELAWARE DENTAL CARE CENTERS
73 Greentree Dr 407 (19904-7646)
PHONE.................................410 474-5520
Jeffrey M Wilson D.d.s., *Prin*
EMP: 5 **EST:** 2009
SALES (est): 182.99K **Privately Held**
SIC: 8021 Dentists' office

(G-2227)
DELAWARE DEPARTMENT FINANCE
Also Called: Delaware State Lottery
1575 Mckee Rd Ste 102 (19904-1382)
PHONE.................................302 739-5291
Vernon Kirk, *Dir*
EMP: 53
SALES (corp-wide): 11.27B **Privately Held**
Web: www.delaware.gov
SIC: 8111 9311 Legal services; Lottery control board, government
HQ: Delaware Department Of Finance
820 N French St Ste 8
Wilmington DE 19801

(G-2228)
DELAWARE DEPARTMENT TRNSP
Also Called: Dart First State
655 S Bay Rd Ste 4g (19904-4656)
PHONE.................................302 577-3278
EMP: 66
SALES (corp-wide): 11.27B **Privately Held**
Web: www.deldot.gov
SIC: 8611 9621 Business associations; Regulation, administration of transportation
HQ: Delaware Department Of Transportation
800 S Bay Rd Ste 1
Dover DE 19901

(G-2229)
DELAWARE DEPT HLTH SOCIAL SVCS
Also Called: James Williams State Svc Ctr
805 River Rd (19901-3753)
PHONE.................................302 857-5000
Linda Melvin, *Dir*
EMP: 8
SALES (corp-wide): 11.27B **Privately Held**
Web: www.delaware.gov
SIC: 8322 8093 9431 Individual and family services; Specialty outpatient clinics, nec; Administration of public health programs, State government
HQ: Delaware Dept Of Health And Social Services
1901 N Dupont Hwy
New Castle DE 19720

(G-2230)
DELAWARE DEPT HLTH SOCIAL SVCS
Division Health Care Comm
410 Federal St Ste 7 (19901-3640)

PHONE.................................302 255-9500
Rosanne Mahaney, *Brnch Mgr*
EMP: 10
SALES (corp-wide): 11.27B **Privately Held**
SIC: 8322 9441 Child related social services; Administration of social and manpower programs, State government
HQ: Delaware Dept Of Health And Social Services
1901 N Dupont Hwy
New Castle DE 19720

(G-2231)
DELAWARE DERMATOLGY PA
Also Called: Andrews, Joseph F MD
737 S Queen St Ste 1 (19904-3529)
PHONE.................................302 736-1800
Joseph Andrews Md, *Owner*
EMP: 5 **EST:** 1986
SALES (est): 447.65K **Privately Held**
Web: www.dederm.com
SIC: 8011 Dermatologist

(G-2232)
DELAWARE DIV HSTRCAL CLTRAL AF (DH)
21 The Grn (19901-3611)
PHONE.................................302 736-7400
James A Stewart, *Admn*
EMP: 13 **EST:** 1931
SALES (est): 2.96MM
SALES (corp-wide): 11.27B **Privately Held**
SIC: 8412 9111 Museum; Executive offices, State government
HQ: Delaware Secretary Of State
401 Federal St Ste 3
Dover DE 19901
302 739-4111

(G-2233)
DELAWARE DRNKING DRVER PROGRAM (PA)
1661 S Dupont Hwy (19901-5129)
PHONE.................................302 736-4326
Walter Mc Cann, *Pr*
Bruce Lorenz, *VP*
EMP: 8 **EST:** 1985
SQ FT: 1,500
SALES (est): 763.08K
SALES (corp-wide): 763.08K **Privately Held**
SIC: 8322 Alcoholism counseling, nontreatment

(G-2234)
DELAWARE ECONOMIC DEV AUTH
99 Kings Hwy (19901-7305)
PHONE.................................302 739-4271
EMP: 5
SALES (est): 577.09K **Privately Held**
SIC: 8748 Economic consultant

(G-2235)
DELAWARE ELECTRIC SIGNAL CO
Also Called: Milford Security Systems
1490 E Lebanon Rd (19901-5833)
PHONE.................................302 422-3916
FAX: 302 734-4878
EMP: 25
SQ FT: 2,800
SALES (est): 1.84MM **Privately Held**
Web: www.decoop.com
SIC: 1731 7382 Fire detection and burglar alarm systems specialization; Burglar alarm maintenance and monitoring

(G-2236)
DELAWARE ENERGY SOLUTIONS
999 Long Point Rd (19901-1200)

PHONE.................................302 242-6315
EMP: 6 **EST:** 2009
SALES (est): 87.74K **Privately Held**
SIC: 1731 Energy management controls

(G-2237)
DELAWARE EYE CARE CENTER (PA)
833 S Governors Ave (19904-4158)
PHONE.................................302 674-1121
Gary Markowitz Md, *Pr*
EMP: 9 **EST:** 1996
SALES (est): 2.74MM
SALES (corp-wide): 2.74MM **Privately Held**
Web: www.delawareeyecare.com
SIC: 8042 Offices and clinics of optometrists

(G-2238)
DELAWARE FFA FOUNDATION INC
35 Commerce Way Ste 1 (19904-5747)
PHONE.................................302 857-6493
Lisa Falconetti, *Pr*
Robert Lawson, *VP*
Amber Bullock, *Sec*
James Testerman, *Treas*
EMP: 9 **EST:** 2009
SALES (est): 89.7K **Privately Held**
Web: www.delawareffa.org
SIC: 8641 Civic and social associations

(G-2239)
DELAWARE FIRST MEDIA CORP
Also Called: Delaware Public Media
1200 N Dupont Hwy (19901-2202)
P.O. Box 455 (19903-0455)
PHONE.................................302 857-7096
EMP: 22 **EST:** 2010
SALES (est): 939.93K **Privately Held**
Web: www.delawarepublic.org
SIC: 4899 Communication services, nec

(G-2240)
DELAWARE FNCL EDCATN ALNCE INC
8 W Loockerman St Ste 200 (19904-7324)
P.O. Box 494 (19903-0494)
PHONE.................................302 674-0288
EMP: 7 **EST:** 1983
SALES (est): 688.65K **Privately Held**
Web: www.dfea.org
SIC: 8299 7389 Educational services; Business Activities at Non-Commercial Site

(G-2241)
DELAWARE GDNCE SVCS FOR CHLDRE
Also Called: Act Program
103 Mont Blanc Blvd (19904-7615)
PHONE.................................302 678-3020
Rhonda Quin, *Dir*
EMP: 30
SALES (corp-wide): 7.01MM **Privately Held**
Web: www.delawareguidance.org
SIC: 8322 Family counseling services
PA: Delaware Guidance Services For Children And Youth, Inc.
1213 Delaware Ave
Wilmington DE 19806
302 652-3948

(G-2242)
DELAWARE HEALTH CARE COMM
410 Federal St Ste 7 (19901)
PHONE.................................302 739-2730
Paula Roy, *Ex Dir*
EMP: 10 **EST:** 2004
SALES (est): 256.31K **Privately Held**
Web: www.delaware.gov

Dover - Kent County (G-2243)   GEOGRAPHIC SECTION

SIC: 8621 Health association

(G-2243)
DELAWARE HEALTH INFO NETWRK
107 Wolf Creek Blvd Ste 2 (19901-4970)
PHONE..................................302 678-0220
EMP: 47 EST: 2010
SALES (est): 10.77MM **Privately Held**
Web: www.dhin.org
SIC: 8621 Health association

(G-2244)
DELAWARE HEART & VASCULAR PA
200 Banning St Ste 340 (19904-3490)
PHONE..................................302 734-1414
Terri Rosetta, *Off Mgr*
Terry Flores, *Pr*
EMP: 8 EST: 2006
SALES (est): 960.83K **Privately Held**
Web: www.bayhealth.org
SIC: 8062 General medical and surgical hospitals

(G-2245)
DELAWARE HOSPICE INC
911 S Dupont Hwy (19901-4468)
PHONE..................................302 678-4444
Judi Tulak, *Mgr*
EMP: 22
SALES (corp-wide): 6.31MM **Privately Held**
Web: www.delawarehospice.org
SIC: 8052 Personal care facility
PA: Delaware Hospice Inc.
     16 Polly Drummond Shpg Ct
     Newark DE 19711
     302 478-5707

(G-2246)
DELAWARE INJURY CARE
240 Beiser Blvd Ste 101 (19904-8208)
PHONE..................................302 678-8866
EMP: 6 EST: 2019
SALES (est): 37.19K **Privately Held**
Web: www.delawareinjurycare.org
SIC: 8041 Offices and clinics of chiropractors

(G-2247)
DELAWARE INTRVNTNAL SPINE ASSO
Also Called: Delaware Spine Institute
1673 S State St Ste B (19901-5148)
PHONE..................................302 674-8444
Ron Lieberman, *Managing Member*
EMP: 7 EST: 2004
SQ FT: 2,000
SALES (est): 585.14K **Privately Held**
Web: www.de-spine.com
SIC: 8011 Physicians' office, including specialists

(G-2248)
DELAWARE LANDSCAPING INC
106 Semans Dr (19904-6460)
P.O. Box 501 (19934-5001)
PHONE..................................302 698-3001
Steve Gedney, *Pr*
EMP: 6 EST: 1998
SQ FT: 6,000
SALES (est): 357.1K **Privately Held**
SIC: 0782 Landscape contractors

(G-2249)
DELAWARE MLTCLTRAL CVIC ORGNZT
365 United Way (19901-3769)
PHONE..................................302 399-6118
Michael H Casson Junior, *Pr*
Enwan Casson, *Prin*
EMP: 10 EST: 2006

SALES (est): 288.06K **Privately Held**
SIC: 8748 Testing service, educational or personnel

(G-2250)
DELAWARE NATIONAL ESTUARINE
818 Kitts Hummock Rd (19901-7093)
PHONE..................................302 739-3436
EMP: 5 EST: 2016
SALES (est): 60.18K **Privately Held**
Web: www.delawarebeautiful.com
SIC: 2721 Magazines: publishing only, not printed on site

(G-2251)
DELAWARE OBGYN & WOMENS HEALTH
1057 S Bradford St (19904-4141)
PHONE..................................302 730-0633
Mark Anthony, *Prin*
EMP: 5 EST: 2009
SALES (est): 388.14K **Privately Held**
Web: www.delawarewomenshealth.com
SIC: 8011 Gynecologist

(G-2252)
DELAWARE PARENTS ASSOCIATION
101 W Loockerman St Ste 3a (19904-7328)
PHONE..................................302 678-9288
EMP: 10 EST: 1985
SALES (est): 406.37K **Privately Held**
Web: www.delparents.org
SIC: 8641 Parent-teachers' association

(G-2253)
DELAWARE PHYSIATRY LLC
Also Called: Delaware Neurorehab
1221 College Park Dr Ste 203
(19904-8727)
PHONE..................................302 387-1407
Jessica Cintron, *Prin*
Haresh Sampathkumar, *Prin*
EMP: 6 EST: 2021
SALES (est): 663.93K **Privately Held**
SIC: 8011 Neurologist

(G-2254)
DELAWARE PLASTIC SURGERY
1695 S State St (19901-5148)
PHONE..................................302 632-7750
EMP: 7 EST: 2019
SALES (est): 167.21K **Privately Held**
SIC: 8011 Plastic surgeon

(G-2255)
DELAWARE PRIMARY CARE LLC
810 New Burton Rd Ste 3 (19904-5488)
PHONE..................................302 730-0554
EMP: 8 EST: 2002
SALES (est): 955.08K **Privately Held**
Web: www.mydeldoc.com
SIC: 8011 General and family practice, physician/surgeon

(G-2256)
DELAWARE RESTAURANT ASSN
420 S State St (19901-6724)
P.O. Box 7838 (19714-7838)
PHONE..................................302 738-2545
Carrie Leishman, *CEO*
Xavier Teixido, *Pr*
EMP: 8 EST: 1965
SALES (est): 565.24K **Privately Held**
Web: www.delawarerestaurant.org
SIC: 8611 Trade associations

(G-2257)
DELAWARE SECRETARY OF STATE
Also Called: Delaware State Hstric Prsrvtio
21 The Grn # A (19901-3611)

PHONE..................................302 736-7400
Timothy Slavin, *Dir*
EMP: 10
SALES (corp-wide): 11.27B **Privately Held**
Web: www.delaware.gov
SIC: 8999 9199 Natural resource preservation service; General government administration
HQ: Delaware Secretary Of State
     401 Federal St Ste 3
     Dover DE 19901
     302 739-4111

(G-2258)
DELAWARE SENIOR OLYMPICS INC
1121 Forrest Ave (19904-3308)
PHONE..................................302 736-5698
Gene J Mirolli, *Pr*
Conny Wertz, *Ex Dir*
EMP: 6 EST: 1991
SALES (est): 94.42K **Privately Held**
Web: www.delawareseniorolympics.org
SIC: 8322 Senior citizens' center or association

(G-2259)
DELAWARE SKATING CENTER LTD
Also Called: Dover Skating Center
2201 S Dupont Hwy (19901-5512)
PHONE..................................302 697-3218
Virgil Dooley, *Mgr*
EMP: 83
SALES (corp-wide): 2.6MM **Privately Held**
Web: www.doverskate.com
SIC: 7999 Roller skating rink operation
PA: Delaware Skating Center Ltd Inc
     801 Christiana Rd
     Newark DE 19713
     302 366-0473

(G-2260)
DELAWARE SOLID WASTE AUTHORITY (PA)
1128 S Bradford St (19904-6919)
P.O. Box 455 (19903-0455)
PHONE..................................302 739-5361
Richard V Pryor, *Ch Bd*
Richard V Pryor, *Ch Bd*
Pasquale S Canzano Pe Dee, *
Joseph Koskey, *
Toby Ryan, *
EMP: 50 EST: 1975
SQ FT: 14,000
SALES (est): 47.22MM
SALES (corp-wide): 47.22MM **Privately Held**
Web: www.dswa.com
SIC: 4953 Recycling, waste materials

(G-2261)
DELAWARE SPINE REHABILITATION
642 S Queen St (19904-3506)
PHONE..................................302 883-2292
EMP: 10 EST: 2017
SALES (est): 73.36K **Privately Held**
SIC: 8093 Rehabilitation center, outpatient treatment

(G-2262)
DELAWARE SSTNBLE ENRGY UTILITY
Also Called: SUSTAINABLE ENERGY
500 W Loockerman St Ste 400
(19904-7309)
PHONE..................................302 883-3038
Tony Deprima, *Prin*
EMP: 20 EST: 2011
SALES (est): 34.79MM **Privately Held**
Web: www.energizedelaware.org
SIC: 8731 Energy research

(G-2263)
DELAWARE STATE EDUCATION ASSN (PA)
136 E Water St (19901-3614)
PHONE..................................302 734-5834
Judy Anderson, *Mgr*
EMP: 14 EST: 1952
SALES (est): 6.13MM
SALES (corp-wide): 6.13MM **Privately Held**
Web: www.dsea.org
SIC: 8631 8742 Labor union; Management consulting services

(G-2264)
DELAWARE STATE PRINTING
110 Galaxy Dr (19901-9262)
PHONE..................................302 228-9431
EMP: 28 EST: 2017
SALES (est): 1.22MM **Privately Held**
SIC: 2752 Commercial printing, lithographic

(G-2265)
DELAWARE STNDRDBRED OWNERS ASS
830 Walker Rd Ste 11-2 (19904-2748)
PHONE..................................302 678-3058
Ralph Holloway, *VP*
Edward Long, *Dir*
Brenda Lewis, *Sec*
Presley Moore, *Treas*
Charles Lockart, *Prin*
EMP: 5 EST: 1997
SQ FT: 1,350
SALES (est): 1.23MM **Privately Held**
Web: www.dsoaonline.com
SIC: 8611 Trade associations

(G-2266)
DELAWARE STORAGE & PIPELINE CO
987 Port Mahon Rd (19901-4833)
P.O. Box 313 (19903-0313)
PHONE..................................302 736-1774
George Steady, *Mgr*
EMP: 8
Web: www.delawarespc.com
SIC: 1389 Pumping of oil and gas wells
HQ: Delaware Storage & Pipeline Co Inc
     400 Amherst St Ste 202
     Nashua NH
     603 886-7300

(G-2267)
DELAWARE STOREFRONTS LLC (PA)
720 S Governors Ave (19904-4106)
PHONE..................................302 697-1850
John E Layton Junior, *Managing Member*
EMP: 5 EST: 2008
SQ FT: 40,000
SALES (est): 505.04K **Privately Held**
Web: www.delawarestorefronts.com
SIC: 1793 Glass and glazing work

(G-2268)
DELAWARE SURGERY CENTER LLC
200 Banning St Ste 110 (19904-3486)
PHONE..................................302 730-0217
Thomas Barnett, *Managing Member*
Stephen Cooper, *
Glen Rowe, *
Eric Shwartz, *
J Hamilton Easter, *
▲ EMP: 48 EST: 2000
SALES (est): 9.95MM **Privately Held**
Web: www.desurgery.com
SIC: 8011 Surgeon

GEOGRAPHIC SECTION
Dover - Kent County (G-2296)

(G-2269)
DELAWARE SURGERY CTR
1326 S Governors Ave Ste C (19904-4800)
PHONE..................................302 730-0217
Shelia Miller, *Mgr*
EMP: 11 **EST:** 2000
SALES (est): 103.83K **Privately Held**
Web: www.desurgery.com
SIC: 8011 Surgeon

(G-2270)
DELAWARE TIRE CENTER INC
207 S Governors Ave (19904-6703)
PHONE..................................302 674-0234
Tom Lindale, *Mgr*
EMP: 10
SALES (corp-wide): 11.11MM **Privately Held**
Web: www.delawaretire.com
SIC: 5531 5014 5013 Automotive tires; Automobile tires and tubes; Automotive batteries
PA: Delaware Tire Center, Inc.
  616 S College Ave
  Newark DE 19713
  302 368-2531

(G-2271)
DELAWARE TRANSPORTATION AUTH
800 S Bay Rd (19901-4685)
PHONE..................................302 760-2000
EMP: 5 **EST:** 2010
SALES (est): 189.2K **Privately Held**
SIC: 4111 Local and suburban transit

(G-2272)
DELAWARE VETERANS POST
720 Pear St (19904-2834)
PHONE..................................302 317-1123
EMP: 6 **EST:** 2017
SALES (est): 237.48K **Privately Held**
Web: www.delvets2.com
SIC: 8641 Veterans' organization

(G-2273)
DELAWARE WIC PROGRAM (PA)
Also Called: Administrative Office
635 S Bay Rd # 1c (19901-4601)
PHONE..................................302 741-2900
Joanne Whire, *Dir*
Joanne White, *Dir*
EMP: 8 **EST:** 1977
SALES (est): 792.82K
SALES (corp-wide): 792.82K **Privately Held**
Web: www.delaware.gov
SIC: 8322 Individual and family services

(G-2274)
DELAWARE WIC PROGRAM
Also Called: Wic State Office of Delaware
805 River Rd (19901-3753)
PHONE..................................302 857-5000
Steve Dettweyler, *Prin*
EMP: 7
SALES (corp-wide): 792.82K **Privately Held**
Web: www.delaware.gov
SIC: 8322 Individual and family services
PA: Delaware Wic Program
  635 S Bay Rd 1c
  Dover DE 19901
  302 741-2900

(G-2275)
DELFAST INC
160 Greentree Dr Ste 101 (19904-7620)
PHONE..................................323 540-5155
EMP: 21
SALES (corp-wide): 162.81K **Privately Held**
Web: www.delfastbikes.com
SIC: 3751 Bicycles and related parts
PA: Delfast Inc.
  13575 Whittier Blvd
  Whittier CA 90605
  323 540-5155

(G-2276)
DELMAR PROCESS SERVERS LLC
8 The Grn Ste 17282 (19901-3618)
PHONE..................................302 306-2805
Marcia Boyer, *Managing Member*
EMP: 10
SALES (est): 348.32K **Privately Held**
SIC: 7389 Process serving service

(G-2277)
DELMARVA EQUINE CLINIC
Also Called: Egli, Michelle D Dvm
1008 S Governors Ave (19904-6902)
PHONE..................................302 735-4735
EMP: 6 **EST:** 1987
SALES (est): 436.38K **Privately Held**
Web: www.delmarva-equine.com
SIC: 0742 Veterinarian, animal specialties

(G-2278)
DELMARVA PROSTHODONTICS
871 S Governors Ave Ste 1 (19904-4115)
PHONE..................................302 674-8331
Christopher David Burns, *Prin*
EMP: 5 **EST:** 2008
SALES (est): 421.35K **Privately Held**
Web: www.delmarvaprosthodontics.com
SIC: 8021 Prosthodontist

(G-2279)
DELMARVA WATER SOLUTIONS
1039 Fowler Ct (19901-4638)
PHONE..................................302 674-0509
John Sensi, *Pr*
Steven Cropper, *VP*
EMP: 5 **EST:** 2012
SALES (est): 404.62K **Privately Held**
Web: www.delmarvawatersolutions.com
SIC: 7389 Water softener service

(G-2280)
DEMC ACADEMIA INSTITUTE ✿
8 The Grn Ste 300 (19901-3618)
PHONE..................................301 215-1056
Antonio Perez, *Pr*
Joseph Rudolph, *Dir*
Luis Colmenares, *Dir*
EMP: 6 **EST:** 2022
SALES (est): 68.89K **Privately Held**
SIC: 7371 Computer software development

(G-2281)
DEMPSEY FARMS LLC
1708 Fast Landing Rd (19901-2718)
PHONE..................................302 734-4937
Alice Mae Jacobs, *Prin*
Charles Dempsey Junior, *Prin*
EMP: 5 **EST:** 2014
SALES (est): 242.34K **Privately Held**
Web: www.dempseyfarms.com
SIC: 0241 7389 Dairy farms; Business services, nec

(G-2282)
DENIM INC
8 The Green Ste #4172 (19901-3618)
PHONE..................................302 401-6502
Nikita Anufriev, *CEO*
Dmitry Gritsenko, *Sec*
EMP: 5 **EST:** 2019
SALES (est): 66.05K **Privately Held**
SIC: 7371 Computer software development and applications

(G-2283)
DENTISTRY AT WALKER SQUARE
882 Walker Rd Ste A (19904-2792)
PHONE..................................302 735-8940
Beth Sadlowski, *Owner*
EMP: 6 **EST:** 2011
SALES (est): 117.18K **Privately Held**
Web: www.walkersquaredental.com
SIC: 8021 Dentists' office

(G-2284)
DERBY SOFTWARE LLC (PA)
8 The Grn Ste A (19901-3618)
PHONE..................................502 435-1371
EMP: 10 **EST:** 2017
SALES (est): 71.56K
SALES (corp-wide): 71.56K **Privately Held**
SIC: 7372 7389 Prepackaged software; Business Activities at Non-Commercial Site

(G-2285)
DERMAL HEALTH SCIENCE LLC
19 Holly Cove Ln (19901-6285)
PHONE..................................302 213-8348
EMP: 6 **EST:** 2020
SALES (est): 362.89K **Privately Held**
SIC: 5122 Cosmetics

(G-2286)
DESEU
500 W Loockerman St Ste 400 (19904-7309)
PHONE..................................302 883-3048
Lisa Gardner, *Prin*
EMP: 8 **EST:** 2018
SALES (est): 76.79K **Privately Held**
Web: www.energizedelaware.org
SIC: 8699 Charitable organization

(G-2287)
DESIRES LINGERIE
4200 N Dupont Hwy (19901-2400)
PHONE..................................302 744-9969
Matt Sinabil, *Owner*
EMP: 5 **EST:** 2017
SALES (est): 68.75K **Privately Held**
SIC: 5137 Lingerie

(G-2288)
DEVON SADLOWSKI DMD
882 Walker Rd Ste A (19904-2792)
PHONE..................................302 735-8940
Devon Sadlowski D.m.d., *Owner*
EMP: 10 **EST:** 1996
SALES (est): 344.9K **Privately Held**
SIC: 8021 Dental surgeon

(G-2289)
DFS CORPORATE SERVICES LLC
34 Starlifter Ave (19901-9245)
PHONE..................................302 735-3902
Richard Palmer, *Mgr*
EMP: 77
SALES (corp-wide): 15.2B **Publicly Held**
Web: www.discoverglobalnetwork.com
SIC: 7389 6153 Credit card service; Short-term business credit institutions, except agricultural
HQ: Dfs Corporate Services Llc
  2500 Lake Cook Rd 2
  Riverwoods IL 60015
  224 405-0900

(G-2290)
DIAMOND ELECTRIC INC
3566 Peachtree Run Rd Ste 1 (19901-7661)
P.O. Box 996 (19903-0996)
PHONE..................................302 697-3296
Tom J Hartley, *Pr*
EMP: 36 **EST:** 1969
SQ FT: 7,500
SALES (est): 11.83MM **Privately Held**
Web: www.diamond-us.com
SIC: 1731 General electrical contractor

(G-2291)
DIAMOND MECHANICAL INC
3588 Peachtree Run Rd (19901-7647)
PHONE..................................302 697-7694
EMP: 20 **EST:** 2018
SALES (est): 1.16MM **Privately Held**
SIC: 8711 Mechanical engineering

(G-2292)
DIAMOND MOTOR SPORTS INC
Also Called: Price Honda
4595 S Dupont Hwy (19901-6034)
PHONE..................................302 697-3222
Warren A Price, *Pr*
Linda Topping, *
EMP: 100 **EST:** 1966
SQ FT: 16,000
SALES (est): 21.92MM **Privately Held**
Web: www.ridedms.com
SIC: 5511 5012 Automobiles, new and used; Automobiles and other motor vehicles

(G-2293)
DIAMOND STATE CLT INC
Also Called: DIAMOND STATE COMMUNITY LAND T
9 E Loockerman St Ste 205 (19901-7347)
P.O. Box 1484 (19903-1484)
PHONE..................................800 282-0477
Van Temple, *Ex Dir*
Amy Walls, *Pr*
EMP: 10 **EST:** 2009
SALES (est): 186.65K **Privately Held**
Web: www.diamondstateclt.org
SIC: 8748 Urban planning and consulting services

(G-2294)
DIAMOND STATE CORPORATION (PA)
Also Called: Berry Van Lines
602 Pear St (19904-2832)
PHONE..................................302 674-1300
W Leland Berry, *Pr*
EMP: 54 **EST:** 1981
SQ FT: 100,000
SALES (est): 12.34MM **Privately Held**
Web: www.berryvanlines.com
SIC: 4213 4214 Trucking, except local; Local trucking with storage

(G-2295)
DIGA FUNDING LLC
8 The Grn Ste B (19901-3618)
PHONE..................................404 631-7127
EMP: 5 **EST:** 2017
SQ FT: 1,200
SALES (est): 286.35K **Privately Held**
SIC: 8742 Management consulting services

(G-2296)
DIGIBOX LLC
8 The Grn Ste A (19901-3618)
PHONE..................................302 203-0088
EMP: 5 **EST:** 2020
SALES (est): 46.16K **Privately Held**
SIC: 7371 5999 Computer software development and applications; Electronic parts and equipment

Dover - Kent County (G-2297)   **GEOGRAPHIC SECTION**

(G-2297)
DIGITALPAYE INC
8 The Grn (19901-3618)
PHONE.................302 232-5116
Helie Guei, *Dir*
EMP: 10
SALES (est): 348.32K **Privately Held**
SIC: 7371 Computer software development and applications

(G-2298)
DIGNISYS INC
8 The Grn Ste R (19901-3618)
PHONE.................845 213-1121
Deepak Sharma, *Pr*
EMP: 12
SALES (est): 433.24K **Privately Held**
SIC: 5734 7389 Software, business and non-game; Business Activities at Non-Commercial Site

(G-2299)
DIPPOLD MARBLE GRANITE
101 Hatchery Rd (19901-1502)
PHONE.................302 734-8505
EMP: 7
SALES (corp-wide): 805.48K **Privately Held**
Web: www.dippoldmarble.com
SIC: 1799 Counter top installation
PA: Dippold Marble Granite
    110 W Main St
    Middletown DE 19709
    302 324-9101

(G-2300)
DIRECTRESTORE LLC
3500 S Dupont Hwy (19901-6041)
PHONE.................650 276-0384
EMP: 21 **EST:** 2008
SALES (est): 493.47K
SALES (corp-wide): 20.76MM **Privately Held**
SIC: 7372 Business oriented computer software
PA: Axcient, Inc.
    707 17th St Ste 3900
    Denver CO 80202
    800 352-0248

(G-2301)
DISCLO INC (PA)
Also Called: Fka Chronically Capable
8 The Grn Ste 8372 (19901-3618)
PHONE.................607 280-8949
Kai Keane, *CPO*
EMP: 6 **EST:** 2021
SALES (est): 264.9K
SALES (corp-wide): 264.9K **Privately Held**
SIC: 7371 7389 Computer software development and applications; Business Activities at Non-Commercial Site

(G-2302)
DISH QUO LLC (PA)
874 Walker Rd (19904-2778)
PHONE.................845 709-1674
Marcos Rojas, *Managing Member*
EMP: 8 **EST:** 2020
SALES (est): 71.56K
SALES (corp-wide): 71.56K **Privately Held**
Web: www.dishquo.com
SIC: 7371 Computer software development and applications

(G-2303)
DISRUPT INDUSTRIES DELEWARE
8 The Grn (19901-3618)
PHONE.................424 229-9300
Gary Elphick, *CEO*
EMP: 3 **EST:** 2017
SALES (est): 85.69K **Privately Held**
SIC: 3949 Sporting and athletic goods, nec

(G-2304)
DISRUPT PHARMA TECH AFRICA INC
Also Called: Disrupt Pharma Tech
8 The Grn Ste A (19901-3618)
PHONE.................312 945-8002
Vivian Nwakah, *Prin*
EMP: 7
SALES (est): 502.76K **Privately Held**
SIC: 5122 Drugs and drug proprietaries

(G-2305)
DITROCCHIO MARIA ANTONETTA
Also Called: Busy Bees Home Learning Center
814 S Governors Ave (19904-4107)
PHONE.................302 450-6790
Ree Ditrocchio, *Prin*
EMP: 5 **EST:** 2010
SALES (est): 85.34K **Privately Held**
SIC: 8351 Child day care services

(G-2306)
DIVERSE GENERATIONS LLC ✪
8 The Grn (19901-3618)
PHONE.................571 248-1806
Andrea Patterson, *CEO*
EMP: 6 **EST:** 2023
SALES (est): 246.7K **Privately Held**
SIC: 8732 Merger, acquisition, and reorganization research

(G-2307)
DIVERSION COMPANY INC
850 New Burton Rd (19904-5785)
PHONE.................415 800-4136
Alexander Medvedovsky, *CEO*
EMP: 8 **EST:** 2021
SALES (est): 306.16K **Privately Held**
SIC: 7371 Software programming applications

(G-2308)
DIVINE ELEMENT HBB
405 W Lebanon Rd (19901-6155)
PHONE.................302 538-5209
Tamara Vicere, *Prin*
EMP: 6 **EST:** 2015
SALES (est): 152.73K **Privately Held**
SIC: 2819 Elements

(G-2309)
DIVINITY ASSETS LLC
Also Called: Divinity Assets
8 The Grn Ste A (19901-3618)
PHONE.................323 508-4130
Christina Woodson, *CEO*
EMP: 6 **EST:** 2020
SALES (est): 71.79K **Privately Held**
SIC: 8742 Real estate consultant

(G-2310)
DIVINITY ASSETS LLC
8 The Grn Ste A (19901-3618)
PHONE.................323 508-4130
Christina Woodson, *Managing Member*
EMP: 60 **EST:** 2020
SALES (est): 1.16MM **Privately Held**
SIC: 8742 7389 Management consulting services; Business services, nec

(G-2311)
DIXON CONTRACTING INC
1614 Seeneytown Rd (19904-4437)
PHONE.................302 653-4623
Lee Dixon, *Pr*
EMP: 8 **EST:** 1999
SQ FT: 5,662
SALES (est): 877.25K **Privately Held**
SIC: 1794 Excavation and grading, building construction

(G-2312)
DIYO INC (PA) ✪
Also Called: Todo
8 The Grn Ste R (19901-3618)
PHONE.................647 354-8859
Niket Soni, *CEO*
EMP: 6 **EST:** 2022
SALES (est): 83.38K
SALES (corp-wide): 83.38K **Privately Held**
SIC: 2099 Food preparations, nec

(G-2313)
DMAI BOYD LLC
8 The Grn # 4000 (19901-3618)
PHONE.................302 330-8293
EMP: 5 **EST:** 2020
SALES (est): 49.23K **Privately Held**
SIC: 7389 Business services, nec

(G-2314)
DNR AUTO
2428 W Denneys Rd (19904-4707)
PHONE.................302 698-7829
EMP: 5 **EST:** 2015
SALES (est): 45.49K **Privately Held**
SIC: 7538 General automotive repair shops

(G-2315)
DNREC AIR WASTE MANAGEMENT
30 S American Ave (19901-7346)
PHONE.................302 739-9406
Wanda Hurley, *Mgr*
EMP: 9 **EST:** 2009
SALES (est): 536.79K **Privately Held**
Web: dnrec.alpha.delaware.gov
SIC: 8741 Management services

(G-2316)
DOC FOALS
1407 Woodmill Dr (19904-7709)
PHONE.................302 632-0424
Lauren Allen, *Prin*
EMP: 4 **EST:** 2017
SALES (est): 84.83K **Privately Held**
Web: www.docfoals.com
SIC: 3949 Sporting and athletic goods, nec

(G-2317)
DOCTORS PATHOLOGY SERVICES PA
1253 College Park Dr (19904-8713)
PHONE.................302 677-0000
Raman Fukumar, *Pr*
EMP: 32 **EST:** 1994
SQ FT: 10,000
SALES (est): 4.74MM **Privately Held**
Web: www.dpspa.com
SIC: 8011 Pathologist

(G-2318)
DOCUMENT ADVISOR INC
Also Called: Ivisa
8 The Grn (19901-3618)
PHONE.................786 206-0756
David Perez, *Pr*
Sergio Marino, *CEO*
EMP: 20 **EST:** 2014
SALES (est): 1.61MM **Privately Held**
Web: www.ivisa.com
SIC: 8231 7389 Documentation center; Business services, nec

(G-2319)
DOKAN INC
8 The Grn (19901-3618)
PHONE.................386 259-8587
Tarek Hasan, *Prin*
EMP: 2
SALES (est): 87.4K **Privately Held**
SIC: 7372 Prepackaged software

(G-2320)
DOMESTIC GEN USA RESOURCES LLC (PA)
8 The Grn Ste R (19901-3618)
PHONE.................312 730-2437
EMP: 7 **EST:** 2019
SALES (est): 947.82K
SALES (corp-wide): 947.82K **Privately Held**
SIC: 7389 Financial services

(G-2321)
DOMINION CARS LLC
624 W Division St (19904-2702)
PHONE.................302 730-3882
EMP: 5 **EST:** 2019
SALES (est): 23.7K **Privately Held**
SIC: 7699 Repair services, nec

(G-2322)
DONALD C SAVOY INC
Also Called: Health Insurance Associates
5158 S Dupont Hwy (19901-6411)
PHONE.................302 697-4100
Jay Moriello, *Brnch Mgr*
EMP: 10
SALES (corp-wide): 10.37MM **Privately Held**
Web: www.savoyassociates.com
SIC: 6411 Insurance brokers, nec
PA: Donald C. Savoy, Inc.
    25b Hanover Rd Ste 220
    Florham Park NJ
    973 377-2220

(G-2323)
DONOVAN CAPITAL GROUP LLC
8 The Grn Ste A (19901-3618)
PHONE.................202 642-4360
Claudio Ochoa, *Managing Member*
EMP: 5 **EST:** 2017
SALES (est): 432.14K **Privately Held**
SIC: 6282 Investment advisory service

(G-2324)
DOPAMINE WORLD INC (PA) ✪
Also Called: Dopamine
3500 S Dupont Hwy (19901-6041)
PHONE.................650 933-8003
Janice Nam, *Pr*
EMP: 8 **EST:** 2023
SALES (est): 312.73K
SALES (corp-wide): 312.73K **Privately Held**
SIC: 7373 Systems software development services

(G-2325)
DOPE VENTURE STUDIO INC ✪
8 The Grn (19901-3618)
PHONE.................302 257-5936
Johannes Le Roux, *Pr*
Andrew Davenport, *VP*
EMP: 3 **EST:** 2023
SALES (est): 135.7K **Privately Held**
SIC: 2086 Bottled and canned soft drinks

(G-2326)
DORI INC
160 Greentree Dr Ste 101 (19904-7620)
PHONE.................858 344-8699

2024 Harris Directory of Delaware Businesses

▲ = Import ▼ = Export
◆ = Import/Export

GEOGRAPHIC SECTION
Dover - Kent County (G-2353)

Nitin Gupta, *CEO*
EMP: 11 **EST:** 2018
SALES (est): 479.82K **Privately Held**
SIC: 7371 Software programming applications

(G-2327)
DOROSHOW PSQALE KRWITZ SGEL BH
Also Called: Law Offices Doroshow Pasquele
500 W Loockerman St Ste 120 (19904-7309)
PHONE..................................302 674-7100
Donald Grogery, *Mgr*
EMP: 11
SALES (corp-wide): 9.95MM **Privately Held**
Web: www.dplaw.com
SIC: 8111 General practice attorney, lawyer
PA: Doroshow Pasquale Krawitz Siegel Bhaya
1202 Kirkwood Hwy
Wilmington DE 19805
302 998-2397

(G-2328)
DOSELVA PBC
838 Walker Rd (19904-2751)
PHONE..................................510 299-7997
Jefferson Shriver, *Prin*
EMP: 40
SALES (est): 1.2MM **Privately Held**
SIC: 2099 Spices, including grinding

(G-2329)
DOT MATRIX INC (PA)
3500 S Dupont Hwy (19901-6041)
PHONE..................................917 657-4918
EMP: 5 **EST:** 2017
SALES (est): 483.54K
SALES (corp-wide): 483.54K **Privately Held**
SIC: 5961 7389 General merchandise, mail order; Business services, nec

(G-2330)
DOVER AFB
442 13th St (19902-6403)
PHONE..................................302 677-3989
EMP: 6
SALES (est): 550.19K **Privately Held**
Web: dover.af.mil
SIC: 1541 Industrial buildings and warehouses

(G-2331)
DOVER AFB
1069 High St (19901-7912)
PHONE..................................321 634-2016
EMP: 6 **EST:** 2019
SALES (est): 321.49K **Privately Held**
Web: www.doverfss.com
SIC: 6512 Nonresidential building operators

(G-2332)
DOVER AFB YOUTH CENTER
864 Center Rd (19901-5908)
PHONE..................................302 677-6376
Gary Winings, *Prin*
EMP: 17 **EST:** 2011
SALES (est): 208.01K **Privately Held**
Web: www.bgclubs.org
SIC: 8322 Youth center

(G-2333)
DOVER ANIMAL HOSPITAL
Also Called: Coon, Chris E Dvm
1151 S Governors Ave (19904-6998)
PHONE..................................302 746-2688
Bernard L Brown D.v.m., *Owner*

A G Howie D.v.m., *VP*
Kathy Study, *Sec*
EMP: 18 **EST:** 1974
SALES (est): 205.47K **Privately Held**
Web: www.vcahospitals.com
SIC: 0742 Animal hospital services, pets and other animal specialties

(G-2334)
DOVER BEHAVORL HLTH 249
725 Horsepond Rd (19901-7232)
PHONE..................................302 741-0140
William Weaver, *Mgr*
EMP: 30 **EST:** 2013
SALES (est): 653.54K **Privately Held**
SIC: 8099 Health and allied services, nec

(G-2335)
DOVER CHIROPRACTIC & REHABILIT
222 S Dupont Hwy Ste 203 (19901-3798)
PHONE..................................302 883-3251
EMP: 6 **EST:** 2017
SALES (est): 193.46K **Privately Held**
Web: www.doverchiropractors.com
SIC: 8041 Offices and clinics of chiropractors

(G-2336)
DOVER COMMONS LLC
Also Called: Dover Commons
1365 N Dupont Hwy Sp 5601 (19901-8710)
PHONE..................................302 678-4000
EMP: 14
Web: www.simon.com
SIC: 6512 Shopping center, property operation only
HQ: Dover Commons, Llc
1365 N Dupont Hwy # 5601
Dover DE 19901

(G-2337)
DOVER COMMUNITY PARTNERSHIP
76 Stevenson Dr (19901-4021)
PHONE..................................302 678-1965
EMP: 5
SALES (est): 36.37K **Privately Held**
SIC: 6531 Real estate agents and managers

(G-2338)
DOVER DOWNS INC
Also Called: Dover Downs Hotel & Casino
1131 N Dupont Hwy (19901-2008)
P.O. Box 843 (19903-0843)
PHONE..................................302 674-4600
Edward Sutor, *Pr*
Denis Mcglynn, *Ch Bd*
Janie Libby, *
Klaus M Belohoubek, *
EMP: 803 **EST:** 1967
SQ FT: 90,000
SALES (est): 107.35MM **Publicly Held**
Web: casinos.ballys.com
SIC: 7999 7011 Gambling machines, operation; Casino hotel
HQ: Premier Entertainment Iii, Llc
1131 N Dupont Hwy
Dover DE 19901
302 674-4600

(G-2339)
DOVER DOWNS GAMING MGT CORP
1131 N Dupont Hwy (19901-2008)
PHONE..................................302 730-3800
EMP: 19 **EST:** 2015
SALES (est): 230.93K **Privately Held**
Web: casinos.ballys.com
SIC: 7011 Casino hotel

(G-2340)
DOVER EDUCATIONAL & CMNTY CTR
744 River Rd (19901-3752)
PHONE..................................302 883-3092
Juliette Jones, *Dir*
EMP: 14 **EST:** 1969
SALES (est): 243.2K **Privately Held**
SIC: 8351 8322 Group day care center; Individual and family services

(G-2341)
DOVER ELECTRIC SUPPLY CO INC (PA)
1631 S Dupont Hwy (19901-5199)
PHONE..................................302 674-0115
Bernard Tudor, *Pr*
Scott Noll, *
Mary Alice Noll, *
EMP: 31 **EST:** 1948
SQ FT: 30,000
SALES (est): 16.07MM
SALES (corp-wide): 16.07MM **Privately Held**
Web: www.doverelectric.com
SIC: 5063 Electrical supplies, nec

(G-2342)
DOVER FAMILY CHIROPRACTIC
119 Stuart Dr (19901-5817)
PHONE..................................302 698-1515
EMP: 6 **EST:** 2013
SALES (est): 74.16K **Privately Held**
SIC: 8041 Offices and clinics of chiropractors

(G-2343)
DOVER FAMILY PHYSICIANS PA
Also Called: Bradley, Michael J Do
1342 S Governors Ave (19904-4804)
PHONE..................................302 734-2500
Jerome L Abrams Md, *Pr*
Michael J Bradley D.o.s., *Treas*
Joseph F Rubacky Iii D.o.s., *Sec*
EMP: 32 **EST:** 1983
SQ FT: 10,000
SALES (est): 2.3MM **Privately Held**
Web: www.doverfamilyphysicians.com
SIC: 8011 General and family practice, physician/surgeon

(G-2344)
DOVER FEDERAL CREDIT UNION (PA)
1075 Silver Lake Blvd (19904-2411)
P.O. Box 2009 (19902-2009)
PHONE..................................302 678-8000
Chaz Rzewnicki, *CEO*
EMP: 80 **EST:** 1958
SQ FT: 12,000
SALES (est): 32.64MM
SALES (corp-wide): 32.64MM **Privately Held**
Web: www.doverfcu.com
SIC: 6061 6062 Federal credit unions; State credit unions

(G-2345)
DOVER GARDEN SUITES
520 Martin Luther King Jr Blvd (19901-3796)
PHONE..................................302 883-2417
EMP: 9 **EST:** 2017
SALES (est): 42.59K **Privately Held**
Web: www.dovergardensuites.net
SIC: 7011 Motels

(G-2346)
DOVER GOLF CENTER
924 Artis Dr (19904-5639)
PHONE..................................302 674-8275

Rick Jones, *Pr*
EMP: 6 **EST:** 1990
SALES (est): 220.54K **Privately Held**
Web: www.doverpar3golf.com
SIC: 7992 Public golf courses

(G-2347)
DOVER HOSPITALITY GROUP LLC
Also Called: Fairfield Inn
655 N Dupont Hwy (19901-3936)
PHONE..................................302 677-0900
Dan Orledge, *Managing Member*
EMP: 33 **EST:** 2002
SALES (est): 874.01K **Privately Held**
Web: fairfield.marriott.com
SIC: 7011 Hotels and motels

(G-2348)
DOVER INTERFAITH MISSION WALTE
1155 Walker Rd (19904-6539)
PHONE..................................302 264-9021
EMP: 5 **EST:** 2014
SALES (est): 61.69K **Privately Held**
SIC: 8322 Social service center

(G-2349)
DOVER INTRFITH MSSION FOR HSIN
630 W Division St (19904-2760)
P.O. Box 1148 (19903-1148)
PHONE..................................302 736-3600
Jeanine Kleimo, *Ch Bd*
Herbert Konowitz, *V Ch Bd*
Dorothy Kashner, *Sec*
Katherine Lessard, *Treas*
EMP: 10 **EST:** 2008
SALES (est): 488.02K **Privately Held**
Web: www.doverinterfaithmission.org
SIC: 8322 Emergency shelters

(G-2350)
DOVER LEASING CO INC
613 Clara St (19904-3011)
P.O. Box 603 (19903-0603)
PHONE..................................302 674-2300
Richard Weyandt, *Pr*
Lynne Bergold, *Treas*
Pam Weyandt, *Sec*
EMP: 12 **EST:** 1955
SQ FT: 5,000
SALES (est): 311.38K **Privately Held**
SIC: 7513 4111 Truck leasing, without drivers ; Bus line operations

(G-2351)
DOVER LITHO PRINTING CO
21 Chadwick Dr (19901-5828)
PHONE..................................302 698-5292
Michael Frebert, *Pr*
EMP: 5 **EST:** 1957
SQ FT: 13,500
SALES (est): 153.91K **Privately Held**
SIC: 2752 Offset printing

(G-2352)
DOVER LUBRICANTS INC
Also Called: Jiffy Lube
236 S Dupont Hwy (19901-4733)
PHONE..................................302 674-8282
Edward Arnold, *Pr*
John Gosnell, *Treas*
Roland Bounds, *Sec*
EMP: 7 **EST:** 1985
SALES (est): 209.48K **Privately Held**
Web: www.jiffylube.com
SIC: 7549 Lubrication service, automotive

(G-2353)
DOVER MALL LLC
Also Called: Dover Security
1365 N Dupont Hwy Ste 5061 (19901-8710)

Dover - Kent County (G-2354)   GEOGRAPHIC SECTION

PHONE..................302 678-4000
Michele Dousette, *Off Mgr*
EMP: 12
Web: www.simon.com
SIC: 6512 Shopping center, property operation only
HQ: Dover Mall, Llc
225 W Washington St
Indianapolis IN 46204

(G-2354)
DOVER MALL LLC
Also Called: Dover Mall
1365 N Dupont Hwy (19901-8710)
PHONE..................302 678-4000
Gregory Eroe, *Brnch Mgr*
EMP: 21
Web: www.simon.com
SIC: 6512 Shopping center, property operation only
HQ: Dover Mall, Llc
225 W Washington St
Indianapolis IN 46204

(G-2355)
DOVER MOTORSPORTS INC (DH)
Also Called: Dover
1131 N Dupont Hwy (19901-2008)
P.O. Box 843 (19903-0843)
PHONE..................302 883-6500
Denis Mcglynn, *Pr*
Michael A Tatoian, *
Timothy R Horne, *
Klaus M Belohoubek, *
Thomas Wintermantel, *
EMP: 51 **EST:** 1969
SALES (est): 38.54MM
SALES (corp-wide): 523.83MM **Privately Held**
Web: www.dovermotorspeedway.com
SIC: 7948 Auto race track operation
HQ: Speedway Motorsports, Llc
5555 Concord Pkwy S
Concord NC 28027

(G-2356)
DOVER NUNAN LLC
Also Called: SERVPRO of Dover/Middletown
607 Otis Dr (19901-4644)
P.O. Box 485 (19903-0485)
PHONE..................302 697-9776
EMP: 9 **EST:** 1976
SQ FT: 2,500
SALES (est): 842.65K **Privately Held**
Web: www.servprodovermiddletown.com
SIC: 7349 Building maintenance services, nec

(G-2357)
DOVER OPHTHALMOLOGY ASC LLC
Also Called: Blue Hen Surgery Center The
655 S Bay Rd Ste 5b (19901-4660)
PHONE..................302 724-4720
Christopher A Holden, *Pr*
EMP: 18 **EST:** 2000
SALES (est): 2.85MM **Publicly Held**
SIC: 8011 Ambulatory surgical center
HQ: Envision Healthcare Corporation
1a Burton Hills Blvd
Nashville TN 37215
615 665-1283

(G-2358)
DOVER ORAL AND MAXILLOFACIAL S
1004 S State St Ste 1 (19901-6901)
PHONE..................302 674-1140
Franklin X Pancko, *Prin*
EMP: 13 **EST:** 2009
SALES (est): 239.78K **Privately Held**
SIC: 8021 Dental surgeon

(G-2359)
DOVER PAVING
1475 S Governors Ave (19904-7017)
PHONE..................302 274-0743
EMP: 6 **EST:** 2019
SALES (est): 108.95K **Privately Held**
Web: www.doverpaving.com
SIC: 1611 Highway and street paving contractor

(G-2360)
DOVER PLUMBING SUPPLY CO
3626 N Dupont Hwy (19901-1500)
P.O. Box 342 (19903-0342)
PHONE..................302 674-0333
Orlan T Kelley Junior, *Pr*
Herbert E Kelley, *Pr*
Megan Kelley, *Sec*
Orlan T Kelly Iii, *Treas*
EMP: 15 **EST:** 1946
SQ FT: 21,000
SALES (est): 4.53MM **Privately Held**
Web: www.doverplumbingsupplycodover.com
SIC: 5074 Plumbing fittings and supplies

(G-2361)
DOVER POOL & PATIO CENTER INC (PA)
1255 S State St Ste 1 (19901-6932)
PHONE..................302 346-7665
Randy D Anderson, *Pr*
Vonda Calhoun, *VP*
EMP: 12 **EST:** 1976
SQ FT: 12,000
SALES (est): 5.19MM
SALES (corp-wide): 5.19MM **Privately Held**
SIC: 1799 5999 Swimming pool construction ; Swimming pool chemicals, equipment, and supplies

(G-2362)
DOVER POST CO INC (PA)
Also Called: Smyrn-Clyton Sn-Tmes Mddltown
609 E Division St (19901-4201)
P.O. Box 664 (19903-0664)
PHONE..................302 653-2083
James A Flood Senior, *Ch*
James A Flood Junior, *Pr*
Fred Kaltreider, *
Mary Kaltreider, *
Donald G Flood, *
EMP: 100 **EST:** 1975
SQ FT: 18,000
SALES (est): 6.21MM
SALES (corp-wide): 6.21MM **Privately Held**
Web: www.delawareonline.com
SIC: 2711 2752 Newspapers, publishing and printing; Offset printing

(G-2363)
DOVER POST CO INC
Also Called: Middletown Transcript
1196 S Little Creek Rd # 101 (19901-4727)
PHONE..................302 378-9531
EMP: 6
SALES (corp-wide): 6.21MM **Privately Held**
Web: www.delawareonline.com
SIC: 2711 Newspapers, publishing and printing
PA: The Dover Post Co Inc
609 E Division St
Dover DE 19901
302 653-2083

(G-2364)
DOVER POST CO INC
Also Called: Dover Post Web Printing
1196 S Little Creek Rd (19901-4727)
PHONE..................302 678-3616
EMP: 34
SALES (corp-wide): 6.21MM **Privately Held**
Web: www.delawareonline.com
SIC: 7383 2791 2789 2752 Press service; Typesetting; Bookbinding and related work; Commercial printing, lithographic
PA: The Dover Post Co Inc
609 E Division St
Dover DE 19901
302 653-2083

(G-2365)
DOVER PULMONARY PA
31 Gooden Ave (19904-4143)
P.O. Box 1297 (19903-1297)
PHONE..................302 734-0400
Brian J Walsh D.o.s., *Pr*
Brian J Walsh, *Pt*
David Jawahar, *Pt*
EMP: 7 **EST:** 1991
SALES (est): 806.38K **Privately Held**
SIC: 8011 Pulmonary specialist, physician/ surgeon

(G-2366)
DOVER RENT-ALL INC
Also Called: Dover Rental
35 Commerce Way Ste 180 (19904-5747)
PHONE..................302 739-0860
George C Clapp Junior, *Pr*
David Clapp, *Sec*
EMP: 23 **EST:** 1973
SALES (est): 2.4MM **Privately Held**
Web: www.collectiveeventgroup.com
SIC: 6512 7359 Commercial and industrial building operation; Equipment rental and leasing, nec

(G-2367)
DOVER SYMPHONY ORCHESTRA INC
P.O. Box 163 (19903-0163)
PHONE..................302 734-1701
Robert Moyer, *Pr*
EMP: 9 **EST:** 2003
SALES (est): 217.97K **Privately Held**
Web: www.doversymphony.org
SIC: 7929 Symphony orchestra

(G-2368)
DOVER VOLKSWAGEN INC
1387 N Dupont Hwy (19901-8702)
PHONE..................302 734-4761
Arthur R Carlson Junior, *Pr*
EMP: 38 **EST:** 1962
SQ FT: 10,000
SALES (est): 1.9MM **Privately Held**
Web: www.winnervw.com
SIC: 5511 7538 Automobiles, new and used; General automotive repair shops

(G-2369)
DOVERS CHILDRENS VILLAG
726 Woodcrest Dr (19904-2439)
PHONE..................302 672-6476
Daisy Callaway, *Dir*
EMP: 19 **EST:** 2006
SALES (est): 496.85K **Privately Held**
SIC: 8351 Group day care center

(G-2370)
DOVERS CHILDRENS VILLAGE TOO
1298 Mckee Rd (19904-1381)
PHONE..................302 674-8142
Daisy Johnson, *Dir*
EMP: 6 **EST:** 2018
SALES (est): 96.69K **Privately Held**
SIC: 8699 Membership organizations, nec

(G-2371)
DR CHRISTOPHER BURNS
871 S Governors Ave Ste 1 (19904-4115)
PHONE..................302 674-8331
EMP: 7 **EST:** 1987
SALES (est): 258.42K **Privately Held**
SIC: 8021 Dentists' office

(G-2372)
DR DAWN GRANDISON DDS
429 S Governors Ave (19904-6707)
PHONE..................302 678-3384
EMP: 11 **EST:** 2018
SALES (est): 66.16K **Privately Held**
Web: www.smiletosmiledentistry.com
SIC: 8021 Dentists' office

(G-2373)
DR HIVEY CORP ◆
8 The Grn Ste 300 (19901-3618)
PHONE..................580 670-2046
Wael Alsmadi, *CEO*
EMP: 5 **EST:** 2022
SALES (est): 199.4K **Privately Held**
SIC: 7371 7389 Software programming applications; Business services, nec

(G-2374)
DR JOHN FONTANA III
910 Walker Rd Ste A (19904-2759)
PHONE..................302 734-1950
EMP: 10 **EST:** 2013
SALES (est): 209.03K **Privately Held**
SIC: 8021 Periodontist

(G-2375)
DR KELLYANN LLC
8 The Grn Ste A (19901-3618)
PHONE..................888 871-2155
Kellyann Petrucci, *Managing Member*
EMP: 200 **EST:** 2020
SALES (est): 5.84MM **Privately Held**
SIC: 8099 Blood related health services

(G-2376)
DR LAWERNCE LEWANDOWSKI
4601 S Dupont Hwy (19901-6405)
PHONE..................302 387-1516
EMP: 6 **EST:** 2016
SALES (est): 54.13K **Privately Held**
SIC: 8011 Neurologist

(G-2377)
DR MARISA E CONTI DO
725 S Queen St (19904-3568)
PHONE..................302 678-4488
Marisa E Conti, *Prin*
EMP: 20 **EST:** 2011
SALES (est): 1.12MM **Privately Held**
SIC: 8031 Offices and clinics of osteopathic physicians

(G-2378)
DR ROBERT WEBSTER
1522 S State St (19901-4950)
PHONE..................302 674-1080
Peter Schaeffer, *Prin*
EMP: 7 **EST:** 2007
SALES (est): 474.39K **Privately Held**
Web: www.webstercosmeticdentistry.com
SIC: 8021 Dentists' office

GEOGRAPHIC SECTION
Dover - Kent County (G-2408)

(G-2379)
DR SHARON M SIFFORD-WILSON MD
38 Chadwick Dr (19901-5827)
PHONE..................................302 698-3725
Sharon M Sifford, *Prin*
EMP: 9 **EST:** 2011
SALES (est): 74.23K **Privately Held**
SIC: 8011 Internal medicine, physician/surgeon

(G-2380)
DREAM FORGE LLC
8 The Grn Ste 4000 (19901-3618)
PHONE..................................802 342-4647
Jacques Lalancette, *Managing Member*
EMP: 5 **EST:** 2020
SALES (est): 105.06K **Privately Held**
SIC: 7371 Computer software development and applications

(G-2381)
DREAM WERKS LLC
100 Carlsons Way (19901-2365)
PHONE..................................302 526-2415
EMP: 6 **EST:** 2015
SALES (est): 318.63K **Privately Held**
SIC: 1521 Single-family housing construction

(G-2382)
DREAMS UNLIMITED LLC ✪
2 Riverside Rd (19904-5723)
PHONE..................................302 747-0527
Howard Gibson, *Managing Member*
EMP: 8 **EST:** 2022
SALES (est): 262.12K **Privately Held**
Web: www.dreamsunlimitedtravel.com
SIC: 1389 7389 Construction, repair, and dismantling services; Business services, nec

(G-2383)
DREAMSPELL LLC
8 The Grn Ste B (19901-3618)
PHONE..................................786 633-1520
Daniel Hernandez, *Managing Member*
EMP: 4
SALES (est): 260.53K **Privately Held**
SIC: 2833 7389 Medicinals and botanicals; Business Activities at Non-Commercial Site

(G-2384)
DREAMSTAGE INC
Also Called: Dreamstage
8 The Grn (19901-3618)
PHONE..................................901 286-5207
Thomas Hesse, *CEO*
Jan Vogler, *Dir*
EMP: 9 **EST:** 2020
SALES (est): 211.76K **Privately Held**
SIC: 7929 Entertainment service

(G-2385)
DREAMTOUCH GAMES LLC ✪
614 N Dupont Hwy Ste 210 (19901-3900)
PHONE..................................408 550-6042
Suchi Muppidi, *Dir*
Imtiaz Hussain, *Ex Dir*
EMP: 5 **EST:** 2023
SALES (est): 199.4K **Privately Held**
SIC: 7371 Computer software development and applications

(G-2386)
DROP FAKE INC
3500 S Dupont Hwy (19901-6041)
PHONE..................................707 563-1529
EMP: 6
SALES (est): 64.94K **Privately Held**

SIC: 7372 Prepackaged software

(G-2387)
DROWSY DIGITAL INC ✪
Also Called: Ozlo Sleepbuds
850 New Burton Rd Ste 201 (19904-5786)
PHONE..................................833 438-6956
N B Patil, *CEO*
Brian Mulcahey, *COO*
EMP: 7 **EST:** 2022
SALES (est): 881.97K **Privately Held**
SIC: 3845 Audiological equipment, electromedical

(G-2388)
DSS - INTEGRITY LLC
1679 S Dupont Hwy Ste 5 (19901-5101)
PHONE..................................302 677-0111
EMP: 10 **EST:** 2012
SQ FT: 1,200
SALES (est): 187.72K **Privately Held**
SIC: 7349 Janitorial service, contract basis

(G-2389)
DSS SERVICES INC
373 W North St Ste B (19904-6748)
PHONE..................................302 677-0111
Dwayne Holmes, *Pr*
Stanford Belfield, *VP*
EMP: 18 **EST:** 2008
SALES (est): 536.53K **Privately Held**
Web: www.dssservicesinc.com
SIC: 7349 Janitorial service, contract basis

(G-2390)
DSS URBAN JOINT VENTURE LLC
373 W North St Ste B (19904-6748)
PHONE..................................302 677-0111
Dwayne Holmes, *Pr*
Stephen Bryant, *Pr*
EMP: 6 **EST:** 2016
SALES (est): 150.08K **Privately Held**
SIC: 7349 Janitorial service, contract basis

(G-2391)
DSU STUDENT HOUSING LLC
430 College Rd (19904-2210)
PHONE..................................302 857-7966
Shekeetah Allan, *Mgr*
EMP: 5 **EST:** 2000
SALES (est): 210.4K **Privately Held**
Web: www.desu.edu
SIC: 7021 Lodging house, except organization

(G-2392)
DUFFIELD ASSOCIATES INC
Also Called: DUFFIELD ASSOCIATES, INC.
1060 S Governors Ave (19904-6920)
PHONE..................................302 747-7156
EMP: 71
SALES (corp-wide): 163.8MM **Privately Held**
Web: www.verdantas.com
SIC: 8711 Consulting engineer
HQ: Duffield Associates, Llc
5400 Limestone Rd
Wilmington DE 19808
302 239-6634

(G-2393)
DUGGAL MANVEEN MD
111 Wolf Creek Blvd Ste 3 (19901-4969)
PHONE..................................302 734-2782
Manveen Duggal, *Prin*
EMP: 8 **EST:** 2017
SALES (est): 218.63K **Privately Held**
SIC: 8011 Offices and clinics of medical doctors

(G-2394)
DUKKA INC
8 The Grn (19901-3618)
PHONE..................................401 659-6948
EMP: 6 **EST:** 2021
SALES (est): 106.88K **Privately Held**
Web: www.dukka.com
SIC: 7371 Computer software development

(G-2395)
DUNAMIS DOMINION LLC
100 Carlsons Way (19901-2365)
P.O. Box 298 (29456-0298)
PHONE..................................302 470-0468
Vanessa Johnson, *CEO*
Vanessa Brinkley, *Managing Member*
EMP: 5 **EST:** 2014
SQ FT: 1,200
SALES (est): 146.36K **Privately Held**
Web: www.dunamisdominionllc.com
SIC: 8322 Emergency shelters

(G-2396)
DVELE PARTNERS LLC
3500 S Dupont Hwy Ste L-101 (19901-6041)
PHONE..................................516 707-9357
Kurt Goodjohn, *Prin*
EMP: 5 **EST:** 2017
SALES (est): 48.49K **Privately Held**
Web: www.dvele.com
SIC: 1521 New construction, single-family houses

(G-2397)
DVFA FOUNDATION
122a S Bradford St (19904-7318)
PHONE..................................302 734-9390
EMP: 5
SALES (est): 32.66K **Privately Held**
Web: www.dvfassn.com
SIC: 8641 Civic and social associations

(G-2398)
E & M ENTERPRISES INC
Also Called: Dover Auto Repair
5102 N Dupont Hwy (19901-2338)
PHONE..................................302 736-6391
Edward Piecuski, *Pr*
EMP: 5 **EST:** 1985
SALES (est): 476.52K **Privately Held**
SIC: 7532 Body shop, automotive

(G-2399)
E N T ASSOCIATES
Also Called: Cooper, Stephen MD
826 S Governors Ave (19904-4107)
PHONE..................................302 674-3752
Stephen Cooper Md, *Pt*
EMP: 21 **EST:** 1985
SALES (est): 1.28MM **Privately Held**
Web: drstephencooper.yourmd.com
SIC: 8011 Eyes, ears, nose, and throat specialist: physician/surgeon

(G-2400)
E-LYTE TRANSPORTATION
8 The Grn (19901-3618)
PHONE..................................808 269-0283
Joel Deners, *Prin*
EMP: 5 **EST:** 2019
SALES (est): 260.96K **Privately Held**
SIC: 4789 Transportation services, nec

(G-2401)
EAGLE HOSPITALITY GROUP LLC
201 Stover Blvd (19901-4675)
P.O. Box 996 (19903-0996)
PHONE..................................302 678-8388
EMP: 9 **EST:** 2008

SALES (est): 442.64K **Privately Held**
SIC: 8741 Hotel or motel management

(G-2402)
EAGLE MEADOWS LLC
4666 Carolina Ave (19901-6321)
PHONE..................................302 698-1073
EMP: 6 **EST:** 2005
SALES (est): 82.73K **Privately Held**
Web: www.eaglemeadowsapts.com
SIC: 6513 Apartment building operators

(G-2403)
EAN HOLDINGS LLC
Also Called: Enterprise Rent-A-Car
580 S Bay Rd (19901-4603)
PHONE..................................302 674-5553
EMP: 8
SALES (corp-wide): 7.04B **Privately Held**
Web: www.enterpriseholdings.com
SIC: 7514 Passenger car rental
HQ: Ean Holdings, Llc
600 Corporate Park Dr
Saint Louis MO 63105

(G-2404)
EANCENTER TELECOM LLC
8 The Grn Ste R (19901-3618)
PHONE..................................302 450-4514
EMP: 5 **EST:** 2016
SALES (est): 89.53K **Privately Held**
SIC: 8748 Business consulting, nec

(G-2405)
EANEREP HOLDINGS LLC
445 Bank Ln Ste 148 (19904-9997)
PHONE..................................888 837-2685
EMP: 4 **EST:** 2020
SALES (est): 10K **Privately Held**
SIC: 2211 Apparel and outerwear fabrics, cotton

(G-2406)
EARLE TEATE MUSIC (PA)
3098 N Dupont Hwy (19901-8793)
PHONE..................................302 736-1937
Dale Teat, *CEO*
Dean Teat, *VP*
Nancy Teat, *Sec*
EMP: 6 **EST:** 1980
SQ FT: 10,000
SALES (est): 1.04MM
SALES (corp-wide): 1.04MM **Privately Held**
Web: www.earleteatmusic.com
SIC: 5736 7922 Organs; Theatrical producers and services

(G-2407)
EARLY CHILDHOOD LAB
1200 N Dupont Hwy (19901-2202)
PHONE..................................302 857-6731
Constance Williams, *Dir*
EMP: 8 **EST:** 1995
SALES (est): 252.37K **Privately Held**
SIC: 8351 Head Start center, except in conjunction with school

(G-2408)
EAST COAST AUTO BODY INC
216 South St (19904-3511)
P.O. Box 432 (19934-0432)
PHONE..................................302 265-6830
Mark Sammak, *Pr*
Norman Mullen, *VP*
EMP: 6 **EST:** 1991
SQ FT: 2,871
SALES (est): 578.1K **Privately Held**
Web: www.eastcoastautobodyinc.com

SIC: 7532 Body shop, automotive

(G-2409)
EAST COAST PAINTING LLC
64 River Chase Dr (19901-4472)
PHONE.................................302 678-9346
Robert Sale, *Prin*
EMP: 5 EST: 2017
SALES (est): 75.52K **Privately Held**
Web: www.stephanieengeln.com
SIC: 1721 Painting and paper hanging

(G-2410)
EAST PARK BRANDS LLC
8 The Grn (19901-3618)
PHONE.................................201 668-7089
Claudio Sanchez, *Managing Member*
EMP: 2
SALES (est): 92.41K **Privately Held**
SIC: 3999 Cigarette and cigar products and accessories

(G-2411)
EASTER SALS DEL MRYLNDS ESTRN
Also Called: Easter Seals
100 Enterprise Pl Ste 1 (19904-8202)
PHONE.................................302 678-3353
EMP: 55
SALES (corp-wide): 27.16MM **Privately Held**
Web: www.easterseals.com
SIC: 8331 8093 Job training and related services; Rehabilitation center, outpatient treatment
PA: Easter Seals Delaware & Marylands Eastern Shore, Inc.
61 Corporate Cir
New Castle DE 19720
302 324-4444

(G-2412)
EASTERN SHORE NATURAL GAS CO
909 Silver Lake Blvd (19904-2409)
PHONE.................................302 734-6716
John R Schimkaitis, *Ch*
Stephen C Thompson, *Pr*
Michael P Mcmasters, *Sr VP*
Paul M Barbas, *Ex VP*
Beth W Cooper, *VP*
EMP: 10 EST: 1955
SQ FT: 4,000
SALES (est): 76.91MM
SALES (corp-wide): 680.7MM **Publicly Held**
Web: www.esng.com
SIC: 4924 Natural gas distribution
PA: Chesapeake Utilities Corporation
500 Energy Ln
Dover DE 19901
302 734-6799

(G-2413)
EASTERN SHORE REAL ESTATE INC
909 Silver Lake Blvd (19904-2409)
PHONE.................................302 734-6799
Joe Steinmetz, *Contrlr*
EMP: 7 EST: 2006
SALES (est): 2.39MM
SALES (corp-wide): 680.7MM **Publicly Held**
SIC: 4924 Natural gas distribution
PA: Chesapeake Utilities Corporation
500 Energy Ln
Dover DE 19901
302 734-6799

(G-2414)
EASTERN SPECIALTY FINANCE INC
Also Called: Check 'n Go 2846
283 N Dupont Hwy Ste B (19901-7532)
PHONE.................................302 736-1348
Scott Davis, *Mgr*
EMP: 10
SALES (corp-wide): 696.24MM **Privately Held**
Web: locations.checkngo.com
SIC: 6141 Personal credit institutions
HQ: Eastern Specialty Finance, Inc.
7755 Montgomery Rd # 400
Cincinnati OH

(G-2415)
EASY TRADE LLC
838 Walker Rd Ste 21-2 (19904-2751)
PHONE.................................334 577-4530
EMP: 7 EST: 2021
SALES (est): 276.06K **Privately Held**
SIC: 8742 Marketing consulting services

(G-2416)
ECOM TECHNOLOGIES LLC
Also Called: Rondevu
8 The Grn Ste A (19901-3618)
PHONE.................................424 362-5155
Nikita Danilov, *Managing Member*
EMP: 12 EST: 2015
SALES (est): 593.25K **Privately Held**
SIC: 7371 Software programming applications

(G-2417)
ECOMO INC
160 Greentree Dr Ste 101 (19904-7620)
PHONE.................................412 567-3867
Zhiqiang Li, *CEO*
EMP: 6 EST: 2016
SALES (est): 402.38K **Privately Held**
Web: www.ecomo.io
SIC: 3571 3823 7389 Electronic computers; Water quality monitoring and control systems; Business services, nec

(G-2418)
ED HUNT INC (PA)
8 The Grn Ste 9487 (19901-3618)
PHONE.................................302 339-8443
Edward E Hunt, *Pr*
EMP: 5 EST: 2019
SALES (est): 50K
SALES (corp-wide): 50K **Privately Held**
SIC: 7032 4789 Sporting camps; Transportation services, nec

(G-2419)
EDEN CARE GROUP HOLDING LLC
8 The Grn (19901-3618)
PHONE.................................929 461-7247
Moses Mukundi, *Managing Member*
EMP: 5
SALES (est): 68.89K **Privately Held**
SIC: 7371 7389 Computer software development; Business services, nec

(G-2420)
EDEN HILL EXPRESS CARE LLC
200 Banning St Ste 170 (19904-3491)
PHONE.................................302 674-1999
Carolyn M Apple, *Dir*
EMP: 8 EST: 2006
SALES (est): 227.84K **Privately Held**
Web: www.edenhillmedicalcenter.com
SIC: 7363 Medical help service

(G-2421)
EDGERITE INC
8 The Grn Ste 8573 (19901-3618)
PHONE.................................302 404-6665
Ken Odiwe, *Prin*
EMP: 5 EST: 2017
SALES (est): 350K **Privately Held**

SIC: 8748 Business consulting, nec

(G-2422)
EDGEWELL PERSONAL CARE LLC
50 N Dupont Hwy (19901-4292)
PHONE.................................302 678-6000
Chris Kroll, *Brnch Mgr*
EMP: 41
SALES (corp-wide): 2.25B **Publicly Held**
Web: www.edgewell.com
SIC: 2676 Tampons, sanitary: made from purchased paper
HQ: Edgewell Personal Care, Llc
1350 Tmbrlake Mnor Pkwy S
Chesterfield MO 63017
314 594-1900

(G-2423)
EDGEWELL PERSONAL CARE COMPANY
185 Saulsbury Rd (19904-2719)
P.O. Box 7016 (19903-1516)
PHONE.................................302 678-6191
Taryn Dalmassi, *Dir*
EMP: 600
SALES (corp-wide): 2.25B **Publicly Held**
Web: www.edgewell.com
SIC: 2676 Panty liners: made from purchased paper
PA: Edgewell Personal Care Company
6 Research Dr Ste 400
Shelton CT 06484
203 944-5500

(G-2424)
EDGILITY INC
Also Called: Heather Ramadoss
108 Lakeland Ave (19901-5109)
PHONE.................................650 382-2346
Balaji Ramadoss, *CEO*
Elizabeth J Lindsay-wood, *Mgr*
EMP: 9 EST: 2013
SALES (est): 517.78K **Privately Held**
SIC: 7371 Custom computer programming services

(G-2425)
EDUQC LLC
3500 S Dupont Hwy (19901-6041)
PHONE.................................800 346-4646
EMP: 19 EST: 2017
SALES (est): 494.87K **Privately Held**
SIC: 7389 Business services, nec

(G-2426)
EDWARD L ALEXANDER MD FACS
724 S New St (19904-3540)
PHONE.................................302 674-4070
Edward L Alexander, *Prin*
EMP: 10 EST: 2011
SALES (est): 130.71K **Privately Held**
SIC: 8011 General and family practice, physician/surgeon

(G-2427)
EDWARDS PAUL CRPT INSTALLATION
Also Called: Paul Edwards Carpet Cleaning
547 Otis Dr (19901-4645)
PHONE.................................302 672-7847
Paul Edwards, *Owner*
EMP: 5 EST: 1977
SQ FT: 1,500
SALES (est): 329.24K **Privately Held**
Web: paul-edwards-complete-carpet.business.site
SIC: 5713 1752 7217 Carpets; Carpet laying ; Carpet and upholstery cleaning on customer premises

(G-2428)
EL LEGACY LLC
8 The Grn Ste B (19901-3618)
PHONE.................................601 790-0636
Crystal Lockett, *Managing Member*
EMP: 5 EST: 2020
SALES (est): 60.13K **Privately Held**
SIC: 8741 Management services

(G-2429)
ELATE PARTNERS LLC
8 The Grn (19901-3618)
PHONE.................................408 335-4582
EMP: 5 EST: 2011
SALES (est): 82.29K **Privately Held**
Web: www.elateinvest.com
SIC: 8742 Business management consultant

(G-2430)
ELDERWOOD VILLAGE DOVER LLC
21 N State St (19901-3802)
PHONE.................................516 496-1505
Lisa Havelow, *Dir*
EMP: 19 EST: 1999
SALES (est): 1.37MM **Privately Held**
SIC: 8361 Aged home

(G-2431)
ELEC INTEGRITY
6253 N Dupont Hwy (19901-2610)
PHONE.................................302 388-3430
EMP: 5 EST: 2013
SALES (est): 141.11K **Privately Held**
SIC: 4911 Electric services

(G-2432)
ELENORE INC ✪
8 The Grn Ste 16591 (19901-3618)
PHONE.................................720 702-9390
Kelly Jakel, *CEO*
Tiffany Ann Bottcher, *COO*
EMP: 2 EST: 2023
SALES (est): 87.4K **Privately Held**
SIC: 7372 7389 Prepackaged software; Business services, nec

(G-2433)
ELEVATE CDB INC
8 The Grn Ste B (19901-3618)
PHONE.................................844 903-4443
Brian Cosgray, *CEO*
EMP: 23 EST: 2020
SALES (est): 1.24MM **Privately Held**
Web: elevate.inc
SIC: 7371 7389 Computer software development and applications; Business services, nec

(G-2434)
ELITE DEVELOPERS GROUP LLC ✪
8 The Grn Ste 8651 (19901-3618)
PHONE.................................615 397-9732
Letijah Johnson, *Managing Member*
EMP: 7 EST: 2023
SALES (est): 84.63K **Privately Held**
SIC: 1521 1522 Single-family housing construction; Residential construction, nec

(G-2435)
ELIYAHNA CREATIVE LLC
8 The Grn (19901-3618)
PHONE.................................530 683-5463
Jesse Vankurin, *Managing Member*
EMP: 3 EST: 2021
SALES (est): 135.7K **Privately Held**
Web: www.eliyahna.com
SIC: 2741 Internet publishing and broadcasting

GEOGRAPHIC SECTION — Dover - Kent County (G-2465)

(G-2436)
ELIZABETH W MURPHEY SCHOOL INC
42 Kings Hwy (19901-3817)
PHONE..................................302 734-7478
EMP: 20 EST: 1922
SALES (est): 3.59MM Privately Held
Web: www.murpheyschool.org
SIC: 8361   Group foster home

(G-2437)
ELOMIA HEALTH INC ✪
8 The Grn (19901-3618)
PHONE..................................302 244-7193
Paras Pohrebniak, Dir
EMP: 8 EST: 2022
SALES (est): 306.16K Privately Held
SIC: 7371   Computer software development and applications

(G-2438)
EMERALD CITY WASH WORLD
730 W Division St (19904-2732)
PHONE..................................302 734-1230
Robin Holt, Pr
EMP: 8 EST: 1997
SALES (est): 294.18K Privately Held
Web: www.emeraldcitywashworld.com
SIC: 7215   Laundry, coin-operated

(G-2439)
EMERITUS CORPORATION
Also Called: Green Meadows At Latrobe
150 Saulsbury Rd (19904-2776)
PHONE..................................302 674-4407
Terry Reardon, Dir
EMP: 149
SALES (corp-wide): 2.83B Publicly Held
Web: www.brookdaleliving.com
SIC: 8051   Skilled nursing care facilities
HQ: Emeritus Corporation
    6737 W Wa St Ste 2300
    Milwaukee WI 53214

(G-2440)
EMIL W TETZNER D M D
804 S State St Ste 1 (19901-4123)
PHONE..................................302 744-9900
Emil Tetzner, Owner
EMP: 7 EST: 1994
SALES (est): 468.84K Privately Held
Web: www.doverperio.com
SIC: 8021   Periodontist

(G-2441)
EMLYN CONSTRUCTION CO
1341 Walnut Shade Rd (19901-7761)
PHONE..................................302 697-8247
Bob Joyner, Pr
EMP: 5 EST: 1977
SQ FT: 7,000
SALES (est): 513.78K Privately Held
SIC: 1791   Structural steel erection

(G-2442)
EMORY MASSAGE THERAPY
155 Willis Rd Apt G (19901-4030)
P.O. Box 422 (19903-0422)
PHONE..................................302 290-0003
Teresa Wilson, Prin
EMP: 7 EST: 2016
SALES (est): 97.78K Privately Held
SIC: 8093   Rehabilitation center, outpatient treatment

(G-2443)
EMPIRE AUTO PROTECT LLC ✪
8 The Grn Ste 11230 (19901-3618)
PHONE..................................888 345-0084
EMP: 5 EST: 2022
SALES (est): 62.38K Privately Held
Web: www.empireautoprotect.com
SIC: 7538   General automotive repair shops

(G-2444)
EMPIRICAL INC
3500 S Dupont Hwy Ste Ek-101 (19901-6041)
PHONE..................................347 828-4528
Lars Williams, CEO
EMP: 6 EST: 2021
SALES (est): 1.04MM Privately Held
SIC: 5182   Wine and distilled beverages

(G-2445)
EMPOWERING GROUP LLC
371 W North St (19904-6713)
PHONE..................................302 450-3065
EMP: 7 EST: 2019
SALES (est): 446.88K Privately Held
SIC: 8322   Individual and family services

(G-2446)
EMPOWERING REALTY LLC
838 Walker Rd Ste 22-1 (19904-2751)
PHONE..................................302 744-8169
Demartrice Kerneal, Managing Member
EMP: 8 EST: 2021
SALES (est): 648.9K Privately Held
SIC: 6531   Real estate brokers and agents

(G-2447)
EMZ PROPERTIES
1447 S Governors Ave (19904-7017)
PHONE..................................302 730-8250
Ennio Zaraeoza, Prin
EMP: 5 EST: 2011
SALES (est): 167.66K Privately Held
SIC: 6512   Nonresidential building operators

(G-2448)
ENDOCRINOLOGY CONSULTANT
111 Wolf Creek Blvd (19901-4969)
PHONE..................................302 734-2782
Judy L Reynolds, Prin
EMP: 7 EST: 2005
SALES (est): 505.75K Privately Held
SIC: 8748   Business consulting, nec

(G-2449)
ENERGY CENTER DOVER LLC
1280 W North St (19904-7756)
PHONE..................................302 678-4666
EMP: 18 EST: 2000
SALES (est): 9.41MM
SALES (corp-wide): 11.19B Publicly Held
SIC: 4911   Generation, electric power
PA: Clearway Energy, Inc.
    300 Carnegie Ctr Ste 300 # 300
    Princeton NJ 08540
    609 608-1525

(G-2450)
ENTE TECHNOLOGIES INC ✪
1111b S Governors Ave Ste 6032 (19904-6903)
PHONE..................................917 924-8450
Vishnu Mohandas, Pr
EMP: 5 EST: 2022
SALES (est): 199.4K Privately Held
Web: www.ente.io
SIC: 7371   Computer software development and applications

(G-2451)
ENVIRONMENTAL PROTECTION AGCY
Also Called: EPA
89 Kings Hwy (19901-7305)
PHONE..................................302 739-9917
John Hues, Dir
EMP: 24
Web: www.epa.gov
SIC: 8731   Environmental research
HQ: Environmental Protection Agency
    1200 Pennsylvania Ave Nw
    Washington DC 20460
    202 564-4700

(G-2452)
ENYUMBA INC
8 The Grn (19901-3618)
PHONE..................................818 272-9383
Paul Kirung, CEO
EMP: 6
SALES (est): 237.56K Privately Held
SIC: 7371   Computer software development and applications

(G-2453)
EOM HEALTHCARE GROUP LLC
555 E Loockerman St Ste 120 (19901-3779)
PHONE..................................917 750-5089
Jacob Jeidel, Managing Member
EMP: 50
SALES (est): 1.21MM Privately Held
SIC: 8741   Nursing and personal care facility management

(G-2454)
EPATRIOTCRM LLC ✪
8 The Grn Ste A (19901-3618)
PHONE..................................419 967-6812
Krunal Pipwala, Managing Member
EMP: 5 EST: 2022
SALES (est): 203.68K Privately Held
SIC: 7379 7389   Computer related consulting services; Business Activities at Non-Commercial Site

(G-2455)
EPHRAIM A AYOOLA M D
4164 N Dupont Hwy (19901-1573)
PHONE..................................302 741-0204
Ephraim Ayoola, Prin
EMP: 9 EST: 2017
SALES (est): 54.13K Privately Held
SIC: 8011   Offices and clinics of medical doctors

(G-2456)
EPIC CHARGING INC
8 The Grn (19901-3618)
PHONE..................................650 250-6811
Ilya Marin, CEO
EMP: 11
SALES (est): 784.04K Privately Held
SIC: 3694   Battery charging generators, automobile and aircraft

(G-2457)
EPISODE INTERACTIVE LLC
3500 S Dupont Hwy (19901-6041)
PHONE..................................858 220-0946
EMP: 7 EST: 2013
SALES (est): 84.19K Privately Held
SIC: 7371   Computer software development and applications

(G-2458)
EQUIDENTAL
21 Wilder Rd (19904-6064)
PHONE..................................302 423-0851
EMP: 9 EST: 2015
SALES (est): 77.64K Privately Held
SIC: 8021   Offices and clinics of dentists

(G-2459)
ERA HARRINGTON REALTY
516 Jefferic Blvd Ste C (19901-2023)
PHONE..................................302 363-1796
Linda Brannock, Brnch Mgr
EMP: 9
SALES (corp-wide): 2.15MM Privately Held
SIC: 6531   Real estate agent, residential
PA: Era Harrington Realty
    1404 Forrest Ave Ste A
    Dover DE 19904
    302 674-4663

(G-2460)
ERA HARRINGTON REALTY (PA)
Also Called: Prudential Emerson and Company
1404 Forrest Ave Ste A (19904-3478)
PHONE..................................302 674-4663
Ralph Pennell Emerson, Pr
EMP: 28 EST: 1974
SQ FT: 2,000
SALES (est): 2.15MM
SALES (corp-wide): 2.15MM Privately Held
SIC: 6531   Real estate agent, residential

(G-2461)
ERANGA CARDIOLOGY PA
200 Banning St Ste 310 (19904-3488)
PHONE..................................302 747-7486
Eranga Haththotuwa, Prin
EMP: 12 EST: 2013
SALES (est): 1.03MM Privately Held
Web: www.erangacardiology.com
SIC: 8011   Cardiologist and cardio-vascular specialist

(G-2462)
ERMAK METALS INC (HQ)
Also Called: Ermak Foundry & Machining
1111 S Governors Ave (19904-6903)
PHONE..................................952 448-2801
Reginald L Zeller, CEO
EMP: 3 EST: 2016
SALES (est): 4.47MM
SALES (corp-wide): 5.54MM Privately Held
Web: www.ermak.com
SIC: 3559   Foundry, smelting, refining, and similar machinery
PA: Canekast Inc.
    1111 S Governors Ave
    Dover DE 19904
    952 448-2801

(G-2463)
ESSENTIAL LUXURIES SPA
255 Webbs Ln Apt B21 (19904-5485)
PHONE..................................302 244-6875
Orline Houston, Prin
EMP: 5 EST: 2018
SALES (est): 29.54K Privately Held
SIC: 7991   Spas

(G-2464)
ESTAREI LLC ✪
838 Walker Rd Ste 1-2 (19904-2751)
PHONE..................................508 494-7260
EMP: 10 EST: 2023
SALES (est): 365.44K Privately Held
SIC: 7372   Business oriented computer software

(G-2465)
ETERNAL WORD TELEVISION INC
173 Continental Dr (19904-2654)
PHONE..................................302 734-8434
Chris Wegemer, Admn

Dover - Kent County (G-2466)

EMP: 6 EST: 2009
SALES (est): 71.67K **Privately Held**
Web: www.ewtn.com
SIC: 4833 Television broadcasting stations

(G-2466)
EVAN W SMITH FUNERAL HOME
518 S Bay Rd (19901-4603)
PHONE.....................302 526-4662
Evan W Smith, *Prin*
EMP: 9 EST: 2016
SALES (est): 210.66K **Privately Held**
Web:
www.evanwsmithfuneralservices.com
SIC: 7261 Funeral home

(G-2467)
EVANDER GREY GROUP LLC
8 The Grn Ste 15251 (19901-3618)
PHONE.....................302 595-1402
Ravien Alexander, *Managing Member*
EMP: 5
SALES (est): 268.9K **Privately Held**
SIC: 8742 Management consulting services

(G-2468)
EVOCATI GROUP CORPORATION
9 E Loockerman St Ste 3a (19901-7316)
PHONE.....................206 551-9087
Alejandro Thornton, *CEO*
EMP: 10 EST: 2015
SALES (est): 500K **Privately Held**
SIC: 8711 7379 Engineering services; Online services technology consultants

(G-2469)
EVOLUTION CLOUD SERVICES INC
8 The Grn Ste 8371 (19901-3618)
PHONE.....................516 507-4026
Arvind Sharma, *CEO*
EMP: 7
SALES (est): 276.06K **Privately Held**
SIC: 8742 7389 Human resource consulting services; Business services, nec

(G-2470)
EWGCS INC
8 The Grn Ste 4755 (19901-3618)
PHONE.....................415 935-5884
EMP: 13 EST: 2018
SALES (est): 255.52K **Privately Held**
Web: www.ewgcs.com
SIC: 7379 Computer related consulting services

(G-2471)
EXCELLA STAFFING SOLUTIONS LLC
8 The Grn Ste A (19901-3618)
P.O. Box 911 (19709-0911)
PHONE.....................302 985-7373
Tammy Zeller, *Managing Member*
EMP: 38 EST: 2018
SALES (est): 2.43MM **Privately Held**
Web: www.goexcella.com
SIC: 7361 7389 Employment agencies; Business Activities at Non-Commercial Site

(G-2472)
EXP REALTY
150 Seacroft Dr (19904-3840)
PHONE.....................302 382-5039
Abby Drobinski, *Prin*
EMP: 22 EST: 2017
SALES (est): 548.22K **Privately Held**
Web: www.exprealty.com
SIC: 6531 Real estate brokers and agents

(G-2473)
EXPONENTIA GLOBAL LLC
8 The Grn Ste 8309 (19901-3618)
PHONE.....................302 330-7967
EMP: 25 EST: 2019
SALES (est): 864.65K **Privately Held**
Web: www.exponentiaglobal.com
SIC: 8748 Telecommunications consultant

(G-2474)
EYE SPECIALISTS OF DELAWARE
200 Banning St Ste 130 (19904-3486)
PHONE.....................302 450-3028
Janet Sturts, *Prin*
EMP: 11 EST: 2021
SALES (est): 1.38MM **Privately Held**
Web: www.eyesde.com
SIC: 8011 Opthalmologist

(G-2475)
EZ INVESTMENT GROUP LLC
8 The Grn Ste A (19901-3618)
PHONE.....................917 215-9887
EMP: 5 EST: 2020
SALES (est): 212.6K **Privately Held**
SIC: 6798 Real estate investment trusts

(G-2476)
EZRA CONSULTING LLC ◆
8 The Grn Ste A (19901-3618)
PHONE.....................912 695-5925
Onur Kilic, *Managing Member*
EMP: 10 EST: 2023
SALES (est): 360.94K **Privately Held**
SIC: 7379 7389 Online services technology consultants; Business services, nec

(G-2477)
F & F PNTG FAITH & FORTUNE LLC
219 N Queen St (19904-3151)
PHONE.....................302 344-2512
Frank Cuffee, *Prin*
EMP: 5 EST: 2017
SALES (est): 59.29K **Privately Held**
SIC: 1721 Painting and paper hanging

(G-2478)
F H EVERETT & ASSOCIATES INC
Also Called: Life Reach / Eap Systems
1151 Walker Rd Ste 100 (19904-6600)
PHONE.....................302 674-2380
Frank H Everett, *Pr*
EMP: 8 EST: 1994
SALES (est): 289.62K **Privately Held**
SIC: 8322 8011 General counseling services ; Psychiatrist

(G-2479)
FAIR MORTGAGE CO
8 The Grn (19901-3618)
PHONE.....................202 904-4843
EMP: 7
SALES (est): 318.41K **Privately Held**
SIC: 6162 Mortgage companies, urban

(G-2480)
FAITHFUL SERVANT INC ◆
8 The Grn Ste 16161 (19901-3618)
PHONE.....................302 597-6387
Shayanda Jasper, *CEO*
EMP: 4 EST: 2023
SALES (est): 182.59K **Privately Held**
Web: www.faithful-servants.com
SIC: 5961 2389 General merchandise, mail order; Apparel and accessories, nec

(G-2481)
FAMILY DENTAL ASSOCIATES INC
385 Saulsbury Rd (19904-2722)
PHONE.....................302 674-8810
Chris A Nacrelli, *Pr*
EMP: 13 EST: 1976
SALES (est): 484.02K **Privately Held**
Web: www.familydentaldover.com
SIC: 8021 Dentists' office

(G-2482)
FAMILY FIRST FUNERAL SVCS LLC
614 S Dupont Hwy (19901-4518)
PHONE.....................800 377-6949
EMP: 6
SALES (corp-wide): 58.7K **Privately Held**
Web:
www.familyfirstfuneralservices.com
SIC: 7261 Funeral home
PA: Family First Funeral Services Llc
212 E Justis St
Newport DE 19804
800 377-6949

(G-2483)
FAMILY FREIGHT LLC
8 The Grn Ste 1 (19901-3618)
PHONE.....................302 212-0708
EMP: 6
SALES (est): 76.63K **Privately Held**
SIC: 4213 Trucking, except local

(G-2484)
FAMILY HEALTH DELAWARE INC
640 S Queen St (19904-3565)
PHONE.....................302 734-2444
EMP: 7 EST: 1995
SALES (est): 663.54K **Privately Held**
Web: www.familyhealthofdelaware.com
SIC: 8011 General and family practice, physician/surgeon

(G-2485)
FAMILY MEDICAL CENTRE PA
111 Wolf Creek Blvd Ste 2 (19901-4969)
PHONE.....................302 678-0510
Jose Austria Md, *Prin*
EMP: 13 EST: 2010
SALES (est): 835.04K **Privately Held**
Web: www.familymedicalcentrepa.com
SIC: 8011 Medical centers

(G-2486)
FARMERS HARVEST INC
Also Called: Sweet Potato Equipments
2826 Seven Hickories Rd (19904-1687)
PHONE.....................302 734-7708
▲ EMP: 2 EST: 1997
SALES (est): 493.44K **Privately Held**
Web: www.farmersharvestinc.com
SIC: 3523 5999 Farm machinery and equipment; Farm equipment and supplies

(G-2487)
FAST INTRCNNECT TCHOLOGIES INC
73 Greentree Dr Ste 30 (19904-7646)
PHONE.....................302 465-5344
R Balasubramanian, *Prin*
EMP: 5 EST: 2004
SALES (est): 171.66K **Privately Held**
SIC: 8732 Business research service

(G-2488)
FAVORED CHILDCARE ACADEMY INC
2319 S Dupont Hwy (19901-5514)
PHONE.....................302 698-1266
Vincent Ikwuagwu, *Pr*
EMP: 8 EST: 2013
SALES (est): 31.13K **Privately Held**
Web: www.favoredacademy.com
SIC: 8299 8351 Airline training; Group day care center

(G-2489)
FAW CASSON & CO LLP
Also Called: Faw Casson & Co
160 Greentree Dr Ste 203 (19904-7620)
PHONE.....................302 674-4305
Lisa Hastings, *Mng Pt*
James Arthur, *Pt*
Alison Houck, *Pt*
Lauren Harper, *Pt*
Tammy Ordway, *Pt*
EMP: 36 EST: 1944
SALES (est): 5.36MM **Privately Held**
Web: www.fawcasson.com
SIC: 8721 Accounting services, except auditing

(G-2490)
FEARS PROMOTIONS LLC
32 W Loockerman St Ste 109 (19904-7352)
PHONE.....................302 437-6364
EMP: 6
SALES (est): 119.28K **Privately Held**
Web: www.fearspromotions.com
SIC: 7941 7922 Boxing and wrestling arena; Entertainment promotion

(G-2491)
FEDERAL TECHNICAL ASSOCIATES
50 Westview Ave (19901-6229)
PHONE.....................302 697-7951
Frank Minnick, *Owner*
EMP: 5 EST: 1997
SALES (est): 153.07K **Privately Held**
SIC: 7389 Pipeline and power line inspection service

(G-2492)
FERGUSON ENTERPRISES LLC
10 Maggies Way (19901-4887)
PHONE.....................302 747-2032
EMP: 7
SALES (corp-wide): 2.67MM **Privately Held**
Web: www.ferguson.com
SIC: 5074 3432 Plumbing fittings and supplies; Plumbing fixture fittings and trim
HQ: Ferguson Enterprises, Llc
751 Lakefront Cmns
Newport News VA 23606
757 969-4011

(G-2493)
FF GROUP LLC
8 The Grn (19901-3618)
PHONE.....................302 608-0609
Levon Grigoryan, *Managing Member*
EMP: 10
SALES (est): 348.32K **Privately Held**
SIC: 7389 4731 Business Activities at Non-Commercial Site; Freight transportation arrangement

(G-2494)
FILTH-FIGHTERS CLG SVCS LLC
4514a New Jersey Dr (19901-6369)
PHONE.....................302 423-4684
Sandra Murphy, *Prin*
EMP: 5 EST: 2016
SALES (est): 46.89K **Privately Held**
SIC: 7699 Cleaning services

(G-2495)
FINAL TOUCH CLEANING
2682 Seven Hickories Rd (19904-1638)
PHONE.....................302 730-1495
Martha Miller, *Prin*
EMP: 5 EST: 2015
SALES (est): 64.76K **Privately Held**
SIC: 7699 Cleaning services

GEOGRAPHIC SECTION
Dover - Kent County (G-2527)

(G-2496)
FINDERS ENTERTAINMENT LLC
8 The Grn Ste A (19901-3618)
PHONE.................................407 765-1826
EMP: 5 **EST:** 2021
SALES (est): 68.89K **Privately Held**
SIC: 7371 Computer software development and applications

(G-2497)
FIRESIDE PARTNERS INC
60 Starlifter Ave (19901-9220)
P.O. Box 213 (19903-0213)
PHONE.................................302 613-2165
Don Chupp, *CEO*
Donald Chupp, *Pr*
EMP: 9 **EST:** 2016
SALES (est): 976.79K **Privately Held**
Web: www.firesideteam.com
SIC: 8748 Safety training service

(G-2498)
FIRST COMMAND BRKG SVCS INC
4608 S Dupont Hwy Ste 1 (19901-6408)
PHONE.................................302 535-8132
Cliff Weddington, *Brnch Mgr*
EMP: 6
SALES (corp-wide): 469.75MM **Privately Held**
Web: www.firstcommand.com
SIC: 6282 Investment advice
HQ: First Command Brokerage Services, Inc.
  1 Firstcomm Plz
  Fort Worth TX 76109
  817 731-8621

(G-2499)
FIRST STATE CMNTY ACTION AGCY
655 S Bay Rd Ste 4j (19901-4656)
PHONE.................................302 674-1355
Bernice Edwards, *Brnch Mgr*
EMP: 29
SALES (corp-wide): 9.7MM **Privately Held**
Web: www.firststatecaa.org
SIC: 8322 Social service center
PA: First State Community Action Agency Inc
  308 N Railroad Ave
  Georgetown DE 19947
  302 856-7761

(G-2500)
FIRST STATE COIN CO
53 Greentree Dr (19904-2685)
PHONE.................................302 734-7776
Ray Gesualdo, *Pr*
Kathleen Gesualdo, *Sec*
EMP: 5 **EST:** 1972
SALES (est): 556.17K **Privately Held**
Web: www.firststatecoins.com
SIC: 5094 5999 5944 Precious metals; Coins ; Jewelry, precious stones and precious metals

(G-2501)
FIRST STATE CPAS LLC
18 S State St (19901-7312)
PHONE.................................302 736-6657
Kathy Sarchett, *Managing Member*
EMP: 6 **EST:** 2010
SALES (est): 425.57K **Privately Held**
Web: www.firststatecpas.com
SIC: 8721 Certified public accountant

(G-2502)
FIRST STATE DME LLC
4115 N Dupont Hwy (19901-1561)
PHONE.................................302 394-0301
EMP: 7 **EST:** 2021
SALES (est): 358.3K **Privately Held**
Web: www.firststatedme.com
SIC: 5047 Medical equipment and supplies

(G-2503)
FIRST STATE FEDERAL CREDIT UN
58 Carver Rd (19904-2716)
PHONE.................................302 674-5281
Bea Conrad, *Pr*
EMP: 10 **EST:** 1972
SQ FT: 1,500
SALES (est): 925.26K **Privately Held**
Web: www.firststatefcu.org
SIC: 6061 Federal credit unions

(G-2504)
FIRST STATE GASTROENTEROLOGY A
644 S Queen St Ste 106 (19904-3543)
PHONE.................................302 677-1617
EMP: 13 **EST:** 2015
SALES (est): 1.13MM **Privately Held**
Web: www.delawaregi.org
SIC: 8011 Gastronomist

(G-2505)
FIRST STATE HOSPITALITY LLC
88 Wildswood Rd (19901-5764)
PHONE.................................302 538-5858
Marybel Johnson, *Prin*
EMP: 15 **EST:** 2014
SALES (est): 169.32K **Privately Held**
SIC: 7011 Hotels and motels

(G-2506)
FIRST STATE INFCTIOUS DISEASES
200 Banning St Ste 230 (19904-3487)
PHONE.................................302 535-4608
Ramesh Vemulapalli, *Prin*
EMP: 10 **EST:** 2018
SALES (est): 477.23K **Privately Held**
SIC: 8011 Offices and clinics of medical doctors

(G-2507)
FIRST STATE MNFCTRED HSING INS
1675 S State St Ste E (19901-5140)
PHONE.................................302 674-5868
EMP: 10 **EST:** 2010
SALES (est): 130.61K **Privately Held**
Web: www.firststatemha.org
SIC: 8611 Trade associations

(G-2508)
FIRST STATE ORAL MXLLFCIAL SRG
1004 S State St Ste 1 (19901-6901)
PHONE.................................302 674-4450
Wanda Connors, *Mgr*
Douglas Ditty D.m.d. Md, *Pr*
EMP: 5 **EST:** 2007
SALES (est): 944.75K **Privately Held**
Web: www.firststateoms.com
SIC: 8021 Dental surgeon

(G-2509)
FIRST STATE PODIATRY LLC
1177 S Governors Ave (19904-6903)
PHONE.................................302 678-4612
EMP: 5 **EST:** 2020
SALES (est): 201.39K **Privately Held**
SIC: 8043 Offices and clinics of podiatrists

(G-2510)
FIRST STATE SIGNS INC
2015 S Dupont Hwy (19901-5508)
PHONE.................................302 744-9990
Dale Mccalister, *Pr*
EMP: 13 **EST:** 2002
SALES (est): 461.2K **Privately Held**
Web: www.firststatesigns.com
SIC: 3993 Electric signs

(G-2511)
FIST FIT
17 Manor Dr (19901-5142)
PHONE.................................302 399-7095
EMP: 6 **EST:** 2016
SALES (est): 29.54K **Privately Held**
SIC: 7991 Physical fitness facilities

(G-2512)
FIZUL H BACCHUS
863 Buttner Pl (19904-2406)
PHONE.................................302 734-3331
Fizul H Bacchus, *Owner*
EMP: 9 **EST:** 2015
SALES (est): 197.74K **Privately Held**
SIC: 8011 Psychiatric clinic

(G-2513)
FIZZ MEDIA CORPORATION
160 Greentree Dr Ste 101 (19904-7620)
PHONE.................................630 730-7200
EMP: 8 **EST:** 2018
SALES (est): 126.96K **Privately Held**
SIC: 4899 Communication services, nec

(G-2514)
FLAWLESS INBOUND LLC
8 The Grn Ste A (19901-3618)
PHONE.................................929 324-1132
EMP: 12 **EST:** 2019
SALES (est): 647.15K **Privately Held**
Web: www.flawlessinbound.ca
SIC: 2051 Bakery: wholesale or wholesale/ retail combined

(G-2515)
FLEX FANTASY INC ✪
874 Walker Rd Ste C (19904-2778)
PHONE.................................201 417-7692
Joel Cettina, *CEO*
EMP: 5 **EST:** 2022
SALES (est): 104.08K **Privately Held**
SIC: 7999 Amusement and recreation, nec

(G-2516)
FLIP APP LLC (PA)
8 The Grn Ste R (19901-3618)
PHONE.................................248 662-6875
EMP: 8 **EST:** 2021
SALES (est): 214.78K
SALES (corp-wide): 214.78K **Privately Held**
SIC: 7371 Computer software development and applications

(G-2517)
FLIPRIDE INC
1221 College Park Dr # 116 (19904-8726)
PHONE.................................208 471-0007
EMP: 6 **EST:** 2019
SALES (est): 98.54K **Privately Held**
Web: www.flipride.com
SIC: 7371 Computer software development and applications

(G-2518)
FLORIDA PUB UTL CO
909 Silver Lake Blvd (19904-2409)
PHONE.................................561 838-1813
EMP: 9 **EST:** 2019
SALES (est): 271.2K **Privately Held**
SIC: 8611 Public utility association

(G-2519)
FLOU HOLDING INC
8 The Grn (19901-3618)
PHONE.................................832 267-3372
Alejandro Lara Jimenez, *Managing Member*

EMP: 5 **EST:** 2019
SALES (est): 130K **Privately Held**
SIC: 4789 Pipeline terminal facilities, independently operated

(G-2520)
FLUTTERBY STITCHES & EMB
203 Doveview Dr Unit 403 (19904-3699)
PHONE.................................302 531-7784
Paulette Leggs, *Prin*
EMP: 4 **EST:** 2015
SALES (est): 52.26K **Privately Held**
SIC: 2395 Embroidery and art needlework

(G-2521)
FLUTTERING BUTTERFLY LLC ✪
8 The Grn Ste 4000 (19901-3618)
PHONE.................................267 974-7812
EMP: 5 **EST:** 2022
SALES (est): 68.89K **Privately Held**
SIC: 8748 Business consulting, nec

(G-2522)
FOLDERLY INC
8 The Grn Ste 10781 (19901-3618)
PHONE.................................302 966-9083
EMP: 12 **EST:** 2020
SALES (est): 46.16K **Privately Held**
Web: www.folderly.com
SIC: 7371 Computer software development and applications

(G-2523)
FONBNK INC
8 The Grn (19901-3618)
PHONE.................................703 585-3288
Christian Duffus, *CEO*
Christian Duffus, *Managing Member*
EMP: 10 **EST:** 2019
SALES (est): 314.57K **Privately Held**
SIC: 7299 Information services, consumer

(G-2524)
FONDEADORA INC (PA)
8 The Grn Ste 10849 (19901-3618)
PHONE.................................925 413-3654
Rene Omar Serrano Ocampo, *Prin*
Norman Mller Vergara, *Prin*
EMP: 7 **EST:** 2017
SALES (est): 46.16K
SALES (corp-wide): 46.16K **Privately Held**
SIC: 7371 Computer software development and applications

(G-2525)
FORECAST INC
8 The Grn Ste A (19901-3618)
PHONE.................................302 413-0675
Tawanna Dabney, *CEO*
EMP: 8 **EST:** 2017
SALES (est): 321.66K **Privately Held**
Web: www.weather.gov
SIC: 4833 Television broadcasting stations

(G-2526)
FOREVER FIT FOUNDATION
1510 E Lebanon Rd (19901-5834)
P.O. Box 44 (19934-0044)
PHONE.................................302 698-5201
Nancy Hawkins-rigg, *Pr*
EMP: 5 **EST:** 1994
SALES (est): 242.53K **Privately Held**
Web: www.foreverfitfoundation.com
SIC: 7991 Health club

(G-2527)
FORMIDABLE FOODS INC (PA)
3500 S Dupont Hwy (19901-6041)
PHONE.................................415 877-9691
Tilen Travnik, *Pr*

Dover - Kent County (G-2528)   GEOGRAPHIC SECTION

Major Hrovat, *Dir*
Luka Sincek, *Dir*
EMP: 2 **EST:** 2021
SALES (est): 279.16K
SALES (corp-wide): 279.16K **Privately Held**
SIC: 3556 Food products machinery

(G-2528)
FORREST AVENUE ANIMAL HOSPITAL
3156 Forrest Ave (19904-5317)
PHONE..................302 736-3000
Vance Sciver, *Pr*
Kim Geines, *VP*
EMP: 19 **EST:** 2000
SQ FT: 2,561
SALES (est): 840.94K **Privately Held**
Web: www.forrestaveanimal.com
SIC: 0742 Animal hospital services, pets and other animal specialties

(G-2529)
FOUR C PAINTING
190 Mannering Dr (19901-5889)
PHONE..................302 242-2497
Jeffery Chandler, *Prin*
EMP: 5 **EST:** 2017
SALES (est): 95.03K **Privately Held**
SIC: 1721 Painting and paper hanging

(G-2530)
FOX POINTE
352 Fox Pointe Dr (19904-1415)
PHONE..................302 744-9442
EMP: 4 **EST:** 2019
SALES (est): 112.48K **Privately Held**
SIC: 2452 Prefabricated wood buildings

(G-2531)
FRACTAL MOBIUS LLC
8 The Grn Ste A (19901-3618)
PHONE..................646 209-8559
EMP: 2 **EST:** 2020
SALES (est): 153.02K **Privately Held**
SIC: 3674 Thin film circuits

(G-2532)
FRANKLIN PANCKO DDS
712 S Governors Ave (19904-4106)
PHONE..................302 674-1140
EMP: 7 **EST:** 2018
SALES (est): 67.3K **Privately Held**
SIC: 8021 Dentists' office

(G-2533)
FRATERNAL ORDER OF POLICE
Kitts Hummock Rd (19901)
PHONE..................302 674-3673
Harry Marvel, *Mgr*
EMP: 7 **EST:** 1998
SALES (est): 85.48K **Privately Held**
Web: www.fop.net
SIC: 8641 Fraternal associations

(G-2534)
FRECKLE HOLDINGS LLC
8 The Grn Ste 12441 (19901-3618)
PHONE..................302 260-6385
Nicole Hubbard, *Managing Member*
EMP: 6
SALES (est): 243.21K **Privately Held**
SIC: 7371 Computer software development and applications

(G-2535)
FREDERICK DIMEO
540 S Governors Ave # 201 (19904-3530)
PHONE..................302 674-3970
Frederick Dimeo, *Prin*

EMP: 6 **EST:** 2017
SALES (est): 66.41K **Privately Held**
SIC: 8049 Offices of health practitioner

(G-2536)
FRESENIUS MEDICAL CARE SOUTHER
Also Called: Fresenius Kidney Care N Dover
80 Salt Creek Dr (19901-2436)
PHONE..................302 678-2181
Mary Garber, *Prin*
EMP: 20 **EST:** 2018
SALES (est): 302.14K **Privately Held**
SIC: 8011 Offices and clinics of medical doctors

(G-2537)
FRIENDS OF OLD DOVER
Also Called: Historical Society of Dover
323 S State St (19901-6729)
PHONE..................302 674-1787
Mary Mason, *Prin*
Helene Altevogt, *Prin*
Bill Burton, *Prin*
Ann Baker-horsey, *Prin*
Cindy Christiansen, *Prin*
EMP: 5 **EST:** 2017
SALES (est): 55.75K **Privately Held**
Web: www.friendsofolddover.org
SIC: 8699 Membership organizations, nec

(G-2538)
FRONTIERX INC ◊
3500 S Dupont Hwy (19901-6041)
PHONE..................201 313-6998
Jonathan Begg, *CEO*
Andrew Gilbert, *CSO*
Andrew Perkins, *CFO*
EMP: 24 **EST:** 2023
SALES (est): 629.49K **Privately Held**
SIC: 7371 Computer software development

(G-2539)
FSA NETWORK INC
60 Starlifter Avenue (19901-9254)
PHONE..................302 316-3200
EMP: 8 **EST:** 2017
SALES (est): 86.35K **Privately Held**
Web: www.fsalogistix.com
SIC: 4212 Delivery service, vehicular

(G-2540)
FSHERY MID-ATLNTIC MGT COUNCIL
800 N State St Ste 201 (19901-3925)
PHONE..................302 674-2331
Doctor C M Moore, *Ex Dir*
Christopher Moore, *Ex Dir*
Kathy Collins, *Operations Officer*
Jan Saunders, *Asstg*
EMP: 13 **EST:** 2015
SALES (est): 488.45K **Privately Held**
Web: www.mafmc.org
SIC: 8748 Environmental consultant

(G-2541)
FSVAP USA INC ◊
108 Lakeland Ave (19901-5109)
PHONE..................248 639-8635
Francois Tardif, *CEO*
Kathleen Boll, *Sec*
EMP: 10 **EST:** 2024
SALES (est): 1.2MM
SALES (corp-wide): 100.93MM **Privately Held**
SIC: 3714 Motor vehicle engines and parts
HQ: Clarion Corporation Of America
15951 Technology Dr
Northville MI 48168
248 724-5100

(G-2542)
FULCRUM ASSETS LLC
8 The Grn Ste A (19901-3618)
PHONE..................615 278-0969
EMP: 5 **EST:** 2020
SALES (est): 71.79K **Privately Held**
Web: www.fulcrumassets.com
SIC: 8742 Marketing consulting services

(G-2543)
FULLER AERIAL SOLUTIONS LLC
7 Nixon Ln (19901-4043)
PHONE..................302 734-1541
Stephen F Fuller, *Prin*
EMP: 5 **EST:** 2015
SALES (est): 96.43K **Privately Held**
SIC: 8713 Ariel digital imaging

(G-2544)
FUN BAKERY LLC
3500 S Dupont Hwy (19901-6041)
PHONE..................858 220-0946
Rhonda Woerner, *Mgr*
EMP: 5 **EST:** 2013
SALES (est): 110K **Privately Held**
SIC: 7372 Home entertainment computer software

(G-2545)
FUNK & BOLTON PA
426 S State St (19901-6724)
P.O. Box 1366 (19903-1366)
PHONE..................302 735-8400
Joshua Twilley, *CEO*
EMP: 6 **EST:** 2010
SALES (est): 131.56K **Privately Held**
Web: www.fblaw.com
SIC: 8111 General practice attorney, lawyer

(G-2546)
FURRS TIRE SERVICE INC
1251 S Bay Rd (19901-4613)
P.O. Box 943 (19903-0943)
PHONE..................302 678-0800
Frank F Furr, *Pr*
Frank Furr Iii, *Pr*
EMP: 5 **EST:** 1983
SQ FT: 3,500
SALES (est): 501.67K **Privately Held**
Web: www.furrstire.com
SIC: 5531 7538 Automotive tires; General automotive repair shops

(G-2547)
FUTURE 50 INC
8 The Grn Ste A (19901-3618)
PHONE..................302 648-4665
Christopher Mau, *CEO*
EMP: 4
SALES (est): 180.26K **Privately Held**
SIC: 3556 Food products machinery

(G-2548)
FUTURE ANALYTICA SOFTWARE INC
8 The Grn (19901-3618)
PHONE..................437 771-2947
Dhiraj Kumar, *Pr*
EMP: 10
SALES (est): 454.47K **Privately Held**
SIC: 5045 7389 Computer software; Business Activities at Non-Commercial Site

(G-2549)
FUTURE BRIGHT PEDIATRICS
Also Called: BRIGHT FUTURE PEDIATRICS
938 S Bradford St (19904-4140)
P.O. Box 1082 (19903-1082)
PHONE..................302 883-3266
Mamoon Mahmoud, *Brnch Mgr*
EMP: 50

SALES (corp-wide): 2.47MM **Privately Held**
Web: www.brightfuturepediatrics.com
SIC: 8011 Pediatrician
PA: Future Bright Pediatrics Llc
120 Old Camden Rd Ste B
Camden DE 19934
302 538-6258

(G-2550)
FYVE BY CORP ◊
611 S Dupont Hwy Ste 102 (19901-4507)
PHONE..................770 862-9152
Benjamin Youngstrom, *CEO*
EMP: 4 **EST:** 2022
SALES (est): 171.34K **Privately Held**
SIC: 7372 Prepackaged software

(G-2551)
G L K INC (PA)
Also Called: Milford Stitching Co
55 Beloit Ave (19901-5704)
PHONE..................302 697-3838
Herbert Konowitz, *Pr*
EMP: 12 **EST:** 1952
SQ FT: 75,000
SALES (est): 2.16MM
SALES (corp-wide): 2.16MM **Privately Held**
SIC: 2392 2391 Bedspreads and bed sets: made from purchased materials; Draperies, plastic and textile: from purchased materials

(G-2552)
GABRIELLE FREELS
200 Banning St Ste 200 (19904-3487)
PHONE..................213 808-4907
Dacm Gabrielle Freels L Ac, *Prin*
EMP: 6 **EST:** 2019
SALES (est): 109.74K **Privately Held**
SIC: 8049 Offices of health practitioner

(G-2553)
GAICHU MANAGED SERVICES LLC
8 The Grn Ste 11236 (19901-3618)
PHONE..................302 232-8420
EMP: 6 **EST:** 2020
SALES (est): 36.24K **Privately Held**
Web: www.gaichuservices.com
SIC: 8711 Engineering services

(G-2554)
GALAXY PLUS FUND - LRR MSTR FU
850 New Burton Rd Ste 201 (19904-5786)
PHONE..................312 504-0096
EMP: 9 **EST:** 2016
SALES (est): 82.35K **Privately Held**
SIC: 7389 Financial services

(G-2555)
GALAXYWORKS LLC
8 The Grn Ste 5008 (19901-3618)
PHONE..................404 894-8703
Mike Sauria, *Pt*
EMP: 11 **EST:** 2018
SALES (est): 445.15K **Privately Held**
Web: www.galaxyworks.io
SIC: 7371 8243 8731 Software programming applications; Software training, computer; Biological research

(G-2556)
GAP INNOVATIONS PBC
8 The Grn Ste B (19901-3618)
PHONE..................203 464-7048
Mark Roithmayr, *CEO*
EMP: 30 **EST:** 2020
SALES (est): 1.18MM **Privately Held**
SIC: 2834 Pharmaceutical preparations

GEOGRAPHIC SECTION
Dover - Kent County (G-2586)

(G-2557)
GARDE-ROBE INC ✪
874 Walker Rd Ste C (19904-2778)
PHONE......................347 986-0455
Sarah Findlay, *CEO*
EMP: 3 **EST:** 2022
SALES (est): 128.34K **Privately Held**
SIC: 7372 Prepackaged software

(G-2558)
GARRETT MECHANICAL & ADVANCED
134 S Shore Dr (19901-5739)
PHONE......................302 632-6261
EMP: 10 **EST:** 2018
SALES (est): 461.98K **Privately Held**
SIC: 8711 Engineering services

(G-2559)
GARRISON CALPINE
450 Garrison Oak Dr (19901-3369)
PHONE......................302 562-5661
EMP: 6 **EST:** 2015
SALES (est): 241.97K **Privately Held**
SIC: 4911 Generation, electric power

(G-2560)
GARRITZ ADVERTISING LLC
8 The Grn Ste 6322 (19901-3618)
PHONE......................347 607-7030
EMP: 5 **EST:** 2017
SALES (est): 98.59K **Privately Held**
Web: www.garritz.com
SIC: 8742 Marketing consulting services

(G-2561)
GARY QUIROGA
34 S Fairfield Dr (19901-5723)
PHONE......................302 697-3352
Gary T Quiroga Md, *Owner*
EMP: 5 **EST:** 1990
SALES (est): 249.08K **Privately Held**
SIC: 8011 Internal medicine, physician/surgeon

(G-2562)
GAS & GO INC
Also Called: Westside Car Wash
805 Forest St (19904-3417)
PHONE......................302 734-8234
Vic Giangrant, *Pr*
Lynn Giangrant, *Sec*
EMP: 7 **EST:** 1981
SQ FT: 800
SALES (est): 910.53K **Privately Held**
Web: www.westsidecarwashde.com
SIC: 7542 7532 Carwash, automatic; Top and body repair and paint shops

(G-2563)
GASTRO GIRL INC
Also Called: GI Ondemand
8 The Grn Unit 8109 (19901-3618)
PHONE......................202 579-1057
Jacqueline Gaulin, *CEO*
EMP: 5 **EST:** 2015
SALES (est): 50.45K **Privately Held**
SIC: 7371 Computer software development and applications

(G-2564)
GATEHOUSE MEDIA INC
Also Called: Dover Post News Paper
1196 S Little Creek Rd (19901-4727)
P.O. Box 664 (19903-0664)
PHONE......................302 678-3616
Mike Reed, *Pr*
EMP: 30 **EST:** 2001
SALES (est): 670.5K **Privately Held**
SIC: 2711 Newspapers, publishing and printing

(G-2565)
GDK SERVICES LLC
8 The Grn Ste 11464 (19901-3618)
PHONE......................929 242-8422
EMP: 35 **EST:** 2021
SALES (est): 920.45K **Privately Held**
Web: www.gdkserv.com
SIC: 7371 Computer software systems analysis and design, custom

(G-2566)
GEARHALO US INC
8 The Grn (19901-3618)
PHONE......................780 239-2120
Demetrius Bazos, *Pr*
EMP: 2 **EST:** 2018
SALES (est): 100K **Privately Held**
SIC: 2842 Sanitation preparations, disinfectants and deodorants

(G-2567)
GEARHART CONSTRUCTION INC
Also Called: J & L Construction Co
5075 N Dupont Hwy (19901-2346)
PHONE......................302 674-5466
Jerry Gearhart, *Pr*
Linda Gearhart, *Sec*
EMP: 6 **EST:** 1975
SALES (est): 676.04K **Privately Held**
SIC: 1761 1531 Roofing contractor; Speculative builder, single-family houses

(G-2568)
GEEKSOFT INC ✪
Also Called: Geeksoft
8 The Grn Ste 11988 (19901-3618)
PHONE......................669 278-8022
Ming Fu, *CEO*
EMP: 6 **EST:** 2022
SALES (est): 237.56K **Privately Held**
SIC: 7371 Computer software development and applications

(G-2569)
GEMINI QULTY FRT SOLUTIONS LLC ✪
8 The Grn Ste 16368 (19901-3618)
PHONE......................302 219-3310
EMP: 6 **EST:** 2023
SALES (est): 280.62K **Privately Held**
SIC: 4731 Transportation agents and brokers

(G-2570)
GENEX STRATEGIES
73 Greentree Dr (19904-7646)
PHONE......................302 356-1522
Roger Proctor, *Prin*
EMP: 6 **EST:** 2010
SALES (est): 210.09K **Privately Held**
Web: www.genexcapital.com
SIC: 8748 Business consulting, nec

(G-2571)
GEO B SCHREPPLER III
1425 New Burton Rd (19904-5462)
PHONE......................302 678-5959
George Schreppler, *Owner*
EMP: 6 **EST:** 2009
SALES (est): 61.84K **Privately Held**
Web: www.schrepplerchiropracticde.com
SIC: 8041 Offices and clinics of chiropractors

(G-2572)
GEOLOGICAL SURVEY US DEPT
Also Called: GEOLOGICAL SURVEY, UNITED STATES DEPARTMENT OF
300 S New St (19904-6726)
PHONE......................302 734-2506
EMP: 14
Web: www.usgs.gov
SIC: 8742 Business planning and organizing services
HQ: United States Dept Of Geological Survey
  12201 Sunrise Valley Dr Ms10
  Reston VA 20192

(G-2573)
GEORGE & LYNCH INC (PA)
150 Lafferty Ln (19901-7205)
PHONE......................302 736-3031
Christopher Baker, *CEO*
William B Robinson, *
Dennis J Dinger, *
David W Mcguigan, *VP*
Jeffrey I Norman, *
EMP: 96 **EST:** 1923
SQ FT: 12,000
SALES (est): 47.84MM
SALES (corp-wide): 47.84MM **Privately Held**
Web: www.geolyn.com
SIC: 1623 1611 1629 1731 Water, sewer, and utility lines; Highway and street construction; Marine construction; Environmental system control installation

(G-2574)
GEORVE V SAWYER
Also Called: Buck's Barber Shop
2296 Forrest Ave (19904-5308)
PHONE......................302 736-1474
George V Sawyer, *Owner*
EMP: 7 **EST:** 1992
SALES (est): 95.63K **Privately Held**
Web: www.buckscountybarbershop.com
SIC: 7241 Barber shops

(G-2575)
GETCARRIER LLC
8 The Grn Ste 7362 (19901-3618)
PHONE......................302 763-3040
EMP: 7 **EST:** 2017
SALES (est): 241.94K **Privately Held**
Web: www.getcarrier.com
SIC: 4213 Contract haulers

(G-2576)
GETRENTACAR INC (PA)
9 E Loockerman St (19901-8306)
PHONE......................786 460-8707
EMP: 6
SALES (est): 81.77K
SALES (corp-wide): 81.77K **Privately Held**
Web: www.getrentacar.com
SIC: 7514 Passenger car rental

(G-2577)
GEVME INC
8 The Grn Ste A (19901-3618)
PHONE......................302 335-7150
Gungadin Shastri, *Prin*
EMP: 3
SALES (est): 128.34K **Privately Held**
SIC: 7372 Prepackaged software

(G-2578)
GGA CONSULTING GROUP LLC ✪
8 The Grn Ste 16721 (19901-3618)
PHONE......................302 307-3443
Gevorg Arutyunyan, *Managing Member*
EMP: 10 **EST:** 2023
SALES (est): 355.79K **Privately Held**
SIC: 7379 Online services technology consultants

(G-2579)
GGA GLOBAL CONSULTING LLC ✪
8 The Grn # 16722 (19901-3618)
PHONE......................302 238-1751
Gevorg A, *Managing Member*
EMP: 10 **EST:** 2023
SALES (est): 362.6K **Privately Held**
Web: www.ggaglobalconsulting.com
SIC: 7376 Computer facilities management

(G-2580)
GGB SOLUTIONS INC
8 The Grn Ste G (19901-3618)
PHONE......................202 999-5313
Francisco Gomez, *Prin*
EMP: 3 **EST:** 2019
SALES (est): 80.37K **Privately Held**
SIC: 3568 Power transmission equipment, nec

(G-2581)
GI ASSOCIATES OF DELAWARE
Also Called: G I Associates of Delaware
742 S Governors Ave Ste 3 (19904-4111)
PHONE......................302 678-5008
Natwarlal V Ramani Md, *CEO*
EMP: 7 **EST:** 1994
SQ FT: 5,000
SALES (est): 674.03K **Privately Held**
Web: www.gidelaware.com
SIC: 8011 Gastronomist

(G-2582)
GIFTED HANDS 2 LLC
500 Isabelle Isle Apt 106 (19904-5493)
PHONE......................302 643-2005
Krystal Cowan, *CEO*
EMP: 6 **EST:** 2021
SALES (est): 245.98K **Privately Held**
SIC: 7389 Business Activities at Non-Commercial Site

(G-2583)
GIFTPASS APP INC
1675 S State St Ste B (19901-5140)
PHONE......................310 529-7566
Maliha Naeem, *CEO*
EMP: 5 **EST:** 2021
SALES (est): 107.01K **Privately Held**
SIC: 7371 Computer software development and applications

(G-2584)
GIGAHUB INC
8 The Grn Ste A (19901-3618)
PHONE......................916 304-4710
Ali Baghchehsara, *CEO*
EMP: 8 **EST:** 2020
SALES (est): 388.37K **Privately Held**
SIC: 7373 Computer integrated systems design

(G-2585)
GIL VANSCIVER
3156 Forrest Ave (19904-5317)
PHONE......................302 736-3000
Gil Van Sciver, *Pr*
EMP: 5 **EST:** 2016
SALES (est): 55.54K **Privately Held**
SIC: 0741 Veterinarian, livestock

(G-2586)
GINA HEALTH LLC
8 The Grn Ste R (19901-3618)
PHONE......................573 529-9858
EMP: 6 **EST:** 2020
SALES (est): 85.87K **Privately Held**
SIC: 8011 Dermatologist

Dover - Kent County (G-2587) GEOGRAPHIC SECTION

(G-2587)
GIVE BACK BEAUTY LLC
8 The Grn Ste 4220 (19901-3618)
PHONE..................571 439-2321
EMP: 13 EST: 2021
SALES (est): 859.41K **Privately Held**
Web: www.givebackbeauty.com
SIC: 7231 Beauty shops

(G-2588)
GIVESENDGO LLC
Also Called: Givesendgo
8 The Grn Ste A (19901-3618)
PHONE..................302 404-6778
EMP: 6 EST: 2014
SALES (est): 373.34K **Privately Held**
Web: www.givesendgo.com
SIC: 7389 Fund raising organizations

(G-2589)
GLEN D ROWE DR
1093 S Governors Ave (19904-6901)
PHONE..................302 730-4366
Glen D Rowe Md, *Owner*
EMP: 8 EST: 2005
SALES (est): 317.63K **Privately Held**
SIC: 8011 Offices and clinics of medical doctors

(G-2590)
GLIMPSE GLOBAL INC
8 The Grn Ste A (19901-3618)
PHONE..................305 216-7667
Reinaldo Ramos, *Prin*
EMP: 7 EST: 2018
SALES (est): 37.59K **Privately Held**
SIC: 2741 Internet publishing and broadcasting

(G-2591)
GLOBAL INFRSTRCTURE SLTONS INC
1675 S State St Ste B (19901-5140)
PHONE..................808 381-3666
Jeffrey M Kissel, *CEO*
EMP: 5 EST: 2016
SALES (est): 30.77K **Privately Held**
SIC: 8742 Management consulting services

(G-2592)
GLOBAL TELLINK
300 W Water St (19904-6743)
PHONE..................302 672-7867
EMP: 5 EST: 2010
SALES (est): 45.24K **Privately Held**
SIC: 4813 Local and long distance telephone communications

(G-2593)
GLOBAL TOUCH CO
8 The Grn (19901-3618)
PHONE..................302 321-5844
Larry Adams, *Ex Dir*
EMP: 50 EST: 2021
SALES (est): 1.37MM **Privately Held**
Web: www.globaltouch.com
SIC: 1531 Townhouse developers

(G-2594)
GLOBALING INC (PA)
Also Called: Globaling.io
3500 S Dunpont Hwy (19901)
PHONE..................619 657-0070
Eduardo Suarez Sanchez, *CEO*
EMP: 9 EST: 2021
SALES (est): 522.71K
SALES (corp-wide): 522.71K **Privately Held**
SIC: 7371 Computer software development and applications

(G-2595)
GLOBALLY SRCED VHCLES PRTS LLC
8 The Grn Ste 8544 (19901-3618)
PHONE..................240 755-4935
EMP: 25
SALES (est): 2.2MM **Privately Held**
SIC: 3714 7389 Motor vehicle parts and accessories; Business Activities at Non-Commercial Site

(G-2596)
GLOBE ELECTRIC COMPANY USA INC
874 Walker Rd Ste C (19904-2778)
PHONE..................514 694-0444
Edward Weinstein, *CEO*
Howard Tafler, *CFO*
EMP: 4 EST: 2002
SALES (est): 577.86K **Privately Held**
SIC: 5063 3648 Electrical apparatus and equipment; Outdoor lighting equipment

(G-2597)
GLYCOMIRA LLC
160 Greentree Dr Ste 101 (19904-7620)
PHONE..................704 651-9789
EMP: 2 EST: 2008
SALES (est): 150.79K **Privately Held**
SIC: 2834 Pharmaceutical preparations

(G-2598)
GMW HABERDASHERY LLC
8 The Grn Ste A (19901-3618)
PHONE..................718 864-7817
George Washington, *Managing Member*
EMP: 2
SALES (est): 92.41K **Privately Held**
SIC: 2329 Men's and boy's clothing, nec

(G-2599)
GOLANCE INC
8 The Grn Ste 4753 (19901-3618)
PHONE..................888 478-0358
Michael Brooks, *CEO*
EMP: 22 EST: 2016
SALES (est): 1.22MM **Privately Held**
Web: www.golance.com
SIC: 7371 Computer software development and applications

(G-2600)
GOLDEN CHARIOT TRANSPORTAION
622 W Division St (19904-2702)
PHONE..................302 730-3882
Adamolekun Olukayode, *Pr*
EMP: 8 EST: 2003
SALES (est): 631.14K **Privately Held**
SIC: 7514 Hearse or limousine rental, without drivers

(G-2601)
GOLDFINCH GROUP INC
9 E Loockerman St Ste 3a (19901-7316)
PHONE..................646 300-0716
Dion Clark, *Ch Bd*
EMP: 5 EST: 2013
SALES (est): 249.24K **Privately Held**
SIC: 8111 7389 Corporate, partnership and business law; Business services, nec

(G-2602)
GOOD 4 LEGACY ◊
8 The Grn (19901-3618)
PHONE..................302 690-4515
Tayo Woolford, *Pr*
EMP: 5 EST: 2024
SALES (est): 164.52K **Privately Held**
SIC: 7389 Business Activities at Non-Commercial Site

(G-2603)
GOOD DRIVER MUTUALITY INC
8 The Grn Ste R (19901-3618)
PHONE..................713 979-8257
Ray Zhong, *Pr*
EMP: 50
SALES (est): 1.14MM **Privately Held**
SIC: 7371 Computer software development

(G-2604)
GOOD MANUFACTURING PRACTICES
80 Coventry Ct (19901-6552)
PHONE..................302 222-6808
EMP: 4 EST: 2017
SALES (est): 82.79K **Privately Held**
SIC: 3999 Manufacturing industries, nec

(G-2605)
GOODBLUE INC
8 The Grn (19901-3618)
PHONE..................801 755-5301
Dallan Koyle, *Pr*
EMP: 2
SALES (est): 92.41K **Privately Held**
SIC: 2399 Pet collars, leashes, etc.: non-leather

(G-2606)
GOODNESS ENTERPRISES LLC
4200 N Dupont Hwy (19901-2400)
PHONE..................302 674-1400
EMP: 5 EST: 2018
SALES (est): 260.58K **Privately Held**
SIC: 7389 Business services, nec

(G-2607)
GOODNESS FOR LIFE CENTER INC
8 The Grn Ste 5312 (19901-3618)
PHONE..................302 922-5055
Tauheedah Bronner, *Prin*
EMP: 5 EST: 2017
SALES (est): 69.04K **Privately Held**
Web: www.gflc.org
SIC: 8399 Advocacy group

(G-2608)
GOTIT INC
3500 S Dupont Hwy (19901-6041)
PHONE..................408 382-1300
Tal Agassi, *CEO*
EMP: 12 EST: 2013
SALES (est): 714.59K **Privately Held**
SIC: 7371 Computer software development and applications

(G-2609)
GOVBIZCONNECT INC
850 New Burton Rd (19904-5451)
PHONE..................860 341-1925
Tom Skypek, *CEO*
EMP: 3 EST: 2018
SALES (est): 86.51K **Privately Held**
SIC: 2741 Internet publishing and broadcasting

(G-2610)
GOVERNORS AVE ANIMAL HOSPITAL
Also Called: The Dog House
1008 S Governors Ave (19904-6902)
PHONE..................302 734-5588
EMP: 24 EST: 1987
SALES (est): 1.45MM **Privately Held**
Web: www.governorsavenueanimalhospital.com
SIC: 0742 Animal hospital services, pets and other animal specialties

(G-2611)
GOVERNORS FAMILY PRACTICE
1177 S Governors Ave (19904-6903)
PHONE..................302 734-9150
Thuya Aye, *Dir*
EMP: 7 EST: 2018
SALES (est): 199.39K **Privately Held**
Web: www.governorsfamilypractice.com
SIC: 8011 General and family practice, physician/surgeon

(G-2612)
GOVPLUS LLC
Also Called: Citizens Bank
1399 Forrest Ave (19904-3312)
PHONE..................302 734-0231
Vicky Shockley, *Mgr*
EMP: 6
SALES (corp-wide): 9.07B **Publicly Held**
Web: www.govplus.com
SIC: 6022 State trust companies accepting deposits, commercial
HQ: Citizens Bank, National Association
   1 Citizens Plz
   Providence RI 02903

(G-2613)
GOVWELL TECHNOLOGIES INC (PA)
614 N Dupont Hwy Ste 210 (19901-3900)
PHONE..................920 360-4496
Troy Lecaire, *CEO*
EMP: 2 EST: 2023
SALES (est): 87.4K
SALES (corp-wide): 87.4K **Privately Held**
SIC: 7372 Prepackaged software

(G-2614)
GR GROUP HOLDINGS INC (PA) ◊
Also Called: Grgh
108 Lakeland Ave (19901)
PHONE..................416 618-2676
Graham Read, *CEO*
EMP: 6 EST: 2022
SALES (est): 84.59K
SALES (corp-wide): 84.59K **Privately Held**
SIC: 3999 Manufacturing industries, nec

(G-2615)
GRAB DC LLC ◊
8 The Grn Ste A (19901-3618)
PHONE..................310 866-0560
EMP: 15 EST: 2022
SALES (est): 530.21K **Privately Held**
SIC: 4212 Delivery service, vehicular

(G-2616)
GRACE FOR DOVER
350 Mckee Rd (19904-8701)
P.O. Box 862 (19903-0862)
PHONE..................302 319-4433
Paige Baione, *Prin*
EMP: 8 EST: 2017
SALES (est): 216.39K **Privately Held**
Web: www.gracefordover.org
SIC: 8399 Advocacy group

(G-2617)
GRACEFUL BODY & WELLNESS LLC ◊
2714 Kitts Hummock Rd (19901-7034)
PHONE..................302 612-3356
Ranay Wilson, *Managing Member*
EMP: 5 EST: 2023
SALES (est): 113.46K **Privately Held**
SIC: 7299 Personal appearance services

GEOGRAPHIC SECTION
Dover - Kent County (G-2647)

(G-2618)
GRADY & HAMPTON LLC
6 N Bradford St (19904-3102)
PHONE.................302 678-1265
John S Grady, *Managing Member*
EMP: 6 **EST:** 1969
SQ FT: 700
SALES (est): 908.24K **Privately Held**
Web: www.gradyhampton.com
SIC: 8111 General practice attorney, lawyer

(G-2619)
GRANDE APARTMENTS
201 Doveview Dr Unit 101 (19904-3598)
PHONE.................302 734-8344
EMP: 5 **EST:** 2016
SALES (est): 123.52K **Privately Held**
Web: www.liveatthegrande.com
SIC: 6513 Apartment building operators

(G-2620)
GRATZ LLC ✪
611 S Dupont Hwy Ste 102 (19901-4507)
PHONE.................719 581-9645
Don Lebert, *Managing Member*
EMP: 3 **EST:** 2022
SALES (est): 128.34K **Privately Held**
SIC: 7372 Prepackaged software

(G-2621)
GREEN CLINICS LABORATORY LLC
1633 Sorghum Mill Rd (19901-6810)
PHONE.................302 734-5050
Fady J Gerges, *Pr*
EMP: 35 **EST:** 2015
SALES (est): 2.12MM **Privately Held**
Web: www.greenclinics.net
SIC: 8099 8071 Health and allied services, nec; Medical laboratories

(G-2622)
GREEN CRESCENT LLC
Also Called: Green Crescent Translations
8 The Grn Ste 4710 (19901-3618)
P.O. Box 19912 (49019-0912)
PHONE.................800 735-9620
Jonathan W Fabian, *Managing Member*
EMP: 5 **EST:** 2003
SALES (est): 216.89K **Privately Held**
Web: www.greencrescent.com
SIC: 7389 7336 Translation services; Graphic arts and related design

(G-2623)
GREEN EYES LANDSCAPING INC
158 Attix Dr (19904-1081)
PHONE.................302 653-3800
Chad Scroggs, *Owner*
EMP: 6 **EST:** 2011
SALES (est): 93.94K **Privately Held**
Web: www.greeneyeslandscaping.com
SIC: 5261 4959 0782 0781 Retail nurseries and garden stores; Snowplowing; Landscape contractors; Landscape services

(G-2624)
GREEN INTEREST ENTERPRISES LLC
81 Rye Oak Ct (19904)
PHONE.................228 355-0708
EMP: 6 **EST:** 2010
SALES (est): 343.36K **Privately Held**
Web: www.greeninterestent.com
SIC: 8742 Management consulting services

(G-2625)
GREEN STANDARDS LLC
1675 S State St Ste B (19901-5140)
PHONE.................855 632-8036
Richard Beaumont, *Managing Member*
EMP: 35 **EST:** 2020
SALES (est): 1.63MM **Privately Held**
Web: www.greenstandardsltd.com
SIC: 8748 Environmental consultant

(G-2626)
GREENE BUSINESS SUPPORT S
3 Heritage Dr (19904-6518)
PHONE.................302 480-3725
EMP: 5 **EST:** 2018
SALES (est): 44.6K **Privately Held**
Web: business.delaware.gov
SIC: 8399 Advocacy group

(G-2627)
GREENLIGHT CONNECTIONS LLC
8 The Grn Ste B (19901-3618)
PHONE.................843 209-1675
EMP: 6
SALES (est): 242.66K **Privately Held**
SIC: 7361 Employment agencies

(G-2628)
GREYNOTE LLC (PA)
8 The Grn Ste B (19901-3618)
PHONE.................646 287-0705
EMP: 7 **EST:** 2018
SALES (est): 144.01K
SALES (corp-wide): 144.01K **Privately Held**
SIC: 7371 7389 Computer software development and applications; Business Activities at Non-Commercial Site

(G-2629)
GRNMETA INC ✪
874 Walker Rd (19904-2778)
PHONE.................425 362-3228
Julia Marhan, *CEO*
EMP: 4 **EST:** 2022
SALES (est): 89.67K **Privately Held**
SIC: 7372 Application computer software

(G-2630)
GROOM KINGS LLC
331 W Loockerman St (19904-3249)
PHONE.................302 744-9444
Abbe Watson, *Owner*
EMP: 6 **EST:** 2016
SALES (est): 25.84K **Privately Held**
SIC: 0752 Boarding services, kennels

(G-2631)
GROUPE EHC LLC
Also Called: Ehc Group
3500 S Dupont Hwy (19901-6041)
PHONE.................302 309-9154
Marc Garibaldi, *Managing Member*
Pierre Hagimanoli, *
EMP: 11 **EST:** 2004
SQ FT: 150
SALES (est): 173.58K **Privately Held**
SIC: 7381 Security guard service

(G-2632)
GULAB MANAGEMENT INC (PA)
Also Called: Dover Budget Inn
1426 N Dupont Hwy (19901-2213)
PHONE.................302 734-4433
Ernest Gulab, *Pr*
Asim Gulab, *Treas*
EMP: 20 **EST:** 1991
SALES (est): 2.41MM **Privately Held**
Web: www.wyndhamhotels.com
SIC: 7011 Hotels and motels

(G-2633)
GULF COAST INVESTMENTS INC
8 The Grn (19901-3618)
PHONE.................929 359-4439
Dharmesh Patel, *Pr*
EMP: 10 **EST:** 2019
SALES (est): 499.55K **Privately Held**
SIC: 6799 Real estate investors, except property operators

(G-2634)
GUTTER CONNECTION LLC
2559 Mckee Rd (19904-1217)
PHONE.................302 736-0105
Debra Carney, *Pr*
EMP: 12 **EST:** 2015
SALES (est): 235.6K **Privately Held**
Web: www.gutterconnectionllc.net
SIC: 7349 Building maintenance services, nec

(G-2635)
GUY & LADY BARREL LLC
Also Called: Guy & Lady Barrel Cigars
198 Hatteras Dr (19904-3883)
PHONE.................302 399-3069
EMP: 5 **EST:** 2012
SALES (est): 425.93K **Privately Held**
Web: www.alcoholinfusedcigars.com
SIC: 5993 5194 7389 Cigar store; Cigars; Business Activities at Non-Commercial Site

(G-2636)
GUY BUG
1017 Westview Ter (19904-4344)
PHONE.................302 242-5254
Jean Taylor, *Owner*
EMP: 7 **EST:** 2014
SALES (est): 249.22K **Privately Held**
Web: www.thebugguydelaware.com
SIC: 7342 Pest control in structures

(G-2637)
GYM STARZ LLC
155 Commerce Way Ste D (19904-8308)
PHONE.................302 747-7218
EMP: 5 **EST:** 2017
SALES (est): 64.86K **Privately Held**
Web: www.gymstarzde.com
SIC: 7999 Gymnastic instruction, non-membership

(G-2638)
H & A ELECTRIC CO
59 Roosevelt Ave (19901-4459)
PHONE.................302 678-8252
Richard W Arndt, *Pr*
Patricia Arndt, *Sec*
EMP: 9 **EST:** 1973
SQ FT: 700
SALES (est): 908.23K **Privately Held**
SIC: 1731 General electrical contractor

(G-2639)
H & H CONSTRUCTION COMPANY LLC
1365 N Dupont Hwy (19901-8710)
PHONE.................936 825-6774
Matthew Husfeed, *Prin*
EMP: 5 **EST:** 2014
SALES (est): 59K **Privately Held**
SIC: 1521 Single-family housing construction

(G-2640)
H H BUILDERS INC
3947 Forrest Ave (19904-5216)
PHONE.................302 735-9900
H Lbaker, *Prin*
EMP: 7 **EST:** 2013
SALES (est): 996.23K **Privately Held**
Web: www.h-hbuildersinc.com
SIC: 1521 New construction, single-family houses

(G-2641)
H S TROYER
351 Rose Valley School Rd (19904-5527)
PHONE.................302 678-2694
H S Troyer, *Prin*
EMP: 5 **EST:** 2009
SALES (est): 110.35K **Privately Held**
SIC: 7389 Auctioneers, fee basis

(G-2642)
H&B EXPRESS LOGISTICS ✪
8 The Grn (19901-3618)
PHONE.................815 201-0915
Michael Holman, *CEO*
EMP: 7 **EST:** 2024
SALES (est): 247.74K **Privately Held**
SIC: 1541 7389 Warehouse construction; Business Activities at Non-Commercial Site

(G-2643)
HAASS FAMILY BUTCHER SHOP
Also Called: West Dover Butcher Shop
3997 Hazletville Rd (19904-5615)
PHONE.................302 734-5447
Jeffrey Dean Haass, *CEO*
▲ **EMP:** 6 **EST:** 1969
SALES (est): 785.72K **Privately Held**
Web: www.haassmeats.com
SIC: 5421 5147 Meat markets, including freezer provisioners; Meats, fresh

(G-2644)
HAIR DAY
2459 S State St (19901-6304)
PHONE.................302 538-5198
Nam Eunsook, *Prin*
EMP: 5 **EST:** 2014
SALES (est): 54.99K **Privately Held**
SIC: 7231 Hairdressers

(G-2645)
HALPERN EYE ASSOCIATES INC (PA)
Also Called: Halpern Eye Care
885 S Governors Ave (19904-4158)
P.O. Box 762 (19903-0762)
PHONE.................302 734-5861
Ryan Halpern, *Pr*
Troy Raber, *
EMP: 25 **EST:** 1946
SQ FT: 1,000
SALES (est): 9.06MM
SALES (corp-wide): 9.06MM **Privately Held**
Web: www.myeyedr.com
SIC: 8042 Specialized optometrists

(G-2646)
HALPERN EYE CARE
1404 Forrest Ave Ste 1 (19904-3478)
PHONE.................302 346-2020
Ryan Halpern, *Mgr*
EMP: 9 **EST:** 2018
SALES (est): 47.44K **Privately Held**
Web: www.eyesde.com
SIC: 8042 Offices and clinics of optometrists

(G-2647)
HALPERN OPTHALMOLOGY ASSOC
Also Called: Halpern Medical
200 Banning St (19904-3485)
PHONE.................302 678-2210
Dawn Wolford, *Pr*
EMP: 5 **EST:** 2009
SALES (est): 488.38K **Privately Held**
Web: www.halpernoa.com
SIC: 8011 Opthalmologist

Dover - Kent County (G-2648)   GEOGRAPHIC SECTION

(G-2648)
HAMPTON INN-DOVER
Also Called: Hampton Inn Dover
1568 N Dupont Hwy (19901-2215)
PHONE..................................302 736-3500
EMP: 7 **EST:** 1994
SALES (est): 482.15K **Privately Held**
Web: www.hilton.com
SIC: 7011 Hotels and motels

(G-2649)
HANDS ON DECK MOVING CO LLC
312 Loganberry Ter (19901-1769)
PHONE..................................302 489-9251
Chad Williams, *Managing Member*
EMP: 9 **EST:** 2015
SALES (est): 459.57K **Privately Held**
Web: www.handsondeckmovingcompany.com
SIC: 4789 Cargo loading and unloading services

(G-2650)
HANK TECHNOLOGIES INC
8 The Grn (19901-3618)
PHONE..................................812 223-5984
Fejiro Agbodje, *Pr*
EMP: 7
SALES (est): 264.9K **Privately Held**
SIC: 7371 Computer software development and applications

(G-2651)
HAPPYROBOT INC ◆
1111b S Governors Ave Ste 6189 (19904-6903)
PHONE..................................972 837-9213
Javier Rodriguez Palafox, *Pr*
Pablo Rodriguez Palafox, *CEO*
EMP: 3 **EST:** 2022
SALES (est): 128.34K **Privately Held**
Web: www.happyrobot.ai
SIC: 7372 Business oriented computer software

(G-2652)
HARMATTAN DESIGN LLC
3500 S Dupont Hwy (19901-6041)
PHONE..................................609 385-1041
EMP: 5 **EST:** 2015
SALES (est): 25.81K **Privately Held**
Web: www.harmattandesign.com
SIC: 7336 Art design services

(G-2653)
HAROLD L SCOTT SR
2148 Lockwood Chapel Rd (19904-5004)
PHONE..................................302 343-9217
Harold Scott, *Prin*
EMP: 5 **EST:** 2005
SALES (est): 238.64K **Privately Held**
SIC: 1522 Residential construction, nec

(G-2654)
HARRINGTON REALTY INC (PA)
Also Called: ERA
516 Jefferic Blvd Ste C (19901-2023)
PHONE..................................302 736-0800
Michael Harrington Senior, *Pr*
Donna Harrington, *
EMP: 50 **EST:** 1972
SALES (est): 9.68MM
SALES (corp-wide): 9.68MM **Privately Held**
SIC: 6411 6531 Insurance agents, brokers, and service; Real estate agents and managers

(G-2655)
HARRINGTON REALTY INC
Also Called: ERA
494 N Dupont Hwy (19901-3906)
PHONE..................................302 422-2424
Michael Harrington Junior, *Mgr*
EMP: 18
SALES (corp-wide): 9.68MM **Privately Held**
SIC: 6531 Real estate agent, residential
PA: Harrington Realty Inc
    516 Jefferic Blvd Ste C
    Dover DE 19901
    302 736-0800

(G-2656)
HARRIS TOWING AND AUTO SERVICE
5360 N Dupont Hwy (19901-2340)
P.O. Box 347 (19936-0347)
PHONE..................................302 736-9901
EMP: 7 **EST:** 1986
SALES (est): 509K **Privately Held**
Web: www.harristowing.com
SIC: 7549 7538 Towing service, automotive; General automotive repair shops

(G-2657)
HARROCK PROPERTIES LLC
Also Called: Facibus
8 The Grn Ste 8334 (19901-3618)
PHONE..................................302 202-1321
EMP: 3 **EST:** 2019
SALES (est): 211.95K **Privately Held**
SIC: 5122 6799 2023 5734 Cosmetics; Real estate investors, except property operators; Dietary supplements, dairy and non-dairy based; Software, business and non-game

(G-2658)
HARRY LOUIES LAUNDRY & DRY CLG
Also Called: Louie Harry Laundry & Dry Clg
129 S Governors Ave (19904-3222)
PHONE..................................302 734-8195
David Mercer Louie, *Owner*
EMP: 6 **EST:** 1949
SQ FT: 3,204
SALES (est): 191.49K **Privately Held**
SIC: 7216 7211 7219 Drycleaning plants, except rugs; Power laundries, family and commercial; Laundry, except power and coin-operated

(G-2659)
HARSHA TANKALA MD
Also Called: Patel, Ashok MD
1055 S Bradford St (19904-4141)
PHONE..................................302 674-1818
Ashok Patel Md, *Pt*
Ashok Patel Md, *Owner*
Harsha Tankala, *Pt*
EMP: 8 **EST:** 1982
SALES (est): 306.4K **Privately Held**
SIC: 8011 Internal medicine, physician/ surgeon

(G-2660)
HART GROUP LLC
8 The Grn Ste A (19901-3618)
PHONE..................................302 782-9742
EMP: 8 **EST:** 2018
SALES (est): 277.22K **Privately Held**
SIC: 7389 Financial services

(G-2661)
HASTEN INC (PA) ◆
8 The Grn Ste R (19901-3618)
PHONE..................................818 867-8151
Giovanni Petrantoni, *CEO*
EMP: 9 **EST:** 2022
SALES (est): 658.98K
SALES (corp-wide): 658.98K **Privately Held**
SIC: 7371 Computer software development and applications

(G-2662)
HATJIS CHRISTOS G MD
1060 S Governors Ave (19904-6920)
PHONE..................................302 744-6220
Christos Hatjis, *Prin*
EMP: 8 **EST:** 2017
SALES (est): 54.13K **Privately Held**
SIC: 8011 Offices and clinics of medical doctors

(G-2663)
HAULEET INC
8 The Grn # 10713 (19901-3618)
PHONE..................................302 434-6384
Abdul Oluwole, *Prin*
EMP: 13 **EST:** 2020
SALES (est): 520.61K **Privately Held**
Web: www.hauleet.com
SIC: 4789 Transportation services, nec

(G-2664)
HAZARDOUS WASTE
89 Kings Hwy (19901-7305)
PHONE..................................302 739-9403
Nancy Marker, *Mgr*
EMP: 9 **EST:** 2010
SALES (est): 244.59K **Privately Held**
Web: www.cleanmanagement.com
SIC: 4959 Environmental cleanup services

(G-2665)
HEALTHSOURCE OF DOVER SOUTH
737 S Governors Ave (19904-4105)
PHONE..................................302 744-8526
EMP: 5 **EST:** 2017
SALES (est): 75.39K **Privately Held**
SIC: 8041 Offices and clinics of chiropractors

(G-2666)
HEART TO HEART HEALTH SVCS LLC
896 S State St (19901-4148)
PHONE..................................302 603-3976
Theressa Milhouse, *Managing Member*
EMP: 3 **EST:** 2020
SALES (est): 100K **Privately Held**
SIC: 3821 8731 Laboratory equipment: fume hoods, distillation racks, etc.; Commercial research laboratory

(G-2667)
HEAVENLY EFFECTS LLC ◆
8 The Grn Ste 13403 (19901-3618)
PHONE..................................302 446-3521
Nevaeh Edwards, *CEO*
EMP: 5 **EST:** 2022
SALES (est): 191.21K **Privately Held**
SIC: 7389 8742 Styling of fashions, apparel, furniture, textiles, etc.; Management consulting services

(G-2668)
HEAVENLY FILMS LLC
8 The Grn Ste 8571 (19901-3618)
PHONE..................................302 232-8988
EMP: 5 **EST:** 2008
SALES (est): 130.19K **Privately Held**
Web: www.heavenlyfilms.com
SIC: 7812 7336 Motion picture production; Graphic arts and related design

(G-2669)
HEAVENLY HARVEST LLC
8 The Grn Ste R (19901-3618)
PHONE..................................302 487-0974
EMP: 5
SALES (est): 86.31K **Privately Held**
SIC: 5141 Food brokers

(G-2670)
HEDGE CAPITAL MARKETS INC
8 The Grn Ste A (19901-3618)
PHONE..................................714 515-2645
Kyle Al-rawi, *CEO*
EMP: 14 **EST:** 2021
SALES (est): 651.12K **Privately Held**
SIC: 7371 Custom computer programming services

(G-2671)
HEL ECRANE INC
8 The Grn Ste A (19901-3618)
PHONE..................................604 519-0200
Mohamed Arif Dewji, *Ex Dir*
EMP: 7 **EST:** 2019
SALES (est): 248.05K **Privately Held**
SIC: 3721 Helicopters

(G-2672)
HELP INITIATIVE INC
101 W Loockerman St Ste 1b (19904-7328)
PHONE..................................302 236-7773
Charles T Kistler, *Ex Dir*
Harold Stafford, *Prin*
EMP: 7 **EST:** 2016
SALES (est): 1.67MM **Privately Held**
Web: www.helpinitiativede.org
SIC: 8699 Charitable organization

(G-2673)
HELTON AND MOOREHEAD TRNSP LLC ◆
12 Royal Grant Way (19901-6108)
PHONE..................................443 842-3360
EMP: 5 **EST:** 2022
SALES (est): 213K **Privately Held**
SIC: 4789 7389 Transportation services, nec ; Business Activities at Non-Commercial Site

(G-2674)
HEMBAL LABS INC ◆
1221 College Park Dr (19904-8726)
PHONE..................................800 414-4741
Joshua Dunn, *CEO*
EMP: 5 **EST:** 2022
SALES (est): 354.78K **Privately Held**
SIC: 2023 Baby formulas

(G-2675)
HERTZ LOCAL EDITION CORP
Also Called: Hertz
1679 S Dupont Hwy Ste 17 (19901-5114)
PHONE..................................302 678-0700
Luke Parson, *Mgr*
EMP: 6
SALES (corp-wide): 9.37B **Publicly Held**
Web: www.hertz.com
SIC: 7514 Rent-a-car service
HQ: Hertz Local Edition Corp.
    170 Weston St
    Hartford CT 06120
    239 301-7000

(G-2676)
HIBNER GROUP INC
8 The Grn (19901-3618)
PHONE..................................717 281-1918
EMP: 5
SALES (est): 68.89K **Privately Held**

GEOGRAPHIC SECTION
Dover - Kent County (G-2705)

SIC: **8748** 7389 Industrial development planning; Business Activities at Non-Commercial Site

(G-2677)
HICKORY HILL METAL FABRICATION
2134 Seven Hickories Rd (19904-1645)
PHONE.................................302 382-6727
EMP: 4 EST: 2008
SALES (est): 111.08K **Privately Held**
SIC: **3499** Fabricated metal products, nec

(G-2678)
HIGH GROUND CREATIVE LLC
401 Cassidy Dr Ste F (19901-4975)
PHONE.................................302 505-1367
Fredrik Ruhe, *Prin*
EMP: 5 EST: 2021
SALES (est): 74.23K **Privately Held**
Web: www.highgroundcreative.com
SIC: **7311** Advertising agencies

(G-2679)
HIGHLIFE ENTRMT GROUP LLC
141 Stone Ridge Dr (19901-8204)
PHONE.................................478 250-1862
EMP: 6 EST: 2021
SALES (est): 80K **Privately Held**
SIC: **7929** Entertainment service

(G-2680)
HILLIS-CARNES ENGRG ASSOC INC
1277 Mcd Dr (19901-4639)
PHONE.................................302 744-9855
Tom Schick, *Brnch Mgr*
EMP: 14
SQ FT: 2,312
SALES (corp-wide): 40.53MM **Privately Held**
Web: www.hcea.com
SIC: **8711** Consulting engineer
PA: Hillis-Carnes Engineering Associates, Inc.
   10975 Guilford Rd Ste A
   Annapolis Junction MD 20701
   410 880-4788

(G-2681)
HIRSH INDUSTRIES INC
631 Ridgely St (19904-2772)
PHONE.................................302 678-4990
▼ EMP: 2
SALES (corp-wide): 174.55MM **Privately Held**
Web: www.hirshindustries.com
SIC: **3999** Barber and beauty shop equipment
PA: Hirsh Industries, Inc.
   3636 Westown Pkwy Ste 100
   West Des Moines IA 50266
   515 299-3200

(G-2682)
HIRSH INDUSTRIES INC
1525 Mckee Rd (19904-1380)
PHONE.................................302 678-3456
EMP: 2
SALES (corp-wide): 174.55MM **Privately Held**
Web: www.hirshindustries.com
SIC: **2522** Filing boxes, cabinets, and cases: except wood
PA: Hirsh Industries, Inc.
   3636 Westown Pkwy Ste 100
   West Des Moines IA 50266
   515 299-3200

(G-2683)
HNH HOLDINGS LLC
8 The Grn A (19901-3618)
PHONE.................................415 548-3871
EMP: 6 EST: 2021
SALES (est): 71.79K **Privately Held**
SIC: **8742** Management consulting services

(G-2684)
HOCKEY LABS INC
8 The Grn Ste 12995 (19901-3618)
PHONE.................................929 909-6607
Yannick Spreen, *Pr*
EMP: 6
SALES (est): 68.89K **Privately Held**
SIC: **7371** Computer software development and applications

(G-2685)
HODGES INTERNATIONAL INC
8 The Grn (19901-3618)
PHONE.................................310 874-8516
Deanna Hodges, *Pr*
EMP: 4 EST: 2017
SALES (est): 176.92K **Privately Held**
SIC: **2299** Textile goods, nec

(G-2686)
HOEK FLOWERS USA INC
160 Greentree Dr (19904-7620)
PHONE.................................786 999-5767
EMP: 6 EST: 2018
SALES (est): 79.09K **Privately Held**
SIC: **5193** Flowers and florists supplies

(G-2687)
HOME BUILDERS ASSN DEL INC
109 E Division St (19901-7303)
PHONE.................................302 678-1520
Steven Lefebvre, *Prin*
EMP: 11 EST: 1954
SALES (est): 343.56K **Privately Held**
Web: www.brad-de.org
SIC: **8611** Contractors' association

(G-2688)
HOME DEPOT USA INC
Also Called: Home Depot, The
801 N Dupont Hwy (19901-2002)
PHONE.................................302 735-8864
Herb Speech, *Mgr*
EMP: 90
SALES (corp-wide): 157.4B **Publicly Held**
Web: www.homedepot.com
SIC: **5211** 7359 Home centers; Tool rental
HQ: Home Depot U.S.A., Inc.
   2455 Paces Ferry Rd Se
   Atlanta GA 30339

(G-2689)
HOME HEALTH CORP AMERICA INC
Also Called: Professional Home Health Care
1221 College Park Dr Ste 203 (19904-8727)
PHONE.................................302 678-4764
EMP: 58
SALES (corp-wide): 24.28MM **Privately Held**
SIC: **8082** Home health care services
PA: Home Health Corporation Of America, Inc.
   425 Se 26th Ave
   Fort Lauderdale FL

(G-2690)
HOME INSTEAD SENIOR CARE
755 Walker Rd Ste A (19904-2801)
P.O. Box 39 (19934-0039)
PHONE.................................302 697-6435
Robert Ware, *Prin*
EMP: 18 EST: 2016
SALES (est): 2.39MM **Privately Held**
Web: www.homeinstead.com
SIC: **8082** Home health care services

(G-2691)
HOMNI HEALTH SOLUTION INC
1221 College Park Dr # 116 (19904-8726)
PHONE.................................408 469-4956
Vishwajith Ramesh, *CEO*
Nadir Weibel, *VP*
EMP: 5 EST: 2021
SALES (est): 104.73K **Privately Held**
SIC: **7389** Business Activities at Non-Commercial Site

(G-2692)
HONEYBEE ARTS LLC
6 Barrington Way (19904-9128)
PHONE.................................646 664-5511
EMP: 5 EST: 2019
SALES (est): 30K **Privately Held**
Web: www.honeybeearts.org
SIC: **7929** Entertainment service

(G-2693)
HONORABLE MYRON T STEELE
800 N State St Ste 401 (19901-3925)
PHONE.................................302 739-4214
Myron T Steele, *Mgr*
EMP: 6 EST: 2017
SALES (est): 93.25K **Privately Held**
SIC: **8111** Legal services

(G-2694)
HOPPSCOTCH LLC
8 The Grn Ste A (19901-3618)
PHONE.................................858 395-1737
EMP: 5 EST: 2020
SALES (est): 46.43K **Privately Held**
SIC: **7299** Consumer purchasing services

(G-2695)
HORTY & HORTY PA
3702 N Dupont Hwy (19901-1555)
PHONE.................................302 730-4560
Doug Phillips, *Brnch Mgr*
EMP: 13
SALES (corp-wide): 2.4MM **Privately Held**
Web: www.horty.com
SIC: **8721** 7291 Certified public accountant; Tax return preparation services
PA: Horty & Horty, P.A.
   503 Carr Rd Ste 120
   Wilmington DE 19809
   302 652-4194

(G-2696)
HOURLY INC
3500 S Dupont Hwy (19901-6041)
PHONE.................................844 800-2211
Tomer Sagi, *CEO*
EMP: 102 EST: 2019
SALES (est): 3.5MM **Privately Held**
SIC: **7372** Application computer software

(G-2697)
HOW MEDICAL MARKETING INC
8 The Grn Ste B (19901-3618)
PHONE.................................302 283-9565
Christopher Hilinsky, *Pr*
EMP: 15
SALES (est): 1.1MM **Privately Held**
SIC: **8742** 7389 Marketing consulting services; Business Activities at Non-Commercial Site

(G-2698)
HOWARD MORRIS GROUP LLC
910 Walker Rd Ste B (19904-2759)
PHONE.................................877 296-4726
Robert Howard, *Managing Member*
EMP: 6 EST: 2020
SALES (est): 334.51K **Privately Held**
Web: www.howardmorrisgroup.com
SIC: **8742** Management consulting services

(G-2699)
HOWARD Z ARIAN M D
95 Wolf Creek Blvd Ste 1 (19901-4965)
PHONE.................................302 674-2390
Howard Arian, *Prin*
EMP: 8 EST: 2017
SALES (est): 57.59K **Privately Held**
SIC: **8011** Offices and clinics of medical doctors

(G-2700)
HUB ASSOCIATES
222 S Dupont Hwy (19901-3797)
PHONE.................................302 674-2200
Greg Kramedas, *Owner*
EMP: 9 EST: 1956
SALES (est): 1.57MM **Privately Held**
Web: www.10xventureshub.com
SIC: **6513** Residential hotel operation

(G-2701)
HUBERT HEADEN
295 Tea Party Trl (19901-8881)
PHONE.................................347 952-9250
Hubert Headen, *Prin*
EMP: 6 EST: 2017
SALES (est): 48.95K **Privately Held**
SIC: **8042** Specialized optometrists

(G-2702)
HUDSON JNES JAYWORK FISHER LLC (PA)
225 S State St (19901-6756)
PHONE.................................302 734-7401
Michelle Belt, *Off Mgr*
Ronald D Smith, *Pt*
John Terence Jaywork, *Pt*
R Brandon Jones, *Pt*
Harry M Fisher Iii, *Pt*
EMP: 24 EST: 1964
SALES (est): 3.82MM
SALES (corp-wide): 3.82MM **Privately Held**
Web: www.delawarelaw.com
SIC: **8111** General practice attorney, lawyer

(G-2703)
HULING COVE HOUSING CORP
18 The Grn (19901-3612)
PHONE.................................302 739-4263
Christopher Whaley, *Prin*
Anas Ben Addi, *Pr*
Cynthia Karnai Crossan, *VP*
Annette Miller, *Treas*
EMP: 7 EST: 2016
SALES (est): 481.1K **Privately Held**
Web: www.destatehousing.com
SIC: **8748** Urban planning and consulting services

(G-2704)
HULLO INC
3500 S Dupont Hwy (19901-6041)
PHONE.................................415 939-6534
Taher Khorakiwala, *CEO*
Angad Nadkarni, *COO*
EMP: 4 EST: 2015
SALES (est): 282.37K **Privately Held**
SIC: **7372** Application computer software

(G-2705)
HUMANDATA INC
Also Called: Humandata
8 The Grn Ste 11370 (19901-3618)
PHONE.................................302 698-1287
EMP: 3 EST: 2020

Dover - Kent County (G-2706) — GEOGRAPHIC SECTION

SALES (est): 56.54K **Privately Held**
SIC: 7372 Prepackaged software

(G-2706)
HUNT ENERGY NETWRK LAND CO LLC
1675 S State St Ste B (19901-5140)
PHONE..................214 978-8000
EMP: 5 EST: 2020
SALES (est): 230K **Privately Held**
SIC: 3825 Energy measuring equipment, electrical

(G-2707)
HUNTER GREEN INC
260 Fieldcrest Dr (19904-1079)
PHONE..................973 986-3114
Mary Grace Hunter, *Ch*
EMP: 10 EST: 2020
SALES (est): 461.18K **Privately Held**
SIC: 7389 Business services, nec

(G-2708)
HUSTLEOFFICIAL247 LLC
544 N Bradford St (19904-7206)
PHONE..................302 465-8965
EMP: 7 EST: 2021
SALES (est): 76.4K **Privately Held**
SIC: 5999 7389 Miscellaneous retail stores, nec; Business services, nec

(G-2709)
HYBRIDTHORY DIGITAL ENTRMT LLC
8 The Grn (19901-3618)
PHONE..................864 973-5753
Chenxi Guo, *Managing Member*
EMP: 5
SALES (est): 199.4K **Privately Held**
SIC: 7371 Computer software development

(G-2710)
HYGIEIA SHIELD INC
47 S West St (19904-3265)
PHONE..................302 388-7350
Ralf Conrad, *Pr*
EMP: 12 EST: 2020
SALES (est): 577.23K **Privately Held**
Web: www.hygieiashield.com
SIC: 3842 Surgical appliances and supplies

(G-2711)
HYPEBEAST INC
Also Called: Hbnyc
3500 S Dupont Hwy (19901-6041)
PHONE..................714 791-0755
Huan Nguyen, *Pr*
EMP: 30 EST: 2016
SQ FT: 1,600
SALES (est): 1.85MM **Privately Held**
SIC: 2721 Magazines: publishing and printing

(G-2712)
HYPERTEC USA INC
73 Greentree Dr (19904-7646)
PHONE..................480 626-9000
Robert Ahdoot, *Pr*
EMP: 9 EST: 2014
SALES (est): 347.02K **Privately Held**
Web: www.hypertec.com
SIC: 5045 Computer peripheral equipment

(G-2713)
I BARRY GUERKE
116 E Water St (19901-3614)
PHONE..................302 450-1098
I Guerke, *Prin*
EMP: 6 EST: 2017
SALES (est): 87.97K **Privately Held**
Web: www.pgslegal.com
SIC: 8111 General practice attorney, lawyer

(G-2714)
I HEART MEDIA
1575 Mckee Rd Ste 206 (19904-1382)
PHONE..................302 730-3783
Valerie Allston, *Prin*
EMP: 5 EST: 2017
SALES (est): 34.59K **Privately Held**
SIC: 4832 Radio broadcasting stations

(G-2715)
IAYAM FINANCIAL LLC
8 The Grn (19901-3618)
PHONE..................800 585-5315
Ivy Mathews, *Managing Member*
EMP: 5
SALES (est): 199.4K **Privately Held**
SIC: 8748 Business consulting, nec

(G-2716)
IBIDD HOLDINGS LLC
8 The Grn Ste A12044 (19901-3618)
PHONE..................800 960-9221
EMP: 5
SALES (est): 68.89K **Privately Held**
SIC: 7371 Computer software development and applications

(G-2717)
ICG ENTERPRISES INC
234 Red Tail Dr (19904-5562)
PHONE..................302 373-7136
Iris C Gibbs, *Asst Sec*
EMP: 5 EST: 2018
SALES (est): 65.69K **Privately Held**
Web: www.icgenterprises.org
SIC: 8399 Social services, nec

(G-2718)
IEG GLBAL MDIA INVSTMNTS ACQST
8 The Grn Ste 10184 (19901-3618)
PHONE..................720 290-9347
Jerry A Randolph, *Prin*
EMP: 5 EST: 2020
SIC: 6719 Holding companies, nec

(G-2719)
IFCF LLC
Also Called: Metodo Fspa - Grriere In Forma
3500 S Dupont Hwy (19901-6041)
PHONE..................351 773-4853
Alessandro Borzi, *CEO*
EMP: 6 EST: 2021
SALES (est): 237.56K **Privately Held**
SIC: 7389 Business Activities at Non-Commercial Site

(G-2720)
IGT INC
1281 Mcd Dr (19901-4639)
PHONE..................302 674-3177
Chuck Mathewson, *Prin*
EMP: 376
SALES (corp-wide): 4.22B **Privately Held**
Web: www.igt.com
SIC: 5099 Game machines, coin-operated
HQ: Igt Inc.
    9295 Prototype Dr
    Reno NV 89521

(G-2721)
III JOHN F GLENN MD
737 S Queen St Ste 2 (19904-3529)
P.O. Box 576 (19903-0576)
PHONE..................302 735-8650
John F Glenn Iii Md, *Owner*
EMP: 7 EST: 2002
SALES (est): 206.22K **Privately Held**
SIC: 8011 General and family practice, physician/surgeon

(G-2722)
IN A STITCH
526 Rose Dale Ln (19904-1606)
PHONE..................302 678-2260
Lisa Mummert, *Owner*
EMP: 4 EST: 2011
SALES (est): 60.16K **Privately Held**
SIC: 2395 Embroidery and art needlework

(G-2723)
IN10SITY FITNESS UNITED
73 First Tenth Ct (19901-6118)
P.O. Box 1158 (08094-5158)
PHONE..................302 677-1010
Reginald Brown, *Ch Bd*
EMP: 2 EST: 2017
SALES (est): 81.76K **Privately Held**
Web: shop.in10sityfitnessunited.com
SIC: 2023 Dietary supplements, dairy and non-dairy based

(G-2724)
INAMCO AIR LLC
Also Called: Inamco Defense
9 E Loockerman St Ste 3a221 (19901-8306)
PHONE..................630 830-4007
EMP: 9 EST: 2008
SALES (est): 149.66K **Privately Held**
SIC: 6211 Brokers, security

(G-2725)
INBOUND IGNITE LLC
8 The Grn Ste 17013 (19901-3618)
PHONE..................866 314-4499
EMP: 8
SALES (est): 306.16K **Privately Held**
SIC: 7389 7311 Business Activities at Non-Commercial Site; Advertising agencies

(G-2726)
INDEPENDENT BB FELLOWSHIP CH
Also Called: Because We Care
48 Mckee Rd Ste A (19904-2229)
PHONE..................302 734-2301
Reverend Gloria Cherry, *Dir*
EMP: 5 EST: 1992
SALES (est): 56.64K **Privately Held**
SIC: 8661 8351 Miscellaneous denomination church; Child day care services

(G-2727)
INDEPENDENT METAL STRAP CO INC
883 Horsepond Rd (19901-7214)
PHONE..................516 621-0030
Paul Maslar, *Pr*
Michael Maslar, *Sr VP*
▲ EMP: 20 EST: 1907
SQ FT: 40,000
SALES (est): 2.18MM **Privately Held**
Web: www.indmetalstrap.com
SIC: 3499 Fire- or burglary-resistive products

(G-2728)
INDEPENDENT NEWSMEDIA INC USA
Also Called: Delaware State News
110 Galaxy Dr (19901-9262)
P.O. Box 737 (19903-0737)
PHONE..................302 674-3600
Mike Pelrine, *Mgr*
EMP: 31
Web: www.baytobaynews.com
SIC: 2711 Newspapers, publishing and printing
HQ: Independent Newsmedia Inc. Usa
    110 Galaxy Dr
    Dover DE 19901
    302 674-3600

(G-2729)
INDEPENDENT NEWSMEDIA INC USA (HQ)
Also Called: Daily News-Sun
110 Galaxy Dr (19901-9262)
PHONE..................302 674-3600
Joe Smyth, *Ch Bd*
Edward Dulin, *
Wanda Ford-waring, *VP*
Toni Jackson, *
▲ EMP: 90 EST: 1953
SALES (est): 47.49MM **Privately Held**
Web: www.newszap.com
SIC: 2711 2752 Newspapers: publishing only, not printed on site; Offset printing
PA: Ini Holdings, Inc.
    110 Galaxy Dr
    Dover DE 19901

(G-2730)
INFARM - INDOOR URBAN FRMING U (PA)
8 The Grn Ste 7929 (19901-3618)
PHONE..................201 616-1441
Erez Galonska, *CEO*
EMP: 24 EST: 2019
SALES (est): 23.35MM
SALES (corp-wide): 23.35MM **Privately Held**
Web: www.infarm.com
SIC: 3999 Hydroponic equipment

(G-2731)
INFO TITAN LLC
32 Loockerman Plz Ste 109 (19901-7328)
PHONE..................510 495-4117
EMP: 3 EST: 2012
SALES (est): 85.58K **Privately Held**
SIC: 2711 Newspapers

(G-2732)
INFUSION SOLUTIONS OF DE
1100 Forrest Ave (19904-3309)
PHONE..................302 674-4627
Robert Anthony Moyer, *Prin*
EMP: 22 EST: 2006
SALES (est): 957.37K **Privately Held**
Web: www.infusede.com
SIC: 8011 Internal medicine, physician/surgeon

(G-2733)
INGENUITY 213 LLC
8 The Grn Ste B (19901-3618)
PHONE..................647 303-5116
EMP: 2
SALES (est): 92.41K **Privately Held**
SIC: 3799 Transportation equipment, nec

(G-2734)
INI HOLDINGS INC (PA)
110 Galaxy Dr (19901-9262)
PHONE..................302 674-3600
Joe Smith, *Pr*
Chris Engel, *Dir*
EMP: 4 EST: 1991
SALES (est): 47.49MM **Privately Held**
SIC: 2752 2711 Offset printing; Newspapers: publishing only, not printed on site

(G-2735)
INK THERAPY TATTOO STUDIOS LLC
155 N Dupont Hwy Ste 2 (19901-4213)
PHONE..................302 674-1900
Carrie Rodriguez, *Asst Sec*
EMP: 5 EST: 2018

GEOGRAPHIC SECTION

Dover - Kent County (G-2764)

SALES (est): 64.18K **Privately Held**
SIC: 7299 Tattoo parlor

(G-2736)
INNOVA BUS APPLICATIONS INC
8 The Grn Ste 12898 (19901-3618)
PHONE..................405 845-6871
Dennis Herrera, *CEO*
EMP: 4
SALES (est): 73.93K **Privately Held**
SIC: 7372 7389 Prepackaged software; Business services, nec

(G-2737)
INSIGHTXPERTS LLC
8 The Grn Ste 4000 (19901-3618)
PHONE..................412 608-4346
EMP: 5 **EST:** 2021
SALES (est): 10K **Privately Held**
SIC: 8699 Membership organizations, nec

(G-2738)
INSLEY INSUR & FINANIAL SVCS
Also Called: Nationwide
20 E Division St Ste B (19901-7366)
PHONE..................302 677-1888
Raymond Book, *Prin*
EMP: 6 **EST:** 2012
SALES (est): 71.84K **Privately Held**
Web: www.nationwide.com
SIC: 6411 Insurance agents, nec

(G-2739)
INSTABASE INC (PA)
3500 S Dupont Hwy (19901-6041)
PHONE..................628 261-7600
Anant Bhardwaj, *CEO*
EMP: 16 **EST:** 2016
SALES (est): 6.21MM
SALES (corp-wide): 6.21MM **Privately Held**
Web: www.instabase.com
SIC: 7389 Personal service agents, brokers, and bureaus

(G-2740)
INSTANT GLOBAL SERVICES CORP
8 The Grn Ste 8301 (19901-3618)
PHONE..................302 514-1047
Christopher A Palmer Junior, *Pr*
EMP: 9 **EST:** 2018
Web: instant-global-services-corp.business.site
SIC: 6719 Holding companies, nec

(G-2741)
INSTASAFE INC
3500 S Dupont Hwy (19901-6041)
PHONE..................408 400-3673
EMP: 5 **EST:** 2019
SALES (est): 104.58K **Privately Held**
SIC: 7382 8211 7371 Confinement surveillance systems maintenance and monitoring; Computer software development and applications

(G-2742)
INTEGRATED HEALTH ASSOC LLC
Also Called: Silver Lining Home Healthcare
24 Hiawatha Ln (19904-2401)
PHONE..................302 264-1021
Tiffany Rubin, *Prin*
EMP: 16 **EST:** 2013
SALES (est): 1.36MM **Privately Held**
Web: www.silverlininghealthcare.com
SIC: 8099 Health and allied services, nec

(G-2743)
INTELLECTUAL LLC
8 The Grn Ste 7213 (19901-3618)
PHONE..................202 769-1986
Daniel G Rego, *Managing Member*
EMP: 11 **EST:** 2010
SALES (est): 556.52K **Privately Held**
Web: www.intellectual.co
SIC: 8742 7379 Management consulting services; Computer related consulting services

(G-2744)
INTELLIGENT CHANGE LLC (PA)
8 The Grn Ste 4000 (19901-3618)
PHONE..................818 997-7712
EMP: 6 **EST:** 2019
SALES (est): 891.87K
SALES (corp-wide): 891.87K **Privately Held**
Web: www.intelligentchange.com
SIC: 5112 Stationery

(G-2745)
INTERMEDIA ANALYTICS LLC (PA)
Also Called: Intermedia
160 Greentree Dr Ste 101 (19904-7620)
PHONE..................305 921-9647
Federico Val, *Managing Member*
EMP: 13 **EST:** 2015
SALES (est): 3.38MM
SALES (corp-wide): 3.38MM **Privately Held**
SIC: 7371 Computer software development and applications

(G-2746)
INTERNAL MEDICINE DOVER PA
725 S Queen St (19904-3568)
PHONE..................302 678-4488
Pam Poore, *Off Mgr*
EMP: 13 **EST:** 2016
SALES (est): 2.12MM **Privately Held**
Web: www.dovermapd.com
SIC: 8011 General and family practice, physician/surgeon

(G-2747)
INTERNATIONAL CLOUD COMPANY
8th Green St (19901)
PHONE..................858 472-9648
James Cloud, *CEO*
EMP: 7 **EST:** 2018
SQ FT: 1,000
SALES (est): 280.04K **Privately Held**
SIC: 8748 Business consulting, nec

(G-2748)
INTERNATIONAL TRADE FIN LLC
8 The Grn Ste 5232 (19901-3618)
PHONE..................302 440-1492
Jasan Morgan, *Pr*
EMP: 10 **EST:** 2016
SALES (est): 76.52K **Privately Held**
Web: www.intltradefinance.com
SIC: 7389 Financial services

(G-2749)
INTOUCH INC
8 The Grn Ste B (19901-3618)
PHONE..................332 223-0720
Shannon Rajkitkul, *CEO*
EMP: 3 **EST:** 2018
SALES (est): 180.16K **Privately Held**
Web: www.briive.com
SIC: 2741 7371 Internet publishing and broadcasting; Computer software development and applications

(G-2750)
INTROSPCTION CUNSELING CTR LLC (PA)
8 The Grn Ste 12921 (19901-3618)
PHONE..................302 213-6158
Dierdra Oretade-branch, *CEO*
EMP: 8 **EST:** 2021
SALES (est): 635.71K
SALES (corp-wide): 635.71K **Privately Held**
Web: www.introspectioncounseling.com
SIC: 8093 7389 Mental health clinic, outpatient; Business Activities at Non-Commercial Site

(G-2751)
IPWE INC
160 Greentree Dr Ste 101 (19904-7620)
PHONE..................214 438-0820
Leann Pinto, *CEO*
Pascal Asselot, *Dir*
Vincent Fitzsimmons, *COO*
EMP: 23 **EST:** 2018
SALES (est): 1.38MM **Privately Held**
Web: www.ipwe.com
SIC: 8742 8748 7389 Management consulting services; Business consulting, nec; Patent brokers

(G-2752)
IRIS DIAGNOSTICS INCORPORATED
8 The Grn Ste 6527 (19901-3618)
PHONE..................877 292-4747
Jason Ryan, *Pr*
EMP: 10 **EST:** 2019
SALES (est): 545.59K **Privately Held**
Web: www.iris-diagnostics.com
SIC: 8742 Management consulting services

(G-2753)
ISPAPP INC
8 The Grn Ste R (19901-3618)
PHONE..................302 310-5009
David Dean, *Pr*
EMP: 10 **EST:** 2019
SALES (est): 535.45K **Privately Held**
Web: www.ispapp.co
SIC: 7371 Computer software development

(G-2754)
IT TAKES A VILLAGE PRESCHOOL
346 W Wind Dr (19901-6688)
PHONE..................302 241-3988
EMP: 6 **EST:** 2017
SALES (est): 97.3K **Privately Held**
SIC: 8351 Preschool center

(G-2755)
ITALTEC GOLD & COMMODITIES INC
8 The Grn Ste A (19901-3618)
PHONE..................302 446-3207
Amari Stringfield, *CEO*
EMP: 10 **EST:** 1999
SALES (est): 1.16MM **Privately Held**
Web: www.boazcapitalservices.com
SIC: 6221 1499 Commodity brokers, contracts; Precious stones mining, nec

(G-2756)
ITCONNECTUS INC
3500 S Dupont Hwy Ste O-101 (19901-6041)
PHONE..................302 531-1139
Yash Pal, *Dir*
EMP: 5
SALES (corp-wide): 3.33MM **Privately Held**
Web: www.itconnectus.com
SIC: 7389 Mailing and messenger services
PA: Itconnectus Inc.
101 E Park Blvd Ste 600
Plano TX 75074
732 789-4834

(G-2757)
ITDW GROUP LLC ✪
8 The Grn Ste 15153 (19901-3618)
PHONE..................917 503-3574
Nir Fatael, *CEO*
EMP: 3 **EST:** 2023
SALES (est): 135.7K **Privately Held**
SIC: 3571 7389 Computers, digital, analog or hybrid; Business Activities at Non-Commercial Site

(G-2758)
J & J BUS SERVICE
315 Billy Mitchell Ln E209 (19901-5390)
PHONE..................302 744-9002
Terry Grim Junior, *Owner*
EMP: 10 **EST:** 2005
SALES (est): 334.34K **Privately Held**
SIC: 4789 Transportation services, nec

(G-2759)
J NICHOLS ENTERPRISES LLC
8 The Grn (19901-3618)
PHONE..................302 579-0720
Janiska Nichols, *Managing Member*
EMP: 5
SALES (est): 220.71K **Privately Held**
SIC: 5331 7389 Variety stores; Business services, nec

(G-2760)
J P BLANDIN BASEBALL LLC
56 W Fairfield Dr (19901-5729)
PHONE..................302 535-8694
Sherri Blandin, *Prin*
EMP: 6 **EST:** 2009
SALES (est): 50.65K **Privately Held**
SIC: 7997 Baseball club, except professional and semi-professional

(G-2761)
J R WILLIAMSON DDS
Also Called: Richard Williamson
900 Forest St (19904-3402)
PHONE..................302 734-8887
Jesse R Williamson D.d.s., *Owner*
EMP: 5 **EST:** 1995
SALES (est): 309.99K **Privately Held**
Web: www.wdssmiles.com
SIC: 8021 Dentists' office

(G-2762)
JACKS LIFE MANAGEMENT INC ✪
8 The Grn Ste 8107 (19901-3618)
PHONE..................347 757-0720
Richard Belczynski, *Dir*
Kirk Seubert, *Dir*
EMP: 2 **EST:** 2022
SALES (est): 92.55K **Privately Held**
SIC: 7372 7389 Prepackaged software; Business services, nec

(G-2763)
JACKSON CONTRACTING INC
7242 Pearsons Corner Rd (19904-0928)
PHONE..................302 678-2011
Gary Jackson, *Pr*
Joe Corrado, *VP*
EMP: 13 **EST:** 1997
SALES (est): 399.4K **Privately Held**
Web: www.jacksoncontractingsite.com
SIC: 8748 Business consulting, nec

(G-2764)
JACKSON HEWITT
Also Called: Jackson Hewitt Tax Service
36 Jerome Dr (19901-2300)
PHONE..................302 382-2140
EMP: 5 **EST:** 2018
SALES (est): 63.32K **Privately Held**

Dover - Kent County (G-2765) — GEOGRAPHIC SECTION

Web: www.jacksonhewitt.com
SIC: 7291 Tax return preparation services

(G-2765)
JAG INDUSTRIALS LLC
8 The Grn (19901-3618)
PHONE....................267 334-7999
EMP: 7 EST: 2021
SALES (est): 1.11MM **Privately Held**
Web: www.jag.network
SIC: 5065 Electronic parts and equipment, nec

(G-2766)
JAIMIE STAFFORD
621 W Division St (19904-2701)
PHONE....................302 336-8307
Jaimie Stafford, *Mgr*
EMP: 7 EST: 2018
SALES (est): 98.12K **Privately Held**
SIC: 8049 Offices of health practitioner

(G-2767)
JAM AIR LLC
60 Twin Oak Dr (19904-1907)
P.O. Box 237 (19934-0237)
PHONE....................302 270-8236
EMP: 6 EST: 2003
SALES (est): 581.49K **Privately Held**
SIC: 1711 7623 Heating systems repair and maintenance; Air conditioning repair

(G-2768)
JAMES S PILLSBURY DDS
125 Greentree Dr # B (19904-7656)
PHONE....................302 734-0330
James S Pillsbury D.d.s., *Owner*
EMP: 7 EST: 1992
SALES (est): 237.11K **Privately Held**
Web: www.pillsburydentalassociates.com
SIC: 8021 Dentists' office

(G-2769)
JAMMIN PRODUCTIONS
2178 S State St (19901-6315)
PHONE....................302 670-7302
Jeff Neitzelt, *Owner*
EMP: 5 EST: 1990
SALES (est): 99.66K **Privately Held**
Web: www.jamminpro.com
SIC: 7929 Entertainment service

(G-2770)
JAMROXK LLC ◇
32 W Loockerman St (19904-7352)
PHONE....................302 423-5377
EMP: 5 EST: 2022
SALES (est): 63.67K **Privately Held**
SIC: 7231 7389 Beauty shops; Business Activities at Non-Commercial Site

(G-2771)
JAPAN MODERN ART LLC
8 The Grn Ste A (19901-3618)
PHONE....................832 458-1536
EMP: 2 EST: 2020
SALES (est): 173.18K **Privately Held**
SIC: 2211 Apparel and outerwear fabrics, cotton

(G-2772)
JARRELL BENSON GILES & SWEENEY
Also Called: Giles, Christopher MD
725 S Queen St (19904-3568)
PHONE....................302 678-4488
T Noble Jarrell, *Pt*
EMP: 13 EST: 1990
SALES (est): 456.37K **Privately Held**
SIC: 8011 Internal medicine practitioners

(G-2773)
JAZZERCISE
33 Turningleaf Ct (19904-1901)
PHONE....................302 730-8177
EMP: 5 EST: 2018
SALES (est): 29.54K **Privately Held**
Web: www.jazzercise.com
SIC: 7991 Aerobic dance and exercise classes

(G-2774)
JAZZERCISE
Also Called: Jazzercise
911 S Governors Ave (19904-4109)
PHONE....................302 698-3020
EMP: 5 EST: 2018
SALES (est): 35.37K **Privately Held**
Web: www.jazzercise.com
SIC: 7991 Aerobic dance and exercise classes

(G-2775)
JB FOR OFFICE) HOGAN
539 Blue Heron Rd (19904-4729)
PHONE....................302 922-0000
Tyler H Hogan, *Asst Sec*
EMP: 5 EST: 2018
SALES (est): 46.65K **Privately Held**
SIC: 8641 Civic and social associations

(G-2776)
JC MARKS INVESTMENTS LLC
8 The Grn Ste A (19901-3618)
PHONE....................302 602-4021
EMP: 5 EST: 2020
SALES (est): 266.3K **Privately Held**
SIC: 6799 Real estate investors, except property operators

(G-2777)
JC&A TRUST
8 The Grn Unit 8215 (19901-3618)
PHONE....................302 579-0886
Justin Beck-el, *Prin*
EMP: 25
SALES (est): 668.72K **Privately Held**
SIC: 8742 Financial consultant

(G-2778)
JEFFERSON URIAN DANE STRNER PA
107 Wolf Creek Blvd Ste 1 (19901-4970)
P.O. Box 830 (19947-0830)
PHONE....................302 678-1425
David Doan, *Pr*
EMP: 10
SALES (corp-wide): 5.15MM **Privately Held**
Web: www.juds.com
SIC: 8721 Certified public accountant
PA: Jefferson, Urian, Doane & Sterner, P.A.
651 N Bedford St
Georgetown DE 19947
302 856-3900

(G-2779)
JEM THERAPEUTICS PBC
8 The Grn (19901-3618)
PHONE....................561 462-1809
Michael Kaplan, *CEO*
EMP: 5
SALES (est): 258.29K **Privately Held**
SIC: 5122 Biotherapeutics

(G-2780)
JENNIFER C DOMBROSKI MSW LCSW
1001 S Bradford St Ste 8 (19904-4153)
PHONE....................302 422-3811
Jennifer Cullen Dombroski, *Prin*
EMP: 7 EST: 2012
SALES (est): 80.5K **Privately Held**
SIC: 8322 Social worker

(G-2781)
JENNIFER F DIVITA
97 Commerce Way Ste 101 (19904-7794)
PHONE....................302 734-8000
Jennifer Divita, *Prin*
EMP: 10 EST: 2014
SALES (est): 48.75K **Privately Held**
Web: www.esopt.com
SIC: 8049 Physical therapist

(G-2782)
JERRY L BURKERT
1244 Forrest Ave (19904-3311)
PHONE....................302 736-1116
EMP: 6 EST: 2009
SALES (est): 254.13K **Privately Held**
SIC: 5091 Sporting and recreation goods

(G-2783)
JESSE JMES SAFOOD BARBEQUE LLC
1030 S Dupont Hwy (19901-4422)
PHONE....................302 883-3518
Jesse T Rhodes, *Prin*
EMP: 5 EST: 2008
SALES (est): 189.1K **Privately Held**
SIC: 5146 Seafoods

(G-2784)
JESSE W STONE
1144 S Bay Rd (19901-4633)
PHONE....................302 677-0500
Jesse Stone, *Owner*
EMP: 5 EST: 2012
SALES (est): 40.53K **Privately Held**
SIC: 7241 Hair stylist, men

(G-2785)
JET GREEN TRANSPORTERS LLC
1001 White Oak Rd Apt C31 (19901-7448)
PHONE....................302 861-8918
Stephen Deshields, *Managing Member*
EMP: 7
SALES (est): 313.65K **Privately Held**
SIC: 4789 7389 Transportation services, nec ; Business Activities at Non-Commercial Site

(G-2786)
JG ALLSTAR TRUCKING LLC (PA) ◇
611 S Dupont Hwy Ste 102 (19901-4507)
PHONE....................609 372-8636
Joe Green, *Managing Member*
EMP: 10 EST: 2022
SALES (est): 410.42K
SALES (corp-wide): 410.42K **Privately Held**
SIC: 4213 Trucking, except local

(G-2787)
JG SERVICES
3650 Upper King Rd (19904-6426)
PHONE....................302 480-1900
James Green, *Prin*
EMP: 5 EST: 2017
SALES (est): 102.08K **Privately Held**
SIC: 1521 Single-family housing construction

(G-2788)
JHANA INC (PA) ◇
850 New Burton Rd Ste 201 (19901-5786)
PHONE....................530 863-7269
Benjamin Hoffner Brodsky, *CEO*
EMP: 3 EST: 2022
SALES (est): 128.34K
SALES (corp-wide): 128.34K **Privately Held**
SIC: 7372 Prepackaged software

(G-2789)
JIM HUTCHISON
50 Billings Dr (19901-2102)
PHONE....................302 739-4758
Jim Hutchison, *Owner*
EMP: 5 EST: 2016
SALES (est): 83.1K **Privately Held**
SIC: 1799 Special trade contractors, nec

(G-2790)
JIRA LLC
8 The Grn (19901-3618)
PHONE....................302 202-4615
EMP: 7 EST: 2021
SALES (est): 312.02K **Privately Held**
Web: www.atlassian.com
SIC: 8742 7389 Retail trade consultant; Business services, nec

(G-2791)
JK TANGLES HAIR SALON
Also Called: Ciseaux Hair Design Studio
1151 E Lebanon Rd Ste E (19901-5829)
PHONE....................302 698-1006
EMP: 5 EST: 1991
SALES (est): 62.16K **Privately Held**
Web: jktangleshairsalon.mysalononline.com
SIC: 7231 Hairdressers

(G-2792)
JKB CORP
Also Called: Two Men and A Truck
1169 S Dupont Hwy (19901-4423)
PHONE....................302 734-5017
Jeremy Brown, *Pr*
EMP: 35 EST: 2014
SQ FT: 2,400
SALES (est): 1.72MM **Privately Held**
Web: www.twomenandatruck.com
SIC: 4212 4225 Moving services; Warehousing, self storage

(G-2793)
JLQUICK PHOTOGRAPHY
104 Quail Hollow Dr (19904-6532)
PHONE....................302 674-3794
Jodi Quick, *Prin*
EMP: 5 EST: 2012
SALES (est): 67.33K **Privately Held**
SIC: 7221 Photographer, still or video

(G-2794)
JOEL R TEMPLE MD
9 E Loockerman St Ste 303 (19901-8305)
PHONE....................302 678-1343
Joel Temple Md, *Owner*
▲ EMP: 5 EST: 1977
SALES (est): 486.41K **Privately Held**
SIC: 8011 Allergist

(G-2795)
JOFF CAPITAL LLC
8 The Grn (19901-3618)
PHONE....................216 682-6822
EMP: 5 EST: 2021
SALES (est): 124.81K **Privately Held**
SIC: 8742 7389 Financial consultant; Business Activities at Non-Commercial Site

(G-2796)
JOHN BORDEN
Also Called: State Farm Insurance
450 S Dupont Hwy Ofc B (19901-4502)
PHONE....................302 674-2992

GEOGRAPHIC SECTION — Dover - Kent County (G-2828)

EMP: 5 EST: 1985
SALES (est): 424.3K **Privately Held**
Web: www.statefarm.com
SIC: 6411 Insurance agents and brokers

(G-2797)
JOHN BUTLER MD
1380 S State St (19901-4946)
PHONE.................302 674-8066
EMP: 8 EST: 2017
SALES (est): 54.13K **Privately Held**
SIC: 8011 Offices and clinics of medical doctors

(G-2798)
JOHN W PETROFSKE
3211 Kenton Rd (19904-1386)
PHONE.................410 422-1545
John W Petrofske, *Prin*
EMP: 5 EST: 2012
SALES (est): 212.94K **Privately Held**
SIC: 1522 Residential construction, nec

(G-2799)
JOHNS PREMIER SERVICES LLC ✪
8 The Grn Ste A (19901-3618)
PHONE.................347 992-3783
Curtis John, *Managing Member*
EMP: 8 EST: 2022
SALES (est): 1MM **Privately Held**
SIC: 4731 Freight forwarding

(G-2800)
JOINCUBE INC
3500 S Dupont Hwy (19901-6041)
PHONE.................214 532-9997
Mariano Rodriguez, *CEO*
EMP: 10 EST: 2013
SALES (est): 462.64K **Privately Held**
SIC: 7371 Computer software development and applications

(G-2801)
JONES LOGISTICS LLC
4486 N Dupont Hwy (19901-1556)
PHONE.................302 724-5663
EMP: 7 EST: 2019
SALES (est): 128.21K **Privately Held**
Web: www.joneslogistics.com
SIC: 4789 Transportation services, nec

(G-2802)
JONNY NICHOLS LDSCP MAINT INC
273 Walnut Shade Rd (19904-6474)
P.O. Box 419 (19980-0419)
PHONE.................302 697-2200
Jon Nichols Junior, *Pr*
Jon Nichols Senior, *VP*
EMP: 9 EST: 1994
SALES (est): 838.96K **Privately Held**
Web: www.jonnynichols.com
SIC: 0782 Landscape contractors

(G-2803)
JOSEPH PARISE DO
793 S Queen St (19904-3568)
PHONE.................302 735-8855
EMP: 5 EST: 2002
SALES (est): 409.09K **Privately Held**
SIC: 8031 Offices and clinics of osteopathic physicians

(G-2804)
JOSHUAS PAVING
100 Isabelle Isle (19904-5269)
PHONE.................302 396-1321
EMP: 5 EST: 2018
SALES (est): 147.21K **Privately Held**
SIC: 1611 Surfacing and paving

(G-2805)
JOY CHOOSE FOUNDATION
1360 Old White Oak Rd (19901-4084)
PHONE.................302 286-7560
Theresa Morris, *Ex Dir*
Harry Morris Iii, *Prin*
EMP: 6 EST: 2015
SALES (est): 103.91K **Privately Held**
SIC: 8641 Civic and social associations

(G-2806)
JP GRAPHICS
58 Sienna Ct (19904-0983)
PHONE.................302 678-0335
EMP: 6 EST: 2011
SALES (est): 60.64K **Privately Held**
Web: www.jp-graphics.com
SIC: 7336 Commercial art and graphic design

(G-2807)
JR ANESTHESIA LLC
30 Chadwick Dr (19901-5827)
PHONE.................302 678-0725
Natwarlal V Ramani, *Owner*
EMP: 9 EST: 2012
SALES (est): 118.51K **Privately Held**
SIC: 8011 Offices and clinics of medical doctors

(G-2808)
JR BOARD OF KENT GEN HOSPITAL
640 S State St (19901-3530)
PHONE.................302 744-7128
EMP: 6
SALES (est): 157.07K **Privately Held**
SIC: 8062 General medical and surgical hospitals

(G-2809)
JS AUTOMOTIVE AAMCO
Also Called: AAMCO Transmissions
3729 N Dupont Hwy (19901-1574)
PHONE.................302 678-5660
John Snyder, *Owner*
EMP: 6 EST: 2005
SALES (est): 478.86K **Privately Held**
Web: www.greaterdoveraamco.com
SIC: 7537 Automotive transmission repair shops

(G-2810)
JSC VENTURES LLC
9 E Loockerman St Ste 202-664 (19901-7347)
PHONE.................302 336-8151
EMP: 65 EST: 2014
SALES (est): 2.27MM **Privately Held**
Web: www.jscventures.com
SIC: 6799 Venture capital companies

(G-2811)
JSD MANAGEMENT INC
Also Called: James, Stevens & Daniels
1283 College Park Dr (19904-8713)
PHONE.................302 735-4628
Kelly Hedrick, *Pr*
EMP: 48 EST: 1997
SQ FT: 8,000
SALES (est): 8.53MM **Privately Held**
Web: www.jsdinc.net
SIC: 7322 Collection agency, except real estate

(G-2812)
JUAN SAUCEDO
Also Called: Saucedos Landscaping
1133 S Little Creek Rd (19901-4772)
PHONE.................302 233-4539
Juan Saucedo, *Prin*
EMP: 6 EST: 2012
SALES (est): 450.77K **Privately Held**
SIC: 0781 Landscape services

(G-2813)
JUDAH ROAD PRODUCTIONS LLC
1221 College Park Dr (19904-8726)
PHONE.................508 640-5022
EMP: 5
SALES (est): 203.68K **Privately Held**
SIC: 7335 Commercial photography

(G-2814)
JUDITH RIPPERT
200 Banning St (19904-3485)
PHONE.................302 734-1414
Judith Rippert, *Prin*
EMP: 10 EST: 2010
SALES (est): 82.72K **Privately Held**
SIC: 8011 Cardiologist and cardio-vascular specialist

(G-2815)
JUEGA LLC
8 The Grn (19901-3618)
PHONE.................716 256-3186
Tania Vaca, *Managing Member*
EMP: 3
SALES (est): 128.34K **Privately Held**
SIC: 7372 7389 Application computer software; Business services, nec

(G-2816)
JULIA C GORMAN
99 Wolf Creek Blvd Ste 2 (19901-4968)
PHONE.................302 734-8000
Julia Gorman, *Ofcr*
EMP: 10 EST: 2017
SALES (est): 224.96K **Privately Held**
Web: www.esopt.com
SIC: 8049 Physical therapist

(G-2817)
JULIE LEWICKI
1991 S State St (19901-5811)
PHONE.................302 531-0763
Julie Elizabeth Lewicki, *Prin*
EMP: 10 EST: 2006
SALES (est): 76.69K **Privately Held**
SIC: 8093 Respiratory therapy clinic

(G-2818)
JULIE Q NIES DDS
1380 S State St (19901-4946)
PHONE.................302 242-9085
Julie Nies, *Prin*
EMP: 10 EST: 2013
SALES (est): 102.53K **Privately Held**
Web: www.quinnchildrensdentistry.com
SIC: 8021 Offices and clinics of dentists

(G-2819)
JUNCTION EXPERT INSIGHTS CORP (PA)
3500 S Dupont Hwy (19901-6041)
PHONE.................202 710-9258
Thomas Jeng, *CEO*
EMP: 6 EST: 2018
SALES (est): 50K
SALES (corp-wide): 50K **Privately Held**
SIC: 7371 7389 Computer software development and applications; Business services, nec

(G-2820)
JUNGLE GYM LLC
1418 S State St (19901-4948)
P.O. Box 1983 (19903-1983)
PHONE.................302 734-1515
EMP: 7 EST: 2007
SALES (est): 230.16K **Privately Held**
Web: www.thejunglegymrehab.com
SIC: 8322 Rehabilitation services

(G-2821)
JUSTIN CONNOR MD LLC
1059 S Bradford St Ste B (19904-4141)
PHONE.................302 483-7115
Justin Connor, *Pr*
EMP: 7 EST: 2018
SALES (est): 110.61K **Privately Held**
SIC: 8011 Offices and clinics of medical doctors

(G-2822)
JUSTIN ONEILL
1990 Fast Landing Rd (19901-2720)
PHONE.................631 346-7333
Justin Oneill, *Prin*
EMP: 6 EST: 2017
SALES (est): 29.71K **Privately Held**
SIC: 7538 General automotive repair shops

(G-2823)
K BS PLUMBING INCORPORATED
518 Lochmeath Way (19904-6452)
PHONE.................302 678-2757
EMP: 5 EST: 1999
SQ FT: 1,850
SALES (est): 481.26K **Privately Held**
Web: www.kbsplumbing.com
SIC: 1711 Plumbing contractors

(G-2824)
K W LANDS NORTH LLC
Also Called: Holiday Inn
1780 N Dupont Hwy (19901-2219)
PHONE.................302 678-0600
EMP: 51 EST: 1998
SALES (est): 989.17K **Privately Held**
Web: www.hiexpress.com
SIC: 7011 Hotels and motels

(G-2825)
K&L ENTERPRISE LLC ✪
1155 E Lebanon Rd (19901-5830)
PHONE.................302 514-1136
Lucien Powell, *Managing Member*
EMP: 5 EST: 2022
SALES (est): 235.55K **Privately Held**
SIC: 4789 Transportation services, nec

(G-2826)
K2 TRUCKING LLC
1609 S State St (19901-5148)
PHONE.................302 257-3135
EMP: 5 EST: 2020
SALES (est): 190.49K **Privately Held**
SIC: 4212 Timber trucking, local

(G-2827)
K9 SERVICE COMPANION INC
8 The Grn Ste A (19901-3618)
PHONE.................716 804-3830
Michael Kornake, *CEO*
EMP: 5
SALES (est): 95.72K **Privately Held**
SIC: 0752 Animal specialty services

(G-2828)
KA ANALYTICS & TECH LLC
1024 Avocado Ave (19901-7908)
PHONE.................800 520-8178
Kankoe Assiongbon, *CEO*
Doctor Kankoe Assiongbon, *CEO*
EMP: 6 EST: 2011
SALES (est): 330.03K **Privately Held**
Web: www.analyticsummit.com
SIC: 8732 Business analysis

Dover - Kent County (G-2829) **GEOGRAPHIC SECTION**

(G-2829)
KAIROS HOME PROS LLC
8 The Grn Ste 8086 (19901-3618)
PHONE..................................302 233-7044
Warren Falden, CEO
EMP: 5 EST: 2016
SALES (est): 288.23K **Privately Held**
SIC: 1521 General remodeling, single-family houses

(G-2830)
KAPPA BIOSCIENCE USA INC
Also Called: Kappa Ingredients Usa, Inc.
850 New Burton Rd Ste 201 (19904-5786)
PHONE..................................609 201-1459
Jorg Buttinghaus, Pr
Kai Schrder, Sec
EMP: 3 EST: 2020
SALES (est): 988.2K **Privately Held**
SIC: 2023 Dietary supplements, dairy and non-dairy based
HQ: Kappa Bioscience As
4. Etasje Silurveien 2b
Oslo 0380

(G-2831)
KAREN Y VCKS LAW OFFCES OF LLC
500 W Loockerman St Ste 102
(19904-7309)
PHONE..................................302 674-1100
EMP: 6 EST: 2007
SQ FT: 1,000
SALES (est): 520.27K **Privately Held**
Web: www.vickslaw.com
SIC: 8111 General practice law office

(G-2832)
KARMA THEORY TATTOO & GALLERY
1022 Lafferty Ln (19901-4642)
PHONE..................................302 526-2096
Paul Todd, Prin
EMP: 5 EST: 2014
SALES (est): 59.81K **Privately Held**
SIC: 7299 Tattoo parlor

(G-2833)
KATHAIROS SOLUTIONS US INC ◆
8 The Grn Ste 4000 (19901-3618)
PHONE..................................855 285-2010
D Brown, CEO
EMP: 20 EST: 2022
SALES (est): 1.89MM **Privately Held**
Web: www.kathairos.com
SIC: 8748 Environmental consultant

(G-2834)
KATHRYN L FORD FMLY PRACTICE
44 Deborah Dr (19901-6403)
PHONE..................................302 674-8088
Paul W Ford, Pt
EMP: 8 EST: 1986
SALES (est): 677.16K **Privately Held**
SIC: 8011 General and family practice, physician/surgeon

(G-2835)
KAZA MEDICAL GROUP INC
Also Called: Kaza, Janaki B MD
810 New Burton Rd (19904-5488)
PHONE..................................302 674-2616
EMP: 21 EST: 1978
SALES (est): 2.05MM **Privately Held**
Web: www.kazamedicalgroup.com
SIC: 8011 General and family practice, physician/surgeon

(G-2836)
KEARNS BRINEN & MONAGHAN INC
371 W North St (19904-6713)
P.O. Box 923 (19903-0923)
PHONE..................................302 736-6481
Mark Lefevre, Pr
EMP: 23 EST: 2004
SALES (est): 2.31MM **Privately Held**
Web: www.kbmcollect.com
SIC: 7322 Collection agency, except real estate

(G-2837)
KEGLERS KORNER PRO SHOP
1600 S Governors Ave (19904-7004)
PHONE..................................302 526-2249
Brian Knauer, Owner
EMP: 7 EST: 2011
SALES (est): 120.95K **Privately Held**
Web: www.keglerskornerproshop.com
SIC: 7933 Bowling centers

(G-2838)
KELITCH INC
8 The Grn Ste 114 (19901-3618)
PHONE..................................847 910-6620
Yanyu Chen, CEO
EMP: 8 EST: 2013
SALES (est): 331.17K **Privately Held**
SIC: 5099 Durable goods, nec

(G-2839)
KELLER WILLIAMS REALTY CE
Also Called: Keller Williams Realtors
1671 S State St (19901-5148)
PHONE..................................302 653-3624
Doreen Lucas, Prin
EMP: 5 EST: 2008
SALES (est): 818.45K **Privately Held**
Web: www.kw.com
SIC: 6531 Real estate agent, residential

(G-2840)
KEN CREST SERVICES
318 Hiawatha Ln (19904-2470)
PHONE..................................302 741-0256
EMP: 9 EST: 2019
SALES (est): 68.44K **Privately Held**
Web: www.kencrest.org
SIC: 7361 Employment agencies

(G-2841)
KENCREST SERVICES
6 Bellrive Ct (19904-2306)
PHONE..................................302 735-1664
Sheena Givens, Pr
EMP: 8 EST: 2018
SALES (est): 189.39K **Privately Held**
Web: www.kencrest.org
SIC: 8748 Business consulting, nec

(G-2842)
KENNETH DALE RALOSKY
Also Called: Dales Lawn Care,
2823 Lockwood Chapel Rd (19904-5014)
PHONE..................................302 343-9464
Kenneth Dale Ralosky, Prin
EMP: 6 EST: 2011
SALES (est): 135.91K **Privately Held**
SIC: 0782 Lawn care services

(G-2843)
KENNETH J HURLEY
3998 Bayside Dr (19901-7169)
PHONE..................................302 734-3251
Kenneth J Hurley, Prin
EMP: 5 EST: 2015
SALES (est): 123.16K **Privately Held**
SIC: 0782 Lawn services

(G-2844)
KENNHARR LLC
8 The Grn Ste 4000 (19901-3618)
PHONE..................................800 692-7970
EMP: 6
SALES (est): 65.1K **Privately Held**
SIC: 7299 Miscellaneous personal service

(G-2845)
KENNY K VU
811 S Governors Ave (19904-4158)
PHONE..................................302 678-0510
Kenny K Vu, Prin
EMP: 9 EST: 2009
SALES (est): 133.29K **Privately Held**
SIC: 8011 General and family practice, physician/surgeon

(G-2846)
KENNY VU
111 Wolf Creek Blvd Ste 2 (19901-4969)
PHONE..................................302 526-2361
EMP: 7 EST: 2019
SALES (est): 83.03K **Privately Held**
SIC: 8011 General and family practice, physician/surgeon

(G-2847)
KENT CNTY CMNTY ACTION AGCY IN
120a S Governors Ave (19904-3223)
PHONE..................................302 678-1949
Sara Butler, Ex Dir
Reverend Larry Blinon, Treas
EMP: 11 EST: 1979
SALES (est): 514.04K **Privately Held**
SIC: 8322 Childrens' aid society

(G-2848)
KENT COUNTY COMMUNITY SCHOOL
117 Saulsbury Rd (19904-2719)
PHONE..................................302 734-9011
EMP: 5 EST: 2019
SALES (est): 65.91K **Privately Held**
Web: kccs.capital.k12.de.us
SIC: 7999 Instruction schools, camps, and services

(G-2849)
KENT FAMILY MEDICINE
960 Forest St (19904-3470)
PHONE..................................302 747-7903
EMP: 5 EST: 2016
SALES (est): 50.87K **Privately Held**
SIC: 8099 Health and allied services, nec

(G-2850)
KENT GENERAL HOSPITAL
Also Called: Saint Jnes Ctr For Bhvral Hlth
725 Horsepond Rd (19901-7232)
PHONE..................................302 744-7688
Janis Chester, Dir
EMP: 832
Web: www.bayhealth.org
SIC: 8062 General medical and surgical hospitals
HQ: Kent General Hospital
640 S State St
Dover DE 19901
302 674-4700

(G-2851)
KENT GENERAL HOSPITAL (HQ)
Also Called: Milford Memorial Hospital
640 S State St (19901-3599)
PHONE..................................302 674-4700
Terry M Murphy, Pr
EMP: 81 EST: 1921
SQ FT: 335,000
SALES (est): 322.56MM **Privately Held**
Web: www.bayhealth.org
SIC: 8062 Hospital, affiliated with AMA residency
PA: Bayhealth Medical Center, Inc.
640 S State St
Dover DE 19901

(G-2852)
KENT LEASING COMPANY INC
2181 S Dupont Hwy (19901-5556)
P.O. Box 456 (19903-0456)
PHONE..................................302 697-3000
John W Whitby Junior, Pr
Audrey Whitby, *
EMP: 9 EST: 1972
SQ FT: 3,000
SALES (est): 152.02K **Privately Held**
SIC: 7514 Rent-a-car service

(G-2853)
KENT PEDIATRICS
748 S New St Ofc 1 (19904-3573)
PHONE..................................302 747-7279
EMP: 8 EST: 2018
SALES (est): 249.77K **Privately Held**
Web: www.kentpediatrics.com
SIC: 8011 Pediatrician

(G-2854)
KENT PEDIATRICS LLC
1102 S Dupont Hwy Ste 1 (19901-4493)
PHONE..................................302 264-9691
Osama Hussein, Prin
EMP: 10 EST: 2013
SALES (est): 370.33K **Privately Held**
Web: www.kentpediatrics.com
SIC: 8011 Pediatrician

(G-2855)
KENT PULMONARY ASSOCIATES LLC
807 S Bradford St (19904-4137)
PHONE..................................302 674-7155
David A Jawahar, Prin
EMP: 5 EST: 2006
SALES (est): 942.9K **Privately Held**
Web: www.kentpulmonaryllc.com
SIC: 8011 Pulmonary specialist, physician/surgeon

(G-2856)
KENT SIGN COMPANY INC
2 E Bradys Ln (19901-6310)
PHONE..................................302 697-2181
Riley Mccalister, VP
William S Craven, Pr
Leona Cravens, Sec
Kim Diehl, Sec
EMP: 10 EST: 1958
SALES (est): 919.03K **Privately Held**
Web: www.kentsigns.net
SIC: 5046 1799 7539 3993 Signs, electrical; Sign installation and maintenance; Electrical services; Electric signs

(G-2857)
KENT SUSSEX AUTO CARE INC
145 Burning Tree Rd (19904-9447)
PHONE..................................302 422-3337
Sam Shah, Pr
EMP: 7 EST: 2005
SALES (est): 223.86K **Privately Held**
Web: www.kentsussexautocarede.com
SIC: 7538 General automotive repair shops

(G-2858)
KENT SUSSEX COMMUNITY SERVICES
1241 College Park Dr (19904-8713)

GEOGRAPHIC SECTION   Dover - Kent County (G-2888)

PHONE..............................302 384-6926
EMP: 28 EST: 2017
SALES (est): 4.88MM Privately Held
Web: www.kscs.org
SIC: 8093 Mental health clinic, outpatient

(G-2859)
KENTON CHILD CARE
1298 Mckee Rd (19904-1381)
P.O. Box 340 (19955-0340)
PHONE..............................302 674-8142
Donna Revel, Owner
EMP: 9 EST: 2008
SALES (est): 195.38K Privately Held
SIC: 8351 Child day care services

(G-2860)
KETURAHS CLEANING
403 Dogwood Ave (19904-4807)
PHONE..............................302 242-3967
Adalyn Neal, Prin
EMP: 5 EST: 2017
SALES (est): 50.83K Privately Held
SIC: 7699 Cleaning services

(G-2861)
KEYSTONE FUNDING INC
Also Called: Rock Rates
519 S Red Haven Ln (19901-6483)
PHONE..............................484 798-9084
Mark Succarotte, Brnch Mgr
EMP: 10
Web: www.keystonefunding.com
SIC: 6162 Mortgage bankers and loan correspondents
PA: Keystone Funding, Inc
523 S Red Hven Ln Ste 101
Dover DE 19901

(G-2862)
KEYSTONE FUNDING INC (PA)
Also Called: Keystone Funding Fairfax Co
523 S Red Haven Ln Ste 101 (19901)
PHONE..............................610 644-6423
Jared Martin, Pr
EMP: 12 EST: 2006
SALES (est): 4.55MM Privately Held
Web: www.keystonefunding.com
SIC: 6162 Mortgage bankers and loan correspondents

(G-2863)
KGS DIGITAL INC
8 The Grn (19901-3618)
PHONE..............................302 213-3979
Tom Anderson, Dir
EMP: 5
SALES (est): 199.4K Privately Held
SIC: 7371 Computer software development and applications

(G-2864)
KID AGAINS INC
33 Lindley Dr (19904-3807)
PHONE..............................631 830-5228
Frank Ko, CEO
Michael Prendergast, Pr
▲ EMP: 2 EST: 2013
SALES (est): 98.96K Privately Held
SIC: 3944 7389 Board games, puzzles, and models, except electronic; Business services, nec

(G-2865)
KIDD ROBERT W III DDS
850 S State St (19901-4113)
P.O. Box 657 (19903-0657)
PHONE..............................302 678-1440
Robert W Kidd Iii D.d.s., Owner
EMP: 15 EST: 1968

SQ FT: 1,800
SALES (est): 302.63K Privately Held
SIC: 8021 Orthodontist

(G-2866)
KIDS R US LEARNING CENTER INC
Also Called: Kids-R-Us Learning Center
425 Webbs Ln (19904-5439)
PHONE..............................302 678-1234
Sylvia Davis, Prin
EMP: 6 EST: 2011
SALES (est): 361.88K Privately Held
SIC: 8351 Child day care services

(G-2867)
KIDS TEENS PEDIATRICS OF DOVER
125 Greentree Dr Ste 1 (19904-7656)
PHONE..............................302 538-5624
Amal Ouad, Prin
EMP: 6 EST: 2014
SALES (est): 910.81K Privately Held
Web: www.ktpdover.com
SIC: 8011 Pediatrician

(G-2868)
KIDS UNIVERSITY LLC
535 Schooner Way (19901-8604)
PHONE..............................302 514-8187
EMP: 6 EST: 2021
SALES (est): 268.08K Privately Held
SIC: 7389 Business Activities at Non-Commercial Site

(G-2869)
KIEFA INC (PA) ✪
614 N Dupont Hwy Ste 210 (19901-3900)
PHONE..............................845 803-5924
Peter Heidrich, CEO
EMP: 2 EST: 2022
SALES (est): 71.36K
SALES (corp-wide): 71.36K Privately Held
SIC: 7372 Business oriented computer software

(G-2870)
KIM GAINES
3156 Forrest Ave (19904-5317)
PHONE..............................302 736-3000
Kim Gaines, Pr
EMP: 5 EST: 2016
SALES (est): 263.39K Privately Held
SIC: 0742 Veterinarian, animal specialties

(G-2871)
KINDRED KIDS YOGA
43 Sherwood Ct (19904-6819)
PHONE..............................302 741-2240
Gwen Senato, Prin
EMP: 5 EST: 2015
SALES (est): 29.16K Privately Held
SIC: 7999 Yoga instruction

(G-2872)
KING JOSIAH COMPANIES LLC
9 E Loockerman St Ste 202-665 (19901-8306)
PHONE..............................855 312-3700
Robert Griffie, Managing Member
EMP: 7 EST: 2016
SALES (est): 461K Privately Held
Web: www.kingjoco.com
SIC: 6531 Real estate agents and managers

(G-2873)
KING OF SWEETS INC
47 S West St (19904-3265)
PHONE..............................302 730-8200
Janine Altenkirch, Pr
EMP: 15 EST: 2013
SALES (est): 744.64K Privately Held

Web: www.kingofsweetsonline.com
SIC: 5441 5145 Candy; Confectionery

(G-2874)
KING OF SWEETS DISTRIBUTION
47 S West St (19904-3265)
PHONE..............................302 730-8200
Ralf Conrad, CEO
EMP: 8 EST: 2010
SALES (est): 243.46K Privately Held
Web: www.kingofsweetsonline.com
SIC: 5149 Chocolate

(G-2875)
KING OF SWEETS ONLINE INC
47 S West St (19904-3265)
PHONE..............................302 730-8200
Ralf Conrad, CEO
Janine Altenkirch, Sec
EMP: 10 EST: 2010
SALES (est): 694.58K Privately Held
Web: www.kingofsweetsonline.com
SIC: 5149 Chocolate

(G-2876)
KING-EDWARDS RESIDENCES LLC
8 The Grn Ste D (19901-3618)
PHONE..............................646 389-5830
EMP: 7 EST: 2021
SALES (est): 454.58K Privately Held
SIC: 6799 6531 Real estate investors, except property operators; Real estate leasing and rentals

(G-2877)
KINGS SEALCOATING
416 Dogwood Ave (19904-4879)
PHONE..............................302 674-1568
Ryan Cushman, Prin
EMP: 7 EST: 2019
SALES (est): 230.52K Privately Held
Web: www.kingssealcoating.com
SIC: 2952 Asphalt felts and coatings

(G-2878)
KINSTA INC
838 Walker Rd Ste 21-2 (19904-2751)
PHONE..............................310 736-9306
Mark Gavalda, CEO
Jonathan Penland, *
David R D Young, *
EMP: 35 EST: 2019
SALES (est): 1.54MM Privately Held
Web: www.kinsta.com
SIC: 7374 Data processing service

(G-2879)
KIWETINOHK MARKETING US CORP
1675 S State St Ste B (19901-5140)
PHONE..............................403 827-6958
Pat Carlson, CEO
EMP: 7 EST: 2021
SALES (est): 81.96K Privately Held
SIC: 1311 Crude petroleum and natural gas

(G-2880)
KNEPPER & STRATTON
309 S State St Ste C (19901-6753)
PHONE..............................302 658-1717
EMP: 6
Web: www.knepperstratton.com
SIC: 8111 General practice attorney, lawyer
PA: Knepper & Stratton
1228 N King St
Wilmington DE 19801

(G-2881)
KNRP LLC
30 Chadwick Dr (19901-5827)
PHONE..............................408 480-8501

John Schaible, VP
EMP: 5 EST: 2011
SALES (est): 94.81K Privately Held
SIC: 7389 Design services

(G-2882)
KODO DIGITAL SYSTEMS INC
8 The Grn Ste A (19901-3618)
PHONE..............................909 843-0946
Arputham Ganesan, CEO
Kiran Asola, Dir
EMP: 5 EST: 2021
SALES (est): 107.01K Privately Held
SIC: 7371 Custom computer programming services

(G-2883)
KOHERIC LLC
8 The Grn (19901-3618)
PHONE..............................646 801-6741
EMP: 3
SALES (est): 128.34K Privately Held
SIC: 7372 Prepackaged software

(G-2884)
KORTEX ENTERPRISES LLC ✪
896 S State St Unit 613 (19901-4148)
PHONE..............................678 551-8260
Daniel Koenigsleb, CEO
Joseph Doughty, COO
EMP: 15 EST: 2023
SALES (est): 518.76K Privately Held
SIC: 7372 Prepackaged software

(G-2885)
KPKM INC
Also Called: Maaco Collision Repr Auto Pntg
1062 Lafferty Ln (19901-4642)
P.O. Box 1852 (19903-1852)
PHONE..............................302 678-0271
Mark Lopisz, Pr
EMP: 8 EST: 2006
SALES (est): 499.82K Privately Held
SIC: 7532 Body shop, automotive

(G-2886)
KRAFT HEINZ COMPANY
Kraft Foods
1250 W North St (19904-7756)
PHONE..............................302 734-6100
Randy Klongland, Mgr
EMP: 800
SALES (corp-wide): 26.48B Publicly Held
Web: stats.mktplacegateway.com
SIC: 2099 2066 2051 2041 Gelatin dessert preparations; Chocolate and cocoa products; Bread, cake, and related products; Flour and other grain mill products
PA: The Heinz Kraft Company
1 Ppg Pl Ste 3400
Pittsburgh PA 15222
412 456-5700

(G-2887)
KRH TRUCKING LLC
112 Wilder Rd (19904-6056)
PHONE..............................302 535-8407
Keshawn Hopkins, Prin
EMP: 5 EST: 2015
SALES (est): 273.95K Privately Held
SIC: 4213 Trucking, except local

(G-2888)
KSRE CAPITAL LLC
8 The Grn Ste A (19901-3618)
PHONE..............................281 501-3777
EMP: 10 EST: 2020
SIC: 6719 Holding companies, nec

Dover - Kent County (G-2889) GEOGRAPHIC SECTION

(G-2889)
KURRENSY INC
8 The Grn Ste 10386 (19901-3618)
PHONE.............................347 228-9306
Sabrina Abraham, *CEO*
EMP: 3 **EST:** 2020
SALES (est): 71.13K **Privately Held**
SIC: 7372 Educational computer software

(G-2890)
KURTZ CONSTRUCTION LLC
506 Rose Dale Ln (19904-1606)
PHONE.............................302 943-4754
EMP: 7 **EST:** 2018
SALES (est): 473.1K **Privately Held**
SIC: 1521 Single-family housing construction

(G-2891)
KW GARDEN
Also Called: Sleep Inn
1784 N Dupont Hwy (19901-2219)
PHONE.............................302 735-7770
Tad Fox, *Genl Mgr*
EMP: 16 **EST:** 2009
SALES (est): 237.06K **Privately Held**
Web: www.choicehotels.com
SIC: 7011 Hotels and motels

(G-2892)
L & W INSURANCE INC
Also Called: Nationwide
1154 S Governors Ave (19904-6904)
P.O. Box 918 (19903-0918)
PHONE.............................302 674-3500
Gary Wyatt, *Acctnt*
EMP: 29 **EST:** 2004
SALES (est): 3.76MM **Privately Held**
Web: www.lwinsurance.com
SIC: 6411 Insurance agents, nec

(G-2893)
L2 TRADE LLC
Also Called: D2cmed
8 The Grn Ste B (19901-3618)
PHONE.............................603 921-7930
Gs Reddy, *Managing Member*
EMP: 11 **EST:** 2021
SALES (est): 911.76K **Privately Held**
Web: www.d2cmed.com
SIC: 5122 7389 Drugs, proprietaries, and sundries; Business services, nec

(G-2894)
L3D LLC
1671 S State St (19901-5148)
PHONE.............................302 677-0031
EMP: 6 **EST:** 2004
SALES (est): 440.34K **Privately Held**
SIC: 6531 Multiple listing service, real estate

(G-2895)
LA BELLA VITA SALON & DAY SPA
525 S Red Haven Ln (19901-6483)
PHONE.............................302 883-2597
Dawn Dicecco, *Owner*
EMP: 6 **EST:** 2010
SALES (est): 367.26K **Privately Held**
Web: www.labellavitaofde.com
SIC: 7991 Spas

(G-2896)
LACONIC INNOVATIONS CO
8 The Grn Ste A (19901-3618)
PHONE.............................302 501-6069
Anan Suliman, *CEO*
EMP: 10 **EST:** 2020
SALES (est): 420.91K **Privately Held**
SIC: 7371 Software programming applications

(G-2897)
LADDER MART USA LLC
9 E Loockerman St Ste 311 (19901-8305)
PHONE.............................866 524-4536
Ryan Torrie, *CEO*
EMP: 22 **EST:** 2021
SALES (est): 1.19MM **Privately Held**
SIC: 5085 Industrial supplies

(G-2898)
LADY LIFTERS GYM
5734 Forrest Ave (19904-5113)
PHONE.............................302 222-2321
EMP: 6 **EST:** 2016
SALES (est): 57.02K **Privately Held**
Web: www.ladyliftersgym.com
SIC: 7999 Gymnastic instruction, non-membership

(G-2899)
LADYCAR LLC ✪
8 The Grn Ste B (19901-3618)
PHONE.............................984 389-9913
Anais Bermond, *Prin*
EMP: 5 **EST:** 2022
SALES (est): 206.44K **Privately Held**
SIC: 4121 Taxicabs

(G-2900)
LAKE PROPERTIES GROUP LLC
8 The Grn (19901-3618)
PHONE.............................516 695-1441
EMP: 5
SALES (est): 300.36K **Privately Held**
SIC: 6531 7389 Real estate leasing and rentals; Business services, nec

(G-2901)
LANDINGS
479 Chevron St (19902-5062)
PHONE.............................302 233-8421
EMP: 5 **EST:** 2014
SALES (est): 124.9K **Privately Held**
Web: www.doverfss.com
SIC: 7299 Tuxedo rental

(G-2902)
LANDMARK HOMES
68 Representative Ln (19904-2491)
P.O. Box 1037 (19709-7037)
PHONE.............................302 388-8557
EMP: 7 **EST:** 2014
SALES (est): 396.4K **Privately Held**
Web: www.lmkhomes.com
SIC: 6799 Investors, nec

(G-2903)
LANGDON GROUP LLC (PA)
8 The Grn Ste A (19901-3618)
PHONE.............................240 578-5400
Kamel Ismail, *Pr*
EMP: 7 **EST:** 2020
SALES (est): 145.26K
SALES (corp-wide): 145.26K **Privately Held**
SIC: 6519 7389 Real property lessors, nec; Business services, nec

(G-2904)
LASER & PLASTIC SURGERY CENTER
200 Banning St Ste 230 (19904-3487)
PHONE.............................302 674-4865
David Smith Doctor, *Pr*
EMP: 5 **EST:** 1974
SQ FT: 5,750
SALES (est): 227.43K **Privately Held**
SIC: 8011 Plastic surgeon

(G-2905)
LASHEDBYINDIE LLC ✪
400 Isabelle Isle Apt 304 (19904-5299)
PHONE.............................267 734-4850
Rasheena Muhammad, *Managing Member*
EMP: 2 **EST:** 2022
SALES (est): 92.41K **Privately Held**
SIC: 3999 7389 Eyelashes, artificial; Business services, nec

(G-2906)
LATAM CORPORATE SERVICES LLC
8 The Grn Ste B (19901-3618)
PHONE.............................301 375-0714
EMP: 10 **EST:** 2018
SALES (est): 631.29K **Privately Held**
SIC: 8748 7379 7389 Business consulting, nec; Computer related consulting services; Business services, nec

(G-2907)
LAURA B MOYLAN MD
200 Banning St Ste 320 (19904-3488)
PHONE.............................302 674-0223
EMP: 11 **EST:** 2017
SALES (est): 275.68K **Privately Held**
Web: www.dedicatedtowomenobgyn.com
SIC: 8011 Gynecologist

(G-2908)
LAURA CASTILLO
885 S Governors Ave (19904-4158)
PHONE.............................302 734-5861
EMP: 5 **EST:** 2019
SALES (est): 47.44K **Privately Held**
SIC: 8042 Offices and clinics of optometrists

(G-2909)
LAURA M GRAVELIN M D
200 Banning St Ste 340 (19904-3490)
PHONE.............................302 734-1414
Laura Gravelin, *Mgr*
EMP: 8 **EST:** 2015
SALES (est): 82.61K **Privately Held**
SIC: 8011 Cardiologist and cardio-vascular specialist

(G-2910)
LAVOISIER INC
8 The Grn Ste 10885 (19901-3618)
PHONE.............................302 446-3244
Shuai Wang, *CEO*
EMP: 3 **EST:** 2020
SALES (est): 700K **Privately Held**
SIC: 2834 Pharmaceutical preparations

(G-2911)
LAW OFFICE LAURA A YIENGST LLC
314 S State St (19901-6730)
PHONE.............................302 264-9780
Donna Juhrden, *Pr*
EMP: 6 **EST:** 2010
SALES (est): 477.14K **Privately Held**
Web: www.yiengstlaw.com
SIC: 8111 General practice attorney, lawyer

(G-2912)
LAW OFFICES GARY R DODGE PA
250 Beiser Blvd Ste 202 (19904-7795)
PHONE.............................302 674-5400
Gary R Dodge, *Pr*
EMP: 5 **EST:** 1983
SALES (est): 398.41K **Privately Held**
Web: www.curleydodgefunk.com
SIC: 8111 General practice law office

(G-2913)
LAW OFFICES OF SEAN M LYNN PA
308 S State St (19901-6730)
PHONE.............................302 734-2000
Sean M Lynn, *Owner*
EMP: 9 **EST:** 2016
SALES (est): 373.49K **Privately Held**
Web: www.bentonlynnlaw.com
SIC: 8111 General practice attorney, lawyer

(G-2914)
LAWALL PROSTHETICS - ORTHOTICS
514 N Dupont Hwy (19901-3961)
PHONE.............................302 677-0693
Doug Davis, *Mgr*
EMP: 5
Web: www.lawall.com
SIC: 8011 8069 Specialized medical practitioners, except internal; Childrens' hospital
PA: Lawall Prosthetics - Orthotics Inc.
1822 Augustine Cut Off
Wilmington DE 19803

(G-2915)
LAWRENCE A LOUIE DMD
250 Beiser Blvd Ste 101 (19904-7795)
PHONE.............................302 674-5437
Lawrence A Louie D.m.d., *Owner*
EMP: 6 **EST:** 1991
SALES (est): 303.86K **Privately Held**
SIC: 8021 Pedodontist

(G-2916)
LAWRENCE M LEWANDOSKI MD
4601 S Dupont Hwy Ste 2 (19901-6405)
PHONE.............................302 698-1100
Lawrence M Lewandoski Md, *Prin*
EMP: 5 **EST:** 2005
SALES (est): 155.86K **Privately Held**
SIC: 8011 General and family practice, physician/surgeon

(G-2917)
LAWTER PLANNING GROUP INC
1305 S Governors Ave (19904-4803)
P.O. Box 1457 (19903-1457)
PHONE.............................302 736-6065
Dallas A Lawter, *Pr*
Sandra Lawter O'toole, *VP*
EMP: 8 **EST:** 1987
SALES (est): 647.45K **Privately Held**
Web: www.lawterotoolewealth.com
SIC: 6282 Investment advisory service

(G-2918)
LEAD ECONOMY LLC
8 The Grn Ste 8162 (19901-3618)
PHONE.............................914 355-1671
Michael Rongo, *Dir*
EMP: 50 **EST:** 2017
SALES (est): 2.33MM
SALES (corp-wide): 5.6MM **Privately Held**
SIC: 7311 Advertising agencies
PA: Trend Capital Holdings Inc.
655 W Columbia Way # 300
Vancouver WA 98660
360 521-9342

(G-2919)
LEAD STOCK
207 W Loockerman St (19904-3247)
PHONE.............................424 306-2700
EMP: 9
SALES (est): 118.11K **Privately Held**
Web: www.theleadstock.com
SIC: 8742 Marketing consulting services

(G-2920)
LEADIFIC SOLUTIONS LLC
850 New Burton Rd Ste 201 (19904-5786)
PHONE.............................866 265-0771
Russell J Gohl, *Managing Member*

GEOGRAPHIC SECTION

Dover - Kent County (G-2950)

EMP: 5 EST: 2021
SALES (est): 350K **Privately Held**
SIC: 7371 Software programming applications

(G-2921)
LEARNING YEARS PRESCHOOL
2 Riverside Rd (19904-5723)
PHONE..................................302 241-4781
Kattie R Gibson, *Owner*
EMP: 5 EST: 2013
SALES (est): 70.07K **Privately Held**
SIC: 8351 Preschool center

(G-2922)
LECHIA INC
8 The Grn Ste 11532 (19901-3618)
PHONE..................................302 261-5733
Nicholas Molnar, *CEO*
EMP: 4 EST: 2020
SALES (est): 289.55K **Privately Held**
Web: www.lechia.co
SIC: 2026 Fluid milk

(G-2923)
LEE LYNN INC
Also Called: Melvin's Sunoco
1020 S State St (19901-6925)
PHONE..................................302 678-9978
James C Davis, *Pr*
Lisa Davis, *VP*
EMP: 10 EST: 1971
SQ FT: 3,000
SALES (est): 982.61K **Privately Held**
Web: www.melvins-sc.com
SIC: 7699 7538 Engine repair and replacement, non-automotive; General automotive repair shops

(G-2924)
LEE M DENNIS MD
960 Forest St (19904-3470)
PHONE..................................302 735-1888
Lee M Dennis Md, *Owner*
Lee M Dennis, *Owner*
▲ EMP: 5 EST: 1991
SALES (est): 486.43K **Privately Held**
Web: www.leemdennismd.com
SIC: 8011 General and family practice, physician/surgeon

(G-2925)
LEE NAILS
63 Greentree Dr (19904-2685)
PHONE..................................302 674-5001
EMP: 5 EST: 1995
SALES (est): 73.7K **Privately Held**
SIC: 7231 Manicurist, pedicurist

(G-2926)
LEGACY GLOBAL DEVELOPMENTS LLC
8 The Grn Ste A (19901-3618)
PHONE..................................310 929-9862
Yaw Darko, *Managing Member*
EMP: 5 EST: 2021
SALES (est): 216.6K **Privately Held**
SIC: 6799 Venture capital companies

(G-2927)
LEGALNATURE LLC (PA)
8 The Grn Ste 1 (19901-3618)
PHONE..................................888 881-1139
Corey Bray, *CEO*
Bernard Bray, *Prin*
EMP: 9 EST: 2016
SALES (est): 935.56K
SALES (corp-wide): 935.56K **Privately Held**
Web: www.legalnature.com

SIC: 8111 Legal services

(G-2928)
LEMPAT FOODS LLC
19 Holly Cove Ln (19901-6285)
PHONE..................................914 449-1803
EMP: 2 EST: 2020
SALES (est): 35K **Privately Held**
Web: www.lempatfoods.com
SIC: 2499 Food handling and processing products, wood

(G-2929)
LETS GATHER LLC
8 The Grn Ste B (19901-3618)
PHONE..................................607 210-0581
Sheridan Lilly, *Managing Member*
EMP: 5 EST: 2021
SALES (est): 60.12K **Privately Held**
SIC: 7929 Entertainers and entertainment groups

(G-2930)
LEVEL FUNDED HLTH PARTNERS LLC
9 E Loockerman St Ste 215 (19901-7347)
PHONE..................................847 310-8190
Russell Carpel, *CEO*
EMP: 7 EST: 2016
SALES (est): 242.77K **Privately Held**
Web: www.levelfunded.com
SIC: 8099 Health and allied services, nec

(G-2931)
LEVELS EXPRESS LOGISTICS LLC
565 Harvest Grove Trl (19901-2796)
PHONE..................................302 760-3750
EMP: 10 EST: 2020
SALES (est): 619.47K **Privately Held**
SIC: 4215 Courier services, except by air

(G-2932)
LEVINES ENTERPRISES LLC
8 The Grn (19901-3618)
PHONE..................................203 212-8441
EMP: 10 EST: 2019
SALES (est): 570.44K **Privately Held**
SIC: 7311 Advertising consultant

(G-2933)
LIBERATED WORLD LLC
8 The Grn Ste 8 (19901-3618)
PHONE..................................347 688-4943
EMP: 7
SALES (est): 78.16K **Privately Held**
SIC: 2389 Apparel and accessories, nec

(G-2934)
LIBERTO DEVELOPMENT LTD
Also Called: Chruch Creek
1500 E Lebanon Rd (19901-5834)
PHONE..................................302 698-1104
EMP: 7 EST: 1986
SALES (est): 1.41MM **Privately Held**
Web: www.libertoplaza.com
SIC: 1521 Prefabricated single-family house erection

(G-2935)
LIBERTY CONSULTANCY FIRM LLC ✪
1041 N Dupont Hwy (19901-2006)
PHONE..................................302 493-4344
Andre Halley, *CEO*
EMP: 20 EST: 2023
SALES (est): 612.9K **Privately Held**
SIC: 8742 7389 Management consulting services

(G-2936)
LIBERTY PEST CONTROL LLC
72 Lynnhaven Dr (19904-6929)
PHONE..................................302 734-1507
EMP: 6 EST: 2016
SALES (est): 45.55K **Privately Held**
SIC: 7342 Pest control in structures

(G-2937)
LIBERTY TAX
1636 S Governors Ave (19904-7004)
PHONE..................................302 678-3101
EMP: 5 EST: 2019
SALES (est): 18.45K **Privately Held**
Web: www.libertytax.com
SIC: 7291 Tax return preparation services

(G-2938)
LICE LIFTERS DISTRIBUTION LLC ✪
Also Called: Health & Beauty
8 The Grn Ste R (19901-3618)
P.O. Box 280 (29304-0280)
PHONE..................................864 680-4030
EMP: 5 EST: 2023
SALES (est): 175K **Privately Held**
SIC: 5122 Cosmetics

(G-2939)
LIDS CORPORATION
Also Called: Hat World
1365 N Dupont Hwy Ste 4018 (19901-8723)
PHONE..................................302 736-8465
Daniel Andrews, *Mgr*
EMP: 4
Web: www.lids.com
SIC: 5699 2395 Caps and gowns (academic vestments); Embroidery products, except Schiffli machine
PA: Lids Corporation
     7676 Interactive Way # 300
     Indianapolis IN 46278

(G-2940)
LIFE CHOICE
240 Norwich Way (19901-1626)
PHONE..................................302 526-2080
Donna Bolger, *Prin*
EMP: 5 EST: 2016
SALES (est): 60.74K **Privately Held**
SIC: 8399 Advocacy group

(G-2941)
LIFESOURCE CONSULTING SVCS LLC
8 The Grn Ste 8155 (19901-3618)
PHONE..................................302 257-6247
EMP: 15 EST: 2018
SALES (est): 500K **Privately Held**
SIC: 8742 Management consulting services

(G-2942)
LIFESQUARED INC
1679 S Dupont Hwy (19901-5101)
PHONE..................................415 475-9090
Zhou Yu, *CEO*
Tingting Hu, *Prin*
Zhou Yu, *Prin*
EMP: 2 EST: 2013
SALES (est): 99.7K **Privately Held**
SIC: 7379 7372 7389 Online services technology consultants; Application computer software; Business services, nec

(G-2943)
LIFETIME FINANCIAL SVCS LLC
292 Evelyndale Dr (19901-1825)
PHONE..................................302 678-1300
EMP: 6 EST: 2013
SALES (est): 123.86K **Privately Held**

SIC: 7389 Financial services

(G-2944)
LIFETOUCH PORTRAIT STUDIOS INC
Also Called: Lifetouch
5000 Dover Mall (19901-8726)
PHONE..................................302 734-9870
EMP: 10
SALES (corp-wide): 2.47B **Privately Held**
Web: www.lifetouch.com
SIC: 7221 Photographer, still or video
HQ: Lifetouch Portrait Studios Inc.
    11000 Viking Dr
    Eden Prairie MN 55344
    952 826-4335

(G-2945)
LIGHTBOX JEWELRY INC
3500 S Dupont Hwy (19901-6041)
PHONE..................................833 270-3737
EMP: 10 EST: 2017
SALES (est): 41.02K **Privately Held**
Web: www.lightboxjewelry.com
SIC: 3911 Jewelry, precious metal

(G-2946)
LIGUORI MORRIS & REDDIN
46 The Grn (19901-3612)
PHONE..................................302 678-9900
Jim Liguori, *Pt*
Gregg Morris, *Pt*
Lori Reddin, *Pt*
EMP: 8 EST: 1999
SALES (est): 750.02K **Privately Held**
SIC: 8111 General practice attorney, lawyer

(G-2947)
LIKEHOOP INC (PA)
8 The Grn Ste A (19901-3618)
PHONE..................................646 643-7738
Guillermo Anthony Coste, *Prin*
EMP: 5 EST: 2015
SALES (est): 575.79K
SALES (corp-wide): 575.79K **Privately Held**
Web: www.likehoop.com
SIC: 7371 7389 Computer software development and applications; Business services, nec

(G-2948)
LILY INTRNL MEDICINE ASSCS LLC
811 Monroe Ter (19904-4117)
PHONE..................................302 424-1000
Ifeanyi A Udezulu, *Prin*
EMP: 5 EST: 2009
SALES (est): 197.87K **Privately Held**
SIC: 8099 Health and allied services, nec

(G-2949)
LIME CCNUT DATA INTLLGNCE LCDI
Also Called: Lcdi
8 The Grn Ste A (19901-3618)
PHONE..................................302 272-2858
Valentin Broeksmit, *Pr*
EMP: 5 EST: 2020
SALES (est): 109.09K **Privately Held**
SIC: 7371 Computer software development

(G-2950)
LINCARE
5 Maggies Way Ste 4 (19901-4893)
PHONE..................................302 736-1210
Jolene Ward, *Prin*
EMP: 7 EST: 2018
SALES (est): 92.61K **Privately Held**
Web: www.lincare.com
SIC: 7352 Medical equipment rental

Dover - Kent County (G-2951)

(G-2951)
LINDA BRANNOCK
1671 S State St (19901-5148)
PHONE..................................302 346-3124
Linda Brannock, *Prin*
EMP: 5 EST: 2017
SALES (est): 88.43K **Privately Held**
Web: lindabrannock.kw.com
SIC: 6531 Real estate brokers and agents

(G-2952)
LINKERS INC
8 The Grn (19901-3618)
PHONE..................................408 757-0021
Ganna Kravets, *CEO*
EMP: 15
SALES (est): 494.46K **Privately Held**
SIC: 7371 7389 Computer software development and applications; Business Activities at Non-Commercial Site

(G-2953)
LINX REALTY 2 LLC (PA)
8 The Grn Ste A (19901-3618)
PHONE..................................888 233-8901
EMP: 6 EST: 2016
SALES (est): 209.95K
SALES (corp-wide): 209.95K **Privately Held**
SIC: 6799 7389 Real estate investors, except property operators; Business services, nec

(G-2954)
LINX SECURITY INC
850 New Burton Rd (19904-5785)
PHONE..................................302 907-9848
Evrona Katzman, *CEO*
EMP: 10
SALES (est): 355.79K **Privately Held**
SIC: 7382 Security systems services

(G-2955)
LISA PRISCO PT
810 New Burton Rd Ste 2 (19904-5488)
PHONE..................................302 698-4256
Lisa Prisco, *CEO*
EMP: 6 EST: 2017
SALES (est): 26.84K **Privately Held**
SIC: 8049 Offices of health practitioner

(G-2956)
LITHOS CARBON INC ◇
1111b S Governors Ave # 6084 (19904-6903)
PHONE..................................425 274-3276
Mary Yap, *CEO*
EMP: 10 EST: 2023
SALES (est): 437.1K **Privately Held**
SIC: 8731 Agricultural research

(G-2957)
LITTLE SCHOOL INC
Also Called: Afternoon Little
105 Mont Blanc Blvd (19904-7615)
PHONE..................................302 734-3040
EMP: 12 EST: 1976
SALES (est): 219.63K **Privately Held**
Web: dover.kidscottage.com
SIC: 8351 Preschool center

(G-2958)
LIV180 INC (PA) ◇
Also Called: Azie.ai
8 The Grn Ste A (19901-3618)
PHONE..................................561 235-9669
Azgari Lipshy, *CEO*
EMP: 8 EST: 2023
SALES (est): 343.22K
SALES (corp-wide): 343.22K **Privately Held**

SIC: 7372 7389 Application computer software; Business services, nec

(G-2959)
LIVING GREAT MEDICAL ASSOC LLC
1027 S Bradford St (19904-4141)
PHONE..................................302 734-9200
Rosalie Vargas, *Pr*
EMP: 7 EST: 2014
SALES (est): 97.72K **Privately Held**
Web: www.timeisonyourside.com
SIC: 8099 Health and allied services, nec

(G-2960)
LIZARD SOFT INC
8 The Grn Ste 5447 (19901-3618)
PHONE..................................619 618-0368
EMP: 5 EST: 2016
SALES (est): 75.92K **Privately Held**
Web: www.ls-intranet.net
SIC: 7371 Computer software development

(G-2961)
LKB MANAGEMENT GROUP LLC (PA) ◇
8 The Grn Ste 13680 (19901-3618)
PHONE..................................919 561-2815
EMP: 6 EST: 2022
SALES (est): 76.03K
SALES (corp-wide): 76.03K **Privately Held**
SIC: 5961 7389 Electronic shopping; Business Activities at Non-Commercial Site

(G-2962)
LKQ NORTHEAST INC
1575 Mckee Rd Ste 5 (19904-1382)
PHONE..................................800 223-0171
EMP: 4 EST: 2019
SALES (est): 937.6K
SALES (corp-wide): 12.79B **Publicly Held**
SIC: 5093 5015 3714 Automotive wrecking for scrap; Motor vehicle parts, used; Motor vehicle parts and accessories
PA: Lkq Corporation
500 W Madison St Ste 2800
Chicago IL 60661
312 621-1950

(G-2963)
LLC SMART BEAN ◇
8 The Grn Ste A (19901-3618)
PHONE..................................302 894-2323
Fengjun Sun, *Prin*
EMP: 5 EST: 2023
SALES (est): 199.4K **Privately Held**
SIC: 7371 Custom computer programming services

(G-2964)
LOAD BALANCER CREW LLC
8 The Grn Ste A (19901-3618)
PHONE..................................805 202-9953
EMP: 5 EST: 2018
SALES (est): 500K **Privately Held**
SIC: 7379 Online services technology consultants

(G-2965)
LOAD MILES INC
8 The Grn (19901-3618)
PHONE..................................323 842-7038
Pratapa R Koppula, *CEO*
EMP: 14 EST: 2021
SALES (est): 512.85K **Privately Held**
SIC: 5734 7389 Software, business and non-game; Business services, nec

(G-2966)
LOANMAX
5455 N Dupont Hwy (19901-2600)

PHONE..................................302 747-2005
EMP: 5 EST: 2014
SALES (est): 191.88K **Privately Held**
Web: www.loanmaxtitleloans.net
SIC: 6141 Automobile and consumer finance companies

(G-2967)
LOCAL MOBILE LLC
8 The Grn (19901-3618)
PHONE..................................619 759-0114
Randi Rogers, *Managing Member*
EMP: 10
SALES (est): 251.04K **Privately Held**
SIC: 5999 7389 Miscellaneous retail stores, nec; Business services, nec

(G-2968)
LOCAL VERTICAL
69 Oakcrest Dr (19901-5730)
PHONE..................................302 242-2552
EMP: 5 EST: 2014
SALES (est): 65.54K **Privately Held**
SIC: 2591 Blinds vertical

(G-2969)
LOCALSORG INC
8 The Grn Ste B (19901-3618)
PHONE..................................650 441-6464
EMP: 7 EST: 2020
SALES (est): 106.08K **Privately Held**
Web: www.locals.org
SIC: 8699 Charitable organization

(G-2970)
LOCKHEED MARTIN CORPORATION
Also Called: Lockheed Martin
Dover Afb (19901)
P.O. Box 1634 (19903-1634)
PHONE..................................302 741-2004
John Burgess Managing, *Brnch Mgr*
EMP: 2
Web: www.gyrocamsystems.com
SIC: 3812 Search and navigation equipment
PA: Lockheed Martin Corporation
6801 Rockledge Dr
Bethesda MD 20817

(G-2971)
LOGICJUNCTION INC
8 The Grn Ste 1 (19901-3618)
PHONE..................................216 292-5760
Mark Jowell, *CEO*
EMP: 7 EST: 2000
SALES (est): 796.47K **Privately Held**
SIC: 7371 Computer software development

(G-2972)
LOGOS COMMUNITY DEV CORP
19 Liberty Dr (19904-2641)
PHONE..................................302 349-2779
Donell Winder, *Prin*
EMP: 9 EST: 2019
SALES (est): 313.8K **Privately Held**
SIC: 8069 Specialty hospitals, except psychiatric

(G-2973)
LOKALISE INC (PA)
3500 S Dupont Hwy Ste Bz-101 (19901-6041)
PHONE..................................302 498-9091
Ustinovs Nikolajs, *CEO*
EMP: 7 EST: 2016
SALES (est): 3.04MM
SALES (corp-wide): 3.04MM **Privately Held**
Web: www.lokalise.com
SIC: 7371 Computer software development

(G-2974)
LONE STAR GLOBAL SERVICES INC
9 E Loockerman St Ste 3a (19901-7316)
PHONE..................................302 744-9800
Markus Vogt, *Pr*
EMP: 2 EST: 2012
SALES (est): 86.37K **Privately Held**
SIC: 1389 Oil and gas field services, nec

(G-2975)
LOOCKERMANS TREE STUMP REMOVAL
225 Northdown Dr (19904-9745)
P.O. Box 997 (19903-0997)
PHONE..................................302 745-6446
Ron Loockerman, *Owner*
EMP: 5 EST: 2010
SALES (est): 234.63K **Privately Held**
SIC: 0783 Removal services, bush and tree

(G-2976)
LORGUS ENTERPRISES INC
68 N Sandpiper Dr (19901-7106)
PHONE..................................610 431-7453
Joan L Lorgus, *Prin*
EMP: 5 EST: 2019
SALES (est): 45.28K **Privately Held**
SIC: 7231 Beauty shops

(G-2977)
LOVE MY DOG INC
1102 S Dupont Hwy (19901-4493)
PHONE..................................240 441-7267
EMP: 5 EST: 2019
SALES (est): 111.69K **Privately Held**
SIC: 0752 Grooming services, pet and animal specialties

(G-2978)
LOVE N LEARN NURSERY TOO
1598 Forrest Ave (19904-3329)
PHONE..................................302 678-0445
Yvonne Biddle, *Mgr*
EMP: 9 EST: 1972
SALES (est): 137.51K **Privately Held**
SIC: 8351 Group day care center

(G-2979)
LOWES HOME CENTERS LLC
Also Called: Lowe's
1450 N Dupont Hwy (19901-2213)
PHONE..................................302 735-7500
Craig Hurd, *Prin*
EMP: 117
SQ FT: 2,014
SALES (corp-wide): 97.06B **Publicly Held**
Web: www.lowes.com
SIC: 5211 5031 5722 5064 Home centers; Building materials, exterior; Household appliance stores; Electrical appliances, television and radio
HQ: Lowe's Home Centers, Llc
1000 Lowes Blvd
Mooresville NC 28117
336 658-4000

(G-2980)
LUMINOUS ENERGY CORPORATION
8 The Grn # 6741 (19901-3618)
PHONE..................................866 475-7504
David Bryson, *Pr*
EMP: 9 EST: 2017
SALES (est): 162.01K
SALES (corp-wide): 5.62MM **Privately Held**
SIC: 8742 Business management consultant
PA: Luminous Energy Group Limited
Hartham Park
Corsham WILTS SN13
333 577-0190

GEOGRAPHIC SECTION   Dover - Kent County (G-3013)

(G-2981)
LURIWARE CONSULTING AGRICULTUR
155 S Bradford St Ste 200a (19904-7367)
PHONE..................................302 244-1947
EMP: 5 EST: 2017
SALES (est): 144.57K Privately Held
Web: www.luriware.org
SIC: 8711 Consulting engineer

(G-2982)
LUTHER MARTIN FOUNDATION DOVER
430 Kings Hwy Ofc 727 (19901-7521)
PHONE..................................302 674-1408
Arthur Kringel, Pr
EMP: 5 EST: 2005
SALES (est): 97.98K Privately Held
SIC: 6531 Rental agent, real estate

(G-2983)
LUTHER TOWERS III DOVER INC
430 Kings Hwy (19901-7512)
PHONE..................................302 674-1408
EMP: 12 EST: 2011
SALES (est): 373.48K Privately Held
Web: www.luthertowersofdover.com
SIC: 6513 Retirement hotel operation

(G-2984)
LUTHER TOWERS IV DOVER INC
430 Kings Hwy Ofc 1021 (19901-7512)
PHONE..................................302 674-1408
Gary Coy, Ex Dir
EMP: 10 EST: 2008
SALES (est): 319.4K Privately Held
Web: www.luthertowersofdover.com
SIC: 6513 Retirement hotel operation

(G-2985)
LUTHER TOWERS OF DOVER INC
430 Kings Hwy Ofc 727 (19901-7521)
PHONE..................................302 674-1408
EMP: 10 EST: 2011
SALES (est): 645.11K Privately Held
Web: www.luthertowersofdover.com
SIC: 6513 Retirement hotel operation

(G-2986)
LUTHER VILLAGE I DOVER INC
430 Kings Hwy Ofc 727 (19901-7521)
PHONE..................................302 674-1408
Gary Coy, Ex Dir
EMP: 10 EST: 2008
SALES (est): 527.66K Privately Held
SIC: 6513 Retirement hotel operation

(G-2987)
LUTHER VILLAGE II DOVER INC
430 Kings Hwy (19901-7512)
PHONE..................................302 674-1408
Gary Coy, Ex Dir
EMP: 10 EST: 2008
SALES (est): 290.85K Privately Held
Web: www.luthertowersofdover.com
SIC: 6513 Retirement hotel operation

(G-2988)
LUTHERAN SENIOR SVCS OF DOVER
Also Called: LUTHER TOWERS OF DOVER
430 Kings Hwy Ofc 727 (19901-7521)
PHONE..................................302 674-1408
  Robert E Bunnell, Dir
  Gary Coy, Dir
  Arthur Kringel, Pr
  Elizabeth Barrett, VP
EMP: 24 EST: 1979
SQ FT: 135,000
SALES (est): 2.13MM Privately Held

Web: www.luthertowersofdover.com
SIC: 6531 Housing authority operator

(G-2989)
LYNDON B CAGAMPAN
830 Walker Rd (19904-2748)
PHONE..................................302 730-8848
EMP: 14 EST: 2011
SALES (est): 164.38K Privately Held
SIC: 8011 Orthopedic physician

(G-2990)
M K CUSTOMER ELEVATOR PADS
1644 Sorghum Mill Rd (19901-6813)
PHONE..................................302 698-3110
Minet Bhagwandin, Owner
EMP: 2 EST: 2012
SALES (est): 169.8K Privately Held
SIC: 3534 Elevators and moving stairways

(G-2991)
M SCOTT BOVELSKY MD
200 Banning St Ste 320 (19904-3488)
PHONE..................................302 674-0223
EMP: 9 EST: 2017
SALES (est): 56.81K Privately Held
SIC: 8011 Gynecologist

(G-2992)
M WILSON ACCNTING BKKPING SVC
580 S Bay Rd (19901-4603)
PHONE..................................302 735-1537
EMP: 6 EST: 2009
SALES (est): 51.65K Privately Held
Web: www.mwilsonaccounting.com
SIC: 8721 Accounting, auditing, and bookkeeping

(G-2993)
M&S GROUP INTERNATIONAL LLC ✪
8 The Grn Ste 1289 (19901-3618)
P.O. Box 2263 (33101-2263)
PHONE..................................302 592-6006
Ivan Wolstencroft, Managing Member
EMP: 5 EST: 2022
SALES (est): 130.21K Privately Held
Web: www.msgroupinternational.com
SIC: 7382 Security systems services

(G-2994)
MADDCITYLIVE LLC
8 The Grn Ste 16129 (19901-3618)
PHONE..................................302 591-3471
N D Brennan, Managing Member
EMP: 7 EST: 2019
SALES (est): 127.31K Privately Held
Web: www.maddcitymedia.com
SIC: 7929 Entertainment service

(G-2995)
MAESTRO MEDIA HOLDINGS INC
8 The Grn Ste A (19901-3618)
PHONE..................................855 313-3337
Ronald Marshall, Managing Member
EMP: 13
SIC: 6719 Holding companies, nec

(G-2996)
MAGNOLIA HOME THEATRE
1165 N Dupont Hwy (19901-2016)
PHONE..................................302 677-7215
Gabriel Torres, Mgr
EMP: 5 EST: 2014
SALES (est): 49.12K Privately Held
SIC: 7922 Theatrical companies

(G-2997)
MAGUS LLC
8 The Grn Ste R (19901-3618)
PHONE..................................213 332-9117
EMP: 5 EST: 2020
SALES (est): 496.64K Privately Held
Web: www.maguslc.com
SIC: 5045 Computers, peripherals, and software

(G-2998)
MAIN STREET STAFFING AGCY LLC
4 Grand Hall (19904-2621)
PHONE..................................302 608-7052
EMP: 5 EST: 2021
SALES (est): 47.02K Privately Held
SIC: 7349 Cleaning service, industrial or commercial

(G-2999)
MAINSTAY SUITES
Also Called: MainStay Suites
201 Stover Blvd (19901-4675)
PHONE..................................302 678-8383
Francine Dobson, Ofcr
EMP: 25 EST: 2008
SALES (est): 464.22K Privately Held
Web: www.choicehotels.com
SIC: 7011 Hotels and motels

(G-3000)
MAKATUU INC
8 The Grn (19901-3618)
PHONE..................................650 431-5582
John Maka, CEO
EMP: 8 EST: 2020
SALES (est): 30.65MM Privately Held
SIC: 8743 7389 Promotion service; Business services, nec

(G-3001)
MAKAVE INTERNATIONAL TRDG LLC
8 The Grn Ste A (19901-3618)
PHONE..................................302 288-0670
EMP: 26 EST: 2017
SALES (est): 644.84K Privately Held
SIC: 7371 Computer software development and applications

(G-3002)
MAKE IT NEW CONSTRUCTION LLC
40 Sienna Ct (19904-0983)
PHONE..................................302 423-7794
EMP: 5 EST: 2015
SALES (est): 147.64K Privately Held
SIC: 1521 Single-family housing construction

(G-3003)
MAKKARI GLOBL VSION A SRIES LL
8 The Grn Ste A (19901-3618)
PHONE..................................571 308-6032
EMP: 2 EST: 2018
SALES (est): 77.45K Privately Held
SIC: 3161 Clothing and apparel carrying cases

(G-3004)
MALAVE PROPERTY GROUP LLC
9 E Loockerman St # 202820 (19901-8306)
PHONE..................................844 203-4610
Mya Malave, Managing Member
EMP: 7 EST: 2021
SALES (est): 304.09K Privately Held
SIC: 6531 Real estate agents and managers

(G-3005)
MAMASTE DOULA AND BIRTH SVCS
429 W Denneys Rd (19904-4954)
PHONE..................................302 670-3188
EMP: 6 EST: 2017

SALES (est): 67.65K Privately Held
SIC: 8099 Childbirth preparation clinic

(G-3006)
MANAGEMENT 24 LLC (PA)
8 The Grn Ste A (19901-3618)
PHONE..................................646 820-5224
Maria Lloyd, Managing Member
EMP: 5 EST: 2015
SALES (est): 242.42K
SALES (corp-wide): 242.42K Privately Held
SIC: 8742 Marketing consulting services

(G-3007)
MANAGEMENT CHEMICAL CO
Also Called: Hanker, James W.
281 Debs Way (19901-2940)
P.O. Box 390 (20657-0390)
PHONE..................................410 326-0964
James Hanker, Owner
EMP: 2 EST: 1968
SALES (est): 116.63K Privately Held
SIC: 2899 5169 Water treating compounds; Chemicals and allied products, nec

(G-3008)
MANE ATTRACTION
604 Forest St (19904-3204)
PHONE..................................302 526-2013
EMP: 5 EST: 2020
SALES (est): 19.5K Privately Held
SIC: 7231 Hairdressers

(G-3009)
MANNERS BRAND LLC (PA) ✪
8 The Grn Ste 8 (19901-3618)
PHONE..................................470 830-1114
Julien Ford, Managing Member
EMP: 6 EST: 2023
SALES (est): 76.37K
SALES (corp-wide): 76.37K Privately Held
SIC: 5961 7389 Catalog and mail-order houses; Business services, nec

(G-3010)
MANOA FRESH FOOD LLC ✪
8 The Grn Ste B (19901-3618)
PHONE..................................561 453-0521
Herman Alejandro, Managing Member
EMP: 5 EST: 2022
SALES (est): 342.88K Privately Held
SIC: 5146 Seafoods

(G-3011)
MANOJ ORNAMENTS INC ✪
8 The Grn Ste A (19901-3618)
PHONE..................................916 779-7916
EMP: 5 EST: 2022
SALES (est): 78.16K Privately Held
SIC: 3911 Jewelry apparel

(G-3012)
MANUFACTURED HOUSING
555 S Bay Rd (19901-4617)
PHONE..................................302 744-2383
EMP: 7 EST: 2019
SALES (est): 122.77K Privately Held
SIC: 3999 Manufacturing industries, nec

(G-3013)
MANUFACTURERS & TRADERS TR CO
Also Called: M&T
1001 E Lebanon Rd (19901-5855)
PHONE..................................302 735-2020
EMP: 10
SALES (corp-wide): 8.6B Publicly Held
Web: ir.mtb.com

(PA)=Parent Co (HQ)=Headquarters
✪ = New Business established in last 2 years

2024 Harris Directory of Delaware Businesses

Dover - Kent County (G-3014)   GEOGRAPHIC SECTION

SIC: 6022 State commercial banks
HQ: Manufacturers And Traders Trust Company
1 M&T Plz Fl 3
Buffalo NY 14203
716 842-4200

(G-3014)
MANUFACTURERS & TRADERS TR CO
Also Called: M&T
139 S State St (19901-7313)
PHONE.....................302 735-2010
Gail Fink, *Mgr*
EMP: 7
SALES (corp-wide): 8.6B **Publicly Held**
Web: ir.mtb.com
SIC: 6022 State trust companies accepting deposits, commercial
HQ: Manufacturers And Traders Trust Company
1 M&T Plz Fl 3
Buffalo NY 14203
716 842-4200

(G-3015)
MANVEEN DUGGAL MD
Also Called: TP Indira and Mdpa
874 Walker Rd Ste B (19904-2778)
PHONE.....................302 734-5438
Senbhab Kumar Md, *Pr*
EMP: 6 EST: 2001
SALES (est): 309.47K **Privately Held**
SIC: 8011 Endocrinologist

(G-3016)
MAR FITNESS ENTERPRISES INC
Also Called: Planet Fitness
1005 N State St (19901-3904)
PHONE.....................302 730-1234
EMP: 6 EST: 2017
SALES (est): 29.54K **Privately Held**
Web: www.planetfitness.com
SIC: 7991 Physical fitness facilities

(G-3017)
MARENOS LANDSCAPING
122 Lakshman Trl (19904-0977)
PHONE.....................302 531-7009
Michael Mareno, *Prin*
EMP: 5 EST: 2015
SALES (est): 135.82K **Privately Held**
SIC: 0781 Landscape services

(G-3018)
MARIANAS ENERGY COMPANY LLC
Also Called: (Marianas Energy Company is a wholly owned subsidiary of Power Solutions
Duns 855023819)
160 Greentree Dr (19904-7620)
PHONE.....................671 477-3060
Rino Manzano, *Managing Member*
EMP: 42 EST: 1996
SQ FT: 5,000
SALES (est): 10.2MM **Privately Held**
SIC: 4911 Electric services
PA: Power Solutions, Llc
180 Cabras Hwy
Piti 96915

(G-3019)
MARK ONE LLC
Also Called: Best Western
1700 E Lebanon Rd (19901-5845)
PHONE.....................302 735-4700
EMP: 36 EST: 1990
SQ FT: 18,000
SALES (est): 340.2K **Privately Held**
Web: www.bestwestern.com

SIC: 7011 Hotels and motels

(G-3020)
MARKETFORCE TECHNOLOGIES INC
8 The Grn Ste A (19901-3618)
PHONE.....................339 674-0529
Mutethia Mbaabu, *CEO*
Collins Mesongo Sibuti, *
EMP: 600 EST: 2020
SALES (est): 750K **Privately Held**
SIC: 7371 Computer software development and applications

(G-3021)
MARKETING PLUS LLC
8 The Grn Ste R (19901-3618)
PHONE.....................205 952-6602
EMP: 9
SALES (est): 320.01K **Privately Held**
SIC: 7311 Advertising agencies

(G-3022)
MARTEL & SON FOREIGN CAR CTR
1161 Horsepond Rd (19901-7218)
PHONE.....................302 674-5556
EMP: 5 EST: 1986
SALES (est): 243.03K **Privately Held**
Web: www.martelsforeigncar.com
SIC: 7538 7549 General automotive repair shops; Towing service, automotive

(G-3023)
MARTEL INC
702 Dundee Rd (19904-6104)
P.O. Box 625 (19903-0625)
PHONE.....................302 674-5660
Mark Carlson, *Pr*
EMP: 8 EST: 1984
SALES (est): 960.05K **Privately Held**
Web: www.martelinc.com
SIC: 7629 1731 Telephone set repair; Communications specialization

(G-3024)
MARTHANN PRINT CENTER LLC
1130 Charles Dr (19904-4328)
PHONE.....................267 884-8130
Yaya G Bruce, *Prin*
EMP: 5 EST: 2016
SALES (est): 97.33K **Privately Held**
SIC: 2752 Offset printing

(G-3025)
MASC FARMING LLC
6479 Bayside Dr (19901-3429)
PHONE.....................302 734-3602
Mark Cartanza, *Prin*
EMP: 5 EST: 2010
SALES (est): 54.91K **Privately Held**
SIC: 0191 General farms, primarily crop

(G-3026)
MASSTECH AMERICAS INC
Also Called: Masstech
850 New Burton Rd Ste 201 (19904-5786)
PHONE.....................905 946-5700
George Kilpatrick, *CEO*
Sharon Yuan, *
EMP: 75 EST: 2016
SALES (est): 1.83MM **Privately Held**
SIC: 7371 Computer software development

(G-3027)
MASTER KIT INC
160 Greentree Dr Ste 101 (19904-7620)
PHONE.....................650 743-5126
EMP: 5 EST: 2019
SALES (est): 61.22K **Privately Held**

SIC: 7371 Computer software development and applications

(G-3028)
MASTERCRAFT WELDING
4010 S Dupont Hwy (19901-6007)
P.O. Box 101 (19980-0101)
PHONE.....................302 697-3932
Chuck Moller, *Owner*
EMP: 5 EST: 1981
SQ FT: 5,000
SALES (est): 419.71K **Privately Held**
SIC: 3444 1761 7692 Sheet metalwork; Sheet metal work, nec; Welding repair

(G-3029)
MASTERCRAFTERS INC
1234 S Governors Ave Ste A (19904-4895)
PHONE.....................302 678-1470
Brian Larson, *Pr*
Marilyn Larson, *
EMP: 25 EST: 1993
SQ FT: 5,000
SALES (est): 2.37MM **Privately Held**
Web: www.mastercrafters.com
SIC: 1751 1799 Cabinet building and installation; Counter top installation

(G-3030)
MATHLETICS INC
117 Lady Bug Dr (19901-8843)
PHONE.....................302 724-0619
Michael Greene, *Prin*
EMP: 5 EST: 2016
SALES (est): 58.65K **Privately Held**
Web: www.mathletics.com
SIC: 8699 Athletic organizations

(G-3031)
MATIUM INC
1111b S Governors Ave Ste 6245 (19904-6903)
PHONE.....................703 457-9997
Bailey Robin, *CEO*
EMP: 5 EST: 2021
SALES (est): 255.13K **Privately Held**
Web: www.matium.io
SIC: 7371 Computer software development and applications

(G-3032)
MATRIXPORT INC
850 New Burton Rd Ste 201 (19904-5786)
PHONE.....................626 474-8738
EMP: 6 EST: 2021
SALES (est): 264.65K **Privately Held**
SIC: 7389 Financial services

(G-3033)
MATTERN & PICCIONI MD PA
260 Beiser Blvd Ste 101 (19904-5773)
PHONE.....................302 730-8060
Michael L Mattern, *Pr*
EMP: 13 EST: 1981
SALES (est): 769.34K **Privately Held**
SIC: 8011 Orthopedic physician

(G-3034)
MATTERN AND ASSOCIATES MD
1675 S State St Ste A (19901-5140)
PHONE.....................302 724-5062
EMP: 6 EST: 2013
SALES (est): 67.8K **Privately Held**
SIC: 8011 Offices and clinics of medical doctors

(G-3035)
MATTHEW SMITH BUS SERVICE
206 N Queen St (19904-3152)
PHONE.....................302 734-9311

Matthew Smith, *Pr*
EMP: 5 EST: 1988
SALES (est): 179.8K **Privately Held**
SIC: 4131 4142 Intercity and rural bus transportation; Bus charter service, except local

(G-3036)
MATTHEWS PIERCE & LLOYD INC (PA)
830 Walker Rd Ste 12 (19904-2748)
PHONE.....................302 678-5500
Alan Nadler, *Pr*
EMP: 20 EST: 2001
SQ FT: 3,200
SALES (est): 2.44MM
SALES (corp-wide): 2.44MM **Privately Held**
Web: www.mpli.net
SIC: 7322 Collection agency, except real estate

(G-3037)
MAUNA SERVICES LLC
8 The Grn (19901-3618)
PHONE.....................302 446-4409
EMP: 6 EST: 2017
SALES (est): 236.42K **Privately Held**
Web: www.maunaservices.com
SIC: 7378 Computer and data processing equipment repair/maintenance

(G-3038)
MAVIS TIRE EXPRESS SVCS CORP
Also Called: Mavis Tire 2104
280 Cowgill St (19901-4500)
PHONE.....................727 440-5435
EMP: 14
SALES (corp-wide): 2.41B **Privately Held**
SIC: 5014 Tires and tubes
HQ: Mavis Tire Express Services Corp.
358 Saw Mill River Rd
Millwood NY 10546
919 330-0690

(G-3039)
MAYA VIRTUAL INC
Also Called: Maya.net
8 The Grn Ste 13521 (19901-3618)
PHONE.....................213 587-7995
Daniel Fry, *CEO*
EMP: 9 EST: 2015
SQ FT: 4,326
SALES (est): 136.65K **Privately Held**
Web: www.maya.net
SIC: 4813 4899 Internet host services; Data communication services

(G-3040)
MC HUNTER LLC
1246 S Little Creek Rd (19901-4729)
PHONE.....................302 672-0072
Mike Hunter, *CEO*
EMP: 6 EST: 2018
SALES (est): 190.93K **Privately Held**
Web: www.mrhunterllc.com
SIC: 1521 Patio and deck construction and repair

(G-3041)
MC2 THERAPEUTICS INC
8 The Grn Ste 8321 (19901-3618)
PHONE.....................202 505-0891
Jesper J Lange, *CEO*
Christopher Bills, *CCO*
Morten Prstegaard, *COO*
EMP: 6 EST: 2018
SALES (est): 96.45K **Privately Held**
Web: www.mc2therapeutics.com

GEOGRAPHIC SECTION
Dover - Kent County (G-3071)

SIC: 2834   Pharmaceutical preparations

(G-3042)
MCA - MDSG CONS ASSOC USA INC
874 Walker Rd Ste C (19904-2778)
PHONE.....................800 465-4755
Steve Kineree, *Pr*
EMP: 6 EST: 2020
SALES (est): 71.79K **Privately Held**
SIC: 8742   Merchandising consultant

(G-3043)
MCCOVE CONSTRUCTION INC
615 Sharon Hill Rd (19904-4666)
P.O. Box 1184 (19903-1184)
PHONE.....................302 363-0528
Marvin K Mccove Senior, *Prin*
▲ EMP: 5 EST: 2004
SALES (est): 235.33K **Privately Held**
SIC: 1521   Single-family housing construction

(G-3044)
MCLEAN MASONRY CONTRACTORS LLC
46 Parkers Dr (19904-1465)
PHONE.....................215 349-0719
Sean Mclean, *Asst Sec*
EMP: 5 EST: 2018
SALES (est): 51.85K **Privately Held**
Web: www.mcleanmasonrycontractors.com
SIC: 7699   Cleaning services

(G-3045)
MDAAS GLOBAL CORP
160 Greentree Dr (19904-7620)
PHONE.....................410 905-1213
Oluwasoga Oni, *Pr*
EMP: 5 EST: 2017
SALES (est): 30.27K **Privately Held**
SIC: 7389   Design services

(G-3046)
MDNEWSLINE INC
28 Old Rudnick Ln (19901-4912)
PHONE.....................773 759-4363
Jeffrey O Osuji, *Prin*
EMP: 6 EST: 2019
SALES (est): 223.98K **Privately Held**
Web: www.mdnewsline.com
SIC: 7389   Courier or messenger service

(G-3047)
MEANINGTEAM INC
3500 S Dupont Hwy (19901-6041)
PHONE.....................213 669-5804
Yishay Carmiel, *CEO*
EMP: 12
SALES (est): 251.15K **Privately Held**
SIC: 7371   Software programming applications

(G-3048)
MECATECH INDUS EQUIPMENTS LLC
8 The Grn Ste B (19901-3618)
PHONE.....................617 586-4224
Jo Lefevre, *Pr*
EMP: 5 EST: 2019
SALES (est): 255.22K **Privately Held**
SIC: 5084   Industrial machinery and equipment

(G-3049)
MEDARCH INC
8 The Grn (19901-3618)
PHONE.....................405 638-3126
Kaustubh Narkhede, *Prin*
EMP: 10
SALES (est): 348.32K **Privately Held**

SIC: 7389   Business Activities at Non-Commercial Site

(G-3050)
MEDBLOB INC
8 The Grn (19901-3618)
PHONE.....................813 308-9273
Richard Tannenbaum, *CEO*
Jonathan Rapaport, *CFO*
Joseph Hasson, *COO*
EMP: 5 EST: 2018
SQ FT: 2,500
SALES (est): 376.07K **Privately Held**
Web: www.medblob.com
SIC: 8733 7372 8011   Medical research; Application computer software; Primary care medical clinic

(G-3051)
MEDEVICE SERVICES LLC
3500 S Dupont Hwy (19901-6041)
PHONE.....................877 202-1588
EMP: 8 EST: 2010
SALES (est): 414.14K **Privately Held**
SIC: 8748   Business consulting, nec

(G-3052)
MEDICAL SUP SUPPORT SVCS LLC
8 The Grn Ste 8095 (19901-3618)
PHONE.....................302 446-3658
Uzoma Ajeroh, *Managing Member*
EMP: 10 EST: 2021
SALES (est): 3.8MM **Privately Held**
SIC: 3841 2834 7389   IV transfusion apparatus; Pharmaceutical preparations; Business Activities at Non-Commercial Site

(G-3053)
MEDICAL TECHNOLOGIES INTL
8 The Grn Ste 1 (19901-3618)
PHONE.....................760 837-4778
Gary Thompson, *Pr*
EMP: 10 EST: 2005
SALES (est): 539.53K **Privately Held**
SIC: 5047   Medical equipment and supplies

(G-3054)
MEDTIX LLC
Also Called: Unknown
1006 College Rd (19904-6513)
PHONE.....................302 736-0172
EMP: 5
SALES (corp-wide): 25.49MM **Privately Held**
SIC: 5047   Medical and hospital equipment
PA: Medtix Llc
      221 S Rehoboth Blvd
      Milford DE 19963
      302 645-8070

(G-3055)
MEGARA INC
8 The Grn (19901-3618)
PHONE.....................914 487-4702
Christopher Francia, *CEO*
EMP: 10 EST: 2021
SALES (est): 503 **Privately Held**
Web: www.megaraentertainment.com
SIC: 7999 7922   Amusement and recreation, nec; Theatrical producers and services

(G-3056)
MEKHALA LIVING INC
8 The Grn (19901-3618)
PHONE.....................650 443-8235
Daphne Hedley, *CEO*
EMP: 6
SALES (est): 86.31K **Privately Held**

SIC: 5149 7389   Groceries and related products, nec; Business Activities at Non-Commercial Site

(G-3057)
MELENTO INC
8 The Grn Ste A (19901-3618)
PHONE.....................571 989-1300
Krupesha Chidambara, *Dir*
EMP: 10 EST: 2020
SALES (est): 348.32K **Privately Held**
SIC: 7371   Custom computer programming services

(G-3058)
MEME US HOLDINGS LLC
8 The Grn Ste B (19901-3618)
PHONE.....................619 342-4340
Steve Warren, *CEO*
EMP: 5 EST: 2016
SALES (est): 56.54K **Privately Held**
SIC: 7372   Prepackaged software

(G-3059)
MENDOTA MERCHANTS LLC
8 The Grn Ste 7347 (19901-3618)
PHONE.....................302 401-6453
EMP: 5 EST: 2018
SALES (est): 228.49K **Privately Held**
SIC: 8611   Merchants' association

(G-3060)
MENEHARIYA LLC
8 The Grn (19901-3618)
PHONE.....................240 432-0082
Mekbeb Scyoum, *Managing Member*
EMP: 10
SALES (est): 348.32K **Privately Held**
SIC: 7371   Computer software development and applications

(G-3061)
MENTAL EDGE COUNSELING
1198 S Governors Ave Ste 201 (19904-6930)
PHONE.....................302 382-8698
EMP: 35 EST: 2015
SALES (est): 1.23MM **Privately Held**
Web: www.mentaledgecounseling.com
SIC: 8322   General counseling services

(G-3062)
MERCHANT GLOBAL ASSISTANCE LLC
8 The Grn (19901-3618)
PHONE.....................914 522-4871
Bryan Cohen, *Managing Member*
EMP: 9 EST: 2019
SALES (est): 72.62K **Privately Held**
SIC: 7389   Business services, nec

(G-3063)
MERCY CARE FOR WNS HLTH OB/GYN
819 S Governors Ave (19904-4158)
PHONE.....................302 883-3677
EMP: 6 EST: 2019
SALES (est): 140.86K **Privately Held**
Web: www.mercycareobgyn.com
SIC: 8011   Gynecologist

(G-3064)
MERIDIAN LIMO LLC
8 The Grn (19901-3618)
PHONE.....................800 462-1550
EMP: 6 EST: 2010
SALES (est): 563.34K **Privately Held**
Web: test11.eaqaratdevelopers.com
SIC: 4789   Transportation services, nec

(G-3065)
MERRILL LYNCH PRCE FNNER SMITH
Also Called: Merrill Lynch
55 Kings Hwy (19901-3816)
P.O. Box 1367 (19903-1367)
PHONE.....................302 736-7700
Lisa Primeck, *Mgr*
EMP: 5
SALES (corp-wide): 94.95B **Publicly Held**
Web: www.ml.com
SIC: 6211   Security brokers and dealers
HQ: Merrill Lynch, Pierce, Fenner & Smith Incorporated
      111 8th Ave
      New York NY 10011
      800 637-7455

(G-3066)
MERRY MAIDS INC
Also Called: Merry Maids
30 S American Ave (19901-7346)
PHONE.....................302 698-9038
EMP: 12 EST: 1988
SALES (est): 220.58K **Privately Held**
Web: www.merrymaids.com
SIC: 7349   Maid services, contract or fee basis

(G-3067)
MESSINA CHARLES PLBG & ELC CO
3681 S Little Creek Rd (19901-4864)
PHONE.....................302 674-5696
EMP: 65 EST: 1985
SALES (est): 4.7MM **Privately Held**
Web: www.callmessina.com
SIC: 1711   Plumbing contractors

(G-3068)
MESYS INC
8 The Grn Ste A (19901-3618)
PHONE.....................917 566-7011
Harry Epstein, *Prin*
EMP: 2
SALES (est): 92.41K **Privately Held**
SIC: 3499   Fabricated metal products, nec

(G-3069)
META MIND GLOBAL CORP LLC (PA) ✪
8 The Grn Ste A (19901-3618)
PHONE.....................267 471-3616
EMP: 5 EST: 2022
SALES (est): 113.46K
SALES (corp-wide): 113.46K **Privately Held**
SIC: 8999 8711 1799 8748   Communication services; Consulting engineer; Special trade contractors, nec; Business consulting, nec

(G-3070)
METANIUM CORP
8 The Grn (19901-3618)
PHONE.....................302 669-9084
Tuan Vo, *CEO*
EMP: 50
SALES (est): 1.14MM **Privately Held**
SIC: 7371   Computer software development

(G-3071)
METANODE INC ✪
8 The Grn Ste D (19901-3618)
PHONE.....................302 782-9758
Hoang Vuan Vo, *Pr*
EMP: 3 EST: 2022
SALES (est): 128.34K **Privately Held**
Web: www.metanode.co
SIC: 7372   Prepackaged software

Dover - Kent County (G-3072) — GEOGRAPHIC SECTION

(G-3072)
METATRON INC (PA)
160 Greentree Dr Ste 101 (19904-7620)
PHONE.................................619 550-4668
EMP: 3 EST: 1992
SALES (est): 721.07K **Publicly Held**
Web: www.metatroninc.com
SIC: 3699 Photographic control systems, electronic

(G-3073)
METLIFE SVCS & SOLUTIONS LLC
Also Called: MetLife
160 Greentree Dr Ste 105 (19904-7620)
PHONE.................................302 734-5803
Rick Walker, *Mgr*
EMP: 10
SALES (corp-wide): 69.9B **Publicly Held**
Web: www.metlife.com
SIC: 6411 Insurance agents and brokers
HQ: Metropolitan Life Insurance Company
200 Park Ave Fl 4
New York NY 10166
908 253-1000

(G-3074)
METRO BY T-MOBILE
431 S New St (19904-6715)
PHONE.................................302 724-7494
EMP: 5 EST: 2018
SALES (est): 87.47K **Privately Held**
SIC: 4812 Cellular telephone services

(G-3075)
METRO BY T-MOBILE
1616 S Governors Ave (19904-7004)
PHONE.................................302 744-8473
EMP: 5 EST: 2018
SALES (est): 120.87K **Privately Held**
SIC: 4812 Cellular telephone services

(G-3076)
MGMIS
1567 Mckee Rd (19904-1380)
PHONE.................................302 744-8645
EMP: 6 EST: 2019
SALES (est): 91.6K **Privately Held**
Web: www.mgm-is.com
SIC: 7379 Computer related consulting services

(G-3077)
MH SOFTWARE INC
614 N Dupont Hwy (19901-3900)
PHONE.................................919 306-0163
Michael Harrison, *CEO*
EMP: 2
SALES (est): 87.4K **Privately Held**
SIC: 7372 Prepackaged software

(G-3078)
MICHAEL FRANKOS
Also Called: Nationwide
375 W North St (19904-6748)
PHONE.................................302 531-0831
Michael Frankos, *Prin*
EMP: 7 EST: 2014
SALES (est): 234.73K **Privately Held**
Web: www.nationwide.com
SIC: 6411 Insurance agents, nec

(G-3079)
MICHAEL G SWEENEY M D
725 S Queen St (19904-3568)
PHONE.................................302 678-4488
Michael Sweeney, *Pr*
EMP: 9 EST: 2018
SALES (est): 105.21K **Privately Held**
SIC: 8011 Offices and clinics of medical doctors

(G-3080)
MICHAEL L MATTERN MD PA
724 S New St (19904-3540)
PHONE.................................302 734-3416
Michael L Mattern Md, *Pr*
EMP: 7 EST: 1981
SQ FT: 4,646
SALES (est): 192.28K **Privately Held**
SIC: 8011 Orthopedic physician

(G-3081)
MICHAEL ZARAGOZA MD FACS
200 Banning St (19904-3485)
PHONE.................................302 736-1320
EMP: 8 EST: 2018
SALES (est): 138.8K **Privately Held**
Web: www.urologydelaware.com
SIC: 8011 Offices and clinics of medical doctors

(G-3082)
MICHAELANGELOS HAIR DESIGNS
696 N Dupont Hwy (19901-3937)
PHONE.................................302 734-8343
Michael Williams, *Pr*
EMP: 7 EST: 2005
SALES (est): 147.17K **Privately Held**
Web: www.michaelangeloshairdesigns.com
SIC: 7231 Hairdressers

(G-3083)
MICROPETS LLC
850 New Burton Rd (19904-5785)
PHONE.................................925 341-2398
Nick Smith, *CEO*
Ryan Hodge, *Managing Member**
EMP: 35 EST: 2021
SALES (est): 1.47MM **Privately Held**
SIC: 7371 Computer software development and applications

(G-3084)
MID ATLANTIC FARM CREDIT ACA
1410 S State St (19901-4948)
PHONE.................................302 734-7534
Robert Frazee, *CEO*
EMP: 7 EST: 1989
SALES (est): 185.27K **Privately Held**
SIC: 6159 6111 Production credit association, agricultural; Federal Land Banks

(G-3085)
MID DELAWARE IMAGING INC
710 S Queen St (19904-3567)
PHONE.................................302 734-9888
Mahendra Parikh, *Pr*
Bharati Parikh, *Sec*
EMP: 54 EST: 1990
SQ FT: 7,000
SALES (est): 8.09MM **Privately Held**
Web: www.radnet.com
SIC: 8011 Radiologist

(G-3086)
MID-ATLANTIC PACKAGING COMPANY
14 Starlifter Ave (19901-9200)
PHONE.................................800 284-1332
Herbert Glanden, *Pr*
Donald T Glanden, *
Andrew Pierson, *
Kimberly Glanden, *
◆ EMP: 30 EST: 1981
SQ FT: 32,000
SALES (est): 9.65MM **Privately Held**
Web: www.midatlanticpackaging.com
SIC: 5199 Packaging materials

(G-3087)
MID-ATLNTIC DISMANTLEMENT CORP
913 Horsepond Rd (19901-7221)
P.O. Box 1192 (19903-1192)
PHONE.................................302 678-9300
Mathew Mitten, *Pr*
Matthew Mitten, *Pr*
EMP: 20 EST: 1999
SALES (est): 1.65MM **Privately Held**
Web: mid-atlantic-dismantlement-corp.hub.biz
SIC: 1795 Demolition, buildings and other structures

(G-3088)
MIDDLESEX WATER COMPANY
1100 S Little Creek Rd (19904-4727)
PHONE.................................302 376-1501
EMP: 7
SALES (corp-wide): 162.43MM **Publicly Held**
Web: www.middlesexwater.com
SIC: 4941 Water supply
PA: Middlesex Water Company
485c Route 1 S Ste 400
Iselin NJ 08830
732 634-1500

(G-3089)
MIGHTYINVOICE LLC
Also Called: Invoicegenius
8 The Grn Ste B (19901-3618)
PHONE.................................302 415-3000
David Reynier, *Managing Member*
EMP: 5 EST: 2017
SALES (est): 214.34K **Privately Held**
SIC: 7371 Computer software development and applications

(G-3090)
MILFORD HOUSING DEVELOPMENT
200 Harmony Ln (19904-6601)
PHONE.................................302 678-0300
EMP: 30
SALES (corp-wide): 10.61MM **Privately Held**
Web: www.milfordhousing.com
SIC: 6513 Apartment building operators
PA: Milford Housing Development Corp
977 E Masten Cir
Milford DE 19963
302 422-8255

(G-3091)
MILFORD RENTAL CENTER INC
1679 S Dupont Hwy (19901-5101)
PHONE.................................302 422-0315
Joseph Wiley, *Pr*
EMP: 6 EST: 1986
SQ FT: 6,000
SALES (est): 843.4K **Privately Held**
SIC: 7353 Heavy construction equipment rental

(G-3092)
MILLENNIUM HOMES
4227 N Dupont Hwy (19901-1560)
P.O. Box 94 (19977-0094)
PHONE.................................302 678-2393
Blair Schwepfinger, *Prin*
EMP: 9 EST: 2009
SALES (est): 538.29K **Privately Held**
Web: www.millenniumhomesdelaware.com
SIC: 1521 Single-family housing construction

(G-3093)
MILLS JAMES MD
540 S Governors Ave Ste 100a (19904-3530)
PHONE.................................302 526-1470
James Mills, *Prin*
EMP: 8 EST: 2017
SALES (est): 63.09K **Privately Held**
SIC: 8011 Offices and clinics of medical doctors

(G-3094)
MILLS ELECTRIC LLC
261 N Caroline Pl (19904-7735)
PHONE.................................302 257-8403
Tyrece Mills, *Prin*
EMP: 7 EST: 2015
SALES (est): 127.23K **Privately Held**
SIC: 1731 General electrical contractor

(G-3095)
MIMESIS SIGNS
1035 Fowler Ct (19901-4638)
PHONE.................................302 674-5566
EMP: 5 EST: 2019
SALES (est): 158.77K **Privately Held**
Web: www.mimesisgraphics.com
SIC: 3993 Signs and advertising specialties

(G-3096)
MIMIX COMPANY
8 The Grn Ste 6236 (19901-3618)
PHONE.................................305 916-8602
David Bethune, *Pr*
Xavier Bethune, *VP*
EMP: 3 EST: 2018
SALES (est): 71.13K **Privately Held**
SIC: 7372 Prepackaged software

(G-3097)
MIND AND BODY CONSORTIUM LLC
156 S State St (19901-7314)
PHONE.................................302 674-2380
Lisa Leidy, *Mgr*
Lisa A Gantt, *Prin*
EMP: 78 EST: 2009
SALES (est): 2.45MM **Privately Held**
Web: www.mindandbodyde.com
SIC: 8322 8011 8049 General counseling services; Psychiatrist; Psychiatric social worker

(G-3098)
MINERS SUPPLY CO LLC ✪
8 The Grn Ste 14017 (19901-3618)
PHONE.................................541 203-6826
EMP: 8 EST: 2022
SALES (est): 25K **Privately Held**
SIC: 7373 Value-added resellers, computer systems

(G-3099)
MIRAGE HEALTH SERVICES LLC
1575 Mckee Rd Ste 203 (19904-1382)
PHONE.................................302 349-7227
EMP: 22
SALES (est): 1.08MM **Privately Held**
SIC: 8082 Home health care services

(G-3100)
MISAKA NETWORK INC
8 The Grn Ste 6288 (19901-3618)
PHONE.................................323 999-1409
EMP: 5 EST: 2019
SALES (est): 90.84K **Privately Held**
Web: www.misaka.io
SIC: 7371 Computer software development and applications

(G-3101)
MISSION SUPPORT SERVICES LLC
8 The Grn Ste A (19901-3618)
PHONE.................................813 494-0795
Ireneusz Iskrzycki, *Prin*

GEOGRAPHIC SECTION

Dover - Kent County (G-3131)

Ireneusz Iskrzycki, *CEO*
Jed Owen, *Ofcr*
EMP: 10 **EST:** 2019
SALES (est): 119.87K **Privately Held**
Web: www.oescgroup.com
SIC: 8711 Engineering services

(G-3102)
MISTY RIVERS LTD
505 Brookfield Dr (19901-6534)
PHONE.................315 415-2826
EMP: 6 **EST:** 2016
SALES (est): 83.62K **Privately Held**
SIC: 4493 Marinas

(G-3103)
MITTEN & WINTERS CPA
119 W Loockerman St (19904-7325)
P.O. Box 492 (19903-0492)
PHONE.................302 736-6100
William Winters, *Pt*
David Mitten, *Pt*
EMP: 10 **EST:** 1988
SALES (est): 904.61K **Privately Held**
Web: www.mittenwinters.com
SIC: 8721 Certified public accountant

(G-3104)
MITTEN CONSTRUCTION CO
1420 E Lebanon Rd (19901-5833)
P.O. Box 904 (19903-0904)
PHONE.................302 697-2124
William B Mitten Iii, *Prin*
Wendy Mitten, *VP*
Jacqueline M Robert, *Sec*
Eben P Roberts, *Treas*
EMP: 15 **EST:** 1968
SQ FT: 2,000
SALES (est): 1.23MM **Privately Held**
Web: www.mittenconstruction.net
SIC: 1611 1542 1541 Highway and street paving contractor; Commercial and office building, new construction; Industrial buildings, new construction, nec

(G-3105)
MITUSHA INTERNATIONAL CORP
626 Roberta Ave (19901-4612)
PHONE.................302 674-2977
Amit Kalyani, *Pr*
▲ **EMP:** 5 **EST:** 1990
SALES (est): 704.66K **Privately Held**
Web: www.mitusha.in
SIC: 5084 5085 Industrial machine parts; Industrial fittings

(G-3106)
MIZU BUSINESS SERVICES INC
8 The Grn Ste 5384 (19901-3618)
PHONE.................302 321-5001
Lisa Reid, *Pr*
EMP: 9 **EST:** 2020
SALES (est): 391.58K **Privately Held**
SIC: 6411 Pension and retirement plan consultants

(G-3107)
MLK EDUCATIONAL COMMUNITY CTR
719 W North St (19904-3458)
PHONE.................302 242-1165
Alex Cropper, *Pr*
EMP: 6 **EST:** 2015
SALES (est): 52.04K **Privately Held**
SIC: 8322 Community center

(G-3108)
MNR INDUSTRIES LLC
200 Banning St Ste 170 (19904-3491)
PHONE.................443 485-6213
EMP: 3 **EST:** 2017
SALES (est): 69.46K **Privately Held**
SIC: 3999 Manufacturing industries, nec

(G-3109)
MOBILE DIRECT LLC
8 The Grn Ste A (19901-3618)
PHONE.................908 342-8994
EMP: 17
SALES (est): 1MM **Privately Held**
SIC: 4813 Telephone communication, except radio

(G-3110)
MOBILE MAGIC PRESSURE WASHING
50 E Darby Cir (19904-6000)
PHONE.................302 697-1230
Lorenzo Hopkins, *Prin*
EMP: 5 **EST:** 2016
SALES (est): 65.23K **Privately Held**
SIC: 1799 Special trade contractors, nec

(G-3111)
MOBILITY ROUTE INC
8 The Grn Ste 11251 (19901-3618)
PHONE.................302 273-0770
Justin Alderman, *Pr*
EMP: 6
SALES (est): 253.86K **Privately Held**
SIC: 7371 Computer software development

(G-3112)
MOBILITY UNBOUND LLC ✪
800 N State St Ste 304 (19901-3925)
PHONE.................786 925-4411
Curtis Englert, *Managing Member*
EMP: 6 **EST:** 2023
SALES (est): 280.62K **Privately Held**
SIC: 4731 Freight transportation arrangement

(G-3113)
MOBIO GLOBAL INC ✪
850 New Burton Rd Ste 201 (19904-5786)
PHONE.................484 263-4845
Sergei Konovalov, *CEO*
EMP: 8 **EST:** 2022
SALES (est): 284.57K **Privately Held**
SIC: 7371 Computer software development

(G-3114)
MOCEAN ENERGY CORP
8 The Grn Ste 10928 (19901-3618)
PHONE.................410 449-4286
James Cameron Mcnatt, *Prin*
EMP: 5 **EST:** 2018
SALES (est): 55.93K **Privately Held**
Web: www.mocean.energy
SIC: 4911 Electric services

(G-3115)
MODERN MATURITY CENTER INC
1121 Forrest Ave (19904-3308)
PHONE.................302 734-1200
Carolyn Fredricks, *Ex Dir*
EMP: 49 **EST:** 1969
SQ FT: 73,000
SALES (est): 7.66MM **Privately Held**
Web: www.modern-maturity.org
SIC: 8322 Senior citizens' center or association

(G-3116)
MODISE IMPORTS & EXPORTS LLC
8 The Grn (19901-3618)
PHONE.................800 274-1240
EMP: 5 **EST:** 2016
SALES (est): 332.98K **Privately Held**
SIC: 5199 Nondurable goods, nec

(G-3117)
MOHAN CONSULTING LLC
614 N Dupont Hwy (19901-3900)
PHONE.................314 583-9140
Sundar Shrestha, *Managing Member*
EMP: 5 **EST:** 2021
SALES (est): 203.68K **Privately Held**
SIC: 7379 Online services technology consultants

(G-3118)
MONEY EX POS SOLUTIONS US INC
1675 S State St Ste B (19901-5140)
PHONE.................866 946-6773
EMP: 50 **EST:** 2021
SALES (est): 20MM **Privately Held**
Web: www.monexgroup.com
SIC: 7389 Credit card service

(G-3119)
MONEY FACTORY LLC ✪
Also Called: Money Factory, The
8 The Grn (19901-3618)
PHONE.................620 755-5215
Trevor Pope, *Managing Member*
EMP: 5 **EST:** 2023
SALES (est): 199.4K **Privately Held**
SIC: 7371 Computer software development

(G-3120)
MONICA BUMBREY
Also Called: Archer Sweets
401 Harmony Ln Unit 5 (19904-6618)
PHONE.................302 538-1942
Monica Bumbrey, *Owner*
EMP: 5 **EST:** 2021
SALES (est): 104.73K **Privately Held**
SIC: 7389 Business services, nec

(G-3121)
MONTRAE DENORRIS JONES LLC ✪
8 The Grn # A (19901-3618)
PHONE.................770 851-3836
Montrae Jones, *CEO*
EMP: 5 **EST:** 2023
SALES (est): 164.52K **Privately Held**
SIC: 7389 Business Activities at Non-Commercial Site

(G-3122)
MORALES SCREEN PRINTING
201 Cassidy Dr Ste C (19901-4899)
PHONE.................302 465-8179
EMP: 4 **EST:** 2017
SALES (est): 83.91K **Privately Held**
SIC: 2752 Commercial printing, lithographic

(G-3123)
MORNING REPORT RESEARCH INC
Also Called: Gaming Morning Report
144 Kings Hwy (19901-7308)
P.O. Box 1676 (19903-1676)
PHONE.................302 730-3793
Frank Fantini, *Pr*
EMP: 7 **EST:** 2005
SALES (est): 1.22MM **Privately Held**
Web: www.fantiniresearch.com
SIC: 2711 8742 Commercial printing and newspaper publishing combined; Management consulting services

(G-3124)
MORRIS JAMES LLP
Also Called: Morris, James
850 New Burton Rd (19904-5786)
PHONE.................302 678-8815
Glenn E Hitchens, *Mgr*
EMP: 7
SALES (corp-wide): 24.52MM **Privately Held**
Web: www.morrisjamespersonalinjurylawyers.com
SIC: 8111 General practice attorney, lawyer
PA: Morris James Llp
500 Delaware Ave Ste 1500
Wilmington DE 19801
302 888-6800

(G-3125)
MOSAIC MEDIA HOLDINGS INC
8 The Grn Ste A (19901-3618)
PHONE.................888 379-3553
EMP: 13
SALES (est): 705.5K **Privately Held**
SIC: 8742 Marketing consulting services

(G-3126)
MOSQUITO AUTHORITY
999 Long Point Rd (19901-1200)
PHONE.................302 346-2970
Matthew Rotuno, *Managing Member*
EMP: 16 **EST:** 2014
SALES (est): 402.66K **Privately Held**
Web: www.mosquito-authority.com
SIC: 7342 Pest control services

(G-3127)
MOTIVATED JUICERY LLC
1365 N Dupont Hwy Ste 4016 (19901-8725)
PHONE.................302 603-4619
EMP: 2 **EST:** 2020
SALES (est): 251.93K **Privately Held**
SIC: 3556 Juice extractors, fruit and vegetable: commercial type

(G-3128)
MOUNTAIN CONSULTING INC
103 S Bradford St (19904-7317)
P.O. Box 558 (19903-0558)
PHONE.................302 744-9875
Kim Adams, *CEO*
Troy Adams, *VP*
EMP: 23 **EST:** 2003
SALES (est): 4.43MM **Privately Held**
Web: www.mountainconsultinginc.net
SIC: 8711 8742 Civil engineering; Construction project management consultant

(G-3129)
MOVING EXPERIENCE DELAWARE
27 W Loockerman St Lowr Lowr (19904-8300)
PHONE.................302 241-0899
EMP: 9 **EST:** 2014
SALES (est): 505.71K **Privately Held**
Web: www.themovingexperiencede.com
SIC: 4789 Transportation services, nec

(G-3130)
MS NEAT CLEANING SERVICES LLC ✪
73 Greentree Dr Pmb 414 (19904-7646)
P.O. Box 188 (19938-0188)
PHONE.................302 535-7236
Melanie Stancell, *Managing Member*
EMP: 5 **EST:** 2022
SALES (est): 113.98K **Privately Held**
SIC: 7349 7389 Building and office cleaning services; Business services, nec

(G-3131)
MSGG LLC
8 The Grn Ste A (19901-3618)
PHONE.................917 565-8306
Mesut Akcin, *Managing Member*
EMP: 2
SALES (est): 92.41K **Privately Held**

Dover - Kent County (G-3132) — **GEOGRAPHIC SECTION**

SIC: 3949 7389 Sporting and athletic goods, nec; Business Activities at Non-Commercial Site

(G-3132)
MURGENCY INC
Also Called: Murgency
3500 S Dupont Hwy Ste Ak101 (19901-6041)
PHONE..............................650 308-9964
Mohammed Mather, *Ch Bd*
EMP: 24 EST: 2014
SALES (est): 4.72MM **Privately Held**
Web: www.murgency.com
SIC: 8999 8721 Personal services; Billing and bookkeeping service

(G-3133)
MURRYS CASH & CARRY
40 Quillen St (19904-5686)
PHONE..............................302 736-6508
C Shah, *Mgr*
EMP: 5 EST: 2007
SALES (est): 91.26K **Privately Held**
SIC: 4812 Cellular telephone services

(G-3134)
MY CARESHARE LLC
160 Greentree Dr Ste 101 (19904-7620)
PHONE..............................901 848-5988
EMP: 7
SALES (est): 208.03K **Privately Held**
SIC: 8059 Rest home, with health care

(G-3135)
MY EYE DR OPTOMETRISTS LLC
Also Called: Myeyedr
1404 Forrest Ave (19904-3478)
PHONE..............................302 346-4992
EMP: 6
SALES (corp-wide): 100.43MM **Privately Held**
Web: www.myeyedr.com
SIC: 8042 Offices and clinics of optometrists
PA: My Eye Dr. Optometrists, Llc
8614 Wstwd Ctr Dr Ste 900
Vienna VA 22182
703 847-8899

(G-3136)
MY EYE DR OPTOMETRISTS LLC
Also Called: Myeyedr
885 S Governors Avenue (19904-4158)
PHONE..............................302 734-5861
EMP: 6
SALES (corp-wide): 100.43MM **Privately Held**
Web: www.myeyedr.com
SIC: 8042 Offices and clinics of optometrists
PA: My Eye Dr. Optometrists, Llc
8614 Wstwd Ctr Dr Ste 900
Vienna VA 22182
703 847-8899

(G-3137)
MY HEALTH GROUP INC
1151 Walker Rd (19904-6600)
PHONE..............................401 400-0015
Ryan Marincowitz, *CEO*
EMP: 37
SALES (est): 626.16K **Privately Held**
SIC: 8322 7371 Individual and family services; Computer software development and applications

(G-3138)
MY LIFE CARE LLC
8 The Grn Ste A (19901-3618)
PHONE..............................302 760-9248
Vintila Severica, *CEO*
EMP: 80 EST: 2018
SALES (est): 3.47MM **Privately Held**
SIC: 3631 Household cooking equipment

(G-3139)
MY ROOTS LLC
9 W Loockerman St (19904-7323)
PHONE..............................302 883-2693
EMP: 5 EST: 2017
SALES (est): 98.19K **Privately Held**
SIC: 7231 Beauty shops

(G-3140)
MYRUCK INC
8 The Grn (19901-3618)
PHONE..............................310 462-3342
Victor Hill, *CEO*
Bradley Clark, *Prin*
Maurice Carrier, *Prin*
EMP: 3 EST: 2021
SALES (est): 71.13K **Privately Held**
SIC: 7372 Prepackaged software

(G-3141)
MYSEGMENTER TECHNOLOGIES INC
8 The Grn (19901-3618)
PHONE..............................302 549-2288
Ketan Jajal, *Pr*
EMP: 2
SALES (est): 87.4K **Privately Held**
SIC: 7372 Prepackaged software

(G-3142)
N DAISY JAX INC
1585 Mckee Rd Ste 3 (19904-1380)
PHONE..............................302 387-3543
Tina Dennis, *CEO*
George Dennis, *Pr*
EMP: 20 EST: 2014
SQ FT: 9,000
SALES (est): 2.03MM **Privately Held**
Web: www.jaxndaisy.com
SIC: 2844 Shampoos, rinses, conditioners: hair

(G-3143)
NABU CASA INC
8 The Grn Ste 12630 (19901-3618)
PHONE..............................747 477-3105
Paulus Schoutsen, *CEO*
EMP: 20 EST: 2018
SALES (est): 441.64K **Privately Held**
Web: www.nabucasa.com
SIC: 7389 Business services, nec

(G-3144)
NAF DOVER AFB
520 Main Gate Way Rm 202 (19902-5520)
P.O. Box 2066 (19902-2066)
PHONE..............................302 677-6950
Lynn M Utz, *Mgr*
EMP: 5 EST: 2006
SALES (est): 150K **Privately Held**
SIC: 8721 Accounting, auditing, and bookkeeping

(G-3145)
NAIL IT DOWN GENERAL CONTRS
Also Called: Nail It Down General Contrs
1474 E Lebanon Rd (19901-5833)
PHONE..............................302 698-3073
Jess Manning, *Pr*
Kim Dawson, *Mgr*
Brian Dawson, *CEO*
EMP: 7 EST: 2000
SALES (est): 560.85K **Privately Held**
SIC: 1522 Residential construction, nec

(G-3146)
NAIL PROS
94 Jessica Lyn Dr (19904-1491)
PHONE..............................302 674-2988
Pat Tang, *Owner*
EMP: 5 EST: 1998
SALES (est): 99.28K **Privately Held**
SIC: 7231 Manicurist, pedicurist

(G-3147)
NAIL SPA BY TR
1188 Forrest Ave (19904-3379)
PHONE..............................302 678-2122
Tr Rowe, *Pr*
EMP: 6 EST: 2015
SALES (est): 47.57K **Privately Held**
Web: the-nail-spa-by-tr.edan.io
SIC: 7991 Spas

(G-3148)
NAKUURUQ SOLUTIONS
206 Atlantic St (19902-5206)
PHONE..............................302 526-2223
EMP: 3 EST: 2012
SALES (est): 185K **Privately Held**
SIC: 3728 Aircraft training equipment

(G-3149)
NAOMI RISING INC
4021 Hemlock Ct (19901-7946)
PHONE..............................803 840-1874
EMP: 5 EST: 2019
SALES (est): 61.99K **Privately Held**
SIC: 8361 Residential care

(G-3150)
NARLEYAPPS INC
8 The Grn Ste A (19901-3618)
PHONE..............................323 744-1398
Troy Wooten, *CEO*
EMP: 5 EST: 2012
SALES (est): 294.54K **Privately Held**
SIC: 7371 2731 Computer software development and applications; Books, publishing and printing

(G-3151)
NASHVILLE SPEEDWAY USA INC
Also Called: Nashville Super Speedway
1131 N Dupont Hwy (19901-2008)
PHONE..............................615 547-7500
Dennis Mcglenn, *Pr*
Cliff Hawks, *
EMP: 40 EST: 2000
SQ FT: 3,200
SALES (est): 2.61MM
SALES (corp-wide): 523.83MM **Privately Held**
Web: casinos.ballys.com
SIC: 7948 Racing, including track operation
HQ: Dover Motorsports, Inc.
1131 N Dupont Hwy
Dover DE 19901
302 883-6500

(G-3152)
NATIONAL AFRICAN AMERICAN COAL
Also Called: Naacaht
18 The Grn (19901-3612)
P.O. Box 2628 (20604-2628)
PHONE..............................301 395-9033
Kelly Cody, *Pr*
EMP: 6
SQ FT: 500
SALES (est): 36.04K **Privately Held**
SIC: 8399 Advocacy group

(G-3153)
NATIONAL ASSOCIATION REALTO
1986 Horsepond Rd (19901-7231)
PHONE..............................302 674-8640
Elisabeth Mcguire, *Prin*
EMP: 5 EST: 2010
SALES (est): 58K **Privately Held**
SIC: 8699 Membership organizations, nec

(G-3154)
NATIONAL CNCIL ON AG LF LBOR R (PA)
363 Saulsbury Rd (19904-2722)
PHONE..............................302 678-9400
Joe L Myer, *Ex Dir*
EMP: 28 EST: 1976
SQ FT: 6,000
SALES (est): 5.84MM
SALES (corp-wide): 5.84MM **Privately Held**
Web: www.neighborgoodpartners.org
SIC: 8748 Urban planning and consulting services

(G-3155)
NATIONAL SOCIETY OF SONS
Also Called: Caesar Rodney Chapter Sar
121 Meetinghouse Ln (19904-2655)
PHONE..............................443 614-5437
EMP: 6 EST: 2014
SALES (est): 110K **Privately Held**
SIC: 8641 Civic associations

(G-3156)
NATIONAL VINYL PRODUCTS INC
1886 Lynnbury Woods Rd (19904-1801)
PHONE..............................817 913-5991
EMP: 14
SALES (corp-wide): 32.72B **Privately Held**
Web: www.nvpfence.com
SIC: 3315 1799 Fence gates, posts, and fittings: steel; Fence construction
HQ: National Vinyl Products Inc.
1277 N 200 W
Nephi UT 84648
435 623-2750

(G-3157)
NATIONWIDE INSURANCE
Also Called: Nationwide
57 Saulsbury Rd Frnt (19904-3472)
PHONE..............................919 644-6535
EMP: 6 EST: 2019
SALES (est): 134.07K **Privately Held**
Web: www.nationwide.com
SIC: 6411 Insurance agents, nec

(G-3158)
NATIONWIDE INSURANCE CO
1252 Forrest Ave (19904-3311)
PHONE..............................302 678-2223
EMP: 6 EST: 1986
SALES (est): 399.94K **Privately Held**
Web: www.nationwide.com
SIC: 6411 Insurance agents, nec

(G-3159)
NATIVE GRID LLC (PA)
8 The Grn Ste A (19901-3618)
PHONE..............................917 893-7544
EMP: 8 EST: 2020
SALES (est): 112.77K
SALES (corp-wide): 112.77K **Privately Held**
SIC: 7371 Computer software development and applications

GEOGRAPHIC SECTION

Dover - Kent County (G-3191)

(G-3160)
NAUTICAL FLFLLMENT LGSTICS LLC
8 The Grn Ste A (19901-3618)
PHONE................................816 810-3118
EMP: 5 **EST:** 2017
SALES (est): 110.13K **Privately Held**
SIC: 7389 Business services, nec

(G-3161)
NAVALT INC
8 The Grn Ste R (19901-3618)
PHONE................................551 273-2773
Sandith Thandasherry, *CEO*
EMP: 2
SALES (est): 92.41K **Privately Held**
Web: www.navaltboats.com
SIC: 3731 Shipbuilding and repairing

(G-3162)
NAVENU INC
8 The Grn (19901-3618)
PHONE................................416 543-9617
Richard Sutin, *Sec*
EMP: 8
SALES (est): 294.17K **Privately Held**
SIC: 7371 Computer software development and applications

(G-3163)
NAZAR DOVER LLC
Also Called: Holiday Inn
561 N Dupont Hwy (19901-3960)
PHONE................................302 747-5050
Muhammad Zulfiqar, *CEO*
EMP: 30 **EST:** 2015
SALES (est): 500.61K **Privately Held**
Web: www.holidayinn.com
SIC: 7011 Hotels and motels

(G-3164)
NAZHAT ENTERPRISES HOLDINGS
8 The Grn Ste 7361 (19901-3618)
PHONE................................302 450-1418
Enayat Nazhat, *CEO*
EMP: 5 **EST:** 2017
SIC: 6719 Holding companies, nec

(G-3165)
NED DAVIS ASSOCIATES INC
314 N Governors Ave (19904-3006)
PHONE................................302 670-5307
EMP: 6 **EST:** 2017
SALES (est): 141.22K **Privately Held**
Web: www.neddavis.com
SIC: 8742 Management consulting services

(G-3166)
NEENEE WEES DAYCARE
208 Mifflin Rd (19904-3321)
PHONE................................302 730-3630
Patricia Williams, *Prin*
EMP: 5 **EST:** 2010
SALES (est): 92.35K **Privately Held**
SIC: 8351 Group day care center

(G-3167)
NEILSEN CLOTHING INC
3500 S Dupont Hwy (19901-6041)
PHONE................................302 342-1370
EMP: 6
SALES (est): 67.05K **Privately Held**
Web: neilsen-clothing.myshopify.com
SIC: 2385 Waterproof outerwear

(G-3168)
NEMOURS DPONT PEDIATRICS DOVER
201 Towne Centre Dr Ste 500 (19904)
PHONE................................302 672-5650
EMP: 7 **EST:** 2020
SALES (est): 207.37K **Privately Held**
Web: www.nemours.org
SIC: 8011 Pediatrician

(G-3169)
NEODATA LLC ✪
8 The Grn Ste A (19901-3618)
PHONE................................302 666-2848
EMP: 25 **EST:** 2022
SALES (est): 641.67K **Privately Held**
SIC: 7371 7389 Computer software development and applications; Business services, nec

(G-3170)
NEON FUN LLC
3500 S Dupont Hwy (19901-6041)
PHONE................................858 220-0946
Rhonda Woerner, *Mgr*
EMP: 5 **EST:** 2012
SALES (est): 166.6K **Privately Held**
SIC: 7372 Home entertainment computer software

(G-3171)
NEON USA LLC ✪
3500 S Dupont Hwy (19901-6041)
PHONE................................360 433-7512
Andre Madeira, *Pr*
EMP: 10 **EST:** 2022
SALES (est): 348.32K **Privately Held**
SIC: 7371 Computer software development

(G-3172)
NERD BOY LLC
800 N State St Ste 402 (19901-3925)
P.O. Box 383 (07058-0383)
PHONE................................302 857-0243
Deniz Turgut, *Managing Member*
EMP: 5 **EST:** 2017
SALES (est): 192.14K **Privately Held**
SIC: 7372 Prepackaged software

(G-3173)
NET JOURNEY LLC (PA)
8 The Grn Ste A (19901-3618)
PHONE................................818 584-2519
Lalo Mantilla, *CEO*
EMP: 7 **EST:** 2017
SALES (est): 71.56K
SALES (corp-wide): 71.56K **Privately Held**
SIC: 7371 Computer software development and applications

(G-3174)
NET MERGE LTD
4115 N Dupont Hwy (19901-1561)
PHONE................................631 816-1145
Everel A Morris, *Pr*
EMP: 5 **EST:** 2020
SALES (est): 307.32K **Privately Held**
SIC: 5045 Computer software

(G-3175)
NETERRA COMMUNICATIONS LLC ✪
500 W Loockerman St Ste 469 (19904-7309)
PHONE................................302 497-3881
George Tomova, *Prin*
EMP: 10 **EST:** 2022
SALES (est): 563.75K **Privately Held**
Web: www.neterra.net
SIC: 4813 Telephone communication, except radio

(G-3176)
NEUROSCIENCE SOFTWARE INC
Also Called: Brainify.ai
8 The Grn Ste 12017 (19901-3618)
PHONE................................855 712-1818
Mariam Khayretdinova, *CEO*
EMP: 9 **EST:** 2021
SALES (est): 500K **Privately Held**
SIC: 7371 8731 Computer software development and applications; Biotechnical research, commercial

(G-3177)
NEUTEC CORP
29 Emerson Dr (19901-5819)
PHONE................................302 697-6752
Lachhman Gupta, *Pr*
Surender Gupta, *VP*
EMP: 5 **EST:** 1996
SALES (est): 328.78K **Privately Held**
Web: www.neutecgroup.com
SIC: 7371 Computer software development and applications

(G-3178)
NEW BODY BY TOMORROW LLC
8 The Grn Ste 4000 (19901-3618)
PHONE................................706 816-9255
EMP: 20
SALES (est): 446.52K **Privately Held**
SIC: 8093 Weight loss clinic, with medical staff

(G-3179)
NEW LEAF PUBLISHING INC (PA)
8 The Grn Ste A (19901-3618)
PHONE................................408 502-8706
Yi Jia, *Prin*
EMP: 8
SALES (est): 643.57K
SALES (corp-wide): 643.57K **Privately Held**
Web: www.nlpg.com
SIC: 2731 Book publishing

(G-3180)
NEW LIFE MEDICALS LLC
3500 S Dupont Hwy (19901-6041)
PHONE................................610 615-1483
EMP: 5 **EST:** 2016
SALES (est): 53.41K **Privately Held**
Web: www.newlifemedicals.com
SIC: 2834 Pharmaceutical preparations

(G-3181)
NEW LIFE SPINAL CENTERS
737 S Governors Ave (19904-4105)
PHONE................................302 883-2504
EMP: 7 **EST:** 2017
SALES (est): 37.19K **Privately Held**
SIC: 8041 Offices and clinics of chiropractors

(G-3182)
NEW YORK BLOOD CTR INC D/B/A B
Also Called: NEW YORK BLOOD CENTER, INC. D/B/A BLOOD BANK OF DELMARVA
221 Saulsbury Rd (19904-2720)
PHONE................................302 734-4100
Elizabeth Mcquail, *CEO*
EMP: 18
SALES (corp-wide): 29.61MM **Privately Held**
Web: www.delmarvablood.org
SIC: 8099 Blood bank
PA: New York Blood Center, Inc.
100 Hygeia Dr
Newark DE 19713
302 737-8405

(G-3183)
NEWPHOENIX SCREEN PRINTING
305 Lotus St (19901-4461)
PHONE................................302 747-8991
Wayne L Newsome Senior, *Owner*
EMP: 4 **EST:** 2015
SALES (est): 104.75K **Privately Held**
Web: www.newphoenixscreenprinting.com
SIC: 2759 Screen printing

(G-3184)
NEXT HYDROGEN USA INC
1675 S State St Ste B (19901-5140)
PHONE................................416 953-6657
Raveel Afzaal, *CEO*
Kasia Malz, *CFO*
Jim Hinatsu, *COO*
EMP: 40 **EST:** 2021
SALES (est): 2.54MM **Privately Held**
SIC: 3599 Industrial machinery, nec

(G-3185)
NEXT LEVEL STAFFING SOLUTIONS ✪
53 Doty Dr (19901-6840)
PHONE................................302 281-4777
Rasheeta Guinyard, *Prin*
EMP: 10 **EST:** 2023
SALES (est): 150K **Privately Held**
SIC: 7361 7389 Employment agencies; Business Activities at Non-Commercial Site

(G-3186)
NEXT PACE TECHNOLOGIES INC
8 The Grn Ste R (19901-3618)
PHONE................................415 900-0876
Rahul Verma, *CEO*
EMP: 5 **EST:** 2019
SALES (est): 100K **Privately Held**
Web: www.nextpacetechnologies.com
SIC: 7379 Computer related consulting services

(G-3187)
NEXTHOME PREFER
144 Kings Hwy (19901-7308)
PHONE................................302 526-2886
EMP: 5 **EST:** 2019
SALES (est): 86.73K **Privately Held**
SIC: 6531 Real estate brokers and agents

(G-3188)
NICOLE A FISHER
200 Banning St Ste 200 (19904-3487)
PHONE................................302 674-0600
Nicole A Fisher Pa, *Owner*
EMP: 8 **EST:** 2017
SALES (est): 144.71K **Privately Held**
SIC: 8049 Offices of health practitioner

(G-3189)
NIKKI SYKES TAX PREPARATION AS
55 Loockerman Plz (19903-8084)
P.O. Box 1285 (19903-1285)
PHONE................................302 399-6363
EMP: 6 **EST:** 2015
SALES (est): 18.45K **Privately Held**
SIC: 7291 Tax return preparation services

(G-3190)
NINA WOOF LLC
8 The Grn (19901-3618)
PHONE................................210 492-6617
EMP: 3 **EST:** 2021
SALES (est): 135.7K **Privately Held**
Web: www.ninawoof.com
SIC: 2399 7389 Pet collars, leashes, etc.; non-leather; Business services, nec

(G-3191)
NOBLE EAGLE SALES LLC
Also Called: Shooter's Choice
5105 N Dupont Hwy (19901-2345)

Dover - Kent County (G-3192) GEOGRAPHIC SECTION

PHONE.................302 736-5166
Beth Parsons, *Mgr*
EMP: 7 **EST:** 2012
SALES (est): 238.84K **Privately Held**
SIC: 5941 7999 Firearms; Shooting range operation

(G-3192)
NOBLE PROPERTY LLC ◆
8 The Grn (19901-3618)
PHONE.................718 502-4806
Nabil Nahlah, *CEO*
EMP: 50 **EST:** 2023
SALES (est): 1.16MM **Privately Held**
SIC: 6531 7389 Real estate agents and managers; Business Activities at Non-Commercial Site

(G-3193)
NOHOTEL ENTERPRISES LLC
8 The Grn Ste 7756 (19901-3618)
PHONE.................917 970-1974
Dea Muriqi, *Managing Member*
EMP: 6 **EST:** 2019
SALES (est): 211.31K **Privately Held**
SIC: 6513 Apartment hotel operation

(G-3194)
NORMAN M LIPPMAN DDS
712 S Governors Ave (19904-4106)
PHONE.................302 674-1140
Norman Lippman D.d.s., *Owner*
Norman Lippman, *Owner*
EMP: 8 **EST:** 1983
SALES (est): 234.66K **Privately Held**
SIC: 8021 Dentists' office

(G-3195)
NORMAN NIELSEN GROUP INC ◆
8 The Grn Ste 14572 (19901-3618)
PHONE.................415 685-4230
Kara Pernice, *Pr*
Sarah Gibbons, *
Hoa Loranger, *
Kate Moran, *
Raluca Budiu, *
EMP: 30 **EST:** 2023
SALES (est): 1.21MM **Privately Held**
SIC: 7372 Business oriented computer software

(G-3196)
NORTH EAST HTG AC
25 Maggies Way Ste 3 (19901-4896)
PHONE.................410 299-1773
EMP: 6 **EST:** 2019
SALES (est): 971.44K **Privately Held**
SIC: 5074 Plumbing fittings and supplies

(G-3197)
NORTH EASTERN WAFFLES LLC
4003 S Dupont Hwy # 1753 (19901-6005)
PHONE.................302 697-2226
Lance Clark, *Ofcr*
EMP: 11 **EST:** 2009
SALES (est): 77.23K **Privately Held**
SIC: 8059 Nursing and personal care, nec

(G-3198)
NORTHNODE GROUP COUNSELING LLC
1609 S State St (19901-5148)
PHONE.................302 257-3135
EMP: 15 **EST:** 2016
SALES (est): 1.11MM **Privately Held**
Web: www.northnodecounseling.com
SIC: 8322 General counseling services

(G-3199)
NORTHWESTERN MUTL FINCL NETWRK
450 S Dupont Hwy Ofc B (19901-4502)
PHONE.................414 299-2508
EMP: 7 **EST:** 2016
SALES (est): 56.53K **Privately Held**
Web: www.northwesternmutual.com
SIC: 6311 Life insurance

(G-3200)
NOT YOUR MOTHERS MAKEUP
34 Brayton Pl (19904-3905)
PHONE.................302 538-1612
Sharon Strand, *Prin*
EMP: 8 **EST:** 2018
SALES (est): 19.3K **Privately Held**
SIC: 7231 Cosmetologist

(G-3201)
NOTCH INSURANCE INC
Also Called: Notch
850 New Burton Rd (19904-5785)
PHONE.................616 622-2554
Rafael Broshi, *CEO*
EMP: 20 **EST:** 2021
SALES (est): 1.79MM **Privately Held**
SIC: 6411 Insurance brokers, nec

(G-3202)
NOVA WAVE CREDIT LLC
8 The Grn Ste A (19901-3618)
PHONE.................929 263-4212
EMP: 6 **EST:** 2020
SALES (est): 277.54K **Privately Held**
Web: www.novawavecredit.com
SIC: 6411 Insurance information and consulting services

(G-3203)
NOVACARE REHABILITATION
128 Greentree Dr (19904-7648)
PHONE.................302 674-4192
EMP: 5 **EST:** 2018
SALES (est): 80.53K **Privately Held**
SIC: 8049 Physical therapist

(G-3204)
NOVACARE REHABILITATION DOVER
230 Beiser Blvd Ste 103 (19904-7791)
PHONE.................302 760-9966
EMP: 6 **EST:** 2017
SALES (est): 73.36K **Privately Held**
SIC: 8093 Rehabilitation center, outpatient treatment

(G-3205)
NOVO FINANCIAL CORP
850 New Burton Rd Ste 201 (19904-5786)
PHONE.................844 260-6800
Tyler Mcintyre, *Pr*
EMP: 10 **EST:** 2016
SALES (est): 931.03K **Privately Held**
SIC: 7371 7389 Computer software development; Financial services

(G-3206)
NOW THATS A PARTY LLC
356 Fork Branch Rd (19904-1225)
PHONE.................302 465-0928
EMP: 5 **EST:** 2015
SALES (est): 22.93K **Privately Held**
Web: www.nowthatsapartyde.com
SIC: 7299 Party planning service

(G-3207)
NOWADAYS INC PBC
614 N Dupont Hwy (19901-3900)

PHONE.................415 279-6802
Max Elder, *CEO*
EMP: 3 **EST:** 2020
SALES (est): 223.47K **Privately Held**
SIC: 5142 2037 Frozen vegetables and fruit products; Frozen fruits and vegetables

(G-3208)
NRAI SERVICES LLC
160 Greentree Dr Ste 101 (19904-7620)
PHONE.................302 674-4089
EMP: 19 **EST:** 2000
SQ FT: 3,000
SALES (est): 2.11MM **Privately Held**
Web: www.nraiservices.com
SIC: 7389 Document storage service

(G-3209)
NSIDE WRESTLING
158 Derby Wood Cir (19904-6490)
PHONE.................302 697-9633
Jermaine Mccove, *Prin*
EMP: 5 **EST:** 2014
SALES (est): 45.94K **Privately Held**
SIC: 7941 Boxing and wrestling arena

(G-3210)
NU ATTITUDE STYLING SALON LTD
49 S Dupont Hwy (19901-7430)
PHONE.................302 734-8638
EMP: 9 **EST:** 1991
SALES (est): 141.51K **Privately Held**
SIC: 7231 Unisex hair salons

(G-3211)
NURSES NEXT STAFFING LLC
8 The Grn Ste 7689 (19901-3618)
PHONE.................302 446-3200
EMP: 12 **EST:** 2014
SALES (est): 300K **Privately Held**
SIC: 7361 Nurses' registry

(G-3212)
NURSING BOARD
861 Silver Lake Blvd (19904-2467)
PHONE.................302 744-4500
Iva Boardman, *Ex Dir*
EMP: 21 **EST:** 2010
SALES (est): 842.89K **Privately Held**
SIC: 8051 Skilled nursing care facilities

(G-3213)
OASM CORP
8 The Grn (19901-3618)
PHONE.................203 679-9124
Cymone Jones, *CEO*
EMP: 13
SALES (est): 408.19K **Privately Held**
SIC: 8748 7389 Business consulting, nec; Business services, nec

(G-3214)
OB-GYN ASSOCIATES OF DOVER P A
200 Banning St Ste 320 (19904-3488)
PHONE.................302 674-0223
Robert Scacheri Md, *Pr*
Robert H Radnick Md, *VP*
EMP: 20 **EST:** 1963
SALES (est): 584.97K **Privately Held**
Web: www.dedicatedtowomenobgyn.com
SIC: 8011 Obstetrician

(G-3215)
OCEANVIEW CAPITAL INDS LLC
8 The Grn (19901-3618)
PHONE.................813 397-3706
James Finley, *Managing Member*
EMP: 15 **EST:** 2020
SALES (est): 560.49K **Privately Held**

SIC: 4731 Transportation agents and brokers

(G-3216)
OCONNOR ORTHODONTICS
1004 S State St (19901-6901)
PHONE.................302 678-1441
Oconnor Orthodontics, *Prin*
EMP: 9 **EST:** 2013
SALES (est): 171.98K **Privately Held**
Web: www.aoortho.com
SIC: 8021 Orthodontist

(G-3217)
OINK OINK LLC
Also Called: Oink Financial Services
8 The Grn Ste A (19901-3618)
PHONE.................302 924-5034
EMP: 8 **EST:** 2019
SALES (est): 795.84K **Privately Held**
Web: en.oinkoink.us
SIC: 6099 6153 7389 7299 Money order issuance; Factoring services; Financial services; Personal financial services

(G-3218)
OJO INVESTMENTS LLC (PA) ◆
8 The Grn Ste 10541 (19901-3618)
PHONE.................215 934-0855
David Ojo, *Managing Member*
EMP: 7 **EST:** 2022
SALES (est): 76.37K
SALES (corp-wide): 76.37K **Privately Held**
SIC: 6799 Investors, nec

(G-3219)
OLD REPUBLIC NAT TITLE INSUR
Also Called: Old Republic
32 The Grn (19901-3612)
PHONE.................302 734-3570
Kathy B Endicott, *Mgr*
EMP: 6
SALES (corp-wide): 8.08B **Publicly Held**
Web: www.oldrepublictitle.com
SIC: 6361 Real estate title insurance
HQ: Old Republic National Title Insurance Company
11055 Wayzata Blvd # 250
Hopkins MN 55305
612 371-1111

(G-3220)
OLSON REALTY
614 N Dupont Hwy Ste 300 (19901-3900)
PHONE.................302 448-6000
James Olson, *Prin*
EMP: 6 **EST:** 2016
SALES (est): 240.46K **Privately Held**
Web: www.olsonrealty.net
SIC: 6531 Real estate agent, residential

(G-3221)
OLUWASEYI DAVID POPOOLA
896 S State St Unit 384 (19901-4148)
PHONE.................302 331-3684
Oluwaseyi Popoola, *Owner*
EMP: 2
SALES (est): 74.83K **Privately Held**
SIC: 5611 2329 Men's and boys' clothing stores; Men's and boy's clothing, nec

(G-3222)
OMAREVA ENERGY INC
3500 S Dupont Hwy (19901-6041)
PHONE.................514 660-0291
Essam Ibrahim, *Pr*
EMP: 3
SALES (est): 135.7K **Privately Held**
SIC: 3691 Storage batteries

GEOGRAPHIC SECTION Dover - Kent County (G-3254)

(G-3223)
OME LAKE VISTA III & IV LLC (PA)
1675 S State St Ste B (19901-5140)
PHONE.................619 787-5592
EMP: 7 EST: 2019
SALES (est): 116.66K
SALES (corp-wide): 116.66K Privately Held
SIC: 6531 Real estate leasing and rentals

(G-3224)
OMEGA INDUSTRIES INC
7 Messina Hill Rd (19904-1831)
P.O. Box 407 (19936-0407)
PHONE.................302 734-3835
George Diakos, Pr
Peter Diakos, Sec
EMP: 9 EST: 1991
SALES (est): 972.69K Privately Held
SIC: 3585 Air conditioning equipment, complete

(G-3225)
OMNISETS LLC
8 The Grn (19901-3618)
PHONE.................425 229-1592
EMP: 4
SALES (est): 73.93K Privately Held
SIC: 7372 7389 Prepackaged software; Business Activities at Non-Commercial Site

(G-3226)
ON GLO LLC (PA) ✪
8 The Grn Ste A (19901-3618)
PHONE.................205 567-3434
Gloria Mencer, Managing Member
EMP: 6 EST: 2023
SALES (est): 76.63K
SALES (corp-wide): 76.63K Privately Held
SIC: 5651 7532 Unisex clothing stores; Mobile home and trailer repair

(G-3227)
ON Q FINANCIAL
20 E Division St Ste C (19901-7366)
PHONE.................866 667-3279
EMP: 6 EST: 2019
SALES (est): 94.36K Privately Held
Web: www.onqfinancial.com
SIC: 6162 Mortgage bankers and loan correspondents

(G-3228)
ONE SENTENTIA LTD
8 The Grn Ste A (19901-3618)
PHONE.................646 284-0321
Zhang Yong, Prin
EMP: 5
SALES (est): 164.52K Privately Held
SIC: 7371 Computer software development

(G-3229)
ONEBILL INC (PA)
8 The Grn Ste 4518 (19901-3618)
PHONE.................619 292-8493
EMP: 6 EST: 2019
SALES (est): 58.42K
SALES (corp-wide): 58.42K Privately Held
SIC: 7371 Computer software development and applications

(G-3230)
ONENGINE CORP
8 The Grn (19901-3618)
PHONE.................949 872-0339
EMP: 8
SALES (est): 306.16K Privately Held
SIC: 7371 Computer software development

(G-3231)
ONLINE CATALYST LLC (PA) ✪
8 The Grn Ste G (19901-3618)
PHONE.................916 990-3150
Camo Sarner, Managing Member
EMP: 6 EST: 2022
SALES (est): 75.41K
SALES (corp-wide): 75.41K Privately Held
SIC: 8742 Marketing consulting services

(G-3232)
ONOLLO INC
8 The Grn Ste R (19901-3618)
PHONE.................925 286-4797
Artin Bogdanov, CEO
Artin Bogdanov, Managing Member
EMP: 5 EST: 2021
SALES (est): 214.47K Privately Held
SIC: 7372 7389 Business oriented computer software; Business services, nec

(G-3233)
OOBLA INC
8 The Grn (19901-3618)
PHONE.................416 230-9119
Jubril Juma, Pr
EMP: 7 EST: 2021
SALES (est): 264.9K Privately Held
SIC: 7389 Financial services

(G-3234)
OOGA TECHNOLOGIES INC
3500 S Dupont Hwy (19901-6041)
PHONE.................585 503-6047
Ajay Pasupuleti, Pr
EMP: 5 EST: 2020
SALES (est): 256.68K Privately Held
SIC: 4785 Inspection services connected with transportation

(G-3235)
OOSO DRINKS CO LLC ✪
611 S Dupont Hwy Ste 102 (19901-4507)
P.O. Box 220130 (11222-0130)
PHONE.................919 808-7605
Sophia Racciatti, Prin
EMP: 2 EST: 2023
SALES (est): 92.41K Privately Held
SIC: 2086 Bottled and canned soft drinks

(G-3236)
OPEN COURT TV LLC
8 The Grn (19901-3618)
PHONE.................646 975-1509
Adrian Gant, Managing Member
EMP: 3
SALES (est): 86.51K Privately Held
SIC: 2741 Internet publishing and broadcasting

(G-3237)
OPENEXO INC
3500 S Dupont Hwy (19901-6041)
PHONE.................617 965-5057
Salim Ismail, Pr
Lawrence Pensack, CFO
EMP: 10 EST: 2017
SALES (est): 791.42K Privately Held
SIC: 8742 Management consulting services

(G-3238)
OPUSAI INC ✪
8 The Grn Ste A (19901-3618)
PHONE.................817 440-4609
Adnan Younas, CEO
EMP: 20 EST: 2022
SALES (est): 600.73K Privately Held
SIC: 7379 Online services technology consultants

(G-3239)
ORBIXPLAY LLC ✪
Also Called: Orbixplay
1111b S Governors Ave Ste 7336 (19904-6903)
PHONE.................408 337-6490
Ezio Amodio, Managing Member
EMP: 10 EST: 2023
SALES (est): 348.32K Privately Held
SIC: 7371 Custom computer programming services

(G-3240)
ORISHUN COMPANY LLC
Also Called: Orishun Filmworks Intl
8 The Grn Ste 10876 (19901-3618)
PHONE.................302 538-2120
Leiba Solomon, CEO
EMP: 20 EST: 2017
SALES (est): 247.06K Privately Held
Web: www.orishuncompany.com
SIC: 7822 7812 Film exchange, for television: motion picture; Motion picture production

(G-3241)
ORTH & KOWALICK PA
1991 S State St (19901-5811)
PHONE.................302 697-2159
P William Orth, Pr
Raymond J Kowalick, Prin
EMP: 5 EST: 1979
SALES (est): 380.46K Privately Held
Web: www.okcpas.com
SIC: 8721 Certified public accountant

(G-3242)
ORTHODONTICS ON SILVER LAKE PA
Also Called: Stephanie E Steckel DDS, Ms
42 Hiawatha Ln (19904-2401)
PHONE.................302 672-7776
EMP: 7 EST: 1995
SALES (est): 247.7K Privately Held
Web: www.beachbraces.com
SIC: 8021 Orthodontist

(G-3243)
ORTHOPAEDIC CONSULTANTS PA
487 S Queen St (19904-3572)
PHONE.................302 724-5062
EMP: 5 EST: 2015
SALES (est): 123.62K Privately Held
SIC: 8999 Scientific consulting

(G-3244)
ORTHOPAEDIC SPECIALISTS
230 Beiser Blvd (19904-7793)
PHONE.................302 730-0840
Richard Dushuttle, Prin
EMP: 9 EST: 2010
SALES (est): 189.54K Privately Held
Web: www.delortho.com
SIC: 8011 Orthopedic physician

(G-3245)
ORTHOPEDIC SPINE CENTER P A
260 Beiser Blvd (19904-5773)
PHONE.................302 734-9700
Stephen L Malone, Prin
EMP: 5 EST: 2009
SALES (est): 465.35K Privately Held
Web: www.orthopaedicspinecenter.com
SIC: 8011 Orthopedic physician

(G-3246)
ORVILLE SAMMONS ARDENS
4272 Judith Rd (19904-5069)
PHONE.................302 492-8620
Orville Sammons, Owner
EMP: 5 EST: 1976
SALES (est): 297.4K Privately Held
SIC: 3479 Painting, coating, and hot dipping

(G-3247)
OTIS KAMARA
Also Called: Veteran Owned Cleaning Svcs
General Delivery (19901)
P.O. Box 960 (19903-0960)
PHONE.................443 207-2643
Otis Kamara, Owner
EMP: 5 EST: 2017
SALES (est): 62.99K Privately Held
Web: www.delawarerestaurant.org
SIC: 7349 Janitorial service, contract basis

(G-3248)
OUR MAIDS INC
8 The Grn Ste 7637 (19901-3618)
PHONE.................302 389-5221
Antonio V Moreno, Ex Dir
EMP: 7 EST: 2020
SALES (est): 100K Privately Held
Web: www.ourmaids.com
SIC: 7699 Cleaning services

(G-3249)
OUTLAND ART INC
8 The Grn Ste 12603 (19901-3618)
PHONE.................800 918-1587
Zhongyuan Li, CEO
EMP: 10
SALES (est): 348.32K Privately Held
SIC: 7371 Computer software development

(G-3250)
OUTMARCH INC
8 The Grn Ste R (19901-3618)
PHONE.................508 289-1233
Uma Killedar, Prin
EMP: 8
SALES (est): 306.16K Privately Held
SIC: 7371 Computer software development and applications

(G-3251)
OUTPATIENT PROCEDURE CTRS LLC
240 Beiser Blvd Ste 201f (19904-8208)
PHONE.................302 734-7246
Ganesh Balu, Prin
EMP: 8 EST: 2013
SALES (est): 77.41K Privately Held
SIC: 8011 Offices and clinics of medical doctors

(G-3252)
OUTREACH TEAM LLC
8 The Grn Ste R (19901-3618)
PHONE.................302 744-9550
EMP: 6 EST: 2017
SALES (est): 113.34K Privately Held
SIC: 8322 Outreach program

(G-3253)
OWENS MANOR LTD PARTNERSHIP
76 Stevenson Dr (19901-4021)
PHONE.................302 678-1065
Pamela Smith, Genl Mgr
EMP: 5 EST: 2001
SALES (est): 149.34K Privately Held
SIC: 6513 Apartment building operators

(G-3254)
OWLII INC
3500 S Dupont Hwy (19901-6041)
PHONE.................626 695-6607
Wen Ziyu, Dir
Zhao Qianyun, Prin
EMP: 5 EST: 2016

Dover - Kent County (G-3255) GEOGRAPHIC SECTION

SALES (est): 86K **Privately Held**
SIC: **7371** Custom computer programming services

(G-3255)
OXI FRESH DOVER CARPET CLG
753 Walker Rd (19904-2724)
PHONE..................302 526-5035
EMP: 10 EST: 2018
SALES (est): 106.53K **Privately Held**
Web: www.oxifresh.com
SIC: **7217** Carpet and upholstery cleaning

(G-3256)
OXYPAPER INC
8 The Grn (19901-3618)
PHONE..................302 202-4897
Niall Alli, CEO
EMP: 312 EST: 2019
SALES (est): 12.12MM **Privately Held**
SIC: **2621 2671 2674 2672** Paper mills; Paper; coated and laminated packaging; Paper bags: made from purchased materials; Paper; coated and laminated, nec

(G-3257)
P A CNMRI
Also Called: Cnmri
1095 S Bradford St (19904-4141)
PHONE..................302 678-8100
Robert Varipapa, Pr
John Coll, *
Audry Lenox, *
EMP: 90 EST: 1988
SALES (est): 9.79MM **Privately Held**
Web: www.cnmri.com
SIC: **8011** 7389 Neurologist; Business services, nec

(G-3258)
PACIFIC GREEN TECHNOLOGIES INC (PA)
Also Called: Pacific Green Technologies
8 The Grn Ste 1 (19901-3618)
PHONE..................302 601-4659
Scott Poulter, CEO
James Tindal-robertson, CFO
EMP: 19 EST: 1994
SALES (est): 7.64MM
SALES (corp-wide): 7.64MM **Publicly Held**
Web: www.pacificgreen.com
SIC: **4953** Refuse systems

(G-3259)
PACO CONSTRUCTION & LDSCPG LLC
221 Kentwood Dr (19901-8737)
PHONE..................302 359-2432
Augusto Ramirez, Prin
EMP: 5 EST: 2016
SALES (est): 31.52K **Privately Held**
Web: paco-contruction.business.site
SIC: **0781** Landscape services

(G-3260)
PAIN MGT & REHABILITATION CTR
240 Beiser Blvd Ste 201a (19904-8208)
PHONE..................302 734-7246
Ganesh Balu, Owner
EMP: 14 EST: 2003
SALES (est): 202.82K **Privately Held**
SIC: **8011** Orthopedic physician

(G-3261)
PAINTING SOLUTIONS LLC
6244 Pearsons Corner Rd (19904-0918)
PHONE..................302 736-6483
James Surtrenant, Prin
EMP: 5 EST: 2016

SALES (est): 44.19K **Privately Held**
SIC: **1721** Painting and paper hanging

(G-3262)
PALM NFT STUDIO INC
874 Walker Rd Ste C (19904-2778)
PHONE..................216 870-9066
EMP: 5 EST: 2021
SALES (est): 451.7K **Privately Held**
Web: www.palmnftstudio.com
SIC: **7389** Design services

(G-3263)
PAMPER PERFECT MOBILE SPA
1033 Harvest Grove Trl (19901-2793)
PHONE..................866 947-9994
Allison Garrett, Owner
EMP: 5 EST: 2015
SALES (est): 77.57K **Privately Held**
Web: www.pamperperfectmobilespa.com
SIC: **7231** Manicurist, pedicurist

(G-3264)
PANAMERICAN COFFEE TRDG CO LLC ◊
874 Walker Rd Ste C (19904-2778)
PHONE..................786 538-9547
EMP: 6 EST: 2022
SALES (est): 265.18K **Privately Held**
SIC: **5149** Coffee, green or roasted

(G-3265)
PANTHEON TECHNOLOGIES LLC
8 The Grn Ste 10236 (19901-3618)
PHONE..................855 927-9387
EMP: 5 EST: 2011
SALES (est): 46.16K **Privately Held**
SIC: **7371** Computer software development

(G-3266)
PANTHERA SENIOR LIVING LLC
8 The Grn Ste A (19901-3618)
PHONE..................786 540-0040
Snorre Eliassen, CEO
EMP: 6 EST: 2021
SALES (est): 76.37K **Privately Held**
SIC: **6733** Personal investment trust management

(G-3267)
PAPEN FARMS INC
847 Papen Ln (19904-5733)
PHONE..................302 697-3291
Jeffrey Papen, Pr
Richard G Papen, VP
Janet Meyer, Sec
EMP: 16 EST: 1926
SALES (est): 971.61K **Privately Held**
SIC: **0161** Cabbage farm

(G-3268)
PAPERBASKET LLC
8 The Grn Ste A (19901-3618)
PHONE..................516 360-3500
Dulcina Belcher, CEO
Tammy Farrell, Prin
EMP: 2
SALES (est): 56.54K **Privately Held**
Web: www.paperbasket.com
SIC: **7372** Educational computer software

(G-3269)
PAR 3 INC
924 Artis Dr (19904-5639)
PHONE..................302 674-8275
Rick Jones, Pr
EMP: 8 EST: 2005
SALES (est): 145.41K **Privately Held**
Web: www.doverpar3golf.com

SIC: **7992** Public golf courses

(G-3270)
PARAMOUNT INSTALLATIONS
28 Tudor Ct (19901-6129)
PHONE..................302 607-4243
William Jennings, Prin
EMP: 5 EST: 2014
SALES (est): 67.1K **Privately Held**
SIC: **1799** Special trade contractors, nec

(G-3271)
PARCELS INC
Also Called: Delaware Document Retrieval
1111 B S Govenanvce Ave (19904)
PHONE..................302 736-1777
Shelly Miles, Brnch Mgr
EMP: 7
SALES (corp-wide): 12.95MM **Privately Held**
Web: www.parcelsinc.com
SIC: **4215** Package delivery, vehicular
PA: Parcels, Inc.
230 N Market St
Wilmington DE 19801
302 888-1718

(G-3272)
PARCLY LLC
8 The Grn (19901-3618)
PHONE..................347 305-6820
Ceil Mcinerney, Mgr
EMP: 4
SALES (est): 92.16K **Privately Held**
SIC: **7389** 7372 Business Activities at Non-Commercial Site; Application computer software

(G-3273)
PARKOBILITY LLC
8 The Grn (19901-3618)
PHONE..................877 298-5550
EMP: 20
SALES (est): 566.73K **Privately Held**
SIC: **7521** 7389 Parking lots; Business services, nec

(G-3274)
PARKOWSKI GUERKE & SWAYZE PA (PA)
Also Called: Dunkle, Mark F
116 W Water St (19904-6739)
P.O. Box 598 (19903-0598)
PHONE..................302 678-3262
F Michael Parkowski, Pr
EMP: 19 EST: 1975
SALES (est): 2.81MM
SALES (corp-wide): 2.81MM **Privately Held**
Web: www.pgslegal.com
SIC: **8111** General practice law office

(G-3275)
PARKS ASSOCIATES
740 Bicentennial Blvd (19904-7604)
PHONE..................302 674-3267
EMP: 7 EST: 2018
SALES (est): 49.79K **Privately Held**
Web: www.parksassociates.com
SIC: **8732** Market analysis or research

(G-3276)
PARTS PLUS MORE LLC
8 The Grn Ste 4469 (19901-3618)
PHONE..................302 480-1495
EMP: 30 EST: 2018
SALES (est): 2.46MM **Privately Held**
SIC: **5015** Automotive supplies, used: wholesale and retail

(G-3277)
PASADENA DIGITAL INC (PA) ◊
850 New Burton Rd Ste 201 (19904-5786)
PHONE..................310 774-6740
Clotilde Fournier, COO
EMP: 4 EST: 2023
SALES (est): 212.9K
SALES (corp-wide): 212.9K **Privately Held**
SIC: **3812** Aircraft/aerospace flight instruments and guidance systems

(G-3278)
PATEL SANDIP
1760 N Dupont Hwy (19901-2219)
PHONE..................302 363-9761
Sandip Patel, Brnch Mgr
EMP: 5 EST: 2016
SALES (est): 531.21K **Privately Held**
SIC: **6799** Investors, nec

(G-3279)
PATPET LLC
8 The Grn Ste A (19901-3618)
PHONE..................855 888-9922
EMP: 5 EST: 2021
SALES (est): 61.22K **Privately Held**
Web: www.patpet.com
SIC: **5099** Durable goods, nec

(G-3280)
PATRICEA AND CO LLC
820 Carvel Dr Apt E4 (19901-6661)
PHONE..................929 374-9761
EMP: 3 EST: 2021
SALES (est): 30K **Privately Held**
SIC: **3111** Accessory products, leather

(G-3281)
PATRICIA CHAVARRY DR
492 Stone Ridge Dr (19901-8211)
PHONE..................302 747-7895
Patricia Chavar, Prin
EMP: 9 EST: 2008
SALES (est): 216.43K **Privately Held**
SIC: **8011** Physicians' office, including specialists

(G-3282)
PATRIOT AUTO & TRUCK CARE LLC
Also Called: General Automotive Repair
497 S Dupont Hwy (19901-4513)
PHONE..................302 257-5715
EMP: 5 EST: 2011
SALES (est): 452.06K **Privately Held**
Web: www.patriotautoandtruckcare.com
SIC: **7538** General automotive repair shops

(G-3283)
PATTERSON 3 INV GROUP LLC ◊
8 The Grn (19901-3618)
P.O. Box 1041 (19903-1041)
PHONE..................302 469-4783
Dwayne Patterson, CEO
Dwayne L Patterson, CEO
EMP: 8 EST: 2022
SALES (est): 375.88K **Privately Held**
SIC: **8741** 8748 Management services; Business consulting, nec

(G-3284)
PATTERSON-SCHWARTZ & ASSOC INC
Also Called: Patterson Schwartz Real Estate
140 Greentree Dr (19904-7648)
PHONE..................302 672-9400
EMP: 65
SQ FT: 3,543
SALES (corp-wide): 24.38MM **Privately Held**
Web: www.pattersonschwartz.com

GEOGRAPHIC SECTION

Dover - Kent County (G-3314)

SIC: 6531 Real estate agent, residential
PA: Patterson-Schwartz And Associates, Inc.
7234 Lancaster Pike
Hockessin DE 19707
302 234-5250

(G-3285)
PAUL J GITLIN MD
103 Mont Blanc Blvd (19904-7615)
PHONE..................................302 678-3020
Paul Gitlin, *Prin*
EMP: 10 **EST**: 2013
SALES (est): 107.56K **Privately Held**
SIC: 8011 Internal medicine, physician/surgeon

(G-3286)
PAYSHIGA TECHNOLOGIES INC
8 The Grn (19901-3618)
PHONE..................................214 447-0677
Oseni Oluwatobi, *CEO*
EMP: 20
SALES (est): 588.11K **Privately Held**
SIC: 7371 Computer software development and applications

(G-3287)
PBL & 5JS HOLDINGS INC
8 The Grn Ste A (19901-3618)
PHONE..................................404 832-5038
Patrick L Allen Senior, *CEO*
EMP: 8 **EST**: 2018
SALES (est): 463.84K **Privately Held**
SIC: 6799 Real estate investors, except property operators

(G-3288)
PEAK EQUIPMENT REPAIR
2061 Bayside Dr (19901-7191)
PHONE..................................302 526-4729
EMP: 5 **EST**: 2017
SALES (est): 247.29K **Privately Held**
SIC: 7699 Repair services, nec

(G-3289)
PEG GILSON MEMBERSHIP CHAIR
224 Winterberry Dr (19904-4886)
PHONE..................................302 734-5190
Peg Gilson, *Prin*
EMP: 5 **EST**: 2011
SALES (est): 108.57K **Privately Held**
SIC: 4911 Electric services

(G-3290)
PENDULUM IT LLC
19 Holly Cove Ln (19901-6285)
PHONE..................................302 480-9343
EMP: 5 **EST**: 2021
SALES (est): 241.32K **Privately Held**
SIC: 7379 7374 Computer related consulting services; Data processing and preparation

(G-3291)
PENGLAI BIOVENTURES LLC (PA)
8 The Grn Ste 16376 (19901-3618)
PHONE..................................302 219-3259
Michael Bell, *Managing Member*
EMP: 6
SALES (est): 87.5K
SALES (corp-wide): 87.5K **Privately Held**
SIC: 5047 Medical laboratory equipment

(G-3292)
PENINSULA ALLERGY AND ASTHMA
200 Banning St Ste 280 (19904-3489)
PHONE..................................302 734-4344
Shankar L Lakhani, *Prin*
EMP: 14 **EST**: 2008
SALES (est): 972.93K **Privately Held**
Web: www.faacconline.com
SIC: 8011 Allergist

(G-3293)
PENINSULA ENERGY SVCS CO INC (HQ)
Also Called: Pesco Energy
909 Silver Lake Blvd (19904-2409)
P.O. Box 615 (19903-0615)
PHONE..................................302 734-6799
Stephen C Thompson, *Pr*
Paul Barbas, *VP*
William C Boyles, *Sec*
Beth W Cooper, *Treas*
Ralph J Askins, *Dir*
EMP: 9 **EST**: 2004
SALES (est): 5.35MM
SALES (corp-wide): 680.7MM **Publicly Held**
SIC: 4932 Gas and other services combined
PA: Chesapeake Utilities Corporation
500 Energy Ln
Dover DE 19901
302 734-6799

(G-3294)
PENNSYLVANIA BRAND CO
550 S New St (19904-3536)
PHONE..................................302 674-5774
EMP: 6 **EST**: 2011
SALES (est): 104.14K **Privately Held**
SIC: 2051 Bread, cake, and related products

(G-3295)
PEOPLES PLACE II INC
165 Commerce Way (19904-8224)
PHONE..................................302 730-1321
Linda Burris, *Mgr*
EMP: 78
SALES (corp-wide): 8.66MM **Privately Held**
Web: www.peoplesplace2.com
SIC: 8351 Child day care services
PA: People's Place Ii, Inc.
1129 Airport Rd
Milford DE 19963
302 422-8033

(G-3296)
PERCEBE MUSIC INC
8 The Grn Ste A (19901-3618)
PHONE..................................850 341-9594
Pitagoras Goncalves, *Pr*
Joel Becker, *Prin*
EMP: 6 **EST**: 2016
SALES (est): 58.59K **Privately Held**
Web: www.percebemusic.com
SIC: 2741 7372 7389 Music book and sheet music publishing; Educational computer software; Business services, nec

(G-3297)
PERCERI LLC
160 Greentree Dr Ste 101 (19904-7620)
PHONE..................................217 721-8731
David Tarvin, *Mgr*
Aaron Wiener, *Mgr*
Sean Mccrimmon, *Mgr*
EMP: 8 **EST**: 2012
SALES (est): 120K **Privately Held**
Web: www.perceri.com
SIC: 7372 7389 Business oriented computer software; Business services, nec

(G-3298)
PERFORMANCE ENHANCEMENT PROFES
1255 S State St Ste 7 (19901-6932)
PHONE..................................302 423-0236
Glenn Brown, *Ofcr*
EMP: 6 **EST**: 2017
SALES (est): 24.4K **Privately Held**
SIC: 8049 Physical therapist

(G-3299)
PERISPHERE INC (PA) ✪
8 The Grn (19901-3618)
PHONE..................................908 581-8058
Evan William Robinson, *Pr*
EMP: 4 **EST**: 2022
SALES (est): 171.34K
SALES (corp-wide): 171.34K **Privately Held**
SIC: 7372 7389 Application computer software; Business services, nec

(G-3300)
PERIVISION USA INC ✪
8 The Grn # 17008 (19901-3618)
PHONE..................................302 665-0866
Patrick Kessel, *Prin*
EMP: 10 **EST**: 2023
SALES (est): 406.01K **Privately Held**
SIC: 3841 Surgical and medical instruments

(G-3301)
PERRY ENTERPRISE LLC ✪
8 The Grn (19901-3618)
PHONE..................................302 505-4458
Tabari Perry, *CEO*
EMP: 5 **EST**: 2022
SALES (est): 275.66K **Privately Held**
SIC: 4212 2542 Delivery service, vehicular; Carrier cases and tables, mail: except wood

(G-3302)
PERSANTE SLEEP CENTER
103 Wolf Creek Blvd Ste 2 (19901-4967)
PHONE..................................302 724-5128
EMP: 14 **EST**: 2014
SALES (est): 70.5K **Privately Held**
Web: www.persante.com
SIC: 8011 Offices and clinics of medical doctors

(G-3303)
PERSHA LLC
950 Bedford Dr (19904-3406)
PHONE..................................786 925-2952
Jameson Germain, *Managing Member*
EMP: 5
SALES (est): 136.96K **Privately Held**
SIC: 4215 7389 Package delivery, vehicular; Business services, nec

(G-3304)
PET SHOP LLC
8 The Grn Ste A (19901-3618)
PHONE..................................646 345-8844
EMP: 2 **EST**: 2019
SALES (est): 62.54K **Privately Held**
SIC: 3999 Pet supplies

(G-3305)
PETES PLUMBING LLC
106 Elm Ter (19901-3606)
PHONE..................................302 270-4990
Michael Olson, *Prin*
EMP: 6 **EST**: 2011
SALES (est): 141.16K **Privately Held**
SIC: 1711 Plumbing contractors

(G-3306)
PETMEX COMPANY LLC ✪
8 The Grn (19901-3618)
PHONE..................................800 829-4943
EMP: 6 **EST**: 2023
SALES (est): 78.16K **Privately Held**
SIC: 2047 Dog and cat food

(G-3307)
PETROLEUM EQUIPMENT INC (PA)
Also Called: Poores Propane Gas Service
3799 N Dupont Hwy (19901-1574)
P.O. Box 1000 (19936-1000)
PHONE..................................302 734-7433
Donald Steiner, *Pr*
Micheal Steiner, *VP*
▲ **EMP**: 20 **EST**: 1988
SQ FT: 4,000
SALES (est): 51.22MM **Privately Held**
Web: www.poorespropane.com
SIC: 5172 5984 Petroleum products, nec; Liquefied petroleum gas dealers

(G-3308)
PETROLEUM EQUIPMENT INC
Also Called: Poore's Propane Gas Service
3799 N Dupont Hwy (19901-1574)
P.O. Box 658 (19903-0658)
PHONE..................................302 422-4281
EMP: 15
Web: www.poorespropane.com
SIC: 5172 Petroleum products, nec
PA: Petroleum Equipment, Inc.
3799 N Dupont Hwy
Dover DE 19901

(G-3309)
PETROVICH MASONRY
214 Carter Rd (19901-5521)
PHONE..................................302 697-2379
Adam Petrovich, *Prin*
EMP: 5 **EST**: 2015
SALES (est): 78.65K **Privately Held**
SIC: 1741 Masonry and other stonework

(G-3310)
PFS LTD
8 The Grn (19901-3618)
PHONE..................................202 709-9755
Wajdi Saoud, *CEO*
EMP: 6
SALES (est): 68.89K **Privately Held**
SIC: 7371 Computer software development

(G-3311)
PHARMD LIVE CORPORATION
8 The Grn Ste 10486 (19901-3618)
PHONE..................................908 803-3311
Cynthia Chioma Nwaubani, *CEO*
EMP: 66 **EST**: 2019
SALES (est): 610.28K **Privately Held**
SIC: 8099 Health and allied services, nec

(G-3312)
PHIL HILL
Also Called: State Farm Insurance
3728 N Dupont Hwy (19901-1555)
PHONE..................................302 678-0499
EMP: 5 **EST**: 1985
SALES (est): 388.54K **Privately Held**
Web: www.philhillagency.com
SIC: 6411 Insurance agents and brokers

(G-3313)
PHILANTHROVEST LLC (PA) ✪
8 The Grn Ste A (19901-3618)
PHONE..................................201 563-9179
EMP: 10 **EST**: 2022
SALES (est): 724.98K
SALES (corp-wide): 724.98K **Privately Held**
SIC: 6799 Investors, nec

(G-3314)
PHOENIX GLOBAL SHOP LLC
8 The Grn (19901-3618)
PHONE..................................347 227-2519
EMP: 10 **EST**: 2021

Dover - Kent County (G-3315)

SALES (est): 1000K **Privately Held**
Web: www.phoenixglobalcommerce.com
SIC: 8742 Retail trade consultant

(G-3315)
PHOENIX INTELLIGENCE INC
8 The Grn Ste 5638 (19901-3618)
PHONE.................................844 663-4799
EMP: 6 EST: 2019
SALES (est): 80.98K **Privately Held**
Web: www.phoenix-intelligence.com
SIC: 8099 Health and allied services, nec

(G-3316)
PHRST
802 Silver Lake Blvd Ste 200 (19904-2488)
PHONE.................................302 739-2260
EMP: 5 EST: 2019
SALES (est): 99.75K **Privately Held**
Web: employeeselfservice.omb.delaware.gov
SIC: 7361 Employment agencies

(G-3317)
PHYSICAL THERAPY SERVICES INC
(PA)
725 Walker Rd (19904-2724)
PHONE.................................302 678-3100
Gary T Nowell, *Owner*
Vincent Deleo, *
Phillip N Barkins, *
Jean T Deleo, *
Gary Nowle, *
EMP: 26 EST: 1984
SQ FT: 4,800
SALES (est): 912.68K
SALES (corp-wide): 912.68K **Privately Held**
Web: www.ptstn.net
SIC: 8049 Physiotherapist

(G-3318)
PHYSICIANS BEAUTY GROUP LLC
9 E Loockerman St Ste 202 (19901-7347)
PHONE.................................866 270-9290
Gregory Socherman, *Pr*
EMP: 30 EST: 2016
SALES (est): 4.76MM **Privately Held**
SIC: 5122 Cosmetics, perfumes, and hair products

(G-3319)
PHYSIOTHERAPY ASSOCIATES INC
Also Called: Barker-Mtrix Thrapy Rhbltation
642 S Queen St Ste 101 (19904)
PHONE.................................302 674-1269
David Wylderman, *Mgr*
EMP: 10
Web: www.selectphysicaltherapy.com
SIC: 8049 Physical therapist
HQ: Physiotherapy Associates, Inc.
   680 American Ave Ste 200
   King Of Prussia PA 19406
   610 644-7824

(G-3320)
PICK WINNERS INC ◯
8 The Grn Ste A (19901-3618)
PHONE.................................516 206-0777
Ramon Rivera, *CEO*
EMP: 10 EST: 2023
SALES (est): 348.32K **Privately Held**
SIC: 7371 Custom computer programming services

(G-3321)
PIERCE FENCE COMPANY INC
5751 N Dupont Hwy (19901-2603)
PHONE.................................302 674-1996
Robert Pierce, *Pr*

EMP: 13 EST: 1971
SQ FT: 5,000
SALES (est): 1.91MM **Privately Held**
Web: www.piercefence.com
SIC: 1799 Fence construction

(G-3322)
PII GROUP INC ◯
8 The Grn Ste A (19901-3618)
P.O. Box 678 (10031-0678)
PHONE.................................917 455-7438
Elizabeth Barrow, *Pr*
Elizabeth Barrow, *Managing Member*
EMP: 5 EST: 2022
SALES (est): 276.55K **Privately Held**
SIC: 6514 Residential building, four or fewer units: operation

(G-3323)
PIKCHABOX LLC
8 The Grn Ste B (19901-3618)
PHONE.................................302 207-1770
EMP: 10 EST: 2020
SALES (est): 467.31K **Privately Held**
Web: www.pikchabox.com
SIC: 8742 Marketing consulting services

(G-3324)
PINEAL CONSULTING GROUP LLC
8 The Grn Unit 6431 (19901-3618)
PHONE.................................302 446-3794
EMP: 7 EST: 2019
SALES (est): 547.56K **Privately Held**
Web: www.pinealconsulting.com
SIC: 5015 8748 8742 Automotive supplies, used: wholesale and retail; Business consulting, nec; Management consulting services

(G-3325)
PIONEER PRODUCTS
752 Long Point Rd (19901-1201)
PHONE.................................302 678-0331
EMP: 6 EST: 2014
SALES (est): 141.4K **Privately Held**
Web: www.pioneerproducts.com
SIC: 1771 Concrete work

(G-3326)
PIVOT PHYSICAL THERAPY
1015 S Governors Ave (19904-6901)
PHONE.................................302 730-4800
EMP: 16 EST: 2018
SALES (est): 231.04K **Privately Held**
Web: www.pivotphysicaltherapy.com
SIC: 8049 Physical therapist

(G-3327)
PK FIRE LLC
8 The Grn (19901-3618)
PHONE.................................253 880-9025
Steve Kang, *Managing Member*
EMP: 6
SALES (est): 86.31K **Privately Held**
SIC: 5182 Wine and distilled beverages

(G-3328)
PLATFORMAVR INC
8 The Grn Ste 5915 (19901-3618)
PHONE.................................302 330-8980
Daniel Sobko, *CEO*
EMP: 8 EST: 2018
SALES (est): 332.41K **Privately Held**
SIC: 8742 7389 Management information systems consultant; Business Activities at Non-Commercial Site

(G-3329)
PLATINUM CNSTR RENOVATIONS LLC ◯

8 The Grn Ste 13137 (19901-3618)
PHONE.................................302 288-0670
Andre Green, *Prin*
EMP: 2 EST: 2022
SALES (est): 72.83K **Privately Held**
Web: platinum-construction-and-renovations-llc.ueniweb.com
SIC: 1389 Construction, repair, and dismantling services

(G-3330)
PLATINUM HERITAGE ENTPS LLC
8 The Grn Ste A (19901-3618)
PHONE.................................469 563-0411
EMP: 5 EST: 2019
SALES (est): 464.36K **Privately Held**
SIC: 1522 Residential construction, nec

(G-3331)
PLATINUM WORLD LLC
8 The Grn Ste 7679 (19901-3618)
PHONE.................................302 321-5040
Farraz Patel, *Managing Member*
EMP: 6 EST: 2021
SALES (est): 644.29K **Privately Held**
Web: www.theplatinumworld.com
SIC: 8011 7389 5047 Health maintenance organization; Business Activities at Non-Commercial Site; Medical and hospital equipment

(G-3332)
PLAY US MEDIA LLC
Also Called: Wild Bets
8 The Grn Ste 8136 (19901)
PHONE.................................302 924-5034
Cesar Espitia, *Managing Member*
EMP: 8 EST: 2018
SALES (est): 275.31K **Privately Held**
Web: www.playusmedia.com
SIC: 7371 7372 7373 7379 Computer software development and applications; Application computer software; Systems software development services; Online services technology consultants

(G-3333)
PLAYHOUSE NURSERY SCHOOL
1925 S Dupont Hwy (19901-5152)
PHONE.................................302 747-7007
Colleen Endicott, *Dir*
EMP: 9 EST: 1981
SALES (est): 152.28K **Privately Held**
SIC: 8351 Nursery school

(G-3334)
PLAYPHONE INC
3500 S Dupont Hwy (19901-6041)
PHONE.................................415 307-0246
Ron Czerny, *CEO*
EMP: 5 EST: 2006
SALES (est): 517.68K **Privately Held**
SIC: 7371 Computer software development and applications
PA: Gungho Online Entertainment, Inc.
   1-11-1, Marunouchi
   Chiyoda-Ku TKY 100-0

(G-3335)
PLAYPOWER LABS INC
8 The Grn Ste 12465 (19901-3618)
PHONE.................................917 544-4171
James Lomas, *CEO*
EMP: 10 EST: 2012
SALES (est): 372.14K **Privately Held**
SIC: 7389 Design services

(G-3336)
PLAYTEX MANUFACTURING INC
(DH)
50 N Dupont Hwy (19901-4292)
PHONE.................................302 678-6000
Michael R Gallagher, *CEO*
EMP: 52 EST: 1995
SALES (est): 94.39MM
SALES (corp-wide): 2.25B **Publicly Held**
SIC: 2676 2844 2842 Sanitary paper products; Perfumes, cosmetics and other toilet preparations; Polishes and sanitation goods
HQ: Playtex Products, Llc
   6 Research Dr Ste 400
   Shelton CT 06484
   203 944-5500

(G-3337)
PLAYTEX MARKETING CORP
800 Silver Lake Blvd Ste 103 (19904-2402)
P.O. Box 7016 (19903-1516)
PHONE.................................302 678-6000
Michael Gallagher, *Ch*
Donald J Franceschini, *VP*
Calvin J Gauss, *VP*
Hercules P Sotos, *VP*
Glenn A Forbes, *Treas*
◆ EMP: 7 EST: 1988
SIC: 6719 Personal holding companies, except banks

(G-3338)
PLUGDIN INC
8 The Grn Ste A (19901-3618)
PHONE.................................347 726-1831
David J Montini, *CEO*
EMP: 5 EST: 2017
SALES (est): 50K **Privately Held**
SIC: 7336 Creative services to advertisers, except writers

(G-3339)
PLX PHARMA WINDDOWN CORP
(PA)
8 The Grn Ste 11895 (19901-3618)
PHONE.................................973 381-7408
Lawrence Perkins, *Restruct*
Natasha Giordano, *Pr*
Michael J Valentino, *Ex Ch Bd*
Rita O'connor, *CFO*
Efthymios Deliargyris, *CMO*
EMP: 8 EST: 2002
SQ FT: 4,695
SALES (est): 8.21MM
SALES (corp-wide): 8.21MM **Publicly Held**
Web: www.plxpharma.com
SIC: 2834 Pharmaceutical preparations

(G-3340)
PLYMA ENTERTAINMENT LLC
8 The Grn Ste R (19901-3618)
PHONE.................................302 248-4567
EMP: 10 EST: 2020
SALES (est): 100K **Privately Held**
SIC: 7929 Entertainers and entertainment groups

(G-3341)
PNC BANK NATIONAL ASSOCIATION
Also Called: PNC
87 Greentree Dr (19904-7647)
PHONE.................................302 735-2160
Aaron Bowers, *Mgr*
EMP: 10
SALES (corp-wide): 23.54B **Publicly Held**
Web: www.pncbank.com

GEOGRAPHIC SECTION

Dover - Kent County (G-3369)

SIC: 6021 National trust companies with deposits, commercial
HQ: Pnc Bank, National Association
300 5th Ave
Pittsburgh PA 15222
877 762-2000

(G-3342)
PNC BANK NATIONAL ASSOCIATION
Also Called: PNC
3 Loockerman Plz Frnt (19901-7335)
PHONE.................302 735-3117
June Allin, *Brnch Mgr*
EMP: 6
SALES (corp-wide): 23.54B **Publicly Held**
Web: www.pncbank.com
SIC: 6021 National commercial banks
HQ: Pnc Bank, National Association
300 5th Ave
Pittsburgh PA 15222
877 762-2000

(G-3343)
PNEUMA WELLNESS & SPA LLC
149 S Governors Ave (19904-3205)
PHONE.................302 990-8907
EMP: 5 EST: 2017
SALES (est): 89.3K **Privately Held**
Web: www.pneumawellnessspa.com
SIC: 8099 Health and allied services, nec

(G-3344)
POBBLES CORPORATION ✪
8 The Grn (19901-3618)
PHONE.................510 371-1627
Sida Lu, *CEO*
EMP: 2 EST: 2023
SALES (est): 87.4K **Privately Held**
SIC: 7372 Prepackaged software

(G-3345)
POC INC
8 The Grn Ste 15060 (19901-3618)
PHONE.................415 853-4762
EMP: 10 EST: 2020
SALES (est): 598.92K **Privately Held**
Web: poc.llc
SIC: 7371 7379 8711 8732 Custom computer programming services; Computer related consulting services; Engineering services; Commercial nonphysical research

(G-3346)
POLARO INC
8 The Grn Ste E (19901-3618)
PHONE.................415 240-0442
Alexander Ledovskiy, *CEO*
EMP: 10
SALES (est): 348.32K **Privately Held**
SIC: 7371 Computer software development and applications

(G-3347)
POLE BUILDINGS UNLIMITED
117 W Reed St (19904-7321)
PHONE.................302 399-3058
Gary Sensenig, *Owner*
EMP: 6 EST: 2017
SALES (est): 183.03K **Privately Held**
Web: pole-buildings-unlimited-inc.business.site
SIC: 1799 Special trade contractors, nec

(G-3348)
POLICE OFFCER MSES WLKER JR IN
131 Nob Hill Rd (19901-8849)
PHONE.................215 268-4146
EMP: 5 EST: 2017

SALES (est): 50.16K **Privately Held**
SIC: 8322 Individual and family services

(G-3349)
POLIQUIN FIRM LLC
1475 S Governors Ave (19904-7017)
PHONE.................302 702-5501
Maria C Tedeman-poliquin Esq, *Prin*
EMP: 6 EST: 2018
SALES (est): 375.7K **Privately Held**
Web: www.doverlawoffice.com
SIC: 8111 General practice law office

(G-3350)
PONY UP INC
8 The Grn (19901-3618)
PHONE.................323 205-7669
Zachary Elardo, *Pr*
EMP: 2
SALES (est): 87.4K **Privately Held**
SIC: 7372 7389 Application computer software; Business Activities at Non-Commercial Site

(G-3351)
POPULUS LLC ✪
8 The Grn Ste R (19901-3618)
PHONE.................412 973-2340
EMP: 7 EST: 2022
SALES (est): 103.03K **Privately Held**
SIC: 7361 Employment agencies

(G-3352)
PORTABLE SHEDS PAUL YODER
1288 Rose Valley School Rd (19904-5514)
PHONE.................302 734-2681
Harvey Yoder, *Prin*
EMP: 5 EST: 2011
SALES (est): 148.49K **Privately Held**
SIC: 1522 Residential construction, nec

(G-3353)
PORTER BROADCASTING
1991 S State St (19901-5811)
PHONE.................302 535-8809
EMP: 5 EST: 2014
SALES (est): 101.27K **Privately Held**
SIC: 4832 Radio broadcasting stations

(G-3354)
POSHLIFE ACQUISITIONS LLC ✪
8 The Grn Ste 4000 (19901-3618)
PHONE.................516 376-7402
EMP: 5 EST: 2022
SALES (est): 204.28K **Privately Held**
SIC: 7389 Business services, nec

(G-3355)
POST ACUTE MEDICAL LLC
1240 Mckee Rd (19904-1381)
PHONE.................717 731-9660
EMP: 69
Web: www.pamhealth.com
SIC: 8051 Skilled nursing care facilities
PA: Post Acute Medical, Llc
1828 Good Hope Rd Ste 102
Enola PA 17025

(G-3356)
POWER PLUS ELEC CONTG INC
10 Janis Dr (19901-5752)
PHONE.................302 736-5070
EMP: 13 EST: 1995
SALES (est): 575.49K **Privately Held**
SIC: 1731 General electrical contractor

(G-3357)
PPG ARCHITECTURAL FINISHES INC
Also Called: Glidden Professional Paint Ctr
177 179 N Dupont Hwy (19901)

PHONE.................302 736-6081
Carrie Jellus, *Brnch Mgr*
EMP: 6
SALES (corp-wide): 17.65B **Publicly Held**
Web: www.silvercanyonrc.com
SIC: 2851 Paints and allied products
HQ: Ppg Architectural Finishes, Inc.
1 Ppg Pl
Pittsburgh PA 15272
412 434-3131

(G-3358)
PRECIOUS MMNTS EDCATN CMNTY CT
4607 S Dupont Hwy (19901-6413)
PHONE.................302 697-9374
Angela C Wilson, *Pr*
EMP: 10 EST: 2002
SQ FT: 3,171
SALES (est): 231.69K **Privately Held**
SIC: 8322 Community center

(G-3359)
PREMIER CAPITAL HOLDING (PA)
1675 S State St (19901-5140)
PHONE.................302 730-1010
Hanh Nguyen, *Prin*
EMP: 6 EST: 2006
SALES (est): 400.79K **Privately Held**
Web: www.nacaloans.com
SIC: 6162 Mortgage bankers

(G-3360)
PREMIER ENTERTAINMENT III LLC (HQ)
Also Called: Dover Downs Gaming & Entrmt
1131 N Dupont Hwy (19901-2008)
PHONE.................302 674-4600
George Papanier, *Pr*
John E Taylor Junior, *Ofcr*
Stephen Capp, *
Craig Eaton, *
EMP: 931 EST: 1969
SALES (est): 122.76MM **Publicly Held**
Web: casinos.ballys.com
SIC: 7929 7999 7011 7948 Entertainment service; Card and game services; Hotels; Racing, including track operation
PA: Bally's Corporation
100 Westminster St
Providence RI 02903

(G-3361)
PREMIER MRTIAL ARTS NSHVLLE LL
321 Independence Blvd Ste B (19904-7626)
PHONE.................302 674-1985
Roxanne Nichols, *Prin*
EMP: 8
SALES (corp-wide): 6.77MM **Privately Held**
Web: www.premiermartialarts.com
SIC: 7999 Martial arts school, nec
PA: Premier Martial Arts Nashville Llc
2350 Airport Fwy
Bedford TX 76022
865 312-9971

(G-3362)
PREMIER PHYSICAL THERAPY
97 Commerce Way Ste 101 (19904-7794)
PHONE.................302 724-6344
EMP: 7 EST: 2019
SALES (est): 183.96K **Privately Held**
Web: www.premierptsp.com
SIC: 8049 Physical therapist

(G-3363)
PREMIER SPINE & REHAB
111 S West St (19904-3219)
PHONE.................302 730-4878
Roberto Thelusma, *Pr*
EMP: 9 EST: 2016
SALES (est): 186.39K **Privately Held**
SIC: 8093 Rehabilitation center, outpatient treatment

(G-3364)
PREMIUM BRANDS INC
8 The Grn Ste R (19901-3618)
PHONE.................925 566-8863
Elena Florova, *Pr*
EMP: 6 EST: 2014
SALES (est): 579.09K **Privately Held**
SIC: 5141 5812 Food brokers; Contract food services

(G-3365)
PRESBYTERIAN HOMES INC
Also Called: Westminster Village Health Ctr
1175 Mckee Rd (19904-2268)
PHONE.................302 744-3600
Rob Kratz, *Dir*
EMP: 300
Web: www.presbyterianseniorliving.org
SIC: 8059 8069 8051 Nursing home, except skilled and intermediate care facility; Specialty hospitals, except psychiatric; Skilled nursing care facilities
HQ: Presbyterian Homes, Inc.
1 Trinity Dr E Ste 201
Dillsburg PA 17019
717 502-8840

(G-3366)
PRESIDIUM USA INC
874 Walker Rd Ste C (19904-2778)
PHONE.................203 803-2980
Jeffery Ritz, *CEO*
EMP: 6 EST: 2016
SALES (est): 898.83K **Privately Held**
SIC: 2821 Plastics materials and resins

(G-3367)
PRESSLEY RIDGE FOUNDATION
Also Called: Treatment Foster Care - Newark
942 Walker Rd Ste A (19904-2757)
PHONE.................302 366-0490
Chatanya Lankford, *Mgr*
EMP: 6
Web: www.pressleyridge.org
SIC: 8211 8361 School for physically handicapped, nec; Group foster home
PA: Pressley Ridge Foundation
5500 Corporate Dr Ste 400
Pittsburgh PA 15237

(G-3368)
PRESSLEY RIDGE FOUNDATION
Also Called: Pressley Ridge of Delaware
942 Walker Rd Ste A (19904-2757)
PHONE.................302 677-1590
Cha-tanya Lankford, *Dir*
EMP: 6
Web: www.pressleyridge.org
SIC: 8322 Child related social services
PA: Pressley Ridge Foundation
5500 Corporate Dr Ste 400
Pittsburgh PA 15237

(G-3369)
PRESTIGE BUILDING CO
992 Whatcoat Dr (19904-2750)
PHONE.................302 744-8282
EMP: 7 EST: 2016
SALES (est): 68.04K **Privately Held**
Web: www.prestigebuildingco.com

Dover - Kent County (G-3370)   **GEOGRAPHIC SECTION**

SIC: 1799 Special trade contractors, nec

(G-3370)
PRESTIGE LABS INC
8 The Grn Ste 7491 (19901-3618)
PHONE..................917 698-3453
EMP: 5
SALES (est): 68.89K **Privately Held**
SIC: 7371 Computer software development and applications

(G-3371)
PRIMARY CARE DELAWARE L L C
200 Banning St Ste 210 (19904-3487)
PHONE..................302 744-9645
EMP: 6 EST: 2002
SALES (est): 581.93K **Privately Held**
Web: www.edenhillmedicalcenter.com
SIC: 8049 Offices of health practitioner

(G-3372)
PRIME INSIGHTS GROUP LLC ✪
8 The Grn Ste R (19901-3618)
PHONE..................407 289-1577
Benjamin Ritzka, *CEO*
EMP: 15 EST: 2022
SALES (est): 515.3K **Privately Held**
SIC: 8742 Marketing consulting services

(G-3373)
PRINTIT SOLUTIONS LLC
1155 E Lebanon Rd (19901-5830)
PHONE..................302 380-3838
EMP: 3 EST: 2017
SALES (est): 54.68K **Privately Held**
SIC: 2752 Offset printing

(G-3374)
PRIVADO INC (PA)
8 The Grn Ste A (19901-3618)
PHONE..................916 730-4522
EMP: 6 EST: 2020
SALES (est): 316.71K
SALES (corp-wide): 316.71K **Privately Held**
Web: www.privado.ai
SIC: 8742 Management consulting services

(G-3375)
PRIVATE MASSAGE BODYWORK
450 S Dupont Hwy (19901-4502)
PHONE..................302 387-7199
Bin Lin, *Prin*
EMP: 6 EST: 2019
SALES (est): 24.86K **Privately Held**
SIC: 8049 Massage Therapist

(G-3376)
PROCTER & GAMBLE PAPER PDTS CO
Also Called: Procter & Gamble
1340 W North St (19904-7796)
P.O. Box 7010 (19903-1510)
PHONE..................302 678-2600
Laytrice Henson, *Mgr*
EMP: 2699
SALES (corp-wide): 82.01B **Publicly Held**
Web: us.pg.com
SIC: 2676 Towels, paper: made from purchased paper
HQ: The Procter & Gamble Paper Products Company
1 Procter And Gamble Plz
Cincinnati OH 45202
513 983-1100

(G-3377)
PROGRESSIVE CASUALTY INSUR CO
Also Called: Progressive Insurance
1241 N Dupont Hwy (19901-8703)
PHONE..................302 734-7360
Mark Bushy, *Brnch Mgr*
EMP: 7
SALES (corp-wide): 49.61B **Publicly Held**
Web: www.progressive.com
SIC: 6331 6411 Fire, marine, and casualty insurance; Insurance agents and brokers
HQ: Progressive Casualty Insurance Company
6300 Wilson Mills Rd
Mayfield Village OH 44143
855 347-3939

(G-3378)
PROGRESSIVE RADIOLOGY
1306 S Dupont Hwy (19901-4404)
PHONE..................302 730-9300
Doug Pollock, *Mgr*
EMP: 16 EST: 2013
SALES (est): 140.6K **Privately Held**
SIC: 8011 Radiologist

(G-3379)
PROLIFIC CONSULTANTS LLC (PA) ✪
8 The Grn Ste A (19901-3618)
PHONE..................302 219-0958
Isiah Taylor, *Managing Member*
EMP: 6 EST: 2023
SALES (est): 71.79K
SALES (corp-wide): 71.79K **Privately Held**
SIC: 8742 Management consulting services

(G-3380)
PROLIFIC PROFESSIONALS LLC (PA) ✪
Also Called: Plentyy Cleaning
8 The Grn Ste 15082 (19901-3618)
PHONE..................302 497-4136
Isiah Taylor, *Managing Member*
EMP: 6 EST: 2023
SALES (est): 70.36K
SALES (corp-wide): 70.36K **Privately Held**
SIC: 7349 Building cleaning service

(G-3381)
PROOFED INC
8 The Grn (19901-3618)
PHONE..................888 851-8179
Adam Harvey, *CEO*
EMP: 6 EST: 2017
SALES (est): 120.73K **Privately Held**
Web: www.proofed.com
SIC: 2741 Miscellaneous publishing

(G-3382)
PROSPECT DE
1524 E Lebanon Rd (19901-5834)
PHONE..................302 382-6579
Kristy Mast, *Prin*
EMP: 5 EST: 2016
SALES (est): 105.82K **Privately Held**
Web: www.prospectwallet.com
SIC: 7389 Building inspection service

(G-3383)
PROSPECT INSPECTION SERVICES
1524 E Lebanon Rd (19901-5834)
PHONE..................302 381-0110
EMP: 11 EST: 2013
SALES (est): 447.03K **Privately Held**
Web: www.pro-spectde.com
SIC: 7389 Building inspection service

(G-3384)
PROTECH LABS INC
8 The Grn (19901-3618)
PHONE..................201 328-7856
Jiabing Xu, *CEO*
EMP: 8 EST: 2020
SALES (est): 424.57K **Privately Held**
SIC: 8742 Sales (including sales management) consultant

(G-3385)
PROVAXUS INC
8 The Grn Ste B (19901-3618)
PHONE..................773 832-8015
Kevin White, *Pr*
Dan Sheehan, *Sec*
Viktor Stolc, *Dir*
EMP: 5 EST: 2020
SALES (est): 104.73K **Privately Held**
SIC: 7389 Business Activities at Non-Commercial Site

(G-3386)
PROVIDENT FEDERAL CREDIT UNION
401 S New St (19904-6715)
PHONE..................302 734-1133
Francine Wilson, *Mgr*
EMP: 10 EST: 1964
SALES (est): 716.03K **Privately Held**
Web: www.providentfcu.com
SIC: 6061 6163 Federal credit unions; Loan brokers

(G-3387)
PRUDENT TECHNOLOGY & SVCS LLC
8 The Grn Ste 5068 (19901-3618)
PHONE..................302 481-6399
Deborah Isukapati, *Managing Member*
Gupta Govindraj, *Off Mgr*
EMP: 14 EST: 2018
SALES (est): 364.22K **Privately Held**
SIC: 7371 7389 Custom computer programming services; Business services, nec

(G-3388)
PSYCHOTHERAPEUTIC SERVICES
942 Walker Rd Ste B (19904-2757)
PHONE..................302 678-9962
Sherry Debra Jones, *Owner*
EMP: 42
Web: www.psychotherapeuticservices.com
SIC: 8049 Acupuncturist
HQ: Psychotherapeutic Services Inc
870 High St Ste 2
Chestertown MD 21620
410 778-1933

(G-3389)
PSYCHOTHERAPEUTIC SERVICES
630 W Division St Ste D (19904-2760)
PHONE..................302 672-7159
Lamont J, *Pr*
EMP: 42
Web: www.psychotherapeuticservices.com
SIC: 8093 Mental health clinic, outpatient
HQ: Psychotherapeutic Services Inc
870 High St Ste 2
Chestertown MD 21620
410 778-1933

(G-3390)
PSYCHOTHERAPEUTIC SVC ASSN INC
Also Called: Felton Residential Trtmnt Ctr
2015 Peachtree Run Rd (19901-7733)
PHONE..................302 284-8370
Nakita Sy, *Brnch Mgr*
EMP: 5
Web: www.psychotherapeuticservices.com
SIC: 8093 Mental health clinic, outpatient
HQ: Psychotherapeutic Service Association, Inc.
870 High St Ste 2
Chestertown MD 21620

(G-3391)
PTCI MANAGEMENT
442 Voshells Mill Star Hill Rd (19901-7608)
PHONE..................302 538-6996
EMP: 5 EST: 2017
SALES (est): 72.76K **Privately Held**
SIC: 8741 Management services

(G-3392)
PTERIS GLOBAL (USA) INC
615 S Dupont Hwy (19901-4517)
PHONE..................516 593-5633
Vince Tong, *Dir*
EMP: 10 EST: 2013
SALES (est): 3.67MM **Privately Held**
Web: pmb.pasca.isi.ac.id
SIC: 4731 Foreign freight forwarding
HQ: Pteris Global Limited
28 Quality Road
Singapore 61882

(G-3393)
PUBLIC MINT INC
8 The Grn Ste A (19901-3618)
PHONE..................833 386-0182
EMP: 10
SALES (est): 46.16K **Privately Held**
Web: www.publicmint.com
SIC: 7371 Computer software development and applications

(G-3394)
PUGHS SERVICE INC
728 Dover Leipsic Rd (19901-2055)
PHONE..................302 678-2408
Horrace Pugh Junior, *Pr*
EMP: 10 EST: 1946
SQ FT: 500
SALES (est): 486.76K **Privately Held**
Web: www.pughsservice.com
SIC: 7538 7549 7699 5261 Engine repair; Towing services; Lawn mower repair shop; Lawn and garden equipment

(G-3395)
PUMAS-AI INC ✪
3500 S Dupont Hwy Ste Gt-101 (19901-6041)
PHONE..................551 207-6084
Vijay Ivaturi, *CEO*
EMP: 50 EST: 2023
SALES (est): 1.69MM **Privately Held**
SIC: 7371 5122 Computer software systems analysis and design, custom; Pharmaceuticals

(G-3396)
PURE ANATOLIA LLC
8 The Grn Ste A (19901-3618)
PHONE..................571 660-0007
EMP: 3 EST: 2019
SALES (est): 244.68K **Privately Held**
Web: www.pureanatolia.us
SIC: 2099 Food preparations, nec

(G-3397)
PURI VINEET MD
200 Banning St Ste 210 (19904-3487)
PHONE..................302 744-9645
Vineet Puri, *Ofcr*
EMP: 7 EST: 2018
SALES (est): 138.06K **Privately Held**
Web: www.edenhillmedicalcenter.com
SIC: 8011 Offices and clinics of medical doctors

GEOGRAPHIC SECTION
Dover - Kent County (G-3427)

(G-3398)
PURPLE WIFI INC
8 The Grn Ste 1 (19901-3618)
PHONE..................877 286-2631
Pete Lee, *Dir*
EMP: 6 **EST:** 2019
SALES (est): 275.52K **Privately Held**
SIC: 7371 Computer software development and applications

(G-3399)
PURPLENOW INC ○
Also Called: Purplenow
8 The Grn Ste B (19901-3618)
PHONE..................302 751-5226
Ravikanth Varigonda, *Pr*
EMP: 21 **EST:** 2022
SALES (est): 613.44K **Privately Held**
SIC: 7373 7371 Systems engineering, computer related; Computer software development

(G-3400)
PURSE MONEY TECHNOLOGIES LLC ○
Also Called: Purse Money
8 The Grn Ste A (19901-3618)
PHONE..................302 208-0184
Michael Nyananyo, *VP*
EMP: 15 **EST:** 2023
SALES (est): 501.62K **Privately Held**
SIC: 7371 Custom computer programming services

(G-3401)
PXE GROUP LLC
8 The Grn Ste A (19901-3618)
PHONE..................561 295-1451
Robert Scaduto, *Mng Pt*
EMP: 8 **EST:** 2017
SQ FT: 500
SALES (est): 598.18K **Privately Held**
Web: www.stopzilla.com
SIC: 7371 Computer software development

(G-3402)
PYTHON SOFTWARE FOUNDATION
8 The Grn Ste R (19901-3618)
P.O. Box 1151 (60048-4151)
PHONE..................970 305-9455
Ewa Jodlowska, *Ex Dir*
Guido Van Rossum, *Pr*
Naomi Ceder, *Ch*
Jackie Kazil, *Vice Chairman*
EMP: 10 **EST:** 2001
SALES (est): 1.11MM **Privately Held**
Web: www.python.org
SIC: 8621 8733 7389 Professional organizations; Physical research, noncommercial; Business services, nec

(G-3403)
QCORTEX LLC
8 The Grn Ste A (19901-3618)
PHONE..................213 257-4004
EMP: 30 **EST:** 2020
SALES (est): 516.5K **Privately Held**
SIC: 7371 Computer software systems analysis and design, custom

(G-3404)
QISSTPAY INC
1675 S State St (19901-5140)
PHONE..................817 239-3900
Jordan Olivas, *CEO*
EMP: 8 **EST:** 2021
SALES (est): 100K **Privately Held**
SIC: 7389 Financial services

(G-3405)
QODEBOTICS LLC
8 The Grn (19901-3618)
PHONE..................617 312-7733
EMP: 5 **EST:** 2020
SALES (est): 107.01K **Privately Held**
SIC: 7371 Software programming applications

(G-3406)
QUADROSENSE LLC
4 The Grn (19901-3617)
PHONE..................302 608-0779
EMP: 3
SALES (est): 128.34K **Privately Held**
SIC: 7372 7389 Application computer software; Business Activities at Non-Commercial Site

(G-3407)
QUAIL TECHNOLOGIES ○
850 New Burton Rd Ste 201 (19904-5786)
PHONE..................201 497-4902
Andrew Fischer, *Pr*
EMP: 5 **EST:** 2022
SALES (est): 209.21K **Privately Held**
SIC: 7372 Application computer software

(G-3408)
QUANTUMFLY LLC
9 E Loockerman St Ste 215 (19901-7347)
PHONE..................312 618-5739
Suri Surinder, *CEO*
EMP: 10
SALES (est): 493.63K **Privately Held**
SIC: 7375 On-line data base information retrieval

(G-3409)
QUEEN B TBL CHAIR RENTALS LLC
8 The Grn # 8105 (19901-3618)
PHONE..................215 960-6303
EMP: 5 **EST:** 2019
SALES (est): 242.47K **Privately Held**
SIC: 7359 Equipment rental and leasing, nec

(G-3410)
QUIC-PRO INC (PA)
8 The Grn Ste A (19901-3618)
PHONE..................302 883-8305
Egor Zudin, *CEO*
EMP: 6
SALES (est): 547.65K
SALES (corp-wide): 547.65K **Privately Held**
SIC: 8748 Telecommunications consultant

(G-3411)
QUINN PEDIATRIC DENTISTRY
1380 S State St (19901-4946)
PHONE..................302 674-8000
Richard M Quinn, *Prin*
EMP: 11 **EST:** 2013
SALES (est): 899.95K **Privately Held**
Web: www.quinnchildrensdentistry.com
SIC: 8011 Pediatrician

(G-3412)
QUINTASIAN LLC
Also Called: Hilton
1706 N Dupont Hwy (19901-2219)
PHONE..................302 674-3784
Andrew Cheung, *Managing Member*
Dorothy Cheung, *
EMP: 35 **EST:** 2015
SALES (est): 1.55MM **Privately Held**
Web: dover.hgi.com
SIC: 7011 Hotels and motels

(G-3413)
QUOTANDA LLC (PA)
3500 S Dupont Hwy (19901-6041)
PHONE..................917 971-7585
Grant Taylor, *Prin*
EMP: 5 **EST:** 2014
SALES (est): 205.05K
SALES (corp-wide): 205.05K **Privately Held**
SIC: 7389 Credit card service

(G-3414)
R E MICHEL COMPANY LLC
550 S Queen St (19904-3563)
PHONE..................302 678-0250
Eric Smith, *Mgr*
EMP: 5
SALES (corp-wide): 1.43B **Privately Held**
Web: www.remichel.com
SIC: 5075 5078 Warm air heating equipment and supplies; Refrigeration equipment and supplies
PA: R. E. Michel Company, Llc
     1 Re Michel Dr
     Glen Burnie MD 21060
     410 760-4000

(G-3415)
R M QUINN DDS
1380 S State St Ste 2 (19901-4911)
PHONE..................302 674-8000
Richard M Quinn, *Owner*
EMP: 12 **EST:** 1984
SALES (est): 189.63K **Privately Held**
SIC: 8021 Dentists' office

(G-3416)
R&O DRYWALL LLC
1061 S Little Creek Rd Trlr 83 (19901-5000)
PHONE..................302 399-9480
Abel Rivas Ortiz, *Asst Sec*
EMP: 9 **EST:** 2014
SALES (est): 489.65K **Privately Held**
SIC: 1742 Drywall

(G-3417)
RA HARRISON PAVING
1679 S Dupont Hwy Ste 100 (19901-5164)
PHONE..................302 363-7344
Christine C Hall, *Owner*
EMP: 6 **EST:** 2016
SALES (est): 146.28K **Privately Held**
Web: www.raharrison.net
SIC: 1611 Surfacing and paving

(G-3418)
RACHEL L FARLEY
99 Wolf Creek Blvd Ste 2 (19901-4968)
PHONE..................302 734-8000
Rachel Farley, *Ofcr*
EMP: 6 **EST:** 2017
SALES (est): 106.72K **Privately Held**
Web: www.associatesinternational.com
SIC: 8049 Physical therapist

(G-3419)
RAH BOOKS INTERNATIONAL
9 E Loockerman St (19901-8306)
PHONE..................917 288-1064
Douglas Thomas, *VP*
EMP: 4
SALES (est): 160K **Privately Held**
SIC: 2731 Books, publishing and printing

(G-3420)
RAMANI NATWARLAL V MD
742 S Governors Ave Ste 2 (19904-4111)
PHONE..................302 465-3002
Natwarlal Ramani, *Mgr*

EMP: 8 **EST:** 2018
SALES (est): 59.55K **Privately Held**
SIC: 8011 Gastronomist

(G-3421)
RAMESH VEMULAPALLI MD
31 Gooden Ave (19904-4143)
PHONE..................302 674-9141
Ramesh Vemulapalli, *Pr*
EMP: 8 **EST:** 2018
SALES (est): 107.83K **Privately Held**
SIC: 8011 Offices and clinics of medical doctors

(G-3422)
RAMPING TECHNOLOGY LLC
160 Greentree Dr Ste 101 (19904-7620)
PHONE..................954 893-2909
Pablo Orlando, *Managing Member*
EMP: 5
SALES (est): 32.18K **Privately Held**
SIC: 7379 Online services technology consultants

(G-3423)
RANGELAND NM LLC
1675 S State St Ste B (19901-5140)
PHONE..................800 316-6660
Christopher W Keene, *CEO*
Paul Broker, *Ex VP*
EMP: 4 **EST:** 2013
SALES (est): 540.04K **Publicly Held**
SIC: 1382 Oil and gas exploration services
HQ: Rio Andeavor Holdings Llc
     2150 Town Square Pl # 700
     Sugar Land TX 77479

(G-3424)
RAPID HMMNGBIRD HOMEBUYERS LLC
8 The Grn Ste 11127 (19901-3618)
P.O. Box 1846 (10008-1846)
PHONE..................347 671-7761
EMP: 7 **EST:** 2020
SALES (est): 403.3K **Privately Held**
SIC: 6799 Real estate investors, except property operators

(G-3425)
RAYMOND F BOOK III (HQ)
Also Called: Ray Book & Co
220 Beiser Blvd (19904-7790)
PHONE..................302 734-5826
Raymond F Book Iii, *Owner*
EMP: 10 **EST:** 1994
SALES (est): 2.27MM **Privately Held**
Web: www.rfbookcpas.com
SIC: 8721 Certified public accountant
PA: Savant Capital, Llc
     190 Buckley Dr
     Rockford IL 61107

(G-3426)
RBS AUTO REPAIR INC
Also Called: Meineke Car Care Center
1312 S Dupont Hwy (19901-4404)
PHONE..................302 678-8803
James R Kramer Junior, *Pr*
EMP: 6 **EST:** 2007
SALES (est): 559.38K **Privately Held**
Web: www.meineke.com
SIC: 7538 General automotive repair shops

(G-3427)
RC&PS LLC
8 The Grn Ste 15196 (19901-3618)
PHONE..................516 984-8184
Richard Clinton, *Managing Member*
EMP: 15
SALES (est): 349.53K **Privately Held**

SIC: 8099 Medical services organization

(G-3428)
RE/MAX HORIZONS INC
Also Called: Re/Max
1198 S Governors Ave (19904-6930)
PHONE..................................302 678-4300
Edward Hammond Junior, *Pr*
EMP: 19 EST: 1991
SALES (est): 931.82K **Privately Held**
Web: www.remax.com
SIC: 6531 Real estate agent, residential

(G-3429)
REACH APPS INC
8 The Grn Ste A (19901-3618)
PHONE..................................707 812-0285
Norris Chebl, *CEO*
EMP: 5 EST: 2020
SALES (est): 46.16K **Privately Held**
SIC: 7371 Software programming applications

(G-3430)
REACHABLE SOLUTIONS INC
8 The Grn (19901-3618)
PHONE..................................908 962-8076
Ravi Gandhi, *CEO*
EMP: 6 EST: 2020
SALES (est): 253.79K **Privately Held**
SIC: 7389 Design services

(G-3431)
READHOWYOUWANT LLC
3702 N Dupont Hwy (19901-1555)
PHONE..................................302 730-4560
Ann Fitts, *Rep*
EMP: 2 EST: 2004
SALES (est): 52.84K **Privately Held**
Web: www.readhowyouwant.com
SIC: 8211 8732 2731 Specialty education; Commercial sociological and educational research; Book publishing

(G-3432)
READMARK INC
8 The Grn Ste A (19901-3618)
PHONE..................................650 450-9110
Junyu Wang, *Prin*
EMP: 5 EST: 2021
SALES (est): 107.01K **Privately Held**
SIC: 7371 Computer software development and applications

(G-3433)
READY 4 WORK LLC
28 S Kirkwood St (19904-3240)
PHONE..................................302 229-9701
Stephen Walker, *Prin*
EMP: 13 EST: 2016
SALES (est): 1.67MM **Privately Held**
Web: www.imready4work.com
SIC: 7361 Employment agencies

(G-3434)
READYB INC
8 The Grn Ste A (19901-3618)
PHONE..................................323 813-8710
Edna Mimran, *Prin*
EMP: 3 EST: 2019
SALES (est): 71.13K **Privately Held**
Web: www.readyb.com
SIC: 7372 Prepackaged software

(G-3435)
REALASSIST INC ◊
8 The Grn Ste 4000 (19901-3618)
PHONE..................................888 309-1114
Bilal Shafi, *Pr*
EMP: 15 EST: 2022

SQ FT: 3,000
SALES (est): 496.68K **Privately Held**
SIC: 7389 7371 Business Activities at Non-Commercial Site; Custom computer programming services

(G-3436)
REALM SOFTWARE INC ◊
850 New Burton Rd (19904-5785)
PHONE..................................734 799-0793
Tejas Ravishankar, *CEO*
EMP: 6 EST: 2022
SALES (est): 252.85K **Privately Held**
SIC: 7372 Application computer software

(G-3437)
REALTY MOGUL 14 LLC
73 Greentree Dr Ste 77 (19904-7646)
PHONE..................................877 977-2776
EMP: 5 EST: 2016
SALES (est): 212.91K **Privately Held**
SIC: 6531 Real estate agent, commercial

(G-3438)
RED BARN INC
Also Called: Maaco Auto Painting
1062 Lafferty Ln (19901-4642)
P.O. Box 1852 (19903-1852)
PHONE..................................302 678-0271
Elmore Smith, *Pr*
EMP: 12 EST: 1982
SQ FT: 6,200
SALES (est): 238.52K **Privately Held**
Web: www.maaco.com
SIC: 7532 Paint shop, automotive

(G-3439)
RED BUFFER LLC ◊
8 The Grn Ste 4645 (19901-3618)
PHONE..................................628 228-6024
EMP: 5 EST: 2023
SALES (est): 87.5K **Privately Held**
SIC: 5045 Computer software

(G-3440)
RED SPEAR LLC
8 The Grn Ste 7142 (19901-3618)
PHONE..................................757 301-1052
EMP: 5 EST: 2017
SALES (est): 85.58K **Privately Held**
Web: www.redspearllc.com
SIC: 7822 Motion picture and tape distribution

(G-3441)
REDARC CORPORATION
Also Called: Redarc Electronics
1675 S State St Ste B (19901-5140)
PHONE..................................704 247-5150
EMP: 7 EST: 2018
SALES (est): 88.38K **Privately Held**
SIC: 3625 Motor starters and controllers, electric

(G-3442)
REELVE INC
8 The Grn (19901-3618)
PHONE..................................312 459-2669
Rafael Rios, *CEO*
EMP: 3
SALES (est): 121.3K **Privately Held**
SIC: 3621 Motors, electric

(G-3443)
REFIX COMMODITIES LLC
160 Greentree Dr Ste 101 (19904-7620)
PHONE..................................888 465-8020
EMP: 7 EST: 2009
SALES (est): 200.15K **Privately Held**
Web: www.refixcommodities.com

SIC: 5141 Groceries, general line

(G-3444)
REFORM LLC
1675 S State St Ste B (19901-5140)
PHONE..................................813 299-5726
EMP: 8 EST: 2018
SALES (est): 313.1K **Privately Held**
SIC: 7372 Application computer software

(G-3445)
REGAL CONTRACTORS LLC
13 Nobles Pond Xing (19904-1296)
PHONE..................................302 736-5000
EMP: 6 EST: 2007
SALES (est): 1.15MM **Privately Held**
Web: www.regalbuilders.com
SIC: 1542 Custom builders, non-residential

(G-3446)
REGIONAL MEDICAL ASSOCIATES PA
240 Beiser Blvd Ste 201 (19904-8208)
PHONE..................................302 734-7246
Ganesh Balu, *CEO*
EMP: 5 EST: 1998
SALES (est): 450K **Privately Held**
SIC: 8011 Physicians' office, including specialists

(G-3447)
REGULATORY INSURANCE SERVICES
841 Silver Lake Blvd Ste 201 (19904-2465)
P.O. Box 835 (19903-0835)
PHONE..................................302 678-2004
John T Tinsley Iii, *Pr*
Tony Meisenheimer, *Sec*
George Donhauser, *VP*
EMP: 5 EST: 1993
SALES (est): 905.12K **Privately Held**
Web: risdelaware.wordpress.com
SIC: 6411 Insurance information and consulting services

(G-3448)
RELIABLE HANDYMAN SERVICES LLC
2807 Peachtree Run Rd (19901-7725)
PHONE..................................302 943-0166
Henry Stephan, *Prin*
EMP: 5 EST: 2014
SALES (est): 66.84K **Privately Held**
SIC: 7299 Handyman service

(G-3449)
RELIG STAFFING INC
32 W Loockerman St Ste 108 (19904-7352)
PHONE..................................312 219-6786
Juzar Motorwala, *Dir*
Ankit Rathod, *Dir*
Jwalant Patel, *Dir*
EMP: 20 EST: 2017
SALES (est): 1.47MM **Privately Held**
Web: www.religstaffing.com
SIC: 7361 Employment agencies

(G-3450)
RELYTV LLC
8 The Grn Ste 8422 (19901-3618)
PHONE..................................213 373-5988
Eric Vasquez, *Managing Member*
EMP: 4 EST: 2018
SALES (est): 275K **Privately Held**
SIC: 7372 Home entertainment computer software

(G-3451)
REMEDY RESTORE AESTHETICS LLC
45 Chadwick Dr (19901-5828)
PHONE..................................302 538-5261
Stephanie D Duphily, *Prin*
EMP: 5 EST: 2019
SALES (est): 142.15K **Privately Held**
SIC: 1799 Special trade contractors, nec

(G-3452)
RENAISSANCE SQUARE LLC
1534 S Governors Ave Ste B (19901-7054)
PHONE..................................302 943-5118
EMP: 7 EST: 2015
SALES (est): 420.79K **Privately Held**
SIC: 8748 Business consulting, nec

(G-3453)
RENAL CARE GROUP INC
748 S New St (19904-3573)
PHONE..................................302 678-8744
Sharon Simmons, *Brnch Mgr*
EMP: 86
SALES (corp-wide): 20.15B **Privately Held**
Web: www.renalcaregroup.com
SIC: 8092 Kidney dialysis centers
HQ: Renal Care Group, Inc.
2525 West End Ave Ste 600
Nashville TN 37203

(G-3454)
RENDERAPPS LLC
8 The Grn Ste A (19901-3618)
PHONE..................................919 274-0582
Bobby Ren, *Managing Member*
EMP: 5 EST: 2016
SALES (est): 10K **Privately Held**
SIC: 7372 7389 Prepackaged software; Business Activities at Non-Commercial Site

(G-3455)
RENE DELYN DESIGNS INC
Also Called: Rene Delyn Hair Design Studio
1744 N Dupont Hwy (19901-2219)
PHONE..................................302 736-6070
Rene Brickman, *Pr*
Jacob R Brickman, *VP*
Gladys T Brickman, *Pt*
EMP: 10 EST: 1987
SALES (est): 463.5K **Privately Held**
Web: www.renedelyndesigns.com
SIC: 7231 Hairdressers

(G-3456)
RENEWABLE ENERGY HOLDINGS LLC
8 The Grn Ste 8357 (19901-3618)
PHONE..................................817 213-6041
Ave Isa, *CEO*
Jackson Lawrence, *
EMP: 40 EST: 2016
SALES (est): 4.08MM **Privately Held**
SIC: 4911 Generation, electric power

(G-3457)
RENT CO INC
35 Commerce Way Ste 180 (19904-5747)
PHONE..................................302 739-0860
George C Clapp Junior, *Pr*
David W Clapp, *Sec*
EMP: 24 EST: 1987
SQ FT: 8,500
SALES (est): 825.36K **Privately Held**
SIC: 7359 Party supplies rental services

(G-3458)
REPUBLIX SOURCESTRIKE CORP
850 New Burton Rd Ste 201 (19904-5786)
PHONE..................................647 206-1503

GEOGRAPHIC SECTION
Dover - Kent County (G-3490)

Thomas Le Maguer, *VP*
EMP: 10 **EST:** 2020
SALES (est): 66.29K **Privately Held**
SIC: 8299 7379 Schools and educational services, nec; Computer related services, nec

(G-3459)
RESERVATION CENTRE LLC
8 The Grn Ste A (19901-3618)
PHONE...................888 284-0908
Deep Prakash, *CEO*
EMP: 50 **EST:** 2021
SALES (est): 2MM **Privately Held**
SIC: 4724 7389 Travel agencies; Business services, nec

(G-3460)
RESIDENCE INN DOVER
600 Jefferic Blvd (19901-2019)
PHONE...................302 677-0777
Diana Carter, *Prin*
EMP: 25 **EST:** 2007
SALES (est): 421.07K **Privately Held**
SIC: 7011 Hotels

(G-3461)
REVER CRE INC
8 The Grn Ste 10664 (19901-3618)
Rural Route 8 Thr Grn Ste (19901)
PHONE...................201 380-4566
Frederick B Krom Iv, *CEO*
Mark F Hammit, *CFO*
EMP: 15 **EST:** 2020
SALES (est): 505.06K **Privately Held**
SIC: 7375 On-line data base information retrieval

(G-3462)
REVOLUTIONARY IDENTITY ELUSION ✪
9 E Loockerman St (19901-8306)
PHONE...................618 780-1755
EMP: 5 **EST:** 2023
SALES (est): 164.52K **Privately Held**
SIC: 7389 Business Activities at Non-Commercial Site

(G-3463)
RFX ANALYST INC
8 The Grn # 5875 (19901-3618)
PHONE...................302 244-5650
Ryan Champion, *Pr*
EMP: 5 **EST:** 2017
SALES (est): 323.3K **Privately Held**
SIC: 7372 7374 7375 Business oriented computer software; Data processing service ; Data base information retrieval

(G-3464)
RHD DE PROGRAM
1305 Mcd Dr (19901-4699)
PHONE...................302 883-2926
EMP: 9 **EST:** 2017
SALES (est): 101.95K **Privately Held**
SIC: 8049 Speech specialist

(G-3465)
RICH RISING ENTERPRISE LLC
8 The Grn (19901-3618)
PHONE...................302 592-6697
EMP: 5
SALES (est): 207.81K **Privately Held**
SIC: 8742 Marketing consulting services

(G-3466)
RICHARD A PARSONS AGENCY INC
57 Saulsbury Rd Ste C (19904-3472)
PHONE...................302 674-2810
Richard Parsons, *Pr*

Kristin Parsons, *VP*
EMP: 6 **EST:** 1973
SALES (est): 758.74K **Privately Held**
SIC: 6411 Insurance agents, nec

(G-3467)
RICHARD BRATCHER
39 Stuart Dr (19901-5815)
PHONE...................803 786-7322
EMP: 5 **EST:** 1996
SALES (est): 193.74K **Privately Held**
SIC: 1521 Single-family housing construction

(G-3468)
RICHARD L ENGLE JR & ASSOC PA
1651 S Dupont Hwy (19901-5129)
PHONE...................302 674-5685
Richard Engle, *Ofcr*
EMP: 5 **EST:** 1987
SALES (est): 228.1K **Privately Held**
Web: www.englepa.com
SIC: 8721 Certified public accountant

(G-3469)
RICHARDSON BUILDING DNREC
89 Kings Hwy (19901-7305)
PHONE...................772 215-7625
EMP: 7 **EST:** 2017
SALES (est): 26.09K **Privately Held**
Web: dnrec.alpha.delaware.gov
SIC: 7999 Fishing boats, party: operation

(G-3470)
RIFTWALKER GAME STUDIO INC
8 The Grn Ste 12437 (19901-3618)
PHONE...................213 215-7165
Andrew Habers, *Prin*
EMP: 8
SALES (est): 306.16K **Privately Held**
SIC: 7371 Computer software development and applications

(G-3471)
RIGHT AS RAIN SEAMLESS RAIN GU
41 N Edgehill Ave (19901-4211)
PHONE...................302 272-2135
Jason Huebner, *Prin*
EMP: 6 **EST:** 2015
SALES (est): 155.83K **Privately Held**
SIC: 1761 Gutter and downspout contractor

(G-3472)
RINGLET LLC (PA) ✪
Also Called: Ringlet Technologies LLC
8 The Grn Ste B (19901-3618)
PHONE...................802 238-5858
Emily Bogue, *Managing Member*
EMP: 2 **EST:** 2022
SALES (est): 94.65K
SALES (corp-wide): 94.65K **Privately Held**
SIC: 7372 Prepackaged software

(G-3473)
RISLEUS PROPERTIES LLC (PA) ✪
8000 Pistachio Pl (19901-5929)
PHONE...................302 353-1255
EMP: 10 **EST:** 2022
SALES (est): 579.08K
SALES (corp-wide): 579.08K **Privately Held**
SIC: 1521 7389 Single-family housing construction; Business Activities at Non-Commercial Site

(G-3474)
ROAR PEDAL LLC
8 The Grn Ste B (19901-3618)
PHONE...................412 301-6002
EMP: 5 **EST:** 2020
SALES (est): 78.16K **Privately Held**

Web: www.roarpedal.com
SIC: 3559 Automotive related machinery

(G-3475)
ROBERT L FOX MST CPA
325 S Shore Dr (19901-5742)
PHONE...................302 697-7889
Christine Fox, *Prin*
EMP: 5 **EST:** 2012
SALES (est): 129.48K **Privately Held**
SIC: 8721 Certified public accountant

(G-3476)
ROCKET EXPRESS LLC ✪
509 Fairnest Ct (19904-9786)
PHONE...................609 854-6705
EMP: 10 **EST:** 2022
SALES (est): 543.01K **Privately Held**
SIC: 4789 Transportation services, nec

(G-3477)
ROCKIN REIKI AND MASSAGE LLC
116 Old Mill Rd (19901-6296)
PHONE...................302 423-3214
Shaston Gorman, *Prin*
EMP: 6 **EST:** 2016
SALES (est): 23.52K **Privately Held**
SIC: 8049 Massage Therapist

(G-3478)
ROCKOLY INC
54 Merion Rd (19904-2321)
P.O. Box 723 (19903-0723)
PHONE...................508 527-1939
EMP: 12 **EST:** 2020
SALES (est): 46.16K **Privately Held**
Web: www.rockoly.com
SIC: 7371 Computer software development and applications

(G-3479)
RODERICK M RELOVA DO
100 Scull Ter (19901-3577)
PHONE...................302 346-3171
Roderick Relova, *Ofcr*
EMP: 8 **EST:** 2017
SALES (est): 107.39K **Privately Held**
SIC: 8011 Offices and clinics of medical doctors

(G-3480)
RONALD A BEARD
44 Carver Rd (19904-2716)
PHONE...................302 883-7883
Ronald A Beard, *Owner*
EMP: 8 **EST:** 2018
SALES (est): 71K **Privately Held**
SIC: 8011 Offices and clinics of medical doctors

(G-3481)
RONALD F FEINBERG MD
200 Banning St Ste 130 (19904-3486)
PHONE...................302 674-1390
Joseph Ortiz, *Prin*
EMP: 11 **EST:** 2014
SALES (est): 251.51K **Privately Held**
Web: www.radfertility.com
SIC: 8011 Opthalmologist

(G-3482)
RONALD MIDAUGH
Also Called: Jackson Hewitt Tax Service
1030 Forrest Ave Ste 104 (19904-3382)
PHONE...................410 860-1040
EMP: 10
Web: www.jacksonhewitt.com
SIC: 7291 Tax return preparation services
PA: Ronald Midaugh
13600 Annapolis Rd

Bowie MD 20720

(G-3483)
ROO OFFICIAL LLC
Also Called: Roo Official
305 Bluecoat St (19901-8863)
PHONE...................267 614-2811
Jennifer Ruiz, *CEO*
EMP: 2 **EST:** 2021
SALES (est): 6K **Privately Held**
Web: www.rooofficialmerch.com
SIC: 2389 Apparel and accessories, nec

(G-3484)
ROOAH LLC
768 Townsend Blvd Ste 3 (19901-2515)
PHONE...................305 233-7557
Robert Njoku, *Prin*
EMP: 5 **EST:** 2017
SALES (est): 294.4K **Privately Held**
Web: www.rooah.xyz
SIC: 7371 Computer software development and applications

(G-3485)
ROSAS GREEK BTQ
338 Blue Heron Rd (19904-4724)
PHONE...................302 678-2147
Rosa Smith, *Owner*
EMP: 2 **EST:** 1984
SALES (est): 149.89K **Privately Held**
Web: www.rosasgreekboutique.com
SIC: 3999 Models, general, except toy

(G-3486)
ROSEDALE DEVELOPMENT LLC
9 E Loockerman St Ste 202 (19901-7347)
PHONE...................281 968-9426
EMP: 25 **EST:** 2020
SALES (est): 1.05MM **Privately Held**
SIC: 6531 Real estate agents and managers

(G-3487)
ROUNDROBIN CORPORATION (PA)
Also Called: Atlas Privacy
8 The Grn (19901-3618)
PHONE...................212 634-9193
Joseph Carlucci, *CEO*
EMP: 7 **EST:** 2021
SALES (est): 500K
SALES (corp-wide): 500K **Privately Held**
SIC: 7371 Software programming applications

(G-3488)
ROXANNE RXNNE CNSLTING GROUP L
8 The Grn (19901-3618)
PHONE...................470 333-8553
EMP: 5 **EST:** 2019
SALES (est): 60K **Privately Held**
SIC: 8742 Management consulting services

(G-3489)
ROZDOUM INC
8 The Grn (19901-3618)
PHONE...................315 707-7517
EMP: 6 **EST:** 2020
SALES (est): 67.98K **Privately Held**
Web: www.rozdoum.com
SIC: 7371 Computer software development

(G-3490)
RPM AUTOMOTIVE OF DOVER LLC
101 Weston Dr Ste 3 (19904-2767)
PHONE...................302 734-9495
EMP: 6 **EST:** 2020
SALES (est): 570.37K **Privately Held**
SIC: 7538 General automotive repair shops

Dover - Kent County (G-3491) — GEOGRAPHIC SECTION

(G-3491)
RPS LLC
16 Waterview Ln (19904-1048)
PHONE....................302 653-2598
Joseph Eric Richardson, *Asst Sec*
EMP: 5 EST: 2018
SALES (est): 125.3K **Privately Held**
SIC: 3699 Electrical equipment and supplies, nec

(G-3492)
RSM CONSTRUCTION
1471 Central Church Rd (19904-4753)
PHONE....................302 270-7099
Ryan Meisinger, *Prin*
EMP: 7 EST: 2010
SALES (est): 155.75K **Privately Held**
Web: www.rsmus.com
SIC: 1521 Single-family housing construction

(G-3493)
RUBY MORIARTY LLC
1221 College Park Dr (19904-8726)
PHONE....................917 587-1511
Terence Culver, *Managing Member*
EMP: 5 EST: 2020
SALES (est): 91.39K **Privately Held**
SIC: 7379 Online services technology consultants

(G-3494)
RUGGERIO WILLSON & ASSOC LLC
109 E Division St (19901-7303)
PHONE....................302 345-8468
EMP: 5 EST: 2014
SALES (est): 49.56K **Privately Held**
Web: www.ruggerio.com
SIC: 8743 Lobbyist

(G-3495)
RUMBLE LEAGUE STUDIOS INC
614 S Dupont Hwy Ste 210 (19901-4518)
PHONE....................800 564-5300
Nicholas Vale, *Prin*
EMP: 8 EST: 2021
SALES (est): 321.21K **Privately Held**
SIC: 7372 Prepackaged software

(G-3496)
S & B PRO SECURITY LLC
Also Called: Electronic Security
1300 E Lebanon Rd (19901-5832)
PHONE....................800 841-9907
EMP: 8 EST: 2010
SALES (est): 867.06K **Privately Held**
Web: www.sbprosecurity.com
SIC: 7382 5065 Protective devices, security; Security control equipment and systems

(G-3497)
S & S WINES AND SPIRITS
1007 Walker Rd (19904-6572)
PHONE....................302 678-9987
Ralph Mills, *Pr*
EMP: 5 EST: 2010
SALES (est): 299.73K **Privately Held**
SIC: 5182 Wine

(G-3498)
S D NEMCIC DDS
910 Walker Rd Ste A (19904-2759)
PHONE....................302 734-1950
EMP: 6 EST: 1985
SALES (est): 238.86K **Privately Held**
SIC: 8021 Specialized dental practitioners

(G-3499)
S G WILLIAMS OF DOVER INC
580 Lafferty Ln (19901-7201)
PHONE....................302 678-1080
John D Griffith, *Pr*
Helen Griffith, *VP*
William M Kinnamon, *Sec*
EMP: 16 EST: 1976
SQ FT: 20,000
SALES (est): 2.45MM
SALES (corp-wide): 6.88MM **Privately Held**
Web: www.sgwilliamssupply.com
SIC: 5033 Roofing and siding materials
PA: S. G. Williams & Bros. Co.
301 N Tatnall St
Wilmington DE 19801
302 656-8167

(G-3500)
SABI AI CORP
850 New Burton Rd Ste 201 (19904-5785)
PHONE....................415 800-4641
William Gaultier, *Managing Member*
EMP: 5 EST: 2021
SALES (est): 289.52K **Privately Held**
SIC: 7375 Data base information retrieval

(G-3501)
SAFAHI CORP
1151 Walker Rd (19904-6600)
PHONE....................925 503-4551
Samuel Safahi, *CEO*
EMP: 7 EST: 2021
SALES (est): 347.42K **Privately Held**
SIC: 6211 Investment firm, general brokerage

(G-3502)
SAFE DRIVER CORPORATION (PA) ◊
838 Walker Rd (19904-2751)
PHONE....................601 207-1164
Etienne Jambou, *CEO*
EMP: 6 EST: 2023
SALES (est): 71.79K
SALES (corp-wide): 71.79K **Privately Held**
SIC: 8742 Marketing consulting services

(G-3503)
SAFEAGAIN INC
8 The Grn (19901-3618)
PHONE....................929 276-2732
Don Bosco, *CEO*
EMP: 5
SALES (est): 68.89K **Privately Held**
SIC: 7371 Computer software development and applications

(G-3504)
SAFELITE GLASS CORP
Also Called: Safelite Autoglass
4200 N Dupont Hwy Ste 6 (19901-2400)
PHONE....................877 800-2727
Kim Cordrey, *Mgr*
EMP: 5
SALES (corp-wide): 3.16B **Privately Held**
Web: www.safelite.com
SIC: 7536 5013 Automotive glass replacement shops; Automobile glass
HQ: Safelite Glass Corp.
7400 Safelite Way
Columbus OH 43235
614 210-9000

(G-3505)
SAFRAX INC
8 The Grn Ste 4000 (19901-3618)
PHONE....................302 404-0388
Y Sierraalta, *Ofcr*
G Elias, *Ofcr*
EMP: 20 EST: 2020
SALES (est): 8MM **Privately Held**
SIC: 2812 Chlorine, compressed or liquefied

(G-3506)
SAISHA SPICES LLC ◊
8 The Grn # B (19901-3618)
PHONE....................786 288-3344
EMP: 5 EST: 2023
SALES (est): 199.4K **Privately Held**
SIC: 7389 Business Activities at Non-Commercial Site

(G-3507)
SALLY BEAUTY SUPPLY LLC
Also Called: Sally Beauty Supply 712
283 N Dupont Hwy Ste D (19901-7532)
PHONE....................302 674-2201
Erin Dudley, *Mgr*
EMP: 7
Web: www.sallybeauty.com
SIC: 5087 Beauty parlor equipment and supplies
HQ: Sally Beauty Supply Llc
3001 Colorado Blvd
Denton TX 76210
940 898-7500

(G-3508)
SANDPIPER ENERGY INC
909 Silver Lake Blvd (19904-2409)
PHONE....................302 736-7656
Thomas Mahn, *Treas*
EMP: 15 EST: 2013
SQ FT: 8,000
SALES (est): 8.99MM
SALES (corp-wide): 680.7MM **Publicly Held**
Web: www.chpk.com
SIC: 4923 Gas transmission and distribution
PA: Chesapeake Utilities Corporation
500 Energy Ln
Dover DE 19901
302 734-6799

(G-3509)
SAPERE
8 The Grn (19901-3618)
PHONE....................888 727-3731
David Koster, *Mng Pt*
EMP: 5
SALES (est): 314.55K **Privately Held**
Web: www.saperesecure.com
SIC: 1731 Safety and security specialization

(G-3510)
SARAH B NEELY-COLLINS
526 Great Geneva Dr (19901-5847)
PHONE....................814 282-6013
Sarah Neely-collins, *Owner*
EMP: 6 EST: 2017
SALES (est): 61.81K **Privately Held**
SIC: 8049 Offices of health practitioner

(G-3511)
SARATOGA FOOD SPECIALTIES LLC (HQ) ◊
Also Called: Saratoga Food Specialties
850 New Burton Rd (19904-5785)
PHONE....................951 270-9600
Michael Marks, *Pr*
EMP: 19 EST: 2022
SALES (est): 106.26MM
SALES (corp-wide): 106.26MM **Privately Held**
SIC: 2099 Seasonings and spices
PA: Solina U.S. Holding Inc.
850 New Burton Rd Ste 20
Dover DE 19904
414 764-1220

(G-3512)
SAVVY HAIR STUDIOS
3847 N Dupont Hwy Ste 1 (19901-2200)
PHONE....................302 724-5629
EMP: 5 EST: 2014
SALES (est): 43.24K **Privately Held**
SIC: 7231 Hairdressers

(G-3513)
SB&B WELLNESS LLC
108 Overlook Pl (19901-4302)
PHONE....................484 681-1411
EMP: 5 EST: 2020
SALES (est): 75.9K **Privately Held**
SIC: 8099 Health and allied services, nec

(G-3514)
SCHMITTINGER AND RODRIGUEZ PA (PA)
414 S State St (19901-6702)
PHONE....................302 674-0140
Nicholas H Rodriguez, *CEO*
Douglas B Catts, *
Paul H Boswell, *
John J Schmittinger, *
Bruce C Ennis, *
EMP: 79 EST: 1973
SQ FT: 9,000
SALES (est): 6.67MM
SALES (corp-wide): 6.67MM **Privately Held**
Web: www.schmittrod.com
SIC: 8111 General practice attorney, lawyer

(G-3515)
SCHUTTE PARK
10 Electric Ave (19904-5772)
PHONE....................302 349-4898
Wayne Voshell, *Ofcr*
EMP: 7 EST: 2020
SALES (est): 71.96K **Privately Held**
Web: www.cityofdover.com
SIC: 7999 Amusement and recreation, nec

(G-3516)
SCHWARTZ ERIC MD
230 Beiser Blvd Ste 100 (19904-7791)
PHONE....................302 730-0840
Eric Schwartz, *Prin*
EMP: 8 EST: 2018
SALES (est): 65.5K **Privately Held**
SIC: 8011 Orthopedic physician

(G-3517)
SCHWARTZ CENTER FOR ARTS
118 S Bradford St (19904-7318)
PHONE....................302 678-3583
Frank A Santini, *Prin*
EMP: 5 EST: 2010
SALES (est): 59.98K **Privately Held**
SIC: 7389 6512 Advertising, promotional, and trade show services; Theater building, ownership and operation

(G-3518)
SCHWARTZ SCHWRTZ ATTYS AT LAW
1140 S State St (19901-6926)
P.O. Box 541 (19903-0541)
PHONE....................302 678-8700
Steven Schwartz, *Pr*
EMP: 6 EST: 1986
SALES (est): 992.05K **Privately Held**
Web: www.schwartzandschwartz.com
SIC: 8111 General practice attorney, lawyer

(G-3519)
SCORE REVIVE LLC
9 E Loockerman St Ste 202 (19901-7347)
PHONE....................302 455-2100
EMP: 5 EST: 2019
SALES (est): 250K **Privately Held**

GEOGRAPHIC SECTION
Dover - Kent County (G-3549)

SIC: 6141 Personal credit institutions

(G-3520)
SCOTT ENGINEERING INC
22 Old Rudnick Ln Ste 2 (19901-4912)
PHONE.................302 736-3058
EMP: 5 EST: 1993
SQ FT: 5,000
SALES (est): 569.94K Privately Held
Web: www.scottengineering.com
SIC: 8711 8713 Consulting engineer; Surveying services

(G-3521)
SCREEN ZONE ENTERPRISES LLC
8 The Grn Ste 6484 (19901-3618)
PHONE.................302 316-0705
Roddry Dickerson, Managing Member
EMP: 20 EST: 2020
SALES (est): 200K Privately Held
SIC: 7371 Software programming applications

(G-3522)
SCUBA WORLD INC
Also Called: Commercial Residential Contrs
4004 S Dupont Hwy Ste B (19901-6077)
PHONE.................302 698-1117
Darrell Louder, Pr
Tracy Louder, Sec
EMP: 8 EST: 1989
SQ FT: 1,200
SALES (est): 410.42K Privately Held
Web: www.scubaworldinc.com
SIC: 5941 1522 Skin diving, scuba equipment and supplies; Residential construction, nec

(G-3523)
SE LAVI PRODUCTIONS LLC (PA)
3500 S Dupont Hwy (19901-6041)
PHONE.................727 457-2625
EMP: 7 EST: 2021
SALES (est): 234.33K
SALES (corp-wide): 234.33K Privately Held
SIC: 2782 Record albums

(G-3524)
SEABRIX LLC
8 The Grn Ste A (19901-3618)
PHONE.................224 578-3191
Steve Chan, Mgr
EMP: 7 EST: 2016
SALES (est): 294.4K Privately Held
SIC: 2731 Books, publishing and printing

(G-3525)
SEARS HEATING AND AC
15 Loockerman Plz (19901-7327)
PHONE.................302 480-1382
EMP: 5 EST: 2018
SALES (est): 71.73K Privately Held
SIC: 1711 Warm air heating and air conditioning contractor

(G-3526)
SECOND TECHNOLOGIES INC
8 The Grn (19901-3618)
PHONE.................310 774-3518
Owen Vries, CEO
EMP: 5
SALES (est): 297.36K Privately Held
SIC: 4789 7371 Transportation services, nec; Computer software development

(G-3527)
SEDATION CENTER PA
429 S Governors Ave (19904-6707)
PHONE.................302 678-3384
Dawn M Grandison, Prin
EMP: 5 EST: 2011
SALES (est): 381.12K Privately Held
Web: www.smiletosmiledentistry.com
SIC: 8021 Dentists' office

(G-3528)
SEKHON TRAVELS LLC (PA) ✪
8 The Grn Ste B (19901-3618)
PHONE.................661 706-6459
Mavjot Sekhon, Managing Member
EMP: 6 EST: 2023
SALES (est): 76.02K
SALES (corp-wide): 76.02K Privately Held
SIC: 7011 Vacation lodges

(G-3529)
SELECT PHYSICAL THERAPY
230 Beiser Blvd Ste 100 (19904-7791)
PHONE.................302 760-9966
EMP: 15
SALES (corp-wide): 24.48MM Privately Held
Web: www.selectphysicaltherapy.com
SIC: 8049 Nutritionist
PA: Select Physical Therapy Holdings, Inc.
680 American Ave Fl 2
King Of Prussia PA 19406
800 331-8840

(G-3530)
SENTRYPPE INC
8 The Grn Ste 10596 (19901-3618)
PHONE.................480 250-1721
Doctor James Chao, Ch Bd
EMP: 8 EST: 2020
SALES (est): 774.99K Privately Held
SIC: 5047 Medical equipment and supplies

(G-3531)
SENZORS INC
3500 S Dupont Hwy (19901-6041)
PHONE.................866 736-9677
EMP: 4 EST: 2019
SALES (est): 194.87K Privately Held
Web: www.senzors.com
SIC: 3823 Process control instruments

(G-3532)
SEPARE INC
529 Weaver Dr (19901-1377)
PHONE.................302 736-5000
Harry Miller, Pr
EMP: 9 EST: 1996
SALES (est): 238.31K Privately Held
Web: www.wildmeadowshomes.com
SIC: 1522 Residential construction, nec

(G-3533)
SEPER 8 MOTEL
Also Called: Red Carpet Inn
348 N Dupont Hwy (19901-3935)
PHONE.................302 734-5701
Pradip Parikh, Pr
EMP: 20 EST: 2005
SALES (est): 361.9K Privately Held
Web: www.stayhihotels.com
SIC: 7011 Hotels and motels

(G-3534)
SERVICE ENERGY LLC (PA)
3799 N Dupont Hwy (19901-1574)
P.O. Box 1000 (19936-1000)
PHONE.................302 734-7433
Edward Steiner, *
EMP: 77 EST: 1954
SQ FT: 5,000
SALES (est): 52.14MM Privately Held
Web: www.serviceenergy.com
SIC: 5172 5983 5411 Petroleum products, nec; Fuel oil dealers; Convenience stores

(G-3535)
SERVICE OIL COMPANY
Also Called: Poores Propane
3799 N Dupont Hwy (19901-1574)
P.O. Box 279 (19963-0279)
PHONE.................302 734-7433
Don Steiner, Owner
EMP: 6
SALES (corp-wide): 22.1MM Privately Held
Web: www.poorespropane.com
SIC: 5171 Petroleum bulk stations and terminals
HQ: Service Oil Company
Cedar Beach Rd
Milford DE 19963
302 422-6631

(G-3536)
SEWELL C BIGGS TRUST
406 Federal St (19901-3615)
P.O. Box 711 (19903-0711)
PHONE.................302 674-2111
EMP: 10 EST: 1993
SALES (est): 2.11MM Privately Held
Web: www.biggsmuseum.org
SIC: 8412 Museum

(G-3537)
SHADE MERCHANT LLC
8 The Grn (19901-3618)
PHONE.................571 634-0670
EMP: 5 EST: 2017
SALES (est): 511.24K Privately Held
SIC: 4213 Trucking, except local

(G-3538)
SHADYBROOK FARMS LLC
6401 Bayside Dr (19901-3429)
PHONE.................302 734-9966
Sandra Cartanza, Owner
EMP: 11 EST: 1957
SQ FT: 3,000
SALES (est): 406.53K Privately Held
SIC: 0115 0134 0111 0116 Corn; Irish potatoes; Wheat; Soybeans

(G-3539)
SHAKTI YOGA LLC
1030 Forrest Ave Ste 100 (19904-3382)
PHONE.................302 696-2288
EMP: 6 EST: 2018
SALES (est): 74.04K Privately Held
Web: www.shaktiyogallc.com
SIC: 7999 Yoga instruction

(G-3540)
SHANNLLS CRTIVE STYLES BRIDS L (PA) ✪
8 The Grn Ste A (19901-3618)
PHONE.................302 508-9215
EMP: 6 EST: 2023
SALES (est): 76.4K
SALES (corp-wide): 76.4K Privately Held
SIC: 7231 7389 Unisex hair salons; Business services, nec

(G-3541)
SHELATIA J DENNIS
9 E Loockerman St Ste 302 (19901-8305)
PHONE.................302 465-0630
Shelatia J Dennis Lcsw, Owner
EMP: 6 EST: 2019
SALES (est): 46.71K Privately Held
SIC: 8322 Social worker

(G-3542)
SHEPHERD PLACE INC
1362 S Governors Ave (19904-4804)
PHONE.................302 678-1909
Lakena Hammond, Ex Dir
EMP: 9 EST: 2002
SALES (est): 403.31K Privately Held
Web: www.shepherdplace.org
SIC: 8322 Social service center

(G-3543)
SHES FILMING PRODUCTIONS LLC ✪
27 S Bradford St (19904-7315)
PHONE.................302 563-0336
Shereen Williams, Managing Member
EMP: 5 EST: 2022
SALES (est): 62.02K Privately Held
SIC: 7812 7389 Television film production; Business services, nec

(G-3544)
SHINING STAR DAYCARE
365 Mimosa Ave (19904-4838)
PHONE.................302 393-7775
Talia Hickman, Prin
EMP: 8 EST: 2016
SALES (est): 49.98K Privately Held
SIC: 8351 Child day care services

(G-3545)
SHIPSERV INC
3500 S Dupont Hwy (19901-6041)
PHONE.................732 738-6500
EMP: 10 EST: 2000
SALES (est): 712.25K Privately Held
Web: www.shipserv.com
SIC: 4731 Freight transportation arrangement

(G-3546)
SHIV BABA LLC
Also Called: Wireless Traders
100 Carlsons Way Ste 15 (19901-2365)
PHONE.................703 314-1203
Mayam Patel, Managing Member
Pandre Prabhu, Managing Member
EMP: 10 EST: 2018
SALES (est): 424.7K Privately Held
SIC: 3661 Telephone dialing devices, automatic

(G-3547)
SHIV SAGAR INC
Also Called: Microtel
1703 E Lebanon Rd (19901-5844)
PHONE.................302 674-3800
Nita Patel, Prin
EMP: 10 EST: 2013
SALES (est): 251.33K Privately Held
Web: www.wyndhamhotels.com
SIC: 7011 Hotels and motels

(G-3548)
SHOOTERS CHOICE INC
5105 N Dupont Hwy (19901-2345)
PHONE.................302 736-5166
EMP: 9 EST: 1994
SQ FT: 7,000
SALES (est): 944.53K Privately Held
Web: www.shooterschoicede.com
SIC: 5941 7999 Firearms; Shooting range operation

(G-3549)
SHORECARE OF DELAWARE
874 Walker Rd Ste D (19904-2778)
PHONE.................302 724-5235
EMP: 10 EST: 2019
SALES (est): 149.96K Privately Held
Web: www.shorecareofdelaware.com

Dover - Kent County (G-3550)   **GEOGRAPHIC SECTION**

SIC: 8082 Home health care services

(G-3550)
SHORTCUTZ LAWN AND LANDSCA
47 Heatherfield Way (19904-9751)
P.O. Box 871 (19903-0871)
PHONE...................302 736-0906
EMP: 7 EST: 2008
SALES (est): 127.84K **Privately Held**
Web: www.shortcutzlandscape.com
SIC: 0782 Lawn care services

(G-3551)
SHORTCUTZ LAWN CARE INC
198 S Shore Dr (19901-5739)
PHONE...................302 538-6007
EMP: 5
SALES (est): 113.06K **Privately Held**
Web: www.shortcutzlandscape.com
SIC: 0781 Landscape services

(G-3552)
SHREE LALJI LLC
Also Called: Red Roof Inn
652 N Dupont Hwy (19901-3937)
PHONE...................302 730-8009
Vinaykumar Patel, *Prin*
Vijay Shroff, *Prin*
EMP: 9 EST: 2013
SQ FT: 45,000
SALES (est): 472.11K **Privately Held**
Web: www.redroof.com
SIC: 7011 Hotels and motels

(G-3553)
SHRI SAI DOVER LLC
Also Called: Holiday Inn
561 N Dupont Hwy (19901-3960)
PHONE...................302 747-5050
EMP: 37 EST: 2009
SALES (est): 657.36K **Privately Held**
Web: www.holidayinn.com
SIC: 7011 Hotels and motels

(G-3554)
SIA NETJER CORP
8 The Grn Ste 8590 (19901-3618)
PHONE...................302 319-5190
Tendai Ndlovu, *Admn*
EMP: 10 EST: 2021
SIC: 6719 Holding companies, nec

(G-3555)
SIGNALL TECHNOLOGIES INC
3500 S Dupont Hwy (19901-6041)
PHONE...................240 623-5800
Zsolt Robotka, *CEO*
EMP: 9 EST: 2020
SALES (est): 181.42K **Privately Held**
Web: www.signall.us
SIC: 7371 Computer software development

(G-3556)
SIGNATURE STITCHES
216 N Caroline Pl (19904-7736)
PHONE...................302 736-6500
Jay Reynolds, *Prin*
EMP: 2 EST: 2006
SALES (est): 98.74K **Privately Held**
Web: www.signaturestitches.com
SIC: 2395 Embroidery products, except Schiffli machine

(G-3557)
SIGNATUREONE MEDIA LLC
8 The Grn Ste 1706 (19901-3618)
PHONE...................347 849-3740
Michael Akande, *Managing Member*
EMP: 5
SALES (est): 220.1K **Privately Held**

SIC: 2741 7371 Miscellaneous publishing; Computer software development and applications

(G-3558)
SIGNS BY TOMORROW
Also Called: Signs By Tomorrow
90 Sunwood Dr (19901-7736)
PHONE...................302 744-9396
Carolyn Phinney, *Pr*
EMP: 6 EST: 2009
SALES (est): 77.22K **Privately Held**
Web: www.signsbytomorrow.com
SIC: 3993 Signs and advertising specialties

(G-3559)
SIGNUP SOFTWARE INC
3500 S Dupont Hwy Ste Dn (19901-6041)
PHONE...................302 531-1139
Michael Medipor, *CEO*
EMP: 2 EST: 2021
SALES (est): 56.54K **Privately Held**
SIC: 7372 Business oriented computer software

(G-3560)
SIGPA
550 Otis Dr (19901-4630)
PHONE...................302 678-8780
Rory Talamini, *Prin*
EMP: 6 EST: 2011
SALES (est): 59.74K **Privately Held**
SIC: 8399 Social services, nec

(G-3561)
SILVER LAKE RESTORATION
16 Ironwood Cir (19904-6522)
PHONE...................302 241-3931
Michael Barr, *Prin*
EMP: 6 EST: 2016
SALES (est): 188.88K **Privately Held**
Web: www.silverlakede.com
SIC: 1799 Special trade contractors, nec

(G-3562)
SIMPLELIFE APPS INC
8 The Grn Ste A (19901-3618)
PHONE...................954 591-8413
Alexander Ilinskiy, *Dir*
EMP: 5
SALES (est): 46.16K **Privately Held**
Web: www.simple.life
SIC: 7371 Computer software development and applications

(G-3563)
SIMPLIIGENCE INC (PA)
8 The Grn Ste A (19901-3618)
PHONE...................404 528-7646
Raghu Seetharam Ra, *Pr*
EMP: 54 EST: 2019
SALES (est): 3.22MM
SALES (corp-wide): 3.22MM **Privately Held**
Web: www.simpliigence.com
SIC: 7371 7389 Software programming applications; Business services, nec

(G-3564)
SIMPLY CLEAN JANTR SVCS INC
Also Called: Simply Clean
100 Carlsons Way Ste 6 (19901-2365)
PHONE...................302 744-9100
Michael Devault, *VP*
EMP: 6 EST: 2000
SALES (est): 97.45K **Privately Held**
Web: www.simplycleanjanitorialservices.com
SIC: 7349 Janitorial service, contract basis

(G-3565)
SIMPLYLAB INC
8 The Grn Ste A (19901)
PHONE...................919 663-2800
Ilya Zubarev, *Prin*
Aleksand Sherbakob, *Prin*
Sergu Krukov, *Prin*
EMP: 12 EST: 2021
SALES (est): 406.37K **Privately Held**
Web: www.simplyex.io
SIC: 7371 Computer software development and applications

(G-3566)
SIMPSONS LOG HOMES INC
126 Lafferty Ln (19901-7205)
PHONE...................302 674-1900
Richard Aslin, *CEO*
EMP: 4 EST: 1989
SALES (est): 355.61K **Privately Held**
SIC: 2452 8712 6531 Log cabins, prefabricated, wood; House designer; Broker of manufactured homes, on site

(G-3567)
SINAPI LLC
3500 S Dupont Hwy Ste 300 (19901-6041)
PHONE...................650 265-7180
Matias Yakimovsky, *Managing Member*
Daniel Campos, *Dir*
Federico Colombo, *Mktg Dir*
EMP: 30 EST: 2014
SALES (est): 824.69K **Privately Held**
SIC: 8742 Marketing consulting services

(G-3568)
SINGH PRIYA C MD
640 S State St (19901-3530)
PHONE...................302 674-4700
Priya Singh, *Prin*
EMP: 8 EST: 2018
SALES (est): 155.48K **Privately Held**
Web: www.bayhealth.org
SIC: 8011 Offices and clinics of medical doctors

(G-3569)
SIRQIL LLC
8 The Grn Ste A (19901-3618)
PHONE...................213 204-9333
EMP: 10 EST: 2021
SALES (est): 348.32K **Privately Held**
SIC: 7371 7389 Software programming applications; Business Activities at Non-Commercial Site

(G-3570)
SISTER SISTER COVID CLEAN LLC
259 Fawn Haven Walk (19901-6591)
PHONE...................267 467-8803
EMP: 5 EST: 2021
SALES (est): 104.73K **Privately Held**
SIC: 7389 Business Activities at Non-Commercial Site

(G-3571)
SKILLFI LLC
8 The Grn (19901-3618)
PHONE...................469 701-9614
EMP: 5 EST: 2020
SALES (est): 124.81K **Privately Held**
Web: www.skillfi.com
SIC: 8742 Human resource consulting services

(G-3572)
SKIPJACK INC
861 Silver Lake Blvd Ste 200 (19904-2467)
PHONE...................302 734-6755
Alfonso Giovannucci, *Prin*

EMP: 53 EST: 1993
SALES (est): 234.26K
SALES (corp-wide): 680.7MM **Publicly Held**
SIC: 6531 Real estate agents and managers
HQ: Chesapeake Service Company
500 Energy Ln Ste 400
Dover DE 19901

(G-3573)
SKIPWITH ORGANICS LLC
8 The Grn Ste A (19901-3618)
PHONE...................908 573-2930
EMP: 2 EST: 2020
SALES (est): 100K **Privately Held**
Web: www.skipwithorganics.com
SIC: 2023 Dietary supplements, dairy and non-dairy based

(G-3574)
SKYWARD SOLUTIONS LLC
8 The Grn Ste A (19901-3618)
PHONE...................469 563-0411
EMP: 5 EST: 2019
SALES (est): 104.37K **Privately Held**
SIC: 7379 Online services technology consultants

(G-3575)
SLACUM & DOYLE TAX SERVICE LLC
Also Called: Liberty Tax Service
838 Walker Rd Ste 22-2 (19904-2751)
PHONE...................302 734-1850
Scott Slacum, *
EMP: 8 EST: 2004
SALES (est): 142.03K **Privately Held**
Web: www.libertytax.com
SIC: 7291 Tax return preparation services

(G-3576)
SMART PROFESSIONS INC
8 The Grn Ste 7712 (19901-3618)
PHONE...................603 289-6263
EMP: 24 EST: 2020
SALES (est): 1.44MM **Privately Held**
SIC: 5511 7371 Trucks, tractors, and trailers: new and used; Computer software development

(G-3577)
SMART-THE TILE RICK SPECIALIST
79 Chatham Ct (19901-3934)
PHONE...................302 331-5529
Rick Smart, *Owner*
EMP: 5 EST: 2017
SALES (est): 54.48K **Privately Held**
SIC: 1743 Tile installation, ceramic

(G-3578)
SMARTIS
Also Called: Home Theater
73 Greentree Dr (19904-7646)
PHONE...................302 653-8355
Christopher Hargett, *Pr*
EMP: 5 EST: 2004
SALES (est): 493.04K **Privately Held**
Web: www.smartisinc.com
SIC: 7373 1731 Systems integration services; Sound equipment specialization

(G-3579)
SMITH COHEN & ROSENBERG LLC
838 Walker Rd (19904-2751)
PHONE...................302 260-8007
EMP: 13 EST: 2016
SALES (est): 1.14MM **Privately Held**
Web: www.scrsolutions.net
SIC: 7322 Collection agency, except real estate

GEOGRAPHIC SECTION

Dover - Kent County (G-3610)

(G-3580)
SNIFFIES LLC ✪
8 The Grn Ste B (19901-3618)
PHONE.................................302 265-4101
Blake Gallagher, *Managing Member*
EMP: 6 **EST:** 2023
SALES (est): 66.98K **Privately Held**
SIC: 7299 Dating service

(G-3581)
SOARES DR NEHA M
212 Portmarnock Ct (19904-9430)
PHONE..................................248 707-4931
Neha M Soares Md, *Prin*
EMP: 6 **EST:** 2019
SALES (est): 60.43K **Privately Held**
SIC: 8011 Offices and clinics of medical doctors

(G-3582)
SOCCER NETWORK LLC
152 Greenview Dr (19901-5746)
PHONE.................................302 724-6951
Lewis Atkinson, *Prin*
EMP: 8 **EST:** 2012
SALES (est): 63.38K **Privately Held**
Web: www.soccernetwork.eu
SIC: 7941 Sports clubs, managers, and promoters

(G-3583)
SOCIAL AFRICA INC
614 N Dupont Hwy (19901-3900)
PHONE.................................763 670-3452
Otis Zeon, *CEO*
EMP: 20 **EST:** 2021
SALES (est): 585.99K **Privately Held**
SIC: 7371 Software programming applications

(G-3584)
SOCIAL HEALTH INNOVATIONS INC
8 The Grn Ste 5175 (19901-3618)
PHONE.................................917 476-9355
Amanda Johnstone, *CEO*
EMP: 8 **EST:** 2016
SALES (est): 82.28K **Privately Held**
Web: www.transhumaninc.com
SIC: 8063 Psychiatric hospitals

(G-3585)
SOCIAL KEYBOARD INC ✪
8 The Grn Ste R (19901-3618)
PHONE.................................650 519-8383
Devon Thomas, *Pr*
EMP: 10 **EST:** 2022
SALES (est): 348.32K **Privately Held**
SIC: 7371 7389 Software programming applications; Business Activities at Non-Commercial Site

(G-3586)
SOCIAL WORK HELPER PBC
8 The Grn Ste 8043 (19901-3618)
PHONE.................................302 233-7422
Deona Cooper, *Pr*
EMP: 9
SALES (est): 612.69K **Privately Held**
Web: www.swhelper.org
SIC: 7313 Electronic media advertising representatives

(G-3587)
SONIC SIGHTS INCORPORATED
8 The Grn Ste A (19901-3618)
PHONE.................................312 498-9977
Todd Robinson, *CEO*
EMP: 4 **EST:** 2020
SALES (est): 250K **Privately Held**
SIC: 2741 Internet publishing and broadcasting

(G-3588)
SOROPTOMIST FOUNDATION INC
1851 Windswept Cir (19901-5852)
PHONE.................................302 698-3686
Mardi Pyott, *Prin*
EMP: 5 **EST:** 2011
SALES (est): 47.05K **Privately Held**
SIC: 8641 Civic and social associations

(G-3589)
SOUTHERN DELAWARE MED GROUP
200 Banning St Ste 380 (19904-3493)
P.O. Box 337 (19963-0337)
PHONE.................................302 424-3900
EMP: 7 **EST:** 2009
SALES (est): 154.53K **Privately Held**
SIC: 8031 8011 Offices and clinics of osteopathic physicians; Offices and clinics of medical doctors

(G-3590)
SOUTHERN DELAWARE ROLLER DERBY
2201 S Dupont Hwy (19901-5512)
PHONE.................................410 253-9798
Jenny Wyatt, *Prin*
EMP: 5 **EST:** 2018
SALES (est): 63.76K **Privately Held**
SIC: 7941 Sports clubs, managers, and promoters

(G-3591)
SOUTHERN RIVERS MANAGEMENT LLC (PA)
160 Greentree Dr Ste 101 (19904-7620)
PHONE.................................302 674-4089
Robert Fitzgerald, *Prin*
EMP: 6 **EST:** 2017
SALES (est): 793.73K
SALES (corp-wide): 793.73K **Privately Held**
SIC: 8741 Management services

(G-3592)
SPACE INDUSTRIES INC
8 The Grn Ste R (19901-3618)
PHONE.................................510 219-1005
Joshua Letcher, *CEO*
EMP: 5 **EST:** 2020
SALES (est): 390.74K **Privately Held**
SIC: 3761 Space vehicles, complete

(G-3593)
SPANA GREGORY MD
200 Banning St Ste 150 (19904-3491)
PHONE.................................302 736-1320
Gregory Spana, *Prin*
EMP: 8 **EST:** 2014
SALES (est): 68.39K **Privately Held**
SIC: 8011 Urologist

(G-3594)
SPARKSPHERE SOLUTIONS LLC ✪
838 Walker Rd Ste 21-2124 (19904-2751)
PHONE.................................302 742-9048
Khawaja Haroon Nazim, *CEO*
Khawaja Haroon Nazim, *Managing Member*
EMP: 5 **EST:** 2023
SALES (est): 203.68K **Privately Held**
SIC: 7379 Computer related consulting services

(G-3595)
SPEEDRID LTD
625 S Dupont Hwy (19901-4504)
PHONE.................................213 550-5462
Guiyun Wang, *Managing Member*
EMP: 98 **EST:** 2017
SALES (est): 1.31MM **Privately Held**
SIC: 7371 Computer software development and applications

(G-3596)
SPENCES BAZAAR & AUCTION LLC
550 S New St (19904-3536)
PHONE.................................302 734-3441
EMP: 8 **EST:** 1933
SALES (est): 182.49K **Privately Held**
SIC: 7389 Auctioneers, fee basis

(G-3597)
SPIN4SPIN INC
8 The Grn (19901-3618)
PHONE.................................720 547-2126
Vladislav Chibinov, *Pr*
EMP: 5 **EST:** 2021
SALES (est): 61.22K **Privately Held**
SIC: 7389 Business Activities at Non-Commercial Site

(G-3598)
SPINRACK CORP
8 The Grn (19901-3618)
PHONE.................................209 965-7746
Melissa Mcginnis, *CEO*
EMP: 6
SALES (est): 317.04K **Privately Held**
SIC: 7372 Prepackaged software

(G-3599)
SPORT CLIPS HRCUTS DVER - DPON
Also Called: Sport Clips
1211 N Dupont Hwy Ste C (19901-2250)
PHONE.................................302 677-1622
EMP: 5 **EST:** 2016
SALES (est): 22.84K **Privately Held**
Web: www.haircutmendupontighwaydoverde.com
SIC: 7231 Unisex hair salons

(G-3600)
SPORTERA EVENTS USA INC
874 Walker Rd Ste C (19904-2778)
PHONE.................................514 978-2648
EMP: 6 **EST:** 2020
SALES (est): 261.6K **Privately Held**
SIC: 7389 Business services, nec

(G-3601)
SQUARE ONE ELECTRIC SERVICE CO
347 Fork Branch Rd (19904-1230)
PHONE.................................302 678-0400
Ed Crumbock, *Pr*
EMP: 18 **EST:** 1981
SQ FT: 12,000
SALES (est): 7.17MM **Privately Held**
Web: www.sqone.com
SIC: 5084 7699 3462 Water pumps (industrial); Industrial machinery and equipment repair; Iron and steel forgings

(G-3602)
ST DELWARE ELECTRICAL
245 Mckee Rd (19904-2232)
PHONE.................................302 857-5316
EMP: 6 **EST:** 2018
SALES (est): 333.04K **Privately Held**
SIC: 4911 Electric services

(G-3603)
STALLION TRUCKING INC
8 The Grn Ste 13936 (19901-3618)
PHONE.................................803 757-4366
Anthony Daley, *CEO*
Jenny Daley, *Pr*
EMP: 6 **EST:** 2007
SALES (est): 494.9K **Privately Held**
SIC: 4212 Local trucking, without storage

(G-3604)
STANDARD DISTRIBUTING CO INC
Horse Pond Rd & Lafferty Ln (19901)
PHONE.................................302 674-4591
Steven Tigani, *Mgr*
EMP: 34
SALES (corp-wide): 40.77MM **Privately Held**
Web: www.standardde.com
SIC: 4225 General warehousing
PA: Standard Distributing Co Inc
100 Mews Dr
New Castle DE 19720
302 655-5511

(G-3605)
STATE EDCATN AGCY DIRS ARTS ED
Also Called: SEADAE
401 Federal St Ste 2 (19901-3639)
PHONE.................................302 739-4111
Ana Luisa Cardona, *Pr*
Debora Hanses, *Sec*
Lynn Tuttle, *Treas*
EMP: 8 **EST:** 2007
SALES (est): 479.7K **Privately Held**
SIC: 8621 Professional organizations

(G-3606)
STATE FARM
Also Called: State Farm Insurance
50 N Dupont Hwy (19901-4292)
PHONE.................................302 678-5656
EMP: 8 **EST:** 2018
SALES (est): 245.3K **Privately Held**
Web: www.statefarm.com
SIC: 6411 Insurance agents and brokers

(G-3607)
STATE JANITORIAL SUPPLY CO
540 Otis Dr # 1 (19901-4630)
PHONE.................................302 734-4814
Chris Lebendig, *Pr*
EMP: 8 **EST:** 1960
SALES (est): 2.37MM **Privately Held**
Web: www.statejanitorialsupply.com
SIC: 5087 Janitors' supplies

(G-3608)
STATE SENIOR CARE LLC
21 N State St (19901-3802)
PHONE.................................302 674-2144
Martin Steinberger, *Prin*
EMP: 7 **EST:** 2017
SALES (est): 32.92K **Privately Held**
SIC: 8322 Senior citizens' center or association

(G-3609)
STATE STREET INN
228 N State St (19901-3837)
PHONE.................................302 734-2294
Yvonne Hall, *Prin*
EMP: 7 **EST:** 2005
SALES (est): 272.11K **Privately Held**
Web: www.statestreetinn.com
SIC: 7011 Bed and breakfast inn

(G-3610)
STEADFAST INSURANCE COMPANY (DH)
2 Loockerman Plz Ste 202 (19901-7328)
PHONE.................................847 605-6000
Michael Foley, *Regional*
Martin Senn, *CEO*
Thomas Buss, *VP*
David A Bowers, *VP*

Dover - Kent County (G-3611) GEOGRAPHIC SECTION

Wayne Fisher, *VP*
EMP: 7 **EST:** 1973
SALES (est): 134.79MM **Privately Held**
SIC: 6411 Insurance agents, brokers, and service
HQ: Zurich American Insurance Company
2860 S Circle Dr Ste 320
Colorado Springs CO 80906
800 987-3373

(G-3611)
STEPH1OFFICIAL INC
8 The Grn (19901-3618)
PHONE..................................302 744-0990
Bayek Braswell, *CEO*
EMP: 13 **EST:** 2015
SALES (est): 45.73K **Privately Held**
SIC: 7819 7389 Personnel services, motion picture production; Business services, nec

(G-3612)
STEPHEN DEVARY
591 Squawigm Rd (19901-3032)
PHONE..................................302 674-4560
EMP: 5 **EST:** 2018
SALES (est): 366.19K **Privately Held**
SIC: 4911 Electric services

(G-3613)
STORMX INC
8 The Grn Ste 1 (19901-3618)
PHONE..................................425 998-8762
EMP: 11 **EST:** 2016
SALES (est): 51.29K **Privately Held**
Web: www.stormx.io
SIC: 7371 Computer software development and applications

(G-3614)
STR8UP GAMES INC ✪
8 The Grn Ste A (19901-3618)
PHONE..................................315 523-8216
Milton Gray Junior, *CEO*
EMP: 15 **EST:** 2023
SALES (est): 581.23K **Privately Held**
SIC: 3944 Electronic games and toys

(G-3615)
STRATEGIC WEALTH CONS INC (PA) ✪
8 The Grn Ste B (19901-3618)
PHONE..................................601 715-4174
Britney Smith, *CEO*
EMP: 6 **EST:** 2023
SALES (est): 75.41K
SALES (corp-wide): 75.41K **Privately Held**
SIC: 8742 Retail trade consultant

(G-3616)
STREET & ELLIS P A
426 S State St (19901-6724)
PHONE..................................302 735-8408
Gerald I Street, *Pr*
John I Ellis Attorney, *Prin*
EMP: 9 **EST:** 1977
SQ FT: 2,500
SALES (est): 822.45K **Privately Held**
Web: www.streetellislaw.com
SIC: 8111 General practice law office

(G-3617)
STUDIO302
3046 Hazlettville Rd (19904-5601)
PHONE..................................302 462-0857
Brooke Gomez, *Prin*
EMP: 11 **EST:** 2017
SALES (est): 63.11K **Privately Held**
SIC: 7011 Hotels and motels

(G-3618)
STYLERE LLC
8 The Grn Ste A (19901-3618)
PHONE..................................650 206-7721
Ryan Lawrence, *Managing Member*
EMP: 10 **EST:** 2021
SALES (est): 451.08K **Privately Held**
SIC: 5734 7389 Software, business and non-game; Business Activities at Non-Commercial Site

(G-3619)
SUGARDUMPLIN
316 Peach Peddler Path (19901-6532)
PHONE..................................302 423-8810
EMP: 5 **EST:** 2014
SALES (est): 64.92K **Privately Held**
SIC: 4812 Cellular telephone services

(G-3620)
SUK-YOUNG CARR DDS
850 S State St Ste 2 (19901-4113)
PHONE..................................302 736-6631
Suk-young Carr, *Owner*
EMP: 9 **EST:** 2017
SALES (est): 102.7K **Privately Held**
SIC: 8021 Endodontist

(G-3621)
SUMTHIN3LSE
8 The Grn Ste 11105 (19901-3618)
PHONE..................................302 272-5435
Darwin-nicho Hayle, *Pr*
Nicole Hayle, *Pr*
Darwin Hayle, *VP*
EMP: 7 **EST:** 2015
SALES (est): 352.02K **Privately Held**
SIC: 7389 8742 7336 ; Management consulting services; Commercial art and graphic design

(G-3622)
SUN PHARMACEUTICALS CORP
Also Called: Banana Boat Products
50 S Dupont Hwy (19901-7431)
PHONE..................................302 678-6000
Max Recone, *Pr*
Glenn Forbes, *Treas*
William B Stammer, *Sec*
◆ **EMP:** 38 **EST:** 1981
SQ FT: 10,000
SALES (est): 1.11MM
SALES (corp-wide): 2.25B **Publicly Held**
SIC: 2844 Cosmetic preparations
HQ: Playtex Products, Llc
6 Research Dr Ste 400
Shelton CT 06484
203 944-5500

(G-3623)
SUNNYFIELD CONTRACTORS INC
Also Called: Bartsch John C
150 Sunnyfield Ln (19904-1657)
PHONE..................................302 674-8610
John Bartsch, *Pr*
Jeffery Bartsch, *VP*
EMP: 11 **EST:** 1981
SALES (est): 407.58K **Privately Held**
SIC: 1799 Building site preparation

(G-3624)
SUNSHINE HOME CHILDCARE
370 Mimosa Ave (19904-4839)
PHONE..................................302 674-2009
EMP: 7 **EST:** 2014
SALES (est): 80.58K **Privately Held**
Web: www.sunshinehomechildcarede.com
SIC: 8351 Group day care center

(G-3625)
SUNU CONSULTING LLC
8 The Grn Ste A (19901-3618)
PHONE..................................202 534-5864
Mark Briscoe, *Prin*
John Gogos, *CFO*
EMP: 5 **EST:** 2020
SALES (est): 103.81K **Privately Held**
SIC: 8111 General practice attorney, lawyer

(G-3626)
SUPER EIGHT DOVER
Also Called: Super 8 Motel
348 N Dupont Hwy (19901-3935)
PHONE..................................302 734-5701
Chirayush Parikh, *Mgr*
EMP: 7 **EST:** 2009
SALES (est): 271.7K **Privately Held**
Web: www.wyndhamhotels.com
SIC: 7011 Hotels and motels

(G-3627)
SUPERSTAR HOLDINGS INC
8 The Grn Ste A (19901-3618)
PHONE..................................302 289-8931
Tameisha Johnson, *CEO*
EMP: 5 **EST:** 2021
SALES (est): 233.08K **Privately Held**
SIC: 8742 7389 Retail trade consultant; Business services, nec

(G-3628)
SUPPORT SERVICES GROUP INC
8 The Grn Ste A (19901-3618)
PHONE..................................404 939-1782
EMP: 5 **EST:** 2021
SALES (est): 77.06K **Privately Held**
Web: www.supportservicesgroup.co
SIC: 7379 Computer related consulting services

(G-3629)
SURGICAL ASSOCIATES PA
Also Called: Eden Hill Medical Center
200 Banning St Ste 200 (19904-3487)
P.O. Box 855 (19903-0855)
PHONE..................................302 346-4502
Tina Mitelmal, *Prin*
EMP: 25 **EST:** 1998
SALES (est): 2.07MM **Privately Held**
Web: www.surgicalassociatespa.com
SIC: 8011 Surgeon

(G-3630)
SVEA REAL ESTATE GROUP LLC (PA)
1675 S State St Ste B (19901-5140)
PHONE..................................855 262-9665
EMP: 15 **EST:** 2016
SALES (est): 2.33MM
SALES (corp-wide): 2.33MM **Privately Held**
SIC: 6799 Real estate investors, except property operators

(G-3631)
SWEAT SOCIAL LLC
8 The Grn Ste 7379 (19901-3618)
PHONE..................................504 510-1973
Rupa Mohan, *Managing Member*
EMP: 5 **EST:** 2015
SALES (est): 219.65K **Privately Held**
SIC: 8742 7372 Hospital and health services consultant; Application computer software

(G-3632)
SWITCH ENTERPRISES LLC (DH)
Also Called: Switch, The
3500 S Dupont Hwy (19901-6041)
PHONE..................................212 227-9191

Eric Cooney, *Managing Member*
Scott Beers, *
Eric Pfaff, *
Areeg Eluri, *
EMP: 25 **EST:** 1990
SALES (est): 43.26MM **Privately Held**
Web: www.theswitch.tv
SIC: 8999 4813 Communication services; Telephone/video communications
HQ: Tata Communications (Netherlands) B.V.
Herikerbergweg 238 Luna Arena
Amsterdam NH
205755600

(G-3633)
SYMPHONY OF MIND COUNSELING
1300 S Farmview Dr G21 (19904-3374)
PHONE..................................302 747-7286
Danielle R May, *Prin*
EMP: 6 **EST:** 2016
SALES (est): 32.92K **Privately Held**
SIC: 8322 General counseling services

(G-3634)
SYNCOGAI CORP ✪
8 The Grn Ste A (19901-3618)
PHONE..................................302 307-4500
Brent Lollis, *Prin*
EMP: 8 **EST:** 2023
SALES (est): 306.16K **Privately Held**
SIC: 7371 Custom computer programming services

(G-3635)
SYNNOVE ENERGY CORPORATION LLC (PA)
160 Greentree Dr Ste 101 (19904-7620)
PHONE..................................805 215-8600
Fred Sisson, *Managing Member*
EMP: 9 **EST:** 2013
SALES (est): 1.13MM
SALES (corp-wide): 1.13MM **Privately Held**
SIC: 1711 Solar energy contractor

(G-3636)
SZOVET & CO LLC
8 The Grn Ste A (19901-3618)
PHONE..................................908 656-5114
EMP: 2 **EST:** 2021
SALES (est): 73.4K **Privately Held**
SIC: 2299 Fabrics: linen, jute, hemp, ramie

(G-3637)
T & J MURRAY WORLDWIDE SVCS
283 Persimmon Tree Ln (19901-1308)
P.O. Box 214 (19903-0214)
PHONE..................................302 736-1790
▼ **EMP:** 10 **EST:** 2001
SALES (est): 961.23K **Privately Held**
Web: www.tnjmurray.com
SIC: 5531 5013 3713 Auto and truck equipment and parts; Truck parts and accessories; Truck bodies and parts

(G-3638)
T J LANE CONSTRUCTION INC
267 Fork Branch Rd (19904-1231)
PHONE..................................302 734-1099
EMP: 5
SIC: 1521 New construction, single-family houses
PA: T J Lane Construction Inc
711 Sharon Hill Rd
Dover DE 19904

(G-3639)
T&B LOGISTICS INC
8 The Grn (19901-3618)

GEOGRAPHIC SECTION
Dover - Kent County (G-3670)

PHONE..................301 304-3255
Terry Alford, *CEO*
EMP: 2
SALES (est): 247.44K **Privately Held**
SIC: 3537 7389 Trucks, tractors, loaders, carriers, and similar equipment; Business services, nec

(G-3640)
T&T CLEANING LLC
2888 Fast Landing Rd (19901-3106)
PHONE..................609 575-0458
EMP: 12 **EST**: 2017
SALES (est): 208.01K **Privately Held**
SIC: 7699 Cleaning services

(G-3641)
T-MOBILE USA INC
Also Called: T-Mobile Store 9730
1141 N Dupont Hwy Ste 3 (19901-2024)
PHONE..................302 736-1980
EMP: 6
SALES (corp-wide): 79.57B **Publicly Held**
Web: www.t-mobile.com
SIC: 4812 Cellular telephone services
HQ: T-Mobile Usa, Inc.
12920 Se 38th St
Bellevue WA 98006
425 378-4000

(G-3642)
TABLETOPIA CORP
850 New Burton Rd Ste 201 (19904-5786)
PHONE..................305 548-8407
Timofey Bokarev, *Pr*
EMP: 12 **EST**: 2020
SALES (est): 406.37K **Privately Held**
SIC: 7371 Computer software development and applications

(G-3643)
TAI GROUP LLC
8 The Grn (19901-3618)
PHONE..................561 819-4231
Adriana Ferreyr, *Managing Member*
EMP: 50 **EST**: 2020
SALES (est): 500K **Privately Held**
Web: www.taigroup.com
SIC: 8742 7389 Marketing consulting services; Business services, nec

(G-3644)
TAILOR MADE GROUP LLC
8 The Grn Ste 11198 (19901-3618)
PHONE..................347 824-0325
Christian Davis, *CEO*
EMP: 5 **EST**: 2016
SALES (est): 139.06K **Privately Held**
SIC: 7389 Business Activities at Non-Commercial Site

(G-3645)
TALENT OLA INC
8 The Grn Ste A (19901-3618)
PHONE..................732 421-3216
Kshma Garg, *CEO*
EMP: 33 **EST**: 2021
SALES (est): 442.88K **Privately Held**
SIC: 8742 Human resource consulting services

(G-3646)
TALENTLAB INC
8 The Grn Ste D (19901-3618)
PHONE..................310 999-4320
Mikhael Cook, *Dir*
EMP: 5
SALES (est): 199.4K **Privately Held**
SIC: 7389 Business services, nec

(G-3647)
TALENTS DIGITAL SERVICES CORP
8 The Grn (19901-3618)
PHONE..................888 508-2503
Yasser Zaki, *CEO*
EMP: 40
SALES (est): 1.06MM **Privately Held**
SIC: 7371 Computer software development

(G-3648)
TALKPUSH LLC
8 The Grn Ste 0424 (19901-3618)
PHONE..................415 818-5083
Max Armbruster, *Managing Member*
EMP: 57 **EST**: 2018
SALES (est): 1.9MM **Privately Held**
Web: www.talkpush.com
SIC: 7373 Systems software development services

(G-3649)
TANGOME INC
Also Called: Tango Live
3500 S Dupont Hwy (19901-6041)
P.O. Box 969 (94042-0969)
PHONE..................650 362-8086
▲ **EMP**: 10 **EST**: 2009
SALES (est): 3.61MM **Privately Held**
Web: www.tango.me
SIC: 7371 Computer software development and applications

(G-3650)
TANKALA HARSHA MD
1125 Forrest Ave Ste 203 (19904-3483)
PHONE..................302 346-0101
Harsha Tankala Md, *Owner*
EMP: 7 **EST**: 2018
SALES (est): 54.13K **Privately Held**
SIC: 8011 Offices and clinics of medical doctors

(G-3651)
TAPPEDN HOLDINGS LLC
8 The Grn (19901-3618)
PHONE..................404 877-2525
EMP: 5
SALES (est): 68.89K **Privately Held**
SIC: 8748 Business consulting, nec

(G-3652)
TAQ INCORPORATED
800 N State St (19901-3925)
PHONE..................302 734-8300
Michael Barr, *Pr*
EMP: 5 **EST**: 2004
SALES (est): 496.12K **Privately Held**
Web: www.unitedcorporate.com
SIC: 8732 Business economic service

(G-3653)
TARA K ADAMS MRS
144 Kings Hwy Ste 302 (19901-7308)
PHONE..................302 450-3936
Tara K Adams Physl Thrp, *Prin*
EMP: 5 **EST**: 2018
SALES (est): 47.22K **Privately Held**
SIC: 8049 Offices of health practitioner

(G-3654)
TAX-E LOGISTICS INC
199 Dorian Dr (19904-5889)
PHONE..................877 829-3669
Priscilla Rainey, *Prin*
Watkins Williams, *Prin*
EMP: 5 **EST**: 2021
SALES (est): 198.09K **Privately Held**
SIC: 4213 Trucking, except local

(G-3655)
TAYLOR WOODWORKS
34 Clearview Dr (19901-5713)
PHONE..................302 745-2049
Jeff Taylor, *Prin*
EMP: 2 **EST**: 2008
SALES (est): 131.67K **Privately Held**
SIC: 2434 Wood kitchen cabinets

(G-3656)
TAZELAAR ROOFING SERVICE INC
Also Called: Tazelaar Roofing Service
4869 S Dupont Hwy (19901-6430)
PHONE..................302 697-2643
John J Tazelaar, *Owner*
John J Tazelaar, *Pr*
Sharon Tazelaar, *Sec*
EMP: 7 **EST**: 1947
SALES (est): 457.02K **Privately Held**
SIC: 1761 Roofing contractor

(G-3657)
TCP/IP SOLUTIONS LLC
8 The Grn B (19901-3618)
PHONE..................302 219-0224
EMP: 19 **EST**: 2020
SALES (est): 616.4K **Privately Held**
SIC: 7373 Computer-aided system services

(G-3658)
TD FOR W GAMES
784 Walker Rd (19904-2725)
PHONE..................302 883-3627
EMP: 5 **EST**: 2014
SALES (est): 60.74K **Privately Held**
SIC: 8399 Advocacy group

(G-3659)
TDOCK SERVICES & HOLDING INC
8 The Grn Ste A (19901-3618)
PHONE..................305 924-3653
EMP: 4 **EST**: 2021
SALES (est): 452.38K **Privately Held**
SIC: 3999 Manufacturing industries, nec

(G-3660)
TDP WIRELESS INC
34 Salt Creek Dr (19901-2436)
PHONE..................302 424-1900
Tajesh Patel, *Owner*
EMP: 9 **EST**: 2007
SALES (est): 297.86K **Privately Held**
SIC: 4812 Cellular telephone services

(G-3661)
TEAL CONSTRUCTION INC
612 Mary St (19904-3024)
P.O. Box 779 (19903-0779)
PHONE..................302 276-6034
Robert Edgell, *Pr*
EMP: 70 **EST**: 1968
SQ FT: 1,200
SALES (est): 15.12MM **Privately Held**
Web: www.tealconstruction.com
SIC: 1611 1623 Highway and street paving contractor; Sewer line construction

(G-3662)
TECHNOLOGY STUDENT ASSOCIATION
401 Federal St Bldg Townsend (19901-3639)
PHONE..................302 857-3336
EMP: 14 **EST**: 2011
SALES (est): 300.04K **Privately Held**
Web: www.detsa.org
SIC: 8611 Business associations

(G-3663)
TEERHUB INC
8 The Grn Ste D (19901-3618)
PHONE..................281 223-3466
Pranit Shah, *Admn*
EMP: 5 **EST**: 2020
SALES (est): 245.78K **Privately Held**
SIC: 7371 Computer software systems analysis and design, custom

(G-3664)
TELAMON CORPORATION
195 Willis Rd (19901-4085)
PHONE..................302 736-5933
Yolanda Evans, *Mgr*
EMP: 8
SALES (corp-wide): 85.01MM **Privately Held**
Web: www.telamon.org
SIC: 8351 Head Start center, except in conjunction with school
PA: Telamon Corporation
5560 Munford Rd Ste 201
Raleigh NC 27612
919 851-7611

(G-3665)
TELCAST NETWORKS LLC
8 The Grn Ste 7044 (19901-3618)
PHONE..................833 835-2278
Talal Khalid, *CEO*
EMP: 6 **EST**: 2017
SALES (est): 17.11K **Privately Held**
Web: www.telcastnetworks.com
SIC: 8999 Communication services

(G-3666)
TELOS LEGAL CORP
1012 College Rd Ste 201 (19904-6506)
P.O. Box 953 (19943-0953)
PHONE..................302 242-4815
EMP: 5 **EST**: 2019
SALES (est): 206.43K **Privately Held**
Web: www.teloslegalcorp.com
SIC: 8111 Legal services

(G-3667)
TEMPLE MASONIC
Also Called: Union Lodge 7
38 South St (19904-3527)
PHONE..................302 734-4147
Gary Laing, *Sec*
EMP: 20 **EST**: 1857
SALES (est): 140.92K **Privately Held**
SIC: 8641 Civic associations

(G-3668)
TENDER HEARTS
1339 S Governors Ave (19904-4803)
PHONE..................302 674-2565
Linda Ohlig, *Pr*
EMP: 10 **EST**: 1999
SALES (est): 474.85K **Privately Held**
SIC: 8351 Child day care services

(G-3669)
TENDER TOUCH SUPPORT LLC
34 Tammie Dr (19904-1910)
PHONE..................302 272-1638
Victorine Burns, *Prin*
EMP: 5 **EST**: 2017
SALES (est): 54.96K **Privately Held**
SIC: 8399 Advocacy group

(G-3670)
TEPUYI LLC
8 The Grn (19901-3618)
PHONE..................954 991-0749
EMP: 10
SALES (est): 348.32K **Privately Held**

Dover - Kent County (G-3671)   GEOGRAPHIC SECTION

SIC: **8748** Business consulting, nec

(G-3671)
TERSIN ENTERPRISES LLC (PA)
55 Loockerman Plz (19903-8084)
PHONE..............................614 260-3215
EMP: **7** EST: 1019
SALES (est): 263.62K
SALES (corp-wide): 263.62K **Privately Held**
SIC: **1611** Concrete construction: roads, highways, sidewalks, etc.

(G-3672)
TESLA NOOTROPICS INC
8 The Grn Ste 5757 (19901-3618)
PHONE..............................514 718-2270
EMP: **2** EST: 2017
SALES (est): 300K **Privately Held**
SIC: **2023** Dietary supplements, dairy and non-dairy based

(G-3673)
THE LRNING TREE CHLD ACDEMY LL
403 W Loockerman St (19904-3251)
PHONE..............................302 841-0194
Jonnell Singh, *Managing Member*
EMP: **7** EST: 2019
SALES (est): 350K **Privately Held**
Web: the-learning-tree-childrens-academy.ueniweb.com
SIC: **8351** Preschool center

(G-3674)
THERESA LITTLE MD
Also Called: Little Thresa P MD Fmly Mdcine
1001 S Bradford St Ste 5 (19904-4153)
PHONE..............................302 735-1616
EMP: **9** EST: 1997
SALES (est): 274.31K **Privately Held**
SIC: **8011** General and family practice, physician/surgeon

(G-3675)
THIRDWAVE SYSTEMS INC ◊
1111 S Governors Ave (19904-6903)
PHONE..............................650 804-1385
Peter Jonas, *CEO*
EMP: **6** EST: 2022
SALES (est): 321.42K **Privately Held**
SIC: **7389** Business Activities at Non-Commercial Site

(G-3676)
THIRTEEN SVNTY SIX CPITL MGT L
8 The Grn Ste A (19901-3618)
PHONE..............................561 247-1521
James Horace, *Managing Member*
EMP: **5** EST: 2020
SALES (est): 256.47K **Privately Held**
SIC: **6799** Venture capital companies

(G-3677)
THIS IS CALA INC
1111 S Governors Ave (19904-6903)
PHONE..............................512 900-4746
Marc Sourour, *Prin*
EMP: **13** EST: 2016
SALES (est): 864.2K **Privately Held**
SIC: **7389** Styling of fashions, apparel, furniture, textiles, etc.

(G-3678)
THOMAS E MOORE INC (PA)
696 S Bay Rd (19901-4626)
P.O. Box 794 (19903-0794)
PHONE..............................302 674-1500
Thomas Cullen, *Pr*
James Michael Cullen Junior, *VP*
▲ EMP: **10** EST: 1923
SQ FT: 3,000
SALES (est): 4.17MM
SALES (corp-wide): 4.17MM **Privately Held**
SIC: **5191** 5083 5148 Chemicals, agricultural ; Farm equipment parts and supplies; Vegetables

(G-3679)
THOMAS FAMILY DENTIST LLC
1981 S State St (19901-5811)
PHONE..............................302 697-1152
EMP: **10** EST: 2020
SALES (est): 585.95K **Privately Held**
Web: www.thomasfamilydentist.com
SIC: **8021** Dentists' office

(G-3680)
THOMAS W MERCER DMD
Also Called: Mercer Dental Associates
77 Saulsbury Rd (19904-3444)
PHONE..............................302 678-2942
Thomas W Mercer D.m.d., *Prin*
EMP: **6** EST: 1980
SALES (est): 898.17K **Privately Held**
Web: www.mercersydelldental.com
SIC: **8021** Dentists' office

(G-3681)
THREADS N DENIMS
8 Senator Ave (19901-5243)
PHONE..............................302 678-0642
Herbert Watkins, *Prin*
EMP: **5** EST: 2014
SALES (est): 59.11K **Privately Held**
SIC: **2211** Denims

(G-3682)
THREATMATE INC ◊
8 The Grn Ste 14359 (19901-3618)
PHONE..............................302 219-4714
Stan Ivanov, *CEO*
EMP: **10** EST: 2023
SALES (est): 531.18K **Privately Held**
SIC: **5045** 7389 Computer software; Business Activities at Non-Commercial Site

(G-3683)
THROAT THREADS APPAREL USA INC
874 Walker Rd Ste C (19904-2778)
PHONE..............................905 681-8437
Russell Fearon, *CEO*
EMP: **58** EST: 2015
SALES (est): 12.1MM **Privately Held**
SIC: **5136** 5137 Men's and boy's clothing; Women's and children's clothing

(G-3684)
TIDEMARK LLC
117 W Reed St (19904-7321)
PHONE..............................302 747-7737
EMP: **8** EST: 2017
SALES (est): 809.01K **Privately Held**
Web: www.tidemarkde.com
SIC: **1521** New construction, single-family houses

(G-3685)
TIDEWATER ENVMTL SVCS INC
1100 S Little Creek Rd (19901-4727)
PHONE..............................302 674-8056
Dian Taylor, *CEO*
EMP: **8** EST: 2004
SALES (est): 913.15K
SALES (corp-wide): 98.9MM **Publicly Held**
SIC: **4941** Water supply

HQ: Artesian Wastewater Management, Inc.
664 Churchmans Rd
Newark DE 19702
302 453-6900

(G-3686)
TIDEWATER UTILITIES INC
1100 S Little Creek Rd (19901-4727)
PHONE..............................302 674-8056
Bruce O'connor, *Pr*
Bruce Patrick, *
Ken Quinn, *
EMP: **100** EST: 1964
SQ FT: 7,000
SALES (est): 23.12MM
SALES (corp-wide): 162.43MM **Publicly Held**
Web: www.middlesexwater.com
SIC: **4941** Water supply
PA: Middlesex Water Company
485c Route 1 S Ste 400
Iselin NJ 08830
732 634-1500

(G-3687)
TILEBOX INC
1111 B S Governers Ave 6076 (19904-6903)
PHONE..............................206 741-0883
Gerard Baptiste, *CEO*
EMP: **6**
SALES (est): 68.89K **Privately Held**
SIC: **7371** Computer software development and applications

(G-3688)
TIMBER HEART LEARNING CENTER
1339 S Governors Ave (19904-4803)
PHONE..............................302 674-2565
Lindy Ohaig, *Owner*
EMP: **8** EST: 1970
SALES (est): 88.96K **Privately Held**
SIC: **8351** Head Start center, except in conjunction with school

(G-3689)
TIMON FINANCIALS INC
8 The Grn Ste R (19901-3618)
PHONE..............................620 464-4247
Chizaram Ucheaga, *CEO*
EMP: **5**
SALES (est): 235.55K **Privately Held**
SIC: **4724** Travel agencies

(G-3690)
TIMOTHY S EARLY
83 Upland Ave (19901-4242)
PHONE..............................302 387-7374
EMP: **5** EST: 2019
SALES (est): 66.63K **Privately Held**
SIC: **8322** Individual and family services

(G-3691)
TLE VENTURES LTD
8 The Grn Ste A (19901-3618)
PHONE..............................800 794-3867
Teresa Espina, *CEO*
EMP: **8** EST: 2018
SALES (est): 518.72K **Privately Held**
SIC: **8748** Business consulting, nec

(G-3692)
TMC TRANSFORMERS USA INC ◊
874 Walker Rd (19904-2778)
PHONE..............................716 548-0825
Cristiano Palladini, *CEO*
EMP: **2** EST: 2022
SALES (est): 167.88K **Privately Held**
SIC: **3612** Power transformers, electric

(G-3693)
TNJD DIAMOND LLC
351 N New St (19904-3030)
PHONE..............................614 902-9431
EMP: **5**
SALES (est): 136.96K **Privately Held**
SIC: **4231** Trucking terminal facilities

(G-3694)
TNT GRAND LUX LLC ◊
8 The Grn Ste 212 (19901-3618)
PHONE..............................443 228-3193
Tiffany Daniels, *CEO*
EMP: **8** EST: 2023
SALES (est): 613.79K **Privately Held**
SIC: **4789** 7299 Transportation services, nec ; Facility rental and party planning services

(G-3695)
TOBOLA HEALTH CARE SVCS INC
1012 College Rd Ste 105 (19904-6506)
PHONE..............................302 389-8448
Oluyemi Awodiya, *CEO*
EMP: **74** EST: 2014
SALES (est): 3.7MM **Privately Held**
Web: www.tobolainc.com
SIC: **8082** Home health care services

(G-3696)
TOBY W MILLER
674 Rose Valley School Rd (19904-5507)
PHONE..............................302 270-1057
EMP: **5** EST: 2010
SALES (est): 106.88K **Privately Held**
SIC: **1799** Special trade contractors, nec

(G-3697)
TONY ASHBURN INC
872 Walker Rd Ste A (19904-2700)
PHONE..............................302 677-1940
Tony Ashburn, *Pr*
Theresa Ashburn, *VP*
EMP: **7** EST: 1978
SALES (est): 1.54MM **Privately Held**
Web: www.ashburnhomes.com
SIC: **1522** Residential construction, nec

(G-3698)
TOOZE & EASTER MD PA
Also Called: Moyer, Robert A MD
720 S Queen St (19904-3500)
P.O. Box 1416 (19903-1416)
PHONE..............................302 735-8700
J Hamilton Easter Md, *Prin*
EMP: **13** EST: 1994
SALES (est): 505.97K **Privately Held**
SIC: **8011** General and family practice, physician/surgeon

(G-3699)
TOP IMPACT LLC
8 The Grn (19901-3618)
PHONE..............................646 830-4324
EMP: **4** EST: 2020
SALES (est): 39.69K **Privately Held**
SIC: **3999** Education aids, devices and supplies

(G-3700)
TOP TIER TRUCKING INC
365 Northdown Dr (19904-5743)
PHONE..............................917 545-5170
Sheldine Edwards, *Pr*
EMP: **5** EST: 2021
SALES (est): 150K **Privately Held**
SIC: **4213** Trucking, except local

GEOGRAPHIC SECTION
Dover - Kent County (G-3731)

(G-3701)
TOPPERS SPA
1131 N Dupont Hwy (19901-2008)
PHONE..................302 857-2020
Judi Little, *Prin*
EMP: 10 **EST:** 2007
SALES (est): 68.01K **Privately Held**
Web: www.toppersspa.com
SIC: 7991 Spas

(G-3702)
TOPTEL INC
8 The Grn Ste D (19901-3618)
PHONE..................310 999-4320
Mikhael Cook, *Dir*
EMP: 5
SALES (est): 209.24K **Privately Held**
SIC: 4813 7389 Online service providers; Business Activities at Non-Commercial Site

(G-3703)
TORBERT FNRL CHPEL AMBLNCE SVC
61 S Bradford St (19904-7315)
PHONE..................302 734-3341
EMP: 7 **EST:** 2015
SALES (est): 73.57K **Privately Held**
Web: www.torbertfuneral.com
SIC: 7261 Funeral home

(G-3704)
TORBERT FUNERAL CHAPEL INC
Also Called: Capital Crematorium
61 S Bradford St (19904-7315)
PHONE..................302 734-3341
William Covell Torbert, *Pr*
EMP: 14 **EST:** 1918
SQ FT: 1,200
SALES (est): 499.2K **Privately Held**
Web: www.torbertfuneral.com
SIC: 7261 Funeral home

(G-3705)
TOSHIKO N RECKNER RPH
36 Holly Cove Ln (19901-6286)
PHONE..................302 697-6407
Toshiko N Reckner, *Prin*
EMP: 8 **EST:** 2012
SALES (est): 93.68K **Privately Held**
SIC: 8011 Medical centers

(G-3706)
TOWLES ELECTRIC INC
621 W Division St (19904)
P.O. Box 1012 (19903-1012)
PHONE..................302 674-4985
Nick Sebastian, *Pr*
EMP: 5 **EST:** 1978
SALES (est): 906.13K **Privately Held**
Web: www.towleselectric.com
SIC: 1731 General electrical contractor

(G-3707)
TOWNSEND BROS INC
21 Emerson Dr (19901-5819)
PHONE..................302 674-0100
Jeffrey S Townsend Senior, *Pr*
Ebe S Townsend Junior, *VP*
Wanda Townsend, *
EMP: 14 **EST:** 1930
SQ FT: 32,000
SALES (est): 2.18MM **Privately Held**
SIC: 5511 5013 Automobiles, new and used; Automotive supplies and parts

(G-3708)
TOXTRAP INC
12 S Springview Dr (19901-5550)
P.O. Box 241 (19962-0241)
PHONE..................302 698-1400
Donald R Wilkinson, *Pr*
Carol Wilkinson, *Sec*
J Robert Zettle, *VP*
EMP: 5 **EST:** 1981
SQ FT: 1,300
SALES (est): 400.43K **Privately Held**
Web: www.toxtrap.com
SIC: 3829 5049 Breathalyzers; Law enforcement equipment and supplies

(G-3709)
TP IT GROUP LLC ✪
8 The Grn Ste A (19901-3618)
PHONE..................302 444-0441
EMP: 5 **EST:** 2022
SALES (est): 207.81K **Privately Held**
SIC: 8742 7389 Management consulting services; Business Activities at Non-Commercial Site

(G-3710)
TPP ACQUISITION INC
1365 N Dupont Hwy Ste 4012 (19901-8710)
PHONE..................302 674-4805
EMP: 12
SALES (corp-wide): 49.93MM **Privately Held**
SIC: 7221 Photographer, still or video
PA: Tpp Acquisition Inc
    1155 Kas Dr
    Richardson TX 75081
    972 265-7721

(G-3711)
TRADE INVESTORS LLC
160 Greentree Dr Ste 101 (19904-7620)
PHONE..................888 579-0286
EMP: 9 **EST:** 2004
SALES (est): 150K **Privately Held**
SIC: 6282 Investment advice

(G-3712)
TRANQUIL SPIRIT MASSAGE & SPA
9 E Loockerman St Ste 208 (19901-7347)
PHONE..................302 538-1135
Holly Overmyer, *Owner*
EMP: 5 **EST:** 2017
SALES (est): 47.53K **Privately Held**
Web: tranquilspirit.vpweb.com
SIC: 7299 Massage parlor

(G-3713)
TRANSLATEAI LLC ✪
8 The Grn Ste A (19901-3618)
PHONE..................213 675-6702
Haihuai Shen, *Managing Member*
EMP: 20 **EST:** 2023
SALES (est): 593.07K **Privately Held**
SIC: 7371 Computer software development

(G-3714)
TRANSPORTTEE INC
8 The Grn Ste A (19901-3618)
PHONE..................302 330-8912
Sonji Arline, *Ex Dir*
EMP: 30 **EST:** 2020
SALES (est): 511.19K **Privately Held**
SIC: 8742 Transportation consultant

(G-3715)
TRANSSTATE JET SERVICE INC
139 Davis Cir (19904-3466)
PHONE..................302 346-3102
EMP: 12 **EST:** 2002
SALES (est): 149.94K **Privately Held**
SIC: 2911 Jet fuels

(G-3716)
TRAPS PLUMBING HEATING A/C
Also Called: Honeywell Authorized Dealer
1851 S Dupont Hwy (19901-5128)
PHONE..................302 677-1775
Trap Tracksem, *Owner*
EMP: 5 **EST:** 2001
SALES (est): 485.48K **Privately Held**
Web: www.honeywell.com
SIC: 1711 Warm air heating and air conditioning contractor

(G-3717)
TRAUMA FILM PRODUCTION PR LLC
8 The Grn Ste A (19901-3618)
PHONE..................623 582-2287
EMP: 6 **EST:** 2016
SALES (est): 560.52K **Privately Held**
SIC: 7822 Motion picture and tape distribution

(G-3718)
TRAVELORY INC ✪
8 The Grn Ste B (19901-3618)
PHONE..................925 216-0718
Arpit Gattani, *Pr*
EMP: 5 **EST:** 2022
SALES (est): 74.79K **Privately Held**
SIC: 7372 Prepackaged software

(G-3719)
TRAVLY US LLC (PA) ✪
Also Called: Travly
850 New Burton Rd Ste 201 (19904-5786)
PHONE..................901 228-5882
EMP: 6 **EST:** 2023
SALES (est): 81.26K
SALES (corp-wide): 81.26K **Privately Held**
SIC: 4724 Travel agencies

(G-3720)
TRENDZ SALON AND SPA
47 Greentree Dr (19904-2685)
PHONE..................302 632-3045
EMP: 9 **EST:** 2016
SALES (est): 222.44K **Privately Held**
Web: www.trendzscb.com
SIC: 7231 Cosmetology and personal hygiene salons

(G-3721)
TRESSES HAIR STUDIO
16 Squire Cir (19901-6113)
PHONE..................302 670-7356
EMP: 5 **EST:** 2018
SALES (est): 75.85K **Privately Held**
SIC: 7231 Hairdressers

(G-3722)
TRI COUNTY MATERIALS
3700 S Bay Rd (19901-5905)
PHONE..................302 677-0156
Mike Handy, *Owner*
EMP: 8 **EST:** 2015
SALES (est): 252.18K **Privately Held**
SIC: 1771 Blacktop (asphalt) work

(G-3723)
TRIAGONS LLC
8 The Grn Ste B (19901-3618)
PHONE..................619 761-0797
EMP: 5
SALES (est): 199.4K **Privately Held**
SIC: 7371 Computer software systems analysis and design, custom

(G-3724)
TRIANGLE HM IMPRVMNT CNTRCTRL
1410 Lochmeath Way (19901-6515)
PHONE..................302 883-4943
Thomas Marciano, *Owner*
EMP: 5 **EST:** 2012
SALES (est): 101.75K **Privately Held**
SIC: 1521 Single-family housing construction

(G-3725)
TRIBETECH SOLUTIONS LLC ✪
8 The Grn Ste A (19901-3618)
PHONE..................302 597-7890
Bianca Ackermann, *Managing Member*
EMP: 5 **EST:** 2023
SALES (est): 199.4K **Privately Held**
SIC: 7371 Custom computer programming services

(G-3726)
TRIDGE TRADE INC
8 The Grn Ste B (19901-3618)
PHONE..................954 512-3734
Hosik Shin, *CEO*
EMP: 10 **EST:** 2018
SALES (est): 3.14MM **Privately Held**
Web: www.tridge.com
SIC: 2037 Frozen fruits and vegetables
PA: Tridge Co., Ltd.
    1,2,4,5,6/F Nexen Gangnam Tower
    Seoul 06584

(G-3727)
TRIKORP INC ✪
Also Called: Triko
8 The Grn Ste A (19901-3618)
PHONE..................970 690-6285
Nicolas Parra, *CEO*
EMP: 7 **EST:** 2022
SALES (est): 355.22K **Privately Held**
SIC: 5045 7372 Computer software; Prepackaged software

(G-3728)
TRIPLEONE INC
8 The Grn Ste 8063 (19901-3618)
PHONE..................833 391-0111
James William Awad, *Managing Member*
EMP: 100 **EST:** 2018
SALES (est): 5MM **Privately Held**
SIC: 6719 Investment holding companies, except banks

(G-3729)
TRIVEDI FOUNDATION LLC
104 Overlook Pl (19901-4302)
PHONE..................302 678-4629
Michael Meyer, *Admn*
EMP: 5 **EST:** 2015
SALES (est): 40.68K **Privately Held**
SIC: 8641 Civic and social associations

(G-3730)
TROPOSPHERE TECHNOLOGIES LLC (PA)
8 The Grn Ste 5258 (19901-3618)
PHONE..................613 833-0984
Arnold Villeneuve, *Managing Member*
EMP: 7 **EST:** 2018
SALES (est): 100K
SALES (corp-wide): 100K **Privately Held**
Web: www.troposphere.tech
SIC: 7379 Online services technology consultants

(G-3731)
TROUTMAN MACHINE COMPANY INC
Also Called: A M T General Contracting
1175 S Governors Ave (19904-6903)

PHONE..................302 674-3540
EMP: 4 EST: 1992
SALES (est): 467.26K Privately Held
Web:
www.troutmanmachinecompany.com
SIC: 3599 Machine shop, jobbing and repair

(G-3732)
TRUCK STORE LLC
423 S Dupont Hwy (19901-4513)
PHONE..................302 724-5918
EMP: 6 EST: 2016
SALES (est): 90.5K Privately Held
Web: www.thetruckstore.com
SIC: 7549 High performance auto repair and service

(G-3733)
TUDOR ELECTRIC INC
801 Otis Dr (19901-4647)
PHONE..................302 736-1444
Robert H Tudor Ii, Pr
Robert H Tudor, VP
Patty Brough, *
Susan P Tudor, *
EMP: 24 EST: 1952
SQ FT: 8,400
SALES (est): 960.77K Privately Held
Web: www.tudorelectricinc.com
SIC: 1731 General electrical contractor

(G-3734)
TULA YOGA REIKI PROFESSIONALS
419 N Bradford St (19904-7203)
PHONE..................302 359-9790
Anoma Russum, Prin
EMP: 5 EST: 2015
SALES (est): 247.66K Privately Held
Web: www.tulayoganrp.com
SIC: 7999 Yoga instruction

(G-3735)
TWASH LLC
292 Trafalgar Dr (19904-9794)
PHONE..................302 488-0248
Travis Washington, Managing Member
EMP: 2
SALES (est): 92.41K Privately Held
SIC: 3069 Clothing, vulcanized rubber or rubberized fabric

(G-3736)
TWIN HEARTS MANAGEMENT LLC
200 Banning St Ste 340 (19904-3490)
PHONE..................302 777-5700
Anthony Alfieri, Prin
EMP: 5 EST: 2010
SALES (est): 192.26K Privately Held
SIC: 8741 Management services

(G-3737)
TYTRIX INC
8 The Grn (19901-3618)
PHONE..................877 489-8749
Syed Hyder, CEO
EMP: 22
SALES (est): 656.03K Privately Held
Web: www.tytrix.com
SIC: 8742 7389 Management consulting services; Business services, nec

(G-3738)
U AND I BUILDERS INC
1200 S Bay Rd (19901-4634)
PHONE..................302 697-1645
Usman Sandhu, Pr
EMP: 6 EST: 2008
SALES (est): 942.06K Privately Held
Web: www.uandibuilder.com
SIC: 1521 New construction, single-family houses

(G-3739)
U S FIRE FORCES INC
8 The Grn Ste 8068 (19901-3618)
PHONE..................302 270-8294
Schuyler Cudd, CEO
EMP: 10 EST: 2020
SALES (est): 500K Privately Held
SIC: 0851 Fire fighting services, forest

(G-3740)
U TAN INC
650 S Bay Rd Ste 11 (19901-4636)
PHONE..................302 674-8040
Lillian Kingsford, Pr
Aaron Kingsford, VP
EMP: 6 EST: 1990
SQ FT: 1,400
SALES (est): 104.9K Privately Held
Web: www.tan-u.net
SIC: 7299 Tanning salon

(G-3741)
UBLERB
9 E Loockerman St Ste 215 (19901-7347)
PHONE..................773 569-9686
Gerard Hartman, CEO
Keith Harris, CFO
EMP: 6 EST: 2014
SQ FT: 500
SALES (est): 320.28K Privately Held
SIC: 7379 Online services technology consultants

(G-3742)
UDR INC
Also Called: Cedar Chase Apartments
1700 N Dupont Hwy Ste 1 (19901-7812)
PHONE..................302 674-8887
Tracey Lund, Brnch Mgr
EMP: 7
SALES (corp-wide): 1.52B Publicly Held
Web: www.udr.com
SIC: 6513 Apartment building operators
PA: Udr, Inc.
1745 Shea Center Dr # 200
Highlands Ranch CO 80129
720 283-6120

(G-3743)
UKAP TRADING LLC
8 The Grn Ste A (19901-3618)
PHONE..................617 447-6490
Chaoneng Lv, Pr
EMP: 10 EST: 2017
SALES (est): 345.82K Privately Held
SIC: 5621 7389 Boutiques; Business Activities at Non-Commercial Site

(G-3744)
UKRAINE POWER RESOURCES LLC
8 The Grn Ste 11279 (19901-3618)
PHONE..................508 280-6910
Peter A Gish, CEO
Geoffrey Berlin, Prin
EMP: 2 EST: 2017
SALES (est): 88.38K Privately Held
Web: www.ukrainepowerresources.com
SIC: 3621 Windmills, electric generating

(G-3745)
ULTRA FITNESS INC
8 The Grn (19901-3618)
PHONE..................310 890-9025
EMP: 6
SALES (est): 96.94K Privately Held
SIC: 7371 Computer software development and applications

(G-3746)
UMIYA INC
Also Called: Dover Inn
428 N Dupont Hwy (19901-3906)
PHONE..................302 674-4011
Ram Patel, Pr
EMP: 6 EST: 1987
SALES (est): 361.32K Privately Held
SIC: 7011 Motels

(G-3747)
UNCHARTED WATERS LLC ◊
8 The Grn Ste 5608 (19901-3618)
PHONE..................302 213-6354
Anthony Baker, Managing Member
EMP: 30 EST: 2023
SALES (est): 1.17MM Privately Held
SIC: 8742 7336 7389 Management consulting services; Commercial art and graphic design; Business services, nec

(G-3748)
UNCORKED CANVAS PARTIES
125 W Loockerman St (19904-7325)
PHONE..................302 724-7625
EMP: 5 EST: 2015
SALES (est): 71.92K Privately Held
Web: www.uncorkedcanvasparties.com
SIC: 2211 Canvas

(G-3749)
UNIKIE INC
615 S Dupont Hwy (19901-4517)
PHONE..................408 839-1920
Seppo Kolari, Ch Bd
EMP: 10 EST: 2015
SALES (est): 426.06K Privately Held
Web: www.unikie.com
SIC: 7371 7389 Software programming applications; Business services, nec

(G-3750)
UNIQUE MASSAGE THERAPY
124 Lynnbroom Ln (19904-1463)
PHONE..................302 359-5982
Nnenna Amadi, Prin
EMP: 8 EST: 2015
SALES (est): 105.93K Privately Held
SIC: 8093 Rehabilitation center, outpatient treatment

(G-3751)
UNITED ELECTRIC SUPPLY CO INC
551 S Dupont Hwy (19901-4515)
PHONE..................302 674-8351
Mike Caloway, Brnch Mgr
EMP: 10
SALES (corp-wide): 244.47MM Privately Held
Web: www.unitedelectric.com
SIC: 5063 Electrical supplies, nec
PA: United Electric Supply Company, Inc.
10 Bellecor Dr
New Castle DE 19720
800 322-3374

(G-3752)
UNIVERSAL ALGORITHM INC
8 The Grn Ste 8167 (19901-3618)
PHONE..................302 446-3562
Pauletta Thompson, Prin
Amber Bruns, Prin
Tiara Thomas, Prin
Brandi Doyle, Prin
Jelani Finley, Prin
EMP: 6 EST: 2020
SALES (est): 267.4K Privately Held
SIC: 7371 Computer software development

(G-3753)
UNIVERSAL ASSEMBLING ENTP LLC
738 N Dupont Hwy (19901-3939)
PHONE..................302 543-3629
EMP: 10 EST: 2020
SALES (est): 203.25K Privately Held
Web: www.universalassembling.com
SIC: 7299 Home improvement and renovation contractor agency

(G-3754)
UNIVERSAL EXTERIORS LLC
164 Hatteras Dr (19904-3883)
PHONE..................302 563-7900
EMP: 5 EST: 2014
SALES (est): 238.73K Privately Held
SIC: 1542 Nonresidential construction, nec

(G-3755)
UNIVERSUM INC ◊
614 N Dupont Hwy Ste 210 (19901-3900)
PHONE..................973 873-2636
Jan Domozilov, Pr
EMP: 7 EST: 2024
SALES (est): 264.9K Privately Held
SIC: 7371 Custom computer programming services

(G-3756)
UPBOUND GROUP INC
Also Called: Rent-A-Center
655 S Bay Rd Ste 204 (19901-4680)
PHONE..................302 734-2094
Scott Johnson, Brnch Mgr
EMP: 5
Web: www.rentacenter.com
SIC: 7311 7359 Advertising agencies; Appliance rental
PA: Upbound Group, Inc.
5501 Headquarters Dr
Plano TX 75024

(G-3757)
UPBOUND GROUP INC
Also Called: Rent-A-Center
137 Jerome Dr Ste 170 (19901-2369)
PHONE..................302 678-4676
Wandfa Hill, Mgr
EMP: 5
Web: www.rentacenter.com
SIC: 7359 Appliance rental
PA: Upbound Group, Inc.
5501 Headquarters Dr
Plano TX 75024

(G-3758)
UPBOUND GROUP INC
Also Called: Rent-A-Center
1688 S Governors Ave (19904-7004)
PHONE..................302 734-3505
EMP: 5
Web: www.rentacenter.com
SIC: 7359 Appliance rental
PA: Upbound Group, Inc.
5501 Headquarters Dr
Plano TX 75024

(G-3759)
UPLIFT BARBERSHOP
1534 S Governors Ave Ste B (19904-7054)
PHONE..................302 883-3001
Andre Boggerty, Owner
EMP: 5 EST: 2013
SALES (est): 41.01K Privately Held
SIC: 7241 Barber shops

(G-3760)
UPPERCUT INC
Also Called: Upper Cut The
119 S Dupont Hwy (19901-7432)

GEOGRAPHIC SECTION
Dover - Kent County (G-3790)

PHONE.................302 736-1661
Carol Brennan, *Pr*
EMP: 8 **EST:** 1986
SALES (est): 245.79K **Privately Held**
Web: www.uppercut.com
SIC: 7231 Hairdressers

(G-3761)
URBIE INC
8 The Grn (19901-3618)
PHONE.................302 572-4243
Bilain Jouni, *CEO*
EMP: 5 **EST:** 2020
SALES (est): 359.65K **Privately Held**
SIC: 3634 Electric housewares and fans

(G-3762)
UROLOGY ASSOCIATES DOVER PA
200 Banning St Ste 250 (19904-3492)
PHONE.................302 674-1728
J Henry Kim, *Pr*
Doctor Jason Walther, *Treas*
EMP: 30 **EST:** 1963
SQ FT: 3,000
SALES (est): 2.67MM **Privately Held**
Web: www.urologydelaware.com
SIC: 8011 Urologist

(G-3763)
US CHERRY LLC
Also Called: US Cherry
8 The Grn Ste B (19901-3618)
PHONE.................305 339-5318
Nicolas Reyes T, *CEO*
EMP: 5 **EST:** 2019
SALES (est): 436.57K **Privately Held**
Web: www.uscherry.com
SIC: 6282 Investment advice

(G-3764)
US DEPT OF THE AIR FORCE
Also Called: 436th Medical Group
300 Tuskegee Blvd Ste 1b22 (19902-5003)
PHONE.................302 677-2525
Timothy Tendergrass, *Mgr*
EMP: 31
Web: www.af.mil
SIC: 8093 9711 Specialty outpatient clinics, nec; Air Force
HQ: The United States Department Of Air Force
10690 Air Force Pentagon
Washington DC 20330

(G-3765)
US RAVENS LOGISTICS INC
8 The Grn Ste B (19901-3618)
PHONE.................302 401-4033
Varinder Rajoria, *Pr*
Alex Christian, *Operations MNG*
Harvey Walton, *Dir Opers*
EMP: 80 **EST:** 2021
SALES (est): 2MM **Privately Held**
Web: www.usravens.com
SIC: 4731 7389 Brokers, shipping; Business Activities at Non-Commercial Site

(G-3766)
USA FULFILLMENT
1870 Lynnbury Woods Rd (19904-1801)
PHONE.................410 810-0880
EMP: 9 **EST:** 2019
SALES (est): 225.66K **Privately Held**
Web: www.usafill.com
SIC: 4225 General warehousing

(G-3767)
USA FULFILLMENT INC
1870 Lynnbury Woods Rd (19904-1801)
PHONE.................410 810-0880

EMP: 15 **EST:** 1986
SALES (est): 528.08K **Privately Held**
Web: www.usafill.com
SIC: 4225 General warehousing

(G-3768)
UZIN UTZ MANUFACTURING N AMER
200 Garrison Oak Dr (19901-3365)
PHONE.................336 456-4624
Phillip Utz, *Mgr*
EMP: 10 **EST:** 2015
SALES (est): 526.17K **Privately Held**
Web: us.uzin-utz.com
SIC: 3999 Manufacturing industries, nec

(G-3769)
UZIN UTZ NORTH AMERICA INC
Also Called: Ufloor Systems
200 Garrison Oak Dr (19901-3365)
PHONE.................302 450-1715
Matthias Liebert, *Brnch Mgr*
EMP: 97
Web: us.uzin.com
SIC: 7389 Automobile recovery service
HQ: Uzin Utz North America, Inc.
14509 E 33rd Pl Ste G
Aurora CO 80011

(G-3770)
UZUAKOLI DEV & CULTURAL ASSN
2319 S Dupont Hwy (19901-5514)
PHONE.................302 465-3266
Ihuoma Chuks, *VP*
EMP: 21
SIC: 8399 Community development groups
PA: Uzuakoli Development And Cultural Association
10311 Adams St
Omaha NE 68127

(G-3771)
VAL CAPITAL HOLDINGS LLC
767 Walker Rd Ste 20 (19904-2753)
PHONE.................800 997-4166
Veronica Vera, *Managing Member*
EMP: 25 **EST:** 2019
SALES (est): 250K **Privately Held**
SIC: 7389 Business services, nec

(G-3772)
VALLEY LANDSCAPING AND CON INC
8 The Grn (19901-3618)
PHONE.................302 922-5020
Paul Kantner, *Pr*
EMP: 5 **EST:** 2016
SALES (est): 335.02K **Privately Held**
SIC: 3271 Blocks, concrete: landscape or retaining wall

(G-3773)
VANGUARD CONSTRUCTION INC
2089 S Dupont Hwy (19901-5566)
PHONE.................302 697-9187
William L Stayton Junior, *Pr*
EMP: 7 **EST:** 1989
SQ FT: 1,000
SALES (est): 1.47MM **Privately Held**
SIC: 1542 1521 Commercial and office building, new construction; New construction, single-family houses

(G-3774)
VANGUARD VENTURE GROUP LLC
8 The Grn Ste B (19901-3618)
PHONE.................954 324-8736
EMP: 5 **EST:** 2021
SALES (est): 207.81K **Privately Held**
SIC: 8742 Marketing consulting services

(G-3775)
VARIGLE LLC
8 The Grn Ste A (19901-3618)
PHONE.................858 336-9471
EMP: 12 **EST:** 2017
SALES (est): 535.58K **Privately Held**
SIC: 3524 Lawn and garden equipment

(G-3776)
VAULT OIL & GAS LLC
850 New Burton Rd Ste 201 (19904-5786)
PHONE.................303 731-0080
EMP: 5 **EST:** 2019
SALES (est): 67.62K **Privately Held**
SIC: 1382 Oil and gas exploration services

(G-3777)
VCG LLC
9 E Loockerman St Ste 3a-522 (19901-8306)
PHONE.................302 336-8151
Frank Johnson, *Managing Member*
EMP: 5 **EST:** 2013
SQ FT: 600
SALES (est): 245.47K **Privately Held**
SIC: 8742 Construction project management consultant

(G-3778)
VEEGLIFE LLC
3500 S Dupont Hwy (19901-6041)
PHONE.................310 866-8249
EMP: 3 **EST:** 2021
SALES (est): 250K **Privately Held**
SIC: 7372 Application computer software

(G-3779)
VEEZYS HOLDING COMPANY LLC (PA) ✪
8 The Grn Ste A (19901-3618)
PHONE.................302 307-2418
Rayvon Bush, *Managing Member*
EMP: 11 **EST:** 2023
SALES (est): 512.42K
SALES (corp-wide): 512.42K **Privately Held**
SIC: 6531 7389 Real estate agents and managers; Business Activities at Non-Commercial Site

(G-3780)
VEIN CENTER AT EDEN H
200 Banning St Ste 300 (19904-3488)
P.O. Box 576 (19903-0576)
PHONE.................302 735-8850
EMP: 8 **EST:** 2018
SALES (est): 163K **Privately Held**
Web: www.veincenterdelaware.com
SIC: 8011 Cardiologist and cardio-vascular specialist

(G-3781)
VENDING SOLUTIONS LLC
131 Rosemary Rd (19901-7245)
P.O. Box 400 (19903-0400)
PHONE.................302 674-2222
Schuyler Sills, *CEO*
EMP: 7 **EST:** 2017
SALES (est): 740.08K **Privately Held**
SIC: 5999 5046 5087 5962 Alarm and safety equipment stores; Vending machines, coin-operated; Vending machines and supplies; Candy and snack food vending machines

(G-3782)
VERBSPACE SOLUTIONS INC
8 The Grn Ste A (19901-3618)
P.O. Box 573 (91740-0573)
PHONE.................626 524-3003
Jibril Ellams, *Pr*

EMP: 10 **EST:** 2009
SALES (est): 647.73K **Privately Held**
SIC: 7379 Online services technology consultants

(G-3783)
VERGE INTERNET INC
8 The Grn Ste A (19901-3618)
PHONE.................202 827-5120
Christopher Wolff, *CEO*
EMP: 5 **EST:** 2020
SALES (est): 33.14K **Privately Held**
SIC: 4813 Internet connectivity services

(G-3784)
VERIDIAN SOLUTIONS LLC
8 The Grn Ste 8189 (19901-3618)
PHONE.................832 867-7263
EMP: 11 **EST:** 2018
SALES (est): 493.21K **Privately Held**
Web: www.veridian.info
SIC: 7379 Computer related consulting services

(G-3785)
VERISOFT INC
48 Kings Hwy (19901-3817)
PHONE.................602 908-7151
Robert Almoney, *Pr*
Jeanette Almoney, *Sec*
EMP: 2 **EST:** 1999
SALES (est): 143.79K **Privately Held**
Web: www.verisoftgroup.com
SIC: 3589 Water treatment equipment, industrial

(G-3786)
VERNON GREEN HYDROGEN LLC ✪
8 The Grn (19901-3618)
PHONE.................609 772-7979
Vishal Shah, *Managing Member*
EMP: 5 **EST:** 2023
SALES (est): 78.16K **Privately Held**
SIC: 2813 Industrial gases

(G-3787)
VERY LLC
160 Greentree Dr Ste 101 (19904-7620)
PHONE.................630 945-5539
Ryan Prosser, *Managing Member*
EMP: 90 **EST:** 2021
SALES (est): 1.85MM **Privately Held**
SIC: 7373 Systems software development services

(G-3788)
VETERANS UNTD OUTREACH DEL INC
726 E Division St (19901-4204)
PHONE.................302 678-1285
Michael Snyder, *Prin*
EMP: 5 **EST:** 2010
SALES (est): 56.5K **Privately Held**
Web: www.veteransunitedoutreach.com
SIC: 8322 Outreach program

(G-3789)
VIACOM LIMITED
1221 College Park Dr # 203 (19904-8726)
PHONE.................484 857-7116
Qixian Chen, *Pr*
EMP: 16 **EST:** 2021
SALES (est): 184.99K **Privately Held**
SIC: 7822 Motion picture and tape distribution

(G-3790)
VICDANIA HEALTH SERVICES LLC
Also Called: Vicdania Health Svc
1006 College Rd Ste 101 (19904-6569)

(PA)=Parent Co (HQ)=Headquarters
✪ = New Business established in last 2 years

2024 Harris Directory of Delaware Businesses

Dover - Kent County (G-3791) — GEOGRAPHIC SECTION

PHONE..............................302 672-0139
Dannette Moore, Mgr
EMP: 50 EST: 2013
SALES (est): 1.74MM Privately Held
Web: www.vicdaniahomehealth.com
SIC: 8082 Home health care services

(G-3791)
VICKS COMMERCIAL CLG & MAINT
378 Mannering Dr (19901-5407)
P.O. Box 1433 (19903-1433)
PHONE..............................302 697-9591
Leah Dickerson, Prin
EMP: 7 EST: 2009
SALES (est): 124.22K Privately Held
SIC: 7349 Building maintenance services, nec

(G-3792)
VICTORY CLEANING LLC
18 Mifflin Mdws (19901-6438)
PHONE..............................267 330-9422
Sakarah Bey, Mgr
EMP: 5
SALES (est): 70.85K Privately Held
SIC: 7699 7389 Cleaning services; Business Activities at Non-Commercial Site

(G-3793)
VIDEO SCENE OF DELAWARE INC (PA)
Also Called: Video Scene
Bay Rd Rr 113 (19901)
P.O. Box 794 (19903-0794)
PHONE..............................302 678-8526
James Michael Cullen Junior, Pr
James Michael Cullen Junior, Pr
Thomas D Cullen, VP
EMP: 5 EST: 1984
SQ FT: 7,000
SALES (est): 1.82MM
SALES (corp-wide): 1.82MM Privately Held
SIC: 7841 5735 Video disk/tape rental to the general public; Video tapes, prerecorded

(G-3794)
VIDFLUENCER LLC
8 The Grn Ste A (19901-3618)
PHONE..............................917 745-3713
EMP: 5 EST: 2017
SALES (est): 58.42K Privately Held
SIC: 7812 Video production

(G-3795)
VIE INCORPORATED
8 The Grn Ste A (19901-3618)
PHONE..............................512 200-7638
Jake Bass, Prin
EMP: 5
SALES (est): 68.89K Privately Held
SIC: 7389 Business services, nec

(G-3796)
VILLAGE AT BLUE HEN
400 Haslet St (19901-4258)
PHONE..............................302 450-1265
EMP: 8 EST: 2013
SALES (est): 89.16K Privately Held
Web: www.pettinaro.com
SIC: 6513 Apartment building operators

(G-3797)
VILLAGES OF NOBLES POND PHASE
13 Nobles Pond Xing (19904-1296)
PHONE..............................302 736-5000
Harry D Miller Iii, Prin
EMP: 8 EST: 2013
SALES (est): 277.13K Privately Held
Web: www.noblespondlifestyle.com
SIC: 6552 Subdividers and developers, nec

(G-3798)
VINCENT ABBRESCIA
200 Banning St (19904-3485)
PHONE..............................302 734-1414
Vincent Abbrescia, Prin
EMP: 9 EST: 2010
SALES (est): 222.44K Privately Held
Web: www.edenhillmedicalcenter.com
SIC: 8011 Internal medicine practitioners

(G-3799)
VINISIA INC
8 The Grn Ste A (19901-3618)
PHONE..............................252 297-6730
Mohammed Mansour, CEO
EMP: 10 EST: 2021
SALES (est): 458.35K Privately Held
Web: www.vinisiaco.com
SIC: 5331 7389 Variety stores; Business services, nec

(G-3800)
VISAVIS INC
8 The Grn (19901-3618)
PHONE..............................858 952-4175
Bridget Regan, CEO
EMP: 5
SALES (est): 70.36K Privately Held
SIC: 7379 Online services technology consultants

(G-3801)
VISIONARY CNSLTING PRTNERS LLC
301 Doveview Dr Unit 204 (19904-3496)
PHONE..............................302 487-4200
EMP: 5 EST: 2020
SALES (est): 204.19K Privately Held
SIC: 7379 Online services technology consultants

(G-3802)
VISIONARY ENERGY SYSTEMS INC
325 Alder Rd (19904-4819)
PHONE..............................410 739-4342
Steven R Rock, Pr
EMP: 3 EST: 2009
SALES (est): 132.86K Privately Held
SIC: 3499 Fabricated metal products, nec

(G-3803)
VISIONQUEST EYE CARE CENTER
Also Called: Visionquest Eye Care Center
820 Walker Rd (19904-2727)
PHONE..............................302 678-3545
Philip Gross, Prin
EMP: 45 EST: 1990
SALES (est): 1.2MM Privately Held
Web: www.vqeyecare.com
SIC: 8042 Offices and clinics of optometrists

(G-3804)
VISIONQUEST NONPROFIT CORP
1001 S Bradford St Ste 1 (19904-4153)
PHONE..............................302 735-1666
Marlene Devonshire, Mgr
EMP: 18
SIC: 8361 Residential care
PA: Visionquest Nonprofit Corporation
600 N Swan Rd
Tucson AZ 85711

(G-3805)
VISITING ANGELS OF DOVER
850 New Burton Rd (19904-5785)
PHONE..............................302 346-7777
EMP: 12 EST: 2017
SALES (est): 61.69K Privately Held
Web: www.visitingangels.com
SIC: 8082 Home health care services

(G-3806)
VOICELY SOCIAL INC ◆
8 The Grn Ste A (19901-3618)
PHONE..............................302 446-4011
Aleksandr Malshakov, CEO
EMP: 10 EST: 2022
SALES (est): 501.99K Privately Held
Web: www.voicely.me
SIC: 4899 Communication services, nec

(G-3807)
VOIP SUPPLIER LLC
8 The Grn Ste 7879 (19901-3618)
PHONE..............................302 760-9237
Ambrose Zaffar, Prin
EMP: 5 EST: 2018
SALES (est): 77.06K Privately Held
Web: www.thevoipsupplier.com
SIC: 4813 Internet connectivity services

(G-3808)
VOITLEX CORP
8 The Grn Ste A (19901-3618)
PHONE..............................302 288-0670
Aliaksandr Vaitovich, Prin
EMP: 10 EST: 2017
SALES (est): 349.02K Privately Held
SIC: 7389 Business services, nec

(G-3809)
VOLUMETRIC FORMAT ASSOCIATION
8 The Grn Ste 11383 (19901-3618)
PHONE..............................760 803-8720
Lisa Robotti, Prin
EMP: 5 EST: 2020
SALES (est): 128K Privately Held
Web: www.volumetricformat.org
SIC: 8741 Business management

(G-3810)
VOSHELL BROS WELDING INC
Also Called: Voshell Brothers
1769 Kenton Rd (19904-1350)
PHONE..............................302 674-1414
Gale Voshell, Pr
Diana Voshell, *
EMP: 49 EST: 1957
SQ FT: 10,000
SALES (est): 5.58MM Privately Held
SIC: 1623 1611 Oil and gas pipeline construction; Highway and street paving contractor

(G-3811)
VOX AI INC ◆
Also Called: Sharly.ai
8 The Grn Ste A (19901-3618)
PHONE..............................302 288-0670
Simone Maria Macario, Prin
EMP: 2 EST: 2022
SALES (est): 87.4K Privately Held
SIC: 7372 Prepackaged software

(G-3812)
VSHIELD SOFTWARE CORP
3500 S Dupont Hwy (19901-6041)
PHONE..............................302 531-0855
Marino Kriheli, Prin
EMP: 8 EST: 2009
SALES (est): 85.91K Privately Held
Web: corp.delaware.gov
SIC: 7372 Prepackaged software

(G-3813)
VTMS LLC
Also Called: Mymortgageready.com
3 Mineral Ct (19904-3704)
PHONE..............................302 264-9094
EMP: 6 EST: 2010
SALES (est): 360K Privately Held
SIC: 8748 8742 7389 Business consulting, nec; Marketing consulting services; Business services, nec

(G-3814)
VTRADERIO LLC
1221 College Park Dr (19904-8726)
PHONE..............................646 952-1189
Stephen Gregory, Managing Member
EMP: 5
SALES (est): 81.29K Privately Held
SIC: 6221 Commodity contracts brokers, dealers

(G-3815)
VUE EVENTS INC
Also Called: Orcavue
8 The Grn Ste 4202 (19901-3618)
P.O. Box 16601 (22215-1601)
PHONE..............................301 812-3800
Daniel Rosenberry, CEO
EMP: 6 EST: 2018
SALES (est): 219.13K Privately Held
SIC: 7389 Business services, nec

(G-3816)
W H THOMAS DDS
1981 S State St (19901-5811)
PHONE..............................302 697-1152
W H Thomas D.d.s., Owner
W H Thomas, Owner
EMP: 6 EST: 1985
SALES (est): 241.28K Privately Held
Web: www.thomasfamilydentist.com
SIC: 8021 Dentists' office

(G-3817)
WALLACE LAMARR
137 S Queen St (19904-3294)
PHONE..............................202 460-3377
Lamarr Wallace, Owner
EMP: 2
SALES (est): 62.23K Privately Held
SIC: 1389 7389 Construction, repair, and dismantling services; Business services, nec

(G-3818)
WALNUT GROVE CABINETS LLC
308 Rose Valley School Rd (19904-5504)
PHONE..............................302 678-2694
EMP: 2 EST: 2009
SALES (est): 215.51K Privately Held
SIC: 2434 Wood kitchen cabinets

(G-3819)
WALTER L FOX POST 2 INC
835 S Bay Rd (19901-4632)
PHONE..............................302 674-1741
Danny Seeman, Pr
Michael Cohill, *
EMP: 8 EST: 1985
SALES (est): 376.11K Privately Held
SIC: 8641 Veterans' organization

(G-3820)
WARD & TAYLOR LLC
83 Greentree Dr (19904-7646)
PHONE..............................302 346-7000
Katie Boulden, Brnch Mgr
EMP: 5
Web: www.wardtaylor.com
SIC: 8111 Legal services

GEOGRAPHIC SECTION
Dover - Kent County (G-3850)

PA: Ward & Taylor, Llc
2710 Centerville Rd # 210
Wilmington DE 19808

(G-3821)
WARRING NATION INC
1221 College Park Dr # 116 (19904-8726)
PHONE..............................757 323-6312
Ethan Warring, *Pr*
EMP: 5 **EST:** 2020
SALES (est): 56.54K **Privately Held**
SIC: 7372 Application computer software

(G-3822)
WATCHDOGDEVELOPMENTCOM LLC
614 N Dupont Hwy Ste 210 (19901-3900)
P.O. Box 3508 (84323-3508)
PHONE..............................888 488-7531
Sean Buffington, *CEO*
EMP: 5 **EST:** 2015
SALES (est): 204.89K **Privately Held**
Web: www.watchdog.dev
SIC: 7373 Systems software development services

(G-3823)
WE DESERVE IT SHS FOR KIDS INC
363 Frear Dr (19901-6612)
PHONE..............................302 521-7255
Jackie Yates, *CEO*
EMP: 5 **EST:** 2015
SALES (est): 85.22K **Privately Held**
SIC: 8322 Childrens' aid society

(G-3824)
WEALTH MANAGEMENT GROUP
220 Beiser Blvd (19904-7790)
PHONE..............................302 734-5826
EMP: 9 **EST:** 2019
SALES (est): 1.49MM **Privately Held**
Web: www.wmgadvisors.com
SIC: 6282 Investment advisory service
PA: Savant Capital, Llc
190 Buckley Dr
Rockford IL 61107

(G-3825)
WEB DATA SOLUTIONS LLC
160 Greentree Dr Ste 101 (19904-7620)
PHONE..............................888 407-5089
Abraham Smilowitz, *Managing Member*
EMP: 50 **EST:** 2016
SALES (est): 407.4K **Privately Held**
SIC: 7299 Dating service

(G-3826)
WEBBER TITLE LLC
556 Fieldcrest Dr (19904-1088)
PHONE..............................302 218-0911
Daniel Webber, *Prin*
EMP: 5 **EST:** 2008
SALES (est): 151.5K **Privately Held**
SIC: 6541 Title and trust companies

(G-3827)
WEBEETA LLC ✪
8 The Grn (19901-3618)
PHONE..............................720 316-1876
EMP: 20 **EST:** 2022
SALES (est): 600.73K **Privately Held**
SIC: 7379 Online services technology consultants

(G-3828)
WEBER GALLAGHER SIMPSON (PA)
19 S State St Ste 102 (19901-7318)
PHONE..............................302 346-6377
Mary Sherlock, *Mgr*
EMP: 5 **EST:** 2011
SALES (est): 411.6K
SALES (corp-wide): 411.6K **Privately Held**
Web: www.wglaw.com
SIC: 8111 General practice attorney, lawyer

(G-3829)
WELLABS INC
8 The Grn Ste 300 (19901-3618)
PHONE..............................816 774-4030
Nikita Stolyarov, *Pr*
Evgeniy Matyitsin, *Prin*
EMP: 3 **EST:** 2021
SALES (est): 132.42K **Privately Held**
Web: www.shopwellabs.com
SIC: 2023 Dietary supplements, dairy and non-dairy based

(G-3830)
WELLFORD CORPORATION
8 The Grn Ste 8174 (19901-3618)
PHONE..............................302 288-0670
Turhan Karadas, *Pr*
EMP: 7 **EST:** 2004
SALES (est): 322.35K **Privately Held**
SIC: 7371 Software programming applications

(G-3831)
WELLTHY INVESTORS LLC
191 Fawn Haven Walk (19901-6592)
PHONE..............................267 847-3486
Cinarda Hamilton, *CEO*
EMP: 4 **EST:** 2021
SALES (est): 180.26K **Privately Held**
SIC: 2731 5942 2844 5999 Pamphlets: publishing and printing; Children's books; Perfumes, cosmetics and other toilet preparations; Cosmetics

(G-3832)
WELTIO LLC
8 The Grn (19901-3618)
PHONE..............................305 307-9815
EMP: 10
SALES (est): 636.63K **Privately Held**
SIC: 6141 7389 Consumer finance companies; Business Activities at Non-Commercial Site

(G-3833)
WELTRI INC
8 The Grn Ste 12596 (19901-3618)
PHONE..............................818 962-8834
Gajaba Hewamadduma, *CEO*
EMP: 12 **EST:** 2021
SALES (est): 65.76K **Privately Held**
SIC: 7999 Physical fitness instruction

(G-3834)
WENDY DIXON LLC
63 Sweetflag Dr (19904-1444)
PHONE..............................302 387-7103
Wendy Dixon, *Managing Member*
EMP: 7
SALES (est): 76.69K **Privately Held**
SIC: 3471 Cleaning, polishing, and finishing

(G-3835)
WESLEY PLAY CARE CENTER
Also Called: Wesley Preschool
209 S State St (19901-6727)
PHONE..............................302 678-8987
Debbie Deburr, *Dir*
EMP: 18 **EST:** 1974
SALES (est): 127.31K **Privately Held**
Web: www.wesleyumc-dover.com
SIC: 8351 Child day care services

(G-3836)
WEST DOVER DENTAL LLC
125 Greentree Dr Ste 2 (19904-7656)
PHONE..............................302 734-0330
EMP: 12 **EST:** 2019
SALES (est): 387.03K **Privately Held**
Web: www.westdoverdental.com
SIC: 8021 Dentists' office

(G-3837)
WESTLAND ENTERTAINMENT LLC
1221 College Park Dr (19904-8726)
PHONE..............................630 988-9684
EMP: 6 **EST:** 2020
SALES (est): 90.22K **Privately Held**
SIC: 7929 Entertainment service

(G-3838)
WESTSIDE FAMILY HEALTHCARE INC
1020 Forrest Ave (19904-2799)
PHONE..............................302 678-4622
Shannon Bartow, *Mgr*
EMP: 35
Web: www.westsidehealth.org
SIC: 8011 Clinic, operated by physicians
PA: Westside Family Healthcare, Inc.
300 Water St Ste 200
Wilmington DE 19801

(G-3839)
WESTWARD LLC
8 The Grn (19901-3618)
PHONE..............................570 609-3500
EMP: 5
SALES (est): 117.43K **Privately Held**
SIC: 5999 7389 Miscellaneous retail stores, nec; Business services, nec

(G-3840)
WHATARETHOSE INC ✪
8 The Grn Ste B (19901-3618)
PHONE..............................443 467-3687
Soumya Pattanayak, *Prin*
EMP: 2 **EST:** 2023
SALES (est): 87.4K **Privately Held**
SIC: 7372 Prepackaged software

(G-3841)
WHATCOAT CHRISTIAN PRESCHOOL
16 Main St (19901-1708)
PHONE..............................302 698-2108
Leanne Jackson, *Dir*
Lee Anne Jackson, *Dir*
EMP: 7 **EST:** 2007
SALES (est): 194.81K **Privately Held**
Web: www.whatcoat.com
SIC: 8351 Preschool center

(G-3842)
WHATCOAT SOCIAL SERVICE AGENCY
Also Called: Ruth N Dorsey Relief Shelter
381 College Rd (19904-2236)
PHONE..............................302 734-0319
Ruth Pugh, *Dir*
EMP: 21 **EST:** 1977
SALES (est): 234.08K **Privately Held**
Web: www.peoplesplace2.com
SIC: 8322 Social service center

(G-3843)
WHATCOAT VILLAGE ASSOC LLC
992 Whatcoat Dr Apt 12 (19904-2755)
P.O. Box 994 (08053-0994)
PHONE..............................856 596-0500
John J O'donnell, *Pr*
Michael J Levitt, *VP*
EMP: 10
SQ FT: 69,000
SALES (est): 459.07K **Privately Held**
Web: www.liveatwhatcoat.com
SIC: 6513 Apartment building operators

(G-3844)
WHISPERING MEADOWS LLC
4110b Connecticut Ln (19901-6337)
PHONE..............................302 698-1073
EMP: 8 **EST:** 2006
SQ FT: 950
SALES (est): 1.14MM
SALES (corp-wide): 661.26MM **Privately Held**
SIC: 8741 Management services
HQ: Hunt Elp, Ltd
4401 N Mesa St
El Paso TX 79902
915 298-0474

(G-3845)
WHITE OAK HEAD START
195 Willis Rd (19901-4085)
PHONE..............................302 736-5933
EMP: 5 **EST:** 2010
SALES (est): 78.56K **Privately Held**
SIC: 8351 Head Start center, except in conjunction with school

(G-3846)
WHSTLE CORPORATION ✪
8 The Grn Ste 300 (19901-3618)
PHONE..............................925 413-3316
Matthew Lasker, *CEO*
EMP: 2 **EST:** 2022
SALES (est): 87.4K **Privately Held**
SIC: 7372 7389 Prepackaged software; Business services, nec

(G-3847)
WIBDI AVIATION CO CORP
8 The Grn (19901-3618)
PHONE..............................305 677-9685
Abdirahman Rage, *CEO*
EMP: 10 **EST:** 2021
SALES (est): 621.63K **Privately Held**
SIC: 3429 7389 Aircraft hardware; Business services, nec

(G-3848)
WIGGINS GROUP LLC
8 The Grn Ste 10359 (19901-3618)
PHONE..............................800 590-8070
Kenneth Wiggins, *Prin*
Tynieka Wiggins, *Prin*
EMP: 12 **EST:** 2020
SALES (est): 697.09K **Privately Held**
SIC: 4214 Local trucking with storage

(G-3849)
WILD MEADOWS HOMES
529 Weaver Dr (19901-1377)
PHONE..............................302 730-4700
Harry Miller, *Owner*
EMP: 5 **EST:** 2001
SALES (est): 198.03K **Privately Held**
SIC: 6514 Residential building, four or fewer units: operation

(G-3850)
WILKISONS MARKING SERVICE INC
22 Stevens St (19901-5533)
PHONE..............................302 697-3669
Robert Wilkison, *Pr*
Patricia Faye Adcox, *VP*
EMP: 5 **EST:** 1970
SQ FT: 3,500
SALES (est): 425.61K **Privately Held**
Web: www.wilkisonmarkingservice.com

SIC: 1721 Residential painting

(G-3851)
WILLIAM HEYDT
767 Walker Rd (19904-2753)
PHONE..................................302 678-1161
William Heydt, *Owner*
EMP: 5 EST: 2017
SALES (est): 89.8K **Privately Held**
SIC: 6411 Insurance agents, brokers, and service

(G-3852)
WILLIES AUTO DETAIL SERVICE
17 Weston Dr (19904-2713)
PHONE..................................302 734-1010
Willie Mills, *Owner*
EMP: 5 EST: 1978
SALES (est): 237.61K **Privately Held**
SIC: 7542 Washing and polishing, automotive

(G-3853)
WILLIS GROUP LLC
4 The Grn (19901-3617)
PHONE..................................302 632-9898
Lincoln Willis, *CEO*
EMP: 5 EST: 2016
SALES (est): 166.67K **Privately Held**
Web: www.thewillisgroupllc.com
SIC: 8743 Lobbyist

(G-3854)
WILLIS LAW LLC
117 W Reed St (19904-7321)
PHONE..................................302 535-3200
Laura Willis, *Prin*
EMP: 5 EST: 2018
SALES (est): 233.46K **Privately Held**
SIC: 8111 General practice attorney, lawyer

(G-3855)
WILMINGTON SAVINGS FUND SOC
1486 Forrest Ave (19904-3380)
PHONE..................................302 677-1891
Diane Simone, *Mgr*
EMP: 6
SALES (corp-wide): 963.95MM **Publicly Held**
Web: www.wsfsbank.com
SIC: 6022 State commercial banks
HQ: Wilmington Savings Fund Society
500 Delaware Ave
Wilmington DE 19801
302 792-6000

(G-3856)
WILSON DUNES CONDO COUNCI
220 Beiser Blvd (19904-7790)
PHONE..................................302 542-1899
EMP: 7 EST: 2009
SALES (est): 71.28K **Privately Held**
SIC: 8641 Condominium association

(G-3857)
WINDSWEPT ENTERPRISES
Also Called: Windswept Enterprising
251 N Dupont Hwy (19901-7539)
PHONE..................................302 678-0805
William Mcpoyle, *Owner*
EMP: 7 EST: 1991
SALES (est): 582.91K **Privately Held**
Web: www.windsweptenterprises.com
SIC: 2752 Offset printing

(G-3858)
WINDY INC
8 The Grn Ste A (19901-3618)
PHONE..................................224 707-0442
EMP: 10 EST: 2018
SALES (est): 348.76K **Privately Held**
SIC: 7389 Financial services

(G-3859)
WINNER DOVER 1387 LLC
1387 N Dupont Hwy (19901-8702)
PHONE..................................302 257-3500
EMP: 19 EST: 2019
SALES (est): 460.34K **Privately Held**
SIC: 7011 Hotels and motels

(G-3860)
WINNER FORD OF DOVER LTD
Also Called: Winner Ford of Dover
591 S Dupont Hwy (19901-4515)
PHONE..................................302 734-0444
John Hynansky, *Pr*
EMP: 374 EST: 1981
SQ FT: 6,000
SALES (est): 49.87MM
SALES (corp-wide): 49.87MM **Privately Held**
Web: www.winnerfordofdover.com
SIC: 5511 7538 Automobiles, new and used; General automotive repair shops
PA: Winner Group, Inc
911 N Tatnall St
Wilmington DE 19801
302 764-5900

(G-3861)
WIS INTERNATIONAL
1203 College Park Dr (19904-8703)
PHONE..................................302 264-9343
EMP: 5 EST: 2014
SALES (est): 70.02K **Privately Held**
Web: www.wisintl.com
SIC: 7389 Inventory computing service

(G-3862)
WIZARD MEDIA INC ◎
8 The Grn (19901-3618)
PHONE..................................610 653-9722
Georgia Austin, *CEO*
EMP: 5 EST: 2022
SALES (est): 109.09K **Privately Held**
SIC: 8742 Marketing consulting services

(G-3863)
WIZE MONKEY USA INC
9 E Loockerman St (19901-8306)
PHONE..................................604 839-7640
Max Rivest, *CEO*
EMP: 3
SALES (est): 135.7K **Privately Held**
SIC: 2086 Carbonated beverages, nonalcoholic: pkged. in cans, bottles

(G-3864)
WOJO HOME CLEANING LLC
160 Beech Dr (19904-9439)
PHONE..................................302 241-5866
Suzanne Wojtkiewicz, *Prin*
EMP: 5 EST: 2016
SALES (est): 46.35K **Privately Held**
SIC: 7699 Cleaning services

(G-3865)
WOLF CREEK SURGEONS PA
1371 S State St (19901-4945)
PHONE..................................302 678-3627
Wendy Newell, *Prin*
EMP: 10 EST: 2007
SALES (est): 648.14K **Privately Held**
Web: www.wolfcreeksurgeons.com
SIC: 8011 Surgeon

(G-3866)
WONG PETER MD
200 Banning St Ste 320 (19904-3488)
PHONE..................................302 674-0223
Peter Wong, *Prin*
EMP: 10 EST: 2018
SALES (est): 347.11K **Privately Held**
SIC: 8011 Offices and clinics of medical doctors

(G-3867)
WOODS HOLE GROUP INC
301 Cassidy Dr Ste D (19901-4973)
PHONE..................................302 222-6720
Stephen O'malley, *Mgr*
EMP: 29
SALES (corp-wide): 2.23MM **Privately Held**
Web: www.woodsholegroup.com
SIC: 8748 Environmental consultant
HQ: The Woods Hole Group Inc
107 Waterhouse Rd
Bourne MA 02532
301 925-4411

(G-3868)
WOOHOO INC ◎
8 The Grn Ste 12103 (19901-3618)
PHONE..................................302 233-7272
Angel Orrantia, *CEO*
EMP: 5 EST: 2022
SALES (est): 81.29K **Privately Held**
SIC: 7389

(G-3869)
WOOLLEYENTERPRISESMX LLC
160 Greentree Dr (19904-7620)
PHONE..................................302 674-4089
EMP: 5 EST: 2007
SALES (est): 84.84K **Privately Held**
SIC: 7389 Business services, nec

(G-3870)
WORKBETTERAI INC
8 The Grn Ste A (19901-3618)
PHONE..................................805 825-5216
Matthew Nolan, *CEO*
EMP: 10 EST: 2021
SALES (est): 346.52K **Privately Held**
SIC: 8748 Business consulting, nec

(G-3871)
WORKFAR INC
Also Called: Olympic Gate
8 The Grn Ste A (19901-3618)
PHONE..................................650 800-3990
EMP: 10 EST: 2020
SALES (est): 475.08K **Privately Held**
Web: www.workfar.com
SIC: 8742 Manufacturing management consultant

(G-3872)
WORKWEEK INC
160 Greentree Dr Ste 101 (19904-7620)
PHONE..................................423 708-4565
Travis Dunn, *CEO*
EMP: 5 EST: 2017
SALES (est): 50K **Privately Held**
SIC: 7371 Computer software development and applications

(G-3873)
WORLD FOODS USA LLC
Also Called: Daily Cart
8 The Grn Ste A (19901-3618)
PHONE..................................302 288-0670
EMP: 5 EST: 2021
SALES (est): 413.66K **Privately Held**
SIC: 5141 Groceries, general line

(G-3874)
WORLD TRANSMISSIONS INC
2860 N Dupont Hwy (19901-8783)
PHONE..................................302 735-5535
EMP: 5 EST: 1992
SALES (est): 473.61K **Privately Held**
Web: www.worldtransmissions.pro
SIC: 7537 Automotive transmission repair shops

(G-3875)
WORLD WEB TECHNOLOGY PVT LTD
8 The Grn (19901-3618)
PHONE..................................646 755-9276
Sanjay Ghinaiya, *Managing Member*
EMP: 50
SALES (est): 1.14MM **Privately Held**
SIC: 7371 7389 Computer software development and applications; Business services, nec

(G-3876)
WUJI INC
8 The Grn Ste A (19901-3618)
PHONE..................................815 274-6777
Stephen M Cutter, *CEO*
Brenden Dougherty, *COO*
EMP: 5 EST: 2017
SALES (est): 104.73K **Privately Held**
SIC: 7389 Business Activities at Non-Commercial Site

(G-3877)
WUTOPIA GROUP US LTD
Also Called: Wutopia Comics
8 The Grn Ste 501 (19901-3618)
PHONE..................................302 488-0248
Jingping Lai, *CEO*
EMP: 11 EST: 2019
SALES (est): 400K **Privately Held**
SIC: 2721 7371 Comic books: publishing and printing; Computer software development and applications

(G-3878)
WWWLAWFRMLLNCORG ASSN JIM CYLE
615 S Dupont Hwy (19901-4517)
PHONE..................................803 212-4978
Beath Seabright, *Prin*
EMP: 5 EST: 2017
SALES (est): 93.36K **Privately Held**
SIC: 8699 Membership organizations, nec

(G-3879)
WYNDHAM FRANCHISOR LLC
Also Called: Wyndham Garden Dover
561 N Dupont Hwy (19901-3960)
PHONE..................................302 487-0234
EMP: 23 EST: 2017
SALES (est): 389.48K **Privately Held**
Web: www.wyndhamhotels.com
SIC: 7011 Hotels and motels

(G-3880)
XCUTIVESCOM INC
3500 S Dupont Hwy (19901-6041)
PHONE..................................888 245-9996
EMP: 23
SALES (corp-wide): 475.18K **Privately Held**
Web: www.xcutives.com
SIC: 8742 General management consultant
PA: Xcutives.Com Inc.
1510 Oakridge Ct
Decatur GA 30033
888 245-9996

GEOGRAPHIC SECTION

Ellendale - Sussex County (G-3910)

(G-3881)
XLR8 LOGISTICS LLC (PA) ✪
8 The Grn Ste 14393 (19901-3618)
PHONE..................................682 622-1546
Leonard Sowell, *Managing Member*
EMP: 9 **EST:** 2023
SALES (est): 410.42K
SALES (corp-wide): 410.42K **Privately Held**
SIC: 4212 Furniture moving, local: without storage

(G-3882)
XPERT TEK SOLUTIONS INC
306 Topaz Cir (19904-3709)
PHONE..................................302 724-4857
EMP: 5 **EST:** 2011
SALES (est): 202.69K **Privately Held**
Web: www.xpertteksolutions.com
SIC: 8748 Business consulting, nec

(G-3883)
XYNOMIC PHARMACEUTICALS INC
3500 S Dupont Hwy Ste Ss101 (19901-6041)
PHONE..................................650 430-7561
Mark Xu, *Pr*
Yong Cui, *VP*
Wentao Wu, *CFO*
EMP: 12 **EST:** 2017
SALES (est): 875.57K **Privately Held**
Web: www.xynomicpharma.com
SIC: 5122 Pharmaceuticals

(G-3884)
YEEZIE HOLDINGS LLC
8 The Grn Ste 7756 (19901-3618)
PHONE..................................917 970-1974
Marc Russo, *CEO*
Dea Muriqi, *Managing Member*
EMP: 8 **EST:** 2017
SALES (est): 250.88K **Privately Held**
SIC: 8748 Urban planning and consulting services

(G-3885)
YELLOW AND GREEN MACHINERY LLC ✪
8 The Grn Ste E (19901-3618)
PHONE..................................302 526-4990
EMP: 6 **EST:** 2022
SALES (est): 87.5K **Privately Held**
SIC: 5082 5083 5084 Construction and mining machinery; Farm and garden machinery; Industrial machinery and equipment

(G-3886)
YEVMA INC ✪
8 The Grn Ste A (19901-3618)
PHONE..................................888 338-2221
EMP: 5 **EST:** 2022
SALES (est): 358.77K **Privately Held**
SIC: 7371 Computer software development and applications

(G-3887)
YIELD NEXUS LLC
1679 S Dupont Hwy Ste 100 (19901-5164)
PHONE..................................308 380-3788
Omer Latif, *CEO*
Loren Wilson, *Pr*
EMP: 10 **EST:** 2016
SALES (est): 623.93K **Privately Held**
Web: www.yieldnexus.com
SIC: 7313 Electronic media advertising representatives

(G-3888)
YODERS CENTRAL AIR
615 Central Church Rd (19904-4761)
PHONE..................................302 674-5144
EMP: 6 **EST:** 2019
SALES (est): 407.73K **Privately Held**
SIC: 1711 Warm air heating and air conditioning contractor

(G-3889)
YODERS GREENHOUSE
5070 Pearsons Corner Rd (19904-4966)
PHONE..................................302 678-3530
Raymond Yoder, *Prin*
EMP: 5 **EST:** 2010
SALES (est): 94.99K **Privately Held**
SIC: 0181 Bulbs and seeds

(G-3890)
YOMI ENTERTAINMENT INC
1221 College Park Dr # 116 (19904-8726)
PHONE..................................838 588-8888
EMP: 5 **EST:** 2021
SALES (est): 59.87K **Privately Held**
SIC: 7929 Entertainers and entertainment groups

(G-3891)
YOUNG & MCNELIS
300 S State St (19901-6730)
PHONE..................................302 674-8822
Jeff Young, *Pn*
Brian Mcnelis, *Pt*
EMP: 7 **EST:** 1995
SALES (est): 755.82K **Privately Held**
Web: www.youngandmcnelis.com
SIC: 8111 General practice law office

(G-3892)
YOUNG AND MALMBERG PA
Also Called: Malmberg Firm, The
30 The Grn (19901-3612)
PHONE..................................302 672-5600
Kenneth Young, *Pt*
Constantine F Malmberg Iii, *Pt*
EMP: 10 **EST:** 1996
SALES (est): 968.32K **Privately Held**
SIC: 8111 General practice attorney, lawyer

(G-3893)
YOUR CBD STORE
222 S Dupont Hwy (19901-3797)
PHONE..................................302 480-4474
EMP: 6 **EST:** 2020
SALES (est): 109.61K **Privately Held**
Web: www.getsunmed.com
SIC: 8049 Offices of health practitioner

(G-3894)
YOUSHOP INC
3500 S Dupont Hwy (19901-6041)
PHONE..................................302 526-0521
Ke Wang, *CEO*
EMP: 5 **EST:** 2014
SALES (est): 82.13K **Privately Held**
SIC: 7371 Computer software development and applications

(G-3895)
YVONNE HALL INC
Also Called: Yvonne Hall Realty
1671 S State St (19901-5148)
PHONE..................................302 677-1300
Yvonne Hall, *CEO*
EMP: 5 **EST:** 2005
SALES (est): 299.26K **Privately Held**
SIC: 6531 Real estate brokers and agents

(G-3896)
ZEHDEN PROPERTIES LLC
8 The Grn Ste R (19901-3618)
PHONE..................................310 773-8529
Michael Zehden, *Managing Member*
EMP: 5
SALES (est): 76.37K **Privately Held**
SIC: 6799 Real estate investors, except property operators

(G-3897)
ZELCORE TECHNOLOGIES INC
8 The Grn Ste A (19901-3618)
PHONE..................................408 829-6352
Parker Honeyman, *Ch Bd*
EMP: 5 **EST:** 2020
SALES (est): 224.89K **Privately Held**
Web: www.zelcore.io
SIC: 7371 Computer software development and applications

(G-3898)
ZENIND INC
8 The Grn Ste R (19901-3618)
PHONE..................................845 300-3310
Yuhan Fu, *Admn*
EMP: 5 **EST:** 2020
SALES (est): 192.43K **Privately Held**
SIC: 7389 Business Activities at Non-Commercial Site

(G-3899)
ZERIBON HOLDING GROUP LLC ✪
8 The Grn Ste B (19901-3618)
PHONE..................................844 205-1999
Arghoon Dar, *Prin*
EMP: 235 **EST:** 2022
SALES (est): 11.41MM **Privately Held**
Web: www.zeribon.com
SIC: 8712 8742 8748 9651 Architectural engineering; Management engineering; Communications consulting; Regulation, miscellaneous commercial sectors

(G-3900)
ZHANG SHUNLI MD
640 S State St (19901-3530)
PHONE..................................302 744-7050
EMP: 10 **EST:** 2018
SALES (est): 247.44K **Privately Held**
SIC: 8011 Offices and clinics of medical doctors

(G-3901)
ZIGGYFLI LLC
1041 N Dupont Hwy (19901-2006)
PHONE..................................302 503-5582
Balanze Bey, *Managing Member*
EMP: 11
SALES (est): 413.76K **Privately Held**
SIC: 8742 Business management consultant

(G-3902)
ZIPLINE XPRESS CORP
1041 N Dupont Hwy (19901-2006)
PHONE..................................302 531-6417
EMP: 6
SALES (est): 82.43K **Privately Held**
SIC: 4731 Freight transportation arrangement

(G-3903)
ZOBER CONTRACTING SERVICES INC
155 Old Mill Rd (19901-6255)
PHONE..................................302 270-3078
Rosalie A Zober, *Pr*
EMP: 5 **EST:** 2006
SALES (est): 1.17MM **Privately Held**
SIC: 1623 Water, sewer, and utility lines

(G-3904)
ZOLAK INC ✪
1111b S Governors Ave Ste 6259 (19904-6903)
PHONE..................................302 889-0556
Hanna Herysh, *CEO*
EMP: 2 **EST:** 2023
SALES (est): 87.4K **Privately Held**
SIC: 7372 Prepackaged software

(G-3905)
ZONE LASER TAG INC
419 Webbs Ln (19904-5439)
PHONE..................................302 730-8888
Adnrew L Jiranek, *Admn*
EMP: 16 **EST:** 2017
SALES (est): 1.62MM **Privately Held**
Web: www.lasertag.com
SIC: 7929 Entertainment service

(G-3906)
ZONE SYSTEMS INC
419 Webbs Ln (19904-5439)
PHONE..................................302 730-8888
Kate Holmes, *Pr*
Simon Willetts, *VP*
Pat Holmes, *VP*
Erik Guthrie, *VP*
▲ **EMP:** 30 **EST:** 2000
SQ FT: 5,000
SALES (est): 696.24K **Privately Held**
Web: www.lasertag.com
SIC: 3944 Electronic game machines, except coin-operated
HQ: P & C Micros Pty. Ltd.
Unit C5 756 Blackburn Road
Clayton VIC 3168

(G-3907)
ZOWIE INC
8 The Grn Ste 10893 (19901-3618)
PHONE..................................725 201-0590
Maja Schaefer, *CEO*
EMP: 75
SALES (est): 1.18MM **Privately Held**
SIC: 7371 Computer software development

(G-3908)
ZUHATREND LLC
207 W Loockerman St (19904-3247)
PHONE..................................302 883-2656
EMP: 2 **EST:** 2009
SALES (est): 245.83K **Privately Held**
Web: www.zuhatrend.com
SIC: 2311 Tuxedos: made from purchased materials

(G-3909)
ZURI HAIR COLLECTION LLC
17 Medinah Ct (19904-7106)
PHONE..................................804 296-7534
Tameka Brown-maddox, *Prin*
EMP: 5 **EST:** 2018
SALES (est): 19.5K **Privately Held**
SIC: 7231 Hairdressers

Ellendale
Sussex County

(G-3910)
BELLA TERRA NURSERY & GRDN CTR
13482 Spicer Rd (19941-2710)
PHONE..................................302 422-9000
EMP: 9 **EST:** 2017
SALES (est): 776.69K **Privately Held**
Web: www.bellaterrade.com
SIC: 0781 Landscape services

Ellendale - Sussex County (G-3911)　　GEOGRAPHIC SECTION

(G-3911)
BRIGGS SERVICES LLC
14546 S Old State Rd (19941-3340)
PHONE.....................302 569-5230
EMP: 6 EST: 2014
SALES (est): 221.42K Privately Held
SIC: 7349 Janitorial service, contract basis

(G-3912)
CRETEWORK LLC
16505 Beach Hwy (19941-2845)
PHONE.....................302 424-9970
EMP: 5 EST: 2020
SALES (est): 83.04K Privately Held
SIC: 1522 Residential construction, nec

(G-3913)
DELMARVA AUTOMOTIVE EQP INC
14247 Oakley Rd (19941-3012)
PHONE.....................302 349-9411
Susanne Webb, Prin
EMP: 5 EST: 2019
SALES (est): 211.49K Privately Held
SIC: 5046 Commercial equipment, nec

(G-3914)
DELMARVA CLERGY UNITED INC
Also Called: Delmarva Clrgy Untd In Scial A
13724 S Old State Rd (19941-3330)
PHONE.....................302 422-2350
Bhisop M Foster, CEO
EMP: 11 EST: 1986
SALES (est): 447.42K Privately Held
Web: delmarva-clergy-united-in-social-action.hub.biz
SIC: 8331 Community service employment training program

(G-3915)
DONNIE JONES FOUNDATION INC
200 Main St (19941-2144)
PHONE.....................302 745-6946
Heather Jones, Pr
Thomas Perry, Dir
EMP: 5 EST: 2015
SALES (est): 52.86K Privately Held
SIC: 8641 Civic and social associations

(G-3916)
DRYZONE LLC
16507 Beach Hwy (19941-2845)
PHONE.....................302 684-5034
EMP: 8 EST: 2006
SALES (est): 1.01MM Privately Held
Web: www.dryzone.com
SIC: 1799 Waterproofing

(G-3917)
FAMGLAM LLC
Also Called: Queen Bee Fashions
20100 Reynolds Pond Rd (19941-2631)
P.O. Box 732 (19963-0732)
PHONE.....................302 930-0026
Marquon Brady, VP
EMP: 11 EST: 2012
SALES (est): 853.45K Privately Held
SIC: 5999 6719 Alarm and safety equipment stores; Investment holding companies, except banks

(G-3918)
FINGER LAKES METROLOGY LLC
13478 Mustang Dr (19941-2571)
PHONE.....................607 742-7240
EMP: 5 EST: 2016
SALES (est): 222.5K Privately Held
Web: www.flmet.com
SIC: 5084 Industrial machinery and equipment

(G-3919)
GRACEFULL HANDS CLEANING LLC
Also Called: Graceful Hands Cleaning Svc
702 Main St (19941-2066)
PHONE.....................302 228-3841
EMP: 6 EST: 2010
SALES (est): 91.29K Privately Held
SIC: 7699 Cleaning services

(G-3920)
HAND -N- HAND EARLY LRNG CTR
13724 S Old State Rd Unit 3 (19941-3330)
PHONE.....................302 422-0702
Cassie Malinger, Dir
Major Chairm Foster, Prin
EMP: 10 EST: 2012
SALES (est): 150.93K Privately Held
SIC: 8351 Group day care center

(G-3921)
HOWELL JUANQUETTA
201 King Aly (19941-2121)
PHONE.....................302 682-1602
Juanquetta Howell, CEO
EMP: 5 EST: 2017
SALES (est): 57.5K Privately Held
Web: www.aficionauto.com
SIC: 8049 Offices of health practitioner

(G-3922)
J DEAN PUSEY CONTRACTOR INC
22548 Reynolds Pond Rd (19941-2677)
P.O. Box 529 (19968-0529)
PHONE.....................302 245-0432
EMP: 5 EST: 2009
SALES (est): 191.43K Privately Held
SIC: 1799 Special trade contractors, nec

(G-3923)
J&R AUTO REPAIR
100 Maggies (19941-2100)
PHONE.....................240 863-8653
Roberto Figueroa, Prin
EMP: 5 EST: 2018
SALES (est): 44.75K Privately Held
SIC: 7538 General automotive repair shops

(G-3924)
JOSE A FERNANDEZ
511 Main St (19941-2063)
PHONE.....................302 422-5903
Jose A Fernandez, Prin
EMP: 6 EST: 2009
SALES (est): 107.16K Privately Held
SIC: 1611 General contractor, highway and street construction

(G-3925)
KEITH PERRY
13299 Spicer Rd (19941-2750)
PHONE.....................302 841-1514
Keith Perry, Pr
EMP: 6 EST: 2017
SALES (est): 22.18K Privately Held
SIC: 8049 Offices of health practitioner

(G-3926)
LEFT FOR DEAD
22350 Reynolds Pond Rd (19941-2653)
PHONE.....................302 684-4320
Robert E Massey, Owner
EMP: 5 EST: 2016
SALES (est): 66.91K Privately Held
SIC: 8399 Advocacy group

(G-3927)
NEW HOPE RCREATION DEV CTR INC
12564 N Old State Rd (19941-2820)
P.O. Box 310 (19941-0310)
PHONE.....................302 424-0767
Paulline Emory, Pr
Kendal Tyre, Ex Dir
EMP: 10
SALES (est): 31.22K Privately Held
Web: www.nhrdc.org
SIC: 8322 Individual and family services

(G-3928)
PHILADLPHIA ARMS TOWN HMES INC
18527 Pentecostal St (19941-3359)
PHONE.....................302 503-7216
Leah Brown, Ex Dir
EMP: 10 EST: 2016
SALES (est): 293.9K Privately Held
SIC: 1521 Single-family housing construction

(G-3929)
SANTAY TRUCKING INC
14296 Dupont Blvd (19941-3300)
PHONE.....................302 245-6012
EMP: 7 EST: 2017
SALES (est): 247.52K Privately Held
SIC: 4212 Local trucking, without storage

Elsmere
New Castle County

(G-3930)
ALBERTO BAEZ
Also Called: Al's Additional Restoration
119 Beech Ave (19805-5006)
PHONE.....................302 543-1212
Alberto Baez, Prin
EMP: 5 EST: 2010
SALES (est): 120.51K Privately Held
SIC: 1799 Special trade contractors, nec

(G-3931)
TERA TECHNOLOGY GROUP
328 New Rd (19805-1914)
PHONE.....................302 994-0500
EMP: 5 EST: 2019
SALES (est): 50.78K Privately Held
Web: www.teratechnologygroup.com
SIC: 7379 Computer related consulting services

Farmington
Sussex County

(G-3932)
AUTO PARTS OF GREENWOOD
8316 Greenwood Rd (19950-4845)
P.O. Box 630 (19950-0630)
PHONE.....................302 349-9601
Devin Johnson, Owner
EMP: 5 EST: 2004
SALES (est): 260.58K Privately Held
Web: www.lkqparts.net
SIC: 5015 Automotive parts and supplies, used

(G-3933)
BAY TO BEACH BUILDERS INC
11582 Sussex Hwy (19950)
PHONE.....................302 349-5099
Derrick Parker, Pr
EMP: 6 EST: 2004
SALES (est): 1.53MM Privately Held
Web: www.baytobeachbuilders.com
SIC: 1521 New construction, single-family houses

(G-3934)
CARLISLE FARMS INC
12733 Shawnee Rd (19950-5327)
PHONE.....................302 349-5692
Keith H Carlisle, Pr
EMP: 5 EST: 2006
SALES (est): 120.06K Privately Held
SIC: 0191 General farms, primarily crop

(G-3935)
DIAMOND STATE MACHINING INC (PA)
207 Main St (19950-2183)
PHONE.....................302 398-8437
Donald Huey, Pr
Joann Huey, Sec
EMP: 13 EST: 1977
SQ FT: 32,000
SALES (est): 2.2MM
SALES (corp-wide): 2.2MM Privately Held
Web: www.diamondstatemachining.com
SIC: 3599 Machine shop, jobbing and repair

(G-3936)
WILLARD AGRI SERVICE GREENW
22272 S Dupont Hwy (19950-2311)
PHONE.....................302 349-4100
Ken Fry, Prin
EMP: 6 EST: 2004
SALES (est): 1.05MM Privately Held
Web: www.willardag.com
SIC: 5083 Agricultural machinery and equipment

Felton
Kent County

(G-3937)
AAA ENVIRONMENTAL SERVICES
257 Deerwood Farm Ln (19943-3709)
PHONE.....................302 284-4334
Michael Stallings, Prin
EMP: 5 EST: 2010
SALES (est): 230.44K Privately Held
SIC: 6411 Insurance agents, nec

(G-3938)
ADAM HOBBS & SON INC
344 Fitzbrian Dr (19943-3377)
PHONE.....................302 697-2090
EMP: 10 EST: 1983
SALES (est): 457.5K Privately Held
SIC: 4213 Trucking, except local

(G-3939)
ALBAN TRACTOR LLC
Also Called: Caterpillar Authorized Dealer
13074 S Dupont Hwy (19943-4027)
PHONE.....................302 284-4100
TOLL FREE: 800
Ed Mosley, Mgr
EMP: 7
SALES (corp-wide): 724.07MM Privately Held
Web: www.caterpillar.com
SIC: 5082 General construction machinery and equipment
HQ: Alban Tractor, Llc
8531 Pulaski Hwy
Baltimore MD 21237
410 686-7777

(G-3940)
ALL COUNTY CLEANING
104 Lake Dr (19943-5112)
P.O. Box 205 (19946-0205)
PHONE.....................302 504-4719
Michael Lunn, Prin
EMP: 7 EST: 2015

SALES (est): 239.24K **Privately Held**
Web: www.allcountycleaning.org
SIC: 7699 Cleaning services

(G-3941)
APEX TRANSPORTATION SVCS LLC
Also Called: Transportation
12600 S Dupont Hwy (19943-4847)
PHONE..................................302 284-7463
Lefeisha Cannon, *Managing Member*
EMP: 30 **EST:** 2017
SALES (est): 2.21MM **Privately Held**
Web: www.transportationapex.com
SIC: 4789 Transportation services, nec

(G-3942)
ASSET KEY MANAGEMENT LLC
125 Dickens Ln (19943-9287)
PHONE..................................302 505-4603
Keith Penawell, *Prin*
EMP: 6 **EST:** 2019
SALES (est): 230.75K **Privately Held**
SIC: 8741 Financial management for business

(G-3943)
ATLANTIC CONTROL SYSTEMS INC
7873 S Dupont Hwy Ste 2 (19943-5700)
PHONE..................................302 284-9700
Gary Reddish, *Pr*
EMP: 8 **EST:** 1987
SALES (est): 1.01MM **Privately Held**
Web: www.acsd.net
SIC: 3613 Control panels, electric

(G-3944)
AVID BUILDERS LLC
1054 Paradise Alley Rd (19943-4011)
PHONE..................................302 233-0148
EMP: 5 **EST:** 2015
SALES (est): 130.98K **Privately Held**
SIC: 1521 New construction, single-family houses

(G-3945)
AZTECH CONTRACTING INC
68 Elijah Ln (19943-7362)
P.O. Box 701 (19943-0701)
PHONE..................................302 526-2145
Henry Mast, *Pr*
EMP: 15 **EST:** 2009
SQ FT: 100
SALES (est): 1.59MM **Privately Held**
Web: www.aztechcontracting.com
SIC: 1799 Service station equipment

(G-3946)
BK RENTALS
7667 Canterbury Rd (19943-5216)
PHONE..................................302 331-1984
Katherine Twardus, *Prin*
EMP: 5 **EST:** 2011
SALES (est): 245.51K **Privately Held**
Web: www.bkpartyrentals.com
SIC: 7359 Party supplies rental services

(G-3947)
BRASS SALES COMPANY INC (PA)
Also Called: Mobile Home Supply
8092 S Dupont Hwy (19943-5712)
PHONE..................................302 284-4574
EMP: 12 **EST:** 1948
SALES (est): 4.55MM
SALES (corp-wide): 4.55MM **Privately Held**
Web: www.brasssalesinc.com
SIC: 5074 5072 Plumbing fittings and supplies; Hardware

(G-3948)
BRYANT TECHNOLOGIES INC
2368 Paradise Alley Rd (19943-4133)
PHONE..................................302 289-2044
Jeannette Bryant, *Pr*
EMP: 5 **EST:** 2007
SALES (est): 255.17K **Privately Held**
Web: www.bryant-technologies.com
SIC: 7371 Computer software development

(G-3949)
BURKE EQUIPMENT COMPANY (PA)
Also Called: Kubota Authorized Dealer
54 Andrews Lake Rd (19943-4633)
PHONE..................................302 697-3200
Mark Babbitt, *Pr*
Lucienne Babbitt, *Treas*
EMP: 12 **EST:** 1949
SQ FT: 8,000
SALES (est): 8.93MM
SALES (corp-wide): 8.93MM **Privately Held**
Web: www.burkeequipment.com
SIC: 5261 7359 5083 Lawnmowers and tractors; Equipment rental and leasing, nec; Farm and garden machinery

(G-3950)
C&M CUSTOM HOMES LLC
7344 S Dupont Hwy Ste 1 (19943-5715)
PHONE..................................302 736-5824
EMP: 6 **EST:** 2019
SALES (est): 499.63K **Privately Held**
Web: www.cmcustomhomes.com
SIC: 1521 New construction, single-family houses

(G-3951)
CARL DEPUTY & SON BUILDERS LLC
981 Tomahawk Ln (19943-6232)
PHONE..................................302 284-3041
EMP: 7 **EST:** 1986
SALES (est): 972.93K **Privately Held**
Web: www.deputybuilders.com
SIC: 1521 1542 New construction, single-family houses; Commercial and office building, new construction

(G-3952)
CENTER FOR A PSTIVE HMNITY LLC
Also Called: Williams-Garcia & Associates
86 Ludlow Ln (19943-1764)
PHONE..................................302 703-1036
Ronald Williams-garcia, *Prin*
EMP: 5 **EST:** 2013
SALES (est): 106.09K **Privately Held**
Web: www.cfaph.org
SIC: 8322 7389 General counseling services

(G-3953)
CHARLES R REED
93 Paradise Cove Way (19943-4000)
PHONE..................................302 284-3353
Charles R Reed, *Prin*
EMP: 5 **EST:** 2005
SALES (est): 115.64K **Privately Held**
SIC: 1521 New construction, single-family houses

(G-3954)
CHEERSRX INC ✪
13 W Main St (19943)
P.O. Box 953 (19943-0953)
PHONE..................................801 210-1658
Jonathan Chen, *Owner*
EMP: 5 **EST:** 2024
SALES (est): 145.92K **Privately Held**
SIC: 7371 Computer software development and applications

(G-3955)
CHESAPEAKE SUPPLY & EQP CO
12915 S Dupont Hwy (19943-4854)
PHONE..................................302 284-1000
TOLL FREE: 800
Dave Goulet, *Brnch Mgr*
EMP: 9
SALES (corp-wide): 4.56MM **Privately Held**
Web: www.equipmentbychesapeake.com
SIC: 5082 7359 7353 General construction machinery and equipment; Equipment rental and leasing, nec; Heavy construction equipment rental
PA: Chesapeake Supply & Equipment Company
8366 Washington Blvd
Savage MD

(G-3956)
DAG RESIDENTIAL COML SVCS LLC
1129 Barney Jenkins Rd (19943-5763)
PHONE..................................302 513-6646
EMP: 5 **EST:** 2019
SALES (est): 101.79K **Privately Held**
Web: www.dagrcs.com
SIC: 7699 Cleaning services

(G-3957)
DC CHAMBERS CONSTRUCTION LLC
1054 Paradise Alley Rd (19943-4011)
PHONE..................................302 233-0148
John Chambers, *Prin*
EMP: 5 **EST:** 2013
SALES (est): 148.83K **Privately Held**
SIC: 1521 Single-family housing construction

(G-3958)
DEL-STATE CLEANING SERVICES
41 Rockwood Blvd (19943-7208)
PHONE..................................302 563-0606
EMP: 5 **EST:** 2017
SALES (est): 26.07K **Privately Held**
SIC: 7699 Cleaning services

(G-3959)
DELAWARE SIGN CO
411 E Railroad Ave (19943-7354)
PHONE..................................302 469-5656
EMP: 4 **EST:** 2017
SALES (est): 46.67K **Privately Held**
Web: www.delawaresign.com
SIC: 3993 Signs and advertising specialties

(G-3960)
DIAMOND STATE POLE BLDGNS LLC (PA)
7288 S Dupont Hwy (19943-5704)
P.O. Box 163 (19962-0163)
PHONE..................................302 387-1710
Nick Alessandro, *Managing Member*
EMP: 5 **EST:** 2008
SALES (est): 2.24MM
SALES (corp-wide): 2.24MM **Privately Held**
Web: www.diamondstatepole.com
SIC: 1522 1542 Residential construction, nec; Commercial and office building contractors

(G-3961)
DOVINGTON TRAINING CENTER LLC
595 Black Swamp Rd (19943-3647)
PHONE..................................302 284-2114
Alan Lovely, *Pr*
Jeffery Franklin, *VP*
Carolyn Franklin, *Treas*
Lorraine Lovely, *Sec*
EMP: 5 **EST:** 2001
SALES (est): 416.88K **Privately Held**
SIC: 0752 Training services, horses (except racing horses)

(G-3962)
DUCTS R US LLC
7686 Burnite Mill Rd (19943-3805)
PHONE..................................302 284-4006
John Caynor, *Prin*
EMP: 5 **EST:** 2008
SALES (est): 64.23K **Privately Held**
Web: www.ductsrusde.com
SIC: 7349 Air duct cleaning

(G-3963)
DWH SYSTEM INC
225 Steamboat Ave (19943-3078)
PHONE..................................551 208-5354
Suchit Kamdar, *Prin*
Chiranjeevi Sigirisetty, *Stockholder*
Shashi Priya Puppala, *Stockholder*
EMP: 16 **EST:** 2013
SALES (est): 260.73K **Privately Held**
Web: www.dwhsystems.com
SIC: 7379 Computer related maintenance services

(G-3964)
EARLS PLACE LLC
12605 S Dupont Hwy (19943-4831)
PHONE..................................302 538-8909
James Knox, *Managing Member*
EMP: 7 **EST:** 2017
SALES (est): 132.31K **Privately Held**
Web: earls-place.business.site
SIC: 7699 Repair services, nec

(G-3965)
EARTHBORNE EQUIPMENT & SVC CO
12915 S Dupont Hwy (19943-4854)
PHONE..................................215 343-2000
EMP: 75
SALES (corp-wide): 177.33K **Privately Held**
SIC: 7389 Business Activities at Non-Commercial Site
PA: Earthborne Equipment & Service Company
100 Titus Ave
Warrington PA
215 343-2000

(G-3966)
ECKELS FAMILY LLC
Also Called: Office Pride
141 Hunters Run Blvd (19943-5772)
PHONE..................................302 465-5224
Kelly Eckels, *
EMP: 31 **EST:** 2014
SALES (est): 562.18K **Privately Held**
Web: www.officepride.com
SIC: 7349 Janitorial service, contract basis

(G-3967)
EDS AUTO REPAIR
1772 Berrytown Rd (19943-6243)
PHONE..................................302 382-0079
EMP: 5 **EST:** 2014
SALES (est): 53.64K **Privately Held**
SIC: 7538 General automotive repair shops

(G-3968)
EXCEDE BRDBAND STLLITE INTRNET
11460 S Dupont Hwy (19943-4835)
PHONE..................................302 289-0147
EMP: 5 **EST:** 2013
SALES (est): 33.14K **Privately Held**
SIC: 4813 Online service providers

Felton - Kent County (G-3969) GEOGRAPHIC SECTION

(G-3969)
FADELY LLC
109 Logan Dr (19943-2962)
PHONE.................................302 284-7389
EMP: 6 EST: 2019
SALES (est): 211.04K Privately Held
Web: fadely-co-roofing-sheet-metal.business.site
SIC: 1761 Roofing contractor

(G-3970)
FAST4WRD TOWING & RECOVERY
98 Sanford St (19943-4673)
PHONE.................................302 331-5157
Christopher Gedney, Prin
EMP: 5 EST: 2010
SALES (est): 133.91K Privately Held
Web: www.fast4wrd.com
SIC: 7549 Towing services

(G-3971)
FELTON COMMUNITY FIRE CO INC
9 E Main St (19943-7323)
P.O. Box 946 (19943-9046)
PHONE.................................302 284-9552
Lawrence R Sipple, Chief
William A Chandler, *
EMP: 46 EST: 1851
SALES (est): 1.33MM Privately Held
Web: www.feltonfirecompany.org
SIC: 4119 Ambulance service

(G-3972)
FELTON LITTLE LEAGUE INC
P.O. Box 132 (19943-0132)
PHONE.................................302 284-3713
Katharine Coleman, Prin
EMP: 7 EST: 2001
SALES (est): 60.47K Privately Held
Web: www.feltonlittleleague.com
SIC: 7997 Baseball club, except professional and semi-professional

(G-3973)
FIRESIDE IT LLC
130 Sumac Dr (19943-6102)
PHONE.................................302 284-4961
EMP: 5 EST: 2011
SALES (est): 79.17K Privately Held
SIC: 4899 Communication services, nec

(G-3974)
FIRST STATE CRANE SERVICE INC
13326 S Dupont Hwy (19943-4030)
PHONE.................................302 398-8885
John P Hayden, Pr
Jim Hauer, Mgr
EMP: 25 EST: 1974
SQ FT: 10,000
SALES (est): 2.35MM Privately Held
Web: www.firststatecrane.com
SIC: 7353 1622 1629 Cranes and aerial lift equipment, rental or leasing; Bridge construction; Pile driving contractor

(G-3975)
FIRST STATE SEALCOATING
4860 Sandtown Rd (19943-2307)
PHONE.................................302 632-7522
Jason Dehorty, Prin
EMP: 6 EST: 2014
SALES (est): 177.92K Privately Held
Web: www.firststatesealcoatingllc.com
SIC: 1611 Surfacing and paving

(G-3976)
FRANCIS BERGOLD
Also Called: By Feel Farms
918 Midstate Rd (19943-4701)
PHONE.................................302 284-8101
Francis Bergold, Owner
EMP: 6 EST: 1949
SALES (est): 283.98K Privately Held
SIC: 0134 0119 0115 Irish potatoes; Barley farm; Corn

(G-3977)
G & B COMP & CREATIVE DESIGN
331 Drapers Mill Rd (19943-2872)
PHONE.................................302 284-3856
George Shinn Junior, Pr
EMP: 8 EST: 1984
SALES (est): 105.78K Privately Held
SIC: 2752 Offset printing

(G-3978)
GERARDI CONSTRUCTION INC
404 Jarrells Rd (19943-3925)
PHONE.................................302 745-6252
EMP: 8 EST: 2019
SALES (est): 474.99K Privately Held
SIC: 1521 Single-family housing construction

(G-3979)
GIBSON GLYNIS
186 Macananny Ln (19943-2500)
PHONE.................................302 730-1300
Glynis Gibson, Prin
EMP: 5 EST: 2013
SALES (est): 168.86K Privately Held
Web: www.gibsonlawde.com
SIC: 8111 General practice law office

(G-3980)
GRANT IRELAND CONTRACTING LLC
622 Mount Olive Cemetery Rd (19943-2556)
PHONE.................................302 265-6112
Grant Ireland, Prin
EMP: 5 EST: 2018
SALES (est): 140.09K Privately Held
SIC: 1799 Special trade contractors, nec

(G-3981)
GREEN DIAMOND BUILDERS INC (PA)
24 Memorial Ave (19943-4602)
PHONE.................................302 284-1177
Stephen Jackson, Pr
EMP: 9 EST: 2004
SALES (est): 955.38K
SALES (corp-wide): 955.38K Privately Held
Web: www.greendiamondbuilders.com
SIC: 1521 New construction, single-family houses

(G-3982)
GREENS CLEANING EXPERT LLC
1129 Barney Jenkins Rd (19943-5763)
PHONE.................................302 697-2848
EMP: 5 EST: 2016
SALES (est): 28.39K Privately Held
SIC: 7699 Cleaning services

(G-3983)
HUGHES DELAWARE MAID SCRAPPLE
8873 Burnite Mill Rd (19943-4552)
PHONE.................................302 284-4370
David Quillen, Pr
Dolly Womack, Sec
EMP: 8 EST: 1978
SALES (est): 943.95K Privately Held
SIC: 5141 Food brokers

(G-3984)
ISOCDE COMMUNITY CTR LOCATION
7953 S Dupont Hwy (19943-5727)
PHONE.................................302 697-7276
Zafar Chaudry, Prin
EMP: 7 EST: 2010
SALES (est): 65.59K Privately Held
SIC: 8322 Community center

(G-3985)
J & M FENCING INC
Also Called: Forrest Fence
68 Elijah Ln (19943-7362)
PHONE.................................302 284-9674
EMP: 5
Web: www.forrestfencing.com
SIC: 1799 Fence construction
PA: J & M Fencing Inc.
    9867 S Dupont Hwy
    Felton DE 19943

(G-3986)
J & M FENCING INC (PA)
Also Called: Forrest Fencing
9867 S Dupont Hwy (19943-5620)
P.O. Box 21 (19943-0021)
PHONE.................................302 284-9674
John Forrest, Pr
John P Forrest, Pr
Karen Forrest, Ofcr
EMP: 5 EST: 2004
SQ FT: 2,100
SALES (est): 1.61MM Privately Held
Web: www.forrestfencing.com
SIC: 1799 5039 Fence construction; Wire fence, gates, and accessories

(G-3987)
J HOOKED TWING RCVERY AUTO REP
2948 Andrews Lake Rd (19943-5362)
PHONE.................................302 335-3043
Shannon Everett, Asst Sec
EMP: 5 EST: 2018
SALES (est): 189.65K Privately Held
SIC: 7699 Repair services, nec

(G-3988)
J R BROOKS CUSTOM FRAMING LLC
Also Called: J R Brooks Custom Framing
1791 Peach Basket Rd (19943-5650)
PHONE.................................302 538-3637
John Brooks, Managing Member
EMP: 4 EST: 2012
SALES (est): 87.1K Privately Held
SIC: 2499 Picture frame molding, finished

(G-3989)
JOHN R STUMP MD
175 Lake Cove Ln (19943-5354)
PHONE.................................302 422-3937
John R Stump Md, Owner
EMP: 6 EST: 1991
SALES (est): 396.15K Privately Held
Web: www.stumpeyecare.com
SIC: 8011 Opthalmologist

(G-3990)
KENCO DRYWALL
Also Called: Kenco Cnstr Drywall Special
7093 S Dupont Hwy (19943-5718)
P.O. Box 957 (19943-0957)
PHONE.................................302 697-6489
Kenneth Collins, Owner
Alyce Collins, Off Mgr
EMP: 5 EST: 1982
SALES (est): 176.41K Privately Held
SIC: 1742 Drywall

(G-3991)
KENNETH H GLADISH
Also Called: Homework
714 Barratts Chapel Rd (19943-5525)
PHONE.................................302 270-2821
Kenneth H Gladish, Prin
EMP: 5 EST: 2012
SALES (est): 248.3K Privately Held
SIC: 1522 Residential construction, nec

(G-3992)
KENT ELECTRICAL SERVICES LLC
112 Lake Dr (19943-5112)
PHONE.................................302 922-4631
Dustin Beckhorn, Prin
EMP: 7 EST: 2018
SALES (est): 179.12K Privately Held
Web: www.kentelectricalservice.com
SIC: 1731 General electrical contractor

(G-3993)
KEVINS MASONRY CONCRETE CO
526 Reeves Crossing Rd (19943-4064)
P.O. Box 827 (19943-0827)
PHONE.................................302 382-7259
Kevin Gay, Prin
EMP: 6 EST: 2010
SALES (est): 219.57K Privately Held
Web: kevinmasonryconcrete.weebly.com
SIC: 1741 Masonry and other stonework

(G-3994)
LAWRENCE E HAUG III
Also Called: Lhaug Painting
101 Pin Oak Ct (19943-9522)
PHONE.................................302 222-7979
Lawrence E Haug Iii, Prin
EMP: 5 EST: 2011
SALES (est): 64.2K Privately Held
SIC: 1721 Painting and paper hanging

(G-3995)
LELAND OAKLEY
785 Paradise Alley Rd (19943-4021)
PHONE.................................302 430-3403
Leland Oakley, Prin
EMP: 2 EST: 2009
SALES (est): 245.23K Privately Held
SIC: 3441 Fabricated structural metal

(G-3996)
LELAND OAKLEY WELDING
93 Paradise Cove Way (19943-4000)
PHONE.................................302 469-5746
Leland Oakley, Prin
EMP: 5 EST: 2017
SALES (est): 25.09K Privately Held
SIC: 7692 Welding repair

(G-3997)
LEROY BETTS CONSTRUCTION INC
4020 Hopkins Cemetery Rd (19943-3729)
PHONE.................................302 284-9193
Leroy Betts, Pr
Mary Lou Betts, Sec
EMP: 9 EST: 1988
SALES (est): 946.67K Privately Held
SIC: 1794 Excavation work

(G-3998)
LIMOUSINE UNLIMITED LLC
Also Called: Transportation
12604 S Dupont Hwy (19943-4847)
PHONE.................................302 284-1100
Lefeisha Cannon, Managing Member
EMP: 11 EST: 1994
SQ FT: 1,600
SALES (est): 450.25K Privately Held
Web: www.limousineunlimited.net

GEOGRAPHIC SECTION

Felton - Kent County (G-4029)

SIC: 4119 Limousine rental, with driver

(G-3999)
LINCARE INC
7012 S Dupont Hwy (19943-5714)
PHONE..............................302 424-8302
Barry Krenbrink, Mgr
EMP: 8
Web: www.lincare.com
SIC: 7352 Medical equipment rental
HQ: Lincare Inc.
19387 Us Highway 19 N
Clearwater FL 33764
727 530-7700

(G-4000)
MANMADE KENNELS LLC
107 Redstone Ct (19943-7411)
PHONE..............................302 272-3625
Edward Perez, Prin
EMP: 5 EST: 2016
SALES (est): 25.84K Privately Held
Web: www.manmadekennels.com
SIC: 0752 Boarding services, kennels

(G-4001)
MARY ANNES LANDSCAPING INC
96 Windward Dr (19943-5356)
PHONE..............................302 335-5433
EMP: 6 EST: 1991
SALES (est): 250.31K Privately Held
SIC: 0782 1711 Landscape contractors; Irrigation sprinkler system installation

(G-4002)
MICHAEL JOSEPH ALEXANDER
420 Reeves Crossing Rd (19943-4063)
PHONE..............................302 670-0993
Michael Alexander, Prin
EMP: 5 EST: 2016
SALES (est): 43.68K Privately Held
SIC: 0191 General farms, primarily crop

(G-4003)
MJM PUBLISHING LLC
719 Tomahawk Ln (19943-6230)
PHONE..............................302 943-3590
EMP: 4 EST: 2017
SALES (est): 41.35K Privately Held
Web: www.motorcycletimes.com
SIC: 2741 Miscellaneous publishing

(G-4004)
MONADNOCK INN
303 Church St (19943-1761)
PHONE..............................603 532-7800
Max Mitchell, Pr
EMP: 13 EST: 2012
SALES (est): 201.45K Privately Held
Web: www.monadnockinn.com
SIC: 7011 Bed and breakfast inn

(G-4005)
NEW CREATION LAWN CARE INC
68 Elijah Ln (19943-7362)
PHONE..............................302 698-0246
Kelvin Smith, Prin
EMP: 8 EST: 2012
SALES (est): 539.33K Privately Held
SIC: 0782 Lawn care services

(G-4006)
NEW DIRECTION COUNSELING SVCS
45 Jubilee Ct (19943-9244)
PHONE..............................302 289-3768
EMP: 5 EST: 2012
SALES (est): 39.43K Privately Held
SIC: 8322 General counseling services

(G-4007)
NEW TRINITY TRANSPORT LLC ✪
192 Fan Branch Dr (19943-9211)
PHONE..............................215 457-5700
EMP: 2 EST: 2022
SALES (est): 93.75K Privately Held
SIC: 3537 Trucks: freight, baggage, etc.: industrial, except mining

(G-4008)
PENWOOD LAWN CARE
125 Dickens Ln (19943-9287)
PHONE..............................302 535-4464
Catherine Nickle, Prin
EMP: 5 EST: 2013
SALES (est): 75.29K Privately Held
Web: www.penwoodlawncarehomeimprovement.com
SIC: 0782 Lawn care services

(G-4009)
PIZZADILI PARTNERS LLC
1683 Peach Basket Rd (19943-5649)
PHONE..............................302 284-9463
EMP: 5 EST: 2007
SALES (est): 386.86K Privately Held
Web: www.pizzadiliwinery.com
SIC: 5921 2084 Wine; Wines

(G-4010)
PURNELLS GENERAL CLG SVCS LLC
76 Belfry Dr (19943-7400)
PHONE..............................302 430-1170
EMP: 10 EST: 2020
SALES (est): 46K Privately Held
SIC: 7349 Janitorial service, contract basis

(G-4011)
R&C CONTRACTORS LLC
Also Called: Site/Tlity /Concrete Gen Contr
11351 S Dupont Hwy (19943-5665)
PHONE..............................302 284-9870
Randy Cole, Pr
EMP: 15 EST: 2020
SALES (est): 2.49MM Privately Held
SIC: 1611 7389 Concrete construction: roads, highways, sidewalks, etc.; Business Activities at Non-Commercial Site

(G-4012)
RAD PETS INC
685 Roesville Rd (19943-4450)
PHONE..............................302 335-5718
Robert Draper Senior, Pr
Robert Draper Ii, VP
EMP: 5 EST: 2001
SALES (est): 240.84K Privately Held
Web: www.radpets.com
SIC: 0752 Grooming services, pet and animal specialties

(G-4013)
RAYS PLUMBING & HEATING SVCS
Also Called: Ray's & Sons
7244 S Dupont Hwy (19943-5704)
P.O. Box 288 (19943-0288)
PHONE..............................302 697-3936
Craig Jones, Pr
Helen Jones, VP
Tamala Jones, Sec
EMP: 10 EST: 1972
SALES (est): 668.89K Privately Held
SIC: 1711 1731 1521 Plumbing contractors; General electrical contractor; New construction, single-family houses

(G-4014)
REGINALD D QUAIL SR
Also Called: Reggies General Contg Svc
3718 Midstate Rd (19943-4934)
PHONE..............................302 335-3145
Reginald D Quail Senior, Prin
EMP: 6 EST: 2010
SALES (est): 115.17K Privately Held
SIC: 1799 Special trade contractors, nec

(G-4015)
RELIABLE TRAILER INC
1603 Andrews Lake Rd (19943-5260)
PHONE..............................856 962-7900
Cory Nelson, Pr
Melissa Nelson, VP
EMP: 10 EST: 1985
SALES (est): 287.64K Privately Held
SIC: 7699 7539 Nautical repair services; Trailer repair

(G-4016)
RICKS ELECTRIC LLC
29 Ridgeway Cir (19943-2900)
PHONE..............................410 924-6764
Richard Bowen, Prin
EMP: 5 EST: 2018
SALES (est): 86K Privately Held
SIC: 1731 General electrical contractor

(G-4017)
RITE WAY DISTRIBUTORS (PA)
Also Called: Value Furniture
7385 S Dupont Hwy (19943-5721)
PHONE..............................302 535-8507
Lucian Szczepanski, Owner
EMP: 25 EST: 1974
SALES (est): 2.29MM
SALES (corp-wide): 2.29MM Privately Held
SIC: 6799 5712 5023 Commodity investors; Furniture stores; Homefurnishings

(G-4018)
RIVERSIDE FARMS LLC
604 Campground Rd (19943-4102)
PHONE..............................302 222-0760
James Wooter, Pr
EMP: 6 EST: 2012
SALES (est): 98.9K Privately Held
SIC: 4212 4789 Local trucking, without storage; Pipeline terminal facilities, independently operated

(G-4019)
ROBERT E DAVIS
72 Sovereignty Dr (19943-4951)
PHONE..............................302 535-9657
Robert E Davis, Prin
EMP: 6 EST: 2005
SALES (est): 481.88K Privately Held
SIC: 1521 Single-family housing construction

(G-4020)
ROBERT MILLER CONSTRUCTION INC
3345 Midstate Rd (19943-4911)
PHONE..............................302 335-4385
Robert Miller, Prin
EMP: 5 EST: 2011
SALES (est): 93.63K Privately Held
SIC: 1521 Single-family housing construction

(G-4021)
ROCK BOTTOM PAVING INC
8191 S Dupont Hwy (19943-5729)
PHONE..............................800 728-3160
EMP: 5 EST: 1999
SALES (est): 884.54K Privately Held
Web: www.rockbottompavingincde.com
SIC: 1611 Surfacing and paving

(G-4022)
RONNIE CARTER
2334 Sandtown Rd (19943-2524)
PHONE..............................302 284-9321
Paul R Carter, Prin
EMP: 5 EST: 2016
SALES (est): 140.91K Privately Held
SIC: 6411 Insurance agents, brokers, and service

(G-4023)
SCHAFFERS MOBILE DETAILING LLC
1539 Andrews Lake Rd (19943-5259)
PHONE..............................302 284-7636
Aaron Schaffer, Prin
EMP: 5 EST: 2014
SALES (est): 84.29K Privately Held
SIC: 7542 Washing and polishing, automotive

(G-4024)
SEAFOOD CITY INC
9996 S Dupont Hwy (19943-5615)
P.O. Box 710 (19943-0710)
PHONE..............................302 284-8486
EMP: 8 EST: 1992
SALES (est): 129.67K Privately Held
SIC: 5421 5146 5812 Seafood markets; Fish and seafoods; Eating places

(G-4025)
SEDOYLE GENERAL CONTRACTOR
9040 Canterbury Rd (19943-5215)
PHONE..............................302 531-5371
Sean Doyle, Prin
EMP: 5 EST: 2010
SALES (est): 85.85K Privately Held
SIC: 1799 Special trade contractors, nec

(G-4026)
SERVICE FIRST CONTAINER LLC
2870 John Hurd Rd (19943-3250)
PHONE..............................302 527-5939
EMP: 6 EST: 2017
SALES (est): 374.09K Privately Held
SIC: 5113 Boxes and containers

(G-4027)
SHAPEUP SALES COACHING
272 Fox Chase Rd (19943-5504)
PHONE..............................850 585-3527
EMP: 5 EST: 2016
SALES (est): 57.92K Privately Held
SIC: 8322 General counseling services

(G-4028)
SHINING TIME DAY CARE CENTER
220 Fox Chase Rd (19943-5504)
PHONE..............................302 335-2770
Michelle Toothman, Owner
EMP: 9 EST: 1992
SALES (est): 192.38K Privately Held
SIC: 8351 Group day care center

(G-4029)
SIGNATURE BUILDERS
1722 Jump School House Rd (19943-2753)
PHONE..............................302 331-9095
Bilders Signature, Pr
EMP: 5 EST: 2017
SALES (est): 89.48K Privately Held
Web: signature-builders-de.hub.biz
SIC: 1521 New construction, single-family houses

(PA)=Parent Co (HQ)=Headquarters
✪ = New Business established in last 2 years

Felton - Kent County (G-4030) GEOGRAPHIC SECTION

(G-4030)
STONEHAMMER CONSTRUCTION
12284 S Dupont Hwy (19943-4843)
PHONE..................302 233-3971
James Mccool, *Prin*
EMP: 5 EST: 2009
SALES (est): 163.32K **Privately Held**
SIC: 1521 Single-family housing construction

(G-4031)
SUPERIOR MAIDS
1391 Chandlers Rd (19943-2457)
PHONE..................302 284-2012
Sharon Creed, *Owner*
EMP: 10 EST: 1999
SALES (est): 194K **Privately Held**
Web: www.atlsuperiormaids.com
SIC: 7699 Cleaning services

(G-4032)
TILE GUY
1847 Barratts Chapel Rd (19943-5319)
PHONE..................302 382-7961
EMP: 5 EST: 2011
SALES (est): 65.24K **Privately Held**
SIC: 1743 Tile installation, ceramic

(G-4033)
TINA TRNER CMT THRPTIC MASSAGE
1365 Black Swamp Rd (19943-3655)
PHONE..................302 242-5114
Michelle Tesznar, *Prin*
EMP: 6 EST: 2015
SALES (est): 26K **Privately Held**
SIC: 8049 Offices of health practitioner

(G-4034)
U HAUL NEIGHBORHOOD DEALER
1408 Willow Grove Rd (19943-2912)
PHONE..................302 284-6051
Jim Martin, *Owner*
EMP: 8 EST: 2017
SALES (est): 50.83K **Privately Held**
Web: www.uhaul.com
SIC: 7513 Truck rental and leasing, no drivers

(G-4035)
UNPRIVILEGED DRINKERS LLC
19 Ponds Edge Ct (19943-7210)
PHONE..................215 800-5475
EMP: 7 EST: 2020
SALES (est): 193.91K **Privately Held**
SIC: 2741 Internet publishing and broadcasting

(G-4036)
W C FARMS LLC
3668 Spectrum Farms Rd (19943-3509)
PHONE..................302 242-1770
Eric Carlson, *Prin*
EMP: 7 EST: 2008
SALES (est): 435.08K **Privately Held**
SIC: 0191 General farms, primarily crop

(G-4037)
WAGNER N J & SONS TRUCKING
5972 Hopkins Cemetery Rd (19943-2365)
PHONE..................302 242-7731
N J Wagner, *Pt*
Emily Wagner, *Pt*
Kenneth Wagner, *Pt*
Christopher Wagner, *Pt*
Matthew Wagner, *Pt*
EMP: 10 EST: 1972
SALES (est): 987.41K **Privately Held**
SIC: 4212 Dump truck haulage

(G-4038)
YENCER BUILDERS INC
925 Marshyhope Rd (19943-3837)
PHONE..................302 284-9977
EMP: 8 EST: 1993
SALES (est): 2.12MM **Privately Held**
Web: www.yencerbuildersinc.com
SIC: 1521 New construction, single-family houses

Fenwick Island
Sussex County

(G-4039)
ACTION ENTERPRISE INC
Also Called: Delmarva Sports Action Mag
27 W Bayard St (19944-4503)
P.O. Box 914 (19930-0914)
PHONE..................302 537-7223
Susan Taylor-walls, *Pr*
EMP: 5 EST: 1987
SALES (est): 208K **Privately Held**
Web: brucewalls.zenfolio.com
SIC: 2721 Magazines: publishing only, not printed on site

(G-4040)
ATLANTIC GENERAL HOSPITAL
1209 Coastal Hwy (19944-4401)
PHONE..................302 539-2399
N Nicholson Borodulia, *Owner*
EMP: 5 EST: 2017
SALES (est): 108.81K **Privately Held**
Web: www.atlanticgeneral.org
SIC: 8099 Health and allied services, nec

(G-4041)
BEAM CONSTRUCTION INC
1 E Atlantic St (19944-4446)
PHONE..................302 537-2787
EMP: 5 EST: 1992
SALES (est): 529.49K **Privately Held**
Web: www.beamhomes.com
SIC: 1521 General remodeling, single-family houses

(G-4042)
BETHANY-FNWICK AREA CHMBER CMM
36913 Coastal Hwy (19944-4079)
PHONE..................302 539-2100
EMP: 5 EST: 1975
SALES (est): 510.9K **Privately Held**
Web: www.thequietresorts.com
SIC: 8611 Chamber of Commerce

(G-4043)
CAROLINA STREET GARDEN & HOME
40118 East South Carolina St (19944)
PHONE..................302 539-2405
Betty Phillips, *Mng Pt*
Paul Phillips, *Mng Pt*
EMP: 6 EST: 1992
SQ FT: 2,000
SALES (est): 449.36K **Privately Held**
Web: www.carolinastreet.com
SIC: 7389 5712 Interior decorating; Furniture stores

(G-4044)
CHESAPEAK INSURANCE ADVISORS
902 S Schulz Rd (19944-4563)
PHONE..................610 793-6885
EMP: 6 EST: 2011
SALES (est): 239.33K **Privately Held**
SIC: 6411 Insurance agents, nec

(G-4045)
COASTAL IMAGES INC
Also Called: Beach-Net.com
711 Coastal Hwy (19944-4416)
P.O. Box 1599 (19930-1599)
PHONE..................302 539-6001
Peter Roenke, *Pr*
Gloria Webster, *VP*
Michelle Roenke, *Sec*
EMP: 7 EST: 1981
SQ FT: 2,000
SALES (est): 639.04K **Privately Held**
Web: www.coastalimagesinc.com
SIC: 4813 2741 Internet host services; Directories, telephone: publishing only, not printed on site

(G-4046)
CORAL SANDS APTS
Bunting Ave (19944)
P.O. Box 281 (19975-0281)
PHONE..................302 539-9559
EMP: 5 EST: 1960
SALES (est): 157.49K **Privately Held**
Web: www.coralsandsapartments.com
SIC: 6513 Apartment building operators

(G-4047)
CYNTHIA DNNIS MTHER FOUNDATION
38892 Bunting Ave (19944-4075)
PHONE..................410 598-3819
EMP: 5 EST: 2011
SALES (est): 46.41K **Privately Held**
SIC: 8699 Charitable organization

(G-4048)
FENWICK ISLAND NAUTICAL SPORTS
300 Coastal Hwy (19944-4490)
PHONE..................443 397-0619
EMP: 5 EST: 2019
SALES (est): 273.15K **Privately Held**
SIC: 5137 5136 Women's and children's sportswear and swimsuits; Men's and boys' sportswear and work clothing

(G-4049)
FENWICK TOWERS CONDO ASSN
40126 Fenwick Towers Rd (19944-4125)
PHONE..................302 281-5025
EMP: 5 EST: 2020
SALES (est): 215.51K **Privately Held**
Web: www.fenwicktowerscondos.com
SIC: 8641 Condominium association

(G-4050)
FISHERS POPCORN FENWICK LLC
37081 Coastal Hwy (19944-4057)
PHONE..................302 539-8833
Martha F Hall, *Prin*
EMP: 35 EST: 1982
SALES (est): 2.73MM **Privately Held**
Web: www.fishers-popcorn.com
SIC: 5441 2096 Popcorn, including caramel corn; Potato chips and similar snacks

(G-4051)
LINDSAY MUMFORD LLC ◆
300 Coastal Hwy Unit 1 (19944-4490)
PHONE..................302 841-2309
Lindsay Mumford, *Managing Member*
EMP: 6 EST: 2022
SALES (est): 72.34K **Privately Held**
SIC: 8743 Public relations services

(G-4052)
LOCATED IN THE VILLAGE FENWICK
300 Coastal Hwy Unit 1 (19944-4490)
PHONE..................302 539-2242
EMP: 5 EST: 2017
SALES (est): 102.03K **Privately Held**
SIC: 6519 Real property lessors, nec

(G-4053)
RAYMOND E TOMASSETTI ESQ (PA)
1209 Coastal Hwy Fl 2 (19944-4401)
PHONE..................302 539-3041
Raymond Tomassetti Junior, *Owner*
EMP: 5 EST: 1989
SALES (est): 944.76K **Privately Held**
SIC: 8111 General practice attorney, lawyer

(G-4054)
SEA PLAY HOMES LLC ◆
1 E Indian St (19944-4430)
PHONE..................302 564-7557
Jeff Mould, *Pr*
EMP: 5 EST: 2022
SALES (est): 463.99K **Privately Held**
SIC: 6531 Real estate agents and managers

(G-4055)
SUNKIST TANNING INC
1300 Coastal Hwy (19944-4481)
PHONE..................302 539-8269
Tanning Sunkissed, *Pr*
EMP: 6 EST: 2010
SALES (est): 76.58K **Privately Held**
SIC: 7299 Tanning salon

(G-4056)
SURF AND SOUL YOGA
1401 Bora Bora St (19944-4511)
PHONE..................302 539-5861
Meghan Hanebutt, *Prin*
EMP: 5 EST: 2016
SALES (est): 22.86K **Privately Held**
SIC: 7999 Yoga instruction

(G-4057)
SUSSEX SANDS INC
Also Called: Sands Motel
1501 Coastal Hwy (19944-4422)
P.O. Box 228 (19975-0228)
PHONE..................302 539-8200
Susan B Caldwell, *Prin*
EMP: 7 EST: 2010
SALES (est): 250.33K **Privately Held**
SIC: 7011 Motels

(G-4058)
WELLNESS BY SEA LLC
1209 Coastal Hwy (19944-4401)
PHONE..................302 278-0093
Kimberly Brasure, *Prin*
EMP: 7 EST: 2018
SALES (est): 236.72K **Privately Held**
Web: www.wellnessbytheseade.com
SIC: 8099 Health and allied services, nec

Frankford
Sussex County

(G-4059)
A & A AIR SERVICES INC (PA)
Also Called: Honeywell Authorized Dealer
35130 Bennett Rd (19945-4061)
P.O. Box 610 (19975-0610)
PHONE..................302 436-4800
Gregory Allen, *Pr*
EMP: 44 EST: 1987
SQ FT: 2,000
SALES (est): 5.4MM **Privately Held**

GEOGRAPHIC SECTION

Frankford - Sussex County (G-4089)

Web: www.aacompanies.com
SIC: **1711** Warm air heating and air conditioning contractor

(G-4060)
ALLISON SCRIVANI LLC
108 Ocean Farm Dr (19945-4757)
PHONE....................302 841-2320
Allison Scrivani, *Prin*
EMP: 8 **EST:** 2011
SALES (est): 100.01K **Privately Held**
SIC: **8011** General and family practice, physician/surgeon

(G-4061)
ASH EDWARD L I
7 Thatcher St (19945-9400)
PHONE....................302 732-9181
Edward L I Ash, *Prin*
EMP: 5 **EST:** 2010
SALES (est): 100.45K **Privately Held**
SIC: **1522** Residential construction, nec

(G-4062)
ATLANTIC COAST BUILDERS LLC
21538 Shell Station Rd (19945-2432)
PHONE....................302 396-7824
Juana Parada, *Prin*
EMP: 8 **EST:** 2017
SALES (est): 407.07K **Privately Held**
SIC: **1521** New construction, single-family houses

(G-4063)
ATLANTIC RESOURCE MANAGEMENT
32717 Lavender Ln (19945-2854)
PHONE....................302 539-2029
Laf Erickson, *Pr*
EMP: 6 **EST:** 1999
SALES (est): 177.49K **Privately Held**
Web: www.atlanticresource.net
SIC: **8748** Environmental consultant

(G-4064)
ATLANTIC RESOURCE MANAGEMENT
32582 Omar Rd (19945-2834)
P.O. Box 869 (19970-0869)
PHONE....................302 539-2029
Lisa Wood, *Owner*
EMP: 10 **EST:** 2006
SALES (est): 563.29K **Privately Held**
Web: www.atlanticresource.net
SIC: **8748** Environmental consultant

(G-4065)
ATTAC CONSULTING GROUP LLC
33968 Monterray Ave (19945-4735)
P.O. Box 563 (19945-0563)
PHONE....................443 766-9079
EMP: 7 **EST:** 2018
SALES (est): 83.37K **Privately Held**
SIC: **8748** Business consulting, nec

(G-4066)
B & E TIRE ALIGNMENT INC
Rr 113 (19945)
P.O. Box 325 (19945-0325)
PHONE....................302 732-6091
Kenneth Evans, *Pr*
EMP: 5 **EST:** 1985
SQ FT: 3,600
SALES (est): 769.74K **Privately Held**
Web: www.bandetireandalignment.com
SIC: **7539** Wheel alignment, automotive

(G-4067)
BARBARA BAKER
37058 Triple B Farm Ln (19945-2325)
PHONE....................302 238-7415
Barbara Baker, *Owner*
EMP: 5 **EST:** 2015
SALES (est): 33.19K **Privately Held**
Web: www.barbarabakerrealty.com
SIC: **7231** Beauty shops

(G-4068)
BARNES CAMP
37171 Camp Barnes Rd (19945-3455)
PHONE....................302 539-7775
Randy Ramirez, *Prin*
EMP: 6 **EST:** 2010
SALES (est): 74K **Privately Held**
Web: www.campbarnes.net
SIC: **7999** Instruction schools, camps, and services

(G-4069)
BAY SPRAY
34199 Dianas Ln (19945-3842)
PHONE....................302 245-2715
EMP: 5 **EST:** 2016
SALES (est): 45.68K **Privately Held**
Web: www.bayspray.com
SIC: **7699** Cleaning services

(G-4070)
BAYSIDE MINI STORAGE
36097 Zion Church Rd (19945-4544)
PHONE....................302 524-2096
EMP: 6 **EST:** 2014
SALES (est): 86.55K **Privately Held**
Web: www.whatwillyoustore.com
SIC: **4225** Miniwarehouse, warehousing

(G-4071)
BETHANY FENWICK AREA CHAM
5 Main St (19945-9516)
PHONE....................302 537-3839
EMP: 5 **EST:** 2018
SALES (est): 84.92K **Privately Held**
Web: www.thequietresorts.com
SIC: **8611** Chamber of Commerce

(G-4072)
BILLIE STEVENS CARLINS
32427 Mccary Rd (19945-4031)
PHONE....................302 436-0856
Billie Carlins, *Prin*
EMP: 5 **EST:** 2009
SALES (est): 42.65K **Privately Held**
SIC: **7231** Beauty shops

(G-4073)
BLADES HVAC SERVICES
Rte 1 Pa (19945-9801)
PHONE....................302 539-4436
EMP: 8 **EST:** 2007
SALES (est): 64.62K **Privately Held**
Web: www.bladeshvac.com
SIC: **1711** Heating and air conditioning contractors

(G-4074)
BOLD INDUSTRIES LLC
37424 Dale Earnhardt Blvd (19945-3676)
PHONE....................302 858-7237
Ashlee Justice, *Prin*
EMP: 4 **EST:** 2018
SALES (est): 107.01K **Privately Held**
SIC: **3999** Manufacturing industries, nec

(G-4075)
BRAD ALLEN CARPENTRY LLC
33133 Jess N Ray Way (19945-2858)
PHONE....................302 228-4256
Brad Allen, *Prin*
EMP: 5 **EST:** 2015
SALES (est): 78.13K **Privately Held**
SIC: **1751** Carpentry work

(G-4076)
BRADFORDS QUALITY CARE INC
32303 Gum Rd (19945-4054)
PHONE....................302 436-2467
Bradford Morris, *Owner*
EMP: 5 **EST:** 2013
SALES (est): 36.55K **Privately Held**
SIC: **7699** Cleaning services

(G-4077)
BRASURES BODY SHOP INC
Rte 113 (19945)
P.O. Box 118 (19945-0118)
PHONE....................302 732-6157
James Brasure, *Pr*
Paulette Brasure, *Sec*
EMP: 6 **EST:** 1983
SQ FT: 4,000
SALES (est): 500.81K **Privately Held**
SIC: **7532** **5521** Body shop, automotive; Automobiles, used cars only

(G-4078)
BRENNAN TITLE COMPANY
31634 Hickory Manor Rd (19945-3142)
PHONE....................302 541-0400
EMP: 5
Web: www.brennantitle.com
SIC: **6541** Title and trust companies
PA: Brennan Title Company
3261 Old Washington Rd # 3040
Waldorf MD 20602

(G-4079)
BRYTON HMES AT FIVE POINTS LLC
30632 Redmon Rd (19945)
PHONE....................302 703-6633
EMP: 5 **EST:** 2014
SALES (est): 147.5K **Privately Held**
Web: www.brytonhomes.com
SIC: **1521** New construction, single-family houses

(G-4080)
BUNTING & BERTRAND INC
15 Hickory St (19945-2032)
P.O. Box 639 (19945-0639)
PHONE....................302 732-6836
Walter H Bunting, *Pr*
EMP: 12 **EST:** 1963
SALES (est): 2.41MM **Privately Held**
Web: www.buntingandbertrand.com
SIC: **5083** Poultry equipment

(G-4081)
C & B COMPLETE CLG SVC INC
Also Called: C&B Complete Cleaning & Cnstr
36007 Zion Church Rd (19945-4544)
PHONE....................302 436-9622
William Craig Conover, *Pr*
EMP: 22 **EST:** 1986
SALES (est): 1.2MM **Privately Held**
Web: www.cbcomplete.com
SIC: **7699** **7217** **7349** **1521** Cleaning services; Carpet and upholstery cleaning; Cleaning service, industrial or commercial; Repairing fire damage, single-family houses

(G-4082)
C M CONSTRUCTION CO LLC
89 Reed St (19945-9799)
PHONE....................302 228-3570
EMP: 5 **EST:** 2018
SALES (est): 221.1K **Privately Held**

SIC: **1521** Single-family housing construction

(G-4083)
CAPPO DENNIS JOHN
32776 Omar Rd (19945-2832)
PHONE....................302 245-2261
Dennis John Cappo, *Owner*
EMP: 5 **EST:** 2006
SALES (est): 369.81K **Privately Held**
SIC: **1522** Residential construction, nec

(G-4084)
CHANDLEE PROJECTS LLC
35145 Chandlee Ln (19945-3586)
PHONE....................717 542-5919
Sara E Chandlee, *Prin*
EMP: 5 **EST:** 2016
SALES (est): 208.27K **Privately Held**
Web: www.chandleeprojects.com
SIC: **1521** New construction, single-family houses

(G-4085)
CHESAPEAKE CLIMATE CONTROL LLC
Also Called: Honeywell Authorized Dealer
34913 Delaware Ave (19945-3890)
PHONE....................302 732-6006
Travis Martin, *Owner*
EMP: 28 **EST:** 2017
SALES (est): 1.84MM **Privately Held**
Web: www.chesapeakeclimatecontrol.net
SIC: **1711** Warm air heating and air conditioning contractor

(G-4086)
CHESAPEAKE FIRE SYSTEMS LLC
34913 Delaware Ave (19945-3890)
PHONE....................302 732-6006
Debbie Chaney, *CFO*
EMP: 10 **EST:** 2019
SALES (est): 665.93K **Privately Held**
SIC: **8741** Management services

(G-4087)
CHESAPEAKE HOME SERVICES LLC
34913 Delaware Ave (19945-3890)
PHONE....................302 732-6006
Travis Martin, *Managing Member*
Jessie Martin, *Managing Member*
EMP: 8 **EST:** 2019
SALES (est): 319.32K **Privately Held**
Web: www.chesapeakehomeservices.com
SIC: **1711** **7349** Plumbing, heating, air-conditioning; Building and office cleaning services

(G-4088)
CHESAPEAKE MANAGEMENT CO LLC
34913 Delaware Ave (19945-3890)
PHONE....................302 732-6006
EMP: 35 **EST:** 2020
SALES (est): 1.78MM **Privately Held**
SIC: **8741** Management services

(G-4089)
CHESAPEAKE PLUMBING & HTG INC
34913 Delaware Ave (19945-3890)
PHONE....................302 732-6006
Travis Martin, *Pr*
Jessie Martin, *
EMP: 27 **EST:** 2004
SALES (est): 15MM **Privately Held**
Web: www.chesapeakehomeservices.com
SIC: **1711** Plumbing contractors

Frankford - Sussex County (G-4090)   GEOGRAPHIC SECTION

(G-4090)
CHUCK COLEMAN
34130 Burton Farm Rd (19945-2951)
PHONE..................................302 537-2071
Chuck Coleman, *Prin*
EMP: 5 **EST:** 2007
SALES (est): 186.24K **Privately Held**
SIC: 1521 New construction, single-family houses

(G-4091)
COASTAL PAINT & REMODELING LLC
153 Clayton Ave (19945-2005)
P.O. Box 547 (19945-0547)
PHONE..................................302 278-5471
EMP: 10 **EST:** 2016
SALES (est): 559.54K **Privately Held**
SIC: 1521 General remodeling, single-family houses

(G-4092)
COASTAL SUN ROMS PRCH ENCLSRES
36017 Pine Bark Ln (19945-3571)
PHONE..................................302 537-3679
David Goodman, *Prin*
EMP: 2 **EST:** 2007
SALES (est): 195.07K **Privately Held**
SIC: 1521 3448 5999 Patio and deck construction and repair; Sunrooms, prefabricated metal; Awnings

(G-4093)
CONNECTIONS DEVELOPMENT CORP
35906 Zion Church Rd (19945-4540)
PHONE..................................302 436-3292
Catherine D Mckay, *CEO*
EMP: 29
SIC: 8351 Group day care center
PA: Connections Development Corp
3821 Lancaster Pike
Wilmington DE 19805

(G-4094)
COZY CRITTERS CHILD CARE CORP
35371 Beaver Dam Rd (19945-3227)
PHONE..................................302 541-8210
Laura Collins, *Dir*
Lora Collins, *Owner*
EMP: 27 **EST:** 2002
SALES (est): 286.11K **Privately Held**
Web: www.cozycritterschildcare.com
SIC: 8351 Group day care center

(G-4095)
CP CASES INC
34607 Dupont Blvd (19945-3870)
PHONE..................................410 352-9450
Peter Gill, *Managing Member*
Bruce Blackway, *Genl Mgr*
EMP: 8 **EST:** 2014
SALES (est): 2.42MM **Privately Held**
Web: www.cpcases.com
SIC: 5084 3444 3089 3161 Materials handling machinery; Sheet metalwork; Cases, plastics; Cases, carrying, nec

(G-4096)
CUSTOM MECHANICAL INC (PA)
Also Called: Honeywell Authorized Dealer
34799 Daisey Rd (19945-3530)
P.O. Box 1479 (19930-1479)
PHONE..................................302 537-1150
Glen S Roberts, *Pr*
Chris Megee, *
Patti Roberts, *
EMP: 40 **EST:** 1981
SQ FT: 3,200
SALES (est): 4.93MM
SALES (corp-wide): 4.93MM **Privately Held**
Web: www.custommechanical.com
SIC: 1711 3444 Mechanical contractor; Sheet metalwork

(G-4097)
CYPRESS TREE CARE
33529 Fox Run (19945-3834)
PHONE..................................302 732-3227
Robert Tunnell, *Prin*
EMP: 5 **EST:** 2016
SALES (est): 242.83K **Privately Held**
Web: www.cypresstreecare.com
SIC: 0783 Planting, pruning, and trimming services

(G-4098)
DAVES TRUCK REPAIR LLC
24434 Cypress Rd (19945-2311)
PHONE..................................302 362-2578
David Craft, *Prin*
EMP: 5 **EST:** 2016
SALES (est): 47.61K **Privately Held**
SIC: 7699 Repair services, nec

(G-4099)
DAVIS TRUCKING & FAMILY LLC
Also Called: Davis Trucking
22181 Charles West Rd (19945-2431)
PHONE..................................302 381-6358
Shannen Davis, *Prin*
Raymond Davis, *Prin*
EMP: 10 **EST:** 2008
SALES (est): 570.6K **Privately Held**
SIC: 4214 Local trucking with storage

(G-4100)
DELMARVA CONCRETE PUMPING INC
34090 Central Ave (19945-3555)
Rural Route 2 Box 174b (19945)
PHONE..................................302 537-4118
Joseph Schroeder, *Pr*
EMP: 12 **EST:** 2000
SALES (est): 487.87K **Privately Held**
Web: www.delmarvaconcretepumping.com
SIC: 1771 Concrete pumping

(G-4101)
DEPENDABLE ELEC SVC & REPR
37680 Hudson Rd (19945-2317)
PHONE..................................302 877-0770
EMP: 5 **EST:** 2013
SALES (est): 185.8K **Privately Held**
Web: www.dependableelectricalservice.com
SIC: 7699 Repair services, nec

(G-4102)
DIRICKSON CREEK CONSTRUCTION L
37377 Dirickson Creek Rd (19945-3430)
PHONE..................................302 604-2482
EMP: 5 **EST:** 2018
SALES (est): 310.29K **Privately Held**
Web: www.dirincksoncreekconstruction.com
SIC: 1521 Single-family housing construction

(G-4103)
DPS CUSTOM PAINTING LLC
33099 Thunder Rd (19945-2917)
PHONE..................................302 732-3232
EMP: 5 **EST:** 2001
SALES (est): 260.52K **Privately Held**
Web: www.dpcustompainting.com
SIC: 1721 Painting and paper hanging

(G-4104)
EAST SUSSEX MOOSE LODGE
35993 Zion Church Rd (19945-4500)
PHONE..................................302 436-2088
Glen Densmore, *Admn*
Glen Densmore, *Admn*
EMP: 5 **EST:** 2008
SALES (est): 278.92K **Privately Held**
Web: www.mdmoose.org
SIC: 8641 8699 Civic associations; Charitable organization

(G-4105)
ESHAM PAINTING LLC
32419 Frankford School Rd (19945-3262)
PHONE..................................302 381-7876
Michael Esham, *Prin*
EMP: 5 **EST:** 2015
SALES (est): 85.87K **Privately Held**
SIC: 1721 Painting and paper hanging

(G-4106)
EUROPEAN COACH WERKES INC
Rte 20 (19945)
PHONE..................................302 436-2277
Jack Barranger, *Pr*
EMP: 6 **EST:** 1991
SQ FT: 6,500
SALES (est): 981.68K **Privately Held**
Web: www.europeancoachwerkes.com
SIC: 5521 7389 Automobiles, used cars only; Automobile recovery service

(G-4107)
FRANCES ANN OWENS
34720 Pyle Center Rd (19945-3272)
PHONE..................................302 436-2333
Frances Ann Owens, *Prin*
EMP: 5 **EST:** 2010
SALES (est): 246.6K **Privately Held**
SIC: 7389 Business Activities at Non-Commercial Site

(G-4108)
FRANKFORD CUSTOM WOODWORKS INC
34139 Dupont Blvd (19945-3807)
PHONE..................................302 732-9570
Maynard Esender, *Pr*
EMP: 8 **EST:** 2007
SALES (est): 331.42K **Privately Held**
Web: www.frankfordcustom.com
SIC: 2431 Millwork

(G-4109)
GARTH ENTERPRISES LTD
37428 Dirickson Creek Rd (19945-3431)
PHONE..................................302 349-2298
Garth Troescher Senior, *Pr*
EMP: 11 **EST:** 2010
SALES (est): 1.36MM **Privately Held**
Web: www.garthenterprises.com
SIC: 1522 1542 Residential construction, nec; Nonresidential construction, nec

(G-4110)
GEARED UP TRUCKS AND MORE
34407 Dupont Blvd (19945-3886)
PHONE..................................302 927-0147
EMP: 5 **EST:** 2019
SALES (est): 479.62K **Privately Held**
Web: www.gearedtrucks.net
SIC: 4212 Local trucking, without storage

(G-4111)
GERONE C HUDSON ELEC CONTR
35944 Bayard Rd (19945-4573)
PHONE..................................302 539-3332
Guy Hudson, *Pr*
Pat Hudson, *Sec*
EMP: 10 **EST:** 1969
SQ FT: 2,500
SALES (est): 261.29K **Privately Held**
SIC: 1731 General electrical contractor

(G-4112)
GUMBORO SERVICE CENTER INC
22181 Charles West Rd (19945-2431)
PHONE..................................302 238-7040
Margarite Davis, *Pr*
EMP: 6 **EST:** 2002
SALES (est): 515.49K **Privately Held**
SIC: 7538 General automotive repair shops

(G-4113)
HITZ MECHANICAL
37300 Dirickson Creek Rd (19945-3429)
PHONE..................................727 742-6315
Thomas Bent, *Prin*
EMP: 6 **EST:** 2018
SALES (est): 35.72K **Privately Held**
SIC: 7349 Building maintenance services, nec

(G-4114)
HK ELECTRIC LLC
36207 Watch Hill Rd (19945-3691)
PHONE..................................302 927-0688
Kevin Curcio, *Prin*
EMP: 5 **EST:** 2019
SALES (est): 197.41K **Privately Held**
SIC: 1731 Electrical work

(G-4115)
HYDROHERO FRANCHISING LLC
34407 Dupont Blvd Unit 8 (19945-3886)
PHONE..................................302 321-7077
Elizabeth Keefer, *Asst Sec*
EMP: 7 **EST:** 2018
SALES (est): 184.27K **Privately Held**
SIC: 1799 Special trade contractors, nec

(G-4116)
INTEGRITY IRRIGATION SERV
20925 Lowes Crossing Rd (19945-2424)
PHONE..................................302 542-7694
EMP: 5 **EST:** 2009
SALES (est): 56.07K **Privately Held**
SIC: 4971 Irrigation systems

(G-4117)
J&M REMODELING
30390 Pepper Trl (19945-3033)
PHONE..................................443 736-0127
Jose Maunel Uscanga, *Prin*
EMP: 5 **EST:** 2016
SALES (est): 78.95K **Privately Held**
SIC: 1521 General remodeling, single-family houses

(G-4118)
JAMES POWELL
Also Called: Robinsons Sewage Disposial
34309 Burton Farm Rd (19945-2957)
PHONE..................................302 539-2351
James R Powell, *Prin*
EMP: 5 **EST:** 2011
SALES (est): 302.81K **Privately Held**
SIC: 4953 Sewage treatment facility

(G-4119)
JUAN DE DIOS PAINTING
21538 Shell Station Rd (19945-2432)
PHONE..................................302 841-0363
Juan Tarda, *Pr*
EMP: 5 **EST:** 2016
SALES (est): 51.62K **Privately Held**
Web: www.juandediospainting.com

GEOGRAPHIC SECTION
Frankford - Sussex County (G-4149)

SIC: 1721 Painting and paper hanging

(G-4120)
KC SERVICE CLEANING
34407 Dupont Blvd (19945-3886)
PHONE..................................410 845-1988
EMP: 5 EST: 2020
SALES (est): 201.97K **Privately Held**
SIC: 7699 Cleaning services

(G-4121)
KEN BERTRAND REALTY REPAIRS
36058 Zion Church Rd (19945-4543)
PHONE..................................302 436-2872
Kenneth Bertrand, *Prin*
EMP: 6 EST: 2008
SALES (est): 161.76K **Privately Held**
SIC: 7699 Repair services, nec

(G-4122)
L MAINTENANCE
32845 Murray Rd (19945-2518)
PHONE..................................302 841-1698
Frederick Manuel, *Prin*
EMP: 5 EST: 2010
SALES (est): 51.23K **Privately Held**
SIC: 7349 Building maintenance services, nec

(G-4123)
LORD AND SONS LANDSCAPING
33999 W Airport Rd (19945-4070)
PHONE..................................302 745-3001
Michael Lord, *Prin*
EMP: 7 EST: 2017
SALES (est): 386.37K **Privately Held**
SIC: 0781 Landscape services

(G-4124)
LOYAL ORDER OF MOOSE
35993 Zion Church Rd (19945-4500)
PHONE..................................302 436-2088
Glen Disnmore, *Mgr*
EMP: 5 EST: 2017
SALES (est): 58.82K **Privately Held**
SIC: 8621 Professional organizations

(G-4125)
MATTS MANAGEMENT FAMILY LLC
Also Called: Matt's Line Painting
32397 Omar Rd (19945-2807)
PHONE..................................302 732-3715
Gary Matthews, *Managing Member*
Angela Matthews, *Managing Member*
EMP: 8 EST: 1983
SALES (est): 690.19K **Privately Held**
Web: www.mattsmanagement.com
SIC: 1611 Highway and street construction

(G-4126)
MELSON FUNERAL SERVICES LTD
Also Called: Melsons Henlipen Creammatury
43 Thatcher St (19945-9400)
P.O. Box 100 (19945-0100)
PHONE..................................302 732-9000
EMP: 5 EST: 1962
SALES (est): 239.53K **Privately Held**
Web: www.melsonfuneralservices.com
SIC: 7261 Funeral director

(G-4127)
MELSONS CAPE HNLOPEN CREMATORY
41 Thatcher St (19945-9400)
P.O. Box 100 (19945-0100)
PHONE..................................302 537-2441
Alvin D Melson, *Dir*
Lisa A Banks, *Sec*
Sharon Melson, *Genl Mgr*
EMP: 9 EST: 1980
SALES (est): 220.94K **Privately Held**
SIC: 7261 Crematory

(G-4128)
MULTI KOASTAL SERVICES
34756 Roxana Rd (19945-3242)
P.O. Box 276 (19970-0276)
PHONE..................................302 436-8822
Kenneth Walsh, *Owner*
EMP: 8 EST: 1985
SALES (est): 836.31K **Privately Held**
Web: www.multikoastal.com
SIC: 7699 Septic tank cleaning service

(G-4129)
OCEAN TOWER CONSTRUCTION LLC
34407 Dupont Blvd Unit 2 (19945-3886)
P.O. Box 270 (19975-0270)
PHONE..................................443 373-7096
Georgiana Cojoearu, *Off Mgr*
EMP: 35 EST: 2010
SALES (est): 2.44MM **Privately Held**
Web: www.oceantowerconstruction.com
SIC: 1521 General remodeling, single-family houses

(G-4130)
OCEAN TOWER CONSTRUCTION LLC
34667 Bethany Dr (19945-4602)
PHONE..................................443 366-5556
Angela Burns, *Prin*
EMP: 5 EST: 2012
SALES (est): 179.62K **Privately Held**
Web: www.oceantowerconstruction.com
SIC: 1521 General remodeling, single-family houses

(G-4131)
PAULS PAVING INC
37425 Dale Earnhardt Blvd (19945-3662)
P.O. Box 232 (19930-0232)
PHONE..................................302 539-9123
Anita Justice, *Pr*
Michael Justice, *VP*
Maureen Justice, *Sec*
EMP: 15 EST: 1974
SALES (est): 483.12K **Privately Held**
Web: www.po-storage.com
SIC: 1771 1629 Driveway contractor; Land clearing contractor

(G-4132)
PEDRO RASCON CIMARRON
Also Called: Pedro Cimarron Rascon LLC
34969 Shockley Town Rd (19945-3041)
PHONE..................................302 448-6806
Pedro Cimarron, *Pr*
EMP: 5 EST: 2011
SALES (est): 232.13K **Privately Held**
SIC: 1521 New construction, single-family houses

(G-4133)
PEN DEL AUTO & MARINE INC
35936 Pen Del Ave (19945-3573)
PHONE..................................302 430-3046
Zach Bedell, *Prin*
EMP: 7 EST: 2016
SALES (est): 49.07K **Privately Held**
Web: www.pen-del.org
SIC: 7538 General automotive repair shops

(G-4134)
PREMIER GLASS & SCREEN INC
Also Called: Premier Porch & Patio
33937 Premire Dr (19945-3830)
PHONE..................................302 732-3101
Joe Kauffman, *Pr*
Frank Tharby, *VP*
EMP: 11 EST: 1990
SQ FT: 6,000
SALES (est): 498.62K **Privately Held**
Web: www.premierglassandscreen.com
SIC: 1793 Glass and glazing work

(G-4135)
PROGRESSIVE SYSTEMS INC
Also Called: PSI
25 Hickory St (19945-2032)
P.O. Box 35 (19945-0035)
PHONE..................................302 732-3321
Joseph P Carney, *Pr*
EMP: 6 EST: 1991
SQ FT: 8,000
SALES (est): 1.44MM **Privately Held**
Web: www.progressivesystemsinc.com
SIC: 5084 5169 7699 Cleaning equipment, high pressure, sand or steam; Chemicals and allied products, nec; Industrial equipment services

(G-4136)
PYLE CHILD DEVELOPMENT CENTER
34314 Pyle Center Rd (19945-3277)
PHONE..................................302 732-1443
EMP: 11 EST: 1992
SALES (est): 232.06K **Privately Held**
SIC: 8351 Child day care services

(G-4137)
RAMAINE&SONS CONTRACTING
35716 Clam Ave (19945-4523)
PHONE..................................302 212-8330
Robert Maine, *Prin*
EMP: 5 EST: 2014
SALES (est): 62.44K **Privately Held**
SIC: 1799 Special trade contractors, nec

(G-4138)
RENOVATE SOLUTIONS
37116 Fairway Dr (19945-5200)
PHONE..................................717 951-4300
Joseph Dopp, *Prin*
EMP: 5 EST: 2015
SALES (est): 59.69K **Privately Held**
SIC: 1721 Painting and paper hanging

(G-4139)
ROBERT GEARS
Also Called: Gears Mechanical Company
34696 Daisey Rd (19945-3531)
PHONE..................................302 690-2590
Robert Gears, *Owner*
EMP: 5 EST: 1992
SQ FT: 1,500
SALES (est): 449.36K **Privately Held**
SIC: 1711 Plumbing contractors

(G-4140)
ROXANA AUTOMOBILE SERVICE CENT
Roxana Rd (19945)
PHONE..................................302 436-6202
EMP: 5 EST: 2004
SALES (est): 61.55K **Privately Held**
SIC: 8699 Automobile owners' association

(G-4141)
SHACKLEFORD FACILITIES INC ✪
33192 Dupont Blvd (19945-3801)
PHONE..................................877 735-3938
Kevin Shackleford, *CEO*
EMP: 10 EST: 2022
SALES (est): 257.53K **Privately Held**
SIC: 0781 4959 8744 1799 Landscape services; Snowplowing; Facilities support services; Parking lot maintenance

(G-4142)
SHOCKER TOWING & RECOVERY
24423 Daisey Rd (19945-2316)
PHONE..................................302 259-1123
Anthony Michael Lagano, *Pr*
EMP: 6 EST: 2015
SALES (est): 245.16K **Privately Held**
Web: www.osvassist.com
SIC: 7549 Towing service, automotive

(G-4143)
SHOCKLEYS AUTO SERVICE
37141 Trixie Ln (19945-3425)
PHONE..................................302 537-7663
Steve Shockley, *Prin*
EMP: 5 EST: 2008
SALES (est): 94.08K **Privately Held**
SIC: 7538 General automotive repair shops

(G-4144)
SIMPLER SURVEYING & ASSOCIATES
32486 Powell Farm Rd (19945-3344)
PHONE..................................302 539-7873
Greg Hook, *Owner*
EMP: 9 EST: 2000
SALES (est): 441.84K **Privately Held**
Web: www.delawaresurveyor.com
SIC: 8713 Surveying services

(G-4145)
SMILE HEATING & AC
34453 Park Cir (19945-3633)
PHONE..................................302 542-7242
Oh Son Young, *Owner*
EMP: 6 EST: 2009
SALES (est): 140.85K **Privately Held**
SIC: 1711 Warm air heating and air conditioning contractor

(G-4146)
SNOW PHARMACEUTICALS LLC
35998 Zion Church Rd (19945-4501)
PHONE..................................302 436-8855
▲ EMP: 6 EST: 1989
SALES (est): 536.94K **Privately Held**
Web: www.snowbalm.com
SIC: 2834 Pharmaceutical preparations

(G-4147)
SOUTH COASTAL
33711 S Coastal Ln (19945-4221)
PHONE..................................302 542-5668
Kevin Vanauken, *Prin*
EMP: 6 EST: 2010
SALES (est): 168.09K **Privately Held**
SIC: 8322 Community center

(G-4148)
STEAM WIZARDS LLC
34575 Dupont Blvd (19945-3945)
PHONE..................................302 548-5942
Liviu Ciobanu, *Managing Member*
EMP: 6
SALES (est): 63.67K **Privately Held**
SIC: 7217 Carpet and rug cleaning plant

(G-4149)
SUN MARINE MAINTENANCE INC
35322 Bayard Rd (19945-4557)
PHONE..................................302 539-6756
Michael R Jahnigen, *Pr*
▼ EMP: 21 EST: 1976
SQ FT: 3,000
SALES (est): 863.84K **Privately Held**
Web: www.sunpilefoundations.com
SIC: 1629 Marine construction

Frankford - Sussex County (G-4150) — GEOGRAPHIC SECTION

(G-4150)
SUN PILEDRIVING EQUIPMENT LLC
35322 Bayard Rd (19945-4557)
PHONE...................302 539-6756
▲ EMP: 6 EST: 2005
SQ FT: 1,500
SALES (est): 2.27MM Privately Held
Web: www.spe-usa.net
SIC: 5082 Road construction equipment

(G-4151)
SUSSEX MARINE CONSTRUCTION INC
32469 Frankford School Rd (19945-3262)
PHONE...................302 436-9680
Jonathan Staehle, Prin
EMP: 5 EST: 2004
SALES (est): 834.73K Privately Held
Web: www.sussexmarineconstruction.com
SIC: 1629 Marine construction

(G-4152)
THOMAS CLARK MASONRY& EXCAV
33722 Clarks Trl (19945-2645)
PHONE...................302 462-6039
Thomas Clark, Prin
EMP: 5 EST: 2011
SALES (est): 142.9K Privately Held
SIC: 1794 Excavation work

(G-4153)
THOMAS PHILLIPS
20952 Shell Station Rd (19945-2404)
PHONE...................302 238-7130
Thomas Phillips, Prin
EMP: 5 EST: 2005
SALES (est): 180K Privately Held
SIC: 7389 Business Activities at Non-Commercial Site

(G-4154)
TROTTYS CONCRETE PUMPING INC
34107 Dupont Blvd (19945-3807)
PHONE...................302 732-3100
Richard Trott, Pr
EMP: 8 EST: 2004
SALES (est): 477.96K Privately Held
SIC: 1771 Concrete pumping

(G-4155)
TRUE NORTH GROUP LLC
35322 Bayard Rd (19945-4557)
PHONE...................302 539-2488
Bradley A Absher, Prin
EMP: 12 EST: 2017
SALES (est): 613.33K Privately Held
Web: www.truenorthls.com
SIC: 8713 Surveying services

(G-4156)
U-HAUL NEIGHBORHOOD DEALER
Also Called: U-Haul
36097 Zion Church Rd (19945-4544)
PHONE...................302 321-6032
EMP: 6 EST: 2014
SALES (est): 72.08K Privately Held
Web: www.uhaul.com
SIC: 7513 Truck rental and leasing, no drivers

(G-4157)
VETERAN SERVICES
32117 Judiths Ln (19945-2826)
PHONE...................302 864-0009
Jack Kessel, Owner
EMP: 59 EST: 2014
SALES (est): 364.38K Privately Held
Web: veterantreeandlandscaping.weebly.com
SIC: 8641 Veterans' organization

(G-4158)
WAYNE BENNETT
Also Called: Bennett Electric
35484 Honeysuckle Rd (19945-4520)
PHONE...................302 436-2379
Wayne Bennett, Owner
EMP: 5 EST: 1980
SALES (est): 390.63K Privately Held
SIC: 1731 General electrical contractor

(G-4159)
WE ARE FAMILY CLEANING SERVICE
32538 Mccary Rd (19945-4030)
PHONE...................302 524-8294
Roxie J Whaley, Owner
EMP: 5 EST: 2017
SALES (est): 48.63K Privately Held
SIC: 7699 Cleaning services

(G-4160)
WEBER SIGN CO
Also Called: Weber Sign & Art Studio
16 Hickory St (19945-2031)
P.O. Box 131 (19939-0131)
PHONE...................302 732-1429
Rick Weber, Owner
EMP: 10 EST: 2001
SALES (est): 483.3K Privately Held
Web: www.webersigns.com
SIC: 3993 Signs and advertising specialties

(G-4161)
WINE WORX LLC
Also Called: Salted Vines Vineyard Winery
32512 Blackwater Rd (19945-2940)
PHONE...................302 436-1500
Adrian Mobilia, Pr
EMP: 20 EST: 2008
SALES (est): 2.73MM Privately Held
Web: www.saltedvines.com
SIC: 5182 2084 Wine; Wines

(G-4162)
WINIFRED ELLEN ERBE
Also Called: Blue Sky Management
38397 Hemlock Dr (19945-4617)
PHONE...................302 541-0889
John Buono, Prin
EMP: 5 EST: 2009
SALES (est): 232.75K Privately Held
SIC: 8741 Management services

Frederica
Kent County

(G-4163)
CATHERINE L KOHLAND
1696 Skeeter Neck Rd (19946-1614)
PHONE...................302 335-1505
Catherine Kohland, Prin
EMP: 5 EST: 2010
SALES (est): 122.99K Privately Held
SIC: 0191 General farms, primarily crop

(G-4164)
DE TURF SPORTS COMPLEX
4000 Bay Rd (19946-2129)
PHONE...................302 330-8873
EMP: 5 EST: 2017
SALES (est): 232.99K Privately Held
Web: www.deturf.com
SIC: 0782 Turf installation services, except artificial

(G-4165)
DELAWARE MUD HENS BASEBALL
584 Otter Way (19946-1878)
PHONE...................703 939-7828
John Mudri, Prin
EMP: 5 EST: 2015
SALES (est): 76.52K Privately Held
SIC: 7997 Baseball club, except professional and semi-professional

(G-4166)
DIANE SPENCE DAY CARE
19 Ruyter Dr (19946-1916)
PHONE...................302 335-4460
Diane Spence, Dir
EMP: 12 EST: 2005
SALES (est): 167.31K Privately Held
SIC: 8351 Child day care services

(G-4167)
FREDERICA SENIOR CENTER INC
216 S Market St (19946-4641)
P.O. Box 165 (19946-0165)
PHONE...................302 335-4555
Wilbur Jones, Pr
Renee Hoffman, Dir
EMP: 8 EST: 1974
SALES (est): 526.28K Privately Held
Web: www.fscnews.org
SIC: 8322 Senior citizens' center or association

(G-4168)
GRAYLING INDUSTRIES INC (HQ)
1 Moonwalker Rd (19946-2080)
PHONE...................770 751-9095
Francis Dinuzzo, CEO
Ken Elston, CFO
▲ EMP: 17 EST: 1986
SQ FT: 20,000
SALES (est): 84.6MM
SALES (corp-wide): 114.92MM Privately Held
Web: www.ilcdover.com
SIC: 5169 2673 3081 2869 Polyurethane products; Plastic bags: made from purchased materials; Unsupported plastics film and sheet; Industrial organic chemicals, nec
PA: Ilc Dover Lp
  1 Moonwalker Rd
  Frederica DE 19946
  302 335-3911

(G-4169)
HABITAT DESIGN GROUP
192 Bowers Beach Rd (19946-1714)
PHONE...................302 335-4452
Coleman Morris Junior, Owner
EMP: 5 EST: 1980
SQ FT: 1,352
SALES (est): 150K Privately Held
SIC: 0781 Landscape planning services

(G-4170)
HARRIS TOWING SERVICE
174 Albacore Dr (19946-2902)
PHONE...................302 736-5473
Jonathan Harris, Pr
EMP: 5 EST: 2017
SALES (est): 35.11K Privately Held
Web: www.harristowing.com
SIC: 7549 Towing service, automotive

(G-4171)
HIGHWATER MANAGEMENT KENT LLC
4000 Bay Rd (19946-2129)
PHONE...................302 245-7570
Scott Kammerer, Pr
EMP: 5 EST: 2021
SALES (est): 225.24K Privately Held
SIC: 8741 Management services

(G-4172)
HUGHES NETWORK SYSTEMS LLC
1 E David St (19946-4617)
PHONE...................302 335-4138
EMP: 5
Web: www.hughes.com
SIC: 4813 Internet connectivity services
HQ: Hughes Network Systems, Llc
  11717 Exploration Ln
  Germantown MD 20876
  301 428-5500

(G-4173)
ILC DOVER LP
Grayling Industries
2 Moonwalker Rd (19946-2080)
PHONE...................302 629-6860
EMP: 288
SALES (corp-wide): 114.92MM Privately Held
Web: www.ilcdover.com
SIC: 3081 Unsupported plastics film and sheet
HQ: Grayling Industries, Inc.
  1 Moonwalker Rd
  Frederica DE 19946
  770 751-9095

(G-4174)
ILC DOVER LP (PA)
Also Called: Ilc
1 Moonwalker Rd (19946-2080)
PHONE...................302 335-3911
William Wallach, Ltd Pt
Fran Dinuzzo, Ltd Pt
▲ EMP: 420 EST: 1984
SQ FT: 270,000
SALES: 114.92MM
SALES (corp-wide): 114.92MM Privately Held
Web: www.ilcdover.com
SIC: 3721 3842 Balloons, hot air (aircraft); Personal safety equipment

(G-4175)
KENT CNTY RGNAL SPT CMPLEX COR
Also Called: De Turf Sports Complex
4000 Bay Rd (19946-2129)
PHONE...................302 330-8873
Christopher Giacomucci, CEO
William Strickland, Pr
EMP: 6 EST: 2012
SALES (est): 3.93MM Privately Held
SIC: 7999 Outfitters, recreation

(G-4176)
KEVIN HANNAH
4417 Barratts Chapel Rd (19946-1536)
PHONE...................302 450-2867
Kevin Hannah, Prin
EMP: 5 EST: 2009
SALES (est): 497.93K Privately Held
Web: www.hannahconstructionde.com
SIC: 1521 General remodeling, single-family houses

(G-4177)
MIKE MEAD CONCRETE LLC
89 Sand Dollar Ln (19946-2308)
PHONE...................816 588-6150
Michael Mead, Prin
EMP: 5 EST: 2016
SALES (est): 77.52K Privately Held
SIC: 1771 Concrete work

GEOGRAPHIC SECTION   Georgetown - Sussex County (G-4208)

(G-4178)
MIKE MORRIS PAINTING LLC
805 Skeeter Neck Rd (19946-1639)
PHONE.............................302 423-3940
Michael Morris, *Prin*
EMP: 5 EST: 2017
SALES (est): 108.48K **Privately Held**
Web: www.mikemorrispainting.com
SIC: 1721 Painting and paper hanging

(G-4179)
NEW ILC DOVER INC (PA)
1 Moonwalker Rd (19946-2080)
PHONE.............................302 335-3911
EMP: 441 EST: 2008
SALES (est): 39.93MM **Privately Held**
Web: www.ilcdover.com
SIC: 3842 Personal safety equipment

(G-4180)
PINNACLE GARAGE DOOR CO LLC
260 Robbins Rd (19946-1954)
PHONE.............................302 505-4531
Shawn Hollar, *Prin*
EMP: 8 EST: 2018
SALES (est): 443.79K **Privately Held**
Web: www.pinnaclegarage302.com
SIC: 1751 7699 2431 5015 Garage door, installation or erection; Garage door repair; Garage doors, overhead, wood; Garage service equipment, used

(G-4181)
ROLL-A-BOUT CORPORATION
3240 Barratts Chapel Rd (19946-1808)
PHONE.............................302 736-6151
Lola Accetta, *Pr*
Susan Accetta, *VP*
EMP: 2 EST: 1994
SALES (est): 200.47K **Privately Held**
Web: www.therollabout.com
SIC: 3842 Crutches and walkers

(G-4182)
S B PORTER SERVICES
4296 Barratts Chapel Rd (19946-1818)
PHONE.............................302 378-0209
Stephen Porter, *Prin*
EMP: 5 EST: 2014
SALES (est): 34.29K **Privately Held**
SIC: 7299 Porter service

(G-4183)
STONE AGE TILE AND FLOORING
90 Channel Xing (19946-2116)
PHONE.............................302 359-2166
Michael Z Postles, *Prin*
EMP: 5 EST: 2017
SALES (est): 106.9K **Privately Held**
SIC: 1743 Tile installation, ceramic

(G-4184)
TAMMI LEA DR
216 N Bayshore Dr (19946-1206)
PHONE.............................302 335-2563
Lea Tammi, *Prin*
EMP: 8 EST: 2008
SALES (est): 95.72K **Privately Held**
SIC: 8011 Offices and clinics of medical doctors

(G-4185)
TM CRIST CONTRACTING INC
250 Buffalo Rd (19946-1537)
P.O. Box 105 (19952-0105)
PHONE.............................302 632-7557
EMP: 5 EST: 2012
SALES (est): 113.65K **Privately Held**
SIC: 1799 Special trade contractors, nec

(G-4186)
VALERIE RIVERA
136 E Poplar St (19946-2207)
PHONE.............................302 387-5334
EMP: 5 EST: 2019
SALES (est): 81.39K **Privately Held**
SIC: 8011 Offices and clinics of medical doctors

(G-4187)
VIVID COLORS CARPET LLC
43 Bayview Ave (19946-1304)
PHONE.............................302 335-3933
EMP: 2 EST: 2002
SALES (est): 249.9K **Privately Held**
Web: www.vividcolorscarpet.com
SIC: 1741 2273 7217 Tuckpointing or restoration; Dyeing and finishing of tufted rugs and carpets; Carpet and upholstery cleaning

---

Georgetown
Sussex County

(G-4188)
302 HEMP CO
18751 Dupont Blvd (19947-3132)
PHONE.............................302 854-4367
EMP: 5 EST: 2020
SALES (est): 82.42K **Privately Held**
SIC: 6719 Holding companies, nec

(G-4189)
A P CROLL & SON INC
22997 Lewes Georgetown Hwy (19947-5301)
P.O. Box 748 (19947-0748)
PHONE.............................302 856-6177
A P Croll Iii, *CEO*
Thomas C Hudson, *
A P Croll Junior, *VP*
EMP: 55 EST: 1921
SQ FT: 2,000
SALES (est): 20.45MM **Privately Held**
Web: www.apcroll.com
SIC: 1611 General contractor, highway and street construction

(G-4190)
A R NAILS
401 College Park Ln (19947-2114)
PHONE.............................302 858-4592
EMP: 5 EST: 2015
SALES (est): 59.37K **Privately Held**
SIC: 7231 Manicurist, pedicurist

(G-4191)
A RODRIGUEZ PAINTING LLC
417 Walter St (19947-2325)
PHONE.............................302 559-7692
Evert Rodriguez, *Prin*
EMP: 5 EST: 2017
SALES (est): 50.13K **Privately Held**
SIC: 1721 Commercial painting

(G-4192)
A&R ENVIRONMENTAL LLC
25200 Governor Stockley Rd (19947-2522)
PHONE.............................302 864-7534
Wesley Macintosh, *Prin*
EMP: 9 EST: 2017
SALES (est): 496.9K **Privately Held**
Web: www.core24services.com
SIC: 8999 Earth science services

(G-4193)
A+ TREE SERVICE LLC
21460 Park Ave (19947-6470)
PHONE.............................302 253-8612
Denise Schmidt, *Prin*
EMP: 7 EST: 2017
SALES (est): 484.32K **Privately Held**
Web: atreeservice.business.site
SIC: 0783 Planting, pruning, and trimming services

(G-4194)
A2Z AUTO RPAIR AUTO MBLE RPAIR
19395 Substation Rd (19947-4760)
PHONE.............................302 856-2219
Celvin De Leon, *Mgr*
EMP: 5 EST: 2009
SALES (est): 47.43K **Privately Held**
SIC: 7699 Repair services, nec

(G-4195)
ABBY L ALLEN FNP
20797 Professional Park Blvd Ste 214 (19947-3198)
PHONE.............................302 856-1773
Abby Allen, *Owner*
EMP: 5 EST: 2010
SALES (est): 131.23K **Privately Held**
SIC: 8011 Allergist

(G-4196)
ACCSS QLTY HEALTHCARE ACCSS
20930 Dupont Blvd (19947-1725)
PHONE.............................302 339-4112
EMP: 5 EST: 2016
SALES (est): 38.22K **Privately Held**
SIC: 8099 Health and allied services, nec

(G-4197)
AD-ART SIGNS GEORGETOWN INC
24383 Mariner Cir (19947-2677)
P.O. Box 750 (19947-0750)
PHONE.............................302 856-7446
EMP: 8 EST: 2011
SALES (est): 424.8K **Privately Held**
Web: www.adartsignsde.com
SIC: 3993 Signs and advertising specialties

(G-4198)
ADAMS CONSTRUCTION & MANAGEMEN
23 Marcella St (19947-9430)
PHONE.............................302 856-2022
EMP: 6 EST: 2008
SALES (est): 451.76K **Privately Held**
SIC: 8741 Construction management

(G-4199)
ADRIANE HOHMANN
501 College Park Ln (19947-2113)
PHONE.............................302 253-2020
Adriane Hohmann, *Prin*
EMP: 8 EST: 2018
SALES (est): 157.34K **Privately Held**
SIC: 8011 Opthalmologist

(G-4200)
AFFORDABLE WEDDING ENTRMT
Also Called: Entertainment
715 Ingramtown Rd (19947-1636)
PHONE.............................302 258-3027
EMP: 5 EST: 2012
SALES (est): 45.09K **Privately Held**
Web: www.affordableweddingent.com
SIC: 7929 Disc jockey service

(G-4201)
AGFIRST FARM CREDIT BANK
20816 Dupont Blvd (19947-3179)
PHONE.............................302 856-9081
Chamayne Busker, *Mgr*
EMP: 8
SALES (corp-wide): 493.46MM **Privately Held**
Web: www.agfirst.com
SIC: 6111 Federal and federally sponsored credit agencies
PA: Agfirst Farm Credit Bank
1901 Main St
Columbia SC 29201
803 799-5000

(G-4202)
AIKEN MASONRY SCOTT TA
22451 Wood Branch Rd (19947-6432)
PHONE.............................302 253-8179
Scott Aiken, *Prin*
EMP: 9 EST: 2010
SALES (est): 387.52K **Privately Held**
SIC: 1741 Masonry and other stonework

(G-4203)
AIR METHODS CORPORATION
Also Called: Air Methods Corporation
21479 Rudder Ln (19947-2024)
PHONE.............................302 363-3168
Aaron Todd, *Brnch Mgr*
EMP: 24
SALES (corp-wide): 1.71B **Privately Held**
Web: www.airmethods.com
SIC: 4119 Ambulance service
HQ: Air Methods Llc
5500 S Quebec St Ste 300
Greenwood Village CO 80111
855 896-9067

(G-4204)
AKU TRANSPORT INC (PA)
24559 Dupont Blvd (19947-2627)
PHONE.............................302 500-8127
Halil Camci, *Pr*
EMP: 5 EST: 2010
SALES (est): 968.72K
SALES (corp-wide): 968.72K **Privately Held**
SIC: 4731 Truck transportation brokers

(G-4205)
ALIAS TECHNOLOGY LLC
25100 Trinity Dr (19947-6585)
PHONE.............................302 856-9488
EMP: 5 EST: 2008
SALES (est): 490.35K **Privately Held**
Web: www.aliastechnology.com
SIC: 7371 8734 Software programming applications; Forensic laboratory

(G-4206)
ALL ABOUT GUTTERS LLC
24531 Bethesda Rd (19947-2549)
PHONE.............................302 853-2645
Christopher M Koenig, *Prin*
EMP: 9 EST: 2015
SALES (est): 494.37K **Privately Held**
Web: www.gutterswithguards.com
SIC: 1761 Gutter and downspout contractor

(G-4207)
ALTERNATIVE SOLUTIONS
532 S Bedford St (19947-1852)
PHONE.............................302 542-9081
Wade Jones, *Prin*
EMP: 6 EST: 2017
SALES (est): 240.03K **Privately Held**
Web: www.alternative-solutions.com
SIC: 8322 General counseling services

(G-4208)
AMERICAN BUILDER LLC
31 Fairway West Dr (19947-9459)
PHONE.............................302 841-2325
Salman Choudhary, *Managing Member*
EMP: 5
SALES (est): 84.63K **Privately Held**

Georgetown - Sussex County (G-4209)

GEOGRAPHIC SECTION

SIC: 1522 7389 Residential construction, nec
; Business services, nec

(G-4209)
AMERICAN HARDSCAPES LLC
20099 Gravel Hill Rd (19947-5359)
PHONE.....................302 253-8237
EMP: 12 EST: 2009
SALES (est): 524.67K **Privately Held**
Web: www.americanhardscapesllc.com
SIC: 8711 Building construction consultant

(G-4210)
AMERICAN LEGION AUXILIARY
25109 Prettyman Rd (19947-5207)
PHONE.....................302 329-9090
EMP: 6 EST: 2018
SALES (est): 74.67K **Privately Held**
Web: www.legion.org
SIC: 8641 Veterans' organization

(G-4211)
ANDREA MEYER
24584 Hollytree Cir (19947-6843)
PHONE.....................302 745-8823
Andrea Meyer, *Owner*
EMP: 6 EST: 2018
SALES (est): 131.04K **Privately Held**
SIC: 8049 Offices of health practitioner

(G-4212)
ARBOR MANAGEMENT ALARM
200 Ingramtown Rd (19947-1626)
PHONE.....................302 856-2876
EMP: 8 EST: 2014
SALES (est): 81.15K **Privately Held**
Web: www.arbormanagement.com
SIC: 8741 Management services

(G-4213)
ASHLEY M OLAND
16 N Bedford St (19947-1463)
PHONE.....................302 854-5406
Ashley M Oland, *Prin*
EMP: 5 EST: 2011
SALES (est): 72.68K **Privately Held**
SIC: 8111 General practice attorney, lawyer

(G-4214)
ATI HOLDINGS LLC
Also Called: ATI Physical Therapy
401 College Park Ln Unit 3 (19947-2114)
PHONE.....................302 253-8296
EMP: 8
SALES (corp-wide): 635.67MM **Publicly Held**
Web: www.atipt.com
SIC: 8049 Physical therapist
HQ: Ati Holdings, Llc
  790 Remington Blvd
  Bolingbrook IL 60440

(G-4215)
ATLANTIC FAMILY PHYSICIAN LLC
2 Lee Ave Unit 103 (19947-2149)
PHONE.....................302 856-4092
Fabricio Alarcon, *Owner*
EMP: 5 EST: 2010
SALES (est): 495.87K **Privately Held**
Web: www.atlanticfamilyphysicians.com
SIC: 8011 General and family practice, physician/surgeon

(G-4216)
ATLANTIC LAW GROUP LLC
512 E Market St (19947-2255)
PHONE.....................302 854-0380
Craig Trumbull, *Brnch Mgr*
EMP: 78
Web: www.orlans.com
SIC: 8111 General practice law office
PA: Atlantic Law Group, Llc
  1602 Vllge Mrkt Se 310
  Leesburg VA 20175

(G-4217)
ATLANTIS INDUSTRIES CORP
21490 Baltimore Ave (19947-6415)
PHONE.....................302 684-8542
Thad Schippereit, *Pr*
Doug Mcgarvey, *VP*
Thorne Gould,
▲ EMP: 86 EST: 2008
SALES (est): 11.33MM **Privately Held**
Web: www.atlantisusa.com
SIC: 3089 Injection molding of plastics

(G-4218)
B & M ELECTRIC INC
19460 Savannah Rd (19947-3094)
PHONE.....................302 745-3807
George Bailey, *Pr*
Lori Bradley, *VP*
EMP: 6 EST: 1994
SALES (est): 532.65K **Privately Held**
Web: www.bmelectricinc.com
SIC: 1731 General electrical contractor

(G-4219)
B WALLS SON HTG & A CONDITIONS
22424 Peterkins Rd (19947-2717)
PHONE.....................302 856-4045
Virginia Walls, *Pr*
Barry Walls, *VP*
Charles Steiner, *Sec*
Robert J Lewis, *VP*
Sharon Lewis, *Prin*
EMP: 14 EST: 1982
SALES (est): 395.74K **Privately Held**
SIC: 1711 Warm air heating and air conditioning contractor

(G-4220)
BACK ROAD STUDIO
23004 Seagull Ln (19947-5805)
PHONE.....................302 381-6060
Kim Pearce, *Prin*
EMP: 5 EST: 2011
SALES (est): 48.07K **Privately Held**
SIC: 7299 Miscellaneous personal service

(G-4221)
BARBOSA MANUFACTURING
24965 Kruger Rd (19947-2640)
PHONE.....................302 856-6343
EMP: 5 EST: 2009
SALES (est): 53.23K **Privately Held**
SIC: 3999 Candles

(G-4222)
BARNETT TOM D LAW FIRM
512 E Market St (19947-2255)
PHONE.....................302 855-9252
EMP: 5 EST: 1985
SALES (est): 263.95K **Privately Held**
SIC: 8111 General practice law office

(G-4223)
BAXTER FARMS INC
23073 Zoar Rd (19947-6801)
PHONE.....................302 856-1818
James H Baxter Junior, *Pr*
Ruth D Baxter, *VP*
James Baxter Iv, *Treas*
EMP: 5 EST: 1908
SQ FT: 5,000
SALES (est): 820K **Privately Held**
Web: www.lizardlickgraphics.com
SIC: 5159 5083 Farm animals; Agricultural machinery and equipment

(G-4224)
BAYHEALTH MEDICAL GROUP ENT
20930 Dupont Boulevard Unit 202 (19947-1725)
PHONE.....................302 339-8040
Michelle Gosnell, *Off Mgr*
EMP: 13 EST: 2017
SALES (est): 219.7K **Privately Held**
Web: www.bayhealth.org
SIC: 8011 Offices and clinics of medical doctors

(G-4225)
BAYSHORE SERVICES LLC
19102 Carey Ln (19947-6378)
PHONE.....................304 596-3788
Matthew Martin, *Prin*
EMP: 5 EST: 2018
SALES (est): 239.77K **Privately Held**
Web: bayshore-services-llc.business.site
SIC: 4789 Transportation services, nec

(G-4226)
BB CUSTOM INSTRUMENTS
300a Nancy St (19947-2324)
PHONE.....................302 339-3826
EMP: 4 EST: 2015
SALES (est): 71.95K **Privately Held**
Web: www.bbcustominstruments.com
SIC: 3931 Musical instruments

(G-4227)
BEACON ENGINEERING LLC
23318 Cedar Ln (19947-2755)
PHONE.....................302 864-8825
Robert Palmer, *Prin*
EMP: 6 EST: 2014
SALES (est): 708.28K **Privately Held**
Web: www.beaconengineeringllc.com
SIC: 8711 Consulting engineer

(G-4228)
BEACON HOSPITALITY
Also Called: Microtel
22297 Dupont Blvd (19947-3182)
PHONE.....................302 249-0502
Chad Moore, *Owner*
EMP: 28 EST: 2014
SALES (est): 436.41K **Privately Held**
Web: www.wyndhamhotels.com
SIC: 7011 7021 Hotels and motels; Dormitory, commercially operated

(G-4229)
BEEBE HEALTHCARE
26179 Manor Way (19947-2597)
PHONE.....................302 249-1448
Kelly Behney R.n., *Prin*
EMP: 12 EST: 2018
SALES (est): 199.6K **Privately Held**
Web: www.beebehealthcare.org
SIC: 8062 General medical and surgical hospitals

(G-4230)
BEEBE LAB EXPRESS GEORGETOWN
21635 Biden Ave Unit 101 (19947-4575)
PHONE.....................302 856-9729
Jan Hickman, *Prin*
EMP: 18 EST: 2007
SALES (est): 213.39K **Privately Held**
Web: www.beebehealthcare.org
SIC: 8062 General medical and surgical hospitals

(G-4231)
BEEBE MEDICAL CENTER INC
Also Called: Beebe Imaging
21635 Biden Ave (19947-4576)
PHONE.....................302 856-9729
EMP: 7
SALES (corp-wide): 581.97MM **Privately Held**
Web: www.beebehealthcare.org
SIC: 8062 8011 General medical and surgical hospitals; Offices and clinics of medical doctors
PA: Beebe Medical Center, Inc.
  424 Savannah Rd
  Lewes DE 19958
  302 645-3300

(G-4232)
BEST CUSTOM EXHAUST
20983 Dupont Blvd (19947-3169)
PHONE.....................302 278-3555
Craig Goldberg, *Prin*
EMP: 5 EST: 2017
SALES (est): 80.77K **Privately Held**
SIC: 7533 Muffler shop, sale or repair and installation

(G-4233)
BIAMBY CLEANING SERVICES
15453 Weigelia Dr (19947-3652)
PHONE.....................302 519-1604
Fern Biamby, *Prin*
EMP: 5 EST: 2015
SALES (est): 71.16K **Privately Held**
SIC: 7699 Cleaning services

(G-4234)
BILL JOHNSON CONTRACTING
29028 Black Pepper Ln (19947-4888)
PHONE.....................302 245-4708
Bill Johnson, *Prin*
EMP: 5 EST: 2016
SALES (est): 76.41K **Privately Held**
Web: www.billjohnsoncontracting.com
SIC: 1799 Special trade contractors, nec

(G-4235)
BLAIR CARMEAN MASONRY
24373 Gravel Hill Rd (19947-6567)
PHONE.....................302 934-6103
Carmean Blair, *Owner*
EMP: 5 EST: 1988
SALES (est): 261.19K **Privately Held**
SIC: 1741 Masonry and other stonework

(G-4236)
BOBS PLUMBING REPAIR LLC
16956 Seashore Hwy (19947-4213)
PHONE.....................302 853-2259
Robert Krause, *Prin*
EMP: 5 EST: 2016
SALES (est): 129.51K **Privately Held**
SIC: 1711 Plumbing contractors

(G-4237)
BONI LANDSCAPING LLC
307 Calhoun St (19947-1207)
PHONE.....................302 569-8852
Bonifacio Ramirez, *Prin*
EMP: 5 EST: 2014
SALES (est): 28.65K **Privately Held**
Web: www.bonilandscape.com
SIC: 0781 Landscape services

(G-4238)
BOYS & GIRLS CLUBS DEL INC
Also Called: Georgetown
115 N Race St (19947-1406)
PHONE.....................302 856-4903
Christopher Couch, *Mgr*
EMP: 10
SALES (corp-wide): 33.26MM **Privately Held**
Web: www.bgclubs.org

GEOGRAPHIC SECTION
Georgetown - Sussex County (G-4264)

SIC: 8641   Youth organizations
PA: Boys & Girls Clubs Of Delaware, Inc.
   669 S Union St
   Wilmington DE 19805
   302 658-1870

(G-4239)
BRAMBLE CONSTRUCTION CO INC
812 E Market St (19947-2224)
PHONE.................................302 856-6723
Sammuel Bramble Iii, *Pr*
Dawn Bramble, *Sec*
EMP: 10 EST: 1993
SALES (est): 1.1MM **Privately Held**
Web: www.brambleconstruction.com
SIC: 1623 1611 1794 Underground utilities contractor; Grading; Excavation work

(G-4240)
BRANDYWINE COUNSELING
528 E Market St (19947-2255)
PHONE.................................302 856-4700
Lynn M Fahey, *Mgr*
EMP: 29
SALES (corp-wide): 16.65MM **Privately Held**
Web: www.brandywinecounseling.com
SIC: 8093 Substance abuse clinics (outpatient)
PA: Brandywine Counseling & Community Services, Inc.
   2713 Lancaster Ave
   Wilmington DE 19805
   302 655-9880

(G-4241)
BY THE SHORE
27303 Road Dawg Ln (19947-6679)
PHONE.................................302 462-0496
EMP: 7 EST: 2012
SALES (est): 61.15K **Privately Held**
SIC: 8082 Home health care services

(G-4242)
C H P T MANUFACTURING INC
Also Called: Chpt Manufacturing
21388 Cedar Creek Ave (19947-6305)
PHONE.................................302 856-7660
Matthew A Koch, *Pr*
Douglas C Hicks, *Pr*
John E Protack, *VP*
EMP: 7 EST: 1991
SQ FT: 4,500
SALES (est): 987.26K **Privately Held**
Web: www.chptmfg.com
SIC: 3561 7699 Pumps and pumping equipment; Industrial machinery and equipment repair

(G-4243)
CAPE CLIMATE INC
26411 Fells St (19947-6744)
PHONE.................................302 858-7160
Adam Cress, *Owner*
EMP: 6 EST: 2012
SALES (est): 137.95K **Privately Held**
SIC: 1711 Heating and air conditioning contractors

(G-4244)
CARVI CARPENTER INC
16562 Seashore Hwy (19947-4206)
PHONE.................................302 722-3352
EMP: 5 EST: 2018
SALES (est): 79.32K **Privately Held**
SIC: 1751 Carpentry work

(G-4245)
CATHOLIC CHARITIES INC
Also Called: Catholic Charities
406 S Bedford St (19947-1853)
PHONE.................................302 856-9578
Teddi Millerline, *Sec*
EMP: 6
SALES (corp-wide): 8.08MM **Privately Held**
Web: www.catholiccharitiesusa.org
SIC: 8322 Social service center
PA: Catholic Charities Inc
   2601 W 4th St
   Wilmington DE 19805
   302 655-9624

(G-4246)
CB THERAPY SERVICES INC
22869 Zoar Rd (19947-2521)
PHONE.................................302 381-7079
Cheryl Bbaxter, *Prin*
EMP: 6 EST: 2011
SALES (est): 54.03K **Privately Held**
SIC: 8049 Offices of health practitioner

(G-4247)
CELSIA INC (PA)
26117 Kits Burrow Ct (19947-5390)
P.O. Box 887 (19947-0887)
PHONE.................................408 577-1407
George Meyer, *CEO*
EMP: 13 EST: 2011
SALES (est): 1.54MM
SALES (corp-wide): 1.54MM **Privately Held**
Web: www.celsiainc.com
SIC: 8731 Electronic research

(G-4248)
CENTRAL AMERICA DISTRS LLC
Also Called: Central Amer Hlth Buty Distrs
11 E Market St Ste 2 (19947-1511)
PHONE.................................302 628-4178
EMP: 10 EST: 2004
SALES (est): 1.88MM **Privately Held**
SIC: 5087 Beauty parlor equipment and supplies

(G-4249)
CHEER INC (PA)
546 S Bedford St (19947-1852)
PHONE.................................302 856-5641
Arlene Littleton, *Ex Dir*
EMP: 13 EST: 1971
SQ FT: 2,500
SALES (est): 7.92MM
SALES (corp-wide): 7.92MM **Privately Held**
Web: www.cheerde.com
SIC: 8322 Senior citizens' center or association

(G-4250)
CHIEF WEB DESIGN
24787 Hollis Rd (19947-5386)
PHONE.................................302 542-8409
Stephen King, *Prin*
EMP: 5 EST: 2010
SALES (est): 66K **Privately Held**
Web: www.chieftechnologies.net
SIC: 7374 Computer graphics service

(G-4251)
CHILD SUPPORT
22 The Cir (19947-1500)
PHONE.................................302 855-7462
Gary Belkot, *Mgr*
EMP: 9 EST: 2017
SALES (est): 44.06K **Privately Held**
Web: www.childsupportoffice.us
SIC: 8322 Individual and family services

(G-4252)
CHILDERS IV HENRY E MD
20930 Dupont Blvd Unit 202 (19947-1725)
PHONE.................................302 258-8853
Henry Childers, *CEO*
EMP: 8 EST: 2017
SALES (est): 119.6K **Privately Held**
SIC: 8011 Offices and clinics of medical doctors

(G-4253)
CHILDREN FMILIES FIRST DEL INC
410 S Bedford St (19947-1850)
PHONE.................................302 856-2388
Al Sneider, *Ex Dir*
EMP: 69
SALES (corp-wide): 17.22MM **Privately Held**
Web: www.cffde.org
SIC: 8069 8322 Alcoholism rehabilitation hospital; Individual and family services
PA: Children & Families First Delaware Inc.
   809 N Washington St
   Wilmington DE 19801
   302 658-5177

(G-4254)
CHILDRENS ADVOCACY CTR OF DEL
410 S Bedford St (19947-1850)
PHONE.................................302 854-0323
Randall Williams, *Brnch Mgr*
EMP: 5
SALES (corp-wide): 1.75MM **Privately Held**
Web: www.cacofde.org
SIC: 8322 Social service center
PA: Children's Advocacy Center Of Delaware Inc
   611 S Dupont Hwy Ste 201
   Dover DE 19901
   302 741-2123

(G-4255)
CHUDASAMA ENTERPRISES LLC
Also Called: Knights Inn
313 N Dupont Hwy (19947)
PHONE.................................302 856-7532
Hitesh Chudasama, *Owner*
EMP: 8
SALES (corp-wide): 441.83K **Privately Held**
Web: www.redlion.com
SIC: 7011 Hotels and motels
PA: Chudasama Enterprises Llc
   521 W Dupont Hwy
   Millsboro DE 19966
   302 934-7968

(G-4256)
CINDY L SZABO
9 N Front St (19947-1413)
P.O. Box 574 (19947-0574)
PHONE.................................302 855-9505
Cindy Szabo, *Mgr*
EMP: 6 EST: 2015
SALES (est): 197.23K **Privately Held**
SIC: 8111 General practice attorney, lawyer

(G-4257)
CLARK & SONS INC
500 W Market St (19947-2322)
PHONE.................................302 856-3372
David J Clark, *Mgr*
EMP: 9
SALES (corp-wide): 8.99MM **Privately Held**
Web: www.clarkandsonsdoors.com
SIC: 1751 Garage door, installation or erection
PA: Clark & Sons, Inc.
   314 E Ayre St
   Wilmington DE 19804
   302 998-7552

(G-4258)
CLAW BLUE MAINTENANCE
27902 Avalon Dr (19947-6728)
PHONE.................................717 487-2808
Roger Greely, *Prin*
EMP: 5 EST: 2017
SALES (est): 22.81K **Privately Held**
SIC: 7349 Building maintenance services, nec

(G-4259)
CLAYTON E BUNTING
107 W Market St (19947-1438)
PHONE.................................302 856-0017
Clayton E Bunting, *Prin*
EMP: 5 EST: 2018
SALES (est): 177.55K **Privately Held**
Web: www.morrisjamespersonalinjurylawyers.com
SIC: 8111 General practice attorney, lawyer

(G-4260)
COATINGS WITH A PURPOSE INC
21166 Greenway Pl (19947-4373)
PHONE.................................302 462-1465
Mark Lyon, *Pr*
EMP: 3 EST: 2014
SALES (est): 379.94K **Privately Held**
Web: www.coatingswithapurpose.com
SIC: 2851 Removers and cleaners

(G-4261)
COMCAST CABLEVISION OF DEL (HQ)
Also Called: Comcast
426a N Dupont Hwy (19947)
PHONE.................................302 856-4591
Henry Pearl, *Genl Mgr*
EMP: 12 EST: 1972
SALES (est): 9.19MM
SALES (corp-wide): 121.43B **Publicly Held**
SIC: 4841 Cable television services
PA: Comcast Corporation
   1 Comcast Ctr
   Philadelphia PA 19103
   215 286-1700

(G-4262)
COMMUNITY AUTO REPAIR
514 W Market St (19947-2322)
PHONE.................................302 856-3333
EMP: 9 EST: 2014
SALES (est): 448.06K **Privately Held**
Web: www.communityautorepairgt.com
SIC: 7538 General automotive repair shops

(G-4263)
COMMUNITY LEGAL AID SOCIETY
Also Called: Disabilities Law Program
20151 Office Cir (19947-3197)
PHONE.................................302 856-0038
Elanoe Kiesel, *Brnch Mgr*
EMP: 12
SALES (corp-wide): 5.71MM **Privately Held**
Web: www.declasi.org
SIC: 8111 Legal aid service
PA: Community Legal Aid Society Inc
   100 W 10th St Ste 801
   Wilmington DE 19801
   302 757-7001

(G-4264)
COMPLETE DISPOSAL SERVICE LLC

Georgetown - Sussex County (G-4265) GEOGRAPHIC SECTION

18265 Deer Forest Rd (19947-3412)
PHONE.....................302 448-1021
EMP: 5 EST: 2018
SALES (est): 252.83K **Privately Held**
Web: www.completedisposalservice.com
SIC: 4953 Rubbish collection and disposal

(G-4265)
CONFLUENT CORPORATION
19640 Buck Run (19947-5336)
PHONE.....................301 440-4100
EMP: 7 EST: 1996
SQ FT: 5,500
SALES (est): 503.01K **Privately Held**
Web: www.confluent.io
SIC: 7378 Computer and data processing equipment repair/maintenance

(G-4266)
CONNOR CHARLES & SONS PAINTING
14219 Road 526 (19947)
P.O. Box 235 (19969-0235)
PHONE.....................302 945-1746
Charles Connor, *Owner*
EMP: 5 EST: 1990
SALES (est): 238.75K **Privately Held**
SIC: 1721 Exterior commercial painting contractor

(G-4267)
CONVENTIONEER PUBG CO INC
Also Called: P & R Printing
24948 Green Fern Dr (19947-2776)
PHONE.....................301 487-3907
David Stein, *Pr*
EMP: 4 EST: 1968
SQ FT: 3,000
SALES (est): 426.47K **Privately Held**
SIC: 2752 Commercial printing, lithographic

(G-4268)
CORINTHIAN HOUSE
219 S Race St (19947-1911)
PHONE.....................302 858-1493
EMP: 5 EST: 2017
SALES (est): 86.23K **Privately Held**
SIC: 8093 Substance abuse clinics (outpatient)

(G-4269)
COUNTY BANK
13 N Bedford St (19947-1497)
PHONE.....................302 855-2000
Robin Parker, *Mgr*
EMP: 7
Web: www.countybankdel.com
SIC: 6022 State commercial banks
PA: County Bank
19927 Shuttle Rd
Rehoboth Beach DE 19971

(G-4270)
COUNTY OF SUSSEX
Also Called: Suffex County Ems
9 S Dupont Hwy (19947)
P.O. Box 589 (19947-0589)
PHONE.....................302 854-5050
Bill Lecates, *Brnch Mgr*
EMP: 10
SALES (corp-wide): 106.35MM **Privately Held**
Web: www.sussexcountyde.gov
SIC: 7363 Medical help service
PA: County Of Sussex
2 The Cir
Georgetown DE 19947
302 855-7700

(G-4271)
CP LAWN AND LANDSCAPE
16963 Hardscrabble Rd (19947-6040)
PHONE.....................302 396-7074
Colby Pfleger, *Prin*
EMP: 5 EST: 2018
SALES (est): 221.79K **Privately Held**
SIC: 0781 Landscape services

(G-4272)
CREATIVE COURTYARDS
20099 Gravel Hill Rd (19947-5359)
PHONE.....................302 253-8237
EMP: 6 EST: 2019
SALES (est): 124.49K **Privately Held**
Web: www.creativecourtyards.com
SIC: 0781 Landscape services

(G-4273)
CROWN EQUINE LLC
14274 Cokesbury Rd (19947-4622)
PHONE.....................302 629-2782
Krystal Lyn Harrell D.v.m., *Prin*
EMP: 5 EST: 2012
SALES (est): 189.08K **Privately Held**
Web: www.crownequine.com
SIC: 0272 Horses and other equines

(G-4274)
CURT M WATKINS M D
20797 Professional Park Boulevard (19947)
PHONE.....................302 856-1773
Curt Watkins, *Pr*
EMP: 9 EST: 2018
SALES (est): 59.55K **Privately Held**
Web: www.theallergyexperts.com
SIC: 8011 Allergist

(G-4275)
DAWSON BEDSWORTH ELEC CONTRS
19291 County Seat Hwy (19947-4824)
PHONE.....................302 854-0210
Jeffrey B Dawson, *Pr*
Greg Besworth, *VP*
Donna Besworth, *Sec*
Cynthis Dawson, *Treas*
EMP: 16 EST: 2001
SALES (est): 2.52MM **Privately Held**
SIC: 1731 General electrical contractor

(G-4276)
DEL COAST EXTERIOR LLC
16732 Seashore Hwy (19947-4209)
PHONE.....................302 752-6678
Duan Ramirez, *Prin*
EMP: 6 EST: 2016
SALES (est): 91.54K **Privately Held**
Web: www.dcexteriorsandrenovationllc.com
SIC: 1761 Roofing contractor

(G-4277)
DEL COAST EXTERIORS
21825 Zoar Rd (19947-2511)
PHONE.....................302 236-5738
Kathryn Ramirez, *Prin*
EMP: 7 EST: 2018
SALES (est): 395.98K **Privately Held**
Web: www.dcexteriorsandrenovationllc.com
SIC: 1761 Siding contractor

(G-4278)
DELAWARE CPA-PAC INC
Also Called: Delaware CPA Services
216 W Market St Unit A (19947-1441)
PHONE.....................302 854-0133
EMP: 6 EST: 1989
SALES (est): 99.79K **Privately Held**

SIC: 8721 Accounting, auditing, and bookkeeping

(G-4279)
DELAWARE DEPARTMENT CORRECTION
Also Called: Sussex Correctional Instn
23203 Dupont Blvd (19947-2664)
P.O. Box 500 (19947-0599)
PHONE.....................302 856-5280
EMP: 137
SALES (corp-wide): 11.27B **Privately Held**
Web: www.delaware.gov
SIC: 8361 9223 Residential care; Correctional institutions
HQ: Delaware Department Of Correction
245 Mckee Rd
Dover DE 19904

(G-4280)
DELAWARE DEPT HLTH SOCIAL SVCS
Also Called: Division Child Spport Enfrcmen
20105 Office Cir (19947-3197)
PHONE.....................302 856-5586
Gary Bellkot, *Dir*
EMP: 8
SALES (corp-wide): 11.27B **Privately Held**
Web: www.delaware.gov
SIC: 8322 9111 Child related social services; Executive offices
HQ: Delaware Dept Of Health And Social Services
1901 N Dupont Hwy
New Castle DE 19720

(G-4281)
DELAWARE DRNKING DRVER PROGRAM
Also Called: Thresholds
6 N Railroad Ave (19947-1242)
PHONE.....................302 856-1835
Andy Burlingame, *Mgr*
EMP: 10
SALES (corp-wide): 763.08K **Privately Held**
SIC: 8322 Alcoholism counseling, nontreatment
PA: Delaware Drinking Driver Program Inc
1661 S Dupont Hwy
Dover DE 19901
302 736-4326

(G-4282)
DELAWARE INTEGRATIVE MEDICAL C
20930 Dupont Blvd Unit 203 (19947-1725)
PHONE.....................302 559-5959
Henry Childers, *Prin*
EMP: 8 EST: 2014
SALES (est): 248K **Privately Held**
Web: www.delawareintegrativemedicine.com
SIC: 8099 Blood related health services

(G-4283)
DELAWARE SMALL BUS DEV CTR
Also Called: Sbdc Sussex County
103 W Pine St (19947-1827)
PHONE.....................302 831-1555
EMP: 6 EST: 1983
SALES (est): 110.28K **Privately Held**
Web: www.delawaresbdc.org
SIC: 8748 Business consulting, nec

(G-4284)
DELAWARE STATE PLICE FDRAL CR
700 N Bedford St (19947-2151)
PHONE.....................800 288-1080
EMP: 10

SALES (est): 87.43K **Privately Held**
Web: www.dspfcu.com
SIC: 6061 Federal credit unions

(G-4285)
DELAWARE STATE PLICE FDRAL CR (PA)
700 N Bedford St (19947-2151)
P.O. Box 717 (19947-0717)
PHONE.....................302 856-3501
EMP: 19 EST: 1960
SQ FT: 6,000
SALES (est): 6.71MM **Privately Held**
Web: www.dspfcu.com
SIC: 6061 Federal credit unions

(G-4286)
DELAWARE TCHNCAL CMNTY COLLEGE
Also Called: Jack F Owens Campus
21179 College Dr (19947-4193)
PHONE.....................302 259-6160
Doctor Ileana Smith, *Dir*
EMP: 35
Web: www.dtcc.edu
SIC: 8222 8111 Junior college; Legal services
PA: Delaware Technical & Community College
100 Campus Dr
Dover DE 19904

(G-4287)
DELAWARE VEIN CENTER
20930 Dupont Blvd Unit 202 (19947-1725)
PHONE.....................302 258-8853
Henry Childers, *Owner*
EMP: 6 EST: 2015
SALES (est): 87.52K **Privately Held**
Web: www.thedelawareveincenter.com
SIC: 8049 Offices of health practitioner

(G-4288)
DELMACO MANUFACTURING INC
21424 Cedar Creek Ave (19947-6305)
PHONE.....................302 856-6345
G Bennett, *Pr*
S Allan Davey, *Ch*
▼ EMP: 14 EST: 1983
SQ FT: 11,200
SALES (est): 1.92MM **Privately Held**
Web: www.delmacomfg.com
SIC: 3499 3495 Reels, cable: metal; Wire springs

(G-4289)
DELMARVA SIGN CO
24835 Lawson Rd (19947-6659)
PHONE.....................302 934-6188
Anna Mcdonough, *Owner*
EMP: 7 EST: 2006
SALES (est): 50.05K **Privately Held**
SIC: 3993 Signs and advertising specialties

(G-4290)
DELMARVA SPRAY FOAM LLC
22976 Sussex Ave (19947-6310)
PHONE.....................302 752-1080
EMP: 13 EST: 2014
SALES (est): 1.89MM
SALES (corp-wide): 23.49MM **Privately Held**
Web: www.delmarvafoam.com
SIC: 1799 1742 Spraying contactor, non-agricultural; Insulation, buildings
PA: Southland Insulators, Inc.
8521 Quarry Rd
Manassas VA 20110
703 368-1965

▲ = Import ▼ = Export
◆ = Import/Export

GEOGRAPHIC SECTION

Georgetown - Sussex County (G-4318)

(G-4291)
DELORES WELCH
Also Called: Dee's Cleaning Service
22812 Cedar Ln (19947-6320)
PHONE...............................302 856-7989
Delores Welch, *Owner*
EMP: 8 **EST:** 1983
SALES (est): 462.86K **Privately Held**
SIC: 7349 Janitorial service, contract basis

(G-4292)
DELTRUST GROUP INC
Also Called: Real Estate Services
115 W Laurel St (19947-1444)
PHONE...............................302 362-9900
Joseph Batres, *CEO*
Heidi Shipe, *CFO*
Laura Lutz, *Prin*
EMP: 7 **EST:** 2019
SALES (est): 340K **Privately Held**
SIC: 6531 Real estate agent, commercial

(G-4293)
DEVERE INSUL HM PRFMCE LLC
22976 Sussex Ave (19947-6310)
PHONE...............................302 854-0344
EMP: 6 **EST:** 2019
SALES (est): 97.12K **Privately Held**
Web:
www.devereinsulationhomeperformance.com
SIC: 1742 Insulation, buildings

(G-4294)
DIANE AUSTIN
15079 Wilson Hill Rd (19947-3630)
PHONE...............................302 856-3369
Diane Austin, *Prin*
EMP: 6 **EST:** 2005
SALES (est): 207.75K **Privately Held**
Web: www.bse-kehl.de
SIC: 1521 Single-family housing construction

(G-4295)
DIY TOOL SUPPLY LLC
23135 Lewes Georgetown Hwy Unit 15 (19947-5395)
PHONE...............................302 253-8461
EMP: 6 **EST:** 2017
SALES (est): 277.31K **Privately Held**
Web: www.diytoolsupply.com
SIC: 3541 Machine tools, metal cutting type

(G-4296)
DONOVAN SALVAGE WORKS INC
20262 Donovans Rd (19947-3006)
PHONE...............................302 856-9501
EMP: 17 **EST:** 2020
SALES (est): 2.44MM **Privately Held**
Web: www.donovansalvageworks.com
SIC: 5015 Automotive parts and supplies, used

(G-4297)
DOREY FINANCIAL SERVICES INC
13 Bridgeville Rd (19947-2105)
PHONE...............................302 856-0970
EMP: 6 **EST:** 2000
SALES (est): 346.44K **Privately Held**
SIC: 8742 Financial consultant

(G-4298)
DRAPER & GOLDBERG PLLC
512 E Market St (19947-2255)
PHONE...............................302 448-4040
Thomas Barnet, *Mgr*
EMP: 6
SALES (corp-wide): 7.35MM **Privately Held**
SIC: 8111 General practice law office
PA: Draper & Goldberg, Pllc
    44050 Ashbrn Shpg Plz
    Ashburn VA 20147
    703 777-7101

(G-4299)
DREAM VIEW EXTERIORS GROUP LLC
201 Primary Ave (19947-2805)
PHONE...............................302 358-9530
EMP: 5 **EST:** 2013
SALES (est): 277.35K **Privately Held**
Web: www.dreamviewexteriors.com
SIC: 1761 Roofing, siding, and sheetmetal work

(G-4300)
DUSTIN DAVIS
25 Bridgeville Rd (19947-2105)
PHONE...............................302 856-2254
Dustin Davis, *Prin*
EMP: 9 **EST:** 2010
SALES (est): 87.08K **Privately Held**
SIC: 8011 Offices and clinics of medical doctors

(G-4301)
DXI CONSTRUCTION INC
22237 Lewes Georgetown Hwy (19947-5526)
PHONE...............................302 858-5007
Keith Jacobi, *Brnch Mgr*
EMP: 212
SALES (corp-wide): 60.86MM **Privately Held**
Web: www.dxiconstruction.com
SIC: 1611 1623 General contractor, highway and street construction; Water, sewer, and utility lines
PA: Dxi Construction, Inc.
    260 Hopewell Rd
    Churchville MD 21028
    410 879-8055

(G-4302)
EAST COAST CSTM CABINETRY LLC
23636 Saulsbury Ln (19947-6389)
PHONE...............................302 245-3040
Kevin Minor, *Prin*
EMP: 4 **EST:** 2009
SALES (est): 184.32K **Privately Held**
SIC: 2434 Wood kitchen cabinets

(G-4303)
EASTER SALS DEL MRYLNDS ESTRN
22317 Dupont Blvd (19947-2153)
PHONE...............................302 856-7364
Pam Reuther, *Mgr*
EMP: 55
SALES (corp-wide): 27.16MM **Privately Held**
Web: www.easterseals.com
SIC: 8331 8399 Job training and related services; Health and welfare council
PA: Easter Seals Delaware & Marylands Eastern Shore, Inc.
    61 Corporate Cir
    New Castle DE 19720
    302 324-4444

(G-4304)
EASTERN AIR SERVICE
26844 Governor Stockley Rd (19947-2598)
PHONE...............................800 921-0392
John Sullivan, *Prin*
EMP: 8 **EST:** 2010
SALES (est): 480.54K **Privately Held**
Web: www.easternairservicesinc.com
SIC: 1711 Warm air heating and air conditioning contractor

(G-4305)
EASTERN SHORE CLEANING LLC
24337 Givens Cir (19947-6852)
P.O. Box 796 (19947-0796)
PHONE...............................302 752-8856
Chris Lee, *CEO*
EMP: 5 **EST:** 2015
SALES (est): 75.79K **Privately Held**
Web: www.easternshorecleaning.com
SIC: 7699 Cleaning services

(G-4306)
EASTERN SHORE POULTRY COMPANY
21724 Broad Creek Ave (19947-6307)
PHONE...............................302 855-1350
Harry Dukes, *Pr*
Edward Pion, *
EMP: 356 **EST:** 1992
SQ FT: 22,000
SALES (est): 29.55MM **Privately Held**
SIC: 2015 Poultry slaughtering and processing

(G-4307)
EILEEN DAVIS DO
201 W Market St (19947-1440)
PHONE...............................302 856-2254
Eileen Davis, *Prin*
EMP: 9 **EST:** 2010
SALES (est): 117.27K **Privately Held**
SIC: 8011 General and family practice, physician/surgeon

(G-4308)
EINSTEINS SCHOOL AGE CENTER
21133 Sterling Ave (19947-5572)
PHONE...............................302 855-5766
EMP: 9 **EST:** 2016
SALES (est): 58.21K **Privately Held**
SIC: 8351 Preschool center

(G-4309)
ENTERPRISE RENT A CAR
22694 Dupont Blvd (19947-8802)
PHONE...............................302 856-6380
Erin Overturs, *Prin*
EMP: 7 **EST:** 2012
SALES (est): 166.03K **Privately Held**
Web: www.enterprise.com
SIC: 7514 Rent-a-car service

(G-4310)
ERIC S BALLIET
Also Called: Lord & Wheeler
212 W Market St (19947-1441)
PHONE...............................302 856-7423
Eric S Balliet, *Prin*
EMP: 10 **EST:** 1968
SQ FT: 2,650
SALES (est): 472.94K **Privately Held**
Web: www.thegeorgetowndental.com
SIC: 8021 Dentists' office

(G-4311)
EXANTUS AND SON HOMES
58 Garden Cir (19947-5619)
PHONE...............................302 745-3468
Ricot Exantus, *Prin*
EMP: 5 **EST:** 2013
SALES (est): 144.32K **Privately Held**
SIC: 1522 Residential construction, nec

(G-4312)
FACILITIES MGMT DIV
5 E Pine St (19947-1903)
PHONE...............................302 856-5817
William Gibbons, *Mgr*
EMP: 5 **EST:** 2013
SALES (est): 83.94K **Privately Held**
SIC: 8741 Management services

(G-4313)
FAMILY MAN CARPENTRY
22236 Breasure Rd (19947-2600)
PHONE...............................302 542-8803
EMP: 5 **EST:** 2020
SALES (est): 148.62K **Privately Held**
SIC: 1751 Carpentry work

(G-4314)
FAMILY PLANNING
544 S Bedford St (19947-1852)
PHONE...............................302 856-5225
Nieca Lietzan, *Prin*
EMP: 9 **EST:** 2014
SALES (est): 163.52K **Privately Held**
SIC: 8093 Specialty outpatient clinics, nec

(G-4315)
FBK MEDICAL TUBING INC
21649 Cedar Creek Ave (19947-6396)
PHONE...............................302 855-0585
Edwin Finch Iii, *Ch Bd*
Jim Kieth, *COO*
Bartlett Bretz, *CEO*
Alan Drenneb Iii, *Sec*
Betty Edkins, *VP Opers*
EMP: 16 **EST:** 1979
SQ FT: 21,750
SALES (est): 495.69K **Privately Held**
Web: www.americanmedicaltubing.com
SIC: 8731 3082 3841 3083 Medical research, commercial; Tubes, unsupported plastics; Surgical and medical instruments; Laminated plastics plate and sheet

(G-4316)
FELLOWSHIP HLTH RESOURCES INC
16 Shortly Rd (19947-4754)
PHONE...............................302 856-7642
EMP: 10
SALES (corp-wide): 33.85MM **Privately Held**
Web: www.fhr.net
SIC: 8361 8661 Halfway group home, persons with social or personal problems; Religious organizations
PA: Fellowship Health Resources, Inc.
    24 Albion Rd Ste 420
    Lincoln RI 02865
    401 333-3980

(G-4317)
FERGUSON ENTERPRISES LLC
25131 Dupont Blvd (19947-2621)
PHONE...............................302 500-8051
EMP: 7
SALES (corp-wide): 2.67MM **Privately Held**
Web: www.ferguson.com
SIC: 5074 Plumbing fittings and supplies
HQ: Ferguson Enterprises, Llc
    751 Lakefront Cmns
    Newport News VA 23606
    757 969-4011

(G-4318)
FERREIRA BUILDERS LLC ✪
22797 Rum Bridge Rd (19947-4511)
PHONE...............................302 296-6014
EMP: 5 **EST:** 2022
SALES (est): 83.04K **Privately Held**
SIC: 1521 7389 Single-family housing construction; Business Activities at Non-Commercial Site

Georgetown - Sussex County (G-4319)

(G-4319)
FERRY JOSEPH & PEARCE PA
6 W Market St (19947-1484)
PHONE...............................302 856-3706
David J Ferry Junior, *Brnch Mgr*
EMP: 14
Web: www.ferryjoseph.com
SIC: 8111 General practice attorney, lawyer
PA: Ferry, Joseph & Pearce Pa
1521 Concord Pike Ste 202
Wilmington DE 19803

(G-4320)
FIRST AMERICAN TITLE INSUR CO
231 S Race St (19947-1911)
PHONE...............................302 855-2120
David Toomey, *Brnch Mgr*
EMP: 10
Web: www.firstam.com
SIC: 6541 Title and trust companies
HQ: First American Title Insurance
Company
1 First American Way
Santa Ana CA 92707
800 854-3643

(G-4321)
FIRST GENERAL
826 E Market St (19947-2224)
PHONE...............................302 381-2581
Roberto Perez, *Prin*
EMP: 9 EST: 2017
SALES (est): 135.42K **Privately Held**
Web: www.fgsna.com
SIC: 1799 Special trade contractors, nec

(G-4322)
FIRST STATE CMNTY ACTION AGCY (PA)
308 N Railroad Ave (19947-1252)
P.O. Box 877 (19947-0877)
PHONE...............................302 856-7761
Bernice Edwards, *Ex Dir*
EMP: 46 EST: 1965
SALES (est): 9.7MM
SALES (corp-wide): 9.7MM **Privately Held**
Web: www.firststatecaa.org
SIC: 8399 8322 Antipoverty board; Individual and family services

(G-4323)
FIRST STATE MANAGEMENT LLC
20856 Dupont Blvd (19947-3180)
P.O. Box 1501 (19971-5501)
PHONE...............................302 648-4600
Cody Ayers, *Managing Member*
EMP: 5 EST: 2018
SALES (est): 200.28K **Privately Held**
Web: www.firststatemgmt.com
SIC: 8741 Management services

(G-4324)
FISHER AUTO PARTS INC
Also Called: Manlove Auto Parts
117 E Market St (19947-1405)
PHONE...............................302 856-2507
Bill Fisher, *Mgr*
EMP: 5
SALES (corp-wide): 525.52MM **Privately Held**
Web: www.fisherautoparts.com
SIC: 5013 Automotive supplies and parts
PA: Fisher Auto Parts, Inc.
512 Greenville Ave
Staunton VA 24201
540 885-8901

(G-4325)
FRANKLIN UTILITIES LLC
14619 Cokesbury Rd (19947-4364)
PHONE...............................302 629-6658
EMP: 7 EST: 2018
SALES (est): 426.43K **Privately Held**
SIC: 1522 Residential construction, nec

(G-4326)
FRETS4VETSORG
300a Nancy St (19947-2324)
PHONE...............................302 382-1426
Isaiah Baker, *Prin*
EMP: 6 EST: 2017
SALES (est): 85.24K **Privately Held**
SIC: 8699 Charitable organization

(G-4327)
FRUITBEARER PUBLISHING LLC
107 Elizabeth St (19947-1427)
PHONE...............................302 856-6649
Candy Abbott, *Mng Pt*
EMP: 4 EST: 2004
SALES (est): 466.65K **Privately Held**
Web: www.fruitbearer.com
SIC: 2741 Miscellaneous publishing

(G-4328)
FULTON BANK NATIONAL ASSN
Also Called: Fulton Financial Advisors
21035 Dupont Blvd (19947-3167)
P.O. Box 520 (19947-0520)
PHONE...............................302 855-2406
Linda Price, *Brnch Mgr*
EMP: 9
SALES (corp-wide): 1.09B **Publicly Held**
Web: www.fultonbank.com
SIC: 6022 State commercial banks
HQ: Fulton Bank, National Association
1 Penn Sq
Lancaster PA 17602
717 581-3166

(G-4329)
FUQUA & YORI P A
Also Called: Fuqua, James A Jr
26 The Cir (19947-1500)
P.O. Box 250 (19947-0250)
PHONE...............................302 856-7777
James Fuqua, *Pr*
EMP: 6 EST: 1977
SALES (est): 361.22K **Privately Held**
Web: www.fwsdelaw.com
SIC: 8111 General practice law office

(G-4330)
GALVIN INDUSTRIES LLC
202 W Laurel St (19947-2308)
PHONE...............................703 505-7860
EMP: 8 EST: 2017
SALES (est): 310.91K **Privately Held**
SIC: 8733 Research institute

(G-4331)
GATOR CONSTRUCTION LLC
26136 Gvernor Stockley Rd (19947-2567)
PHONE...............................302 430-1160
Lisa Polly, *Prin*
EMP: 5 EST: 2010
SALES (est): 78.27K **Privately Held**
SIC: 1521 Single-family housing construction

(G-4332)
GEO-TECHNOLOGY ASSOCIATES INC
Also Called: Gga
21491 Baltimore Ave # 1 (19947-6421)
PHONE...............................302 855-5775
Greg Sauter, *Brnch Mgr*
EMP: 5
Web: www.gtaeng.com
SIC: 8711 Consulting engineer
HQ: Geo-Technology Associates Inc
3445 Box Hll Corp Ctr Dr
Abingdon MD 21009
410 515-9446

(G-4333)
GEORGETOWN AIR SERVICES
21553 Rudder Ln Unit 1 (19947-2029)
P.O. Box 760 (19947-0760)
PHONE...............................302 855-2355
Gerrett Dernoga, *Owner*
EMP: 5 EST: 1998
SALES (est): 320.11K **Privately Held**
SIC: 4581 Aircraft maintenance and repair services

(G-4334)
GEORGETOWN AIR SERVICES LLC
Also Called: Sussex Aero Maintenance
21553 Rudder Ln Unit 1 (19947-2029)
PHONE...............................302 855-2355
John F Kenney, *Prin*
John F Kenney, *Owner*
Lisa Brown, *CFO*
EMP: 10 EST: 2002
SQ FT: 6,400
SALES (est): 681.52K **Privately Held**
Web: www.georgetownair.com
SIC: 4581 Aircraft maintenance and repair services

(G-4335)
GEORGETOWN ANIMAL HOSPITAL PA
20784 Dupont Blvd (19947-3178)
PHONE...............................302 856-2623
John Gooss, *Pt*
Don Gooss Patnr, *Prin*
EMP: 7 EST: 1995
SALES (est): 511.5K **Privately Held**
Web: www.georgetownanimalhospital.com
SIC: 0742 Animal hospital services, pets and other animal specialties

(G-4336)
GEORGETOWN BOYS AND GIRLS CLUB
115 N Race St (19947-1406)
PHONE...............................302 856-4903
Renee Hickman, *Dir*
Geanne Guckes, *Dir*
Adriona Harris, *Program Coordinator*
EMP: 10 EST: 2001
SALES (est): 142.21K **Privately Held**
Web: www.bgclubs.org
SIC: 8641 Youth organizations

(G-4337)
GEORGETOWN CONSTRUCTION CO
25136 Dupont Blvd (19947-2610)
PHONE...............................302 856-7601
Kenneth Adams, *Pr*
Joe Ann Adams, *
EMP: 7 EST: 1952
SALES (est): 420.44K **Privately Held**
SIC: 8748 Business consulting, nec

(G-4338)
GEORGETOWN FAMILY MEDICINE
201 W Market St (19947-1440)
PHONE...............................302 856-4092
Ryan Scot Davis, *Prin*
EMP: 21 EST: 2001
SALES (est): 1.89MM **Privately Held**
Web: www.georgetowndocs.com
SIC: 8011 General and family practice, physician/surgeon

(G-4339)
GEORGETOWN HOTEL LLC
Also Called: Tru By Hilton
301 College Park Ln (19947-2111)
PHONE...............................302 515-2100
Steven Silver, *CEO*
Ron Schaefer, *
EMP: 24 EST: 2019
SALES (est): 593.14K **Privately Held**
Web: www.hilton.com
SIC: 7011 Hotels

(G-4340)
GEORGETOWN MEDICAL ASSOC LLC
20930 Dupont Blvd Unit 101 (19947-1723)
PHONE...............................302 856-3737
Beshara Helou, *Prin*
Stacey Dixon, *Off Mgr*
EMP: 14 EST: 2008
SALES (est): 950.23K **Privately Held**
Web: www.mygeorgetownmd.com
SIC: 8011 General and family practice, physician/surgeon

(G-4341)
GEORGETOWN PLAYGROUND & PK INC
212 Wilson St (19947-2328)
PHONE...............................302 856-7111
Christine Lecates, *Pr*
EMP: 6 EST: 2013
SALES (est): 120.89K **Privately Held**
Web: parks.georgetown.org
SIC: 8399 Fund raising organization, non-fee basis

(G-4342)
GILL EDWARD LAW OFFICES OF
16 N Bedford St (19947-1463)
P.O. Box 824 (19947-0824)
PHONE...............................302 854-5400
EMP: 10 EST: 1995
SALES (est): 432.31K **Privately Held**
Web: www.de-law.com
SIC: 8111 General practice law office

(G-4343)
GODDESS BEAUTY SUPPLY LLC
401 College Park Ln Unit 5 (19947-2114)
PHONE...............................302 858-4649
Charity Sample, *Managing Member*
EMP: 5 EST: 2018
SALES (est): 94.41K **Privately Held**
SIC: 7231 Beauty shops

(G-4344)
GOLDEN CAR CARE
19395 Substation Rd (19947-4760)
PHONE...............................302 856-2219
EMP: 6 EST: 2010
SALES (est): 245.39K **Privately Held**
Web: www.goldencarcare.com
SIC: 7538 General automotive repair shops

(G-4345)
GREAT CLIPS FOR HAIR
Also Called: Great Clips
401 College Park Ln (19947-2114)
PHONE...............................302 858-4871
EMP: 5 EST: 2018
SALES (est): 60.84K **Privately Held**
Web: www.greatclips.com
SIC: 7231 Unisex hair salons

(G-4346)
GREAT OUTDOOR COTTAGES LLC
21498 Baltimore Ave (19947-6415)
PHONE...............................215 760-4971
Todd Burgage, *Managing Member*

GEOGRAPHIC SECTION

Georgetown - Sussex County (G-4374)

Michael Scheid, *COO*
John Longino, *CFO*
EMP: 11 **EST:** 2020
SALES (EST): 490.77K **Privately Held**
Web: www.greatoutdoorcottages.com
SIC: 2452 Log cabins, prefabricated, wood

(G-4347)
GRIMES CONSTRUCTION
22242 Lewes Georgetown Hwy
(19947-5536)
PHONE..............................302 462-6533
Joseph Grimes, *Owner*
EMP: 5 **EST:** 2015
SALES (est): 247.61K **Privately Held**
Web: www.grimesconstructionllc.com
SIC: 1521 New construction, single-family houses

(G-4348)
GUARDIAN ANGEL DAY CARE
25193 Zoar Rd (19947-6523)
PHONE..............................302 934-0130
Shirley Davis, *Pr*
Sharon Moore, *VP*
EMP: 5 **EST:** 1997
SALES (est): 202.52K **Privately Held**
Web: www.daycarecarrollton.org
SIC: 8351 Preschool center

(G-4349)
H & R BLOCK
Also Called: H & R Block
21305 Berlin Rd Unit 1 (19947-3186)
PHONE..............................302 856-3272
EMP: 8 **EST:** 1955
SALES (est): 63.88K **Privately Held**
Web: www.hrblock.com
SIC: 7291 Tax return preparation services

(G-4350)
H P CUSTOM TRIM LLC
22091 Lwes Georgetown Hwy
(19947-5523)
PHONE..............................302 381-0802
Chad Hayes, *Pr*
EMP: 6 **EST:** 2011
SALES (est): 388.9K **Privately Held**
SIC: 1751 1531 1521 1522 Cabinet and finish carpentry; Speculative builder, single-family houses; Single-family home remodeling, additions, and repairs; Hotel/motel and multi-family home renovation and remodeling

(G-4351)
HABITAT FOR HUMANITY INTL INC
Also Called: Habitat For Humanity
107 Depot St (19947-1471)
P.O. Box 759 (19947-0759)
PHONE..............................302 855-1156
Kevin Gilmore, *Ex Dir*
EMP: 6
SALES (corp-wide): 272.79MM **Privately Held**
Web: www.hfhtkc.org
SIC: 8399 Community development groups
PA: Habitat For Humanity International, Inc.
285 Peachtree Center Ave
Atlanta GA 30303
800 422-4828

(G-4352)
HALLER & HUDSON
101 S Bedford St (19947-1843)
PHONE..............................302 856-4525
Karl Haller, *Pt*
Howard Hudson, *Pt*
EMP: 5 **EST:** 1983
SALES (est): 452.79K **Privately Held**
Web: www.mortgagerefinance.com

SIC: 8111 General practice attorney, lawyer

(G-4353)
HARRISON SNIOR LVING GORGETOWN
110 W North St (19947-2144)
PHONE..............................302 856-4574
Carol Daniels, *Admn*
EMP: 5 **EST:** 2007
SALES (est): 10.59MM **Privately Held**
Web: www.harrisonseniorliving.com
SIC: 8051 Skilled nursing care facilities
PA: Harrison Holdings Corporation
300 Strode Ave
Coatesville PA 19320

(G-4354)
HEALTHY OUTCOMES LLC
2 Lee Ave Unit 103 (19947-2149)
PHONE..............................302 856-4022
Jennifer Morelli, *Off Mgr*
EMP: 9 **EST:** 2011
SALES (est): 385.25K **Privately Held**
Web: www.healthy-outcomes.com
SIC: 8011 Offices and clinics of medical doctors

(G-4355)
HERNANDEZ PAINTING
14947 Wilson Hill Rd (19947-3631)
PHONE..............................302 212-8425
Hernandez Miguel Martinez, *Prin*
EMP: 5 **EST:** 2016
SALES (est): 52.88K **Privately Held**
SIC: 1721 Painting and paper hanging

(G-4356)
HIGHWATER MGT SUSSEX LLC
22518 Lewes Georgetown Hwy
(19947-5533)
PHONE..............................302 245-7570
Scott Kammerer, *Pr*
EMP: 5 **EST:** 2021
SALES (est): 457.67K **Privately Held**
SIC: 8741 Management services

(G-4357)
HIPPO TRAILER
14 Evergreen Dr (19947-9483)
PHONE..............................302 854-6661
Walter Hyler, *Pr*
Elaine Hyler, *Sec*
EMP: 2 **EST:** 1999
SALES (est): 129.71K **Privately Held**
SIC: 2451 Mobile homes

(G-4358)
HISTORIC GEORGETOWN ASSN
105 Spicer St (19947-1834)
PHONE..............................302 934-8818
Carlton Moore, *Prin*
EMP: 5 **EST:** 2018
SALES (est): 21.56K **Privately Held**
Web: www.georgetowntrainstation.org
SIC: 8699 Membership organizations, nec

(G-4359)
HOLIDAY HAIR
6 College Park Ln Ste 1 (19947-2179)
PHONE..............................302 856-2575
EMP: 5 **EST:** 2019
SALES (est): 82.46K **Privately Held**
Web: www.signaturestyle.com
SIC: 7231 Unisex hair salons

(G-4360)
HOLLINGSEAD INTERNATIONAL LLC
21583 Baltimore Ave (19947-6313)
PHONE..............................302 855-5888

Sandra Taras, *
Matthew Hill Sales, *Prin*
Christopher Mikola, *
EMP: 300 **EST:** 2011
SQ FT: 100,000
SALES (est): 83.87MM **Privately Held**
Web: www.aloftaeroarchitects.com
SIC: 3679 Electronic switches
HQ: Pats Aircraft, Llc
21652 Nanticoke Ave
Georgetown DE 19947
855 236-1638

(G-4361)
HOME MEDIA ONE LLC
22344 Lewes Georgetown Hwy
(19947-5535)
PHONE..............................302 644-0307
EMP: 5 **EST:** 2004
SALES (est): 133.87K **Privately Held**
Web: www.homemediaone.com
SIC: 4813 Telephone communication, except radio

(G-4362)
HOME MEDIC LLC
24617 Springfield Rd (19947-6330)
PHONE..............................302 841-3861
Paul Stillman, *Prin*
EMP: 10 **EST:** 2019
SALES (est): 844.09K **Privately Held**
SIC: 8099 Health and allied services, nec

(G-4363)
HOMESTEAD CAMPING INC
25165 Prettyman Rd (19947-5207)
PHONE..............................302 684-4278
William Prettyman, *Pr*
Irma Prettyman, *Pr*
EMP: 5 **EST:** 1974
SALES (est): 142.63K **Privately Held**
Web: www.homesteadde.com
SIC: 7033 Campgrounds

(G-4364)
HOMETOWN FENCE LLC
23656 Fox Croft Ln (19947-4567)
PHONE..............................302 629-0415
Craig Brady, *Prin*
EMP: 6 **EST:** 2010
SALES (est): 111.59K **Privately Held**
SIC: 1799 Fence construction

(G-4365)
HORIZON FARM CREDIT
20816 Dupont Blvd (19947-3179)
PHONE..............................302 856-9081
Charmayne Busker, *Brnch Mgr*
EMP: 8
SALES (corp-wide): 93.15MM **Privately Held**
Web: www.horizonfc.com
SIC: 6141 Personal credit institutions
PA: Horizon Farm Credit
300 Winding Creek Blvd
Mechanicsburg PA 17050
888 339-3334

(G-4366)
HOY EN DELAWARE LLC
105 Depot St (19947-1471)
P.O. Box 593 (19947-0593)
PHONE..............................302 854-0240
EMP: 9 **EST:** 2005
SALES (est): 256.19K **Privately Held**
Web: www.hoyendelaware.com
SIC: 2711 Commercial printing and newspaper publishing combined

(G-4367)
HUDSON HOUSE SERVICES
11 W Pine St (19947-1825)
PHONE..............................302 856-4363
Cindy Witt, *Prin*
EMP: 8 **EST:** 2016
SALES (est): 80.69K **Privately Held**
SIC: 8093 Substance abuse clinics (outpatient)

(G-4368)
INFINITY CHOPPERS
24655 Dupont Blvd (19947-2626)
PHONE..............................302 249-7282
Michael Pizzola, *Prin*
EMP: 5 **EST:** 2014
SALES (est): 61K **Privately Held**
Web: www.infinitychoppers.com
SIC: 3751 Motorcycles and related parts

(G-4369)
INFOCUS FINANCIAL ADVISORS INC
406 S Bedford St (19947-1853)
PHONE..............................410 677-4848
EMP: 5 **EST:** 2019
SALES (est): 201.5K **Privately Held**
Web: www.retireinfocus.com
SIC: 6282 Investment advice

(G-4370)
INSIGHT HOMES
17 Frankenberry Dr (19947-3832)
PHONE..............................302 858-4281
EMP: 7 **EST:** 2016
SALES (est): 82.65K **Privately Held**
Web: www.itsjustabetterhouse.com
SIC: 6531 6519 Real estate agents and managers; Real property lessors, nec

(G-4371)
INSPECTION LANES
23737 Dupont Blvd (19947-8805)
PHONE..............................302 853-1003
Pam Smith, *Mgr*
EMP: 7 **EST:** 2010
SALES (est): 79.38K **Privately Held**
Web: dmv.de.gov
SIC: 7933 Ten pin center

(G-4372)
INTERIORS JUDITH DAVIDSON
13 Fairway East Dr (19947-9457)
PHONE..............................302 841-5500
Judith L Davidson, *Prin*
EMP: 5 **EST:** 2007
SALES (est): 143.8K **Privately Held**
Web: www.judithdavidsoninteriors.com
SIC: 7389 Interior designer

(G-4373)
IRON SOURCE LLC
25113 Dupont Blvd (19947-2621)
PHONE..............................302 856-7545
Chess Hedrick, *Managing Member*
▼ **EMP:** 8 **EST:** 2009
SQ FT: 5,500
SALES (est): 8.67MM **Privately Held**
Web: www.ironsourcede.com
SIC: 5082 7353 General construction machinery and equipment; Heavy construction equipment rental

(G-4374)
ISAACS ASPHALT PAVING
24087 Lewes Georgetown Hwy
(19947-5303)
PHONE..............................302 251-2990
A Parker, *Owner*
EMP: 5 **EST:** 2006
SALES (est): 108.95K **Privately Held**

Georgetown - Sussex County (G-4375)   GEOGRAPHIC SECTION

SIC: **1611** Surfacing and paving

(G-4375)
J & P MANAGEMENT INC
Also Called: Comfort Inn
20530 Dupont Blvd (19947-3176)
PHONE.....................302 854-9400
Raj Patel, *CEO*
Sashi Patel, *Pr*
EMP: **30** EST: 1997
SALES (est): 474.86K **Privately Held**
Web: www.choicehotels.com
SIC: **7011** Hotels and motels

(G-4376)
J & V CLEANING LLC
20479 Scott Dr Unit D (19947-6128)
PHONE.....................302 245-5230
Jessica Perez, *Prin*
EMP: **5** EST: 2018
SALES (est): 23.7K **Privately Held**
SIC: **7699** Cleaning services

(G-4377)
JACKIE HECK
21176 Pepper Rd (19947-5825)
PHONE.....................302 856-1598
Jackie Heck, *Prin*
EMP: **6** EST: 2011
SALES (est): 63.48K **Privately Held**
SIC: **0752** Boarding services, horses: racing and non-racing

(G-4378)
JANE L STAYTON CPA
117 S Bedford St (19947-1843)
PHONE.....................302 856-4141
Jane L Stayton, *Owner*
EMP: **10** EST: 2001
SALES (est): 474.66K **Privately Held**
Web: www.staytondickens.com
SIC: **8721** Certified public accountant

(G-4379)
JAYKAL LED SOLUTIONS INC
21499 Baltimore Ave (19947-6419)
PHONE.....................302 295-0015
Sanjay Kapuria, *Pr*
Brian Asher, *Dir*
Frank Gayzur, *Prin*
▲ EMP: **3** EST: 2011
SALES (est): 1.24MM **Privately Held**
Web: www.jaykalusa.com
SIC: **3648** 3674 Lighting fixtures, except electric: residential; Light emitting diodes

(G-4380)
JDJS LLC
Also Called: Jennygems
21348 Cedar Creek Ave (19947-6305)
PHONE.....................844 967-3748
Jennifer Mcmillan, *Managing Member*
EMP: **20** EST: 2015
SALES (est): 1.5MM **Privately Held**
Web: www.jennygems.com
SIC: **5999** 2499 3993 5947 Art, picture frames, and decorations; Signboards, wood ; Signs and advertising specialties; Gift, novelty, and souvenir shop

(G-4381)
JEFFERSON URIAN DANE STRNER PA (PA)
651 N Bedford St (19947-2159)
P.O. Box 830 (19947-0830)
PHONE.....................302 856-3900
David C Doan, *Pr*
David Urian, *
Charles Sterner, *
EMP: **30** EST: 1970
SALES (est): 5.15MM
SALES (corp-wide): 5.15MM **Privately Held**
Web: www.juds.com
SIC: **8721** Certified public accountant

(G-4382)
JENKINS MECHANICAL
3 Fairway Ave (19947-9486)
PHONE.....................302 430-8211
Jay Jenkins, *Prin*
EMP: **6** EST: 2016
SALES (est): 119.4K **Privately Held**
Web: www.plumbingandmechanical.com
SIC: **1711** Plumbing contractors

(G-4383)
JG TOWNSEND JR & CO INC (PA)
316 N Race St (19947-1166)
P.O. Box 430 (19947-0430)
PHONE.....................302 856-2525
Paul G Townsend, *Pr*
EMP: **40** EST: 1937
SQ FT: 52,554
SALES (est): 5.39MM
SALES (corp-wide): 5.39MM **Privately Held**
SIC: **6531** 6519 5099 5142 Selling agent, real estate; Farm land leasing; Timber products, rough; Packaged frozen goods

(G-4384)
JLJ ENTERPRISES INC
16975 Redden Rd (19947-3340)
PHONE.....................302 398-0229
Jerry L Jerman, *Pr*
Elizabeth Jerman, *Sec*
▼ EMP: **13** EST: 1989
SALES (est): 2.42MM **Privately Held**
Web: www.jljenterprises.com
SIC: **5084** Food industry machinery

(G-4385)
JOHN T TEDESCO
19181 Alcott Way (19947-5408)
P.O. Box 9011 (22304-0011)
PHONE.....................703 357-0797
John Tedesco, *Prin*
EMP: **4** EST: 2013
SALES (est): 105.91K **Privately Held**
SIC: **2711** Newspapers, publishing and printing

(G-4386)
JORDY JAEL LAWN CARE
28024 Wagner Rd (19947-6746)
PHONE.....................302 824-3748
EMP: **5** EST: 2018
SALES (est): 171.37K **Privately Held**
SIC: **0782** Lawn care services

(G-4387)
JOSEPH M L SAND & GRAVEL CO
25136 Dupont Blvd (19947-2610)
PHONE.....................302 856-7396
Melvin L Joseph, *Pr*
Joanne Adams, *Sec*
EMP: **25** EST: 1990
SQ FT: 700
SALES (est): 1.97MM **Privately Held**
SIC: **1442** 5191 Sand mining; Farm supplies

(G-4388)
JOSEPH PATRICK FABBER MEML
401 N Bedford St (19947-2197)
PHONE.....................302 858-4040
EMP: **5** EST: 2016
SALES (est): 162.32K **Privately Held**
Web: www.jpfmf.com

SIC: **8641** Civic and social associations

(G-4389)
JUSTIN TANKS LLC
21413 Cedar Creek Ave (19947-6306)
PHONE.....................302 856-3521
EMP: **30** EST: 1974
SQ FT: 35,000
SALES (est): 3.66MM **Privately Held**
Web: www.justintanks.com
SIC: **3089** Plastics and fiberglass tanks

(G-4390)
KARINS ENGINEERING INC
128 W Market St (19947-1416)
PHONE.....................302 856-6699
EMP: **11**
SALES (corp-wide): 5.38MM **Privately Held**
Web: www.karinsengineering.com
SIC: **8711** Civil engineering
PA: Karins Engineering Inc
17 Polly Drummond Ste 201
Newark DE 19711
302 369-2900

(G-4391)
KATHARINE N SNYDER
113 W North St (19947-2134)
PHONE.....................302 381-7283
Katharine N Snyder Lcsw, *Owner*
EMP: **7** EST: 2018
SALES (est): 36.21K **Privately Held**
SIC: **8322** Social worker

(G-4392)
KEITHS BOAT CANVAS
16408 Seashore Hwy (19947-4205)
PHONE.....................302 841-8081
EMP: **4** EST: 2019
SALES (est): 95.58K **Privately Held**
Web: www.keithsboatcanvas.com
SIC: **2211** Canvas

(G-4393)
KEVIN MCDANIEL
22495 Lewes Georgetown Hwy (19947-5528)
PHONE.....................302 236-1351
Kevin Mcdaniel, *Prin*
EMP: **33** EST: 2010
SALES (est): 221.43K **Privately Held**
SIC: **7389** Business Activities at Non-Commercial Site

(G-4394)
KIMBLES AVI LGISTICAL SVCS INC
Also Called: Kimbles DLS
21785 Aviation Ave (19947-5574)
PHONE.....................334 663-4954
Mark Langley, *Pr*
Sean Carroll, *VP*
EMP: **9** EST: 2014
SALES (est): 454.57K **Privately Held**
SIC: **4231** Trucking terminal facilities

(G-4395)
KRUGER FARMS INC
24306 Dupont Blvd (19947-2602)
PHONE.....................302 856-2577
Alvin Kruger, *Pr*
Frank Kruger, *VP*
Paul Kruger, *Sec*
EMP: **5** EST: 1954
SALES (est): 479.09K **Privately Held**
SIC: **0119** Barley farm

(G-4396)
KRUGER TRAILERS INC
24306 Dupont Blvd (19947-2602)

PHONE.....................302 856-2577
Alvin Kruger, *Pr*
Frank Kruger, *VP*
Paul Kruger, *Sec*
EMP: **8** EST: 1958
SQ FT: 15,000
SALES (est): 965.05K **Privately Held**
Web: www.krugertrailers.com
SIC: **3715** 3713 Trailer bodies; Farm truck bodies

(G-4397)
LA ESPERANZA INC
Also Called: LA ESPERANZA COMMUNITY CENTER
216 N Race St (19947-1409)
PHONE.....................302 854-9262
Claudia Pena Porretti, *Ex Dir*
Charles Burton, *OF*
EMP: **13** EST: 1997
SALES (est): 853.18K **Privately Held**
Web: www.laesperanzacenter.org
SIC: **8322** 8111 Social service center; Immigration and naturalization law

(G-4398)
LA RED HEALTH CARE
23659 Saulsbury Ln (19947-6388)
PHONE.....................757 709-5072
Magali Tellez Blancas, *Mgr*
EMP: **10** EST: 2017
SALES (est): 222.15K **Privately Held**
SIC: **8082** Home health care services

(G-4399)
LA RED HEALTH CENTER INC (PA)
21444 Carmean Way (19947-4572)
PHONE.....................302 855-1233
Brian Olson, *CEO*
Beatrice Chiemelu, *CFO*
Judy Johnson, *Treas*
Rosa Rivera, *COO*
Francisco Rodriguez, *Dir*
EMP: **47** EST: 2002
SQ FT: 25,000
SALES (est): 14.82MM
SALES (corp-wide): 14.82MM **Privately Held**
Web: www.laredhealthcenter.org
SIC: **8099** Medical services organization

(G-4400)
LAFOND CONSTRUCTION
24645 Springfield Rd (19947-6330)
PHONE.....................302 430-2834
Christina Lafond, *Prin*
EMP: **5** EST: 2008
SALES (est): 152.57K **Privately Held**
SIC: **1521** Single-family housing construction

(G-4401)
LARRY COVERDALE
120 S King St (19947-1612)
PHONE.....................302 855-9305
Larry Coverdale, *Prin*
EMP: **5** EST: 2009
SALES (est): 38.4K **Privately Held**
SIC: **7241** Barber shops

(G-4402)
LATIN CHAT SERVICES
111 N Race St (19947-1461)
PHONE.....................302 249-4151
Gesel Hernandez, *Prin*
EMP: **5** EST: 2010
SALES (est): 97.69K **Privately Held**
Web: www.slatinosinc.com
SIC: **8111** Immigration and naturalization law

GEOGRAPHIC SECTION

Georgetown - Sussex County (G-4432)

(G-4403)
LAW OFFCES MURRAY PHILLIPS GAY
215 E Market St (19947-1233)
PHONE.................................302 855-9300
EMP: 5 **EST:** 2020
SALES (est): 222.23K **Privately Held**
Web: www.murrayphillipslaw.com
SIC: 8111 General practice attorney, lawyer

(G-4404)
LAW OFFICE OF ANDREW WHITEHEAD
5 W Market St (19947-1492)
PHONE.................................302 248-2000
EMP: 5 **EST:** 2013
SALES (est): 246.31K **Privately Held**
Web: www.whiteheadlawde.com
SIC: 8111 Criminal law

(G-4405)
LEGACY VULCAN LLC
28272 Landfill Ln (19947-6071)
PHONE.................................302 875-0748
EMP: 4
Web: www.vulcanmaterials.com
SIC: 3273 Ready-mixed concrete
HQ: Legacy Vulcan, Llc
1200 Urban Center Dr
Vestavia AL 35242
205 298-3000

(G-4406)
LIFE NET
21479 Rudder Ln (19947-2024)
PHONE.................................302 855-0550
EMP: 5 **EST:** 2010
SALES (est): 56.77K **Privately Held**
SIC: 8099 Organ bank

(G-4407)
LIFESTYLE DOCUMENT MGT INC
22277 Lewes Georgetown Hwy (19947-5526)
P.O. Box 822 (19947-0822)
PHONE.................................302 856-6387
David Parker, *Pr*
EMP: 5 **EST:** 2000
SQ FT: 5,000
SALES (est): 456.95K **Privately Held**
Web: www.lifestyledocumentmanagement.com
SIC: 4226 Document and office records storage

(G-4408)
LISA BARTELS
10 N Front St (19947-1414)
PHONE.................................302 856-9596
Lisa Bartels, *Prin*
EMP: 14 **EST:** 2013
SALES (est): 488.34K **Privately Held**
Web: www.beebehealthcare.org
SIC: 8062 General medical and surgical hospitals

(G-4409)
LUCKY STAR FARMS LLC
15942 Wilson Hill Rd (19947-3509)
PHONE.................................302 841-5177
Mark Briggs, *Managing Member*
EMP: 6 **EST:** 2006
SALES (est): 242.56K **Privately Held**
SIC: 4212 Live poultry haulage

(G-4410)
M DAVIS FARMS LLC
17741 Davis Rd (19947-4430)
PHONE.................................302 856-7018
EMP: 5 **EST:** 2001
SALES (est): 514.89K **Privately Held**
SIC: 0191 General farms, primarily crop

(G-4411)
MACKLYN HOME CARE
6 W Market St (19947-1484)
PHONE.................................302 253-8208
EMP: 7 **EST:** 2017
SALES (est): 61.12K **Privately Held**
Web: www.macklynhomecare.net
SIC: 8082 8059 Home health care services; Personal care home, with health care

(G-4412)
MAID EASY CLEANING DELAWARE
332 S Bedford St (19947-1848)
PHONE.................................302 858-1883
Stacey Dawson, *Prin*
EMP: 5 **EST:** 2016
SALES (est): 94.27K **Privately Held**
SIC: 7699 Cleaning services

(G-4413)
MARINS MED LLC
23334 Frederick Ln (19947-6454)
PHONE.................................302 245-4596
EMP: 2 **EST:** 2017
SALES (est): 103.91K **Privately Held**
Web: www.marinsmed.com
SIC: 3842 Prosthetic appliances

(G-4414)
MARK MENENDEZ
4 Blue Heron Dr (19947-9485)
PHONE.................................302 644-8500
Mark Menendez, *Owner*
EMP: 5 **EST:** 2004
SALES (est): 116.32K **Privately Held**
SIC: 8011 Offices and clinics of medical doctors

(G-4415)
MARK PENUEL
Also Called: State Farm Insurance
522 E Market St (19947-2255)
P.O. Box 384 (19947-0384)
PHONE.................................302 856-7724
Bruce Penuel, *Owner*
EMP: 7 **EST:** 1946
SALES (est): 486.49K **Privately Held**
Web: www.penuelinsurance.com
SIC: 6411 Insurance agents and brokers

(G-4416)
MARK PERRY PRODUCTIONS LLC
5 Par Ct (19947-9471)
PHONE.................................443 521-4382
EMP: 5 **EST:** 2019
SALES (est): 189.42K **Privately Held**
SIC: 7822 Motion picture and tape distribution

(G-4417)
MARKET STREET CENTER INC
Also Called: Barnett, Norman C
9 Chestnut St (19947-1901)
P.O. Box 755 (19947-0755)
PHONE.................................302 856-9024
William Schab, *Pr*
Norman C Barnett, *VP*
EMP: 8 **EST:** 1993
SALES (est): 579.24K **Privately Held**
SIC: 6512 Nonresidential building operators

(G-4418)
MARKETING RESOURCES INC
Also Called: Money Mailer of East Central
23 Fairway Ave (19947-9486)
PHONE.................................302 855-9209
Carol Bazat, *Prin*
EMP: 7 **EST:** 2011
SALES (est): 164.5K **Privately Held**
Web: www.moneymailer.com
SIC: 7331 Direct mail advertising services

(G-4419)
MARTINEZ PAINTING LLC
21859 Hickory Dr (19947-2653)
PHONE.................................302 448-1932
Israel Martinez, *Prin*
EMP: 6 **EST:** 2017
SALES (est): 211.44K **Privately Held**
SIC: 1721 Painting and paper hanging

(G-4420)
MASTERING MRCURY DSIGN ELMENTS
12 Boisenberry Ln (19947-3817)
PHONE.................................302 344-4323
Zack Varrato, *Prin*
EMP: 4 **EST:** 2016
SALES (est): 57.88K **Privately Held**
SIC: 2819 Industrial inorganic chemicals, nec

(G-4421)
MCCABES MECHANICAL SERVICE INC
16689 Seashore Hwy (19947-4221)
P.O. Box 488 (19947-0488)
PHONE.................................302 854-9001
Allen Mc Cabe, *Pr*
Debra Mccabe, *VP*
EMP: 10 **EST:** 1995
SQ FT: 60,000
SALES (est): 2.39MM **Privately Held**
Web: www.mccabesmechanical.com
SIC: 5084 3444 3823 Industrial machinery and equipment; Sheet metalwork; Process control instruments

(G-4422)
MEGEE PLUMBING & HEATING CO
Also Called: Honeywell Authorized Dealer
22965 Lewes Georgetown Hwy (19947-5301)
P.O. Box 745 (19947-0745)
PHONE.................................302 856-6311
B Darrow Mclauchlin, *Pr*
Ernest E Megee Junior, *Sec*
EMP: 65 **EST:** 1936
SQ FT: 18,000
SALES (est): 9.52MM **Privately Held**
Web: www.fhfurr.com
SIC: 1711 1731 Warm air heating and air conditioning contractor; General electrical contractor

(G-4423)
MEGHAN HOUSE INC
210 Rosa St (19947-1248)
PHONE.................................302 253-8261
EMP: 6 **EST:** 2010
SALES (est): 83.51K **Privately Held**
SIC: 8399 Social services, nec

(G-4424)
MELVIN L JOSEPH CNSTR CO
25136 Dupont Blvd (19947-2610)
PHONE.................................302 856-7396
Ken Adams, *Pr*
Melvin L Joseph Senior, *Pr*
Joe Ann Adams, *

EMP: 50 **EST:** 1940
SQ FT: 42,000
SALES (est): 10.63MM **Privately Held**
Web: www.melvinjoseph.com
SIC: 1629 1611 Land clearing contractor; Highway and street paving contractor

(G-4425)
MENTOR DE
19372 Citizens Blvd (19947-4180)
PHONE.................................302 858-4644
EMP: 6 **EST:** 2011
SALES (est): 82.73K **Privately Held**
SIC: 8322 Social service center

(G-4426)
MICHAEL WESCOTT
24265 Dupont Blvd (19947-2630)
PHONE.................................302 423-7094
EMP: 5 **EST:** 2019
SALES (est): 22.86K **Privately Held**
SIC: 7999 Karate instruction

(G-4427)
MID ATLANTIC
403 E Laurel St (19947-2336)
PHONE.................................302 393-4355
Anibal Soto, *Prin*
EMP: 7 **EST:** 2019
SALES (est): 82.42K **Privately Held**
Web: www.midatlanticcare.com
SIC: 0782 Lawn and garden services

(G-4428)
MID ATLANTIC BUILDER INC
22532 Pine Haven Dr (19947-6367)
PHONE.................................302 344-7224
Douglas Catts, *Prin*
EMP: 10 **EST:** 2017
SALES (est): 882.43K **Privately Held**
SIC: 1521 New construction, single-family houses

(G-4429)
MIRACLE BUILDERS LLC
315 Calhoun St (19947-1207)
PHONE.................................302 236-1351
EMP: 5 **EST:** 2009
SALES (est): 136.35K **Privately Held**
Web: www.miraclebuildersllc.com
SIC: 1521 New construction, single-family houses

(G-4430)
MOBILE TAX LLC
7 S King St (19947-1601)
PHONE.................................302 297-8325
EMP: 6 **EST:** 2016
SALES (est): 54.28K **Privately Held**
Web: www.delawaremobiletaxde.com
SIC: 7291 Tax return preparation services

(G-4431)
MOONEY & ANDREW PA
11 S Race St (19947-1907)
PHONE.................................302 856-3070
Eric Mooney, *Owner*
Eric G Mooney, *Owner*
Michael W Andrew, *Prin*
EMP: 6 **EST:** 2005
SALES (est): 472.5K **Privately Held**
Web: www.dedefense.com
SIC: 8111 General practice attorney, lawyer

(G-4432)
MOORE & RUTT PA (PA)
Also Called: Moore J Everett
122 W Market St (19947-1416)
P.O. Box 554 (19947-0554)
PHONE.................................302 856-9568
J E Moore Junior, *Pr*
J Everett Moore Junior, *Pr*
David N Rutt, *Sec*
EMP: 9 **EST:** 1986
SALES (est): 2.38MM
SALES (corp-wide): 2.38MM **Privately Held**

Georgetown - Sussex County (G-4433)   GEOGRAPHIC SECTION

Web: www.mooreandrutt.com
SIC: 8111 General practice attorney, lawyer

(G-4433)
MOORE CLINTON DENVER II
Also Called: Moore's Masonry
24062 Peterkins Rd (19947-2723)
PHONE..................302 856-3385
EMP: 5 EST: 2011
SALES (est): 111.5K Privately Held
SIC: 1741 Masonry and other stonework

(G-4434)
MOORE FARMS
14619 Cokesbury Rd (19947-4364)
PHONE..................302 629-4999
Donald Moore Senior, Pt
Donald Moore Junior, Pt
EMP: 11 EST: 2004
SALES (est): 2.05MM Privately Held
Web: www.moorefarms.net
SIC: 1542 Commercial and office building, new construction

(G-4435)
MORRIS & RITCHIE ASSOC INC
8 W Market St (19947-1437)
PHONE..................302 855-5734
Kenneth Usab, Brnch Mgr
EMP: 22
Web: www.mragta.com
SIC: 8711 8713 Designing: ship, boat, machine, and product; Surveying services
HQ: Morris & Ritchie Associates, Inc.
   3445 Box Hll Corp Ctr Dr B
   Abingdon MD
   410 515-9000

(G-4436)
MORRIS JAMES PER INJURY GROUP
107 W Market St (19947-1438)
PHONE..................302 856-0017
EMP: 5 EST: 2017
SALES (est): 134.09K Privately Held
Web: www.morrisjamespersonalinjurylawyers.com
SIC: 8111 General practice attorney, lawyer

(G-4437)
MR COUNSELING LLC
24680 Shortly Rd (19947-4936)
PHONE..................302 855-9598
Michelle M Robinson, CEO
EMP: 6 EST: 2018
SALES (est): 84K Privately Held
SIC: 8011 Offices and clinics of medical doctors

(G-4438)
MULLIGANS POINTE LLC
22426 Sussex Pines Rd (19947-6445)
PHONE..................302 856-6283
EMP: 11 EST: 2018
SALES (est): 405.08K Privately Held
Web: www.mulliganspointe.com
SIC: 7992 Public golf courses

(G-4439)
MURPHY LAW FIRM
313 N Bedford St (19947-1103)
PHONE..................302 855-1055
Theodore Murphy, Brnch Mgr
EMP: 6
SALES (corp-wide): 949.3K Privately Held
Web: www.murphy-law-firm.com
SIC: 8111 General practice law office
PA: Murphy Law Firm
   320 N High St
   West Chester PA 19380
   610 436-7555

(G-4440)
MY HANDS HANDYMAN LLC
2 Booker St (19947-2002)
PHONE..................302 387-2749
EMP: 5 EST: 2019
SALES (est): 18.95K Privately Held
SIC: 7299 Handyman service

(G-4441)
NANCY HASTINGS
701 E Market St (19947-2221)
PHONE..................302 396-2899
Nancy Hastings, Mgr
EMP: 6 EST: 2017
SALES (est): 59.97K Privately Held
SIC: 8049 Offices of health practitioner

(G-4442)
NATASCHA L HUGHES
528 E Market St (19947-2255)
PHONE..................302 856-4700
Natascha Hughes, Pr
EMP: 6 EST: 2018
SALES (est): 32.92K Privately Held
SIC: 8322 Individual and family services

(G-4443)
NATIONWIDE INSURANCE
Also Called: Nationwide
22836 Dupont Blvd (19947-8804)
PHONE..................302 515-1851
EMP: 5 EST: 2019
SALES (est): 61.44K Privately Held
Web: www.nationwide.com
SIC: 6411 Insurance agents, nec

(G-4444)
NEW YORK BLOOD CTR INC D/B/A B
Also Called: NEW YORK BLOOD CENTER, INC. D/B/A BLOOD BANK OF DELMARVA
N Bedford St Rte 113 (19947)
PHONE..................302 737-8400
Linda Walls, Brnch Mgr
EMP: 10
SALES (corp-wide): 29.61MM Privately Held
Web: www.delmarvablood.org
SIC: 8099 Blood bank
PA: New York Blood Center, Inc.
   100 Hygeia Dr
   Newark DE 19713
   302 737-8405

(G-4445)
NICKLE ELEC COMPANIES INC
540 S Bedford St (19947-1852)
PHONE..................302 856-1006
Steve Dignan, Brnch Mgr
EMP: 38
SALES (corp-wide): 34.24MM Privately Held
Web: www.nickleelectrical.com
SIC: 1731 General electrical contractor
PA: Nickle Electrical Companies, Inc.
   125 Ruthar Dr
   Newark DE 19711
   302 453-4000

(G-4446)
NICOLE LOWE
604 Wagamon Ave Extended (19947-3801)
PHONE..................302 858-4337
Nicole Lowe, Mgr
EMP: 7 EST: 2017
SALES (est): 72.5K Privately Held
SIC: 8049 Offices of health practitioner

(G-4447)
NO NONSENSE OFFICE MCHS LLC
22416 Lewes Georgetown Hwy (19947-5534)
P.O. Box 931 (19947-0931)
PHONE..................302 856-7381
EMP: 5 EST: 2008
SALES (est): 544.1K Privately Held
Web: www.nononsenseoffice.com
SIC: 5044 Office equipment

(G-4448)
NOVA POLYMERS
25 Dewberry Dr (19947-3827)
PHONE..................302 858-4677
EMP: 6 EST: 2016
SALES (est): 121.49K Privately Held
SIC: 2821 Plastics materials and resins

(G-4449)
NOVACARE
2 Lee Ave (19947-2149)
PHONE..................302 500-6363
EMP: 12 EST: 2019
SALES (est): 23.86K Privately Held
Web: www.novacare.com
SIC: 8049 Physical therapist

(G-4450)
OCEAN SUDS LAUNDROMAT
22899 E Trap Pond Rd (19947-4730)
PHONE..................302 856-3002
Kathy Rash, Prin
EMP: 7 EST: 2010
SALES (est): 191.94K Privately Held
SIC: 7215 Laundry, coin-operated

(G-4451)
OLSEN ENTERPRISES INC
26250 Shortly Rd (19947-5839)
PHONE..................443 928-0089
EMP: 9 EST: 2015
SALES (est): 263.4K Privately Held
SIC: 7389 Business services, nec

(G-4452)
OMTRON USA LLC
Also Called: Townsends
22855 Dupont Blvd (19947-8801)
PHONE..................302 855-7131
▼ EMP: 1200
SIC: 2015 Chicken, processed, nsk

(G-4453)
PACKD LLC
Also Called: Homewell Care Services
142 E Market St (19947-1411)
PHONE..................302 467-3443
Cydnei Childers, *
Karlyssa Childers, *
EMP: 45 EST: 2020
SALES (est): 3.5MM Privately Held
Web: www.homewellseniorcare.com
SIC: 8082 Home health care services

(G-4454)
PAINTERSRUS
830 E Market St (19947-2224)
PHONE..................302 855-1317
Juan A Mota, Prin
EMP: 5 EST: 2016
SALES (est): 63.43K Privately Held
SIC: 1721 Painting and paper hanging

(G-4455)
PATRICK AIRCRAFT GROUP LLC
21583 Baltimore Ave (19947-6313)
PHONE..................302 854-9300
EMP: 12 EST: 1999
SALES (est): 309 Privately Held
SIC: 3728 Refueling equipment for use in flight, airplane

(G-4456)
PATS AIRCRAFT LLC (HQ)
Also Called: Aloft Aeroarchitects
21652 Nanticoke Ave (19947-6308)
PHONE..................855 236-1638
Robert Sundin, Pr
Sandra Taras, *
EMP: 63 EST: 2003
SQ FT: 90,000
SALES (est): 124.07MM Privately Held
Web: www.aloftaeroarchitects.com
SIC: 4581 3728 3721 Aircraft upholstery repair; Fuselage assembly, aircraft; Aircraft
PA: Moelis Capital Partners Llc
   399 Park Ave Fl 5
   New York NY 10022

(G-4457)
PAYNE ENTERPRISES LLC
201 Old Laurel Rd (19947-1817)
PHONE..................302 856-2899
EMP: 5 EST: 2018
SALES (est): 203.57K Privately Held
SIC: 1521 Single-family housing construction

(G-4458)
PENINSULA FINANCIAL GROUP INC
13 Bridgeville Rd (19947-2105)
PHONE..................302 856-0970
Ben Bateman, Prin
EMP: 5 EST: 2017
SALES (est): 220.27K Privately Held
Web: www.peninsulafinancialgroup.com
SIC: 6282 Investment advice

(G-4459)
PENINSULA PAVE & SEAL LLC
Also Called: Peninsula Paving
20288 Asphalt Aly (19947-5392)
PHONE..................302 226-7283
David Fletcher Kenton, Prin
EMP: 12 EST: 2014
SALES (est): 1.5MM Privately Held
Web: www.peninsulapavingco.com
SIC: 1611 Highway and street paving contractor

(G-4460)
PEP-UP INC (PA)
Also Called: Pep-Up
24987 Dupont Blvd (19947-2623)
P.O. Box 556 (19947-0556)
PHONE..................302 856-2555
William C Pepper, Pr
Martin Pepper, VP
Bryan Pepper, Sec
EMP: 12 EST: 1977
SQ FT: 3,000
SALES (est): 23.77MM
SALES (corp-wide): 23.77MM Privately Held
Web: www.pepupinc.com
SIC: 5984 5172 Liquefied petroleum gas, delivered to customers' premises; Service station supplies, petroleum

(G-4461)
PERDUE FARMS INCORPORATED
20621 Savannah Rd (19947-2252)
PHONE..................302 855-5635
Jim Perdue, Ch
David Jones, Prin
EMP: 2 EST: 1920
SALES (est): 2.38MM Privately Held
Web: www.perdue.com
SIC: 2015 Poultry slaughtering and processing

GEOGRAPHIC SECTION

Georgetown - Sussex County (G-4491)

(G-4462)
PERFORMNCE INJCTION EQUIPMENTC
24994 Betts Ln (19947-2662)
PHONE.................302 858-5145
Christopher Hitchens, *Prin*
EMP: 2 **EST:** 2009
SALES (est): 262.57K **Privately Held**
Web: www.performanceinjectionequipment.com
SIC: 3714 Motor vehicle parts and accessories

(G-4463)
PERSANTE
2 Lee Ave (19947-2149)
PHONE.................302 253-8740
EMP: 11 **EST:** 2017
SALES (est): 46.62K **Privately Held**
Web: www.persante.com
SIC: 8099 Health and allied services, nec

(G-4464)
PESTEX PEST CONTROL INC
26066 Bethesda Rd (19947-2530)
PHONE.................302 745-8366
EMP: 5 **EST:** 2016
SALES (est): 73.04K **Privately Held**
SIC: 7342 Pest control in structures

(G-4465)
PET BOW TIQUE LLC
18355 County Seat Hwy (19947-4832)
PHONE.................302 856-7297
EMP: 5 **EST:** 2014
SALES (est): 333.97K **Privately Held**
SIC: 0752 Grooming services, pet and animal specialties

(G-4466)
PINEAPPLE STITCHERY
26005 Governor Stockley Rd (19947-2568)
PHONE.................302 500-8050
Stacy L Henningan, *Owner*
EMP: 4 **EST:** 2017
SALES (est): 55.38K **Privately Held**
SIC: 2395 Embroidery and art needlework

(G-4467)
PLANT RETRIEVERS WHL NURS
13418 Seashore Hwy (19947-4395)
PHONE.................302 337-9833
John Briggs, *Pt*
EMP: 8 **EST:** 2005
SALES (est): 498.16K **Privately Held**
Web: www.plantretrieversnursery.com
SIC: 0782 Landscape contractors

(G-4468)
PNC BANK NATIONAL ASSOCIATION
Also Called: PNC
Rt 113 Alfred St (19947)
PHONE.................302 855-0400
EMP: 9
SALES (corp-wide): 23.54B **Publicly Held**
Web: www.pnc.com
SIC: 6021 National trust companies with deposits, commercial
HQ: Pnc Bank, National Association
300 5th Ave
Pittsburgh PA 15222
877 762-2000

(G-4469)
POWELL CONSTRUCTION L L C
100 Murrays Ln (19947-2232)
PHONE.................302 745-1146
Bruce Powell, *Prin*
EMP: 5 **EST:** 2008

SALES (est): 341.61K **Privately Held**
SIC: 1521 Single-family housing construction

(G-4470)
PRECIOUS MOMENTS DAY CARE
18943 Shingle Point Rd (19947-5233)
PHONE.................302 856-2346
Lester Maloney, *Prin*
EMP: 5 **EST:** 2000
SALES (est): 134.8K **Privately Held**
SIC: 8351 Preschool center

(G-4471)
PREMIER STAFFING SOLUTIONS INC (PA)
123 W Market St (19947-1415)
PHONE.................302 344-5996
Christopher Washington, *CEO*
Cameron Scotton, *Pr*
EMP: 22 **EST:** 2015
SALES (est): 4.06MM
SALES (corp-wide): 4.06MM **Privately Held**
Web: www.premierstaffingsolutions.net
SIC: 7361 Labor contractors (employment agency)

(G-4472)
PRESSLEY RIDGE FOUNDATION
Also Called: Treatment Fster Care - Grgtown
20461 Dupont Blvd Ste 2 (19947-3174)
PHONE.................302 854-9782
Cha-tanya Lankford, *Dir*
EMP: 6
Web: www.pressleyridge.org
SIC: 8699 8299 Charitable organization; Educational service, nondegree granting: continuing educ.
PA: Pressley Ridge Foundation
5500 Corporate Dr Ste 400
Pittsburgh PA 15237

(G-4473)
PRIMEROS PASOS INC
Also Called: First Steps Primeros Pasos
20648 Savannah Rd (19947-2261)
PHONE.................302 856-7406
Ann Camasso, *Pr*
EMP: 5 **EST:** 1996
SALES (est): 481.81K **Privately Held**
Web: www.primerospasosde.org
SIC: 8351 Preschool center

(G-4474)
PROFESSNAL ARFICATION SVCS INC
4 Hollyberry Dr (19947-9427)
PHONE.................302 752-7003
Benito A Peta, *Pr*
Benito Peta, *Pr*
EMP: 7 **EST:** 2004
SALES (est): 283.11K **Privately Held**
SIC: 0782 Lawn services

(G-4475)
PUBLIC HEALTH NURSING
544 S Bedford St (19947-1852)
PHONE.................302 856-5136
John Kennedy, *Prin*
EMP: 14 **EST:** 2008
SALES (est): 209.49K **Privately Held**
SIC: 8051 Skilled nursing care facilities

(G-4476)
QUESTAR CAPITAL CORPORATION
13 Bridgeville Rd (19947-2105)
PHONE.................302 856-9778
Michael Johnson, *Pr*
Terry Dorey, *Prin*
EMP: 7 **EST:** 2010

SALES (est): 467.13K **Privately Held**
SIC: 6799 Investors, nec

(G-4477)
R & R CONTRACTORS LLC
25115 Mary Rd (19947-2670)
PHONE.................302 344-6580
Madelin Rodas, *Prin*
EMP: 5 **EST:** 2016
SALES (est): 74.47K **Privately Held**
SIC: 1721 Painting and paper hanging

(G-4478)
R & R POWER WASHING
3 N Front St (19947-1413)
PHONE.................302 259-4012
Devon Richardson, *Prin*
EMP: 5 **EST:** 2017
SALES (est): 51.58K **Privately Held**
SIC: 7349 Building cleaning service

(G-4479)
R AND H FILTER CO INC
21646 Baltimore Ave (19947-6311)
PHONE.................302 856-2129
David F Davidson, *Pr*
Renee Davidson, *VP*
Mamie E Reese, *Stockholder*
EMP: 3 **EST:** 1955
SQ FT: 4,100
SALES (est): 496.94K **Privately Held**
Web: www.glassfilterde.com
SIC: 3229 Scientific glassware

(G-4480)
R R COMMERCIAL REALTY
20461 Dupont Blvd (19947-3174)
PHONE.................302 856-4000
EMP: 6 **EST:** 2019
SALES (est): 86.87K **Privately Held**
Web: www.randrcommercialrealty.com
SIC: 6531 Real estate agent, commercial

(G-4481)
RANDYS TREE SERVICE
20185 Dupont Blvd (19947-3138)
PHONE.................302 856-7244
EMP: 8 **EST:** 2010
SALES (est): 681.25K **Privately Held**
SIC: 0783 Planting, pruning, and trimming services

(G-4482)
REDI CALL CORP
Also Called: Redi-Call Communications
543 S Bedford St (19947-1851)
P.O. Box 571 (19947-0571)
PHONE.................302 856-9000
TOLL FREE: 800
Randy K Murray, *Pr*
Aubrey P Murray, *VP*
Sharyn A Murray, *Sec*
EMP: 10 **EST:** 1973
SQ FT: 1,500
SALES (est): 486.69K **Privately Held**
Web: www.redi-call.com
SIC: 5731 4812 Radio, television, and electronic stores; Cellular telephone services

(G-4483)
RETIRED SENIOR VOLUNTEER PROG
546 S Bedford St (19947-1852)
PHONE.................302 856-5815
Mary Hook, *Mgr*
EMP: 8 **EST:** 2013
SALES (est): 69.65K **Privately Held**
SIC: 8322 Geriatric social service

(G-4484)
REYES PAINTING LLC
25203 Zoar Rd (19947-6522)
PHONE.................302 470-1961
EMP: 5 **EST:** 2016
SALES (est): 243.73K **Privately Held**
SIC: 1721 Painting and paper hanging

(G-4485)
RIAR JEHAN MD
25 Bridgeville Rd (19947-2105)
PHONE.................302 855-1349
Riar Jehan, *Pr*
EMP: 9 **EST:** 2017
SALES (est): 65.5K **Privately Held**
SIC: 8011 General and family practice, physician/surgeon

(G-4486)
RICHARD ALLEN COALITION
16950 Deer Forest Rd (19947-3404)
P.O. Box 624 (19947-0624)
PHONE.................302 258-7182
Jane Hovington, *Prin*
EMP: 5 **EST:** 2016
SALES (est): 81.25K **Privately Held**
Web: www.richardallenschoolgeorgetown.com
SIC: 8399 Advocacy group

(G-4487)
RICHELLE L CLARK
401 N Bedford St (19947-2197)
PHONE.................302 448-8094
Richelle L Clark, *Prin*
EMP: 7 **EST:** 2019
SALES (est): 97.03K **Privately Held**
SIC: 8011 Offices and clinics of medical doctors

(G-4488)
RIGID BUILDERS LLC
24491 Blackberry Dr (19947-2780)
PHONE.................732 425-3443
EMP: 12 **EST:** 2017
SALES (est): 482.36K **Privately Held**
SIC: 1711 Solar energy contractor

(G-4489)
ROGER C PERRY
22957 Deep Branch Rd (19947-6518)
PHONE.................302 604-7912
Roger C Perry, *Prin*
EMP: 8 **EST:** 2009
SALES (est): 55.45K **Privately Held**
SIC: 7699 Repair services, nec

(G-4490)
ROGERS GRAPHICS INC (PA)
Also Called: Copy Print
32 Bridgeville Rd (19947-2106)
PHONE.................302 856-0028
Charles J Rogers, *Pr*
Frank E Rogers, *VP*
EMP: 18 **EST:** 1983
SQ FT: 12,000
SALES (est): 2.11MM
SALES (corp-wide): 2.11MM **Privately Held**
Web: www.rogersgraphics.com
SIC: 2752 Offset printing

(G-4491)
RONALD D JR ATTORNEY AT LAW
Also Called: Murrayphillipspa
215 E Market St (19947-1233)
PHONE.................302 856-9860
Ronald D Phillips Junior, *Prin*
EMP: 6 **EST:** 2010
SALES (est): 439.46K **Privately Held**

Georgetown - Sussex County (G-4492)

Web: www.murrayphillipslaw.com
SIC: 8111 Criminal law

(G-4492)
ROSA HEALTH CENTER INC
10 N Froht St (19947-1414)
PHONE.................................302 858-4381
Rama Dasika Peri, Pr
EMP: 8 EST: 2015
SALES (est): 264.2K Privately Held
Web: www.rosahealthcenter.org
SIC: 8099 Medical services organization

(G-4493)
ROTTEN APPLES CIDER CO LLC
23656 Fox Croft Ln (19947-4567)
PHONE.................................609 602-7811
Christina Brady, Prin
EMP: 4 EST: 2021
SALES (est): 78.16K Privately Held
SIC: 2084 Wines, brandy, and brandy spirits

(G-4494)
ROUTE 9 AUTO CENTER
23422 Park Ave (19947-6370)
PHONE.................................302 856-3941
Robert Lawson, Pr
Diana Lawson, VP
EMP: 6 EST: 1999
SALES (est): 486.26K Privately Held
Web: www.rt9autocenter.com
SIC: 7538 General automotive repair shops

(G-4495)
ROWE INDUSTRIES INC
21649 Cedar Creek Ave (19947-6396)
P.O. Box 189 (21404-0189)
PHONE.................................443 458-5569
Gerald L Rowe, Prin
EMP: 6 EST: 2014
SALES (est): 178.97K Privately Held
Web: www.roweindustries.com
SIC: 3999 Manufacturing industries, nec

(G-4496)
S WILSON AUTO REPAIR
15388 Wilson Hill Rd (19947-3503)
PHONE.................................302 856-3839
Richard E Wilson, Prin
EMP: 5 EST: 2009
SALES (est): 163.29K Privately Held
SIC: 7538 General automotive repair shops

(G-4497)
SAFELITE FULFILLMENT INC
Also Called: Safelite Autoglass
314 S Dupont Hwy (19947-8804)
PHONE.................................302 856-7175
Raymond Plymire, Brnch Mgr
EMP: 7
SALES (corp-wide): 3.16B Privately Held
Web: www.safelite.com
SIC: 7536 Automotive glass replacement shops
HQ: Safelite Fulfillment, Inc.
7400 Safelite Way
Columbus OH 43235
614 210-9000

(G-4498)
SANDY HILL GREENHOUSES INC
18303 Sand Hill Rd (19947-3726)
PHONE.................................302 856-2412
Mark Folke, Pr
Maria Folke, VP
EMP: 10 EST: 1974
SALES (est): 531.8K Privately Held
Web: sandy-hill-greenhouses.business.site
SIC: 0181 Flowers: grown under cover (e.g., greenhouse production)

(G-4499)
SCCHS
110 N Railroad Ave (19947-1244)
PHONE.................................302 856-7524
EMP: 10 EST: 2010
SALES (est): 91.16K Privately Held
Web: www.scchsinc.org
SIC: 8322 Social service center

(G-4500)
SCHAB & BARNETT PA
Also Called: Schab & Barnett
9 Chestnut St (19947-1901)
PHONE.................................302 856-9024
Norman Barnett, Pt
William Schab, Pt
EMP: 7 EST: 1981
SALES (est): 245.73K Privately Held
Web: www.schabbarnett.com
SIC: 8111 General practice attorney, lawyer

(G-4501)
SCHELL BROTHERS
19640 Buck Run (19947-5336)
PHONE.................................302 242-8334
EMP: 6 EST: 2019
SALES (est): 228.98K Privately Held
Web: www.schellbrothers.com
SIC: 1521 New construction, single-family houses

(G-4502)
SCHFH RESTORE
206 Academy St (19947-1947)
PHONE.................................302 855-1156
EMP: 8 EST: 2015
SALES (est): 84.82K Privately Held
Web: www.sussexcountyhabitat.org
SIC: 8399 Community development groups

(G-4503)
SCHUSTER JACHETTI LLP (PA)
20632 Dupont Blvd (19947-3177)
PHONE.................................302 856-2400
Joseph Jachetti, Pt
EMP: 6 EST: 2017
SALES (est): 249.25K
SALES (corp-wide): 249.25K Privately Held
Web: www.mydelawarelawyer.com
SIC: 8111 General practice law office

(G-4504)
SENTINEL INSURANCE
20254 Dupont Blvd (19947-3105)
PHONE.................................302 858-4962
David Drandorff, Owner
EMP: 7 EST: 2016
SALES (est): 61.44K Privately Held
Web: www.waggingtailspetresort.com
SIC: 6411 Insurance agents, brokers, and service

(G-4505)
SERGOVIC & ELLIS PA
9 N Front St (19947-1413)
PHONE.................................302 855-9500
John A Sergovic Junior, Pr
Steven P Ellis, Pt
EMP: 14 EST: 1988
SALES (est): 1.01MM Privately Held
Web: www.sussexattorney.com
SIC: 8111 General practice law office

(G-4506)
SERGOVIC CRMEAN WDMAN MCCRTNEY
25 Chestnut St (19947-1931)
PHONE.................................302 855-1260
EMP: 6 EST: 2020
SALES (est): 218.61K Privately Held
Web: www.sussexattorney.com
SIC: 8111 General practice law office

(G-4507)
SERVICE GENERAL CORPORATION
Also Called: Crestwood Garden Apts
120 N Race St (19947-1483)
PHONE.................................302 218-4279
Bamdad Bahar, Pr
EMP: 13 EST: 2001
SQ FT: 50,000
SALES (est): 1.09MM Privately Held
Web: www.servicegeneral.net
SIC: 6513 8741 7361 3582 Apartment building operators; Management services; Employment agencies; Washing machines, laundry: commercial, incl. coin-operated

(G-4508)
SERVICE GENERAL CORPORATION
13 E Laurel St (19947-1435)
PHONE.................................302 856-3500
EMP: 5 EST: 2019
SALES (est): 233.95K Privately Held
Web: www.servicegeneral.net
SIC: 7363 Help supply services

(G-4509)
SERVICEXPRESS CORPORATION (PA)
120 N Ray St (19947)
PHONE.................................302 856-3500
EMP: 24 EST: 2007
SALES (est): 25MM Privately Held
Web: www.serviceexpressworks.net
SIC: 7361 Labor contractors (employment agency)

(G-4510)
SHADY OAK MOBILE HOME CMNTY
21159 Airport Rd (19947-5549)
PHONE.................................302 245-4324
Richard Clendaniel, Prin
EMP: 5 EST: 2017
SALES (est): 58.62K Privately Held
Web: shadyoakde.business.site
SIC: 8399 Community development groups

(G-4511)
SHORE ANSWER LLC
Also Called: Telephone Answering Service
543 S Bedford St (19947-1851)
PHONE.................................302 253-8381
EMP: 8 EST: 2003
SALES (est): 266.88K Privately Held
Web: www.shoreanswer.com
SIC: 7389 Telephone answering service

(G-4512)
SHURE LINE ELECTRICAL INC
24207 Dupont Blvd (19947-2630)
P.O. Box 249 (19955-0249)
PHONE.................................302 856-3110
Ed Hitch, Prin
EMP: 8 EST: 2011
SALES (est): 1.41MM Privately Held
Web: www.shure-line.com
SIC: 1731 General electrical contractor

(G-4513)
SMART LAUNDROMAT
110 N Race St Ste 1010 (19947-1474)
PHONE.................................302 854-0300
EMP: 5 EST: 2016
SALES (est): 123.73K Privately Held

SIC: 7215 Coin-operated laundries and cleaning

(G-4514)
SMITH FNBERG MCCRTNEY BERL LLP (PA)
406 S Bedford St (19947-1853)
P.O. Box 588 (19947-0588)
PHONE.................................302 856-7082
Richard E Berl, Mng Pt
George Smith, Pt
EMP: 18 EST: 1998
SALES (est): 2.45MM Privately Held
Web: www.sussexattorney.com
SIC: 8111 General practice law office

(G-4515)
SOFT DIG LLC
14619 Cokesbury Rd. (19947-4364)
PHONE.................................302 629-6658
EMP: 6 EST: 2012
SALES (est): 183.7K Privately Held
SIC: 8611 Public utility association

(G-4516)
SOFTBALL WORLD LLC
Also Called: Sports At The Beach
22518 Lewes Georgetown Hwy (19947-5533)
PHONE.................................302 856-7922
Ronald Barrows, Owner
EMP: 6 EST: 2003
SALES (est): 1.09MM Privately Held
Web: www.sportsatthebeach.com
SIC: 7997 Baseball club, except professional and semi-professional

(G-4517)
SOUTH WELLINGTON LLC
30 E Pine St (19947-1904)
PHONE.................................954 736-7418
Sebastian Btesh, Managing Member
EMP: 6 EST: 2017
SALES (est): 63.12K Privately Held
SIC: 7389 Personal service agents, brokers, and bureaus

(G-4518)
SOUTHERN DELAWARE DENTAL SPEC
20785 Professional Park Blvd (19947)
PHONE.................................302 855-9499
EMP: 9 EST: 2017
SALES (est): 102.23K Privately Held
Web: www.dentaldelaware.com
SIC: 8021 Offices and clinics of dentists

(G-4519)
SOUTHERN DELAWARE HORSE
22532 Pine Haven Dr (19947-6367)
PHONE.................................302 856-1598
Jackie Heck, Prin
EMP: 6 EST: 2011
SALES (est): 116.13K Privately Held
Web: www.visitsoutherndelaware.com
SIC: 5159 Horses

(G-4520)
SOUTHLAND INSULATORS DEL LLC
Also Called: Delmarva Insulation
22976 Sussex Ave (19947-6310)
PHONE.................................302 854-0344
Gerald Palmer, *
EMP: 89 EST: 2002
SALES (est): 4.84MM Privately Held
Web: www.delmarvainsulation.com
SIC: 1742 Insulation, buildings

GEOGRAPHIC SECTION
Georgetown - Sussex County (G-4549)

(G-4521)
SPCA SUSSEX CHAPTER
22918 Dupont Blvd (19947-8803)
PHONE..................................302 856-6361
Gerald Linkerhof, *Mgr*
EMP: 10 **EST:** 2011
SALES (est): 205.15K **Privately Held**
Web: www.animalshelter.net
SIC: 8699 Animal humane society

(G-4522)
SPLASH LNDRMAT LLC - GORGETOWN
201 E Laurel St (19947-1202)
PHONE..................................302 249-8231
Enrique Nunez, *Prin*
EMP: 6 **EST:** 2018
SALES (est): 259.1K **Privately Held**
Web: www.laundrydelaware.com
SIC: 7215 Laundry, coin-operated

(G-4523)
STAG RUN FARM LLC
Also Called: Chrissy Bees Honey
23656 Fox Croft Ln (19947-4567)
PHONE..................................302 270-8435
Craig Brady, *Managing Member*
EMP: 5 **EST:** 2015
SALES (est): 69.4K **Privately Held**
SIC: 0175 Deciduous tree fruits

(G-4524)
STARS ON 9 DANCE CENTER LLC
205 N Race St (19947-1408)
PHONE..................................302 855-9595
Susan Fortier, *Prin*
EMP: 7 **EST:** 2015
SALES (est): 23.23K **Privately Held**
Web: www.starson9.com
SIC: 7911 Dance studio and school

(G-4525)
STAYTON AND DICKENS LLP
117 S Bedford St (19947-1843)
PHONE..................................302 856-4141
EMP: 7 **EST:** 2015
SALES (est): 236.27K **Privately Held**
Web: www.staytondickens.com
SIC: 8721 Certified public accountant

(G-4526)
STOCKLEY MATERIALS LLC
25154 Dupont Blvd (19947-2610)
PHONE..................................302 856-7601
Joe Adams, *Owner*
EMP: 10 **EST:** 2012
SALES (est): 852.1K **Privately Held**
Web: www.stockleymaterials.com
SIC: 2499 3531 1446 Mulch or sawdust products, wood; Pavers; Industrial sand

(G-4527)
STONEGATE GRANITE
25029 Dupont Blvd (19947-2622)
PHONE..................................302 500-8081
Naim Celik, *Owner*
EMP: 8 **EST:** 2015
SALES (est): 440.96K **Privately Held**
Web: www.stonegategranite.com
SIC: 1741 Masonry and other stonework

(G-4528)
STUMPF VICKERS AND SANDY
8 W Market St (19947-1437)
PHONE..................................302 856-3561
Vincent Vickers, *Pt*
John Sandy, *Pt*
Tom Gay, *Pt*
Brian Dolan, *Pt*
Thomas J Stumpf, *Pt*
EMP: 9 **EST:** 1998
SALES (est): 157.93K **Privately Held**
Web: www.svslaw.com
SIC: 8111 General practice law office

(G-4529)
SUFFEX CONSERVATION
23818 Shortly Rd (19947-4755)
PHONE..................................302 856-2105
Debbie Absher, *Mgr*
EMP: 8 **EST:** 1999
SALES (est): 486.6K **Privately Held**
Web: www.sussexconservation.org
SIC: 8748 Environmental consultant

(G-4530)
SUN BEHAVIORAL DELAWARE LLC
21655 Biden Ave (19947-4573)
PHONE..................................732 747-1800
Ann Wayne, *CEO*
EMP: 22 **EST:** 2017
SALES (est): 18.75MM
SALES (corp-wide): 24.12MM **Privately Held**
Web: www.sunbehavioral.com
SIC: 8099 Health and allied services, nec
HQ: Sun Behavioral Health, Inc.
  12 Broad St Ste 403
  Red Bank NJ 07701
  732 747-1800

(G-4531)
SURE LINE ELECTRICAL INC
281 W Commerce St (19947)
PHONE..................................302 856-3110
Ed Hitch, *Pr*
EMP: 6 **EST:** 2004
SALES (est): 84.15K **Privately Held**
SIC: 1731 General electrical contractor

(G-4532)
SUSSEX CMNTY CRSIS HSING SVCS
204 E North St (19947-1243)
PHONE..................................302 856-2246
Marie Morole, *CEO*
EMP: 15 **EST:** 1981
SALES (est): 216K **Privately Held**
Web: www.scchsinc.org
SIC: 8322 Social service center

(G-4533)
SUSSEX CNTY HBTAT FOR HMNITY I
206 Academy St (19947-1947)
P.O. Box 759 (19947-0759)
PHONE..................................302 855-1153
Kevin Gilmore, *Ex Dir*
EMP: 8 **EST:** 2006
SALES (est): 5MM **Privately Held**
Web: www.sussexcountyhabitat.org
SIC: 1521 Single-family housing construction

(G-4534)
SUSSEX CNTY SNIOR SVCS ADULT D
Also Called: Sand Hill Adult Program
20520 Sand Hill Rd (19947-5504)
PHONE..................................302 854-2882
A S Littleton, *Ex Dir*
Arlene S Littleton, *Ex Dir*
EMP: 5 **EST:** 2010
SALES (est): 149.39K **Privately Held**
SIC: 8322 Senior citizens' center or association

(G-4535)
SUSSEX CONSERVATION DISTRICT
23818 Shortly Rd (19947-4755)
PHONE..................................302 856-2105
Debra Absher, *Pr*
EMP: 26 **EST:** 1944
SALES (est): 4.6MM **Privately Held**
Web: www.sussexconservation.org
SIC: 8999 Natural resource preservation service

(G-4536)
SUSSEX COUNTY VOLUNTEER
546 S Bedford St (19947-1852)
PHONE..................................302 515-3020
David M Hudson, *Pr*
Roberta Bass, *CEO*
Ann Gorrin, *Admn*
EMP: 7 **EST:** 2015
SALES (est): 157.93K **Privately Held**
Web: www.delawareonline.com
SIC: 8611 Business associations

(G-4537)
SUSSEX EYE CENTER PA (PA)
502 W Market St (19947-2322)
P.O. Box 400 (19947-0400)
PHONE..................................302 856-2020
Carl Maschauer, *Owner*
EMP: 6 **EST:** 1997
SALES (est): 2.32MM
SALES (corp-wide): 2.32MM **Privately Held**
Web: www.sussexeyecenter.com
SIC: 8042 Specialized optometrists

(G-4538)
SUSSEX FAMILY COUNSELING LLC
26114 Kits Burrow Ct (19947-5390)
PHONE..................................302 864-7970
Matthew W Turley, *Owner*
EMP: 5 **EST:** 2018
SALES (est): 42.46K **Privately Held**
SIC: 8322 Family counseling services

(G-4539)
SUSSEX HOME IMPRV CONTR LLC
14 Evergreen Dr (19947-9483)
PHONE..................................302 855-9679
Lancelot Johnson, *Prin*
EMP: 5 **EST:** 2015
SALES (est): 100.15K **Privately Held**
SIC: 1521 Single-family housing construction

(G-4540)
SUSSEX PAIN RELIEF CENTER LLC
18229 Dupont Blvd (19947-3127)
PHONE..................................302 519-0100
Antony Manonmani, *Managing Member*
EMP: 24 **EST:** 2010
SALES (est): 793.25K **Privately Held**
Web: www.sussexpainrelief.com
SIC: 8041 8011 Offices and clinics of chiropractors; Physicians' office, including specialists

(G-4541)
SUSSEX PINES COUNTRY CLUB
22426 Sussex Pines Rd (19947-6445)
PHONE..................................302 856-6283
Jim King, *Pr*
Tom Love, *
Dennis Fitzgerald, *
EMP: 15 **EST:** 1965
SALES (est): 871.19K **Privately Held**
Web: www.sussexpines.com
SIC: 7997 Country club, membership

(G-4542)
SUSSEX PREGNANCY CARE CENTER
5 Burger King Dr (19947-2176)
PHONE..................................302 856-4344
Rita Denney, *Dir*
EMP: 5 **EST:** 1985
SALES (est): 364.51K **Privately Held**
Web: www.sussexpregnancy.com
SIC: 8322 8093 Crisis center; Family planning clinic

(G-4543)
SUSSEX REGEN SPECIALISTS
18229 Dupont Blvd (19947-3127)
PHONE..................................302 727-6669
EMP: 8 **EST:** 2016
SALES (est): 80.39K **Privately Held**
SIC: 8011 Neurologist

(G-4544)
T & M EXHAUST HOOD CLEANING
12 Jacqueline Dr (19947-2184)
PHONE..................................302 362-8816
Tayron Orozco, *Prin*
EMP: 5 **EST:** 2017
SALES (est): 60.77K **Privately Held**
SIC: 7699 Cleaning services

(G-4545)
TAYLOR & SONS INC
26511 E Trap Pond Rd (19947-5721)
PHONE..................................302 856-6962
EMP: 6 **EST:** 1977
SALES (est): 466.45K **Privately Held**
Web: www.taylorpaint.com
SIC: 1721 Painting and paper hanging

(G-4546)
TC TRANS INC
24557 Dupont Blvd (19947)
PHONE..................................302 339-7952
Ismail Sen, *Pr*
EMP: 8 **EST:** 2011
SQ FT: 1,000
SALES (est): 800K **Privately Held**
Web: www.tctransport.com
SIC: 4731 Freight forwarding

(G-4547)
TEFF INC
Also Called: SERVPRO
109 E Laurel St (19947-1429)
P.O. Box 70 (19947-0070)
PHONE..................................302 856-9768
Raymond T Hopkins, *Pr*
Kathleen Hargrove, *Ofcr*
Joanne Hopkins, *VP*
EMP: 10 **EST:** 1979
SALES (est): 830.9K **Privately Held**
Web: www.servprosussexcounty.com
SIC: 7349 Building maintenance services, nec

(G-4548)
TELAMON CORP/EARLY CHLDHD PGRM
26351 Patriots Way (19947-2575)
PHONE..................................302 934-1642
Nancy Shaffer, *Prin*
EMP: 5 **EST:** 2005
SALES (est): 234.59K **Privately Held**
SIC: 8331 Job training services

(G-4549)
TELAMON CORPORATION
308 N Railroad Ave (19947-1252)
PHONE..................................302 934-0925
Miguelina Cruz, *Brnch Mgr*
EMP: 6
SALES (corp-wide): 85.01MM **Privately Held**
Web: www.telamon.org
SIC: 8331 Job training services
PA: Telamon Corporation
  5560 Munford Rd Ste 201
  Raleigh NC 27612
  919 851-7611

Georgetown - Sussex County (G-4550)

(G-4550)
TELAMON DELAWARE HEAD START
26351 Patriots Way (19947-2575)
PHONE.................................302 934-1642
EMP: 19 EST: 2019
SALES (est): 630.22K **Privately Held**
SIC: 8331 Job training services

(G-4551)
THERESA HAYES
16 N Bedford St (19947-1463)
PHONE.................................302 854-5406
Theresa Hayes, *Prin*
EMP: 6 EST: 2011
SALES (est): 88.09K **Privately Held**
Web: www.de-law.com
SIC: 8111 General practice attorney, lawyer

(G-4552)
THERMOPLASTIC PROCESSES INC
21649 Cedar Creek Ave (19947-6396)
PHONE.................................888 554-6400
Brooke Kinney, *CEO*
EMP: 12 EST: 1949
SALES (est): 347.72K **Privately Held**
SIC: 3082 Unsupported plastics profile shapes

(G-4553)
THOMAS F ALLEN
115 W Market St (19947-1415)
PHONE.................................302 604-3357
Thomas Allen, *Prin*
EMP: 15 EST: 2005
SALES (est): 67.07K **Privately Held**
SIC: 8059 Home for the mentally retarded, ex. skilled or intermediate

(G-4554)
THOROUGHBRED SOFTWARE INTL
22536 Lakeshore Dr (19947-2563)
PHONE.................................302 339-8383
Charles Gilman, *Prin*
EMP: 5 EST: 2010
SALES (est): 63.19K **Privately Held**
SIC: 7372 Prepackaged software

(G-4555)
TIER TWO CONTRACTING LLC
26250 Shortly Rd (19947-5839)
PHONE.................................443 928-0089
Patrick Olsen, *Prin*
EMP: 5 EST: 2018
SALES (est): 83.88K **Privately Held**
SIC: 1799 Special trade contractors, nec

(G-4556)
TKO PAINTING
1 Oak St (19947-5617)
PHONE.................................302 259-9450
Fabricio Sanchez, *Prin*
EMP: 5 EST: 2015
SALES (est): 72.44K **Privately Held**
SIC: 1721 Painting and paper hanging

(G-4557)
TOP NOTCH CLEANING SERVICE
16562 Seashore Hwy (19947-4206)
PHONE.................................302 854-6611
Delphine Rideau, *Prin*
EMP: 5 EST: 2015
SALES (est): 26.07K **Privately Held**
Web: www.top-notchclean.com
SIC: 7699 Cleaning services

(G-4558)
TPI PARTNERS INC (PA)
Also Called: Thermoplastic Processes
21649 Cedar Creek Ave (19947-6396)
PHONE.................................302 855-0139
D Brooke Kinney, *Prin*
EMP: 27 EST: 2003
SALES (est): 22.67MM
SALES (corp-wide): 22.67MM **Privately Held**
Web: www.thermoplasticprocesses.com
SIC: 3082 Tubes, unsupported plastics

(G-4559)
TREATMENT ACCESS CTR
21309 Berlin Rd Unit 7 (19947-3185)
PHONE.................................302 856-5487
EMP: 8 EST: 2016
SALES (est): 59.22K **Privately Held**
SIC: 8011 Offices and clinics of medical doctors

(G-4560)
TRIANGLE ELECTRICAL SVC CO
22180 Lewes Georgetown Hwy (19947-5537)
PHONE.................................302 856-7880
David George, *Mgr*
EMP: 5 EST: 2008
SALES (est): 118.19K **Privately Held**
SIC: 1731 General electrical contractor

(G-4561)
TRIGGER ACTION LLC
Also Called: Integrity Pest Solutions
16992 Redden Rd (19947-3332)
PHONE.................................302 858-8629
Keith Ruark, *Owner*
EMP: 6 EST: 2017
SALES (est): 34.22K **Privately Held**
Web: www.integrity-pestsolutions.com
SIC: 7342 Pest control in structures

(G-4562)
TROPACOOL
23738 Heavens Walk Way (19947-5269)
PHONE.................................302 245-4078
Chris Bennett, *Prin*
EMP: 5 EST: 2017
SALES (est): 108.14K **Privately Held**
SIC: 1522 Residential construction, nec

(G-4563)
TUNNELL & RAYSOR PA (PA)
30 E Pine St (19947-1904)
P.O. Box 151 (19947-0151)
PHONE.................................302 856-7313
Harold E Dukes Junior, *Pr*
Kelly Dunn Gelof, *VP*
Heidi Balliet, *VP*
EMP: 48 EST: 1880
SALES (est): 5.89MM
SALES (corp-wide): 5.89MM **Privately Held**
Web: www.tunnellraysor.com
SIC: 8111 General practice attorney, lawyer

(G-4564)
TURNKEY ELECTRIC LLC
24648 Zoar Rd (19947-6817)
PHONE.................................302 858-3726
Brandon Miller, *Prin*
EMP: 5 EST: 2018
SALES (est): 167.05K **Privately Held**
SIC: 1522 Residential construction, nec

(G-4565)
UNDERGROUND LOCATING SERVICES
24497 Dupont Blvd (19947-2628)
PHONE.................................302 856-9626
Alton Stack, *Prin*
EMP: 9 EST: 2004
SALES (est): 1.1MM **Privately Held**
SIC: 1623 Underground utilities contractor

(G-4566)
UPBOUND GROUP INC
Also Called: Rent-A-Center
12 Georgetown Plz (19947-2300)
PHONE.................................302 856-9200
Jennifer Aguirre, *Mgr*
EMP: 6
Web: www.rentacenter.com
SIC: 7359 Appliance rental
PA: Upbound Group, Inc.
5501 Headquarters Dr
Plano TX 75024

(G-4567)
VANGUARD CONSTRUCTION MGT
9 Hollyberry Dr (19947-9427)
PHONE.................................302 462-2161
EMP: 6 EST: 2014
SALES (est): 70.39K **Privately Held**
SIC: 8741 Construction management

(G-4568)
VERDE LOMA LLC
401 N Bedford St (19947-2197)
PHONE.................................302 858-4040
EMP: 5 EST: 2019
SALES (est): 486.59K **Privately Held**
Web: www.vlcounselingservices.com
SIC: 8093 Specialty outpatient clinics, nec

(G-4569)
VEST MANAGEMENT INC
18591 Sand Hill Rd (19947-3723)
PHONE.................................302 856-3100
EMP: 5 EST: 2008
SALES (est): 225.38K **Privately Held**
SIC: 8741 Management services

(G-4570)
VOICE RADIO LLC
20254 Dupont Blvd (19947-3105)
PHONE.................................302 858-5118
Kevin Andrade, *Dir*
EMP: 13 EST: 2015
SALES (est): 643.26K **Privately Held**
Web: www.max953.com
SIC: 4832 Radio broadcasting stations

(G-4571)
WAHOO REPAIR LLC
24094 Lawson Rd (19947-6634)
PHONE.................................302 430-4588
George Griffith, *Prin*
EMP: 5 EST: 2009
SALES (est): 67.88K **Privately Held**
SIC: 7699 Repair services, nec

(G-4572)
WALTER T WILSON
23422 Winding Pines Ln (19947-5569)
PHONE.................................302 542-6753
Walter T Wilson, *Prin*
EMP: 5 EST: 2011
SALES (est): 140.15K **Privately Held**
SIC: 6519 Real property lessors, nec

(G-4573)
WALTON FARM & TRUCK REPAIR
15209 S Old State Rd (19947-3304)
PHONE.................................302 245-3479
G K Walton, *Prin*
EMP: 5 EST: 2016
SALES (est): 57.34K **Privately Held**
SIC: 7699 Repair services, nec

(G-4574)
WILSON CONSTRUCTION CO INC
23054 Park Ave (19947-6364)
PHONE.................................302 856-3115
Richard Wilson, *Pr*
Joan Wilson, *Sec*
EMP: 5 EST: 1972
SALES (est): 687.62K **Privately Held**
SIC: 1521 New construction, single-family houses

(G-4575)
WILSON HALBROOK & BAYARD PA
Also Called: Bayard, Eugene H
107 W Market St (19947-1438)
P.O. Box 690 (19947-0690)
PHONE.................................302 856-0015
Eugene H Bayard, *Pr*
Clayton E Bunting, *VP*
Dennis L Schrader, *Sec*
Robert G Gibbs, *Sec*
Eric C Howard, *Dir*
EMP: 51 EST: 1930
SALES (est): 2.41MM **Privately Held**
Web: www.morrisjames.com
SIC: 8111 General practice law office

(G-4576)
WIRENUT LLC
240 S Bedford St (19947-1870)
PHONE.................................302 858-7027
Vince Leager, *Prin*
EMP: 6 EST: 2019
SALES (est): 332.72K **Privately Held**
SIC: 1522 Residential construction, nec

(G-4577)
WN BUILDERS INC
18456 Gravel Hill Rd (19947-5270)
P.O. Box 734 (19958-0734)
PHONE.................................302 253-8640
EMP: 8 EST: 2014
SALES (est): 236.81K **Privately Held**
Web: www.wnbuildersinc.com
SIC: 1521 New construction, single-family houses

(G-4578)
WOODLAND FERRY BEAGLE CLUB
26858 Johnson Rd (19947-6610)
PHONE.................................302 856-2186
Paul Eckrich, *Prin*
EMP: 10 EST: 2010
SALES (est): 125.45K **Privately Held**
SIC: 7997 Membership sports and recreation clubs

(G-4579)
WOODS GENERAL CONTRACTING INC
22403 Peterkins Rd (19947-2733)
P.O. Box 240 (19966-0240)
PHONE.................................302 856-4047
William B Wood, *Pr*
Karen Wood, *VP*
EMP: 5 EST: 1983
SQ FT: 3,200
SALES (est): 876.59K **Privately Held**
SIC: 1542 1521 Commercial and office building, new construction; New construction, single-family houses

(G-4580)
WORKMANS INC
20135 Hardscrabble Rd (19947-6124)
PHONE.................................302 934-9228
Mark Workman, *Pr*
Charles Workman, *VP*
EMP: 5 EST: 1978
SQ FT: 5,500

GEOGRAPHIC SECTION

Greenwood - Sussex County (G-4609)

SALES (est): 468.88K **Privately Held**
SIC: 0111 0115 0116 0119 Wheat; Corn; Soybeans; Barley farm

(G-4581)
WORLDWIDE CLINICAL TRIALS INC
22510 Lakeshore Dr (19947-2563)
PHONE.....................317 297-2208
EMP: 6 EST: 2019
SALES (est): 72.85K **Privately Held**
Web: www.worldwide.com
SIC: 8733 Medical research

(G-4582)
ZCORP PROPERTY CONSULTANTS LLC
14288 Brandy Ln (19947-4563)
PHONE.....................302 864-8581
Barry Zeigler, *Prin*
EMP: 5 EST: 2017
SALES (est): 234.9K **Privately Held**
SIC: 8748 Business consulting, nec

Greenville
New Castle County

(G-4583)
ASTORIA BUILDERS LLC
1107 Hillside Rd (19807-2215)
PHONE.....................302 892-9211
Ronald Stevens, *CEO*
Zai Stevens, *VP*
EMP: 8 EST: 2018
SALES (est): 442.92K **Privately Held**
Web: www.astoriabuildersllc.com
SIC: 1521 New construction, single-family houses

(G-4584)
GERARD JOSEPH CAPANO
Also Called: Split Racing
1105 Hillside Rd (19807-2215)
PHONE.....................302 658-3505
EMP: 6 EST: 2009
SALES (est): 107.69K **Privately Held**
SIC: 7948 Racing, including track operation

Greenwood
Sussex County

(G-4585)
A & B ELECTRIC
25 Adamsville Rd (19950-8400)
PHONE.....................302 349-4050
Alan Warren, *Pr*
Andrew Warren, *VP*
Brenda Warren, *Sec*
EMP: 9 EST: 2005
SALES (est): 891.39K **Privately Held**
Web: www.atkelectric.com
SIC: 1731 General electrical contractor

(G-4586)
A DISH NETWORK
2 Schulze Rd (19950-5357)
PHONE.....................302 495-5709
EMP: 5 EST: 2017
SALES (est): 81.71K **Privately Held**
Web: www.dish.com
SIC: 4841 Direct broadcast satellite services (DBS)

(G-4587)
A TO Z FIRST BUILDERS LLC
87 Gardenia Blvd (19950-2511)
PHONE.....................302 393-9761
EMP: 7 EST: 2013
SALES (est): 252.29K **Privately Held**
Web: www.atozfirstbuilders.com
SIC: 1521 New construction, single-family houses

(G-4588)
ABC DRYWALL
14432 Owens Rd (19950-5629)
PHONE.....................302 249-0389
Abidail Cifuentes, *Prin*
EMP: 7 EST: 2019
SALES (est): 474.2K **Privately Held**
SIC: 1742 Drywall

(G-4589)
ADANDY FARM
13450 Adandy Farm Ln (19950-5766)
P.O. Box 2016 (19950-0606)
PHONE.....................302 349-5116
Cathrine Vincent, *Owner*
EMP: 5 EST: 1975
SALES (est): 404.43K **Privately Held**
Web: www.adandyfarm.com
SIC: 0752 Training services, horses (except racing horses)

(G-4590)
AHMAD FAMILY FARM LLC
14699 B&R Rd (19950)
PHONE.....................302 349-5500
Mohammed Ahmad, *Pt*
EMP: 5 EST: 2015
SALES (est): 217.99K **Privately Held**
SIC: 0191 General farms, primarily crop

(G-4591)
ASAP CLEANING SERVICES
14198 Cart Branch Rd (19950-6016)
PHONE.....................302 519-6607
EMP: 6 EST: 2014
SALES (est): 50.28K **Privately Held**
SIC: 7699 Cleaning services

(G-4592)
ATLANTIC ALUMINUM PRODUCTS INC
12136 Sussex Hwy (19950-5414)
PHONE.....................302 349-9091
Daniel Schlabach, *Pr*
Harold Sylvester, *Prin*
EMP: 57 EST: 1996
SQ FT: 165,000
SALES (est): 13.37MM **Privately Held**
Web: www.atlanticaluminumproducts.com
SIC: 3089 3446 2431 Fences, gates, and accessories: plastics; Railings, banisters, guards, etc: made from metal pipe; Staircases, stairs and railings

(G-4593)
ATLANTIC BUSINESS CONTRACTING
9599 Nanticoke Business Park Dr (19950-5448)
PHONE.....................302 337-7490
EMP: 6 EST: 2014
SALES (est): 454.27K **Privately Held**
Web: www.coastalcountertops.net
SIC: 1799 Counter top installation

(G-4594)
ATLANTIC CONTRACTING SVCS LLC
Also Called: Coastal Hearth and Home
9599 Nanticoke Business Park Dr (19950-5448)
PHONE.....................302 337-8360
EMP: 20 EST: 2016
SALES (est): 462.1K **Privately Held**
Web: www.coastalhearthandhome.com

SIC: 1742 Insulation, buildings

(G-4595)
BEAVERDAM PET FOOD
12933 Sussex Hwy (19950-6070)
PHONE.....................302 349-5299
EMP: 8 EST: 2003
SALES (est): 1.27MM **Privately Held**
Web: www.beaverdampetfood.com
SIC: 5149 Pet foods

(G-4596)
BENDER FARMS LLC
13060 Bender Farm Rd (19950-5050)
PHONE.....................302 349-5574
EMP: 6 EST: 2008
SALES (est): 396.84K **Privately Held**
SIC: 0191 General farms, primarily crop

(G-4597)
BERACAH HOMES INC
9590 Nanticoke Business Park Dr (19950-5453)
PHONE.....................302 349-4561
Wayne Collison, *CEO*
Jeffrey Bowers, *
EMP: 50 EST: 2002
SALES (est): 21.55MM **Privately Held**
Web: www.beracahhomes.com
SIC: 1521 2452 New construction, single-family houses; Prefabricated buildings, wood

(G-4598)
BILLY WARREN & SON LLC
7040 Hickman Rd (19950-4808)
PHONE.....................302 349-5767
EMP: 8 EST: 1978
SALES (est): 778.02K **Privately Held**
Web: www.billywarrenandson.com
SIC: 5093 5084 Ferrous metal scrap and waste; Industrial machinery and equipment

(G-4599)
BLUE HEN MASONRY INC
3296 Andrewville Rd (19950-2206)
PHONE.....................302 398-8737
Norman Woodall, *Pr*
Jason W Woodall, *VP*
EMP: 6 EST: 1993
SALES (est): 359.02K **Privately Held**
SIC: 1741 Masonry and other stonework

(G-4600)
BLUE HERON CONTRACTING LLC ✪
45 Amanda Ave (19950-2419)
PHONE.....................302 526-0648
Greg Pritchett, *Managing Member*
EMP: 9 EST: 2022
SALES (est): 527.72K **Privately Held**
SIC: 7389 1771 1791 3272 Business Activities at Non-Commercial Site; Concrete work; Concrete reinforcement, placing of; Concrete structural support and building material

(G-4601)
BYRON OUTTEN PLUMBING
10004 Woodyard Rd (19950-5439)
PHONE.....................302 236-4727
EMP: 5 EST: 2018
SALES (est): 56.99K **Privately Held**
SIC: 1711 Plumbing contractors

(G-4602)
C&F CONTRACTORS SERVICE LLC
21033 S Dupont Hwy (19950-2376)
PHONE.....................302 480-3002
Darrin Willis, *Prin*

EMP: 5 EST: 2018
SALES (est): 56.76K **Privately Held**
SIC: 1799 Special trade contractors, nec

(G-4603)
CARLISLE FARMS INC
12733 Shawnee Rd (19950-5327)
PHONE.....................302 349-5692
Keith Carlisle, *Pr*
Richard Carlisle, *VP*
Carol Carlisle, *Sec*
EMP: 8 EST: 1964
SALES (est): 678.92K **Privately Held**
SIC: 0191 General farms, primarily crop

(G-4604)
COMCAST CORPORATION
2 Schulze Rd (19950-5357)
PHONE.....................302 495-5612
EMP: 5
SALES (corp-wide): 121.43B **Publicly Held**
Web: corporate.comcast.com
SIC: 4841 Cable television services
PA: Comcast Corporation
1 Comcast Ctr
Philadelphia PA 19103
215 286-1700

(G-4605)
COUNTERPARTS LLC
12952 Sussex Hwy (19950-6006)
P.O. Box 580 (19950-0580)
PHONE.....................302 349-0400
EMP: 5 EST: 2008
SALES (est): 278.83K **Privately Held**
Web: www.counterpartsllc.com
SIC: 2541 Counter and sink tops

(G-4606)
COUNTING HOUSE
94 Mcewen Dr (19950-2480)
PHONE.....................302 249-5596
EMP: 5 EST: 2018
SALES (est): 98.55K **Privately Held**
SIC: 7291 Tax return preparation services

(G-4607)
COUNTRY COOP INC
16048 Long Branch Rd (19950-5806)
PHONE.....................302 249-1985
Matthew Ellis, *Prin*
EMP: 6 EST: 2016
SALES (est): 418.13K **Privately Held**
SIC: 4911 Distribution, electric power

(G-4608)
COUNTRY KIDS CHILD CARE LRNG C
Also Called: Country Kids Child Care
14352 Staytonville Rd (19950-5008)
P.O. Box 46 (19950-0046)
PHONE.....................302 349-5888
EMP: 5 EST: 1985
SALES (est): 166.98K **Privately Held**
Web: www.gosmallbusiness.org
SIC: 8351 Group day care center

(G-4609)
CUSTOM CABINET SHOP INC
Also Called: Campbell's Custom Cabinet Shop
Rte 13 (19950)
P.O. Box 2 (19950-0002)
PHONE.....................302 337-8241
Gerald Campbell, *Pr*
Valerie Campbell, *Sec*
EMP: 14 EST: 1964
SQ FT: 3,000
SALES (est): 876.86K **Privately Held**

Greenwood - Sussex County (G-4610)   GEOGRAPHIC SECTION

Web: www.customcabinetshopde.com
SIC: **2434** 5211 Wood kitchen cabinets; Lumber and other building materials

(G-4610)
D & D SCREEN PRINTING
12794 Shawnee Rd (19950-5331)
PHONE.................................302 349-4231
David Friedel, *Prin*
EMP: 2 EST: 2007
SALES (est): 103.19K **Privately Held**
Web: www.ddscreenprinting.com
SIC: **2752** Offset printing

(G-4611)
DANIEL SHEA
1859 Elliott Ln (19950-4215)
PHONE.................................302 349-5599
Daniel Shea, *Prin*
EMP: 5 EST: 2006
SALES (est): 149.65K **Privately Held**
SIC: **1522** Residential construction, nec

(G-4612)
DBA HEATING PARTS HUB
6953 Hickman Rd (19950-4807)
PHONE.................................302 381-3705
Amy Schlabach, *Prin*
EMP: 6 EST: 2018
SALES (est): 234.19K **Privately Held**
SIC: **1711** Heating and air conditioning contractors

(G-4613)
DELAWARE ELECTRIC COOPERATIVE INC
Also Called: D E C
14198 Sussex Hwy (19950-6009)
P.O. Box 600 (19950-0600)
PHONE.................................302 349-9090
EMP: 141 EST: 1936
SALES (est): 226.82MM **Privately Held**
Web: www.delaware.coop
SIC: **4911** Distribution, electric power

(G-4614)
DELMARVA AUTO REPAIR LLC
12313 Sussex Hwy (19950-5419)
PHONE.................................302 727-3237
Paul Webb Junior, *Owner*
EMP: 6 EST: 2014
SALES (est): 248.93K **Privately Held**
Web: www.delmarvaautorepair.com
SIC: **7549** High performance auto repair and service

(G-4615)
DELMARVA ROOFING & COATING INC
12982 Mennonite School Rd (19950-5310)
P.O. Box 489 (19950-0489)
PHONE.................................302 349-5174
Sheldon L Swartzentruber, *Pr*
Verle D Schlabach, *VP*
EMP: 22 EST: 1988
SQ FT: 12,000
SALES (est): 2.12MM **Privately Held**
Web: www.delmarvaroofing.com
SIC: **1761** 1799 Roofing contractor; Waterproofing

(G-4616)
DELMARVA TRANSPORTATION INC
101 Maryland Ave (19950-7728)
PHONE.................................302 349-0840
Debbie Freeman, *Pr*
EMP: 8 EST: 2001
SALES (est): 865.1K **Privately Held**
Web: www.delmarvatransportation.com

SIC: **4111** Local and suburban transit

(G-4617)
DFS CORPORATE SERVICES LLC
502 E Market St (19950-9700)
PHONE.................................302 349-4512
EMP: 31 EST: 2014
SALES (est): 835.06K
SALES (corp-wide): 15.2B **Publicly Held**
SIC: **6061** Federal credit unions
PA: Discover Financial Services
      2500 Lake Cook Rd
      Riverwoods IL 60015
      224 405-0900

(G-4618)
DISCOVER BANK (HQ)
502 E Market St (19950-9700)
PHONE.................................302 349-4512
EMP: 144 EST: 1911
SALES (est): 14.32B
SALES (corp-wide): 15.2B **Publicly Held**
Web: www.discover.com
SIC: **6022** State trust companies accepting deposits, commercial
PA: Discover Financial Services
      2500 Lake Cook Rd
      Riverwoods IL 60015
      224 405-0900

(G-4619)
DISTINCTIVE LANDSCAPING LLC
12101 Tuckers Rd (19950-5615)
PHONE.................................410 971-8466
EMP: 5 EST: 2016
SALES (est): 121.93K **Privately Held**
Web: www.distinctivelandscaping.pro
SIC: **0781** Landscape services

(G-4620)
DLC DRYWALL
1044 Abbotts Pond Rd (19950-2411)
PHONE.................................302 382-2213
Miriam Carmona, *Pr*
EMP: 6 EST: 2010
SALES (est): 113.03K **Privately Held**
SIC: **1742** Drywall

(G-4621)
DONS TREE FARM
6396 Hickman Rd (19950-4504)
P.O. Box 7 (19950-0007)
PHONE.................................302 349-0555
Don Hallowell, *Mgr*
EMP: 5 EST: 2011
SALES (est): 178.09K **Privately Held**
Web: www.donstreefarm.com
SIC: **0811** Tree farm

(G-4622)
DOUGLAS HOMEWOOD
12005 Woodbridge Rd (19950-4557)
PHONE.................................302 349-5964
Douglas Homewood, *Prin*
EMP: 6 EST: 2011
SALES (est): 116.43K **Privately Held**
SIC: **1721** Painting and paper hanging

(G-4623)
EAST COAST MACHINE WORKS
12773 Tuckers Rd (19950-5609)
PHONE.................................302 349-5180
George Mihalik, *Owner*
EMP: 5 EST: 1974
SALES (est): 305.93K **Privately Held**
SIC: **3599** 3444 7692 Machine shop, jobbing and repair; Sheet metalwork; Welding repair

(G-4624)
EASY LAWN INC
9599 Nanticoke Business Park Dr Ste 1 (19950)
P.O. Box 316 (19933-0316)
PHONE.................................302 815-6500
Robert N Lisle, *Pr*
Marcia Lisle, *
▼ EMP: 47 EST: 1976
SQ FT: 80,000
SALES (est): 670.29K **Privately Held**
Web: www.epicmanufacturing.com
SIC: **3524** 3563 3423 3523 Lawn and garden equipment; Air and gas compressors ; Hand and edge tools, nec; Farm machinery and equipment

(G-4625)
ELVIN SCHROCK AND SONS INC
10725 Beach Hwy (19950-5710)
PHONE.................................302 349-4384
Merlin Schrock, *Pr*
Marlin J Schrock, *VP*
Linda Schrock, *Sec*
EMP: 8 EST: 1951
SALES (est): 662.05K **Privately Held**
SIC: **1711** Plumbing contractors

(G-4626)
ENSINGER PENN FIBRE INC
220 S Church & Snider St (19950)
P.O. Box 160 (19950-0160)
PHONE.................................302 349-4505
Jimmy Walls, *Brnch Mgr*
EMP: 45
SALES (corp-wide): 632.07MM **Privately Held**
Web: www.pennfibre.com
SIC: **3089** Injection molding of plastics
HQ: Ensinger Penn Fibre, Inc.
      2434 Bristol Rd
      Bensalem PA 19020
      215 702-9551

(G-4627)
ENSINGER PENN FIBRE INC
221 S Church St (19950)
PHONE.................................302 349-4505
EMP: 16 EST: 2019
SALES (est): 5.44MM **Privately Held**
Web: www.ensingerplastics.com
SIC: **5064** Television sets

(G-4628)
EXECUTIVE TRANSPORTATION INC
12643 Rock Rd (19950-5364)
PHONE.................................302 337-3455
Robin Lynn Mullins, *Pr*
EMP: 8 EST: 1997
SALES (est): 227.84K **Privately Held**
Web: www.executivetransportationde.net
SIC: **4119** Limousine rental, with driver

(G-4629)
FAIRCHILD RENTAL PRPTS LLC
12916 Oak Rd (19950-5503)
PHONE.................................302 745-1144
Tamara Fairchild, *Prin*
EMP: 5 EST: 2015
SALES (est): 192.06K **Privately Held**
SIC: **6512** Nonresidential building operators

(G-4630)
FOCAL POINT PRODUCTS
9706 Nanticoke Business Park Dr (19950-5455)
PHONE.................................800 662-5550
Afshan Khan, *CEO*
EMP: 7 EST: 2016
SALES (est): 241.66K **Privately Held**

Web: www.focalpointproducts.com
SIC: **7389** Design services

(G-4631)
FONZIS LLC
13149 Mennonite School Rd (19950-5313)
PHONE.................................302 858-8024
Frank Bolles, *Prin*
EMP: 6 EST: 2011
SALES (est): 142.45K **Privately Held**
SIC: **7699** Repair services, nec

(G-4632)
GRIMM FARMS LLC
12620 Hunters Cove Rd (19950-5548)
PHONE.................................302 841-8381
Yvonne Krause, *Prin*
EMP: 5 EST: 2017
SALES (est): 213.58K **Privately Held**
SIC: **0191** General farms, primarily crop

(G-4633)
GROFF TRACTOR & EQUIPMENT LLC
12420 Sussex Hwy (19950-5447)
P.O. Box 338 (19950-0338)
PHONE.................................302 349-5760
Mike Youse, *Prin*
EMP: 10
SALES (corp-wide): 120.35MM **Privately Held**
Web: www.grofftractor.com
SIC: **5084** 7699 7359 Industrial machinery and equipment; Industrial machinery and equipment repair; Equipment rental and leasing, nec
PA: Groff Tractor & Equipment, Llc
      6779 Carlisle Pike
      Mechanicsburg PA 17050
      717 766-7671

(G-4634)
H & C INSULATION LLC
14329 Saint Johnstown Rd (19950-6055)
PHONE.................................302 448-0777
Joseph Caudell, *Owner*
EMP: 6 EST: 2012
SALES (est): 236.86K **Privately Held**
SIC: **1742** Insulation, buildings

(G-4635)
HCLINTON FOUNDATION
12363 Sussex Hwy (19950-5418)
PHONE.................................302 393-1448
Tigran Mesropyan, *Prin*
EMP: 5 EST: 2017
SALES (est): 53.54K **Privately Held**
SIC: **8641** Civic and social associations

(G-4636)
HOME SWEET
202 Governors Ave (19950-6097)
PHONE.................................302 353-9733
Jennifer Nelson, *Prin*
EMP: 8 EST: 2009
SALES (est): 214.18K **Privately Held**
SIC: **8082** Home health care services

(G-4637)
HUMPHRIES CONSTRUCTION COMPANY
11533 Holly Tree Ln (19950-5458)
PHONE.................................302 349-9277
Danny Humphries, *Pr*
EMP: 5 EST: 2011
SALES (est): 911.26K **Privately Held**
Web: www.excelconstruction.group
SIC: **1542** 1521 Farm building construction; Single-family housing construction

GEOGRAPHIC SECTION
Greenwood - Sussex County (G-4666)

(G-4638)
HYDROSEEDING COMPANY LLC
Also Called: Epic Manufacturing
9599 Nanticoke Business Park Dr Ste 3 (19950-5448)
PHONE.................302 815-6500
EMP: 30 EST: 2010
SQ FT: 2,000
SALES (est): 2.5MM **Privately Held**
SIC: 3524 5999 Lawn and garden equipment; Farm equipment and supplies

(G-4639)
INSPIRATION EMPIRE
13747 Wolf Rd (19950-5533)
PHONE.................302 535-9920
Bryant C Bundick, *Prin*
EMP: 5 EST: 2016
SALES (est): 41.38K **Privately Held**
SIC: 7991 Spas

(G-4640)
INSTALLED BUILDING PDTS INC
Also Called: 1st State Insulation
9796 Nanticoke Business Park Dr (19950-5455)
PHONE.................302 480-1520
EMP: 17
SALES (corp-wide): 2.67B **Publicly Held**
Web: www.installedbuildingproducts.com
SIC: 1742 Insulation, buildings
PA: Installed Building Products, Inc.
495 S High St Ste 50
Columbus OH 43215
614 221-3399

(G-4641)
J B S CONSTRUCTION LLC
8801 Greenwood Rd (19950-4878)
PHONE.................302 349-5705
Bruce Wardwell, *Managing Member*
EMP: 7 EST: 2002
SQ FT: 3,500
SALES (est): 1.23MM **Privately Held**
Web: www.jbsconstructionllc.com
SIC: 1521 New construction, single-family houses

(G-4642)
J E BAILEY & SONS INC
2135 Seashore Hwy (19950-4146)
PHONE.................302 349-4376
Jeffery Bailey, *Pr*
Alan Bailey, *Asst Tr*
EMP: 5 EST: 1962
SALES (est): 412.46K **Privately Held**
SIC: 0241 0254 Milk production; Chicken hatchery

(G-4643)
JAGER TRANSPORT LLC
14206 Blanchard Rd (19950-4340)
PHONE.................302 858-2962
Kenneth Jager, *Prin*
EMP: 7 EST: 2017
SALES (est): 489.62K **Privately Held**
SIC: 4789 Transportation services, nec

(G-4644)
JAMES THOMPSON & COMPANY INC
301 S Church St (19950-7726)
P.O. Box 2013 (19950-0603)
PHONE.................302 349-4501
Steve Luchansky, *Mgr*
EMP: 35
SQ FT: 135,000
SALES (corp-wide): 8.34MM **Privately Held**
Web: www.jamesthompson.com
SIC: 2843 2269 2261 Textile finishing agents; Finishing plants, nec; Finishing plants, cotton
PA: James Thompson & Company, Inc.
463 7th Ave Rm 1603
New York NY 10018
212 686-4242

(G-4645)
JEFFREY GLENN MINOR
7557 Lindale Rd (19950-4916)
PHONE.................302 422-3403
Jeffrey Minor, *Prin*
EMP: 5 EST: 2004
SALES (est): 125.38K **Privately Held**
SIC: 7389 Business Activities at Non-Commercial Site

(G-4646)
JEREMEY M WEDDLE
Also Called: Weddle Contracting
8028 Hidden Meadow Ln (19950-4920)
PHONE.................410 829-7224
Jeremey M Weddle, *Prin*
EMP: 6 EST: 2011
SALES (est): 87.56K **Privately Held**
SIC: 1799 Special trade contractors, nec

(G-4647)
JUDY TIM FUEL INC
12386 Beach Hwy (19950-5728)
PHONE.................302 349-5895
Timothy F Judy, *Owner*
EMP: 7 EST: 2009
SALES (est): 228.09K **Privately Held**
SIC: 2869 Fuels

(G-4648)
LINDALE PLUMBING LLC
15020 Abbotts Pond Rd (19950-4901)
PHONE.................302 242-2493
EMP: 5 EST: 2019
SALES (est): 257.88K **Privately Held**
Web: www.lindaleplumbing.com
SIC: 1711 Plumbing contractors

(G-4649)
LINEAGE BJJ
6 E Market St (19950-9732)
PHONE.................201 788-8167
EMP: 5 EST: 2017
SALES (est): 47.77K **Privately Held**
Web: www.lineagebjj.com
SIC: 7999 Martial arts school, nec

(G-4650)
M/S HOLLOW METAL WHOLESALE LLC
9644 Nanticoke Business Park Dr (19950-5454)
PHONE.................302 349-9471
Jim Schroeder, *Genl Mgr*
EMP: 9 EST: 2005
SALES (est): 542.85K **Privately Held**
Web: www.mshollowmetal.com
SIC: 5031 Windows

(G-4651)
MCBROOM JR ROGER DALE
Also Called: 1st Choice Service
13505 Bender Farm Rd (19950-5046)
PHONE.................302 228-0998
Roger Mcbroom Junior, *Prin*
EMP: 5 EST: 2011
SALES (est): 79.52K **Privately Held**
SIC: 0119 Cash grains, nec

(G-4652)
MIKES EXPERT DETAILING
13448 Sun St (19950-4978)
PHONE.................302 853-5368
Michael Ross, *Prin*
EMP: 5 EST: 2010
SALES (est): 42.63K **Privately Held**
SIC: 7542 Washing and polishing, automotive

(G-4653)
MJ WEBB FARMS INC
12608 Webb Farm Rd (19950-5111)
PHONE.................302 349-4453
M J Webb, *Pr*
M J Webb Iii, *VP*
Michael B Webb, *Treas*
Louise Webb, *Sec*
EMP: 7 EST: 1976
SQ FT: 2,400
SALES (est): 728.68K **Privately Held**
SIC: 0191 General farms, primarily crop

(G-4654)
NAEGELE HEATING & COOLING
14160 Staytonville Rd (19950-5006)
PHONE.................443 996-1881
George Naegele, *Prin*
EMP: 5 EST: 2018
SALES (est): 137.33K **Privately Held**
SIC: 1711 Warm air heating and air conditioning contractor

(G-4655)
NANTICOKE CONSULTING INC
Also Called: Nanticoke Consulting and McHy
7707 Lindale Rd (19950-4914)
PHONE.................302 424-0750
Kevin Huey, *CEO*
Brent Huey, *VP*
EMP: 9 EST: 1996
SALES (est): 912.25K **Privately Held**
SIC: 3599 7389 Machine shop, jobbing and repair; Business services, nec

(G-4656)
NATIONAL CONCRETE PRODUCTS LLC
9466 Beach Hwy (19950-5302)
P.O. Box 2001 (19950-0501)
PHONE.................302 349-5528
EMP: 23 EST: 2000
SALES (est): 1.18MM **Privately Held**
SIC: 3272 Steps, prefabricated concrete

(G-4657)
NEW PROCESS FIBRE COMPANY
12655 First St (19950-4864)
P.O. Box 2009 (19950-0510)
PHONE.................302 349-4535
Carl Peters, *Pr*
Carl Peters, *Pr*
William Rust, *
EMP: 88 EST: 1927
SQ FT: 65,000
SALES (est): 10.52MM **Privately Held**
Web: www.newprocess.com
SIC: 3089 3053 2396 2821 Washers, plastics; Gaskets and sealing devices; Fabric printing and stamping; Thermoplastic materials

(G-4658)
OTHER SIDE LLC
9802 Nanticoke Business Park Dr (19950-5450)
PHONE.................410 829-1053
EMP: 6 EST: 2019
SALES (est): 841.4K **Privately Held**
SIC: 5199 Nondurable goods, nec

(G-4659)
PAINTINGS BY SARA
362 Abbotts Pond Rd (19950-2404)
PHONE.................302 424-0376
Sara Gallagher, *Prin*
EMP: 5 EST: 2018
SALES (est): 96.66K **Privately Held**
SIC: 1721 Painting and paper hanging

(G-4660)
PB TRUCKING INC
8940 Greenwood Rd (19950-4861)
PHONE.................302 841-3209
Perry Butler, *Pr*
Nicole Callahan, *Mgr*
EMP: 10 EST: 1983
SALES (est): 971.21K **Privately Held**
SIC: 4212 Local trucking, without storage

(G-4661)
PET STOP OF DELAWARE
938 Todds Chapel Rd (19950-1851)
PHONE.................302 922-7572
Kathleen Lewis, *Prin*
EMP: 5 EST: 2009
SALES (est): 76.6K **Privately Held**
Web: www.zieglerreports.com
SIC: 5039 Construction materials, nec

(G-4662)
PRESSURE WASHING
14514 Tull Rd (19950-4612)
PHONE.................302 393-0879
EMP: 5 EST: 2014
SALES (est): 68.84K **Privately Held**
SIC: 1799 Cleaning building exteriors, nec

(G-4663)
RELAXING TOURS LLC
11546 Adamsville Rd (19950-4202)
PHONE.................610 905-3852
Hildegard Rieger, *Pr*
EMP: 7 EST: 2017
SALES (est): 105.09K **Privately Held**
SIC: 8093 Rehabilitation center, outpatient treatment

(G-4664)
RIFENBURG TRUCKING INC
6525 Hickman Rd (19950-4509)
PHONE.................302 349-5969
Mike Rifenburg, *Pr*
Nicole Rifenburg, *VP*
EMP: 15 EST: 1994
SALES (est): 681.9K **Privately Held**
Web: www.rifenburgtrucking.com
SIC: 4212 Local trucking, without storage

(G-4665)
ROBERT T MINNER JR
Also Called: Rt Minner & Sons
2181 Deep Grass Ln (19950-2450)
P.O. Box 63 (19954-0063)
PHONE.................302 422-9206
Robert T Minner Junior, *Owner*
EMP: 5 EST: 1972
SALES (est): 523.06K **Privately Held**
SIC: 5148 Fruits

(G-4666)
SAM YODER AND SON LLC
9387 Memory Rd (19950-4924)
PHONE.................302 398-4711
Sam Yoder, *Ch*
Maylon Mast, *
Ronald Yoder, *
Ramona Carter, *
Rhonda Brenneman, *

Greenwood - Sussex County (G-4667)   GEOGRAPHIC SECTION

EMP: 114 EST: 2010
SQ FT: 57,200
SALES (est): 9.06MM **Privately Held**
Web: www.samyoder.com
SIC: **2439** Trusses, wooden roof

(G-4667)
SEASIDE PRESSURE WASH LLC
4840 Shirleys Rd (19950-4318)
PHONE..................................302 470-4035
EMP: **5** EST: 2018
SALES (est): 131.82K **Privately Held**
Web: www.seasidepressurewash.com
SIC: **1799** Cleaning building exteriors, nec

(G-4668)
SHIRKEY TRUCKING CORP
734 Cattail Branch Rd (19950-1704)
PHONE..................................302 349-2791
EMP: **5** EST: 2008
SALES (est): 365.8K **Privately Held**
SIC: **4212** Local trucking, without storage

(G-4669)
SPARKYS AUTO REPAIR LLC
12630 Sussex Hwy (19950-6074)
PHONE..................................302 495-7525
EMP: **5** EST: 2018
SALES (est): 241.38K **Privately Held**
Web: sparkys-auto-repair-llc.business.site
SIC: **7538** General automotive repair shops

(G-4670)
TED JOHNSON ENTERPRISES
14403 Adamsville Rd (19950-4110)
PHONE..................................302 349-5925
Ted Johnson, *Owner*
EMP: **6** EST: 2003
SALES (est): 160.03K **Privately Held**
SIC: **3663** Space satellite communications equipment

(G-4671)
THAT GRANITE PLACE LLC
9599 Nanticoke Business Park Dr (19950-5448)
PHONE..................................302 337-7490
EMP: **6** EST: 2008
SALES (est): 972.23K **Privately Held**
Web: www.coastalcountertops.net
SIC: **1799** Counter top installation

(G-4672)
TRANSITIONAL YOUTH
8748 Greenwood Rd (19950-4858)
PHONE..................................302 423-7543
Shannies Felipa, *Prin*
EMP: **10** EST: 2008
SALES (est): 99.03K **Privately Held**
Web: www.transitionalyouth.org
SIC: **8322** Social service center

(G-4673)
U-HAUL NEIGHBORHD DEALR BUDGET
12847 Sussex Hwy (19950-6071)
PHONE..................................302 349-2167
Dan Schlabach, *Owner*
EMP: **8** EST: 2010
SALES (est): 92.19K **Privately Held**
Web: www.uhaul.com
SIC: **7513** 4225 Truck rental and leasing, no drivers; Miniwarehouse, warehousing

(G-4674)
WILLIAM C LEAGER
13600 Hewish Pkwy (19950-4980)
PHONE..................................302 398-7525
William Leager, *Prin*

EMP: **5** EST: 2005
SALES (est): 165.6K **Privately Held**
SIC: **7389** Business Activities at Non-Commercial Site

(G-4675)
WM COMPANIES LLC
8961 Greenwood Rd (19950-4860)
PHONE..................................302 228-5122
Sarah Jessica Stanley, *Prin*
EMP: **8** EST: 2013
SALES (est): 486.9K **Privately Held**
SIC: **1522** Residential construction, nec

(G-4676)
WOODBRDGE HIGH SCHL PRFRMG ART
608 Schlabach Rd (19950-2379)
PHONE..................................302 495-7025
Kim Wharton, *Asst Sec*
EMP: **5** EST: 2018
SALES (est): 85.95K **Privately Held**
SIC: **8399** Social services, nec

(G-4677)
YELLOW LIGHT PUBLISHING LLC
25 Governors Ave (19950-6090)
PHONE..................................302 242-0990
EMP: **5** EST: 2017
SALES (est): 83.39K **Privately Held**
SIC: **2741** Miscellaneous publishing

(G-4678)
YODER AND SONS CNSTR LLC
10222 Woodyard Rd (19950-5436)
PHONE..................................302 349-0444
Gerald Yoder, *Mgr*
EMP: **10** EST: 2016
SALES (est): 883.25K **Privately Held**
Web: www.yoderandsonsconstruction.com
SIC: **1521** New construction, single-family houses

Harbeson
Sussex County

(G-4679)
A SMARTER CLEAN LLC
21 Pinewater Dr (19951-9477)
PHONE..................................302 841-8419
Dawn Stewart, *Pr*
EMP: **11** EST: 2016
SALES (est): 413.64K **Privately Held**
Web: www.asmarterclean.com
SIC: **7699** Cleaning services

(G-4680)
ADAMS CUSTOM LEATHER
22089 Harbeson Rd (19951-2912)
PHONE..................................302 462-0187
EMP: **7** EST: 2017
SALES (est): 31.81K **Privately Held**
Web: www.adamscustomleather.com
SIC: **7699** Motorcycle repair service

(G-4681)
ALLEN HARIM FOODS LLC
18752 Harbeson Rd (19951-2802)
P.O. Box 1380 (19966-5380)
PHONE..................................302 684-1640
Donnie Pierce, *CEO*
EMP: **22** EST: 2017
SALES (est): 4.12MM **Privately Held**
Web: www.allenharimllc.com
SIC: **2011** Meat packing plants

(G-4682)
ALLSERVE ALLSCPES ALLSTRCTURES
26539 Lewes Georgetown Hwy (19951-2861)
PHONE..................................302 684-1414
EMP: **5** EST: 2010
SALES (est): 56K **Privately Held**
SIC: **7538** General automotive repair shops

(G-4683)
ARTISAN WOODWORKS LLC
28205 Johnson Ln (19951-2827)
PHONE..................................302 841-5182
EMP: **6** EST: 2013
SALES (est): 72.53K **Privately Held**
SIC: **2499** Decorative wood and woodwork

(G-4684)
ASPHALT PAVING EQP & SUPS
26822 Lewes Georgetown Hwy (19951-2856)
PHONE..................................302 683-0105
Andy Pennington, *Owner*
EMP: **8** EST: 2014
SALES (est): 433.79K **Privately Held**
SIC: **5032** Paving materials

(G-4685)
BARBER SHOP AT REHOBOTH BEACH
20187 Doddtown Rd (19951-2847)
PHONE..................................240 743-9064
Amy Ferro, *Prin*
EMP: **5** EST: 2015
SALES (est): 56.06K **Privately Held**
SIC: **7241** Barber shops

(G-4686)
BRENDA RADICK
11 Multiflora Dr (19951-9422)
PHONE..................................302 945-8982
Brenda Radick, *Prin*
EMP: **7** EST: 2009
SALES (est): 60.65K **Privately Held**
SIC: **8361** 7349 Residential care; Cleaning service, industrial or commercial

(G-4687)
CERAMIC TILE SUPPLY CO
26836 Lewes Georgetown Hwy Ste B1c (19951-2856)
PHONE..................................302 684-5691
Sharon Hazzard, *Brnch Mgr*
EMP: **9**
SALES (corp-wide): 28.9MM **Privately Held**
Web: www.bathkitchenandtile.com
SIC: **1751** Cabinet and finish carpentry
PA: Ceramic Tile Supply Co.
103 Greenbank Rd
Wilmington DE 19808
302 992-9200

(G-4688)
COAM EXTERIOR INC
26826 Lewes Georgetown Hwy (19951-2856)
PHONE..................................302 329-9545
EMP: **6** EST: 2014
SALES (est): 278.88K **Privately Held**
SIC: **1761** Siding contractor

(G-4689)
COASTAL CONCRETE WORKS LLC
27220 Buckskin Trl (19951-2717)
PHONE..................................302 381-5261
EMP: **5** EST: 2015
SALES (est): 159.53K **Privately Held**

Web: coastalconcreteworksllc.business.site
SIC: **1771** Concrete work

(G-4690)
COMPASS POINT ASSOCIATES LLC
26373 Lewes Georgetown Hwy (19951-2869)
P.O. Box 246 (19951-0246)
PHONE..................................302 684-2980
Mary Walch, *Managing Member*
EMP: **5** EST: 2004
SQ FT: 2,800
SALES (est): 432.29K **Privately Held**
Web: www.compasspointassoc.com
SIC: **8713** Surveying services

(G-4691)
COSTLINE CLEANING SERVICE
22791 Dozer Ln Unit 5 (19951-3023)
PHONE..................................302 420-3000
EMP: **6** EST: 2013
SALES (est): 112.71K **Privately Held**
Web: www.coastlinepoolservices.com
SIC: **7699** Cleaning services

(G-4692)
COUNTRY LAWN CARE & MAINT
30435 Hollymount Rd (19951-2938)
PHONE..................................302 593-3393
Jerry Dougherty, *Prin*
EMP: **10** EST: 2010
SALES (est): 479.19K **Privately Held**
Web: www.clclawns.com
SIC: **0782** Lawn care services

(G-4693)
CREATIVE BUILDERS INC
20593 Rust Rd (19951-2828)
PHONE..................................302 228-8153
Brian Ware, *Pr*
EMP: **5** EST: 1992
SQ FT: 4,000
SALES (est): 500.53K **Privately Held**
SIC: **1531** Speculative builder, single-family houses

(G-4694)
CUSTOM FRAMERS INC
Also Called: At The Bch Repr & Maintainance
26526 Lewes Georgetown Hwy (19951-2858)
P.O. Box 261 (19951-0261)
PHONE..................................302 684-5377
William Payden, *Pt*
Tom Shinn, *Pt*
Karen Payden, *Pt*
EMP: **10** EST: 1990
SALES (est): 403.25K **Privately Held**
SIC: **2499** 1799 Picture frame molding, finished; Athletic and recreation facilities construction

(G-4695)
DELMARVA CRAWL SPACE SLTNS
28323 Johnson Ln (19951-2826)
PHONE..................................302 265-0637
EMP: **6** EST: 2016
SALES (est): 126.92K **Privately Held**
Web: www.delmarvacrawlspacesolutions.com
SIC: **1799** Waterproofing

(G-4696)
FLEXERA INC
22791 Dozer Ln Unit 8 (19951-3023)
P.O. Box 884 (19975-0884)
PHONE..................................302 945-6870
Robert Light, *CEO*
Brian Lisiewski, *Pr*
Alice Lisiewski, *COO*

GEOGRAPHIC SECTION   Harrington - Kent County (G-4725)

Benjamin Farr, *VP*
EMP: 12 **EST:** 2006
SQ FT: 1,000
SALES (est): 1.48MM **Privately Held**
Web: www.flexera.net
SIC: 8748 Energy conservation consultant

(G-4697)
GOAT JOY LLC
22114 Ritter Ln (19951-3013)
PHONE..................302 542-1062
Laura Ritter, *Asst Sec*
EMP: 5 **EST:** 2018
SALES (est): 50.9K **Privately Held**
Web: www.goatjoy.com
SIC: 7999 Yoga instruction

(G-4698)
HELLENS HEATING & AIR I
20949 Harbeson Rd (19951-2914)
PHONE..................302 945-1875
Mike Hellen, *Prin*
EMP: 6 **EST:** 2006
SALES (est): 473.73K **Privately Held**
SIC: 1711 Warm air heating and air conditioning contractor

(G-4699)
HLS EVENT SOLUTIONS LLC
21577 Capitan Loop (19951-3066)
PHONE..................484 293-4272
EMP: 8 **EST:** 2019
SALES (est): 25.14K **Privately Held**
SIC: 7231 Beauty shops

(G-4700)
HOT SHOT CONCEPTS
4 Sassafras Ln (19951-9469)
PHONE..................302 947-1808
Karin Snoots, *Owner*
EMP: 2 **EST:** 2008
SALES (est): 82.12K **Privately Held**
SIC: 3953 Stencils, painting and marking

(G-4701)
HYETT REFRIGERATION INC
Also Called: Honeywell Authorized Dealer
26451 Lewes Georgetown Hwy (19951-2860)
PHONE..................302 684-4600
Ernest Hyett, *Pr*
EMP: 11 **EST:** 1999
SQ FT: 4,000
SALES (est): 466.43K **Privately Held**
Web: www.hyettrefrigeration.com
SIC: 1711 Warm air heating and air conditioning contractor

(G-4702)
J D MASONRY INC
Rte 5 (19951)
P.O. Box 111 (19951-0111)
PHONE..................302 684-1009
John Davison, *Pr*
EMP: 21 **EST:** 1978
SALES (est): 1.03MM **Privately Held**
SIC: 1741 Masonry and other stonework

(G-4703)
JOES AUTO AND EQUIPMENT REPAIR
26527 Lewes Georgetown Hwy (19951-2861)
PHONE..................302 990-5845
EMP: 5 **EST:** 2019
SALES (est): 71.92K **Privately Held**
SIC: 7538 General automotive repair shops

(G-4704)
K&D INC
Also Called: Stretched Out Trucking
26873 Anderson Corner Rd (19951-2922)
PHONE..................302 945-7036
Deanne M Welsh, *Pr*
EMP: 5 **EST:** 2005
SALES (est): 256.52K **Privately Held**
SIC: 7389 Business Activities at Non-Commercial Site

(G-4705)
LANE BUILDERS INC
1009 Road 268 (19951)
P.O. Box 202 (19951-0202)
PHONE..................302 644-1182
Gary Mc Crea, *Prin*
EMP: 5 **EST:** 2011
SALES (est): 176.16K **Privately Held**
Web: www.lanebuilders.com
SIC: 1521 New construction, single-family houses

(G-4706)
LULLABY LEARNING CENTER INC
Also Called: CHILD CARE
26324 Lewes Georgetown Hwy (19951-2867)
PHONE..................302 703-2871
Sheri Gebbia, *Ex Dir*
Joseph Gebbia, *Pr*
EMP: 15 **EST:** 2016
SQ FT: 4,500
SALES (est): 968.52K **Privately Held**
Web: www.lullabylearningcenter.com
SIC: 8351 Group day care center

(G-4707)
MAKO SWIM CLUB LLC
P.O. Box 231 (19951-0231)
PHONE..................631 682-2131
EMP: 5 **EST:** 2017
SALES (est): 93.33K **Privately Held**
SIC: 7997 Membership sports and recreation clubs

(G-4708)
MIDWAY LIONS CLUB INC
1 Mulberry Ln (19951-9470)
PHONE..................302 945-5525
EMP: 6 **EST:** 2014
SALES (est): 44.58K **Privately Held**
SIC: 8641 Civic associations

(G-4709)
MJ BRUNIN LLC
23382 Greenbank Dr (19951-3006)
PHONE..................302 945-9467
Michael Bruzdzinski, *Prin*
EMP: 5 **EST:** 2019
SALES (est): 131.22K **Privately Held**
Web: www.mjbrunin.com
SIC: 7699 Cleaning services

(G-4710)
OLD WOOD & CO LLC
26804 Lewes Georgetown Hwy (19951-2856)
PHONE..................302 684-3600
Martin Bueneman, *Managing Member*
EMP: 10 **EST:** 2004
SALES (est): 449.05K **Privately Held**
Web: www.oldwoodde.com
SIC: 2426 Flooring, hardwood

(G-4711)
PENINSULA MASONRY INC
26822 Lewes Georgetown Hwy (19951-2856)
P.O. Box 9174 (19714-9174)
PHONE..................302 684-3410
EMP: 8 **EST:** 1994
SQ FT: 2,500
SALES (est): 261.98K **Privately Held**
SIC: 1741 1771 Masonry and other stonework; Concrete work

(G-4712)
R F GENTNER & SON
22797 Dozer Ln Unit 15 (19951-3024)
PHONE..................302 947-2733
Richard F Gentner, *Owner*
EMP: 5 **EST:** 1992
SALES (est): 294.8K **Privately Held**
SIC: 1741 Masonry and other stonework

(G-4713)
ROGERS GRAPHICS INC
26836 Lewes Georgetown Hwy (19951-2856)
P.O. Box 231 (19963-0231)
PHONE..................302 422-6694
EMP: 2
SALES (corp-wide): 2.11MM **Privately Held**
Web: www.rogersgraphics.com
SIC: 2752 Offset printing
PA: Rogers Graphics Inc
32 Bridgeville Rd
Georgetown DE 19947
302 856-0028

(G-4714)
RW HEATING & AIR INC
20801 Doddtown Rd (19951-2845)
P.O. Box 385 (19947-0385)
PHONE..................302 856-4330
Ronald Witke, *Pr*
EMP: 7 **EST:** 1998
SALES (est): 498.78K **Privately Held**
Web: www.rwheatingandair.com
SIC: 1711 Warm air heating and air conditioning contractor

(G-4715)
SHORE PROPERTY MAINTENANCE
28828 Four Of Us Rd (19951-2890)
PHONE..................302 947-4440
Ted Nowakowski, *Owner*
EMP: 11 **EST:** 2004
SALES (est): 226.16K **Privately Held**
Web: www.shorepropertyde.com
SIC: 0781 Landscape services

(G-4716)
SHORE TINT & MORE INC
22797 Dozer Ln Unit 13 (19951-3024)
PHONE..................302 947-4624
Jared Becker, *Pr*
EMP: 5 **EST:** 2016
SALES (est): 530.2K **Privately Held**
Web: www.shoretintandmore.com
SIC: 7549 1799 Glass tinting, automotive; Glass tinting, architectural or automotive

(G-4717)
SUNDEW PAINTING INC
26836 Lewes Georgetown Hwy Ste B1e (19951-2856)
PHONE..................302 684-5858
Dino Mardo, *Pr*
Jenny Wottes, *Sec*
Nardo Nick, *Pr*
EMP: 11 **EST:** 2001
SALES (est): 560.33K **Privately Held**
SIC: 1721 Residential painting

(G-4718)
WEBSTUDY INC (PA)
30649 Hollymount Rd (19951-3010)
PHONE..................888 326-4058
Joseph Curt Corbi, *CEO*
Michael Adams, *Pr*
EMP: 5 **EST:** 2001
SALES (est): 831.77K
SALES (corp-wide): 831.77K **Privately Held**
SIC: 7371 7372 7373 7374 Computer software development; Prepackaged software; Computer integrated systems design; Data processing and preparation

(G-4719)
WILLIAM V GALLERY DR
16 Chester Ct (19951-9741)
PHONE..................302 945-5943
William Gallery, *Prin*
EMP: 9 **EST:** 2004
SALES (est): 64.96K **Privately Held**
SIC: 8011 Offices and clinics of medical doctors

Harrington
Kent County

(G-4720)
A LITTLE VETERINARY CLINIC PA
6902 Milford Harrington Hwy (19952)
PHONE..................302 398-3367
Sharon Little D.v.m., *Pr*
EMP: 10 **EST:** 2001
SALES (est): 653.67K **Privately Held**
Web: www.alittlevet.com
SIC: 0742 Animal hospital services, pets and other animal specialties

(G-4721)
A1 HANDYMAN SERVICES
2199 Brownsville Rd (19952-5029)
PHONE..................302 398-4235
Matthew Layton, *Prin*
EMP: 5 **EST:** 2017
SALES (est): 27.46K **Privately Held**
SIC: 7299 Handyman service

(G-4722)
ABOUT - PER RUSH ADVENTURES
1211 Sandbox Rd (19952-2674)
PHONE..................302 270-7886
Lisa Callaway, *Prin*
EMP: 6 **EST:** 2017
SALES (est): 48.64K **Privately Held**
SIC: 7999 Amusement and recreation, nec

(G-4723)
AGRO LAB
101 Clukey Dr (19952-2372)
PHONE..................302 265-2734
EMP: 11
SALES (est): 265.73K **Privately Held**
Web: www.agrolab.us
SIC: 8071 Testing laboratories

(G-4724)
AGROLAB INC
101 Clukey Dr (19952)
PHONE..................302 535-6591
Bill Rohrer, *Pr*
EMP: 7 **EST:** 2010
SALES (est): 460.41K **Privately Held**
Web: www.agrolab.us
SIC: 0711 Soil preparation services

(G-4725)
ALPHA CARE MEDICAL LLC (PA)
1000 Midway Dr Ste 3 (19952-2448)
PHONE..................302 398-0888
EMP: 8 **EST:** 2017
SALES (est): 4.74MM

Harrington - Kent County (G-4726) GEOGRAPHIC SECTION

SALES (corp-wide): 4.74MM **Privately Held**
Web: www.alphacaremedical.net
SIC: 8011 Primary care medical clinic

(G-4726)
ALWAYS INSURANCE AGENCY LLC
16190 S Dupont Hwy (19952-3122)
PHONE.................................302 566-6529
EMP: 5 **EST:** 2015
SALES (est): 120.44K **Privately Held**
SIC: 6411 Insurance agents, nec

(G-4727)
AMERICAN FINANCE LLC
17507 S Dupont Hwy (19952-2378)
PHONE.................................302 674-0365
Frank Moore, *Pr*
EMP: 60 **EST:** 1996
SQ FT: 22,000
SALES (est): 27MM **Privately Held**
Web: www.americanfinancellc.com
SIC: 6159 Agricultural credit institutions

(G-4728)
AMERICAN LEGION
Also Called: American Legion Ckrt Post 7
17448 S Dupont Hwy (19952-2481)
PHONE.................................302 398-3566
Chris Werner, *Prin*
EMP: 5 **EST:** 1972
SALES (est): 368.36K **Privately Held**
Web: www.legion.org
SIC: 8641 Veterans' organization

(G-4729)
AMERICINN BY WYNDHAM
Also Called: AmericInn
1259 Corn Crib Rd (19952-2266)
PHONE.................................302 398-3900
Nancy Roberts, *Mgr*
EMP: 10
SALES (corp-wide): 1.5B **Publicly Held**
Web: www.wyndhamhotels.com
SIC: 7011 Hotels and motels
HQ: Americinn International, Llc
250 Lake Dr E
Chanhassen MN 55317

(G-4730)
AMES MUSIC STUDIO
16 Fleming St (19952-1162)
PHONE.................................302 222-4648
Nathan Ames, *Owner*
EMP: 5 **EST:** 2010
SALES (est): 48.44K **Privately Held**
SIC: 7389 Recording studio, noncommercial records

(G-4731)
ANTHONYS COLLISION CSTM WORKS
10 Clark St (19952-1211)
PHONE.................................302 542-2489
EMP: 5 **EST:** 2017
SALES (est): 150.4K **Privately Held**
SIC: 7532 Body shop, automotive

(G-4732)
ANTOINETTE XAVIER
17573 S Dupont Hwy (19952-2370)
PHONE.................................980 549-3272
EMP: 15
SALES (est): 653.06K **Privately Held**
SIC: 5136 7389 Men's and boy's clothing; Business services, nec

(G-4733)
ANYTHINGS POSSIBLE CNSTR
1211 Sandbox Rd (19952-2674)
PHONE.................................302 233-2357
James Callaway, *Prin*
EMP: 5 **EST:** 2017
SALES (est): 173.49K **Privately Held**
SIC: 1521 Single-family housing construction

(G-4734)
AP IRRIGATION INC
1211 Sandbox Rd (19952-2674)
PHONE.................................302 233-2357
James Callaway, *Prin*
EMP: 6 **EST:** 2019
SALES (est): 125.27K **Privately Held**
SIC: 4971 Irrigation systems

(G-4735)
ARCADIA FENCING INC
166 Hopkins Cemetery Rd (19952-3235)
P.O. Box 97 (19952-0097)
PHONE.................................302 398-7700
Steve Scott, *Pr*
EMP: 5 **EST:** 2000
SALES (est): 557.57K **Privately Held**
Web: www.ashleyfencellc.com
SIC: 1799 Fence construction

(G-4736)
ARUNDEL TRAILER SALES
344 Jefferson Woods Dr (19952-6032)
PHONE.................................302 398-6288
Bill Hoovler, *CEO*
EMP: 5 **EST:** 2005
SALES (est): 477.79K **Privately Held**
Web: www.arundeltrailersales.com
SIC: 5013 5015 Trailer parts and accessories; Trailer parts and accessories, used

(G-4737)
ATI HOLDINGS LLC
Also Called: ATI Physical Therapy
16819 S Dupont Hwy Ste 500 (19952-3192)
PHONE.................................302 786-3008
EMP: 8
SALES (corp-wide): 635.67MM **Publicly Held**
Web: www.atipt.com
SIC: 8049 Physical therapist
HQ: Ati Holdings, Llc
790 Remington Blvd
Bolingbrook IL 60440

(G-4738)
BAY 2 BAY BUILDERS
396 Hayfield Rd (19952-5733)
PHONE.................................302 632-7222
John Bauer, *Owner*
EMP: 5 **EST:** 2009
SALES (est): 132.38K **Privately Held**
Web: www.bay2baybuilders.com
SIC: 1521 New construction, single-family houses

(G-4739)
BEACHY TRANSPORTATION
177 Plummer Ln (19952-5659)
PHONE.................................302 284-7202
Jason Raksnis, *Mgr*
EMP: 7 **EST:** 2017
SALES (est): 503.72K **Privately Held**
Web: www.richasshit.com
SIC: 4789 Transportation services, nec

(G-4740)
BI-STATE FEEDERS LLC
16054 S Dupont Hwy (19952-3121)
PHONE.................................302 398-3408
EMP: 7 **EST:** 2002
SALES (est): 563.05K **Privately Held**
SIC: 0213 2048 Hog feedlot; Feed supplements

(G-4741)
BRS CONSULTING INC
293 Jackson Ditch Rd (19952-2432)
P.O. Box 237 (19952-0237)
PHONE.................................302 786-2326
Robin Schurman, *Pr*
Brian Schurman, *VP*
EMP: 8 **EST:** 2013
SALES (est): 791.44K **Privately Held**
Web: www.brsconinc.com
SIC: 8742 1542 Construction project management consultant; Nonresidential construction, nec

(G-4742)
BURRIS LOGISTICS
Burris Retail Food System
111 Reese Ave (19952-1316)
PHONE.................................302 398-5050
Larry Passwater, *VP*
EMP: 148
SQ FT: 200,000
SALES (corp-wide): 1.24B **Privately Held**
Web: www.burrislogistics.com
SIC: 4225 5143 5142 General warehousing and storage; Dairy products, except dried or canned; Packaged frozen goods
PA: Burris Logistics
501 Se 5th St
Milford DE 19963
302 839-4531

(G-4743)
BW ELECTRIC INC
Also Called: Bwe Electric
15342 S Dupont Hwy (19952-3114)
PHONE.................................302 566-6248
Bryon S Warren, *Pr*
Kelly Warren, *
EMP: 44 **EST:** 2007
SQ FT: 2,500
SALES (est): 7.87MM **Privately Held**
Web: www.bwelectricinc.com
SIC: 1731 General electrical contractor

(G-4744)
CALEB G STEVENS
Also Called: Sealguard
118 Mechanic St (19952-1008)
PHONE.................................302 535-4202
Caleb G Stevens, *Prin*
EMP: 7 **EST:** 2011
SALES (est): 143.63K **Privately Held**
SIC: 1611 Surfacing and paving

(G-4745)
CALLAWAY FURNITURE INC
15152 S Dupont Hwy (19952-3112)
PHONE.................................302 398-8858
Paul S Callaway, *Pr*
Paul R Callaway, *Pr*
EMP: 8 **EST:** 1947
SQ FT: 15,000
SALES (est): 1.58MM **Privately Held**
Web: www.callawayfurniture.com
SIC: 5712 2394 5713 Office furniture; Awnings, fabric: made from purchased materials; Carpets

(G-4746)
CAMPBELLS
332 Weiner Ave (19952-1141)
PHONE.................................302 359-9918
Anthony Campbell, *Owner*
EMP: 6 **EST:** 2013
SALES (est): 241.09K **Privately Held**

SIC: 7538 General automotive repair shops

(G-4747)
CEDAR ROCK CONSTRUCTION
5513 Whiteleysburg Rd (19952-3660)
PHONE.................................302 430-1276
Kenneth Bendfeldt, *Prin*
EMP: 5 **EST:** 2017
SALES (est): 82.72K **Privately Held**
Web: www.cedarrockde.com
SIC: 1521 General remodeling, single-family houses

(G-4748)
CHICK HARNESS & SUPPLY INC (PA)
Also Called: Equine Wholesalers
18011 S Dupont Hwy (19952-2135)
PHONE.................................302 398-4630
Robert L Fleming, *Pr*
Linda Chick, *
◆ **EMP:** 30 **EST:** 1975
SQ FT: 20,000
SALES (est): 8.87MM
SALES (corp-wide): 8.87MM **Privately Held**
Web: www.chicksaddlery.com
SIC: 5941 5699 5661 5191 Saddlery and equestrian equipment; Western apparel; Men's boots; Equestrian equipment

(G-4749)
CHOICES FOR COMMUNITY LIVING (PA)
100 Kings Ct (19952-2553)
PHONE.................................302 398-0446
Belinda Smith, *Mgr*
EMP: 5 **EST:** 2004
SALES (est): 237.55K
SALES (corp-wide): 237.55K **Privately Held**
Web: www.ccldelaware.org
SIC: 8361 Residential care for the handicapped

(G-4750)
CLASSIC AUTO RESTORATION SVCS
2782 Jackson Ditch Rd (19952-2454)
PHONE.................................302 398-9652
Kenneth Cannon, *Prin*
EMP: 5 **EST:** 2015
SALES (est): 101.8K **Privately Held**
SIC: 7538 General automotive repair shops

(G-4751)
COASTAL PUMP & TANK INC
17401 S Dupont Hwy (19952-2312)
PHONE.................................302 398-3061
William E Towers Junior, *Pr*
William Thompson, *Treas*
EMP: 9 **EST:** 1990
SQ FT: 1,500
SALES (est): 487.48K **Privately Held**
SIC: 1799 Gasoline pump installation

(G-4752)
COLLINS MECHANICAL INC
15294 S Dupont Hwy (19952-3113)
PHONE.................................302 398-8877
Bruce Collins, *Pr*
Gregory Collins, *
Barbara Collins, *
Sara Collins, *
EMP: 40 **EST:** 1979
SQ FT: 2,200
SALES (est): 4.74MM **Privately Held**
Web: www.collinsmech.com
SIC: 5999 1711 Plumbing and heating supplies; Plumbing contractors

Harrington - Kent County (G-4779)

(G-4753)
CONNECTONS CSP0110 W LBERTY ST
110 W Liberty St (19952-1006)
PHONE..................302 566-6078
EMP: 5 EST: 2016
SALES (est): 59.38K **Privately Held**
SIC: 8361 Residential care

(G-4754)
COUNTY SEAT CRUISERS INC
158 Central Park Dr (19952-2256)
PHONE..................302 398-8999
Mabel E Kelly, *Prin*
EMP: 5 EST: 2017
SALES (est): 77.28K **Privately Held**
SIC: 7997 Membership sports and recreation clubs

(G-4755)
CUTTING EDGE TREATMENT CENTER
1000 Midway Dr Ste 3 (19952-2448)
P.O. Box 91 (19952-0091)
PHONE..................302 258-5710
Jamie Everton, *Prin*
EMP: 6 EST: 2014
SALES (est): 63.11K **Privately Held**
SIC: 7241 Barber shops

(G-4756)
D A B PRODUCTIONS
Also Called: Axe Bail Bonds
604 Fernwood Dr (19952-6012)
PHONE..................302 670-9407
Dwayne Breeding, *Prin*
EMP: 5 EST: 2011
SALES (est): 175.66K **Privately Held**
Web: www.axebailbonds.com
SIC: 7389 Bail bonding

(G-4757)
DELAWARE RURAL WATER ASSN
27 Commerce St Ste 27c (19952-1500)
PHONE..................302 398-9633
EMP: 8 EST: 1996
SQ FT: 500
SALES (est): 310.01K **Privately Held**
SIC: 7699 Waste cleaning services

(G-4758)
DELAWARE STATE FAIR INC (PA)
18500 S Dupont Hwy (19952-2107)
P.O. Box 28 (19952-0028)
PHONE..................302 398-3269
Brent M Adams Junior, *Ch Bd*
W Leroy Betts, *
R Ronald Draper, *
R Bruce Betts, *
John M Short, *
EMP: 5 EST: 1919
SQ FT: 15,000
SALES (est): 10.08MM
SALES (corp-wide): 10.08MM **Privately Held**
Web: www.delawarestatefair.com
SIC: 7999 Agricultural fair

(G-4759)
DELMARVA CHIROPRACTIC WEL
1000 Midway Dr (19952-2448)
PHONE..................302 682-7975
EMP: 5 EST: 2019
SALES (est): 168.28K **Privately Held**
Web: www.delmarvawellness.com
SIC: 8041 Offices and clinics of chiropractors

(G-4760)
DELMARVA PLASTICS CO
800 Pine Pitch Rd (19952-3432)
PHONE..................302 398-1000
Dirk Gleysteen, *Pr*
EMP: 5 EST: 2002
SQ FT: 1,000
SALES (est): 912.43K **Privately Held**
SIC: 2821 Plastics materials and resins

(G-4761)
DENNIS M HUGHES
597 Gallo Rd (19952-4469)
PHONE..................302 632-4503
Dennis Hughes, *Prin*
EMP: 6 EST: 2015
SALES (est): 27.25K **Privately Held**
SIC: 7299 Handyman service

(G-4762)
DFA DAIRY BRANDS FLUID LLC
Also Called: HI Grade Dairy
17267 S Dupont Hwy (19952-2484)
PHONE..................302 398-8321
Steve Moore, *Brnch Mgr*
EMP: 11
SALES (corp-wide): 24.52B **Privately Held**
Web: www.dfamilk.com
SIC: 2026 5143 5149 Milk processing (pasteurizing, homogenizing, bottling); Milk; Juices
HQ: Dfa Dairy Brands Fluid, Llc
1405 N 98th St
Kansas City KS 66111
816 801-6455

(G-4763)
DISCOUNT CIGARETTE DEPOT
1 Liberty Plz (19952-1248)
PHONE..................302 398-4447
Askol Patel, *Owner*
EMP: 2 EST: 2004
SALES (est): 75.51K **Privately Held**
SIC: 3999 Cigar and cigarette holders

(G-4764)
DOVER MILLWORK INC
Also Called: Dover Windows and Doors
10862 Shawnee Rd (19952-6836)
PHONE..................302 349-5070
Larry Yoder, *Pr*
Jeanette Yoder, *VP*
▲ EMP: 18 EST: 1982
SALES (est): 3.06MM **Privately Held**
Web: www.doverwindows.com
SIC: 2431 Doors and door parts and trim, wood

(G-4765)
DYNAMIC THERAPY SERVICES LLC
2000 Midway Dr (19952-2449)
PHONE..................302 566-6624
EMP: 6 EST: 2016
SALES (est): 73.19K **Privately Held**
SIC: 8093 Rehabilitation center, outpatient treatment

(G-4766)
ENVIROCORP INC
51 Clark St (19952-1242)
PHONE..................302 398-3869
H Joseph Gannon Junior, *Pr*
H Jpseph Gannon Iii, *VP*
EMP: 10 EST: 1984
SQ FT: 5,000
SALES (est): 1.64MM **Privately Held**
Web: www.envirocorplabs.com
SIC: 8734 Water testing laboratory

(G-4767)
ERCO CEILINGS & INTERIORS INC
Also Called: Erco Ceilings & Blinds
512 Shaw Ave (19952-1233)
PHONE..................302 398-3200
EMP: 15
SALES (corp-wide): 23.8MM **Privately Held**
Web: www.ercoonline.com
SIC: 5039 5211 Ceiling systems and products; Lumber and other building materials
HQ: Erco Ceilings & Interiors Inc
2 S Dupont Rd
Wilmington DE 19805
302 994-6200

(G-4768)
FAIRWAY MANUFACTURING COMPANY (HQ)
51 Clark St (19952-1242)
PHONE..................302 398-4630
Linda Chick, *Pr*
James Fleming, *VP*
Rebecca Fleming, *Treas*
Scott Fleming, *Sec*
Frank Chick, *Stockholder*
EMP: 10 EST: 1980
SALES (est): 632.89K
SALES (corp-wide): 3.96MM **Privately Held**
Web: www.fairwaymfg.com
SIC: 3199 2399 3111 Equestrian related leather articles; Horse blankets; Saddlery leather
PA: Chick Harness & Supply, Inc.
18011 S Dupont Hwy
Harrington DE 19952
302 398-4630

(G-4769)
FFI IONIX INC
299 Cluckey Dr Ste A (19952-2376)
PHONE..................302 629-5768
Paul Browning, *Pr*
EMP: 18 EST: 2021
SALES (est): 1.25MM **Privately Held**
SIC: 3677 Filtration devices, electronic
HQ: Fortescue Future Industries Pty Ltd
L 2 87 Adelaide Tce
Perth East WA 6004

(G-4770)
FIRST STATE PETROLEUM SERVICES
714 Gallo Rd (19952-4454)
PHONE..................302 398-9704
Stacey Gallo, *Pr*
Carmine Gallo, *Stockholder*
Frank Gallo, *VP*
Helen Gallo, *Sec*
Fred Gallo, *VP*
EMP: 7 EST: 1989
SALES (est): 950.68K **Privately Held**
SIC: 1799 Gasoline pump installation

(G-4771)
GAMING ENTERTAINMENT DEL LLC
15 W Rider Rd (19952-3322)
PHONE..................302 398-4920
EMP: 7 EST: 2011
SALES (est): 116.86K **Privately Held**
SIC: 7929 Entertainers and entertainment groups

(G-4772)
GARY P SIMPSON CONTRACTING LLC
1994 Fox Hunters Rd (19952-4063)
PHONE..................302 398-7733
Gary Simpson, *Managing Member*
EMP: 6 EST: 2004
SALES (est): 992.34K **Privately Held**
Web: www.harringtondedemolitioncontractor.com
SIC: 1542 Commercial and office building contractors

(G-4773)
GEORGE K HOREIS
3822 Fox Hunters Rd (19952-3610)
PHONE..................302 398-8684
George K Horeis, *Prin*
EMP: 5 EST: 2011
SALES (est): 84.87K **Privately Held**
SIC: 8699 Charitable organization

(G-4774)
GOODE CLEANING LLC (PA)
229 Beaver Pond Rd (19952-1983)
PHONE..................302 398-4520
Denise Goodegreen, *Prin*
EMP: 7 EST: 2012
SALES (est): 496.94K
SALES (corp-wide): 496.94K **Privately Held**
Web: www.goodecleaning.com
SIC: 7699 Cleaning services

(G-4775)
GRIFFITH ROOFING AND
205 Hanley St (19952-1327)
PHONE..................302 275-7123
EMP: 5 EST: 2017
SALES (est): 109.26K **Privately Held**
SIC: 1761 Roofing contractor

(G-4776)
GULAB MANAGEMENT INC
Also Called: Super 8 Motel
17101 Dupont Hwy (19952)
PHONE..................302 398-4206
Asim Gulab, *Mgr*
EMP: 5
Web: www.wyndhamhotels.com
SIC: 7011 Hotels and motels
PA: Gulab Management Inc
1426 N Dupont Hwy
Dover DE 19901

(G-4777)
GULLWING CONTRACTING INC
728 Toby Collins Ln (19952-5940)
P.O. Box 158 (19962-0158)
PHONE..................302 943-0133
EMP: 15 EST: 2009
SALES (est): 1.72MM **Privately Held**
Web: www.gullwingcontracting.com
SIC: 1741 Masonry and other stonework

(G-4778)
H & R BLOCK
Also Called: H & R Block
16819 S Dupont Hwy Ste 200 (19952-3193)
PHONE..................302 398-8730
Linda H Niehorster, *Prin*
EMP: 9 EST: 2008
SALES (est): 38.36K **Privately Held**
Web: www.hrblock.com
SIC: 7291 Tax return preparation services

(G-4779)
HARRINGTON RACEWAY INC
15 W Rider Rd (19952-3322)
P.O. Box 28 (19952-0028)
PHONE..................302 398-4920
William Chasanov, *Pr*
Leroy Detts, *VP*
▲ EMP: 15 EST: 1946

Harrington - Kent County (G-4780)

SQ FT: 12,000
SALES (est): 6.11MM
SALES (corp-wide): 10.08MM **Privately Held**
Web: casino.harringtonraceway.com
SIC: 7948 0752 Harness horse racing; Animal specialty services
PA: The Delaware State Fair Inc
18500 S Dupont Hwy
Harrington DE 19952
302 398-3269

(G-4780)
HARRINGTON RACEWAY INC
Also Called: Harrington Raceway and Casino
Rte 13-2nd Gate (19952)
P.O. Box 310 (19952-0310)
PHONE..................................302 398-5346
EMP: 100 EST: 1996
SQ FT: 72,000
SALES (est): 10.3MM **Privately Held**
Web: casino.harringtonraceway.com
SIC: 7999 7993 5813 5812 Gambling and lottery services; Gambling establishments operating coin-operated machines; Drinking places; Eating places

(G-4781)
HARRINGTON SENIOR CENTER INC
102 Fleming St (19952-1145)
PHONE..................................302 398-4224
Karen Crouse, *Ex Dir*
EMP: 5 EST: 1967
SALES (est): 346.08K **Privately Held**
Web: www.harringtonseniorcenter.org
SIC: 8322 Senior citizens' center or association

(G-4782)
HEAD START HARRINGTON
112 East St (19952-3375)
PHONE..................................302 398-9196
Cheryl Pritchett, *Prin*
EMP: 5 EST: 2010
SALES (est): 126.86K **Privately Held**
SIC: 8351 Head Start center, except in conjunction with school

(G-4783)
HEATHER BAKER
4320 Vernon Rd (19952-4213)
PHONE..................................302 382-7466
Heather Baker, *Prin*
EMP: 5 EST: 2018
SALES (est): 22.82K **Privately Held**
Web: www.bakerthompsonassoc.co.uk
SIC: 7221 Photographer, still or video

(G-4784)
HENSCO LLC
Also Called: Hensco Glass Company
155 Argos Choice (19952-2641)
PHONE..................................302 423-1638
Kenneth Bailey, *Pr*
Joseph Scott, *VP*
EMP: 5 EST: 2000
SALES (est): 250.85K **Privately Held**
SIC: 3231 6519 1742 Insulating glass; made from purchased glass; Real property lessors, nec; Plastering, drywall, and insulation

(G-4785)
HOLIDAY INN EXPRESS
Also Called: Holiday Inn
17271 S Dupont Hwy (19952-2484)
PHONE..................................302 398-8800
Alina Keller, *Genl Mgr*
EMP: 28 EST: 2003
SALES (est): 297.44K **Privately Held**
Web: www.hiexpress.com
SIC: 7011 Hotels and motels

(G-4786)
HOT ROD WELDING
258 Sika Dr (19952-1705)
PHONE..................................302 725-5485
EMP: 3 EST: 2017
SALES (est): 52.15K **Privately Held**
SIC: 7692 Welding repair

(G-4787)
HRUPSA FARMS LTD PARTNERSHIP
3418 Hopkins Cemetery Rd (19952-3522)
PHONE..................................302 270-1817
Frank G Hrupsa, *Prin*
EMP: 7 EST: 2009
SALES (est): 487.66K **Privately Held**
SIC: 0191 General farms, primarily crop

(G-4788)
HUGHY INC
111 E Center St (19952-1105)
PHONE..................................302 398-8826
Ron Hughes, *Owner*
EMP: 5 EST: 2011
SALES (est): 28.92K **Privately Held**
Web: www.hughyrt.com
SIC: 7231 Manicurist, pedicurist

(G-4789)
J & B MD CRABS
784 Gallo Rd (19952-4454)
PHONE..................................302 387-2161
EMP: 6 EST: 2016
SALES (est): 63.16K **Privately Held**
SIC: 8011 Offices and clinics of medical doctors

(G-4790)
JD SIGN COMPANY LLC
515 Smith Ave (19952-1227)
P.O. Box 937 (19943-0937)
PHONE..................................302 786-2761
Jason Dean, *Pr*
EMP: 2 EST: 2009
SALES (est): 300.77K **Privately Held**
Web: www.delawaresign.com
SIC: 3993 Electric signs

(G-4791)
JJS LEARNING EXPERIENCE LLC
17001 S Dupont Hwy (19952-2486)
PHONE..................................302 398-9000
Keith Shawanda, *Managing Member*
EMP: 15 EST: 2018
SALES (est): 904.69K **Privately Held**
SIC: 8351 Child day care services

(G-4792)
JOSEPH T RICHARDSON INC
105 E Center St (19952-1105)
P.O. Box 269 (19952-0269)
PHONE..................................302 398-8101
John Dunbar, *Pr*
Virginia Richardson, *Sec*
EMP: 21 EST: 1952
SALES (est): 2.4MM **Privately Held**
SIC: 1711 Plumbing contractors

(G-4793)
K L VINCENT WELDING SVC INC
19456 S Dupont Hwy (19952-2116)
PHONE..................................302 398-9357
Kenneth L Vincent, *Pr*
EMP: 15 EST: 1992
SALES (est): 2.5MM **Privately Held**
Web: www.klvincentwelding.com
SIC: 7692 Welding repair

(G-4794)
KIRBY & HOLLOWAY PROVISIONS CO
Also Called: K & H Provision Co
966 Jackson Ditch Rd (19952-2417)
P.O. Box 222 (19952-0222)
PHONE..................................302 398-3705
Russell Kirby Ii, *Pr*
Blanche Kirby, *
EMP: 50 EST: 1946
SQ FT: 5,000
SALES (est): 4.59MM **Privately Held**
SIC: 2013 Sausages, from purchased meat

(G-4795)
LAKE FOREST SCHOOL DISTRICT
Also Called: Delaware Early Childhood Ctr
100 W Mispillion St (19952-1027)
PHONE..................................302 398-8945
Janet Cornwell, *Dir*
EMP: 48
SALES (corp-wide): 47.09MM **Privately Held**
Web: www.lf.k12.de.us
SIC: 8211 8351 Public special education school; Child day care services
PA: Lake Forest School District
5423 Killens Pond Rd
Felton DE 19943
302 284-3020

(G-4796)
LANDSLIDE FARM LLP
2638 Woodyard Rd (19952-1931)
PHONE..................................302 566-6418
Denise Corcoran, *Prin*
EMP: 5 EST: 2016
SALES (est): 229.58K **Privately Held**
SIC: 0191 General farms, primarily crop

(G-4797)
LARIMORE INC
2504 High Stump Rd (19952-4581)
PHONE..................................302 632-3618
Patrick Larimore, *Pr*
EMP: 7 EST: 2016
SALES (est): 212.65K **Privately Held**
SIC: 0191 General farms, primarily crop

(G-4798)
LDMASONRY
1665 Sandbox Rd (19952-2670)
PHONE..................................302 270-3386
Debra Phillippi, *Prin*
EMP: 7 EST: 2017
SALES (est): 143.25K **Privately Held**
Web: www.ldmasonry.com
SIC: 1741 Masonry and other stonework

(G-4799)
MARSHALL ANTHONY JR
Roads 111 (19952)
PHONE..................................302 398-3043
Anthony Marshall Junior, *Prin*
EMP: 5 EST: 2004
SALES (est): 154.64K **Privately Held**
SIC: 0119 Cash grains, nec

(G-4800)
MEDICAL CENTER OF HARRINGTON
Also Called: Harrington Medical & Optical
203 Shaw Ave # 205 (19952-1220)
P.O. Box 179 (19952-0179)
PHONE..................................302 398-8704
Vincent Lobo D.o.s., *Owner*
EMP: 6 EST: 1965
SALES (est): 285.63K **Privately Held**
SIC: 8062 General medical and surgical hospitals

(G-4801)
MESSICKS MOBILE HOMES INC
17959 S Dupont Hwy (19952-2136)
PHONE..................................302 398-9166
Ronald Messick, *Pr*
EMP: 10 EST: 1980
SALES (est): 685.23K **Privately Held**
SIC: 4213 1799 Mobile homes transport; Mobile home site set up and tie down

(G-4802)
MICHAEL MATTHEW SPONAUGLE
Also Called: Happy Hoofer
2427 Flatiron Rd (19952-3926)
PHONE..................................302 566-1010
Michael Sponaugle, *Owner*
EMP: 7 EST: 2009
SALES (est): 215.63K **Privately Held**
Web: www.thehappywoofer.com
SIC: 7699 0752 Horseshoeing; Training services, horses (except racing horses)

(G-4803)
MID DEL CHARITY FOUNDATION
15 W Rider Rd (19952-3322)
PHONE..................................302 398-7223
EMP: 7 EST: 2010
SALES (est): 197.5K **Privately Held**
Web: casino.harringtonraceway.com
SIC: 8699 Charitable organization

(G-4804)
MIDWAY SLOTS & SIMULCAST
15 W Rider Rd (19952-3322)
P.O. Box 310 (19952-0310)
PHONE..................................302 398-4920
EMP: 7 EST: 2019
SALES (est): 122.13K **Privately Held**
Web: www.midwayslots.com
SIC: 7993 Coin-operated amusement devices

(G-4805)
MOUNTAIRE FARMS DELAWARE INC
Also Called: Mountaire Farms
615 Fairground Rd (19952-3318)
P.O. Box 218 (19952-0218)
PHONE..................................302 398-3296
Scott Brittingham, *Mgr*
EMP: 5
SALES (corp-wide): 2.07B **Privately Held**
Web: www.mountaire.com
SIC: 5153 Grain elevators
HQ: Mountaire Farms Of Delaware, Inc.
1901 Napa Valley Dr
Little Rock AR 72212
501 372-6524

(G-4806)
MUNCIE INS & FNCL SVCS INC
Also Called: Nationwide
17067 S Dupont Hwy (19952-7403)
PHONE..................................302 398-9100
Marvin Muncie, *Owner*
EMP: 6 EST: 2012
SALES (est): 101.52K **Privately Held**
Web: www.muncieinsurance.net
SIC: 6411 Insurance agents, nec

(G-4807)
OBRYAN WOODWORKS
5400 Vernon Rd (19952-4166)
PHONE..................................302 398-8202
Robert Obryan, *Prin*
EMP: 5 EST: 2016
SALES (est): 64.06K **Privately Held**
SIC: 2431 Millwork

GEOGRAPHIC SECTION   Harrington - Kent County (G-4838)

(G-4808)
PARKER BUILDERS LLC
101 W Mispillion St (19952-1026)
PHONE.....................................302 398-6182
Micah Parker, *Prin*
EMP: 5 **EST:** 2010
SALES (est): 105.77K **Privately Held**
SIC: 1521 New construction, single-family houses

(G-4809)
PERFECT FINISH POWDER COATING
3845 Whiteleysburg Rd (19952-5334)
PHONE.....................................302 566-6189
Steve Curtiss, *Pr*
EMP: 5 **EST:** 2013
SALES (est): 410.38K **Privately Held**
Web: www.perfectfinishde.com
SIC: 3479 Coating of metals and formed products

(G-4810)
PET STOP OF DELMARVA
2416 Flatiron Rd (19952-3903)
PHONE.....................................302 943-2310
Brian A Lewis, *Prin*
EMP: 7 **EST:** 2015
SALES (est): 92.63K **Privately Held**
Web: www.petstopofdelmarva.com
SIC: 1799 Fence construction

(G-4811)
PETROSERV INC
17436 S Dupont Hwy (19952)
PHONE.....................................302 398-3260
William Thompson, *Pr*
EMP: 5 **EST:** 1990
SALES (est): 517.58K **Privately Held**
SIC: 5051 5072 5085 Pipe and tubing, steel; Nozzles; Drums, new or reconditioned

(G-4812)
PHOENIX FITNESS LLC
124 Lucky Ben Dr (19952-6047)
PHONE.....................................302 786-2435
Christina Moritz, *Prin*
EMP: 5 **EST:** 2019
SALES (est): 37.08K **Privately Held**
SIC: 7991 Physical fitness facilities

(G-4813)
PORTER SAND & GRAVEL INC
640 Sandbox Rd (19952-2707)
PHONE.....................................302 335-5132
Frank Porter, *Pr*
EMP: 8 **EST:** 1956
SALES (est): 1.09MM **Privately Held**
Web: porter-sand-gravel.business.site
SIC: 5032 Gravel

(G-4814)
PUCKETTS HEATING ADN AIR ✪
427 Vernon Rd (19952-4737)
PHONE.....................................443 239-2129
David Puckett, *Pr*
EMP: 9 **EST:** 2022
SALES (est): 667.49K **Privately Held**
SIC: 1711 7389 Heating and air conditioning contractors; Business services, nec

(G-4815)
QUALITY EXTERIORS INC
60 Hopkins Cemetery Rd (19952-3149)
P.O. Box 9303 (02889-0303)
PHONE.....................................302 398-9283
Micheal Makdad, *Pr*
EMP: 23 **EST:** 1981
SALES (est): 2.08MM **Privately Held**
Web: www.qexteriorsinc.com

SIC: 1761 Roofing contractor

(G-4816)
R S BAUER LLC
14380 S Dupont Hwy (19952-3104)
PHONE.....................................302 398-4668
EMP: 16 **EST:** 1994
SALES (est): 2.3MM **Privately Held**
Web: www.rsbauerhvac.com
SIC: 1711 Hydronics heating contractor

(G-4817)
R STANLEY COLLIER & SON INC
1832 Brownsville Rd (19952-5017)
PHONE.....................................302 398-7855
R Stanley Collier Junior, *Pr*
R Thomas Collier, *VP*
Faye Collier, *Sec*
EMP: 5 **EST:** 1964
SALES (est): 400.56K **Privately Held**
SIC: 0241 Dairy farms

(G-4818)
RAPID RENOVATION AND REPR LLC
79 Pleasant Pine Ct (19952-6403)
PHONE.....................................302 475-5400
EMP: 5 **EST:** 2011
SALES (est): 243.12K **Privately Held**
Web: www.rapidrenovationandrepair.com
SIC: 1521 General remodeling, single-family houses

(G-4819)
RED TARGET LLC
Also Called: Scj Commercial Financial Svcs
17507 S Dupont Hwy (19952-2378)
PHONE.....................................302 752-4449
EMP: 14 **EST:** 2019
SALES (est): 2.5MM **Privately Held**
Web: www.scjinc.net
SIC: 6153 Purchasers of accounts receivable and commercial paper

(G-4820)
RHONDA REPLOGLE HORSES
281 Marjorie Ln (19952-2525)
PHONE.....................................301 730-3100
EMP: 11 **EST:** 2000
SALES (est): 243.09K **Privately Held**
SIC: 8011 Offices and clinics of medical doctors

(G-4821)
RONS MOBILE HOME SALES INC
17959 S Dupont Hwy (19952-2136)
PHONE.....................................302 398-9166
Michael Smith, *Contrlr*
EMP: 5 **EST:** 1989
SQ FT: 3,000
SALES (est): 448.44K **Privately Held**
Web: www.ronsmobilehomes.com
SIC: 5271 1521 Mobile home dealers; Single-family housing construction

(G-4822)
ROUTZHAN JESSMAN
Also Called: Super 8 Motel
17010 S Dupont Hwy (19952-2477)
PHONE.....................................302 398-4206
EMP: 25 **EST:** 1995
SALES (est): 210.18K **Privately Held**
Web: www.wyndhamhotels.com
SIC: 7011 5812 Hotels and motels; Eating places

(G-4823)
RP HOSPITALITY LLC
17010 S Dupont Hwy (19952-2477)
PHONE.....................................302 398-4206
EMP: 11 **EST:** 2013

SALES (est): 135.36K **Privately Held**
SIC: 7011 Hotels and motels

(G-4824)
RYDER TRUCK
111 Reese Ave (19952-1316)
PHONE.....................................302 398-5106
EMP: 7 **EST:** 2018
SALES (est): 46.21K **Privately Held**
Web: www.ryder.com
SIC: 7513 Truck rental, without drivers

(G-4825)
S BROWN APPRAISALS LLC
16819 S Dupont Hwy Ste 300 (19952-3192)
PHONE.....................................302 672-0694
Scott Brown, *Managing Member*
EMP: 9 **EST:** 2018
SALES (est): 384.58K **Privately Held**
Web: sbrownappraisals.appraiserxsites.com
SIC: 7389 Appraisers, except real estate

(G-4826)
SAMANTHA HUDRAN MASSAGE
231 Delaware Ave (19952-1238)
PHONE.....................................302 382-5851
Samantha J Hudran, *Prin*
EMP: 5 **EST:** 2010
SALES (est): 40K **Privately Held**
Web: www.samanthahudran.com
SIC: 7299 Massage parlor

(G-4827)
SCHATZ MESSICK ENTERPRISES LLC
705 Andrewville Rd (19952-4443)
PHONE.....................................302 398-8646
John Schatzschneider, *Prin*
EMP: 8 **EST:** 2008
SALES (est): 429.45K **Privately Held**
Web: www.schatzmessick.com
SIC: 8748 Business consulting, nec

(G-4828)
SCHIFF FARMS INC (PA)
16054 S Dupont Hwy (19952-3121)
PHONE.....................................302 398-8014
James Schiff, *Pr*
Carol Schiff, *Sec*
EMP: 10 **EST:** 1949
SALES (est): 4.96MM
SALES (corp-wide): 4.96MM **Privately Held**
Web: www.schifffarms.com
SIC: 0212 0115 0116 0111 Beef cattle, except feedlots; Corn; Soybeans; Wheat

(G-4829)
SCHIFF TRANSPORT LLC
16054 S Dupont Hwy (19952-3121)
PHONE.....................................302 398-8014
Terrence Schiff, *Prin*
EMP: 17 **EST:** 2011
SALES (est): 873.28K **Privately Held**
SIC: 4789 Transportation services, nec

(G-4830)
SHARON ALGER-LITTLE DR
6902 Milford Harrington Hwy (19952)
PHONE.....................................302 398-3367
Sharon Alger-little, *Owner*
EMP: 6 **EST:** 1997
SALES (est): 57.48K **Privately Held**
Web: www.alittlevet.com
SIC: 0742 Animal hospital services, pets and other animal specialties

(G-4831)
SHARP RAINGUTTERS
Rte 36 (19952)
PHONE.....................................302 398-4873
EMP: 10 **EST:** 1987
SALES (est): 398.21K **Privately Held**
SIC: 1761 Gutter and downspout contractor

(G-4832)
SHELLS CHILD CARE CENTER III
5332 Milford Harrington Hwy (19952)
PHONE.....................................302 398-9778
Michelle Malavet, *Owner*
EMP: 13 **EST:** 2003
SALES (est): 74.15K **Privately Held**
Web: www.shellschildcare.com
SIC: 8351 Group day care center

(G-4833)
SMITTYS AUTO REPAIR INC
17378 S Dupont Hwy (19952-2464)
PHONE.....................................302 398-8419
Anthony W Smith, *Pr*
EMP: 5 **EST:** 2006
SALES (est): 490.51K **Privately Held**
SIC: 7538 General automotive repair shops

(G-4834)
SMOOTH SOUND DANCE BAND
201 Dorman St (19952-1002)
PHONE.....................................302 398-8467
Tony Perrone, *Dir*
EMP: 5 **EST:** 2010
SALES (est): 39.39K **Privately Held**
SIC: 7929 Dance band

(G-4835)
STAPLES & ASSOCIATES INSURANCE
Also Called: Nationwide
35 Commerce St (19952-1055)
PHONE.....................................302 398-3276
EMP: 6 **EST:** 2017
SALES (est): 103.79K **Privately Held**
Web: www.staplesagency.com
SIC: 6282 6411 Investment advice; Insurance agents, brokers, and service

(G-4836)
STEVENS & JAMES INC
15602 S Dupont Hwy (19952-3117)
PHONE.....................................302 398-6066
Jim Kossman, *Mgr*
EMP: 30 **EST:** 2003
SQ FT: 1,875
SALES (est): 907.39K **Privately Held**
SIC: 7322 Collection agency, except real estate

(G-4837)
SUNNY HOSPITALITY LLC
Also Called: AmericInn
1259 Corn Crib Rd (19952-2266)
PHONE.....................................302 398-3900
Nancy Roberts, *Genl Mgr*
EMP: 41 **EST:** 1995
SALES (est): 236.33K **Privately Held**
Web: www.wyndhamhotels.com
SIC: 7011 Hotels and motels

(G-4838)
SYLVESTER CUSTOM CABINETRY
16869 S Dupont Hwy (19952-2488)
PHONE.....................................302 398-6050
Greg Sylvester, *Owner*
EMP: 4 **EST:** 2010
SALES (est): 222.35K **Privately Held**
Web: www.sylvestercustomcabinetry.com

Harrington - Kent County (G-4839)

SIC: **2434** 3261 Wood kitchen cabinets; Closet bowls, vitreous china

(G-4839)
TAYLOR AND MESSICK INC
Also Called: John Deere Authorized Dealer
325 Walt Messick Rd (19952-3300)
PHONE..................................302 398-3729
James W Messick, *Pr*
Maryann Wilson, *Sec*
Rhonda Lee Shalzschnider, *Treas*
EMP: 23 **EST:** 1951
SQ FT: 7,000
SALES (est): 2.45MM **Privately Held**
Web: www.taylormessick.com
SIC: 5083 Agricultural machinery and equipment

(G-4840)
TELAMON CORPORATION
112 East St (19952-3375)
PHONE..................................302 398-9196
Lurys Fuhrman, *Mgr*
EMP: 6
SALES (corp-wide): 85.01MM **Privately Held**
Web: www.telamon.org
SIC: 8331 Job training services
PA: Telamon Corporation
  5560 Munford Rd Ste 201
  Raleigh NC 27612
  919 851-7611

(G-4841)
TIDEWATER PHYSCL THRPY AND REB
610 Gordon St (19952-1217)
PHONE..................................302 398-7982
Patrick Mckenzie, *Brnch Mgr*
EMP: 6
Web: www.tidewaterpt.com
SIC: 8049 Physical therapist
PA: Tidewater Physical Therapy And Rehabilitation Associates Pa
  406 Marvel Ct
  Easton MD 21601

(G-4842)
UNITED STTES HARN WRTERS ASSOC
5582 Milford Harrington Hwy (19952)
PHONE..................................215 681-0697
Steve Wolf, *BD*
EMP: 5 **EST:** 2017
SALES (est): 35.68K **Privately Held**
Web: www.ushwa.net
SIC: 8631 Labor union

(G-4843)
USA TRANSPORT LLC (PA)
121 Mechanic St (19952-1007)
PHONE..................................302 273-0806
EMP: 6
SALES (est): 159.23K
SALES (corp-wide): 159.23K **Privately Held**
SIC: 4789 Transportation services, nec

(G-4844)
VEER HOTELS INC
Also Called: Quality Inn
1259 Corn Crib Rd (19952-2266)
PHONE..................................302 398-3900
Jigar Patel, *Pr*
EMP: 8 **EST:** 2013
SALES (est): 645.14K **Privately Held**
Web: www.choicehotels.com
SIC: 7011 Hotels and motels

(G-4845)
VINCENT LOBO DR PA
203 Shaw Ave # 205 (19952-1220)
P.O. Box 179 (19952-0179)
PHONE..................................302 398-8163
Vincent Lobo Junior, *Pr*
EMP: 5 **EST:** 1966
SQ FT: 2,400
SALES (est): 151.04K **Privately Held**
SIC: 8031 Offices and clinics of osteopathic physicians

(G-4846)
WESTMOR INDUSTRIES
17409 S Dupont Hwy (19952-2312)
P.O. Box 219 (19933-0219)
PHONE..................................302 398-3253
EMP: 8 **EST:** 2016
SALES (est): 95.39K **Privately Held**
Web: www.westmor-ind.com
SIC: 3999 Manufacturing industries, nec

(G-4847)
WILSON MASONRY CORP
1229 Staytonville Rd (19952-1849)
PHONE..................................302 398-8240
Linda Wilson, *Owner*
EMP: 14 **EST:** 1998
SALES (est): 1.77MM **Privately Held**
SIC: 1741 Masonry and other stonework

(G-4848)
WONDER YEARS KIDS CLUB
17629 S Dupont Hwy (19952-2369)
PHONE..................................302 398-0563
Denise Halcomb, *Dir*
Judy Williams, *Owner*
Kathleen Kagle, *Owner*
EMP: 10 **EST:** 2001
SALES (est): 312.4K **Privately Held**
SIC: 8351 Group day care center

(G-4849)
WRIGHT ROBERT STEELE
1783 Whiteleysburg Rd (19952-5151)
PHONE..................................302 423-2093
Robert Wright, *Prin*
EMP: 5 **EST:** 2013
SALES (est): 114.4K **Privately Held**
SIC: 1522 Residential construction, nec

(G-4850)
WTM BUILDERS
1262 Gun And Rod Club Rd (19952-2028)
PHONE..................................302 398-9522
William Moffett, *Prin*
EMP: 5 **EST:** 2017
SALES (est): 116.29K **Privately Held**
SIC: 1521 New construction, single-family houses

(G-4851)
WYATT & BROWN INC
15602 S Dupont Hwy (19952-3117)
PHONE..................................302 786-2793
EMP: 8 **EST:** 2010
SALES (est): 462.8K **Privately Held**
SIC: 7322 Collection agency, except real estate

(G-4852)
XTREME CLEANING
820 Cedar Grove Church Rd (19952-5638)
PHONE..................................302 331-1084
Kimberly Cohee, *Prin*
EMP: 6 **EST:** 2016
SALES (est): 49.23K **Privately Held**
Web: www.xtremecleaningrestoration.com
SIC: 7699 Cleaning services

Hartly
Kent County

(G-4853)
ABC CONTRACTORS LLC
4491 Arthursville Rd (19953-3124)
PHONE..................................302 492-1116
Arthur Brewer, *Prin*
EMP: 10 **EST:** 2014
SALES (est): 182.46K **Privately Held**
SIC: 8611 Contractors' association

(G-4854)
AFFORD-A-TREE SVC & LDSCPG LLC
118 Downes Dr (19953-2051)
PHONE..................................302 670-4154
EMP: 8 **EST:** 2021
SALES (est): 96.48K **Privately Held**
SIC: 0783 7389 Ornamental shrub and tree services; Business Activities at Non-Commercial Site

(G-4855)
AIR DOCTORX INC
Also Called: Honeywell Authorized Dealer
4639 Halltown Rd Ste B (19953-2614)
P.O. Box 267 (19953-0267)
PHONE..................................302 492-1333
EMP: 10 **EST:** 1989
SALES (est): 951.34K **Privately Held**
Web: www.airdoctorx.com
SIC: 1711 Warm air heating and air conditioning contractor

(G-4856)
AMANDA F BODINE
1652 Hourglass Rd (19953-2809)
PHONE..................................302 270-5579
James Bodine, *Prin*
EMP: 5 **EST:** 2017
SALES (est): 174.51K **Privately Held**
Web: www.bodinefarm.com
SIC: 0191 General farms, primarily crop

(G-4857)
BOOTH WYN HEATING & AC
1052 Everetts Corner Rd (19953-3440)
PHONE..................................302 737-7170
Tom Deandrea, *Prin*
EMP: 6 **EST:** 2007
SALES (est): 154.81K **Privately Held**
SIC: 1711 Warm air heating and air conditioning contractor

(G-4858)
BOOTHWYN HEATING & AC INC
1052 Everetts Corner Rd (19953-3440)
PHONE..................................302 284-2772
Thomas D'andreamatteo, *Pr*
Linda D'andreamatteo, *Sec*
EMP: 13 **EST:** 1975
SALES (est): 494.12K **Privately Held**
SIC: 1711 Warm air heating and air conditioning contractor

(G-4859)
BOYDS CUSTOM REMODELING INC
2429 Tower Rd (19953-1956)
PHONE..................................302 698-1739
EMP: 6 **EST:** 2007
SALES (est): 471.5K **Privately Held**
Web: www.boydscustomremodelinginc.com
SIC: 1521 General remodeling, single-family houses

(G-4860)
CANNON IRON AND METAL INC
3221 Hartly Rd (19953-2744)
PHONE..................................302 492-8091
EMP: 5 **EST:** 2019
SALES (est): 98.68K **Privately Held**
SIC: 4953 Recycling, waste materials

(G-4861)
CARING HEARTS HOME CARE LLC
971 Burris Rd (19953-3515)
PHONE..................................302 734-9000
EMP: 11 **EST:** 2014
SALES (est): 449.21K **Privately Held**
SIC: 8082 Home health care services

(G-4862)
CASEY BATTLES CONCRETE
1423 Everetts Corner Rd (19953-3464)
PHONE..................................302 312-3905
Casey Battles, *Prin*
EMP: 8 **EST:** 2018
SALES (est): 484.44K **Privately Held**
Web: www.caseybattlesconcrete.com
SIC: 1771 Concrete work

(G-4863)
CENTRAL HEATING A CONDTIONING
2114 Fords Corner Rd (19953-3536)
PHONE..................................302 492-1169
Roland Timmons, *Prin*
EMP: 7 **EST:** 2008
SALES (est): 177K **Privately Held**
SIC: 1711 Warm air heating and air conditioning contractor

(G-4864)
D GINGERICH CONCRETE & MASNRY
952 Myers Dr (19953-3034)
P.O. Box 242 (19953-0242)
PHONE..................................302 492-8662
Connie Gingerich, *Pr*
David Ginerich, *VP*
EMP: 14 **EST:** 1987
SQ FT: 500
SALES (est): 695.48K **Privately Held**
SIC: 1771 Concrete work

(G-4865)
D S BUILDERS
1325 Tuxward Rd (19953-1979)
PHONE..................................302 242-3308
EMP: 8 **EST:** 2019
SALES (est): 104.3K **Privately Held**
Web: www.dsbuilders.org
SIC: 1521 New construction, single-family houses

(G-4866)
DAN H BEACHY & SONS INC
1298 Lockwood Chapel Rd (19953-3050)
PHONE..................................302 492-1493
Alva Beachy, *Pr*
EMP: 9 **EST:** 1980
SALES (est): 1.02MM **Privately Held**
Web: www.danhbeachy.com
SIC: 1542 1541 Farm building construction; Warehouse construction

(G-4867)
DAN MILLER AND SONS CNSTR LLC
5790 Halltown Rd (19953-2539)
PHONE..................................302 492-8116
Dan J Miller, *Owner*
EMP: 5 **EST:** 2012
SALES (est): 78.21K **Privately Held**
SIC: 1521 Single-family housing construction

GEOGRAPHIC SECTION
Hartly - Kent County (G-4900)

(G-4868)
DESS MACHINE & MANUFACTURING
1426 Pearsons Corner Rd (19953-2335)
PHONE....................302 736-7457
Martin Graham, *Pr*
Susan Graham, *VP*
Evan Graham, *Treas*
Stacey Graham, *Sec*
EMP: 2 **EST:** 1987
SALES (est): 241.87K **Privately Held**
Web: www.dessmachine.com
SIC: 3599 Machine shop, jobbing and repair

(G-4869)
DETWEILERS LIGHTING
285 Pearsons Corner Rd R (19953-2364)
PHONE....................302 678-5804
EMP: 2 **EST:** 2010
SALES (est): 226.37K **Privately Held**
SIC: 3648 Lighting equipment, nec

(G-4870)
DREAM STRUCTURES LLC
1998 Tower Rd (19953-1950)
PHONE....................302 943-3974
John Sapp Junior, *Prin*
EMP: 7 **EST:** 2018
SALES (est): 407.67K **Privately Held**
SIC: 1522 Residential construction, nec

(G-4871)
DYNAMIC AIR LLC
3354 Arthursville Rd (19953-3106)
PHONE....................302 612-1412
Stephen Yoder, *Managing Member*
EMP: 5
SALES (est): 267.9K **Privately Held**
SIC: 1711 Heating and air conditioning contractors

(G-4872)
EDWARD KRUPKA
Also Called: Genesis Deer Farm
1079 Lockwood Chapel Rd (19953-3153)
PHONE....................302 492-0833
Edward Krupka, *Prin*
EMP: 5 **EST:** 2011
SALES (est): 52.85K **Privately Held**
SIC: 0191 General farms, primarily crop

(G-4873)
ELECTRICAL ASSOCIATES INC
959 Hazletville Rd (19953-2417)
P.O. Box 381 (19934-0381)
PHONE....................302 678-1068
William Webb, *Pr*
Glenn Cillen, *VP*
EMP: 5 **EST:** 2000
SALES (est): 398.08K **Privately Held**
SIC: 1731 General electrical contractor

(G-4874)
EVERGREEN WOOD PRODUCTS LLC
4763 Halltown Rd (19953-2613)
PHONE....................302 697-2588
EMP: 5 **EST:** 2017
SALES (est): 215.54K **Privately Held**
Web: www.evergreenwoodproducts.com
SIC: 5099 Wood and wood by-products

(G-4875)
HARTLY FAMILY LEARNING CTR LLC
21 North St (19953-2936)
P.O. Box 138 (19953-0138)
PHONE....................302 492-1152
Connie Richards, *Owner*
EMP: 12 **EST:** 2004
SALES (est): 223.47K **Privately Held**
Web: www.hartlyfamily.org

SIC: 8351 Preschool center

(G-4876)
HB WINE MERCHANTS LLC
Also Called: Hbwm
884 Arthursville Rd (19953-3301)
PHONE....................302 384-5991
▲ **EMP:** 5 **EST:** 2002
SALES (est): 941.64K **Privately Held**
Web: www.hbwinemerchants.com
SIC: 5182 Wine

(G-4877)
HERITAGE SPORTS RDO NETWRK LLC
1841 Bryants Corner Rd (19953-2247)
PHONE....................302 492-1132
David Jones, *Prin*
EMP: 9 **EST:** 2007
SALES (est): 711.91K **Privately Held**
Web: www.hsrn.com
SIC: 4832 Radio broadcasting stations

(G-4878)
HILLANDALE FARMS DELAWARE INC
Also Called: Sydell-Hillandale Farms
149 Sydell Dr (19953-3584)
P.O. Box 269 (19953-0269)
PHONE....................302 492-3644
Ian Sydell, *Genl Mgr*
Chuck Vincent, *
Rita Fabi, *
EMP: 30 **EST:** 2001
SALES (est): 3.07MM **Privately Held**
SIC: 2499 Food handling and processing products, wood

(G-4879)
INSIDE & OUT PROPERTY MGT LLC
386 Main St (19953-4007)
P.O. Box 165 (19953-0165)
PHONE....................302 632-4467
Mark Maguire, *Prin*
EMP: 5 **EST:** 2016
SALES (est): 85.09K **Privately Held**
SIC: 8741 Management services

(G-4880)
JADE LOGISTICS INC
5 Sherwood Forest Way (19953-3000)
PHONE....................302 724-2649
Joshua Davis, *Pr*
EMP: 6
SALES (est): 82.43K **Privately Held**
SIC: 4731 Freight transportation arrangement

(G-4881)
JAMES RAY FAMILY & FRIENDS LLC
5102 Halltown Rd (19953-2533)
PHONE....................302 670-0305
Dallas L Ray, *Prin*
EMP: 5 **EST:** 2012
SALES (est): 113.88K **Privately Held**
SIC: 7389 Business services, nec

(G-4882)
JOHN J MAST
2777 Hartly Rd (19953-2749)
PHONE....................302 492-1356
John Mast, *Prin*
EMP: 5 **EST:** 2012
SALES (est): 108.74K **Privately Held**
SIC: 1522 Residential construction, nec

(G-4883)
JOHN MOBILE SNDBLST & PAIN
683 Hartly Rd (19953-2922)
PHONE....................302 270-5627
EMP: 8 **EST:** 2009

SALES (est): 352.15K **Privately Held**
SIC: 1721 Painting and paper hanging

(G-4884)
JOHNS WOODWORKING LLC
84 Tack Shop Ln (19953-1860)
PHONE....................302 492-3527
EMP: 5 **EST:** 2018
SALES (est): 78.48K **Privately Held**
SIC: 2431 Millwork

(G-4885)
JOSEPH SMITH & SONS INC
3221 Hartly Rd (19953-2744)
PHONE....................302 492-8091
Ronald Demoss, *Brnch Mgr*
EMP: 7
Web: www.smithindustriesgroup.com
SIC: 5093 Metal scrap and waste materials
HQ: Joseph Smith & Sons, Inc.
2001 Kenilworth Ave
Capitol Heights MD 20743
301 773-1266

(G-4886)
JOSHUA S STEVENS
Also Called: Josh's Contracting Services
1385 Lockwood Chapel Rd (19953-3060)
PHONE....................302 492-3450
Joshua S Stevens, *Prin*
EMP: 10 **EST:** 2010
SALES (est): 457.45K **Privately Held**
SIC: 1799 Special trade contractors, nec

(G-4887)
JT ENTERPRISE LLC
1752 Halltown Rd (19953-1765)
PHONE....................302 492-8119
Jamie Cassidy, *Mgr*
EMP: 8 **EST:** 2003
SALES (est): 336.11K **Privately Held**
SIC: 1623 Underground utilities contractor

(G-4888)
JUSTIN MAYNARD
567 Tuxward Rd (19953-1929)
PHONE....................302 233-6086
Maynard Justin, *Prin*
EMP: 5 **EST:** 2012
SALES (est): 170.53K **Privately Held**
SIC: 1522 Residential construction, nec

(G-4889)
KENT CONTRACTING LLC
882 Tappahana Bridge Rd (19953-1739)
PHONE....................302 233-3157
Charles Daniel, *Prin*
EMP: 5 **EST:** 2016
SALES (est): 94.38K **Privately Held**
SIC: 1799 Special trade contractors, nec

(G-4890)
KINGDOM KIDS DAY CARE
Also Called: Kingdom of God Fellowship
2899 Arthursville Rd (19953-3141)
P.O. Box 196 (19953-0196)
PHONE....................302 492-0207
Judy P Nazelrod, *Dir*
EMP: 10 **EST:** 1991
SALES (est): 219.42K **Privately Held**
SIC: 8351 Group day care center

(G-4891)
KINGS MASONRY LLC
2685 Hartly Rd (19953-2750)
PHONE....................302 632-6783
EMP: 5 **EST:** 2011
SALES (est): 146.97K **Privately Held**
SIC: 1741 Masonry and other stonework

(G-4892)
KOVACH S CONSTRUCTION
55 Sherwood Forest Way (19953-3000)
PHONE....................302 363-4130
James Kovach, *Owner*
EMP: 5 **EST:** 2009
SALES (est): 151.33K **Privately Held**
SIC: 1521 Single-family housing construction

(G-4893)
KRISS CONTRACTING INC
1523 Gunter Rd (19953)
P.O. Box 246 (19953-0246)
PHONE....................302 492-3502
Veronica Kriss, *Pr*
Kathleen Kriss, *VP*
EMP: 20 **EST:** 1979
SALES (est): 1.92MM **Privately Held**
SIC: 1731 7389 Electrical work; Business Activities at Non-Commercial Site

(G-4894)
M&M SMALL ENGINE REPAIR
1254 Gunter Rd (19953-1717)
PHONE....................302 270-3941
Mark Shahan, *Prin*
EMP: 5 **EST:** 2016
SALES (est): 56.2K **Privately Held**
SIC: 7538 Engine repair

(G-4895)
MAYHORNS COLLISIONANDRESTORATN
3002 Judith Rd (19953-3010)
PHONE....................302 779-2177
Greg Mayhorn, *Prin*
EMP: 5 **EST:** 2017
SALES (est): 105.32K **Privately Held**
SIC: 1799 Special trade contractors, nec

(G-4896)
MIA BELLAS CANDLES
697 Judith Rd (19953-2663)
PHONE....................302 331-7038
Dawn Walker, *Prin*
EMP: 4 **EST:** 2018
SALES (est): 39.69K **Privately Held**
SIC: 3999 Candles

(G-4897)
MILLERS MASONRY & BLOCK LLC
1780 Yoder Dr (19953-2445)
PHONE....................302 222-4091
EMP: 6 **EST:** 2009
SALES (est): 135.67K **Privately Held**
SIC: 1741 Masonry and other stonework

(G-4898)
MILLERS ROOFING & COATING LLC
305 Pine Tree Rd (19953-2135)
PHONE....................302 943-8988
EMP: 6 **EST:** 2019
SALES (est): 268.51K **Privately Held**
SIC: 1761 Roofing contractor

(G-4899)
MORNING AFTER INC
5006 Halltown Rd (19953-2532)
PHONE....................302 562-5190
Harriet W Glover, *Ex Dir*
EMP: 5 **EST:** 2009
SALES (est): 45.56K **Privately Held**
SIC: 8699 7389 Charitable organization; Business services, nec

(G-4900)
NATIONWIDE INVENTORY SVCS INC
P.O. Box 264 (19953-0264)
PHONE....................888 741-3039
EMP: 6 **EST:** 2013

Hartly - Kent County (G-4901)

SALES (est): 78.74K **Privately Held**
Web: www.nationwideinv.com
SIC: 8742 Materials mgmt. (purchasing, handling, inventory) consultant

(G-4901)
NORMAN YODER CONSTRUCTION
1875 Pearsons Corner Rd (19953-2530)
PHONE.....................................302 492-3516
Norman Yoder, *Owner*
EMP: 7 EST: 2005
SALES (est): 209.64K **Privately Held**
SIC: 1521 Single-family housing construction

(G-4902)
PHYSICAL THRAPY BOKKEEPING LLC
645 Hazlettville Rd (19953-2344)
PHONE.....................................302 505-5721
Alyssa Hermosisima, *Prin*
EMP: 6 EST: 2017
SALES (est): 53.71K **Privately Held**
SIC: 8049 Physical therapist

(G-4903)
PONY RUN KITCHENS LLC
Also Called: Pony Run Kitchens
5066 Westville Rd (19953-2106)
PHONE.....................................302 492-3006
EMP: 5 EST: 2008
SALES (est): 265.71K **Privately Held**
SIC: 2514 3089 3263 Kitchen cabinets: metal; Kitchenware, plastics; Kitchen articles, semivitreous earthenware

(G-4904)
PRECISION LDSCPG & LAWN CARE
286 Judith Rd (19953-2648)
PHONE.....................................302 492-1583
Mike Nagyiski, *Mng Pt*
EMP: 9 EST: 2004
SALES (est): 503.71K **Privately Held**
Web: www.precisionlandscapingandlawncare.com
SIC: 0781 Landscape services

(G-4905)
PURPLE MOON HERBS STUDIES LLC
1841 Bryants Corner Rd (19953-2247)
PHONE.....................................302 270-5095
EMP: 6 EST: 2019
SALES (est): 246.89K **Privately Held**
Web: www.purplemoonherbstudies.com
SIC: 8399 Advocacy group

(G-4906)
REXMEX DRYWALL LLC
449 Gibbs Chapel Rd (19953-3427)
PHONE.....................................302 343-9140
EMP: 7 EST: 2010
SALES (est): 219.55K **Privately Held**
SIC: 1742 Drywall

(G-4907)
ROBERT C THOMPSON
Also Called: Thompson's Farm
671 Bryants Corner Rd (19953-1974)
PHONE.....................................302 492-1053
Robert C Thompson, *Owner*
EMP: 5 EST: 2002
SQ FT: 3,288
SALES (est): 647.69K **Privately Held**
SIC: 0141 Dairy farms

(G-4908)
SJ BUILDERS LLC
1578 Fords Corner Rd (19953-3530)
PHONE.....................................302 242-8222
EMP: 8 EST: 2017
SALES (est): 474.48K **Privately Held**
SIC: 1521 New construction, single-family houses

(G-4909)
SWARTZENTRUBER SAWMILL CO
1191 Pearsons Corner Rd (19953-2355)
PHONE.....................................302 492-1665
Norman Wilkerson, *Pr*
Henry Swartzentruber, *VP*
Gertrude Swartzentruber, *Sec*
EMP: 8 EST: 1945
SALES (est): 465.37K **Privately Held**
SIC: 2421 Sawmills and planing mills, general

(G-4910)
TUDOR ENTERPRISES L L C
Also Called: Tudor Enterprises
4405 Arthursville Rd (19953-3124)
PHONE.....................................302 736-8255
EMP: 5 EST: 1983
SALES (est): 451.22K **Privately Held**
Web: www.tudorenterprisesllc.com
SIC: 6512 Commercial and industrial building operation

(G-4911)
U-HAUL NEIGHBORHOOD DEALER
Also Called: U-Haul
324 Main St (19953-4007)
PHONE.....................................302 343-7497
EMP: 6 EST: 2016
SALES (est): 63.6K **Privately Held**
Web: www.uhaul.com
SIC: 7513 Truck rental and leasing, no drivers

(G-4912)
WJ MCDOUGALL RACING INC
215 Hartly Rd (19953-2927)
PHONE.....................................302 492-8248
J Y Mcdougall, *Prin*
EMP: 6 EST: 2006
SALES (est): 34.85K **Privately Held**
SIC: 7948 Racing, including track operation

(G-4913)
YODERS MAINTENANCE
488 Myers Dr (19953-3029)
PHONE.....................................302 492-0203
Chrles Yoder, *Prin*
EMP: 5 EST: 2014
SALES (est): 25.41K **Privately Held**
SIC: 7349 Building maintenance services, nec

Historic New Castle
New Castle County

(G-4914)
3D EXHIBITS INC
200 Centerpoint Blvd Ste A (19720-4175)
PHONE.....................................302 319-1051
EMP: 6 EST: 2019
SALES (est): 63.76K **Privately Held**
Web: www.3dexhibits.com
SIC: 7389 Advertising, promotional, and trade show services

(G-4915)
730 ENTERPRISES LLC
730 Ferry Cut Off St (19720-5072)
PHONE.....................................216 355-3008
Steven Velitsakis, *Owner*
EMP: 5 EST: 2016
SALES (est): 231.12K **Privately Held**
SIC: 7389 Business services, nec

(G-4916)
855 INC
Also Called: Anthony D'S Auto Repair
464 Moores Ln (19720-4481)
PHONE.....................................302 325-9100
Doug Salter, *Prin*
EMP: 5 EST: 2014
SALES (est): 89.17K **Privately Held**
SIC: 8721 Accounting services, except auditing

(G-4917)
A DUIE PYLE INC
204 Quigley Blvd (19720-4106)
PHONE.....................................302 326-9440
Duie Latta, *Pr*
EMP: 63
SALES (corp-wide): 308.57MM **Privately Held**
Web: www.aduiepyle.com
SIC: 4213 Trucking, except local
PA: A. Duie Pyle Inc.
650 Westtown Rd
West Chester PA 19382
610 696-5800

(G-4918)
AAA MIDATLANTIC INC
19 Lukens Dr Ste 100 (19720-2787)
PHONE.....................................800 999-4952
EMP: 14 EST: 2011
SALES (est): 229.33K **Privately Held**
SIC: 6411 Insurance agents, nec

(G-4919)
ACTION UNLIMITED RESOURCES INC
230 Quigley Blvd (19720-4106)
PHONE.....................................302 323-1455
Aaron Glazar, *Pr*
EMP: 21 EST: 1982
SQ FT: 35,000
SALES (est): 5.66MM **Privately Held**
Web: www.actioncleanup.com
SIC: 7359 2621 5169 Stores and yards equipment rental; Paper mills; Chemicals and allied products, nec

(G-4920)
ADAM R NECELIS CPA LLC
700 Delaware St (19720-5060)
PHONE.....................................302 322-1135
EMP: 5 EST: 2018
SALES (est): 230.32K **Privately Held**
Web: www.neceliscpa.com
SIC: 8721 Certified public accountant

(G-4921)
ADT LLC
140 Quigley Blvd (19720-4104)
PHONE.....................................302 613-4745
Eric Orosco, *Mgr*
EMP: 134
SALES (corp-wide): 6.4B **Publicly Held**
Web: www.adt.com
SIC: 7382 Burglar alarm maintenance and monitoring
HQ: Adt Llc
1501 W Yamato Rd
Boca Raton FL 33431
561 988-3600

(G-4922)
ADVANCE OFFICE INSTLLTIONS INC
37 Lukens Dr Ste B (19720-7710)
PHONE.....................................302 777-5599
Joseph Culter, *VP*
EMP: 40 EST: 2005
SALES (est): 4.54MM **Privately Held**
Web: www.aoi-inc.us
SIC: 1799 4214 7641 4225 Office furniture installation; Furniture moving and storage, local; Office furniture repair and maintenance; General warehousing and storage

(G-4923)
AFFORDABLE CONTRACTOR
400 Delaware St (19720-5040)
PHONE.....................................302 670-5699
EMP: 5 EST: 2014
SALES (est): 124.82K **Privately Held**
SIC: 1799 Special trade contractors, nec

(G-4924)
AFFORDABLE HEATING & AC
1700 Wilmington Rd (19720-2749)
PHONE.....................................302 328-9220
William J Burns, *Pr*
EMP: 5 EST: 1990
SALES (est): 497.28K **Privately Held**
Web: www.affordableair.org
SIC: 1711 Warm air heating and air conditioning contractor

(G-4925)
AGILENT TECHNOLOGIES INC
500 Ships Landing Way (19720-4578)
PHONE.....................................302 633-7337
Dave Terry, *Pr*
EMP: 9 EST: 2014
SALES (est): 190.06K **Privately Held**
Web: www.agilent.com
SIC: 3545 Precision measuring tools

(G-4926)
AIRCRAFTERS LLC ◆
259 Quigley Blvd Ste 12-18 (19720-4186)
PHONE.....................................302 777-5000
Jim Hicks, *Pr*
EMP: 15 EST: 2022
SALES (est): 1.12MM
SALES (corp-wide): 32.9MM **Privately Held**
SIC: 5088 Aircraft and space vehicle supplies and parts
PA: Aero 3, Inc.
41 Tinker Ave
Londonderry NH 03053
603 657-7336

(G-4927)
ALLSTON CHEMICAL SUPPLY INC
Also Called: Philip Rosenau
264 Quigley Blvd (19720-4106)
PHONE.....................................302 322-3952
Phillip Rosenau, *Pr*
EMP: 8 EST: 1965
SQ FT: 5,000
SALES (est): 730K **Privately Held**
SIC: 5087 Janitors' supplies

(G-4928)
ALMARS OUTBOARD SERVICE & SLS
701 Washington St (19720-6046)
PHONE.....................................302 328-8541
Albert Marinelli Junior, *Pr*
EMP: 9 EST: 1980
SQ FT: 16,000
SALES (est): 928.04K **Privately Held**
Web: www.almarsoutboards.net
SIC: 7699 5551 Marine engine repair; Outboard motors

(G-4929)
ALPHA OMEGA COMMUNITY SVC CTR
806 Tremont St (19720-6045)
PHONE.....................................302 323-1311

Robert Godwin, *Pr*
EMP: 5 **EST:** 2010
SALES (est): 109.97K **Privately Held**
SIC: 8322 Community center

(G-4930)
AMAZONCOM SERVICES LLC
Also Called: Amazon.Com
1 Centerpoint Blvd (19720-4172)
PHONE.................206 266-1000
Mark Masadrea, *Brnch Mgr*
EMP: 94
Web: www.amazon.com
SIC: 4225 General warehousing and storage
HQ: Amazon.Com Services Llc
410 Terry Ave N
Seattle WA 98109
206 266-1000

(G-4931)
AMERICAN TRAFFIC PD LLC
122 Delaware St (19720-4814)
PHONE.................302 883-7263
EMP: 45 **EST:** 2019
SALES (est): 1.55MM **Privately Held**
SIC: 7359 Work zone traffic equipment (flags, cones, barrels, etc.)

(G-4932)
ANIXTER POWER SOLUTIONS INC
Also Called: Anixter
599 Ships Landing Way (19720-4578)
PHONE.................302 298-3601
EMP: 12
Web: www.distributiondynamics.com
SIC: 5063 Electrical apparatus and equipment
HQ: Anixter Power Solutions Inc.
2301 Patriot Blvd
Glenview IL 60026

(G-4933)
APRIL MRIES HAIR DESIGN STUDIO
202 E 6th St Ste D (19720-4566)
PHONE.................302 981-3386
April Briseno, *Prin*
EMP: 5 **EST:** 2010
SALES (est): 68K **Privately Held**
SIC: 7231 Hairdressers

(G-4934)
ARS NEW CASTLE LLC
263 Quigley Blvd Ste 1b (19720-8126)
PHONE.................302 323-9400
Daniel Ennis, *Managing Member*
EMP: 13 **EST:** 2010
SALES (est): 964.02K **Privately Held**
Web: www.arshealth.com
SIC: 8069 Drug addiction rehabilitation hospital

(G-4935)
ARS OF RIO GRANDE LLC
263 Quigley Blvd (19720-8112)
PHONE.................302 323-9400
EMP: 49
SALES (corp-wide): 457.73K **Privately Held**
SIC: 8069 Drug addiction rehabilitation hospital
PA: Ars Of Rio Grande Llc
150 Onix Dr
Kennett Square PA
302 427-8181

(G-4936)
ASW MACHINERY INC (DH)
Also Called: Felder USA
2 Lukens Dr Ste 300 (19720-2796)
PHONE.................866 792-5288
◆ **EMP:** 16 **EST:** 1995
SQ FT: 7,800
SALES (est): 10.97MM
SALES (corp-wide): 12.59MM **Privately Held**
SIC: 5084 Woodworking machinery
HQ: Felder Kg
Kr-Felder-StraBe 1
Hall In Tirol 6060
522358500

(G-4937)
AXESS CORPORATION (PA)
91 Lukens Dr Ste E (19720-2799)
PHONE.................302 292-8500
Richard Giacco, *Pr*
EMP: 3 **EST:** 1990
SALES (est): 4.76MM **Privately Held**
Web: www.empowermaterials.com
SIC: 3826 3089 3081 Analytical instruments; Plastics containers, except foam; Unsupported plastics film and sheet

(G-4938)
BATTLE AXE LLC
616 Delaware St (19720-5058)
PHONE.................302 437-4283
Michael Evans, *Prin*
EMP: 5 **EST:** 2018
SALES (est): 61.76K **Privately Held**
SIC: 7999 Amusement and recreation, nec

(G-4939)
BEAST OF EAST BASEBALL LLC
916 Gray St (19720-6036)
PHONE.................302 545-9094
EMP: 5 **EST:** 2018
SALES (est): 101.36K **Privately Held**
Web: www.beastoftheeast.org
SIC: 7997 Baseball club, except professional and semi-professional

(G-4940)
BENCHMARK TRANSMISSIONS
1 Merit Dr (19720-3683)
PHONE.................302 221-5380
Joseph Principe, *Mgr*
EMP: 6 **EST:** 2018
SALES (est): 43.2K **Privately Held**
Web: www.benchmarkonline.biz
SIC: 7537 Automotive transmission repair shops

(G-4941)
BEST WAREHOUSE AND TRNSP LLC
350 Anchor Mill Rd (19720-4574)
PHONE.................302 328-5371
Winston Mcdonald Junior, *CEO*
EMP: 9 **EST:** 2016
SALES (est): 445.31K **Privately Held**
Web: www.bestwtc.com
SIC: 4789 Transportation services, nec

(G-4942)
BEVS CRAFTING SUPPLIES LLC
147 Quigley Blvd (19720-4103)
PHONE.................302 252-7583
EMP: 5 **EST:** 2021
SALES (est): 20K **Privately Held**
SIC: 2051 Bakery: wholesale or wholesale/retail combined

(G-4943)
BLUE MARBLE LOGISTICS LLC
263 Quigley Blvd Ste 3 (19720-8112)
PHONE.................302 221-4674
Bill Rinick, *Brnch Mgr*
EMP: 6
SALES (corp-wide): 2.84MM **Privately Held**
Web: bluemarbledd.homestead.co
SIC: 4215 Courier services, except by air
PA: Blue Marble Logistics Llc
800 N King St Ste 102
Wilmington DE 19801
302 661-4390

(G-4944)
BOLLINGER CLEANING SERVICE LLC
1403 Wilmington Rd (19720-3614)
P.O. Box 878 (21922-0878)
PHONE.................410 620-1953
Steven Bollinger, *Mgr*
EMP: 5 **EST:** 2009
SALES (est): 91.44K **Privately Held**
SIC: 7699 Cleaning services

(G-4945)
BRIDGEWATER JEWELERS
318 Delaware St (19720-5038)
P.O. Box 44 (19720-0044)
PHONE.................302 328-2101
Mary F Lenhoff, *Owner*
EMP: 5 **EST:** 1883
SQ FT: 2,000
SALES (est): 387.24K **Privately Held**
Web: www.bridgewaterjewelers.com
SIC: 7631 5944 Watch repair; Watches

(G-4946)
BROWNSTONE LLC
200 Centerpoint Blvd Ste A (19720-4175)
PHONE.................302 300-4370
EMP: 6 **EST:** 2016
SALES (est): 374.29K **Privately Held**
SIC: 8741 Business management

(G-4947)
BUCHI CORPORATION (HQ)
19 Lukens Dr Ste 400 (19720-2787)
PHONE.................302 652-3000
Thomas Liner, *CEO*
Herve Lacombe, *
▲ **EMP:** 37 **EST:** 2000
SALES (est): 30.38MM **Privately Held**
Web: www.buchi.com
SIC: 5049 Laboratory equipment, except medical or dental
PA: Buchi Labortechnik Ag
Meierseggstrasse 40
Flawil SG 9230

(G-4948)
BURRIS LOGISTICS
Also Called: Burris Refrigerated Logistics
1000 Centerpoint Blvd (19720-8124)
PHONE.................302 221-4100
Eric Fears, *Brnch Mgr*
EMP: 118
SALES (corp-wide): 1.24B **Privately Held**
Web: www.burrislogistics.com
SIC: 4225 4222 4213 General warehousing and storage; Storage, frozen or refrigerated goods; Refrigerated products transport
PA: Burris Logistics
501 Se 5th St
Milford DE 19963
302 839-4531

(G-4949)
BYERS ELECTRICAL CONSTRUC
508 South St (19720-5024)
PHONE.................302 420-8700
EMP: 9 **EST:** 2017
SALES (est): 430.18K **Privately Held**
Web: www.byersindustrial.com
SIC: 1521 Single-family housing construction

(G-4950)
CAD IMPORT INC
650 Centerpoint Blvd (19720-8108)
PHONE.................302 628-4178
Vicky Deleon, *null ACCT RECB*
Tanya Roblero, *
▲ **EMP:** 30 **EST:** 2010
SALES (est): 8.21MM **Privately Held**
Web: www.pharmadelusa.com
SIC: 5087 7389 Beauty parlor equipment and supplies; Labeling bottles, cans, cartons, etc.

(G-4951)
CANDOR TRADING CORP
122 Delaware St (19720-4814)
PHONE.................302 268-6800
Alex Schmidt, *CEO*
EMP: 5 **EST:** 2014
SALES (est): 169.93K **Privately Held**
SIC: 5199 Nondurable goods, nec

(G-4952)
CARTER PRINTING AND DESIGN
427 Martin Dr (19720-2759)
PHONE.................302 655-2343
Robert Carter, *Pr*
EMP: 3 **EST:** 2008
SALES (est): 117.01K **Privately Held**
Web: www.delawarescreenprint.com
SIC: 2261 Screen printing of cotton broadwoven fabrics

(G-4953)
CEDAR LANE INC
Also Called: Oak Knoll Books
310 Delaware St (19720-5038)
PHONE.................302 328-7232
Robert D Fleck Junior, *Pr*
Mildred Fleck, *VP*
▲ **EMP:** 10 **EST:** 1976
SQ FT: 15,000
SALES (est): 912.46K **Privately Held**
Web: www.oakknoll.com
SIC: 5961 2731 Book club, mail order; Book publishing

(G-4954)
CEVA LOGISTICS
800 Ships Landing Way (19720-4575)
PHONE.................512 356-1700
EMP: 12 **EST:** 2016
SALES (est): 2.98MM **Privately Held**
Web: www.cevalogistics.com
SIC: 4731 Freight forwarding

(G-4955)
CHAMPIONX LLC
204 Quigley Blvd (19720-4106)
PHONE.................856 423-6417
Brian Devlin, *Brnch Mgr*
EMP: 5
SALES (corp-wide): 3.76B **Publicly Held**
Web: www.championx.com
SIC: 2899 Corrosion preventive lubricant
HQ: Championx Llc
2445 Tech Frest Blvd Bldg
The Woodlands TX 77381
281 632-6500

(G-4956)
CHIMES INC
Also Called: New Beginnings
130 Quigley Blvd (19720-4104)
PHONE.................302 382-4500
EMP: 26
Web: www.chimes.org
SIC: 8331 Vocational training agency
HQ: The Chimes Inc
4815 Seton Dr

Historic New Castle - New Castle County (G-4957)   GEOGRAPHIC SECTION

Baltimore MD 21215
410 358-6400

(G-4957)
CHIMES METRO INC
323 E 14th St (19720-4509)
PHONE..................302 452-3400
EMP: 530
Web: www.chimes.org
SIC: 3699 Chimes, electric
HQ: Chimes Metro, Inc.
  514 Interchange Blvd
  Newark DE 19711

(G-4958)
CHRISTIANA HOSPITAL
9 W 9th St (19720-6002)
PHONE..................203 645-2903
Rani Beharry, Prin
EMP: 8 EST: 2019
SALES (est): 94.25K Privately Held
Web: www.christianacare.org
SIC: 8062 General medical and surgical hospitals

(G-4959)
COASTAL FUNDING CORPORATION (PA)
216 Delaware St (19720-4816)
PHONE..................302 328-4113
John Fiore, Pr
EMP: 7 EST: 1990
SALES (est): 975.3K Privately Held
SIC: 6531 6513 7991 Real estate agents and managers; Apartment building operators; Physical fitness facilities

(G-4960)
COLONIAL ELECTRIC SUPPLY CO
Also Called: Brite Lite Supply
88 Quigley Blvd (19720-4150)
PHONE..................302 998-9993
John Przychodzien, Mgr
EMP: 10
SALES (corp-wide): 218.53MM Privately Held
Web: www.colonialelectricsupply.com
SIC: 5063 5719 Lighting fixtures; Lighting fixtures
PA: The Colonial Electric Supply Company
  201 W Church Rd Ste 100
  King Of Prussia PA 19406
  610 312-8100

(G-4961)
COLONIAL INCOME TAX SERVICE
700 Delaware St (19720-5060)
PHONE..................302 322-6881
EMP: 5 EST: 2010
SALES (est): 44K Privately Held
Web: www.colonialincometax.com
SIC: 7291 Tax return preparation services

(G-4962)
COMMUNITY CLLABORATION DEL INC
621 Delaware St (19720-5073)
PHONE..................302 824-6896
David Salter, Ex Dir
Chris Devaney, COO
EMP: 8 EST: 2019
SALES (est): 101.33K Privately Held
SIC: 8322 Individual and family services

(G-4963)
COMMUNITY PWERED FEDERAL CR UN
4 Quigley Blvd (19720-4150)
PHONE..................302 324-1441
John Watterson, Brnch Mgr

EMP: 99
SALES (corp-wide): 5.19MM Privately Held
Web: www.cpwrfcu.org
SIC: 6061 Federal credit unions
PA: Community Powered Federal Credit Union
  1758 Pulaski Hwy
  Bear DE 19701
  302 368-2396

(G-4964)
COOLERSMART
88 Quigley Blvd (19720-4150)
PHONE..................302 323-2100
EMP: 5 EST: 2019
SALES (est): 140.87K Privately Held
SIC: 1711 Plumbing, heating, air-conditioning

(G-4965)
CPR CONSTRUCTION INC
106 E 14th St (19720-4506)
P.O. Box 10845 (19850-0845)
PHONE..................302 322-5770
EMP: 7 EST: 1983
SALES (est): 635.66K Privately Held
SIC: 1521 New construction, single-family houses

(G-4966)
CROZIER FINE ARTS
1400 Johnson Way (19720-8125)
PHONE..................302 325-2071
EMP: 6
Web: www.crozierfinearts.com
SIC: 8412 Art gallery
HQ: Crozier Fine Arts
  8712 Jericho City Dr
  Landover MD 20785

(G-4967)
DANNYS GARAGE LLC
606 Cherry St (19720-5035)
PHONE..................702 752-9964
Daie Nortey, Managing Member
EMP: 5 EST: 2017
SALES (est): 104.73K Privately Held
SIC: 7389 Business Activities at Non-Commercial Site

(G-4968)
DATA MGT INTERNATIONALE INC (PA)
Also Called: D M I
55 Lukens Dr Ste A (19720-2788)
PHONE..................302 656-1151
TOLL FREE: 800
Carol Swezey, CEO
William Swezey Senior, Sec
▲ EMP: 33 EST: 1977
SQ FT: 50,000
SALES (est): 8.99MM
SALES (corp-wide): 8.99MM Privately Held
Web: www.imagingservices.com
SIC: 7389 Microfilm recording and developing service

(G-4969)
DELAWARE FLOORING SUPPLY INC
Also Called: Eztread
520 South St (19720-5024)
PHONE..................302 276-0031
Max T Maurer, Pr
Sharon Maurer, CFO
EMP: 7 EST: 2005
SQ FT: 13,000
SALES (est): 762.25K Privately Held
Web: www.eztread.com

SIC: 3446 5031 Stairs, staircases, stair treads: prefabricated metal; Building materials, interior

(G-4970)
DELAWARE HOME PROS LLC
710 Wilmington Rd Ste 1 (19720-3685)
PHONE..................302 894-7098
EMP: 5 EST: 2018
SALES (est): 200.96K Privately Held
Web: www.dehomepros.com
SIC: 1521 General remodeling, single-family houses

(G-4971)
DELAWARE LAST MILE LGSTICS DLM
1500 Johnson Way (19720-8110)
PHONE..................302 407-1415
EMP: 5 EST: 2019
SALES (est): 71.79K Privately Held
SIC: 8742 Transportation consultant

(G-4972)
DELAWARE SPINE REHABILITATION
216 E 2nd St (19720-3602)
PHONE..................302 563-7442
EMP: 5 EST: 2017
SALES (est): 74.22K Privately Held
SIC: 8093 Rehabilitation center, outpatient treatment

(G-4973)
DENN CON LLC ◊
702 Delaware St (19720-5060)
PHONE..................443 941-4279
EMP: 10 EST: 2022
SALES (est): 554.69K Privately Held
SIC: 1771 Concrete work

(G-4974)
DIGITIZING AMERICA LLC
147 Quigley Blvd Ste 12006 (19720-4103)
P.O. Box 32875 (48232-0875)
PHONE..................315 882-9516
EMP: 5 EST: 2016
SALES (est): 208.15K Privately Held
SIC: 8721 4899 8011 Accounting, auditing, and bookkeeping; Data communication services; Offices and clinics of medical doctors

(G-4975)
DIMARQUEZ INTL MINISTRIES INC
Also Called: Bells of Hope
417 Moores Ln (19720-4476)
PHONE..................302 256-4847
EMP: 8 EST: 2010
SALES (est): 45.36K Privately Held
SIC: 8322 Individual and family services

(G-4976)
DMC POWER INC
98 Quigley Blvd (19720-4150)
PHONE..................302 276-0303
EMP: 15
Web: www.dmcpower.com
SIC: 3643 Current-carrying wiring services
PA: Dmc Power, Inc.
  623 E Artesia Blvd
  Carson CA 90746

(G-4977)
DREAM CHASERS GYMNASTICS
245 Quigley Blvd (19720-4192)
PHONE..................302 276-0457
EMP: 5 EST: 2017
SALES (est): 61.76K Privately Held
Web: www.dreamchasersgym.com

SIC: 7999 Gymnastic instruction, non-membership

(G-4978)
DURALEX USA INC
Also Called: Duralex USA
802 Centerpoint Blvd (19720-8123)
PHONE..................302 326-4804
Alan Senior, Pr
Jacques Henry, Stockholder
▲ EMP: 18 EST: 2009
SQ FT: 44,000
SALES (est): 507.76K Privately Held
Web: www.duralexusa.com
SIC: 5023 Glassware

(G-4979)
EASTERN INDUSTRIAL SVCS INC
Also Called: Eisi
196 Quigley Blvd Ste A (19720-4176)
PHONE..................302 455-1400
Louis Pete Faverio, CEO
Tim Shelton,
EMP: 80 EST: 2000
SALES (est): 13.69MM Privately Held
Web: www.eastern-industrial.com
SIC: 1742 1799 Insulation, buildings; Coating, caulking, and weather, water, and fireproofing

(G-4980)
ELECTRIC MOTOR REPAIR SVC
263 Quigley Blvd Ste 12 (19720-8112)
PHONE..................302 322-1179
Caroline Kauffman, Prin
EMP: 5 EST: 2016
SALES (est): 210.97K Privately Held
SIC: 7694 Electric motor repair

(G-4981)
ELECTRONICS EXCHANGE INC
282 Quigley Blvd (19720-4163)
P.O. Box 7550 (19803-0550)
PHONE..................302 322-5401
Roberta Mostovoy, Pr
Stanley Mostovoy, Sec
EMP: 7 EST: 1978
SQ FT: 2,500
SALES (est): 2.18MM Privately Held
Web: www.eedelaware.com
SIC: 5065 Electronic parts

(G-4982)
ELIZABETH BEVERAGE COMPANY LLC
Also Called: Elizabeth Bottling Company
650 Ships Landing Way (19720-4577)
PHONE..................302 322-9895
Robert Dalvano, VP
EMP: 9 EST: 2005
SALES (est): 2.37MM Privately Held
SIC: 5149 Soft drinks
PA: Elizco Inc
  650 Ships Landing Way
  New Castle DE 19720

(G-4983)
ET COMMUNICATIONS LLC
270 Quigley Blvd (19720-4106)
PHONE..................302 322-2222
Eddie Traynham, Prin
EMP: 15 EST: 1999
SALES (est): 934.24K Privately Held
Web: www.etcommun.com
SIC: 7622 Communication equipment repair

(G-4984)
EVOQUA WATER TECHNOLOGIES LLC
259 Quigley Blvd (19720-4186)

PHONE..............302 322-6247
EMP: 6
Web: www.evoqua.com
SIC: 3589 Water treatment equipment, industrial
HQ: Evoqua Water Technologies Llc
210 6th Ave Ste 3300
Pittsburgh PA 15222
724 772-0044

(G-4985)
EXCELLENT HOME CARE
122 Delaware St (19720-4814)
PHONE..............302 327-0147
EMP: 8 EST: 2017
SALES (est): 513.92K Privately Held
SIC: 8082 Home health care services

(G-4986)
EZTZ INC
263 Quigley Blvd Ste 9 (19720-8112)
PHONE..............302 376-5641
Tom Zabielski, Mgr
EMP: 6 EST: 2019
SALES (est): 771.59K Privately Held
SIC: 5141 Groceries, general line

(G-4987)
FIBERSTATE LLC ✪
122 Delaware St Ste B8 (19720-4814)
PHONE..............800 575-8921
Brianna Bohanon, Managing Member
EMP: 30 EST: 2022
SALES (est): 1.02MM Privately Held
SIC: 4899 4813 Data communication services; Data telephone communications

(G-4988)
FIRST CHOICE HOME MED EQUIPT (PA)
259 Quigley Blvd Ste 1 (19720-4186)
PHONE..............302 323-8700
Michael Eddy, *
Richard Kreider, *
EMP: 24 EST: 2005
SALES (est): 9.91MM Privately Held
Web: www.adapthealth.com
SIC: 5047 Medical equipment and supplies

(G-4989)
FLOWRITE
1620 Wilmington Rd (19720-3619)
PHONE..............302 544-4042
EMP: 5 EST: 2015
SALES (est): 162.78K Privately Held
Web: www.flowritedelaware.com
SIC: 1711 Plumbing contractors

(G-4990)
FOX SPECIALTIES INC
Also Called: Encompass Elements
1500 Johnson Way (19720-8110)
PHONE..............302 322-5200
Phillip Murray, Brnch Mgr
EMP: 14
SALES (corp-wide): 20.16MM Privately Held
Web: www.encompasselements.com
SIC: 2789 Binding only: books, pamphlets, magazines, etc.
PA: Fox Specialties, Inc.
2750 Morris Rd Ste C
Lansdale PA 19446
215 822-5175

(G-4991)
FRANCIS ENTERPRISES LLC
Also Called: Sheep Skin Gifts
261 Quigley Blvd Ste 10 (19720-4187)
PHONE..............302 276-1316
▲ EMP: 12 EST: 2011
SALES (est): 1.03MM Privately Held
Web: www.sheepskin.com
SIC: 5699 5199 Leather garments; Leather, leather goods, and furs

(G-4992)
FRESENIUS MEDICAL CARE N AMER
Also Called: First State
608 Ferry Cut Off St (19720-4549)
PHONE..............302 328-9044
John Grandson, Brnch Mgr
EMP: 15
SALES (corp-wide): 20.15B Privately Held
Web: www.fmcna.com
SIC: 8092 Kidney dialysis centers
HQ: Fresenius Usa Manufacturing, Inc.
920 Winter St
Waltham MA 02451

(G-4993)
FRITZ STAFFING GROUP LLC (PA)
508 South St Bldg D (19720-5024)
PHONE..............844 581-5873
Nicholas Wagner, Managing Member
EMP: 16 EST: 2020
SALES (est): 7.65MM
SALES (corp-wide): 7.65MM Privately Held
SIC: 7363 Manpower pools

(G-4994)
FSCOM INC
Also Called: Fiberstore
380 Centerpoint Blvd (19720-8100)
PHONE..............888 468-7419
Daniel Xiang, CEO
Wei Xiang, Ch Bd
EMP: 100 EST: 2018
SALES (est): 154.76MM Privately Held
SIC: 5999 4841 Telephone and communication equipment; Cable and other pay television services

(G-4995)
FUJIFILM IMAGING COLORANTS INC
109 Lukens Dr (19720-2747)
PHONE..............302 472-1298
EMP: 60
Web: www.fujifilmic.com
SIC: 7389 Business Activities at Non-Commercial Site
HQ: Fujifilm Imaging Colorants, Inc.
233 Cherry Ln
New Castle DE 19720

(G-4996)
GLOBAL CONTAINER & CHASSIS LLC
607 Deemer Pl (19720-5043)
PHONE..............302 608-0822
EMP: 9 EST: 2019
SALES (est): 716.89K Privately Held
SIC: 4731 Freight forwarding

(G-4997)
GLOBAL SHOPAHOLICS LLC
243 Quigley Blvd Ste E (19720-4191)
PHONE..............302 725-0586
Muhammad Zulqarnain, Admn
EMP: 10 EST: 2017
SALES (est): 1.03MM Privately Held
Web: www.globalshopaholics.com
SIC: 4731 Freight forwarding

(G-4998)
GREEN RECOVERY TECH LLC
42 Lukens Dr Ste 100 (19720-2700)
PHONE..............302 317-0062
Kenneth Laubsch, Pr
EMP: 6 EST: 2011
SALES (est): 916.92K Privately Held
Web: www.greenrecoverytech.com
SIC: 2048 Prepared feeds, nec

(G-4999)
GREENTEC LABORATORIES LLC
122 Delaware St Ste F7 (19720-4814)
PHONE..............301 744-7336
Kendel Covington, CEO
EMP: 5 EST: 2016
SALES (est): 1MM Privately Held
Web: www.greenteclabs.com
SIC: 2911 Fuel additives

(G-5000)
HARBOUR TEXTILE RENTAL SVC INC
259 Quigley Blvd Ste 8 (19720-4186)
PHONE..............302 656-2300
Donald L Struminger, Ch Bd
David M Struminger, Pr
Nancy Alley V, President Contract
John Crockford, VP
EMP: 7 EST: 1992
SALES (est): 905.44K
SALES (corp-wide): 48.52MM Privately Held
Web: www.yourlinenservice.com
SIC: 7213 7218 7211 Linen supply; Industrial uniform supply; Power laundries, family and commercial
PA: Mohenis Services, Inc.
875 E Bank St
Petersburg VA 23803
800 879-3315

(G-5001)
HARRY KENYON INCORPORATED
259 Quigley Blvd Ste 1 (19720-4186)
PHONE..............302 762-7776
E Kenyon Still, Pr
Betty Lee Bradley, *
John H Still, *
Harry K Still, *
EMP: 26 EST: 1875
SQ FT: 30,000
SALES (est): 830.43K Privately Held
Web: www.kenyon.edu
SIC: 5194 5145 Cigars; Confectionery

(G-5002)
HARTZELL INDUSTRIES INC
Also Called: Kad Industrial Rubber Products
115 Quigley Blvd (19720-4103)
PHONE..............302 322-4900
Jay Williams, Pr
Marion Williams, Treas
EMP: 7 EST: 2001
SALES (est): 977.51K Privately Held
Web: www.omniservices.com
SIC: 5085 Hose, belting, and packing

(G-5003)
HERMANN WAREHOUSE CORPORATION ✪
400 Anchor Mill Rd (19720-4573)
PHONE..............732 297-5333
Jeff Hermann, CEO
EMP: 15 EST: 2023
SALES (est): 498.38K Privately Held
SIC: 4225 General warehousing

(G-5004)
HIBBERT COMPANY
Also Called: Hibbert Group, The
890 Ships Landing Way (19720-4575)
PHONE..............609 394-7500
Paul Zukowski, Brnch Mgr
EMP: 116
SALES (corp-wide): 56.65MM Privately Held
Web: www.hibbert.com
SIC: 7331 Direct mail advertising services
PA: The Hibbert Company
400 Pennington Ave
Trenton NJ 08618
609 392-0478

(G-5005)
HISTORICAL SOCIETY OF DELAWARE
Also Called: George Read II House
42 The Strand (19720-4826)
PHONE..............302 322-8411
Michelle Ainstine, Mgr
EMP: 29
SALES (corp-wide): 2.63MM Privately Held
Web: www.dehistory.org
SIC: 8412 Museum
PA: The Historical Society Of Delaware
505 N Market St
Wilmington DE 19801
302 655-7161

(G-5006)
HOSPITAL BLLING CLLCTN SVC LTD (PA)
Also Called: Hbcs
118 Lukens Dr (19720-2727)
PHONE..............302 552-8000
Brain J Wasilewski, Pr
Kevin Haggerty, *
Brain J Wasilewski, Pr
Joseph Dudek, *
Maureen Dieleuterio, *
EMP: 370 EST: 1984
SQ FT: 43,000
SALES (est): 52.98MM
SALES (corp-wide): 52.98MM Privately Held
Web: www.hbcsrevcycle.com
SIC: 8721 Billing and bookkeeping service

(G-5007)
IEXPERIENCEILEARN LLC
66 Buttonwood Ave (19720-3604)
PHONE..............718 704-4870
EMP: 2 EST: 2015
SALES (est): 107.3K Privately Held
SIC: 7372 Educational computer software

(G-5008)
INTEGRITY TESTLABS LLC (PA)
258 Quigley Blvd (19720-4106)
PHONE..............302 325-2365
EMP: 55 EST: 2002
SQ FT: 5,000
SALES (est): 2.44MM Privately Held
Web: www.integritytestlabsllc.com
SIC: 8734 Testing laboratories

(G-5009)
J & L BUILDING MATERIALS INC
59 Lukens Dr (19720-2718)
PHONE..............302 504-0350
John Rash, Prin
EMP: 26
SALES (corp-wide): 59.54MM Privately Held
Web: www.jlbuilding.com
SIC: 5033 Roofing, asphalt and sheet metal
PA: J & L Building Materials, Inc.
600 Lancaster Ave
Malvern PA 19355
610 644-6311

Historic New Castle - New Castle County (G-5010)

(G-5010)
JCR SYSTEMS LLC
621 Delaware St (19720-5073)
PHONE..................................302 420-6072
Doug Salter, *Managing Member*
Mark Lumer, *Mgr*
EMP: 2 **EST:** 2013
SALES (est): 185.23K **Privately Held**
Web: www.jcrsystems.net
SIC: 2493 2899 Insulation and roofing material, reconstituted wood; Waterproofing compounds

(G-5011)
JOHN F ELDER
Also Called: J Elder Gerenal Contracting
1011 Deemers Lndg (19720-7218)
PHONE..................................302 544-6569
John Elder, *Owner*
Connie Wilson, *Prin*
EMP: 5 **EST:** 2012
SALES (est): 71.33K **Privately Held**
SIC: 1751 Carpentry work

(G-5012)
JUDITH A SMITH
38 W 4th St (19720-5093)
PHONE..................................302 322-9396
Judith A Smith, *Prin*
EMP: 5 **EST:** 2012
SALES (est): 36.03K **Privately Held**
SIC: 7291 Tax return preparation services

(G-5013)
JUICEPLUS+
15 W 3rd St (19720-5009)
PHONE..................................302 322-2616
Marilyn Del Duca, *Prin*
EMP: 4 **EST:** 2011
SALES (est): 66.53K **Privately Held**
SIC: 2037 Fruit juices

(G-5014)
KAUL GLOVE AND MFG CO
Also Called: Choctaw- Kaul Distribution Co
599 Ships Landing Way (19720-4578)
PHONE..................................302 292-2660
Judy Mcdilda, *Mgr*
EMP: 89
SALES (corp-wide): 102.58MM **Privately Held**
SIC: 2381 3151 5136 Fabric dress and work gloves; Gloves, leather: work; Work clothing, men's and boys'
PA: Kaul Glove And Mfg. Co.
3540 Vinewood St
Detroit MI 48208
313 894-9494

(G-5015)
KNOTTS INCORPORATED
700 Wilmington Rd (19720-3698)
PHONE..................................302 322-0554
Edna J Knotts, *Pr*
Paul H Knotts, *
Philip L Knotts, *
EMP: 20 **EST:** 1977
SQ FT: 14,500
SALES (est): 417.52K **Privately Held**
Web: www.knotts.com
SIC: 4151 School buses

(G-5016)
LEHANES BUS SERVICE INC
1705 Wilmington Rd (19720-2750)
P.O. Box 349 (19720-0349)
PHONE..................................302 328-7100
EMP: 17 **EST:** 1994
SQ FT: 10,000
SALES (est): 746.21K **Privately Held**
SIC: 4151 School buses

(G-5017)
LEKUE USA INC
802 Centerpoint Blvd (19720-8123)
PHONE..................................302 326-4805
Alan Senior, *Pr*
Charles Quinn, *
Patrick Lobo, *
▲ **EMP:** 16 **EST:** 2011
SQ FT: 60,000
SALES (est): 889.53K **Privately Held**
SIC: 5023 Kitchen tools and utensils, nec

(G-5018)
LIMO EXCHANGE
Also Called: Limo Exchange, The
800 Washington St (19720-6049)
PHONE..................................302 322-1200
Greg Zelano, *Pr*
EMP: 10 **EST:** 1999
SALES (est): 584.76K **Privately Held**
Web: www.limo-exchange.com
SIC: 4119 Limousine rental, with driver

(G-5019)
LOYAL ORDER OF MOOSE
2 Victorian Ct (19720-4534)
PHONE..................................302 378-2624
John Wather, *Mgr*
EMP: 5 **EST:** 2017
SALES (est): 39.99K **Privately Held**
SIC: 8641 Civic associations

(G-5020)
LUCILA CARMICHAEL RN
1101 Delaware St (19720-6033)
PHONE..................................302 324-8901
Lucila Carmichael, *Prin*
EMP: 6 **EST:** 2017
SALES (est): 65.76K **Privately Held**
SIC: 8049 Offices of health practitioner

(G-5021)
LUMBER JACKS AXE CLUB LLC
44 E 4th St (19720-5014)
PHONE..................................215 900-0318
EMP: 10 **EST:** 2018
SALES (est): 88.09K **Privately Held**
SIC: 7997 Outdoor field clubs

(G-5022)
M & M AUTOMOTIVE LLC
800 Frenchtown Rd (19720-4102)
PHONE..................................302 325-8140
EMP: 5 **EST:** 2017
SALES (est): 339.76K **Privately Held**
Web: www.mandmautomotivellc.com
SIC: 7538 General automotive repair shops

(G-5023)
MAGIC TOUCH
1707 New Castle Ave (19720-7711)
PHONE..................................302 655-6430
Richard M Collins, *Pt*
Richard F Hickman, *Pt*
EMP: 7 **EST:** 1979
SALES (est): 258.88K **Privately Held**
SIC: 7542 Washing and polishing, automotive

(G-5024)
MATERIAL HANDLING SUPPLY INC
Also Called: MHS Lift of Delaware
243 Quigley Blvd Ste I (19720-4191)
PHONE..................................302 571-0176
Dave Brown, *Mgr*
EMP: 15
SALES (corp-wide): 40.99MM **Privately Held**
Web: www.mhslift.com
SIC: 5084 7359 Materials handling machinery; Equipment rental and leasing, nec
PA: Material Handling Supply, Llc
6965 Airport Highway Ln
Pennsauken NJ 08109
877 647-9320

(G-5025)
MAUVIEL USA INC
802 Centerpoint Blvd (19720-8123)
PHONE..................................302 326-4800
Alan Senior, *Genl Mgr*
Charles Quinn, *
▲ **EMP:** 30 **EST:** 2003
SQ FT: 44,000
SALES (est): 1.2MM **Privately Held**
SIC: 3263 Cookware, fine earthenware

(G-5026)
MCLAREN HEALTH CARE CORP
55 Lukens Dr (19720-2788)
PHONE..................................214 257-7012
EMP: 9 **EST:** 2019
SALES (est): 235.89K **Privately Held**
SIC: 8099 Health and allied services, nec

(G-5027)
MID ATLANTIC TIRE ADI
600 Ships Landing Way (19720-4577)
PHONE..................................302 221-2000
Bob Zattaterrini, *Prin*
EMP: 5 **EST:** 2018
SALES (est): 197.26K **Privately Held**
SIC: 5015 Motor vehicle parts, used

(G-5028)
MID-ATLANTIC ENVMTL LABS INC
30 Lukens Dr Ste A (19720-2700)
PHONE..................................302 654-1340
Akhter Mehmood, *Pr*
Nuzhat Mehmood, *Sec*
EMP: 15 **EST:** 1998
SQ FT: 3,200
SALES (est): 2.3MM **Privately Held**
Web: www.maelinc.com
SIC: 8748 Environmental consultant

(G-5029)
MINER LTD
2 Lukens Dr (19720-2796)
PHONE..................................302 516-7791
EMP: 115
SALES (corp-wide): 595.89MM **Privately Held**
Web: www.minercorp.com
SIC: 1751 Window and door installation and erection
HQ: Miner, Ltd
11827 Tech Com Ste 115
San Antonio TX 78233

(G-5030)
MULDOONS DIESEL PRFMCE LLC
610 South St (19720-5026)
PHONE..................................302 276-2882
EMP: 4 **EST:** 2013
SALES (est): 342.94K **Privately Held**
Web: www.muldoonsdiesel.com
SIC: 3714 Transmissions, motor vehicle

(G-5031)
MUNICIPAL SERVICES COMMISSION (PA)
216 Chestnut St (19720-4834)
P.O. Box 208 (19720-0208)
PHONE..................................302 323-2330
Chip Patterson, *Sec*
Robert S Appleby, *Pr*
George Freebery, *Commsnr*
Hickman Rolling, *Commsrs*
EMP: 9 **EST:** 1921
SALES (est): 9.79MM
SALES (corp-wide): 9.79MM **Privately Held**
Web: www.newcastlemsc.com
SIC: 4911 4941 Distribution, electric power; Water supply

(G-5032)
NATIONAL DENTEX LLC
Also Called: Ndx Dodd
24 Lukens Dr (19720-2700)
P.O. Box 1005 (19720-7005)
PHONE..................................302 661-6000
Roy Levine, *Brnch Mgr*
EMP: 132
SALES (corp-wide): 339.71MM **Privately Held**
Web: www.nationaldentex.com
SIC: 8072 Crown and bridge production
HQ: National Dentex, Llc
1701 Military Trl Ste 150
Jupiter FL 33458
800 678-4140

(G-5033)
NATIONAL RSTRTION FCLTY SVCS I
30 Lukens Dr # B (19720-2700)
PHONE..................................856 401-0100
John Marroni, *Pr*
Kimberly Marroni, *
EMP: 25 **EST:** 2008
SALES (est): 2.04MM **Privately Held**
SIC: 1521 1542 Repairing fire damage, single-family houses; Commercial and office buildings, renovation and repair

(G-5034)
NEW CASTLE COUNTER
55 Lukens Dr (19720-2788)
PHONE..................................302 421-3940
Paul Jackson, *Mgr*
EMP: 7 **EST:** 2015
SALES (est): 75.84K **Privately Held**
Web: newcastlecity.delaware.gov
SIC: 1731 General electrical contractor

(G-5035)
NEW CASTLE HISTORICAL SOCIETY
30 Market St (19720-4830)
PHONE..................................302 322-2794
Michael Connolly, *Ex Dir*
EMP: 10 **EST:** 1934
SALES (est): 225.14K **Privately Held**
Web: www.newcastlenhhistoricalsociety.org
SIC: 8412 Historical society

(G-5036)
NEW CASTLE INSURANCE LTD
Also Called: Nationwide
621 Delaware St Ste 100 (19720-5073)
PHONE..................................302 328-6111
Dennis Salter, *Pr*
Patricia Flynn, *Sec*
Michelle Fidance, *Mgr*
EMP: 16 **EST:** 1991
SQ FT: 5,600
SALES (est): 2.29MM **Privately Held**
Web: www.newcastleinsure.com
SIC: 6411 Insurance agents, nec

(G-5037)
NEW CASTLE RX LLC
363 Quigley Blvd Ste B (19720-4107)
PHONE..................................302 356-5600
EMP: 6 **EST:** 2008
SALES (est): 411.43K **Privately Held**

SIC: 5122 Drugs, proprietaries, and sundries

(G-5038)
NEW CSTLE CNTY SCHL EMPLYEES F
Also Called: Nccsefcu
113 W 6th St (19720-5070)
P.O. Box 232 (19720-0232)
PHONE.................302 613-5330
Terri L Keene, *Genl Mgr*
EMP: 20 **EST:** 1953
SALES (est): 1.77MM **Privately Held**
Web: www.edufcu.org
SIC: 6061 Federal credit unions

(G-5039)
NIXON UNF RNTL SVC OF LNCASTER (PA)
42 Lukens Dr Ste 100 (19720-2700)
PHONE.................302 656-2774
Brian Bear, *Pr*
EMP: 5 **EST:** 1989
SQ FT: 23,000
SALES (est): 4.49MM **Privately Held**
SIC: 7299 Clothing rental services

(G-5040)
NIXON UNIFORM SERVICE INC (PA)
Also Called: Nixon Uniform Service & Med Wr
500 Centerpoint Blvd (19720-8106)
PHONE.................302 325-2875
TOLL FREE: 800
Jason Berstein, *Pr*
Robert L Schecter, *
Jason Berstein, *COO*
EMP: 170 **EST:** 1969
SQ FT: 75,000
SALES (est): 36.71MM
SALES (corp-wide): 36.71MM **Privately Held**
Web: www.nixonmedical.com
SIC: 7218 2326 Industrial equipment launderers; Medical and hospital uniforms, men's

(G-5041)
NPMHE LOCAL 308
147 Quigley Blvd (19720-4103)
PHONE.................302 322-2430
EMP: 5 **EST:** 2014
SALES (est): 85.81K **Privately Held**
SIC: 8631 Labor union

(G-5042)
OFFICE SERVICE SOLUTIONS LLC
710 Wilmington Rd # A (19720-3685)
PHONE.................302 420-3958
Candice Knotts, *Prin*
EMP: 7 **EST:** 2015
SALES (est): 345.22K **Privately Held**
Web: www.officeservicesolutions.com
SIC: 8721 Billing and bookkeeping service

(G-5043)
ONE TECH SOL LLC
243 Quigley Blvd Ste E (19720-4191)
PHONE.................302 551-6777
Arslan Ali, *CEO*
Nighat Shaheen, *VP*
Waleed Falak, *VP*
Nabeel Falak, *VP*
EMP: 3 **EST:** 2021
SALES (est): 255.72K **Privately Held**
SIC: 3571 Electronic computers

(G-5044)
OVER RAINBOW DAYCARE
713 W 12th St (19720-4947)
PHONE.................302 328-6574
Robert Gibbons, *Prin*
EMP: 9 **EST:** 2008
SALES (est): 83.44K **Privately Held**
SIC: 8351 Group day care center

(G-5045)
PAGODA HOTEL INC
Also Called: Pagoda Hotel & Floating Rest
599 Ships Landing Way (19720-4578)
PHONE.................808 922-1233
Herbert T Hayashi, *Ch Bd*
Harry Hayashi, *VP*
Kery Kamita, *Treas*
John Hayashi, *Sec*
EMP: 17 **EST:** 1963
SALES (est): 880.89K
SALES (corp-wide): 48.57MM **Privately Held**
SIC: 5812 7011 Restaurant, family: independent; Hotels
PA: Hth Asset Management, Llc
1668 S King St Fl 2
Honolulu HI 96826
808 469-4111

(G-5046)
PETES BIG TVS INC (PA)
22 Lukens Dr (19720-2700)
P.O. Box 1156 (21044-0156)
PHONE.................302 328-3551
Peter Daniel, *Pr*
Guy Benjamin, *VP*
▲ **EMP:** 6 **EST:** 2002
SQ FT: 44,000
SALES (est): 2.55MM
SALES (corp-wide): 2.55MM **Privately Held**
Web: www.petesbigtvs.com
SIC: 7812 Audio-visual program production

(G-5047)
PHARMADEL LLC
600 Ships Landing Way (19720-4577)
PHONE.................302 322-1329
▲ **EMP:** 7 **EST:** 2010
SQ FT: 28,000
SALES (est): 160.31K **Privately Held**
Web: www.pharmadel.com
SIC: 5122 Cosmetics

(G-5048)
PHILIP ROSENAU CO INC
Also Called: Allston Chemical
264 Quigley Blvd (19720-4106)
PHONE.................302 322-3952
EMP: 6
SALES (corp-wide): 1.65B **Privately Held**
Web: www.imperialdade.com
SIC: 5087 Janitors' supplies
HQ: Lcjn, Inc.
750 Jacksonville Rd
Warminster PA 18974
215 956-1980

(G-5049)
PIFFERT INC
19 Lukens Dr Ste 300 (19720-2787)
PHONE.................302 407-6185
Hamza Inatz, *CEO*
EMP: 10 **EST:** 2020
SALES (est): 958.71K **Privately Held**
SIC: 5141 Groceries, general line

(G-5050)
PODS INC NEW CASTLE
299 Anchor Mill Rd (19720-4582)
PHONE.................856 217-4685
EMP: 5 **EST:** 2017
SALES (est): 95.81K **Privately Held**
SIC: 6519 Real property lessors, nec

(G-5051)
POSITIVE ENERGY ELECTRIC
21 Holcomb Ln (19720-3624)
PHONE.................267 902-1655
Ralph Goldsborough, *Prin*
EMP: 5 **EST:** 2017
SALES (est): 95.09K **Privately Held**
SIC: 1731 General electrical contractor

(G-5052)
PREVENT ALARM COMPANY LLC
Also Called: Prevent Security and Tech
91 Lukens Dr Ste B (19720-2799)
PHONE.................302 478-6647
EMP: 6 **EST:** 1999
SALES (est): 1.13MM
SALES (corp-wide): 177.79MM **Privately Held**
SIC: 7382 Burglar alarm maintenance and monitoring
PA: Unified Door And Hardware Group, Llc
1650 Suckle Hwy Ste A
Pennsauken NJ 08110
856 320-4868

(G-5053)
PREZOOM LLC
262 Quigley Blvd (19720-9004)
PHONE.................732 837-1170
Claire Davids, *Managing Member*
EMP: 7 **EST:** 2012
SQ FT: 12,000
SALES (est): 662.48K **Privately Held**
Web: www.prezoom.com
SIC: 3086 Packaging and shipping materials, foamed plastics

(G-5054)
PRINTCUREMENT
122 Delaware St Ste 300 (19720-4814)
PHONE.................302 249-6100
EMP: 3 **EST:** 2018
SALES (est): 67.82K **Privately Held**
SIC: 2752 Commercial printing, lithographic

(G-5055)
PROMOFILL
800 Centerpoint Blvd (19720-8123)
PHONE.................302 276-2700
EMP: 8 **EST:** 2017
SALES (est): 85.17K **Privately Held**
Web: www.promofill.com
SIC: 7389 Packaging and labeling services

(G-5056)
PTM MANUFACTURING LLC
196 Quigley Blvd Ste A (19720-4176)
PHONE.................302 455-9733
Pete Faverio Iv, *Managing Member*
▲ **EMP:** 8 **EST:** 1998
SALES (est): 1.83MM **Privately Held**
Web: www.ptmmanufacturing.com
SIC: 3564 Air cleaning systems

(G-5057)
PULSAR PRINT LLC
243 Quigley Blvd Ste K (19720-4191)
PHONE.................302 394-9202
EMP: 6 **EST:** 2016
SALES (est): 290.71K **Privately Held**
Web: www.pulsarprint.com
SIC: 2752 Commercial printing, lithographic

(G-5058)
QUALITY FINISHERS INC
1 Merit Dr (19720-3683)
P.O. Box 288 (19720-0288)
PHONE.................302 325-1963
John Stachowski, *Pr*
Korang Stachowski, *Treas*
EMP: 8 **EST:** 1985
SQ FT: 5,000
SALES (est): 790.31K **Privately Held**
Web: www.qualityfinishers.com
SIC: 1721 1521 Exterior residential painting contractor; General remodeling, single-family houses

(G-5059)
QUICK TO GO SHIPPING CENTER
Also Called: Quick Togo
260 Quigley Blvd (19720-9012)
PHONE.................302 327-0399
Bai Jennifer, *Prin*
EMP: 6 **EST:** 2010
SALES (est): 220.65K **Privately Held**
Web: www.firststatemail.com
SIC: 5088 Ships

(G-5060)
RODNEY PRATT FRAMING GALLERY
204 Delaware St Ste A (19720-4880)
PHONE.................302 593-6108
EMP: 4 **EST:** 2016
SALES (est): 62.25K **Privately Held**
SIC: 2499 Picture frame molding, finished

(G-5061)
ROLLINS INC
101 Johnson Way (19720-8115)
PHONE.................302 325-4410
EMP: 123 **EST:** 2011
SALES (est): 314.29K
SALES (corp-wide): 2.7B **Publicly Held**
Web: www.rollins.com
SIC: 7342 Exterminating and fumigating
PA: Rollins, Inc.
2170 Piedmont Rd Ne
Atlanta GA 30324
404 888-2000

(G-5062)
ROSLE U S A CORP
802 Centerpoint Blvd (19720-8123)
PHONE.................302 326-4801
Eric Jones, *Genl Mgr*
▲ **EMP:** 33 **EST:** 1997
SALES (est): 3.2MM **Privately Held**
SIC: 5023 Kitchen tools and utensils, nec

(G-5063)
ROYAL INSTRUMENTS INC
266 Quigley Blvd (19720-4106)
PHONE.................302 328-5900
Dominick Paladinetti, *Mgr*
EMP: 6
SALES (corp-wide): 2.49MM **Privately Held**
Web: www.royalinstruments.com
SIC: 5085 Valves and fittings
PA: Royal Instruments Inc
835 Industrial Hwy Ste 2
Cinnaminson NJ 08077
856 829-9888

(G-5064)
RTX CORPORATION
276 Quigley Blvd (19720-4106)
PHONE.................800 227-7437
Doug Ergod, *Brnch Mgr*
EMP: 2
SALES (corp-wide): 67.07B **Publicly Held**
Web: www.rtx.com
SIC: 3724 Aircraft engines and engine parts
PA: Rtx Corporation
1000 Wilson Blvd
Arlington VA 22209
781 522-3000

Historic New Castle - New Castle County (G-5065) GEOGRAPHIC SECTION

(G-5065)
SAKER ENERGY SOLUTIONS INC
122 Delaware St Ste F-15 (19720-4814)
PHONE.............................808 398-8326
Raymond King, *CEO*
Salvatore Leone, *Pr*
Frank Zarrelli, *CFO*
Jonathan Georgis, *CLO*
EMP: 3 **EST:** 2018
SALES (est): 240.13K **Privately Held**
SIC: 3586 Gasoline pumps, measuring or dispensing

(G-5066)
SAVARNA INC
259 Quigley Blvd Ste 15 (19720-4186)
PHONE.............................757 446-0101
Daniel Singh, *Prin*
EMP: 7 **EST:** 2015
SALES (est): 223.16K **Privately Held**
SIC: 7231 Beauty shops

(G-5067)
SAVVY ARTISTRY LLC
1016 Clayton St (19720-6026)
PHONE.............................302 339-1712
EMP: 5 **EST:** 2016
SALES (est): 102.16K **Privately Held**
SIC: 7231 Beauty shops

(G-5068)
SER TRUCKING INC
703 W 11th St (19720-4915)
PHONE.............................302 328-0782
Susan E Reed, *Prin*
EMP: 5 **EST:** 2012
SALES (est): 245.67K **Privately Held**
SIC: 4212 Local trucking, without storage

(G-5069)
SGM SOCHER INC
144 Quigley Blvd (19720-4199)
PHONE.............................718 484-4253
Yosef Greenwald, *Prin*
EMP: 5
SALES (est): 272.71K **Privately Held**
SIC: 5065 Electronic parts and equipment, nec

(G-5070)
SIEMENS CORPORATION
800 Centerpoint Blvd Ste A (19720-8123)
PHONE.............................302 220-1544
EMP: 21
SALES (corp-wide): 84.48B **Privately Held**
Web: www.siemens.com
SIC: 3661 Telephones and telephone apparatus
HQ: Siemens Corporation
300 New Jersey Ave Nw # 100
Washington DC 20001
202 434-4800

(G-5071)
SIEMENS HLTHCARE DGNOSTICS INC
200 Centerpoint Blvd (19720-4175)
PHONE.............................302 631-8006
Tony Oleck, *Brnch Mgr*
EMP: 4
SALES (corp-wide): 84.48B **Privately Held**
Web: www.siemens.com
SIC: 2835 Diagnostic substances
HQ: Siemens Healthcare Diagnostics Inc.
511 Benedict Ave
Tarrytown NY 10591
914 631-8000

(G-5072)
SIEMENS INDUSTRY INC
259 Quigley Blvd (19720-4186)
PHONE.............................302 322-6247
EMP: 17
SALES (corp-wide): 84.48B **Privately Held**
Web: www.siemens.com
SIC: 4941 Water supply
HQ: Siemens Industry, Inc.
100 Technology Dr
Alpharetta GA 30005
847 215-1000

(G-5073)
SNICKERS DITCH TRUNK COMPANY
182 E 4th St (19720-4539)
PHONE.............................302 325-1762
Kenneth Sturgis, *Owner*
EMP: 5 **EST:** 2012
SALES (est): 212.14K **Privately Held**
SIC: 3161 Trunks

(G-5074)
SPEAKMAN COMPANY
400 Anchor Mill Rd (19720-4573)
PHONE.............................302 765-0204
EMP: 11 **EST:** 2019
SALES (est): 932.88K **Privately Held**
Web: www.speakman.com
SIC: 3432 Plumbing fixture fittings and trim

(G-5075)
SPEC SIMPLE INC
16 W 4th St (19720-5018)
P.O. Box 211 (19720-0211)
PHONE.............................212 352-2002
Suzanne Swift, *Prin*
EMP: 10 **EST:** 2008
SALES (est): 274.45K **Privately Held**
Web: vlibrary.specsimple.com
SIC: 7389 Personal service agents, brokers, and bureaus

(G-5076)
SPEEDER SOLUTIONS LLC
330 Centerpoint Blvd (19720-8100)
PHONE.............................302 448-8668
Shucheng Gong, *Prin*
Lu Zan, *Prin*
EMP: 14 **EST:** 2017
SALES (est): 2.17MM **Privately Held**
Web: www.speedersolutions.com
SIC: 7389 Courier or messenger service

(G-5077)
SUNLITE ENERGY INTLL
112 The Strand Apt C (19720-4863)
P.O. Box 30286 (19805-7286)
PHONE.............................302 598-2984
Jean Weaver, *Owner*
EMP: 5 **EST:** 2015
SALES (est): 380.13K **Privately Held**
SIC: 5171 Petroleum bulk stations and terminals

(G-5078)
T P COMPOSITES INC
1600 Johnson Way (19720-8199)
PHONE.............................610 358-9001
Anna Romanowski, *Prin*
EMP: 5 **EST:** 2016
SALES (est): 82.8K **Privately Held**
SIC: 2821 Plastics materials and resins

(G-5079)
TA INSTRUMENTS - WATERS LLC (DH)
Also Called: Ta Instruments
159 Lukens Dr (19720-2795)
PHONE.............................302 427-4000
Jonathan M Pratt, *Pr*
▲ **EMP:** 200 **EST:** 1990
SQ FT: 200,000
SALES (est): 89.82MM **Publicly Held**
Web: www.tainstruments.com
SIC: 3826 Instruments measuring thermal properties
HQ: Waters Technologies Corporation,
34 Maple St
Milford MA 01757
508 478-2000

(G-5080)
TA INSTRUMENTS-WATERS LLC (PA)
Also Called: Lasercomp Ta
159 Lukens Dr (19720-2795)
PHONE.............................781 233-1717
EMP: 10 **EST:** 1990
SALES (est): 1.61MM **Privately Held**
SIC: 3826 Thermal analysis instruments, laboratory type

(G-5081)
TALOSTECH LLC
274 Quigley Blvd (19720-4106)
PHONE.............................302 332-9236
Hansan Liu, *Pr*
EMP: 4 **EST:** 2016
SALES (est): 496.38K **Privately Held**
Web: www.talostechllc.com
SIC: 3691 3692 Storage batteries; Primary batteries, dry and wet

(G-5082)
TERMINIX INTL CO LTD PARTNR
Also Called: Terminix
284 Quigley Blvd (19720-4106)
PHONE.............................302 653-4866
Brian Searle, *Mgr*
EMP: 15
SALES (corp-wide): 4.47B **Privately Held**
Web: www.terminix.com
SIC: 7342 Pest control services
HQ: The Terminix International Company Limited Partnership
150 Peabody Pl
Memphis TN 38103
901 766-1400

(G-5083)
TESLA INDUSTRIES INC (PA)
Also Called: Tesla
101 Centerpoint Blvd (19720-4180)
PHONE.............................302 324-8910
David Masilotti, *Pr*
▲ **EMP:** 14 **EST:** 1991
SQ FT: 20,000
SALES (est): 8.98MM **Privately Held**
Web: www.teslaind.com
SIC: 3724 3812 Starting vibrators, aircraft engine; Aircraft control instruments

(G-5084)
THINK CLEAN & GROUNDS UP LLC
11 W 9th St (19720-6002)
PHONE.............................904 250-1614
EMP: 10 **EST:** 2019
SALES (est): 147.78K **Privately Held**
SIC: 7342 Disinfecting services

(G-5085)
THOMAS A COCHRAN & SONS INC
807 Washington St (19720-6079)
PHONE.............................302 656-6054
John Cochren, *Pr*
EMP: 12 **EST:** 2019
SALES (est): 1.97MM **Privately Held**
Web: www.cochranandson.com
SIC: 1711 Warm air heating and air conditioning contractor

(G-5086)
TIMKEN GEARS & SERVICES INC
Also Called: Philadelphia Gear
100 Anchor Mill Rd (19720-4572)
PHONE.............................302 633-4600
Rich Chrivnowski, *Mgr*
EMP: 23
SALES (corp-wide): 4.5B **Publicly Held**
Web: www.philagear.com
SIC: 3462 Gear and chain forgings
HQ: Timken Gears & Services Inc.
935 1st Ave Ste 200
King Of Prussia PA 19406

(G-5087)
TIRE RACK INC
300 Anchor Mill Rd (19720-4574)
PHONE.............................302 325-8260
Chris Lagkowski, *Mgr*
EMP: 23
SALES (corp-wide): 3.69B **Privately Held**
Web: www.tirerack.com
SIC: 5014 Tires and tubes
HQ: The Tire Rack Inc
7101 Vorden Pkwy
South Bend IN 46628
888 541-1777

(G-5088)
TOWER BUSINESS MACHINES INC
Also Called: Tower Business Systems
278 Quigley Blvd (19720-4106)
PHONE.............................302 395-1445
Kevin Laird, *Pr*
EMP: 5 **EST:** 1979
SQ FT: 2,500
SALES (est): 817.39K **Privately Held**
Web: www.towerbiz.com
SIC: 5734 5999 7378 7629 Computer peripheral equipment; Business machines and equipment; Computer maintenance and repair; Business machine repair, electric

(G-5089)
TOWN AND COUNTRY SALON
18 E 5th St (19720-5090)
PHONE.............................302 322-2929
Marissa Collurafici, *Prin*
EMP: 5 **EST:** 2010
SALES (est): 41.2K **Privately Held**
SIC: 7231 Beauty shops

(G-5090)
TRANS PLUS INC
423 W 7th St (19720-4904)
PHONE.............................302 323-3051
Charles Cox, *Pr*
EMP: 5 **EST:** 2015
SALES (est): 174.04K **Privately Held**
Web: www.transplusdelaware.com
SIC: 7537 Automotive transmission repair shops

(G-5091)
TRIANGLE FASTENER CORPORATION
243 Quigley Blvd Ste C (19720-4191)
PHONE.............................302 322-0600
Tony Gutowski, *Mgr*
EMP: 10
SQ FT: 12,500
SALES (corp-wide): 57.3MM **Privately Held**
Web: www.trianglefastener.com
SIC: 5085 Fasteners, industrial: nuts, bolts, screws, etc.
PA: Triangle Fastener Corporation
1925 Preble Ave
Pittsburgh PA 15233
412 321-5021

GEOGRAPHIC SECTION
Hockessin - New Castle County (G-5117)

(G-5092)
TRIMARK INC
621 Delaware St Ste 200 (19720-5073)
P.O. Box 10530 (19850-0530)
PHONE.............................302 322-2143
John E Kinch, *Pr*
EMP: 5 **EST:** 1987
SQ FT: 46,000
SALES (est): 529.06K **Privately Held**
SIC: 7331 Direct mail advertising services

(G-5093)
TZ DISTRIBUTORS
263 Quigley Blvd Ste B (19720-8112)
PHONE.............................302 562-1029
EMP: 5 **EST:** 2017
SALES (est): 205.17K **Privately Held**
Web: www.tzdistributors.com
SIC: 5199 Nondurable goods, nec

(G-5094)
ULTRACHEM INC
900 Centerpoint Blvd (19720-8121)
PHONE.............................302 325-9880
Robert Whiting, *Pr*
Bruce Jewett, *VP*
Jonathan Rickner D.o.s., *Prin*
◆ **EMP:** 17 **EST:** 1965
SQ FT: 58,000
SALES (est): 20.69M **Privately Held**
Web: www.ultracheminc.com
SIC: 5172 Lubricating oils and greases

(G-5095)
UNITED GROUP REAL ESTATE LLC
607 Deemer Pl (19720-5043)
PHONE.............................929 999-1277
Thamer Alamry, *Managing Member*
EMP: 25 **EST:** 2019
SALES (est): 679.61K **Privately Held**
SIC: 6531 Real estate leasing and rentals

(G-5096)
UNIVERSAL DESIGN COMPANY
18 Baldt Ave (19720-4512)
PHONE.............................302 328-8391
James Dugan, *Prin*
EMP: 5 **EST:** 2001
SALES (est): 77.47K **Privately Held**
SIC: 8351 Group day care center

(G-5097)
VERITABLE USA INC
802 Centerpoint Blvd (19720-8123)
PHONE.............................302 326-4800
Laurent Berp, *Prin*
EMP: 65 **EST:** 2020
SALES (est): 2.96MM **Privately Held**
SIC: 5023 Kitchenware

(G-5098)
W W GRAINGER INC
Also Called: Grainger 595
117 Quigley Blvd (19720-4188)
PHONE.............................302 322-1840
Rick Bliss, *Mgr*
EMP: 6
SALES (corp-wide): 15.23B **Publicly Held**
Web: www.johnsoncontrols.com
SIC: 5063 5084 5075 5078 Motors, electric; Fans, industrial; Warm air heating equipment and supplies; Refrigeration equipment and supplies
PA: W.W. Grainger, Inc.
   100 Grainger Pkwy
   Lake Forest IL 60045
   847 535-1000

(G-5099)
WAHID CONSULTANTS LLC
147 Quigley Blvd Unit 12006 (19720-4103)
P.O. Box 32875 (48232-0875)
PHONE.............................315 400-0955
Asma Rashid, *Managing Member*
Farham Dafar, *
EMP: 26 **EST:** 2016
SALES (est): 733.02K **Privately Held**
SIC: 7379 7389 7291 7382 Computer related consulting services; Business Activities at Non-Commercial Site; Tax return preparation services; Security systems services

(G-5100)
WALKER INTERNATIONAL TRNSP LLC
700 Centerpoint Blvd (19720-8120)
PHONE.............................302 325-4180
Mike Zandier, *Brnch Mgr*
EMP: 10
SALES (corp-wide): 99.2MM **Privately Held**
Web: www.walkerscm.com
SIC: 4731 Freight forwarding
HQ: Walker International Transportation Llc
   70 E Sunrise Hwy Ste 611
   Valley Stream NY 11581
   516 568-2080

(G-5101)
WHITAKER & RAGO
316 Delaware St (19720-5038)
PHONE.............................302 414-0056
EMP: 5 **EST:** 2016
SALES (est): 178.86K **Privately Held**
Web: www.wrtaxes.com
SIC: 8721 Certified public accountant

(G-5102)
WILMINGTON FIBRE SPECIALTY CO
700 Washington St (19720-6065)
P.O. Box 192 (19720-0192)
PHONE.............................302 328-7525
John W Morris Iii, *Ch Bd*
B Scott Morris, *
Stephanie Stevens Stkholder, *Prin*
▲ **EMP:** 30 **EST:** 1904
SQ FT: 40,000
SALES (est): 4.81MM **Privately Held**
Web: www.wilmfibre.com
SIC: 3089 3081 3714 Thermoformed finished plastics products, nec; Polyethylene film; Motor vehicle parts and accessories

(G-5103)
ZENITH HOME CORP (DH)
Also Called: Zhc
400 Lukens Dr (19720-2772)
PHONE.............................302 326-8200
Andre Tarant, *CFO*
EMP: 21 **EST:** 2015
SQ FT: 20,000
SALES (est): 96.46MM
SALES (corp-wide): 6.08MM **Privately Held**
Web: www.zenith-products.com
SIC: 5023 Decorative home furnishings and supplies
HQ: Decolin Inc
   9150 Av Du Parc
   Montreal QC H2N 1
   514 384-2910

(G-5104)
ZENITH HOME CORP
499 Ships Landing Way (19720-4579)
PHONE.............................302 322-2190
EMP: 528
SALES (corp-wide): 6.08MM **Privately Held**
Web: www.mayzon.com
SIC: 4225 General warehousing
HQ: Zenith Home Corp.
   400 Lukens Dr
   Historic New Castle DE 19720
   302 326-8200

(G-5105)
ZENITH PRODUCTS
499 Ships Landing Way (19720-4579)
PHONE.............................302 322-2190
EMP: 2
SALES (corp-wide): 6.08MM **Privately Held**
Web: www.mayzon.com
SIC: 2434 Vanities, bathroom: wood
HQ: Maytex Mills
   9150 Av Du Parc
   Montreal QC H2N 1
   514 384-2910

(G-5106)
ZWD PRODUCTS CORPORATION (DH)
Also Called: India Ink
400 Lukens Dr (19720-2728)
PHONE.............................302 326-8200
Richard Benaron, *Pr*
◆ **EMP:** 470 **EST:** 1939
SQ FT: 480,000
SALES (est): 74.32MM
SALES (corp-wide): 6.08MM **Privately Held**
SIC: 2434 2514 Vanities, bathroom: wood; Medicine cabinets and vanities: metal
HQ: Maytex Mills
   9150 Av Du Parc
   Montreal QC H2N 1
   514 384-2910

Hockessin
New Castle County

(G-5107)
100 ST CLIRE DRV OPRATIONS LLC
Also Called: Brackenville Center
100 Saint Claire Dr (19707-8906)
PHONE.............................610 444-6350
J Richard Edwards, *Treas*
Michael Sherman, *
EMP: 762 **EST:** 2014
SALES (est): 52.33MM **Privately Held**
SIC: 8051 Skilled nursing care facilities
HQ: Genesis Healthcare Llc
   101 E State St
   Kennett Square PA 19348

(G-5108)
3D TECH LLC
7454 Lancaster Pike # 308 (19707-9399)
PHONE.............................610 268-2350
Thomas E Boyle, *Managing Member*
EMP: 5 **EST:** 1998
SALES (est): 294.4K **Privately Held**
Web: www.3dtechllc.com
SIC: 7379 Data processing consultant

(G-5109)
924 INC
Also Called: Brandywine Technology
724 Yorklyn Rd Ste 305 (19707-8739)
PHONE.............................302 656-6100
Joel Pierson, *Pr*
Anne Keehan, *VP*
Sean Palat, *Dir*
EMP: 27 **EST:** 1999
SQ FT: 2,600
SALES (est): 4.68MM **Privately Held**
Web: www.brandywinetechnology.com
SIC: 8742 7373 7361 Business management consultant; Computer integrated systems design; Employment agencies

(G-5110)
A2Z PROPERTY MANAGEMENT LLC
2 White Briar Cir (19707-2027)
P.O. Box 1376 (19707-5376)
PHONE.............................302 239-6000
Joseph F Hackman, *Prin*
EMP: 5 **EST:** 2007
SALES (est): 238.21K **Privately Held**
Web: www.a2zpmc.com
SIC: 6531 Real estate managers

(G-5111)
ACHIEVE SOLUTIONS
1 Foxview Cir (19707-2503)
PHONE.............................302 598-1457
Justin Dinorscia, *Prin*
EMP: 6 **EST:** 2010
SALES (est): 92.95K **Privately Held**
SIC: 8322 Community center

(G-5112)
ACHIEVING PHYSIQUES INC
207 Hobson Dr (19707-2135)
PHONE.............................302 593-7067
Joe Deascanis, *Prin*
EMP: 6 **EST:** 2008
SALES (est): 95.52K **Privately Held**
Web: www.achievingphysiques.com
SIC: 7991 Physical fitness facilities

(G-5113)
AD BITS ADVERTISING AND PR
754 Morris Rd (19707-9697)
PHONE.............................954 467-8420
EMP: 5 **EST:** 2017
SALES (est): 74.23K **Privately Held**
SIC: 7311 Advertising agencies

(G-5114)
ADD-INSCOM LLC
144 Dewberry Dr (19707-2118)
PHONE.............................302 584-1771
Mamdouh Barakat, *Pr*
EMP: 5 **EST:** 2010
SALES (est): 135.9K **Privately Held**
Web: www.add-ins.com
SIC: 8721 Accounting services, except auditing

(G-5115)
ADVIK REPUBLIC INC
7209 Lancaster Pike Ste 4-1112 (19707-9292)
PHONE.............................844 987-4238
Gunnar Advik, *Pr*
EMP: 9 **EST:** 2019
SALES (est): 125.47K **Privately Held**
SIC: 4953 Refuse collection and disposal services

(G-5116)
AFFINITY WOMENS HEALTH LLC
614 Loveville Rd Ste F1a (19707-1623)
PHONE.............................302 234-8982
Samuel H Blumberg, *Prin*
EMP: 10 **EST:** 2011
SALES (est): 140K **Privately Held**
Web: www.affinitywomens.com
SIC: 8099 Health and allied services, nec

(G-5117)
AIM RESEARCH CO
5936 Limestone Rd Ste 302 (19707-8932)
PHONE.............................302 235-5940

Hockessin - New Castle County (G-5118)

Dian Y Lee, *Pr*
Diana Z Lee, *COO*
EMP: 8 **EST:** 1998
SQ FT: 600
SALES (est): 853K **Privately Held**
Web: www.aimresearchcompany.com
SIC: 3825 Lab standards, electric: resistance, inductance, capacitance

(G-5118)
ALARM SYSTEMS CO OF DELAWARE
735 Montgomery Woods Dr (19707-9324)
PHONE.................302 239-7754
Thomas S Hounsell, *Pr*
EMP: 5 **EST:** 1974
SALES (est): 346.88K **Privately Held**
SIC: 1731 Fire detection and burglar alarm systems specialization

(G-5119)
ALDAS REFINISHING COMPANY
Also Called: Aldas Refinishing
606 Chanin Ct (19707-9541)
PHONE.................302 528-5028
German Aldas Junior, *Pr*
Juan Aldas, *VP*
EMP: 3 **EST:** 2005
SALES (est): 137.64K **Privately Held**
SIC: 2431 7389 Millwork; Business Activities at Non-Commercial Site

(G-5120)
AMERICAN LEGION AUXILIARY
62 Wesley Dr (19707-9628)
PHONE.................302 235-0878
Lisamarie Mccarley, *Prin*
EMP: 6 **EST:** 2015
SALES (est): 46.86K **Privately Held**
Web: www.legion.org
SIC: 8641 Veterans' organization

(G-5121)
AMERICAN UNVRSAL-HOCKESSIN LLC
Also Called: AMERICAN RENAL
5936 Limestone Rd Ste 101 (19707-8931)
PHONE.................302 239-4106
John Mcdonough, *Mgr*
EMP: 44 **EST:** 2015
SALES (est): 1.26MM
SALES (corp-wide): 822.52MM **Privately Held**
SIC: 8052 Intermediate care facilities
HQ: American Renal Associates Holdings, Inc.
500 Cummings Ctr Ste 6550
Beverly MA 01915

(G-5122)
AMERIPRISE FINANCIAL INC
Also Called: Ameriprise Financial Services
103 Brook Run (19707-2405)
PHONE.................302 235-5765
Paul Gibler, *Admn*
EMP: 5 **EST:** 2019
SALES (est): 230.28K **Privately Held**
Web: www.ameriprise.com
SIC: 6282 Investment advice

(G-5123)
AMSTEL BARBERSHOP LLC
7313 Lancaster Pike Ste 4 (19707-9278)
PHONE.................302 635-7686
EMP: 5 **EST:** 2016
SALES (est): 34.13K **Privately Held**
Web: www.amstelbarbershop.com
SIC: 7241 Barber shops

(G-5124)
AMY CHILIMIDOS C O BOA
108 Haddington Way (19707-1810)
PHONE.................302 388-1880
Amy Chilimidos, *Prin*
EMP: 5 **EST:** 2011
SALES (est): 154.1K **Privately Held**
SIC: 1521 Single-family housing construction

(G-5125)
ANGELO JOSEPH CHIARI RPH
516 Defoe Rd (19707-1132)
PHONE.................302 239-5949
Angelo Joseph Chiari, *Prin*
EMP: 8 **EST:** 2012
SALES (est): 68.93K **Privately Held**
SIC: 8011 Medical centers

(G-5126)
ANGITA PHARMARD LLC
24 Tall Oaks Dr (19707-2041)
PHONE.................302 234-6794
EMP: 2 **EST:** 2006
SQ FT: 1,000
SALES (est): 14.91K **Privately Held**
SIC: 2834 Pharmaceutical preparations

(G-5127)
ANHUI XNCHENG HIGH SCHL ALMNI
115 Hockessin Dr (19707-2071)
PHONE.................302 234-4351
Min Zhang, *Pr*
EMP: 5 **EST:** 2014
SALES (est): 38.73K **Privately Held**
SIC: 8641 Civic and social associations

(G-5128)
ANYTIME FITNESS MAIN LINE
Also Called: Anytime Fitness
702 Lantana Dr (19707-8810)
PHONE.................302 239-4800
Julie Panaro, *Pr*
EMP: 9 **EST:** 2017
SALES (est): 62.73K **Privately Held**
Web: www.anytimefitness.sg
SIC: 7991 7299 Physical fitness clubs with training equipment; Personal appearance services

(G-5129)
ARCHADECK OF DELAWARE
Also Called: Archadeck
7465 Lancaster Pike (19707-9583)
PHONE.................302 766-3698
EMP: 11 **EST:** 2019
SALES (est): 474.89K **Privately Held**
Web: www.archadeck.com
SIC: 1521 Patio and deck construction and repair

(G-5130)
BASHER & SON ENTERPRISES INC
Also Called: Basher & Son Welding
1072 Yorklyn Rd (19707-9769)
P.O. Box 1615 (19707-5615)
PHONE.................302 239-6584
Warren Basher, *Pr*
Kim Mavil, *Treas*
EMP: 4 **EST:** 1972
SALES (est): 280K **Privately Held**
SIC: 7549 7692 Trailer maintenance; Welding repair

(G-5131)
BATHOLITE NATURAL STONE INC
302 Wellspring Ct (19707-2096)
PHONE.................206 707-2298
Harishu Koya, *Dir*
EMP: 6 **EST:** 2014
SALES (est): 81.78K **Privately Held**

SIC: 5032 Granite building stone

(G-5132)
BERKSHIRE HATAWAY HOME SVCS
88 Lantana Dr (19707-8814)
PHONE.................302 235-6431
EMP: 21 **EST:** 2014
SALES (est): 159.86K **Privately Held**
Web: www.foxroach.com
SIC: 6531 Real estate agent, residential

(G-5133)
BILL BURRIS INSURANCE
7217 Lancaster Pike Ste B (19707-9587)
PHONE.................302 239-6661
EMP: 5 **EST:** 2017
SALES (est): 167.91K **Privately Held**
Web: www.billburrisinsurance.com
SIC: 6411 Insurance agents and brokers

(G-5134)
BLUE HEN ROOFING LLC
503 Hemingway Dr (19707-1117)
PHONE.................302 545-2349
Edward Szczerba Junior, *Prin*
EMP: 5 **EST:** 2015
SALES (est): 74.36K **Privately Held**
SIC: 1761 Roofing contractor

(G-5135)
BOB PRESTON CARPENTRY
433 Bishop Dr (19707-9708)
PHONE.................302 234-8659
Bob Preston, *Prin*
EMP: 5 **EST:** 2016
SALES (est): 71.78K **Privately Held**
SIC: 1751 Carpentry work

(G-5136)
BOB REYNOLDS BACKHOE SERVICES
1124 Old Wilmington Rd (19707-9367)
PHONE.................302 239-4711
Bob Reynolds, *Mgr*
EMP: 5 **EST:** 2017
SALES (est): 62.55K **Privately Held**
SIC: 3531 Backhoes

(G-5137)
BONNA-AGELA TECHNOLOGIES INC
217 Cherry Blossom Pl (19707-2047)
PHONE.................302 438-8798
Zhixin Yang, *Mgr*
EMP: 77
Web: www.agela.com
SIC: 3826 Analytical instruments
PA: Bonna-Agela Technologies Inc
2038a Telegraph Rd
Wilmington DE 19808

(G-5138)
BORSELLO INC
720 Yorklyn Rd Ste 5 (19707-8729)
P.O. Box 970 (19707-0970)
PHONE.................302 472-2600
Thomas M Borsello Junior, *Pr*
Tammy Booth-rice, *Off Mgr*
EMP: 20 **EST:** 2009
SALES (est): 1.45MM **Privately Held**
Web: www.borsellolandscaping.com
SIC: 0781 0782 Landscape services; Landscape contractors

(G-5139)
BOWMAN FAMILY FOUNDATION
7234 Lancaster Pike Ste 300a (19707-9295)
PHONE.................302 234-5750
EMP: 8 **EST:** 1994
SALES (est): 457.31K **Privately Held**

SIC: 8699 Charitable organization

(G-5140)
BRANDYWINE ART
809 Grande Ln (19707-9350)
PHONE.................302 234-7874
Michael Romano, *Prin*
EMP: 7 **EST:** 2013
SALES (est): 35.01K **Privately Held**
Web: www.thebrandywine.com
SIC: 7999 Art gallery, commercial

(G-5141)
BRANDYWINE TRUST CO
7234 Lancaster Pike Ste 300a (19707-9295)
PHONE.................302 234-5750
Richard E Carlson, *Pr*
W Scott Campbell, *
Jeffrey S Becker, *
EMP: 88 **EST:** 1911
SALES (est): 11.97MM **Privately Held**
Web: www.brandywinetrust.com
SIC: 6733 Trusts, except educational, religious, charity: management

(G-5142)
BRENDEN BLEY CHANL VFW POST 58
Also Called: VFW Post 5892
7620 Lancaster Pike (19707-9755)
P.O. Box 231 (19707-0231)
PHONE.................302 239-0797
Gayle Bledens, *Pr*
EMP: 6 **EST:** 1946
SALES (est): 147.7K **Privately Held**
SIC: 8641 Veterans' organization

(G-5143)
BRIGHTSIDE PEST SERVICES INC
27 Wesley Dr (19707-9624)
PHONE.................302 893-5858
EMP: 5 **EST:** 2015
SALES (est): 67.11K **Privately Held**
Web: www.brightsidepest.com
SIC: 7342 Pest control in structures

(G-5144)
BRUCE E MATTHEWS DDS PA
451 Hockessin Cors (19707-9586)
PHONE.................302 234-2440
Daniel E Matthews, *Prin*
EMP: 5
SALES (corp-wide): 994.93K **Privately Held**
Web: www.drmatthewswilmington.com
SIC: 8021 Dentists' office
PA: Bruce E Matthews Dds Pa
1403 Silverside Rd Ste A
Wilmington DE 19810
302 475-9220

(G-5145)
BURTON CONSTRUCTION CO LLC
530 Schoolhouse Rd Ste E (19707-9526)
PHONE.................302 327-8650
EMP: 6 **EST:** 2020
SALES (est): 925.8K **Privately Held**
Web: www.burtonconstructionllc.com
SIC: 1521 Single-family housing construction

(G-5146)
C WALLACE & ASSOCIATES
Also Called: Wallce & Associates
805 Grande Ln (19707-9350)
PHONE.................302 528-2182
Charles N Wallace, *Pr*
Brady Harris, *Mng Pt*
EMP: 6 **EST:** 2009
SALES (est): 597.45K **Privately Held**

Hockessin - New Castle County (G-5175)

SIC: 1521 General remodeling, single-family houses

(G-5147)
CACC MONTESSORI SCHOOL
1313 Little Baltimore Rd (19707-9701)
P.O. Box 892 (19707-0892)
PHONE.....................302 239-2917
Elizabeth Simmon, Dir
EMP: 12 EST: 1982
SALES (est): 261.89K Privately Held
Web: www.caccmont.org
SIC: 8211 8351 Private elementary and secondary schools; Child day care services

(G-5148)
CAMBRIDGE CLB ASSOC LTD PARTNR
726 Yorklyn Rd Ste 200 (19707-8701)
PHONE.....................302 674-3500
EMP: 9 EST: 2004
SALES (est): 355.24K Privately Held
SIC: 7997 Membership sports and recreation clubs

(G-5149)
CARRIE CONSTRUCTION INC
403 Hockessin Hills Rd (19707-9699)
PHONE.....................302 239-5386
Robert Wilkinson, Pr
Frederick Charles Wilkinson, VP
EMP: 5 EST: 1979
SALES (est): 520K Privately Held
SIC: 1521 General remodeling, single-family houses

(G-5150)
CARTESSA AESTHETICS
210 Peoples Way (19707-1904)
PHONE.....................302 332-1991
Joe Amon, Prin
EMP: 8 EST: 2017
SALES (est): 28.8K Privately Held
Web: www.cartessaaesthetics.com
SIC: 7231 Cosmetology and personal hygiene salons

(G-5151)
CASE HNDYMAN SVCS W CHSTER LLC
510 Thorndale Dr (19707-2332)
PHONE.....................302 234-6558
EMP: 6 EST: 2004
SALES (est): 497.92K Privately Held
Web: www.casedesign.com
SIC: 1521 General remodeling, single-family houses

(G-5152)
CATALYST FITNESS LLC
40 Pierson Dr (19707-1030)
PHONE.....................302 379-3883
Catherine Scherer, Prin
EMP: 5 EST: 2018
SALES (est): 157.59K Privately Held
Web: www.catalystfitnessde.com
SIC: 7991 Physical fitness facilities

(G-5153)
CAVEMAN DESIGN INC
359 Lower Snuff Mill Rd (19707-9389)
P.O. Box 235 (19736-0235)
PHONE.....................302 234-9969
Tom Long, Pr
EMP: 3 EST: 1996
SALES (est): 232.48K Privately Held
Web: www.caveman3.com
SIC: 3841 Medical instruments and equipment, blood and bone work

(G-5154)
CDB VENTURES INC
Also Called: The Goddard School
157 Lantana Dr (19707-8808)
PHONE.....................302 235-0414
Genelle Craig, Pr
Christian Craig, *
EMP: 22 EST: 1997
SALES (est): 426.18K Privately Held
Web: www.goddardschool.com
SIC: 8351 Preschool center

(G-5155)
CEO-HQCOM LLC
Also Called: Consulting Experts Online
7209 Lancaster Pike # 41023 (19707-9292)
PHONE.....................302 883-8555
EMP: 6 EST: 2015
SALES (est): 155.85K Privately Held
SIC: 8741 Business management

(G-5156)
CHARLES SLANINA
724 Yorklyn Rd Ste 210 (19707-8704)
PHONE.....................302 234-1605
Charles Slanina, Owner
EMP: 5 EST: 2007
SALES (est): 234.84K Privately Held
Web: www.delawgroup.com
SIC: 8111 General practice attorney, lawyer

(G-5157)
CHEAP-SCAPE INC
Also Called: Borsello Landscaping
720 Yorklyn Rd Ste 5 (19707-8729)
P.O. Box 970 (19707-0970)
PHONE.....................302 472-2600
Thomas M Borsello Junior, Pr
EMP: 16 EST: 2001
SQ FT: 3,000
SALES (est): 1.33MM Privately Held
Web: www.borsellolandscaping.com
SIC: 0781 Landscape services

(G-5158)
CHERYL WAGNER
7217 Lancaster Pike (19707-9585)
PHONE.....................302 635-7632
EMP: 9 EST: 2018
SALES (est): 271.8K Privately Held
Web: www.wagnerreg.com
SIC: 8748 Environmental consultant

(G-5159)
CHILIMIDOS LLC
7209 Lancaster Pike Ste 4 # 314 (19707-9292)
PHONE.....................302 388-1880
EMP: 6 EST: 2005
SALES (est): 938.45K Privately Held
SIC: 1542 Nonresidential construction, nec

(G-5160)
CHIP DESIGN SYSTEMS INC
12 Longacre Ct (19707-2068)
PHONE.....................302 494-6220
Michelle Mcgee, Prin
EMP: 10 EST: 1994
SALES (est): 1.02MM Privately Held
Web: www.chipdesignsystems.com
SIC: 8748 Business consulting, nec

(G-5161)
CHIP DESIGN SYSTEMS LLC
12 Longacre Ct (19707-2068)
PHONE.....................302 307-6731
Emir Kiamilev, Prin
Fouad Kiamilev, Prin
Chandra Kiamilev, Prin
Hamzah Ahmed, Prin
Rodney Mcgee, Prin
EMP: 23 EST: 2013
SALES (est): 1.07MM Privately Held
SIC: 8711 Engineering services

(G-5162)
CHOICE RMDLG & RESTORATION INC
110 Ramunno Cir (19707-9743)
PHONE.....................717 917-0601
John Paoletti, Pr
EMP: 5 EST: 2009
SALES (est): 937.36K Privately Held
SIC: 1521 General remodeling, single-family houses

(G-5163)
CHRISTOPHER H WENDEL MD PA
P.O. Box 14155 (33408-0155)
PHONE.....................302 540-2979
Christopher Wendel, Prin
EMP: 10 EST: 2002
SALES (est): 229.19K Privately Held
SIC: 8011 General and family practice, physician/surgeon

(G-5164)
CMC CORPORATION OF HOCKESSIN
Also Called: U S Male Mens Hair Care Ctrs
721 Yorklyn Rd (19707-9279)
P.O. Box 1269 (19707-5269)
PHONE.....................302 239-1960
Clinton Vick Senior, Pr
EMP: 7 EST: 1990
SQ FT: 1,200
SALES (est): 129.9K Privately Held
SIC: 7231 7241 Beauty shops; Barber shops

(G-5165)
CODY H HAFNER
100 Fitness Way (19707-2423)
PHONE.....................302 234-1030
Cody Hafner, Prin
EMP: 7 EST: 2017
SALES (est): 94.68K Privately Held
SIC: 8049 Offices of health practitioner

(G-5166)
COFFEE RUN CONDO COUNCIL INC
614 Loveville Rd (19707-1623)
PHONE.....................302 239-4134
John Bryans, Pr
EMP: 5 EST: 1973
SQ FT: 800
SALES (est): 484.19K Privately Held
SIC: 8641 Condominium association

(G-5167)
COMFORT SUITES MOTEL
Also Called: Comfort Suites
181 Thompson Dr (19707-1913)
PHONE.....................302 266-6600
Paresh Patel, Owner
EMP: 7 EST: 1998
SALES (est): 348.02K Privately Held
Web: www.choicehotels.com
SIC: 7011 Hotel, franchised

(G-5168)
COMMUNITY CONSULTING CORPS
3 Larchmont Ct (19707-9682)
P.O. Box 68 (19736-0068)
PHONE.....................614 348-7823
EMP: 5 EST: 2018
SALES (est): 34.23K Privately Held
Web: www.karaoke-dj.com
SIC: 8748 Business consulting, nec

(G-5169)
CRAIG SMUCKER MD ORTHOPAEDICS
5936 Limestone Rd Ste 202 (19707-8931)
PHONE.....................610 869-5757
Craig G Smucker, Pr
EMP: 7 EST: 2017
SALES (est): 129.06K Privately Held
Web: www.eandjheatingcooling.com
SIC: 8011 Offices and clinics of medical doctors

(G-5170)
CREATIVE SOLUTIONS INTL (HQ)
724 Yorklyn Rd Ste 240 (19707-8732)
PHONE.....................302 234-7400
EMP: 7 EST: 1996
SALES (est): 246.45K
SALES (corp-wide): 5.78MM Privately Held
SIC: 7336 Creative services to advertisers, except writers
PA: De Novo Corporation
1011 Centre Rd Ste 104
Wilmington DE 19805
302 234-7407

(G-5171)
CROSSLAND & ASSOCIATES LLC
724 Yorklyn Rd Ste 100 (19707-8734)
PHONE.....................302 409-0120
Daniel Crossland, Owner
EMP: 13 EST: 2012
SALES (est): 878.22K Privately Held
Web: www.macelree.com
SIC: 8111 General practice attorney, lawyer

(G-5172)
CROSSLAND AND ASSOCIATES
724 Yorklyn Rd Ste 100 (19707-8734)
PHONE.....................302 658-2100
EMP: 5
SALES (est): 477.18K Privately Held
Web: www.macelree.com
SIC: 8111 General practice attorney, lawyer

(G-5173)
CRUISE HOLIDAYS BRANDYWINE VLY
Also Called: Cruise Holidays
7460 Lancaster Pike Ste 6 (19707-9276)
PHONE.....................302 239-6400
Shirley Mccreary, Owner
James Mccreary, Prin
EMP: 10 EST: 1994
SALES (est): 630K Privately Held
Web: www.cruisedel.com
SIC: 4724 Tourist agency arranging transport, lodging and car rental

(G-5174)
CS WEBB DAUGHTERS & SON INC
1028 Yorklyn Rd (19707-9769)
P.O. Box 84 (19736-0084)
PHONE.....................302 239-2801
EMP: 6 EST: 1962
SALES (est): 470.69K Privately Held
SIC: 1711 Septic system construction

(G-5175)
DAVID P ROSER INC (PA)
19 Roser Ln (19707-9551)
P.O. Box 104 (19707-0104)
PHONE.....................302 239-7605
David P Roser, Pr
EMP: 20 EST: 1965
SALES (est): 3.16MM
SALES (corp-wide): 3.16MM Privately Held

Hockessin - New Castle County (G-5176)

SIC: 1794 Excavation and grading, building construction

(G-5176)
DAVITRON LLC
20 Longacre Ct (19707-2068)
PHONE..............................302 239-1383
Susan Davies, *Prin*
EMP: 8 EST: 2011
SALES (est): 101.15K **Privately Held**
Web: www.output.net
SIC: 6519 Real property lessors, nec

(G-5177)
DEATON MCCUE & CO INC
724 Yorklyn Rd (19707-8736)
PHONE..............................302 658-7789
Sean Mccue, *Pr*
Stephen Deaton, *CFO*
EMP: 8 EST: 1990
SALES (est): 897.63K **Privately Held**
Web: www.deatonmccue.com
SIC: 6531 Real estate managers

(G-5178)
DELAWARE CRDOVASCULAR ASSOC PA
5936 Limestone Rd (19707-8930)
PHONE..............................302 235-4100
EMP: 12
Web: www.decardio.com
SIC: 8011 Cardiologist and cardio-vascular specialist
PA: Delaware Cardiovascular Associates, P.A.
1403 Foulk Rd Ste 101a
Wilmington DE 19803

(G-5179)
DELAWARE HEALTH AND FITNES LLC
204 Lantana Dr (19707-8805)
PHONE..............................302 584-7531
EMP: 7 EST: 2019
SALES (est): 76K **Privately Held**
SIC: 8099 Health and allied services, nec

(G-5180)
DELAWARE MECH CONTRS ASSOC
P.O. Box 1692 (19707-5692)
PHONE..............................302 235-2813
EMP: 6 EST: 2011
SALES (est): 188 **Privately Held**
SIC: 1711 Mechanical contractor

(G-5181)
DELAWARE MONUMENT AND VAULT
203 Wyndtree Ct S (19707-2316)
PHONE..............................302 540-2387
EMP: 3 EST: 2011
SALES (est): 120.37K **Privately Held**
SIC: 3272 Burial vaults, concrete or precast terrazzo

(G-5182)
DELAWARE NATURE SOCIETY (PA)
3511 Barley Mill Rd (19707-9393)
P.O. Box 700 (19707-0700)
PHONE..............................302 239-1283
Bernard Dempsey, *Pr*
Nancy Frederick, *
Thomas Shey, *
George Fisher, *
EMP: 43 EST: 1962
SALES (est): 3.64MM
SALES (corp-wide): 3.64MM **Privately Held**
Web: www.delawarenaturesociety.org

SIC: 8631 8641 8733 Labor organizations; Civic and social associations; Noncommercial research organizations

(G-5183)
DELAWARE OUTDOOR ADVERTISING
207 Golding Ct (19707-1356)
PHONE..............................302 234-1975
Brendan Killeen, *Owner*
EMP: 6 EST: 1976
SALES (est): 70.41K **Privately Held**
Web: www.delawareoutdoor.com
SIC: 7312 Billboard advertising

(G-5184)
DELAWARE SPRAY FOAM INC
585 Hemingway Dr (19707-1153)
P.O. Box 168 (19736-0168)
PHONE..............................302 234-4050
EMP: 6 EST: 2012
SALES (est): 121.97K **Privately Held**
Web: www.delawaresprayfoam.com
SIC: 1742 Insulation, buildings

(G-5185)
DELAWARE VALLEY PATHOLOGY
22 Withers Way (19707-2510)
PHONE..............................302 239-3729
Al A Nabil, *Prin*
EMP: 10 EST: 2010
SALES (est): 173.17K **Privately Held**
SIC: 8011 Pathologist

(G-5186)
DIAMOND STATE CURLING CLUB
8 E Aldine Dr (19707-1814)
PHONE..............................856 577-3747
Frank Sharp, *Pr*
EMP: 6 EST: 2017
SALES (est): 65.78K **Privately Held**
Web: www.diamondstatecurling.org
SIC: 7997 Membership sports and recreation clubs

(G-5187)
DIAMOND STATE EXPRESS LLC
105 E Bridle Path (19707-9409)
PHONE..............................302 563-3514
EMP: 43 EST: 2012
SALES (est): 728K **Privately Held**
SIC: 7241 Barber shops

(G-5188)
DMG CLEARANCES INC
7209 Lancaster Pike Ste 4-330 (19707-9292)
PHONE..............................302 239-6337
EMP: 6 EST: 1996
SALES (est): 843.5K **Privately Held**
Web: www.dmgclearances.com
SIC: 7389 Music distribution systems

(G-5189)
DOMINIQUE HO
252 Pond Dr (19707-9239)
PHONE..............................302 234-2971
Dominique Ho, *Prin*
EMP: 5 EST: 2019
SALES (est): 40.67K **Privately Held**
SIC: 8641 Environmental protection organization

(G-5190)
DON BAAG MD
722 Yorklyn Rd (19707-8718)
PHONE..............................302 235-2351
Don Baag, *Prin*
EMP: 11 EST: 2001
SALES (est): 133.66K **Privately Held**

SIC: 8011 General and family practice, physician/surgeon

(G-5191)
DONOVAN PROPERTY SERVICE INC
15 Foxview Cir (19707-2503)
PHONE..............................917 841-2396
EMP: 5 EST: 2019
SALES (est): 638.04K **Privately Held**
SIC: 6512 Nonresidential building operators

(G-5192)
DR KAZ FMLY COSMTC DENTISTRY
5936 Limestone Rd Ste 201 (19707-8931)
PHONE..............................302 235-7645
Robert Kaz, *Owner*
EMP: 6 EST: 2014
SALES (est): 192.56K **Privately Held**
Web: www.drkazde.com
SIC: 8021 Dentists' office

(G-5193)
DSOUZA AND ASSOCIATES INC
530 Schoolhouse Rd Ste A (19707-9526)
PHONE..............................302 239-2300
Mabel Dsouza, *Pr*
Rudy D'souza, *VP*
EMP: 28 EST: 1989
SQ FT: 1,400
SALES (est): 4.25MM **Privately Held**
Web: www.dsouzainc.com
SIC: 8721 Billing and bookkeeping service

(G-5194)
DT TRANSIT LLC
7209 Lancaster Pike (19707-9292)
PHONE..............................302 216-3547
Johnny Miango, *Managing Member*
EMP: 6
SALES (est): 76.63K **Privately Held**
SIC: 4215 Courier services, except by air

(G-5195)
E2E LLC
177 Thompson Dr Ste 888 (19707-1913)
PHONE..............................703 906-5353
EMP: 5 EST: 2006
SALES (est): 228.07K **Privately Held**
SIC: 7379 7371 Computer related consulting services; Computer software development and applications

(G-5196)
EARLY LEARNING CENTER
7250 Lancaster Pike (19707-9263)
PHONE..............................302 239-3033
Kelly Mervine, *Dir*
Kim Simmons, *Dir*
EMP: 18 EST: 1977
SALES (est): 244.8K **Privately Held**
Web: www.hockessinumc.org
SIC: 8351 Preschool center

(G-5197)
EASTERN ATHLETIC CLUBS LLC
Also Called: Hockessin Athletic Club
100 Fitness Way (19707-2423)
PHONE..............................302 239-6688
EMP: 115 EST: 2005
SALES (est): 17.82MM **Privately Held**
Web: www.hachealthclub.com
SIC: 7991 Health club

(G-5198)
ECONOMIC LAUNDRY SOLUTIONS
Also Called: Alpha Chemicals
14 Cinnamon Dr (19707-1349)
PHONE..............................302 234-7627
Michael Schulte, *Owner*
EMP: 4 EST: 2002

SALES (est): 62.6K **Privately Held**
SIC: 2899 Household tints or dyes

(G-5199)
EMERALD BIOAGRICULTURE CORP (PA)
726 Yorklyn Rd Ste 420 (19707-8700)
PHONE..............................517 882-7370
John Mcintyre, *Pr*
John L Mcintyre, *Pr*
◆ EMP: 10 EST: 2000
SQ FT: 6,500
SALES (est): 2.8MM **Privately Held**
SIC: 2875 5191 8748 Fertilizers, mixing only; Chemicals, agricultural; Agricultural consultant

(G-5200)
EMW PUBLICATIONS
351 Mockingbird Hill Rd (19707-9723)
P.O. Box 400 (19707-0400)
PHONE..............................302 438-9879
Edith M Warren, *Owner*
EMP: 4 EST: 2017
SALES (est): 48.91K **Privately Held**
SIC: 2741 Miscellaneous publishing

(G-5201)
EN PROPERTIES LLC
11 Foxview Cir (19707-2503)
P.O. Box 1221 (19707-5221)
PHONE..............................302 738-4201
Nazir Nisar, *Prin*
EMP: 6 EST: 2016
SALES (est): 222.78K **Privately Held**
SIC: 6531 Real estate agents and managers

(G-5202)
ENVISION PROPERTY SOLVERS LLC
7209 Lancaster Pike (19707-9292)
PHONE..............................888 478-0744
Camille Dorsey, *CEO*
EMP: 5 EST: 2019
SALES (est): 254.54K **Privately Held**
SIC: 6512 Nonresidential building operators

(G-5203)
ESHOPPERLISTS COM INC
114 Hockessin Dr (19707-2070)
PHONE..............................302 235-5743
Surya Chitra, *Prin*
EMP: 5 EST: 2013
SALES (est): 85.77K **Privately Held**
SIC: 7371 Computer software development

(G-5204)
EXCLUSIVELY LEGAL INC
7301 Lancaster Pike Ste 2 (19707-9589)
P.O. Box 1436 (19707-5436)
PHONE..............................302 239-5990
Sueann M Hall, *Pr*
EMP: 10 EST: 2004
SALES (est): 652.06K **Privately Held**
Web: www.justlegalinc.com
SIC: 7361 Placement agencies

(G-5205)
F & H MECHANICAL LLC
10 Arthur Dr (19707-1010)
PHONE..............................302 932-8034
EMP: 5 EST: 2018
SALES (est): 180.45K **Privately Held**
Web: www.fhmechanical.com
SIC: 1711 Mechanical contractor

(G-5206)
FAIRVILLE MANAGEMENT CO LLC (PA)
726 Yorklyn Rd Ste 200 (19707-8701)
PHONE..............................302 489-2000

GEOGRAPHIC SECTION

Hockessin - New Castle County (G-5236)

EMP: 5 **EST:** 2002
SALES (est): 2.12MM
SALES (corp-wide): 2.12MM **Privately Held**
Web: www.fairvillemanagement.com
SIC: 6531 Rental agent, real estate

(G-5207)
FAMILY PRACTICE HOCKESSIN PA
5936 Limestone Rd Ste 202 (19707-8931)
PHONE..................302 239-4500
Alessandro Bianchi, *Prin*
EMP: 5 **EST:** 2009
SALES (est): 437.28K **Privately Held**
SIC: 8031 8011 Offices and clinics of osteopathic physicians; General and family practice, physician/surgeon

(G-5208)
FIELDS & COMPANY INC
7460 Lancaster Pike Ste 3 (19707-9276)
PHONE..................302 234-2775
William F Fields Junior, *Pr*
EMP: 5 **EST:** 1992
SALES (est): 207.76K **Privately Held**
Web: www.billfieldscpa.com
SIC: 8721 Certified public accountant

(G-5209)
FIRST CHOICE REAL ESTATE SVCS
724 Yorklyn Rd (19707-8704)
PHONE..................302 525-4970
Stacie L Marchese, *Owner*
EMP: 7 **EST:** 2011
SALES (est): 306.14K **Privately Held**
Web: www.firstchoicerellc.com
SIC: 6531 Real estate agent, residential

(G-5210)
FIRST STATE ORTHOPAEDICS PA
304 Lantana Dr (19707-8807)
PHONE..................302 234-2600
Charles L Lockwood, *Brnch Mgr*
EMP: 6
SALES (corp-wide): 31.54MM **Privately Held**
Web: www.firststateortho.com
SIC: 8011 Orthopedic physician
PA: First State Orthopaedics, P.A.
  4745 Ogltn Stntn Rd # 225
  Newark DE 19713
  302 731-2888

(G-5211)
FIRST STATE ROBOTICS INC
106 Meriden Dr (19707-1702)
P.O. Box 116 (19707-0116)
PHONE..................302 584-7152
John Larock, *Prin*
EMP: 6 **EST:** 2019
SALES (est): 107.86K **Privately Held**
Web: www.firststaterobotics.org
SIC: 8731 Commercial physical research

(G-5212)
FIX IT NOW
13 Rivendell Ct (19707-2400)
PHONE..................302 293-7748
EMP: 5 **EST:** 2014
SALES (est): 90.23K **Privately Held**
Web: www.fix-it-now-services.com
SIC: 1521 General remodeling, single-family houses

(G-5213)
FLO MECHANICAL LLC
507 Baxter Ct (19707-1916)
PHONE..................302 239-7299
EMP: 28 **EST:** 2011
SALES (est): 2.1MM **Privately Held**
Web: www.flomechanical.com
SIC: 1711 Mechanical contractor

(G-5214)
FRESENIUS MED CARE NTHRN DEL L
Also Called: Fresenius Kidney Care Lantana
214 Lantana Dr (19707-8805)
PHONE..................302 239-4704
Elizabeth Beer, *Brnch Mgr*
EMP: 25
SALES (corp-wide): 2.09MM **Privately Held**
Web: www.freseniuskidneycare.com
SIC: 8092 Kidney dialysis centers
PA: Fresenius Medical Care Northern Delaware, Llc
  920 Winter St
  Waltham MA 02451
  781 699-4404

(G-5215)
FRIENDS HCKSSIN CLRED SCHL 107
4266 Mill Creek Rd (19707-9101)
PHONE..................302 540-5959
EMP: 7 **EST:** 2017
SALES (est): 926.67K **Privately Held**
Web: www.hockessincoloredschool107.org
SIC: 8699 Charitable organization

(G-5216)
G FEDALE GENERAL CONTRS LLC
Also Called: G Fedale Roofing & Siding
160 Thompson Dr (19707-1911)
PHONE..................302 225-7663
EMP: 22 **EST:** 2008
SALES (est): 1.56MM **Privately Held**
SIC: 1761 Roofing contractor

(G-5217)
GARDEN DESIGN GROUP INC
787 Valley Rd (19707-9150)
P.O. Box 1143 (19707-5143)
PHONE..................302 234-3000
EMP: 8 **EST:** 1992
SALES (est): 777.23K **Privately Held**
Web: www.gardendesigngroup.com
SIC: 0781 Landscape architects

(G-5218)
GARRY F KUHLMAN GEN CONTRACTOR
1580 Snuff Mill Rd (19707-9641)
PHONE..................302 482-3535
Garry F Kuhlman, *Prin*
EMP: 5 **EST:** 2016
SALES (est): 90.64K **Privately Held**
SIC: 1799 Special trade contractors, nec

(G-5219)
GENERAL MERCHANDISE & SVCS LLC
11 Mccormick Dr (19707-2107)
PHONE..................302 690-8662
Jinfeng Gu, *Prin*
EMP: 5 **EST:** 2017
SALES (est): 125.23K **Privately Held**
SIC: 7699 Industrial machinery and equipment repair

(G-5220)
GENESIS PSYCHOLOGICAL SERVICES
7503 Lancaster Pike (19707-9593)
PHONE..................302 513-7156
EMP: 5 **EST:** 2017
SALES (est): 71.67K **Privately Held**
SIC: 8049 Clinical psychologist

(G-5221)
GENOVESIUS SOLUTIA LLC
521 Cabot Dr (19707-1138)
PHONE..................302 252-7506
EMP: 5 **EST:** 2014
SALES (est): 245.18K **Privately Held**
Web: www.genosolutia.com
SIC: 8742 7379 Quality assurance consultant; Computer related consulting services

(G-5222)
GLOBAL WELLNESS
17 Raphael Rd (19707-2209)
PHONE..................302 234-6550
EMP: 8 **EST:** 2008
SALES (est): 140K **Privately Held**
Web: www.5pillarswellness.com
SIC: 8099 Health and allied services, nec

(G-5223)
GLOBE ELECTRIC COMPANY
28 Longbow Ter (19707-1527)
PHONE..................302 328-8809
EMP: 6 **EST:** 2015
SALES (est): 84.45K **Privately Held**
SIC: 1731 General electrical contractor

(G-5224)
GOM TECHNOLOGIES LLC
724 Yorklyn Rd Ste 250 (19707-8736)
PHONE..................410 275-8029
Michael Hollins, *Pr*
EMP: 5 **EST:** 2017
SALES (est): 21.57K **Privately Held**
SIC: 8731 Commercial physical research

(G-5225)
GONCE WILLIAM E DR DDS PA
1127 Valley Rd Ste 4 (19707-8515)
PHONE..................302 235-2400
William E Gonce D.d.s., *Owner*
EMP: 5 **EST:** 1999
SALES (est): 409.22K **Privately Held**
Web: www.dentistryofhockessin.com
SIC: 8021 Dentists' office

(G-5226)
GOVPLUS LLC
Also Called: GOVPLUS LLC
128 Lantana Dr (19707-8800)
PHONE..................302 235-4321
Jennifer Lyons, *Brnch Mgr*
EMP: 10
SALES (corp-wide): 9.07B **Publicly Held**
Web: www.govplus.com
SIC: 6022 State commercial banks
HQ: Citizens Bank, National Association
  1 Citizens Plz
  Providence RI 02903

(G-5227)
GREAT CLIPS FOR HAIR
Also Called: Great Clips
6292 Limestone Rd (19707-9738)
PHONE..................302 235-2887
EMP: 5 **EST:** 2018
SALES (est): 69.96K **Privately Held**
Web: www.greatclips.com
SIC: 7231 Unisex hair salons

(G-5228)
GREEN RIVER CONSULTING LLC
P.O. Box 669 (19707-0669)
PHONE..................302 494-4497
EMP: 7 **EST:** 2017
SALES (est): 59.92K **Privately Held**
SIC: 8742 Management consulting services

(G-5229)
GREG ELECT
547 Ashland Ridge Rd (19707-9662)
PHONE..................215 651-1477
George Eichelberger, *Prin*
EMP: 5 **EST:** 2009
SALES (est): 352.91K **Privately Held**
SIC: 1796 Installing building equipment

(G-5230)
GULU PROJECT INC
123 Dantes Dr (19707-2201)
PHONE..................302 547-8106
EMP: 5 **EST:** 2017
SALES (est): 56.05K **Privately Held**
Web: www.theguluproject.us
SIC: 8641 Civic and social associations

(G-5231)
GUNNAR ADVIK EL
7209 Lancaster Pike Ste 4-1112 (19707-9292)
PHONE..................302 867-0424
Gunnar Advik El, *Pr*
EMP: 9 **EST:** 2020
SALES (est): 537.89K **Privately Held**
SIC: 6082 Foreign trade and international banks

(G-5232)
H DEAN MCSPADDEN DDS
500 Lantana Dr (19707-8813)
PHONE..................302 239-5917
H Dean Mcspadden, *Prin*
EMP: 9 **EST:** 2014
SALES (est): 111.74K **Privately Held**
Web: www.dentalassociatesofdelaware.com
SIC: 8021 Dentists' office

(G-5233)
HCSG REGAL HGHTS REGAL41
6525 Lancaster Pike (19707-9582)
PHONE..................302 998-0181
Ben Friedman, *Prin*
EMP: 14 **EST:** 2007
SALES (est): 575.68K **Privately Held**
SIC: 8011 Clinic, operated by physicians

(G-5234)
HEALING INTENTIONS LLC
120 Farm Meadows Ln (19707-3400)
PHONE..................302 690-3270
Nancy Pribble, *Prin*
EMP: 6 **EST:** 2010
SALES (est): 72.55K **Privately Held**
SIC: 8049 Offices of health practitioner

(G-5235)
HEALTHY FOOT CARE INC
124 Lantana Dr (19707-8800)
PHONE..................302 235-7799
Jing Zhang, *Asst Sec*
EMP: 5 **EST:** 2018
SALES (est): 110.53K **Privately Held**
Web: www.healthyfootcarede.com
SIC: 7299 Massage parlor

(G-5236)
HECKESSIN HEALTH PARTNERS
5850 Limestone Rd (19707-9819)
PHONE..................302 234-2597
EMP: 6 **EST:** 2014
SALES (est): 193.67K **Privately Held**
SIC: 8099 Physical examination and testing services

Hockessin - New Castle County (G-5237)

(G-5237)
HENAGHAN INSURANCE
1302 Old Lancaster Pike (19707-9557)
PHONE...................................302 235-3111
EMP: 5 EST: 2012
SALES (est): 240.95K **Privately Held**
SIC: **6411** Insurance agents, nec

(G-5238)
HERBERT R MARTIN ASSOCIATES
489 Valley Brook Dr (19707-9113)
PHONE...................................302 239-1700
EMP: 5 EST: 1984
SALES (est): 251.72K **Privately Held**
Web: www.childassist.com
SIC: **7376** Computer facilities management

(G-5239)
HOCKESSIN
7503 Lancaster Pike (19707-9593)
PHONE...................................302 234-4100
Laurie Matamoros, *Owner*
EMP: 6 EST: 2014
SALES (est): 117.19K **Privately Held**
Web: www.hockessin19.com
SIC: **6513** Apartment building operators

(G-5240)
HOCKESSIN ANIMAL HOSPITAL
Also Called: Windcrest Animal Hospital
643 Yorklyn Rd (19707-9248)
PHONE...................................302 239-9464
Bruce Damme D.v.m., *Owner*
EMP: 6 EST: 1980
SALES (est): 415.59K **Privately Held**
Web: www.hockessinanimal.com
SIC: **0742** Animal hospital services, pets and other animal specialties

(G-5241)
HOCKESSIN CHRPRACTIC CENTRE PA
Also Called: Blossic, Tamara DC
724 Yorklyn Rd Ste 150 (19707-8735)
PHONE...................................302 239-8550
Tamara Blossic, *Pr*
EMP: 9 EST: 1991
SALES (est): 378.24K **Privately Held**
Web: www.hockessinchiro.com
SIC: **8041** 5499 8049 Offices and clinics of chiropractors; Health and dietetic food stores; Massage Therapist

(G-5242)
HOCKESSIN ELECTRIC INC
6 Fritze Ct (19707-1042)
P.O. Box 72 (19707-0072)
PHONE...................................302 239-9332
Mark Denney, *Pr*
Paul Dieleuterio, *VP*
EMP: 8 EST: 1993
SALES (est): 805.82K **Privately Held**
Web: www.hockessinelectric.com
SIC: **1731** Electrical work

(G-5243)
HOCKESSIN FAMILY PRACTICE MED
726 Yorklyn Rd Ste 100 (19707-8745)
PHONE...................................302 234-5770
Tom Short, *Mgr*
EMP: 11 EST: 2018
SALES (est): 238.89K **Privately Held**
SIC: **8011** General and family practice, physician/surgeon

(G-5244)
HOCKESSIN MONTESSORI SCHOOL
1000 Old Lancaster Pike (19707-9522)
PHONE...................................302 234-1240
Marcia Kinnamen, *Pr*
EMP: 49 EST: 1963
SQ FT: 24,000
SALES (est): 2.64MM **Privately Held**
Web: www.thehms.org
SIC: **8351** Montessori child development center

(G-5245)
HOCKESSIN SALON
117 Pumpkin Patch Ln (19707-8940)
PHONE...................................302 740-3638
Maryalice Lavoie, *Prin*
EMP: 5 EST: 2015
SALES (est): 17.73K **Privately Held**
Web: www.salonbydominic.com
SIC: **7231** Hairdressers

(G-5246)
HOCKESSIN SOCCER CLUB
740 Evanson Rd (19707-9114)
PHONE...................................302 234-1444
Pete Hayes, *Pr*
Tom Braatz, *VP*
Justin Romano, *Admn*
EMP: 9 EST: 1991
SALES (est): 948.9K **Privately Held**
Web: www.hockessinsoccerclub.com
SIC: **7941** Soccer club

(G-5247)
HOCKESSIN TRACTOR INC
Also Called: Gravely Hockessin
654 Yorklyn Rd (19707-9688)
P.O. Box 203 (19707-0203)
PHONE...................................302 239-4201
John Langille, *Pr*
Louise Langille, *VP*
Betty Rector, *Sec*
EMP: 8 EST: 1968
SQ FT: 10,000
SALES (est): 757.84K **Privately Held**
Web: www.gravelyhockessin.com
SIC: **5261** 7699 Lawnmowers and tractors; Tractor repair

(G-5248)
IN VISION EYE CARE INC
Also Called: Fairfax Vision Center
210 Lantana Dr (19707-8805)
PHONE...................................302 235-7031
Roger D Ammon, *Pr*
EMP: 6 EST: 2009
SALES (est): 124.34K **Privately Held**
Web: eyeworks.optometry.net
SIC: **8042** Specialized optometrists

(G-5249)
INDEPENDENT TRANSFER OPERATORS
P.O. Box 1443 (19707-5443)
PHONE...................................302 420-4289
EMP: 7 EST: 2010
SALES (est): 695.16K **Privately Held**
SIC: **4953** Refuse collection and disposal services

(G-5250)
INDEPNDNCE WEALTH ADVISORS INC
726 Yorklyn Rd Ste 300 (19707-8701)
PHONE...................................302 763-1180
Louanne Hammer, *Prin*
EMP: 9 EST: 1994
SALES (est): 585.45K **Privately Held**
SIC: **6282** Investment advisory service

(G-5251)
INFINITY ELECTRIC LLC
1264 Old Wilmington Rd (19707-9371)
PHONE...................................302 635-4388
EMP: 5 EST: 2013
SALES (est): 66.97K **Privately Held**
Web: www.infinityelectricnd.com
SIC: **1731**. General electrical contractor

(G-5252)
IRWIN LANDSCAPING INC
1080 Old Lancaster Pike (19707-9514)
P.O. Box 186 (19707-0186)
PHONE...................................302 239-9229
Peter D Irwin, *Pr*
EMP: 9 EST: 1989
SQ FT: 3,000
SALES (est): 382.35K **Privately Held**
Web: www.irwinlandscaping.com
SIC: **0781** 0782 Landscape services; Landscape contractors

(G-5253)
IS2 LLC
780 Brookwood Ln (19707-9536)
PHONE...................................302 379-1265
EMP: 12 EST: 2011
SALES (est): 146.63K **Privately Held**
SIC: **7389** Design services

(G-5254)
J M INDUSTRIES
845 Old Public Rd (19707-9631)
PHONE...................................302 893-0363
EMP: 5 EST: 2018
SALES (est): 90.83K **Privately Held**
SIC: **3999** Manufacturing industries, nec

(G-5255)
J&D MANAGEMENT
1174 Old Wilmington Rd (19707-9368)
PHONE...................................302 239-2489
Donna Malloy, *Prin*
EMP: 5 EST: 2008
SALES (est): 90.41K **Privately Held**
SIC: **8741** Management services

(G-5256)
J&J SYSTEMS
10 Ridgewood Dr (19707-1413)
PHONE...................................302 239-2969
Frank Jaksky, *Owner*
EMP: 6 EST: 1974
SALES (est): 981.97K **Privately Held**
Web: www.jjsystemsirrigation.com
SIC: **1521** Patio and deck construction and repair

(G-5257)
JACK KELLYS LDSCPG & TREE SVC
Also Called: Jack Kelly's Landscaping
6 Crest Dr (19707-9772)
PHONE...................................302 239-7185
Jack Kelly, *Pr*
EMP: 5 EST: 1980
SALES (est): 225.24K **Privately Held**
Web: www.jackkellylandscaping.com
SIC: **0781** Landscape services

(G-5258)
JAN PATRICK RES
17 Ridon Dr (19707-1035)
PHONE...................................302 234-6046
George Patrick, *Prin*
EMP: 6 EST: 2010
SALES (est): 96.21K **Privately Held**
Web: www.janpatrick.com
SIC: **6531** Real estate agent, residential

(G-5259)
JEFFKO INC
Also Called: Snap Fitness
7209 Lancaster Pike Ste 1 (19707-9292)
PHONE...................................302 235-2180
EMP: 11 EST: 2009
SALES (est): 97.74K **Privately Held**
Web: www.snapfitness.com
SIC: **7991** Physical fitness facilities

(G-5260)
JILLANN I HOUNSELL DDS
7197 Lancaster Pike (19707-9270)
PHONE...................................302 239-5917
Jillann Hounsell, *Prin*
EMP: 10 EST: 2013
SALES (est): 98.86K **Privately Held**
SIC: **8021** Dentists' office

(G-5261)
JOHN CAMPANELLI & SONS INC
7460 Lancaster Pike (19707-9294)
PHONE...................................302 239-8573
John E Campanelli, *Pr*
Mary Jane Campanelli, *Sec*
EMP: 6 EST: 1966
SALES (est): 660K **Privately Held**
SIC: **1521** 1522 1542 New construction, single-family houses; Apartment building construction; Commercial and office building contractors

(G-5262)
JOHN KOZIOL INC
Also Called: Nationwide
7209 Lancaster Pike Ste 4-1178 (19707-9292)
PHONE...................................302 234-5430
John Koziol, *Pr*
EMP: 7 EST: 2019
SQ FT: 1,500
SALES (est): 684.06K **Privately Held**
Web: www.johnkoziolinc.com
SIC: **6282** 6411 Investment advice; Insurance agents, brokers, and service

(G-5263)
JSI GROUP LLC
7217 Lancaster Pike Ste 6 (19707-9585)
P.O. Box 1092 (19707-5092)
PHONE...................................267 582-5850
Joel Iagovino, *Managing Member*
EMP: 512 EST: 2015
SALES (est): 13.21MM **Privately Held**
Web: www.jsigroupllc.co
SIC: **4813** Telephone communication, except radio

(G-5264)
KAREN BERRIE
1209 Madison Ln (19707-9418)
PHONE...................................201 906-9789
Karen Berrie, *Prin*
EMP: 6 EST: 2017
SALES (est): 63.74K **Privately Held**
SIC: **8049** Offices of health practitioner

(G-5265)
KAT POSTCARD SOLUTIONS INC
3 Heatherstone Way (19707-9405)
PHONE...................................614 288-1733
EMP: 4 EST: 2017
SALES (est): 58.61K **Privately Held**
SIC: **2741** Miscellaneous publishing

(G-5266)
KATS MEOW INC
1 Wintercorn Cir (19707-1402)
PHONE...................................302 383-5412
Katina Geralis, *Prin*
EMP: 5 EST: 2011
SALES (est): 97.4K **Privately Held**
SIC: **6531** Real estate agents and managers

GEOGRAPHIC SECTION
Hockessin - New Castle County (G-5296)

(G-5267)
KELLYS LAWN CARE
7 Slashpine Cir (19707-9206)
PHONE.................302 584-1045
EMP: 5 EST: 2017
SALES (est): 246.04K **Privately Held**
SIC: 0782 Lawn care services

(G-5268)
KENDALL JAMES ADVISORS LLC
12 Elderberry Ct (19707-2122)
PHONE.................302 463-0720
John Paul Gulli, *Prin*
EMP: 5 EST: 2016
SALES (est): 249.92K **Privately Held**
SIC: 6282 Investment advice

(G-5269)
KINDERCARE LEARNING CTRS LLC
Also Called: Hockessin Kinder Care 1633
6696 Lancaster Pike (19707-9596)
PHONE.................302 234-8680
Heather Schorah, *Dir*
EMP: 17
SALES (corp-wide): 967.64MM **Privately Held**
Web: www.kindercare.com
SIC: 8351 Group day care center
HQ: Kindercare Learning Centers, Llc
  650 Ne Holladay St # 1400
  Portland OR 97232

(G-5270)
KINGS KIDS
536 Hemingway Dr (19707-1110)
PHONE.................302 239-4961
Donna Zeberkiewicz, *Prin*
EMP: 11 EST: 2010
SALES (est): 71.56K **Privately Held**
SIC: 8351 Child day care services

(G-5271)
KLM CONSULTING LLC
Also Called: Kompli
28 Staten Dr (19707-1339)
PHONE.................302 763-2174
Kristin Marinelli, *Prin*
EMP: 5 EST: 2017
SALES (est): 254.3K **Privately Held**
Web: www.kompli.com
SIC: 8748 Business consulting, nec

(G-5272)
KUBOTA RESEARCH ASSOCIATES
100 Hobson Dr (19707-2106)
PHONE.................302 683-0199
Masanori Kubota, *Pr*
Ayako Kubota, *CFO*
EMP: 5 EST: 2000
SQ FT: 1,500
SALES (est): 489.24K **Privately Held**
SIC: 8711 Consulting engineer

(G-5273)
L & D INSURANCE SERVICES LLC
Also Called: Nationwide
1 Isabella Ct (19707-9298)
PHONE.................302 235-2288
EMP: 5 EST: 2015
SALES (est): 404.63K **Privately Held**
Web: www.ldinsurance.net
SIC: 6411 Insurance agents, nec

(G-5274)
LA PETITE ACADEMY INC
Also Called: La Petite Academy
5986 Limestone Rd (19707-9157)
PHONE.................877 271-6466
Valerie Miller, *Dir*
EMP: 18
Web: www.lapetite.com
SIC: 8351 Preschool center
HQ: La Petite Academy, Inc.
  21333 Haggerty Rd Ste 300
  Novi MI 48375
  877 861-5078

(G-5275)
LANTANA VETERINARY CENTER INC
306 Lantana Dr (19707-8807)
PHONE.................302 234-3275
EMP: 10 EST: 1998
SALES (est): 487.14K **Privately Held**
Web: www.lantanavetcenter.com
SIC: 0742 Animal hospital services, pets and other animal specialties

(G-5276)
LASTING LOOKS
447 Hockessin Cors (19707-9586)
PHONE.................302 635-7327
EMP: 6 EST: 2019
SALES (est): 29.54K **Privately Held**
Web: www.lastinglooksforyou.com
SIC: 7231 Cosmetology and personal hygiene salons

(G-5277)
LAURAS CHILD CARE
4 Pine Grove Ln (19707-2012)
PHONE.................302 690-1283
Laura Baker, *Prin*
EMP: 8 EST: 2016
SALES (est): 56.84K **Privately Held**
SIC: 8351 Child day care services

(G-5278)
LAW OF MICHELE D
724 Yorklyn Rd (19707-8704)
PHONE.................302 234-8600
Michele D Allen, *Prin*
EMP: 5 EST: 2013
SALES (est): 183.18K **Privately Held**
SIC: 8111 General practice attorney, lawyer

(G-5279)
LC ASSOCIATES LLC
726 Yorklyn Rd Ste 150 (19707-8701)
PHONE.................302 235-2500
EMP: 10 EST: 2013
SALES (est): 626.38K **Privately Held**
SIC: 6799 Real estate investors, except property operators

(G-5280)
LENS TOLIC LLC
7209 Lancaster Pike (19707-9292)
PHONE.................800 343-5697
EMP: 5 EST: 2013
SALES (est): 381.49K **Privately Held**
Web: www.lenstolic.com
SIC: 8748 Business consulting, nec

(G-5281)
LIMESTONE VETERINARY HOSPITAL
6102 Limestone Rd (19707-9158)
PHONE.................302 239-5415
John Williams, *Owner*
EMP: 10 EST: 1987
SALES (est): 751.64K **Privately Held**
Web: www.limestonevet.com
SIC: 0742 Animal hospital services, pets and other animal specialties

(G-5282)
LISA A DELEONARDO
614 Loveville Rd (19707-1622)
PHONE.................302 234-3443
Lisa Deleonardo, *Ofcr*
EMP: 7 EST: 2017
SALES (est): 93.99K **Privately Held**
SIC: 8049 Clinical psychologist

(G-5283)
LITHO-PRINT INC
205 S Pond Rd (19707-2325)
PHONE.................302 239-1341
William F Talarowski, *Pr*
Dianne Thomas, *Stockholder*
Louise Jones, *Stockholder*
EMP: 7 EST: 1950
SQ FT: 20,000
SALES (est): 419.26K **Privately Held**
SIC: 2752 Offset printing

(G-5284)
LYNN VICTORIA COSM&MED SKIN
830 Stockbridge Dr (19707-1435)
PHONE.................302 388-5459
Lynn Esdale, *Prin*
EMP: 5 EST: 2015
SALES (est): 106.85K **Privately Held**
SIC: 7991 Spas

(G-5285)
M LEVEL INC
Also Called: Mig Soccer
14 Stuyvesant Dr (19707-1341)
PHONE.................302 762-3910
EMP: 5 EST: 2011
SALES (est): 86.59K **Privately Held**
SIC: 7941 Soccer club

(G-5286)
M W FOGARTY INC
22 Bernard Blvd (19707-9756)
PHONE.................302 658-5547
Michael W Fogarty, *Pr*
EMP: 5 EST: 1983
SALES (est): 964.05K **Privately Held**
SIC: 1521 1542 General remodeling, single-family houses; Commercial and office buildings, renovation and repair

(G-5287)
MAC CONCUSSION CENTER
5936 Limestone Rd Ste 301b (19707-8931)
PHONE.................302 379-1027
EMP: 6 EST: 2019
SALES (est): 58.87K **Privately Held**
Web: www.macconcussion.com
SIC: 8099 Health and allied services, nec

(G-5288)
MAC PHYSICIAN LLC
5936 Limestone Rd Ste 301b (19707-8930)
PHONE.................302 235-8808
EMP: 5 EST: 2018
SALES (est): 81.65K **Privately Held**
SIC: 8011 Offices and clinics of medical doctors

(G-5289)
MACKNYFE SPECIALTIES
Also Called: Macknife Specialties
862 Auburn Mill Rd (19707-8502)
PHONE.................302 239-4904
C J Mclaughlin Iii, *Owner*
EMP: 2 EST: 1971
SALES (est): 82.27K **Privately Held**
Web: www.macknyfe.com
SIC: 3421 3523 3999 Scissors, shears, clippers, snips, and similar tools; Clippers, for animal use: hand or electric; Manufacturing industries, nec

(G-5290)
MACON RENOVATIONS LLC
4040 Mill Creek Rd (19707-9740)
PHONE.................302 244-9161
EMP: 7 EST: 2018
SALES (est): 459.94K **Privately Held**
Web: www.maconrenovation.com
SIC: 1521 General remodeling, single-family houses

(G-5291)
MACROSTAT INC
307 Blue Jay Dr (19707-2049)
PHONE.................302 239-7442
Bing Zhang, *Owner*
EMP: 10 EST: 2016
SALES (est): 23.79K **Privately Held**
Web: www.macrostat.com
SIC: 7299 Miscellaneous personal service

(G-5292)
MAGIC CAR WASH
108 S Colts Neck Way (19707-9798)
PHONE.................302 750-2197
Ginger Emerson, *Prin*
EMP: 6 EST: 2019
SALES (est): 186.65K **Privately Held**
Web: www.magiccarwashinc.com
SIC: 7542 Washing and polishing, automotive

(G-5293)
MALINS JIM E PLUMBING & HTG
538 Basher Ln (19707-2415)
P.O. Box 1135 (19707-5135)
PHONE.................302 239-2755
James E Malin, *CEO*
James E Malin, *Pr*
Eileen M Malin, *Sec*
EMP: 6 EST: 1990
SALES (est): 797.65K **Privately Held**
Web: www.jimmalinplumbing.net
SIC: 1711 Plumbing contractors

(G-5294)
MALLARD ADVISORS LLC
7234 Lancaster Pike Ste 220a (19707-9295)
PHONE.................302 239-1654
Paul S Baumbach, *Brnch Mgr*
EMP: 15
SALES (corp-wide): 164.45MM **Privately Held**
Web: www.merceradvisors.com
SIC: 8742 6282 Financial consultant; Investment advisory service
HQ: Mallard Advisors Llc
  750 Barksdale Rd Ste 3
  Newark DE 19711
  302 239-1654

(G-5295)
MANUFACTURERS & TRADERS TR CO
Also Called: M&T
151 Lantana Dr (19707-8808)
PHONE.................302 472-3177
Gale Dibble, *Mgr*
EMP: 10
SALES (corp-wide): 8.6B **Publicly Held**
Web: ir.mtb.com
SIC: 6022 State commercial banks
HQ: Manufacturers And Traders Trust Company
  1 M&T Plz Fl 3
  Buffalo NY 14203
  716 842-4200

(G-5296)
MARIA LAZAR MD
102 Harvest Ct (19707-2114)
PHONE.................302 838-2210
Maria Lazar Md, *Owner*
Maria Lazar, *Owner*
EMP: 5 EST: 1998

Hockessin - New Castle County (G-5297)   GEOGRAPHIC SECTION

SALES (est): 198.34K **Privately Held**
SIC: 8071 Medical laboratories

(G-5297)
MARIACHI HOUSE
7313 Lancaster Pike Ste 3 (19707-9278)
PHONE...................302 635-7361
Carlos Rivera, *Owner*
EMP: 3 EST: 2011
SALES (est): 161.56K **Privately Held**
SIC: 2032 Mexican foods, nec: packaged in cans, jars, etc.

(G-5298)
MARIAN THURRELL
533 Holly Knoll Rd (19707-9749)
PHONE...................302 239-1269
Marian Thurrell, *Prin*
EMP: 8 EST: 2010
SALES (est): 71.16K **Privately Held**
SIC: 8011 Offices and clinics of medical doctors

(G-5299)
MARK GOSSER
2083 Brackenville Rd (19707-9569)
PHONE...................302 388-8395
Mark Gosser, *Prin*
EMP: 6 EST: 2010
SALES (est): 164.88K **Privately Held**
SIC: 1521 New construction, single-family houses

(G-5300)
MARK VENTRESCA ASSOCIATES INC
19 Bernard Blvd (19707-9758)
PHONE...................302 239-3925
Mark Ventresca, *Prin*
EMP: 5 EST: 1997
SALES (est): 468.98K **Privately Held**
SIC: 1521 1751 5211 Single-family home remodeling, additions, and repairs; Carpentry work; Door and window products

(G-5301)
MARSHA NEAL STUDIO LLC
56 Kings Grant Rd (19707-1203)
PHONE...................302 559-6781
Marsha Minutella, *Prin*
EMP: 5 EST: 2010
SALES (est): 119.26K **Privately Held**
Web: marshanealstudio.blogspot.com
SIC: 7299 Miscellaneous personal service

(G-5302)
MATCHAPRO INC
7209 Lancaster Pike (19707-9292)
PHONE...................213 573-9882
EMP: 6
SALES (est): 68.89K **Privately Held**
SIC: 7371 Computer software development and applications

(G-5303)
MATTER GRAY SECURITY LLC
118 Juneberry Ct (19707-2116)
PHONE...................302 235-8627
Patricia Kingery, *Prin*
EMP: 5 EST: 2016
SALES (est): 82.9K **Privately Held**
SIC: 7381 Guard services

(G-5304)
MAX RE CENTRAL
Also Called: Re/Max
1302 Old Lancaster Pike (19707-9557)
PHONE...................302 234-3800
John Ford, *Mgr*
EMP: 10
SALES (corp-wide): 2.27MM **Privately Held**
Web: www.remax.com
SIC: 6531 Real estate agent, residential
PA: Max Re Central
228 Suburban Dr
Newark DE

(G-5305)
MCCAULEY ENTERPRISES LLC
7209 Lancaster Pike Ste 4 (19707-9292)
PHONE...................217 454-7056
EMP: 5 EST: 2019
SALES (est): 750K **Privately Held**
SIC: 8742 Retail trade consultant

(G-5306)
MEADOW EDGE CORP
313 Blue Jay Dr (19707-2049)
PHONE...................302 530-7339
EMP: 5 EST: 2011
SALES (est): 165.3K **Privately Held**
SIC: 6531 Real estate agents and managers

(G-5307)
MEDI-WEIGHTLOSS CLINICS
502 Lantana Dr (19707-8813)
PHONE...................302 763-3455
EMP: 9
SALES (est): 73.36K **Privately Held**
Web: www.mediweightloss.com
SIC: 8093 Weight loss clinic, with medical staff

(G-5308)
MEENAKSHI HINDU CHARITABLE
146 Pumpkin Patch Ln (19707-8942)
PHONE...................302 588-0686
Palaniappan S Chetty, *Prin*
EMP: 5 EST: 2017
SALES (est): 34.78K **Privately Held**
SIC: 8699 Charitable organization

(G-5309)
MIKE MOLITOR CONTRACTOR LLC
754 Morris Rd (19707-9697)
PHONE...................302 528-6300
EMP: 5 EST: 2010
SALES (est): 313.19K **Privately Held**
SIC: 1542 Nonresidential construction, nec

(G-5310)
MONETRAN LLC
501 Pershing Ct (19707-1108)
PHONE...................732 984-1983
Don Bielak, *Prin*
EMP: 5 EST: 2018
SALES (est): 87.48K **Privately Held**
Web: www.monetran.com
SIC: 7371 Computer software development and applications

(G-5311)
MONSECO LEATHER LLC
724 Yorklyn Rd Ste 260 (19707-8738)
PHONE...................302 235-1777
▲ EMP: 5 EST: 1981
SQ FT: 20,000
SALES (est): 240.19K **Privately Held**
SIC: 5199 Leather and cut stock

(G-5312)
MSCOOPERHOMELOANS
1037 Old Wilmington Rd (19707-9565)
PHONE...................302 494-7712
Alisha Cooper, *Pr*
EMP: 11 EST: 2020
SALES (est): 450K **Privately Held**
SIC: 8742 Marketing consulting services

(G-5313)
MT CUBA CENTER INC
3120 Barley Mill Rd (19707-9579)
P.O. Box 3570 (19807-0570)
PHONE...................302 239-4244
Stephen Martinez, *Pr*
EMP: 109 EST: 1953
SALES (est): 9.71MM **Privately Held**
Web: www.mtcubacenter.org
SIC: 7389 Fund raising organizations

(G-5314)
MYFURTRIBE INC
515 Wilson Dr (19707-1918)
PHONE...................210 904-3036
Amir Rady, *Ex Dir*
EMP: 2
SALES (est): 87.4K **Privately Held**
SIC: 7372 7389 Prepackaged software; Business Activities at Non-Commercial Site

(G-5315)
MYMEDCHOICES INC
407 Valley Brook Dr (19707-9113)
PHONE...................302 932-1920
Mary Schreiber Swenson, *Pr*
EMP: 7 EST: 2017
SALES (est): 466.6K **Privately Held**
SIC: 8011 7371 Offices and clinics of medical doctors; Computer software development

(G-5316)
NATIONAL COMMUNICATIONS IN
14 Longacre Ct (19707-2068)
PHONE...................302 235-0677
Dawn Wilson, *Owner*
EMP: 5 EST: 2015
SALES (est): 35.32K **Privately Held**
Web: www.slicecommunications.com
SIC: 4812 Radiotelephone communication

(G-5317)
NATIONWIDE MUTUAL INSURANCE CO
Also Called: Nationwide
724 Yorklyn Rd Ste 200 (19707-8732)
PHONE...................302 234-5430
EMP: 10
SALES (corp-wide): 18.35B **Privately Held**
Web: www.nationwide.com
SIC: 6411 Insurance agents, nec
PA: Nationwide Mutual Insurance Company
1 Nationwide Plz
Columbus OH 43215
614 249-7111

(G-5318)
NATURAL SALON
6284 Limestone Rd (19707-9738)
PHONE...................302 239-5000
Son Nguyen, *Prin*
EMP: 5 EST: 2014
SALES (est): 37.86K **Privately Held**
SIC: 7231 Manicurist, pedicurist

(G-5319)
NAUDAIN ENTERPRISES LLC
5840 Limestone Rd (19707-9731)
PHONE...................302 239-6840
EMP: 10 EST: 1977
SALES (est): 660.64K **Privately Held**
SIC: 1611 Highway and street paving contractor

(G-5320)
NICOLE L SCOTT NP-C ADULT PRMR
45 Forest Creek Dr (19707-2017)
PHONE...................302 690-1692
Nicole L Scott, *Asst Sec*
EMP: 9 EST: 2018
SALES (est): 156.46K **Privately Held**
SIC: 8059 Nursing and personal care, nec

(G-5321)
NIMBIS DESIGNS LLC
16 Piersons Rdg (19707-9290)
PHONE...................302 494-7584
Vinayak Rajendran, *Prin*
EMP: 10 EST: 2019
SALES (est): 188.04K **Privately Held**
Web: www.nimbis.com
SIC: 7389 Design services

(G-5322)
NINJANURSE LLC
703 Walnut Hill Rd (19707-9609)
PHONE...................302 750-6666
Paul Hoffman, *Prin*
EMP: 6 EST: 2011
SALES (est): 64.58K **Privately Held**
SIC: 8049 Nurses, registered and practical

(G-5323)
NO TAX MALL LLC
1 Barclay Dr (19707-8913)
PHONE...................215 554-5380
EMP: 5 EST: 2014
SALES (est): 22.33K **Privately Held**
Web: www.notaxmall.com
SIC: 7291 Tax return preparation services

(G-5324)
NOOR FOUNDATION INTERNATIONAL
249 Peoples Way (19707-1908)
PHONE...................302 234-8860
EMP: 5 EST: 2009
SALES (est): 76.42K **Privately Held**
Web: www.noorherbals.com
SIC: 8641 Civic and social associations

(G-5325)
NORTH STAR PTA
1340 Little Baltimore Rd (19707-9733)
PHONE...................302 234-7200
EMP: 9 EST: 2010
SALES (est): 124.64K **Privately Held**
Web: www.nspta.com
SIC: 8641 Parent-teachers' association

(G-5326)
NOUVEAU INC
100 Fitness Way (19707-2423)
PHONE...................302 235-4961
Lawrence D Chang, *Prin*
EMP: 11 EST: 2010
SALES (est): 159.28K **Privately Held**
Web: www.nouveaucosmeticcenter.com
SIC: 8011 Plastic surgeon

(G-5327)
NURSE ANGELS LLC
448 Stella Dr (19707-1901)
PHONE...................302 765-8093
Stephanie Dumpson, *Prin*
EMP: 7 EST: 2017
SALES (est): 48.08K **Privately Held**
SIC: 8082 Home health care services

(G-5328)
OASIS SENIOR ADVISORS DELAWARE
Also Called: Oasis Senior Advisors
7209 Lancaster Pike (19707-9292)
PHONE...................302 668-0298
EMP: 6 EST: 2015
SALES (est): 215.07K **Privately Held**
Web: www.oasisserioradvisors.com

GEOGRAPHIC SECTION

Hockessin - New Castle County (G-5355)

SIC: 8322 Geriatric social service

(G-5329)
ONEILLS FLY FISHING LLC
516 Garrick Rd (19707-1121)
PHONE..................302 898-6911
Tim Oneill, *Prin*
EMP: 6 **EST:** 2018
SALES (est): 94.14K **Privately Held**
Web: www.oneillsflyfishing.com
SIC: 7999 Fishing boats, party: operation

(G-5330)
OTOLARYNGOLOGY CONSULTANTS (PA)
Also Called: New Castle Hearing Speech Ctr
10 Foxview Cir (19707-2504)
PHONE..................302 328-1331
Emilio Valdes Junior Md, *Pr*
EMP: 15 **EST:** 1972
SQ FT: 5,000
SALES (est): 1.54MM
SALES (corp-wide): 1.54MM **Privately Held**
SIC: 8011 Ears, nose, and throat specialist: physician/surgeon

(G-5331)
OWCP CLAIMS CONSULTING LLC
315 Sheringham Dr (19707-1928)
PHONE..................302 559-7501
Toby Rubenstein, *Prin*
EMP: 5 **EST:** 2011
SALES (est): 223.49K **Privately Held**
Web: www.owcpclaimsconsulting.com
SIC: 8748 Business consulting, nec

(G-5332)
PAT T CLEAN INC
519 Cabot Dr (19707-1138)
PHONE..................302 239-5354
Pat Turtoro, *Pr*
Pat Tuney, *Mgr*
Josepg Turtoro, *VP*
EMP: 5 **EST:** 1980
SALES (est): 106.9K **Privately Held**
SIC: 7699 Cleaning services

(G-5333)
PATTERSON-SCHWARTZ & ASSOC INC
Also Called: Patterson Schwartz Real Estate
7234 Lancaster Pike Ste 302b (19707-9295)
PHONE..................302 234-3606
Donna Greenspan, *Brnch Mgr*
EMP: 19
SALES (corp-wide): 24.38MM **Privately Held**
Web: www.pattersonschwartz.com
SIC: 8741 6531 Management services; Real estate brokers and agents
PA: Patterson-Schwartz And Associates, Inc.
7234 Lancaster Pike
Hockessin DE 19707
302 234-5250

(G-5334)
PATTERSON-SCHWARTZ & ASSOC INC (PA)
Also Called: Patterson-Schwartz Real Estate
7234 Lancaster Pike (19707-9295)
PHONE..................302 234-5250
Richard Christopher, *Pr*
Christopher Patterson, *
Susan Cleal, *
Charles Schwartz Ii, *Sec*
EMP: 124 **EST:** 1961
SALES (est): 24.38MM
SALES (corp-wide): 24.38MM **Privately Held**
Web: www.pattersonschwartz.com
SIC: 6531 Real estate agent, residential

(G-5335)
PENINSULA UNTD MTHDST HMES INC (PA)
Also Called: Pumh
726 Loveville Rd Ste 3000 (19707-1536)
PHONE..................302 235-6800
Robert Supper, *Rgnl VP*
EMP: 8 **EST:** 1954
SQ FT: 11,000
SALES (est): 30.23MM
SALES (corp-wide): 30.23MM **Privately Held**
SIC: 8361 Aged home

(G-5336)
PENINSULA UNTD MTHDST HMES INC
Also Called: Cokesbury Village
726 Loveville Rd Ste 3000 (19707-1536)
PHONE..................302 235-6810
TOLL FREE: 800
Alan Johnson, *CEO*
EMP: 259
SALES (corp-wide): 24.28MM **Privately Held**
SIC: 8051 Skilled nursing care facilities
PA: Peninsula United Methodist Homes, Inc.
726 Loveville Rd Ste 3000
Hockessin DE 19707
302 235-6800

(G-5337)
PENNOCK INSURANCE INC
761 Whitebriar Rd (19707-9345)
PHONE..................302 235-8258
Edwin J Minner Junior, *Prin*
EMP: 6 **EST:** 2011
SALES (est): 86.79K **Privately Held**
Web: www.pennockins.com
SIC: 6411 Insurance agents, nec

(G-5338)
PERFORMANCE LUBRICANTS INC
7460 Lancaster Pike Ste 4 (19707-9276)
PHONE..................302 239-5661
EMP: 6 **EST:** 2010
SALES (est): 2.46MM **Privately Held**
SIC: 5172 Lubricating oils and greases

(G-5339)
PERFORMANCE PHYSCL THERAPY INC (PA)
720 Yorklyn Rd Ste 150 (19707-8729)
PHONE..................302 234-2288
Steve Rapposelli, *Pr*
Rosann Bryant, *CFO*
EMP: 10 **EST:** 1991
SALES (est): 3.48MM **Privately Held**
Web: www.pptandfitness.com
SIC: 8049 Physical therapist

(G-5340)
PERFORMANCE PT SOLUTIONS LLC
720 Yorklyn Rd Ste 150 (19707-8729)
PHONE..................302 202-3155
EMP: 8 **EST:** 2019
SALES (est): 84.45K **Privately Held**
Web: www.sportpump.com
SIC: 8049 Physical therapist

(G-5341)
PERKWIZ INC
7209 Lancaster Pike (19707-9292)
PHONE..................702 866-9122
Leon Lapel, *CEO*
EMP: 7 **EST:** 2019
SALES (est): 458.77K **Privately Held**
SIC: 7389 7371 Credit card service; Computer software development and applications

(G-5342)
PERRY AND ASSOCIATES INC
540 Waterford Rd (19707-9545)
P.O. Box 1521 (19707-5521)
PHONE..................302 898-2327
Yvonne Dollar-perry, *Pr*
Yvonne Dollar-perry, *Pr*
EMP: 10 **EST:** 2009
SALES (est): 645.59K **Privately Held**
SIC: 8742 Management consulting services

(G-5343)
PETER DUNCKLEY
4 Bent Tree Cir (19707-2028)
PHONE..................302 234-1561
Peter Dunckley, *Prin*
EMP: 8 **EST:** 2007
SALES (est): 87.07K **Privately Held**
SIC: 8011 8049 Physicians' office, including specialists; Offices of health practitioner

(G-5344)
PHARMA E MARKET LLC
Also Called: Monitor For Hire. Com
726 Loveville Rd Apt 99 (19707-1524)
PHONE..................302 737-3711
Louis Freedman, *Managing Member*
Scott Freedman, *Managing Member*
EMP: 11 **EST:** 2000
SALES (est): 837.29K **Privately Held**
SIC: 2834 Pharmaceutical preparations

(G-5345)
PIEDMONT BASEBALL LEAGUE INC
102 Wyeth Way (19707-1200)
P.O. Box 425 (19707-0425)
PHONE..................302 234-9437
Ron Pena, *Pr*
Roger Leach, *Sec*
EMP: 5 **EST:** 1982
SALES (est): 320.66K **Privately Held**
Web: www.piedmontbaseball.com
SIC: 8699 Athletic organizations

(G-5346)
POLYMART INC
710 Yorklyn Rd Ste 200 (19707-8749)
PHONE..................302 656-1470
Don Priester, *Mgr*
EMP: 6
SIC: 5162 5085 Plastics materials, nec; Rubber goods, mechanical
PA: Polymart Inc
129 Ridgway Dr
Bordentown NJ 08505

(G-5347)
PORSCHE CLUB AMERICA DEL REG
201 Louis Ln (19707-9767)
P.O. Box 911 (19707-0911)
PHONE..................302 588-3511
Sam Dali, *Pr*
EMP: 6 **EST:** 2018
SALES (est): 64.73K **Privately Held**
Web: www.delawarepca.net
SIC: 8641 Civic and social associations

(G-5348)
POSH CUPCAKE
50 Westwoods Blvd (19707-2062)
PHONE..................302 234-4451
Tricia Matthews, *Prin*
EMP: 5 **EST:** 2010
SALES (est): 56.86K **Privately Held**
SIC: 2051 Bread, cake, and related products

(G-5349)
POSTAL CONNECTIONS INC
7209 Lancaster Pike (19707-9292)
PHONE..................302 239-1129
Rick Martin, *Pr*
EMP: 5 **EST:** 2014
SALES (est): 187.62K **Privately Held**
Web: www.postalconnections234.com
SIC: 7389 Mailbox rental and related service

(G-5350)
POWER BROKERS HOLDINGS LLC
3 Longacre Ct (19707-2069)
PHONE..................800 901-8483
Andre Ward Senior, *Managing Member*
EMP: 5
SALES (est): 271.26K **Privately Held**
SIC: 8741 Management services

(G-5351)
PRADHAN ENERGY PROJECTS
Also Called: Peppl
104 Hawthorne Ct W (19707-1800)
PHONE..................305 428-2123
Ravi Pradhan, *CEO*
Maya Pradhan, *Pr*
Vinay Pradhan, *VP*
EMP: 8 **EST:** 2010
SALES (est): 425.38K **Privately Held**
SIC: 1796 7389 Pollution control equipment installation; Business Activities at Non-Commercial Site

(G-5352)
PRIMEX COMPOSITES LLC
P.O. Box 460 (19707-0460)
PHONE..................302 981-1470
Dan White, *Pr*
EMP: 6 **EST:** 2020
SALES (est): 593.07K
SALES (corp-wide): 1.34MM **Privately Held**
SIC: 3699 Electrical equipment and supplies, nec
PA: Thermal Transfer Composites, Llc
724 Yorklyn Rd Ste 200
Hockessin DE 19707
302 635-7156

(G-5353)
RALPH DEL SIGNORE JR
Also Called: Delone
516 Erickson Ave (19707-1130)
PHONE..................302 239-0803
Ralph Del Signore Junior, *Prin*
EMP: 5 **EST:** 2011
SALES (est): 162.62K **Privately Held**
SIC: 1522 Residential construction, nec

(G-5354)
RAMA CORPORATION
181 Thompson Dr (19707-1913)
PHONE..................302 266-6600
EMP: 22 **EST:** 1991
SALES (est): 236.21K **Privately Held**
Web: www.ramacorporation.com
SIC: 7011 Hotel, franchised

(G-5355)
RAW TENNIS INC
127 Dewberry Dr (19707-2119)
PHONE..................302 507-8687
EMP: 5 **EST:** 2012
SALES (est): 38.23K **Privately Held**
SIC: 7999 Tennis services and professionals

Hockessin - New Castle County (G-5356)

(G-5356)
RAYCO AUTO & MARINE UPHL INC
113 Carriage Dr (19707-1329)
PHONE..................302 323-8844
EMP: 5 EST: 2014
SALES (est): 336.85K **Privately Held**
Web: www.delawareupholstery.com
SIC: **4581** 7532 Aircraft upholstery repair; Upholstery and trim shop, automotive

(G-5357)
RAYMOND L PARA DDS
720 Yorklyn Rd Ste 120 (19707-8730)
PHONE..................302 234-2728
Raymond L Para D.d.s., *Owner*
Linda Dicampli, *Mgr*
EMP: 10 EST: 1992
SALES (est): 641.77K **Privately Held**
Web: www.stonemilldental.com
SIC: **8021** Dentists' office

(G-5358)
RECOVERY DESTINATION SERVICES
853 Stockbridge Dr (19707-1436)
PHONE..................302 559-1010
Lorraine Smith, *Prin*
EMP: 6 EST: 2018
SALES (est): 42.88K **Privately Held**
SIC: **8322** General counseling services

(G-5359)
RED CLAY CONSOLIDATED SCHL DST
2025 Graves Rd (19707-9128)
PHONE..................302 235-6600
Linda Ennis, *Brnch Mgr*
EMP: 17
SALES (corp-wide): 130.58MM **Privately Held**
Web: www.redclayschools.com
SIC: **8641** Parent-teachers' association
PA: Red Clay Consolidated School District
  1502 Spruce Ave
  Wilmington DE 19805
  302 552-3700

(G-5360)
RED CLAY INC
2388 Brackenville Rd (19707-9306)
PHONE..................302 239-2018
David Ford, *Pr*
Susan Ford, *Sec*
EMP: 2 EST: 1979
SALES (est): 232.06K **Privately Held**
SIC: **3599** 8731 8742 Machine shop, jobbing and repair; Commercial physical research; Industrial and labor consulting services

(G-5361)
REGAL HTS HLTHCARE RHAB CTR LL
6525 Lancaster Pike (19707-9582)
PHONE..................302 998-0181
Meir Gelley, *Managing Member*
Ben Friedman,
EMP: 99 EST: 2006
SALES (est): 18.18MM **Privately Held**
Web: www.regalheightshealthcare.com
SIC: **8051** Convalescent home with continuous nursing care

(G-5362)
RH GALLERY AND STUDIOS
1304 Old Lancaster Pike Ste D (19707-8806)
PHONE..................302 218-5182
EMP: 5 EST: 2018
SALES (est): 50.52K **Privately Held**
SIC: **8412** Art gallery

(G-5363)
RIGGIN GROUP
530 Schoolhouse Rd Ste E (19707-9526)
PHONE..................302 235-2903
Eddie Riggin, *Owner*
EMP: 6 EST: 2001
SALES (est): 367.24K **Privately Held**
SIC: **6531** Real estate agent, residential

(G-5364)
RIGHT-AWAY AUTO ASSISTANCE LLC
7209 Lancaster Pike 4-1 (19707-9292)
PHONE..................302 438-9970
David Crosby, *Managing Member*
EMP: 5 EST: 2021
SALES (est): 63.79K **Privately Held**
SIC: **7549** Road service, automotive

(G-5365)
RITA GASZ REAL ESTATE
7234 Lancaster Pike (19707-9295)
PHONE..................302 234-6043
Rita Gasz, *Owner*
EMP: 8 EST: 1968
SALES (est): 117.85K **Privately Held**
Web: www.pattersonschwartz.com
SIC: **6531** Real estate agent, residential

(G-5366)
RK ADVISORS LLC
104 Country Center Ln (19707-9335)
PHONE..................302 561-5258
Richard Klumpp, *Prin*
EMP: 6 EST: 2016
SALES (est): 371.13K **Privately Held**
Web: www.rkadvisorsllc.com
SIC: **6282** Investment advice

(G-5367)
ROBERT A CHAGNON
726 Loveville Rd Rm A55 (19707-1535)
PHONE..................302 489-1932
Robert A Chagnon, *Prin*
EMP: 5 EST: 2006
SALES (est): 222.92K **Privately Held**
SIC: **8711** Consulting engineer

(G-5368)
ROBERT A STEELE M D
304 Lantana Dr (19707-8807)
PHONE..................302 234-2600
Robert Steele, *Prin*
EMP: 8 EST: 2018
SALES (est): 112.96K **Privately Held**
SIC: **8011** Orthopedic physician

(G-5369)
ROCKHAM 5G PA LP
136 Lantana Dr (19707-8800)
PHONE..................302 239-1250
EMP: 6 EST: 2010
SALES (est): 149.47K **Privately Held**
SIC: **8621** Professional organizations

(G-5370)
ROGER SUMMERS LAWN CARE INC
364 Skyline Orchard Dr (19707-9354)
PHONE..................302 218-3319
Roger Summers, *Prin*
EMP: 5 EST: 2005
SALES (est): 213.21K **Privately Held**
Web: www.rogersummerslawncare.com
SIC: **0782** Lawn care services

(G-5371)
ROLL OUT TRANSIT LLC
3 Longacre Ct (19707-2069)
PHONE..................800 233-1680
Andre Ward, *Managing Member*
EMP: 5
SALES (est): 207.81K **Privately Held**
SIC: **8742** 7389 Transportation consultant; Business Activities at Non-Commercial Site

(G-5372)
ROLUVA PAINTING
106 Pumpkin Patch Ln (19707-8940)
PHONE..................610 470-5207
Rolando Luna, *Prin*
EMP: 5 EST: 2015
SALES (est): 57.71K **Privately Held**
SIC: **1721** Painting and paper hanging

(G-5373)
ROSS CAPITAL PARTNERS LLC
724 Yorklyn Rd (19707-8704)
PHONE..................302 300-4220
EMP: 5 EST: 2019
SALES (est): 463.3K **Privately Held**
Web: www.rosscapitalpartners.com
SIC: **6799** Investors, nec

(G-5374)
RSG CLEANING SERVICES
101 Wooden Carriage Dr (19707-1430)
PHONE..................302 650-3702
Sandra Gavidia, *Prin*
EMP: 5 EST: 2017
SALES (est): 45.31K **Privately Held**
SIC: **7699** Cleaning services

(G-5375)
RYAN GALLO TREE SERVICE INC
Also Called: Gallo Tree Service
1536 Brackenville Rd (19707-9525)
P.O. Box 549 (19707-0549)
PHONE..................302 239-1001
Ryan Gallo, *Pr*
EMP: 10 EST: 1997
SALES (est): 248.34K **Privately Held**
Web: www.gallotreeserviceinc.com
SIC: **0783** 0781 1629 Planting, pruning, and trimming services; Landscape services; Land clearing contractor

(G-5376)
RYZENLINK TECHNOLOGIES LLC
7209 Lancaster Pike Ste 4 (19707-9292)
PHONE..................786 536-0349
Jose Padron, *Managing Member*
EMP: 6
SALES (est): 75.18K **Privately Held**
SIC: **5734** 7371 Computer software and accessories; Computer software development

(G-5377)
SABO LOGISTICS LLC
1074 Yorklyn Rd Unit E (19707-9769)
PHONE..................302 440-4544
EMP: 5 EST: 2015
SALES (est): 195.58K **Privately Held**
SIC: **4789** Cargo loading and unloading services

(G-5378)
SALON BY DOMINIC
130 Lantana Dr (19707-8800)
PHONE..................302 239-8282
Dominic Rappuci, *Owner*
EMP: 21 EST: 1992
SALES (est): 588.27K **Privately Held**
Web: www.salonbydominic.com
SIC: **7231** Hairdressers

(G-5379)
SCHWARTZ ERIC WM MD
726 Yorklyn Rd Ste 100 (19707-8745)
PHONE..................302 234-5770
Eric Schwartz, *Prin*
Doctor Eric Schwartz Md, *Prin*
EMP: 10 EST: 1993
SALES (est): 144.37K **Privately Held**
SIC: **8011** General and family practice, physician/surgeon

(G-5380)
SERVICE QUEST
217 Louis Ln (19707-9767)
P.O. Box 1637 (19707-5637)
PHONE..................302 235-0173
P Fitzharris, *Prin*
EMP: 6 EST: 2003
SALES (est): 116.35K **Privately Held**
SIC: **8331** Job training and related services

(G-5381)
SHARON MD
724 Yorklyn Rd Ste 375 (19707-8738)
PHONE..................302 239-2600
EMP: 6 EST: 2016
SALES (est): 87.64K **Privately Held**
SIC: **8011** Psychiatrist

(G-5382)
SHASHI PATEL
2 Stuyvesant Dr (19707-1341)
PHONE..................302 737-5074
Sheel Patel, *Prin*
EMP: 8 EST: 2010
SALES (est): 226.09K **Privately Held**
SIC: **8011** Offices and clinics of medical doctors

(G-5383)
SHERPA FINANCIAL SERVICES
722 Yorklyn Rd Ste 300 (19707-8703)
PHONE..................302 235-1284
Peter Succoso, *Prin*
EMP: 10 EST: 2017
SALES (est): 503.39K **Privately Held**
Web: www.sherpafinancial.com
SIC: **8742** Financial consultant

(G-5384)
SLAM AQUATICS LLC
528 Wayland Dr (19707-9724)
PHONE..................302 668-0186
Michael Wind, *Prin*
EMP: 6 EST: 2018
SALES (est): 194.8K **Privately Held**
Web: www.slamaquatics.com
SIC: **8422** Botanical and zoological gardens

(G-5385)
SOCIABLE CONSULTING LLC
113 Brook Run (19707-2407)
PHONE..................302 546-2750
EMP: 6 EST: 2020
SALES (est): 150K **Privately Held**
Web: www.sociableconsulting.com
SIC: **8742** Marketing consulting services

(G-5386)
SPECIALTY REHABILITATION INC
26 Wesley Dr (19707-9624)
PHONE..................302 709-0440
Lisa Marshall, *Dir*
EMP: 10 EST: 2003
SALES (est): 207.24K **Privately Held**
Web: www.specialtyrehab.net
SIC: **8049** Physical therapist

(G-5387)
SPEECH THERAPEUTICS INC
15 Elderberry Ct (19707-2131)
PHONE..................302 234-9226
Judy Roberson, *Owner*
EMP: 7 EST: 1993

GEOGRAPHIC SECTION
Hockessin - New Castle County (G-5419)

SALES (est): 238.31K **Privately Held**
SIC: 8049 Speech specialist

(G-5388)
SQUEAKY CLEAN & DRY
7 Eynon Ct (19707-9217)
PHONE...................302 327-6240
Jim Richardson, *Owner*
EMP: 6 EST: 2017
SALES (est): 26.07K **Privately Held**
Web: www.squeakycleananddry.com
SIC: 7699 Cleaning services

(G-5389)
STARRETT DESIGN BUILD
1304 Old Lancaster Pike D (19707-8806)
PHONE...................302 598-6607
EMP: 6
SALES (est): 255.63K **Privately Held**
Web: www.starrettdesignbuild.com
SIC: 1799 Special trade contractors, nec

(G-5390)
STATE DRYWALL CO INC
12 Ridon Dr (19707-1002)
P.O. Box 717 (19707-0717)
PHONE...................302 239-2843
Eugene R Radka, *VP*
EMP: 8 EST: 1965
SALES (est): 444.56K **Privately Held**
SIC: 1742 Drywall

(G-5391)
STOKELAN ESTATE WINERY LLC
4 Thornberry Ln (19707-9786)
PHONE...................609 451-5535
EMP: 5 EST: 2018
SALES (est): 69.63K **Privately Held**
SIC: 6552 Subdividers and developers, nec

(G-5392)
STREET CORE UTILITY SERVICE
501 Erickson Ave (19707-1129)
PHONE...................302 239-4110
Scott Bell, *Pr*
Michael Mcmahon, *VP*
EMP: 10 EST: 2006
SALES (est): 617.86K **Privately Held**
SIC: 3448 Farm and utility buildings

(G-5393)
STRETCHPLEX LLC
722 Yorklyn Rd Ste 200 (19707-8703)
PHONE...................302 696-5966
EMP: 6 EST: 2021
SALES (est): 131.75K **Privately Held**
SIC: 8049 Physical therapist

(G-5394)
SUI TRADING CO
Also Called: Reima Sportswear
406 Hawthorne Ct E (19707-1805)
P.O. Box 1720 (19707-5720)
PHONE...................302 239-2012
EMP: 6 EST: 1993
SALES (est): 853.17K **Privately Held**
SIC: 5136 Gloves, men's and boys'

(G-5395)
SUMMERS LOGGING LLC
364 Skyline Orchard Dr (19707-9354)
PHONE...................302 234-8725
EMP: 4 EST: 2018
SALES (est): 81.72K **Privately Held**
SIC: 2411 Logging

(G-5396)
SUMMIT AT HOCKESSIN
Also Called: Summit
5850 Limestone Rd (19707-9819)
PHONE...................302 235-8388
EMP: 20 EST: 2015
SALES (est): 7.72MM **Privately Held**
Web: www.thesummitretirement.com
SIC: 8051 Skilled nursing care facilities

(G-5397)
SUMMIT RETIREMENT COMMUNITY
5850 Limestone Rd Ofc 1 (19707-9828)
PHONE...................888 933-2300
EMP: 14 EST: 2015
SALES (est): 194.98K **Privately Held**
SIC: 8051 Skilled nursing care facilities

(G-5398)
SUPERIOR EXTERIOR CONTRACTING
1261 Old Wilmington Rd (19707-9672)
PHONE...................302 287-8391
Daniel Krajewski, *Prin*
EMP: 5 EST: 2017
SALES (est): 63.03K **Privately Held**
SIC: 1799 Special trade contractors, nec

(G-5399)
SUPERIOR YARDWORKS INC
211 Cherry Blossom Pl (19707-2047)
PHONE...................610 274-2255
Christopher Kane, *Pr*
EMP: 6 EST: 1993
SALES (est): 302.82K **Privately Held**
Web: www.superioryardworks.com
SIC: 0781 Landscape architects

(G-5400)
SUSAN C OVER PC
724 Yorklyn Rd Ste 250 (19707-8736)
PHONE...................302 660-2913
Susan Over, *Prin*
EMP: 6 EST: 2010
SALES (est): 432.57K **Privately Held**
Web: www.susancoverlaw.com
SIC: 8111 General practice attorney, lawyer

(G-5401)
SUSAN S BRYDE
700 Lantana Dr (19707-8810)
PHONE...................302 239-2343
EMP: 5 EST: 2010
SALES (est): 168.76K **Privately Held**
Web: www.suebryde.com
SIC: 6531 Real estate agent, residential

(G-5402)
TECHWORLD CORPORATION INC
6 Spring Meadow Ln (19707-9606)
PHONE...................302 757-3866
Weineng Zuo, *Prin*
EMP: 7 EST: 2016
SALES (est): 125.73K **Privately Held**
SIC: 8099 Health and allied services, nec

(G-5403)
THERAPY SERVICES OF DELAW
24 Gates Cir (19707-9686)
PHONE...................302 239-2285
EMP: 7 EST: 2018
SALES (est): 175.41K **Privately Held**
SIC: 8093 Rehabilitation center, outpatient treatment

(G-5404)
THERMAL TRANSF COMPOSITES LLC (PA)
724 Yorklyn Rd Ste 200 (19707-8732)
P.O. Box 460 (19707-0460)
PHONE...................302 635-7156
EMP: 4 EST: 2004
SALES (est): 1.34MM
SALES (corp-wide): 1.34MM **Privately Held**

SIC: 3699 Electrical equipment and supplies, nec

(G-5405)
TIMBER RIDGE INC
710 Yorklyn Rd (19707-8747)
PHONE...................302 239-9239
Matt Minker, *Pr*
Mark Price, *
Robert Blanck, *
Kevin Lucas, *
Carol Minker, *
EMP: 14 EST: 1983
SQ FT: 6,000
SALES (est): 210.37K **Privately Held**
SIC: 7363 Help supply services

(G-5406)
TOLTON BUILDERS INC
7301 Lancaster Pike (19707-9588)
P.O. Box 811 (19707-0811)
PHONE...................302 239-5357
Randy R Tolton, *Pr*
EMP: 5 EST: 1983
SQ FT: 200
SALES (est): 900K **Privately Held**
SIC: 1521 New construction, single-family houses

(G-5407)
TOM WRIGHT REAL ESTATE
7234 Lancaster Pike Ste 101 (19707-9295)
PHONE...................302 234-6026
Tom Wright, *Owner*
EMP: 8 EST: 1993
SALES (est): 134.69K **Privately Held**
Web: www.implantinfo.com
SIC: 6531 Real estate agent, residential

(G-5408)
TOP NOTCH CLEANING
6 Quail Hollow Dr (19707-1404)
PHONE...................302 893-7643
Leslie C Yacovella, *Owner*
EMP: 5 EST: 2014
SALES (est): 69.14K **Privately Held**
SIC: 7699 Cleaning services

(G-5409)
TP WIRELESS INC
122 Lantana Dr (19707-8800)
PHONE...................302 235-0402
EMP: 5 EST: 2015
SALES (est): 144.71K **Privately Held**
SIC: 4812 Cellular telephone services

(G-5410)
TRI STATE FOOT ANKLE CENT
6300 Limestone Rd (19707-9178)
PHONE...................302 239-1625
EMP: 12 EST: 2008
SALES (est): 276.36K **Privately Held**
Web: www.tristatefootandankle.com
SIC: 8043 Offices and clinics of podiatrists

(G-5411)
TRITEK CORPORATION
Also Called: Tritek Technologies
103 E Bridle Path (19707-9409)
PHONE...................302 239-1638
James Malatesta, *Pr*
EMP: 10 EST: 1990
SALES (est): 891.49K **Privately Held**
Web: www.tritek.com
SIC: 3579 Mailing, letter handling, and addressing machines

(G-5412)
TRITEK TECHNOLOGIES INC (PA)
Also Called: Tritek

103 E Bridle Path (19707-9409)
PHONE...................302 239-1638
James Malatesta, *Pr*
EMP: 7 EST: 1997
SALES (est): 1.27MM
SALES (corp-wide): 1.27MM **Privately Held**
Web: www.tritek.com
SIC: 3579 Mailing, letter handling, and addressing machines

(G-5413)
TWO COUGARS LLC
6 Wyndom Ct (19707-2511)
PHONE...................302 358-0197
EMP: 5 EST: 2013
SALES (est): 165.39K **Privately Held**
SIC: 7389

(G-5414)
US MALE MODERN BARBERSHOP
7197 Lancaster Pike (19707-9270)
PHONE...................302 635-7370
EMP: 11 EST: 2012
SALES (est): 318.94K **Privately Held**
Web: www.usmalemodernbarbershop.com
SIC: 7241 7231 Barber shops; Beauty shops

(G-5415)
UTOPIA ALLEY LLC
56 Westwoods Blvd (19707-2062)
PHONE...................302 218-3108
Kaven Didehvar, *CEO*
▲ EMP: 5 EST: 2015
SALES (est): 152.24K **Privately Held**
Web: www.utopiaalley.com
SIC: 1542 Design and erection, combined: non-residential

(G-5416)
VEGAN SKIN CLINIC LLC
407 Valley Brook Dr (19707-9113)
PHONE...................302 932-1920
Mary Schreiber Swenson, *Managing Member*
EMP: 5 EST: 2021
SALES (est): 286.64K **Privately Held**
SIC: 2844 7389 Perfumes, cosmetics and other toilet preparations; Business services, nec

(G-5417)
VEL MICRO WORKS INCORPORATED
133 Cheltenham Rd (19707-1807)
PHONE...................302 239-4661
Sakthi Vel, *Pr*
Kamatchi Vel, *VP*
EMP: 7 EST: 1996
SALES (est): 710.52K **Privately Held**
Web: www.velmicro.com
SIC: 7371 Computer software development

(G-5418)
VETERAN IT PRO LLC
37 Staten Dr (19707-1338)
PHONE...................302 824-3111
Luke Bernhardt, *CEO*
Amrinder Romana, *COO*
EMP: 10 EST: 2016
SALES (est): 260.57K **Privately Held**
SIC: 8742 7389 7375 7371 Management consulting services; Information retrieval services; Custom computer programming services

(G-5419)
VICTORIA MEWS LP DELNWARE VALL
722 Yorklyn Rd Ste 350 (19707-8740)

Hockessin - New Castle County (G-5420)

GEOGRAPHIC SECTION

PHONE.................................302 489-2000
EMP: 6 EST: 2013
SALES (est): 473.33K Privately Held
SIC: 6513 Apartment building operators

(G-5420)
VILLA TOKEN INC
7209 Lancaster Pike (19707-9292)
PHONE.................................831 227-9878
Allison Peck, Pr
EMP: 5 EST: 2018
SALES (est): 32.18K Privately Held
SIC: 7379 Online services technology consultants

(G-5421)
WEBSTER DERMATOLOGY PA
720 Yorklyn Rd Ste 10 (19707-8730)
PHONE.................................302 234-9305
EMP: 10 EST: 2020
SALES (est): 485.31K Privately Held
Web: www.websterdermatology.com
SIC: 8011 Dermatologist

(G-5422)
WELLS FARGO BANK NATIONAL ASSN
Also Called: Wells Fargo
5801 Limestone Rd (19707-9732)
PHONE.................................302 235-4304
Pat Ponzo, Prin
EMP: 8
SALES (corp-wide): 82.86B Publicly Held
Web: www.wellsfargo.com
SIC: 6021 National commercial banks
HQ: Wells Fargo Bank, National Association
420 Montgomery St San
San Francisco CA 94104
605 575-6900

(G-5423)
WELLS FARGO HOME MORTGAGE INC
Also Called: Wells Fargo
7465 Lancaster Pike (19707-9583)
PHONE.................................302 239-6300
Chritopher Tally, Brnch Mgr
EMP: 6
SALES (corp-wide): 82.86B Publicly Held
Web: www.wellsfargo.com
SIC: 6021 National commercial banks
HQ: Wells Fargo Home Mortgage Inc
1 Home Campus
Des Moines IA 50328
515 324-3707

(G-5424)
WELSH FAMILY DENTISTRY
Also Called: Sharon A Welsh DDS
34 Withers Way (19707-2514)
PHONE.................................302 836-3711
Sharon Welsh, Owner
EMP: 8 EST: 1999
SALES (est): 374.07K Privately Held
SIC: 8072 Dental laboratories

(G-5425)
WIDE RANGE INC (PA)
108 Bellfield Ct (19707-2322)
P.O. Box 392 (19970-0392)
PHONE.................................302 234-1193
Gary S Wilkinson Ph.d., Pr
Mary Ann Wilkinson, VP
EMP: 7 EST: 1993
SQ FT: 2,400
SALES (est): 520.89K Privately Held
SIC: 2741 Miscellaneous publishing

(G-5426)
WILLIS NORTH AMERICA INC
Also Called: Willis Hrh
512 Garrick Rd (19707-1121)
PHONE.................................302 239-2416
EMP: 49
Web: www.wtwco.com
SIC: 8742 Management consulting services
HQ: Willis North America Inc.
200 Liberty St Fl 7
New York NY 10281
212 915-8888

(G-5427)
WINDSOR PLACE
6677 Lancaster Pike (19707-9503)
PHONE.................................302 239-3200
John Place, Prin
EMP: 8 EST: 2013
SALES (est): 123.22K Privately Held
SIC: 8361 Residential care

(G-5428)
WM H JEPPE DR
103 Dennison Ln (19707-9637)
PHONE.................................302 234-1785
Wm Jeppe, Prin
EMP: 9 EST: 2002
SALES (est): 71.22K Privately Held
SIC: 8011 Physicians' office, including specialists

(G-5429)
WOMEN FIRST LLC
6300 Limestone Rd (19707-9178)
PHONE.................................302 635-9800
EMP: 8 EST: 2009
SALES (est): 218.26K Privately Held
Web: www.wlwobgyn.com
SIC: 8011 Gynecologist

(G-5430)
WOODCHUCK ENTERPRISES INC
1070 Sharpless Rd (19707-9664)
PHONE.................................302 239-8336
John Fauerbach, Prin
EMP: 6 EST: 2011
SALES (est): 96.93K Privately Held
SIC: 2421 Sawmills and planing mills, general

(G-5431)
WRITE TO POINT
6 Liveoak Ct (19707-9202)
PHONE.................................302 235-7149
Catherine Kaser, Owner
EMP: 5 EST: 2014
SALES (est): 97.16K Privately Held
SIC: 7999 Amusement and recreation, nec

(G-5432)
YELLOWFIN CONSTRUCTION LLC
3903 Mill Creek Rd (19707-9105)
PHONE.................................302 293-0028
EMP: 11 EST: 2019
SALES (est): 2.33MM Privately Held
Web: www.yellowfinco.com
SIC: 1521 Single-family housing construction

(G-5433)
YORKLYN HOME LLC
211 Gun Club Rd (19707-8201)
PHONE.................................302 584-1219
Jj Wicks, Owner
EMP: 5 EST: 2018
SALES (est): 137.39K Privately Held
Web: www.yorklynhome.com
SIC: 1521 General remodeling, single-family houses

Houston
Kent County

(G-5434)
A&J PRODUCTS INC
2860 Williamsville Rd (19954-2526)
PHONE.................................302 424-0750
Kevin Huey, Pr
Brent Huey, VP
EMP: 12 EST: 1994
SQ FT: 7,000
SALES (est): 1.1MM Privately Held
Web: www.intermoldcorp.com
SIC: 3089 Injection molding of plastics

(G-5435)
AGAPE LEARNING ACADEMY
283 School St (19954-2205)
PHONE.................................302 491-4890
Jennie Hess, Prin
EMP: 6 EST: 2016
SALES (est): 60.05K Privately Held
Web: www.agapelearningacademy.org
SIC: 8299 7999 Schools and educational services, nec; Martial arts school, nec

(G-5436)
APEX ARABIANS INC
Also Called: Apex Stable
671 Williamsville Rd (19954-2618)
PHONE.................................302 242-6272
P O Robichaud, Pr
Pamela Onusko, Pr
Nancy Onusko, Sec
Edward Robichaud, Prin
EMP: 6 EST: 2000
SQ FT: 40,000
SALES (est): 449.15K Privately Held
Web: www.apexarabians.com
SIC: 0752 Breeding services, horses: racing and non-racing

(G-5437)
BROTHERS GANNON INC
31 Oakglade Dr (19954-9633)
PHONE.................................302 422-2734
Garrett M Gannon, Prin
EMP: 5 EST: 2008
SALES (est): 57.97K Privately Held
SIC: 7389 Auctioneers, fee basis

(G-5438)
CARRILLOS AUTO CARE
7 Sleepy Hollow Dr (19954-9600)
PHONE.................................302 339-7234
Jose Carrillo, Prin
EMP: 5 EST: 2016
SALES (est): 28.25K Privately Held
SIC: 7538 General automotive repair shops

(G-5439)
CONVENTIONAL BUILDERS INC
846 School St (19954-2018)
P.O. Box 47 (19954-0047)
PHONE.................................302 422-2429
Gregory Thompson, Pr
W Pierce Thompson Senior, Pr
W Pierce Thompson Junior, VP
Dawn Layton, Sec
EMP: 14 EST: 1975
SQ FT: 10,000
SALES (est): 2.5MM Privately Held
Web: www.conventionalbuildersinc.com
SIC: 1542 1541 Commercial and office building, new construction; Industrial buildings, new construction, nec

(G-5440)
EMOTINAL WLLNESS CUNSELING LLC
818 Williamsville Rd (19954-2619)
PHONE.................................302 865-8098
EMP: 7 EST: 2014
SALES (est): 159.12K Privately Held
Web: www.ewcdelaware.com
SIC: 8099 Health and allied services, nec

(G-5441)
FIRST STATE RENTAL COMPANY LLC
4414 Williamsville Rd (19954-2402)
P.O. Box 198 (19954-0198)
PHONE.................................302 632-5699
EMP: 5 EST: 2014
SALES (est): 86.44K Privately Held
Web: www.firststaterentalcompany.com
SIC: 7359 1799 1629 0783 Equipment rental and leasing, nec; Construction site cleanup; Land clearing contractor; Removal services, bush and tree

(G-5442)
GEORGE W OPPEL
3202 Gun And Rod Club Rd (19954-2601)
PHONE.................................302 398-4433
George W Oppel, Owner
EMP: 5 EST: 2002
SALES (est): 343.57K Privately Held
SIC: 4213 Trucking, except local

(G-5443)
HELEN MALONEY
184 Broad St (19954-2014)
PHONE.................................302 422-5359
Helen Maloney, Prin
EMP: 6 EST: 2007
SALES (est): 96K Privately Held
SIC: 8049 Nurses and other medical assistants

(G-5444)
HOUSTON SELF STORAGE
Mill St (19954)
P.O. Box 146 (19954-0146)
PHONE.................................302 422-9660
Thomas Cain, Owner
EMP: 5 EST: 2004
SALES (est): 68.33K Privately Held
SIC: 5932 4226 Furniture, secondhand; Household goods and furniture storage

(G-5445)
MILFORD MACHINE LLC
10 The Mead (19954-9632)
PHONE.................................410 924-3211
Jason Potocki, Prin
EMP: 5 EST: 2019
SALES (est): 149.21K Privately Held
SIC: 7699 Industrial machinery and equipment repair

(G-5446)
NANTICOKE CONSULTING INC
2856 Williamsville Rd (19954-2526)
PHONE.................................302 245-3465
EMP: 6 EST: 2019
SALES (est): 471.8K Privately Held
SIC: 8748 Business consulting, nec

(G-5447)
PTS PROFESSIONAL WELDING
609 Broad St (19954-2009)
PHONE.................................302 632-2079
Philip Taubler, Prin
EMP: 2 EST: 2013
SALES (est): 151.48K Privately Held
SIC: 7692 Welding repair

GEOGRAPHIC SECTION

Laurel - Sussex County (G-5474)

(G-5448)
R J K TRANSPORTATION INC
1118 School St (19954-2303)
PHONE..............................302 422-3188
Robert J Koppenhaver, *Pr*
Mary Koppenhaver, *VP*
EMP: 9 EST: 1985
SALES (est): 407.17K **Privately Held**
SIC: 4141 Local bus charter service

(G-5449)
RE CALLOWAY TRNSP INC
897 School St (19954-2019)
PHONE..............................302 422-2471
Barbara J Calloway, *Pr*
EMP: 22 EST: 1969
SALES (est): 938.82K **Privately Held**
SIC: 4131 Intercity highway transport, special service

(G-5450)
ROCK RANCH AUTO LLC
592 Broad St (19954-2008)
PHONE..............................302 670-9992
Thomas Postles, *Prin*
EMP: 5 EST: 2017
SALES (est): 28.25K **Privately Held**
SIC: 7538 General automotive repair shops

Hst Newcastle
New Castle County

(G-5451)
PADRINO RECORDS LLC ✪
419 W 9th St Apt 503 (19720-6086)
PHONE..............................609 353-4683
EMP: 4 EST: 2022
SALES (est): 154.19K **Privately Held**
SIC: 3651 7389 Music distribution apparatus ; Business services, nec

Kenton
Kent County

(G-5452)
COUNTRY STORE
11 S Main St (19955)
P.O. Box 328 (19955-0328)
PHONE..............................302 653-5111
Nona Porter, *Owner*
EMP: 9 EST: 1971
SQ FT: 2,500
SALES (est): 465.4K **Privately Held**
SIC: 5399 0251 Country general stores; Broiling chickens, raising of

(G-5453)
ROOS FOODS INC
251 Roos Ln (19955)
PHONE..............................302 653-0600
Ana Roos, *Pr*
▲ EMP: 19 EST: 1989
SQ FT: 3,683
SALES (est): 1MM **Privately Held**
SIC: 2026 2022 Cream, sour; Cheese; natural and processed

(G-5454)
SHURE-LINE CONSTRUCTION INC
Also Called: Electric
281 W Commerce St (19955)
PHONE..............................302 653-4610
J A Stoneberger, *Pr*
Vernon Wright, *
Ron Pryor, *
Gary Everett, *
EMP: 45 EST: 1991
SQ FT: 4,600
SALES (est): 24.89MM **Privately Held**
Web: www.shure-line.com
SIC: 1542 Commercial and office buildings, renovation and repair

(G-5455)
SMALLEYS AUTOMOTIVE GROUP INC
196 S Main St Ste 211 (19955)
PHONE..............................302 450-0983
Robert Iii, *CEO*
EMP: 5
SALES (est): 106.32K **Privately Held**
SIC: 7538 General automotive repair shops

(G-5456)
THOMAS E MOORE INC
6 Maryland Ave (19955)
PHONE..............................302 674-1500
Thomas D Cullen, *VP*
EMP: 10
SALES (corp-wide): 4.17MM **Privately Held**
SIC: 5148 5141 Vegetables; Food brokers
PA: Thomas E. Moore, Inc.
   696 S Bay Rd
   Dover DE 19901
   302 674-1500

Laurel
Sussex County

(G-5457)
3D MICROWAVE LLC
7795 Bethel Rd (19956-3921)
PHONE..............................302 497-0223
EMP: 2 EST: 2011
SALES (est): 148.74K **Privately Held**
Web: www.3dmicrowave.com
SIC: 3663 Radio and t.v. communications equipment

(G-5458)
A&T CLEANING SERVICES
117 Washington St (19956-1155)
PHONE..............................302 752-5520
Renee Brewington, *Prin*
EMP: 5 EST: 2018
SALES (est): 56.93K **Privately Held**
SIC: 7699 Cleaning services

(G-5459)
ABOVE & BEYOND SERVICES
Also Called: Honeywell Authorized Dealer
14461 Johnson Rd (19956-2939)
P.O. Box 1018 (19956-6018)
PHONE..............................443 614-2068
Gary Mitchell, *Prin*
EMP: 14 EST: 2016
SALES (est): 925.42K **Privately Held**
Web: www.abovenbeyondservices.com
SIC: 1711 Warm air heating and air conditioning contractor

(G-5460)
ACCURATE PEST CONTROL COMPANY
Also Called: Accurate Termite & Pest Ctrl
30139 Sussex Hwy (19956-3826)
P.O. Box 1686 (21802-1686)
PHONE..............................302 875-2725
Gordon R Benson, *Pr*
David Register, *
Mary Register, *
Ruth Ann Taylor, *
EMP: 17 EST: 1995
SQ FT: 1,500
SALES (est): 963.42K **Privately Held**
Web: www.accurate.pro
SIC: 7342 Pest control in structures

(G-5461)
AEG INTERNATIONAL LLC
30931 Sussex Hwy (19956-4426)
P.O. Box 461 (19939-0461)
PHONE..............................302 750-6411
Asher Gulab, *Managing Member*
EMP: 3 EST: 2005
SALES (est): 201.9K **Privately Held**
Web: www.aeginternational.com
SIC: 4789 7372 Transportation services, nec ; Application computer software

(G-5462)
AFFORDABLE CUSTOM CARPENTRY
525 King St (19956-1510)
PHONE..............................302 853-5582
EMP: 5 EST: 2017
SALES (est): 54.73K **Privately Held**
SIC: 1751 Carpentry work

(G-5463)
AMERICAN MASONRY
9602 Chris Ave (19956-4562)
PHONE..............................302 362-9962
David Mcbroom, *Prin*
EMP: 5 EST: 2017
SALES (est): 90.07K **Privately Held**
Web: www.americanmasonryllc.com
SIC: 1741 Masonry and other stonework

(G-5464)
ARMIGERS AUTO CENTER INC (PA)
28866 Sussex Hwy (19956-3825)
PHONE..............................302 875-7642
Jay E Armiger, *Pr*
Jed E Armiger, *VP*
Judith Armiger, *Sec*
Junior E Armiger, *Stockholder*
EMP: 6 EST: 1958
SQ FT: 2,400
SALES (est): 2.42MM
SALES (corp-wide): 2.42MM **Privately Held**
Web: www.armigers.com
SIC: 5521 7532 Automobiles, used cars only ; Body shop, automotive

(G-5465)
AZTEK TILE
Road 451 (19956)
PHONE..............................302 875-0690
John Mackinnis, *Owner*
EMP: 7 EST: 2004
SALES (est): 152.8K **Privately Held**
SIC: 1743 Tile installation, ceramic

(G-5466)
BANK OF DELMARVA
200 E Market St (19956-1535)
PHONE..............................302 875-5901
EMP: 5
Web: www.linkbank.com
SIC: 6022 6029 State trust companies accepting deposits, commercial; Commercial banks, nec
PA: The Bank Of Delmarva
   2245 Northwood Dr
   Salisbury MD 21801

(G-5467)
BAYNUM ENTERPRISES INC
Also Called: Pizza King
403 N Central Ave Unit A (19956-1127)
PHONE..............................302 875-4477
EMP: 34
SALES (corp-wide): 9.15MM **Privately Held**
Web: www.pizzakingde.com
SIC: 5812 6514 Pizza restaurants; Dwelling operators, except apartments
PA: Baynum Enterprises, Inc.
   300 W Stein Hwy
   Seaford DE 19973
   302 629-6104

(G-5468)
BCG INC
30739 Sussex Hwy (19956-4425)
P.O. Box 311 (19956-0311)
PHONE..............................302 875-6013
EMP: 6 EST: 2018
SALES (est): 114.3K **Privately Held**
Web: www.bcg.com
SIC: 8742 Business management consultant

(G-5469)
BETTER HOMES LAUREL II INC
Also Called: Carvel Gardens Annex
2900 Daniel St (19956)
P.O. Box 635 (19956-0635)
PHONE..............................302 875-4282
EMP: 5 EST: 1981
SALES (est): 329.05K **Privately Held**
SIC: 6531 Real estate agents and managers

(G-5470)
BONES INNOVATIONS IN ART
9645 Chris Ave (19956-4563)
PHONE..............................302 430-3592
Kenneth Rathbone, *Prin*
EMP: 5 EST: 2016
SALES (est): 34.26K **Privately Held**
SIC: 7999 Art gallery, commercial

(G-5471)
BOS CONSTRUCTION COMPANY
7045 Sharptown Rd (19956-4153)
PHONE..............................302 875-9120
EMP: 2 EST: 1995
SALES (est): 131.56K **Privately Held**
SIC: 3531 Buckets, excavating: clamshell, concrete, dragline, etc.

(G-5472)
BOYS & GIRLS CLUBS OF AMERICA
454 Central Ave (19956-1128)
PHONE..............................302 875-1200
Brian Daisey, *Dir*
EMP: 9
SALES (corp-wide): 128.99MM **Privately Held**
Web: www.bgca.org
SIC: 8641 Youth organizations
PA: Boys & Girls Clubs Of America
   1275 Peachtree St Ne # 100
   Atlanta GA 30309
   404 487-5700

(G-5473)
BRAHAM PLUMBING LLC
10682 Dorothy Rd (19956-4613)
PHONE..............................302 448-5708
Katrina Braham, *Prin*
EMP: 5 EST: 2014
SALES (est): 150.7K **Privately Held**
SIC: 1711 Plumbing contractors

(G-5474)
BROTHERS LANDSCAPING LLC
31871 Old Hickory Rd (19956-4225)
PHONE..............................360 609-8131
Ismar H Chun Castro, *Prin*
EMP: 5 EST: 2013
SALES (est): 84.36K **Privately Held**
SIC: 0781 Landscape services

Laurel - Sussex County (G-5475)   **GEOGRAPHIC SECTION**

(G-5475)
BULLFEATHERS AUTO SOUND INC
28368 Beaver Dam Branch Rd
(19956-2548)
PHONE.............................302 846-0434
EMP: 6 EST: 1991
SQ FT: 2,700
SALES (est): 699.65K Privately Held
Web: www.bullfeathersautosound.com
SIC: 5511 7538 New and used car dealers; General automotive repair shops

(G-5476)
C&S FARMS INC
8947 Woodland Ferry Rd (19956-3887)
PHONE.............................302 249-0458
Scot Bennett Givens, Pr
EMP: 5 EST: 2009
SALES (est): 553.93K Privately Held
SIC: 0191 General farms, primarily crop

(G-5477)
CABLE CONNECTIONS LLC
28838 E Trap Pond Rd (19956-2521)
PHONE.............................302 397-9014
EMP: 11 EST: 2019
SALES (est): 498.02K Privately Held
Web: www.cable-connections.com
SIC: 4841 Cable television services

(G-5478)
CAREYS INC
Also Called: Careys Towing
30986 Sussex Hwy (19956-4429)
PHONE.............................302 875-5674
Robert Carey, Pr
Grace Carey, Sec
EMP: 16 EST: 1981
SQ FT: 5,080
SALES (est): 791.26K Privately Held
Web: www.careystowing.com
SIC: 7538 5541 7549 Diesel engine repair; automotive; Filling stations, gasoline; Towing service, automotive

(G-5479)
CATHY ANN MITCHELL
31894 Mitchell Ln (19956-3484)
PHONE.............................302 875-7018
Cathy Ann Mitchell, Prin
EMP: 5 EST: 2011
SALES (est): 38.95K Privately Held
SIC: 7231 Beauty shops

(G-5480)
CBD PRO LLC
6625 Millcreek Rd (19956-3221)
PHONE.............................443 736-9002
Barrett Morrison, Prin
EMP: 5 EST: 2016
SALES (est): 107.74K Privately Held
SIC: 3999

(G-5481)
CHESAPEAKE DESIGN CENTER LLC
32852 Sussex Hwy (19956-4564)
PHONE.............................302 875-8570
Warren Reid, Managing Member
EMP: 9 EST: 2006
SALES (est): 280.21K Privately Held
Web: www.chesapeakedesigncenter.com
SIC: 7389 Design services

(G-5482)
CHILDRENS PLACE
Also Called: Children's Place
12034 County Seat Hwy (19956-2634)
PHONE.............................302 875-7733
Fracis Arriola, Dir
EMP: 8 EST: 2017
SALES (est): 54.62K Privately Held
Web: www.childrensplace.com
SIC: 8351 Child day care services

(G-5483)
CLARAVALL ODILON
1124 S Central Ave (19956-1418)
PHONE.............................302 875-7753
Odilon Claravall Md, Pt
Antonio Pedro Md, Pt
EMP: 6 EST: 1972
SALES (est): 291.07K Privately Held
Web: www.lmgdoctors.net
SIC: 8011 Internal medicine, physician/surgeon

(G-5484)
COMMON SENSE SOLUTIONS LLC
14127 Rottwaller Rd (19956-2746)
PHONE.............................302 875-4510
EMP: 14 EST: 2012
SALES (est): 2.49MM Privately Held
Web: www.css-de.com
SIC: 0782 Landscape contractors

(G-5485)
COMMUNICATIONS CNSTR GROUP LLC
1158 S Central Ave (19956-1418)
PHONE.............................302 280-6926
EMP: 42 EST: 2016
SALES (est): 337.44K
SALES (corp-wide): 3.81B Publicly Held
Web: www.ccgcatv.com
SIC: 4899 1521 Communication services, nec; Single-family housing construction
PA: Dycom Industries, Inc.
11780 Us Highway 1 # 600
Palm Beach Gardens FL 33408
561 627-7171

(G-5486)
COOL BRANCH ASSOCIATES LLC
31052 Shady Acres Ln (19956-3572)
PHONE.............................302 629-5363
EMP: 4 EST: 1996
SALES (est): 475.83K Privately Held
Web: www.coolbranch.com
SIC: 2452 Modular homes, prefabricated, wood

(G-5487)
CR LUBE RUN LLC
30053 Fire Tower Rd (19956-2703)
PHONE.............................302 875-1641
Laura Ryan, Prin
EMP: 6 EST: 2013
SALES (est): 116.89K Privately Held
SIC: 7549 Lubrication service, automotive

(G-5488)
CRAFTSMAN BUILDERS OF DE
16101 Willow Way (19956-3098)
PHONE.............................302 542-0731
Aaron Deitzel, Prin
EMP: 5 EST: 2014
SALES (est): 118.92K Privately Held
Web: www.craftsmanbuildersofdelaware.com
SIC: 1521 New construction, single-family houses

(G-5489)
CURTIS A SMITH
314 S Central Ave (19956-1525)
PHONE.............................302 875-6800
Curtis Smith, Owner
EMP: 8 EST: 1989
SALES (est): 493.62K Privately Held
Web: de-laurel.doctors.at.com
SIC: 8011 General and family practice, physician/surgeon

(G-5490)
D & J SWEEPING LLC
7119 Airport Rd (19956-4239)
PHONE.............................302 875-3393
Jaime Hooks, Managing Member
EMP: 7 EST: 2016
SALES (est): 535.99K Privately Held
SIC: 4959 4212 Sanitary services, nec; Dump truck haulage

(G-5491)
DADS WORKWEAR INC (PA)
Also Called: Dad's Workwear
11480 Commercial Ln (19956-4585)
PHONE.............................302 663-0068
Mitchell Brittingham, Pr
Anissa Brittingham, VP
EMP: 2 EST: 2005
SALES (est): 558.69K
SALES (corp-wide): 558.69K Privately Held
Web: www.dadsworkwear.com
SIC: 3842 5611 Personal safety equipment; Men's and boys' clothing stores

(G-5492)
DANIEL GEORGE BEBEE INC
Also Called: Tri County Electrical Services
32353 Cobbs Creek Rd (19956-4087)
PHONE.............................443 359-1542
Dan Bebee, Pr
EMP: 9 EST: 2005
SALES (est): 801.4K Privately Held
Web: www.tri-countyelectrical.com
SIC: 1731 General electrical contractor

(G-5493)
DAVES AUTO RESTORATION
28327 Woods Ln (19956-2678)
PHONE.............................302 258-7981
David Peterson, Prin
EMP: 5 EST: 2018
SALES (est): 89.42K Privately Held
SIC: 7538 General automotive repair shops

(G-5494)
DAVID G HORSEY & SONS INC
Also Called: Horsey Family, The
28107 Beaver Dam Branch Rd
(19956-2543)
PHONE.............................302 875-3033
David G Horsey, Pr
Michael A Horsey, *
Patricia L Horsey, *
EMP: 75 EST: 1985
SALES (est): 23.11MM Privately Held
SIC: 1611 1794 7389 Surfacing and paving; Excavation work; Business services, nec

(G-5495)
DELAWARE SCUBA LLC
31785 Katum Dr (19956-4524)
PHONE.............................302 236-6350
James Brittingham, Prin
EMP: 7 EST: 2018
SALES (est): 123.27K Privately Held
SIC: 8011 Offices and clinics of medical doctors

(G-5496)
DELMARVA BATH LLC
32097 Lous Discount Ln (19956-4587)
PHONE.............................302 278-1717
EMP: 7 EST: 2003
SALES (est): 118.41K Privately Held
SIC: 1799 Kitchen and bathroom remodeling

(G-5497)
DELMARVA HARDWOOD PRODUCTS INC
28950 Seaford Rd (19956-3868)
PHONE.............................302 349-4101
Ben Gordy, Pr
EMP: 10 EST: 2004
SALES (est): 639.18K Privately Held
SIC: 2426 Lumber, hardwood dimension

(G-5498)
DELMARVA IRRIGATION INC
11027 Delaware Ave (19956-4402)
PHONE.............................302 490-1588
Robert Mapp, CEO
Amanda Mapp, COO
Jim Walsh, CFO
EMP: 12 EST: 2020
SALES (est): 1.1MM Privately Held
Web: www.delmarvairr.com
SIC: 4971 7389 Water distribution or supply systems for irrigation; Business Activities at Non-Commercial Site

(G-5499)
DELMARVA SOAP & POWERWASH SLS
10759 N Laurel Plaza Rd (19956-3874)
PHONE.............................302 875-2012
Matt Windsor, Prin
EMP: 6 EST: 2008
SALES (est): 53K Privately Held
SIC: 7349 Building maintenance services, nec

(G-5500)
DEVASTATOR GAME CALLS LLC
12009 Lahoba Ln (19956-2776)
PHONE.............................302 875-5328
EMP: 2 EST: 2008
SALES (est): 150K Privately Held
SIC: 3949 Game calls

(G-5501)
DONALD R CORDREY JR
33258 Shockley Rd (19956-4058)
PHONE.............................302 875-4939
Donald R Cordrey Junior, Prin
EMP: 5 EST: 2012
SALES (est): 93.09K Privately Held
SIC: 1522 Residential construction, nec

(G-5502)
DSI LAUREL LLC
Also Called: US Renal Care Laurel Dialysis
30214 Sussex Hwy (19956-3880)
P.O. Box 638754 (45263-8754)
PHONE.............................302 715-3060
Stephen Pirri, Pr
EMP: 58 EST: 2015
SALES (est): 4.58MM Privately Held
SIC: 8092 Kidney dialysis centers
HQ: Dialysis Newco, Llc
424 Church St Ste 1900
Nashville TN 37219

(G-5503)
DVR INTERNATIONAL INC (PA) ✪
12062 Laurel Rd (19956-3534)
P.O. Box 561 (19703-0561)
PHONE.............................800 958-9000
Johnny Nguyen, Pr
Binh Prung, VP
EMP: 10 EST: 2023
SALES (est): 1.19MM
SALES (corp-wide): 1.19MM Privately Held
SIC: 6221 Commodity traders, contracts

GEOGRAPHIC SECTION

Laurel - Sussex County (G-5534)

(G-5504)
DYNAMIC THERAPY SERVICES LLC
400 S Central Ave (19956-1571)
PHONE..................................302 280-6953
Patricia Petrecca, *Prin*
EMP: 9 **EST:** 2012
SALES (est): 181.36K **Privately Held**
SIC: 8093 Rehabilitation center, outpatient treatment

(G-5505)
EASTERN LIFT TRUCK CO INC
11512 Commercial Ln (19956-4585)
PHONE..................................302 875-4031
Peggy Berest, *Brnch Mgr*
EMP: 48
SALES (corp-wide): 193.26MM **Privately Held**
Web: www.easternlifttruck.com
SIC: 5084 Materials handling machinery
PA: Eastern Lift Truck Co., Inc.
549 E Linwood Ave
Maple Shade NJ 08052
856 779-8880

(G-5506)
EASTERN SHORE VETERINARY HOSP
32384 Sussex Hwy (19956-4642)
P.O. Box 586 (19956-0586)
PHONE..................................302 875-5941
Sarah Dykstra, *Pr*
EMP: 14 **EST:** 1998
SQ FT: 8,700
SALES (est): 996.97K **Privately Held**
Web: www.easternshoreveterinaryhospitals.com
SIC: 0742 Animal hospital services, pets and other animal specialties

(G-5507)
EDGE RACING LLC
34772 Hill Hvn (19956-4279)
PHONE..................................302 519-6680
Brandi Willey, *Prin*
EMP: 6 **EST:** 2014
SALES (est): 86.42K **Privately Held**
SIC: 7948 Racing, including track operation

(G-5508)
EJ CONSTRUCTIONS
14726 Shiloh Church Rd (19956-2810)
PHONE..................................302 272-2101
Elmer Bartolon, *Prin*
EMP: 5 **EST:** 2018
SALES (est): 121.44K **Privately Held**
SIC: 1521 Single-family housing construction

(G-5509)
EMECA/SPE USA LLC
200 W 10th St (19956-1966)
PHONE..................................302 875-0760
▲ **EMP:** 5 **EST:** 2008
SALES (est): 838.19K **Privately Held**
Web: www.emeca-speusa.com
SIC: 3317 Steel pipe and tubes

(G-5510)
END RESULT GYM
28167 Seaford Rd (19956-3704)
PHONE..................................302 280-6387
Phil Depenna, *Prin*
EMP: 6 **EST:** 2012
SALES (est): 72.97K **Privately Held**
SIC: 7991 Athletic club and gymnasiums, membership

(G-5511)
EVAN HOOPER
400 Park Ln (19956-1071)
PHONE..................................302 682-5617
Evan Hooper, *Prin*
EMP: 5 **EST:** 2018
SALES (est): 110.12K **Privately Held**
SIC: 7299 Handyman service

(G-5512)
FIGGSY BUILDERS
5656 Broad Dr (19956-3235)
PHONE..................................302 875-2505
Mark Figgs, *Prin*
EMP: 5 **EST:** 2017
SALES (est): 104.16K **Privately Held**
SIC: 1521 New construction, single-family houses

(G-5513)
FLEMINGS ELECTRICAL SERVICE
15199 Trap Pond Rd (19956-3133)
PHONE..................................302 258-9386
Brandon Fleming, *Prin*
EMP: 6 **EST:** 2017
SALES (est): 233.54K **Privately Held**
Web: www.flemingselectricalservice.com
SIC: 4911 Electric services

(G-5514)
FOWLER & WILLIAMS INC
314 S Central Ave (19956-1525)
P.O. Box 526 (19956-0526)
PHONE..................................302 875-7518
Greg N Johnson, *Pr*
Edward L Fowler, *VP*
John L Downes, *Treas*
EMP: 10 **EST:** 1900
SQ FT: 1,850
SALES (est): 625.94K **Privately Held**
SIC: 6411 Insurance agents, brokers, and service

(G-5515)
FROMMS AUTOMOTIVE
14519 Arvey Rd (19956-3107)
PHONE..................................717 202-9918
Michael Fromm, *Prin*
EMP: 5 **EST:** 2017
SALES (est): 123.64K **Privately Held**
SIC: 7538 General automotive repair shops

(G-5516)
FUN 2 LEARN DAY CARE
7119 Airport Rd (19956-4239)
PHONE..................................302 875-3393
EMP: 6 **EST:** 2015
SALES (est): 56.11K **Privately Held**
SIC: 8351 Child day care services

(G-5517)
GARRET THOMAS PUSEY LLC
412 E 4th St (19956-1552)
PHONE..................................302 875-9146
Garret Thomas Pusey, *Prin*
EMP: 5 **EST:** 2009
SALES (est): 153.64K **Privately Held**
SIC: 1522 Residential construction, nec

(G-5518)
GAS CONTRACTING INC
16091 Willow Way (19956-3086)
PHONE..................................302 875-2302
Michael Granger, *Prin*
EMP: 6 **EST:** 2014
SALES (est): 209.8K **Privately Held**
SIC: 1799 Special trade contractors, nec

(G-5519)
GENERATIONS WLDG & CONTG LLC
14716 Laurel Rd (19956-3156)
PHONE..................................302 430-4099
Carrie Coleman, *Prin*
EMP: 8 **EST:** 2017
SALES (est): 462.79K **Privately Held**
SIC: 1799 Special trade contractors, nec

(G-5520)
GETER DONE MECHANICAL
231 Lewis Dr (19956-1147)
PHONE..................................302 727-3291
Scott Demarest, *Prin*
EMP: 5 **EST:** 2016
SALES (est): 62.69K **Privately Held**
SIC: 1711 Mechanical contractor

(G-5521)
GOOD BEGINNINGS PRESCHOOL
10024 Woodland Ferry Rd (19956-3860)
PHONE..................................302 875-5507
Hazel P Glover, *Prin*
EMP: 5 **EST:** 2005
SALES (est): 79.16K **Privately Held**
Web: www.goodbeginningspreschool.com
SIC: 8351 Preschool center

(G-5522)
GOOD SAMARITAN AID
Also Called: GOOD SAMARITAN THRIFT SHOP, TH
115 W Market St (19956-1001)
P.O. Box 643 (19956-0643)
PHONE..................................302 875-2425
Henretta Koch, *Mgr*
Dale Doice, *Pr*
EMP: 9 **EST:** 1976
SALES (est): 192.49K **Privately Held**
SIC: 8322 5947 Individual and family services; Gift shop

(G-5523)
GOP PRECISION MACHINING
5583 Watson Rd (19956-4041)
PHONE..................................302 875-8875
Elena David, *Owner*
EMP: 6 **EST:** 1995
SALES (est): 339.93K **Privately Held**
SIC: 3549 Wiredrawing and fabricating machinery and equipment, ex. die

(G-5524)
GORDYS LUMBER INC
28950 Seaford Rd (19956-3868)
PHONE..................................302 875-3502
John B Gordy, *Pr*
EMP: 10 **EST:** 1973
SALES (est): 139.08K **Privately Held**
SIC: 2421 2426 Sawmills and planing mills, general; Hardwood dimension and flooring mills

(G-5525)
GREGORY A WILLIAMS JR EDUC
104 E 6th St (19956-1545)
PHONE..................................302 875-1218
Gregory Williams, *Prin*
EMP: 5 **EST:** 2010
SALES (est): 66.87K **Privately Held**
SIC: 8641 Civic and social associations

(G-5526)
HABITAT AMERICA LLC
100 Laurel Commons Ln (19956-1408)
PHONE..................................302 875-3525
EMP: 19
Web: www.habitatamerica.com
SIC: 6512 Nonresidential building operators
PA: Habitat America Llc
180 Admiral Cochrane Dr
Annapolis MD 21401

(G-5527)
HANDS OF HOPE
32104 S Spring Ct (19956-2023)
PHONE..................................302 519-2706
Victoria Snell, *Prin*
EMP: 10 **EST:** 2016
SALES (est): 32.92K **Privately Held**
SIC: 8322 Individual and family services

(G-5528)
HANNIGAN SHORT DISHAROONK
700 West St (19956-1928)
PHONE..................................302 875-3637
Holly Hannigan, *Owner*
EMP: 6 **EST:** 2010
SALES (est): 273.04K **Privately Held**
Web: www.hsdfuneralhome.com
SIC: 7261 Funeral home

(G-5529)
HOG SLAT INCORPORATED
Also Called: Eastern Shore Poultry Services
30709 Sussex Hwy (19956-4425)
PHONE..................................302 875-0889
Larry Hill, *Brnch Mgr*
EMP: 21
SALES (corp-wide): 538.94MM **Privately Held**
Web: www.hogslat.com
SIC: 3523 Farm machinery and equipment
PA: Hog Slat, Incorporated
206 Fayetteville St
Newton Grove NC 28366
800 949-4647

(G-5530)
HOGS HEROES FOUNDATION DE CH1
31799 Katum Dr (19956-4524)
PHONE..................................443 754-0343
Sherry Williamson, *Prin*
EMP: 5 **EST:** 2017
SALES (est): 50.47K **Privately Held**
Web: www.hogsheroesfoundation.com
SIC: 8641 Civic and social associations

(G-5531)
HOMES FOR LAUREL II INC
100 Laurel Commons Ln (19956-1408)
PHONE..................................302 875-3525
Cathy Murphy, *Prin*
EMP: 5 **EST:** 2011
SALES (est): 144.45K **Privately Held**
SIC: 1521 Single-family housing construction

(G-5532)
HORSEY TURF FARM LLC
28107 Beaver Dam Branch Rd (19956-2543)
PHONE..................................302 875-7299
Robert Horsey, *Managing Member*
EMP: 14 **EST:** 1999
SALES (est): 1.41MM **Privately Held**
SIC: 0782 Sodding contractor

(G-5533)
HUMMELL JAMES MD
30867 Al Jan Dr (19956-3239)
PHONE..................................302 875-8127
James Hummell, *Owner*
EMP: 7 **EST:** 2017
SALES (est): 54.13K **Privately Held**
SIC: 8011 Offices and clinics of medical doctors

(G-5534)
INSURANCE MARKET INC (PA)
450 N Central Ave (19956-1128)
P.O. Box 637 (19956-0637)
PHONE..................................302 875-7591

Laurel - Sussex County (G-5535) GEOGRAPHIC SECTION

Stephen Hartstein, *Pr*
James J Hartstein, *
Edward Fowler, *Sec*
John L Downes, *
EMP: 14 **EST:** 1940
SQ FT: 2,000
SALES (est): 4.82MM
SALES (corp-wide): 4.82MM **Privately Held**
Web: www.insurancechoices.com
SIC: 6411 Insurance agents, nec

(G-5535)
INTELEXMICRO INC
Also Called: Lexatys,
10253 Stone Creek Dr # 1 (19956-4700)
PHONE.................................302 907-9545
Walter Gordon, *Pr*
EMP: 3 **EST:** 2012
SALES (est): 246.56K **Privately Held**
Web: www.intelexmicro.com
SIC: 3679 Microwave components

(G-5536)
INTERNET BUSINESS PUBG CORP
Also Called: Delmarva Digital Media Group
220 Laureltowne (19956)
PHONE.................................302 875-7700
Tim Smith, *Pr*
Alan Cole, *VP*
EMP: 12 **EST:** 1997
SALES (est): 637.7K **Privately Held**
SIC: 7373 Computer integrated systems design

(G-5537)
JOHNNY JANOSIK INC (PA)
Also Called: Johnny Janosik World Furniture
11151 Trussum Pond Rd (19956-4522)
PHONE.................................302 875-5955
David Koehler, *CEO*
Lori J Morrison, *
Dan Ringer, *
▲ **EMP:** 200 **EST:** 1953
SQ FT: 80,000
SALES (est): 50.28MM
SALES (corp-wide): 50.28MM **Privately Held**
Web: www.johnnyjanosik.com
SIC: 5712 7389 Beds and accessories; Design services

(G-5538)
JOLLY JOES CLEANING SERVICE
913 West St (19956-1931)
PHONE.................................302 853-5681
Joseph Pastic, *Prin*
EMP: 5 **EST:** 2017
SALES (est): 45.01K **Privately Held**
SIC: 7699 Cleaning services

(G-5539)
K C CONTRACTING
11041 County Seat Hwy (19956-3656)
PHONE.................................302 875-4661
Kenneth M Chase, *Prin*
EMP: 5 **EST:** 2015
SALES (est): 118.12K **Privately Held**
SIC: 1799 Special trade contractors, nec

(G-5540)
K E SMART & SONS INC
29110 Discount Land Rd (19956-3662)
PHONE.................................302 875-7002
Kenneth Smart, *Pr*
Joyce Smart, *Sec*
EMP: 5 **EST:** 1970
SALES (est): 505.59K **Privately Held**
SIC: 1521 General remodeling, single-family houses

(G-5541)
KAREN SCHREIBER
Also Called: Discovery Cove Learning Center
12034 County Seat Hwy (19956-2634)
PHONE.................................302 875-7733
Karen Schreiber, *Owner*
EMP: 9 **EST:** 2015
SALES (est): 164.31K **Privately Held**
Web: www.sussexpreschools.org
SIC: 8351 Preschool center

(G-5542)
L & J SHEET METAL
8095 Airport Rd (19956-4218)
PHONE.................................302 875-2822
Leroy Smith, *Owner*
EMP: 10 **EST:** 1987
SALES (est): 653.96K **Privately Held**
SIC: 1761 7692 3444 Sheet metal work, nec; Welding repair; Sheet metalwork

(G-5543)
LAKESIDE FARMS INC
32206 Hastings Dr (19956-4320)
PHONE.................................302 841-8843
John T Hastings, *Pr*
EMP: 7 **EST:** 2017
SALES (est): 444.02K **Privately Held**
SIC: 0191 General farms, primarily crop

(G-5544)
LAKESIDE GREENHOUSES INC (PA)
Also Called: Windsors Flowers Plants Shrubs
31494 Greenhouse Ln (19956-3583)
PHONE.................................302 875-2457
James C Windsor, *Pr*
Janet Windsor, *VP*
EMP: 5 **EST:** 1972
SALES (est): 693.23K
SALES (corp-wide): 693.23K **Privately Held**
Web: www.lakeside-greenhouses.com
SIC: 5992 5193 0181 Flowers, fresh; Flowers, fresh; Flowers: grown under cover (e.g., greenhouse production)

(G-5545)
LAKESIDE PHYSICAL THERAPY LLC
404 E Front St (19956-1741)
PHONE.................................302 280-6920
Metodio A Pamplona, *Prin*
Rowena Pamplona, *Prin*
EMP: 10 **EST:** 2009
SALES (est): 494.6K **Privately Held**
Web: www.mylakesidept.com
SIC: 8049 8011 Physical therapist; Offices and clinics of medical doctors

(G-5546)
LAUREL DENTAL
10250 Stone Creek Dr Unit 1 (19956-4707)
PHONE.................................302 875-4271
Richard Tananis, *Owner*
EMP: 8 **EST:** 2013
SALES (est): 195.53K **Privately Held**
Web: www.laureldental.net
SIC: 8021 Dentists' office

(G-5547)
LAUREL GRAIN COMPANY
10717 Georgetown Rd (19956-3823)
P.O. Box 422 (19956-0422)
PHONE.................................302 875-4231
Burton Massick, *Pr*
Craig Truitt, *Bd of Dir*
EMP: 5 **EST:** 1965
SQ FT: 20,000
SALES (est): 666.38K **Privately Held**
Web: www.laurelgrain.com
SIC: 5153 Grains

(G-5548)
LAUREL HIGHSCHOOL WELLNESS CTR
1133 S Central Ave (19956-1417)
PHONE.................................302 875-6164
Karen L Hearn, *Dir*
EMP: 7 **EST:** 2004
SALES (est): 435.58K **Privately Held**
SIC: 8099 Medical services organization

(G-5549)
LAUREL LIONS CLUB FOUNDATION
P.O. Box 10 (19956-0010)
PHONE.................................302 875-9178
Barry Munoz, *Prin*
EMP: 5 **EST:** 2010
SALES (est): 79.1K **Privately Held**
SIC: 8641 Civic associations

(G-5550)
LAUREL MEDICAL GROUP
1124 S Central Ave (19956-1418)
PHONE.................................302 875-7753
Kathy Tyler, *Mgr*
EMP: 5 **EST:** 2006
SALES (est): 407.59K **Privately Held**
Web: www.lmgdoctors.net
SIC: 8011 Internal medicine, physician/surgeon

(G-5551)
LAUREL REDEVELOPMENT CORP
202 E Front St (19956-1736)
P.O. Box 333 (19956-0333)
PHONE.................................302 875-0601
Ed Hannigan, *Prin*
EMP: 6 **EST:** 2020
SALES (est): 1.03MM **Privately Held**
Web: www.laurelredevelopment.com
SIC: 1542 Nonresidential construction, nec

(G-5552)
LAUREL SENIOR CENTER INC
Also Called: LAUREL ADULT DAY CARE
113 N Central Ave (19956-1723)
P.O. Box 64 (19956-0064)
PHONE.................................302 875-2536
Dee Renshaw, *Pr*
Robbin Lecates, *Dir*
Harriet Tulliet, *Prin*
EMP: 5 **EST:** 1984
SALES (est): 328.86K **Privately Held**
Web: www.pgparks.com
SIC: 8322 Senior citizens' center or association

(G-5553)
LAYTONS UMBRELLAS
35527 Jami Ave (19956-4602)
PHONE.................................302 249-1958
EMP: 4 **EST:** 2011
SALES (est): 166.68K **Privately Held**
Web: www.laytonsumbrellas.com
SIC: 3999 5021 Manufacturing industries, nec; Furniture

(G-5554)
LBG HOMES LLC
10912 County Seat Hwy (19956-3688)
PHONE.................................302 542-4221
Lisa Horsey, *Prin*
EMP: 5 **EST:** 2011
SALES (est): 250.86K **Privately Held**
Web: www.lbghomes.com
SIC: 8742 Financial consultant

(G-5555)
LEXATYS LLC
10253 Stone Creek Dr # 1 (19956-4700)
PHONE.................................302 715-5029

Walter E Gordon, *Prin*
EMP: 18 **EST:** 2003
SALES (est): 2.08MM **Privately Held**
Web: www.lexatys.com
SIC: 3679 Electronic circuits

(G-5556)
LINCOLN FINANCIAL ADVISORS
Also Called: Lincoln Financial
214 E Front St (19956-1736)
PHONE.................................302 875-8300
Matthew T Parker, *Pr*
EMP: 5 **EST:** 2017
SALES (est): 92.58K **Privately Held**
Web: www.lincolnfinancial.com
SIC: 6282 Investment advice

(G-5557)
LOWER SUSSEX MASONRY LLC
34888 Chelton Dr (19956-3380)
PHONE.................................302 249-3275
EMP: 5 **EST:** 2017
SALES (est): 97.05K **Privately Held**
SIC: 1741 Masonry and other stonework

(G-5558)
M C CHIROPRACTIC CLINIC INC
116 E Front St Ste C (19956-1725)
P.O. Box 998 (19956-0998)
PHONE.................................302 715-5035
Maxene Canton, *Dir*
EMP: 6 **EST:** 2017
SALES (est): 49.5K **Privately Held**
SIC: 8041 Offices and clinics of chiropractors

(G-5559)
MANUFACTURERS & TRADERS TR CO
Also Called: M&T
101 W Market St (19956-1001)
PHONE.................................302 855-2873
Nancy Hearn, *Mgr*
EMP: 8
SALES (corp-wide): 8.6B **Publicly Held**
Web: ir.mtb.com
SIC: 6022 State commercial banks
HQ: Manufacturers And Traders Trust Company
1 M&T Plz Fl 3
Buffalo NY 14203
716 842-4200

(G-5560)
MARY BRYAN INC
4679 Old Sharptown Rd (19956-4013)
PHONE.................................302 875-2087
EMP: 8 **EST:** 2010
SALES (est): 234.58K **Privately Held**
Web: www.marybryaninc.com
SIC: 6411 Insurance agents, nec

(G-5561)
MAXINES HAIR HAPPENINGS INC
206 Laureltowne (19956)
PHONE.................................302 875-4055
Maxine Lynch, *Pr*
EMP: 5 **EST:** 1985
SALES (est): 139.15K **Privately Held**
SIC: 7231 Hairdressers

(G-5562)
MCV MICROWAVE EAST INC
11307 Trussum Pond Rd (19956-4520)
PHONE.................................302 877-8079
Edward Liang, *CEO*
EMP: 25 **EST:** 2019
SALES (est): 15MM **Privately Held**
Web: www.mcv-microwave.com
SIC: 3629 Electronic generation equipment

GEOGRAPHIC SECTION
Laurel - Sussex County (G-5592)

(G-5563)
MICHAEL C RAPA
Also Called: Mk Krawlers
10596 Georgetown Rd (19956-3820)
PHONE..............................302 236-4423
Michael C Rapa, *Owner*
EMP: 2 **EST:** 2010
SALES (est): 98.99K **Privately Held**
SIC: 3799 Off-road automobiles, except recreational vehicles

(G-5564)
MIDDLE DEPT INSPTN AGCY INC
11508 Commercial Ln (19956-4582)
PHONE..............................302 875-4514
Sam Trice, *Mgr*
EMP: 11
SALES (corp-wide): 4.75MM **Privately Held**
Web: www.mdia.us
SIC: 7389 Building inspection service
PA: Middle Department Inspection Agency, Inc.
  1337 W Chester Pike
  West Chester PA 19382
  610 696-3900

(G-5565)
MILLER FNRL HM & CREMATION SVC
11475 Commercial Ln Unit C (19956-4657)
PHONE..............................302 947-1144
Robert Miller, *Owner*
EMP: 5 **EST:** 2016
SALES (est): 82.76K **Privately Held**
Web: www.millerfuneralandcremation.com
SIC: 7261 Funeral home

(G-5566)
MORRIS FARMS LLC
27955 Beaver Dam Branch Rd (19956-2584)
PHONE..............................302 875-1518
EMP: 5 **EST:** 2014
SALES (est): 435.99K **Privately Held**
SIC: 0191 General farms, primarily crop

(G-5567)
MR APPLIANCE SUSSEX COUNTY
32672 Bi State Blvd (19956-4529)
PHONE..............................302 752-3747
Joe Szczepanski, *Owner*
EMP: 5 **EST:** 2017
SALES (est): 48.8K **Privately Held**
Web: www.mrappliance.com
SIC: 7629 Electrical household appliance repair

(G-5568)
MR CUSTOM RENOVATIONS LLC
34542 Branch School Rd (19956-4194)
PHONE..............................302 521-9663
Ryan A Parkin, *Prin*
EMP: 5 **EST:** 2019
SALES (est): 131.27K **Privately Held**
SIC: 1521 General remodeling, single-family houses

(G-5569)
NANTICOKE IMMEDIATE CARE
30549 Sussex Hwy (19956-3891)
PHONE..............................302 715-5214
EMP: 8 **EST:** 2019
SALES (est): 310.91K **Privately Held**
Web: www.tidalhealth.org
SIC: 8062 General medical and surgical hospitals

(G-5570)
NORTHEAST AGRI SYSTEMS INC
28527 Boyce Rd (19956-3877)
PHONE..............................302 875-1886
Frank Pusey, *Brnch Mgr*
EMP: 7
SALES (corp-wide): 26.88MM **Privately Held**
Web: www.neagri.com
SIC: 5083 Agricultural machinery and equipment
PA: Northeast Agri Systems, Inc.
  139a W Airport Rd
  Lititz PA 17543
  717 569-2702

(G-5571)
NR HUDSON CONSULTING INC
14617 Arvey Rd (19956-3069)
PHONE..............................302 875-5276
Nathan R Hudson, *Prin*
EMP: 7 **EST:** 2005
SALES (est): 554.63K **Privately Held**
Web: www.nrhudsonconsulting.com
SIC: 8748 Business consulting, nec

(G-5572)
ONE THE SPOT
30993 Tail Feather Run (19956-3285)
PHONE..............................302 858-2957
Michael J Wilson, *Owner*
EMP: 5 **EST:** 2016
SALES (est): 43.5K **Privately Held**
SIC: 7542 Carwash, self-service

(G-5573)
PENINSULA POULTRY EQP CO INC
30709 Sussex Hwy (19956-4425)
PHONE..............................302 875-0889
Larry Hill, *Owner*
EMP: 29
Web: www.expiredwixdomain.com
SIC: 5083 Poultry equipment
PA: Peninsula Poultry Equipment Company, Inc.
  201 N Dual Hwy
  Laurel DE 19956

(G-5574)
PENINSULA POULTRY EQP CO INC (PA)
201 N Dual Hwy (19956)
P.O. Box 249 (19956-0249)
PHONE..............................302 875-0886
EMP: 5 **EST:** 1994
SALES (est): 907.34K **Privately Held**
Web: www.expiredwixdomain.com
SIC: 5083 Poultry equipment

(G-5575)
PERDUE FARMS INC
Also Called: Laurel DMV North Growout Off
10262 Stone Creek Dr Unit 3 (19956-4701)
PHONE..............................302 855-5681
Marilyn O'neal, *Brnch Mgr*
EMP: 35
SALES (corp-wide): 1.24B **Privately Held**
Web: www.perdue.com
SIC: 0251 Broiler, fryer, and roaster chickens
PA: Perdue Farms Incorporated
  31149 Old Ocean City Rd
  Salisbury MD 21804
  800 473-7383

(G-5576)
PHILLIPS FABRICATION
32846 Shockley Rd (19956-4047)
PHONE..............................302 875-4424
Bruce Phlps, *Owner*
Bruce Phillips, *Owner*
EMP: 3 **EST:** 1990
SQ FT: 1,700
SALES (est): 201.16K **Privately Held**
Web: www.phillipsfab.com
SIC: 3444 3441 Sheet metal specialties, not stamped; Fabricated structural metal

(G-5577)
PLANNED POULTRY RENOVATION
28667 Sussex Hwy (19956-3730)
PHONE..............................302 875-4196
Jay James, *Pt*
Brian Ramey, *Pt*
EMP: 32 **EST:** 1995
SALES (est): 2.11MM **Privately Held**
Web: www.plannedpoultryrenovations.com
SIC: 1796 Machinery installation

(G-5578)
PREDATOR RECOVERY & TOWING LLC
31531 Jestice Farm Rd (19956-2955)
PHONE..............................302 381-2135
Michael Milligan, *Prin*
EMP: 7 **EST:** 2013
SALES (est): 484.81K **Privately Held**
SIC: 7549 Towing service, automotive

(G-5579)
PRIDE CLEANING
6121 Millcreek Rd (19956-3217)
PHONE..............................302 228-0755
Carol Caudill, *Prin*
EMP: 8 **EST:** 2015
SALES (est): 55.39K **Privately Held**
Web: www.officepride.com
SIC: 7349 Janitorial service, contract basis

(G-5580)
PROXIMITY MALT LLC
33222 Bi State Blvd (19956-4644)
PHONE..............................414 755-8388
Matt Musial, *Brnch Mgr*
EMP: 16
SALES (corp-wide): 11.15MM **Privately Held**
Web: www.proximitymalt.com
SIC: 2083 Barley malt
PA: Proximity Malt, Llc
  644 S 5th St
  Milwaukee WI 53204
  414 755-8388

(G-5581)
QUALITY CRAWLSPACE & MORE LLC
32250 Mount Pleasant Rd (19956-3263)
PHONE..............................443 944-5163
Torrez Spence, *Prin*
EMP: 5 **EST:** 2016
SALES (est): 144.93K **Privately Held**
SIC: 7622 Radio and television repair

(G-5582)
R & J WELDING & FABRICATION
32812 Bi State Blvd (19956-4533)
PHONE..............................302 236-5618
EMP: 4 **EST:** 2009
SALES (est): 48.26K **Privately Held**
SIC: 7692 Welding repair

(G-5583)
R J BAKER DISTILLERY
34171 Rider Rd (19956-4067)
PHONE..............................302 745-0967
EMP: 4 **EST:** 2014
SALES (est): 112.79K **Privately Held**
SIC: 2085 Distilled and blended liquors

(G-5584)
RAM ELECTRIC INC
34779 Whaleys Rd (19956-3015)
P.O. Box 1680 (19973-8980)
PHONE..............................302 875-2356
Rodney A Morton, *Pr*
EMP: 9 **EST:** 2005
SALES (est): 803.1K **Privately Held**
SIC: 1731 General electrical contractor

(G-5585)
RAMCO SOLUTIONS LLC
28667 Sussex Hwy (19956-3730)
PHONE..............................302 715-5432
EMP: 3 **EST:** 2020
SALES (est): 460.04K **Privately Held**
Web: www.ramco-solutions.com
SIC: 3444 Sheet metalwork

(G-5586)
REAL ESTATE MARKET
405 N Central Ave (19956-1127)
PHONE..............................302 715-5640
EMP: 5 **EST:** 2017
SALES (est): 240.16K **Privately Held**
Web: www.realestatemarket.pro
SIC: 6531 Real estate brokers and agents

(G-5587)
REDHEAD FARMS LLC
34102 Rider Rd (19956-4062)
PHONE..............................443 235-3990
EMP: 3 **EST:** 2007
SALES (est): 277.46K **Privately Held**
SIC: 3523 Driers (farm): grain, hay, and seed

(G-5588)
RELAX INN
30702 Sussex Hwy (19956-4424)
PHONE..............................302 875-1554
Rk Gadani, *Prin*
EMP: 7 **EST:** 2007
SALES (est): 234.56K **Privately Held**
SIC: 7011 Inns

(G-5589)
RESURRECTED ELECTRIC LLC
9248 Sharptown Rd (19956-4310)
PHONE..............................302 841-8989
John Porter, *Prin*
EMP: 5 **EST:** 2019
SALES (est): 238.37K **Privately Held**
SIC: 4911 Electric services

(G-5590)
RICHARD HARRISON JR PAVING
4705 Phillips Landing Rd (19956-3289)
PHONE..............................302 875-4206
EMP: 9 **EST:** 2010
SALES (est): 288.94K **Privately Held**
SIC: 1611 Surfacing and paving

(G-5591)
RICHARD J TANANIS DDS LLC
10250 Stone Creek Dr Unit 1 (19956-4703)
PHONE..............................302 875-4271
Richard J Tananis, *Asstg*
EMP: 5 **EST:** 2008
SALES (est): 405.89K **Privately Held**
Web: www.laureldental.net
SIC: 8021 Dentists' office

(G-5592)
RISEN SERVICES
32531 Samuel Hill Rd (19956-2903)
PHONE..............................302 858-8840
Robert Cooper, *Prin*
EMP: 5 **EST:** 2017
SALES (est): 219.24K **Privately Held**
Web: www.risenservces.com

Laurel - Sussex County (G-5593) GEOGRAPHIC SECTION

SIC: **1522** Residential construction, nec

(G-5593)
RIVERA TRANSPORTATION INC
205 W 7th St (19956-1939)
PHONE..................................302 258-9023
Erlin I Rivera, *Prin*
EMP: 8 EST: 2010
SALES (est): 359.84K **Privately Held**
SIC: **4789** Transportation services, nec

(G-5594)
ROLAND E TICE
32888 Bi State Blvd (19956-4533)
PHONE..................................302 629-3674
Roland E Tice, *Pr*
EMP: 5 EST: 2017
SALES (est): 67.44K **Privately Held**
SIC: **8641** Civic and social associations

(G-5595)
ROSEMONT WEALTH MANAGEMENT
214 E Front St (19956-1736)
P.O. Box 818 (19956-0818)
PHONE..................................302 875-8300
EMP: 5 EST: 2017
SALES (est): 249.45K **Privately Held**
Web: www.rosemontwealth.com
SIC: **8741** Management services

(G-5596)
ROSSAKATUM RANCH INC
12487 Salt Barn Rd (19956-3337)
PHONE..................................302 875-5707
EMP: 7 EST: 2009
SALES (est): 437.7K **Privately Held**
SIC: **0291** General farms, primarily animals

(G-5597)
ROYAL FARMS
11112 Laurel Rd (19956-3564)
PHONE..................................410 725-9100
EMP: 8 EST: 2017
SALES (est): 171.4K **Privately Held**
Web: www.royalfarms.com
SIC: **0191** General farms, primarily crop

(G-5598)
ROYAL MISSION & MINISTRIES
9751 Randall St (19956-4315)
PHONE..................................302 249-8863
Gerry Royal, *Prin*
EMP: 5 EST: 2008
SALES (est): 78.61K **Privately Held**
SIC: **8399** Social services, nec

(G-5599)
SMITH-SPINELLA ELECTRIC LLC
28988 Seaford Rd (19956-3868)
PHONE..................................302 228-4865
EMP: 6 EST: 2010
SALES (est): 53.94K **Privately Held**
Web: smithspinellaelect8.wixsite.com
SIC: **1731** Electrical work

(G-5600)
SMW SALES LLC
11432 Trussum Pond Rd (19956-3412)
PHONE..................................302 875-7958
Richard Carmine, *Prin*
EMP: 21 EST: 2007
SALES (est): 4.49MM **Privately Held**
Web: www.smwsales.net
SIC: **3272** **3531** **3594** Irrigation pipe, concrete ; Rakes, land clearing; mechanical; Fluid power pumps and motors

(G-5601)
SNK ENTERPRISES INC
34650 Hudson Rd (19956-3060)
PHONE..................................443 783-5717
Scott L Whaley, *Pr*
EMP: 6 EST: 1985
SALES (est): 71.28K **Privately Held**
SIC: **8741** Management services

(G-5602)
SNYDERS HVAC SERVICES LLC
14835 Arvey Rd (19956-3084)
PHONE..................................302 236-2517
EMP: 5 EST: 2013
SALES (est): 94.49K **Privately Held**
SIC: **1711** Warm air heating and air conditioning contractor

(G-5603)
SOLID IMAGE INC
11244 Whitesville Rd (19956-3318)
PHONE..................................302 877-0901
Warren Reid, *Pr*
EMP: 22 EST: 2013
SALES (est): 1.44MM **Privately Held**
SIC: **2541** Counter and sink tops

(G-5604)
SOUTHERN DEL TRCK GROWERS ASSN
Dual Hwy & Georgetown Rd (19956)
PHONE..................................302 875-3147
George Collins, *Pr*
Robert L Whaley, *VP*
Thomas Wright, *Sec*
Joseph C O'neal, *Treas*
EMP: 8 EST: 1940
SALES (est): 171.13K **Privately Held**
SIC: **7389** Auctioneers, fee basis

(G-5605)
SPORTZ TEES
16536 Adams Rd (19956-2922)
PHONE..................................302 280-6076
Chris Otwell, *Owner*
EMP: 6 EST: 2012
SALES (est): 146.57K **Privately Held**
Web: www.shopsportztees.com
SIC: **2759** Screen printing

(G-5606)
SSMMD LLC
Also Called: Laurel Tire Center
29092 Sussex Hwy (19956-3878)
PHONE..................................302 249-1045
EMP: 2 EST: 2014
SALES (est): 181.68K **Privately Held**
SIC: **5015** **7534** Tires, used: retail only; Tire repair shop

(G-5607)
STATE LINE MACHINE INC
1154 S Central Ave (19956-1418)
P.O. Box 667 (19706-0667)
PHONE..................................302 875-2248
EMP: 17 EST: 2019
SALES (est): 2.52MM **Privately Held**
Web: www.statelinemachine.com
SIC: **3599** Machine shop, jobbing and repair

(G-5608)
SUPERIOR DEDICATED SVCS LLC
10957 Salt Barn Rd (19956-3327)
PHONE..................................443 497-4410
EMP: 10 EST: 2020
SALES (est): 1.52MM **Privately Held**
SIC: **4213** Trucking, except local

(G-5609)
SUSSEX DIESEL INC
31051 Old Sailor Rd (19956-3918)
PHONE..................................302 877-0330
Jeffrey Givens, *Prin*
EMP: 6 EST: 2017
SALES (est): 207.37K **Privately Held**
SIC: **7538** General automotive repair shops

(G-5610)
SUSSEX MACHINE WORKS INC
11432 Trussum Pond Rd (19956-3412)
PHONE..................................302 875-7958
Richard Charmina, *Pr*
EMP: 8 EST: 1972
SALES (est): 923.97K **Privately Held**
SIC: **1799** Welding on site

(G-5611)
SUSSEX PLUMBING & HEATING
14320 Shiloh Way (19956-3163)
PHONE..................................302 344-2199
EMP: 6 EST: 2015
SALES (est): 241.06K **Privately Held**
SIC: **1711** Plumbing contractors

(G-5612)
SYNERGY EMPOWERMENT COACHING
6334 Phillips Landing Rd (19956-3247)
PHONE..................................302 362-0054
Shelley Hastings, *Prin*
EMP: 7 EST: 2019
SALES (est): 41.55K **Privately Held**
Web: www.synergyempowermentcoaching.com
SIC: **8322** General counseling services

(G-5613)
TABITHA MEDICAL CARE LLC
30668 Sussex Hwy (19956-4421)
PHONE..................................302 251-8870
EMP: 6 EST: 2019
SALES (est): 737.48K **Privately Held**
Web: www.tabithamedicalcare.com
SIC: **8099** Health and allied services, nec

(G-5614)
TARACHAND BEHARRY
18250 Laurel Rd (19956-2938)
PHONE..................................302 875-0684
Tarachand Beharry, *Prin*
EMP: 5 EST: 2010
SALES (est): 194.93K **Privately Held**
SIC: **0191** General farms, primarily crop

(G-5615)
TELAMON CORPORATION HEADSTART
Also Called: Telamon - Laurel Head Start
30125 Discount Land Rd (19956-3679)
PHONE..................................302 875-7718
Selina Houston, *Prin*
EMP: 10 EST: 2006
SALES (est): 259.01K **Privately Held**
SIC: **8331** Job training services

(G-5616)
TROPIC FEVER TANNING SALON
303 S Poplar St Ste 1 (19956-1065)
PHONE..................................302 875-1500
David Thomas, *Owner*
EMP: 6 EST: 2016
SALES (est): 25.22K **Privately Held**
Web: www.tropicfevertanning.com
SIC: **7299** Tanning salon

(G-5617)
UNIQUE AUTO ACCESSORIES LLC
28042 Seaford Rd (19956-3772)
PHONE..................................302 841-0983
Evens Janvier, *Pr*
EMP: 8 EST: 2017
SALES (est): 489.18K **Privately Held**
Web: www.uniqueautosalesandservice.com
SIC: **7538** General automotive repair shops

(G-5618)
VANY PRODUCTIONS LOGISTICS LLC ◯
2700 Daniel St #2708 (19956-1776)
PHONE..................................443 397-2949
Varnel Edmond, *CEO*
EMP: 5 EST: 2022
SALES (est): 288.66K **Privately Held**
SIC: **4789** **7389** Transportation services, nec ; Business Activities at Non-Commercial Site

(G-5619)
VINCENT FARMS INC
12487 Salt Barn Rd (19956-3337)
P.O. Box 219 (19940-0219)
PHONE..................................302 875-5707
EMP: 125 EST: 1978
SQ FT: 25,000
SALES (est): 9.93MM **Privately Held**
Web: www.vincentfamilyfarms.com
SIC: **0191** **4971** General farms, primarily crop ; Irrigation systems

(G-5620)
WARREN REID
Also Called: Warren A Reid Custon Builders
14234 Sycamore Rd (19956-2738)
PHONE..................................302 877-0901
Warren A Reid, *Pr*
EMP: 25 EST: 1999
SALES (est): 1.29MM **Privately Held**
SIC: **1522** Residential construction, nec

(G-5621)
WASTE MANAGEMENT DELAWARE INC
11323 Trussum Pond Rd (19956-4520)
PHONE..................................302 854-5301
EMP: 8
SALES (corp-wide): 20.43B **Publicly Held**
SIC: **4953** Refuse systems
HQ: Waste Management Of Delaware Inc.
1001 Fannin St Ste 4000
Houston TX 77002
713 512-6200

(G-5622)
WASTEFLO LLC
207 N Poplar St (19956-1009)
PHONE..................................410 202-0802
EMP: 5 EST: 2011
SALES (est): 237.49K **Privately Held**
SIC: **4212** **4953** Garbage collection and transport, no disposal; Rubbish collection and disposal

(G-5623)
WHALEYS SEED STORE INC
106 W 8th St (19956-1900)
PHONE..................................302 875-7833
W Douglas Whaley, *Pr*
Patricia Whaley, *Sec*
Lisa Jester, *VP*
EMP: 6 EST: 1946
SALES (est): 770K **Privately Held**
SIC: **5191** **5083** **7349** Farm supplies; Garden machinery and equipment, nec; Building maintenance services, nec

GEOGRAPHIC SECTION   Lewes - Sussex County (G-5653)

(G-5624)
WHAYLAND COMPANY INC
30613 Sussex Hwy (19956-4420)
PHONE.................................302 875-5445
Robert Wheatley, *Pr*
EMP: 12 **EST:** 1993
SQ FT: 1,200
SALES (est): 4.38MM **Privately Held**
Web: www.whayland.com
SIC: 1542 1541 Commercial and office building, new construction; Industrial buildings, new construction, nec

(G-5625)
WHAYLAND COMPANY LLC
100 W 10th St (19956-1904)
PHONE.................................302 875-5445
Steven Hentschel, *Pr*
EMP: 12 **EST:** 2013
SALES (est): 4.87MM **Privately Held**
Web: www.whayland.com
SIC: 1542 Commercial and office building, new construction

(G-5626)
WILLEY AND CO
11588 Commercial Ln (19956-4640)
P.O. Box 60 (19973-0060)
PHONE.................................302 629-3327
Micheal Willey, *Owner*
EMP: 9 **EST:** 1974
SALES (est): 918.09K **Privately Held**
Web: www.willeyco.com
SIC: 1711 1389 Heating systems repair and maintenance; Cleaning wells

(G-5627)
ZAT3 TRANSPORT LLC ✪
33221 Horsey Church Rd (19956-4356)
PHONE.................................302 470-6172
Terell Jones, *Managing Member*
EMP: 7 **EST:** 2022
SALES (est): 502.74K **Privately Held**
SIC: 5088 7389 Transportation equipment and supplies; Business Activities at Non-Commercial Site

(G-5628)
ZINGER ENTERPRIZES INC
9224 Sharptown Rd (19956-4310)
PHONE.................................302 381-6761
Carl Schirtzinger, *CEO*
EMP: 5 **EST:** 2004
SALES (est): 317.55K **Privately Held**
Web: www.zingerenterprizes.com
SIC: 8733 Research institute

Leipsic
Kent County

(G-5629)
CAREYS DIESEL INC
168 Denny St (19901-1763)
PHONE.................................302 678-3797
John J Carey, *Pr*
Louise Carey, *Sec*
◆ **EMP:** 10 **EST:** 1989
SALES (est): 540.3K **Privately Held**
Web: www.careysdiesel.com
SIC: 7538 5084 Diesel engine repair: automotive; Engines and parts, diesel

(G-5630)
DELAWARE BLUE CLAWS
354 Main St (19901-1703)
PHONE.................................302 674-3123
Alan Pleasanton, *Prin*
EMP: 7 **EST:** 2010
SALES (est): 64.04K **Privately Held**

SIC: 0752 Boarding services, kennels

(G-5631)
DONA E ORTELLI SLP
228 Front St (19901-1735)
PHONE.................................302 734-2606
Donne Ortelli, *Prin*
EMP: 7 **EST:** 2011
SALES (est): 63.64K **Privately Held**
SIC: 8049 Speech pathologist

(G-5632)
EASTERN SHORE ONSITE SVCS LLC
265 Front St (19901-1736)
PHONE.................................302 736-0366
Samuel J Fox Iv, *Prin*
EMP: 5 **EST:** 2012
SALES (est): 171.14K **Privately Held**
SIC: 7389 Inspection and testing services

(G-5633)
SAWYERS SANITATION SERVICE
184 Front St (19901-1715)
P.O. Box 538 (19977-0538)
PHONE.................................302 678-8240
Daniel Fox, *Owner*
EMP: 5 **EST:** 1971
SALES (est): 337.29K **Privately Held**
SIC: 7699 Cesspool cleaning

Lewes
Sussex County

(G-5634)
1 KONTO INC
16192 Coastal Hwy (19958-3608)
PHONE.................................215 783-8166
Edwin Handschuh, *CEO*
EMP: 13
SALES (est): 536.92K **Privately Held**
SIC: 6289 Financial reporting

(G-5635)
114 AI INC
16192 Coastal Hwy (19958-3608)
PHONE.................................719 394-0606
Vinayak Dalmia, *CEO*
EMP: 5 **EST:** 2020
SALES (est): 46.16K **Privately Held**
SIC: 7371 Computer software systems analysis and design, custom

(G-5636)
1TOUCH PAINTING LLC
17527 Nassau Commons Blvd (19958-6283)
PHONE.................................302 703-6027
EMP: 8 **EST:** 2018
SALES (est): 249.54K **Privately Held**
Web: www.1touchpainting.com
SIC: 1721 Painting and paper hanging

(G-5637)
208 SOCIAL
17270 N Village Main Blvd (19958-7219)
PHONE.................................610 762-3793
EMP: 6 **EST:** 2018
SALES (est): 47.42K **Privately Held**
SIC: 7389 Tourist information bureau

(G-5638)
360 DIGITAL MARKETING LLC
16192 Coastal Hwy (19958-3608)
PHONE.................................214 247-7153
EMP: 8 **EST:** 2015
SALES (est): 241.14K **Privately Held**
Web: www.360digimarketing.com

SIC: 8742 Marketing consulting services

(G-5639)
4 GREEN SOLUTIONS INC (PA)
16192 Coastal Hwy (19958-3608)
PHONE.................................954 770-5157
Daniel Lsr Dawson, *Pr*
EMP: 6 **EST:** 2016
SALES (est): 549.18K
SALES (corp-wide): 549.18K **Privately Held**
SIC: 8082 Home health care services

(G-5640)
4GURUS LLC (PA)
Also Called: Event Guru Software
33621 Union Cir (19958-9433)
PHONE.................................571 789-0012
Mark Williams, *Mgr*
EMP: 4 **EST:** 2014
SALES (est): 433.84K
SALES (corp-wide): 433.84K **Privately Held**
Web: www.eventgurusoftware.com
SIC: 7372 7389 Business oriented computer software; Business services, nec

(G-5641)
6 8 MEDICAL SOLUTIONS LLC
16192 Coastal Hwy (19958-3608)
PHONE.................................843 481-5550
EMP: 5
SALES (est): 76.37K **Privately Held**
SIC: 6794 Patent owners and lessors

(G-5642)
8MESH INC
16192 Coastal Hwy (19958-3608)
PHONE.................................888 627-4331
Ta Cheng Hsu, *Pr*
EMP: 5 **EST:** 2020
SALES (est): 60.69K **Privately Held**
SIC: 4813 Internet connectivity services

(G-5643)
A & TC BUILDERS INC
32808 Pear Tree Ct (19958-3724)
PHONE.................................443 736-0099
Timothy Charles Duval, *Prin*
EMP: 5 **EST:** 2019
SALES (est): 82.12K **Privately Held**
SIC: 1521 New construction, single-family houses

(G-5644)
A CHANCE TO WRITE IT LLC
16192 Coastal Hwy (19958-3608)
PHONE.................................202 256-4524
EMP: 7
SALES (est): 295.19K **Privately Held**
SIC: 2731 Book publishing

(G-5645)
A CHILDS POTENTIAL
12 Gosling Dr (19958-9570)
PHONE.................................302 249-6929
Candace Shetzler, *Prin*
EMP: 5 **EST:** 2010
SALES (est): 90.29K **Privately Held**
Web: www.vistaprint.com
SIC: 8351 Montessori child development center

(G-5646)
A M CLAY ONROE INC
1143 Savannah Rd (19958-1516)
PHONE.................................302 645-6565
EMP: 5 **EST:** 2020
SALES (est): 229.01K **Privately Held**
Web: www.clayamonroe.com

SIC: 6411 Insurance agents, nec

(G-5647)
A-ONE TOWING INC
22467 John J Williams Hwy (19958-4337)
PHONE.................................302 853-2326
Satinder Singh, *Pt*
EMP: 6 **EST:** 2016
SALES (est): 357.66K **Privately Held**
SIC: 7549 Towing services

(G-5648)
A2A INTGRTED PHRMCEUTICALS LLC
16192 Coastal Hwy (19958-3608)
PHONE.................................270 202-2461
EMP: 5 **EST:** 2019
SALES (est): 340.79K **Privately Held**
SIC: 2834 5122 7389 Druggists' preparations (pharmaceuticals); Pharmaceuticals; Business services, nec

(G-5649)
ABA TRAVL & ENT INC
16192 Coastal Hwy (19958-3608)
PHONE.................................800 696-0838
Wenceslao Lora, *CEO*
EMP: 5 **EST:** 1989
SQ FT: 1,100
SALES (est): 570.02K **Privately Held**
Web: www.abatr.com
SIC: 4724 Travel agencies

(G-5650)
ACCENDUSTRY LLC
16192 Coastal Hwy (19958-3608)
PHONE.................................469 777-6186
Wei Ke, *Managing Member*
EMP: 2
SALES (est): 87.4K **Privately Held**
SIC: 7372 Prepackaged software

(G-5651)
ACCESS PURCHASING NETWORK INC (PA)
16192 Coastal Hwy (19958-3608)
EMP: 6 **EST:** 1979
SQ FT: 5,000
SALES (est): 1.49MM
SALES (corp-wide): 1.49MM **Privately Held**
SIC: 8742 Management consulting services

(G-5652)
ACCESS4U INC
510 Railroad Ave (19958-1432)
P.O. Box 2535 (15068-0747)
PHONE.................................800 355-7025
Robert B Heffernan, *Pr*
Kirit Patel, *VP*
EMP: 15 **EST:** 2005
SALES (est): 1.32MM **Privately Held**
Web: www.rampsaccess4u.com
SIC: 3446 Stairs, staircases, stair treads: prefabricated metal

(G-5653)
ACCURATE MEDIA LLC
14689 Pleasant Pond Way (19958-5927)
PHONE.................................301 943-9428
EMP: 4 **EST:** 2013
SQ FT: 2,700
SALES (est): 359.7K **Privately Held**
Web: www.accuratemediallc.com
SIC: 8742 7372 Marketing consulting services; Prepackaged software

Lewes - Sussex County (G-5654) GEOGRAPHIC SECTION

(G-5654)
ACCURATE-ENERGY LLC
35180 South Dr (19958-3244)
P.O. Box 293 (19958-0293)
PHONE..................................302 947-9560
EMP: 4 **EST:** 2008
SALES (est): 498.32K **Privately Held**
Web: www.accurate-energy.com
SIC: 1389 Oil field services, nec

(G-5655)
ACT MEDIA
16192 Coastal Hwy (19958-3608)
PHONE..................................888 666-0786
EMP: 6 **EST:** 2014
SALES (est): 113.91K **Privately Held**
SIC: 7336 Graphic arts and related design

(G-5656)
ACTION TRACK USA
33217 W Edgemoor St (19958-7227)
PHONE..................................610 780-2290
Doug Rose, *Prin*
EMP: 5 **EST:** 2017
SALES (est): 83.54K **Privately Held**
SIC: 7948 Racing, including track operation

(G-5657)
ACTIV PEST & LAWN INC
16861 New Rd (19958-3706)
PHONE..................................302 645-1502
Bailey Mcmahon, *Owner*
EMP: 18 **EST:** 2005
SALES (est): 870.81K **Privately Held**
Web: www.activpestsolutions.com
SIC: 7342 Pest control in structures

(G-5658)
ACTIVE LIFE ACUPUNCTURE
33044 E Light Dr (19958-4657)
PHONE..................................302 827-2691
Denise Demback, *Prin*
EMP: 6 **EST:** 2017
SALES (est): 22.18K **Privately Held**
Web: www.activelifeacupuncture.com
SIC: 8049 Acupuncturist

(G-5659)
ACTUAL VEGGIES LLC
17500 Slipper Shell Way Unit 12
(19958-6318)
PHONE..................................818 825-0531
Jason Rosenbaum, *Managing Member*
EMP: 8 **EST:** 2020
SALES (est): 1.08MM **Privately Held**
Web: www.actualveggies.com
SIC: 2099 Food preparations, nec

(G-5660)
ADRION & CO LLC
16192 Coastal Hwy (19958-3608)
PHONE..................................302 313-1392
EMP: 2 **EST:** 2018
SALES (est): 250K **Privately Held**
SIC: 2844 Cosmetic preparations

(G-5661)
ADVANCED BEHAVIORAL CARE INC
19 Cedarwood Dr (19958-9583)
PHONE..................................410 599-7400
Leonard Francis Stielper, *Prin*
EMP: 8 **EST:** 2008
SALES (est): 75.94K **Privately Held**
SIC: 8093 Mental health clinic, outpatient

(G-5662)
ADVANTAGE FUTURETECH COMPANY
16192 Coastal Hwy (19958-3608)
PHONE..................................347 592-5667
Gaurav Malhotra, *Admn*
Gaurav Malhotra, *Pr*
Rajat Khare, *Prin*
EMP: 2 **EST:** 2021
SALES (est): 86.08K **Privately Held**
SIC: 3728 7389 Aircraft parts and equipment, nec; Business services, nec

(G-5663)
AERONA SOLUTIONS INC ✪
16192 Coastal Hwy (19958-3608)
PHONE..................................302 601-4332
Farid Mullah, *Pr*
EMP: 4 **EST:** 2023
SALES (est): 171.34K **Privately Held**
SIC: 7372 Application computer software

(G-5664)
AESTHETICS CENTER
34172 Citizen Dr (19958-4777)
PHONE..................................302 827-2125
Abdollah Malek, *Prin*
EMP: 8 **EST:** 2012
SALES (est): 233.16K **Privately Held**
Web: www.aestheticcenter.com
SIC: 7299 Personal appearance services

(G-5665)
AGITEK SOFTWORKS INC
16192 Coastal Hwy (19958-3608)
PHONE..................................240 356-3034
EMP: 6 **EST:** 2019
SALES (est): 103.81K **Privately Held**
Web: www.agitek.io
SIC: 7371 Computer software development

(G-5666)
AIGC GAMES INC
16192 Coastal Hwy (19958-3608)
PHONE..................................214 499-8654
Mohammed Ammous, *CEO*
Maram Amous, *VP*
EMP: 7 **EST:** 2015
SQ FT: 2,000
SALES (est): 350K **Privately Held**
SIC: 7373 Computer integrated systems design

(G-5667)
AIRLOCK389 INC
16192 Postal Hwy (19958)
PHONE..................................213 393-1785
Chris Cooper, *CEO*
EMP: 2 **EST:** 2020
SALES (est): 107.44K **Privately Held**
Web: www.airlock389.com
SIC: 3564 Air purification equipment

(G-5668)
AK ELECTRIC INC
31575 Gooseberry Way (19958-5829)
PHONE..................................302 379-3728
Andrezej Klosowski, *Prin*
EMP: 6 **EST:** 2011
SALES (est): 113.35K **Privately Held**
SIC: 1731 Electrical work

(G-5669)
ALAWAR ENTERTAINMENT INC (PA)
16192 Coastal Hwy (19958-3608)
PHONE..................................646 413-5757
EMP: 7 **EST:** 2019
SALES (est): 96.39K
SALES (corp-wide): 96.39K **Privately Held**
Web: www.universidades-rusia.com
SIC: 7929 Entertainers and entertainment groups

(G-5670)
ALBION INVESTMENTS LLC (PA)
16192 Coastal Hwy (19958-3608)
PHONE..................................876 575-7371
EMP: 6
SALES (est): 46.16K
SALES (corp-wide): 46.16K **Privately Held**
SIC: 7371 Computer software development and applications

(G-5671)
ALCOSM LLC
16192 Coastal Hwy (19958-3608)
PHONE..................................302 703-7635
EMP: 4 **EST:** 2020
SALES (est): 199.62K **Privately Held**
SIC: 2842 Disinfectants, household or industrial plant

(G-5672)
ALL CLIMATE STORAGE CENTE
17485 Shady Rd (19958-6234)
PHONE..................................302 645-0006
Steve Twigg, *Mgr*
EMP: 7 **EST:** 2006
SALES (est): 103.44K **Privately Held**
Web: www.allclimatestorage.com
SIC: 4226 Special warehousing and storage, nec

(G-5673)
ALL LOGISTICS LLC
30862 Saddleridge Way (19958-5594)
PHONE..................................800 748-4891
EMP: 10 **EST:** 2020
SALES (est): 500K **Privately Held**
Web: www.allusalogistics.com
SIC: 4731 Freight transportation arrangement

(G-5674)
ALL PRO MAIDS INC
1546 Savannah Rd (19958-1624)
PHONE..................................302 645-9247
James Sprinkle, *Pr*
Michele Sprinkle, *
EMP: 30 **EST:** 1991
SALES (est): 938.38K **Privately Held**
Web: www.allprolewes.com
SIC: 7349 Janitorial service, contract basis

(G-5675)
ALLERFREE CLEANING
428 W 4th St (19958-1241)
PHONE..................................302 593-6261
David Scholz, *Pr*
EMP: 5 **EST:** 2016
SALES (est): 51.68K **Privately Held**
SIC: 7699 Cleaning services

(G-5676)
ALLISON VEITH LPCMH
31168 Learning Ln (19958-3685)
PHONE..................................302 645-5338
Allison Rhue, *Prin*
EMP: 7 **EST:** 2016
SALES (est): 52.15K **Privately Held**
Web: www.delawareguidance.org
SIC: 8322 Family counseling services

(G-5677)
ALLSTATE INSURANCE
Also Called: Allstate
19413 Jingle Shell Way (19958-6307)
PHONE..................................302 248-8500
Paul Sarnak, *Owner*
EMP: 6 **EST:** 2012
SALES (est): 179.41K **Privately Held**
Web: www.allstate.com
SIC: 6411 Insurance agents, brokers, and service

(G-5678)
ALLTEMP AIR INC
21171 John J Williams Hwy (19958-4329)
PHONE..................................302 945-5734
EMP: 10 **EST:** 2020
SALES (est): 625.09K **Privately Held**
Web: www.alltempairinc.com
SIC: 1521 General remodeling, single-family houses

(G-5679)
ALLURE OUTDOOR LIGHTING LLC
20187 Beaver Dam Rd (19958-5525)
PHONE..................................302 226-2532
EMP: 5 **EST:** 2018
SALES (est): 108.09K **Privately Held**
Web: www.allureoutdoorlighting.com
SIC: 0781 Landscape services

(G-5680)
AMADA SENIOR CARE SOUTHERN DEL
Also Called: Amada Senior Care
1 Ashford Dr (19958-8955)
PHONE..................................302 272-9500
EMP: 10 **EST:** 2012
SALES (est): 70.2K **Privately Held**
Web: www.amadaseniorcare.com
SIC: 8082 Home health care services

(G-5681)
AMALIPO SMARTDUKA LTD
16192 Coastal Hwy (19958-3608)
PHONE..................................857 452-1692
Marc Bouviere, *CEO*
EMP: 12 **EST:** 2016
SALES (est): 206.95K **Privately Held**
Web: www.smartduka.com
SIC: 8999 Communication services

(G-5682)
AMBER DRAGON ACUPUNCTURE
1143 Savannah Rd Ste 4 (19958-1515)
P.O. Box 104 (19969-0104)
PHONE..................................206 227-0641
Amber M Novak, *Prin*
EMP: 6 **EST:** 2010
SALES (est): 114.88K **Privately Held**
Web: www.amberdragonacu.com
SIC: 8049 Acupuncturist

(G-5683)
AMERICAN CEDAR & MILLWORK INC (PA)
Also Called: American Cedar & Millwork
17993 American Way (19958-4799)
PHONE..................................302 645-9580
TOLL FREE: 800
Michael Neal, *Pr*
Julie A Neal, *Sec*
John Ritson, *CFO*
EMP: 34 **EST:** 1984
SQ FT: 24,000
SALES (est): 24.56MM
SALES (corp-wide): 24.56MM **Privately Held**
Web: www.millwork1.com
SIC: 5031 5211 Building materials, interior; Lumber and other building materials

(G-5684)
AMERICAN CLASSIC GOLF CLUB LLC
18485 Bethpage Dr Ste 1 (19958-4853)
PHONE..................................302 703-6662
Bonnie Morrison, *Prin*
Harry Morrison Junior, *Prin*
EMP: 8 **EST:** 2012
SALES (est): 445.31K **Privately Held**
Web: www.americanclassicgolf.com

GEOGRAPHIC SECTION

Lewes - Sussex County (G-5715)

SIC: 7992 Public golf courses

(G-5685)
AMERICAN ELECTRIC LLC
31019 Edgewood Dr (19958-3836)
PHONE................302 632-6724
EMP: 5 EST: 2008
SALES (est): 92.64K Privately Held
SIC: 1731 General electrical contractor

(G-5686)
AMERICAN ELI TRUCK NETWORK INC
16192 Coastal Hwy (19958-3608)
PHONE................210 842-2134
Christopher John, CEO
EMP: 21
SALES (est): 1.05MM Privately Held
SIC: 4449 Transportation (freight) on bays and sounds of the ocean

(G-5687)
AMERICAN RESPONDER SVCS LLC
Also Called: Best Shot
16797 Coastal Hwy (19958-3653)
PHONE................302 567-2530
EMP: 7 EST: 2018
SALES (est): 187.87K Privately Held
Web: www.bestshotde.com
SIC: 7999 Shooting range operation

(G-5688)
AMINO MEDICAL SCIENCE INC
16192 Coastal Hwy Ste 102 (19958-3608)
PHONE................213 232-8619
Frederick Wolfe, CEO
EMP: 10
SALES (est): 254.87K Privately Held
Web: www.aminoco.com
SIC: 8731 Biotechnical research, commercial

(G-5689)
AMY DONOVAN
32855 Ocean Reach Dr (19958-4666)
PHONE................302 245-8957
Amy Donovan, Pr
EMP: 6 EST: 2017
SALES (est): 65.76K Privately Held
SIC: 8049 Offices of health practitioner

(G-5690)
AMY GABEL
18370 Alpine Loop (19958-9703)
PHONE................703 598-0763
Amy Gabel, CEO
EMP: 5 EST: 2017
SALES (est): 38.73K Privately Held
SIC: 8641 Civic and social associations

(G-5691)
ANGELIC THERAPY
17436 Slipper Shell Way Unit 11 (19958-6319)
PHONE................717 870-4618
Angel Ic Therapy, Prin
EMP: 7 EST: 2017
SALES (est): 75.69K Privately Held
Web: www.angelictouchtherapyanimals.com
SIC: 8093 Rehabilitation center, outpatient treatment

(G-5692)
ANGOLA BY THE BAY PRPRTY OWNER
33457 Woodland Cir (19958-5179)
PHONE................302 945-2700
Kim Rogers, Genl Mgr
EMP: 10 EST: 1968
SQ FT: 1,200
SALES (est): 770.52K Privately Held
Web: www.angolabythebay.org
SIC: 8641 Homeowners' association

(G-5693)
ANNABELLA TECHNOLOGIES INC ✪
16192 Coastal Hwy (19958-3608)
PHONE................833 716-1909
Uri Yaffe, Prin
EMP: 15 EST: 2023
SALES (est): 518.76K Privately Held
SIC: 7372 Prepackaged software

(G-5694)
ANYTIME FITNESS
17400 N Village Main Blvd (19958-7239)
PHONE................302 212-6151
EMP: 10 EST: 2018
SALES (est): 39.63K Privately Held
Web: www.anytimefitness.sg
SIC: 7991 Physical fitness clubs with training equipment

(G-5695)
AQUACARE PHYSICAL
34434 King Street Row (19958-4987)
PHONE................302 200-9159
EMP: 6 EST: 2017
SALES (est): 109.68K Privately Held
Web: www.aquacarephysicaltherapy.com
SIC: 8049 Physical therapist

(G-5696)
AQUAMARINE BOUTIQUE LLC
Also Called: Aquamarine On Market
114 2nd St (19958-1324)
PHONE................302 644-4550
EMP: 8 EST: 2006
SALES (est): 580.24K Privately Held
SIC: 5137 Women's and children's clothing

(G-5697)
ARDEUN BIOMETRICS CORP LLC
16192 Coastal Hwy (19958-3608)
PHONE................949 662-1096
EMP: 11
SALES (est): 397.02K Privately Held
Web: www.ardeun.com
SIC: 7371 Computer software systems analysis and design, custom

(G-5698)
ARENA SIGNS
34696 Jiffy Way (19958-4931)
PHONE................302 644-8300
Ed Martin, Owner
EMP: 2 EST: 2010
SALES (est): 203.86K Privately Held
Web: www.arena-signs.com
SIC: 3993 Signs, not made in custom sign painting shops

(G-5699)
ARLENE WEISMAN
119 W 3rd St (19958-1315)
PHONE................302 569-2822
Arlene Weisman, Owner
EMP: 5 EST: 2017
SALES (est): 103.73K Privately Held
Web: www.eastcoastseedconnection.com
SIC: 8322 Social worker

(G-5700)
ARMIN MAREFAT DO
33663 Bayview Medical Dr (19958-1663)
PHONE................302 645-9725
Armin Marefat, Mgr
EMP: 14 EST: 2017
SALES (est): 54.13K Privately Held
SIC: 8011 Endocrinologist

(G-5701)
ART FOR A PURPOSE
102 Savannah Rd (19958-1485)
PHONE................302 245-4528
EMP: 5 EST: 2016
SALES (est): 44.2K Privately Held
SIC: 8641 Civic and social associations

(G-5702)
ARTISAN ELECTRICAL INC
119 S Washington Ave (19958-1443)
PHONE................302 645-5844
EMP: 5 EST: 1963
SALES (est): 820.58K Privately Held
SIC: 5064 1731 Fans, household: electric; Electrical work

(G-5703)
ARTISTIC DESIGNS SALON
20361 John J Williams Hwy (19958-4305)
PHONE................302 644-2009
Arlin Berlinger, Pr
EMP: 8 EST: 2004
SALES (est): 277.21K Privately Held
Web: www.artisticdesignsdelaware.com
SIC: 7231 Hairdressers

(G-5704)
ARUNA NETWORK INC
16192 Coastal Hwy (19958-3608)
PHONE................832 303-3628
Phillip Rossi, Managing Member
EMP: 6
SALES (est): 76.63K Privately Held
SIC: 4214 Local trucking with storage

(G-5705)
ARYA LIFE COACHING LLC ✪
16192 Coastal Hwy (19958-3608)
PHONE................610 590-1440
Gauravbhai Doshi, Dir
EMP: 5 EST: 2022
SALES (est): 199.4K Privately Held
SIC: 7389 Business Activities at Non-Commercial Site

(G-5706)
ASPIRA HEALTH LLC
18068 Coastal Hwy (19958-4901)
PHONE................302 567-1500
William Albanese, CEO
EMP: 100 EST: 2020
SALES (est): 3.84MM Privately Held
Web: www.atracare.com
SIC: 8099 Health and allied services, nec

(G-5707)
ASSOCIATES IN MEDICINE PA
1302 Savannah Rd (19958-1526)
PHONE................302 645-6644
Mark Schatz, Mgr
EMP: 8 EST: 2005
SALES (est): 395.14K Privately Held
SIC: 8011 General and family practice, physician/surgeon

(G-5708)
ASTER BOUQUET FLOWER SHOP LLC ✪
Also Called: Aster Bouquet Flower Shop
624 Pilottown Rd (19958-1236)
PHONE................302 258-9242
Kurt Wehberg, Managing Member
EMP: 5 EST: 2022
SALES (est): 199.4K Privately Held
SIC: 3993 7389 Advertising artwork; Business services, nec

(G-5709)
ASTON DIGITAL LLC
16192 Coastal Hwy (19958-3608)
PHONE................323 286-4365
Matthew Addison, Managing Member
EMP: 40 EST: 2021
SALES (est): 1.11MM Privately Held
SIC: 8742 Management consulting services

(G-5710)
ATI HOLDINGS LLC
Also Called: ATI Physical Therapy
17252 N Village Main Blvd Unit 2 (19958)
PHONE................302 827-5123
Joe Skocypec, Brnch Mgr
EMP: 15
SALES (corp-wide): 635.67MM Publicly Held
Web: www.atipt.com
SIC: 8049 Physical therapist
HQ: Ati Holdings, Llc
 790 Remington Blvd
 Bolingbrook IL 60440

(G-5711)
ATLANTIC ADULT & PEDIATRIC
34453 King Street Row Ste 1 (19958-4787)
PHONE................302 644-1300
Charles Stanislav, Owner
EMP: 10 EST: 2006
SALES (est): 516.03K Privately Held
Web: www.atlanticapmed.com
SIC: 8011 Pediatrician

(G-5712)
ATLANTIC ADULT PDTRICS MDCINE
34435 King Street Row # 1 (19958-4787)
PHONE................302 644-1300
EMP: 6 EST: 2020
SALES (est): 202.52K Privately Held
SIC: 8099 Health and allied services, nec

(G-5713)
ATLANTIC CABINETRY CORPORATION
17527 Nassau Commons Blvd (19958-6283)
PHONE................302 644-1407
Mark Woodruff, Pr
Mickey Brown, Sec
Richard Doyle, Sec
Wayne Bister, Sec
Richard A Reed, VP
EMP: 12 EST: 1998
SQ FT: 5,000
SALES (est): 1MM Privately Held
Web: www.atlanticmillwork.com
SIC: 2434 Wood kitchen cabinets

(G-5714)
ATLANTIC HOMES LLC
20684 John J Williams Hwy Ste 1 (19958-4393)
PHONE................302 947-0223
Mark Grahne, Managing Member
Linda Grahne, Admn
EMP: 5 EST: 1992
SQ FT: 256
SALES (est): 580.07K Privately Held
Web: www.bethanybeachcustomhomes.net
SIC: 1521 New construction, single-family houses

(G-5715)
ATLANTIC KITCHEN & BATH LLC
18355 Coastal Hwy (19958-4778)
PHONE................302 947-9001
Mark Grahne, Managing Member
EMP: 7 EST: 2009

Lewes - Sussex County (G-5716) — GEOGRAPHIC SECTION

SALES (est): 485.66K **Privately Held**
Web: www.atlantickb.com
SIC: **1799** Kitchen and bathroom remodeling

(G-5716)
ATLANTIC MLLWK CABINETRY CORP
17527 Nassau Commons Blvd (19958-6283)
PHONE..............................302 644-1405
Mark Woodruff, *Pr*
EMP: 30 EST: 2002
SALES (est): 3.35MM **Privately Held**
Web: www.atlanticmillwork.com
SIC: **5031 1751** Lumber, plywood, and millwork; Carpentry work

(G-5717)
ATLANTIC REFRIGERATION INC
Also Called: Atlantic Refrigeration & AC
17553 Nassau Commons Blvd (19958-6284)
PHONE..............................302 645-9321
David Jones, *Pr*
EMP: 32 EST: 2001
SALES (est): 9.35MM **Privately Held**
Web: www.atlanticrefrigeration.com
SIC: **1711** Warm air heating and air conditioning contractor

(G-5718)
ATLANTIC SOURCE CONTG INC
35 Bridle Ridge Cir (19958)
PHONE..............................302 645-5207
Michael Mattia, *Pr*
Linda Mattia, *VP*
EMP: 2 EST: 2005
SALES (est): 416.33K **Privately Held**
Web: www.atlanticsource.net
SIC: **3088 1799** Shower stalls, fiberglass and plastics; Closet organizers, installation and design

(G-5719)
AURELIUM INC
16192 Coastal Hwy (19958-3608)
PHONE..............................415 636-6892
Harpreet Singh, *CEO*
EMP: 26
SALES (est): 782.95K **Privately Held**
SIC: **7372** Prepackaged software

(G-5720)
AUSPICE RISK LLC
11286 Hall Rd (19958-6547)
PHONE..............................484 467-1963
Michael P Dever, *Pt*
EMP: 5 EST: 2013
SALES (est): 120.38K **Privately Held**
Web: www.auspicerisk.com
SIC: **6411** Insurance agents, nec

(G-5721)
AUTO WORKS COLLISION CTR LLC
1145 Savannah Rd (19958-1524)
PHONE..............................302 732-3902
EMP: 17 EST: 2002
SALES (est): 935.15K **Privately Held**
Web: www.autoworkscoll.com
SIC: **7532** Body shop, automotive

(G-5722)
AUXILITY INC
Also Called: Auxility
16192 Coastal Hwy (19958-3608)
PHONE..............................610 245-8053
EMP: 30 EST: 2019
SALES (est): 764.29K **Privately Held**
SIC: **7371** Custom computer programming services

(G-5723)
AVANTISH CLEANERS
20231 Wil King Rd (19958-4507)
PHONE..............................302 947-1632
Michele Battle, *Prin*
EMP: 5 EST: 2017
SALES (est): 32.06K **Privately Held**
SIC: **7699** Cleaning services

(G-5724)
AVATAR INSTRUMENTS INC
16587 Coastal Hwy (19958-3605)
P.O. Box 496 (19958-0496)
PHONE..............................302 703-6865
Paul Evalds, *Pr*
EMP: 5 EST: 1990
SQ FT: 8,000
SALES (est): 728.93K **Privately Held**
Web: www.avatarinstruments.com
SIC: **3829** Measuring and controlling devices, nec

(G-5725)
AVELLO HOLDINGS LLC
16192 Coastal Hwy Ste 1 (19958-3608)
PHONE..............................631 533-2634
EMP: 5 EST: 2019
SALES (est): 119.02K **Privately Held**
SIC: **6531** Real estate managers

(G-5726)
AVOKADIO INC
Also Called: Avokadio,
19162 Coastal Hwy (19958)
PHONE..............................302 291-4080
Mustafaunus Konmaz, *CEO*
EMP: 5 EST: 2021
SALES (est): 125.33K **Privately Held**
Web: www.avokad.io
SIC: **5731 7371** Radio, television, and electronic stores; Computer software development and applications

(G-5727)
AWAKEN ATUSKY LLC
16192 Coastal Hwy (19958-3608)
PHONE..............................302 231-0818
Sheng Yu, *Managing Member*
Caylee Cooper, *Prin*
EMP: 38 EST: 2020
SALES (est): 2.9MM **Privately Held**
SIC: **5064** Electrical appliances, television and radio

(G-5728)
AWESOME CLEANING SERVICES LLC
31587 Siham Rd (19958-2026)
PHONE..............................302 585-3115
Whitney Diggs, *Prin*
EMP: 5 EST: 2017
SALES (est): 55.41K **Privately Held**
SIC: **7699** Cleaning services

(G-5729)
AWL LLC
16192 Coastal Hwy (19958-3608)
PHONE..............................610 299-3322
Richard Puleo, *Managing Member*
EMP: 7 EST: 2021
SALES (est): 126.53K **Privately Held**
Web: www.awltransport.com
SIC: **7941** Sports clubs, managers, and promoters

(G-5730)
AXA ZARA LLC
16192 Coastal Hwy (19958-3608)
PHONE..............................513 206-4606
EMP: 9

SALES (est): 313.29K **Privately Held**
Web: www.axazara.com
SIC: **7371** Software programming applications

(G-5731)
AXXESS MARINE LLC
16192 Coastal Hwy (19958-3608)
PHONE..............................954 225-1744
Dennis Sokke, *Managing Member*
EMP: 5 EST: 2014
SALES (est): 977.14K **Privately Held**
Web: www.axxess-marine.com
SIC: **4899** Data communication services

(G-5732)
B&P BROWN & PARTNERS CORP
16192 Coastal Hwy (19958-3608)
PHONE..............................302 703-0522
Alexander Bell, *Pr*
Ursula Bell, *Dir Fin*
EMP: 6 EST: 2002
SALES (est): 121.48K **Privately Held**
Web: www.docsuisseconsult.com
SIC: **8742** Management consulting services

(G-5733)
B-DUN CLEANING
33980 Yoshino Dr (19958-5777)
P.O. Box 704 (19958-0704)
PHONE..............................302 542-7869
Brandon Dunsmore, *Prin*
EMP: 5 EST: 2018
SALES (est): 133.13K **Privately Held**
SIC: **7699** Cleaning services

(G-5734)
BAIRD MANDALAS BROCKSTEDT LLC
1413 Savannah Rd Unit 1 (19958-1792)
PHONE..............................302 644-0302
Kevin M Baird, *Brnch Mgr*
EMP: 13
SALES (corp-wide): 5.98MM **Privately Held**
Web: www.bmbde.com
SIC: **8111** General practice attorney, lawyer
PA: Baird Mandalas Brockstedt Llc
6 S State St Ste 6 # 6
Dover DE 19901
302 677-0061

(G-5735)
BASE-2 SOLUTIONS LLC
Also Called: Base-2 Solutions
12211 Collins Rd (19958-4982)
PHONE..............................202 215-2152
Tysen Leckie, *VP*
Dylan Leckie, *
EMP: 60 EST: 2016
SALES (est): 4.82MM **Privately Held**
Web: www.base-2solutions.com
SIC: **7379 7371 7373 8742** Computer related consulting services; Custom computer programming services; Computer integrated systems design; Management consulting services

(G-5736)
BASEMENT UNLIMITED LLC
17667 Gate Dr Unit 3 (19958-6540)
PHONE..............................302 569-2211
EMP: 6 EST: 2017
SALES (est): 287.57K **Privately Held**
Web: www.basementunlimited4u.com
SIC: **1521** General remodeling, single-family houses

(G-5737)
BASKET FUNDAMENTALS LLC
16192 Coastal Hwy (19958-3608)
PHONE..............................302 360-8617
EMP: 6 EST: 2017
SALES (est): 34.16K **Privately Held**
SIC: **7032** Youth camps

(G-5738)
BASTION RESEARCH LTD
16192 Coastal Hwy (19958-3608)
PHONE..............................307 370-3767
Dmitry Dotol, *CEO*
EMP: 8
SALES (est): 306.16K **Privately Held**
SIC: **7371** Computer software development

(G-5739)
BAY ROSE HOMES
31767 Marsh Island Ave (19958-3350)
PHONE..............................302 945-9510
EMP: 6 EST: 2017
SALES (est): 98.24K **Privately Held**
Web: www.schellbrothers.com
SIC: **6531** Real estate agents and managers

(G-5740)
BAYSIDE HEALTH ASSN CHARTERED (PA)
Also Called: Bahtiarian, Gregory Do
1535 Savannah Rd (19958-1611)
P.O. Box 538 (19966-0538)
PHONE..............................302 645-4700
Vincent B Killeen Md, *Pr*
Susan L Rogers Md, *Sec*
Newell R Washburn Md, *Treas*
Gina Hunsicker, *Dir Opers*
EMP: 56 EST: 1988
SQ FT: 5,000
SALES (est): 6.28MM **Privately Held**
SIC: **8011** Obstetrician

(G-5741)
BAYSIDE PAINTING
111 American Legion Rd (19958-1159)
PHONE..............................302 344-6910
EMP: 5 EST: 2009
SALES (est): 48.53K **Privately Held**
SIC: **1721** Painting and paper hanging

(G-5742)
BAYVIEW ENDOSCOPY CENTER
Also Called: Eastern Shore Gastroenterology
33663 Bayview Medical Dr # 3 (19958)
PHONE..............................302 644-0455
EMP: 25 EST: 1995
SALES (est): 490.26K **Privately Held**
SIC: **8062** General medical and surgical hospitals

(G-5743)
BEACH TIME
32191 Nassau Rd (19958-3762)
PHONE..............................302 644-2850
Greg Christmas, *Owner*
EMP: 8 EST: 2015
SALES (est): 410.03K **Privately Held**
Web: www.beachtimedistilling.com
SIC: **2085** Distilled and blended liquors

(G-5744)
BEACHVIEW MGMT INC
Also Called: Sign-A-Rama
33045 E Light Dr (19958-4661)
PHONE..............................302 227-3280
Gwen Osborne, *Owner*
Pamela K Handy, *Pr*
Gwendolyn Osborne, *VP*
EMP: 4 EST: 2006
SALES (est): 410.76K **Privately Held**

GEOGRAPHIC SECTION

Lewes - Sussex County (G-5772)

Web: www.signarama.com
SIC: 8741 3993 Management services; Advertising artwork

(G-5745)
BEACON MOTEL
514 E Savannah Rd (19958-1161)
PHONE..................302 645-4888
Janice Lingo, Owner
EMP: 9 EST: 1997
SALES (est): 215.18K Privately Held
Web: www.beaconinnlewes.com
SIC: 7011 Motels

(G-5746)
BEE WISE LLC
Also Called: Nexthome Tomorrow Realty
20028 John J Williams Hwy (19958-4300)
PHONE..................302 601-4171
Erinann Beebe, Managing Member
Craig A Beebe, Managing Member
EMP: 5 EST: 2020
SALES (est): 266.06K Privately Held
Web: www.nexthometomorrowrealty.com
SIC: 6531 Real estate brokers and agents

(G-5747)
BEEBE HOSPITAL HS
424 E Savannah Rd (19958-1133)
PHONE..................302 645-3565
Andrew Fitzee, Owner
EMP: 18 EST: 2015
SALES (est): 1.1MM Privately Held
SIC: 8062 General medical and surgical hospitals

(G-5748)
BEEBE MEDICAL CENTER INC (PA)
Also Called: Beebe Medical Ctr HM Hlth Svc
424 Savannah Rd (19958-1462)
P.O. Box 226 (19958-0226)
PHONE..................302 645-3300
David Tam, Pr
David A Herbert, *
Paul T Cowan, *
Ashley Foster, CPO*
Christopher J Weeks, *
EMP: 800 EST: 1916
SQ FT: 196,556
SALES (est): 581.97MM
SALES (corp-wide): 581.97MM Privately Held
Web: www.beebehealthcare.org
SIC: 8062 General medical and surgical hospitals

(G-5749)
BEEBE MEDICAL CENTER INC
440 Market St (19958-1308)
PHONE..................302 645-3300
EMP: 28
SALES (corp-wide): 581.97MM Privately Held
Web: www.beebehealthcare.org
SIC: 8062 General medical and surgical hospitals
PA: Beebe Medical Center, Inc.
424 Savannah Rd
Lewes DE 19958
302 645-3300

(G-5750)
BEEBE MEDICAL CENTER INC
Also Called: Beebe Healthcare
431 Savannah Rd Bldg C (19958-1460)
PHONE..................302 645-3629
James Bartle, Brnch Mgr
EMP: 136
SALES (corp-wide): 581.97MM Privately Held
Web: www.beebehealthcare.org
SIC: 8062 General medical and surgical hospitals
PA: Beebe Medical Center, Inc.
424 Savannah Rd
Lewes DE 19958
302 645-3300

(G-5751)
BEEBE PHYSICIAN NETWORK INC
Also Called: BEEBE MEDICAL CENTER HOME HEAL
1515 Savannah Rd Ste 103 (19958-1675)
P.O. Box 226 (19958-0226)
PHONE..................302 645-1805
EMP: 428 EST: 1999
SALES (est): 57.62MM
SALES (corp-wide): 581.97MM Privately Held
SIC: 8062 General medical and surgical hospitals
PA: Beebe Medical Center, Inc.
424 Savannah Rd
Lewes DE 19958
302 645-3300

(G-5752)
BEEBE SCHOOL OF NURSING
424 Savannah Rd (19958-1462)
PHONE..................302 645-3251
Connie Bushey, Prin
EMP: 33 EST: 2002
SALES (est): 1.4MM Privately Held
Web: www.beebehealthcare.org
SIC: 8051 Skilled nursing care facilities

(G-5753)
BEEJUG GAMES LLC
16192 Coastal Hwy (19958-3608)
PHONE..................310 382-0746
EMP: 5 EST: 2020
SALES (est): 46.16K Privately Held
SIC: 7371 Computer software development and applications

(G-5754)
BELL MANUFACTURING COMPANY INC
31971 Carneros Ave (19958-2501)
PHONE..................302 703-2684
Thomas Bell, Owner
EMP: 2 EST: 2010
SALES (est): 116.18K Privately Held
SIC: 3999 Manufacturing industries, nec

(G-5755)
BERKELYN INC
16192 Coastal Hwy (19958-3608)
PHONE..................360 609-4981
Jacob Irwin, CEO
EMP: 7 EST: 2020
SALES (est): 281.11K Privately Held
SIC: 8748 Business consulting, nec

(G-5756)
BESECURE LLC
16192 Coastal Hwy (19958-3608)
PHONE..................855 897-0650
EMP: 25 EST: 2008
SALES (est): 624.36K Privately Held
Web: www.besecuregroup.com
SIC: 7382 Security systems services

(G-5757)
BETHANY FOREST HOA
34634 Bay Crossing Blvd (19958-2737)
PHONE..................302 645-7242
EMP: 6 EST: 2016
SALES (est): 65.14K Privately Held
SIC: 8641 Homeowners' association

(G-5758)
BETHEL UNITED METHODIST CHURCH
Also Called: United Methodist Church
129 W 4th St (19958-1333)
PHONE..................302 645-9426
Reverend Fred W Duncan, Pastor
Donna Dickey, Adm/Asst
EMP: 11 EST: 1900
SALES (est): 445.35K Privately Held
Web: www.bethellewes.org
SIC: 8661 8351 Methodist Church; Nursery school

(G-5759)
BETTAN TRUCKING LLC
19347 Beaver Dam Rd (19958-5539)
PHONE..................302 841-3834
EMP: 20 EST: 2019
SALES (est): 500K Privately Held
SIC: 4731 Freight transportation arrangement

(G-5760)
BETWORKS CORPORATION (PA)
Also Called: Bet.works
16192 Coastal Hwy (19958-3608)
PHONE..................310 866-0365
David Wang, CEO
Quinton Singleton, COO
EMP: 11 EST: 2018
SALES (est): 2.33MM
SALES (corp-wide): 2.33MM Privately Held
Web: www.bet.works
SIC: 7371 Computer software development and applications

(G-5761)
BHASKAR PALEKAR MD PA
1526 Savannah Rd Ste 1 (19958-1683)
P.O. Box 519 (19947-0519)
PHONE..................302 645-1805
Bhaskar Palekar Md, Owner
EMP: 8 EST: 1976
SALES (est): 424.44K Privately Held
SIC: 8062 General medical and surgical hospitals

(G-5762)
BIBLION
205 2nd St Ste 6 (19958-1354)
PHONE..................302 644-2210
Jen Mason, Owner
EMP: 5 EST: 2010
SALES (est): 124.28K Privately Held
Web: www.biblionbooks.com
SIC: 5942 8999 Comic books; Editorial service

(G-5763)
BID ON ENERGY LLC
16192 Coastal Hwy (19958-3608)
PHONE..................302 360-8110
EMP: 10 EST: 2018
SALES (est): 1.27MM Privately Held
Web: www.bidonenergy.org
SIC: 4911 Electric services

(G-5764)
BIHBRAND INC
16192 Coastal Hwy (19958-3608)
PHONE..................302 223-4330
Grace Enow Maximuangu, Dir
EMP: 10
SALES (est): 109.11K Privately Held
SIC: 7929 Entertainers and entertainment groups

(G-5765)
BILL M DOUTHAT JR
Also Called: Unicare Transport Service
17468 Slipper Shell Way Unit 16 (19958-6316)
P.O. Box 677802 (32867-7802)
PHONE..................407 977-2273
Bill Douthat Junior, Owner
EMP: 5 EST: 1995
SALES (est): 125.36K Privately Held
SIC: 4119 Ambulance service

(G-5766)
BIO RIOT TECHNOLOGIES MFG INC
16192 Coastal Hwy (19958-3608)
PHONE..................407 399-3413
Michael Laible, CEO
EMP: 2 EST: 2020
SALES (est): 262.12K Privately Held
SIC: 3272 Concrete products, nec

(G-5767)
BIYA GLOBAL LLC
16192 Coastal Hwy (19958-3608)
PHONE..................302 645-7400
EMP: 8 EST: 2020
SALES (est): 290.91K Privately Held
SIC: 7389 Financial services

(G-5768)
BLAIR A JONES DDS
34359 Carpenters Way (19958-4910)
PHONE..................302 226-1115
Blair Jones, Ofcr
EMP: 8 EST: 2017
SALES (est): 117.82K Privately Held
Web: www.thedentalgrouplewes.com
SIC: 8021 Dentists' office

(G-5769)
BLAK MPIRE LLC
16192 Coastal Hwy (19958-3608)
PHONE..................803 966-7648
Shaquille Cantey, Prin
Tonya Lane, Prin
Joseph Jeffrey, Prin
Charles Lane, Prin
Maleek Collins, Prin
EMP: 7 EST: 2020
SALES (est): 263.5K Privately Held
SIC: 7389 Business Activities at Non-Commercial Site

(G-5770)
BLUE HERON ACUPUNCTURE & HERBS
1307 Savannah Rd (19958-1514)
PHONE..................302 344-7333
Lauren Mund, Prin
EMP: 5 EST: 2017
SALES (est): 204.63K Privately Held
Web: www.blueheronacuherbs.com
SIC: 8049 Acupuncturist

(G-5771)
BLUENT LLC
16192 Coastal Hwy (19958-3608)
PHONE..................832 476-8459
Sajeel Khanna, Managing Member
◆ EMP: 24 EST: 2003
SQ FT: 6,000
SALES (est): 657.41K Privately Held
Web: www.bluent.net
SIC: 7379 7373 Computer related consulting services; Computer-aided system services

(G-5772)
BLUEPOINT SYSTEMS LLC
16192 Coastal Hwy (19958-3608)
PHONE..................817 714-2320

Lewes - Sussex County (G-5773) GEOGRAPHIC SECTION

EMP: 5 EST: 2011
SALES (est): 85.68K **Privately Held**
SIC: **7389** Business services, nec

(G-5773)
BLUEWATER WIND LLC
700 Pilottown Rd (19958-1242)
PHONE..................302 731-7020
EMP: 20 EST: 2005
SALES (est): 2.3MM **Publicly Held**
SIC: **5083** Wind machines (frost protection equipment)
PA: Nrg Energy, Inc.
  910 Louisiana St Ste B200
  Houston TX 77002

(G-5774)
BOBOT ROBOTICS INC
16192 Coastal Hwy (19958-3608)
PHONE..................501 301-0612
EMP: 5 EST: 2018
SALES (est): 112.87K **Privately Held**
SIC: **1799** Appliance installation

(G-5775)
BOOMN INC (PA)
Also Called: Boomn
16192 Coastal Hwy (19958-3608)
PHONE..................844 808-2666
Daniel Sado, CEO
EMP: 8 EST: 2021
SALES (est): 505.33K
SALES (corp-wide): 505.33K **Privately Held**
SIC: **7373** **7389** Computer systems analysis and design; Business services, nec

(G-5776)
BRAND IQ GROUP INC
16192 Coastal Hwy (19958-3608)
PHONE..................302 924-8558
EMP: 9 EST: 2018
SALES (est): 176.64K **Privately Held**
Web: www.brandiq.com
SIC: **7389**

(G-5777)
BRI US LLC
16192 Coastal Hwy (19958-3608)
PHONE..................408 550-6354
EMP: 5 EST: 2017
SALES (est): 164.36K **Privately Held**
SIC: **6799** Venture capital companies

(G-5778)
BRIDGEWAY DIGITAL LLC ◆
16192 Coastal Hwy (19958-3608)
PHONE..................212 684-6931
EMP: 5 EST: 2022
SALES (est): 203.68K **Privately Held**
SIC: **7373** Value-added resellers, computer systems

(G-5779)
BS INSURANCE LLC
17527 Nassau Commons Blvd (19958-6283)
PHONE..................302 645-2356
Bob Sonchen, Pr
EMP: 20
SALES (corp-wide): 6.14MM **Privately Held**
Web: www.ifs-benefits.com
SIC: **6411** Insurance agents, nec
PA: Bs Insurance, Llc
  220 Continental Dr # 209
  Newark DE 19713

(G-5780)
BURKE DERMATOLOGY
353 Savannah Rd (19958-1438)
PHONE..................302 703-6585
EMP: 48
SALES (corp-wide): 2.17MM **Privately Held**
Web: www.burkedermatology.com
SIC: **8011** Dermatologist
PA: Burke Dermatology
  774 Christiana Rd Ste 107
  Newark DE 19713
  302 230-3376

(G-5781)
BURKE PAINTING CO INC
119 E Quail Trl (19958-1636)
PHONE..................302 998-8500
Robert Burke, Pr
EMP: 5 EST: 1980
SALES (est): 249.19K **Privately Held**
Web: www.burkepaintingco.com
SIC: **1721** Exterior commercial painting contractor

(G-5782)
BUSINESS AT INTERNATIONAL LLC
16192 Coastal Hwy (19958-3608)
PHONE..................605 610-4885
EMP: 20 EST: 2019
SALES (est): 483.25K **Privately Held**
Web: www.bizbrokersintl.com
SIC: **7389** Financial services

(G-5783)
BUTTERFIELD INSPECTION SERVICE
113 Dewey Ave (19958-1712)
PHONE..................301 322-1644
Merrill Johnson, Owner
EMP: 6 EST: 2011
SALES (est): 15.97K **Privately Held**
SIC: **8351** Child day care services

(G-5784)
BYTE TECHNOLOGY SYSTEMS INC
16192 Coastal Hwy (19958-3608)
PHONE..................347 687-7240
Syed Safeeullah Shah, CEO
EMP: 5 EST: 2019
SALES (est): 100K **Privately Held**
SIC: **7371** Computer software development

(G-5785)
C AND C ALPACA FACTORY
17219 Sweetbriar Rd (19958-4028)
PHONE..................609 752-7894
Christian Addor, Prin
EMP: 5 EST: 2011
SALES (est): 65.85K **Privately Held**
SIC: **2211** Alpacas, cotton

(G-5786)
CAMBRIA LLC
16826 Forest Dr (19958-4846)
PHONE..................703 898-9989
Michael Rowlands, Prin
EMP: 9 EST: 2018
SALES (est): 292.96K **Privately Held**
SIC: **1521** Single-family housing construction

(G-5787)
CAMPUS ELCTION ENGGMENT PRJ IN
16192 Coastal Hwy (19958-3608)
PHONE..................614 735-1460
EMP: 8 EST: 2020
SALES (est): 27.98K **Privately Held**
Web: www.civicinfluencers.org
SIC: **8399** Advocacy group

(G-5788)
CANADIAN SUNPAL POWER LLC
16192 Coastal Hwy (19958-3608)
PHONE..................905 926-6681
Dennis Andrew Gittins, CEO
EMP: 5 EST: 2021
SALES (est): 219.01K **Privately Held**
Web: www.canadiansolarwindpower.ca
SIC: **5961** **8742** Electronic shopping; Management engineering

(G-5789)
CANDICE RYDER
17432 Slipper Shell Way # 1 (19958-6320)
PHONE..................954 296-5709
Candice Ryder, Mgr
EMP: 6 EST: 2017
SALES (est): 24.4K **Privately Held**
SIC: **8049** Offices of health practitioner

(G-5790)
CANDYMAN INDUSTRIES INC
16192 Coastal Hwy (19958-3608)
PHONE..................970 319-8404
Shawn Honaker, CEO
EMP: 5
SALES (est): 78.16K **Privately Held**
SIC: **2064** Candy and other confectionery products

(G-5791)
CAPB INFOTEK LLC
16192 Coastal Hwy (19958-3608)
PHONE..................347 277-7125
EMP: 6 EST: 2010
SALES (est): 175.51K **Privately Held**
Web: www.capbinfotek.com
SIC: **7371** Custom computer programming services

(G-5792)
CAPE ENT PA
17005 Old Orchard Rd (19958-4828)
PHONE..................717 269-3106
A Aukamp Credentialing, Mgr
EMP: 10 EST: 2018
SALES (est): 473.87K **Privately Held**
Web: www.capemedicalde.com
SIC: **8621** Professional organizations

(G-5793)
CAPE FINANCIAL SERVICES INC
Also Called: CFS Construction
16117 Willow Creek Rd (19958-3620)
P.O. Box 758 (19958-0758)
PHONE..................302 645-6274
L Thomas Miller, Pr
Linda F Miller, VP
Kevin Miller, VP
EMP: 10 EST: 1983
SQ FT: 3,200
SALES (est): 933.08K **Privately Held**
Web: www.cfsconstruction.net
SIC: **1521** **1531** **1542** New construction, single-family houses; Speculative builder, single-family houses; Commercial and office building, new construction

(G-5794)
CAPE GAZETTE LTD
17585 Nassau Commons Blvd Ste 6 (19958-6286)
P.O. Box 213 (19958-0213)
PHONE..................302 645-7700
Dennis Forney, Pr
EMP: 25 EST: 1993
SALES (est): 3MM **Privately Held**
Web: www.capegazette.com
SIC: **2711** Newspapers, publishing and printing

(G-5795)
CAPE MEDICAL ASSOCIATES PA
Also Called: Cape Orthopedic
701 Savannah Rd Ste B (19958-1557)
PHONE..................302 645-2805
James Marvel Junior Md, Pr
Paul J Harriot Md, Prin
Mark J Boytim, Prin
EMP: 19 EST: 1980
SQ FT: 2,500
SALES (est): 985.12K **Privately Held**
SIC: **8011** Orthopedic physician

(G-5796)
CAPE SPINE & DISC
1540 Savannah Rd Ste B (19958-1682)
PHONE..................302 644-2473
Frank Joseph Mrazeck, Owner
EMP: 10 EST: 2015
SALES (est): 238.99K **Privately Held**
Web: www.piranhaems.com
SIC: **8041** Offices and clinics of chiropractors

(G-5797)
CAPE WATER TAXI
107 Anglers Rd (19958-1109)
PHONE..................302 644-7334
EMP: 7 EST: 2016
SALES (est): 51.52K **Privately Held**
Web: www.capewatertaxi.com
SIC: **7999** Fishing boats, party: operation

(G-5798)
CAPE WATER TOURS & TAXI
22549 Rocky Rd (19958-5771)
PHONE..................302 245-4794
David Green, Prin
EMP: 5 EST: 2019
SALES (est): 158.9K **Privately Held**
Web: www.capewatertaxi.com
SIC: **4725** Tours, conducted

(G-5799)
CAPSTONE HOMES LLC
33712 Wescoats Rd Unit 5 (19958-4926)
P.O. Box 212 (19958-0212)
PHONE..................302 644-0300
EMP: 14 EST: 2006
SALES (est): 791.64K **Privately Held**
Web: www.capstone-homes.com
SIC: **8748** Business consulting, nec

(G-5800)
CAPSTONE HOMES LLC
28855 Lewes Georgetown Hwy (19958)
PHONE..................302 644-0300
EMP: 40 EST: 2006
SALES (est): 6.32MM **Privately Held**
Web: www.capstone-homes.com
SIC: **1521** New construction, single-family houses

(G-5801)
CARDIOLOGY CONSULTANTS
16704 Kings Hwy (19958-4929)
PHONE..................302 645-1233
Judy Callaghan, Brnch Mgr
EMP: 47
SQ FT: 9,000
Web: www.cvcde.com
SIC: **8011** Cardiologist and cardio-vascular specialist
PA: Cardiology Consultants
  35141 Atlantic Ave Unit 3
  Millville DE 19967

(G-5802)
CARL KING TIRE CO INC
96 Tulip Dr (19958-1689)
PHONE..................302 644-4070

GEOGRAPHIC SECTION

Lewes - Sussex County (G-5831)

Carl King, *CEO*
EMP: 10
SALES (corp-wide): 8.39MM **Privately Held**
SIC: 5014 5531 Automobile tires and tubes; Automotive tires
PA: Carl King Tire Co., Inc.
109 S Main St
Camden DE 19934
302 697-9506

(G-5803)
CAROL BOYD HERON
Also Called: Peninsula Gallery
520 E Savannah Rd (19958-1161)
PHONE.................................302 645-0551
EMP: 2 **EST:** 1996
SALES (est): 120.09K **Privately Held**
Web: www.peninsula-gallery.com
SIC: 2499 5999 Picture frame molding, finished; Alcoholic beverage making equipment and supplies

(G-5804)
CARPAL ENTERPRISE INC
16192 Coastal Hwy (19958-3608)
PHONE.................................917 985-8293
EMP: 18
SALES (est): 583.41K **Privately Held**
SIC: 7371 Computer software development and applications

(G-5805)
CARTER POOL MANAGEMENT LLC
35740 Cutter Ct (19958-5020)
P.O. Box 288 (19958-0288)
PHONE.................................302 236-6952
EMP: 6 **EST:** 2002
SALES (est): 98.1K **Privately Held**
SIC: 7389 Swimming pool and hot tub service and maintenance

(G-5806)
CARUSO RICHARD F MD PA
Also Called: Seaside Gstrointerology Conslt
130 Savannah Rd Ste B (19958-1463)
P.O. Box 472 (19958-0472)
PHONE.................................302 645-6698
EMP: 8 **EST:** 1993
SALES (est): 715.02K **Privately Held**
SIC: 8011 Gastronomist

(G-5807)
CASPER HOSTING LLC
Also Called: Sitecanix
16192 Coastal Hwy (19958-3608)
PHONE.................................480 442-7112
Jaime Phillips, *CEO*
EMP: 5 **EST:** 2014
SALES (est): 226.36K **Privately Held**
Web: www.casperhosting.com
SIC: 7373 7374 7379 8742 Value-added resellers, computer systems; Computer processing services; Computer related consulting services; Business management consultant

(G-5808)
CASTLE CARE INC
22530 Waterview Rd (19958-5703)
PHONE.................................302 947-2377
Lyn Mox, *Owner*
EMP: 6 **EST:** 2007
SALES (est): 199.82K **Privately Held**
Web: www.castlecare.us
SIC: 1521 New construction, single-family houses

(G-5809)
CHAS MEDICINE
34435 King Street Row (19958-4787)
PHONE.................................302 644-5870
EMP: 7 **EST:** 2019
SALES (est): 351.72K **Privately Held**
SIC: 8099 Health and allied services, nec

(G-5810)
CHATTY PRESS
31210 Ringtail Dr (19958-3409)
PHONE.................................617 712-3882
Jen Pepper, *Prin*
EMP: 3 **EST:** 2017
SALES (est): 102.94K **Privately Held**
Web: www.chattypress.com
SIC: 2741 Miscellaneous publishing

(G-5811)
CHAUKISS LLC (PA) ✪
16192 Coastal Hwy (19958-3608)
PHONE.................................551 655-5181
EMP: 2 **EST:** 2022
SALES (est): 103.59K
SALES (corp-wide): 103.59K **Privately Held**
SIC: 2771 Greeting cards

(G-5812)
CHILDRENS BEACH HOUSE INC
1800 Bay Ave (19958-1859)
PHONE.................................302 645-9184
EMP: 23
SALES (corp-wide): 3.09MM **Privately Held**
Web: www.cbhinc.org
SIC: 7999 8351 Instruction schools, camps, and services; Preschool center
PA: Children's Beach House Inc
100 W 10th St Ste 411
Wilmington DE 19801
302 655-4288

(G-5813)
CHILDS PLAY AT HOME LLC
11 Hartford Way (19958-9419)
PHONE.................................302 644-3445
Alisha Melesky, *Prin*
EMP: 5 **EST:** 2009
SALES (est): 138.3K **Privately Held**
Web: www.childsplayathome.com
SIC: 8351 Group day care center

(G-5814)
CHILDS PLAY BY BAY
1510 Savannah Rd (19958-1624)
PHONE.................................302 703-6234
Alisia Melesky, *Owner*
Sarah Dickey, *Owner*
EMP: 8 **EST:** 2005
SALES (est): 247.78K **Privately Held**
Web: www.childsplaylewes.com
SIC: 8351 Child day care services

(G-5815)
CHILLAX INN AT LEWES BEACH
4 Camden Ave (19958-1805)
PHONE.................................302 685-8845
EMP: 7 **EST:** 2019
SALES (est): 63.04K **Privately Held**
Web: www.chillaxinnlewesbeach.com
SIC: 7011 Inns

(G-5816)
CHOCOLETTE DISTRIBUTION LLC
16192 Coastal Hwy (19958-3608)
PHONE.................................917 547-8905
Arnold W Vahrenwald Ea, *Managing Member*
EMP: 5 **EST:** 2018
SALES (est): 1.01MM **Privately Held**
SIC: 5149 Chocolate

(G-5817)
CHPT MFG INC
100 Dock Dr (19958-1190)
PHONE.................................302 645-4314
Hicks Douglas, *Owner*
EMP: 2 **EST:** 2004
SALES (est): 78.97K **Privately Held**
SIC: 3599 Machine shop, jobbing and repair

(G-5818)
CHRIST CARE CARDIAC SURGERY
400 Savannah Rd Ste C (19958-1499)
PHONE.................................302 644-4282
EMP: 5 **EST:** 2007
SALES (est): 254.58K **Privately Held**
SIC: 8062 General medical and surgical hospitals

(G-5819)
CHT HOLDINGS LLC
16192 Coastal Hwy (19958-3608)
PHONE.................................954 864-2008
Harrison Vargas, *Managing Member*
EMP: 8 **EST:** 2013
SQ FT: 1,500
SALES (est): 179.41K **Privately Held**
SIC: 8741 Business management

(G-5820)
CIRCUS ASSOCIATES INTELLIGENCE
Also Called: Circus Associates, The
16192 Coastal Hwy (19958-3608)
PHONE.................................757 663-7864
EMP: 41 **EST:** 2018
SALES (est): 2.21MM **Privately Held**
Web: www.neolore.com
SIC: 8742 8732 Business management consultant; Research services, except laboratory

(G-5821)
CITIZENS BANK NATIONAL ASSN
Also Called: Citizens Bank
34161 Citizen Dr (19958-4722)
PHONE.................................302 645-2024
Dennise Durton, *Brnch Mgr*
EMP: 7
SALES (corp-wide): 9.07B **Publicly Held**
Web: www.govplus.com
SIC: 6022 State commercial banks
HQ: Citizens Bank, National Association
1 Citizens Plz
Providence RI 02903

(G-5822)
CIVIC INFLUENCERS INC
16192 Coastal Hwy (19958-3608)
PHONE.................................302 644-5757
Maxim Thorne, *Prin*
EMP: 6 **EST:** 2020
SALES (est): 55.48K **Privately Held**
SIC: 8651 Political fundraising

(G-5823)
CJS BEACH BAYS INC
33711 Wescoats Rd (19958-5097)
PHONE.................................302 645-8478
Carlton Bailey, *Pr*
Renee Bailey, *Sec*
EMP: 10 **EST:** 2005
SALES (est): 744.15K **Privately Held**
Web: www.cjsbeachbays.com
SIC: 7538 General automotive repair shops

(G-5824)
CLEAN CONSCIENCE LLC
20883 Iris Rd (19958-2611)
PHONE.................................410 746-1315
EMP: 5 **EST:** 2018
SALES (est): 32.62K **Privately Held**
Web: www.conscienceit.com
SIC: 7699 Cleaning services

(G-5825)
CLEANERS SUNNY
17601 Coastal Hwy (19958-6217)
PHONE.................................302 827-2095
Sunhui Seo, *Owner*
EMP: 5 **EST:** 2008
SALES (est): 105.47K **Privately Held**
SIC: 7349 Building and office cleaning services

(G-5826)
CLEARED FOR USE INC (PA)
16192 Coastal Hwy (19958-3608)
PHONE.................................206 636-5222
Nidhi Dutt, *CEO*
EMP: 6 **EST:** 2021
SALES (est): 60.47K
SALES (corp-wide): 60.47K **Privately Held**
Web: www.delawarellc.com
SIC: 7371 Computer software development and applications

(G-5827)
CLERK CHAT INC ✪
Also Called: Clerk Chat
16192 Coastal Hwy (19958-3608)
PHONE.................................415 943-6084
Alexander Haque, *Managing Member*
EMP: 9 **EST:** 2022
SALES (est): 512.95K **Privately Held**
SIC: 7372 7389 Utility computer software; Business services, nec

(G-5828)
CLIKTRUCOM
20487 Old Meadow Ln (19958-7307)
PHONE.................................302 827-1103
EMP: 5 **EST:** 2018
SALES (est): 77.44K **Privately Held**
Web: www.cliktru.com
SIC: 8742 Marketing consulting services

(G-5829)
CLINIC BY SEA
16295 Willow Creek Rd (19958-3614)
PHONE.................................302 644-0999
Zeina Jeha, *Prin*
EMP: 6 **EST:** 2006
SALES (est): 570.98K **Privately Held**
Web: www.clinicbythesea.org
SIC: 8011 Cardiologist and cardio-vascular specialist

(G-5830)
CLOUDBEES INC (PA)
Also Called: Cloudbees
16192 Coastal Hwy (19958-3608)
PHONE.................................323 842-7783
EMP: 15 **EST:** 2010
SALES (est): 40.07MM **Privately Held**
Web: www.cloudbees.com
SIC: 7371 Computer software development

(G-5831)
CLS COUNSELING LLC
20268 Plantations Rd (19958-4622)
PHONE.................................302 644-2633
EMP: 6 **EST:** 2019
SALES (est): 34.55K **Privately Held**
SIC: 8322 Individual and family services

Lewes - Sussex County (G-5832) GEOGRAPHIC SECTION

(G-5832)
CLS TRUCKING & LOGISTICS INC
16192 Coastal Hwy (19958-3608)
PHONE.................................609 380-3399
Divya Singh, *CEO*
EMP: 4 **EST:** 2020
SALES (est): 271.87K **Privately Held**
SIC: 3537 Trucks, tractors, loaders, carriers, and similar equipment

(G-5833)
CLYMENE LLC
16192 Coastal Hwy (19958-3608)
PHONE.................................888 679-3310
Kambiz Behi, *Dir*
EMP: 5 **EST:** 2015
SALES (est): 250.58K **Privately Held**
Web: www.clymeneenterprises.com
SIC: 7371 Custom computer programming services

(G-5834)
CM BEACH LLC
19830 Beaver Dam Rd (19958-5128)
PHONE.................................202 521-1493
Chase Beach, *Pr*
EMP: 6 **EST:** 2016
SALES (est): 252.53K **Privately Held**
SIC: 1522 Residential construction, nec

(G-5835)
CNCT APP INC (PA)
16192 Coastal Hwy (19958-3608)
PHONE.................................724 288-3212
David Tennent, *Pr*
EMP: 8 **EST:** 2021
SALES (est): 29.29K
SALES (corp-wide): 29.29K **Privately Held**
SIC: 7371 Computer software development and applications

(G-5836)
COAST SURVEY
32261 Nassau Rd (19958-4071)
P.O. Box 117 (19969-0117)
PHONE.................................302 645-7184
EMP: 6 **EST:** 1985
SALES (est): 400.45K **Privately Held**
SIC: 8713 Surveying services

(G-5837)
COASTAL CHEM-DRY
34043 Clematis St (19958-2625)
PHONE.................................302 645-2800
Stephanie Todd, *Prin*
EMP: 5 **EST:** 2016
SALES (est): 38.17K **Privately Held**
Web: www.coastalchemdry.com
SIC: 7217 Carpet and upholstery cleaning

(G-5838)
COASTAL CHEM-DRY
112 Breakwater Reach (19958-3124)
PHONE.................................302 234-0200
EMP: 4 **EST:** 2020
SALES (est): 27.95K **Privately Held**
Web: www.coastalchemdry.com
SIC: 7349 2842 Building maintenance services, nec; Polishes and sanitation goods

(G-5839)
COASTAL CLUB SCHELL BROTHERS
31605 Exeter Way (19958-5827)
PHONE.................................302 966-0063
EMP: 7 **EST:** 2015
SALES (est): 56.38K **Privately Held**
Web: www.schellbrothers.com
SIC: 7997 Membership sports and recreation clubs

(G-5840)
COASTAL COATINGS INC
17993 American Way (19958-4799)
PHONE.................................302 645-1399
EMP: 7 **EST:** 2010
SALES (est): 125.13K **Privately Held**
Web: www.coastalcoatings.net
SIC: 3479 Metal coating and allied services

(G-5841)
COASTAL CONCERTS INC
Bethel United Methodist Church Hall Fourth & Market Streets (19958)
P.O. Box 685 (19958-0685)
PHONE.................................302 645-1539
Denise Emery, *Pr*
Edna V Ellett, *Ex Dir*
EMP: 9 **EST:** 2008
SALES (est): 127.81K **Privately Held**
Web: www.coastalconcerts.org
SIC: 7929 Entertainers and entertainment groups

(G-5842)
COASTAL CTTAGE RENOVATIONS LLC
344 Pilottown Rd (19958-1200)
PHONE.................................302 727-2443
EMP: 5 **EST:** 2017
SALES (est): 158.59K **Privately Held**
Web: www.coastalcottagerenos.com
SIC: 1521 General remodeling, single-family houses

(G-5843)
COASTAL DIRECT PRMRY CARE LLC
1409 Savannah Rd (19958-1610)
PHONE.................................786 897-2550
Christine Degnon, *Prin*
EMP: 8 **EST:** 2018
SALES (est): 532.58K **Privately Held**
Web: www.coastaldpc.com
SIC: 8011 General and family practice, physician/surgeon

(G-5844)
COASTAL LIFE PATIOS
9 Greystone Dr (19958-9450)
PHONE.................................301 944-4005
Michael Rhine, *Prin*
EMP: 5 **EST:** 2017
SALES (est): 438.66K **Privately Held**
Web: www.coastallifepatios.com
SIC: 0781 Landscape services

(G-5845)
COASTAL PAIN CARE PHYSCIANS PA
1606 Savannah Rd Ste 8 (19958-1656)
PHONE.................................302 644-8330
Gabriel Somori, *Prin*
Gabriel Somori, *Dir*
EMP: 8 **EST:** 2005
SALES (est): 136.32K **Privately Held**
Web: www.coastal-paincare.com
SIC: 8011 Medical centers

(G-5846)
COASTAL SEAFOOD LLC
34527 Maple Dr (19958-4711)
PHONE.................................302 242-6659
Mike Meibaum, *Prin*
EMP: 8 **EST:** 2015
SALES (est): 252.76K **Privately Held**
Web: www.coastalseafoods.com
SIC: 0782 Lawn care services

(G-5847)
COASTAL TOWING INC
33012 Cedar Grove Rd (19958-4644)
PHONE.................................302 645-6300
EMP: 9 **EST:** 1990
SALES (est): 1.08MM **Privately Held**
Web: www.coastaltowingandautode.com
SIC: 7549 7539 7538 Towing service, automotive; Automotive repair shops, nec; General truck repair

(G-5848)
CODESHIP INC
16192 Coastal Hwy (19958-3608)
PHONE.................................617 515-3664
Moritz Plassnig, *Pr*
Daniel Curtis, *CFO*
EMP: 20 **EST:** 2013
SQ FT: 2,000
SALES (est): 1.63MM **Privately Held**
Web: www.cloudbees.com
SIC: 7371 Computer software development
PA: Cloudbees, Inc.
  16192 Coastal Hwy
  Lewes DE 19958

(G-5849)
COFINET LLC
16192 Coastal Hwy (19958-3608)
PHONE.................................614 301-8082
EMP: 13 **EST:** 2020
SALES (est): 568.45K **Privately Held**
Web: www.cofinet.com.au
SIC: 2095 Roasted coffee
PA: Cofinet Pty Ltd
  157 Victoria Rd
  Marrickville NSW

(G-5850)
COGNITRO LLC
16192 Coastal Hwy (19958-3608)
PHONE.................................347 983-9785
EMP: 7 **EST:** 2009
SALES (est): 300K **Privately Held**
Web: www.cognitro.ai
SIC: 7374 Data entry service

(G-5851)
COLONIAL EAST LP
16 Manor House Ln (19958-4165)
PHONE.................................302 644-4758
Stevan Class, *Pt*
EMP: 11 **EST:** 1972
SALES (est): 436.38K **Privately Held**
Web: colonialeast.communitysite.com
SIC: 6515 Mobile home site operators

(G-5852)
COLORWISE AND MORE
34732 Bookhammer Landing Rd (19958-5721)
PHONE.................................302 703-6330
Adel Baghouli, *Pr*
EMP: 5 **EST:** 2010
SALES (est): 75.47K **Privately Held**
Web: www.colorwiseandmore.com
SIC: 1721 Interior residential painting contractor

(G-5853)
COMMTRAK CORPORATION
17493 Nassau Commons Blvd (19958-6283)
P.O. Box 390355 (32739-0355)
PHONE.................................302 644-1600
Gene Wilson, *Pr*
Roger Miersch, *VP*
EMP: 8 **EST:** 1988
SQ FT: 1,800
SALES (est): 865.12K **Privately Held**
Web: www.commtrak.com
SIC: 7322 7371 Collection agency, except real estate; Custom computer programming services

(G-5854)
COMMUNITY BANK DELAWARE (PA)
16982 Kings Hwy (19958-4785)
P.O. Box 742 (19958-0742)
PHONE.................................302 348-8600
Jack Riddle, *Pr*
Angie Warrell, *CFO*
EMP: 22 **EST:** 2005
SALES (est): 11.97MM **Privately Held**
Web: www.communitybankdelaware.com
SIC: 6022 State trust companies accepting deposits, commercial

(G-5855)
COMRADE TECHNOLOGIES INC
16192 Coastal Hwy (19958-3608)
PHONE.................................888 575-1225
Sami Baddar, *CEO*
EMP: 6
SALES (est): 70.36K **Privately Held**
Web: www.cmrd.com
SIC: 7311 Advertising agencies

(G-5856)
CONCIERGE BY SEA INC
36269 Tarpon Dr (19958-5054)
PHONE.................................302 228-2014
Aildasani Pishu, *Prin*
EMP: 5 **EST:** 2010
SALES (est): 73.87K **Privately Held**
SIC: 7299 Miscellaneous personal service

(G-5857)
CONSTRUCTION RESOURCE MGT INC
101 Quaker Rd (19958-1708)
P.O. Box 3424 (19804-0264)
PHONE.................................302 778-2335
David Green, *Pr*
EMP: 6 **EST:** 2008
SALES (est): 122.79K **Privately Held**
SIC: 1521 Single-family housing construction

(G-5858)
CONWAY CONSTRUCTION CO
29893 Vincent Ave (19958-4041)
PHONE.................................302 598-5019
Joe Conway, *Owner*
EMP: 5 **EST:** 2020
SALES (est): 80.45K **Privately Held**
Web: www.conwayconstruction.net
SIC: 1521 Single-family housing construction

(G-5859)
CORAL TECHNOLOGY LLC (PA)
16192 Coastal Hwy (19958-3608)
PHONE.................................201 793-7127
Doug Calahan, *CEO*
Natasha Matskovich, *COO*
EMP: 5 **EST:** 2014
SALES (est): 890.69K
SALES (corp-wide): 890.69K **Privately Held**
Web: www.coralmsp.com
SIC: 7371 Computer software development

(G-5860)
COREY KENNEDY
31607 Exeter Way (19958-5827)
PHONE.................................201 233-8054
Corey Kennedy, *Owner*
EMP: 6 **EST:** 2017
SALES (est): 22.18K **Privately Held**
SIC: 8049 Offices of health practitioner

GEOGRAPHIC SECTION   Lewes - Sussex County (G-5893)

(G-5861)
COSINE SOLUTIONS LLC
16192 Coastal Hwy (19958-3608)
PHONE.................................267 398-8995
Russ Holmes, *CEO*
EMP: 25 EST: 2019
SALES (est): 967.56K **Privately Held**
Web: www.cosine-solutions.com
SIC: **7372** Application computer software

(G-5862)
COTT ELECTRONICS LLC
16192 Coastal Hwy (19958-3608)
PHONE.................................302 520-2838
EMP: 99 EST: 2021
SALES (est): 3.12MM **Privately Held**
SIC: **3559** Semiconductor manufacturing machinery

(G-5863)
COTTAGE AT CURRY MANOR
6 Seashell Pl (19958-3123)
PHONE.................................202 258-7674
EMP: 8 EST: 2016
SALES (est): 69.3K **Privately Held**
SIC: **8361** Aged home

(G-5864)
COUNTY BANK
Also Called: Five Points
1609 Savannah Rd (19958-1625)
PHONE.................................302 645-8880
Gavin Radka, *Mgr*
EMP: 9
Web: www.countybankdel.com
SIC: **6022** State commercial banks
PA: County Bank
   19927 Shuttle Rd
   Rehoboth Beach DE 19971

(G-5865)
COUNTY WOMEN S JOURNAL
17252 N Village Main Blvd Unit 9
(19958-6292)
P.O. Box 57 (19958-0057)
PHONE.................................302 236-1435
EMP: 4 EST: 2008
SALES (est): 206.91K **Privately Held**
SIC: **2711** Newspapers, publishing and printing

(G-5866)
COVERED BRIDGE INN
30249 Fisher Rd (19958-5536)
PHONE.................................302 542-9605
EMP: 10 EST: 2017
SALES (est): 179.81K **Privately Held**
Web: www.hopkinsheartland.com
SIC: **7011** Bed and breakfast inn

(G-5867)
CREATIVE IMPRESSIONS ART
17303 N Village Main Blvd (19958-7220)
PHONE.................................858 722-2252
Philip Gallelli, *Prin*
EMP: 5 EST: 2019
SALES (est): 73.75K **Privately Held**
Web: www.creativeimpressionsartgallery.com
SIC: **8412** Art gallery

(G-5868)
CREATOR STUDIOS INC
16192 Coastal Hwy (19958-3608)
PHONE.................................323 992-4350
Nicholas Jarecki, *Mgr*
EMP: 5
SALES (est): 199.4K **Privately Held**
SIC: **7371** Computer software development and applications

(G-5869)
CRUISE PLANNERS
22424 S Acorn Way (19958-4556)
PHONE.................................302 858-1996
EMP: 5 EST: 2018
SALES (est): 153.84K **Privately Held**
Web: www.cruiseplanners.com
SIC: **4724** Travel agencies

(G-5870)
CRUISE PLANNERS
24343 Zinfandel Ln Unit 107 (19958-1884)
PHONE.................................302 381-9249
Cindy Husbands, *Owner*
EMP: 5 EST: 2007
SALES (est): 230K **Privately Held**
Web: www.cruiseplanners.com
SIC: **4724** Travel agencies

(G-5871)
CRUISINGAPP LLC (PA) ✪
16192 Coastal Hwy (19958-3608)
PHONE.................................302 645-7400
EMP: 6 EST: 2023
SALES (est): 68.89K
SALES (corp-wide): 68.89K **Privately Held**
SIC: **7371** Computer software development and applications

(G-5872)
CRYPTLEX LLC
16192 Coastal Hwy (19958-3608)
PHONE.................................786 269-0931
EMP: 7 EST: 2016
SALES (est): 174.71K **Privately Held**
Web: www.cryptlex.com
SIC: **7371** Computer software development

(G-5873)
CS SERVICES LLC
30757 Conleys Chapel Rd (19958-5508)
PHONE.................................302 841-9420
EMP: 6 EST: 2012
SALES (est): 222.03K **Privately Held**
Web: www.csservicesde.com
SIC: **1711** Warm air heating and air conditioning contractor

(G-5874)
CURRENT CARE ANALYTICS INC
16192 Coastal Hwy (19958-3608)
PHONE.................................248 425-3973
Brandon Busuito, *Prin*
EMP: 6 EST: 2017
SALES (est): 72.91K **Privately Held**
SIC: **8071** Medical laboratories

(G-5875)
CYCOLOGY 202 LLC (PA)
23924 Sunny Cove Ct (19958-5695)
PHONE.................................610 202-0518
EMP: 12 EST: 2018
SALES (est): 331.51K
SALES (corp-wide): 331.51K **Privately Held**
SIC: **7991** 7389 Exercise facilities; Business services, nec

(G-5876)
CYDALLIA INC (PA)
16192 Coastal Hwy (19958-3608)
PHONE.................................860 682-0947
Sawsan Hubaishy, *Pr*
EMP: 2 EST: 2021
SALES (est): 244.73K
SALES (corp-wide): 244.73K **Privately Held**
SIC: **3841** 7389 Surgical and medical instruments; Business services, nec

(G-5877)
D STEVEN CALDWELL
34444 King Street Row (19958-4787)
PHONE.................................302 245-9713
D Steven Caldwell Lmt, *Owner*
EMP: 6 EST: 2017
SALES (est): 87.57K **Privately Held**
SIC: **8049** Offices of health practitioner

(G-5878)
DALE F SUTHERLAND MD LLC
35573 Peregrine Rd (19958-7042)
PHONE.................................302 827-4376
Dale F Sutherland Md, *Prin*
EMP: 10 EST: 2016
SALES (est): 194.83K **Privately Held**
SIC: **8011** Offices and clinics of medical doctors

(G-5879)
DANIEL HALVORSEN
33095 Nassau Loop (19958-3730)
PHONE.................................302 645-1761
Daniel Halvorsen, *Prin*
EMP: 5 EST: 2008
SALES (est): 49.97K **Privately Held**
SIC: **7231** Beauty shops

(G-5880)
DANNY THACH
17601 Coastal Hwy (19958-6217)
PHONE.................................302 645-7779
Danny Thach, *Prin*
EMP: 6 EST: 2010
SALES (est): 27.22K **Privately Held**
SIC: **7231** Beauty shops

(G-5881)
DARLENE R N SHEERAN
31247 Temple Rd (19958-3422)
PHONE.................................845 297-9704
Darlene Sheeran R.n., *Owner*
EMP: 6 EST: 2018
SALES (est): 100.41K **Privately Held**
SIC: **8049** Offices of health practitioner

(G-5882)
DATA UNBLOCKED INC ✪
16192 Coastal Hwy (19958-3608)
PHONE.................................540 424-0801
Ash Ashtiani, *Pr*
EMP: 7 EST: 2022
SALES (est): 264.9K **Privately Held**
SIC: **7371** Computer software development and applications

(G-5883)
DATAMOLA LLC
16192 Coastal Hwy (19958-3608)
PHONE.................................347 474-1003
Kyrla Bucha, *Managing Member*
EMP: 5
SALES (est): 303.02K **Privately Held**
SIC: **7371** Computer software development

(G-5884)
DDH (NORTH AMERICA) INC
1100 Louisiana St Ste 2750 (19958-3608)
PHONE.................................617 893-9004
Karina Walters, *Genl Mgr*
EMP: 7 EST: 2020
SALES (est): 1.02MM **Privately Held**
SIC: **7374** 7389 Data processing service; Business Activities at Non-Commercial Site

(G-5885)
DEBAY SURGICAL SERVICE
Also Called: Delaware Surgical Service
33664 Bayview Medical Dr (19958-1687)
PHONE.................................302 644-4954
Mayer Catz, *Pr*
EMP: 15 EST: 1990
SALES (est): 1.44MM **Privately Held**
SIC: **8011** Orthopedic physician

(G-5886)
DEEPTRACE INC
16192 Coastal Hwy (19958-3608)
PHONE.................................424 413-8787
Jonas Gavelis, *Pr*
EMP: 50
SALES (est): 1.17MM **Privately Held**
SIC: **7374** Data processing service

(G-5887)
DEL MARVA HAND SPECIALISTS LLC
701 Savannah Rd Ste B (19958-1550)
PHONE.................................302 644-0940
Scott M Schulze, *Owner*
EMP: 24 EST: 2013
SALES (est): 816.95K **Privately Held**
Web: www.delawarebonedocs.com
SIC: **8011** Orthopedic physician

(G-5888)
DELAWARE ARTHRITIS
20268 Plantations Rd (19958-4622)
PHONE.................................302 644-2633
EMP: 6 EST: 2019
SALES (est): 295.78K **Privately Held**
Web: www.delawarearthritis.com
SIC: **8049** Offices of health practitioner

(G-5889)
DELAWARE BAY & RIVER
700 Pilottown Rd (19958-1242)
PHONE.................................302 645-7861
Gene Johnson, *Pr*
EMP: 7 EST: 2006
SALES (est): 182.71K **Privately Held**
Web: www.dbrcinc.org
SIC: **8748** Environmental consultant

(G-5890)
DELAWARE BAY SURGICAL SVC PA
33664 Bayview Medical Dr Ste 2
(19958-1933)
PHONE.................................302 645-5650
Mayer M Katz, *Pr*
EMP: 22 EST: 1992
SALES (est): 401.07K **Privately Held**
SIC: **8062** General medical and surgical hospitals

(G-5891)
DELAWARE BEACH STORAGE CENTER
333 Market St (19958-1335)
PHONE.................................302 644-7774
EMP: 5 EST: 2015
SALES (est): 269.51K **Privately Held**
Web: www.debeachstorage.com
SIC: **4225** Warehousing, self storage

(G-5892)
DELAWARE CONCRETE COATINGS
17569 Nassau Commons Blvd
(19958-6284)
PHONE.................................302 864-4014
EMP: 8 EST: 2017
SALES (est): 679.55K **Privately Held**
Web: www.delawareconcretecoatings.com
SIC: **1771** Concrete work

(G-5893)
DELAWARE CONSULTING SERVI
19082 Robinsonville Rd (19958-4494)
PHONE.................................302 945-7936

EMP: 5 EST: 2018
SALES (est): 78.44K **Privately Held**
SIC: 8748 Business consulting, nec

(G-5894)
DELAWARE CRAWL SPACE CO INC
37101 Suzanne Ln (19958-2532)
PHONE..................................302 930-0386
EMP: 6 EST: 2018
SALES (est): 112.91K **Privately Held**
Web:
www.delawarecrawlspacecompany.com
SIC: 1799 Waterproofing

(G-5895)
DELAWARE CRDOVASCULAR ASSOC PA
34453 King Street Row (19958-4787)
PHONE..................................302 644-7676
Grace Walls D.o.s., *Mgr*
EMP: 27
Web: www.decardio.com
SIC: 8011 Cardiologist and cardio-vascular specialist
PA: Delaware Cardiovascular Associates, P.A.
1403 Foulk Rd Ste 101a
Wilmington DE 19803

(G-5896)
DELAWARE CUSTOM TILE
125b Beach Plum Pl (19958-1737)
PHONE..................................302 841-9215
EMP: 8 EST: 2017
SALES (est): 212.21K **Privately Held**
Web: www.tilemarketofde.com
SIC: 1743 Tile installation, ceramic

(G-5897)
DELAWARE EYE CLINICS
31059 Sycamore Dr (19958-3883)
PHONE..................................302 645-2338
Edward Jaoude, *Prin*
EMP: 9 EST: 2017
SALES (est): 411.73K **Privately Held**
Web: www.delawareeyeclinics.com
SIC: 8099 Health and allied services, nec

(G-5898)
DELAWARE HOME & ENVMTL SVCS
16141 Willow Creek Rd (19958-3620)
PHONE..................................302 313-2899
EMP: 5 EST: 2016
SALES (est): 71.44K **Privately Held**
Web:
www.delawarehomeenvironmentalservices.com
SIC: 1799 Asbestos removal and encapsulation

(G-5899)
DELAWARE OTOLARYNGOLOGY CONSUL
17316 Coastal Hwy (19958-6209)
PHONE..................................302 644-2232
EMP: 10 EST: 2014
SALES (est): 467.02K **Privately Held**
Web: www.delawareoto.com
SIC: 8011 Ears, nose, and throat specialist: physician/surgeon

(G-5900)
DELAWARE PSYCHOLOGICAL SVCS LLC
16287 Willow Creek Rd (19958-3614)
PHONE..................................302 703-6332
Katherine Elder, *CEO*
EMP: 9 EST: 2014
SALES (est): 489.55K **Privately Held**
Web:
www.delawarepsychologicalservices.com
SIC: 8049 Clinical psychologist

(G-5901)
DELAWARE TITLE LOANS INC
17672 Coastal Hwy (19958-6214)
PHONE..................................302 644-3640
EMP: 11
SALES (corp-wide): 820.18K **Privately Held**
Web: www.delawaretitleloansinc.com
SIC: 6163 Loan agents
PA: Delaware Title Loans, Inc.
8601 Dunwoody Pl Ste 406
Atlanta GA 30350
770 552-9840

(G-5902)
DELCOMPS LLC
Also Called: Delcomps
31059 Sycamore Dr (19958-3883)
PHONE..................................302 754-1543
EMP: 6 EST: 2012
SALES (est): 73.89K **Privately Held**
Web: www.delcomps.com
SIC: 7379 Computer related consulting services

(G-5903)
DELMARVA COMMUNITY WELLNET
1307 Savannah Rd (19958-1514)
PHONE..................................704 779-3280
EMP: 5 EST: 2019
SALES (est): 147.93K **Privately Held**
SIC: 8641 Civic and social associations

(G-5904)
DELMARVA FURNITURE SVCS LLC
Also Called: Services
16192 Coastal Hwy (19958-3608)
PHONE..................................302 644-4970
Emilia Sikorska, *Prin*
EMP: 11 EST: 2009
SALES (est): 1.52MM **Privately Held**
Web: www.hsws.com
SIC: 7379 Computer related consulting services

(G-5905)
DELMARVA GROUP
1632 Savannah Rd Ste 2 (19958-1659)
PHONE..................................302 200-9053
EMP: 7 EST: 2019
SALES (est): 85.26K **Privately Held**
SIC: 6531 Real estate agents and managers

(G-5906)
DELMARVA INSURANCE GROUP
19413 Jingle Shell Way (19958-6307)
PHONE..................................302 248-8500
EMP: 6 EST: 2018
SALES (est): 490.57K **Privately Held**
SIC: 6411 Insurance agents, nec

(G-5907)
DELMARVA REPAIR
16557 Coastal Hwy (19958-3605)
PHONE..................................302 313-6900
EMP: 5 EST: 2015
SALES (est): 88.6K **Privately Held**
Web: www.delmarvarepair.com
SIC: 7699 Repair services, nec

(G-5908)
DELMARVA SURGERY ASSOC
36031 Tarpon Dr (19958-5059)
PHONE..................................302 644-8880
EMP: 8 EST: 2019
SALES (est): 247.38K **Privately Held**
SIC: 8011 Surgeon

(G-5909)
DELMARVAVOIP LLC
16557 Coastal Hwy (19958-3605)
PHONE..................................855 645-8647
EMP: 9 EST: 2017
SALES (est): 165.56K **Privately Held**
Web: www.thinksecurenet.com
SIC: 7379 Online services technology consultants

(G-5910)
DELTA KAPPA GAMMA SOCIETY
33676 Woodland Cir (19958-5163)
PHONE..................................302 945-7174
Susan F Lore, *Prin*
EMP: 5 EST: 2011
SALES (est): 120K **Privately Held**
SIC: 8641 University club

(G-5911)
DENTAL GROUP
Also Called: Barnhart, Ryan DDS
34359 Carpenters Way (19958-4910)
PHONE..................................302 645-8993
Blair A Jones, *Prin*
Blair A Jones D.m.d., *Prin*
EMP: 8 EST: 1992
SALES (est): 973.92K **Privately Held**
Web: www.thedentalgrouplewes.com
SIC: 8021 Dentists' office

(G-5912)
DESTINY RESCUE INTL INC
16192 Coastal Hwy (19958-3608)
P.O. Box 25684 (46825-0684)
PHONE..................................574 529-2238
Tony Kirwan, *Pr*
EMP: 7 EST: 2015
SALES (est): 77.32K **Privately Held**
Web: www.destinyrescue.org
SIC: 8999 Search and rescue service

(G-5913)
DEVSTRINGX TECHNOLOGIES INC
16192 Coastal Hwy (19958-3608)
PHONE..................................650 209-7815
Manan Sharma, *Prin*
EMP: 7 EST: 2021
SALES (est): 18.95K **Privately Held**
Web: www.devstringx.com
SIC: 7299 Information services, consumer

(G-5914)
DICK ENNIS INC
22357 John J Williams Hwy (19958-4370)
PHONE..................................302 945-2627
Harold R Ennis Junior, *Pr*
Richard Ennis, *Pr*
EMP: 6 EST: 1987
SALES (est): 654.94K **Privately Held**
Web: www.dickennis.com
SIC: 5211 1389 0782 4492 Modular homes; Construction, repair, and dismantling services; Lawn care services; Marine towing services

(G-5915)
DIEHL & CO CPA
18306 Coastal Hwy (19958-4772)
PHONE..................................302 644-4441
Mark Diehl, *Owner*
EMP: 5 EST: 2005
SALES (est): 128.89K **Privately Held**
Web: www.dfcpasllc.com
SIC: 8721 Certified public accountant

(G-5916)
DIEHL FORAKER CPAS LLC
18306 Coastal Hwy (19958-4772)
PHONE..................................800 748-0354
EMP: 5 EST: 2014
SALES (est): 70.26K **Privately Held**
SIC: 8721 Accounting, auditing, and bookkeeping

(G-5917)
DIGIAPP LLC
16192 Coastal Hwy (19958-3608)
PHONE..................................855 217-2744
EMP: 6 EST: 2020
SALES (est): 198.85K **Privately Held**
SIC: 7389 Business services, nec

(G-5918)
DIGITALZONE INC
16192 Coastal Hwy (19958-3608)
PHONE..................................646 771-6969
Rishikkes Pawar, *CEO*
EMP: 40 EST: 2016
SALES (est): 15.48MM **Privately Held**
Web: www.digitalzone.com
SIC: 5199 Advertising specialties

(G-5919)
DILLONS DRIFTWOOD ENTP LLC
18282 Coastal Hwy (19958-4773)
PHONE..................................302 645-7500
EMP: 7 EST: 2018
SALES (est): 123.86K **Privately Held**
SIC: 7011 Motels

(G-5920)
DIMITRIOS M D BARMPOULETOS
34453 King Street Row (19958-4787)
PHONE..................................302 644-7676
Dimitrios Barmpouletos, *Mgr*
EMP: 8 EST: 2017
SALES (est): 54.13K **Privately Held**
Web: www.decardio.com
SIC: 8011 Cardiologist and cardio-vascular specialist

(G-5921)
DIRT WORKS INC
22547 Waterview Rd (19958-5749)
P.O. Box 511 (19958-0511)
PHONE..................................302 947-2429
Clint Fluharty, *Pr*
EMP: 16 EST: 1999
SALES (est): 970.96K **Privately Held**
SIC: 1794 Excavation work

(G-5922)
DISAB LLC
805 Savannah Rd (19958-1522)
PHONE..................................302 645-6987
Mario Pdisabatino, *Prin*
EMP: 5 EST: 2010
SALES (est): 94.72K **Privately Held**
SIC: 6519 Real property lessors, nec

(G-5923)
DIVVZ INC
16192 Coastal Hwy (19958-3608)
PHONE..................................571 238-1722
Doug Steele, *CEO*
EMP: 3 EST: 2020
SALES (est): 139.91K **Privately Held**
SIC: 7372 Application computer software

(G-5924)
DL HOLDING AND DESIGN INC
16192 Coastal Hwy (19958-3608)
PHONE..................................302 219-4922
Michael Dailey, *Pr*
EMP: 12 EST: 2019

GEOGRAPHIC SECTION

Lewes - Sussex County (G-5956)

SALES (est): 500K **Privately Held**
SIC: **7299** Home improvement and renovation contractor agency

(G-5925)
DOC REO MEDIA LLC
Also Called: Ahmir Media
16192 Coastal Hwy (19958-3608)
PHONE..................................818 824-2885
Mareo-ahmir Lawson, *Managing Member*
EMP: 5 EST: 2016
SALES (est): 229.59K **Privately Held**
Web: www.ahmirmedia.com
SIC: **4899** Communication services, nec

(G-5926)
DOGFISH INN
105 Savannah Rd (19958-1437)
PHONE..................................302 644-8292
EMP: 17 EST: 2014
SALES (est): 384.08K **Privately Held**
Web: www.dogfish.com
SIC: **7011** Inns

(G-5927)
DON WLLAMS GROUP - KLLER WLLAM
18344 Coastal Hwy (19958-4772)
PHONE..................................302 545-6859
EMP: 5 EST: 2017
SALES (est): 75.13K **Privately Held**
Web: www.viewdelawarehomes.com
SIC: **6531** Real estate agent, residential

(G-5928)
DONNA MARIE KEMP
17232 N Village Main Blvd (19958-6287)
PHONE..................................302 645-7088
Donna M Kemp Pharmd, *Owner*
EMP: 6 EST: 2018
SALES (est): 78.25K **Privately Held**
SIC: **8049** Offices of health practitioner

(G-5929)
DOUBLE R HOLDINGS INC
1009 Kings Hwy (19958-1731)
PHONE..................................302 645-5555
Robert Burton, *Pr*
Jeffrey Burton, *VP*
EMP: 5 EST: 2003
SALES (est): 283.75K **Privately Held**
SIC: **6519** Real property lessors, nec

(G-5930)
DOUGLAS DITTY DMD MD
37718 Wescoats Rd (19958)
PHONE..................................302 644-2977
Douglas Ditty, *Prin*
EMP: 10 EST: 2007
SALES (est): 92.49K **Privately Held**
Web: www.firststateoms.com
SIC: **8021** Dental surgeon

(G-5931)
DOUGLAS RANDALL INC
20684 John J Williams Hwy Ste 1 (19958-4393)
PHONE..................................302 448-5826
EMP: 6 EST: 2019
SALES (est): 468.13K **Privately Held**
Web: www.randall-douglas.com
SIC: **1522** Residential construction, nec

(G-5932)
DR BETH DUNCAN
17316 Coastal Hwy (19958-6209)
PHONE..................................302 644-2232
Beth Duncan, *Owner*
EMP: 9 EST: 2014
SALES (est): 131.52K **Privately Held**
Web: www.delawareoto.com
SIC: **8011** Offices and clinics of medical doctors

(G-5933)
DR SCOTT SCHULZE
701 Savannah Rd Ste B (19958-1550)
PHONE..................................302 644-0940
Scott Schulze, *Prin*
EMP: 9 EST: 2008
SALES (est): 100.13K **Privately Held**
SIC: **8011** Orthopedic physician

(G-5934)
DREAM AMERICA LLC
16192 Coastal Hwy (19958-3608)
PHONE..................................305 509-9201
Chris Innes, *Prin*
EMP: 5 EST: 2019
SALES (est): 311.55K **Privately Held**
Web: www.dreamamerica.com
SIC: **6531** Real estate brokers and agents

(G-5935)
DREAMVILLE LLC
16192 Coastal Hwy (19958-3608)
PHONE..................................662 524-0917
EMP: 6
SALES (est): 300.65K **Privately Held**
SIC: **8742** 6531 Management consulting services; Real estate leasing and rentals

(G-5936)
DRIFTWOOD CABINETRY LLC
1009 Kings Hwy (19958-1731)
PHONE..................................302 645-4876
EMP: 2 EST: 2010
SALES (est): 139.94K **Privately Held**
SIC: **2434** Wood kitchen cabinets

(G-5937)
DRW CONSTRUCTION
30777 Steeple Chase Run (19958-5522)
PHONE..................................302 945-9055
Danny Wilson, *Prin*
EMP: 5 EST: 2010
SALES (est): 146.16K **Privately Held**
SIC: **1521** Single-family housing construction

(G-5938)
DUNG BEETLE TRUCKING LLC
16192 Coastal Hwy (19958-3608)
PHONE..................................312 843-1118
EMP: 4 EST: 2017
SALES (est): 30K **Privately Held**
SIC: **3537** Trucks: freight, baggage, etc.: industrial, except mining

(G-5939)
DYNAMIC MOBILE IMAGING
17527 Nassau Commons Blvd (19958-6283)
PHONE..................................302 645-2142
EMP: 11 EST: 2014
SALES (est): 266.49K **Privately Held**
Web: www.dynamicmobileimaging.com
SIC: **8071** Ultrasound laboratory

(G-5940)
DYTE INC
16192 Coastal Hwy (19958-3608)
PHONE..................................669 577-4571
Abhishek Kankani, *Prin*
EMP: 6 EST: 2020
SALES (est): 69.44K **Privately Held**
SIC: **7371** Computer software development and applications

(G-5941)
E-BERK CORPORATION
16192 Coastal Hwy (19958-3608)
PHONE..................................925 643-2375
Ozgur Ozudogru, *CEO*
Kenan Poyraz, *CFO*
EMP: 2 EST: 2020
SALES (est): 95.58K **Privately Held**
Web: www.eberk-usa.com
SIC: **3531** Tunneling machinery

(G-5942)
E2LINGO INC
16192 Coastal Hwy (19958-3608)
PHONE..................................800 345-2677
Amro Elsayed Fathelbab, *Pr*
EMP: 5 EST: 2020
SALES (est): 56.54K **Privately Held**
SIC: **7372** Educational computer software

(G-5943)
EAGER GEAR
19413 Jingle Shell Way # 6 (19958-6307)
PHONE..................................302 727-5831
EMP: 5 EST: 2015
SALES (est): 71.01K **Privately Held**
Web: www.eagergear.com
SIC: **3462** Gear and chain forgings

(G-5944)
EAST COAST
909 Pilottown Rd (19958-1274)
PHONE..................................302 249-8867
EMP: 5 EST: 2015
SALES (est): 121.75K **Privately Held**
Web: www.eastcoastx.org
SIC: **7641** Upholstery work

(G-5945)
EASTERN ALLRGY ASTHMA SPCLSTS
750 Kings Hwy Ste 102 (19958-1772)
PHONE..................................732 789-7982
EMP: 6
SALES (est): 73.18K **Privately Held**
Web: www.eaasde.com
SIC: **8011** Allergist

(G-5946)
EASY BREEZY BEAUTY
12 Pinewood Dr (19958-9107)
PHONE..................................302 562-6751
Bree Helwich, *Prin*
EMP: 5 EST: 2018
SALES (est): 56.41K **Privately Held**
SIC: **8049** Offices of health practitioner

(G-5947)
ECOLISTIC LIVING INC
Also Called: Ecolistic Cleaning
17046 Oak Ct (19958-3864)
PHONE..................................888 432-6547
Courtney Sunborn, *CEO*
EMP: 23 EST: 2003
SALES (est): 628K **Privately Held**
Web: www.ecolisticcleaning.com
SIC: **7699** Cleaning services

(G-5948)
EDC LLC
Also Called: Element Design Group
115 W Market St Fl 2 (19958-1309)
PHONE..................................302 645-0777
Katie Harp, *Off Mgr*
Douglas Warner, *Managing Member*
EMP: 8 EST: 2005
SALES (est): 1.3MM **Privately Held**
Web: www.elementdg.com

(G-5949)
EDOKK LLC
16192 Coastal Hwy (19958-3608)
PHONE..................................305 434-7227
EMP: 8 EST: 2019
SALES (est): 288.82K **Privately Held**
SIC: **7389** Business services, nec

(G-5950)
EDUARDO MCEDO LITE DE OLIVEIRA ✪
16192 Coastal Hwy (19958-3608)
PHONE..................................302 476-2285
EMP: 5 EST: 2022
SALES (est): 76.63K **Privately Held**
SIC: **4225** General warehousing and storage

(G-5951)
EGNM LLC
17015 Old Orchard Rd Unit 4 (19958-4849)
PHONE..................................302 644-3466
EMP: 10 EST: 2019
SALES (est): 446.31K **Privately Held**
SIC: **8011** Offices and clinics of medical doctors

(G-5952)
EGW CAPITAL INC
16192 Coastal Hwy (19958-3608)
PHONE..................................302 261-2008
EMP: 5 EST: 2017
SALES (est): 115.43K **Privately Held**
SIC: **6799** Investors, nec

(G-5953)
EICE INTERNATIONAL LLC
Also Called: Eice Texas
31794 Marsh Island Ave (19958-3351)
PHONE..................................281 451-7328
EMP: 6 EST: 2017
SALES (est): 329.49K **Privately Held**
Web: www.eiceinternational.com
SIC: **7371** Custom computer programming services

(G-5954)
ELCHEMY INC ✪
16192 Coastal Hwy (19958-3608)
PHONE..................................908 663-8750
Hardik Seth, *Dir*
EMP: 6 EST: 2022
SALES (est): 86.31K **Privately Held**
SIC: **5169** Chemicals and allied products, nec

(G-5955)
ELDERSAFE TECHNOLOGIES INC (PA)
Also Called: Sparrow
16192 Coastal Hwy (19958-3608)
PHONE..................................617 852-3018
Thomas Goulding, *Pr*
EMP: 5 EST: 2014
SALES (est): 194.08K
SALES (corp-wide): 194.08K **Privately Held**
SIC: **8733** Noncommercial research organizations

(G-5956)
ELEMENT
115 W Market St (19958-1309)
PHONE..................................302 645-0777
Douglas M Warner, *Prin*
EMP: 5 EST: 2011
SALES (est): 200.01K **Privately Held**

SIC: **8712** 8711 0781 Architectural services; Structural engineering; Landscape architects

Lewes - Sussex County (G-5957) GEOGRAPHIC SECTION

Web: www.elementdg.com
SIC: 2819 Industrial inorganic chemicals, nec

(G-5957)
ELITE CLEANING SERVICES LLC
13 Amberwood Way (19958-9467)
PHONE..................................571 359-7751
Camila Carneiro, *Prin*
EMP: 5 **EST:** 2018
SALES (est): 52K **Privately Held**
Web: www.oceanside-elite.com
SIC: 7699 Cleaning services

(G-5958)
ELITE NAILS
34005 Wescoats Rd Unit 4 (19958-4928)
PHONE..................................302 745-5988
Dina Donofrio, *Prin*
EMP: 5 **EST:** 2010
SALES (est): 226.08K **Privately Held**
SIC: 7231 Manicurist, pedicurist

(G-5959)
ELZUFON AUSTIN REARDON TARLOV
1413 Savannah Rd Unit 1 (19958-1792)
PHONE..................................302 644-0144
Edward A Tarlov, *Pr*
EMP: 5
SALES (corp-wide): 5.17MM **Privately Held**
Web: www.elzufon.com
SIC: 8111 General practice attorney, lawyer
PA: Elzufon Austin Reardon Tarlov & Mondell, P.A.
300 Delaware Ave Ste 1700
Wilmington DE 19801
302 428-3181

(G-5960)
EMERGING IMPACT GROUP CORP
16192 Coastal Hwy Apt 1 (19958-3608)
PHONE..................................404 625-1530
Robert Thomas Greenfield, *CEO*
Jonathan Lewis, *Prin*
Sandra Hart, *Prin*
EMP: 5
SALES (est): 104.73K **Privately Held**
SIC: 7389 Business Activities at Non-Commercial Site

(G-5961)
ENCLAVE DIGITAL DEVELOPMENT CO (PA)
16192 Coastal Hwy (19958-3608)
PHONE..................................203 807-0400
Rory John Diverall Semple, *Pr*
EMP: 7 **EST:** 2019
SALES (est): 50K
SALES (corp-wide): 50K **Privately Held**
SIC: 7372 7389 Application computer software; Business services, nec

(G-5962)
ENDLESSPENS LLC
16192 Coastal Hwy (19958-3608)
PHONE..................................813 550-5501
Avery K, *Managing Member*
EMP: 15 **EST:** 2018
SALES (est): 1.01MM **Privately Held**
Web: www.endlesspens.com
SIC: 5112 Pens and/or pencils

(G-5963)
ENVIROTECH ENVMTL CONSULTING
17605 Nassau Commons Blvd (19958-6284)
PHONE..................................302 684-5201
EMP: 6 **EST:** 2002
SQ FT: 1,500
SALES (est): 1.03MM **Privately Held**
Web: www.envirotechecinc.com
SIC: 8748 Environmental consultant

(G-5964)
ENVIRTECH ENVIROMENTAL CONSLTG
34634 Bay Crossing Blvd (19958-2737)
PHONE..................................302 645-6491
Todd Fritchman, *Pr*
Kelly Fritchman, *Sec*
EMP: 9 **EST:** 2003
SALES (est): 555.45K **Privately Held**
Web: www.envirotechecinc.com
SIC: 8748 Environmental consultant

(G-5965)
ENVISION HEALTHCARE CORP
Also Called: Seaside Endoscopy Pavillion
1451 Kings Hwy Ste 4a (19958)
PHONE..................................302 644-3852
Sandy Kennedy, *Brnch Mgr*
EMP: 10
Web: www.envisionhealth.com
SIC: 8062 General medical and surgical hospitals
HQ: Envision Healthcare Corporation
1a Burton Hills Blvd
Nashville TN 37215
615 665-1283

(G-5966)
EP SUPPLY CORP
16192 Coastal Hwy (19958-3608)
PHONE..................................909 969-5122
Brun Stephane, *Prin*
EMP: 6 **EST:** 2017
SALES (est): 120.53K **Privately Held**
SIC: 5063 Batteries

(G-5967)
EPD TECH LLC
16192 Coastal Hwy (19958-3608)
PHONE..................................415 508-7580
EMP: 5 **EST:** 2014
SALES (est): 46.16K **Privately Held**
SIC: 7371 Computer software development and applications

(G-5968)
EPIX INDUSTRIES INC
16192 Coastal Hwy (19958-3608)
PHONE..................................302 550-9007
EMP: 4 **EST:** 2020
SALES (est): 105.38K **Privately Held**
SIC: 3999 Manufacturing industries, nec

(G-5969)
ERIC KAFKA PSYCHOLOGIST
216 W 3rd St (19958-1328)
PHONE..................................302 644-8891
Eric Kafka, *Prin*
EMP: 6 **EST:** 2007
SALES (est): 89.74K **Privately Held**
SIC: 8049 Clinical psychologist

(G-5970)
ERIK M D STANCOFSKI
431 Savannah Rd (19958-1460)
PHONE..................................302 645-7050
E Stancofski, *Asstg*
EMP: 13 **EST:** 2016
SALES (est): 336.1K **Privately Held**
Web: www.beebehealthcare.org
SIC: 8062 General medical and surgical hospitals

(G-5971)
ERNEST SOFFRONOFF DR
36315 Tarpon Dr (19958-5056)
PHONE..................................302 827-2284
Ernest Soffronoff Md, *Owner*
EMP: 8 **EST:** 2018
SALES (est): 84.88K **Privately Held**
SIC: 8011 Offices and clinics of medical doctors

(G-5972)
EROS TECHNOLOGIES INC
16192 Coastal Hwy (19958-3608)
PHONE..................................650 242-9262
EMP: 31 **EST:** 2017
SALES (est): 714.5K **Privately Held**
Web: www.erostechnologies.com
SIC: 7379 Online services technology consultants

(G-5973)
ESCAPE REHOBOTH
510 Kings Hwy (19958-1422)
PHONE..................................302 645-7653
Diane Thornberg, *Prin*
EMP: 5 **EST:** 2017
SALES (est): 88.85K **Privately Held**
SIC: 7999 Amusement and recreation, nec

(G-5974)
ESCHBACH JR LEO H DO
1535 Savannah Rd (19958-1611)
PHONE..................................302 645-4700
Leo Eschbach Junior D.o.s., *Prin*
EMP: 10 **EST:** 2015
SALES (est): 137.75K **Privately Held**
SIC: 8011 Obstetrician

(G-5975)
ESPINO LLC
16192 Coastal Hwy (19958-3608)
PHONE..................................855 506-3862
EMP: 10 **EST:** 2020
SALES (est): 366.79K **Privately Held**
SIC: 8741 Financial management for business

(G-5976)
EV USA INC
16192 Coastal Hwy (19958-3608)
PHONE..................................973 674-1326
Richard Cobbinah, *Pr*
EMP: 2
SALES (est): 92.41K **Privately Held**
SIC: 3694 7371 Automotive electrical equipment, nec; Computer software development and applications

(G-5977)
EVAGORAS G ECONOMIDES
16704 Kings Hwy (19958-4929)
PHONE..................................302 645-1233
Rosa R Alberto, *Prin*
EMP: 6 **EST:** 2010
SALES (est): 57.88K **Privately Held**
SIC: 8011 Offices and clinics of medical doctors

(G-5978)
EVERLIFT WIND TECHNOLOGY
Also Called: Everlift
31798 Carneros Ave (19958-2523)
PHONE..................................240 683-9787
EMP: 4 **EST:** 2011
SALES (est): 125.83K **Privately Held**
SIC: 3511 Turbines and turbine generator sets

(G-5979)
EVON ELECTRIC ENTERPRISE INC
16192 Coastal Hwy (19958-3608)
PHONE..................................909 997-9599
Charles Cox, *CEO*
James Bryan, *CFO*
EMP: 11 **EST:** 2020
SALES (est): 444.7K **Privately Held**
SIC: 3694 Battery charging generators, automobile and aircraft

(G-5980)
EXCEL THROUGH ACTION
17021 Old Orchard Rd # 1 (19958-4832)
PHONE..................................302 569-9564
EMP: 6 **EST:** 2016
SALES (est): 85.9K **Privately Held**
SIC: 8049 Physical therapist

(G-5981)
EXPOTRADE INC
Also Called: Milestone
16192 Coastal Hwy (19958-3608)
PHONE..................................818 212-8905
Lydmila Korobkin, *CEO*
Volodymyr Chobotarov, *Sec*
EMP: 5 **EST:** 2020
SALES (est): 506.87K **Privately Held**
Web: www.milestonetl.com
SIC: 4731 Transportation agents and brokers

(G-5982)
F AND S COMMERCIAL CLEANING
32789 Ocean Reach Dr (19958-4663)
PHONE..................................302 250-1736
EMP: 8 **EST:** 2012
SALES (est): 241.66K **Privately Held**
SIC: 7699 Cleaning services

(G-5983)
F S PROPERTY MANAGEMENT
2500 Savannah West Sq (19958-9495)
PHONE..................................302 644-4403
Pat Bachelor, *Pr*
EMP: 5 **EST:** 2009
SALES (est): 172.95K **Privately Held**
SIC: 8741 Management services

(G-5984)
FACTORY SPORTS
17543 Nassau Commons Blvd (19958-6284)
PHONE..................................302 313-4186
EMP: 6 **EST:** 2016
SALES (est): 178.81K **Privately Held**
Web: www.factoryhoops.com
SIC: 7997 Membership sports and recreation clubs

(G-5985)
FAITH FMLY FRIENDS HOLDG LLC
16192 Coastal Hwy (19958-3608)
PHONE..................................202 256-4524
EMP: 10
SIC: 6719 Holding companies, nec

(G-5986)
FAMILY PRACTICE CENTER
7 Dunes Ter (19958-3128)
PHONE..................................302 645-2833
Connie Groll, *Asstg*
EMP: 10 **EST:** 2005
SALES (est): 166.99K **Privately Held**
Web: www.familypracticecenter.us
SIC: 8011 General and family practice, physician/surgeon

GEOGRAPHIC SECTION
Lewes - Sussex County (G-6017)

(G-5987)
FARKAS CONCRETE
31632 Sarah Rd (19958-2045)
PHONE..................302 249-9172
Jeremy Farkas, *Prin*
EMP: 5 **EST:** 2010
SALES (est): 136.34K **Privately Held**
SIC: 1771 Concrete work

(G-5988)
FARMA QUIMICA LLC
16192 Coastal Hwy (19958-3608)
PHONE..................703 537-9789
EMP: 3 **EST:** 2008
SALES (est): 257.78K **Privately Held**
SIC: 2835 Diagnostic substances

(G-5989)
FARPATH FOUNDATION
800 Bay Ave (19958-1005)
PHONE..................302 645-8328
Clifford Diver, *Dir*
EMP: 6 **EST:** 2005
SALES (est): 82.08K **Privately Held**
SIC: 8641 Civic and social associations

(G-5990)
FARR FAMILY FOUNDATION INC
16192 Coastal Hwy (19958-3608)
PHONE..................540 349-4103
EMP: 5 **EST:** 2017
SALES (est): 372.14K **Privately Held**
SIC: 8641 Civic and social associations

(G-5991)
FAUST SHEET METAL WORKS INC
1636 Savannah Rd Ste A (19958-1657)
P.O. Box 181 (19958-0181)
PHONE..................302 645-9509
Mike Faust, *Pr*
EMP: 2 **EST:** 1930
SQ FT: 2,400
SALES (est): 214.7K **Privately Held**
Web: www.faustsheetmetal.com
SIC: 3444 Metal ventilating equipment

(G-5992)
FBINAA
7 Anser Ln (19958-8956)
P.O. Box 350 (19958-0350)
PHONE..................302 344-7700
EMP: 7 **EST:** 2018
SALES (est): 198.92K **Privately Held**
Web: www.fbinaa.org
SIC: 8641 Civic and social associations

(G-5993)
FEMMEPAL CORPORATION
Also Called: Underground
16192 Coastal Hwy (19958-3608)
PHONE..................888 406-0804
Andrew Linney, *CEO*
Rebecca Knuth, *
EMP: 5 **EST:** 2012
SALES (est): 200.17K **Privately Held**
SIC: 8742 Management consulting services

(G-5994)
FERGUSON ENTERPRISES LLC
Also Called: Ferguson Enterprises 784
32325 Lewes Georgetown Hwy
(19958-1676)
PHONE..................302 732-0940
EMP: 5
SALES (corp-wide): 2.67MM **Privately Held**
Web: www.ferguson.com
SIC: 5074 Plumbing fittings and supplies
HQ: Ferguson Enterprises, Llc
751 Lakefront Cmns
Newport News VA 23606
757 969-4011

(G-5995)
FIORANO SOFTWARE INC
16192 Coastal Hwy (19958-3608)
PHONE..................650 326-1136
Atul Saini, *CEO*
Anjali Saini, *
Annie D.o.s., *Off Mgr*
◆ **EMP:** 85 **EST:** 1993
SALES (est): 2.97MM **Privately Held**
Web: www.fiorano.com
SIC: 7372 7371 Prepackaged software; Custom computer programming services

(G-5996)
FIRST ATLANTIC MRTG SVCS LLC
Also Called: First Atlantic Mortgage Svcs
16678 Kings Hwy Ste 2 (19958-4927)
PHONE..................302 841-8435
EMP: 6 **EST:** 1996
SALES (est): 506.99K **Privately Held**
SIC: 6163 Mortgage brokers arranging for loans, using money of others

(G-5997)
FIRST SHIPMENT INC ✪
16192 Coastal Hwy (19958-3608)
PHONE..................206 747-1237
Shashank Pant, *CEO*
EMP: 8 **EST:** 2022
SALES (est): 306.16K **Privately Held**
SIC: 7389 Business Activities at Non-Commercial Site

(G-5998)
FIRST STATE DISPOSAL
15 Bridle Ridge Cir (19958-8912)
PHONE..................302 644-3885
Tom Grogas, *Owner*
EMP: 6 **EST:** 2007
SALES (est): 162.22K **Privately Held**
SIC: 4953 Refuse collection and disposal services

(G-5999)
FIRST STATE TROLLEY CO LLC
32099 Conleys Chapel Rd (19958-6057)
PHONE..................302 500-0526
Tyler Donovan, *Prin*
EMP: 5 **EST:** 2018
SALES (est): 97.72K **Privately Held**
Web: www.firststatetrolley.com
SIC: 4119 Limousine rental, with driver

(G-6000)
FIRSTCHOICE GROUP AMERICA LLC
16192 Coastal Hwy (19958-3608)
PHONE..................425 242-8626
Suresh Jagtiani, *Managing Member*
EMP: 6
Web: www.firstchoiceamerica.net
SIC: 5084 Industrial machinery and equipment
PA: Firstchoice Group America Llc
169 Lewfield Cir Ste 169 # 169
Winter Park FL 32792

(G-6001)
FIRSTCOLLECT INC
12000 Old Vine Blvd (19958-1700)
P.O. Box 102 (19958-0102)
PHONE..................302 644-6804
Tracy M Hynes, *Prin*
EMP: 8 **EST:** 2009
SALES (est): 731.5K **Privately Held**
Web: www.firstcollect.com
SIC: 7322 Collection agency, except real estate

(G-6002)
FIVE STAR HOME DELIVERY LLC
16192 Coastal Hwy (19958-3608)
PHONE..................302 213-3535
EMP: 10 **EST:** 2019
SALES (est): 300K **Privately Held**
Web: www.fivestarhomefoods.com
SIC: 8742 Restaurant and food services consultants

(G-6003)
FLAGPOLE CORP
16192 Coastal Hwy (19958-3608)
PHONE..................302 261-5170
EMP: 7
SALES (est): 68.89K **Privately Held**
Web: www.flagpolesetc.com
SIC: 7371 Computer software development and applications

(G-6004)
FLEX WORLD FITNESS LLC
6 Nicole Way (19958-9744)
PHONE..................302 856-7771
Heidi Helou, *Prin*
EMP: 7 **EST:** 2010
SALES (est): 84.2K **Privately Held**
Web: www.flexworldfitness.com
SIC: 7991 Health club

(G-6005)
FLY BY JING INC
16192 Coastal Hwy (19958-3608)
PHONE..................646 875-2465
Jing Gao, *Prin*
EMP: 10 **EST:** 2018
SALES (est): 542.86K **Privately Held**
Web: www.flybyjing.com
SIC: 2099 Food preparations, nec

(G-6006)
FLYINGPARTS INTERNATIONAL INC
Also Called: Aroma
16192 Coastal Hwy (19958-3608)
PHONE..................610 400-1110
Paul Prior, *Prin*
EMP: 2 **EST:** 2017
SALES (est): 57.88K **Privately Held**
Web: www.flying-parts.com
SIC: 3599 Machine shop, jobbing and repair

(G-6007)
FME LIGHTING LLC
34005 Wescoats Rd Unit A2 (19958-4928)
P.O. Box 488 (19707-0488)
PHONE..................877 234-8460
Patrick Mckeefery, *Managing Member*
EMP: 2 **EST:** 2016
SALES (est): 1.5MM **Privately Held**
Web: www.fmelighting.com
SIC: 3645 Residential lighting fixtures

(G-6008)
FOCUS BEHAVIORAL HEALTH
33712 Wescoats Rd Unit 4 (19958-4926)
PHONE..................302 827-4206
Ranga Ram Md, *Prin*
EMP: 8 **EST:** 2016
SALES (est): 339.72K **Privately Held**
SIC: 8049 Speech specialist

(G-6009)
FOOT LIGHT PRODUCTION INC
516 Kings Hwy (19958-1456)
PHONE..................302 645-7220
John Warrener, *Pr*
EMP: 10 **EST:** 1998
SALES (est): 151.83K **Privately Held**
SIC: 7832 Motion picture theaters, except drive-in

(G-6010)
FRANCHISE CO LLC USA
16192 Coastal Hwy (19958-3608)
PHONE..................868 280-5272
Lee Romany, *Managing Member*
EMP: 5
SALES (est): 76.34K **Privately Held**
SIC: 6531 Real estate leasing and rentals

(G-6011)
FREE PDF TECHNOLOGIES INC ✪
16192 Coastal Hwy (19958-3608)
PHONE..................872 204-6733
Yu Xiao, *CEO*
EMP: 16 **EST:** 2023
SALES (est): 543.62K **Privately Held**
SIC: 7389 Business services, nec

(G-6012)
FREE PROPERTIES
31443 Falmouth Way (19958-5836)
PHONE..................914 474-1980
Jim Farr, *Prin*
EMP: 5 **EST:** 2017
SALES (est): 93.22K **Privately Held**
Web: www.farr-engineering.com
SIC: 6512 Nonresidential building operators

(G-6013)
FREE SPIRITED FOUNDATION
23951 Creek Ln (19958-3340)
PHONE..................614 946-7358
Athena Allread, *Prin*
EMP: 6 **EST:** 2016
SALES (est): 49.17K **Privately Held**
SIC: 8641 Civic and social associations

(G-6014)
FREEDOM BOAT CLUB DELAWARE
909 Pilottown Rd (19958-1274)
PHONE..................302 219-3549
EMP: 7 **EST:** 2019
SALES (est): 118.72K **Privately Held**
SIC: 4493 Marinas

(G-6015)
FRESH INDUSTRIES LTD
Also Called: Juicefresh
18388 Coastal Hwy Unit 10 (19958-4204)
PHONE..................205 737-3747
David Harrison, *Prin*
EMP: 6 **EST:** 2012
SALES (est): 495.36K **Privately Held**
Web: www.juicefresh.net
SIC: 2033 Vegetable juices: fresh

(G-6016)
FRESH JUICE PARTNERS LLC
Also Called: Wellness Connections
18388 Coastal Hwy Unit 10 (19958-4204)
PHONE..................302 364-0909
EMP: 6 **EST:** 2017
SALES (est): 238.01K **Privately Held**
Web: www.juicefresh.net
SIC: 5812 7991 5499 Eating places; Physical fitness facilities; Vitamin food stores

(G-6017)
FRINGE HAIR STUDIO
1509 Savannah Rd (19958-1611)
PHONE..................302 313-5213
Allfather Marlyn, *Prin*
EMP: 5 **EST:** 2013
SALES (est): 67.09K **Privately Held**
SIC: 7231 Hairdressers

Lewes - Sussex County (G-6018) GEOGRAPHIC SECTION

(G-6018)
FT MILES HISTORIC SITE
15099 Cape Henlopen Dr (19958-3153)
PHONE..................302 644-5007
John Marta, *Owner*
EMP: 8 **EST:** 2013
SALES (est): 62.77K **Privately Held**
Web: www.fortmiles.org
SIC: 8412 Museum

(G-6019)
FTL TECHNOLOGIES CORPORATION
Also Called: Silis Security Group
16192 Coastal Hwy (19958-3608)
PHONE..................703 634-6910
Robert Bass, *Ex Dir*
Alexandra Maria Gomez-gamboa, *Admn*
EMP: 50 **EST:** 2019
SALES (est): 1.51MM **Privately Held**
SIC: 7371 7374 7375 7372 Custom computer programming services; Data processing and preparation; Information retrieval services; Prepackaged software

(G-6020)
FUINRE INC
16192 Coastal Hwy (19958-3608)
PHONE..................402 480-6465
Ha Nguyen Van, *CEO*
EMP: 20 **EST:** 2021
SALES (est): 1.04MM **Privately Held**
SIC: 6289 Financial reporting

(G-6021)
FULTON BANK NATIONAL ASSN
Also Called: Fulton Financial Advisors
34346 Carpenters Way (19958-4910)
PHONE..................302 644-4900
Adrianne Morre, *Brnch Mgr*
EMP: 5
SALES (corp-wide): 1.09B **Publicly Held**
Web: www.fultonbank.com
SIC: 6022 State commercial banks
HQ: Fulton Bank, National Association
1 Penn Sq
Lancaster PA 17602
717 581-3166

(G-6022)
FUN FIT VIBE LLC
1604 Savannah Rd Unit A (19958-1664)
PHONE..................302 249-8000
Gregory Mervine, *Prin*
EMP: 5 **EST:** 2012
SALES (est): 93.33K **Privately Held**
Web: www.funfitvibe.com
SIC: 7991 Physical fitness facilities

(G-6023)
FUND FOR THE WALKING WOUNDED
21338 N Acorn Way (19958-4545)
PHONE..................302 947-9056
Ralph Patterson, *Prin*
EMP: 5 **EST:** 2015
SALES (est): 61.12K **Privately Held**
Web: www.walkingwounded.org
SIC: 8399 Advocacy group

(G-6024)
FUTURE CMPUS - TECH INNVTION L
16192 Coastal Hwy (19958-3608)
PHONE..................737 217-0321
Adriano Martins, *Pr*
EMP: 12
SALES (est): 251.15K **Privately Held**
SIC: 7371 Custom computer programming services

(G-6025)
G M CONSTRUCTION LLC
21618 W Conley Cir (19958-6020)
PHONE..................302 462-5871
Buck Mclamb, *Owner*
EMP: 8 **EST:** 2005
SALES (est): 110.22K **Privately Held**
Web: www.buildingdelmarva.com
SIC: 1799 Special trade contractors, nec

(G-6026)
GAMEFORT LLC
16192 Coastal Hwy (19958-3608)
PHONE..................302 645-7400
EMP: 30
SALES (est): 1.02MM **Privately Held**
SIC: 4832 7371 Sports; Computer software development and applications

(G-6027)
GARRISON CUSTOM HOMES
19413 Jingle Shell Way Unit 5 (19958-6307)
PHONE..................302 644-4008
Jeffrey M Garrison, *Owner*
EMP: 8 **EST:** 2004
SALES (est): 1.4MM **Privately Held**
Web: www.garrisonhomes.com
SIC: 1521 New construction, single-family houses

(G-6028)
GBS BACKUP LLC
16192 Coastal Hwy (19958-3608)
PHONE..................302 907-9099
EMP: 7 **EST:** 2017
SALES (est): 46.16K **Privately Held**
Web: www.gbsbackup.com
SIC: 7371 Computer software systems analysis and design, custom

(G-6029)
GENESIS CLEANERS
17601 Coastal Hwy (19958-6217)
PHONE..................302 827-2095
Sunny Seo, *Owner*
EMP: 6 **EST:** 2015
SALES (est): 42.79K **Privately Held**
SIC: 7699 Cleaning services

(G-6030)
GEORGE W PLUMMER & SON INC
18370 Coastal Hwy (19958-4772)
PHONE..................302 645-9531
George Plummer Iii, *Pr*
Greg E Plummer, *Sec*
▲ **EMP:** 7 **EST:** 1947
SQ FT: 8,000
SALES (est): 930.56K **Privately Held**
Web: www.georgeplummerandson.com
SIC: 7692 Welding repair

(G-6031)
GERALDINE M VOTA
33712 Wescoats Rd Unit 4 (19958-4926)
PHONE..................302 762-2283
Geraldine M Vota Lacmh, *Owner*
EMP: 6 **EST:** 2018
SALES (est): 85.91K **Privately Held**
SIC: 8322 Individual and family services

(G-6032)
GET TAKEOUT LLC
Also Called: Gettakeout.com
16192 Coastal Hwy (19958-3608)
P.O. Box 25653 (97298-0653)
PHONE..................800 785-6218
Frank Halpin, *Mng Pt*
EMP: 3 **EST:** 2008
SALES (est): 208.35K **Privately Held**
SIC: 7372 7389 Business oriented computer software; Business services, nec

(G-6033)
GETBIT TECHNOLOGIES INC ✪
Also Called: Getbit.money
16192 Coastal Hwy (19958-3608)
PHONE..................425 647-3121
Abhay Agarwal, *CEO*
EMP: 7 **EST:** 2022
SALES (est): 264.9K **Privately Held**
SIC: 7371 Custom computer programming services

(G-6034)
GETBLEND INC
16192 Coastal Hwy (19958-3608)
PHONE..................800 720-3722
Lior Libman, *Pr*
EMP: 5 **EST:** 2014
SALES (est): 618.12K **Privately Held**
Web: www.getblend.com
SIC: 7389 Translation services
PA: Getblend Ltd
13 Shontzino
Tel Aviv-Jaffa 67216

(G-6035)
GIGKLOUD INC
16192 Coastal Hwy (19958-3608)
PHONE..................301 375-5008
D William Zero, *CEO*
Brett Nelson, *OK Vice President*
Bradley Sackmann, *OF STRATEGIC PARTNERSHIPS*
Brandon Robinson, *OF CLIENT ACQUISITIONS*
Jaime Wong Luna, *OF LATINO USER ACQUISITIONS*
EMP: 10 **EST:** 2018
SALES (est): 571.57K **Privately Held**
Web: www.gigkloud.com
SIC: 7371 Computer software development and applications

(G-6036)
GL FLUHARTY JR CONCRETE LLC
3 Felicia Ln (19958-8922)
PHONE..................302 745-1290
Krista Fluharty, *Prin*
EMP: 5 **EST:** 2018
SALES (est): 133.52K **Privately Held**
SIC: 1771 Concrete work

(G-6037)
GLEN PLAYA INC
16192 Coastal Hwy (19958-3608)
PHONE..................302 703-7512
Heather Hargett, *CEO*
EMP: 8 **EST:** 2010
SALES (est): 476.46K **Privately Held**
Web: www.lanamarkscantpayherbills.com
SIC: 8741 Financial management for business

(G-6038)
GLOBAL BRIDGING CORP
16192 Coastal Hwy (19958-3608)
PHONE..................202 318-7119
EMP: 7 **EST:** 2019
SALES (est): 68.89K **Privately Held**
Web: www.handelnine.com
SIC: 8748 7379 Telecommunications consultant; Online services technology consultants

(G-6039)
GLOBAL MARINE NETWORKS LLC
205 E Savannah Rd (19958-1128)
PHONE..................215 327-2814
EMP: 5 **EST:** 2019
SALES (est): 76.58K **Privately Held**
Web: www.pivotel.com
SIC: 4813 Internet connectivity services

(G-6040)
GMDH INC
16192 Coastal Hwy (19958-3608)
PHONE..................347 470-4634
EMP: 7 **EST:** 2020
SALES (est): 264.76K **Privately Held**
Web: www.gmdhsoftware.com
SIC: 7371 Computer software development

(G-6041)
GMETRI INC
16192 Coastal Hwy (19958-3608)
PHONE..................704 260-6116
Utsav Mathur, *CEO*
EMP: 12 **EST:** 2019
SALES (est): 251.15K **Privately Held**
Web: www.gmetri.com
SIC: 7371 Software programming applications

(G-6042)
GNZ LLC (HQ)
Also Called: Renewable energies
16192 Coastal Hwy (19958-3608)
PHONE..................302 499-2024
EMP: 183 **EST:** 2019
SALES (est): 272.71MM
SALES (corp-wide): 391.62MM **Privately Held**
Web: www.gnzenergy.com
SIC: 1731 Energy management controls
PA: Gcg Capital Llc
16192 Coastal Hwy
Lewes DE 19958
302 703-7610

(G-6043)
GO UNDERGROUND LLC
16192 Coastal Hwy (19958-3608)
PHONE..................732 740-1127
EMP: 8 **EST:** 2008
SALES (est): 411.76K **Privately Held**
SIC: 4789 Transportation services, nec

(G-6044)
GO-GIVERS LLC
16192 Coastal Hwy (19958-3608)
PHONE..................302 703-9293
EMP: 5
SALES (est): 137.74K **Privately Held**
SIC: 8743 Sales promotion

(G-6045)
GOLDEN COASTAL REALTY
33815 Clay Rd Ste 5 (19958-6297)
PHONE..................302 360-0226
Carol Golden, *Owner*
EMP: 10 **EST:** 2005
SALES (est): 542.83K **Privately Held**
Web: www.goldencoastalrealty.com
SIC: 6531 Real estate agent, residential

(G-6046)
GOLDEN INC ✪
16192 Coastal Hwy (19958-3608)
PHONE..................408 384-9136
Jalen Wall, *Prin*
EMP: 10 **EST:** 2022
SALES (est): 348.32K **Privately Held**
SIC: 7371 7372 Computer software development; Prepackaged software

GEOGRAPHIC SECTION   Lewes - Sussex County (G-6079)

(G-6047)
GOLDEN TV INC
16192 Coastal Hwy (19958-3608)
PHONE.....................213 260-0070
Takashi Cheng, *CEO*
EMP: 4
SALES (est): 73.93K **Privately Held**
SIC: 7372 Application computer software

(G-6048)
GOOD GOOD NTURAL SWEETNESS LLC
16192 Coastal Hwy (19958-3608)
PHONE.....................302 364-0015
▲ **EMP:** 9 **EST:** 2018
SALES (est): 2.21MM **Privately Held**
SIC: 5149 Health foods

(G-6049)
GOVPLUS LLC
Also Called: GOVPLUS LLC
34161 Citizen Dr (19958-4722)
PHONE.....................302 360-6101
Erin Baker, *Brnch Mgr*
EMP: 10
SALES (corp-wide): 9.07B **Publicly Held**
Web: www.govplus.com
SIC: 6022 State commercial banks
HQ: Citizens Bank, National Association
   1 Citizens Plz
   Providence RI 02903

(G-6050)
GR DISPATCH INC
16192 Coastal Hwy (19958-3608)
PHONE.....................888 985-3440
Denis Zamylin, *Managing Member*
EMP: 6
SALES (est): 312.15K **Privately Held**
SIC: 7371 Software programming applications

(G-6051)
GRACEBLOOD LLC
417 E Cape Shores Dr (19958-3109)
PHONE.....................302 703-2524
Karen A Blood, *Prin*
EMP: 19 **EST:** 2016
SALES (est): 194.4K **Privately Held**
SIC: 7379 Computer related consulting services

(G-6052)
GRASSROTS DATA INNOVATIONS INC
16192 Coastal Hwy (19958-3608)
PHONE.....................267 664-9905
Nicholas Lagnese, *CEO*
EMP: 2 **EST:** 2020
SALES (est): 130.82K **Privately Held**
SIC: 7372 Educational computer software

(G-6053)
GRAULICH BUILDERS
34697 Jiffy Way (19958-4932)
PHONE.....................302 313-4882
EMP: 8 **EST:** 2017
SALES (est): 330.34K **Privately Held**
Web: www.graulichbuilders.com
SIC: 1521 New construction, single-family houses

(G-6054)
GRAVITY-TECHINC LLC
16192 Coastal Hwy (19958-3608)
PHONE.....................346 258-1597
EMP: 19 **EST:** 2021
SALES (est): 71.79K **Privately Held**
SIC: 8742 Management consulting services

(G-6055)
GREAT STEMPORIUM
18388 Coastal Hwy Unit 10 (19958-4204)
PHONE.....................302 313-5139
EMP: 5 **EST:** 2019
SALES (est): 47.16K **Privately Held**
Web: www.greatstem.com
SIC: 7999 Amusement and recreation, nec

(G-6056)
GREATER LEWES COMMUNITY VLG
16686 Kings Hwy # B (19958-4904)
PHONE.....................302 703-2568
EMP: 5 **EST:** 2017
SALES (est): 138.82K **Privately Held**
Web: www.greaterlewescommunityvillage.org
SIC: 8322 Senior citizens' center or association

(G-6057)
GREEN ACRES FARM INC
18186 Dairy Farm Rd (19958-4505)
PHONE.....................302 645-8652
Walter C Hopkins, *Senior President*
Walter C Hopkins Senior, *Pr*
Walter C Hopkins Junior, *Sec*
EMP: 17 **EST:** 1946
SALES (est): 999.1K **Privately Held**
Web: www.hopkinsfarmcreamery.com
SIC: 0191 General farms, primarily crop

(G-6058)
GREEN ROOTS LLC
16192 Coastal Hwy (19958-3608)
PHONE.....................516 643-2621
EMP: 5 **EST:** 2019
SALES (est): 100K **Privately Held**
SIC: 5149 Organic and diet food

(G-6059)
GREENLEAF SERVICES INC
20393 John J Williams Hwy (19958-4305)
PHONE.....................302 836-9050
Joseph B Winemiller, *Pr*
EMP: 7 **EST:** 1992
SALES (est): 973.07K **Privately Held**
Web: www.greenleafservicesinc.net
SIC: 0782 Landscape contractors

(G-6060)
GREP BIOGAS I LLC
16192 Coastal Hwy (19958-3608)
PHONE.....................212 390-8110
EMP: 5 **EST:** 2020
SALES (est): 206.05K **Privately Held**
SIC: 2813 Industrial gases

(G-6061)
GREYSTONE BED & BREAKFA
303 Market St (19958-1305)
PHONE.....................302 645-0699
William Stevenson, *Prin*
EMP: 14 **EST:** 2006
SALES (est): 50.63K **Privately Held**
SIC: 7011 Bed and breakfast inn

(G-6062)
GRISWOLD HOME CARE
18335 Coastal Hwy Ste A (19958-2738)
PHONE.....................302 703-0130
EMP: 9 **EST:** 2020
SALES (est): 398.52K **Privately Held**
Web: www.griswoldhomecare.com
SIC: 8082 Home health care services

(G-6063)
GRIZZLYS LANDSCAPE SUP & SVCS
20144 John J Williams Hwy (19958-4339)
PHONE.....................302 644-0654

Richard Pack, *Prin*
EMP: 8 **EST:** 2005
SALES (est): 352.75K **Privately Held**
Web: www.grizzlycompost.com
SIC: 0782 Landscape contractors

(G-6064)
GRIZZLYS LANDSCAPE SUPL & SVC
18412 The Narrow Rd (19958-3955)
P.O. Box 203 (19958-0203)
PHONE.....................302 644-0654
EMP: 7 **EST:** 2018
SALES (est): 105.56K **Privately Held**
Web: www.grizzlycompost.com
SIC: 0781 Landscape services

(G-6065)
GRLLA GMNG LLC
16192 Coastal Hwy (19958-3608)
PHONE.....................302 291-2075
J Weiss, *Pr*
EMP: 5
SALES (est): 235.33K **Privately Held**
SIC: 7371 Computer software development and applications

(G-6066)
GRO-CONNECTCOM INC
Also Called: AG Wholesale Marketplace
16192 Coastal Hwy (19958-3608)
PHONE.....................347 918-7437
Lee Seward, *CEO*
EMP: 7 **EST:** 2019
SALES (est): 950K **Privately Held**
SIC: 5734 0139 0182 5193 Software, business and non-game; Food crops; Food crops grown under cover; Nursery stock

(G-6067)
GUARDIAN PROPERTY MGT LLC
17298 Coastal Hwy Unit 1 (19958-6226)
PHONE.....................302 227-7878
EMP: 10 **EST:** 2004
SALES (est): 978.32K **Privately Held**
SIC: 6531 Real estate managers

(G-6068)
GULL HOUSE ADULT ACTIVITY
34382 Carpenters Way Ste 1 (19958-4919)
PHONE.....................302 226-2160
Kay Edman, *Ex Dir*
Kathy Schlitter, *Dir*
EMP: 7 **EST:** 1987
SALES (est): 244.66K **Privately Held**
SIC: 8322 Adult day care center

(G-6069)
HAGUE SURFBOARDS
102 Gosling Creek Rd (19958-9592)
PHONE.....................302 745-9336
EMP: 4 **EST:** 2008
SALES (est): 53.23K **Privately Held**
SIC: 3949 Surfboards

(G-6070)
HALE J ERIC MD
1305 Savannah Rd (19958-1501)
PHONE.....................302 644-2064
J Hale, *Ofcr*
EMP: 13 **EST:** 2017
SALES (est): 607.62K **Privately Held**
Web: www.beebehealthcare.org
SIC: 8062 General medical and surgical hospitals

(G-6071)
HALLEY LLC
16192 Coastal Hwy (19958-3608)
PHONE.....................650 628-8501
Bruno Ruyu, *Managing Member*

EMP: 2
SALES (est): 87.4K **Privately Held**
SIC: 7372 Application computer software

(G-6072)
HALLIGAN INC
16192 Coastal Hwy (19958-3608)
PHONE.....................314 488-9400
Alexander Montgomery, *Pr*
Alexander Krill, *Treas*
EMP: 2 **EST:** 2016
SALES (est): 104.98K **Privately Held**
SIC: 7372 Application computer software

(G-6073)
HANBRUN LLC
16192 Coastal Hwy (19958-3608)
PHONE.....................929 302-6393
EMP: 5 **EST:** 2019
SALES (est): 104.39K **Privately Held**
SIC: 7389

(G-6074)
HANDYMAN HOUSECALLS INC
34417 Skyler Dr (19958-5685)
PHONE.....................302 245-3816
Charles Wisely, *Prin*
EMP: 5 **EST:** 2016
SALES (est): 234.25K **Privately Held**
SIC: 1521 Single-family housing construction

(G-6075)
HAP LLC
16192 Coastal Hwy (19958-3608)
PHONE.....................302 645-7400
Eyal Ramakrishnan, *Managing Member*
EMP: 5 **EST:** 2014
SALES (est): 209.38K **Privately Held**
SIC: 7374 Computer processing services

(G-6076)
HARBOR HLTHCARE RHBLTATION CTR
301 Ocean View Blvd (19958-1270)
PHONE.....................302 645-4664
Ronald Schafer, *Pr*
Stephen Silver, *
EMP: 300 **EST:** 1988
SQ FT: 65,000
SALES (est): 14.65MM **Privately Held**
Web: www.harbor.care
SIC: 8051 Convalescent home with continuous nursing care

(G-6077)
HARBOUR TOWNE ASSOCIATES LP
34232 Woods Edge Dr Unit 313
(19958-4912)
PHONE.....................302 645-1003
Linda Chantler, *Prin*
EMP: 5 **EST:** 2005
SALES (est): 177.49K **Privately Held**
SIC: 6513 Apartment building operators

(G-6078)
HARLEM WATCH COMPANY LLC
16192 Coastal Hwy (19958-3608)
PHONE.....................646 354-7644
Dwight Richards, *Managing Member*
EMP: 2 **EST:** 2020
SALES (est): 120K **Privately Held**
SIC: 3915 Jewel preparing: instruments, tools, watches, and jewelry

(G-6079)
HAROLD DUTTON JR
Also Called: Harold Dutton Builder
14 Schaffer Ln (19958-9030)
PHONE.....................302 644-2992
Harold Dutton Junior, *Prin*

Lewes - Sussex County (G-6080)

EMP: 5 EST: 2009
SALES (est): 109.32K **Privately Held**
SIC: **1521** New construction, single-family houses

(G-6080)
HART TO HEART AMBULANCE
32413 Lewes Georgetown Hwy (19958-1646)
PHONE.................................302 697-9395
Beth Thompson, Mgr
EMP: 6 EST: 2016
SALES (est): 77.76K **Privately Held**
Web: www.harttohearttransportation.com
SIC: **4119** Ambulance service

(G-6081)
HARVARD BUSINESS SERVICES INC (PA)
Also Called: Hbs
16192 Coastal Hwy (19958-3608)
PHONE.................................302 645-7400
Richard Bell, CEO
Michael Bell, *
EMP: 29 EST: 1981
SQ FT: 8,500
SALES (est): 12.71MM
SALES (corp-wide): 12.71MM **Privately Held**
Web: www.delawareinc.com
SIC: **8111** Specialized legal services

(G-6082)
HASHOUT TECHNOLOGIES INC
16192 Coastal Hwy (19958-3608)
PHONE.................................703 622-1689
EMP: 5 EST: 2018
SALES (est): 63.63K **Privately Held**
SIC: **7389** Business services, nec

(G-6083)
HAZZARD AUTO REPAIRS INC
1141 Savannah Rd (19958-1524)
PHONE.................................302 645-4543
Michael Hazzard, Pr
EMP: 6 EST: 1989
SALES (est): 930.82K **Privately Held**
Web: www.hazzardautorepair.com
SIC: **7538** 7549 Engine rebuilding: automotive; Towing service, automotive

(G-6084)
HAZZARD ELECTRICAL CONTRS INC
Also Called: Hazzard Electric
111 American Legion Rd (19958-1159)
P.O. Box 252 (19958-0252)
PHONE.................................302 645-8457
David Hazzard, Pr
John Hazzard, VP
EMP: 8 EST: 1946
SQ FT: 3,000
SALES (est): 980.78K **Privately Held**
Web: www.hazzardelectric.com
SIC: **1731** General electrical contractor

(G-6085)
HCSG HARBOR HC HARBO44
301 Ocean View Blvd (19958-1269)
PHONE.................................302 645-4664
EMP: 6 EST: 2013
SALES (est): 145.72K **Privately Held**
SIC: **8099** Health and allied services, nec

(G-6086)
HEART TO HAND DAYCARE LLC
16192 Coastal Hwy (19958-3608)
PHONE.................................202 256-4524
EMP: 6
SALES (est): 126.48K **Privately Held**
SIC: **8351** Child day care services

(G-6087)
HELICAL SOFTWARE CORP
16192 Coastal Hwy (19958-3608)
PHONE.................................323 544-5348
Robin Young, CEO
EMP: 2
SALES (est): 64.53K **Privately Held**
SIC: **7372** 7374 Prepackaged software; Data processing and preparation

(G-6088)
HENLOPEN DESIGN LLC
16192 Coastal Hwy (19958-3608)
PHONE.................................302 265-4330
EMP: 2 EST: 2011
SALES (est): 87.29K **Privately Held**
SIC: **2721** Periodicals

(G-6089)
HENLOPEN HOMES INC
17644 Coastal Hwy (19958-6257)
P.O. Box 476 (19947-0476)
PHONE.................................302 684-0860
Tim Parker, Pr
EMP: 5 EST: 2005
SALES (est): 458.11K **Privately Held**
Web: www.henlopenhomes.com
SIC: **1521** 2452 New construction, single-family houses; Modular homes, prefabricated, wood

(G-6090)
HENLOPEN MUSIC THERAPY SE
31618 Holly Ct (19958-2051)
PHONE.................................302 593-7784
EMP: 5 EST: 2018
SALES (est): 73.36K **Privately Held**
SIC: **8093** Rehabilitation center, outpatient treatment

(G-6091)
HENLOPEN OVERHEAD DOOR
31547 N Conley Cir (19958-6016)
PHONE.................................302 228-0561
Jim Bachman, Prin
EMP: 8 EST: 2016
SALES (est): 102.16K **Privately Held**
Web: www.henlopenoverheaddoor.com
SIC: **1751** Window and door installation and erection

(G-6092)
HERRING CREEK BUILDERS INC
23130 Prince George Dr (19958-5241)
PHONE.................................302 684-3015
Alan Steele, Pr
Allen Steel, Pr
EMP: 8 EST: 1979
SALES (est): 991.75K **Privately Held**
Web: www.herringcreekbuilders.com
SIC: **1521** New construction, single-family houses

(G-6093)
HIGH5 GLOBAL CORPORATION (PA) ✪
16192 Coastal Hwy (19958-3608)
PHONE.................................732 248-1900
Bipin Thakur, Pr
EMP: 15 EST: 2023
SALES (est): 505.06K
SALES (corp-wide): 505.06K **Privately Held**
SIC: **7361** Employment agencies

(G-6094)
HOENEN & MITCHELL INC
18548 Arabian Acres Rd (19958-3920)
PHONE.................................302 645-6193
Richard Hoenen, Pr
Wayne Mitchell, VP
EMP: 6 EST: 1984
SALES (est): 788.65K **Privately Held**
Web: www.hoenenandmitchell.com
SIC: **1521** New construction, single-family houses

(G-6095)
HOLA AMERICA LLC
16192 Coastal Hwy (19958-3608)
PHONE.................................302 261-3460
Mapa Del Sitio, Prin
EMP: 9 EST: 2008
SALES (est): 206.26K **Privately Held**
Web: www.holaamerica.com
SIC: **4812** Radiotelephone communication

(G-6096)
HOLA MEDIA NETWORK LLC
17818 Cape Dr (19958-4670)
PHONE.................................302 228-8942
Edwin Andrade, Prin
EMP: 5 EST: 2012
SALES (est): 111.53K **Privately Held**
Web: www.humusolver.com
SIC: **4899** Communication services, nec

(G-6097)
HOME INNOVATIONS
17693 Coastal Hwy (19958-1685)
PHONE.................................302 448-9555
EMP: 5 EST: 2014
SALES (est): 172.63K **Privately Held**
SIC: **5045** 7371 Computer software; Computer software development

(G-6098)
HOME2 SUITES BY HILTON
17388 Ocean One Plz (19958-1897)
PHONE.................................302 291-1616
EMP: 15 EST: 2020
SALES (est): 228.61K **Privately Held**
Web: www.hilton.com
SIC: **7011** Hotels

(G-6099)
HOMEFIX
17667 Gate Dr Unit 3 (19958-6540)
PHONE.................................302 682-3837
Paulina Owedyk, Prin
EMP: 9 EST: 2015
SALES (est): 183.41K **Privately Held**
Web: www.homefixcustomremodeling.com
SIC: **1522** Residential construction, nec

(G-6100)
HOMEWATCH CAREGIVERS
17527 Nassau Commons Blvd (19958-6283)
PHONE.................................302 644-1888
EMP: 12 EST: 2014
SALES (est): 245.48K **Privately Held**
Web: www.homewatchcaregivers.com
SIC: **8082** Home health care services

(G-6101)
HONEY ALTERATION
17370 Coastal Hwy (19958-6209)
PHONE.................................302 519-2031
Honey Kang, Prin
EMP: 5 EST: 2017
SALES (est): 45.99K **Privately Held**
SIC: **7219** Garment making, alteration, and repair

(G-6102)
HONEYS FARM FRESH
329 Savannah Rd (19958-1438)
P.O. Box 953 (19971-0953)
PHONE.................................302 644-8400
Mark Grabowski, Pr
EMP: 8 EST: 2014
SALES (est): 486.13K **Privately Held**
Web: www.honeysfresh.farm
SIC: **0191** General farms, primarily crop

(G-6103)
HOOK PR GROUP
135 2nd St Fl 2 (19958-1347)
PHONE.................................302 858-5055
EMP: 8 EST: 2018
SALES (est): 208.85K **Privately Held**
Web: www.hookpr.com
SIC: **8742** Marketing consulting services

(G-6104)
HOPKINS HENLOPEN HOMESTEAD
18186 Dairy Farm Rd (19958-4505)
PHONE.................................202 695-9302
Amy Hopkins, Prin
EMP: 5 EST: 2015
SALES (est): 200.42K **Privately Held**
Web: www.hopkinsfarmcreamery.com
SIC: **0191** General farms, primarily crop

(G-6105)
HOTEL RODNEY
142 2nd St Unit 1 (19958-1396)
PHONE.................................302 645-6466
EMP: 8 EST: 2018
SALES (est): 35.85K **Privately Held**
Web: www.hotelrodneydelaware.com
SIC: **7011** Hotels

(G-6106)
HOUSE CALL DENTISTRY INC
3 Bay Oak Dr (19958-5757)
PHONE.................................866 686-4423
Dawn Simpson, Ex Dir
EMP: 6
SALES (est): 136.6K **Privately Held**
SIC: **8021** Specialized dental practitioners

(G-6107)
HUDSON JONES JAYWORK FISHER
34382 Carpenters Way # 3 (19958-4919)
PHONE.................................302 645-7999
EMP: 5
SALES (est): 70.03K **Privately Held**
Web: www.delawarelaw.com
SIC: **8111** General practice attorney, lawyer

(G-6108)
HUMMINGBIRD HILL PSYCHOLOGICAL
1143 Savannah Rd Ste 4 (19958-1515)
PHONE.................................302 864-8818
Laura L Epstein, Prin
EMP: 9 EST: 2015
SALES (est): 42.04K **Privately Held**
SIC: **8049** Psychologist, psychotherapist and hypnotist

(G-6109)
HYATT HSE LEWES / REHOBOTH BCH
17254 Five Points Sq (19958-6289)
PHONE.................................302 783-1000
EMP: 11
SALES (est): 304.27K **Privately Held**
SIC: **7011** Hotels and motels

GEOGRAPHIC SECTION

Lewes - Sussex County (G-6141)

(G-6110)
HYDROSHIELD DELMARVA
30723 Molly B Rd (19958-3853)
PHONE..................302 542-5923
EMP: 5 **EST:** 2017
SALES (est): 26.07K **Privately Held**
Web: 45j.d19.myftpupload.com
SIC: 7699 General household repair services

(G-6111)
HYPER GIZMO LLC
16192 Coastal Hwy (19958-3608)
PHONE..................888 487-1550
EMP: 5 **EST:** 2019
SALES (est): 77.06K **Privately Held**
Web: www.getuvpod.com
SIC: 5047 Medical equipment and supplies

(G-6112)
IBOPE MEDIA LLC
16192 Coastal Hwy (19958-3608)
PHONE..................305 529-0062
EMP: 7 **EST:** 2010
SALES (est): 470K **Privately Held**
SIC: 8732 Market analysis or research

(G-6113)
ICASE LLC
16192 Coastal Hwy (19958-3608)
PHONE..................302 703-7854
Usama Shahzad, *Prin*
EMP: 15
SALES (est): 386.99K **Privately Held**
SIC: 7389 Business Activities at Non-Commercial Site

(G-6114)
IDENTISOURCE LLC
16192 Coastal Hwy (19958-3608)
PHONE..................888 716-7498
EMP: 3 **EST:** 2004
SALES (est): 234.13K **Privately Held**
Web: www.identisource.net
SIC: 3955 Carbon paper and inked ribbons

(G-6115)
IGNIS GROUP LLC
16192 Coastal Hwy (19958-3608)
PHONE..................302 645-7400
EMP: 21 **EST:** 2018
SALES (est): 661.52K **Privately Held**
SIC: 8742 Management consulting services

(G-6116)
ILJ INTERNATIONAL LLC
16192 Coastal Hwy (19958-3608)
PHONE..................786 332-8535
EMP: 6 **EST:** 2021
SALES (est): 87.81K **Privately Held**
Web: ilj.law.indiana.edu
SIC: 2741 Miscellaneous publishing

(G-6117)
IMAGIC LLC
16192 Coastal Hwy (19958-3608)
PHONE..................628 600-5244
Ahmed Albarbawil, *CEO*
EMP: 5
SALES (est): 199.4K **Privately Held**
Web: www.magicbytes.com
SIC: 7371 Computer software development and applications

(G-6118)
IMPROVE SUSSEX LLC
22948 Pine Rd (19958-5651)
PHONE..................302 864-8350
EMP: 5 **EST:** 2016
SALES (est): 111.98K **Privately Held**
Web: www.improvesussex.com

(G-6119)
IN THE NEST QUILTING
32905 Nassau Ct S (19958-3726)
PHONE..................302 644-7316
Susan Wimmer, *Prin*
EMP: 5 **EST:** 2010
SALES (est): 22.69K **Privately Held**
SIC: 7299 Quilting for individuals

(G-6120)
INCLIND INC
119 W 3rd St Ste 6 (19958-1315)
P.O. Box 265 (19968-0265)
PHONE..................302 856-2802
Shaun Tyndall, *Pr*
EMP: 8 **EST:** 1999
SQ FT: 2,250
SALES (est): 1.61MM **Privately Held**
Web: www.inclind.com
SIC: 7371 7373 Computer software systems analysis and design, custom; Systems software development services

(G-6121)
INCREDO US LLC
16192 Coastal Hwy (19958-3608)
PHONE..................530 586-8995
EMP: 6 **EST:** 2019
SALES (est): 87.55K **Privately Held**
Web: www.incredo.co
SIC: 8742 Marketing consulting services

(G-6122)
INDELIBLE BLUE INC
16192 Coastal Hwy (19958-3608)
PHONE..................302 231-5200
Valerie Kestenbaum, *VP*
Victor Oppleman, *Dir*
EMP: 10 **EST:** 2015
SQ FT: 3,000
SALES (est): 401.46K **Privately Held**
Web: www.indelibleblue.net
SIC: 7373 Computer systems analysis and design

(G-6123)
INETWORKZ LLC
16192 Coastal Hwy (19958-3608)
PHONE..................407 401-9384
EMP: 10 **EST:** 2009
SALES (est): 439.37K **Privately Held**
SIC: 7379 7389 Computer related consulting services; Business services, nec

(G-6124)
INITITIVE FOR MED ACCESS KNWLD
16192 Coastal Hwy (19958-3608)
PHONE..................917 455-6601
EMP: 6 **EST:** 2011
SALES (est): 724.02K **Privately Held**
Web: www.i-mak.org
SIC: 8399 Advocacy group

(G-6125)
INNOVTIVE CPITL CNSLTING GROUP
16192 Coastal Hwy (19958-3608)
PHONE..................202 670-0797
Nicole Newman, *Managing Member*
EMP: 5 **EST:** 2018
SALES (est): 60K **Privately Held**
SIC: 8742 Financial consultant

(G-6126)
INPUTSOFT INC
16192 Coastal Hwy (19958-3608)
PHONE..................312 358-4509
Anastasiia Smyk, *CEO*
EMP: 7

SALES (est): 277.92K **Privately Held**
SIC: 7372 Prepackaged software

(G-6127)
INRG OF DELAWARE INC
16949 Hudsons Turn (19958-4840)
PHONE..................302 369-1412
Bill Mccarten, *Pr*
EMP: 5 **EST:** 1996
SALES (est): 378.35K **Privately Held**
SIC: 8748 Business consulting, nec

(G-6128)
INSIGHTZEN LLC
16192 Coastal Hwy (19958-3608)
PHONE..................647 227-9325
Xiaomei Wang, *CEO*
Michael Loh Cvo, *Prin*
EMP: 5 **EST:** 2017
SALES (est): 46.16K **Privately Held**
SIC: 7371 Computer software development and applications

(G-6129)
INSTOCKING LLC
16192 Coastal Hwy (19958-3608)
PHONE..................302 595-1595
EMP: 8 **EST:** 2020
SALES (est): 510.61K **Privately Held**
Web: www.instocking.com
SIC: 5099 Durable goods, nec

(G-6130)
INTELHOUSE MARKETING LLC
16192 Coastal Hwy (19958-3608)
PHONE..................213 438-9667
EMP: 10
SALES (est): 363K **Privately Held**
Web: www.intelhouse.net
SIC: 8742 Marketing consulting services

(G-6131)
IRENA C VIOLA MD PA
30900 Stallion Ln (19958-4065)
PHONE..................302 645-7257
Irena Viola, *Prin*
EMP: 10 **EST:** 2004
SALES (est): 100.8K **Privately Held**
SIC: 8011 General and family practice, physician/surgeon

(G-6132)
IT TIGERS LLC
16192 Coastal Hwy (19958-3608)
PHONE..................732 898-2793
EMP: 5 **EST:** 2018
SALES (est): 294.44K **Privately Held**
Web: www.ittigers.com
SIC: 8742 7379 Management information systems consultant; Online services technology consultants

(G-6133)
ITEA INC
Also Called: Springhaus Landscape Company
12006 Collins Rd (19958-4977)
PHONE..................302 328-3716
Steve Price, *Pr*
Debbie Mulholland, *VP*
George Price, *Prin*
EMP: 9 **EST:** 1932
SALES (est): 877.26K **Privately Held**
SIC: 0782 5261 Landscape contractors; Nursery stock, seeds and bulbs

(G-6134)
J G M ASSOCIATES
Also Called: John Mancuso and Associates
17569 Nassau Commons Blvd (19958-6284)

PHONE..................302 645-2159
John Mancuso, *Owner*
EMP: 6 **EST:** 2000
SALES (est): 480.74K **Privately Held**
Web: www.jgmcustompainting.com
SIC: 1721 Residential painting

(G-6135)
JACK LINGO INC REALTOR
1240 Kings Hwy (19958-1735)
P.O. Box 789 (19958-0789)
PHONE..................302 947-9030
John Lingo, *Mgr*
EMP: 30
SALES (corp-wide): 10.96MM **Privately Held**
Web: www.jacklingo.com
SIC: 6531 Real estate brokers and agents
PA: Jack Lingo Inc Realtor
246 Rehoboth Ave
Rehoboth Beach DE 19971
302 227-3883

(G-6136)
JACK LINGO REALTOR
1240 Kings Hwy (19958-1735)
PHONE..................302 645-2207
Paul Townsend, *Prin*
EMP: 10 **EST:** 1999
SALES (est): 610.17K **Privately Held**
Web: www.jacklingo.com
SIC: 6531 Real estate brokers and agents

(G-6137)
JEANINE ODONNELL
16583 Coastal Hwy (19958-3605)
PHONE..................302 644-3276
Jeanine O'donnell, *Mgr*
EMP: 5 **EST:** 2011
SALES (est): 191.05K **Privately Held**
Web: www.lewesinsurance.com
SIC: 6411 Insurance agents and brokers

(G-6138)
JGM & ASSOCIATES CUSTOM PNTG
17569 Nassau Commons Blvd (19958-6284)
PHONE..................302 645-2159
John Mantuso, *Pr*
EMP: 10 **EST:** 2016
SALES (est): 408.38K **Privately Held**
Web: www.jgmcustompainting.com
SIC: 1721 Residential painting

(G-6139)
JILL RILEY
23715 Driftwood Ln (19958-5339)
PHONE..................802 272-7310
Jill Riley, *Pr*
EMP: 6 **EST:** 2017
SALES (est): 24.4K **Privately Held**
SIC: 8049 Offices of health practitioner

(G-6140)
JKINGS MINING COMPANY LLC ✪
16192 Coastal Hwy (19958-3608)
PHONE..................628 600-9522
Abdul Kamara, *Managing Member*
EMP: 10 **EST:** 2022
SALES (est): 348.32K **Privately Held**
SIC: 7371 Computer software development and applications

(G-6141)
JMJ ASSOC
31699 Alsace Ct (19958-2513)
PHONE..................410 320-0890
EMP: 6 **EST:** 2018
SALES (est): 60.8K **Privately Held**
Web: www.jmj.com

(PA)=Parent Co (HQ)=Headquarters
✪ = New Business established in last 2 years

2024 Harris Directory of Delaware Businesses

Lewes - Sussex County (G-6142)   GEOGRAPHIC SECTION

SIC: 8742 Business management consultant

(G-6142)
JOAN A PROCACCIO INC
32180 Oak Dr (19958-3663)
PHONE..................302 542-6394
EMP: 6 EST: 2013
SALES (est): 83.19K **Privately Held**
SIC: 8011 Offices and clinics of medical doctors

(G-6143)
JOBES LANDSCAPE INC
20934 Robinsonville Rd (19958-6045)
PHONE..................302 945-0195
Joy Tomer, Pr
Jobe Tomer, Sec
EMP: 9 EST: 2005
SALES (est): 493.98K **Privately Held**
Web: www.jobeslandscape.com
SIC: 0781 4971 Landscape services; Irrigation systems

(G-6144)
JOHN LI-AMERIPRISE FINVL SRVCS
102 2nd St (19958-1324)
PHONE..................302 200-9548
EMP: 5 EST: 2018
SALES (est): 193.19K **Privately Held**
SIC: 7389 Financial services

(G-6145)
JOHN M COOPER REVERAND
Tall Pines (19958)
PHONE..................302 684-8639
John Cooper, Prin
EMP: 5 EST: 2004
SALES (est): 105K **Privately Held**
SIC: 2389 Clergymen's vestments

(G-6146)
JOHN S KASSEES INC
30024 W Barrier Reef Blvd (19958-6830)
PHONE..................302 838-1976
John Kassees, Prin
EMP: 5 EST: 2002
SALES (est): 63.66K **Privately Held**
SIC: 1752 Floor laying and floor work, nec

(G-6147)
JOHN SNOW LABS INC
16192 Coastal Hwy (19958-3608)
PHONE..................302 786-5227
John Snow, Pr
EMP: 39 EST: 2015
SQ FT: 5,000
SALES (est): 1.42MM **Privately Held**
Web: www.johnsnowlabs.com
SIC: 7374 Data processing service

(G-6148)
JOHN W BATEMAN
30723 Molly B Rd (19958-3853)
PHONE..................302 644-1177
John Bateman, Prin
EMP: 5 EST: 2010
SALES (est): 180.04K **Privately Held**
SIC: 1522 Residential construction, nec

(G-6149)
JOHNS EL FAMILY INDUSTRIES INC (PA) ✪
16192 Coastal Hwy (19958-3608)
PHONE..................310 701-5678
Azuree Johns El, Pr
EMP: 5 EST: 2023
SALES (est): 250.49K
SALES (corp-wide): 250.49K **Privately Held**

SIC: 8322 5651 Family counseling services; Unisex clothing stores

(G-6150)
JOSE A PANDO MD
Also Called: Rheumatology Consultant Del
20268 Plantations Rd (19958-4622)
PHONE..................302 644-2302
Jose Pando, Owner
EMP: 10 EST: 2006
SALES (est): 1.01MM **Privately Held**
Web: www.delawarearthritis.com
SIC: 8011 Rheumatology specialist, physician/surgeon

(G-6151)
JOSE H AUSTRIA MD
10 Pilot Pt (19958-1154)
PHONE..................302 645-8954
Jose Austria Md, Owner
EMP: 6 EST: 1977
SALES (est): 172.66K **Privately Held**
SIC: 8011 Offices and clinics of medical doctors

(G-6152)
JOSELOW BETH LPCMH
1307 Savannah Rd (19958-1514)
PHONE..................302 644-0130
Loretta Higgins, Prin
EMP: 10 EST: 2007
SALES (est): 197.48K **Privately Held**
SIC: 8093 Mental health clinic, outpatient

(G-6153)
JOSEPH M FARRELL DO
1606 Savannah Rd Ste 1 (19958-1656)
PHONE..................302 424-4141
Joseph M Farrell, Prin
EMP: 7 EST: 2018
SALES (est): 237.91K **Privately Held**
SIC: 8011 Orthopedic physician

(G-6154)
JOURNALNAME LLC
16192 Coastal Hwy (19958-3608)
PHONE..................302 522-7680
Mahibur Rahman, Managing Member
EMP: 6
SALES (est): 71.79K **Privately Held**
SIC: 8742 Marketing consulting services

(G-6155)
JULIE GRITTON TEAM LLC
800 Kings Hwy (19958-1706)
PHONE..................302 645-1111
EMP: 5 EST: 2018
SALES (est): 158.99K **Privately Held**
Web: www.selltheshore.com
SIC: 6531 Real estate agent, residential

(G-6156)
JUST BREATHE HOME THERAPY
18210 Hickory Ln (19958-4707)
PHONE..................919 270-3347
Angelina Salas, Prin
EMP: 6 EST: 2012
SALES (est): 34.8K **Privately Held**
SIC: 8049 Offices of health practitioner

(G-6157)
K BANK
17021 Old Orchard Rd Ste A (19958-4832)
PHONE..................302 645-9700
Julie Brown, Brnch Mgr
EMP: 5
SALES (corp-wide): 35.49MM **Privately Held**
Web: www.mtb.com

SIC: 6029 6022 Commercial banks, nec; State commercial banks
PA: K Bank
11407 Cronhill Dr Ste N
Owings Mills MD 21117
443 271-6491

(G-6158)
KAIRON CORP
16192 Coastal Hwy (19958-3608)
PHONE..................347 688-3993
Justin T, CEO
Nahrie Chung, COO
EMP: 10 EST: 2019
SALES (est): 380.63K **Privately Held**
SIC: 7389 Business Activities at Non-Commercial Site

(G-6159)
KANCAPI LLC
16192 Coastal Hwy (19958-3608)
PHONE..................949 508-0350
Preetika Judge, CEO
EMP: 20 EST: 2021
SALES (est): 570.87K **Privately Held**
SIC: 7389 Business Activities at Non-Commercial Site

(G-6160)
KAPLAN SOFTWARE GROUP
15649 Simpson Dr (19958-4953)
PHONE..................646 498-8275
Stanley Kaplan, Ofcr
EMP: 5 EST: 2018
SALES (est): 240.19K **Privately Held**
SIC: 7371 Computer software development

(G-6161)
KASMO CLOUD INC
16192 Coastal Hwy (19958-3608)
PHONE..................302 319-9952
EMP: 5 EST: 2017
SALES (est): 65.78K **Privately Held**
SIC: 8742 Management consulting services

(G-6162)
KATHRYN M GEHRET
Also Called: Kate Gehret Ms
17124 Poplar Dr (19958-3873)
PHONE..................610 420-7233
Kathryn M Gehret, Prin
EMP: 6 EST: 2012
SALES (est): 88.66K **Privately Held**
SIC: 8049 Clinical psychologist

(G-6163)
KATHY J KING PA
17527 Nassau Commons Blvd (19958-6283)
PHONE..................302 827-4740
Kathy J King, Pr
EMP: 6 EST: 2014
SALES (est): 106.07K **Privately Held**
Web: www.kathykingcounselor.com
SIC: 8621 Professional organizations

(G-6164)
KELLER WILLIAMS REALTY
Also Called: Keller Williams Realtors
18344 Coastal Hwy (19958-4772)
PHONE..................302 360-0300
Brigit Taylor, Owner
EMP: 9 EST: 2020
SALES (est): 223.52K **Privately Held**
Web: loyemiller.kw.com
SIC: 6531 Real estate agent, residential

(G-6165)
KELLI ARMSTRONG MD
480 E Market St (19958-1123)

PHONE..................203 783-9632
Kelli Armstrong Md, Owner
EMP: 5 EST: 1998
SALES (est): 301.41K **Privately Held**
Web: www.lonearmadillo.com
SIC: 8042 Specialized optometrists

(G-6166)
KELLIES HAIR PLACE
17018 Bristol Rd (19958-3887)
PHONE..................302 827-2715
Kellie Wallace, Owner
EMP: 5 EST: 2010
SALES (est): 31.37K **Privately Held**
SIC: 7231 Hairdressers

(G-6167)
KINGSTOWN LLC
33672 Bayview Medical Dr (19958-1687)
PHONE..................302 645-7050
EMP: 8 EST: 2015
SALES (est): 327.16K **Privately Held**
SIC: 8011 Surgeon

(G-6168)
KITSCHY STITCH
18419 Berkeley Rd (19958-4692)
PHONE..................302 200-9889
EMP: 3 EST: 2018
SALES (est): 48.88K **Privately Held**
SIC: 2395 Embroidery and art needlework

(G-6169)
KLH INDUSTRIES LLC
16192 Coastal Hwy (19958-3608)
PHONE..................800 348-0758
EMP: 2 EST: 2015
SALES (est): 86.89K **Privately Held**
Web: www.klhindustries.com
SIC: 3999 Barber and beauty shop equipment

(G-6170)
KNOWT INC
16192 Coastal Hwy (19958-3608)
PHONE..................848 391-0575
EMP: 11 EST: 2019
SALES (est): 760.25K **Privately Held**
Web: www.knowt.io
SIC: 7371 7372 7389 Computer software development and applications; Application computer software; Business Activities at Non-Commercial Site

(G-6171)
KO GUTTERS LLC
33499 Aster St (19958-5335)
PHONE..................302 943-8293
EMP: 6 EST: 2018
SALES (est): 231.75K **Privately Held**
Web: www.koguttersllc.com
SIC: 1761 Gutter and downspout contractor

(G-6172)
KRATOM FOUNDATION
16192 Coastal Hwy (19958-3608)
PHONE..................302 645-7400
EMP: 5 EST: 2016
SALES (est): 306K **Privately Held**
SIC: 5099 Durable goods, nec

(G-6173)
KS NAIL AND SPA
1551 Savannah Rd Ste C (19958-1681)
PHONE..................302 703-6158
Hanh Giang, Owner
EMP: 5 EST: 2015
SALES (est): 52.92K **Privately Held**
SIC: 7231 Manicurist, pedicurist

GEOGRAPHIC SECTION
Lewes - Sussex County (G-6203)

(G-6174)
KZY GROUP INC
16192 Coastal Hwy (19958-3608)
PHONE....................302 684-3078
EMP: 6 **EST:** 2018
SALES (est): 1.11MM **Privately Held**
SIC: 4213 Trucking, except local

(G-6175)
LAIMA V ANTHANEY DMD
1200 Savannah Rd (19958-1525)
PHONE....................302 645-4726
Anthaney Laima, *Owner*
EMP: 5 **EST:** 1990
SALES (est): 203.77K **Privately Held**
Web: www.anthaneydmd.com
SIC: 8021 Dentists' office

(G-6176)
LANDMARK ASSOCIATES OF DEL
Also Called: Piper, Glenn T
9 Bradford Ln (19958-9511)
PHONE....................302 645-7070
EMP: 5 **EST:** 1993
SALES (est): 314.32K **Privately Held**
Web: www.landmarkassociates.net
SIC: 6531 Appraiser, real estate

(G-6177)
LANDVILLE GROUP LLC (PA) ✪
16192 Coastal Hwy (19958-3608)
PHONE....................727 557-6149
Robert Vaughan, *Managing Member*
EMP: 10 **EST:** 2022
SALES (est): 415.33K
SALES (corp-wide): 415.33K **Privately Held**
SIC: 6719 Holding companies, nec

(G-6178)
LANE BUILDERS LLC
1009 Kings Hwy (19958-1731)
PHONE....................302 645-5555
Jeff Burtun, *Managing Member*
EMP: 16 **EST:** 1999
SALES (est): 2.33MM **Privately Held**
Web: www.lanebuilders.com
SIC: 1521 New construction, single-family houses

(G-6179)
LANTRANSIT ENTERPRISES LLC
Also Called: U S Mail Transport
16192 Coastal Hwy (19958-3608)
PHONE....................302 722-4800
Madison Walsh, *Ch*
Deborah Holcomb, *Pr*
Linda Portrum, *Ex VP*
EMP: 5 **EST:** 2008
SQ FT: 1,500
SALES (est): 119.87K **Privately Held**
SIC: 4789 Freight car loading and unloading

(G-6180)
LAOHIO HOLDINGS LLC
16192 Coastal Hwy (19958-3608)
PHONE....................302 200-9685
EMP: 5
SIC: 6719 Investment holding companies, except banks

(G-6181)
LASH BEAUTY BAR
34005 Wescoats Rd Unit 3 (19958-4928)
PHONE....................302 827-2160
Barbara Lindner, *Owner*
EMP: 6 **EST:** 2008
SALES (est): 52.09K **Privately Held**
Web: www.lashandbeautybar.com
SIC: 7231 Cosmetology and personal hygiene salons

(G-6182)
LAUGHING HORSE LLC
16192 Coastal Hwy (19958-3608)
PHONE....................917 513-5255
EMP: 10 **EST:** 2021
SALES (est): 68.89K **Privately Held**
SIC: 7011 Bed and breakfast inn

(G-6183)
LE ARTIST LUCRATIF N AMER LLC
16192 Coastal Hwy (19958-3608)
PHONE....................438 223-3788
EMP: 5
SALES (est): 230.11K **Privately Held**
SIC: 7371 Computer software development and applications

(G-6184)
LEAK STOPPERS LLC
29029 Lewes Georgetown Hwy (19958-3909)
PHONE....................302 236-1652
Joseph Crispin, *Prin*
EMP: 5 **EST:** 2017
SALES (est): 96.81K **Privately Held**
Web: www.theleakstoppers.com
SIC: 1799 Waterproofing

(G-6185)
LEARNING CORE LLC
16192 Coastal Hwy (19958-3608)
PHONE....................628 600-9644
EMP: 20 **EST:** 2021
SALES (est): 612.9K **Privately Held**
SIC: 8742 Training and development consultant

(G-6186)
LEE ANN WILKINSON GROUP
16698 Kings Hwy Ste A (19958-4936)
PHONE....................302 645-6664
Beth Heid, *Prin*
EMP: 8 **EST:** 2017
SALES (est): 242.15K **Privately Held**
Web: www.leeanngroup.com
SIC: 6531 Real estate agent, residential

(G-6187)
LEFTYS ALLEY & EATS
36450 Plaza Blvd (19958-4211)
PHONE....................302 864-6000
EMP: 16 **EST:** 2017
SALES (est): 725.77K **Privately Held**
Web: www.iloveleftys.com
SIC: 7933 Ten pin center

(G-6188)
LEGUM & NORMAN MID-WEST LLC
Also Called: Legum & Norman Realty
12000 Old Vine Blvd Unit 114 (19958-1717)
PHONE....................302 227-8448
EMP: 6
SALES (corp-wide): 22.03MM **Privately Held**
Web: www.legumnorman.com
SIC: 6531 Real estate brokers and agents
PA: Legum & Norman Mid-West, Llc
3130 Frview Pk Dr Ste 200
Falls Church VA 22042
703 600-6000

(G-6189)
LEMONFACE TECHNOLOGIES CORP ✪
16192 Coastal Hwy (19958-3608)
PHONE....................844 615-3666
Rolf Barandun, *CEO*
EMP: 7 **EST:** 2023
SALES (est): 264.9K **Privately Held**
SIC: 7371 Software programming applications

(G-6190)
LESSARD CUSTOM HOMES
33673 E Hunters Run (19958-4844)
PHONE....................302 645-7444
EMP: 5 **EST:** 2018
SALES (est): 90.93K **Privately Held**
Web: www.lessardbuilders.com
SIC: 1521 New construction, single-family houses

(G-6191)
LEWES BODY WORKS INC
16205 New Rd (19958-3707)
PHONE....................302 645-5595
Richard Perez, *Pr*
EMP: 6 **EST:** 2004
SALES (est): 492.88K **Privately Held**
Web: www.lewesbodyworks.com
SIC: 7532 Body shop, automotive

(G-6192)
LEWES CHIROPRACTIC CENTER
Also Called: Elrod, Michael E DC
1527 Savannah Rd (19958-1611)
PHONE....................302 645-9171
EMP: 5 **EST:** 1990
SALES (est): 145.71K **Privately Held**
Web: www.leweschiro.com
SIC: 8041 Offices and clinics of chiropractors

(G-6193)
LEWES COUNSELING LLC
32413 Lewes Georgetown Hwy (19958-1646)
P.O. Box 588 (19969-0588)
PHONE....................302 430-2127
Jeanne Doe Dukes, *Prin*
EMP: 5 **EST:** 2014
SALES (est): 61.39K **Privately Held**
Web: www.lewescounseling.com
SIC: 8322 General counseling services

(G-6194)
LEWES DAIRY INC
660 Pilottown Rd (19958-1299)
P.O. Box 207 (19958-0207)
PHONE....................302 645-6281
Archie Brittingham Junior, *Pr*
Robert E Brittingham, *VP*
Judy B Bye, *Treas*
Henry L Brittingham, *Sec*
Lonie Di Joseph, *Mgr*
EMP: 10 **EST:** 1946
SQ FT: 20,000
SALES (est): 184.78K **Privately Held**
Web: www.lewesdairy.com
SIC: 0241 Dairy farms

(G-6195)
LEWES EXPRESSIVE THERAPY
105 Dove Dr (19958-1622)
PHONE....................302 727-3275
Sarah Smith, *Prin*
EMP: 7 **EST:** 2016
SALES (est): 79.08K **Privately Held**
SIC: 8093 Rehabilitation center, outpatient treatment

(G-6196)
LEWES FISHHOUSE & PRODUCE INC
17696 Coastal Hwy (19958-6214)
PHONE....................302 827-7074
EMP: 25 **EST:** 1994
SQ FT: 1,500
SALES (est): 4.28MM **Privately Held**
Web: www.lewesfishhouse.com
SIC: 5147 5421 5146 Meats and meat products; Meat and fish markets; Fish and seafoods

(G-6197)
LEWES MEINEKE
16753 Coastal Hwy (19958-3653)
PHONE....................302 827-2054
EMP: 9
SALES (est): 741.14K **Privately Held**
SIC: 7533 Muffler shop, sale or repair and installation

(G-6198)
LEWES MONTESSORI SCHOOL
32234 Conleys Chapel Rd (19958-6023)
PHONE....................302 644-7482
Lisa Desombre, *Prin*
EMP: 5 **EST:** 2011
SALES (est): 114.14K **Privately Held**
SIC: 8351 Montessori child development center

(G-6199)
LEWES ORTHOPEDIC CTR
16704 Kings Hwy # 2 (19958-4929)
PHONE....................302 645-4939
EMP: 5 **EST:** 1996
SALES (est): 497.25K **Privately Held**
SIC: 8062 General medical and surgical hospitals

(G-6200)
LEWES SENIOR CITIZENS CENTER
Also Called: LEWES SENIOR CENTER
32083 Janice Rd (19958-2004)
PHONE....................302 645-9293
Dennis Nealen, *Dir*
EMP: 5 **EST:** 1967
SALES (est): 834.52K **Privately Held**
Web: www.lewesseniorcenter.org
SIC: 8322 8699 Senior citizens' center or association; Charitable organization

(G-6201)
LEWES SURGERY CENTER
17015 Old Orchard Rd Unit 4 (19958-4849)
P.O. Box 495 (19958-0495)
PHONE....................302 644-3466
John E Spieker, *Mng Pt*
Gina Mcclanahan, *Pt*
Wilson Choy, *Pt*
EMP: 8 **EST:** 2006
SQ FT: 5,000
SALES (est): 1.02MM **Privately Held**
Web: www.delawarebonedocs.com
SIC: 8011 Surgeon

(G-6202)
LEWES WELLNESS CENTER
20268 Plantations Rd (19958-4622)
PHONE....................302 313-9990
EMP: 6 **EST:** 2015
SALES (est): 153.92K **Privately Held**
Web: www.lewes-wellness-center.com
SIC: 8099 Childbirth preparation clinic

(G-6203)
LEWES YOGA & MEDITATION CENTER
17605 Nassau Commons Blvd Unit B (19958)
PHONE....................302 245-6133
EMP: 5 **EST:** 2016
SALES (est): 25.15K **Privately Held**
Web: www.lewesyoga.com
SIC: 7999 Yoga instruction

Lewes - Sussex County (G-6204)　　　　GEOGRAPHIC SECTION

(G-6204)
LEWIS LETTERING CO
15 Sussex Dr (19958-1506)
PHONE.....................610 209-0998
EMP: 4 EST: 2018
SALES (est): 131.49K Privately Held
SIC: 3993 Signs and advertising specialties

(G-6205)
LICENSING ASSURANCE LLC
16192 Coastal Hwy (19958-3608)
PHONE.....................305 851-3545
Dimitri Largaespada, CEO
EMP: 30 EST: 2014
SALES (est): 1.6MM Privately Held
Web: www.licensingassurance.com
SIC: 5045 Computer software

(G-6206)
LIFE-SCIENCE AI LLC
16192 Coastal Hwy (19958-3608)
PHONE.....................438 833-8504
EMP: 5 EST: 2021
SALES (est): 250K Privately Held
SIC: 8733 Research institute

(G-6207)
LIFENET INC
36871 Crooked Hammock Way (19958-4943)
PHONE.....................973 698-6881
EMP: 9 EST: 2017
SALES (est): 50.13K Privately Held
Web: www.lifenetems.org
SIC: 4119 Ambulance service

(G-6208)
LIGHTHOUSE MASONRY INC
20090 Beaver Dam Rd (19958-5517)
PHONE.....................302 945-1392
James Mcilreavy Junior, Pr
EMP: 7 EST: 2002
SALES (est): 686.89K Privately Held
SIC: 1741 Masonry and other stonework

(G-6209)
LINDNER LLC
34005 Wescoats Rd Unit 3 (19958-4928)
PHONE.....................302 827-2160
Barbara Lindner, Owner
EMP: 6 EST: 2010
SALES (est): 47.73K Privately Held
Web: www.lindner-group.com
SIC: 7231 Beauty shops

(G-6210)
LINK ROAD LOGISTICS INC
16192 Coastal Hwy (19958-3608)
P.O. Box 262 (19490-0262)
PHONE.....................267 283-9370
John Andrew, CEO
EMP: 5
SALES (est): 238.96K Privately Held
SIC: 4731 Freight transportation arrangement

(G-6211)
LISA INSURTECH LLC
16192 Coastal Hwy (19958-3608)
PHONE.....................612 470-1009
EMP: 8 EST: 2021
SALES (est): 87.5K Privately Held
Web: www.lisainsurtech.com
SIC: 5045 Computer software

(G-6212)
LISA M ANDERSEN
1201 Savannah Rd (19958-1553)
PHONE.....................302 644-3668
Lisa M Andersen, Prin
EMP: 5 EST: 2006

SALES (est): 85.63K Privately Held
SIC: 8111 Real estate law

(G-6213)
LITTLE WORLD LLC
4 Henlopen Ct (19958-1768)
PHONE.....................302 644-1530
Patrick Snyder, Prin
EMP: 7 EST: 2017
SALES (est): 104.04K Privately Held
Web: www.littleworldima.com
SIC: 8351 Preschool center

(G-6214)
LIVETRADE LTD
16192 Coastal Hwy (19958-3608)
PHONE.....................302 305-1797
EMP: 5 EST: 2019
SALES (est): 63.87K Privately Held
Web: www.livetrade.io
SIC: 7371 Computer software development

(G-6215)
LOAD 2 GO INC
16192 Coastal Hwy (19958-3608)
PHONE.....................302 722-8844
Kristina Berezovska, CEO
EMP: 25
SALES (est): 709.65K Privately Held
SIC: 4212 Local trucking, without storage

(G-6216)
LOCAL HANDS-CRAFTED IN AMERICA
118 2nd St (19958-1324)
PHONE.....................302 645-9100
Brenda L Murr, Prin
EMP: 6 EST: 2008
SALES (est): 84.44K Privately Held
SIC: 8631 Labor organizations

(G-6217)
LONG AND FOSTER
35115 Roebuck Ln (19958-7011)
PHONE.....................925 699-4783
Daniel Dellegrotti, Prin
EMP: 5 EST: 2017
SALES (est): 115.77K Privately Held
Web: www.longandfoster.com
SIC: 6531 Real estate brokers and agents

(G-6218)
LONG LIFE FOOD SAFETY PDTS LLC ✪
16192 Coastal Hwy (19958-3608)
PHONE.....................302 229-1207
David Keezer, Managing Member
EMP: 5 EST: 2022
SALES (est): 220.1K Privately Held
SIC: 2673 Food storage and frozen food bags, plastic

(G-6219)
LONJEW LLC
16192 Coastal Hwy (19958-3608)
PHONE.....................803 994-9888
EMP: 6 EST: 2020
SALES (est): 50K Privately Held
SIC: 3089 Organizers for closets, drawers, etc.: plastics

(G-6220)
LORETTA A HIGGINS
34431 King Street Row (19958-4787)
PHONE.....................302 645-2666
Loretta Higgins, Ofcr
EMP: 12 EST: 2017
SALES (est): 71.12K Privately Held
Web: www.beebehealthcare.org

SIC: 8049 Offices of health practitioner

(G-6221)
LORI RYAN SKYE
31672 Siham Rd (19958-2027)
PHONE.....................302 588-2588
Lori Ryan, Mgr
EMP: 6 EST: 2017
SALES (est): 22.18K Privately Held
SIC: 8049 Offices of health practitioner

(G-6222)
LORICA STRATEGY PARTNERS LLC ✪
16192 Coastal Hwy (19958-3608)
PHONE.....................301 535-8263
Richard Milner, Managing Member
EMP: 5 EST: 2023
SALES (est): 331.57K Privately Held
SIC: 8742 Management consulting services

(G-6223)
LOSS PAY INC ✪
16192 Coastal Hwy (19958-3608)
PHONE.....................833 567-7729
Priest Fletcher, CEO
EMP: 9 EST: 2022
SALES (est): 358.33K Privately Held
SIC: 6411 Insurance agents and brokers

(G-6224)
LOVE CITY PRINTS LLC
33497 Creekside Dr (19958-3722)
PHONE.....................302 245-5702
EMP: 4 EST: 2013
SALES (est): 77.35K Privately Held
SIC: 2752 Commercial printing, lithographic

(G-6225)
LOVE CREEK MARINA MBL HM SITE (PA)
Also Called: Laurel Storage Center
31136 Conleys Chapel Rd (19958-5511)
PHONE.....................302 448-6492
Milton Chaski Junior, Pr
Mary Lee Chaski, Sec
Diana Chaski, VP
Joanne Middleton, Stockholder
Eugenia Roskos, Stockholder
EMP: 10 EST: 1964
SQ FT: 10,000
SALES (est): 1.25MM
SALES (corp-wide): 1.25MM Privately Held
SIC: 5271 6515 4493 4225 Mobile home dealers; Mobile home site operators; Marinas; Miniwarehouse, warehousing

(G-6226)
LOWES HOME CENTERS LLC
Also Called: Lowe's
20364 Plantations Rd (19958-5814)
PHONE.....................302 645-0900
Kerilyn Urvan, Brnch Mgr
EMP: 108
SALES (corp-wide): 97.06B Publicly Held
Web: www.lowes.com
SIC: 5211 5031 5722 5064 Home centers; Building materials, exterior; Household appliance stores; Electrical appliances, television and radio
HQ: Lowe's Home Centers, Llc
1000 Lowes Blvd
Mooresville NC 28117
336 658-4000

(G-6227)
LOYAL ORDER MOSE LWES REHOBOTH
28971 Lewes Georgetown Hwy (19958-3910)

PHONE.....................302 684-4004
EMP: 5 EST: 2010
SALES (est): 139.22K Privately Held
Web: www.mdmoose.org
SIC: 8641 Civic associations

(G-6228)
LUMIA HOME LLC
16192 Coastal Hwy (19958-3608)
PHONE.....................516 373-5269
Zihao Liu, Prin
EMP: 10 EST: 2021
SALES (est): 349.48K Privately Held
SIC: 2254 Nightwear (nightgowns, negligees, pajamas), knit

(G-6229)
LUTINX INC
16192 Coastal Hwy (19958-3608)
PHONE.....................718 502-6961
Civati Alessandro, CEO
EMP: 10 EST: 2021
SALES (est): 433.11K Privately Held
SIC: 7371 Software programming applications

(G-6230)
LUTTRELL GUITARS
23199 Bridgeway Dr W (19958-5117)
PHONE.....................404 325-7977
Ralph Luttrell, Prin
EMP: 5 EST: 2017
SALES (est): 52.37K Privately Held
Web: www.luttrellguitars.com
SIC: 7699 Repair services, nec

(G-6231)
LUX MEDICAL SOLUTIONS LLC
16192 Coastal Hwy (19958-3608)
PHONE.....................302 440-4557
EMP: 5 EST: 2018
SALES (est): 220.52K Privately Held
SIC: 8099 Health and allied services, nec

(G-6232)
M & P ADVENTURES INC
Also Called: Lighthuse Rest At Fshrmans Wha
Corner Of Savannah Angler (19958)
P.O. Box 623 (19958-0623)
PHONE.....................302 645-6271
Paul Buchness, Pr
Mary Buchness, VP
EMP: 6 EST: 1982
SALES (est): 92.75K Privately Held
SIC: 7299 5812 Banquet hall facilities; Eating places

(G-6233)
M&M PURE AIR SYSTEMS LLC
Also Called: Woodyknows
16192 Coastal Hwy (19958-3608)
PHONE.....................403 801-2925
Xinyu Xu, Owner
EMP: 6 EST: 2012
SALES (est): 247.89K Privately Held
SIC: 3842 Respiratory protection equipment, personal

(G-6234)
MACINTOSH ENGINEERING
32191 Nassau Rd Unit 2 (19958-3762)
PHONE.....................302 448-2000
James Baker, Pr
EMP: 7 EST: 2017
SALES (est): 230.49K Privately Held
Web: www.macintosheng.com
SIC: 8711 Civil engineering

GEOGRAPHIC SECTION

Lewes - Sussex County (G-6263)

(G-6235)
MAD DELAWARE CHAPTER
34013 Woodland Cir (19958-5212)
PHONE.................910 284-6286
Hector Reyes, *Prin*
EMP: 5 **EST:** 2016
SALES (est): 58.08K **Privately Held**
SIC: 8399 Advocacy group

(G-6236)
MAGIC BYTES LLC
16192 Coastal Hwy (19958-3608)
PHONE.................813 995-7343
Thomas Meiertoberens, *CEO*
EMP: 12 **EST:** 2013
SALES (est): 251.15K **Privately Held**
Web: www.magicbytes.com
SIC: 7371 Computer software development and applications

(G-6237)
MAID FOR SHORE
22 Chesterfield Dr (19958-9407)
PHONE.................302 344-1857
Juliana Vantol, *Prin*
EMP: 5 **EST:** 2007
SALES (est): 169.42K **Privately Held**
Web: www.maidforshore.com
SIC: 7349 Cleaning service, industrial or commercial

(G-6238)
MAKEUP & LOVE
17277 Queen Anne Way (19958-3763)
PHONE.................856 524-1966
Danielle Gaudiosi, *Prin*
EMP: 5 **EST:** 2015
SALES (est): 24.56K **Privately Held**
Web: www.aestheticcenter.com
SIC: 7231 Cosmetology and personal hygiene salons

(G-6239)
MALWATION INC
16192 Coastal Hwy (19958-3608)
PHONE.................302 208-9661
Kagan Isildak, *Managing Member*
EMP: 10
SALES (est): 348.32K **Privately Held**
SIC: 7371 Custom computer programming services

(G-6240)
MANUFACTURERS & TRADERS TR CO
Also Called: M&T
32547 Lewes Georgetown Hwy (19958)
PHONE.................302 855-2218
EMP: 8
SALES (corp-wide): 8.6B **Publicly Held**
Web: ir.mtb.com
SIC: 6022 State commercial banks
HQ: Manufacturers And Traders Trust Company
  1 M&T Plz Fl 3
  Buffalo NY 14203
  716 842-4200

(G-6241)
MARCHES JEWELERS INC
34508 Spring Brook Ave (19958-5992)
PHONE.................856 858-4463
Joe Marche, *Pr*
EMP: 6 **EST:** 1964
SALES (est): 568.02K **Privately Held**
Web: www.joemarchebythesea.com
SIC: 5944 5094 Jewelry, precious stones and precious metals; Jewelry

(G-6242)
MARGARITA MAN
34397 Skyler Dr (19958-5685)
PHONE.................302 947-4000
Kevin Cunningham, *Owner*
EMP: 6 **EST:** 2004
SALES (est): 116.96K **Privately Held**
Web: www.margaritamande.com
SIC: 7359 Party supplies rental services

(G-6243)
MARIE WILLOW & CO
18422 Coastal Hwy (19958-4776)
PHONE.................302 632-0831
EMP: 5 **EST:** 2018
SALES (est): 239.81K **Privately Held**
Web: willow-marie-co.myshopify.com
SIC: 0191 General farms, primarily crop

(G-6244)
MARKET RESEARCH REPORTS INC
16192 Coastal Hwy (19958-3608)
PHONE.................302 703-9904
Ambarish Kumar Verma, *Pr*
EMP: 8 **EST:** 2012
SALES (est): 27.3K **Privately Held**
Web: www.verifiedmarketresearch.com
SIC: 8732 Market analysis or research

(G-6245)
MARQUIS CONSULTING LLC
16192 Coastal Hwy (19958-3608)
PHONE.................480 438-5582
EMP: 5 **EST:** 2016
SALES (est): 800K **Privately Held**
SIC: 8748 Business consulting, nec

(G-6246)
MARTIN GREY LLC
16192 Coastal Hwy (19958-3608)
PHONE.................302 990-0675
EMP: 3 **EST:** 2019
SALES (est): 158.64K **Privately Held**
Web: www.martingrey.app
SIC: 2099 Tea blending

(G-6247)
MARYLAND CENTER FOR THERAPEUTI
28763 Valley View Ln (19958-6859)
PHONE.................302 727-8832
Debra Davies, *Ofcr*
EMP: 8 **EST:** 2013
SALES (est): 54.13K **Privately Held**
SIC: 8011 Offices and clinics of medical doctors

(G-6248)
MATADOR COMPANIES LLC
16192 Coastal Hwy (19958-3608)
PHONE.................855 303-4229
EMP: 5 **EST:** 2017
SIC: 6719 Investment holding companies, except banks

(G-6249)
MATRIX LIFE SCIENCE INC
16192 Coastal Hwy (19958-3608)
PHONE.................281 419-7942
Anuj Kabra, *Admn*
EMP: 5 **EST:** 2021
SALES (est): 1.1MM **Privately Held**
SIC: 5122 Vitamins and minerals
PA: Matrix Life Science Private Limited
  12 Shilpnagar Railway Station Road
  Aurangabad MH 43100

(G-6250)
MATT S AUTO CARE
18013 Robinsonville Rd (19958-4401)
PHONE.................302 226-2407
Matt Wiedmann, *Pr*
EMP: 5 **EST:** 2010
SALES (est): 80.34K **Privately Held**
SIC: 7538 General automotive repair shops

(G-6251)
MATTS FISH CAMP LEWES DE LLC
34401 Tenley Ct (19958-4200)
PHONE.................302 539-4415
Jack Temple, *Genl Mgr*
EMP: 11 **EST:** 2016
SALES (est): 60.51K **Privately Held**
Web: www.mattsfishcamplewes.com
SIC: 7032 Sporting and recreational camps

(G-6252)
MAX SEAL INC
Also Called: Teleborg Pipe Seals US
16192 Coastal Hwy (19958-3608)
PHONE.................619 946-2650
Alan Guzowski, *Pr*
Alejandro Castro, *Prin*
▼ **EMP:** 10 **EST:** 2006
SQ FT: 10,000
SALES (est): 2.47MM **Privately Held**
SIC: 2891 Sealing compounds, synthetic rubber or plastic

(G-6253)
MAXILLOFACIAL SOUTHERN DE ORAL
17605 Nassau Commons Blvd # 1 (19958-6284)
P.O. Box 400 (19969-0400)
PHONE.................302 644-2977
Bruce D Fisher, *Prin*
EMP: 24 **EST:** 2004
SALES (est): 505.56K **Privately Held**
SIC: 8021 Oral pathologist

(G-6254)
MCCLAIN CUSTODIAL SERVICE
418 Burton Ave (19958-1238)
PHONE.................302 645-6597
Tacolla Mc Clain, *Owner*
EMP: 5 **EST:** 1972
SALES (est): 124.57K **Privately Held**
SIC: 7349 Janitorial service, contract basis

(G-6255)
MCMAHON HEATING & AC
20378 John J Williams Hwy (19958-4303)
PHONE.................302 945-4300
Rick Mcmahon, *Owner*
EMP: 10 **EST:** 2001
SALES (est): 350.69K **Privately Held**
SIC: 1711 Heating and air conditioning contractors

(G-6256)
MEALS ON WHEELS OF LWES RHOBOTH
Also Called: MEALS ON WHEELS
32409 Lewes Georgetown Hwy (19958-1646)
PHONE.................302 645-7449
Kathleen Keuski, *Ex Dir*
Robert Derrickson, *Pr*
EMP: 5 **EST:** 1970
SALES (est): 1.04MM **Privately Held**
Web: www.mealsonwheels-lr.org
SIC: 8322 Meal delivery program

(G-6257)
MEDFLUENCERS INC ✪
21215 Dauphine St (19958-8915)
PHONE.................518 813-2788
Adam Goodcoff, *CEO*
Adam Goodcoff, *Managing Member*
EMP: 10 **EST:** 2022
SALES (est): 501.88K **Privately Held**
SIC: 8742 Marketing consulting services

(G-6258)
MEDTIX LLC
16337 Coastal Hwy (19958-3607)
P.O. Box 188 (19701-0188)
PHONE.................302 265-4550
Jack Berberian, *Prin*
EMP: 15
SALES (corp-wide): 9.06MM **Privately Held**
SIC: 5047 Medical equipment and supplies
PA: Medtix Llc
  221 S Rehoboth Blvd
  Milford DE 19963
  302 645-8070

(G-6259)
MEINEKE MUFFLER
Also Called: Meineke Discount Mufflers
213 W Cape Shores Dr (19958-3103)
PHONE.................302 644-8544
EMP: 5 **EST:** 2019
SALES (est): 44.38K **Privately Held**
Web: www.meineke.com
SIC: 7533 Muffler shop, sale or repair and installation

(G-6260)
MELCHIORRE AND MELCHIORRE
Also Called: J Melchiore & Sons
17352 Coastal Hwy (19958-6209)
PHONE.................302 645-6311
J G Melchiorre Senior, *Pr*
EMP: 10 **EST:** 1981
SQ FT: 6,000
SALES (est): 875.33K **Privately Held**
SIC: 6512 6514 Commercial and industrial building operation; Residential building, four or fewer units: operation

(G-6261)
MELISSA A WOLF
18512 Belle Grove Rd # 6 (19958-4699)
PHONE.................716 465-7093
Melissa Wolf, *Owner*
EMP: 5 **EST:** 2018
SALES (est): 65.76K **Privately Held**
SIC: 8049 Offices of health practitioner

(G-6262)
MEN IN BLACK WDDING OFFICIANTS
36000 Chester Ct (19958-5277)
PHONE.................302 945-6903
Kenneth Warne, *Prin*
EMP: 5 **EST:** 2017
SALES (est): 64.78K **Privately Held**
Web: www.meninblackofficiants.com
SIC: 7299 Wedding consultant

(G-6263)
MERESTONE CONSULTANTS INC
33516 Crossing Ave Unit 1 (19958-1697)
PHONE.................302 226-5880
Mike Early, *Brnch Mgr*
EMP: 10
SALES (corp-wide): 2.14MM **Privately Held**
Web: www.merestoneconsultants.com
SIC: 8713 8711 Surveying services; Construction and civil engineering

Lewes - Sussex County (G-6264) **GEOGRAPHIC SECTION**

PA: Merestone Consultants, Inc.
5215 W Woodmill Dr Ste 38
Wilmington DE 19808
302 992-7900

(G-6264)
MERIDA AEROSPACE INC (PA) ◊
16192 Coastal Hwy (19958-3608)
PHONE.....................305 396-1471
Fallon Velasco, *Pr*
EMP: 10 **EST:** 2023
SALES (est): 812.86K
SALES (corp-wide): 812.86K **Privately Held**
SIC: 3761 Guided missiles and space vehicles

(G-6265)
MERIX LLC (PA)
16192 Coastal Hwy (19958-3608)
PHONE.....................425 659-1425
Nithin Yadav, *Dir*
EMP: 7 **EST:** 2018
SALES (est): 264.34K
SALES (corp-wide): 264.34K **Privately Held**
SIC: 7372 7375 7389 Application computer software; On-line data base information retrieval; Business services, nec

(G-6266)
MERMAN MANAGEMENT INC
109 W Market St (19958-1346)
PHONE.....................302 644-6990
Elizabeth S Copeland, *Dir*
EMP: 5 **EST:** 2016
SALES (est): 107.33K **Privately Held**
SIC: 8741 Management services

(G-6267)
META HUMANS LTD ◊
16192 Coastal Hwy (19958-3608)
PHONE.....................904 690-1589
J Dsouza, *Ch Bd*
EMP: 10 **EST:** 2022
SALES (est): 670.97K **Privately Held**
SIC: 5045 Computer software

(G-6268)
MEXIGAS GROUP LLC
16192 Coastal Hwy (19958-3608)
PHONE.....................302 645-7400
Edgardo Armando P Robert, *Prin*
Pedro A Martinez, *Prin*
EMP: 12 **EST:** 2020
SALES (est): 132K **Privately Held**
SIC: 4923 Gas transmission and distribution

(G-6269)
MICHAEL ROBERT MEIBAUM
34527 Maple Dr (19958-4711)
PHONE.....................302 212-9969
EMP: 6 **EST:** 2018
SALES (est): 239.37K **Privately Held**
Web: www.meibaumlandscaping.com
SIC: 1794 Excavation work

(G-6270)
MICHELANGELO TECHNOLOGIES INC
16192 Coastal Hwy (19958-3608)
PHONE.....................949 382-1899
Ana O Tovar, *CEO*
EMP: 50 **EST:** 2017
SALES (est): 3.27MM **Privately Held**
SIC: 6361 Real estate title insurance

(G-6271)
MID ATLANTIC COMPOST & RE
33718 Wescoats Rd (19958-4902)
PHONE.....................302 644-2977
Bruce Fisher, *Prin*
EMP: 5 **EST:** 2007
SALES (est): 128.66K **Privately Held**
SIC: 4953 Recycling, waste materials

(G-6272)
MID-ATLANTIC FMLY PRACTICE LLC (PA)
20251 John J Williams Hwy (19958-4314)
P.O. Box 465 (19958-0465)
PHONE.....................302 644-6860
EMP: 11 **EST:** 2003
SALES (est): 6.65MM
SALES (corp-wide): 6.65MM **Privately Held**
Web: www.mafp.net
SIC: 8011 General and family practice, physician/surgeon

(G-6273)
MIDGE SMITH FINE ART GALLERY
135 2nd St Fl 2 (19958-1347)
PHONE.....................302 245-4528
Midge Smith, *Prin*
EMP: 7 **EST:** 2011
SALES (est): 53.63K **Privately Held**
SIC: 8412 Art gallery

(G-6274)
MILLENNIUM MARKETING SOLUTIONS
Also Called: Millennium Printing & Graphics
31015 Sycamore Dr (19958-3883)
PHONE.....................301 725-8000
Janice Tippett, *Pr*
EMP: 20 **EST:** 1980
SALES (est): 2.33MM **Privately Held**
Web: imk.ironmarkusa.com
SIC: 2752 Offset printing

(G-6275)
MILTON FAMILY PRACTICE
16529 Coastal Hwy (19958-3696)
PHONE.....................302 684-2000
Charles G Wagner, *Prin*
EMP: 11 **EST:** 2012
SALES (est): 1.73MM **Privately Held**
Web: www.miltonfamilypractice.com
SIC: 8011 General and family practice, physician/surgeon

(G-6276)
MILWOOD HYDROGEN LLC
16192 Coastal Hwy (19958-3608)
PHONE.....................424 330-5739
Jacques Fumento, *Ex Dir*
EMP: 60 **EST:** 2021
SALES (est): 7.7MM **Privately Held**
SIC: 2813 Hydrogen

(G-6277)
MINDER FOUNDATION
16192 Coastal Hwy (19958-3608)
PHONE.....................917 477-7661
Natalie Moore, *Dir*
EMP: 5 **EST:** 2016
SALES (est): 107.6K **Privately Held**
SIC: 8733 Research institute

(G-6278)
MINFON GROUP INC
16192 Coastal Hwy (19958-3608)
P.O. Box 592 (95015-0592)
PHONE.....................408 930-2190
Ken Chang, *CEO*
EMP: 15 **EST:** 2007
SALES (est): 1.28MM **Privately Held**
SIC: 5099 Durable goods, nec

(G-6279)
MIRANDAS CARPENTRY
18272 Magnolia Ln (19958-4770)
PHONE.....................302 245-0298
Fernando Miranda, *Prin*
EMP: 5 **EST:** 2017
SALES (est): 65.22K **Privately Held**
SIC: 1751 Carpentry work

(G-6280)
MITCHELL C STICKLER MD INC (PA)
Also Called: Cape Hnlpen Nntcoke Drmatology
750 Kings Hwy Ste 110 (19958-1772)
PHONE.....................302 644-6400
EMP: 16 **EST:** 1991
SALES (est): 1.28MM **Privately Held**
Web: www.beachderm.com
SIC: 8011 Dermatologist

(G-6281)
MJLINKCOM INC
16192 Coastal Hwy (19958-3608)
PHONE.....................303 324-7668
EMP: 5 **EST:** 2020
SALES (est): 46.16K **Privately Held**
Web: www.mjlink.com
SIC: 7371 Computer software development and applications

(G-6282)
MNBOOST CORP (PA)
16192 Coastal Hwy (19958)
PHONE.....................302 645-7400
EMP: 6
SALES (est): 72.36K
SALES (corp-wide): 72.36K **Privately Held**
SIC: 7371 Computer software development and applications

(G-6283)
MOBEASY LLC
16192 Coastal Hwy (19958-3608)
PHONE.....................628 251-1274
EMP: 5 **EST:** 2021
SALES (est): 46.16K **Privately Held**
Web: www.mobeasy.com
SIC: 7371 Computer software development and applications

(G-6284)
MOBILE ENGAGEMENT LLC
16192 Coastal Hwy (19958-3608)
PHONE.....................646 583-2775
Mark Hadleigh, *Managing Member*
EMP: 5 **EST:** 2020
SALES (est): 130.5K **Privately Held**
Web: www.save.social
SIC: 2741 Internet publishing and broadcasting

(G-6285)
MOBILE HOME REMEDIES LLC
17144 Holly Rd (19958-6260)
PHONE.....................717 879-9176
Christopher Burhans, *Prin*
EMP: 5 **EST:** 2008
SALES (est): 118.06K **Privately Held**
SIC: 6515 Mobile home site operators

(G-6286)
MODENA SOFTWARE INC
16192 Coastal Hwy (19958-3608)
PHONE.....................650 326-1136
Kunal Puri, *Prin*
EMP: 5 **EST:** 2012
SALES (est): 93.08K **Privately Held**
Web: www.modenasoftware.com
SIC: 5045 Computer software

(G-6287)
MOHANDIS ENTERPRISES LLC ◊
16192 Coastal Hwy (19958-3608)
PHONE.....................302 261-2821
Ahmad Khan, *Managing Member*
EMP: 5 **EST:** 2023
SALES (est): 207.81K **Privately Held**
SIC: 8742 Human resource consulting services

(G-6288)
MONSTER GAMING LLC
16192 Coastal Hwy (19958-3608)
PHONE.....................251 281-8906
Meng Wu, *Dir*
EMP: 16
SALES (est): 543.62K **Privately Held**
SIC: 7371 Computer software development and applications

(G-6289)
MOON SHOT ENERGY LLC
16192 Coastal Hwy (19958-3608)
PHONE.....................512 297-2626
EMP: 3 **EST:** 2013
SALES (est): 375.75K **Privately Held**
SIC: 2086 Bottled and canned soft drinks

(G-6290)
MOORINGS AT LEWES
17028 Cadbury Cir (19958-7022)
PHONE.....................302 644-6382
EMP: 80 **EST:** 1999
SALES (est): 15.08MM **Privately Held**
Web: www.mooringsatlewes.org
SIC: 8361 Aged home

(G-6291)
MORE FOUNDATION GROUP
210 Priscilla Cir (19958-8920)
PHONE.....................302 645-4669
James J Riordan, *Pr*
EMP: 8 **EST:** 2011
SALES (est): 543.37K **Privately Held**
Web: www.morefoundationgroup.org
SIC: 8699 Charitable organization

(G-6292)
MORTON ELECTRIC CO
Also Called: U-Haul
16867 Kings Hwy (19958-4783)
PHONE.....................302 645-9414
Todd Fritchman, *Pr*
EMP: 5 **EST:** 2011
SALES (est): 197.94K **Privately Held**
Web: www.mortonelectric.com
SIC: 7519 7513 7359 7629 Utility trailer rental; Truck rental and leasing, no drivers; Equipment rental and leasing, nec; Electrical repair shops

(G-6293)
MOTAMEET LLC
16192 Coastal Hwy (19958-3608)
PHONE.....................302 242-4483
EMP: 5 **EST:** 2016
SALES (est): 46.16K **Privately Held**
SIC: 7371 Computer software development and applications

(G-6294)
MOVEMENT MORTGAGE LLC
19413 Jingle Shell Way Unit 2 (19958)
PHONE.....................302 344-6758
Trish Raber, *Brnch Mgr*
EMP: 11
Web: www.movement.com
SIC: 6162 Mortgage bankers and loan correspondents
PA: Movement Mortgage, Llc

GEOGRAPHIC SECTION

Lewes - Sussex County (G-6324)

8024 Calvin Hall Rd
Fort Mill SC 29707

(G-6295)
MSD BUSINESS SOLUTIONS LLC
16192 Coastal Hwy (19958-3608)
PHONE..................609 375-8461
Rajavel Selvaraj, *Managing Member*
EMP: 6 **EST:** 2021
SALES (est): 358.14K **Privately Held**
SIC: 7371 Computer software development and applications

(G-6296)
MURPHY ELECTRIC INC
30731 Sassafras Dr (19958-3875)
P.O. Box 392 (19958-0392)
PHONE..................302 644-0404
June Murphy, *Pr*
James Murphy, *VP*
EMP: 9 **EST:** 2000
SALES (est): 429K **Privately Held**
Web: www.murphyelectricde.com
SIC: 1731 General electrical contractor

(G-6297)
MUSIC ART & CULTURE FOUNDATION
Also Called: Culcha Foundation
16192 Coastal Hwy (19958-3608)
PHONE..................347 746-9047
Sharon Abrams, *Managing Member*
Shawn Griffith, *Prin*
EMP: 5 **EST:** 2019
SALES (est): 50.66K **Privately Held**
SIC: 8322 8011 8399 8299 Outreach program; Health maintenance organization; Health systems agency; Meditation therapy

(G-6298)
MY BEACH AGENT REALTY GROUP
16392 Coastal Hwy (19958-3611)
PHONE..................302 858-2370
EMP: 5 **EST:** 2018
SALES (est): 152.56K **Privately Held**
SIC: 6531 Real estate brokers and agents

(G-6299)
MY KASE LLC
16192 Coastal Hwy (19958-3608)
PHONE..................647 686-7202
Vimosan Nanthakuran, *Prin*
EMP: 20 **EST:** 2021
SALES (est): 588.11K **Privately Held**
SIC: 7371 Computer software development and applications

(G-6300)
MY LIP STUFF
21002 Robinsonville Rd (19958-6069)
PHONE..................302 945-5922
My Lip Stuff, *Prin*
EMP: 2 **EST:** 2008
SALES (est): 174.65K **Privately Held**
Web: www.mylipstuff.com
SIC: 2844 Perfumes, cosmetics and other toilet preparations

(G-6301)
MY SEASIDE SPA
17021 Old Orchard Rd (19958-4832)
PHONE..................302 313-5174
Mei Lin, *Prin*
EMP: 6 **EST:** 2015
SALES (est): 37.51K **Privately Held**
SIC: 7991 Spas

(G-6302)
MYRALON WEBB MS
18494 Foxfield Ln (19958-3949)
PHONE..................302 684-3841
Myralon Ms Webb, *Prin*
EMP: 6 **EST:** 2010
SALES (est): 121.5K **Privately Held**
SIC: 1623 Underground utilities contractor

(G-6303)
NABEEL AND HUZAIF LLC
16192 Coastal Hwy (19958-3608)
PHONE..................302 445-7483
EMP: 2
SALES (est): 92.41K **Privately Held**
SIC: 2844 Depilatories (cosmetic)

(G-6304)
NANCY A MONDERO DO
110 Anglers Rd Unit 103 (19958-1192)
PHONE..................302 644-9641
Nancy Mondero, *Prin*
EMP: 7 **EST:** 2017
SALES (est): 54.13K **Privately Held**
SIC: 8011 Offices and clinics of medical doctors

(G-6305)
NANCY A UNION MD
Also Called: Aponte, Lourdes MD
1302 Savannah Rd (19958-1526)
PHONE..................302 645-6644
EMP: 9 **EST:** 1984
SALES (est): 452.07K **Privately Held**
Web: www.beaconinvest.com
SIC: 8062 General medical and surgical hospitals

(G-6306)
NASSAU VLY VINEYARDS & WINERY
32165 Winery Way (19958-6326)
PHONE..................302 645-9463
Margaret Raley, *Owner*
EMP: 4 **EST:** 1995
SALES (est): 251.45K **Privately Held**
Web: www.nassauvalley.com
SIC: 2084 Wines

(G-6307)
NATURAL STACKS INC
16192 Coastal Hwy (19958-3608)
PHONE..................855 678-2257
Abelard Lindsay, *Dir*
Ryan Munsey, *Chief*
EMP: 5 **EST:** 2014
SALES (est): 317.82K **Privately Held**
Web: www.naturalstacks.com
SIC: 2834 Vitamin, nutrient, and hematinic preparations for human use

(G-6308)
NEFTALI AYERAS MARTINEZ MD
31674 Grenache Ct (19958-2516)
PHONE..................302 827-2330
Neftali Ayeras Martinez, *Prin*
EMP: 8 **EST:** 2011
SALES (est): 82.72K **Privately Held**
SIC: 8011 Physicians' office, including specialists

(G-6309)
NETSKYADS MEDIA LLC
16192 Coastal Hwy (19958-3608)
PHONE..................302 476-2277
Gong Hao, *Managing Member*
EMP: 10 **EST:** 2018
SALES (est): 341.86K **Privately Held**
Web: www.netskyads.com
SIC: 7311 Advertising agencies

(G-6310)
NEVER NVER LAND KNNEL CTTERY I
34377 Neverland Rd (19958-4651)
PHONE..................302 645-6140
Allen Quillen, *Pr*
Dorothy Guillen, *Pr*
EMP: 5 **EST:** 1975
SALES (est): 266.86K **Privately Held**
Web: www.neverlandkennel.com
SIC: 0752 Boarding services, kennels

(G-6311)
NEW LIVE VENTURES INC
Also Called: Strave
16192 Coastal Hwy (19958-3608)
PHONE..................914 960-1877
Brent Lavitt, *Pr*
EMP: 5
SALES (est): 46.16K **Privately Held**
SIC: 7371 Computer software development and applications

(G-6312)
NEWREZ LLC
17723 Coastal Hwy Unit 2 (19958-6322)
PHONE..................240 475-4741
EMP: 7 **EST:** 2008
SALES (est): 57.87K **Privately Held**
Web: www.newrez.com
SIC: 8111 Legal services

(G-6313)
NICOIN TELECOM LLC
16192 Coastal Hwy (19958-3608)
PHONE..................800 914-6177
Mirta Cedeo, *Managing Member*
EMP: 24
SALES (est): 1.45MM **Privately Held**
SIC: 1623 Transmitting tower (telecommunication) construction

(G-6314)
NICOLA PIZZA INC
Also Called: Nic-O-Boli
17323 Ocean One Plz (19958-1898)
PHONE..................302 227-6211
Nicholas S Caggiano, *Pr*
Nicholas S Caggiano Junior, *VP*
Joan Caggiano, *
EMP: 30 **EST:** 1971
SALES (est): 2.2MM **Privately Held**
Web: www.nicolapizza.com
SIC: 5812 2038 Pizza restaurants; Frozen specialties, nec

(G-6315)
NIKKO CAPITAL INVESTMENTS LTD
16192 Coastal Hwy (19958-3608)
PHONE..................832 324-5335
Phong Lai, *CEO*
EMP: 9 **EST:** 2014
SALES (est): 121.63K **Privately Held**
Web: www.nikkocapital.com
SIC: 6799 Venture capital companies

(G-6316)
NIRU LLC
Also Called: Nitespot
16192 Coastal Hwy (19958-3608)
PHONE..................617 893-7317
EMP: 5 **EST:** 2021
SALES (est): 191.53K **Privately Held**
Web: www.nirugroup.com
SIC: 7389 7929 Business Activities at Non-Commercial Site; Entertainment service

(G-6317)
NO CODE SOFTWARE INC
16192 Coastal Hwy (19958-3608)
PHONE..................833 366-2633
EMP: 10 **EST:** 2020
SALES (est): 428.62K **Privately Held**
SIC: 7371 Computer software development and applications

(G-6318)
NOBLE BUILDERS & DEVELOPERS LL
16694 Blue Marlin Ct (19958-9148)
PHONE..................203 948-9396
EMP: 5 **EST:** 2018
SALES (est): 251.89K **Privately Held**
SIC: 1521 New construction, single-family houses

(G-6319)
NORTHWEST TITLE PLANET INC
16192 Coastal Hwy (19958-3608)
PHONE..................248 278-4080
Hariprasad Ky, *Pr*
EMP: 5 **EST:** 2020
SALES (est): 365.07K **Privately Held**
SIC: 6361 Real estate title insurance

(G-6320)
NORWEX
402 Samantha Dr (19958-4146)
PHONE..................817 691-7759
EMP: 5 **EST:** 2018
SALES (est): 74.09K **Privately Held**
Web: www.norwex.biz
SIC: 7699 Cleaning services

(G-6321)
NOVA RE & BUS CONSULTING LLC
Also Called: Nova Real Estate
16192 Coastal Hwy (19958-3608)
PHONE..................302 258-2193
EMP: 9 **EST:** 2006
SQ FT: 1,200
SALES (est): 338.77K **Privately Held**
SIC: 8742 Management consulting services

(G-6322)
NUTRA4HEALTH LLC
16192 Coastal Hwy (19958-3608)
PHONE..................704 223-8677
EMP: 8 **EST:** 2018
SALES (est): 622.09K **Privately Held**
Web: www.nutra4.com
SIC: 8099 Health and allied services, nec

(G-6323)
NUYKA INC (PA)
Also Called: Nuyka
16192 Coastal Hwy (19958-3608)
PHONE..................707 400-5444
Bhavin Patel, *CEO*
EMP: 25 **EST:** 2013
SQ FT: 1,100
SALES (est): 9.65MM
SALES (corp-wide): 9.65MM **Privately Held**
Web: www.nuyka.com
SIC: 7371 7376 8731 Computer software development and applications; Computer facilities management; Computer (hardware) development

(G-6324)
OAK CONSTRUCTION
788 Kings Hwy (19958-1704)
PHONE..................302 703-2013
Michael Purnell, *Prin*
EMP: 5 **EST:** 2008
SALES (est): 875.22K **Privately Held**

Lewes - Sussex County (G-6325)   GEOGRAPHIC SECTION

Web: www.oakconstructioncompany.com
SIC: 1521 New construction, single-family houses

(G-6325)
OAKLEAF INC
Also Called: Oakleaf Personal Care Home
31859 Carneros Ave (19958-2506)
PHONE..................................412 881-8194
EMP: 20 **EST:** 1996
SALES (est): 1.99MM **Privately Held**
Web: www.oakleafpersonalcarehome.com
SIC: 8052 Personal care facility

(G-6326)
OBHOST LLC
16192 Coastal Hwy (19958-3608)
PHONE..................................302 440-1447
Mohammad Owais, *Prin*
EMP: 8 **EST:** 2019
SALES (est): 322.19K **Privately Held**
Web: www.obhost.net
SIC: 7373 4813 Systems integration services; Internet host services

(G-6327)
OCEAN RACH INTRNAL MEDICINE PA
32796 Ocean Reach Dr (19958-4662)
PHONE..................................302 644-7472
Gary E Raffel, *Prin*
EMP: 7 **EST:** 2018
SALES (est): 134.01K **Privately Held**
SIC: 8099 Health and allied services, nec

(G-6328)
OCEANIC VENTURES INC
32292 Nassau Rd Unit 1 (19958-3721)
PHONE..................................302 645-5872
EMP: 8 **EST:** 1995
SQ FT: 5,000
SALES (est): 835.49K **Privately Held**
Web: www.oceanic-cabinetry.com
SIC: 1751 Cabinet and finish carpentry

(G-6329)
OCEANSIDE ELITE CLG BLDG SVCS
33033 Nassau Loop (19958-3730)
PHONE..................................302 339-7777
Noreen Kushner, *Prin*
EMP: 25 **EST:** 2017
SQ FT: 250
SALES (est): 427.69K **Privately Held**
Web: www.oceanside-elite.com
SIC: 7349 7217 Building and office cleaning services; Carpet and upholstery cleaning on customer premises

(G-6330)
OCEANSIDE SEAFOOD MKT DELI LLC
109 Savannah Rd (19958-1475)
PHONE..................................302 313-5158
Christine Becker, *Prin*
EMP: 14 **EST:** 2014
SALES (est): 94.68K **Privately Held**
SIC: 5812 5146 Delicatessen (eating places); Fish and seafoods

(G-6331)
OCIETY LLC (PA)
16192 Coastal Hwy (19958-3608)
PHONE..................................760 408-1992
Manfred Swarovski, *CEO*
EMP: 6 **EST:** 2020
SALES (est): 101.16K
SALES (corp-wide): 101.16K **Privately Held**

SIC: 7371 Computer software development and applications

(G-6332)
OFC OF PREACHESS VELLAH MD
36377 Tarpon Dr (19958-5056)
PHONE..................................302 645-2245
EMP: 8 **EST:** 2012
SALES (est): 105.22K **Privately Held**
SIC: 8011 General and family practice, physician/surgeon

(G-6333)
OMOGS GROUP CORP ✪
16192 Coastal Hwy (19958-3608)
PHONE..................................302 645-7400
Shu Lu, *Prin*
EMP: 5 **EST:** 2022
SALES (est): 68.89K **Privately Held**
SIC: 7389 Business services, nec

(G-6334)
ONE VENTURES EAST LLC
16192 Coastal Hwy (19958-3608)
PHONE..................................412 477-2754
EMP: 5
SALES (est): 76.37K **Privately Held**
SIC: 6799 Commodity contract trading companies

(G-6335)
ONECALL SERVICES INC
341 Highway One (19958)
PHONE..................................302 645-9008
EMP: 10 **EST:** 1999
SALES (est): 258.34K **Privately Held**
Web: www.onecallservices.biz
SIC: 1521 Single-family home remodeling, additions, and repairs

(G-6336)
ONEILL WOODWORKING LLC
23292 Bridgeway Dr W (19958-5115)
PHONE..................................443 669-3458
EMP: 3 **EST:** 2018
SALES (est): 82.89K **Privately Held**
SIC: 2431 Millwork

(G-6337)
OPEN HEART STUDIO LLC
32191 Nassau Rd Unit 3 (19958-3762)
PHONE..................................302 381-0212
Karen L Barwick, *Prin*
EMP: 5 **EST:** 2009
SALES (est): 101.4K **Privately Held**
SIC: 7299 Miscellaneous personal service

(G-6338)
OPPAMEET LLC
Also Called: Oppa
16192 Coastal Hwy (19958-3608)
PHONE..................................732 540-0308
Hung C Ho, *CEO*
EMP: 6
SQ FT: 6,486
SALES (est): 258.94K **Privately Held**
SIC: 7372 Application computer software

(G-6339)
ORGANIZATION INNOVATIONS
18393 Dunes Way (19958-5906)
PHONE..................................443 280-3009
Stephanie Brooks, *Prin*
EMP: 6 **EST:** 2013
SALES (est): 129.18K **Privately Held**
Web: www.organizationinnovations.com
SIC: 8699 Personal interest organization

(G-6340)
ORTHOPDIC ASSOC SUTHERN DEL PA
12100 Black Swan Dr Ste 201 (19958-4991)
PHONE..................................302 644-3311
David Blaeuer, *Executive Administrator*
EMP: 406 **EST:** 1990
SALES (est): 9.22MM
SALES (corp-wide): 31.54MM **Privately Held**
Web: www.delawarebonedocs.com
SIC: 8011 Orthopedic physician
PA: First State Orthopaedics, P.A.
4745 Ogltn Stntn Rd # 225
Newark DE 19713
302 731-2888

(G-6341)
OVERFALLS MARITIME MUSEUM
219 Pilottown Road (19958)
P.O. Box 413 (19958-0413)
PHONE..................................302 644-8050
EMP: 60
SALES (corp-wide): 93.41K **Privately Held**
Web: www.overfalls.org
SIC: 8412 Museum
PA: Overfalls Maritime Museum
13 Harborview Rd
Lewes DE 19958
302 645-0761

(G-6342)
OVERSCOUT INC
16192 Coastal Hwy (19958-3608)
PHONE..................................415 687-3005
EMP: 5 **EST:** 2020
SALES (est): 46.16K **Privately Held**
Web: www.overscout.com
SIC: 7371 Computer software development and applications

(G-6343)
P A ABA INTL INC
Also Called: Aba PA
16192 Coastal Hwy (19958-3608)
PHONE..................................800 979-5106
Manuel P Lora, *CEO*
Aycher Carbonell, *Sec*
EMP: 9 **EST:** 1985
SQ FT: 1,500
SALES (est): 451.5K **Privately Held**
SIC: 8742 Banking and finance consultant

(G-6344)
P&A RIVER GALLERY PROMOTION
33189 Cherry Ct (19958-5227)
PHONE..................................302 947-1805
Pat Matero, *Prin*
EMP: 5 **EST:** 2006
SALES (est): 236.55K **Privately Held**
SIC: 5199 Advertising specialties

(G-6345)
PACBAK INC ✪
16192 Coastal Hwy (19958-3608)
PHONE..................................907 268-0802
Brian Mckinnon, *Pr*
EMP: 10 **EST:** 2023
SALES (est): 406.01K **Privately Held**
SIC: 3429 Ice chests or coolers, portable, except foam plastic

(G-6346)
PAGETECH
20418 Oakney St (19958-5820)
PHONE..................................845 624-4911
EMP: 3 **EST:** 2019
SALES (est): 59.63K **Privately Held**

SIC: 2741 Miscellaneous publishing

(G-6347)
PAINT BY BILL LLC
30897 Best Ln (19958-3659)
PHONE..................................302 565-9013
William Lemon, *Prin*
EMP: 5 **EST:** 2017
SALES (est): 72.55K **Privately Held**
Web: www.paintbybill.biz
SIC: 1721 Painting and paper hanging

(G-6348)
PAPALEO ROSEN CHELF & PINDER
135 2nd St (19958-1347)
PHONE..................................302 644-8600
Harry Papaleo, *Pr*
EMP: 8 **EST:** 2005
SALES (est): 221.44K **Privately Held**
Web: www.prccpa.com
SIC: 7291 8721 Tax return preparation services; Accounting, auditing, and bookkeeping

(G-6349)
PARALLELDOTS INC
16192 Coastal Hwy (19958-3608)
PHONE..................................224 587-0022
Angam Parashar, *Dir*
EMP: 18 **EST:** 2017
SALES (est): 554.57K **Privately Held**
Web: www.paralleldots.com
SIC: 7371 Computer software development

(G-6350)
PARKINSONS EDCATN SPPORT GROUP
17000 Black Marlin Cir (19958-5026)
P.O. Box 56 (19958-0056)
PHONE..................................302 644-3465
Denise Demback, *Prin*
EMP: 5 **EST:** 2016
SALES (est): 63.68K **Privately Held**
Web: www.delmarvaparkinsonsalliance.org
SIC: 8399 Social services, nec

(G-6351)
PARSELL FUNERAL ENTPS INC
Also Called: Parsell Fnrl Homes Crematorium
16961 Kings Hwy (19958-4782)
PHONE..................................302 645-9520
Keith Parsell, *Pr*
Andrea Parsell, *VP*
Andrew Parsell, *Prin*
Johnathan Parsell, *Prin*
EMP: 7 **EST:** 1895
SALES (est): 955.14K **Privately Held**
Web: www.parsellfuneralhomes.com
SIC: 7261 Funeral home

(G-6352)
PAT & RAY ENTERPRISES
22907 Dogwood Dr (19958-5222)
PHONE..................................302 945-1367
Raymond Deskins, *Prin*
EMP: 5 **EST:** 2008
SALES (est): 88K **Privately Held**
SIC: 7389 Business services, nec

(G-6353)
PATIO SYSTEMS INC
16083 New Rd (19958-3710)
PHONE..................................302 644-6540
Ronald Simmons, *Pr*
Karen Truitt, *Sec*
EMP: 5 **EST:** 2001
SQ FT: 1,300
SALES (est): 1.38MM **Privately Held**
Web: www.patiosystems.com

GEOGRAPHIC SECTION

Lewes - Sussex County (G-6383)

SIC: 1799 Awning installation

(G-6354)
PATRICK SWIER MDPA KAR
1400 Savannah Rd (19958-1623)
PHONE..................302 645-7737
Patrick Swier, *Prin*
EMP: 5 **EST:** 2005
SALES (est): 612.11K **Privately Held**
Web: www.theswierclinic.com
SIC: 8011 Plastic surgeon

(G-6355)
PAUL C CUNNINGHAM & ASSOC LLC
18700 Arabian Acres Rd (19958-3923)
PHONE..................302 258-4163
Paul C Cunningham, *Managing Member*
EMP: 5 **EST:** 2009
SALES (est): 114.08K **Privately Held**
SIC: 8742 7389 Management consulting services; Business services, nec

(G-6356)
PDING LLC ✪
16192 Coastal Hwy (19958-3608)
PHONE..................252 201-8458
Woojin Jo, *Managing Member*
EMP: 7 **EST:** 2023
SALES (est): 270.58K **Privately Held**
SIC: 7379 Computer related services, nec

(G-6357)
PEAK PRFMCE GLOBL SVCS LLC
18261 Alpine Loop (19958-9702)
PHONE..................610 554-4773
EMP: 10 **EST:** 2013
SALES (est): 330.09K **Privately Held**
Web: www.peakperformanceglobalservices.com
SIC: 0741 Veterinary services for livestock

(G-6358)
PEAR MEDIA LLC
16192 Coastal Hwy (19958-3608)
PHONE..................505 932-6555
Rachit Madan, *Managing Member*
EMP: 35 **EST:** 2020
SALES (est): 2MM **Privately Held**
SIC: 7311 Advertising consultant

(G-6359)
PEMBINA HEALTH INC
16192 Coastal Hwy (19958-3608)
PHONE..................701 314-7895
Jenn Klym, *Pr*
EMP: 10 **EST:** 2021
SALES (est): 541.18K **Privately Held**
SIC: 2051 Bakery: wholesale or wholesale/retail combined

(G-6360)
PEPPERS INC (PA)
17601 Coastal Hwy Unit 1 (19958-6217)
PHONE..................302 645-0812
Chip Hearn, *Pr*
Luther Hearn, *VP*
EMP: 5 **EST:** 1986
SALES (est): 2.82MM
SALES (corp-wide): 2.82MM **Privately Held**
Web: www.peppers.com
SIC: 5149 Sauces

(G-6361)
PEPPERS INC
15608 Coastal Hwy (19958)
PHONE..................302 644-6900
Nicole Cooper, *Off Mgr*
EMP: 10
SALES (corp-wide): 2.82MM **Privately Held**

Web: www.peppers.com
SIC: 5149 Sauces
PA: Peppers Inc
   17601 Coastal Hwy Unit 1
   Lewes DE 19958
   302 645-0812

(G-6362)
PEPPERSCOM INC
17601 Coastal Hwy Unit 1 (19958-6217)
PHONE..................302 703-6355
Ruth Spepper, *Prin*
EMP: 6 **EST:** 2013
SALES (est): 199.26K **Privately Held**
Web: www.peppers.com
SIC: 5149 Sauces

(G-6363)
PERRYFILMS PRODUCTION CO LLC
16192 Coastal Hwy (19958-3608)
PHONE..................302 505-4458
Tabari Perry, *Managing Member*
EMP: 4 **EST:** 2021
SALES (est): 61.77K **Privately Held**
Web: www.perryfilmsproduction.com
SIC: 7335 3861 Commercial photography; Photographic paper and cloth, all types, nec

(G-6364)
PETAL PUSHERS LLC
31341 Kendale Rd (19958-4480)
PHONE..................302 945-0350
Harriet Allen, *Prin*
EMP: 4 **EST:** 2008
SALES (est): 100K **Privately Held**
Web: www.petalpushers.us
SIC: 3545 Pushers

(G-6365)
PHILLIP T BRADLEY INC
33057 Angola Rd (19958-5699)
PHONE..................302 947-2741
Phillip Bradley, *Prin*
EMP: 5 **EST:** 2006
SALES (est): 487.22K **Privately Held**
SIC: 1522 Residential construction, nec

(G-6366)
PHYSICANS DSPNSING SLTONS LWES
33664 Bayview Medical Dr (19958-1933)
PHONE..................302 313-4883
EMP: 7 **EST:** 2017
SALES (est): 90.11K **Privately Held**
SIC: 8011 Offices and clinics of medical doctors

(G-6367)
PIEHOLETV LLC
16192 Coastal Hwy (19958-3608)
PHONE..................415 287-3566
EMP: 9 **EST:** 2019
SALES (est): 261.31K **Privately Held**
Web: www.piehole.tv
SIC: 7812 Video production

(G-6368)
PIIS GLOBAL LLC
16192 Coastal Hwy (19958-3608)
PHONE..................628 600-5249
EMP: 30 **EST:** 2021
SALES (est): 788.31K **Privately Held**
SIC: 7389 Business Activities at Non-Commercial Site

(G-6369)
PILOTS ASSN FOR BAY RIVER DEL
41 Cape Henlopen Dr (19958-3142)
PHONE..................302 645-2229
John Vaughn, *Dir*

EMP: 31
SALES (corp-wide): 3.22MM **Privately Held**
Web: www.delpilots.org
SIC: 3812 Search and navigation equipment
PA: Pilots Association For The Bay And River Delaware
   800 S Columbus Blvd
   Philadelphia PA
   215 465-2851

(G-6370)
PINE ACRES INC
Also Called: Leisure Pt MBL HM Pk Cmpground
34385 Carpenters Way # B (19958-5094)
PHONE..................302 945-2000
George H Harrison Junior, *Pr*
Judith Harrison, *VP*
Thelma Corso, *Sec*
EMP: 15 **EST:** 1967
SALES (est): 225.4K **Privately Held**
SIC: 7033 6515 Campsite; Mobile home site operators

(G-6371)
PIRATE POOLS LLC
31325 Red Mill Cir (19958-4178)
PHONE..................302 519-0624
EMP: 6 **EST:** 2018
SALES (est): 245.75K **Privately Held**
Web: www.piratepools.net
SIC: 1799 Swimming pool construction

(G-6372)
PIRATES OF LEWES EXPEDITIONS
400 Anglers Rd (19958-3145)
PHONE..................302 249-3538
EMP: 6 **EST:** 2013
SALES (est): 33.75K **Privately Held**
Web: www.lewespirates.com
SIC: 7999 Fishing boats, party: operation

(G-6373)
PIXSTORY GLOBAL HOLDING INC
16192 Coastal Hwy (19958-3608)
PHONE..................202 615-6777
EMP: 5
SALES (est): 247.21K **Privately Held**
Web: www.pixstory.com
SIC: 3629 Electrical industrial apparatus, nec

(G-6374)
PJHJ LLC
17569 Nassau Commons Blvd (19958-6284)
PHONE..................302 645-2159
EMP: 7 **EST:** 2011
SALES (est): 262.42K **Privately Held**
SIC: 1721 Painting and paper hanging

(G-6375)
PKS & COMPANY PA
1143 Savannah Rd Ste 1 (19958-1515)
PHONE..................302 645-5757
Ronald E Derr, *Bmch Mgr*
EMP: 6
SALES (corp-wide): 5MM **Privately Held**
Web: www.pkscpa.com
SIC: 8721 Auditing services
PA: Pks & Company, P.A.
   1801 Sweetbay Dr
   Salisbury MD 21804
   410 219-3345

(G-6376)
PLACIDIFY INC
16192 Coastal Hwy (19958-3608)
PHONE..................833 752-2434
Paul Gneco, *CEO*

EMP: 20 **EST:** 2016
SALES (est): 594.77K **Privately Held**
Web: www.placidify.com
SIC: 8748 Business consulting, nec

(G-6377)
PLASTIC CSMTC PRIPH NRVE SRGER
1400 Savannah Rd (19958-1623)
PHONE..................302 645-7737
Patrick Swier, *Prin*
EMP: 10 **EST:** 2010
SALES (est): 97.49K **Privately Held**
Web: www.theswierclinic.com
SIC: 8011 Plastic surgeon

(G-6378)
PLATINUM ROOFS
29029 Lewes Georgetown Hwy (19958-3909)
PHONE..................302 226-4510
Joe Crispin, *Pr*
EMP: 7 **EST:** 2017
SALES (est): 67.02K **Privately Held**
Web: www.platinumroofs.com
SIC: 1761 Roofing contractor

(G-6379)
PNC BANK NATIONAL ASSOCIATION
Also Called: PNC
17725 Coastal Hwy (19958-6215)
PHONE..................302 645-4500
David Crouse, *Mgr*
EMP: 5
SALES (corp-wide): 23.54B **Publicly Held**
Web: www.pnc.com
SIC: 6021 National trust companies with deposits, commercial
HQ: Pnc Bank, National Association
   300 5th Ave
   Pittsburgh PA 15222
   877 762-2000

(G-6380)
POCKET FM CORP
Also Called: Pocket FM
16192 Coastal Hwy (19958-3608)
PHONE..................408 896-7038
Rohan Nayak, *CEO*
EMP: 30 **EST:** 2021
SALES (est): 430.88K **Privately Held**
SIC: 7812 Audio-visual program production

(G-6381)
POLAR STRATEGY INC
16192 Coastal Hwy (19958-3608)
PHONE..................703 628-0001
Omar Mahmood, *Prin*
EMP: 5
SQ FT: 150
SALES (est): 230.53K **Privately Held**
Web: www.polarstrategy.com
SIC: 7371 7373 Computer software systems analysis and design, custom; Value-added resellers, computer systems

(G-6382)
POPEYCO LLC
16192 Coastal Hwy (19958-3608)
PHONE..................202 368-3842
EMP: 6
SALES (est): 87.5K **Privately Held**
SIC: 5045 Computer software

(G-6383)
PORT LEWES ASSOC UNIT OWNER
34382 Carpenters Way Ste 6 (19958-4919)
PHONE..................302 645-6110
EMP: 6 **EST:** 2004

Lewes - Sussex County (G-6384)   GEOGRAPHIC SECTION

SALES (est): 219.55K **Privately Held**
SIC: **8611** Business associations

(G-6384)
POWER ON US INC
Also Called: Power On
16192 Coastal Hwy (19958-3608)
PHONE..................212 317-1010
Per Solli, *CEO*
EMP: 40 EST: 2016
SQ FT: 2,000
SALES (est): 3MM
SALES (corp-wide): 51.78MM **Privately Held**
SIC: **7371** Computer software development
PA: Insightsoftware, Llc
   8529 Six Forks Rd
   Raleigh NC 27615
   919 872-7800

(G-6385)
POWERS INTERACTIVE DIGITAL LLC
16192 Coastal Hwy (19958-3608)
PHONE..................267 334-6306
EMP: 6 EST: 2021
SALES (est): 70.36K **Privately Held**
SIC: **7319** Display advertising service

(G-6386)
PREMIER PHYSICAL THERAPY AND
20268 Plantations Rd Ste B (19958-4622)
PHONE..................302 727-0075
Richard Binstein, *Prin*
EMP: 11 EST: 2018
SALES (est): 215.47K **Privately Held**
Web: www.premierptsp.com
SIC: **8049** Physical therapist

(G-6387)
PREMIER RESTORATION INC
145 Heather Dr (19958-6042)
PHONE..................302 645-1611
William Baughman, *Pr*
Bill Baughman, *Pr*
EMP: 10 EST: 2003
SALES (est): 988.15K **Privately Held**
SIC: **1521** Repairing fire damage, single-family houses

(G-6388)
PRESIDIO HOLDINGS LLC
6 Lake Shore Dr (19958-9100)
PHONE..................240 219-8351
EMP: 12
SALES (corp-wide): 1.13MM **Privately Held**
SIC: **8742** Management consulting services
PA: Presidio Holdings, Llc
   522 W 158th St Apt 34
   New York NY 10032
   646 228-9610

(G-6389)
PRESTWICK COMMUNITY CORP
17298 Coastal Hwy (19958-6226)
PHONE..................302 227-7878
EMP: 5 EST: 2017
SALES (est): 51.35K **Privately Held**
Web: www.hpsmanagement.com
SIC: **8322** Community center

(G-6390)
PRIDESTAFFING LLC
16192 Coastal Hwy (19958)
PHONE..................302 525-2561
Shagun Duggal, *Managing Member*
EMP: 20 EST: 2020
SALES (est): 100K **Privately Held**
Web: www.pridstaffing.com

SIC: **7361** Employment agencies

(G-6391)
PRINT COAST 2 COAST
33073 E Light Dr (19958-4661)
PHONE..................302 381-4610
Melody Diaz, *Prin*
EMP: 4 EST: 2013
SALES (est): 168.43K **Privately Held**
Web: www.printcoast2coast.com
SIC: **2752** Offset printing

(G-6392)
PRO REHAB CHIROPRACTIC
105 W 4th St (19958-1311)
PHONE..................302 200-9102
EMP: 7 EST: 2016
SALES (est): 73.36K **Privately Held**
Web: www.prorehabchiro.com
SIC: **8093** 8041 Rehabilitation center, outpatient treatment; Offices and clinics of chiropractors

(G-6393)
PROCINO WELLS & WOODLAND LLC
1519 Savannah Rd (19958-1611)
PHONE..................302 313-5934
Michele Procino-wells, *Prin*
EMP: 9 EST: 2014
SALES (est): 235.8K **Privately Held**
Web: www.pwwlaw.com
SIC: **8111** General practice attorney, lawyer

(G-6394)
PROGAR & CO
Also Called: Progar & Company PA
33815 Clay Rd Ste 1 (19958-6297)
PHONE..................302 645-6216
Gary A Progar, *Prin*
EMP: 8 EST: 2001
SALES (est): 478.06K **Privately Held**
Web: www.1040pro.com
SIC: **8721** Certified public accountant

(G-6395)
PROPERTY MAINTENANCE
32206 Sandpiper Dr (19958-3640)
PHONE..................302 645-5921
EMP: 7 EST: 2013
SALES (est): 52.51K **Privately Held**
Web: www.tidewaterproperty.com
SIC: **7349** Building maintenance services, nec

(G-6396)
PRUDENTIAL GALLO REALTY
16712 Kings Hwy (19958-4929)
PHONE..................302 645-6661
Salvatore Gallo, *Owner*
EMP: 10 EST: 1978
SALES (est): 474.51K **Privately Held**
Web: beachrentals.penfedrealty.com
SIC: **6531** 6512 6513 6514 Real estate agent, residential; Commercial and industrial building operation; Apartment building operators; Dwelling operators, except apartments

(G-6397)
PSC TECHNOLOGY INCORPORATED (PA)
16192 Coastal Hwy (19958-3608)
PHONE..................866 866-1466
Paul Brooks, *Pr*
EMP: 10 EST: 2008
SALES (est): 2.13MM
SALES (corp-wide): 2.13MM **Privately Held**
Web: www.psctechnologyinc.com

SIC: **8059** Personal care home, with health care

(G-6398)
QUAKERTOWN WELLNESS CENTER
1143 Savannah Rd Ste 4 (19958-1515)
PHONE..................302 644-0130
Sally Laux, *Dir*
EMP: 8 EST: 2014
SALES (est): 315.95K **Privately Held**
SIC: **8099** Blood related health services

(G-6399)
QUALITY CARE HOMES LLC
20366 Hopkins Rd (19958-5533)
PHONE..................302 858-3999
Dominic Drummond, *Prin*
EMP: 15 EST: 2015
SALES (est): 1.97MM **Privately Held**
Web: www.qualitycarehomes.net
SIC: **8059** Nursing and personal care, nec

(G-6400)
QUANTCONNECT CORPORATION
16192 Coastal Hwy (19958-3608)
PHONE..................917 327-0556
Jared Broad, *CEO*
EMP: 10 EST: 2013
SALES (est): 534.43K **Privately Held**
Web: www.quantconnect.com
SIC: **7371** Computer software development

(G-6401)
QUESKR INC
16192 Coastal Hwy (19958-3608)
PHONE..................302 527-6007
EMP: 6 EST: 2016
SALES (est): 46.16K **Privately Held**
Web: www.queskr.com
SIC: **7371** Computer software development and applications

(G-6402)
QUICK CARE WALK IN AND MEDICAL
17274 Coastal Hwy (19958-6324)
PHONE..................302 313-4660
EMP: 5 EST: 2016
SALES (est): 38.22K **Privately Held**
SIC: **8099** Health and allied services, nec

(G-6403)
R E MICHEL COMPANY LLC
32258 Janice Rd (19958-2003)
PHONE..................302 645-0585
Carl Mears, *Mgr*
EMP: 7
SALES (corp-wide): 1.43B **Privately Held**
Web: www.remichel.com
SIC: **5075** 5078 Warm air heating equipment and supplies; Refrigeration equipment and supplies
PA: R. E. Michel Company, Llc
   1 Re Michel Dr
   Glen Burnie MD 21060
   410 760-4000

(G-6404)
R M BELL INDUSTRIES INC
1504 Savannah Rd (19958-1624)
PHONE..................302 542-3747
EMP: 4 EST: 2012
SALES (est): 94.53K **Privately Held**
SIC: **3999** Manufacturing industries, nec

(G-6405)
RACE ADVISORS LLC
21914 Back Bay Ln (19958-5756)
PHONE..................302 245-1895
Lauren P Brueckner, *Prin*

EMP: 5 EST: 2016
SALES (est): 148.2K **Privately Held**
SIC: **6282** Investment advice

(G-6406)
RAILBUS INC
16192 Coastal Hwy (19958-3608)
PHONE..................302 725-3185
EMP: 6 EST: 2021
SALES (est): 46.16K **Privately Held**
Web: www.railbus.com
SIC: **7371** Computer software development and applications

(G-6407)
RAMACHANDRA U HOSMANE MD
1408 Savannah Rd (19958-1623)
P.O. Box 648 (19958-0648)
PHONE..................302 645-2274
Ramachandra U Hosmane Md, *Owner*
EMP: 6 EST: 1977
SQ FT: 1,000
SALES (est): 707.75K **Privately Held**
SIC: **8011** Surgeon

(G-6408)
RANUBA INC
16192 Coastal Hwy (19958-3608)
PHONE..................870 360-3372
Rachael Bynum, *CEO*
EMP: 6
SALES (est): 63.67K **Privately Held**
SIC: **7299** Facility rental and party planning services

(G-6409)
RAVE BUSINESS SYSTEMS LLC
16192 Coastal Hwy (19958-3608)
PHONE..................302 407-2270
EMP: 15 EST: 2018
SALES (est): 1.1MM **Privately Held**
Web: www.ravebizz.com
SIC: **7379** 7373 Online services technology consultants; Systems software development services

(G-6410)
RAVIS CAR DETAILING
23524 Elmwood Ave W (19958-5249)
PHONE..................302 945-8253
Joel Ortiz, *Owner*
EMP: 5 EST: 2017
SALES (est): 28.21K **Privately Held**
SIC: **7542** Washing and polishing, automotive

(G-6411)
REAL MATTER LLC
16192 Coastal Hwy (19958-3608)
PHONE..................302 291-2562
EMP: 5 EST: 2020
SALES (est): 746.92K **Privately Held**
SIC: **4731** Freight transportation arrangement

(G-6412)
REBATUS INC
16192 Coastal Hwy (19958-3608)
PHONE..................929 393-5529
EMP: 5
SALES (est): 46.16K **Privately Held**
SIC: **7371** 7389 Computer software development and applications; Business services, nec

(G-6413)
RED STONE USA INC
16192 Coastal Hwy (19958-3608)
PHONE..................919 931-5078
EMP: 32
SALES (corp-wide): 389.55K **Privately Held**

GEOGRAPHIC SECTION
Lewes - Sussex County (G-6444)

SIC: 7389 Business Activities at Non-Commercial Site
PA: Red Stone Usa Inc.
20 River Ct Apt 2907
Jersey City NJ 07310
919 931-5078

(G-6414)
REDDIX TRANSPORTATION INC
31014 Oak Leaf Dr (19958-5596)
PHONE..................................302 249-9331
George I Reddix, *Prin*
EMP: 10 EST: 2007
SALES (est): 714.4K **Privately Held**
SIC: 4789 Pipeline terminal facilities, independently operated

(G-6415)
REGAL TECHNOLOGIES LLC
16192 Coastal Hwy (19958-3608)
PHONE..................................321 695-4142
Armand Nannicola, *Prin*
EMP: 7 EST: 2020
SALES (est): 230.79K **Privately Held**
SIC: 7371 Custom computer programming services

(G-6416)
REMORA COMPANY ✪
16192 Coastal Hwy (19958-3608)
PHONE..................................845 532-5172
Shahinda Ghaly, *CEO*
EMP: 4 EST: 2023
SALES (est): 73.93K **Privately Held**
SIC: 7372 Application computer software

(G-6417)
RESORT BROADCASTING CO LP
Also Called: Wgmd
31549 Dutton Ln (19958-4512)
P.O. Box 530 (19971-0530)
PHONE..................................302 945-2050
David Schoumacher, *Pt*
Joseph Giuliani, *Genl Pt*
EMP: 19 EST: 1975
SALES (est): 1.87MM **Privately Held**
Web: www.wgmd.com
SIC: 4832 Radio broadcasting stations, music format

(G-6418)
RESORT CUSTOM HOMES
18355 Coastal Hwy (19958-4778)
PHONE..................................302 645-8222
EMP: 6 EST: 2017
SALES (est): 400.24K **Privately Held**
Web: www.resortcustomhomes.com
SIC: 1522 Residential construction, nec

(G-6419)
RESTORE SSSEX CNTY HBTAT FOR H
18501 Stamper Dr (19958-3947)
PHONE..................................302 703-6388
EMP: 8 EST: 2017
SALES (est): 43.61K **Privately Held**
Web: www.sussexcountyhabitat.org
SIC: 8399 Community development groups

(G-6420)
RETOUCH SALON LLC (PA)
16192 Coastal Hwy (19958-3608)
PHONE..................................929 247-7095
Solveig Galbo, *CEO*
EMP: 5 EST: 2018
SALES (est): 351.81K
SALES (corp-wide): 351.81K **Privately Held**
SIC: 7371 Computer software development and applications

(G-6421)
REVOLTION FREEDOM PLATFORM LLC
16192 Coastal Hwy (19958-3608)
PHONE..................................301 653-9207
EMP: 10
SALES (est): 348.32K **Privately Held**
SIC: 7371 Computer software development and applications

(G-6422)
RICHARD C PAUL
34431 King Street Row (19958-4787)
PHONE..................................302 645-2666
Richard Paul, *Prin*
EMP: 25 EST: 2011
SALES (est): 217.3K **Privately Held**
Web: www.beebehealthcare.org
SIC: 8011 Internal medicine, physician/surgeon

(G-6423)
RIVERSIDE FOODS INC
16192 Coastal Hwy (19958-3608)
PHONE..................................888 546-8810
Bo Liu, *CEO*
EMP: 6
SALES (est): 86.31K **Privately Held**
SIC: 5142 Vegetables, frozen

(G-6424)
ROAD SITE CONSTRUCTION INC
Also Called: Clean Cut Interlocking Pavers
16192 Coastal Hwy (19958-3608)
PHONE..................................302 645-1922
Rich Bell, *Pr*
EMP: 36 EST: 1995
SQ FT: 24,001
SALES (est): 5.34MM **Privately Held**
Web: www.cleancutpaversandpools.com
SIC: 1611 Surfacing and paving

(G-6425)
ROBERT WESTLEY
Also Called: Details Cleaning Service
115 S Washington Ave (19958-1443)
PHONE..................................302 645-2301
Robert Westley, *Prin*
EMP: 5 EST: 2010
SALES (est): 50K **Privately Held**
SIC: 7699 Cleaning services

(G-6426)
ROBIN S WRIGHT
Also Called: Lotus Blossom Learning Center
19305 Beaver Dam Rd (19958-5539)
PHONE..................................302 249-2105
Robin Wright, *Dir*
Robin Wright, *Owner*
EMP: 5 EST: 2012
SALES (est): 219.43K **Privately Held**
SIC: 8351 Child day care services

(G-6427)
ROCKAWAY AUTO REPAIR
19738 Bernard Dr (19958-3515)
PHONE..................................302 644-1485
Mike Hruska, *Owner*
EMP: 5 EST: 2013
SALES (est): 78.24K **Privately Held**
SIC: 7538 General automotive repair shops

(G-6428)
ROCKET SIGNS
18388 Coastal Hwy Unit 4 (19958-4204)
P.O. Box 332 (19969-0332)
PHONE..................................302 645-1425
Rocket Arena, *Prin*
EMP: 2 EST: 2011
SALES (est): 139.35K **Privately Held**
SIC: 3993 Signs and advertising specialties

(G-6429)
ROCKEY & ASSOCIATES INC
Also Called: Rockteam
18306 Coastal Hwy (19958-4772)
P.O. Box 1538 (19971-5538)
PHONE..................................800 338-7734
Patience Rockey, *Pr*
EMP: 5 EST: 1986
SQ FT: 6,000
SALES (est): 445.78K **Privately Held**
SIC: 7371 Computer software systems analysis and design, custom

(G-6430)
ROI INTERNATIONAL LLC (PA)
16192 Coastal Hwy (19958-3608)
PHONE..................................704 340-1289
Melissa Ursi, *Managing Member*
EMP: 9
SALES (est): 554.44K
SALES (corp-wide): 554.44K **Privately Held**
SIC: 7379 Computer related consulting services

(G-6431)
RON DURR MECHANICAL
36851 Crooked Hammock Way (19958-4939)
PHONE..................................215 643-6990
Ronald P Durr, *Prin*
EMP: 5 EST: 2008
SALES (est): 119.56K **Privately Held**
SIC: 1711 Mechanical contractor

(G-6432)
ROSIES PH LLC
16192 Coastal Hwy (19958-3608)
PHONE..................................630 222-5155
EMP: 5 EST: 2021
SALES (est): 44.12K **Privately Held**
SIC: 8699 Food co-operative

(G-6433)
ROSS BICYCLES LLC (PA)
16192 Coastal Hwy (19958-3608)
PHONE..................................888 392-5628
Shaun Ross, *CEO*
EMP: 8 EST: 2017
SALES (est): 907.96K
SALES (corp-wide): 907.96K **Privately Held**
SIC: 3751 Bicycles and related parts

(G-6434)
RUDYS EUROPEAN MOTORCARS
17493 Nassau Commons Blvd (19958-6283)
PHONE..................................302 645-6410
Ken Rudy, *Prin*
EMP: 6 EST: 2012
SALES (est): 291.69K **Privately Held**
Web: www.rudyseurocars.com
SIC: 7538 General automotive repair shops

(G-6435)
RXBENEFITS INC
32907 Ocean Blf (19958-4683)
PHONE..................................724 525-9080
EMP: 6 EST: 2018
SALES (est): 49.66K **Privately Held**
Web: www.rxbenefits.com
SIC: 8748 Business consulting, nec

(G-6436)
S FINNEY HOME IMPROVEMENTS
31110 Mills Chase Dr (19958-5908)
PHONE..................................302 358-4562
EMP: 5 EST: 2016
SALES (est): 100.11K **Privately Held**
Web: sfinneyhomeimprove.wix.com
SIC: 1521 Single-family housing construction

(G-6437)
S S I GROUP LLC
16192 Coastal Hwy (19958-3608)
PHONE..................................877 778-7099
Haley Paul, *Prin*
EMP: 6 EST: 2010
SALES (est): 498.73K **Privately Held**
SIC: 8748 Business consulting, nec

(G-6438)
SAASANT INC
16192 Coastal Hwy (19958-3608)
PHONE..................................619 377-0977
Aravinth Chandrasekhar, *CEO*
EMP: 39 EST: 2021
SALES (est): 1.13MM **Privately Held**
SIC: 7372 Business oriented computer software

(G-6439)
SABRS HOME COMFORT
17815 Sandcastle Cv (19958-4680)
PHONE..................................302 379-8133
Jeff Gross, *Prin*
EMP: 8 EST: 2016
SALES (est): 674.97K **Privately Held**
Web: www.sabrsheatingandair.com
SIC: 1711 Warm air heating and air conditioning contractor

(G-6440)
SAF ENGINEERING LLC
16192 Coastal Hwy (19958-3608)
PHONE..................................302 645-7400
EMP: 5 EST: 2016
SALES (est): 500K **Privately Held**
SIC: 8711 Acoustical engineering

(G-6441)
SAFEUP US LLC
16192 Coastal Hwy (19958-3608)
PHONE..................................480 526-5152
EMP: 7 EST: 2020
SALES (est): 105.28K **Privately Held**
Web: www.safeup.co
SIC: 7371 Computer software development and applications

(G-6442)
SAHRA INTL HOLDINGS INC
16192 Coastal Hwy (19958-3608)
PHONE..................................202 660-0090
EMP: 5
SALES (est): 50K **Privately Held**
SIC: 8732 Merger, acquisition, and reorganization research

(G-6443)
SAHRA INTL HOLDINGS INC
Also Called: Sahra International Holdings
16192 Coastal Hwy Ste 100 (19958-3608)
PHONE..................................202 660-0090
S Alex Azimi, *CEO*
M Sahra Azimi, *Pr*
EMP: 5 EST: 2015
SALES (est): 252.6K **Privately Held**
SIC: 4731 Freight consolidation

(G-6444)
SAM8SARA INC
16192 Coastal Hwy (19958-3608)
PHONE..................................347 605-0693
Sanzhar Rakhmetzhanov, *CEO*
EMP: 15 EST: 2021
SALES (est): 501.62K **Privately Held**

Lewes - Sussex County (G-6445)   GEOGRAPHIC SECTION

SIC: 7371 8999 Custom computer programming services; Psychological consultant

(G-6445)
SAND DOLLAR DEWEY LLC
30972 Sycamore Dr (19958-3893)
PHONE..................302 858-7030
EMP: 5 EST: 2019
SALES (est): 143.21K **Privately Held**
Web: www.sanddollarcruises.com
SIC: 7999 Fishing boats, party: operation

(G-6446)
SANDRA M CMPOS RESTORATION LLC
30209 Regatta Bay Blvd (19958-6803)
PHONE..................302 883-7663
Sandra Campos, *Prin*
EMP: 5 EST: 2014
SALES (est): 104.2K **Privately Held**
SIC: 1799 Special trade contractors, nec

(G-6447)
SAVANNAH ELECTRIC
2039 Savannah Cir (19958-1542)
PHONE..................302 645-5906
Richard Kroon, *Owner*
EMP: 6 EST: 2013
SALES (est): 153.44K **Privately Held**
SIC: 1731 Electrical work

(G-6448)
SAVANNAH INN
55 N Atlantic Dr (19958-1765)
PHONE..................302 645-0330
Gina Kaye, *Prin*
EMP: 15 EST: 2008
SALES (est): 203.98K **Privately Held**
Web: www.thesavannahlewes.com
SIC: 7011 Bed and breakfast inn

(G-6449)
SAVEMUNCH INC
16192 Coastal Hwy (19958-3608)
PHONE..................469 473-1601
EMP: 5 EST: 2020
SALES (est): 400K **Privately Held**
SIC: 7379 7389 Online services technology consultants; Business services, nec

(G-6450)
SCANTA INC
16192 Coastal Hwy (19958-3608)
PHONE..................302 645-7400
Chaitanya Hiremath, *CEO*
EMP: 22 EST: 2017
SALES (est): 613.53K **Privately Held**
SIC: 7371 Computer software development and applications

(G-6451)
SCHOLARJET PBC
16192 Coastal Hwy (19958-3608)
PHONE..................617 407-9851
Tuan Ho, *CEO*
Joseph Alim, *CEO*
EMP: 2 EST: 2016
SALES (est): 56.54K **Privately Held**
SIC: 7372 Educational computer software

(G-6452)
SCOTT CHARLES FORESMAN
124 Gosling Creek Rd (19958-9594)
PHONE..................302 644-8418
Scott Foresman, *Prin*
EMP: 6 EST: 2011
SALES (est): 243.33K **Privately Held**
SIC: 1522 Residential construction, nec

(G-6453)
SEA BARRE FITNESS
34410 Tenley Ct Unit 2 (19958-4202)
PHONE..................610 202-0518
Ellen Spell, *Prin*
EMP: 7 EST: 2017
SALES (est): 58.02K **Privately Held**
Web: www.seabarrefitness.com
SIC: 7991 Physical fitness facilities

(G-6454)
SEAGREEN BICYCLE
209 Monroe Ave (19958-1429)
PHONE..................302 645-7008
EMP: 5 EST: 2015
SALES (est): 27.66K **Privately Held**
Web: www.seagreenbicycle.com
SIC: 7999 5091 Bicycle rental; Bicycles

(G-6455)
SEASIDE SERVICE LLC
36360 Tarpon Dr (19958-5055)
PHONE..................302 827-3775
EMP: 8 EST: 2016
SALES (est): 261.47K **Privately Held**
Web: www.seasideservicellc.com
SIC: 3444 3312 Casings, sheet metal; Structural shapes and pilings, steel

(G-6456)
SECURENETMD LLC (PA)
16557 Coastal Hwy (19958-3605)
PHONE..................302 645-7770
EMP: 23 EST: 2010
SALES (est): 4.45MM
SALES (corp-wide): 4.45MM **Privately Held**
Web: www.thinksecurenet.com
SIC: 7379 Computer related consulting services

(G-6457)
SELISAV CORPORATION
16192 Coastal Hwy (19958-3608)
PHONE..................702 888-2175
Michelangelo Lamonaca, *CEO*
EMP: 10 EST: 2021
SALES (est): 363K **Privately Held**
SIC: 8742 Marketing consulting services

(G-6458)
SENHASEGURA USA LLC
16192 Coastal Hwy (19958-3608)
PHONE..................469 620-7643
EMP: 5
SALES (est): 257.14K **Privately Held**
Web: www.senhasegura.com
SIC: 7371 Software programming applications

(G-6459)
SENSO DYNAMICS LLC
16192 Coastal Hwy (19958-3608)
PHONE..................302 257-5926
Oleg Kovalev, *Managing Member*
EMP: 8 EST: 2019
SALES (est): 555.09K **Privately Held**
Web: www.senso-dynamics.com
SIC: 6082 5084 Foreign trade and international banks; Industrial machinery and equipment

(G-6460)
SERVICE ENERGY LLC
Also Called: Service Energy
47 Clay Rd (19958-1741)
P.O. Box 24 (19963-0024)
PHONE..................302 645-9050
EMP: 10
Web: www.serviceenergy.com
SIC: 5172 5983 Petroleum products, nec; Fuel oil dealers
PA: Service Energy, L.L.C.
3799 N Dupont Hwy
Dover DE 19901

(G-6461)
SHAMROCK SERVICES LLC
Also Called: Shamrock Taxi
22576 Waterview Rd (19958-5703)
PHONE..................302 519-7609
Jason Wells, *Mgr*
EMP: 16 EST: 2011
SALES (est): 187.53K **Privately Held**
SIC: 4111 Local and suburban transit

(G-6462)
SHEETS AT BEACH
31114 Beaver Cir (19958-5503)
PHONE..................302 362-0876
Vera Bailey, *Prin*
EMP: 5 EST: 2016
SALES (est): 248.8K **Privately Held**
Web: www.sheetsatthebeach.com
SIC: 7359 Equipment rental and leasing, nec

(G-6463)
SHERIFF ELECTRONIC LLC
16192 Coastal Hwy (19958-3608)
PHONE..................302 654-8090
EMP: 4 EST: 2020
SALES (est): 100K **Privately Held**
SIC: 3571 Electronic computers

(G-6464)
SHOOTLE INC
16192 Coastal Hwy (19958-3608)
PHONE..................941 866-2135
Tajudeen Osaba, *Pr*
Melisha Masek, *Sec*
EMP: 7 EST: 2008
SALES (est): 118.84K **Privately Held**
SIC: 7629 Telecommunication equipment repair (except telephones)

(G-6465)
SHORE ELECTRIC INC
34697 Jiffy Way Unit 4 (19958-4932)
PHONE..................302 645-4503
Joseph Johnson, *Pr*
EMP: 6 EST: 1995
SALES (est): 625.08K **Privately Held**
Web: www.shoreelectricde.com
SIC: 1731 General electrical contractor

(G-6466)
SHORE MECHANICAL SERVICES
30420 E Barrier Reef Blvd (19958-6820)
PHONE..................302 519-6540
EMP: 6 EST: 2019
SALES (est): 76.51K **Privately Held**
SIC: 1711 Mechanical contractor

(G-6467)
SHOULDR LLC
16192 Coastal Hwy (19958-3608)
PHONE..................917 331-1384
Mohashin Azad, *CEO*
Adam Thiessen, *COO*
EMP: 5
SALES (est): 107.01K **Privately Held**
SIC: 7371 Computer software development and applications

(G-6468)
SIGNATURE PROPERTY MANAGEMENT
20375 John J Williams Hwy (19958-4305)
PHONE..................302 212-2381
Harry Burroughs, *Owner*
EMP: 12 EST: 2014
SALES (est): 521.02K **Privately Held**
Web: www.tidewaterproperty.com
SIC: 6531 Real estate managers

(G-6469)
SIGNATURE SQUARE LLC
16192 Coastal Hwy (19958-3608)
PHONE..................866 216-5792
Diana Rose, *Managing Member*
EMP: 8
SALES (est): 319.06K **Privately Held**
SIC: 8742 Management consulting services

(G-6470)
SILICON PARTNERS INC
16192 Coastal Hwy (19958-3608)
PHONE..................646 571-2324
EMP: 11 EST: 2017
SALES (est): 82.63K **Privately Held**
Web: www.thesiliconpartners.com
SIC: 7379 Computer related consulting services

(G-6471)
SILK GRASS HOLDINGS US LLC
16192 Coastal Hwy (19958-3608)
PHONE..................610 943-3047
Mandy Cabot, *Managing Member*
EMP: 12 EST: 2019
SALES (est): 180.69K **Privately Held**
SIC: 0191 General farms, primarily crop

(G-6472)
SIMBULL SPORTS EXCHANGE INC
16192 Coastal Hwy (19958-3608)
PHONE..................319 899-6223
Kenneth Giles, *CEO*
EMP: 6
SALES (est): 123.52K **Privately Held**
SIC: 7371 Computer software development and applications

(G-6473)
SIMPLECODE LLC
16192 Coastal Hwy (19958-3608)
PHONE..................302 703-7231
EMP: 5 EST: 2020
SALES (est): 46.16K **Privately Held**
Web: www.simplecodesoftware.com
SIC: 7371 Computer software development

(G-6474)
SKYLINE ROOFING & CNSTR LLC
33126 Perrydale Grn (19958-9200)
PHONE..................610 929-4135
David C Barth, *Prin*
EMP: 5 EST: 2007
SALES (est): 317K **Privately Held**
Web: www.skylineroofingandconstruction.com
SIC: 1761 1741 1711 1542 Roofing contractor; Masonry and other stonework; Plumbing, heating, air-conditioning; Nonresidential construction, nec

(G-6475)
SKYLINES ONE LLC
16192 Coastal Hwy (19958-3608)
PHONE..................646 400-0535
EMP: 6 EST: 2020
SALES (est): 179.36K **Privately Held**
SIC: 7389 Business services, nec

(G-6476)
SLEEP DISORDERS CENTER
424 Savannah Rd (19958-1462)
PHONE..................302 645-3186
Jeffrey Freed, *CEO*
EMP: 5 EST: 1993

GEOGRAPHIC SECTION
Lewes - Sussex County (G-6506)

SALES (est): 240K **Privately Held**
SIC: 8099 Health screening service

(G-6477)
SLEEP INN & SUITES
Also Called: Sleep Inn
18451 Coastal Hwy (19958-4930)
PHONE.............................302 645-6464
Tom Kramedas, *Owner*
EMP: 17 EST: 2001
SALES (est): 426.04K **Privately Held**
Web: www.choicehotels.com
SIC: 7011 Hotels and motels

(G-6478)
SMALL WONDERS
47 Sussex Dr (19958-1506)
PHONE.............................302 645-8410
Judith Davidson, *Owner*
EMP: 8 EST: 2015
SALES (est): 21.43K **Privately Held**
SIC: 8351 Child day care services

(G-6479)
SMAPPY INC
16192 Coastal Hwy (19958-3608)
PHONE.............................650 360-0713
Iuliia Grebeshok, *CEO*
EMP: 5 EST: 2020
SALES (est): 56.54K **Privately Held**
SIC: 7372 Application computer software

(G-6480)
SMART ALTCOINS INC ✪
Also Called: Mpay
16192 Coastal Hwy (19958-3608)
PHONE.............................626 540-9415
Chan Wai Chun, *Dir*
EMP: 5 EST: 2022
SALES (est): 234.69K **Privately Held**
SIC: 6231 7389 Security and commodity exchanges; Business services, nec

(G-6481)
SMART CHOICE TRUCKING INC
31791 Marsh Island Ave (19958-3350)
PHONE.............................302 945-7100
Paul F Troccoli, *Pr*
EMP: 8 EST: 2014
SALES (est): 458.33K **Privately Held**
SIC: 4212 Local trucking, without storage

(G-6482)
SMART FIT LLC
Also Called: Smart Fit Studio
17601 Coastal Hwy (19958-6217)
PHONE.............................302 200-9803
EMP: 6 EST: 2006
SALES (est): 69.54K **Privately Held**
Web: www.smartfit.com.br
SIC: 7991 Physical fitness facilities

(G-6483)
SMART UNION BLOCKCHAIN LLC ✪
16192 Coastal Hwy (19958-3608)
PHONE.............................919 872-5631
Jagmohan Singh, *Managing Member*
EMP: 10 EST: 2023
SALES (est): 348.32K **Privately Held**
SIC: 7371 Computer software development

(G-6484)
SMARTWNNR INC ✪
16192 Coastal Hwy (19958-3608)
PHONE.............................415 534-9794
EMP: 45 EST: 2022
SALES (est): 1.21MM **Privately Held**
SIC: 7372 Prepackaged software

(G-6485)
SOCAL AUTO SUPPLY INC (PA)
16192 Postal Hwy (19958)
PHONE.............................818 717-9982
EMP: 19 EST: 2006
SQ FT: 5,000
SALES (est): 1.24MM **Privately Held**
SIC: 7213 2676 Towel supply; Towels, napkins, and tissue paper products

(G-6486)
SOCIAL MONEY INC
16192 Coastal Hwy (19958-3608)
PHONE.............................212 810-7540
Steve Ghiassi, *CEO*
EMP: 5 EST: 2020
SALES (est): 199.4K **Privately Held**
SIC: 7371 Computer software development and applications

(G-6487)
SOCIALPILOT TECHNOLOGIES INC
16192 Coastal Hwy (19958-3608)
PHONE.............................415 450-6060
EMP: 9 EST: 2018
SALES (est): 92.36K **Privately Held**
Web: www.socialpilot.co
SIC: 7371 Computer software development

(G-6488)
SOCIETY FOR ACPUNCTURE RES INC
108 Dewey Ave (19958-1713)
PHONE.............................302 222-1832
Rosa Schnyer, *Pr*
Richard Harris, *VP*
Roni D Posner, *Ex Dir*
EMP: 6 EST: 1995
SALES (est): 34.16K **Privately Held**
Web: www.acupunctureresearch.org
SIC: 8733 7389 Noncommercial research organizations; Business Activities at Non-Commercial Site

(G-6489)
SOFP
251 Lakeside Dr (19958-8993)
PHONE.............................302 354-3643
EMP: 6 EST: 2017
SALES (est): 135.18K **Privately Held**
SIC: 8011 Psychiatrist

(G-6490)
SOLID CONSTRUCTION LLC
202 Lakeside Dr (19958-8938)
PHONE.............................571 451-4727
Anatoly Kitaev, *Prin*
EMP: 5 EST: 2017
SALES (est): 121.63K **Privately Held**
Web: www.solidconstructionllc.work
SIC: 1521 Single-family housing construction

(G-6491)
SOLID IDEA SOLUTIONS LLC
16192 Coastal Hwy (19958-3608)
PHONE.............................646 982-2890
Travis Vance, *CEO*
EMP: 5 EST: 2017
SALES (est): 225.2K **Privately Held**
SIC: 7379 Computer related consulting services

(G-6492)
SOUCIALIZE INC
16192 Coastal Hwy (19958-3608)
PHONE.............................916 803-1057
Monique Rice, *CEO*
EMP: 7 EST: 2019
SALES (est): 228.3K **Privately Held**

SIC: 7929 1522 8641 7011 Entertainment service; Hotel/motel and multi-family home construction; Social club, membership; Hotels

(G-6493)
SOUTH PAW ACRES
34465 Bookhammer Landing Rd (19958-5746)
PHONE.............................302 945-1092
Todd Connie, *Prin*
EMP: 5 EST: 2009
SALES (est): 42.51K **Privately Held**
SIC: 0752 Animal training services

(G-6494)
SOUTHERN DELAWARE IMAGING LLP
Also Called: Southern Del Imaging Assoc
17503 Nassau Commons Blvd (19958-6283)
P.O. Box 97 (19969-0097)
PHONE.............................302 645-7919
Norman Boyer Md, *Pt*
Ellen Bahtiarian, *Pt*
EMP: 22 EST: 1977
SALES (est): 854.95K **Privately Held**
SIC: 8011 Radiologist

(G-6495)
SOUTHERN DELAWARE SIGNS
18388 Coastal Hwy Unit 4 (19958-4204)
PHONE.............................302 645-1425
EMP: 6 EST: 2014
SALES (est): 50.69K **Privately Held**
Web: www.southerndelawaresigns.com
SIC: 3993 Signs and advertising specialties

(G-6496)
SPARE CS INC
16192 Coastal Hwy (19958-3608)
PHONE.............................424 744-0155
D'ontra Hughes, *CEO*
EMP: 11 EST: 2015
SALES (est): 213.92K **Privately Held**
SIC: 7371 4731 3669 Computer software development and applications; Transportation agents and brokers; Transportation signaling devices

(G-6497)
SPECIAL CARE INC
16698 Kings Hwy Ste D (19958-4936)
PHONE.............................302 644-6990
Cheryl Jankowski, *Brnch Mgr*
EMP: 7
SALES (corp-wide): 22.56MM **Privately Held**
Web: www.griswoldsa.com
SIC: 8082 Home health care services
PA: Special Care, Inc.
    800 Bethlehem Pike
    Glenside PA 19038
    215 402-0200

(G-6498)
SPECIAL SUPPORT TECH INC
16192 Coastal Hwy (19958-3608)
PHONE.............................804 620-6072
Eden Levinson, *Pr*
EMP: 5 EST: 2020
SALES (est): 408.23K **Privately Held**
SIC: 3812 Defense systems and equipment

(G-6499)
SPEED AUTO SYSTEMS LLC
16192 Coastal Hwy (19958-3608)
PHONE.............................888 446-7102
EMP: 25 EST: 2017
SALES (est): 693.23K **Privately Held**

Web: www.speedautosystems.com
SIC: 7371 Computer software development

(G-6500)
SPI PHARMA INC
40 Cape Henlopen Dr (19958-1168)
PHONE.............................302 360-7200
EMP: 4
SALES (corp-wide): 24.92B **Privately Held**
Web: www.spipharma.com
SIC: 2834 Pharmaceutical preparations
HQ: Spi Pharma, Inc.
    503 Carr Rd Ste 210
    Wilmington DE 19809

(G-6501)
SPICER BROS CONSTRUCTION INC
34634 Bay Crossing Blvd Unit 4 (19958-2742)
PHONE.............................302 703-6754
Brian Spicer, *Prin*
EMP: 7 EST: 2014
SALES (est): 134.32K **Privately Held**
Web: www.spicerbros.com
SIC: 1521 General remodeling, single-family houses

(G-6502)
SPIRO HEALTH INC
16192 Coastal Hwy (19958-3608)
PHONE.............................302 645-7400
Artem Spiridonov, *CEO*
EMP: 5 EST: 2019
SALES (est): 46.16K **Privately Held**
SIC: 7371 Software programming applications

(G-6503)
SPRINGPOINT AT LEWES INC
17028 Cadbury Cir (19958-7022)
PHONE.............................732 430-3660
Sunny Taragin, *Prin*
EMP: 20 EST: 1999
SALES (est): 14.58MM **Privately Held**
Web: www.springpointsl.org
SIC: 8361 Aged home

(G-6504)
SRUPLEX LLC
16192 Coastal Hwy (19958-3608)
PHONE.............................331 901-0011
Daniyal Naseer, *Managing Member*
EMP: 15 EST: 2019
SALES (est): 639.83K **Privately Held**
SIC: 7379 Online services technology consultants

(G-6505)
STACKADAPT US INC
16192 Coastal Hwy (19958-3608)
PHONE.............................647 385-7698
Ildar Shar, *CEO*
Vitaly Pecherskiy, *COO*
Mehmet Shah, *CFO*
Richard Jones, *CRO*
EMP: 236 EST: 2014
SALES (est): 36.32MM
SALES (corp-wide): 172.94MM **Privately Held**
Web: www.stackadapt.com
SIC: 7319 7371 Media buying service; Custom computer programming services
PA: Stackadapt Inc
    100 University Ave 5 Fl
    Toronto ON M5J 1
    416 435-5781

(G-6506)
STARKIT STUDIO LLC
16192 Coastal Hwy (19958-3608)

Lewes - Sussex County (G-6507)   GEOGRAPHIC SECTION

PHONE.................302 467-2017
EMP: 5 EST: 2020
SALES (est): 46.16K Privately Held
Web: www.starkitstudio.com
SIC: 7371 Computer software development and applications

(G-6507)
STEAMBOAT LANDING
Coastal Hwy 1 (19958)
P.O. Box 300 (19958-0300)
PHONE.................302 645-6500
Linda Pride, Owner
EMP: 5 EST: 1970
SALES (est): 242.78K Privately Held
Web: www.steamboatrvandmarina.com
SIC: 7033 Campgrounds

(G-6508)
STEEL BUILDINGS INC
Also Called: Northern Steel International
17515 Nassau Commons Blvd (19958-6283)
PHONE.................302 644-0444
Joss Hudson, Pr
EMP: 2 EST: 1996
SQ FT: 4,500
SALES (est): 192.71K Privately Held
SIC: 3448 Buildings, portable: prefabricated metal

(G-6509)
STEERR INC
16192 Coastal Hwy (19958-3608)
PHONE.................412 303-5840
EMP: 5 EST: 2019
SALES (est): 53.48K Privately Held
Web: www.steerr.com
SIC: 7538 General automotive repair shops

(G-6510)
STEIMEL CONSTRUCTION LLC
26 Canterbury Ct (19958-8900)
P.O. Box 217 (19969-0217)
PHONE.................302 827-2471
EMP: 7 EST: 2008
SALES (est): 452.3K Privately Held
SIC: 1521 Single-family housing construction

(G-6511)
STEVEN P COPP
Also Called: Copp Seafood
Rr 3 Box 254a (19958)
PHONE.................302 645-9112
EMP: 6 EST: 1972
SALES (est): 95.48K Privately Held
SIC: 2092 Seafoods, frozen: prepared

(G-6512)
STI LANDSCAPE SOLUTIONS
20144 John J Williams Hwy (19958-4339)
PHONE.................302 645-6262
EMP: 7 EST: 2010
SALES (est): 240.74K Privately Held
Web: www.sussextreeinc.com
SIC: 0782 Landscape contractors

(G-6513)
STONEWORKS LAPIDARY
23604 Woods Dr (19958-3313)
PHONE.................814 528-1468
Frank Navecky, Pr
EMP: 6 EST: 2011
SALES (est): 154.42K Privately Held
SIC: 1741 Masonry and other stonework

(G-6514)
STORAGE SQUAD LLC
16192 Coastal Hwy (19958-3608)
PHONE.................830 200-0269
Nicholas J Huber, Prin
EMP: 10 EST: 2013
SALES (est): 1.08MM Privately Held
Web: www.storagesquad.com
SIC: 4225 Warehousing, self storage

(G-6515)
STRANG & EDSON LLC (PA) ◊
16192 Coastal Hwy (19958-3608)
PHONE.................917 664-0298
Kwame Kusi, Managing Member
EMP: 6 EST: 2023
SALES (est): 73.91K
SALES (corp-wide): 73.91K Privately Held
SIC: 7379 Computer related consulting services

(G-6516)
STRATEGYBRIX LLC (PA) ◊
16192 Coastal Hwy (19958-3608)
PHONE.................312 804-6768
Jasvinder Randhawa, CEO
Jasvinder Randhawa, Managing Member
EMP: 10 EST: 2022
SALES (est): 572.11K
SALES (corp-wide): 572.11K Privately Held
SIC: 8742 Management consulting services

(G-6517)
STREAMEQ INC (PA) ◊
16192 Coastal Hwy (19958-3608)
PHONE.................951 807-4938
EMP: 4 EST: 2023
SALES (est): 180.26K
SALES (corp-wide): 180.26K Privately Held
SIC: 2741 7371 Internet publishing and broadcasting; Computer software development and applications

(G-6518)
STRIKE EXCHANGE INC
Also Called: Strike Social
16192 Coastal Hwy (19958-3608)
PHONE.................310 995-5653
Patrick Mckenna, CEO
Tim Helfrey, Prin
EMP: 6 EST: 2013
SALES (est): 102.26K Privately Held
SIC: 7389

(G-6519)
STUDIO ON 24 INC
20231 John J Williams Hwy (19958-4314)
PHONE.................302 644-4424
Debra Applebey, Pr
EMP: 3 EST: 2000
SALES (est): 198.61K Privately Held
Web: www.thestudioon24.com
SIC: 3229 Pressed and blown glass, nec

(G-6520)
SUMMIT ORTHOPAEDIC HM CARE LLC
35745 Black Marlin Dr (19958-5043)
PHONE.................302 703-0800
Eric Reinhold, Managing Member
EMP: 20 EST: 2014
SALES (est): 2.1MM Privately Held
Web: www.summit-homehealth.com
SIC: 8011 Orthopedic physician

(G-6521)
SUN CONSTRUCTION INC
22465 Holly Oak Ln (19958-5451)
PHONE.................267 767-5047
EMP: 6 EST: 2018
SALES (est): 108.7K Privately Held
Web: www.sunconstruction.com
SIC: 1521 Single-family housing construction

(G-6522)
SUN EXCHANGE INC (PA)
16192 Coastal Hwy 1 (19958-3608)
PHONE.................917 747-9527
Abraham Campbridge, CEO
Lawrence Temlock, CFO
EMP: 5 EST: 2016
SALES (est): 363.75K
SALES (corp-wide): 363.75K Privately Held
Web: www.thesunexchange.com
SIC: 7389 Financial services

(G-6523)
SUNRISE RE PARTNERS LLC
18334 Coastal Hwy (19958-4772)
PHONE.................302 644-0300
Jeff Bowers, Owner
EMP: 5 EST: 2013
SALES (est): 228.55K Privately Held
Web: www.sunrisesells.com
SIC: 6531 Real estate agent, residential

(G-6524)
SUNSHINE NUT COMPANY LLC (PA)
16192 Coastal Hwy (19958-3608)
PHONE.................781 352-7766
▲ EMP: 5 EST: 2011
SALES (est): 196.69K Privately Held
Web: www.sunshinenuts.com
SIC: 2068 Salted and roasted nuts and seeds

(G-6525)
SUNSHINE NUTRITION LLC
16192 Coastal Hwy (19958-3608)
PHONE.................971 456-1000
EMP: 7 EST: 2015
SALES (est): 56.38K Privately Held
Web: www.sunshinenutrition.us
SIC: 5122 Vitamins and minerals

(G-6526)
SURGE AUTOMATED INC
16192 Coastal Hwy (19958-3608)
PHONE.................800 457-9713
Joseph Long, Pr
EMP: 5 EST: 2019
SALES (est): 107.01K Privately Held
SIC: 7371 Software programming applications

(G-6527)
SUSAN KELLY MD
431 Savannah Rd (19958-1460)
PHONE.................302 644-9080
EMP: 9 EST: 2015
SALES (est): 116.56K Privately Held
SIC: 8011 General and family practice, physician/surgeon

(G-6528)
SUSAN PEET RN
21476 Willow Ln (19958-6031)
PHONE.................302 945-5228
Susan Peet, Owner
EMP: 6 EST: 2018
SALES (est): 73.21K Privately Held
SIC: 8049 Offices of health practitioner

(G-6529)
SUSSEX AMATEUR RADIO ASSN
22907 Dogwood Dr (19958-5222)
PHONE.................302 629-4949
Raymond Deskins Junior, Prin
EMP: 5 EST: 2019
SALES (est): 38.05K Privately Held
Web: www.sussexamateurradio.com
SIC: 4832 Radio broadcasting stations

(G-6530)
SUSSEX EYE CARE & MEDICAL ASSO
1306 Savannah Rd (19958-1526)
PHONE.................302 644-8007
▲ EMP: 9 EST: 2007
SALES (est): 675.17K Privately Held
Web: www.atlanticeyecare.com
SIC: 8011 Opthalmologist

(G-6531)
SUSSEX PODIATRY GROUP
Also Called: Kulina, Patrick F MD
1532 Savannah Rd (19958-1624)
PHONE.................302 645-8555
Patrick F Kulina, Pr
EMP: 8 EST: 1992
SALES (est): 373.78K Privately Held
SIC: 8043 Offices and clinics of podiatrists

(G-6532)
SUTE MEDIA INC (PA) ◊
16192 Coastal Hwy (19958-3608)
PHONE.................617 774-9499
Cameron Mulvey, CEO
EMP: 3 EST: 2022
SALES (est): 255.87K
SALES (corp-wide): 255.87K Privately Held
SIC: 7372 Prepackaged software

(G-6533)
SWELLINFOCOM
221 Lakeside Dr (19958-8939)
PHONE.................302 588-6241
EMP: 7 EST: 2012
SALES (est): 74.61K Privately Held
Web: www.swellinfo.com
SIC: 7999 Amusement and recreation, nec

(G-6534)
SWIPES INCORPORATED
16192 Coastal Hwy (19958-3608)
PHONE.................650 686-0223
EMP: 5 EST: 2013
SALES (est): 163.25K Privately Held
SIC: 7371 Computer software development and applications

(G-6535)
SWYPE INC
16192 Coastal Hwy (19958-3608)
PHONE.................619 736-1410
EMP: 2
SALES (est): 100K Privately Held
SIC: 7372 Prepackaged software

(G-6536)
SYNCCORE INC
16192 Coastal Hwy (19958-3608)
PHONE.................833 612-0999
EMP: 6 EST: 2018
SALES (est): 64.74K Privately Held
Web: www.synccore.io
SIC: 7379 Online services technology consultants

(G-6537)
SYNCOLOGI LLC ◊
16192 Coastal Hwy (19958-3608)
PHONE.................408 549-9559
Abdulaziz Sema, Ex Dir
EMP: 50 EST: 2022
SALES (est): 1.14MM Privately Held
SIC: 7371 Software programming applications

GEOGRAPHIC SECTION
Lewes - Sussex County (G-6567)

(G-6538)
TAFFY TUBES LLC
110 New Rd (19958-9573)
PHONE.................................302 200-9255
EMP: 5 EST: 2017
SALES (est): 92.36K Privately Held
Web: www.taffytubes.com
SIC: 5051 Steel

(G-6539)
TALENTS LIST INC
16192 Coastal Hwy (19958-3608)
PHONE.................................650 618-1040
Claudia Lucena, Prin
EMP: 5 EST: 2017
SALES (est): 324.76K Privately Held
Web: www.talentslist.com
SIC: 4899 Communication services, nec

(G-6540)
TALK AWARE LLC
16192 Coastal Hwy (19958-3608)
PHONE.................................302 645-7400
EMP: 2
SQ FT: 1,500
SALES (est): 56.54K Privately Held
SIC: 7372 Operating systems computer software

(G-6541)
TALL PINES ASSOCIATES LLC
Also Called: Tall Pines Campground
29551 Persimmon Rd (19958-3954)
P.O. Box 221 (19958-0221)
PHONE.................................302 684-0300
Richard Berman, Pr
EMP: 12 EST: 1994
SALES (est): 212.79K Privately Held
Web: www.tallpines-del.com
SIC: 7033 Campgrounds

(G-6542)
TARO MEDICAL INCORPORATED
16192 Coastal Hwy (19958-3608)
PHONE.................................818 245-2202
EMP: 12 EST: 2021
SALES (est): 46.16K Privately Held
SIC: 3841 Surgical and medical instruments

(G-6543)
TCONCEPTS RESOURCES INC ✪
16192 Coastal Hwy (19958-3608)
PHONE.................................302 309-2490
Suresh Karampudi, Pr
EMP: 10 EST: 2022
SALES (est): 355.79K Privately Held
SIC: 7379 Online services technology consultants

(G-6544)
TDC PARTNERS LTD
31781 Marsh Island Ave (19958-3350)
PHONE.................................302 827-2137
Theodore R Ferragut, Pr
EMP: 5 EST: 2008
SALES (est): 83.22K Privately Held
SIC: 8741 Business management

(G-6545)
TEAM SYSTEMS INTERNATIONAL LLC
16192 Coastal Hwy (19958-3608)
PHONE.................................703 217-7648
Deborah Evans Mott, Managing Member
Christopher Mott, OF BUS AND DEVELOP
EMP: 5 EST: 2001
SALES (est): 315.11K Privately Held
SIC: 8748 1623 8744 Telecommunications consultant; Cable laying construction; Facilities support services

(G-6546)
TECHNO GOOBER
17527 Nassau Commons Blvd Ste 213 (19958)
PHONE.................................302 645-7177
Frank Payton, Owner
EMP: 10 EST: 2013
SALES (est): 553.3K Privately Held
Web: www.technogoober.com
SIC: 7374 Computer graphics service

(G-6547)
TECTANIC LLC
16192 Coastal Hwy (19958-3608)
PHONE.................................302 440-2788
EMP: 6 EST: 2020
SALES (est): 46.16K Privately Held
Web: www.tectanic.com
SIC: 7371 Computer software development and applications

(G-6548)
TELECOM CONSULTING GROUP INC
16192 Coastal Hwy (19958-3608)
PHONE.................................302 645-7400
EMP: 5 EST: 1999
SALES (est): 150.85K Privately Held
SIC: 8742 Business management consultant

(G-6549)
TELORCA LLC
16192 Coastal Hwy (19958-3608)
PHONE.................................315 693-8488
EMP: 6 EST: 2021
SALES (est): 46.16K Privately Held
Web: www.telorca.com
SIC: 7371 Software programming applications

(G-6550)
TENON TOURS LLC (PA)
17515 Nassau Commons Blvd (19958-6283)
PHONE.................................781 435-0425
Bryan D Lewis, Managing Member
EMP: 5 EST: 2012
SALES (est): 975.6K
SALES (corp-wide): 975.6K Privately Held
Web: www.tenontours.com
SIC: 4724 Travel agencies

(G-6551)
TERANETWORK LLC
16192 Coastal Hwy (19958-3608)
PHONE.................................302 257-7782
EMP: 5 EST: 2020
SALES (est): 27.98K Privately Held
SIC: 7379 Computer related consulting services

(G-6552)
TERRAN GLOBAL CORPORATION
Also Called: Global Space Organization
16192 Coastal Hwy (19958-3608)
PHONE.................................702 626-5704
Caed Aldwych, CEO
Kevin Mcghee, Prin
Paul Kelly, Prin
Michael Brunn, Prin
Latoya Stephenson, Prin
EMP: 6 EST: 2012
SALES (est): 619.99K Privately Held
Web: www.terrancorp.com
SIC: 3829 8731 Measuring and controlling devices, nec; Commercial physical research

(G-6553)
TFT MEDIA LLC
16192 Coastal Hwy (19958-3608)
PHONE.................................302 645-7400

EMP: 5 EST: 2020
SALES (est): 171.12K Privately Held
SIC: 2721 Magazines: publishing only, not printed on site

(G-6554)
THE NORTH TRUCKERS INC ✪
16192 Coastal Hwy (19958-3608)
PHONE.................................302 309-0786
Meenakshijit Jauhra, Pr
Meenakshijit Jauhra, Pr
Sumeet Jaurha, Dir
EMP: 12 EST: 2022
SALES (est): 1.01MM Privately Held
SIC: 4731 Freight transportation arrangement

(G-6555)
THERAPY AT BEACH
34444 King Street Row (19958-4787)
PHONE.................................302 313-5555
EMP: 6 EST: 2015
SALES (est): 179.68K Privately Held
Web: www.delawarehyperbarics.com
SIC: 7299 Massage parlor

(G-6556)
THINKSECURENET
16557 Coastal Hwy (19958-3605)
PHONE.................................302 703-9717
EMP: 19 EST: 2019
SALES (est): 644.91K Privately Held
Web: www.thinksecurenet.com
SIC: 7371 Computer software development

(G-6557)
THRESHOLDS INC
17577 Nassau Commons Blvd Ste 202 (19958-6288)
PHONE.................................302 827-4478
EMP: 29 EST: 2012
SALES (est): 639.27K Privately Held
SIC: 8069 Drug addiction rehabilitation hospital

(G-6558)
TIDEWATER PHYSCL THRPY AND REB
20750 John J Williams Hwy Unit 1 (19958-4399)
PHONE.................................302 945-5111
EMP: 8
Web: www.tidewaterpt.com
SIC: 8049 8093 Physical therapist; Rehabilitation center, outpatient treatment
PA: Tidewater Physical Therapy And Rehabilitation Associates Pa
406 Marvel Ct
Easton MD 21601

(G-6559)
TIDY TECHNOLOGIES INC (PA)
Also Called: Tidy App
16192 Coastal Hwy (19958-3608)
PHONE.................................888 788-2445
Derrick Agyiri, Pr
EMP: 5 EST: 2019
SALES (est): 734.14K
SALES (corp-wide): 734.14K Privately Held
SIC: 7371 Software programming applications

(G-6560)
TILE MARKET OF DELAWARE INC
Also Called: TILE MARKET OF DELAWARE, INC.
17701 Dartmouth Dr Unit 1 (19958-4205)
PHONE.................................302 644-7100
Paul Anderson, Genl Mgr
EMP: 28

SALES (corp-wide): 42.97MM Privately Held
Web: www.tilemarketofde.com
SIC: 1743 Tile installation, ceramic
HQ: Tile Market Of Delaware Llc
405 Marsh Ln Ste 3
Wilmington DE 19804

(G-6561)
TIPLAB INC
16192 Coastal Hwy (19958-3608)
PHONE.................................917 586-9649
Frederick Olsen, Prin
EMP: 3 EST: 2021
SALES (est): 71.13K Privately Held
SIC: 7372 Application computer software

(G-6562)
TIS GROUP INC ✪
Also Called: Tis Group
1692 Coastal Hwy (19958)
PHONE.................................929 322-8811
Irakli Koblianidze, Dir
EMP: 12 EST: 2022
SALES (est): 173.23K Privately Held
SIC: 7699 7371 Cleaning services; Computer software development and applications

(G-6563)
TKXAI LLC
16192 Coastal Hwy (19958-3608)
PHONE.................................202 670-8818
Keith Casscells Hamby, Managing Member
EMP: 5 EST: 2021
SALES (est): 53.68K Privately Held
SIC: 7922 Entertainment promotion

(G-6564)
TLBC LLC
Also Called: Lewes Building Co, The
105 2nd St (19958-1356)
PHONE.................................302 797-8700
Jeff Dawson, Owner
EMP: 5 EST: 2011
SALES (est): 523.3K Privately Held
Web: www.lewesbuildingco.com
SIC: 1521 New construction, single-family houses

(G-6565)
TNT DRYWALL LLC
17870 Callaway Dr (19958-3681)
PHONE.................................302 381-0114
Kyle Travis, Prin
EMP: 5 EST: 2017
SALES (est): 81.13K Privately Held
SIC: 1742 Drywall

(G-6566)
TOBACK BUILDERS
20375 John J Williams Hwy (19958-4305)
PHONE.................................302 644-1015
Mat Toback, Owner
EMP: 6 EST: 2016
SALES (est): 587.07K Privately Held
Web: www.tobackbuilders.com
SIC: 1521 New construction, single-family houses

(G-6567)
TODD R WILLIAMS
Also Called: Tectonics
22337 Dorman Rd (19958-4360)
PHONE.................................302 945-3662
Andrea Williams, Prin
EMP: 5 EST: 2009
SALES (est): 240.17K Privately Held
SIC: 1522 Residential construction, nec

(PA)=Parent Co (HQ)=Headquarters
✪ = New Business established in last 2 years

2024 Harris Directory of Delaware Businesses

Lewes - Sussex County (G-6568) GEOGRAPHIC SECTION

(G-6568)
TOLEDO&GIRON USA LLC ◆
16192 Coastal Hwy (19958-3608)
PHONE.................................302 261-3771
Kleyner Aguilar, *Managing Member*
EMP: 5 **EST:** 2022
SALES (est): 78.16K **Privately Held**
Web: www.toledogiron.com
SIC: 3566 Speed changers, drives, and gears

(G-6569)
TOM RAINEY BUILDERS LLC
31503 S Conley Cir (19958-6018)
PHONE.................................302 381-5339
Thomas Rainey, *Owner*
EMP: 5 **EST:** 2011
SALES (est): 156.82K **Privately Held**
SIC: 1521 New construction, single-family houses

(G-6570)
TOOKUAI INC
16192 Coastal Hwy (19958-3608)
PHONE.................................302 291-1505
Charles Wang, *CEO*
EMP: 5
SALES (est): 206.44K **Privately Held**
SIC: 4121 Taxicabs

(G-6571)
TOP NOTCH HTG & A C & RFRGN
33806 Dreamweaver Ln (19958-1653)
P.O. Box 9 (19947-0009)
PHONE.................................302 645-7171
Robert Willin, *Prin*
EMP: 6 **EST:** 2008
SALES (est): 464.61K **Privately Held**
Web: www.topnotchheating.com
SIC: 1711 Warm air heating and air conditioning contractor

(G-6572)
TOP OF THE LINE JANTR SVCS
19602 Mulberry Knoll Rd (19958-4358)
P.O. Box 668 (19958-0668)
PHONE.................................302 645-2668
Robert W Shipe, *Pr*
Sandra Shipe, *Treas*
EMP: 8 **EST:** 1975
SALES (est): 234.3K **Privately Held**
SIC: 7349 Janitorial service, contract basis

(G-6573)
TOSPAY INC
16192 Coastal Hwy (19958-3608)
PHONE.................................347 474-0402
Daud Suleiman, *Pr*
EMP: 42 **EST:** 2019
SALES (est): 558.96K **Privately Held**
SIC: 7389 Financial services

(G-6574)
TOUCH OF ITALY BAKERY LLC
33323 E Chesapeake St Unit 31 (19958-7242)
PHONE.................................302 827-2132
EMP: 8 **EST:** 2012
SALES (est): 956.54K **Privately Held**
Web: www.touchofitaly.com
SIC: 5149 Bakery products

(G-6575)
TPW MANAGEMENT LLC
Also Called: Tpw Management
17577 Nassau Commons Blvd Ste 103 (19958-6288)
PHONE.................................302 227-7878
EMP: 11
Web: www.tpw.com

SIC: 8741 Management services
PA: Tpw Management Llc
4903 Main St
Manchester Center VT 05255

(G-6576)
TRACY B HARRIS
Also Called: Lighthouse Cleaning
18002 Ebb Tide Dr (19958-4185)
PHONE.................................302 644-1477
EMP: 5 **EST:** 2009
SALES (est): 72.89K **Privately Held**
SIC: 7699 Cleaning services

(G-6577)
TRADEALLY INCORPORATED (PA) ◆
16192 Coastal Hwy (19958-3608)
PHONE.................................832 997-2582
Tonye Membere Otaji, *Pr*
EMP: 20 **EST:** 2023
SALES (est): 1.22MM
SALES (corp-wide): 1.22MM **Privately Held**
SIC: 4731 Freight forwarding

(G-6578)
TRAVELBOOK INC (PA)
16192 Coastal Hwy (19958-3608)
PHONE.................................646 575-6731
Dean Kelly, *CEO*
EMP: 7 **EST:** 2016
SALES (est): 1.25MM
SALES (corp-wide): 1.25MM **Privately Held**
Web: www.travelbook.com
SIC: 4724 Travel agencies

(G-6579)
TREVCON CONSTRUCTION CO
33915 Mcnicol Rd (19958-6220)
PHONE.................................908 413-7001
Frederic Price, *Prin*
EMP: 8 **EST:** 2018
SALES (est): 92.16K **Privately Held**
Web: www.trevconconstruction.com
SIC: 1521 Single-family housing construction

(G-6580)
TROVETY INC
16192 Coastal Hwy (19958-3608)
P.O. Box 434 (70748-0434)
PHONE.................................302 291-2252
Clifton Green, *Pr*
Clifton E Green, *Pr*
EMP: 5 **EST:** 2019
SALES (est): 50K **Privately Held**
SIC: 5199 5999 General merchandise, non-durable; Miscellaneous retail stores, nec

(G-6581)
TRUCK LAGBE INC
16192 Coastal Hwy (19958-3608)
PHONE.................................860 810-8677
Anayet Rashid, *CEO*
EMP: 42 **EST:** 2018
SALES (est): 1.43MM **Privately Held**
SIC: 7371 Computer software development and applications

(G-6582)
TRUITT INSURANCE AGENCY INC
Also Called: Nationwide
365 Savannah Rd (19958-1438)
P.O. Box 248 (19958-0248)
PHONE.................................302 645-9344
Thad Truitt, *Pr*
EMP: 5 **EST:** 1965
SQ FT: 2,200
SALES (est): 446.54K **Privately Held**
Web: www.nationwide.com

SIC: 6411 Insurance agents, nec

(G-6583)
TRUMOVE INC
16192 Coastal Hwy (19958-3608)
PHONE.................................917 379-7427
Chiao-wei Lee, *Dir*
EMP: 3 **EST:** 2016
SALES (est): 144.06K **Privately Held**
SIC: 7372 Application computer software

(G-6584)
TUNNELL & RAYSOR PA
770 Kings Hwy (19958-1704)
PHONE.................................302 644-4442
Heidi Balliet, *Brnch Mgr*
EMP: 5
SALES (corp-wide): 5.89MM **Privately Held**
Web: www.tunnellraysor.com
SIC: 8111 General practice attorney, lawyer
PA: Tunnell & Raysor, P.A.
30 E Pine St
Georgetown DE 19947
302 856-7313

(G-6585)
TWISTY SYSTEMS LLC
16192 Coastal Hwy (19958-3608)
PHONE.................................571 331-7093
EMP: 7 **EST:** 2017
SALES (est): 120.25K **Privately Held**
Web: www.twistysystems.com
SIC: 7371 Computer software development

(G-6586)
U-HAUL NEIGHBORHOOD DEALER
33012 Cedar Grove Rd (19958-4644)
PHONE.................................302 644-4316
EMP: 7 **EST:** 2018
SALES (est): 134.94K **Privately Held**
Web: www.uhaul.com
SIC: 7513 Truck rental and leasing, no drivers

(G-6587)
U-HAUL NEIGHBORHOOD DEALER
17649 Coastal Hwy (19958-6213)
PHONE.................................302 703-0376
EMP: 7 **EST:** 2018
SALES (est): 135.21K **Privately Held**
Web: www.uhaul.com
SIC: 7513 Truck rental and leasing, no drivers

(G-6588)
UNIQUE BIOTECH INC
16192 Coastal Hwy (19958-3608)
PHONE.................................888 478-2799
Joshua Iii, *Managing Member*
EMP: 2
SALES (est): 92.41K **Privately Held**
SIC: 2048 Prepared feeds, nec

(G-6589)
UNIQUE MNDS CHANGING LIVES INC
17584 Stingey Ln (19958-4997)
P.O. Box 103 (19969-0103)
PHONE.................................302 943-1945
Helena Gibbs, *Pr*
EMP: 5
SALES (est): 107.26K **Privately Held**
SIC: 8399 Community development groups

(G-6590)
UNITED SUN SYSTEMS US INC
16192 Coastal Hwy (19958-3608)
PHONE.................................650 460-8707
EMP: 6 **EST:** 2018

SALES (est): 120.02K **Privately Held**
SIC: 1711 Solar energy contractor

(G-6591)
UPON A ONCE TILE INC
16192 Coastal Hwy (19958-3608)
PHONE.................................646 992-1376
Michael Pavarini, *CEO*
EMP: 5 **EST:** 2019
SALES (est): 77.06K **Privately Held**
SIC: 1743 Tile installation, ceramic

(G-6592)
US ENGINEERING CORPORATION
16192 Coastal Hwy (19958-3608)
PHONE.................................302 645-7400
EMP: 10
SALES (est): 631.87K **Privately Held**
SIC: 3533 Oil and gas field machinery

(G-6593)
US LAWNS DOVER
Also Called: US Lawns
16856 Ketch Ct (19958-5012)
PHONE.................................302 703-2818
Bruce Maloomian, *Prin*
EMP: 9 **EST:** 2012
SALES (est): 133.75K **Privately Held**
Web: www.uslawns.com
SIC: 0782 Lawn care services

(G-6594)
USACARRECORDCOM LLC
16192 Coastal Hwy (19958-3608)
PHONE.................................302 645-7400
EMP: 5 **EST:** 2017
SALES (est): 37.46K **Privately Held**
Web: usacarrecord.com.usitestat.com
SIC: 7374 Data processing service

(G-6595)
USS WIND TECHNOLOGIES LLC (PA)
16192 Coastal Hwy (19958-3608)
PHONE.................................646 770-6265
EMP: 5 **EST:** 2020
SALES (est): 2.48MM
SALES (corp-wide): 2.48MM **Privately Held**
SIC: 4911 Electric services

(G-6596)
UTILISITE INC
20721 Robinsonville Rd (19958-6044)
PHONE.................................302 945-5022
Sharon Hart, *Pr*
EMP: 12 **EST:** 2004
SALES (est): 1.65MM **Privately Held**
Web: www.utilisiteinc.com
SIC: 1623 Water, sewer, and utility lines

(G-6597)
UTOPIE TECHNOLOGIES INC
16192 Coastal Hwy (19958-3608)
PHONE.................................628 251-1312
Stephen Konigbagbe, *CEO*
EMP: 10
SALES (est): 348.32K **Privately Held**
SIC: 7371 Computer software development

(G-6598)
VALIU INC
16192 Coastal Hwy (19958-3608)
PHONE.................................317 853-5081
Simon Chamorro, *CEO*
EMP: 6 **EST:** 2018
SALES (est): 284.12K **Privately Held**
SIC: 7374 Data processing service

GEOGRAPHIC SECTION

Lewes - Sussex County (G-6630)

(G-6599)
VERDANTAS LLC
1143 Savannah Rd Ste 1a (19958-1515)
PHONE..................................302 239-6634
EMP: 5 EST: 2021
SALES (est): 73.03K **Privately Held**
SIC: 8711 Engineering services

(G-6600)
VERTRIUS CORP
16192 Coastal Hwy (19958-3608)
PHONE..................................800 770-1913
Joe Ruiz, *CEO*
EMP: 10 EST: 2016
SQ FT: 7,500
SALES (est): 484.11K **Privately Held**
Web: www.vertrius.com
SIC: 7371 Computer software development

(G-6601)
VETERANS DEVELOPMENT CO LLC
23171 Albertson Ct (19958-5274)
PHONE..................................302 945-5281
France Shelton, *Prin*
EMP: 5 EST: 2016
SALES (est): 60.42K **Privately Held**
SIC: 8641 Veterans' organization

(G-6602)
VETERANS STORY PROJECT INC
308 Ocean View Blvd (19958-1296)
PHONE..................................302 644-4600
EMP: 5 EST: 2017
SALES (est): 46.83K **Privately Held**
Web: www.veteransstoryproject.com
SIC: 8641 Veterans' organization

(G-6603)
VIC VICTOR IMAGINATION CO LLC ✪
16192 Coastal Hwy (19958-3608)
PHONE..................................714 262-4326
Victor Guiza, *Managing Member*
EMP: 6 EST: 2022
SALES (est): 216.16K **Privately Held**
SIC: 7374 8742 Computer graphics service; Marketing consulting services

(G-6604)
VIEWBIX INC (HQ)
16192 Coastal Hwy (19958-3608)
PHONE..................................302 645-7400
Amihay Hadad, *CEO*
Yoram Bauman, *Ch Bd*
Shahar Marom, *CFO*
EMP: 10 EST: 1985
SALES (est): 96.6MM **Privately Held**
SIC: 7372 Prepackaged software
PA: Gix Internet Ltd
    14 Shenkar Arie
    Herzliya 46725

(G-6605)
VIINEX INC
16192 Coastal Hwy (19958-3608)
PHONE..................................510 443-5114
German Zhyvotnikov, *CEO*
Andrey Kireev, *CFO*
EMP: 8 EST: 2019
SALES (est): 83K **Privately Held**
Web: www.viinex.com
SIC: 7371 Computer software development

(G-6606)
VINCENT B KILLEEN M D
1535 Savannah Rd (19958-1611)
PHONE..................................302 645-4700
EMP: 9 EST: 2018
SALES (est): 143.24K **Privately Held**
SIC: 8011 Offices and clinics of medical doctors

(G-6607)
VIVIANS STYLE
33516 Crossing Ave Unit 2 (19958-1697)
PHONE..................................302 645-9444
Vivan Mills, *CEO*
EMP: 5 EST: 2004
SALES (est): 100.88K **Privately Held**
Web: www.viviansstyle.com
SIC: 7231 Hairdressers

(G-6608)
VIZZIE 360 (PA)
16192 Coastal Hwy (19958-3608)
PHONE..................................323 239-0690
Arie Lofton, *CEO*
EMP: 4 EST: 2016
SALES (est): 231.58K
SALES (corp-wide): 231.58K **Privately Held**
SIC: 7389 8999 7389 Business Activities at Non-Commercial Site; Application computer software; Medical research

(G-6609)
VOLVOX BIOLOGIC INC
16192 Coastal Hwy (19958-3608)
PHONE..................................801 722-5942
Nigel Reuel, *CEO*
EMP: 6 EST: 2012
SALES (est): 59K **Privately Held**
SIC: 8731 8999 7389 Biological research; Scientific consulting; Business services, nec

(G-6610)
VPS INTERNATIONAL LLC
16192 Coastal Hwy (19958-3608)
PHONE..................................800 493-9356
Carlos Sanchez, *Managing Member*
EMP: 6 EST: 2012
SALES (est): 113.36K **Privately Held**
SIC: 4813 Telephone communication, except radio

(G-6611)
VRTII CORPORATION
16192 Coastal Hwy (19958-3608)
PHONE..................................703 401-8963
Andrew Lovegrove, *Ch Bd*
EMP: 6 EST: 2014
SQ FT: 1,000
SALES (est): 84.51K **Privately Held**
Web: www.vrtiiapp.com
SIC: 7311 Advertising agencies

(G-6612)
VULCAN WIZARD LLC
16192 Coastal Hwy (19958-3608)
PHONE..................................914 326-0023
EMP: 2
SALES (est): 92.41K **Privately Held**
SIC: 2023 Dietary supplements, dairy and non-dairy based

(G-6613)
WAGNER & PRIGG FAMILY MEDICINE
16529 Coastal Hwy (19958-3696)
PHONE..................................302 684-2000
EMP: 8 EST: 2017
SALES (est): 494.05K **Privately Held**
Web: www.lewesdoctor.com
SIC: 8011 General and family practice, physician/surgeon

(G-6614)
WALK BY FAITH LLC
16192 Coastal Hwy (19958-3608)
PHONE..................................737 529-5869
EMP: 10 EST: 2021
SALES (est): 820K **Privately Held**
Web: www.shopwalkbyfaith.com
SIC: 6531 Real estate leasing and rentals

(G-6615)
WASH-N-WAG
34680 Jiffy Way (19958-4931)
PHONE..................................302 644-2466
Joyce Stillwel, *Pr*
Joyce Stillwel, *Prin*
EMP: 5 EST: 2000
SALES (est): 116.96K **Privately Held**
Web: www.wagnwash.com
SIC: 0752 Grooming services, pet and animal specialties

(G-6616)
WASTECOST CORPORATION
16192 Coastal Hwy (19958-3608)
PHONE..................................512 562-0888
Ivan Gribin, *CEO*
EMP: 5 EST: 2020
SALES (est): 86.19K **Privately Held**
SIC: 7929 Musician

(G-6617)
WATERFRONT LDSCPG IRRIGATION
1604 Savannah Rd (19958-1662)
PHONE..................................302 645-8100
EMP: 5 EST: 2018
SALES (est): 208.71K **Privately Held**
SIC: 0781 Landscape services

(G-6618)
WEALTH CAPITAL INVESTORS LLC
7 Canary Dr (19958-2317)
PHONE..................................202 596-2280
EMP: 5 EST: 2014
SALES (est): 151.06K **Privately Held**
SIC: 6799 Investors, nec

(G-6619)
WEBTRIT INC
16192 Coastal Hwy (19958-3608)
PHONE..................................954 364-8888
Andriy Zhylenko, *CEO*
EMP: 5
SALES (est): 199.4K **Privately Held**
SIC: 7371 Software programming applications

(G-6620)
WEKEEP TRAVEL SERVICES LLC ✪
16192 Coastal Hwy (19958-3608)
PHONE..................................786 814-0722
EMP: 5 EST: 2022
SALES (est): 63.4K **Privately Held**
SIC: 7371 Computer software development and applications

(G-6621)
WELCOME ABOARD TRAVEL LTD
405 Lakeside Dr (19958-8950)
PHONE..................................302 678-9480
Shelley Brocklehurst, *Pr*
EMP: 5 EST: 1981
SALES (est): 767.22K **Privately Held**
Web: www.welcomeaboard.net
SIC: 4724 Tourist agency arranging transport, lodging and car rental

(G-6622)
WELLNESS FROM WITHIN
33253 Waterview Ct (19958-5317)
PHONE..................................717 884-3908
Emma Newman, *Prin*
EMP: 6 EST: 2016
SALES (est): 76K **Privately Held**
SIC: 8099 Health and allied services, nec

(G-6623)
WELTRON TECHNOLOGY LTD CO
16192 Coastal Hwy (19958-3608)
PHONE..................................508 353-6752
Binrong Yang, *CEO*
EMP: 6
SALES (est): 237.56K **Privately Held**
SIC: 7371 Computer software development

(G-6624)
WESTCHESTER COMMUNICATIONS SVC
18561 Rose Ct (19958-5912)
PHONE..................................302 827-2939
William Luongo, *Pr*
EMP: 5 EST: 2013
SALES (est): 43.15K **Privately Held**
SIC: 4899 Communication services, nec

(G-6625)
WESTERN KENTUCKY AMBULATORY
210 Tanglewood Dr (19958-9545)
PHONE..................................302 542-2770
Eric Lee, *Prin*
EMP: 8 EST: 2012
SALES (est): 68.94K **Privately Held**
SIC: 8011 Surgeon

(G-6626)
WHAT IS YOUR VOICE INC
17583 Shady Rd (19958-6237)
PHONE..................................443 653-2067
Jacqueline Sterbach, *CEO*
Walter Sterbach, *VP*
Steve Folsom, *Treas*
Maria Grace Folsom, *OF EMPOWERMENT PROGRAMS*
EMP: 15 EST: 2014
SALES (est): 216.62K **Privately Held**
SIC: 8699 Charitable organization

(G-6627)
WHOOP LABS INC
16192 Coastal Hwy (19958-3608)
PHONE..................................425 442-2137
Victor Huang, *CEO*
EMP: 3 EST: 2020
SALES (est): 100K **Privately Held**
Web: www.whoop.com
SIC: 7372 Business oriented computer software

(G-6628)
WHUUPS LLC
16192 Coastal Hwy (19958-3608)
PHONE..................................808 393-6240
EMP: 2 EST: 2021
SALES (est): 56.54K **Privately Held**
Web: www.whuups.com
SIC: 7372 Application computer software

(G-6629)
WIFIESTA INC (PA)
16192 Coastal Hwy (19958-3608)
PHONE..................................206 923-9206
Baker Garbawi, *Pr*
EMP: 10 EST: 2017
SALES (est): 733.02K
SALES (corp-wide): 733.02K **Privately Held**
SIC: 7371 Computer software development and applications

(G-6630)
WILGUS ASSOCIATES INC
1520 Savannah Rd (19958-1624)
PHONE..................................302 644-2960
Joe Polichetti, *Mgr*
EMP: 8

Lewes - Sussex County (G-6631)

SALES (corp-wide): 8.51MM **Privately Held**
Web: www.wilgusassociates.com
SIC: 6411 6519 6531 Insurance brokers, nec; Real property lessors, nec; Real estate agents and managers
PA: Wilgus Associates Inc
32904 Coastal Hwy
Bethany Beach DE 19930
302 539-7511

(G-6631)
WILLIAM CRAFT
20433 Wil King Rd (19958-4510)
PHONE.................302 945-5798
Steven Craft, *Prin*
EMP: 5 EST: 2005
SALES (est): 51.32K **Privately Held**
SIC: 7538 General automotive repair shops

(G-6632)
WILLIAMSON BUILDING CORP
130 New Rd (19958-9573)
PHONE.................302 644-0605
EMP: 5 EST: 1992
SALES (est): 492.66K **Privately Held**
SIC: 1521 7389 Single-family home remodeling, additions, and repairs; Business Activities at Non-Commercial Site

(G-6633)
WILLOW TREE EQUITY HOLDING LLC
16192 Coastal Hwy (19958-3608)
PHONE.................213 479-4077
EMP: 10 EST: 2017
Web: www.shopwillow.net
SIC: 6719 Holding companies, nec

(G-6634)
WIRELISITY INC
16192 Coastal Hwy (19958-3608)
PHONE.................213 816-1957
EMP: 5 EST: 2018
SALES (est): 88.38K **Privately Held**
SIC: 3629 Battery chargers, rectifying or nonrotating

(G-6635)
WITT BUTCH INC
16192 Coastal Hwy (19958-3608)
PHONE.................706 883-0539
Eshovo Oga, *Pr*
EMP: 5 EST: 2020
SALES (est): 46.16K **Privately Held**
Web: www.wittbutch.com
SIC: 7371 Computer software development and applications

(G-6636)
WIXFI INC
16192 Coastal Hwy (19958-3608)
PHONE.................415 504-2607
Nikolay Klimov, *CEO*
EMP: 6 EST: 2020
SALES (est): 170K **Privately Held**
SIC: 7371 Computer software development

(G-6637)
WOMEN LEADING INNOVATION INC
16192 Coastal Hwy (19958-3608)
PHONE.................540 798-4023
Lorena Gonzalez, *CEO*
Patricia C Lopez, *CFO*
EMP: 3 EST: 2021
SALES (est): 128.34K **Privately Held**
SIC: 7372 Prepackaged software

(G-6638)
WOMENS HEALTH CENTER
24351 Zinfandel Ln # 202 (19958-1888)
PHONE.................517 437-5390
EMP: 5 EST: 2020
SALES (est): 54.13K **Privately Held**
SIC: 8011 Offices and clinics of medical doctors

(G-6639)
WONDERLUST LLC
16192 Coastal Hwy (19958-3608)
PHONE.................662 312-8390
EMP: 9 EST: 2020
SALES (est): 399.13K **Privately Held**
SIC: 7371 Computer software development and applications

(G-6640)
WORLD ECONOMIC MAGAZINE INC
16192 Coastal Hwy (19958-3608)
PHONE.................302 499-2016
EMP: 5 EST: 2020
SALES (est): 73.16K **Privately Held**
Web: www.worldecomag.com
SIC: 2721 Magazines: publishing and printing

(G-6641)
WRUFF WRYDER PRODUCTIONS
112 Seagull Dr (19958-3793)
PHONE.................602 803-7620
Eric Davison, *Prin*
EMP: 5 EST: 2017
SALES (est): 65.29K **Privately Held**
SIC: 7819 Developing and laboratory services, motion picture

(G-6642)
X LEADER LLC
16192 Coastal Hwy (19958-3608)
PHONE.................800 345-2677
EMP: 2 EST: 2018
SALES (est): 71.5K **Privately Held**
Web: www.delawareinc.com
SIC: 2741 Internet publishing and broadcasting

(G-6643)
XENOPIA LLC
16192 Coastal Hwy (19958-3608)
PHONE.................302 703-7050
◆ EMP: 5 EST: 2001
SALES (est): 318.18K **Privately Held**
SIC: 5999 7389 Electronic parts and equipment; Business services, nec

(G-6644)
XWIND SERVICES LTD
16192 Coastal Hwy (19958-3608)
PHONE.................916 367-2994
EMP: 6 EST: 2019
SALES (est): 70.4K **Privately Held**
SIC: 1796 Installing building equipment

(G-6645)
XWIND SERVICES LTD
16192 Coastal Hwy (19958-3608)
PHONE.................418 563-5453
Jason Tozer, *Pr*
Marc Poirier, *
EMP: 28 EST: 2019
SALES (est): 1.3MM **Privately Held**
SIC: 1796 Power generating equipment installation

(G-6646)
YUMITOS LLC
16192 Coastal Hwy (19958-3608)
PHONE.................704 819-6745
Charlie Green, *Managing Member*
EMP: 3 EST: 2020
SALES (est): 91.38K **Privately Held**
Web: www.yumitos.com
SIC: 2051 Bakery, for home service delivery

(G-6647)
ZAWADIUS INC
16192 Coastal Hwy (19958-3608)
PHONE.................888 979-6929
Mustafa Salemwalla, *CEO*
EMP: 5 EST: 2021
SALES (est): 550.12K **Privately Held**
SIC: 5023 Decorating supplies

(G-6648)
ZEEQUEST INC (PA)
16192 Coastal Hwy (19958-3608)
PHONE.................760 212-7378
EMP: 5 EST: 2016
SALES (est): 282.76K
SALES (corp-wide): 282.76K **Privately Held**
Web: www.zeequest.com
SIC: 2833 Medicinals and botanicals

(G-6649)
ZEINA JEHA MD MPH
16295 Willow Creek Rd (19958-3614)
PHONE.................302 503-4200
EMP: 7 EST: 2018
SALES (est): 118.67K **Privately Held**
SIC: 8011 Offices and clinics of medical doctors

(G-6650)
ZIPHEALTH INC
16192 Coastal Hwy (19958-3608)
PHONE.................561 207-7140
EMP: 5 EST: 2018
SALES (est): 214.11K **Privately Held**
SIC: 8099 Health and allied services, nec

(G-6651)
ZK TECHNOLOGIES LLC
16192 Coastal Hwy (19958-3608)
PHONE.................980 246-4090
EMP: 5 EST: 2020
SALES (est): 500K **Privately Held**
Web: www.zktechinc.com
SIC: 7299 Information services, consumer

(G-6652)
ZWAANENDAEL LLC
142 2nd St (19958-1396)
PHONE.................302 645-6466
EMP: 9 EST: 1952
SQ FT: 20,000
SALES (est): 609.73K **Privately Held**
SIC: 7261 7011 6513 6514 Funeral home; Hotels; Apartment building operators; Residential building, four or fewer units: operation

---

Lincoln
Sussex County

(G-6653)
ACP TECHNOLOGIES INC
218 W Holly Dr (19960-9637)
PHONE.................302 981-5976
EMP: 5 EST: 2011
SALES (est): 82.01K **Privately Held**
Web: www.acptechnologies.com
SIC: 8731 Commercial physical research

(G-6654)
AGE ELECTRIC LTD
8768 Clendaniel Pond Rd (19960-2947)
PHONE.................302 632-2968
Wesley Spruill, *Prin*
EMP: 5 EST: 2019
SALES (est): 241.3K **Privately Held**
Web: www.ageelectricde.com
SIC: 4911 Electric services

(G-6655)
ALL CREATURES VET SERVICES
10395 Clendaniel Pond Rd (19960-3012)
PHONE.................302 398-3367
EMP: 5 EST: 2014
SALES (est): 222.03K **Privately Held**
SIC: 0742 Animal hospital services, pets and other animal specialties

(G-6656)
ANDREWS CONSTRUCTION LLC
126 Major St (19960-2814)
PHONE.................302 604-8166
Kevin Andrews, *Managing Member*
EMP: 6 EST: 2020
SALES (est): 350.56K **Privately Held**
SIC: 1521 Single-family housing construction

(G-6657)
ARBOR CARE
21429 Bella Terra Dr (19960-3725)
PHONE.................302 491-4392
Richard Thurman, *Owner*
EMP: 7 EST: 2014
SALES (est): 119.36K **Privately Held**
Web: www.arborcarede.com
SIC: 0783 Planting, pruning, and trimming services

(G-6658)
BELLA TERRA LANDSCAPES LLC
21429 Bella Terra Dr (19960-3725)
PHONE.................302 422-9000
Mike Schimmel, *Managing Member*
Katharine Schimmel, *Managing Member*
EMP: 12 EST: 2003
SALES (est): 385.76K **Privately Held**
Web: www.bellaterrade.com
SIC: 0781 Landscape services

(G-6659)
CEDARCREEKLANDINGCGCOM
8295 Brick Granary Rd (19960-3845)
PHONE.................302 491-6614
EMP: 9 EST: 2016
SALES (est): 58.9K **Privately Held**
Web: www.delawarejellystone.com
SIC: 7033 Campgrounds

(G-6660)
CHANGING FACES INC
19500 Pine Rd (19960-3016)
PHONE.................302 397-4164
Deneen Smith-roe, *Prin*
EMP: 7 EST: 2007
SALES (est): 58.44K **Privately Held**
Web: www.changingfaces.net
SIC: 8361 Residential care

(G-6661)
CLUB MANTIS BOXING LLC
16424 Fitzgeralds Rd (19960-3220)
PHONE.................302 943-2580
Christopher Johnson, *Prin*
EMP: 5 EST: 2017
SALES (est): 42.37K **Privately Held**
SIC: 7997 Membership sports and recreation clubs

(G-6662)
DELAWARE BEACHES JELLYSTONE PK
22444 Holly Branch Way (19960-3844)

GEOGRAPHIC SECTION
Lincoln - Sussex County (G-6692)

PHONE..................302 491-4531
EMP: 11 **EST:** 2014
SALES (est): 56.82K **Privately Held**
Web: www.delawarejellystone.com
SIC: 7033 Campgrounds

(G-6663)
DELAWARE TERRY FARRELL FUND
18578 Sherman Ave (19960-3163)
PHONE..................302 242-4341
Ryan Knowles, *Prin*
EMP: 6 **EST:** 2017
SALES (est): 203.2K **Privately Held**
Web: www.terryfund.org
SIC: 8641 Civic and social associations

(G-6664)
DELRAY FOUNDATIONS INC
7411 Marshall St (19960-3108)
PHONE..................302 503-3341
EMP: 22 **EST:** 2016
SALES (est): 469.84K **Privately Held**
Web: www.delarayfoundations.com
SIC: 8641 Civic and social associations

(G-6665)
EMPOWERMENT GROUP INC
22761 Slaughter Neck Rd (19960-3908)
PHONE..................302 930-8080
Bryant Hazzard, *Prin*
EMP: 5 **EST:** 2018
SALES (est): 93.22K **Privately Held**
SIC: 8641 Civic and social associations

(G-6666)
EVANS HANDYMAN SERVICES
228 W Holly Dr (19960-9682)
PHONE..................302 422-2758
Brett A Evans Senior, *Prin*
EMP: 5 **EST:** 2012
SALES (est): 58.59K **Privately Held**
SIC: 7299 Handyman service

(G-6667)
F & N VAZQUEZ CONCRETE LLC
18679 Sherman Ave (19960-3133)
PHONE..................302 725-5305
Fernando Vazquez, *Prin*
EMP: 13 **EST:** 2010
SALES (est): 827.31K **Privately Held**
Web: www.fn-concrete.com
SIC: 1771 Concrete work

(G-6668)
FAMILY OTRACH MLT-PRPOSE CMNTY
19227 Young Ln (19960-2941)
PHONE..................302 422-2158
Stephanie Dukes, *Ex Dir*
EMP: 8 **EST:** 2009
SALES (est): 138.21K **Privately Held**
Web: www.familyoutreach.us
SIC: 8399 Community development groups

(G-6669)
FITZGERALD AUTO SALVAGE INC
17115 Fitzgeralds Rd (19960-3265)
P.O. Box 26 (19960-0026)
PHONE..................302 422-7584
John Fitzgerald Junior, *Pr*
Karen Fitzgerald, *
Kim Attix, *
Scott Fitzgerald, *
EMP: 70 **EST:** 1959
SQ FT: 2,000
SALES (est): 7.32MM **Privately Held**
Web: www.fitzgeralds.us
SIC: 5013 5531 5015 Automotive supplies and parts; Automotive parts; Automotive parts and supplies, used

(G-6670)
GGC INC
Also Called: Delight Housing Complex
19544 Pine Rd (19960-3016)
P.O. Box 113 (19960-0113)
PHONE..................267 893-8052
Krystal Blackwell, *Pr*
EMP: 5 **EST:** 2016
SALES (est): 496.69K **Privately Held**
SIC: 8399 Neighborhood development group

(G-6671)
GIBBONS INNOVATIONS INC
10633 W Yellowood Dr (19960-3627)
P.O. Box 99 (19960-0099)
PHONE..................302 265-4220
Christopher Gibbons, *Pr*
EMP: 3 **EST:** 2011
SALES (est): 238.98K **Privately Held**
Web: www.gibbonsinnovations.com
SIC: 3429 Hardware, nec

(G-6672)
GLENS EXTERIOR CLEANING
10316 Greentop Rd (19960-2914)
PHONE..................302 725-7222
Glen Evans, *Owner*
EMP: 5 **EST:** 2016
SALES (est): 82.97K **Privately Held**
SIC: 7699 Cleaning services

(G-6673)
HACCP NAVIGATOR LLC
10256 Webb Farm Rd (19960-3434)
PHONE..................302 531-7922
EMP: 7 **EST:** 2015
SALES (est): 342.34K **Privately Held**
Web: frontlineoffoodsafety.wildapricot.org
SIC: 8742 Food and beverage consultant

(G-6674)
HAPPYLAND CHILDCARE
18073 Johnson Rd (19960-3209)
PHONE..................302 424-3868
Sharon Mcphatter, *Prin*
EMP: 9 **EST:** 2010
SALES (est): 56.02K **Privately Held**
SIC: 8351 Child day care services

(G-6675)
HAROLD D SHOCKLEY
Also Called: Shockley Motorsports
14686 Staytonville Rd (19960-3522)
PHONE..................302 275-8500
Harold D Shockley, *Prin*
EMP: 5 **EST:** 2012
SALES (est): 38.28K **Privately Held**
SIC: 7549 High performance auto repair and service

(G-6676)
HOOD MAN LLC
10421 Jasmine Dr (19960-3634)
PHONE..................302 422-4564
Rob Hill, *Prin*
EMP: 5 **EST:** 2006
SALES (est): 108.25K **Privately Held**
Web: www.hoodmanusa.com
SIC: 7349 Exhaust hood or fan cleaning

(G-6677)
JBM PETROLEUM SERVICE LLC
8913 Clendaniel Pond Rd (19960-2979)
PHONE..................302 752-6105
Dean Vincent, *Prin*
EMP: 3 **EST:** 2013
SALES (est): 353.69K **Privately Held**
SIC: 1799 7389 7699 1389 Petroleum storage tanks, pumping and draining; Petroleum refinery inspection service; Service station equipment repair; Testing, measuring, surveying, and analysis services

(G-6678)
KEYS R US LLC
20415 Spangler Dr (19960-2672)
PHONE..................619 886-8774
Rhonda L Craddolph, *Prin*
Yvette Radin-brown, *Prin*
Stacy Burwell, *Prin*
Valerie Ellis, *Prin*
Nina Graves, *Prin*
EMP: 5 **EST:** 2019
SALES (est): 104.73K **Privately Held**
SIC: 7389 Business Activities at Non-Commercial Site

(G-6679)
LARRIMORE LOGISTICS LLC
10879 Heritage Rd (19960-4022)
PHONE..................302 265-2290
James Larrimore, *CEO*
EMP: 5 **EST:** 2007
SALES (est): 483.03K **Privately Held**
SIC: 4789 4213 Transportation services, nec; Trucking, except local

(G-6680)
LBM PAINTING LLC
9204 E Mayhew Dr (19960-2734)
PHONE..................302 569-1506
Juan C Benitez Rodriguez, *Prin*
EMP: 5 **EST:** 2015
SALES (est): 44.83K **Privately Held**
SIC: 1721 Painting and paper hanging

(G-6681)
LINCOLN COMMUNITY HALL INC
18881 Washington St (19960-3131)
P.O. Box 77 (19960-0077)
PHONE..................302 242-1747
EMP: 9
SALES (est): 11K **Privately Held**
SIC: 8641 Civic and social associations

(G-6682)
MARK H DAVIDSON
8684 Cedar Creek Rd (19960-2766)
PHONE..................302 422-0646
Mark H Davidson, *Prin*
EMP: 7 **EST:** 2012
SALES (est): 87.84K **Privately Held**
Web: www.lozenlaw.com
SIC: 6519 Real property lessors, nec

(G-6683)
MARTHA MARIE CHARTERS
8965 Clendaniel Pond Rd (19960-2979)
PHONE..................302 222-5637
EMP: 5 **EST:** 2011
SALES (est): 101.2K **Privately Held**
Web: www.marthamariecharters.com
SIC: 7999 Fishing boats, party: operation

(G-6684)
MELS WELLS LLC
8468 Hollybrook Dr (19960-3451)
PHONE..................302 393-9017
EMP: 8 **EST:** 2015
SALES (est): 239.22K **Privately Held**
Web: www.melswellsllc.com
SIC: 1711 Plumbing contractors

(G-6685)
MIDWAY SERVICES INC
9446 Willow Pond Ln (19960-2778)
PHONE..................302 422-8603
Robert Bower, *Pr*
EMP: 5 **EST:** 1974
SALES (est): 489.01K **Privately Held**
Web: www.midwayseptics.com
SIC: 1711 1794 Septic system construction; Excavation work

(G-6686)
MILFORD GUTTER GUYS LLC
7074 Marshall St (19960-3155)
PHONE..................302 424-1931
Randolph Adams, *Managing Member*
EMP: 5 **EST:** 2003
SALES (est): 413.08K **Privately Held**
Web: www.thegutterguys.com
SIC: 1761 Gutter and downspout contractor

(G-6687)
MILFORD LIONS CLUB SVC FDN
9400 Benson Rd (19960-3049)
P.O. Box 25 (19963-0025)
PHONE..................302 422-2861
EMP: 6 **EST:** 2011
SALES (est): 59.25K **Privately Held**
SIC: 8641 Civic associations

(G-6688)
MISSION MOVEMENT TRANSPORT LLC
8604 First Born Church Rd (19960-3235)
PHONE..................302 480-9401
Tonya Snead, *Prin*
EMP: 5 **EST:** 2016
SALES (est): 235.91K **Privately Held**
SIC: 7389

(G-6689)
MITCHELL E MORTON
Also Called: Developers Concrete Con
12087 N Union Church Rd (19960-3512)
PHONE..................302 236-0878
Mitchell E Morton, *Prin*
EMP: 6 **EST:** 2009
SALES (est): 149.84K **Privately Held**
SIC: 1771 Concrete work

(G-6690)
MOBILE MECHANICAL SERVICES
10014 N Union Church Rd (19960-3339)
P.O. Box 127 (19960-0127)
PHONE..................302 503-7441
EMP: 6 **EST:** 2019
SALES (est): 59.1K **Privately Held**
Web: www.mobilemechanical.com
SIC: 1711 Mechanical contractor

(G-6691)
MYOSITIS SPPORT UNDRSTNDING AS
9125 N Old State Rd (19960-3654)
PHONE..................888 696-7273
Jerry Williams, *Pr*
Lynn Wilson, *VP*
Shirley Peters, *Treas*
Benita Moyers, *Sec*
Manuel Lubinus Science, *Ofcr*
EMP: 12 **EST:** 2015
SALES (est): 67.38K **Privately Held**
Web: www.understandingmyositis.org
SIC: 8099 Medical services organization

(G-6692)
ONEALS MILLWRIGHT SERVICES LLC
18063 Johnson Rd (19960-3209)
PHONE..................302 542-5811
EMP: 8 **EST:** 2017
SALES (est): 472.25K **Privately Held**
SIC: 1796 Millwright

Lincoln - Sussex County (G-6693)   GEOGRAPHIC SECTION

(G-6693)
PRIORITY CLEANING LLC
10119 Greentop Rd (19960-2918)
PHONE..................................302 519-4998
Henry Nesmith, Prin
EMP: 5 EST: 2018
SALES (est): 68.01K Privately Held
SIC: 7699 Cleaning services

(G-6694)
PRO QUALITY EAST COAST PNTG
214 Misty Ln (19960-2849)
PHONE..................................302 745-7753
Diego Rodriguez, Prin
EMP: 5 EST: 2018
SALES (est): 96.59K Privately Held
Web: www.l-j-east-coast-painting.com
SIC: 1721 Painting and paper hanging

(G-6695)
R W MORGAN FARMS INC
18126 Haflinger Rd (19960-3318)
PHONE..................................302 542-7740
Ron W Morgan, Pr
Ron Morgan, Pr
EMP: 5 EST: 1998
SALES (est): 310.34K Privately Held
SIC: 4213 Trucking, except local

(G-6696)
RICHARD Y JOHNSON & SON INC
18404 Johnson Rd (19960-3112)
P.O. Box 105 (19960-0105)
PHONE..................................302 422-3732
Dean Johnson, CEO
EMP: 25 EST: 1939
SQ FT: 2,000
SALES (est): 4.26MM Privately Held
Web: www.ryjson.com
SIC: 1542 1521 Commercial and office building, new construction; New construction, single-family houses

(G-6697)
SAPPS WELDING SERVICE
8547 Sophies Way (19960-2679)
PHONE..................................302 491-6319
EMP: 5 EST: 2017
SALES (est): 201.06K Privately Held
SIC: 7692 Welding repair

(G-6698)
SEBASTIANS PAINTING
9072 Greentop Rd (19960-2908)
PHONE..................................302 725-8023
Kevin Sebastian, Prin
EMP: 5 EST: 2017
SALES (est): 42.66K Privately Held
SIC: 1721 Painting and paper hanging

(G-6699)
SHOCKLEY BROTHERS CONSTRUCTION
8772 Herring Branch Rd (19960-3933)
PHONE..................................302 424-3255
Vernon Shockley, Pr
Marvel Shockley, VP
Ivan Shockley, Sec
EMP: 5 EST: 1965
SQ FT: 388
SALES (est): 875.22K Privately Held
SIC: 1521 Single-family housing construction

(G-6700)
SHORE CONCIERGE INC
18060 Morgan Dr (19960-3353)
PHONE..................................302 500-1162
EMP: 5 EST: 2014
SALES (est): 62.23K Privately Held

SIC: 7299 Miscellaneous personal service

(G-6701)
SILBEREISEN S PAINTING LLC
8923 Detwiler Ln (19960-2770)
PHONE..................................302 396-8135
Brandon Silbereisen, Prin
EMP: 5 EST: 2017
SALES (est): 42.66K Privately Held
SIC: 1721 Painting and paper hanging

(G-6702)
SITE-ON AUTO INC
16906 Staytonville Rd (19960-3736)
PHONE..................................302 505-5100
Ryan Graham, Pr
EMP: 5 EST: 2016
SALES (est): 32.24K Privately Held
SIC: 7538 General automotive repair shops

(G-6703)
SLAUGHTER NECK EDUCATIONAL AND
22942 Slaughter Neck Rd (19960-3911)
PHONE..................................302 684-1834
Roslyn Harris, Dir
Ellen Parker, VP
Grace A Young, Pr
EMP: 6 EST: 1988
SALES (est): 151.71K Privately Held
SIC: 8351 Group day care center

(G-6704)
SPACECON SPECIALTY CONTRACTORS
7254 Cedar Creek Rd (19960-2601)
PHONE..................................302 503-3824
EMP: 12 EST: 2017
SALES (est): 65.03K Privately Held
Web: www.spacecon.com
SIC: 1799 Special trade contractors, nec

(G-6705)
SWAIN EXCAVATION INC
18678 Sherman Ave Unit 1 (19960-3132)
P.O. Box 46 (19960-0046)
PHONE..................................302 422-4349
Lee Chaney, Pr
Robert Bower, VP
EMP: 7 EST: 1994
SQ FT: 7,500
SALES (est): 751.16K Privately Held
SIC: 1794 Excavation work

(G-6706)
TORRESDRYWALL LLC
305 Cubbage Dr (19960-2830)
PHONE..................................302 228-6450
Jose Torres Martinez, Prin
EMP: 5 EST: 2016
SALES (est): 55.51K Privately Held
SIC: 1742 Drywall

(G-6707)
TTI INC
Also Called: Rfmw
20420 Spangler Dr (19960-2675)
PHONE..................................302 725-5189
Ralph Baquol, Mgr
EMP: 5
SALES (corp-wide): 302.09B Publicly Held
Web: www.tti.com
SIC: 5065 Electronic parts
HQ: Tti, Inc.
    2441 Northeast Pkwy
    Fort Worth TX 76106
    817 740-9000

(G-6708)
WHITE DRILLING CORP
Us 113 (19960)
PHONE..................................302 422-4057
Roy White, Pr
R Allen White, Sec
Francis White, Treas
EMP: 7 EST: 1972
SALES (est): 713.6K Privately Held
SIC: 1781 1799 Water well drilling; Hydraulic equipment, installation and service

(G-6709)
WILSONS AUCTION SALES INC
10120 Dupont Blvd (19960-3604)
P.O. Box 84 (19960-0084)
PHONE..................................302 422-3454
David Wilson, Pr
EMP: 7 EST: 1968
SQ FT: 22,000
SALES (est): 585.77K Privately Held
Web: www.wilsonsauction.com
SIC: 7389 6531 Auctioneers, fee basis; Real estate agents and managers

(G-6710)
WORTHYS PROPERTY MGT LLC
8989 Herring Branch Rd (19960-3930)
PHONE..................................302 265-8301
Tykesha Garland, Prin
EMP: 15 EST: 2016
SALES (est): 101.22K Privately Held
SIC: 7217 Carpet and furniture cleaning on location

(G-6711)
YOGI BEAR CAMPGROUND
8295 Brick Granary Rd (19960-3845)
PHONE..................................302 491-6614
EMP: 10 EST: 2017
SALES (est): 100.11K Privately Held
Web: www.delawarejellystone.com
SIC: 7033 Campgrounds

Magnolia
Kent County

(G-6712)
A PAIR OF PAINTERS
191 Ponderosa Dr (19962-1211)
PHONE..................................302 526-6761
Christy Wilson, Prin
EMP: 5 EST: 2017
SALES (est): 64.89K Privately Held
SIC: 1721 Painting and paper hanging

(G-6713)
ABBEY HAIR STYLING
1309 Ponderosa Dr (19962-1165)
PHONE..................................302 697-1186
Myrtle Stapleford, Owner
EMP: 5 EST: 2017
SALES (est): 17.73K Privately Held
SIC: 7231 Hairdressers

(G-6714)
ADVANCED HOME SERVICES INC
126 Hunters Ridge Way (19962-1588)
PHONE..................................302 339-7600
EMP: 5 EST: 2012
SALES (est): 108.69K Privately Held
SIC: 1711 Plumbing contractors

(G-6715)
ALL COUNTY CLEANING
122 Church Creek Dr (19962-2218)
PHONE..................................914 497-1177
EMP: 5 EST: 2019

SALES (est): 166.08K Privately Held
Web: www.allcountycleaning.org
SIC: 7699 Cleaning services

(G-6716)
ALLPRO SERVICES GROUP INC
529 Tullamore Rd (19962-2619)
P.O. Box 461 (19903-0461)
PHONE..................................302 750-1112
EMP: 5 EST: 2017
SALES (est): 223.85K Privately Held
Web: www.allproservicesgroup.com
SIC: 1799 Special trade contractors, nec

(G-6717)
ANOINTED TO CLEAN
135 Winding Wood Dr (19962-1757)
PHONE..................................302 284-7243
Camilla Christopher, Prin
EMP: 5 EST: 2016
SALES (est): 43.77K Privately Held
SIC: 7699 Cleaning services

(G-6718)
ANTHEM GRAPHIX
10 Cinnamon Way (19962-3649)
PHONE..................................302 270-5111
Kelly Hurlburt, Prin
EMP: 4 EST: 2018
SALES (est): 81.59K Privately Held
Web: www.anthemgraphix.com
SIC: 2759 Screen printing

(G-6719)
ATLANTIC H&S CONSULTING
247 Cider Run (19962-1668)
PHONE..................................302 222-5526
EMP: 6 EST: 2012
SALES (est): 106.34K Privately Held
SIC: 8742 Hospital and health services consultant

(G-6720)
AUTOMATION MACHINE DESIGN SE
164 Dogwood Dr (19962-1602)
PHONE..................................302 335-3911
EMP: 5 EST: 2015
SALES (est): 49.23K Privately Held
SIC: 7389 Design services

(G-6721)
BLUE HORIZON PROPERTIES LLC
49 Heartleaf Ln (19962-3603)
PHONE..................................347 731-5570
EMP: 7 EST: 2018
SALES (est): 355.53K Privately Held
SIC: 8742 Real estate consultant

(G-6722)
BONK FARMS LLC
472 Barkers Landing Rd (19962-1105)
PHONE..................................302 542-2431
Brandon Pbonk, Prin
EMP: 9 EST: 2011
SALES (est): 477.98K Privately Held
SIC: 0191 General farms, primarily crop

(G-6723)
C & H CONTRACTING LLC
3404 Irish Hill Rd (19962-1516)
PHONE..................................302 883-4339
Christopher Snyder, Prin
EMP: 5 EST: 2017
SALES (est): 56.76K Privately Held
SIC: 1799 Special trade contractors, nec

(G-6724)
C & W AUTO PARTS CO INC
851 Sorghum Mill Rd (19962-1228)
PHONE..................................302 697-2684

GEOGRAPHIC SECTION

Magnolia - Kent County (G-6756)

Craig Conner, *Pr*
EMP: 9 **EST:** 1958
SQ FT: 5,600
SALES (est): 731.9K **Privately Held**
SIC: 5013 5531 Automotive supplies and parts; Automotive parts

(G-6725)
C&M CONSTRUCTION COMPANY LLC
Also Called: C & M Roofing & Siding
49 Doris Ct (19962-3824)
PHONE.............................302 663-0936
Cindy Cruz, *Managing Member*
EMP: 24 **EST:** 2016
SALES (est): 2.28MM **Privately Held**
Web: www.candm-roofingsiding.com
SIC: 1521 General remodeling, single-family houses

(G-6726)
CAMPBELL HOME EXTERIORS LLC
276 Jury Dr (19962-2315)
PHONE.............................302 526-9663
EMP: 6 **EST:** 2014
SALES (est): 113.28K **Privately Held**
SIC: 1761 Roofing, siding, and sheetmetal work

(G-6727)
CANT WAIT OVERHEAD DOOR LLC ✪
1554 Walnut Shade Rd (19962-1833)
PHONE.............................302 546-3667
John Schulties, *Managing Member*
EMP: 7 **EST:** 2023
SALES (est): 76.51K **Privately Held**
SIC: 1751 Garage door, installation or erection

(G-6728)
CHAMPIONS CLUB
488 Augusta National Dr (19962-3199)
PHONE.............................215 380-1273
EMP: 6 **EST:** 2016
SALES (est): 41.98K **Privately Held**
Web: www.55kentcounty.com
SIC: 7997 Membership sports and recreation clubs

(G-6729)
CHERYL L CHAMBERS
689 Golf Links Ln (19962-1173)
PHONE.............................302 393-3854
Cheryl Chambers, *Mgr*
EMP: 6 **EST:** 2017
SALES (est): 59.01K **Privately Held**
SIC: 8322 Individual and family services

(G-6730)
CHILD INC
Also Called: Children's Place, The
776 Tullamore Ct (19962-2602)
PHONE.............................302 335-8652
EMP: 10 **EST:** 1990
SALES (est): 248.78K **Privately Held**
Web: www.childinc.com
SIC: 8351 Child day care services

(G-6731)
CLEANITH LLC
348 Cinnamon Way (19962-3719)
PHONE.............................571 269-8212
Latavia Jefferson, *CEO*
EMP: 5 **EST:** 2021
SALES (est): 47.02K **Privately Held**
SIC: 7349 Building maintenance services, nec

(G-6732)
COASTAL ALUMINUM PRODUCTS
814 Evergreen Rd (19962-1232)
PHONE.............................302 242-4868
EMP: 6 **EST:** 2018
SALES (est): 60.2K **Privately Held**
Web: www.coastaluminum.com
SIC: 5051 Steel

(G-6733)
COLEMAN CLEANING SERVICES INC
Also Called: Coleman Cleaning Services
831 Lexington Mill Rd (19962-1597)
PHONE.............................302 335-1868
EMP: 5 **EST:** 1988
SALES (est): 94.16K **Privately Held**
SIC: 7349 Cleaning service, industrial or commercial

(G-6734)
CONNECTIONS CSP
27 Medal Way (19962-1281)
PHONE.............................302 535-8330
EMP: 5 **EST:** 2015
SALES (est): 43.61K **Privately Held**
SIC: 8399 Social services, nec

(G-6735)
CONVENTION COACH
554 Lexington Mill Rd (19962-1545)
PHONE.............................302 335-5459
Cynthia Baker, *Owner*
EMP: 7 **EST:** 1997
SALES (est): 403.2K **Privately Held**
SIC: 5199 7311 Advertising specialties; Advertising consultant

(G-6736)
CROSSFIT DOVER LLC
177 Windrow Way (19962-3617)
PHONE.............................302 242-5400
EMP: 5 **EST:** 2012
SALES (est): 97.3K **Privately Held**
Web: www.crossfitdover.com
SIC: 7991 Health club

(G-6737)
DAVID IRA JENKINS
117 Barkers Landing Rd (19962-1117)
PHONE.............................302 335-3309
EMP: 5 **EST:** 2010
SALES (est): 77K **Privately Held**
SIC: 1522 Residential construction, nec

(G-6738)
DAVIS A SCOTT
Also Called: Pestpro
57 Snowdrift Cir (19962-1649)
PHONE.............................302 535-0570
EMP: 6 **EST:** 2011
SALES (est): 110.03K **Privately Held**
Web: www.pestpro1.com
SIC: 7342 Pest control in structures

(G-6739)
DEL HOMES INC (PA)
1309 Ponderosa Dr (19962-1165)
P.O. Box 8 (19962-0008)
PHONE.............................302 697-8204
Jacquelyn I West, *Pr*
John T Beiser, *Stockholder*
EMP: 17 **EST:** 1964
SALES (est): 3.42MM
SALES (corp-wide): 3.42MM **Privately Held**
SIC: 1521 1542 1531 6552 New construction, single-family houses; Commercial and office building, new construction; Condominium developers; Subdividers and developers, nec

(G-6740)
DESHIELDS CONSTRUCTION
281 Sunny Meadow Dr (19962-1779)
PHONE.............................302 331-5214
Troy Deshields, *Owner*
EMP: 5 **EST:** 2010
SALES (est): 208.72K **Privately Held**
Web: www.deshieldsconstruction.com
SIC: 1521 Single-family housing construction

(G-6741)
DEYAS HONEST SOLUTIONS LLC
199 Wildflower Cir N (19962-9359)
PHONE.............................302 682-1830
Gmecia Gil, *Prin*
EMP: 5 **EST:** 2015
SALES (est): 63.07K **Privately Held**
SIC: 7819 Services allied to motion pictures

(G-6742)
E K LONG GENERAL CONTRACTORS
154 Loquitur Ln (19962-2326)
PHONE.............................302 883-1463
Eric Long, *Prin*
EMP: 5 **EST:** 2016
SALES (est): 56.76K **Privately Held**
Web: www.eklong.com
SIC: 1799 Special trade contractors, nec

(G-6743)
ECR COMMUNICATIONS LLC
190 Galway Ct (19962-2627)
PHONE.............................302 865-3118
EMP: 5 **EST:** 2017
SALES (est): 138.45K **Privately Held**
SIC: 4899 Communication services, nec

(G-6744)
EXCELLING LLC
5121 S State St (19962-1467)
PHONE.............................302 276-3908
EMP: 5
SALES (est): 65.94K **Privately Held**
SIC: 7371 Computer software development

(G-6745)
EXQUISITE TASTE VENDING LLC ✪
745 Chestnut Ridge Dr (19962-1767)
PHONE.............................856 278-3091
EMP: 4 **EST:** 2022
SALES (est): 187.9K **Privately Held**
SIC: 3581 Automatic vending machines

(G-6746)
FUTURE BRIGHT PEDIATRICS
121 Windrow Way (19962-3617)
PHONE.............................609 744-2265
Deborah Delgiorno, *Prin*
EMP: 8 **EST:** 2019
SALES (est): 159.59K **Privately Held**
Web: www.brightfuturepediatrics.com
SIC: 8011 Pediatrician

(G-6747)
GRACELAND DAYCARE
342 Ponderosa Dr (19962-1204)
PHONE.............................302 698-0414
Alfred Wieczorek, *Prin*
EMP: 5 **EST:** 2010
SALES (est): 65.55K **Privately Held**
SIC: 8351 Group day care center

(G-6748)
GREEN BLADE IRRIGATION & TURF
2203 Ponderosa Dr (19962-1256)
PHONE.............................302 736-8873
Todd Burger, *Prin*
EMP: 8 **EST:** 2007
SALES (est): 435.5K **Privately Held**
SIC: 0782 Turf installation services, except artificial

(G-6749)
GREENSBORO HEATING & AIR
126 Mystic Ln (19962-1436)
PHONE.............................302 598-5568
Luke Vannicola, *Prin*
EMP: 5 **EST:** 2017
SALES (est): 56.99K **Privately Held**
SIC: 1711 Plumbing, heating, air-conditioning

(G-6750)
H G INVESTMENTS LLC
Also Called: Two Men and A Truck
27 E Walnut St (19962-9304)
PHONE.............................302 734-5017
EMP: 11 **EST:** 2006
SQ FT: 1,500
SALES (est): 226.03K **Privately Held**
Web: www.twomenandatruck.com
SIC: 4212 Moving services

(G-6751)
HERITAGE PAINTING
595 Augusta National Dr (19962-3144)
PHONE.............................302 270-2008
Charlie Heritage, *Owner*
EMP: 5 **EST:** 2017
SALES (est): 56.76K **Privately Held**
SIC: 1799 Special trade contractors, nec

(G-6752)
INSPIRIT STUDIOS
190 Dogwood Dr (19962-1602)
PHONE.............................302 222-4804
Anita Brown, *Prin*
EMP: 5 **EST:** 2011
SALES (est): 109.65K **Privately Held**
Web: www.inspiritstudios.com
SIC: 8049 Acupuncturist

(G-6753)
JGREENBERGCONSULTING LLC
280 Wildflower Cir N (19962-9358)
PHONE.............................610 572-2729
Jeff Greenburb, *Prin*
EMP: 10 **EST:** 2018
SALES (est): 476.86K **Privately Held**
Web: www.jgreenbergconsulting.com
SIC: 8748 Business consulting, nec

(G-6754)
JONATHAN LOPEZ
Also Called: Absolute Locksmith
331 Sedgewick Dr (19962-3203)
PHONE.............................302 752-5229
Jonathan Lopez, *Prin*
EMP: 5 **EST:** 2010
SALES (est): 165.96K **Privately Held**
Web: www.fs5uz.com
SIC: 7389 Swimming pool and hot tub service and maintenance

(G-6755)
JONATHANS LANDING
Also Called: Jonathans Landing Pub Golf CLB
1309 Ponderosa Dr (19962-1165)
PHONE.............................302 697-8204
Jack Beiser, *Owner*
EMP: 22
SALES (est): 373.4K **Privately Held**
Web: www.jonathanslandinggolf.com
SIC: 7992 Public golf courses

(G-6756)
KANGA REW SOFTWARE
167 Carnation Dr (19962-1584)
PHONE.............................302 335-3546
EMP: 5 **EST:** 2008

Magnolia - Kent County (G-6757)

SALES (est): 110K **Privately Held**
SIC: **7372** Prepackaged software

(G-6757)
KENNETH E BARRETT
2308 Woodlytown Rd (19962-1447)
PHONE..........................302 270-6056
Kenneth E Barrett, *Prin*
EMP: **7** EST: 2006
SQ FT: 3,580
SALES (est): 408.44K **Privately Held**
SIC: **1521** New construction, single-family houses

(G-6758)
KING SNIPERS DRYWALL LLC
121 Daffodil Dr (19962-9330)
PHONE..........................302 452-4515
Juan Carrillo, *Prin*
EMP: **5** EST: 2018
SALES (est): 87.81K **Privately Held**
SIC: **1742** Drywall

(G-6759)
LIGHTHOUSE CONSTRUCTION INC
859 Golf Lane Ste1 (19962)
PHONE..........................302 677-1965
EMP: **14** EST: 1997
SALES (est): 4.84MM **Privately Held**
Web: www.lhconstruction.com
SIC: **1542** **8741** Commercial and office building contractors; Construction management

(G-6760)
LINKSIDE APTS LLC
56 W Birdie Ln Ste 5 (19962-1402)
PHONE..........................302 697-0378
EMP: **7** EST: 2008
SALES (est): 325.45K **Privately Held**
Web: www.linksideapt.com
SIC: **6513** Apartment building operators

(G-6761)
LINKSIDE LLC
25 Flagstick Ln (19962-3128)
PHONE..........................302 697-8312
EMP: **5** EST: 2007
SALES (est): 83.61K **Privately Held**
Web: www.linksideapt.com
SIC: **6513** Apartment building operators

(G-6762)
LIONS GROUP LLC
3435 Irish Hill Rd (19962-1529)
PHONE..........................302 535-6584
Lori Conner, *Managing Member*
EMP: **5** EST: 2021
SALES (est): 74.09K **Privately Held**
SIC: **1522** **7389** Hotel/motel and multi-family home renovation and remodeling; Business Activities at Non-Commercial Site

(G-6763)
MAINTENANCE UNLIMITED LLC
73 Moores Dr (19962-2074)
PHONE..........................302 387-1868
Mark S Mcguire, *Prin*
EMP: **5** EST: 2010
SALES (est): 42.95K **Privately Held**
SIC: **7349** Building maintenance services, nec

(G-6764)
MCH CONSTRUCTION LLC
170 Plain Dealing Rd (19962-1120)
PHONE..........................302 249-2765
EMP: **5** EST: 2020
SALES (est): 199.63K **Privately Held**
Web: www.mycustomhome.net

SIC: **1521** Single-family housing construction

(G-6765)
MICHAEL J MUNROE
811 Augusta National Dr (19962-3257)
PHONE..........................804 240-7188
J Munroe, *Prin*
EMP: **4** EST: 2018
SALES (est): 57.85K **Privately Held**
SIC: **3999** Manufacturing industries, nec

(G-6766)
MID ATLANTIC ATHC PROMOTIONS
814 Evergreen Rd (19962-1232)
PHONE..........................302 535-8472
Richard Hawkins, *Prin*
EMP: **5** EST: 2016
SALES (est): 95.8K **Privately Held**
SIC: **8743** Promotion service

(G-6767)
MIND MECHANIX LLC
583 W Birdie Ln (19962-3116)
PHONE..........................302 313-1288
EMP: **6** EST: 2020
SALES (est): 109.75K **Privately Held**
Web: www.mindmechanixllc.com
SIC: **8049** Offices of health practitioner

(G-6768)
MISTER SPARKY
165 Barkers Landing Rd (19962-1117)
PHONE..........................302 751-6363
EMP: **5** EST: 2020
SALES (est): 81.61K **Privately Held**
Web: www.mistersparky.com
SIC: **1731** General electrical contractor

(G-6769)
MOMMAS MOUNTAIN LLC
Also Called: Mommas Mountain
558 Tullamore Rd (19962-2601)
PHONE..........................410 236-6717
Gregory Danylyk, *CEO*
EMP: **2** EST: 2015
SALES (est): 28.84K **Privately Held**
SIC: **5961** 5499 2836 2834 Mail order house, nec; Spices and herbs; Vaccines and other immunizing products; Pharmaceutical preparations

(G-6770)
NARROW GATE1
30 Plica Cir (19962-3604)
PHONE..........................302 387-1838
Shanett L Hynson, *Prin*
EMP: **7** EST: 2012
SALES (est): 50.16K **Privately Held**
SIC: **8322** General counseling services

(G-6771)
NOBLES HVAC DUCT CLEANING
160 Whitetail Ln (19962-2160)
PHONE..........................302 538-5909
Anthony Noble, *Prin*
EMP: **5** EST: 2014
SALES (est): 36.17K **Privately Held**
Web: www.airductcleaningdover.com
SIC: **7699** Cleaning services

(G-6772)
PATTERSON MRS DARNETTA L
49 Macintosh Cir (19962-3647)
PHONE..........................215 828-2597
Darnetta L Patterson, *Prin*
EMP: **6** EST: 2019
SALES (est): 82.07K **Privately Held**
SIC: **8049** Offices of health practitioner

(G-6773)
PEAK PERFORMANCE ATHLETICS
48 Merganser Dr (19962-2509)
PHONE..........................443 404-6049
Timothy Bowie, *Prin*
EMP: **6** EST: 2014
SALES (est): 55.51K **Privately Held**
SIC: **8699** Athletic organizations

(G-6774)
PILLAR TO POST
145 Bay Hill Ln (19962-1285)
PHONE..........................410 804-8626
Jim Williams, *Owner*
EMP: **6** EST: 2017
SALES (est): 124.53K **Privately Held**
Web: www.pillartopost.com
SIC: **7389** Building inspection service

(G-6775)
PLUME SERUM LLC
1059 Ponderosa Dr (19962-1168)
PHONE..........................302 697-9044
Daniel Dunkleberger, *Prin*
EMP: **5** EST: 2015
SALES (est): 74.42K **Privately Held**
SIC: **2836** Serums

(G-6776)
PRISTINE CLEAN CO
126 Carnation Dr (19962-1577)
PHONE..........................302 465-8274
EMP: **6** EST: 2019
SALES (est): 67.35K **Privately Held**
Web: www.pristineclean.com
SIC: **7699** Cleaning services

(G-6777)
PROPERTY DOCTORS LLC
309 Millchop Ln (19962-2008)
PHONE..........................302 249-7731
James Shuford, *Prin*
EMP: **8** EST: 2016
SALES (est): 229.26K **Privately Held**
SIC: **1389** Construction, repair, and dismantling services

(G-6778)
PURPLE4S INC
Also Called: Purple4s
40 Bushel Cir (19962-3637)
PHONE..........................443 504-9755
Marcellus Hunter, *Pr*
EMP: **2** EST: 2015
SALES (est): 61.68K **Privately Held**
SIC: **2842** Sanitation preparations, disinfectants and deodorants

(G-6779)
ROBERTS ELECTRIC INC
165 Barkers Landing Rd (19962-1117)
PHONE..........................302 233-3017
Mike Roberts, *Pr*
EMP: **5** EST: 2004
SALES (est): 405.93K **Privately Held**
Web: www.robertselectricservices.com
SIC: **1731** General electrical contractor

(G-6780)
ROCK SOLID SERVICING LLC
89 Mandrake Dr (19962-3670)
PHONE..........................302 233-2569
EMP: **4** EST: 2014
SALES (est): 84.59K **Privately Held**
SIC: **1389** Roustabout service

(G-6781)
S B TRAILER PARK
72 Mabel Dr (19962-1904)
PHONE..........................302 697-0699

Richard Parson, *Prin*
EMP: **7** EST: 2009
SALES (est): 36.19K **Privately Held**
SIC: **7033** Trailer park

(G-6782)
SERVICE AIR TECH HVAC
3998 Irish Hill Rd (19962-1522)
PHONE..........................302 335-8334
EMP: **6** EST: 2009
SALES (est): 106.95K **Privately Held**
SIC: **1711** Heating and air conditioning contractors

(G-6783)
SOULES MANAGEMENT INC
1674 Mcginnis Pond Rd (19962-1554)
PHONE..........................302 335-1980
Michael Soules, *Prin*
EMP: **6** EST: 2015
SALES (est): 229.73K **Privately Held**
SIC: **8741** Management services

(G-6784)
SOUTHERN MEADOW
109 Lavender Dr (19962-2513)
PHONE..........................302 677-0800
EMP: **5** EST: 2018
SALES (est): 61.78K **Privately Held**
Web: www.i-realty.com
SIC: **8322** Community center

(G-6785)
STOCKMARKET
2573 Woodlytown Rd (19962-1452)
PHONE..........................302 697-8878
Bruce Ney, *Prin*
EMP: **5** EST: 2004
SALES (est): 100.61K **Privately Held**
SIC: **3484** Shotguns or shotgun parts, 30 mm. and below

(G-6786)
SUMURI LLC
40 S Main St (19962-6205)
P.O. Box 121 (19962-0121)
PHONE..........................302 570-0015
EMP: **25** EST: 2010
SALES (est): 8.2MM **Privately Held**
Web: www.sumuri.com
SIC: **3571** 3669 5045 7372 Mainframe computers; Emergency alarms; Computer peripheral equipment; Application computer software

(G-6787)
TAILORED CARE LLC
85 Point Landing Ln (19962-2800)
PHONE..........................302 883-1761
EMP: **6** EST: 2019
SALES (est): 252.18K **Privately Held**
Web: www.tailoredcarellc.com
SIC: **8082** Home health care services

(G-6788)
VERSION 40 SOFTWARE LLC
662 Tullamore Ct (19962-2603)
PHONE..........................302 270-0245
EMP: **2** EST: 2011
SALES (est): 91.54K **Privately Held**
SIC: **7372** Application computer software

(G-6789)
VETEX CONSTRUCTION LLC
65 Douglas Fir Rd (19962-1274)
PHONE..........................302 670-0989
Gerardo Arriola, *Prin*
EMP: **5** EST: 2017
SALES (est): 169.87K **Privately Held**

GEOGRAPHIC SECTION

Middletown - New Castle County (G-6819)

SIC: 1521 Single-family housing construction

(G-6790)
WALKERS CONTRACTING LLC
756 Millchop Ln (19962-1960)
PHONE..................................302 331-0425
Ricky Walker, *Owner*
EMP: 6 EST: 2013
SALES (est): 66.65K **Privately Held**
SIC: 1799 Special trade contractors, nec

(G-6791)
WILLIAMS ENGRG SOLUTIONS LLC
24 W Chestnut Ridge Dr (19962-1676)
PHONE..................................302 670-4841
Brian Williams Junior, *CEO*
EMP: 3 EST: 2020
SALES (est): 50K **Privately Held**
SIC: 3625 Electric controls and control accessories, industrial

(G-6792)
YEBO ALPHA INC
184 Winners Cir (19962-9749)
PHONE..................................302 335-8887
Anna Ryan, *CEO*
EMP: 7 EST: 2020
SALES (est): 499.8K **Privately Held**
SIC: 8742 Business management consultant

(G-6793)
ZACS INC
31 Par Ct (19962-1153)
PHONE..................................302 242-4653
Billy Zaccardelli, *Prin*
EMP: 5 EST: 2008
SQ FT: 37,000
SALES (est): 281.33K **Privately Held**
SIC: 1542 Commercial and office buildings, renovation and repair

(G-6794)
ZWEEMERS PAV & SEALCOATING LLC
46 Records Dr (19962-4604)
PHONE..................................302 363-6116
James Zweemer, *Prin*
EMP: 8 EST: 2018
SALES (est): 482.78K **Privately Held**
SIC: 1611 Surfacing and paving

Marydel
Kent County

(G-6795)
BALANCED PLATES & WEIGHTS
1883 Westville Rd (19964-2050)
PHONE..................................302 632-0953
Esther Miller, *Prin*
EMP: 5 EST: 2019
SALES (est): 29.54K **Privately Held**
SIC: 7991 Physical fitness facilities

(G-6796)
DELMARVA PUMP CENTER INC (PA)
Also Called: Dpc Emergency Equipment
335 Strauss Ave (19964-2218)
P.O. Box 340 (19964-0340)
PHONE..................................302 492-1245
Richard Strauss Junior, *Pr*
Richard Strauss Senior, *VP*
Mary Pardee, *
EMP: 17 EST: 1990
SQ FT: 25,000
SALES (est): 2.55MM **Privately Held**
Web: www.dpcemergency.com
SIC: 7538 5511 5012 General truck repair; New and used car dealers; Fire trucks

(G-6797)
DURHAM PLUMBING SERVICE LLC
555 Parkers Chapel Rd (19964-2015)
PHONE..................................302 653-5601
David Durham, *Prin*
EMP: 6 EST: 2017
SALES (est): 112.41K **Privately Held**
SIC: 1711 Plumbing contractors

(G-6798)
GRACIOUS HART NURSING SVCS LLC
1884 Westville Rd (19964-2026)
PHONE..................................302 343-9083
Sharon Burton-young, *Prin*
Darneisha Young, *Prin*
EMP: 7 EST: 2015
SALES (est): 285.1K **Privately Held**
Web: www.gracioushearthnursing.com
SIC: 8051 Skilled nursing care facilities

(G-6799)
HARVEST RIDGE WINERY LLC
447 Westville Rd (19964-1820)
PHONE..................................302 250-6583
Chuck Nunan, *Managing Member*
Chris Nunan, *Managing Member*
EMP: 7 EST: 2011
SALES (est): 743.05K **Privately Held**
Web: www.harvestridgewinery.com
SIC: 2084 Wines

(G-6800)
HIDDEN ACRES REST HOME INC
265 Mowely Ln (19964-1839)
PHONE..................................302 492-1962
EMP: 6 EST: 2010
SALES (est): 104.06K **Privately Held**
SIC: 8399 Social services, nec

(G-6801)
INTEGRITY CONSTRUCTION LLC
Also Called: INTEGRITY CONSTRUCTION OF MARY
91 Selheimer Ln (19964-2255)
P.O. Box 9 (19964-0009)
PHONE..................................302 241-6429
Alexander Adjoodani, *Pr*
Christopher Adjoodani, *Pr*
EMP: 5 EST: 2014
SALES (est): 101.67K **Privately Held**
SIC: 1521 Single-family housing construction

(G-6802)
K C FARMS LLC
232 Westville Rd (19964-1872)
PHONE..................................302 492-3439
EMP: 5 EST: 2017
SALES (est): 456.57K **Privately Held**
SIC: 0191 General farms, primarily crop

(G-6803)
KRISS CONTRACTING INC
1523 Gunter Rd (19964-2236)
PHONE..................................302 492-3502
Veronica Kriss, *Pr*
EMP: 6 EST: 1979
SALES (est): 87.77K **Privately Held**
SIC: 1731 Electrical work

(G-6804)
LLOYDS STONEWORKS
927 Grygo Rd (19964-1709)
PHONE..................................302 492-0847
William Lloyd, *Prin*
EMP: 5 EST: 2016
SALES (est): 167.58K **Privately Held**
SIC: 1522 Residential construction, nec

(G-6805)
M & G PRO SERVICES LLC
135 Blackberry Cir (19964-2174)
PHONE..................................302 420-1428
Michael Banning, *Prin*
EMP: 5 EST: 2014
SALES (est): 46.34K **Privately Held**
SIC: 1522 Residential construction, nec

(G-6806)
M D PLUMBING DRAIN CLEANING
1500 Gunter Rd (19964-2251)
PHONE..................................302 492-8880
Mike Megill, *Pr*
Tammy Megill, *VP*
EMP: 9 EST: 2002
SALES (est): 725.44K **Privately Held**
Web: www.mdplumbinganddrain.com
SIC: 1711 Plumbing contractors

(G-6807)
MARY DEL RANCH INC
449 Tappahannak Trl (19964-1754)
PHONE..................................302 492-8866
Shelton Weiner, *Owner*
EMP: 5 EST: 2005
SALES (est): 57.09K **Privately Held**
SIC: 0291 General farms, primarily animals

(G-6808)
NATIONAL DCUMENT MGT SOLUTIONS
301 Westville Rd (19964-1821)
PHONE..................................302 535-9263
EMP: 5 EST: 2011
SALES (est): 123.09K **Privately Held**
SIC: 7374 Data processing service

(G-6809)
PLATINUM LLC
523 Halltown Rd (19964-2149)
PHONE..................................302 492-1850
Jenna Reece, *Prin*
EMP: 5 EST: 2016
SALES (est): 29.31K **Privately Held**
SIC: 7231 Hairdressers

(G-6810)
SMITH ELECTRICAL SERVICES
150 East St (19964-2154)
PHONE..................................302 423-5994
Adam Smith, *Prin*
EMP: 5 EST: 2015
SALES (est): 64.48K **Privately Held**
SIC: 1731 General electrical contractor

(G-6811)
SPG INTERNATIONAL LLC
841 Mud Mill Rd (19964-1921)
PHONE..................................404 823-3934
EMP: 5 EST: 2017
SALES (est): 87.46K **Privately Held**
SIC: 3441 Fabricated structural metal

(G-6812)
THOMAS FAMILY FARMS LLC
896 Sandy Bend Rd (19964-1948)
PHONE..................................302 492-3688
John W Thomas, *Pt*
Carolyn Thomas, *Pt*
EMP: 7
SALES (est): 458.38K **Privately Held**
SIC: 0191 General farms, primarily crop

Middletown
New Castle County

(G-6813)
01 HIRE INC
651 N Broad St (19709-6400)
PHONE..................................408 599-2693
Shoaib Ahmad, *CEO*
EMP: 22 EST: 2020
SALES (est): 699.69K **Privately Held**
SIC: 7379 Online services technology consultants

(G-6814)
1000X LLC ✪
651 N Broad St (19709-6400)
PHONE..................................919 584-5420
Mohammad Agha, *Managing Member*
EMP: 12 EST: 2022
SALES (est): 406.37K **Privately Held**
SIC: 7371 Custom computer programming services

(G-6815)
333 REI LLC
651 N Broad St Ste 205 (19709-6402)
PHONE..................................808 758-3095
El Boyd, *Managing Member*
EMP: 10 EST: 2021
SALES (est): 473.6K **Privately Held**
SIC: 6798 Real estate investment trusts

(G-6816)
3D INTERNET GROUP INC
609 Colchester Ct (19709-2139)
PHONE..................................302 376-7900
Ian Frisbie, *Pr*
EMP: 5 EST: 1997
SALES (est): 290.91K **Privately Held**
Web: www.newsdart.com
SIC: 4813 Internet connectivity services

(G-6817)
3DSTEEL INC
651 N Broad St Ste 206 (19709-6402)
PHONE..................................713 677-2027
EMP: 5 EST: 2020
SALES (est): 62.63K **Privately Held**
Web: www.3dsteelinc.com
SIC: 3291 Abrasive metal and steel products

(G-6818)
6CLICKS INC (PA)
651 N Broad St Ste 206 (19709-6402)
PHONE..................................925 699-6304
Anthony Stevens, *CEO*
Michelle Torrey-teunissen, *CRO*
Doctor Heather Buker, *CCO*
George Mcmillan, *CFO*
EMP: 13 EST: 2020
SALES (est): 448.95K
SALES (corp-wide): 448.95K **Privately Held**
SIC: 7371 Software programming applications

(G-6819)
911 RESTORATION OF DELAWARE
Also Called: 911 Restoration
105 E Lockwood St (19709-1126)
PHONE..................................302 331-2033
EMP: 5 EST: 2017
SALES (est): 76.84K **Privately Held**
Web: www.911restorationdelaware.com
SIC: 1799 Fireproofing buildings

Middletown - New Castle County (G-6820)

(G-6820)
9JUNIO INC ◊
651 N Broad St (19709-6400)
PHONE.................................239 946-6374
Jimmy Fuentes, *CEO*
EMP: 5 EST: 2022
SALES (est): 199.4K Privately Held
SIC: 7371 Computer software development

(G-6821)
A AND J WELDING
4401 Summit Bridge Rd Ste 1 (19709)
PHONE.................................302 229-2000
Al Biliski, *Prin*
EMP: 4 EST: 2019
SALES (est): 63.56K Privately Held
SIC: 7692 Welding repair

(G-6822)
A FARM INC
1482 Levels Rd (19709-9084)
PHONE.................................610 496-1504
EMP: 6 EST: 2017
SALES (est): 467.84K Privately Held
SIC: 0191 General farms, primarily crop

(G-6823)
A G M GENERAL CONTRACTOR INC
600 N Broad St Ste 5 (19709-1032)
PHONE.................................215 558-6880
Antonio Montgomery, *CEO*
EMP: 25 EST: 2015
SALES (est): 2.34MM Privately Held
SIC: 1531 Operative builders

(G-6824)
A S JACONO LLC
865 Vance Neck Rd (19709-9135)
PHONE.................................302 378-3000
EMP: 5 EST: 2013
SALES (est): 499.79K Privately Held
Web: www.asjacono.com
SIC: 1521 Single-family housing construction

(G-6825)
AA MEDIA INC
307 S Cass St (19709-1308)
PHONE.................................302 729-2882
Adam Animasaun, *CEO*
EMP: 5 EST: 2020
SALES (est): 714.79K Privately Held
Web: www.aamediainc.com
SIC: 8742 Marketing consulting services

(G-6826)
AA SMITH & ASSOCIATES LLC
364 E Main St Ste 403 (19709-1482)
PHONE.................................973 477-3052
Alvin Smith, *Managing Member*
EMP: 12 EST: 2016
SALES (est): 493.3K Privately Held
SIC: 8742 Management consulting services

(G-6827)
AARON AUTO GLASS
651 N Broad St (19709-6400)
PHONE.................................302 297-8008
EMP: 6 EST: 2017
SALES (est): 82.6K Privately Held
SIC: 7536 Automotive glass replacement shops

(G-6828)
ABLED DIRECTIONS LLC
1017 Ashland St (19709-1747)
PHONE.................................206 265-3928
EMP: 12
SALES (est): 215.17K Privately Held
SIC: 8361 7389 Residential care; Business services, nec

(G-6829)
ABOVE ALL GUTTER SVC
301 Senator Dr (19709-8021)
PHONE.................................302 561-0709
Paul Eiermann, *Prin*
EMP: 5 EST: 2017
SALES (est): 66.28K Privately Held
SIC: 1761 Gutter and downspout contractor

(G-6830)
ABRA AUTO BODY & GLASS LP
Also Called: ABRA Autobody & Glass
5077 Summit Bridge Rd (19709-9591)
PHONE.................................302 279-1007
Michael Levasseur, *Brnch Mgr*
EMP: 6
Web: www.abraauto.com
SIC: 7532 Body shop, automotive
HQ: Abra Auto Body & Glass Lp
7225 Northland Dr N # 110
Brooklyn Park MN 55428
888 872-2272

(G-6831)
AC TAX GROUP LLC
Also Called: Accounting
801 Mapleton Ave (19709-0057)
PHONE.................................844 378-1040
Anthony Colonnello, *Pr*
EMP: 5 EST: 2017
SALES (est): 226.24K Privately Held
Web: www.actaxgroup.com
SIC: 7291 Tax return preparation services

(G-6832)
ACCESS IT SERVICES INC
651 N Broad St Ste 206 (19709-6402)
PHONE.................................408 520-9069
Kris Nair, *CEO*
EMP: 7 EST: 2020
SALES (est): 324.73K Privately Held
SIC: 7379 Online services technology consultants

(G-6833)
ACUHEALTH & WELLNESS
134 Tywyn Dr (19709-8701)
PHONE.................................302 438-4493
Patricia Yancey, *Prin*
EMP: 6 EST: 2018
SALES (est): 210.62K Privately Held
SIC: 8099 Health and allied services, nec

(G-6834)
ADAMS BUSINESS DEVELOPMEN
17 Palmer Dr (19709-9371)
PHONE.................................302 698-1709
EMP: 8 EST: 2015
SALES (est): 57.89K Privately Held
Web: www.maccde.com
SIC: 8611 Chamber of Commerce

(G-6835)
ADECTRA LLC
651 N Broad St (19709-6400)
PHONE.................................203 424-2800
Austin Stierler, *Managing Member*
EMP: 10 EST: 2010
SALES (est): 341.77K Privately Held
SIC: 7379 4813 Computer related consulting services; Internet connectivity services

(G-6836)
ADVANCED METAL CONCEPTS INC
1823 Choptank Rd (19709-9047)
PHONE.................................302 421-9905
Greg Sachetta, *Pr*
Beth Sachetta, *VP*
EMP: 12 EST: 2001
SQ FT: 2,000
SALES (est): 959.92K Privately Held
Web: advancedmetalconceptsde.business.site
SIC: 3545 Precision tools, machinists'

(G-6837)
AERO DYNAMIC SERVICES INC
18 Manassas Dr (19709-3802)
PHONE.................................302 737-4920
EMP: 5 EST: 2008
SALES (est): 61.24K Privately Held
SIC: 8721 Payroll accounting service

(G-6838)
AFLAC
334 Senator Dr (19709-8022)
PHONE.................................302 376-9880
Greg Tash, *Pr*
EMP: 6 EST: 2003
SALES (est): 108.17K Privately Held
Web: www.aflac.com
SIC: 6411 Insurance agents, brokers, and service

(G-6839)
AFRICAN WOOD INC
274 Liborio Dr (19709-3109)
PHONE.................................302 884-6738
David Amakobe, *Pr*
EMP: 5 EST: 2005
SQ FT: 200
SALES (est): 569.58K Privately Held
Web: www.amakobe.com
SIC: 5159 5211 8748 Oil nuts, kernels, seeds ; Solar heating equipment; Business consulting, nec

(G-6840)
AG6 ENGINEERING & DEFENSE LLC
651 N Broad St Ste 2054626 (19709-6400)
PHONE.................................609 480-4823
EMP: 6 EST: 2021
SALES (est): 289.43K Privately Held
SIC: 8711 Engineering services

(G-6841)
AGILE LEGAL
651 N Broad St Ste 308 (19709-6403)
PHONE.................................302 376-6710
EMP: 21 EST: 2015
SALES (est): 1.12MM Privately Held
Web: www.agilelegal.com
SIC: 8111 Legal services

(G-6842)
AIKYM ESSENTIALS LLC
1051 Sherbourne Rd (19709-5301)
PHONE.................................215 910-9479
EMP: 4
SALES (est): 74.42K Privately Held
Web: www.aikym.com
SIC: 2844 Perfumes, cosmetics and other toilet preparations

(G-6843)
AIM GOD SOCIETY ◊
Also Called: Aims.gg
651 N Broad St Ste 206 (19709-6402)
PHONE.................................207 299-3881
Dawson Gray, *CEO*
EMP: 19 EST: 2022
SALES (est): 659.45K Privately Held
SIC: 3577 Computer peripheral equipment, nec

(G-6844)
AIRNAV GROUP LLC
651 N Broad St Ste 206 (19709-6402)
PHONE.................................954 798-5509
Christian Marquez, *Prin*

EMP: 7 EST: 2020
SALES (est): 324.47K Privately Held
SIC: 3714 Motor vehicle parts and accessories

(G-6845)
AJAM INC
10 Willow Grove Mill Dr (19709-8619)
PHONE.................................267 323-5005
EMP: 6 EST: 2012
SALES (est): 144.1K Privately Held
Web: www.ajamsonic.com
SIC: 3931 Musical instruments

(G-6846)
AJWADATES INC
651 N Broad St (19709-6400)
PHONE.................................323 999-1998
Khaled Almohammadi, *CEO*
EMP: 2 EST: 2020
SALES (est): 100K Privately Held
SIC: 2034 Dates, dried

(G-6847)
ALBERT T WOOD III
350 Noxontown Rd (19709-1621)
PHONE.................................302 463-5386
Albert T Wood Atc, *Owner*
EMP: 15 EST: 2018
SALES (est): 225.23K Privately Held
Web: www.standrews-de.org
SIC: 8049 Offices of health practitioner

(G-6848)
ALERIC INTERNATIONAL INC
116 Saint Andrews Ct (19709-8851)
PHONE.................................302 547-4846
Alain Ratsimbazafy, *Pr*
Eric Ratsimbazafy, *Dir*
EMP: 10 EST: 1989
SALES (est): 774.11K Privately Held
Web: www.aleric.biz
SIC: 7379 Computer related consulting services

(G-6849)
ALISI HOME CARE LLC
108 Patriot Dr Ste A (19709-8803)
PHONE.................................302 268-8686
Shuna Lanier, *Mgr*
EMP: 5 EST: 2021
SALES (est): 46.65K Privately Held
SIC: 8082 Home health care services

(G-6850)
ALL AMERICAN FENCING
6 Jersey Ct (19709-6813)
PHONE.................................302 530-8155
Dale Wingo, *Prin*
EMP: 5 EST: 2007
SALES (est): 151.52K Privately Held
Web: www.allamericanfence.net
SIC: 1799 Fence construction

(G-6851)
ALLEN SPOLDEN LLC ◊
651 N Broad St Ste 205 (19709-6402)
PHONE.................................267 226-2160
EMP: 12 EST: 2022
SALES (est): 615.24K Privately Held
SIC: 7361 Employment agencies

(G-6852)
ALLIED PRECISION INC
106 Sleepy Hollow Dr Ste C (19709-9191)
PHONE.................................302 376-6844
John R Lees, *Pr*
Sandee Hartzel, *CFO*
EMP: 6 EST: 1991
SQ FT: 5,000

SALES (est): 1.3MM **Privately Held**
Web: www.alliedprecisionusa.com
SIC: **7692** 3444 3599 Welding repair; Sheet metalwork; Machine shop, jobbing and repair

(G-6853)
ALLSTATE INSUR RYAN NICHOLS
Also Called: Allstate
704 Ash Blvd (19709-8871)
PHONE.................................302 864-2230
Ryan Nichols, *Pr*
EMP: 7 **EST:** 2017
SALES (est): 241.01K **Privately Held**
Web: www.allstate.com
SIC: **6399** 6331 Bank deposit insurance; Associated factory mutuals, fire and marine insurance

(G-6854)
ALLTECH PRO CORPORATION
651 N Broad St Ste 205 (19709-6402)
PHONE.................................323 457-3225
Jay Wilson, *Pr*
EMP: 45 **EST:** 2020
SALES (est): 2.6MM **Privately Held**
SIC: **1611** General contractor, highway and street construction

(G-6855)
ALTAIRIS TECH PARTNERS LLC
257 Milford Dr (19709-9469)
PHONE.................................302 354-0662
EMP: 5 **EST:** 2018
SALES (est): 87.03K **Privately Held**
SIC: **7379** Computer related consulting services

(G-6856)
AMALGAMA DIGITAL INC
651 N Broad St Ste 206 (19709-6402)
PHONE.................................302 387-0140
EMP: 6 **EST:** 2021
SALES (est): 46.16K **Privately Held**
Web: landing.amalgama.co
SIC: **7371** Custom computer programming services

(G-6857)
AMATUZIO APPRAISAL SVCS INC
409 Waltham Dr (19709-2195)
PHONE.................................302 378-9654
Thomas Amatuzio, *Owner*
EMP: 5 **EST:** 2009
SALES (est): 36.24K **Privately Held**
SIC: **8711** Engineering services

(G-6858)
AMERICAN BUILDERS INC
1212 Pimpernell Path (19709-7506)
PHONE.................................856 287-0840
EMP: 6 **EST:** 2013
SALES (est): 75.52K **Privately Held**
Web: www.americanbuilders.com
SIC: **1521** New construction, single-family houses

(G-6859)
AMERICAN K9 DGGIE DYCARE TRNIN
128 Patriot Dr Unit 12 (19709-8770)
PHONE.................................302 376-9663
Laurie Brown, *Managing Member*
EMP: 10 **EST:** 2008
SALES (est): 312.04K **Privately Held**
Web: www.ak9training.com
SIC: **0752** Boarding services, kennels

(G-6860)
AMIRA SPRAY FOAM
548 Red Fox Cir S (19709-6075)
PHONE.................................302 464-0644
EMP: 5 **EST:** 2017
SALES (est): 62.44K **Privately Held**
Web: www.amiracontracting.com
SIC: **1799** Special trade contractors, nec

(G-6861)
AMSTEL BARBER SHOP
2484 N Dupont Pkwy (19709-9653)
PHONE.................................302 696-2300
EMP: 5 **EST:** 2019
SALES (est): 16.07K **Privately Held**
Web: www.amstelbarbershop.com
SIC: **7241** Barber shops

(G-6862)
AMSTEL BARBER SHOP
712 Ash Blvd (19709-8871)
PHONE.................................302 378-5300
EMP: 6 **EST:** 2015
SALES (est): 25.89K **Privately Held**
Web: www.amstelbarbershop.com
SIC: **7241** Hair stylist, men

(G-6863)
ANDREW HAYDEN
306 Seamans Ct (19709-6823)
PHONE.................................302 562-9236
Andrew Hayden, *Mgr*
EMP: 5 **EST:** 2017
SALES (est): 22.18K **Privately Held**
SIC: **8049** Offices of health practitioner

(G-6864)
ANGEL NAILS
480 Middletown Warwick Rd (19709-9192)
PHONE.................................302 449-5067
Tony Nguyen, *Owner*
EMP: 16 **EST:** 2004
SALES (est): 259.69K **Privately Held**
SIC: **7231** Manicurist, pedicurist

(G-6865)
ANGRY REELS INC
651 N Broad St Ste 205 (19709-6402)
PHONE.................................336 906-1797
Shalimar Gilbert, *Pr*
EMP: 15 **EST:** 2020
SALES (est): 255.71K **Privately Held**
SIC: **7812** Television film production

(G-6866)
ANTHOGO ENTERPRISES
535 Maiden Ct (19709-2197)
PHONE.................................302 378-0235
EMP: 5 **EST:** 2009
SALES (est): 129.58K **Privately Held**
SIC: **8748** Business consulting, nec

(G-6867)
APEX CHIROPRACTIC SERVICES
404 N Hampton Ct (19709-7944)
PHONE.................................302 598-9404
EMP: 6 **EST:** 2014
SALES (est): 247.3K **Privately Held**
SIC: **8041** Offices and clinics of chiropractors

(G-6868)
APPGENIUS LABS LLC ✿
651 N Broad St Ste 201 (19709-6402)
PHONE.................................412 953-5064
Joemar Ayuban, *Managing Member*
EMP: 10 **EST:** 2023
SALES (est): 365.44K **Privately Held**
SIC: **7372** Prepackaged software

(G-6869)
APPOINTIV INC
651 N Broad St (19709-6400)
PHONE.................................415 877-4339
Jason Wallis, *CEO*
EMP: 8
SALES (est): 306.16K **Privately Held**
SIC: **7371** Software programming applications

(G-6870)
APPOQNMINK COUNSELING SVCS LLC
11 Crawford St (19709-1116)
PHONE.................................302 898-1616
Dawn M Schatz, *Prin*
EMP: 5 **EST:** 2009
SALES (est): 173.76K **Privately Held**
Web: www.appocounseling.com
SIC: **8322** General counseling services

(G-6871)
APPOQUINIMINK DEVELOPMENT INC
Also Called: Norris Village
103 E Park Pl (19709-1429)
PHONE.................................302 378-0878
EMP: 7 **EST:** 1996
SALES (est): 449.6K **Privately Held**
SIC: **6513** Apartment building operators

(G-6872)
ARC SEMINARS LLC
406 S Cass St (19709-1311)
P.O. Box 72 (08051-0072)
PHONE.................................856 776-6758
Ruth Polillo, *Prin*
EMP: 6 **EST:** 2017
SALES (est): 58.45K **Privately Held**
Web: www.arcseminars.net
SIC: **8093** Rehabilitation center, outpatient treatment

(G-6873)
ARROWTECH LLC
651 N Broad St (19709-6400)
PHONE.................................704 833-8777
Richard Fields, *Managing Member*
EMP: 10 **EST:** 2019
SALES (est): 494.64K **Privately Held**
SIC: **7379** Online services technology consultants

(G-6874)
ARTSENSE INC
651 N Broad St Ste 206 (19709-6402)
PHONE.................................302 613-1870
Taras Maslov, *CEO*
EMP: 5 **EST:** 2020
SALES (est): 104.73K **Privately Held**
SIC: **7389** Business services, nec

(G-6875)
ARUANNO ENTERPRISES INC
524 E Creek Ln (19709-8836)
PHONE.................................302 530-1217
Deanne Smith, *Mgr*
Michael Aruanno, *Pr*
EMP: 8 **EST:** 2017
SALES (est): 760.28K **Privately Held**
SIC: **1522** 1521 Remodeling, multi-family dwellings; Single-family home remodeling, additions, and repairs

(G-6876)
ASTEC INC
1554 Lorewood Grove Rd (19709-9480)
PHONE.................................302 378-2717
Io J Betley, *Pr*
Thomas P Betley, *VP*
EMP: 9 **EST:** 1989
SQ FT: 2,200
SALES (est): 488.92K **Privately Held**
Web: www.astecenviro.com
SIC: **1799** Asbestos removal and encapsulation

(G-6877)
AT&E DEVELOPERS LTD
600 N Broad St (19709-1032)
PHONE.................................302 467-1100
Charles Graham, *Prin*
EMP: 10 **EST:** 2005
SQ FT: 5,000
SALES (est): 237.83K **Privately Held**
Web: www.precisioncurbing.com
SIC: **6552** Subdividers and developers, nec

(G-6878)
ATI HOLDINGS LLC
Also Called: ATI Physical Therapy
114 Sandhill Dr Ste 103 (19709-5805)
PHONE.................................302 285-0700
Kevin Calvey, *Dir*
EMP: 7
SALES (corp-wide): 635.67MM **Publicly Held**
Web: www.atipt.com
SIC: **8049** Physical therapist
HQ: Ati Holdings, Llc
790 Remington Blvd
Bolingbrook IL 60440

(G-6879)
ATI HOLDINGS LLC
224 Dove Run Centre Dr (19709-7971)
PHONE.................................302 696-1924
EMP: 6
SALES (corp-wide): 635.67MM **Publicly Held**
Web: www.atipt.com
SIC: **8049** Physical therapist
HQ: Ati Holdings, Llc
790 Remington Blvd
Bolingbrook IL 60440

(G-6880)
ATLANTIC BULK CARRIERS
364 E Main St (19709-1482)
PHONE.................................302 378-6300
George Smith, *VP*
EMP: 9 **EST:** 2006
SALES (est): 433.34K **Privately Held**
Web: www.atlanticbulkltd.com
SIC: **4213** Trucking, except local

(G-6881)
ATLANTIC BULK CARRIERS INC
Also Called: Van Smith Co.
1600 Belts Rd (19709-8604)
PHONE.................................302 378-4522
George Smith, *Pr*
EMP: 13 **EST:** 2018
SALES (est): 496.36K **Privately Held**
Web: www.atlanticbulk.com
SIC: **4213** Trucking, except local

(G-6882)
ATLANTIC BULK LTD
421 Boyds Corner Rd (19709-9547)
PHONE.................................302 378-6300
Jennifer Rice, *Pr*
EMP: 8 **EST:** 2015
SALES (est): 425.46K **Privately Held**
Web: www.atlanticbulkltd.com
SIC: **4789** Cargo loading and unloading services

Middletown - New Castle County (G-6883)

GEOGRAPHIC SECTION

(G-6883)
ATLANTIC VETERINARY SVCS INC
Also Called: Atlantic Veterinary Center
411 Weston Dr (19709-1715)
PHONE...............................302 376-7506
John Weiher, *Pr*
EMP: 6 **EST:** 1997
SALES (est): 502.59K **Privately Held**
Web: www.atlanticvetcenter.com
SIC: 0742 Animal hospital services, pets and other animal specialties

(G-6884)
ATLAS WORLD EXPRESS LLC
119 Plymouth Pl (19709-8314)
PHONE...............................202 536-5238
Fred M Scott Iii, *Prin*
EMP: 5 **EST:** 2011
SALES (est): 219.16K **Privately Held**
SIC: 4212 Delivery service, vehicular

(G-6885)
ATOM TECH INC
221 N Broad St Ste 3 (19709-1070)
PHONE...............................510 789-3045
EMP: 5 **EST:** 1987
SALES (est): 131.36K **Privately Held**
SIC: 8742 Management consulting services

(G-6886)
ATR ELECTRICAL SERVICES INC
14 Manassas Dr (19709-3802)
PHONE...............................302 373-7769
Sean Mccarron, *Prin*
EMP: 15 **EST:** 2013
SQ FT: 2,500
SALES (est): 994.68K **Privately Held**
Web: www.atrelectricde.com
SIC: 1731 7389 Electrical work; Business Activities at Non-Commercial Site

(G-6887)
AUTOMATION ALLIANCE GROUP LLC
651 N Broad St Ste 206 (19709-6402)
PHONE...............................302 202-5433
EMP: 5 **EST:** 2020
SALES (est): 110.63K **Privately Held**
Web: www.automationalliance.net
SIC: 8748 Business consulting, nec

(G-6888)
AUTOMOTIVE ACCOUNTING SERVICE
680 N Broad St (19709-1030)
P.O. Box 5000 (19709-5000)
PHONE...............................302 378-9551
James Duckworth, *Pr*
William Stackhouse, *VP*
EMP: 20 **EST:** 1958
SQ FT: 2,000
SALES (est): 867.41K
SALES (corp-wide): 22.1B **Publicly Held**
SIC: 8721 Accounting services, except auditing
PA: Genuine Parts Company
2999 Wildwood Pkwy
Atlanta GA 30339
678 934-5000

(G-6889)
AUTOTYPE HOLDINGS (USA) INC
701 Industrial Dr (19709-1085)
PHONE...............................302 378-3100
Frank J Monteiro, *Pr*
John L Cordanis, *
▲ **EMP:** 61 **EST:** 1975
SALES (est): 2.26MM
SALES (corp-wide): 2.55B **Publicly Held**

SIC: 5043 5084 Printing apparatus, photographic; Industrial machinery and equipment
PA: Element Solutions Inc
500 E Broward Blvd # 1860
Fort Lauderdale FL 33394
561 207-9600,

(G-6890)
AVENUE 121
809 Marsh Hawk Ct (19709-2237)
PHONE...............................302 354-1839
EMP: 5 **EST:** 2019
SALES (est): 458.18K **Privately Held**
Web: www.avenue121.com
SIC: 5199 Advertising specialties

(G-6891)
AVIER UNLTD LLC
651 N Broad St Ste 206 (19709-6402)
PHONE...............................909 436-6964
EMP: 2 **EST:** 2021
SALES (est): 92.41K **Privately Held**
SIC: 2329 Athletic clothing, except uniforms: men's, youths' and boys'

(G-6892)
AVNI ADTECH INC ◊
651 N Broad St (19709-6400)
PHONE...............................628 600-5009
Pradeep Vallat, *CEO*
EMP: 13 **EST:** 2022
SALES (est): 445.76K **Privately Held**
SIC: 7371 Computer software development

(G-6893)
AVS SOLUTIONS LLC
730 Wood Duck Ct (19709-6112)
PHONE...............................302 562-0642
Sanjeev Walia, *Prin*
EMP: 5 **EST:** 2017
SALES (est): 246.64K **Privately Held**
SIC: 8748 Business consulting, nec

(G-6894)
AVVINUE INC (PA)
651 N Broad St Ste 20 (19709-6400)
PHONE...............................929 444-0554
EMP: 6 **EST:** 2021
SALES (est): 64.46K
SALES (corp-wide): 64.46K **Privately Held**
Web: www.avvinue.com
SIC: 4724 Travel agencies

(G-6895)
B RICH ENTERPRISES
808 Sweet Hollow Ct (19709-8645)
PHONE...............................302 530-6865
David Rich, *CEO*
Veronica Rich, *Admn*
EMP: 5 **EST:** 2005
SALES (est): 233.46K **Privately Held**
SIC: 8748 Business consulting, nec

(G-6896)
B&B TRANSPORTS LLC
651 N Broad St Ste 201 (19709-6402)
PHONE...............................223 877-6812
Antonio Shelton, *Managing Member*
EMP: 6 **EST:** 2021
SALES (est): 242.66K **Privately Held**
SIC: 7363 Truck driver services

(G-6897)
B&S HOME IMPRV ENVMTL UNVRSAL
600 N Broad St 5 (19709-1032)
PHONE...............................302 310-4374
Bethel Mansaray, *Prin*
Abu Mansaray, *Pr*

EMP: 5 **EST:** 2016
SQ FT: 350
SALES (est): 584.35K **Privately Held**
Web: www.bandsgeneralservice.com
SIC: 1521 General remodeling, single-family houses

(G-6898)
BACK CREEK GOLF CLUB
Also Called: Back Creek Golf Course
101 Back Creek Dr (19709-8843)
PHONE...............................302 378-6499
Allen Liddicoat, *Genl Pt*
EMP: 24 **EST:** 1997
SALES (est): 1.54MM **Privately Held**
Web: www.backcreekgc.com
SIC: 7992 Public golf courses

(G-6899)
BACKDOOR ENTERTAINMENT LLC
137 Betsy Rawls Dr (19709-9378)
PHONE...............................215 514-0915
Harry Jeudy, *Prin*
EMP: 7 **EST:** 2006
SALES (est): 52.12K **Privately Held**
SIC: 8999 Services, nec

(G-6900)
BACKDOOR GLOBAL INC ◊
651 N Broad St Ste 201 (19709-6402)
PHONE...............................386 465-2646
E I Villamizar Penaloza, *CEO*
Euder Isaac Villamizar Penaloz a, *CEO*
EMP: 5 **EST:** 2022
SALES (est): 199.4K **Privately Held**
SIC: 7371 Software programming applications

(G-6901)
BADILLO TRUCKING LLC
103 Night Heron Ln (19709-2208)
PHONE...............................302 368-4207
Pedro Badillo Junior, *Prin*
EMP: 5 **EST:** 2018
SALES (est): 229.02K **Privately Held**
SIC: 4212 Local trucking, without storage

(G-6902)
BAGEL TECHNOLOGIES INC
651 N Broad St Ste 206 (19709-6400)
PHONE...............................650 410-8018
Ohad Biron, *CEO*
EMP: 6
SALES (est): 237.56K **Privately Held**
SIC: 7371 Computer software development

(G-6903)
BAKER & SONS PAVING
116 Bakerfield Dr (19709-9451)
PHONE...............................302 945-6333
William Baker, *Pr*
EMP: 8 **EST:** 2011
SALES (est): 975.26K **Privately Held**
Web: www.bakerandsonspaving.com
SIC: 1611 Surfacing and paving

(G-6904)
BALANCED MIND CNSELING CTR LLC
115 N Broad St Ste 4a (19709-1045)
PHONE...............................302 377-6911
Jennifer Ewald, *Prin*
EMP: 10 **EST:** 2015
SALES (est): 222.7K **Privately Held**
Web: www.balancedmindcounseling.com
SIC: 8322 General counseling services

(G-6905)
BANG BANG MEDIA CORP (HQ)
651 N Broad St Ste 308 (19709-6403)
PHONE...............................213 374-0555
Roopak Singh Saluja, *Pr*
EMP: 6 **EST:** 2021
SALES (est): 145.56K **Privately Held**
SIC: 7922 Entertainment promotion
PA: Bang Bang Mediacorp Private Limited
Flat 7a,Saturn Chs,4th Flr,Plot No
C/729 Pali Mala Rd,Bandra(W)
Mumbai MH

(G-6906)
BBI-FIBER LLC (PA)
364 E Main St Ste 410 (19709-1482)
PHONE...............................224 633-1288
Tasha Davis-burroughs, *Managing Member*
EMP: 7 **EST:** 2018
SALES (est): 236.32K
SALES (corp-wide): 236.32K **Privately Held**
SIC: 4813 Internet connectivity services

(G-6907)
BECOMING BIO INC ◊
651 N Broad St Ste 201 (19709-6402)
PHONE...............................415 980-9796
Divya Cohen, *CEO*
EMP: 5 **EST:** 2022
SALES (est): 270.98K **Privately Held**
SIC: 8731 Biological research

(G-6908)
BEE A QUEEN INC
73 Cantwell Dr (19709-6835)
PHONE...............................267 235-8415
Charde Hines, *Pr*
EMP: 5 **EST:** 2017
SALES (est): 38.82K **Privately Held**
SIC: 8699 Charitable organization

(G-6909)
BEEBZ INC
221 N Broad St Ste 3a (19709-1070)
PHONE...............................832 692-7558
Habeeb Ayangbade, *CEO*
EMP: 5
SALES (est): 206.44K **Privately Held**
SIC: 4119 Local passenger transportation, nec

(G-6910)
BEELINE SERVICES LLC
865 Vance Neck Rd (19709-9135)
PHONE...............................302 376-7399
Steve Jacono, *Managing Member*
EMP: 5 **EST:** 2007
SALES (est): 508.57K **Privately Held**
SIC: 1751 7389 Carpentry work; Automobile recovery service

(G-6911)
BELLA MIA AESTHETICS LLC
111 W Main St (19709-1018)
PHONE...............................302 548-0660
Marla Chiarelli, *Managing Member*
EMP: 6 **EST:** 2021
SALES (est): 65.1K **Privately Held**
SIC: 7231 Beauty shops

(G-6912)
BENEREE INC
651 N Broad St Ste 201 (19709-6400)
PHONE...............................814 526-4238
EMP: 6
SALES (est): 237.56K **Privately Held**
SIC: 7371 Computer software development

GEOGRAPHIC SECTION

Middletown - New Castle County (G-6944)

(G-6913)
BENO INC
651 N Broad St (19709-6400)
PHONE.................................814 796-7686
EMP: 5 **EST**: 2020
SALES (est): 211.01K **Privately Held**
Web: www.reevobikes.com
SIC: 3751 Motorcycles, bicycles and parts

(G-6914)
BERRY GLOBAL INC
801 Industrial Dr (19709-1066)
PHONE.................................302 378-9853
EMP: 22
Web: www.berryglobal.com
SIC: 3089 Plastics containers, except foam
HQ: Berry Global, Inc.
101 Oakley St
Evansville IN 47710

(G-6915)
BETH A RENZULLI M D
102 Sleepy Hollow Dr Ste 200
(19709-5841)
PHONE.................................302 449-0420
Beth Renzulli, *Prin*
EMP: 8 **EST**: 2017
SALES (est): 97.45K **Privately Held**
SIC: 8011 General and family practice, physician/surgeon

(G-6916)
BETHESDA CHILD DEVMNT CTR
116 E Main St (19709-1428)
PHONE.................................302 378-8435
Christine Poehlmann, *Ofcr*
EMP: 13 **EST**: 1900
SALES (est): 17.57K **Privately Held**
Web: www.middletownhope.com
SIC: 8351 Child day care services

(G-6917)
BETTER DAYS PROPERTIES LLC
204 Sheats Ln (19709-9262)
PHONE.................................718 644-0163
EMP: 5 **EST**: 2019
SALES (est): 75.67K **Privately Held**
SIC: 6512 Nonresidential building operators

(G-6918)
BIG MOOSE EXTERIOR LLC
1057 Boyds Corner Rd (19709-9227)
PHONE.................................302 722-1969
EMP: 6 **EST**: 2010
SALES (est): 804.05K **Privately Held**
SIC: 7371 Computer software development and applications

(G-6919)
BIGTHINX INC (PA)
651 N Broad St (19709-6400)
PHONE.................................401 300-0494
Shivang Desai, *CEO*
EMP: 2
SALES (est): 87.4K
SALES (corp-wide): 87.4K **Privately Held**
SIC: 7372 Prepackaged software

(G-6920)
BIOBX LTD
651 N Broad St Ste 205-1772 (19709-6400)
PHONE.................................626 898-5814
Kevin Yu, *Pr*
Samson Ly, *VP*
EMP: 5 **EST**: 2020
SALES (est): 246.58K **Privately Held**
Web: www.biobx.co
SIC: 8742 Management consulting services

(G-6921)
BIPGO INC
651 N Broad St Ste 206 (19709-6402)
PHONE.................................708 586-9016
Angel Da Silva, *Prin*
EMP: 15 **EST**: 2020
SALES (est): 535.04K **Privately Held**
SIC: 7371 Software programming applications

(G-6922)
BIZZY BEES HOME DAYCARE LLC
815 S Cass St (19709-1334)
PHONE.................................302 376-9245
EMP: 8 **EST**: 2014
SALES (est): 53.13K **Privately Held**
Web: 654095.site123.me
SIC: 8351 Child day care services

(G-6923)
BJC-5 LLC
7 Jackie Cir (19709-9369)
PHONE.................................302 230-6733
Admiral Bumble B Hauling, *Prin*
EMP: 5 **EST**: 2021
SALES (est): 131.93K **Privately Held**
SIC: 4212 7389 Local trucking, without storage; Business services, nec

(G-6924)
BLIPS DIGITAL INC
651 N Broad St (19709-6400)
PHONE.................................661 520-1539
Archie Peterson, *CEO*
EMP: 10
SALES (est): 346.52K **Privately Held**
SIC: 7371 Computer software development and applications

(G-6925)
BLOOMFIELD TRUCKING INC
P.O. Box 1284 (19709-7284)
PHONE.................................302 834-6922
EMP: 5 **EST**: 2012
SALES (est): 188.1K **Privately Held**
SIC: 4213 Trucking, except local

(G-6926)
BLUE HEN ROUTE LLC
1102 White Ibis Ct (19709-2228)
PHONE.................................347 863-5534
Bilal Gondal, *Pr*
EMP: 30 **EST**: 2019
SALES (est): 1.62MM **Privately Held**
SIC: 4789 Transportation services, nec

(G-6927)
BLUE MONEY MUSIC GROUP INC
651 N Broad St Ste 205 (19709-6402)
PHONE.................................302 413-1304
Raquim D Watson, *Pr*
EMP: 10 **EST**: 2021
SALES (est): 100K **Privately Held**
SIC: 7922 Entertainment promotion

(G-6928)
BNJS LLC
Also Called: Bnj's Trucking
910 Benalli Dr (19709-6120)
PHONE.................................302 465-6105
Binyamin Salis, *Pr*
EMP: 6 **EST**: 2011
SALES (est): 772.05K **Privately Held**
SIC: 4212 Local trucking, without storage

(G-6929)
BOLDIFY INC
651 N Broad St Ste 206 (19709-6402)
PHONE.................................240 396-0247
EMP: 7 **EST**: 2018
SALES (est): 1.11MM **Privately Held**
Web: www.getboldify.com
SIC: 2844 Hair preparations, including shampoos

(G-6930)
BOOMERANG RETURNS LTD
651 N Broad St (19709-6400)
PHONE.................................347 205-1275
Benjamin Freedman, *Managing Member*
EMP: 6
SALES (est): 252.17K **Privately Held**
SIC: 7371 Computer software development and applications

(G-6931)
BOOTCAMP HELICOPTERS LLC
364 E Main St Ste 985 (19709-1482)
PHONE.................................301 717-5455
EMP: 5 **EST**: 2010
SALES (est): 55.89K **Privately Held**
Web: www.bootcamphelicopters.com
SIC: 4581 Airports, flying fields, and services

(G-6932)
BOT WORKSHOP LLC
600 N Broad St Ste 5 # 3349 (19709-1032)
PHONE.................................888 228-8799
EMP: 5
SALES (est): 134.3K **Privately Held**
Web: www.faidoe.com
SIC: 8742 Marketing consulting services

(G-6933)
BOTIX INC (PA) ✪
651 N Broad St Ste 205 (19709-6402)
PHONE.................................239 600-8116
Ardian Preci, *CEO*
EMP: 6 **EST**: 2022
SALES (est): 287.06K
SALES (corp-wide): 287.06K **Privately Held**
SIC: 7371 Software programming applications

(G-6934)
BRADFORD ENTERPRISES INC
503 Aspen Ct (19709-9311)
PHONE.................................302 378-0662
Susan Bradford, *Prin*
EMP: 5 **EST**: 2016
SALES (est): 169.96K **Privately Held**
SIC: 6531 Real estate managers

(G-6935)
BRADLEYS AUTO CENTER INC
1167 Bohemia Mill Rd (19709-9755)
PHONE.................................302 762-2247
Robert Bradley, *Pr*
EMP: 5 **EST**: 1974
SALES (est): 437.03K **Privately Held**
Web: www.bradleysautocenter.com
SIC: 7538 Engine rebuilding: automotive

(G-6936)
BREAKTHRU BEVERAGE GROUP LLC
Also Called: Breakthru Beverage Delaware
922 Levels Rd (19709-9074)
PHONE.................................443 631-2597
Michele Jankowski, *Mgr*
EMP: 429
SALES (corp-wide): 2.8B **Privately Held**
Web: www.breakthrubev.com
SIC: 5182 Wine
PA: Breakthru Beverage Group, Llc
60 E 42nd St Ste 1915
New York NY 10165
212 699-7000

(G-6937)
BREWSTER PRODUCTS
205 Ruth Dr (19709-9470)
PHONE.................................302 463-3531
EMP: 5 **EST**: 2010
SALES (est): 179.05K **Privately Held**
Web: www.brewsterproducts.com
SIC: 7822 Motion picture and tape distribution

(G-6938)
BRIAN MCALLISTER DDS
200 Cleaver Farms Rd Ste 101
(19709-1630)
PHONE.................................302 376-0617
EMP: 5 **EST**: 2003
SALES (est): 236.26K **Privately Held**
Web: www.bmcallisterdds.com
SIC: 8021 Dentists' office

(G-6939)
BRIANNA RAFETTO DMD PA
Also Called: Bright Dental
600 N Broad St Ste 7 (19709-1032)
PHONE.................................302 376-7882
Doctor Brianna Rafetto, *Pr*
EMP: 10 **EST**: 2015
SALES (est): 494.51K **Privately Held**
Web: www.jeffreyabright.com
SIC: 8021 Dentists' office

(G-6940)
BRIGHT BEGINNINGS INC
341 W Windmill Way (19709-9669)
PHONE.................................302 376-8001
EMP: 9 **EST**: 2010
SALES (est): 83.94K **Privately Held**
Web: www.bbidc.org
SIC: 8351 Preschool center

(G-6941)
BRIGHT FUTURES INC
125 Sleepy Hollow Dr (19709-8895)
PHONE.................................610 905-0506
Jessica Deshong, *CEO*
EMP: 20 **EST**: 2017
SALES (est): 462.94K **Privately Held**
Web: www.brightfuturesea.com
SIC: 8351 Preschool center

(G-6942)
BRIGHT STARS HOME DAYCARE
302 Northhampton Way (19709-8338)
PHONE.................................302 378-8142
Reshina Wells, *Prin*
EMP: 5 **EST**: 2010
SALES (est): 96.14K **Privately Held**
SIC: 8351 Group day care center

(G-6943)
BRILLIANT LITTLE MINDS
102 Sandhill Dr (19709-5806)
PHONE.................................302 376-9889
Jennifer Phipps, *Dir*
EMP: 5 **EST**: 2009
SALES (est): 665.56K **Privately Held**
Web: www.brilliantlittleminds.com
SIC: 8351 Preschool center

(G-6944)
BROADMEADOW INVESTMENT LLC
Also Called: Broadmeadow Healthcare
500 S Broad St (19709-1443)
PHONE.................................302 449-3400
EMP: 42 **EST**: 2005
SALES (est): 14.56MM **Privately Held**
Web: www.cadiahealthcare.com
SIC: 8051 Convalescent home with continuous nursing care

Middletown - New Castle County (G-6945) — GEOGRAPHIC SECTION

(G-6945)
BROTHERS PAINTING AND DRYWALL
709 Waterbird Ln (19709-2233)
PHONE................................302 737-9600
EMP: 7 EST: 2019
SALES (est): 475.44K **Privately Held**
SIC: 1742 Drywall

(G-6946)
BULL HEAD TRANSPORT LLC
8 Chase Ln (19709-9612)
PHONE................................302 650-8544
EMP: 6 EST: 2017
SALES (est): 494.84K **Privately Held**
SIC: 4789 Transportation services, nec

(G-6947)
BUNKER HILL EQUESTRIAN CENTER
1239 Bunker Hill Rd (19709-9031)
PHONE................................302 312-9890
Susan Natrin, Prin
EMP: 5 EST: 2010
SALES (est): 40.98K **Privately Held**
SIC: 7999 Riding academy and school

(G-6948)
BUZZSPARK LABS LLC ◇
651 N Broad St Ste 201 (19709-6402)
PHONE................................302 828-0969
EMP: 5 EST: 2022
SALES (est): 63.4K **Privately Held**
SIC: 7371 Computer software development and applications

(G-6949)
BY LORE TECH SOLUTIONS INC ◇
743 Ashington Dr (19709-7521)
PHONE................................302 202-9499
Sridevi Nekkalapu, Pr
EMP: 5 EST: 2023
SALES (est): 203.68K **Privately Held**
SIC: 7379 7389 Computer related consulting services; Business services, nec

(G-6950)
CAHILL CONTRACTING
Also Called: Cahill Electrical Contractors
104 Sleepy Hollow Dr Ste 201 (19709-5842)
PHONE................................302 378-9650
Kevin Cahill, Pr
EMP: 10 EST: 1987
SQ FT: 6,700
SALES (est): 950.33K **Privately Held**
Web: www.cahillelectric.com
SIC: 1731 General electrical contractor

(G-6951)
CALIBER COLLISION
5077 Summit Bridge Rd (19709-9591)
PHONE................................302 279-1007
EMP: 6 EST: 2019
SALES (est): 234.42K **Privately Held**
Web: www.caliber.com
SIC: 7536 7532 Automotive glass replacement shops; Top and body repair and paint shops

(G-6952)
CALIBER HOME LOANS
107 Brooks Ct (19709-9188)
PHONE................................302 584-0580
Gary Huegel, Prin
EMP: 6 EST: 2018
SALES (est): 117.31K **Privately Held**
Web: www.caliberhomeloans.com
SIC: 6162 Mortgage bankers and loan correspondents

(G-6953)
CAMP ADVENTURELAND LLC
112 Patriot Dr Ste C (19709-8997)
PHONE................................302 449-2267
Phil Nannay, Prin
EMP: 7 EST: 2019
SALES (est): 106.69K **Privately Held**
Web: www.campadventureland.com
SIC: 7999 Amusement and recreation, nec

(G-6954)
CAMP CHIROPRACTIC INC
272 Carter Dr Ste 120 (19709-5850)
PHONE................................302 378-2899
EMP: 7 EST: 1991
SALES (est): 396.49K **Privately Held**
Web: www.campchiropractic.com
SIC: 8041 8011 Offices and clinics of chiropractors; Physicians' office, including specialists

(G-6955)
CARE CONSTITUTION LLC ◇
651 N Broad St (19709-6400)
PHONE................................201 240-3661
Jennifer Kirkland, Managing Member
EMP: 5 EST: 2022
SALES (est): 199.4K **Privately Held**
SIC: 7389 8099 Business Activities at Non-Commercial Site; Health screening service

(G-6956)
CAREBNB INC
651 N Broad St Ste 206 (19709-6402)
PHONE................................904 303-6825
Demetrio Guilardi, CEO
EMP: 6 EST: 2020
SALES (est): 100K **Privately Held**
SIC: 7371 Software programming applications

(G-6957)
CAREKRAKEN LLC
221 N Broad St Ste 3a (19709-1070)
PHONE................................410 808-0333
EMP: 5 EST: 2020
SALES (est): 104.73K **Privately Held**
SIC: 7389 Business services, nec

(G-6958)
CARIBBEAN CLTURE AWARENESS INC (PA)
610 Wesley Ct (19709-2192)
PHONE................................888 595-1259
Eveann Metelus, CEO
EMP: 6 EST: 2021
SALES (est): 60.12K
SALES (corp-wide): 60.12K **Privately Held**
SIC: 7929 Entertainers and entertainment groups

(G-6959)
CARIBE TECHNOLOGIES INC
651 N Broad St (19709-6400)
PHONE................................205 590-5767
EMP: 7 EST: 2021
SALES (est): 272.09K **Privately Held**
SIC: 7389 Business services, nec

(G-6960)
CARING MINDS MEDICAL CENTER
2 Hogan Cir (19709-9367)
PHONE................................267 243-9102
Florence Akouegnon, Prin
EMP: 9 EST: 2017
SALES (est): 313.87K **Privately Held**
Web: www.caringmindsmedicalcenter.com
SIC: 8011 Medical centers

(G-6961)
CARTED INC
651 N Broad St Ste 206 (19709-6402)
PHONE................................415 967-8691
Holly Cardew, Managing Member
EMP: 7 EST: 2020
SALES (est): 264.9K **Privately Held**
SIC: 7371 Custom computer programming services

(G-6962)
CASTING ARABIA LLC (PA)
221 N Broad St Ste 3a (19709-1070)
PHONE................................917 832-5287
EMP: 8 EST: 2020
SALES (est): 29.29K
SALES (corp-wide): 29.29K **Privately Held**
SIC: 7371 Computer software development and applications

(G-6963)
CASUS CONSULTING LLC (PA)
651 N Broad St Ste 201 (19709-6402)
PHONE................................972 532-6357
Roslyn Gillespie, Managing Member
EMP: 5 EST: 2021
SALES (est): 264.97K
SALES (corp-wide): 264.97K **Privately Held**
SIC: 8748 Business consulting, nec

(G-6964)
CAVALIER LAWN CARE & LDSCPG
724 New Brighton Ct (19709-7926)
PHONE................................302 838-2005
EMP: 5 EST: 2018
SALES (est): 493.1K **Privately Held**
SIC: 0782 Lawn care services

(G-6965)
CAYTU INC ◇
651 N Broad St Ste 206 (19709-6402)
PHONE................................202 670-9288
Sidy Ndao, Prin
EMP: 6 EST: 2022
SALES (est): 249.24K **Privately Held**
SIC: 7372 Prepackaged software

(G-6966)
CAYUGA CENTERS
292 Carter Dr Ste A (19709-5846)
PHONE................................302 257-5848
EMP: 14 EST: 2019
SALES (est): 47.22K **Privately Held**
Web: www.cayugacenters.org
SIC: 8322 Social service center

(G-6967)
CCCI- CELEBRANTS CHRISTN CHPEL
410 N Ramunno Dr # 2304 (19709-3003)
PHONE................................302 690-4890
Rex Adzadu, Prin
EMP: 5 EST: 2015
SALES (est): 105.68K **Privately Held**
SIC: 7261 Funeral home

(G-6968)
CELERA SERVICES INC
364 E Main St (19709-1482)
PHONE................................302 378-7778
Linda Lushbaugh, Pr
Ed Lushbaugh, VP Opers
EMP: 6 EST: 2005
SALES (est): 540K **Privately Held**
SIC: 7359 Home appliance, furniture, and entertainment rental services

(G-6969)
CENTER FOR CONSCIOUS HEALING
101 W Park Pl (19709-1324)
PHONE................................302 376-6144
Colleen M Mcginnis, Owner
EMP: 7 EST: 2014
SALES (est): 66.37K **Privately Held**
Web: www.center-for-conscious-healing.com
SIC: 8049 Offices of health practitioner

(G-6970)
CERTIFIED CODE INC
651 N Broad St (19709-6400)
PHONE................................347 508-6396
EMP: 5 EST: 2021
SALES (est): 68.89K **Privately Held**
Web: www.certifiedcode.us
SIC: 7371 Computer software development

(G-6971)
CHAS POOLS INC
600 N Broad St Ste 11 (19709-1032)
PHONE................................302 376-5840
Joseph Chas Ii, Owner
Joseph Chas Ii, Pr
Kathleen M Chas, VP
EMP: 10 EST: 2000
SALES (est): 419.36K **Privately Held**
Web: www.chaspools.com
SIC: 1799 Swimming pool construction

(G-6972)
CHEON IL GUK INCORPORATED
500 Ethel Ct (19709-9410)
PHONE................................302 332-2672
Andrea Mylar, Prin
EMP: 6 EST: 2015
SALES (est): 7.05K **Privately Held**
Web: www.cheon-il-guk.org
SIC: 8322 Individual and family services

(G-6973)
CHICHESTER BUSINESS PARK LLC
108 Patriot Dr Ste A (19709-8803)
PHONE................................302 685-2997
EMP: 5 EST: 2008
SALES (est): 285.7K **Privately Held**
Web: www.maccde.com
SIC: 6531 Real estate leasing and rentals

(G-6974)
CHIEFFO ELECTRIC INC
108 W Cedarwood Dr (19709-4022)
PHONE................................302 292-6813
Joseph F Chieffo, Pr
EMP: 9 EST: 1988
SALES (est): 931.12K **Privately Held**
SIC: 1731 General electrical contractor

(G-6975)
CHOICES FOR COMMUNITY
30 W Main St (19709-1039)
PHONE................................302 378-3821
EMP: 5 EST: 2017
SALES (est): 48.01K **Privately Held**
SIC: 8322 Community center

(G-6976)
CHRISTIANA CARE HEALTH SYS INC
124 Sleepy Hollow Dr Ste 203 (19709-5838)
PHONE................................302 449-3000
Todd S Cumming, Pt
EMP: 228
SALES (corp-wide): 666.58K **Privately Held**
Web: www.christianacare.org
SIC: 8062 General medical and surgical hospitals

GEOGRAPHIC SECTION

Middletown - New Castle County (G-7007)

HQ: Christiana Care Health System, Inc.
200 Hygeia Dr
Newark DE 19713
302 733-1000

(G-6977)
CHRISTIANA CENTER-ORAL SURGERY
114 Saint Annes Church Rd (19709-1495)
PHONE...............................302 376-3700
Cheryl Harris, *Mgr*
EMP: 10 **EST:** 2017
SALES (est): 216.55K **Privately Held**
Web: www.christianaoms.com
SIC: 8021 Dental surgeon

(G-6978)
CHRISTIANA MECHANICAL INC
Also Called: CMI
109 Sleepy Hollow Dr Ste A (19709-8895)
PHONE...............................302 378-7308
EMP: 13 **EST:** 1995
SQ FT: 1,200
SALES (est): 4.63MM **Privately Held**
Web: www.christianamechanical.com
SIC: 1711 Mechanical contractor

(G-6979)
CHRISTINE METZING
413 Meadow Ln (19709-9693)
PHONE...............................302 376-5148
Christine E Metzing Md, *Owner*
EMP: 7 **EST:** 2018
SALES (est): 117.58K **Privately Held**
SIC: 8011 Offices and clinics of medical doctors

(G-6980)
CHRISTOPHERS HAIR DESIGN
Also Called: Christopher's Salon & Spa
423 N Broad St Ste 5 (19709-1092)
PHONE...............................302 378-1988
EMP: 8 **EST:** 1994
SALES (est): 209.44K **Privately Held**
SIC: 7231 7991 Hairdressers; Spas

(G-6981)
CIMI ENTERPRISES LLC
108 Patriot Dr (19709-8803)
PHONE...............................302 803-2210
Lisa Prince, *CEO*
EMP: 11 **EST:** 2018
SALES (est): 566.68K **Privately Held**
Web: www.cimibas.com
SIC: 8093 Rehabilitation center, outpatient treatment

(G-6982)
CINDYS HOME AWAY FROM HME FAM
22 Canary Ct (19709-2184)
PHONE...............................302 378-0487
Cindy Shaw, *Prin*
EMP: 8 **EST:** 2010
SALES (est): 129.74K **Privately Held**
SIC: 8082 Home health care services

(G-6983)
CIVIL CONSULTING ENGINEERS LLC
8 Berton Ct (19709-9934)
PHONE...............................302 824-6041
Jason Halpin, *Prin*
EMP: 5 **EST:** 2017
SALES (est): 66.92K **Privately Held**
SIC: 8711 Consulting engineer

(G-6984)
CIVIL ENGINEERING ASSOC LLC
55 W Main St (19709-1017)
PHONE...............................302 376-8833
EMP: 5 **EST:** 2006
SQ FT: 2,880
SALES (est): 781.94K **Privately Held**
Web: www.cea-de.com
SIC: 8711 Civil engineering

(G-6985)
CKQ PROPERTIES LLC
5197 Summit Bridge Rd (19709-8821)
PHONE...............................302 378-2560
EMP: 6 **EST:** 2011
SALES (est): 210.19K **Privately Held**
Web: www.sqjohnson.com
SIC: 6512 Nonresidential building operators

(G-6986)
CLARIOS LLC
Also Called: Johnson Controls
50 Patriot Dr (19709-8769)
PHONE...............................302 696-3221
EMP: 117
SALES (corp-wide): 1.54B **Privately Held**
Web: www.clarios.com
SIC: 3691 Storage batteries
HQ: Clarios, Llc
5757 N Green Bay Ave
Milwaukee WI 53209

(G-6987)
CLASSIC FINANCIAL LLC
764 Ashington Dr Ste 100 (19709-7518)
PHONE...............................302 476-0948
Derek Cunningham, *Ex Dir*
EMP: 25 **EST:** 2019
SALES (est): 360K **Privately Held**
SIC: 6531 Real estate managers

(G-6988)
CLEANPRO DETAIL CENTER
5221 Summit Bridge Rd (19709-8823)
PHONE...............................302 464-1017
EMP: 5 **EST:** 2017
SALES (est): 100.16K **Privately Held**
Web: www.cleanprodetailcenter.com
SIC: 8322 Individual and family services

(G-6989)
CLEAT LRNG & COMMUNICATIONS
218 Wilgus Ct (19709-8306)
PHONE...............................845 527-3754
Tom Peters, *Prin*
EMP: 6 **EST:** 2017
SALES (est): 73.11K **Privately Held**
SIC: 4899 Communication services, nec

(G-6990)
CLICOH INC ✪
651 N Broad St Ste 206 (19709-6402)
PHONE...............................415 987-3261
Juan Altamirano, *COO*
EMP: 5 **EST:** 2023
SALES (est): 488.14K **Privately Held**
SIC: 5088 Transportation equipment and supplies

(G-6991)
CLIFFORD L ANZILOTTI DDS PC
112 Saint Annes Church Rd (19709-1495)
PHONE...............................302 378-2778
Doctor Clifford Anzilotti, *Brnch Mgr*
EMP: 7
SALES (corp-wide): 1.08MM **Privately Held**
Web: www.anzilottiortho.com
SIC: 8021 Orthodontist
PA: Clifford L Anzilotti Dds Pc
2101 Foulk Rd
Wilmington DE 19810
302 475-2050

(G-6992)
CLIFTON ENTERPRISES LLC
651 N Broad St Ste 205 (19709-6400)
PHONE...............................630 220-7435
Robert Boling, *Managing Member*
EMP: 5
SALES (est): 68.89K **Privately Held**
SIC: 7371 Computer software development and applications

(G-6993)
CLIFTON L BAKHSH JR INC
Also Called: Bakhsh Surveyors
4450 Summit Bridge Rd (19709-9344)
PHONE...............................302 378-8009
Clifton L Bakhsh Junior, *Pr*
Sue Bakhsh, *VP*
EMP: 14 **EST:** 1985
SQ FT: 2,000
SALES (est): 527.82K **Privately Held**
Web: www.cbakhsh.com
SIC: 8713 Surveying services

(G-6994)
CLINE LABS INC
651 N Broad St (19709-6400)
PHONE...............................901 834-5102
Boma Josiah, *CEO*
EMP: 9
SALES (est): 313.29K **Privately Held**
SIC: 7371 Computer software development

(G-6995)
CLINTON CRADDOCK
Also Called: Delaware Protection Agency
511 Cilantro Ct (19709-8783)
PHONE...............................267 505-2671
Clinton Craddock, *Owner*
EMP: 10 **EST:** 2019
SALES (est): 180.69K **Privately Held**
SIC: 7389 Business Activities at Non-Commercial Site

(G-6996)
CLIPPING BEAST LLC
364 E Main St Ste 1011 (19709-1482)
PHONE...............................850 312-8223
Udit Mandal, *CEO*
EMP: 5 **EST:** 2017
SALES (est): 86.49K **Privately Held**
Web: www.clippingbeast.com
SIC: 7389 Press clipping service

(G-6997)
CLOUD CYSTEMS LLC ✪
651 N Broad St Ste 201 (19709-6402)
PHONE...............................815 797-9929
Ahmad Mushtaq, *Managing Member*
EMP: 10 **EST:** 2022
SALES (est): 348.32K **Privately Held**
SIC: 8748 Business consulting, nec

(G-6998)
CLOUDBRST LAWN SPRNKLR SYSTEMS
212 Wilmore Dr (19709-8359)
PHONE...............................302 375-0446
EMP: 7 **EST:** 2017
SALES (est): 59.19K **Privately Held**
Web: www.cloudburstsprinkler.com
SIC: 1711 Irrigation sprinkler system installation

(G-6999)
CLOVER LOGISTICS LLC
651 N Broad St (19709-6400)
PHONE...............................713 474-4094
EMP: 2 **EST:** 2021
SALES (est): 85.99K **Privately Held**

(G-7000)
COACH AK ENTERPRISES LLC
651 N Broad St Ste 205 (19709-6402)
PHONE...............................617 433-7560
EMP: 12 **EST:** 2020
SALES (est): 75K **Privately Held**
SIC: 8748 Business consulting, nec

(G-7001)
COFFEEDGE INC
651 N Broad St Ste 206 (19709-6402)
PHONE...............................585 294-2726
Gustav Renman, *Pr*
EMP: 6 **EST:** 2020
SALES (est): 800K **Privately Held**
SIC: 2522 Office chairs, benches, and stools, except wood

(G-7002)
COINTIGO LLC
651 N Broad St Ste 205 # 647 (19709-6402)
PHONE...............................817 681-7131
EMP: 10 **EST:** 2019
SALES (est): 455.88K **Privately Held**
SIC: 7389 Business Activities at Non-Commercial Site

(G-7003)
COLOR ME CRAZY HAIR LLC (PA)
27 W Main St (19709-1189)
PHONE...............................484 838-6027
EMP: 6 **EST:** 2016
SALES (est): 72.21K
SALES (corp-wide): 72.21K **Privately Held**
Web: colormecrazyhairextensions.bigcartel.com
SIC: 7231 Hairdressers

(G-7004)
COMMUNITY PUBLICATIONS INC
Also Called: Greenville Community Newspaper
24 W Main St (19709-1039)
P.O. Box 536 (19707-0536)
PHONE...............................302 239-4644
Joseph Amom, *Pr*
EMP: 17 **EST:** 1987
SALES (est): 173.26K **Privately Held**
Web: www.delawareonline.com
SIC: 2711 Newspapers, publishing and printing

(G-7005)
COMPASS GRAPHICS
137 Back Creek Dr (19709-8843)
PHONE...............................302 378-1977
D Clendening, *Prin*
EMP: 2 **EST:** 2003
SALES (est): 146.8K **Privately Held**
SIC: 2759 Commercial printing, nec

(G-7006)
COMPASSNATE HLTH INTATIVES INC
Also Called: CHI
717 Dairy Dr (19709-3078)
PHONE...............................302 765-8256
Robert Onyango, *Pr*
Steve Kabiru, *Admn*
Maurice Ojwang, *Treas*
EMP: 11 **EST:** 2019
SALES (est): 87.93K **Privately Held**
SIC: 8399 Social services, nec

(G-7007)
COMPASSONATE CERTIFICATION CTR
364 E Main St Ste 2001 (19709-1482)

Middletown - New Castle County (G-7008) GEOGRAPHIC SECTION

PHONE..................................888 316-9085
Bryan Doner, *Owner*
EMP: 7 **EST:** 2016
SALES (est): 217.21K **Privately Held**
Web: www.compassionatecertificationcenters.com
SIC: 8099 Health and allied services, nec

(G-7008)
COMPLETE ACCIDENT RELIEF
222 Carter Dr Ste 103 (19709-5856)
PHONE..................................302 375-5019
Patricia Wendel, *Prin*
EMP: 7 **EST:** 2014
SALES (est): 243.34K **Privately Held**
Web: www.motchiropractic.com
SIC: 8041 Offices and clinics of chiropractors

(G-7009)
CONFIDNTIAL EXEC TRNSP INTL IN
651 N Broad St Ste 205-1082 (19709-6400)
PHONE..................................800 316-0802
Jose Pinell, *Pr*
EMP: 8 **EST:** 2019
SALES (est): 262.88K **Privately Held**
SIC: 4119 Local passenger transportation, nec

(G-7010)
CONREP INC
292 Carter Dr Ste C (19709-5846)
PHONE..................................302 528-8383
EMP: 22 **EST:** 2010
SALES (est): 882.44K **Privately Held**
Web: www.conrep.com
SIC: 7371 Computer software development

(G-7011)
COOK G LEGIH DDS& COOK JEFRY
12 Pennington St Ste 300 (19709-1026)
PHONE..................................302 378-4416
Gordon Leigh Cook D.d.s., *Pt*
Doctor G Leigh Cook D.d.s., *Pt*
Doctor Jeffrey L Cook, *Pt*
▲ **EMP:** 6 **EST:** 1978
SQ FT: 650
SALES (est): 418.07K **Privately Held**
SIC: 8021 Dentists' office

(G-7012)
COOK HAULING LLC
350 Misty Vale Dr (19709-2124)
PHONE..................................302 378-6451
EMP: 5 **EST:** 1998
SALES (est): 248.36K **Privately Held**
SIC: 1442 Construction sand and gravel

(G-7013)
COOPER-WILBERT VAULT CO INC
4971 Summit Bridge Rd (19709-8819)
PHONE..................................302 376-1331
Paul Cooper, *Genl Mgr*
EMP: 4
SALES (corp-wide): 4.33MM **Privately Held**
Web: www.coopervault.com
SIC: 3272 Burial vaults, concrete or precast terrazzo
PA: Cooper-Wilbert Vault Co Inc
    621 Atlantic Ave
    Barrington NJ 08007
    856 547-8405

(G-7014)
CORNERSTONE RBE CONTG LLC
911 Lansdowne Rd (19709-8391)
PHONE..................................443 480-6674
Sarah Christophel, *Prin*
EMP: 5 **EST:** 2016
SALES (est): 56.76K **Privately Held**
SIC: 1799 Special trade contractors, nec

(G-7015)
COUNTRMSRES ASSSSMENT SEC EXPR
Also Called: Case
36 E Sarazen Dr (19709-7960)
PHONE..................................302 322-9600
Ernest Frazier Senior, *Managing Member*
EMP: 7 **EST:** 2004
SALES (est): 775.71K **Privately Held**
Web: www.caseexperts.com
SIC: 8748 8742 8111 Business consulting, nec; Business planning and organizing services; Legal services

(G-7016)
COUNTY BUILDING SERVICES INC
8 Knightsbridge Rd (19709-9706)
PHONE..................................302 377-4213
Jack Reede, *Pr*
EMP: 5 **EST:** 2012
SALES (est): 51.97K **Privately Held**
SIC: 7349 Building cleaning service

(G-7017)
CRAB MEAT FOR KIDS
482 Brick Mill Rd (19709-8954)
P.O. Box 360 (19709-0360)
PHONE..................................302 378-1327
Jerry Thompson, *Prin*
EMP: 5 **EST:** 2009
SALES (est): 49.39K **Privately Held**
SIC: 8641 Youth organizations

(G-7018)
CRAIG MAURER
791 Idlewyld Dr (19709-7848)
PHONE..................................302 293-2365
Craig Maurer, *Prin*
EMP: 5 **EST:** 2010
SALES (est): 200.96K **Privately Held**
SIC: 1521 Single-family housing construction

(G-7019)
CRAZY COATINGS
4783 Summit Bridge Rd (19709-8815)
PHONE..................................302 378-0888
Dave Seemans, *Mgr*
EMP: 5 **EST:** 2011
SALES (est): 109.22K **Privately Held**
Web: www.crazycoatings.com
SIC: 3479 Coating of metals and formed products

(G-7020)
CREATIVE DEVICES INC
361 Misty Vale Dr (19709-2125)
PHONE..................................302 378-5433
Robert Urstadt, *Pr*
Sandra Urstadt, *Sec*
▲ **EMP:** 2 **EST:** 1990
SALES (est): 248.01K **Privately Held**
Web: www.creativedevices.com
SIC: 3826 Analytical optical instruments

(G-7021)
CREATIVITY DIVERSIFIED LLC
141 Gillespie Ave (19709-8362)
PHONE..................................302 897-5961
EMP: 5 **EST:** 2021
SALES (est): 257.42K **Privately Held**
Web: www.creativitydiversified.com
SIC: 8748 8742 7389 Communications consulting; Marketing consulting services; Design services

(G-7022)
CUBIC SCT INC ✪
600 N Broad St (19709-1032)
PHONE..................................845 977-3240
Oran Sever, *CEO*
EMP: 12 **EST:** 2023
SALES (est): 690.21K **Privately Held**
SIC: 4731 Freight transportation arrangement

(G-7023)
CYBERDEFENDERS INC
651 N Broad St (19709-6400)
PHONE..................................510 999-3490
Mohammad Alharmeel, *CEO*
EMP: 8
SALES (est): 347.57K **Privately Held**
SIC: 1731 7371 Safety and security specialization; Computer software development and applications

(G-7024)
CYBERLETE INC
651 N Broad St (19709-6400)
PHONE..................................440 983-8647
Geoffrey Maunus, *COO*
EMP: 3
SALES (est): 128.34K **Privately Held**
SIC: 7372 Application computer software

(G-7025)
CYPROTECK INC
651 N Broad St Ste 201 (19709-6400)
PHONE..................................860 890-1889
Cherie Dunn, *Prin*
EMP: 10
SALES (est): 355.79K **Privately Held**
SIC: 7382 Security systems services

(G-7026)
D & C BATH LLC
600 N Broad St Ste 4 (19709-1032)
PHONE..................................888 323-2284
EMP: 8
SALES (est): 347.57K **Privately Held**
Web: www.dcbathllc.com
SIC: 1799 Kitchen and bathroom remodeling

(G-7027)
DAMA INTERNATIONAL LLC
364 E Main St Ste 157 (19709-1482)
P.O. Box 477 (60106-0477)
PHONE..................................813 778-5495
Loretta Mahon Smith, *Managing Member*
EMP: 11 **EST:** 2005
SALES (est): 130.4K **Privately Held**
Web: www.dama.org
SIC: 7371 Computer software development

(G-7028)
DANDREA CONTRACTING
230 Milford Dr (19709-9417)
PHONE..................................302 893-4183
EMP: 5 **EST:** 2018
SALES (est): 56.76K **Privately Held**
SIC: 1799 Special trade contractors, nec

(G-7029)
DATALOGY BUS SOLUTIONS INC
651 N Broad St Ste 206 (19709-6402)
PHONE..................................832 713-4790
Khrystle Riley, *CEO*
EMP: 5 **EST:** 2020
SALES (est): 100K **Privately Held**
Web: www.maccde.com
SIC: 7322 Collection agency, except real estate

(G-7030)
DATWYLER PHARMA PACKG USA INC
571 Merrimac Ave (19709-4647)
PHONE..................................302 603-8020
EMP: 15
Web: www.datwyler.com
SIC: 3841 Surgical instruments and apparatus
HQ: Datwyler Pharma Packaging Usa Inc.
    9012 Pennsauken Hwy
    Pennsauken NJ 08110
    856 663-2202

(G-7031)
DAWN L CONLY
266 Bucktail Dr (19709-6131)
PHONE..................................302 378-1890
Dawn L Conly, *Prin*
EMP: 11 **EST:** 2010
SALES (est): 100.03K **Privately Held**
SIC: 8351 Child day care services

(G-7032)
DAWN SOMER FITNESS
706 Worcester Ave (19709-8348)
PHONE..................................229 325-9173
Somer Phoebus, *Prin*
EMP: 5 **EST:** 2015
SALES (est): 35.74K **Privately Held**
Web: www.somerdawnfitness.com
SIC: 7991 Physical fitness facilities

(G-7033)
DE PROPERTY MAINTENANCE LLC
110 W Green St (19709-1317)
PHONE..................................302 241-5567
Tami Golt, *Prin*
EMP: 5 **EST:** 2017
SALES (est): 20.74K **Privately Held**
Web: www.depropmaint.com
SIC: 7349 Building maintenance services, nec

(G-7034)
DEANNE NAPLES FAMILY DAYCARE
225 Manchester Way (19709-2131)
PHONE..................................302 376-1408
David Naples, *Prin*
EMP: 5 **EST:** 2009
SALES (est): 71.43K **Privately Held**
Web: www.wakeup.com
SIC: 8351 Group day care center

(G-7035)
DEDICATED TO WOMEN OBGYN
209 E Main St (19709-1449)
PHONE..................................302 285-5545
Michelle H Cooper, *Pt*
EMP: 10 **EST:** 2013
SALES (est): 512.5K **Privately Held**
Web: www.dedicatedtowomenobgyn.com
SIC: 8011 Gynecologist

(G-7036)
DEEPEN INC ✪
651 N Broad St Ste 201 (19709-6402)
PHONE..................................813 813-9053
EMP: 6 **EST:** 2023
SALES (est): 68.89K **Privately Held**
SIC: 7371 Computer software development

(G-7037)
DELA BELLE INV GROUP CORP
651 N Broad St Ste 205 (19709-6402)
PHONE..................................901 279-2742
Juanita Wilson, *COO*
Tehren Wilson, *VP*
EMP: 6 **EST:** 2019
SALES (est): 245.36K **Privately Held**

SIC: 7514 Rent-a-car service

(G-7038)
DELAWARE CONSTRUCTIONOLOGY
314 White Pine Dr (19709-9779)
PHONE..................................302 827-3072
Richard Edwards, *Pt*
EMP: 5 **EST:** 2014
SALES (est): 97.18K **Privately Held**
SIC: 1521 Single-family housing construction

(G-7039)
DELAWARE DEPARTMENT TRNSP
Also Called: Highway Operations
5369 Summit Bridge Rd (19709-1493)
PHONE..................................302 653-4128
EMP: 41
SALES (corp-wide): 11.27B **Privately Held**
Web: www.deldot.gov
SIC: 1611 9621 Highway and street maintenance; Regulation, administration of transportation
HQ: Delaware Department Of Transportation
800 S Bay Rd Ste 1
Dover DE 19901

(G-7040)
DELAWARE HLTH EQITY CLTION INC ✪
239 Wickerberry Dr (19709-7810)
PHONE..................................302 383-1701
Gina Kilgore, *Prin*
EMP: 5 **EST:** 2022
SALES (est): 72.52K **Privately Held**
SIC: 8011 7389 Physicians' office, including specialists; Business Activities at Non-Commercial Site

(G-7041)
DELAWARE IMAGING NETWORK
Also Called: Papastavros Assoc Med Imaging
114 Sandhill Dr Ste 201 (19709-5805)
PHONE..................................302 449-5400
Dick Palmer, *Mgr*
EMP: 5
Web: www.papastavros.com
SIC: 8011 8071 Radiologist; X-ray laboratory, including dental
HQ: Papastavros' Associates Medical Imaging L.L.C.
40 Polly Drummond Hill Rd
Newark DE 19711
302 652-3016

(G-7042)
DELAWARE JUNETEENTH ASSN
139 Asbury Loop (19709-8655)
PHONE..................................302 530-1605
EMP: 6 **EST:** 2014
SALES (est): 80.22K **Privately Held**
Web: www.delawarejuneteenth.org
SIC: 8699 Membership organizations, nec

(G-7043)
DELAWARE MILLWORK
110 W Green St (19709-1317)
PHONE..................................302 376-8324
EMP: 5 **EST:** 2019
SALES (est): 369.35K **Privately Held**
Web: www.delawaremillwork.com
SIC: 2431 Millwork

(G-7044)
DELAWARE SCREEN PRINTING INC
Also Called: Delaware Screen Printing
350 Strawberry Ln (19709-9641)
PHONE..................................302 378-4321
Dennis Cowan, *Pr*
EMP: 3 **EST:** 1973
SALES (est): 191.88K **Privately Held**
Web: www.delawarescreenprinting.com
SIC: 2759 2752 2396 Commercial printing, nec; Commercial printing, lithographic; Automotive and apparel trimmings

(G-7045)
DELAWARE SIGNING SERVICES LLC
163 Tywyn Dr (19709-8741)
PHONE..................................302 464-5038
EMP: 5 **EST:** 2021
SALES (est): 104.73K **Privately Held**
SIC: 7389 Notary publics

(G-7046)
DELAWARE SLEEP DISORDER C
108 Patriot Dr Ste A (19709-8803)
PHONE..................................302 407-3349
EMP: 10 **EST:** 2019
SALES (est): 1.64MM **Privately Held**
Web: www.delsleep.com
SIC: 8093 Specialty outpatient clinics, nec

(G-7047)
DELAWARE SMILE CENTER
201 Carter Dr Ste A (19709-5833)
PHONE..................................302 285-7645
Saqib Usmani, *Prin*
EMP: 15 **EST:** 2007
SALES (est): 633.85K **Privately Held**
Web: www.desmilecenter.com
SIC: 8021 Dentists' office

(G-7048)
DELAWARE WOMENS GOLF ASSN
800 Shallcross Lake Rd (19709-9439)
PHONE..................................302 598-0566
Linda Knorr Sullivan, *Prin*
EMP: 6 **EST:** 2018
SALES (est): 23.29K **Privately Held**
SIC: 7999 Golf services and professionals

(G-7049)
DELAWARE WOOD RENEWAL INC
Also Called: Nhance
2 Rebecca Ct (19709-9016)
PHONE..................................302 750-5167
EMP: 7 **EST:** 2009
SALES (est): 230.56K **Privately Held**
Web: www.nhance.com
SIC: 1752 Floor laying and floor work, nec

(G-7050)
DELMARVA CENTRAL RAILROAD
1275 Lorewood Grove Rd (19709-9481)
PHONE..................................302 449-1576
EMP: 6 **EST:** 2019
SALES (est): 243.11K **Privately Held**
Web: www.carloadexpress.com
SIC: 4011 Railroads, line-haul operating

(G-7051)
DELSTAR TECHNOLOGIES INC (DH)
Also Called: Delnet
601 Industrial Dr (19709-1083)
PHONE..................................302 378-8888
Mark Abrahams, *Pr*
James Dickson, *Corporate Vice President*
William Geissler, *
Timothy Cullen, *
Dennis Eckels, *Corporate Vice President*
◆ **EMP:** 130 **EST:** 1946
SQ FT: 145,000
SALES (est): 93.3MM **Publicly Held**
Web: www.swmintl.com
SIC: 3081 Polypropylene film and sheet
HQ: Delstar Holding Corp.
100 N Point Ctr E Ste 600
Alpharetta GA 30022
800 514-0186

(G-7052)
DEMCO
102 E Kilts Ln (19709-8745)
PHONE..................................302 399-6118
EMP: 5 **EST:** 2014
SALES (est): 56.91K **Privately Held**
Web: www.demcoinc.net
SIC: 5021 Furniture

(G-7053)
DEMO EASEL LLC
221 N Broad St Ste 3a (19709-1070)
PHONE..................................408 242-2770
Kenneth Philipp, *Genl Pt*
EMP: 2 **EST:** 2012
SALES (est): 89K **Privately Held**
SIC: 7372 Prepackaged software

(G-7054)
DENALI CANNING LLC
221 N Broad St 3a (19709-1070)
PHONE..................................272 226-6464
Trent Pezzano, *Managing Member*
EMP: 3 **EST:** 2021
SALES (est): 239.1K **Privately Held**
Web: www.denalicanning.com
SIC: 2033 Canned fruits and specialties

(G-7055)
DESIGNER BRAIDS AND TRADE
148 Vincent Cir (19709-3059)
PHONE..................................718 783-9078
Marion Council-george, *Pr*
Anita Hill, *VP*
EMP: 6 **EST:** 1987
SQ FT: 1,700
SALES (est): 80.11K **Privately Held**
SIC: 7231 5999 5611 5621 Hairdressers; Hair care products; Clothing, male: everyday, except suits and sportswear; Women's clothing stores

(G-7056)
DIALOG ENGINEERS INC
600 N Broad St Ste 5 (19709-1032)
PHONE..................................302 581-8080
Matther Hamer, *CEO*
EMP: 5
SALES (est): 107.01K **Privately Held**
Web: www.dialogengineers.com
SIC: 7371 Computer software development and applications

(G-7057)
DIAMOND STATE SRGCAL ASSOC LLC
102 Sleepy Hollow Dr Ste 101 (19709-5841)
PHONE..................................302 449-9660
Sasha Barrow, *Mgr*
EMP: 10 **EST:** 2017
SALES (est): 179.71K **Privately Held**
Web: www.diamondstatesurgical.com
SIC: 8099 Health and allied services, nec

(G-7058)
DIANN JONES AGCY - NATIONWIDE
226 Horseshoe Dr (19709-1364)
PHONE..................................302 530-1234
Diann Jones, *Prin*
EMP: 5 **EST:** 2012
SALES (est): 89.22K **Privately Held**
SIC: 6411 Insurance agents, nec

(G-7059)
DIAVAEH LUXURY CAR RENTAL LLC
1317 Darling Dr (19709-8508)
PHONE..................................302 497-3443
Dezene Thompson-powell, *Managing Member*
EMP: 5 **EST:** 2021
SALES (est): 81.73K **Privately Held**
SIC: 7514 7389 Passenger car rental; Business services, nec

(G-7060)
DIENAY DISTRIBUTION CORP
101 Trupenny Turn Ste 1b (19709-8965)
PHONE..................................732 766-0814
EMP: 5 **EST:** 2011
SALES (est): 466.27K **Privately Held**
SIC: 5047 Medical and hospital equipment

(G-7061)
DIGILENCE LLC ✪
651 N Broad St Ste 201 (19709-6402)
PHONE..................................678 296-9198
Jessica Beeland, *Managing Member*
EMP: 7 **EST:** 2022
SALES (est): 264.9K **Privately Held**
SIC: 7371 Computer software development

(G-7062)
DIPPOLD MARBLE GRANITE (PA)
110 W Main St (19709-1040)
PHONE..................................302 324-9101
Emmitt Dippold, *Prin*
EMP: 5 **EST:** 2004
SALES (est): 805.48K
SALES (corp-wide): 805.48K **Privately Held**
Web: www.dippoldmarble.com
SIC: 1743 5211 Tile installation, ceramic; Masonry materials and supplies

(G-7063)
DISCOVER PERMACULTURE LLC
651 N Broad St Ste 206 (19709-6402)
PHONE..................................850 970-7376
Mohmad Marei, *Managing Member*
EMP: 6 **EST:** 2020
SALES (est): 119.81K **Privately Held**
SIC: 8299 8742 Educational services; Marketing consulting services

(G-7064)
DIVINE LEGACY GROUP LLC
1025 Sherbourne Rd (19709-8396)
PHONE..................................973 986-7896
EMP: 7
SALES (est): 298.45K **Privately Held**
SIC: 6799 7389 Investment clubs; Business services, nec

(G-7065)
DMAC ENTERPRISES LLC
221 N Broad St (19709-1070)
PHONE..................................917 504-4529
Dara Mcdoanld, *Managing Member*
EMP: 22
SIC: 6719 Personal holding companies, except banks

(G-7066)
DOC OPTICS CENTER
272 Carter Dr (19709-5852)
PHONE..................................302 477-2626
EMP: 8 **EST:** 2017
SALES (est): 95.69K **Privately Held**
Web: www.delawareeyes.com
SIC: 8011 Opthalmologist

(G-7067)
DOG STOP
108 Sleepy Hollow Dr Ste 100 (19709-5848)
PHONE..................................302 376-9006
EMP: 6 **EST:** 2017
SALES (est): 150.21K **Privately Held**
Web: www.thedogstop.com

Middletown - New Castle County (G-7068) GEOGRAPHIC SECTION

SIC: 0752 Grooming services, pet and animal specialties

(G-7068)
DOMAIN HR SOLUTIONS
364 E Main St Ste 1012 (19709-1482)
PHONE...................302 357-9401
Irshad Beg, *Acctg Mgr*
EMP: 10 EST: 2016
SALES (est): 74.08K **Privately Held**
SIC: 7218 Industrial equipment launderers

(G-7069)
DONALD BRIGGS
Also Called: Don Noel Professional Services
400 W Harvest Ln (19709-3046)
PHONE...................267 476-2712
Donald Briggs, *Owner*
EMP: 5 EST: 2012
SALES (est): 126.56K **Privately Held**
SIC: 7538 7549 General automotive repair shops; High performance auto repair and service

(G-7070)
DORIS V OBENSHAIN
Also Called: Doris Obenshain Counseling
100 W Green St (19709-1398)
PHONE...................302 448-1450
Doris Venetta Obenshain, *Prin*
EMP: 5 EST: 2011
SALES (est): 106.96K **Privately Held**
Web: www.daybreakcounseling.org
SIC: 8093 Mental health clinic, outpatient

(G-7071)
DOVER SURGICENTER LLC
108 Patriot Dr Ste A (19709-8803)
PHONE...................302 346-3171
Larry Piccioni, *Prin*
EMP: 22 EST: 2005
SALES (est): 1.79MM **Privately Held**
Web: www.doversurgicenter.com
SIC: 8011 Ambulatory surgical center

(G-7072)
DREYA INC
651 N Broad St Ste 205 # 5784 (19709-6402)
PHONE...................302 265-0759
Rameek Sims, *CEO*
EMP: 7 EST: 2021
SALES (est): 246.26K **Privately Held**
SIC: 7812 Video production

(G-7073)
DS EXPRESS LLC
108 Peachtree Ln (19709-9397)
PHONE...................302 494-4957
EMP: 9 EST: 2019
SALES (est): 469.17K **Privately Held**
SIC: 8099 Health and allied services, nec

(G-7074)
DSR DREW SPARKS REALTY LLC
408 Commodore Dr (19709-8608)
PHONE...................302 743-1210
Drew Sparks, *Prin*
EMP: 5 EST: 2018
SALES (est): 218.4K **Privately Held**
SIC: 6531 Real estate brokers and agents

(G-7075)
DUTCH NECK LAWN AND LDSCP LLC
1210 Dutch Neck Rd (19709-9496)
PHONE...................302 562-3651
Bill Greer, *Owner*
EMP: 6 EST: 2017
SALES (est): 31.52K **Privately Held**
Web: www.dutchnecklawnandlandscape.com
SIC: 0781 Landscape services

(G-7076)
DYNASTY CAR COLLECTION LLC
651 N Broad St Ste 205 (19709-6402)
PHONE...................855 700-6530
Asaru El Bey, *Managing Member*
EMP: 25 EST: 2019
SALES (est): 1MM **Privately Held**
SIC: 4119 Automobile rental, with driver

(G-7077)
EAN HOLDINGS LLC
Also Called: Enterprise Rent-A-Car
5207 Summit Bridge Rd (19709-8823)
PHONE...................302 376-5606
Anthony Jacobs, *Brnch Mgr*
EMP: 8
SALES (corp-wide): 7.04B **Privately Held**
Web: www.enterpriseholdings.com
SIC: 7514 Passenger car rental
HQ: Ean Holdings, Llc
    600 Corporate Park Dr
    Saint Louis MO 63105

(G-7078)
EASYDMARC INC
651 N Broad St Ste 206 (19709-6402)
PHONE...................888 563-5277
EMP: 7 EST: 2020
SALES (est): 558.39K **Privately Held**
Web: www.easydmarc.com
SIC: 8741 Business management

(G-7079)
EAZIFUNDS INC
651 N Broad St Ste 206 (19709-6402)
PHONE...................909 697-6422
O Abdulrahman Okusi, *CEO*
EMP: 15 EST: 2020
SALES (est): 351.35K **Privately Held**
SIC: 7389 Financial services

(G-7080)
ECO CENTRIC SALON
317 W Main St (19709-1766)
PHONE...................302 378-1988
Carla Jennings, *Prin*
EMP: 8 EST: 2019
SALES (est): 210.33K **Privately Held**
Web: www.ecocentricbeauty.com
SIC: 7231 Hairdressers

(G-7081)
ECONAT INC
651 N Broad St Ste 206 (19709-6402)
PHONE...................302 504-4207
Selcuk Yesil, *Pr*
EMP: 3 EST: 2017
SALES (est): 291.28K **Privately Held**
Web: www.econatinc.com
SIC: 3634 Heating units, for electric appliances

(G-7082)
EDFEED FOUNDATION
909 Benalli Dr (19709-6121)
PHONE...................917 459-2762
Jude Onicha, *Ch Bd*
EMP: 11 EST: 2021
SALES (est): 122.59K **Privately Held**
SIC: 8641 Civic and social associations

(G-7083)
EDGE CASE LLC
651 N Broad St (19709-6400)
PHONE...................302 207-1291
EMP: 20

SALES (est): 588.11K **Privately Held**
SIC: 7371 Software programming applications

(G-7084)
EDUCUP INC
651 N Broad St Ste 206 (19709-6402)
PHONE...................305 504-1073
EMP: 4
SALES (est): 56.54K **Privately Held**
SIC: 7372 Educational computer software

(G-7085)
EDWARD HACKENDORN
417 N Broad St (19709-1037)
PHONE...................302 981-5000
Edward Hackendorn, *Prin*
EMP: 6 EST: 2009
SALES (est): 164.31K **Privately Held**
Web: www.hackendornelectric.com
SIC: 1731 Electrical work

(G-7086)
EIGHTH STREET ENTERPRISES LLC
12 W Main St (19709-1000)
PHONE...................302 376-8222
EMP: 5 EST: 2012
SALES (est): 420.98K **Privately Held**
SIC: 8748 Business consulting, nec

(G-7087)
EJ USA INC
401 Industrial Dr (19709)
P.O. Box 510 (19709-0510)
PHONE...................302 378-1100
EMP: 20
Web: www.ejco.com
SIC: 3321 Manhole covers, metal
HQ: Ej Usa, Inc.
    301 Spring St
    East Jordan MI 49727
    800 874-4100

(G-7088)
EL MANAGEMENT GROUP LLC
651 N Broad St (19709-6400)
PHONE...................844 263-3335
EMP: 5
SALES (est): 212.45K **Privately Held**
SIC: 8741 Administrative management

(G-7089)
ELAINE LEONARD
Also Called: Early Essntals Prschool Innvti
111 Patriot Dr Ste A&B (19709-8771)
PHONE...................302 376-5553
Elaine Leonard, *Owner*
EMP: 5 EST: 2016
SALES (est): 74.72K **Privately Held**
SIC: 8351 Preschool center

(G-7090)
ELAYNE JAMES SALON & SPA LLC
221 Porky Oliver Dr (19709-9381)
PHONE...................302 376-5290
James Galoff, *Prin*
EMP: 6 EST: 2008
SALES (est): 247.87K **Privately Held**
Web: www.elaynejamessalon.com
SIC: 7231 Hairdressers

(G-7091)
ELEVATUM CONSULTING LLC ✪
221 N Broad St Ste 3a (19709-1070)
PHONE...................571 330-9016
Audry Okyere, *Managing Member*
EMP: 6 EST: 2022
SALES (est): 204.35K **Privately Held**
SIC: 8721 Auditing services

(G-7092)
ELITE AUTO LLC
364 E Main St Ste 204 (19709-1482)
PHONE...................302 690-2948
Maurice Curtis, *CEO*
EMP: 5 EST: 2011
SALES (est): 223.39K **Privately Held**
SIC: 7538 General automotive repair shops

(G-7093)
ELITE AUTO TRANSPORT
1327 Darling Dr (19709-8508)
PHONE...................302 252-5847
Richmond Alimoh, *Prin*
EMP: 5 EST: 2019
SALES (est): 231.71K **Privately Held**
Web: www.autotransport.co
SIC: 4789 Transportation services, nec

(G-7094)
ELITE FEET LLC
5238 Summit Bridge Rd (19709-8822)
PHONE...................302 464-1028
Jason Hunt, *Managing Member*
EMP: 8 EST: 2014
SALES (est): 904.73K **Privately Held**
Web: www.elitefeet302.com
SIC: 5139 5661 Footwear; Footwear, athletic

(G-7095)
ELITE PROPERTY MAINTENANCE
137 Pine Valley Dr (19709-9789)
PHONE...................302 836-8878
EMP: 6 EST: 2014
SALES (est): 72.94K **Privately Held**
Web: www.elite-property-maintenance.net
SIC: 7349 Building maintenance services, nec

(G-7096)
ELKTON MDDLTOWN ASHTMA ALLERGY
Also Called: Nashed PA
12 Pennington St Ste 100 (19709-1026)
PHONE...................302 378-1887
FAX: 302 378-5130
EMP: 9
SALES (corp-wide): 607.54K **Privately Held**
SIC: 8011 Specialized medical practitioners, except internal
PA: Elkton & Middletown Ashtma & Allergy
    111 W High St Ste 311
    Elkton MD

(G-7097)
ELLI CREATORS INC
651 N Broad St Ste 201 (19709-6400)
PHONE...................269 742-4057
Dalia Ghoush, *CEO*
EMP: 10
SALES (est): 385.96K **Privately Held**
SIC: 4813 Proprietary online service networks

(G-7098)
ELLIE TAX INC
909 Benalli Dr (19709-6121)
PHONE...................917 459-2762
Chia Yu Chang, *CEO*
EMP: 5 EST: 2021
SALES (est): 500K **Privately Held**
SIC: 8721 Accounting, auditing, and bookkeeping

(G-7099)
EMERALD GREEN
992 Port Penn Rd (19709-8932)
PHONE...................302 836-6909

GEOGRAPHIC SECTION
Middletown - New Castle County (G-7128)

Laura Moyer, *Mgr*
EMP: 5 **EST:** 2005
SALES (est): 437.16K **Privately Held**
Web: www.emeraldgreenlawns.com
SIC: 0782 Lawn care services

(G-7100)
ENCLOSED AUTO SOLUTIONS LLC
229 Liborio Dr (19709-3108)
PHONE.............................302 437-9858
EMP: 6 **EST:** 2017
SALES (est): 225.87K **Privately Held**
SIC: 7538 General automotive repair shops

(G-7101)
ENCOMPASS HEALTH CORPORATION
Also Called: HealthSouth
250 E Hampden Rd (19709-5303)
PHONE.............................302 464-3400
EMP: 12
SALES (corp-wide): 4.35B **Publicly Held**
Web: www.encompasshealth.com
SIC: 8093 Rehabilitation center, outpatient treatment
PA: Encompass Health Corporation
9001 Liberty Pkwy
Birmingham AL 35242
205 967-7116

(G-7102)
ENTERPRISE RENT-A-CAR
Also Called: Enterprise Rent-A-Car
753 N Broad St (19709-1171)
PHONE.............................302 376-5606
EMP: 7 **EST:** 1957
SALES (est): 101.15K **Privately Held**
Web: www.enterprise.com
SIC: 7514 Rent-a-car service

(G-7103)
ENVIRONMENTAL CONSULTING SVCS (PA)
100 S Cass St (19709-1354)
P.O. Box 138 (19709-0138)
PHONE.............................302 378-9881
Alvin Maiden, *Pr*
Gary A Hayes, *VP*
EMP: 12 **EST:** 1984
SQ FT: 3,800
SALES (est): 2.19MM
SALES (corp-wide): 2.19MM **Privately Held**
Web: www.ecsi-del.com
SIC: 8731 8748 Environmental research; Environmental consultant

(G-7104)
ENVIRONMENTAL TESTING INC
100 S Cass St (19709-1354)
P.O. Box 138 (19709-0138)
PHONE.............................302 378-5341
Gary Hayes, *Pr*
A L Maiden, *Sec*
C C Miller, *VP*
EMP: 6 **EST:** 1988
SQ FT: 3,800
SALES (est): 1.02MM
SALES (corp-wide): 2.19MM **Privately Held**
Web: www.envirosureinc.com
SIC: 8748 8731 Environmental consultant; Natural resource research
PA: Environmental Consulting Services, Inc
100 S Cass St
Middletown DE 19709
302 378-9881

(G-7105)
EPIC MARKETING CONS CORP
10 Jackie Cir (19709-9369)
PHONE.............................302 285-9790
Nancy Dibert, *CEO*
Donald Dibert, *Pr*
EMP: 20 **EST:** 2009
SALES (est): 2.22MM **Privately Held**
Web: www.epicmc2.com
SIC: 7311 8742 Advertising agencies; Marketing consulting services

(G-7106)
EPTIKAR IT SOLUTIONS INC
651 N Broad St (19709-6400)
PHONE.............................720 422-8441
Mohanad Ali, *Pr*
EMP: 12
SALES (est): 251.15K **Privately Held**
Web: www.eptikar.com
SIC: 7371 Computer software development and applications

(G-7107)
EQUINE TECHNOLOGIES INC ✪
651 N Broad St Ste 205 (19709-6402)
PHONE.............................669 306-6009
Matthew Greenleaf, *Prin*
EMP: 3 **EST:** 2022
SALES (est): 128.34K **Privately Held**
SIC: 7372 Prepackaged software

(G-7108)
EROSION CTRL SPECIALISTS INC
364 E Main St Pmb 332 (19709-1482)
PHONE.............................302 367-6649
EMP: 9 **EST:** 2006
SALES (est): 174.9K **Privately Held**
Web: erosion-control-specialist.business.site
SIC: 0783 Ornamental shrub and tree services

(G-7109)
ESQUIRE PLUMBING & HEATING CO
7 Wood St (19709-1048)
P.O. Box 441 (19709-0441)
PHONE.............................302 378-7001
Virginia Briccotto, *Pr*
Robert Briccotto Junior, *VP*
Virginia Briccotto, *Pr*
EMP: 7 **EST:** 1971
SQ FT: 3,500
SALES (est): 989.67K **Privately Held**
SIC: 1711 Warm air heating and air conditioning contractor

(G-7110)
ESSEN TECHNOLOGIES INC
651 N Broad St (19709-6400)
PHONE.............................617 959-9595
EMP: 5 **EST:** 2020
SALES (est): 46.16K **Privately Held**
SIC: 7371 Computer software development and applications

(G-7111)
EVANIX ENTERPRISES LLC
49 W Sarazen Dr (19709-9358)
PHONE.............................302 384-1806
EMP: 5 **EST:** 2016
SALES (est): 399.83K **Privately Held**
SIC: 4731 Freight forwarding

(G-7112)
EVERETT INC
47 W Main St (19709-1017)
PHONE.............................302 378-7038
Christopher Everett, *Ofcr*
EMP: 6 **EST:** 2001

SALES (est): 197.07K **Privately Held**
Web: www.everetttheatre.com
SIC: 7832 Motion picture theaters, except drive-in

(G-7113)
EVOLUTION ENTERPRISE LLC
610 Wesley Ct (19709-2192)
PHONE.............................302 602-1875
EMP: 5 **EST:** 2019
SALES (est): 53.68K **Privately Held**
SIC: 7922 Entertainment promotion

(G-7114)
EXERCOMM INC
335 Jessica Dr (19709-4013)
PHONE.............................302 438-6130
Keith Yocum, *Owner*
EMP: 5 **EST:** 2009
SALES (est): 244.86K **Privately Held**
SIC: 7389 Business Activities at Non-Commercial Site

(G-7115)
EXPERT HOME CARE LLC
504 Silverhill Xing (19709-6842)
PHONE.............................856 870-6691
Agememnon M Davis, *Mgr*
EMP: 9 **EST:** 2018
SALES (est): 164.84K **Privately Held**
SIC: 8082 Home health care services

(G-7116)
EZANGACOM INC
222 Carter Dr Ste 201 (19709-5857)
PHONE.............................888 439-2642
Richard K Kahn, *Pr*
Beth Kahn, *
EMP: 42 **EST:** 2004
SQ FT: 7,500
SALES (est): 5.86MM **Privately Held**
Web: www.ezanga.com
SIC: 7374 Computer graphics service

(G-7117)
F AND D EQUIPMENT & REPAIR LLC
213 W Lake St Unit F (19709-1757)
PHONE.............................302 378-1999
EMP: 4 **EST:** 2016
SALES (est): 57.61K **Privately Held**
SIC: 7694 Motor repair services

(G-7118)
F PETE LISINSKI LAND SURVEYOR
1848 Choptank Rd (19709-9648)
PHONE.............................302 378-3200
F Pete Lisinski, *Prin*
EMP: 5 **EST:** 2007
SALES (est): 134.39K **Privately Held**
SIC: 8713 Surveying services

(G-7119)
FAMILY CARE CONNECTIONS
225 Armata Dr (19709-9824)
PHONE.............................856 579-7303
Bruce Betner, *Prin*
EMP: 12 **EST:** 2019
SALES (est): 110.65K **Privately Held**
Web: www.azfcc.org
SIC: 8322 General counseling services

(G-7120)
FAMILY DEPOSITORY ALLIANCE
651 N Broad St Ste 201 (19709-6402)
PHONE.............................888 332-6275
Kevin Winters, *Pr*
EMP: 10 **EST:** 2020
SALES (est): 500K **Privately Held**
SIC: 7941 Sports promotion

(G-7121)
FARAMOVE INC
651 N Broad St (19709-6400)
PHONE.............................815 674-3114
Adewale Opaleye, *CEO*
EMP: 10
SALES (est): 414.81K **Privately Held**
SIC: 4731 7371 Freight transportation arrangement; Computer software development and applications

(G-7122)
FARANARIUM INC
600 N Broad St Ste 5 (19709-1032)
PHONE.............................716 235-5950
Stanislav Honcharinko, *Pr*
EMP: 14 **EST:** 2021
SALES (est): 200K **Privately Held**
SIC: 1799 Cleaning building exteriors, nec

(G-7123)
FARRELL ROOFING INC
201 W Lake St (19709-1755)
PHONE.............................302 378-7663
T Paul Farrell, *Pr*
Paula J Farrel, *VP*
Frank E Clark, *Dir*
EMP: 22 **EST:** 2007
SQ FT: 5,000
SALES (est): 4.56MM **Privately Held**
Web: www.farrellroofinginc.com
SIC: 1761 1799 Roofing contractor; Waterproofing

(G-7124)
FELIXCHEM CORP INC
110 W Main St (19709-1040)
PHONE.............................302 376-0199
EMP: 7 **EST:** 2010
SALES (est): 243.94K **Privately Held**
Web: www.felixchem.com
SIC: 1743 Tile installation, ceramic

(G-7125)
FERGUSON VENTURES
600 N Broad St (19709-1032)
PHONE.............................484 561-3510
Clarence Ferguson, *CEO*
EMP: 5
SALES (est): 103.98K **Privately Held**
SIC: 7542 Carwashes

(G-7126)
FILE RIGHT LLC
364 E Main St (19709-1482)
PHONE.............................302 757-7107
Justin Workman, *Prin*
EMP: 7 **EST:** 2011
SALES (est): 246.26K **Privately Held**
Web: www.fileright.com
SIC: 7371 Computer software development and applications

(G-7127)
FILEC SERVICES LLC
680 Port Penn Rd (19709-9435)
P.O. Box 227 (19730-0227)
PHONE.............................302 328-7188
EMP: 14 **EST:** 2010
SALES (est): 1.16MM **Privately Held**
Web: www.filecservices.com
SIC: 1731 General electrical contractor

(G-7128)
FINNCHAT INC
651 N Broad St Ste 206 (19709-6402)
PHONE.............................517 258-6991
Theophilus Ederaro, *CEO*
EMP: 5 **EST:** 2020
SALES (est): 100K **Privately Held**

Middletown - New Castle County (G-7129)

SIC: 7371 Software programming applications

(G-7129)
FIRESTONE COMPLETE AUTO C ◆
202 Casa Dr (19709-5839)
PHONE..................................302 437-0497
EMP: 7 EST: 2023
SALES (est): 64.69K **Privately Held**
Web: www.bridgestonetire.com
SIC: 7538 General automotive repair shops

(G-7130)
FIRST LOVE MINISTRIES INC
853 Bullen Dr (19709-8973)
PHONE..................................302 655-1776
Susan Napier, *Pr*
EMP: 5 EST: 2021
SALES (est): 46.17K **Privately Held**
SIC: 8661 7389 Religious organizations; Business services, nec

(G-7131)
FIRST STATE BREWING CO LLC
109 Patriot Dr (19709-8760)
PHONE..................................302 285-9535
Paul Hester, *Managing Member*
EMP: 40 EST: 2014
SALES (est): 2.72MM **Privately Held**
Web: www.firststatebrewing.com
SIC: 2082 5813 5812 Malt beverages; Drinking places; Eating places

(G-7132)
FIRST STATE INSPECTION AGENCY
811 N Broad St Ste 201 (19709-1173)
PHONE..................................302 449-5383
Robert Smith, *Brnch Mgr*
EMP: 5
SALES (corp-wide): 2.24MM **Privately Held**
Web: www.firststateinspection.com
SIC: 7389 Building inspection service
PA: First State Inspection Agency Inc
1001 Mattlind Way
Milford DE 19963
302 422-3859

(G-7133)
FIRST STATE NEUROLOGY LLC
114 Sandhill Dr Ste 201a (19709-5807)
PHONE..................................302 293-7524
Richard J Schumann, *Prin*
EMP: 9 EST: 2009
SALES (est): 154.86K **Privately Held**
SIC: 8011 Neurologist

(G-7134)
FIRST STATE PATRIOTS INC
103 Avian Way (19709-9296)
PHONE..................................302 378-6092
EMP: 5 EST: 2011
SALES (est): 37.06K **Privately Held**
Web: www.firststatepatriots.com
SIC: 8699 Charitable organization

(G-7135)
FITAR INC
651 N Broad St Ste 201 (19709-6400)
PHONE..................................416 347-8099
Matthew Collie, *CEO*
EMP: 5
SALES (est): 101.79K **Privately Held**
SIC: 7999 Physical fitness instruction

(G-7136)
FIVE STARS EMBROIDERY
224 Milford Dr (19709-9417)
PHONE..................................443 466-9692
Tamara Lewis, *Owner*

Marion Hughes, *Owner*
EMP: 2 EST: 2004
SALES (est): 111.2K **Privately Held**
SIC: 2395 Embroidery products, except Schiffli machine

(G-7137)
FLORIAN P LISINSKI INC
1848 Choptank Rd (19709-9648)
PHONE..................................302 378-3200
F Lisinski, *Prin*
EMP: 5 EST: 2017
SALES (est): 44.22K **Privately Held**
SIC: 8713 Surveying services

(G-7138)
FOR THEM INC
651 N Broad St Ste 206 (19709-6402)
PHONE..................................646 623-4041
Chloe Freeman, *CEO*
EMP: 10 EST: 2021
SALES (est): 276.87K **Privately Held**
SIC: 7922 Theatrical producers

(G-7139)
FOREVER INC
Also Called: Fulton Paper
328 E Main St (19709-1482)
PHONE..................................302 449-2100
Lisa Stoddard, *Pr*
EMP: 7
SALES (corp-wide): 2.26MM **Privately Held**
Web: www.fultonparty.com
SIC: 5113 Paper, wrapping or coarse, and products
PA: Forever, Inc.
1006 W 27th St
Wilmington DE 19802
302 594-0400

(G-7140)
FREEDOM TECH CONSULTING LLC
221 N Broad St Ste 3a (19709-1070)
PHONE..................................215 485-7383
David Judge, *CEO*
David Judge, *Managing Member*
EMP: 5 EST: 2021
SALES (est): 60.47K **Privately Held**
SIC: 8748 7389 Business consulting, nec; Business services, nec

(G-7141)
FRIGHTLAND LLC
309 Port Penn Rd (19709-9732)
PHONE..................................302 838-0256
EMP: 9 EST: 2011
SALES (est): 207.88K **Privately Held**
Web: www.frightland.com
SIC: 7999 Amusement and recreation, nec

(G-7142)
FROG HOLLOW GOLF COURSE
1 Wittington Way (19709-7906)
PHONE..................................302 376-6500
Alan Liddicoat, *Pt*
Ken Kershaw, *Pt*
EMP: 15 EST: 2000
SALES (est): 440.23K **Privately Held**
Web: www.froghollowgolfclub.com
SIC: 7992 Public golf courses

(G-7143)
FROM TOP LTD (PA) ◆
651 N Broad St Ste 201 (19709-6402)
PHONE..................................310 626-0090
Joey Winshman, *CEO*
EMP: 8 EST: 2022
SALES (est): 312.73K
SALES (corp-wide): 312.73K **Privately Held**

SIC: 7311 Advertising agencies

(G-7144)
FULTON BANK NATIONAL ASSN
Also Called: Fulton Financial Advisors
468 W Main St (19709-1063)
PHONE..................................302 378-4575
EMP: 9
SALES (corp-wide): 1.09B **Publicly Held**
Web: www.fultonbank.com
SIC: 6022 State commercial banks
HQ: Fulton Bank, National Association
1 Penn Sq
Lancaster PA 17602
717 581-3166

(G-7145)
G B TECH INC
651 N Broad St Ste 301 (19709-6403)
PHONE..................................302 378-5600
Sudheer Bathula, *Pr*
EMP: 50 EST: 1997
SALES (est): 2.41MM **Privately Held**
Web: www.gbtechinc.com
SIC: 7379 Online services technology consultants

(G-7146)
G G + A LLC
1050 Industrial Dr Ste 110 (19709-2801)
PHONE..................................302 376-6122
EMP: 24 EST: 2005
SALES (est): 2.45MM **Privately Held**
SIC: 1521 General remodeling, single-family houses

(G-7147)
G TS FOODS INC
428 E Main St (19709-1462)
PHONE..................................302 376-3555
Theresa A Ambrosine, *Prin*
EMP: 6 EST: 2016
SALES (est): 124.27K **Privately Held**
SIC: 1541 Food products manufacturing or packing plant construction

(G-7148)
G5 CYBER SECURITY (USA) INC
651 N Broad St Ste 206 (19709-6402)
PHONE..................................302 570-0905
Gavin Dennis, *Pr*
EMP: 20 EST: 2020
SALES (est): 1.03MM **Privately Held**
Web: www.g5cybersecurity.com
SIC: 8742 Management consulting services

(G-7149)
GAMBERS LLC
221 N Broad St (19709-1070)
PHONE..................................402 218-7929
Christopher Chambers, *Managing Member*
EMP: 2 EST: 2021
SALES (est): 92.41K **Privately Held**
SIC: 2824 Acrylic fibers

(G-7150)
GAMERSUNITE INC ◆
601 N Broad St Ste 201 (19709-1052)
PHONE..................................760 284-5588
Nicolas Brstilo, *Genl Mgr*
EMP: 18 EST: 2022
SALES (est): 583.41K **Privately Held**
SIC: 7371 Custom computer programming services

(G-7151)
GARCIAS AUTO REPAIR
213 W Lake St (19709-1754)
PHONE..................................302 464-1118
EMP: 7 EST: 2016

SALES (est): 210.03K **Privately Held**
SIC: 7538 General automotive repair shops

(G-7152)
GB JACOBS LLC
Also Called: Grow & Learn Childcare Center
2486 N Dupont Pkwy (19709-9653)
PHONE..................................302 378-9100
Kari Kroll, *Mgr*
EMP: 15 EST: 2016
SQ FT: 5,500
SALES (est): 246.48K **Privately Held**
SIC: 8351 Group day care center

(G-7153)
GEM SCHOOL INC
100 Patriot Dr (19709-8763)
PHONE..................................302 464-1711
Clarissa Paterson D.o.s., *Prin*
EMP: 10 EST: 2017
SALES (est): 231.38K **Privately Held**
SIC: 8351 Preschool center

(G-7154)
GENE GUARD INC (PA)
651 N Broad St Ste 206 (19709-6402)
PHONE..................................248 479-3623
Radu Andrei Tanasa, *CEO*
EMP: 6 EST: 2021
SALES (est): 556.36K
SALES (corp-wide): 556.36K **Privately Held**
Web: www.geneguard.bio
SIC: 8731 Biotechnical research, commercial

(G-7155)
GEORGE PRODUCTS COMPANY INC
110 Sleepy Hollow Dr (19709-8894)
PHONE..................................302 449-0199
Fred Land, *Pr*
Dawn Land, *VP*
George Kreshock, *Treas*
EMP: 18 EST: 1951
SQ FT: 20,000
SALES (est): 2.62MM
SALES (corp-wide): 2.62MM **Privately Held**
Web: www.georgeproducts.com
SIC: 3469 Ornamental metal stampings
PA: Junia Holdings Inc.
110 Sleepy Hollow Dr
Middletown DE 19709
302 449-0199

(G-7156)
GERALD 1MCCARTHY
1061 Dutch Neck Rd (19709-9493)
PHONE..................................302 836-3171
Gerald Mccarthy, *Prin*
EMP: 5 EST: 2012
SALES (est): 127.86K **Privately Held**
Web: www.mccarthytreefarm.com
SIC: 0191 General farms, primarily crop

(G-7157)
GFC LEASING LLC
4783 Summit Bridge Rd (19709-8815)
PHONE..................................302 449-5006
Terri Seemans, *Prin*
EMP: 5 EST: 2019
SALES (est): 460.92K **Privately Held**
SIC: 7359 Equipment rental and leasing, nec

(G-7158)
GGA CONSTRUCTION
1285 Cedar Lane Rd (19709-9636)
PHONE..................................302 376-5193
EMP: 5 EST: 2016
SALES (est): 92.1K **Privately Held**
Web: www.ggabuilds.com

GEOGRAPHIC SECTION
Middletown - New Castle County (G-7188)

SIC: **1521** Single-family housing construction

(G-7159)
GGA CONSTRUCTION
1130 Industrial Dr (19709-1187)
PHONE..................................302 376-6122
EMP: 23 **EST:** 2018
SALES (est): 9.76MM **Privately Held**
Web: www.ggabuilds.com
SIC: **1542** Commercial and office building, new construction

(G-7160)
GILBERT ARCHITECTS INC
100 S Broad St (19709-1467)
PHONE..................................302 449-2492
Thomas Gilbert, *CEO*
EMP: 10 **EST:** 2017
SALES (est): 164.68K **Privately Held**
Web: www.gilbertarchitects.com
SIC: **8712** Architectural engineering

(G-7161)
GILBERT PERRY CENTER FOR ARTS
51 W Main St (19709-1017)
PHONE..................................302 378-2932
EMP: 7 **EST:** 2016
SALES (est): 48.34K **Privately Held**
Web: www.theeverett.org
SIC: **8412** Arts or science center

(G-7162)
GLANCE CAPITAL INC
651 N Broad St (19709-6400)
PHONE..................................800 825-9889
EMP: 6
SALES (est): 216.97K **Privately Held**
Web: www.glancecapital.com
SIC: **6141** Consumer finance companies

(G-7163)
GLOBAL COMPUTERS NETWORKS LLC
718 Pinewood Dr Ste 2 (19709-8643)
PHONE..................................484 686-8374
Dominique Pereira, *Prin*
Harlen King, *Prin*
EMP: 7
SALES (est): 103.89K **Privately Held**
SIC: **8243** 7372 Repair training, computer; Application computer software

(G-7164)
GLOBAL EXTERIOR
325 Clayton Manor Dr (19709-8859)
P.O. Box 842 (19709-0842)
PHONE..................................302 449-1559
EMP: 5 **EST:** 2018
SALES (est): 472.49K **Privately Held**
SIC: **1522** Residential construction, nec

(G-7165)
GLOBAL PHI TRADING COMPANY LLC
651 N Broad St Ste 206 (19709-6402)
PHONE..................................404 759-8409
Yida Gao, *Managing Member*
EMP: 5 **EST:** 2020
SALES (est): 294.95K **Privately Held**
SIC: **5047** Industrial safety devices: first aid kits and masks

(G-7166)
GM REALESTATE
503 S Broad St (19709-1464)
PHONE..................................302 376-9362
Laura Johnson, *Prin*
EMP: 5 **EST:** 2015
SALES (est): 85.03K **Privately Held**

SIC: **6531** Real estate brokers and agents

(G-7167)
GO GO PROF CLG SVCS LLC
1117 Westown Way (19709-9545)
P.O. Box 242 (19710-0242)
PHONE..................................302 729-2883
EMP: 10 **EST:** 2021
SALES (est): 197.57K **Privately Held**
SIC: **7349** Janitorial service, contract basis

(G-7168)
GO TEES LLC
101 Arcadia Pkwy (19709-1329)
PHONE..................................708 703-1788
Christine Degliobizzi, *Prin*
EMP: 4 **EST:** 2016
SALES (est): 125.48K **Privately Held**
SIC: **2759** Screen printing

(G-7169)
GOLDEN GATE INVESTMENTS LLC
651 N Broad St Ste 205 (19709-6402)
PHONE..................................302 894-8922
EMP: 5 **EST:** 2021
SALES (est): 256.55K **Privately Held**
Web: www.goldengatecap.com
SIC: **6799** Real estate investors, except property operators

(G-7170)
GORDON C HONIG DMD PA
104 Sleepy Hollow Dr (19709-5842)
PHONE..................................302 696-4020
EMP: 5
SALES (corp-wide): 977.23K **Privately Held**
Web: www.honigorthodontics.com
SIC: **8021** Orthodontist
PA: Gordon C Honig Dmd Pa
2707 Kirkwood Hwy
Newark DE 19711
302 737-6333

(G-7171)
GOURMETCARTE INC
600 N Broad St (19709-1032)
PHONE..................................631 418-6170
David Zhong, *CEO*
EMP: 5
SALES (est): 199.4K **Privately Held**
SIC: **7371** Computer software development and applications

(G-7172)
GOVPLUS LLC
Also Called: GOVPLUS LLC
460 E Main St (19709-1462)
PHONE..................................302 376-3641
Danielle Cummins, *Mgr*
EMP: 7
SALES (corp-wide): 9.07B **Publicly Held**
Web: www.govplus.com
SIC: **6022** State commercial banks
HQ: Citizens Bank, National Association
1 Citizens Plz
Providence RI 02903

(G-7173)
GRC & ASSOCIATES LLC
1419 Westown Way (19709-9615)
PHONE..................................770 484-9082
Raelyn Coleman, *Pr*
EMP: 6 **EST:** 2015
SALES (est): 77.45K **Privately Held**
SIC: **7291** 8721 Tax return preparation services; Accounting services, except auditing

(G-7174)
GREAT NEW BGNNNGS MDDLTOWN INC
Also Called: Early Education
210 Cleaver Farms Rd Ste 3 (19709-1670)
PHONE..................................302 378-5555
Linda Clark, *Pr*
Kristin Tomczak, *
Jessica Coleman, *
Pamela Maiorano, *
EMP: 30 **EST:** 2019
SALES (est): 377.35K **Privately Held**
Web: www.gnbkids.com
SIC: **8351** Preschool center

(G-7175)
GREAT THING INC
651 N Broad St Ste 201 (19709-6400)
PHONE..................................302 314-3909
Borja Terol, *CEO*
EMP: 2
SALES (est): 87.4K **Privately Held**
SIC: **7372** Business oriented computer software

(G-7176)
GREENHILL CAR WASH
890 Middletown Warwick Rd (19709-9542)
PHONE..................................302 420-5961
Doug Rogers, *Prin*
EMP: 7 **EST:** 2017
SALES (est): 97.97K **Privately Held**
Web: www.greenhillcarwash.com
SIC: **7542** Washing and polishing, automotive

(G-7177)
GREENHILL EXPRESS CAR WASH
299 E Main St (19709-1449)
PHONE..................................302 464-1031
EMP: 7 **EST:** 2015
SALES (est): 86.27K **Privately Held**
Web: www.greenhillcarwash.com
SIC: **7542** Washing and polishing, automotive

(G-7178)
GREENWICH AEROGROUP INC
4200 Summit Bridge Rd (19709-9340)
P.O. Box 258 (19709-0258)
PHONE..................................302 834-5400
EMP: 12 **EST:** 2011
SALES (est): 1.4MM
SALES (corp-wide): 11.17B **Publicly Held**
Web: www.greenwichaerogroup.com
SIC: **3724** Research and development on aircraft engines and parts
PA: W. R. Berkley Corporation
475 Steamboat Rd Fl 1
Greenwich CT 06830
203 629-3000

(G-7179)
GROWING PALACE
111 Patriot Dr Ste A (19709-8771)
PHONE..................................302 376-5553
Drexann Fields, *Prin*
EMP: 10 **EST:** 2016
SALES (est): 165.59K **Privately Held**
SIC: **8351** Child day care services

(G-7180)
GROWING PALACE III
Also Called: Growing Palace 3, The
111 Patriot Dr Ste A (19709-8771)
PHONE..................................302 376-5553
Ranika Holmes, *Owner*
EMP: 13 **EST:** 2018
SALES (est): 168.35K **Privately Held**

SIC: **8351** Child day care services

(G-7181)
GT DESIGNS INC
109 Wellington Way (19709-9406)
PHONE..................................302 275-8100
Greg Tweddell, *Pr*
EMP: 5 **EST:** 2008
SALES (est): 248.35K **Privately Held**
Web: www.ceogt-designs.com
SIC: **7389** Design services

(G-7182)
GUARDIAN FENCE COMPANY
4783 Summit Bridge Rd (19709-8815)
PHONE..................................302 834-3044
Ruth Ann Seemans, *Pr*
David Seemans, *VP*
Terri Seemans, *Sec*
EMP: 12 **EST:** 1957
SALES (est): 2.18MM **Privately Held**
Web: www.guardian-fence.com
SIC: **1799** Fence construction

(G-7183)
H & E TRUCKING CO LLC
581 Old State Rd (19709-9182)
PHONE..................................302 287-2113
EMP: 6 **EST:** 2001
SALES (est): 520K **Privately Held**
SIC: **4231** Trucking terminal facilities

(G-7184)
H & R BLOCK
Also Called: H & R Block
705 Middletown Warwick Rd (19709-9095)
PHONE..................................302 378-1538
EMP: 7 **EST:** 2018
SALES (est): 111.02K **Privately Held**
Web: www.hrblock.com
SIC: **7291** Tax return preparation services

(G-7185)
H & R BLOCK INC
Also Called: H & R Block
Middletown Shopping Ctr (19709)
PHONE..................................302 378-8931
George Manz, *Mgr*
EMP: 5
SALES (corp-wide): 3.47B **Publicly Held**
Web: www.hrblock.com
SIC: **7291** Tax return preparation services
PA: H & R Block, Inc.
1 H And R Block Way
Kansas City MO 64105
816 854-3000

(G-7186)
H B P INC (PA)
110 W Green St (19709-1317)
PHONE..................................302 378-9693
EMP: 31 **EST:** 1994
SALES (est): 5.89MM **Privately Held**
Web: www.phb-inc.com
SIC: **1521** New construction, single-family houses

(G-7187)
H&H CUSTOMS INC
708 Lorewood Grove Rd (19709-9428)
PHONE..................................302 378-0810
EMP: 2 **EST:** 1999
SALES (est): 138.88K **Privately Held**
SIC: **2449** Rectangular boxes and crates, wood

(G-7188)
H+TRACE INC
651 N Broad St (19709-6400)
PHONE..................................954 381-1400

Emiliano Buitrago, *CEO*
EMP: 7 EST: 2021
SALES (est): 155.65K **Privately Held**
SIC: **8049** Offices of health practitioner

(G-7189)
HAIR YARD
11 Wood St Ste D (19709-1098)
P.O. Box 144 (19709-0144)
PHONE..................................302 264-0594
Toni Rice, *Owner*
EMP: 5 EST: 2017
SALES (est): 57.67K **Privately Held**
SIC: **7231** Hairdressers

(G-7190)
HALPERN EYE ASSOCIATES INC
223 E Main St (19709-1449)
PHONE..................................302 734-5861
Joel Halpern, *Owner*
EMP: 5
SALES (corp-wide): 9.06MM **Privately Held**
Web: www.myeyedr.com
SIC: **8042** Contact lens specialist optometrist
PA: Halpern Eye Associates, Inc.
    885 S Governors Ave
    Dover DE 19904
    302 734-5861

(G-7191)
HAMPTON INN MIDDLETOWN
Also Called: Hampton By Hilton
117 Sandhill Dr (19709-5813)
PHONE..................................302 378-5656
Linda Dunn, *Mgr*
EMP: 26 EST: 2008
SALES (est): 459.37K **Privately Held**
Web: www.hilton.com
SIC: **7011** Hotels and motels

(G-7192)
HAND STONE MASSAGE FACIAL SPA
401 S Ridge Ave (19709-4688)
PHONE..................................302 643-2991
EMP: 6 EST: 2018
SALES (est): 66.82K **Privately Held**
Web: www.handandstone.com
SIC: **7299** Massage parlor

(G-7193)
HANDY HANDYMAN
630 Vivaldi Dr (19709-6618)
PHONE..................................267 307-5206
Mario Bercholc, *Prin*
EMP: 5 EST: 2018
SALES (est): 141.56K **Privately Held**
SIC: **7299** Handyman service

(G-7194)
HANDYTECH SOLUTIONS LLC
308 John Randal Dr (19709-9263)
PHONE..................................302 449-4497
Christian Maldonado, *Prin*
EMP: 6 EST: 2010
SALES (est): 81K **Privately Held**
Web: www.handytechsolutions.com
SIC: **7378** Computer and data processing equipment repair/maintenance

(G-7195)
HAPPY PL CHILD CARE MDDLTOWN L
4922 Summit Bridge Rd (19709-8818)
PHONE..................................302 449-3311
Sam Tawfik, *CEO*
EMP: 14 EST: 2018
SALES (est): 200.51K **Privately Held**
Web: www.happyplacedaycare.net

SIC: **8351** Preschool center

(G-7196)
HARDWOOD DIRECT LLC
4390 Summit Bridge Rd Ste 5 (19709)
PHONE..................................302 378-3692
John Demers, *Managing Member*
Lorraine Demers, *CFO*
EMP: 4 EST: 2013
SQ FT: 1,200
SALES (est): 487.28K **Privately Held**
Web: www.hardwooddirectllc.com
SIC: **5999** 2426 Alarm signal systems; Blanks, wood: bowling pins, handles, etc.

(G-7197)
HARMON LARHONDA
734 Rothwell Dr (19709-1749)
PHONE..................................302 747-0700
La-rhonda Harmon, *Owner*
EMP: 6 EST: 2017
SALES (est): 50.16K **Privately Held**
SIC: **8322** General counseling services

(G-7198)
HBM APPS INC
51 N Broad St (19709-1033)
PHONE..................................302 387-0052
Ashraf Mourad, *Pr*
EMP: 6
SALES (est): 237.56K **Privately Held**
SIC: **7371** Computer software development

(G-7199)
HC SALON HOLDINGS INC
Also Called: Hair Cuttery
659 Middletown Warwick Rd (19709-9639)
PHONE..................................302 378-8565
EMP: 25
SALES (corp-wide): 95.49MM **Privately Held**
Web: www.haircuttery.com
SIC: **7231** Unisex hair salons
PA: Hc Salon Holdings, Inc.
    1640 Boro Pl Fl 4
    Mc Lean VA 22102
    917 751-8869

(G-7200)
HEADQUARTER BARBER SHOP
217 E Main St (19709-1449)
PHONE..................................302 378-7372
Pheob Milford, *Owner*
EMP: 5 EST: 2011
SALES (est): 56.77K **Privately Held**
SIC: **7241** Barber shops

(G-7201)
HEALTHY SNACKS HOLDINGS INC
Also Called: Pink Panda
651 N Broad St Ste 206 (19709-6402)
PHONE..................................917 540-6588
Noah Bernett, *CEO*
Ron Hinkle, *Dir*
EMP: 5 EST: 2021
SALES (est): 675.51K **Privately Held**
SIC: **1541** Food products manufacturing or packing plant construction

(G-7202)
HEART AND VASCULAR CLINIC PA
118 Sandhill Dr Ste 104 (19709-5859)
PHONE..................................302 261-8200
EMP: 9 EST: 2019
SALES (est): 120.19K **Privately Held**
Web: www.heartandvascularclinic.com
SIC: **8011** Cardiologist and cardio-vascular specialist

(G-7203)
HELIX INC TA AUDIOWORKS
478 Middletown Warwick Rd (19709-9192)
PHONE..................................302 285-0555
Ben Holland, *Prin*
EMP: 4 EST: 2006
SALES (est): 57.88K **Privately Held**
SIC: **3651** Audio electronic systems

(G-7204)
HELIX SERVICES LLC
651 N Broad St Ste 205-1930 (19709-6400)
PHONE..................................302 306-4880
Jafar Shah, *Managing Member*
EMP: 5
SALES (est): 74.44K **Privately Held**
SIC: **1321** Natural gas liquids

(G-7205)
HEMPVILLE INC
651 N Broad St Ste 206 (19709-6402)
PHONE..................................336 862-0107
Taimour Azhar, *CEO*
EMP: 2 EST: 2020
SALES (est): 116.46K **Privately Held**
SIC: **2282** Acetate filament yarn: throwing, twisting, winding, spooling

(G-7206)
HERDIFY LLC
651 N Broad St Ste 205 (19709-6402)
PHONE..................................619 405-3952
EMP: 7 EST: 2021
SALES (est): 268.74K **Privately Held**
SIC: **7371** Computer software systems analysis and design, custom

(G-7207)
HERMS FREIGHT LLC
651 N Broad St Ste 205 (19709-6400)
PHONE..................................321 417-4884
EMP: 5
SALES (est): 392.44K **Privately Held**
SIC: **4731** Freight transportation arrangement

(G-7208)
HETRICK-DRAKE ASSOCIATES INC
Also Called: Hetrick, C H Associates
1220 N Olmsted Pkwy (19709-9993)
PHONE..................................302 998-7500
Peter Drake, *Pr*
John Walsh, *Sec*
Dennis Dorsey, *Stockholder*
EMP: 9 EST: 1948
SALES (est): 820.97K **Privately Held**
Web: www.chhetrick.com
SIC: **6411** Insurance claim adjusters, not employed by insurance company

(G-7209)
HEY LOGISTICS LLC
651 N Broad St (19709-6400)
PHONE..................................706 350-5539
EMP: 10
SALES (est): 414.81K **Privately Held**
SIC: **4731** Freight transportation arrangement

(G-7210)
HILTON GARDEN INN DOVER
Also Called: Hilton Garden Inns
416 Tartan Dr (19709-1641)
PHONE..................................302 465-3061
Wendy Stephens, *Prin*
EMP: 11 EST: 2018
SALES (est): 35.85K **Privately Held**
Web: www.hilton.com
SIC: **7011** Hotels and motels

(G-7211)
HIREWISE INC
Also Called: Adeva
651 N Broad St (19709-6400)
PHONE..................................888 899-4980
EMP: 9 EST: 2019
SALES (est): 107.46K **Privately Held**
Web: www.hirewise.com
SIC: **7371** Computer software development and applications

(G-7212)
HIVEMQ INC ◊
600 N Broad St Ste 5 (19709-1032)
PHONE..................................888 803-3966
Christian Meinerding, *CEO*
EMP: 6 EST: 2022
SALES (est): 73.93K **Privately Held**
SIC: **7372** Prepackaged software

(G-7213)
HOMEVIEW GROUP LLC ◊
651 N Broad St Ste 205 (19709-6400)
PHONE..................................508 686-6669
Antonio Banson, *Admn*
EMP: 10 EST: 2022
SALES (est): 444.15K **Privately Held**
SIC: **6513** Apartment building operators

(G-7214)
HOOBER INC
Also Called: Hoober Equipment
1130 Middletown Warwick Rd (19709-9096)
PHONE..................................717 768-8231
Charles Hoober, *Brnch Mgr*
EMP: 24
SALES (corp-wide): 24.92MM **Privately Held**
Web: www.hoober.com
SIC: **5083** Farm implements
PA: Hoober, Inc.
    3452 Old Philadelphia Pike
    Intercourse PA 17534
    717 768-8231

(G-7215)
HOPE HEALTH SYSTEMS INC
417 E Main St (19709-1463)
PHONE..................................302 376-9619
EMP: 9 EST: 2016
SALES (est): 127.21K **Privately Held**
Web: www.hopehealthsystems.com
SIC: **8099** Health and allied services, nec

(G-7216)
HOPSHOP INC ◊
651 N Broad St Ste 201 (19709-6402)
PHONE..................................323 745-1115
Tigran Chakhalyan, *Prin*
EMP: 8 EST: 2022
SALES (est): 306.16K **Privately Held**
SIC: **7371** Computer software development

(G-7217)
HORTON HOLDINGS INC
651 N Broad St Ste 205 (19709-6402)
PHONE..................................855 501-5834
Zachary Horton, *CEO*
EMP: 36
SIC: **6719** Holding companies, nec

(G-7218)
HOSPITALITY ESSENTIALS LLC
811 N Broad St Ste 203 (19709-1173)
PHONE..................................732 874-0048
EMP: 5 EST: 2017
SALES (est): 2.09MM **Privately Held**
Web: www.hospitalityessentials.com

GEOGRAPHIC SECTION

Middletown - New Castle County (G-7250)

SIC: **5046** 1522 Hotel equipment and supplies; Hotel/motel and multi-family home renovation and remodeling

(G-7219)
HUDSON FARM SUPPLY CO INC
Also Called: Souther States Co-Op
318 W Windmill Way (19709-9667)
PHONE..............................302 398-3654
E Ruth Hudson, *Pr*
EMP: 7 **EST:** 1938
SALES (est): 990.18K **Privately Held**
SIC: **5261** 5191 Nursery stock, seeds and bulbs; Farm supplies

(G-7220)
ID BY OLIVER LLC
651 N Broad St Ste 20523 (19709-6400)
PHONE..............................202 643-5536
EMP: 3 **EST:** 2020
SALES (est): 100K **Privately Held**
SIC: **3161** Clothing and apparel carrying cases

(G-7221)
IEXPERTO INC
651 N Broad St (19709-6400)
PHONE..............................347 808-3708
Ainal Haque, *CEO*
EMP: 8
SALES (est): 306.16K **Privately Held**
SIC: **7371** Computer software development

(G-7222)
IFI TECHSOLUTIONS INC
651 N Broad St Ste 206 (19709-6402)
PHONE..............................332 456-0765
Ankur Garg, *Pr*
EMP: 5 **EST:** 2020
SALES (est): 105.52K **Privately Held**
Web: dev.ifi.tech
SIC: **7373** Value-added resellers, computer systems

(G-7223)
IHEART DANCE STUDIO LLC
600 N Broad St Ste 20 (19709-1032)
P.O. Box 323 (19709-0323)
PHONE..............................267 249-8367
Chablis Reese, *Prin*
EMP: 6 **EST:** 2014
SALES (est): 21.12K **Privately Held**
Web: www.iheartdancestudio.com
SIC: **7911** Dance studio and school

(G-7224)
IN WELLNESS WE WIN
350 Noxontown Rd (19709-1621)
PHONE..............................917 509-5414
Stacey Duprey, *Prin*
EMP: 7 **EST:** 2018
SALES (est): 247.92K **Privately Held**
SIC: **8099** Health and allied services, nec

(G-7225)
INFINIT VENTURES LLC
651 N Broad St (19709-6400)
PHONE..............................800 966-9023
Sheldon Hanson, *Managing Member*
EMP: 5 **EST:** 2020
SALES (est): 20K **Privately Held**
SIC: **5099** Souvenirs

(G-7226)
INSIDER INSIGHT LLC
Also Called: Management Consulting
221 N Broad St Ste 3a (19709-1070)
PHONE..............................480 548-0440
Celaya Brown, *CEO*
EMP: 6

SALES (est): 226.9K **Privately Held**
SIC: **7389** Business services, nec

(G-7227)
INSPEKTLABS INC
651 N Broad St Ste 20 (19709-6400)
PHONE..............................302 601-7191
EMP: 10 **EST:** 2019
SALES (est): 128.71K **Privately Held**
Web: www.inspektlabs.com
SIC: **8071** Testing laboratories

(G-7228)
INTELLITEK INC
411 Weston Dr (19709-1715)
PHONE..............................856 381-7650
John Weiher, *Pr*
EMP: 9 **EST:** 2012
SALES (est): 188.02K **Privately Held**
SIC: **1731** Fiber optic cable installation

(G-7229)
INTERNAL MEDICINE DELAWARE LLC
411 Hawks Nest Ct (19709-4107)
PHONE..............................302 261-2269
EMP: 19 **EST:** 2010
SALES (est): 223.88K **Privately Held**
SIC: **8011** General and family practice, physician/surgeon

(G-7230)
INTRINSIC REALTY LLC
216 Rutland Ave (19709-9971)
PHONE..............................302 425-1025
Taylor Martin, *Managing Member*
EMP: 7 **EST:** 2021
SALES (est): 352.13K **Privately Held**
SIC: **8742** 7389 Management consulting services; Business Activities at Non-Commercial Site

(G-7231)
IOANNIS KEHAGIAS-ATHANA MD
222 Carter Dr Ste 101 (19709-5856)
PHONE..............................302 378-5494
Ioannis Kehagias, *Owner*
EMP: 8 **EST:** 2017
SALES (est): 65.5K **Privately Held**
SIC: **8011** General and family practice, physician/surgeon

(G-7232)
J & D CUSTOM GOLF CARTS LLC
141 Netherlands Dr (19709-9679)
PHONE..............................302 218-1505
EMP: 5 **EST:** 2011
SALES (est): 178.29K **Privately Held**
SIC: **5088** Golf carts

(G-7233)
J & G ACOUSTICAL CO
Also Called: J&G Building Group
216 E Dickerson Ln (19709-8824)
PHONE..............................302 285-3630
Gladys D King, *CEO*
Paul A King, *
G Keith Hopkins, *
EMP: 25 **EST:** 1984
SALES (est): 2.23MM **Privately Held**
Web: www.jgbuildinggroup.com
SIC: **1742** 1799 Acoustical and ceiling work; Demountable partition installation

(G-7234)
J & S - LOE INCORPORATED
651 N Broad St Ste 205 (19709-6402)
PHONE..............................302 608-7858
Shinobi Harris, *Admn*
EMP: 5 **EST:** 2020

SALES (est): 500K **Privately Held**
SIC: **8742** Management consulting services

(G-7235)
J A S LOGISTIC INC
410 N Ramunno Dr Unit 211 (19709-3091)
PHONE..............................302 339-1825
EMP: 5 **EST:** 2011
SALES (est): 114.16K **Privately Held**
SIC: **4731** Freight forwarding

(G-7236)
JAFFERY & JAFFERY CONTRACTORS
422 Naughty Ln (19709-3053)
PHONE..............................302 766-3795
Syed Jaffery, *Prin*
EMP: 5 **EST:** 2017
SALES (est): 108.32K **Privately Held**
SIC: **1799** Special trade contractors, nec

(G-7237)
JAKL BEER WORKS LLC
160 Gillespie Ave (19709-8361)
PHONE..............................610 442-0878
EMP: 2 **EST:** 2020
SALES (est): 212.74K **Privately Held**
Web: www.jaklbeerworks.com
SIC: **2082** Beer (alcoholic beverage)

(G-7238)
JAMES & PATRICIA BOOTH
725 Wood Duck Ct (19709-6114)
PHONE..............................302 378-9139
James Booth, *Prin*
EMP: 5 **EST:** 2008
SALES (est): 142.4K **Privately Held**
SIC: **7389** Business Activities at Non-Commercial Site

(G-7239)
JAMES W MCKEE
305 Beech Ln (19709-9521)
PHONE..............................302 540-9191
Jim Mckee, *Prin*
EMP: 5 **EST:** 2012
SALES (est): 82.91K **Privately Held**
SIC: **1522** Residential construction, nec

(G-7240)
JANA ANALYSIS INC
651 N Broad St Ste 2051916 (19709-6400)
PHONE..............................724 584-0545
Manoharan Duraisamy, *CEO*
EMP: 20 **EST:** 2020
SALES (est): 562.51K **Privately Held**
Web: www.janaanalysis.com
SIC: **7371** Computer software development

(G-7241)
JANE CHOUNG
410 N Cass St (19709-1038)
PHONE..............................302 378-8740
Jane Choung, *Prin*
EMP: 13 **EST:** 2014
SALES (est): 202.11K **Privately Held**
SIC: **8021** Dentists' office

(G-7242)
JAQUEZ CONCRETE LLC
4 Bryant Ct (19709-1647)
PHONE..............................302 379-1148
EMP: 7 **EST:** 2017
SALES (est): 483.1K **Privately Held**
Web: www.jaquezco.com
SIC: **1771** Concrete work

(G-7243)
JC CONTRACTORS LLC
318 White Pine Dr (19709-9779)
PHONE..............................302 420-9338
Kristen Nicole Lloyd, *Prin*
EMP: 8 **EST:** 2015
SALES (est): 421.86K **Privately Held**
SIC: **1799** Special trade contractors, nec

(G-7244)
JEFFREY A BRIGHT DMD
600 N Broad St Ste 7 (19709-1032)
PHONE..............................302 832-1371
Jeffrey A Bright D.m.d., *Pr*
EMP: 15 **EST:** 1992
SALES (est): 247.64K **Privately Held**
Web: www.brightdental.net
SIC: **8021** Dentists' office

(G-7245)
JENNIFER M EWALD
120 W Main St (19709-1040)
PHONE..............................302 377-6911
Jennifer Ewald, *Owner*
EMP: 5 **EST:** 2015
SALES (est): 44.18K **Privately Held**
SIC: **8322** Social worker

(G-7246)
JEREMIAH 29 11 FITNESS LLC
521 Wheelmen St (19709-0027)
PHONE..............................302 376-1287
Jeremiah O Guy, *Prin*
EMP: 5 **EST:** 2020
SALES (est): 59.71K **Privately Held**
SIC: **7991** Physical fitness facilities

(G-7247)
JESCO INC
Also Called: John Deere Authorized Dealer
1001 Industrial Dr (19709-1097)
PHONE..............................302 376-6946
EMP: 118
SALES (corp-wide): 2.84B **Privately Held**
Web: www.jesco.us
SIC: **5046** 5082 Commercial equipment, nec; Construction and mining machinery
HQ: Jesco, Inc.
2020 Mccullough Blvd
Tupelo MS 38801
662 842-3240

(G-7248)
JH CONTRACTING INC
807 Laurelwood Ct (19709-9257)
PHONE..............................302 893-4766
Joseph C Harrington, *CEO*
EMP: 10 **EST:** 2014
SALES (est): 474K **Privately Held**
Web: www.jhcontractingde.com
SIC: **1799** Special trade contractors, nec

(G-7249)
JIGA INC
651 N Broad St (19709-6400)
PHONE..............................408 878-3213
Assaf Geuz, *Prin*
EMP: 11
SALES (est): 405.54K **Privately Held**
SIC: **7363** Help supply services

(G-7250)
JMT SERVICES INC
808 Lorewood Grove Rd (19709-9236)
PHONE..............................302 530-2807
EMP: 11
SALES (corp-wide): 536.21K **Privately Held**
Web: www.jmt.com

Middletown - New Castle County (G-7251)

SIC: **1711** 7389 Ventilation and duct work contractor; Business services, nec
PA: Jmt Services Inc.
520 Robinson Ln
Wilmington DE 19805
302 407-5978

(G-7251)
JO STEFANIE ARMOUR
Also Called: SA Medical Billing
101 Bakerfield Dr (19709-9453)
PHONE.................................302 838-5311
Stefanie Armour, *Prin*
EMP: 8 EST: 2010
SALES (est): 121.13K **Privately Held**
SIC: **8099** Health and allied services, nec

(G-7252)
JOANNE PARKER-HENRY INC
102 Joshua Ct (19709-8850)
PHONE.................................302 378-7251
John Parker, *Owner*
EMP: 7 EST: 2010
SALES (est): 92.85K **Privately Held**
SIC: **8322** Individual and family services

(G-7253)
JOSEPH D ALLEN
861 Shallcross Lake Rd (19709-8937)
PHONE.................................302 685-4230
Joseph Allen, *Prin*
EMP: 5 EST: 2017
SALES (est): 125.98K **Privately Held**
SIC: **1522** Residential construction, nec

(G-7254)
JOSHUA TILGHMAN
207 E Crail Ct (19709-8723)
PHONE.................................302 582-1491
Joshua Tilghman, *Owner*
EMP: 6
SALES (est): 191.04K **Privately Held**
SIC: **4213** 7389 Trucking, except local; Business services, nec

(G-7255)
JS CARPENTER IMPROVEMENTS
342 Jessica Dr (19709-4018)
PHONE.................................302 540-0590
John Carpenter, *Prin*
EMP: 5 EST: 2013
SALES (est): 62.35K **Privately Held**
SIC: **1751** Carpentry work

(G-7256)
K AND W PAINTING
23 Fairview Ave (19709-3819)
PHONE.................................302 598-5663
William Todd, *Prin*
EMP: 5 EST: 2016
SALES (est): 64.74K **Privately Held**
Web: www.kandwpainting.com
SIC: **1721** Residential painting

(G-7257)
K LUSH EXTENSIONS LLC
282 Wilmore Dr (19709-8388)
PHONE.................................347 274-4353
EMP: 3 EST: 2019
SALES (est): 39.69K **Privately Held**
SIC: **3999** Hair and hair-based products

(G-7258)
K WOLF CUSTOM HOMES CNSTR INC
507 Red Oak Dr (19709-9580)
PHONE.................................302 598-2899
EMP: 5 EST: 2017
SALES (est): 110.29K **Privately Held**

SIC: **1521** New construction, single-family houses

(G-7259)
KAEBOX LLC
651 N Broad St Ste 206 (19709-6402)
PHONE.................................919 777-3939
EMP: 5 EST: 2020
SALES (est): 46.16K **Privately Held**
SIC: **7371** 4215 Computer software development and applications; Courier services, except by air

(G-7260)
KAGOAL TECHNOLOGY LLC
651 N Broad St Ste 2056367 (19709-6400)
PHONE.................................617 818-0588
Hussein Zahran, *Managing Member*
EMP: 5 EST: 2021
SALES (est): 199.4K **Privately Held**
SIC: **7371** 7373 7379 Computer software development and applications; Systems integration services; Computer related consulting services

(G-7261)
KARL MARINACCIO CPA
4705 Astaire Pl (19709-6613)
PHONE.................................914 736-0772
Karl Marinaccio, *Prin*
EMP: 5 EST: 2016
SALES (est): 31.93K **Privately Held**
SIC: **8721** Certified public accountant

(G-7262)
KASA ENTERPRISE LLC (PA) ◊
221 N Broad St Ste 3a (19709-1070)
PHONE.................................302 634-0138
EMP: 8 EST: 2022
SALES (est): 394.7K
SALES (corp-wide): 394.7K **Privately Held**
SIC: **7021** Rooming and boarding houses

(G-7263)
KATHERINE M KING RN
555 Hyetts Corner Rd (19709-8907)
PHONE.................................302 449-3625
Katherine M King, *Prin*
EMP: 9 EST: 2012
SALES (est): 88.67K **Privately Held**
SIC: **8011** Offices and clinics of medical doctors

(G-7264)
KAYS NAIL & SPA LLC
17 Wood St (19709-1048)
PHONE.................................302 376-7788
EMP: 5 EST: 2016
SALES (est): 108.57K **Privately Held**
Web: www.kaysnailsandspa.com
SIC: **7231** Manicurist, pedicurist

(G-7265)
KENNETH D MORRIS
528 Wheelmen St (19709-0026)
PHONE.................................415 760-0791
Kenneth Morris, *Prin*
EMP: 5 EST: 2004
SALES (est): 114.41K **Privately Held**
SIC: **8049** Clinical psychologist

(G-7266)
KENT GENERAL HOSPITAL
Also Called: Bayhealth Medical Center
209 E Main St (19709-1449)
PHONE.................................302 378-1199
Deana Rigby, *Dir*
EMP: 8
Web: www.bayhealth.org

SIC: **8062** General medical and surgical hospitals
HQ: Kent General Hospital
640 S State St
Dover DE 19901
302 674-4700

(G-7267)
KENZZ INC ◊
651 N Broad St (19709-6400)
PHONE.................................310 254-6927
Ahmad Atef, *CEO*
EMP: 40 EST: 2022
SALES (est): 1.06MM **Privately Held**
SIC: **7371** Custom computer programming services

(G-7268)
KERSHAW INDUSTRIES
110 W Main St (19709-1040)
PHONE.................................302 464-1051
EMP: 4 EST: 2015
SALES (est): 69.14K **Privately Held**
SIC: **3999** Manufacturing industries, nec

(G-7269)
KEYSTONE NFP MIDDLETOWN LLC
703 N Broad St (19709-1166)
PHONE.................................302 378-2777
EMP: 5 EST: 2019
SALES (est): 63.4K **Privately Held**
SIC: **7991** Physical fitness clubs with training equipment

(G-7270)
KIARA M MOORE
421 Cicero Xing (19709-9860)
PHONE.................................412 953-2791
Kiara Moore Lpcmh, *Owner*
EMP: 7 EST: 2018
SALES (est): 93.54K **Privately Held**
SIC: **8011** Offices and clinics of medical doctors

(G-7271)
KIDS CLUBHOUSE
5350 Summit Bridge Rd (19709-4801)
PHONE.................................302 464-1134
EMP: 5 EST: 2017
SALES (est): 80.07K **Privately Held**
SIC: **7997** Membership sports and recreation clubs

(G-7272)
KIDZ INK
125 Sleepy Hollow Dr (19709-8895)
PHONE.................................302 376-1700
Phil Kitson, *Owner*
EMP: 5
SALES (corp-wide): 4.11MM **Privately Held**
Web: www.kidzearlylearning.com
SIC: **8351** Preschool center
PA: Kidz Ink
1703 Porter Rd
Bear DE 19701
302 838-1500

(G-7273)
KIM SIMPSON REALTY GROUP
104 W Main St Ste B (19709-4400)
PHONE.................................302 690-0245
Kim Simpson, *Pr*
EMP: 6 EST: 2017
SALES (est): 110.18K **Privately Held**
Web: www.thymerealestateco.com
SIC: **6531** Real estate brokers and agents

(G-7274)
KIMBERLY TUCKER
Also Called: K&D Maintenance Service
249 E Crail Ct (19709-8727)
PHONE.................................302 358-0574
Kimerly Tucker, *Owner*
EMP: 6 EST: 2017
SALES (est): 22.81K **Privately Held**
SIC: **7349** Building maintenance services, nec

(G-7275)
KIND-CHARITY INC
651 N Broad St Ste 206 (19709-6402)
PHONE.................................302 867-6042
Andrei Vashchenko, *Pr*
EMP: 5 EST: 2021
SALES (est): 40.03K **Privately Held**
SIC: **8641** Community membership club

(G-7276)
KINDHEART HOME CARE INC
207 Parker Dr (19709-2623)
PHONE.................................484 479-6582
Oluyemi Taiwo, *Prin*
EMP: 7 EST: 2019
SALES (est): 246.85K **Privately Held**
Web: www.kindheart-homecare.com
SIC: **8082** Home health care services

(G-7277)
KINGDOM SPA INC
5 Emerson Ct (19709-1646)
PHONE.................................302 897-8255
Minh Bui, *Pr*
EMP: 6 EST: 2015
SALES (est): 237.25K **Privately Held**
SIC: **7991** Spas

(G-7278)
KJAN INNOVATIONS LLC ◊
Also Called: Kjan Innovations
364 E Main St (19709-1482)
PHONE.................................954 388-1293
EMP: 8 EST: 2022
SALES (est): 306.16K **Privately Held**
SIC: **7389** Business services, nec

(G-7279)
KLF MUSIC FACTORY
809 Marsh Hawk Ct (19709-2237)
PHONE.................................302 598-8770
EMP: 6 EST: 2014
SALES (est): 58.46K **Privately Held**
SIC: **7929** Musical entertainers

(G-7280)
KLIP-IT LLC ◊
651 N Broad St (19709-6400)
PHONE.................................888 202-0533
Matthew Davis, *CEO*
EMP: 2 EST: 2022
SALES (est): 87.4K **Privately Held**
SIC: **7372** 7319 Application computer software; Coupon distribution

(G-7281)
KOOL BOIZ FOUNDATION LLC
603 E Glen Mare Dr (19709-8774)
PHONE.................................614 404-2396
Bruce Rushton, *Prin*
EMP: 5 EST: 2015
SALES (est): 229.12K **Privately Held**
Web: www.koolboizfoundation.org
SIC: **8641** Civic and social associations

(G-7282)
KOVAN STUDIO INC
600 N Broad St (19709-1032)
PHONE.................................855 964-3748

EMP: 10
SALES (est): 454.47K **Privately Held**
SIC: 5045 Computer software

(G-7283)
KRISTINA BRANDIS
208 Wickerberry Dr (19709-7806)
PHONE.................516 457-2717
Kristina Brandis, *Prin*
EMP: 6 EST: 2017
SALES (est): 46.71K **Privately Held**
SIC: 8322 Individual and family services

(G-7284)
KUEST INC
651 N Broad St Ste 206 (19709-6402)
PHONE.................786 840-0842
EMP: 5 EST: 2020
SALES (est): 68.89K **Privately Held**
SIC: 7371 Computer software development

(G-7285)
KUTBU LLC ✪
651 N Broad St Ste 201 (19709-6402)
PHONE.................848 225-8848
Muhammed Yalcinkaya, *Managing Member*
EMP: 3 EST: 2023
SALES (est): 128.34K **Privately Held**
SIC: 7372 Prepackaged software

(G-7286)
LA BANCA
1 W Main St (19709-1017)
PHONE.................302 464-3005
EMP: 6 EST: 2017
SALES (est): 102.2K **Privately Held**
SIC: 2024 Ice cream and frozen deserts

(G-7287)
LAND LOCK LLC
600 N Broad St (19709-1032)
PHONE.................302 747-6124
Alexia Lopez, *CEO*
EMP: 5 EST: 2020
SALES (est): 148.14K **Privately Held**
SIC: 7389 Business Activities at Non-Commercial Site

(G-7288)
LANDELL LABS LLC ✪
651 N Broad St Ste 201 (19709-6402)
PHONE.................917 722-5166
Daniel Vargas, *Managing Member*
EMP: 6 EST: 2023
SALES (est): 69.69K **Privately Held**
SIC: 7371 Computer software development and applications

(G-7289)
LARGER STORY INC
117 Shannon Blvd (19709-2193)
PHONE.................302 834-5712
James Swalm Junior, *Prin*
EMP: 6 EST: 2016
SALES (est): 205.5K **Privately Held**
Web: www.largerstory.com
SIC: 4832 Radio broadcasting stations

(G-7290)
LAUNCHARM INC
651 N Broad St Ste 206 (19709-6402)
PHONE.................320 520-3818
Yong Wang, *VP*
EMP: 8 EST: 2021
SALES (est): 306.16K **Privately Held**
SIC: 7371 Custom computer programming services

(G-7291)
LAUREL COMMUNITY HARDWARE INC
420 Draper Ln (19709-8018)
PHONE.................302 598-0454
EMP: 11 EST: 2013
SALES (est): 305.97K **Privately Held**
SIC: 8322 Community center

(G-7292)
LEARN GAME LLC (PA)
Also Called: Learn The Game App
221 N Broad St Ste 3a (19709-1070)
PHONE.................484 841-9709
EMP: 10 EST: 2020
SALES (est): 690.87K
SALES (corp-wide): 690.87K **Privately Held**
SIC: 8299 7371 Educational services; Computer software development and applications

(G-7293)
LEARNING TREE ACADEMY
400 N Ramunno Dr (19709-3001)
PHONE.................302 449-1711
Megan Coats, *Dir*
EMP: 10 EST: 2019
SALES (est): 212.17K **Privately Held**
Web: www.learningtreede.com
SIC: 8351 Preschool center

(G-7294)
LEGION TRANSFORMATION CENTER
128 Patriot Dr Unit 8 (19709-8770)
PHONE.................302 464-1081
EMP: 6 EST: 2017
SALES (est): 55.32K **Privately Held**
Web: www.legiontransform.com
SIC: 7991 Physical fitness facilities

(G-7295)
LES NAILS
372 E Main St (19709-1482)
PHONE.................302 449-5290
Le Le, *Prin*
EMP: 6 EST: 2005
SALES (est): 84.58K **Privately Held**
Web: www.lesnailsmiddletown.com
SIC: 7231 Manicurist, pedicurist

(G-7296)
LEVEL UP CONSULTING GROUP INC
651 N Broad St Ste 205 # 4768 (19709-6402)
PHONE.................855 967-5550
Jerrell Lewis, *Managing Member*
EMP: 5 EST: 2021
SALES (est): 131.34K **Privately Held**
SIC: 7379 8742 Online services technology consultants; Management consulting services

(G-7297)
LIBERTY TAX
419 E Main St (19709-1463)
PHONE.................302 526-1611
EMP: 6 EST: 2018
SALES (est): 26.47K **Privately Held**
Web: www.libertytax.com
SIC: 7291 Tax return preparation services

(G-7298)
LIESKE E2E HOME HLTH CARE INC
Also Called: Shorecare of Delaware
53 Meadow Dr (19709-4103)
PHONE.................302 898-1563
Jacqueline Lieske, *Pr*
EMP: 9 EST: 2009
SALES (est): 249.1K **Privately Held**
SIC: 8082 Home health care services

(G-7299)
LIFE STRONG FITNESS LLC
216 W Old Squaw Rd (19709-9152)
PHONE.................302 312-9673
Kirk Phang, *Prin*
EMP: 5 EST: 2017
SALES (est): 35.37K **Privately Held**
SIC: 7991 Physical fitness facilities

(G-7300)
LIFESCORE INC
108 Patriot Dr Ste A (19709-8803)
PHONE.................808 780-4645
EMP: 5 EST: 2020
SALES (est): 68.89K **Privately Held**
SIC: 7389 Business services, nec

(G-7301)
LIFESTYLE COMMUNITIES LLC
111 Patriot Dr Ste A (19709-8771)
PHONE.................302 376-3066
Rick Woodin, *Mgr*
EMP: 22 EST: 2001
SQ FT: 14,268
SALES (est): 4.33MM **Privately Held**
Web: www.lifestylehomes.us
SIC: 1521 New construction, single-family houses

(G-7302)
LIFETIME SKILLS SERVICES LLC
Also Called: Digen Auto Group
300 Brady Ln (19709-9010)
PHONE.................302 378-2911
Digen Ballayan, *Managing Member*
EMP: 8 EST: 2015
SALES (est): 190.38K **Privately Held**
SIC: 8082 5521 Home health care services; Automobiles, used cars only

(G-7303)
LIGHTNING PAINTING LLC
326 Ellenwood Dr (19709-7861)
PHONE.................302 521-6033
EMP: 6 EST: 2016
SALES (est): 240.67K **Privately Held**
Web: www.lightning-painting.com
SIC: 1721 Painting and paper hanging

(G-7304)
LILA KESHAV HOSPITALITY LLC
Also Called: Holiday Inn Express & Suites
315 Auto Park Dr (19709-9983)
PHONE.................302 696-2272
EMP: 15 EST: 2016
SALES (est): 713.41K **Privately Held**
Web: www.hiexpress.com
SIC: 7011 Hotels and motels

(G-7305)
LILA LABS INC
600 N Broad St Ste 5-802 (19709-1032)
PHONE.................949 371-3978
Errick Williams, *COO*
Matthew Cohen, *COO*
EMP: 6 EST: 2019
SALES (est): 86.05K **Privately Held**
SIC: 8731 Biotechnical research, commercial

(G-7306)
LISA JOHANNSEN
4485 Summit Bridge Rd (19709-9549)
PHONE.................302 270-5082
Lisa Johannsen, *Prin*
EMP: 5 EST: 2018
SALES (est): 149.88K **Privately Held**
Web: www.psredelaware.com
SIC: 6531 Real estate brokers and agents

(G-7307)
LISA R SHANNON LMT
5 Bridge Ct (19709-9285)
PHONE.................302 468-9416
Lisa R Shannon Lmt, *Owner*
EMP: 6 EST: 2018
SALES (est): 72.69K **Privately Held**
SIC: 8049 Massage Therapist

(G-7308)
LITTLE PEOPLE DAY CARE
17 Cole Blvd (19709-1617)
PHONE.................302 528-4336
EMP: 8 EST: 2012
SALES (est): 54.54K **Privately Held**
SIC: 8351 Child day care services

(G-7309)
LITTLE TROOPER DAY CARE
329 Senator Dr (19709-8023)
PHONE.................302 378-7355
Bonnie Aube, *Dir*
EMP: 5 EST: 2009
SALES (est): 154.25K **Privately Held**
SIC: 8351 Child day care services

(G-7310)
LIVEBOARD INC
651 N Broad St Ste 206 (19709-6402)
PHONE.................888 412-8882
EMP: 5 EST: 2020
SALES (est): 68.89K **Privately Held**
Web: www.liveboard.online
SIC: 7371 Computer software development

(G-7311)
LLC CUTLER PARRISH
639 Swansea Dr (19709-0202)
PHONE.................609 744-9871
Jane C Yepez, *Prin*
EMP: 5 EST: 2019
SALES (est): 72.25K **Privately Held**
SIC: 7311 Advertising consultant

(G-7312)
LONGWOOD ASSETS LLC ✪
651 N Broad St Ste 201 (19709-6400)
PHONE.................617 906-8882
Melissa Andrews, *Managing Member*
EMP: 5 EST: 2022
SALES (est): 413.25K **Privately Held**
SIC: 8748 Business consulting, nec

(G-7313)
LOVE HARRISBURG LLC
651 N Broad St (19709-6400)
PHONE.................717 710-1556
Mayya Poprotska, *CEO*
EMP: 5 EST: 2021
SALES (est): 107.26K **Privately Held**
SIC: 8399 Community development groups

(G-7314)
LOVE N FUN FAMILY DAYCARE
246 Wilgus Ct (19709-8307)
PHONE.................302 601-3629
Charlotte Goode, *Prin*
EMP: 9 EST: 2018
SALES (est): 74.97K **Privately Held**
Web: www.lovenfunfamilydaycare.com
SIC: 8351 Group day care center

(G-7315)
LOWES HOME CENTERS LLC
Also Called: Lowe's
500 W Main St (19709-9651)
PHONE.................302 376-3006
Paul Bateman, *Brnch Mgr*

Middletown - New Castle County (G-7316) GEOGRAPHIC SECTION

EMP: 73
SALES (corp-wide): 97.06B **Publicly Held**
Web: www.lowes.com
SIC: 5211 5031 5722 5064 Home centers; Building materials, exterior; Household appliance stores; Electrical appliances, television and radio
HQ: Lowe's Home Centers, Llc
1000 Lowes Blvd
Mooresville NC 28117
336 658-4000

(G-7316)
LUPOLI GENERAL CONTRACTING
28 Kirkcaldy Ln (19709-8738)
P.O. Box 582 (19709-0582)
PHONE...............302 449-1533
Jeannette Lupoli, *Owner*
EMP: 5 **EST**: 2011
SALES (est): 130.75K **Privately Held**
Web: www.lupolihomeimprovements.com
SIC: 1799 Special trade contractors, nec

(G-7317)
M O T SENIOR CITIZEN CENTER
300 S Scott St (19709-1355)
PHONE...............302 378-3041
Maxine Barton, *Ex Dir*
Jack Tellman, *Pr*
EMP: 10 **EST**: 1967
SQ FT: 2,500
SALES (est): 243.92K **Privately Held**
Web: www.motseniorcenter.com
SIC: 8322 Senior citizens' center or association

(G-7318)
M O T YOUTH FTBALL & CHEERLDNG
P.O. Box 793 (19709-0793)
PHONE...............302 345-6182
Ken Anderson, *Pr*
EMP: 8 **EST**: 2008
SALES (est): 228.17K **Privately Held**
SIC: 7941 Football club

(G-7319)
M&M COURIER SERVICE LLC
305 Jefferson St (19709-1132)
PHONE...............302 430-2740
Michael D Middleton, *Prin*
EMP: 5 **EST**: 2010
SALES (est): 101.09K **Privately Held**
SIC: 4215 Courier services, except by air

(G-7320)
MAAD AFRICA INC
651 N Broad St (19709-6400)
PHONE...............847 927-0519
Jessica Long, *CEO*
EMP: 60
SALES (est): 1.11MM **Privately Held**
SIC: 7371 Computer software development

(G-7321)
MAGGIE MAGPIE INC
7 Redding Cir (19709-1150)
PHONE...............302 331-5061
Sabrina Desir, *Prin*
EMP: 6 **EST**: 2020
SALES (est): 300K **Privately Held**
SIC: 8299 7389 Educational services; Business Activities at Non-Commercial Site

(G-7322)
MAHAFFY & ASSOCIATES INC
4 Brightham Ln (19709-2112)
PHONE...............302 656-8381
Hugh Mahaffy, *Pr*
Edward Fayda, *VP*
Scott D Parlow, *VP*
EMP: 20 **EST**: 1916
SALES (est): 1.29MM **Privately Held**
Web: www.mahaffyengineers.com
SIC: 8711 Consulting engineer

(G-7323)
MAIDPRO
4442 Summit Bridge Rd 12 (19709-9344)
PHONE...............302 327-4250
EMP: 8 **EST**: 2018
SALES (est): 55.59K **Privately Held**
Web: www.maidpro.com
SIC: 7349 Cleaning service, industrial or commercial

(G-7324)
MAIL EXPRESS
600 N Broad St Ste 5 (19709-1032)
PHONE...............302 376-5151
EMP: 5 **EST**: 2018
SALES (est): 165.42K **Privately Held**
Web: www.mymailexp.com
SIC: 7389 Packaging and labeling services

(G-7325)
MANATEC ELECTRONICS LLC
651 N Broad St Ste 205 # 1405 (19709-6402)
PHONE...............248 653-1245
EMP: 6 **EST**: 2019
SALES (est): 388.85K **Privately Held**
SIC: 3999 3559 Wheelchair lifts; Wheel balancing equipment, automotive

(G-7326)
MANUFACTURERS & TRADERS TR CO
Also Called: M&T
405 W Main St (19709-1064)
PHONE...............302 449-2780
Betty Whitlock, *Mgr*
EMP: 8
SALES (corp-wide): 8.6B **Publicly Held**
Web: ir.mtb.com
SIC: 6022 State commercial banks
HQ: Manufacturers And Traders Trust Company
1 M&T Plz Fl 3
Buffalo NY 14203
716 842-4200

(G-7327)
MANUFACTURERS & TRADERS TR CO
Also Called: M&T
399 E Main St (19709-1450)
PHONE...............302 285-3277
Dona Jester, *Mgr*
EMP: 9
SALES (corp-wide): 8.6B **Publicly Held**
Web: ir.mtb.com
SIC: 6022 State trust companies accepting deposits, commercial
HQ: Manufacturers And Traders Trust Company
1 M&T Plz Fl 3
Buffalo NY 14203
716 842-4200

(G-7328)
MARK E CASE M D
272 Carter Dr Ste 200 (19709-5851)
PHONE...............302 449-1710
Mark Case, *Owner*
EMP: 5 **EST**: 2001
SALES (est): 59.55K **Privately Held**
SIC: 8011 Offices and clinics of medical doctors

(G-7329)
MARQUIS DORSEY LLC
651 N Broad St Ste 205 # 6054 (19709-6402)
PHONE...............832 693-0260
EMP: 13 **EST**: 2021
SALES (est): 597.27K **Privately Held**
SIC: 7311 Advertising consultant

(G-7330)
MARTIAL INDUSTRIES LLC
526 Barrymore Pkwy (19709-6614)
PHONE...............302 983-5742
EMP: 3 **EST**: 2016
SALES (est): 64.76K **Privately Held**
SIC: 3999 Manufacturing industries, nec

(G-7331)
MATIV HOLDINGS INC
Also Called: Mativ
601 Industrial Dr (19709-1083)
PHONE...............302 378-8888
EMP: 12
SIC: 3081 Unsupported plastics film and sheet
PA: Mativ Holdings, Inc.
100 Kimball Pl Ste 600
Alpharetta GA 30009

(G-7332)
MAYSE PAINTING & CONTG LLC
2250 Audubon Trl (19709-9844)
PHONE...............443 553-6503
EMP: 5 **EST**: 2018
SALES (est): 404.88K **Privately Held**
SIC: 1721 Residential painting

(G-7333)
MCCORMICK ASSOC MIDDLETOWN LLC
5350 Summit Bridge Rd Ste 107 (19709)
PHONE...............302 449-0710
Caren Coffy-mccormick, *Prin*
EMP: 5 **EST**: 2011
SALES (est): 192.14K **Privately Held**
Web: www.mccormickandassociatesofmiddletown.com
SIC: 8093 Mental health clinic, outpatient

(G-7334)
MCKEE GROUP MCKEE MANAGEMENT
1467 Whispering Woods Rd (19709-3305)
PHONE...............302 449-0778
EMP: 5 **EST**: 2019
SALES (est): 89.97K **Privately Held**
Web: www.mckeegroup.net
SIC: 8741 Management services

(G-7335)
MCKENZIE PAVING INC
114 Bakerfield Dr (19709-9451)
PHONE...............302 376-8560
Margaret Mckenzie, *Pr*
EMP: 14 **EST**: 2005
SALES (est): 982.18K **Privately Held**
Web: www.mckenziepavinginc.com
SIC: 1611 Surfacing and paving

(G-7336)
MCROGGE LLC (PA) ✪
651 N Broad St (19709-6400)
PHONE...............215 300-7975
Sean Rogge, *Prin*
EMP: 5 **EST**: 2022
SALES (est): 69.5K
SALES (corp-wide): 69.5K **Privately Held**
SIC: 1521 7389 Single-family home remodeling, additions, and repairs; Business services, nec

(G-7337)
MEDZOOMER INC
600 N Broad St Ste 5 (19709-1032)
PHONE...............239 595-8899
Marvin Kloss, *CEO*
EMP: 5 **EST**: 2019
SALES (est): 288.3K **Privately Held**
Web: www.medzoomer.com
SIC: 7371 Computer software development and applications

(G-7338)
MEGAN AITKEN TEAM LLC
831 Kingswood Path (19709-7523)
PHONE...............302 376-9836
Megan Aitken, *Prin*
EMP: 5 **EST**: 2019
SALES (est): 217.36K **Privately Held**
Web: www.delawarelistings.com
SIC: 6531 Real estate brokers and agents

(G-7339)
MELLON CARE INC (PA) ✪
651 N Broad St Ste 201 (19709-6402)
PHONE...............800 406-0281
Austin Grisham, *Pr*
Benjamin Bimanywaruhanga, *Pr*
EMP: 6 **EST**: 2023
SALES (est): 278.65K
SALES (corp-wide): 278.65K **Privately Held**
SIC: 5122 5961 5999 2023 Cosmetics; Cosmetics and perfumes, mail order; Toiletries, cosmetics, and perfumes; Dietary supplements, dairy and non-dairy based

(G-7340)
MENAINFOSEC INC
651 N Broad St Ste 206 (19709-6402)
PHONE...............217 650-7167
Faisal Al Farsi, *Pr*
Maitham Alwati,
EMP: 30 **EST**: 2020
SALES (est): 1.35MM **Privately Held**
Web: www.menainfosec.com
SIC: 7379 Online services technology consultants

(G-7341)
MERCURY RESEARCH LLC
651 N Broad St (19709-6400)
PHONE...............860 532-3480
George Alexander, *Managing Member*
EMP: 16
SALES (est): 657.74K **Privately Held**
SIC: 6411 Research services, insurance

(G-7342)
MERCY LAND ACADEMY INC
211 E Main St (19709-1449)
PHONE...............302 378-2013
Adeola Salako, *Prin*
EMP: 5 **EST**: 2019
SALES (est): 235.96K **Privately Held**
SIC: 8351 Child day care services

(G-7343)
MESA JAME CORP
120 Laks Dr (19709-9390)
PHONE...............302 528-9106
EMP: 8 **EST**: 2015
SALES (est): 476.95K **Privately Held**
SIC: 4899 Communication services, nec

GEOGRAPHIC SECTION

Middletown - New Castle County (G-7375)

(G-7344)
METANOIA COUNSELING LLC
101 W Park Pl (19709-1324)
PHONE.....................302 559-4421
EMP: 7 **EST:** 2018
SALES (est): 41.33K **Privately Held**
SIC: 8322 General counseling services

(G-7345)
METRO BY T-MOBILE
859 N Broad St (19709-1197)
PHONE.....................302 378-3559
EMP: 5 **EST:** 2019
SALES (est): 33.14K **Privately Held**
SIC: 4812 Cellular telephone services

(G-7346)
MIDDLETOWN CAR CARE
133 Leanne Dr (19709-9102)
PHONE.....................302 449-1550
Sean J Mcdade, *Owner*
Sean Mcdade, *Owner*
EMP: 5 **EST:** 2010
SALES (est): 383.42K **Privately Held**
Web: www.middletowncarcarede.com
SIC: 7538 General automotive repair shops

(G-7347)
MIDDLETOWN CHIROPRACTIC & REHA
421 E Main St Ste 6 (19709-1463)
PHONE.....................302 376-5830
EMP: 8 **EST:** 2018
SALES (est): 37.19K **Privately Held**
Web: www.middletownchiropractic.net
SIC: 8041 Offices and clinics of chiropractors

(G-7348)
MIDDLETOWN COUNSELING
401 N Broad St (19709-1037)
PHONE.....................302 376-0621
Sandra Lee Lnauer, *Prin*
EMP: 8 **EST:** 2008
SALES (est): 477.65K **Privately Held**
Web: www.middletowncounseling.com
SIC: 8322 General counseling services

(G-7349)
MIDDLETOWN DE
520 Middletown Warwick Rd (19709-8873)
PHONE.....................302 449-2547
EMP: 5 **EST:** 2018
SALES (est): 138.16K **Privately Held**
Web: middletown.delaware.gov
SIC: 2711 Newspapers, publishing and printing

(G-7350)
MIDDLETOWN DE
252 Carter Dr Ste 101 (19709-5858)
PHONE.....................302 655-9494
EMP: 6 **EST:** 2019
SALES (est): 64.15K **Privately Held**
Web: middletown.delaware.gov
SIC: 2711 Newspapers, publishing and printing

(G-7351)
MIDDLETOWN FAMILY DENTIST
122 Sandhill Dr Ste 101 (19709-5861)
PHONE.....................302 376-1959
Scott Anthony Arrighi, *Prin*
EMP: 16 **EST:** 2007
SALES (est): 2.31MM **Privately Held**
Web: www.middletownfamilydentistry.com
SIC: 8021 Dentists' office

(G-7352)
MIDDLETOWN FAMILY MEDICINE CTR
124 Sleepy Hollow Dr Ste 203 (19709-5838)
PHONE.....................302 449-3030
EMP: 12 **EST:** 2019
SALES (est): 424.65K **Privately Held**
SIC: 8011 Medical centers

(G-7353)
MIDDLETOWN INK LLC
126 Patriot Dr (19709-8762)
PHONE.....................302 725-0705
Megan Haines, *Owner*
Brian Haines, *Owner*
▲ **EMP:** 2 **EST:** 2008
SALES (est): 86.9K **Privately Held**
Web: middletown.delaware.gov
SIC: 2759 Screen printing

(G-7354)
MIDDLETOWN KITCHEN & BATH LLC
111 Patriot Dr Ste C (19709-8771)
PHONE.....................302 464-1236
Mark Gandy, *Managing Member*
EMP: 11 **EST:** 2015
SALES (est): 438.89K **Privately Held**
Web: www.mkbde.com
SIC: 1799 Kitchen and bathroom remodeling

(G-7355)
MIDDLETOWN KITCHEN AND BATH
987 Marl Pit Rd (19709-9604)
PHONE.....................302 376-5766
EMP: 6 **EST:** 2015
SALES (est): 792.23K **Privately Held**
Web: www.mkbde.com
SIC: 5023 Kitchenware

(G-7356)
MIDDLETOWN MOSQUITO CTRL LLC
229 Oak Dr (19709-9514)
PHONE.....................302 378-3378
Michael Mahoney, *Prin*
EMP: 5 **EST:** 2016
SALES (est): 95.37K **Privately Held**
Web: www.middletownmosquito.com
SIC: 7342 Pest control services

(G-7357)
MIDDLETOWN PAINTING LLC
1027 Sherbourne Rd (19709-8396)
PHONE.....................302 376-5419
Wilmer Torrealba, *Prin*
EMP: 5 **EST:** 2017
SALES (est): 236.39K **Privately Held**
Web: www.middletownpainting.us
SIC: 1721 Painting and paper hanging

(G-7358)
MIDDLETOWN SPORTS COMPLEX LLC
407 Draper Ln (19709-8017)
PHONE.....................302 299-8630
EMP: 10 **EST:** 2012
SALES (est): 84.12K **Privately Held**
Web: www.middletownsc.com
SIC: 7997 Membership sports and recreation clubs

(G-7359)
MIDDLETOWN TENT RENTALS INC
7 E Cochran St (19709-1410)
PHONE.....................302 376-7010
Thomas A Pavonarius, *Prin*
EMP: 5 **EST:** 2003
SALES (est): 111.48K **Privately Held**
SIC: 7359 Party supplies rental services

(G-7360)
MIDDLETOWN VETERINARY HOSPITAL
366 Warwick Rd (19709-9537)
PHONE.....................302 378-2342
David Beste D.v.m., *Owner*
EMP: 6 **EST:** 1982
SALES (est): 980.88K **Privately Held**
Web: www.bestvetyet.com
SIC: 0742 Animal hospital services, pets and other animal specialties

(G-7361)
MIDDLETOWN YMCA
Also Called: YMCA
404 N Cass St (19709-1038)
PHONE.....................302 510-1166
EMP: 11 **EST:** 2018
SALES (est): 242.83K **Privately Held**
Web: www.ymcade.org
SIC: 8641 Youth organizations

(G-7362)
MIDDLTOWN AREA CHMBER COMMERCE
1050 Industrial Dr Ste 110 (19709-2801)
PHONE.....................302 376-0222
EMP: 10 **EST:** 2019
SALES (est): 241.57K **Privately Held**
Web: www.maccde.com
SIC: 8611 Chamber of Commerce

(G-7363)
MIDDLTOWN FAMILYCARE ASSOC LLC
114 Sandhill Dr Ste 101 (19709-5805)
PHONE.....................302 378-4779
Lax Dedhia, *Managing Member*
Lax Dedhia Md, *Managing Member*
Guni Dedhia, *Off Mgr*
EMP: 21 **EST:** 1997
SALES (est): 4.44MM **Privately Held**
Web: www.middletownfamilycare.com
SIC: 8011 General and family practice, physician/surgeon

(G-7364)
MIDDLTOWN ODSSA TWNSEND SNIOR
Also Called: MOT SENIOR CENTER
300 S Scott St (19709-1355)
PHONE.....................302 378-4758
Cecillai Rocunalski, *Dir*
EMP: 20 **EST:** 1967
SALES (est): 799.39K **Privately Held**
Web: www.motseniorcenter.com
SIC: 8322 Senior citizens' center or association

(G-7365)
MIDDLTOWN SNIOR LVING PRTNERS
820 Middletown Odessa Rd (19709-9049)
PHONE.....................302 828-0988
EMP: 6 **EST:** 2018
SALES (est): 61.12K **Privately Held**
SIC: 8082 Home health care services

(G-7366)
MIDDLTOWN VLG CMNTY FOUNDATION
194 Vincent Cir (19709-3061)
PHONE.....................857 544-3954
EMP: 5 **EST:** 2017
SALES (est): 51.38K **Privately Held**
SIC: 8641 Civic and social associations

(G-7367)
MIDWAY LLC
Also Called: Midway
102 Dungarvan Dr (19709-9455)
PHONE.....................302 378-9156
EMP: 7 **EST:** 1976
SIC: 6719 Investment holding companies, except banks

(G-7368)
MILANA COLORS LLC ✪
651 N Broad St (19709-6400)
PHONE.....................872 274-4321
EMP: 2 **EST:** 2022
SALES (est): 92.41K **Privately Held**
SIC: 2869 Laboratory chemicals, organic

(G-7369)
MILE FOR MELANOMA DE
P.O. Box 954 (19709-0954)
PHONE.....................302 540-8073
Anna Farro, *Prin*
EMP: 6 **EST:** 2011
SALES (est): 75.21K **Privately Held**
Web: www.delawaremelanoma.org
SIC: 8699 Charitable organization

(G-7370)
MILLENIUM SERVICES LLC
651 N Broad St (19709-6400)
PHONE.....................888 507-9473
Fabien Charlot, *Managing Member*
EMP: 10 **EST:** 2021
SALES (est): 460.39K **Privately Held**
SIC: 8748 Business consulting, nec

(G-7371)
MILLER HEATING & COOLING LLC
108 Patriot Dr Ste E (19709-8803)
P.O. Box 168 (19730-0168)
PHONE.....................302 750-2409
EMP: 17 **EST:** 2019
SALES (est): 2.29MM **Privately Held**
Web: www.reddogac.com
SIC: 1711 Warm air heating and air conditioning contractor

(G-7372)
MILLER JW WLDG BOILER REPR CO
Also Called: J W Miller Wldg Boiler Repr Co
4917 Summit Bridge Rd (19709-8819)
P.O. Box 862 (19709-0862)
PHONE.....................302 449-1575
James Butch W Miller, *Pr*
Grace Miller, *Treas*
EMP: 6 **EST:** 1996
SALES (est): 198.33K **Privately Held**
SIC: 7692 Welding repair

(G-7373)
MINT & NEEDLE LLC
Also Called: Mint & Needle
219 W Green St (19709-1333)
PHONE.....................302 696-2484
Brandi Gregge, *Managing Member*
EMP: 7 **EST:** 2018
SALES (est): 603.95K **Privately Held**
Web: www.mintandneedle.com
SIC: 8011 Offices and clinics of medical doctors

(G-7374)
MJP ENTERPRISES
117 Dungarvan Dr (19709-9456)
PHONE.....................302 584-4736
Debra W Petro, *Owner*
EMP: 5 **EST:** 2011
SALES (est): 67.12K **Privately Held**
SIC: 8748 Business consulting, nec

(G-7375)
MOHAMMAD A KHAN MD
212 Carter Dr (19709-5837)

PHONE.................302 449-5791
Mohammad Khan, *Prin*
EMP: 9 **EST:** 2007
SALES (est): 130.47K **Privately Held**
SIC: 8011 Pediatrician

(G-7376)
MOLINAS CONTRACTING LLC
553 Maple Ave (19709-1242)
PHONE.................302 378-9316
EMP: 5 **EST:** 2019
SALES (est): 96.9K **Privately Held**
SIC: 1799 Special trade contractors, nec

(G-7377)
MONRO INC
Also Called: Mr. Tire
430 Haveg Rd (19709-1723)
PHONE.................302 378-3801
EMP: 43
SALES (corp-wide): 1.33B **Publicly Held**
Web: www.monro.com
SIC: 7538 General automotive repair shops
PA: Monro, Inc.
  200 Holleder Pkwy
  Rochester NY 14615
  585 647-6400

(G-7378)
MONSTER INCORPORATION INC ✪
651 N Broad St Ste 201 (19709-6402)
PHONE.................920 349-7947
Harinderpreet Singh, *Prin*
EMP: 2 **EST:** 2022
SALES (est): 87.4K **Privately Held**
SIC: 7372 Prepackaged software

(G-7379)
MOORE QUALITY WELDING FAB
328 W Dickerson Ln (19709-8832)
PHONE.................302 250-7136
Dan Moore, *Prin*
EMP: 4 **EST:** 2018
SALES (est): 88.73K **Privately Held**
SIC: 7692 Welding repair

(G-7380)
MOORES CABINET REFINISHING INC
939 Bethel Church Rd (19709-9757)
PHONE.................302 378-3055
John D Moore, *Pr*
Joanne Moore, *Sec*
EMP: 4 **EST:** 1976
SALES (est): 468.42K **Privately Held**
Web: www.moorescabinets.com
SIC: 2434 Wood kitchen cabinets

(G-7381)
MOSQUITO AUTHORITY WILMINGTON
Also Called: Mosquito Authority
106 Newbury Ct (19709-2106)
PHONE.................302 299-5299
Deborah Nolan, *Prin*
EMP: 8 **EST:** 2013
SALES (est): 85.46K **Privately Held**
Web: www.mosquito-authority.com
SIC: 7342 Pest control services

(G-7382)
MOT CNC WORKS LLC
110 Patriot Dr Ste H (19709-8901)
PHONE.................302 379-2114
EMP: 5 **EST:** 2019
SALES (est): 117.59K **Privately Held**
SIC: 3541 Machine tools, metal cutting type

(G-7383)
MOT COMMUNITY FUND INC
5240 Summit Bridge Rd (19709-8822)
PHONE.................302 378-5494
EMP: 5 **EST:** 2001
SALES (est): 71.05K **Privately Held**
SIC: 8399 Community chest

(G-7384)
MOT FAMILY CHIROPRACTIC -
222 Carter Dr Ste 103 (19709-5856)
PHONE.................302 378-9191
EMP: 6 **EST:** 2018
SALES (est): 132.41K **Privately Held**
Web: www.motchiropractic.com
SIC: 8041 Offices and clinics of chiropractors

(G-7385)
MOVARNA LLC
651 N Broad St Ste 205 (19709-6400)
PHONE.................805 501-5821
EMP: 3
SALES (est): 121.77K **Privately Held**
SIC: 3011 Motorcycle inner tubes

(G-7386)
MOXELLE INC (PA)
651 N Broad St Ste 201 (19709-6402)
PHONE.................646 226-9430
Gjorge Lazarov, *CEO*
EMP: 6 **EST:** 2021
SALES (est): 72.36K
SALES (corp-wide): 72.36K **Privately Held**
SIC: 7371 Computer software development and applications

(G-7387)
MSI
238 Casper Way (19709-7942)
PHONE.................302 449-5508
Larry Hart, *Prin*
EMP: 7 **EST:** 2011
SALES (est): 130.24K **Privately Held**
Web: www.msilab.com
SIC: 8734 Testing laboratories

(G-7388)
MUMFORD AND MILLER CON INC
1005 Industrial Dr (19709-1097)
PHONE.................302 378-7736
Richard L Mumford, *Pr*
Bernadette Mumford, *
EMP: 140 **EST:** 1976
SQ FT: 11,500
SALES (est): 48.96MM **Privately Held**
Web: www.mumfordandmiller.com
SIC: 1629 1611 1771 Land preparation construction; Highway and street construction; Concrete work

(G-7389)
MUSE GLOBAL CONSULTING INC
651 N Broad St (19709-6400)
PHONE.................325 221-3634
Sofia Shved, *CEO*
EMP: 25 **EST:** 2019
SALES (est): 673.89K **Privately Held**
SIC: 8743 Public relations and publicity

(G-7390)
MUSICK LLC
211 N Broad St Ste 3a (19709-1035)
PHONE.................201 962-0023
EMP: 3 **EST:** 2020
SALES (est): 71.13K **Privately Held**
SIC: 7372 Application computer software

(G-7391)
NANOSKIN LLC
651 N Broad St Ste 206 (19709-6402)
PHONE.................310 345-4768
EMP: 2 **EST:** 2021
SALES (est): 99.28K **Privately Held**
Web: www.nanoskinusa.com
SIC: 2834 Dermatologicals

(G-7392)
NAPA M3 INC
221 N Broad St Ste 3a (19709-1070)
PHONE.................719 660-6263
EMP: 2 **EST:** 2011
SALES (est): 177.38K **Privately Held**
SIC: 3714 5511 5571 Motor vehicle parts and accessories; Automobiles, new and used; Motorcycle dealers

(G-7393)
NASHED MAHER MD
12 Pennington St Ste 100 (19709-1026)
PHONE.................302 378-1887
Maher Nashed Md, *Prin*
EMP: 9 **EST:** 2001
SALES (est): 130.8K **Privately Held**
Web: www.allergyasthmaimmunologyofdelaware.com
SIC: 8011 Allergist

(G-7394)
NDON JORDONA
941 Lansdowne Rd (19709-8395)
PHONE.................609 254-2620
Jordona Ndon, *Owner*
EMP: 5 **EST:** 2018
SALES (est): 68.91K **Privately Held**
SIC: 8049 Offices of health practitioner

(G-7395)
NEST PROPERTIES LLC
412 Reading Ln (19709-2136)
PHONE.................302 373-8015
Dianne Platt, *Prin*
EMP: 5 **EST:** 2016
SALES (est): 137.62K **Privately Held**
SIC: 6531 Real estate brokers and agents

(G-7396)
NEURAL HEAVEN INC ✪
651 N Broad St Ste 201 (19709-6402)
PHONE.................631 485-4205
Gaurav Upadhyay, *Dir*
EMP: 12 **EST:** 2022
SALES (est): 406.37K **Privately Held**
SIC: 7371 Computer software development and applications

(G-7397)
NEURASTACK INC
651 N Broad St Ste 9566 (19709-6400)
PHONE.................512 760-3149
Cameron Jackson, *CEO*
EMP: 2
SALES (est): 92.41K **Privately Held**
SIC: 3571 Electronic computers

(G-7398)
NEW COVENANT ELEC SVCS INC
Also Called: Nces
806 Old School House Rd (19709-9066)
PHONE.................302 454-1165
Kimberly Creek, *Pr*
Kimberly Irene Creek, *Pr*
Kevin Elwood Creek, *VP*
EMP: 9 **EST:** 2005
SALES (est): 744.41K **Privately Held**
Web: www.ncesi.com

SIC: 8748 Business consulting, nec

(G-7399)
NEWPORT VENTURES INC
Also Called: Exxon
512 Barrymore Pkwy (19709-6614)
PHONE.................302 998-1693
Robert Weber, *CEO*
Joseph Fitzgerald, *Pr*
Richard Kemske, *VP*
Beatrice Schneckenburger, *Stockholder*
Bonnie Kemske, *Stockholder*
EMP: 17 **EST:** 1981
SALES (est): 822.72K **Privately Held**
Web: corporate.exxonmobil.com
SIC: 5541 7542 5411 Filling stations, gasoline; Carwash, self-service; Convenience stores, independent

(G-7400)
NEWS IN BULLETS LLC
600 N Broad St Ste 52185 (19709-1032)
PHONE.................831 250-6955
EMP: 20 **EST:** 2020
SALES (est): 602.8K **Privately Held**
SIC: 4832 News

(G-7401)
NEWTON MANAGEMENT HOLDING INC ✪
600 N Broad St Ste 5 (19709-1032)
PHONE.................800 784-8714
Shamar Newton, *CEO*
EMP: 10 **EST:** 2022
SALES (est): 494.72K **Privately Held**
Web: www.newtonmanagementholdinginc.com
SIC: 7389 8742 Business Activities at Non-Commercial Site; Business management consultant

(G-7402)
NEWTONE COMMUNICATIONS INC
651 N Broad St (19709-6400)
PHONE.................650 727-0998
Jin Zhang, *CEO*
EMP: 5
SALES (est): 107.01K **Privately Held**
SIC: 7371 Computer software development

(G-7403)
NEXTDNS INC
651 N Broad St Ste 206 (19709-6402)
PHONE.................831 854-7227
Romain Cointetas, *CEO*
EMP: 20 **EST:** 2000
SALES (est): 851.11K **Privately Held**
Web: www.nextdns.io
SIC: 4813 Online service providers

(G-7404)
NEXTERA ROBOTIC SYSTEMS INC
651 N Broad St (19709-6400)
PHONE.................617 899-7323
Svetlana Graf, *CEO*
EMP: 15
SALES (est): 494.46K **Privately Held**
SIC: 7371 Software programming applications

(G-7405)
NICKELS ARCADE LLC
118 Sleepy Hollow Dr (19709-5836)
PHONE.................800 979-3224
EMP: 5 **EST:** 2006
SALES (est): 80.56K **Privately Held**
SIC: 7389 Business services, nec

GEOGRAPHIC SECTION

Middletown - New Castle County (G-7435)

(G-7406)
NICKLES ARCADE LLC
356 Norwalk Way (19709-8310)
PHONE.....................302 376-1794
EMP: 14 **EST:** 2014
SALES (est): 1.14MM **Privately Held**
SIC: 5023 5961 Kitchenware; Arts and crafts equipment and supplies, mail order

(G-7407)
NOBLE CONTRACTING GROUP LLC
625 Warren Dr (19709-1704)
PHONE.....................302 219-4006
EMP: 5 **EST:** 2019
SALES (est): 228.98K **Privately Held**
SIC: 1799 Special trade contractors, nec

(G-7408)
NODE TECHNOLOGIES INC (PA)
651 N Broad St Ste 206 (19709-6402)
PHONE.....................866 366-1862
EMP: 6 **EST:** 2021
SALES (est): 46.16K
SALES (corp-wide): 46.16K **Privately Held**
SIC: 7371 Computer software development and applications

(G-7409)
NORBERTINE FATHERS
1269 Bayview Rd (19709-2147)
PHONE.....................302 449-1840
John Logan, *Manager*
EMP: 8 **EST:** 2004
SALES (est): 468.91K **Privately Held**
Web: www.perumission.ca
SIC: 8699 Charitable organization

(G-7410)
NORKRISSERVICES
534 Maiden Ct (19709-2198)
PHONE.....................302 450-6108
EMP: 5 **EST:** 2019
SALES (est): 110.84K **Privately Held**
SIC: 8093 Mental health clinic, outpatient

(G-7411)
NORTHEASTERN SUPPLY INC
Also Called: Northeastern Supply
104 Patriot Dr (19709-8762)
PHONE.....................302 378-7880
Jarrod Moore, *Brnch Mgr*
EMP: 5
SALES (corp-wide): 195.02MM **Privately Held**
Web: www.northeastern.com
SIC: 5074 Plumbing fittings and supplies
PA: Northeastern Supply, Inc.
    8323 Pulaski Hwy
    Baltimore MD 21237
    410 574-0010

(G-7412)
NURDSOFT LLC ✪
221 N Broad St 3a (19709-1070)
PHONE.....................332 203-2920
Abhishake Pathak, *Prin*
EMP: 5 **EST:** 2022
SALES (est): 199.4K **Privately Held**
SIC: 7371 Custom computer programming services

(G-7413)
OHM LSHREE FOUNDATION
767 Wood Duck Ct (19709-6114)
PHONE.....................302 652-2900
Samir Patel, *Prin*
EMP: 5 **EST:** 2018
SALES (est): 55.4K **Privately Held**
SIC: 8641 Civic and social associations

(G-7414)
OMNIMAVEN INC
103 Cazier Dr (19709-8852)
PHONE.....................302 378-8918
Manuel Duarte, *Prin*
EMP: 5 **EST:** 2002
SALES (est): 460.07K **Privately Held**
Web: www.omnimaven.com
SIC: 8731 7373 Computer (hardware) development; Systems software development services

(G-7415)
ONE OFF ROD & CUSTOM INC
118 Sleepy Hollow Dr Ste 5& (19709-5836)
PHONE.....................302 449-1489
Ray Bartlett, *Pr*
Garyson Corkell, *Pr*
Theresa Faust, *VP*
EMP: 14 **EST:** 2009
SALES (est): 891.81K **Privately Held**
Web: www.oneoffhotrod.com
SIC: 7532 Antique and classic automobile restoration

(G-7416)
ONNEC USA INC
108 Patriot Dr Ste A (19709-8803)
PHONE.....................703 309-7338
EMP: 6 **EST:** 2020
SALES (est): 183.76K **Privately Held**
Web: www.onnecgroup.com
SIC: 7371 Computer software systems analysis and design, custom

(G-7417)
OPTIMA IQ INVESTMENTS INC
Also Called: Investments
600 N Broad St Ste 5-403 (19709-1032)
PHONE.....................302 279-5750
Kelvin Burton Junior, *CEO*
Kelvyon Burton, *
Aleasha Coleman, *
Galean Jack, *
EMP: 35 **EST:** 2020
SALES (est): 2MM **Privately Held**
SIC: 6799 5962 Real estate investors, except property operators; Beverage vending machines

(G-7418)
OPTIONS OR FAST CASH INC
651 N Broad St (19709-6400)
PHONE.....................310 867-9171
EMP: 5
SALES (est): 286.41K **Privately Held**
SIC: 6411 Insurance information and consulting services

(G-7419)
ORANGETHEORY FITNESS
476 Middletown Warwick Rd (19709-9192)
PHONE.....................302 426-2284
EMP: 6 **EST:** 2019
SALES (est): 29.54K **Privately Held**
Web: www.orangetheory.com
SIC: 7991 Physical fitness clubs with training equipment

(G-7420)
ORIGINAL SHOPPERS THE LLC ✪
600 N Broad St Ste 569 (19709-1032)
PHONE.....................866 838-3224
Jacob Williamson, *Managing Member*
EMP: 5 **EST:** 2022
SALES (est): 203.87K **Privately Held**
SIC: 8742 Marketing consulting services

(G-7421)
PADI TECHNOLOGY LTD (PA) ✪
651 N Broad St Ste 201 (19709-6402)
PHONE.....................832 646-6926
Osagie Otoikhine, *CEO*
EMP: 9 **EST:** 2023
SALES (est): 470.79K
SALES (corp-wide): 470.79K **Privately Held**
SIC: 7389 Financial services

(G-7422)
PAGOS SOLUTIONS INC
651 N Broad St Ste 206 (19709-6402)
PHONE.....................310 245-3591
Klas Back, *CEO*
EMP: 18 **EST:** 2020
SALES (est): 588.75K **Privately Held**
Web: www.pagos.com
SIC: 7389 Financial services

(G-7423)
PALLINO ASSET MANAGEMENT LLC
651 N Broad St (19709-6400)
PHONE.....................302 378-0686
EMP: 9 **EST:** 2004
SALES (est): 244.74K **Privately Held**
SIC: 8741 Financial management for business

(G-7424)
PAPONA LLC ✪
651 N Broad St Ste 206 (19709-6402)
PHONE.....................302 285-9559
Ahmad Al Nees, *Managing Member*
EMP: 10 **EST:** 2022
SALES (est): 456.18K **Privately Held**
SIC: 5199 Nondurable goods, nec

(G-7425)
PARAMUNT HLTHCARE RSOURCES LLC
833 Llanelli Dr (19709-1546)
PHONE.....................302 722-5484
EMP: 10
SALES (est): 348.32K **Privately Held**
SIC: 7389 7361 Business Activities at Non-Commercial Site; Employment agencies

(G-7426)
PARCHIVE ANALYTICS INC
Also Called: Parchive Analytics
651 N Broad St Ste 206 (19709-6402)
PHONE.....................903 683-5878
Oluyinka Oginni, *CEO*
EMP: 7 **EST:** 2021
SALES (est): 302.13K **Privately Held**
SIC: 7371 Computer software development and applications

(G-7427)
PARTY PRINCESS PRODUCTIONS
332 Misty Vale Dr (19709-2124)
PHONE.....................302 378-7127
Pamela Cichocki, *Prin*
EMP: 5 **EST:** 2018
SALES (est): 42.51K **Privately Held**
Web: www.partyprincessproductions.com
SIC: 7299 Party planning service

(G-7428)
PARTY PRINCESS PRODUCTIONS
364 E Main St Ste 420 (19709-1482)
PHONE.....................302 307-3804
EMP: 5 **EST:** 2017
SALES (est): 50.74K **Privately Held**
Web: wilmington.partyprincessproductions.com
SIC: 7822 Motion picture and tape distribution

(G-7429)
PATRICK GAYDOS
117 Night Heron Ln (19709-2208)
PHONE.....................302 378-8753
Patrick Gaydos, *Prin*
EMP: 5 **EST:** 2008
SALES (est): 88.99K **Privately Held**
SIC: 7389 Business Activities at Non-Commercial Site

(G-7430)
PATTERSON-SCHWARTZ & ASSOC INC
Also Called: Patterson Schwartz Real Estate
4417 Summit Bridge Rd (19709-9549)
PHONE.....................302 285-5100
Michael C Dunning, *Mgr*
EMP: 74
SALES (corp-wide): 24.38MM **Privately Held**
Web: www.pattersonschwartz.com
SIC: 6531 Real estate agent, residential
PA: Patterson-Schwartz And Associates, Inc.
    7234 Lancaster Pike
    Hockessin DE 19707
    302 234-5250

(G-7431)
PAUL A LANGE
7 Claddagh Ct (19709-9003)
PHONE.....................302 378-1706
EMP: 4 **EST:** 1956
SALES (est): 159.26K **Privately Held**
SIC: 3541 Machine tools, metal cutting type

(G-7432)
PAUL DVIS EMRGNCY SVCS NEW CST
519 Diamond Dr (19709-1363)
PHONE.....................302 364-3139
EMP: 5 **EST:** 2017
SALES (est): 167.24K **Privately Held**
Web: new-castle.pauldavis.com
SIC: 1521 Repairing fire damage, single-family houses

(G-7433)
PAWS & PEOPLE TOO
4390 Summit Bridge Rd Ste 4 (19709-9828)
PHONE.....................302 376-8234
Theresa Overbey, *Owner*
EMP: 5 **EST:** 2001
SALES (est): 312.42K **Privately Held**
Web: www.pawsandpeopletoo.org
SIC: 0752 Grooming services, pet and animal specialties

(G-7434)
PAWS FOR LIFE INC
4466 Summit Bridge Rd (19709-9344)
PHONE.....................302 376-7297
Tracie Simon, *Prin*
EMP: 6 **EST:** 1998
SALES (est): 98.74K **Privately Held**
Web: www.pawsforlife.org
SIC: 8699 0752 Animal humane society; Animal specialty services

(G-7435)
PCK ASSOCIATES INC
Also Called: Candyland Farm
1343 Bohemia Mill Rd (19709-9021)
PHONE.....................302 378-7192
Herbert Moelis, *Pr*
Ellen Moelis, *Sec*

Middletown - New Castle County (G-7436) — GEOGRAPHIC SECTION

EMP: 5 **EST:** 1986
SALES (est): 414.2K **Privately Held**
SIC: 0272 Horses and other equines

(G-7436)
PEARCE & MORETTO INC
1060 Industrial Dr (19709-2800)
PHONE.....................302 326-0707
Earl Pearce, *Pr*
Joseph Moretto, *
EMP: 30 **EST:** 2000
SALES (est): 7.56MM **Privately Held**
Web: www.pearce-moretto.com
SIC: 1794 Excavation work

(G-7437)
PEBBLE STACK LLC
651 N Broad St Ste 206 (19709-6402)
PHONE.....................732 910-9701
Prabodh Maisuri, *Managing Member*
EMP: 5 **EST:** 2020
SALES (est): 46.16K **Privately Held**
SIC: 7371 Computer software development and applications

(G-7438)
PEIRCE JAMES TOWNSEND III
Also Called: A & J Custom Woodworking
19 Canary Ct (19709-2183)
PHONE.....................302 449-2279
James Peirce, *Prin*
EMP: 2 **EST:** 2011
SALES (est): 115.03K **Privately Held**
SIC: 2431 Millwork

(G-7439)
PENSKE TRUCK LEASING CORP
Also Called: Penske
921 Middletown Warwick Rd (19709-9099)
PHONE.....................302 449-9294
EMP: 5
SALES (corp-wide): 5.16B **Privately Held**
Web: www.pensketruckrental.com
SIC: 7513 4214 Truck rental and leasing, no drivers; Local trucking with storage
HQ: Penske Truck Leasing Corporation
2675 Morgantown Rd
Reading PA 19607
610 775-6000

(G-7440)
PEOPLES FIRST INSURANCE INC
292 Carter Dr Ste C (19709-5846)
PHONE.....................302 449-4777
EMP: 5 **EST:** 2014
SALES (est): 242K **Privately Held**
SIC: 6411 Insurance agents, nec

(G-7441)
PERFECTION LAWNCARE LTD
129 Gazebo Ln (19709-4601)
PHONE.....................215 624-7410
Walt Beuttenmuller, *Owner*
EMP: 9 **EST:** 1990
SALES (est): 191.26K **Privately Held**
SIC: 0782 Lawn care services

(G-7442)
PERSHING FOUNDATION
23 Palmer Dr (19709-9371)
PHONE.....................636 352-7122
EMP: 6 **EST:** 2019
SALES (est): 65.91K **Privately Held**
SIC: 8641 Civic and social associations

(G-7443)
PETCY INC
Also Called: Petcy
651 N Broad St Ste 206 (19709-6402)
PHONE.....................920 240-4312
Kashif Ahmad Khan, *CEO*
EMP: 5
SALES (est): 46.16K **Privately Held**
SIC: 7371 Computer software development and applications

(G-7444)
PETER ZORACH
495 E Main St (19709-1463)
PHONE.....................302 377-5874
Peter Zorach, *Owner*
EMP: 5 **EST:** 2015
SALES (est): 59.55K **Privately Held**
SIC: 8011 Psychiatric clinic

(G-7445)
PHILADLPHIA PRTECTION UNIT LLC
511 Cilantro Ct (19709-8783)
PHONE.....................267 505-2671
Clinton Craddock, *CEO*
EMP: 5 **EST:** 2013
SALES (est): 94.58K **Privately Held**
SIC: 7381 Security guard service

(G-7446)
PHILLIPS TRUCK AND TRAILER
14 W Reybold Dr (19709-1500)
PHONE.....................302 502-5046
Joshua Phillips, *Prin*
EMP: 5 **EST:** 2017
SALES (est): 75.98K **Privately Held**
Web: www.bgtruckandtrailer.com
SIC: 7538 General truck repair

(G-7447)
PHYSICAL THERAPIST
503 Pierce Ct (19709-9697)
PHONE.....................302 983-4151
Amy Delaney, *Prin*
EMP: 6 **EST:** 2016
SALES (est): 71.36K **Privately Held**
Web: www.thrivemiddletown.com
SIC: 8049 Physical therapist

(G-7448)
PIERCE TOTAL COMFORT LLC
Also Called: Honeywell Authorized Dealer
21 S Broad St (19709-1404)
PHONE.....................302 378-7714
EMP: 12 **EST:** 2009
SALES (est): 1.03MM **Privately Held**
Web: www.piercetotalcomfort.com
SIC: 1711 Warm air heating and air conditioning contractor

(G-7449)
PINE VALLEY CORVETTES
108 Pine Valley Dr (19709-9793)
PHONE.....................302 834-1268
EMP: 6 **EST:** 2011
SALES (est): 221.63K **Privately Held**
Web: www.vetteclub.org
SIC: 7532 Top and body repair and paint shops

(G-7450)
PIVOT PHYSICAL THERAPY
120 Sandhill Dr (19709-5864)
PHONE.....................302 449-7792
EMP: 12 **EST:** 2017
SALES (est): 244.77K **Privately Held**
Web: www.pivotphysicaltherapy.com
SIC: 8049 Physical therapist

(G-7451)
PJK GOLF OPERATIONS LLC
1 Wittington Way (19709-7906)
PHONE.....................302 376-6500
EMP: 6 **EST:** 2019
SALES (est): 20.78K **Privately Held**
SIC: 7999 Golf professionals

(G-7452)
PLANE JAMES AND JANES LLC
606 E Glen Mare Dr (19709-8776)
PHONE.....................267 716-6723
EMP: 5 **EST:** 2021
SALES (est): 288.66K **Privately Held**
SIC: 4724 Travel agencies

(G-7453)
PLANE SOFTWARE INC ◊
651 N Broad St Ste 201 (19709-6402)
PHONE.....................857 693-9321
Vamsi Kurama, *CEO*
Vihar Kurama, *COO*
EMP: 20 **EST:** 2023
SALES (est): 588.11K **Privately Held**
SIC: 7371 Computer software development

(G-7454)
PLANET FITNESS
703 N Broad St (19709-1166)
PHONE.....................302 378-2777
EMP: 9 **EST:** 2018
SALES (est): 32.49K **Privately Held**
Web: www.planetfitness.com
SIC: 7991 Physical fitness facilities

(G-7455)
PLANET IOT INC
651 N Broad St Ste 206 (19709-6402)
PHONE.....................314 585-9924
Muhammad Bilal, *CEO*
EMP: 10 **EST:** 2020
SALES (est): 247.5K **Privately Held**
SIC: 3564 Air purification equipment

(G-7456)
PLATINUM PLUS ENTERPRISE LLC
Also Called: Platinum Plus Enterprise
405 Champs Ln (19709-3119)
PHONE.....................302 200-2257
Majid Razzaq, *Prin*
EMP: 6 **EST:** 2017
SALES (est): 358.66K **Privately Held**
SIC: 7389 Business services, nec

(G-7457)
PLAY BETTER INC
651 N Broad St Ste 206 (19709-6402)
PHONE.....................407 815-2719
Marielle Du Toit, *Pr*
EMP: 5
SALES (est): 73.93K **Privately Held**
SIC: 7372 Prepackaged software

(G-7458)
PLUG TRANSPORTATION LLC
600 N Broad St Ste 5483 (19709-1032)
PHONE.....................302 644-5511
EMP: 2 **EST:** 2021
SALES (est): 100K **Privately Held**
SIC: 3537 Trucks, tractors, loaders, carriers, and similar equipment

(G-7459)
PNC BANK NATIONAL ASSOCIATION
Also Called: PNC
460 W Main St (19709-1063)
PHONE.....................302 378-4441
William Neal, *Mgr*
EMP: 5
SALES (corp-wide): 23.54B **Publicly Held**
Web: www.pnc.com
SIC: 6021 National trust companies with deposits, commercial
HQ: Pnc Bank, National Association
300 5th Ave
Pittsburgh PA 15222
877 762-2000

(G-7460)
POSHSISTAHS HAIR LLC
912 Janvier Ct (19709-1733)
PHONE.....................302 464-2469
EMP: 10 **EST:** 2016
SALES (est): 283.15K **Privately Held**
SIC: 3999 Hair and hair-based products

(G-7461)
POSTLY TECHNOLOGIES INC ◊
651 N Broad St Ste 201 (19709-6402)
PHONE.....................315 215-0320
Paul Onu, *CEO*
EMP: 10 **EST:** 2022
SALES (est): 365.44K **Privately Held**
Web: www.postly.ai
SIC: 7372 Prepackaged software

(G-7462)
POWER TRANSMISSION SVCS INC
501 Industrial Dr (19709-1081)
PHONE.....................302 378-7925
Charles R Russell, *Pr*
EMP: 6 **EST:** 1990
SALES (est): 1.05MM **Privately Held**
Web: www.powertransmissionservices.com
SIC: 3566 Gears, power transmission, except auto

(G-7463)
PREMIER COMPREHENSIVE DENTAL
212 Celebration Ct (19709-8777)
PHONE.....................302 378-3131
Kate Oshea, *Prin*
EMP: 5 **EST:** 2010
SALES (est): 292.49K **Privately Held**
Web: www.premiercdental.com
SIC: 8021 Dentists' office

(G-7464)
PREMIER PRO CLEANING SOLUTIONS
507 Pythagoras Path (19709-9862)
PHONE.....................302 743-5337
EMP: 6 **EST:** 2015
SALES (est): 242.58K **Privately Held**
Web: www.premierproclean.com
SIC: 7699 Cleaning services

(G-7465)
PREMIER PROPERTY & POOL MGT
106 Sandhill Dr Unit C (19709-5849)
PHONE.....................302 357-6321
EMP: 8 **EST:** 2018
SALES (est): 161.99K **Privately Held**
Web: www.premierpropertyandpool.com
SIC: 8741 Management services

(G-7466)
PREMIER RESTORATION CNSTR INC (PA)
Also Called: Premier Restorations
703 Industrial Dr (19709-1085)
PHONE.....................302 832-1288
EMP: 5 **EST:** 2009
SALES (est): 460.69K **Privately Held**
SIC: 1741 Tuckpointing or restoration

(G-7467)
PREMIERE HAIR DESIGN
117 Marathon Dr (19709-7603)
PHONE.....................302 368-7711
Barbie Mooney, *Pt*
EMP: 6 **EST:** 1990
SALES (est): 130.38K **Privately Held**

GEOGRAPHIC SECTION

Middletown - New Castle County (G-7497)

SIC: **7231** Cosmetology and personal hygiene salons

(G-7468)
PRESS MEDIA GROUP INC (PA)
600 N Broad St (19709-1032)
PHONE..................................323 205-5488
Alberto Marzan, *CEO*
EMP: **5** EST: **2016**
SQ FT: **2,105**
SALES (est): **1.06MM**
SALES (corp-wide): **1.06MM Privately Held**
Web: www.vumatv.com
SIC: **2741** 7812 Internet publishing and broadcasting; Motion picture production

(G-7469)
PRIME SECURITY CORP
600 N Broad St Ste 5 (19709-1032)
PHONE..................................803 281-0378
Chengbeili Li, *Prin*
EMP: **5**
SALES (est): **107.01K Privately Held**
SIC: **7371** Computer software development and applications

(G-7470)
PRIV SOCIAL INC
651 N Broad St Ste 206 (19709-6402)
PHONE..................................501 301-4197
Juan Carlos Lopez Pendas, *Pr*
EMP: **5**
SALES (est): **23.63K Privately Held**
SIC: **7374** Data processing and preparation

(G-7471)
PRO RFP INC ✪
221 N Broad St Ste 3a (19709-1070)
PHONE..................................302 265-3786
Tom Fillaus, *CEO*
EMP: **6** EST: **2022**
SALES (est): **72.34K Privately Held**
SIC: **8732** Business analysis

(G-7472)
PRODUCTIONS FOR PURPOSE INC
10 Little Cir (19709-7956)
PHONE..................................302 388-9883
Dawn Mosley, *Ex Dir*
EMP: **6** EST: **2014**
SALES (est): **149.83K Privately Held**
SIC: **7812** Motion picture and video production

(G-7473)
PROFESSIONAL SECURITY CO
625 Swansea Dr (19709-0202)
PHONE..................................302 383-7142
EMP: **5** EST: **2016**
SALES (est): **59.36K Privately Held**
SIC: **7381** Security guard service

(G-7474)
PROGLO 2 LLC
651 N Broad St Ste 205 (19709-6402)
PHONE..................................702 494-7877
Rakesh Arunachalam, *Managing Member*
EMP: **10** EST: **2021**
SALES (est): **355.79K Privately Held**
SIC: **7379** Online services technology consultants

(G-7475)
PROPERTIES FOR LIFE LLC
5403 Proust Pl (19709-3209)
PHONE..................................302 293-9465
Jim Willis, *Prin*
EMP: **5** EST: **2010**
SALES (est): **137.87K Privately Held**

SIC: **6512** Nonresidential building operators

(G-7476)
PROSPERITY UNLIMITED ENTE
32 E Sarazen Dr (19709-7960)
PHONE..................................302 379-2494
EMP: **5** EST: **2010**
SALES (est): **194.57K Privately Held**
SIC: **8741** Management services

(G-7477)
PROVEN PASS INC
221 N Broad St (19709-1070)
PHONE..................................888 404-2775
Peter Gallic, *CEO*
EMP: **10**
SALES (est): **208.73K Privately Held**
SIC: **7371** Computer software development and applications

(G-7478)
PRYSM FINANCIAL TECHNOLOGY INC
651 N Broad St (19709-6400)
PHONE..................................323 333-7698
Ari Stiegler, *CEO*
EMP: **15**
SALES (est): **857.15K Privately Held**
SIC: **7389** Business services, nec

(G-7479)
PUGLISI EGG FARMS DELAWARE LLC
1881 Middle Neck Rd (19709-9646)
PHONE..................................302 376-1200
John Puglisi, *Pr*
Paul Puglisi, *VP*
Michael Puglisi, *Sec*
EMP: **35** EST: **1999**
SALES (est): **3.48MM**
SALES (corp-wide): **4.66MM Privately Held**
SIC: **0252** 5144 Chicken eggs; Eggs
PA: Three Puglisi Brothers, Inc.
75 Easy St
Howell NJ 07731
732 938-2373

(G-7480)
PUMPKIN SPACE LATTE CO
651 N Broad St Ste 206 (19709-6402)
PHONE..................................765 326-0517
EMP: **5** EST: **2021**
SALES (est): **107.01K Privately Held**
SIC: **7371** Custom computer programming services

(G-7481)
PUMPKIN SPICE LATTE CO
651 N Broad St Ste 206 (19709-6402)
PHONE..................................765 326-0517
Juliana Hill, *CEO*
EMP: **5** EST: **2021**
SALES (est): **107.01K Privately Held**
SIC: **7371** Custom computer programming services

(G-7482)
PUPPY PLAYDATE CO
651 N Broad St Ste 206 (19709-6402)
PHONE..................................765 326-0517
Juliana Hill, *CEO*
EMP: **5** EST: **2021**
SALES (est): **40.03K Privately Held**
SIC: **8641** Social club, membership

(G-7483)
PURE SELF COACHING LLC
160 Shannon Blvd (19709-2190)
PHONE..................................302 345-0356

Camille Pilgrim Haynes, *Prin*
EMP: **5** EST: **2016**
SALES (est): **41.48K Privately Held**
SIC: **7999** Amusement and recreation, nec

(G-7484)
PURE WELLNESS LLC
708 Ash Blvd (19709-8871)
PHONE..................................302 449-0149
EMP: **7**
SALES (corp-wide): **2.76MM Privately Held**
Web: www.purewellchiro.com
SIC: **8041** Offices and clinics of chiropractors
PA: Pure Wellness, Llc
550 Stanton Christn Rd # 302
Newark DE 19713
302 365-5470

(G-7485)
QUADIX LLC
364 E Main St Ste 212 (19709-1482)
PHONE..................................877 669-8680
David Estes, *Owner*
EMP: **8** EST: **2014**
SQ FT: **20,000**
SALES (est): **169.48K Privately Held**
SIC: **4813** 4899 Internet host services; Communication signal enhancement network services

(G-7486)
QUALITY CONTRACTING & DEVELOPM
605 Louis Ln (19709-3115)
PHONE..................................302 438-0874
EMP: **5** EST: **2008**
SALES (est): **130.29K Privately Held**
SIC: **1799** Special trade contractors, nec

(G-7487)
QUALITY POOL CARE
100 E Green St (19709-1423)
PHONE..................................302 378-7486
Noah Shumate, *Owner*
EMP: **7** EST: **2009**
SALES (est): **143.02K Privately Held**
Web: www.qualitypoolcareinc.com
SIC: **7389** Swimming pool and hot tub service and maintenance

(G-7488)
QUALITY RESIDE LLC
651 N Broad St Ste 205 (19709-6400)
PHONE..................................484 957-0564
EMP: **8**
SALES (est): **65.81K Privately Held**
SIC: **7011** Vacation lodges

(G-7489)
QUANTUM TEMPLE INC
651 N Broad St Ste 206 (19709-6402)
PHONE..................................917 900-7452
Hunter Soik, *CEO*
EMP: **20** EST: **2021**
SALES (est): **744.67K Privately Held**
SIC: **6799** Commodity investors

(G-7490)
QUANTUM TRANSFORMATION INC ✪
651 N Broad St Ste 206 (19709-6402)
PHONE..................................315 795-4427
Paul Carey, *Prin*
EMP: **6** EST: **2022**
SALES (est): **65.1K Privately Held**
SIC: **7299** Miscellaneous personal service

(G-7491)
QUEST DIAGNOSTICS INCORPORATED
Also Called: Quest Diagnostics
114 Sandhill Dr Ste 202 (19709-5807)
PHONE..................................302 376-8675
Bijoy Ghosh, *Brnch Mgr*
EMP: **5**
SALES (corp-wide): **9.88B Publicly Held**
Web: www.questdiagnostics.com
SIC: **8071** Testing laboratories
PA: Quest Diagnostics Incorporated
500 Plaza Dr Ste G
Secaucus NJ 07094
973 520-2700

(G-7492)
QUILTED HEIRLOOMS
123 Back Creek Dr (19709-8843)
PHONE..................................302 354-6061
Michelle Smith, *Prin*
EMP: **5** EST: **2010**
SALES (est): **102.75K Privately Held**
SIC: **2511** Wood household furniture

(G-7493)
QWICK TIME LOGISTICS LLC
651 N Broad St Ste 205 (19709-6402)
PHONE..................................985 413-2217
Brandon Tunson, *CEO*
EMP: **5** EST: **2021**
SALES (est): **115K Privately Held**
SIC: **4789** Transportation services, nec

(G-7494)
R & L PROPERTY MANAGEMENT LLC
212 Murphy Dr (19709-7502)
PHONE..................................267 825-3570
Rekiya Bell, *Prin*
EMP: **5** EST: **2016**
SALES (est): **234.53K Privately Held**
SIC: **8741** Management services

(G-7495)
R D ARNOLD CONSTRUCTION INC
33 E Stonewall Dr (19709-3810)
P.O. Box 26 (19347-0026)
PHONE..................................610 255-4739
Rudy Arnold, *Pr*
Greg Fletcher, *VP*
Christy Kane, *Sec*
Chris Gordon, *Sec*
EMP: **8** EST: **1986**
SALES (est): **754.95K Privately Held**
SIC: **1521** New construction, single-family houses

(G-7496)
R&M REAL ESTATE COMPANY LLC (PA) ✪
651 N Broad St Ste 205 (19709-6402)
PHONE..................................610 715-0906
EMP: **7** EST: **2022**
SALES (est): **273.99K**
SALES (corp-wide): **273.99K Privately Held**
Web: www.rmrealestatecompany.com
SIC: **6513** Apartment building operators

(G-7497)
RABBANI-TEHRANI SHAHARIAR
Also Called: Hummingbird Lawn Care
1401 Pole Bridge Rd (19709-2167)
PHONE..................................302 376-1081
Rabbani-tehrani Shahariar, *Prin*
EMP: **5** EST: **2010**
SALES (est): **73.65K Privately Held**
SIC: **0782** Lawn care services

Middletown - New Castle County (G-7498)

GEOGRAPHIC SECTION

(G-7498)
RACHEL ANNE BEASTON
460 E Main St (19709-1462)
PHONE.....................302 449-1875
Rachel Beaston, *Prin*
EMP: 6 EST: 2017
SALES (est): 66.18K **Privately Held**
SIC: 8049 Offices of health practitioner

(G-7499)
RAGE RECORDING STUDIO LLC
651 N Broad St Ste 20530 (19709-6400)
PHONE.....................302 313-1699
EMP: 5 EST: 2020
SALES (est): 104.73K **Privately Held**
SIC: 7389 Music recording producer

(G-7500)
RAM TECH SYSTEMS INC (PA)
1050 Industrial Dr Ste 110 (19709-2802)
P.O. Box 778 (19701-0778)
PHONE.....................302 832-6600
Srinivas Lokula, *CEO*
EMP: 41 EST: 1994
SQ FT: 1,300
SALES (est): 2.29MM
SALES (corp-wide): 2.29MM **Privately Held**
Web: www.rtsiusa.com
SIC: 7371 7373 7372 7629 Computer software systems analysis and design, custom; Value-added resellers, computer systems; Prepackaged software; Business machine repair, electric

(G-7501)
RAMIGLOT INC
651 N Broad St (19709-6400)
PHONE.....................929 203-5115
Rami Abusalah, *CEO*
EMP: 5 EST: 2021
SALES (est): 46.43K **Privately Held**
SIC: 7299 Information services, consumer

(G-7502)
RARE ROYALS INCORPORATED
651 N Broad St (19709-6400)
PHONE.....................833 288-7171
John A Annan-forson, *CEO*
EMP: 5 EST: 2021
SALES (est): 270.26K **Privately Held**
SIC: 7389 5661 Business Activities at Non-Commercial Site; Shoe stores

(G-7503)
RASTAN ENTERPRISES LLC
651 N Broad St (19709-6400)
PHONE.....................443 691-0232
EMP: 8
SALES (est): 319.06K **Privately Held**
SIC: 8742 Transportation consultant

(G-7504)
RATED10 LLC ◆
651 N Broad St (19709-6400)
PHONE.....................310 699-9537
Mert Akanay, *Managing Member*
EMP: 2 EST: 2023
SALES (est): 87.4K **Privately Held**
SIC: 7372 Application computer software

(G-7505)
RAVANA C STARKS CLEANING SVCS
506 Pythagoras Path (19709-9863)
PHONE.....................215 647-2467
Natalie Price, *Prin*
EMP: 6 EST: 2018
SALES (est): 100.44K **Privately Held**
SIC: 7699 Cleaning services

(G-7506)
RDU INSTAHOTELS LLC
651 N Broad St Ste 205 No7146 (19709-6400)
PHONE.....................919 297-8399
EMP: 5 EST: 2021
SALES (est): 55.75K **Privately Held**
Web: www.rduinstahotels.com
SIC: 7011 Vacation lodges

(G-7507)
REDFLAG MARKETING CORP
600 N Broad St Ste 5 (19709-1032)
PHONE.....................302 464-8116
Simon Jenkins, *CEO*
Fadia Miari, *CFO*
EMP: 5
SALES (est): 205.24K **Privately Held**
SIC: 8742 Marketing consulting services

(G-7508)
REEL INC
651 N Broad St Ste 201 (19709-6400)
PHONE.....................302 319-3522
Jake Vogel, *CEO*
EMP: 10
SALES (est): 406.01K **Privately Held**
SIC: 2741 Internet publishing and broadcasting

(G-7509)
REGIS CORPORATION
705 Middletown Warwick Rd (19709-9095)
PHONE.....................302 376-6165
Lucy Martinez, *Brnch Mgr*
EMP: 8
SALES (corp-wide): 233.33MM **Publicly Held**
Web: www.regiscorp.com
SIC: 7231 Unisex hair salons
PA: Regis Corporation
    3701 Wayzata Blvd Ste 500
    Minneapolis MN 55416
    952 947-7777

(G-7510)
REHABILITATION SERVICE
124 Sleepy Hollow Dr Ste 101 (19709-5838)
PHONE.....................302 449-3050
Todd Cumming, *Prin*
EMP: 10 EST: 2016
SALES (est): 120.15K **Privately Held**
SIC: 8049 Physical therapist

(G-7511)
REMARLE LLC
427 Smee Rd (19709-9539)
PHONE.....................215 245-6448
Renee Lemasney, *Prin*
EMP: 7 EST: 2011
SALES (est): 226.89K **Privately Held**
Web: www.remarlellc.com
SIC: 2844 Lotions, shaving

(G-7512)
REMAX 1ST CHOICE LLC
Also Called: Re/Max
100 S Broad St (19709-1467)
PHONE.....................302 378-8700
EMP: 5 EST: 1999
SALES (est): 969.53K **Privately Held**
Web: www.remax.com
SIC: 6531 Real estate agent, residential

(G-7513)
RENEGADE ENTRMT & MEDIA CO
651 N Broad St Ste 201 (19709-6402)
PHONE.....................904 789-2897
Torrence Ray, *CEO*
Torrence Ray, *Prin*
Allen Ray, *Prin*
EMP: 10 EST: 2018
SALES (est): 872.36K **Privately Held**
SIC: 4899 7929 7922 2711 Communication services, nec; Entertainers and entertainment groups; Entertainment promotion; Newspapers: publishing only, not printed on site

(G-7514)
RENEGADE ENTRMT & MEDIA CO LLC
651 N Broad St Ste 205 (19709-6402)
PHONE.....................267 648-7916
Torrence Ray, *Managing Member*
EMP: 15 EST: 2020
SALES (est): 188.44K **Privately Held**
SIC: 7929 Entertainers and entertainment groups

(G-7515)
RENOVATE LLC
786 Old School House Rd (19709-9692)
PHONE.....................302 378-1768
Michael Biliunas, *Prin*
EMP: 8 EST: 2011
SALES (est): 496.14K **Privately Held**
Web: www.renovatedelaware.com
SIC: 1542 Commercial and office buildings, renovation and repair

(G-7516)
RESEMBLE AI INC
651 N Broad St Ste 201 (19709-6402)
PHONE.....................401 255-6004
EMP: 9 EST: 2020
SALES (est): 304.44K
SALES (corp-wide): 2.26MM **Privately Held**
SIC: 8742 Management consulting services
PA: Resemble Ai Inc
    233 Mountainberry Rd
    Brampton ON L6R 1

(G-7517)
RESUME TECH CORP
651 N Broad St (19709-6400)
PHONE.....................800 403-5610
Nofel Izz, *CEO*
EMP: 12 EST: 2020
SALES (est): 600K **Privately Held**
SIC: 7338 Resume writing service

(G-7518)
RESURREKTION ATHLETICS INC
651 N Broad St Ste 205 # 2478 (19709-6402)
PHONE.....................302 300-1900
M Williams, *Ex Dir*
EMP: 25 EST: 2020
SALES (est): 1.15MM **Privately Held**
SIC: 3949 Sporting and athletic goods, nec

(G-7519)
ROBERT W NAGOWSKI
Also Called: Bob's Touch of The Brush
304 Pheasant Dr (19709-9201)
PHONE.....................302 584-2326
Robert W Nagowski, *Prin*
EMP: 7 EST: 2012
SALES (est): 78.96K **Privately Held**
Web: www.bobstouchofthebrush.com
SIC: 1721 Painting and paper hanging

(G-7520)
ROCK ROOFING
304 E Main St 308 (19709-1482)
PHONE.....................302 757-2350
Ted Rock, *Prin*
EMP: 6 EST: 2010
SALES (est): 156.54K **Privately Held**
Web: www.rockroofingde.com
SIC: 1761 Roofing contractor

(G-7521)
RODNEY BALTAZAR
Also Called: Baltazar Women's Care
120 Sandhill Dr (19709-5864)
PHONE.....................302 283-3300
Rodney Baltazar, *Owner*
EMP: 5 EST: 2001
SALES (est): 256.51K **Privately Held**
SIC: 8011 Endocrinologist

(G-7522)
RON ENGLISH ENTERPRISES INC
1775 Pole Bridge Rd (19709-2173)
PHONE.....................302 981-9276
Ronald J English Senior, *Pr*
EMP: 5 EST: 2015
SALES (est): 37.24K **Privately Held**
SIC: 7389 Business services, nec

(G-7523)
ROPHE LIVING INC
721 Marian Dr (19709-3124)
PHONE.....................302 500-9238
Andre Hlliard, *CEO*
EMP: 5 EST: 2020
SALES (est): 55K **Privately Held**
SIC: 2023 Dietary supplements, dairy and non-dairy based

(G-7524)
ROTOBOT AI LLC
651 N Broad St Ste 201 (19709-6400)
PHONE.....................978 305-5794
EMP: 8
SALES (est): 306.16K **Privately Held**
SIC: 7371 Computer software development and applications

(G-7525)
ROYAL PEST MANAGEMENT INC
755 N Broad St (19709-1171)
PHONE.....................302 376-8243
EMP: 6 EST: 2006
SALES (est): 77.22K **Privately Held**
SIC: 7342 Pest control in structures

(G-7526)
RUAN TRANSPORT CORPORATION
50 Patriot Dr (19709-8769)
PHONE.....................302 696-3270
EMP: 54
SALES (corp-wide): 7.23MM **Privately Held**
Web: www.ruan.com
SIC: 4213 Contract haulers
HQ: Ruan Transport Corporation
    666 Grand Ave Ste 3100
    Des Moines IA 50309
    515 245-2500

(G-7527)
RUSHSTAN GROUP LLC
603 E Glen Mare Dr (19709-8774)
PHONE.....................302 376-0259
EMP: 5 EST: 2018
SALES (est): 212.57K **Privately Held**
SIC: 4899 Communication services, nec

(G-7528)
RUTKOSKE BROS INC
819 Middletown Warwick Rd (19709-9097)
P.O. Box 227 (19709-0227)
PHONE.....................302 378-8181
Felix Rutkoske, *Pr*
Mark A Rutkoske, *VP*

GEOGRAPHIC SECTION

Middletown - New Castle County (G-7558)

EMP: 7 EST: 1973
SALES (est): 856.79K **Privately Held**
SIC: **0134** 0115 Irish potatoes; Corn

(G-7529)
RUTLEDGE DENTAL ASSOC INC
410 N Cass St (19709-1038)
PHONE..................................302 378-8705
Jane C Rutledge, *Sec*
EMP: 14 EST: 2014
SALES (est): 818.3K **Privately Held**
Web: www.rutledgedental.com
SIC: **8021** Dentists' office

(G-7530)
S & J HAFTL INC
519 Diamond Dr (19709-1363)
PHONE..................................302 378-7571
Stephen Haftl, *Prin*
EMP: 5 EST: 2015
SALES (est): 123.35K **Privately Held**
SIC: **3732** Boatbuilding and repairing

(G-7531)
S & S MGNT CO LLC
307 Bald Eagle Way (19709-4112)
PHONE..................................302 353-9249
EMP: 5 EST: 2021
SALES (est): 260.14K **Privately Held**
SIC: **8742** 7389 Management consulting services; Business services, nec

(G-7532)
S&N LOGISTICS LLC ✪
600 N Broad St Ste 5 (19709-1032)
PHONE..................................302 303-3037
Nasheen Isoke Hill, *Managing Member*
EMP: 3 EST: 2022
SALES (est): 135.7K **Privately Held**
SIC: **3537** Trucks: freight, baggage, etc.: industrial, except mining

(G-7533)
S3STAFFINGUSA INC (PA)
651 N Broad St Ste 205-156 (19709-6400)
PHONE..................................248 986-6062
Swapnika Darla, *Pr*
EMP: 11
SALES (est): 987.15K
SALES (corp-wide): 987.15K **Privately Held**
Web: www.s3staffingusa.com
SIC: **7389** Business services, nec

(G-7534)
SACHETTA MACHINE & DEVELOPMENT
1823 Choptank Rd (19709-9047)
PHONE..................................302 378-5468
Gregory L Sachetta, *Pr*
Pamela Sue Sachetta, *Sec*
EMP: 10 EST: 1985
SQ FT: 6,200
SALES (est): 673.97K **Privately Held**
SIC: **3599** Machine shop, jobbing and repair

(G-7535)
SAGGIO MANAGEMENT GROUP INC
102 Sleepy Hollow Dr (19709-5841)
PHONE..................................302 696-2036
EMP: 12 EST: 2017
SALES (est): 744.26K **Privately Held**
Web: www.saggioaccounting.com
SIC: **8741** Management services

(G-7536)
SALON 828 LLC
600 N Broad St Ste 8 (19709-1032)
PHONE..................................302 376-8282
Don Christ, *Mgr*

EMP: 6 EST: 2016
SALES (est): 75.33K **Privately Held**
Web: www.salon828.com
SIC: **7231** Hairdressers

(G-7537)
SANAD CASH INC
651 N Broad St (19709-6400)
PHONE..................................302 314-8170
EMP: 6
SALES (est): 257.27K **Privately Held**
Web: www.sanadcash.com
SIC: **7389** Business services, nec

(G-7538)
SAVANNAH LOGISTICS LLC
278 Liborio Dr (19709-3109)
PHONE..................................302 893-7251
Njenga Benson, *Prin*
EMP: 5 EST: 2012
SALES (est): 173.26K **Privately Held**
SIC: **4789** Transportation services, nec

(G-7539)
SBR ENTERPRISES LLC
992 Port Penn Rd (19709-8932)
PHONE..................................302 836-6909
EMP: 5 EST: 2019
SALES (est): 247.18K **Privately Held**
SIC: **7389** Business services, nec

(G-7540)
SCASSOCIATES INC
651 N Broad St Ste 103 (19709-6401)
PHONE..................................302 454-1100
Sharron Cirillo, *Pr*
EMP: 10 EST: 2005
SQ FT: 3,000
SALES (est): 1.83MM **Privately Held**
Web: www.scassoc.net
SIC: **8721** Certified public accountant

(G-7541)
SCHAGRIN GAS CO (PA)
Also Called: Schagringas Company
1000 N Broad St (19709-1062)
P.O. Box 427 (19709-0427)
PHONE..................................302 378-2000
Eric Levinson, *Pr*
Margarete Levinson, *
Andrew Levinson, *
EMP: 35 EST: 1932
SQ FT: 4,000
SALES (est): 15.72MM
SALES (corp-wide): 15.72MM **Privately Held**
Web: www.schagrins.com
SIC: **5984** 5722 5074 Propane gas, bottled; Gas household appliances; Water purification equipment

(G-7542)
SCHMITTINGER & RODRIGUEZ ATTYS
651 N Broad St (19709-6401)
PHONE..................................302 378-1697
Scott Chambers, *Mgr*
EMP: 7 EST: 2010
SALES (est): 237.49K **Privately Held**
Web: www.schmittrod.com
SIC: **8111** General practice attorney, lawyer

(G-7543)
SCHWARZ PROPERTIES LLC
203 Cheshire Dr (19709-8880)
PHONE..................................302 376-1696
EMP: 5 EST: 2016
SALES (est): 76.43K **Privately Held**
SIC: **6512** Nonresidential building operators

(G-7544)
SCIMEDICO LLC
221 N Broad St Ste 3a (19709-1070)
PHONE..................................302 375-7500
EMP: 6 EST: 2021
SALES (est): 82.28K **Privately Held**
Web: www.scimedico.com
SIC: **8062** General medical and surgical hospitals

(G-7545)
SCOTT MUFFLER LLC
308 W Main St (19709-1701)
PHONE..................................302 378-9247
EMP: 8
SALES (corp-wide): 929.47K **Privately Held**
Web: www.scottimufflercentermiddletown.com
SIC: **7538** 7537 5013 General automotive repair shops; Automotive transmission repair shops; Automotive supplies and parts
PA: Scott Muffler Llc
1465 S Governors Ave
Dover DE 19904
302 674-8280

(G-7546)
SCOUT LEVEL LLC (PA) ✪
651 N Broad St Ste 205 (19709-6402)
PHONE..................................336 500-2067
Steven Carter, *Managing Member*
EMP: 6 EST: 2023
SALES (est): 76.69K
SALES (corp-wide): 76.69K **Privately Held**
SIC: **6799** Investment clubs

(G-7547)
SECURE AMERICAS FUTURE ECONOMY
115 Dungarvan Dr (19709-9456)
PHONE..................................302 464-2687
William Whipple, *Pr*
EMP: 8 EST: 2007
SALES (est): 163.93K **Privately Held**
SIC: **8699** Charitable organization

(G-7548)
SECURELAYER7 LLC
364 E Main St 1010 (19709-1482)
PHONE..................................302 391-0803
EMP: 16 EST: 2016
SALES (est): 419.54K **Privately Held**
Web: www.securelayer7.net
SIC: **7379** 7371 Computer related consulting services; Computer software development and applications

(G-7549)
SECURITY SATELLITE
Also Called: Security Satellite Systems
5101 Summit Bridge Rd (19709-8821)
P.O. Box 12 (19709-0012)
PHONE..................................302 376-0241
Steve Kacprzyk, *Pr*
Steve Kacpryzyk, *Pr*
EMP: 2 EST: 1996
SALES (est): 121.87K **Privately Held**
SIC: **3643** Current-carrying wiring services

(G-7550)
SEE THE WORLD TRAVEL AGENCY
425 Maplewood Dr (19709-4011)
PHONE..................................302 559-4514
Catherine L Short, *Prin*
EMP: 5 EST: 2015
SALES (est): 117.31K **Privately Held**
SIC: **4724** Travel agencies

(G-7551)
SENDLINK INC (PA)
651 N Broad St Ste 206 (19709-6402)
PHONE..................................650 505-5299
Daniil Titov, *CEO*
EMP: 7 EST: 2020
SALES (est): 317.7K
SALES (corp-wide): 317.7K **Privately Held**
SIC: **7371** Software programming applications

(G-7552)
SENSIAI INC
651 N Broad St Ste 206 (19709-6402)
PHONE..................................646 665-7668
EMP: 5 EST: 2021
SALES (est): 127.09K **Privately Held**
SIC: **7371** Computer software development and applications

(G-7553)
SEOTWIX LLC
651 N Broad St (19709-6400)
PHONE..................................877 849-8777
Yulian Fediukov, *Managing Member*
EMP: 20
SALES (est): 612.9K **Privately Held**
SIC: **8742** Marketing consulting services

(G-7554)
SERENITY GARDENS ASSISTED LIVI
Also Called: Serenity Grdns Assisted Living
207 Ruth Dr (19709-9470)
P.O. Box 9541 (19809-0541)
PHONE..................................302 442-5330
Heather Bressi, *Ex Dir*
EMP: 11 EST: 2004
SQ FT: 4,000
SALES (est): 581.37K **Privately Held**
SIC: **8059** Personal care home, with health care

(G-7555)
SERVICE CLEANING
33 Browning Cir (19709-1662)
PHONE..................................302 376-7258
Brian Carey, *Prin*
EMP: 5 EST: 2015
SALES (est): 117.1K **Privately Held**
Web: www.forevercleanmaryland.com
SIC: **7699** Cleaning services

(G-7556)
SEVEN TECH LLC
600 N Broad St (19709-1032)
PHONE..................................302 464-6488
EMP: 5 EST: 2019
SALES (est): 100K **Privately Held**
SIC: **7371** Software programming applications

(G-7557)
SEVO INDUS FIRE PROTECTION LLC
221 N Broad St Ste 3a (19709-1070)
PHONE..................................913 677-1112
EMP: 8 EST: 2020
SALES (est): 401.63K **Privately Held**
SIC: **1711** Fire sprinkler system installation

(G-7558)
SHALEX INDUSTRIES US CORP
364 E Main St Ste 1012 (19709-1482)
PHONE..................................323 540-5586
Stephen Uther, *Prin*
EMP: 5 EST: 2019
SALES (est): 107.29K **Privately Held**
SIC: **3999** Manufacturing industries, nec

Middletown - New Castle County (G-7559)

(G-7559)
SHARP FARM
1214 Sharp Ln (19709-8806)
PHONE..................302 378-9606
Michael Zwiesler, *Mgr*
EMP: 10
SALES (corp-wide): 681.36K **Privately Held**
Web: www.thesharpfoundation.com
SIC: 0752 7948 Breeding services, horses: racing and non-racing; Horses, racing
PA: Sharp Farm
5727 Kennett Pike
Wilmington DE 19807
302 652-7729

(G-7560)
SHERPA BROKERS LLC
651 N Broad St Ste 205 (19709-6402)
PHONE..................917 455-0094
Carlos Diaz, *CEO*
EMP: 12 EST: 2021
SIC: 6719 Investment holding companies, except banks

(G-7561)
SHIRE CIVICS CO ◊
600 N Broad St (19709-1032)
PHONE..................423 520-6705
Samantha Boucher, *CEO*
EMP: 3 EST: 2022
SALES (est): 128.34K **Privately Held**
SIC: 7372 Prepackaged software

(G-7562)
SHORE ACCOUNTANTS MD INC
18 Manassas Dr (19709-3802)
PHONE..................410 758-6900
Christopher Acevedo, *Prin*
EMP: 6 EST: 2017
SALES (est): 138.92K **Privately Held**
Web: www.shoreaccountants.com
SIC: 8011 Offices and clinics of medical doctors

(G-7563)
SIBACPAY INC
651 N Broad St (19709-6400)
PHONE..................302 257-5784
Izukanji Silwimba, *Pr*
EMP: 5
SALES (est): 198.37K **Privately Held**
SIC: 7389 Business services, nec

(G-7564)
SIGMA THETA TAU INC
302 Green Ct (19709-6803)
PHONE..................302 584-5908
Megan Holdrigde, *Prin*
EMP: 5 EST: 2010
SALES (est): 42.44K **Privately Held**
SIC: 8641 University club

(G-7565)
SIGNATURE CLEAN SOLUTIONS LLC
651 N Broad St (19709-6400)
PHONE..................571 565-1270
EMP: 5 EST: 2020
SALES (est): 214.26K **Privately Held**
SIC: 7349 7699 Janitorial service, contract basis; Cleaning services

(G-7566)
SILPADA DESIGNS
410 Bluebird Hvn (19709-9599)
PHONE..................302 376-6964
EMP: 5 EST: 2019
SALES (est): 55.18K **Privately Held**
SIC: 7389 Design services

(G-7567)
SILVERBULLET USA INC
651 N Broad St (19709-6400)
PHONE..................203 216-2414
Umberto Torrielli, *Ex Dir*
EMP: 11
SALES (est): 405.54K **Privately Held**
SIC: 7379 Online services technology consultants

(G-7568)
SIMS TEAM CLEANING LLC
651 N Broad St Ste 205 (19709-6402)
PHONE..................610 990-1950
EMP: 20 EST: 2020
SALES (est): 250K **Privately Held**
SIC: 7349 Cleaning service, industrial or commercial

(G-7569)
SINKOR BEAUTY SALON
4446 Summit Bridge Rd (19709-9399)
PHONE..................302 464-3292
EMP: 7 EST: 2017
SALES (est): 259.04K **Privately Held**
Web: www.sinkorhair.com
SIC: 7231 Hairdressers

(G-7570)
SKY ZONE TRAMPOLINE PARK
120 Laks Dr (19709-9390)
PHONE..................302 449-1252
EMP: 7 EST: 2020
SALES (est): 81.28K **Privately Held**
Web: www.skyzone.com
SIC: 7999 Amusement and recreation, nec

(G-7571)
SLAVIA TRANSPORTATION
7 Tami Trl (19709-9391)
PHONE..................302 218-4474
Milenko Radovanovic, *Prin*
EMP: 5 EST: 2013
SALES (est): 250.55K **Privately Held**
SIC: 4789 Transportation services, nec

(G-7572)
SLAY BY JERE
408 Afton Dr (19709-9818)
PHONE..................302 723-0034
Jere Davis, *Prin*
EMP: 7 EST: 2017
SALES (est): 70.07K **Privately Held**
SIC: 8011 Offices and clinics of medical doctors

(G-7573)
SLEEPAGOTCHI INC ◊
651 N Broad St Ste 201 (19709-6402)
PHONE..................617 852-7380
Anton Kraminkin, *Prin*
EMP: 10 EST: 2022
SALES (est): 348.32K **Privately Held**
SIC: 7371 Custom computer programming services

(G-7574)
SLIMS SPORTS COMPLEX LLC
938 Middletown Warwick Rd (19709-9092)
PHONE..................302 464-1058
EMP: 7 EST: 2018
SALES (est): 374.03K **Privately Held**
Web: www.slimssc.com
SIC: 7997 Membership sports and recreation clubs

(G-7575)
SMACKERALS BY MICHELLE LLC
109 Fox Hunt Ln (19709-8996)
PHONE..................302 376-8272
EMP: 3 EST: 2009
SALES (est): 211.02K **Privately Held**
Web: www.smackeralsbymichelle.com
SIC: 2051 Bread, cake, and related products

(G-7576)
SMARKETICS INC
651 N Broad St Ste 206 (19709-6400)
PHONE..................929 265-0177
Alexis Ponte, *CEO*
EMP: 5
SALES (est): 107.01K **Privately Held**
Web: www.smarketics.com
SIC: 7371 Software programming applications

(G-7577)
SMART TIRE COMPANY INC
651 N Broad St Ste 205 # 3318 (19709-6402)
PHONE..................909 358-0987
Earl Cole, *CEO*
EMP: 2 EST: 2020
SALES (est): 57.88K **Privately Held**
Web: www.smarttirecompany.com
SIC: 3011 Tires, semi-pneumatic

(G-7578)
SMARTPROFYL LLC
651 N Broad St Ste 205 (19709-6402)
PHONE..................832 412-5803
EMP: 2 EST: 2020
SALES (est): 66K **Privately Held**
Web: www.smartprofyl.com
SIC: 7372 7371 8243 8742 Educational computer software; Computer software systems analysis and design, custom; Software training, computer; Human resource consulting services

(G-7579)
SMILES JOLLY PA
102 Sleepy Hollow Dr Ste 100 (19709-5841)
PHONE..................302 378-3384
Jeena M Jolly, *Owner*
EMP: 5 EST: 2009
SALES (est): 388.94K **Privately Held**
Web: www.jollysmiles.com
SIC: 8021 Dentists' office

(G-7580)
SMILEY SHINEY
320 Price Dr (19709-9933)
PHONE..................215 601-6036
Shiney Smiley Motr L, *Owner*
EMP: 9 EST: 2018
SALES (est): 100.04K **Privately Held**
SIC: 8052 Intermediate care facilities

(G-7581)
SNEAKYLINKS COM INC
Also Called: Sneaky Links
651 N Broad St Ste 205 (19709-6402)
PHONE..................470 312-3827
Daniel Gamble, *Prin*
EMP: 10 EST: 2021
SALES (est): 365.44K **Privately Held**
SIC: 7372 Prepackaged software

(G-7582)
SOCALLOVA LLC
610 Wesley Ct (19709-2192)
PHONE..................347 721-6416
EMP: 10 EST: 2019
SALES (est): 270K **Privately Held**
SIC: 7929 Entertainers and entertainment groups

(G-7583)
SOCIAL MEDIA GRABS
600 N Broad St (19709-1032)
PHONE..................281 603-2803
Penelope Hutchens, *CEO*
EMP: 5 EST: 2021
SALES (est): 327.89K **Privately Held**
SIC: 4899 Communication services, nec

(G-7584)
SOCRADAR CYBER INTELLIGENCE
651 N Broad St Ste 205 (19709-6402)
PHONE..................571 249-4598
EMP: 14 EST: 2019
SALES (est): 63.38K **Privately Held**
SIC: 7371 Software programming applications

(G-7585)
SOLACE LIFESCIENCES INC
122 Willow Grove Mill Dr (19709-8637)
PHONE..................830 792-3123
Allen David, *Dir*
EMP: 8 EST: 2012
SALES (est): 198.92K **Privately Held**
SIC: 8082 Home health care services

(G-7586)
SOLACE LIFESCIENCES INC
122 Willow Grove Mill Dr (19709-8637)
PHONE..................302 383-1450
EMP: 5 EST: 2019
SALES (est): 82.33K **Privately Held**
SIC: 8082 Home health care services

(G-7587)
SOLAR FRONTIERS CORP
22 W Minglewood Dr (19709-2408)
PHONE..................302 588-7600
Joseph Della Valle, *Prin*
EMP: 6 EST: 2019
SALES (est): 101.38K **Privately Held**
SIC: 1711 Solar energy contractor

(G-7588)
SOSA PAINTING LLC
336 Hostetter Blvd (19709-1249)
PHONE..................302 437-9282
Arianna Fonseca, *Prin*
EMP: 5 EST: 2018
SALES (est): 42.66K **Privately Held**
SIC: 1721 Painting and paper hanging

(G-7589)
SOUF MODE LLC
221 N Broad St (19709-1070)
PHONE..................332 220-6189
EMP: 8 EST: 2021
SALES (est): 40.94K **Privately Held**
SIC: 7929 Musician

(G-7590)
SOUTHEAST DELCO EDUCATION ASSN
416 Hope Dr (19709-9204)
PHONE..................302 420-4888
Rose Marie Knox, *Pr*
EMP: 5 EST: 2017
SALES (est): 71.09K **Privately Held**
SIC: 8699 Membership organizations, nec

(G-7591)
SOUTHGATE CONCRETE COMPANY
600 Industrial Dr (19709-1082)
PHONE..................302 376-5280
Dennis Partrillo, *Mgr*
EMP: 14
SIC: 3273 Ready-mixed concrete
PA: Southgate Concrete Company
204 Marsh Ln

New Castle DE

(G-7592)
SOUTRON GLOBAL INC
Also Called: Bloomvp Spav2 Co.
600 N Broad St Ste 5-3477 (19709-1032)
PHONE..............................760 519-3328
Tony Saadat, *CEO*
Ryan Khan, *CFO*
EMP: 10 **EST:** 2021
SALES (est): 348.32K **Privately Held**
Web: www.soutron.com
SIC: 7371 Software programming applications

(G-7593)
SPARTAN CLEANING
443 Boxwood Ln (19709-9659)
PHONE..............................302 345-7591
EMP: 6 **EST:** 2017
SALES (est): 63.73K **Privately Held**
SIC: 7699 Cleaning services

(G-7594)
SPRINGMILL COMMUNITY ASSOC
2 Windmill Ln (19709-5844)
PHONE..............................302 376-5466
EMP: 5 **EST:** 2004
SALES (est): 127.03K **Privately Held**
Web: www.springmilldelaware.org
SIC: 8641 Homeowners' association

(G-7595)
SPUNKCHILD LLC
221 N Broad St (19709-1070)
PHONE..............................917 504-4529
Dara A Mcdonald, *Managing Member*
EMP: 15 **EST:** 2021
SALES (est): 581.23K **Privately Held**
SIC: 2211 Apparel and outerwear fabrics, cotton

(G-7596)
STAR SERVICES LLC
218 Appoquin Dr S (19709-9175)
PHONE..............................302 373-5210
Steven Costa, *Owner*
EMP: 5 **EST:** 2009
SALES (est): 70.44K **Privately Held**
Web: www.starservicesllc.net
SIC: 7363 Help supply services

(G-7597)
STATE OF DE
112 Netherlands Dr (19709-9676)
PHONE..............................302 376-5125
EMP: 8 **EST:** 2018
SALES (est): 58.21K **Privately Held**
SIC: 8011 Offices and clinics of medical doctors

(G-7598)
STELLA C OHANENYE OD LLC
600 N Broad St Ste 12 (19709-1032)
PHONE..............................302 388-7288
Uchay Ohanenye, *Prin*
EMP: 6 **EST:** 2019
SALES (est): 218.18K **Privately Held**
SIC: 8042 Offices and clinics of optometrists

(G-7599)
STEPHEN J DUGGAN DO
124 Sleepy Hollow Dr Ste 203 (19709-5838)
PHONE..............................302 449-3030
Connie Graham, *Prin*
EMP: 11 **EST:** 2006
SALES (est): 89.03K **Privately Held**
SIC: 8011 8031 General and family practice, physician/surgeon; Offices and clinics of osteopathic physicians

(G-7600)
STONE EXPRESS
5093 Summit Bridge Rd (19709-9591)
PHONE..............................302 376-8876
EMP: 8 **EST:** 2004
SALES (est): 245.35K **Privately Held**
SIC: 3281 Marble, building: cut and shaped

(G-7601)
STORESKIPPER INC
651 N Broad St Ste 206 (19709-6402)
PHONE..............................505 850-5878
Stephen Tapia, *CEO*
EMP: 3 **EST:** 2020
SALES (est): 32.77K **Privately Held**
SIC: 7372 Application computer software

(G-7602)
STRATEGIC INTEGRATION LLC
651 N Broad St (19709-6400)
PHONE..............................714 227-0142
EMP: 10 **EST:** 2019
SALES (est): 409.63K **Privately Held**
SIC: 8742 Marketing consulting services

(G-7603)
STUCCO REPAIRS
114 Willow Grove Mill Dr (19709-8637)
PHONE..............................302 442-0795
EMP: 5 **EST:** 2017
SALES (est): 216.93K **Privately Held**
SIC: 5032 Stucco

(G-7604)
STUDIO 13 SKIN BY CHRISTINA
13 Shallcross Pl (19709-1024)
PHONE..............................302 258-4205
Christina Bradham, *Prin*
EMP: 8 **EST:** 2016
SALES (est): 54.13K **Privately Held**
Web: www.skinbychristina.com
SIC: 8011 Offices and clinics of medical doctors

(G-7605)
STUMPYS HATCHET HOUSE
819 Middletown Warwick Rd Unit E2 (19709-9097)
PHONE..............................302 378-4737
EMP: 9 **EST:** 2019
SALES (est): 137.56K **Privately Held**
Web: www.stumpyshh.com
SIC: 7999 Amusement and recreation, nec

(G-7606)
SUMMIT CENTRE TR
2143 Choptank Rd (19709-9660)
PHONE..............................302 690-7235
Karen Garland, *Prin*
EMP: 6 **EST:** 2017
SALES (est): 63.48K **Privately Held**
Web: www.summitcentre4tr.com
SIC: 8699 Charitable organization

(G-7607)
SUMMIT TAX SOLUTIONS LLC
5 Brady Cir (19709-1713)
PHONE..............................302 464-1016
Craig Sparacino, *Prin*
EMP: 5 **EST:** 2015
SALES (est): 209.99K **Privately Held**
Web: www.summittaxde.com
SIC: 7291 Tax return preparation services

(G-7608)
SUN GAS & DIESEL
1228 Middletown Warwick Rd (19709-9098)
PHONE..............................302 376-8200
Jimmy Dhaliwal, *Owner*
EMP: 7 **EST:** 2016
SALES (est): 273.72K **Privately Held**
SIC: 7538 General automotive repair shops

(G-7609)
SUNDAE BODY LLC
221 N Broad St Ste 3a (19709-1070)
PHONE..............................480 430-5675
EMP: 10 **EST:** 2021
SALES (est): 183.81K **Privately Held**
SIC: 7231 Beauty shops

(G-7610)
SUNDARI KULA LLC
Also Called: Serenity Yoga
5244 Summit Bridge Rd (19709-8822)
PHONE..............................302 373-7538
EMP: 12 **EST:** 2021
SALES (est): 77.11K **Privately Held**
Web: www.serenityogastudio.com
SIC: 7999 Yoga instruction

(G-7611)
SUNWISE DRMATOLOGY SURGERY LLC
102 Sleepy Hollow Dr Ste 203 (19709-5841)
PHONE..............................302 378-7981
Jennifer Larusso, *Owner*
EMP: 16 **EST:** 2017
SALES (est): 1.98MM **Privately Held**
Web: www.sunwisederm.com
SIC: 8011 Dermatologist

(G-7612)
SUPER SERVICE AUTOMOTIVE INC
610 Tower Ln (19709-1767)
PHONE..............................302 464-1149
Nicholas Gadaleta, *Pr*
EMP: 16 **EST:** 2017
SALES (est): 869.82K **Privately Held**
SIC: 7539 Automotive repair shops, nec

(G-7613)
SURGICAL FOCUS
20 W Kilts Ln (19709-8712)
PHONE..............................215 518-2138
Jerome Upchurch, *Prin*
EMP: 7 **EST:** 2017
SALES (est): 96.81K **Privately Held**
SIC: 8011 Medical centers

(G-7614)
SYMBIANCEHR LLC
364 E Main St (19709-1482)
PHONE..............................302 276-3302
EMP: 6 **EST:** 2019
SALES (est): 467.63K **Privately Held**
Web: www.tahrservices.com
SIC: 7299 Miscellaneous personal service

(G-7615)
SYSTEMONEX INC (PA)
364 E Main St Ste 1001 (19709-1482)
PHONE..............................201 688-7663
Tarun Kumar Singh, *Prin*
EMP: 6 **EST:** 2017
SALES (est): 551.64K
SALES (corp-wide): 551.64K **Privately Held**
Web: www.systemonex.com
SIC: 7379 Computer related consulting services

(G-7616)
T & B INVSTGTIONS SEC AGCY LLC
68 Haggis Rd (19709-8751)
PHONE..............................302 476-4087
EMP: 7 **EST:** 2017
SALES (est): 74.86K **Privately Held**
SIC: 7381 7389 Security guard service; Personal investigation service

(G-7617)
T & M PROPERTY MAINTENANCE LLC
2 Bristle Cone Dr (19709-9785)
PHONE..............................302 462-1080
EMP: 5 **EST:** 2018
SALES (est): 239.68K **Privately Held**
SIC: 7349 Building maintenance services, nec

(G-7618)
TAGLATAM INC
Also Called: Mutari
651 N Broad St Ste 206 (19709-6402)
PHONE..............................302 314-9898
Andres Conejo, *CEO*
EMP: 7 **EST:** 2020
SALES (est): 276.06K **Privately Held**
SIC: 8742 Marketing consulting services

(G-7619)
TAJAN HLDINGS INVESTMENTS INC
600 N Broad St Ste 5 # 3166 (19709-1032)
PHONE..............................302 300-1183
Latoya Roberts, *CEO*
EMP: 2 **EST:** 2019
SALES (est): 90.89K **Privately Held**
SIC: 3324 Steel investment foundries

(G-7620)
TARGET INTEGRATION INC
600 N Broad St Ste 53593 (19709-1032)
PHONE..............................254 845-5684
EMP: 5 **EST:** 2021
SALES (est): 49.23K **Privately Held**
Web: www.targetintegration.com
SIC: 7379 Computer related consulting services
HQ: Target Integration Consultancy Private Limited
B-52, Ground Floor, Street No.7
New Delhi DL 11009

(G-7621)
TATTOO BLUE MOON
4446 Summit Bridge Rd Unit 8 (19709-9399)
PHONE..............................302 449-1551
Jim Whitby, *Mgr*
EMP: 5 **EST:** 2015
SALES (est): 34.75K **Privately Held**
SIC: 7299 Tattoo parlor

(G-7622)
TAX GIANTS LLC
364 E Main St Ste 337 (19709-1482)
PHONE..............................908 822-1090
Julane Miller-armbrister, *Prin*
EMP: 5 **EST:** 2016
SALES (est): 86.4K **Privately Held**
SIC: 7291 Tax return preparation services

(G-7623)
TAX WITH US LLC
357 Misty Vale Dr (19709-2125)
PHONE..............................302 378-2627
Kyle Gorman, *Prin*
EMP: 5 **EST:** 2019
SALES (est): 18.45K **Privately Held**
Web: www.taxwithus.net

Middletown - New Castle County (G-7624)   GEOGRAPHIC SECTION

SIC: 7291 Tax return preparation services

(G-7624)
TEACHEDISON INC
651 N Broad St Ste 206 (19709-6400)
PHONE.................................973 902-8026
Deepak Murugaian, *CEO*
EMP: 6 EST: 2020
SALES (est): 68.89K **Privately Held**
Web: www.teachedison.com
SIC: 7371 Computer software development and applications

(G-7625)
TEAM HORNE LLC
357 Canvasback Rd (19709-9161)
PHONE.................................302 376-0579
Kimberly Horne, *Prin*
EMP: 5 EST: 2015
SALES (est): 122.23K **Privately Held**
SIC: 7997 Membership sports and recreation clubs

(G-7626)
TECHNICAL MEDIA SOLUTIONS
116 Sleepy Hollow Dr (19709-5816)
PHONE.................................302 376-7588
EMP: 6 EST: 2018
SALES (est): 302.83K **Privately Held**
SIC: 7379 Computer related consulting services

(G-7627)
TEK ELECTRONICS LLC
Also Called: Tek Electronics
865 Bullen Dr (19709-8973)
P.O. Box 853 (19709-0853)
PHONE.................................302 449-6947
Tom Voytek, *Prin*
EMP: 7 EST: 2010
SALES (est): 781.13K **Privately Held**
Web: www.tekelectronicsllc.com
SIC: 8748 Systems engineering consultant, ex. computer or professional

(G-7628)
TEK INTERNATIONAL INC
811 N Broad St Ste 217 (19709-1173)
PHONE.................................302 543-8035
EMP: 9 EST: 2018
SALES (est): 609.91K **Privately Held**
Web: www.tekinternational.net
SIC: 7379 Computer related consulting services

(G-7629)
TEKGEMINUS SOLUTIONS INC ◊
221 N Broad St Ste 3a (19709-1070)
PHONE.................................503 336-5259
Piyush Desai, *Ex Dir*
EMP: 5 EST: 2023
SALES (est): 199.4K **Privately Held**
SIC: 7371 Computer software development

(G-7630)
TELEMIND CLINIC
600 N Broad St (19709-1032)
PHONE.................................253 332-4110
EMP: 6 EST: 2018
SALES (est): 112.76K **Privately Held**
Web: www.telemind.com
SIC: 8099 Health and allied services, nec

(G-7631)
TELEMIND INC
600 N Broad St (19709-1032)
PHONE.................................725 333-2411
Anton Fisher, *CEO*
EMP: 7 EST: 2018
SALES (est): 480.91K **Privately Held**
Web: www.telemind.com
SIC: 8049 Offices of health practitioner

(G-7632)
TELESONIC PC INC (PA)
260 Milford Dr (19709-9417)
PHONE.................................302 658-6945
Bernard Katz, *Pr*
EMP: 7 EST: 2003
SALES (est): 759.18K
SALES (corp-wide): 759.18K **Privately Held**
Web: www.telesoniconline.com
SIC: 3565 Packaging machinery

(G-7633)
TELLERONE INC (PA) ◊
651 N Broad St Ste 206 (19709-6402)
PHONE.................................302 261-9062
Olajuwon Olaniyi, *CEO*
EMP: 10 EST: 2023
SALES (est): 500.3K
SALES (corp-wide): 500.3K **Privately Held**
Web: www.tellerone.co
SIC: 7372 Prepackaged software

(G-7634)
TEN TALENTS ENTERPRISES INC (PA)
Also Called: ABG Designs
316 Braemar St (19709-8733)
PHONE.................................302 409-0718
Jessica J Hallman, *Prin*
Jason Clifton, *Pr*
Jessica Clifton, *VP*
◆ EMP: 3 EST: 2009
SALES (est): 252.29K **Privately Held**
SIC: 2759 7359 Screen printing; Home cleaning and maintenance equipment rental services

(G-7635)
TENDER LOVING KARE
400 N Ramunno Dr (19709-3001)
PHONE.................................302 464-1014
Megan Coats, *Dir*
Samuel Q Johnson, *Pr*
EMP: 21 EST: 2004
SALES (est): 466.14K **Privately Held**
Web: www.cadence-education.com
SIC: 8351 Preschool center

(G-7636)
TERRANCE R HESTER
Also Called: Hester Winery
447 Georgiana Dr (19709-2612)
PHONE.................................856 905-8196
Terrance R Hester, *Owner*
EMP: 2 EST: 2021
SALES (est): 67K **Privately Held**
SIC: 2084 Wines

(G-7637)
TESIS TIME INC
651 N Broad St (19709-6400)
PHONE.................................302 613-0789
Johnniel Rojas, *CEO*
EMP: 5
SALES (est): 104.37K **Privately Held**
SIC: 7379 Online services technology consultants

(G-7638)
THELUXESTAY LLC
651 N Broad St (19709-6400)
PHONE.................................802 234-1410
April Moore, *Managing Member*
EMP: 12
SALES (est): 64.36K **Privately Held**
SIC: 7011 Vacation lodges

(G-7639)
THOROUGHBRED CHARITIES-AMERICA
1343 Bohemia Mill Rd (19709-9021)
PHONE.................................302 376-6289
Herb Moelis, *Mgr*
EMP: 5 EST: 2001
SALES (est): 65.61K **Privately Held**
SIC: 0272 Horses and other equines

(G-7640)
THREE LITTLE BUILDERS
123 Pine Valley Dr (19709-9786)
PHONE.................................302 317-1969
EMP: 5 EST: 2016
SALES (est): 82.72K **Privately Held**
Web: www.threelittlebuilders.com
SIC: 1521 New construction, single-family houses

(G-7641)
THREE SHEEP AND A MILL LLC
651 N Broad St Ste 205 (19709-6402)
PHONE.................................616 820-5668
EMP: 5 EST: 2020
SALES (est): 378.36K **Privately Held**
Web: www.threesheepandamill.com
SIC: 7389 5149 Textile and apparel services; Coffee, green or roasted

(G-7642)
THRIVE PHYSICAL THERAPY INC
Also Called: Thrive Pt
834 Kohl Ave (19709-4703)
PHONE.................................302 834-8400
Kevin Calvey, *CEO*
EMP: 11 EST: 2018
SALES (est): 276.33K **Privately Held**
Web: www.thrivemiddletown.com
SIC: 8049 7371 Physical therapist; Computer software development

(G-7643)
THRIVE REAL LF INDPENDENCE LLC
252 Carter Dr Ste 200 (19709-2859)
PHONE.................................302 261-2139
Yvonne F Coleman, *Prin*
EMP: 7 EST: 2012
SALES (est): 123.07K **Privately Held**
SIC: 6531 Real estate brokers and agents

(G-7644)
TICKET TO TRAVEL
7 E Sarazen Dr (19709-7939)
PHONE.................................302 442-0225
Anita Pagliasso, *Pr*
EMP: 7 EST: 2013
SALES (est): 89.88K **Privately Held**
Web: www.wanderu.com
SIC: 4724 Travel agencies

(G-7645)
TIGER LLC
100 S Broad St (19709-1467)
PHONE.................................302 378-8700
EMP: 7 EST: 2018
SALES (est): 960.62K **Privately Held**
Web: www.gotiger.com
SIC: 6029 Commercial banks, nec

(G-7646)
TITAN RETAIL LLC
651 N Broad St (19709-6400)
PHONE.................................205 291-1305
Jermaine Nathan, *Managing Member*
EMP: 10
SALES (est): 387.73K **Privately Held**
SIC: 6552 Land subdividers and developers, commercial

(G-7647)
TJS & ASSOCIATES LLC
198 Bonnybrook Rd (19709-1638)
PHONE.................................302 563-5593
EMP: 20 EST: 2020
SALES (est): 500K **Privately Held**
SIC: 5961 7389 7313 Electronic shopping; Business services, nec; Electronic media advertising representatives

(G-7648)
TLK
2356 Dupont Pkwy (19709-9334)
PHONE.................................302 376-8554
EMP: 9 EST: 2018
SALES (est): 84.76K **Privately Held**
SIC: 8351 Group day care center

(G-7649)
TODD YERGER TA
1681 Choptank Rd (19709-9043)
PHONE.................................302 378-4196
Abbie Yerger, *Prin*
EMP: 5 EST: 2011
SALES (est): 246.06K **Privately Held**
SIC: 1521 Single-family housing construction

(G-7650)
TODDS JANITORIAL SERVICE INC
407 E Lake St (19709-1137)
PHONE.................................302 378-8212
Charmaine Todd Butcher, *Owner*
Unitas Todd, *Pr*
Norman H Todd Junior, *VP*
Devin M Todd, *VP*
EMP: 9 EST: 1966
SALES (est): 152.46K **Privately Held**
SIC: 7349 Janitorial service, contract basis

(G-7651)
TOMASI USA LLC
1232 Choptank Rd (19709-9038)
PHONE.................................302 449-6492
EMP: 6 EST: 2019
SALES (est): 275.31K **Privately Held**
Web: www.tomasiusa.com
SIC: 3556 Food products machinery

(G-7652)
TOOSACOM INC
600 N Broad St Ste 5 (19709-1032)
PHONE.................................415 240-0442
Alexaner Ledovskiy, *Pr*
EMP: 9 EST: 2021
SALES (est): 328.69K **Privately Held**
SIC: 7372 Application computer software

(G-7653)
TOUCH CLASS CLEANING SERVICE
410 N Ramunno Dr Unit 1705 (19709-3003)
PHONE.................................302 482-5357
Kelly Torrenegra, *Prin*
EMP: 5 EST: 2018
SALES (est): 76.79K **Privately Held**
SIC: 7699 Cleaning services

(G-7654)
TOURETTE SYNDROME
112 E Kilts Ln (19709-8745)
PHONE.................................302 547-6306
EMP: 11 EST: 2014
SALES (est): 48.55K **Privately Held**
Web: www.tourette.org
SIC: 8699 Charitable organization

GEOGRAPHIC SECTION Middletown - New Castle County (G-7685)

(G-7655)
TOWN & COUNTRY HOMES OF KELLER
755 N Broad St (19709-1171)
PHONE..................................302 252-5911
EMP: 5 EST: 2011
SALES (est): 107.95K Privately Held
Web: www.himado.com
SIC: 5099 Durable goods, nec

(G-7656)
TOWN OF MIDDLETOWN
Also Called: Middletown Police Department
130 Hampden Rd (19709-5302)
PHONE..................................302 376-9950
Daniel Yeager, *Chief*
EMP: 37
SALES (corp-wide): 20.15MM Privately Held
Web: middletown.delaware.gov
SIC: 9221 7371 Police protection, Local government; Custom computer programming services
PA: Town Of Middletown
   19 W Green St
   Middletown DE 19709
   302 378-1171

(G-7657)
TRANQUIL SOLUTIONS FOR A
550 Janvier Dr (19709-1738)
PHONE..................................302 383-5011
Dawn Paramore, *Prin*
EMP: 5 EST: 2016
SALES (est): 64.47K Privately Held
Web: www.acenteredmind.com
SIC: 8399 Advocacy group

(G-7658)
TRANSCORE LP
Also Called: Transcore
2111 Dupont Pkwy (19709-9332)
PHONE..................................302 838-7429
Joseph Morris, *Brnch Mgr*
EMP: 5
Web: www.transcore.com
SIC: 4731 Domestic freight forwarding
HQ: Transcore, Lp
   150 4th Ave N Ste 1200
   Nashville TN 37219
   800 923-4824

(G-7659)
TRANSLUCENCE RESEARCH INC
651 N Broad St Ste 206 (19709-6402)
PHONE..................................425 753-8886
Benjamin Fisch, *CEO*
Charles Lu, *Prin*
Benjamin Fisch, *Prin*
Karl Benedikt Bnz, *Prin*
EMP: 20 EST: 2020
SALES (est): 775.64K Privately Held
SIC: 7371 Computer software development and applications

(G-7660)
TREINTA INC
Also Called: Treinta
651 N Broad St Ste 206 (19709-6402)
PHONE..................................786 400-2430
Man Hei Lou, *Prin*
EMP: 200
SALES (est): 12.03MM Privately Held
SIC: 7371 Custom computer programming services

(G-7661)
TRINITY HALTHCARE STAFFING LLC
707 Pinewood Dr (19709-8644)
PHONE..................................302 420-3782
John Onyoni, *Prin*
EMP: 5 EST: 2019
SALES (est): 237.65K Privately Held
SIC: 7361 Employment agencies

(G-7662)
TRU AMERICAN ENTERPRISES LLC ✪
651 N Broad St (19709-6400)
PHONE..................................801 404-1124
Rebecca Morgan, *Managing Member*
Linn Wright, *Mgr*
EMP: 6 EST: 2023
SALES (est): 87.5K Privately Held
SIC: 5047 Medical and hospital equipment

(G-7663)
TRU BEAUTI LLC
Also Called: Bodied By Tru
307 Bald Eagle Way (19709-4112)
PHONE..................................302 353-9249
Sharmayne Weatherbee, *Managing Member*
EMP: 30 EST: 2019
SQ FT: 2,000
SALES (est): 980K Privately Held
SIC: 7991 7299 Spas; Massage parlor

(G-7664)
TRUE LEGACY RENTALS LLC
651 N Broad St Ste 205713 (19709-6400)
PHONE..................................844 857-2271
EMP: 6 EST: 2021
SALES (est): 85.72K Privately Held
SIC: 7514 Rent-a-car service

(G-7665)
TRUE PEST CONTROL SERVICES (PA)
48 Loblolly Ln (19709-9781)
PHONE..................................302 834-0867
Bruce York, *Pr*
EMP: 5 EST: 1980
SALES (est): 199.02K
SALES (corp-wide): 199.02K Privately Held
SIC: 7342 Pest control in structures

(G-7666)
TRUEHOST CLOUD LLC ✪
651 N Broad St Ste 205 # 927 (19709-6402)
PHONE..................................972 674-3814
EMP: 4 EST: 2022
SALES (est): 73.93K Privately Held
Web: www.truehost.cloud
SIC: 7372 Business oriented computer software

(G-7667)
TUFF TASKS LLC
317 Great Oak Dr (19709-9721)
PHONE..................................302 983-5990
EMP: 5 EST: 2014
SALES (est): 79.86K Privately Held
SIC: 7549 Do-it-yourself garages

(G-7668)
U-HAUL NEIGHBORHOOD DEALER
1228 Middletown Warwick Rd (19709-9098)
PHONE..................................302 376-6858
Todd Levine, *Prin*
EMP: 7 EST: 2018
SALES (est): 46.21K Privately Held
Web: www.uhaul.com
SIC: 7513 Truck rental and leasing, no drivers

(G-7669)
U-HAUL NEIGHBORHOOD DEALER
5101 Summit Bridge Rd (19709-8821)
PHONE..................................302 449-7379
EMP: 7 EST: 2018
SALES (est): 196.16K Privately Held
Web: www.uhaul.com
SIC: 7513 Truck rental and leasing, no drivers

(G-7670)
UA SERVICES CORP
221 N Broad St Ste 1 (19709-1070)
PHONE..................................302 467-3700
Henry Boyce, *CEO*
EMP: 9 EST: 1998
SIC: 6719 Personal holding companies, except banks

(G-7671)
ULTAHOST INC
651 N Broad St Ste 201 (19709-6402)
PHONE..................................302 966-3941
EMP: 6 EST: 2021
SALES (est): 70.36K Privately Held
Web: www.ultahost.com
SIC: 4813 Internet host services

(G-7672)
UNIMRKT RESPONSE INC
651 N Broad St (19709-6400)
PHONE..................................646 712-9302
Dilip Singh, *Managing Member*
EMP: 6
SALES (est): 68.94K Privately Held
SIC: 8732 Market analysis, business, and economic research

(G-7673)
UNIVERSAL BEV IMPORTERS LLC
505 E Glen Mare Dr (19709-8773)
PHONE..................................302 276-0619
Alexander Rivera, *Managing Member*
EMP: 7 EST: 2016
SALES (est): 381.62K Privately Held
Web: www.ubiimports.com
SIC: 2084 Wine coolers (beverages)

(G-7674)
UNREAL VAPORS LLC
520 Middletown Warwick Rd (19709-8873)
PHONE..................................302 449-2547
Kevin Christianson, *Mng Pt*
EMP: 5 EST: 2014
SALES (est): 142.15K Privately Held
Web: www.unrealvapors.com
SIC: 5194 Smokeless tobacco

(G-7675)
UPSIDE GAMING INC ✪
Also Called: Upside Gaming
651 N Broad St Ste 205 (19709-6402)
PHONE..................................937 475-6908
Aaron Rucker, *CEO*
EMP: 5 EST: 2022
SALES (est): 199.4K Privately Held
SIC: 7389 Business Activities at Non-Commercial Site

(G-7676)
UR WORLD INC (PA) ✪
651 N Broad St Ste 201 (19709-6402)
PHONE..................................313 241-0060
EMP: 2 EST: 2022
SALES (est): 94.65K
SALES (corp-wide): 94.65K Privately Held
SIC: 7372 Prepackaged software

(G-7677)
V P CUSTOM FINISHERS IN
339 W Dickerson Ln (19709-8829)
PHONE..................................302 415-0002
EMP: 7 EST: 2019
SALES (est): 197.11K Privately Held
SIC: 1751 Carpentry work

(G-7678)
V POWER FIT INC
651 N Broad St Ste 206 (19709-6402)
PHONE..................................832 743-7116
V Renee Shepherd, *Managing Member*
EMP: 5 EST: 2019
SALES (est): 52.77K Privately Held
SIC: 7999 Physical fitness instruction

(G-7679)
V QUINTON INC
400 N Ramunno Dr (19709-3001)
PHONE..................................302 449-1711
Samuel Q Johnson, *Prin*
EMP: 17 EST: 2005
SALES (est): 467.47K Privately Held
SIC: 8351 Group day care center

(G-7680)
VA MEDICAL CTR WILMINGTON DE
720 Pinewood Dr (19709-8643)
PHONE..................................302 563-6024
Deborah Jones, *Prin*
EMP: 8 EST: 2010
SALES (est): 94.68K Privately Held
SIC: 8099 8011 Health and allied services, nec; Medical centers

(G-7681)
VALUEWRITE
204 Tralee Dr (19709-9006)
PHONE..................................302 593-0694
Valerie Stewart, *Prin*
EMP: 5 EST: 2009
SALES (est): 77.03K Privately Held
Web: www.valuewrite.com
SIC: 3269 Pottery florists' articles

(G-7682)
VANGO PAINTING
4106 Laughton Ln (19709-6601)
PHONE..................................302 689-8071
EMP: 5 EST: 2017
SALES (est): 109.25K Privately Held
Web: www.vangopaint.com
SIC: 1721 Painting and paper hanging

(G-7683)
VEER TRUCKING LLC
Also Called: VT
1234 Hook Dr (19709-9913)
PHONE..................................484 802-1452
Gurinder Saini, *Pr*
EMP: 5 EST: 2016
SALES (est): 235.35K Privately Held
SIC: 4212 Local trucking, without storage

(G-7684)
VELOCITY EU INC
Also Called: Velocity Eu
651 N Broad St Ste 206 (19709-6402)
PHONE..................................331 226-1818
Alexandar Trifonov, *CEO*
EMP: 10 EST: 2020
SALES (est): 441.85K Privately Held
SIC: 7372 5065 Application computer software; Modems, computer

(G-7685)
VENTURA MAINTENANCE COMPANY
101 E Green St (19709-1422)
PHONE..................................302 376-9060

Middletown - New Castle County (G-7686) — GEOGRAPHIC SECTION

EMP: 10 **EST:** 2015
SALES (est): 244.58K **Privately Held**
SIC: 7349 Building maintenance services, nec

(G-7686)
VERIFIEDLY LLC (PA)
651 N Broad St Ste 205 (19709-6402)
PHONE..................240 708-9025
Samuel Ailemen, *Managing Member*
EMP: 6 **EST:** 2020
SALES (est): 193.75K
SALES (corp-wide): 193.75K **Privately Held**
Web: www.stack-ft.com
SIC: 7371 Software programming applications

(G-7687)
VERITAS JUDGMENT RECOVERY
412 Benjamin Wright Dr (19709-9272)
PHONE..................302 376-7076
Theodore J Davis, *Prin*
EMP: 7 **EST:** 2016
SALES (est): 115.39K **Privately Held**
SIC: 8093 Substance abuse clinics (outpatient)

(G-7688)
VINYO INC (PA) ◊
651 N Broad St Ste 201 (19709-6402)
PHONE..................856 493-2042
Gerald Stephens, *Prin*
EMP: 6 **EST:** 2022
SALES (est): 87.88K
SALES (corp-wide): 87.88K **Privately Held**
SIC: 5045 Computer software

(G-7689)
VIRO INC
651 N Broad St (19709-6400)
PHONE..................857 207-8174
Usman Khalid, *CEO*
EMP: 5 **EST:** 2020
SALES (est): 425.64K **Privately Held**
SIC: 5047 Medical equipment and supplies

(G-7690)
VISUEATS IMAGERY SOLUTIONS LLC
651 N Broad St Ste 2051480 (19709-6400)
PHONE..................954 687-5112
EMP: 3 **EST:** 2019
SALES (est): 71.13K **Privately Held**
Web: www.visueats.com
SIC: 7372 Application computer software

(G-7691)
VITAL-GH MEDIA GROUP LLC (PA) ◊
600 N Broad St Ste 750 (19709-1032)
PHONE..................302 437-4258
Kwame Sapah, *Managing Member*
EMP: 5 **EST:** 2022
SALES (est): 456.2K
SALES (corp-wide): 456.2K **Privately Held**
SIC: 3663 Studio equipment, radio and television broadcasting

(G-7692)
VOICELOFT INC
651 N Broad St Ste 206 (19709-6402)
PHONE..................678 882-5024
Toghrul Samadov, *CEO*
EMP: 12 **EST:** 2021
SALES (est): 251.15K **Privately Held**
SIC: 7371 Software programming applications

(G-7693)
VOICEMIX INC
651 N Broad St (19709-6400)
PHONE..................305 981-0518
EMP: 5 **EST:** 2020
SALES (est): 68.89K **Privately Held**
SIC: 7371 Computer software development

(G-7694)
VOLUNTEER BREWING COMPANY LLC
120 W Main St (19709-1040)
PHONE..................610 721-2836
EMP: 7 **EST:** 2015
SALES (est): 424.18K **Privately Held**
Web: www.volunteerbrewing.com
SIC: 2082 Malt beverages

(G-7695)
VORA LABS INC ◊
600 N Broad St (19709-1032)
PHONE..................860 559-8985
Leo Sarian, *CEO*
EMP: 5 **EST:** 2023
SALES (est): 209.42K **Privately Held**
SIC: 8734 Testing laboratories

(G-7696)
VPS SERVICES LLC
651 N Broad St Ste 308 (19709-6403)
PHONE..................302 376-6710
EMP: 9 **EST:** 2013
SALES (est): 653.42K **Privately Held**
SIC: 8111 Legal services

(G-7697)
VTECH ENGINEERING GROUP LLC
1050 Industrial Dr # 110 (19709-2802)
PHONE..................267 253-2576
Lori Grayson, *Prin*
EMP: 8 **EST:** 2015
SALES (est): 241.72K **Privately Held**
SIC: 1521 Single-family housing construction

(G-7698)
VVARDIS INC
651 N Broad St (19709-6400)
PHONE..................917 940-3009
Sven Kaufmann, *Pr*
Stan Kosyakovskiy, *Prin*
EMP: 2 **EST:** 2022
SALES (est): 74.42K **Privately Held**
Web: www.vvardis.com
SIC: 2844 Toothpastes or powders, dentifrices

(G-7699)
VYZER INC ◊
651 N Broad St Ste 201 (19709-6402)
PHONE..................530 446-2568
Litan Yahav, *CEO*
EMP: 13 **EST:** 2022
SALES (est): 320.59K **Privately Held**
SIC: 7299 Personal financial services

(G-7700)
W P D TRANSPORT INC
605 Nesting Ln (19709-6126)
PHONE..................302 449-3260
EMP: 9 **EST:** 2005
SALES (est): 629.48K **Privately Held**
SIC: 4789 Transportation services, nec

(G-7701)
W500G INC
274 Liborio Dr (19709-3109)
PHONE..................302 252-7279
David Fredrick Amakobe, *CEO*
Moody Amakobe, *Cnslt*
EMP: 5
SALES (est): 119.92K **Privately Held**
SIC: 8732 Commercial nonphysical research

(G-7702)
WAGEFI INC
651 N Broad St Ste 206 (19709-6400)
PHONE..................646 853-0165
Prshant Batra, *CEO*
EMP: 5
SALES (est): 68.89K **Privately Held**
SIC: 7371 Computer software development and applications

(G-7703)
WAJBA CORP
221 N Broad St (19709-1070)
PHONE..................650 307-0070
Muhannad Taslaq, *CEO*
EMP: 5
SALES (est): 107.01K **Privately Held**
SIC: 7371 Computer software development and applications

(G-7704)
WALLACE INVESTMENTS GROUP LLC
651 N Broad St Ste 205 (19709-6402)
PHONE..................323 407-2889
EMP: 5 **EST:** 2020
SALES (est): 200K **Privately Held**
SIC: 8742 Management consulting services

(G-7705)
WALLIS REPAIR INC
106 Patriot Dr (19709-8762)
PHONE..................302 378-4301
Norman Wallis, *Pr*
Phyllis Wallis, *VP*
EMP: 8 **EST:** 1991
SQ FT: 20,000
SALES (est): 924.59K **Privately Held**
SIC: 7538 General automotive repair shops

(G-7706)
WALTER W SNYDER
Also Called: W W Snyder Excavating & Masnry
1844 Choptank Rd (19709-9648)
PHONE..................302 378-1817
Walter W Snyder, *Owner*
EMP: 5 **EST:** 1980
SALES (est): 330K **Privately Held**
SIC: 1741 1794 Masonry and other stonework; Excavation work

(G-7707)
WARD & TAYLOR LLC
242 Dove Run Dr (19709-7971)
PHONE..................302 225-3350
Katie Boulden, *Prin*
EMP: 5
Web: www.wardtaylor.com
SIC: 8111 Real estate law
PA: Ward & Taylor, Llc
2710 Centerville Rd # 210
Wilmington DE 19808

(G-7708)
WARTIMEACTION LLC
221 N Broad St Ste 3a (19709-1070)
PHONE..................203 685-8868
EMP: 10 **EST:** 2020
SALES (est): 369.13K **Privately Held**
SIC: 7389 Business Activities at Non-Commercial Site

(G-7709)
WE ARE FRIENDS INC
651 N Broad St Ste 206 (19709-6402)
PHONE..................302 501-7521
Signe Naessing, *CEO*
EMP: 6 **EST:** 2020
SALES (est): 46.16K **Privately Held**
SIC: 7371 Computer software development and applications

(G-7710)
WE ARE FUTURE TECH INC
651 N Broad St Ste 205 (19709-6402)
PHONE..................832 224-5528
Daniel Sloan, *Dir*
EMP: 25 **EST:** 2020
SALES (est): 641.67K **Privately Held**
SIC: 7371 Custom computer programming services

(G-7711)
WEAREXALT LLC (PA)
221 N Broad St (19709-1070)
PHONE..................203 913-5286
Catherine Mullen, *Managing Member*
EMP: 10
SALES (est): 348.32K
SALES (corp-wide): 348.32K **Privately Held**
SIC: 7371 Computer software development

(G-7712)
WEBILL INC
651 N Broad St Ste 206 (19709-6400)
PHONE..................628 227-7780
Serafim Korablev, *CEO*
EMP: 14
SALES (est): 535.57K **Privately Held**
SIC: 7371 Computer software development and applications

(G-7713)
WEBSAYS INC ◊
651 N Broad St Ste 201 (19709-6402)
PHONE..................424 385-9361
Oscar Aguilar, *CEO*
EMP: 8 **EST:** 2023
SALES (est): 306.16K **Privately Held**
SIC: 7371 Software programming applications

(G-7714)
WEEDIM INC
651 N Broad St (19709-6400)
PHONE..................202 773-9244
Yacoub Abshir, *Pr*
EMP: 5 **EST:** 2021
SALES (est): 259.56K **Privately Held**
SIC: 5045 Computer software

(G-7715)
WELL PRIMARY CARE LLC
102 Sleepy Hollow Dr Ste 200 (19709-5841)
PHONE..................302 449-0070
EMP: 7 **EST:** 2018
SALES (est): 479.15K **Privately Held**
Web: www.wellprimarycare.com
SIC: 8011 General and family practice, physician/surgeon

(G-7716)
WELLS FARGO BANK NATIONAL ASSN
310 Dove Run Centre Dr (19709-7912)
PHONE..................302 449-5485
Joan B Hitchens, *Brnch Mgr*
EMP: 8
SALES (corp-wide): 82.86B **Publicly Held**
Web: www.wellsfargo.com
SIC: 6021 National commercial banks
HQ: Wells Fargo Bank, National Association
420 Montgomery St San
San Francisco CA 94104
605 575-6900

GEOGRAPHIC SECTION
Middletown - New Castle County (G-7748)

(G-7717)
WESTOVER CARDIOLOGY
222 Carter Dr (19709-5854)
PHONE..................302 482-2035
EMP: 7 **EST:** 2012
SALES (est): 153.5K **Privately Held**
SIC: 8011 Cardiologist and cardio-vascular specialist

(G-7718)
WESTOWN DENTAL LLC
818 Kohl Ave (19709-4703)
PHONE..................302 376-3750
Glen Goleburn, *Managing Member*
EMP: 7
SALES (est): 155.65K **Privately Held**
SIC: 8021 Dental clinics and offices

(G-7719)
WESTOWN MOVIES LLC
Also Called: Westown Movies
150 Commerce Dr (19709-9039)
PHONE..................330 244-1633
EMP: 5 **EST:** 2013
SALES (est): 222.93K **Privately Held**
Web: www.westownmovies.com
SIC: 7832 Motion picture theaters, except drive-in

(G-7720)
WEXMON LLC
Also Called: Amrelieve
651 N Broad St Ste 205 # 1983 (19709-6402)
PHONE..................302 746-2472
EMP: 8 **EST:** 2020
SALES (est): 448.46K **Privately Held**
Web: www.amrelieve.com
SIC: 5047 Medical equipment and supplies

(G-7721)
WHAGONS NORTH AMERICA INC
Also Called: Software As A Service Saas
651 N Broad St Ste 206 (19709-6402)
PHONE..................781 241-5946
Matthias Malek, *Prin*
EMP: 20 **EST:** 2021
SALES (est): 677.83K **Privately Held**
SIC: 7372 Prepackaged software

(G-7722)
WHITE EAGLE ELECTRICAL CONTG
709 Guido Dr (19709-1480)
PHONE..................302 378-3366
Al Rutkowski, *Pr*
EMP: 10 **EST:** 1997
SALES (est): 833.03K **Privately Held**
Web: www.paglenstudio.com
SIC: 1731 Electrical work

(G-7723)
WHITE EAGLE INTEGRATIONS
635 Lorewood Grove Rd (19709-9235)
PHONE..................302 464-0550
Walter White, *Prin*
EMP: 9 **EST:** 2010
SALES (est): 938.35K **Privately Held**
Web: www.whiteeagleintegrations.com
SIC: 1542 7299 Commercial and office building contractors; Home improvement and renovation contractor agency

(G-7724)
WICKED PAY LLC ✪
651 N Broad St Ste 201 (19709-6402)
PHONE..................646 785-1143
Pooja Lama, *Managing Member*
EMP: 2 **EST:** 2023
SALES (est): 87.4K **Privately Held**

SIC: 7372 Prepackaged software

(G-7725)
WICKET WIRELESS LLC
653 Nesting Ln (19709-6129)
PHONE..................302 376-1788
Kunal Manekporia, *Admn*
EMP: 5 **EST:** 2016
SALES (est): 68.17K **Privately Held**
SIC: 4812 Cellular telephone services

(G-7726)
WILLIAM H BURKHARDT
342 Clayton Manor Dr (19709-8868)
PHONE..................302 376-1193
William H Burkhardt, *Prin*
EMP: 5 **EST:** 2014
SALES (est): 62K **Privately Held**
SIC: 7389 Business services, nec

(G-7727)
WILLIAMS FAMILY
655 Warren Dr (19709-1704)
PHONE..................302 378-9493
EMP: 8 **EST:** 2017
SALES (est): 17.9K **Privately Held**
SIC: 8351 Child day care services

(G-7728)
WILLOW GRACE VTRINARY HOSP LLC
311 W Main St (19709-1766)
PHONE..................302 378-9800
EMP: 7 **EST:** 2020
SALES (est): 269.66K **Privately Held**
Web: www.willowgraceveterinaryhospital.com
SIC: 0742 Animal hospital services, pets and other animal specialties

(G-7729)
WILLOW WINTERS PUBLISHING LLC
164 N Bayberry Pkwy (19709-9855)
PHONE..................570 885-2513
Shawn Van Nort, *Managing Member*
EMP: 2 **EST:** 2018
SALES (est): 104.44K **Privately Held**
SIC: 2741 Miscellaneous publishing

(G-7730)
WIREGATEIT LLC
909 Benalli Dr (19709-6121)
PHONE..................302 538-1304
EMP: 2 **EST:** 2020
SALES (est): 160K **Privately Held**
SIC: 3674 Integrated circuits, semiconductor networks, etc.

(G-7731)
WIRELESS NATION
38 W Sarazen Dr (19709-9357)
PHONE..................443 841-0116
EMP: 5
SALES (est): 35.32K **Privately Held**
Web: www.wirelessnation.com
SIC: 4812 Cellular telephone services

(G-7732)
WOLFE ASSOCIATES LLC
122 Sandhill Dr Ste 203 (19709-5862)
PHONE..................302 668-6178
Erica Wolfe, *Prin*
EMP: 8 **EST:** 2017
SALES (est): 994.98K **Privately Held**
Web: www.wolfe-associates.com
SIC: 8111 Legal services

(G-7733)
WOMENS HARMONY BRIGADE ASSN
300 Fox Hound Ct (19709-8611)
PHONE..................610 659-0096
Jennifer Newman, *Pr*
EMP: 5 **EST:** 2015
SALES (est): 55.39K **Privately Held**
SIC: 8699 Charitable organization

(G-7734)
WONDER YEARS PRESCHOOL LLC
111 Patriot Dr Ste A (19709-8771)
PHONE..................302 376-5553
Dwight Fields, *Managing Member*
EMP: 13 **EST:** 2019
SALES (est): 385.47K **Privately Held**
SIC: 8351 Preschool center

(G-7735)
WOODIN + ASSOCIATES LLC
111 Patriot Dr Ste D (19709-8771)
PHONE..................302 378-7300
EMP: 11 **EST:** 1988
SQ FT: 3,000
SALES (est): 489.62K **Privately Held**
Web: www.woodinassociates.com
SIC: 8711 8713 Civil engineering; Surveying services

(G-7736)
WOODWARD ENTERPRISES INC
Also Called: Woodward Outdoor Equipment
226 W Main St (19709-1041)
PHONE..................302 378-2849
Christopher Woodward, *CEO*
Ray Woodward, *VP*
Susan Woodward, *Sec*
EMP: 13 **EST:** 1940
SQ FT: 6,000
SALES (est): 1.31MM **Privately Held**
Web: www.woodwardoutdoor.com
SIC: 5261 7699 5083 Lawnmowers and tractors; General household repair services; Lawn and garden machinery and equipment

(G-7737)
X TRILLION INC
651 N Broad St (19709-6400)
PHONE..................347 370-9117
Jelani English, *CEO*
EMP: 6 **EST:** 2021
SIC: 6719 Investment holding companies, except banks

(G-7738)
XANADU CONCEPTS LLC
104 W Main St Ste 4a (19709-4400)
PHONE..................302 449-2677
Andrea Patterson, *Managing Member*
EMP: 5 **EST:** 2010
SQ FT: 1,200
SALES (est): 119.92K **Privately Held**
Web: www.xanadusalononline.com
SIC: 7231 Hairdressers

(G-7739)
XI GLOBAL LLC
651 N Broad St Ste 201 (19709-6400)
PHONE..................332 456-6969
Jan Rokita, *CEO*
EMP: 11
SALES (est): 390.81K **Privately Held**
SIC: 7371 Computer software development

(G-7740)
XPEDIENT FREIGHT LLC
Also Called: 2678266170
211 N Broad St Ste 3a (19709-1035)
PHONE..................267 826-6170
Lorenzo Woods, *Managing Member*
EMP: 2 **EST:** 2021
SALES (est): 208.38K **Privately Held**
SIC: 4731 4213 3537 Freight transportation arrangement; Trucking, except local; Trucks, tractors, loaders, carriers, and similar equipment

(G-7741)
XTALOS LLC
651 N Broad St Ste 20533 (19709-6400)
PHONE..................800 383-0662
EMP: 5 **EST:** 2020
SALES (est): 129.73K **Privately Held**
SIC: 7373 Computer systems analysis and design

(G-7742)
YALLA MARKETING LLC ✪
651 N Broad St Ste 201 (19709-6402)
PHONE..................209 201-0313
EMP: 5 **EST:** 2022
SALES (est): 59.87K **Privately Held**
SIC: 8742 Marketing consulting services

(G-7743)
YALLERY INC
651 N Broad St Ste 206 (19709-6402)
PHONE..................571 351-3820
Dzhavid Babakishiiev, *CEO*
EMP: 2 **EST:** 2020
SALES (est): 100K **Privately Held**
SIC: 7372 Application computer software

(G-7744)
YENASYS LLC
651 N Broad St Ste 205 (19709-6400)
PHONE..................302 956-9277
EMP: 8
SALES (est): 512.29K **Privately Held**
Web: www.yenasys.com
SIC: 7371 Software programming applications

(G-7745)
YENTAL EMPIRE LLC
600 N Broad St Ste 3119 (19709-1032)
PHONE..................404 423-0454
EMP: 5 **EST:** 2011
SALES (est): 277.43K **Privately Held**
SIC: 4731 5932 Freight transportation arrangement; Used merchandise stores

(G-7746)
YESAMERICA CORPORATION
651 N Broad St Ste 205-908 (19709-6400)
PHONE..................800 872-1548
Kirill Zhukov, *CEO*
EMP: 10 **EST:** 2019
SALES (est): 500K **Privately Held**
SIC: 7379 Online services technology consultants

(G-7747)
YHK ELM CLEANERS INC
400 W Main St (19709-1063)
PHONE..................302 378-2017
EMP: 5 **EST:** 2012
SALES (est): 190.24K **Privately Held**
SIC: 7699 Cleaning services

(G-7748)
YORSTON AND CO LLC
651 Nesting Ln (19709-6129)
PHONE..................302 415-1925
Kara Yorston, *Prin*
EMP: 8 **EST:** 2018
SALES (est): 103.34K **Privately Held**
Web: www.yorstonandassociates.com
SIC: 8748 Business consulting, nec

Middletown - New Castle County (G-7749) GEOGRAPHIC SECTION

(G-7749)
YOU ARE NOT ALONE VTRANS FNDTI
224 Ann Dr (19709-2606)
PHONE.....................302 287-8533
EMP: 10 EST: 2009
SALES (est): 136.09K **Privately Held**
SIC: 8641 Veterans' organization

(G-7750)
ZEROANT INC
651 N Broad St Ste 206 (19709-6402)
PHONE.....................567 342-1530
Michael Piper, CEO
EMP: 5 EST: 2021
SALES (est): 107.01K **Privately Held**
SIC: 7371 Computer software development and applications

(G-7751)
ZODIAC INC
651 N Broad St Ste 205-22 (19709-6400)
PHONE.....................800 969-4170
Hero Huggins, CEO
EMP: 2 EST: 1996
SALES (est): 126.22K **Privately Held**
SIC: 7372 Application computer software

(G-7752)
ZULUDYNASTY LLC
651 N Broad St Ste 2054236 (19709-6400)
PHONE.....................815 909-4236
EMP: 5 EST: 2020
SALES (est): 100K **Privately Held**
SIC: 6719 Investment holding companies, except banks

Milford
Sussex County

(G-7753)
500 SUTH DPONT BLVD OPRTONS LL
Also Called: Milford Place
500 S Dupont Blvd (19963-1758)
PHONE.....................302 422-8700
EMP: 313
SALES (est): 19.06MM **Privately Held**
SIC: 8051 Convalescent home with continuous nursing care
HQ: Genesis Healthcare Llc
   101 E State St
   Kennett Square PA 19348

(G-7754)
700 MARVEL ROAD OPERATIONS LLC
Also Called: Milford Center
700 Marvel Rd (19963-1740)
PHONE.....................302 422-3303
Shirlyn Shafer, Managing Member
EMP: 322
SALES (est): 27.99MM **Privately Held**
SIC: 8051 Convalescent home with continuous nursing care
HQ: Genesis Healthcare Llc
   101 E State St
   Kennett Square PA 19348

(G-7755)
887 THE BRIDGE
1977 Bay Rd (19963-6134)
P.O. Box 680 (19963-0680)
PHONE.....................302 422-6909
William T Sammons, Genl Mgr
EMP: 11 EST: 2010
SALES (est): 155.63K **Privately Held**
Web: www.wearethebridge.org

SIC: 4832 Radio broadcasting stations

(G-7756)
A BETTER CHNCE FOR OUR CHLDREN
805 S Dupont Blvd (19963-2232)
PHONE.....................302 725-5008
EMP: 14 EST: 2011
SALES (est): 97.43K **Privately Held**
Web: www.abcfoc.org
SIC: 8351 Child day care services

(G-7757)
A PLUMBER
5923 Old Shawnee Rd (19963-3368)
PHONE.....................302 249-7606
Paul Mcconnell, Prin
EMP: 5 EST: 2017
SALES (est): 60.42K **Privately Held**
SIC: 1711 Plumbing contractors

(G-7758)
AAA COMPUTING
306 S Washington St (19963-2815)
PHONE.....................302 430-9048
Joseph Zimmerman, Prin
EMP: 5 EST: 2016
SALES (est): 28.27K **Privately Held**
SIC: 7378 Computer maintenance and repair

(G-7759)
ADDUS HEALTHCARE INC
1675 S State Street (19963)
PHONE.....................302 424-4842
EMP: 133
Web: www.addus.com
SIC: 8082 Home health care services
HQ: Addus Healthcare, Inc.
   2300 Warrenville Rd
   Downers Grove IL 60515
   630 296-3400

(G-7760)
ADKINS MANAGEMENT COMPANY
421 Kings Hwy (19963-1763)
P.O. Box 316 (19963-0316)
PHONE.....................302 684-3000
Chris Adkins, Prin
EMP: 18 EST: 1990
SALES (est): 436.18K **Privately Held**
SIC: 7997 Golf club, membership

(G-7761)
ADVANCED HEALING INC
919 Se 2nd St (19963-1577)
PHONE.....................302 363-5839
William Matthews, Prin
EMP: 6 EST: 2016
SALES (est): 22.85K **Privately Held**
Web: www.advanced-healing.net
SIC: 8049 Offices of health practitioner

(G-7762)
AIM INC
506 Heath Row (19963-1634)
P.O. Box 332 (19963-0332)
PHONE.....................302 424-1424
D Gardner, Owner
EMP: 8 EST: 2014
SALES (est): 145.37K **Privately Held**
SIC: 6411 Insurance agents, brokers, and service

(G-7763)
ALL ABOUT ME DAY CARE
104 Mccoy St (19963-2310)
PHONE.....................302 424-8322
Cherie Kersey, Owner
EMP: 10 EST: 1991
SALES (est): 303.03K **Privately Held**

SIC: 8351 Child day care services

(G-7764)
ALL PRO PROPERTY MAINT LLC
410 East St (19963-2507)
PHONE.....................302 531-6811
EMP: 5 EST: 2018
SALES (est): 20.74K **Privately Held**
SIC: 7349 Janitorial service, contract basis

(G-7765)
ALORA LLC
5995 Williamsville Rd (19963-6314)
PHONE.....................302 670-3066
Jeremy Dickerson, Owner
EMP: 5 EST: 2016
SALES (est): 243.97K **Privately Held**
Web: www.alora.biz
SIC: 7299 Massage parlor

(G-7766)
AMAZON STEEL CONSTRUCTION INC
2537 Bay Rd (19963-6020)
PHONE.....................302 751-1146
Martin Heesh, Pr
▼ EMP: 9 EST: 2003
SQ FT: 13,000
SALES (est): 1.68MM **Privately Held**
Web: www.amazonsteelconstruction.com
SIC: 1799 1796 3441 1791 Welding on site; Millwright; Fabricated structural metal; Structural steel erection

(G-7767)
AMERICAN NEON PRODUCTS COMPANY
Also Called: Tetrus Led Co
720 Mccolley St (19963-2393)
PHONE.....................302 856-3400
EMP: 10 EST: 1988
SALES (est): 1.59MM **Privately Held**
Web: www.tetrus.com
SIC: 5063 Lighting fixtures, commercial and industrial

(G-7768)
ANDREW PIPON
Also Called: Embroidery Enterprises
8231 Woods Edge Cir (19963-4803)
PHONE.....................949 337-2249
Andrew Pipon, Owner
EMP: 4 EST: 2017
SALES (est): 113.11K **Privately Held**
SIC: 2395 Embroidery and art needlework

(G-7769)
ANDY IS MY COACH LLC
21 General Torbert Dr (19963-2547)
PHONE.....................302 943-4819
Andy Stevens, Prin
EMP: 5 EST: 2017
SALES (est): 66.61K **Privately Held**
Web: www.andyismycoach.com
SIC: 7819 Developing and laboratory services, motion picture

(G-7770)
AP LINENS INC
Also Called: A P Linen Service
713 S Washington St (19963-2305)
PHONE.....................302 430-0851
Michael G Attix, Pr
EMP: 26 EST: 1999
SALES (est): 1.04MM **Privately Held**
Web: www.aplinens.com
SIC: 7211 Power laundries, family and commercial

(G-7771)
APEX EXTERIORS INC
497 Bowman Rd (19963-5353)
PHONE.....................302 858-1699
EMP: 5 EST: 2017
SALES (est): 112.21K **Privately Held**
Web: www.delawaremetalroofingsystems.com
SIC: 1761 Roofing contractor

(G-7772)
ARTISANS BANK INC
100 Aerenson Dr (19963-1236)
PHONE.....................302 430-7681
Kathleen Cooper, Mgr
EMP: 7
SALES (corp-wide): 25.62MM **Privately Held**
Web: www.artisansbank.com
SIC: 6036 6029 State savings banks, not federally chartered; Commercial banks, nec
PA: Artisans Bank Inc
   2961 Centerville Rd # 101
   Wilmington DE 19808
   302 658-6881

(G-7773)
AT HOME CABINETRY & DESIGN LLC
219 S Walnut St (19963-1957)
PHONE.....................302 853-5305
Brian Walp, Prin
EMP: 5 EST: 2014
SALES (est): 391.7K **Privately Held**
Web: www.athomecabinetry.com
SIC: 2434 Wood kitchen cabinets

(G-7774)
ATI HOLDINGS LLC
Also Called: ATI Physical Therapy
941 N Dupont Blvd Ste C (19963-1069)
PHONE.....................302 422-6670
Jennifer Hilliard, Brnch Mgr
EMP: 6
SALES (corp-wide): 635.67MM **Publicly Held**
Web: www.atipt.com
SIC: 8049 Physical therapist
HQ: Ati Holdings, Llc
   790 Remington Blvd
   Bolingbrook IL 60440

(G-7775)
ATLANTIC CHIROPRACTIC ASSOC
509 Lakeview Ave (19963-2917)
PHONE.....................302 422-3100
Andrew Riddle, Owner
EMP: 21 EST: 2019
SALES (est): 1.57MM **Privately Held**
Web: www.atlanticchiropractic.net
SIC: 8041 Offices and clinics of chiropractors

(G-7776)
ATLANTIC CHIROPRACTIC ASSOCIAT (PA)
375 Mullet Run (19963-5373)
PHONE.....................302 422-3100
Andrew W Riddle, Owner
EMP: 10 EST: 2007
SALES (est): 848.48K **Privately Held**
Web: www.atlanticchiropractic.net
SIC: 8041 Offices and clinics of chiropractors

(G-7777)
ATLANTIC CONCRETE COMPANY INC (PA)
New Wharf Rd (19963)
P.O. Box 321 (19963-0321)
PHONE.....................302 422-8017
David A Jones, Pr
Cynthia Jones, *

GEOGRAPHIC SECTION
Milford - Sussex County (G-7805)

EMP: 60 EST: 1946
SQ FT: 10,000
SALES (est): 8.28MM
SALES (corp-wide): 8.28MM **Privately Held**
Web: www.atlanticconcrete.com
SIC: 3273 Ready-mixed concrete

(G-7778)
ATLANTIC PHYSICIANS BILLING
9 Lake Crest Dr (19963-9659)
PHONE..................914 490-3741
Melissa Nieli, *Prin*
EMP: 8 EST: 2019
SALES (est): 240.47K **Privately Held**
SIC: 8011 Offices and clinics of medical doctors

(G-7779)
ATTITUDE LLC NONE
617 N Dupont Blvd (19963-1099)
PHONE..................302 422-3356
Cheryl O'connor, *Mgr*
EMP: 5 EST: 2007
SALES (est): 240.4K **Privately Held**
Web: www.attitudesmedicalspa.com
SIC: 8011 Dermatologist

(G-7780)
AVE PRESCHOOL
20 N Church Ave (19963-1021)
PHONE..................302 422-8775
Cheryl Waldon, *Dir*
EMP: 21 EST: 2002
SALES (est): 358.59K **Privately Held**
Web: www.avenuepreschool.org
SIC: 8351 Preschool center

(G-7781)
BALTIMORE AIRCOIL COMPANY INC
Also Called: B A C
1162 Holly Hill Rd (19963-6339)
P.O. Box 402 (19963-0402)
PHONE..................302 424-2583
Richard Green, *Brnch Mgr*
EMP: 140
SQ FT: 60,000
SALES (corp-wide): 189K **Privately Held**
Web: www.baltimoreaircoil.com
SIC: 3585 3443 3498 Evaporative condensers, heat transfer equipment; Heat exchangers: coolers (after, inter), condensers, etc.; Fabricated pipe and fittings
HQ: Baltimore Aircoil Company, Inc.
7600 Dorsey Run Rd
Jessup MD 20794
410 799-6200

(G-7782)
BANK HOUSE
5879 Old Shawnee Rd (19963-3369)
PHONE..................302 422-4824
Denise Morris, *Prin*
EMP: 11 EST: 2018
SALES (est): 53.06K **Privately Held**
Web: www.bankhousemilford.com
SIC: 7011 Bed and breakfast inn

(G-7783)
BAY HEALTH FREZZA CHARLES
21 W Clarke Ave (19963-1849)
PHONE..................302 430-5565
Charles Frezza, *Prin*
EMP: 11 EST: 2013
SALES (est): 149.41K **Privately Held**
Web: www.bayhealth.org
SIC: 8099 Health and allied services, nec

(G-7784)
BAYADA HOME HEALTH CARE INC
1016 N Walnut St (19963-1244)
PHONE..................302 424-8200
Steve P Flannery, *Brnch Mgr*
EMP: 74
SALES (corp-wide): 694.21MM **Privately Held**
Web: www.bayada.com
SIC: 8082 8049 8011 Visiting nurse service; Nurses and other medical assistants; Pediatrician
PA: Bayada Home Health Care, Inc.
1 W Main St
Moorestown NJ 08057
856 231-1000

(G-7785)
BAYADA HOME HEALTH CARE INC
100 Silicato Pkwy Suite 104 (19963-1271)
PHONE..................302 351-1244
EMP: 61
SALES (corp-wide): 694.21MM **Privately Held**
Web: www.bayada.com
SIC: 8082 Visiting nurse service
PA: Bayada Home Health Care, Inc.
1 W Main St
Moorestown NJ 08057
856 231-1000

(G-7786)
BAYHEALTH BARIATRIC PROGRAM
100 Wellness Way (19963-4364)
PHONE..................302 430-5454
EMP: 12 EST: 2019
SALES (est): 196.11K **Privately Held**
Web: www.bayhealth.org
SIC: 8099 Health and allied services, nec

(G-7787)
BAYHEALTH HEMATOLOGY ONCOLOGY
21 W Clarke Ave (19963-1849)
PHONE..................302 430-5072
Dennis Klima, *CEO*
EMP: 14 EST: 2017
SALES (est): 184.27K **Privately Held**
Web: www.bayhealth.org
SIC: 8011 Oncologist

(G-7788)
BAYPRO CONTRACTING
211 S Walnut St (19963-1957)
PHONE..................703 593-7673
Francis Culotta, *Prin*
EMP: 5 EST: 2015
SALES (est): 68.68K **Privately Held**
Web: www.bayprorestore.com
SIC: 1799 Athletic and recreation facilities construction

(G-7789)
BCB DIESEL MECHANICS LLC
404 Milford Harrington Hwy (19963)
PHONE..................302 422-3787
EMP: 5 EST: 2018
SALES (est): 209.71K **Privately Held**
SIC: 7538 General automotive repair shops

(G-7790)
BEEBE MEDICAL CENTER INC
810 Seabury Ave (19963-2223)
PHONE..................302 393-2056
EMP: 31
SALES (corp-wide): 581.97MM **Privately Held**
Web: www.beebehealthcare.org
SIC: 8062 General medical and surgical hospitals
PA: Beebe Medical Center, Inc.
424 Savannah Rd
Lewes DE 19958
302 645-3300

(G-7791)
BEGINNING
303 Moyer Cir W (19963-9614)
PHONE..................302 491-6545
Angela Jefferson, *Prin*
EMP: 5 EST: 2011
SALES (est): 44.03K **Privately Held**
SIC: 7299 Massage parlor

(G-7792)
BENNETT FARMS INC
24139 Sugar Hill Rd (19963-4713)
PHONE..................302 684-1627
Fred Bennett, *Prin*
EMP: 5 EST: 2009
SALES (est): 553.65K **Privately Held**
SIC: 0191 General farms, primarily crop

(G-7793)
BETTYS
140 N Landing Dr (19963-5382)
PHONE..................302 233-2675
EMP: 5 EST: 2012
SALES (est): 212.88K **Privately Held**
Web: www.bettylous.net
SIC: 2087 Beverage bases

(G-7794)
BL OWN UP LLC
Also Called: Logistics
18 Little Pond Dr (19963-3903)
PHONE..................609 509-8388
Steven L Jones Junior, *Managing Member*
EMP: 8 EST: 2020
SALES (est): 599.21K **Privately Held**
SIC: 4213 Trucking, except local

(G-7795)
BLESSNGS GRNHSES CMPOST FCILTY
9372 Draper Rd (19963-4670)
P.O. Box 512 (19963-0512)
PHONE..................302 684-8890
EMP: 15 EST: 1999
SALES (est): 529.01K **Privately Held**
Web: www.blessingsblends.com
SIC: 0181 8744 Flowers: grown under cover (e.g., greenhouse production); Facilities support services

(G-7796)
BLUE HEN INSULATION INC
2844 Deer Valley Rd (19963-6234)
PHONE..................302 424-4482
Joann Carter, *Pr*
Constance Warren, *VP*
John P Carter, *Stockholder*
EMP: 8 EST: 1984
SALES (est): 576.06K **Privately Held**
SIC: 1742 Insulation, buildings

(G-7797)
BLUE HEN LINES INC
404 Milford Harrington Hwy (19963)
PHONE..................302 422-6206
Dewey C Lynch, *Pr*
John R Lynch, *VP*
EMP: 25 EST: 1940
SQ FT: 5,000
SALES (est): 1.2MM **Privately Held**
SIC: 4213 Trucking, except local

(G-7798)
BLUE HEN SPRING WORKS INC
112 N Rehoboth Blvd (19963-1339)
PHONE..................302 422-6600
Billie Lynn Thompson, *Pr*
Mathew Thompson, *Sec*
EMP: 10 EST: 1981
SALES (est): 468.26K **Privately Held**
Web: www.bluehensprings.com
SIC: 7539 7538 Brake repair, automotive; General truck repair

(G-7799)
BMA MILFORD
656 N Dupont Blvd Ste D (19963-1002)
PHONE..................302 424-0552
Allison Jenks, *Mgr*
EMP: 8 EST: 2016
SALES (est): 54.13K **Privately Held**
SIC: 8011 Offices and clinics of medical doctors

(G-7800)
BOUTIQUE THE BRIDAL LTD
2454 Bay Rd (19963-6003)
PHONE..................302 335-5948
Patricia S Davis, *Owner*
EMP: 8 EST: 1985
SALES (est): 427.71K **Privately Held**
Web: www.the-bridal-boutique-ltd.com
SIC: 5621 7299 Bridal shops; Tuxedo rental

(G-7801)
BOYS & GIRLS CLUB OF MILFORD
105 Ne Front St (19963-1429)
PHONE..................302 422-4453
Maria Edgerton, *Prin*
EMP: 6 EST: 2013
SALES (est): 119.43K **Privately Held**
SIC: 8641 Youth organizations

(G-7802)
BRANDYWINE CENTER FOR AUTISM
1010 Mattlind Way (19963-5300)
PHONE..................302 503-3120
EMP: 10 EST: 2016
SALES (est): 36.21K **Privately Held**
Web: www.brandywinecenterforautism.com
SIC: 8322 Social services for the handicapped

(G-7803)
BRANDYWINE CNSELING CMNTY SVCS
769 E Masten Cir (19963-1091)
PHONE..................302 856-4700
EMP: 7 EST: 2020
SALES (est): 235.37K **Privately Held**
Web: www.brandywinecounseling.com
SIC: 8011 Medical centers

(G-7804)
BREAKWATER FENCE AND DECK
9565 Bay Shore Dr (19963)
PHONE..................302 684-3333
Jerry Little, *Prin*
EMP: 5 EST: 2008
SALES (est): 61.05K **Privately Held**
Web: www.breakwaterfence.com
SIC: 1799 Fence construction

(G-7805)
BRIDGESTONE RET OPERATIONS LLC
Also Called: Firestone
103 Causey Ave Bldg 103 (19963-1933)
PHONE..................302 422-4508
Brandy Ward, *Mgr*
EMP: 7

Web: www.bridgestoneamericas.com
SIC: **5531** 5014 5013 Automotive tires; Automobile tires and tubes; Automotive supplies and parts
HQ: Bridgestone Retail Operations, Llc
333 E Lake St Ste 300
Bloomingdale IL 60108
630 259-9000

(G-7806)
BRIGHTEN UP PAINTING
2 W Thrush Dr (19963-3919)
PHONE...............................302 424-4591
David Wschleigh, *Prin*
EMP: 5 EST: 2010
SALES (est): 84.61K **Privately Held**
SIC: **1721** Painting and paper hanging

(G-7807)
BURRIS FREIGHT MANAGEMENT LLC
501 Se 5th St (19963-2022)
PHONE...............................800 805-8135
Nick Falk, *Pr*
Anthony Megale, *VP*
EMP: 9 EST: 2015
SALES (est): 2.02MM
SALES (corp-wide): 1.24B **Privately Held**
Web: www.burrislogistics.com
SIC: **4731** Transportation agents and brokers
PA: Burris Logistics
501 Se 5th St
Milford DE 19963
302 839-4531

(G-7808)
BURRIS LOGISTICS (PA)
Also Called: Burris Retail Logistics
501 Se 5th St (19963-2022)
P.O. Box 219 (19963-0219)
PHONE...............................302 839-4531
Donnan R Burris, *Pr*
Jeff Swain, *
Don Mcentaffer, *Ex VP*
Margaret E Owens, *
◆ **EMP:** 60 **EST:** 1925
SQ FT: 10,000
SALES (est): 1.24B
SALES (corp-wide): 1.24B **Privately Held**
Web: www.burrislogistics.com
SIC: **4789** Freight car loading and unloading

(G-7809)
C & B CONSTRUCT
150 Vickers Rd (19963-5393)
PHONE...............................302 378-9862
EMP: 5 EST: 2011
SALES (est): 576.63K **Privately Held**
SIC: **1521** New construction, single-family houses

(G-7810)
C & S CONSULTANTS INC
6 E Clarke Ave (19963-1803)
PHONE...............................302 236-5211
Chuck Culotta, *Pr*
EMP: 5 EST: 1984
SALES (est): 413.87K **Privately Held**
Web: www.ronclearfield.com
SIC: **8741** Construction management

(G-7811)
CANINE CTURE EXPRT GROMING LLC
217 N Rehoboth Blvd (19963-1303)
PHONE...............................302 500-1814
Loren R Hill, *Asst Sec*
EMP: 5 EST: 2017
SALES (est): 78.05K **Privately Held**
Web: www.caninecoutureeg.com
SIC: **0752** Grooming services, pet and animal specialties

(G-7812)
CAROLS
7082 Pleasanton Dr (19963-3489)
PHONE...............................302 448-0734
Carol Collins, *Prin*
EMP: 5 EST: 2017
SALES (est): 27.74K **Privately Held**
SIC: **7231** Hairdressers

(G-7813)
CASCADES LLC
151 Cascades Ln (19963-6481)
PHONE...............................856 662-1730
Brad Ingerman, *Managing Member*
EMP: 5 EST: 2011
SALES (est): 237.08K **Privately Held**
Web: www.livewillows.com
SIC: **6513** Apartment building operators

(G-7814)
CEDAR CREEK CSTM CABINETS LLC
7816 Cedar Creek Ct (19963-4784)
PHONE...............................302 542-7794
Brandon Ritter, *Prin*
EMP: 5 EST: 2018
SALES (est): 53.79K **Privately Held**
SIC: **2434** Wood kitchen cabinets

(G-7815)
CEDAR CREEK MARKET INC
20728 Sapp Rd (19963-4247)
PHONE...............................302 249-0725
Joel Peterman, *Pr*
EMP: 5 EST: 2020
SALES (est): 400K **Privately Held**
SIC: **4151** School buses

(G-7816)
CENTER FOR COMMUNITY JUSTICE
1129 Airport Rd (19963-6418)
PHONE...............................302 424-0890
Natalie Way, *Dir*
EMP: 5 EST: 1996
SALES (est): 281.49K **Privately Held**
Web: www.peoplesplace2.com
SIC: **7389** Arbitration and conciliation service

(G-7817)
CENTER FOR NEUROLOGY
Also Called: Physical Medical Rehab Assoc
111 Neurology Way (19963-5368)
PHONE...............................302 422-0800
Peter Koveleski, *Mgr*
EMP: 11 EST: 1999
SALES (est): 494.99K **Privately Held**
Web: www.cnmri.com
SIC: **8011** Neurologist

(G-7818)
CENTER OF EXCELLENCE IN
305 Jefferson Ave (19963-1800)
PHONE...............................302 503-0741
EMP: 10 EST: 2015
SALES (est): 416.58K **Privately Held**
Web: www.dceobgyn.com
SIC: **8011** Gynecologist

(G-7819)
CENTRAL AND SOUTHERN DELAWARE
221 S Rehoboth Blvd (19963-1568)
PHONE...............................302 545-8067
Paul Lakeman, *Ex Dir*
EMP: 9 EST: 2006
SALES (est): 250.06K **Privately Held**
SIC: **8621** Health association

(G-7820)
CHARLENE WEBB
Also Called: Allstate
915 N Dupont Blvd Ste 102 (19963-1093)
PHONE...............................302 424-8490
Louis Sevrin, *Owner*
EMP: 6 EST: 2011
SALES (est): 69.28K **Privately Held**
Web: www.allstate.com
SIC: **6411** Insurance agents, brokers, and service

(G-7821)
CHARLES H WEST FARMS INC
Also Called: Charles H West Farms
2953 Tub Mill Pond Rd (19963-5910)
PHONE...............................302 335-3936
Stanley West, *Pr*
Charles West, *Ex VP*
Lorraine B West, *Sec*
Sandra L Mitchell, *Treas*
Steven H West, *Sec*
EMP: 17 EST: 1953
SQ FT: 1,500
SALES (est): 950.3K **Privately Held**
SIC: **0161** 0119 Rooted vegetable farms; Feeder grains

(G-7822)
CHARLES TAYLOR CONSULTING INC
8485 Glade Dr (19963-4802)
PHONE...............................703 200-8057
Charles Taylor, *Owner*
EMP: 5 EST: 2017
SALES (est): 80.57K **Privately Held**
Web: www.charlestaylor.com
SIC: **8748** Business consulting, nec

(G-7823)
CHAYIL HEALTHCARELLC
26 Patrick Henry Ln (19963-4004)
PHONE...............................302 399-0991
Dandrea Kittles, *Prin*
EMP: 7 EST: 2015
SALES (est): 138.76K **Privately Held**
SIC: **8099** Health and allied services, nec

(G-7824)
CHEMSTAR CORP
686 N Dupont Blvd (19963-1002)
PHONE...............................302 465-3175
EMP: 7 EST: 2018
SALES (est): 245.47K **Privately Held**
SIC: **2951** Asphalt and asphaltic paving mixtures (not from refineries)

(G-7825)
CHITIKI DHADHA GAUTAMY MD
517 S Dupont Blvd (19963-1757)
PHONE...............................302 393-5006
G Chitiki Dhadham Md, *Owner*
EMP: 9 EST: 2018
SALES (est): 112.1K **Privately Held**
SIC: **8011** Offices and clinics of medical doctors

(G-7826)
CHOY WILSON CDGN
Also Called: Waverly Orthopaedic
329 Mullet Run (19963-5373)
PHONE...............................302 424-4141
Wilson Choy, *Prin*
EMP: 7 EST: 2011
SALES (est): 131.95K **Privately Held**
Web: www.delawarebonecare.com
SIC: **3842** Prosthetic appliances

(G-7827)
CHRISTOPHER FORTIN DDS
214 S Walnut St (19963-1958)
PHONE...............................302 422-9791
Christopher Fortin, *Prin*
EMP: 9 EST: 2017
SALES (est): 67.67K **Privately Held**
SIC: **8021** Dentists' office

(G-7828)
CITIFINANCIAL CREDIT COMPANY
Also Called: Citifinancial
660 N Dupont Blvd (19963-1002)
PHONE...............................302 422-9657
Debra Hoopengardner, *Mgr*
EMP: 6
SALES (corp-wide): 101.08B **Publicly Held**
SIC: **6141** Consumer finance companies
HQ: Citifinancial Credit Company
300 Saint Paul Pl Fl 3
Baltimore MD 21202
410 332-3000

(G-7829)
CITY OF MILFORD
Also Called: Electric Department
180 Vickers Rd (19963-5393)
PHONE...............................302 422-1110
Rick Carmean, *Superintnt*
EMP: 29
Web: www.cityofmilford.com
SIC: **4911** Electric services
PA: Milford, City Of (Inc)
201 S Walnut St
Milford DE 19963
302 424-3712

(G-7830)
CLEAN CUT THREAD
125 Causey Ave (19963-1909)
PHONE...............................302 491-4336
EMP: 5 EST: 2014
SALES (est): 62.26K **Privately Held**
SIC: **7699** Cleaning services

(G-7831)
CLEAN SWEEP
5862 Old Shawnee Rd (19963-3352)
PHONE...............................302 422-6085
Ernest Hostedler, *Owner*
EMP: 5 EST: 1981
SALES (est): 333.98K **Privately Held**
Web: www.delawarecleansweep.com
SIC: **1741** 7349 Chimney construction and maintenance; Chimney cleaning

(G-7832)
CLEAR DEFINITION LLC
110 N Rehoboth Blvd (19963-1339)
PHONE...............................302 503-7560
EMP: 8 EST: 2019
SALES (est): 437.05K **Privately Held**
Web: www.cleardefdetailing.com
SIC: **7532** Body shop, automotive

(G-7833)
CLEARVIEW WINDOWS LLC
Also Called: Fish Window Cleaning Services
600 Ne Front Street Ext Ste H (19963-1395)
PHONE...............................302 491-6768
EMP: 5 EST: 2010
SALES (est): 160.34K **Privately Held**
Web: www.fishwindowcleaning.com
SIC: **7349** 5031 Window cleaning; Doors and windows

GEOGRAPHIC SECTION
Milford - Sussex County (G-7861)

(G-7834)
CLENDANIEL CONSTRUCTION
7632 N Union Church Rd (19963-3629)
PHONE..........................302 422-7415
Frank C Clendaniel, *Prin*
EMP: 5 **EST:** 2011
SALES (est): 190.01K **Privately Held**
SIC: 1521 Single-family housing construction

(G-7835)
CLIFTON FARMS INC
306 Warner Rd (19963-5834)
PHONE..........................302 242-8806
William Clifton, *Prin*
William Clifton, *Pr*
William Donald Clifton, *Sr VP*
Ruth Ellen Clifton, *Sec*
EMP: 5 **EST:** 2004
SALES (est): 414.68K **Privately Held**
SIC: 0722 0723 0762 0116 Vegetables and melons, machine harvesting services; Vegetable crops market preparation services; Farm management services; Soybeans

(G-7836)
CLOSE CUTS LAWN SVC & LDSCPG
24 Ne 10th St (19963-1363)
PHONE..........................302 422-2248
Cyle Hostedler, *Owner*
EMP: 5 **EST:** 2009
SALES (est): 62.02K **Privately Held**
Web: www.closecutslandscaping.com
SIC: 3999 Grasses, artificial and preserved

(G-7837)
CNMRI
111 Neurology Way (19963-5368)
PHONE..........................302 422-0800
EMP: 7 **EST:** 2019
SALES (est): 228.82K **Privately Held**
Web: www.cnmri.com
SIC: 8011 Neurologist

(G-7838)
COASTLINE MEDICAL CTR MILFORD
907 N Dupont Blvd (19963-1060)
PHONE..........................302 265-2893
Aaron Block, *Owner*
EMP: 10 **EST:** 2010
SALES (est): 178.5K **Privately Held**
Web: www.coastlinemedical.org
SIC: 8011 Medical centers

(G-7839)
COLDWELL BANKER RESORT REALTY
711 N Dupont Blvd (19963-1003)
PHONE..........................302 422-8200
EMP: 8 **EST:** 2019
SALES (est): 206.34K **Privately Held**
Web: www.coldwellbanker.com
SIC: 6531 Real estate agent, residential

(G-7840)
COMMUNITY INTEGRATED SERVICES
24 Nw Front St Ste 300 (19963-1463)
PHONE..........................215 238-7411
Susan Schonfeld, *Ex Dir*
EMP: 50
SALES (corp-wide): 14.57MM **Privately Held**
Web: www.cisworks.org
SIC: 7361 Employment agencies
PA: Community Integrated Services
441 N 5th St Ste 210
Philadelphia PA 19123
215 238-7411

(G-7841)
COUNTRY LIFE HOMES MILFORD DE
610 Marshall St (19963-2308)
PHONE..........................302 265-2257
Elmer Fannin, *Prin*
EMP: 5 **EST:** 2009
SALES (est): 905.94K **Privately Held**
Web: www.countrylifehomes.com
SIC: 1521 New construction, single-family houses

(G-7842)
COUNTRY VILLA MOTEL
1036 N Walnut St (19963-1222)
PHONE..........................814 938-8330
Monica Haag, *Owner*
EMP: 7 **EST:** 1950
SALES (est): 158.11K **Privately Held**
SIC: 7011 5812 5813 Motels; Restaurant, family: independent; Bar (drinking places)

(G-7843)
COUNTY BANK
100 E Masten Cir (19963-1062)
PHONE..........................302 424-2500
EMP: 6
Web: www.countybankdel.com
SIC: 6022 State commercial banks
PA: County Bank
19927 Shuttle Rd
Rehoboth Beach DE 19971

(G-7844)
CRUISE PLANNERS
115 N Walnut St (19963-1472)
PHONE..........................302 503-3694
Susan Austin, *Pr*
EMP: 6 **EST:** 2017
SALES (est): 126.78K **Privately Held**
Web: www.cruiseplanners.com
SIC: 4724 Travel agencies

(G-7845)
D & J RECYCLING INC
5688 Betty St (19963-3304)
P.O. Box 411 (19963-0411)
PHONE..........................302 422-0163
Duane A Kenton, *Pr*
Joyce A Kenton, *VP*
EMP: 6 **EST:** 1982
SALES (est): 556.72K **Privately Held**
Web: d-j-recycling-inc.hub.biz
SIC: 4953 Recycling, waste materials

(G-7846)
D&N BUS SERVICE INC
140 Vickers Rd (19963-5393)
PHONE..........................302 422-3869
Neil Moore, *Pr*
EMP: 10 **EST:** 1995
SQ FT: 1,500
SALES (est): 691.59K **Privately Held**
SIC: 4151 School buses

(G-7847)
DAVIS BOWEN & FRIEDEL INC
1 Park Ave (19963-1441)
PHONE..........................302 424-1441
Brenda Horstic, *Mgr*
EMP: 33
SALES (corp-wide): 9.27MM **Privately Held**
Web: www.dbfinc.com
SIC: 8713 8712 Surveying services; Architectural engineering
PA: Davis, Bowen & Friedel, Inc.
601 E Main St Ste 100
Salisbury MD 21804
410 543-9091

(G-7848)
DEANS BUS SERVICE INC
1891 Fork Landing Rd (19963-5946)
PHONE..........................302 335-5095
Delbert Mills Junior, *Prin*
EMP: 5 **EST:** 2008
SALES (est): 99.18K **Privately Held**
SIC: 4141 Local bus charter service

(G-7849)
DEL RAY FOUNDATINS LLC
48 Goosebriar Ln (19963-6348)
PHONE..........................302 272-6153
Raynold Garcia, *Prin*
EMP: 8 **EST:** 2012
SALES (est): 165.47K **Privately Held**
SIC: 8641 Civic and social associations

(G-7850)
DEL-ONE FEDERAL CREDIT UNION
100 Credit Union Way (19963-1071)
PHONE..........................302 424-2969
Amy Vest, *Mgr*
EMP: 6
Web: www.del-one.org
SIC: 6061 Federal credit unions
PA: Del-One Federal Credit Union
270 Beiser Blvd
Dover DE 19904

(G-7851)
DELAWARE ANIMAL PRODUCTS LLC
Also Called: Dap
662 Log Cabin Rd (19963-6952)
PHONE..........................302 423-7754
Scott Peterman, *Managing Member*
Brian Shanklin, *Managing Member*
EMP: 2 **EST:** 2015
SALES (est): 105.96K **Privately Held**
SIC: 2499 Mulch or sawdust products, wood

(G-7852)
DELAWARE ARCHITECTS LLC
16558 Retreat Cir (19963-3028)
PHONE..........................302 491-6047
EMP: 5 **EST:** 2010
SALES (est): 458.15K **Privately Held**
Web: www.delawarearchitectsllc.com
SIC: 8712 Architectural services

(G-7853)
DELAWARE BAY LAUNCH SERVICE
100 Passwaters Dr (19963-4921)
PHONE..........................302 422-7604
H Hickman Rowland Junior, *Pr*
Christopher Rowland, *Treas*
EMP: 14 **EST:** 1973
SALES (est): 2.14MM
SALES (corp-wide): 6.74MM **Privately Held**
Web: www.delawarebaylaunch.com
SIC: 4493 4489 4449 Marinas; Water taxis; River transportation, except on the St. Lawrence Seaway
PA: Tug Wilmington Inc
11 Gist Rd Ste 200
Wilmington DE 19801
302 652-1666

(G-7854)
DELAWARE BUILDING SUPPLY CORP
141 Mullet Run (19963-5376)
PHONE..........................302 424-3505
Darin Hobbs, *Pr*
Kelly Hobbs, *VP*
EMP: 20 **EST:** 1991
SQ FT: 30,000
SALES (est): 7.41MM **Privately Held**
Web: www.debuildingsupply.com
SIC: 5031 Building materials, exterior

(G-7855)
DELAWARE COAST LINE RR CO (PA)
8266 N Union Church Rd (19963-3633)
PHONE..........................302 422-9200
Elaine Herholdt, *Pr*
Michael Herholdt, *Pr*
Dan Herholdt, *Treas*
EMP: 5 **EST:** 1982
SQ FT: 500
SALES (est): 948.15K
SALES (corp-wide): 948.15K **Privately Held**
SIC: 4011 Railroads, line-haul operating

(G-7856)
DELAWARE HOSPICE INC
100 Patriots Way (19963-5800)
PHONE..........................302 856-7717
EMP: 22
SALES (corp-wide): 6.31MM **Privately Held**
Web: www.delawarehospice.org
SIC: 8052 Personal care facility
PA: Delaware Hospice Inc.
16 Polly Drummond Shpg Ct
Newark DE 19711
302 478-5707

(G-7857)
DELAWARE RIVER ADVENTURES LLC
21 Nw Front St (19963-1439)
PHONE..........................302 422-2000
Amy Perfetti, *Asst Sec*
EMP: 6 **EST:** 2018
SALES (est): 49.2K **Privately Held**
Web: www.delawareriveradventures.com
SIC: 7999 Tour and guide services

(G-7858)
DELAWARE RURAL WATER ASSN
210 Vickers Rd (19963-5374)
PHONE..........................302 424-3792
Allen Atkins, *Pr*
Richard A Duncan, *Ex Dir*
David Baird, *VP*
EMP: 9 **EST:** 1990
SALES (est): 1.38MM **Privately Held**
Web: www.drwa.org
SIC: 8621 Professional organizations

(G-7859)
DELAWARE THRMPLASTIC SPECIALTY
720 Mccolley St Ste D (19963-2393)
PHONE..........................302 424-4722
John Dorofee Junior, *Pr*
EMP: 2 **EST:** 1974
SALES (est): 195.63K **Privately Held**
Web: www.delawarethermoplastics.com
SIC: 2821 Plastics materials and resins

(G-7860)
DELAWARE VETERANS HOME INC
100 Delaware Veterans Blvd (19963-5395)
PHONE..........................302 424-6000
EMP: 47 **EST:** 2006
SQ FT: 110,000
SALES (est): 568.5K **Privately Held**
Web: vethome.delaware.gov
SIC: 8641 Veterans' organization

(G-7861)
DELMARVA METAL ROOFING
497 Bowman Rd (19963-5353)
PHONE..........................302 858-1699
EMP: 6 **EST:** 2020
SALES (est): 349.04K **Privately Held**

Milford - Sussex County (G-7862)

Web: www.delmarvametalroofing.com
SIC: 1761 Roofing and gutter work

(G-7862)
DELMARVA PRECISION GRINDING
906 Se 2nd St (19963-1514)
PHONE..................................302 393-3008
Mary Jo Hill, Owner
EMP: 2 EST: 2012
SALES (est): 95.4K Privately Held
Web: www.delmarvagrinding.com
SIC: 3599 Grinding castings for the trade

(G-7863)
DELMARVA RV CENTER INC
702 Milford Harrington Hwy (19963-5308)
PHONE..................................302 424-4505
Ryan Clough, CEO
Louis Clough, CEO
George Kover, CFO
EMP: 23 EST: 1993
SQ FT: 15,000
SALES (est): 2.11MM Privately Held
Web: www.delmarvarvcenter.com
SIC: 7538 5561 Recreational vehicle repairs; Camper and travel trailer dealers

(G-7864)
DENTSPLY SIRONA INC
Dentsply Caulk
38 W Clarke Ave (19963-1805)
P.O. Box 359 (19963-0359)
PHONE..................................302 422-4511
Eugene Dorff, Brnch Mgr
EMP: 100
SALES (corp-wide): 3.92B Publicly Held
Web: www.dentsplysirona.com
SIC: 3843 Dental equipment and supplies
PA: Dentsply Sirona Inc.
    13320 Balntyn Corp Pl
    Charlotte NC 28277
    844 848-0137

(G-7865)
DENTSPLY SIRONA INC
779 E Masten Cir (19963-1030)
P.O. Box 359 (19963-0359)
PHONE..................................302 422-1043
EMP: 10
SALES (corp-wide): 3.92B Publicly Held
Web: www.dentsplysirona.com
SIC: 3843 Dental equipment and supplies
PA: Dentsply Sirona Inc.
    13320 Balntyn Corp Pl
    Charlotte NC 28277
    844 848-0137

(G-7866)
DENTSPLY SIRONA INC
Dentsply Caulk
412 Mccolley St (19963-2068)
PHONE..................................302 430-7474
EMP: 5
SALES (corp-wide): 3.92B Publicly Held
Web: www.dentsplysirona.com
SIC: 3843 Dental equipment and supplies
PA: Dentsply Sirona Inc.
    13320 Balntyn Corp Pl
    Charlotte NC 28277
    844 848-0137

(G-7867)
DENTSPLY SIRONA INC
38 W Clarke Ave (19963-1805)
PHONE..................................302 422-4511
Robert Size, Brnch Mgr
EMP: 5
SALES (corp-wide): 3.92B Publicly Held
Web: www.dentsplysirona.com

SIC: 5047 5999 Dental equipment and supplies; Medical apparatus and supplies
PA: Dentsply Sirona Inc.
    13320 Balntyn Corp Pl
    Charlotte NC 28277
    844 848-0137

(G-7868)
DESTORAGE
1001 E Masten Cir (19963-1205)
PHONE..................................302 424-6902
Jerry Hill, Mgr
EMP: 5 EST: 2018
SALES (est): 194.41K Privately Held
Web: www.destorage.com
SIC: 4225 Warehousing, self storage

(G-7869)
DIAMOND STATE DENTISTRY
215 W Liberty Way (19963-5399)
PHONE..................................302 424-7976
Lucinda K Bunting, Owner
EMP: 17 EST: 2011
SALES (est): 538.3K Privately Held
Web: www.diamondstatedentistry.com
SIC: 8021 Dentists' office

(G-7870)
DOROSHOW PSQALE KRWITZ SGEL BH
903 Lakeview Ave (19963-1731)
PHONE..................................302 424-7744
Eric Doroshow Pt, Brnch Mgr
EMP: 8
SALES (corp-wide): 10.59MM Privately Held
Web: www.dplaw.com
SIC: 8111 General practice attorney, lawyer
PA: Doroshow Pasquale Krawitz Siegel Bhaya
    1202 Kirkwood Hwy
    Wilmington DE 19805
    302 998-2397

(G-7871)
DOVER POST INC
12 S Walnut St (19963-1954)
PHONE..................................304 222-6025
John Trumpower, Prin
EMP: 6 EST: 2004
SALES (est): 67.5K Privately Held
SIC: 2711 Newspapers, publishing and printing

(G-7872)
DSP BUILDERS
7587 Shawnee Rd (19963-3531)
PHONE..................................302 422-3515
Steve Parson, Owner
EMP: 7 EST: 2015
SALES (est): 86.28K Privately Held
Web: www.dspbuilders.com
SIC: 1521 New construction, single-family houses

(G-7873)
E D S OF MILFORD INC
Also Called: EDS
2542 Deer Valley Rd (19963-6206)
PHONE..................................302 245-8813
EMP: 5 EST: 2012
SALES (est): 55,01K Privately Held
SIC: 7538 General automotive repair shops

(G-7874)
E MARK JOHNSON
802 N Dupont Blvd (19963-1006)
PHONE..................................302 422-6050
Phil Chapman, Prin
EMP: 10 EST: 2010

SALES (est): 90.84K Privately Held
SIC: 8011 Cardiologist and cardio-vascular specialist

(G-7875)
EAN HOLDINGS LLC
Also Called: Enterprise Rent-A-Car
411 N Rehoboth Blvd (19963-1307)
PHONE..................................302 422-1167
Michael Bryant, Brnch Mgr
EMP: 8
SALES (corp-wide): 7.04B Privately Held
Web: www.enterpriseholdings.com
SIC: 7514 Passenger car rental
HQ: Ean Holdings, Llc
    600 Corporate Park Dr
    Saint Louis MO 63105

(G-7876)
EAST COAST POURED WALLS INC
331 S Rehoboth Blvd (19963-1531)
PHONE..................................302 430-0630
Fred Fowler, Pr
EMP: 14 EST: 2002
SALES (est): 815.05K Privately Held
SIC: 1771 Concrete work

(G-7877)
EASTERN SHORE PAINTERS
405 Wisseman Ave (19963-1667)
PHONE..................................443 373-3119
EMP: 5 EST: 2017
SALES (est): 42.66K Privately Held
Web: www.easternshorepainting.com
SIC: 1721 Painting and paper hanging

(G-7878)
EDWARD HU MD
110 Ne Front St (19963-1430)
PHONE..................................302 422-5155
Edward Hu, Prin
EMP: 9 EST: 2006
SALES (est): 54.13K Privately Held
SIC: 8011 Opthalmologist

(G-7879)
EL NOPALITO DISTRIBUTORS INC
656 N Dupont Blvd Unit G (19963-1002)
PHONE..................................302 393-2050
Francisco Uscanga, Prin
Jerson Guox, Prin
EMP: 10 EST: 2018
SALES (est): 1.12MM Privately Held
SIC: 5141 Groceries, general line

(G-7880)
EMERALD LAWN AND LDSCPG LLC
701 Lindsay Ln (19963-2130)
PHONE..................................302 228-1468
John Davis, Pr
EMP: 5 EST: 2012
SALES (est): 248.95K Privately Held
Web: www.emeraldlandscapingde.com
SIC: 0781 Landscape services

(G-7881)
END IMPORTS INC
656 N Dupont Blvd Unit G (19963-1002)
PHONE..................................302 393-2050
EMP: 5
SALES (est): 63.12K Privately Held
SIC: 7389

(G-7882)
ERANGA CARDIOLOGY
113 Neurology Way (19963-5368)
PHONE..................................302 422-2496
EMP: 9 EST: 2014
SALES (est): 32.48K Privately Held
Web: www.erangacardiology.com

SIC: 8011 Cardiologist and cardio-vascular specialist

(G-7883)
ESTHER V GRAHAM
Also Called: Milford Early Learning Center
901 N Dupont Blvd (19963-1092)
PHONE..................................302 422-6667
Oleta Fullmun, Dir
EMP: 5 EST: 2009
SALES (est): 254.07K Privately Held
SIC: 8351 Child day care services

(G-7884)
EUPHORIC HRBALS APOTHECARY LLC
Also Called: Euphoric Herbals
621 N Dupont Blvd (19963-1099)
PHONE..................................302 491-4443
Cindy Collins, Managing Member
EMP: 5 EST: 2018
SALES (est): 87.17K Privately Held
Web: www.euphoricherbals.com
SIC: 2899 2833 Essential oils; Drugs and herbs: grading, grinding, and milling

(G-7885)
EVOLVE HEALTH AND FITNESS LLC
1004 Mattlind Way (19963-5300)
PHONE..................................302 265-2560
EMP: 6 EST: 2018
SALES (est): 168.68K Privately Held
Web: www.evolvehf.com
SIC: 7991 Physical fitness facilities

(G-7886)
F D HAMMOND ENTERPRISES INC
Also Called: Trans Products
1111 N Dupont Blvd (19963-1075)
P.O. Box 898 (19963-0898)
PHONE..................................302 424-8455
Wyatt F Hammond, Pr
Elizabeth A Hammond, VP
EMP: 10 EST: 1957
SQ FT: 7,200
SALES (est): 827.93K Privately Held
Web: www.transproducts.com
SIC: 8742 5961 Business management consultant; Mail order house, nec

(G-7887)
F M REPAIRS
19840 Beaver Dam Rd (19963-4207)
PHONE..................................302 422-7229
Francis Morris, Owner
EMP: 5 EST: 2009
SALES (est): 41.11K Privately Held
SIC: 7699 Repair services, nec

(G-7888)
FAMILY DENTISTRY MILFORD PA
100 Sussex Ave (19963-1823)
PHONE..................................302 422-6924
John Bausch D.d.s., Pr
EMP: 8 EST: 1991
SQ FT: 2,200
SALES (est): 628.46K Privately Held
Web: www.jitenpateldds.com
SIC: 8021 Dentists' office

(G-7889)
FAMILY SERVICES
247 Ne Front St (19963-1431)
PHONE..................................302 422-1400
Barbarra Westfall, Mgr
EMP: 14 EST: 2011
SALES (est): 68.64K Privately Held
Web: kids.delaware.gov
SIC: 8322 Child related social services

GEOGRAPHIC SECTION
Milford - Sussex County (G-7916)

(G-7890)
FELLOWSHIP HLTH RESOURCES INC
7549 Wilkins Rd (19963-4106)
PHONE..................................302 422-6699
Antonio Ojongtambia, *Dir*
EMP: 9
SALES (corp-wide): 33.85MM **Privately Held**
Web: www.fhr.net
SIC: 8093 Mental health clinic, outpatient
PA: Fellowship Health Resources, Inc.
   24 Albion Rd Ste 420
   Lincoln RI 02865
   401 333-3980

(G-7891)
FIRST CARE PHYSICIANS PA
124 Ivy Ln (19963-6370)
PHONE..................................302 424-6995
Harvey Y Lee, *Prin*
EMP: 8 **EST:** 2008
SALES (est): 131.3K **Privately Held**
SIC: 8011 General and family practice, physician/surgeon

(G-7892)
FIRST CHOICE HOME MED EQUIPT
1013 Mattlind Way (19963-5369)
PHONE..................................302 424-2510
Craig Rotenberry, *Pr*
EMP: 9
Web: www.adapthealth.com
SIC: 5047 Medical equipment and supplies
PA: First Choice Home Medical Equiptment, Llc
   259 Quigley Blvd Ste 1
   Historic New Castle DE 19720

(G-7893)
FIRST STATE ACADEMY OF D
107 S Maple Ave Rm Main (19963-1951)
PHONE..................................302 422-2633
Mairia Fry, *Owner*
EMP: 7 **EST:** 2008
SALES (est): 137.24K **Privately Held**
Web: www.firststatedance.com
SIC: 7911 Dance studio and school

(G-7894)
FIRST STATE BMX
1045 N Walnut St (19963-1201)
P.O. Box 239 (19952-0239)
PHONE..................................302 422-4133
Shawn Mallak, *Pr*
Denise Morris, *Treas*
Garey Morris, *VP*
Donita Mallak, *Sec*
EMP: 7 **EST:** 2005
SALES (est): 244.72K **Privately Held**
Web: www.firststatebmx.com
SIC: 8699 Athletic organizations

(G-7895)
FIRST STATE INSPECTION AGENCY (PA)
1001 Mattlind Way (19963-5369)
PHONE..................................302 422-3859
Theodore Morrison, *Pr*
Frances Morrison, *VP*
EMP: 9 **EST:** 1985
SQ FT: 720
SALES (est): 2.24MM
SALES (corp-wide): 2.24MM **Privately Held**
Web: www.firststateinspection.com
SIC: 7389 Industrial and commercial equipment inspection service

(G-7896)
FIRST STATE MANUFACTURING INC
301 Se 4th St (19963-2011)
PHONE..................................302 424-4520
Eliseo Valenzuela, *CEO*
Eliseo Valenzuela, *Pr*
Cheryl Valenzuela, *
EMP: 63 **EST:** 1998
SQ FT: 5,000
SALES (est): 9.71MM **Privately Held**
Web: www.firststatemfg.com
SIC: 2396 Automotive trimmings, fabric

(G-7897)
FIRST STEPS PRESCHOOL-MILFORD
104 Mccoy St (19963-2310)
PHONE..................................302 424-4470
Carrie Singer, *Dir*
EMP: 5 **EST:** 2012
SALES (est): 155.52K **Privately Held**
Web: www.myfirststepspreschool.com
SIC: 8351 Preschool center

(G-7898)
FISH WHISPERER CHARTERS
14 Rogers Dr (19963-1063)
PHONE..................................302 363-2597
Rodney Jones, *Prin*
EMP: 6 **EST:** 2012
SALES (est): 53.99K **Privately Held**
SIC: 7999 Fishing boats, party: operation

(G-7899)
FLOOD RESCUE LLC
7851 Sugar Maple Dr (19963-4786)
PHONE..................................302 547-4092
Robert Gerlitz, *Managing Member*
EMP: 7
SALES (est): 84.48K **Privately Held**
SIC: 1623 Water, sewer, and utility lines

(G-7900)
FOOD BANK OF DELAWARE INC
1040 Mattlind Way (19963-5366)
PHONE..................................302 424-3301
Patricia Bebe, *Pr*
EMP: 50
SALES (corp-wide): 35MM **Privately Held**
Web: www.fbd.org
SIC: 8399 Community development groups
PA: Food Bank Of Delaware, Inc.
   222 Lake Dr
   Newark DE 19702
   302 292-1305

(G-7901)
FOTO VIDEO GENESIS
635 Adams Dr (19963-2405)
PHONE..................................302 422-6988
Adolfo Sorcia, *Prin*
EMP: 5 **EST:** 2010
SALES (est): 53.48K **Privately Held**
SIC: 7841 Video tape rental

(G-7902)
FOUR EVER GREEN INC
Also Called: Goodnew Natural Foods
1 N Walnut St (19963-1456)
PHONE..................................302 424-2393
Richard Collins, *Pr*
EMP: 5 **EST:** 2010
SALES (est): 133.69K **Privately Held**
SIC: 5149 Natural and organic foods

(G-7903)
FRANCISCO J RODRIGUEZ
806 Seabury Ave (19963-2223)
PHONE..................................302 424-7522
Francisco J Rodriguez, *Prin*
EMP: 9 **EST:** 2010
SALES (est): 93.43K **Privately Held**
SIC: 8011 Internal medicine, physician/surgeon

(G-7904)
FUR BABY
301 Ne Front St (19963-1433)
PHONE..................................302 725-5078
Sherry Shaffer, *Prin*
EMP: 6 **EST:** 2011
SALES (est): 279.02K **Privately Held**
Web: www.furbabypetresort.com
SIC: 5999 0752 Pets; Grooming services, pet and animal specialties

(G-7905)
G & S TV & ANTENNA
20450 Sapp Rd (19963-4243)
PHONE..................................302 422-5733
Eugene D Smith Junior, *Pt*
Sue Smith, *Pt*
EMP: 5 **EST:** 1981
SALES (est): 495.32K **Privately Held**
SIC: 7622 5731 Television repair shop; Television sets

(G-7906)
GALLERY 37
8 S Walnut St (19963-1954)
PHONE..................................413 297-2690
EMP: 5 **EST:** 2012
SALES (est): 70.93K **Privately Held**
Web: www.marciareedpainting.com
SIC: 7999 Art gallery, commercial

(G-7907)
GANDER CONSTRUCTION
510 Caulk Rd (19963-2902)
PHONE..................................302 424-4007
Tom Humes, *Prin*
EMP: 5 **EST:** 2010
SALES (est): 106.44K **Privately Held**
SIC: 1521 New construction, single-family houses

(G-7908)
GENESIS HEALTHCARE CORPORATION
Also Called: GENESIS HEALTHCARE CORPORATION
700 Marvel Rd (19963-1740)
PHONE..................................302 422-3754
EMP: 5
SALES (corp-wide): 5.86B **Publicly Held**
Web: www.genesishcc.com
SIC: 8051 Convalescent home with continuous nursing care
HQ: Genesis Hc Llc
   101 E State St
   Kennett Square PA 19348
   610 444-6350

(G-7909)
GOODEN FLORAL SP & GREENHOUSES
909 N Walnut St (19963-1235)
PHONE..................................302 422-4961
James A Gooden, *Pr*
EMP: 6 **EST:** 1946
SALES (est): 142.03K **Privately Held**
SIC: 0181 Flowers: grown under cover (e.g., greenhouse production)

(G-7910)
GOVPLUS LLC
Also Called: Citizens Bank
610 N Dupont Blvd (19963-1002)
PHONE..................................302 422-5010
Michelle Cavello, *Mgr*
EMP: 6
SALES (corp-wide): 9.07B **Publicly Held**
Web: www.govplus.com
SIC: 6022 State commercial banks
HQ: Citizens Bank, National Association
   1 Citizens Plz
   Providence RI 02903

(G-7911)
GRAY RENTAL PROPERTIES LLC
4771 Mills Rd (19963-4331)
PHONE..................................302 382-0439
EMP: 5 **EST:** 2017
SALES (est): 79.36K **Privately Held**
SIC: 7359 Equipment rental and leasing, nec

(G-7912)
GROWMARK FS LLC
Also Called: Shopworks
339 Milford Harrington Hwy (19963)
PHONE..................................302 422-3001
EMP: 5
SALES (corp-wide): 7.54B **Privately Held**
Web: www.growmarkfs.com
SIC: 2874 5191 Phosphatic fertilizers; Pesticides
HQ: Growmark Fs, Llc
   308 Ne Front St
   Milford DE 19963
   302 422-3002

(G-7913)
GROWMARK FS LLC (HQ)
Also Called: Milford Fertilizer
308 Ne Front St (19963-1434)
PHONE..................................302 422-3002
◆ **EMP:** 75 **EST:** 1937
SQ FT: 351,500
SALES (est): 98.14MM
SALES (corp-wide): 7.54B **Privately Held**
Web: www.growmarkfs.com
SIC: 2875 2873 2874 5191 Fertilizers, mixing only; Nitrogenous fertilizers; Phosphatic fertilizers; Pesticides
PA: Growmark, Inc.
   1705 Towanda Ave
   Bloomington IL 61701
   309 557-6000

(G-7914)
GULAB MANAGEMENT INC
Also Called: Super 8 Motel
729 Bay Rd (19963-6122)
PHONE..................................302 934-6126
Asim Gulab, *Mgr*
EMP: 35
Web: www.wyndhamhotels.com
SIC: 7011 Hotels and motels
PA: Gulab Management Inc
   1426 N Dupont Hwy
   Dover DE 19901

(G-7915)
GULAB MANAGEMENT INC
Also Called: Travelers Inn
1036 N Walnut St (19963-1222)
PHONE..................................302 422-8089
Asim Gulab, *Treas*
EMP: 10
Web: www.wyndhamhotels.com
SIC: 7011 Resort hotel
PA: Gulab Management Inc
   1426 N Dupont Hwy
   Dover DE 19901

(G-7916)
GUYS GUTTER
466 Bay Rd (19963-6103)
PHONE..................................302 424-1931
EMP: 8 **EST:** 2019
SALES (est): 239.12K **Privately Held**
Web: www.thegutterguys.com

Milford - Sussex County (G-7917)

SIC: 1761 Gutter and downspout contractor

(G-7917)
HALPERN EYE ASSOCIATES INC
Also Called: Helpern Eye Associates
771 E Masten Cir Ste 109 (19963-1088)
PHONE..................302 422-2020
Juan Rodriguez, *Mgr*
EMP: 7
SALES (corp-wide): 9.06MM **Privately Held**
Web: www.myeyedr.com
SIC: 8042 Specialized optometrists
PA: Halpern Eye Associates, Inc.
  885 S Governors Ave
  Dover DE 19904
  302 734-5861

(G-7918)
HALPERN EYE CARE
1197 Airport Rd (19963-6491)
PHONE..................302 678-1700
Deb Farley Blunt, *Prin*
EMP: 6 **EST:** 2018
SALES (est): 47.44K **Privately Held**
SIC: 8042 Offices and clinics of optometrists

(G-7919)
HAMMOND ENTERPRISES INC
1111 N Dupont Blvd (19963-1075)
P.O. Box 820 (19966-0820)
PHONE..................302 934-1700
Ricky Hammond, *Owner*
EMP: 7 **EST:** 2003
SALES (est): 827.83K **Privately Held**
Web: www.transproducts.com
SIC: 5015 Tires, used: retail only

(G-7920)
HAMPTON INN
800 Karken Pit Rd (19963)
PHONE..................302 422-4320
Jenifer Barto, *Genl Mgr*
EMP: 22 **EST:** 2010
SALES (est): 419.85K **Privately Held**
Web: www.hilton.com
SIC: 7011 Hotels and motels

(G-7921)
HARVEST POWER INC
1977 Bay Rd (19963-6134)
PHONE..................270 765-6268
EMP: 5 **EST:** 2019
SALES (est): 152.62K **Privately Held**
SIC: 6552 Subdividers and developers, nec

(G-7922)
HARVEY Y LEE M D
21 W Clarke Ave (19963-1849)
PHONE..................302 682-4155
EMP: 9 **EST:** 2017
SALES (est): 62.49K **Privately Held**
Web: www.pediatriccardiologymd.com
SIC: 8011 Cardiologist and cardio-vascular specialist

(G-7923)
HAVEN LAKE ANIMAL HOSPITAL
300 Milford Harrington Hwy (19963-5304)
PHONE..................302 422-8100
Chris Coon, *Owner*
EMP: 13 **EST:** 1999
SALES (est): 471.48K **Privately Held**
Web: www.havenlakeanimalhospital.com
SIC: 0742 Animal hospital services, pets and other animal specialties

(G-7924)
HEALTHSTAT INC
1162 Holly Hill Rd (19963-6339)
PHONE..................704 936-5546
Warren Hutton, *COO*
EMP: 7 **EST:** 2018
SALES (est): 58.21K **Privately Held**
Web: www.eversidehealth.com
SIC: 8011 Offices and clinics of medical doctors

(G-7925)
HEARSAY SERVICES OF DELAWARE
104 Ne Front St (19963-1430)
PHONE..................302 422-3312
Pamela J P Robinson, *Pr*
Ronniere Robinson, *VP*
EMP: 5 **EST:** 2007
SALES (est): 383.94K **Privately Held**
Web: www.hearsayservices.com
SIC: 8011 5999 Ears, nose, and throat specialist: physician/surgeon; Hearing aids

(G-7926)
HENDERSON SERVICES INC
Also Called: Pools & Spas Unlimited Milford
219 N Rehoboth Blvd (19963-1303)
PHONE..................302 424-1999
Mark Henderson, *Pr*
Susan Henderson, *VP*
EMP: 10 **EST:** 1991
SALES (est): 1.07MM **Privately Held**
Web: www.swimdelmarva.com
SIC: 7389 1799 Swimming pool and hot tub service and maintenance; Athletic and recreation facilities construction

(G-7927)
HERITAGE AT MILFORD
500 S Dupont Blvd (19963-1758)
PHONE..................302 422-8700
Eileen Hanhauser, *Prin*
EMP: 16 **EST:** 2008
SALES (est): 968.45K **Privately Held**
Web: www.watergateatmilford.com
SIC: 8361 Aged home

(G-7928)
HERTRICH COLLISION CTR OF
1449 Bay Rd (19963-6129)
PHONE..................302 839-0550
EMP: 11 **EST:** 2013
SALES (est): 205.23K **Privately Held**
Web: www.hertrichcollision.com
SIC: 7532 Collision shops, automotive

(G-7929)
HH CONCRETE LLC
4927 Mills Rd (19963-4333)
PHONE..................302 242-6342
Jeremy Harrington, *Prin*
EMP: 6 **EST:** 2016
SALES (est): 88.07K **Privately Held**
SIC: 1771 Concrete work

(G-7930)
HICKMAN OVERHEAD DOOR COMPANY
Also Called: Springhill Seamless Gutter
1625 Bay Rd (19963-6131)
PHONE..................302 422-4249
Phyllis Walker, *Pr*
Paul E Walker Junior, *VP*
Phillip E Hickman, *Treas*
EMP: 17 **EST:** 1978
SALES (est): 3.73MM **Privately Held**
Web: www.hickmandoor.com
SIC: 5211 7699 5031 1761 Garage doors, sale and installation; Garage door repair; Doors, garage; Gutter and downspout contractor

(G-7931)
HIGHBRED HORSE RACING
624 Cicada Ln (19963-6050)
PHONE..................302 519-6676
William Reilly, *Prin*
EMP: 5 **EST:** 2017
SALES (est): 44.19K **Privately Held**
SIC: 7948 Racing, including track operation

(G-7932)
HITHER CREEK PRESS
197 Meadow Brook Ln (19963-3020)
PHONE..................603 387-3444
EMP: 4 **EST:** 2018
SALES (est): 70.34K **Privately Held**
SIC: 2741 Miscellaneous publishing

(G-7933)
HOLLINGSWORTH HEATING & AC
719 S Dupont Blvd (19963-2230)
P.O. Box 493 (21629-0493)
PHONE..................302 422-7525
EMP: 8 **EST:** 1981
SALES (est): 601.2K **Privately Held**
SIC: 1711 Warm air heating and air conditioning contractor

(G-7934)
HOOK EM & COOK EM LLC
24603 Bay Ave (19963-4900)
PHONE..................302 226-8220
EMP: 5 **EST:** 2004
SALES (est): 226.63K **Privately Held**
Web: www.hookemcookemoutfitters.com
SIC: 7999 Fishing boats, party: operation

(G-7935)
HORSE POWER SHOW HUNTERS LLC
307 Hall Pl (19963-1808)
PHONE..................302 265-2881
Heather Hudson, *Prin*
EMP: 5 **EST:** 2016
SALES (est): 23.29K **Privately Held**
SIC: 7999 Horse shows

(G-7936)
HOWARD M JOSEPH INC (PA)
3235 Bay Rd (19963-6027)
PHONE..................302 335-1300
Howard M Joseph, *Pr*
Nadina Joseph, *Sec*
EMP: 8 **EST:** 1973
SQ FT: 8,000
SALES (est): 1.26MM
SALES (corp-wide): 1.26MM **Privately Held**
SIC: 6531 2452 Broker of manufactured homes, on site; Prefabricated buildings, wood

(G-7937)
HUDSON JNES JYWORK FSHER ATTYS
995 N Dupont Blvd (19963-1072)
PHONE..................302 839-1153
EMP: 5 **EST:** 2019
SALES (est): 57.87K **Privately Held**
SIC: 8111 General practice attorney, lawyer

(G-7938)
IG BURTON & COMPANY INC (PA)
Also Called: I G Burton Imports
793 Bay Rd (19963-6122)
PHONE..................302 422-3041
Charles Burton, *Pr*
Irwin G Burton Iii, *VP*
Pete Renzi, *
EMP: 70 **EST:** 1960
SQ FT: 25,000
SALES (est): 51.18MM
SALES (corp-wide): 51.18MM **Privately Held**
Web: www.igburton.com
SIC: 5511 7538 Automobiles, new and used; General automotive repair shops

(G-7939)
IG BURTON & COMPANY INC
Also Called: I G Burton Chrysler
605 Bay Rd (19963-6121)
PHONE..................302 424-3041
EMP: 88
SALES (corp-wide): 51.18MM **Privately Held**
Web: www.igburtonchrysler.com
SIC: 5511 7538 5531 Automobiles, new and used; General automotive repair shops; Automotive parts
PA: I.G. Burton & Company, Inc.
  793 Bay Rd
  Milford DE 19963
  302 422-3041

(G-7940)
IMPERIAL NUTRITION
229 Ne Front St (19963-1431)
PHONE..................302 752-8220
Tammey Merix, *Prin*
EMP: 6 **EST:** 2018
SALES (est): 93.42K **Privately Held**
SIC: 8049 Nutrition specialist

(G-7941)
INDEPENDENT NEWSMEDIA INC USA
Chronicle The
37a Walnut St (19963)
PHONE..................302 422-1200
Gwen Guerke, *Mgr*
EMP: 8
SQ FT: 4,000
Web: www.newszap.com
SIC: 2711 Newspapers, publishing and printing
HQ: Independent Newsmedia Inc. Usa
  110 Galaxy Dr
  Dover DE 19901
  302 674-3600

(G-7942)
INTERNET WORKING TECHNOLOGIES
12 S Walnut St # A (19963-1954)
P.O. Box 852 (19963-0852)
PHONE..................302 424-1855
David Dolan, *Pr*
James Allen Wagaman, *VP*
EMP: 8 **EST:** 1995
SQ FT: 2,500
SALES (est): 743.24K **Privately Held**
SIC: 7379 Computer related consulting services

(G-7943)
IVEH LATINO FAMILY SERVIC
125 Causey Ave (19963-1909)
PHONE..................302 381-0762
EMP: 6 **EST:** 2018
SALES (est): 32.92K **Privately Held**
SIC: 8322 Individual and family services

(G-7944)
J & J SERVICES
2908 Milford Harrington Hwy Ste 1 (19963)
PHONE..................302 422-2684
Jonathan J Plump, *Owner*
EMP: 10 **EST:** 2014
SALES (est): 537.58K **Privately Held**
Web: www.jandjserv.com

GEOGRAPHIC SECTION
Milford - Sussex County (G-7974)

SIC: 7699 Cleaning services

(G-7945)
J & V SHOOTERS SUPPLY LP
7369 Shawnee Rd (19963-3436)
PHONE..................................302 422-5417
EMP: 2 EST: 1981
SALES (est): 121.07K Privately Held
SIC: 3949 Shooting equipment and supplies, general

(G-7946)
J C WELLS & SONS LP
7481 Wells Rd (19963-4728)
PHONE..................................302 422-4732
Mark Wells, Pr
Mark Wells, Pt
Dawn Wells, Pt
EMP: 5 EST: 1980
SALES (est): 342.83K Privately Held
SIC: 8748 Agricultural consultant

(G-7947)
J E PARSLEY ELECTRIC LLC
605 Abbott Dr (19963-2401)
PHONE..................................302 396-9642
EMP: 6 EST: 2011
SALES (est): 125.56K Privately Held
SIC: 1731 Electrical work

(G-7948)
J MAMASIAN & CO LLC ✪
3 E Bullrush Dr (19963-3926)
PHONE..................................302 219-2880
EMP: 5 EST: 2022
SALES (est): 243.18K Privately Held
SIC: 7389 Business Activities at Non-Commercial Site

(G-7949)
JACK ENNIS CUSTOM LAWN
Rural Route 5 Box 740 (19963-9805)
PHONE..................................302 422-8577
Jack Ennis, Owner
EMP: 5 EST: 1997
SALES (est): 63.51K Privately Held
SIC: 0782 Lawn care services

(G-7950)
JAY J DAVE DO
111 Neurology Way (19963-5368)
PHONE..................................302 422-0800
Jay Dave, Prin
EMP: 6 EST: 2018
SALES (est): 58.22K Privately Held
Web: www.cnmri.com
SIC: 8011 Neurologist

(G-7951)
JD ASPHALT
933 N Dupont Blvd (19963-1045)
PHONE..................................302 514-7325
EMP: 11 EST: 2019
SALES (est): 500.35K Privately Held
Web: www.jdasphaltinc.com
SIC: 1771 Blacktop (asphalt) work

(G-7952)
JERRYS INC
17776 Oak Hill Dr (19963-3400)
PHONE..................................302 422-7676
Jerry Kovach, CEO
Jan Kovach, VP
EMP: 20 EST: 1990
SALES (est): 777.73K Privately Held
Web: www.jerryspaving.com
SIC: 1794 1611 Excavation work; Surfacing and paving

(G-7953)
JEWELS CLEANING SERVICE
5616 Betty St (19963-3304)
PHONE..................................302 841-2948
Julia Vecchioni, Prin
EMP: 5 EST: 2015
SALES (est): 23.7K Privately Held
SIC: 7699 Cleaning services

(G-7954)
JITEN PATEL DDS
100 Sussex Ave (19963-1823)
PHONE..................................302 690-8629
EMP: 9 EST: 2019
SALES (est): 147.01K Privately Held
Web: www.jitenpateldds.com
SIC: 8021 Dentists' office

(G-7955)
JOHN EISENBREY III
Also Called: Olde Tyme Chimney Sweeps
16 Delaware Ave (19963-2319)
PHONE..................................302 422-5845
John Eisenbrey Iii, Owner
EMP: 7 EST: 1981
SALES (est): 183.87K Privately Held
Web: www.jceisenbrey.com
SIC: 7349 5074 Chimney cleaning; Oil burners

(G-7956)
JOHN T MALCYNSKI MD
Also Called: Atlantic Surgical
100 Wellness Way (19963-4364)
P.O. Box 412 (19963-0412)
PHONE..................................302 424-7522
David Clooney Md, Owner
EMP: 7 EST: 2000
SALES (est): 616.85K Privately Held
Web: www.bayhealth.org
SIC: 8011 Surgeon

(G-7957)
JONATHAN L PATTERSON MD
3 Victoria Dr (19963-9661)
PHONE..................................302 242-6176
Jonathan L Patterson, Prin
EMP: 9 EST: 2012
SALES (est): 105.58K Privately Held
SIC: 8011 Offices and clinics of medical doctors

(G-7958)
JOR-LIN INC
Also Called: Jor-Lin Charter Bus Service
309 S Rehoboth Blvd (19963-1531)
PHONE..................................302 424-4445
EMP: 17 EST: 1994
SALES (est): 982.93K Privately Held
Web: www.jor-lin.com
SIC: 4142 Bus charter service, except local

(G-7959)
JOSE M SAEZ DO
201 W Liberty Way (19963-5399)
PHONE..................................302 424-3694
Jose Saez, Prin
EMP: 8 EST: 2014
SALES (est): 85.07K Privately Held
SIC: 8011 Nephrologist

(G-7960)
JOSEPHINE KEIR LIMITED
27 S Walnut St (19963-1953)
PHONE..................................302 422-0270
EMP: 5 EST: 2016
SALES (est): 117.22K Privately Held
Web: www.josephinekeir.com
SIC: 2273 Carpets and rugs

(G-7961)
KD NAILS
1053 N Walnut St (19963-1242)
PHONE..................................302 422-0998
EMP: 5 EST: 2013
SALES (est): 147.44K Privately Held
Web: k-d-nails-nail-salon.business.site
SIC: 7231 Manicurist, pedicurist

(G-7962)
KENT GENERAL HOSPITAL
Also Called: Milford Memorial Hospital
100 Wellness Way (19963-4364)
PHONE..................................302 430-5731
Joe Whiting, COO
EMP: 832
Web: www.bayhealth.org
SIC: 8062 General medical and surgical hospitals
HQ: Kent General Hospital
640 S State St
Dover DE 19901
302 674-4700

(G-7963)
KENT GENERAL HOSPITAL INC
Also Called: KENT GENERAL HOSPITAL, INC
301 Jefferson Ave (19963-1800)
PHONE..................................302 430-5705
Craig Crouch, Owner
EMP: 749
Web: www.bayhealth.org
SIC: 8099 8011 Blood related health services ; Clinic, operated by physicians
HQ: Kent General Hospital
640 S State St
Dover DE 19901
302 674-4700

(G-7964)
KENT-SUSSEX INDUSTRIES INC
Also Called: KSI CARTRIDGE SERVICE
301 N Rehoboth Blvd (19963-1305)
PHONE..................................302 422-4014
B Craig Crouch, CEO
EMP: 313 EST: 1962
SQ FT: 75,000
SALES (est): 7.49MM Privately Held
Web: www.ksiinc.org
SIC: 3955 Print cartridges for laser and other computer printers

(G-7965)
KIDS INC
613 Lakeview Ave (19963-2919)
PHONE..................................302 422-9099
Mary Wilson, Prin
EMP: 5 EST: 2006
SALES (est): 80.32K Privately Held
Web: www.reformation-lutheran.net
SIC: 8351 Group day care center

(G-7966)
KIRKWOOD PAIN & INJURY CHIROPR
600 Ne Front Street Ext Ste D (19963-1395)
PHONE..................................302 422-2329
Jean Laine, Pr
EMP: 6 EST: 2015
SALES (est): 40.91K Privately Held
SIC: 8041 Offices and clinics of chiropractors

(G-7967)
KOAM CORP
209b Ne Front St (19963-1431)
PHONE..................................302 422-4848
EMP: 5 EST: 2019
SALES (est): 114.3K Privately Held
SIC: 4731 Freight transportation arrangement

(G-7968)
KUSTOM KUTZ
1007 N Walnut St (19963-1201)
PHONE..................................302 424-7556
Joetta Hopkins, Owner
Joetta Lowbray, Owner
EMP: 6 EST: 1996
SALES (est): 78.03K Privately Held
SIC: 7231 Hairdressers

(G-7969)
LA BELLA
628 Milford Harrington Hw (19963-5370)
PHONE..................................302 644-2572
Janice Ervin, Prin
EMP: 5 EST: 2016
SALES (est): 22.25K Privately Held
SIC: 0752 Grooming services, pet and animal specialties

(G-7970)
LAKESIDE PHYSCL THRAPY METODIO
907 N Dupont Blvd (19963-1060)
PHONE..................................302 422-2518
George Rodriguera, Prin
EMP: 7 EST: 2018
SALES (est): 91.82K Privately Held
Web: www.mylakesidept.com
SIC: 8049 Physical therapist

(G-7971)
LANK JOHNSON AND TULL (PA)
268 Milford Harrington Hwy (19963-5303)
P.O. Box 253 (19963-0253)
PHONE..................................302 422-3308
Robert B Lank, Pt
Terrance Johnson, Pt
Richard Tull, Pt
EMP: 8 EST: 1982
SALES (est): 2.38MM
SALES (corp-wide): 2.38MM Privately Held
Web: www.ljtcpa.com
SIC: 8721 Accounting services, except auditing

(G-7972)
LAW OFFICES PATRICK SCANLON PA
203 Ne Front St (19963-1431)
PHONE..................................302 424-1996
Patrick Scanlon, Pr
EMP: 7 EST: 2014
SALES (est): 219.54K Privately Held
Web: www.delcollections.com
SIC: 8111 Legal services

(G-7973)
LAWRENCE LEGATES MASNRY CO INC
2891 Milford Harrington Hwy (19963)
P.O. Box 199 (19954-0199)
PHONE..................................302 422-8043
Lawrence D Legates, Pr
Margaret Legates, VP
EMP: 6 EST: 1976
SALES (est): 503.5K Privately Held
SIC: 1741 Masonry and other stonework

(G-7974)
LAYTON BUILDERS
2135 Milford Harrington Hwy (19963)
PHONE..................................302 491-4571
EMP: 5 EST: 2018
SALES (est): 129.01K Privately Held
Web: www.laytonbuilders.com

Milford - Sussex County (G-7975) GEOGRAPHIC SECTION

SIC: 1521 New construction, single-family houses

(G-7975)
LISA HARKINS
3103i E Brookmyer Dr (19963-4034)
PHONE.................302 388-2856
Lisa Harkins, Prin
EMP: 6 EST: 2017
SALES (est): 61.45K Privately Held
SIC: 8049 Offices of health practitioner

(G-7976)
LONG & FOSTER REAL ESTATE INC
995 N Dupont Blvd (19963-1072)
PHONE.................302 542-0811
Daniel Shockley, Prin
EMP: 5 EST: 2017
SALES (est): 123.12K Privately Held
Web: www.longandfoster.com
SIC: 6531 Real estate brokers and agents

(G-7977)
LOVE LEARN & PLAY DC
16758 Shawnee Pl Apt B (19963-3411)
PHONE.................302 236-9888
Debbie Case, Dir
EMP: 8 EST: 2017
SALES (est): 103.91K Privately Held
SIC: 8351 Child day care services

(G-7978)
LUFF & ASSOCIATES CPA PA
Also Called: Luff & Associates PA
223 S Rehoboth Blvd (19963-1568)
PHONE.................302 422-9699
George Luff, Pr
EMP: 7 EST: 1993
SALES (est): 495.14K Privately Held
Web: www.luffcpas.com
SIC: 8721 Certified public accountant

(G-7979)
LUIS L DAVID MD PA
204 S Walnut St (19963-1958)
P.O. Box 482 (19963-0482)
PHONE.................302 422-9768
Luis L David, Pr
EMP: 6 EST: 1968
SALES (est): 270.92K Privately Held
SIC: 8011 Pediatrician

(G-7980)
LYNCH HEIGHTS FUEL CORP
840 Bay Rd (19963-6107)
PHONE.................302 422-9195
Liz Garcia, Mgr
EMP: 8 EST: 2009
SALES (est): 902.73K Privately Held
SIC: 2869 Fuels

(G-7981)
M D N BILLING CONSULTING LLC
9 Lake Crest Dr (19963-9659)
PHONE.................914 376-6100
Melissa Nieli, Ofcr
EMP: 6 EST: 2013
SALES (est): 34.55K Privately Held
Web: www.statesideservices.org
SIC: 8721 Billing and bookkeeping service

(G-7982)
MAN AROUND HOUSE
618 Evans Dr (19963-2404)
PHONE.................302 531-5124
Meridith Jones, Prin
EMP: 5 EST: 2016
SALES (est): 106.9K Privately Held
SIC: 1521 Single-family housing construction

(G-7983)
MANUFACTURERS & TRADERS TR CO
Also Called: M&T
673 N Dupont Blvd (19963-1001)
PHONE.................302 855-2160
Gail Dickerson, Mgr
EMP: 6
SALES (corp-wide): 8.6B Publicly Held
Web: ir.mtb.com
SIC: 6022 State trust companies accepting deposits, commercial
HQ: Manufacturers And Traders Trust Company
1 M&T Plz Fl 3
Buffalo NY 14203
716 842-4200

(G-7984)
MARC KATTELMAN DO
100 Delaware Veterans Blvd (19963-5395)
PHONE.................260 485-4580
Marc Kattelman, Mgr
EMP: 8 EST: 2017
SALES (est): 74.11K Privately Held
SIC: 8011 Offices and clinics of medical doctors

(G-7985)
MARSHALL MANOR LP
977 E Masten Cir (19963-1085)
PHONE.................302 422-8255
David Moore, CEO
EMP: 6
SALES (est): 415.5K Privately Held
SIC: 6531 Real estate agents and managers

(G-7986)
MARVEL AGENCY INC
Also Called: Allstate
15 N Walnut St (19963-1445)
P.O. Box 358 (19963-0358)
PHONE.................302 422-7844
Harvey G Marvel Junior, Pr
Randy Marvel, Treas
Annette Cerasaro, Sec
EMP: 9 EST: 1947
SQ FT: 5,000
SALES (est): 450.78K Privately Held
Web: www.marvelagency.com
SIC: 6411 6531 Insurance agents, brokers, and service; Real estate brokers and agents

(G-7987)
MARYLOU SHEAFFER
Also Called: Harmony Yoga
432 Kings Hwy (19963-1768)
PHONE.................302 422-4118
Marylou Sheaffer, Prin
EMP: 7 EST: 2011
SALES (est): 75.42K Privately Held
SIC: 7999 Amusement and recreation, nec

(G-7988)
MASTER INTERIORS INC
156 Mullet Run (19963-5367)
PHONE.................302 368-9361
Lyle Humpton, Mgr
EMP: 21
SALES (corp-wide): 9.86MM Privately Held
Web: www.masterinteriors.com
SIC: 1742 Acoustical and ceiling work
PA: Master Interiors, Inc.
113 Sandy Dr
Newark DE 19713
302 368-9361

(G-7989)
MATRIX REHABILITATION DELAWARE
Also Called: Barker Therapy Rehabilitation
800 Airport Rd Ste 102 (19963-6469)
PHONE.................302 424-1714
Courtney Twilley, Owner
EMP: 6 EST: 2009
SALES (est): 632.56K
SALES (corp-wide): 5.53B Publicly Held
SIC: 8049 Physical therapist
PA: Select Medical Holdings Corporation
4714 Gettysburg Rd
Mechanicsburg PA 17055
717 972-1100

(G-7990)
MATTRESS FIRM MILFORD
Also Called: Mattress Firm
945a N Dupont Blvd Ste D (19963-1072)
PHONE.................302 422-6585
EMP: 7 EST: 2016
SALES (est): 101.79K Privately Held
Web: www.mattressfirm.com
SIC: 2519 5712 Household furniture, nec; Beds and accessories

(G-7991)
MDN BILLING CONSULTING SVCS
24 Nw Front St (19963-1463)
PHONE.................914 376-6100
EMP: 5 EST: 2020
SALES (est): 233.27K Privately Held
SIC: 8721 Billing and bookkeeping service

(G-7992)
MEDHAT ISKANDER
1197 Airport Rd Ste 1 (19963-6491)
PHONE.................302 422-2020
EMP: 7 EST: 2018
SALES (est): 54.13K Privately Held
SIC: 8011 Offices and clinics of medical doctors

(G-7993)
MEDICAL ALTERNATIVE CARE
301 Jefferson Ave (19963-1800)
PHONE.................302 430-5705
Sandy Fox, Prin
EMP: 7 EST: 2010
SALES (est): 86.14K Privately Held
SIC: 8099 Blood related health services

(G-7994)
MEDTIX LLC (PA)
Also Called: Medtix Medical Supply
221 S Rehoboth Blvd (19963-1568)
P.O. Box 188 (19701-0188)
PHONE.................302 645-8070
EMP: 20 EST: 2009
SALES (est): 9.06MM
SALES (corp-wide): 9.06MM Privately Held
SIC: 5047 Medical equipment and supplies

(G-7995)
MICHELLE HAND
Also Called: Massage By Hand
123 School Pl (19963-1821)
PHONE.................302 422-0622
Michelle Hand, Prin
EMP: 5 EST: 2010
SALES (est): 40.09K Privately Held
SIC: 7299 Massage parlor

(G-7996)
MID ATLANTIC PAIN INSTITUTE
550 S Dupont Blvd Ste C (19963-1704)
PHONE.................302 369-1700
Rhonda Biddle, Prin

EMP: 6 EST: 2013
SALES (est): 85.42K Privately Held
Web: www.midatlanticspine.com
SIC: 8733 Noncommercial research organizations

(G-7997)
MIDATLNTIC AUTO RSTRATION SUPS
6930 Shawnee Rd (19963-3430)
PHONE.................302 422-3812
Fred Golden, Owner
EMP: 7 EST: 1989
SALES (est): 394.1K Privately Held
SIC: 5099 Durable goods, nec

(G-7998)
MILDFORD NECK FARMS
7343 Big Stone Beach Rd (19963-7444)
PHONE.................302 422-6432
Thomas Webb, Prin
EMP: 6 EST: 2010
SALES (est): 262.25K Privately Held
SIC: 0191 General farms, primarily crop

(G-7999)
MILFORD BOWLING LANES INC
809 N Dupont Blvd (19963-1066)
PHONE.................302 422-9456
Ernest Fry, Pr
Doris Fry, Sec
EMP: 14 EST: 1957
SQ FT: 30,000
SALES (est): 397.65K Privately Held
Web: www.milfordbowl.com
SIC: 7933 Ten pin center

(G-8000)
MILFORD COMMUNITY BAND INC
616 Cedarwood Ave (19963-2357)
PHONE.................302 422-6304
Joe Lear, Mgr
EMP: 5 EST: 2005
SALES (est): 87.84K Privately Held
Web: www.milfordcommunityband.org
SIC: 7929 Musical entertainers

(G-8001)
MILFORD HOUSING DEVELOPMENT (PA)
977 E Masten Cir (19963-1085)
PHONE.................302 422-8255
David Moore, CEO
Russel Huxtable, VP
EMP: 18 EST: 1977
SALES (est): 10.61MM
SALES (corp-wide): 10.61MM Privately Held
Web: www.milfordhousing.com
SIC: 6531 Real estate managers

(G-8002)
MILFORD LITTLE LEAGUE
944 Bay Rd (19963-6108)
PHONE.................302 424-3100
EMP: 6 EST: 2007
SALES (est): 45.86K Privately Held
SIC: 7997 Baseball club, except professional and semi-professional

(G-8003)
MILFORD LODGING LLC
Also Called: AmericInn
699 N Dupont Blvd (19963-1001)
PHONE.................302 839-5000
EMP: 35 EST: 2003
SALES (est): 233.95K Privately Held
Web: www.wyndhamhotels.com
SIC: 7011 Hotels and motels

Milford - Sussex County (G-8032)

(G-8004)
MILFORD MEDICAL ASSOCIATES PA (PA)
310 Mullet Run (19963-5371)
PHONE....................302 424-0600
G Mitchell Edmondson Md, *Pt*
Susan Sufit Md, *Pt*
Mary Lynn Hawkins Md, *Pt*
Loretta I Edmondson, *Pt*
EMP: 10 **EST:** 1999
SALES (est): 1.38MM
SALES (corp-wide): 1.38MM Privately Held
Web: www.milfordmedical.org
SIC: 8011 General and family practice, physician/surgeon

(G-8005)
MILFORD MICROTEL LLC
Also Called: Microtel Inn Stes By Wyndham M
106 Silicato Pkwy (19963-1266)
PHONE....................302 503-7615
Chad Moore, *Managing Member*
Robert Moore, *Managing Member*
EMP: 13 **EST:** 2021
SALES (est): 495.5K Privately Held
Web: www.wyndhamhotels.com
SIC: 7011 Hotels

(G-8006)
MILFORD PRIMARY CARE ASSOC LLC
301 Jefferson Ave (19963-1800)
PHONE....................302 536-2580
Cindy Siu, *Admn*
EMP: 13 **EST:** 2021
SALES (est): 505.97K Privately Held
Web: www.milfordlive.com
SIC: 8011 Primary care medical clinic

(G-8007)
MILFORD PULMONARY ASSOC LLC
39 W Clarke Ave (19963-1839)
PHONE....................302 424-3100
Angela Messick, *Pr*
EMP: 9 **EST:** 2017
SALES (est): 449.63K Privately Held
Web: www.milfordpulmonary.com
SIC: 8011 Pulmonary specialist, physician/surgeon

(G-8008)
MILFORD SENIOR CENTER INC
111 Park Ave (19963-1443)
PHONE....................302 422-3385
Daphne Bumbrey, *Ex Dir*
EMP: 16 **EST:** 1973
SALES (est): 847.85K Privately Held
Web: www.milfordseniorcenter.net
SIC: 8322 Senior citizens' center or association

(G-8009)
MILFORD VETERANS OF FOREIGN WA
77 Veterans Cir (19963-6352)
PHONE....................302 422-4412
EMP: 5 **EST:** 2011
SALES (est): 45.23K Privately Held
SIC: 8641 Veterans' organization

(G-8010)
MILFORDLIVECOM
805 Joshua Dr (19963-2131)
PHONE....................302 542-9231
Bryan Shupe, *Prin*
EMP: 6 **EST:** 2011
SALES (est): 105.54K Privately Held
Web: www.milfordlive.com
SIC: 7389 Design services

(G-8011)
MILLER INVESTMENTS LLC
10 Nw 10th St (19963-1221)
PHONE....................949 836-2511
EMP: 5 **EST:** 2019
SALES (est): 638.85K Privately Held
SIC: 6799 Investors, nec

(G-8012)
MILLMAR CONTRACTING
411 Wisseman Ave (19963-1667)
PHONE....................302 222-0823
Nicholas Marvel, *Prin*
EMP: 5 **EST:** 2019
SALES (est): 62.44K Privately Held
SIC: 1799 Special trade contractors, nec

(G-8013)
MIND MECHANIX
556 S Dupont Blvd Ste I (19963-1706)
PHONE....................302 503-5142
EMP: 6 **EST:** 2019
SALES (est): 96.18K Privately Held
Web: www.mindmechanixllc.com
SIC: 8099 Health and allied services, nec

(G-8014)
MINDY BODY CONSORTIUM
993 N Dupont Blvd (19963-1072)
PHONE....................302 424-1322
Lori Malloy, *Prin*
EMP: 7 **EST:** 2017
SALES (est): 36.21K Privately Held
Web: www.mindandbodyde.com
SIC: 8322 General counseling services

(G-8015)
MISPILLION ART LEAGUE INC
5 N Walnut St (19963-1456)
PHONE....................302 430-7646
EMP: 9 **EST:** 2007
SALES (est): 116.5K Privately Held
Web: www.mispillionarts.org
SIC: 8699 Art council

(G-8016)
MISPILLION III
504 Mispillion Apts (19963-2348)
PHONE....................302 422-4429
Arthur W Edwards, *CEO*
Arthur Edwards, *Owner*
EMP: 5 **EST:** 2006
SALES (est): 385.21K Privately Held
Web: www.mispillionarts.org
SIC: 6513 Apartment building operators

(G-8017)
MODERN MIXTURE LLC
37 Meadow Lark Dr (19963-3910)
PHONE....................302 249-6183
EMP: 5 **EST:** 2012
SALES (est): 104.51K Privately Held
SIC: 8111 Legal services

(G-8018)
MOHAWK ELECTRICAL SYSTEMS INC
Also Called: Mohawk
251 S Rehoboth Blvd (19963-1568)
P.O. Box 630 (19963-0630)
PHONE....................302 422-2500
Scott Welch, *Pr*
Scott M Welch, *
EMP: 25 **EST:** 1979
SQ FT: 24,000
SALES (est): 4.88MM Privately Held
Web: www.mohawk-usa.com
SIC: 3699 Electrical equipment and supplies, nec

(G-8019)
MOM HOME DAYCARE
8351 Collett Ln (19963-3666)
PHONE....................302 265-2668
M Maldonado-hernandez, *Prin*
EMP: 9 **EST:** 2013
SALES (est): 67.16K Privately Held
SIC: 8351 Group day care center

(G-8020)
MORRIS CAROL JAMIE DO
517 S Dupont Blvd (19963-1757)
PHONE....................302 393-5006
Carol J Morris D.o.s., *Owner*
EMP: 9 **EST:** 2017
SALES (est): 54.13K Privately Held
SIC: 8011 Offices and clinics of medical doctors

(G-8021)
MOSO NORTH AMERICA INC
203 Se Front St Ste 101 (19963-1945)
PHONE....................855 343-8444
Mark Liston, *VP*
EMP: 5 **EST:** 2017
SALES (est): 176.98K Privately Held
Web: www.moso-bamboo.com
SIC: 5031 Lumber, plywood, and millwork

(G-8022)
MUDIWA MUNYIKWA MD
39 W Clarke Ave (19963-1839)
PHONE....................302 645-7050
EMP: 12 **EST:** 2017
SALES (est): 280.33K Privately Held
Web: www.capesurgical.com
SIC: 8062 General medical and surgical hospitals

(G-8023)
MY EYE DR OPTOMETRISTS LLC
Also Called: Myeyedr
1197 Airport Rd (19963-6491)
PHONE....................302 422-2020
EMP: 6
SALES (corp-wide): 100.43MM Privately Held
Web: www.myeyedr.com
SIC: 8042 Offices and clinics of optometrists
PA: My Eye Dr. Optometrists, Llc
  8614 Wstwd Ctr Dr Ste 900
  Vienna VA 22182
  703 847-8899

(G-8024)
MY TOUCH WORKS MASSAGE
125 Causey Ave Ste 103 (19963-1910)
PHONE....................302 943-9783
EMP: 5 **EST:** 2014
SALES (est): 59.37K Privately Held
SIC: 8049 Massage Therapist

(G-8025)
NATIONWIDE INSURANCE
Also Called: Nationwide
100 Credit Union Way (19963-1071)
PHONE....................302 402-5188
EMP: 5 **EST:** 2019
SALES (est): 92.77K Privately Held
Web: www.nationwide.com
SIC: 6411 Insurance agents, nec

(G-8026)
NEMOURS FOUNDATION
Also Called: Nemours Senior Care, Milford
101 Wellness Way (19963-4394)
PHONE....................302 424-5420
EMP: 10
SALES (corp-wide): 1.94B Privately Held
Web: www.nemours.org
SIC: 8051 Skilled nursing care facilities
PA: Nemours Foundation
  10140 Centurion Pkwy N
  Jacksonville FL 32256
  904 697-4100

(G-8027)
NEMOURS FOUNDATION
Also Called: Nemours Dpont Pdatrics Milford
101 Wellness Way (19963-4394)
PHONE....................302 422-4559
Susan Wagenhoffer, *Mgr*
EMP: 7
SALES (corp-wide): 1.94B Privately Held
Web: www.nemours.org
SIC: 8011 Pediatrician
PA: Nemours Foundation
  10140 Centurion Pkwy N
  Jacksonville FL 32256
  904 697-4100

(G-8028)
NEW LIFE MOVING INC
1 N Maple Ave (19963-1073)
PHONE....................704 969-0858
Roger Wood, *CEO*
EMP: 5 **EST:** 2020
SALES (est): 77.16K Privately Held
Web: www.newlifemovingandstorage.com
SIC: 4789 Transportation services, nec

(G-8029)
NKS DISTRIBUTORS INC
759 E Masten Cir (19963-1030)
P.O. Box 758 (19720-0758)
PHONE....................302 422-1220
Edward Walsen, *Opers Mgr*
EMP: 17
SALES (corp-wide): 24.65MM Privately Held
Web: www.nksdistributors.com
SIC: 5181 Beer and other fermented malt liquors
PA: N.K.S. Distributors, Inc.
  205 Big Woods Rd
  Smyrna DE 19977
  302 322-1811

(G-8030)
NOEL ANUPOL
305 Jefferson Ave (19963-1800)
P.O. Box 199 (19963-0199)
PHONE....................302 424-6511
Noel Anupol, *Prin*
EMP: 10 **EST:** 2007
SALES (est): 181.62K Privately Held
Web: www.obgyncenterofexcellence.com
SIC: 8011 8031 Gynecologist; Offices and clinics of osteopathic physicians

(G-8031)
NORMAN S STEWARD DDS PA
214 S Walnut St (19963-1958)
PHONE....................302 422-9791
Norman S Steward D.d.s., *Owner*
EMP: 8 **EST:** 1997
SALES (est): 538.13K Privately Held
Web: www.drstewarddds.net
SIC: 8021 Dentists' office

(G-8032)
NOVACARE RHABILITATION MILFORD
800 Airport Rd Ste 102 (19963-6469)
PHONE....................302 393-5889
EMP: 5 **EST:** 2017
SALES (est): 54.13K Privately Held
SIC: 8049 Physical therapist

Milford - Sussex County (G-8033)

(G-8033)
NURSES N KIDS INC
Also Called: Nurses N Kids Southern Del
21 W Clarke Ave Ste 1005 (19963-1849)
PHONE..................................302 424-1770
EMP: 50
SALES (corp-wide): 4.77MM **Privately Held**
Web: www.nursesnkids.com
SIC: 8082 Home health care services
PA: Nurses N Kids, Inc
      11 Reads Way
      New Castle DE 19720
      302 323-1118

(G-8034)
NUTRIEN AG SOLUTIONS INC
200 N Rehoboth Blvd (19963-1304)
PHONE..................................302 422-3570
Jimmy Warren, Brnch Mgr
EMP: 10
SALES (corp-wide): 27.71B **Privately Held**
Web: www.nutrienagsolutions.com
SIC: 5191 Fertilizer and fertilizer materials
HQ: Nutrien Ag Solutions, Inc.
      3005 Rocky Mountain Ave
      Loveland CO 80538
      970 685-3300

(G-8035)
OCCUPTNL THRPY OF DELAWARE
550 S Dupont Blvd (19963-1704)
PHONE..................................302 491-4813
EMP: 11 EST: 2016
SALES (est): 558.96K **Privately Held**
Web: www.otdelaware.com
SIC: 8093 Rehabilitation center, outpatient treatment

(G-8036)
ODD FELLOWS CMTRY OF MILFORD
300 S Rehoboth Blvd (19963-1532)
PHONE..................................302 422-4619
James Greenly, Pr
Bill Sipple, Pr
EMP: 6 EST: 1991
SALES (est): 333.08K **Privately Held**
Web: www.sipplemonuments.com
SIC: 6553 Cemetery subdividers and developers

(G-8037)
ONE STOP MEDICAL INC
515 S Dupont Blvd Bldg C (19963-1757)
PHONE..................................302 450-4479
Alisa Miller, VP
Dorothy Harmon, Prin
EMP: 8 EST: 2019
SALES (est): 407.58K **Privately Held**
SIC: 8099 Health and allied services, nec

(G-8038)
ONSITE SEMI TRUCK REPAIR
18 Sw Front St (19963-1948)
PHONE..................................302 526-0517
Kimmy Kardash, Prin
EMP: 5 EST: 2016
SALES (est): 28.25K **Privately Held**
SIC: 7538 General automotive repair shops

(G-8039)
OVERHEAD DOOR CO DELMAR INC
Also Called: Overhead Doors
603 Marshall St (19963-2307)
PHONE..................................302 424-4400
Robert S Gross, Pr
Paul Cummings Iii, VP
EMP: 20 EST: 1989
SQ FT: 8,000
SALES (est): 2.38MM **Privately Held**
Web: www.overheaddoordelmar.com
SIC: 1751 Garage door, installation or erection

(G-8040)
P2 DENTAL PA
100 Sussex Ave (19963-1823)
PHONE..................................302 422-6924
EMP: 9 EST: 2018
SALES (est): 200.27K **Privately Held**
SIC: 8021 Offices and clinics of dentists

(G-8041)
PACKAGING MANIA (NOT INC) ✪
114 Manor Ln `(19963-2382)
PHONE..................................917 410-6835
EMP: 6 EST: 2022
SALES (est): 86.31K **Privately Held**
Web: www.packagingmania.com
SIC: 5199 7389 Packaging materials; Business services, nec

(G-8042)
PATRICK SCANLON PA
203 Ne Front St Ste 101 (19963-1431)
PHONE..................................302 424-1996
Patrick Scanlon, Pr
EMP: 7 EST: 2002
SALES (est): 629.93K **Privately Held**
Web: www.delcollections.com
SIC: 8111 Debt collection law

(G-8043)
PEACHY KEEN SLON + BUTY BAR LL
606 Milford Harrington Hwy (19963)
PHONE..................................302 519-5572
EMP: 9 EST: 2019
SALES (est): 181.12K **Privately Held**
SIC: 7231 Beauty shops

(G-8044)
PENINSULA POLYMERS INC
640 Marshall St (19963-2308)
PHONE..................................302 422-2002
Dirk Gleysteen, VP
EMP: 8 EST: 2013
SALES (est): 509.34K **Privately Held**
Web: www.penpoly.com
SIC: 5046 Commercial equipment, nec

(G-8045)
PEOPLES PLACE II INC (PA)
1129 Airport Rd (19963-6418)
PHONE..................................302 422-8033
Michael Kersteter, Ex Dir
Del Failing, Dir
Bev Lawson, Dir
Cherelyn Homlish, Dir
EMP: 7 EST: 1972
SALES (est): 8.66MM
SALES (corp-wide): 8.66MM **Privately Held**
Web: www.peoplesplace2.com
SIC: 8322 Social service center

(G-8046)
PERDUE FARMS INC
Also Called: Perdue Farms
225 S Rehoboth Blvd (19963-1568)
PHONE..................................302 424-2600
EMP: 567
SALES (corp-wide): 1.24B **Privately Held**
Web: www.perdue.com
SIC: 2015 Poultry, processed, nsk
PA: Perdue Farms Incorporated
      31149 Old Ocean City Rd
      Salisbury MD 21804
      800 473-7383

(G-8047)
PERDUE WELLNESS CENTER
255 N Rehoboth Blvd (19963-1303)
PHONE..................................302 424-2663
EMP: 7 EST: 2019
SALES (est): 197.65K **Privately Held**
SIC: 8099 Health and allied services, nec

(G-8048)
PEST PRO LLC
Also Called: Pest Pro Pest Control
100 Kona Cir (19963-5459)
PHONE..................................877 737-8360
EMP: 6 EST: 2018
SALES (est): 266.75K **Privately Held**
Web: www.pestpro1.com
SIC: 7342 Pest control in structures

(G-8049)
PETER RENZI
793 Bay Rd (19963-6122)
PHONE..................................302 265-1309
Peter Renzi, CEO
EMP: 5 EST: 2017
SALES (est): 233.25K **Privately Held**
SIC: 6411 Insurance agents, brokers, and service

(G-8050)
PNC BANK NATIONAL ASSOCIATION
Also Called: PNC
655 N Dupont Blvd (19963-1001)
PHONE..................................302 422-1015
Wayne Davis, Genl Mgr
EMP: 5
SALES (corp-wide): 23.54B **Publicly Held**
Web: www.pnc.com
SIC: 6021 National commercial banks
HQ: Pnc Bank, National Association
      300 5th Ave
      Pittsburgh PA 15222
      877 762-2000

(G-8051)
PRECISION JEWELRY INC
Also Called: EKA Jewelers
607 N Dupont Blvd (19963-1099)
PHONE..................................302 422-7138
Robert Addonizio, Pr
EMP: 5 EST: 1981
SQ FT: 1,100
SALES (est): 477.42K **Privately Held**
Web: www.ekajewelers.com
SIC: 5944 7631 Jewelry, precious stones and precious metals; Watch, clock, and jewelry repair

(G-8052)
PRO BENEFITS PLUS
569 Bay Ave (19963-4915)
PHONE..................................302 683-5546
Ed St Jean, Prin
EMP: 5 EST: 2018
SALES (est): 264.46K **Privately Held**
Web: www.probenefitsplus.com
SIC: 8748 Business consulting, nec

(G-8053)
PRO FABRICATING INC
1011 Mattlind Way (19963-5369)
P.O. Box 409 (19946-0409)
PHONE..................................302 424-7700
Walter Breeding, Pr
EMP: 5 EST: 1998
SALES (est): 365.24K **Privately Held**
SIC: 3714 Motor vehicle engines and parts

(G-8054)
PRO PHYSICAL THERAPY
941 N Dupont Blvd Ste C (19963-1069)
PHONE..................................302 422-6670
Jim Langejans, Prin
EMP: 5 EST: 2007
SALES (est): 61.05K **Privately Held**
SIC: 8748 8049 Business consulting, nec; Physical therapist

(G-8055)
PROUSE ENTERPRISES LLC
Also Called: Old Mill Crab House
120 Mullet Run (19963-5367)
PHONE..................................302 846-9000
EMP: 4 EST: 2008
SALES (est): 45.2K **Privately Held**
SIC: 3949 Scoops, crab and fish

(G-8056)
PT WORKS DE LLC
907 N Dupont Blvd (19963-1060)
PHONE..................................410 446-2589
EMP: 7 EST: 2018
SALES (est): 102.13K **Privately Held**
Web: www.ptworksdelaware.com
SIC: 8049 Physical therapist

(G-8057)
R L WLKERSON ASSOC LTD A/K/A R
150a Vickers Rd (19963-5393)
PHONE..................................302 503-3207
R Wilkerson, CEO
EMP: 5 EST: 2017
SALES (est): 83.8K **Privately Held**
Web: www.rlwilkersonassociates.com
SIC: 1721 Painting and paper hanging

(G-8058)
RALPH E WILLIS
690 Tub Mill Pond Rd (19963-5807)
PHONE..................................302 422-7167
Ralph E Willis, Prin
EMP: 5 EST: 2010
SALES (est): 44.19K **Privately Held**
SIC: 7299 Handyman service

(G-8059)
RAZOR RICK
18 W Saratoga Rd (19963-2106)
PHONE..................................302 604-1339
Rick Barclay, Prin
EMP: 5 EST: 2015
SALES (est): 47.21K **Privately Held**
Web: www.razorick.com
SIC: 7699 Taxidermists

(G-8060)
REAGAN-WATSON AUCTIONS LLC
115 N Washington St (19963-1457)
PHONE..................................302 422-2392
EMP: 5 EST: 2010
SALES (est): 229.7K **Privately Held**
Web: www.reagan-watsonauctions.com
SIC: 7389 Auctioneers, fee basis

(G-8061)
REGIS CORPORATION
939 N Dupont Blvd (19963-1072)
PHONE..................................302 430-0881
Peggy Tice, Brnch Mgr
EMP: 8
SALES (corp-wide): 233.33MM **Publicly Held**
Web: www.regiscorp.com
SIC: 7231 Unisex hair salons
PA: Regis Corporation
      3701 Wayzata Blvd Ste 500
      Minneapolis MN 55416
      952 947-7777

GEOGRAPHIC SECTION

Milford - Sussex County (G-8091)

(G-8062)
RENZI RUST INC
Also Called: Almost Home Child Care Center
6722 Griffith Lake Dr (19963-3510)
PHONE...................................302 424-4470
Christine Rust, Pr
EMP: 10 EST: 2002
SALES (est): 59.51K Privately Held
SIC: 8351 Group day care center

(G-8063)
RESPONSE COMPUTER GROUP INC
213 W Liberty Way (19963-5399)
PHONE...................................302 335-3400
Robert Stone, Pr
Randy Ennis, Sec
EMP: 10 EST: 1981
SQ FT: 2,500
SALES (est): 959.56K Privately Held
Web: www.rcgweb.com
SIC: 7378 5734 Computer and data processing equipment repair/maintenance; Computer and software stores

(G-8064)
RESTORATION GUYS LLC
717 S Washington St (19963-2305)
P.O. Box 805 (19963-0805)
PHONE...................................302 542-4045
Josh Muncy, Managing Member
EMP: 7 EST: 2019
SALES (est): 1.27MM Privately Held
Web: www.trg247.com
SIC: 1521 New construction, single-family houses

(G-8065)
RHEUMATOLOGY CONSULTANTS
509 Lakeview Ave (19963-2917)
PHONE...................................302 491-6659
EMP: 5 EST: 2019
SALES (est): 74.99K Privately Held
SIC: 8748 Business consulting, nec

(G-8066)
RHOADES & MORROW LLC
30 Nw 10th St (19963-1267)
PHONE...................................302 422-6705
Stephen Morrow, Pr
EMP: 5 EST: 2015
SALES (est): 148.78K Privately Held
Web: www.rhoadeslegal.com
SIC: 8111 General practice attorney, lawyer

(G-8067)
RHUE & ASSOCIATES INC
Also Called: Rhue Insurance
628 Milford Harrington Hwy Ste 3 (19963)
P.O. Box 569 (19963-0569)
PHONE...................................302 422-3058
Edward B Rhue, Pr
Nancy C Rhue, Sec
EMP: 5 EST: 1975
SALES (est): 530.29K Privately Held
SIC: 6411 Insurance agents, nec

(G-8068)
RICHARD ADDINGTON CO
316 N Rehoboth Blvd (19963-1306)
PHONE...................................302 422-2668
EMP: 6 EST: 1992
SALES (est): 1.07MM Privately Held
Web: www.raddingtonco.com
SIC: 5511 7542 New and used car dealers; Washing and polishing, automotive

(G-8069)
ROBERT G STARKEY CPA
1043 N Walnut St (19963-1201)
PHONE...................................302 422-0108
EMP: 5 EST: 1996
SALES (est): 270.41K Privately Held
Web: www.starkeyandcompany.com
SIC: 8721 Certified public accountant

(G-8070)
ROBERT GRANT INC
Also Called: Grant & Sons Roofing & Siding
606 Milford Harrington Hwy (19963)
PHONE...................................302 422-6090
Robert Grant, Pr
EMP: 18 EST: 1969
SALES (est): 941.64K Privately Held
Web: www.grantroofing.com
SIC: 1761 Roofing contractor

(G-8071)
ROBERT L GRZONKA M D
200 Kings Hwy Ste 7 (19963-1854)
PHONE...................................302 503-2460
Robert Grzonka, Pr
EMP: 8 EST: 2017
SALES (est): 54.13K Privately Held
SIC: 8011 Offices and clinics of medical doctors

(G-8072)
ROOKERY GOLF COURSES SOUTH
6152 S Rehoboth Blvd (19963-4140)
PHONE...................................302 422-7010
Glenda Adkins, Mgr
EMP: 10 EST: 2013
SALES (est): 194.51K Privately Held
Web: www.rookerygolf.com
SIC: 7992 Public golf courses

(G-8073)
ROWE INDUSTRIES INC
12 S Walnut St (19963-1954)
PHONE...................................302 855-0585
EMP: 7 EST: 2019
SALES (est): 172.89K Privately Held
Web: www.roweindustries.com
SIC: 3069 Fabricated rubber products, nec

(G-8074)
ROWE ROBERT L DR REV
206 Se Front St (19963-1946)
PHONE...................................302 422-8814
Robert Rowe, Prin
EMP: 8 EST: 2007
SALES (est): 72.54K Privately Held
SIC: 8011 Physicians' office, including specialists

(G-8075)
RUMPSTICH MACHINE WORKS INC
305 S Rehoboth Blvd (19963-1531)
PHONE...................................302 422-4816
John L Allen, Pr
Joan A Maloney, Sec
Ronald R Allen, VP
EMP: 5 EST: 1931
SQ FT: 3,600
SALES (est): 406.46K Privately Held
SIC: 3599 Machine shop, jobbing and repair

(G-8076)
RYAN HOMES
7305 Clubhouse Dr (19963-2231)
PHONE...................................302 491-4442
Michael Schaffer, Ofcr
EMP: 5 EST: 2020
SALES (est): 103.18K Privately Held
Web: www.ryanhomes.com
SIC: 1521 New construction, single-family houses

(G-8077)
S J PASSWATER GENERAL CNSTR
715a S Washington St (19963-2341)
PHONE...................................302 422-1061
Samuel Passwater, Owner
EMP: 5 EST: 1986
SALES (est): 453.87K Privately Held
SIC: 1521 General remodeling, single-family houses

(G-8078)
SAD ENTERPRISES INC
Also Called: H & R Block-Milford
915 N Dupont Blvd Ste 101 (19963-1076)
PHONE...................................302 422-6100
Linda H Niehorster, Mgr
EMP: 7 EST: 2009
SALES (est): 81.87K Privately Held
Web: www.hrblock.com
SIC: 7291 Tax return preparation services

(G-8079)
SAI RAM HOSPITALITY INC
1036 N Walnut St (19963-1222)
PHONE...................................302 422-8089
Jigar Patel, Prin
EMP: 16 EST: 2014
SALES (est): 252.65K Privately Held
SIC: 7011 Hotels and motels

(G-8080)
SAINT HOME HEALTH CARE
1017 Mattlind Way (19963-5369)
PHONE...................................302 514-9597
Tina Chambers, CEO
EMP: 12 EST: 2011
SALES (est): 185.9K Privately Held
SIC: 8082 Home health care services

(G-8081)
SAMAHA MICHEL R MD
39 W Clarke Ave (19963-1839)
PHONE...................................302 422-3100
Michel Samaha, Prin
EMP: 5 EST: 2011
SALES (est): 165.48K Privately Held
SIC: 8011 Offices and clinics of medical doctors

(G-8082)
SAMEENA MALHAN
21 W Clarke Ave (19963-1840)
PHONE...................................302 422-3311
Sameena Malhan, Prin
EMP: 10 EST: 2011
SALES (est): 80.89K Privately Held
SIC: 8011 Offices and clinics of medical doctors

(G-8083)
SANDRA S GULLEDGE CPA
107 N Walnut St (19963-1447)
PHONE...................................302 422-5005
Sandra Gulledge, Prin
EMP: 5 EST: 2006
SALES (est): 98.4K Privately Held
Web: www.taxchicks.com
SIC: 8721 Certified public accountant

(G-8084)
SARAH WOLFE LCSW
509 Lakeview Ave (19963-2917)
PHONE...................................302 744-8046
EMP: 7 EST: 2018
SALES (est): 36.21K Privately Held
SIC: 8322 Individual and family services

(G-8085)
SATTERFIELD & RYAN INC
8266 N Union Church Rd (19963-3633)
PHONE...................................302 422-4919
Michael Herholdt, Pr
Michael D Herholdt Junior, Treas
EMP: 19 EST: 1931
SQ FT: 30,000
SALES (est): 898.9K Privately Held
Web: www.satterfieldandryan.com
SIC: 1731 General electrical contractor

(G-8086)
SCHANNE MARK STATE FARM INSUR
Also Called: State Farm Insurance
915 S Dupont Blvd (19963-2234)
PHONE...................................302 422-7231
Mark Schanne, Owner
EMP: 8 EST: 1985
SALES (est): 773.39K Privately Held
Web: www.sfdelaware.com
SIC: 6411 Insurance agents and brokers

(G-8087)
SCOTT A HAMMER MD FAAFP
119 Neurology Way (19963-5368)
PHONE...................................302 725-2033
EMP: 6 EST: 2019
SALES (est): 54.13K Privately Held
SIC: 8011 Offices and clinics of medical doctors

(G-8088)
SEASCAPE LAB
628 Milford Harrington Hwy Ste 5 (19963-5370)
PHONE...................................760 807-7983
Richard Wilson, Prin
EMP: 9 EST: 2019
SALES (est): 176.59K Privately Held
Web: www.labatseascape.com
SIC: 8099 Health and allied services, nec

(G-8089)
SERVICEXPRESS CORPORATION
340 Ne Front St (19963-1434)
PHONE...................................302 424-3500
Bamdad Bahar, Brnch Mgr
EMP: 546
Web: www.serviceexpressworks.net
SIC: 7361 Labor contractors (employment agency)
PA: Servicexpress Corporation
120 N Ray St
Georgetown DE 19947

(G-8090)
SHALINI SEHGAL MD
200 Kings Hwy Ste 1 (19963-1850)
PHONE...................................302 424-3694
Shalini Sehgal, Prin
EMP: 10 EST: 2007
SALES (est): 145.17K Privately Held
Web: www.delawarekidney.com
SIC: 8011 Nephrologist

(G-8091)
SHEA CONCRETE LTD
4th & Montgomery St (19963)
P.O. Box 264 (19963-0264)
PHONE...................................302 422-7221
Mike Shea, Pr
EMP: 9 EST: 1980
SQ FT: 5,400
SALES (est): 401.31K Privately Held
SIC: 1771 Concrete work

Milford - Sussex County (G-8092)

(G-8092)
SHREE KISHNA INC
699 N Dupont Blvd (19963-1001)
PHONE.....................302 839-5000
Arvid Patel, *Pr*
EMP: 10 EST: 2013
SALES (est): 930.39K **Privately Held**
SIC: 7011 Motel, franchised

(G-8093)
SKJALDBORG ARTISANS LLC
803 N Dupont Blvd (19963-1005)
PHONE.....................302 698-7552
Joshua White, *Pr*
EMP: 5 EST: 2021
SALES (est): 164.52K **Privately Held**
SIC: 7389 Business Activities at Non-Commercial Site

(G-8094)
SMITH CONCRETE INC
Also Called: Smith Concrete
8473 N Union Church Rd (19963-3638)
PHONE.....................302 270-9251
EMP: 5 EST: 1990
SALES (est): 321.27K **Privately Held**
Web: www.smithconcreteinc.com
SIC: 1771 Concrete work

(G-8095)
SOUND-N-SECURE INC
20444 Pingue Dr (19963-4276)
PHONE.....................302 424-3670
Melissa E Pingue, *CEO*
Robert Pingue, *VP*
EMP: 7 EST: 1997
SQ FT: 20,000
SALES (est): 2.01MM **Privately Held**
Web: www.sound-n-secure.com
SIC: 7382 3651 Burglar alarm maintenance and monitoring; Audio electronic systems

(G-8096)
SOUTH BOWERS LADIES AUXILIARY
57 Scotts Corner Rd (19963-7129)
P.O. Box 314 (19963-0314)
PHONE.....................302 335-4135
Jo Ann Webb, *Pr*
Michele Melvin, *Pr*
EMP: 7 EST: 1999
SALES (est): 47.42K **Privately Held**
Web: www.southbowers57.com
SIC: 8641 Civic and social associations

(G-8097)
SOUTH BOWERS VOLUNTEER FIRE CO
57 Scotts Corner Rd (19963-7129)
P.O. Box 314 (19963-0314)
PHONE.....................302 335-4666
EMP: 8 EST: 2006
SALES (est): 908.01K **Privately Held**
Web: www.southbowers57.com
SIC: 8711 Fire protection engineering

(G-8098)
SOUTHERN DELAWARE MED GROUP PA
100 Silicato Pkwy Ste 301 (19963-1272)
P.O. Box 337 (19963-0337)
PHONE.....................302 424-3900
EMP: 18 EST: 2007
SALES (est): 840.42K **Privately Held**
Web: www.southerndelawaremedicalgroup.com
SIC: 8011 General and family practice, physician/surgeon

(G-8099)
SPECIALIZED CARIER SYSTEMS INC
256 N Rehoboth Blvd (19963-1304)
P.O. Box 198 (19963-0198)
PHONE.....................302 424-4548
Tom Noll, *Pr*
EMP: 5 EST: 1987
SQ FT: 12,000
SALES (est): 500.06K **Privately Held**
SIC: 4212 7389 Local trucking, without storage; Crane and aerial lift service

(G-8100)
SPLASH LAUNDROMAT
668 N Dupont Blvd (19963-1002)
PHONE.....................302 503-3325
EMP: 6 EST: 2017
SALES (est): 115.51K **Privately Held**
Web: www.laundrydelaware.com
SIC: 7215 Laundry, coin-operated

(G-8101)
SPRINT SPECTRUM LP
Also Called: Sprint
120 Aerenson Dr (19963-1236)
PHONE.....................302 393-2060
EMP: 10
SALES (corp-wide): 79.57B **Publicly Held**
SIC: 4813 Local and long distance telephone communications
HQ: Sprint Spectrum L.P.
6800 Sprint Pkwy
Overland Park KS 66251

(G-8102)
STAFFMARK INVESTMENT LLC
242 S Rehoboth Blvd (19963-1569)
PHONE.....................302 422-0606
Brenda Bill, *Prin*
EMP: 9
Web: www.staffmarkexecutivesearch.com
SIC: 7361 Labor contractors (employment agency)
HQ: Staffmark Investment Llc
201 E 4th St
Cincinnati OH 45202

(G-8103)
STEVEN ALBAN DDS PA
3 Sussex Ave (19963-1853)
PHONE.....................302 422-9637
Steven Michael Alban, *Prin*
EMP: 5 EST: 2008
SALES (est): 441.76K **Privately Held**
Web: www.albandental.com
SIC: 8021 Dentists' office

(G-8104)
STEVEN ROGERS
6918 Shawnee Rd (19963-3430)
PHONE.....................302 422-6285
Steven Rogers, *Prin*
EMP: 5 EST: 2007
SALES (est): 100.79K **Privately Held**
SIC: 1521 Single-family housing construction

(G-8105)
STEVENSON VENTURES LLC
Also Called: Scj
26 N Walnut St (19963-1446)
PHONE.....................302 752-4449
EMP: 8 EST: 2015
SQ FT: 2,450
SALES (est): 289.54K **Privately Held**
Web: www.scjinc.net
SIC: 7322 Collection agency, except real estate

(G-8106)
STUDIO B MILFORD LLC ✪
110 Ne Front St (19963-1430)
PHONE.....................302 491-7910
Brianna Westover, *Pr*
EMP: 2 EST: 2023
SALES (est): 68.89K **Privately Held**
SIC: 7389 2752 5947 Notary publics; Commercial printing, lithographic; Gift, novelty, and souvenir shop

(G-8107)
SUN DAZED TANNING
280 N Rehoboth Blvd (19963-1304)
PHONE.....................302 430-0150
EMP: 5 EST: 2019
SALES (est): 230.68K **Privately Held**
Web: www.sundazedde.com
SIC: 7299 Tanning salon

(G-8108)
SUPERCUTS
Also Called: Supercuts
28257 Lexus Dr (19963-2200)
PHONE.....................302 422-8448
EMP: 5 EST: 2016
SALES (est): 19.5K **Privately Held**
Web: www.supercuts.com
SIC: 7231 Unisex hair salons

(G-8109)
SURVEY SUPPLY INC
726 Mccolley St (19963-2314)
P.O. Box 403 (19963-0403)
PHONE.....................302 422-3338
Jerry H Mcpherson, *Pr*
Kevin S Mcpherson, *VP*
EMP: 6 EST: 2000
SQ FT: 10,000
SALES (est): 852.1K **Privately Held**
Web: www.surveysupplyinc.com
SIC: 5049 Surveyor's instruments

(G-8110)
SUSSEX POST
37 N Walnut St (19963-1445)
PHONE.....................302 629-5505
Kitt Parker, *Mgr*
EMP: 5 EST: 2009
SALES (est): 102.06K **Privately Held**
Web: www.sussexcountypost.com
SIC: 2711 Newspapers, publishing and printing

(G-8111)
SVASTIJAYA DAVIRATANASILP MD
201 W Liberty Way (19963-5399)
PHONE.....................302 424-3694
Svastijaya Daviratanasilp, *Prin*
EMP: 8 EST: 2014
SALES (est): 75.29K **Privately Held**
SIC: 8011 Nephrologist

(G-8112)
SWITCHGEARUS LLC
Also Called: Great American Switchgear
123 Isaacs Shore Dr Ste 500 (19963-4930)
PHONE.....................302 232-3209
Ellen Barag, *CEO*
Donia Krause, *Pr*
Bill Krause, *Ex VP*
EMP: 20 EST: 2021
SALES (est): 3.44MM
SALES (corp-wide): 3.44MM **Privately Held**
SIC: 5063 7389 Electrical supplies, nec; Business Activities at Non-Commercial Site
PA: Hireli Llc
123 Isaacs Shore Dr # 30
Milford DE 19963
302 232-3220

(G-8113)
T J IRVIN TRUCKING
6250 Griffith Lake Dr (19963-3506)
PHONE.....................302 270-8475
EMP: 5 EST: 2018
SALES (est): 424.67K **Privately Held**
SIC: 4212 Local trucking, without storage

(G-8114)
TAYLOR ELECTRIC SERVICE INC
8 Columbia St (19963-1536)
PHONE.....................302 422-3966
William C Taylor Junior, *Pr*
Michael Taylor, *VP*
EMP: 5 EST: 1969
SALES (est): 486.02K **Privately Held**
SIC: 1731 General electrical contractor

(G-8115)
TELAMON CORPORATION
Also Called: Telamon Corp Lincoln Hs
518 N Church Ave (19963-1129)
PHONE.....................302 424-2335
Sedonia Worthy, *Brnch Mgr*
EMP: 6
SALES (corp-wide): 85.01MM **Privately Held**
Web: www.telamon.org
SIC: 8331 Job training services
PA: Telamon Corporation
5560 Munford Rd Ste 201
Raleigh NC 27612
919 851-7611

(G-8116)
TERESA H KELLER MD
16 S Dupont Blvd (19963-1027)
PHONE.....................302 422-2022
Teresa H Keller Md, *Owner*
EMP: 6 EST: 1984
SALES (est): 249.85K **Privately Held**
SIC: 8011 General and family practice, physician/surgeon

(G-8117)
TESLA BIOHEALING INC
111 Mccoy St (19963-2309)
PHONE.....................302 265-2213
James Z Liu Ph.d., *CEO*
EMP: 45 EST: 2019
SALES (est): 4.98MM **Privately Held**
SIC: 2834 Solutions, pharmaceutical

(G-8118)
THAT GRANITE PLACE
6832 Shawnee Rd (19963-3429)
PHONE.....................302 236-0820
EMP: 5 EST: 2018
SALES (est): 56.76K **Privately Held**
Web: www.coastalcountertops.net
SIC: 1799 Counter top installation

(G-8119)
TJS REPAIR LLC
201 Marshall St (19963-2055)
PHONE.....................302 422-8383
EMP: 5 EST: 2018
SALES (est): 151.83K **Privately Held**
Web: tjsrepair.mechanicnet.com
SIC: 7699 Repair services, nec

(G-8120)
TROYER CONSTRUCTION INC
6650 Shawnee Rd (19963-3426)
PHONE.....................302 422-0745
Thomas Trice, *Asst Sec*
EMP: 5 EST: 2018
SALES (est): 154.95K **Privately Held**
SIC: 1521 Single-family housing construction

(G-8121)
TURNING POINT AT PEOPLES PLACE
1131 Airport Rd (19963-6418)
PHONE..............................302 424-2420
EMP: 8 **EST:** 1996
SALES (est): 508.43K **Privately Held**
Web: www.peoplesplace2.com
SIC: 8322 Social service center

(G-8122)
TWIN CREEK FARMS LLC
638 Canterbury Rd (19963-5328)
PHONE..............................302 249-2294
EMP: 5 **EST:** 2015
SALES (est): 229.46K **Privately Held**
SIC: 0119 7389 Cash grains, nec; Business Activities at Non-Commercial Site

(G-8123)
U HAUL CO INDEPENDENT DEALERS
Also Called: U-Haul
601 Marshall St (19963-2307)
PHONE..............................302 424-3189
Joe Wiley, *Owner*
Gerald Wiley, *Owner*
EMP: 5 **EST:** 2002
SALES (est): 322.43K **Privately Held**
Web: www.uhaul.com
SIC: 7513 Truck rental and leasing, no drivers

(G-8124)
U HAUL NEIGHBORHOOD DEALER
1001 E Masten Cir (19963-1205)
PHONE..............................302 393-2999
Jerry Hill, *Owner*
EMP: 8 **EST:** 2014
SALES (est): 95.84K **Privately Held**
Web: www.uhaul.com
SIC: 7513 Truck rental and leasing, no drivers

(G-8125)
U-HAUL NEIGHBORHOOD DEALER
340 Ne Front St (19963-1434)
PHONE..............................302 725-4525
EMP: 6 **EST:** 2018
SALES (est): 142.82K **Privately Held**
Web: www.uhaul.com
SIC: 7513 Truck rental and leasing, no drivers

(G-8126)
UNDER/COMM INC
198 Mullet Run (19963-5367)
P.O. Box 881 (19963-0881)
PHONE..............................302 424-1554
EMP: 15 **EST:** 1993
SQ FT: 480
SALES (est): 2.27MM **Privately Held**
Web: www.assurancemedia.com
SIC: 4813 Telephone communication, except radio

(G-8127)
UNITED STATES COLD STORAGE INC
Also Called: American Ice
419 Milford Harrington Hwy (19963)
P.O. Box 242 (19963-0242)
PHONE..............................302 422-7536
Ron Longhany, *Mgr*
EMP: 20
SALES (corp-wide): 17.24B **Privately Held**
Web: www.uscold.com
SIC: 4222 Warehousing, cold storage or refrigerated
HQ: United States Cold Storage, Inc.
2 Aquarium Dr Ste 400
Camden NJ 08103
856 354-8181

(G-8128)
UNITED STATES COLD STORAGE INC
P.O. Box 242 (19963-0242)
PHONE..............................302 422-7536
Ron Linghany, *Brnch Mgr*
EMP: 10
SALES (corp-wide): 17.24B **Privately Held**
Web: www.uscold.com
SIC: 4222 Warehousing, cold storage or refrigerated
HQ: United States Cold Storage, Inc.
2 Aquarium Dr Ste 400
Camden NJ 08103
856 354-8181

(G-8129)
UNITRACK INDUSTRIES INC
967 E Masten Cir (19963-1085)
PHONE..............................302 424-5050
Clayton Marchetti, *Pr*
EMP: 30 **EST:** 1937
SQ FT: 34,000
SALES (est): 1.69MM **Privately Held**
Web: www.unitrack.com
SIC: 8711 Engineering services

(G-8130)
UNITY PERSPECTIVES INC
702 North St (19963-2708)
P.O. Box 555 (19963-0555)
PHONE..............................302 265-2854
EMP: 9 **EST:** 2010
SALES (est): 104.77K **Privately Held**
Web: upi.unityperspectives.com
SIC: 8322 Individual and family services

(G-8131)
UPBOUND GROUP INC
Also Called: Rent-A-Center
678 N Dupont Blvd (19963-1002)
PHONE..............................302 422-1230
EMP: 5
Web: www.rentacenter.com
SIC: 7359 Appliance rental
PA: Upbound Group, Inc.
5501 Headquarters Dr
Plano TX 75024

(G-8132)
UPTOWN PET PAWS GROOMING
1001 N Walnut St (19963-1201)
PHONE..............................302 422-2229
Lori Baker, *Owner*
EMP: 5 **EST:** 2008
SALES (est): 77.76K **Privately Held**
SIC: 0752 Grooming services, pet and animal specialties

(G-8133)
USS DELAWARE
204 Charles St (19963-2037)
PHONE..............................908 910-4812
EMP: 7 **EST:** 2016
SALES (est): 97.16K **Privately Held**
Web: www.milfordlive.com
SIC: 8699 Membership organizations, nec

(G-8134)
VERIZON DELAWARE LLC
Also Called: Verizon
2 S Industrial Ln (19963-1080)
PHONE..............................302 422-1430
Janice Porter, *Genl Mgr*
EMP: 81
SALES (corp-wide): 133.97B **Publicly Held**
Web: www.delaware.gov
SIC: 4813 Telephone communication, except radio
HQ: Verizon Delaware Llc
901 N Tatnall St Fl 2
Wilmington DE 19801
302 571-1571

(G-8135)
VFW POST 6483
Also Called: VFW
77 Veterans Cir (19963-6352)
PHONE..............................302 422-4412
EMP: 7 **EST:** 2010
SALES (est): 230K **Privately Held**
SIC: 8641 Veterans' organization

(G-8136)
WAFL WYUS BROADCASTING INC
Also Called: Eagle 97.7 FM
1666 Blairs Pond Rd (19963-5263)
PHONE..............................302 422-7575
Melody Booker, *Pr*
EMP: 7 **EST:** 1981
SQ FT: 2,500
SALES (est): 121.51K **Privately Held**
Web: www.foreverdelmarva.com
SIC: 4832 Radio broadcasting stations

(G-8137)
WALLS FARM AND GARDEN CTR INC
833 S Dupont Blvd (19963-2232)
PHONE..............................302 422-4565
Robert E Walls, *Pr*
Robert B Walls, *General Vice President*
Bonnie Walls, *Treas*
Lisa Walls, *Sec*
EMP: 5 **EST:** 2000
SQ FT: 5,000
SALES (est): 1.19MM **Privately Held**
SIC: 5571 5012 5261 5719 All-terrain vehicles; Recreation vehicles, all-terrain; Lawnmowers and tractors; Fireplaces and wood burning stoves

(G-8138)
WALLS IRRIGATION INC (PA)
833 S Dupont Blvd (19963-2232)
PHONE..............................302 422-2262
EMP: 7 **EST:** 1996
SQ FT: 10,000
SALES (est): 3.48MM **Privately Held**
Web: www.wallsirrigation.com
SIC: 5083 Irrigation equipment

(G-8139)
WALLS SERVICE CENTER INC
220 Ne Front St (19963-1432)
PHONE..............................302 422-8110
Colin Walls, *Pr*
John W Walls Junior, *Pr*
EMP: 6 **EST:** 1956
SQ FT: 3,000
SALES (est): 970.44K **Privately Held**
Web: www.wallsservicecenter.com
SIC: 7537 7533 5541 Automotive transmission repair shops; Muffler shop, sale or repair and installation; Gasoline service stations

(G-8140)
WALSH CHIROPRACTIC CENTER
800 Airport Rd Ste 103 (19963-6469)
PHONE..............................302 422-0622
Lynn Walsh, *Owner*
EMP: 5 **EST:** 1981
SALES (est): 116.82K **Privately Held**
SIC: 8041 Offices and clinics of chiropractors

(G-8141)
WALTER SCOTT
606 Milford Harrington Hwy (19963)
PHONE..............................302 265-2383
Walter Scott, *Prin*
EMP: 8 **EST:** 2015
SALES (est): 68.93K **Privately Held**
SIC: 8021 Dentists' office

(G-8142)
WARFEL CONSTRUCTION CO INC
246 S Rehoboth Blvd (19963-1569)
PHONE..............................302 422-8927
Rob Warfel, *Pr*
Jay Schlabach, *
Weston Yutzy, *
EMP: 20 **EST:** 1972
SQ FT: 14,000
SALES (est): 1.35MM **Privately Held**
Web: www.warfelconstruction.com
SIC: 1521 1542 New construction, single-family houses; Farm building construction

(G-8143)
WATSONS AUCTION & REALTY SVC
Also Called: Re/Max Twin Counties
115 N Washington St (19963-1457)
PHONE..............................302 422-2392
EMP: 5 **EST:** 1993
SALES (est): 518.65K **Privately Held**
Web: www.remax.com
SIC: 6531 Real estate agent, residential

(G-8144)
WE CARE NEPHROLOGY LLC
100 Kings Hwy (19963-1812)
PHONE..............................302 242-0531
EMP: 6 **EST:** 2018
SALES (est): 170.86K **Privately Held**
Web: www.wecarenephrologydoc.com
SIC: 8011 Nephrologist

(G-8145)
WE CLEAN FOR A REASON
109 N Walnut St (19963-1447)
PHONE..............................302 930-0237
EMP: 5 **EST:** 2015
SALES (est): 64.1K **Privately Held**
SIC: 7699 Cleaning services

(G-8146)
WEBBIT
6200 Kirby Rd (19963-4146)
PHONE..............................302 725-6024
EMP: 5 **EST:** 2010
SALES (est): 181.77K **Privately Held**
SIC: 7379 Computer related consulting services

(G-8147)
WELLNESS HEALTH INC
Also Called: Wellness Health Center
106 Nw Front St (19963-1023)
P.O. Box 618132 (32861-8132)
PHONE..............................302 424-4100
Pierre Moise, *Owner*
EMP: 5 **EST:** 2013
SALES (est): 184.36K **Privately Held**
SIC: 8041 8049 Offices and clinics of chiropractors; Physical therapist

(G-8148)
WELLS FARMS INC
7481 Wells Rd (19963-4728)
PHONE..............................302 422-4732
EMP: 6 **EST:** 1981
SALES (est): 507.33K **Privately Held**
SIC: 0191 General farms, primarily crop

Milford - Sussex County (G-8149) GEOGRAPHIC SECTION

(G-8149)
WILKINS FUEL CO
701 S Washington St (19963-2305)
P.O. Box 167 (19963-0167)
PHONE......................302 422-5597
Howard C Wilkins Ii, *Pr*
Aileen Wilkins, *Sec*
EMP: 6 EST: 1947
SQ FT: 1,500
SALES (est): 944.19K **Privately Held**
Web: www.wilkinsfuel.com
SIC: 5983 1711 Fuel oil dealers; Heating systems repair and maintenance

(G-8150)
WILLIAM STELE WLDG FABRICATION
200 Mullet Run (19963-5372)
PHONE......................302 422-7444
Steele William, *Owner*
EMP: 4 EST: 2004
SALES (est): 300.54K **Privately Held**
Web: mobile.wmsteelewelding.comcastbiz.net
SIC: 7692 Welding repair

(G-8151)
WILLIAM T WADKINS GARAGE INC
Also Called: U-Save Auto
402 Ne Front St (19963-1436)
PHONE......................302 422-0265
William T Wadkins, *Pr*
EMP: 7 EST: 1987
SALES (est): 746.35K **Privately Held**
Web: wadkinsgarage.mechanicnet.com
SIC: 7538 General automotive repair shops

(G-8152)
WILSON FLEET & EQUIPMENT
961 E Masten Cir (19963-1085)
PHONE......................302 422-7159
Rick Wilson, *Pt*
EMP: 7 EST: 2000
SALES (est): 571.57K **Privately Held**
Web: www.wilsonfleetandequipment.com
SIC: 7549 Automotive services, nec

(G-8153)
WOMENS CENTER AT MILFORD MEML
200 Kings Hwy Ste 3 (19963-1854)
PHONE......................302 430-5540
John Stump, *Owner*
EMP: 8 EST: 2015
SALES (est): 61.7K **Privately Held**
SIC: 8011 Offices and clinics of medical doctors

(G-8154)
X SCREEN GRAPHIX
1514 Bay Rd (19963-6114)
P.O. Box 6 (19963-0006)
PHONE......................302 422-4550
Richard Dix, *Owner*
EMP: 2 EST: 1977
SALES (est): 120K **Privately Held**
SIC: 3993 Signs and advertising specialties

(G-8155)
YANKEE CLIPPERS HAIR DESIGNER
30 Nw 10th St Ste A (19963-1267)
PHONE......................302 422-2748
EMP: 5 EST: 1996
SALES (est): 86.64K **Privately Held**
SIC: 7231 Hairdressers

(G-8156)
ZARRAGA & ZARRAGA INTERNL MEDC
219 S Walnut St (19963-1957)
P.O. Box 258 (19963-0258)
PHONE......................302 422-9140
Antonio Zarraga, *Pr*
Cindy Zarraga, *VP*
EMP: 8 EST: 2000
SALES (est): 638.88K **Privately Held**
SIC: 8011 Infectious disease specialist, physician/surgeon

Millsboro
Sussex County

(G-8157)
A E MOORE INCORPORATED
25872 W State St (19966-1551)
P.O. Box 638 (19966-0638)
PHONE......................302 934-7055
Steve Kern, *Pr*
Tom White, *VP*
David Wharton, *Sec*
EMP: 15 EST: 1988
SQ FT: 10,000
SALES (est): 5.82MM **Privately Held**
Web: www.aemoorejanitorial.com
SIC: 5169 5113 5145 Specialty cleaning and sanitation preparations; Paper, wrapping or coarse, and products; Confectionery

(G-8158)
AAA TREE WORK LLC
28334 Wynikako Ave (19966-2529)
PHONE......................302 213-2917
EMP: 5 EST: 2005
SALES (est): 44.55K **Privately Held**
Web: www.aaatreework.com
SIC: 0783 Planting, pruning, and trimming services

(G-8159)
ABRAXAS MASSAGE AND BODYWORK
33010 Circle Dr (19966-4809)
PHONE......................910 992-0350
Carolyn Stewart, *Prin*
EMP: 6 EST: 2016
SALES (est): 41.29K **Privately Held**
SIC: 8049 Massage Therapist

(G-8160)
ABSOLUTELY FLAWLESS WOMEN INC
19845 Lowes Crossing Rd (19966-2953)
PHONE......................410 845-6930
EMP: 6
SALES (est): 52.77K **Privately Held**
Web: www.flawlesswomeninc.com
SIC: 8322 Individual and family services

(G-8161)
ACCESS QUALITY HEALTHCARE
32026 Long Neck Rd (19966-6228)
PHONE......................302 947-4437
Aaron Green, *Prin*
EMP: 5 EST: 2007
SALES (est): 258.07K **Privately Held**
Web: www.accessqualityhealthcare.com
SIC: 8099 Health and allied services, nec

(G-8162)
ACCORD RESTORATION INC
28368 John J Williams Hwy (19966-4005)
PHONE......................302 933-0991
Frank Nemshick, *Brnch Mgr*
EMP: 5
SALES (corp-wide): 5.43MM **Privately Held**
Web: www.accordrestoration.com
SIC: 1521 Repairing fire damage, single-family houses
PA: Accord Restoration, Inc.
4510 Paxton St Ste 100
Harrisburg PA 17111
302 933-0991

(G-8163)
AIR ONE HTG COOLING PROS
34712 Ringbolt Ave (19966-6167)
PHONE......................908 623-6154
EMP: 5 EST: 2019
SALES (est): 249.72K **Privately Held**
Web: www.aironepros.com
SIC: 1711 Warm air heating and air conditioning contractor

(G-8164)
ALL ABOUT PINK INC
28903 Harmons Hill Rd (19966-6419)
PHONE......................302 947-0309
Antionette Johnson, *Prin*
EMP: 10 EST: 2010
SALES (est): 111.12K **Privately Held**
SIC: 8052 Intermediate care facilities

(G-8165)
ALLEN BIOTECH LLC
Also Called: Allen Harim
29984 Pinnacle Way (19966)
P.O. Box 1380 (19966-5380)
PHONE......................302 629-9136
EMP: 1000 EST: 2011
SALES (est): 144.16MM
SALES (corp-wide): 345.31MM **Privately Held**
Web: www.allenharimllc.com
SIC: 2015 Poultry, processed, nsk
HQ: Allen Harim Foods, Llc
29984 Pinnacle Way
Millsboro DE 19966
302 629-9136

(G-8166)
ALLEN HARIM FARMS LLC
29984 Pinnacle Way (19966)
PHONE......................302 629-9136
EMP: 41 EST: 2011
SALES (est): 3.38MM **Privately Held**
Web: www.allenharimllc.com
SIC: 0751 Poultry services

(G-8167)
ALLEN HARIM FOODS LLC (HQ)
Also Called: Allen Harim
29984 Pinnacle Way (19966)
PHONE......................302 629-9136
Joe Moran, *Managing Member*
EMP: 40 EST: 2011
SALES (est): 144.16MM
SALES (corp-wide): 345.31MM **Privately Held**
Web: www.allenharimllc.com
SIC: 0251 Broiler, fryer, and roaster chickens
PA: Harim Usa, Ltd
126 N Shipley St
Seaford DE 19973
302 629-9136

(G-8168)
ALPHA ROOFING & SIDING INC
29758 Colonial Estates Ave (19966-4250)
PHONE......................302 249-2491
Jose Alvardo, *Prin*
EMP: 8 EST: 2021
SALES (est): 252.94K **Privately Held**
Web: www.alpharoofingde.com
SIC: 1761 Roofing contractor

(G-8169)
ALS FARE GREEN
98 Rudder Rd (19966-6665)
PHONE......................302 500-1871
Alvaro Perez, *Prin*
EMP: 7 EST: 2020
SALES (est): 242.38K **Privately Held**
Web: als-fare-green-landscaping-llc.business.site
SIC: 0781 Landscape services

(G-8170)
AMVETS POST 22
32369 Long Neck Rd Unit 18 (19966-6681)
PHONE......................302 945-2599
EMP: 6 EST: 2019
SALES (est): 194.37K **Privately Held**
SIC: 8641 Veterans' organization

(G-8171)
AQUIA INC
24408 Shady Ln (19966-4423)
PHONE......................530 215-7158
David Maskeroni, *CEO*
John Sasser, *COO*
EMP: 19 EST: 2021
SALES (est): 1.09MM **Privately Held**
Web: www.aquia.us
SIC: 7371 Computer software development

(G-8172)
AQUIA NAVA II LLC ◆
24408 Shady Ln (19966-4423)
PHONE......................410 245-8990
David Maskeroni, *Managing Member*
EMP: 35 EST: 2023
SALES (est): 1.03MM **Privately Held**
SIC: 7382 7389 Security systems services; Business Activities at Non-Commercial Site

(G-8173)
ARK OF REFUGE MISSION-SHELTER
29687 Millsboro Hwy (19966-3622)
PHONE......................302 381-2143
Larry R Joseph, *Prin*
EMP: 12 EST: 2010
SALES (est): 74.11K **Privately Held**
SIC: 7011 Hotels and motels

(G-8174)
ARK RECRUITING SOLUTIONS INC
27185 Barefoot Blvd (19966-7138)
PHONE......................302 947-1877
Anne F Knudsen, *Dir*
EMP: 5 EST: 2018
SALES (est): 184.06K **Privately Held**
Web: www.arkrecruiting.com
SIC: 7361 Executive placement

(G-8175)
ARMSTRONG PAINTING INC
25216 Harmony Woods Dr (19966-3784)
PHONE......................302 420-0415
Raymond Armstrong, *Prin*
EMP: 5 EST: 2018
SALES (est): 184.41K **Privately Held**
SIC: 1721 Painting and paper hanging

(G-8176)
ATI HOLDINGS LLC
Also Called: ATI Physical Therapy
28535 Dupont Blvd Unit 1 (19966-4799)
PHONE......................302 297-0700
Dave Pinkerton, *Dir*
EMP: 13
SALES (corp-wide): 635.67MM **Publicly Held**
Web: www.atipt.com
SIC: 8049 Physical therapist
HQ: Ati Holdings, Llc
790 Remington Blvd
Bolingbrook IL 60440

GEOGRAPHIC SECTION
Millsboro - Sussex County (G-8205)

(G-8177)
ATLANTIC CELLULAR
Also Called: Verizon Wreless Authorized Ret
31507 Trading Post Plz Unit 9
(19966-4873)
PHONE.............................302 945-3334
EMP: 6 **EST:** 2015
SALES (est): 67.67K **Privately Held**
Web: www.verizon.com
SIC: 4812 Cellular telephone services

(G-8178)
ATLANTIC PHYSCL THRAPY RHBLTTI
358 E Dupont Hwy (19966-1920)
PHONE.............................302 934-0304
EMP: 136
SIC: 8049 Physical therapist
PA: Atlantic Physical Therapy,
  Rehabilitation And Sports Medicine Inc.
  303 W Market St
  Snow Hill MD 21863

(G-8179)
BACK BAY PLUMBING
34140 Meadow Ln (19966-6360)
PHONE.............................302 945-1210
Craig Rahn, Owner
EMP: 7 **EST:** 2004
SALES (est): 254.02K **Privately Held**
SIC: 1711 Plumbing contractors

(G-8180)
BACK POWER SERVICE LLC
25252 Summer Rd (19966-3528)
PHONE.............................302 934-1901
EMP: 6 **EST:** 2020
SALES (est): 238.02K **Privately Held**
Web: www.powerbackllc.com
SIC: 1711 Plumbing, heating, air-conditioning

(G-8181)
BARRACUDA CARPENTRY LLC
9 Nelsa Ln (19966-8911)
PHONE.............................302 415-1588
Robert Buckley, Prin
EMP: 5 **EST:** 2016
SALES (est): 53.36K **Privately Held**
SIC: 1751 Carpentry work

(G-8182)
BARSGR LLC
Also Called: Holly Lake Campsite
32087 Holly Lake Rd (19966-4472)
P.O. Box 141 (19966-0141)
PHONE.............................302 945-3410
Kenny Hopkins, Mgr
EMP: 16
SALES (corp-wide): 776.43K **Privately Held**
Web: www.hollylakecampsites.com
SIC: 7033 Campsite
PA: Barsgr Llc
  32193 Winery Way
  Lewes DE 19958
  302 645-6665

(G-8183)
BAYNUM ENTERPRISES INC
Also Called: T/A Pizza King
28632 Dupont Blvd Unit 20 (19966-4793)
PHONE.............................302 934-8699
EMP: 34
SALES (corp-wide): 9.15MM **Privately Held**
Web: www.pizzakingde.com
SIC: 5812 6514 Pizza restaurants; Dwelling operators, except apartments
PA: Baynum Enterprises, Inc.
  300 W Stein Hwy
  Seaford DE 19973
  302 629-6104

(G-8184)
BAYSIDE FITNESS
24784 Shoreline Dr (19966-7201)
PHONE.............................302 231-8982
Melissa Whitman, Prin
EMP: 7 **EST:** 2017
SALES (est): 79.19K **Privately Held**
Web: www.baysidefitness.org
SIC: 7991 Health club

(G-8185)
BAYSIDE LIMOUSINE
34026 Annas Way Unit 1 (19966-3213)
PHONE.............................302 644-6999
Tyrone Gale, Pr
Tyrone Gale, Prin
EMP: 10 **EST:** 2006
SALES (est): 349.88K **Privately Held**
SIC: 4119 Limousine rental, with driver

(G-8186)
BAYWOOD GREENS GOLF CLUB
24 Ofc Rt (19966)
PHONE.............................302 947-9225
Robert Tunnell Junior, Brnch Mgr
EMP: 31
SALES (corp-wide): 1.87MM **Privately Held**
Web: www.baywoodgreens.com
SIC: 7992 5941 5812 Public golf courses; Golf goods and equipment; Eating places
PA: Baywood Greens Golf Club
  32267 Clubhouse Way
  Millsboro DE 19966
  302 947-9800

(G-8187)
BAYWOOD GREENS GOLF CLUB (PA)
32267 Clubhouse Way (19966-6259)
PHONE.............................302 947-9800
Robert Tunnell Junior, Pr
EMP: 7 **EST:** 1998
SALES: 1.87MM
SALES (corp-wide): 1.87MM **Privately Held**
Web: www.baywoodgreens.com
SIC: 7992 Public golf courses

(G-8188)
BAYWOOD GREENS GOLF MNTNC
25258 Banks Rd (19966-7403)
PHONE.............................757 460-5584
Warren Golde, Dir
EMP: 8 **EST:** 1948
SALES (est): 111.47K **Privately Held**
Web: www.baywoodgreens.com
SIC: 7992 Public golf courses

(G-8189)
BEACH MOBILE HOME SUPPLY
32695 Long Neck Rd Unit 1 (19966-6693)
P.O. Box 361 (19966-0361)
PHONE.............................302 945-5611
EMP: 4 **EST:** 2019
SALES (est): 79.98K **Privately Held**
Web: www.brasssalesinc.com
SIC: 3585 Refrigeration and heating equipment

(G-8190)
BECKS MASONRY
26395 W Pintail Rd (19966-5836)
PHONE.............................302 231-5485
Thomas Beckham, Prin
EMP: 6 **EST:** 2010
SALES (est): 177.82K **Privately Held**
SIC: 1741 Masonry and other stonework

(G-8191)
BEEBE HEALTHCARE
28538 Dupont Blvd Unit 2 (19966-4791)
PHONE.............................302 934-5052
EMP: 10 **EST:** 2019
SALES (est): 980.7K **Privately Held**
Web: www.beebehealthcare.org
SIC: 8062 General medical and surgical hospitals

(G-8192)
BEEBE LAB EXPRESS MILLBORO
28538 Dupont Blvd Unit 2 (19966-4791)
PHONE.............................302 934-5052
EMP: 17 **EST:** 2007
SALES (est): 187.97K **Privately Held**
SIC: 8062 General medical and surgical hospitals

(G-8193)
BEEBE MEDICAL CENTER INC
Long Neck Rd (19966)
PHONE.............................302 947-9767
EMP: 26
SALES (corp-wide): 581.97MM **Privately Held**
Web: www.beebehealthcare.org
SIC: 8062 General medical and surgical hospitals
PA: Beebe Medical Center, Inc.
  424 Savannah Rd
  Lewes DE 19958
  302 645-3300

(G-8194)
BENNIE SMITH FUNERAL HOME INC
216 S Washington St (19966-8426)
PHONE.............................302 934-9019
Bennie Smith, Mgr
EMP: 6
Web: www.benniesmithfuneralhome.com
SIC: 7261 Funeral director
PA: Bennie Smith Funeral Home, Inc.
  717 W Division St
  Dover DE 19904

(G-8195)
BEST VETERINARY SOLUTIONS INC
1381 Northern Ave (19966-3875)
PHONE.............................302 934-1109
Kenny Hawkins, Mgr
EMP: 19
SALES (corp-wide): 11.12MM **Privately Held**
Web: www.bestvetsolutions.com
SIC: 2048 Feed premixes
PA: Best Veterinary Solutions, Inc.
  1716 Detroit St
  Ellsworth IA 50075
  515 836-4001

(G-8196)
BETHANY TRAVEL INC
Also Called: Dream Vacations
28436 Dupont Blvd (19966-1226)
PHONE.............................302 933-0955
EMP: 5 **EST:** 1996
SQ FT: 800
SALES (est): 874.3K **Privately Held**
Web: www.bethanytravel.net
SIC: 4724 Travel agencies

(G-8197)
BINGNEAR CLEANING
26034 Redwing Ln (19966-6968)
PHONE.............................302 519-7318
Linda Bingnear, Prin
EMP: 5 **EST:** 2017
SALES (est): 49.62K **Privately Held**
SIC: 7699 Cleaning services

(G-8198)
BIOCHEK USA CORP
109 Woodland Way (19966-1516)
PHONE.............................302 521-5554
EMP: 5 **EST:** 2017
SALES (est): 54.83K **Privately Held**
Web: www.biochek.com
SIC: 8734 Testing laboratories

(G-8199)
BLAIR CARMEAN & SONS MASONRY
26624 Gravel Hill Rd (19966-3418)
PHONE.............................302 249-5783
Blair Carmean, Prin
EMP: 7 **EST:** 2017
SALES (est): 418.53K **Privately Held**
SIC: 1741 Masonry and other stonework

(G-8200)
BLUE HEN BZZRDS DSPOSE-ALL INC
34026 Annas Way Unit 3 (19966-3213)
PHONE.............................302 945-3500
Shannon Argo, Pr
EMP: 50 **EST:** 2010
SALES (est): 19MM **Privately Held**
Web: www.bluehendisposal.com
SIC: 4953 Recycling, waste materials

(G-8201)
BLUE MASSAGE
28408 Dupont Blvd (19966-4776)
PHONE.............................302 934-7378
EMP: 5 **EST:** 2016
SALES (est): 30.51K **Privately Held**
SIC: 7299 Massage parlor

(G-8202)
BOWDEN LANDSCAPING
25831 Gravel Hill Rd (19966-3421)
PHONE.............................302 934-6567
William Valeria Bowden, Prin
EMP: 5 **EST:** 2011
SALES (est): 116.13K **Privately Held**
Web: www.bowdenslawnlandscapect.com
SIC: 0782 Landscape contractors

(G-8203)
BOYS AND GIRLS
32615 Oak Orchard Rd # 3 (19966-4886)
PHONE.............................302 947-4600
EMP: 5 **EST:** 2017
SALES (est): 49.99K **Privately Held**
SIC: 8641 Youth organizations

(G-8204)
BRADLEYLEMONDPM LEMON
28253 Dupont Blvd (19966-1223)
PHONE.............................302 934-7100
EMP: 6 **EST:** 2016
SALES (est): 68.03K **Privately Held**
SIC: 8043 Offices and clinics of podiatrists

(G-8205)
BREAKWATER CONSTRUCTION ENVMTL
4 Chief Joseph Trl (19966-2018)
PHONE.............................302 945-5800
John Fink, Pr
Shaun Fink, VP
EMP: 20 **EST:** 2016
SALES (est): 2.43MM **Privately Held**
SIC: 1629 Athletic and recreation facilities construction

Millsboro - Sussex County (G-8206)

(G-8206)
BRICK HOTEL ON THE CIRCLE
32344 River Rd (19966-2550)
PHONE..................302 745-0115
Lynn Lester, *Prin*
EMP: 14 EST: 2017
SALES (est): 243.36K **Privately Held**
SIC: 7011 Hotels

(G-8207)
BRIDGESTONE CON & MASNRY LLC
24242 Kent Dr (19966-3631)
PHONE..................302 462-5422
William Hardy, *Prin*
EMP: 5 EST: 2016
SALES (est): 104.79K **Privately Held**
SIC: 1771 Concrete work

(G-8208)
BRIGHT BGNNNGS CHILD CARE CTR
29753 John J Williams Hwy (19966-3921)
PHONE..................302 934-1249
Catlina Bright, *Prin*
EMP: 5 EST: 2015
SALES (est): 245.92K **Privately Held**
SIC: 8351 Group day care center

(G-8209)
BROWN ELECTRICAL SERVICES LLC
28881 Harmons Hill Rd (19966-6418)
PHONE..................302 245-4593
EMP: 6 EST: 2012
SALES (est): 75.61K **Privately Held**
Web: www.brown-electrical.com
SIC: 1731 General electrical contractor

(G-8210)
BURTON REALTY INC
24808 John J Williams Hwy (19966-4983)
PHONE..................302 945-5100
Kathrine Louheed, *Pr*
EMP: 5 EST: 1994
SALES (est): 279.36K **Privately Held**
Web: www.burtonrealtyinc.com
SIC: 6531 Real estate agent, commercial

(G-8211)
BWB INC
24115 Cari Dr (19966-4442)
P.O. Box 7582 (17113-0582)
PHONE..................717 939-3679
John G Slabonik, *Pr*
Joseph Reagen, *Asst Tr*
Matthew Slabonik, *VP*
Greg Sholly, *VP*
EMP: 13 EST: 1968
SALES (est): 447.79K **Privately Held**
Web: www.bwbdemolition.com
SIC: 1794 Excavation and grading, building construction

(G-8212)
BY THE SEA CONTRACTING LLC
32641 W Carteret Ct (19966-4828)
PHONE..................302 569-9701
Mark Holmes, *Prin*
EMP: 5 EST: 2017
SALES (est): 109.95K **Privately Held**
SIC: 1799 Special trade contractors, nec

(G-8213)
C & C CONTRACTORS LLC
11 Beacon Cir (19966-8709)
PHONE..................302 934-1134
Charles S Herrmann, *Prin*
EMP: 5 EST: 2010
SALES (est): 63.64K **Privately Held**
SIC: 1799 Special trade contractors, nec

(G-8214)
CADIA REHABILITATION RNSSNC
26002 John J Williams Hwy (19966-4948)
PHONE..................302 947-4200
Janet Mahoney, *Prin*
EMP: 10 EST: 2016
SALES (est): 228.71K **Privately Held**
Web: www.cadiahealthcare.com
SIC: 8331 Job training and related services

(G-8215)
CANDLELIGHT BRIDAL FORMAL TLRG
314 Main St (19966-8414)
P.O. Box 777 (19966-0777)
PHONE..................302 934-8009
Hope T Mitchell, *Pt*
Julia R Cornell, *Pt*
EMP: 6 EST: 1987
SQ FT: 1,800
SALES (est): 499.83K **Privately Held**
Web: www.candlelightbridalandformal.com
SIC: 5699 7219 7299 Formal wear; Tailor shop, except custom or merchant tailor; Clothing rental services

(G-8216)
CARROLL BROTHERS ELECTRIC LLC
24853 Rivers Edge Rd (19966-7217)
PHONE..................302 947-4754
John Ehartshorn, *Prin*
EMP: 5 EST: 2011
SALES (est): 142.88K **Privately Held**
Web: www.elitevehicle.com
SIC: 4911 Electric services

(G-8217)
CEDAR TREE SURGICAL CENTER
32711 Long Neck Rd (19966-6678)
PHONE..................302 945-9766
Barbara Campilano, *Dir*
EMP: 22 EST: 2006
SALES (est): 482.36K **Privately Held**
SIC: 8062 General medical and surgical hospitals

(G-8218)
CELLCO PARTNERSHIP
Also Called: Verizon Wireless
26676 Centerview Dr (19966-3750)
PHONE..................302 933-0514
EMP: 14
SALES (corp-wide): 133.97B **Publicly Held**
Web: www.verizonwireless.com
SIC: 4812 Cellular telephone services
HQ: Cellco Partnership
   1 Verizon Way
   Basking Ridge NJ 07920

(G-8219)
CGM REPAIR
22638 Bethel Rd (19966-3134)
PHONE..................302 344-4222
Charles Marnati, *Owner*
EMP: 5 EST: 2017
SALES (est): 68.18K **Privately Held**
SIC: 7699 Repair services, nec

(G-8220)
CHESAPAKE SLVER CRNET BRASS BA
Also Called: Chesapeake Brass Band
23674 Samuel Adams Cir (19966-8204)
PHONE..................302 530-2915
Richard B Fischer, *Pr*
Robert Warren Campbell, *VP*
EMP: 5 EST: 2003
SALES (est): 51.07K **Privately Held**
Web: www.chesapeakebrassband.org
SIC: 7929 Orchestras or bands, nec

(G-8221)
CHILDRENS PLACE CHILD DEV CE
32362 Long Neck Rd (19966-9062)
PHONE..................302 947-4808
EMP: 10 EST: 2015
SALES (est): 23.38K **Privately Held**
SIC: 8351 Child day care services

(G-8222)
CHIMES INC
28393 Dupont Blvd (19966-4789)
PHONE..................302 934-1450
Darrin Sheppard, *Ofcr*
EMP: 8 EST: 2018
SALES (est): 102.32K **Privately Held**
Web: www.chimes.org
SIC: 8322 Individual and family services

(G-8223)
CHIP VICKIO
30845 Phillips Branch Rd (19966-6405)
PHONE..................302 448-0211
EMP: 9 EST: 2018
SALES (est): 70.56K **Privately Held**
SIC: 2741 Miscellaneous publishing

(G-8224)
CHRISTOPHER BURKE
20766 Brunswick Ln (19966-7553)
PHONE..................410 603-7450
Christopher Burke, *Prin*
EMP: 6 EST: 2017
SALES (est): 24.4K **Privately Held**
SIC: 8049 Offices of health practitioner

(G-8225)
CHRISTOPHER HANDY
Also Called: Handy Man Maintenance
24872 Doe Bridge Ln (19966-1670)
PHONE..................302 934-1018
Christopher Handy, *Prin*
EMP: 6 EST: 2011
SALES (est): 86.85K **Privately Held**
SIC: 7349 Building maintenance services, nec

(G-8226)
CHUCK HALL AGT
29787 John J Williams Hwy (19966-4097)
PHONE..................302 934-8083
Chuck Hall, *Prin*
EMP: 6 EST: 2017
SALES (est): 154.62K **Privately Held**
Web: www.chuckhallinsurance.com
SIC: 6411 Insurance agents and brokers

(G-8227)
CHUDASAMA ENTERPRISES LLC (PA)
Also Called: Best Value Inn
521 W Dupont Hwy (19966-1712)
PHONE..................302 934-7968
G C Chudafama, *Managing Member*
Gharmbhirsinh C Chudafama, *Managing Member*
EMP: 5 EST: 1957
SQ FT: 7,000
SALES (est): 441.83K
SALES (corp-wide): 441.83K **Privately Held**
Web: www.redlion.com
SIC: 7011 Hotels and motels

(G-8228)
CIFUENTES LANDSCAPING LLC
29314 Ed Morris Ln (19966-3983)
PHONE..................302 344-8108
Adler Cifuentes, *Prin*
EMP: 5 EST: 2017
SALES (est): 30.5K **Privately Held**
SIC: 0781 Landscape services

(G-8229)
CLAUDIO M MOREL
31309 Olney Way (19966-1815)
PHONE..................917 584-5236
Claudio M Morel, *Prin*
EMP: 6 EST: 2015
SALES (est): 68.62K **Privately Held**
SIC: 8049 Offices of health practitioner

(G-8230)
CLEARBLUE POOLS & SPAS LLC
26046 Matthews St (19966-3599)
PHONE..................888 630-7665
Alia Abrams, *Managing Member*
EMP: 10
SALES (est): 628.58K **Privately Held**
Web: www.bestpoolcompany.com
SIC: 5091 7389 Swimming pools, equipment and supplies; Business services, nec

(G-8231)
COASTAL CARE & DERMATOLOGY LLC
230 Mitchell St Ste B (19966-9402)
PHONE..................302 542-4999
EMP: 10 EST: 2016
SALES (est): 400.07K **Privately Held**
SIC: 8011 Dermatologist

(G-8232)
COASTAL CLEANING SERVICES INC
24832 John J Williams Hwy (19966-4997)
PHONE..................302 858-8857
Nicole Finney, *Prin*
EMP: 9 EST: 2007
SALES (est): 76.39K **Privately Held**
SIC: 7349 Building cleaning service

(G-8233)
COASTAL COUNSELING LLC
330 Blossom Way (19966-4287)
P.O. Box 1741 (19966-5741)
PHONE..................302 542-4271
Florence White, *Prin*
EMP: 6 EST: 2018
SALES (est): 47.71K **Privately Held**
SIC: 8322 General counseling services

(G-8234)
COASTAL TILE AND HARDWOOD
28509 Ok Waw Ave (19966-2507)
PHONE..................302 339-7772
Jason Condit, *Prin*
EMP: 5 EST: 2018
SALES (est): 54.48K **Privately Held**
SIC: 1743 Tile installation, ceramic

(G-8235)
COFFEE ARTISAN LLC
718 Phillips Hill Dr (19966-1764)
PHONE..................302 297-8800
◆ EMP: 2 EST: 2008
SALES (est): 180.36K **Privately Held**
SIC: 3589 Coffee brewing equipment

(G-8236)
COLDWELL BANKER RESORT REALTY
100 White Pine Dr (19966-8749)
PHONE..................302 645-2881

▲ = Import ▼ = Export
◆ = Import/Export

GEOGRAPHIC SECTION
Millsboro - Sussex County (G-8267)

Joanie Hannigan, *Prin*
EMP: 7 **EST:** 2015
SALES (est): 97.81K **Privately Held**
Web: www.cbanker.com
SIC: 6531 Real estate agent, residential

(G-8237)
COMPLETE TREE CARE INC
Also Called: Complete Lawn Care
30598 Cordrey Rd (19966-4041)
PHONE..................302 945-8289
Dan Atkinson, *Pr*
EMP: 6 **EST:** 2006
SALES (est): 703.82K **Privately Held**
Web: www.completetreecarede.com
SIC: 0783 Planting, pruning, and trimming services

(G-8238)
CONTRACTOR MASONARY
30983 Phillips Branch Rd (19966-6403)
PHONE..................302 945-1930
EMP: 5 **EST:** 2008
SALES (est): 82.36K **Privately Held**
SIC: 1741 Masonry and other stonework

(G-8239)
CORDREY CHARITIES INC
70 Creek Dr (19966-9679)
PHONE..................302 945-5855
EMP: 7 **EST:** 2019
SALES (est): 171.63K **Privately Held**
Web: www.eastcoastgardencenter.com
SIC: 0191 General farms, primarily crop

(G-8240)
COSMIC CUSTOM SCREEN PRINTING
Also Called: COSMIC CUSTOM SCREEN PRINTING
28116 John J Williams Hwy (19966-4002)
PHONE..................302 933-0920
EMP: 2
Web: www.logomotivede.com
SIC: 2759 Screen printing
PA: Cosmic Custom Screen Printing Llc
935 S Black Horse Pike
Williamstown NJ 08094

(G-8241)
COUNTRYSIDE MASONRY LLC
28248 Cannon St (19966-2588)
PHONE..................302 945-5642
Frank Miller, *Prin*
EMP: 5 **EST:** 2014
SALES (est): 93.21K **Privately Held**
SIC: 1741 Masonry and other stonework

(G-8242)
COUNTY BANK
25933 School Ln (19966-6265)
PHONE..................302 947-7300
Kathy Coffin, *Brnch Mgr*
EMP: 7
Web: www.countybankdel.com
SIC: 6022 State commercial banks
PA: County Bank
19927 Shuttle Rd
Rehoboth Beach DE 19971

(G-8243)
COUNTY OF SUSSEX
Inland Bays Rgnal Wstwter Fclt
29445 Inland Bay Rd (19966-2632)
PHONE..................302 947-0864
Justin Mitchell, *Dist Mgr*
EMP: 13
SALES (corp-wide): 106.35MM **Privately Held**
Web: www.sussexcountyde.gov

SIC: 4971 Water distribution or supply systems for irrigation
PA: County Of Sussex
2 The Cir
Georgetown DE 19947
302 855-7700

(G-8244)
CRESTVIEW SERVICES LLC
26212 Tucks Rd (19966-4962)
PHONE..................302 569-4909
EMP: 5 **EST:** 2019
SALES (est): 232.48K **Privately Held**
Web: crestview-services-llc.business.site
SIC: 1799 Special trade contractors, nec

(G-8245)
CROSSROADS LAND TECH LLC
34364 Fox Hound Ln (19966-2932)
PHONE..................302 841-0654
Ray Ellis, *Prin*
EMP: 11 **EST:** 2017
SALES (est): 876.08K **Privately Held**
Web: www.crossroadslandtech.com
SIC: 1521 Single-family housing construction

(G-8246)
CRYSTAL CLEAN
22235 Westwoods Rd (19966-3035)
PHONE..................302 864-4032
Crystal Baldwin, *Prin*
EMP: 9 **EST:** 2018
SALES (est): 44.72K **Privately Held**
Web: www.crystal-clean.com
SIC: 7699 Cleaning services

(G-8247)
CTM MEDICAL ASSOCIATES LLC
32711 Long Neck Rd (19966-6678)
PHONE..................302 945-9730
EMP: 19
SALES (corp-wide): 145.3K **Privately Held**
SIC: 8011 Offices and clinics of medical doctors
PA: Ctm Medical Associates Llc
109 Heronwood Dr
Milton DE 19968
302 645-8587

(G-8248)
CW MOBILE AUTOMOTIVE REPA
26693 Jersey Rd (19966-3902)
PHONE..................302 663-0035
EMP: 6 **EST:** 2014
SALES (est): 55.05K **Privately Held**
SIC: 7538 General automotive repair shops

(G-8249)
CYNTHIA R DREW NP
28467 Dupont Blvd Unit 6 (19966-3749)
PHONE..................302 933-0111
Cynthia Drew, *Ofcr*
EMP: 6 **EST:** 2017
SALES (est): 72.1K **Privately Held**
SIC: 8049 Offices of health practitioner

(G-8250)
CZAPP MASONRY INC
36171 Victory Ln (19966-3001)
PHONE..................302 238-7007
EMP: 5 **EST:** 2011
SALES (est): 112.36K **Privately Held**
SIC: 1741 Masonry and other stonework

(G-8251)
D & F BUSSING INC
231 Laurel Rd (19966-1732)
PHONE..................302 934-9461
C Dlingo, *Prin*
EMP: 5 **EST:** 2012

SALES (est): 245.42K **Privately Held**
SIC: 7389 Business services, nec

(G-8252)
D S AUTO
23108 Country Living Rd (19966-2844)
PHONE..................302 542-3023
David Smith, *Mgr*
EMP: 6 **EST:** 2014
SALES (est): 121.49K **Privately Held**
SIC: 7538 General automotive repair shops

(G-8253)
DANIEL A KINSLER
Also Called: Kinsler Electrical
28426 Wynikako Ave (19966-2528)
PHONE..................302 947-9790
Angela Kinsler, *Prin*
EMP: 7 **EST:** 2011
SALES (est): 119.69K **Privately Held**
SIC: 1731 Electrical work

(G-8254)
DAVID DUKES
29622 Dirt Ln (19966-4243)
PHONE..................302 841-9481
David Dukes, *Prin*
EMP: 5 **EST:** 2012
SALES (est): 161.7K **Privately Held**
SIC: 1522 Residential construction, nec

(G-8255)
DAVID G MAJOR ASSOCIATES INC
Also Called: Ci Centre
30165 Ethan Allen Ct (19966-8300)
PHONE..................703 642-7450
EMP: 5 **EST:** 1997
SALES (est): 419.95K **Privately Held**
SIC: 8742 Training and development consultant

(G-8256)
DAVID M SHOWALTER
4 Scott Dr (19966-1321)
PHONE..................302 462-5264
David M Showalter, *Prin*
EMP: 5 **EST:** 2009
SALES (est): 176.04K **Privately Held**
SIC: 1522 Residential construction, nec

(G-8257)
DAVID V MARTINI MD
32711 Long Neck Rd (19966-6678)
PHONE..................302 945-9730
David Martini, *Owner*
EMP: 9 **EST:** 2017
SALES (est): 135.25K **Privately Held**
SIC: 8011 Offices and clinics of medical doctors

(G-8258)
DEBORRA M TRRES MSN PMHNP LTD
32853 Circle Dr (19966-4810)
PHONE..................609 500-4018
Deborra M Torres, *Prin*
EMP: 6 **EST:** 2012
SALES (est): 66.19K **Privately Held**
SIC: 8049 Nurses, registered and practical

(G-8259)
DEL COAST EXTERIORS
35430 Sussex Ln (19966-5881)
PHONE..................302 542-8979
Tyrone Romano Junior, *Prin*
EMP: 5 **EST:** 2017
SALES (est): 88.38K **Privately Held**
Web: www.dcexteriorsandrenovationllc.com

SIC: 1761 Roofing contractor

(G-8260)
DELAWARE CON FNDTONS SLABS LLC
31241 Barnacle Blvd (19966-7305)
PHONE..................302 945-1223
EMP: 7 **EST:** 2010
SALES (est): 450.94K **Privately Held**
SIC: 8641 Civic and social associations

(G-8261)
DELAWARE HOME VALUATIONS PA
305 Laurel Rd (19966-1733)
PHONE..................302 933-8607
Michael Marino, *Prin*
EMP: 5 **EST:** 2017
SALES (est): 92.98K **Privately Held**
Web: www.delawarehomeappraiser.com
SIC: 8621 Professional organizations

(G-8262)
DELAWARE HOSPICE
315 Old Landing Rd Unit 1 (19966-1210)
PHONE..................302 934-9018
Sandy Farrell, *Admn*
EMP: 20 **EST:** 2007
SALES (est): 326.78K **Privately Held**
Web: www.delawarehospice.org
SIC: 8052 Personal care facility

(G-8263)
DELAWARE MOBILE SIGNINGS LLC
Also Called: DELAWARE MOBILE SIGNINGS
26976 Bethesda Rd (19966-1680)
PHONE..................302 316-3926
Marcia Boyer, *CEO*
EMP: 5 **EST:** 2020
SALES (est): 69.34K **Privately Held**
SIC: 7389 7299 7381 Notary publics; Wedding consultant; Fingerprint service

(G-8264)
DELAWARE SURF FISHING LLC
25728 Whispering Wind Ln (19966-2603)
PHONE..................302 296-7812
Rich King, *Prin*
EMP: 6 **EST:** 2019
SALES (est): 60.12K **Privately Held**
Web: www.delaware-surf-fishing.com
SIC: 7999 Fishing boats, party: operation

(G-8265)
DELCO MODULAR
23581 Godwin School Rd (19966-2857)
PHONE..................302 934-7704
EMP: 5 **EST:** 2018
SALES (est): 114.19K **Privately Held**
SIC: 7389 Design services

(G-8266)
DELMARVA COASTAL CNSTR LLC
28464 Nanticoke Ave (19966-2519)
PHONE..................302 259-5593
Michael Marciano Junior, *Managing Member*
EMP: 6 **EST:** 2020
SALES (est): 545.72K **Privately Held**
SIC: 1751 Carpentry work

(G-8267)
DELMARVA SERVICES
28528 Warwick Rd (19966-4019)
PHONE..................302 934-8750
EMP: 5 **EST:** 2012
SALES (est): 486.58K **Privately Held**
SIC: 4923 Gas transmission and distribution

Millsboro - Sussex County (G-8268) GEOGRAPHIC SECTION

(G-8268)
DELMARVA SHORE MAINTENANCE
35487 Skipjack Ln (19966-6865)
PHONE..................302 519-8657
Anthony Wesley, *Prin*
EMP: 5 **EST:** 2016
SALES (est): 60.42K **Privately Held**
SIC: 7349 Building maintenance services, nec

(G-8269)
DELMARVA SPACE SCNCES FNDATION
Also Called: Dssf
10046 Iron Pointe Drive Ext (19966-4264)
PHONE..................302 236-2761
Michael Potter, *Prin*
Bob Lingo, *Pr*
Ryan Goodwin, *Prin*
Jeff Geidel, *Prin*
Jeremy Kirkendall, *Prin*
EMP: 5 **EST:** 2017
SALES (est): 107.29K **Privately Held**
Web: www.delmarvaspace.org
SIC: 8641 Civic and social associations

(G-8270)
DENNEY ELECTRIC SUPPLY DEL INC
Also Called: Denney Electric Supply
28635 Dupont Blvd (19966-4784)
PHONE..................302 934-8885
John Mccormick, *Pr*
Mark Mccormick, *Treas*
EMP: 9 **EST:** 1984
SQ FT: 12,000
SALES (est): 11.9MM **Privately Held**
Web: www.denneyelectric.com
SIC: 5063 5999 5719 Electrical supplies, nec; Electronic parts and equipment; Lighting fixtures

(G-8271)
DIAMOND STATE CABINETRY
32627 Millsboro Hwy (19966-3010)
PHONE..................302 250-3531
EMP: 5 **EST:** 2012
SALES (est): 109.6K **Privately Held**
Web: www.diamondstatecabinetry.com
SIC: 2434 Wood kitchen cabinets

(G-8272)
DIVERSE SUPPLY SOLUTIONS LLC
35486 Bayview Ln (19966-6957)
PHONE..................215 588-8300
Kathleen Gorman, *CEO*
EMP: 5 **EST:** 2018
SALES (est): 453.3K **Privately Held**
Web: www.diversesupplysolutions.net
SIC: 5099 Durable goods, nec

(G-8273)
DO IT UP DESIGNS LLC
27569 Mayfield Rd (19966-7041)
PHONE..................484 269-6142
EMP: 5
SALES (est): 373.88K **Privately Held**
SIC: 1389 7389 Construction, repair, and dismantling services; Business Activities at Non-Commercial Site

(G-8274)
DONALD GREBE
31790 Schooner Dr (19966-4531)
PHONE..................302 945-7975
Donald Grebe, *Prin*
EMP: 5 **EST:** 2005
SALES (est): 163.43K **Privately Held**
Web: www.dongrebeconstruction.com
SIC: 1522 Residential construction, nec

(G-8275)
DONAWAY CORPORATION (PA)
Also Called: Donaway Service Station
Route 24 (19966)
PHONE..................302 934-6226
Bart Donaway, *Pr*
EMP: 8 **EST:** 1980
SALES (est): 992.04K
SALES (corp-wide): 992.04K **Privately Held**
Web: www.donawayhomes.com
SIC: 7692 7538 Automotive welding; General automotive repair shops

(G-8276)
DOROSHOW PSQALE KRWITZ SGEL BH
Also Called: Doroshow Pasquale Law Offices
28535 Dupont Blvd Unit 2 (19966-4799)
PHONE..................302 934-9400
Debra Aldrich, *Mgr*
EMP: 12
SQ FT: 2,194
SALES (corp-wide): 9.95MM **Privately Held**
Web: www.dplaw.com
SIC: 8111 General practice attorney, lawyer
PA: Doroshow Pasquale Krawitz Siegel Bhaya
1202 Kirkwood Hwy
Wilmington DE 19805
302 998-2397

(G-8277)
DOUBLE DIAMONE BUILDERS INC
25187 Banks Rd (19966-4482)
PHONE..................302 945-2512
Brandee East, *Pr*
EMP: 10 **EST:** 2005
SALES (est): 948.33K **Privately Held**
SIC: 1521 New construction, single-family houses

(G-8278)
E&A DRYWALL AND PAINTING INC ◊
27324 John J Williams Hwy (19966-4033)
PHONE..................302 393-1743
Amalia Rodriguez, *Pr*
EMP: 5 **EST:** 2022
SALES (est): 307.98K **Privately Held**
SIC: 1721 7389 Painting and paper hanging; Business Activities at Non-Commercial Site

(G-8279)
EAST COAST COMPUTER CONS
295 Pond Rd (19966-9538)
PHONE..................302 945-5089
Mike Phoebus, *Owner*
EMP: 6 **EST:** 2012
SALES (est): 74.8K **Privately Held**
SIC: 8742 Management consulting services

(G-8280)
EDWARD A FUFARO INC
29728 Springwood Dr (19966-2892)
PHONE..................302 934-6595
Edward A Fufaro, *Prin*
EMP: 5 **EST:** 2005
SALES (est): 49.65K **Privately Held**
SIC: 0851 Forestry services

(G-8281)
EMPIRE DATA VOICE NETWORKS LLC
30851 Fowlers Path (19966-7316)
PHONE..................702 613-4900
Yasir Mccarroll, *Pr*
Yasir Mccarroll, *Managing Member*
EMP: 2 **EST:** 2016
SALES (est): 54.38K **Privately Held**
SIC: 7371 1389 7349 7299 Custom computer programming services; Construction, repair, and dismantling services; Cleaning service, industrial or commercial; Information services, consumer

(G-8282)
ENTERPRISE RENT-A-CAR
Also Called: Enterprise Rent-A-Car
28656 Dupont Blvd (19966-4794)
PHONE..................302 934-1216
EMP: 5 **EST:** 2018
SALES (est): 122.18K **Privately Held**
Web: www.enterprise.com
SIC: 7514 Rent-a-car service

(G-8283)
ERIC M DOROSHOW
213 E Dupont Hwy (19966)
PHONE..................302 934-9400
Eric Doroshow, *Owner*
EMP: 7 **EST:** 2003
SALES (est): 406.51K **Privately Held**
Web: www.deworkinjury.com
SIC: 8111 General practice attorney, lawyer

(G-8284)
EYE WORX LLC
28544 Dupont Blvd Unit 1 (19966-4792)
PHONE..................302 934-9679
EMP: 13 **EST:** 2018
SALES (est): 822.29K **Privately Held**
SIC: 8042 Offices and clinics of optometrists

(G-8285)
EZ LOANS INC (PA)
28273 Dupont Blvd (19966-4747)
PHONE..................302 934-5563
John Adkins, *Pr*
EMP: 12 **EST:** 2001
SALES (est): 4.59MM
SALES (corp-wide): 4.59MM **Privately Held**
Web: www.ezloansdelmarva.com
SIC: 6141 Personal credit institutions

(G-8286)
FARMERS BANK OF WILLARDS
Also Called: Farmers Bank
28656 Dupont Blvd (19966-4794)
PHONE..................302 934-6300
Justin Gray, *Pr*
EMP: 8
SALES (corp-wide): 21.35MM **Privately Held**
Web: www.fbwbank.com
SIC: 6022 State trust companies accepting deposits, commercial
PA: The Farmers Bank Of Willards
7484 Market St
Willards MD 21874
410 835-8404

(G-8287)
FARRELL HOME RENOVATIONS LLC
26310 Portside Ln (19966-6980)
PHONE..................443 386-0885
Andrew Farrell, *Prin*
EMP: 7 **EST:** 2017
SALES (est): 248.7K **Privately Held**
SIC: 1521 General remodeling, single-family houses

(G-8288)
FERGUSON ENTERPRISES LLC
28520 Dupont Blvd (19966-4739)
PHONE..................302 934-6040
EMP: 11
SALES (corp-wide): 2.67MM **Privately Held**
Web: www.ferguson.com
SIC: 5074 Plumbing fittings and supplies
HQ: Ferguson Enterprises, Llc
751 Lakefront Cmns
Newport News VA 23606
757 969-4011

(G-8289)
FIRST CLASS HEATING & AC INC
28418 Dupont Blvd (19966-1226)
P.O. Box 1264 (19966-5264)
PHONE..................302 934-8900
Tim Pulice, *Pr*
Tim Tulice, *
EMP: 60 **EST:** 1987
SALES (est): 4.9MM **Privately Held**
Web: www.firstclasshvac.com
SIC: 1711 Warm air heating and air conditioning contractor

(G-8290)
FIRST STATE ROOF EXTRIOR CLEAN
29257 Revel Rd (19966-4721)
PHONE..................302 751-0439
Daniel Wanamaker, *Prin*
EMP: 6 **EST:** 2018
SALES (est): 233.93K **Privately Held**
Web: www.1statecleaning.com
SIC: 7699 Cleaning services

(G-8291)
FISHER AUTO PARTS INC
Also Called: Federated Auto Parts
422 Union St (19966-1203)
P.O. Box 592 (19966-0592)
PHONE..................302 934-8088
John Clifton, *Mgr*
EMP: 5
SALES (corp-wide): 525.52MM **Privately Held**
Web: www.fisherautoparts.com
SIC: 5013 5531 Automotive supplies and parts; Auto and truck equipment and parts
PA: Fisher Auto Parts, Inc.
512 Greenville Ave
Staunton VA 24401
540 885-8901

(G-8292)
FISHERS AUTO PARTS INC
Also Called: NAPA
422 Union St (19966-1203)
PHONE..................302 934-8088
Wayne Nagee, *Mgr*
EMP: 5
SALES (corp-wide): 2.84MM **Privately Held**
Web: www.napaonline.com
SIC: 5531 5013 Automotive parts; Automotive supplies and parts
PA: Fisher's Auto Parts Inc
211 W Market St
Georgetown DE 19947
302 856-9591

(G-8293)
FOCUS REHABILITATION & FITNESS
34814 Long Neck Rd (19966-4323)
PHONE..................302 231-8982
Kayla Holland, *Owner*
EMP: 7 **EST:** 2016
SALES (est): 122.37K **Privately Held**
SIC: 8099 8093 Nutrition services; Rehabilitation center, outpatient treatment

(G-8294)
FOOT & ANKLE CTR OF DELAWARE
26744 John J Williams Hwy (19966-4667)
PHONE..................302 945-1221
James Palmer Dpm, *Prin*
EMP: 7 **EST:** 2012

SALES (est): 109.29K **Privately Held**
Web: www.sodelfootandankle.com
SIC: 8043 Offices and clinics of podiatrists

(G-8295)
FRESH CUT LNDSCPING MINTENANCE
314 Country Pl (19966-1657)
PHONE..................302 841-1848
Marquie Brady, *Prin*
EMP: 5 EST: 2016
SALES (est): 54.69K **Privately Held**
SIC: 7349 Building maintenance services, nec

(G-8296)
FRESH HARVEST HYDROPONICS
25345 Gravel Hill Rd (19966-3423)
PHONE..................302 934-7506
EMP: 5 EST: 2013
SALES (est): 252.63K **Privately Held**
SIC: 7389 Business Activities at Non-Commercial Site

(G-8297)
GENERAL COATINGS LLC
26492 Shasta Way (19966-4305)
PHONE..................302 841-7958
EMP: 6 EST: 2010
SALES (est): 63.68K **Privately Held**
SIC: 3479 Metal coating and allied services

(G-8298)
GEORGE & LYNCH INC
20631 Betts Rd (19966-4115)
PHONE..................302 238-7289
Will Robbinson, *Brnch Mgr*
EMP: 19
SALES (corp-wide): 47.84MM **Privately Held**
Web: www.geolyn.com
SIC: 1521 Single-family housing construction
PA: George & Lynch, Inc.
150 Lafferty Ln
Dover DE 19901
302 736-3031

(G-8299)
GIGGLEBUGS EARLY LEARNING CTR
213 W State St (19966-1510)
PHONE..................302 934-5347
Jennifer Spinks, *Prin*
EMP: 13 EST: 2015
SALES (est): 275.35K **Privately Held**
Web: www.cadence-education.com
SIC: 8351 Preschool center

(G-8300)
GLENEAGLE HOMES LLC
32653 Seaview Loop (19966-7132)
PHONE..................914 262-1402
Edward Alexander, *Prin*
EMP: 5 EST: 2004
SALES (est): 108.28K **Privately Held**
SIC: 1521 Single-family housing construction

(G-8301)
GOOD OLE BOY FOUNDATION INC
20529 Laurel Rd (19966-2973)
PHONE..................302 249-0307
EMP: 5 EST: 2018
SALES (est): 97.19K **Privately Held**
Web: www.goodoleboyfoundation.com
SIC: 8641 Civic and social associations

(G-8302)
GOODWILL
28595 Dupont Blvd Unit 1 (19966-4797)
PHONE..................302 934-9146
EMP: 11 EST: 2019
SALES (est): 21.32K **Privately Held**
Web: www.goodwillde.org
SIC: 8331 Vocational rehabilitation agency

(G-8303)
GOT A DOC - WALK IN MED CTR
25935 Plaza Dr Unit 1 (19966-6289)
PHONE..................302 947-4111
EMP: 8 EST: 2019
SALES (est): 54.13K **Privately Held**
SIC: 8011 Medical centers

(G-8304)
GRAHAMS WIRELESS SOLUTIONS INC
24817 Rivers Edge Rd (19966-7216)
PHONE..................717 943-0717
Joseph Graham, *Pr*
EMP: 6 EST: 2004
SALES (est): 114.9K **Privately Held**
SIC: 4812 7389 Cellular telephone services; Business services, nec

(G-8305)
GREEN ACRES HEALTH SYSTEMS
Also Called: Green Valley Terrance
231 S Washington St (19966-1236)
PHONE..................302 934-7300
Allen Segal, *Pr*
EMP: 480
SALES (corp-wide): 9.92MM **Privately Held**
SIC: 8051 Extended care facility
PA: Green Acres Health Systems Inc
4 Ivybrook Blvd
Warminster PA

(G-8306)
GREEN VALLEY TERRACE SNF LLC
Also Called: Atlantic Shres Rhblttion Hlth
231 S Washington St (19966-1236)
PHONE..................302 934-7300
Allen Segal, *Pr*
Gary Segal, *
EMP: 185 EST: 1960
SQ FT: 37,020
SALES (est): 21.62MM **Privately Held**
Web: www.atlanticrhc.com
SIC: 8051 Convalescent home with continuous nursing care

(G-8307)
GREENER CLEANER SUSSEX CORP
31007 Conaway Rd (19966-3685)
PHONE..................302 497-7123
EMP: 5 EST: 2010
SALES (est): 106.36K **Privately Held**
Web: www.sussexchemdry.com
SIC: 7217 Carpet and upholstery cleaning

(G-8308)
GREYSTONE BUSINESS CREDIT
27191 Barefoot Blvd (19966-7138)
PHONE..................410 456-6559
Jim Pierce, *Prin*
EMP: 5 EST: 2016
SALES (est): 120.76K **Privately Held**
SIC: 6159 Miscellaneous business credit institutions

(G-8309)
GUARDIAN INVESTMENTS
28371 Dupont Blvd Unit 3 (19966-1224)
PHONE..................302 541-2114
EMP: 7 EST: 2019
SALES (est): 226.62K **Privately Held**
Web: www.guardmyplan.com
SIC: 6799 Investors, nec

(G-8310)
H & R BLOCK INC
Also Called: H & R Block
28417 Dupont Blvd Unit 4 (19966-1209)
PHONE..................302 934-6178
Elizabeth Whetler, *Owner*
EMP: 5
SALES (corp-wide): 3.47B **Publicly Held**
Web: www.hrblock.com
SIC: 7291 Tax return preparation services
PA: H & R Block, Inc.
1 H And R Block Way
Kansas City MO 64105
816 854-3000

(G-8311)
HAGY LANDSCAPING INC
16 Lenape Ln (19966-9215)
PHONE..................707 935-6119
Bob Hagy, *Owner*
EMP: 5 EST: 1990
SALES (est): 402.27K **Privately Held**
Web: www.hagylandscaping.com
SIC: 0782 Landscape contractors

(G-8312)
HAIR STUDIO II
Long Neck Rd (19966)
P.O. Box 12 (19966-0012)
PHONE..................302 945-5110
Pam Johnston, *Owner*
EMP: 5 EST: 1992
SALES (est): 120K **Privately Held**
Web: www.hairstudioii.com
SIC: 7241 7231 Barber shops; Beauty shops

(G-8313)
HARRY CASWELL INC
32645 Long Neck Rd (19966-6677)
PHONE..................302 945-5322
Lynne Caswell, *Pr*
Harry Caswell, *
EMP: 49 EST: 1989
SQ FT: 15,000
SALES (est): 8.23MM **Privately Held**
Web: www.harrycaswell.com
SIC: 1711 Plumbing contractors

(G-8314)
HARRYS NUTS AND THEN SOME
32645 Long Neck Rd (19966-6677)
PHONE..................302 947-1344
EMP: 6 EST: 2016
SALES (est): 61.69K **Privately Held**
Web: harryshardwarelongneck.wordpress.com
SIC: 1711 Plumbing contractors

(G-8315)
HATFIELD MEDICAL INSTRS INC (PA)
Also Called: Hmi
29186 Baylis Ave (19966-7476)
PHONE..................301 468-0011
Robert Hatfield, *Pr*
Robert Hatfield, *Pr*
Audrey Hatfield, *VP*
EMP: 5 EST: 1987
SALES (est): 523.79K **Privately Held**
Web: www.hatfieldmedical.com
SIC: 7352 Medical equipment rental

(G-8316)
HEALTHY DIRECTIONS WELLNESS
6 Arrowhead Trl (19966-2022)
PHONE..................302 420-3927
EMP: 6 EST: 2014
SALES (est): 42.59K **Privately Held**
Web: www.healthydirectionswellness.com
SIC: 8099 Health and allied services, nec

(G-8317)
HENNINGER PRINTING CO INC
208 Main St (19966-8411)
P.O. Box 550 (19966-0550)
PHONE..................302 934-8119
Judith M Henninger, *Pr*
Paul Henninger Junior, *VP*
EMP: 6 EST: 1959
SQ FT: 4,000
SALES (est): 493.44K **Privately Held**
Web: www.henningerprinting.com
SIC: 2621 5943 5999 5947 Stationary, envelope and tablet papers; Stationery stores; Flags; Party favors

(G-8318)
HOSE PROS
270 W State St (19966-1585)
PHONE..................302 663-0016
Sean Swain, *Owner*
EMP: 7 EST: 2013
SALES (est): 990.09K **Privately Held**
SIC: 5085 Hose, belting, and packing

(G-8319)
HUNT WANDENDALE CLUB
34068 Village Way (19966-6728)
PHONE..................302 945-3369
Hank Gonelli, *Pr*
EMP: 6 EST: 2011
SALES (est): 43.92K **Privately Held**
SIC: 7997 Membership sports and recreation clubs

(G-8320)
INDIAN RIVER GOLF CARS DR WLDG
26246 Kathys Way (19966-3218)
PHONE..................302 947-2044
Mike M Curdy, *Prin*
EMP: 3 EST: 2010
SALES (est): 291.51K **Privately Held**
Web: www.indianrivergolfcars.com
SIC: 8011 7692 5511 Offices and clinics of medical doctors; Welding repair; New and used car dealers

(G-8321)
INSURANCE MARKET INC
17 Main St (19966-8408)
P.O. Box 312 (19947-0312)
PHONE..................302 934-9006
Terri L Moor, *Mgr*
EMP: 5
SALES (corp-wide): 4.82MM **Privately Held**
Web: www.insurancechoices.com
SIC: 6411 Insurance agents, nec
PA: The Insurance Market Inc
450 N Central Ave
Laurel DE 19956
302 875-7591

(G-8322)
ISAACS LANDSCAPING & GARDENING
Also Called: Long Neck Garden Center
Rr1 372 Longneck Rd (19966-9801)
PHONE..................302 947-1414
David Isaacs, *Owner*
EMP: 5 EST: 1996
SALES (est): 135.37K **Privately Held**
SIC: 5261 0782 Retail nurseries and garden stores; Garden services

(G-8323)
J A RIBINSKY BUILDERS
33827 Lawton Ln (19966-4400)

Millsboro - Sussex County (G-8324) GEOGRAPHIC SECTION

PHONE.....................302 542-7014
Joseph Ribinsky, *Prin*
EMP: 11 **EST:** 2016
SALES (est): 859.79K **Privately Held**
SIC: 1521 New construction, single-family houses

(G-8324)
JACK DONOVAN
Also Called: Donovan, Jack, Seminars
23868 Samuel Adams Cir (19966-8206)
PHONE.....................410 715-0504
Jack Donovan, *Owner*
EMP: 5 **EST:** 1985
SALES (est): 255.91K **Privately Held**
SIC: 8742 Programmed instruction service

(G-8325)
JACKSON HEWITT TAX SERVICE INC
Also Called: Jackson Hewitt Tax Service
320 W Dupont Hwy Ste 102 (19966-1715)
PHONE.....................302 934-7430
Joyce Rosas, *Mgr*
EMP: 6
Web: www.jacksonhewitt.com
SIC: 7291 Tax return preparation services
PA: Jackson Hewitt Tax Service Inc.
10 Exchange Pl Fl 27
Jersey City NJ 07302

(G-8326)
JAG PAYMENTS INC
30567 Flycatcher Ct (19966-7383)
PHONE.....................800 261-0240
Tracy Neidens, *Prin*
EMP: 5 **EST:** 2015
SALES (est): 192.85K **Privately Held**
SIC: 8721 Accounting, auditing, and bookkeeping

(G-8327)
JAMC LLC
20479 Asheville Dr (19966-7565)
P.O. Box 448 (21661-0448)
PHONE.....................410 639-2224
EMP: 5 **EST:** 2010
SALES (est): 103.33K **Privately Held**
SIC: 4493 7011 Marinas; Motels

(G-8328)
JAMES MAINTENANCE SERVICES LLC
12 Ward Way (19966-1506)
PHONE.....................302 934-7625
James Revel, *Prin*
EMP: 5 **EST:** 2008
SALES (est): 64.69K **Privately Held**
SIC: 7349 Building maintenance services, nec

(G-8329)
JAY LYNN CNSTR SOLUTIONS LLC
136 Laurel Rd (19966-1731)
PHONE.....................302 349-5799
Derek J Hall, *Prin*
EMP: 5 **EST:** 2008
SALES (est): 98.45K **Privately Held**
SIC: 1521 Single-family housing construction

(G-8330)
JEANS LOVE-N-CARE CHILDCARE
27294 Dogwood Ln (19966-1667)
PHONE.....................302 934-5665
EMP: 8 **EST:** 2017
SALES (est): 19.13K **Privately Held**
SIC: 8351 Child day care services

(G-8331)
JET FAST LOANS
28544 Dupont Blvd Unit 9 (19966-4792)
PHONE.....................302 934-6794
Tammy Adkins, *Prin*
EMP: 5 **EST:** 2000
SALES (est): 125.33K **Privately Held**
Web: www.jetfastloans.com
SIC: 6162 Mortgage bankers and loan correspondents

(G-8332)
JL SOLIS LLC
25709 Whispering Wind Ln (19966-2603)
PHONE.....................302 212-9521
Jose Solis-marin, *Prin*
EMP: 5 **EST:** 2014
SALES (est): 108.22K **Privately Held**
SIC: 1522 Residential construction, nec

(G-8333)
JOSE MANUEL HERNANDEZ-ALVAREZ
Also Called: Hernandez Contractor
24922 Gravel Hill Rd (19966-3459)
PHONE.....................302 265-7873
EMP: 9 **EST:** 2009
SALES (est): 469.82K **Privately Held**
Web: www.hernandezcontractor.net
SIC: 1761 Roofing contractor

(G-8334)
JUMARALLY CHANDRA
32750 Curley Dr (19966-2905)
PHONE.....................302 212-7027
Chandra Jumarally, *Prin*
EMP: 5 **EST:** 2006
SALES (est): 140K **Privately Held**
SIC: 0119 Pea and bean farms (legumes)

(G-8335)
KAAN CAKES LLC
314 Wilson Hwy (19966-1216)
PHONE.....................302 260-0647
Emine Pomakoglu, *CEO*
Grace Kearns, *Pr*
John Kearns, *VP*
Kaan Pomakoglu, *Sec*
EMP: 7 **EST:** 2020
SALES (est): 188.31K **Privately Held**
Web: www.kaanbakery.com
SIC: 2051 5812 5461 Cakes, bakery; except frozen; Coffee shop; Retail bakeries

(G-8336)
KCS TOTAL LAWN CARE LLC
33427 Marina Bay Cir (19966-7085)
P.O. Box 873 (19966-0873)
PHONE.....................732 331-2454
EMP: 5 **EST:** 2016
SALES (est): 236.78K **Privately Held**
SIC: 0782 Lawn care services

(G-8337)
KEN FIBBLE PROFESSIONAL SVCS
35373 Bay Winds Ln (19966-6951)
PHONE.....................302 947-2430
Kenneth Fibble, *Prin*
EMP: 5 **EST:** 2016
SALES (est): 62.18K **Privately Held**
SIC: 8621 Professional organizations

(G-8338)
KENT & O CONNOR INC
Also Called: Kent & O'Connor
26333 Timbercreek Ln (19966-8105)
PHONE.....................703 351-6222
Pat O'connor, *Pr*
Jon Kent, *Ch Bd*
▲ **EMP:** 7 **EST:** 1979

SALES (est): 514.71K **Privately Held**
Web: www.kentoconnor.com
SIC: 8743 Lobbyist

(G-8339)
KENYA GATHER FOUNDATION
23246 Country Living Rd (19966-2848)
PHONE.....................302 382-8227
Alayna Aiken, *Prin*
Karen Johnson, *Prin*
Tom Angote, *Prin*
EMP: 15 **EST:** 2018
SALES (est): 159.95K **Privately Held**
SIC: 8399 Social services, nec

(G-8340)
KIM JONES AGCY STATE FRM INSUR
29848 Millsboro Hwy (19966-3604)
PHONE.....................302 934-9393
Kim Jones, *Admn*
EMP: 5 **EST:** 2015
SALES (est): 126.88K **Privately Held**
Web: www.kimbenton.com
SIC: 6411 Insurance agents and brokers

(G-8341)
KINSLER LANDSCAPING LLC
32172 Robin Hoods Loop (19966-6205)
PHONE.....................302 745-0269
Christopher Kinsler, *Prin*
EMP: 5 **EST:** 2018
SALES (est): 85.91K **Privately Held**
SIC: 0781 Landscape services

(G-8342)
KNAUER ASSOCIATION LLC
37145 Sandpiper Rd (19966-6838)
PHONE.....................302 947-2531
Lewis Knauer, *Prin*
EMP: 5 **EST:** 2014
SALES (est): 46.67K **Privately Held**
SIC: 8699 Membership organizations, nec

(G-8343)
KNEESAVERELECTRICALBOX
27936 Home Farm Dr (19966-3392)
PHONE.....................732 239-7514
Alexander Ruggiero, *Prin*
EMP: 5 **EST:** 2016
SALES (est): 76.69K **Privately Held**
SIC: 1521 Single-family housing construction

(G-8344)
LARRY BAKER LLC
26279 W Mallard Rd (19966-5838)
PHONE.....................302 703-2127
Larry Wiley, *Prin*
EMP: 7 **EST:** 2011
SALES (est): 155.98K **Privately Held**
Web: www.cbintouch.com
SIC: 1522 Residential construction, nec

(G-8345)
LAST NICKEL INN LLC
10 Valley Rd (19966-8729)
PHONE.....................302 945-4880
Thomas Mahler, *Prin*
EMP: 11 **EST:** 2017
SALES (est): 82.29K **Privately Held**
SIC: 7011 Inns

(G-8346)
LAUDATO HOME IMPROVEMENTS LLC
28226 Sloop Ave (19966-6178)
PHONE.....................610 656-2944
EMP: 5 **EST:** 2014
SALES (est): 104.59K **Privately Held**
Web: www.laudatohomeimprovements.com

SIC: 1521 General remodeling, single-family houses

(G-8347)
LEWES SURGICAL AND MED ASSOC
Also Called: Cedar Tree Medical Center
32711 Long Neck Rd (19966-6678)
PHONE.....................302 945-9730
Semaan M Abboud, *Prin*
EMP: 17 **EST:** 2004
SALES (est): 2.5MM **Privately Held**
SIC: 8011 Internal medicine, physician/surgeon

(G-8348)
LEWIS SAND AND GRAVEL LLC
38227 Firemans Rd (19966-3122)
PHONE.....................302 238-0169
Ray Lewis, *Owner*
EMP: 6 **EST:** 2006
SALES (est): 497.06K **Privately Held**
Web: www.minotchrysler.com
SIC: 1442 Construction sand and gravel

(G-8349)
LITTLE EINSTEINS PRESCHOOL
28253 Dupont Blvd (19966-1223)
PHONE.....................302 933-0600
Lindsey Cannon, *Dir*
EMP: 9 **EST:** 2013
SALES (est): 135.18K **Privately Held**
SIC: 8351 Preschool center

(G-8350)
LOAN TILL PAYDAY LLC
28521 Dupont Blvd Unit 3 (19966-3751)
PHONE.....................302 536-2183
EMP: 8
Web: www.loantillpaydaydelaware.com
SIC: 6141 Personal credit institutions
PA: Loan Till Payday Llc
1901 W 4th St &Lincln
Wilmington DE

(G-8351)
LONG NECK WATER CO
32783 Long Neck Rd Unit 6 (19966-6692)
PHONE.....................302 947-9600
Jim Mooney, *Dir*
Jim Mooney, *Dir Opers*
EMP: 8 **EST:** 1997
SALES (est): 959.35K **Privately Held**
Web: www.longneckwater.com
SIC: 4941 Water supply

(G-8352)
LONGNECK FAMILY PRACTICE
26744 John J Williams Hwy Unit 3 (19966)
PHONE.....................302 947-9767
Jeffrey Hawtof, *Prin*
Jeffrey Hawtof Md, *Prin*
EMP: 8 **EST:** 2002
SALES (est): 208.13K **Privately Held**
SIC: 8011 General and family practice, physician/surgeon

(G-8353)
LOOKS NEW POWERWASHING LLC
Also Called: Looks New Powerwashing
30306 Hickory Hill Rd (19966-3501)
PHONE.....................302 569-0172
Tyler Hundley, *Prin*
EMP: 5 **EST:** 2016
SALES (est): 60.92K **Privately Held**
SIC: 7699 Cleaning services

(G-8354)
LOWES HOME CENTERS LLC
Also Called: Lowe's
26688 Centerview Dr (19966-3750)

PHONE..............................302 934-3740
Frank Guidry, Mgr
EMP: 99
SALES (corp-wide): 97.06B Publicly Held
Web: www.lowes.com
SIC: 5211 5031 5722 5064 Home centers; Building materials, exterior; Household appliance stores; Electrical appliances, television and radio
HQ: Lowe's Home Centers, Llc
1000 Lowes Blvd
Mooresville NC 28117
336 658-4000

(G-8355)
LWECO GROUP LLC
Also Called: Master Industrial Catalog
28428 Cedar Ridge Dr (19966-2710)
P.O. Box 368 (19966-0368)
PHONE..............................302 296-8035
EMP: 6 EST: 2010
SQ FT: 1,500
SALES (est): 507.84K Privately Held
SIC: 5084 Materials handling machinery

(G-8356)
M M MARINE SERVICE
24530 Hollyville Rd (19966-2600)
PHONE..............................302 841-7689
Mike Henderson, Owner
EMP: 5 EST: 2008
SALES (est): 104.75K Privately Held
SIC: 7699 Boat repair

(G-8357)
M&L CLEANING SERVICE
24572 Straight Arrow Rd (19966-1695)
PHONE..............................302 249-8634
Iva West, Prin
EMP: 5 EST: 2018
SALES (est): 58.33K Privately Held
SIC: 7699 Cleaning services

(G-8358)
MA TRANSPORTATION LLC
34016 Sea Otter Way (19966-6465)
PHONE..............................302 588-5435
Murtada Alatta, Managing Member
EMP: 8 EST: 2013
SALES (est): 460.73K Privately Held
SIC: 4731 Freight transportation arrangement

(G-8359)
MAID MY DAY CLEANING SVC
Mariners Way (19966)
PHONE..............................302 947-9355
Carl Pearson, Prin
EMP: 5 EST: 2004
SALES (est): 80.88K Privately Held
SIC: 7349 Janitorial service, contract basis

(G-8360)
MAIL STOP
24832 John J Williams Hwy Unit 1
(19966-4997)
PHONE..............................302 947-4704
Laura Gregory, Mgr
EMP: 5 EST: 2011
SALES (est): 409.32K Privately Held
Web: www.mailstopde.com
SIC: 7389 Mailbox rental and related service

(G-8361)
MALONE BAYSIDE MARINA
Long Neck Rd (19966)
PHONE..............................302 947-0334
EMP: 6 EST: 1996
SALES (est): 269.4K Privately Held
SIC: 6515 Mobile home site operators

(G-8362)
MANUFACTURERS & TRADERS TR CO
Also Called: M&T
207 E Dupont Hwy (19966-4798)
PHONE..............................302 855-2891
Lenny Brittingham, Mgr
EMP: 8
SALES (corp-wide): 8.6B Publicly Held
Web: ir.mtb.com
SIC: 6022 State commercial banks
HQ: Manufacturers And Traders Trust Company
1 M&T Plz Fl 3
Buffalo NY 14203
716 842-4200

(G-8363)
MANUFCTURED HSING CONCEPTS LLC
Also Called: Longneck Housing Specialist
28862 Dupont Blvd (19966-4781)
P.O. Box 1048 (19966-1048)
PHONE..............................302 934-8848
EMP: 64
SALES (est): 2.32MM Privately Held
SIC: 6531 Broker of manufactured homes, on site

(G-8364)
MARGARET WRIGHT-STASI
213 E State St (19966-1117)
PHONE..............................302 745-1509
Margaret Wright-stasi, CEO
EMP: 6 EST: 2018
SALES (est): 59.7K Privately Held
SIC: 8049 Offices of health practitioner

(G-8365)
MARGARITA MAN OF DELAWARE
32353 Turnstone Ct (19966-9042)
PHONE..............................302 344-5837
Kevin Cunningham, Prin
EMP: 5 EST: 2017
SALES (est): 184.71K Privately Held
Web: www.margaritamande.com
SIC: 7359 Party supplies rental services

(G-8366)
MARK NEUROLOGY LLC
22998 Springwood Cir (19966-2897)
P.O. Box 860 (19966-0860)
PHONE..............................302 933-0111
EMP: 9 EST: 2008
SALES (est): 230.41K Privately Held
SIC: 8011 Neurologist

(G-8367)
MASSEYS LANDING PARK INC
Also Called: Resort At Massey's Landing
20628 Long Beach Dr (19966-4331)
PHONE..............................302 947-2600
Patricia Lavanceau, Pr
EMP: 13 EST: 2001
SALES (est): 211.01K Privately Held
Web: www.sunoutdoors.com
SIC: 7033 Campgrounds

(G-8368)
MASTER PAINTING AND REMODELING
29538 Millsboro Hwy (19966-3601)
PHONE..............................302 604-8978
Deysy Ojeda Perez, Owner
EMP: 5 EST: 2014
SALES (est): 67.96K Privately Held
Web: www.masterpaintingandremodeling.com
SIC: 1721 Painting and paper hanging

(G-8369)
MASTERMARK WOODWORKING INC
25205 Mastermark Ln (19966-2615)
PHONE..............................302 945-9131
Mark K Miller, Prin
EMP: 2 EST: 2011
SALES (est): 176.6K Privately Held
SIC: 2431 Millwork

(G-8370)
MC CREATIVE GROUP
25935 Plaza Dr Unit 2 (19966-6289)
PHONE..............................302 348-8977
Kariane Christophel, Pr
EMP: 12 EST: 2015
SALES (est): 998.5K Privately Held
Web: www.mccreativegroup.com
SIC: 8748 8742 7311 Business consulting, nec; Marketing consulting services; Advertising agencies

(G-8371)
MCNEIL PAVING
32758 Spring Water Dr (19966-7126)
PHONE..............................302 945-7131
Jimmy Neal, Prin
EMP: 8 EST: 2008
SALES (est): 615.88K Privately Held
SIC: 1611 Surfacing and paving

(G-8372)
MEDICAL REIMBURSEMENT SOL
29517 Glenwood Dr (19966-7503)
PHONE..............................516 809-6812
Paul Newman, Prin
EMP: 5 EST: 2010
SALES (est): 457.41K Privately Held
SIC: 8099 Health and allied services, nec

(G-8373)
MEHER HEALTH SERVICES
32362 Long Neck Rd (19966-9062)
PHONE..............................302 947-0333
Percy Dhamodiwala, Mgr
EMP: 7 EST: 2015
SALES (est): 175.8K Privately Held
SIC: 8099 Health and allied services, nec

(G-8374)
MELS HTG & A/C
33736 Lawton Ln (19966-4401)
PHONE..............................302 947-1979
Mel Mousley, Owner
EMP: 6 EST: 2006
SALES (est): 149.14K Privately Held
SIC: 1711 Heating and air conditioning contractors

(G-8375)
MELSON FUNERAL SERVICES
Longneck Rd (19966)
P.O. Box 100 (19945-0100)
PHONE..............................302 945-9000
A Douglas Melson, Owner
EMP: 6 EST: 1992
SALES (est): 313.1K Privately Held
Web: www.melsonfuneralservices.com
SIC: 7261 Funeral home

(G-8376)
MENTON ELIZABETH A CRNA PC
28881 Harmons Hill Rd (19966-6418)
PHONE..............................443 694-6769
Elizabeth Ann Menton, Prin
EMP: 8 EST: 2011
SALES (est): 240.9K Privately Held
SIC: 8049 Nurses, registered and practical

(G-8377)
MERCK & CO INC
Also Called: Merck
29160 Intervet Ln (19966-4217)
PHONE..............................302 934-8051
Rose Collins, Brnch Mgr
▲ EMP: 34
SALES (corp-wide): 59.28B Publicly Held
Web: www.merck.com
SIC: 2834 Pharmaceutical preparations
PA: Merck & Co., Inc.
126 E Lincoln Ave
Rahway NJ 07065
908 740-4000

(G-8378)
MID SUSSEX RESCUE SQUAD INC
31738 Indian Mission Rd (19966-4911)
PHONE..............................302 945-2680
Raymond Johnson, Pr
Captain Jerry Johnson, Prin
EMP: 17 EST: 1972
SALES (est): 1.53MM Privately Held
Web: www.midsussexrescuesquad.com
SIC: 8999 Search and rescue service

(G-8379)
MID-ATLANTIC ELEC SVCS INC
24556 Betts Pond Rd (19966-1560)
PHONE..............................302 945-2555
Joseph Noble, Pr
EMP: 27 EST: 2010
SQ FT: 3,200
SALES (est): 1.22MM Privately Held
Web: www.maes1.com
SIC: 1731 General electrical contractor

(G-8380)
MID-COUNTY ELECTRIC INC
24556 Betts Pond Rd (19966-1560)
P.O. Box 951 (19966-0951)
PHONE..............................302 934-8304
Judith K Doughty, Pr
EMP: 10 EST: 1977
SQ FT: 1,600
SALES (est): 253.14K Privately Held
SIC: 1731 General electrical contractor

(G-8381)
MILLSBORO
26744 John J Williams Hwy Unit 4
(19966-4667)
PHONE..............................302 231-1152
EMP: 7 EST: 2019
SALES (est): 166.36K Privately Held
Web: www.millsboropd.com
SIC: 8611 Chamber of Commerce

(G-8382)
MILLSBORO
30265 Commerce Dr Unit 201
(19966-3593)
PHONE..............................302 934-0300
EMP: 6 EST: 2019
SALES (est): 68.87K Privately Held
Web: www.millsborochamber.com
SIC: 8611 Chamber of Commerce

(G-8383)
MILLSBORO FAMILY PRACTICE PA
201 Laurel Rd (19966-1732)
PHONE..............................302 934-5626
Lisa A Martin Md, Pr
EMP: 7 EST: 2004
SALES (est): 541.79K Privately Held
SIC: 8011 General and family practice, physician/surgeon

Millsboro - Sussex County (G-8384)

(G-8384)
MILLSBORO FITNESS LLC
28632 Dupont Blvd Unit 14 (19966-4793)
PHONE....................302 933-0722
EMP: 53
SALES (est): 191.69K **Privately Held**
SIC: 7991 Physical fitness facilities

(G-8385)
MILLSBORO HSING FOR PRGRESS IN
701 Stanford Bratton Dr (19966-1268)
PHONE....................302 934-6491
William Duffy, *Pr*
Elva Allen, *Prin*
Vanessa Deloach, *Prin*
Robert Drain, *Prin*
Tina Midgete, *Prin*
EMP: 7 EST: 1971
SALES (est): 1.02MM **Privately Held**
SIC: 6513 Apartment building operators

(G-8386)
MILLSBORO LANDING INC
29320 White St (19966-1124)
P.O. Box 177 (19966-0177)
PHONE....................302 934-6073
William Duffy Junior, *Pr*
Patricia Kelleher, *Pr*
Vaness Deloach, *Treas*
Elva Allen, *Sec*
EMP: 10 EST: 2018
SALES (est): 89.15K **Privately Held**
Web: www.millsboro.org
SIC: 7997 Membership sports and recreation clubs

(G-8387)
MILLSBORO LANES INC
Also Called: Millsboro Bowling Center
213 Mitchell St (19966-9402)
PHONE....................302 934-0400
Craig Smith, *Pt*
EMP: 13 EST: 1989
SQ FT: 20,000
SALES (est): 464.01K **Privately Held**
SIC: 7933 5813 Ten pin center; Bar (drinking places)

(G-8388)
MILLSBORO LITTLE LEAGUE
262 W State St (19966-1507)
PHONE....................302 934-1806
EMP: 10
SALES (est): 69.93K **Privately Held**
SIC: 7997 Membership sports and recreation clubs

(G-8389)
MILLSBORO VILLAGE I LLC
701 Stanford Bratton Dr (19966-1268)
PHONE....................302 678-9400
EMP: 9 EST: 2009
SALES (est): 518.67K **Privately Held**
SIC: 6513 Apartment building operators

(G-8390)
MOORE & LIND INC
Also Called: Indian River Land Company
28448 Dupont Blvd (19966-4707)
PHONE....................302 934-8818
Lynn W Moore, *Pr*
Cathi Lind, *VP*
Judy A Moore, *Sec*
Terry L Lind, *Treas*
Susan C Moore, *Sec*
EMP: 5 EST: 1969
SQ FT: 2,000
SALES (est): 467.15K **Privately Held**
Web: www.indianriverland.com
SIC: 6531 Real estate agent, commercial

(G-8391)
MOTHER GOOSE CH!LDRENS CENTER
27275 Dagsboro Rd (19966-3721)
P.O. Box 233 (19966-0233)
PHONE....................302 934-8454
Sarah Thoroughgood, *Pr*
EMP: 5 EST: 1971
SALES (est): 289.84K **Privately Held**
SIC: 8351 Preschool center

(G-8392)
MOUNTAIRE FARMS LLC
Also Called: MOUNTAIRE FARMS, L.L.C.
Rte 24 E (19966)
PHONE....................302 934-3011
EMP: 84
SALES (corp-wide): 2.07B **Privately Held**
Web: www.mountaire.com
SIC: 0191 General farms, primarily crop
HQ: Mountaire Farms Inc.
1901 Napa Valley Dr
Little Rock AR 72212
501 372-6524

(G-8393)
MOUNTAIRE FARMS DELAWARE INC
29005 John J Williams Hwy (19966-4095)
PHONE....................302 934-1100
◆ EMP: 1565
SALES (corp-wide): 2.07B **Privately Held**
Web: www.mountaire.com
SIC: 0191 General farms, primarily crop
HQ: Mountaire Farms Of Delaware, Inc.
1901 Napa Valley Dr
Little Rock AR 72212
501 372-6524

(G-8394)
MOUNTAIRE FARMS INC
29529 John J Williams Hwy (19966-3920)
PHONE....................302 934-1100
Pihlipp Plylar, *Pr*
EMP: 200
SALES (corp-wide): 2.07B **Privately Held**
Web: www.mountaire.com
SIC: 2015 Poultry slaughtering and processing
HQ: Mountaire Farms Inc.
1901 Napa Valley Dr
Little Rock AR 72212
501 372-6524

(G-8395)
MOUNTAIRE FARMS INC
29106 John J Williams Hwy (19966-4008)
PHONE....................302 934-1100
EMP: 113
SALES (corp-wide): 2.07B **Privately Held**
Web: www.mountaire.com
SIC: 2015 Poultry slaughtering and processing
HQ: Mountaire Farms Inc.
1901 Napa Valley Dr
Little Rock AR 72212
501 372-6524

(G-8396)
MSB ENTERPRISE PARTNERS LLC
24912 Pot Bunker Way (19966-6279)
PHONE....................302 947-0736
EMP: 5 EST: 2001
SALES (est): 216.81K **Privately Held**
SIC: 7389 Purchasing service

(G-8397)
NAILS AT TAORMINA
36932 Silicato Dr Unit 4 (19966-5004)
PHONE....................302 519-7528
Mai Le, *Prin*
EMP: 5 EST: 2019
SALES (est): 185.11K **Privately Held**
SIC: 7231 Manicurist, pedicurist

(G-8398)
NANTICOKE INDIAN MUSEUM
27073 John J Williams Hwy (19966-4642)
PHONE....................302 945-7022
Herman Robbins, *Chief*
Leoya Wright, *Dir*
EMP: 5 EST: 1984
SALES (est): 134.81K **Privately Held**
Web: www.nanticokeindians.org
SIC: 8412 Museum

(G-8399)
NANTICOKE SHORES ASSOC LLC
Also Called: Rehoboth Shores
26335 Goosepond Rd (19966-6945)
PHONE....................302 945-1500
EMP: 6 EST: 1994
SALES (est): 499.28K **Privately Held**
Web: www.rehobothshores.com
SIC: 6515 6531 Mobile home site operators; Real estate agents and managers

(G-8400)
NARDI CABINETRY LLC
26429 Creekwood Cir (19966-5927)
PHONE....................302 945-7918
EMP: 2
SALES (est): 145.24K **Privately Held**
SIC: 2434 Wood kitchen cabinets

(G-8401)
NATIONAL MENTOR HOLDINGS INC
Also Called: Delaware Mentor
230 Mitchell St (19966-9402)
PHONE....................302 934-0512
EMP: 588
SALES (corp-wide): 1.67B **Privately Held**
Web: www.sevitahealth.com
SIC: 8082 8361 Home health care services; Mentally handicapped home
HQ: National Mentor Holdings, Inc.
313 Congress St Fl 5
Boston MA 02210
617 790-4800

(G-8402)
NCD REMODELING LLC
29460 Glenwood Dr (19966-7500)
PHONE....................302 604-3971
Nick Demopoulos, *Owner*
EMP: 5 EST: 2011
SALES (est): 154.73K **Privately Held**
SIC: 1521 General remodeling, single-family houses

(G-8403)
NEMOURS PEDIATRICS
30265 Commerce Dr (19966-3593)
PHONE....................302 934-6073
EMP: 14 EST: 2019
SALES (est): 200K **Privately Held**
Web: www.nemours.org
SIC: 8011 Pediatrician

(G-8404)
NEW RELAXATION INC
28544 Dupont Blvd Unit 14 (19966-4792)
PHONE....................302 934-9344
EMP: 5 EST: 2014
SALES (est): 60.47K **Privately Held**
SIC: 7991 Spas

(G-8405)
NO PRESSURE LLC
Also Called: No Pressure
26055 Saint Hayes Blvd (19966-4771)
PHONE....................347 693-3116
EMP: 2 EST: 2021
SALES (est): 92.41K **Privately Held**
SIC: 3799 Transportation equipment, nec

(G-8406)
NORTHEAST RALLY CLUB
213 Dodd St (19966-1138)
P.O. Box 547 (19966-0547)
PHONE....................302 934-1246
EMP: 5 EST: 2010
SALES (est): 43.18K **Privately Held**
Web: www.northeastrallyclub.com
SIC: 7997 Membership sports and recreation clubs

(G-8407)
NOVACARE REHABILITATION
36932 Silicato Dr (19966-5003)
PHONE....................302 947-0781
EMP: 6 EST: 2018
SALES (est): 220.28K **Privately Held**
Web: www.novacare.com
SIC: 8049 Physical therapist

(G-8408)
NRG ENERGY INC
Burton Island Rd (19966)
PHONE....................302 934-3537
Jim Spencer, *Brnch Mgr*
EMP: 15
Web: www.nrg.com
SIC: 4911 Electric services
PA: Nrg Energy, Inc.
910 Louisiana St Ste B200
Houston TX 77002

(G-8409)
NU-TECH MASONRY INC
Rd 2 Box 332f (19966)
P.O. Box 806 (19966-0806)
PHONE....................302 934-5660
Steven Short, *Pr*
EMP: 9 EST: 1992
SALES (est): 499.13K **Privately Held**
SIC: 1741 Masonry and other stonework

(G-8410)
OLD LANDING II LP
29320 White St Unit 400 (19966-1124)
PHONE....................302 934-1871
William Duffy, *Prin*
EMP: 8 EST: 2015
SALES (est): 315.32K **Privately Held**
SIC: 6513 Apartment building operators

(G-8411)
OLD TOWNE PT - MILLSBORO
32695 Long Neck Rd (19966-6693)
PHONE....................302 945-5300
EMP: 5 EST: 2019
SALES (est): 92.76K **Privately Held**
SIC: 8049 Physical therapist

(G-8412)
PARADISE GRILL
27344 Bay Walk (19966-6392)
PHONE....................302 945-4500
EMP: 10 EST: 2014
SALES (est): 1.3MM **Privately Held**
Web: www.paradisegrillde.com
SIC: 5099 Durable goods, nec

Millsboro - Sussex County (G-8441)

(G-8413)
PARKER BLOCK CO INC (HQ)
30234 Millsboro Hwy (19966)
PHONE.................302 934-9237
Marvin Mccray, *Prin*
Jimmy Conley, *
Mike Tang, *
Brad Black, *
Doug Clarke, *
EMP: 25 **EST:** 1929
SQ FT: 1,000
SALES (est): 11.1MM
SALES (corp-wide): 50.7MM **Privately Held**
Web: www.ernestmaier.com
SIC: 5032 Brick, stone, and related material
PA: Ernest Maier, Inc.
4700 Annapolis Rd
Bladensburg MD 20710
301 927-8300

(G-8414)
PARSONS PAINTING&DRYWALL LLC
113 Moores Xing Unit 50 (19966-3815)
PHONE.................302 462-6169
Joseph Parsons, *Prin*
EMP: 5 **EST:** 2016
SALES (est): 70.29K **Privately Held**
SIC: 1742 Drywall

(G-8415)
PATRICIA DEGIROLANO DAY CARE
32909 Long Neck Rd (19966-6690)
P.O. Box 344 (19966-0344)
PHONE.................302 947-2874
Patricia Degirolano, *Prin*
EMP: 5 **EST:** 2003
SALES (est): 76.95K **Privately Held**
SIC: 8351 Group day care center

(G-8416)
PATTERSON & SCHWARTZ
28600 Gazebo Way Unit 76 (19966-4676)
PHONE.................302 945-5568
Mike Porro, *Pr*
EMP: 10 **EST:** 1989
SALES (est): 530K **Privately Held**
Web: www.pattersonschwartz.com
SIC: 6531 Real estate agent, residential

(G-8417)
PEARL CLINIC LLC
28539 Dupont Blvd (19966-4798)
P.O. Box 489 (19939-0489)
PHONE.................302 648-2099
Sherin Ibrahim, *Prin*
EMP: 5 **EST:** 2011
SALES (est): 457.7K **Privately Held**
Web: www.pearlclinicllc.com
SIC: 8099 Health and allied services, nec

(G-8418)
PELICAN BAY GROUP INC
Also Called: Sea Esta Motel 2
100 Rudder Rd (19966-6636)
P.O. Box 4 (19966-0004)
PHONE.................302 945-5900
George A Metz Iii, *Pr*
EMP: 8 **EST:** 2007
SQ FT: 325
SALES (est): 231.75K **Privately Held**
SIC: 7011 Motels

(G-8419)
PENINSULA
Also Called: Peninsula Community Assn
26937 Bay Farm Rd (19966-7134)
PHONE.................410 342-8111
EMP: 7 **EST:** 2019
SALES (est): 118.44K **Privately Held**
Web: www.peninsula-delaware.com
SIC: 7992 Public golf courses

(G-8420)
PENINSULA AT LONG NECK LLC
468 Bay Farm Rd (19966)
PHONE.................302 947-4717
EMP: 8 **EST:** 2002
SALES (est): 240.77K **Privately Held**
SIC: 7992 Public golf courses

(G-8421)
PENINSULA DENTAL LLC
26670 Centerview Dr Unit 19 (19966-3584)
PHONE.................302 297-3750
John Moore, *Prin*
Marisol Vega, *Prin*
EMP: 5 **EST:** 2009
SALES (est): 495.76K **Privately Held**
Web: www.peninsuladentalmillsboro.com
SIC: 8021 Dentists' office

(G-8422)
PENINSULA HEALTH LLC
26744 John J Williams Hwy Unit 7 (19966-4667)
PHONE.................302 945-0440
EMP: 5 **EST:** 2009
SALES (est): 586.58K **Privately Held**
Web: www.tidalhealth.org
SIC: 8099 Health and allied services, nec

(G-8423)
PENINSULA PLASTIC SURGERY PC
30265 Commerce Dr Unit 208 (19966-3593)
PHONE.................302 663-0119
EMP: 9 **EST:** 1995
SALES (est): 481.71K **Privately Held**
Web: www.penplasticsurgery.com
SIC: 8011 Plastic surgeon

(G-8424)
PENINSULA VETERINARY SVCS LLC
32038 Long Neck Rd (19966-6228)
PHONE.................302 947-0719
EMP: 5 **EST:** 2017
SALES (est): 410.63K **Privately Held**
Web: www.peninsulaveterinaryservices.com
SIC: 0742 Animal hospital services, pets and other animal specialties

(G-8425)
PENSKE TRUCK RENTAL
25920 Plaza Dr (19966-4998)
PHONE.................302 648-3199
EMP: 6 **EST:** 2017
SALES (est): 46.21K **Privately Held**
Web: www.pensketruckrental.com
SIC: 7513 Truck rental and leasing, no drivers

(G-8426)
PEOPLES PLACE II INC
30265 Commerce Dr Unit 201 (19966-3593)
PHONE.................302 934-0300
Del Failing Junior, *Brnch Mgr*
EMP: 78
SALES (corp-wide): 8.66MM **Privately Held**
Web: www.peoplesplace2.com
SIC: 8351 Child day care services
PA: People's Place Ii, Inc.
1129 Airport Rd
Milford DE 19963
302 422-8033

(G-8427)
PETITE HAIR DESIGNS
Long Neck Rd Plmer Shopg Palmer (19966)
P.O. Box 388 (19966-0388)
PHONE.................302 945-2595
Terry Roberts Beiner, *Owner*
Terry Roberts-beiner, *Owner*
EMP: 8 **EST:** 1992
SALES (est): 128.48K **Privately Held**
SIC: 7231 Hairdressers

(G-8428)
PILLAR TO POST
26244 E Old Gate Dr (19966-3775)
PHONE.................908 319-4493
Michael Brown, *Pr*
EMP: 5 **EST:** 2011
SALES (est): 68.3K **Privately Held**
Web: www.pillartopost.com
SIC: 7389 Building inspection service

(G-8429)
PLANTATION LAKES HOMEOWNERS
29787 Plantation Lakes Blvd (19966)
PHONE.................302 934-5200
Keith Hines, *Prin*
EMP: 7 **EST:** 2016
SALES (est): 245.84K **Privately Held**
SIC: 8641 Homeowners' association

(G-8430)
PLAZA MEXICO
26506 Victorias Landing Rd Unit 5 (19966-7064)
PHONE.................301 643-5701
EMP: 5 **EST:** 2017
SALES (est): 61.35K **Privately Held**
SIC: 7999 Recreation services

(G-8431)
PNC BANK NATIONAL ASSOCIATION
Also Called: PNC
104 Main St (19966-8409)
P.O. Box 507 (19966-0507)
PHONE.................302 934-3106
Scott E Bagshaw, *Brnch Mgr*
EMP: 5
SALES (corp-wide): 23.54B **Publicly Held**
Web: www.pncbank.com
SIC: 6021 National trust companies with deposits, commercial
HQ: Pnc Bank, National Association
300 5th Ave
Pittsburgh PA 15222
877 762-2000

(G-8432)
POSITIVE GROWTH ALLIANCE INC
28612 Cynthia Marie Dr (19966-1549)
PHONE.................302 381-1610
EMP: 6 **EST:** 2009
SALES (est): 74.77K **Privately Held**
Web: www.makingdelawaregreat.com
SIC: 8399 Community development groups

(G-8433)
POT-NETS BAYSIDE LLC
34026 Annas Way Unit 1 (19966-3213)
PHONE.................302 945-9300
EMP: 50 **EST:** 2004
SALES (est): 2.51MM **Privately Held**
Web: www.potnets.com
SIC: 8742 Management consulting services

(G-8434)
POT-NETS BYWOOD VACATION RENTL
Also Called: Pot-Nets
34026 Annas Way Unit 2 (19966-3213)
PHONE.................302 945-9300
Robert Tunnell, *Prin*
EMP: 19
SALES (est): 1.71MM
SALES (corp-wide): 9.27MM **Privately Held**
Web: www.potnets.com
SIC: 7021 Lodging house, except organization
PA: Tunnell Companies, L.P.
34026 Annas Way Unit 1
Millsboro DE 19966
302 945-9300

(G-8435)
POWERBACK SERVICE LLC
30148 Mitchell St (19966)
PHONE.................302 934-1901
Matt Williams, *Owner*
EMP: 7 **EST:** 2008
SALES (est): 890.29K **Privately Held**
Web: www.powerbackllc.com
SIC: 5063 Generators

(G-8436)
POWERS PUBLISHING GROUP
29549 Whitstone Ln (19966-4752)
PHONE.................302 519-8575
Bryan Powers, *Prin*
EMP: 6 **EST:** 2012
SALES (est): 72.2K **Privately Held**
SIC: 2741 Miscellaneous publishing

(G-8437)
PREFERRED TAX SVC INC
32369 Long Neck Rd Unit 13 (19966-6681)
PHONE.................302 945-3700
Eddie Swan, *Mgr*
EMP: 5 **EST:** 2017
SALES (est): 73.45K **Privately Held**
Web: www.preferredtax.com
SIC: 7291 Tax return preparation services

(G-8438)
PRO CARPET LLC
26315 Miller St (19966-3475)
PHONE.................443 757-7320
EMP: 7 **EST:** 2018
SALES (est): 461.96K **Privately Held**
SIC: 1521 Single-family housing construction

(G-8439)
QUALITY HOME SOLUTIONS LLC
65 Creek Dr (19966-9678)
PHONE.................330 717-6793
EMP: 5 **EST:** 2015
SALES (est): 245.45K **Privately Held**
SIC: 1521 General remodeling, single-family houses

(G-8440)
QUANTAE L JENNINGS
Also Called: Richmen Trucking
26497 Mount Joy Rd (19966-3438)
PHONE.................561 537-0821
Quantae L Jennings, *Owner*
EMP: 5 **EST:** 2021
SALES (est): 68.92K **Privately Held**
SIC: 4212 Local trucking, without storage

(G-8441)
REIKI EXPERIENCE
128 Wharton St (19966-1702)
PHONE.................704 526-7092
Patricia Gilmore, *Prin*
EMP: 6 **EST:** 2017
SALES (est): 61.03K **Privately Held**
SIC: 8049 Massage Therapist

Millsboro - Sussex County (G-8442) — GEOGRAPHIC SECTION

(G-8442)
RENEW YOUR HEART AND MIND LLC
23321 Country Living Rd (19966-2850)
PHONE..............................302 344-7519
EMP: 8 EST: 2017
SALES (est): 66.65K Privately Held
Web: www.renewyourheartandmind.net
SIC: 8322 General counseling services

(G-8443)
RENTZ PAINTING LLC
32473 E Penn Ct (19966-4823)
PHONE..............................302 363-6619
Russell Rowe, Prin
EMP: 5 EST: 2015
SALES (est): 42.66K Privately Held
SIC: 1721 Painting and paper hanging

(G-8444)
REYES PAINTING LLC
28936 John J Williams Hwy (19966-4007)
PHONE..............................302 519-4538
EMP: 5 EST: 2012
SALES (est): 97.19K Privately Held
SIC: 1721 Painting and paper hanging

(G-8445)
RICHARD D WHALEY CNSTR LLC
29952 Lewis Rd (19966-4740)
PHONE..............................302 934-9525
EMP: 5 EST: 2003
SQ FT: 2,400
SALES (est): 572.43K Privately Held
SIC: 1521 1771 Single-family housing construction; Concrete work

(G-8446)
RIVERDALE PARK LLC
28301 Chief Rd (19966-4582)
PHONE..............................302 945-2475
Kenneth S Clark Senior, Owner
EMP: 5 EST: 1920
SQ FT: 600
SALES (est): 168.95K Privately Held
SIC: 7011 0191 Resort hotel; General farms, primarily crop

(G-8447)
RKB FUNERALS INC
P.O. Box 125 (19966-0125)
PHONE..............................302 934-7842
EMP: 5 EST: 2009
SALES (est): 137.58K Privately Held
SIC: 7261 Funeral home

(G-8448)
ROBERT HOYT & CO
Also Called: Hoyt, Robert M & Co LLC CPA
218 N Dupont (19966)
P.O. Box 818 (19966-0818)
PHONE..............................302 934-6688
W H Pusey, Owner
EMP: 8 EST: 1989
SALES (est): 491.95K Privately Held
Web: www.rmhoytco.com
SIC: 8721 Certified public accountant

(G-8449)
ROBINSON EXPORT & IMPORT CORP
Also Called: Reico Kitchen & Bath
28412 Dupont Blvd Ste 106 (19966-1227)
PHONE..............................410 219-7200
Tessa Hammer, Brnch Mgr
EMP: 5
SALES (corp-wide): 103.5MM Privately Held
Web: www.reico.com
SIC: 1799 Kitchen and bathroom remodeling
PA: Robinson Export And Import Corporation
6790 Commercial Dr
Springfield VA 22151
703 245-8322

(G-8450)
ROUTE 24 GOT JUNK
31788 Schooner Dr (19966-4531)
PHONE..............................302 258-7990
EMP: 5 EST: 2015
SALES (est): 110.49K Privately Held
SIC: 4953 Rubbish collection and disposal

(G-8451)
SAB HEATING & AIR
24430 Shady Ln (19966-4423)
P.O. Box 6 (19966-0006)
PHONE..............................302 945-3117
EMP: 5 EST: 1990
SALES (est): 140.67K Privately Held
SIC: 1711 Heating and air conditioning contractors

(G-8452)
SALTWATER COWGIRLS
26563 Jersey Rd (19966-3901)
PHONE..............................302 745-3632
EMP: 5 EST: 2017
SALES (est): 67.42K Privately Held
Web: www.saltwatercowgirlssurf.com
SIC: 7997 Membership sports and recreation clubs

(G-8453)
SALVATION ARMY
Also Called: Salvation Army
559 E Dupont Hwy (19966-1914)
PHONE..............................302 934-3730
Christy Cugno, Brnch Mgr
EMP: 16
SALES (corp-wide): 2.41B Privately Held
Web: www.saconnects.org
SIC: 8322 8661 Individual and family services; Religious organizations
HQ: The Salvation Army
440 W Nyack Rd Ofc
West Nyack NY 10994
845 620-7200

(G-8454)
SARA ELIZABETH NOVY DPT
32310 Bayshore Dr (19966-9058)
PHONE..............................201 783-5082
Sara Novy, Prin
EMP: 6 EST: 2016
SALES (est): 34.6K Privately Held
SIC: 8049 Offices of health practitioner

(G-8455)
SCHELL BROS AT PENINSULA LAKES
30965 Fowlers Path (19966-7318)
PHONE..............................302 228-4488
EMP: 8 EST: 2017
SALES (est): 139.47K Privately Held
Web: www.schellbrothers.com
SIC: 1521 New construction, single-family houses

(G-8456)
SCHRIDER ENTERPRISES INC
398 W State St (19966)
PHONE..............................302 934-1900
EMP: 7 EST: 1995
SALES (est): 91.31K Privately Held
SIC: 7539 7549 Automotive repair shops, nec ; Lubrication service, automotive

(G-8457)
SHADOW PROTECTIVE SERVICES
25906 Country Meadows Dr (19966-3485)
PHONE..............................410 903-3455
Matthew Miller, Prin
EMP: 5 EST: 2017
SALES (est): 96.05K Privately Held
SIC: 7381 Detective and armored car services

(G-8458)
SHELTER CONST
23431 Godwin School Rd (19966-2856)
PHONE..............................302 829-8310
EMP: 6 EST: 2018
SALES (est): 195.18K Privately Held
Web: www.shelterconstructionde.com
SIC: 1521 Single-family housing construction

(G-8459)
SHORE IRRIGATION SERVICES
22009 Dots Rd (19966-3111)
PHONE..............................302 542-1206
Cody Collins, Prin
EMP: 13 EST: 2019
SALES (est): 2.33MM Privately Held
SIC: 4971 Irrigation systems

(G-8460)
SHORE MASONRY INC
32405 Mermaid Run (19966-4462)
PHONE..............................302 945-5933
EMP: 7 EST: 1990
SALES (est): 624.86K Privately Held
SIC: 1741 1771 Masonry and other stonework; Concrete work

(G-8461)
SHORE PRIDE ALL-STARS INC
34267 Pear Tree Rd (19966-3152)
PHONE..............................302 245-1347
Christina Mccoy, Prin
EMP: 7 EST: 2015
SALES (est): 157.69K Privately Held
Web: www.shoreprideallstars.com
SIC: 7991 Physical fitness facilities

(G-8462)
SHORE SHUTTERS AND SHADE
35736 S Gloucester Cir (19966-3202)
PHONE..............................302 569-1738
Todd Ellis, Prin
EMP: 6 EST: 2018
SALES (est): 196.47K Privately Held
SIC: 3442 Shutters, door or window: metal

(G-8463)
SHUTTLE RUNNERS
29852 Plantation Lakes Blvd (19966)
PHONE..............................302 245-0945
Clay Snead, Prin
EMP: 5 EST: 2018
SALES (est): 65.13K Privately Held
Web: www.shuttlerunners.net
SIC: 4111 Local and suburban transit

(G-8464)
SIGNATURE RENOVATIONS
31885 Schooner Dr (19966-4536)
PHONE..............................302 858-2955
Neal Colvard, Prin
EMP: 5 EST: 2017
SALES (est): 78.56K Privately Held
SIC: 1521 General remodeling, single-family houses

(G-8465)
SOUTHERN DELAWARE FOOT & ANKLE
28253 Dupont Blvd Unit 2 (19966-1223)
PHONE..............................302 629-3000
Bradley Lemon, Pr
EMP: 7 EST: 2014
SALES (est): 231.82K Privately Held
Web: www.sodelfootandankle.com
SIC: 8043 Offices and clinics of podiatrists

(G-8466)
SPLASH DAY
36773 Millsboro Hwy (19966-3023)
PHONE..............................302 238-7457
EMP: 8 EST: 2014
SALES (est): 144.34K Privately Held
Web: www.splashdayschool.com
SIC: 8099 Health and allied services, nec

(G-8467)
STATE FARM INSURANCE
Also Called: State Farm Insurance
29787 John J Williams Hwy Unit 1 (19966-4097)
PHONE..............................302 934-8083
Chuck Hall, Owner
EMP: 5 EST: 2014
SALES (est): 55.85K Privately Held
Web: www.statefarm.com
SIC: 6411 Insurance agents and brokers

(G-8468)
STOP TRAFFIC
408 Circle Rd (19966-8730)
PHONE..............................302 604-1176
EMP: 3 EST: 2016
SALES (est): 98.36K Privately Held
Web: www.producebanners.com
SIC: 3993 Signs and advertising specialties

(G-8469)
STRANDS PRPRTY PRSERVATION LLC
26035 Oak St Ste 101 (19966-3430)
PHONE..............................302 381-9792
EMP: 8 EST: 2011
SALES (est): 283.28K Privately Held
SIC: 8741 7389 Business management; Business Activities at Non-Commercial Site

(G-8470)
SUNRISE MEDICAL CENTER
Also Called: Office of Ruben Tejeira MD The
29339 Iron Branch Rd (19966-4211)
PHONE..............................302 854-9006
Lilian Vassallo, Off Mgr
Ruben Tejeira Md, Prin
EMP: 6 EST: 2003
SALES (est): 493.31K Privately Held
SIC: 8099 Childbirth preparation clinic

(G-8471)
SUPERCUTS
Also Called: Supercuts
26670 Centerview Dr (19966-3584)
PHONE..............................302 934-6534
EMP: 8 EST: 2009
SALES (est): 68.39K Privately Held
Web: www.supercuts.com
SIC: 7231 Unisex hair salons

(G-8472)
SURRENDER HOUSE
28124 Layton Davis Rd (19966-4623)
PHONE..............................302 249-6830
Quadree Burden, Prin
EMP: 5 EST: 2016
SALES (est): 44.37K Privately Held
SIC: 8641 Civic and social associations

GEOGRAPHIC SECTION

Millsboro - Sussex County (G-8501)

(G-8473)
SUSAN DONGES
32060 Long Neck Rd (19966-6228)
PHONE.................302 645-3100
EMP: 7 **EST:** 2018
SALES (est): 87.85K **Privately Held**
SIC: 8322 Social worker

(G-8474)
SUSSEX FENCE CO
32524 Morning View Ln (19966-4982)
PHONE.................302 945-7008
Robert Haas, *Pr*
EMP: 9 **EST:** 1981
SALES (est): 222.2K **Privately Held**
Web: www.sussexfence.com
SIC: 1799 Fence construction

(G-8475)
SUSSEX FENCING
John J Williams Hwy (19966)
PHONE.................302 945-7008
Rob Haas, *Owner*
EMP: 5 **EST:** 1982
SALES (est): 340.56K **Privately Held**
Web: www.sussexfence.com
SIC: 1799 Fence construction

(G-8476)
SUSSEX HEATING AND AIR LLC
153 Teal Dr (19966-8769)
PHONE.................302 231-8446
Shawn Hatton, *Prin*
EMP: 5 **EST:** 2017
SALES (est): 129.5K **Privately Held**
SIC: 1711 Warm air heating and air conditioning contractor

(G-8477)
SUSSEX SUPERIOR TOOLS INC
25269 Mastermark Ln (19966-2615)
PHONE.................302 752-6817
Karen Sauers, *Prin*
EMP: 5 **EST:** 2016
SALES (est): 143.07K **Privately Held**
SIC: 4789 Transportation services, nec

(G-8478)
SWAMPS PROPERTY MAINT LLC
34604 Lynch Rd (19966-3056)
PHONE.................302 841-1162
EMP: 6 **EST:** 2018
SALES (est): 227.56K **Privately Held**
SIC: 7349 Building maintenance services, nec

(G-8479)
T & C ENTERPRISE INCORPORATED
Also Called: Tri-State Mobile Home Supply
26007 Pugs Xing (19966-3995)
PHONE.................302 934-8080
Greson Duox, *Pr*
Patricia L Taylor, *Pr*
Willie Taylor, *VP*
EMP: 5 **EST:** 1988
SQ FT: 6,400
SALES (est): 1.15MM **Privately Held**
SIC: 5039 5271 5072 Mobile homes; Mobile home equipment; Builders' hardware, nec

(G-8480)
TAIL BANGERS INC
24546 Betts Pond Rd (19966-1560)
PHONE.................302 947-4900
Lisa Sinclair, *Pr*
EMP: 10 **EST:** 2005
SQ FT: 5,000
SALES (est): 2.14MM **Privately Held**
Web: www.tailbangers.com
SIC: 5149 Dog food

(G-8481)
TAILBANGERS INC
24546 Betts Pond Rd (19966-1560)
PHONE.................302 934-1125
Lisa St Clair, *Prin*
EMP: 10 **EST:** 2014
SALES (est): 3.18MM **Privately Held**
Web: www.tailbangers.com
SIC: 5149 Dog food

(G-8482)
TH WHITE GENERAL CONTRACT
32783 Long Neck Rd Unit 2 (19966-6692)
PHONE.................302 945-1829
Thomas H White, *Prin*
EMP: 5 **EST:** 2006
SALES (est): 681.45K **Privately Held**
SIC: 5082 General construction machinery and equipment

(G-8483)
TH WHITE GENERAL CONTRACTOR
31687 Messiah Ln (19966-4963)
PHONE.................302 945-1829
EMP: 7 **EST:** 2020
SALES (est): 469.89K **Privately Held**
Web: www.thwhitegeneralcontractor.com
SIC: 1521 General remodeling, single-family houses

(G-8484)
THE OAK ORCHRD-RVRDALE POST 28
Also Called: OAK ORCHARD AM LEGION 28
31768 Legion Rd (19966-7114)
PHONE.................302 945-1673
Casmere Stasack, *Pr*
EMP: 10 **EST:** 1981
SQ FT: 1,600
SALES (est): 1.4MM **Privately Held**
Web: www.alpost28.com
SIC: 8641 Veterans' organization

(G-8485)
THELMA STANLEY
Also Called: Tms Asphalt Maintenance
32189 Steele Dr (19966-6221)
PHONE.................302 604-8481
Stanley Thelma, *Prin*
EMP: 6 **EST:** 2011
SALES (est): 367.65K **Privately Held**
Web: www.tmsasphaltmaintenance.com
SIC: 1611 Surfacing and paving

(G-8486)
TJ S PLUMBING HEATING L
32605 Millsboro Hwy (19966-3010)
PHONE.................302 228-7129
Travis Lee Justice Senior, *Pr*
EMP: 10 **EST:** 2014
SALES (est): 453.92K **Privately Held**
SIC: 1711 Plumbing contractors

(G-8487)
TRIPLE A CLEANING SERVICES INC
32277 Pelican Ct (19966-9026)
P.O. Box 49 (19966-0049)
PHONE.................302 236-0407
William Hopkins, *Prin*
EMP: 5 **EST:** 2016
SALES (est): 30.18K **Privately Held**
SIC: 7699 Cleaning services

(G-8488)
TUNNELL COMPANIES LP (PA)
Also Called: Tunnel Industries
34026 Annas Way Unit 1 (19966-3213)
PHONE.................302 945-9300
Robert Tunnell Junior, *Genl Pt*
Robert W Tunnell Iii, *Pt*
EMP: 19 **EST:** 1981
SQ FT: 10,000
SALES (est): 9.27MM
SALES (corp-wide): 9.27MM **Privately Held**
Web: www.baywoodgreens.com
SIC: 6515 6531 6519 Mobile home site operators; Real estate agents and managers; Real property lessors, nec

(G-8489)
U-HAUL INTERNATIONAL
Also Called: U-Haul
327 Main St (19966-8413)
PHONE.................302 934-1601
Liann Burroughs, *Mgr*
EMP: 8 **EST:** 2010
SALES (est): 94.27K **Privately Held**
Web: www.uhaul.com
SIC: 7513 Truck rental and leasing, no drivers

(G-8490)
UPBOUND GROUP INC
Also Called: Rent-A-Center
28544 Dupont Blvd Unit 9 (19966-4792)
PHONE.................302 934-6700
EMP: 5
Web: www.rentacenter.com
SIC: 7359 Appliance rental
PA: Upbound Group, Inc.
5501 Headquarters Dr
Plano TX 75024

(G-8491)
URIS LLC (PA)
Also Called: Uris Salvage Auto Inspections
32783 Long Neck Rd Unit 3 (19966-6692)
PHONE.................302 469-7000
Leo Sticinski, *Pr*
EMP: 5 **EST:** 2013
SALES (est): 263.15K
SALES (corp-wide): 263.15K **Privately Held**
Web: www.look.live
SIC: 7549 Inspection and diagnostic service, automotive

(G-8492)
VAN BUREN MORTGAGE LLC
26506 Victorias Landing Rd (19966-7064)
PHONE.................302 945-1109
EMP: 8
Web: www.jgwentworth.com
SIC: 6163 Mortgage brokers arranging for loans, using money of others
HQ: Van Buren Mortgage, Llc
3350 Commission Ct
Woodbridge VA 22192
888 349-3773

(G-8493)
VECTOR ENGINEERING SVCS CORP
27045 Firefly Blvd (19966-7092)
PHONE.................609 947-2580
Pete A Geradino, *Prin*
EMP: 5 **EST:** 2016
SALES (est): 247.25K **Privately Held**
SIC: 8711 Structural engineering

(G-8494)
VICTIMS VOICES HEARD INC
32449 Back Nine Way (19966-6283)
PHONE.................302 242-1108
Kimberly L Book, *Prin*
EMP: 5 **EST:** 2017
SALES (est): 66.31K **Privately Held**
Web: www.victimsvoicesheard.org
SIC: 8399 Advocacy group

(G-8495)
VIRGIL P ELLWANGER
Mllsboro Vlg Grn Rr 24 (19966)
P.O. Box 216 (19966-0216)
PHONE.................302 934-8083
Virgil Ellwanger, *Owner*
EMP: 6 **EST:** 1967
SALES (est): 339.02K **Privately Held**
SIC: 6411 Insurance agents, nec

(G-8496)
VOGUE ON 24 SALON & SPA LLC
36908 Silicato Dr Unit 11 (19966-5006)
PHONE.................302 947-5667
Robert Brandon Tatum-poole, *Prin*
EMP: 6 **EST:** 2020
SALES (est): 98.71K **Privately Held**
Web: www.vogueon24.com
SIC: 7991 Spas

(G-8497)
W POWELL INVESTMENTS
20437 Laurel Rd (19966-2947)
PHONE.................443 523-2476
William J Powell, *Prin*
EMP: 5 **EST:** 2017
SALES (est): 229.88K **Privately Held**
SIC: 6799 Investors, nec

(G-8498)
W T SCHRIDER & SONS INC
24572 Betts Pond Rd (19966-1560)
PHONE.................302 934-1900
William Schrider, *Pr*
EMP: 10 **EST:** 2009
SQ FT: 6,000
SALES (est): 1.58MM **Privately Held**
Web: www.inandouttires.com
SIC: 5085 Industrial supplies

(G-8499)
WARRIOR COMMUNITY CONNECT INC
22165 S Preservation Dr (19966-7160)
PHONE.................202 309-5729
Walt Ellenberger, *Ch Bd*
EMP: 5 **EST:** 2020
SALES (est): 70K **Privately Held**
Web: www.warriorcommunityconnect.org
SIC: 8641 Civic and social associations

(G-8500)
WASTE INDUSTRIES DELAWARE LLC
Also Called: Gfl Environmental
28471 John J Williams Hwy (19966-4098)
PHONE.................302 934-1364
EMP: 5
SIC: 4953 Garbage: collecting, destroying, and processing
HQ: Waste Industries Of Delaware, Llc
604 Cannery Ln
Townsend DE 19734
302 378-5400

(G-8501)
WATSON FUNERAL HOME INC
Also Called: Rkb Fnral Trdg As Wtson Fnrl H
211 S Washington St (19966-8425)
P.O. Box 125 (19966-0125)
PHONE.................302 934-7842
Robert Herrington, *Pr*
Tia Watson, *Treas*
EMP: 10 **EST:** 1944
SALES (est): 495.69K **Privately Held**
Web: www.watsonfh.com
SIC: 7261 Funeral home

Millsboro - Sussex County (G-8502) GEOGRAPHIC SECTION

(G-8502)
WE R WIRELESS
Also Called: Verizon Wireless Authorized Ret
28665 Dupont Blvd (19966-4784)
PHONE...................443 880-0308
EMP: 6 EST: 2015
SALES (est): 66.3K **Privately Held**
Web: www.verizon.com
SIC: 4812 Cellular telephone services

(G-8503)
WELLNESS AND REJUVENATION
30996 Puseys Rd (19966-2913)
PHONE...................732 977-6958
Tiffany Siegler, *Prin*
EMP: 6 EST: 2017
SALES (est): 84.4K **Privately Held**
Web: www.firststatemedspa.com
SIC: 8099 Health and allied services, nec

(G-8504)
WESTWOOD FARMS INCORPORATED
21906 Esham Ln (19966-3032)
PHONE...................302 238-7141
Bruce Esham, *Pr*
EMP: 10 EST: 1979
SALES (est): 1.92MM **Privately Held**
SIC: 1542 0111 0251 Farm building construction; Wheat; Broiler, fryer, and roaster chickens

(G-8505)
WHITE HOUSE BEACH INC
35266 Fishermans Rd Unit 2 (19966-7282)
PHONE...................302 945-3032
William H Showell, *Pr*
Sam Showell, *VP*
John Showell, *Sec*
EMP: 10 EST: 1959
SALES (est): 752.05K **Privately Held**
Web: www.whitehousebeach.net
SIC: 6515 Mobile home site operators

(G-8506)
WILGUS INSUR AGCY INC - MLLSBO
400 Delaware Ave Ste 103 (19966-1763)
PHONE...................302 934-1502
EMP: 8 EST: 1977
SALES (est): 50.78K **Privately Held**
Web: www.wilgusins.com
SIC: 6411 Insurance agents, nec

(G-8507)
WOOLEY BULLY INC
Also Called: Labrador, The
25605 Rogers Rd (19966-4943)
PHONE...................302 542-3613
Roger B Wooleyhan Junior, *Pr*
Elizebeth M Wooleyhan, *Sec*
EMP: 6 EST: 2004
SALES (est): 797.12K **Privately Held**
SIC: 5146 Fish and seafoods

(G-8508)
WWC III TRUCKING LLC
34564 Pear Tree Rd (19966-3040)
PHONE...................302 238-7778
EMP: 4 EST: 2010
SALES (est): 488.86K **Privately Held**
SIC: 3537 Industrial trucks and tractors

(G-8509)
XPRESS CONTRACTING
26182 Flying Bridge Ct (19966-6935)
P.O. Box 279 (19951-0279)
PHONE...................703 932-8565
Brian Carneiro, *Prin*
EMP: 6 EST: 2016
SALES (est): 256.01K **Privately Held**
SIC: 1799 Special trade contractors, nec

(G-8510)
YELLOWFINS
36908 Silicato Dr Unit 14 (19966-5006)
PHONE...................302 381-2569
Josh Fallon, *Prin*
EMP: 5 EST: 2018
SALES (est): 132.24K **Privately Held**
SIC: 8621 Bar association

(G-8511)
ZEGLINS AUTOMOTIVE INC
25374 Townsend Rd (19966-2620)
PHONE...................302 947-1414
William Zeglin, *Prin*
EMP: 5 EST: 2010
SALES (est): 100.2K **Privately Held**
SIC: 7538 General automotive repair shops

Millville
Sussex County

(G-8512)
AFTERGLO BEAUTY SPA
22 Cedar Dr (19967)
PHONE...................302 537-7546
Sheila Rebbingham, *Owner*
EMP: 6 EST: 2011
SALES (est): 133.5K **Privately Held**
Web: www.afterglospa.com
SIC: 7991 7231 Spas; Beauty shops

(G-8513)
ALICIA KENDORSKI NCC
32630 Cedar Dr Unit A (19967-6946)
PHONE...................302 448-5054
Alicia Kendorski, *Prin*
EMP: 8 EST: 2016
SALES (est): 50.14K **Privately Held**
SIC: 8011 Offices and clinics of medical doctors

(G-8514)
ALL ABOUT U EVADA CONCEPT (PA)
35825 Atlantic Ave (19967-6908)
PHONE...................302 539-1925
Cathy Lynch, *Owner*
EMP: 6 EST: 2005
SALES (est): 240.59K **Privately Held**
Web: www.allaboutusalonandspa.com
SIC: 7231 Unisex hair salons

(G-8515)
ATLANTIC AUTO REPAIR LLC
35252 Atlantic Ave (19967-6902)
PHONE...................302 539-7352
Kevin Martin, *Managing Member*
EMP: 7 EST: 2017
SALES (est): 407.75K **Privately Held**
Web: www.atlanticautorepair.net
SIC: 7538 General automotive repair shops

(G-8516)
BAYSIDE RESORT GOLF CLUB
31854 Mill Run Drive (19970-3807)
PHONE...................410 652-7705
Jennifer Idzi, *Prin*
EMP: 15 EST: 2016
SALES (est): 32.59K **Privately Held**
Web: www.golfbayside.com
SIC: 7011 Resort hotel

(G-8517)
BEACHVIEW FAMILY HEALTH
550 Atlantic Ave (19967-6901)
PHONE...................302 537-8318
Julie Hattier D.o.s., *Prin*
EMP: 5 EST: 2006
SALES (est): 315.06K **Privately Held**
SIC: 8099 Health and allied services, nec

(G-8518)
BEAR TRAP SPIRITS INC
38014 Town Center Dr (19967-6970)
PHONE...................302 537-8008
EMP: 5 EST: 2019
SALES (est): 236.46K **Privately Held**
SIC: 2085 Distilled and blended liquors

(G-8519)
BEEBE MEDICAL CENTER INC
32550 Docs Pl (19967-6975)
PHONE...................302 541-4175
EMP: 21
SALES (corp-wide): 581.97MM **Privately Held**
Web: www.beebehealthcare.org
SIC: 8062 General medical and surgical hospitals
PA: Beebe Medical Center, Inc.
424 Savannah Rd
Lewes DE 19958
302 645-3300

(G-8520)
BETHANY BCH HAIR SNIPPERY INC
Also Called: Hair Snippery
32566 Docs Pl Unit 6 (19967-6959)
P.O. Box 923 (19930-0923)
PHONE...................302 539-8344
John Scordo, *Pr*
EMP: 5 EST: 1982
SALES (est): 83.38K **Privately Held**
SIC: 7241 7231 Barber shops; Beauty shops

(G-8521)
BONNIE L BURNQUIST MD PA
118 Atlantic Ave (19970-9163)
PHONE...................302 537-2260
EMP: 6 EST: 2004
SALES (est): 137.56K **Privately Held**
Web: www.bonnielburnquistmdpa.net
SIC: 8011 General and family practice, physician/surgeon

(G-8522)
CHRISTOPHER COMPANIES
39008 Seascape Ct (19967-6841)
PHONE...................302 539-2888
EMP: 5 EST: 2015
SALES (est): 142.95K **Privately Held**
SIC: 1542 Nonresidential construction, nec

(G-8523)
COASTAL RENTALS HYDRAULICS LLC
35283 Atlantic Ave (19967-6912)
PHONE...................302 251-3103
EMP: 6 EST: 2009
SALES (est): 996.51K **Privately Held**
Web: www.coastalrentalsde.com
SIC: 7359 Equipment rental and leasing, nec

(G-8524)
COASTAL TENTED EVENTS
35283 Atlantic Ave (19967-6912)
PHONE...................302 539-5211
EMP: 5 EST: 2019
SALES (est): 78.05K **Privately Held**
Web: www.tentedeventsde.com
SIC: 7359 Party supplies rental services

(G-8525)
COLDWELL BANKER
Also Called: Coldwell Banker
35786 Atlantic Ave Unit 2 (19967-6955)
PHONE...................302 541-5790
EMP: 5 EST: 2019
SALES (est): 74.37K **Privately Held**
Web: www.coldwellbanker.com
SIC: 6531 Real estate agent, residential

(G-8526)
COUNTY BANK
10 Old Mill Dr (19967-6951)
PHONE...................302 537-0900
Dick Reed, *Mgr*
EMP: 6
Web: www.countybankdel.com
SIC: 6021 6029 National commercial banks; Commercial banks, nec
PA: County Bank
19927 Shuttle Rd
Rehoboth Beach DE 19971

(G-8527)
DR JULIE HATTIER
35202 Atlantic Ave (19967-6901)
PHONE...................302 539-7063
Julie Hattier, *Prin*
EMP: 10 EST: 2013
SALES (est): 107.05K **Privately Held**
Web: www.rejuvenationskinwellness.com
SIC: 8011 Dermatologist

(G-8528)
EXCEL PROPERTY MANAGEMENT LLC
35370 Atlantic Ave (19967-6903)
P.O. Box 808 (19970-0808)
PHONE...................302 541-5312
EMP: 9 EST: 2001
SQ FT: 1,500
SALES (est): 835.07K **Privately Held**
Web: www.excelpmllc.com
SIC: 6531 Real estate managers

(G-8529)
FRIENDS & FAMILY PRACTICE
609 Atlantic Ave Ste A (19967)
PHONE...................302 537-3740
Kimberly Gallagher, *Dir*
EMP: 6 EST: 2002
SALES (est): 475.89K **Privately Held**
SIC: 8062 General medical and surgical hospitals

(G-8530)
GO CURVES LADIES
33077 Deer Trl (19967-6928)
PHONE...................302 541-4681
Nancy Maupai, *Prin*
EMP: 5 EST: 2015
SALES (est): 74.36K **Privately Held**
SIC: 7991 Exercise salon

(G-8531)
GULFSTREAM DEVELOPMENT CORP
35477 Atlantic Ave (19967-6990)
PHONE...................302 539-6178
Mark Zduriencik, *Ch*
Robert Harris Junior, *Pr*
EMP: 5 EST: 1988
SALES (est): 891.37K **Privately Held**
SIC: 1521 6552 New construction, single-family houses; Land subdividers and developers, residential

(G-8532)
HALPERN EYE ASSOCIATES INC
142 Atlantic Ave Ste A (19967-6955)
PHONE...................302 537-0234
P Zakrochimski, *Brnch Mgr*
EMP: 8

GEOGRAPHIC SECTION

Milton - Sussex County (G-8562)

SALES (corp-wide): 9.06MM **Privately Held**
Web: www.myeyedr.com
SIC: 8042 Specialized optometrists
PA: Halpern Eye Associates, Inc.
885 S Governors Ave
Dover DE 19904
302 734-5861

(G-8533)
HC SALON HOLDINGS INC
Also Called: Hair Cuttery
38069 Town Center Dr (19967-6968)
PHONE.................................302 537-4624
Jessica Johnson, Brnch Mgr
EMP: 25
SALES (corp-wide): 95.49MM **Privately Held**
Web: www.haircuttery.com
SIC: 7231 Unisex hair salons
PA: Hc Salon Holdings, Inc.
1640 Boro Pl Fl 4
Mc Lean VA 22102
917 751-8869

(G-8534)
HELEN DELVECCHIO LPN
30237 Seashore Park Dr (19967-6788)
PHONE.................................914 472-3837
Helen Delvecchio, Mgr
EMP: 6 EST: 2017
SALES (est): 22.18K **Privately Held**
SIC: 8049 Offices of health practitioner

(G-8535)
KELLER WLLAMS RLTY - LSKO TO B
Also Called: Keller Williams Realtors
35091 Atlantic Ave (19970-3522)
PHONE.................................302 581-9101
EMP: 5 EST: 2019
SALES (est): 208.44K **Privately Held**
Web: www.kw.com
SIC: 6531 Real estate agent, residential

(G-8536)
LIFELINE BLTMORE MD MLLVLLE DE
33367 Lone Cedar Lndg (19967-6774)
PHONE.................................410 262-0875
EMP: 6 EST: 2017
SALES (est): 64.83K **Privately Held**
SIC: 8011 Offices and clinics of medical doctors

(G-8537)
LOCCHIO EYECARE LLC
32566 Docs Pl (19967-6959)
PHONE.................................302 644-1039
EMP: 7 EST: 2019
SALES (est): 259.27K **Privately Held**
Web: www.locchio-lewes.com
SIC: 8042 Offices and clinics of optometrists

(G-8538)
LORDS LANDSCAPING INC
315 Atlantic Ave (19967-6961)
PHONE.................................302 539-6119
William Lord, Pr
Donna Lord, VP
EMP: 20 EST: 1978
SQ FT: 7,000
SALES (est): 910.56M **Privately Held**
Web: www.lordslandscaping.com
SIC: 0782 5261 Landscape contractors; Garden supplies and tools, nec

(G-8539)
MARK T DRONEY
31322 Railway Rd (19967-6962)
PHONE.................................302 537-2305
Mark T Droney, Prin

EMP: 9 EST: 2014
SALES (est): 496K **Privately Held**
SIC: 7538 General automotive repair shops

(G-8540)
MERCANTILE PROCESSING INC
32695 Roxana Rd (19967)
PHONE.................................302 524-8000
Kyle Morgan, Pr
EMP: 33 EST: 2008
SALES (est): 4.24MM **Privately Held**
Web: www.mpiprocessing.com
SIC: 7389 Credit card service

(G-8541)
MICHAEL MCCARTHY STONES
35283 Atlantic Ave (19967-6912)
PHONE.................................302 539-8056
EMP: 7 EST: 2016
SALES (est): 1.11MM **Privately Held**
Web: www.mccarthystones.com
SIC: 5032 Brick, stone, and related material

(G-8542)
MIKEN BUILDERS INC
32782 Cedar Dr Unit 1 (19967-6919)
PHONE.................................302 537-4444
T Michael Nally, CEO
Mike Mckone, Pr
Mike Cummings, *
EMP: 28 EST: 1986
SALES (est): 9.56MM **Privately Held**
Web: www.mikenbuilders.com
SIC: 1542 1541 1521 Commercial and office building, new construction; Industrial buildings, new construction, nec; New construction, single-family houses

(G-8543)
MILLVILLE REHABILITATION SVC
32566 Docs Pl Unit 7 (19967-6959)
PHONE.................................302 645-3100
Timothy Phelps, Prin
EMP: 16 EST: 1998
SALES (est): 59.88K **Privately Held**
SIC: 8322 Rehabilitation services

(G-8544)
MILLVLLE BY THE SEA MSTR CMNTY
30794 Endless Summer Dr (19967-6839)
PHONE.................................302 539-2888
EMP: 6 EST: 2019
SALES (est): 54.83K **Privately Held**
Web: www.christophercompanies.com
SIC: 8699 Membership organizations, nec

(G-8545)
REJUVNTION SKIN WLLNESS ASTHTI
35202 Atlantic Ave (19967-6901)
PHONE.................................302 537-8318
Amanda Dempsey Donaway, Managing Member
EMP: 10 EST: 2017
SALES (est): 377.38K **Privately Held**
Web: www.rejuvenationskinwellness.com
SIC: 7231 Beauty shops

(G-8546)
RESORT INVESTIGATION & PATROL
19 Pine St (19970)
PHONE.................................302 539-5808
Joseph J Kansak Senior, Pr
Janet Rae Kansak, *
EMP: 7 EST: 1971
SALES (est): 196.04K **Privately Held**
SIC: 7381 Detective agency

(G-8547)
SAVVYDERM SKIN CLINIC LLC
32782 Cedar Dr Ste 2 (19967-6919)
PHONE.................................302 257-5089
EMP: 11 EST: 2021
SALES (est): 255.33K **Privately Held**
SIC: 8011 Dermatologist

(G-8548)
SUZETTE NOECKER
Also Called: Bloom 415
27066 Lightning Run (19967-6892)
PHONE.................................301 814-8003
Suzette Noecker, Owner
EMP: 5 EST: 2006
SALES (est): 150.47K **Privately Held**
Web: bloom415.carlsoncraft.com
SIC: 7389 Advertising, promotional, and trade show services

(G-8549)
TIDALHLTH PNNSULA REGIONAL INC
142 Atlantic Ave Ste C (19967)
PHONE.................................302 537-1457
EMP: 145
SALES (corp-wide): 1.18MM **Privately Held**
Web: www.tidalhealth.org
SIC: 8099 Childbirth preparation clinic
HQ: Tidalhealth Peninsula Regional, Inc.
100 E Carroll St
Salisbury MD 21801
410 546-6400

(G-8550)
TRANSFORMING WELLNESS LLC
35802 Atlantic Ave (19967-6907)
PHONE.................................302 249-2526
Marcia Moon, Prin
EMP: 6 EST: 2016
SALES (est): 78.07K **Privately Held**
Web: www.avlandhardscaping.com
SIC: 8099 Health and allied services, nec

(G-8551)
WHITES CREEK MANOR POA
430 Jackie Dr (19970-9784)
PHONE.................................302 541-9422
EMP: 5 EST: 2018
SALES (est): 46.16K **Privately Held**
Web: wcmanor.wordpress.com
SIC: 8641 Homeowners' association

Milton
Sussex County

(G-8552)
1825 INN
26285 Broadkill Rd (19968-2944)
PHONE.................................717 838-8282
EMP: 10 EST: 2019
SALES (est): 32.59K **Privately Held**
SIC: 7011 Bed and breakfast inn

(G-8553)
A & V LDSCPG & HARDSCAPING LLC
704 Chestnut St (19968-1324)
PHONE.................................302 684-8609
EMP: 8
SALES (est): 256.47K **Privately Held**
Web: www.avlandhardscaping.com
SIC: 0781 Landscape services

(G-8554)
A&V LANDSCAPING
704 Chestnut St (19968-1324)
PHONE.................................302 684-8609

Victor Gomez, Prin
EMP: 9 EST: 2015
SALES (est): 397.39K **Privately Held**
Web: www.avlandhardscaping.com
SIC: 0781 Landscape services

(G-8555)
ADMEAL INC
124 Broadkill Rd (19968-1008)
P.O. Box 771 (19968-0771)
PHONE.................................954 758-8699
Bakhrom Kholmatov, Pr
EMP: 6
SALES (est): 68.24K **Privately Held**
SIC: 8399 Social services, nec

(G-8556)
ALLAN FOR DELAWARE
13288 Sunland Dr (19968-2990)
PHONE.................................410 920-2493
Donald Allan, Prin
EMP: 5 EST: 2017
SALES (est): 54.21K **Privately Held**
SIC: 8399 Advocacy group

(G-8557)
ALLEN CHORMAN & SON INC
30475 E Mill Run (19968-3457)
PHONE.................................302 684-2770
Allen Chorman, Pr
Jeffrey A Chorman, VP
EMP: 12 EST: 1966
SALES (est): 938.73K **Privately Held**
SIC: 0721 Crop dusting services

(G-8558)
ALWAYS BEST CARE
624 Mulberry St (19968-1516)
PHONE.................................302 409-3710
EMP: 10 EST: 2018
SALES (est): 135.86K **Privately Held**
Web: www.alwaysbestcare.com
SIC: 8082 Home health care services

(G-8559)
AMERICAN INDUSTRIES LLC
124 Broadkill Rd Ste 436 (19968-1008)
PHONE.................................302 585-0129
EMP: 5 EST: 2018
SALES (est): 190.74K **Privately Held**
Web: www.americanindustries.com
SIC: 3999 Manufacturing industries, nec

(G-8560)
AMY KELLENBERGER INC
22542 Hartschorn Dr (19968-2935)
PHONE.................................302 381-7901
Amy Kellenberger, Asst Sec
EMP: 14 EST: 2018
SALES (est): 264.09K **Privately Held**
Web: www.activeadultsdelaware.com
SIC: 6512 Nonresidential building operators

(G-8561)
ANYTIME FITNESS LEWES
Also Called: Anytime Fitness
23574 Holly Oak Dr (19968-4533)
PHONE.................................856 340-9252
EMP: 8 EST: 2017
SALES (est): 74.17K **Privately Held**
Web: www.anytimefitness.sg
SIC: 7991 Physical fitness clubs with training equipment

(G-8562)
AR CAMPAGNONE LLC
14928 Hudson Rd (19968-3601)
PHONE.................................302 329-9323
Alfred Campagnone, Prin
EMP: 5 EST: 2012

Milton - Sussex County (G-8563)   GEOGRAPHIC SECTION

SALES (est): 100.01K **Privately Held**
SIC: 1522 Residential construction, nec

(G-8563)
ART AND THERAPY SERVICES
120 S White Cedar Dr (19968-9700)
PHONE..................302 329-9794
Nicole Luther, *Prin*
EMP: 7 EST: 2014
SALES (est): 37.9K **Privately Held**
SIC: 8093 Rehabilitation center, outpatient treatment

(G-8564)
ARTESIAN WATER COMPANY INC
14701 Coastal Hwy (19968-3721)
PHONE..................800 332-5114
EMP: 14
SALES (corp-wide): 98.9MM **Publicly Held**
Web: www.artesianwater.com
SIC: 4941 Water supply
HQ: Artesian Water Company, Inc.
664 Churchmans Rd
Newark DE 19702
302 453-6900

(G-8565)
ATLANTIC SCREEN & MFG INC
Also Called: A S I
142 Broadkill Rd (19968-1008)
PHONE..................302 684-3197
Patricia Lawson, *Pr*
Jeffrey Lawson, *Sec*
Bill Lawson, *VP*
EMP: 4 EST: 1980
SQ FT: 28,000
SALES (est): 722.43K **Privately Held**
Web: www.atlantic-screen.com
SIC: 3444 3569 3498 Irrigation pipe, sheet metal; Filters and strainers, pipeline; Pipe sections, fabricated from purchased pipe

(G-8566)
AVAMER ROOFING INC
26483 Cave Neck Rd (19968-3002)
PHONE..................302 228-8673
EMP: 8 EST: 2011
SALES (est): 449.36K **Privately Held**
Web: www.avamerroofinginc.com
SIC: 1761 Roofing contractor

(G-8567)
BAILEY BUILDERS LLC
29615 Woodgate Dr (19968-3313)
PHONE..................302 236-0035
EMP: 5 EST: 2010
SALES (est): 116.86K **Privately Held**
Web: www.baileybuilders.net
SIC: 1531 Speculative builder, single-family houses

(G-8568)
BAYHEALTH PRIMARY CARE
18383 Hudson Rd (19968-3103)
PHONE..................302 855-1349
EMP: 10 EST: 2019
SALES (est): 106.95K **Privately Held**
Web: www.bayhealth.org
SIC: 8011 General and family practice, physician/surgeon

(G-8569)
BEACH HOUSE SERVICES
26 Cripple Creek Run (19968-9731)
PHONE..................302 645-2554
Rick Trasati, *Owner*
EMP: 7 EST: 2002
SALES (est): 249.31K **Privately Held**
SIC: 7011 Resort hotel

(G-8570)
BEACHES PLUMBING PLUS
14955 Orth Ln (19968-2459)
PHONE..................302 841-0171
Tim Houser, *Prin*
EMP: 5 EST: 2016
SALES (est): 56.99K **Privately Held**
SIC: 1711 Plumbing contractors

(G-8571)
BERACAH SALES OFFICE
18427 Josephs Rd (19968-3269)
PHONE..................302 854-6700
Pam Parker, *Mgr*
EMP: 5 EST: 2014
SALES (est): 47.37K **Privately Held**
SIC: 1521 New construction, single-family houses

(G-8572)
BLACKWELLS WELDING INC
15491 Lavinia St (19968-2858)
P.O. Box 1417 (20725-1417)
PHONE..................301 498-5277
William P Blackwell, *Pr*
Margaret Anne Blackwell, *Sec*
EMP: 2 EST: 1985
SALES (est): 200.06K **Privately Held**
Web: www.blackwellweldinginc.com
SIC: 1799 7692 Welding on site; Welding repair

(G-8573)
BOOZER EXCAVATION CO INC
18208 Beech Tree Path (19968-2618)
PHONE..................302 542-0290
Douglas L Boozer, *Prin*
EMP: 12 EST: 2015
SALES (est): 525.5K **Privately Held**
SIC: 1771 Concrete work

(G-8574)
BRIAN PATTERSON PA
122 Main Sail Dr (19968-1138)
P.O. Box 330 (19701-0330)
PHONE..................203 466-9972
Brian Patterson, *Pr*
EMP: 6 EST: 2021
SALES (est): 49.23K **Privately Held**
SIC: 7389 Business Activities at Non-Commercial Site

(G-8575)
BRIDGES4KIDS
110 W Shore Dr (19968-1148)
PHONE..................302 841-3700
EMP: 5 EST: 2015
SALES (est): 98.96K **Privately Held**
Web: www.bridges4kids.org
SIC: 8322 Individual and family services

(G-8576)
BUILT FITNESS LLC
29634 Woodgate Dr (19968-3316)
PHONE..................302 645-1932
EMP: 5 EST: 2015
SALES (est): 84.19K **Privately Held**
SIC: 7991 Physical fitness clubs with training equipment

(G-8577)
BULTON PROPERTIES LLC
29161 Stockley Rd (19968-3245)
PHONE..................302 945-0967
Huseyin Senturk, *Asst Sec*
EMP: 5 EST: 2018
SALES (est): 206.62K **Privately Held**
SIC: 6512 Nonresidential building operators

(G-8578)
BYZANTIUM SKY PRESS
27567 Bristol Ct (19968-3742)
PHONE..................302 258-6116
EMP: 3 EST: 2018
SALES (est): 65.95K **Privately Held**
SIC: 2741 Miscellaneous publishing

(G-8579)
CAMCO TIRE & AUTO LLC
200 Business Park Ln (19968-1063)
PHONE..................302 664-1264
EMP: 5 EST: 2018
SALES (est): 390.73K **Privately Held**
Web: www.camcotireandauto.com
SIC: 7538 General automotive repair shops

(G-8580)
CATHOLIC CHARITIES INC
Also Called: Casa San Francisco
127 Broad St (19968-1601)
P.O. Box 38 (19968-0038)
PHONE..................302 684-8694
Melinda Wolf, *Mgr*
EMP: 7
SALES (corp-wide): 8.08MM **Privately Held**
Web: www.ccwilm.org
SIC: 8322 Social service center
PA: Catholic Charities Inc
2601 W 4th St
Wilmington DE 19805
302 655-9624

(G-8581)
CENTRAL BACKHOE SERVICE
28247 Round Pole Bridge Rd (19968-3093)
PHONE..................302 398-6420
Debbie Craft, *Prin*
EMP: 3 EST: 2007
SALES (est): 173.66K **Privately Held**
Web: www.centralseptic.com
SIC: 3531 1794 Backhoes; Excavation work

(G-8582)
CHELSEA KING
Also Called: Turning Point Yoga
108 Bangor Ln (19968-2568)
PHONE..................302 684-5227
Chelsea King, *Prin*
EMP: 6 EST: 2011
SALES (est): 28.18K **Privately Held**
SIC: 7999 Yoga instruction

(G-8583)
CITYSTLECOLLECTIONS LLC
124 Broadkill Rd (19968-1008)
PHONE..................302 219-0259
Verneda Hunter, *Managing Member*
EMP: 7
SALES (est): 78.16K **Privately Held**
SIC: 3999 Eyelashes, artificial

(G-8584)
CLEAN DELAWARE INC
Rte 404 (19968)
P.O. Box 123 (19968-0123)
PHONE..................302 684-4221
Gerry Desmonz, *Mgr*
EMP: 9 EST: 1981
SQ FT: 3,000
SALES (est): 495.6K **Privately Held**
Web: www.cleandelaware.com
SIC: 4953 7699 1794 Liquid waste, collection and disposal; Septic tank cleaning service; Excavation and grading, building construction

(G-8585)
CLENDANIEL PLBG HTG & COOLG
Also Called: Clendaniel Plbg Htg & Coolg
14677 Oyster Rocks Rd (19968-3752)
PHONE..................302 684-3152
Arthur Clendaniel, *Owner*
EMP: 8 EST: 1960
SALES (est): 591.22K **Privately Held**
Web: www.clendanielplumbingheating.com
SIC: 1711 Plumbing contractors

(G-8586)
COASTAL CONCRETE WORKS LL
14298 Isaacs Rd (19968-2454)
P.O. Box 331 (19968-0331)
PHONE..................302 684-2872
EMP: 9 EST: 2018
SALES (est): 913.18K **Privately Held**
Web: www.coastalccw.com
SIC: 1771 Concrete work

(G-8587)
COBALT ART STUDIO
16394 Samuel Paynter Blvd (19968-3560)
PHONE..................201 819-9087
Siobhan Duggan, *Prin*
EMP: 6 EST: 2015
SALES (est): 39.83K **Privately Held**
SIC: 7999 Art gallery, commercial

(G-8588)
COMFORT ZONE JAZZ LLC
30515 Osprey Rd (19968-3467)
PHONE..................302 745-2019
EMP: 7 EST: 2008
SALES (est): 57.92K **Privately Held**
SIC: 7929 Entertainers and entertainment groups

(G-8589)
COMPLETE CONCRETE SYSTEMS
27403 Walking Run (19968-3086)
PHONE..................302 396-0013
EMP: 6 EST: 2016
SALES (est): 238.61K **Privately Held**
Web: www.completeconcretesystem.com
SIC: 1771 Concrete work

(G-8590)
CONTINENTAL INSIGHT
124 Broadkill Rd (19968-1008)
PHONE..................302 273-4458
EMP: 7 EST: 2018
SALES (est): 155.28K **Privately Held**
SIC: 8011 Offices and clinics of medical doctors

(G-8591)
CORE & MAIN LP
25414 Primehook Rd Ste 100 (19968-2706)
PHONE..................302 684-3054
EMP: 5
SALES (corp-wide): 6.65B **Publicly Held**
Web: www.coreandmain.com
SIC: 5074 4941 4952 Plumbing fittings and supplies; Water supply; Sewerage systems
HQ: Core & Main Lp
1830 Craig Park Ct
Saint Louis MO 63146

(G-8592)
COUNTY BANK
140 Broadkill Rd (19968-1008)
PHONE..................302 684-2300
Sonja Davis, *VP*
EMP: 7
Web: www.countybankdel.com
SIC: 6022 State commercial banks
PA: County Bank

GEOGRAPHIC SECTION   Milton - Sussex County (G-8623)

19927 Shuttle Rd
Rehoboth Beach DE 19971

(G-8593)
CTM MEDICAL ASSOCIATES LLC (PA)
109 Heronwood Dr (19968-3660)
PHONE.................................302 645-8587
Semaan Abboud, *Asst Sec*
EMP: 7 **EST:** 2018
SALES (est): 145.3K
SALES (corp-wide): 145.3K **Privately Held**
SIC: 8099 Health and allied services, nec

(G-8594)
CURTISS CONTRACTING LLC
807 Atlantic Ave (19968-1265)
PHONE.................................302 604-1071
William Curtiss, *Prin*
EMP: 5 **EST:** 2017
SALES (est): 61.77K **Privately Held**
SIC: 1799 Special trade contractors, nec

(G-8595)
CUSTOM CONCRETE FINISHES
103 W Apollo Ln (19968-9780)
PHONE.................................302 463-0635
Shane Mayhew, *Prin*
EMP: 5 **EST:** 2018
SALES (est): 96.58K **Privately Held**
SIC: 1771 Concrete work

(G-8596)
DEBRA ROSE
506 Union St (19968-1047)
PHONE.................................302 519-3029
Debra Rose, *Prin*
EMP: 6 **EST:** 2017
SALES (est): 22.18K **Privately Held**
SIC: 8049 Offices of health practitioner

(G-8597)
DEL BAY CHARTER FISHING LLC
23602 Harvest Run Reach (19968-2470)
PHONE.................................302 542-1930
Richard M Cornell, *Prin*
EMP: 7 **EST:** 2008
SALES (est): 249.95K **Privately Held**
SIC: 7999 Fishing boats, party: operation

(G-8598)
DELAWARE BEACH BOOK LLC
19401 Hunter Dr (19968-3201)
PHONE.................................302 249-1030
EMP: 5 **EST:** 2015
SALES (est): 51.29K **Privately Held**
Web: www.delawarebeachbook.com
SIC: 5192 Books

(G-8599)
DELAWARE MEDICAL COURIER
17048 W Holly Dr (19968-3435)
PHONE.................................302 670-1247
EMP: 5 **EST:** 2011
SALES (est): 161.9K **Privately Held**
SIC: 4215 Courier services, except by air

(G-8600)
DELEWARE EYE CLINICS
28322 Lewes Georgetown Hwy Unit 1 (19968-3117)
PHONE.................................302 684-2020
EMP: 6 **EST:** 2008
SALES (est): 148.68K **Privately Held**
SIC: 8042 Offices and clinics of optometrists

(G-8601)
DELMARVA 2000 LTD
21 Shay Ln (19968-3048)
PHONE.................................302 645-2226
Chuck Betyeman, *Pr*
Katrina Bethard, *Sec*
John Marsillo, *VP*
EMP: 8 **EST:** 2016
SALES (est): 421.09K **Privately Held**
Web: www.delmarva2000.com
SIC: 3843 Dental equipment and supplies

(G-8602)
DESIGN CONSULTANTS GROUP LLC
10872d Davidson Dr (19968)
PHONE.................................302 684-8030
EMP: 20 **EST:** 1998
SALES (est): 1.01MM **Privately Held**
SIC: 8713 Photogrammetric engineering

(G-8603)
DEWEY BEER COMPANY LLC
21241 Iron Throne Dr (19968-3024)
PHONE.................................302 329-9759
Jon Schorah, *Prin*
EMP: 6 **EST:** 2019
SALES (est): 117.59K **Privately Held**
SIC: 2082 Malt beverages

(G-8604)
DIAMOND STATE WELDING LLC
13307 Jefferson Rd (19968-2988)
PHONE.................................302 644-8489
Christopher O'callaghan, *Prin*
EMP: 5 **EST:** 2008
SALES (est): 49.92K **Privately Held**
SIC: 7692 Welding repair

(G-8605)
DIGITAL WISH INC (PA)
Also Called: Digital Wish
15187 Hudson Rd (19968-3616)
P.O. Box 255 (19968-0255)
PHONE.................................802 375-6721
Heather Chirtea, *Ch Bd*
Gordon Woodrow, *Ex Dir*
EMP: 5 **EST:** 2009
SQ FT: 600
SALES (est): 498.79K **Privately Held**
Web: www.digitalwish.com
SIC: 8732 Commercial nonphysical research

(G-8606)
DIGITLOGY LLC DBA EXPRTTEXTING
124 Broadkill Rd (19968-1008)
PHONE.................................302 703-9672
Ahmed Reza, *Managing Member*
EMP: 5 **EST:** 2016
SALES (est): 212.62K **Privately Held**
Web: www.digitalogy.us
SIC: 7371 8748 Computer software development; Telecommunications consultant

(G-8607)
DISTINCTION LLC
22467 Ridgecrest Dr (19968-3377)
PHONE.................................302 362-7574
Thomas Costello, *Owner*
EMP: 30 **EST:** 2012
SALES (est): 2.5MM **Privately Held**
SIC: 1521 1541 General remodeling, single-family houses; Renovation, remodeling and repairs: industrial buildings

(G-8608)
DISTINCTIVE STATIONERY LLC
18801 Riverwalk Dr (19968-3319)
PHONE.................................410 247-5600
EMP: 6 **EST:** 2004
SALES (est): 423.94K **Privately Held**
Web: www.distinctivestationery.com

SIC: 2759 Commercial printing, nec

(G-8609)
DOGFISH HEAD COMPANIES LLC
6 Cannery Vlg (19968-1308)
PHONE.................................302 684-1000
Nick Benz, *CEO*
EMP: 226 **EST:** 2017
SALES (est): 2.34MM **Privately Held**
Web: www.dogfish.com
SIC: 2085 Distilled and blended liquors

(G-8610)
DOGFISH HEAD CRAFT BREWERY LLC
6 Cannery Vlg (19968-1308)
PHONE.................................302 684-1000
Sam Calagione, *CEO*
George Pastrana, *
Mariah Calagione, *
Michael G Andrews, *
▲ **EMP:** 220 **EST:** 1995
SQ FT: 102,000
SALES (est): 66.38MM **Publicly Held**
Web: www.dogfish.com
SIC: 2082 Ale (alcoholic beverage)
HQ: Boston Beer Corporation
1 Design Center Pl # 850
Boston MA 02210
617 368-5000

(G-8611)
DR JAMES SOOR
6 Meadowridge Ln (19968-9694)
PHONE.................................302 684-4682
James Soor, *Prin*
EMP: 8 **EST:** 2009
SALES (est): 136.43K **Privately Held**
SIC: 8011 Physicians' office, including specialists

(G-8612)
DUKES SEPTIC
16653 Sand Hill Rd (19968-2525)
PHONE.................................302 362-6010
Victor Daniels, *Prin*
EMP: 6 **EST:** 2017
SALES (est): 61.94K **Privately Held**
SIC: 7699 Septic tank cleaning service

(G-8613)
E A ZANDO CUSTOM DESIGNS INC
Also Called: Zando Custom Designs
210 Chandler St (19968-1236)
PHONE.................................302 684-4601
Elizabeth A Zando, *Pr*
EMP: 10 **EST:** 1980
SALES (est): 325.81K **Privately Held**
Web: www.zandodesigns.com
SIC: 0781 1522 Landscape planning services ; Residential construction, nec

(G-8614)
EAGLE NEST DAYCARE
Zion Church Rd (19968)
PHONE.................................302 684-2765
Lucy Dutton, *Dir*
EMP: 11 **EST:** 1998
SALES (est): 197.35K **Privately Held**
SIC: 8351 Child day care services

(G-8615)
EDWARD S JAOUDE
28322 Lewes Georgetown Hwy (19968-3117)
PHONE.................................302 684-2020
Edward Jaoude, *Owner*
EMP: 11 **EST:** 2010
SALES (est): 97.9K **Privately Held**
Web: www.delawareeyeclinics.com

SIC: 8011 Internal medicine, physician/surgeon

(G-8616)
EISELE CELINE
Also Called: Shell Recreation Center
225 Bayport Business Park (19968)
P.O. Box 277 (19968-0277)
PHONE.................................302 684-3201
EMP: 8 **EST:** 1993
SALES (est): 190.12K **Privately Held**
Web: www.shellschildcare.com
SIC: 8351 Group day care center

(G-8617)
EMENTUM INC (PA)
2841 S Bay Shore Dr (19968)
PHONE.................................866 984-1999
Carolyn Merek, *Pr*
EMP: 9 **EST:** 1999
SQ FT: 3,000
SALES (est): 2.32MM
SALES (corp-wide): 2.32MM **Privately Held**
Web: www.ementum.com
SIC: 8748 Business consulting, nec

(G-8618)
EMPIRE CONSTRUCTION
221 Milton Ellendale Hwy (19968-1507)
PHONE.................................302 329-9256
EMP: 6 **EST:** 2016
SALES (est): 504.76K **Privately Held**
SIC: 1521 Single-family housing construction

(G-8619)
EMPIRE CONSTRUCTION GROUP LLC
16791 Hudson Rd (19968-3634)
PHONE.................................302 223-9208
Aaron Rogers, *Owner*
EMP: 5 **EST:** 2014
SALES (est): 237.18K **Privately Held**
SIC: 1521 Single-family housing construction

(G-8620)
ENF VENTURES LLC ✪
21884 Spring Forest Way (19968-3311)
PHONE.................................443 475-0175
Lauron Torsiello, *Pr*
EMP: 5 **EST:** 2022
SALES (est): 176.88K **Privately Held**
SIC: 7389 Business Activities at Non-Commercial Site

(G-8621)
ESPOSITOS WOODWORKING & CNSTR
99 Falls Rd (19968-9374)
PHONE.................................302 245-5474
EMP: 6 **EST:** 2019
SALES (est): 206.79K **Privately Held**
Web: www.espositoswoodworking.com
SIC: 2431 Millwork

(G-8622)
EVANS TRUCKING INC
Also Called: Welton Evans
604 Mulberry St (19968-1516)
P.O. Box 525 (19968-0525)
PHONE.................................302 344-9375
Welton Evans, *Prin*
EMP: 7 **EST:** 2008
SALES (est): 398.64K **Privately Held**
SIC: 4212 Local trucking, without storage

(G-8623)
FIRE ALARM SUPPLIER LLC
124 Broadkill Rd Ste 600 (19968-1008)
PHONE.................................302 444-0801

Milton - Sussex County (G-8624) GEOGRAPHIC SECTION

EMP: 8 EST: 2020
SALES (est): 1.35MM
SALES (corp-wide): 10.92MM **Privately Held**
Web: www.thefirealarmsupplier.us
SIC: 5063 Fire alarm systems
PA: Jem Security Llc
21410 N 15th Ln Ste 114
Phoenix AZ 85027
877 215-7579

(G-8624)
FIRST STATE HEALTH & WELLNESS
113 Union St Unit A (19968-1600)
PHONE..................302 684-1995
EMP: 6 EST: 2013
SALES (est): 76K **Privately Held**
Web: www.firststatehealth.com
SIC: 8099 Health and allied services, nec

(G-8625)
FOOTCARE TECHNOLOGIES INC
124 Broadkill Rd Ste 472 (19968-1008)
PHONE..................704 301-6966
Tyler Mccracken, *Pr*
EMP: 4 EST: 2019
SALES (est): 66.43K **Privately Held**
SIC: 3999 Manufacturing industries, nec

(G-8626)
FOOTPRNTS PROF WRTING SVCS LLC
22607 Deep Woods Rd (19968-3367)
PHONE..................917 324-6941
Carole James, *Pr*
EMP: 6 EST: 2016
SALES (est): 42.18K **Privately Held**
SIC: 8099 Health and allied services, nec

(G-8627)
GARY CHORMAN
29545 Canvasback Xing (19968-3686)
PHONE..................302 645-2972
Gary Chorman, *Prin*
EMP: 5 EST: 2011
SALES (est): 100.28K **Privately Held**
SIC: 7389 Business Activities at Non-Commercial Site

(G-8628)
GRACE VISITATION SERVICES
Also Called: Visiting Angel of Sussex, De
28350 Lewes Georgetown Hwy (19968-3115)
PHONE..................302 329-9475
David Forman, *Pr*
Karen Reed, *
EMP: 60 EST: 2011
SALES (est): 4.72MM **Privately Held**
SIC: 8082 Home health care services

(G-8629)
GRAPHITES
12200 Cadet Dr (19968-2753)
PHONE..................302 329-9182
Colleen Dayton, *Prin*
EMP: 5 EST: 2010
SALES (est): 73.9K **Privately Held**
SIC: 7299 Handyman service

(G-8630)
GREEN TEAM
405 Behringer Ave (19968-1227)
PHONE..................302 344-4512
Christopher Woodall, *Prin*
EMP: 5 EST: 2018
SALES (est): 46.84K **Privately Held**
Web: www.historicmilton.com
SIC: 8611 Chamber of Commerce

(G-8631)
GREENS AT BROADVIEW LLC
Also Called: Rookery, The
27052 Broadkill Rd (19968-3736)
PHONE..................302 684-3000
EMP: 22 EST: 2000
SALES (est): 875.11K **Privately Held**
Web: www.rookerygolf.com
SIC: 7992 Public golf courses

(G-8632)
GREENVILLE TRAVEL AGENCY INC
16923 Beulah Blvd (19968-3814)
PHONE..................302 658-3585
Frank Martinez Junior, *Pr*
Jean Martinez, *Sec*
Glen Hey, *Prin*
EMP: 8 EST: 1948
SALES (est): 967.88K **Privately Held**
Web: www.greenvilletravel.com
SIC: 4724 Tourist agency arranging transport, lodging and car rental

(G-8633)
HALF PINT INK
114 Falls Rd (19968-9370)
PHONE..................302 381-5561
EMP: 7 EST: 2011
SALES (est): 237.21K **Privately Held**
Web: www.halfpintink.com
SIC: 7299 Tattoo parlor

(G-8634)
HD SUPPLY WATERWORKS LTD
Also Called: HD SUPPLY WATERWORKS LTD
25414 Primehook Rd # 100 (19968-2706)
PHONE..................302 684-3054
EMP: 10
SALES (corp-wide): 7.5B **Privately Held**
SIC: 5074 Plumbing and hydronic heating supplies
HQ: Core & Main Lp
1830 Craig Park Ct
Saint Louis MO 63146
314 432-4700

(G-8635)
HEALTH CARE ASSOC PA
616 Mulberry St (19968-1516)
PHONE..................302 684-2033
EMP: 7 EST: 2007
SALES (est): 370.45K **Privately Held**
SIC: 8011 Internal medicine, physician/surgeon

(G-8636)
HENLOPEN HOMES LLC
18427 Josephs Rd (19968-3269)
P.O. Box 476 (19947-0476)
PHONE..................302 684-0860
Timothy Parker, *Mng Pt*
EMP: 5 EST: 2013
SALES (est): 298.47K **Privately Held**
Web: www.henlopenhomes.com
SIC: 1522 Residential construction, nec

(G-8637)
HENLOPEN MASONRY INC
20072 Cool Spring Rd (19968-3231)
PHONE..................302 947-9900
Susan Fluharty, *Pr*
George Fluharty, *VP*
EMP: 7 EST: 1997
SALES (est): 247.13K **Privately Held**
SIC: 1741 Masonry and other stonework

(G-8638)
HOLLY ANN SEMANCHIK PA
30241 Whitehall Dr (19968-3781)
PHONE..................908 672-1163
Holly Semanchik, *Prin*
EMP: 6 EST: 2018
SALES (est): 22.18K **Privately Held**
SIC: 8049 Offices of health practitioner

(G-8639)
HOWARD PAUL MD LLP
506 Union St (19968-1047)
PHONE..................302 644-2232
Paul E Howard, *Ofcr*
EMP: 12 EST: 2009
SALES (est): 240.89K **Privately Held**
SIC: 8011 General and family practice, physician/surgeon

(G-8640)
HTS 20 LLP
Also Called: Hts
16394 Samuel Paynter Blvd Unit 103 (19968-3560)
PHONE..................800 690-2029
EMP: 6 EST: 2013
SQ FT: 900
SALES (est): 235.69K **Privately Held**
SIC: 1731 7389 Sound equipment specialization; Business services, nec

(G-8641)
HUDSON MANAGEMENT & ENTPS LLC
30045 Eagles Crest Rd (19968-3624)
PHONE..................302 645-9464
EMP: 9 EST: 1974
SALES (est): 1.58MM **Privately Held**
Web: www.hudmgt.com
SIC: 1531 Condominium developers

(G-8642)
HYDROLOGICAL SOLUTIONS
27394 Round Pole Bridge Rd (19968-3040)
PHONE..................302 841-4444
Ryan Bunting, *Prin*
EMP: 6 EST: 2010
SALES (est): 263.99K **Privately Held**
Web: www.hydrological.org
SIC: 8741 Management services

(G-8643)
IRON WORKS INC
14726 Gravel Hill Rd # 1 (19968-2449)
PHONE..................302 684-1887
Robert Klerlein, *Pr*
EMP: 15 EST: 2003
SQ FT: 1,500
SALES (est): 2.22MM **Privately Held**
Web: www.ironworksde.com
SIC: 3441 Fabricated structural metal

(G-8644)
J L CARPENTER FARMS LLC
27113 Carpenter Rd (19968-3129)
PHONE..................302 684-8601
James L Carpenter Junior, *Pr*
EMP: 8 EST: 2008
SALES (est): 480.03K **Privately Held**
SIC: 0115 0161 7389 Corn; Vegetables and melons; Business services, nec

(G-8645)
J&A ELECTRICAL SERVICES LLC
12737 Reynolds Rd (19968-2972)
PHONE..................302 943-9894
Adam Klemanski, *Pr*
EMP: 6 EST: 2017
SALES (est): 235.38K **Privately Held**
SIC: 1731 General electrical contractor

(G-8646)
JACO LLC
Also Called: Macan Manufacturing
21 Shay Ln (19968-3048)
PHONE..................302 645-8068
EMP: 8 EST: 2008
SALES (est): 992.17K **Privately Held**
Web: www.macanmanufacturing.com
SIC: 5047 Medical equipment and supplies

(G-8647)
JAMES L CARPENTER & SON INC
27113 Carpenter Rd (19968-3129)
PHONE..................302 684-8601
James L Carpenter Junior, *Pr*
Kay C Dukes, *Sec*
EMP: 7 EST: 1950
SALES (est): 701.79K **Privately Held**
SIC: 0241 0161 0119 Dairy farms; Vegetables and melons; Feeder grains

(G-8648)
JANI UDAY
28312 Lewes Georgetown Hwy (19968-3115)
P.O. Box 340 (19969-0340)
PHONE..................302 684-0990
Uday Jani, *Internal Medicine*
EMP: 8 EST: 2017
SALES (est): 65.5K **Privately Held**
Web: www.udayjanimd.com
SIC: 8011 Internal medicine, physician/surgeon

(G-8649)
JOHN L BRIGGS & CO
Also Called: Briggs Company
29111 Stockley Rd (19968-3245)
PHONE..................302 856-7033
Charles D Dolson, *Pr*
W F Carlsten, *Sec*
EMP: 15 EST: 1947
SALES (est): 472.61K **Privately Held**
SIC: 1542 1541 Commercial and office building, new construction; Industrial buildings, new construction, nec

(G-8650)
KELLER WILLIAMS AT BEACH RLTY
Also Called: Keller Williams Realtors
16880 Ole Grist Run (19968-3401)
PHONE..................302 363-0453
Sherri Bigelow, *Prin*
EMP: 6 EST: 2010
SALES (est): 98.87K **Privately Held**
Web: www.kw.com
SIC: 6531 Real estate agent, residential

(G-8651)
KEYSTONE SWINE SERVICES
14356 Clydes Dr (19968-2987)
PHONE..................302 329-9731
Mike Mullady, *Owner*
EMP: 6 EST: 2004
SALES (est): 223.96K **Privately Held**
SIC: 0213 Hogs

(G-8652)
KLH ENTERPRISES
29099 Stockley Rd (19968-3244)
PHONE..................302 245-0712
Kevin Hendershot, *Prin*
EMP: 11 EST: 2019
SALES (est): 737.1K **Privately Held**
Web: www.klhenterprises.com
SIC: 1522 Residential construction, nec

(G-8653)
LAWSON HOME SERVICES LLC
115 Atlantic Ave (19968-1205)

GEOGRAPHIC SECTION
Milton - Sussex County (G-8683)

P.O. Box 228 (19968-0228)
PHONE.................302 684-3418
David Lawson, *Prin*
EMP: 7 **EST:** 2010
SALES (est): 833.79K **Privately Held**
Web: www.lawsonhomeservices.com
SIC: 1742 Insulation, buildings

(G-8654)
LISA MATHENA GROUP
16154 Hudson Rd (19968-3605)
PHONE.................302 645-4804
Melissa Mathena, *Owner*
EMP: 13 **EST:** 2011
SALES (est): 457.68K **Privately Held**
Web: www.lisamathena.com
SIC: 8748 Business consulting, nec

(G-8655)
LOCKWOOD DESIGN CONSTRUCTION
26412 Broadkill Rd 1st Fl (19968-2955)
PHONE.................302 684-4844
Donald H Lockwood, *CEO*
Don A Lockwood, *Pr*
EMP: 7 **EST:** 1978
SQ FT: 9,000
SALES (est): 1.11MM **Privately Held**
Web: www.lockwooddesigns.com
SIC: 1542 1521 Commercial and office building, new construction; New construction, single-family houses

(G-8656)
LOWELL SCOTT MD PA
611 Federal St Ste 3 (19968-1157)
PHONE.................302 684-1119
Scott Lowell, *Prin*
EMP: 5 **EST:** 2008
SALES (est): 496.28K **Privately Held**
Web: www.scottpediatrics.com
SIC: 8011 Pediatrician

(G-8657)
LUTHERAN SNIOR SVCS OF SSSEX C
Also Called: LUTHER TOWERS OF MILTON,THE
500 Palmer St (19968-1006)
PHONE.................302 684-1668
John Ranney, *Pr*
John Barton, *VP*
Sandra Wachter-myers, *Sec*
EMP: 6 **EST:** 1991
SALES (est): 582.38K **Privately Held**
Web: www.historicmilton.com
SIC: 6513 Retirement hotel operation

(G-8658)
M T O CLEAN OF SUSSEX COUNTY
2 N Aquarius Way (19968-9483)
PHONE.................302 854-0204
Sandra Connelly, *Pr*
Rodney Connelly, *Sr VP*
April Connelly, *VP*
EMP: 6 **EST:** 2004
SALES (est): 142.24K **Privately Held**
SIC: 7349 Maid services, contract or fee basis

(G-8659)
MAJOR LEAGUE BOCCE LLC
303 Walnut St (19968-1449)
PHONE.................240 476-3801
Rachael Preston, *Prin*
EMP: 7 **EST:** 2013
SALES (est): 198.82K **Privately Held**
Web: www.majorleaguebocce.com
SIC: 7997 Membership sports and recreation clubs

(G-8660)
MANUFACTURERS & TRADERS TR CO
Also Called: M&T
107 Front St (19968-1427)
P.O. Box 217 (19968-0217)
PHONE.................302 855-2184
Beverly White, *Mgr*
EMP: 6
SALES (corp-wide): 8.6B **Publicly Held**
Web: ir.mtb.com
SIC: 6022 State commercial banks
HQ: Manufacturers And Traders Trust Company
1 M&T Plz Fl 3
Buffalo NY 14203
716 842-4200

(G-8661)
MARTECH COMMUNICATIONS
16233 John Rowland Trl (19968-3537)
PHONE.................703 989-6390
EMP: 6 **EST:** 2015
SALES (est): 54.99K **Privately Held**
Web: www.martechcomm.com
SIC: 4899 Communication services, nec

(G-8662)
MARY ZIOMEK DDS
317 Mariners Cir (19968-2236)
PHONE.................301 984-9646
Mary Ziomek, *Prin*
EMP: 9 **EST:** 2008
SALES (est): 221.47K **Privately Held**
SIC: 8021 Dentists' office

(G-8663)
MAWS TAILS MFG
29621 Riverstone Dr (19968-3927)
PHONE.................302 740-7664
EMP: 4 **EST:** 2018
SALES (est): 94.61K **Privately Held**
SIC: 3999 Manufacturing industries, nec

(G-8664)
MCILVAIN LAWN MOWING MORE LLC
26564 Carpenter Rd (19968-3123)
PHONE.................302 684-4213
William R Mcilvain Junior, *Prin*
EMP: 5 **EST:** 2008
SALES (est): 67.08K **Privately Held**
SIC: 0782 Mowing services, lawn

(G-8665)
MECHAM MECHANICAL
30202 Whitehall Dr (19968-3778)
PHONE.................302 645-2793
Linda Mecham, *Prin*
EMP: 6 **EST:** 2008
SALES (est): 114.03K **Privately Held**
SIC: 1711 Mechanical contractor

(G-8666)
MEDICINE WOMAN
503 Canning House Row (19968-1314)
PHONE.................302 684-8048
EMP: 5 **EST:** 2017
SALES (est): 76K **Privately Held**
SIC: 8099 Health and allied services, nec

(G-8667)
MERCER DENTAL ASSOCIATES
Also Called: Mercer and Sydell Dental
524 Union St (19968-1016)
PHONE.................302 664-1385
Sean M Mercer, *Prin*
EMP: 5 **EST:** 2012
SALES (est): 405.06K **Privately Held**
Web: www.mercersydelldental.com

SIC: 8021 Dentists' office

(G-8668)
MILLSBORO EYE CARE LLC
Also Called: Delaware Eye Clinic
28322 Lewes Georgetown Hwy Unit 1 (19968-3117)
PHONE.................302 684-2020
EMP: 29 **EST:** 2003
SALES (est): 1.2MM **Privately Held**
Web: www.delawareeyeclinics.com
SIC: 8011 Opthalmologist

(G-8669)
MILTON ENTERPRISES INC
Also Called: Milton Family Practice
424 Mulberry St Ste 2 (19968-1628)
PHONE.................302 684-2000
Charles G Wagner Md, *Pr*
EMP: 6 **EST:** 1981
SALES (est): 592.33K **Privately Held**
Web: www.sugarfreekids.org
SIC: 8062 General medical and surgical hospitals

(G-8670)
MILTON GARDEN CLUB
14354 Sand Hill Rd (19968-2562)
P.O. Box 203 (19968-0203)
PHONE.................302 684-8315
EMP: 7 **EST:** 2018
SALES (est): 38.16K **Privately Held**
Web: www.themiltongardenclub.org
SIC: 7997 Membership sports and recreation clubs

(G-8671)
MILTON HISTORICAL SOCIETY
210 Union St (19968-1620)
P.O. Box 112 (19968-0112)
PHONE.................302 684-1010
Melinda Huff, *Dir*
EMP: 10 **EST:** 1970
SALES (est): 181.97K **Privately Held**
Web: www.historicmilton.org
SIC: 8412 Museum

(G-8672)
MILTON MAIL BOXES
124 Broadkill Rd (19968-1008)
PHONE.................302 664-2623
EMP: 5 **EST:** 2019
SALES (est): 238.01K **Privately Held**
Web: www.miltonmailboxes.com
SIC: 7389 Mailbox rental and related service

(G-8673)
MILTON THEATRE
101 Pond Dr (19968-1155)
PHONE.................302 684-4232
EMP: 6 **EST:** 2013
SALES (est): 43.11K **Privately Held**
Web: www.miltontheatre.com
SIC: 7922 Theatrical companies

(G-8674)
MOD VELLUM INC
22167 Arbor Cir (19968-3356)
PHONE.................415 310-7354
EMP: 5 **EST:** 2018
SALES (est): 463.02K **Privately Held**
SIC: 5087 Service establishment equipment

(G-8675)
MOTTO MORTGAGE PROSPERITY LLC
16394 Samuel Paynter Blvd (19968-3560)
PHONE.................302 313-5145
EMP: 5 **EST:** 2018
SALES (est): 245.19K **Privately Held**

SIC: 6162 Mortgage bankers and loan correspondents

(G-8676)
NEW EDGE ENTERPRISES LLC
26095 Marys Ln (19968-4547)
PHONE.................908 892-2856
Brian Baker, *Managing Member*
EMP: 6
SALES (est): 76.37K **Privately Held**
SIC: 6799 Real estate investors, except property operators

(G-8677)
OCEAN MEDICAL IMAGING DEL LLC
611 Federal St Ste 4 (19968-1157)
PHONE.................302 684-5151
EMP: 13 **EST:** 2007
SALES (est): 910.89K **Privately Held**
Web: www.oceanmedicalimaging.net
SIC: 8011 Radiologist

(G-8678)
OCEANSIDE CLEANING INC
30237 Whitehall Dr (19968-3781)
PHONE.................302 526-4400
Noreen Kushner, *Prin*
EMP: 5 **EST:** 2014
SALES (est): 83.88K **Privately Held**
Web: www.oceanside-elite.com
SIC: 7699 Cleaning services

(G-8679)
OE PERFORMANCE REPR MAINT INC
100 Business Park Ln (19968-1035)
PHONE.................302 664-1264
Christopher White, *Prin*
EMP: 6 **EST:** 2016
SALES (est): 149.77K **Privately Held**
Web: www.camcotireandauto.com
SIC: 7349 Building maintenance services, nec

(G-8680)
OUT-TRAIN FITNESS & PRFMCE LLC
18499 Harbeson Rd (19968-2836)
PHONE.................610 470-3196
EMP: 6 **EST:** 2020
SALES (est): 38.22K **Privately Held**
Web: www.outtrainfp.com
SIC: 8099 7991 7389 7997 Health and allied services, nec; Health club; Business services, nec; Membership sports and recreation clubs

(G-8681)
PATRICIA AYERS
15629 Walker Dr (19968-2847)
PHONE.................302 841-9909
Patricia Ayers Mha R.n., *Prin*
EMP: 6 **EST:** 2018
SALES (est): 34.6K **Privately Held**
SIC: 8049 Offices of health practitioner

(G-8682)
PEACEWORKS
16909 Jays Way (19968-3462)
PHONE.................302 727-2464
Mary Brett, *Prin*
EMP: 5 **EST:** 2018
SALES (est): 61.31K **Privately Held**
Web: www.peacework.org
SIC: 8699 Charitable organization

(G-8683)
PEDIATRIC & ADOLESCENT CENTER
424 Mulberry St (19968-1628)
PHONE.................302 684-0561
John Ludwicki, *Pr*

Milton - Sussex County (G-8684) GEOGRAPHIC SECTION

EMP: 16 EST: 2009
SALES (est): 2.42MM **Privately Held**
Web: www.pacpediatrics.com
SIC: 8011 Pediatrician

(G-8684)
PETTYJOHN FARMS INC
16771 Gravel Hill Rd (19968-2515)
PHONE.....................302 684-4383
Arthur Pettyjohn, *Pr*
EMP: 5 EST: 1940
SALES (est): 341.83K **Privately Held**
SIC: 0111 Wheat

(G-8685)
PHOENIX CONSTRUCTION LLC
Also Called: Phoenix Construction
16880 Ole Grist Run (19968-3401)
PHONE.....................302 363-0453
Sherri Bigelow, *Prin*
EMP: 6 EST: 2016
SALES (est): 140.06K **Privately Held**
SIC: 1521 Single-family housing construction

(G-8686)
PIONEER DISTRIBUTORS INC
16612 Howard Millman Ln (19968-3528)
P.O. Box 90 (19973-0090)
PHONE.....................302 644-0791
EMP: 7 EST: 1995
SQ FT: 5,000
SALES (est): 680K **Privately Held**
SIC: 5149 Bakery products

(G-8687)
PORTABLE PILOT SOLUTIONS LLC
28 Cripple Creek Run (19968-9731)
PHONE.....................302 644-2775
Stephen A Roberts, *Prin*
EMP: 5 EST: 2008
SALES (est): 173.04K **Privately Held**
SIC: 5088 Aircraft equipment and supplies, nec

(G-8688)
PREMIER CENTRE FOR ARTS LLC
110 Union St (19968-1618)
PHONE.....................302 684-3038
Henry F Munzert, *Managing Member*
EMP: 8 EST: 2002
SALES (est): 240.78K **Privately Held**
SIC: 7911 7922 Dance studio and school; Theatrical companies

(G-8689)
PREMIER RESTORATION
30616 Overbrook Center Way Unit 1 (19968-3798)
PHONE.....................302 645-1611
EMP: 5 EST: 2020
SALES (est): 239.49K **Privately Held**
SIC: 1799 Special trade contractors, nec

(G-8690)
PRESTON & REMODELING
201 Lavinia St (19968-1127)
PHONE.....................302 604-0760
EMP: 5 EST: 2017
SALES (est): 196.14K **Privately Held**
Web: www.prestonbuilding.com
SIC: 1521 General remodeling, single-family houses

(G-8691)
PRO EXTERIORS
221 Milton Ellendale Hwy (19968-1507)
PHONE.....................302 664-1700
EMP: 5 EST: 2018
SALES (est): 245.54K **Privately Held**
Web: www.askproexteriors.com
SIC: 0782 Lawn and garden services

(G-8692)
QUICK SURFACE SOLUTIONS LLC
30015 Gatehouse Dr (19968-3396)
PHONE.....................302 236-6941
EMP: 10 EST: 2017
SALES (est): 392.64K **Privately Held**
SIC: 8062 General medical and surgical hospitals

(G-8693)
REAL WORLD ENDO
29602 Vincent Village Dr (19968-3808)
PHONE.....................302 827-4816
EMP: 6 EST: 2017
SALES (est): 108.94K **Privately Held**
Web: www.realworldendo.com
SIC: 8748 Business consulting, nec

(G-8694)
REED TRUCKING COMPANY
522 Chestnut St (19968-1320)
P.O. Box 216 (19968-0216)
PHONE.....................302 684-8585
Blake Reed, *Pr*
George Reed, *"*
Beulah Reed, *"*
Nancy Reed, *"*
EMP: 60 EST: 1933
SQ FT: 1,800
SALES (est): 7.11MM **Privately Held**
Web: www.reed-trucking.com
SIC: 4213 Trucking, except local

(G-8695)
REMENTER BROTHERS INC
Also Called: Budget Blinds
28348 Lewes Georgetown Hwy (19968-3115)
PHONE.....................302 249-4250
Christopher Rementer, *Pr*
Anthony Rementer, *VP*
EMP: 6 EST: 2005
SALES (est): 597.6K **Privately Held**
Web: www.budgetblinds.com
SIC: 5719 1751 Window furnishings; Cabinet and finish carpentry

(G-8696)
RICHARD L TODD PHD
28312 Lewes Georgetown Hwy (19968-3115)
PHONE.....................302 853-0559
Richard L Todd, *Prin*
EMP: 8 EST: 2011
SALES (est): 135.33K **Privately Held**
SIC: 8093 Mental health clinic, outpatient

(G-8697)
RICHARD M WHITE WELDING
14443 Collins St (19968-2640)
PHONE.....................302 684-4461
Richard White, *Owner*
EMP: 5 EST: 2011
SALES (est): 65.16K **Privately Held**
SIC: 7692 Welding repair

(G-8698)
RICHERT INC (PA)
Also Called: Accent Drapery Div Richert Inc
2836 S Bay Shore Dr (19968-9451)
PHONE.....................302 684-0696
Allyn I Richert, *Pr*
EMP: 10 EST: 1975
SQ FT: 2,500
SALES (est): 2.41MM
SALES (corp-wide): 2.41MM **Privately Held**
SIC: 5021 Office furniture, nec

(G-8699)
RICKS FITNESS & HEALTH INC
22893 Neptune Rd (19968-2536)
PHONE.....................302 684-0316
Richard G Moore, *Pr*
EMP: 6 EST: 1998
SALES (est): 130.03K **Privately Held**
Web: www.ricksfitness.net
SIC: 7991 8011 Health club; Offices and clinics of medical doctors

(G-8700)
RMV WORKFORCE CORP
124 Broadkill Rd Ste 380 (19968-1008)
PHONE.....................302 408-1061
Rohit Sood, *Prin*
EMP: 10 EST: 2018
SALES (est): 1.03MM **Privately Held**
Web: www.rmvworkforce.com
SIC: 7361 Employment agencies

(G-8701)
ROBERT MCMANN
Also Called: Frst State Ceramics & Marble
13259 Sunland Dr (19968-2992)
PHONE.....................302 329-9413
Robert Mcmann, *Prin*
EMP: 5 EST: 2010
SALES (est): 117.16K **Privately Held**
SIC: 3269 Pottery products, nec

(G-8702)
ROCKLES SERVICES LLC
14404 Russell St (19968-2643)
PHONE.....................302 258-5357
John Rockle, *Prin*
EMP: 5 EST: 2017
SALES (est): 51.8K **Privately Held**
SIC: 1522 Residential construction, nec

(G-8703)
ROGERS SIGN COMPANY INC
110 Lavinia St (19968-1126)
PHONE.....................302 684-8338
Lynn Rogers, *Pr*
Keith Revelle, *VP*
Linda Rogers, *Sec*
EMP: 10 EST: 1969
SQ FT: 14,000
SALES (est): 396.48K **Privately Held**
Web: www.rogerssign.com
SIC: 3993 Signs and advertising specialties

(G-8704)
RON LANK/CASH
209 Atlantic St (19968-1403)
PHONE.....................302 684-4667
Ronald Lank, *Prin*
EMP: 5 EST: 2011
SALES (est): 74.91K **Privately Held**
SIC: 8611 Contractors' association

(G-8705)
S AND S LLC
22855 Milton Ellendale Hwy (19968-2625)
PHONE.....................302 344-5990
EMP: 6 EST: 2019
SALES (est): 139.4K **Privately Held**
SIC: 1522 Residential construction, nec

(G-8706)
SANDHILL DEVELOPMENT GROUP LLC
16181 Hudson Rd (19968-3612)
PHONE.....................302 703-2140
Anthony D Sposato, *Asst Sec*
EMP: 6 EST: 2017
SALES (est): 255.75K **Privately Held**
SIC: 1522 Residential construction, nec

(G-8707)
SANGREE CONSTRUCTION INC
315 Union St (19968-1621)
PHONE.....................717 576-7144
T Allen, *Ofcr*
EMP: 5 EST: 2008
SALES (est): 63.02K **Privately Held**
SIC: 1799 Special trade contractors, nec

(G-8708)
SCOTT PEDIATRICS
611 Federal St Ste 3 (19968-1157)
PHONE.....................302 684-1119
EMP: 7 EST: 2020
SALES (est): 196.5K **Privately Held**
Web: www.scottpediatrics.com
SIC: 8011 Pediatrician

(G-8709)
SECURITY INSTRUMENT CORP DEL
28226 Lewes Georgetown Hwy (19968-3107)
PHONE.....................302 674-2891
Mike Cork, *Mgr*
EMP: 10
SALES (corp-wide): 52.15K **Privately Held**
Web: www.securityinstrument.com
SIC: 1731 Fire detection and burglar alarm systems specialization
PA: Security Instrument Corp Of Delaware
  309 W Newport Pike
  Wilmington DE 19804
  302 998-2261

(G-8710)
SENSOFUSION INC
30061 Clam Shell Ln (19968-3793)
PHONE.....................570 239-4912
Kaveh Haroun Mahdavi, *VP*
EMP: 15 EST: 2016
SALES (est): 1.09MM **Privately Held**
SIC: 7373 7371 7389 Systems software development services; Computer software development and applications; Business Activities at Non-Commercial Site
HQ: Sensofusion Oy
  Hakamaenkuja 1
  Vantaa 01510
  985619420

(G-8711)
SHERMAN HEATING OILS INC
223 Bay Front Rd # G (19968-9563)
P.O. Box 206 (19968-0206)
PHONE.....................302 684-4008
Harold Sheets Junior, *Dir*
EMP: 9
Web: www.shonet.net
SIC: 5172 Gases, liquefied petroleum (propane)
PA: Sherman Heating Oils Inc
  223g Bay Ave
  Milton DE 19968

(G-8712)
SLEIGH FINANCIAL INC
28266 Lewes Georgetown Hwy (19968-3107)
PHONE.....................302 684-2929
Randy Reed, *Pr*
EMP: 7 EST: 2004
SQ FT: 5,000
SALES (est): 976.16K **Privately Held**
Web: www.georgetownfsbo.com
SIC: 5182 Wine and distilled beverages

GEOGRAPHIC SECTION
New Castle - New Castle County (G-8742)

(G-8713)
SPOSATO IRRIGATION COMPANY
16181 Hudson Rd (19968-3612)
PHONE..................302 645-4773
David Anthony Sposato, *Prin*
John Frederick Sposato, *Prin*
EMP: 46 **EST:** 1998
SALES (est): 2.13MM **Privately Held**
Web: www.sposatoirrigation.com
SIC: 0781 Landscape services

(G-8714)
SPOSATO LANDSCAPE COMPANY INC
16181 Hudson Rd (19968-3612)
PHONE..................302 645-4773
Tony Sposato, *Owner*
EMP: 50 **EST:** 2014
SALES (est): 9.93MM **Privately Held**
Web: www.sposatolandscape.com
SIC: 0781 Landscape services

(G-8715)
SPOSATO LAWN CARE
Rd 4 Box 265-B (19968)
PHONE..................302 645-4773
David Sposato, *Owner*
EMP: 5 **EST:** 1992
SALES (est): 226.98K **Privately Held**
SIC: 0782 Lawn care services

(G-8716)
STRAIGHT LINE STRIPING LLC
18473 Harbeson Rd (19968-2836)
PHONE..................302 228-3335
William Robert Hall Iii, *Pr*
EMP: 10 **EST:** 2017
SALES (est): 2.23MM **Privately Held**
Web: www.slsde.com
SIC: 1611 Surfacing and paving

(G-8717)
SUBURBAN FARMHOUSE
107 Federal St (19968-1602)
PHONE..................302 250-6254
Kristen Latham, *Prin*
EMP: 6 **EST:** 2017
SALES (est): 483.92K **Privately Held**
SIC: 0191 General farms, primarily crop

(G-8718)
TCS INC
433 Main Sail Ln (19968-1534)
PHONE..................302 858-1389
Jeff Shade, *Prin*
EMP: 6 **EST:** 2010
SALES (est): 72.94K **Privately Held**
SIC: 7378 Computer maintenance and repair

(G-8719)
TEE IT UP GOLF CAMP
22222 Saw Mill Rd (19968-2420)
PHONE..................302 684-1808
Wendy Stenger, *Prin*
EMP: 8 **EST:** 2016
SALES (est): 73.82K **Privately Held**
Web: www.shamrockpar3golf.com
SIC: 7992 Public golf courses

(G-8720)
TIDEWATER PHYSCL THRPY AND REB
611 Federal St (19968-1157)
PHONE..................302 684-2829
Richard Recicar, *Brnch Mgr*
EMP: 6
Web: www.tidewaterpt.com
SIC: 8049 8322 Physical therapist; Rehabilitation services
PA: Tidewater Physical Therapy And Rehabilitation Associates Pa
406 Marvel Ct
Easton MD 21601

(G-8721)
TIMOTHY P COLLORD
22926 Donovan Rd (19968-2434)
PHONE..................302 448-9577
Timothy P Collord, *Prin*
EMP: 5 **EST:** 2010
SALES (est): 244.11K **Privately Held**
SIC: 1522 Residential construction, nec

(G-8722)
TRENTON BLOCK DELAWARE INC
701 Federal St (19968-1117)
PHONE..................302 684-0112
Richard Kilian, *Pr*
EMP: 10 **EST:** 2017
SALES (est): 494.9K **Privately Held**
SIC: 1741 Masonry and other stonework

(G-8723)
TRI STATE CLEANING
30181 E Mill Run (19968-3459)
PHONE..................302 644-6554
EMP: 5 **EST:** 2012
SALES (est): 139.33K **Privately Held**
Web: www.tri-statecleaning.com
SIC: 7217 Carpet and upholstery cleaning

(G-8724)
URBAN DWELLER
338 Union St (19968-1643)
PHONE..................973 402-7400
Mark Polo, *Owner*
Mark Polo, *Prin*
EMP: 3 **EST:** 2007
SALES (est): 218.97K **Privately Held**
SIC: 2499 5023 8412 Picture frame molding, finished; Frames and framing, picture and mirror; Art gallery

(G-8725)
VIAPROGRAM TECHNOLOGY INC (PA)
124 Broadkill Rd Ste 480 (19968-1008)
PHONE..................917 292-5433
EMP: 6 **EST:** 2019
SALES (est): 62.54K
SALES (corp-wide): 62.54K **Privately Held**
Web: www.viagood.app
SIC: 7371 Computer software development and applications

(G-8726)
VIDALYTICS
124 Broadkill Rd Pmb 728 (19968-1008)
PHONE..................303 500-5715
Patrick Stiles, *CEO*
EMP: 10 **EST:** 2016
SALES (est): 441.66K **Privately Held**
Web: www.vidalytics.com
SIC: 7372 7371 Prepackaged software; Software programming applications

(G-8727)
VINNYS HANDYMAN SERVIES
27619 Dunstan Ct (19968-3740)
PHONE..................302 265-9196
Vincent Denney, *Prin*
EMP: 5 **EST:** 2017
SALES (est): 20.84K **Privately Held**
SIC: 7299 Handyman service

(G-8728)
WE DEM BOYS TRANSPORTATION LLC
16620 Gravel Hill Rd (19968-2503)
PHONE..................302 727-6164
Orice L Hayes Senior, *Pr*
EMP: 5 **EST:** 2015
SALES (est): 311.1K **Privately Held**
SIC: 4111 Local and suburban transit

(G-8729)
WELLNESS WAHINE
19868 Mayas Ln (19968-3385)
PHONE..................302 841-4988
Jessica Sander Peden, *Prin*
EMP: 6 **EST:** 2019
SALES (est): 72.89K **Privately Held**
Web: www.wellnesswahine.com
SIC: 8099 Health and allied services, nec

(G-8730)
WORCESTER GOLF CLUB INC
121 W Shore Dr (19968-1145)
PHONE..................610 222-0200
EMP: 10 **EST:** 1996
SQ FT: 2,500
SALES (est): 279.82K **Privately Held**
Web: www.worcestergolfclub.com
SIC: 7992 7299 Public golf courses; Banquet hall facilities

(G-8731)
WRIGHTS LAWN CARE INC
14174 Union Street Ext (19968-2662)
PHONE..................302 684-3058
Jill Wright, *Pr*
Bill Wright, *VP*
EMP: 10 **EST:** 1996
SALES (est): 467.47K **Privately Held**
Web: www.wrightslawncare.org
SIC: 0782 Lawn care services

(G-8732)
WYOMING MILLWORK CO
23000 Tracks End Ln (19968-2620)
PHONE..................302 684-3150
EMP: 2
Web: www.wyomingmillwork.com
SIC: 2431 Millwork
PA: Wyoming Millwork Co.
140 Vepco Blvd
Camden DE 19934

(G-8733)
Y AND Y GARDEN ASSOCIATES INC
17430 Red Gate Ln (19968-2547)
PHONE..................302 684-0383
James Sidney, *Registered Agent*
EMP: 5 **EST:** 1990
SALES (est): 105.49K **Privately Held**
SIC: 6552 Subdividers and developers, nec

(G-8734)
YOLOHA YOGA
16182 Hudson Rd (19968-3605)
PHONE..................443 223-8651
EMP: 5 **EST:** 2014
SALES (est): 27.27K **Privately Held**
Web: www.yolohayoga.com
SIC: 7999 Yoga instruction

Montchanin
New Castle County

(G-8735)
CHARLES GRAEF INC
1302 Old Lancaster Pike (19710)
P.O. Box 196 (19710-0196)
PHONE..................302 239-7924
Charles Graef, *Prin*
EMP: 5 **EST:** 2010
SALES (est): 102K **Privately Held**
Web: www.charlesgraef.com
SIC: 8742 Real estate consultant

(G-8736)
DAN LICALE
Also Called: Inn At Montchanin Village, The
Corner Kirk Rd And 100 (19710)
P.O. Box 130 (19710-0130)
PHONE..................302 888-2133
EMP: 17 **EST:** 1997
SALES (est): 179.11K **Privately Held**
Web: www.montchanin.com
SIC: 7011 Bed and breakfast inn

(G-8737)
DAVIS INSURANCE GROUP INC
Rte 100 And Rockland Rd (19710)
P.O. Box 215 (19710-0215)
PHONE..................302 652-4700
William H Davis Junior, *CEO*
Robert H Davis Junior, *Pr*
Robert Davis, *Pr*
EMP: 9 **EST:** 1948
SQ FT: 3,500
SALES (est): 892.51K **Privately Held**
Web: www.davisinsurancegroup.com
SIC: 6411 Insurance agents, nec

(G-8738)
MEGAN GORELICK INTERIORS INC
100 W Rockland Rd (19710-2006)
PHONE..................302 482-1325
EMP: 7 **EST:** 2020
SALES (est): 396.68K **Privately Held**
Web: www.megangorelickinteriors.com
SIC: 7389 Interior designer

(G-8739)
MORROW LIMITED
4 W Rockland Rd (19710-2008)
PHONE..................213 631-3534
Lan Fu, *Sls Mgr*
EMP: 61 **EST:** 2018
SALES (est): 1.31MM **Privately Held**
Web: www.morrowsodali.com
SIC: 7371 Computer software development and applications

Nassau
Sussex County

(G-8740)
CAPE HENLOPEN ELKS LODGE
P.O. Box 68 (19969-0068)
PHONE..................302 645-7016
John Souder, *Owner*
EMP: 5 **EST:** 2001
SALES (est): 406.57K **Privately Held**
Web: www.capehenlopenelks.org
SIC: 8641 Civic associations

(G-8741)
IMMANUEL SHELTER INC
17601 Coastal Hwy (19969-2004)
P.O. Box 431 (19969-0431)
PHONE..................302 227-7743
Ann Bailey, *Prin*
EMP: 7 **EST:** 2017
SALES (est): 125.6K **Privately Held**
Web: www.immanuelshelter.org
SIC: 8322 Social service center

New Castle
New Castle County

(G-8742)
1-800-BY-MULCH
1715 River Rd (19720-5197)

New Castle - New Castle County (G-8743) — GEOGRAPHIC SECTION

PHONE..................302 325-2257
Robert Gallo, *Mgr*
EMP: 5 **EST:** 2013
SALES (est): 57.21K **Privately Held**
Web: www.1800bymulch.net
SIC: 0782 Landscape contractors

(G-8743)
13 LAUNDROMAT
329 S Dupont Hwy (19720-4641)
PHONE..................302 322-1910
Sophia Kim, *Prin*
EMP: 5 **EST:** 2016
SALES (est): 50.19K **Privately Held**
SIC: 7215 Laundry, coin-operated

(G-8744)
166TH MEDICAL SQUADRON
2600 Spruance Dr (19720-1615)
PHONE..................302 323-3385
Rick Collier, *Mgr*
EMP: 10 **EST:** 2010
SALES (est): 375.35K **Privately Held**
SIC: 8099 Health and allied services, nec

(G-8745)
300 GATEWAY LLC
1200 West Ave (19720-6249)
PHONE..................302 655-4100
EMP: 12 **EST:** 2013
SALES (est): 238.69K **Privately Held**
SIC: 7011 Hotels and motels

(G-8746)
3E VENTURES INC
410 Churchmans Rd (19720-3157)
PHONE..................302 773-8658
John Sweigart, *CEO*
EMP: 8
SALES (est): 176.86K **Privately Held**
SIC: 7532 Collision shops, automotive

(G-8747)
4DIMENSIONS LLC
402 Rolling Green Ave (19720-4792)
PHONE..................302 339-0082
Qaisar Mehmood, *Managing Member*
EMP: 70 **EST:** 2021
SALES (est): 2.9MM **Privately Held**
SIC: 8111 7389 Legal services; Business Activities at Non-Commercial Site

(G-8748)
A B FAB & MACHINING LLC
170 Earland Dr (19720)
PHONE..................302 293-4945
EMP: 2 **EST:** 2005
SQ FT: 23,000
SALES (est): 129.78K **Privately Held**
SIC: 3499 Machine bases, metal

(G-8749)
A M TOWING CO
91 Villas Dr Apt 10 (19720-2838)
PHONE..................302 357-5159
Alan Mou, *Prin*
EMP: 5 **EST:** 2016
SALES (est): 52.24K **Privately Held**
SIC: 7549 Towing service, automotive

(G-8750)
A S T B ANALYTICAL SERVICES
4027 New Castle Ave (19720-1414)
PHONE..................302 571-8882
Richard Rowe, *Pr*
EMP: 42 **EST:** 1987
SALES (est): 3.4MM **Privately Held**
SIC: 8734 Testing laboratories

(G-8751)
A STITCH IN TIME
101 Harrison Ave (19720-2526)
PHONE..................302 395-1306
EMP: 4 **EST:** 1991
SALES (est): 298.48K **Privately Held**
SIC: 2395 Embroidery products, except Schiffli machine

(G-8752)
A-1 SANITATION SERVICE INC
1009 River Rd (19720-5103)
P.O. Box 336 (19720-0336)
PHONE..................302 322-1074
Anthony Smiertka Junior, *Pr*
Joanne Smiertka, *Sec*
Anthony A Smiertka Junior, *VP*
Steven Smiertka, *VP*
EMP: 25 **EST:** 1968
SQ FT: 3,800
SALES (est): 1.23MM **Privately Held**
Web: www.a1sanitation.com
SIC: 7359 7699 Portable toilet rental; Sewer cleaning and rodding

(G-8753)
A22 COMMUNITY CONNECTIONS
125 Rodney Dr (19720-2729)
PHONE..................302 213-9426
EMP: 5 **EST:** 2017
SALES (est): 57.69K **Privately Held**
SIC: 8322 Community center

(G-8754)
AARON ANDERSON ◊
973 Red Lion Rd (19720-5204)
PHONE..................804 986-1666
EMP: 2 **EST:** 2023
SALES (est): 92.41K **Privately Held**
SIC: 3714 Motor vehicle engines and parts

(G-8755)
AB CARPENTRY SERVICES INC
217 Sykes Rd (19720-1813)
PHONE..................302 276-2457
David Ashley, *Pr*
EMP: 6 **EST:** 2014
SALES (est): 73.06K **Privately Held**
SIC: 1751 Carpentry work

(G-8756)
ABC DELAWARE
31 Blevins Dr Ste B (19720-4170)
PHONE..................302 858-2185
EMP: 9 **EST:** 2013
SALES (est): 501.72K **Privately Held**
Web: www.abcdelaware.com
SIC: 8611 Contractors' association

(G-8757)
ABCO MECH HTG & COOLG LLC
14 Rambleton Dr (19720-4042)
PHONE..................302 353-4336
EMP: 5 **EST:** 2019
SALES (est): 109.82K **Privately Held**
SIC: 1711 Warm air heating and air conditioning contractor

(G-8758)
ABUWEN ANESTHESIA SERVICES LLC
516 Bluebill Dr (19720-8931)
PHONE..................301 526-4584
Celestine Atangcho, *Prin*
EMP: 9 **EST:** 2017
SALES (est): 243.03K **Privately Held**
SIC: 8011 Anesthesiologist

(G-8759)
ACADIA HEALTHCARE COMPANY INC
Also Called: PHC Meadowwood
575 S Dupont Hwy (19720-4606)
PHONE..................302 328-3330
EMP: 13
Web: www.meadowwoodhospital.com
SIC: 8099 Childbirth preparation clinic
PA: Acadia Healthcare Company, Inc.
6100 Tower Cir Ste 1000
Franklin TN 37067

(G-8760)
ACCESS LABOR SERVICE INC (PA)
2203 N Dupont Hwy (19720-6302)
PHONE..................302 326-2575
Butch Brooks, *Pr*
EMP: 29 **EST:** 1999
SALES (est): 4.74MM
SALES (corp-wide): 4.74MM **Privately Held**
Web: www.accesslaborservice.com
SIC: 7361 Placement agencies

(G-8761)
ACE HOME SOLUTIONS CORP
5 Camino Ct (19720-8627)
PHONE..................302 743-8995
Jonathan Edler, *Prin*
EMP: 5 **EST:** 2016
SALES (est): 214.81K **Privately Held**
SIC: 1521 New construction, single-family houses

(G-8762)
ADECCO USA INC
40 Reads Way (19720-1649)
PHONE..................302 669-4005
Sandie Milligan, *Brnch Mgr*
EMP: 7
Web: www.adeccousa.com
SIC: 7363 Temporary help service
HQ: Adecco Usa, Inc.
4800 Deerwood Campus Pkwy # 800
Jacksonville FL 32246
904 360-2000

(G-8763)
ADERYN WOODWORKS
11 Villas Dr Apt 9 (19720-2846)
PHONE..................219 229-5070
Sean Billups, *Prin*
EMP: 4 **EST:** 2018
SALES (est): 65.83K **Privately Held**
SIC: 2431 Millwork

(G-8764)
ADESIS INC
27 Mccullough Dr (19720-2080)
PHONE..................302 323-4880
Charles Chuck Beard, *CEO*
Linda Choi Macdonald, *
▲ **EMP:** 40 **EST:** 2005
SALES (est): 10.93MM **Publicly Held**
Web: www.adesisinc.com
SIC: 2834 Medicines, capsuled or ampuled
PA: Universal Display Corporation
250 Phillips Blvd
Ewing NJ 08618

(G-8765)
ADVANCED LOGISTICS LLC
13 Erbitea Ln (19720-4655)
PHONE..................302 345-8921
EMP: 5 **EST:** 2021
SALES (est): 210.36K **Privately Held**
Web: www.advancedlogistics.us

SIC: 4789 7389 Transportation services, nec ; Business Activities at Non-Commercial Site

(G-8766)
ADVANCED MACHINERY SALES INC
Also Called: Advanced Machinery
2 Mccullough Dr Ste 2 (19720-2092)
P.O. Box 312 (19720-0312)
PHONE..................302 322-2226
Wolfgang Derke, *Pr*
Hanns J Derke, *VP*
▲ **EMP:** 9 **EST:** 1975
SQ FT: 11,000
SALES (est): 455.22K **Privately Held**
Web: www.advmachinery.com
SIC: 5084 Sawmill machinery and equipment

(G-8767)
ADVANCED POWER CONTROL INC (HQ)
Also Called: Albireo Energy
15 Reads Way Ste 101 (19720-1600)
PHONE..................302 368-0443
Paul E Czerwin, *Pr*
Joan Czerwin, *
Ronald Myers, *
EMP: 64 **EST:** 1980
SALES (est): 32.86MM
SALES (corp-wide): 141.55MM **Privately Held**
SIC: 1731 Energy management controls
PA: Albireo Energy, Llc
3 Ethel Rd Ste 300
Edison NJ 08817
732 512-9100

(G-8768)
AERO WAYS INC
Also Called: Fly Advanced
131 N Dupont Hwy (19720-3135)
PHONE..................302 324-9970
Regis De Ramel, *Pr*
Charles Belmont, *
Ron Beckson, *
Ronald M Beckson, *
Edward T Bohn, *
EMP: 125 **EST:** 2000
SQ FT: 24,000
SALES (est): 17.15MM **Privately Held**
Web: www.flyadvanced.com
SIC: 7363 Pilot service, aviation

(G-8769)
AEROSPACE DSIGN COMPLIANCE LLC
10 Corporate Cir Ste 225 (19720-2403)
PHONE..................302 407-6825
EMP: 5 **EST:** 2017
SALES (est): 217.71K **Privately Held**
Web: www.aerodcllc.com
SIC: 7389 Design services

(G-8770)
AEROTEK INC
Also Called: AEROTEK, INC.
100 W Commons Blvd Ste 425 (19720)
PHONE..................302 561-6300
Matt Bramblett, *Pr*
EMP: 5
SALES (corp-wide): 15.88B **Privately Held**
Web: www.aerotek.com
SIC: 7363 Temporary help service
HQ: Aerotek Affiliated Services, Inc.
7301 Parkway Dr
Hanover MD 21076
410 694-5100

GEOGRAPHIC SECTION

New Castle - New Castle County (G-8799)

(G-8771)
AFFORDABLE DELIVERY SVCS LLC
Also Called: ADS
217 Lisa Dr Ste D (19720-8404)
PHONE.............................302 276-0246
EMP: 20 **EST:** 2010
SALES (est): 1.81MM **Privately Held**
SIC: 4212 1799 Delivery service, vehicular; Office furniture installation

(G-8772)
AGENTS OF DELAWARE INC
257 Old Churchmans Rd (19720-1529)
PHONE.............................302 544-2467
EMP: 11 **EST:** 2016
SALES (est): 432.89K **Privately Held**
Web: www.agentsofdelaware.com
SIC: 8111 Legal services

(G-8773)
AGROREFINER LLC ✪
51 Steel Dr Unit B (19720-7709)
PHONE.............................212 651-4865
Howard Matz, *Prin*
EMP: 6 **EST:** 2022
SALES (est): 335.15K **Privately Held**
Web: www.agroref.com
SIC: 8734 Testing laboratories

(G-8774)
AIA
4058 New Castle Ave (19720-1434)
PHONE.............................302 407-2252
Brian Darby, *Owner*
EMP: 6 **EST:** 2018
SALES (est): 121.8K **Privately Held**
SIC: 2759 Commercial printing, nec

(G-8775)
AIR TEMP SOLUTIONS LLC
101 J And M Dr (19720-3147)
PHONE.............................302 276-0532
EMP: 12 **EST:** 2011
SALES (est): 861.43K **Privately Held**
Web: www.air-tempsolutions.com
SIC: 1711 7371 Warm air heating and air conditioning contractor; Computer software development and applications

(G-8776)
AJACKS TIRE SERVICE INC
819 S Dupont Hwy (19720-4610)
PHONE.............................302 834-5200
Anthony Micucio Junior, *Pr*
EMP: 4 **EST:** 1976
SQ FT: 2,400
SALES (est): 277.49K **Privately Held**
SIC: 7534 5531 Tire repair shop; Automotive tires

(G-8777)
ALDERMAN AUTOMOTIVE ENTERPRISE
Also Called: Alderman Automotive Machine Sp
2317 N Dupont Hwy (19720-6304)
PHONE.............................302 652-3733
George Alderman, *Pr*
Paul Alderman, *VP*
EMP: 6 **EST:** 1983
SALES (est): 751.34K **Privately Held**
Web: www.aldermanmachine.com
SIC: 7538 General automotive repair shops

(G-8778)
ALL BRIGHT CLEANING SVCS LLC
117 Malcolm Forest Rd (19720-8740)
PHONE.............................302 219-7016
Byron Hinson, *Managing Member*
Byron B Hinson, *Prin*
EMP: 15 **EST:** 2017
SALES (est): 649.01K **Privately Held**
Web: www.allbrightcleanings.com
SIC: 7699 Cleaning services

(G-8779)
ALL FOR FUN PARTY RENTALS
200 Lisa Dr (19720-4167)
PHONE.............................302 322-3844
EMP: 5 **EST:** 2018
SALES (est): 230.1K **Privately Held**
Web: www.allforfunpartyrentals.com
SIC: 7359 Party supplies rental services

(G-8780)
ALL JS CLEANING SERVICES INC
21 Jennings Ct (19720-3908)
PHONE.............................302 299-9916
Johneshia Kornegay, *CEO*
EMP: 8 **EST:** 2018
SALES (est): 500.04K **Privately Held**
Web: www.alljscleaning.com
SIC: 7389 7699 7349 Business Activities at Non-Commercial Site; Cleaning services; Building and office cleaning services

(G-8781)
ALL RIGHT PAINTING
185 Edge Ave (19720-2016)
PHONE.............................302 983-7761
EMP: 5 **EST:** 2014
SALES (est): 42.66K **Privately Held**
Web: www.rightincorporated.com
SIC: 1721 Painting and paper hanging

(G-8782)
ALL STAR SHREDDING LP
6 Dock View Dr Ste 1000 (19720-2206)
PHONE.............................302 325-9998
EMP: 15
SIC: 7389 4953 Document and office record destruction; Recycling, waste materials

(G-8783)
ALL STAR TOWING LLC
4030 New Castle Ave (19720-1455)
PHONE.............................302 388-4221
EMP: 5 **EST:** 2018
SALES (est): 180.78K **Privately Held**
SIC: 7549 Towing service, automotive

(G-8784)
ALL TYPES CONCRETE
63 Meadow Rd (19720-1513)
PHONE.............................302 613-8400
Thomas Kreske, *Prin*
EMP: 5 **EST:** 2014
SALES (est): 101.68K **Privately Held**
SIC: 1771 Concrete work

(G-8785)
ALLIED PRINTING CO INC
2 Penns Way Ste 301 (19720-2407)
PHONE.............................503 626-0669
EMP: 9 **EST:** 2019
SALES (est): 83.91K **Privately Held**
SIC: 2752 Offset printing

(G-8786)
ALLMARK DOOR COMPANY LLC
502 Churchmans Rd (19720-3155)
PHONE.............................302 323-4999
Kelly Vanquez, *Brnch Mgr*
EMP: 10
Web: www.allmarkdoors.com
SIC: 2431 3442 Garage doors, overhead, wood; Garage doors, overhead: metal
PA: Allmark Door Company Llc
      15 Stern Ave
      Springfield NJ 07081

(G-8787)
ALPHA OMEGA SCIENTIFIC LLC
129 Freedom Trl (19720-3849)
PHONE.............................302 415-4499
Emmanuel Troumouhis, *Prin*
Emmanuel Troumouhis, *Pr*
Saki Koudis, *VP*
EMP: 5 **EST:** 2019
SALES (est): 222.08K **Privately Held**
SIC: 8731 Biotechnical research, commercial

(G-8788)
ALSCO INC
30 Mccullough Dr (19720-2066)
PHONE.............................302 322-2136
Jared Wantoch, *Genl Mgr*
EMP: 31
SALES (corp-wide): 540.5MM **Privately Held**
Web: www.alsco.com
SIC: 7213 Uniform supply
PA: Alsco Inc
      505 E 200 S
      Salt Lake City UT 84102
      801 328-8831

(G-8789)
ALVINS PROFESSIONAL SERVICES
Also Called: APS Cleaning Services
241 Old Churchmans Rd (19720-1529)
PHONE.............................302 544-6634
Alvin R Emory Junior, *Pr*
Brandt Emory, *VP*
EMP: 10 **EST:** 2003
SALES (est): 342.85K **Privately Held**
Web: www.apscleaning.org
SIC: 7349 7699 Janitorial service, contract basis; Cleaning services

(G-8790)
AMARCH LLC
1023 Matthew Way (19720-5651)
PHONE.............................484 478-1034
Singh Manvinder, *Prin*
EMP: 5 **EST:** 2014
SALES (est): 237.92K **Privately Held**
SIC: 4789 Transportation services, nec

(G-8791)
AMBIENCE OF EXCELLENCE LLC
9 Liborio Ln (19720-4653)
P.O. Box 12442 (19850-2442)
PHONE.............................302 751-0778
Rita Bell, *CEO*
EMP: 7 **EST:** 2017
SALES (est): 106.12K **Privately Held**
SIC: 7299 Party planning service

(G-8792)
AMEDEE ENTERPRISES LLC ✪
1 E Saxony Dr (19720-8806)
PHONE.............................302 482-7442
Paulinus Amedee, *Managing Member*
Jinesha Amedee, *Pr*
EMP: 5 **EST:** 2022
SALES (est): 233.47K **Privately Held**
SIC: 6519 Real property lessors, nec

(G-8793)
AMEMG INC
Also Called: Adventres In Lrng Erly Chldhoo
32 Phoebe Farms Ln (19720-8769)
PHONE.............................302 220-7132
Joanne Steicher, *Pr*
EMP: 10 **EST:** 2006
SALES (est): 93.77K **Privately Held**
SIC: 8351 Child day care services

(G-8794)
AMER MASONRY T A MARINO
Also Called: Marino & Sons
811 Reybold Dr (19720-4616)
PHONE.............................302 834-1511
Thomas Marino Junior, *Pr*
EMP: 5 **EST:** 1983
SALES (est): 417.75K **Privately Held**
SIC: 1741 Masonry and other stonework

(G-8795)
AMERI AUTO LLC
150 Malcolm Forest Rd (19720-8746)
PHONE.............................302 607-9113
Charles Davis, *Prin*
EMP: 5 **EST:** 2015
SALES (est): 30.91K **Privately Held**
SIC: 7538 General automotive repair shops

(G-8796)
AMERICAN FDRTION STATE CNTY MN
100 Churchmans Rd (19720-3108)
PHONE.............................302 323-2600
Michael Begatto, *Prin*
EMP: 7 **EST:** 2010
SALES (est): 87.63K **Privately Held**
SIC: 8631 Labor union

(G-8797)
AMERICAN FDRTION STATE CNTY MN
Also Called: Afscme-Council 81
91 Christiana Rd (19720-3104)
PHONE.............................302 323-2121
Michael Beagetto, *Ex Dir*
EMP: 10
SALES (corp-wide): 140.24MM **Privately Held**
Web: www.afscme.org
SIC: 8631 Labor union
PA: American Federation Of State County
      & Municipal Employees
      1625 L St Nw
      Washington DC 20036
      202 429-1000

(G-8798)
AMERICAN FURNITURE RENTALS INC
Also Called: A F R
490 W Basin Rd (19720-6408)
PHONE.............................302 323-1682
Frank Mccall, *Brnch Mgr*
EMP: 23
SALES (corp-wide): 144.59MM **Privately Held**
Web: www.rentfurniture.com
SIC: 7359 Furniture rental
PA: American Furniture Rentals, Inc.
      720 Hylton Rd
      Pennsauken NJ 08110
      856 406-1200

(G-8799)
AMERICAN MINERALS INC
301 Pigeon Point Rd (19720-1400)
PHONE.............................302 652-3301
Jim Murphy, *Mgr*
EMP: 8
SALES (corp-wide): 1.88B **Privately Held**
Web: www.vibrantz.com
SIC: 1446 3313 Silica sand mining; Electrometallurgical products
HQ: American Minerals Inc
      21 W 46th St Fl 14
      New York NY 10036
      646 747-4222

New Castle - New Castle County (G-8800) — GEOGRAPHIC SECTION

(G-8800)
AMERICAN MINERALS PARTNERSHIP
301 Pigeon Point Rd (19720-1400)
PHONE..................302 652-3301
Frank Nefoske, *Prin*
▲ EMP: 15 EST: 1987
SALES (est): 1.03MM **Privately Held**
SIC: **1061** 1011 1099 Manganese ores mining; Iron ores; Bauxite mining

(G-8801)
AMERICAN STANDARD
66 Southgate Blvd (19720-2068)
PHONE..................302 326-1349
EMP: 9 EST: 2019
SALES (est): 126.67K **Privately Held**
Web: staging-asa.irapis.com
SIC: **1711** Warm air heating and air conditioning contractor

(G-8802)
AMERIMAX INC
3025 Bowlarama Dr (19720-1316)
PHONE..................951 710-0899
EMP: 5 EST: 2015
SALES (est): 101.59K **Privately Held**
SIC: **1761** Gutter and downspout contractor

(G-8803)
AMSTEL MECHANICAL CONTRS INC
Also Called: Honeywell Authorized Dealer
1183 S Dupont Hwy (19720-5203)
PHONE..................302 836-6469
John Nobel, *Pr*
EMP: 8 EST: 1991
SQ FT: 5,000
SALES (est): 883.43K **Privately Held**
Web: www.amstelmechanical.net
SIC: **1711** Warm air heating and air conditioning contractor

(G-8804)
AMTRAK MATERIAL CONTROL
5 Boulden Cir (19720-3400)
PHONE..................302 319-7270
EMP: 9 EST: 2019
SALES (est): 801.1K **Privately Held**
SIC: **7389** Business services, nec

(G-8805)
AMY CORBITT
632 Dane Ct (19720-5636)
PHONE..................302 635-7233
Amy Corbitt, *Prin*
EMP: 10 EST: 2014
SALES (est): 251.26K **Privately Held**
SIC: **8099** Health and allied services, nec

(G-8806)
ANALYTICAL BIOLOGICAL SVCS INC
Also Called: ABS
2 Reads Way (19720-1602)
PHONE..................302 654-4492
Charles Saller, *Pr*
EMP: 20 EST: 1990
SQ FT: 10,000
SALES (est): 5.44MM **Privately Held**
Web: www.absbio.com
SIC: **2836** 8733 Biological products, except diagnostic; Medical research

(G-8807)
ANCHOR ELECTRIC INC
185 Old Churchmans Rd (19720-3115)
P.O. Box 12591 (19850-2591)
PHONE..................302 221-6111
Charles Saxton, *Pr*
EMP: 8 EST: 2007
SALES (est): 948.73K **Privately Held**
Web: www.anchorelectric.us
SIC: **1731** General electrical contractor

(G-8808)
ANGELS IN ACTION INC
Also Called: Angels Interaction
23 Elks Trl (19720-3856)
PHONE..................302 397-7061
Balki Yousiffou, *Prin*
EMP: 6 EST: 2011
SALES (est): 79.94K **Privately Held**
Web: www.ainachildcare.com
SIC: **8699** Charitable organization

(G-8809)
ANGELS LINDAS
6 Parkway Ct (19720-4020)
PHONE..................302 328-3700
Linda Bright, *Owner*
EMP: 9 EST: 2002
SALES (est): 79.43K **Privately Held**
SIC: **8351** Group day care center

(G-8810)
ANIXTER INC
51 Steel Dr (19720-7700)
PHONE..................302 325-2590
EMP: 5
Web: www.anixter.com
SIC: **5063** Electrical apparatus and equipment
HQ: Anixter Inc.
2301 Patriot Blvd
Glenview IL 60026
800 323-8167

(G-8811)
ANN M CAMPAGNA
2 Boulden Cir Ste 1 (19720-3492)
PHONE..................302 395-8950
Ann M Campagna Rph, *Owner*
EMP: 5 EST: 2018
SALES (est): 22.18K **Privately Held**
SIC: **8049** Offices of health practitioner

(G-8812)
ANOINTED CREATIVE CREATIONS
15 Meadow Rd (19720-1544)
PHONE..................302 650-7033
Shanika Cotton, *CEO*
EMP: 6 EST: 2017
SALES (est): 51.56K **Privately Held**
SIC: **7299** Party planning service

(G-8813)
ANTHONYS AUTOMOTIVE
252 Bassett Ave (19720-1828)
PHONE..................302 420-9804
Anthony Claudio Black, *Prin*
EMP: 5 EST: 2016
SALES (est): 49.76K **Privately Held**
SIC: **7538** General automotive repair shops

(G-8814)
APPLE CLEANING SYSTEMS LLC
34 Blevins Dr Ste 1 (19720-4177)
PHONE..................302 368-7507
EMP: 13 EST: 2004
SALES (est): 469.65K **Privately Held**
Web: www.applecleaningsystems.net
SIC: **7349** 7217 Cleaning service, industrial or commercial; Carpet and upholstery cleaning

(G-8815)
APPLEBY APARTMENTS ASSOC LP
401 Bedford Ln (19720-3936)
PHONE..................302 219-5014
Trudy Carter, *Mgr*
EMP: 5 EST: 1988
SALES (est): 484.24K **Privately Held**
SIC: **6513** Apartment hotel operation

(G-8816)
APRIA HEALTHCARE LLC
1 Mccullough Dr (19720-2007)
PHONE..................302 737-7979
William Guidetti, *Brnch Mgr*
EMP: 12
Web: www.apria.com
SIC: **7352** Medical equipment rental
HQ: Apria Healthcare Llc
7353 Company Dr
Indianapolis IN 46237
949 639-2000

(G-8817)
AQUATICA PLUMBING GROUP INC
414 Greenwood Dr (19720)
PHONE..................866 606-2782
EMP: 5 EST: 2014
SALES (est): 18.09K **Privately Held**
Web: www.aquaticausa.com
SIC: **3261** Bathroom accessories/fittings, vitreous china or earthenware

(G-8818)
ARCADE SERVICES INC ◆
257 Old Churchmans Rd (19720-1529)
PHONE..................630 777-8092
EMP: 19 EST: 2022
SALES (est): 583.41K **Privately Held**
SIC: **7371** Computer software development and applications

(G-8819)
ARCHITECTURAL SOLUTIONS
23 Grady Ln (19720-7643)
PHONE..................302 230-1809
EMP: 5 EST: 2019
SALES (est): 91.02K **Privately Held**
SIC: **8621** Architect association

(G-8820)
ARGO FINANCIAL SERVICES INC
Also Called: United Check Cashing
104 Penn Mart Shopping Ctr (19720-4209)
PHONE..................302 322-7788
EMP: 6 EST: 1994
SQ FT: 1,000
SALES (est): 740.7K **Privately Held**
Web: www.unitedcheckcashing.com
SIC: **6099** Check cashing agencies

(G-8821)
ARISE AFRICA FOUNDATION INC
10 Elks Trl (19720-3855)
PHONE..................877 829-5500
Damilola Junaid, *Pr*
Archit Joshi, *Dir*
EMP: 6 EST: 2016
SALES (est): 95.64K **Privately Held**
SIC: **8641** Civic and social associations

(G-8822)
ARKION LIFE SCIENCES LLC (PA)
Also Called: Arkion
551 Mews Dr Ste J (19720-2798)
PHONE..................800 468-6324
Earnest W Porta, *CEO*
Lanny Weaver, *VP*
Rick L Stejskal, *CFO*
Kenneth Ballinger Agricultural Crop, *Mgr*
▲ EMP: 13 EST: 2001
SQ FT: 7,998
SALES (est): 8.55MM
SALES (corp-wide): 8.55MM **Privately Held**
Web: www.arkionls.com
SIC: **2879** 8731 Pesticides, agricultural or household; Biological research

(G-8823)
ARMSTRONG TRNSF STOR INC/ RMSTR
20 E Commons Blvd (19720-1734)
PHONE..................302 323-9000
EMP: 326
SALES (corp-wide): 64.12MM **Privately Held**
Web: www.armstrongrelocation.com
SIC: **4212** Moving services
PA: Armstrong Transfer And Storage Co., Inc./Armstrong Relocation Company, Memphis
3927 Winchester Rd
Memphis TN 38118
901 363-1914

(G-8824)
ARS FLEET SERVICE
501 Lambson Ln (19720-2101)
PHONE..................302 482-1305
EMP: 9 EST: 2018
SALES (est): 253.04K **Privately Held**
Web: www.arsfleetservice.com
SIC: **7538** General automotive repair shops

(G-8825)
ARTISTRY SALON STUDIO
210 Sterling Ave (19720-4730)
PHONE..................302 513-9225
Tahra Clarke, *Prin*
EMP: 5 EST: 2016
SALES (est): 248.89K **Privately Held**
Web: www.artistrysalonstudio.com
SIC: **7231** Hairdressers

(G-8826)
ASSURANCE PLUMBING COMPNAY
87 Skyline Dr (19720-2944)
PHONE..................302 324-0403
Douglas C Riley, *Prin*
EMP: 5 EST: 2014
SALES (est): 121.93K **Privately Held**
Web: www.assuranceplumbingcompany.com
SIC: **1711** Plumbing contractors

(G-8827)
ASTER DRYWALL
103 Wedgefield Dr (19720-3717)
PHONE..................302 757-5876
Eric Moore, *Pr*
EMP: 6 EST: 2012
SALES (est): 280.31K **Privately Held**
Web: www.asterdrywall.com
SIC: **1742** Drywall

(G-8828)
AT HOME PROPERTY MGT LLC
39 Winburne Dr (19720-3721)
PHONE..................623 216-8052
EMP: 5
SALES (est): 119.02K **Privately Held**
SIC: **6531** Real estate leasing and rentals

(G-8829)
ATELEIR ART SERVICES INC
71 Southgate Blvd (19720-2069)
PHONE..................302 669-6400
EMP: 6 EST: 2015
SALES (est): 230.44K **Privately Held**
SIC: **8999** Art restoration

(G-8830)
ATI HOLDINGS LLC
Also Called: ATI Physical Therapy
2032 New Castle Ave (19720-7703)

GEOGRAPHIC SECTION

New Castle - New Castle County (G-8856)

PHONE...................302 654-1700
EMP: 8
SALES (corp-wide): 635.67MM **Publicly Held**
Web: www.atipt.com
SIC: 8049 Physical therapist
HQ: Ati Holdings, Llc
 790 Remington Blvd
 Bolingbrook IL 60440

(G-8831)
ATLANTIC WATER PRODUCTS
74 Southgate Blvd (19720-2068)
PHONE...................302 326-1166
Curtis Wunder, *Owner*
Timothy Way, *Genl Mgr*
EMP: 21 **EST:** 2000
SALES (est): 781.5K **Privately Held**
Web: www.atlanticwaterproducts.com
SIC: 7389 4971 Water softener service; Water distribution or supply systems for irrigation

(G-8832)
ATLAS WLDG & FABRICATION INC
Also Called: Atlas Welding
728 Grantham Ln (19720-4802)
PHONE...................302 326-1900
Christopher Ramsey, *Pr*
Tracey Schmid, *Sec*
EMP: 21 **EST:** 1974
SQ FT: 3,000
SALES (est): 5.92MM **Privately Held**
Web: www.atlasfab.net
SIC: 3444 1791 Sheet metalwork; Structural steel erection

(G-8833)
AUDIT TEAM LLC
1 Bassett Ave (19720-2088)
PHONE...................302 322-0452
John D Travis, *Prin*
EMP: 5 **EST:** 2013
SALES (est): 51.02K **Privately Held**
SIC: 8721 Auditing services

(G-8834)
AUTOPORT INC
203 Pigeon Point Rd (19720-2177)
PHONE...................302 658-5100
Roy Kirchner, *Pr*
John Lovett, *
D Ick Johnson, *
▼ **EMP:** 40 **EST:** 1981
SQ FT: 29,000
SALES (est): 4.89MM **Privately Held**
Web: www.autoportinc.com
SIC: 7532 7549 5012 3714 Top and body repair and paint shops; Automotive customizing services, nonfactory basis; Truck bodies; Acceleration equipment, motor vehicle

(G-8835)
AVIS RENT A CAR SYSTEM LLC
Also Called: Avis Rent A Car Systems
151 N Dupont Hwy (19720-3136)
PHONE...................302 322-2092
Pat Boyer, *Prin*
EMP: 5
SALES (corp-wide): 11.99B **Publicly Held**
Web: www.avis.com
SIC: 7514 Rent-a-car service
HQ: Avis Rent A Car System, Llc
 6 Sylvan Way Ste 1
 Parsippany NJ 07054
 973 496-3500

(G-8836)
AVS INDUSTRIES LLC
21 Bellecor Dr Ste C (19720-1743)
PHONE...................302 221-1705
David Sydow, *CEO*
◆ **EMP:** 7 **EST:** 2004
SALES (est): 2.32MM **Privately Held**
Web: www.avsind.com
SIC: 5023 Sheets, textile

(G-8837)
AXIS GEOSPATIAL
40 Mccullough Dr (19720-2227)
PHONE...................302 276-0160
EMP: 5 **EST:** 2016
SALES (est): 101.22K **Privately Held**
SIC: 8713 Surveying services

(G-8838)
AZEXTENSIONS LLC
96 Freedom Trl (19720-3847)
PHONE...................609 202-2098
Arionna Callaway, *Mng Pt*
EMP: 3 **EST:** 2021
SALES (est): 17.21K **Privately Held**
SIC: 3999 Hair and hair-based products

(G-8839)
B & F TOWING CO
449 Old Airport Rd (19720-1001)
PHONE...................302 328-4146
Robert Fenimore, *Pr*
Henry Fenimore, *
EMP: 32 **EST:** 1967
SQ FT: 3,000
SALES (est): 2.29MM **Privately Held**
Web: www.bftowing.com
SIC: 7549 7538 Towing service, automotive; General truck repair

(G-8840)
B G HALKO & SONS INC
204 Old Churchmans Rd (19720-1530)
PHONE...................302 322-2020
Thomas G Halko, *Pr*
EMP: 6 **EST:** 1970
SQ FT: 4,000
SALES (est): 991.53K **Privately Held**
Web: www.bghalkoandsons.com
SIC: 1799 Fence construction

(G-8841)
BABOON BUBBLE INC ✪
406 John Vineyards Ln (19720-8729)
PHONE...................302 307-2979
Silver Lin, *CFO*
EMP: 3 **EST:** 2022
SALES (est): 135.7K **Privately Held**
SIC: 2087 7389 Beverage bases; Business services, nec

(G-8842)
BABY BEAR EDUCARE
202 Remi Dr (19720-5622)
PHONE...................302 981-9571
Tanisha Holmes, *Prin*
EMP: 8 **EST:** 2018
SALES (est): 62.46K **Privately Held**
SIC: 8351 Child day care services

(G-8843)
BABY BUBBA DJ & EVENT PLANNING
18 Crippen Dr (19720-3243)
PHONE...................302 373-4653
Brian Connor, *Owner*
EMP: 5 **EST:** 2010
SALES (est): 48.05K **Privately Held**
Web: www.bigbangdjservice.com
SIC: 7231 Beauty shops

(G-8844)
BACK 2 HEALTHY NUTRITION LLC
20 Blyth Ct (19720-3734)
PHONE...................302 857-9818
Edith Chewning, *Asst Sec*
EMP: 6 **EST:** 2018
SALES (est): 85.12K **Privately Held**
SIC: 8049 Nutrition specialist

(G-8845)
BACK IN ACTION CHIROPRACTIC
819 Churchmans Road Ext (19720-3152)
PHONE...................302 322-3304
Brian R Chandler, *Prin*
EMP: 5 **EST:** 2009
SALES (est): 205.68K **Privately Held**
Web: www.backinactioncenter.com
SIC: 8041 Offices and clinics of chiropractors

(G-8846)
BANK OF NEW CASTLE
12 Reads Way (19720-1649)
PHONE...................800 347-3301
Beverly Ballard, *Prin*
EMP: 45 **EST:** 2000
SALES (est): 316K
SALES (corp-wide): 15.2B **Publicly Held**
SIC: 6141 Personal credit institutions
PA: Discover Financial Services
 2500 Lake Cook Rd
 Riverwoods IL 60015
 224 405-0900

(G-8847)
BATTAGLIA ELECTRIC INC
11 Industrial Blvd (19720-2087)
P.O. Box 630 (19720-0630)
PHONE...................302 325-6100
Gene Battaglia, *Pr*
Louis J Orsini, *
George Lazorick, *
EMP: 175 **EST:** 1981
SQ FT: 20,000
SALES (est): 25.43MM **Privately Held**
Web: www.battag.com
SIC: 1731 1711 General electrical contractor; Mechanical contractor

(G-8848)
BATTAGLIA MANAGEMENT INC
11 Industrial Blvd Ste B (19720-2087)
PHONE...................302 325-6100
B Eugene Battaglia, *Prin*
EMP: 10 **EST:** 1997
SALES (est): 175.66K **Privately Held**
Web: www.battag.com
SIC: 6531 Real estate agents and managers

(G-8849)
BATTAGLIA MECHANICAL INC
11 Industrial Blvd (19720-2087)
P.O. Box 630 (19720-0630)
PHONE...................302 325-6100
Eugene Battaglia, *Pr*
Jean Battaglia, *
Anthony Iori, *
EMP: 21 **EST:** 1997
SQ FT: 20,000
SALES (est): 479.39K **Privately Held**
Web: www.battag.com
SIC: 1521 Single-family housing construction

(G-8850)
BAY SHIPPERS LLC
1535 Matassino Rd (19720-3353)
P.O. Box 18 (19373-0018)
PHONE...................302 652-5005
Robert Higgins, *Prin*
EMP: 8 **EST:** 2005
SALES (est): 582.69K **Privately Held**
Web: www.bayshippers.com
SIC: 4789 Cargo loading and unloading services

(G-8851)
BAYADA HOME HEALTH CARE INC
15 Reads Way Ste 205 (19720-1600)
PHONE...................302 322-2300
Mary Agnes, *Brnch Mgr*
EMP: 5
SALES (corp-wide): 694.21MM **Privately Held**
Web: www.bayada.com
SIC: 8082 Visiting nurse service
PA: Bayada Home Health Care, Inc.
 1 W Main St
 Moorestown NJ 08057
 856 231-1000

(G-8852)
BAYETE CORP
10 Shadwell Ct (19720-4423)
PHONE...................302 562-7415
Marcus Stevens, *Asst Sec*
EMP: 5 **EST:** 2018
SALES (est): 55.94K **Privately Held**
SIC: 7299 Miscellaneous personal service

(G-8853)
BAYSHORE FORD TRUCK SALES INC (PA)
Also Called: Quick Lane
4003 N Dupont Hwy (19720-6323)
P.O. Box 627 (19720-0627)
PHONE...................302 656-3160
Dale Brewer, *Pr*
▼ **EMP:** 69 **EST:** 1976
SQ FT: 26,000
SALES (est): 16.1MM
SALES (corp-wide): 16.1MM **Privately Held**
Web: www.bayshoreford.com
SIC: 7513 5511 7538 Truck rental and leasing, no drivers; Automobiles, new and used; General automotive repair shops

(G-8854)
BEACON AIR INC
23 Parkway Cir Ste 9 (19720-4019)
P.O. Box 10806 (19850-0806)
PHONE...................302 323-1688
Dennis Mellott, *Pr*
EMP: 8 **EST:** 1984
SALES (est): 1.02MM **Privately Held**
Web: www.beaconheatingandair.com
SIC: 1711 Warm air heating and air conditioning contractor

(G-8855)
BEAR MATERIALS LLC (PA)
4048 New Castle Ave (19720-1455)
PHONE...................302 658-5241
EMP: 4 **EST:** 1998
SQ FT: 8,000
SALES (est): 6.84MM
SALES (corp-wide): 6.84MM **Privately Held**
SIC: 1442 Construction sand and gravel

(G-8856)
BEAUTY BY JAMIE
8 Nieole Ave (19720-1207)
PHONE...................302 784-5311
Jamie Shanklin, *Prin*
EMP: 5 **EST:** 2010
SALES (est): 46.12K **Privately Held**
SIC: 7231 Beauty shops

New Castle - New Castle County (G-8857)

(G-8857)
BEGINNING BLSSNGS CHLDCARE LLC
Also Called: Beginning Blessings Daycare
23 Karen Ct (19720-5171)
PHONE..................................302 893-1726
Deborah Omowunmi, *Pr*
Rotimi Omowunmi, *Prin*
EMP: 5 **EST:** 2004
SALES (est): 98.45K **Privately Held**
SIC: 8351 Child day care services

(G-8858)
BENZ HYDRAULICS INC (PA)
Also Called: Benz Hydraulic Service
153 S Dupont Hwy (19720-4127)
PHONE..................................302 328-6648
TOLL FREE: 800
Timothy J Dougherty, *Pr*
Shelley Dougherty, *VP*
EMP: 10 **EST:** 1984
SQ FT: 3,800
SALES (est): 3.39MM **Privately Held**
Web: www.benzhydraulics.com
SIC: 5084 Hydraulic systems equipment and supplies

(G-8859)
BERMAN DEVELOPMENT CORP
Also Called: Scotch Hills Apartments
30 Highland Blvd (19720-6980)
PHONE..................................302 323-1197
Sara Farmer, *Mgr*
EMP: 5
SALES (corp-wide): 5.01MM **Privately Held**
Web: www.scotchhills.com
SIC: 6513 Apartment building operators
PA: Berman Development Corp
  901 S Trooper Rd
  Valley Forge PA

(G-8860)
BERRODIN SOUTH INC
20 Mccullough Dr (19720-2066)
PHONE..................................302 575-0500
John Berrodin, *Pr*
James Berrodin, *Sec*
Lou Berrodin, *VP*
EMP: 20 **EST:** 1967
SQ FT: 25,000
SALES (est): 5.88MM
SALES (corp-wide): 9.59MM **Privately Held**
Web: www.berrodin.com
SIC: 5013 Truck parts and accessories
PA: Berrodin Co.
  790 Burmont Rd
  Drexel Hill PA 19026
  610 259-8700

(G-8861)
BEST CHOICE LLC
209 Skelton Dr (19720-4428)
PHONE..................................302 722-4249
EMP: 5 **EST:** 2012
SALES (est): 49.03K **Privately Held**
SIC: 7699 Cleaning services

(G-8862)
BEST STUCCO LLC
304 Jefferson Ave (19720-2506)
PHONE..................................302 650-3620
Edgar Morales, *Prin*
EMP: 6 **EST:** 2012
SALES (est): 69.93K **Privately Held**
SIC: 3299 Stucco

(G-8863)
BESTRANS INC
19 Davidson Ln Frnt Frnt (19720-2207)
PHONE..................................302 824-0909
Brian E Simmons, *Pr*
Tracey Simmons, *
EMP: 68 **EST:** 1996
SQ FT: 4,000
SALES (est): 9.44MM **Privately Held**
Web: www.bestransinc.com
SIC: 4953 Hazardous waste collection and disposal

(G-8864)
BETHRANT INDUSTRIES LLC
7 Midfield Rd (19720-3439)
PHONE..................................484 343-5435
Ashly Bethrant, *Managing Member*
EMP: 2 **EST:** 2014
SQ FT: 1,500
SALES (est): 95.21K **Privately Held**
SIC: 2392 Household furnishings, nec

(G-8865)
BETTER BUSINESS BUREAU OF DE
60 Reads Way (19720-1649)
PHONE..................................302 221-5255
Frances West, *Pr*
EMP: 7 **EST:** 1965
SALES (est): 640.43K **Privately Held**
Web: www.bbb.org
SIC: 8611 Better Business Bureau

(G-8866)
BGDEDGE INC
Also Called: Instant Imprints of Delaware
62 Southgate Blvd (19720-2090)
PHONE..................................302 477-1734
Brian Drysdale, *Pr*
EMP: 2 **EST:** 2009
SALES (est): 254.73K **Privately Held**
Web: www.instantimprints.com
SIC: 2752 Commercial printing, lithographic

(G-8867)
BIG WLLY STYLE PRODUCTIONS LLC
5 Nicole Ct (19720-3760)
PHONE..................................973 897-8661
Latysse Mckinzie-mack, *Prin*
EMP: 5 **EST:** 2017
SALES (est): 50.23K **Privately Held**
SIC: 7819 Developing and laboratory services, motion picture

(G-8868)
BIOTEK REMEDYS INC (PA)
2 Penns Way Ste 404 (19720-2407)
PHONE..................................877 246-9104
Chai Gadde, *CEO*
EMP: 40 **EST:** 2011
SQ FT: 5,000
SALES (est): 14.08MM
SALES (corp-wide): 14.08MM **Privately Held**
Web: www.biotekrx.com
SIC: 8082 Home health care services

(G-8869)
BLUCHILL INC
19 Davidson Ln Bldg 7 (19720-2207)
PHONE..................................302 658-2638
Bob Onorato, *Pr*
Carl Warren, *VP*
EMP: 5 **EST:** 2007
SQ FT: 5,000
SALES (est): 557.59K **Privately Held**
Web: www.bluchill.com
SIC: 3585 Refrigeration equipment, complete

(G-8870)
BLUE HEN UTILITY SERVICES INC
473 Old Airport Rd Bldg 4 (19720-1017)
PHONE..................................302 273-3167
Michele Reynolds, *Pr*
Ted Kelly, *VP*
Mike Reynolds, *VP*
EMP: 6 **EST:** 2014
SQ FT: 7,000
SALES (est): 722.83K **Privately Held**
SIC: 4911 Distribution, electric power

(G-8871)
BLUE SKIES SOLAR & WIND POWER
261 Airport Rd (19720-1540)
PHONE..................................302 326-0856
Bruce Wanex, *Owner*
EMP: 6 **EST:** 2007
SALES (est): 179.64K **Privately Held**
Web: www.wanex.com
SIC: 1711 7629 Solar energy contractor; Electrical repair shops

(G-8872)
BODY MATRIX
13 Oakmont Dr (19720-1320)
PHONE..................................302 220-8406
Tocarra Moore, *Owner*
EMP: 5 **EST:** 2019
SALES (est): 262.92K **Privately Held**
SIC: 5091 7389 Sporting and recreation goods; Business services, nec

(G-8873)
BOJ GLOBAL SERVICES LLC ◆
152 N Katrin Cir (19720-3582)
PHONE..................................302 325-4018
Richard Ojedukun, *Managing Member*
EMP: 10 **EST:** 2022
SALES (est): 547.9K **Privately Held**
SIC: 4731 Freight forwarding

(G-8874)
BOMBONAIS CABLE TECH LLC
218 Mccallmont Rd (19720-3332)
PHONE..................................302 444-1199
Salvador Gonzalez, *Pr*
EMP: 10 **EST:** 2011
SALES (est): 903.25K **Privately Held**
SIC: 4841 Cable television services

(G-8875)
BORDERX LAB INC
1140 River Rd (19720-5106)
PHONE..................................510 203-3974
EMP: 7 **EST:** 2019
SALES (est): 97.52K **Privately Held**
SIC: 8734 Testing laboratories

(G-8876)
BORNE LEGACY LOGISTICS LLC ◆
7 E Lexton Rd (19720-8826)
PHONE..................................609 346-0380
EMP: 5 **EST:** 2022
SALES (est): 220.1K **Privately Held**
SIC: 2519 7389 Household furniture, nec; Business services, nec

(G-8877)
BOUNDARIES NEW
103 E Hazeldell Ave Ste A (19720-1300)
PHONE..................................302 658-3486
EMP: 6 **EST:** 2007
SALES (est): 69.52K **Privately Held**
SIC: 7231 Beauty shops

(G-8878)
BOWLERAMA INC
3031 New Castle Ave (19720-2297)
PHONE..................................302 654-0263
Mark Mattei, *Pr*
EMP: 35 **EST:** 1959
SQ FT: 55,000
SALES (est): 2.64MM **Privately Held**
Web: www.bowlerama.us
SIC: 7933 Ten pin center

(G-8879)
BOWMAN GROUP LLC
1207 Canvasback Dr (19720-8934)
PHONE..................................302 494-7476
Maryjo Bowman, *Prin*
EMP: 5 **EST:** 2009
SALES (est): 110K **Privately Held**
SIC: 4213 Trucking, except local

(G-8880)
BOXWOOD ELECTRIC INC
10 King Ave (19720-1512)
PHONE..................................302 368-3257
David Fink, *Prin*
EMP: 8 **EST:** 2005
SALES (est): 422.94K **Privately Held**
SIC: 1731 Electrical work

(G-8881)
BOYS & GIRLS CLUBS DEL INC
Also Called: New Castle Boys & Girls Clubs
19 Lambson Ln (19720-2118)
PHONE..................................302 655-8569
Leandra Brown, *Mgr*
EMP: 10
SALES (corp-wide): 33.26MM **Privately Held**
Web: www.bgclubs.org
SIC: 8641 Youth organizations
PA: Boys & Girls Clubs Of Delaware, Inc.
  669 S Union St
  Wilmington DE 19805
  302 658-1870

(G-8882)
BRAIN WORKS & MIND MATTERS LLC
42 Reads Way Ste 135-136 (19720-1612)
PHONE..................................302 324-5255
Myrna F Moxham, *Owner*
EMP: 7 **EST:** 2018
SALES (est): 73.36K **Privately Held**
SIC: 8093 Specialty outpatient clinics, nec

(G-8883)
BRANDYWINE CHEMICAL COMPANY
600 Terminal Ave (19720-1457)
PHONE..................................302 656-5428
Valerie C Hahn, *Pr*
Ken Shockley, *VP*
Betty Schockley, *Sec*
EMP: 2 **EST:** 1977
SQ FT: 23,000
SALES (est): 156.2K **Privately Held**
SIC: 4225 2819 Warehousing, self storage; Industrial inorganic chemicals, nec

(G-8884)
BRANDYWINE CONSTRUCTION CO
101 Pigeon Point Rd (19720-2197)
PHONE..................................302 571-9773
Kathleen Thomas, *Pr*
John Olson, *
EMP: 80 **EST:** 1957
SQ FT: 8,000
SALES (est): 11.01MM **Privately Held**
Web: www.bccico.com
SIC: 1794 1623 1611 Excavation and grading, building construction; Water, sewer, and utility lines; Surfacing and paving

GEOGRAPHIC SECTION

New Castle - New Castle County (G-8909)

(G-8885)
BRANDYWINE CONTRACTORS INC
Also Called: BCI
34 Industrial Blvd (19720-2091)
PHONE.................................302 325-2700
Michael J Peters, *Pr*
Michael Pergeorelis, *
EMP: 30 **EST:** 1998
SQ FT: 1,000
SALES (est): 7.6MM **Privately Held**
Web: www.bci-online.com
SIC: 1542 Commercial and office building, new construction

(G-8886)
BRANDYWINE CONTRACTORS INC
34 Industrial Blvd (19720-2091)
PHONE.................................302 325-2700
EMP: 8 **EST:** 2007
SALES (est): 950.75K **Privately Held**
Web: www.bci-online.com
SIC: 1521 1542 1711 8741 New construction, single-family houses; Nonresidential construction, nec; Plumbing, heating, air-conditioning; Construction management

(G-8887)
BRANDYWINE VALLEY SPCA
290 Churchmans Rd (19720-3110)
PHONE.................................302 516-1000
EMP: 10 **EST:** 2019
SALES (est): 222.78K **Privately Held**
Web: www.bvspca.org
SIC: 8699 Animal humane society

(G-8888)
BRASS UNLIMITED
441 Park Ave (19720-4793)
PHONE.................................302 322-2529
EMP: 5 **EST:** 2018
SALES (est): 46.31K **Privately Held**
SIC: 7922 Theatrical producers and services

(G-8889)
BRAVO BUILDING SERVICES INC
34 Blevins Dr Ste 7 (19720-4177)
PHONE.................................302 322-5959
Sally Denton, *VP*
EMP: 1471
SALES (corp-wide): 620.83MM **Privately Held**
Web: www.bravobuildingservices.com
SIC: 7349 Janitorial service, contract basis
HQ: Bravo Building Services, Inc.
   1140 Rte 22 Ste 202
   Bridgewater NJ 08807
   732 465-0707

(G-8890)
BREAKTHRU BEVERAGE GROUP LLC
Also Called: Breakthru Beverage Delaware
411 Churchmans Rd (19720-3156)
P.O. Box 10370 (19850-0370)
PHONE.................................302 356-3500
Paul Tigani, *Mgr*
EMP: 80
SALES (corp-wide): 2.8B **Privately Held**
Web: www.breakthrubev.com
SIC: 2085 2869 Rum (alcoholic beverage); Alcohols, non beverage
PA: Breakthru Beverage Group, Llc
   60 E 42nd St Ste 1915
   New York NY 10165
   212 699-7000

(G-8891)
BRESLIN CONTRACTING INC
18 King Ct (19720-1519)
PHONE.................................302 322-0320
Patrick Breslin, *Pr*
Anita Breslin, *
Carol Breslin, *
Peter Breslin, *
EMP: 43 **EST:** 1968
SQ FT: 6,000
SALES (est): 11.56MM **Privately Held**
Web: www.breslincorp.com
SIC: 1541 1542 Renovation, remodeling and repairs: industrial buildings; Commercial and office buildings, renovation and repair

(G-8892)
BRIDGESTONE RET OPERATIONS LLC
Also Called: Firestone
2098 New Castle Ave (19720-7704)
PHONE.................................302 656-2529
Brian Williams, *Mgr*
EMP: 7
Web: www.bridgestoneamericas.com
SIC: 5531 7534 Automotive tires; Rebuilding and retreading tires
HQ: Bridgestone Retail Operations, Llc
   333 E Lake St Ste 300
   Bloomingdale IL 60108
   630 259-9000

(G-8893)
BRISTOL INDUSTRIAL CORPORATION
1010 River Rd (19720-5104)
P.O. Box 12304 (19850-2304)
PHONE.................................302 322-1100
Felicia Enuha, *Pr*
EMP: 10 **EST:** 1997
SALES (est): 2.49MM **Privately Held**
Web: www.bristol-indcorp.com
SIC: 1541 5074 5085 5082 Industrial buildings, new construction, nec; Plumbing and heating valves; Hydraulic and pneumatic pistons and valves; Bailey bridges

(G-8894)
BRUCE INDUSTRIAL CO INC
4049 New Castle Ave (19720-1496)
P.O. Box 10485 (19850-0485)
PHONE.................................302 655-9616
Christian Johnston, *Pr*
▲ **EMP:** 75 **EST:** 1947
SQ FT: 50,000
SALES (est): 22.32MM **Privately Held**
Web: www.bruceindustrial.com
SIC: 5084 7699 1796 Materials handling machinery; Industrial machinery and equipment repair; Machinery installation

(G-8895)
BRUSH OF COLOR LLC
28 Yorktown Rd (19720-4222)
PHONE.................................302 932-0005
Cristina Lorenzoni, *Prin*
EMP: 5 **EST:** 2017
SALES (est): 69.98K **Privately Held**
Web: www.brushofcolor.team
SIC: 1721 Painting and paper hanging

(G-8896)
BUDGET RENT A CAR
Also Called: Budget Rent-A-Car
151 N Dupont Hwy (19720-3136)
PHONE.................................302 322-2026
EMP: 6 **EST:** 2018
SALES (est): 108.94K **Privately Held**
Web: www.budget.com
SIC: 7514 Rent-a-car service

(G-8897)
BUDGET ROOTER INC
1015 River Rd (19720-5103)
P.O. Box 1708 (19701-7708)
PHONE.................................302 322-3011
Suzanne Palady, *Pr*
Jeffrey Palady, *VP*
Andrea Myers, *Sec*
EMP: 10 **EST:** 1998
SQ FT: 4,000
SALES (est): 2MM **Privately Held**
Web: www.budgetrooterinc.com
SIC: 1711 7699 Plumbing contractors; Sewer cleaning and rodding

(G-8898)
BUDGET TRUCK RENTAL
Also Called: Budget Rent-A-Car
211 S Dupont Hwy (19720-4129)
PHONE.................................302 325-9111
EMP: 6 **EST:** 2018
SALES (est): 62.7K **Privately Held**
Web: www.budget.com
SIC: 7514 Rent-a-car service

(G-8899)
BUDGET TRUCK RENTAL
Also Called: Budget Rent-A-Car
103 N Dupont Hwy (19720-3101)
PHONE.................................302 328-1282
EMP: 6 **EST:** 2018
SALES (est): 95.59K **Privately Held**
Web: www.budget.com
SIC: 7514 Rent-a-car service

(G-8900)
BUDS AUTO
632 Dane Ct (19720-5636)
PHONE.................................302 690-3838
EMP: 5 **EST:** 2018
SALES (est): 64.58K **Privately Held**
Web: www.budsautosales.com
SIC: 7538 General automotive repair shops

(G-8901)
BURNS & MCBRIDE INC (HQ)
Also Called: Burns & McBride
18 Boulden Cir Ste 30 (19720-3494)
P.O. Box 11287 (19850-1287)
PHONE.................................302 656-5110
Thomas G Mc Bride, *Pr*
James R Mc Bride, *
Terrace Mc Bride, *
EMP: 60 **EST:** 1949
SQ FT: 8,000
SALES (est): 11.16MM
SALES (corp-wide): 35.28MM **Privately Held**
Web: www.burnsandmcbride.com
SIC: 1711 5983 7623 7699 Boiler and furnace contractors; Fuel oil dealers; Air conditioning repair; Oil burner repair service
PA: Sila Services, Llc
   900 E 8th Ave Ste 106
   King Of Prussia PA 19406
   610 491-9409

(G-8902)
BUSHWICK METALS LLC
100 Steel Dr (19720-7708)
PHONE.................................302 328-0590
EMP: 8 **EST:** 2017
SALES (est): 2.12MM
SALES (corp-wide): 302.09B **Publicly Held**
Web: www.bushwickmetals.com
SIC: 5051 Steel
PA: Berkshire Hathaway Inc.
   3555 Farnam St Ste 1440
   Omaha NE 68131
   402 346-1400

(G-8903)
BUSINESS INSURANCE SERVICES
Also Called: Nationwide
100 W Commons Blvd (19720-2419)
P.O. Box 4380 (19807-0380)
PHONE.................................302 655-5300
Joe Chambers, *Pr*
Janet Hess, *Treas*
EMP: 7 **EST:** 1979
SALES (est): 933.96K **Privately Held**
Web: www.bisiagency.com
SIC: 6411 Insurance agents, nec

(G-8904)
BUSINESS MOVE SOLUTIONS INC
Also Called: Office Movers
11 Boulden Cir (19720-3400)
PHONE.................................302 324-0080
David Greenblatt, *Pr*
Betty Greenblatt, *
EMP: 30 **EST:** 2007
SQ FT: 53,000
SALES (est): 1.46MM **Privately Held**
Web: www.meyerinc.com
SIC: 7389 Relocation service

(G-8905)
BYRD GROUP DELAWARE
10 Corporate Cir Ste 215 (19720-2418)
PHONE.................................302 757-8300
Bob Byrd, *Prin*
EMP: 5 **EST:** 2014
SALES (est): 188.77K **Privately Held**
Web: www.byrdgomes.com
SIC: 8748 Business consulting, nec

(G-8906)
C & N FREIGHT LLC
354 Hackberry Dr (19720-7696)
PHONE.................................302 897-4061
EMP: 5 **EST:** 2021
SALES (est): 259.56K **Privately Held**
SIC: 5088 7389 Transportation equipment and supplies; Business services, nec

(G-8907)
C B JOE TV & APPLIANCES INC
348 Churchmans Rd (19720-3112)
PHONE.................................302 322-7600
Joseph M Williams, *Pr*
Alice Williams, *VP*
EMP: 9 **EST:** 1972
SQ FT: 6,000
SALES (est): 410.48K **Privately Held**
Web: www.cbjoe.com
SIC: 5722 5731 7622 Electric household appliances, major; Radios, two-way, citizens band, weather, short-wave, etc.; Radio repair shop, nec

(G-8908)
C&C WELDING
50 N Purdue Ave (19720-4315)
PHONE.................................402 414-2485
Cesar J Torres Junior, *Prin*
EMP: 4 **EST:** 2015
SALES (est): 33.85K **Privately Held**
SIC: 7692 Welding repair

(G-8909)
C-MET INC
Also Called: Midas Muffler
1604 N Dupont Hwy (19720-1904)
PHONE.................................302 652-1884
Ernest Natal, *Pr*
EMP: 8 **EST:** 1988
SALES (est): 905.13K **Privately Held**
Web: www.midas.com
SIC: 7533 Muffler shop, sale or repair and installation

New Castle - New Castle County (G-8910)   GEOGRAPHIC SECTION

(G-8910)
CAM-K TRANSPORT LLC
550 S Dupont Hwy Apt 15 (19720-5123)
PHONE.....................267 693-1797
EMP: 6 EST: 2019
SALES (est): 273.08K **Privately Held**
SIC: 4789 Transportation services, nec

(G-8911)
CANNON SLINE INDUSTRIAL INC (DH)
103 Carroll Dr (19720-4873)
PHONE.....................302 658-1420
Mark Chuplis, *Pr*
EMP: 16 EST: 2003
SALES (est): 20.4MM
SALES (corp-wide): 2.72B **Privately Held**
SIC: 1799 1761 Coating of metal structures at construction site; Roofing contractor
HQ: K2 Industrial Services, Inc.
  2552 Industrial Dr
  Highland IN 46322
  219 933-1100

(G-8912)
CANNON SLINE LLC
103 Carroll Dr (19720-4873)
PHONE.....................302 658-1420
Mark Chuplis, *Pr*
Glenn Baughman, *
Rich Bartell, *
Ted Mansfield, *
Marcy Miller, *
EMP: 124 EST: 2000
SQ FT: 5,000
SALES (est): 2.13MM
SALES (corp-wide): 2.72B **Privately Held**
SIC: 1721 Industrial painting
HQ: K2 Industrial Services, Inc.
  2552 Industrial Dr
  Highland IN 46322
  219 933-1100

(G-8913)
CARING FOR LIFE INC
Also Called: Comfort Keepers
92 Reads Way Ste 207 (19720-1631)
PHONE.....................302 892-2214
Sharon Powell, *Pr*
Jim Powell, *
EMP: 13 EST: 2002
SALES (est): 236.58K **Privately Held**
Web: www.comfortkeepers.com
SIC: 8082 Home health care services

(G-8914)
CARLYLE COCOA CO LLC (PA)
23 Harbor View Dr (19720-2179)
PHONE.....................302 428-3800
◆ EMP: 6 EST: 1999
SQ FT: 20,000
SALES (est): 3.22MM
SALES (corp-wide): 3.22MM **Privately Held**
Web: www.gcbcocoa.com
SIC: 2099 Food preparations, nec

(G-8915)
CARROW CONSTRUCTION LLC
1685 River Rd (19720-5194)
PHONE.....................302 376-0520
EMP: 6 EST: 2019
SALES (est): 788.74K **Privately Held**
Web: www.carrowconstruction.com
SIC: 1521 Single-family housing construction

(G-8916)
CARTER ASTON
100 W Commons Blvd (19720-2419)
PHONE.....................302 561-6315
EMP: 5 EST: 2018
SALES (est): 120.88K **Privately Held**
SIC: 7361 Executive placement

(G-8917)
CASE TOUR DUTY
77 Mccullough Dr Ste 6 (19720-2089)
PHONE.....................302 668-6998
EMP: 5 EST: 2010
SALES (est): 479.03K **Privately Held**
Web: www.tourdutycases.com
SIC: 4725 Tours, conducted

(G-8918)
CASSIDY PAINTING INC
17 Bellecor Dr (19720-1755)
PHONE.....................302 683-0710
Michael Cassidy, *Pr*
EMP: 40 EST: 1985
SALES (est): 6.36MM **Privately Held**
Web: www.cassidypainting.com
SIC: 1721 1799 Residential painting; Sandblasting of building exteriors

(G-8919)
CASSIDY PAINTING INC
3128 New Castle Ave (19720-2162)
PHONE.....................302 326-2412
EMP: 14
SALES (est): 1.3MM **Privately Held**
SIC: 1721 Painting and paper hanging

(G-8920)
CASTLE CONSTRUCTION DEL INC
185 Old Churchmans Rd (19720-3115)
PHONE.....................302 326-3600
Dennis W Yanick, *Pr*
EMP: 33 EST: 1987
SQ FT: 4,000
SALES (est): 4.48MM **Privately Held**
Web: www.montana-signs.com
SIC: 1794 Excavation work

(G-8921)
CAYLEY J CARSON
Also Called: New Castle Gunsmithing
1 Lasalle Ave (19720-4309)
PHONE.....................302 328-2561
Cayley J Carson, *Prin*
EMP: 5 EST: 2012
SALES (est): 68.52K **Privately Held**
SIC: 7699 Gunsmith shop

(G-8922)
CBI SERVICES LLC
24 Reads Way (19720-1649)
PHONE.....................302 325-8400
Alan Black, *Brnch Mgr*
EMP: 10
SALES (corp-wide): 712.88MM **Privately Held**
SIC: 1629 Marine construction
HQ: Cbi Services, Llc
  8900 Frbanks N Houston Rd
  Houston TX 77064
  713 896-5900

(G-8923)
CBM INSURANCE AGENCY LLC (PA)
Also Called: Nationwide
100 W Commons Blvd Ste 302 (19720)
PHONE.....................302 322-2261
Brandon Baffone, *Pr*
EMP: 20 EST: 2009
SALES (est): 7.11MM
SALES (corp-wide): 7.11MM **Privately Held**
Web: www.cbmins.com
SIC: 6411 Insurance agents, nec

(G-8924)
CHAMBERS INSURANCE AGENCY INC
100 W Commons Blvd (19720-2419)
P.O. Box 4380 (19807-0380)
PHONE.....................302 655-5300
Joe Chambers, *Pr*
EMP: 9 EST: 1972
SALES (est): 839.66K **Privately Held**
Web: www.chambersinsurance.com
SIC: 6411 Insurance agents, nec

(G-8925)
CHAMBERS LDSCPG & LAWNCARE INC
41 Don Ave (19720-1507)
PHONE.....................302 328-1312
Woodrow Chambers, *Pr*
EMP: 8 EST: 1997
SALES (est): 494.56K **Privately Held**
Web: www.chamberslandscapinginc.com
SIC: 0782 Lawn care services

(G-8926)
CHE STUDIO INC
103 E Hazeldell Ave (19720-1300)
PHONE.....................856 246-8440
Sinise Gould, *Prin*
EMP: 6 EST: 2018
SALES (est): 40.5K **Privately Held**
Web: www.che-studio.com
SIC: 7231 Hairdressers

(G-8927)
CHEAPS TREE SERVICE
110 Paisley Ln (19720-3841)
PHONE.....................302 750-4590
Luis Ceballas, *Prin*
EMP: 5 EST: 2010
SALES (est): 52.42K **Privately Held**
SIC: 0783 Planting, pruning, and trimming services

(G-8928)
CHELTEN PRESERVATION ASSOC LLC
Also Called: Chelten Apartments
431 Old Forge Rd (19720-3764)
PHONE.....................302 322-6323
William Demarco, *Mng Pt*
William Demarco, *VP*
EMP: 5 EST: 2015
SALES (est): 97.05K **Privately Held**
SIC: 6514 Dwelling operators, except apartments

(G-8929)
CHEMAX MANUFACTURING CORP
1025 River Rd (19720-5103)
PHONE.....................302 328-2440
Susan H Rappa, *Pr*
Charles J Rappa, *VP*
EMP: 4 EST: 1953
SQ FT: 2,000
SALES (est): 468.53K **Privately Held**
Web: www.chemax.com
SIC: 3999 Barber and beauty shop equipment

(G-8930)
CHERRY ISLAND LLC
4048 New Castle Ave (19720-1455)
PHONE.....................302 658-5241
Maryann Kowalski, *Off Mgr*
EMP: 16 EST: 2009
SALES (est): 739.7K **Privately Held**
SIC: 4953 Sanitary landfill operation

(G-8931)
CHESAPEAKE INSURANCE ADVISORS
10 Corporate Cir Ste 215 (19720-2418)
PHONE.....................302 544-6900
Michael V Buchler, *Pr*
Linda Dean, *Treas*
Robert Houser, *Pr*
EMP: 12 EST: 2002
SQ FT: 5,000
SALES (est): 365.72K **Privately Held**
Web: www.thechesapeakecompanies.com
SIC: 6411 Insurance agents, nec

(G-8932)
CHESCO CORING & CUTNG DEL LLC
473 Old Airport Rd (19720-1005)
PHONE.....................302 276-7900
EMP: 6 EST: 2018
SALES (est): 165.06K **Privately Held**
Web: ccwp.chescocoringandcutting.com
SIC: 1771 Concrete work

(G-8933)
CHESTER ROSS
Also Called: Imprint Genetics
113 Stanley Ln (19720-2739)
PHONE.....................267 461-1568
Chester Ross, *Owner*
EMP: 4 EST: 2020
SALES (est): 147.6K **Privately Held**
SIC: 2221 Apparel and outerwear fabric, manmade fiber or silk

(G-8934)
CHILDREN YUTH THEIR FMLIES DEL
Also Called: Terry Chld Psychiatric Ctr
10 Central Ave (19720-1152)
PHONE.....................302 577-4270
Sterling Seemans, *Prin*
EMP: 12
SALES (corp-wide): 11.27B **Privately Held**
Web: kids.delaware.gov
SIC: 8063 9431 Psychiatric hospitals; Administration of public health programs
HQ: Children, Youth & Their Families, Delaware Dept Of Services For
  1825 Faulkland Rd
  Wilmington DE 19805

(G-8935)
CHIROPRACTIC COLONIAL
105 Penn Mart Shopping Ctr (19720-4208)
PHONE.....................302 328-1444
EMP: 6 EST: 2019
SALES (est): 229.48K **Privately Held**
Web: www.colonialchiropractic.org
SIC: 8041 Offices and clinics of chiropractors

(G-8936)
CHOPTANK EXCAVATION LLC
1715 River Rd (19720-5197)
PHONE.....................302 420-0354
Keith Biddle, *VP*
Stacey Biddle, *Pr*
EMP: 7 EST: 2009
SALES (est): 905.11K **Privately Held**
Web: www.choptankexcavation.com
SIC: 1794 Excavation work

(G-8937)
CHRISTANA CARE HM HLTH CMNTY S (HQ)
Also Called: Christana Care Vsting Nrse Ass
1 Reads Way Ste 100 (19720-1605)
PHONE.....................302 327-5583
Lynn Jones, *Pr*
Gerald Manley, *
Brenda K Pierce Esq, *Sec*

GEOGRAPHIC SECTION

New Castle - New Castle County (G-8959)

EMP: 300 EST: 1922
SQ FT: 22,000
SALES (est): 42.5MM
SALES (corp-wide): 666.58K **Privately Held**
Web: www.christianacare.org
SIC: 8082 Visiting nurse service
PA: Christiana Care Health Services, Inc.
4755 Ogletown Stanton Rd
Newark DE 19718
302 733-1000

(G-8938)
CHRISTIANA CARE HEALTH SYS INC
Also Called: Cchs Logistics Center
11 Boulden Cir (19720-3400)
PHONE...............................302 623-3970
Janice E Nevin, *CEO*
EMP: 250
SALES (corp-wide): 666.58K **Privately Held**
Web: www.christianacare.org
SIC: 4119 Ambulance service
HQ: Christiana Care Health System, Inc.
200 Hygeia Dr
Newark DE 19713
302 733-1000

(G-8939)
CHRISTIANA CARE HLTH SVCS INC
Also Called: Information Services
1 Reads Way Ste 200 (19720-1605)
PHONE...............................302 327-3959
Lynn Jones, *Brnch Mgr*
EMP: 200
SALES (corp-wide): 666.58K **Privately Held**
Web: www.christianacare.org
SIC: 8062 General medical and surgical hospitals
PA: Christiana Care Health Services, Inc.
4755 Ogletown Stanton Rd
Newark DE 19718
302 733-1000

(G-8940)
CHRISTIANA MOTOR FREIGHT INC (PA)
520 Terminal Ave Ste C (19720-1459)
P.O. Box 668 (19720-0668)
PHONE...............................302 655-6271
Imari Bollman, *Pr*
Herbert Bollman, *Pr*
Evelyn Bollman, *Sec*
EMP: 10 EST: 1981
SQ FT: 15,000
SALES (est): 1.29MM
SALES (corp-wide): 1.29MM **Privately Held**
Web: www.cmcresto.com
SIC: 4213 4214 Trucking, except local; Local trucking with storage

(G-8941)
CHRISTIANA WOOD LLC
Also Called: Villas Apartments
21- 8 Villas Dr (19720)
PHONE...............................302 322-1172
EMP: 6 EST: 1980
SALES (est): 494.41K **Privately Held**
SIC: 6513 Apartment building operators

(G-8942)
CIM CONCEPTS INCORPORATED
100 W Commons Blvd Ste 101 (19720)
PHONE...............................302 613-5400
Randall C Herbein, *Pr*
Joachim Hirche, *VP*
EMP: 16 EST: 1988
SQ FT: 2,500
SALES (est): 1.35MM **Privately Held**

Web: www.cimconcepts.com
SIC: 7373 7371 Systems integration services; Custom computer programming services

(G-8943)
CIRILLO BROS INC
761 Grantham Ln (19720-4801)
PHONE...............................302 326-1540
Michael Cirillo, *Pr*
Mark Cirillo, *
EMP: 50 EST: 1985
SQ FT: 1,000
SALES (est): 14.94MM **Privately Held**
Web: www.cirillobros.com
SIC: 1794 1542 1522 Excavation and grading, building construction; Commercial and office building contractors; Residential construction, nec

(G-8944)
CITIBANK NATIONAL ASSOCIATION
Also Called: Citibank
1 Penns Way (19721-2300)
PHONE...............................302 477-5418
Vickram Pandit, *Pr*
EMP: 6
SALES (corp-wide): 101.08B **Publicly Held**
Web: www.citigroup.com
SIC: 6021 National commercial banks
HQ: Citibank, National Association
701 E 60th St N
Sioux Falls SD 57104
605 331-2626

(G-8945)
CITIBANK OVERSEAS INV CORP (DH)
Also Called: Citibank
1 Penns Way (19720-2408)
PHONE...............................302 323-3600
EMP: 11 EST: 2013
SALES (est): 105.19MM
SALES (corp-wide): 101.08B **Publicly Held**
SIC: 6211 Investment bankers
HQ: Citibank, National Association
701 E 60th St N
Sioux Falls SD 57104
605 331-2626

(G-8946)
CITICORP BANKING CORPORATION (HQ)
Also Called: Citigroup
One Penn's Way (19721-2300)
PHONE...............................302 323-3140
Richard Collins, *Pr*
Edward Salvitti, *
David M Baginsky, *
EMP: 200 EST: 1979
SALES (est): 2.28B
SALES (corp-wide): 101.08B **Publicly Held**
Web: www.citigroup.com
SIC: 6021 National commercial banks
PA: Citigroup Inc.
388 Greenwich St Fl 38
New York NY 10013
212 559-1000

(G-8947)
CITICORP DEL-LEASE INC (HQ)
Also Called: Citicorp
1 Penn's Wy (19721-2300)
PHONE...............................302 323-3801
William Silver, *Pr*
Timothy Cormany, *VP*
Robert Goldberg, *Sec*
Nick Lamour, *Treas*
EMP: 100 EST: 1986

SALES (est): 106.06MM
SALES (corp-wide): 101.08B **Publicly Held**
SIC: 6022 6311 6321 State commercial banks; Life insurance; Disability health insurance
PA: Citigroup Inc.
388 Greenwich St Fl 38
New York NY 10013
212 559-1000

(G-8948)
CITICORP DELAWARE SERVICES INC
1 Penns Way (19721-2300)
PHONE...............................302 323-3124
William Wolf, *Pr*
EMP: 10 EST: 1981
SALES (est): 4.74MM
SALES (corp-wide): 101.08B **Publicly Held**
SIC: 6021 National commercial banks
HQ: Citicorp Banking Corporation
1 Penns Way
New Castle DE 19721
302 323-3140

(G-8949)
CITIGROUP ASIA PCF HOLDG CORP (DH)
Also Called: Citibank
1 Penns Way Street 1st Fl (19721-2300)
PHONE...............................302 323-3100
Edward C Salvitti, *Pr*
Peter Hagertty, *VP*
William H Wolf, *Ex VP*
Micahel F Brisgone, *VP*
Michael P Humes, *VP*
▲ EMP: 5 EST: 1964
SQ FT: 1,000
SALES (est): 15.06MM
SALES (corp-wide): 101.08B **Publicly Held**
Web: www.citigroup.com
SIC: 6021 National commercial banks
HQ: Citibank, National Association
701 E 60th St N
Sioux Falls SD 57104
605 331-2626

(G-8950)
CITY MIST LLC
Also Called: City Mist Logistics
1005 Willings Way (19720-3955)
PHONE...............................302 342-1377
EMP: 8 EST: 2014
SQ FT: 5,000
SALES (est): 501.36K **Privately Held**
Web: www.citymistlogistics.com
SIC: 4213 4731 Trucking, except local; Freight transportation arrangement

(G-8951)
CITY TOWING SERVICES
415 Old Airport Rd (19720-1001)
PHONE...............................302 561-7979
EMP: 5 EST: 2020
SALES (est): 227.26K **Privately Held**
SIC: 7549 Towing service, automotive

(G-8952)
CLARIOS LLC
Also Called: Johnson Controls
18 Boulden Cir Ste 24 (19720-3494)
PHONE...............................302 996-0309
EMP: 120
SALES (corp-wide): 1.54B **Privately Held**
Web: www.clarios.com
SIC: 2531 Seats, automobile
HQ: Clarios, Llc
5757 N Green Bay Ave

Milwaukee WI 53209

(G-8953)
CLARKS GLASGOW POOLS INC (PA)
Also Called: Clarks Pool and Spa
109 J And M Dr (19720-3147)
PHONE...............................302 834-0200
Cary Pitman, *Pr*
EMP: 20 EST: 1990
SQ FT: 10,000
SALES (est): 2.2MM **Privately Held**
Web: www.clarkspools.com
SIC: 1799 1771 Swimming pool construction; Blacktop (asphalt) work

(G-8954)
CLYDE SPINELLI
Also Called: Pinevalley Apartments
500 S Dupont Hwy Apt 225 (19720-4631)
PHONE...............................302 328-7679
Clyde Spinelli, *Owner*
EMP: 6 EST: 1969
SALES (est): 392.49K **Privately Held**
SIC: 6513 Apartment building operators

(G-8955)
CMC-KUHNKE INC
40 Mccullough Dr (19720-2228)
PHONE...............................302 613-5600
Renee Butz, *Prin*
EMP: 7 EST: 2018
SALES (est): 244.24K **Privately Held**
Web: www.industrialphysics.com
SIC: 8742 Marketing consulting services

(G-8956)
COLLABRTIVE EFFORT TO RNFRCE T (PA)
Also Called: C.E.R.T.S.
52 Reads Way (19720-1649)
PHONE...............................302 731-0301
Vivian Turner, *Dir*
EMP: 5 EST: 2007
SALES (est): 1.46MM
SALES (corp-wide): 1.46MM **Privately Held**
Web: www.forwardjourney.org
SIC: 8051 8049 Skilled nursing care facilities; Physical therapist

(G-8957)
COLONIAL MARBLE OF DELAWARE
240 S Dupont Hwy Ste 100 (19720-8403)
PHONE...............................302 328-1735
EMP: 8 EST: 2015
SALES (est): 81.24K **Privately Held**
Web: www.colonialmarble.net
SIC: 1799 Counter top installation

(G-8958)
COLONIAL SCHOOL DISTRICT
Also Called: Transportation Department
1617 Matassino Rd (19720-2086)
PHONE...............................302 323-2700
Donald R Hartwig, *Dir*
EMP: 47
SALES (corp-wide): 96.75MM **Privately Held**
Web: www.colonialschooldistrict.org
SIC: 4151 School buses
PA: Colonial School District
318 E Basin Rd
New Castle DE 19720
302 323-2700

(G-8959)
COLOR WORKS PAINTING INC
251 Edwards Ave (19720-4857)
PHONE...............................302 324-8411

Sean O Histed, *Pr*
EMP: 10 EST: 1993
SQ FT: 5,500
SALES (est): 1.19MM **Privately Held**
Web: www.colorworkspainting.com
SIC: **1721** Painting and paper hanging

(G-8960)
COMCAST CABLEVISION OF DEL
Also Called: Comcast
5 Bellecor Dr (19720-1763)
PHONE.................................302 661-4465
Jim Maguire, *Mgr*
EMP: 26
SALES (corp-wide): 121.57B **Publicly Held**
SIC: **4841** Cable television services
HQ: Comcast Cablevision Of Delaware Inc
426a N Dupont Hwy
Georgetown DE 19947
302 856-4591

(G-8961)
COMCAST CBLE CMMUNICATIONS LLC
Also Called: Comcast
22 Reads Way (19720-1649)
PHONE.................................302 323-9200
EMP: 5
SALES (corp-wide): 121.57B **Publicly Held**
Web: www.cmcsa.com
SIC: **4841** Cable television services
HQ: Comcast Cable Communications, Llc
1701 John F Kennedy Blvd
Philadelphia PA 19103

(G-8962)
COMMUNITY SYSTEMS AND SVCS INC
2 Penns Way Ste 301 (19720-2407)
PHONE.................................302 325-1500
David Paige, *Brnch Mgr*
EMP: 180
SQ FT: 400
SALES (corp-wide): 9.8MM **Privately Held**
Web: www.communitysystems.org
SIC: **8052** Home for the mentally retarded, with health care
PA: Community Systems And Services, Inc.
7926 Jones Branch Dr # 105
Mc Lean VA 22102
703 448-0606

(G-8963)
COMPACT MEMBRANE SYSTEMS INC
15 Reads Way (19720-1600)
PHONE.................................302 999-7996
Doctor Stuart Nemser, *Ch*
John Bowser, *Pr*
EMP: 22 EST: 1993
SALES (est): 5.76MM **Privately Held**
Web: www.compactmembrane.com
SIC: **8734** Testing laboratories

(G-8964)
CONCEPCION PROPERTIES LLC
141 Sweetbay Ln (19720-7677)
PHONE.................................302 691-9233
EMP: 5 EST: 2018
SALES (est): 212.07K **Privately Held**
SIC: **6512** Property operation, retail establishment

(G-8965)
CONNECTIONS
204 Gordy Pl (19720-4704)
PHONE.................................302 221-6605
Catheryn Murry, *Mgr*
EMP: 10 EST: 2008
SALES (est): 107.29K **Privately Held**
SIC: **8093** Mental health clinic, outpatient

(G-8966)
CONNECTIONS CSP INC
550 S Dupont Hwy (19720-5193)
PHONE.................................302 327-0122
EMP: 7 EST: 2019
SALES (est): 182.91K **Privately Held**
SIC: **8082** Home health care services

(G-8967)
CONNOLLY OPTIONS LLC
Also Called: Two Men and A Truck
83 Christiana Rd (19720-3104)
PHONE.................................302 998-2016
EMP: 12 EST: 2005
SALES (est): 542.61K **Privately Held**
Web: www.twomenandatruck.com
SIC: **4212** Moving services

(G-8968)
CONSTANCE P DEPTULA LCSW
85 Commonwealth Blvd (19720-3432)
PHONE.................................302 323-0345
Constance P Deptula, *Prin*
EMP: 7 EST: 2012
SALES (est): 57.13K **Privately Held**
SIC: **8322** Social worker

(G-8969)
CONTINENTAL GREEN JANITORIAL
296 Churchmans Rd (19720-3110)
P.O. Box 10445 (19850-0445)
PHONE.................................302 324-8063
Jeffrey Minner, *Prin*
EMP: 5 EST: 2016
SALES (est): 33.41K **Privately Held**
SIC: **7349** Janitorial service, contract basis

(G-8970)
CONTRACTOR MATERIALS LLC
Also Called: Contractors Materials
4048 New Castle Ave (19720-1455)
PHONE.................................302 658-5241
EMP: 27 EST: 1997
SALES (est): 2.44MM **Privately Held**
SIC: **3443** Mixers, for hot metal

(G-8971)
CONWAY MANAGEMENT GROUP
2801 Stonebridge Blvd (19720-6738)
PHONE.................................302 323-9522
Jim Conway, *Pr*
EMP: 6 EST: 2008
SALES (est): 120.91K **Privately Held**
SIC: **8741** Management services

(G-8972)
COOPER BROS INC
62 Southgate Blvd Frnt Frnt (19720)
PHONE.................................302 323-0717
Walter D Cooper, *Pr*
George Cooper, *VP*
Sandra L Cooper, *Treas*
Debra Scully, *Sec*
EMP: 10 EST: 1963
SQ FT: 5,200
SALES (est): 462.71K **Privately Held**
SIC: **1711** Plumbing contractors

(G-8973)
CORPORATE INTERIORS INC
240 Lisa Dr (19720-4174)
PHONE.................................800 690-9101
Janice Leone, *Brnch Mgr*
EMP: 11
Web: www.corporate-interiors.com
SIC: **5021** 2521 Furniture; Wood office furniture
PA: Corporate Interiors, Inc.
223 Lisa Dr
New Castle DE 19720

(G-8974)
CORPORATE INTERIORS INC (PA)
Also Called: Corporate Interiors Delaware
223 Lisa Dr (19720-4193)
PHONE.................................302 322-1008
▲ EMP: 81 EST: 1985
SALES (est): 78.77MM **Privately Held**
Web: www.corporate-interiors.com
SIC: **5021** 2521 Office furniture, nec; Wood office furniture

(G-8975)
CORRADO AMERICAN LLC
200 Marsh Ln (19720-1175)
PHONE.................................302 655-6501
EMP: 50 EST: 1945
SQ FT: 16,366
SALES (est): 10.41MM **Privately Held**
Web: www.corradoamerican.com
SIC: **1794** 1741 Excavation and grading, building construction; Foundation building

(G-8976)
CORRADO CONSTRUCTION CO LLC
210 Marsh Ln (19720-1175)
PHONE.................................302 652-3339
EMP: 66 EST: 2007
SQ FT: 9,180
SALES (est): 10.46MM **Privately Held**
Web: www.corradoconstruction.com
SIC: **1794** Excavation and grading, building construction

(G-8977)
CORRADO MANAGEMENT SVCS LLC
204 Marsh Ln (19720-1175)
PHONE.................................302 225-0700
Terri L Bertrando, *
Adrienne Allison, *
EMP: 35 EST: 2006
SQ FT: 21,309
SALES (est): 2.82MM **Privately Held**
Web: www.corrado.com
SIC: **8741** Financial management for business

(G-8978)
COTTMAN TRANSMISSION
1600 N Dupont Hwy (19720-1904)
PHONE.................................302 322-4600
Greg Dittbrenner, *Owner*
Carolyn Dittbrenner, *Genl Mgr*
EMP: 6 EST: 1983
SALES (est): 755.95K **Privately Held**
Web: www.cottmanofnewcastle.com
SIC: **7537** Automotive transmission repair shops

(G-8979)
COUNTY ENVIRONMENTAL INC
Also Called: County Group Companies
461 Churchmans Rd (19720-3156)
PHONE.................................302 322-8946
James W Bently, *Pr*
Larry Johnson, *
Mary Jean Betley, *
EMP: 40 EST: 1996
SQ FT: 10,000
SALES (est): 7.46MM **Privately Held**
Web: www.countygrp.com
SIC: **1799** 4959 Asbestos removal and encapsulation; Environmental cleanup services

(G-8980)
COUNTY INSULATION CO
461 Churchmans Rd (19720-3186)
PHONE.................................302 322-8946
James W Betley, *Pr*
Larry C Johnson, *
Mary Jean Betley, *
EMP: 80 EST: 1971
SQ FT: 12,000
SALES (est): 9.15MM **Privately Held**
Web: www.countygrp.com
SIC: **1799** Insulation of pipes and boilers

(G-8981)
COUNTY OF NEW CASTLE
26 Karlyn Dr (19720-1235)
PHONE.................................302 571-4004
Captain Steward Snyder, *Pr*
EMP: 10
SALES (corp-wide): 339.15MM **Privately Held**
Web: www.newcastlede.gov
SIC: **7991** Physical fitness facilities
PA: County Of New Castle
87 Reads Way
New Castle DE 19720
302 395-5555

(G-8982)
COURTESY TRNSP SVCS INC
Also Called: Global Logistics and Trnsp
4 Parkway Cir (19720-4077)
PHONE.................................302 322-9722
Henry Kamau, *Pr*
EMP: 10 EST: 2002
SQ FT: 10,000
SALES (est): 447.69K **Privately Held**
SIC: **4212** Local trucking, without storage

(G-8983)
COUTURE DENIM LLC
Also Called: MSA
3 Silsbee Rd (19720-3227)
PHONE.................................302 220-8339
EMP: 5 EST: 2010
SALES (est): 295.5K **Privately Held**
SIC: **5712** 7389 Furniture stores; Business services, nec

(G-8984)
CRAVITYSCI LLC
19 Bellecor Dr (19720-1761)
PHONE.................................571 208-6421
Wenyu Zhang, *Managing Member*
EMP: 6 EST: 2021
SALES (est): 270.3K **Privately Held**
SIC: **3843** Dental equipment and supplies

(G-8985)
CRICKET WIRELESS LLC
1405 N Dupont Hwy (19720-1843)
PHONE.................................302 276-0496
Taina Rivera, *Prin*
EMP: 92 EST: 2016
SALES (est): 249.59K
SALES (corp-wide): 120.74B **Publicly Held**
SIC: **4812** Cellular telephone services
PA: At&T Inc.
208 S Akard St
Dallas TX 75202
210 821-4105

(G-8986)
CRODA INC
315 Cherry Ln (19720-2780)
PHONE.................................302 429-5200
EMP: 3
SALES (corp-wide): 2.52B **Privately Held**
Web: www.croda.com

GEOGRAPHIC SECTION

New Castle - New Castle County (G-9015)

SIC: **5169** 2899 Industrial chemicals; Chemical preparations, nec
HQ: Croda, Inc.
777 Scudders Mill Rd
Plainsboro NJ 08536
609 212-2500

(G-8987)
CRODA INC
321 Cherry Ln (19720-2780)
PHONE.................................302 429-5249
EMP: 5
SALES (corp-wide): 2.52B **Privately Held**
Web: www.croda.com
SIC: **2899** Chemical preparations, nec
HQ: Croda, Inc.
777 Scudders Mill Rd
Plainsboro NJ 08536
609 212-2500

(G-8988)
CRODA UNIQEMA INC
Also Called: Croda Atlas Point
315 Cherry Ln (19720-2780)
PHONE.................................302 429-5599
Kevin Gallagher, *Pr*
▲ EMP: 66 EST: 2003
SALES (est): 9.29MM
SALES (corp-wide): 2.52B **Privately Held**
Web: www.croda.com
SIC: **1629** Chemical plant and refinery construction
PA: Croda International Public Limited Company
Cowick Hall
Goole N HUMBS DN14
140 586-0551

(G-8989)
CRUMPTON STARLINE
5 Greenfield Dr (19720-7671)
PHONE.................................302 832-1342
Crumpton Starline, *Prin*
EMP: 5 EST: 2010
SALES (est): 48.68K **Privately Held**
SIC: **7231** Beauty shops

(G-8990)
CRYSTAL KLEEN INC
32 Appleby Rd (19720-3748)
P.O. Box 1046 (19720-7046)
PHONE.................................302 326-1140
John Beardsley, *Pr*
Wanda Beardsley, *VP*
EMP: 6 EST: 2004
SALES (est): 118.75K **Privately Held**
SIC: **7217** 7699 Carpet and upholstery cleaning; Antique repair and restoration, except furniture, autos

(G-8991)
CUSTOM CREAMS LLC
128 Sunset Blvd Pmb 1211 (19720-4100)
PHONE.................................302 582-8862
Ashley Cook Smith, *Managing Member*
EMP: 5 EST: 2021
SALES (est): 240.13K **Privately Held**
SIC: **5149** Bakery products

(G-8992)
D C S COMPANY
233 Gordy Pl (19720-4733)
PHONE.................................302 328-5138
Debra Wolfe, *Pt*
Robert Wolfe, *Pt*
EMP: 8 EST: 1986
SALES (est): 156.12K **Privately Held**
SIC: **7349** Cleaning service, industrial or commercial

(G-8993)
DAB DEODORANT LLC
6 Tulip Ln Apt 36 (19720-5813)
PHONE.................................973 512-2703
EMP: 2 EST: 2021
SALES (est): 92.41K **Privately Held**
SIC: **2844** 7389 Deodorants, personal; Business services, nec

(G-8994)
DAISY CONSTRUCTION COMPANY
3128 New Castle Ave (19720-2162)
PHONE.................................302 658-4417
EMP: 9 EST: 2019
SALES (est): 215.81K **Privately Held**
Web: www.sovproperties.com
SIC: **1521** Single-family housing construction

(G-8995)
DALE INSULATION CO OF DELAWARE
13 King Ct Ste 5 (19720-1523)
PHONE.................................302 324-9332
Thomas J Dale Junior, *Pr*
EMP: 9 EST: 1990
SQ FT: 2,100
SALES (est): 777.4K **Privately Held**
Web: www.daleinsulation.com
SIC: **1742** Insulation, buildings

(G-8996)
DANCEWORKS DANCE STUDIO LLC
Also Called: Danceworks Studio
187 Penn Mart Shopping Ctr (19720-4208)
PHONE.................................302 244-8570
Amanda Pollard, *Managing Member*
EMP: 5 EST: 2015
SALES (est): 57.26K **Privately Held**
Web: www.danceworksde.net
SIC: **7911** Dance studio and school

(G-8997)
DANIS HOME CLEANING SERVICES
6 Cresson Ave (19720-1103)
PHONE.................................302 525-8286
EMP: 7 EST: 2019
SALES (est): 111.01K **Privately Held**
Web: www.danishomecleaningservices.com
SIC: **7699** Cleaning services

(G-8998)
DART CONTAINER SALES COMPANY
2451 Bear Corbitt Rd (19720-5685)
PHONE.................................305 759-5044
EMP: 6 EST: 2019
SALES (est): 311.58K **Privately Held**
Web: www.dartcontainer.com
SIC: **3086** Plastics foam products

(G-8999)
DASSAULT AIRCRAFT SVCS CORP
191 N Dupont Hwy (19720-3121)
PHONE.................................302 322-7000
EMP: 154
SIC: **5088** Aircraft and parts, nec
HQ: Dassault Aircraft Services Corp.
200 Riser Rd
Little Ferry NJ 07643

(G-9000)
DASSAULT FALCON JET - WILMINGTON CORP
191 N Dupont Hwy (19720-3121)
PHONE.................................302 322-7000
EMP: 250 EST: 2000
SALES (est): 57.15MM **Privately Held**
Web: www.dassaultfalcon.com
SIC: **3721** 3728 Aircraft; Aircraft parts and equipment, nec
HQ: Dassault Falcon Jet Corp.
200 Riser Rd
Little Ferry NJ 07643
201 440-6700

(G-9001)
DAVIDSON LANE LLC
761 Grantham Ln (19720-4801)
PHONE.................................302 326-1540
EMP: 5 EST: 2010
SALES (est): 78.2K **Privately Held**
Web: www.davidsonlane.com
SIC: **6519** Real property lessors, nec

(G-9002)
DAWN ARROW INC
602 Brant Ave (19720)
PHONE.................................302 328-9695
Donald Dalton, *Pr*
EMP: 5 EST: 1983
SALES (est): 96.17K **Privately Held**
SIC: **4212** Local trucking, without storage

(G-9003)
DAY SCHOOL FOR CHILDREN
3071 New Castle Ave (19720-2245)
PHONE.................................302 652-4651
R Dorsey, *Ex Dir*
EMP: 5 EST: 2004
SALES (est): 135.28K **Privately Held**
Web: www.thedayschoolforchildrenprep.com
SIC: **8351** Preschool center

(G-9004)
DE ALCOHOLIC BEVERAGE WHL ASSN
411 Churchmans Rd (19720-3156)
PHONE.................................302 356-3500
Robert Trostel, *Pr*
EMP: 5 EST: 2016
SALES (est): 226.15K **Privately Held**
SIC: **5099** Durable goods, nec

(G-9005)
DE CHEAPER TRASH LLC
22 Mark Dr (19720-1756)
PHONE.................................302 325-0670
EMP: 5 EST: 2010
SALES (est): 304.69K **Privately Held**
SIC: **4212** Garbage collection and transport, no disposal

(G-9006)
DEARNG SAFETY OFFICE
1 Vavala Way (19720-2417)
PHONE.................................302 326-7100
EMP: 5 EST: 2018
SALES (est): 121.36K **Privately Held**
SIC: **8748** Business consulting, nec

(G-9007)
DEBRA MCAFEE
Also Called: Nationwide
2323 N Dupont Hwy (19720-6304)
PHONE.................................302 655-7999
Debra Mcafee, *Ofcr*
EMP: 8 EST: 2018
SALES (est): 115.62K **Privately Held**
Web: www.nationwide.com
SIC: **6411** Insurance agents, nec

(G-9008)
DECO CRETE INC
550 S Dupont Hwy (19720-5193)
PHONE.................................302 367-0151
EMP: 6 EST: 2011
SALES (est): 176.76K **Privately Held**
Web: www.decocreteremodel.com

SIC: **1521** General remodeling, single-family houses

(G-9009)
DEDICATED TO HOME CARE LLC
2 Yorktown Rd (19720-4222)
PHONE.................................484 470-5013
Haywood Lewis, *Prin*
EMP: 7 EST: 2017
SALES (est): 61.12K **Privately Held**
Web: www.dedicatedtohomecare.com
SIC: **8082** Home health care services

(G-9010)
DEJOUR REIGN CL & AP CO LLC
107 Hillview Ave (19720-2236)
PHONE.................................302 981-2568
EMP: 3 EST: 2020
SALES (est): 116.13K **Privately Held**
SIC: **2211** Apparel and outerwear fabrics, cotton

(G-9011)
DELASOFT INC
92 Reads Way Ste 204 (19720-1631)
PHONE.................................302 533-7912
Sateesh Dola, *Pr*
Jyothsna Dola, *
EMP: 175 EST: 2002
SQ FT: 2,400
SALES (est): 13.44MM **Privately Held**
Web: www.delasoft.com
SIC: **7379** Computer related consulting services

(G-9012)
DELAWARE ACDEMY PUB SAFETY SEC
179 Stanton Christiana Road (19720)
PHONE.................................302 377-1465
Charles Hughes, *Prin*
EMP: 8 EST: 2016
SALES (est): 180.92K **Privately Held**
SIC: **7381** Guard services

(G-9013)
DELAWARE APARTMENT ASSOCIATION
1627 New Jersey Ave (19720-1933)
PHONE.................................302 998-0322
Daniel Darring, *Prin*
EMP: 5 EST: 2013
SALES (est): 89.27K **Privately Held**
Web: www.apartmentassociations.com
SIC: **8699** Membership organizations, nec

(G-9014)
DELAWARE BUS LEADERSHIP NETWRK
13 Reads Way Ste 101 (19720-1609)
PHONE.................................302 314-5070
Danielle Guest, *Prin*
EMP: 7 EST: 2015
SALES (est): 74.66K **Privately Held**
Web: www.debln.org
SIC: **8331** Job training and related services

(G-9015)
DELAWARE BUSINESS SYSTEMS INC
Also Called: D B S
191 Airport Rd (19720-2379)
PHONE.................................302 395-0900
Bernard L Pankowski, *Sec*
Mike Hynson, *
EMP: 31 EST: 1983
SQ FT: 10,000
SALES (est): 7.36MM **Privately Held**
Web: www.dbs4pos.com

New Castle - New Castle County (G-9016)   GEOGRAPHIC SECTION

SIC: 7373 Value-added resellers, computer systems

(G-9016)
DELAWARE CITY REFINING CO LLC
4550 Wrangle Hill Rd (19720-5509)
P.O. Box 7000 (19706-7000)
PHONE..................302 834-6000
Thomas Nimbley, *Brnch Mgr*
EMP: 489
SALES (corp-wide): 46.83B **Publicly Held**
Web: www.pbfenergy.com
SIC: 1629 Oil refinery construction
HQ: Delaware City Refining Company Llc
1 Sylvan Way Ste 2
Parsippany NJ 07054

(G-9017)
DELAWARE DEPT HLTH SOCIAL SVCS
Also Called: Delaware Industries For Blind
1901 N Dupont Hwy (19720-1100)
PHONE..................302 255-9855
Edna Newsome, *Brnch Mgr*
EMP: 8
SALES (corp-wide): 11.27B **Privately Held**
Web: www.delaware.gov
SIC: 9431 8331 3993 2752 Administration of public health programs, State government; Job training and related services; Signs and advertising specialties; Commercial printing, lithographic
HQ: Delaware Dept Of Health And Social Services
1901 N Dupont Hwy
New Castle DE 19720

(G-9018)
DELAWARE DEPT HLTH SOCIAL SVCS
Also Called: Delaware Psychiatric Center
1901 N Dupont Hwy (19720-1100)
PHONE..................302 255-2700
Elizabeth Hurley, *Mgr*
EMP: 82
SALES (corp-wide): 11.27B **Privately Held**
Web: www.delaware.gov
SIC: 8063 Psychiatric hospitals
HQ: Delaware Dept Of Health And Social Services
1901 N Dupont Hwy
New Castle DE 19720

(G-9019)
DELAWARE DEPT HLTH SOCIAL SVCS
Also Called: Delaware State Hospital
1901 N Dupont Hwy Fl 1 (19720-1100)
PHONE..................302 255-2700
EMP: 74
SALES (corp-wide): 11.27B **Privately Held**
Web: www.delaware.gov
SIC: 8063 9431 Psychiatric hospitals; Administration of public health programs
HQ: Delaware Dept Of Health And Social Services
1901 N Dupont Hwy
New Castle DE 19720

(G-9020)
DELAWARE DEPT HLTH SOCIAL SVCS
Also Called: Division For Visually Impaired
1901 N Dupont Hwy (19720-1100)
PHONE..................302 255-9800
Alan Wingrove, *Prin*
EMP: 80
SALES (corp-wide): 11.27B **Privately Held**
Web: www.delaware.gov

SIC: 8331 3993 2752 2396 Job training and related services; Signs and advertising specialties; Commercial printing, lithographic; Automotive and apparel trimmings
HQ: Delaware Dept Of Health And Social Services
1901 N Dupont Hwy
New Castle DE 19720

(G-9021)
DELAWARE DEPT HLTH SOCIAL SVCS
Division Svcs For Aging Adlts
1901 N Dupont Hwy Annex Entrance (19720-1100)
PHONE..................302 391-3505
Herman Holloway, *Dir*
EMP: 13
SALES (corp-wide): 11.27B **Privately Held**
Web: www.delaware.gov
SIC: 8322 9441 9431 Geriatric social service; Administration of social and manpower programs; Administration of public health programs
HQ: Delaware Dept Of Health And Social Services
1901 N Dupont Hwy
New Castle DE 19720

(G-9022)
DELAWARE ENTERPRISES INC
Also Called: Buffalo Consulting Group
42 Reads Way Ste B (19720-1612)
P.O. Box 539 (19347-0539)
PHONE..................302 324-5660
Kurt Sarac, *CEO*
EMP: 10 EST: 1999
SQ FT: 800
SALES (est): 491.13K **Privately Held**
SIC: 8742 New products and services consultants

(G-9023)
DELAWARE FILTER CORP
4 Bellecor Dr (19720-1763)
PHONE..................302 326-3950
Alan Karpo, *Prin*
EMP: 8 EST: 2018
SALES (est): 168.85K **Privately Held**
Web: www.dfcind.com
SIC: 5084 Industrial machinery and equipment

(G-9024)
DELAWARE HOTEL-MOTEL ASSN (PA)
1612 N Dupont Hwy (19720-1904)
PHONE..................302 674-0630
Harriett Donofrio, *Prin*
EMP: 5 EST: 2009
SALES (est): 209.76K
SALES (corp-wide): 209.76K **Privately Held**
Web: www.delawarelodging.org
SIC: 7011 Motels

(G-9025)
DELAWARE IMPORTERS INC
615 Lambson Ln (19720-2100)
P.O. Box 10887 (19850-0887)
PHONE..................302 656-4487
Edward J Stegemeier, *Pr*
Roger B Hart, *
Kenneth Beach, *
▲ EMP: 59 EST: 1933
SQ FT: 100,000
SALES (est): 4.05MM **Privately Held**
Web: www.delaware.gov
SIC: 5182 5181 Liquor; Beer and other fermented malt liquors

(G-9026)
DELAWARE LAWNANDLANDSCAPE
467 Old Airport Rd (19720-1001)
PHONE..................302 276-1060
Michael Jerry Neal, *Pr*
EMP: 5 EST: 2015
SALES (est): 34.64K **Privately Held**
Web: www.delawnandlandscape.com
SIC: 0782 Lawn and garden services

(G-9027)
DELAWARE MOTEL AND RV PARK
235 S Dupont Hwy (19720-4141)
PHONE..................302 328-3114
David Shah, *Owner*
EMP: 5 EST: 1955
SALES (est): 166.55K **Privately Held**
SIC: 7033 7011 Trailer park; Motels

(G-9028)
DELAWARE NAT GARD YUTH FNDTION
Also Called: DNG YOUTH FOUNDATION
1 Vavala Way (19720-2417)
PHONE..................302 326-7582
Christine Kubik, *Ch*
Christine Kubik, *Ch Bd*
EMP: 8
SALES (est): 36.63K **Privately Held**
SIC: 8322 Child related social services

(G-9029)
DELAWARE OBS LLC
305 Pennewill Dr (19720-1811)
PHONE..................302 743-4798
EMP: 7 EST: 2018
SALES (est): 54.13K **Privately Held**
SIC: 8011 Offices and clinics of medical doctors

(G-9030)
DELAWARE PREMIER TRNSP
30 Lanford Rd (19720-3837)
PHONE..................616 617-2598
Angelo Grant, *Prin*
EMP: 6 EST: 2018
SALES (est): 91.83K **Privately Held**
Web: www.delawarepremiertransportation.com
SIC: 4119 Limousine rental, with driver

(G-9031)
DELAWARE PUBLIC AUTO AUCTION
2323 N Dupont Hwy (19720-6304)
PHONE..................302 656-0500
Doug Powell, *Owner*
EMP: 13 EST: 1998
SALES (est): 966.55K **Privately Held**
Web: www.dpaa2.com
SIC: 5012 5521 Automobile auction; Used car dealers

(G-9032)
DELAWARE RECYCLABLE PRODUCTS
246 Marsh Ln (19720-1175)
PHONE..................302 655-1360
Matt Williams, *Ch Bd*
Jonathan Barber, *Prin*
Chris Isakov, *Dist Mgr*
EMP: 23 EST: 1991
SALES (est): 8.74MM
SALES (corp-wide): 20.43B **Publicly Held**
SIC: 4953 Recycling, waste materials
PA: Waste Management, Inc.
800 Capitol St Ste 3000
Houston TX 77002
713 512-6200

(G-9033)
DELAWARE RECYCLING CENTER
1101 Lambson Ln (19720-2186)
PHONE..................215 921-7508
EMP: 6 EST: 2019
SALES (est): 209.21K **Privately Held**
Web: www.dswa.com
SIC: 4953 Recycling, waste materials

(G-9034)
DELAWARE RIVER & BAY AUTHORITY (PA)
2162 New Castle Ave (19720-2009)
P.O. Box 71 (19720-0071)
PHONE..................302 571-6303
Scott A Green, *Ex Dir*
Joseph Larotonda, *Dir Fin*
William Lowe, *Vice Chairman*
Vincent P Meconi, *COO*
EMP: 200 EST: 1962
SALES (est): 189.98MM
SALES (corp-wide): 189.98MM **Privately Held**
Web: www.drba.net
SIC: 4785 Toll bridge operation

(G-9035)
DELAWARE RVER BAY AUTH EMPLYEE
P.O. Box 71 (19720-0071)
PHONE..................302 571-6320
Scott W Reese Junior, *Pr*
Jack Cawman, *Pr*
Rich Standarowsky, *VP*
Frances Sweeney, *Dir*
Joe Carson, *Sec*
EMP: 7 EST: 1963
SALES (est): 94.99K **Privately Held**
SIC: 6061 Federal credit unions

(G-9036)
DELAWARE SAFETY COUNCIL INC
2 Penns Way Ste 201 (19720-2407)
PHONE..................302 276-0660
Stacey Inglis, *Ex Dir*
Frances M West, *Pr*
Harry Roosevelt, *Dir*
R B Swayze, *VP*
John A Reed Junior, *Sec*
EMP: 8 EST: 1919
SALES (est): 465.4K **Privately Held**
Web: www.delawaresafety.org
SIC: 8748 Safety training service

(G-9037)
DELAWARE SCHL COUNSELORS ASSN
713 E Basin Rd (19720-4201)
PHONE..................302 323-2821
Shirin Skovronski, *Pr*
EMP: 9 EST: 2017
SALES (est): 108.25K **Privately Held**
SIC: 8699 Membership organizations, nec

(G-9038)
DELAWARE STATE PLICE FDRAL CR
235 Christiana Rd (19720-2907)
P.O. Box 717 (19947-0717)
PHONE..................302 324-8141
Lexine Starling, *Mgr*
EMP: 5
Web: www.dspfcu.com
SIC: 6061 Federal credit unions
PA: Delaware State Police Federal Credit Union
700 N Bedford St
Georgetown DE 19947

GEOGRAPHIC SECTION

New Castle - New Castle County (G-9065)

(G-9039)
DELAWARE TITLE LOANS INC
505 N Dupont Hwy (19720-6442)
PHONE.................302 328-7482
EMP: 11
SALES (corp-wide): 820.18K **Privately Held**
Web: www.delawaretitleloansinc.com
SIC: 6159 General and industrial loan institutions
PA: Delaware Title Loans, Inc.
     8601 Dunwoody Pl Ste 406
     Atlanta GA 30350
     770 552-9840

(G-9040)
DELAWARE UNION
214 Harlequin Dr (19720-8900)
PHONE.................484 645-7064
Sean Corbett, *Prin*
EMP: 5 EST: 2017
SALES (est): 52.78K **Privately Held**
Web: www.delawareunion.com
SIC: 7997 Membership sports and recreation clubs

(G-9041)
DELCARD ASSOCIATES INC
31 Blevins Dr Ste C (19720-4170)
PHONE.................302 221-4822
EMP: 195 EST: 1984
SALES (est): 9.87MM
SALES (corp-wide): 4.14B **Publicly Held**
SIC: 1711 Mechanical contractor
PA: Comfort Systems Usa, Inc.
     675 Bering Dr Ste 400
     Houston TX 77057
     713 830-9600

(G-9042)
DELMARVA COMMUNICATIONS INC
113 J And M Dr (19720-3142)
P.O. Box 11725 (19850-1725)
PHONE.................302 324-1230
Jeff D Tillinghast, *Pr*
EMP: 10 EST: 1991
SQ FT: 9,500
SALES (est): 2.91MM **Privately Held**
Web: www.delmarvacom.com
SIC: 5065 5731 8999 1731 Radio and television equipment and parts; Radios, two-way, citizens band, weather, short-wave, etc.; Communication services; Electrical work

(G-9043)
DELPA BUILDERS LLC
10 King Ave (19720-1512)
PHONE.................302 731-7304
Larry Zeccola, *Managing Member*
EMP: 14 EST: 2013
SALES (est): 2.15MM **Privately Held**
SIC: 1521 New construction, single-family houses

(G-9044)
DELPORT HOLDING COMPANY
529 Terminal Ave (19720-1426)
PHONE.................302 655-7300
James B Thomas Senior, *Ch*
Mary Thomas, *Pr*
Margaret Knotts, *Sec*
Madeleine Tucker, *Treas*
EMP: 6 EST: 1960
SALES (est): 562.18K **Privately Held**
Web: www.portcontractors.com
SIC: 6512 Nonresidential building operators

(G-9045)
DELTA ENGINEERING CORPORATION
13 Drba Way (19720-3129)
PHONE.................302 325-9320
EMP: 28 EST: 1992
SALES (est): 5.98MM **Privately Held**
Web: www.delta-engineering.com
SIC: 8711 5088 Aviation and/or aeronautical engineering; Aircraft equipment and supplies, nec

(G-9046)
DEPENDABLE CMNTY HM CARE LLC
8 Peachleaf Trl (19720-7672)
PHONE.................302 893-3779
EMP: 6 EST: 2020
SALES (est): 242.42K **Privately Held**
Web: www.dchc-de.com
SIC: 8082 Home health care services

(G-9047)
DEPENDABLE TRUCKING INC
520 Terminal Ave (19720-1459)
P.O. Box 668 (19720-0668)
PHONE.................302 655-6271
Herbert Bollman, *Pr*
E Marie Bollman, *Sec*
EMP: 15 EST: 1978
SQ FT: 15,000
SALES (est): 378.01K
SALES (corp-wide): 1.29MM **Privately Held**
SIC: 7513 4212 Truck leasing, without drivers; Local trucking, without storage
PA: Christiana Motor Freight, Inc
     520 Terminal Ave Ste C
     New Castle DE 19720
     302 655-6271

(G-9048)
DFC INDUSTRIES INC
Also Called: Dfc Industries
4 Bellecor Dr Unit B (19720-2218)
PHONE.................215 292-1572
Jeffrey D Wright, *Pr*
EMP: 6 EST: 1978
SQ FT: 14,000
SALES (est): 944.81K **Privately Held**
Web: www.dfcind.com
SIC: 5085 Filters, industrial

(G-9049)
DFS CORPORATE SERVICES LLC
Also Called: Discover Financial Services
12 Reads Way (19720-1649)
PHONE.................302 323-7191
Richard Howard, *Mgr*
EMP: 155
SALES (corp-wide): 15.2B **Publicly Held**
Web: www.discoverglobalnetwork.com
SIC: 7389 Credit card service
HQ: Dfs Corporate Services Llc
     2500 Lake Cook Rd 2
     Riverwoods IL 60015
     224 405-0900

(G-9050)
DIAMOND HILL INC
34 Industrial Blvd # 104 (19720-2091)
PHONE.................302 999-0302
Michael E Sheehan, *Pr*
EMP: 25 EST: 2004
SALES (est): 7.31MM **Privately Held**
Web: www.diamond-hill.com
SIC: 1542 Commercial and office building, new construction

(G-9051)
DIAMOND STATE GRAPHICS INC
200 Century Park (19720-3122)
PHONE.................302 325-1100
David Hood, *Pr*
Douglas Hood, *VP*
EMP: 14 EST: 1988
SQ FT: 5,500
SALES (est): 1.04MM **Privately Held**
Web: www.diamondstategraphics.com
SIC: 2759 Screen printing

(G-9052)
DIAMOND STATE TRUCK CENTER LLC
29 E Commons Blvd Ste 300 (19720-1736)
PHONE.................302 275-9050
Jeff Layton, *Managing Member*
EMP: 7 EST: 2005
SALES (est): 134.73K **Privately Held**
SIC: 7538 5531 5511 5012 General truck repair; Truck equipment and parts; Trucks, tractors, and trailers: new and used; Trucks, commercial

(G-9053)
DIAMOND STATE WTERPROOFING SYS
13 King Ct Ste 5 (19720-1523)
PHONE.................302 325-0866
Thomas Dale Junior, *Pr*
EMP: 5 EST: 1991
SQ FT: 2,100
SALES (est): 486.88K **Privately Held**
Web: diamond-state-waterproofing-company-inc.hub.biz
SIC: 1799 Waterproofing

(G-9054)
DIJITRU INC ✪
257 Old Churchmans Rd (19720-1529)
PHONE.................903 345-4878
Rakesh Patel, *CEO*
EMP: 7 EST: 2022
SALES (est): 264.9K **Privately Held**
SIC: 7371 Computer software development

(G-9055)
DIMENSIONAL STONE PRODUCTS LLC
76 Southgate Blvd (19720-2068)
PHONE.................302 322-3900
EMP: 12 EST: 2000
SQ FT: 4,000
SALES (est): 750K **Privately Held**
SIC: 1411 Granite dimension stone

(G-9056)
DIMO CORP
46 Industrial Blvd (19720-2091)
PHONE.................302 324-8100
EMP: 28 EST: 1994
SQ FT: 18,500
SALES (est): 14.2MM **Privately Held**
Web: www.dimo.com
SIC: 5088 5599 Aircraft and parts, nec; Aircraft instruments, equipment or parts

(G-9057)
DIVISION SVCS FOR AGING ADLTS
1901 N Dupont Hwy Fl 1 (19720-1100)
PHONE.................302 255-9390
Guy Peroppi, *Dir*
EMP: 9 EST: 2004
SALES (est): 110.18K **Privately Held**
SIC: 8322 Senior citizens' center or association

(G-9058)
DJ FIRST CLASS
20 Robins Nest Ln (19720-1860)
P.O. Box 961 (19720-0961)
PHONE.................302 345-0602
Valerie C Chaney, *CEO*
EMP: 10 EST: 2010
SALES (est): 87.71K **Privately Held**
SIC: 7929 8999 Entertainment service; Music arranging and composing

(G-9059)
DONKEY TRUCKING LLC ✪
117 W Harvest Dr (19720-5607)
PHONE.................302 507-2380
EMP: 5 EST: 2022
SALES (est): 220.71K **Privately Held**
SIC: 4212 4213 7389 Local trucking, without storage; Trucking, except local; Business Activities at Non-Commercial Site

(G-9060)
DOVER PARKS MANAGEMENT LLC
761 Grantham Ln (19720-4801)
PHONE.................302 326-1540
EMP: 5 EST: 2015
SALES (est): 269.04K **Privately Held**
SIC: 8741 Management services

(G-9061)
DR THOMAS C SCOTT DO
11 Hodgkins Pl (19720-4707)
PHONE.................302 328-0650
Thomas C Scott D.o.s., *Owner*
EMP: 7 EST: 2018
SALES (est): 76.15K **Privately Held**
SIC: 8011 Offices and clinics of medical doctors

(G-9062)
DRBA POLICE FUND
Route 9 And I-295 (19720)
PHONE.................302 571-6326
James T Johnson Junior, *Dir*
EMP: 10 EST: 2004
SALES (est): 171.28K **Privately Held**
Web: www.drba.net
SIC: 4785 Inspection and fixed facilities

(G-9063)
DREAM GRAPHICS
9 King Ave (19720-1511)
PHONE.................302 328-6264
Kathy Stabley, *Pt*
Susan Rawheiser, *Pt*
EMP: 2 EST: 1995
SALES (est): 241.26K **Privately Held**
Web: www.dreamgraphicsde.com
SIC: 2759 Screen printing

(G-9064)
DRIVEWAY SEALCOATING
12 Appleby Trlr Ct (19720-5406)
PHONE.................302 203-7451
Peter Simpson, *Prin*
EMP: 6 EST: 2018
SALES (est): 96.58K **Privately Held**
SIC: 1771 Driveway contractor

(G-9065)
DRYWALL INC
13 King Ct Ste 3 (19720-1523)
PHONE.................302 838-6500
Bryan Hannum, *Owner*
EMP: 35 EST: 2007
SALES (est): 5.64MM **Privately Held**
Web: www.drywallinc.com
SIC: 1742 Drywall

New Castle - New Castle County (G-9066) GEOGRAPHIC SECTION

(G-9066)
DUMONT AIRCRAFT CHARTER LLC
Also Called: Dumont Jets
1 Boulden Cir (19720-3400)
PHONE.....................610 266-1369
Dan Piraino, *Managing Member*
EMP: 18 **EST:** 2015
SALES (est): 977.28K **Privately Held**
Web: www.dumontaviation.com
SIC: 4581 Hangars and other aircraft storage facilities

(G-9067)
DUMONT AVIATION GROUP INC
Also Called: Dumont Aviation
1 Boulden Cir (19720-3400)
PHONE.....................302 777-1003
Amber Martin, *Mgr*
EMP: 7 **EST:** 2014
SALES (est): 1.84MM **Privately Held**
Web: www.dumontaviation.com
SIC: 4581 Airports, flying fields, and services

(G-9068)
DUMONT AVIATION GROUP INC
15 Penns Way (19720-2437)
PHONE.....................302 777-1003
EMP: 10 **EST:** 2014
SALES (est): 73.65K **Privately Held**
Web: www.dumontaviation.com
SIC: 4581 Airports, flying fields, and services

(G-9069)
DUPONT AVIATION CORP
199 N Dupont Hwy (19720-3121)
PHONE.....................302 996-8000
Keith Shelburn, *Dir*
EMP: 35 **EST:** 2009
SALES (est): 4.8MM
SALES (corp-wide): 17.23B **Publicly Held**
SIC: 8711 Aviation and/or aeronautical engineering
HQ: Eidp, Inc.
9330 Zionsville Rd
Indianapolis IN 46268
833 267-8382

(G-9070)
DUTCH VILLAGE MOTEL INC
Also Called: Rodeway Inn
111 S Dupont Hwy (19720-4127)
PHONE.....................302 328-6246
Harshad Amin, *Pr*
Pierre Peter L Olivero, *Pr*
Margaret L Olivero, *VP*
EMP: 32 **EST:** 1950
SQ FT: 21,000
SALES (est): 205.94K **Privately Held**
Web: www.dutchinnde.net
SIC: 7011 Motels

(G-9071)
DYCOM INDUSTRIES INC
34 Blevins Dr Ste 5 (19720-4177)
PHONE.....................302 613-0958
Jeff Drzymala, *Prin*
EMP: 6 **EST:** 2016
SALES (est): 201.09K **Privately Held**
Web: www.princetelecom.com
SIC: 1623 Underground utilities contractor

(G-9072)
E-CARAUCTIONS LLC (PA)
1602 N Dupont Hwy (19720-1904)
P.O. Box 272 (19899-0272)
PHONE.....................302 677-1552
Kathleen Stevenson, *Prin*
EMP: 5 **EST:** 2005
SALES (est): 239.92K
SALES (corp-wide): 239.92K **Privately Held**

SIC: 7389 Auction, appraisal, and exchange services

(G-9073)
EACH ONE TEACH ONE INC
550 S Dupont Hwy Apt 55w (19720-5184)
PHONE.....................302 345-8744
EMP: 7 **EST:** 2018
SALES (est): 60.72K **Privately Held**
Web: www.eachoneteachone.is
SIC: 8399 Advocacy group

(G-9074)
EAGLE EXPRESS
101 J And M Dr Ste 101 (19720-3147)
PHONE.....................302 898-2247
EMP: 7 **EST:** 2017
SALES (est): 114.3K **Privately Held**
Web: www.eagleexpressfcu.com
SIC: 4213 Trucking, except local

(G-9075)
EAGLE LIMOUSINE INC (PA)
Also Called: Eagle Transportation
77 Mccullough Dr Ste 5 (19720-2089)
PHONE.....................302 325-4200
Kristin Aulendach, *Pr*
EMP: 150 **EST:** 1991
SQ FT: 15,000
SALES (est): 5.12MM **Privately Held**
Web: www.eaglelimo.com
SIC: 4119 Limousine rental, with driver

(G-9076)
EAGLE POWER AND EQUIPMENT CORP
2211 N Dupont Hwy (19720-6302)
P.O. Box 889 (19720-0889)
PHONE.....................302 652-3028
Bob Mccullough, *Mgr*
EMP: 10
Web: www.eaglepowerandequipment.com
SIC: 5082 7353 General construction machinery and equipment; Heavy construction equipment rental
PA: Eagle Power And Equipment Corp.
953 Bethlehem Pike
Montgomeryville PA 18936

(G-9077)
EAST COAST ERECTORS INC
1144 River Rd (19720-5106)
P.O. Box 448 (19720-0448)
PHONE.....................302 323-1800
Michael A Williams, *Pr*
Thomas Williams, *
William Zern, *
EMP: 19 **EST:** 1985
SALES (est): 937.69K **Privately Held**
Web: www.eastcoasterectors.com
SIC: 1791 3441 Structural steel erection; Fabricated structural metal

(G-9078)
EASTER SALS DEL MRYLNDS ESTRN (PA)
61 Corporate Cir (19720-2439)
PHONE.....................302 324-4444
Kenan J Sklenar, *CEO*
EMP: 75 **EST:** 1949
SQ FT: 20,000
SALES (est): 27.16MM
SALES (corp-wide): 27.16MM **Privately Held**
Web: www.easterseals.com
SIC: 8322 8331 Social services for the handicapped; Vocational training agency

(G-9079)
EASTERN HOSPITALITY MANAGEMENT
Also Called: Super 8 Motel
215 S Dupont Hwy (19720-4141)
PHONE.....................302 322-9480
EMP: 20
Web: www.wyndhamhotels.com
SIC: 7011 Hotels and motels
PA: Eastern Hospitality Management, Inc
1910 8th Ave Ne
Aberdeen SD 57401

(G-9080)
EBANKS CONSTRUCTION LLC
507 Florence Fields Ln (19720-8752)
PHONE.....................302 420-7584
EMP: 6 **EST:** 2008
SALES (est): 993.93K **Privately Held**
SIC: 1542 1522 Commercial and office building, new construction; Residential construction, nec

(G-9081)
ECOLAB PEST ELIMINATION
53 Mccullough Dr (19720-2080)
PHONE.....................302 322-3600
EMP: 12 **EST:** 2019
SALES (est): 337.57K **Privately Held**
Web: www.ecolab.com
SIC: 2841 Soap and other detergents

(G-9082)
EDWARDS LAWN CARE
258 Bassett Ave (19720-1828)
PHONE.....................302 981-7751
Angelica Ledesma, *Prin*
EMP: 5 **EST:** 2009
SALES (est): 88.27K **Privately Held**
Web: www.edwardsgrass.com
SIC: 0782 Lawn care services

(G-9083)
EGM LLC
42 Valley Forge Rd (19720-4241)
PHONE.....................302 932-1700
Volkan Alev, *Managing Member*
EMP: 2 **EST:** 2013
SALES (est): 68.07K **Privately Held**
SIC: 7371 2037 Computer software development and applications; Frozen fruits and vegetables

(G-9084)
EIDP INC
Also Called: Dupont
1001 Lambson Ln (19720-2107)
PHONE.....................302 772-0016
EMP: 4
SALES (corp-wide): 17.23B **Publicly Held**
Web: www.dupont.com
SIC: 2911 5171 5541 Petroleum refining; Petroleum bulk stations and terminals; Gasoline service stations
HQ: Eidp, Inc.
9330 Zionsville Rd
Indianapolis IN 46268
833 267-8382

(G-9085)
EKEO GROUP LLC ◆
128 Sunset Blvd (19720-4100)
P.O. Box 1039 (19720-7039)
PHONE.....................973 489-1962
Osagieoduwa Ekenezar, *Managing Member*
EMP: 7 **EST:** 2022
SALES (est): 540.86K **Privately Held**
Web: www.ekeogroup.com
SIC: 7361 Placement agencies

(G-9086)
ELCRITON INC
15 Reads Way (19720-1600)
PHONE.....................864 921-5146
Eleftherios Papoutsakis, *Pr*
Bryan Tracy, *CEO*
Shawn Jones, *Research & Development*
Daniel Mitchell, *Research & Development*
Carrissa Kesler, *Research & Development*
EMP: 4 **EST:** 2009
SALES (est): 868.72K **Privately Held**
Web: www.superbrewedfood.com
SIC: 2869 Industrial organic chemicals, nec

(G-9087)
ELECTRICAL INTEGRITY LLC
117 J And M Dr (19720-3147)
PHONE.....................302 388-3430
EMP: 10 **EST:** 2012
SALES (est): 1.85MM **Privately Held**
Web: www.elecintegrity.com
SIC: 4911 Electric services

(G-9088)
ELECTRICAL POWER SYSTEMS INC (PA)
240a Churchmans Rd (19720-3110)
PHONE.....................302 325-3502
Stephen Yovanov, *Pr*
EMP: 5 **EST:** 1988
SQ FT: 2,700
SALES (est): 2.42MM **Privately Held**
Web: www.epsibiz.com
SIC: 1731 General electrical contractor

(G-9089)
ELECTRO-ART SIGN COMPANY
107 J And M Dr (19720-3147)
P.O. Box 281 (19720-0281)
PHONE.....................302 322-1108
Thomas Rash Junior, *Pr*
Tony Tettoruto, *VP*
Nick Tettoruto, *Treas*
Dave Tettoruto, *Sec*
EMP: 6 **EST:** 1980
SQ FT: 3,000
SALES (est): 419.63K **Privately Held**
Web: www.instasignsplus.com
SIC: 3993 Electric signs

(G-9090)
EMORY HILL & COMPANY (PA)
10 Corporate Cir Ste 100 (19720-2418)
PHONE.....................302 322-4400
Robert H Hill, *Pr*
Carmen Facciolo Junior, *VP*
EMP: 59 **EST:** 1981
SQ FT: 4,000
SALES (est): 14.95MM
SALES (corp-wide): 14.95MM **Privately Held**
Web: www.naiemoryhill.com
SIC: 8742 Construction project management consultant

(G-9091)
EMORY HILL RE SVCS INC (PA)
10 Corporate Cir Ste 100 (19720-2418)
PHONE.....................302 322-9500
Carmen J Facciolo Junior, *Pr*
Robert H Hill, *
EMP: 55 **EST:** 1981
SQ FT: 3,500
SALES (est): 5.1MM **Privately Held**
Web: www.naiemoryhill.com
SIC: 6512 Commercial and industrial building operation

GEOGRAPHIC SECTION

New Castle - New Castle County (G-9122)

(G-9092)
EMPIRE BLUE
315 Schafer Blvd (19720-8859)
PHONE.................302 324-1015
Tierra N Greenlea, *Prin*
EMP: 5 EST: 2016
SALES (est): 87.89K **Privately Held**
SIC: 7379 Computer related consulting services

(G-9093)
EMPIRE INVESTMENTS INC
Also Called: Empire
201 Jestan Blvd (19720-5214)
PHONE.................302 838-0631
Pasquale Muzzi, *Pr*
Sylvester Aiello, *Sec*
EMP: 7 EST: 1980
SQ FT: 3,000
SALES (est): 1.07MM **Privately Held**
Web: www.empirebuilds.com
SIC: 1521 1542 New construction, single-family houses; Nonresidential construction, nec

(G-9094)
ENCORE LASHES LASH LOUNGE LLC ✪
15 Dalton Ct (19720-5674)
PHONE.................844 408-0004
Lori Angelique Hutson, *CEO*
EMP: 9 EST: 2022
SALES (est): 317.82K **Privately Held**
SIC: 7389 7231 Business Activities at Non-Commercial Site; Beauty shops

(G-9095)
ENERGY SERVICES GROUP
2 King Ct Ste A (19720-1518)
PHONE.................302 324-8400
EMP: 11 EST: 2019
SALES (est): 842.71K **Privately Held**
Web: www.energysvc.com
SIC: 7699 General household repair services

(G-9096)
ENERGY SYSTEMS TECH INC
15 Reads Way Ste 101a (19720-1611)
PHONE.................302 368-0443
Paul E Czerwin, *Pr*
Joan Czerwin, *Sec*
EMP: 5 EST: 2006
SALES (est): 1.06MM
SALES (corp-wide): 141.55MM **Privately Held**
Web: www.estdistribution.com
SIC: 3822 Environmental controls
PA: Albireo Energy, Llc
3 Ethel Rd Ste 300
Edison NJ 08817
732 512-9100

(G-9097)
ENGLAND COLLISION CENTER LLC
19 King Ct (19720-1519)
PHONE.................240 440-1111
EMP: 5 EST: 2016
SALES (est): 207.62K **Privately Held**
SIC: 7532 Collision shops, automotive

(G-9098)
ENVIRONMENTAL SERVICES INC
461 Churchmans Rd (19720-3156)
PHONE.................302 669-6812
EMP: 6 EST: 2009
SALES (est): 639.49K **Privately Held**
Web: www.esi-green.com
SIC: 8748 Environmental consultant

(G-9099)
EPSTEIN KPLAN OPTHLMLOGIST LLP
169 Christiana Rd (19720-3040)
PHONE.................302 322-4444
EMP: 8 EST: 2010
SALES (est): 336.88K **Privately Held**
Web: www.goodeyecarede.com
SIC: 8042 Offices and clinics of optometrists

(G-9100)
ESSENTIAL MINERALS LLC
901 Lambson Ln (19720-2135)
PHONE.................602 377-9878
EMP: 5 EST: 2017
SALES (est): 1MM **Privately Held**
Web: www.essentialminerals.com
SIC: 2819 Industrial inorganic chemicals, nec

(G-9101)
ESTELLES CHILD DEV CTR INC
132 Colesbery Dr (19720-3204)
PHONE.................302 792-9065
Estelle Turner, *CEO*
EMP: 10 EST: 2005
SALES (est): 236.27K **Privately Held**
SIC: 8351 Head Start center, except in conjunction with school

(G-9102)
EVAN H CRAIN M D
239 Christiana Rd (19720-2907)
PHONE.................302 322-3400
EMP: 18 EST: 2017
SALES (est): 238.68K **Privately Held**
Web: www.firststateortho.com
SIC: 8011 Orthopedic physician

(G-9103)
EVELYN M FALKOWSKI
335 Pennewill Dr (19720-1811)
PHONE.................302 328-3125
Evelyn M Falkowski, *Prin*
EMP: 6 EST: 2012
SALES (est): 55.03K **Privately Held**
SIC: 8049 Offices of health practitioner

(G-9104)
EVENTSBYNYE LLC
6 Carvel Ave (19720-2667)
PHONE.................302 256-3971
EMP: 6
SALES (est): 63.67K **Privately Held**
SIC: 7299 7389 Facility rental and party planning services; Business services, nec

(G-9105)
EVERGREEN APARTMENT GROUP INC
Also Called: Hampton Walk Apartments
1627 New Jersey Ave (19720-1933)
PHONE.................302 998-0322
Kevin Wolfgang, *CEO*
EMP: 20 EST: 2010
SALES (est): 737.88K **Privately Held**
Web: www.evergreenapartments.com
SIC: 6513 Apartment building operators

(G-9106)
EVERGREEN PROPERTIES MGT INC
1627 New Jersey Ave (19720-1933)
PHONE.................302 998-0322
Gregory Wolfgang, *CFO*
EMP: 9 EST: 2009
SALES (est): 249.95K **Privately Held**
Web: www.evergreenapartments.com
SIC: 6513 Apartment building operators

(G-9107)
EVERGREEN WASTE SERVICES LLC
619 Lambson Ln (19720-2166)
PHONE.................302 635-7055
Raphael Morado, *
EMP: 30 EST: 2010
SALES (est): 2.77MM **Privately Held**
Web: www.evergreenws.com
SIC: 4953 Garbage: collecting, destroying, and processing

(G-9108)
EXCEDE BRDBAND STLLITE INTRNET
905 E Basin Rd (19720-4253)
PHONE.................302 613-0669
EMP: 5 EST: 2013
SALES (est): 90.89K **Privately Held**
SIC: 4813 Online service providers

(G-9109)
EXIT KING REALTY
Also Called: Exit Realty
18 Lovelace Ave (19720-1141)
PHONE.................941 961-4925
Erin Savidge, *Prin*
EMP: 5 EST: 2016
SALES (est): 72.98K **Privately Held**
Web: www.exitrealty.com
SIC: 6531 Real estate brokers and agents

(G-9110)
EXPERT BASEMENT WATERPROO
745 Cox Neck Rd (19720-5701)
PHONE.................302 655-8202
EMP: 5 EST: 2018
SALES (est): 120.2K **Privately Held**
Web: www.ebwaterproofing.com
SIC: 1799 Waterproofing

(G-9111)
EXTRAVAGANZA INTERNATIONAL INC
257 Old Churchmans Rd (19720-1529)
PHONE.................302 321-7117
EMP: 5 EST: 2019
SALES (est): 46.16K **Privately Held**
Web: www.extravaganza-intl.us
SIC: 7371 Computer software development and applications

(G-9112)
EZ CONSTRUCTION CO
4 Bellecor Dr (19720-1763)
PHONE.................302 723-5730
EMP: 5 EST: 2018
SALES (est): 75.19K **Privately Held**
SIC: 1521 Single-family housing construction

(G-9113)
F W D INC
Also Called: Overhead Door Grter Wilmington
502 Churchmans Rd (19720-3155)
P.O. Box 2600 (19805-0600)
PHONE.................302 323-4999
Frank W Diver Iii, *Pr*
Frank W Diver Junior, *VP*
EMP: 16 EST: 1968
SQ FT: 12,000
SALES (est): 929.4K **Privately Held**
Web: www.overheaddoor.com
SIC: 1751 Garage door, installation or erection

(G-9114)
F&M CUSTOM PAINTING LLC
1208 Stonebridge Blvd (19720-6722)
PHONE.................302 391-4017
Felipe Martinez, *Prin*
EMP: 5 EST: 2018
SALES (est): 42.66K **Privately Held**
SIC: 1721 Painting and paper hanging

(G-9115)
FACEPAINTING
260 Christiana Rd Apt F10 (19720-2970)
PHONE.................302 344-3145
Daria Lewis, *Prin*
EMP: 5 EST: 2016
SALES (est): 66.33K **Privately Held**
SIC: 1721 Painting and paper hanging

(G-9116)
FAITHFUL FRIENDS INC
Also Called: Faithful Friends Animal Soc
165 Airport Rd (19720-2382)
PHONE.................302 427-8514
Jane Pierantozzi, *Ex Dir*
EMP: 60 EST: 2001
SALES (est): 5.07MM **Privately Held**
Web: www.faithfulfriends.us
SIC: 8699 Animal humane society

(G-9117)
FAMILY HEATING & COOLING LLC
11 Hardy Rd (19720-2324)
PHONE.................302 229-4716
Matthew Kolf, *Prin*
EMP: 7 EST: 2017
SALES (est): 471.83K **Privately Held**
SIC: 1711 Warm air heating and air conditioning contractor

(G-9118)
FAMOUS WSI RESULTS
12 Penns Way (19720-2414)
PHONE.................302 407-0430
Matthew Doyle, *Pr*
EMP: 6 EST: 2015
SALES (est): 79.87K **Privately Held**
Web: www.famouswsiresults.com
SIC: 7311 Advertising agencies

(G-9119)
FANTASTIC GREEN CLEANING SVC
32 Valley Forge Rd (19720-4240)
PHONE.................302 981-8259
Abel Aguilar, *Prin*
EMP: 5 EST: 2017
SALES (est): 46.52K **Privately Held**
SIC: 7699 Cleaning services

(G-9120)
FEDCAP REHABILITATION SERVICES
241 Old Churchmans Rd (19720-1529)
PHONE.................302 544-6634
EMP: 11 EST: 2019
SALES (est): 32.92K **Privately Held**
Web: www.fedcap.org
SIC: 8322 Rehabilitation services

(G-9121)
FEDDLY JEANNITON
4 Bellecor Dr (19720-1763)
PHONE.................302 325-1000
Feddly Jeanniton, *Owner*
EMP: 6 EST: 2017
SALES (est): 255.83K **Privately Held**
SIC: 7378 Computer maintenance and repair

(G-9122)
FEDERAL EXPRESS CORPORATION
Also Called: Fedex
2 W Commons Blvd (19720-2497)
PHONE.................800 463-3339
EMP: 13
SALES (corp-wide): 90.16B **Publicly Held**
Web: www.fedex.com
SIC: 4513 Package delivery, private air
HQ: Federal Express Corporation

3610 Hacks Cross Rd
Memphis TN 38125
901 369-3600

(G-9123)
FEDERAL MECHANICAL CONTRACTORS
Also Called: Cochran Oil
229 Hillview Ave (19720-2204)
PHONE..................................302 656-2998
Thomas H Cochran Junior, *Pr*
EMP: 10 EST: 1978
SQ FT: 6,000
SALES (est): 1.06MM **Privately Held**
Web: www.cochranoil.com
SIC: 1711 Plumbing contractors

(G-9124)
FELIXCEM CORPORATION INC
314 Bay West Blvd (19720-5195)
PHONE..................................302 324-9101
Earl Pearce, *Prin*
EMP: 3 EST: 2003
SALES (est): 170K **Privately Held**
SIC: 3471 Cleaning, polishing, and finishing

(G-9125)
FIERCE DANCE ACADEMY
608 E Basin Rd (19720-4202)
PHONE..................................302 414-9191
EMP: 8 EST: 2013
SALES (est): 259.45K **Privately Held**
Web: www.fiercedanceacademy.com
SIC: 7911 Dance studio and school

(G-9126)
FIRST CALIBER SERVICES LLC
144 Dutton Ct (19720-5415)
PHONE..................................302 328-3049
Chris Shipkowski, *Prin*
EMP: 5 EST: 2010
SALES (est): 31.4K **Privately Held**
SIC: 7699 Repair services, nec

(G-9127)
FIRST STATE AUTOMATION LLC
34 Blevins Dr Ste 3 (19720-4177)
PHONE..................................302 743-4798
EMP: 5 EST: 2009
SALES (est): 359.84K **Privately Held**
SIC: 5084 Industrial machinery and equipment

(G-9128)
FIRST STATE ELECTRIC CO
25 King Ct (19720-1519)
PHONE..................................302 322-0140
Nicola J Aievoli, *Pr*
Edward P Twitchell, *Sec*
EMP: 22 EST: 1979
SQ FT: 6,000
SALES (est): 799.53K **Privately Held**
Web: support.website-creator.org
SIC: 1731 General electrical contractor

(G-9129)
FIRST STATE FLEET SERVICE INC
100 Carroll Dr (19720-4873)
PHONE..................................302 598-9500
Arthur F Mcguire Iii, *Pr*
EMP: 8 EST: 2010
SALES (est): 250.31K **Privately Held**
SIC: 7538 General truck repair

(G-9130)
FIRST STATE PLASTICS INC
955 River Rd (19720-4837)
PHONE..................................302 325-3700
EMP: 50 EST: 2004
SQ FT: 50,000
SALES (est): 5.47MM **Privately Held**
SIC: 4953 Recycling, waste materials

(G-9131)
FIRST STATE PLUMBING & HEATING
47 Dunsinane Dr (19720-2316)
PHONE..................................302 275-9746
Willam B Hall Junior, *Owner*
EMP: 6 EST: 2008
SALES (est): 64.85K **Privately Held**
SIC: 7699 1711 Boiler and heating repair services; Plumbing contractors

(G-9132)
FIRST STATE STEEL DRUM CO
4030 New Castle Ave (19720-1455)
PHONE..................................302 655-2422
John D Ryan Iii, *Pt*
William R Ryan, *Pt*
Robert S Ryan, *Pt*
Jane Ryan, *Pt*
EMP: 6 EST: 1960
SQ FT: 2,000
SALES (est): 987.24K **Privately Held**
Web: www.firststatesteeldrum.com
SIC: 5085 Drums, new or reconditioned

(G-9133)
FIRST STATE TOWING LLC
431 Old Airport Rd (19720-1001)
PHONE..................................302 322-1777
EMP: 6 EST: 2018
SALES (est): 499.31K **Privately Held**
Web: www.firststatetowing.com
SIC: 4953 Recycling, waste materials

(G-9134)
FIRST STATE WAREHOUSING
Also Called: Diamond State Whsng & Dist
300 Pigeon Blvd (19720)
PHONE..................................302 426-0802
Patrick Bastian, *Owner*
EMP: 6 EST: 2005
SALES (est): 443.23K **Privately Held**
Web: www.firststatewarehousing.com
SIC: 4225 General warehousing

(G-9135)
FLOATER PAINTING
36 Roxeter Rd (19720-3525)
PHONE..................................302 290-8520
Ricardo Brown, *Prin*
EMP: 5 EST: 2015
SALES (est): 70.32K **Privately Held**
SIC: 1721 Painting and paper hanging

(G-9136)
FLOOR COATINGS ETC INC
110 J And M Dr (19720-3147)
P.O. Box 310 (19720-0310)
PHONE..................................302 322-4177
Bill Deveney, *CEO*
John Pennington, *
Anthony Watkins, *
EMP: 25 EST: 1995
SQ FT: 3,000
SALES (est): 5.13MM **Privately Held**
Web: www.floorcoatingsetc.com
SIC: 1752 Floor laying and floor work, nec

(G-9137)
FLOOR GUY SUPPLY LLC
12 Mccullough Dr Ste 10 (19720-2076)
PHONE..................................302 325-3801
EMP: 5 EST: 2005
SALES (est): 675.84K **Privately Held**
Web: www.myfgsupply.com
SIC: 5961 2842 General merchandise, mail order; Floor waxes

(G-9138)
FOCUS HEALTH CARE DELAWARE LLC
Also Called: Meadowwood Behavioral Health
575 S Dupont Hwy (19720-4606)
PHONE..................................302 395-1111
Admiral Patty Wright, *Prin*
EMP: 64 EST: 2002
SALES (est): 13.04MM **Privately Held**
Web: www.meadowwoodhospital.com
SIC: 8093 Mental health clinic, outpatient

(G-9139)
FORCEBEYOND LLC (PA)
261 Quigley Blvd Ste 18 (19720-9039)
PHONE..................................302 995-6588
Steve Bai, *Managing Member*
EMP: 19 EST: 2018
SALES (est): 3.57MM
SALES (corp-wide): 3.57MM **Privately Held**
Web: www.forcebeyond.com
SIC: 5085 Industrial supplies

(G-9140)
FOREVER GREEN LANDSCAPING INC
340 Churchmans Rd (19720-3112)
PHONE..................................302 322-9535
Elly Nadot, *Pr*
EMP: 18 EST: 1994
SALES (est): 903.63K **Privately Held**
Web: www.forevergreenlandscapinginc.com
SIC: 0782 Landscape contractors

(G-9141)
FOUNDATION DELAWARE ISLAMIC
249 Appleby Rd (19720-5403)
PHONE..................................302 325-4149
Mustafa Tuncer, *Prin*
EMP: 7 EST: 2013
SALES (est): 59.34K **Privately Held**
Web: www.diyanetmosque.org
SIC: 8641 Civic and social associations

(G-9142)
FOUR SEASONS PROPERTY MANAGEME
162 Christiana Rd (19720-3003)
PHONE..................................302 275-4816
EMP: 5 EST: 2014
SALES (est): 367.35K **Privately Held**
SIC: 8741 Management services

(G-9143)
FOUR STATES LLC
520 Terminal Ave Ste G (19720-1447)
P.O. Box 891 (19720-0891)
PHONE..................................302 655-3400
Jim Byrne, *Owner*
EMP: 10 EST: 2003
SQ FT: 25,000
SALES (est): 605.97K **Privately Held**
Web: www.fourstatesllc.com
SIC: 7538 5084 Truck engine repair, except industrial; Trucks, industrial

(G-9144)
FRANK DERAMO & SON INC
10 King Ct (19720-1519)
PHONE..................................302 328-0102
S Elizabeth Deramo, *Pr*
Frank Deramo Junior, *Stockholder*
EMP: 10 EST: 1978
SQ FT: 3,480
SALES (est): 500K **Privately Held**
SIC: 1771 Concrete work

(G-9145)
FREEHOLD CARTAGE INC
350 Pigeon Point Rd (19720-1464)
PHONE..................................302 658-2005
EMP: 38
SALES (corp-wide): 49.32MM **Privately Held**
Web: www.freeholdcartage.com
SIC: 4789 Pipeline terminal facilities, independently operated
PA: Freehold Cartage Inc.
825 State Route 33
Freehold NJ 07728
732 462-1001

(G-9146)
FRIENDS OF BELLACA AIRFIELD
Rt 273 Ctr Pt Blvd (19720)
PHONE..................................302 322-3816
Sally Monigle, *VP*
EMP: 5 EST: 2006
SALES (est): 99.38K **Privately Held**
Web: www.bellancamuseum.org
SIC: 8412 Museum

(G-9147)
FRIENDS OF COLONIAL
318 E Basin Rd (19720-4214)
PHONE..................................302 323-2746
EMP: 5 EST: 2015
SALES (est): 114.24K **Privately Held**
SIC: 8641 Civic and social associations

(G-9148)
FRONTLINE CROSSFIT
4060 N Dupont Hwy # 1 (19720-6325)
PHONE..................................302 229-6467
EMP: 6 EST: 2015
SALES (est): 81.96K **Privately Held**
Web: www.frontlinecf.com
SIC: 7991 Health club

(G-9149)
FUJI FILM
233 Cherry Ln (19720-2779)
PHONE..................................302 477-8000
Brian Meldrum, *Prin*
EMP: 37 EST: 2002
SALES (est): 3.39MM **Privately Held**
Web: www.fujifilmic.com
SIC: 3081 Photographic and X-ray film and sheet

(G-9150)
FUJIFILM IMAGING COLORANTS INC (DH)
233 Cherry Ln (19720-2779)
PHONE..................................800 552-1609
Ian Wilkinson, *Pr*
◆ EMP: 30 EST: 2005
SQ FT: 5,000
SALES (est): 39.01MM **Privately Held**
Web: global.fujifilm.com
SIC: 2893 Printing ink
HQ: Fujifilm Corporation
9-7-3, Akasaka
Minato-Ku TKY 107-0

(G-9151)
FUJIFILM IMAGING COLORANTS INC
Also Called: Fujifilm
233 Cherry Ln (19720-2779)
PHONE..................................302 472-1245
EMP: 60
Web: global.fujifilm.com
SIC: 7384 Photofinish laboratories
HQ: Fujifilm Imaging Colorants, Inc.
233 Cherry Ln
New Castle DE 19720

GEOGRAPHIC SECTION

New Castle - New Castle County (G-9178)

(G-9152)
FUSCO ENTERPRISES (PA)
200 Airport Rd (19720-1520)
PHONE.....................302 328-6251
Anthony Fusco, *Owner*
EMP: 5 **EST:** 2008
SALES (est): 720.89K
SALES (corp-wide): 720.89K **Privately Held**
Web: www.fuscomanagement.com
SIC: 6512 Shopping center, property operation only

(G-9153)
FUSCO MANAGEMENT INC
Also Called: Fusco Enterprises
200 Airport Rd (19720-1520)
P.O. Box 665 (19720-0665)
PHONE.....................302 328-6251
Anthony Fusco, *Pr*
Catherine Fusco, *
EMP: 29 **EST:** 1984
SQ FT: 26,000
SALES (est): 2.17MM **Privately Held**
Web: www.fuscomanagement.com
SIC: 6512 Commercial and industrial building operation

(G-9154)
FUTURE LEGACY OF DANCE
401 Llangollen Blvd (19720-4751)
PHONE.....................610 400-7433
Harold Dorsey, *Prin*
EMP: 6 **EST:** 2014
SALES (est): 50.26K **Privately Held**
SIC: 7911 Dance studios, schools, and halls

(G-9155)
G & E WELDING SUPPLY CO
Also Called: G & E Welding Supply
281 Airport Rd (19720-1540)
PHONE.....................302 322-9353
Wayne E Rapine, *Pr*
Pam S Rapine, *VP*
EMP: 15 **EST:** 1975
SQ FT: 4,000
SALES (est): 3.44MM **Privately Held**
Web: www.geweldingsupply.com
SIC: 5084 5085 Welding machinery and equipment; Welding supplies

(G-9156)
G CUSTOM WORK LLC
186 N Dupont Hwy Ste 27 (19720-3138)
PHONE.....................302 353-2137
Roberto Diaz Ortega, *Managing Member*
EMP: 5 **EST:** 2018
SALES (est): 289.69K **Privately Held**
Web: g-custom-work.business.site
SIC: 7538 General automotive repair shops

(G-9157)
GABY AUTO
425 Stahl Ave (19720-3217)
PHONE.....................856 469-1378
Gabriel Rivera, *Prin*
EMP: 5 **EST:** 2013
SALES (est): 62.49K **Privately Held**
SIC: 7538 General automotive repair shops

(G-9158)
GALMAN GROUP LTD
30 Highland Blvd (19720-6980)
PHONE.....................302 328-8149
EMP: 10
SALES (corp-wide): 24.26MM **Privately Held**
Web: www.galmangroup.com
SIC: 6519 Real property lessors, nec
PA: Galman Group, Ltd.

261 Old York Rd Ste 110
Jenkintown PA 19046
215 886-2000

(G-9159)
GC NEW CASTLE INC
Also Called: Great Clips Hair Cut Salon
1508 Beaver Brook Plz (19720)
PHONE.....................302 544-6128
EMP: 8 **EST:** 2010
SQ FT: 1,600
SALES (est): 61.6K **Privately Held**
SIC: 7231 Unisex hair salons

(G-9160)
GEMINI KUSTOMS LLC
105 Fowler Ct (19720-5409)
PHONE.....................267 318-4121
EMP: 2 **EST:** 2020
SALES (est): 67.05K **Privately Held**
SIC: 2329 Men's and boy's clothing, nec

(G-9161)
GENERAL SERVICE CONTRS LLC
729 Grantham Ln (19720-4897)
PHONE.....................302 220-1946
EMP: 9 **EST:** 2018
SALES (est): 493.04K **Privately Held**
SIC: 1522 Residential construction, nec

(G-9162)
GEO TRANSPORT AUTO EXPORT LLC
235 S Dupont Hwy (19720-4141)
PHONE.....................302 322-9001
EMP: 9 **EST:** 2014
SALES (est): 458.53K **Privately Held**
SIC: 7538 General automotive repair shops

(G-9163)
GEO-TECHNOLOGY ASSOCIATES INC
18 Boulden Cir Ste 36 (19720-3494)
PHONE.....................302 326-2100
Chris Reith, *Brnch Mgr*
EMP: 7
Web: www.gtaeng.com
SIC: 8748 8734 Environmental consultant; Soil analysis
HQ: Geo-Technology Associates Inc
  3445 Box Hll Corp Ctr Dr
  Abingdon MD 21009
  410 515-9446

(G-9164)
GEORGE SCOTT PAVING
502 Isadore Dr (19720-5629)
PHONE.....................302 588-0024
EMP: 5 **EST:** 2018
SALES (est): 61.41K **Privately Held**
SIC: 4213 Trucking, except local

(G-9165)
GEORGETOWN MANOR APARTMENTS
260 Christiana Rd Ofc B4 (19720-2964)
PHONE.....................302 328-6231
Pam Abel, *Mgr*
EMP: 8 **EST:** 2000
SALES (est): 536.28K **Privately Held**
Web: www.thegeorgetownmanor.com
SIC: 6513 Apartment building operators

(G-9166)
GERARDOS MARBLE & GRANITE LLC
314 Bay West Blvd (19720-5195)
PHONE.....................302 344-2150
EMP: 5 **EST:** 2014

SALES (est): 231.13K **Privately Held**
SIC: 5032 Marble building stone

(G-9167)
GIRLS AUTO CLINIC LLC
35 Antioch Ct (19720-3704)
P.O. Box 686 (19710-0686)
PHONE.....................484 679-6394
Patrice Banks, *Pr*
Crystal Lewis, *Managing Member*
EMP: 7 **EST:** 2013
SALES (est): 181.29K **Privately Held**
Web: www.girlsautoclinic.com
SIC: 7538 7231 General automotive repair shops; Cosmetology and personal hygiene salons

(G-9168)
GIVE FROM THE HEART-THE DOROTH
6 Fairhaven Ct (19720-3931)
PHONE.....................302 322-7808
Robin Johnson, *Prin*
EMP: 5 **EST:** 2010
SALES (est): 140K **Privately Held**
SIC: 8641 Civic and social associations

(G-9169)
GLITZY AND GLAMOUR HAIR SALON
265 N Dupont Hwy (19720-6400)
PHONE.....................302 325-9565
EMP: 6 **EST:** 2015
SALES (est): 90.96K **Privately Held**
SIC: 7231 Beauty shops

(G-9170)
GLOBAL LIME & LUMBER CO INC
732 Grantham Ln (19720-4802)
PHONE.....................609 579-1778
James Storm, *Pr*
EMP: 5 **EST:** 2020
SALES (est): 261.83K **Privately Held**
SIC: 5031 7389 Lumber, plywood, and millwork; Business services, nec

(G-9171)
GOLD STAR SERVICES LLC
21a Industrial Blvd (19720)
PHONE.....................610 444-3333
EMP: 7 **EST:** 2012
SALES (est): 359.59K **Privately Held**
SIC: 1711 Heating and air conditioning contractors

(G-9172)
GORDY MANAGEMENT INC
Also Called: Gordy Enterprises
265 N Dupont Hwy Fl 2 (19720-6400)
P.O. Box 687 (19720-0687)
PHONE.....................302 322-3723
Ralph E Gordy Junior, *Pr*
Peter Gordy, *VP*
EMP: 5 **EST:** 1971
SALES (est): 458.65K **Privately Held**
Web: www.gordymanagement.com
SIC: 6512 Commercial and industrial building operation

(G-9173)
GORE FUNERAL SERVICES
Also Called: GORE FUNERAL SERVICES
812 Arthur Springs Ln (19720-8771)
PHONE.....................610 364-9900
Derick Gore, *Owner*
EMP: 7
SALES (corp-wide): 236.17K **Privately Held**
Web: www.gorefuneralservices.com
SIC: 7261 Funeral director
PA: Gore Funeral Services, Llc

406 Marsh Rd
Wilmington DE 19809
610 364-9900

(G-9174)
GOVPLUS LLC
Also Called: GOVPLUS LLC
130 N Dupont Hwy (19720-3102)
PHONE.....................302 322-0525
Jennifer Mckenna, *Brnch Mgr*
EMP: 10
SALES (corp-wide): 9.07B **Publicly Held**
Web: www.govplus.com
SIC: 6022 State commercial banks
HQ: Citizens Bank, National Association
  1 Citizens Plz
  Providence RI 02903

(G-9175)
GRACELAWN MEMORIAL PARK INC (PA)
2220 N Dupont Hwy (19720-6319)
P.O. Box 714 (19720-0714)
PHONE.....................302 654-6158
Lee W Hagenbach, *Pr*
EMP: 24 **EST:** 1934
SQ FT: 5,000
SALES (est): 1.61MM
SALES (corp-wide): 1.61MM **Privately Held**
Web: www.gracelawn.com
SIC: 6553 Cemeteries, real estate operation

(G-9176)
GRAY AUDOGRAPH AGENCY INC
2340 N Dupont Hwy (19720-6327)
P.O. Box 726 (19720-0726)
PHONE.....................302 658-1700
John P Collins, *Pr*
John P Collins, *Pr*
Paul J Collins, *Treas*
Pea Marshall, *Sec*
EMP: 12 **EST:** 1966
SQ FT: 8,000
SALES (est): 296.88K **Privately Held**
SIC: 1731 1799 5999 Telephone and telephone equipment installation; Office furniture installation; Business machines and equipment

(G-9177)
GRAYBAR ELECTRIC COMPANY INC
43 Boulden Blvd (19720-2082)
PHONE.....................302 322-2200
Robert Gibson, *Mgr*
EMP: 57
SALES (corp-wide): 8.77B **Privately Held**
Web: www.graybar.com
SIC: 5063 Electrical supplies, nec
PA: Graybar Electric Company, Inc.
  34 N Meramec Ave
  Saint Louis MO 63105
  855 347-2839

(G-9178)
GREAT I AM PROD STUDIOS INC
Also Called: Great I AM
25 Rose Ln (19720-2140)
P.O. Box 30412 (19805-7412)
PHONE.....................302 463-2483
Candy Watkins, *CEO*
EMP: 5 **EST:** 1999
SALES (est): 205.5K **Privately Held**
Web: www.thegreatiamproductionstudio.com
SIC: 7389 Recording studio, noncommercial records

New Castle - New Castle County (G-9179)

GEOGRAPHIC SECTION

(G-9179)
GREEN PEST MANAGEMENT LLC
18 Boulden Cir Ste 22 (19720-3494)
PHONE.....................302 777-2390
Justin Butler, *Managing Member*
EMP: 14 **EST:** 2014
SALES (est): 614.4K Privately Held
Web: www.greenpestmgmt.com
SIC: 7342 Pest control in structures

(G-9180)
GREGGO & FERRARA INC (PA)
4048 New Castle Ave (19720-1498)
PHONE.....................302 658-5241
EMP: 200 **EST:** 1946
SALES (est): 36.39MM
SALES (corp-wide): 36.39MM Privately Held
Web: www.houndspound.com
SIC: 1611 1622 1542 General contractor, highway and street construction; Bridge construction; Commercial and office building contractors

(G-9181)
GRINDSTONE AVIATION LLC
13 1/2 Penns Way (19720-2437)
PHONE.....................302 324-1993
EMP: 7 **EST:** 1998
SALES (est): 86.08K Privately Held
SIC: 3721 Aircraft

(G-9182)
GSZ ASSOCIATES INC
7 Dunsinane Dr (19720-2316)
PHONE.....................302 824-2572
Glenn Prichard, *Pr*
Shelbie Prichard, *Treas*
EMP: 5 **EST:** 2016
SALES (est): 100.09K Privately Held
SIC: 1521 Single-family home remodeling, additions, and repairs

(G-9183)
GUARDIAN CONSTRUCTION CO INC (HQ)
1617 Matassino Rd (19720-2086)
P.O. Box 11607 (19850-1607)
PHONE.....................302 834-1000
Nona J Cunane, *Ch Bd*
Joseph Cunane Junior, *Ex VP*
Bradley C Leto, *
Paul Dimino, *
Teresa Miller, *
EMP: 90 **EST:** 1976
SQ FT: 50,000
SALES (est): 32.2MM Privately Held
Web: www.guardianco.com
SIC: 1542 Commercial and office building, new construction
PA: Guardian Companies, Inc.
   101 Rogers Rd Ste 101 # 101
   Wilmington DE 19801

(G-9184)
GURUKRUPA INC
Also Called: Knights Inn
133 S Dupont Hwy (19720-4127)
PHONE.....................302 328-6691
Raman Patel, *Pr*
Amball Patel, *Stockholder*
EMP: 6 **EST:** 1961
SQ FT: 5,400
SALES (est): 226.28K Privately Held
Web: www.relaxinn-de.com
SIC: 7011 Hotels and motels

(G-9185)
H & R BLOCK
Also Called: H & R Block
287 Christiana Rd Ste 24 (19720-2978)
PHONE.....................302 324-1040
EMP: 18 **EST:** 2015
SALES (est): 18.45K Privately Held
Web: www.hrblock.ca
SIC: 7291 Tax return preparation services

(G-9186)
H & R BLOCK INC
Also Called: H & R Block
196 Penn Mart Shopping Ctr Unit 11 (19720-4209)
PHONE.....................302 328-7320
Bernie Brittingham, *Brnch Mgr*
EMP: 5
SALES (corp-wide): 3.47B Publicly Held
Web: www.hrblock.com
SIC: 7291 Tax return preparation services
PA: H & R Block, Inc.
   1 H And R Block Way
   Kansas City MO 64105
   816 854-3000

(G-9187)
H & R BLOCK INC
Also Called: H & R Block
232 New Castle Ave (19720-2701)
PHONE.....................302 652-3286
Bernie Brittingham, *Mgr*
EMP: 5
SALES (corp-wide): 3.47B Publicly Held
Web: www.hrblock.com
SIC: 7291 8244 Tax return preparation services; Business and secretarial schools
PA: H & R Block, Inc.
   1 H And R Block Way
   Kansas City MO 64105
   816 854-3000

(G-9188)
H & R HEATING & AC
7 King Ct (19720-1519)
PHONE.....................302 323-9919
Rodney Husfelt, *Pr*
Charles Reeve, *
EMP: 40 **EST:** 1995
SALES (est): 4.2MM Privately Held
Web: www.newcastlehvacservice.com
SIC: 1711 Warm air heating and air conditioning contractor

(G-9189)
H T G CONSULTING LLC
2 Penns Way Ste 300 (19720-2407)
PHONE.....................302 322-4100
EMP: 5 **EST:** 1998
SALES (est): 452.15K Privately Held
SIC: 6531 Real estate agents and managers

(G-9190)
H&H SERVICES ELECTRICAL CONTRS
507 Sterling Ave (19720-4780)
PHONE.....................302 373-4950
James J Howard, *Prin*
EMP: 5 **EST:** 2017
SALES (est): 174.54K Privately Held
SIC: 7539 Electrical services

(G-9191)
HAINES CONTRACTING INC
1055 Lower Twin Lane Rd (19720-5502)
PHONE.....................443 877-7103
EMP: 6 **EST:** 2019
SALES (est): 245.01K Privately Held
Web: www.hainescontracting.org
SIC: 1799 Special trade contractors, nec

(G-9192)
HAIR EXPERIENCE
11 Calwell Dr (19720-4211)
PHONE.....................302 293-0359
Edtrina Jones, *Prin*
EMP: 5 **EST:** 2010
SALES (est): 53.18K Privately Held
Web: www.thehairexperiencedelaware.com
SIC: 7231 Hairdressers

(G-9193)
HAIR SENSATIONS INC
55 Herbert Dr (19720-3231)
PHONE.....................302 731-0920
Renee Greenlee, *Pr*
EMP: 7 **EST:** 1976
SQ FT: 1,600
SALES (est): 145.28K Privately Held
Web: www.hairsensationsinc.com
SIC: 7231 Hairdressers

(G-9194)
HANDS HEALING MASSAGE DAY SPA
42 Reads Way (19720-1612)
PHONE.....................302 689-3183
Sonya Johnson, *Prin*
EMP: 6 **EST:** 2018
SALES (est): 22.18K Privately Held
SIC: 8049 Massage Therapist

(G-9195)
HANDY LOGISTICS LLC
319 Elizabeth Sweetbriar Ln (19720-8757)
PHONE.....................570 905-4173
Kathi Handy, *Managing Member*
EMP: 2 **EST:** 2021
SALES (est): 307.5K Privately Held
SIC: 3537 7389 Trucks, tractors, loaders, carriers, and similar equipment; Business Activities at Non-Commercial Site

(G-9196)
HARDCORE CMPSTES OPRATIONS LLC
Also Called: Hardcore Composites
618 Lambson Ln (19720-2187)
PHONE.....................302 442-5900
Scott Hemphill, *Pt*
EMP: 17 **EST:** 1985
SQ FT: 108,000
SALES (est): 403.96K Privately Held
Web: hardcore-composites-operations.sbcontract.com
SIC: 3441 8711 Fabricated structural metal for bridges; Engineering services

(G-9197)
HARRISON HSE CMNTY PRGRAMS INC
6 Halcyon Dr (19720-1239)
PHONE.....................302 427-8438
Lateasa L Scott, *Pr*
EMP: 5 **EST:** 1991
SQ FT: 18,500
SALES (est): 2.06MM Privately Held
SIC: 8322 Community center

(G-9198)
HARRY L ADAMS INC
23 Parkway Cir Ste 14 (19720-4019)
PHONE.....................302 328-5268
Lee Adams, *Pr*
EMP: 6 **EST:** 1955
SALES (est): 498.26K Privately Held
SIC: 1711 Warm air heating and air conditioning contractor

(G-9199)
HARRYMRMAX LGSTICS CRIER SVCS
26 Bellecor Dr Ste B (19720-2188)
P.O. Box 10364 (19850-0364)
PHONE.....................302 784-5578
EMP: 5 **EST:** 2010
SALES (est): 121.72K Privately Held
SIC: 4789 4215 Cargo loading and unloading services; Courier services, except by air

(G-9200)
HARTLE BRIAN STATE FARM AGENCY
Also Called: State Farm Insurance
239 Christiana Rd Ste C (19720-2907)
PHONE.....................302 322-1741
Brian Hartle, *Owner*
EMP: 5 **EST:** 2007
SALES (est): 491.86K Privately Held
Web: www.brianhartle.com
SIC: 6411 Insurance agents and brokers

(G-9201)
HARVEY DEVELOPMENT CO
29 E Commons Blvd Ste 100 (19720-1736)
PHONE.....................302 323-9300
Edgar Thomas Harvey Iii, *Pr*
Debra Harvey, *
EMP: 20 **EST:** 1993
SALES (est): 399.41K Privately Held
SIC: 8741 6531 Management services; Real estate agents and managers

(G-9202)
HARVEY MACK SALES & SVC INC (PA)
Also Called: Harvey Truck Center
29 E Commons Blvd Ste 300 (19720-1739)
PHONE.....................302 324-8340
TOLL FREE: 800
Debrah Layton-harvey, *Pr*
Jeffrey Layton, *
EMP: 50 **EST:** 1990
SQ FT: 34,000
SALES (est): 9.26MM Privately Held
Web: www.harveytruckcenter.com
SIC: 5012 5013 5511 Trailers for trucks, new and used; Truck parts and accessories; Pickups, new and used

(G-9203)
HEALING ARTS LLC
25 Jay Dr (19720-1717)
PHONE.....................302 530-9152
Susan Brown, *Prin*
EMP: 6 **EST:** 2017
SALES (est): 53.45K Privately Held
SIC: 8049 Offices of health practitioner

(G-9204)
HEART 2 HEART SERVICES LLC
442 Pigeon View Ln (19720-7686)
PHONE.....................302 293-0124
Christina Crawford, *Managing Member*
EMP: 6
SALES (est): 79.97K Privately Held
SIC: 8082 Home health care services

(G-9205)
HEAVY EQUIPMENT RENTAL INC
Also Called: Corrado Fleet Services
218 Marsh Ln (19720-1175)
PHONE.....................302 654-5716
Frank L Corrado, *Pr*
Joseph J Corrado Senior, *VP*
EMP: 17 **EST:** 1984
SALES (est): 2.49MM Privately Held

GEOGRAPHIC SECTION

SIC: 7353 7699 Heavy construction equipment rental; Construction equipment repair

(G-9206)
HELEN WILLIAMS INC
Also Called: Helen's Psychic Readings
179 S Dupont Hwy (19720-4140)
PHONE.....................302 328-9656
Helen Williams, *Pr*
EMP: 5 **EST:** 1992
SALES (est): 64K **Privately Held**
SIC: 7299 Massage parlor

(G-9207)
HELP IS ON WAY
211 Llangollen Blvd (19720-4711)
PHONE.....................302 328-4510
Mary Graybeal, *Prin*
EMP: 5 **EST:** 2011
SALES (est): 52.6K **Privately Held**
SIC: 8399 Fund raising organization, non-fee basis

(G-9208)
HELPING HANDS CHILD CARE
4 Capo Ln (19720-7674)
PHONE.....................302 438-1656
EMP: 8 **EST:** 2019
SALES (est): 19.32K **Privately Held**
Web: www.helpinghandsfamilychildcare.com
SIC: 8351 Preschool center

(G-9209)
HENRY M MCELDUFF
117 Rodney Dr (19720-2763)
PHONE.....................302 656-5561
Henry M Mcelduff, *Prin*
EMP: 5 **EST:** 2010
SALES (est): 90K **Privately Held**
SIC: 1721 Painting and paper hanging

(G-9210)
HERMAN/TURNER GROUP
2 Penns Way Ste 300 (19720-2407)
PHONE.....................302 322-4100
EMP: 7 **EST:** 2019
SALES (est): 242.75K **Privately Held**
Web: www.htgconsultants.com
SIC: 6531 Appraiser, real estate

(G-9211)
HERNANDEZ & SONS
308 Elwood Pl (19720-3657)
PHONE.....................302 765-8476
Saul Hernandez, *Prin*
EMP: 5 **EST:** 2017
SALES (est): 56.76K **Privately Held**
SIC: 1799 Special trade contractors, nec

(G-9212)
HERTZ CORPORATION
Also Called: Hertz
131 N Dupont Hwy (19720-3135)
PHONE.....................302 428-0637
EMP: 23
SALES (corp-wide): 9.37B **Publicly Held**
Web: www.hertz.com
SIC: 7514 Rent-a-car service
HQ: The Hertz Corporation
    8501 Williams Rd
    Estero FL 33928
    239 301-7000

(G-9213)
HERTZ CORPORATION
Also Called: Hertz
120 Old Churchmans Rd (19720-3116)
PHONE.....................302 428-0637
EMP: 23
SALES (corp-wide): 9.37B **Publicly Held**
Web: www.hertz.com
SIC: 7514 Rent-a-car service
HQ: The Hertz Corporation
    8501 Williams Rd
    Estero FL 33928
    239 301-7000

(G-9214)
HILLMAN/DOVER LTD PARTNERSHIP
100 W Cmmons Blvd Ste 303 (19720)
PHONE.....................302 655-4133
EMP: 5 **EST:** 2015
SALES (est): 119.69K **Privately Held**
SIC: 6733 Private estate, personal investment and vacation fund trusts

(G-9215)
HITRUST LLC
Also Called: Hitrust Hair
1140 River Rd (19720-5106)
PHONE.....................302 525-6223
EMP: 9 **EST:** 2017
SALES (est): 142.11K
SALES (corp-wide): 3.93MM **Privately Held**
Web: www.shophitrusthair.com
SIC: 7231 Hairdressers
PA: Qingdao Hitrust Import And Export Co., Ltd.
    Rm A2705, Top Yihe Int'l, No.10
    Hongkong Middle Road, Shinan Dis
    Qingdao SD 26607
    53285039391

(G-9216)
HOLMAN MOVING SYSTEMS LLC (PA)
Also Called: Holman Moving Systems
20 E Commons Blvd (19720-1734)
P.O. Box 3043 (19804-0043)
PHONE.....................302 323-9000
TOLL FREE: 800
◆ **EMP:** 50 **EST:** 1885
SQ FT: 60,000
SALES (est): 9.55MM
SALES (corp-wide): 9.55MM **Privately Held**
Web: www.holmanmoving.com
SIC: 4213 4214 Trucking, except local; Local trucking with storage

(G-9217)
HOLMES SMITH CONSULTING SVCS
19 Lambson Ln (19720-2118)
PHONE.....................302 407-6691
EMP: 5 **EST:** 2015
SALES (est): 104.24K **Privately Held**
Web: www.holmessmithconsulting.com
SIC: 8999 Scientific consulting

(G-9218)
HOME DEPOT USA INC
Also Called: Home Depot, The
138 Sunset Blvd (19720-4100)
PHONE.....................302 395-1260
Rob Garbacz, *Mgr*
EMP: 115
SALES (corp-wide): 157.4B **Publicly Held**
Web: www.homedepot.com
SIC: 5211 7359 Home centers; Tool rental
HQ: Home Depot U.S.A., Inc.
    2455 Paces Ferry Rd Se
    Atlanta GA 30339

(G-9219)
HOME PRMNT PEST CTRL CMPNIES I
Also Called: Paramount Pest Control
769 S Dupont Hwy (19720-4609)
PHONE.....................302 894-9201
Jeff Fuge, *Mgr*
EMP: 6
SALES (corp-wide): 55.27MM **Privately Held**
Web: www.homeparamount.com
SIC: 7342 Pest control in structures
PA: Home Paramount Pest Control Companies, Inc.
    2011 Rock Spring Rd
    Forest Hill MD 21050
    410 638-0800

(G-9220)
HONEYWELL INTERNATIONAL INC
Also Called: Honeywell
3 Boulden Cir (19720-3400)
PHONE.....................302 322-4071
EMP: 2
SALES (corp-wide): 35.47B **Publicly Held**
Web: www.honeywell.com
SIC: 3724 Aircraft engines and engine parts
PA: Honeywell International Inc.
    855 S Mint St
    Charlotte NC 28202
    704 627-6200

(G-9221)
HOUSE OF KINGS INC ✿
1511 N Dupont Hwy (19720-1900)
PHONE.....................302 319-8724
EMP: 6 **EST:** 2023
SALES (est): 64.59K **Privately Held**
SIC: 7241 Barber shops

(G-9222)
HOWARD WESTON SENIOR CENTER
1 Bassett Ave Ste 1 (19720-2088)
PHONE.....................302 328-6425
EMP: 5 **EST:** 1978
SALES (est): 838.33K **Privately Held**
Web: www.westonseniorcenter.org
SIC: 8322 Senior citizens' center or association

(G-9223)
HSBC BANK USA NATIONAL ASSN
90 Christiana Rd (19720-3118)
PHONE.....................800 975-4722
EMP: 5
SALES (corp-wide): 93.79B **Privately Held**
Web: www.hsbc.com
SIC: 6029 Commercial banks, nec
HQ: Hsbc Bank Usa, National Association
    1800 Tysons Blvd Ste 560
    Mc Lean VA 22102

(G-9224)
HYPE HAIR LLC
550 S Dupont Hwy Apt 8i (19720-5193)
PHONE.....................302 898-3145
EMP: 6 **EST:** 2017
SALES (est): 42.26K **Privately Held**
Web: www.mailchi.mp
SIC: 7231 Hairdressers

(G-9225)
I AM MY SISTERS KEEPER
207 Highland Blvd Apt D (19720-3984)
PHONE.....................302 304-1070
Melody Phillips, *Prin*
EMP: 8 **EST:** 2017
SALES (est): 40.5K **Privately Held**
Web: www.iammsk.org
SIC: 8699 Charitable organization

(G-9226)
IAA INC
Also Called: IAA, INC.
417 Old Airport Rd (19720-1001)
PHONE.....................302 322-1808
Paul Weeks, *Brnch Mgr*
EMP: 6
SALES (corp-wide): 1.73B **Privately Held**
Web: www.iaai.com
SIC: 5012 Automobile auction
HQ: Insurance Auto Auctions, Inc.
    2 Westbrook Corp Ctr Fl 1
    Westchester IL 60154
    708 492-7000

(G-9227)
IBG ENTERPRISE INC
9 Nieole Ave (19720-1206)
PHONE.....................302 494-5017
EMP: 6 **EST:** 2011
SALES (est): 180.92K **Privately Held**
SIC: 8999 Music arranging and composing

(G-9228)
ICONIX LLC
34 Dunsinane Dr (19720-2323)
PHONE.....................215 850-9337
Kamil Dixon, *Prin*
EMP: 5 **EST:** 2016
SALES (est): 55.22K **Privately Held**
SIC: 6799 Investors, nec

(G-9229)
II EXTREME ENTERTAINMENT
100 Schafer Blvd (19720-4722)
P.O. Box 293 (19938-0293)
PHONE.....................302 389-8525
Warner Knowland, *Owner*
EMP: 7 **EST:** 2008
SALES (est): 1.46K **Privately Held**
SIC: 7911 Dance studio and school

(G-9230)
INDUSTRIAL PHYSICS INC (HQ)
Also Called: Testing Machines
40 Mccullough Dr (19720-2227)
PHONE.....................302 613-5600
Barry Lyon, *CEO*
Lance Reisman, *Ch Bd*
Matthew Weinmann, *Pr*
EMP: 25 **EST:** 2014
SALES (est): 189.36MM **Publicly Held**
Web: www.industrialphysics.com
SIC: 3829 Testing equipment: abrasion, shearing strength, etc.
PA: Kkr & Co. Inc.
    30 Hudson Yards
    New York NY 10001

(G-9231)
INDUSTRIAL PRODUCTS OF DEL
153 S Dupont Hwy (19720-4127)
PHONE.....................302 328-6648
John E Dougherty, *Pr*
Timothy J Dougherty, *VP*
EMP: 4 **EST:** 1959
SALES (est): 966.27K **Privately Held**
SIC: 5085 5082 3441 Industrial supplies; General construction machinery and equipment; Fabricated structural metal
PA: Benz Hydraulics, Inc.
    153 S Dupont Hwy
    New Castle DE 19720

(G-9232)
INDUSTRIAL STL STRUCTURES INC
4049 New Castle Ave (19720-1414)
PHONE.....................302 275-8892
EMP: 30 **EST:** 2012
SALES (est): 3.06MM **Privately Held**
SIC: 5051 Steel

New Castle - New Castle County (G-9233) — GEOGRAPHIC SECTION

(G-9233)
INDUSTRIAL VALVES & FITTINGS
Also Called: I V F
55 Mccullough Dr (19720-2080)
PHONE..................302 326-2494
Julio C Daponte Senior, Pr
Maureen L Daponte, VP
EMP: 14 EST: 1981
SQ FT: 10,000
SALES (est): 4.54MM Privately Held
Web: www.ivfinc.com
SIC: 3052 5085 Rubber and plastics hose and beltings; Hose, belting, and packing

(G-9234)
INSTA SIGNS PLUS INC
107 J And M Dr (19720-3147)
PHONE..................302 324-8800
Anthony Pettoruto, Pr
David Pettoruto, VP
EMP: 18 EST: 1991
SQ FT: 4,500
SALES (est): 1.42MM Privately Held
Web: www.instasignsplus.com
SIC: 3993 Signs, not made in custom sign painting shops

(G-9235)
INSURANCE & FINANCIAL SVCS INC
Also Called: Nationwide
100 W Commons Blvd Ste 302 (19720)
PHONE..................302 239-5895
Richard H Lapenta, CEO
John R Davis, VP
EMP: 20 EST: 1932
SALES (est): 4.5MM Privately Held
Web: www.cbmins.com
SIC: 6411 Insurance agents, nec

(G-9236)
INTEGRATED HOME LLC
12 Penns Way (19720-2414)
PHONE..................302 656-1624
Jeffrey Brooks, Prin
EMP: 5 EST: 2010
SALES (est): 300.35K Privately Held
Web: www.ihomellc.com
SIC: 7374 Computer graphics service

(G-9237)
INTEGRATED TECH SYSTEMS LLC
42 Reads Way (19720-1649)
PHONE..................302 613-2111
Daniela Santos, Dir
EMP: 5 EST: 2014
SALES (est): 143.85K Privately Held
Web: www.integratedtechsystems.com
SIC: 7382 Security systems services

(G-9238)
INTEREBAR FABRICATORS LLC
20 Davidson Ln (19720-2214)
PHONE..................513 310-1782
Chris Motley, Brnch Mgr
EMP: 14
SALES (corp-wide): 2.43MM Privately Held
Web: www.interebar.com
SIC: 3441 Fabricated structural metal
PA: Interebar Fabricators, Llc
10800 Biscayne Blvd # 830
Miami FL 33161
305 705-0208

(G-9239)
INTERIM HEALTH CARE
Also Called: Interim Services
2 Reads Way Ste 209 (19720-1630)
PHONE..................302 322-2743
Lynda Kupishke, Pr
EMP: 6 EST: 1966
SALES (est): 767.78K Privately Held
Web: www.interimhealthcare.com
SIC: 8082 Home health care services

(G-9240)
INTERNTNAL BRTHD ELEC WKRS LCA
Also Called: LOCAL 313 IBEW ELECTRICIANS
814 W Basin Rd (19720-1708)
PHONE..................302 328-0773
Paul F Campbell, Pr
Douglas Drumman, Pr
EMP: 6 EST: 1960
SALES (est): 2.39MM Privately Held
Web: www.ibew313.org
SIC: 8631 Labor union

(G-9241)
IPM INC (HQ)
247 Old Churchmans Rd (19720-1529)
PHONE..................302 328-4030
EMP: 13 EST: 2010
SALES (est): 797.86K Publicly Held
SIC: 3296 2952 Fiberglass insulation; Asphalt felts and coatings
PA: Owens Corning
1 Owens Corning Pkwy
Toledo OH 43659

(G-9242)
IRIDESCENT DANCE ALLIANCE ASSN
187 Penn Mart Shopg Ctr (19720-4208)
PHONE..................302 244-8570
Amanda Pollard, Prin
EMP: 5 EST: 2020
SALES (est): 56.93K Privately Held
SIC: 8699 Charitable organization

(G-9243)
ISAAC FAIR CORPORATION
100 W Commons Blvd Ste 400 (19720)
PHONE..................302 324-8015
EMP: 4
SALES (corp-wide): 1.51B Publicly Held
Web: www.fico.com
SIC: 7372 3575 Operating systems computer software; Computer terminals
PA: Fair Isaac Corporation
5 W Mendenhall St Ste 105
Bozeman MT 59715
406 982-7276

(G-9244)
ISTORAGE NEW CASTLE
4016 N Dupont Hwy (19720-6314)
PHONE..................302 396-6224
EMP: 7 EST: 2018
SALES (est): 104.8K Privately Held
Web: www.istorage.com
SIC: 4225 General warehousing and storage

(G-9245)
ITSKINS AMERICAS INC ◆
257 Old Churchmans Rd (19720-1529)
PHONE..................805 422-6700
Christopher Jakobuco, CEO
EMP: 6 EST: 2022
SALES (est): 270.3K Privately Held
SIC: 3089 7389 Cases, plastics; Business services, nec

(G-9246)
J CHANCE PRODUCTIONS
5 Stevens Ave (19720-4046)
PHONE..................302 322-2251
Jabari Chancey, Prin
EMP: 5 EST: 2010
SALES (est): 116.14K Privately Held
SIC: 7822 Motion picture and tape distribution

(G-9247)
J J WHITE INC
250 Edwards Ave (19720-4875)
PHONE..................215 722-1000
James J White Iv, Pr
EMP: 672
Web: www.jjwhiteinc.com
SIC: 1711 Mechanical contractor
HQ: J. J. White, Inc.
5500 Bingham St
Philadelphia PA 19120
215 722-1000

(G-9248)
J R FORSHEY DMD PA
702 E Basin Rd Ste 1 (19720-4263)
PHONE..................302 322-0245
James R Forshey D.m.d., Pr
Jennifer Greenley D.d.s., VP
EMP: 10 EST: 1977
SALES (est): 486.04K Privately Held
Web: www.forsheygreenleydentistry.com
SIC: 8021 Dentists' office

(G-9249)
J&J FLEET SERVICE
729 Grantham Ln Ste 7 (19720-4898)
PHONE..................484 632-1647
Jeremy Wertz, Prin
EMP: 12 EST: 2017
SALES (est): 367.66K Privately Held
Web: www.jjfleetservice.com
SIC: 7538 General automotive repair shops

(G-9250)
JACKS CLEANING SERVICES LLC
803 Quinn Ct (19720-5679)
PHONE..................302 494-8887
EMP: 5 EST: 2018
SALES (est): 77.04K Privately Held
SIC: 7699 Cleaning services

(G-9251)
JACKSON ED HOME IMPROVEMENTS
45 Skyline Dr (19720-2924)
PHONE..................302 322-1566
Edward Jackson, Prin
EMP: 5 EST: 2011
SALES (est): 106K Privately Held
SIC: 1521 General remodeling, single-family houses

(G-9252)
JAMES SUTTON
Also Called: Training Center, The
807 Churchmans Road Ext (19720-3152)
PHONE..................302 328-5438
James Sutton, Owner
EMP: 10 EST: 1986
SALES (est): 1.08MM Privately Held
Web: www.tcgym.com
SIC: 5091 Fitness equipment and supplies

(G-9253)
JATC LOCAL UNION 313
814 W Basin Rd (19720-1708)
PHONE..................302 322-5089
EMP: 7 EST: 2018
SALES (est): 226.15K Privately Held
Web: www.ibew313.org
SIC: 8631 Labor union

(G-9254)
JAY AMBE INC
Also Called: Days Inn
3 Memorial Dr (19720-1310)
PHONE..................302 654-5400
Pramod Patel, Pr
EMP: 10 EST: 1989
SQ FT: 50,000
SALES (est): 2.6MM Privately Held
Web: www.budgetinnnewcastle.com
SIC: 7011 Motels

(G-9255)
JAY DEVI INC
Also Called: Fairfield Inn Stes Wlmngton New
2117 N Dupont Hwy (19720-6308)
PHONE..................302 777-4700
Mehul Patel, Pr
Chetan Patel, Prin
Dhruv Jani, Prin
EMP: 45 EST: 2009
SALES (est): 496.05K Privately Held
Web: fairfield.marriott.com
SIC: 7011 Motels

(G-9256)
JBS KITCHEN LLC
123 Hunn Rd (19720-1807)
PHONE..................302 487-3830
EMP: 7
SALES (est): 67.43K Privately Held
SIC: 5812 7389 Eating places; Business services, nec

(G-9257)
JEFFREY BOWERSOX
290 Churchmans Rd (19720-3110)
PHONE..................302 322-6933
Jeffrey Bowersox, Prin
EMP: 6 EST: 2010
SALES (est): 116.02K Privately Held
SIC: 0742 Veterinarian, animal specialties

(G-9258)
JENNIFER SELLITTO-PENOZA LCSW
15 Angola Rd (19720-3518)
PHONE..................302 328-4936
J Sellitto-penoza Lcsw, Owner
EMP: 7 EST: 2013
SALES (est): 54.04K Privately Held
SIC: 8322 Social worker

(G-9259)
JERRYS HANDYMAN LLC
36 Lanford Rd (19720-3836)
PHONE..................302 357-1589
Gerardo Padilla, Prin
EMP: 5 EST: 2017
SALES (est): 34.16K Privately Held
SIC: 7299 Handyman service

(G-9260)
JM GENERAL CONTRACTOR
152 Freedom Trl (19720-3850)
PHONE..................302 464-9730
Rojas Juan Alvardo, Prin
EMP: 5 EST: 2016
SALES (est): 56.76K Privately Held
Web: www.jmgeneralcontractors.com
SIC: 1799 Special trade contractors, nec

(G-9261)
JOE COOVER CONTRACTING INC
306 Llangollen Blvd (19720-4750)
PHONE..................302 540-5806
Joe Coover, Pr
EMP: 5 EST: 2015
SALES (est): 89.6K Privately Held
SIC: 1799 Special trade contractors, nec

GEOGRAPHIC SECTION
New Castle - New Castle County (G-9287)

(G-9262)
JOHN R SEIBERLICH INC
Also Called: Seiberlich Trane
66 Southgate Blvd (19720-2068)
PHONE.................................302 356-2400
  John Seiberlich, *Pr*
  Lorraine Seiberlich, *
  Ronald Hess, *
EMP: 72 **EST:** 1960
SQ FT: 24,000
SALES (est): 23.02MM **Privately Held**
Web: www.seiberlich.com
SIC: 5063 5065 5075 5078   Electronic wire and cable; Capacitors, electronic; Air filters; Commercial refrigeration equipment

(G-9263)
JOHNSON CNTRLS SEC SLTIONS LLC
18 Boulden Cir Ste 24 (19720-3494)
PHONE.................................302 328-2800
  Pat Feeley, *Mgr*
EMP: 66
Web: datasource.johnsoncontrols.com
SIC: 7382   Burglar alarm maintenance and monitoring
HQ: Johnson Controls Security Solutions Llc
  6600 Congress Ave
  Boca Raton FL 33487
  561 264-2071

(G-9264)
JORC INDUSTRIAL LLC
1146 River Rd Ste 100 (19720-5106)
PHONE.................................302 395-0310
▲ **EMP:** 7 **EST:** 1996
SQ FT: 4,500
SALES (est): 1.38MM **Privately Held**
Web: www.jorc.com
SIC: 5084   Compressors, except air conditioning

(G-9265)
JOSEPH DEVANE ENTERPRISES INC
Also Called: Allstate
240 S Dupont Hwy Ste 200 (19720-8403)
PHONE.................................302 703-0493
  Joseph Devane, *Pr*
EMP: 10 **EST:** 2003
SALES (est): 1.09MM **Privately Held**
SIC: 1521   Single-family home remodeling, additions, and repairs

(G-9266)
JOSEPH J SHEERAN INC (HQ)
Also Called: Sheeran Direct
71 Southgate Blvd (19720-2069)
PHONE.................................302 324-0200
  Peggy Sheeran, *Pr*
  Mitchell R Dickinson, *
  Linda K Dickinson, *
  Sean Malone, *
◆ **EMP:** 50 **EST:** 1964
SQ FT: 150,000
SALES (est): 9.85MM **Privately Held**
SIC: 7331 7389 8742 7371   Direct mail advertising services; Telemarketing services ; Management consulting services; Custom computer programming services
PA: Echodata Group
  121 N Shirk Rd
  New Holland PA 17557

(G-9267)
JOSEPH RIZZO & SONS CNSTR CO
13 Rizzo Ave (19720-2139)
PHONE.................................302 656-8136
  Anthony A Rizzo, *Pr*
  Anthony Rizzo, *
  John Rizzo, *
  Mark Rizzo, *
EMP: 30 **EST:** 1942
SQ FT: 3,000
SALES (est): 2.25MM **Privately Held**
Web: www.jrizzoandsons.com
SIC: 1741   Stone masonry

(G-9268)
JOSEPH T HARDY & SON INC (PA)
Also Called: Hardy Environmental Services
425 Old Airport Rd (19720-1001)
PHONE.................................302 328-9457
  Jack J Hardy, *Pr*
  John J Hardy, *
  Robert P Hopkins, *
EMP: 39 **EST:** 1921
SQ FT: 2,000
SALES (est): 9.77MM
SALES (corp-wide): 9.77MM **Privately Held**
Web: www.hardyservices.com
SIC: 1623 8748   Underground utilities contractor; Environmental consultant

(G-9269)
JRS HOMES LLC
439 Wynthorpe Rd (19720-8845)
PHONE.................................302 544-5911
  Donald Solomon, *Prin*
EMP: 5 **EST:** 2010
SALES (est): 76.45K **Privately Held**
SIC: 1521   Single-family housing construction

(G-9270)
JULIO DRYWALL INC
851 Cornstalk Dr (19720-7659)
PHONE.................................302 218-8596
EMP: 5 **EST:** 2010
SALES (est): 207.91K **Privately Held**
SIC: 1742   Drywall

(G-9271)
JUNE MEDICAL USA INC
257 Old Churchmans Rd (19720-1529)
PHONE.................................302 408-0084
  Angela Spang, *CEO*
EMP: 5 **EST:** 2019
SALES (est): 100K **Privately Held**
Web: www.junemedical.com
SIC: 5047   Medical equipment and supplies

(G-9272)
K AND C CLEANING SERVICES
59 Landers Ln (19720-2041)
PHONE.................................302 897-8661
EMP: 5 **EST:** 2012
SALES (est): 45.2K **Privately Held**
SIC: 7699   Cleaning services

(G-9273)
K V ASSOCIATES INC
Also Called: Family Care Associates
191 Christiana Rd Ste 3 (19720-3024)
PHONE.................................302 322-1353
  Khaja G Yezdani, *Pr*
  Doctor Vijaya Yezdani, *VP*
EMP: 7 **EST:** 1981
SALES (est): 798.3K **Privately Held**
SIC: 8011   General and family practice, physician/surgeon

(G-9274)
KAESER COMPRESSORS INC
77 Mccullough Dr Ste 3 (19720-2079)
PHONE.................................410 242-8793
  Dan Leviness, *Brnch Mgr*
EMP: 8
SALES (corp-wide): 1.42B **Privately Held**
Web: us.kaeser.com
SIC: 5084   Compressors, except air conditioning
HQ: Kaeser Compressors, Inc.
  511 Sigma Dr
  Fredericksburg VA 22408
  540 898-5500

(G-9275)
KATY AUKAMP MEM FOUNDATION
245 Riveredge Dr (19720-8705)
PHONE.................................302 328-6446
  Jack Aukamp, *Prin*
EMP: 6 **EST:** 2010
SALES (est): 92.76K **Privately Held**
SIC: 8641   Civic and social associations

(G-9276)
KEEN COMPRESSED GAS CO
4063 New Castle Ave (19720-1497)
PHONE.................................302 594-4545
  Bryan Keen, *Brnch Mgr*
EMP: 40
SALES (corp-wide): 38.14MM **Privately Held**
Web: www.keengas.com
SIC: 5085 5169 5984 2813   Welding supplies ; Gases, compressed and liquefied; Propane gas, bottled; Industrial gases
PA: Keen Compressed Gas Co.
  101 Rogers Rd Ste 200
  Wilmington DE 19801
  302 594-4545

(G-9277)
KEEN COMPRESSED GAS CO (PA)
Also Called: Keen Cmprssed Gas - Wilmington
4063 New Castle Ave (19720-1497)
P.O. Box 15146 (19850-5146)
PHONE.................................302 594-4545
  Bryan Keen, *Pr*
  Peter Giorgi, *Pr*
  Carol Giorgi, *Sec*
EMP: 18 **EST:** 2019
SQ FT: 3,500
SALES (est): 5.68MM
SALES (corp-wide): 5.68MM **Privately Held**
Web: www.keengas.com
SIC: 2813   Industrial gases

(G-9278)
KELLER WILLIAMS REALTY CENTRAL
Also Called: Keller Williams Realtors
80 Christiana Rd (19720-3118)
PHONE.................................302 465-7562
EMP: 5 **EST:** 2019
SALES (est): 72.84K **Privately Held**
Web: www.kw.com
SIC: 6531   Real estate agent, residential

(G-9279)
KELLY SERVICES INC
Also Called: Kelly Services
34 Reads Way (19720-1649)
PHONE.................................302 323-4748
  George Freas, *Mgr*
EMP: 5
SALES (corp-wide): 4.97B **Publicly Held**
Web: www.kellyservices.com
SIC: 7363   Temporary help service
PA: Kelly Services, Inc.
  999 W Big Beaver Rd
  Troy MI 48084
  248 362-4444

(G-9280)
KEYSTONE GRANITE AND TILE INC
217 Lisa Dr Ste C (19720-8404)
PHONE.................................302 323-0200
▲ **EMP:** 11 **EST:** 2014
SALES (est): 494.93K **Privately Held**
Web: www.keystone-granite.com
SIC: 1743 3281   Tile installation, ceramic; Granite, cut and shaped

(G-9281)
KHAJA YEZDANI MD
191 Christiana Rd Ste 3 (19720-3024)
PHONE.................................302 322-1794
  Khaja Yezdani Md, *Owner*
EMP: 10 **EST:** 1998
SALES (est): 334.86K **Privately Held**
SIC: 8011   General and family practice, physician/surgeon

(G-9282)
KINDERCARE LEARNING CTRS LLC
Also Called: Kindercare Learning Centers
327 Old State Rd (19720-4618)
PHONE.................................302 322-3102
  Megan Williams, *Brnch Mgr*
EMP: 14
SALES (corp-wide): 967.64MM **Privately Held**
Web: www.kindercare.com
SIC: 8351   Group day care center
HQ: Kindercare Learning Centers, Llc
  650 Ne Holladay St # 1400
  Portland OR 97232

(G-9283)
KING LA EXPRESS
13 Chaddwyck Blvd (19720-8834)
PHONE.................................215 607-9997
  Trenton David Laborde, *Prin*
EMP: 5 **EST:** 2018
SALES (est): 224.86K **Privately Held**
SIC: 4789   Transportation services, nec

(G-9284)
KIRKIN ROOFING LLC
1053 Lower Twin Lane Rd (19720-5502)
PHONE.................................302 832-7663
EMP: 11 **EST:** 2015
SALES (est): 768.03K **Privately Held**
Web: www.kirkinroofing.com
SIC: 1761   Roofing contractor

(G-9285)
KIWANIS INTERNATIONAL INC
Also Called: Kiwanis Club of Wilmington
202 W Franklin Ave (19720-2515)
P.O. Box 1873 (19899-1873)
PHONE.................................302 325-0778
  Coleman Bye, *Brnch Mgr*
EMP: 8
SALES (corp-wide): 20.12MM **Privately Held**
Web: www.kiwanis.org
SIC: 8641   Civic associations
PA: Kiwanis International, Inc.
  3636 Woodview Trce
  Indianapolis IN 46268
  317 875-8755

(G-9286)
KLD TRUCKING CORPORATION
550 S Dupont Hwy Apt 14s (19720-5122)
PHONE.................................347 399-7619
  Desire Komliapoe, *Prin*
EMP: 5 **EST:** 2015
SALES (est): 98.18K **Privately Held**
SIC: 4212   Local trucking, without storage

(G-9287)
KLOECKNER METALS
20 Davidson Ln (19720-2214)
PHONE.................................302 652-3326
EMP: 10 **EST:** 2019

New Castle - New Castle County (G-9288)

SALES (est): 815.31K **Privately Held**
Web: www.kloecknermetals.com
SIC: 5051 Steel

(G-9288)
KOKOSZKA & SONS INC
68 Skyline Dr (19720-2943)
PHONE....................302 328-4807
Edward Kokoszka Senior, *Pr*
EMP: 5 EST: 1970
SALES (est): 554.03K **Privately Held**
SIC: 1521 1731 1721 New construction, single-family houses; General electrical contractor; Wallcovering contractors

(G-9289)
KOMPRESSED AIR DELAWARE INC
21 Blevins Dr (19720-4153)
PHONE....................302 275-1985
Jay Williams, *CEO*
Jay Williams, *Pr*
Marian Williams, *VP*
EMP: 8 EST: 1988
SQ FT: 14,000
SALES (est): 2.42MM **Privately Held**
Web: www.kompressedair.net
SIC: 5075 7699 Compressors, air conditioning; Compressor repair

(G-9290)
KRISTA J ANDERSON MRS
24 Fithian Dr (19720-3208)
PHONE....................239 247-1170
Krista J Anderson R.n., *Prin*
EMP: 5 EST: 2019
SALES (est): 64K **Privately Held**
SIC: 8049 Offices of health practitioner

(G-9291)
KUEHNE CHEMICAL COMPANY INC
Chloramone Co
1645 River Rd (19720-5194)
P.O. Box 294 (19706-0294)
PHONE....................302 834-4557
Charles Mccun, *Brnch Mgr*
EMP: 45
SQ FT: 30,000
SALES (corp-wide): 86.48MM **Privately Held**
Web: www.kuehnecompany.com
SIC: 2812 2819 Chlorine, compressed or liquefied; Industrial inorganic chemicals, nec
PA: Kuehne Chemical Company, Inc.
86 N Hackensack Ave
Kearny NJ 07032
973 589-0700

(G-9292)
L F SYSTEMS CORP
249 Old Churchmans Rd (19720-1529)
PHONE....................302 322-0460
Gerald Holmes, *Pr*
EMP: 11 EST: 1983
SQ FT: 9,800
SALES (est): 1.89MM **Privately Held**
Web: www.lfsystems.com
SIC: 5021 3821 Furniture; Laboratory furniture

(G-9293)
LA BENDICION CLEANING SVCS LL
209 May Ave (19720-3663)
PHONE....................302 276-6468
German Santizo, *Prin*
EMP: 5 EST: 2014
SALES (est): 46.62K **Privately Held**
SIC: 7699 Cleaning services

(G-9294)
LAMART DRYWALL LLC
32 Cahalan Rd (19720-2114)
PHONE....................302 723-8751
Jose Lara-martinez, *Pr*
EMP: 5 EST: 2017
SALES (est): 198.26K **Privately Held**
SIC: 1742 Drywall

(G-9295)
LARRY SHELTON
Also Called: Holy See Global District
128 Sunset Blvd (19720-4100)
PHONE....................678 948-6096
Larry Shelton, *CEO*
Larry Shelton, *Owner*
Freddie Rivera, *Prin*
Richard Steward, *Prin*
Laremy Wade, *Prin*
EMP: 11 EST: 2018
SALES (est): 450.69K **Privately Held**
Web: www.larryshelton.net
SIC: 6732 9111 8661 8299 Trusts: educational, religious, etc.; Executive offices, level of government; Religious organizations; Religious school

(G-9296)
LAUREL LINEN SERVICE INC
17 Harbor View Dr (19720-2179)
PHONE....................804 732-3315
Donald Struminger, *Ch Bd*
David M Struminger, *Pr*
Nancy Pugh, *VP*
John Crockford, *VP*
EMP: 15 EST: 1939
SALES (est): 459.78K
SALES (corp-wide): 48.52MM **Privately Held**
SIC: 7213 7211 Linen supply; Power laundries, family and commercial
PA: Mohenis Services, Inc.
875 E Bank St
Petersburg VA 23803
800 879-3315

(G-9297)
LAW OFFICE OF MELISSA GREEN
910 W Basin Rd Ste 100 (19720-1015)
PHONE....................302 998-2049
EMP: 5 EST: 2016
SALES (est): 58.3K **Privately Held**
Web: www.delawaredisability.com
SIC: 8111 General practice attorney, lawyer

(G-9298)
LE SALONE HAIR SALON
68 Briarcliff Dr (19720-1339)
PHONE....................302 384-6788
Lisa Beach, *Prin*
EMP: 5 EST: 2010
SALES (est): 44.11K **Privately Held**
SIC: 7231 Beauty shops

(G-9299)
LEES BEST CAR WASH
194 S Dupont Hwy (19720-4265)
PHONE....................302 328-0770
Sung Lee, *Pr*
EMP: 7 EST: 2017
SALES (est): 31.02K **Privately Held**
SIC: 7539 Automotive repair shops, nec

(G-9300)
LEGACY MARTIAL ARTS
32 Yale Ave (19720-4328)
PHONE....................302 345-8515
Annaliza Setyanto, *Prin*
EMP: 5 EST: 2015
SALES (est): 50.44K **Privately Held**
Web: www.legacymtc.com
SIC: 7999 Martial arts school, nec

(G-9301)
LEGEND TRANSPORTATION LLC
323 Wooddale Ave (19720-4737)
PHONE....................215 713-7472
EMP: 30 EST: 2021
SALES (est): 950K **Privately Held**
SIC: 4789 Freight car loading and unloading

(G-9302)
LEHIGH TESTING LABORATORIES
308 W Basin Rd (19720-6406)
PHONE....................302 328-0500
J Barry Mccrudden, *Pr*
Jeffrey L Donaldson, *Sec*
EMP: 8 EST: 1955
SQ FT: 13,625
SALES (est): 350.98K
SALES (corp-wide): 4.1MM **Privately Held**
Web: www.lehightesting.com
SIC: 8734 Testing laboratories
PA: The Mmr Group Inc
308 W Basin Rd
New Castle DE 19720
302 328-0500

(G-9303)
LEIGHTNER ELECTRICAL CONTRACTO
21 Arden Ave (19720-3433)
PHONE....................302 723-1507
Albert Leightner, *Prin*
EMP: 6 EST: 2008
SALES (est): 128.49K **Privately Held**
SIC: 1731 General electrical contractor

(G-9304)
LEITERS TOOLS LLC
51 Saratoga Dr (19720-4234)
PHONE....................302 538-3284
EMP: 5 EST: 2018
SALES (est): 229.42K **Privately Held**
SIC: 8748 Business consulting, nec

(G-9305)
LENAR DETECTIVE AGENCY INC
Also Called: Colonial Security Services
714 Grantham Ln (19720-4802)
PHONE....................302 322-3700
EMP: 75
SALES (corp-wide): 8.73MM **Privately Held**
Web: www.colonialsecurityservices.com
SIC: 7381 Security guard service
PA: Lenar Detective Agency Inc
170 Us Highway 206
Hillsborough NJ 08844
908 298-0012

(G-9306)
LEON N WEINER & ASSOCIATES INC
Also Called: Chelten Apartments
431 Old Forge Rd Ofc Ofc (19720-3765)
PHONE....................302 322-6323
William Demarco, *VP*
EMP: 34
SALES (corp-wide): 73.09K **Privately Held**
Web: www.lnwa.com
SIC: 6513 Apartment building operators
PA: Leon N. Weiner & Associates, Inc.
1 Fox Pt Ctr 4 Denny Rd
Wilmington DE 19809
302 656-1354

(G-9307)
LEONARDS EXPRESS INC
300 Pigeon Point Rd (19720-1418)
PHONE....................302 426-0802
Richard Bastian, *Pr*
EMP: 32
SALES (corp-wide): 234.86MM **Privately Held**
Web: www.leonardsexpress.com
SIC: 4731 Freight transportation arrangement
PA: Leonard's Express, Inc.
6070 Collett Rd Bldg 2
Farmington NY 14425
585 924-8140

(G-9308)
LEONS GARDEN WORLD EJ INC
137 S Dupont Hwy (19720-4127)
PHONE....................410 392-8630
Evan Macguinness, *Prin*
EMP: 12 EST: 2016
SALES (est): 875.49K **Privately Held**
SIC: 5261 5191 0781 Retail nurseries and garden stores; Garden supplies; Landscape services

(G-9309)
LEWIS ENVIRONMENTAL GROUP INC
101 Carroll Dr (19720-4873)
P.O. Box 639 (19468-0639)
PHONE....................302 669-6010
EMP: 14
Web: www.discoverlewis.com
SIC: 6512 Commercial and industrial building operation
PA: Lewis Environmental Group, Inc.
155 Railroad Plz Ste 3
Royersford PA 19468

(G-9310)
LINARDUCCI & BUTLER PA
910 W Basin Rd Ste 100 (19720-1015)
PHONE....................302 325-2400
EMP: 8 EST: 1995
SALES (est): 526K **Privately Held**
Web: www.delawaredisability.com
SIC: 8111 General practice attorney, lawyer

(G-9311)
LINDAS ANGELS CHLDCARE DEV CTR
6 Parkway Ct (19720-4020)
PHONE....................302 328-3700
Linda Bright, *Owner*
EMP: 16 EST: 2010
SALES (est): 455.7K **Privately Held**
SIC: 8351 Child day care services

(G-9312)
LINDE NORTH AMERICA
315 Cherry Ln (19720-2780)
PHONE....................302 654-9348
Linde North, *Ofcr*
EMP: 13 EST: 2017
SALES (est): 435.53K **Privately Held**
SIC: 8661 5084 Religious organizations; Blanks, tips, and inserts

(G-9313)
LINEAGE AUTO GROUP L L C ◆
7 Marlin Ct (19720-7634)
PHONE....................302 595-2119
Jeanine Taylor, *CEO*
EMP: 5 EST: 2023
SALES (est): 107.71K **Privately Held**
SIC: 7538 7389 General automotive repair shops; Business services, nec

(G-9314)
LITTLE FRIENDS LRNG ACADEMY
122 Memorial Dr (19720-1336)
PHONE....................302 655-0725
Christina Mccoy, *Owner*

GEOGRAPHIC SECTION
New Castle - New Castle County (G-9343)

EMP: 17 EST: 2010
SALES (est): 762.02K **Privately Held**
Web: www.littlefriendslearningacademy.com
SIC: 8351 Preschool center

(G-9315)
LITTLE GIGGLES
58 Charles Dr (19720-4670)
PHONE..................................678 770-2089
Kesha Stroman, *Prin*
EMP: 5 EST: 2019
SALES (est): 63.33K **Privately Held**
SIC: 8351 Child day care services

(G-9316)
LITTLE LEAGUE BASEBALL INC
23 Blount Rd (19720-3221)
PHONE..................................302 276-0375
James Raab, *Brnch Mgr*
EMP: 9
SALES (corp-wide): 31.78MM **Privately Held**
Web: www.littleleague.org
SIC: 8699 7997 Athletic organizations; Membership sports and recreation clubs
PA: Little League Baseball Inc
    539 Us Route 15 Hwy
    Williamsport PA 17702
    570 326-1921

(G-9317)
LITTLE PEOPLE CHILD DEV CTR 3
1169 S Dupont Hwy (19720-5203)
PHONE..................................302 832-1891
EMP: 6 EST: 2019
SALES (est): 91.46K **Privately Held**
SIC: 8351 Preschool center

(G-9318)
LIVEO RESEARCH INC (DH)
1389 School House Rd (19720-5524)
P.O. Box 537 (19706-0537)
PHONE..................................302 838-3200
Kevin Stevens, *Pr*
◆ EMP: 136 EST: 2005
SALES (est): 51.08MM
SALES (corp-wide): 260.22MM **Privately Held**
Web: www.liveoresearch.com
SIC: 2821 Vinyl resins, nec
HQ: Liveo Research Gmbh
    Radebeulstr. 1
    Staufen Im Breisgau BW 79219
    76338110

(G-9319)
LIVINGSTON ENTERPRISE
205 S Booth Dr (19720-3325)
PHONE..................................302 588-5722
Jeanette Livingston, *Managing Member*
EMP: 6 EST: 2007
SALES (est): 85.31K **Privately Held**
Web: www.livingstonenterprise.com
SIC: 6531 Real estate brokers and agents

(G-9320)
LL RENOVATION LLC
7 3rd Ave (19720-4119)
PHONE..................................302 250-6449
Lloyd Loller, *Owner*
EMP: 6 EST: 2010
SALES (est): 237.64K **Privately Held**
Web: www.llrenovation.com
SIC: 1521 General remodeling, single-family houses

(G-9321)
LOANMAX
1517 N Dupont Hwy (19720-1901)
PHONE..................................302 326-0123
Mickey Brochett, *Prin*
EMP: 9 EST: 2007
SALES (est): 116.86K **Privately Held**
Web: www.loanmaxtitleloans.net
SIC: 6141 Personal credit institutions

(G-9322)
LOGAN & ASSOCIATES LLC
100 W Commons Blvd Ste 300 (19720)
PHONE..................................302 325-3555
Steven Rombach, *Dir*
EMP: 9 EST: 2007
SALES (est): 222.86K **Privately Held**
Web: www.bmbde.com
SIC: 8111 Legal services

(G-9323)
LOGIQUE INC
257 Old Churchmans Rd (19720-1529)
PHONE..................................302 330-8866
EMP: 6 EST: 2021
SALES (est): 249.97K **Privately Held**
SIC: 7371 Custom computer programming services

(G-9324)
LONNIE WRIGHT
83 Charles Dr (19720-4679)
PHONE..................................302 655-1632
Lonnie Wright, *Owner*
EMP: 6 EST: 2015
SALES (est): 46.9K **Privately Held**
SIC: 8611 Business associations

(G-9325)
LOPEZ GENERAL CONTRACTORS LLC
404 Llangollen Blvd (19720-4700)
PHONE..................................302 377-2591
EMP: 5 EST: 2017
SALES (est): 56.76K **Privately Held**
SIC: 1799 Special trade contractors, nec

(G-9326)
LORRAINE S DAYCARE
3 N Independence Blvd (19720-4457)
PHONE..................................302 328-1333
EMP: 8 EST: 2018
SALES (est): 84.71K **Privately Held**
SIC: 8351 Child day care services

(G-9327)
LOST AND FOUND DOG RESCUE ADOP
70 Ivy Ln (19720-2339)
PHONE..................................302 613-0394
Marleen Oetzel, *Prin*
EMP: 5 EST: 2009
SALES (est): 137.2K **Privately Held**
Web: www.lnfdogs.org
SIC: 8322 Adoption services

(G-9328)
LOWES HOME CENTERS LLC
Also Called: Lowe's
2225 Hessler Blvd (19720-6305)
PHONE..................................302 252-3228
EMP: 80
SALES (corp-wide): 97.06B **Publicly Held**
Web: www.lowes.com
SIC: 5211 5031 5722 5064 Home centers; Building materials, exterior; Household appliance stores; Electrical appliances, television and radio
HQ: Lowe's Home Centers, Llc
    1000 Lowes Blvd
    Mooresville NC 28117
    336 658-4000

(G-9329)
LUCYS CLEANING SERVICE
28 Mifflin Ave (19720-1157)
PHONE..................................302 893-9946
EMP: 5 EST: 2018
SALES (est): 108.02K **Privately Held**
Web: www.lucyshousecleaners.com
SIC: 7699 Cleaning services

(G-9330)
LYNNE FARDELL & ASSOCIATES LLC
58 The Strand (19720-4826)
PHONE..................................302 276-1541
EMP: 5 EST: 2011
SALES (est): 63.96K **Privately Held**
SIC: 8742 Management consulting services

(G-9331)
M & W TRUCKING INC
44 Glen Ave (19720-2008)
PHONE..................................302 655-6994
Willie L Mc Reynolds, *Pr*
Marjorie Mc Reynolds, *VP*
EMP: 6 EST: 1984
SALES (est): 494.45K **Privately Held**
SIC: 4212 Local trucking, without storage

(G-9332)
M G HAMEX CORPORATION
1063 Twin Lane Rd (19720-5502)
PHONE..................................302 832-9072
Michael Hamm, *Prin*
Michael Hamm, *Pr*
Georgia Hamm, *VP*
EMP: 12 EST: 1997
SQ FT: 2,250
SALES (est): 1.08MM **Privately Held**
SIC: 1794 Excavation work

(G-9333)
M P LOGISTICS INC
232 Harlequin Dr (19720-8900)
PHONE..................................302 562-0420
EMP: 6 EST: 2018
SALES (est): 585.25K **Privately Held**
SIC: 4789 Transportation services, nec

(G-9334)
MAGCO KISSNER MILLING CO
341 Pigeon Point Rd (19720-1448)
PHONE..................................913 713-0612
EMP: 7 EST: 2016
SALES (est): 945.71K **Privately Held**
Web: www.kissner.com
SIC: 5169 Chemicals and allied products, nec

(G-9335)
MAGIC YRS CHILD CARE LRNG CNTR
327 Old State Rd (19720-4618)
PHONE..................................302 322-3102
Madeline Robinson, *Dir*
EMP: 10
SALES (corp-wide): 967.64MM **Privately Held**
SIC: 8351 Child day care services
HQ: Magic Yrs Child Care & Lrng Cntr Inc
    560 B St
    King Of Prussia PA

(G-9336)
MAGNUS ENVIRONMENTAL CORP
220 Marsh Ln (19720-1175)
PHONE..................................302 655-4443
EMP: 9 EST: 1995
SQ FT: 70,000
SALES (est): 481K **Privately Held**
Web: www.magnusenvironmental.com

SIC: 4953 Recycling, waste materials

(G-9337)
MAICHLE S HEATING AIR
105 J And M Dr (19720-3147)
PHONE..................................302 328-4822
Donna Maichle, *Owner*
EMP: 16 EST: 2008
SALES (est): 2.29MM **Privately Held**
Web: www.maichlesvac.com
SIC: 1711 Warm air heating and air conditioning contractor

(G-9338)
MAIDS FOR YOU INC
3 Scottie Ln (19720-3922)
PHONE..................................302 328-9050
Joe Mc Donald, *VP*
EMP: 7 EST: 1986
SQ FT: 750
SALES (est): 56.08K **Privately Held**
SIC: 7349 Maid services, contract or fee basis

(G-9339)
MAILLIE LLP
15 Reads Way Ste 200 (19720-1600)
P.O. Box 11847 (19850-1847)
PHONE..................................302 324-0780
EMP: 14
SALES (corp-wide): 5.12MM **Privately Held**
Web: www.maillie.com
SIC: 8721 Certified public accountant
PA: Maillie Llp
    140 Whitaker Ave Ste A
    Mont Clare PA
    610 935-1420

(G-9340)
MAINTENANCE TECH
10 Strawbridge Ave (19720-1536)
PHONE..................................302 322-6410
Rita Skinner, *Mgr*
EMP: 5 EST: 2008
SALES (est): 231.41K **Privately Held**
Web: www.maintenance-tech.net
SIC: 7349 Building maintenance services, nec

(G-9341)
MALIKS AUTO REPAIR
95 Christiana Rd (19720-3104)
PHONE..................................302 325-2555
Anadil Aslam, *Owner*
EMP: 7 EST: 2010
SALES (est): 881.94K **Privately Held**
Web: www.newcastleautorepair.com
SIC: 7538 General automotive repair shops

(G-9342)
MANCON INC
100 Churchmans Rd (19720-3108)
PHONE..................................302 395-5376
EMP: 9 EST: 2015
SALES (est): 164.33K **Privately Held**
Web: www.manconinc.com
SIC: 8742 Management consulting services

(G-9343)
MANUFACTURERS & TRADERS TR CO
Also Called: M&T
287 Christiana Rd Ste 16 (19720-2978)
PHONE..................................302 472-3249
Katrine Hutchison, *Brnch Mgr*
EMP: 5
SALES (corp-wide): 8.6B **Publicly Held**
Web: ir.mtb.com

New Castle - New Castle County (G-9344) — GEOGRAPHIC SECTION

SIC: **6022** State commercial banks
HQ: Manufacturers And Traders Trust Company
1 M&T Plz Fl 3
Buffalo NY 14203
716 842-4200

(G-9344)
MAP HAUILING
5 Surrey Dr (19720-8829)
PHONE..................267 235-6712
Melvin Presha, *Prin*
EMP: **5** EST: 2019
SALES (est): 101.38K **Privately Held**
SIC: **7699** Cleaning services

(G-9345)
MARINIS BROS INC
755 Grantham Ln (19720-4801)
PHONE..................302 322-9663
Nick Marinis, *Pr*
Sothiere Marinis, *VP*
Sophia Marinis, *Sec*
EMP: **10** EST: 1966
SALES (est): 1.2MM **Privately Held**
Web: www.marinisbros.com
SIC: **1721** Bridge painting

(G-9346)
MARITA F FALLORINA MD
1 Catherine St Ste 1 (19720-3001)
PHONE..................302 322-0660
Marita F Fallorina Md, *Owner*
EMP: **5** EST: 1999
SALES (est): 493.98K **Privately Held**
SIC: **8011** General and family practice, physician/surgeon

(G-9347)
MARKET BLACK LLC
Also Called: Market Black Trucking
304 7th St (19720-6201)
PHONE..................267 257-3017
Rasheim Hagwood, *Managing Member*
Malaika Hagwood, *Managing Member*
EMP: **2** EST: 2020
SALES (est): 113.59K **Privately Held**
SIC: **7372** Application computer software

(G-9348)
MARLEX PHARMACEUTICALS INC
65 Lukens Dr (19720)
PHONE..................302 328-3355
Amrish Patel, *Pr*
Samir Patel, *Sec*
EMP: **40** EST: 1992
SQ FT: 80,000
SALES (est): 8.05MM **Privately Held**
Web: www.marlexpharm.com
SIC: **4783** 2834 Packing goods for shipping; Pharmaceutical preparations

(G-9349)
MAROSA SURGICAL INDUSTRIES
Also Called: Avenue Medical
42 Reads Way Ste A (19720-1612)
PHONE..................302 674-0907
Adam Samuel, *Pr*
EMP: **11** EST: 1975
SALES (est): 2.47MM **Privately Held**
Web: www.avenuemedical.com
SIC: **5047** 5999 Medical equipment and supplies; Medical apparatus and supplies

(G-9350)
MARTINEZ AUTOMOTIVE
260 Christiana Rd Apt N5 (19720-2962)
PHONE..................302 250-5933
Richard Martinez, *Prin*
EMP: **5** EST: 2018
SALES (est): 227.32K **Privately Held**
Web: martinez-automotive.business.site
SIC: **7538** General automotive repair shops

(G-9351)
MARVELOUS LGHTS PRDUCTIONS LLC (PA)
3 Evlon Ct (19720-5421)
PHONE..................215 678-2013
Michael Gaskins, *Prin*
EMP: **9** EST: 2021
SALES (est): 393.32K
SALES (corp-wide): 393.32K **Privately Held**
Web: www.marvelouslight.tv
SIC: **7812** Motion picture and video production

(G-9352)
MASTERS TOUCH CLEANING LLC
118 Colesbery Dr (19720-3204)
PHONE..................302 650-8165
Tim Visser, *Owner*
EMP: **5** EST: 2008
SALES (est): 151.15K **Privately Held**
SIC: **7699** Cleaning services

(G-9353)
MATERIAL TRANSIT INC
Also Called: Material Supply
255 Airport Rd (19720-1539)
PHONE..................302 395-0556
Blaise Saienni, *Pr*
William Saienni Junior, *Sec*
Quinton Saienni, *VP*
William Saienni Senior, *Stockholder*
Elmer Saienne, *Stockholder*
EMP: **21** EST: 1947
SQ FT: 5,000
SALES (est): 240.7K **Privately Held**
SIC: **1442** 3273 4213 Construction sand and gravel; Ready-mixed concrete; Heavy hauling, nec

(G-9354)
MAYFLOWER LAUNDRY AND LIN SUPS
10 Dock View Dr (19720-2180)
PHONE..................302 652-1416
EMP: **9** EST: 2019
SALES (est): 390.86K **Privately Held**
Web: www.mayflowerlaundries.com
SIC: **7213** Linen supply

(G-9355)
MECHANICS PARADISE INC
Also Called: Tools & More
2335 N Dupont Hwy (19720-6304)
PHONE..................302 652-8863
William Bill Baron, *CEO*
Suzanne Baron, *Treas*
EMP: **10** EST: 1984
SALES (est): 2.39MM **Privately Held**
Web: www.toolsandmorestore.com
SIC: **5084** 5211 5251 Industrial machinery and equipment; Lumber and other building materials; Hardware stores

(G-9356)
MEDLAB-HAVERTOWN INC (PA)
212 Cherry Ln (19720-2776)
PHONE..................302 655-5227
EMP: **6**
SALES (est): 604.37K
SALES (corp-wide): 604.37K **Privately Held**
SIC: **8071** Testing laboratories

(G-9357)
MEMORIAL SUPER FUEL
3006 New Castle Ave (19720-2244)
PHONE..................215 512-1012
Jassveer Singh, *Mgr*
EMP: **9** EST: 2011
SALES (est): 487.84K **Privately Held**
SIC: **2869** Fuels

(G-9358)
MERAKEY USA
2 Penns Way (19720-2407)
PHONE..................302 325-3540
Rose Stewart, *Brnch Mgr*
EMP: **47**
SALES (corp-wide): 60.74MM **Privately Held**
Web: www.merakey.org
SIC: **8322** Social service center
PA: Merakey Usa
620 Germantown Pike
Lafayette Hill PA 19444
610 260-4600

(G-9359)
METAL PARTNERS REBAR LLC
Also Called: Metal Partners International
20 Davidson Ln (19720-2214)
PHONE..................215 791-3491
Mike Poff, *Brnch Mgr*
EMP: **12**
SIC: **5051** Steel
PA: Metal Partners Rebar, Llc
3933 75th St Ste 101
Aurora IL 60504

(G-9360)
METAL-TECH INC
265 Airport Rd (19720-1540)
PHONE..................302 322-7770
TOLL FREE: 800
Tony Morris, *Pr*
Hugh Hood, *Pr*
Erika Hood, *VP*
EMP: **22** EST: 1969
SQ FT: 50,000
SALES (est): 4.08MM **Privately Held**
Web: www.metaltech-de.com
SIC: **3599** 3444 7692 3479 Machine shop, jobbing and repair; Sheet metalwork; Welding repair; Painting of metal products

(G-9361)
METRO STEEL INCORPORATED
4049 New Castle Ave (19720-1414)
P.O. Box 12808 (19850-2808)
PHONE..................302 778-2288
Robert Cordrey, *Pr*
EMP: **20** EST: 1998
SQ FT: 5,000
SALES (est): 2.03MM **Privately Held**
Web: www.metrosteelusa.com
SIC: **1791** Structural steel erection

(G-9362)
METROPOLITAN REVENUE ASSOC LLC
Also Called: Metropolitan Revenue Assoc
29 E Commons Blvd Ste 100 (19720-1736)
P.O. Box 47 (19709-0047)
PHONE..................302 449-7490
John P Eldridge, *Prin*
EMP: **8** EST: 2011
SALES (est): 659.02K **Privately Held**
SIC: **8742** Hospital and health services consultant

(G-9363)
MICHAEL D JOHNSON M D
810 Brant Dr (19720-8905)
PHONE..................267 760-7195
Michael Johnson, *Pr*
EMP: **8** EST: 2017
SALES (est): 232.05K **Privately Held**
SIC: **8011** Offices and clinics of medical doctors

(G-9364)
MICHAELS HOME REPAIR SERVICES
550 S Dupont Hwy Apt 22k (19720-5135)
PHONE..................302 333-2235
Michael Dobey, *VP*
EMP: **6** EST: 2017
SALES (est): 248.6K **Privately Held**
SIC: **1521** General remodeling, single-family houses

(G-9365)
MID ATLANTIC GRAND PRIX LLC
Also Called: Mid Atlantic Grand Prix
4060 N Dupont Hwy Ste 11 (19720-6325)
PHONE..................302 656-5278
EMP: **9** EST: 2005
SALES (est): 481.58K **Privately Held**
Web: www.xtremezone.com
SIC: **7929** 8741 7999 Entertainers and entertainment groups; Management services; Indoor court clubs

(G-9366)
MID ATLANTIC WASTE SYSTEM
314 Bay West Blvd Ste 3 (19720-5195)
PHONE..................610 497-2405
Richard Weinstein, *Owner*
EMP: **7** EST: 2005
SALES (est): 183.46K **Privately Held**
Web: www.mawaste.com
SIC: **4953** Recycling, waste materials

(G-9367)
MID ATLNTIC SCIENTIFIC SVC INC
62 Southgate Blvd Ste A (19720-2075)
P.O. Box 880 (19720-0880)
PHONE..................302 328-4440
James Twenge, *CEO*
Robert Reissman, *Pr*
Lorie Twenge, *COO*
EMP: **5** EST: 1995
SQ FT: 6,000
SALES (est): 990K **Privately Held**
Web: www.midatlanticscientificservice.com
SIC: **7699** 5999 Scientific equipment repair service; Medical apparatus and supplies

(G-9368)
MID-ATLANTIC STEEL LLC
1144 River Rd (19720-5106)
PHONE..................302 323-1800
EMP: **36** EST: 2003
SALES (est): 3.25MM **Privately Held**
Web: www.midatlanticsteel.com
SIC: **3441** Fabricated structural metal

(G-9369)
MIDDLE ROOM LLC
637 Country Path Dr (19720-7663)
PHONE..................302 220-9979
Kena Williams, *CEO*
Kena Williams, *Managing Member*
EMP: **6** EST: 2016
SALES (est): 279.64K **Privately Held**
SIC: **5651** 7389 Unisex clothing stores; Business Activities at Non-Commercial Site

(G-9370)
MILES RS SON ROOFING
113 J And M Dr (19720-3142)
PHONE..................302 250-4992
Robert Miles, *Prin*

GEOGRAPHIC SECTION

New Castle - New Castle County (G-9399)

EMP: 6 EST: 2010
SALES (est): 115.28K **Privately Held**
SIC: 1761 Roofing contractor

(G-9371)
MILLERS GUN CENTER INC
97 Jackson Ave (19720-6431)
PHONE...............................302 328-9747
John Miller Junior, *Pr*
Robert Miller, *VP*
EMP: 9 EST: 1959
SQ FT: 2,500
SALES (est): 961.41K **Privately Held**
Web: www.millersguncenter.com
SIC: 5941 5091 Firearms; Firearms, sporting

(G-9372)
MINDSET NUTRITION & FITNESS
19 Highland Blvd Apt A (19720-6919)
PHONE...............................302 219-0777
Leah Brown, *CEO*
EMP: 5 EST: 2016
SALES (est): 39.53K **Privately Held**
SIC: 7991 Physical fitness facilities

(G-9373)
MITCHELL ASSOCIATES INC (PA)
100 W Commons Blvd Ste 300 (19720)
PHONE...............................302 594-9400
Louis B Rosenberg, *Pr*
William Endicott, *Sec*
Sheree L Jones, *VP*
Kim Leborys, *Treas*
EMP: 25 EST: 1965
SALES (est): 5.44MM
SALES (corp-wide): 5.44MM **Privately Held**
Web: www.mitchellai.com
SIC: 7389 7336 Interior designer; Graphic arts and related design

(G-9374)
MITEK HOLDINGS INC (DH)
42 Reads Way # C (19720-1612)
PHONE...............................302 429-1816
Susan Besley, *Admn Mgr*
EMP: 95 EST: 1988
SALES (est): 1.28MM
SALES (corp-wide): 302.09B **Publicly Held**
SIC: 7389 Financial services
HQ: Mitek Industries, Inc.
   16023 Swinly Rdg
   Chesterfield MO 63017
   314 434-1200

(G-9375)
MMR GROUP INC (PA)
Also Called: Connecticut Metallurgical
308 W Basin Rd (19720-6406)
PHONE...............................302 328-0500
Francis S Shoreys, *Pr*
Jennifer Wegner, *
EMP: 22 EST: 1961
SQ FT: 25,000
SALES (est): 4.1MM
SALES (corp-wide): 4.1MM **Privately Held**
Web: www.lehightesting.com
SIC: 8731 8734 Commercial physical research; Metallurgical testing laboratory

(G-9376)
MOBETTA BOOKS LLC
68 Valley Forge Rd (19720-4242)
PHONE...............................904 762-3043
Djuan Frazier, *Managing Member*
EMP: 2
SALES (est): 92.41K **Privately Held**
SIC: 2731 Books, publishing only

(G-9377)
MODERN CONTROLS INC
26 Bellecor Dr Ste A (19720-2188)
PHONE...............................302 325-6800
Michael Peet, *Pr*
EMP: 145 EST: 1989
SALES (est): 30.62MM **Privately Held**
Web: www.moderncontrols.com
SIC: 1711 7699 7629 Mechanical contractor; Pumps and pumping equipment repair; Electrical repair shops

(G-9378)
MODERN WATER INC
15 Reads Way Ste 100 (19720-1600)
PHONE...............................302 669-6900
EMP: 23 EST: 2011
SALES (est): 3.28MM **Privately Held**
Web: www.modernwater.com
SIC: 8731 Commercial physical research

(G-9379)
MODULAR CARPET RECYCLING INC
239 Lisa Dr (19720-4193)
PHONE...............................484 885-5890
Ron Simonetti, *CEO*
EMP: 10 EST: 2008
SALES (est): 427.9K **Privately Held**
SIC: 4953 1752 Recycling, waste materials; Carpet laying

(G-9380)
MONSTER KING CONGLOMERATE LLC (PA)
106 Memorial Dr (19720-1336)
PHONE...............................302 222-9742
EMP: 7 EST: 2021
SALES (est): 351.38K
SALES (corp-wide): 351.38K **Privately Held**
SIC: 4731 Freight forwarding

(G-9381)
MORAN ENVIRONMENTAL RECOVERY
314 Bay West Blvd Ste 8 (19720-5195)
PHONE...............................302 322-6008
Justin Woodard, *Mgr*
EMP: 8 EST: 1998
SALES (est): 97.71K **Privately Held**
Web: www.moranenvironmental.com
SIC: 8748 Environmental consultant

(G-9382)
MORRIS & RITCHIE ASSOC INC
18 Boulden Cir Ste 36 (19720-3494)
PHONE...............................302 326-2200
Phillip Tolliver, *Mgr*
EMP: 18
Web: www.mragta.com
SIC: 8711 8713 Designing: ship, boat, machine, and product; Surveying services
HQ: Morris & Ritchie Associates, Inc.
   3445 Box Hill Corp Ctr Dr B
   Abingdon MD
   410 515-9000

(G-9383)
MOVE MINT ✪
503 Paisley Ln (19720-3828)
PHONE...............................267 289-4545
Jessica Rieman, *CEO*
EMP: 5 EST: 2022
SALES (est): 248.42K **Privately Held**
SIC: 4212 Moving services

(G-9384)
MOVING CLUB LLC (PA) ✪
600 Garrison Ct (19720)
PHONE...............................929 377-9332

EMP: 6 EST: 2022
SALES (est): 83.38K
SALES (corp-wide): 83.38K **Privately Held**
SIC: 2519 7389 Household furniture, nec; Business services, nec

(G-9385)
MR KLEEN II
272 Christiana Rd (19720-2965)
PHONE...............................302 324-8797
EMP: 5 EST: 2015
SALES (est): 26.07K **Privately Held**
Web: www.mrkleenlaundromat.com
SIC: 7699 Cleaning services

(G-9386)
MS KIMS DAY CARE
10 Westbury Dr (19720-8813)
PHONE...............................304 689-8023
EMP: 8 EST: 2018
SALES (est): 110.11K **Privately Held**
SIC: 8351 Child day care services

(G-9387)
MSP EQUIP RENTAL
3128 New Castle Ave (19720-2162)
PHONE...............................302 322-5394
Mike Cassidy, *Owner*
EMP: 13 EST: 2017
SALES (est): 236.45K **Privately Held**
SIC: 7353 Heavy construction equipment rental

(G-9388)
MTC DELAWARE LLC
2 Dock View Dr (19720-2180)
PHONE...............................302 654-3400
Harry Halpert, *Pr*
EMP: 19 EST: 2012
SALES (est): 3.11MM **Privately Held**
SIC: 4731 Freight forwarding
HQ: Lineage Logistics, Llc
   46500 Humboldt Dr
   Novi MI 48377
   248 863-4400

(G-9389)
N R O DRYWALL
221 E Hazeldell Ave (19720-1348)
PHONE...............................302 293-8811
Nereo Tovar, *Prin*
EMP: 5 EST: 2017
SALES (est): 73.69K **Privately Held**
SIC: 1742 Drywall

(G-9390)
NABERTHERM INC
64 Reads Way (19720-1649)
PHONE...............................302 322-3665
Martin Naber, *Ch*
▲ EMP: 5 EST: 1997
SALES (est): 2.28MM
SALES (corp-wide): 75.96MM **Privately Held**
Web: www.nabertherm.com
SIC: 3567 Industrial furnaces and ovens
HQ: Nabertherm Gmbh
   Bahnhofstr. 20
   Lilienthal NI 28865
   42989220

(G-9391)
NAES CORPORATION
13 Reads Way Ste 100 (19720-1609)
PHONE...............................856 299-0020
Steve Goers, *Mgr*
EMP: 25
Web: www.naes.com
SIC: 4911 Electric services
HQ: Naes Corporation
   1180 Nw Maple St Ste 200
   Issaquah WA 98027
   425 961-4700

(G-9392)
NANNYS HEAVENLY DAYCARE
5 Skyline Dr (19720-2924)
PHONE...............................302 276-7149
EMP: 6 EST: 2017
SALES (est): 17.57K **Privately Held**
SIC: 8351 Group day care center

(G-9393)
NATIONAL ASSN ELEC DISTR
10 Bellecor Dr (19720-1763)
PHONE...............................302 322-3333
Pat Mcfarland, *Prin*
EMP: 5 EST: 2015
SALES (est): 47.27K **Privately Held**
SIC: 8611 Trade associations

(G-9394)
NATIONAL ASSN OF HISPNC NRSES
213 Shetland Dr (19720-8800)
PHONE...............................302 325-9292
Maria T Villot, *Prin*
EMP: 5 EST: 2011
SALES (est): 47.53K **Privately Held**
SIC: 8641 Civic and social associations

(G-9395)
NATIONAL FINANCIAL LLC
1511 N Dupont Hwy (19720-1900)
PHONE...............................302 328-1370
EMP: 6 EST: 2019
SALES (est): 380.86K **Privately Held**
SIC: 6282 Investment advice

(G-9396)
NATIONAL GUARD ASSOCIATION DEL
1 Vavala Way (19720-2417)
PHONE...............................302 326-7125
Leonard Gratteri, *CEO*
David Rice, *Prin*
EMP: 15 EST: 2017
SALES (est): 789.78K **Privately Held**
Web: www.delawareonline.com
SIC: 8699 Membership organizations, nec

(G-9397)
NATIONAL HVAC SERVICE
Also Called: Honeywell Authorized Dealer
42a Southgate Blvd (19720-2068)
PHONE...............................302 323-1776
Pat Cunningham, *Genl Mgr*
EMP: 7
Web: www.nationalhvacservice.com
SIC: 1711 Warm air heating and air conditioning contractor
PA: National H.V.A.C. Service, Ltd
   624 Grassmere Park Ste 8
   Nashville TN 37211

(G-9398)
NATIONAL OPPRTNITIES UNLIMITED
42 Reads Way Ste 5 (19720-1612)
PHONE...............................913 905-2261
Joshua Landy, *Pr*
EMP: 5 EST: 2001
SALES (est): 169.69K **Privately Held**
SIC: 7389 Financial services

(G-9399)
NAVAS PAINTING LLC
3 Freeport Rd (19720-3016)
PHONE...............................302 685-1474
EMP: 5 EST: 2016
SALES (est): 42.66K **Privately Held**

New Castle - New Castle County (G-9400) — **GEOGRAPHIC SECTION**

SIC: 1721 Painting and paper hanging

(G-9400)
NEGRI BOSSI NORTH AMERICA INC
311 Carroll Dr (19720-4858)
PHONE..................302 328-8020
John Stone, Contrlr
Sandra Ryan, Acctg Mgr
▲ EMP: 2 EST: 2013
SALES (est): 742.04K **Privately Held**
Web: www.negribossi.com
SIC: 3089 Injection molded finished plastics products, nec

(G-9401)
NEGRI BOSSI USA INC
311 Carroll Dr # 100 (19720-4858)
PHONE..................302 328-8020
Luca Berrone, Pr
▲ EMP: 47 EST: 2003
SALES (est): 4.56MM **Privately Held**
Web: www.negribossi.com
SIC: 3559 Plastics working machinery
HQ: Negri Bossi Spa
   Viale Europa 64
   Cologno Monzese MI 20093
   022 734-8323

(G-9402)
NEITAO EXPRESS NAILS
77 Mccullough Dr (19720-2089)
PHONE..................302 276-1027
EMP: 5 EST: 2016
SALES (est): 19.07K **Privately Held**
SIC: 7231 Manicurist, pedicurist

(G-9403)
NESO TRUCKING LLC
65 Buena Vista Dr (19720-8629)
PHONE..................302 358-7878
EMP: 2
SALES (est): 95.58K **Privately Held**
SIC: 3537 7389 Trucks: freight, baggage, etc.: industrial, except mining; Business Activities at Non-Commercial Site

(G-9404)
NEUROSTAR INC
303 S Booth Dr (19720-4329)
PHONE..................302 778-0100
EMP: 5 EST: 2017
SALES (est): 224.88K **Privately Held**
SIC: 8011 Psychiatrist

(G-9405)
NEW CAR CONNECTION
174 N Dupont Hwy (19720-3103)
PHONE..................302 328-7000
Chris Dagesse, Owner
Ron Miller, Owner
EMP: 8 EST: 1975
SALES (est): 237.35K **Privately Held**
SIC: 5511 7538 7532 7515 Automobiles, new and used; General automotive repair shops; Top and body repair and paint shops; Passenger car leasing

(G-9406)
NEW CASTLE CNTY SHOPPERS GUIDE
Also Called: Shopper's Guide
950 W Basin Rd (19720-1008)
PHONE..................302 325-6600
Curtis Riddle, Pr
EMP: 9 EST: 1986
SALES (est): 158.15K **Privately Held**
SIC: 8748 2741 Business consulting, nec; Miscellaneous publishing

(G-9407)
NEW CASTLE DENTAL ASSOC PA
Also Called: Chamish, Steven E
92 Reads Way Ste 200 (19720-1631)
PHONE..................302 328-1513
Steven Chamish, Pr
EMP: 18 EST: 1964
SALES (est): 246.06K **Privately Held**
Web: www.newcastledental.net
SIC: 8021 Dentists' office

(G-9408)
NEW CASTLE ENGRAVING CO
133 Festone Ave (19720-2049)
PHONE..................302 652-7551
Jim Cain, Owner
EMP: 2 EST: 1971
SALES (est): 128.48K **Privately Held**
SIC: 3089 Engraving of plastics

(G-9409)
NEW CASTLE GLASS INC
38 Lesley Ln (19720-3340)
P.O. Box 10984 (19850-0984)
PHONE..................302 322-6164
George R Glanden, Pr
Joanne Glanden, Treas
EMP: 8 EST: 1989
SQ FT: 1,400
SALES (est): 700K **Privately Held**
Web: www.newcastleglassde.com
SIC: 1793 Glass and glazing work

(G-9410)
NEW CASTLE LODGING CORPORATION
Also Called: Travelodge
1213 West Ave (19720-6250)
PHONE..................302 654-5544
Peter Bhai, Pr
Pinky Bhai, Sec
EMP: 73 EST: 1989
SALES (est): 242.18K **Privately Held**
Web: www.wyndhamhotels.com
SIC: 7011 Motels

(G-9411)
NEW CASTLE PRECISION MCH LLC
729 Grantham Ln Bldg 2ad (19720-4898)
PHONE..................302 650-7849
Guy Anderson, Managing Member
EMP: 7 EST: 2019
SALES (est): 211.49K **Privately Held**
Web: www.newcastleprecisionmachine.com
SIC: 3599 Machine shop, jobbing and repair

(G-9412)
NEW CASTLE SHOP RENTAL INC
34 Yeates Dr (19720-3230)
PHONE..................302 328-8346
Jon Rogers, Prin
EMP: 5 EST: 2015
SALES (est): 32.23K **Privately Held**
SIC: 7241 Barber shops

(G-9413)
NEW CASTLE SHUTTLE AND TAXI SE
38 Stevens Ave (19720-4047)
PHONE..................302 326-1855
Carolyn Propson, Owner
EMP: 7 EST: 2004
SALES (est): 239.74K **Privately Held**
Web: www.newcastleshuttleandtaxi.com
SIC: 4119 Limousine rental, with driver

(G-9414)
NEW CSTLE CNTY DEL EMPLYEES FD
100 Churchmans Rd (19720-3108)
PHONE..................302 395-5350
Merideth Jefferies, CEO
EMP: 10 EST: 2016
SALES (est): 569.68K **Privately Held**
Web: www.nccdefcu.com
SIC: 6061 7371 Federal credit unions; Computer software development

(G-9415)
NEW CSTLE CNTY EMPLYEES PNSION
87 Reads Way (19720-1648)
PHONE..................302 395-5555
EMP: 8 EST: 2014
SALES (est): 517.44K **Privately Held**
Web: www.newcastlede.gov
SIC: 6371 Pensions

(G-9416)
NEW CSTLE HLTH RHBLTTION CTR L
Also Called: NEW CASTLE HEALTH & REHABILITA
32 Buena Vista Dr (19720-4660)
PHONE..................302 328-2580
Richard Powell, Mgr
EMP: 126 EST: 2018
SALES (est): 12.57MM **Privately Held**
Web: www.saberhealth.com
SIC: 8051 Skilled nursing care facilities

(G-9417)
NEWS-JOURNAL COMPANY
950 W Basin Rd (19720-1006)
PHONE..................302 324-2500
Jane Amari, Prin
EMP: 124 EST: 2011
SALES (est): 2.96MM **Privately Held**
Web: www.delawareonline.com
SIC: 2711 Commercial printing and newspaper publishing combined

(G-9418)
NEXGEN TECHNICAL SUPPORT GROUP
5 Walker Dr (19720-4683)
PHONE..................302 345-1330
Manuel Peralta, Prin
EMP: 5 EST: 2016
SALES (est): 88.35K **Privately Held**
SIC: 8399 Advocacy group

(G-9419)
NICASTROS INC
489 Old Airport Rd (19720-1001)
PHONE..................302 425-5555
Vince Nicastro, Pr
EMP: 5 EST: 2015
SALES (est): 55.86K **Privately Held**
SIC: 7549 Automotive services, nec

(G-9420)
NICHOLLS PHOTOGRAPHY
104 Callow Pl (19720-8711)
PHONE..................302 543-3879
EMP: 6 EST: 2017
SALES (est): 67.61K **Privately Held**
SIC: 7221 Photographer, still or video

(G-9421)
NO JOKE I LLC
Also Called: Champion Builders
16 Stockton Dr (19720-4318)
PHONE..................302 395-0882
Micheal Stewart, Managing Member
EMP: 7 EST: 2005
SALES (est): 420.59K **Privately Held**

SIC: 1531 7389 Operative builders; Business Activities at Non-Commercial Site

(G-9422)
NORTH AMERICAN TRNSPT CO INC
92 Reads Way Ste 202 (19720-1631)
PHONE..................856 696-5483
Stephanie Wood, Brnch Mgr
EMP: 5
SALES (corp-wide): 9.55MM **Privately Held**
Web: www.americantransport.com
SIC: 4731 Truck transportation brokers
PA: North American Transport Company Inc.
   1830 Gallagher Dr Ste 101
   Vineland NJ 08360
   856 696-5483

(G-9423)
NORTH ATL INTL OCEAN CARIER
35 Davidson Ln (19720-2213)
PHONE..................786 275-5352
Olga Fred, Genl Mgr
EMP: 27 EST: 2016
SALES (est): 693.66K **Privately Held**
Web: www.gruponorthatlantic.com
SIC: 3711 Motor vehicles and car bodies

(G-9424)
NORTH ATLANTIC OCEAN SHIP
19 Davidson Ln (19720-2246)
PHONE..................302 652-3782
Efren Jimenez, Prin
EMP: 6 EST: 2006
SALES (est): 444.68K **Privately Held**
SIC: 4789 Cargo loading and unloading services

(G-9425)
NORTH EAST HOME INTERIORS LLC
6 N Booth Dr (19720-3302)
PHONE..................302 388-6262
EMP: 5 EST: 2015
SALES (est): 238.34K **Privately Held**
SIC: 1771 1799 Flooring contractor; Kitchen and bathroom remodeling

(G-9426)
NORTH EAST POOL PLUMBING
226 Harlequin Dr (19720-8900)
PHONE..................302 740-5071
Royce R Knabe, Pr
EMP: 5 EST: 2016
SALES (est): 87.44K **Privately Held**
SIC: 1711 Plumbing contractors

(G-9427)
NORTHEASTERN TITLE LOANS
Also Called: Select Management Resources
1560 N Dupont Hwy (19720-1902)
PHONE..................302 326-2210
Rod Aycox, Pr
John Henry, Genl Mgr
EMP: 9 EST: 1992
SALES (est): 655.62K **Privately Held**
Web: www.northeasterntitleloans.net
SIC: 6141 Personal finance licensed loan companies, small

(G-9428)
NOTHING BUT NET INC
83 Charles Dr (19720-4679)
PHONE..................302 476-0453
Lonnie Wright, Prin
EMP: 5 EST: 2017
SALES (est): 58.05K **Privately Held**
SIC: 7999 Basketball instruction school

▲ = Import ▼ = Export
◆ = Import/Export

GEOGRAPHIC SECTION

New Castle - New Castle County (G-9457)

(G-9429)
NU FRIENDSHIP OUTREACH
622 Country Path Dr (19720-7662)
PHONE.................................302 354-1517
Kevin Evans, *Prin*
EMP: 8 **EST:** 2010
SALES (est): 68K **Privately Held**
Web: www.nufoutreach.org
SIC: 8322 Outreach program

(G-9430)
NUR TEMPLE AAONMS
198 S Dupont Hwy (19720-4149)
PHONE.................................302 328-6100
Mick Schroder, *Prin*
EMP: 7 **EST:** 1993
SALES (est): 108.64K **Privately Held**
SIC: 7299 8699 Banquet hall facilities; Charitable organization

(G-9431)
NURSES N KIDS INC (PA)
11 Reads Way (19720-1648)
PHONE.................................302 323-1118
Janet Carroll, *CEO*
Janet Carroll, *Pr*
Melissa Cappelli, *
Charles Carroll, *
David Carroll, *
EMP: 50 **EST:** 1987
SALES (est): 4.77MM
SALES (corp-wide): 4.77MM **Privately Held**
Web: www.nursesnkids.com
SIC: 8351 Child day care services

(G-9432)
OAK HRC NEW CASTLE LLC
Also Called: New Cstle Hlth Rhblitation Ctr
32 Buena Vista Dr (19720-4660)
PHONE.................................302 328-2580
Karen Thomas, *Admn*
Howard Jaffe, *
Wayne Barrett, *
EMP: 18 **EST:** 2014
SQ FT: 40,000
SALES (est): 481.62K **Privately Held**
SIC: 8051 Mental retardation hospital

(G-9433)
ON-BOARD ENGINEERING CORP
2 Penns Way Ste 400 (19720-2407)
PHONE.................................302 613-5030
Richard Jervis, *Mgr*
EMP: 13
SALES (corp-wide): 21.08MM **Privately Held**
Web: www.onboardusa.com
SIC: 8711 Consulting engineer
PA: On-Board Engineering Corporation
50 Millstone Rd Bldg 300
East Windsor NJ 08520
609 945-8000

(G-9434)
ONLY GODS SPEED LLC
150 Karlyn Dr (19720-1309)
PHONE.................................302 367-8366
EMP: 10 **EST:** 2020
SALES (est): 394.17K **Privately Held**
SIC: 8748 Urban planning and consulting services

(G-9435)
OPPORTUNITY CENTER INC (PA)
Also Called: OCI
13 Reads Way Ste 101 (19720-1609)
P.O. Box 254 (19899-0254)
PHONE.................................302 762-0300
Janet Samuelson, *Pr*
Mark Hall, *
David Hodge, *
Bruce Patterson, *
Lisa Ward, *
EMP: 100 **EST:** 1957
SALES (est): 8.78MM
SALES (corp-wide): 8.78MM **Privately Held**
SIC: 8331 7361 Job counseling; Placement agencies

(G-9436)
ORCHARD PARK GROUP INC
42 Reads Way (19720-1612)
PHONE.................................302 356-1139
Ray Garcia, *Pr*
EMP: 6 **EST:** 2007
SALES (est): 155.84K **Privately Held**
SIC: 8748 Business consulting, nec

(G-9437)
ORDER DEPARTMENT
615 Lambson Ln (19720-2103)
PHONE.................................302 654-3116
Lynn Haskins, *Prin*
EMP: 5 **EST:** 2016
SALES (est): 66.64K **Privately Held**
SIC: 5182 Wine

(G-9438)
OSKI INDUSTRIES
34 Blevins Dr Ste 10 (19720-4177)
PHONE.................................646 369-5799
EMP: 8 **EST:** 2020
SALES (est): 271.05K **Privately Held**
SIC: 3999 Manufacturing industries, nec

(G-9439)
OTR 2 OTR DISPATCHING LLC
20 Penn Mart Shopping Ctr (19720-4207)
PHONE.................................862 249-9407
EMP: 6
SALES (est): 81.26K **Privately Held**
SIC: 4789 Transportation services, nec

(G-9440)
OUTSIDE CREATIONS
83 Charles Dr (19720-4679)
PHONE.................................302 757-5944
EMP: 5 **EST:** 2010
SALES (est): 252.96K **Privately Held**
SIC: 0782 Landscape contractors

(G-9441)
OVERNIGHT MOVERS LLC
102 Robinson Dr (19720-1824)
PHONE.................................302 345-1142
EMP: 10 **EST:** 2020
SALES (est): 316.02K **Privately Held**
SIC: 4212 Moving services

(G-9442)
P & C ROOFING INC
35 Southgate Blvd (19720-2069)
PHONE.................................302 322-6767
Angela Papa Mariano, *Pr*
Peter A Papa Junior, *VP*
Vincent Papa, *
Randy Mariano, *
Mathew Papa, *
EMP: 45 **EST:** 1971
SQ FT: 30,000
SALES (est): 7.18MM **Privately Held**
Web: www.pcroofinginc.com
SIC: 1761 Roofing contractor

(G-9443)
P A ANESTHESIA SERVICES
100 W Commons Blvd Ste 400 (19720)
PHONE.................................302 709-4709
Richard Stern, *Prin*
EMP: 6 **EST:** 2008
SALES (est): 2.58MM **Privately Held**
Web: www.aspa-de.com
SIC: 8011 Anesthesiologist

(G-9444)
PADENS HAIR STUDIO
28 Scottie Ln (19720-3923)
PHONE.................................267 718-8109
Tiana Paden, *Prin*
EMP: 5 **EST:** 2018
SALES (est): 70.35K **Privately Held**
SIC: 7231 Hairdressers

(G-9445)
PALACE LAUNDRY INC
Also Called: Linens of The Week
30 Mccullough Dr (19720-2066)
PHONE.................................302 322-2136
TOLL FREE: 800
Ken Bubes, *Brnch Mgr*
EMP: 612
SALES (corp-wide): 20.11MM **Privately Held**
Web: www.firmdalehotels.com
SIC: 7213 Uniform supply
PA: Palace Laundry, Inc.
713 Lamont St Nw
Washington DC 20010
202 291-9200

(G-9446)
PANDA EARLY EDUCATION CTR INC
1169 S Dupont Hwy (19720-5203)
PHONE.................................302 328-1481
EMP: 10
SIC: 8351 Preschool center
PA: Early Panda Education Center Inc
105 Emerald Ridge Dr
Bear DE 19701

(G-9447)
PANELMATIC INC
11 Southgate Blvd (19720-2069)
P.O. Box 141 (45071-0141)
PHONE.................................302 324-9193
EMP: 7
SALES (corp-wide): 42.48MM **Privately Held**
Web: www.panelmatic.com
SIC: 3613 8711 Control panels, electric; Designing: ship, boat, machine, and product
PA: Panelmatic, Inc.
258 Donald Dr
Fairfield OH 45014
513 829-3666

(G-9448)
PANELMATIC EAST INC
11 Southgate Blvd (19720-2069)
P.O. Box 141 (45071-0141)
PHONE.................................302 324-9193
Richard Leach, *Pr*
David D Adamson, *Sec*
▼ **EMP:** 10 **EST:** 1977
SALES (est): 2.08MM
SALES (corp-wide): 42.48MM **Privately Held**
Web: www.panelmatic.com
SIC: 3613 8711 Control panels, electric; Designing: ship, boat, machine, and product
PA: Panelmatic, Inc.
258 Donald Dr
Fairfield OH 45014
513 829-3666

(G-9449)
PARK SIDE UTILITY CONSTRUCTION
718 Grantham Ln (19720-4802)
PHONE.................................302 322-9760
EMP: 19 **EST:** 2016
SALES (est): 73.67K **Privately Held**
SIC: 1521 Single-family housing construction

(G-9450)
PARKWAY GRAVEL INC
4048 New Castle Ave (19720-1455)
PHONE.................................302 658-5241
Nicholas Ferrara Junior, *Pr*
Henry S Alisa, *
EMP: 99 **EST:** 2006
SALES (est): 4.73MM **Privately Held**
SIC: 6519 6552 6512 Real property lessors, nec; Subdividers and developers, nec; Nonresidential building operators

(G-9451)
PARKWAY GRAVEL INC
13 Parkway Cir (19720-4077)
PHONE.................................302 326-0554
EMP: 5 **EST:** 2018
SALES (est): 179.52K **Privately Held**
SIC: 1442 Construction sand and gravel

(G-9452)
PARTNERS PLUS INC
2 Tenns Way Ste 403 (19720)
PHONE.................................302 529-3700
William Hogan, *Pr*
EMP: 5 **EST:** 1991
SALES (est): 1.24MM **Privately Held**
Web: www.partnersplus.com
SIC: 7379 Computer related consulting services

(G-9453)
PARTYRITE EVENTS & RENTALS ✪
622 E Basin Rd # A (19720-4202)
PHONE.................................302 743-5691
Ceceile Binns, *CEO*
EMP: 5 **EST:** 2023
SALES (est): 272.75K **Privately Held**
SIC: 4899 Communication services, nec

(G-9454)
PASCALE INDUSTRIES INC
National Roll Kote
55 Harbor View Dr (19720-2179)
PHONE.................................302 421-9400
Joe Ferma, *Brnch Mgr*
EMP: 10
Web: www.enyarns.com
SIC: 3069 5084 Rubber rolls and roll coverings; Industrial machinery and equipment
PA: Pascale Industries, Inc.
4301 Pratt Remmel Rd
Little Rock AR 72206

(G-9455)
PASSION CARE SERVICES
604 Highpointe Dr (19720-5645)
PHONE.................................302 834-9585
EMP: 6 **EST:** 2019
SALES (est): 15.97K **Privately Held**
SIC: 8351 Child day care services

(G-9456)
PASSION DRIVEN LLC
4a King Ave (19720-1512)
PHONE.................................302 293-5960
EMP: 5 **EST:** 2016
SALES (est): 140.71K **Privately Held**
SIC: 7299 Tattoo parlor

(G-9457)
PATIO PRINTING CO INC
197 Airport Rd (19720-2379)
PHONE.................................302 328-6881
George T Fox Ii, *Pr*

New Castle - New Castle County (G-9458)

EMP: 3 EST: 1981
SQ FT: 2,600
SALES (est): 232.98K **Privately Held**
Web: www.patioprinting.com
SIC: **2752** Offset printing

(G-9458)
PATRIOT GENERAL CONTRACTORS
205 Adele Pl (19720-2706)
P.O. Box 85 (19720-0085)
PHONE..................................302 287-9000
EMP: 6 EST: 2015
SALES (est): 106.89K **Privately Held**
SIC: **1521** Single-family housing construction

(G-9459)
PATRIOT TRUCKING LLC
111 Cross Ave (19720-2001)
PHONE..................................302 469-3774
Lori Welsh, *Prin*
EMP: 7 EST: 2016
SALES (est): 70.31K **Privately Held**
SIC: **4212** Local trucking, without storage

(G-9460)
PATS MANAGEMENT
602 E Basin Rd (19720-4202)
PHONE..................................302 322-3442
EMP: 63 EST: 2014
SALES (est): 767.9K **Privately Held**
Web: www.patspizzapasta.com
SIC: **8741** Management services

(G-9461)
PAUL DVIS RSTORATION NTHRN DEL
Also Called: Paul Davis Restoration
1061 Lower Twin Lane Rd (19720-5502)
PHONE..................................302 449-6941
EMP: 7 EST: 2019
SALES (est): 271.39K **Privately Held**
Web: northern-delaware.pauldavis.com
SIC: **1799** Post disaster renovations

(G-9462)
PAULS PLASTERING INC
19 Davidson Ln (19720-2210)
PHONE..................................302 654-5583
Donald L Jester, *Pr*
Ken P Jester, *VP*
Helen Marie Jester, *Sec*
EMP: 17 EST: 1952
SQ FT: 2,500
SALES (est): 930.87K **Privately Held**
Web: www.paulsplastering.com
SIC: **1742** Plastering, plain or ornamental

(G-9463)
PENN ACRES CIVIC ASSOCIATION
19 Silsbee Rd (19720-3236)
P.O. Box 1178 (19720-7178)
PHONE..................................302 328-8500
Kenneth J Lagowski, *Prin*
EMP: 5 EST: 2010
SALES (est): 68.76K **Privately Held**
SIC: **8699** Membership organizations, nec

(G-9464)
PENN DEL CARRIERS LLC
110 W Edinburgh Dr (19720-2317)
PHONE..................................484 424-3768
Raymond Lamont Butts, *Managing Member*
EMP: 6 EST: 2003
SALES (est): 934.65K **Privately Held**
Web: www.penndelcarriers.com
SIC: **4731** Freight transportation arrangement

(G-9465)
PENNY COOPER SPORTSWEAR & EMB
204 Christiana Rd (19720-3010)
PHONE..................................302 325-3710
Penny Weingardner, *Owner*
EMP: 6 EST: 1997
SALES (est): 276.38K **Privately Held**
SIC: **2395** Embroidery products, except Schiffli machine

(G-9466)
PENOBSCOT PROPERTIES LLC (PA)
135 N Dupont Hwy (19720-3135)
PHONE..................................302 322-4477
EMP: 9 EST: 1996
SALES (est): 1.43MM **Privately Held**
SIC: **4512** 4522 4513 Air transportation, scheduled; Air transportation, nonscheduled ; Air courier services

(G-9467)
PENSKE TRUCK LEASING CO LP
Also Called: Penske
51 Boulden Blvd (19720-2065)
PHONE..................................302 325-9290
Bill Mc Anally, *Brnch Mgr*
EMP: 6
SALES (corp-wide): 2.11B **Privately Held**
Web: www.pensketruckrental.com
SIC: **7513** 7519 7359 Truck rental and leasing, no drivers; Utility trailer rental; Equipment rental and leasing, nec
PA: Penske Truck Leasing Co., L.P.
2675 Morgantown Rd
Reading PA 19607
610 775-6000

(G-9468)
PEOPLE IN TRANSITION INC
39 Thorn Ln (19720-2151)
PHONE..................................302 784-5214
Doreen S Watson, *Dir*
EMP: 8 EST: 2005
SALES (est): 136.09K **Privately Held**
SIC: **8361** Residential care

(G-9469)
PEOPLE TECH GROUP INC
42 Reads Way (19720-1612)
PHONE..................................833 202-3555
EMP: 5 EST: 2018
SALES (est): 94.52K **Privately Held**
Web: www.peopletechcorp.com
SIC: **7371** Custom computer programming services

(G-9470)
PHC INC (HQ)
Also Called: Pioneer Behavioral Health
575 S Dupont Hwy (19720-4606)
PHONE..................................313 831-3500
Bruce A Shear, *Pr*
EMP: 50 EST: 2019
SALES (est): 7.25MM **Publicly Held**
SIC: **8063** 8322 Psychiatric hospitals; Rehabilitation services
PA: Acadia Healthcare Company, Inc.
6100 Tower Cir Ste 1000
Franklin TN 37067

(G-9471)
PHILADELPHIA PLUMBING
100 Garfield Ave (19720-6418)
PHONE..................................302 327-8545
EMP: 5 EST: 2016
SALES (est): 75.28K **Privately Held**
SIC: **1711** Plumbing contractors

(G-9472)
PHOTON PROGRAMMING
58 Stockton Dr (19720-4318)
PHONE..................................302 328-2925
Thomas Shustack, *Prin*
EMP: 2 EST: 2008
SALES (est): 86.14K **Privately Held**
SIC: **3661** Fiber optics communications equipment

(G-9473)
PJ FITZPATRICK INC (PA)
Also Called: Rt Stover
21 Industrial Blvd (19720-2087)
PHONE..................................302 325-2360
Rick Stover, *Pr*
Scott Schmoyer, *
EMP: 68 EST: 1980
SQ FT: 26,500
SALES (est): 25.71MM
SALES (corp-wide): 25.71MM **Privately Held**
Web: www.pjfitz.com
SIC: **1761** 1521 Siding contractor; Single-family home remodeling, additions, and repairs

(G-9474)
PLANET FITNESS
148 Sunset Blvd (19720-4100)
PHONE..................................302 501-7220
EMP: 15 EST: 2019
SALES (est): 264.27K **Privately Held**
Web: www.planetfitness.com
SIC: **7991** Physical fitness facilities

(G-9475)
PLANET PAYMENT INC (PA)
100 W Commons Blvd Ste 200 (19720-2419)
PHONE..................................516 670-3200
Robert J Cox, *Pr*
Raymond D'aponte, *CFO*
EMP: 90 EST: 1999
SALES (est): 53.75MM
SALES (corp-wide): 53.75MM **Privately Held**
Web: www.planetpayment.com
SIC: **7389** Credit card service

(G-9476)
PLANET PAYMENT SOLUTIONS INC
100 W Commons Blvd Ste 200 (19720)
PHONE..................................516 670-3200
EMP: 40
Web: www.planetpayment.com
SIC: **7374** 6411 Data processing service; Insurance agents, brokers, and service

(G-9477)
PNC BANK NATIONAL ASSOCIATION
Also Called: PNC
1 Penn Mart Shopping Ctr (19720-4206)
PHONE..................................302 326-4710
Rick Modell, *Prin*
EMP: 6
SALES (corp-wide): 23.54B **Publicly Held**
Web: www.pnc.com
SIC: **6021** National commercial banks
HQ: Pnc Bank, National Association
300 5th Ave
Pittsburgh PA 15222
877 762-2000

(G-9478)
PNC BANK NATIONAL ASSOCIATION
Also Called: PNC
1 E Basin Rte (19720-4264)
PHONE..................................302 326-4701
Pedro Viero Junior, *Brnch Mgr*
EMP: 5
SALES (corp-wide): 23.54B **Publicly Held**
Web: www.pnc.com
SIC: **6021** National commercial banks
HQ: Pnc Bank, National Association
300 5th Ave
Pittsburgh PA 15222
877 762-2000

(G-9479)
POINT HOPE BRAIN INJURY SPPORT
34 Blevins Dr Ste 5 (19720-4177)
PHONE..................................302 731-7676
Damian Robinson, *Prin*
EMP: 10 EST: 2017
SALES (est): 267.08K **Privately Held**
Web: www.point-of-hope.com
SIC: **8093** Mental health clinic, outpatient

(G-9480)
POINT OF HOPE INC
34 Blevins Dr Ste 5 (19720-4177)
PHONE..................................302 731-7676
EMP: 49 EST: 2007
SALES (est): 624.14K **Privately Held**
Web: www.point-of-hope.com
SIC: **8322** Social service center

(G-9481)
POLICE & FIRE ROD & GUN CLUB
1 Glen Ave (19720-3528)
PHONE..................................302 655-0304
Fred Durham, *Pr*
EMP: 5 EST: 1955
SALES (est): 282.51K **Privately Held**
SIC: **7997** 5941 Gun club, membership; Firearms

(G-9482)
POLICE ATHLETIC LEAGUE DEL INC (PA)
26 Karlyn Dr (19720-1253)
PHONE..................................302 656-9501
Jimmy Riggs, *Ex Dir*
Captain Steward Snyder, *Pr*
EMP: 5 EST: 1984
SALES (est): 1.62MM **Privately Held**
Web: www.palde.org
SIC: **8641** Youth organizations

(G-9483)
POLITE CONSTRUCTION JAY
138 Louise Rd (19720-1758)
PHONE..................................302 328-0390
Jay Polite, *Prin*
EMP: 5 EST: 2011
SALES (est): 140K **Privately Held**
SIC: **1521** Single-family housing construction

(G-9484)
PORT TO PORT INTL CORP
32 Pyles Ln (19720-1467)
PHONE..................................302 654-2444
Anabel Panayotti, *Pr*
Gwen North, *
◆ EMP: 40 EST: 1998
SALES (est): 9.64MM **Privately Held**
Web: www.ptpshipping.com
SIC: **4731** Foreign freight forwarding

(G-9485)
PORT TO PORT LOGISTICS LLC
32 Pyles Ln (19720-1420)
PHONE..................................302 654-2444
EMP: 6
SALES (est): 280.62K **Privately Held**
SIC: **4731** Freight transportation arrangement

New Castle - New Castle County (G-9515)

(G-9486)
POWER OVER PAIN CRPS FNDTION I
1 Ferris Ct (19720-5169)
PHONE..................................302 983-6412
Sharron Snavely, *Prin*
EMP: 5 **EST:** 2016
SALES (est): 52.93K **Privately Held**
SIC: 8641 Civic and social associations

(G-9487)
PQS LANDSCAPING
19 Caxton Dr (19720-2332)
PHONE..................................302 690-6505
EMP: 6 **EST:** 2014
SALES (est): 31.52K **Privately Held**
SIC: 0781 Landscape services

(G-9488)
PRATT-FIELDS HOME PLEASE INC
220 Remi Dr (19720-5622)
PHONE..................................215 868-9028
Janice Pratt-fields, *CEO*
Daryl Field, *CEO*
Harriet Waddy King, *Sec*
Abbie Holliday, *Treas*
Sabrina Malrura, *Prin*
EMP: 6 **EST:** 2018
SALES (est): 98.94K **Privately Held**
SIC: 8052 Intermediate care facilities

(G-9489)
PRECISION FLOW LLC
62 Southgate Blvd Ste L (19720-2090)
P.O. Box 875 (08021-0875)
PHONE..................................302 544-4417
EMP: 10 **EST:** 2001
SALES (est): 1.68MM **Privately Held**
Web: www.precisionflow.net
SIC: 5085 Valves and fittings

(G-9490)
PREFERRED CONSTRUCTION INC
505 Churchmans Rd (19720-3154)
PHONE..................................302 322-9568
Joseph A Sparco, *Pr*
John Paul, *VP*
EMP: 8 **EST:** 1999
SQ FT: 1,500
SALES (est): 1.7MM **Privately Held**
Web: www.preferredinc.net
SIC: 1542 1522 Commercial and office building contractors; Residential construction, nec

(G-9491)
PREFERRED ELECTRIC INC
505 Churchmans Rd (19720-3154)
PHONE..................................302 322-1217
Catherine L Sparco, *Pr*
John Paul Sparco, *
Joseph Sparco, *
EMP: 70 **EST:** 2000
SQ FT: 15,000
SALES (est): 13.17MM **Privately Held**
Web: www.preferredinc.net
SIC: 1731 General electrical contractor

(G-9492)
PRESS FITNESS LLC
260 Christiana Rd Apt L2 (19720-2973)
PHONE..................................973 441-9397
Andrei Francis, *Prin*
EMP: 5 **EST:** 2016
SALES (est): 40.67K **Privately Held**
SIC: 7991 Physical fitness facilities

(G-9493)
PRIME BEVERAGE GROUP LLC
200 Lisa Dr (19720-4167)
PHONE..................................302 327-0002
Valentine Orock, *Asst Sec*
EMP: 5 **EST:** 2018
SALES (est): 248.49K **Privately Held**
SIC: 5181 Beer and ale

(G-9494)
PRINCE TELECOM LLC (HQ)
Also Called: Leading Communication Contrs
551 Mews Dr Ste A (19720-2798)
PHONE..................................302 324-1800
EMP: 60 **EST:** 1989
SQ FT: 6,000
SALES (est): 270.88MM
SALES (corp-wide): 3.81B **Publicly Held**
Web: www.princetelecom.com
SIC: 1731 Cable television installation
PA: Dycom Industries, Inc.
  11780 Us Highway 1 # 600
  Palm Beach Gardens FL 33408
  561 627-7171

(G-9495)
PRINTPACK INC
Also Called: Flexible Packaging Group
600 Grantham Ln (19720-4852)
P.O. Box 110 (19720-0110)
PHONE..................................302 323-4000
Steve Aguillard, *Brnch Mgr*
EMP: 134
SALES (corp-wide): 1.3B **Privately Held**
Web: www.printpack.com
SIC: 2673 3081 2671 Bags: plastic, laminated, and coated; Plastics film and sheet; Paper; coated and laminated packaging
HQ: Printpack, Inc.
  2800 Overlook Pkwy Ne
  Atlanta GA 30339
  404 460-7000

(G-9496)
PRO PHYSICAL THERAPY PA
Also Called: ATI
2032 New Castle Ave (19720-7703)
PHONE..................................302 654-1700
Matthew Haney, *Pr*
EMP: 10 **EST:** 2003
SALES (est): 164.1K **Privately Held**
SIC: 8049 Physical therapist

(G-9497)
PRO WORKS INC DH
177 Old Churchmans Rd (19720-3115)
PHONE..................................302 221-4200
EMP: 12 **EST:** 2018
SALES (est): 937.11K **Privately Held**
SIC: 1711 Plumbing contractors

(G-9498)
PRODUCT SERVICE AND REPAIR
17 Bellecor Dr # 11a (19720-1755)
PHONE..................................443 466-0566
EMP: 5 **EST:** 2019
SALES (est): 193.31K **Privately Held**
SIC: 7699 Repair services, nec

(G-9499)
PROMO MARKETING
950 W Basin Rd (19720-1008)
PHONE..................................302 324-2650
EMP: 5 **EST:** 2014
SALES (est): 155.31K **Privately Held**
Web: search.printandpromomarketing.com
SIC: 7311 Advertising agencies

(G-9500)
PUBLIC SYSTEMS INC
Also Called: P S I Maximus
2 Penns Way Ste 406 (19720-2407)
PHONE..................................302 326-4500
Clark Brown Senior, *Pr*
Michael Moore, *
Reese Robinson, *
EMP: 5 **EST:** 1989
SALES (est): 138.64K **Privately Held**
SIC: 7373 Systems software development services

(G-9501)
PUREBRED LLC
157 Riverview Dr (19720-2721)
PHONE..................................929 777-7770
EMP: 2 **EST:** 2020
SALES (est): 62.54K **Privately Held**
SIC: 3999 Pet supplies

(G-9502)
PYRAMID EDUCATIONAL CONS
350 Churchmans Rd Ste B (19720-3146)
PHONE..................................302 368-2515
Andrew Bondy, *Pr*
EMP: 28 **EST:** 1992
SALES (est): 4.75MM **Privately Held**
Web: www.pecs.com
SIC: 8748 Educational consultant

(G-9503)
PYRAMID GROUP MGT SVCS CO
350 Churchmans Rd Ste A (19720-3146)
PHONE..................................302 355-1760
EMP: 8 **EST:** 2017
SALES (est): 319.98K **Privately Held**
Web: www.pecs.com
SIC: 8741 Management services

(G-9504)
QORO LLC
Also Called: Qoro
166 S Dupont Hwy Ste B (19720-4159)
PHONE..................................302 322-5900
E William Jensen, *Pr*
Katherine Griffith, *Sec*
Colonel Frank D Davis, *CEO*
EMP: 7 **EST:** 1991
SALES (est): 541.1K **Privately Held**
Web: www.qoro.com
SIC: 2741 Art copy and poster publishing

(G-9505)
QUALITY CONSTRUCTION DE LLC
811 Moores Ln (19720-3480)
PHONE..................................302 757-6185
EMP: 9 **EST:** 2014
SALES (est): 258.19K **Privately Held**
Web: www.corradoconstruction.com
SIC: 1521 Single-family housing construction

(G-9506)
QUALITY ROFG SUP LANCASTER INC
Also Called: Quality Roofing Supply
9 Parkway Cir (19720-4077)
PHONE..................................302 322-8322
Todd Doussard, *Mgr*
EMP: 9
SALES (corp-wide): 8.43B **Publicly Held**
Web: www.becn.com
SIC: 5033 Roofing, asphalt and sheet metal
HQ: Quality Roofing Supply Company Of Lancaster, Inc.
  737 Flory Mill Rd
  Lancaster PA 17601
  717 569-2661

(G-9507)
QUANTUM ALCHEMY LLC ✪
94 Karlyn Dr (19720-1235)
PHONE..................................484 299-8016
Demetri Williams, *CEO*
EMP: 5 **EST:** 2022
SALES (est): 78.16K **Privately Held**
SIC: 3572 7389 Computer storage devices; Business Activities at Non-Commercial Site

(G-9508)
QUICK SERVER HOSTING LLC
122 Delaware Ave Ste B8 (19720-6414)
PHONE..................................800 586-6126
James Mcough, *Pr*
EMP: 33 **EST:** 2019
SALES (est): 1.25MM **Privately Held**
SIC: 4813 Internet host services

(G-9509)
QWINTRY LLC
Also Called: Qwintry Logistics
1620 Johnson Way (19720)
PHONE..................................844 794-6879
EMP: 5 **EST:** 2017
SALES (est): 247.15K **Privately Held**
Web: www.qwintry.global
SIC: 7371 Computer software development

(G-9510)
R & E EXCAVATION LLC
226 Harlequin Dr (19720-8900)
PHONE..................................302 750-5226
EMP: 8 **EST:** 2011
SALES (est): 458.48K **Privately Held**
Web: www.randeexcavation.com
SIC: 1794 Excavation work

(G-9511)
R A CHANCE PLUMBING INC
23 Parkway Cir Ste 5 (19720-4019)
PHONE..................................302 324-8200
EMP: 8 **EST:** 1988
SALES (est): 694.89K **Privately Held**
Web: www.rachance.com
SIC: 1711 Plumbing contractors

(G-9512)
RCD TIMBER PRODUCTS INC (PA)
1699 Matassino Rd (19720-2086)
PHONE..................................302 778-5700
Robert C Donehower, *Pr*
Joanne Donehower, *Sec*
EMP: 6 **EST:** 1991
SALES (est): 2.3MM **Privately Held**
Web: www.rcdtimber.com
SIC: 2448 5031 Pallets, wood; Pallets, wood

(G-9513)
RCD TIMBER PRODUCTS INC
4093 New Castle Ave (19720-1414)
PHONE..................................302 384-6243
EMP: 3
Web: www.rcdtimber.com
SIC: 2448 Pallets, wood
PA: Rcd Timber Products, Inc
  1699 Matassino Rd
  New Castle DE 19720

(G-9514)
RCS MUFFLERS INC
Also Called: Meineke Discount Mufflers
120 N Dupont Hwy (19720-3102)
PHONE..................................302 328-7788
EMP: 7 **EST:** 2010
SALES (est): 261.54K **Privately Held**
Web: www.meineke.com
SIC: 7533 Muffler shop, sale or repair and installation

(G-9515)
RECYCLING SWIFT & DEMOLITION
469 Old Airport Rd (19720-1001)
PHONE..................................302 328-8283
EMP: 6 **EST:** 2016

New Castle - New Castle County (G-9516)

SALES (est): 41.54K **Privately Held**
Web:
www.swiftrecyclinganddemolition.com
SIC: 4953 Recycling, waste materials

(G-9516)
REDRUM CITY PRODUCTIONS
110 Hillview Ave (19720-2237)
PHONE.................................313 389-6836
Darrell Hervey, *CEO*
EMP: 5 EST: 2014
SALES (est): 240.66K **Privately Held**
SIC: 8748 Business consulting, nec

(G-9517)
REFINING CO
4550 Wrangle Hill Rd (19720-5509)
PHONE.................................302 832-1099
Dave Pino, *Ofcr*
EMP: 10 EST: 2015
SALES (est): 258.3K **Privately Held**
Web: www.ncccc.com
SIC: 8611 Chamber of Commerce

(G-9518)
RELIABLE AID INC
2 Commonwealth Blvd (19720-4431)
PHONE.................................302 419-3558
Khyon Church, *Admn*
Ellie Ortman, *
Khyon Church, *Contrlr*
EMP: 40 EST: 2015
SALES (est): 1.29MM **Privately Held**
Web: www.reliableaidinc.com
SIC: 8742 Marketing consulting services

(G-9519)
RENAL CARE CTR
63 University Ave (19720-4319)
PHONE.................................302 453-8834
Patti French, *Mgr*
EMP: 7 EST: 2011
SALES (est): 88.34K **Privately Held**
SIC: 8099 Health and allied services, nec

(G-9520)
RENEWED ENVIRONMENTS
223 Lisa Dr (19720-4193)
PHONE.................................302 323-9100
Kevin Ennis, *Dir*
EMP: 10 EST: 2015
SALES (est): 583.92K **Privately Held**
Web: www.corporate-interiors.com
SIC: 5021 Office furniture, nec

(G-9521)
RENNIES ROLLED ICE CREAM LLC
501 Central Ave (19720-5920)
PHONE.................................551 273-8925
Renieal Campbell, *Prin*
EMP: 2
SALES (est): 72.72K **Privately Held**
SIC: 2656 7389 Frozen food and ice cream containers; Business services, nec

(G-9522)
REPROGRAPHICS CENTER INC
Also Called: Rci
298 Churchmans Rd (19720-3110)
PHONE.................................302 328-5019
Joan A Janis, *Pr*
Michael J Janis, *VP*
EMP: 8 EST: 1959
SQ FT: 6,000
SALES (est): 968.88K **Privately Held**
Web: www.rciplot.com
SIC: 7334 5049 Blueprinting service; Drafting supplies

(G-9523)
RESH LLC
206 Jestan Blvd (19720-5214)
PHONE.................................302 543-5469
Sherell Flagg, *Managing Member*
EMP: 13 EST: 2009
SALES (est): 973.85K **Privately Held**
Web: www.myresh.com
SIC: 7231 5122 Cosmetologist; Cosmetics, perfumes, and hair products

(G-9524)
RESOURCE INTL INC
Also Called: Mishimoto
7 Boulden Cir (19720-3400)
PHONE.................................302 762-4501
Michael Sullivan, *Pr*
▲ EMP: 10 EST: 2005
SQ FT: 3,000
SALES (est): 2.37MM **Privately Held**
Web: www.mishimoto.com
SIC: 3089 Automotive parts, plastic

(G-9525)
RESTORING LF RSTRTION CTR CORP
Also Called: Restoring Life
109 Arnell Ct (19720-5407)
PHONE.................................862 772-5148
Laverne Booker-kornegay, *Prin*
Joseph Kornegay, *Prin*
Gabrielle Montlouis, *Prin*
Evans Montlouis, *Prin*
EMP: 5 EST: 2016
SALES (est): 96.78K **Privately Held**
SIC: 8322 Individual and family services

(G-9526)
RESTU STAY LLC
128 Sunset Blvd (19720-4100)
PHONE.................................347 522-0919
No Jimmy, *Managing Member*
EMP: 5
SALES (est): 219.88K **Privately Held**
SIC: 6531 Real estate leasing and rentals

(G-9527)
REVOLUTION RECOVERY DEL LLC
1101 Lambson Ln (19720-2186)
PHONE.................................302 356-3000
Fern Gookin, *Dir*
EMP: 23 EST: 2012
SALES (est): 2.38MM **Privately Held**
SIC: 2611 Pulp manufactured from waste or recycled paper

(G-9528)
REYBOLD GROUP OF COMPANIES INC
950 Red Lion Rd (19720-5205)
PHONE.................................302 838-7405
EMP: 44
SALES (corp-wide): 10.3MM **Privately Held**
Web: www.reybold.com
SIC: 4226 Special warehousing and storage, nec
PA: The Reybold Group Of Companies Inc
116 E Scotland Dr
Bear DE 19701
302 832-7100

(G-9529)
REYBOLD HOMES INC
960 Red Lion Rd (19720-5205)
PHONE.................................302 834-3000
Lex Burkett, *Mgr*
EMP: 118
SALES (corp-wide): 8.2MM **Privately Held**
Web: www.reybold.com
SIC: 1521 Single-family housing construction
PA: Reybold Homes, Inc.
116 E Scotland Dr
Bear DE 19701
302 832-7100

(G-9530)
REYES REBECA
Also Called: Kidd Mc
1303 Goldeneye Dr (19720-8923)
PHONE.................................302 276-9132
Rebeca Reyes, *Owner*
Ivalisse King, *Prin*
EMP: 5 EST: 2016
SALES (est): 104.73K **Privately Held**
SIC: 7389 Business Activities at Non-Commercial Site

(G-9531)
RHINO FENCE
10 Mcgaughy Dr (19720-4034)
PHONE.................................302 544-5225
EMP: 5 EST: 2011
SALES (est): 93.87K **Privately Held**
SIC: 1799 Fence construction

(G-9532)
RICHARD L CRUZ MD
10 Central Ave (19720-1152)
PHONE.................................302 577-4270
Richard Cruz, *Prin*
EMP: 7 EST: 2013
SALES (est): 54.13K **Privately Held**
SIC: 8011 Offices and clinics of medical doctors

(G-9533)
RICHARD S BROWN
Also Called: Rickcools
70 University Ave (19720-4347)
PHONE.................................302 438-6885
Richard S Brown, *Prin*
EMP: 5 EST: 2012
SALES (est): 83.85K **Privately Held**
SIC: 1711 Warm air heating and air conditioning contractor

(G-9534)
RITA PORTER DARNETTA
Also Called: Born Again Beautiful Entps
25 Aquilla Dr (19720-1301)
PHONE.................................302 419-3877
Rita D Johnson, *Owner*
EMP: 5 EST: 2010
SALES (est): 35.15K **Privately Held**
SIC: 7231 Beauty shops

(G-9535)
RITTENHOUSE SQ FINE ART SHOW
28 Bradbury Rd (19720-2328)
PHONE.................................610 299-1343
Steve Oliver, *Prin*
EMP: 5 EST: 2017
SALES (est): 45.8K **Privately Held**
Web: www.rittenhousesquareart.com
SIC: 7999 Art gallery, commercial

(G-9536)
RJR RECYCLING CO
955 River Rd (19720-4837)
PHONE.................................610 647-1555
EMP: 6 EST: 2018
SALES (est): 170.94K **Privately Held**
SIC: 4953 Recycling, waste materials

(G-9537)
RNS CONTRACTING
810 Liberty Blvd (19720-1137)
PHONE.................................302 384-4633
Bernabe Reyes, *Prin*
EMP: 5 EST: 2018
SALES (est): 86.22K **Privately Held**
SIC: 1799 Special trade contractors, nec

(G-9538)
ROBERT J PEOPLES INC
3020 Bowlarama Dr (19720-1317)
P.O. Box 65 (19720-0065)
PHONE.................................302 984-2017
Steven M Pedrick, *Owner*
Felix Pedrick, *Prin*
Sandra Pedrick, *Prin*
EMP: 12 EST: 1918
SALES (est): 436.63K **Privately Held**
Web: www.rjpeoples.com
SIC: 1721 Painting and paper hanging

(G-9539)
ROBERT P HART DDS
92 Reads Way Ste 101 (19720-1631)
PHONE.................................302 328-1513
Robert P Hart D.m.d., *Owner*
EMP: 8 EST: 2017
SALES (est): 67.67K **Privately Held**
SIC: 8021 Dentists' office

(G-9540)
RON ENGLISH TRUCKING INC
512 Golding Ave (19720-1461)
P.O. Box 248 (19720-0248)
PHONE.................................302 328-2059
EMP: 15 EST: 1999
SALES (est): 2.28MM **Privately Held**
Web: www.ronenglishtrucking.com
SIC: 4212 Local trucking, without storage

(G-9541)
ROSE HILL COMMUNITY CENTER
19 Lambson Ln (19720-2118)
PHONE.................................302 656-8513
Deborah Deubert, *Admn*
EMP: 12 EST: 1980
SQ FT: 47,000
SALES (est): 1.18MM **Privately Held**
Web: www.rosehillcommunitycenter.org
SIC: 8322 8299 8351 Senior citizens' center or association; Educational services; Head Start center, except in conjunction with school

(G-9542)
ROUND TABLE MEN LLC (PA) ◎
13 Constitution Blvd (19720-4403)
PHONE.................................302 287-8200
Terrance Wallace, *Managing Member*
EMP: 6 EST: 2022
SALES (est): 74.93K
SALES (corp-wide): 74.93K **Privately Held**
SIC: 6799 7389 Investors, nec; Business services, nec

(G-9543)
ROYAL PEST SOLUTIONS INC
53 Mccullough Dr (19720-2080)
PHONE.................................302 322-6665
Roy Richardson, *Pr*
Roger Richardson, *
James Conroy, *
EMP: 35 EST: 1991
SALES (est): 9.67MM
SALES (corp-wide): 14.19B **Publicly Held**
Web: www.royalpest.com
SIC: 7342 Pest control in structures
PA: Ecolab Inc.
1 Ecolab Pl
Saint Paul MN 55102
800 232-6522

GEOGRAPHIC SECTION

New Castle - New Castle County (G-9573)

(G-9544)
ROYAL RSDNTIAL RENOVATIONS LLC
131 Karlyn Dr (19720-1308)
PHONE..................302 377-0128
EMP: 6 EST: 2020
SALES (est): 260.62K **Privately Held**
SIC: 1521 Single-family housing construction

(G-9545)
ROYAL TERMITE & PEST CTRL INC
Also Called: Royal Termite and Pest Control
53 Mccullough Dr (19720-2080)
PHONE..................302 322-3600
Roy Richardson, *Pr*
Donna Richardson, *
EMP: 24 EST: 1977
SQ FT: 1,800
SALES (est): 363.77K **Privately Held**
SIC: 7342 Pest control in structures

(G-9546)
ROYAL VANITY HAIR STUDIO
1506 Beaver Brook Plz (19720-8633)
PHONE..................302 322-4680
Deshaun V Chancy, *Owner*
EMP: 5 EST: 2016
SALES (est): 21.46K **Privately Held**
SIC: 7231 Hairdressers

(G-9547)
ROYALROSE302 LLC
108 Talbot Dr (19720-1816)
PHONE..................800 259-7918
Johnathan Jackson, *CEO*
EMP: 6 EST: 2021
SALES (est): 230.09K **Privately Held**
SIC: 5651 7389 Unisex clothing stores; Business Activities at Non-Commercial Site

(G-9548)
RUSH AUTO LLC
6 Elks Trl (19720-3855)
PHONE..................302 323-9070
Aole Kunte Phillips, *Prin*
EMP: 5 EST: 2016
SALES (est): 28.25K **Privately Held**
SIC: 7538 General automotive repair shops

(G-9549)
RYES HVAC LLC
12 Pembroke Ln (19720-3806)
PHONE..................302 981-7851
Ryan Lawson, *Managing Member*
EMP: 5
SALES (est): 77.62K **Privately Held**
SIC: 1711 7389 Heating and air conditioning contractors; Business Activities at Non-Commercial Site

(G-9550)
RYLA REAL ESTATE OPTIONS LLC
23 W Lexton Rd (19720-8824)
PHONE..................302 397-7402
Vernon Broussard, *CEO*
EMP: 5 EST: 2007
SALES (est): 287.95K **Privately Held**
SIC: 1521 Single-family housing construction

(G-9551)
SAMUEL CORALUZZO CO INC
729 Grantham Ln (19720-4897)
PHONE..................302 322-1195
EMP: 24
SALES (corp-wide): 79.64MM **Privately Held**
Web: www.coraluzzo.com
SIC: 4212 Local trucking, without storage
PA: Samuel Coraluzzo Co Inc
   1713 N Main Rd
   Vineland NJ 08360
   856 691-1142

(G-9552)
SANTOS AIRCRAFT LLC
15 Penns Way (19720-2437)
PHONE..................302 608-6637
EMP: 9 EST: 2014
SALES (est): 354.5K **Privately Held**
SIC: 3721 3724 Aircraft; Aircraft engines and engine parts

(G-9553)
SAVAREN CORPORATE ARCFT SVCS
120 Old Churchmans Rd (19720-3116)
PHONE..................443 207-1372
EMP: 5 EST: 2019
SALES (est): 296.28K **Privately Held**
Web: www.sca-ilg.com
SIC: 4581 Airports, flying fields, and services

(G-9554)
SCOTTISH VENTURES LLC
5 Wildfire Ln (19720-3859)
PHONE..................302 382-6057
EMP: 8 EST: 2009
SALES (est): 741.34K **Privately Held**
Web: www.andrewmcdannels.com
SIC: 8742 7389 6799 Marketing consulting services; Business services, nec; Real estate investors, except property operators

(G-9555)
SECURE SELF STORAGE (PA)
1020 Bear Rd (19720-4602)
PHONE..................302 832-0400
Ken Newberry, *Prin*
EMP: 7 EST: 2007
SALES (est): 462.95K
SALES (corp-wide): 462.95K **Privately Held**
Web: www.secureselfstorage.com
SIC: 4225 4226 Warehousing, self storage; Household goods and furniture storage

(G-9556)
SEENEY ELECTRIC LLC
223 Heron Cir (19720-4974)
PHONE..................302 494-3686
EMP: 5 EST: 2019
SALES (est): 164.34K **Privately Held**
Web: www.seeneyelectricllc.com
SIC: 0782 Lawn and garden services

(G-9557)
SEIBERLICH TRANE ENERGY SVCS
66 Southgate Blvd (19720-2068)
PHONE..................302 395-0200
John Seiberlich, *Owner*
EMP: 55 EST: 2020
SALES (est): 1.76MM **Privately Held**
Web: www.seiberlich.com
SIC: 1711 Warm air heating and air conditioning contractor

(G-9558)
SERVICE UNLIMITED INC
Also Called: S U I
19 Southgate Blvd Unit A (19720-2231)
PHONE..................302 326-2665
Carl R Wolf, *Pr*
Ralph R Rose, *
Brian Martinenza Junior, *VP*
EMP: 36 EST: 1962
SQ FT: 15,000
SALES (est): 9.79MM **Privately Held**
Web: www.suihvac.com
SIC: 1711 1731 Warm air heating and air conditioning contractor; Electronic controls installation

(G-9559)
SERVICESOURCE INC
13 Reads Way (19720-1609)
PHONE..................302 322-0904
EMP: 7 EST: 2019
SALES (est): 180.31K **Privately Held**
Web: www.servicesource.org
SIC: 7361 Employment agencies

(G-9560)
SEVYS AUTO SERVICE INC
245 Christiana Rd (19720-2907)
PHONE..................302 328-0839
Allan Hammond, *Owner*
EMP: 6 EST: 1966
SALES (est): 486.27K **Privately Held**
Web: www.sevysautorepair.com
SIC: 7538 7539 General automotive repair shops; Brake services

(G-9561)
SEYMOUR SASHA RENE C N A
34 Tuckahoe Rd (19720-4433)
PHONE..................302 543-1180
Sasha R Seymour C, *Owner*
EMP: 6 EST: 2018
SALES (est): 59.97K **Privately Held**
SIC: 8011 Offices and clinics of medical doctors

(G-9562)
SF EXPRESS CORPORATION
1140 River Rd (19720-5106)
PHONE..................302 407-6155
EMP: 9 EST: 2014
SALES (est): 280.39K **Privately Held**
SIC: 4212 Delivery service, vehicular

(G-9563)
SF LOGISTICS LIMITED
1140 River Rd (19720-5106)
PHONE..................302 317-3954
Boris Tikhonov, *Dir*
EMP: 50 EST: 2015
SALES (est): 1.92MM **Privately Held**
SIC: 4731 Freight transportation arrangement

(G-9564)
SH HAUGHTON TRUCKING MOVING CO
36 Lesley Ln (19720-3328)
PHONE..................302 324-9505
Solomon Haughton, *Prin*
EMP: 5 EST: 2015
SALES (est): 274.4K **Privately Held**
Web: www.shhaughtonmoving.com
SIC: 4212 Moving services

(G-9565)
SHAVONE LOVES KIDS DAY CARE
Also Called: Little Sunshines
6 Darien Ct (19720-3804)
PHONE..................302 544-6170
Kevin Thomas, *Prin*
EMP: 5 EST: 2009
SALES (est): 87.49K **Privately Held**
SIC: 8351 Group day care center

(G-9566)
SHELTON LADAY HAMMOND JR
58 Charles Dr (19720-4670)
PHONE..................302 832-6257
Shelton Laday Hammond Junior, *Owner*
EMP: 6 EST: 2021
SALES (est): 184.93K **Privately Held**
SIC: 7389 Business Activities at Non-Commercial Site

(G-9567)
SHRIJI HOSPITALITY (NOT LLC)
Also Called: Travelodge
1213 West Ave (19720-6250)
PHONE..................302 654-5544
EMP: 56 EST: 2001
SQ FT: 600
SALES (est): 187.92K **Privately Held**
Web: www.wyndhamhotels.com
SIC: 7011 Hotels and motels

(G-9568)
SIECK WHOLESALE FLORIST INC
11 Southgate Blvd (19720-2069)
P.O. Box 1166 (19707-5166)
PHONE..................302 356-2000
Don Freeburn, *Pr*
EMP: 6 EST: 2011
SALES (est): 221K **Privately Held**
SIC: 5193 Nursery stock

(G-9569)
SIGNATURE CNSTR SVCS LLC
Also Called: Signature Cnstr & Design
3029 Bowlarama Dr (19720-1316)
P.O. Box 10285 (19850-0285)
PHONE..................302 691-1010
Eric Holloway, *Prin*
EMP: 10 EST: 2000
SALES (est): 1.31MM **Privately Held**
Web: www.signaturegroup.us
SIC: 1521 Single-family home remodeling, additions, and repairs

(G-9570)
SIGNATURE FURNITURE SVCS LLC
Also Called: Signature Construction Svcs
3029 Bowlarama Dr (19720-1316)
P.O. Box 10285 (19850-0285)
PHONE..................302 691-1010
EMP: 40 EST: 2001
SQ FT: 54,000
SALES (est): 9.51MM **Privately Held**
Web: www.signaturefurnitureservices.com
SIC: 1542 Commercial and office building contractors

(G-9571)
SIMPLEX TIME RECORDER LLC
Also Called: Simplex Time Recorder 557
18 Boulden Cir Ste 36 (19720-3494)
PHONE..................302 325-6300
EMP: 5
Web: www.simplexfire.com
SIC: 5063 1731 Fire alarm systems; Electrical work
HQ: Simplex Time Recorder Llc
   50 Technology Dr
   Westminster MA 01441

(G-9572)
SKYWAYS MOTOR LODGE CORP
Also Called: Quality Inn
147 N Dupont Hwy (19720-3135)
PHONE..................302 328-6666
Alan Spiro, *Pr*
Mark Mattei, *Sec*
EMP: 36 EST: 1961
SQ FT: 8,000
SALES (est): 357.67K **Privately Held**
Web: www.choicehotels.com
SIC: 7011 Hotels and motels

(G-9573)
SMARTDRIVE FOUNDATION
3029 Bowlarama Dr (19720-1316)

PHONE.....................302 463-6543
Guy Vanderlek, *Prin*
EMP: 9 **EST:** 2016
SALES (est): 91.61K **Privately Held**
Web: www.smartdriveusa.org
SIC: 8641 Civic and social associations

(G-9574)
SMARTER HOME & OFFICE LLC
18 Monticello Blvd (19720-3404)
PHONE.....................302 723-9313
EMP: 5 **EST:** 2009
SALES (est): 259.41K **Privately Held**
SIC: 1542 Nonresidential construction, nec

(G-9575)
SMITHS WORK AT HM SLUTIONS LLC
Also Called: Swahs
17 Irwin Ave (19720-1176)
PHONE.....................302 367-6671
Cherise Smith, *Managing Member*
EMP: 7 **EST:** 2016
SALES (est): 267.95K **Privately Held**
Web: www.swahsllc.com
SIC: 7361 7389 Employment agencies; Business services, nec

(G-9576)
SOLAR FOUNDATIONS USA INC (PA)
1142 River Rd (19720-5106)
PHONE.....................855 738-7200
Michael Zuritis, *Pr*
Paul Lapinski, *VP*
EMP: 6 **EST:** 2009
SALES (est): 4.11MM
SALES (corp-wide): 4.11MM **Privately Held**
Web: www.solarfoundationsusa.com
SIC: 3433 1711 Solar heaters and collectors; Solar energy contractor

(G-9577)
SOLO CUP OPERATING CORPORATION
2451 Bear Corbitt Rd (19720-5685)
PHONE.....................800 248-5960
EMP: 317
SALES (corp-wide): 1.16B **Privately Held**
Web: www.solocup.com
SIC: 3089 2656 Plastics kitchenware, tableware, and houseware; Paper cups, plates, dishes, and utensils
HQ: Solo Cup Operating Corporation
500 Hogsback Rd
Mason MI 48854
800 248-5960

(G-9578)
SOLUTION ON-CALL SERVICES LLC
19 Lambson Ln Ste 108-B (19720-2118)
PHONE.....................302 353-4328
EMP: 11 **EST:** 2009
SQ FT: 160
SALES (est): 937.89K **Privately Held**
Web: www.solutiononcallservices.com
SIC: 8082 Home health care services

(G-9579)
SOS PERSONNEL LTD LIABILITY CO
100 Mcmullen Ave Unit 1022 (19720-8046)
P.O. Box 1022 (19720-7022)
PHONE.....................267 357-9124
Tanisha Wilson, *Prin*
EMP: 9 **EST:** 2014
SALES (est): 82.81K **Privately Held**
Web: www.sossubs.org
SIC: 7361 Employment agencies

(G-9580)
SOURCE SUPPLY INC (PA)
6 Bellecor Dr Ste 104 (19720-1744)
P.O. Box 3318 (19804-4318)
PHONE.....................302 328-5110
Dave Brown, *Pr*
EMP: 8 **EST:** 2000
SALES (est): 4.61MM
SALES (corp-wide): 4.61MM **Privately Held**
Web: www.sourcesupplycompany.com
SIC: 5087 Janitors' supplies

(G-9581)
SOUTHERN GLZERS WINE SPRITS LL
615 Lambson Ln (19720-2103)
PHONE.....................302 656-4487
Jim Miller, *Genl Mgr*
EMP: 30
SALES (corp-wide): 7.22B **Privately Held**
Web: www.southernglazers.com
SIC: 5181 5182 Beer and ale; Bottling wines and liquors
PA: Southern Glazer's Wine And Spirits, Llc
1600 Nw 163rd St
Miami FL 33169
866 375-9555

(G-9582)
SOUTHERN WINE SPIRITS DEL LLC
Also Called: Southern Glazers Wine Spirits
615 Lambson Ln (19720-2103)
PHONE.....................800 292-7890
▲ **EMP:** 24 **EST:** 2007
SALES (est): 2.66MM **Privately Held**
Web: www.delimporters.com
SIC: 5182 Wine

(G-9583)
SPACECON LLC (HQ)
292 Churchmans Rd (19720-3110)
PHONE.....................302 322-9285
B G Dicarlo, *Sec*
EMP: 11 **EST:** 1983
SALES (est): 1.91MM
SALES (corp-wide): 20.14MM **Privately Held**
Web: www.spacecon.com
SIC: 1742 1752 Drywall; Floor laying and floor work, nec
PA: Smucker Company
15 Newport Rd
Leola PA 17540
717 396-8900

(G-9584)
SPARK
950 W Basin Rd (19720-1008)
PHONE.....................302 324-2203
Kelly Housen, *Prin*
EMP: 9 **EST:** 2007
SALES (est): 141.86K **Privately Held**
Web: www.delawareonline.com
SIC: 2711 Newspapers, publishing and printing

(G-9585)
SPICER MULLIKIN FUNERAL HOMES (PA)
1000 N Dupont Hwy (19720-2537)
PHONE.....................302 368-9500
Harvey C Smith Junior, *Pr*
Frank C Mayer Junior, *VP*
EMP: 9 **EST:** 1906
SQ FT: 8,000
SALES (est): 2.27MM
SALES (corp-wide): 2.27MM **Privately Held**
Web: www.spicermullikin.com

SIC: 7261 Funeral home

(G-9586)
SPINLIFECOM LLC
773 S Dupont Hwy (19720-4609)
PHONE.....................888 398-2267
EMP: 14
SALES (corp-wide): 12.67MM **Privately Held**
Web: www.spinlife.com
SIC: 3999 Wheelchair lifts
HQ: Spinlife.Com, Llc
330 W Spring St Ste 303
Columbus OH 43215
614 564-1400

(G-9587)
SPRINT SPECTRUM LP
Also Called: Sprint
118 N Dupont Hwy (19720-3102)
PHONE.....................302 322-1712
Jonathon Yi, *Brnch Mgr*
EMP: 11
SALES (corp-wide): 78.56B **Publicly Held**
SIC: 4812 Cellular telephone services
HQ: Sprint Spectrum L.P.
6800 Sprint Pkwy
Overland Park KS 66251

(G-9588)
SSS CLUTCH COMPANY INC
610 W Basin Rd (19720-6448)
PHONE.....................302 322-8080
Morgan Hendry, *Pr*
◆ **EMP:** 7 **EST:** 1984
SQ FT: 10,000
SALES (est): 1.08MM **Privately Held**
Web: www.sssclutch.com
SIC: 3568 Clutches, except vehicular

(G-9589)
STAGING DIMENSIONS INC
Also Called: Mathias
31 Blevins Dr Ste A (19720-4170)
PHONE.....................302 328-4100
Scott Humphrey, *Pr*
EMP: 26 **EST:** 2001
SQ FT: 8,000
SALES (est): 3.63MM **Privately Held**
Web: www.stagingdimensionsinc.com
SIC: 3999 Stage hardware and equipment, except lighting

(G-9590)
STANDARD DISTRIBUTING CO INC (PA)
100 Mews Dr (19720-2792)
PHONE.....................302 655-5511
Eugene M Tigani, *Pr*
J Vincent Tigani Junior, *VP*
Stephen D Tigani, *
J Paul Tigani, *
F Gregory Tigani, *
▲ **EMP:** 100 **EST:** 1933
SQ FT: 115,000
SALES (est): 40.77MM
SALES (corp-wide): 40.77MM **Privately Held**
Web: www.standardde.com
SIC: 5181 5182 Beer and other fermented malt liquors; Wine

(G-9591)
STANDARD INSURANCE COMPANY
10 Corporate Cir (19720-2418)
PHONE.....................302 322-9922
J Greg Ness, *Brnch Mgr*
EMP: 71
Web: www.standard.com

SIC: 6411 Insurance agents, nec
HQ: Standard Insurance Company
900 Sw 5th Ave Ste 400
Portland OR 97204
971 321-7000

(G-9592)
STANLEY STEEMER INTL INC
Also Called: Wilmington 102
31 Southgate Blvd (19720-2069)
PHONE.....................302 293-2879
Carlton Morrison, *Brnch Mgr*
EMP: 34
SALES (corp-wide): 263.72MM **Privately Held**
Web: www.stanleysteemer.com
SIC: 7217 Carpet and furniture cleaning on location
PA: Stanley Steemer International, Inc.
5800 Innovation Dr
Dublin OH 43016
614 764-2007

(G-9593)
STATE OF DE
36 Herbert Dr (19720-3233)
P.O. Box 906 (19720-0906)
PHONE.....................302 328-3573
EMP: 9 **EST:** 2018
SALES (est): 636.43K **Privately Held**
Web: www.newcastlede.gov
SIC: 7361 Employment agencies

(G-9594)
STATE OF DELAWARE
84 Christiana Rd Ste A (19720-2223)
PHONE.....................302 322-2303
Art Caldwell, *Ofcr*
EMP: 26 **EST:** 2004
SALES (est): 2.62MM **Privately Held**
Web: statefiremarshal.delaware.gov
SIC: 8099 Health and allied services, nec

(G-9595)
STONE TECHNOLOGIES
110 Rodney Dr (19720-2764)
PHONE.....................302 379-1759
Nathan Stone, *Prin*
EMP: 6 **EST:** 2016
SALES (est): 92.36K **Privately Held**
Web: www.stonetechnology.com
SIC: 1771 Concrete work

(G-9596)
STONES AND CABINETS CITY LLC ✪
93 Christiana Rd (19720-3104)
PHONE.....................302 729-4201
EMP: 6 **EST:** 2022
SALES (est): 75.18K **Privately Held**
Web: www.stonesandcabinets.com
SIC: 2434 Wood kitchen cabinets

(G-9597)
STORAGE RENTALS OF AMERICA
950 Red Lion Rd (19720-5205)
PHONE.....................302 838-7405
EMP: 5 **EST:** 2018
SALES (est): 74.77K **Privately Held**
Web: www.sroa.com
SIC: 4225 Warehousing, self storage

(G-9598)
SUBCOOL HEATING & AIR INC
112 E Van Buren Ave (19720-3322)
PHONE.....................302 442-5658
EMP: 13 **EST:** 2018
SALES (est): 483.72K **Privately Held**
Web: www.subcoolheatingandair.com
SIC: 1711 Warm air heating and air conditioning contractor

GEOGRAPHIC SECTION

New Castle - New Castle County (G-9625)

(G-9599)
SUMMIT STEEL INC
201 Edwards Ave (19720-4857)
P.O. Box 730 (19720-0730)
PHONE....................302 325-3220
Jerry Tompkins, *Pr*
Joseph L Irwin, *
EMP: 55 **EST:** 1987
SQ FT: 13,000
SALES (est): 8.48MM **Privately Held**
Web: www.summitsteelde.com
SIC: 3441 1791 Building components, structural steel; Structural steel erection

(G-9600)
SUN HOTEL INC
Also Called: Econo Lodge
232 S Dupont Hwy (19720-4130)
PHONE....................302 322-0711
Debbie Patel, *Genl Mgr*
EMP: 8 **EST:** 1987
SQ FT: 34,000
SALES (est): 495.95K **Privately Held**
Web: www.choicehotels.com
SIC: 7011 Motels

(G-9601)
SUNBELT RENTALS INC
3120 New Castle Ave (19720-2162)
PHONE....................302 322-5394
Christopher Craig, *Brnch Mgr*
EMP: 9
SALES (corp-wide): 9.67B **Privately Held**
Web: www.sunbeltrentals.com
SIC: 7353 Heavy construction equipment rental
HQ: Sunbelt Rentals, Inc.
 1799 Innovation Pt
 Fort Mill SC 29715
 803 578-5811

(G-9602)
SUNBELT RENTALS INC
453 Pulaski Hwy (19720-3901)
PHONE....................302 669-0595
EMP: 9
SALES (corp-wide): 9.67B **Privately Held**
Web: www.sunbeltrentals.com
SIC: 7353 Heavy construction equipment rental
HQ: Sunbelt Rentals, Inc.
 1799 Innovation Pt
 Fort Mill SC 29715
 803 578-5811

(G-9603)
SUNNYVILLE RESORT LLC (PA) ✪
128 Sunset Blvd Ste 1365 (19720-4100)
PHONE....................706 255-9765
EMP: 6 **EST:** 2022
SALES (est): 271.25K
SALES (corp-wide): 271.25K **Privately Held**
SIC: 6531 Real estate agent, commercial

(G-9604)
SUNSTATES SECURITY LLC
10 Corporate Cir Ste 220 (19720-2418)
PHONE....................866 710-2019
EMP: 23 **EST:** 2019
SALES (est): 220.2K **Privately Held**
Web: www.sunstatessecurity.com
SIC: 1731 Safety and security specialization

(G-9605)
SUPER HEAT
26 Parkway Cir (19720-4070)
PHONE....................302 276-0689
EMP: 5 **EST:** 2019
SALES (est): 65.83K **Privately Held**
SIC: 1711 Warm air heating and air conditioning contractor

(G-9606)
SUPERBREWED FOOD INC (PA)
239 Lisa Dr (19720-4193)
PHONE....................302 220-4760
Bryan Tracy, *CEO*
Aharon Ari Eyal, *CSO*
EMP: 13 **EST:** 2011
SALES (est): 2.52MM
SALES (corp-wide): 2.52MM **Privately Held**
Web: www.superbrewedfood.com
SIC: 8731 Biotechnical research, commercial

(G-9607)
SUSAN R AUSTIN
Also Called: Guiding Hearts Family Daycare
103 Lesley Ln (19720-3329)
PHONE....................302 322-4685
EMP: 5 **EST:** 2009
SALES (est): 54.62K **Privately Held**
SIC: 8351 Child day care services

(G-9608)
SUSTAINABLE ENVMTL MGT LLC
755 Governor Lea Rd (19720-5512)
P.O. Box 987 (19720-0987)
PHONE....................302 832-8000
EMP: 44 **EST:** 2015
SALES (est): 10.46MM
SALES (corp-wide): 10.46MM **Privately Held**
Web: www.trashtech.com
SIC: 4953 Garbage: collecting, destroying, and processing
PA: Rpj Waste Services, Inc.
 453 Pier Head Blvd
 Smyrna DE 19977
 302 653-9999

(G-9609)
SWARTHMORE FINANCIAL SVCS LLC
15 Reads Way Ste 210 (19720-1600)
PHONE....................302 325-0700
Charles Pass, *Prin*
EMP: 9 **EST:** 2004
SALES (est): 485.94K **Privately Held**
Web: www.precisionwealthpartners.com
SIC: 8742 Financial consultant

(G-9610)
SWIFT SERVICES INC
2 3rd Ave (19720-4120)
PHONE....................302 328-1145
Michael Salemi, *Pr*
EMP: 7 **EST:** 1981
SALES (est): 278.48K **Privately Held**
Web: www.swiftservices.pro
SIC: 7349 Chimney cleaning

(G-9611)
SWIFT TOWING & RECOVERY
469 Old Airport Rd (19720-1001)
PHONE....................302 650-4579
Ron Bennett, *Owner*
EMP: 6 **EST:** 2005
SALES (est): 499.6K **Privately Held**
SIC: 7549 Towing services

(G-9612)
SYNERFAC INC (PA)
Also Called: Synerfac Technical Staffing
100 W Commons Blvd Ste 100 (19720)
PHONE....................302 324-9400
EMP: 15 **EST:** 1987
SALES (est): 23.12MM
SALES (corp-wide): 23.12MM **Privately Held**
Web: www.synerfac.com
SIC: 8711 7389 7361 7363 Consulting engineer; Drafting service, except temporary help; Placement agencies; Labor resource services

(G-9613)
T SHANE PALMER DC
Also Called: Palmer Chiropractic
1 Pleasant Pl (19720-3005)
PHONE....................302 328-2656
T Shane Palmer D.c., *Owner*
EMP: 5 **EST:** 1990
SALES (est): 239.91K **Privately Held**
Web: www.palmerchiropracticlifecenter.com
SIC: 8041 Offices and clinics of chiropractors

(G-9614)
TAB WELLNESS INC
38 Walker Dr (19720-4682)
PHONE....................914 396-4316
EMP: 5 **EST:** 2013
SALES (est): 60.47K **Privately Held**
SIC: 8099 Health and allied services, nec

(G-9615)
TABOR AUTO PARTS INC (PA)
Also Called: Berrodin Auto Parts
20 Mccullough Dr (19720-2066)
PHONE....................302 395-1100
John Berrodin, *Pr*
▲ **EMP:** 25 **EST:** 2013
SALES (est): 7.09MM
SALES (corp-wide): 7.09MM **Privately Held**
Web: www.berrodin.com
SIC: 5013 Automotive supplies and parts

(G-9616)
TARABICOS GROSSO
100 W Commons Blvd Ste 415 (19720-2419)
PHONE....................302 757-7800
Larry J Tarabicos, *Prin*
EMP: 16 **EST:** 2013
SALES (est): 6.29MM **Privately Held**
Web: www.tarabicosgrosso.com
SIC: 8111 General practice attorney, lawyer

(G-9617)
TAXES ITS YOUR MONEY
1 Bassett Ave Ste 1211 (19720-2088)
PHONE....................302 322-0452
John D Travis, *Prin*
EMP: 5 **EST:** 2009
SALES (est): 126.58K **Privately Held**
SIC: 7291 Tax return preparation services

(G-9618)
TAYLOR KLINE INC
298b Churchmans Rd (19720-3110)
PHONE....................302 328-8306
Jeffrey Kline, *Pr*
Gary Place, *VP*
EMP: 15 **EST:** 1956
SQ FT: 6,400
SALES (est): 4.62MM **Privately Held**
Web: www.taylorkline.com
SIC: 1542 Commercial and office building, new construction

(G-9619)
TD AUTOMOTIVE
9 University Ave (19720-4319)
PHONE....................443 794-3453
Tim Dever, *Prin*
EMP: 5 **EST:** 2018
SALES (est): 163.61K **Privately Held**
SIC: 7538 General automotive repair shops

(G-9620)
TDW DELAWARE INC (HQ)
43 Harbor View Dr (19720-2179)
PHONE....................302 594-9880
Richard B Williamson, *Pr*
EMP: 12 **EST:** 1988
SALES (est): 1.8MM
SALES (corp-wide): 499.09MM **Privately Held**
SIC: 3533 Gas field machinery and equipment
PA: T. D. Williamson, Inc.
 6120 S Yale Ave Ste 1700
 Tulsa OK 74136
 918 493-9494

(G-9621)
TEC-CON INC
Also Called: Keen Compressed Gas
4063 New Castle Ave (19720-1414)
PHONE....................610 583-8770
Rich Fleming, *Brnch Mgr*
EMP: 3 **EST:** 2010
SALES (est): 107K **Privately Held**
SIC: 1389 Gas compressing (natural gas) at the fields

(G-9622)
TECHNLOGY EXPLRATION GROUP INC
257 Old Churchmans Rd (19720-1529)
PHONE....................202 222-0794
EMP: 6 **EST:** 2011
SALES (est): 291.23K **Privately Held**
Web: www.technologyexplorationgroup.com
SIC: 7379 7371 7374 Computer related services, nec; Custom computer programming services; Data processing and preparation

(G-9623)
TELE-HELP INC
Also Called: Telehelp24/7
216 Remi Dr (19720-5622)
PHONE....................888 247-5767
Robert L Adams Junior, *CEO*
EMP: 8 **EST:** 2020
SALES (est): 220.19K **Privately Held**
Web: www.telehelp247.org
SIC: 8093 Mental health clinic, outpatient

(G-9624)
TELEPLAN VDEOCOM SOLUTIONS INC
100 W Commons Blvd Ste 415 (19720)
PHONE....................302 323-8503
Joe Neff, *CEO*
EMP: 21 **EST:** 2005
SALES (est): 535.61K **Privately Held**
SIC: 7378 Computer maintenance and repair
HQ: Teleplan International B.V.
 Spicalaan 1
 Hoofddorp NH
 852733674

(G-9625)
TESTING MACHINES INC (PA)
Also Called: T M I Div
40 Mccullough Dr Unit A (19720-2228)
PHONE....................302 613-5600
John L Sullivan, *Pr*
▲ **EMP:** 30 **EST:** 1931
SQ FT: 15,000
SALES (est): 12.93MM
SALES (corp-wide): 12.93MM **Privately Held**
Web: www.industrialphysics.com

SIC: 3829 5084 Physical property testing equipment; Measuring and testing equipment, electrical

(G-9626)
THDXNGRP LLC
34 Dunsinane Dr (19720-2323)
PHONE.....................443 993-6414
Kamil Dixon, *Managing Member*
EMP: 6 EST: 2020
SALES (est): 315.88K **Privately Held**
SIC: 6733 Private estate, personal investment and vacation fund trusts

(G-9627)
THRUPORE TECHNOLOGIES INC (PA)
Also Called: Thrupore Technologies
15 Reads Way Ste 107 (19720-1600)
PHONE.....................205 657-0714
Franchessa Sayler, *CEO*
Martin G Bakker, *COO*
EMP: 8 EST: 2018
SALES (est): 815.66K
SALES (corp-wide): 815.66K **Privately Held**
Web: www.thrupore.com
SIC: 2899 Chemical preparations, nec

(G-9628)
TMI REALTY LLC
40 Mccullough Dr (19720-2227)
PHONE.....................302 613-5600
John Sullivan, *Pr*
EMP: 12 EST: 2010
SALES (est): 807.31K **Privately Held**
Web: www.industrialphysics.com
SIC: 6531 Real estate brokers and agents

(G-9629)
TOTALTRANSLOGISTICS LLC
8 Mccullough Dr (19720-2066)
PHONE.....................302 325-4245
EMP: 6 EST: 2011
SQ FT: 6,500
SALES (est): 460.88K **Privately Held**
SIC: 8741 Business management

(G-9630)
TOTALTRAX INC
920 W Basin Rd Ste 400 (19720-1013)
PHONE.....................302 514-0600
Frank Cavallaro, *CEO*
Neil O'connell, *COO*
Anthony Andriano, *
Philip B Van Wormer, *
Larry G Mahan, *
▲ EMP: 60 EST: 2009
SALES (est): 8.67MM **Privately Held**
Web: www.totaltraxinc.com
SIC: 3822 3621 5084 Building services monitoring controls, automatic; Control equipment for buses or trucks, electric; Safety equipment

(G-9631)
TOUCHSTONE SYSTEMS INC
42 Reads Way C (19720-1612)
PHONE.....................302 324-5322
Sanford S Stone, *Pr*
EMP: 10 EST: 1993
SALES (est): 556.28K **Privately Held**
Web: www.touchstone-systems.com
SIC: 7371 Computer software development

(G-9632)
TRANE US INC
Also Called: Trane
66 Southgate Blvd (19720-2068)
PHONE.....................302 395-0200
Mark Cresitello, *Sec*
EMP: 8
Web: www.trane.com
SIC: 3585 Refrigeration and heating equipment
HQ: Trane U.S. Inc.
  800 Beaty St Ste E
  Davidson NC 28036
  704 655-4000

(G-9633)
TRANSAXLE LLC
4060 N Dupont Hwy Ste 6 (19720-6325)
PHONE.....................302 322-8300
Sam Palmucci, *Brnch Mgr*
EMP: 5
SALES (corp-wide): 91.27MM **Privately Held**
Web: www.transaxle.com
SIC: 5013 5531 Truck parts and accessories ; Truck equipment and parts
PA: Transaxle Llc
  2501 Route 73
  Cinnaminson NJ 08077
  856 665-4445

(G-9634)
TRANSCARE
6 Bellecor Dr (19720-1741)
PHONE.....................302 322-2454
Josh Rhoads, *Mgr*
EMP: 6 EST: 2017
SALES (est): 119.68K **Privately Held**
SIC: 4119 Ambulance service

(G-9635)
TRANSITIONAL FISHER
10 Denby Ct (19720-5400)
PHONE.....................302 322-4124
EMP: 8 EST: 2011
SALES (est): 54.68K **Privately Held**
Web: www.fishertransitionalservices.org
SIC: 8322 Individual and family services

(G-9636)
TRAVEL INN NEW
232 S Dupont Hwy (19720-4130)
PHONE.....................302 322-4500
EMP: 11 EST: 2016
SALES (est): 67.41K **Privately Held**
Web: www.travelinnnewcastle.com
SIC: 7011 Inns

(G-9637)
TRIAD CONSTRUCTION COMPANY LLC
Also Called: Triad Construction Co
210 Marsh Ln (19720-1175)
PHONE.....................302 652-3339
Christopher Modesto, *Pr*
Marty Bienkowski, *
Jerry Denney, *
EMP: 9 EST: 1998
SALES (est): 234.43K **Privately Held**
SIC: 1771 Blacktop (asphalt) work

(G-9638)
TRIBUTARYMARINECOM LLC
265 Airport Rd (19720-1540)
PHONE.....................443 553-9485
EMP: 3 EST: 2018
SALES (est): 150K **Privately Held**
SIC: 3999 Manufacturing industries, nec

(G-9639)
TRICON CONSTRUCTION MGT INC
13 King Ct Ste 3 (19720-1523)
PHONE.....................302 838-6500
James Marcus, *CFO*
EMP: 50 EST: 2007

SALES (est): 5.19MM **Privately Held**
Web: www.tricontristate.com
SIC: 1521 Single-family housing construction

(G-9640)
TRINITY LOGISTICS INC
23 Fantail Ct (19720-4674)
PHONE.....................302 595-2116
Dismas Makori, *Brnch Mgr*
EMP: 10
SALES (corp-wide): 1.24B **Privately Held**
Web: www.trinitylogistics.com
SIC: 4731 Freight transportation arrangement
HQ: Trinity Logistics, Inc.
  50 Fallon Ave
  Seaford DE 19973
  302 253-3900

(G-9641)
TRITON CONSTRUCTION CO INC
101 Pigeon Point Rd (19720-2108)
PHONE.....................516 780-8100
EMP: 13 EST: 1999
SQ FT: 1,800
SALES (est): 668.63K **Privately Held**
Web: www.bccico.com
SIC: 1623 Water, sewer, and utility lines

(G-9642)
TRUCK TECH INC
1600 Matassino Rd (19720-2085)
P.O. Box 987 (19720-0987)
PHONE.....................302 832-8000
Kevin Shegog, *Pr*
EMP: 9 EST: 2009
SALES (est): 449.63K **Privately Held**
SIC: 7538 7692 General truck repair; Welding repair

(G-9643)
TRUE MOBILITY INC
773 S Dupont Hwy (19720-4609)
PHONE.....................302 836-4110
EMP: 6 EST: 2010
SALES (est): 990K **Privately Held**
Web: www.spinlife.com
SIC: 5999 7699 5531 Medical apparatus and supplies; Recreational vehicle repair services; Auto and truck equipment and parts

(G-9644)
TRUE-PACK LTD (PA)
Also Called: Mail Box Outlet
420 Churchmans Rd (19720-3157)
PHONE.....................302 326-2222
William Warren Bane Iii, *Pr*
William W Bane Iii, *Pr*
Theresa Groves, *VP*
EMP: 18 EST: 1982
SQ FT: 35,000
SALES (est): 4.89MM
SALES (corp-wide): 4.89MM **Privately Held**
Web: www.truepack.com
SIC: 2653 5999 Boxes, corrugated: made from purchased materials; Packaging materials: boxes, padding, etc.

(G-9645)
U S EXPRESS TAXI COMPANY LLC
260 Christiana Rd Apt N18 (19720-2963)
PHONE.....................302 357-1908
Abdoulaye Kamagate, *Prin*
EMP: 5 EST: 2015
SALES (est): 58.36K **Privately Held**
Web: www.expressus.kg
SIC: 4121 Taxicabs

(G-9646)
U-HAUL INTERNATIONAL INC
906 S Dupont Hwy (19720-5210)
PHONE.....................336 667-0147
EMP: 6 EST: 2019
SALES (est): 99.2K **Privately Held**
Web: www.uhaul.com
SIC: 7513 Truck rental and leasing, no drivers

(G-9647)
U-HAUL NEIGHBORHOOD DEALER
3006 New Castle Ave (19720-2244)
PHONE.....................302 250-4422
EMP: 7 EST: 2018
SALES (est): 46.21K **Privately Held**
Web: www.uhaul.com
SIC: 7513 Truck rental and leasing, no drivers

(G-9648)
U-HAUL NEIGHBORHOOD DEALER
327 Airport Rd (19720-1007)
PHONE.....................302 544-9178
Kathy De Angelis, *Owner*
EMP: 6 EST: 2018
SALES (est): 46.21K **Privately Held**
Web: www.uhaul.com
SIC: 7513 Truck rental and leasing, no drivers

(G-9649)
UKHI LLC
128 Sunset Blvd (19720-4100)
PHONE.....................833 511-1977
EMP: 2
SALES (est): 77.45K **Privately Held**
SIC: 3161 7389 Clothing and apparel carrying cases; Business Activities at Non-Commercial Site

(G-9650)
UKRAINE EXPRESS INC
78 Mccullough Dr (19726-2079)
PHONE.....................973 253-0050
EMP: 8 EST: 2014
SALES (est): 779.29K **Privately Held**
Web: www.ukraine-express.com
SIC: 4731 Shipping documents preparation

(G-9651)
UNI PRINTING SOLUTIONSLLC
42 Reads Way (19720-1612)
PHONE.....................631 438-6045
EMP: 4 EST: 2018
SALES (est): 214.14K **Privately Held**
Web: www.etcommun.com
SIC: 2752 Commercial printing, lithographic

(G-9652)
UNION BUILDING TRADES FCU
814 W Basin Rd (19720-1708)
PHONE.....................973 263-0001
EMP: 6 EST: 2019
SALES (est): 208.47K **Privately Held**
Web: www.ubtfcu.org
SIC: 5199 Nondurable goods, nec

(G-9653)
UNITED ELECTRIC SUPPLY CO INC (PA)
10 Bellecor Dr (19720-1763)
P.O. Box 10287 (19850-0287)
PHONE.....................800 322-3374
TOLL FREE: 800
George Vorwick, *CEO*
Gayle Davis, *
EMP: 112 EST: 1965
SQ FT: 80,000
SALES (est): 244.47MM

GEOGRAPHIC SECTION
New Castle - New Castle County (G-9681)

SALES (corp-wide): 244.47MM **Privately Held**
Web: www.westwayelectricsupply.com
SIC: 5063 Electrical supplies, nec

(G-9654)
UNITED LEMON SALES LLC
2 Dock View Dr (19720-2180)
PHONE.................513 368-6107
Michael Dubrul, *Prin*
Jeffrey G Stagnaro, *Prin*
EMP: 10 EST: 2013
SALES (est): 276.12K **Privately Held**
SIC: 2037 Fruit juice concentrates, frozen

(G-9655)
UNITED REFRIGERATION INC
Also Called: Johnson Contrls Authorized Dlr
818 W Basin Rd (19720-1708)
PHONE.................302 322-1836
William Stapleton, *Mgr*
EMP: 9
SALES (corp-wide): 736.55MM **Privately Held**
Web: www.johnsoncontrols.com
SIC: 5078 5075 Refrigeration equipment and supplies; Warm air heating and air conditioning
PA: United Refrigeration, Inc.
  11401 Roosevelt Blvd
  Philadelphia PA 19154
  215 698-9100

(G-9656)
UNITED RENTALS NORTH AMER INC
Also Called: United Rentals
248 S Dupont Hwy (19720-4130)
PHONE.................302 328-2900
Mike Roberts, *Mgr*
EMP: 20
SALES (corp-wide): 14.33B **Publicly Held**
Web: www.unitedrentals.com
SIC: 7359 Rental store, general
HQ: United Rentals (North America), Inc.
  100 Frst Stmford Pl Ste 7
  Stamford CT 06902
  203 622-3131

(G-9657)
UNITED TESTING SYSTEMS INC
40 Mccullough Dr (19720-2227)
PHONE.................714 638-2322
Jim Neville, *CEO*
Sean Kohl, *
▲ EMP: 31 EST: 1964
SALES (est): 6.56MM **Privately Held**
Web: www.industrialphysics.com
SIC: 3829 8734 5084 Hardness testing equipment; Calibration and certification; Industrial machinery and equipment

(G-9658)
UNITED TRNSP UN INSUR ASSN
12 Varmar Dr (19720-2036)
PHONE.................302 655-6084
Nelson Seeney, *Brnch Mgr*
EMP: 10
SALES (corp-wide): 17.68MM **Privately Held**
Web: www.utuia.org
SIC: 8631 Labor union
PA: United Transportation Union Insurance Association
  6060 Rckside Woods Blvd N
  Independence OH 44131
  216 228-9400

(G-9659)
UNIVERSAL BEV IMPORTERS LLC
200 Lisa Dr Ste D (19720-4182)
PHONE.................302 322-7900
EMP: 6 EST: 2018
SALES (est): 344.17K **Privately Held**
Web: www.ubiimports.com
SIC: 5182 Wine

(G-9660)
UNIVERSALFLEET
2019 Walmsley Dr (19720)
PHONE.................302 428-0661
Gary Merritt, *Owner*
EMP: 5 EST: 2007
SALES (est): 237.6K **Privately Held**
Web: www.carolinabarns.com
SIC: 7538 General truck repair

(G-9661)
UNREAL VAPORS
1418 N Dupont Hwy (19720-1844)
PHONE.................302 322-2600
Vapor Hexed, *Prin*
EMP: 5 EST: 2018
SALES (est): 136.79K **Privately Held**
SIC: 5194 Smokeless tobacco

(G-9662)
URBAN AVENUE INC
44 Hillary Cir (19720-8620)
PHONE.................302 420-1105
Bruce David Junior, *Pr*
EMP: 6 EST: 2008
SALES (est): 72.87K **Privately Held**
SIC: 7361 Employment agencies

(G-9663)
URBAN CHANGE INCORPORATED
725 Staghorn Dr (19720-7653)
PHONE.................215 749-2049
Nickisha Lingham, *Prin*
EMP: 5 EST: 2016
SALES (est): 40.33K **Privately Held**
SIC: 8641 Civic and social associations

(G-9664)
URBAN ENGINEERS INC
2 Penns Way Ste 400 (19720-2407)
PHONE.................302 689-0260
John Pietrobono, *Brnch Mgr*
EMP: 5
SALES (corp-wide): 87.47MM **Privately Held**
Web: www.urbanengineers.com
SIC: 8711 Consulting engineer
PA: Urban Engineers, Inc.
  530 Walnut St Fl 7
  Philadelphia PA 19106
  215 922-8080

(G-9665)
US GREEN BATTERY INC
157 S Dupont Hwy 2nd Fl (19720-4138)
PHONE.................347 723-5963
Falguni R Trivedi, *VP*
EMP: 2 EST: 2018
SALES (est): 69.39K **Privately Held**
SIC: 3999 Manufacturing industries, nec

(G-9666)
VANNIES HATS
4 Andover Ct (19720-3905)
PHONE.................302 765-7094
EMP: 3 EST: 2015
SALES (est): 76.56K **Privately Held**
SIC: 2353 Hats, caps, and millinery

(G-9667)
VEHATTIRE LLC
174 N Dupont Hwy (19720-3103)
PHONE.................302 221-2000
EMP: 8 EST: 2003
SQ FT: 12,000
SALES (est): 854.5K **Privately Held**
Web: www.vehattire.com
SIC: 5015 Automotive accessories, used, nec

(G-9668)
VELOCITY MAINT SOLUTIONS LLC
6 Drba Way (19720-3141)
PHONE.................844 538-8349
EMP: 21 EST: 2021
SALES (est): 545.34K **Privately Held**
Web: www.velocitymaintenancesolutions.com
SIC: 8748 Business consulting, nec

(G-9669)
VERISIGN INC
21 Boulden Cir (19720-3400)
PHONE.................571 325-7916
EMP: 27 EST: 1995
SALES (est): 316.29K **Privately Held**
Web: www.verisign.com
SIC: 7371 Custom computer programming services

(G-9670)
VETERINARY SPECIALTY CTR DEL PA
Also Called: Veterinary Emergency Ctr Del
290 Churchmans Rd (19720-3110)
PHONE.................302 322-6933
Mark Cofone, *Pr*
Robin Pullen, *Sec*
Mike Miller, *VP*
R Jankowski, *Stockholder*
Shirley A Lockhart, *Dir*
EMP: 53 EST: 2000
SALES (est): 3.04MM **Privately Held**
Web: www.bluepearlvet.com
SIC: 0742 Animal hospital services, pets and other animal specialties

(G-9671)
VILLAGE GREEN INC
Also Called: Tropic Wholesale
62 Southgate Blvd (19720-2090)
PHONE.................302 764-2234
Scott Weiler, *Pr*
Sharon Weiler, *
EMP: 26 EST: 1975
SALES (est): 2.47MM **Privately Held**
Web: www.villagegreeninc.com
SIC: 7389 5992 5193 Plant care service; Florists; Plants, potted

(G-9672)
VIRTUAL ENTERPRISES INC
42 Reads Way Ste C (19720-1612)
PHONE.................302 324-5322
Paul Boudrye, *Pr*
EMP: 10 EST: 1995
SALES (est): 122.27K **Privately Held**
SIC: 7373 Computer integrated systems design

(G-9673)
VIVIS DAYCARE AND PRESCHOOL
200 Hazlett Rd (19720-1804)
PHONE.................302 607-4478
Viviana Oyola, *Prin*
EMP: 8 EST: 2017
SALES (est): 15.97K **Privately Held**
SIC: 8351 Preschool center

(G-9674)
WANEX ELECTRICAL SERVICE LLC
261 Airport Rd (19720-1540)
PHONE.................302 326-1700
EMP: 16 EST: 1994
SALES (est): 2.21MM **Privately Held**
Web: www.wanex.com
SIC: 1731 General electrical contractor

(G-9675)
WASTE INDUSTRIES
903 Lambson Ln (19720-2259)
PHONE.................302 367-5511
EMP: 7 EST: 2018
SALES (est): 221.87K **Privately Held**
SIC: 4953 Recycling, waste materials

(G-9676)
WASTE MANAGEMENT MICHIGAN INC
Also Called: Waste Management
246 Marsh Ln (19720-1175)
PHONE.................302 655-1360
Anne Krolicki, *Brnch Mgr*
EMP: 18
SALES (corp-wide): 19.7B **Publicly Held**
SIC: 4953 Garbage: collecting, destroying, and processing
HQ: Waste Management Of Michigan, Inc.
  48797 Alpha Dr Ste 100
  Wixom MI 48393
  586 574-2760

(G-9677)
WASTE MASTERS SOLUTIONS LLC
Also Called: Waste Masters
19 Davidson Ln (19720-2246)
PHONE.................302 824-0909
Brian Simmons, *Pr*
EMP: 6 EST: 2010
SALES (est): 2.52MM **Privately Held**
Web: www.wastemasters.com
SIC: 4953 Rubbish collection and disposal

(G-9678)
WATKINS SYSTEM INC
Also Called: Watkins Dealership
4031 New Castle Ave (19720-1414)
PHONE.................302 658-8561
Stan Lenanski, *Mgr*
EMP: 44
SALES (corp-wide): 18.99MM **Privately Held**
SIC: 7513 Truck rental and leasing, no drivers
PA: Watkins System Inc
  1516 Rt 202
  Concordville PA

(G-9679)
WEBSTAURANT STORE INC
705 Moorehouse Rd (19720-1370)
PHONE.................302 654-1247
EMP: 19 EST: 2014
SALES (est): 194.18K **Privately Held**
Web: www.webstaurantstore.com
SIC: 5046 Restaurant equipment and supplies, nec

(G-9680)
WELLS FARGO BANK NATIONAL ASSN
1424 N Dupont Hwy (19720-1844)
PHONE.................302 326-4304
Susan Robinson, *Mgr*
EMP: 18
SALES (corp-wide): 82.86B **Publicly Held**
Web: www.wellsfargo.com
SIC: 6021 National commercial banks
HQ: Wells Fargo Bank, National Association
  420 Montgomery St San
  San Francisco CA 94104
  605 575-6900

(G-9681)
WHITEOPTICS LLC
Also Called: White Optics

19 Blevins Dr (19720-4153)
PHONE..................................302 476-2055
▲ EMP: 4
Web: whiteoptics.acuitybrands.com
SIC: 3646 Commercial lighting fixtures

(G-9682)
WILCOX LANDSCAPING INC
230 S Dupont Hwy (19720-4130)
P.O. Box 629 (19720-0629)
PHONE..................................302 322-3002
Tom Wilcox, *Owner*
EMP: 50 EST: 2001
SALES (est): 2.02MM **Privately Held**
Web: www.twilcoxlandscaping.com
SIC: 0782 Landscape contractors

(G-9683)
WILLIS HSPITALITY PARTNERS LLC
63 Queen Ave (19720-2072)
PHONE..................................302 544-5054
Andrew Willis, *Prin*
EMP: 11 EST: 2016
SALES (est): 45.84K **Privately Held**
SIC: 7011 Hotels and motels

(G-9684)
WILMINGTON AQUATIC CLUB INC
Also Called: Wac
212 W Grant Ave (19720-2525)
PHONE..................................302 322-2487
EMP: 8 EST: 2011
SALES (est): 192.42K **Privately Held**
SIC: 7997 Membership sports and recreation clubs

(G-9685)
WILMINGTON MANOR LIONS SERVICE
320 N Dupont Hwy (19720-6434)
P.O. Box 569 (19720-0569)
PHONE..................................302 322-3250
EMP: 10 EST: 2010
SALES (est): 62.56K **Privately Held**
Web: www.wilmu.edu
SIC: 8699 Charitable organization

(G-9686)
WIZ ELECTRIC
56 Aidone Dr (19720-4623)
PHONE..................................302 293-0403
Marvin Butler, *Prin*
EMP: 6 EST: 2010
SALES (est): 109.29K **Privately Held**
SIC: 1731 Electrical work

(G-9687)
WJC OF DELAWARE LLC (PA)
Also Called: Johnstone Supply
19 E Commons Blvd Ste 3 (19720-2262)
PHONE..................................302 323-9600
Richard Comunale, *CEO*
Dean Mader, *Mgr*
EMP: 10 EST: 2013
SALES (est): 927.21K
SALES (corp-wide): 927.21K **Privately Held**
SIC: 5075 Warm air heating and air conditioning

(G-9688)
WOLF STONE ENTERPRISES LLC
18 Lea Rd (19720-1908)
PHONE..................................302 765-7456
Ahmad Johnson, *Managing Member*
EMP: 7
SALES (est): 78.16K **Privately Held**
SIC: 3581 Automatic vending machines

(G-9689)
WORKHORSE II LLC
152 S Dupont Hwy (19720-4149)
PHONE..................................302 533-5342
EMP: 11
SALES (est): 425.73K **Privately Held**
SIC: 4212 Local trucking, without storage

(G-9690)
WORKS OF ART
13 Ridge Dr (19720-2303)
PHONE..................................302 562-3597
George Neuberger, *Prin*
EMP: 5 EST: 2019
SALES (est): 90.83K **Privately Held**
Web: www.gneuberger.com
SIC: 7999 Art gallery, commercial

(G-9691)
WORTH CO
19 E Commons Blvd Ste C (19720-2260)
PHONE..................................302 221-4822
EMP: 9 EST: 2018
SALES (est): 120.82K **Privately Held**
Web: www.worthandcompany.com
SIC: 1711 Mechanical contractor

(G-9692)
WS ONE INVESTMENT USA LLC
Also Called: Ws1.com
298 Cherry Ln (19720-2776)
PHONE..................................302 317-2610
Donald Godwin, *Brnch Mgr*
EMP: 15
SALES (corp-wide): 9.75MM **Privately Held**
Web: www.ws1.com
SIC: 6799 Investors, nec
PA: Ws One Investment Usa, Llc
  1263 S Chillicothe Rd
  Aurora OH 44202
  855 895-3728

(G-9693)
WSFS FINANCIAL CORPORATION
2080 New Castle Ave (19720-2777)
PHONE..................................302 254-3569
EMP: 15
SALES (corp-wide): 641.85MM **Publicly Held**
Web: www.wsfsbank.com
SIC: 7389 Financial services
PA: Wsfs Financial Corporation
  500 Delaware Ave
  Wilmington DE 19801
  302 792-6000

(G-9694)
YEAHER INC
51 Steel Dr Unit A (19720-7709)
PHONE..................................513 293-4347
Rongyu Yuan, *CEO*
EMP: 32 EST: 2013
SALES (est): 1.03MM **Privately Held**
SIC: 3571 Electronic computers

(G-9695)
YOUNG DIVAS LLC
Also Called: Young Divas Spa 4 Girlz
216 Harlequin Dr (19720-8900)
PHONE..................................302 354-6232
Sabrina Young, *Prin*
EMP: 5 EST: 2010
SALES (est): 26.57K **Privately Held**
SIC: 7231 Cosmetology and personal hygiene salons

(G-9696)
YOUTH SPORTS INSTITUTE DEL INC
153 S Dupont Hwy (19720-4127)
PHONE..................................302 275-5947
EMP: 7 EST: 2016
SALES (est): 333.63K **Privately Held**
Web: www.youthsportsinstitutede.org
SIC: 8733 Noncommercial research organizations

(G-9697)
ZENDO MEDICAL LLC
606 E Basin Rd (19720-4202)
PHONE..................................302 322-3442
George Degermentzidis, *Prin*
EMP: 7 EST: 2015
SALES (est): 38.22K **Privately Held**
SIC: 8099 Health and allied services, nec

(G-9698)
ZEON ENTERPRISES INC
806 Wildel Ave (19720-6149)
PHONE..................................302 898-7167
Otis Zeon, *Pr*
EMP: 10 EST: 2019
SALES (est): 383.34K **Privately Held**
SIC: 6799 7371 6719 Venture capital companies; Software programming applications; Investment holding companies, except banks

(G-9699)
ZIMNY & ASSOCIATES PA
92 Reads Way Ste 104 (19720-1631)
PHONE..................................302 325-6900
EMP: 7 EST: 2004
SQ FT: 3,800
SALES (est): 877.26K **Privately Held**
Web: www.zimnycpa.com
SIC: 8721 Certified public accountant

(G-9700)
ZUMINEX INC
217 Lisa Dr Ste A (19720-8404)
PHONE..................................302 325-3200
Jose Zuniga, *Prin*
EMP: 8 EST: 2012
SALES (est): 474.65K **Privately Held**
SIC: 5199 Advertising specialties

(G-9701)
ZZHOUSE INC
34 Blevins Dr Ste 1 (19720-4177)
PHONE..................................302 354-3474
EMP: 10 EST: 2018
SALES (est): 392.97K **Privately Held**
SIC: 2759 Commercial printing, nec

Newark
New Castle County

(G-9702)
100 COMMERCE LLC
100 Commerce Dr (19713-2878)
PHONE..................................302 738-3038
EMP: 5 EST: 2015
SALES (est): 116.28K **Privately Held**
SIC: 8611 Business associations

(G-9703)
160 ENGINEERS
1001 Ogletown Rd (19711-5413)
PHONE..................................302 326-7441
EMP: 7 EST: 2018
SALES (est): 135.94K **Privately Held**
SIC: 8711 Engineering services

(G-9704)
1ST STATE PALLETS LLC
2911 Frazer Rd (19702-4809)
PHONE..................................302 743-3993
EMP: 2 EST: 2020
SALES (est): 86.73K **Privately Held**
SIC: 2448 Pallets, wood

(G-9705)
2 GUYS PRESSURE WASHING
113 Meadowood Dr (19711-7237)
PHONE..................................302 250-3721
Spencer Malcom Iii, *Prin*
EMP: 5 EST: 2009
SALES (est): 90K **Privately Held**
SIC: 1799 Cleaning building exteriors, nec

(G-9706)
2NU PHOTONICS LLC
113 E Main St Unit 404 (19711-7380)
PHONE..................................302 388-2261
EMP: 3 EST: 2018
SALES (est): 121.3K **Privately Held**
SIC: 3661 Fiber optics communications equipment

(G-9707)
3-D FABRICATIONS INC
100 Gabor Dr (19711-6629)
PHONE..................................302 292-3501
Greg Brant, *Pr*
Steve Friedman,
EMP: 32 EST: 1986
SQ FT: 17,500
SALES (est): 2.81MM **Privately Held**
Web: www.3dfab.biz
SIC: 2541 Cabinets, except refrigerated: show, display, etc.: wood

(G-9708)
302 PROPERTIES LLC
250 Corporate Blvd Ste L (19702-3329)
PHONE..................................302 525-4302
Lou Honick, *Managing Member*
EMP: 7 EST: 2009
SALES (est): 615.92K **Privately Held**
Web: www.302properties.com
SIC: 6512 1521 6514 Nonresidential building operators; General remodeling, single-family houses; Residential building, four or fewer units: operation

(G-9709)
30215 MOTORSPORTS
715 Stanton Christiana Rd (19713-2141)
PHONE..................................302 293-6193
EMP: 6 EST: 2019
SALES (est): 136.98K **Privately Held**
SIC: 7549 High performance auto repair and service

(G-9710)
360WISE LIVE INC ◊
254 Chapman Rd (19702-5413)
PHONE..................................844 360-9473
Robert Alexander, *CEO*
EMP: 3 EST: 2023
SALES (est): 135.7K **Privately Held**
SIC: 2741 Internet publishing and broadcasting

(G-9711)
3D CAD DESIGN
12 Bunker Hill Ct (19702-5208)
PHONE..................................302 373-7750
Joe Vercammen, *Prin*
EMP: 7 EST: 2010
SALES (est): 55.77K **Privately Held**
Web: www.treatstock.com
SIC: 7389 Design services

(G-9712)
3M COMPANY
Also Called: 3M

GEOGRAPHIC SECTION

Newark - New Castle County (G-9740)

650 Dawson Dr (19713-3412)
PHONE.................302 286-2480
Tom Flaherty, *Prin*
EMP: 150
SALES (corp-wide): 34.23B **Publicly Held**
Web: www.3m.com
SIC: 3537 Industrial trucks and tractors
PA: 3m Company
3m Center
Saint Paul MN 55144
651 733-1110

(G-9713)
4-H
461 Wyoming Rd (19716-5901)
PHONE.................302 831-8161
Katie Daly-jones, *Mgr*
EMP: 9 **EST:** 2016
SALES (est): 94.7K **Privately Held**
Web: www.4-h.org
SIC: 8641 Youth organizations

(G-9714)
4RB LOGISTICS LLC ✪
8 Bergen Ct (19702-4243)
PHONE.................302 290-8187
EMP: 5 **EST:** 2023
SALES (est): 235.55K **Privately Held**
SIC: 4789 7389 Transportation services, nec; Business services, nec

(G-9715)
6 STAR FUNDRAISING LLC
16 Revelstone Ct (19711-2981)
P.O. Box 1435 (19707-5435)
PHONE.................302 250-5085
Doug Mostrom, *Sls Dir*
EMP: 7 **EST:** 2011
SALES (est): 206.44K **Privately Held**
SIC: 7389 Fund raising organizations

(G-9716)
7ELEMENTS INC
308 Suburban Dr (19711-3599)
PHONE.................302 294-1791
Laura Wu, *Prin*
EMP: 10 **EST:** 2016
SALES (est): 899.08K **Privately Held**
SIC: 2819 Elements

(G-9717)
9193 4323 QUEBEC INC
Also Called: Dml Creation
2915 Ogletown Rd Unit 2385 (19713-1927)
PHONE.................855 824-0795
Ron De Moor, *Pr*
EMP: 2
SALES (corp-wide): 177.54K **Privately Held**
Web: www.dmlcreation.com
SIC: 3993 7336 Signs and advertising specialties; Graphic arts and related design
PA: 9193-4323 Quebec Inc
800 Rue Price
Saint-Jerome QC J7Y 4
514 750-0795

(G-9718)
9ROUND
2826 Pulaski Hwy (19702-3913)
PHONE.................302 365-5590
EMP: 6 **EST:** 2018
SALES (est): 29.54K **Privately Held**
Web: www.9round.com
SIC: 7991 Physical fitness facilities

(G-9719)
A & F MACHINE & DEVELOPMENT
129 Sandy Dr (19713-1149)
PHONE.................302 368-4303
Doug Ahearn, *Pr*
EMP: 13 **EST:** 1975
SQ FT: 9,600
SALES (est): 347.85K **Privately Held**
Web: www.afmachine.net
SIC: 3599 Machine shop, jobbing and repair

(G-9720)
A & H METALS INC
249 E Chestnut Hill Rd (19713-3734)
PHONE.................302 366-7540
Brian Perry, *Pr*
Antoinette Armento, *
Anne Farnan, *
EMP: 35 **EST:** 1971
SQ FT: 26,000
SALES (est): 6.39MM **Privately Held**
Web: www.ahmetals.com
SIC: 3444 Sheet metal specialties, not stamped

(G-9721)
A 1 AT YOUR SERVICE
74 Albe Dr (19702-1350)
PHONE.................302 369-7000
EMP: 5 **EST:** 2007
SALES (est): 39.39K **Privately Held**
SIC: 0781 Landscape architects

(G-9722)
A C M S INC
14 Thomas Ln N (19711-4865)
PHONE.................302 738-6036
EMP: 10 **EST:** 2008
SALES (est): 110K **Privately Held**
SIC: 8322 Individual and family services

(G-9723)
A CARING DOCTOR MINNESOTA PA
1291 Churchmans Rd (19713-2149)
PHONE.................302 266-0122
Jessica Berkeridge, *Brnch Mgr*
EMP: 14
SALES (corp-wide): 42.84B **Privately Held**
SIC: 0742 Animal hospital services, pets and other animal specialties
HQ: A Caring Doctor Minnesota Pa
8000 Ne Tillamook St
Portland OR 97213
503 922-5000

(G-9724)
A DISH NETWORK
668 Paper Mill Rd (19711-7516)
PHONE.................302 565-4175
EMP: 6 **EST:** 2013
SALES (est): 100.4K **Privately Held**
Web: www.dish.com
SIC: 4841 Direct broadcast satellite services (DBS)

(G-9725)
A JS FENCE BUILDERS INC
11 Lawrence Ave (19711-7216)
PHONE.................302 731-0000
Ron Janarowicz, *Prin*
EMP: 5 **EST:** 2008
SALES (est): 202.25K **Privately Held**
SIC: 1521 New construction, single-family houses

(G-9726)
A PLUS ELECTRIC & SECURITY
94 Stardust Dr (19702-4771)
PHONE.................302 455-1725
David Johnson, *Owner*
EMP: 6 **EST:** 2001
SALES (est): 302.5K **Privately Held**
SIC: 1731 5065 5999 7382 General electrical contractor; Security control equipment and systems; Alarm and safety equipment stores; Security systems services

(G-9727)
A RALPH WOODROW INC
116 Chadd Rd (19711-5969)
PHONE.................302 655-0297
Woodrow Ralph, *Prin*
EMP: 5 **EST:** 2016
SALES (est): 117.76K **Privately Held**
SIC: 1711 Plumbing, heating, air-conditioning

(G-9728)
A S A P INSULATION INC
3019 Mcdaniel Ln (19702-4506)
PHONE.................302 836-9040
EMP: 5 **EST:** 1993
SALES (est): 179.87K **Privately Held**
SIC: 1742 Insulation, buildings

(G-9729)
A-DEL CONSTRUCTION COMPANY INC
10 Adel Dr (19702-1331)
PHONE.................302 453-8286
Barry J Baker, *Pr*
Sonny Johnson, *
Harry G Johnson, *
EMP: 100 **EST:** 1976
SQ FT: 5,000
SALES (est): 26.98MM **Privately Held**
Web: www.a-del.com
SIC: 1611 Highway and street paving contractor

(G-9730)
A1 STRIPING INC
902 Irish Bank Rd (19702-2135)
P.O. Box 3 (19701-0003)
PHONE.................302 738-5016
Joseph Shortlidge, *Prin*
EMP: 8 **EST:** 2001
SALES (est): 928.11K **Privately Held**
Web: www.a1striping.net
SIC: 1721 4959 7349 Pavement marking contractor; Sweeping service: road, airport, parking lot, etc.; Building maintenance services, nec

(G-9731)
AAA CLUB ALLIANCE INC
200 Commerce Dr (19713-6804)
PHONE.................302 368-8175
Janyce Smalley, *Brnch Mgr*
EMP: 52
SALES (corp-wide): 1.03B **Privately Held**
Web: mwg.aaa.com
SIC: 8699 Automobile owners' association
PA: Aaa Club Alliance Inc.
1 River Pl
Wilmington DE 19801
302 299-4700

(G-9732)
AAA CLUB ALLIANCE INC
200 Continental Dr Ste 402 (19713-4334)
PHONE.................302 283-4300
Margret Mary Burke, *Brnch Mgr*
EMP: 39
SALES (corp-wide): 1.03B **Privately Held**
Web: mwg.aaa.com
SIC: 6411 Insurance agents, nec
PA: Aaa Club Alliance Inc.
1 River Pl
Wilmington DE 19801
302 299-4700

(G-9733)
AAL DRTC
200 Gbc Dr (19702-2462)
PHONE.................302 229-5891
Christian Dussarrat, *Pr*
EMP: 17 **EST:** 2010
SALES (est): 3.09MM **Privately Held**
SIC: 2813 Oxygen, compressed or liquefied

(G-9734)
AARK NETWORK INC
1142 Elkton Rd (19711-3509)
PHONE.................302 399-3945
Pradip Saha, *Pr*
EMP: 8 **EST:** 2007
SALES (est): 361.52K **Privately Held**
Web: www.aark.us
SIC: 8741 Restaurant management

(G-9735)
AARON B POLECK DDS
50 Omega Dr (19713-2060)
PHONE.................302 533-7649
Aaron B Poleck, *Prin*
EMP: 8 **EST:** 2018
SALES (est): 203.91K **Privately Held**
Web: www.christianafamilydentalcare.com
SIC: 8021 Dentists' office

(G-9736)
AB GROUP PACKAGING INC
1800 Ogletown Rd (19711-5472)
PHONE.................302 607-3281
◆ **EMP:** 19 **EST:** 2015
SALES (est): 2.41MM
SALES (corp-wide): 566.42K **Privately Held**
SIC: 5199 Packaging materials
PA: Premier Liveaboard Diving Limited
74 Ashby Road
Spilsby LINCS PE23
777 526-9547

(G-9737)
ABBEY LEIN INC
28 Meteor Ct (19711-3026)
PHONE.................302 239-2712
Jeff Robinson, *Pr*
EMP: 5 **EST:** 1998
SALES (est): 242.14K **Privately Held**
SIC: 3949 Golf equipment

(G-9738)
ABBY MEDICAL CENTER
Also Called: Gold Care Center
1 Centurian Dr Ste 301 (19713-2127)
PHONE.................302 999-0003
Arlen D Stone, *Pt*
EMP: 5 **EST:** 2007
SALES (est): 1MM **Privately Held**
Web: www.gocaredelaware.com
SIC: 8011 8031 Medical centers; Offices and clinics of osteopathic physicians

(G-9739)
ABC LENDING CORP
1007 S College Ave (19713-2305)
PHONE.................302 369-5626
Aneesah Michael, *Prin*
EMP: 5 **EST:** 2005
SALES (est): 242.87K **Privately Held**
SIC: 6163 Mortgage brokers arranging for loans, using money of others

(G-9740)
ABC SYSTEMS INC
92 White Clay Cres (19711-4847)
PHONE.................302 528-8875
Steve French, *Pr*

(PA)=Parent Co (HQ)=Headquarters
✪ = New Business established in last 2 years

Newark - New Castle County (G-9741) GEOGRAPHIC SECTION

EMP: 8 EST: 2004
SALES (est): 523.01K **Privately Held**
SIC: 8748 Telecommunications consultant

(G-9741)
ABIGAIL FAMILY MEDICINE LLC
Also Called: Abbycare
412 Suburban Dr (19711-3564)
P.O. Box 147 (19715-0147)
PHONE..................302 738-3770
Christine Horah, *Owner*
EMP: 6 EST: 1999
SALES (est): 446.62K **Privately Held**
SIC: 8011 General and family practice, physician/surgeon

(G-9742)
ABOUT ANGELA ANGELAS HOME LN
22 Polly Drummond Hill Rd (19711-5703)
PHONE..................302 598-7799
EMP: 5 EST: 2018
SALES (est): 140.38K **Privately Held**
Web: www.angelashomeloans.com
SIC: 6162 Mortgage bankers and loan correspondents

(G-9743)
ABOVE AND BEYOND CLEANING SVCS
904 Vinings Way (19702-7613)
PHONE..................484 206-5101
Yazmin Derrickson, *CEO*
EMP: 50 EST: 2018
SALES (est): 200K **Privately Held**
SIC: 7349 Janitorial service, contract basis

(G-9744)
ABRI SPAC 2 INC
40 E Main St 1009 (19711-4639)
PHONE..................424 732-1021
Jeffrey Tirman, *Ch Bd*
Nima Montazeri, *Ex VP*
Christopher Hardt, *CFO*
Peter Bakker, *VP*
Amy Wall, *VP*
EMP: 5 EST: 2021
SIC: 6799 Investors, nec

(G-9745)
ABSOLUTE COMPUTER SUPPORT LLC
249 E Main St Bldg 1 (19711-7317)
PHONE..................717 917-8900
EMP: 9 EST: 1990
SQ FT: 1,000
SALES (est): 239.78K **Privately Held**
SIC: 7376 Computer facilities management

(G-9746)
ABSOLUTELY GREEN INC
Also Called: Lawn Doctor of Newark
995 S Chapel St Ste 3 (19713-3441)
P.O. Box 8130 (19714-8130)
PHONE..................302 731-1616
Brian Singleton, *Pr*
EMP: 8 EST: 1972
SQ FT: 4,200
SALES (est): 455.81K **Privately Held**
Web: www.lawndoctor.com
SIC: 0782 Lawn care services

(G-9747)
ACADEMY DOG TRAINING & AGILITY
89b Albe Dr (19702-1321)
PHONE..................302 588-4636
Don Brown, *Prin*
EMP: 5 EST: 2008
SALES (est): 200.63K **Privately Held**
Web: www.academyofdogtraining.com

SIC: 0752 Training services, pet and animal specialties (not horses)

(G-9748)
ACCELERATE MORTGAGE LLC
750 Prides Xing Ste 303 (19713)
PHONE..................866 986-1245
Michael Kacor, *Mgr*
EMP: 25 EST: 2018
SALES (est): 3.83MM **Privately Held**
SIC: 6162 Mortgage bankers and loan correspondents

(G-9749)
ACCELERATED VIRTUAL SOLUTIONS
57 E Periwinkle Ln (19711-6216)
PHONE..................302 494-3215
EMP: 5 EST: 2010
SALES (est): 200.15K **Privately Held**
SIC: 3674 Semiconductors and related devices

(G-9750)
ACCUDYNE SYSTEMS INC (PA)
210 Executive Dr Ste 5 (19702-3335)
PHONE..................302 369-5390
EMP: 21 EST: 1996
SQ FT: 15,000
SALES (est): 10.39MM **Privately Held**
Web: www.accudyne.com
SIC: 5084 Industrial machinery and equipment

(G-9751)
ACCUGENIX INC
223 Lake Dr (19702-3320)
PHONE..................302 292-8888
Douglas Smith, *Pr*
Michael Waddington, *
Patricia Wray, *
Joseph Martini, *
EMP: 41 EST: 1990
SQ FT: 12,000
SALES (est): 7.81MM
SALES (corp-wide): 4.13B **Publicly Held**
Web: www.criver.com
SIC: 8731 Biotechnical research, commercial
HQ: Charles River Laboratories, Inc.
251 Ballardvale St
Wilmington MA 01887
781 222-6000

(G-9752)
ACCURATE AUTO SERVICE INC
233 E Main St (19711-7314)
PHONE..................302 737-7998
EMP: 9 EST: 2004
SALES (est): 478.42K **Privately Held**
Web: www.accurateautonewark.com
SIC: 7538 General automotive repair shops

(G-9753)
ACCUSHEETS
218 W General Grey Ct (19702-3831)
PHONE..................302 266-1047
EMP: 5 EST: 2018
SALES (est): 73.45K **Privately Held**
SIC: 8721 Certified public accountant

(G-9754)
ACCUVENTION LLC
210 Executive Dr (19702-3335)
PHONE..................302 369-5390
Joy Waibel, *Pr*
EMP: 6 EST: 2011
SALES (est): 81.74K **Privately Held**
Web: www.accuvention.com
SIC: 6519 Real property lessors, nec

(G-9755)
ACE RENT-A-CAR INC
915 S Chapel St (19713-3419)
PHONE..................302 368-5950
EMP: 13
SALES (corp-wide): 9.7MM **Privately Held**
Web: www.acerentacar.com
SIC: 7514 Rent-a-car service
PA: Ace Rent-A-Car, Inc.
4529 W 96th St
Indianapolis IN 46268
317 243-6336

(G-9756)
ACOPIA LLC
220 Continental Dr Ste 203 (19713-4312)
PHONE..................302 286-5172
EMP: 78
SALES (corp-wide): 51.42MM **Privately Held**
Web: www.acopiahomeloans.com
SIC: 6799 Investors, nec
PA: Acopia, Llc
306 Northcreek Blvd # 100
Goodlettsville TN 37072
615 859-5537

(G-9757)
ACORN FITNES WELL-BEING LLC
903 Pickett Ln (19711-2641)
PHONE..................302 545-3032
Antonette Maring, *Asst Sec*
EMP: 5 EST: 2017
SALES (est): 57.51K **Privately Held**
SIC: 7991 Physical fitness facilities

(G-9758)
ACOSH ENTERPRISE LLC
1107 Lauren Pl (19702-6926)
PHONE..................631 767-4501
EMP: 4
SALES (est): 78.16K **Privately Held**
SIC: 3999 2841 5812 7389 Candles; Soap: granulated, liquid, cake, flaked, or chip; Caterers; Business Activities at Non-Commercial Site

(G-9759)
ACT & ASSOCIATES LLC
3 Francis Cir (19711-2625)
PHONE..................302 318-6842
EMP: 5 EST: 2019
SALES (est): 99.91K **Privately Held**
SIC: 2999 Petroleum and coal products, nec

(G-9760)
ACTION RENTAL INC
8 Mill Park Ct (19713-1986)
PHONE..................302 366-0749
Gregory Kerstey, *Pr*
EMP: 5 EST: 1969
SALES (est): 400.93K **Privately Held**
SIC: 7359 7513 Party supplies rental services; Truck rental, without drivers

(G-9761)
ACTION SECURITY
100 Peoples Dr (19702-1306)
PHONE..................302 838-2852
Michael Doto, *Chief*
EMP: 6 EST: 2011
SALES (est): 176.61K **Privately Held**
Web: www.actionsecurityusa.com
SIC: 7382 Security systems services

(G-9762)
ADAMS KEMP ASSOCIATES INC
17 Polly Drummond Shpg Ctr Ste 201 (19711-4820)
PHONE..................302 856-6699

Charles E Adams Junior, *Pr*
Roy B Kemp, *Sec*
EMP: 5 EST: 1982
SALES (est): 594.27K **Privately Held**
Web: www.adamskemp.com
SIC: 8713 Photogrammetric engineering

(G-9763)
ADECCO USA INC
Also Called: Adecco Staffing
1000 Samoset Dr (19713-6000)
PHONE..................302 457-4059
EMP: 7
Web: www.adeccousa.com
SIC: 7363 Temporary help service
HQ: Adecco Usa, Inc.
4800 Deerwood Campus Pkwy # 800
Jacksonville FL 32246
904 360-2000

(G-9764)
ADEL CONSTRUCTION
300 Creek View Rd (19711-8546)
PHONE..................302 286-7676
EMP: 9 EST: 2019
SALES (est): 195.69K **Privately Held**
Web: www.a-del.com
SIC: 1521 Single-family housing construction

(G-9765)
ADEOX TECHNOLOGIES INC
226 W Park Pl Ste 14 (19711-4516)
PHONE..................347 884-7131
EMP: 5 EST: 2018
SALES (est): 134.79K **Privately Held**
Web: www.adeox.com
SIC: 4813 Internet host services

(G-9766)
ADJUVANT RESEARCH SERVICES INC
1 Innovation Way Ste 400 (19711-5463)
PHONE..................302 737-5513
James Cinquina, *Pr*
EMP: 11 EST: 1993
SQ FT: 1,000
SALES (est): 435.9K **Privately Held**
Web: www.adjres.com
SIC: 8742 Industry specialist consultants

(G-9767)
ADMIN-SUPPORT
12 Top View Ct (19702-1623)
PHONE..................302 368-6441
Veda Harris, *Prin*
EMP: 5 EST: 2012
SALES (est): 41.17K **Privately Held**
SIC: 8399 Advocacy group

(G-9768)
ADRIEL INC
2035 Sunset Lake Rd Ste B2 (19702-2600)
PHONE..................860 595-4602
EMP: 10 EST: 2018
SALES (est): 282.89K **Privately Held**
SIC: 7389 Business services, nec
PA: Adriel
Rm 1605
Seoul 03158

(G-9769)
ADRIENNE B NEITHARDT MD
4735 Ogletown Stanton Rd Ste 3217 (19713-2094)
PHONE..................302 623-4242
Adrienne Neithardt, *Ofcr*
EMP: 11 EST: 2017
SALES (est): 65.15K **Privately Held**
SIC: 8011 Gynecologist

GEOGRAPHIC SECTION
Newark - New Castle County (G-9796)

(G-9770)
ADT LLC
Also Called: Protection One
130 Executive Dr Ste 2 (19702-3349)
PHONE..................................302 918-1016
Jamie R Haenggi, *Ofcr*
EMP: 124
SALES (corp-wide): 6.4B **Publicly Held**
Web: www.adt.com
SIC: 7382 Security systems services
HQ: Adt Llc
 1501 W Yamato Rd
 Boca Raton FL 33431
 561 988-3600

(G-9771)
ADVANCE INC
Also Called: Advance Windows
645 Dawson Dr Ste A (19713-3443)
PHONE..................................302 324-8890
Gary Derrick, *Pr*
EMP: 16 **EST:** 1991
SALES (est): 1.75MM **Privately Held**
Web: www.advancemyhome.com
SIC: 1521 Single-family home remodeling, additions, and repairs

(G-9772)
ADVANCE WNDW/SPRIOR SIDING INC
11 Mcmillan Way Ste A (19713-3456)
PHONE..................................302 324-8890
Gary Derrick, *Pr*
Doug Derrick, *VP*
Audery Derrick, *Sec*
EMP: 8 **EST:** 1990
SQ FT: 5,500
SALES (est): 883.65K **Privately Held**
SIC: 1521 General remodeling, single-family houses

(G-9773)
ADVANCED CNSTR TECHNIQUES INC
Also Called: Advanced Cnstrctons Techniques
2860 Ogletown Rd (19713-1857)
PHONE..................................302 273-2617
EMP: 84
SALES (corp-wide): 9.41MM **Privately Held**
Web: www.advancedconstructiontechniques.com
SIC: 1629 Dams, waterways, docks, and other marine construction
HQ: Advanced Construction Techniques Inc.
 1403 N Charlotte Ave
 Monroe NC 28110

(G-9774)
ADVANCED COATINGS ENGRG LLC
2915 Ogletown Rd (19713-1927)
PHONE..................................888 607-0000
EMP: 33 **EST:** 2018
SALES (est): 1.62MM **Privately Held**
SIC: 1731 Safety and security specialization

(G-9775)
ADVANCED FOOT & ANKLE CENTER
774 Christiana Rd Ste 105 (19713-4248)
PHONE..................................302 355-0056
Raymond Dipretoro, *Owner*
EMP: 6 **EST:** 2003
SALES (est): 425.55K **Privately Held**
Web: www.advancedfootandanklectr.com
SIC: 8043 Offices and clinics of podiatrists

(G-9776)
ADVANCED HEATING & AIR INC
667 Dawson Dr Ste C (19713-3437)
PHONE..................................302 731-1000
Bill Tidaback, *Pt*
EMP: 8 **EST:** 2009
SALES (est): 152.07K **Privately Held**
SIC: 1711 Heating systems repair and maintenance

(G-9777)
ADVANCED MODERN CARE LLC
16 N Bellwoode Dr (19702-3415)
PHONE..................................267 235-6922
EMP: 10
SALES (est): 253.03K **Privately Held**
SIC: 8082 7389 Home health care services; Business Activities at Non-Commercial Site

(G-9778)
ADVANCED NETWORKING
36 Brookhill Dr (19702-1301)
PHONE..................................302 368-7552
EMP: 7 **EST:** 2017
SALES (est): 47.04K **Privately Held**
Web: www.advnetwork.com
SIC: 1731 Telephone and telephone equipment installation

(G-9779)
ADVANCED PEST MANAGEMENT
955 Dawson Dr Ste 2 (19713-5814)
PHONE..................................410 398-4378
Phillip Kreer, *Prin*
EMP: 5 **EST:** 2000
SALES (est): 107.07K **Privately Held**
SIC: 7342 Pest control in structures

(G-9780)
ADVANCED PLASTIC SURGERY CENTE
4735 Ogletown Stanton Rd (19713-2072)
PHONE..................................302 623-4004
Theresa A Adams, *Prin*
EMP: 11 **EST:** 2007
SALES (est): 1.43MM **Privately Held**
SIC: 8011 Plastic surgeon

(G-9781)
ADVANCED PLASTIC SURGERY CTR
774 Christiana Rd Ste 101 (19713-4248)
PHONE..................................302 355-0005
Shelia Mcguigan, *Mgr*
EMP: 13 **EST:** 1993
SALES (est): 511.2K **Privately Held**
SIC: 8011 Plastic surgeon

(G-9782)
ADVANCED SYSTEMS INC
202 Cheltenham Rd (19711-3681)
P.O. Box 8032 (19714-8032)
PHONE..................................302 368-1211
EMP: 5 **EST:** 1992
SALES (est): 437.42K **Privately Held**
Web: www.advancedsys.com
SIC: 8742 Quality assurance consultant

(G-9783)
ADVANCED TRAINING ACADMEY
9 Prospect Ave (19711-2261)
PHONE..................................302 369-8800
Bowen Wang, *Prin*
EMP: 7 **EST:** 1999
SALES (est): 150K **Privately Held**
SIC: 8331 Skill training center

(G-9784)
ADVANCXING PAIN RHBLTTION CLIN
620 Stanton Christiana Rd Ste 202 (19713-2133)
PHONE..................................302 384-7439
Selina Xing, *Owner*
EMP: 10 **EST:** 2010
SALES (est): 868.71K **Privately Held**
Web: www.advancexing.com
SIC: 8093 Rehabilitation center, outpatient treatment

(G-9785)
ADVANT-DGE SLTONS MDDLE ATL IN
17 Shea Way (19713-3421)
PHONE..................................302 533-6858
Jacqueline Ogborne, *Pr*
Laurie Holland, *VP*
Don Holland, *VP*
EMP: 5 **EST:** 2000
SQ FT: 1,200
SALES (est): 1.56MM **Privately Held**
Web: www.asiwaste.com
SIC: 4953 Recycling, waste materials

(G-9786)
ADVANTDGE HLTHCARE SLTIONS INC
Also Called: ADVANTEDGE HEALTHCARE SOLUTIONS INC.
307 Ruthar Dr (19711-8016)
P.O. Box 41263 (10304-7263)
PHONE..................................302 224-5678
EMP: 14
SALES (corp-wide): 44.77MM **Privately Held**
Web: www.ahsrcm.com
SIC: 8721 Billing and bookkeeping service
PA: Advantedge Healthcare Solutions, Inc.
 30 Technology Dr Ste 1n
 Warren NJ 07059
 908 279-8111

(G-9787)
AEARO TECHNOLOGIES LLC
E-A-R Specialty Composites Div
650 Dawson Dr (19713-3412)
PHONE..................................302 283-5497
George Klett, *Brnch Mgr*
EMP: 255
SALES (corp-wide): 34.23B **Publicly Held**
Web: www.aearotechnologies.com
SIC: 3081 3086 2821 Unsupported plastics film and sheet; Plastics foam products; Plastics materials and resins
HQ: Aearo Technologies Llc
 7911 Zionsville Rd
 Indianapolis IN 46268

(G-9788)
AECOM USA INC
248 Chapman Rd (19702-5447)
PHONE..................................302 781-5963
William Marshall, *Mgr*
EMP: 98
SALES (corp-wide): 14.38B **Publicly Held**
SIC: 8748 8711 Business consulting, nec; Construction and civil engineering
HQ: Aecom Usa, Inc.
 605 3rd Ave
 New York NY 10158
 212 973-2900

(G-9789)
AEROTEK INC
Also Called: AEROTEK, INC.
240 Continental Dr Ste 201 (19713-4312)
PHONE..................................302 318-8760
Nicholas Colangelo, *Brnch Mgr*
EMP: 5
SALES (corp-wide): 15.88B **Privately Held**
Web: www.aerotek.com
SIC: 7363 Temporary help service
HQ: Aerotek Affiliated Services, Inc.
 7301 Parkway Dr
 Hanover MD 21076
 410 694-5100

(G-9790)
AES FOODS
83 Albe Dr Ste F (19702-1374)
P.O. Box 1034 (19701-7034)
PHONE..................................302 420-8377
Patrick Kinyanga, *Pr*
EMP: 2 **EST:** 2014
SALES (est): 234.33K **Privately Held**
Web: www.aesfoods.com
SIC: 2013 Sausages and other prepared meats

(G-9791)
AETNA HOSE HOOK & LADDER CO 9
Also Called: Aetna Banquet Hall
400 Ogletown Rd (19711-5402)
PHONE..................................302 454-3305
EMP: 50
Web: www.aetnahhl.org
SIC: 6324 Health Maintenance Organization (HMO), insurance only
PA: Aetna Hose Hook & Ladder Co.
 31 Academy St
 Newark DE 19711
 302 454-3300

(G-9792)
AETNA HOSE HOOK AND LADDER CO
31 Academy St (19711-4608)
P.O. Box 148 (19715-0148)
PHONE..................................302 454-3300
EMP: 3 **EST:** 2011
SALES (est): 319.45K **Privately Held**
Web: www.aetnahhl.org
SIC: 3711 Fire department vehicles (motor vehicles), assembly of

(G-9793)
AFFILIATED PSYCHOLOGICAL SVC
303 Shisler Ct (19702-1341)
PHONE..................................302 507-3039
Jeffrie J Silverberg, *Mgr*
EMP: 5 **EST:** 2016
SALES (est): 29.52K **Privately Held**
Web: www.consultthedr.com
SIC: 8049 Clinical psychologist

(G-9794)
AFFORDABLE SOD INC
1 S Wynwyd Dr (19711-7426)
PHONE..................................302 545-0275
Stan Spoor, *Owner*
EMP: 5 **EST:** 2006
SALES (est): 195.46K **Privately Held**
SIC: 0181 Sod farms

(G-9795)
AGE ADVANTAGE SENIOR CARE SVCS
2634 Kirkwood Highway (19711-7263)
PHONE..................................302 722-8240
EMP: 10 **EST:** 2017
SALES (est): 232.59K **Privately Held**
Web: www.ageadvantagenewark.com
SIC: 8322 Individual and family services

(G-9796)
AGENT LAUNCH LLC
256 Chapman Rd Ste 1054 (19702-5499)
PHONE..................................302 200-5574
Eric Preston, *Managing Member*
EMP: 19 **EST:** 2021
SALES (est): 583.41K **Privately Held**
SIC: 7371 7389 Computer software development; Business Activities at Non-Commercial Site

Newark - New Castle County (G-9797)

(G-9797)
AHU TECHNOLOGIES INC
Also Called: Ahu Tech
15 Prestbury Sq Ste 11 (19713-2608)
PHONE.................................302 397-7091
Ashan Malik, *Pr*
EMP: 15 **EST:** 2011
SALES (est): 600.76K **Privately Held**
Web: www.ahutech.com
SIC: 7379 Computer related consulting services

(G-9798)
AI WHOO LLC
88 Munro Rd (19711-3559)
PHONE.................................302 494-6952
EMP: 7
SALES (est): 46.16K **Privately Held**
Web: www.aiwhoo.com
SIC: 7371 Computer software development and applications

(G-9799)
AIR LQIDE ADVANCED TECH US LLC
200 Gbc Dr (19702-2462)
PHONE.................................302 225-1100
EMP: 1048
SALES (corp-wide): 101.26MM **Privately Held**
SIC: 2813 Industrial gases
HQ: Air Liquide Advanced Technologies Us Llc
9807 Katy Fwy
Houston TX 77024

(G-9800)
AIR NATURES WAY INC
5 Myers Rd (19713-2316)
PHONE.................................302 738-3063
Patricia Sutton, *Prin*
EMP: 2 **EST:** 1996
SALES (est): 144.75K **Privately Held**
SIC: 3564 Purification and dust collection equipment

(G-9801)
AIRGAS USA LLC
200 Gbc Dr (19702-2462)
PHONE.................................302 286-5400
Patricia Mcqueeney, *Brnch Mgr*
EMP: 21
SALES (corp-wide): 101.26MM **Privately Held**
Web: www.airgas.com
SIC: 5084 Welding machinery and equipment
HQ: Airgas Usa, Llc
259 N Radnor Chester Rd
Radnor PA 19087
216 642-6600

(G-9802)
AIRSLED INC
66 Albe Dr (19702-1322)
PHONE.................................302 292-8911
Bruce F Harvey, *Ch Bd*
Steve Wolfgang, *CEO*
Karen Edwards, *VP*
EMP: 5 **EST:** 1982
SALES (est): 579.19K **Privately Held**
Web: www.airsled.com
SIC: 3535 5084 3537 Conveyors and conveying equipment; Materials handling machinery; Industrial trucks and tractors

(G-9803)
AJEDIUM FILM GROUP LLC
100 Interchange Blvd (19711-3549)
PHONE.................................302 452-6609
Peter Woldson, *CEO*
Richard Giacco, *Pr*
▲ **EMP:** 6 **EST:** 2002
SALES (est): 991.67K **Privately Held**
SIC: 3081 Plastics film and sheet

(G-9804)
AKITA TRUCKING LLC
Also Called: Trucking/Logistics
6 Redwood Ct (19702-3630)
PHONE.................................302 463-8152
Shauna Estep, *CEO*
EMP: 5 **EST:** 2018
SALES (est): 485.55K **Privately Held**
Web: www.akitatrucking.com
SIC: 4212 Local trucking, without storage

(G-9805)
ALAS CLEANERS & ALTERATIONS
430 Old Baltimore Pike (19702-2611)
PHONE.................................302 366-1638
EMP: 5 **EST:** 2010
SALES (est): 80.95K **Privately Held**
SIC: 7699 Cleaning services

(G-9806)
ALBERT DELPIZZO LLC
224 Mercury Rd (19711-3038)
PHONE.................................302 234-2994
Albert Delpizzo, *Prin*
EMP: 5 **EST:** 2011
SALES (est): 176.69K **Privately Held**
SIC: 1522 Residential construction, nec

(G-9807)
ALCHEMY OF HAIR
4633 Ogletown Stanton Rd (19713-2006)
PHONE.................................302 525-6676
EMP: 5 **EST:** 2017
SALES (est): 60.24K **Privately Held**
Web: www.thealchemyofhair.com
SIC: 7231 Hairdressers

(G-9808)
ALEX AND ANI LLC
Also Called: Alex and Ani
132 Christiana Mall (19702-3202)
PHONE.................................302 731-1420
EMP: 3
SALES (corp-wide): 91.95MM **Privately Held**
Web: www.alexandani.com
SIC: 5944 3911 Jewelry, precious stones and precious metals; Jewelry, precious metal
HQ: Alex And Ani, Llc
10 Briggs Dr
East Greenwich RI 02818

(G-9809)
ALEXIS LEGAL SUPPORT SVCS INC
35 Fairway Rd Apt 3a (19711-5654)
PHONE.................................646 494-3289
Dawn Alexis Demby, *Owner*
EMP: 5 **EST:** 2016
SALES (est): 69.19K **Privately Held**
SIC: 8111 Legal services

(G-9810)
ALI S HUSAIN ORTHODONTIST (PA)
Also Called: Husain, Ali S DMD Msd
1400 Peoples Plz Ste 312 (19702-5708)
PHONE.................................302 838-1400
Ali S Husain, *Owner*
EMP: 10 **EST:** 1998
SQ FT: 2,800
SALES (est): 888.98K **Privately Held**
Web: www.delawareorthodontics.com
SIC: 8021 Orthodontist

(G-9811)
ALIVIO HEALTH CORP
256 Chapman Rd (19702-5499)
PHONE.................................754 230-0234
Juan Anzueto, *Prin*
EMP: 8 **EST:** 2021
SALES (est): 306.16K **Privately Held**
SIC: 7371 Computer software development and applications

(G-9812)
ALJSTAR GLOBAL HOLDINGS INC
200 Continental Dr Ste 401-1103 (19714-4334)
PHONE.................................302 565-5249
Anita Jernigan, *CEO*
EMP: 10 **EST:** 2015
SALES (est): 679.87K **Privately Held**
Web: www.aljstarglobalholdingsinc.com
SIC: 8742 Business management consultant

(G-9813)
ALL ABOUT PAIN AND SPINE
2600 Glasgow Ave Ste 102 (19702-5703)
P.O. Box 308 (19701-0308)
PHONE.................................302 595-3670
Mohamed F Ahmed Md, *Prin*
EMP: 7 **EST:** 2015
SALES (est): 328.08K **Privately Held**
Web: www.painandspinede.com
SIC: 8011 Orthopedic physician

(G-9814)
ALL ABOUT WOMEN
2600 Glasgow Ave Ste 120 (19702-4777)
PHONE.................................302 832-8331
Peggy Tracy, *Owner*
EMP: 9 **EST:** 2017
SALES (est): 135.64K **Privately Held**
SIC: 8011 Gynecologist

(G-9815)
ALL ABOUT WOMEN LLC
4735 Ogletown Stanton Rd Ste 2300 (19713-8005)
PHONE.................................302 224-8400
Diane Mccracken, *Prin*
EMP: 24 **EST:** 2007
SALES (est): 3.64MM **Privately Held**
Web: www.aawdocs.com
SIC: 8011 General and family practice, physician/surgeon

(G-9816)
ALL IN HARMONY CHILD CARE
802 S Harmony Rd (19713-3345)
PHONE.................................302 494-3618
EMP: 6 **EST:** 2014
SALES (est): 19.32K **Privately Held**
SIC: 8351 Child day care services

(G-9817)
ALL IN ONE HOME REPAIRS LLC
596 Old Baltimore Pike (19702-1309)
PHONE.................................302 897-3845
EMP: 5 **EST:** 2017
SALES (est): 232.04K **Privately Held**
Web: www.allinone-homerepairs.com
SIC: 1521 General remodeling, single-family houses

(G-9818)
ALL STATE TRANSPORT LLC
200 Continental Dr (19713-4334)
P.O. Box 121 (19956-0121)
PHONE.................................443 735-6453
EMP: 2 **EST:** 2020
SALES (est): 150K **Privately Held**
SIC: 3537 Trucks, tractors, loaders, carriers, and similar equipment

(G-9819)
ALL THE DIFFERENCE INC
119 Saint Regis Dr (19711-3822)
PHONE.................................302 738-6353
Kristina Stroh, *Ex Dir*
EMP: 10 **EST:** 2007
SALES (est): 304.06K **Privately Held**
SIC: 8093 Rehabilitation center, outpatient treatment

(G-9820)
ALL TRANS TRANSMISSION INC
Also Called: Transm
18 Albe Dr (19702-1353)
PHONE.................................302 366-0104
Mark Bulovas, *Pr*
EMP: 5 **EST:** 1980
SALES (est): 450.31K **Privately Held**
Web: www.alltranstransmissions.com
SIC: 7537 Automotiv e transmission repair shops

(G-9821)
ALL WORK SERVICES
2433 Glasgow Ave (19702-4729)
PHONE.................................302 345-2695
EMP: 5 **EST:** 2016
SALES (est): 81.38K **Privately Held**
SIC: 7699 Cleaning services

(G-9822)
ALLEGIANT FIRE PROTECTION LLC
118 Sandy Dr Ste 6 (19713-1177)
PHONE.................................302 276-1300
Frederick Hill, *VP*
EMP: 5 **EST:** 2016
SALES (est): 652.39K **Privately Held**
Web: www.allegiantfireprotection.com
SIC: 7389 Fire protection service other than forestry or public

(G-9823)
ALLERGY ASSOCIATES PA
2600 Glasgow Ave Ste 201 (19702-5704)
PHONE.................................302 834-3401
Micheal Wydila, *CEO*
EMP: 7 **EST:** 2006
SALES (est): 222.78K **Privately Held**
Web: www.wilmington-allergist.com
SIC: 8011 Medical centers

(G-9824)
ALLI INC
250 Pencader Plz (19713-3453)
PHONE.................................302 733-0740
Allison Brown, *Mgr*
EMP: 5 **EST:** 2015
SALES (est): 117.58K **Privately Held**
Web: www.lourdesmont.com
SIC: 3993 Signs and advertising specialties

(G-9825)
ALLIANCE ELECTRIC INC
1003 S Chapel St Ste D (19702-1357)
PHONE.................................302 366-0295
Kevin Morgan, *Pr*
EMP: 12 **EST:** 2001
SQ FT: 2,068
SALES (est): 2.26MM **Privately Held**
Web: www.alliance-electric.net
SIC: 1731 General electrical contractor

(G-9826)
ALLSTATE INSUR AGNT INTGRITY I
230 E Cleveland Ave (19711-3711)
PHONE.................................302 368-6279
EMP: 5 **EST:** 2018
SALES (est): 55.85K **Privately Held**
SIC: 6411 Insurance agents and brokers

GEOGRAPHIC SECTION

Newark - New Castle County (G-9856)

(G-9827)
ALLSTATE VAN & STORAGE CORP
910 Interchange Blvd (19711-3563)
PHONE.....................302 369-0230
Thomas Bennett Iii, *Pr*
EMP: 9 **EST:** 1982
SALES (est): 181.36K **Privately Held**
Web: www.movingandstoragedelaware.com
SIC: 4225 General warehousing and storage

(G-9828)
ALLURA BATH & KITCHEN INC
704 Interchange Blvd (19711-3595)
PHONE.....................302 731-2851
Alan J Pannaccione, *Pr*
EMP: 6 **EST:** 1970
SQ FT: 5,144
SALES (est): 943.27K **Privately Held**
Web: www.alluragroup.com
SIC: 1799 5031 Kitchen and bathroom remodeling; Kitchen cabinets

(G-9829)
ALMA COMPANY
625 Barksdale Rd (19711-4535)
PHONE.....................302 731-4427
Jeffrey Morton, *Pr*
EMP: 5 **EST:** 1958
SALES (est): 268.43K **Privately Held**
SIC: 8721 Accounting services, except auditing

(G-9830)
ALMOST HOME DAY CARE
1129 Capitol Trl (19711-3921)
PHONE.....................302 220-6731
EMP: 6 **EST:** 2012
SALES (est): 106.87K **Privately Held**
SIC: 8082 Home health care services

(G-9831)
ALMOST HOME DAY CARE LLC
201 Cain Rue (19711-3001)
PHONE.....................302 220-6731
EMP: 6 **EST:** 2020
SALES (est): 67.24K **Privately Held**
SIC: 8082 Home health care services

(G-9832)
ALN CONSTRUCTION INC
104 Sandy Dr (19713-1147)
P.O. Box 7959 (19714-7959)
PHONE.....................302 292-1580
Greg Peterson, *Pr*
EMP: 85 **EST:** 2000
SQ FT: 3,500
SALES (est): 4.66MM **Privately Held**
Web: www.alnconstruction.com
SIC: 1742 Drywall

(G-9833)
ALPHA MEDICAL DISTRIBUTION
201 Ruthar Dr Ste 5 (19711-8029)
PHONE.....................302 738-9742
Robert Quinn, *Pr*
EMP: 11 **EST:** 2011
SALES (est): 74.66K **Privately Held**
SIC: 8099 Health and allied services, nec

(G-9834)
ALPHA NET CONSULTING LLC
100 Commerce Dr (19713-2878)
PHONE.....................302 737-2532
Gurderpind Dhillon, *Ofcr*
EMP: 8 **EST:** 2015
SALES (est): 50.76K **Privately Held**
Web: www.anetcorp.com
SIC: 8742 Business management consultant

(G-9835)
ALPHA RAILROAD & PILING
231 Executive Dr Ste 15 (19702-3324)
PHONE.....................318 377-8720
Steven Gorham, *CFO*
EMP: 6 **EST:** 2018
SALES (est): 195.27K **Privately Held**
SIC: 1629 Heavy construction, nec

(G-9836)
ALPHASENSE INC
28 Hillstream Rd (19711-2480)
PHONE.....................302 294-0116
Xin Zhang, *CEO*
EMP: 6 **EST:** 2007
SALES (est): 240.77K **Privately Held**
Web: www.alphasense.net
SIC: 3826 Analytical instruments

(G-9837)
ALTERNATE CMMODITIES INDEX INC ✪
9 Innovation Way (19711-5449)
PHONE.....................302 238-1077
Dato Sheikh Jamal, *CEO*
EMP: 8 **EST:** 2022
SALES (est): 306.16K **Privately Held**
SIC: 7371 Computer software development and applications

(G-9838)
ALTERNATIVE THERAPY LLC
4629 Ogletown Stanton Rd (19713-2006)
PHONE.....................302 368-0800
Rachele Louis, *Managing Member*
EMP: 7 **EST:** 2008
SALES (est): 143.12K **Privately Held**
Web: www.alternativetherapyllc.com
SIC: 7299 7991 Massage parlor; Spas

(G-9839)
AMADEX LLC ✪
254 Chapman Rd Ste 208 # 10451 (19702-5422)
PHONE.....................302 722-6027
Manuel Gonzalez, *Managing Member*
EMP: 6 **EST:** 2022
SALES (est): 252.85K **Privately Held**
SIC: 7372 Prepackaged software

(G-9840)
AMAZON COMMODITIES LLC (PA)
112 Capitol Trl Ste A455 (19711-3716)
PHONE.....................302 715-1427
EMP: 7 **EST:** 2019
SALES (est): 63.57K
SALES (corp-wide): 63.57K **Privately Held**
SIC: 5141 Food brokers

(G-9841)
AMBIENT PROCUREMENT GROUP LLC ✪
300 Creek View Rd Ste 209 (19711-8548)
PHONE.....................718 925-7750
EMP: 14 **EST:** 2023
SALES (est): 558.87K **Privately Held**
SIC: 8748 Business consulting, nec

(G-9842)
AMERICAN ART TATTTOO
114 W Rutherford Dr (19713-2032)
PHONE.....................484 889-1663
Cloudia Hadley, *Prin*
EMP: 5 **EST:** 2015
SALES (est): 41.2K **Privately Held**
Web: www.americanarttattoo.com
SIC: 7999 Art gallery, commercial

(G-9843)
AMERICAN CNCIL FOR AN ENRGY EF
1 Roy Ct (19711-6106)
PHONE.....................202 507-4000
EMP: 7 **EST:** 2019
SALES (est): 37.8K **Privately Held**
Web: www.aceee.org
SIC: 8399 Advocacy group

(G-9844)
AMERICAN CRAFTSMEN LLC
608 S Gerald Dr (19713-3233)
PHONE.....................302 545-3666
Jon Gilbert, *Managing Member*
EMP: 5 **EST:** 2005
SALES (est): 215.93K **Privately Held**
Web: www.americancraftsmenllc.com
SIC: 1522 Residential construction, nec

(G-9845)
AMERICAN HOMEPATIENT INC
Also Called: American Homepatient
701 Interchange Blvd (19711-3594)
PHONE.....................302 454-4941
Joseph Cozza, *Mgr*
EMP: 21
Web: www.ahom.com
SIC: 7352 5999 Medical equipment rental; Medical apparatus and supplies
HQ: American Homepatient, Inc.
19387 Us Highway 19 N
Clearwater FL 33764

(G-9846)
AMERICAN KARATE STUDIOS
Also Called: Academy Bind Body Arts
1150 Capitol Trl (19711-3933)
P.O. Box 9102 (19714-9102)
PHONE.....................302 737-9500
Jim Clapp, *Owner*
EMP: 7 **EST:** 1973
SALES (est): 243.18K **Privately Held**
Web: www.karatenewark.com
SIC: 7999 7991 Martial arts school, nec; Aerobic dance and exercise classes

(G-9847)
AMERICAN SOLUTIONS INC
100 Commerce Dr Ste 103 (19713-2878)
PHONE.....................302 456-9600
Subba Raju Indukuri, *Pr*
EMP: 38 **EST:** 1999
SQ FT: 3,000
SALES (est): 2.18MM **Privately Held**
SIC: 7379 Computer related consulting services

(G-9848)
AMERICAN SPIRIT FEDERAL CR UN
1110 Elkton Rd (19711-3509)
PHONE.....................302 738-4515
Maurice Dawkins, *Pr*
EMP: 25 **EST:** 1963
SALES (est): 3.87MM **Privately Held**
Web: www.americanspirit.org
SIC: 6061 6163 Federal credit unions; Loan brokers

(G-9849)
AMERICAN UNIVERSAL LLC
Also Called: AMERICAN RENAL
1415 Pulaski Hwy Ste 2 (19702-5104)
PHONE.....................302 836-9790
John J Mcdonough, *COO*
EMP: 5 **EST:** 2013
SALES (est): 3.19MM
SALES (corp-wide): 822.52MM **Privately Held**
SIC: 8351 Child day care services
HQ: American Renal Associates Holdings, Inc.
500 Cummings Ctr Ste 6550
Beverly MA 01915

(G-9850)
AMERICAN VAN STORAGE CORP
Also Called: American Records Management
900 Interchange Blvd (19711-3563)
PHONE.....................302 369-0900
Thomas Bennett Iii, *Pr*
EMP: 14 **EST:** 1959
SQ FT: 40,000
SALES (est): 415.35K **Privately Held**
Web: www.movingandstoragedelaware.com
SIC: 4213 4225 Household goods transport; General warehousing

(G-9851)
AMETEK INC
Ametek Process Anlytical Instrs
455 Corporate Blvd (19702-3332)
PHONE.....................302 456-4400
Jim Burns, *Brnch Mgr*
EMP: 79
SALES (corp-wide): 6.15B **Publicly Held**
Web: www.ametek.com
SIC: 3399 3577 3621 3823 Powder, metal; Plotters, computer; Motors and generators; Process control instruments
PA: Ametek, Inc.
1100 Cassatt Rd
Berwyn PA 19312
610 647-2121

(G-9852)
AMFINE CHEMICAL CORP
602 Benham Ct (19711-6015)
PHONE.....................302 559-2948
EMP: 6 **EST:** 2018
SALES (est): 68.47K **Privately Held**
Web: www.amfine.com
SIC: 5169 Industrial chemicals

(G-9853)
AMPLIFIED GCHMICAL IMAGING LLC
210 Executive Dr Ste 1 (19702-3335)
PHONE.....................302 266-2428
Mark Arnold, *Mgr*
EMP: 10 **EST:** 2007
SALES (est): 959.36K **Privately Held**
Web: www.agisurveys.net
SIC: 8713 Ariel digital imaging

(G-9854)
AMSOL INC
100 Commerce Dr Ste 103 (19713-2878)
PHONE.....................302 369-6969
Venkat Indukuri, *Pr*
EMP: 5 **EST:** 2004
SALES (est): 107.71K **Privately Held**
SIC: 8748 Business consulting, nec

(G-9855)
AMSTEL BARBERSHOP LLC
1830 Capitol Trl (19711-5722)
PHONE.....................302 299-5926
EMP: 6 **EST:** 2018
SALES (est): 16.07K **Privately Held**
Web: www.amstelbarbershop.com
SIC: 7241 Barber shops

(G-9856)
AMY M FARRALL OD LLC
317 E Main St (19711-7152)
PHONE.....................302 737-5777
Amy Farrall, *Owner*
Doctor Amy Farrall, *Owner*

Newark - New Castle County (G-9857) GEOGRAPHIC SECTION

EMP: 6 EST: 2007
SALES (est): 446.3K **Privately Held**
SIC: 8042 Offices and clinics of optometrists

(G-9857)
AN INTGRATIVE HLTH CTR MED SPA
19 Haines St (19711-4610)
PHONE..................484 550-2085
Andrea Dean, *Prin*
EMP: 6 EST: 2018
SALES (est): 144.73K **Privately Held**
Web: www.betrulywell.com
SIC: 8099 Health and allied services, nec

(G-9858)
ANACONDA PRTCTIVE CONCEPTS INC
210 Executive Dr Ste 6 (19702-3335)
PHONE..................302 834-1125
Nancy L Dunfee, *Pr*
EMP: 10 EST: 2005
SALES (est): 1.89MM **Privately Held**
Web: www.anacondaprotectiveconcepts.com
SIC: 7382 1731 Burglar alarm maintenance and monitoring; General electrical contractor

(G-9859)
ANALYTICS REALM LLC
43 Anthony Dr (19702-8428)
PHONE..................302 743-0342
Michael Ojo, *CEO*
EMP: 5 EST: 2019
SALES (est): 247.63K **Privately Held**
SIC: 8748 Business consulting, nec

(G-9860)
ANAX DESIGNS
200 Continental Dr (19711-4334)
PHONE..................877 908-8719
EMP: 5 EST: 2019
SALES (est): 224.54K **Privately Held**
Web: www.anaxdesigns.com
SIC: 7389 Design services

(G-9861)
ANCAR ENTERPRISES LLC
Also Called: AlphaGraphics
703 Interchange Blvd (19711-3594)
PHONE..................302 453-2600
Atul Chugh, *Pr*
EMP: 7
SALES (corp-wide): 1.2MM **Privately Held**
Web: www.alphagraphics.com
SIC: 2752 Commercial printing, lithographic
PA: Ancar Enterprises Llc
3411 Silverside Rd 103
Wilmington DE 19810
302 477-1884

(G-9862)
ANCATT COMPANY
20 Findail Dr (19711-2972)
PHONE..................302 897-8366
EMP: 5 EST: 2018
SALES (est): 69.33K **Privately Held**
Web: www.ancatt.com
SIC: 5169 Chemicals and allied products, nec

(G-9863)
ANCHOR PLUMBING INC
207 Brennen Dr (19713-3907)
PHONE..................410 392-6520
Joseph Simmons, *Pr*
Benjamin Haines, *VP*
EMP: 7 EST: 1992
SALES (est): 516.82K **Privately Held**
SIC: 1711 Plumbing contractors

(G-9864)
ANCIENT ORDER OF HIBERNIANS
11 Palmer Pl (19713-1645)
PHONE..................302 368-0264
Michael Quirk, *Pr*
EMP: 5 EST: 2014
SALES (est): 46.71K **Privately Held**
SIC: 8641 Fraternal associations

(G-9865)
ANDRE M D HOFFMAN
1090 Old Churchmans Rd (19713-2102)
PHONE..................302 892-2710
EMP: 8 EST: 2017
SALES (est): 71.02K **Privately Held**
SIC: 8011 Offices and clinics of medical doctors

(G-9866)
ANDY MULRINE
228 Suburban Dr (19711-3596)
PHONE..................302 547-7139
Andy Mulrine, *Prin*
EMP: 5 EST: 2010
SALES (est): 136.67K **Privately Held**
SIC: 6531 Real estate agent, residential

(G-9867)
ANESTHESIOLOGY & PAIN MGT
1080 S Chapel St Ste 100 (19702-1378)
PHONE..................302 235-8074
Bhawna Jha Md, *Pr*
EMP: 5 EST: 2014
SALES (est): 168.71K **Privately Held**
Web: www.epoxyofvirginia.com
SIC: 8741 8011 Business management; Specialized medical practitioners, except internal

(G-9868)
ANGEL HOMEOWNER
25 Sunny Bnd (19702-2324)
PHONE..................302 504-6895
Drew Fioravanti, *Owner*
EMP: 5 EST: 2016
SALES (est): 51.38K **Privately Held**
SIC: 8641 Homeowners' association

(G-9869)
ANGELAS MASSAGE AND BODYWORK
11 O Rourke Ct (19702-6835)
PHONE..................302 547-9390
Angela Giroud, *Prin*
EMP: 5 EST: 2010
SALES (est): 80K **Privately Held**
SIC: 7299 Massage parlor

(G-9870)
ANGLER PLUMBING LLC
37 Dempsey Dr (19713-1930)
PHONE..................302 293-5691
EMP: 7 EST: 2010
SALES (est): 489.45K **Privately Held**
Web: www.anglerplumbing.com
SIC: 1711 Plumbing contractors

(G-9871)
ANGRY 8 LLC (PA)
200 Continental Dr Ste 401-796 (19713-4334)
PHONE..................888 417-5477
EMP: 10 EST: 2018
SALES (est): 2MM
SALES (corp-wide): 2MM **Privately Held**
Web: www.angry8.com
SIC: 5149 Beverages, except coffee and tea

(G-9872)
ANN WHITE
14 Newbrook Rd (19711-5522)
PHONE..................302 365-4664
Ann White, *Prin*
EMP: 8 EST: 2018
SALES (est): 121.98K **Privately Held**
SIC: 8011 Offices and clinics of medical doctors

(G-9873)
ANNS FAMILY DAYCARE
30 Reubens Cir (19702-3034)
PHONE..................302 836-8910
Shawn Ennis, *Prin*
EMP: 9 EST: 2008
SALES (est): 61.68K **Privately Held**
SIC: 8351 Group day care center

(G-9874)
ANP BIOPHARMA LLC
824 Interchange Blvd (19711-3570)
PHONE..................302 283-1730
Ray Yin, *CEO*
William Witham, *Mgr*
EMP: 20 EST: 2016
SALES (est): 978.37K **Privately Held**
Web: www.anptinc.com
SIC: 8731 Biotechnical research, commercial

(G-9875)
ANP TECHNOLOGIES INC
824 Interchange Blvd (19711-3570)
PHONE..................302 283-1730
EMP: 25 EST: 2002
SALES (est): 4.24MM **Privately Held**
Web: www.anptinc.com
SIC: 2835 2834 8731 Diagnostic substances ; Antibiotics, packaged; Biotechnical research, commercial

(G-9876)
ANTENNA HOUSE INC
500 Creek View Rd Ste 107 (19711-8549)
PHONE..................302 566-7225
Tokushige Kobayashi, *Pr*
Michael Miller, *Ex VP*
EMP: 6 EST: 2003
SALES (est): 837.37K **Privately Held**
Web: www.antennahouse.com
SIC: 7379 5734 Computer related maintenance services; Computer and software stores

(G-9877)
ANTHONY A VASILE DO
620 Stanton Christiana Rd (19713-2134)
PHONE..................302 764-2072
Anthony Vasile D.o.s., *Owner*
EMP: 5 EST: 1988
SALES (est): 359.6K **Privately Held**
Web: www.dranthonyvasile.com
SIC: 8031 Offices and clinics of osteopathic physicians

(G-9878)
ANTHONY GIANTINOTO DC
260 Chapman Rd Ste 104e (19702-5410)
PHONE..................302 294-1832
Anthony Giantinoto, *Owner*
EMP: 5 EST: 2018
SALES (est): 120.66K **Privately Held**
Web: www.302relief.com
SIC: 8041 Offices and clinics of chiropractors

(G-9879)
ANTHONY LEE CUCUZZELLA MD
Also Called: Physiatrist Assoc
4735 Ogletown Stanton Rd Ste 3302 (19713-2094)
PHONE..................302 623-4370
Anthony L Cucuzzella, *Owner*
EMP: 7 EST: 1963
SALES (est): 415.95K **Privately Held**
SIC: 8011 Physical medicine, physician/surgeon

(G-9880)
ANTHONY M CARISTO DPM
2600 Glasgow Ave Ste 106 (19702-5703)
PHONE..................302 834-3575
Anthony Caristo, *Ofcr*
EMP: 9 EST: 2017
SALES (est): 376.17K **Privately Held**
Web: www.defootandanklegroup.net
SIC: 8043 Offices and clinics of podiatrists

(G-9881)
ANTONIO C NARVAEZ MD
2602 Eastburn Ctr (19711-7285)
PHONE..................302 453-1002
Antonio C Narvaez Md, *Owner*
EMP: 5 EST: 1999
SALES (est): 114.31K **Privately Held**
SIC: 8011 Offices and clinics of medical doctors

(G-9882)
ANYTIME FITNESS
247 S Main St (19711-4564)
PHONE..................302 533-7773
EMP: 10 EST: 2017
SALES (est): 229.38K **Privately Held**
Web: www.anytimefitness.com
SIC: 7991 Physical fitness clubs with training equipment

(G-9883)
ANYTIME FITNESS
201 Louviers Dr (19711-4164)
PHONE..................302 738-3040
Troy Rinker, *Prin*
EMP: 6 EST: 2007
SALES (est): 210.96K **Privately Held**
Web: www.anytimefitness.com
SIC: 7991 Physical fitness clubs with training equipment

(G-9884)
APEX MANUFACTURING GROUP INC
825 Dawson Dr Ste 1 (19713-3438)
PHONE..................484 888-6252
John Kuklinski, *Prin*
John Kuklinski, *CEO*
Mary Kuklinski, *Sec*
EMP: 3 EST: 2016
SQ FT: 10,000
SALES (est): 392.09K **Privately Held**
Web: www.apexmgi.com
SIC: 3599 Machine shop, jobbing and repair

(G-9885)
APOLLO IMPORTS INC
2915 Ogletown Rd # 3696 (19713-1927)
PHONE..................514 895-9410
Christopher Heathcote-rey, *CEO*
EMP: 48 EST: 2020
SALES (est): 1.48MM **Privately Held**
SIC: 3751 Motor scooters and parts

(G-9886)
APOLLO SCITECH LLC
18 Shea Way Ste 108 (19713-3448)
PHONE..................302 861-6557
Yanping Amy Chen, *Pr*
EMP: 3 EST: 2014
SQ FT: 2,250
SALES (est): 321K **Privately Held**
Web: www.apolloscitech.com

GEOGRAPHIC SECTION

Newark - New Castle County (G-9914)

SIC: 3826 Gas analyzing equipment

(G-9887)
APOLLO SOFTWARE INC
2035 Sunset Lake Rd B2 (19702-2600)
PHONE..............................800 992-0847
Sardor Umrdinov, *CEO*
EMP: 5 **EST:** 2017
SALES (est): 432K **Privately Held**
SIC: 7371 Software programming applications

(G-9888)
APPHIVE INC
2035 Sunset Lake Rd (19702-2600)
PHONE..............................240 898-4661
EMP: 8 **EST:** 2019
SALES (est): 447.04K **Privately Held**
Web: www.apphive.io
SIC: 7371 7389 Computer software development and applications; Business Activities at Non-Commercial Site

(G-9889)
APPHUD INC
200 Continental Dr Ste 401 (19713-4334)
PHONE..............................415 936-8741
EMP: 5 **EST:** 2019
SALES (est): 105.28K **Privately Held**
SIC: 7371 Computer software development

(G-9890)
APPLIED ANALYTICS INC
113 Barksdale Professional Ctr (19711-3258)
PHONE..............................781 791-5005
Giselle Ridderplaat, *Pr*
Grogory Elias, *
Andrea Norton, *
EMP: 30 **EST:** 2010
SQ FT: 12,000
SALES (est): 3.42MM **Privately Held**
Web: www.aai.solutions
SIC: 3823 Industrial process measurement equipment

(G-9891)
APPLIED CONTROL ENGRG INC (PA)
700 Creek View Rd (19711-8544)
P.O. Box 520 (19707-0520)
PHONE..............................302 738-8800
EMP: 60 **EST:** 1991
SQ FT: 20,800
SALES (est): 26.58MM **Privately Held**
Web: www.ace-net.com
SIC: 7371 7373 7379 Custom computer programming services; Computer systems analysis and design; Computer related consulting services

(G-9892)
APPLIED VIRTUAL SOLUTIONS LLC
16 N Bellwoode Dr (19702-3415)
P.O. Box 1625 (19701-7625)
PHONE..............................302 312-8548
EMP: 6 **EST:** 2015
SALES (est): 422.63K **Privately Held**
SIC: 7389 Telephone answering service

(G-9893)
APPLOYE INC
2035 Sunset Lake Rd B2 (19702-2600)
PHONE..............................925 452-6102
EMP: 4 **EST:** 2019
SALES (est): 10K **Privately Held**
Web: www.apploye.com
SIC: 7372 7371 Business oriented computer software; Computer software development and applications

(G-9894)
APRIL L SARVER
Also Called: April's Healing Hand's
303 N Dillwyn Rd (19711-5541)
PHONE..............................302 559-0787
April Sarver, *Prin*
EMP: 7 **EST:** 2011
SALES (est): 52.86K **Privately Held**
SIC: 8049 Offices of health practitioner

(G-9895)
AQUA INFRA REHAB CO LLC
567 Walther Rd (19702-2903)
PHONE..............................610 328-7714
EMP: 6 **EST:** 2014
SALES (est): 70.39K **Privately Held**
SIC: 8322 Rehabilitation services

(G-9896)
AQUA SCIENCE LLC
250 Corporate Blvd Ste K (19702-3329)
PHONE..............................302 757-5241
Iwona Evans, *CEO*
Iwona Evans, *CFO*
Alan Mcquillin, *Prin*
EMP: 6 **EST:** 2020
SALES (est): 956.17K **Privately Held**
Web: www.aqua-sci.com
SIC: 2835 Diagnostic substances

(G-9897)
AQUACAST LINER LLC
100 Lake Dr Ste 200 (19702-3361)
P.O. Box 1187 (19701-7187)
PHONE..............................302 535-3728
EMP: 10 **EST:** 2011
SQ FT: 2,000
SALES (est): 912.63K **Privately Held**
Web: www.aquacastliner.com
SIC: 2899 Waterproofing compounds

(G-9898)
ARBITER INC
2035 Sunset Lake Rd B2 (19702-2600)
PHONE..............................404 939-2826
EMP: 8 **EST:** 2018
SALES (est): 191.89K **Privately Held**
SIC: 8742 Management consulting services

(G-9899)
ARCHADECK OF DELAWARE
Also Called: Archadeck
31 Savoy Rd (19702-8615)
PHONE..............................302 766-3698
EMP: 9 **EST:** 2017
SALES (est): 82.72K **Privately Held**
Web: www.archadeck.com
SIC: 1521 Patio and deck construction and repair

(G-9900)
AREA WIDE PROTECTIVE
12 Mill Park Ct (19713-1986)
PHONE..............................302 455-1900
EMP: 7 **EST:** 2017
SALES (est): 58.4K **Privately Held**
Web: www.awpsafety.com
SIC: 8711 Engineering services

(G-9901)
ARGILLA BREWING COMPANY
2667 Kirkwood Hwy (19711-7242)
PHONE..............................302 731-8200
EMP: 7 **EST:** 2011
SALES (est): 204.11K **Privately Held**
Web: www.argillabrewing.com
SIC: 5181 Beer and ale

(G-9902)
ARIA SOLUTIONS INC
194 Mccormick Blvd (19702-2161)
PHONE..............................302 453-8389
EMP: 7 **EST:** 2012
SALES (est): 63.5K **Privately Held**
SIC: 8748 Business consulting, nec

(G-9903)
ARIVERS CONSTRUCTION
43 Abbey Rd (19702-8611)
PHONE..............................302 299-2288
Arnold Rivers, *Prin*
EMP: 5 **EST:** 2016
SALES (est): 82.72K **Privately Held**
Web: www.ariversconstruction.com
SIC: 1521 Single-family housing construction

(G-9904)
ARLEN D STONE M D
1 Centurian Dr Ste 105 (19713-2154)
PHONE..............................302 999-0933
EMP: 5 **EST:** 2019
SALES (est): 108.5K **Privately Held**
Web: www.gascodrilling.com
SIC: 8011 Offices and clinics of medical doctors

(G-9905)
ARMOR GRAPHICS INC
1102 Ogletown Rd (19711-5416)
P.O. Box 386 (19936-0386)
PHONE..............................302 737-8790
Margaret Allen, *Pr*
David Allen, *VP*
EMP: 5 **EST:** 2001
SQ FT: 1,500
SALES (est): 565.72K **Privately Held**
Web: www.armorgraphicsinc.com
SIC: 2752 Offset printing

(G-9906)
ARNAB MOBILITY INC
2035 Sunset Lake Rd B2 (19702-2600)
PHONE..............................774 316-6767
Hamad Obaid Rashid Obaid, *CEO*
Hamad Obaid Rashid Obaid Alsha msi, *CEO*
EMP: 15 **EST:** 2019
SALES (est): 752.8K **Privately Held**
SIC: 7371 Software programming applications

(G-9907)
ARNOLD INTERNATIONAL INC
573 Bellevue Rd Ste B (19713-5801)
PHONE..............................302 266-4441
John Michael Arnold, *Pr*
Margaret Arnold, *VP*
▲ **EMP:** 5 **EST:** 1996
SQ FT: 4,500
SALES (est): 560K **Privately Held**
SIC: 5084 Machine tools and accessories

(G-9908)
ARROW CHEMICAL INC
4142 Ogletown Stanton Rd (19713-4169)
PHONE..............................302 731-7403
Gary Trief, *Pr*
EMP: 9 **EST:** 2015
SALES (est): 208.65K **Privately Held**
SIC: 5169 Chemicals and allied products, nec

(G-9909)
ARROW EXPRESS INC
26 Chambord Dr (19702-5547)
PHONE..............................302 836-3658
EMP: 5 **EST:** 2018
SALES (est): 99.97K **Privately Held**
Web: www.arrowexpress.com
SIC: 4111 Local and suburban transit

(G-9910)
ARTCOMUN TECHNOLOGIES INC ✪
Also Called: Artcomun
112 Capitol Trl Ste A153 (19711-3716)
PHONE..............................302 266-1521
Osman Dora Kezer, *Prin*
EMP: 6 **EST:** 2023
SALES (est): 63.67K **Privately Held**
SIC: 8999 Artists and artists' studios

(G-9911)
ARTESIAN RESOURCES CORPORATION (PA)
Also Called: Artesian Resources
664 Churchmans Rd (19702-1934)
P.O. Box 15004 (19850-5004)
PHONE..............................302 453-6900
Dian C Taylor, *Ch Bd*
David B Spacht, *CFO*
Joseph A Dinunzio, *Corporate Secretary*
Pierre A Anderson, *CIO*
Jennifer L Finch, *Corporate Treasurer*
EMP: 8 **EST:** 1905
SALES (est): 98.9MM
SALES (corp-wide): 98.9MM **Publicly Held**
Web: www.artesianwater.com
SIC: 4941 Water supply

(G-9912)
ARTESIAN UTILITY DEV INC
664 Churchmans Rd (19702-1934)
P.O. Box 15004 (19850-5004)
PHONE..............................800 332-5114
Dian C Taylor, *CEO*
EMP: 16 **EST:** 2015
SALES (est): 852.57K
SALES (corp-wide): 98.9MM **Publicly Held**
Web: www.artesianwater.com
SIC: 4941 Water supply
PA: Artesian Resources Corporation
664 Churchmans Rd
Newark DE 19702
302 453-6900

(G-9913)
ARTESIAN WASTEWATER MD INC
664 Churchmans Rd (19702-1934)
P.O. Box 15004 (19850-5004)
PHONE..............................302 453-6900
Dian C Taylor, *Pr*
EMP: 32 **EST:** 2015
SALES (est): 1.01MM
SALES (corp-wide): 98.9MM **Publicly Held**
Web: www.artesianwater.com
SIC: 4941 Water supply
PA: Artesian Resources Corporation
664 Churchmans Rd
Newark DE 19702
302 453-6900

(G-9914)
ARTESIAN WATER MARYLAND INC
664 Churchmans Rd (19702-1934)
P.O. Box 15004 (19850-5004)
PHONE..............................302 453-6900
EMP: 32 **EST:** 2015
SALES (est): 2.35MM
SALES (corp-wide): 98.9MM **Publicly Held**
Web: www.artesianwater.com
SIC: 4941 Water supply
PA: Artesian Resources Corporation
664 Churchmans Rd
Newark DE 19702
302 453-6900

(PA)=Parent Co (HQ)=Headquarters
✪ = New Business established in last 2 years

Newark - New Castle County (G-9915)

(G-9915)
ARTHUR L YOUNG DENTIST JR
6 Millbourne Dr (19711-3900)
PHONE..................................302 737-9065
Arthur Young, *Prin*
EMP: 12 EST: 2006
SALES (est): 114.22K **Privately Held**
SIC: 8021 Dentists' office

(G-9916)
ARTIFEX CARPENTRY
40 Fairway Rd Apt 3c (19711-5659)
PHONE..................................484 557-7623
Morgan Waddell, *Prin*
EMP: 5 EST: 2018
SALES (est): 90.94K **Privately Held**
SIC: 1751 Carpentry work

(G-9917)
ARTISANS BANK INC
Also Called: Artisans Bank Clefco Branch
2424 Pulaski Hwy (19702-3906)
PHONE..................................302 838-6700
Alice Candeloro, *Mgr*
EMP: 7
SALES (corp-wide): 25.62MM **Privately Held**
Web: www.artisansbank.com
SIC: 6036 State savings banks, not federally chartered
PA: Artisans Bank Inc
    2961 Centerville Rd # 101
    Wilmington DE 19808
    302 658-6881

(G-9918)
ASCELA
200 Continental Dr Ste 305 (19713-4334)
PHONE..................................888 298-5151
EMP: 20 EST: 2018
SALES (est): 551.47K **Privately Held**
Web: www.ascela.com
SIC: 6411 Insurance agents, nec

(G-9919)
ASCENT TECHNOLOGIES INC
42 Prestbury Sq Ste 12 (19713-2690)
PHONE..................................302 491-0545
Saroja Balla, *Pr*
Srinivas Muppalla, *
EMP: 9 EST: 2005
SQ FT: 750
SALES (est): 176.75K **Privately Held**
Web: www.ascenttechinc.com
SIC: 8748 7371 Business consulting, nec; Computer software development

(G-9920)
ASHBY MANAGEMENT CORPORATION
108 W Main St (19711-3229)
PHONE..................................302 894-1200
Robert E Ashby, *Pr*
EMP: 5 EST: 1986
SALES (est): 903.09K **Privately Held**
SIC: 8741 Restaurant management

(G-9921)
ASHESH I MODI
4745 Ogletown Stanton Rd # 134 (19713-2074)
PHONE..................................302 452-3000
Ashesh I Modi, *Prin*
EMP: 11 EST: 2010
SALES (est): 243.59K **Privately Held**
SIC: 8011 Gastronomist

(G-9922)
ASHISH B PARIKH
Also Called: Heart and Vascular Clinic
620 Stanton Christiana Rd Ste 203 (19713-2130)
PHONE..................................302 338-9444
Ashish B Parikh, *Owner*
EMP: 19 EST: 2010
SQ FT: 1,600
SALES (est): 4.85MM **Privately Held**
Web: www.heartandvascularclinic.com
SIC: 8011 Cardiologist and cardio-vascular specialist

(G-9923)
ASI COMPREHENSIVE WASTE MGT
1 Shea Way (19713-3421)
PHONE..................................302 533-6858
EMP: 9 EST: 2019
SALES (est): 610.35K **Privately Held**
Web: www.asiwaste.com
SIC: 4953 Recycling, waste materials

(G-9924)
ASPIRA OF DELAWARE INC
326 Ruthar Dr (19711-8017)
PHONE..................................302 292-1463
Jari Santana-wynn, *Prin*
Jari Santana-wynn, *VP*
Margaret Rivera, *Ch Bd*
EMP: 5 EST: 1980
SQ FT: 103,000
SALES (est): 15.8MM **Privately Held**
Web: www.aspirade.org
SIC: 8748 Testing service, educational or personnel

(G-9925)
ASPIRE WELLNESS LLC
1220 Capitol Trl (19711-3924)
PHONE..................................302 366-1727
EMP: 7 EST: 2016
SALES (est): 412.97K **Privately Held**
Web: www.aspirewellnessnow.com
SIC: 8099 Health and allied services, nec

(G-9926)
ASPIRING CHANGE LLC
308 Scotland Dr (19702-4055)
PHONE..................................302 689-3138
EMP: 6 EST: 2019
SALES (est): 55.5K **Privately Held**
Web: www.aspiringchangellc.com
SIC: 8322 General counseling services

(G-9927)
ASSANIS & ASSOCIATES INC
47 Kent Way (19711-5201)
PHONE..................................734 277-0846
Dimitris Assanis, *Owner*
EMP: 9 EST: 2000
SALES (est): 46.16K **Privately Held**
Web: www.udel.edu
SIC: 7371 Custom computer programming services

(G-9928)
ASSOCIATION OF CENTERS STUDY O
16 Allison Ln (19711-2607)
PHONE..................................302 831-1724
Danielle Emerling, *Prin*
EMP: 8 EST: 2014
SALES (est): 61.19K **Privately Held**
SIC: 8699 Membership organizations, nec

(G-9929)
ASTRAZENECA PHARMACEUTICALS LP
587 Old Baltimore Pike (19702-1307)
P.O. Box 4520 (19714-4520)
PHONE..................................302 286-3500
W R Matthews, *Mgr*
EMP: 258
SALES (corp-wide): 44.35B **Privately Held**
Web: www.astrazeneca.com
SIC: 2834 Pharmaceutical preparations
HQ: Astrazeneca Pharmaceuticals Lp
    1800 Concord Pike
    Wilmington DE 19850

(G-9930)
ATH SOLUTIONS LLC (PA) ✧
254 Chapman Rd Ste 209 (19702-5413)
PHONE..................................888 861-6657
Braylon Thompson, *Managing Member*
EMP: 5 EST: 2024
SALES (est): 215.18K
SALES (corp-wide): 215.18K **Privately Held**
SIC: 8742 Management consulting services

(G-9931)
ATHENA BIOTECHNOLOGIES INC
1090 Elkton Rd (19711-3507)
PHONE..................................302 224-3450
EMP: 5 EST: 2019
SALES (est): 194.01K **Privately Held**
Web: www.athenabioscience.com
SIC: 5047 Medical equipment and supplies

(G-9932)
ATHENA T JOLLY M D
24 Brookhill Dr (19702-1301)
PHONE..................................302 454-3020
Athena Jolly, *Owner*
EMP: 8 EST: 2017
SALES (est): 85.35K **Privately Held**
SIC: 8011 Offices and clinics of medical doctors

(G-9933)
ATI HOLDINGS LLC
Also Called: ATI Physical Therapy
2600 Glasgow Ave Ste 105 (19702-5703)
PHONE..................................302 838-2165
John Records, *Brnch Mgr*
EMP: 8
SALES (corp-wide): 635.67MM **Publicly Held**
Web: www.atipt.com
SIC: 8049 Physical therapist
HQ: Ati Holdings, Llc
    790 Remington Blvd
    Bolingbrook IL 60440

(G-9934)
ATLANTIC DAWN LTD
Also Called: Little Caboose The
366 Old Baltimore Pike (19702-8412)
PHONE..................................302 737-8854
Ms. Kim B, *Owner*
Michelle Spencer, *Dir*
EMP: 17 EST: 2005
SALES (est): 350K **Privately Held**
Web: www.thelittlecaboose.com
SIC: 8351 Group day care center

(G-9935)
ATLANTIC DUNCAN INC
5 Magil Ct (19702-8636)
PHONE..................................302 383-0740
Janinder Kalsi, *CEO*
EMP: 10 EST: 1999
SALES (est): 501.99K **Privately Held**
SIC: 8748 Business consulting, nec

(G-9936)
ATLANTIC SUN SCREEN PRTG INC
700 Peoples Plz (19702-5601)
PHONE..................................302 731-5100
John Whitehead, *Pr*
EMP: 10 EST: 2013
SALES (est): 523.08K **Privately Held**
Web: www.atsunorders.com
SIC: 2396 7389 Screen printing on fabric articles; Embroidery advertising

(G-9937)
ATLANTIC TRACTOR LLC
Also Called: John Deere Authorized Dealer
2688 Pulaski Hwy (19702-3915)
PHONE..................................302 834-0114
Thomas Patrick, *Genl Mgr*
EMP: 14
SALES (corp-wide): 51.66MM **Privately Held**
Web: www.atlantictractor.net
SIC: 5261 5082 Lawn and garden equipment; Construction and mining machinery
PA: Atlantic Tractor Llc
    720 Wheeler School Rd
    Whiteford MD 21160
    410 457-3696

(G-9938)
ATLANTIC TRAINING LLC
200 Ruthar Dr Ste 4 (19711-8000)
P.O. Box 44 (19709-0044)
PHONE..................................302 464-0341
EMP: 10 EST: 2010
SALES (est): 1.2MM **Privately Held**
Web: www.atlantictraining.com
SIC: 8748 Safety training service

(G-9939)
ATLAS SOFTWARE LLC
200 Continental Dr # 401 (19713-4334)
PHONE..................................312 576-2247
EMP: 10 EST: 2020
SALES (est): 438.01K **Privately Held**
SIC: 7371 Software programming applications

(G-9940)
ATLAS VAN LINES AGENTS
900 Interchange Blvd (19711-3563)
PHONE..................................302 369-0900
Thomas Bennett Iii, *Pr*
EMP: 5 EST: 1955
SALES (est): 113.36K **Privately Held**
SIC: 4783 Packing and crating

(G-9941)
ATM THE BOTTOM LINE LTD
118 Astro Shopping Ctr (19711-7254)
PHONE..................................302 322-0452
EMP: 7 EST: 2015
SALES (est): 467.04K **Privately Held**
Web: www.atmthebottomline.com
SIC: 7291 Tax return preparation services

(G-9942)
ATTERBURY VFW POST 3420
646 Churchmans Rd (19702-1934)
PHONE..................................302 737-6903
EMP: 7 EST: 2010
SALES (est): 80.92K **Privately Held**
SIC: 8641 Veterans' organization

(G-9943)
AUDITBOT
11 Latour Ln (19702-4543)
PHONE..................................302 494-9476
EMP: 8 EST: 2016
SALES (est): 93.78K **Privately Held**
Web: www.auditbots.com
SIC: 7371 Computer software development

GEOGRAPHIC SECTION

Newark - New Castle County (G-9975)

(G-9944)
AUSTIN & BEDNASH CNSTR INC
Also Called: Austin
32 Brookhill Dr (19702-1301)
PHONE..................................302 376-5590
Mike Austin, *Prin*
Sam Bednash, *
EMP: 45 **EST:** 2000
SQ FT: 43,560
SALES (est): 8.92MM **Privately Held**
Web: www.austin-bednash.com
SIC: 1611 General contractor, highway and street construction

(G-9945)
AUTHORITY MEDIA GROUP
2035 Sunset Lake Rd (19702-2600)
PHONE..................................302 894-7700
EMP: 5 **EST:** 2019
SALES (est): 189.06K **Privately Held**
Web: www.authoritymediagroup.com
SIC: 4899 Communication services, nec

(G-9946)
AUTISM DELAWARE INC
924 Old Harmony Rd Ste 201 (19713-4186)
PHONE..................................302 224-6020
Theda Ellis, *Ex Dir*
EMP: 49 **EST:** 2006
SALES (est): 4.99MM **Privately Held**
Web: www.autismdelaware.org
SIC: 8322 Social service center

(G-9947)
AUTOMATION RESEARCH GROUP LLC
929 Crossan Rd (19711-2916)
PHONE..................................302 897-7776
EMP: 5 **EST:** 2007
SALES (est): 119.66K **Privately Held**
Web:
www.automationresearchgroup.com
SIC: 8711 Building construction consultant

(G-9948)
AUTOMOTIVE DIAGNOSTIC SOL
1106 Ogletown Rd (19711-5416)
PHONE..................................443 466-6108
EMP: 5 **EST:** 2015
SALES (est): 28.25K **Privately Held**
Web:
www.automotive-diagnostic-solutions.com
SIC: 7538 General automotive repair shops

(G-9949)
AVALON DENTAL LLC BLDG G4
420 Christiana Medical Ctr (19702-1654)
PHONE..................................302 292-8899
Adeline Farhi, *Prin*
EMP: 13 **EST:** 2012
SALES (est): 265.63K **Privately Held**
Web: www.avalondentalde.com
SIC: 8021 Offices and clinics of dentists

(G-9950)
AVANT DIGITAL INC
254 Chapman Rd (19702-5413)
PHONE..................................660 726-2416
Shivani Saagi, *Managing Member*
EMP: 6
SALES (est): 72.22K **Privately Held**
SIC: 7373 Systems software development services

(G-9951)
AVANTIX LABRATORIES INC
100 Biddle Ave Ste 202 (19702-3983)
PHONE..................................302 832-1008
Linyee Shum Md, *CEO*
Doctor Linyee Shum, *CEO*
EMP: 10 **EST:** 1998
SQ FT: 10,000
SALES (est): 879.62K **Privately Held**
SIC: 8733 Scientific research agency

(G-9952)
AVCO ENERGY LLC
200 Continental Dr (19713-4334)
PHONE..................................302 597-0034
Lee Preston, *Managing Member*
EMP: 7 **EST:** 2020
SALES (est): 309.3K **Privately Held**
SIC: 4924 Natural gas distribution

(G-9953)
AVERY ENTERPRISES LLC
4 Georgian Cir (19711-2550)
PHONE..................................302 750-5468
Benjamin Sowden, *Prin*
EMP: 5 **EST:** 2016
SALES (est): 70.58K **Privately Held**
SIC: 8748 Business consulting, nec

(G-9954)
AVIANT CNSLTNG & RIVA PYMNT
21 Somerset Ln (19711-1900)
PHONE..................................302 584-0549
EMP: 5 **EST:** 2018
SALES (est): 60.84K **Privately Held**
SIC: 8748 Business consulting, nec

(G-9955)
AVIS CAR RENTAL
915 S Chapel St (19713-3419)
PHONE..................................302 368-5950
EMP: 7 **EST:** 2017
SALES (est): 99.82K **Privately Held**
Web: www.avis.com
SIC: 7514 Rent-a-car service

(G-9956)
AVIXIA LLC
254 Chapman Rd Ste 208 Pmb 12750 (19702-5422)
PHONE..................................781 882-2200
Nirmal Patel, *Prin*
EMP: 8 **EST:** 2015
SALES (est): 750K **Privately Held**
Web: www.avixia.com
SIC: 7379 Online services technology consultants

(G-9957)
AWARENESS CENTER
280 E Main St Ste 109 (19711-7324)
PHONE..................................302 426-5050
EMP: 6 **EST:** 2019
SALES (est): 31.25K **Privately Held**
Web: www.mindnbodycenter.com
SIC: 7999 Yoga instruction

(G-9958)
AXESS CORP
100 Interchange Blvd (19711-3549)
PHONE..................................910 270-2077
EMP: 5 **EST:** 2019
SALES (est): 22.22K **Privately Held**
Web: www.empowermaterials.com
SIC: 7381 Detective and armored car services

(G-9959)
AXXIOM ESCAPE ROOMS
284 E Main St (19711-7311)
PHONE..................................732 606-2844
EMP: 6 **EST:** 2018
SALES (est): 139.67K **Privately Held**
Web: www.axxiomnewark.com
SIC: 7999 Amusement and recreation, nec

(G-9960)
AY TECH LLC
117 Ruthar Dr (19711-8025)
PHONE..................................302 861-6610
EMP: 4 **EST:** 2006
SALES (est): 221.43K **Privately Held**
Web: www.aytech.us
SIC: 2241 Narrow fabric mills

(G-9961)
AYON CABLE TECHNOLOGY LLC
72 Hobart Dr Apt C2 (19713-4647)
PHONE..................................302 465-8999
Miguel Aullon, *Prin*
EMP: 5 **EST:** 2017
SALES (est): 234.47K **Privately Held**
SIC: 4841 Cable television services

(G-9962)
AZHAR H KHAN MD
111 Continental Dr Ste 406 (19713-4306)
PHONE..................................302 454-8880
Azhar Khan, *Prin*
EMP: 10 **EST:** 2013
SALES (est): 117.56K **Privately Held**
SIC: 8011 General and family practice, physician/surgeon

(G-9963)
B & W TEK INC
18 Shea Way Ste 103 (19713-3448)
PHONE..................................855 692-9835
▲ **EMP:** 60 **EST:** 1996
SQ FT: 20,000
SALES (est): 14.61MM **Privately Held**
Web: www.bwtek.com
SIC: 3826 Analytical instruments

(G-9964)
B AND B CONTRACTORS INC
503 Stewarton Ct (19702-4076)
PHONE..................................302 836-9207
Thomas D Barker Senior, *Pr*
Shirley Barker, *VP*
EMP: 6 **EST:** 1987
SALES (est): 504.95K **Privately Held**
SIC: 1521 Single-family housing construction

(G-9965)
B E & K INC
Also Called: B E & K, INC.
242 Chapman Rd (19702)
PHONE..................................302 452-9000
Robert Pinson, *Genl Mgr*
EMP: 5
SIC: 8711 Construction and civil engineering
HQ: Be&K, Inc.
2000 International Pk Dr
Birmingham AL 35243

(G-9966)
B FIT ENTERPRISES (PA)
35 Salem Church Rd Ste 23 (19713-4927)
PHONE..................................302 292-1785
Marcellus Beasley, *Owner*
EMP: 5 **EST:** 2005
SALES (est): 452.16K **Privately Held**
Web: www.bfitenterprises.com
SIC: 7991 Health club

(G-9967)
B&H CONTRACTING GROUP
505 W Hummock Ln (19702-1499)
PHONE..................................302 588-9774
Binh Ho, *Prin*
EMP: 5 **EST:** 2018
SALES (est): 56.76K **Privately Held**
SIC: 1799 Special trade contractors, nec

(G-9968)
B+H INSURANCE LLC
Also Called: Nationwide
111 Continental Dr (19713-4313)
PHONE..................................302 995-2247
John Boykin, *Pr*
EMP: 26 **EST:** 2016
SALES (est): 4.76MM **Privately Held**
Web: www.assuredpartners.com
SIC: 6411 7371 Insurance agents, nec; Computer software development and applications
PA: Assuredpartners, Inc.
450 S Orange Ave Fl 4
Orlando FL 32801

(G-9969)
B-SMART LOGISTICS LLC
524 Jacobsen Dr (19702-1587)
PHONE..................................609 388-6622
Akira Smart, *Managing Member*
EMP: 10 **EST:** 2018
SALES (est): 448.29K **Privately Held**
SIC: 4789 Transportation services, nec

(G-9970)
BABY TEL COMMUNICATIONS INC
727 Art Ln (19713-1208)
PHONE..................................302 368-3969
Benjamin Raphael, *Pr*
Catherine P Raphael, *Sec*
EMP: 5 **EST:** 1981
SALES (est): 389.69K **Privately Held**
Web: www.babytel.com
SIC: 1731 Sound equipment specialization

(G-9971)
BACK UP CTR
400 White Clay Center Dr (19711-5468)
PHONE..................................302 758-4500
Nick Antonelli, *CEO*
EMP: 9 **EST:** 2011
SALES (est): 53.53K **Privately Held**
SIC: 8322 Adult day care center

(G-9972)
BACKUPTA INC ✿
2915 Ogletown Rd (19713-1927)
PHONE..................................828 337-8957
Joey Davis, *Pr*
EMP: 5 **EST:** 2023
SALES (est): 209.21K **Privately Held**
SIC: 7372 Prepackaged software

(G-9973)
BAIBI WISE LLC ✿
Also Called: John Nathan Smith Fmly Tr/U/St
4 Peddlers Row Pmb 285 (19702-1525)
PHONE..................................201 375-0170
EMP: 5 **EST:** 2023
SALES (est): 160.26K **Privately Held**
SIC: 7389 Business Activities at Non-Commercial Site

(G-9974)
BAINBRIDGE COMPANY
1 Eaton Pl (19711-2990)
PHONE..................................302 509-3185
EMP: 5 **EST:** 2016
SALES (est): 119.47K **Privately Held**
Web: www.bainbridgecompanies.com
SIC: 5063 Electrical supplies, nec

(G-9975)
BAIR & GOFF SALES LLC
Also Called: Bair & Goff Sales
199 Kenneth Ct (19711-8506)
PHONE..................................302 292-2546
EMP: 22 **EST:** 1994
SQ FT: 1,300

Newark - New Castle County (G-9976)

SALES (est): 2.3MM **Privately Held**
SIC: **5198** 5072 5031 Paints; Hardware; Building materials, exterior

(G-9976)
BAMBOOZLE WEB SERVICES INC
2035 Sunset Lake Rd (19702-2600)
PHONE.................................833 380-4600
Patrick Swoboda, *CEO*
EMP: 7 EST: 2016
SALES (est): 331.74K **Privately Held**
Web: www.bamboozle.at
SIC: **7379** Online services technology consultants

(G-9977)
BAMBU CANDLES LLC
210 Cullen Way (19711-6112)
PHONE.................................917 903-2563
EMP: 3 EST: 2017
SALES (est): 55.54K **Privately Held**
SIC: **3999** Manufacturing industries, nec

(G-9978)
BANCROFT INC
9 Thunder Gulch (19702-2037)
PHONE.................................856 769-1300
EMP: 18 EST: 2019
SALES (est): 173.92K **Privately Held**
Web: www.bancroft.org
SIC: **8099** Blood related health services

(G-9979)
BANCROFT NEURO HEALTH
107 Lauren Pl (19702-2950)
PHONE.................................302 266-7054
EMP: 5 EST: 2014
SALES (est): 75.9K **Privately Held**
SIC: **8099** Health and allied services, nec

(G-9980)
BANGUS BUSINESS SERVICES
18 Marvin Dr Apt B4 (19713-1362)
PHONE.................................302 266-7285
Shu Chow, *Owner*
EMP: 6 EST: 2004
SALES (est): 354.37K **Privately Held**
SIC: **8748** Business consulting, nec

(G-9981)
BANK AMERICA NATIONAL ASSN
1000 Samoset Dr (19713-6000)
PHONE.................................888 550-6433
EMP: 19
SALES (corp-wide): 94.95B **Publicly Held**
Web: www.bankofamerica.com
SIC: **6021** National commercial banks
HQ: Bank Of America, National Association
100 N Tryon St
Charlotte NC 28202
704 386-5681

(G-9982)
BARBARA L MCKINNEY
Also Called: Kiddie Express
5 Knickerbocker Dr (19713-3708)
PHONE.................................302 266-9594
Barbara L Mckinney, *Prin*
EMP: 5 EST: 2009
SALES (est): 87.33K **Privately Held**
SIC: **8351** Child day care services

(G-9983)
BARKSDALE DENTAL ASSOCIATES
625 Barksdale Rd Ste 115-117 (19711)
PHONE.................................302 731-4907
Nathaniel Bent, *Prin*
EMP: 9 EST: 2019
SALES (est): 190.22K **Privately Held**
Web: www.barksdaledental.com

SIC: **8021** Dentists' office

(G-9984)
BARRETTES RUN APARTMENTS
Also Called: Village of Barrett's Run The
100 N Barrett Ln (19702-2927)
PHONE.................................302 368-3400
Lewis Capano, *Owner*
EMP: 8 EST: 1989
SALES (est): 566.1K **Privately Held**
SIC: **6513** Apartment hotel operation

(G-9985)
BARRIER INTEGRATED SYSTEMS LLC
527 Stanton Christiana Rd (19713-2106)
PHONE.................................302 502-2727
Mike Harris, *Pr*
EMP: 8 EST: 2015
SALES (est): 124.64K **Privately Held**
Web: www.barrierintegratedsystems.com
SIC: **5065** Security control equipment and systems

(G-9986)
BARRY KAYNE DDS
58 Omega Dr Ste F58 (19713-2062)
PHONE.................................302 456-0400
Barry Kayne D.d.s., *Owner*
EMP: 7 EST: 1988
SALES (est): 462.63K **Privately Held**
Web: www.delawareperio.com
SIC: **8021** Periodontist

(G-9987)
BASE86 INC
2035 Sunset Lake Rd Ste B2 (19702-2600)
PHONE.................................619 781-2670
Edward Isarevich, *Prin*
EMP: 6 EST: 2019
SALES (est): 104.12K **Privately Held**
Web: www.base86.com
SIC: **7371** Computer software development and applications

(G-9988)
BASEMENT PROS INC
569 Walther Rd (19702-2903)
PHONE.................................302 266-0203
EMP: 7 EST: 2016
SALES (est): 127.02K **Privately Held**
Web: www.basementpros.net
SIC: **1799** Waterproofing

(G-9989)
BASTIANELLI GROUP INC
231 Executive Dr Ste 15 (19702-3324)
PHONE.................................302 658-1500
Paul Bastianelli, *Pr*
EMP: 5 EST: 1995
SALES (est): 460K **Privately Held**
SIC: **8748** 8721 Business consulting, nec; Accounting, auditing, and bookkeeping

(G-9990)
BATH KITCHEN TILE DH
23 Ridgewood Turn (19711-8300)
PHONE.................................302 992-9210
EMP: 8 EST: 2018
SALES (est): 251.55K **Privately Held**
Web: www.bathkitchenandtile.com
SIC: **1743** Tile installation, ceramic

(G-9991)
BATTA INC
6 Garfield Way (19713-3450)
PHONE.................................302 737-3376
Neeraj K Batta, *Pr*
Naresh Batta, *
EMP: 12 EST: 2004

SALES (est): 590.13K **Privately Held**
Web: www.battaenv.com
SIC: **8748** Environmental consultant

(G-9992)
BATTA ENVIRONMENTAL ASSOC INC (PA)
Also Called: Batta Laboratory
6 Garfield Way (19713-9921)
PHONE.................................302 737-3376
Naresh C Batta, *Pr*
Neelam Batta, *
EMP: 24 EST: 1982
SQ FT: 6,000
SALES (est): 8.56MM
SALES (corp-wide): 8.56MM **Privately Held**
Web: www.battaenv.com
SIC: **8748** Environmental consultant

(G-9993)
BAUGUESS ELECTRICAL SVCS INC
1400 Interchange Blvd (19711-1818)
PHONE.................................302 737-5614
Mark Bauguess, *Prin*
EMP: 6 EST: 2010
SALES (est): 956.96K **Privately Held**
Web: www.bauguesselectric.com
SIC: **1731** General electrical contractor

(G-9994)
BAYADA HOME HEALTH CARE INC
Also Called: Bayada Nurses
200 Biddle Ave Ste 101 (19702-3967)
PHONE.................................302 836-1000
EMP: 66
SALES (corp-wide): 694.21MM **Privately Held**
Web: www.bayada.com
SIC: **8082** Visiting nurse service
PA: Bayada Home Health Care, Inc.
1 W Main St
Moorestown NJ 08057
856 231-1000

(G-9995)
BAYSHORE COMMUNICATIONS INC
Also Called: Telsec Answering Service
2839 Ogletown Rd (19713-1837)
PHONE.................................302 737-2164
Mary Lou Bayshore, *Pr*
EMP: 11 EST: 1968
SALES (est): 342.25K **Privately Held**
SIC: **7389** 7311 Telephone answering service; Advertising agencies

(G-9996)
BAYSHORE RECORDS MGT LLC
901 Dawson Dr (19713-3417)
PHONE.................................302 731-4477
EMP: 6 EST: 2007
SALES (est): 311.67K **Privately Held**
Web: www.bayshoreallied.com
SIC: **8741** Management services

(G-9997)
BAYSHORE TRNSP SYS INC (PA)
901 Dawson Dr (19713-5802)
PHONE.................................302 366-0220
Linda L Piazza, *Pr*
Ralph E Piazza, *
Andy Larmore, *
Matt Larmore, *
Mark Muddiman, *
▲ EMP: 60 EST: 1973
SQ FT: 193,500
SALES (est): 18.66MM
SALES (corp-wide): 18.66MM **Privately Held**
Web: www.bayshoreallied.com

SIC: **4213** 4214 Household goods transport; Local trucking with storage

(G-9998)
BAYTOWN PACKHOUSE INC
Also Called: Day Town Pack House
112 Capitol Trl (19711-3716)
PHONE.................................936 340-2122
Laryssa Ferreira, *Mgr*
EMP: 9 EST: 2018
SALES (est): 951.25K **Privately Held**
SIC: **3086** Packaging and shipping materials, foamed plastics

(G-9999)
BBDOTQ USA INC
Also Called: Bb.q Chicken South Main St Plz
165 S Main St Unit 117 (19711-7984)
PHONE.................................302 533-6589
EMP: 138
SALES (corp-wide): 5.2MM **Privately Held**
Web: franchise.bbqchicken.com
SIC: **5812** 6794 Chicken restaurant; Franchises, selling or licensing
PA: Bbdotq Usa Inc.
2134 N Central Rd
Fort Lee NJ 07024
201 461-4580

(G-10000)
BDI INC
706 Enter Chance Blvd (19711)
PHONE.................................570 299-7679
EMP: 103
SALES (corp-wide): 1.51B **Privately Held**
Web: www.bearingdistributors.com
SIC: **5085** Bearings
HQ: Bdi, Inc.
8000 Hub Pkwy
Cleveland OH 44125
216 642-9100

(G-10001)
BE RIGHT THERE CONSULTING LLC
4 Peddlers Row (19702-1525)
PHONE.................................302 727-5047
EMP: 5
SALES (est): 269.61K **Privately Held**
SIC: **8748** Business consulting, nec

(G-10002)
BE TRULY WELL LLC
218 E Main St Ste 112 (19711-7364)
PHONE.................................302 525-4343
Jeffrey West, *Pr*
EMP: 11 EST: 2008
SALES (est): 486.73K **Privately Held**
Web: www.betrulywell.com
SIC: **8041** Offices and clinics of chiropractors

(G-10003)
BEAR EARLY EDUCATION CENTER
2884 Glasgow Ave (19702-4774)
PHONE.................................302 836-5000
Jacqui Mullen, *Prin*
EMP: 5 EST: 2009
SALES (est): 104.48K **Privately Held**
SIC: **8351** Group day care center

(G-10004)
BEAR GLASGOW DENTAL
1290 Peoples Plz (19702-5701)
PHONE.................................302 836-3750
Glen Goleburn, *Pt*
EMP: 20 EST: 1989
SALES (est): 1.98MM **Privately Held**
Web: www.bearglasgowdental.com
SIC: **8021** Dentists' office

GEOGRAPHIC SECTION
Newark - New Castle County (G-10034)

(G-10005)
BEAR INDUSTRIES INC
15 Albe Dr (19702-1321)
P.O. Box 9174 (19714-9174)
PHONE.................................302 368-1311
John R Eisenbrey Junior, *Pr*
Lou Annas Iv, *VP*
Charles Johnston, *
Sue Eisenbrey, *
EMP: 80 **EST:** 1979
SQ FT: 10,000
SALES (est): 8.35MM **Privately Held**
SIC: 1711 Sprinkler contractors

(G-10006)
BEAR-GLASGOW YMCA
Also Called: YMCA
351 George Williams Way (19702-3518)
PHONE.................................302 836-9622
Angie Riley, *Dir*
Terry Mullen, *Owner*
EMP: 5 **EST:** 2009
SALES (est): 999.71K **Privately Held**
Web: www.ymcade.org
SIC: 8641 7991 8351 7032 Youth organizations; Physical fitness facilities; Child day care services; Youth camps

(G-10007)
BEAUTIFUL FLOORS LLC
4 Lynford St (19713-1625)
PHONE.................................302 690-5230
EMP: 6
SALES (est): 204.5K **Privately Held**
SIC: 7389 1771 Business Activities at Non-Commercial Site; Flooring contractor

(G-10008)
BEAUTY BARRETTES LLC
24 Sandalwood Dr (19713-3541)
PHONE.................................302 883-7532
EMP: 3 **EST:** 2021
SALES (est): 72.86K **Privately Held**
Web: www.beautybarrettes.com
SIC: 3999 7389 Barrettes; Business services, nec

(G-10009)
BEECANVAS INC
2035 Sunset Lake Rd Ste B2 (19702-2600)
PHONE.................................415 800-4980
EMP: 6 **EST:** 2017
SALES (est): 121.85K **Privately Held**
SIC: 7389 Business services, nec

(G-10010)
BEETLES PLAYHOUSE DAY CARE
1 Coronet Ct (19713-1975)
PHONE.................................302 593-7321
EMP: 8 **EST:** 2015
SALES (est): 130.48K **Privately Held**
SIC: 8351 Group day care center

(G-10011)
BEHOLDER AGENCY LLC
200 Continental Dr Ste 401 (19713-4334)
PHONE.................................302 455-2351
EMP: 10 **EST:** 2020
SALES (est): 665.8K **Privately Held**
Web: www.beholderagency.com
SIC: 8742 7311 Marketing consulting services; Advertising agencies

(G-10012)
BELCHER-TIMME DR ZOE
52 Omega Dr (19713-2062)
PHONE.................................215 266-5839
Zoe Belcher-timme Psy D, *Prin*
EMP: 5 **EST:** 2019
SALES (est): 88.01K **Privately Held**
SIC: 8049 Offices of health practitioner

(G-10013)
BELL PAINTING AND WALL CVG INC
Also Called: Bell Painting
667 Dawson Dr Ste F (19713-3437)
PHONE.................................302 738-8854
Harry W Bell Junior, *Pr*
Donna Bell, *Sec*
Robert Mark Geary, *VP*
EMP: 11 **EST:** 1978
SALES (est): 498.66K **Privately Held**
SIC: 1721 Residential painting

(G-10014)
BELLA HVAC
3 Linette Ct (19702-6815)
PHONE.................................302 561-4025
EMP: 5 **EST:** 2013
SALES (est): 179.82K **Privately Held**
SIC: 1711 Heating and air conditioning contractors

(G-10015)
BELLAWOOD KENNELS LLC
2131 Pleasant Valley Rd (19702-2103)
PHONE.................................302 738-0864
Casey Guerke, *Prin*
EMP: 5 **EST:** 2019
SALES (est): 247.66K **Privately Held**
Web: www.bellawoodkennels.com
SIC: 0191 General farms, primarily crop

(G-10016)
BELMONT VILLA CONDOMINIUMS
Also Called: Villa Belmont
60 Welsh Tract Rd Ste 2b (19713-2265)
PHONE.................................302 368-1633
Lisa Thornton, *Mgr*
EMP: 8 **EST:** 1979
SALES (est): 920.94K
SALES (corp-wide): 2.49MM **Privately Held**
Web: www.villabelmont.com
SIC: 6513 Apartment building operators
PA: Stoltz Realty Co
3704 Kennett Pike Ste 200
Wilmington DE 19807
302 656-2852

(G-10017)
BELUSKO SIDING & WINDOWS
30 Donegal Ct (19711-3441)
PHONE.................................302 366-8783
Jocelyn Belusko, *Prin*
EMP: 5 **EST:** 2006
SALES (est): 184.51K **Privately Held**
SIC: 1761 Siding contractor

(G-10018)
BEMARK ASSOCIATES
104 W Mill Station Dr (19711-7484)
PHONE.................................302 373-6417
Kim Macknis, *Prin*
EMP: 6 **EST:** 2018
SALES (est): 248.06K **Privately Held**
Web: www.bemark.us
SIC: 5074 Plumbing fittings and supplies

(G-10019)
BEN-DOM PRINTING COMPANY
Also Called: Bendom Printing
35 Salem Church Rd Ste 43e (19713-4924)
PHONE.................................302 737-9144
EMP: 10 **EST:** 1994
SQ FT: 5,500
SALES (est): 689.54K **Privately Held**
Web: www.carladelawarehomes.com
SIC: 2752 2791 2789 Offset printing; Typesetting; Bookbinding and related work

(G-10020)
BENDER
501 E Hanna Dr (19702-2715)
PHONE.................................302 366-8637
Wanda Bender, *Prin*
EMP: 5 **EST:** 2010
SALES (est): 35.01K **Privately Held**
SIC: 7929 Musical entertainers

(G-10021)
BENEFACTORY VENTURES INC
2035 Sunset Lake Rd B2 (19702-2600)
PHONE.................................646 693-6186
EMP: 6 **EST:** 2018
SALES (est): 97.68K **Privately Held**
Web: www.benefactory.live
SIC: 7389 Business services, nec

(G-10022)
BENLICK FREIGHT FORWARDERS LLC
322 Jaymar Blvd (19702-2884)
PHONE.................................302 743-4990
Kefa Mong Are, *Asst Sec*
EMP: 5 **EST:** 2017
SALES (est): 215.38K **Privately Held**
SIC: 4789 Transportation services, nec

(G-10023)
BERKSHIRE HATHAWAY HOME SERVIC
850 Library Ave (19711-7170)
PHONE.................................302 373-7220
EMP: 17 **EST:** 2016
SALES (est): 1.4MM **Privately Held**
Web: www.bhhs.com
SIC: 6531 Real estate agent, residential

(G-10024)
BERNARD HOPKINS BOXING INC
38 Lakewood Cir (19711-2342)
PHONE.................................302 239-7170
Bernard Hopkins, *Pr*
EMP: 6 **EST:** 2011
SALES (est): 67.97K **Privately Held**
SIC: 7941 Boxing and wrestling arena

(G-10025)
BERRY REFRIGERATION CO
Also Called: Honeywell Authorized Dealer
2 Garfield Way (19713-5807)
PHONE.................................302 733-0933
Louis G Perna, *Pr*
Paul Perna, *
Lou Perna Junior, *Stockholder*
EMP: 38 **EST:** 1960
SQ FT: 9,000
SALES (est): 7.09MM **Privately Held**
Web: www.berryrefrigeration.com
SIC: 7623 5075 5078 Air conditioning repair; Warm air heating equipment and supplies; Refrigeration equipment and supplies

(G-10026)
BEST HIGH TECHNOLOGIES LLC
200 Continental Dr Ste 401 (19713-4334)
PHONE.................................917 742-6658
EMP: 54
SALES (corp-wide): 4.53MM **Privately Held**
Web: www.besthtech.com
SIC: 7371 Custom computer programming services
PA: Best High Technologies Llc
13 Roszel Rd Ste C204b
Princeton NJ 08540
917 742-6658

(G-10027)
BETH R SCHUBERT MD
875 Aaa Blvd (19713-3624)
PHONE.................................302 224-9400
Beth Schubert, *Pr*
EMP: 12 **EST:** 2008
SALES (est): 609.4K **Privately Held**
SIC: 8011 Gynecologist

(G-10028)
BETH TRUCKING INC
129 Crikmoe Blvd (19702)
PHONE.................................918 814-2970
Elijah Kamau, *VP*
EMP: 7 **EST:** 2015
SALES (est): 462.33K **Privately Held**
SIC: 4212 Local trucking, without storage

(G-10029)
BETTS TEXACO AND B & G GL INC
Also Called: Betts Garage
2806 Pulaski Hwy (19702-3913)
PHONE.................................302 834-2284
William W Betts Senior, *Prin*
David Betts Junior, *Prin*
EMP: 13 **EST:** 1975
SALES (est): 752.15K **Privately Held**
Web: www.bgautoglass.com
SIC: 7532 Collision shops, automotive

(G-10030)
BF RICH CO INC
Also Called: Benjamin F Rich Company
322 Ruthar Dr (19711-8017)
P.O. Box 6031 (19714-6031)
PHONE.................................302 369-2512
EMP: 240
Web: www.perfectdomain.com
SIC: 3089 3442 Windows, plastics; Casements, aluminum

(G-10031)
BIG CATS FOUNDATION
617 5th St (19711-8716)
PHONE.................................302 897-7140
Leslie Gibbs, *Pr*
EMP: 5 **EST:** 2012
SALES (est): 94.25K **Privately Held**
SIC: 8641 Civic and social associations

(G-10032)
BIGCLOUD SOLUTIONS INC
260 Chapman Rd Ste 206 (19702-5491)
PHONE.................................917 972-6891
Koti Karri, *Pr*
EMP: 5 **EST:** 2018
SALES (est): 268K **Privately Held**
SIC: 7371 Software programming applications

(G-10033)
BILINGUAL ACCESS MEDIA LLC
2 Rolling Dr (19713-2020)
PHONE.................................302 738-4782
Ronald Tello-marzol, *Prin*
EMP: 5 **EST:** 2016
SALES (est): 168.75K **Privately Held**
SIC: 4899 Communication services, nec

(G-10034)
BIO-MDICAL APPLICATIONS OF DEL
Also Called: Fresenius Med Care Brndywine H
4923 Ogletown Stanton Rd Ste 210 (19713-2081)
PHONE.................................302 998-7568
Mary Garber, *Mgr*
EMP: 9 **EST:** 2012
SALES (est): 181.1K **Privately Held**

Newark - New Castle County (G-10035) GEOGRAPHIC SECTION

SIC: 8092 Kidney dialysis centers

(G-10035)
BIOMARKER ASSOCIATES INC
25 Meteor Ct (19711-3026)
PHONE..................302 239-7962
Robert Ballas, *Prin*
EMP: 10 EST: 2010
SALES (est): 129.22K **Privately Held**
Web: www.qps.com
SIC: 8742 Management consulting services

(G-10036)
BIOME BIOPLASTICS INC
200 Continental Dr Ste 401 (19713-4334)
PHONE..................917 724-2850
EMP: 5 EST: 2021
SALES (est): 372.81K **Privately Held**
SIC: 2821 Cellulose acetate (plastics)

(G-10037)
BIOSION USA INC ◆
1 Innovation Way Ste 300 (19711-5490)
PHONE..................302 257-5085
Hugh M Davis Ph.d., *Prin*
EMP: 10 EST: 2022
SALES (est): 1.22MM **Privately Held**
Web: www.biosion.com
SIC: 2834 Pharmaceutical preparations

(G-10038)
BIRTH CNTER HLSTIC WNS HLTH CA
Also Called: Birth Center
620 Churchmans Rd Ste 101 (19702-1945)
PHONE..................302 658-2229
EMP: 19 EST: 1998
SALES (est): 5.91MM **Privately Held**
Web: www.thebirthcenter.com
SIC: 8011 8051 Gynecologist; Skilled nursing care facilities

(G-10039)
BISHOP ASSOCIATES
1235 Peoples Plz (19702-5701)
PHONE..................302 838-1270
Walter Bishop, *Owner*
EMP: 6 EST: 1993
SALES (est): 679.87K **Privately Held**
Web: www.bishopassociates.com
SIC: 6411 Insurance agents, nec

(G-10040)
BITTA MONK ENTERTAINMENT INC
25 Winchester Rd Apt G (19713-3124)
PHONE..................916 969-4430
Marcellus Brady, *Pr*
EMP: 5 EST: 2006
SALES (est): 228.8K **Privately Held**
SIC: 7389 Music recording producer

(G-10041)
BKL VENTURES LLC
22 Cedar Farms Dr (19702-3615)
PHONE..................302 317-2377
EMP: 5 EST: 2021
SALES (est): 104.73K **Privately Held**
SIC: 6799 Investors, nec

(G-10042)
BLAB STUDIOS LLC
2 Hempstead Dr (19702-7712)
PHONE..................302 602-5211
Bryant Richardson, *Prin*
EMP: 5 EST: 2016
SALES (est): 33.77K **Privately Held**
SIC: 7299 Miscellaneous personal service

(G-10043)
BLACK & DECKER INC (DH)
1207 Drummond Plz (19711-5790)
PHONE..................860 827-3861
Charles Fenton, *VP*
EMP: 8 EST: 1978
SQ FT: 220,000
SALES (est): 133.59MM
SALES (corp-wide): 16.95B **Publicly Held**
Web: www.blackanddecker.com
SIC: 3452 3579 3423 3949 Bolts, nuts, rivets, and washers; Stapling machines (hand or power); Garden and farm tools, including shovels; Shafts, golf club
HQ: The Black & Decker Corporation
  701 E Joppa Rd
  Towson MD 21286
  410 716-3900

(G-10044)
BLACK DIAMOND PAVING
252 N Patrice Dr (19702-4126)
PHONE..................302 333-1987
Eric Y Esquivel-jimenez, *Prin*
EMP: 6 EST: 2015
SALES (est): 115.72K **Privately Held**
Web: www.blackdiamondpavingde.com
SIC: 1611 Surfacing and paving

(G-10045)
BLACK DOG CONSTRUCTION LLC
1104 Oakland Ct (19711-3450)
PHONE..................302 530-4967
EMP: 5 EST: 2013
SALES (est): 329.84K **Privately Held**
SIC: 1521 Single-family housing construction

(G-10046)
BLACK DRAGON CORPORATION
40 E Main St 1010 (19711-4639)
PHONE..................617 470-9230
EMP: 7 EST: 2010
SALES (est): 95.79K **Privately Held**
SIC: 7381 Detective and armored car services

(G-10047)
BLACK STAR GENERAL CONTRACTORS
56 Gill Dr (19713-2367)
PHONE..................302 275-4533
EMP: 5 EST: 2012
SALES (est): 115.21K **Privately Held**
SIC: 1799 Special trade contractors, nec

(G-10048)
BLACKTOP SEALCOATING INC
511 Paisley Pl (19711-3453)
PHONE..................302 234-2243
Thomas P Harkins, *Prin*
EMP: 5 EST: 2009
SALES (est): 287.71K **Privately Held**
Web: www.blacktopsealcoatinginc.com
SIC: 1611 Surfacing and paving

(G-10049)
BLAIR COMPUTING SYSTEMS INC
500 Creek View Rd Ste 200 (19711-8549)
PHONE..................302 453-8947
Mark Blair, *Pr*
EMP: 12 EST: 1986
SALES (est): 1.11MM **Privately Held**
Web: www.laurelbridge.com
SIC: 7371 Computer software development

(G-10050)
BLAZE SYSTEMS CORPORATION
300 Creek View Rd Ste 204 (19711-8548)
PHONE..................302 733-7235
Lawrence E Deheer, *Pr*
Kevin M Winter, *Stockholder*
EMP: 9 EST: 1992
SALES (est): 1.01MM **Privately Held**
Web: www.blazesystems.com
SIC: 7372 7371 Prepackaged software; Computer software development

(G-10051)
BLENHEIM MANAGEMENT COMPANY
Also Called: Blenheim Homes
220 Continental Dr Ste 410 (19713-4315)
PHONE..................302 254-0100
Jay Sonecha, *Pr*
EMP: 38 EST: 1983
SQ FT: 2,800
SALES (est): 16.08MM **Privately Held**
Web: www.blenheimhomes.com
SIC: 1521 New construction, single-family houses

(G-10052)
BLIX INC
40 E Main St Ste 556 (19711-4639)
PHONE..................347 753-8035
Dotan Volach, *Pr*
EMP: 40 EST: 2019
SALES (est): 852.75K **Privately Held**
SIC: 7371 Computer software development and applications

(G-10053)
BLOG EXPECTING MIRACLES LLC
500 Christiana Medical Ctr (19702-1655)
PHONE..................302 533-6682
EMP: 5 EST: 2018
SALES (est): 170.7K **Privately Held**
Web: www.expectingmiraclesllc.com
SIC: 8071 Ultrasound laboratory

(G-10054)
BLOKHAUS INC
200 Continental Dr Ste 401 (19713-4334)
PHONE..................302 932-7704
Mark Soares, *Pr*
EMP: 25 EST: 2021
SALES (est): 7.78MM **Privately Held**
SIC: 8742 Marketing consulting services

(G-10055)
BLOOM DAILY PLANNERS INC
500 Creek View Rd Ste 302 (19711-8549)
PHONE..................302 607-2580
John Rafanello, *Dir*
EMP: 14 EST: 2018
SALES (est): 241.63K **Privately Held**
Web: www.bloomplanners.com
SIC: 2741 Miscellaneous publishing

(G-10056)
BLOOM ENERGY CORPORATION
Also Called: Manufacturing Center
200 Christina Pkwy (19713-4000)
PHONE..................408 543-1227
EMP: 7
SALES (corp-wide): 1.2B **Publicly Held**
Web: www.bloomenergy.com
SIC: 3674 Fuel cells, solid state
PA: Bloom Energy Corporation
  4353 N 1st St
  San Jose CA 95134
  408 543-1500

(G-10057)
BLUE FALLS GROVE INC
913 Kenilworth Ave (19711-2637)
PHONE..................610 926-4017
Doug Mehrkam, *Pr*
EMP: 7 EST: 1982
SALES (est): 109.14K **Privately Held**
SIC: 7999 7299 Recreation services; Banquet hall facilities

(G-10058)
BLUE HEN CAR WASH
1008 Capitol Trl (19711-3920)
PHONE..................302 273-2100
EMP: 8 EST: 2015
SALES (est): 162.2K **Privately Held**
Web: www.bluehencarwash.com
SIC: 7542 Washing and polishing, automotive

(G-10059)
BLUE HEN HOTEL LLC
400 David Hollowell Dr (19716-7448)
PHONE..................302 266-0354
Tracy Holmes, *Mgr*
EMP: 22 EST: 2004
SALES (est): 140.6K **Privately Held**
SIC: 7011 Hotel, franchised

(G-10060)
BLUE HEN PHYSICAL THERAPY INC
Also Called: Novacare Rehabilitation
407 New London Rd (19711-7009)
PHONE..................302 453-1588
Jim Taylor, *Dir*
EMP: 50 EST: 1991
SALES (est): 968.26K
SALES (corp-wide): 5.53B **Publicly Held**
SIC: 8049 Physiotherapist
HQ: Select Medical Corporation
  4714 Gettysburg Rd
  Mechanicsburg PA 17055
  717 972-1100

(G-10061)
BLUE LEVEL INC
2915 Ogletown Rd Ste 3546 (19713-1927)
PHONE..................337 623-4442
Conner Schryver, *CEO*
EMP: 6 EST: 2020
SALES (est): 471.74K **Privately Held**
Web: www.blueleveltraining.com
SIC: 8742 Training and development consultant

(G-10062)
BLUE MOUNTAIN APPAREL LA LLC
40 E Main St Ste 899 (19711-4639)
PHONE..................646 787-5679
Dennis Slapo, *Pr*
EMP: 9 EST: 2012
SQ FT: 2,000
SALES (est): 687.79K **Privately Held**
SIC: 2325 Jeans: men's, youths', and boys'

(G-10063)
BLUE SKY WEB SOLUTIONS INC
200 Continental Dr # 401 (19713-4334)
PHONE..................302 261-2654
EMP: 5 EST: 2018
SALES (est): 97.7K **Privately Held**
SIC: 7373 Systems integration services

(G-10064)
BLUMATTER INC
Also Called: Cleverx
2035 Sunset Lake Rd (19702-2600)
PHONE..................415 318-6857
Sharekh Shaikh, *Prin*
EMP: 7 EST: 2019
SALES (est): 136.43K **Privately Held**
SIC: 5045 Computer software

(G-10065)
BOCA RATON EXCH FOUNDATION INC
333 Stamford Dr (19711-2728)

GEOGRAPHIC SECTION

Newark - New Castle County (G-10093)

PHONE...................302 286-6067
Douglas G Gordon, *Prin*
EMP: 5 **EST:** 2010
SALES (est): 44.98K **Privately Held**
SIC: 8641 Civic and social associations

(G-10066)
BODY EASE THERAPY
105 Louviers Dr (19711-4163)
PHONE...................610 314-0780
Rachel Gottesman Oc, *Independent SP*
EMP: 5 **EST:** 2017
SALES (est): 73.36K **Privately Held**
Web: www.bodyeasetherapy.com
SIC: 8093 Rehabilitation center, outpatient treatment

(G-10067)
BODY WORKS
78 Albe Dr Ste 1 (19702-1366)
PHONE...................302 275-2750
Harry Villanueva, *Prin*
EMP: 5 **EST:** 2018
SALES (est): 29.95K **Privately Held**
SIC: 7532 Body shop, automotive

(G-10068)
BOOK EM DANNI LOGISTICS LLC
42 Teal Cir (19702-4210)
PHONE...................302 983-2921
EMP: 5 **EST:** 2021
SALES (est): 235.55K **Privately Held**
SIC: 4789 Transportation services, nec

(G-10069)
BOOKKEEPING SOLUTIONS
414 Stafford Ave (19711-5514)
P.O. Box 729 (21922-0729)
PHONE...................302 650-5058
EMP: 5 **EST:** 2018
SALES (est): 83.93K **Privately Held**
Web: www.bookkeepingsolutions-de.com
SIC: 8721 Billing and bookkeeping service

(G-10070)
BOOTHS SERVICES PLBG HTG & AC
1088 1/2 S Chapel St (19702-1304)
PHONE...................302 454-7385
EMP: 9 **EST:** 1989
SQ FT: 3,900
SALES (est): 884.97K **Privately Held**
SIC: 1711 Plumbing, heating, air-conditioning

(G-10071)
BOTHUB AI LIMITED
113 Darksdale Prof Ctr (19711)
PHONE...................669 278-7485
Wenhao Xu, *CEO*
EMP: 10 **EST:** 2017
SALES (est): 500K **Privately Held**
SIC: 7373 Systems software development services

(G-10072)
BOULDEN BROTHERS
107 Sandy Dr Unit 700 (19713-1198)
PHONE...................302 368-3848
Timothy Boulden, *Pr*
EMP: 48 **EST:** 2007
SALES (est): 2.03MM **Privately Held**
Web: www.bouldenbrothers.com
SIC: 7389 1711 1731 Water softener service; Plumbing, heating, air-conditioning; Electrical work

(G-10073)
BOULDEN SERVICES LLC
Also Called: Boulden Brothers
107 Sandy Dr Unit 700 (19713-1198)

PHONE...................302 368-0100
EMP: 23 **EST:** 2005
SALES (est): 497.84K **Privately Held**
SIC: 1711 1731 Warm air heating and air conditioning contractor; Electrical work

(G-10074)
BOUNDED BITS LLC (PA)
2035 Sunset Lake Rd B2 (19702-2600)
PHONE...................949 291-7358
EMP: 7 **EST:** 2019
SALES (est): 100K
SALES (corp-wide): 100K **Privately Held**
SIC: 7371 Computer software development and applications

(G-10075)
BOWMANS REPAIR AND HAULING
107 Burningbush Dr (19711-6801)
PHONE...................302 803-0098
Andrew Bowman, *Prin*
EMP: 5 **EST:** 2018
SALES (est): 221.51K **Privately Held**
SIC: 4212 Light haulage and cartage, local

(G-10076)
BOYER
110 Anglin Dr (19713-4014)
PHONE...................302 368-8489
Scott Boyer, *Prin*
EMP: 9 **EST:** 2010
SALES (est): 86.74K **Privately Held**
SIC: 8641 Civic and social associations

(G-10077)
BRANDYWINE BALUSTRADES
1225 Old Coochs Bridge Rd (19713-2333)
PHONE...................302 893-1837
Keith Fleming, *Prin*
EMP: 7 **EST:** 2007
SALES (est): 500.92K **Privately Held**
Web: www.brandywinebalustrades.com
SIC: 3534 Elevators and moving stairways

(G-10078)
BRANDYWINE CNSLING CMNTY SVCS
Also Called: Brandywine Counseling
24 Brookhill Dr (19702-1301)
PHONE...................302 454-3020
Lynn M Fahey, *Mgr*
EMP: 30
SALES (corp-wide): 16.65MM **Privately Held**
Web: www.brandywinecounseling.com
SIC: 8093 Substance abuse clinics (outpatient)
PA: Brandywine Counseling & Community Services, Inc.
2713 Lancaster Ave
Wilmington DE 19805
302 655-9880

(G-10079)
BRANDYWINE COSMETIC SURGERY
Medical Arts Pavilion Ste 137 (19713)
PHONE...................302 652-3331
Christopher Saunders Md, *Brnch Mgr*
EMP: 5
SALES (corp-wide): 1MM **Privately Held**
Web: www.chrissaundersmd.com
SIC: 8011 Plastic surgeon
PA: Brandywine Cosmetic Surgery
410 Foulk Rd Ste 201
Wilmington DE 19804
302 652-3331

(G-10080)
BRANDYWINE UROLOGY CONS PA
4701 Ogletown Stanton Rd Ste 4500 (19713-2055)

PHONE...................302 652-8990
EMP: 5
SALES (corp-wide): 3.3MM **Privately Held**
Web: www.brandywineuc.com
SIC: 8011 Urologist
PA: Brandywine Urology Consultants, P.A.
2000 Foulk Rd Ste F
Wilmington DE 19810
302 652-8990

(G-10081)
BRANNAN CONSTRUCTION LLC
35 Wenark Dr Apt 6 (19713-1445)
PHONE...................302 547-1659
Jeff Brannan, *Owner*
EMP: 5 **EST:** 2011
SALES (est): 137.3K **Privately Held**
SIC: 1521 General remodeling, single-family houses

(G-10082)
BREAST IMAGING CENTER
4735 Ogletown Stanton Rd # 2112 (19713-8000)
P.O. Box 16015 (19718-0001)
PHONE...................302 623-9729
Bob Garrett, *VP*
EMP: 10 **EST:** 1980
SALES (est): 91.87K **Privately Held**
SIC: 8071 X-ray laboratory, including dental

(G-10083)
BREYLACOM
18 Argyle Rd (19713-4049)
PHONE...................302 731-7456
Rose Breyla, *Prin*
EMP: 5 **EST:** 2010
SALES (est): 103.49K **Privately Held**
Web: www.breyla.com
SIC: 8748 Business consulting, nec

(G-10084)
BRIDAL & TUXEDO OUTLET INC (PA)
Also Called: Bridal & Tuxedo Shoppe
124 Astro Shopping Ctr (19711-7254)
PHONE...................302 731-8802
Vaughn Sawdon, *Pr*
Cathy Sawdon, *VP*
EMP: 5 **EST:** 1980
SQ FT: 3,300
SALES (est): 775.82K
SALES (corp-wide): 775.82K **Privately Held**
Web: www.btshoppe.com
SIC: 5621 7299 Bridal shops; Tuxedo rental

(G-10085)
BRIDGEFORCE INC
155 Stanton Christiana Rd (19702-1619)
PHONE...................302 325-7100
Dawn Willey, *CFO*
EMP: 7 **EST:** 2019
SALES (est): 479.06K **Privately Held**
Web: www.bridgeforce.com
SIC: 8748 Business consulting, nec

(G-10086)
BRIGHT HORIZONS CHLD CTRS LLC
Also Called: Bank Amer Child Dev Ctr - Nwar
950 Samoset Dr (19713-6003)
P.O. Box 442 (21014-0442)
PHONE...................302 456-8913
Tracey Kuhn, *Dir*
EMP: 23
SALES (corp-wide): 2.02B **Publicly Held**
Web: www.brighthorizons.com
SIC: 8351 Group day care center
HQ: Bright Horizons Children's Centers Llc
2 Wells Ave Ste 1
Newton MA 02459
617 673-8000

(G-10087)
BRIGHT HORIZONS CHLD CTRS LLC
Also Called: MBNA Bank Great Expectations
1089 Prides Xing (19713-6106)
PHONE...................302 453-2050
Linda Whitehead, *Dir*
EMP: 19
SALES (corp-wide): 2.02B **Publicly Held**
Web: child-care-preschool.brighthorizons.com
SIC: 8351 Group day care center
HQ: Bright Horizons Children's Centers Llc
2 Wells Ave Ste 1
Newton MA 02459
617 673-8000

(G-10088)
BRIGHT KIDZ INC
273 Old Baltimore Pike (19702-1420)
PHONE...................302 369-6929
Medhat Banoub, *Pr*
EMP: 13 **EST:** 2006
SALES (est): 500K **Privately Held**
SIC: 8351 Group day care center

(G-10089)
BRIGHT NEW SCHLARS ACADEMY LLC
355 Corporate Blvd (19702-3305)
PHONE...................302 668-6053
Elizabeth Briggs, *Prin*
EMP: 10 **EST:** 2014
SALES (est): 242.24K **Privately Held**
Web: www.bnsachildcare.com
SIC: 8351 Preschool center

(G-10090)
BRISCOE TRUCKING INC
28 Chambord Dr (19702-5547)
PHONE...................302 836-1327
Brenda Briscoe, *CEO*
Bernard Briscoe, *Pr*
Brian Briscoe, *VP*
EMP: 10 **EST:** 2001
SALES (est): 1.11MM **Privately Held**
SIC: 4731 Freight transportation arrangement

(G-10091)
BROKEN SPOKE OUTFITTERS INC
Also Called: Velofix
40 E Main St Ste 959 (19711-4639)
PHONE...................604 558-0248
Davide Xausa, *CEO*
Chris Guillemet, *
Boris Martin, *
Jennifer Vlek, *
EMP: 34 **EST:** 2014
SALES (est): 2.75MM **Privately Held**
SIC: 7699 Bicycle repair shop

(G-10092)
BRONSWERK MARINE CORP
2915 Ogletown Rd Ste 869 (19713-1927)
PHONE...................619 813-4797
Francis Fontaine, *CEO*
EMP: 5 **EST:** 2010
SALES (est): 55.53K **Privately Held**
SIC: 8711 1711 Heating and ventilation engineering; Heating and air conditioning contractors

(G-10093)
BROOKSIDE LAUNDROMAT
69 Marrows Rd (19713-3701)
PHONE...................302 369-3366
Young Choe, *Owner*
EMP: 5 **EST:** 1995
SALES (est): 156.23K **Privately Held**
SIC: 7215 Laundry, coin-operated

Newark - New Castle County (G-10094) GEOGRAPHIC SECTION

(G-10094)
BROOKSIDE PLAZA APARTMENTS LLC
885 Marrows Rd Apt D6 (19713-1571)
P.O. Box 627 (19715-0627)
PHONE..................................302 737-2008
EMP: 5 EST: 1969
SALES (est): 462.81K Privately Held
Web: www.brooksideplaza.com
SIC: 6513 Apartment hotel operation

(G-10095)
BROWN LISHA
Also Called: Sprinkles Christian Daycare
33 Wellington Dr (19702-4225)
PHONE..................................302 832-9529
Lisha Brown, Prin
EMP: 5 EST: 2010
SALES (est): 107.92K Privately Held
SIC: 8351 Group day care center

(G-10096)
BRYAN LONGHENRY MAN
245 S Dillwyn Rd (19711-5549)
PHONE..................................302 369-3369
Diana Longhenry, Prin
EMP: 7 EST: 2015
SALES (est): 115.27K Privately Held
SIC: 8049 Offices of health practitioner

(G-10097)
BRYANT GUERNSEY CNSTR CO
54 Montrose Dr (19713-2550)
PHONE..................................302 737-1841
Gene Guernsey, Owner
EMP: 5 EST: 1989
SALES (est): 213.04K Privately Held
SIC: 1521 New construction, single-family houses

(G-10098)
BUDGET TRUCK LLC
915 S Chapel St (19713-3419)
PHONE..................................302 731-5067
EMP: 6 EST: 2017
SALES (est): 50.83K Privately Held
Web: www.budget.com
SIC: 7514 Rent-a-car service

(G-10099)
BUENO TECHNOLOGIES INC
2035 Sunset Lake Rd Ste B2 (19702-2600)
PHONE..................................559 785-9800
Ankit Kumar Dudhwewala, CEO
EMP: 9 EST: 2017
SALES (est): 167.92K Privately Held
Web: www.callhippo.com
SIC: 7371 Computer software development and applications

(G-10100)
BUILDERS LLC GENERAL
99 Albe Dr Ste A (19702-1363)
PHONE..................................302 533-6528
Jeff Scarangelli, Owner
EMP: 6 EST: 2011
SALES (est): 781.51K Privately Held
Web: www.generalbuildersllc.com
SIC: 1799 Special trade contractors, nec

(G-10101)
BUILDING CONCEPTS AMERICA INC
101 Peoples Dr (19702-1306)
PHONE..................................302 292-0200
Anthony Ferrara, Pr
EMP: 25 EST: 1987
SQ FT: 2,000
SALES (est): 8.88MM Privately Held
Web: www.buildingconceptsofamerica.com

SIC: 5039 1541 Metal buildings; Prefabricated building erection, industrial

(G-10102)
BUILDING FASTENERS INC
955 Dawson Dr Ste 1 (19713-5803)
PHONE..................................302 738-0671
Jeffrey Dalton, Pr
Joseph F Dalton, Pr
Susan Fritsch, Sec
EMP: 8 EST: 1978
SQ FT: 8,000
SALES (est): 1.66MM Privately Held
Web: www.buildingfastenersinc.com
SIC: 5085 5072 Fasteners, industrial: nuts, bolts, screws, etc.; Bolts

(G-10103)
BUKER LIMOUSINE & TRNSP SVC
517 Paisley Pl (19711-3457)
PHONE..................................302 234-7600
Robert Buker, Pr
EMP: 10 EST: 1996
SALES (est): 346.06K Privately Held
Web: www.limo-exchange.com
SIC: 4119 Limousine rental, with driver

(G-10104)
BULWARK BUILDERS INC
15 Bender Dr (19711-3807)
PHONE..................................302 299-3190
Melissa Stalczynski, Pr
EMP: 7 EST: 2014
SALES (est): 223.15K Privately Held
Web: www.bulwark.com
SIC: 1521 New construction, single-family houses

(G-10105)
BURKE DERMATOLOGY (PA)
774 Christiana Rd Ste 107 (19713-4248)
PHONE..................................302 230-3376
Thomas John Burke D.o.s., Pr
EMP: 8 EST: 2015
SALES (est): 2.17MM
SALES (corp-wide): 2.17MM Privately Held
Web: www.burkedermatology.com
SIC: 8011 Dermatologist

(G-10106)
BURRIS LOGISTICS
650 Pencader Dr (19702-3348)
PHONE..................................302 737-5203
EMP: 5
SALES (corp-wide): 1.24B Privately Held
Web: www.burrislogistics.com
SIC: 4789 Freight car loading and unloading
PA: Burris Logistics
501 Se 5th St
Milford DE 19963
302 839-4531

(G-10107)
BUSINESS INTEGRATION SOLUTION
220 Continental Dr Ste 213 (19713-4312)
PHONE..................................302 355-3512
Raju Enduri, CEO
EMP: 8 EST: 2009
SALES (est): 519.09K Privately Held
SIC: 8741 Business management

(G-10108)
BUTT KAMBIZ R MD
111 Continental Dr # 406 (19713-4306)
PHONE..................................708 927-7169
Kambiz Butt, Pr
EMP: 9 EST: 2017
SALES (est): 94.16K Privately Held

SIC: 8011 Offices and clinics of medical doctors

(G-10109)
BUTTER GAMES LLC ✪
254 Chapman Rd Ste 208 (19702-5422)
PHONE..................................650 867-2492
Nishita Surakanti, CEO
EMP: 3 EST: 2023
SALES (est): 128.34K Privately Held
SIC: 7372 Prepackaged software

(G-10110)
BWT LIGHTING INC
825 Dawson Dr Ste 1 (19713-3438)
PHONE..................................302 709-0808
Sean Wang, Ch
Brian Todd, Pr
▲ EMP: 8 EST: 2004
SALES (est): 132.37K Privately Held
SIC: 3646 Commercial lighting fixtures

(G-10111)
C & A INK
42 Stallion Dr (19713-3571)
PHONE..................................302 565-9866
EMP: 4 EST: 2016
SALES (est): 108.47K Privately Held
SIC: 2893 Printing ink

(G-10112)
C & M SERVICE INC
550 S College Ave (19713-1324)
P.O. Box 886 (19715-0886)
PHONE..................................302 453-5228
Charles Mendola Junior, Pr
EMP: 9 EST: 1984
SQ FT: 350
SALES (est): 225.51K Privately Held
SIC: 4212 Local trucking, without storage

(G-10113)
C M D INC
Also Called: Delaware Industrial Supply
62 Albe Dr Ste C (19702-1370)
PHONE..................................302 894-1776
EMP: 7 EST: 1972
SALES (est): 2MM Privately Held
Web: www.wareindustrial.com
SIC: 5072 5085 Hardware; Tools, nec

(G-10114)
C M-TEC INC
1 Innovation Way Ste 100 (19711-5462)
PHONE..................................302 369-6166
Xiaoqun Daniel Wu, Pr
Huifang Chen, Prin
EMP: 6 EST: 2003
SQ FT: 1,000
SALES (est): 610.02K Privately Held
Web: www.cmtec-inc.com
SIC: 8731 Biotechnical research, commercial

(G-10115)
C S CONSULTANTS
4735 Ogletown Stanton Rd (19713-2072)
PHONE..................................302 623-4144
Anthony Cucuzzella, Prin
EMP: 8 EST: 2010
SALES (est): 102.29K Privately Held
Web: www.christianaspinecenter.com
SIC: 8748 Business consulting, nec

(G-10116)
C21 GOLD KEY REALTY
260 E Main St Frnt (19711-7357)
PHONE..................................302 250-6801
Ed Adams, Prin
EMP: 25 EST: 2013
SALES (est): 420.62K Privately Held

Web: www.c21gk.com
SIC: 6531 Real estate agent, residential

(G-10117)
C3 WAVE HOLDINGS LLC
Also Called: C3 Solutions
35 Salem Church Rd Ste 80 (19713-4927)
PHONE..................................412 708-6476
EMP: 7 EST: 2018
SALES (est): 300K Privately Held
SIC: 4789 Transportation services, nec

(G-10118)
CAFECTION CORP
2915 Ogletown Rd (19713-1927)
PHONE..................................800 561-6162
Andrea Zocchi, Pr
EMP: 5 EST: 2014
SALES (est): 450.78K Privately Held
SIC: 5046 5962 Coffee brewing equipment and supplies; Beverage vending machines

(G-10119)
CAHILL PLUMBING & HEATING INC
325 Markus Ct (19713-1157)
P.O. Box 250 (19351-0250)
PHONE..................................302 894-1802
Wendy Cahill, CEO
Paul Cahill, Pr
EMP: 8 EST: 1992
SQ FT: 4,500
SALES (est): 805.15K Privately Held
SIC: 1711 Plumbing contractors

(G-10120)
CALIBER COLLISION
8 Mill Park Ct (19713-1986)
PHONE..................................302 731-1200
EMP: 7 EST: 2017
SALES (est): 247.77K Privately Held
Web: www.caliber.com
SIC: 7532 Body shop, automotive

(G-10121)
CALIBER HOME LOANS INC
200 Continental Dr Ste 201 (19713-4335)
PHONE..................................302 483-7587
EMP: 9 EST: 2019
SALES (est): 467.91K Privately Held
Web: www.caliberhomeloans.com
SIC: 6162 Mortgage bankers and loan correspondents

(G-10122)
CAM PHYSCAL THRAPY WLLNESS SVC (PA)
100 Biddle Ave Ste 101a (19702-3982)
PHONE..................................301 853-0093
EMP: 5 EST: 2007
SALES (est): 839.29K Privately Held
Web: www.camphysicaltherapy.com
SIC: 8049 Physiotherapist

(G-10123)
CAMBRIDGE TRS INC
Also Called: Sonesta Es Wilmington Newark
240 Chapman Rd (19702-5405)
PHONE..................................302 453-9200
EMP: 15 EST: 2018
SALES (est): 225.04K Privately Held
SIC: 7011 Hotels

(G-10124)
CAMERAS ETC INC
Also Called: Cameras Etc TV & Video
165 E Main St (19711-7350)
PHONE..................................302 453-9400
EMP: 6
SALES (corp-wide): 864.44K Privately Held

GEOGRAPHIC SECTION   Newark - New Castle County (G-10152)

Web: www.camerasetc.net
SIC: 5946 7384 Cameras; Film developing and printing
PA: Cameras, Etc Inc
2303 Baynard Blvd
Wilmington DE 19802
302 764-9400

(G-10125)
CAMPBELLS LANDSCAPE SVC INC
22 Deer Run (19711-2424)
P.O. Box 1631 (19707-5631)
PHONE..............................302 266-0117
Jeff Campbell, CEO
EMP: 7 EST: 1994
SALES (est): 512.85K Privately Held
SIC: 0781 Landscape architects

(G-10126)
CAMPUS LIFE
501 Hamlet Way (19711-3646)
PHONE..............................302 294-6520
EMP: 6 EST: 2019
SALES (est): 32.92K Privately Held
SIC: 8322 Individual and family services

(G-10127)
CAN SERVICES LLC
254 Chapman Rd (19702-5413)
PHONE..............................212 920-9348
EMP: 7 EST: 2020
SALES (est): 200K Privately Held
SIC: 8742 Transportation consultant

(G-10128)
CANDLEWOOD SUITES
1101 S College Ave (19713-2307)
PHONE..............................302 266-8184
EMP: 19 EST: 2016
SALES (est): 257.19K Privately Held
Web: www.ihg.com
SIC: 7011 Hotels

(G-10129)
CANNONS CAKE AND CANDY SUPS
Also Called: Cannon's
2638 Kirkwood Hwy (19711)
PHONE..............................302 738-3321
Leah J Cannon, Mng Pt
Leah J Cannon, Pt
Stephen J Cannon, Pt
EMP: 5 EST: 1976
SQ FT: 6,000
SALES (est): 478.53K Privately Held
Web: www.cannonscakes.com
SIC: 5999 5199 Cake decorating supplies; Candy making goods and supplies

(G-10130)
CANON HOSPITALITY MGT LLC
Also Called: Super 8 By Wyndham Newark De
268 E Main St (19711-7390)
PHONE..............................302 737-5050
EMP: 29 EST: 2010
SALES (est): 487.54K Privately Held
Web: www.wyndhamhotels.com
SIC: 7011 Hotels and motels

(G-10131)
CANOPY INTERACTIVE LLC (PA)
2035 Sunset Lake Rd (19702-2600)
PHONE..............................631 258-1352
EMP: 5 EST: 2018
SALES (est): 155.51K
SALES (corp-wide): 155.51K Privately Held
SIC: 7371 Computer software development and applications

(G-10132)
CAPANO MANAGEMENT COMPANY
33 Marrows Rd (19713-3701)
PHONE..............................302 737-8056
Michelle Malizia, CFO
EMP: 51 EST: 1989
SALES (est): 2.77MM Privately Held
Web: www.capanomanagement.com
SIC: 6513 6531 1522 Apartment building operators; Real estate managers; Residential construction, nec

(G-10133)
CAPITAL CONTRACTING LLC
6 Noble Ln (19713-4800)
PHONE..............................302 690-0094
John Giacinto, Prin
EMP: 5 EST: 2017
SALES (est): 66.75K Privately Held
SIC: 1799 Special trade contractors, nec

(G-10134)
CAPITAL TRAIL SERVICE CENTER
1530 Capitol Trl (19711-5716)
PHONE..............................302 731-0999
Robert Teague, Pr
EMP: 5 EST: 1987
SALES (est): 204.48K Privately Held
SIC: 7538 7539 7549 General automotive repair shops; Brake repair, automotive; Lubrication service, automotive

(G-10135)
CAPITOL ENVIRONMENTAL SVCS INC (PA)
200 Biddle Ave Ste 205 (19702-3966)
P.O. Box 9499 (19714-9499)
PHONE..............................302 380-3737
James M Mraz, Pr
Jim Mraz, Pr
Christopher Ward, CFO
▲ EMP: 7 EST: 1988
SQ FT: 2,500
SALES (est): 8.16MM
SALES (corp-wide): 8.16MM Privately Held
Web: www.capitolenv.com
SIC: 8748 Environmental consultant

(G-10136)
CAPITOL ENVIRONMENTAL SVCS INC
Also Called: Capitaql Environmental
200 Biddle Ave Ste 205 (19702-3966)
P.O. Box 9499 (19714-9499)
PHONE..............................302 652-8999
EMP: 6
SALES (corp-wide): 8.16MM Privately Held
Web: www.capitolenv.com
SIC: 8748 Environmental consultant
PA: Capitol Environmental Services, Inc.
200 Biddle Ave Ste 205
Newark DE 19702
302 380-3737

(G-10137)
CAPPA INC
321 Possum Park Rd (19711-3853)
PHONE..............................302 598-4762
EMP: 5 EST: 2010
SALES (est): 62.63K Privately Held
SIC: 8699 Charitable organization

(G-10138)
CAR TECH AUTO CENTER
102 Albe Dr Ste A (19702-1347)
PHONE..............................302 368-4104
Curt Geesaman, Owner
EMP: 7 EST: 2004

SALES (est): 496.1K Privately Held
Web: www.cartechde.com
SIC: 7532 Top and body repair and paint shops

(G-10139)
CARDIAC REHAB
2600 Glasgow Ave Ste 220 (19702-5704)
PHONE..............................302 832-5414
John Records, Prin
EMP: 10 EST: 2016
SALES (est): 136.6K Privately Held
SIC: 8011 Offices and clinics of medical doctors

(G-10140)
CARDIO-KINETICS INC
52 N Chapel St Ste 101 (19711-2363)
PHONE..............................302 738-6635
Tom Hall, CEO
Richard Shaw, Pr
Phillis Mc Gee Addmin, Asstg
EMP: 36 EST: 1979
SQ FT: 6,500
SALES (est): 4.89MM Privately Held
Web: www.cardiokinetics.com
SIC: 8093 8011 Rehabilitation center, outpatient treatment; Offices and clinics of medical doctors

(G-10141)
CARDIOLOGY PHYSICANS PA INC
Also Called: Leidig, Gilbert A MD
1 Centurian Dr Ste 200 (19713-2150)
PHONE..............................302 366-8600
John J Kelly Iii, Pr
EMP: 30 EST: 1995
SQ FT: 10,000
SALES (est): 4.46MM Privately Held
Web: www.cardiocppa.com
SIC: 8011 Cardiologist and cardio-vascular specialist

(G-10142)
CAREPORTMD LLC
100 College Sq (19711-5481)
PHONE..............................302 202-3020
EMP: 5 EST: 2015
SALES (est): 48.07K Privately Held
Web: www.careforcemd.com
SIC: 8099 Health and allied services, nec

(G-10143)
CAREPORTMD LLC (PA)
1 Innovation Way Ste 400 (19711-5463)
PHONE..............................302 283-9001
Ashok Subramanian, CEO
Edward C White, COO
EMP: 8 EST: 2015
SALES (est): 5K
SALES (corp-wide): 5K Privately Held
Web: www.careforcemd.com
SIC: 8049 Offices of health practitioner

(G-10144)
CARGIMEX WORLD LLC
3390 Ogletown Rd (19713)
PHONE..............................514 701-4224
EMP: 5 EST: 2019
SALES (est): 101.15K Privately Held
Web: www.cargimex.com
SIC: 2084 Wines, brandy, and brandy spirits

(G-10145)
CARING FOR WOMENS HEALTH
620 Stanton Christiana Rd (19713-2133)
PHONE..............................302 489-2420
Beth Schubert, Prin
EMP: 10 EST: 2015
SALES (est): 152.46K Privately Held

SIC: 8099 Health and allied services, nec

(G-10146)
CARING N ACTION NURSING
15 Prestbury Sq (19713-2608)
PHONE..............................302 368-2273
Yvette Hall, Managing Member
EMP: 9 EST: 2015
SALES (est): 348.09K Privately Held
Web: www.caringnaction.com
SIC: 7361 Employment agencies

(G-10147)
CARITAS HOME HEALTH SERVICES
30 Prestbury Sq Ste 325 (19713-3237)
PHONE..............................302 525-6331
EMP: 5 EST: 2017
SALES (est): 148.81K Privately Held
SIC: 8099 Health and allied services, nec

(G-10148)
CARL R YACOUB
537 Stanton Christiana Rd Ste 106 (19713-2145)
PHONE..............................302 996-9010
EMP: 10 EST: 2013
SALES (est): 262.54K Privately Held
SIC: 8011 Neurologist

(G-10149)
CARMALT STUART LLC
801 Christiana Rd (19713-3262)
PHONE..............................302 366-8920
EMP: 5 EST: 2014
SALES (est): 218.47K Privately Held
SIC: 5941 7999 Skating equipment; Roller skating rink operation

(G-10150)
CARME LLC
Also Called: School - Del Paul Mitchell
1420 Pulaski Hwy (19702-5108)
PHONE..............................302 832-8418
Trina Carter, Prin
EMP: 10 EST: 2006
SQ FT: 9,000
SALES (est): 496.73K Privately Held
Web: www.paulmitchell.edu
SIC: 7231 Cosmetology school

(G-10151)
CARMINE POTTER & ASSOCIATES
1400 Peoples Plz Ste 104 (19702-5706)
PHONE..............................302 832-6000
Stephen Potter, Brnch Mgr
EMP: 5
SALES (corp-wide): 1.03MM Privately Held
Web: www.pottercarmine.com
SIC: 8111 General practice attorney, lawyer
PA: Carmine Potter & Associates
1719 Delaware Ave Ste 200
Wilmington DE 19806
302 658-8940

(G-10152)
CAROL A TAVANI MD
Also Called: Christiana Psychiatric Svcs
4745 Ogletown Stanton Rd Ste 124 (19713-1390)
PHONE..............................302 454-9900
Carol A Tavani Md, Owner
EMP: 5 EST: 1989
SALES (est): 284.68K Privately Held
Web: www.christianacare.org
SIC: 8011 General and family practice, physician/surgeon

Newark - New Castle County (G-10153) GEOGRAPHIC SECTION

(G-10153)
CARPE DIA ORGANIZATION
241 Goldfinch Turn (19711-4119)
PHONE..................302 333-7546
Martha Essick, *Ex Dir*
EMP: 6 EST: 2015
SALES (est): 130.15K **Privately Held**
SIC: 8322 Rehabilitation services

(G-10154)
CARPER FOR DELAWARE HQ
218 E Main St (19711-7325)
PHONE..................302 328-5774
EMP: 5 EST: 2017
SALES (est): 42.34K **Privately Held**
SIC: 8651 Political campaign organization

(G-10155)
CARTER ASTON
240 Continental Dr (19713-4307)
PHONE..................302 561-6315
EMP: 8 EST: 2018
SALES (est): 75.28K **Privately Held**
Web: www.astoncarter.com
SIC: 7361 Executive placement

(G-10156)
CARTERS INC
3132 Fashion Center Blvd (19702-3246)
PHONE..................302 731-1432
EMP: 3
SALES (corp-wide): 3.21B **Publicly Held**
Web: www.carters.com
SIC: 2361 5641 Girl's and children's dresses, blouses; Children's wear
PA: Carter's, Inc.
3438 Peachtree Rd Ne # 18
Atlanta GA 30326
678 791-1000

(G-10157)
CARVER GARDENS PROPERTIES LLC
482 W Chestnut Hill Rd (19713-1102)
PHONE..................302 420-2662
EMP: 5 EST: 2005
SALES (est): 143.63K **Privately Held**
SIC: 6512 Nonresidential building operators

(G-10158)
CASE CONSTRUCTION INC
Also Called: A Toll Building Systems
17 Mcmillan Way (19713-3420)
PHONE..................302 737-3800
EMP: 8 EST: 1964
SQ FT: 17,000
SALES (est): 249.7K **Privately Held**
SIC: 5211 5251 5085 Lumber and other building materials; Tools; Tools, nec

(G-10159)
CASH CONNECT INC
Also Called: W S M S Bank
700 Prides Xing (19713-6109)
PHONE..................302 283-4100
Thomas E Stevenson, *Pr*
EMP: 30 EST: 1985
SALES (est): 6.19MM **Privately Held**
Web: www.cash-connect.com
SIC: 6099 Automated teller machine (ATM) network

(G-10160)
CAST
500 N Wakefield Dr (19702-5440)
P.O. Box 8139 (19714-8139)
PHONE..................781 245-2212
EMP: 8 EST: 2017
SALES (est): 145.77K **Privately Held**
Web: www.cast.org

SIC: 8742 Management consulting services

(G-10161)
CASTLE MORTAGE SERVICES INC
4 Vantage Ct (19711-4814)
PHONE..................302 366-0912
Jeff Mcgowan, *Pr*
EMP: 10 EST: 1998
SALES (est): 781.43K **Privately Held**
SIC: 6162 Mortgage bankers

(G-10162)
CATARACT AND LASER CENTER LLC
4102 Ogletown Stanton Rd Ste 1 (19713-4183)
PHONE..................302 454-8802
Frank R Owczarek, *Owner*
EMP: 17 EST: 2007
SALES (est): 2.15MM **Privately Held**
Web: www.eyecareofdelaware.com
SIC: 8011 Opthalmologist

(G-10163)
CATHOLIC MNSTRY TO ELDERLY INC
Also Called: Marydale Retirement Village
135 Jeandell Dr (19713-2962)
PHONE..................302 368-2784
W Francis Malooly, *Pr*
Ray Lloyd, *Admn*
EMP: 10 EST: 1979
SALES (est): 348.7K **Privately Held**
Web: www.ccwilm.org
SIC: 8361 Geriatric residential care

(G-10164)
CATHY L HARRIS DDS
220 Christiana Medical Ctr (19702-1652)
PHONE..................302 453-1400
Cathy Harris, *Mgr*
EMP: 8 EST: 2018
SALES (est): 67.67K **Privately Held**
SIC: 8021 Dentists' office

(G-10165)
CAVALIER GROUP
Also Called: Cavalier Apts
25 Golf View Dr Ofc A4 (19702-1721)
PHONE..................302 368-7437
Ann Mcdonald, *Brnch Mgr*
EMP: 20
SALES (corp-wide): 4.45MM **Privately Held**
Web: www.capanomanagement.com
SIC: 6513 Apartment building operators
PA: The Cavalier Group
105 Foulk Rd
Wilmington DE 19803
302 429-8700

(G-10166)
CBI GROUP LLC (PA)
Also Called: Outside In
850 Library Ave Ste 106 (19711-7170)
PHONE..................302 266-0860
EMP: 31 EST: 1994
SALES (est): 11.51MM
SALES (corp-wide): 11.51MM **Privately Held**
Web: www.myplacers.com
SIC: 7361 Executive placement

(G-10167)
CC ENTERPRISES LLC
105 Anita Dr (19713-2341)
PHONE..................302 265-3677
EMP: 11 EST: 2012
SALES (est): 184.54K **Privately Held**
SIC: 1021 Copper ores

(G-10168)
CD INSTALLATION
90 Old Red Mill Rd (19711-6670)
PHONE..................302 588-7678
Chris Diiorio, *Prin*
EMP: 5 EST: 2011
SALES (est): 128.31K **Privately Held**
SIC: 1799 Special trade contractors, nec

(G-10169)
CEASAR RODNEY INSTITUTE
420 Corporate Blvd (19702-3330)
P.O. Box 7619 (19803-0619)
PHONE..................302 542-1781
Shaun Fink, *Prin*
EMP: 11 EST: 2016
SALES (est): 54.82K **Privately Held**
Web: www.caesarrodney.org
SIC: 8733 Noncommercial research organizations

(G-10170)
CELLULAR SALES EP CH
379 E Chestnut Hill Rd (19713-3735)
PHONE..................302 455-1092
EMP: 6 EST: 2017
SALES (est): 43.67K **Privately Held**
SIC: 4812 Cellular telephone services

(G-10171)
CELLULAR SALES KNOXVILLE INC
379 E Chestnut Hill Rd (19713-3735)
PHONE..................302 455-1092
EMP: 6
Web: www.cellularsales.com
SIC: 4812 Cellular telephone services
PA: Cellular Sales Of Knoxville, Inc.
9040 Executive Park Dr
Knoxville TN 37923

(G-10172)
CENTER FOR CHILD DEVELOPEMENT
256 Chapman Rd Ste 201 (19702-5415)
PHONE..................302 292-1334
Lisa R Savage, *Prin*
EMP: 5 EST: 2010
SALES (est): 568.57K **Privately Held**
Web: www.thecenterforchilddevelopment.com
SIC: 8351 Child day care services

(G-10173)
CENTER FOR COSMETIC SURGERY
1 Centurian Dr Ste 301 (19713-2127)
PHONE..................302 994-8492
EMP: 8 EST: 2019
SALES (est): 754.11K **Privately Held**
Web: www.thecentreforcosmeticsurgery.com
SIC: 8011 Plastic surgeon

(G-10174)
CENTER FOR GRWING TLENT BY PMA
1500 Casho Mill Rd (19711-3547)
PHONE..................302 738-7100
Kelsey Palandrani, *Prin*
EMP: 10 EST: 2019
SALES (est): 1.14MM **Privately Held**
SIC: 7911 Dance studios, schools, and halls

(G-10175)
CENTER FOR HUMAN REPRODUCTION (PA)
Also Called: Delaware Inst For Rep
4745 Ogletown Stanton Rd Ste 111 (19713-2067)
PHONE..................302 738-4600
Jeffrey B Russell, *Dir*

Jeffrey Russell, *Pr*
EMP: 18 EST: 1996
SALES (est): 4.87MM
SALES (corp-wide): 4.87MM **Privately Held**
Web: www.ivf-success.com
SIC: 8011 Endocrinologist

(G-10176)
CENTER FOR SURGICAL STUDIES
537 Stanton Christiana Rd Ste 109 (19713-2145)
PHONE..................302 225-0177
Peter Panzer, *Prin*
EMP: 10 EST: 2006
SALES (est): 170.65K **Privately Held**
SIC: 8011 Surgeon

(G-10177)
CENTURY 21 GOLD KEY REALTY
Also Called: Century 21
2 Magil Ct (19702-8636)
PHONE..................405 315-1105
Roopa Reddy, *Prin*
EMP: 5 EST: 2018
SALES (est): 82.25K **Privately Held**
Web: www.century21.com
SIC: 6531 Real estate agent, residential

(G-10178)
CENTURY 21 TOM LIVIZOS INC
Also Called: Century 21
701 Capitol Trl (19711-3913)
PHONE..................302 737-9000
Tom Livizos, *Pr*
EMP: 9 EST: 1954
SQ FT: 3,000
SALES (est): 763.3K **Privately Held**
Web: www.tomlivizosrealestate.com
SIC: 6531 Real estate agent, residential

(G-10179)
CERAMIC TILE SUPPLY CO
375 Bellevue Rd (19713-3429)
PHONE..................302 737-4968
Pauline Campbell, *Brnch Mgr*
EMP: 9
SALES (corp-wide): 28.9MM **Privately Held**
Web: www.bathkitchenandtile.com
SIC: 1743 Tile installation, ceramic
PA: Ceramic Tile Supply Co.
103 Greenbank Rd
Wilmington DE 19808
302 992-9200

(G-10180)
CEST MOI INFINITY INC
13 Brookfield Dr (19702-5941)
PHONE..................267 455-2455
Brenda Bell, *Prin*
EMP: 5 EST: 2010
SALES (est): 47.43K **Privately Held**
SIC: 7231 Beauty shops

(G-10181)
CGC GEOSERVICES LLC
1000 Dawson Dr Ste C (19713-5805)
PHONE..................302 489-2398
EMP: 19 EST: 2008
SALES (est): 1.21MM **Privately Held**
Web: www.cgcgeoservices.com
SIC: 8711 1799 Engineering services; Boring for building construction

(G-10182)
CH ASSOCIATES VIII LLC ◊
Also Called: Sonesta Select Newark
48 Geoffrey Dr (19713-3603)
PHONE..................302 456-3800

GEOGRAPHIC SECTION

Newark - New Castle County (G-10211)

EMP: 11 EST: 2022
SALES (est): 533.91K **Privately Held**
Web: www.sonesta.com
SIC: 7011 Hotels

(G-10183)
CH WILMINGTON LLC
Also Called: Courtyard By Marriott
268 E Main St (19711-7390)
PHONE..................................302 438-4504
EMP: 23 EST: 2015
SALES (est): 515.56K **Privately Held**
Web: courtyard.marriott.com
SIC: 7011 Hotels and motels

(G-10184)
CHA MOON DDS
1290 Peoples Plz (19702-5701)
PHONE..................................302 297-3750
EMP: 10 EST: 2017
SALES (est): 74.43K **Privately Held**
SIC: 8021 Dentists' office

(G-10185)
CHAFFIN CLEANING SERVICE INC
3 Whitfield Rd (19711-4817)
PHONE..................................302 369-2704
Jamie Chaffin, Pr
Robert Chaffin, Genl Mgr
EMP: 5 EST: 1981
SALES (est): 45.39K **Privately Held**
SIC: 7349 Janitorial service, contract basis

(G-10186)
CHAMPIONS FOR CHILDRENS MH
119 Timberline Dr (19711-7443)
PHONE..................................302 249-6788
Barbara Messick, Prin
EMP: 5 EST: 2017
SALES (est): 75.46K **Privately Held**
SIC: 8399 Advocacy group

(G-10187)
CHANCE DE GROUP LLC
262 Chapman Rd Ste 205223
(19702-5448)
PHONE..................................800 667-3082
Ernest Osei-owusu, CEO
Ernest Osei-owusu, Prin
EMP: 5 EST: 2018
SALES (est): 51.91K **Privately Held**
SIC: 8748 Business consulting, nec

(G-10188)
CHANNELPRO MOBILE LLC
19 Kris Ct (19702-6843)
PHONE..................................757 620-4635
EMP: 10 EST: 2018
SALES (est): 363.5K **Privately Held**
SIC: 7371 Custom computer programming services

(G-10189)
CHAPMAN HOSPITALITY INC
Also Called: Ramada Inn
260 Chapman Rd (19702-5490)
PHONE..................................302 738-3400
David Shah, Pr
Pragna Shah, VP
EMP: 91 EST: 1958
SALES (est): 924.44K **Privately Held**
Web: www.wyndhamhotels.com
SIC: 7011 Hotels and motels

(G-10190)
CHARLES L SAULSBERY AGT
226 W Park Pl Ste 12 (19711-4516)
P.O. Box 5320 (19808-0320)
PHONE..................................302 894-1430
Charles Saulsbery, Owner

EMP: 5 EST: 2017
SALES (est): 50.78K **Privately Held**
SIC: 6411 Insurance agents, brokers, and service

(G-10191)
CHARLES RIVER LABS INTL INC
Also Called: Accugenix
614 Interchange Blvd (19711-3560)
PHONE..................................302 292-8888
Gary Merkel, Pr
EMP: 16
SALES (corp-wide): 3.98B **Publicly Held**
Web: www.criver.com
SIC: 8731 Biotechnical research, commercial
PA: Charles River Laboratories
    International, Inc.
    251 Ballardvale St
    Wilmington MA 01887
    781 222-6000

(G-10192)
CHARMED MEDI SPA
48 Omega Dr (19713-2060)
PHONE..................................302 273-2827
Anna Damico, Pr
EMP: 6 EST: 2015
SALES (est): 64.48K **Privately Held**
Web: www.charmedmedispa.com
SIC: 7991 Spas

(G-10193)
CHARMED MEDISPA INC
H48 Omega Dr (19713)
PHONE..................................302 593-1994
Loraine Olson, Owner
EMP: 7 EST: 2015
SALES (est): 82.07K **Privately Held**
Web: www.charmedmedispa.com
SIC: 7991 Spas

(G-10194)
CHEC INC
1100 Helen Dr Apt 107 (19702-1668)
PHONE..................................302 275-4709
Octavia Dryden, Prin
EMP: 6 EST: 2018
SALES (est): 54.68K **Privately Held**
Web: www.checinc.org
SIC: 8322 Individual and family services

(G-10195)
CHEER FORCE
20 Swansea Ln (19702-4287)
PHONE..................................302 218-7384
Kennika Caesar, Prin
EMP: 6 EST: 2010
SALES (est): 66.42K **Privately Held**
SIC: 7999 Gymnastic instruction, non-membership

(G-10196)
CHEMOURS COMPANY
Also Called: Advanced Performance Materials
201 Discovery Blvd (19713-1344)
PHONE..................................302 773-6417
EMP: 12
SALES (corp-wide): 6.79B **Publicly Held**
Web: www.chemours.com
SIC: 8732 Business research service
PA: The Chemours Company
    1007 Market St
    Wilmington DE 19898
    302 773-1000

(G-10197)
CHERRY PSYCHOLOGICAL SERVICES
218 Cullen Way (19711-6112)
PHONE..................................302 528-2235

Kathleen J Cherry, Owner
EMP: 6 EST: 2015
SALES (est): 22.18K **Privately Held**
SIC: 8049 Psychologist, psychotherapist and hypnotist

(G-10198)
CHESAPEAKE REHAB EQUIPMENT INC
810 Interchange Blvd (19711-3570)
PHONE..................................302 266-6234
Kari Queen, Brnch Mgr
EMP: 7
SALES (corp-wide): 770.72MM **Privately Held**
Web: www.numotion.com
SIC: 5999 6321 Medical apparatus and supplies; Health insurance carriers
HQ: Chesapeake Rehab Equipment, Inc.
    2700 Lord Baltimore Dr
    Baltimore MD 21244
    410 298-4555

(G-10199)
CHESTNUT HILL PLAZA
110 Christiana Med Ctr (19702-1697)
PHONE..................................302 731-0643
EMP: 5 EST: 2010
SALES (est): 284.77K **Privately Held**
SIC: 6519 Real property lessors, nec

(G-10200)
CHEVEUX INC
1115 Churchmans Rd (19713-2112)
PHONE..................................302 731-9202
Mario Rispoli, Pr
Lisa Rispoli, VP
Dorothy Rosica, Sec
EMP: 7 EST: 1993
SALES (est): 116.74K **Privately Held**
SIC: 7231 Hairdressers

(G-10201)
CHILAY INC
Also Called: Consumer Injury Alert
40 E Main St 111 (19711-4639)
PHONE..................................302 559-6014
EMP: 6 EST: 2009
SQ FT: 1,000
SALES (est): 497.18K **Privately Held**
SIC: 7311 Advertising agencies

(G-10202)
CHILD INC
148 Flamingo Dr Sparrow Run (19702-4147)
PHONE..................................302 832-5451
Earline Vann, Mgr
EMP: 118
SALES (corp-wide): 5.53MM **Privately Held**
Web: www.childinc.com
SIC: 8322 Social service center
PA: Child, Inc.
    507 Philadelphia Pike
    Wilmington DE 19809
    302 762-8989

(G-10203)
CHILD CARE SERVICE
262 Chapman Rd Ste 202 (19702-5442)
PHONE..................................302 981-1328
Patricia Raynor, Owner
EMP: 13 EST: 2017
SALES (est): 51.15K **Privately Held**
SIC: 8351 Child day care services

(G-10204)
CHILD HELP FOUNDATION
6 Wyncliff Ln (19711-7525)

PHONE..................................302 533-7078
Basilio Bautista, Prin
EMP: 6 EST: 2017
SALES (est): 34.78K **Privately Held**
Web: www.childhelpfoundation.in
SIC: 8699 Charitable organization

(G-10205)
CHILDRENS CHOICE INC
25 S Old Baltimore Pike Ste 101 (19702-1540)
PHONE..................................302 731-9512
Erin Bates, Mgr
EMP: 8
SALES (corp-wide): 178.33K **Privately Held**
Web: www.childrenschoice.org
SIC: 8322 Social service center
PA: Children's Choice, Inc.
    211 Benigno Blvd 100
    Bellmawr NJ 08031
    856 754-0914

(G-10206)
CHIMES INC
514 Interchange Blvd (19711-3557)
PHONE..................................302 452-3400
Pete Dakchunak, Dir
EMP: 38
Web: www.chimes.org
SIC: 8361 Residential care for the handicapped
HQ: The Chimes Inc
    4815 Seton Dr
    Baltimore MD 21215
    410 358-6400

(G-10207)
CHIMES METRO INC (HQ)
514 Interchange Blvd (19711-3557)
PHONE..................................302 838-1202
EMP: 50 EST: 1992
SALES (est): 896.14K **Privately Held**
Web: www.chimes.org
SIC: 7349 Janitorial service, contract basis
PA: Chimes International Limited
    4815 Seton Dr
    Baltimore MD 21215

(G-10208)
CHISTINE E WOODS
111 Continental Dr # 412 (19713-4306)
PHONE..................................302 709-4497
EMP: 10 EST: 2013
SALES (est): 107.91K **Privately Held**
SIC: 8011 Offices and clinics of medical doctors

(G-10209)
CHOPIN BUILDING
258 Chapman Rd (19702-5445)
PHONE..................................302 283-7130
EMP: 7 EST: 2013
SALES (est): 84K **Privately Held**
Web: www.universityofficeplaza.com
SIC: 8099 Health and allied services, nec

(G-10210)
CHRIS HAIST
33 Possum Park Mall (19711-3954)
PHONE..................................302 234-1116
Chris Haist, Prin
EMP: 5 EST: 2013
SALES (est): 82.31K **Privately Held**
SIC: 6411 Insurance agents and brokers

(G-10211)
CHRISTANA CARE VSCLAR SPCALIST
4765 Ogletown Stanton Rd Ste 1e20 (19713-8003)

Newark - New Castle County (G-10212) GEOGRAPHIC SECTION

PHONE.................302 733-5700
Todd F Harad, Pr
Sonya Tuerff Md, Prin
EMP: 10 EST: 1999
SALES (est): 789.4K Privately Held
Web: www.christianacare.org
SIC: 8062 General medical and surgical hospitals

(G-10212)
CHRISTANA CTR FOR WNS WELLNESS
4745 Ogletown Stanton Rd Ste 105 (19713-2067)
PHONE.................302 454-9800
EMP: 13 EST: 2015
SALES (est): 178.45K Privately Held
Web: www.christianacare.org
SIC: 8011 3842 Gynecologist; Supports: abdominal, ankle, arch, kneecap, etc.

(G-10213)
CHRISTANA INST ADVNCED SRGERY
Also Called: Chrias
537 Stanton Christiana Rd Ste 102 (19713-2146)
PHONE.................302 892-9900
Isaias Irgau, Pr
EMP: 27 EST: 2002
SALES (est): 5.71MM Privately Held
Web: www.chrias.com
SIC: 8011 Surgeon

(G-10214)
CHRISTIAN REACHFM RADIO NETWRK
179 Stanton Christiana Rd (19702-1619)
PHONE.................302 731-0690
EMP: 6 EST: 2018
SALES (est): 135.04K Privately Held
SIC: 4832 Radio broadcasting stations

(G-10215)
CHRISTIAN SCIENCE READING ROOM
92 E Main St Ste 7 (19711-4640)
PHONE.................302 456-1428
Peggy Schultz, Religious Leader
Peggy Schultz, Prin
EMP: 7 EST: 1999
SALES (est): 143.69K Privately Held
SIC: 8699 Reading room, religious materials

(G-10216)
CHRISTIANA AUCTION GALLERY
314 E Main St (19711-7128)
PHONE.................570 441-7503
Nicole Veit, Prin
EMP: 5 EST: 2014
SALES (est): 54.43K Privately Held
Web: www.christianaauctiongallery.com
SIC: 7389 Auction, appraisal, and exchange services

(G-10217)
CHRISTIANA CARE CORP
21 Nightingale Cir (19711-3776)
PHONE.................302 738-4596
Dana Guhl, Prin
EMP: 8 EST: 2018
SALES (est): 104.1K Privately Held
Web: www.christianacare.org
SIC: 8062 General medical and surgical hospitals

(G-10218)
CHRISTIANA CARE HEALTH SYS INC
300 Biddle Ave Ste 200 (19702-3972)
PHONE.................302 838-4750
Nancy Howard, Mgr
EMP: 228
SALES (corp-wide): 666.58K Privately Held
Web: www.christianacare.org
SIC: 8062 General medical and surgical hospitals
HQ: Christiana Care Health System, Inc.
200 Hygeia Dr
Newark DE 19713
302 733-1000

(G-10219)
CHRISTIANA CARE HEALTH SYS INC
Also Called: Christana Care Crdiolgy Conslt
252 Chapman Rd Ste 150 (19702-5438)
PHONE.................302 366-1929
Edward Goldenberg, Brnch Mgr
EMP: 9
SALES (corp-wide): 666.58K Privately Held
Web: www.christianacare.org
SIC: 8062 General medical and surgical hospitals
HQ: Christiana Care Health System, Inc.
200 Hygeia Dr
Newark DE 19713
302 733-1000

(G-10220)
CHRISTIANA CARE HEALTH SYS INC (HQ)
Also Called: Christiana Hospital
200 Hygeia Dr (19713-2049)
PHONE.................302 733-1000
Robert Laskowski, Pr
Buddy Elmore, VP Fin
Janice E Nevin, CMO
EMP: 6 EST: 1985
SQ FT: 600,000
SALES (est): 1.72MM
SALES (corp-wide): 666.58K Privately Held
Web: www.christianacare.org
SIC: 8062 General medical and surgical hospitals
PA: Christiana Care Health Services, Inc.
4755 Ogletown Stanton Rd
Newark DE 19718
302 733-1000

(G-10221)
CHRISTIANA CARE HEALTH SYS INC
Also Called: Christiana Care Health System
4755 Ogletown Stanton Rd (19718-2200)
P.O. Box 6001 (19714-6001)
PHONE.................302 733-5700
EMP: 6
SALES (corp-wide): 666.58K Privately Held
Web: www.christianacare.org
SIC: 8062 General medical and surgical hospitals
HQ: Christiana Care Health System, Inc.
200 Hygeia Dr
Newark DE 19713
302 733-1000

(G-10222)
CHRISTIANA CARE HEALTH SYS INC
Also Called: Christianity Care Pathology
4755 Stanton Ogletown Rd Ste Lo308 (19718-0001)
P.O. Box 6001 (19714-6001)
PHONE.................302 733-1601
Cheryle Katz, VP
EMP: 410
SALES (corp-wide): 666.58K Privately Held
Web: www.christianacare.org
SIC: 8741 8071 Hospital management; Pathological laboratory
HQ: Christiana Care Health System, Inc.
200 Hygeia Dr
Newark DE 19713
302 733-1000

(G-10223)
CHRISTIANA CARE HEALTH SYS INC
200 Hygeia Dr (19713-2049)
PHONE.................302 623-0390
Bill Padmonsky, Mgr
EMP: 159
SALES (corp-wide): 666.58K Privately Held
Web: www.christianacare.org
SIC: 8741 8093 Hospital management; Respiratory therapy clinic
HQ: Christiana Care Health System, Inc.
200 Hygeia Dr
Newark DE 19713
302 733-1000

(G-10224)
CHRISTIANA CARE HEALTH SYS INC
Also Called: Christany Care Healthcare
4745 Ogletown Stanton Rd Map 1 Ste 217 (19718-0001)
PHONE.................302 733-2410
EMP: 205
SALES (corp-wide): 666.58K Privately Held
Web: www.christianacare.org
SIC: 8011 Offices and clinics of medical doctors
HQ: Christiana Care Health System, Inc.
200 Hygeia Dr
Newark DE 19713
302 733-1000

(G-10225)
CHRISTIANA CARE HLTH SVCS INC (PA)
Also Called: Christiana Hospital
4755 Ogletown Stanton Rd (19718-2200)
P.O. Box 1668 (19899-1668)
PHONE.................302 733-1000
Robert Laskowski, Pr
Sharon Anderson, Sr VP
Rosa M Colon-kolacko, Sr VP
Thomas L Corrigan, Sr VP
Alan S Greenglass, Sr VP
EMP: 1000 EST: 1965
SQ FT: 1,200,000
SALES (est): 666.58K
SALES (corp-wide): 666.58K Privately Held
Web: www.christianacare.org
SIC: 8062 General medical and surgical hospitals

(G-10226)
CHRISTIANA CARE INFUSION
600 White Clay Center Dr (19711-5455)
PHONE.................302 623-0345
Barbara Knightly, Mgr
EMP: 18 EST: 2010
SALES (est): 210.49K Privately Held
Web: www.christianacare.org
SIC: 8082 Visiting nurse service

(G-10227)
CHRISTIANA CENT
1082 Old Churchmans Rd Ste 100 (19713-2143)
PHONE.................302 368-3257
David Mitchell Fink, Prin
EMP: 15 EST: 2008
SALES (est): 118.63K Privately Held
Web: www.christianacare.org
SIC: 8011 Gynecologist

(G-10228)
CHRISTIANA EXCAVATING COMPANY
2016 Sunset Lake Rd (19702-2630)
PHONE.................302 738-8660
Mike Conner, Pr
Paul Connor, *
EMP: 35 EST: 1987
SQ FT: 5,000
SALES (est): 3.18MM Privately Held
Web: www.cecde.net
SIC: 1794 Excavation and grading, building construction

(G-10229)
CHRISTIANA FAMILY DENTAL CARE
50 Omega Dr (19713-2060)
PHONE.................302 623-4190
EMP: 9 EST: 2017
SALES (est): 170.81K Privately Held
Web: www.christianafamilydentalcare.com
SIC: 8021 Dental clinic

(G-10230)
CHRISTIANA FAMILY DENTAL CARE
4735 Ogletown Stanton Rd Ste 1101 (19713-2089)
PHONE.................302 623-4190
EMP: 8 EST: 2020
SALES (est): 200.22K Privately Held
Web: www.christianafamilydentalcare.com
SIC: 8021 Dental clinic

(G-10231)
CHRISTIANA HERNIA CENTER
550 Stanton Christiana Rd Ste 202 (19713-2125)
PHONE.................302 996-6400
EMP: 7 EST: 2019
SALES (est): 59.55K Privately Held
Web: www.christianaherniacenter.com
SIC: 8011 Surgeon

(G-10232)
CHRISTIANA NEONATAL PRACTICE
4745 Ogletown Stanton Rd Ste 217 (19713-2074)
PHONE.................302 733-2410
Deborah Tuttle, Pt
EMP: 16 EST: 2001
SALES (est): 177.67K Privately Held
Web: www.christianacare.org
SIC: 8011 General and family practice, physician/surgeon

(G-10233)
CHRISTIANA PLEASANT DENTA
72 Omega Dr (19713-2063)
PHONE.................302 738-3666
EMP: 7 EST: 2019
SALES (est): 200.92K Privately Held
Web: www.christianapleasantdental.com
SIC: 8021 Dentists' office

(G-10234)
CHRISTINA EDUCATION ASSN
4135 Ogletown Stanton Rd (19713-4179)
PHONE.................302 454-7700
EMP: 7 EST: 1962
SALES (est): 111.44K Privately Held
Web: www.christinaeducationassociation.org
SIC: 8631 Employees' association

(G-10235)
CHRISTINE W MAYNARD M D
4735 Ogletown Stanton Rd Ste 2300 (19713-2072)

GEOGRAPHIC SECTION

Newark - New Castle County (G-10264)

PHONE.................302 225-6110
Christine Maynard, *Mgr*
EMP: 14 **EST:** 2017
SALES (est): 520.4K **Privately Held**
Web: www.aawdocs.com
SIC: 8011 Gynecologist

(G-10236)
CHRISTOPHER A BOWENS MD
Also Called: Deleware Heart Group
2600 Glasgow Ave Ste 108 (19702-5703)
PHONE.................302 834-3700
Christopher A Bowens Md, *Pt*
Doctor Joseph West, *Pt*
EMP: 8 **EST:** 1992
SALES (est): 335.71K **Privately Held**
SIC: 8011 8049 Cardiologist and cardio-vascular specialist; Offices of health practitioner

(G-10237)
CHRISTOPHER J SEIVERT
3 Andrew Jackson Cir (19702-3081)
PHONE.................302 731-2719
Christopher J Seivert, *Prin*
EMP: 6 **EST:** 2005
SALES (est): 61.66K **Privately Held**
SIC: 1721 Painting and paper hanging

(G-10238)
CHUCK REDSTONE - STATE FARM IN
920 Peoples Plz (19702-5603)
PHONE.................302 832-0345
EMP: 5 **EST:** 2019
SALES (est): 223.11K **Privately Held**
Web: www.chuckredstoneinsurance.com
SIC: 6411 Insurance agents and brokers

(G-10239)
CHURCHMAN DE SNF MGT LLC
Also Called: CHURCHMAN VILLAGE
4949 Ogletown Stanton Rd (19713-2068)
PHONE.................302 998-6900
Justin Weinberg, *CEO*
Kim Blunt, *Ex Dir*
EMP: 99 **EST:** 2020
SALES (est): 9.77MM **Privately Held**
Web: www.churchmanvillage.com
SIC: 8051 Skilled nursing care facilities

(G-10240)
CHURCHMAN VILLAGE CENTER LLC
Also Called: Churman Village Center
4949 Ogletown Stanton Rd (19713-2068)
PHONE.................302 998-6900
Richard Powell, *Ex Dir*
EMP: 21 **EST:** 2007
SQ FT: 90,820
SALES (est): 2.1MM **Privately Held**
Web: www.churchmanvillage.com
SIC: 8051 8361 Convalescent home with continuous nursing care; Geriatric residential care

(G-10241)
CIBT AMERICA INC
200 Continental Dr # 401 (19713-4334)
PHONE.................302 318-1300
Alexander Kedo, *Prin*
EMP: 6 **EST:** 2018
SALES (est): 349.18K **Privately Held**
SIC: 5169 Organic chemicals, synthetic

(G-10242)
CIGARETTE CITY INC (PA)
460 Peoples Plz (19702-4797)
PHONE.................302 836-4889
Frank Speciale, *Pr*
EMP: 10 **EST:** 1993
SALES (est): 1.81MM **Privately Held**
Web: www.delawarecigars.com
SIC: 5194 5993 Cigars; Tobacco stores and stands

(G-10243)
CINDY ELKO PSYD LLC
260 Chapman Rd Ste 205c (19702-5449)
PHONE.................302 229-2110
Cindy Elko, *Prin*
EMP: 6 **EST:** 2016
SALES (est): 22.18K **Privately Held**
SIC: 8049 Clinical psychologist

(G-10244)
CITIGROUP INC
Also Called: Citigroup
500 White Clay Center Dr (19711-5469)
PHONE.................302 631-3530
EMP: 48 **EST:** 2014
SALES (est): 12.28MM
SALES (corp-wide): 101.08B **Publicly Held**
Web: www.citigroup.com
SIC: 6099 7389 Check clearing services; Financial services
PA: Citigroup Inc.
388 Greenwich St Fl 38
New York NY 10013
212 559-1000

(G-10245)
CITY OF NEWARK
Also Called: Parks Rcreation Dept Cy Newark
220 S Main St (19711-4594)
PHONE.................302 366-7060
Charlie Emerson, *Dir*
EMP: 20
SALES (corp-wide): 21.09MM **Privately Held**
Web: www.newarkde.gov
SIC: 9512 7999 Recreational program administration, government; Recreation center
PA: City Of Newark
220 S Main St
Newark DE 19711
302 366-7000

(G-10246)
CITY THEATER CO INC
110 Tanglewood Ln (19711-3120)
PHONE.................302 831-2206
John Suchanec, *Prin*
EMP: 5 **EST:** 2016
SALES (est): 65.64K **Privately Held**
SIC: 2339 Women's and misses' outerwear, nec

(G-10247)
CJM BOOKKEEPING AND TAXES LLC
10 Broadfield Dr (19713-2722)
PHONE.................302 999-8755
Carmen Martinez, *Prin*
EMP: 5 **EST:** 2009
SALES (est): 100.18K **Privately Held**
SIC: 7291 Tax return preparation services

(G-10248)
CKS GLOBAL VENTURES LLC
Also Called: Assetone
792 Jacobsen Cir (19702-1624)
PHONE.................302 355-0511
Kashyap Sanghvi, *CEO*
Chaitali K Sanghvi, *Prin*
EMP: 20 **EST:** 2015
SALES (est): 726.14K **Privately Held**

SIC: **7379** 7376 7373 7371 Computer related maintenance services; Computer facilities management; Computer integrated systems design; Custom computer programming services

(G-10249)
CLAIRE KUBIZNE PT
16 Tremont Ct (19711-1901)
PHONE.................302 521-3305
Claire Kubizne, *Pr*
EMP: 6 **EST:** 2017
SALES (est): 24.86K **Privately Held**
SIC: 8049 Offices of health practitioner

(G-10250)
CLAUDIVA KAE & CO LLC
406 Suburban Dr (19711-3566)
PHONE.................302 283-9803
EMP: 3 **EST:** 2020
SALES (est): 75K **Privately Held**
SIC: 2844 Cosmetic preparations

(G-10251)
CLAY WHITE DENTAL ASSOCIATES
Also Called: Bond, Donald T DDS
12 Polly Drummond Hill Rd (19711-5703)
PHONE.................302 731-4225
Donald Bond, *Pr*
EMP: 10 **EST:** 1994
SALES (est): 970.13K **Privately Held**
Web: www.whiteclaydental.com
SIC: 8021 Dentists' office

(G-10252)
CLAY WHITE ELECTRICAL INC
17 New Haven Dr (19713-2122)
PHONE.................302 994-7748
Heather Good, *Prin*
EMP: 5 **EST:** 2019
SALES (est): 180.6K **Privately Held**
SIC: 4911 Electric services

(G-10253)
CLEAN A LOT LLC
5 Jaymar Blvd (19702-2878)
PHONE.................302 218-2755
EMP: 10 **EST:** 2011
SALES (est): 344.18K **Privately Held**
Web: www.cleanalot.net
SIC: 7699 Cleaning services

(G-10254)
CLEAN BEE
6 Philip Ct (19711-5681)
PHONE.................302 416-1723
Carly Vega, *Prin*
EMP: 5 **EST:** 2018
SALES (est): 64.95K **Privately Held**
SIC: 7699 Cleaning services

(G-10255)
CLEAN PROS
27 Concord Dr (19702-4239)
PHONE.................302 312-5666
Joseph Conti, *Owner*
EMP: 5 **EST:** 2006
SALES (est): 106.32K **Privately Held**
SIC: 1799 Special trade contractors, nec

(G-10256)
CLEANING FRENZY LLC
2860 Ogletown Rd Bldg 6-1 (19713-1820)
PHONE.................302 453-8800
Ashley Dematt, *Managing Member*
EMP: 8 **EST:** 2019
SALES (est): 494.79K **Privately Held**
Web: www.cleaningfrenzyllc.com
SIC: 7699 Cleaning services

(G-10257)
CLEMENTES CLUBHOUSE
321 Shisler Ct (19702-1341)
PHONE.................302 455-0936
EMP: 5 **EST:** 2011
SALES (est): 66.75K **Privately Held**
Web: www.clementesclubhouse.com
SIC: 7997 Membership sports and recreation clubs

(G-10258)
CLG TRUE SOLUTIONS LLC
130 Cannonball Ln (19702-3096)
PHONE.................302 709-1312
EMP: 5
SALES (est): 36.21K **Privately Held**
Web: www.clgtruesolutions.com
SIC: 8322 General counseling services

(G-10259)
CLICKSSL
40 E Main St (19711-4639)
PHONE.................302 355-0692
EMP: 5 **EST:** 2020
SALES (est): 215.81K **Privately Held**
Web: www.clickssl.net
SIC: 4813 Internet host services

(G-10260)
CLIENT MONSTER LLC
1300 Helen Dr Apt 112 (19702-1672)
PHONE.................866 799-5433
EMP: 5 **EST:** 2018
SALES (est): 172.44K **Privately Held**
Web: www.goclientmonster.com
SIC: 7371 Computer software development and applications

(G-10261)
CLINICAL CRDLGY SPCIALISTS LLC
1400 Peoples Plz Ste 111 (19702-5706)
PHONE.................302 834-3700
Christopher A Bowens, *Prin*
EMP: 5 **EST:** 2009
SALES (est): 498.56K **Privately Held**
Web: www.stonerunfamilymedicine.com
SIC: 8011 Cardiologist and cardio-vascular specialist

(G-10262)
CLOUD COLLECTED LLC
Also Called: Cloud
560 Peoples Plz # 312 (19702-4798)
PHONE.................302 273-4010
EMP: 5 **EST:** 2016
SALES (est): 115.68K **Privately Held**
SIC: 3825 Radio frequency measuring equipment

(G-10263)
CLOUDLI COMMUNICATIONS INC ✪
Also Called: Voip Carrier Services
2915 Ogletown Rd (19713-1927)
PHONE.................877 808-8647
Stephen Dorsey, *Pr*
EMP: 12 **EST:** 2022
SALES (est): 2.65MM **Privately Held**
Web: www.cloudli.com
SIC: 4899 Communication services, nec

(G-10264)
CLOVER VIEW INC ✪
254 Chapman Rd Ste 208 (19702-5422)
PHONE.................561 779-2423
Vanessa Greysonyoung, *CEO*
EMP: 2 **EST:** 2023
SALES (est): 87.4K **Privately Held**
SIC: 7372 Business oriented computer software

Newark - New Castle County (G-10265) **GEOGRAPHIC SECTION**

(G-10265)
CMI ELECTRIC INC (PA)
Also Called: CMI Solar Electric
83 Albe Dr Ste A (19702-1373)
PHONE.................................302 731-5556
Dale W Davis, *Pr*
Linda A Davis, *
EMP: 23 EST: 1998
SQ FT: 6,000
SALES (est): 6.47MM
SALES (corp-wide): 6.47MM **Privately Held**
Web: www.cmielectric.com
SIC: **4911** 1711
; Solar energy contractor

(G-10266)
CMP FIRE LLC
1820 Otts Chapel Rd (19702-2016)
PHONE.................................410 620-2062
Samantha Pearce, *Pr*
EMP: 9 EST: 2008
SALES (est): 1.75MM **Privately Held**
Web: www.cmpfire.com
SIC: **1711** 7389 Fire sprinkler system installation; Fire extinguisher servicing

(G-10267)
CNS CONSTRUCTION CORP
116 Sandy Dr Ste B (19713-1187)
PHONE.................................302 224-0450
Charles Showell, *Pr*
EMP: 7 EST: 1998
SQ FT: 500
SALES (est): 240.63K **Privately Held**
SIC: **1521** Single-family housing construction

(G-10268)
CO FS HOLDING COMPANY LLC
502 S College Ave (19713-1338)
PHONE.................................302 894-1244
Bob Pfeifer, *Brnch Mgr*
EMP: 7
SALES (corp-wide): 540.51MM **Privately Held**
SIC: **4213** Automobiles, transport and delivery
HQ: Co Fs Holding Company, Llc
624 Steele St
Denver CO 80206
800 624-3256

(G-10269)
CODE-MASTERS LLC ◯
254 Chapman Rd Ste 208 (19702-5422)
PHONE.................................408 508-9955
Robette Pepa, *Managing Member*
EMP: 9 EST: 2023
SALES (est): 328.69K **Privately Held**
SIC: **7372** Prepackaged software

(G-10270)
COGIR MANAGEMENT USA INC
Also Called: Cogir On NAPA Road
2915 Ogletown Rd (19713-1927)
PHONE.................................916 400-3985
EMP: 5 EST: 2018
SALES (est): 228.13K **Privately Held**
SIC: **8741** Management services

(G-10271)
COLE JANEIKA
Also Called: SIS Stylogy Beauty Salon
6 Lyon Ct (19702-5523)
PHONE.................................302 838-1868
Cole Janeika, *Prin*
EMP: 5 EST: 2011
SALES (est): 37.63K **Privately Held**
SIC: **7231** Beauty shops

(G-10272)
COLECAROL
1217 Churchmans Rd (19713-2149)
PHONE.................................302 313-6698
Carol Cole, *Prin*
EMP: 5 EST: 2015
SALES (est): 90K **Privately Held**
Web: www.carolcolesalonandspa.com
SIC: **7231** Hairdressers

(G-10273)
COLIVING INC
2035 Sunset Lake Rd Ste B2 (19702-2600)
PHONE.................................650 449-4448
Daniel Beck, *CEO*
EMP: 9
SALES (est): 301.02K **Privately Held**
SIC: **7371** Computer software development and applications

(G-10274)
COLLINS ASSOCIATES
38 Peoples Plz (19702-4727)
PHONE.................................302 834-4000
Ronald E Collins D.d.s., *Pt*
Lynn Collins D.d.s., *Pt*
EMP: 18 EST: 1963
SQ FT: 6,636
SALES (est): 1MM **Privately Held**
Web: www.delawarepediatricdentistry.com
SIC: **8021** Dentists' office

(G-10275)
COLON HEALTH CENTERS AMERIC
537 Stanton Christiana Rd (19713-2148)
PHONE.................................302 995-2656
Mark Baumel, *Prin*
EMP: 8 EST: 2008
SALES (est): 217.49K **Privately Held**
SIC: **8099** Medical services organization

(G-10276)
COLON RECTAL SURGERY ASSOC DEL
4745 Ogletown Stanton Rd Ste 216 (19713-2074)
PHONE.................................302 737-5444
Joseph Damico Md, *Pt*
Frederick Denstman Md, *Pt*
Carey Mason, *Pt*
Shanthi Shakamori, *Pt*
EMP: 25 EST: 1978
SALES (est): 2.23MM **Privately Held**
SIC: **8011** Surgeon

(G-10277)
COLONIAL CHPTER OF THE PRLYZED
700 Barksdale Rd Ste 7 (19711-3260)
PHONE.................................302 861-6671
Allyson Swartzentruber, *Admn*
EMP: 5 EST: 2018
SALES (est): 319.82K **Privately Held**
Web: www.colonialpva.org
SIC: **8399** Advocacy group

(G-10278)
COLONIAL RLTY ASSOC LTD PARTNR
Also Called: Colonial Garden Apartments
334 E Main St Bldg B (19711-7151)
PHONE.................................302 737-1254
Jonathan De Young, *Pt*
Philip Pearlstein D.o.s., *Pt*
Mitchell Horenstein D.o.s., *Pt*
Robert Levin D.d.s., *Pt*
EMP: 10 EST: 1969
SALES (est): 655.77K **Privately Held**
SIC: **6513** Apartment building operators

(G-10279)
COLOR DYE SYSTEMS AND CO
Also Called: Trim Shop
663 Dawson Dr Ste B (19713-3461)
PHONE.................................302 454-1754
Greg Culbertson, *Owner*
EMP: 7 EST: 1981
SALES (est): 331.04K **Privately Held**
SIC: **7641** Upholstery work

(G-10280)
COMBAT ZONE WRESTING LLC
208 Spruceglen Dr (19711-7210)
PHONE.................................302 345-1077
EMP: 6 EST: 2011
SALES (est): 237.01K **Privately Held**
SIC: **7941** Sports clubs, managers, and promoters

(G-10281)
COMFORT BOYCE SYSTEMS
134b Sandy Dr (19713-1147)
PHONE.................................302 419-4748
EMP: 10 EST: 2015
SALES (est): 469.94K **Privately Held**
SIC: **7699** Repair services, nec

(G-10282)
COMFORT CARE AT HOME INC
254 Chapman Rd (19702-5489)
PHONE.................................302 737-8078
Adwoa Tina Brew R.n., *Admn*
EMP: 15 EST: 2007
SALES (est): 871.51K **Privately Held**
Web: www.comfortcare-home.com
SIC: **8082** Home health care services

(G-10283)
COMFORT INN & SUITES
Also Called: Comfort Inn
3 Concord Ln (19713-3577)
PHONE.................................302 737-3900
EMP: 21 EST: 2011
SALES (est): 520.49K **Privately Held**
Web: www.choicehotels.com
SIC: **7011** Hotels and motels

(G-10284)
COMMERCIAL INSURANCE ASSOC
256 Chapman Rd Ste 203 (19702-5415)
PHONE.................................610 436-4608
Victoria Tester, *Pr*
EMP: 5 EST: 2007
SQ FT: 10,000
SALES (est): 486.92K **Privately Held**
Web: www.insurance-cia.com
SIC: **6411** Insurance agents, nec

(G-10285)
COMMODITIES PLUS INC
Also Called: Buy and Sell Rags
132 Sandy Dr (19713-1147)
P.O. Box 517 (19709-0517)
PHONE.................................302 376-5219
Lallind Nalwattie, *Pr*
EMP: 5 EST: 2002
SQ FT: 10,000
SALES (est): 6.04K **Privately Held**
Web: www.buyandsellrags.com
SIC: **4953** Recycling, waste materials

(G-10286)
COMMUNCTONS WKRS AMER LCAL 131
350 Gooding Dr (19702-1906)
PHONE.................................302 737-0400
EMP: 5 EST: 2011
SALES (est): 272.56K **Privately Held**
Web: www.cwa13101.org
SIC: **8631** Labor union

(G-10287)
COMMUNICATIONS PRINTING INC
2850 Ogletown Rd (19713-1838)
P.O. Box 7790 (19714-7790)
PHONE.................................302 229-9369
Vincent Mercante, *Pr*
Alice Mercante, *Sec*
EMP: 4 EST: 1969
SQ FT: 1,000
SALES (est): 420.05K **Privately Held**
Web: www.communicationsprinting.com
SIC: **2752** Offset printing

(G-10288)
COMMUNITY BUSINESS DEV CORP
25 Hempstead Dr (19702-7713)
PHONE.................................302 544-1709
Roger Turner, *Pr*
Carlton Gray, *VP*
EMP: 5 EST: 2009
SALES (est): 47.64K **Privately Held**
SIC: **8641** Civic and social associations

(G-10289)
COMMUNITY SERVICES CORPORATION
116 Haines St (19711-5367)
PHONE.................................302 368-4400
Mark Smith Junior, *Pr*
EMP: 13 EST: 1972
SQ FT: 1,400
SALES (est): 329.13K **Privately Held**
Web: www.dewindows.com
SIC: **7299** 7349 Home improvement and renovation contractor agency; Building cleaning service

(G-10290)
COMMUNITY TWERED FEDERAL CR UN (PA)
401 Eagle Run Rd (19702-1602)
P.O. Box 7739 (19714-7739)
PHONE.................................302 368-2396
Anthony Hinds, *Genl Mgr*
Anthony Hinds, *CEO*
Robert Oaks, *Pr*
EMP: 11 EST: 1962
SALES (est): 3.46MM
SALES (corp-wide): 3.46MM **Privately Held**
Web: www.cpwrfcu.org
SIC: **6061** 6062 Federal credit unions; State credit unions

(G-10291)
COMPASS ELECTRIC LLC
935 Rahway Dr (19711-2687)
PHONE.................................302 731-0240
Richard Crouse, *Prin*
EMP: 6 EST: 2014
SALES (est): 162.56K **Privately Held**
SIC: **1731** Electrical work

(G-10292)
COMPREHENSIVE BUS SVCS LLC (PA)
112 Capitol Trl (19711-3716)
PHONE.................................302 994-2000
Dean Brand, *CEO*
Mark Marinzoli, *VP*
Robert Dotey, *Prin*
EMP: 11 EST: 1993
SQ FT: 3,500
SALES (est): 1.03MM
SALES (corp-wide): 1.03MM **Privately Held**
Web: www.cbstaxpro.com

GEOGRAPHIC SECTION
Newark - New Castle County (G-10317)

SIC: 7389 Financial services

(G-10293)
COMPRHENSIVE NEUROLOGY CTR LLC
1114 Drummond Plz (19711-5705)
PHONE..............................302 996-9010
Carl Yacoub, *Owner*
EMP: 8 EST: 2002
SALES (est): 451.63K **Privately Held**
Web: www.newarkneurology.com
SIC: 8011 Neurologist

(G-10294)
COMPUTER AID INC
500 Creek View Rd Ste 201 (19711-8549)
PHONE..............................302 831-5500
Tom Salvaggio, *Mgr*
EMP: 9
SALES (corp-wide): 874.76MM **Privately Held**
Web: www.cai.io
SIC: 7371 7374 Computer software systems analysis and design, custom; Data processing and preparation
PA: Computer Aid, Inc.
1390 Ridgeview Dr Ste 300
Allentown PA 18104
610 530-5000

(G-10295)
COMPUTER SCIENCES CORPORATION
500 Creek View Rd (19711-8549)
PHONE..............................302 391-8347
Anthony Kowal, *Mgr*
EMP: 6
SALES (corp-wide): 14.43B **Publicly Held**
Web: www.dxc.com
SIC: 7379 Computer related consulting services
HQ: Computer Sciences Corporation
20408 Bashan Dr Ste 231
Ashburn VA 20147
855 716-0853

(G-10296)
CONCORD TOWERS INC
Also Called: Holiday Inn
1201 Christiana Rd (19713-3503)
PHONE..............................302 737-2700
Paul Isken, *Pr*
Donald Isken, *
Laura Isken Doyle, *
EMP: 70 EST: 1955
SQ FT: 80,000
SALES (est): 4.55MM **Privately Held**
Web: www.hiexpress.com
SIC: 7011 Hotels and motels

(G-10297)
CONECTIV LLC
375 N Wakefield Dr (19702-5416)
P.O. Box 6066 (19714-6066)
PHONE..............................302 429-3018
Bruce Pawling, *Dir*
EMP: 1404
SALES (corp-wide): 19.08B **Publicly Held**
Web: www.conectiv.com
SIC: 4911 Distribution, electric power
HQ: Conectiv, Llc
500 N Wkfeld Drv Mlsto
Newark DE 19702
202 872-2680

(G-10298)
CONECTIV LLC (HQ)
500 N Wakefield Dr (19702)
PHONE..............................202 872-2680
John M Derrick Junior, *CEO*
Dennis R Wraase, *Pr*
Gary Stockbritge, *Prin*
EMP: 123 EST: 1998
SQ FT: 130,000
SALES (est): 25.41MM
SALES (corp-wide): 19.08B **Publicly Held**
Web: www.conectiv.com
SIC: 4911 4924 1731 5172 Generation, electric power; Natural gas distribution; Electrical work; Crude oil
PA: Exelon Corporation
10 S Dearborn St Fl 52
Chicago IL 60603
800 483-3220

(G-10299)
CONECTIV COMMUNICATIONS INC
500 N Wakefield Dr (19702)
PHONE..............................302 224-1177
Tom Shaw, *Pr*
L Laird Elevison, *
EMP: 50 EST: 1996
SALES (est): 9.27MM
SALES (corp-wide): 19.08B **Publicly Held**
SIC: 1731 7379 4813 Fiber optic cable installation; Computer related maintenance services; Telephone communication, except radio
PA: Exelon Corporation
10 S Dearborn St Fl 52
Chicago IL 60603
800 483-3220

(G-10300)
CONECTIV ENERGY SUPPLY INC (DH)
500 N Wakefield Dr (19702-5440)
P.O. Box 6066 (19714-6066)
PHONE..............................302 454-0300
Howard Cosgrove, *CEO*
Jerrold Jacobs, *
David Hughes, *
EMP: 96 EST: 1998
SQ FT: 2,500
SALES (est): 91.3MM
SALES (corp-wide): 10.07B **Privately Held**
SIC: 5063 1731 4924 4925 Antennas, receiving, satellite dishes; Cable television installation; Natural gas distribution; Gas production and/or distribution
HQ: Calpine Mid-Atlantic Energy, Llc
717 Texas St Ste 1000
Houston TX 77002
713 830-2000

(G-10301)
CONECTIV ENERGY SUPPLY INC
Also Called: Petron Oil
500 N Wakefield Dr (19702)
PHONE..............................302 454-0300
Jerry Aunet, *Dir Fin*
EMP: 50 EST: 1980
SQ FT: 4,000
SALES (est): 27.63MM
SALES (corp-wide): 19.08B **Publicly Held**
SIC: 5172 5541 5983 Gasoline; Gasoline service stations; Fuel oil dealers
PA: Exelon Corporation
10 S Dearborn St Fl 52
Chicago IL 60603
800 483-3220

(G-10302)
CONFERENCE GROUP LLC
254 Chapman Rd Ste 200 (19702-5422)
P.O. Box 420842 (33042-0842)
PHONE..............................302 224-8255
John Riggins, *Managing Member*
EMP: 40 EST: 1999
SQ FT: 6,500
SALES (est): 6.64MM **Privately Held**
Web: www.conferencegroup.com
SIC: 7389 Teleconferencing services

(G-10303)
CONFORMIT CORP
2915 Ogletown Rd Ste 2636 (19713-1927)
PHONE..............................302 451-9167
EMP: 7 EST: 2016
SALES (est): 118.64K **Privately Held**
Web: www.conformit.com
SIC: 7372 Prepackaged software

(G-10304)
CONGRUENCE CONSULTING GROUP
Also Called: Congruence Consulting
87 Madison Dr Ste A (19711-4403)
PHONE..............................320 290-6155
Kelli Collins, *Prin*
EMP: 7 EST: 2013
SALES (est): 294.76K **Privately Held**
SIC: 7361 8742 8748 7379 Labor contractors (employment agency); Human resource consulting services; Business consulting, nec; Computer related consulting services

(G-10305)
CONJURED JEWELLS
Also Called: Iconjured
17 Oakview Dr (19702-2221)
PHONE..............................267 240-2263
Sodette Fox, *Pr*
EMP: 5 EST: 2021
SALES (est): 150.7K **Privately Held**
SIC: 3999 Candles

(G-10306)
CONNECTONS CMNTY SPPORT PRGRAM
1423 Capitol Trl Polly Drummond Plz Bldg 3 (19711)
PHONE..............................302 454-7520
EMP: 99
Web: coras.flywheelsites.com
SIC: 8322 8361 8049 Rehabilitation services; Mentally handicapped home; Psychiatric social worker
PA: Connections Community Support Programs, Inc.
590 Naamans Rd
Claymont DE 19703

(G-10307)
CONNELL CONSTRUCTION CO
808 N Country Club Dr (19711-2751)
PHONE..............................302 738-9428
David Connell, *Owner*
EMP: 6 EST: 1993
SALES (est): 423.38K **Privately Held**
Web: www.connellconstruction.com
SIC: 1521 New construction, single-family houses

(G-10308)
CONSENSUS MEDICAL SYSTEMS
131 Continental Dr (19713-4305)
PHONE..............................302 453-1969
Eileen Selph, *Mgr*
EMP: 9 EST: 2013
SALES (est): 130.75K **Privately Held**
SIC: 8099 Medical services organization

(G-10309)
CONSPIRACY THEORY LLC
200 Continental Dr Ste 401 (19713-4334)
PHONE..............................201 566-1069
Justin Flayer, *Managing Member*
EMP: 5 EST: 2021
SALES (est): 71.79K **Privately Held**
SIC: 8742 Marketing consulting services

(G-10310)
CONSULTTIVE RVIEW RHBILITATION
630 Churchmans Rd Ste 105 (19702-1943)
PHONE..............................302 366-0356
Robert Pare, *Brnch Mgr*
EMP: 11
SQ FT: 1,300
SIC: 8748 Business consulting, nec
PA: Consultative Review And Rehabilitation Inc
20 Lee Ann Dr
Blackwood NJ

(G-10311)
CONTAINER HOME FUND
200 Continental Dr # 401 (19713-4337)
PHONE..............................915 433-4817
EMP: 5 EST: 2017
SALES (est): 74.86K **Privately Held**
SIC: 5113 Boxes and containers

(G-10312)
CONTINENTAL AFRICA LLC
35 Autumnwood Dr (19711-2485)
PHONE..............................302 540-0069
Sam Nyabiosi, *CEO*
EMP: 3 EST: 2016
SALES (est): 215.28K **Privately Held**
SIC: 3612 Transformers, except electric

(G-10313)
CONTINENTAL CASE
64 Shields Ln (19702-3111)
PHONE..............................302 322-1765
James Broomall, *Owner*
Bonnie Broomall, *Sec*
EMP: 3 EST: 1986
SALES (est): 217.8K **Privately Held**
Web: www.continentalcase.com
SIC: 3161 Cases, carrying, nec

(G-10314)
CONTINENTAL CR PROTECTION LLC
121 Continental Dr # 108 (19713-4325)
PHONE..............................302 456-1930
Steve Mcsorley, *Managing Member*
EMP: 5 EST: 2017
SALES (est): 322.85K **Privately Held**
SIC: 7389 Credit card service

(G-10315)
CONTLO INC
200 Continental Dr Ste 401 (19713-4334)
PHONE..............................860 775-7179
EMP: 6 EST: 2021
SALES (est): 69.88K **Privately Held**
SIC: 7371 Computer software development and applications

(G-10316)
CONTRACTUAL CARRIERS INC
104 Alan Dr (19711-8027)
PHONE..............................302 453-1420
Karl E Schneider, *Pr*
Stephen Dawson, *
Karen Thompson, *
Joachim John Schneider, *Treas*
EMP: 27 EST: 1975
SQ FT: 2,000
SALES (est): 1.01MM **Privately Held**
Web: www.wedistribute.com
SIC: 4214 4213 Local trucking with storage; Contract haulers

(G-10317)
CONVERGETEL LLC
112 Capitol Trl Ste A (19711-3716)
PHONE..............................347 688-0922

Newark - New Castle County (G-10318) — GEOGRAPHIC SECTION

Shariq Khan, *Managing Member*
EMP: 5 **EST:** 2021
SALES (est): 32.18K **Privately Held**
Web: www.convergellc.net
SIC: 7379 Online services technology consultants

(G-10318)
CONZURGE INC
2035 Sunset Lake Rd B2 (19702-2600)
PHONE.................................267 507-6039
Jees Raj, *CEO*
EMP: 10 **EST:** 2016
SALES (est): 338.67K **Privately Held**
SIC: 7389 Business services, nec

(G-10319)
COOK PLASTERING INC
1026 Summit View Dr (19713-1124)
PHONE.................................302 737-0778
Steve Cook, *Pr*
EMP: 8 **EST:** 1994
SALES (est): 225.05K **Privately Held**
SIC: 1742 Drywall

(G-10320)
COOL CUSTOMS INC
80 Aleph Dr (19702-1319)
PHONE.................................302 894-0406
EMP: 5 **EST:** 2007
SALES (est): 190K **Privately Held**
SIC: 5012 Automobiles

(G-10321)
CORBALLIS EMERGENCY MEDICINE R
307 Ruthar Dr (19711-8016)
PHONE.................................302 224-5678
EMP: 6
SALES (est): 135.05K **Privately Held**
SIC: 8011 Freestanding emergency medical center

(G-10322)
CORDJIA LLC (PA)
131 Continental Dr Ste 409 (19713-4308)
PHONE.................................302 743-1297
Shane Flynn, *Managing Member*
EMP: 13 **EST:** 2007
SALES (est): 2.45MM **Privately Held**
Web: www.cordjia.com
SIC: 7389 Financial services

(G-10323)
CORE & MAIN LP
22 Garfield Way (19713-3450)
PHONE.................................302 737-1500
EMP: 5
SALES (corp-wide): 6.65B **Publicly Held**
Web: www.coreandmain.com
SIC: 1623 4941 4952 Water, sewer, and utility lines; Water supply; Sewerage systems
HQ: Core & Main Lp
1830 Craig Park Ct
Saint Louis MO 63146

(G-10324)
CORLO SERVICES INC
100 Peoples Dr (19702-1306)
PHONE.................................302 737-3207
EMP: 3 **EST:** 2019
SALES (est): 73.28K **Privately Held**
SIC: 2759 Commercial printing, nec

(G-10325)
CORNERSTONE GROUP LLC
273 E Main St Ste E (19711-7331)
PHONE.................................302 377-7165
Wendy Hassiepen, *Prin*
EMP: 8 **EST:** 2010
SALES (est): 226.13K **Privately Held**
Web: www.cpacornerstone.com
SIC: 7291 Tax return preparation services

(G-10326)
CORPOMAX INC
2915 Ogletown Rd (19713-1927)
PHONE.................................302 266-8200
Vincent Allard, *Pr*
EMP: 20 **EST:** 2007
SALES (est): 220.61K **Privately Held**
Web: www.corpomax.com
SIC: 7389 Paralegal service

(G-10327)
CORPORATE LOYALTY LLC
200 Continental Dr Ste 401 (19713-4334)
PHONE.................................732 455-9266
EMP: 8
SALES (est): 528.29K **Privately Held**
Web: www.corporate-loyalty.com
SIC: 8742 Human resource consulting services

(G-10328)
CORROSION PROBE
6 Verdun Ct (19702-5525)
PHONE.................................302 836-0165
Duane Edwards, *Owner*
EMP: 5 **EST:** 2019
SALES (est): 41.99K **Privately Held**
Web: www.cpiengineering.com
SIC: 8711 Consulting engineer

(G-10329)
CORROSION TESTING LABORATORIES
60 Blue Hen Dr (19713-3406)
PHONE.................................302 454-8200
Richard A Corbett, *Pr*
Barbara Corbett, *Sec*
EMP: 10 **EST:** 1984
SQ FT: 6,500
SALES (est): 1.58MM **Privately Held**
Web: www.corrosionlab.com
SIC: 8711 8734 Engineering services; Testing laboratories

(G-10330)
CORROZI FOUNTAINVIEW LLC
1000 Fountainview Cir (19713-3864)
PHONE.................................302 266-7501
Horacio Lewis Ph.d., *Prin*
EMP: 6 **EST:** 2011
SALES (est): 62.62K **Privately Held**
SIC: 8641 Condominium association

(G-10331)
CORTICALIO USA INC
Also Called: Cortical.io
40 E Main St Ste 737 (19711-4639)
PHONE.................................415 350-8588
Francisco Webber, *CEO*
Daniel Schreiber, *CFO*
Thomas Reinemer, *COO*
EMP: 11 **EST:** 2014
SALES (est): 633.49K **Privately Held**
SIC: 7371 Computer software development

(G-10332)
CORVANT LLC
131 Continental Dr Ste 409 (19713-4308)
PHONE.................................302 299-1570
Navroze Eduljee, *CEO*
Sukumar Narayanan, *COO*
Carol Lambert, *Contrlr*
Michael Frayler D.o.s., *Prin*
EMP: 10 **EST:** 2012
SALES (est): 236.78K **Privately Held**

Web: www.piervantage.com
SIC: 7371 Computer software development

(G-10333)
COUNSELING INSIGHT LLC
254 Chapman Rd Ste 208 (19702-5413)
PHONE.................................805 341-9020
Elijah Lipsky, *Managing Member*
EMP: 3
SALES (est): 128.34K **Privately Held**
SIC: 7372 Prepackaged software

(G-10334)
COUNTRY INNS SUITES
Also Called: Country Suites By Carlson
1024 Old Churchmans Rd (19713-2102)
PHONE.................................302 266-6400
Perry Patel, *Owner*
EMP: 7 **EST:** 2002
SALES (est): 447.21K **Privately Held**
Web: www.radissonhotels.com
SIC: 7011 Hotels and motels

(G-10335)
COUNTRY VINTNER LLC
Also Called: Winebow
310 Ruthar Dr (19711-8036)
PHONE.................................877 946-3620
Dean K Ferrell, *CEO*
EMP: 20 **EST:** 2011
SALES (est): 30MM
SALES (corp-wide): 518.86MM **Privately Held**
Web: www.winebow.com
SIC: 5182 Wine
HQ: The Country Vintner Inc
4800 Cox Rd Ste 300
Glen Allen VA 23060
804 752-3670

(G-10336)
COURTYARD MANAGEMENT CORP
Also Called: Courtyard By Marriott
48 Geoffrey Dr (19713-3603)
PHONE.................................302 456-3800
Jason Abbey, *Genl Mgr*
EMP: 25
SALES (corp-wide): 20.77B **Publicly Held**
Web: courtyard.marriott.com
SIC: 7011 Hotels and motels
HQ: Courtyard Management Llc
7750 Wisconsin Ave
Bethesda MD 20814

(G-10337)
COURTYARD NEWARK AT UD
400 David Hollowell Dr (19716-7448)
PHONE.................................302 737-0900
Bill Sullivan, *Dir*
EMP: 25 **EST:** 2007
SALES (est): 838.49K **Privately Held**
Web: www.udel.edu
SIC: 7011 Motels

(G-10338)
COVANT SOLUTIONS INC
220 Continental Dr Ste 314 (19713-4314)
PHONE.................................302 607-2678
Haris Koya, *Pr*
EMP: 18 **EST:** 2004
SQ FT: 1,500
SALES (est): 1MM **Privately Held**
Web: www.covantsol.com
SIC: 7371 Computer software development

(G-10339)
COVATION BIOMATERIALS LLC
800 Prides Xing Ste 201 (19713)
PHONE.................................865 279-1414
Mike Saltzberg, *CEO*

EMP: 130 **EST:** 2020
SALES (est): 25.68MM **Privately Held**
Web: www.covationbio.com
SIC: 3089 Plastics processing

(G-10340)
COX INDUSTRIES INC
111 Lake Dr Ste C (19702-3334)
PHONE.................................302 332-8470
Alan Cox, *Pr*
EMP: 5 **EST:** 2010
SALES (est): 509.7K **Privately Held**
SIC: 3449 Miscellaneous metalwork

(G-10341)
COZY STAYS LLC
254 Chapman Rd (19702-5413)
PHONE.................................424 207-0157
EMP: 5
SALES (est): 76.34K **Privately Held**
SIC: 6531 Real estate agent, residential

(G-10342)
CR&US LLC
254 Chapman Rd Ste 208 (19702-5413)
PHONE.................................678 429-6293
Issis Newcomb, *Managing Member*
EMP: 6
SALES (est): 247.57K **Privately Held**
SIC: 8742 Management consulting services

(G-10343)
CRAIG D STERNBERG MD
87 Omega Dr (19713-2065)
PHONE.................................302 733-0980
EMP: 11 **EST:** 2017
SALES (est): 68.01K **Privately Held**
Web: www.delawarebackpain.com
SIC: 8011 Orthopedic physician

(G-10344)
CRAMARO TARPAULIN SYSTEMS INC
131 Sandy Dr (19713-1149)
PHONE.................................302 292-2170
Ernie Dempsey, *Mgr*
EMP: 5
Web: www.cramarotarps.com
SIC: 5199 3089 Tarpaulins; Floor coverings, plastics
PA: Cramaro Tarpaulin Systems Inc
600 North Dr
Melbourne FL 32934

(G-10345)
CREAFORM USA INC
220 E Delaware Ave (19711-4607)
PHONE.................................407 732-4103
Charled Mony, *Pr*
EMP: 6 **EST:** 2005
SALES (est): 2.3MM
SALES (corp-wide): 6.15B **Publicly Held**
Web: www.creaform3d.com
SIC: 7374 Optical scanning data service
PA: Ametek, Inc.
1100 Cassatt Rd
Berwyn PA 19312
610 647-2121

(G-10346)
CREATIVBAR LLC
254 Chapman Rd (19702-5413)
PHONE.................................510 260-3011
EMP: 6
SALES (est): 68.89K **Privately Held**
SIC: 7389 Business Activities at Non-Commercial Site

GEOGRAPHIC SECTION

Newark - New Castle County (G-10377)

(G-10347)
CREATIVE CERAMICS LLC
112 Mccormick Blvd (19702-2128)
PHONE..................302 275-9211
EMP: 5 EST: 2009
SALES (est): 96.26K Privately Held
SIC: 1743 Tile installation, ceramic

(G-10348)
CREATIVE FINANCIAL GROUP
111 Continental Dr Ste 305 (19713-4317)
PHONE..................302 738-0888
EMP: 5 EST: 2019
SALES (est): 209.93K Privately Held
Web: www.1creative.com
SIC: 6282 Investment advice

(G-10349)
CREATIVE MICRO DESIGNS INC
645 Dawson Dr Ste B (19713-3443)
PHONE..................302 456-5800
Ralph Page, Pr
Phillip Emms, Ex VP
EMP: 8 EST: 1991
SQ FT: 3,900
SALES (est): 959.12K Privately Held
Web: www.cmdfab.com
SIC: 8748 5734 3577 Systems engineering consultant, ex. computer or professional; Computer peripheral equipment; Computer peripheral equipment, nec

(G-10350)
CREATIVE TRAVEL INC
Also Called: Rainbow Charter Service
908 Old Harmony Rd (19713-4107)
P.O. Box 30798 (19805-7798)
PHONE..................302 658-2900
Bob Older, Pr
EMP: 7 EST: 1994
SALES (est): 394.58K Privately Held
Web: www.creativetravelinc.com
SIC: 4724 Tourist agency arranging transport, lodging and car rental

(G-10351)
CREDIT LIFESTYLE LLC
200 Continental Dr Ste 401 (19713-4337)
PHONE..................302 317-1812
Tamara Holmes, Prin
EMP: 7 EST: 2017
SALES (est): 538.96K Privately Held
Web: www.thecreditlifestyle.com
SIC: 7389 Financial services

(G-10352)
CREEKSIDE COUNSELING & WELLNES
318 N Dillwyn Rd (19711-5505)
PHONE..................302 562-7953
EMP: 5 EST: 2014
SALES (est): 131.04K Privately Held
SIC: 8099 Health and allied services, nec

(G-10353)
CREEKVIEW PSYCHOLOGICAL
300 Creek View Rd Ste 101b (19711-8547)
PHONE..................302 731-3130
EMP: 5 EST: 2019
SALES (est): 131.2K Privately Held
Web: www.apsyd.com
SIC: 8049 Clinical psychologist

(G-10354)
CRIME VICTIMS CTR CHESTER CNTY
720 6th St (19711-8718)
PHONE..................610 692-7340
Beth Watson, Off Mgr
EMP: 5 EST: 2017
SALES (est): 40.38K Privately Held
SIC: 8399 Advocacy group

(G-10355)
CRIMSON GROUP LLC
17 Dubb Dr (19702-6825)
PHONE..................301 252-3779
EMP: 7 EST: 2007
SALES (est): 294.34K Privately Held
Web: www.thecrimsongrp.com
SIC: 1629 Waste water and sewage treatment plant construction

(G-10356)
CROSSFIT PETRAM
20 Shea Way (19713-3447)
PHONE..................302 345-2560
Nick Rybinski, Prin
EMP: 6 EST: 2018
SALES (est): 63.93K Privately Held
SIC: 7991 Physical fitness facilities

(G-10357)
CRUISE PLANNERS
4 High Pond Dr (19711-2597)
PHONE..................302 731-9548
Joanne Raffel, Prin
EMP: 6 EST: 2014
SALES (est): 158.9K Privately Held
Web: www.cruiseplanners.com
SIC: 4724 Travel agencies

(G-10358)
CRUISE SHIP CENTERS
760 Peoples Plz (19702-5601)
PHONE..................302 999-0202
James Devoe, Owner
Dave Devoe, Owner
EMP: 5 EST: 2001
SALES (est): 419.94K Privately Held
SIC: 4724 Tourist agency arranging transport, lodging and car rental

(G-10359)
CRYSTAL DIAMOND PUBLISHING
1 Mabry Ct (19702-2156)
PHONE..................302 737-2130
Delilah Jackson-britt, Prin
EMP: 2 EST: 2009
SALES (est): 90.27K Privately Held
SIC: 2741 Miscellaneous publishing

(G-10360)
CSI SOLUTIONS LLC (PA)
200 Continental Dr Ste 401 (19713-4334)
PHONE..................202 506-7573
Roger Chaufournier, CEO
EMP: 10 EST: 2007
SALES (est): 527.19K Privately Held
SIC: 8742 Management consulting services

(G-10361)
CSOLS INC
750 Prides Xing Ste 305 (19713)
PHONE..................302 731-5290
Kyle Mcduffie, Pr
Sandy Ahmed, *
EMP: 30 EST: 2001
SQ FT: 1,575
SALES (est): 5.69MM Privately Held
Web: www.csolsinc.com
SIC: 7379 Computer related consulting services

(G-10362)
CT PETE CROSSAN INC
420 Terrapin Ln (19711-2118)
PHONE..................302 737-0223
Michael Crossan, Prin
EMP: 5 EST: 2013
SALES (est): 120.05K Privately Held

(G-10363)
CTA ROOFING & WATERPROOFING
91 Blue Hen Dr (19713-3405)
P.O. Box 7109 (19714-7109)
PHONE..................302 454-8551
Mark Cribb, Pr
EMP: 13 EST: 2001
SALES (est): 1.95MM Privately Held
Web: www.ctaroofing.com
SIC: 1799 1761 Waterproofing; Roofing and gutter work

(G-10364)
CUHIANA CARE HEALTH SYSTEM
4755 Ogletown Stanton Rd (19718-2200)
PHONE..................302 733-1780
Anzilotti Kert, Dir
EMP: 15 EST: 2012
SALES (est): 725.13K Privately Held
SIC: 8062 General medical and surgical hospitals

(G-10365)
CURRAN JAMES P LAW OFFICES
Also Called: James P Curran
256 Chapman Rd Ste 107 (19702-5417)
PHONE..................302 894-1111
EMP: 7 EST: 2007
SALES (est): 500.26K Privately Held
Web: www.jcurranlaw.com
SIC: 8111 General practice law office

(G-10366)
CURVATURE INC
Also Called: SMS Systems Maintenance
645 Paper Mill Rd (19711-7515)
PHONE..................302 525-9525
EMP: 8
Web: www.sysmaint.com
SIC: 7378 Computer maintenance and repair
HQ: Curvature Technologies Llc
2810 Coliseum Centre Dr
Charlotte NC 28217
704 921-1620

(G-10367)
CUSTOM DRYWALL INC
Also Called: Larry's Custom Drywall
573 Bellevue Rd Ste C (19713-5801)
PHONE..................302 369-3266
EMP: 9 EST: 1990
SALES (est): 741.83K Privately Held
SIC: 1742 Drywall

(G-10368)
CUSTOM IMPROVERS INC
89 Albe Dr (19702-1321)
PHONE..................302 731-9246
Richard Altemus, Pr
Ann Altemus, Sec
EMP: 5 EST: 1979
SQ FT: 3,800
SALES (est): 699.59K Privately Held
SIC: 1522 1521 Residential construction, nec; General remodeling, single-family houses

(G-10369)
CW SIGNS LLC
812 Pencader Dr Unit E (19702-3365)
PHONE..................302 533-5492
EMP: 3 EST: 2019
SALES (est): 46.08K Privately Held
SIC: 3993 Signs and advertising specialties

(G-10370)
CYBER 20/20 INC
1 Innovation Way Unit 2 (19711-5442)
PHONE..................203 802-8742
N Macdonnell Ulsch, CEO
John Modi, COO
Victoria Kumaran, Ex Dir
EMP: 10 EST: 2015
SALES (est): 457.1K Privately Held
SIC: 7372 7389 Prepackaged software; Business Activities at Non-Commercial Site

(G-10371)
CYNTHIA L CARROLL
262 Chapman Rd Ste 108 (19702-5412)
PHONE..................302 733-0411
Cynthia L Carroll, Owner
EMP: 5 EST: 1999
SALES (est): 395.91K Privately Held
Web: www.cynthiacarrolllaw.com
SIC: 8111 General practice attorney, lawyer

(G-10372)
CYNTHIA L RAE
254 E Main St (19711-7390)
PHONE..................302 985-7069
Cynthia Rae, Mgr
EMP: 7 EST: 2017
SALES (est): 46.31K Privately Held
SIC: 8322 Individual and family services

(G-10373)
D & B PRINTING AND MAILING INC
3 Brookmont Dr (19702-4141)
PHONE..................302 838-7111
Craig Mcclintock, Pr
Ken Kerns, VP
EMP: 5 EST: 1982
SQ FT: 3,600
SALES (est): 439.49K Privately Held
Web: www.dbprinting.net
SIC: 2752 7331 Offset printing; Mailing service

(G-10374)
D & S WAREHOUSING INC
104 Alan Dr (19711-8027)
PHONE..................302 731-7440
Stephen Dawson, Pr
Monika Fulton, *
▲ EMP: 40 EST: 1970
SQ FT: 550,000
SALES (est): 4.5MM Privately Held
Web: www.wedistribute.com
SIC: 4225 General warehousing

(G-10375)
D B MECHANICAL LLC
Also Called: D&B Mechanical
13 Oakknoll Cir (19711-2491)
PHONE..................302 722-0471
Dennis Daniels, Prin
EMP: 5 EST: 2011
SALES (est): 189.85K Privately Held
SIC: 1711 Mechanical contractor

(G-10376)
D H AUTOMOTIVE TOWING
80 Aleph Dr (19702-1319)
PHONE..................302 368-5590
Dave Hudson, Pr
EMP: 8 EST: 2015
SALES (est): 451.11K Privately Held
SIC: 7538 General automotive repair shops

(G-10377)
D H GENERAL CONTRACTING
112 Kenmar Dr (19713-2432)
PHONE..................302 420-5269
EMP: 5 EST: 2011
SALES (est): 219.54K Privately Held
SIC: 1799 Special trade contractors, nec

(G-10378)
D150 FUELING LLC
150 East Chestnut Hill Rd (19713-4058)
PHONE.....................215 559-1132
Amedel Deluca, *Managing Member*
EMP: 42 EST: 2017
SALES (est): 4.97MM **Privately Held**
Web: www.d150fueling.com
SIC: 4731 2911 Freight forwarding; Oils, fuel

(G-10379)
DA VINCI PAINTING
5 Wenark Dr Apt 11 (19713-1410)
PHONE.....................302 229-0644
EMP: 4 EST: 2014
SALES (est): 154.87K **Privately Held**
Web: www.davincipaintingservices.com
SIC: 3993 Signs, not made in custom sign painting shops

(G-10380)
DAIKIN COMFORT TECH MFG LP
230 Executive Dr Ste 5 (19702-3338)
PHONE.....................302 894-1010
Matt Brubraker, *Mgr*
EMP: 6
Web: www.goodmanmfg.com
SIC: 5199 Advertising specialties
HQ: Daikin Comfort Technologies Manufacturing, L.P.
    19001 Kermier Rd
    Waller TX 77484
    877 254-4729

(G-10381)
DAIMLERCHRYSLER N AMRCA FINANC
131 Continental Dr (19713-4305)
PHONE.....................302 292-6840
EMP: 16 EST: 2008
SALES (est): 190.13K **Privately Held**
SIC: 8742 Financial consultant

(G-10382)
DAL CONTRACTORS LLC
50 Albe Dr (19702-1322)
PHONE.....................302 737-3220
EMP: 6 EST: 2010
SALES (est): 187.27K **Privately Held**
Web: dalbuilders.wordpress.com
SIC: 1799 Special trade contractors, nec

(G-10383)
DALE CARNEGIE TRAINING
220 Continental Dr Ste 205 (19713-4311)
PHONE.....................302 368-7292
Katie Iorio, *COO*
EMP: 6 EST: 2019
SALES (est): 37.51K **Privately Held**
Web: www.dalecarnegie.com
SIC: 8742 Training and development consultant

(G-10384)
DALTON PERSONAL TRAINING LLC
218 Megan Ct (19702-2814)
PHONE.....................302 266-7005
Michael Dalton, *Prin*
EMP: 6 EST: 2014
SALES (est): 60.25K **Privately Held**
SIC: 7991 Physical fitness facilities

(G-10385)
DANCEWORKS
413 New London Rd (19711-7009)
PHONE.....................302 286-1492
Amanda Pollard, *Owner*
EMP: 5 EST: 2006
SALES (est): 61.2K **Privately Held**
Web: www.danceworksde.com
SIC: 7911 5632 Dance studio and school; Dancewear

(G-10386)
DANIEL T METZGAR LLC
84 Kenmar Dr (19713-2422)
PHONE.....................302 602-4451
Daniel T Metzgar, *Prin*
EMP: 5 EST: 2010
SALES (est): 90.73K **Privately Held**
SIC: 7389 Business Activities at Non-Commercial Site

(G-10387)
DANOFFICE IT INC
200 Continental Dr Ste 401 (19713-4334)
PHONE.....................703 579-0180
EMP: 6 EST: 2005
SALES (est): 80.05K **Privately Held**
SIC: 7371 Custom computer programming services

(G-10388)
DAPHNE LLC
Also Called: Sonora
3 Chesmar Plz (19713-2461)
PHONE.....................302 525-6010
EMP: 6 EST: 2019
SALES (est): 128.58K **Privately Held**
SIC: 8621 Bar association

(G-10389)
DARLINGTON POSTAL COMPANY LLC
1217 Old Coochs Bridge Rd (19713-2333)
PHONE.....................410 917-4147
EMP: 5
SALES (corp-wide): 492.52K **Privately Held**
Web: www.darlingtonpost.com
SIC: 4215 Courier services, except by air
PA: Darlington Postal Company, Llc
    2434 Shuresville Rd
    Darlington MD 21034
    410 917-4147

(G-10390)
DATA DRUM INC
2035 Sunset Lake Rd (19702-2600)
PHONE.....................347 502-8485
EMP: 5 EST: 2018
SALES (est): 163.44K **Privately Held**
SIC: 7374 Data processing service

(G-10391)
DAVID OPPENHEIMER AND CO I LLC
Also Called: Oppenheimer Group, The
200 Continental Dr Ste 301 (19713-4334)
PHONE.....................302 533-0779
Brett Libke, *Brnch Mgr*
EMP: 35
Web: www.oppy.com
SIC: 5148 Fruits, fresh
HQ: David Oppenheimer And Company I, L.L.C.
    180 Nickerson St Ste 211
    Seattle WA 98109
    206 284-1705

(G-10392)
DAVIS & YODER CONTRACTING SERV
9 Cartier Ct (19711-5951)
PHONE.....................302 369-8888
EMP: 5 EST: 2004
SALES (est): 115.1K **Privately Held**
SIC: 1799 Special trade contractors, nec

(G-10393)
DAYS OF KNIGHTS
173 E Main St Lowr (19711-7330)
PHONE.....................302 366-0963
Daniel W Farrow Iv, *Pr*
John M Corradin, *VP*
Frank Givonnazzi, *Treas*
EMP: 8 EST: 1981
SQ FT: 3,000
SALES (est): 592.21K **Privately Held**
Web: www.daysofknights.com
SIC: 5945 7999 Games (chess, backgammon, and other durable games); Game parlor

(G-10394)
DCB APPAREL LLC
5 Rudloff Ct (19702-2863)
PHONE.....................267 473-0895
Latoya Cunningham, *Managing Member*
EMP: 3
SALES (est): 135.7K **Privately Held**
SIC: 2389 7389 Apparel and accessories, nec; Business services, nec

(G-10395)
DCMFM AT CHRISTIANA CARE
1 Centurian Dr Ste 312 (19713-2127)
PHONE.....................302 543-7543
A C Sciscione, *Pt*
Anthony C Sciscione, *Pt*
EMP: 5 EST: 2011
SALES (est): 949.74K **Privately Held**
Web: www.dcmfm.com
SIC: 8011 Gynecologist

(G-10396)
DCT
230 E Seneca Dr (19702-1932)
PHONE.....................302 420-6350
EMP: 5 EST: 2018
SALES (est): 49.08K **Privately Held**
SIC: 7922 Legitimate live theater producers

(G-10397)
DDH ADVANCED MTLS SYSTEMS INC
625 Dawson Dr Ste B (19713-3433)
PHONE.....................515 441-1313
Yulin Huang, *CEO*
Fei Deng, *VP*
EMP: 2 EST: 2013
SALES (est): 239.67K **Privately Held**
Web: www.ddham.com
SIC: 2819 Catalysts, chemical

(G-10398)
DDUBERRY LLC
200 Continental Dr Ste 401 (19713-4334)
PHONE.....................703 798-5280
EMP: 5 EST: 2019
SALES (est): 100K **Privately Held**
SIC: 4724 8742 Travel agencies; Management consulting services

(G-10399)
DE SALES AND SERVICE
1210 Janice Dr (19713-2355)
PHONE.....................302 456-1660
EMP: 4 EST: 2010
SALES (est): 193.21K **Privately Held**
SIC: 3563 Air and gas compressors

(G-10400)
DEADCOW COMPUTERS
14 Deer Track Ln (19711-2968)
PHONE.....................302 239-5974
EMP: 6 EST: 2016
SALES (est): 73.89K **Privately Held**
SIC: 2621 Paper mills

(G-10401)
DEAN A AMAN LPCMH LLC
260 Chapman Rd Ste 205c (19702-5449)
PHONE.....................302 858-3324
Dean Aman, *Mgr*
EMP: 13 EST: 2017
SALES (est): 398.76K **Privately Held**
Web: www.deanaman.com
SIC: 8322 General counseling services

(G-10402)
DEAUTHORIZED INC (PA)
2035 Sunset Lake Rd B2 (19702-2600)
PHONE.....................512 769-3026
EMP: 5 EST: 2018
SALES (est): 194.82K
SALES (corp-wide): 194.82K **Privately Held**
SIC: 7371 Computer software development and applications

(G-10403)
DEBBIE D TAKATS RN
110 Elma Dr (19711-8524)
PHONE.....................302 737-4552
Debbie D Takats, *Prin*
EMP: 10 EST: 2012
SALES (est): 179.99K **Privately Held**
SIC: 8011 Offices and clinics of medical doctors

(G-10404)
DECISIVEDGE LLC (PA)
131 Continental Dr Ste 409 (19713-4308)
PHONE.....................302 299-1570
Sukumar Narayanan, *
Ken Netzorg, *
EMP: 85 EST: 2007
SALES (est): 7.14MM
SALES (corp-wide): 7.14MM **Privately Held**
Web: www.decisivedge.com
SIC: 7371 8742 Computer software systems analysis and design, custom; Management consulting services

(G-10405)
DEDC LLC
315 S Chapel St (19711-5307)
PHONE.....................302 738-7172
Steven Krinsky, *Managing Member*
Steven Krinsky, *Prin*
EMP: 75 EST: 2010
SALES (est): 3.84MM **Privately Held**
Web: www.dedc-eng.com
SIC: 8711 Consulting engineer

(G-10406)
DEDICATED AND DRIVEN HLG LLC ◆
14 Tarcote Ct (19702-4220)
PHONE.....................404 909-6031
Janiska Nichols, *Managing Member*
EMP: 5 EST: 2022
SALES (est): 312.02K **Privately Held**
SIC: 4212 7389 Light haulage and cartage, local; Business Activities at Non-Commercial Site

(G-10407)
DEER CLIENT HAIR SALON
116 Astro Shopping Ctr (19711-7254)
PHONE.....................302 983-3353
Ann Marie Reed, *Prin*
EMP: 5 EST: 2015
SALES (est): 86.48K **Privately Held**
Web: www.deerclienthairsalon.com
SIC: 7231 Hairdressers

GEOGRAPHIC SECTION
Newark - New Castle County (G-10434)

(G-10408)
DEES LEARNING CARE
128 Auckland Dr (19702-6206)
PHONE.....................908 623-7685
Diedrean Patton, *Prin*
EMP: 8 EST: 2017
SALES (est): 56.41K **Privately Held**
SIC: 8351 Child day care services

(G-10409)
DEGUSSA INTERNATIONAL INC
220 Continental Dr Ste 204 (19713-4362)
PHONE.....................302 731-9250
Eric Dawson, *Sec*
EMP: 8 EST: 2006
SALES (est): 1.8MM
SALES (corp-wide): 2.27B **Privately Held**
SIC: 2819 Industrial inorganic chemicals, nec
HQ: Evonik Corporation
2 Turner Pl
Piscataway NJ 08854
732 982-5000

(G-10410)
DEL HARDBAT LLC
70 Aleph Dr Ste B (19702-1359)
PHONE.....................484 256-0465
EMP: 5 EST: 2016
SALES (est): 83.9K **Privately Held**
SIC: 7991 Physical fitness facilities

(G-10411)
DEL HAVEN OF WILMINGTON INC
Also Called: Jewelers of Wilmington
152 Kane Dr (19702-2801)
PHONE.....................302 999-9040
Leonard Lewkowitz, *Pr*
EMP: 9 EST: 1973
SQ FT: 2,000
SALES (est): 974.94K **Privately Held**
SIC: 5944 7631 Jewelry, precious stones and precious metals; Jewelry repair services

(G-10412)
DEL LAWN SERVICE
5 Matthews Rd (19713-2554)
PHONE.....................302 525-4148
EMP: 5 EST: 2009
SALES (est): 136.68K **Privately Held**
Web: www.dellawnsvc.com
SIC: 0782 Lawn services

(G-10413)
DEL PREMIER CARE INC
Also Called: Senior Helpers
630 Churchmans Rd Ste 107 (19702-1943)
PHONE.....................302 533-5988
EMP: 22 EST: 2019
SALES (est): 1.08MM **Privately Held**
Web: www.seniorhelpers.com
SIC: 8082 Home health care services

(G-10414)
DEL-CHARTER ASSOCIATES LP
200 Continental Dr # 200 (19713-4303)
PHONE.....................302 325-1111
Ernest F Delle Donne G, *Pt*
Ernest F Delle Donne, *Genl Pt*
Paul Jannelli, *Contrlr*
EMP: 7 EST: 1987
SALES (est): 421.83K **Privately Held**
SIC: 6552 Subdividers and developers, nec

(G-10415)
DELAWARE ADLESCENT PROGRAM INC (PA)
Also Called: DAPI
1901 S College Ave (19702-2377)
PHONE.....................302 268-7218
Deborah Bailey, *Ex Dir*
EMP: 25 EST: 1969
SALES (est): 1.52MM
SALES (corp-wide): 1.52MM **Privately Held**
Web: www.dapi.org
SIC: 8299 8099 8351 Prenatal instruction; Childbirth preparation clinic; Child day care services

(G-10416)
DELAWARE ADVANCED VEIN CENTER
40 Omega Dr Bldg G (19713-2059)
PHONE.....................302 737-0857
Anthony Alfieri, *Prin*
EMP: 10 EST: 2012
SALES (est): 100.33K **Privately Held**
Web: www.delawareadvancedveincenter.com
SIC: 8011 Physical medicine, physician/surgeon

(G-10417)
DELAWARE AUTO GLASS
810 Pencader Dr Unit A (19702-3363)
PHONE.....................302 709-2300
Michael Lattomus, *Prin*
EMP: 7 EST: 2019
SALES (est): 209.71K **Privately Held**
Web: www.delawareautoglass.com
SIC: 7536 Automotive glass replacement shops

(G-10418)
DELAWARE BACK PAIN & SPORTS
87 Omega Dr (19713-2065)
PHONE.....................302 733-0980
Gloria Payne, *Mgr*
EMP: 10 EST: 2018
SALES (est): 235.7K **Privately Held**
Web: www.delawarebackpain.com
SIC: 8011 Orthopedic physician

(G-10419)
DELAWARE BACK PAIN AND SPORTS
Also Called: Delaw Back Pain and
2600 Glasgow Ave Ste 210 (19702-5704)
PHONE.....................302 832-3369
EMP: 10 EST: 2010
SALES (est): 130.29K **Privately Held**
Web: www.delawarebackpain.com
SIC: 8031 8322 Offices and clinics of osteopathic physicians; Rehabilitation services

(G-10420)
DELAWARE BARTER CORP
Also Called: Atlantic Barter
4 Mill Park Ct # F (19713-1901)
PHONE.....................800 343-1322
Mattew Hepworth, *Pr*
Renee Skibicki, *Sec*
EMP: 9 EST: 2007
SQ FT: 1,200
SALES (est): 467.85K **Privately Held**
Web: www.atlanticbarter.com
SIC: 7389 Barter exchange

(G-10421)
DELAWARE BRACES LLC
2444 Pulaski Hwy Ste 200 (19702-3906)
PHONE.....................302 365-5971
EMP: 10 EST: 2019
SALES (est): 475.44K **Privately Held**
SIC: 8021 Orthodontist

(G-10422)
DELAWARE CENTER FOR CNSELNG
262 Chapman Rd Ste 100 (19702-5412)
PHONE.....................302 353-7052
Lisa R Savage, *Owner*
EMP: 5 EST: 2018
SALES (est): 176.16K **Privately Held**
Web: www.delawarecenterforcounselingandwellness.com
SIC: 8099 Health and allied services, nec

(G-10423)
DELAWARE CENTER FOR COUNSELING
262 Chapman Rd Ste 100 (19702-5412)
PHONE.....................302 292-1334
EMP: 5 EST: 2018
SALES (est): 155.55K **Privately Held**
Web: www.delawarecenterforcounselingandwellness.com
SIC: 8099 Health and allied services, nec

(G-10424)
DELAWARE CENTER FOR DIGESTIVE
537 Stanton Christiana Rd Ste 203 (19713-2148)
PHONE.....................302 565-6596
EMP: 12 EST: 2016
SALES (est): 1MM **Privately Held**
Web: www.usdigestivehealth.com
SIC: 8399 Advocacy group

(G-10425)
DELAWARE CHPTER OF THE AMRCN A
4765 Ogletown Stanton Rd Ste L10 (19713-8003)
PHONE.....................302 218-1075
Katie Hamilton, *Ex Dir*
EMP: 6 EST: 1975
SALES (est): 95.61K **Privately Held**
Web: www.delawarepas.org
SIC: 8699 Charitable organization

(G-10426)
DELAWARE CLNCAL LAB PHYSCANS P (PA)
4701 Ogletown Stanton Rd Ste 4200 (19713-2055)
PHONE.....................302 737-7700
Gary Witkin, *Pr*
Cynthia Flynn, *VP*
William Kirby, *Sec*
R Bradley Slease, *Treas*
Frank Beardell, *VP*
EMP: 33 EST: 1969
SQ FT: 1,000
SALES (est): 4.3MM
SALES (corp-wide): 4.3MM **Privately Held**
Web: www.christianacare.org
SIC: 8011 General and family practice, physician/surgeon

(G-10427)
DELAWARE CONCRETE SPECIALISTS
26 Kenmar Dr (19713-2421)
PHONE.....................302 507-3038
Kevin Lamborn, *Prin*
EMP: 8 EST: 2016
SALES (est): 105.25K **Privately Held**
SIC: 1771 Concrete work

(G-10428)
DELAWARE CRDOVASCULAR ASSOC PA
537 Stanton Christiana Rd Ste 105 (19713-2146)
PHONE.....................302 993-7676
Missy Henderson, *Brnch Mgr*
EMP: 5
Web: www.decardio.com
SIC: 8011 Cardiologist and cardio-vascular specialist
PA: Delaware Cardiovascular Associates, P.A.
1403 Foulk Rd Ste 101a
Wilmington DE 19803

(G-10429)
DELAWARE CREDIT UNION LEAG INC
262 Chapman Rd Ste 101 (19702-5412)
PHONE.....................302 322-9341
Patrick Mahaney, *Pr*
EMP: 5 EST: 1958
SALES (est): 254.28K **Privately Held**
Web: www.dcul.org
SIC: 8611 Trade associations

(G-10430)
DELAWARE CTR FOR MTRNAL FTAL M
Also Called: Delaware Center For Maternal
1 Centurian Dr Ste 312 (19713-2127)
PHONE.....................302 319-5680
Anthony Sciscione, *Pr*
Elizabeth A Williams, *
EMP: 38 EST: 2007
SALES (est): 9.16MM **Privately Held**
Web: www.dcmfm.com
SIC: 8011 Gynecologist

(G-10431)
DELAWARE DANCE CENTER
11 Foxtail Ct (19711-4377)
PHONE.....................302 229-9334
Jane Griffin, *Prin*
EMP: 29 EST: 2017
SALES (est): 35.66K **Privately Held**
SIC: 7911 Dance studio and school

(G-10432)
DELAWARE DANCE COMPANY INC
168 S Main St Ste 101 (19711-7966)
PHONE.....................302 738-2023
EMP: 27 EST: 1982
SALES (est): 601.71K **Privately Held**
Web: www.delawaredancecompany.org
SIC: 7911 Dance studio and school

(G-10433)
DELAWARE DEPT HLTH SOCIAL SVCS
Also Called: Hudson State Service Center
501 Ogletown Rd (19711-5403)
PHONE.....................302 368-6700
Darleissa Robertson, *Dir*
EMP: 15
SALES (corp-wide): 11.27B **Privately Held**
Web: www.delaware.gov
SIC: 8093 9431 Mental health clinic, outpatient; Administration of public health programs
HQ: Delaware Dept Of Health And Social Services
1901 N Dupont Hwy
New Castle DE 19720

(G-10434)
DELAWARE DEPT HLTH SOCIAL SVCS
Also Called: New Cstle Cmnty Mntal Hlth Ctr
501 Ogletown Rd 3rd Fl (19711-5403)
PHONE.....................302 283-7500
Neil Mclaughlin, *Brnch Mgr*
EMP: 5
SALES (corp-wide): 11.27B **Privately Held**
Web: www.delaware.gov

SIC: 8093 9431 Mental health clinic, outpatient; Administration of public health programs
HQ: Delaware Dept Of Health And Social Services
1901 N Dupont Hwy
New Castle DE 19720

(G-10435)
DELAWARE DESIGN COMPANY
Also Called: Dolphin Design & Communic
29 S Old Baltimore Pike (19702-1533)
P.O. Box 413 (19730-0413)
PHONE..................................302 737-9700
Janice Garbini, Pr
EMP: 5 EST: 1997
SALES (est): 404.71K Privately Held
SIC: 7311 Advertising consultant

(G-10436)
DELAWARE DIAGNOSTIC LABS LLC
1 Centurian Dr Ste 103 (19713-2154)
PHONE..................................302 407-5903
EMP: 45 EST: 2017
SALES (est): 2.58MM Privately Held
Web: www.deldxlabs.com
SIC: 8734 Testing laboratories

(G-10437)
DELAWARE DIY LLC
Also Called: Board & Brush
110 Peoples Plz (19702-4794)
PHONE..................................302 318-8007
James Spofford, Prin
EMP: 5 EST: 2017
SALES (est): 66.53K Privately Held
Web: www.boardandbrush.com
SIC: 7999 Arts and crafts instruction

(G-10438)
DELAWARE EAR NOSE & THROAT HEA
4701 Ogletown Stanton Rd Ste 1200 (19713-2079)
PHONE..................................302 738-6014
Robert L Witt, Prin
EMP: 5 EST: 2007
SALES (est): 429.9K Privately Held
Web: www.doctor-rlwitt.com
SIC: 8011 Ears, nose, and throat specialist; physician/surgeon

(G-10439)
DELAWARE ELEVATOR INC
2907 Ogletown Rd (19713-1927)
PHONE..................................800 787-0436
EMP: 8 EST: 2018
SALES (est): 487.46K Privately Held
Web: www.delawareelevator.com
SIC: 5084 Elevators

(G-10440)
DELAWARE ENGRG & DESIGN CORP
315 S Chapel St (19711-5307)
PHONE..................................302 738-7172
Robert Krinsky, Pr
EMP: 24 EST: 1965
SQ FT: 2,200
SALES (est): 2.4MM Privately Held
Web: www.dedc-eng.com
SIC: 8711 Heating and ventilation engineering

(G-10441)
DELAWARE EXPRESS SHUTTLE INC
Also Called: Delaware Ex Shuttle & Tours
2825 Ogletown Rd (19713-1837)
PHONE..................................302 454-7800
EMP: 150 EST: 1984
SALES (est): 5MM Privately Held
Web: www.delexpress.com
SIC: 4111 4119 Airport limousine, scheduled service; Limousine rental, with driver

(G-10442)
DELAWARE EXPRESS TOURS INC
2825 Ogletown Rd (19713-1837)
PHONE..................................302 454-7800
EMP: 14 EST: 1994
SALES (est): 1.09MM Privately Held
Web: www.delexpress.com
SIC: 4725 Tours, conducted

(G-10443)
DELAWARE FAMILIES FOR HAN
4 Vista Dr (19711-4003)
PHONE..................................302 383-9890
EMP: 5 EST: 2018
SALES (est): 71.02K Privately Held
SIC: 8322 Individual and family services

(G-10444)
DELAWARE FINANCIAL CAPITAL (PA)
22 Polly Drummond Hill Rd (19711-5703)
PHONE..................................302 266-9500
Sam Collins, Pr
Samuel A Collins Iii, Pr
EMP: 7 EST: 1997
SALES (est): 1.35MM
SALES (corp-wide): 1.35MM Privately Held
Web: www.defcc.com
SIC: 6163 Mortgage brokers arranging for loans, using money of others

(G-10445)
DELAWARE FOOT & ANKLE ASSOC
Also Called: Troisi, Ernest DPM PA
2600 Glasgow Ave Ste 101 (19702-5703)
PHONE..................................302 834-3575
Ernest Troisi, Owner
EMP: 6 EST: 1997
SALES (est): 445.92K Privately Held
Web: www.defootandanklegroup.net
SIC: 8043 Offices and clinics of podiatrists

(G-10446)
DELAWARE FREEPORT LLC
111 Alan Dr (19711-8028)
PHONE..................................302 366-1150
David Chaves Preston, Prin
EMP: 11 EST: 2016
SALES (est): 445.02K Privately Held
Web: www.delawarefreeport.com
SIC: 4226 Special warehousing and storage, nec

(G-10447)
DELAWARE FREEPORT HOLDINGS LLC
111 Alan Dr (19711-8028)
PHONE..................................302 366-1150
Fritz Dietl, Managing Member
EMP: 20 EST: 2014
SALES (est): 594.11K Privately Held
Web: www.delawarefreeport.com
SIC: 4225 General warehousing and storage

(G-10448)
DELAWARE GDNCE SVCS FOR CHLDRE
Also Called: Dgs
1 Polly Drummond Shpg Ctr (19711)
PHONE..................................302 455-9333
C Molina, Brnch Mgr
EMP: 30
SALES (corp-wide): 7.01MM Privately Held
Web: www.delawareguidance.org
SIC: 8322 Family counseling services
PA: Delaware Guidance Services For Children And Youth, Inc.
1213 Delaware Ave
Wilmington DE 19806
302 652-3948

(G-10449)
DELAWARE GDNCE SVCS FOR CHLDRE
261 Chapman Rd Ste 102 (19702-5423)
PHONE..................................302 355-0132
C Molina, Owner
EMP: 13 EST: 2017
SALES (est): 135.91K Privately Held
Web: www.delawareguidance.org
SIC: 8322 Family counseling services

(G-10450)
DELAWARE HEALTH MANAGEMENT
Also Called: Newark Chiropractic
1536 Capitol Trl (19711-5716)
PHONE..................................302 454-1200
Stacy Cohen D.c., Pr
Lydia Cohen D.c., VP
EMP: 60 EST: 1984
SALES (est): 4.39MM Privately Held
Web: www.firststatehealth.com
SIC: 8041 Offices and clinics of chiropractors

(G-10451)
DELAWARE HEATING & AC SVCS INC
11 Mcmillan Way (19713-3456)
PHONE..................................302 738-4669
EMP: 40 EST: 1994
SQ FT: 1,500
SALES (est): 2.34MM Privately Held
Web: www.delawareheatandair.com
SIC: 1711 Warm air heating and air conditioning contractor

(G-10452)
DELAWARE HOSPICE INC (PA)
Also Called: Delaware Hospice
16 Polly Drummond Shpg Ctr Ste 2 (19711-4861)
PHONE..................................302 478-5707
John Ward, Pr
Susan Lloyd, *
Sharon Leyhow, *
David Brown, *
EMP: 55 EST: 1981
SQ FT: 10,200
SALES (est): 6.31MM
SALES (corp-wide): 6.31MM Privately Held
Web: www.delawarehospice.org
SIC: 8082 Home health care services

(G-10453)
DELAWARE IMAGING NETWORK
Also Called: Papastavros Assoc Med Imaging
40 Polly Drummond Hill Rd Bldg 4 (19711-5703)
PHONE..................................302 737-5990
Thomas Fiss, Pr
EMP: 76
Web: www.papastavros.com
SIC: 8099 Blood related health services
HQ: Papastavros' Associates Medical Imaging L.L.C.
40 Polly Drummond Hill Rd
Newark DE 19711
302 652-3016

(G-10454)
DELAWARE IMAGING NETWORK
Also Called: Delaware Imaging Network
2600 Glasgow Ave Ste 122 (19702-4777)
PHONE..................................302 836-4200
Anna Allen, Mgr
EMP: 5
Web: www.papastavros.com
SIC: 8011 Radiologist
HQ: Papastavros' Associates Medical Imaging L.L.C.
40 Polly Drummond Hill Rd
Newark DE 19711
302 652-3016

(G-10455)
DELAWARE IMAGING NETWORK INC
Also Called: Mri of Wilmington
40 Polly Drummond Hill Rd # 4 (19711-5703)
PHONE..................................302 427-9855
Kakhy Tze, Prin
EMP: 62 EST: 1996
SALES (est): 2.31MM Publicly Held
SIC: 8011 Radiologist
PA: Radnet, Inc.
1510 Cotner Ave
Los Angeles CA 90025

(G-10456)
DELAWARE JUNIORS VOLLEYBALL
4142 Ogletown Stanton Rd # 229 (19713-4169)
PHONE..................................302 463-4218
Steve Lenderman, Dir
EMP: 7 EST: 2013
SALES (est): 121.38K Privately Held
SIC: 8322 Individual and family services

(G-10457)
DELAWARE LIBERIA ASSOCIATION
27 Sandalwood Dr Apt 8 (19713-4609)
PHONE..................................302 983-2536
Samuel F Kwalalon, Prin
EMP: 5 EST: 2011
SALES (est): 84K Privately Held
SIC: 8699 Membership organizations, nec

(G-10458)
DELAWARE MED CARE ASSOC LLC
550 Stanton Christiana Rd Ste 103 (19713-2131)
PHONE..................................302 633-9033
Hummayun Ismail, Prin
EMP: 5 EST: 2008
SALES (est): 496.79K Privately Held
Web: www.hismailmd.com
SIC: 8099 Health and allied services, nec

(G-10459)
DELAWARE MEDICAL MGT SVCS LLC
Also Called: Dmms
71 Omega Dr (19713-2063)
PHONE..................................302 283-3300
EMP: 21 EST: 1998
SQ FT: 2,500
SALES (est): 4.56MM Privately Held
Web: www.dmms.us
SIC: 8721 Billing and bookkeeping service

(G-10460)
DELAWARE MFG EXT PARTNR INC
Also Called: DEMEP
400 Stanton Christiana Rd Ste 154 (19713-2111)
PHONE..................................302 283-3131
Rustyn Stoops, Ex Dir
EMP: 8 EST: 1993
SQ FT: 1,000
SALES (est): 785.03K Privately Held
Web: www.demep.org

GEOGRAPHIC SECTION Newark - New Castle County (G-10487)

SIC: 8742 Manufacturing management consultant

(G-10461)
DELAWARE MODERN PEDIATRICS
300 Biddle Ave Ste 206 (19702-3972)
PHONE.................................302 392-2077
Janet Storch, *Off Mgr*
EMP: 10 **EST:** 2012
SALES (est): 692.04K **Privately Held**
Web: www.dmpkids.com
SIC: 8011 Pediatrician

(G-10462)
DELAWARE MOSQUITO CONTROL LLC
Also Called: Mosquito Joe of Delaware
4 Cobblestone Xing (19702-1150)
PHONE.................................302 504-6757
Ken Alkire, *Managing Member*
EMP: 6 **EST:** 2014
SALES (est): 467.36K **Privately Held**
Web: delaware.mosquitojoe.com
SIC: 7342 7389 Pest control in structures; Business Activities at Non-Commercial Site

(G-10463)
DELAWARE NUROSURGICAL GROUP PA
774 Christiana Rd Ste 202 (19713-4221)
PHONE.................................302 366-7671
EMP: 10 **EST:** 1996
SALES (est): 2.46MM **Privately Held**
Web: www.delawareneurosurgicalgroup.com
SIC: 8011 Neurosurgeon

(G-10464)
DELAWARE OCCPTNAL HLTH SVCS LL
Also Called: Omega Medical Center
15 Omega Dr Bldg K15 (19713-2057)
PHONE.................................302 368-5100
EMP: 25 **EST:** 1984
SQ FT: 14,500
SALES (est): 2.85MM **Privately Held**
SIC: 8099 8721 6512 Medical services organization; Billing and bookkeeping service; Nonresidential building operators

(G-10465)
DELAWARE OPHTHALMOLOGY CO
401 Eagle Run Rd (19702-1602)
PHONE.................................302 451-5022
EMP: 7 **EST:** 2018
SALES (est): 177.83K **Privately Held**
Web: www.delawareeyes.com
SIC: 8011 Opthalmologist

(G-10466)
DELAWARE ORTHODONTICS
2444 Pulaski Hwy (19702-3906)
PHONE.................................302 838-1400
Brienne Flagg, *Prin*
EMP: 11
SALES (est): 740.17K **Privately Held**
Web: www.delawareorthodontics.com
SIC: 8021 Orthodontist

(G-10467)
DELAWARE OTPTENT CTR FOR SRGER
774 Christiana Rd Ste 2 (19713-4219)
PHONE.................................302 738-0300
Cherrie Records, *Mgr*
EMP: 46 **EST:** 2008
SALES (est): 11.45MM
SALES (corp-wide): 2.54B **Publicly Held**
Web: www.dedocs.com
SIC: 8011 Surgeon

PA: Surgery Partners, Inc.
340 Sven Sprng Way Ste 60
Brentwood TN 37027
615 234-5900

(G-10468)
DELAWARE PARALYZED VETS
700 Barksdale Rd (19711-3260)
PHONE.................................302 861-6671
EMP: 5 **EST:** 2018
SALES (est): 72.73K **Privately Held**
Web: www.colonialpva.org
SIC: 8641 Veterans' organization

(G-10469)
DELAWARE PLASTIC & RECON
Also Called: Delaware Plastic & Recon
1 Centurian Dr Ste 301 (19713-2127)
PHONE.................................302 994-8492
Abdollah Malek Md, *Pr*
EMP: 10 **EST:** 1984
SALES (est): 1.34MM **Privately Held**
Web: www.thecentreforcosmeticsurgery.com
SIC: 8011 Plastic surgeon

(G-10470)
DELAWARE PREP CENTER LLC
250 Executive Dr (19702-3336)
PHONE.................................302 932-1208
Kano Alev, *CEO*
EMP: 48 **EST:** 2019
SALES (est): 3.15MM **Privately Held**
SIC: 4225 General warehousing

(G-10471)
DELAWARE PROF FNRL SVCS INC
Also Called: Strano-Feely Funeral Home
635 Churchmans Rd (19702-2917)
PHONE.................................302 731-5459
Vincent Strano, *Pr*
Joseph Feeley, *VP*
EMP: 20 **EST:** 1998
SALES (est): 1.9MM **Privately Held**
Web: www.stranofeeley.com
SIC: 7261 Funeral home

(G-10472)
DELAWARE PROPERTY MGMT CO LLC
1101 Millstone Dr (19711-1811)
PHONE.................................302 366-0208
Duncan Patterson, *Pr*
EMP: 5 **EST:** 2003
SALES (est): 100.5K **Privately Held**
Web: www.delawarepropertymgt.com
SIC: 8742 Management consulting services

(G-10473)
DELAWARE RACING ASSOCIATION
2701 Kirkwood Hwy (19711-6810)
PHONE.................................302 355-1000
Bill Fasy, *Brnch Mgr*
EMP: 300
SALES (corp-wide): 53.41MM **Privately Held**
Web: www.delawarepark.com
SIC: 7948 7993 Horse race track operation; Slot machine
PA: Delaware Racing Association
777 Delaware Park Blvd
Wilmington DE 19804
302 994-2521

(G-10474)
DELAWARE REAL ESTATE SEARCH
5 Crabapple Ct (19702-3945)
PHONE.................................302 437-6516
EMP: 5 **EST:** 2018
SALES (est): 84.36K **Privately Held**

SIC: 6531 Real estate agent, residential

(G-10475)
DELAWARE S P C A (PA)
455 Stanton Christiana Rd (19713-2119)
P.O. Box 398 (19947-0398)
PHONE.................................302 998-2281
Andrea Terlack, *Dir*
EMP: 35 **EST:** 1873
SQ FT: 3,000
SALES (est): 2.73MM
SALES (corp-wide): 2.73MM **Privately Held**
Web: www.humaneanimalpartners.org
SIC: 8699 8322 0742 0752 Animal humane society; Adoption services; Veterinary services, specialties; Vaccinating services, pet and animal specialties

(G-10476)
DELAWARE SAENGERBUND LIB ASSN
49 Salem Church Rd (19713-2933)
PHONE.................................302 366-9454
Richard Grieb, *Pr*
Crystal Coffee, *Treas*
George Schweiger, *VP*
EMP: 7 **EST:** 1903
SQ FT: 3,000
SALES (est): 628.33K **Privately Held**
Web: www.delawaresaengerbund.org
SIC: 8641 Social club, membership

(G-10477)
DELAWARE SCHOOL FOR DEAF
630 E Chestnut Hill Rd (19713-1828)
PHONE.................................302 454-2301
EMP: 60 **EST:** 2018
SALES (est): 157.06K **Privately Held**
Web: www.dsdeaf.org
SIC: 7999 Instruction schools, camps, and services

(G-10478)
DELAWARE SETTLEMENT SERVICES
930 Old Harmony Rd Ste F1 (19713-4161)
PHONE.................................302 731-2500
EMP: 7 **EST:** 1997
SALES (est): 600.47K **Privately Held**
Web: www.desettle.com
SIC: 6541 Title and trust companies

(G-10479)
DELAWARE SKATING CENTER LTD (PA)
Also Called: Christiana Skating Center
801 Christiana Rd (19713-3262)
PHONE.................................302 366-0473
Charles Wahlig, *Pr*
Constance Wahlig, *
EMP: 40 **EST:** 1979
SALES (est): 2.6MM
SALES (corp-wide): 2.6MM **Privately Held**
Web: www.christianaskatingcenter.com
SIC: 7999 Roller skating rink operation

(G-10480)
DELAWARE SLEEP DSRDERS CTRS LT (PA)
620 Stanton Christiana Rd Ste 101 (19713-2133)
PHONE.................................302 669-6141
EMP: 8 **EST:** 2006
SALES (est): 5.4MM
SALES (corp-wide): 5.4MM **Privately Held**
Web: www.delsleep.com
SIC: 8011 Clinic, operated by physicians

(G-10481)
DELAWARE SMALL BUS DEV CTR
Also Called: Sbdc Lead Center
1 Innovation Way Ste 301 (19711-5490)
PHONE.................................302 831-1555
EMP: 11 **EST:** 1983
SALES (est): 430.52K **Privately Held**
Web: www.delawaresbdc.org
SIC: 8748 Business consulting, nec

(G-10482)
DELAWARE SOC FOR RSPRTORY CARE
111 Marabou Dr (19702-4718)
P.O. Box 5951 (19714-5951)
PHONE.................................302 834-2905
EMP: 7 **EST:** 2010
SALES (est): 54.38K **Privately Held**
Web: www.delawarelung.org
SIC: 8399 Advocacy group

(G-10483)
DELAWARE SPORTS
338 Tamara Cir (19711-6929)
PHONE.................................302 731-1676
Marshal Manlove, *Owner*
EMP: 6 **EST:** 2015
SALES (est): 85.26K **Privately Held**
Web: www.delawaresports.com
SIC: 7812 Video production

(G-10484)
DELAWARE STATE EDUCATION ASSN
4135 Ogletown Stanton Rd Ste 101 (19713-4180)
PHONE.................................302 366-8440
Admiral Laura Rowe, *Brnch Mgr*
EMP: 6
SALES (corp-wide): 6.13MM **Privately Held**
Web: www.dsea.org
SIC: 8631 Labor organizations
PA: Delaware State Education Association Inc
136 E Water St
Dover DE 19901
302 734-5834

(G-10485)
DELAWARE STATE PIPE TRDES ASSN
201 Executive Dr (19702-3316)
PHONE.................................302 636-7400
EMP: 6 **EST:** 2011
SALES (est): 80.09K **Privately Held**
SIC: 8699 Membership organizations, nec

(G-10486)
DELAWARE STATE PISTOL CLUB
36 Mercer Dr (19713-1561)
PHONE.................................302 328-6836
Tom Perry, *Prin*
EMP: 5 **EST:** 2016
SALES (est): 20.78K **Privately Held**
Web: www.delawarestatepistolclub.org
SIC: 7999 Amusement and recreation, nec

(G-10487)
DELAWARE SURGICAL ARTS
537 Stanton Christiana Rd Ste 109 (19713-2145)
PHONE.................................302 225-0177
Peter Panzer, *Prin*
EMP: 5 **EST:** 2010
SALES (est): 410.96K **Privately Held**
SIC: 8011 Internal medicine, physician/surgeon

Newark - New Castle County (G-10488)

(G-10488)
DELAWARE TAX & ACCOUNTING SVCS
284 E Main St (19711-7311)
PHONE..........................302 504-4063
EMP: 5 EST: 2013
SALES (est): 68.68K **Privately Held**
SIC: 7291 Tax return preparation services

(G-10489)
DELAWARE TAX SERVICES
16 Tyre Ave (19711-7142)
PHONE..........................302 453-1040
Walt Twardus, *Prin*
EMP: 7 EST: 2016
SALES (est): 29.38K **Privately Held**
Web: revenue.delaware.gov
SIC: 7291 Tax return preparation services

(G-10490)
DELAWARE TAXES LLC
Also Called: Tax Center
14a Marrows Rd (19713-3702)
PHONE..........................302 368-7040
EMP: 7 EST: 1992
SALES (est): 233.01K **Privately Held**
Web: www.taxcenter.biz
SIC: 7291 7389 8721 Tax return preparation services; Notary publics; Accounting, auditing, and bookkeeping

(G-10491)
DELAWARE TECHNOLOGY PARK INC
1 Innovation Way Ste 300 (19711-5490)
PHONE..........................302 452-1100
J Michael Bowman, *Ch Bd*
J Michael Bowman, *Ch Bd*
EMP: 3 EST: 1991
SALES (est): 4.43MM **Privately Held**
Web: www.deltechpark.org
SIC: 3821 Incubators, laboratory

(G-10492)
DELAWARE TIRE CENTER INC (PA)
616 S College Ave (19713-1314)
PHONE..........................302 368-2531
James Baxter Junior, *CEO*
James P Walling, *VP*
James Jay Baxter Junior, *VP*
EMP: 12 EST: 1957
SQ FT: 15,000
SALES (est): 11.11MM
SALES (corp-wide): 11.11MM **Privately Held**
Web: www.delawaretire.com
SIC: 5531 5014 Automotive tires; Automobile tires and tubes

(G-10493)
DELAWARE TITLE LOANS INC
2431 Pulaski Hwy Ste 1 (19702-3905)
PHONE..........................302 368-2131
EMP: 11
SALES (corp-wide): 820.18K **Privately Held**
Web: www.delawaretitleloansinc.com
SIC: 6159 General and industrial loan institutions
PA: Delaware Title Loans, Inc.
8601 Dunwoody Pl Ste 406
Atlanta GA 30350
770 552-9840

(G-10494)
DELAWARE TRAIL SPINNERS
1013 Tulip Tree Ln (19713-1128)
PHONE..........................302 738-0177
Rick Henry, *Pr*
EMP: 5 EST: 2001

SALES (est): 94.06K **Privately Held**
SIC: 7997 Membership sports and recreation clubs

(G-10495)
DELAWARE VALLEY SAFETY COUNCIL
130 Executive Dr (19702-3349)
PHONE..........................302 607-2758
EMP: 9 EST: 2012
SALES (est): 170K **Privately Held**
Web: www.dvsconline.org
SIC: 7353 Cranes and aerial lift equipment, rental or leasing

(G-10496)
DELAWARES FINEST SERVICES
2914a Ogletown Rd (19713-1928)
PHONE..........................302 607-9288
Andrew L Anderson Junior, *Prin*
EMP: 5 EST: 2015
SALES (est): 71.48K **Privately Held**
Web: www.definestservices.com
SIC: 7699 Cleaning services

(G-10497)
DELEWARE ACUPUNCTURE
7 Greenfield Ct (19713-2003)
PHONE..........................302 273-2807
Barry Gommer, *Owner*
EMP: 5 EST: 2015
SALES (est): 58.13K **Privately Held**
Web: www.delawareacupuncture.com
SIC: 8049 Acupuncturist

(G-10498)
DELL OEM INC
705 Dawson Dr (19713-3413)
PHONE..........................302 294-0060
Guru Singh, *Pr*
EMP: 5 EST: 2017
SALES (est): 110K **Privately Held**
SIC: 5961 7389 Electronic shopping; Business services, nec

(G-10499)
DELMAR CORPORATE CLG SVCS INC
Also Called: Vanguard Cleaning Systems
260 Chapman Rd Ste 104b (19702-5410)
PHONE..........................302 861-8006
EMP: 45
SALES (corp-wide): 281.08K **Privately Held**
Web: www.vanguardcleaning.com
SIC: 8744 7349 Facilities support services; Building maintenance services, nec
PA: Delmar Corporate Cleaning Services, Inc.
913 Ridgebrook Rd Ste 104
Sparks Glencoe MD 21152
443 461-0049

(G-10500)
DELMAR TRUCKING
18 Top View Ct (19702-1623)
PHONE..........................240 353-3553
EMP: 8 EST: 2017
SALES (est): 69.6K **Privately Held**
SIC: 4212 Local trucking, without storage

(G-10501)
DELMARVA PAIN & SPINE CTR LLC
Also Called: Delmarva Pain and Spine Center
1 Centurian Dr Ste 110 (19713-2154)
PHONE..........................302 355-0900
Yogan Patel, *Prin*
EMP: 9 EST: 2017
SALES (est): 240.31K **Privately Held**
Web: www.delmarvapain.com

SIC: 8011 Orthopedic physician

(G-10502)
DELMARVA POWER & LIGHT COMPANY (HQ)
Also Called: EXELON
500 N Wakefield Dr Fl 2 (19702-5440)
Rural Route 805379 (60680)
PHONE..........................302 454-0300
David M Velazquez, *Pr*
Robert Kleczynski, *VP*
Calvin G Butler Junior, *Ch*
EMP: 97 EST: 1909
SALES (est): 1.59B
SALES (corp-wide): 19.08B **Publicly Held**
Web: www.delmarva.com
SIC: 4911 Distribution, electric power
PA: Exelon Corporation
10 S Dearborn St Fl 52
Chicago IL 60603
800 483-3220

(G-10503)
DELMARVA POWER & LIGHT COMPANY
401 Eagle Run Rd (19702-1598)
PHONE..........................302 454-4040
David M Velazquez, *Pr*
EMP: 11
SALES (corp-wide): 19.08B **Publicly Held**
Web: www.delmarva.com
SIC: 4911 Distribution, electric power
HQ: Delmarva Power & Light Company
500 N Wakefield Dr Fl 2
Newark DE 19702
302 454-0300

(G-10504)
DELMARVA POWER & LIGHT COMPANY
Rt 273 & I-95 (19714)
P.O. Box 9239 (19714-9239)
PHONE..........................302 454-4450
Wayne Yerkes, *VP*
EMP: 22
SALES (corp-wide): 19.08B **Publicly Held**
Web: www.delmarva.com
SIC: 4911 Distribution, electric power
HQ: Delmarva Power & Light Company
500 N Wakefield Dr Fl 2
Newark DE 19702
302 454-0300

(G-10505)
DELMARVA SURGERY CENTER
139 E Chestnut Hill Rd (19713-4043)
PHONE..........................302 369-1700
Frank Falco, *Prin*
EMP: 5 EST: 2009
SALES (est): 360.73K **Privately Held**
SIC: 8011 Surgeon

(G-10506)
DELMARVA SURGERY CTR
100 Biddle Ave Ste 101 (19702-3982)
PHONE..........................443 245-3470
Ray Krett, *Off Mgr*
EMP: 8 EST: 2017
SALES (est): 146.34K **Privately Held**
SIC: 8093 Specialty outpatient clinics, nec

(G-10507)
DELMARVA VOICE & INTERNET LLC
432 S Barrington Ct Ste B (19702-2177)
PHONE..........................302 496-0054
EMP: 6
SALES (est): 249.27K **Privately Held**
SIC: 4899 Communication services, nec

(G-10508)
DELT LLC
201 Ruthar Dr Ste 4 (19711-8029)
PHONE..........................215 869-7409
EMP: 5 EST: 2015
SALES (est): 203.02K **Privately Held**
SIC: 7379 Online services technology consultants

(G-10509)
DELTA ENGINEERING CORPORATION
20 Shea Way (19713-3447)
PHONE..........................302 750-1065
EMP: 6 EST: 1992
SALES (est): 270.56K **Privately Held**
SIC: 8711 Engineering services

(G-10510)
DELTRANS INC
759 Old Baltimore Pike (19702-1316)
PHONE..........................302 453-8213
Edward Lee, *Pr*
Susanna Lee, *Sec*
EMP: 6 EST: 1982
SQ FT: 10,000
SALES (est): 954.01K **Privately Held**
Web: www.deltransinc.com
SIC: 5015 5531 Automotive parts and supplies, used; Automotive parts

(G-10511)
DEMPSEYS SERVICE CENTER INC
604 Corner Ketch Rd (19711-2901)
P.O. Box 15114 (19711-0114)
PHONE..........................302 239-4996
William Dempsey, *Pr*
Warren Dempsey, *Sec*
EMP: 8 EST: 1986
SQ FT: 3,000
SALES (est): 896.6K **Privately Held**
Web: www.dempseyservicecenter.com
SIC: 7538 Engine repair

(G-10512)
DEMPSEYS SPECIALIZED SVCS LLC
Also Called: Metal Fabrication / Contractor
304b Markus Ct (19713-1151)
PHONE..........................302 530-7856
EMP: 11 EST: 2014
SALES (est): 938.84K **Privately Held**
Web: www.dssfabrication.com
SIC: 7692 Welding repair

(G-10513)
DENICES RAGGED WREATH
691 Churchmans Rd (19702-1918)
PHONE..........................302 220-7377
Denice Montero, *Prin*
EMP: 4 EST: 2017
SALES (est): 138.14K **Privately Held**
SIC: 3999 Wreaths, artificial

(G-10514)
DENTAL ASSOCIATES OF NEWARK
301 S Chapel St (19711-5307)
PHONE..........................302 737-6761
EMP: 7 EST: 2020
SALES (est): 428.55K **Privately Held**
Web: www.dentalassociatesofdelaware.com
SIC: 8021 Dentists' office

(G-10515)
DEPARTMENT PSYCHLGCAL BRAIN SC
105 The Grn Rm 108 (19716-2596)
PHONE..........................302 831-4591
EMP: 7 EST: 2016
SALES (est): 150.78K **Privately Held**

GEOGRAPHIC SECTION

Newark - New Castle County (G-10545)

SIC: 8049 Clinical psychologist

(G-10516)
DERIDE IGO
28 Findail Dr (19711-2972)
PHONE..................302 234-4121
Kevin Igo, *Prin*
EMP: 5 **EST:** 2002
SALES (est): 105.37K **Privately Held**
SIC: 3613 Distribution cutouts

(G-10517)
DESHONG & SONS CONTRACTORS INC
2606 Ogletown Rd (19713-1824)
P.O. Box 7498 (19714-7498)
PHONE..................302 453-8500
Marc Deshong, *Pr*
Ryan R Deshong, *Sec*
EMP: 7 **EST:** 1972
SQ FT: 4,500
SALES (est): 869.64K **Privately Held**
Web: www.deshongandsons.com
SIC: 1542 1541 1521 Commercial and office building, new construction; Industrial buildings, new construction, nec; New construction, single-family houses

(G-10518)
DETAIL STONE WORKS
113 Pike Creek Rd (19711-6864)
PHONE..................302 357-7065
Gabriel Gonzalez, *Prin*
EMP: 5 **EST:** 2017
SALES (est): 70.88K **Privately Held**
SIC: 7542 Washing and polishing, automotive

(G-10519)
DEVEREUX FOUNDATION
Also Called: Devereux Foundation
930 Old Harmony Rd Ste B (19713-4161)
PHONE..................302 731-2500
EMP: 41
SALES (corp-wide): 516.85MM **Privately Held**
Web: www.devereux.org
SIC: 8093 Mental health clinic, outpatient
PA: Devereux Foundation
444 Devereux Dr
Villanova PA 19085
610 542-3057

(G-10520)
DEW SOFTECH INC
200 Biddle Ave Ste 212 (19702-3966)
PHONE..................302 834-2555
EMP: 16 **EST:** 2007
SQ FT: 1,000
SALES (est): 1.35MM **Privately Held**
Web: www.dewsoftech.com
SIC: 7379 Computer related consulting services

(G-10521)
DGC PUBLISHING LLC ✪
31 Bass Ct (19713-1973)
PHONE..................302 634-0461
EMP: 4 **EST:** 2023
SALES (est): 174.89K **Privately Held**
SIC: 2741 7389 Miscellaneous publishing; Business services, nec

(G-10522)
DIAMOND CHIROPRACTIC INC
Also Called: Diamond State Chiropractic
1101 Twin Ceiling Ln Ste 201 (19713)
PHONE..................302 892-9355
Cristina Holstein, *Pr*
EMP: 10 **EST:** 2000

SALES (est): 463.56K **Privately Held**
Web: www.diamondstatechiropractic.com
SIC: 8041 Offices and clinics of chiropractors

(G-10523)
DIAMOND MATERIALS
394 S Chapel St (19713-3852)
PHONE..................302 292-1100
Richard Pierson, *Prin*
EMP: 8 **EST:** 2018
SALES (est): 497.78K **Privately Held**
Web: www.diamondmaterials.com
SIC: 1611 Guardrail construction, highways

(G-10524)
DIAMOND STATE CHIROPRACTIC
215 Upper Pike Creek Rd (19711-5955)
PHONE..................302 737-6037
Kristina Hollstein, *Prin*
EMP: 5 **EST:** 2016
SALES (est): 37.19K **Privately Held**
Web: www.diamondstatechiropractic.com
SIC: 8041 Offices and clinics of chiropractors

(G-10525)
DIAMOND STATE COUNSELING
2644 Kirkwood Highway Ste 250 (19711-7231)
PHONE..................302 683-1055
Elizabeth Bowman, *Prin*
EMP: 7 **EST:** 2016
SALES (est): 137.14K **Privately Held**
Web: www.diamondstatecounseling.com
SIC: 8322 General counseling services

(G-10526)
DIAMOND STATE FINCL GROUP INC
Also Called: Diamond State Financial Group
900 Prides Xing (19713-6100)
PHONE..................302 366-0366
Raymond F Bree, *Pr*
EMP: 75 **EST:** 1989
SALES (est): 4.82MM **Privately Held**
Web: www.dsfg.com
SIC: 8742 Financial consultant

(G-10527)
DIAMOND STATE HOMES & RMDLG
176 Starr Rd (19711-2002)
PHONE..................302 983-5574
Stephen Dicecco, *Prin*
EMP: 5 **EST:** 2016
SALES (est): 95.86K **Privately Held**
SIC: 1521 General remodeling, single-family houses

(G-10528)
DIAZ DRYWALL LLC
73 Auckland Dr (19702-4253)
PHONE..................302 602-1110
Gilberto Diaz, *Prin*
EMP: 5 **EST:** 2017
SALES (est): 75.95K **Privately Held**
SIC: 1742 Drywall

(G-10529)
DIGITAL GENERATION INC
450 Corporate Blvd (19702-3330)
PHONE..................302 368-0002
Delwin Bothof, *Mgr*
EMP: 25
Web: www.sourceecreative.com
SIC: 7311 Advertising consultant
HQ: Digital Generation, Inc.
75 2nd Ave Ste 720
Needham Heights MA 02494

(G-10530)
DIGITAL OFFICE SOLUTIONS INC
Also Called: Copy Systems
101 Sandy Dr (19713-1148)
PHONE..................302 286-6706
Annette Simms, *Pr*
EMP: 12 **EST:** 1999
SALES (est): 2.48MM **Privately Held**
Web: www.doscorp.net
SIC: 5044 Office equipment

(G-10531)
DIGITAL TECHNOLOGIES
62 Albe Dr Ste B (19702-1370)
PHONE..................302 731-1928
EMP: 5 **EST:** 2019
SALES (est): 118.92K **Privately Held**
SIC: 4841 Cable television services

(G-10532)
DILIGENT BUS SOLUTIONS LLC
1 Marra Pl (19702-5200)
PHONE..................302 897-5993
Vidyashankar Narayanan, *Pt*
EMP: 6 **EST:** 2003
SALES (est): 261.91K **Privately Held**
SIC: 7379 Computer related consulting services

(G-10533)
DINA R ANDERSON
4735 Ogletown Stanton Rd Ste 2310 (19713-2072)
PHONE..................302 623-4144
Dina Anderson, *Owner*
EMP: 12 **EST:** 2017
SALES (est): 82.44K **Privately Held**
Web: www.aawdocs.com
SIC: 8049 Offices of health practitioner

(G-10534)
DINGLE & KANE PA
356 E Main St Ste A (19711-7194)
PHONE..................302 731-5200
EMP: 6 **EST:** 1989
SALES (est): 802.96K **Privately Held**
Web: www.dinglekane.com
SIC: 8721 Certified public accountant

(G-10535)
DIRECT IMPORTER LLC
843 Salem Church Rd (19702-4015)
PHONE..................302 838-2183
EMP: 5 **EST:** 2010
SALES (est): 259.62K **Privately Held**
SIC: 5099 Durable goods, nec

(G-10536)
DIRECT RADIOGRAPHY CORP
600 Technology Dr (19702-2463)
PHONE..................302 631-2700
Peter Soltani, *Sr VP*
▲ **EMP:** 155 **EST:** 1999
SQ FT: 164,000
SALES (est): 16.67MM
SALES (corp-wide): 4.03B **Publicly Held**
Web: www.hologic.com
SIC: 3845 3844 Electromedical equipment; X-ray apparatus and tubes
PA: Hologic, Inc.
250 Campus Dr
Marlborough MA 01752
508 263-2900

(G-10537)
DISASTER RESEARCH CENTER
111 Academy St Rm 166 (19716-7399)
PHONE..................302 831-6618
EMP: 5 **EST:** 2009
SALES (est): 106.81K **Privately Held**

Web: drc.udel.edu
SIC: 8733 Research institute

(G-10538)
DISCIDIUM TECHNOLOGY INC
Also Called: Discidium Technologies
100 Cullen Way (19711-6108)
PHONE..................347 220-5979
Renee Casanova, *Pr*
Joshua Schuller, *Prin*
EMP: 2 **EST:** 2016
SALES (est): 89.23K **Privately Held**
Web: www.discidium.technology
SIC: 7379 8243 7372 7371 Computer related consulting services; Software training, computer; Application computer software; Custom computer programming services

(G-10539)
DIVINE PAINTING AND CNSTR
41 Martindale Dr (19713-2536)
PHONE..................302 983-9405
EMP: 5 **EST:** 2010
SALES (est): 76.14K **Privately Held**
SIC: 1721 Painting and paper hanging

(G-10540)
DIVINE TRANSITIONAL LIFE LLC
23 Eastwind Ct (19713-2825)
PHONE..................215 432-4974
EMP: 5 **EST:** 2020
SALES (est): 100K **Privately Held**
SIC: 8093 Rehabilitation center, outpatient treatment

(G-10541)
DKS SPORTS DEVELOPMENT LLC
24 Stage Rd (19711-4004)
PHONE..................302 222-6184
EMP: 5 **EST:** 2009
SALES (est): 120.76K **Privately Held**
SIC: 8741 Management services

(G-10542)
DNA ROOFING AND SIDING
31 Savoy Rd (19702-8615)
PHONE..................302 455-2180
EMP: 8 **EST:** 2019
SALES (est): 146.65K **Privately Held**
Web: www.dnaroofingsiding.com
SIC: 1761 Roofing contractor

(G-10543)
DO NOTHING CORP ✪
Also Called: Happypath
254 Chapman Rd Ste 208 (19702-5422)
PHONE..................216 780-1910
William Dulude, *Prin*
EMP: 5 **EST:** 2023
SALES (est): 209.21K **Privately Held**
SIC: 7372 Prepackaged software

(G-10544)
DOCTORS FOR EMERGENCY SVC PC
4755 Ogletown Stanton Rd (19718-0001)
P.O. Box 3048 (19804-0048)
PHONE..................302 733-1000
Joseph E Belgrade, *Prin*
EMP: 28 **EST:** 2002
SALES (est): 806.77K **Privately Held**
Web: www.christianacare.org
SIC: 8322 Emergency social services

(G-10545)
DOCUVAULT DELAWARE VALLEY LLC
300 Pencader Dr (19702-3342)
PHONE..................302 366-0220

Matthew Larrmore, *Brnch Mgr*
EMP: 18
SALES (corp-wide): 10.71MM **Privately Held**
Web: www.bayshoreallied.com
SIC: 4214 Household goods moving and storage, local
PA: Docuvault Delaware Valley, Llc.
1395 Imperial Way
West Deptford NJ 08066
856 853-5160

(G-10546)
DOG ANYA
918 Kenilworth Ave (19711-2638)
PHONE..................302 456-0108
Dog Anya, *Prin*
EMP: 2 **EST:** 2011
SALES (est): 93.65K **Privately Held**
SIC: 3999 Pet supplies

(G-10547)
DOG HOUSE VENTURES INC
Also Called: Camp Bow Wow
21 Grosbeak Ln (19711-8309)
PHONE..................302 738-2267
EMP: 16 **EST:** 2009
SALES (est): 962.55K **Privately Held**
Web: www.campbowwow.com
SIC: 0752 Grooming services, pet and animal specialties

(G-10548)
DON D BALCKBURN OD
317 E Main St (19711-7152)
PHONE..................302 737-5777
EMP: 5 **EST:** 2019
SALES (est): 47.44K **Privately Held**
Web: www.visionsource-newark.com
SIC: 8042 Offices and clinics of optometrists

(G-10549)
DONALD C SAVOY INC
200 Continental Dr Ste 209 (19713-4334)
PHONE..................888 992-6755
Chris Handley, *Brnch Mgr*
EMP: 10
SALES (corp-wide): 10.37MM **Privately Held**
Web: www.savoyassociates.com
SIC: 6411 6311 Insurance brokers, nec; Life insurance
PA: Donald C. Savoy, Inc.
25b Hanover Rd Ste 220
Florham Park NJ
973 377-2220

(G-10550)
DONNA D PLANCK
680 S College Ave (19713-1306)
PHONE..................302 733-7056
Donna Planck, *Prin*
EMP: 5 **EST:** 2007
SALES (est): 97.04K **Privately Held**
Web: www.donnaplanck.com
SIC: 6531 Real estate agent, residential

(G-10551)
DONNE DELLE & ASSOCIATES INC (PA)
200 Continental Dr (19713-4303)
PHONE..................302 325-1111
Ernest Delle Donne, *Pr*
EMP: 20 **EST:** 1944
SQ FT: 9,000
SALES (est): 3.41MM
SALES (corp-wide): 3.41MM **Privately Held**
Web: www.dda1.com

SIC: 6552 Land subdividers and developers, commercial

(G-10552)
DORIS HOUSE CLEANING
9 Hillstream Rd (19711-2469)
PHONE..................302 235-8239
EMP: 5 **EST:** 2019
SALES (est): 84.78K **Privately Held**
SIC: 7699 Cleaning services

(G-10553)
DOROTHY A CARROLL
Also Called: Soothing Hands
17 Millwright Dr (19711-8023)
PHONE..................302 455-0243
Dorothy A Carroll, *Prin*
EMP: 5 **EST:** 2012
SALES (est): 32.64K **Privately Held**
SIC: 7299 Massage parlor

(G-10554)
DOUG RICHMONDS BODY SHOP
Also Called: Richmonds Automotive
5 Garfield Way (19713-3457)
PHONE..................302 453-1173
Douglas Richmond, *Owner*
EMP: 8 **EST:** 1976
SALES (est): 393.86K **Privately Held**
SIC: 7532 Body shop, automotive

(G-10555)
DOUGLAS C LOEW & ASSOCIATES
248 E Chestnut Hill Rd Ste 4 (19713-3700)
PHONE..................302 453-0550
Douglas C Loew, *Owner*
EMP: 6 **EST:** 1973
SQ FT: 800
SALES (est): 413.8K **Privately Held**
Web: www.loewassoc.com
SIC: 8742 6411 Financial consultant; Insurance agents, nec

(G-10556)
DOUGLAS J LAVENBURG MD PA (PA)
1 Centurian Dr Ste 114 (19713-2154)
PHONE..................302 993-0722
Douglas J Lavenburg Md, *Pr*
EMP: 10 **EST:** 1984
SALES (est): 1.05MM **Privately Held**
Web: www.delmarvisionandcosmetic.com
SIC: 8042 Offices and clinics of optometrists

(G-10557)
DOW CHEMICAL COMPANY
Also Called: Dow Chemical
231 Lake Dr (19702-3320)
PHONE..................302 366-0500
EMP: 29
SALES (corp-wide): 44.62B **Publicly Held**
Web: www.dow.com
SIC: 2819 2821 Industrial inorganic chemicals, nec; Plastics materials and resins
HQ: The Dow Chemical Company
2211 H H Dow Way
Midland MI 48642
989 636-1000

(G-10558)
DOW CHEMICAL COMPANY
Also Called: Dow Chemical
451 Bellevue Rd Bldg 9 (19713-3431)
PHONE..................302 368-4169
Tony Khouri, *Pr*
EMP: 47
SALES (corp-wide): 44.62B **Publicly Held**
Web: www.dow.com

SIC: 2842 2297 3291 Polishes and sanitation goods; Nonwoven fabrics; Abrasive products
HQ: The Dow Chemical Company
2211 H H Dow Way
Midland MI 48642
989 636-1000

(G-10559)
DPNL LLC
Also Called: Staybrdge Stes - Nwrk/Wlmngton
270 Chapman Rd (19702-5406)
PHONE..................302 366-8097
Michelle Fones, *Genl Mgr*
EMP: 17 **EST:** 2006
SALES (est): 977.37K **Privately Held**
Web: www.staybridgesuites.com
SIC: 7011 Hotels and motels

(G-10560)
DR CAROLINE M WIECZOREK
50 Somerset Ln (19711-1902)
PHONE..................302 635-1430
Caroline M Wieczorek, *Owner*
EMP: 7 **EST:** 2017
SALES (est): 76.15K **Privately Held**
SIC: 8011 Offices and clinics of medical doctors

(G-10561)
DR DEBRA WOLF ENCORE HEALTH
19 Green Meadow Ct (19711-2583)
PHONE..................302 737-1918
EMP: 5 **EST:** 2016
SALES (est): 76K **Privately Held**
SIC: 8099 Health and allied services, nec

(G-10562)
DR DOUGLAS A PALMA MD
1096 Old Churchmans Rd (19713-2102)
PHONE..................302 655-9494
EMP: 10 **EST:** 2016
SALES (est): 68.6K **Privately Held**
Web: www.delortho.com
SIC: 8011 Orthopedic physician

(G-10563)
DR JUNFANG JIAO
179 W Chestnut Hill Rd Ste 1 (19713-2210)
PHONE..................302 453-1342
EMP: 11 **EST:** 2016
SALES (est): 106.11K **Privately Held**
Web: www.entad.org
SIC: 8011 Ears, nose, and throat specialist: physician/surgeon

(G-10564)
DR MAE GASKINS
22 Kayser Ct (19711-1519)
PHONE..................302 731-0439
Mae Gaskins, *Prin*
EMP: 8 **EST:** 2006
SALES (est): 183.44K **Privately Held**
SIC: 8011 Offices and clinics of medical doctors

(G-10565)
DR MICHELE TURLEY
300 Creek View Rd (19711-8546)
PHONE..................302 266-4043
EMP: 7 **EST:** 2017
SALES (est): 115.8K **Privately Held**
Web: www.apsyd.com
SIC: 8049 Clinical psychologist

(G-10566)
DR MONIKA GUPTA PA
314 E Main St Ste 404 (19711-7182)
PHONE..................302 737-5074
Monika Gupta, *Prin*

EMP: 5 **EST:** 2008
SALES (est): 372.47K **Privately Held**
SIC: 8011 General and family practice, physician/surgeon

(G-10567)
DR QUAN NGUYEN
1200 Peoples Plz (19702-5701)
PHONE..................302 453-1342
EMP: 7 **EST:** 2018
SALES (est): 143.72K **Privately Held**
SIC: 8011 Offices and clinics of medical doctors

(G-10568)
DR RENE BADILLO
1450 Pulaski Hwy (19702-5108)
PHONE..................301 827-1800
EMP: 6 **EST:** 2018
SALES (est): 60.66K **Privately Held**
SIC: 8011 Offices and clinics of medical doctors

(G-10569)
DRAFTING BY DESIGN INC
170 E Main St Ste 1 (19711-7318)
P.O. Box 8062 (19714-8062)
PHONE..................302 292-8304
Neil Brenner, *Pr*
EMP: 8 **EST:** 1976
SQ FT: 1,000
SALES (est): 683.88K **Privately Held**
Web: www.draftingbydesign.com
SIC: 8711 7389 Industrial engineers; Design, commercial and industrial

(G-10570)
DREAM HOME REMODELING LLC
147 Woodshade Dr (19702-1413)
PHONE..................302 981-4919
Paul Bartelt, *Pr*
EMP: 5 **EST:** 2017
SALES (est): 113.92K **Privately Held**
SIC: 1521 General remodeling, single-family houses

(G-10571)
DREAMSCAPE DESIGN CONS LLC
Also Called: Landscape Contractor
205 Roseman Ct (19711-6006)
PHONE..................302 893-0984
Alexander Woods, *Pr*
EMP: 5 **EST:** 2018
SALES (est): 28.29K **Privately Held**
SIC: 7389 1799 1741 0782 Business Activities at Non-Commercial Site; Swimming pool construction; Masonry and other stonework; Landscape contractors

(G-10572)
DRS PAHNKE PENMAN & WHITNEY
4701 Ogletown Stanton Rd Ste 1340 (19713-2055)
PHONE..................302 656-1950
Greg R Pahnke, *Prin*
EMP: 10 **EST:** 2010
SALES (est): 166.68K **Privately Held**
SIC: 8011 Surgeon

(G-10573)
DRUMMOND HILL SWIM CLUB
Alton Dr (19711)
PHONE..................302 366-9882
Ed Broadbelt, *Pr*
EMP: 6 **EST:** 1971
SALES (est): 108.05K **Privately Held**
Web: www.drummondhillpool.org
SIC: 7997 Swimming club, membership

GEOGRAPHIC SECTION

Newark - New Castle County (G-10602)

(G-10574)
DRY WALL ASSOCIATES LTD
58 Albe Dr (19702-1375)
PHONE.................................302 737-3220
David Bull, *Pr*
EMP: 60 **EST:** 1980
SQ FT: 5,000
SALES (est): 8.23MM **Privately Held**
SIC: 1542   Commercial and office buildings, renovation and repair

(G-10575)
DUHADAWAY TOOL AND DIE SP INC
801 Dawson Dr (19713-3415)
PHONE.................................302 366-0113
Robert W Duhadaway, *Pr*
Cathy Duhadaway, *
John J O Donnell, *
▲ **EMP:** 80 **EST:** 1957
SQ FT: 49,000
SALES (est): 9.62MM **Privately Held**
Web: www.duhadawaytool.com
SIC: 3544   Special dies and tools

(G-10576)
DUPONT ELECTRONICS & IMAGING
231 Lake Dr (19702-3320)
PHONE.................................302 273-6958
EMP: 8 **EST:** 2020
SALES (est): 1.29MM **Privately Held**
Web: www.dupont.com
SIC: 2879   Agricultural chemicals, nec

(G-10577)
DUPONT SPECIALTY PDTS USA LLC
Also Called: Dupont
350 Bellevue Rd (19713-3430)
P.O. Box 6100 (19714-6100)
PHONE.................................800 972-7252
Robert J Phillip, *Manager*
EMP: 50
SALES (corp-wide): 13.02B **Publicly Held**
Web: www.dupont.com
SIC: 2819   Industrial inorganic chemicals, nec
HQ: Dupont Specialty Products Usa, Llc
   974 Centre Rd
   Wilmington DE 19805
   302 992-2941

(G-10578)
DUPONT SPECIALTY SYSTEMS ✪
231 Lake Dr (19702-3320)
PHONE.................................302 273-6955
EMP: 6 **EST:** 2022
SALES (est): 612.51K **Privately Held**
Web: www.dupont.com
SIC: 2819   Industrial inorganic chemicals, nec

(G-10579)
DWK LLC
53 Cheswold Blvd (19713-4164)
PHONE.................................917 370-7106
Kashif Bookard, *Managing Member*
EMP: 6
SALES (est): 68.89K **Privately Held**
SIC: 7389   Courier or messenger service

(G-10580)
DX TECH SOLUTIONS INC
107 Carriage Wood Ct (19702-1145)
PHONE.................................302 397-3500
Maurice Butler, *Prin*
EMP: 5 **EST:** 2019
SALES (est): 112.3K **Privately Held**
Web: www.dxtechsolutions.org
SIC: 7379   Computer related consulting services

(G-10581)
DXC TECHNOLOGY COMPANY
645 Paper Mill Rd (19711-7515)
PHONE.................................302 391-2762
EMP: 5
SALES (corp-wide): 14.43B **Publicly Held**
Web: www.dxc.com
SIC: 7372   Prepackaged software
PA: Dxc Technology Company
   20408 Bashan Dr Ste 231
   Ashburn VA 20147
   703 245-9700

(G-10582)
DYGITAL TECHNOLOGY LLC
130 Peoples Plz (19702-4794)
PHONE.................................302 283-9160
Zachary Fetterman, *Pr*
EMP: 7 **EST:** 2015
SALES (est): 55.49K **Privately Held**
Web: www.dygitaltechnology.com
SIC: 7371   Computer software development and applications

(G-10583)
DYNAMIC CONVERTERS LLC
122 Sandy Dr Ste F (19713-1188)
PHONE.................................302 454-9203
EMP: 6 **EST:** 1998
SALES (est): 436.15K **Privately Held**
Web: www.dynamicconverters.com
SIC: 7537   Automotive transmission repair shops

(G-10584)
DYNAMIC PACKET CORP
40 E Main St Ste 4000 (19711-4639)
PHONE.................................302 448-2222
Robert Pedraza, *Pr*
EMP: 13 **EST:** 2012
SQ FT: 2,000
SALES (est): 617.72K **Privately Held**
Web: www.dynamicpacket.com
SIC: 8999   Communication services

(G-10585)
DYNAMIC THERAPY SERVICES LLC
Also Called: Dynamic Physical Therapy
2717 Pulaski Hwy (19702-3960)
PHONE.................................302 292-3454
Jody Riddle, *AR Specialist*
EMP: 6
SALES (corp-wide): 23.32MM **Privately Held**
SIC: 8049   Physical therapist
PA: Dynamic Therapy Services Llc
   1501 Blueball Ave
   Linwood PA 19061
   610 859-8850

(G-10586)
DYNASEP LLC
134 Sandy Dr (19713-1147)
PHONE.................................302 368-4540
Brian Waider, *Managing Member*
Mark Gruber, *Sec*
EMP: 2 **EST:** 2008
SALES (est): 18.21K **Privately Held**
SIC: 2899   Chemical preparations, nec

(G-10587)
E C I MOTORSPORTS INC
9 Polaris Dr (19711-3056)
PHONE.................................302 239-6376
EMP: 4 **EST:** 2012
SALES (est): 70.15K **Privately Held**
SIC: 2879   Agricultural chemicals, nec

(G-10588)
E I DU PONT DE NEMOURS & CO
350 Bellevue Rd (19713-3430)
PHONE.................................302 733-8134
EMP: 15 **EST:** 1915
SALES (est): 4.58MM **Privately Held**
Web: www.dupont.com
SIC: 2819   Industrial inorganic chemicals, nec

(G-10589)
E&S HOME IMPROVEMENT LLC
5 Clemson Ct (19711-4301)
PHONE.................................302 559-2340
EMP: 5 **EST:** 2009
SALES (est): 165.53K **Privately Held**
SIC: 1521   Single-family housing construction

(G-10590)
EAR NOSE THROAT & ALLERGY
2600 Glasgow Ave Ste 221 (19702-5704)
PHONE.................................302 998-0300
Michelle O'neil, *Off Mgr*
EMP: 11 **EST:** 2017
SALES (est): 123.07K **Privately Held**
SIC: 8011   Ears, nose, and throat specialist: physician/surgeon

(G-10591)
EAST COAST STAINLESS INC
22 Albe Dr (19702-1322)
PHONE.................................302 366-0675
James Adie, *Pr*
Art Adie, *Ex VP*
Debra Adie, *Ch*
EMP: 7 **EST:** 1992
SALES (est): 3.4MM **Privately Held**
Web: www.eastcoaststainless.com
SIC: 5051   Steel

(G-10592)
EAST COAST STAINLESS & ALLOYS
22 Albe Dr (19702-1322)
PHONE.................................302 366-0675
EMP: 10
SALES (corp-wide): 2.75MM **Privately Held**
SIC: 5051   Steel
PA: East Coast Stainless And Alloys Inc
   26 W Inman Ave Ste 28
   Rahway NJ

(G-10593)
EAST COAST TRANS LLC
Also Called: Transportation
2 Hidlins Way (19713-4923)
PHONE.................................302 740-5458
Clinton Perdue, *Pr*
EMP: 8 **EST:** 2010
SALES (est): 429.58K **Privately Held**
Web: www.eastcoastrans.com
SIC: 8621   Professional organizations

(G-10594)
EASTERN GROUP INC
Also Called: Trailer Parts Superstore
931 S Chapel St (19713-3419)
PHONE.................................302 737-6603
John H Hollingsworth, *Stockholder*
Tom Bidgood, *
Dorothy H Bailey, *
▼ **EMP:** 40 **EST:** 1912
SQ FT: 10,000
SALES (est): 9.13MM **Privately Held**
Web: www.easternmarine.com
SIC: 5551 5088 5091   Marine supplies, nec; Marine supplies; Outboard motors

(G-10595)
EASTERN INSULATION INC
401 Bellevue Rd (19713-3431)
PHONE.................................302 455-1400
Timothy Shelton, *Prin*
EMP: 9 **EST:** 2016
SALES (est): 168.35K **Privately Held**
Web: www.easterninsulation.com
SIC: 1742   Insulation, buildings

(G-10596)
EASTERN LIFT TRUCK CO INC
137 Sandy Dr (19713-1149)
PHONE.................................302 286-6660
Max Bielat, *Mgr*
EMP: 151
SALES (corp-wide): 193.26MM **Privately Held**
Web: www.easternlifttruck.com
SIC: 5084   Materials handling machinery
PA: Eastern Lift Truck Co., Inc.
   549 E Linwood Ave
   Maple Shade NJ 08052
   856 779-8880

(G-10597)
EASTERN METAL SUPPLY
231 Executive Dr Ste 11 (19702-3324)
PHONE.................................302 391-1370
Susie Walsh, *Owner*
EMP: 10 **EST:** 2005
SALES (est): 475.85K **Privately Held**
Web: www.easternmetal.com
SIC: 5051   Metals service centers and offices

(G-10598)
EASTERN METALS INC
679 Dawson Dr (19713-3411)
P.O. Box 674 (19701-0674)
PHONE.................................302 454-7886
Walter J Moulder Junior, *Pr*
Michael J Moulder, *VP*
EMP: 11 **EST:** 1987
SALES (est): 851.44K **Privately Held**
Web: www.easternmetalsinc.com
SIC: 1761 1541   Roofing contractor; Prefabricated building erection, industrial

(G-10599)
EASY LIFT EQUIPMENT CO INC
Also Called: Easy Lift Equipment
2 Mill Park Ct (19713-1986)
PHONE.................................302 737-7000
▲ **EMP:** 20 **EST:** 1982
SALES (est): 6.22MM **Privately Held**
Web: www.easyliftegpt.com
SIC: 5084   Materials handling machinery

(G-10600)
EAVIS AND SONS GARAGE DOORS
9 Ansonia Ct (19711-5901)
PHONE.................................302 893-3783
Amanda Eavis, *Prin*
EMP: 5 **EST:** 2016
SALES (est): 64.58K **Privately Held**
Web: eavis-and-sons-garage-doors.business.site
SIC: 1751   Garage door, installation or erection

(G-10601)
EB RENTAL LTD
2915 Ogletown Rd (19713-1927)
PHONE.................................310 951-8931
EMP: 6 **EST:** 2017
SALES (est): 65.5K **Privately Held**
SIC: 7359   Equipment rental and leasing, nec

(G-10602)
EBENEZER UNITED METHDST CHRUCH
Also Called: Ebenezer Preschool
525 Polly Drummond Hill Rd (19711-4342)

Newark - New Castle County (G-10603)

PHONE....................302 731-9495
Kathleen M Bieri, *Dir*
EMP: 10 **EST:** 1965
SALES (est): 240.44K **Privately Held**
Web: www.ebenezerumcnewark.org
SIC: 8661 8351 Methodist Church; Preschool center

(G-10603)
ECG INDUSTRIES INC (PA)
254 Chapman Rd Ste 203 (19702-5422)
PHONE....................302 453-0535
Enemute Oduaran, *Pr*
EMP: 3 **EST:** 1990
SALES (est): 659.43K **Privately Held**
SIC: 8744 4953 1799 1389 Facilities support services; Sanitary landfill operation; Petroleum storage tanks, pumping and draining; Testing, measuring, surveying, and analysis services

(G-10604)
ECHOFIN INC
2035 Sunset Lake Rd Ste B2 (19702-2600)
PHONE....................844 700-6060
Georgios Lipordezis, *CEO*
EMP: 8 **EST:** 2020
SALES (est): 300K **Privately Held**
Web: www.echofin.com
SIC: 7372 Application computer software

(G-10605)
ECO DENTAL DELAWARE
1400 Peoples Plz Ste 207 (19702-5708)
PHONE....................302 836-3711
EMP: 8 **EST:** 2020
SALES (est): 53.13K **Privately Held**
Web: www.ecodentalde.com
SIC: 8021 Dental clinic

(G-10606)
ECOTRADE GROUP NORTH AMER LLC
2915 Ogletown Rd (19713-1927)
PHONE....................302 724-6975
Valery Hamelet, *CEO*
EMP: 7 **EST:** 2014
SALES (est): 55.39K **Privately Held**
SIC: 5093 Metal scrap and waste materials

(G-10607)
ECSQUARED INC
717 Swarthmore Dr (19711-4927)
PHONE....................302 750-8554
Edward Crowder, *Pr*
Eric Christy, *VP*
EMP: 5 **EST:** 2007
SALES (est): 488.81K **Privately Held**
Web: www.ecsquared.net
SIC: 8742 Hospital and health services consultant

(G-10608)
EDGE FITNESS LLC
2800 Fashion Center Blvd (19702-3251)
PHONE....................302 613-0721
EMP: 7 **EST:** 2019
SALES (est): 107.85K **Privately Held**
Web: www.theedgefitnessclubs.com
SIC: 7991 Health club

(G-10609)
EDISON TRNSPT & LOGISTICS INC
200 Continental Dr Ste 401 (19713-4334)
PHONE....................302 332-6878
Edison Mcpherson, *Asst Sec*
EMP: 8 **EST:** 2018
SALES (est): 241.78K **Privately Held**
Web: www.edison-transport.com
SIC: 4789 Transportation services, nec

(G-10610)
EDMONDS BUSINESS VENTURES LLC
98 S Skyward Dr (19713-2844)
PHONE....................302 772-9112
EMP: 7 **EST:** 2019
SALES (est): 450K **Privately Held**
SIC: 7389 8742 Business services, nec; Management consulting services

(G-10611)
EDS ROAD SERVICE INC
1000 Dawson Dr Ste B (19713-5805)
PHONE....................302 437-4103
William Bishop, *Pr*
EMP: 6 **EST:** 2011
SALES (est): 104.94K **Privately Held**
SIC: 8999 Services, nec

(G-10612)
EDWARD VARNES HARDWOOD FLOORS
634 Old Baltimore Pike (19702-1311)
PHONE....................302 292-0919
Edward Varnes, *Pr*
EMP: 10 **EST:** 1990
SALES (est): 738.12K **Privately Held**
Web: www.edvarnes.com
SIC: 1752 Wood floor installation and refinishing

(G-10613)
EDWIN C KATZMAN MD
Also Called: Kids First Newark
210 Christiana Med Ctr (19702-1652)
PHONE....................302 368-2501
Edwin C Katzman Md, *Prin*
EMP: 5 **EST:** 1968
SALES (est): 491.11K **Privately Held**
SIC: 8011 Pediatrician

(G-10614)
EDWIN S KUIPERS DDS
210 W Park Pl (19711-4519)
PHONE....................302 455-0333
Edwin S Kuipers, *Prin*
EMP: 9 **EST:** 2018
SALES (est): 169.24K **Privately Held**
Web: www.thedentalgroupofdelaware.com
SIC: 8021 Dentists' office

(G-10615)
EF TECHNOLOGIES INC
119b Sandy Dr (19713-1148)
PHONE....................302 451-1088
EMP: 7 **EST:** 1996
SQ FT: 5,000
SALES (est): 1.38MM **Privately Held**
Web: www.eft-inc.com
SIC: 3679 Electronic circuits

(G-10616)
EIDP INC
Also Called: Haskell Laboratory
1090 Elkton Rd (19711-3507)
PHONE....................302 366-5763
Carol Ashman, *Mgr*
EMP: 5
SALES (corp-wide): 17.23B **Publicly Held**
Web: www.dupont.com
SIC: 2813 Industrial gases
HQ: Eidp, Inc.
9330 Zionsville Rd
Indianapolis IN 46268
833 267-8382

(G-10617)
EIDP INC
Also Called: Dupont
6 Meteor Ln (19711-3042)
PHONE....................302 239-9424
Ram Kahanna, *Brnch Mgr*
EMP: 5
SALES (corp-wide): 17.23B **Publicly Held**
Web: www.dupont.com
SIC: 2819 Industrial inorganic chemicals, nec
HQ: Eidp, Inc.
9330 Zionsville Rd
Indianapolis IN 46268
833 267-8382

(G-10618)
EIDP INC
Also Called: Dupont Stine Haskell RES Ctr
1090 Elkton Rd (19711-3507)
PHONE....................302 366-5583
Chuck Corrigan, *Prin*
EMP: 5
SALES (corp-wide): 17.45B **Publicly Held**
Web: www.dupont.com
SIC: 2819 Industrial inorganic chemicals, nec
HQ: Eidp, Inc.
9330 Zionsville Rd
Indianapolis IN 46268
833 267-8382

(G-10619)
EIDP INC
Also Called: Dupont
1090 Elkton Rd (19711-3507)
P.O. Box 30 (19714-0030)
PHONE....................302 266-7101
Debbie Carman, *Prin*
EMP: 30
SALES (corp-wide): 17.23B **Publicly Held**
Web: www.dupont.com
SIC: 2819 Industrial inorganic chemicals, nec
HQ: Eidp, Inc.
9330 Zionsville Rd
Indianapolis IN 46268
833 267-8382

(G-10620)
EIDP INC
Also Called: Dupont
242 Chapman Rd (19702-5405)
P.O. Box 8255 (19714-8255)
PHONE....................302 452-9000
EMP: 10
SALES (corp-wide): 17.23B **Publicly Held**
Web: www.dupont.com
SIC: 2911 Petroleum refining
HQ: Eidp, Inc.
9330 Zionsville Rd
Indianapolis IN 46268
833 267-8382

(G-10621)
EINSTEIN TECHNOLOGIES LLC
Also Called: Einstein Lighting
2035 Sunset Lake Rd B2 (19702-2600)
PHONE....................407 614-7404
EMP: 5 **EST:** 2019
SALES (est): 77.06K **Privately Held**
SIC: 7379 Computer related consulting services

(G-10622)
ELECTRANET ENTERPRISES
4 Belfort Loop (19702-5526)
PHONE....................302 309-8320
EMP: 5 **EST:** 2019
SALES (est): 82.95K **Privately Held**
SIC: 7379 Computer related consulting services

(G-10623)
ELECTRONIC SYSTEMS SPECIALIST
Bldg 16 Polly Drummond Shp Ctr C (19711)
PHONE....................302 738-4165
Matthew Kearns, *Pr*
EMP: 6 **EST:** 1988
SALES (est): 520.15K **Privately Held**
SIC: 1731 Electrical work

(G-10624)
ELEGANT EXTERIORS LLC
47 Wedgewood Rd (19711-2055)
PHONE....................302 218-8378
EMP: 6 **EST:** 2016
SALES (est): 185.26K **Privately Held**
SIC: 1522 Residential construction, nec

(G-10625)
ELEMENTICE INC
2035 Sunset Lake Rd B2 (19702-2600)
PHONE....................302 444-5406
Peter Presneill, *CEO*
EMP: 5 **EST:** 2020
SALES (est): 378.41K **Privately Held**
SIC: 5043 7335 Photographic processing equipment; Photographic studio, commercial

(G-10626)
ELICIN EDELINE
260 Chapman Rd Ste 100b (19702-5410)
PHONE....................973 687-9930
Edeline Elicin, *Owner*
EMP: 7 **EST:** 2018
SALES (est): 32.92K **Privately Held**
SIC: 8322 Individual and family services

(G-10627)
ELITE CHEMICAL AND SUPPLY INC
630 Churchmans Rd Ste 106 (19702-1943)
PHONE....................302 366-8900
Sheryl Ecton, *Prin*
EMP: 6 **EST:** 2011
SALES (est): 62.39K **Privately Held**
SIC: 7699 Cleaning services

(G-10628)
ELITE COMMERCIAL CLEANING INC
Also Called: Elite Cleaning Company
630 Churchmans Rd Ste 106 (19702-1943)
PHONE....................302 366-8900
EMP: 60 **EST:** 2011
SALES (est): 697.19K **Privately Held**
SIC: 7349 Janitorial service, contract basis

(G-10629)
ELITE FACILITY SERVICES LLC
200 Continental Dr Ste 401 (19713-4337)
PHONE....................302 566-7031
EMP: 70 **EST:** 2021
SALES (est): 2.42MM **Privately Held**
SIC: 4173 7349 Maintenance facilities, buses; Janitorial service, contract basis

(G-10630)
ELKTON EXTERMINATING CO INC
1040 S Chapel St (19702-1303)
PHONE....................302 368-9116
Philip Kreer, *Prin*
EMP: 8
SALES (corp-wide): 958.85K **Privately Held**
SIC: 7342 Pest control in structures
PA: Elkton Exterminating Company, Inc.
913 N Bridge St
Elkton MD 21921
410 398-4378

GEOGRAPHIC SECTION

Newark - New Castle County (G-10659)

(G-10631)
ELLINGSEN & ASSOCIATES
113 Barksdale Professional Ctr (19711-3258)
PHONE.............................302 650-6437
Mary Ellingsen, Owner
EMP: 6 EST: 1986
SALES (est): 117.74K Privately Held
Web: www.onlinespeechtherapy.com
SIC: 8049 Speech therapist

(G-10632)
ELMS MANAGEMENT ASSOCIATION
2201 London Way (19713-4407)
PHONE.............................302 738-5225
EMP: 5 EST: 2012
SALES (est): 172.68K Privately Held
SIC: 8611 Business associations

(G-10633)
ELS TIRE SERVICE INC
2724 Pulaski Hwy (19702-3911)
PHONE.............................302 834-1997
El Van Blarcom, Pr
Joyce Van Blarcom, VP
EMP: 15 EST: 1977
SQ FT: 5,200
SALES (est): 1.75MM Privately Held
Web: www.elstireservice.com
SIC: 5531 5014 7539 Automotive tires; Truck tires and tubes; Automotive repair shops, nec

(G-10634)
ELSICON INC
5 Innovation Way Ste 100 (19711-5459)
PHONE.............................302 266-7030
Shao-tang Sun, Pr
Wayne Gibbons, Dir Opers
Eric Fahnoe, Dir Fin
EMP: 6 EST: 1997
SQ FT: 14,000
SALES (est): 224.38K Privately Held
Web: www.elsicon.com
SIC: 5049 Optical goods

(G-10635)
ELUKTRONICS INC
9 Albe Dr Ste E (19702-1380)
PHONE.............................302 380-3242
William Kiryluk, CEO
▲ EMP: 8 EST: 2011
SQ FT: 7,920
SALES (est): 4.88MM Privately Held
Web: www.eluktronics.com
SIC: 5045 Computers, peripherals, and software

(G-10636)
EM BEAUTY BAR INC
24 Prestbury Sq (19713-2609)
PHONE.............................302 525-3933
EMP: 5 EST: 2019
SALES (est): 186.17K Privately Held
Web: www.embeautybar.net
SIC: 8621 Bar association

(G-10637)
EM PHOTONICS INC
51 E Main St Ste 203 (19711-4685)
PHONE.............................302 456-9003
Eric Kelmelis, CEO
Dennis Prather, Pr
EMP: 15 EST: 2001
SQ FT: 1,500
SALES (est): 1.57MM Privately Held
Web: www.emphotonics.com
SIC: 8711 Electrical or electronic engineering

(G-10638)
EMBLEM AT CHRISTIANA CLUBHOUSE
1150 Helen Dr (19702-1650)
PHONE.............................302 525-6692
EMP: 6 EST: 2017
SALES (est): 87.86K Privately Held
Web: www.emblemapt.com
SIC: 7997 Membership sports and recreation clubs

(G-10639)
EMBRACE CHANGE LLC
179 W Chestnut Hill Rd Ste 6 (19713-2210)
PHONE.............................302 286-5288
Luz Del Alba Reynoso, Prin
EMP: 7 EST: 2017
SALES (est): 54.68K Privately Held
SIC: 8322 General counseling services

(G-10640)
EMBRACE THE CHANGE COUNSELING
179 W Chestnut Hill Rd Ste 6 (19713-2210)
PHONE.............................302 358-6237
EMP: 5 EST: 2015
SALES (est): 84.47K Privately Held
SIC: 8322 General counseling services

(G-10641)
EMERICK CONSTRUCTION GROUP LLC
3205 Frazer Rd (19702-4901)
PHONE.............................302 547-0715
Stacia Emerick, Prin
EMP: 5 EST: 2018
SALES (est): 98.74K Privately Held
Web: www.emerick.com
SIC: 1521 Single-family housing construction

(G-10642)
EMPATHY HOME CARE LLC
57 Anglin Dr (19713-4012)
PHONE.............................302 722-1538
EMP: 6 EST: 2016
SALES (est): 54.34K Privately Held
SIC: 8082 Home health care services

(G-10643)
EMPIRE REALTY MANAGEMENT INC
54 Cheswold Blvd (19713-4178)
PHONE.............................302 731-0784
EMP: 5 EST: 2010
SALES (est): 126.49K Privately Held
SIC: 8741 Management services

(G-10644)
ENCOMPASS ACCOUNTING
523 Capitol Trl (19711-3859)
PHONE.............................302 648-5488
Ryan Walsh, Prin
EMP: 6 EST: 2017
SALES (est): 290.17K Privately Held
Web: www.encompassde.com
SIC: 8721 Accounting, auditing, and bookkeeping

(G-10645)
ENCORE DANCE ACADEMY
1150 Capitol Trl (19711-3933)
PHONE.............................302 824-9669
EMP: 6 EST: 2016
SALES (est): 126.69K Privately Held
Web: www.encoredanceacademyde.com
SIC: 7911 Dance studio and school

(G-10646)
ENDLESS PSSBLTIES IN THE CMNTY
54 Winslow Rd (19711-5210)
PHONE.............................302 528-4503
Teresa Hancharick, Pr
EMP: 5 EST: 2017
SALES (est): 99.47K Privately Held
SIC: 8399 Community development groups

(G-10647)
ENDOSCOPY CENTER OF DELAWARE
Also Called: Endoscopy Center of Delaware
1090 Old Churchmans Rd (19713-2102)
PHONE.............................302 892-2710
Joseph S Hacker Iii, Pr
Donald Girard Md, VP
Warren G Butt Md, Sec
George Benes Md, Treas
EMP: 25 EST: 1994
SALES (est): 15.39MM Privately Held
Web: www.endoscopycenterofdelaware.com
SIC: 8062 General medical and surgical hospitals

(G-10648)
ENHANCED CORPORATE PRFMCE LLC
Also Called: McCoy Enterprises
1 Morning Glen Ln (19711-4396)
P.O. Box 5338 (08096-0338)
PHONE.............................302 545-8541
EMP: 6 EST: 2004
SALES (est): 103.43K Privately Held
SIC: 8299 8742 Educational services; Training and development consultant

(G-10649)
ENHANCED HEATING & AC
68 Albe Dr (19702-1322)
PHONE.............................302 836-1921
EMP: 5 EST: 2020
SALES (est): 82.72K Privately Held
Web: www.enhancedheatingandair.net
SIC: 1711 Warm air heating and air conditioning contractor

(G-10650)
ENS LOGISTICS LLC
39 O Rourke Ct (19702-6845)
PHONE.............................302 784-5155
EMP: 5 EST: 2019
SALES (est): 73.24K Privately Held
SIC: 4731 Freight forwarding

(G-10651)
ENT AND ALLERGY DELAWARE LLC (PA)
Also Called: Silverside Medical Center
700 Prides Xing Ste 200 (19713-6109)
PHONE.............................302 478-8467
Rob Goss, Prin
Nurse Practitioner, Prin
EMP: 7 EST: 2010
SALES (est): 5.07MM
SALES (corp-wide): 5.07MM Privately Held
Web: www.entad.org
SIC: 8011 Ears, nose, and throat specialist: physician/surgeon

(G-10652)
ENTERPRISE LSG PHILADELPHIA LLC
Also Called: Enterprise Rent-A-Car
409 E Cleveland Ave (19711-3714)
PHONE.............................302 266-7777
EMP: 6
SALES (corp-wide): 7.04B Privately Held
Web: www.enterprise.com
SIC: 7514 Rent-a-car service
HQ: Enterprise Leasing Company Of Philadelphia, Llc
2434 W Main St 2436
Norristown PA 19403

(G-10653)
ENTERPRISE LSG PHLADELPHIA LLC
Also Called: Enterprise Rent-A-Car
430 Newark Shopping Ctr (19711-7304)
PHONE.............................302 292-0524
EMP: 7
SALES (corp-wide): 7.04B Privately Held
Web: www.enterprise.com
SIC: 7514 Rent-a-car service
HQ: Enterprise Leasing Company Of Philadelphia, Llc
2434 W Main St 2436
Norristown PA 19403

(G-10654)
ENTERPRISE RENT A CAR
2405 Pulaski Hwy (19702-3905)
PHONE.............................302 454-2939
EMP: 6 EST: 2018
SALES (est): 146.77K Privately Held
Web: www.enterprise.com
SIC: 7514 Rent-a-car service

(G-10655)
ENTERTAINMENT FACTORY
810 Broadfield Dr (19713-2726)
PHONE.............................302 824-1428
Matthew Wright, Prin
EMP: 5 EST: 2010
SALES (est): 56.7K Privately Held
Web: entertainmentfactory.yolasite.com
SIC: 7929 Disc jockey service

(G-10656)
ENVISION INFOSOLUTIONS INC
260 Chapman Rd Ste 204d (19702-5491)
PHONE.............................302 565-4289
Aswitha Vempati, Pr
EMP: 25 EST: 2014
SQ FT: 420
SALES (est): 1.26MM Privately Held
Web: www.envisioninfosolutions.com
SIC: 7371 Custom computer programming services

(G-10657)
ENVOY FLIGHT SYSTEMS INC
201 Ruthar Dr Ste 3 (19711-8029)
PHONE.............................302 738-1788
Jason Amato, Prin
EMP: 2 EST: 2013
SQ FT: 2,000
SALES (est): 85.98K Privately Held
SIC: 3728 R and D by manuf., aircraft parts and auxiliary equipment

(G-10658)
EONSCOPE INC
2035 Sunset Lake Rd B2 (19702-2600)
PHONE.............................312 319-4484
EMP: 6 EST: 2018
SALES (est): 94.33K Privately Held
Web: www.eonscope.com
SIC: 7371 Computer software development and applications

(G-10659)
EPEIUS CONTRACTING SERVICE LLC
30 Windy Ct (19713-2821)
PHONE.............................302 533-8753
Daniel Baker, Prin
EMP: 5 EST: 2018
SALES (est): 142.91K Privately Held

Newark - New Castle County (G-10660) — GEOGRAPHIC SECTION

SIC: 1799 Special trade contractors, nec

(G-10660)
EQUINOX CLEANING LLC
520 Capitol Trl (19711-3867)
PHONE..................240 419-9077
Sherry L Hall, *Prin*
EMP: 5 EST: 2019
SALES (est): 62.32K **Privately Held**
SIC: 7699 Cleaning services

(G-10661)
EQUINOX LLC
131 King William St (19711-2546)
PHONE..................856 364-5615
David Yetter, *Prin*
EMP: 5 EST: 2016
SALES (est): 56.74K **Privately Held**
SIC: 7991 Health club

(G-10662)
ER AT HOME LLC
11 Christina Woods Ct Ste B (19702-2724)
PHONE..................540 845-9499
Isaac K Otu Junior, *Prin*
EMP: 8 EST: 2016
SALES (est): 96.95K **Privately Held**
Web: www.careforcemd.com
SIC: 8099 Health and allied services, nec

(G-10663)
ERIC BARSKY
19 Autumnwood Dr (19711-6218)
PHONE..................856 495-6988
Eric Barsky, *Mgr*
EMP: 6 EST: 2017
SALES (est): 72.33K **Privately Held**
SIC: 8049 Offices of health practitioner

(G-10664)
ERICKSON MANAGEMENT
447 Coldspring Run (19711-2466)
PHONE..................302 235-0855
Thomas Erickson, *Prin*
EMP: 6 EST: 2013
SALES (est): 99.31K **Privately Held**
SIC: 8741 Management services

(G-10665)
ERIN N MACKO DDS LLC
625 Barksdale Rd Ste 101 (19711-4535)
PHONE..................302 368-7463
Erin N Macko D.d.s., *Prin*
EMP: 10 EST: 2016
SALES (est): 242.6K **Privately Held**
Web: www.thenewarkdentist.com
SIC: 8021 Offices and clinics of dentists

(G-10666)
ESOURCE SYSTEMS LLC
750 Barksdale Rd Ste 4 (19711-3245)
PHONE..................302 444-4228
EMP: 7 EST: 2013
SALES (est): 49.93K **Privately Held**
SIC: 7389 Design services

(G-10667)
ESTATE SERVICING LLC
901 Barksdale Rd (19711-3205)
PHONE..................302 731-1119
George Zielinski, *Prin*
EMP: 2 EST: 2008
SALES (est): 83.26K **Privately Held**
SIC: 1389 Roustabout service

(G-10668)
ESWAP GLOBAL INC
2035 Sunset Lake Rd (19702-2600)
PHONE..................323 244-2927
EMP: 5

SALES (est): 46.16K **Privately Held**
Web: www.eswap.global
SIC: 7371 Computer software development

(G-10669)
ETAILFLOW LLC ✪
1800 Ogletown Rd Ste B (19711-5474)
PHONE..................302 894-8862
Charles Zhang, *CEO*
EMP: 30 EST: 2023
SALES (est): 2.95MM **Privately Held**
SIC: 5045 Computers, peripherals, and software

(G-10670)
ETEKSERVE INC
100 Biddle Ave Ste 201 (19702-3983)
PHONE..................302 497-4301
EMP: 5 EST: 2021
SALES (est): 68.89K **Privately Held**
SIC: 7389 Business services, nec

(G-10671)
ETS & YCP LLC
113 Barksdale Professional Ctr (19711-3258)
PHONE..................302 525-4111
Tommie Price, *Managing Member*
EMP: 5 EST: 2009
SALES (est): 301.37K **Privately Held**
Web: www.ets-de.com
SIC: 7379 Computer related consulting services

(G-10672)
EUROPEAN WAX CENTER
3162 Fashion Center Blvd (19702-3246)
PHONE..................302 731-2700
EMP: 5 EST: 2018
SALES (est): 149.65K **Privately Held**
Web: locations.waxcenter.com
SIC: 7231 Cosmetology and personal hygiene salons

(G-10673)
EUROPLISH PRCSION FNSHG USA IN
112 Capitol Trl (19711-3716)
PHONE..................302 451-9241
EMP: 6 EST: 2021
SALES (est): 175.43K **Privately Held**
Web: www.europolish.com
SIC: 3471 Cleaning, polishing, and finishing

(G-10674)
EV FLUX INC
2035 Sunset Lake Rd B2 (19702-2600)
PHONE..................510 880-3737
Andrew Krulewitz, *CEO*
EMP: 5 EST: 2018
SALES (est): 150K **Privately Held**
SIC: 6159 Equipment and vehicle finance leasing companies

(G-10675)
EV GG1 LLC ✪
254 Chapman Rd (19702-5413)
PHONE..................313 269-4175
Terry Garvin, *Managing Member*
EMP: 9 EST: 2023
SALES (est): 565.14K **Privately Held**
SIC: 3624 Electric carbons

(G-10676)
EVEREST AUTO REPAIR LLC
690 Capitol Trl (19711-3869)
PHONE..................302 737-8424
Marykay Mills, *Prin*
EMP: 7 EST: 2011
SALES (est): 225.76K **Privately Held**

Web: www.everestautorepair.com
SIC: 7538 General automotive repair shops

(G-10677)
EVEREST AUTOWORKS AUTO SPA LLC
690 Kirkwood Hwy (19711)
PHONE..................302 737-8424
EMP: 5 EST: 2005
SALES (est): 458.67K **Privately Held**
Web: www.everestautorepair.com
SIC: 7538 General automotive repair shops

(G-10678)
EVERNEX USA INC
2915 Ogletown Rd Ste 1844 (19713-1927)
PHONE..................888 630-9396
Bruno Demolin, *CEO*
EMP: 450 EST: 2015
SALES (est): 8.22MM **Privately Held**
SIC: 7379 Computer hardware requirements analysis

(G-10679)
EVOLVE BANK & TRUST
220 Continental Dr Ste 215 (19713-4312)
PHONE..................302 286-7838
Jesse Mcconnell, *Brnch Mgr*
EMP: 16
SALES (corp-wide): 67.78MM **Privately Held**
Web: www.getevolved.com
SIC: 6162 Mortgage bankers and loan correspondents
PA: Evolve Bank & Trust
    6000 Poplar Ave Ste 300
    Memphis TN 38119
    901 624-5500

(G-10680)
EWE-NITED STATES OF FIBER
512 Benham Ct (19711-6014)
PHONE..................302 690-5084
EMP: 3 EST: 2015
SALES (est): 98.32K **Privately Held**
SIC: 2389 Apparel and accessories, nec

(G-10681)
EWINGS TOWING SERVICE INC
30 Aleph Dr (19702-1319)
PHONE..................302 366-8806
Kevin Cox, *Pr*
Joe Reilly, *VP*
Dale Duncan, *Dir*
EMP: 8 EST: 1980
SALES (est): 849.72K **Privately Held**
Web: www.ewingtowing.net
SIC: 7549 7539 Towing service, automotive; Automotive repair shops, nec

(G-10682)
EXAM MASTER CORPORATION
100 Lake Dr Ste 6 (19702-3346)
P.O. Box 9326 (19714-9326)
PHONE..................800 572-3627
EMP: 23 EST: 1994
SALES (est): 3.8MM **Privately Held**
Web: www.exammaster.com
SIC: 8099 Physical examination and testing services

(G-10683)
EXCEL BUSINESS SYSTEMS INC (PA)
201 Ruthar Dr Ste 10 (19711-8029)
PHONE..................302 453-1500
Frank Montisano, *Pr*
Joseph Di Marco, *VP*
EMP: 23 EST: 1984
SQ FT: 5,500

SALES (est): 5.3MM
SALES (corp-wide): 5.3MM **Privately Held**
Web: www.exceldigital.com
SIC: 5999 7629 Business machines and equipment; Business machine repair, electric

(G-10684)
EXCELLENT EDUCATN DAYCARE LLC
Also Called: Lil' Einsteins Lrng Academy
1411 Old Baltimore Pike (19702-2025)
PHONE..................302 565-2200
EMP: 18 EST: 2019
SALES (est): 460.76K **Privately Held**
Web: www.lelaonline.com
SIC: 8351 Child day care services

(G-10685)
EXCEPTIONAL CARE FOR CHILDREN
Also Called: EXCEPTIONAL CARE FOR CHILDREN
11 Independence Way (19713-1159)
PHONE..................302 894-1001
Stephen J Falchek, *Prin*
Annette V Moore, *
EMP: 80 EST: 1998
SALES (est): 17.97MM **Privately Held**
Web: www.exceptionalcare.org
SIC: 8051 Convalescent home with continuous nursing care

(G-10686)
EXCLUSIVE SRCH CONNECTIONS LLC
103 Glen Avon Ct (19702-2082)
PHONE..................610 864-8000
Kevin Cameron, *Prin*
EMP: 5 EST: 2015
SALES (est): 153.04K **Privately Held**
Web: www.talent-connect.net
SIC: 7361 Executive placement

(G-10687)
EXECUTIVE BRDBAND CMMNCTONS LL
Also Called: Executive Brdband Cmmnications
6 Jaymar Blvd (19702-2877)
PHONE..................302 463-4335
EMP: 5 EST: 2010
SALES (est): 455.69K **Privately Held**
Web: www.executive-broadband.com
SIC: 3663 4841 Cable television equipment; Cable television services

(G-10688)
EXEIRE INC
15 Peddlers Row (19702-1525)
PHONE..................302 232-3555
EMP: 5 EST: 2019
SALES (est): 155.76K **Privately Held**
Web: www.exeire.com
SIC: 7389 Business services, nec

(G-10689)
EXODUS ESCAPE ROOMS LLC
280 E Main St (19711-7333)
PHONE..................302 366-8250
EMP: 6 EST: 2017
SALES (est): 299.55K **Privately Held**
Web: www.axxiomescaperooms.com
SIC: 7929 Entertainment service

(G-10690)
EXPANSION PLATFORMS INC
200 Creek View Rd (19711-8539)
PHONE..................866 928-3098
Deshawn Britton, *CEO*

EMP: 20
SALES (est): 588.11K **Privately Held**
SIC: 7371 Computer software development and applications

(G-10691)
EXPEDIA CRUISESHIPCENTERS
5 W Hawthorne Ct (19702-3939)
PHONE.................................484 483-3272
David Diamond, *Prin*
EMP: 5 EST: 2019
SALES (est): 97.39K **Privately Held**
Web: www.expediafranchise.com
SIC: 4724 Travel agencies

(G-10692)
EXPRESS VPN LLC
113 Barksdale Pro Ctr (19711-3258)
PHONE.................................310 601-8492
EMP: 7 EST: 2011
SALES (est): 386.4K **Privately Held**
SIC: 5045 Computer software

(G-10693)
EXTENSIVE HEALTH SERVICES LLC
280 E Main St Ste 112 (19711-7324)
PHONE.................................302 733-0303
EMP: 5 EST: 2019
SALES (est): 126.06K **Privately Held**
Web: www.extensivehealthservices.com
SIC: 8099 Health and allied services, nec

(G-10694)
EXTREME ASPHALT MAINTENANCE
352 Matthew Flocco Dr (19713-2350)
PHONE.................................302 275-8996
Rachel Nichols, *Prin*
EMP: 6 EST: 2016
SALES (est): 190.19K **Privately Held**
Web: ms-paving-and-concrete.business.site
SIC: 1611 Surfacing and paving

(G-10695)
EXTREME AUDIO & VIDEO
19a Albe Dr (19702-1321)
PHONE.................................302 533-7404
Alfred Barone, *Prin*
EMP: 5 EST: 2005
SALES (est): 203.35K **Privately Held**
SIC: 7841 Video tape rental

(G-10696)
EXTREME MACHINING LLC
111 Lake Dr Ste A (19702-3334)
PHONE.................................302 368-7595
EMP: 10 EST: 2004
SQ FT: 80,000
SALES (est): 2.53MM **Privately Held**
Web: www.extrememachining.com
SIC: 3599 Machine shop, jobbing and repair

(G-10697)
EXTREME SCALE SOLUTIONS LLC
260 Chapman Rd (19702-5491)
PHONE.................................302 540-7149
EMP: 16 EST: 2014
SALES (est): 3.8MM **Privately Held**
Web: www.extreme-scale.com
SIC: 7371 Computer software systems analysis and design, custom

(G-10698)
EYE CARE OF DELAWARE
4102 Ogletown Rd Ste 1 (19713)
PHONE.................................302 454-8800
Jane Baker, *Mgr*
EMP: 13 EST: 1993
SALES (est): 3.06MM **Privately Held**
Web: www.eyecareofdelaware.com

SIC: 8011 Opthalmologist

(G-10699)
F SCHUMACHER & CO LLC
Also Called: F S C Wallcoverings
131 Continental Dr Ste 300 (19713-4305)
P.O. Box 7960 (10116-7960)
PHONE.................................302 454-3200
Richard Malin, *Mgr*
EMP: 27
SALES (corp-wide): 100.72MM **Privately Held**
Web: www.schumacher.com
SIC: 5023 5131 5198 Draperies; Yard goods, woven; Paints, varnishes, and supplies
PA: F. Schumacher & Co., Llc
459 Broadway Fl 2
New York NY 10001
212 213-7900

(G-10700)
FABREEKA INTL HOLDINGS INC
Fabreeka-Fablene Division
315 Ruthar Dr (19711-8016)
PHONE.................................302 452-2500
EMP: 5
SALES (corp-wide): 1.32B **Privately Held**
Web: www.fabreeka.com
SIC: 3069 Molded rubber products
HQ: Fabreeka International Holdings, Inc.
1023 Turnpike St
Stoughton MA 02072
781 341-3655

(G-10701)
FACTORY TECHNOLOGIES INC
2035 Sunset Lake Rd Ste 82 (19702-2600)
PHONE.................................302 266-1290
Valentine Oleka, *CEO*
EMP: 9 EST: 2017
SALES (est): 362.09K **Privately Held**
Web: www.serversfactory.com
SIC: 7371 Computer software development

(G-10702)
FAIRNESS INSTITUTE
1000 Fountainview Cir Apt 216 (19713-3864)
PHONE.................................302 559-4074
Horacio Lewis Ph.d., *Prin*
EMP: 7 EST: 2010
SALES (est): 137.08K **Privately Held**
Web: www.horaciolewis.com
SIC: 8733 Noncommercial research organizations

(G-10703)
FAIRWINDS TECHNOLOGIES ENGRG
111 Sandy Dr (19713-1148)
PHONE.................................732 674-0094
EMP: 5 EST: 2018
SALES (est): 36.24K **Privately Held**
Web: www.fairwindstechnologies.com
SIC: 8711 Engineering services

(G-10704)
FAITH FAMILY MANAGEMENT CO
63 Marrows Rd (19713-3701)
PHONE.................................302 832-5936
Lan Nguyen, *Pt*
EMP: 5 EST: 2013
SALES (est): 221.31K **Privately Held**
SIC: 8741 Management services

(G-10705)
FAMILY CARE ASSOCIATES
510 Christiana Medical Ctr (19702-1655)
PHONE.................................302 454-8880
Crystal Mason, *Off Mgr*

EMP: 7 EST: 2017
SALES (est): 219.04K **Privately Held**
SIC: 8049 Offices of health practitioner

(G-10706)
FAMILY CREATIONS
915 Doe Run Rd (19711-2402)
PHONE.................................302 239-4275
EMP: 6 EST: 2014
SALES (est): 47.22K **Privately Held**
Web: www.familycreations.net
SIC: 7389 Design services

(G-10707)
FAMILY DENISTRY
179 W Chestnut Hill Rd # 4 (19713-2210)
PHONE.................................302 368-0054
EMP: 7 EST: 2018
SALES (est): 77.02K **Privately Held**
SIC: 8021 Offices and clinics of dentists

(G-10708)
FAMILY DOCTORS
Also Called: Bilski, William F Do
4 Polly Drummond Hill Rd (19711-5703)
PHONE.................................302 368-3600
EMP: 6 EST: 1990
SALES (est): 461.06K **Privately Held**
SIC: 8031 Offices and clinics of osteopathic physicians

(G-10709)
FAMILY PRCTICE CTR OF NEW CSTL
Also Called: Abby Family Practice
1 Centurian Dr Ste 105 (19713-2154)
PHONE.................................302 999-0933
Arlen D Stone, *Prin*
EMP: 5 EST: 2010
SALES (est): 487.33K **Privately Held**
SIC: 8011 General and family practice, physician/surgeon

(G-10710)
FAMOID TECHNOLOGY LLC
112 Capitol Trl (19711-3716)
PHONE.................................530 601-7284
EMP: 2 EST: 2017
SALES (est): 170.95K **Privately Held**
Web: www.famoid.com
SIC: 7371 7372 5734 Computer software development and applications; Application computer software; Software, business and non-game

(G-10711)
FANTASTIC LANDSCAPING FEN
51 Greenridge Rd (19711-6704)
PHONE.................................302 494-9034
EMP: 5 EST: 2018
SALES (est): 204.35K **Privately Held**
SIC: 0781 Landscape services

(G-10712)
FAR REZOLUTIONS INC
218 Margaux Cir (19702-4548)
PHONE.................................302 547-6850
Steve Resnick, *Pr*
EMP: 5 EST: 2007
SALES (est): 83.65K **Privately Held**
SIC: 7622 Television repair shop

(G-10713)
FAS MART / SHORE STOP 286 LLC
Also Called: Shore Stop Store 286
1400 Capitol Trl (19711-5782)
PHONE.................................302 366-9694
Gene Daunno, *Prin*
EMP: 5 EST: 2011
SALES (est): 223.41K **Privately Held**
SIC: 6799 Investors, nec

(G-10714)
FAST ACTION LANDSCAPING INC
3 Broadfield Dr (19713-2703)
PHONE.................................302 332-7124
Justin Devine, *Pr*
EMP: 5 EST: 2011
SALES (est): 185.8K **Privately Held**
SIC: 0781 Landscape services

(G-10715)
FAST AF INC
2035 Sunset Lake Rd B2 (19702-2600)
PHONE.................................415 770-5235
Domm Holland, *CEO*
EMP: 6 EST: 2018
SALES (est): 277.34K **Privately Held**
SIC: 7371 Software programming applications

(G-10716)
FAST PIPE LINING EAST INC
563 Walther Rd (19702-2903)
P.O. Box 99 (19701-0099)
PHONE.................................302 368-7414
Robin Quinn, *CEO*
EMP: 10 EST: 2016
SALES (est): 517.89K **Privately Held**
Web: fastpipeeast.com.bitverzo.com
SIC: 1623 Water, sewer, and utility lines

(G-10717)
FATANEH M ZIARI MD
2600 Glasgow Ave Ste 212 (19702-5704)
PHONE.................................302 836-8533
Fataneh Ziari Md, *Owner*
EMP: 9 EST: 2001
SALES (est): 501.78K **Privately Held**
Web: www.pediatricspersonalcare.com
SIC: 8011 Pediatrician

(G-10718)
FBBC LLC
8 Spinet Rd (19713-3512)
PHONE.................................302 442-3004
EMP: 8 EST: 2020
SALES (est): 40.94K **Privately Held**
SIC: 7929 Entertainment service

(G-10719)
FE MRAN INC FIRE PRTCTION E
Also Called: F E Moran
301 Ruthar Dr Ste B (19711-8031)
PHONE.................................302 453-9237
William Eder, *Genl Mgr*
EMP: 20
SQ FT: 30,000
SALES (corp-wide): 225.37MM **Privately Held**
Web: www.femoran.com
SIC: 1711 Fire sprinkler system installation
HQ: F.E. Moran, Inc. Fire Protection East Coast
2265 Carlson Dr
Northbrook IL 60062
847 498-4800

(G-10720)
FEATHERS GROUP LLC
13 Sheldrake Rd (19713-3508)
PHONE.................................302 300-5967
EMP: 9 EST: 2013
SALES (est): 238.42K **Privately Held**
SIC: 8011 Offices and clinics of medical doctors

(G-10721)
FEDEX CORPORATION
701 Pencader Dr Ste C (19702-3360)
PHONE.................................302 286-6570
Stephen Radulski, *Prin*

Newark - New Castle County (G-10722)　　　GEOGRAPHIC SECTION

EMP: 6 EST: 1997
SALES (est): 152.21K **Privately Held**
Web: local.fedex.com
SIC: 4513 Package delivery, private air

(G-10722)
FERN CLEANING
605 Coventry Ln (19713-4427)
PHONE..................................302 480-0241
Fernanda Rodriguez, *Prin*
EMP: 5 EST: 2014
SALES (est): 46.57K **Privately Held**
SIC: 7699 Cleaning services

(G-10723)
FERNANDEZ DRYWALL INC
379 Moir St (19702-4195)
PHONE..................................302 521-2760
Gerardo Fernandez, *Prin*
EMP: 5 EST: 2016
SALES (est): 65.43K **Privately Held**
SIC: 1742 Drywall

(G-10724)
FERRANTE & ASSOCIATES INC
501 Paisley Pl (19711-3453)
PHONE..................................781 891-4328
Audrey Ferrante, *Pr*
EMP: 2 EST: 1988
SALES (est): 246.74K **Privately Held**
SIC: 3555 Printing presses

(G-10725)
FERRIS HOME IMPRVS CO LLC
1908 Kirkwood Hwy Ste 3 (19711)
PHONE..................................302 998-4500
EMP: 20 EST: 2009
SALES (est): 5.11MM **Privately Held**
Web: www.ferrishomeimprovements.com
SIC: 1761 1751 1799 1521 Roofing contractor; Window and door installation and erection; Kitchen and bathroom remodeling; Patio and deck construction and repair

(G-10726)
FIBER-ONE INC
2812 Old County Rd (19702-4602)
PHONE..................................302 834-0890
Ruth Filippone, *Pr*
Joseph Filippone, *VP*
EMP: 8 EST: 1996
SALES (est): 156.07K **Privately Held**
SIC: 1731 Communications specialization

(G-10727)
FIREBRAND ENTERTAINMENT INC
503 4th St (19711-8714)
PHONE..................................571 330-8983
Austin Abram, *Prin*
EMP: 5 EST: 2020
SALES (est): 53.68K **Privately Held**
SIC: 7922 Entertainment promotion

(G-10728)
FIRST CLASS HEATING AC
6 Shea Way (19713-3422)
PHONE..................................302 834-1036
EMP: 9 EST: 1994
SALES (est): 152.46K **Privately Held**
SIC: 1711 Warm air heating and air conditioning contractor

(G-10729)
FIRST STATE CNSTR MGT LLC
1802 Chelmsford Cir (19713-2909)
PHONE..................................302 257-5438
EMP: 5 EST: 2021
SALES (est): 110K **Privately Held**

SIC: 8741 Construction management

(G-10730)
FIRST STATE CONTAINER LLC
100 Lake Dr Ste 106 (19702-3351)
PHONE..................................603 888-1315
EMP: 28 EST: 2006
SALES (est): 971.26K **Privately Held**
SIC: 3089 Plastics containers, except foam
PA: Carr Management, Inc.
　　1 Tara Blvd Ste 303
　　Nashua NH 03062

(G-10731)
FIRST STATE GYMNSTICS ATHC ASS
131 John F Campbell Rd (19711-5457)
PHONE..................................302 368-7107
Evelyn Rappaport, *Prin*
EMP: 15 EST: 2008
SALES (est): 9.27K **Privately Held**
Web: www.firststategymnastics.com
SIC: 7999 Gymnastic instruction, non-membership

(G-10732)
FIRST STATE HOBBIES LLC
600 Peoples Plz (19702-5600)
PHONE..................................302 595-2475
EMP: 7 EST: 2019
SALES (est): 129.89K **Privately Held**
Web: www.peoplesplaza.com
SIC: 6512 Shopping center, property operation only

(G-10733)
FIRST STATE ORTHOPAEDICS PA
Also Called: Sabre Building
4051 Ogletown Rd Ste 103 (19713-3101)
PHONE..................................302 322-3400
David Blaeuer, *Brnch Mgr*
EMP: 6
SALES (corp-wide): 31.54MM **Privately Held**
Web: www.firststateortho.com
SIC: 8011 Orthopedic physician
PA: First State Orthopaedics, P.A.
　　4745 Ogltn Stntn Rd # 225
　　Newark DE 19713
　　302 731-2888

(G-10734)
FIRST STATE ORTHOPAEDICS PA (PA)
4745 Ogletown Stanton Rd Ste 225 (19713-1387)
PHONE..................................302 731-2888
Admiral Charles Lockwood, *Prin*
EMP: 20 EST: 1979
SALES (est): 31.54MM
SALES (corp-wide): 31.54MM **Privately Held**
Web: www.firststateortho.com
SIC: 8011 Orthopedic physician

(G-10735)
FIRST STATE ORTHOPAEDICS PA
Also Called: First State Surgery Center
1000 Twin C Ln Ste 200 (19713-2142)
PHONE..................................302 683-0700
William Newcomb, *Brnch Mgr*
EMP: 6
SALES (corp-wide): 31.54MM **Privately Held**
Web: www.firststateortho.com
SIC: 8011 Orthopedic physician
PA: First State Orthopaedics, P.A.
　　4745 Ogltn Stntn Rd # 225
　　Newark DE 19713
　　302 731-2888

(G-10736)
FIRST STATE PEDIATRICS LLC (PA)
210 Christiana Medical Ctr (19702-1695)
PHONE..................................302 292-1559
John W Murphy, *Prin*
EMP: 10 EST: 2009
SALES (est): 6.84MM
SALES (corp-wide): 6.84MM **Privately Held**
Web: www.firststatepediatrics.com
SIC: 8011 Pediatrician

(G-10737)
FIRST STATE PRESS LLC
14 Eileen Dr (19711-3814)
PHONE..................................302 731-9058
John Micklos, *Prin*
EMP: 4 EST: 2015
SALES (est): 74.79K **Privately Held**
Web: www.firststatepress.com
SIC: 2711 Newspapers: publishing only, not printed on site

(G-10738)
FIRST STATE SURGERY CENTER LLC
Also Called: First State Orthopaedics
1000 Twin C Ln Ste 200 (19713-2142)
PHONE..................................302 683-0700
William A Newcomb, *Pt*
EMP: 13 EST: 2000
SQ FT: 12,000
SALES (est): 4.37MM **Privately Held**
Web: www.fssurg.com
SIC: 8011 Surgeon

(G-10739)
FIRST STUDENT INC
Also Called: First Student
750 Stanton Christiana Rd (19713-2028)
PHONE..................................302 995-9607
Joy Miller, *Brnch Mgr*
EMP: 11
Web: www.firststudentinc.com
SIC: 4142 4151 Bus charter service, except local; School buses
PA: First Student, Inc.
　　191 Rosa Parks St Ste 800
　　Cincinnati OH 45202

(G-10740)
FISCAL ASSOCIATES
16 Fairfield Dr (19711-2767)
PHONE..................................302 894-0500
G William Bailey, *Prin*
EMP: 10 EST: 1996
SALES (est): 504.86K **Privately Held**
SIC: 8742 Business management consultant

(G-10741)
FITNESS MANAGEMENT GROUP INC
247 S Main St (19711-4564)
PHONE..................................302 218-5644
EMP: 5 EST: 2020
SALES (est): 250.94K **Privately Held**
SIC: 8741 Management services

(G-10742)
FITNESS PERFORMANCE CORP
2915 Ogletown Rd Ste 2839 (19713-1927)
PHONE..................................866 710-2227
Maxime Gagne, *CEO*
EMP: 5 EST: 2018
SALES (est): 55.34K **Privately Held**
SIC: 7991 Physical fitness facilities

(G-10743)
FIVE 1 FIVE ICE SPORTS GROUP L
101 John F Campbell Rd (19711-5457)
PHONE..................................302 266-0777

EMP: 6 EST: 2019
SALES (est): 38.16K **Privately Held**
SIC: 7997 Ice sports

(G-10744)
FIVE STAR PAINTING
5 Beacon Ln (19711-1904)
PHONE..................................302 743-6515
David Stracke, *Prin*
EMP: 7 EST: 2016
SALES (est): 212.13K **Privately Held**
Web: www.fivestarpainting.com
SIC: 1721 Painting and paper hanging

(G-10745)
FIVE STAR QUALITY CARE INC
Also Called: Somerford House Newark
501 S Harmony Rd (19713-3338)
PHONE..................................302 266-9255
Brenda Cuart, *Brnch Mgr*
EMP: 6
SALES (corp-wide): 934.59MM **Privately Held**
Web: www.somerfordhousenewark.com
SIC: 8051 Skilled nursing care facilities
HQ: Alerislife Inc.
　　255 Washington St Ste 300
　　Newton MA 02458

(G-10746)
FIVE STAR QUALITY CARE INC
Also Called: Millcroft
255 Possum Park Rd (19711-3877)
PHONE..................................302 366-0160
Goeff Henry, *Mgr*
EMP: 8
SALES (corp-wide): 934.59MM **Privately Held**
Web: www.fivestarseniorliving.com
SIC: 8051 Skilled nursing care facilities
HQ: Alerislife Inc.
　　255 Washington St Ste 300
　　Newton MA 02458

(G-10747)
FIVE STAR SENIOR LIVING INC
Also Called: Somerford Place Newark
4175 Ogletown Rd (19713)
PHONE..................................302 283-0540
Sue Russ, *Brnch Mgr*
EMP: 24
SALES (corp-wide): 934.59MM **Privately Held**
Web: www.fivestarseniorliving.com
SIC: 8051 Skilled nursing care facilities
HQ: Alerislife Inc.
　　255 Washington St Ste 300
　　Newton MA 02458

(G-10748)
FIYAH B MUSIC LLC (PA)
Also Called: Fiyah B
140 Songsmith Dr (19702-4458)
PHONE..................................949 656-3246
Andre Austin, *CEO*
Andre Austin, *Managing Member*
EMP: 5 EST: 2019
SALES (est): 161.88K
SALES (corp-wide): 161.88K **Privately Held**
SIC: 7929 7389 Entertainers and entertainment groups; Recording studio, noncommercial records

(G-10749)
FLACKON INC
2035 Sunset Lake Rd Ste B2 (19702-2600)
PHONE..................................701 369-0789
EMP: 6
SALES (est): 63.38K **Privately Held**
Web: www.docupilot.app

GEOGRAPHIC SECTION

Newark - New Castle County (G-10778)

SIC: 7371 Computer software development and applications

(G-10750)
FLAPDOODLES INC (PA)
725 Dawson Dr (19713-3413)
P.O. Box 4675 (19807-4675)
PHONE....................302 731-9793
Marc A Ham, *Pr*
Carole A Bieber, *
EMP: 92 EST: 1985
SQ FT: 60,000
SALES (est): 11.89MM
SALES (corp-wide): 11.89MM **Privately Held**
SIC: 2253 5137 Knit outerwear mills; Children's goods

(G-10751)
FMC CORPORATION
Also Called: F M C Biopolymore
1301 Ogletown Rd (19711-5496)
PHONE....................302 451-0100
James Cronin, *Mgr*
EMP: 100
SALES (corp-wide): 5.8B **Publicly Held**
Web: www.fmc.com
SIC: 2823 2834 Cellulosic manmade fibers; Pharmaceutical preparations
PA: Fmc Corporation
2929 Walnut St
Philadelphia PA 19104
215 299-6000

(G-10752)
FMC CORPORATION
1090 Elkton Rd (19711-3507)
PHONE....................302 366-5107
EMP: 52
SALES (corp-wide): 5.8B **Publicly Held**
Web: www.fmc.com
SIC: 2812 Soda ash, sodium carbonate (anhydrous)
PA: Fmc Corporation
2929 Walnut St
Philadelphia PA 19104
215 299-6000

(G-10753)
FOCUS SOLUTIONS SERVICES INC
262 Chapman Rd Ste 200 (19702-5442)
PHONE....................302 318-1345
Troy Husser, *CEO*
Darrell Hervey, *Pr*
EMP: 10 EST: 2014
SALES (est): 316.96K **Privately Held**
Web: www.focussolutionservices.com
SIC: 7349 8744 Cleaning service, industrial or commercial; Facilities support services

(G-10754)
FOOD BANK OF DELAWARE INC (PA)
222 Lake Dr (19702-3319)
PHONE....................302 292-1305
Patricia Bebe, *Pr*
EMP: 49 EST: 1981
SQ FT: 16,000
SALES (est): 35MM
SALES (corp-wide): 35MM **Privately Held**
Web: www.fbd.org
SIC: 8322 Social service center

(G-10755)
FOOD WORKS MANAGEMENT LLC
560 Peoples Plz Ste 310 (19702-4738)
PHONE....................302 397-3000
EMP: 6 EST: 2016
SALES (est): 268.44K **Privately Held**
Web: www.foodworksmanagement.com

SIC: 8741 Management services

(G-10756)
FOODLINER INC
206 Hansen Ct (19713-1150)
PHONE....................302 368-4204
Bob Houston, *Brnch Mgr*
EMP: 63
SALES (corp-wide): 114.96MM **Privately Held**
Web: www.foodliner.com
SIC: 4213 Contract haulers
PA: Foodliner, Inc.
2099 Southpark Ct Ste 1
Dubuque IA 52003
563 584-2670

(G-10757)
FOOT STEPS TWO HEAVEN DAYCARE
606 Lisbeth Rd (19713-1742)
PHONE....................302 738-5519
EMP: 5 EST: 2010
SALES (est): 114.83K **Privately Held**
SIC: 8351 Child day care services

(G-10758)
FOREIGNERDS INC
2035 Sunset Lake Rd Ste B2 (19702-2600)
PHONE....................201 381-5152
Akshay Tikoo, *Prin*
EMP: 15 EST: 2019
SALES (est): 674.43K **Privately Held**
Web: www.foreignerds.com
SIC: 7371 Custom computer programming services

(G-10759)
FORESEE PHARMA
550 S College Ave (19716-1304)
PHONE....................302 368-1758
EMP: 6 EST: 2018
SALES (est): 404.25K **Privately Held**
SIC: 6512 Commercial and industrial building operation

(G-10760)
FORESEE PHARMACEUTICALS INC
3 Innovation Way Ste 240 (19711-5456)
PHONE....................302 396-5243
Jennifer Yen, *Admn*
EMP: 15 EST: 2014
SALES (est): 465.15K **Privately Held**
Web: www.foreseepharma.com
SIC: 5122 Pharmaceuticals

(G-10761)
FOREST OAK ELEMENTARY PTA
55 S Meadowood Dr (19711-6755)
PHONE....................302 540-2873
EMP: 6 EST: 2010
SALES (est): 68.62K **Privately Held**
SIC: 8641 Parent-teachers' association

(G-10762)
FORESTER COMMUNICATIONS
887 Salem Church Rd (19702-4321)
PHONE....................302 545-6169
Pat Forester, *Prin*
EMP: 5 EST: 2010
SALES (est): 72.45K **Privately Held**
SIC: 4899 Communication services, nec

(G-10763)
FOREWINDS HOSPITALITY LLC (HQ)
507 Thompson Station Rd (19711-7504)
PHONE....................302 368-6640
EMP: 19 EST: 2005
SALES (est): 8.09MM
SALES (corp-wide): 35.8MM **Privately Held**

Web: www.forewindshospitality.com
SIC: 7997 Golf club, membership
PA: Sawyer Property Management Of Maryland, Inc.
9658 Baltimore Ave # 300
College Park MD 20740
781 449-6650

(G-10764)
FORGED BDC INC ✪
254 Chapman Rd Ste 209 (19702-5413)
PHONE....................561 802-8919
Austin Skumanich, *CEO*
EMP: 6 EST: 2023
SALES (est): 83.48K **Privately Held**
SIC: 7389 Telemarketing services

(G-10765)
FORMAL AFFAIRS INC
257 E Main St # 100 (19711-7382)
PHONE....................302 737-1519
Christopher Locke, *Pr*
EMP: 5 EST: 1983
SALES (est): 244.77K **Privately Held**
Web: www.formalaffairsnewark.com
SIC: 7299 5699 Tuxedo rental; Formal wear

(G-10766)
FORTE SPORTS INCORPORATED
314 E Main St Ste 1 (19711-7195)
P.O. Box 422 (19715-0422)
PHONE....................302 731-0776
James L Manniso, *CEO*
Mark Manniso, *Pr*
EMP: 5 EST: 1993
SQ FT: 3,600
SALES (est): 681.37K **Privately Held**
Web: www.fortecreates.com
SIC: 3069 Toys, rubber

(G-10767)
FORWARD SUPPORT LLC
903 S College Ave (19713-2303)
PHONE....................315 292-8770
EMP: 6 EST: 2014
SALES (est): 87.55K **Privately Held**
SIC: 8331 Job training and related services

(G-10768)
FOUNTAIN RESURGENCE LLC
4 Peddlers Row Unit 31 (19702-1525)
PHONE....................302 518-5659
Eboni Fountain, *CEO*
EMP: 12 EST: 2019
SALES (est): 300K **Privately Held**
SIC: 8742 Administrative services consultant

(G-10769)
FOXFIRE PRINTING AND PACKAGING INC
750 Dawson Dr (19713-3414)
PHONE....................302 533-2240
◆ EMP: 200
SIC: 2752 Commercial printing, lithographic

(G-10770)
FRANK GILLEN
9 Stearrett Dr (19702-6823)
PHONE....................302 894-1023
Frank Gillen, *Prin*
EMP: 6 EST: 2010
SALES (est): 40.39K **Privately Held**
SIC: 7999 Tour and guide services

(G-10771)
FRANKLIN AND PROKOPIK
500 Creek View Rd Ste 502 (19713-8549)
PHONE....................302 594-9780
EMP: 7 EST: 2018
SALES (est): 155.56K **Privately Held**

Web: www.fandpnet.com
SIC: 8111 General practice attorney, lawyer

(G-10772)
FRANKLIN JESTER PA
603 Lisbeth Rd (19713-1741)
PHONE....................302 368-3080
EMP: 5 EST: 1996
SALES (est): 364.08K **Privately Held**
Web: www.jesterstaxservice.com
SIC: 2899 Patching plaster, household

(G-10773)
FRAUNHOFER USA INC
Also Called: Fraunhofer Center For Molecula
9 Innovation Way (19711-5449)
PHONE....................302 369-1708
Vidadi Yusibov, *Ex Dir*
EMP: 52
Web: www.fraunhofer.org
SIC: 8731 Biotechnical research, commercial
PA: Fraunhofer Usa, Inc.
44792 Helm St
Plymouth MI 48170

(G-10774)
FREDERICK M WILLIAMS MD
4110 Ogletown Stanton Rd (19713-4169)
PHONE....................302 738-0103
Frederick Williams Md, *Prin*
EMP: 7 EST: 2018
SALES (est): 83.6K **Privately Held**
SIC: 8011 Offices and clinics of medical doctors

(G-10775)
FREEDOM CYCLE LLC
1110 Ogletown Rd (19711-5416)
PHONE....................302 286-6900
EMP: 5 EST: 2001
SALES (est): 385.58K **Privately Held**
Web: www.freedom-cycle.com
SIC: 7699 Motorcycle repair service

(G-10776)
FREEDOM DENTAL MANAGEMENT INC
1290 Peoples Plz (19702-5701)
PHONE....................302 836-3750
EMP: 15 EST: 2015
SALES (est): 2.88MM **Privately Held**
Web: www.sleepytoothgroup.com
SIC: 8021 Offices and clinics of dentists

(G-10777)
FREEDOM DRYWALL SUPPLY LLC (HQ)
Also Called: Freedom Materials
721 Dawson Dr (19713-3413)
PHONE....................302 281-0085
Silvio Ferrari, *Managing Member*
EMP: 27 EST: 2015
SALES (est): 10.12MM
SALES (corp-wide): 125.25K **Privately Held**
Web: www.freedommaterials.com
SIC: 1742 5032 Plaster and drywall work; Drywall materials
PA: Kodiak Building Partners, Llc
9780 Pyramid Ct Ste 300
Englewood CO 80112
303 576-2230

(G-10778)
FREEDOM KITCHEN AND BATH
159 E Green Valley Cir (19711-6791)
PHONE....................302 463-1659
EMP: 7 EST: 2014
SALES (est): 64.87K **Privately Held**
Web: www.bathkitchenandtile.com

Newark - New Castle County (G-10779)

SIC: **1799** Kitchen and bathroom remodeling

(G-10779)
FREEDOM MORTGAGE CORPORATION
220 Continental Dr Ste 315 (19713-4311)
PHONE...................................302 368-7100
EMP: 7
Web: www.freedommortgage.com
SIC: **6162** Mortgage bankers
PA: Freedom Mortgage Corporation
   951 W Yamato Rd Ste 175
   Boca Raton FL 33431

(G-10780)
FREELEE FOUNDATION
1400 Helen Dr Apt 104 (19702-1678)
PHONE...................................302 607-8053
Keonna Freeman, *Pr*
Varleisha Gibbs, *Pr*
Vacinqua Rogers, *Pr*
Lachema Manigault, *Pr*
Renae Pritchett, *Pr*
EMP: 5 EST: 2017
SALES (est): 89.65K **Privately Held**
SIC: **8641** Civic and social associations

(G-10781)
FREMONT HALL
82 Possum Park Rd (19711-3858)
PHONE...................................302 731-2431
EMP: 7 EST: 1957
SALES (est): 135.71K **Privately Held**
SIC: **7299** Banquet hall facilities

(G-10782)
FRESH HEALTHY MARKETS LLC
304 S Chapel St Unit 5 (19711-5378)
PHONE...................................484 748-4791
EMP: 5 EST: 2018
SALES (est): 240.48K **Privately Held**
SIC: **8742** Marketing consulting services

(G-10783)
FRESH START LAWN SERVICES
213 N Oxford Dr (19702-4122)
PHONE...................................302 279-6234
Chris Lafferty, *Prin*
EMP: 6 EST: 2017
SALES (est): 27.59K **Privately Held**
Web: www.freshstartlawnservices.com
SIC: **0782** Lawn care services

(G-10784)
FRESH START TRANSFORMATIONS
4604 Tracy Dr (19702-8104)
PHONE...................................302 219-0221
Joyce Nichols, *CEO*
EMP: 5 EST: 2014
SALES (est): 59.43K **Privately Held**
Web: www.freshstartwithjoyce.com
SIC: **7299** 7389 Personal appearance services; Business services, nec

(G-10785)
FRIDAY GAMES INC
200 Continental Dr Ste 401 (19713-4334)
PHONE...................................847 246-2189
EMP: 20 EST: 2021
SALES (est): 600.31K **Privately Held**
SIC: **7371** Computer software development and applications

(G-10786)
FRIENDS AND SIGN
61 Matthews Rd (19713-2555)
PHONE...................................302 368-4794
Erin Barthel, *Prin*
EMP: 4 EST: 2017
SALES (est): 54.88K **Privately Held**
SIC: **3993** Signs and advertising specialties

(G-10787)
FRIENDSHIP HOUSE NEC
69 E Main St (19711-4645)
PHONE...................................302 731-5338
Randy Weins, *Prin*
EMP: 16 EST: 2010
SALES (est): 44.18K **Privately Held**
Web: www.friendshiphousede.org
SIC: **8322** Social service center

(G-10788)
FROM GROUND UP CONSTRUCTION
26 Evergreen Dr (19702-3712)
PHONE...................................302 747-0996
EMP: 7 EST: 2011
SALES (est): 486.91K **Privately Held**
SIC: **1542** Nonresidential construction, nec

(G-10789)
FRONTIER SCIENTIFIC SVCS INC
Also Called: Asdi
601 Interchange Blvd (19711-3561)
PHONE...................................302 266-6891
W Tim Miller, *Pr*
Bert Israelsen, *CFO*
Kabana Perkins, *Sr VP*
EMP: 33 EST: 2011
SALES (est): 10.02MM **Privately Held**
Web: www.frontierscientific.com
SIC: **8731** 2899 Commercial research laboratory; Chemical preparations, nec

(G-10790)
FULTON BANK NATIONAL ASSN
Also Called: Fulton Financial Advisors
287 E Main St Unit 105 (19711-7569)
PHONE...................................302 737-7766
Deborah Blyskal, *Brnch Mgr*
EMP: 5
SALES (corp-wide): 1.09B **Publicly Held**
Web: www.fultonbank.com
SIC: **6022** State commercial banks
HQ: Fulton Bank, National Association
   1 Penn Sq
   Lancaster PA 17602
   717 581-3166

(G-10791)
FUNSTEP INC
1805 Capitol Trl (19711-5721)
PHONE...................................302 731-9618
Kim Libus, *Dir*
EMP: 22 EST: 2001
SALES (est): 241.34K **Privately Held**
Web: www.funsteps.net
SIC: **8351** Preschool center

(G-10792)
FURRER INC
38 Executive Dr (19702-3370)
PHONE...................................302 273-3109
Caihong He, *CEO*
EMP: 7
SALES (est): 78.16K **Privately Held**
SIC: **3851** Eyeglasses, lenses and frames

(G-10793)
FUTURETECH INV GROUP INC
Also Called: Future Option Trading Company
12 Timber Creek Ln (19711-2606)
PHONE...................................302 476-9529
Wayne L Branch, *Ch Bd*
EMP: 10 EST: 1996
SQ FT: 1,500
SALES (est): 937.28K **Privately Held**
Web: www.ftigi.com
SIC: **6211** Traders, security

(G-10794)
FUZZY FIBERSNET
25 Glencoe Dr (19702-2061)
PHONE...................................302 737-0644
EMP: 5 EST: 2011
SALES (est): 111.32K **Privately Held**
SIC: **4812** Cellular telephone services

(G-10795)
G2 PERFORMANCE
23 Beagle Club Way (19711-6117)
PHONE...................................302 293-1847
EMP: 7 EST: 2019
SALES (est): 134.47K **Privately Held**
Web: www.g2performance.com
SIC: **7929** Entertainers and entertainment groups

(G-10796)
GABBAUD HEALTH LLC
406 Anchorage Ct (19702-4830)
PHONE...................................267 512-1750
Esther Nkrumah, *Managing Member*
EMP: 11 EST: 2021
SALES (est): 300.41K **Privately Held**
SIC: **8011** Offices and clinics of medical doctors

(G-10797)
GAETANO N PASTORE MD
1 Centurian Dr Ste 200 (19713-2150)
PHONE...................................302 994-3685
EMP: 9 EST: 2015
SALES (est): 89.5K **Privately Held**
SIC: **8011** Cardiologist and cardio-vascular specialist

(G-10798)
GAI COMMUNICATIONS INC
560 Peoples Plz 136 (19702-4798)
PHONE...................................609 254-1470
Miguel Graham, *Pr*
EMP: 5 EST: 2004
SALES (est): 251.38K **Privately Held**
SIC: **4899** Data communication services

(G-10799)
GALERIE MEDIA INC
154 W Rutherford Dr (19713-2034)
PHONE...................................917 685-4168
Hans Fleurimont, *Pr*
EMP: 2 EST: 2021
SALES (est): 59.23K **Privately Held**
SIC: **2741** 8748 Miscellaneous publishing; Business consulting, nec

(G-10800)
GALLOWAY ELECTRIC CO INC
19 Albe Dr (19702-1321)
PHONE...................................302 453-8385
J Paul Galloway Junior, *Pr*
Ronald Galloway, *VP*
Janice Galloway, *Sec*
EMP: 14 EST: 1948
SALES (est): 465.29K **Privately Held**
Web: www.gallowayelectric.net
SIC: **1731** General electrical contractor

(G-10801)
GALLOWAY LEASING INC
19 Albe Dr (19702-1321)
PHONE...................................302 453-8385
EMP: 5 EST: 1985
SALES (est): 122.32K **Privately Held**
SIC: **6531** Real estate leasing and rentals

(G-10802)
GALMAN GROUP LTD
Also Called: Cooper's Place
146 Chestnut Crossing Dr (19713-2600)
PHONE...................................215 886-2000
Holly Wessell, *Mgr*
EMP: 10
SALES (corp-wide): 24.26MM **Privately Held**
Web: www.galmangroup.com
SIC: **6513** Apartment building operators
PA: Galman Group, Ltd.
   261 Old York Rd Ste 110
   Jenkintown PA 19046
   215 886-2000

(G-10803)
GALMAN GROUP INC
Also Called: Buckingham Pl Twnhuse Aprtmnts
25b Windsor Cir (19702-1977)
PHONE...................................302 737-5550
Gina Plunto, *Mgr*
EMP: 8 EST: 1986
SALES (est): 502.09K **Privately Held**
Web: www.galmangroup.com
SIC: **6513** Apartment building operators

(G-10804)
GAMERS4GAMERS LLC
40 E Main St Ste 649 (19711-4639)
PHONE...................................302 722-6289
EMP: 6 EST: 2014
SALES (est): 123.52K **Privately Held**
SIC: **7371** 7389 Computer software development and applications; Business Activities at Non-Commercial Site

(G-10805)
GAMESTOP INC
326 Suburban Dr (19711-3599)
PHONE...................................302 266-7362
Bryan Mcmilina, *Mgr*
EMP: 10
Web: www.gamestop.com
SIC: **5092** 5734 5945 Video games; Computer and software stores; Hobby, toy, and game shops
HQ: Gamestop, Inc.
   625 Westport Pkwy
   Grapevine TX 76051

(G-10806)
GANC COMMERCIAL REALTY LLC
105 Briggs Ln (19711-3931)
PHONE...................................302 292-1131
EMP: 5 EST: 2014
SALES (est): 200.18K **Privately Held**
SIC: **6531** Real estate brokers and agents

(G-10807)
GARAGE
132 Christiana Mall (19702-3202)
PHONE...................................302 453-1930
EMP: 4 EST: 2016
SALES (est): 50.8K **Privately Held**
SIC: **5651** 5632 5621 2299 Family clothing stores; Women's dancewear, hosiery, and lingerie; Women's clothing stores; Jute and flax textile products

(G-10808)
GARCIA & SONS LLC
106 Fox Dr (19713-3506)
PHONE...................................302 562-8878
Julina Garcia, *Prin*
EMP: 5 EST: 2017
SALES (est): 179.84K **Privately Held**
SIC: **1522** Residential construction, nec

(G-10809)
GARILE INC
Also Called: Sir Speedy
311 Ruthar Dr (19711-8016)

PHONE..................302 366-0848
EMP: 22 EST: 1995
SQ FT: 3,200
SALES (est): 2.24MM **Privately Held**
Web: www.sirspeedy.com
SIC: **2752** 7334 2791 2789 Commercial printing, lithographic; Photocopying and duplicating services; Typesetting; Bookbinding and related work

(G-10810)
GARRETTS TRUCKING LLC
632 Candlestick Ln (19702-5906)
PHONE..................302 415-1794
EMP: 2 EST: 2020
SALES (est): 95.58K **Privately Held**
SIC: **3537** Trucks, tractors, loaders, carriers, and similar equipment

(G-10811)
GARRI INC
256 Chapman Rd (19702-5499)
PHONE..................319 538-4071
Daniel Temesgen, *CEO*
EMP: 6
SALES (est): 123.52K **Privately Held**
SIC: **7371** Software programming applications

(G-10812)
GARY M MUNCH INC
Also Called: Sign-A-Rama
995 S Chapel St Ste 1 (19713-3441)
PHONE..................302 525-8301
EMP: 3 EST: 1992
SQ FT: 4,000
SALES (est): 44.1K **Privately Held**
Web: www.signarama.com
SIC: **3993** Signs and advertising specialties

(G-10813)
GASTROENTEROLOGY ASSOCIATES PA (PA)
4745 Ogletown Stanton Rd Ste 134 (19713-1342)
PHONE..................302 738-5300
Ira Lobis Md, *Pt*
Ira Lobiz Md, *Pr*
Joseph Hacker, *Treas*
Marciana D Filippone Md, *Sec*
Warren G Butt Md, *VP*
EMP: 20 EST: 1970
SALES (est): 4.27MM
SALES (corp-wide): 4.27MM **Privately Held**
Web: www.delawarecenterfordigestivecare.com
SIC: **8011** Gastronomist

(G-10814)
GATELLO INC
256 Chapman Rd (19702-5499)
PHONE..................725 333-3830
Dennis Vinoba, *CEO*
EMP: 14
SALES (est): 481.04K **Privately Held**
SIC: **7371** Computer software development

(G-10815)
GATHER SOCIAL TECH CORP
300 Creek View Rd (19711-8546)
PHONE..................604 356-0981
EMP: 5
SALES (est): 67.36K **Privately Held**
SIC: **7371** Computer software development and applications

(G-10816)
GDT PROPERTIES INC
302 Gabor Dr (19711-6633)
PHONE..................302 737-3778
EMP: 26
SALES (corp-wide): 1.5B **Privately Held**
Web: www.yaleelectricsupply.com
SIC: **3699** Electrical equipment and supplies, nec
HQ: Gdt Properties, Inc.
    312 N 8th St
    Lebanon PA 17046
    717 273-4514

(G-10817)
GE ENERGY CERAMIC COMPOSITE PRODUCTS LLC
400 Bellevue Rd (19713-3432)
PHONE..................302 631-1300
EMP: 60
SIC: **3253** Ceramic wall and floor tile

(G-10818)
GEM PRODUCTIONS
6 Amaranth Dr (19711-2051)
PHONE..................302 650-6725
Debra Christie, *Prin*
EMP: 5 EST: 2016
SALES (est): 44.15K **Privately Held**
SIC: **7822** Motion picture and tape distribution

(G-10819)
GENERAL ELECTRIC COMPANY
Also Called: GE
400 Bellevue Rd (19713-3432)
PHONE..................302 631-1300
EMP: 240
SALES (corp-wide): 76.56B **Publicly Held**
Web: www.ge.com
SIC: **3724** Aircraft engines and engine parts
PA: General Electric Company
    1 Financial Ctr Ste 3700
    Boston MA 02111
    617 443-3000

(G-10820)
GENOHM INC
2915 Ogletown Rd (19713-1927)
PHONE..................646 616-7531
Frederik Decouttere, *CEO*
Frederik Decouttere, *CEO*
EMP: 7 EST: 2012
SALES (est): 169.56K **Privately Held**
Web: explore.agilent.com
SIC: **7371** Computer software development

(G-10821)
GEO-PLUS CORPORATION
2915 Ogletown Rd (19713-1927)
PHONE..................800 672-1733
Wilfrid Beaupre, *Pr*
EMP: 10 EST: 2004
SALES (est): 32.18K **Privately Held**
Web: www.geo-plus.com
SIC: **7379** 5045 Computer related services, nec; Computer software

(G-10822)
GEODESIC MANAGEMENT LLC
15 Split Rail Ln (19702-8415)
PHONE..................302 737-2151
Keith Ghion, *Prin*
EMP: 7 EST: 2014
SALES (est): 212.25K **Privately Held**
Web: www.geodesicmanagement.com
SIC: **8741** Management services

(G-10823)
GEORGE MINKALIS
104 Lynch Farm Dr (19713-2813)
PHONE..................302 983-6475
George Minkalis, *Prin*

EMP: 5 EST: 2015
SALES (est): 54.16K **Privately Held**
SIC: **7389** Business services, nec

(G-10824)
GEORGE P STEWART
488 Walther Rd (19702-2902)
P.O. Box 1563 (19701-7563)
PHONE..................302 737-4927
George Stewart, *Prin*
EMP: 5 EST: 2005
SALES (est): 465.48K **Privately Held**
SIC: **1611** Surfacing and paving

(G-10825)
GEOSPOT COMMUNITY LLC
211 Amstel Way (19711-7968)
PHONE..................570 504-4115
Jason Bamford, *CEO*
EMP: 5 EST: 2016
SALES (est): 101.81K **Privately Held**
SIC: **7371** Computer software development and applications

(G-10826)
GERIS AUTO FINANCIAL SVCS LLC
23 Geneva Ct Apt B4 (19702-2619)
PHONE..................302 660-9719
Geraldine Rilley, *Pt*
EMP: 6 EST: 2013
SALES (est): 270.82K **Privately Held**
SIC: **6163** Loan agents

(G-10827)
GES-BAY WEST JOINT VENTURE LLC
70 Albe Dr (19702-1322)
PHONE..................302 918-3070
Joseph Cunane, *Pr*
EMP: 6 EST: 2017
SALES (est): 49.4K **Privately Held**
SIC: **8744** Facilities support services

(G-10828)
GETTIER SECURITY
1901 Ogletown Rd (19711-5437)
PHONE..................302 652-2700
Daniel Coe, *Prin*
EMP: 11 EST: 2013
SALES (est): 168.07K **Privately Held**
Web: www.gettiersecurity.com
SIC: **7381** Security guard service

(G-10829)
GFC LOGISTICS LLC
200 Continental Dr Ste 401 (19713-4334)
PHONE..................302 203-9511
Nick Berg, *Managing Member*
EMP: 2 EST: 2018
SALES (est): 225K **Privately Held**
Web: www.gfc-logistics.com
SIC: **3661** Fiber optics communications equipment

(G-10830)
GHT AUTOGLASS
15 Merriman Rd (19713-2514)
PHONE..................302 494-4369
George Terry, *Prin*
EMP: 5 EST: 2018
SALES (est): 29.18K **Privately Held**
Web: www.ghtautoglass1.com
SIC: **7536** Automotive glass replacement shops

(G-10831)
GI SPECIALISTS OF DE
2600 Glasgow Ave Ste 106 (19702-5703)
P.O. Box 5372 (19808-0372)
PHONE..................302 832-1545

EMP: 14 EST: 2014
SALES (est): 1.09MM **Privately Held**
Web: www.delawaregi.com
SIC: **8011** Gastronomist

(G-10832)
GIBELLINO CONSTRUCTION CO INC
1213 Old Coochs Bridge Rd (19713-2333)
PHONE..................302 455-0500
Aldo Gibellino, *Pr*
EMP: 5 EST: 1993
SALES (est): 1.88MM **Privately Held**
Web: www.gibellinoconstruction.com
SIC: **1521** Repairing fire damage, single-family houses

(G-10833)
GIESELA INC
2035 Sunset Lake Rd Ste B2 (19702-2600)
PHONE..................855 556-4338
Shikhir Arora, *Pr*
Simon Berger, *VP*
EMP: 2 EST: 2018
SALES (est): 56.54K **Privately Held**
Web: www.giesela.io
SIC: **7372** 7371 7389 Application computer software; Computer software development; Business services, nec

(G-10834)
GIFTY A NYINAKU LPN
315 Valley Stream Dr (19702-2932)
PHONE..................571 224-2660
Gifty A Nyinaku, *Prin*
EMP: 9 EST: 2012
SALES (est): 206.32K **Privately Held**
SIC: **8011** Offices and clinics of medical doctors

(G-10835)
GILANTE SCIENTIFIC LLC
18 Shea Way Ste 106 (19713-3448)
PHONE..................302 317-6060
EMP: 5 EST: 2016
SALES (est): 138.87K **Privately Held**
Web: www.gilantesci.com
SIC: **5049** Laboratory equipment, except medical or dental

(G-10836)
GILES ENTERPRISE
4142 Ogletown Stanton Rd (19713-4169)
PHONE..................302 559-2577
Jose Giles, *Prin*
EMP: 5 EST: 2010
SALES (est): 82.89K **Privately Held**
SIC: **7389** Business services, nec

(G-10837)
GINCH GONCH CORP
2915 Ogletown Rd (19713-1927)
PHONE..................713 240-9900
Robert Chouecke, *Pr*
Neil Rohr, *Sec*
EMP: 2 EST: 2017
SALES (est): 156.76K **Privately Held**
Web: www.ginchgonch.com
SIC: **2254** Knit underwear mills

(G-10838)
GIRL SCUTS OF CHSPAKE BAY CNCI (PA)
225 Old Baltimore Pike (19702-8409)
PHONE..................302 456-7150
Anne T Hogan, *CEO*
EMP: 32 EST: 1935
SQ FT: 20,000
SALES (est): 4.3MM
SALES (corp-wide): 4.3MM **Privately Held**
Web: www.gscb.org

Newark - New Castle County (G-10839) GEOGRAPHIC SECTION

SIC: **8322** 8641 Youth center; Girl Scout organization

(G-10839)
GIRLEY BELLS LLC
Also Called: Girleybells.com
28 Iris Ln (19702-7402)
PHONE..................347 922-6398
April Beaufort, *Pr*
April Beaufort, *Managing Member*
EMP: 6 **EST:** 2017
SALES (est): 491.36K **Privately Held**
Web: www.girleybells.com
SIC: **5999** 7389 Cosmetics; Business Activities at Non-Commercial Site

(G-10840)
GISCO LOGISTICS LLC
462 Welsh Hill Rd (19702-1000)
PHONE..................800 226-3696
EMP: 5 **EST:** 2020
SALES (est): 79.72K **Privately Held**
SIC: **4789** Transportation services, nec

(G-10841)
GIVE ME SHELTER
209 Megan Ct (19702-2816)
PHONE..................302 420-0402
EMP: 5 **EST:** 2018
SALES (est): 92.61K **Privately Held**
Web: www.givemeshelterllc.com
SIC: **1521** General remodeling, single-family houses

(G-10842)
GJP & SONS LLC
64 Sanford Dr (19713-4029)
PHONE..................302 690-8954
EMP: 5 **EST:** 2010
SALES (est): 68.31K **Privately Held**
SIC: **1751** Carpentry work

(G-10843)
GLASGOW AUTO BODY
2905 Pulaski Hwy (19702-2113)
PHONE..................302 292-1201
EMP: 7 **EST:** 1993
SALES (est): 497.61K **Privately Held**
SIC: **7532** Body shop, automotive

(G-10844)
GLASGOW COURT ENTERPRISES LLC
268 Cornell Dr (19702-4163)
PHONE..................302 834-1633
EMP: 13 **EST:** 1997
SALES (est): 252.51K **Privately Held**
Web: www.glasgowcourt.com
SIC: **7041** Residence club, organization

(G-10845)
GLASGOW IMAGING LLC
40 Polly Drummond Hill Rd (19711-5703)
PHONE..................302 993-2330
Christopher Ciconte, *Prin*
EMP: 19
SALES (corp-wide): 10.63MM **Privately Held**
SIC: **8011** Radiologist
HQ: Glasgow Imaging, L.L.C.
1271 S Creek Rd
West Chester PA 19382

(G-10846)
GLASGOW MEDICAL ASSOCIATES PA (PA)
Also Called: Glasgow Medical Center
2600 Glasgow Ave Ste 126 (19702-4778)
PHONE..................302 836-8350
EMP: 18 **EST:** 1990
SALES (est): 5.14MM **Privately Held**
Web: www.glasgowsurgerycenter.com
SIC: **8011** Physicians' office, including specialists

(G-10847)
GLASGOW MEDICAL ASSOCIATES PA
2600 Glasgow Ave Ste 106 (19702-5703)
PHONE..................302 836-3539
EMP: 9
Web: www.glasgowsurgerycenter.com
SIC: **8011** Surgeon
PA: Glasgow Medical Associates Pa
2600 Glasgow Ave Ste 126
Newark DE 19702

(G-10848)
GLEWED MEDIA LLC
200 Continental Dr Ste 401 (19713-4334)
PHONE..................844 445-3933
Harvey Parsons, *CEO*
Sophie Patrick, *CFO*
Derrick Daniel, *CMO*
EMP: 20 **EST:** 2019
SALES (est): 319.02K **Privately Held**
Web: www.glewed.tv
SIC: **7922** Television program, including commercial producers

(G-10849)
GLOBAL AIR STRATEGY INC
40 E Main St Ste 275 (19711-4639)
PHONE..................302 229-5889
Luiz Sette, *Pr*
S Hughes, *Prin*
EMP: 5 **EST:** 2011
SALES (est): 298.71K **Privately Held**
SIC: **3728** Aircraft parts and equipment, nec

(G-10850)
GLOBAL INSTITUTE
10 Eileen Dr (19711-3814)
P.O. Box 7137 (19714-7137)
PHONE..................732 776-7360
Susanne Richert, *Prin*
EMP: 5 **EST:** 2008
SALES (est): 318.43K **Privately Held**
SIC: **8733** Noncommercial research organizations

(G-10851)
GLOBAL RECRUITERS NETWORK INC
Also Called: Grn Wilmington
3202 Drummond Plz (19711-5746)
PHONE..................302 455-9500
Jamie Mosberg, *Prin*
EMP: 9 **EST:** 2002
SALES (est): 212.93K **Privately Held**
Web: www.grnwilmington.com
SIC: **7361** Executive placement

(G-10852)
GLOBAL RECRUITERS WILMINGTO
Also Called: Jmco
1114 Drummond Plz (19711-5705)
PHONE..................302 455-9500
EMP: 5 **EST:** 2013
SALES (est): 229.6K **Privately Held**
SIC: **7361** Executive placement

(G-10853)
GLOSSGIRL INC (PA)
Also Called: Gloss City
77 E Main St (19711-5000)
PHONE..................302 737-8080
Bethany Keith, *Pr*
Gail R Davis, *Prin*
Bethany Keith, *Prin*

EMP: 5 **EST:** 2015
SALES (est): 466.39K
SALES (corp-wide): 466.39K **Privately Held**
Web: www.salondelaware.com
SIC: **7231** Hairdressers

(G-10854)
GM CAPITAL INVESTMENTS INC ◎
41 Cannon Run (19702-2443)
PHONE..................302 722-0558
Eric Young, *Owner*
Eric Young, *CEO*
EMP: 6 **EST:** 2022
SALES (est): 243.25K **Privately Held**
SIC: **6531** 7389 Real estate managers; Business Activities at Non-Commercial Site

(G-10855)
GM TRUCKING LLC
133 Torington Way (19702-2675)
PHONE..................412 609-8818
Gurnam Singh, *Prin*
EMP: 5 **EST:** 2017
SALES (est): 173.54K **Privately Held**
SIC: **4212** Local trucking, without storage

(G-10856)
GO SHOPPING INC ◎
200 Interchange Blvd (19711-9100)
PHONE..................305 370-4704
EMP: 5 **EST:** 2022
SALES (est): 78.16K **Privately Held**
SIC: **2833** Medicinals and botanicals

(G-10857)
GOBLIN TECHNOLOGIES LLC
100 Discovery Blvd Ste 802 (19713-1325)
PHONE..................302 644-5599
Dale Hoops, *CEO*
Stephen Hoops, *CEO*
Dale Hoops, *CRO*
EMP: 5 **EST:** 2018
SALES (est): 91.27K **Privately Held**
SIC: **7374** Data processing and preparation

(G-10858)
GODDARD SCHOOL
50 Polly Drummond Hill Rd (19711-5703)
PHONE..................302 454-9454
Cindy Rowles, *Admn*
EMP: 16 **EST:** 2017
SALES (est): 437K **Privately Held**
Web: www.goddardschool.com
SIC: **8351** Preschool center

(G-10859)
GOLD KEY REALTY
Also Called: Century 21
122 W Main St (19711-3241)
PHONE..................302 369-5397
EMP: 13 **EST:** 2007
SALES (est): 496.19K **Privately Held**
Web: www.century21.com
SIC: **6531** Real estate agent, residential

(G-10860)
GOLD LABEL TRANSPORTATION LLC
36 Cardenti Ct (19702-6841)
PHONE..................302 668-2383
Corey Brisco-bey, *Prin*
EMP: 5 **EST:** 2015
SALES (est): 201.03K **Privately Held**
SIC: **4111** Airport transportation

(G-10861)
GOLDEN INC
200 Continental Dr Ste 401 (19713-4334)
PHONE..................800 878-1356

Kevin Smith, *CEO*
EMP: 50 **EST:** 2021
SALES (est): 500K **Privately Held**
Web: www.goldenincorporated.com
SIC: **7349** Building maintenance services, nec

(G-10862)
GOLDEN MERGER CORP
Also Called: VCA Hockessin Animal Hospital
245 E Cleveland Ave (19711-3710)
PHONE..................302 737-8100
Shirley Lockhart, *Mgr*
EMP: 10
SALES (corp-wide): 42.84B **Privately Held**
Web: www.vcahospitals.com
SIC: **0742** Animal hospital services, pets and other animal specialties
HQ: Golden Merger Corp
12401 W Olympic Blvd
Los Angeles CA 90064

(G-10863)
GOLDENPGSUS IT CNSLTING SVCS L
112 Capitol Trl Ste A (19711-3716)
PHONE..................804 742-0710
EMP: 5 **EST:** 2021
SALES (est): 71.79K **Privately Held**
SIC: **8742** Management consulting services

(G-10864)
GOLO LLC (PA)
4051 Ogletown Rd Fl 3 (19713-3101)
P.O. Box 247 (19701-0247)
PHONE..................302 781-4260
Christopher Lundin, *Pt*
Chris Lundin, *CEO*
Jennifer Brooks, *Pr*
EMP: 25 **EST:** 2010
SALES (est): 27.31MM
SALES (corp-wide): 27.31MM **Privately Held**
Web: www.golo.com
SIC: **2023** Dietary supplements, dairy and non-dairy based

(G-10865)
GOLO LLC
Also Called: Golo For Life
203 Gabor Dr (19711)
PHONE..................302 781-4260
Chris Lundin, *CEO*
EMP: 39
SALES (corp-wide): 27.31MM **Privately Held**
Web: www.golo.com
SIC: **4225** General warehousing and storage
PA: Golo, Llc
4051 Ogletown Rd Fl 3
Newark DE 19713
302 781-4260

(G-10866)
GOOD STOCKX LLC
12 Timber Creek Ln (19711-2606)
PHONE..................949 609-9533
EMP: 7 **EST:** 2021
SALES (est): 400K **Privately Held**
SIC: **5047** Medical equipment and supplies

(G-10867)
GOODALES NATURALS
84 Warren Dr (19702-6822)
PHONE..................302 743-6455
EMP: 3 **EST:** 2017
SALES (est): 128.02K **Privately Held**
SIC: **2844** Perfumes, cosmetics and other toilet preparations

GEOGRAPHIC SECTION

Newark - New Castle County (G-10894)

(G-10868)
GOODCHILD INC
6 Brookhill Dr (19702-1395)
PHONE..............................302 368-1681
Paul R Goodchild Senior, *Pr*
Paula Henderson Newton, *Sec*
EMP: 6 **EST:** 1963
SQ FT: 11,500
SALES (est): 484.45K **Privately Held**
SIC: 7539 5015 7549 Automotive repair shops, nec; Automotive supplies, used: wholesale and retail; Towing services

(G-10869)
GOODYEAR TIRE & RUBBER COMPANY
Also Called: Goodyear
1929 Kirkwood Hwy (19711)
PHONE..............................302 737-2461
Chris Lee, *Brnch Mgr*
EMP: 5
SALES (corp-wide): 20.8B **Publicly Held**
Web: www.goodyear.com
SIC: 5531 7538 Automotive tires; General automotive repair shops
PA: The Goodyear Tire & Rubber Company
200 E Innovation Way
Akron OH 44316
330 796-2121

(G-10870)
GORDON C HONIG DMD PA (PA)
Also Called: Honig, Gordon C DMD
2707 Kirkwood Hwy (19711-6828)
PHONE..............................302 737-6333
Gordon C Honig, *Owner*
EMP: 5 **EST:** 1980
SALES (est): 977.23K
SALES (corp-wide): 977.23K **Privately Held**
Web: www.honigorthodontics.com
SIC: 8021 Orthodontist

(G-10871)
GOTSHADEONLINE INC
2860 Ogletown Rd (19713-1857)
PHONE..............................302 384-2932
EMP: 3 **EST:** 2017
SALES (est): 55.55K **Privately Held**
SIC: 3993 Signs and advertising specialties

(G-10872)
GOVERNMENT MRKTPLACE LTD LBLTY
200 Continental Dr Ste 401 (19713-4334)
PHONE..............................302 297-9694
Steven Stone, *
EMP: 42 **EST:** 2015
SALES (est): 719.3K **Privately Held**
Web: www.gov-marketplace.com
SIC: 8742 Business management consultant

(G-10873)
GOVPLUS LLC
Also Called: GOVPLUS LLC
100 Suburban Dr (19711-3597)
PHONE..............................302 292-6401
Michael Vaught, *Brnch Mgr*
EMP: 10
SALES (corp-wide): 9.07B **Publicly Held**
Web: www.govplus.com
SIC: 6022 State commercial banks
HQ: Citizens Bank, National Association
1 Citizens Plz
Providence RI 02903

(G-10874)
GOVPLUS LLC
Also Called: GOVPLUS LLC
40 Chestnut Hill Plz (19713-2701)
PHONE..............................302 456-7100
Jonica Clay, *Brnch Mgr*
EMP: 10
SALES (corp-wide): 9.07B **Publicly Held**
Web: www.govplus.com
SIC: 6022 State commercial banks
HQ: Citizens Bank, National Association
1 Citizens Plz
Providence RI 02903

(G-10875)
GOVPLUS LLC
Also Called: GOVPLUS LLC
1 University Plz (19702-1549)
PHONE..............................302 283-5600
Belinda Hawes, *Brnch Mgr*
EMP: 10
SALES (corp-wide): 9.07B **Publicly Held**
Web: www.govplus.com
SIC: 6022 State commercial banks
HQ: Citizens Bank, National Association
1 Citizens Plz
Providence RI 02903

(G-10876)
GPC CONSTRUCTION SERVICES LLC
9 Todd Ln (19713-2851)
PHONE..............................302 390-1257
EMP: 5 **EST:** 2021
SALES (est): 100K **Privately Held**
SIC: 7299 Home improvement and renovation contractor agency

(G-10877)
GPC PRODUCTIONS
38 Abelia Ln (19711-3417)
PHONE..............................302 530-4547
Stephen Mcpeak, *Owner*
EMP: 5 **EST:** 2011
SALES (est): 91.23K **Privately Held**
SIC: 7822 Motion picture and tape distribution

(G-10878)
GRAHAM PACKAGING PET TECH INC
1601 Ogletown Rd (19711-5425)
PHONE..............................302 453-9464
Bob Doyle, *Mgr*
EMP: 27
SIC: 5199 Packaging materials
HQ: Graham Packaging Pet Technologies Inc.
700 Indian Springs Dr # 100
Lancaster PA 17601

(G-10879)
GRAND DESIGNS IT SOLUTIONS LLC
113 Woodland Rd (19702-1473)
PHONE..............................302 299-3500
EMP: 5
SALES (est): 71.79K **Privately Held**
SIC: 8742 Management information systems consultant

(G-10880)
GRANITE CENTRAL DISTRIBUTORS
131 Mute Swan Pl (19711-4115)
PHONE..............................302 521-1584
EMP: 10 **EST:** 2014
SALES (est): 237.24K **Privately Held**
Web: www.granitecentral.net
SIC: 1799 Counter top installation

(G-10881)
GRASS BUSTERS LANDSCAPING CO
935 Rahway Dr (19711-2687)
PHONE..............................302 292-1166
EMP: 50 **EST:** 1988
SALES (est): 2.41MM **Privately Held**
SIC: 0782 Landscape contractors

(G-10882)
GRAVER SEPARATIONS INC
200 Lake Dr (19702-3327)
PHONE..............................302 731-1700
EMP: 12 **EST:** 1994
SQ FT: 6,000
SALES (est): 4.88MM
SALES (corp-wide): 302.09B **Publicly Held**
SIC: 3569 Filters, general line: industrial
HQ: Graver Technologies Llc
200 Lake Dr Frnt
Newark DE 19702

(G-10883)
GRAVER TECHNOLOGIES LLC (DH)
200 Lake Dr Frnt (19702-3355)
PHONE..............................302 731-1700
Bill Cummings, *Pr*
Mike Procyk, *Prin*
James Knoll, *Prin*
Robert Webb, *
John J Goody, *
◆ **EMP:** 200 **EST:** 1866
SQ FT: 43,000
SALES (est): 56.5MM
SALES (corp-wide): 302.09B **Publicly Held**
Web: www.gravertech.com
SIC: 5999 5074 3589 Water purification equipment; Water purification equipment; Water treatment equipment, industrial
HQ: Marmon Industrial Llc
181 W Madison St Fl 26
Chicago IL 60602
312 372-9500

(G-10884)
GRAYDEN APPRAISALS INC
580 Timber Wood Blvd (19702-8439)
PHONE..............................302 598-8511
Cathy Berchock, *Owner*
EMP: 5 **EST:** 2011
SALES (est): 134.44K **Privately Held**
Web: www.graydenappraisal.com
SIC: 6531 Appraiser, real estate

(G-10885)
GREAT CLIPS
212 Suburban Dr (19713-3596)
PHONE..............................302 737-2887
EMP: 6 **EST:** 2017
SALES (est): 60.36K **Privately Held**
Web: www.greatclips.com
SIC: 7231 Unisex hair salons

(G-10886)
GREATER NEWARK BASEBALL L
P.O. Box 7212 (19714-7212)
PHONE..............................302 635-0562
EMP: 5 **EST:** 2009
SALES (est): 48.6K **Privately Held**
SIC: 7997 Baseball club, except professional and semi-professional

(G-10887)
GREDELL & ASSOCIATES PA
725 Art Ln (19713-1208)
PHONE..............................302 996-9500
Gary Gredell, *Prin*
EMP: 5 **EST:** 2011
SALES (est): 91.47K **Privately Held**
SIC: 8742 Management consulting services

(G-10888)
GREEN ACRES LAWN & LDSCPG CORP
39 Brookhill Dr (19702-1320)
PHONE..............................302 332-8239
Joe Kautz, *Mgr*
EMP: 5 **EST:** 2017
SALES (est): 26.36K **Privately Held**
Web: www.greenacresde.com
SIC: 0782 Lawn care services

(G-10889)
GREENE LAWN & LANDSCAPE
6 S Fawn Dr (19711-2545)
PHONE..............................302 379-4425
Andrew Greene, *Owner*
EMP: 5 **EST:** 2015
SALES (est): 116.69K **Privately Held**
SIC: 8711 Engineering services

(G-10890)
GREENLEAF TURF SOLUTIONS INC
9 Albe Dr Ste C (19702-1380)
PHONE..............................302 731-1075
David Greenleaf, *Prin*
EMP: 9 **EST:** 2013
SALES (est): 764.89K **Privately Held**
Web: www.greenleafturfsolutions.com
SIC: 0782 Turf installation services, except artificial
PA: Central Irrigation Supply, Inc.
8 Williams St Fl 2
Elmsford NY 10523

(G-10891)
GREENWAY COMFORT SOLUTIONS
8 Westover Woods Dr (19702-1324)
PHONE..............................302 200-4929
EMP: 9 **EST:** 2018
SALES (est): 491.11K **Privately Held**
Web: www.greenwaycomfort.com
SIC: 1711 Warm air heating and air conditioning contractor

(G-10892)
GREG MOTORS USA INC
2915 Ogletown Rd (19713-1927)
PHONE..............................302 266-8200
Serge Michaud, *Pr*
EMP: 5 **EST:** 2016
SALES (est): 162.52K **Privately Held**
Web: www.phmcgpe.com
SIC: 5012 Automobiles and other motor vehicles

(G-10893)
GREG SMITH EQUIPMENT INC
250 Executive Dr Ste 123 (19702-3336)
PHONE..............................302 894-9333
Greg Smith, *Owner*
▲ **EMP:** 7 **EST:** 2005
SALES (est): 192.35K **Privately Held**
Web: www.tooltopia.com
SIC: 5046 Commercial equipment, nec

(G-10894)
GREG SMITH EQUIPMENT SALES LLC
250 Executive Dr Ste 1 (19702-3336)
PHONE..............................302 894-9333
EMP: 6
SALES (corp-wide): 5.21MM **Privately Held**
Web: www.tooltopia.com
SIC: 5013 Tools and equipment, automotive
PA: Greg Smith Equipment Sales, Llc
6278 W 300 N
Greenfield IN 46140
317 333-8444

Newark - New Castle County (G-10895) — GEOGRAPHIC SECTION

(G-10895)
GREGG ZOARSKI
4755 Ogletown Stanton Rd (19718-2200)
PHONE..................302 733-1487
Gregg Zoarski, *Prin*
EMP: 10 **EST:** 2012
SALES (est): 349.09K **Privately Held**
Web: www.christianacare.org
SIC: 8011 General and family practice, physician/surgeon

(G-10896)
GREGGII INC
200 Continental Dr (19713-4334)
PHONE..................647 606-3348
Mina Ghabryal, *CEO*
EMP: 10
SALES (est): 348.32K **Privately Held**
SIC: 7371 Computer software development and applications

(G-10897)
GREGORY A MAAHS SR
69 S Skyward Dr (19713-2847)
PHONE..................302 359-9077
Gregory A Maahs Senior, *Prin*
EMP: 5 **EST:** 2009
SALES (est): 140.52K **Privately Held**
SIC: 4212 Local trucking, without storage

(G-10898)
GREY ROCK FARMS LLC
189 N Star Rd (19711-2921)
PHONE..................215 847-3478
Dawn Davis, *Prin*
EMP: 5 **EST:** 2019
SALES (est): 174.33K **Privately Held**
SIC: 0191 General farms, primarily crop

(G-10899)
GRIER SIGNS
4 Bridgeview Ct (19711-7454)
PHONE..................302 737-4823
Robert Grier, *Owner*
EMP: 3 **EST:** 1972
SALES (est): 99.12K **Privately Held**
SIC: 3993 Signs and advertising specialties

(G-10900)
GRIME BUSTERS USA INC
3 Misty Ct (19702-4726)
PHONE..................302 834-7006
Edward Wilberg Junior, *Pr*
EMP: 6 **EST:** 1990
SALES (est): 194.81K **Privately Held**
SIC: 7217 5087 Carpet and upholstery cleaning on customer premises; Carpet and rug cleaning equipment and supplies, commercial

(G-10901)
GROFOS INTERNATIONAL LLC (PA)
Also Called: 5 Roads
1 Innovation Way Ste 426 (19711-5463)
PHONE..................302 635-4805
EMP: 6 **EST:** 2013
SALES (est): 5K
SALES (corp-wide): 5K **Privately Held**
Web: www.5-roads.com
SIC: 7299 8742 Information services, consumer; Management consulting services

(G-10902)
GROWING & GLOWING LLC
1 Smalleys Cv (19702-5262)
PHONE..................302 500-9220
Leslie Salazar, *Managing Member*
EMP: 5
SALES (est): 113.46K **Privately Held**
SIC: 7231 7389 Beauty shops; Business services, nec

(G-10903)
GROWTH INC
311 Ruthar Dr (19711-8016)
PHONE..................302 366-0848
John Riley, *CEO*
EMP: 23 **EST:** 2004
SALES (est): 1.53MM **Privately Held**
Web: www.sayyestogrowth.com
SIC: 7336 2759 Commercial art and graphic design; Publication printing

(G-10904)
GROWTH CAVE LLC ◇
254 Chapman Rd Ste 208634 (19702-5413)
PHONE..................323 688-5042
Lucas Lee-tyson, *Managing Member*
EMP: 40 **EST:** 2023
SALES (est): 1.06MM **Privately Held**
SIC: 7371 Computer software development

(G-10905)
GUARD PROSTAMP INC
4 Peddlers Row Unit 299 (19702-1525)
PHONE..................626 290-3357
Bo Liu, *CEO*
EMP: 2
SALES (est): 87.4K **Privately Held**
SIC: 7372 Prepackaged software

(G-10906)
GUARDIAN ANGEL HM HLTH CARE AG
30 Prestbury Sq Ste 301 (19713-3235)
PHONE..................302 476-1281
Beyan Kesselly, *Managing Member*
EMP: 6 **EST:** 2019
SALES (est): 245.39K **Privately Held**
SIC: 8082 Home health care services

(G-10907)
GUARDIAN ENVMTL SVCS CO INC
70 Albe Dr (19702-1322)
PHONE..................302 918-3070
Joseph A Cunane, *Pr*
Herbert G Vandeusen, *
Nona M Vandeusen, *
Sherry Maule, *
EMP: 65 **EST:** 1988
SQ FT: 6,000
SALES (est): 19.72MM **Privately Held**
Web: www.gesoncall.com
SIC: 1541 4959 Industrial buildings, new construction, nec; Environmental cleanup services

(G-10908)
GUSTAVO E ESPINOSA
Also Called: G & A Repairs & Improvements
111 Radcliffe Dr (19711-3146)
PHONE..................302 731-5203
Gustavo E Espinosa, *Prin*
EMP: 5 **EST:** 2009
SALES (est): 98.9K **Privately Held**
SIC: 7699 Repair services, nec

(G-10909)
GWANTEL INTL CORP ENGRG & TECH
Also Called: Gwantel-Usa
21 Hidden Valley Dr Fl B (19711-7463)
PHONE..................302 377-6235
Frank Gao, *Pr*
Harry Wang, *VP*
Gilbert Tellez, *VP*
EMP: 8 **EST:** 2001
SALES (est): 324.48K **Privately Held**
SIC: 8748 Environmental consultant

(G-10910)
GWP GROUP LLC
200 Continental Dr Ste 401 (19713-4334)
PHONE..................888 217-4497
Timothy Patton, *Managing Member*
EMP: 25 **EST:** 2018
SALES (est): 890.27K **Privately Held**
SIC: 8742 Management consulting services

(G-10911)
H & J UNISEX SALON
15 Salem Village Sq (19713-2976)
PHONE..................302 983-6833
Helen Henry, *Owner*
EMP: 5 **EST:** 2013
SALES (est): 40.5K **Privately Held**
SIC: 7231 Beauty shops

(G-10912)
H & R BLOCK
Also Called: H & R Block
561 College Sq (19711-8603)
PHONE..................302 368-7500
EMP: 7 **EST:** 2015
SALES (est): 22.1K **Privately Held**
Web: www.hrblock.com
SIC: 7291 Tax return preparation services

(G-10913)
H I E CONTRACTORS INC
324 Markus Ct (19713-1151)
PHONE..................302 224-3032
James Houston, *CEO*
Judy Houston, *Sec*
EMP: 18 **EST:** 1983
SALES (est): 1.03MM **Privately Held**
SIC: 1623 Sewer line construction

(G-10914)
H K GRIFFITH INC
115 Happy Ln (19711-8020)
PHONE..................302 368-4635
John Mclaughlin, *Pr*
Ronald Jackson, *
EMP: 40 **EST:** 1973
SQ FT: 20,000
SALES (est): 11.13MM **Privately Held**
Web: www.hkgriffith.com
SIC: 1761 Roofing contractor

(G-10915)
H&J TRUCKING CORP
254 Chapman Rd Ste 208 (19702-5413)
PHONE..................516 737-9134
Shamard Gooding, *Admn*
EMP: 7
SALES (est): 532.73K **Privately Held**
SIC: 3537 Trucks, tractors, loaders, carriers, and similar equipment

(G-10916)
HACKNEY BUSINESS SOLUTIONS LLC
930 Alexandria Dr (19711-7701)
PHONE..................843 496-7236
EMP: 9
SALES (est): 401.42K **Privately Held**
SIC: 6311 Life insurance

(G-10917)
HAGERTY HOMES LLC
42 E Periwinkle Ln (19711-6215)
PHONE..................302 234-4268
Kathryn Hagerty, *Prin*
EMP: 7 **EST:** 2014
SALES (est): 229.84K **Privately Held**
SIC: 1522 Residential construction, nec

(G-10918)
HAIR ACADEMY LLC
Also Called: Hair Acdemy Schl Brbering Buty
160 Pencader Plz (19713-3408)
PHONE..................302 738-6251
Raymond Noel, *Managing Member*
EMP: 5 **EST:** 1982
SALES (est): 241.45K **Privately Held**
Web: www.hairacademysbb.edu
SIC: 7231 Beauty schools

(G-10919)
HAIR STUDIO
133 E Elgin Ct (19702-4004)
PHONE..................302 740-4804
Linda Mullins, *Prin*
EMP: 5 **EST:** 2016
SALES (est): 50.29K **Privately Held**
SIC: 7231 Hairdressers

(G-10920)
HAIRCUT & COMPANY INC
Also Called: Haircut & Co
47 Tenby Chase Dr (19711-2440)
PHONE..................302 239-3236
William Gioffre, *Pr*
EMP: 5 **EST:** 1979
SQ FT: 800
SALES (est): 57.43K **Privately Held**
SIC: 7241 Hair stylist, men

(G-10921)
HALE BYRNES HOUSE
606 Stanton Christiana Rd (19713-2109)
PHONE..................302 998-3792
Barbara White, *Ch*
EMP: 6 **EST:** 1750
SALES (est): 11K **Privately Held**
Web: www.halebyrnes.org
SIC: 8412 Museum

(G-10922)
HAMLIN MONA LIZA BSN RN IBCLC
306 Cox Rd (19711-3025)
PHONE..................302 235-8277
Mona Liza Hamlin, *Prin*
EMP: 5 **EST:** 2019
SALES (est): 62.19K **Privately Held**
SIC: 8049 Nurses, registered and practical

(G-10923)
HAMMOND M KNOX DDS
13 Thomas Ln N (19711-4865)
PHONE..................302 383-6696
Hammond Knox, *Pr*
EMP: 8 **EST:** 2017
SALES (est): 69.7K **Privately Held**
SIC: 8021 Dentists' office

(G-10924)
HANBANG GROUP
201 Ruthar Dr (19711-8029)
PHONE..................626 506-7585
EMP: 5 **EST:** 2015
SALES (est): 119.63K **Privately Held**
Web: www.gammascout.com
SIC: 3829 Measuring and controlling devices, nec

(G-10925)
HANDYMAN MARK
213 Mulberry Rd (19711-5519)
PHONE..................302 454-1170
Mark Liebal, *Owner*
EMP: 5 **EST:** 2014
SALES (est): 36.41K **Privately Held**
Web: handymanmarks.wordpress.com
SIC: 7299 Handyman service

GEOGRAPHIC SECTION

Newark - New Castle County (G-10958)

(G-10926)
HAPPY HNDS FEET KIDZ TRNSP LLC
262 Chapman Rd Ste 221 (19702-5448)
PHONE..................302 897-2375
Jessica Davis, *Managing Member*
EMP: 5 EST: 2021
SALES (est): 90K Privately Held
SIC: 4151 School buses

(G-10927)
HAPPY KIDS ACADEMY INC
273 Old Baltimore Pike (19702-1420)
PHONE..................302 369-6929
Mariam Banoub, *Pr*
EMP: 11 EST: 2007
SALES (est): 180.62K Privately Held
Web: www.happykidsplayground.com
SIC: 8351 Preschool center

(G-10928)
HAPPY PLACE DAY CARE LLC
4638 Ogletown Stanton Rd (19713-2007)
PHONE..................302 737-7603
Sameh Tawfik, *Prin*
EMP: 15 EST: 2012
SALES (est): 449.5K Privately Held
SIC: 8351 Child day care services

(G-10929)
HARBOR CLUB APARTMENTS
26 Cheswold Blvd Apt 2a (19713-4135)
PHONE..................302 738-3561
Paul Lawrence, *Mng Pt*
EMP: 5 EST: 1998
SALES (est): 136.13K Privately Held
Web: www.harborclubapts.net
SIC: 6513 Apartment building operators

(G-10930)
HARMONY CONSTRUCTION INC
350 Salem Church Rd (19702-1698)
PHONE..................302 737-8700
William Saienni Junior, *Pr*
Carolyn Hamby, *Sec*
Gerald Denney, *VP*
Joe Cannon, *VP*
EMP: 10 EST: 1995
SALES (est): 2.78MM Privately Held
Web: www.harmonyconst.com
SIC: 1611 1799 Highway and street paving contractor; Building site preparation

(G-10931)
HARMONY MILL LP
26 Cheswold Blvd (19713-4135)
PHONE..................302 731-7948
Jeff Kunkely, *Prin*
EMP: 6 EST: 2009
SALES (est): 153.47K Privately Held
SIC: 6513 Apartment building operators

(G-10932)
HARMONY SPA
550 Stanton Christiana Rd Ste 301 (19713-2132)
PHONE..................302 563-7723
EMP: 8 EST: 2018
SALES (est): 208.9K Privately Held
Web: www.harmonywellspa.com
SIC: 7991 Spas

(G-10933)
HARPER FITNESS
266 Romney Blvd (19702-2670)
PHONE..................302 286-0474
Robert Harper, *Prin*
EMP: 5 EST: 2014
SALES (est): 43.72K Privately Held
SIC: 7991 Physical fitness facilities

(G-10934)
HARRISON HEART DAYCARE
58 Wellington Dr (19702-4223)
PHONE..................302 836-8581
EMP: 6 EST: 2018
SALES (est): 27.63K Privately Held
SIC: 8351 Child day care services

(G-10935)
HARRISON HOUSE CMNTY PROGRAM
1415 Pulaski Hwy (19702-5104)
PHONE..................302 595-3370
Leticia Scott, *Pr*
EMP: 30 EST: 2014
SALES (est): 514.97K Privately Held
SIC: 8699 8351 Charitable organization; Child day care services

(G-10936)
HARRY HE DDS LLC
1400 Peoples Plz Ste 207 (19702-5708)
PHONE..................302 836-3711
EMP: 9 EST: 2016
SALES (est): 244.33K Privately Held
SIC: 8021 Dentists' office

(G-10937)
HART CONSTRUCTION CO INC
Also Called: Hart Management Group
109 Dallas Ave (19711-5125)
P.O. Box 721 (19715-0721)
PHONE..................302 737-7886
William B Hart, *Pr*
Lawrence J Hart, *Ex VP*
EMP: 6 EST: 1969
SQ FT: 900
SALES (est): 223.97K Privately Held
Web: www.hartconstruction.com
SIC: 1542 1541 Commercial and office building, new construction; Industrial buildings, new construction, nec

(G-10938)
HATCHING TIME LLC
305 Ruthar Dr Ste C (19711-8035)
PHONE..................800 511-1369
Ryan Flanagan, *CEO*
Yagiz Aksu, *CEO*
EMP: 11 EST: 2019
SALES (est): 4.1MM Privately Held
Web: www.hatchingtime.com
SIC: 0252 Chicken eggs

(G-10939)
HAWTHORN SUITES HOTELS INTL
410 Eagle Run Rd (19702-1603)
PHONE..................302 369-6212
Joan Payne, *Prin*
EMP: 19 EST: 2011
SALES (est): 80.29K Privately Held
Web: www.wyndhamhotels.com
SIC: 7011 Hotels and motels

(G-10940)
HAYJAY AUTO EXPORTS
900 Old Harmony Rd (19713-4107)
PHONE..................302 266-0266
EMP: 5 EST: 2015
SALES (est): 241.46K Privately Held
SIC: 5199 Nondurable goods, nec

(G-10941)
HEAL AUTISM NOW DEL FOUNDATION
133 Pawnee Ct (19702-1911)
PHONE..................302 456-1735
Eileen Coleman, *Prin*
EMP: 6 EST: 2010
SALES (est): 87K Privately Held
SIC: 8641 Civic and social associations

(G-10942)
HEART MINISTRY RADIO
20 Ricci Ln (19702-1618)
PHONE..................215 847-6664
EMP: 6 EST: 2018
SALES (est): 34.59K Privately Held
Web: www.heartministryradio.com
SIC: 4832 Radio broadcasting stations

(G-10943)
HEATHER BROUJOS AGT
33 Possum Park Mall (19711-3954)
PHONE..................302 368-8080
Heather Broujos, *CEO*
EMP: 7 EST: 2017
SALES (est): 147.4K Privately Held
Web: www.heatherbroujos.com
SIC: 6411 Insurance agents and brokers

(G-10944)
HEDGEFORCE LLC
9 Majestic Dr (19713-3070)
PHONE..................305 600-0085
EMP: 8 EST: 2010
SALES (est): 544.84K Privately Held
SIC: 8748 Business consulting, nec

(G-10945)
HELIUM3 TECH AND SERVICES LLC
197 Harriet Ct (19711-8521)
PHONE..................302 766-2856
EMP: 4 EST: 2018
SALES (est): 135.61K Privately Held
SIC: 2813 Helium

(G-10946)
HELLS KITCHEN SOFTWARE LTD
12 Furman Ct (19713-1611)
PHONE..................302 983-5644
EMP: 3 EST: 2011
SALES (est): 68.97K Privately Held
Web: www.hellskitchensoftware.com
SIC: 7372 Prepackaged software

(G-10947)
HERBSTAR INDUSTRIES LLC
94 Albe Dr Ste 3 (19702-1364)
PHONE..................302 888-9207
EMP: 4 EST: 2021
SALES (est): 355.73K Privately Held
Web: www.herbstarindustries.com
SIC: 3442 Metal doors, sash, and trim

(G-10948)
HERBSTAR INDUSTRIES LLC
94 Albe Dr Ste 3 (19702-1364)
PHONE..................754 273-4204
EMP: 5
SALES (est): 78.16K Privately Held
Web: www.herbstarindustries.com
SIC: 3442 Garage doors, overhead: metal

(G-10949)
HERITAGE INTERIORS INC
113 Sandy Dr (19713-1148)
PHONE..................302 369-3199
Roger Humpton, *Pr*
Jeffrey Faull, *
EMP: 19 EST: 1998
SALES (est): 494.4K Privately Held
Web: www.heritageinteriors.net
SIC: 1742 Drywall

(G-10950)
HERNANDEZ GUSTAVO
Also Called: Hernandez Landscaping
1 Neurys Ln (19702-1616)
PHONE..................302 354-1969
Gustavo Hernandez, *Prin*
EMP: 5 EST: 2011
SALES (est): 216.81K Privately Held
Web: www.hernandezpoetry.com
SIC: 0781 Landscape services

(G-10951)
HIDDEN JEWEL TICKETS LLC
40 E Main St # 830 (19711)
PHONE..................571 425-6522
Christopher Keys, *Managing Member*
EMP: 6 EST: 2016
SALES (est): 113.15K Privately Held
SIC: 7929 Entertainers and entertainment groups

(G-10952)
HIGH TRANSIT US LLC
1263 Old Coochs Bridge Rd (19713-2336)
PHONE..................302 286-5192
EMP: 5 EST: 2018
SALES (est): 95.99K Privately Held
SIC: 4111 Local and suburban transit

(G-10953)
HILLSIDE OIL COMPANY INC
Also Called: Meter Service
40 Brookhill Dr (19702-1328)
PHONE..................302 738-4144
James L Sellers, *Pr*
James Mackenzie, *
EMP: 28 EST: 1970
SQ FT: 3,700
SALES (est): 2.33MM Privately Held
Web: www.hillsidehvac.com
SIC: 5983 1711 Fuel oil dealers; Warm air heating and air conditioning contractor

(G-10954)
HISPANIC PERSONAL DEV LLC
2 Rolling Dr (19713-2020)
PHONE..................302 738-4782
Ronald Tello-marzol, *Prin*
EMP: 5 EST: 2017
SALES (est): 77.07K Privately Held
Web: www.hispanicde.org
SIC: 8399 Advocacy group

(G-10955)
HISPANO MAGAZINE
2 Rolling Dr (19713-2020)
PHONE..................302 668-6118
Ronaldo Tello-marzol, *Dir*
EMP: 6 EST: 2015
SALES (est): 61.75K Privately Held
Web: www.delhispano.com
SIC: 5192 Magazines

(G-10956)
HOCKESSIN LANDSCAPING
24 Donaldson Dr (19713-1783)
PHONE..................302 235-2141
John Kirk, *Prin*
EMP: 5 EST: 2018
SALES (est): 90.64K Privately Held
SIC: 0781 Landscape services

(G-10957)
HOESCHEL INV & INSUR GROUP
106 Haines St Ste A (19711-5365)
PHONE..................302 738-3535
EMP: 10 EST: 1996
SALES (est): 571.79K Privately Held
Web: www.pswealthstrategies.com
SIC: 6411 Insurance agents, nec

(G-10958)
HOLLYWOOD GRILL RESTAURANT
Also Called: Hampton Inn
3 Concord Ln (19713-3577)

Newark - New Castle County (G-10959)

PHONE..................................302 737-3900
Rodney Perkins, Mgr
EMP: 77
SALES (corp-wide): 8.88MM Privately Held
Web: www.hilton.com
SIC: 7011 Hotels and motels
PA: Hollywood Grill Restaurant Inc
3513 Concord Pike # 3300
Wilmington DE 19803
302 655-1348

(G-10959)
HOLLYWOOD TANS OF ELKTON
32 Belfort Loop (19702-5526)
PHONE..................................302 345-2510
Karin Henigan, Prin
EMP: 5 EST: 2010
SALES (est): 51.34K Privately Held
SIC: 7299 Tanning salon

(G-10960)
HOLOGIC INC
18 Bay Blvd (19702-4800)
PHONE..................................302 631-2846
Shusheng He, Mgr
EMP: 55
SALES (corp-wide): 4.03B Publicly Held
Web: www.hologic.com
SIC: 3845 Electromedical equipment
PA: Hologic, Inc.
250 Campus Dr
Marlborough MA 01752
508 263-2900

(G-10961)
HOLOGIC INC
600 Technology Dr (19702-2463)
PHONE..................................302 631-2700
EMP: 65
SALES (corp-wide): 4.03B Publicly Held
Web: www.hologic.com
SIC: 3845 Electromedical equipment
PA: Hologic, Inc.
250 Campus Dr
Marlborough MA 01752
508 263-2900

(G-10962)
HOME DEPOT USA INC
Also Called: Home Depot, The
2000 Peoples Plz (19702-5702)
PHONE..................................302 838-6818
Rob Garbacc, Mgr
EMP: 71
SALES (corp-wide): 157.4B Publicly Held
Web: www.homedepot.com
SIC: 5211 7359 Home centers; Tool rental
HQ: Home Depot U.S.A., Inc.
2455 Paces Ferry Rd Se
Atlanta GA 30339

(G-10963)
HOME SAVINGS AMERICA NEWARK
220 Continental Dr (19713-4311)
PHONE..................................302 286-7814
Jesse Mcconnell, Mgr
EMP: 5 EST: 2011
SALES (est): 258.01K Privately Held
SIC: 6035 Federal savings and loan associations

(G-10964)
HOME SERVICES UNLIMITED
22 Sailboat Cir (19702-2319)
PHONE..................................302 293-8726
Rick Smith, Owner
EMP: 8 EST: 2008
SALES (est): 510.1K Privately Held
Web: www.hsucares.com

SIC: 1761 Siding contractor

(G-10965)
HOMESTEAD NEWARK - CHRISTIANA
333 Continental Dr (19713-4329)
PHONE..................................302 283-0800
Newark Christiana, Ofcr
EMP: 13 EST: 2014
SALES (est): 70.86K Privately Held
SIC: 7011 Hotels

(G-10966)
HOMEWARD BOUND INC
34 Continental Ave (19711-5310)
P.O. Box 9740 (19714-9740)
PHONE..................................302 737-2241
EMP: 10 EST: 1996
SALES (est): 100K Privately Held
Web: www.homewardboundaz.org
SIC: 8399 Social services, nec

(G-10967)
HONESTY SERVICE
2213 Ogletown Rd Ste E (19711-5400)
PHONE..................................302 690-2433
Dan Holman, Managing Member
EMP: 8 EST: 2012
SALES (est): 293.3K Privately Held
Web: www.honestyplumbingservices.com
SIC: 1711 Plumbing contractors

(G-10968)
HOOPES FIRE PREVENTION INC
124 Sandy Dr (19713-1147)
P.O. Box 7839 (19714-7839)
PHONE..................................302 323-0220
Jeff Eastburn, VP
Jaclyn Eastburn, Pr
EMP: 18 EST: 1962
SQ FT: 8,000
SALES (est): 5.44MM Privately Held
Web: www.hoopesfp.com
SIC: 5087 Firefighting equipment

(G-10969)
HOPE WELLNESS OPPORTUNITY
2 Dempsey Dr (19713-1931)
PHONE..................................302 521-6421
EMP: 5 EST: 2014
SALES (est): 49.73K Privately Held
SIC: 8099 Health and allied services, nec

(G-10970)
HORIZON HELICOPTERS INC
2035 Sunset Lake Rd Ste A (19702-2665)
PHONE..................................302 368-5135
Harry Griffith, Pr
Judy Trella, VP
EMP: 8 EST: 1985
SQ FT: 2,000
SALES (est): 833.5K Privately Held
Web: www.horizonhelicopter.com
SIC: 4522 8299 7335 Helicopter carriers, nonscheduled; Flying instruction; Aerial photography, except mapmaking

(G-10971)
HORIZON SERVICES INC
307 Ruthar Dr (19711-8016)
PHONE..................................610 491-8800
Gary Obert Junior, Prin
EMP: 294
Web: www.horizonservices.com
SIC: 1711 Plumbing contractors
PA: Horizon Services, Inc.
320 Century Blvd
Wilmington DE 19808

(G-10972)
HOSPITALISTS OF DELAWARE
5 Deville Ct (19711-5906)
PHONE..................................302 757-1231
Rashmi Mundalmani, Prin
EMP: 7 EST: 2010
SALES (est): 87.28K Privately Held
SIC: 8099 Medical services organization

(G-10973)
HOSPITALITY HOUSE LLC ✪
254 Chapman Rd Ste 208 (19702-5413)
P.O. Box 2776 (10008-2776)
PHONE..................................929 262-1790
EMP: 5 EST: 2022
SALES (est): 258.74K Privately Held
SIC: 6513 Apartment building operators

(G-10974)
HOSTIGGER INC
2035 Sunset Lake Rd Ste B (19702-2600)
PHONE..................................650 618-9818
EMP: 5 EST: 2019
SALES (est): 251.15K Privately Held
Web: www.hostiger.com
SIC: 7372 Prepackaged software

(G-10975)
HOTELRUNNER INC
2035 Sunset Lake Rd Ste B2 (19702-2600)
PHONE..................................650 665-6405
Arden Agopyan, Pr
EMP: 25 EST: 2016
SALES (est): 1.53MM Privately Held
Web: www.hotelrunner.com
SIC: 2741 Internet publishing and broadcasting

(G-10976)
HOUGH ASSOCIATES INC
2605 Eastburn Ctr (19711-7285)
PHONE..................................302 322-7800
Tom Bombico, Pr
James J Cuff, Treas
David Fraczkowski, VP
Mitchell Hill, VP
Lisa Fauser, Sec
EMP: 21 EST: 1977
SQ FT: 10,000
SALES (est): 434.79K Privately Held
Web: www.houghassociates.com
SIC: 8711 Consulting engineer

(G-10977)
HOUSE OF YOGA LLC
7 Haileys Trl (19711-3005)
PHONE..................................302 373-9534
Janvier Kiersten Laushev, Asst Sec
EMP: 5 EST: 2018
SALES (est): 75.58K Privately Held
SIC: 7999 Yoga instruction

(G-10978)
HOUSE TO HOUSE INCORPORATION
157 Chestnut Crossing Dr (19713-2646)
PHONE..................................302 450-8445
Ernesto R Diffut, Prin
EMP: 11 EST: 2015
SALES (est): 52.37K Privately Held
SIC: 7011 Hotels and motels

(G-10979)
HOWARD B STROMWASSER
Also Called: Vision Optik
210 Suburban Dr (19711-3596)
PHONE..................................302 368-4424
Howard B Stromwasser, Owner
EMP: 6 EST: 1976
SQ FT: 1,500
SALES (est): 235.06K Privately Held

SIC: 8042 Specialized optometrists

(G-10980)
HOWARD MANAGEMENT GROUP I
22 N Valley Stream Cir (19702-2962)
PHONE..................................302 562-5051
Howard Karten, Prin
EMP: 5 EST: 2008
SALES (est): 139.59K Privately Held
SIC: 8741 Management services

(G-10981)
HP MOTORS INC
Also Called: H P Electric Motors
38 Albe Dr Ste 14 (19702-1351)
PHONE..................................302 368-4543
Richard Hamory, Pr
Richard Hamory, Pr
Charles Perkins, VP
EMP: 5 EST: 1985
SQ FT: 3,000
SALES (est): 499.05K Privately Held
SIC: 7694 5999 3599 Electric motor repair; Motors, electric; Machine shop, jobbing and repair

(G-10982)
HRC MEDICS LLC
2608 Eastburn Ctr (19711-7285)
PHONE..................................561 856-6180
EMP: 10 EST: 2019
SALES (est): 100K Privately Held
SIC: 5122 Pharmaceuticals

(G-10983)
HRD PRODUCTS INC
68d Omega Dr (19713-2063)
PHONE..................................302 757-3587
Saurabh Sheth, Prin
EMP: 4 EST: 2016
SALES (est): 83.99K Privately Held
SIC: 2899 Chemical preparations, nec

(G-10984)
HSI SERVICE CORP
220 Continental Dr Ste 115 (19713-4311)
PHONE..................................302 369-3709
David Dwire, Pr
EMP: 10 EST: 1999
SIC: 6719 Personal holding companies, except banks

(G-10985)
HUNTER CONSTRUCTION (PA)
560 Peoples Plz 282 (19702-4798)
PHONE..................................410 392-5109
Randy Richardson, Owner
EMP: 6 EST: 2003
SALES (est): 986.66K
SALES (corp-wide): 986.66K Privately Held
SIC: 1521 Single-family housing construction

(G-10986)
HUY M LE
32 Omega Dr (19713-2058)
PHONE..................................302 738-7054
Huy M Le, Prin
EMP: 8 EST: 2010
SALES (est): 221.75K Privately Held
SIC: 8011 General and family practice, physician/surgeon

(G-10987)
HUZALA INC (PA)
Also Called: Weanas
4c Aleph Dr (19702)
PHONE..................................313 404-6941
Wei Zhang, Pr
◆ EMP: 5 EST: 2013

GEOGRAPHIC SECTION   Newark - New Castle County (G-11018)

SQ FT: 5,000
SALES (est): 75.69K
SALES (corp-wide): 75.69K **Privately Held**
Web: www.weanas.com
SIC: **5699** 2329 5137 Sports apparel; Men's and boys' sportswear and athletic clothing; Women's and children's sportswear and swimsuits

(G-10988)
HYLAND RESTORATION LLC
2 Burleigh Ct Apt A5 (19702-2605)
PHONE.................................516 713-6518
EMP: 6 EST: 2015
SALES (est): 65.86K **Privately Held**
Web: www.handymaninsouthjersey.com
SIC: **1799** Special trade contractors, nec

(G-10989)
IAAD
Also Called: Indoor American Assn Del
113 Jupiter Rd (19711-3426)
PHONE.................................302 234-0214
Jitu Asthana, *Pr*
Pidren Tandon, *VP*
Vishal Tandon, *Sec*
EMP: 7 EST: 2000
SALES (est): 196.11K **Privately Held**
Web: www.iaadelaware.org
SIC: **8699** Charitable organization

(G-10990)
IAG SERVICE CORP
200 Continental Dr Ste 401 (19713-4337)
PHONE.................................302 577-1333
EMP: 7 EST: 2016
SALES (est): 243.22K **Privately Held**
Web: www.iag.biz
SIC: **4173** Bus terminal and service facilities

(G-10991)
IAN MYERS MD LLC
2600 Glasgow Ave Ste 218 (19702-5704)
PHONE.................................302 832-7600
Ian Myers, *Prin*
EMP: 16 EST: 2005
SALES (est): 990.41K **Privately Held**
SIC: **8011** General and family practice, physician/surgeon

(G-10992)
IBR GROUP INC
1098 Elkton Rd (19711-3507)
PHONE.................................610 986-8545
Ibrahim Sanni, *Pr*
EMP: 12 EST: 2019
SALES (est): 802K **Privately Held**
SIC: **8742** Management consulting services

(G-10993)
ICLEAN LLC (PA)
2035 Sunset Lake Rd (19702-2600)
PHONE.................................518 573-3446
Carmen Sharpe, *Managing Member*
EMP: 7 EST: 2019
SALES (est): 110K
SALES (corp-wide): 110K **Privately Held**
SIC: **1541** Renovation, remodeling and repairs; industrial buildings

(G-10994)
ICRUSH TECHNOLOGIES LLC (PA)
200 Continental Dr (19713-4334)
PHONE.................................302 613-2500
EMP: 10 EST: 2015
SALES (est): 1.69MM
SALES (corp-wide): 1.69MM **Privately Held**
Web: www.icrushtech.com

SIC: **7379** Online services technology consultants

(G-10995)
IDEAL PROPERTY SOLUTIONS
204 Edjil Dr (19713-2349)
PHONE.................................302 266-0451
Jessica Stiner, *Prin*
EMP: 5 EST: 2015
SALES (est): 245.22K **Privately Held**
Web: www.idealsolutions247.com
SIC: **6512** Nonresidential building operators

(G-10996)
IEC
451 Wyoming Rd (19716-5901)
PHONE.................................302 831-6231
Robert Brikmire, *Dir*
EMP: 9 EST: 2011
SALES (est): 84.64K **Privately Held**
Web: www.interstateequities.com
SIC: **8731** Energy research

(G-10997)
IGAL BIOCHEMICAL LLC
4142 Ogletown Stanton Rd Ste 244 (19713-4169)
PHONE.................................302 525-2090
Igor Shkodin, *Mgr*
EMP: 5 EST: 2010
SALES (est): 155.52K **Privately Held**
SIC: **7699** 5049 Scientific equipment repair service; Scientific instruments

(G-10998)
IGLEISIAS AQUILES
540 S College Ave (19713-1302)
PHONE.................................302 831-7100
Aquiles Igleisias, *Prin*
EMP: 6 EST: 2017
SALES (est): 22.18K **Privately Held**
SIC: **8049** Offices of health practitioner

(G-10999)
IGM LOGISTICS LLC ✿
30 Prestbury Sq Ste 309 (19713-3235)
PHONE.................................302 409-9404
Innocent Mongare, *Managing Member*
EMP: 6 EST: 2022
SALES (est): 511.4K **Privately Held**
SIC: **4213** Trucking, except local

(G-11000)
IGNITE YOUR LIGHT
904 8th St (19711-8731)
PHONE.................................302 766-0982
Kiera White, *Prin*
EMP: 6 EST: 2016
SALES (est): 59.74K **Privately Held**
Web: ignite360.kartra.com
SIC: **8322** General counseling services

(G-11001)
IKKAR INC
1 Chestnut Hill Plz (19713-2761)
PHONE.................................814 351-9394
Pavel Tsyganov, *CEO*
EMP: 10
SALES (est): 348.32K **Privately Held**
SIC: **7371** Computer software development and applications

(G-11002)
ILOVEKICKBOXING-WILMINGTON DE
6 Blackbird Ct (19702-8632)
PHONE.................................518 593-3463
EMP: 6 EST: 2017
SALES (est): 62.93K **Privately Held**
SIC: **7941** Boxing and wrestling arena

(G-11003)
IMPACT SPORTS & HEALTH INC
239 Goldfinch Turn (19711-4119)
PHONE.................................734 678-5726
Mary Van De Kerkhof, *Prin*
EMP: 6 EST: 2013
SALES (est): 91.69K **Privately Held**
SIC: **8099** Health and allied services, nec

(G-11004)
IMPERIAL MUSIC GROUP LLC
7 Bushwick Dr (19702-4247)
PHONE.................................302 289-6145
Gabriel Reyes, *Prin*
EMP: 5 EST: 2017
SALES (est): 57.6K **Privately Held**
SIC: **7389** Music and broadcasting services

(G-11005)
IMPERIAL POPCORN CORP
2915 Ogletown Rd (19713-1927)
PHONE.................................847 641-0991
Marty Faierstain, *Sls Mgr*
Audrey Martel, *
EMP: 40 EST: 2021
SALES (est): 4.5MM **Privately Held**
Web: www.imperialpopcorn.com
SIC: **5145** 7389 Popcorn and supplies; Business services, nec

(G-11006)
IMPERIAL REALTY GROUP LLC
213 Johnce Rd (19711-2290)
PHONE.................................215 850-3142
EMP: 5 EST: 2021
SALES (est): 20K **Privately Held**
SIC: **6799** Real estate investors, except property operators

(G-11007)
IMPLIFY INC
260 Chapman Rd Ste 201c (19702-5491)
PHONE.................................302 533-2345
Ravi Kondapalli, *CEO*
EMP: 21 EST: 2006
SALES (est): 371.52K **Privately Held**
Web: www.implifyinc.com
SIC: **7371** 7379 Computer software development; Data processing consultant

(G-11008)
IN LOVING HANDZ HOME CARE LLC
3 Fairway Rd (19711-5622)
PHONE.................................302 530-6344
Alexis Jones, *Managing Member*
EMP: 6
SALES (est): 71.72K **Privately Held**
SIC: **8082** Home health care services

(G-11009)
INCLUSIVE INNOVATIONS INC
2035 Sunset Lake Rd B2 (19702-2600)
PHONE.................................781 962-9959
Paul Damalie, *CEO*
EMP: 8 EST: 2021
SALES (est): 60.84K **Privately Held**
SIC: **7299** Information services, consumer

(G-11010)
INCREDIBLE ONE ENTERPRISES LLC
560 Peoples Plz Ste 255 (19702-4798)
PHONE.................................888 801-5794
Darnyelle Jervey, *Managing Member*
EMP: 5 EST: 2009
SALES (est): 1.6MM **Privately Held**
Web: www.incredibleoneenterprises.com
SIC: **8748** Business consulting, nec

(G-11011)
INDEPENDENCE SCHOOL INC
1300 Paper Mill Rd (19711-3408)
PHONE.................................302 239-0330
Catherine Pomeroy, *Dir*
EMP: 90 EST: 1978
SQ FT: 60,000
SALES (est): 12.24MM **Privately Held**
Web: www.theindependenceschool.org
SIC: **8211** 8351 Private combined elementary and secondary school; Child day care services

(G-11012)
INDEPENDENT INSUR CONSULTING
31 Golf View Dr Apt C3 (19702-1746)
PHONE.................................302 983-0298
Salathiel M Gaymon, *Pr*
EMP: 8 EST: 2011
SALES (est): 54.13K **Privately Held**
SIC: **8011** Offices and clinics of medical doctors

(G-11013)
INDEPENDENT INVESTORS INC
150 E Main St (19711-7352)
PHONE.................................302 366-1187
EMP: 5 EST: 2010
SALES (est): 144.53K **Privately Held**
SIC: **6799** Investors, nec

(G-11014)
INDO FOREIGN TRADE CRAFT LLC
254 Chapman Rd Ste 208 (19702-5422)
PHONE.................................818 927-2872
Varun Lal, *Managing Member*
EMP: 48 EST: 2021
SALES (est): 2.55MM **Privately Held**
Web: www.iftcglobal.com
SIC: **2273** 5023 Rugs, hand and machine made; Rugs

(G-11015)
INDO-AMERICAN ASSOCIATION DEL
113 Jupiter Rd (19711-3426)
PHONE.................................302 234-0214
Jitender Asthana, *Prin*
EMP: 6 EST: 2000
SALES (est): 85.64K **Privately Held**
SIC: **8641** Educator's association

(G-11016)
INDUSTRIAL TRAINING CONS INC
Also Called: Itc Specialty
13 Garfield Way (19713-3450)
PHONE.................................302 266-6100
Louis M Mene, *Pr*
EMP: 22 EST: 1987
SALES (est): 865.95K **Privately Held**
Web: www.itcsafety.com
SIC: **7311** 8331 7389 Advertising agencies; Skill training center; Product endorsement service

(G-11017)
INFECTIOUS DISEASE ASSOCIATION
Also Called: Bacon, Alfred
78 Omega Dr # C (19713-2064)
PHONE.................................302 368-2883
EMP: 9 EST: 2002
SALES (est): 986.82K **Privately Held**
SIC: **8011** Internal medicine, physician/surgeon

(G-11018)
INFECTIOUS DISEASES CONS PA
537 Stanton Christiana Rd Ste 201 (19713-2146)
PHONE.................................302 994-9692
Marshall T Williams, *Pr*

Newark - New Castle County (G-11019) **GEOGRAPHIC SECTION**

EMP: 10 EST: 1991
SALES (est): 1MM **Privately Held**
Web:
www.infectiousdiseasesdelaware.com
SIC: 8011 Internal medicine, physician/surgeon

(G-11019)
INFLOW NETWORK LLC
112 Capitol Trl (19711-3716)
P.O. Box 19711 (19711)
PHONE....................424 303-0464
Afsin Avci, *Managing Member*
EMP: 7
SALES (est): 298.99K **Privately Held**
SIC: 1731 Communications specialization

(G-11020)
INFORMATION TECHNOLOGY AFFORDA
5 W Kyla Marie Dr (19702-5498)
PHONE....................302 525-6252
John Cassell, *Prin*
EMP: 5 EST: 2016
SALES (est): 90.89K **Privately Held**
SIC: 7378 Computer maintenance and repair

(G-11021)
INN LLC A-1 DASH
380 E Chestnut Hill Rd (19713-2759)
PHONE....................302 368-7964
EMP: 15 EST: 2011
SALES (est): 98.36K **Privately Held**
SIC: 7011 Inns

(G-11022)
INNOSPEC INC
200 Executive Dr (19702-3315)
PHONE....................302 454-8100
EMP: 12 EST: 1994
SQ FT: 13,000
SALES (est): 5.36MM
SALES (corp-wide): 1.95B **Publicly Held**
Web: www.innospec.com
SIC: 2911 Petroleum refining
HQ: Innospec Fuel Specialties Llc
8310 S Valley Hwy Ste 350
Englewood CO 80112
303 792-5554

(G-11023)
INNOVATIVE HEATING & COOLG LLC
24 Lyric Dr (19702-4521)
PHONE....................302 528-4172
John Huhn, *Prin*
EMP: 5 EST: 2016
SALES (est): 116.09K **Privately Held**
SIC: 1711 Warm air heating and air conditioning contractor

(G-11024)
INNOVATIVE MACHINE LLC
53b Mcmillan Way (19713-3420)
PHONE....................302 455-1466
EMP: 6 EST: 2016
SALES (est): 208.79K **Privately Held**
Web: www.innovativemach.com
SIC: 3599 Machine shop, jobbing and repair

(G-11025)
INSLEY INSUR & FINCL SVCS INC
Also Called: Nationwide
110 Christiana Medical Ctr (19702-1697)
PHONE....................302 286-0777
Harry Insley Junior, *Pr*
Brandon Insley, *VP*
Nicholas Insley, *VP*
Anna Insley, *CFO*
EMP: 11 EST: 2009
SALES (est): 2.95MM

SALES (corp-wide): 260.93MM **Privately Held**
Web: www.insleyinsurance.com
SIC: 6411 Insurance agents, nec
PA: Relation Insurance, Inc.
1277 Treat Blvd Ste 400
Walnut Creek CA 94597
925 937-5858

(G-11026)
INSTA ANSWER LLC
200 Continental Dr # 401 (19713-4334)
PHONE....................973 303-1764
EMP: 5 EST: 2017
SALES (est): 106.49K **Privately Held**
SIC: 7389 Telephone answering service

(G-11027)
INSTAWORKS INC
Also Called: Oliv Ai
4 Peddlers Row Unit 44 (19702-1525)
PHONE....................925 389-9799
Ishan Chhabra, *CEO*
EMP: 5 EST: 2017
SALES (est): 257.12K **Privately Held**
SIC: 7372 Prepackaged software

(G-11028)
INSURANCE ASSOCIATES INC
Also Called: Nationwide
720 New London Rd (19711-2100)
PHONE....................302 368-0888
Dennis Barba, *Pr*
EMP: 15 EST: 1980
SQ FT: 4,500
SALES (est): 2.18MM **Privately Held**
Web: www.iai-de.com
SIC: 6411 Insurance agents, nec

(G-11029)
INTECH SERVICES
136 Pawnee Ct (19702-1920)
PHONE....................302 366-1442
Tom Mcnulty, *Owner*
EMP: 5 EST: 2018
SALES (est): 149.8K **Privately Held**
Web: www.intechservices.com
SIC: 3795 Tanks and tank components

(G-11030)
INTECH SERVICES INC
211 Lake Dr Ste J (19702-3320)
PHONE....................302 366-8530
Michael Paterson, *Pr*
▲ EMP: 5 EST: 1992
SQ FT: 6,000
SALES (est): 2.94MM **Privately Held**
Web: www.fluorogistx.com
SIC: 2821 Polytetrafluoroethylene resins, teflon

(G-11031)
INTEGRATED TURF MANAGEMENT SYS
Also Called: I T M S
200 Ruthar Dr Ste 7 (19711-8000)
PHONE....................302 266-8000
Stephen Lange, *Pr*
EMP: 10 EST: 1998
SALES (est): 937.47K **Privately Held**
SIC: 0782 Lawn care services

(G-11032)
INTEGRATION LOGISTICS INC
130 Executive Dr Ste 2a (19702-3349)
P.O. Box 7868 (19714-7868)
PHONE....................302 832-7200
EMP: 30 EST: 2005
SALES (est): 1.76MM **Privately Held**
Web: www.adt.com

SIC: 7373 7382 Local area network (LAN) systems integrator; Security systems services

(G-11033)
INTEGRITY CORPORATION INC
Also Called: Integrity Supply & Service
1 Innovation Way Ste 300 (19711-5490)
PHONE....................410 392-8665
EMP: 10
Web: www.integritysite.com
SIC: 5072 Hardware

(G-11034)
INTEGRITY FIRST MORTGAGE LLC
9 Peddlers Row (19702-1525)
PHONE....................302 318-6858
EMP: 5
SALES (est): 434.6K **Privately Held**
Web: www.integrityfirstmortgage.com
SIC: 6162 Mortgage bankers and loan correspondents

(G-11035)
INTEGRITY HOME HEALTH LLC
111 Rustic Dr (19713-4214)
PHONE....................302 981-4475
EMP: 5 EST: 2015
SALES (est): 46.24K **Privately Held**
Web: www.integrityhomehealthllcpa.com
SIC: 8099 Health and allied services, nec

(G-11036)
INTEGRITY STAFFING SOLUTIONS (PA)
Also Called: Integrity Staffing
700 Prides Xing Ste 300 (19713-6109)
PHONE....................302 661-8770
Todd B Bavol, *Pr*
Sean Montgomery, *
EMP: 1472 EST: 1997
SQ FT: 15,150
SALES (est): 606.41MM
SALES (corp-wide): 606.41MM **Privately Held**
Web: www.integritystaffing.com
SIC: 7361 Employment agencies

(G-11037)
INTEGRITY STAFFING SOLUTIONS
Also Called: Integrity Staffing Solutions
700 Prides Xing Ste 300 (19713-6109)
PHONE....................520 276-7775
EMP: 1041
SALES (corp-wide): 485.1MM **Privately Held**
Web: www.integritystaffing.com
SIC: 7363 Help supply services
PA: Integrity Staffing Solutions Inc
700 Prides Xing Ste 300
Newark DE 19713
302 661-8770

(G-11038)
INTEGRITY TECH SOLUTIONS INC
200 Continental Dr Ste 401 (19713-4334)
PHONE....................302 369-9093
James R Draper, *Pr*
Pam Draper, *VP*
EMP: 5 EST: 2002
SALES (est): 453.81K **Privately Held**
SIC: 1731 General electrical contractor

(G-11039)
INTEGRTIVE PSYCHLOGY GROUP LLC
300 Creek View Rd Ste 101 (19711-8547)
PHONE....................302 307-3702
Christina Zampitella, *Prin*
EMP: 18 EST: 2016

SALES (est): 991.44K **Privately Held**
Web: www.inpsychgroup.com
SIC: 8049 Clinical psychologist

(G-11040)
INTELLIGENT BUILDING MTLS LLC
40 E Main St Ste 611 (19711-4639)
PHONE....................302 261-9922
Bernhard Kinpel, *CEO*
EMP: 2 EST: 2010
SALES (est): 98.02K **Privately Held**
SIC: 3253 3269 Ceramic wall and floor tile; Chemical porcelain

(G-11041)
INTELLITEC SOLUTIONS LLC
750 Prides Xing Ste 100 (19713)
PHONE....................302 652-3480
EMP: 20 EST: 2001
SALES (est): 476.3K **Privately Held**
Web: www.intellitecsolutions.com
SIC: 7379 Computer related consulting services

(G-11042)
INTERACTIVE MARKETING SERVICES
200 University Plz (19702-1550)
PHONE....................302 456-9810
EMP: 30
SIC: 7389 Telemarketing services
PA: Interactive Marketing Services, Inc
2 N Maple Ave
Ridgely MD 21660

(G-11043)
INTERNATIONAL ASSN EMRGNCY
2 Cobblestone Xing (19702-1150)
PHONE....................302 731-5705
Lawrence E Tan, *Prin*
EMP: 5 EST: 2008
SALES (est): 45.51K **Privately Held**
SIC: 8699 Charitable organization

(G-11044)
INTERNATIONAL FOOD CO LLC
11 Salem Village Sq (19713-2976)
PHONE....................404 333-3434
Mohamed Amed, *Managing Member*
EMP: 2 EST: 2009
SALES (est): 108.51K **Privately Held**
SIC: 2051 Bread, cake, and related products

(G-11045)
INTERNATIONAL FRESH PROD ASSN (PA) ◆
1500 Casho Mill Rd (19711-3547)
P.O. Box 6036 (19714-6036)
PHONE....................302 738-7100
Catherine Burns, *CEO*
Felicia Schellinger, *Dir Fin*
EMP: 33 EST: 2022
SALES (est): 46.59MM
SALES (corp-wide): 46.59MM **Privately Held**
SIC: 6221 Commodity traders; contracts

(G-11046)
INTERNATIONAL LITERACY ASSN (PA)
Also Called: ILA
800 Barksdale Rd (19711-3204)
P.O. Box 8139 (19714-8139)
PHONE....................302 731-1600
Marcie Craig Post, *Ex Dir*
Mark Mullen, *
Carol A Dunn Meeting Planner, *Prin*
Patricia Dreyer, *
EMP: 34 EST: 1956
SQ FT: 30,000

GEOGRAPHIC SECTION

Newark - New Castle County (G-11076)

SALES (est): 1.33MM
SALES (corp-wide): 1.33MM **Privately Held**
Web: www.literacyworldwide.org
SIC: **8699** Charitable organization

(G-11047)
INTERNATIONAL N&H USA INC
1301 Ogletown Rd (19711-5419)
PHONE...............................302 451-0176
EMP: 67
SALES (corp-wide): 4.1MM **Privately Held**
Web: www.dupont.com
SIC: **2834** Pharmaceutical preparations
PA: International N&H Usa, Inc.
    2 Boulden Cir Ste 6
    New Castle DE

(G-11048)
INTERSTATE CONSTRUCTION INC
1000 Dawson Dr Ste A (19713-5805)
PHONE...............................302 369-3590
Gordon B Lester, *Pr*
James P Insley, *Prin*
EMP: 20 EST: 1986
SQ FT: 2,000
SALES (est): 2.35MM **Privately Held**
Web: www.interstateconstruction.net
SIC: **1629** Dams, waterways, docks, and other marine construction

(G-11049)
INTERSTATE MORTGAGE CORP INC
Also Called: Lowe, Robert W Agency
1933 Kirkwood Hwy (19711-5708)
PHONE...............................302 733-7620
Robert W Lowe, *Pr*
EMP: 7 EST: 1993
SQ FT: 5,000
SALES (est): 1.12MM **Privately Held**
SIC: **6163** Mortgage brokers arranging for loans, using money of others

(G-11050)
INTERSTATE STEEL CO INC
11 Taylors Farm Dr (19711-2964)
PHONE...............................302 598-5159
William F Drupieski Junior, *Pr*
Laura J Drupieski, *Sec*
EMP: 10 EST: 1984
SALES (est): 401.13K **Privately Held**
SIC: **1761** Siding contractor

(G-11051)
INTUNE AUTOMOTIVE INC
5 Trotters Turn (19711-2030)
PHONE...............................302 824-9893
Michael Till, *Prin*
EMP: 5 EST: 2017
SALES (est): 108.06K **Privately Held**
Web: www.intuneautorepair.com
SIC: **7538** General automotive repair shops

(G-11052)
INVISTA CAPITAL MANAGEMENT LLC
150 Red Mill Rd (19711-6632)
PHONE...............................302 731-6882
EMP: 93
SALES (corp-wide): 36.93B **Privately Held**
Web: www.invista.com
SIC: **2821** Plastics materials and resins
HQ: Invista Capital Management, Llc
    2801 Centerville Rd
    Wilmington DE 19808
    302 683-3000

(G-11053)
INVISTA HOME LLC ✺
200 Continental Dr Ste 401 (19713-4334)
PHONE...............................855 337-3200
Ashley Gershoony, *Managing Member*
EMP: 6 EST: 2023
SALES (est): 262.55K **Privately Held**
SIC: **1761** Roofing contractor

(G-11054)
INVISTAS APPLIED RES CENTRE
150 Red Mill Rd (19711-6632)
PHONE...............................302 731-6800
Greg Weeks, *Prin*
EMP: 6 EST: 2008
SALES (est): 238.53K **Privately Held**
SIC: **2821** Plastics materials and resins

(G-11055)
IPD TECHNOLOGIES LLC
240 Goldfinch Turn (19711-4112)
PHONE...............................302 533-8850
EMP: 2 EST: 2011
SALES (est): 93.37K **Privately Held**
SIC: **3083** Laminated plastics plate and sheet

(G-11056)
IRENE FISHER PHD
87 Omega Dr (19713-2065)
PHONE...............................302 733-0980
Irene Fisher, *Ofcr*
EMP: 10 EST: 2017
SALES (est): 22.18K **Privately Held**
Web: www.delawarebackpain.com
SIC: **8049** Offices of health practitioner

(G-11057)
IRGAU ISAIAS MD
537 Stanton Christiana Rd # 102 (19713-2145)
PHONE...............................302 892-9900
Isaias Irgau, *Prin*
EMP: 7 EST: 2018
SALES (est): 54.13K **Privately Held**
SIC: **8011** Surgeon

(G-11058)
IRON HILL APARTMENTS ASSOC
Also Called: Iron Hill Apartments
2 Burleigh Ct Ofc A4 (19702-2605)
PHONE...............................302 366-8228
Anne Andreas, *Genl Mgr*
Robin Reich, *Genl Mgr*
Arnon Perry, *Sec*
Aaron Pomares, *Genl Pt*
EMP: 6 EST: 1975
SALES (est): 423.51K **Privately Held**
SIC: **6513** Apartment hotel operation

(G-11059)
IRON HILL FENCE
1565 Old Baltimore Pike (19702-2008)
PHONE...............................302 453-9060
David E Waugh, *Owner*
EMP: 5 EST: 1978
SALES (est): 359.64K **Privately Held**
Web: www.ironhillsciencecenter.org
SIC: **1799** Fence construction

(G-11060)
ISHA BROTHERS INC
37 Coach Hill Dr (19711-7637)
PHONE...............................302 299-3156
EMP: 7 EST: 2017
SALES (est): 997.97K **Privately Held**
SIC: **4212** Local trucking, without storage

(G-11061)
ISMAIL HUMMAYUN
537 Stanton Christiana Rd (19713-2146)
PHONE...............................302 633-9033
Hummayun Ismail, *Owner*
EMP: 10 EST: 2016
SALES (est): 180.22K **Privately Held**
Web: www.hismailmd.com
SIC: **8011** Internal medicine, physician/surgeon

(G-11062)
IT RESOURCES INC
220 Continental Dr Ste 104 (19713-4304)
PHONE...............................203 521-6945
Hari Koya, *Dir*
EMP: 32 EST: 2012
SALES (est): 321.75K **Privately Held**
Web: www.it-resinc.com
SIC: **7379** Computer related consulting services

(G-11063)
IUVENTASE BIOSCIENCES INC
2035 Sunset Lake Rd (19702-2600)
PHONE...............................858 302-8583
EMP: 6 EST: 2019
SALES (est): 65.1K **Privately Held**
SIC: **7299** Miscellaneous personal service

(G-11064)
IVAN COHEN & ASSOC LLC
260 Chapman Rd Ste 205c (19702-5449)
PHONE...............................302 428-0205
Ivan Cohen, *Owner*
EMP: 9 EST: 2014
SALES (est): 122.24K **Privately Held**
SIC: **8011** Offices and clinics of medical doctors

(G-11065)
J & A GRINDING INC
307 Markus Ct (19713-1151)
PHONE...............................302 368-8760
Jeff T Coffin, *Pr*
EMP: 15 EST: 1978
SQ FT: 5,000
SALES (est): 894.38K **Privately Held**
Web: www.jagrinding.com
SIC: **3599** Machine shop, jobbing and repair

(G-11066)
J & O BUSINESS INC
122 Blue Ridge Ct (19702-2983)
PHONE...............................917 504-6062
Jing Chen, *Pr*
EMP: 5 EST: 2016
SALES (est): 169.39K **Privately Held**
SIC: **8742** Business management consultant

(G-11067)
J & S MOVING & DLVRY SVC LLC
603 Franklin Bldg (19702-5231)
PHONE...............................302 357-5675
EMP: 6 EST: 2018
SQ FT: 450
SALES (est): 458.58K **Privately Held**
SIC: **4212** Delivery service, vehicular

(G-11068)
J & T CONCRETE INC
84 Salem Church Rd (19702-2935)
PHONE...............................302 368-4949
Julio Vasquez Senior, *Pr*
EMP: 9 EST: 1989
SALES (est): 451.68K **Privately Held**
SIC: **1771** Flooring contractor

(G-11069)
J & W MC CORMICK LTD
Also Called: Maids
310 Ruthar Dr Unit 4 (19711-8036)
PHONE...............................302 798-0336
Wayne Mc Cormick, *Pr*
Jean Mc Cormick, *
EMP: 11 EST: 1985

SALES (est): 189.41K **Privately Held**
Web: www.maids.com
SIC: **7349** Maid services, contract or fee basis

(G-11070)
J BARTLEY STEWART MD
314 E Main St Ste 101 (19711-7180)
PHONE...............................302 737-3281
J Bartley Stewart, *Prin*
EMP: 9 EST: 2016
SALES (est): 77.55K **Privately Held**
Web: www.newarkpeds.com
SIC: **8011** Pediatrician

(G-11071)
J D CONSTRUCTION
5 Radnor Rd (19713-1817)
PHONE...............................302 292-8789
Jeff Denyes, *Owner*
EMP: 5 EST: 2000
SALES (est): 229.57K **Privately Held**
SIC: **1531** Operative builders

(G-11072)
J FREDERICKS & SON ELEC C
16 Flint Hill Dr (19702-2835)
PHONE...............................302 733-0307
V S Marioni, *Prin*
EMP: 5 EST: 2006
SALES (est): 189.65K **Privately Held**
SIC: **4911** Electric services

(G-11073)
J MATTHEW PEARSON LLC
24 Bar Dr (19702-4628)
P.O. Box 708 (19701-0708)
PHONE...............................302 834-4595
EMP: 5 EST: 2011
SALES (est): 175.18K **Privately Held**
SIC: **8712** Architectural engineering

(G-11074)
J MICHAELS PAINTING INC
108 Unami Trl (19711-7507)
P.O. Box 7767 (19714-7767)
PHONE...............................302 738-8465
James Purvis, *Pr*
EMP: 7 EST: 1991
SALES (est): 480.93K **Privately Held**
Web: www.jmichaelspainting.com
SIC: **1721 1742** Painting and paper hanging; Drywall

(G-11075)
J P MORGAN SERVICES INC
500 Stanton Christiana Rd (19713-2105)
PHONE...............................302 634-1000
Rich J Johnson, *Pr*
EMP: 104 EST: 1978
SQ FT: 635,000
SALES (est): 6.27MM
SALES (corp-wide): 154.79B **Publicly Held**
Web: www.jpmorgan.com
SIC: **7374 8741** Data processing service; Management services
PA: Jpmorgan Chase & Co.
    383 Madison Ave
    New York NY 10179
    212 270-6000

(G-11076)
J R RENTS INC (PA)
Also Called: Aaron's Rental Purchase
59 Marrows Rd (19713-3701)
PHONE...............................302 266-8090
EMP: 10 EST: 1996
SALES (est): 2.42MM **Privately Held**
Web: www.aarons.com

Newark - New Castle County (G-11077)   **GEOGRAPHIC SECTION**

SIC: 7359 Furniture rental

(G-11077)
J STEWART PAVING INC
488 Walther Rd (19702-2902)
PHONE..................................610 359-9059
EMP: 5 EST: 2019
SALES (est): 498.59K Privately Held
Web: www.jstewartpaving.com
SIC: 1611 Surfacing and paving

(G-11078)
J T ELECTRIC
16 Rose Cir (19711-4736)
PHONE..................................302 275-6778
James Greenplate, Mgr
EMP: 5 EST: 2018
SALES (est): 59.33K Privately Held
SIC: 1731 General electrical contractor

(G-11079)
J&J STAFFING RESOURCES INC
Also Called: J&J STAFFING RESOURCES, INC
200 Continental Dr Ste 107 (19713-4303)
PHONE..................................302 738-7800
EMP: 5
SALES (corp-wide): 24.94MM Privately Held
Web: www.jjstaff.com
SIC: 7363 Temporary help service
PA: J&J Staffing Resources, Inc.
   1814 Marlton Pike E # 210
   Cherry Hill NJ 08003
   856 751-5050

(G-11080)
JACK R KELLYS LANDSCAPE & TRE
11 Summerknoll Cir (19711-2488)
PHONE..................................302 218-6684
EMP: 6 EST: 2018
SALES (est): 242.66K Privately Held
SIC: 0781 Landscape services

(G-11081)
JACOBS SQUARED
34 Aronimink Dr (19711-3833)
PHONE..................................302 294-6607
Clifford Jacobs, Prin
EMP: 5 EST: 2014
SALES (est): 93.61K Privately Held
SIC: 1522 Hotel/motel and multi-family home renovation and remodeling

(G-11082)
JACQUELINE ALLENS DAYCARE
17 Timberline Dr (19711-7413)
PHONE..................................302 368-3633
Jacqualine Allen, Owner
EMP: 9 EST: 1989
SALES (est): 121.16K Privately Held
SIC: 8351 Child day care services

(G-11083)
JACTA ALEA EST LLC
Also Called: Planet Fitness
53 Marrows Rd (19713-3701)
PHONE..................................302 731-7360
EMP: 12 EST: 2009
SALES (est): 69.87K Privately Held
Web: www.planetfitness.com
SIC: 7991 Physical fitness facilities

(G-11084)
JADALI SEYEDMEHDI MD
324 E Main St Ste 204 (19711-7150)
PHONE..................................302 738-4300
Seyedmehdi Jadali Md, Prin
EMP: 8 EST: 2018
SALES (est): 202.12K Privately Held

SIC: 8011 Offices and clinics of medical doctors

(G-11085)
JAGUAR TUBULARS INC
2915 Ogletown Rd (19713-1927)
PHONE..................................438 778-6535
Anshu Bhatia, CEO
EMP: 8 EST: 2019
SALES (est): 90.89K Privately Held
SIC: 3317 Steel pipe and tubes

(G-11086)
JAM PRODUCTIONS
8 Hillcroft Rd (19711-5513)
P.O. Box 9585 (19714-9585)
PHONE..................................302 369-3629
Jamie Waltz, Prin
EMP: 5 EST: 2010
SALES (est): 49.72K Privately Held
SIC: 7822 Motion picture and tape distribution

(G-11087)
JAMAL G MISLEH M D
4701 Ogletown Stanton Rd Ste 3400 (19713-7007)
PHONE..................................302 658-7533
Jamal Misleh, Mgr
EMP: 8 EST: 2015
SALES (est): 194.45K Privately Held
SIC: 8011 Physicians' office, including specialists

(G-11088)
JAMES A PEEL & SONS INC
Also Called: Peel & Sons
118 Sandy Dr Ste 1 (19713-1177)
PHONE..................................302 738-1468
EMP: 5 EST: 1965
SQ FT: 4,000
SALES (est): 675.68K Privately Held
Web: www.peelbuilt.com
SIC: 1521 General remodeling, single-family houses

(G-11089)
JAMES C WANG
Also Called: Shining Nails
1450 Capitol Trl Ste 112 (19711-5700)
PHONE..................................302 737-6000
James C Wang, Prin
EMP: 5 EST: 2011
SALES (est): 66.41K Privately Held
Web: shining-nails.business.site
SIC: 7231 Manicurist, pedicurist

(G-11090)
JAMES DOCHERTY
47 Aronimink Dr (19711-3801)
PHONE..................................302 983-2653
James Docherty, Prin
EMP: 5 EST: 2018
SALES (est): 230.94K Privately Held
SIC: 1611 Surfacing and paving

(G-11091)
JAMES MORAN DO
4745 Ogletown Stanton Rd # 238 (19713-2074)
PHONE..................................302 731-2888
James Moran, COO
EMP: 13 EST: 2017
SALES (est): 64.64K Privately Held
SIC: 8011 Orthopedic physician

(G-11092)
JAMES RICE JR CONSTRUCTION CO
122 Upper Pike Creek Rd (19711-5802)
P.O. Box 7276 (19714-7276)

PHONE..................................302 731-9323
James Rice Junior, Pr
EMP: 6 EST: 1980
SALES (est): 961.35K Privately Held
Web: www.jamesricejrconstruction.com
SIC: 1521 1542 General remodeling, single-family houses; Commercial and office buildings, renovation and repair

(G-11093)
JAMESTOWN PAINTING & DCTG INC
830 Dawson Dr (19713-3416)
PHONE..................................302 454-7344
Christopher S Blackwell, Pr
EMP: 50 EST: 1985
SALES (est): 18.48MM Privately Held
Web: www.jamestownpainting.com
SIC: 1721 Interior residential painting contractor

(G-11094)
JAMESTOWN SPORTS
6 Shea Way (19713-3422)
PHONE..................................302 328-2770
EMP: 6 EST: 2016
SALES (est): 81.94K Privately Held
SIC: 8641 Youth organizations

(G-11095)
JAMIE LABER
226 W Park Pl Ste 1a (19711-4530)
PHONE..................................302 373-7890
Jamie Laber, Prin
EMP: 5 EST: 2015
SALES (est): 50.78K Privately Held
SIC: 6411 Insurance agents, brokers, and service

(G-11096)
JANICE JAMES & JOAN LLC ◆
254 Chapman Rd (19702-5413)
PHONE..................................845 682-1886
Ayesha Mitchell, Managing Member
EMP: 2 EST: 2023
SALES (est): 92.41K Privately Held
SIC: 2331 7389 Women's and misses' blouses and shirts; Business services, nec

(G-11097)
JANICE TILDON-BURTON MD (PA)
2600 Glasgow Ave Ste 207 (19702-5704)
PHONE..................................302 832-1124
Janice Tildon-burton, Owner
EMP: 5 EST: 1992
SALES (est): 786.42K Privately Held
SIC: 8011 Pediatrician

(G-11098)
JANIES ANGEL LLC
109 Cannonball Ln (19702-3097)
PHONE..................................302 669-1516
Janique Kearse, Prin
EMP: 5 EST: 2017
SALES (est): 113.59K Privately Held
SIC: 7699 Cleaning services

(G-11099)
JASON BELL DR
1 Centurian Dr Ste 101 (19713-2154)
PHONE..................................302 993-0722
Jason Bell, Prin
EMP: 9 EST: 2007
SALES (est): 244.53K Privately Held
SIC: 8043 Offices and clinics of podiatrists

(G-11100)
JAY J HARRIS PC
Also Called: Wild Smiles
220 Christiana Medical Ctr (19702-1652)
PHONE..................................302 453-1400

Jay J Harris, Owner
Jay Harris, Prin
EMP: 8 EST: 1984
SALES (est): 498.22K Privately Held
Web: www.wildsmiles4kids.com
SIC: 8021 Dentists' office

(G-11101)
JAYS AUTO REPAIR LLC
61 Blue Hen Dr (19713-3403)
PHONE..................................302 273-2811
Julius Wilkinson, Prin
EMP: 6 EST: 2018
SALES (est): 194.05K Privately Held
SIC: 7538 General automotive repair shops

(G-11102)
JEANES RADIOLOGY ASSOCIATES PC
Also Called: Delaware Open M R I
42 Omega Dr Ste H (19713-2078)
PHONE..................................302 738-1700
Linda Collin, Mgr
EMP: 8
SALES (corp-wide): 826.13MM Privately Held
SIC: 8011 Radiologist
HQ: Jeanes Radiology Associates, Llc
   888 Fox Chase Rd
   Jenkintown PA 19046
   215 728-3767

(G-11103)
JEFFREY L COOK D M D
16 Peddlers Row Ste 16 (19702-1525)
PHONE..................................302 453-8700
EMP: 10 EST: 2013
SALES (est): 241.52K Privately Held
SIC: 8021 Dentists' office

(G-11104)
JENNIFER
31 Hillcroft Rd (19711-5559)
PHONE..................................302 738-3020
▼ EMP: 9 EST: 2007
SALES (est): 144.81K Privately Held
SIC: 8011 Offices and clinics of medical doctors

(G-11105)
JENNIFER TROLIO LCSW
136 Cann Rd (19702-4765)
PHONE..................................302 836-1131
Jennifer Trolio Lcsw, Prin
EMP: 7 EST: 2010
SALES (est): 42.88K Privately Held
SIC: 8322 Social worker

(G-11106)
JENNIFERS SPA
4 S Merriment Dr (19702-5300)
PHONE..................................302 740-6363
Jennifer Allegretti, Prin
EMP: 6 EST: 2010
SALES (est): 113.64K Privately Held
Web: www.jensspa.com
SIC: 7991 Spas

(G-11107)
JEROME C KAYATTA DDS
192 Kenneth Ct (19711-8504)
PHONE..................................302 737-6761
Jerome Kayatta, Owner
EMP: 7 EST: 1989
SALES (est): 246.2K Privately Held
SIC: 8021 Dentists' office

▲ = Import ▼ = Export
◆ = Import/Export

GEOGRAPHIC SECTION

Newark - New Castle County (G-11134)

(G-11108)
JERRY L CASE DR
430 Christiana Medical Ctr (19702-1654)
PHONE..................302 368-5500
Jerry L Case Md, *Owner*
EMP: 8 **EST:** 2017
SALES (est): 105.76K **Privately Held**
SIC: 8011 Offices and clinics of medical doctors

(G-11109)
JET CARRIER
19 Shea Way Ste 308 (19713-3452)
PHONE..................908 759-6938
EMP: 5 **EST:** 2020
SALES (est): 451.29K **Privately Held**
Web: www.jetcarrier.com
SIC: 4731 Freight forwarding

(G-11110)
JEWELL ENTERPRISES INC
Also Called: Maaco Auto Painting
729 Dawson Dr (19713-3413)
PHONE..................302 737-8460
William Jewell, *Pr*
William H Jewell Senior, *Treas*
EMP: 11 **EST:** 1984
SQ FT: 12,000
SALES (est): 496.17K **Privately Held**
Web: www.maaco.com
SIC: 7532 Paint shop, automotive

(G-11111)
JFM ENTERPRISES LLC
525 Hambleton Ln (19702-4313)
PHONE..................302 836-4107
Joseph F Martin, *Prin*
EMP: 5 **EST:** 2010
SALES (est): 74.62K **Privately Held**
SIC: 8748 Business consulting, nec

(G-11112)
JIM KNNAS OPTMTRSTS OPTCANS IN
40 E Main St # 854 (19711-4639)
PHONE..................302 722-6197
Jim Kounnas, *Pr*
EMP: 19
SALES (corp-wide): 2.3MM **Privately Held**
Web: www.kuonopt.com
SIC: 3851 5995 5048 Frames, lenses, and parts, eyeglass and spectacle; Eyeglasses, prescription; Frames, ophthalmic
PA: Jim Kounnas Optometrists & Opticians Inc.
501 Silverside Rd 105-3
Wilmington DE 19809
302 722-6197

(G-11113)
JOEL CHODOS DR
930 Old Harmony Rd Ste D (19713-4161)
PHONE..................302 455-1980
EMP: 6 **EST:** 2020
SALES (est): 226.82K **Privately Held**
SIC: 8011 Gastronomist

(G-11114)
JOHN LOVETT INC
Also Called: Prime America
520 Christiana Medical Ctr (19702-1655)
PHONE..................302 455-9460
Steele Lovett, *Pr*
EMP: 10 **EST:** 1983
SALES (est): 392.17K **Privately Held**
Web: www.johnlovett.com

SIC: 6163 6153 6141 6211 Mortgage brokers arranging for loans, using money of others; Working capital financing; Consumer finance companies; Mortgages, buying and selling

(G-11115)
JOHN M D MURPHY
210 Christiana Medical Ctr (19702-1652)
PHONE..................302 368-2501
EMP: 6 **EST:** 2019
SALES (est): 109.91K **Privately Held**
SIC: 8011 Offices and clinics of medical doctors

(G-11116)
JOHN M OTTO OD
Also Called: Christiana Hosp Satellite Off
200 Hygeia Dr Ste 1420 (19713-2049)
PHONE..................302 623-0170
John M Otto, *Prin*
EMP: 5 **EST:** 1998
SALES (est): 166.13K **Privately Held**
SIC: 8042 Offices and clinics of optometrists

(G-11117)
JOHN NISTA DDS
74 Omega Dr (19713-2063)
PHONE..................302 292-1552
John Nista, *Prin*
EMP: 11 **EST:** 1995
SALES (est): 95.29K **Privately Held**
Web: www.firststatesmiles.com
SIC: 8021 Dentists' office

(G-11118)
JOHN WASNIEWSKI DMD
103 Louviers Dr (19714-4163)
PHONE..................302 266-0200
John Wasniewski Iii D.m.d., *Prin*
EMP: 10 **EST:** 2015
SALES (est): 396.49K **Privately Held**
Web: www.drwasniewski.com
SIC: 8021 Dentists' office

(G-11119)
JOHNS FARM FRESH PRODUCE
3055 Old County Rd (19702-4510)
PHONE..................302 834-3747
John Conner, *Prin*
EMP: 5 **EST:** 2010
SALES (est): 72.16K **Privately Held**
SIC: 0191 General farms, primarily crop

(G-11120)
JOHNSON MIRMIRAN THOMPSON INC
Also Called: Jmt
121 Continental Dr Ste 300 (19713-4342)
PHONE..................302 266-9600
Dave Duplessis, *VP*
EMP: 12
SALES (corp-wide): 362.51MM **Privately Held**
Web: www.jmt.com
SIC: 8711 Civil engineering
PA: Johnson, Mirmiran & Thompson, Inc.
40 Wight Ave
Hunt Valley MD 21030
410 329-3100

(G-11121)
JOHNSTON ASSOCIATES
5 Winsome Way (19702-6311)
PHONE..................302 521-2984
Dean Johnston, *Prin*
EMP: 5 **EST:** 2010
SALES (est): 229.2K **Privately Held**
Web: www.johnstonandassoc.com

SIC: 8742 Management consulting services

(G-11122)
JOINT ANLYTCL SYSTMS (AMRCS)
134a Sandy Dr (19713-1147)
PHONE..................302 607-0088
Joachim Gerstel, *Owner*
Ken Ellis, *Svc Mgr*
EMP: 4 **EST:** 2002
SALES (est): 945.57K
SALES (corp-wide): 166.62K **Privately Held**
Web: www.jas.de
SIC: 3826 5049 Chromatographic equipment, laboratory type; Analytical instruments
HQ: Joint Analytical Systems Gmbh
Carl-Zeiss-Str. 49
Moers NW 47445
28419871100

(G-11123)
JOLTTEK INC
200 Biddle Ave Ste 206 (19702-3966)
PHONE..................302 204-7629
EMP: 5 **EST:** 2021
SALES (est): 71.79K **Privately Held**
Web: www.jolttek.com
SIC: 8742 Management consulting services

(G-11124)
JOOLALA LLC
24 Polly Drummond Hill Rd (19711-5703)
PHONE..................302 444-0178
Ronny Keren Cohen, *CEO*
Mordhay Paz, *CFO*
EMP: 42 **EST:** 2021
SALES (est): 1.15MM **Privately Held**
Web: www.joolala.com
SIC: 5961 3911 Jewelry, mail order; Jewelry, precious metal

(G-11125)
JOOZOOR IPTV LLC
200 Continental Dr Ste 401 (19713-4334)
PHONE..................302 635-4092
Keiry Basilious, *Managing Member*
EMP: 13
SALES (est): 484.71K **Privately Held**
SIC: 7371 7812 Computer software development and applications; Motion picture production and distribution

(G-11126)
JOSE PICAZO M D P A
600 Christiana Medical Ctr (19702-1656)
PHONE..................302 738-6535
Jose Picazo, *Prin*
EMP: 5 **EST:** 2007
SALES (est): 396.77K **Privately Held**
SIC: 8011 Obstetrician

(G-11127)
JOSEPH J THORNTON
2600 Glasgow Ave Ste 107 (19702-5703)
PHONE..................302 355-0055
Joseph Thornton, *Owner*
EMP: 9 **EST:** 2002
SALES (est): 211.25K **Privately Held**
Web: www.thorntonplasticsurgery.com
SIC: 8011 Plastic surgeon

(G-11128)
JOSEPH STRAIGHT MD
4745 Ogletown Stanton Rd (19713-2067)
PHONE..................302 731-2888
Joseph J Straight, *Prin*
EMP: 18 **EST:** 2011
SALES (est): 244.01K **Privately Held**
Web: www.firststateortho.com

SIC: 8011 Orthopedic physician

(G-11129)
JOSEPH T RYERSON & SON INC
Also Called: Ryerson Thypin Steel
700 Pencader Dr (19702-3310)
PHONE..................215 736-8970
Amro Elsabbagh, *Mgr*
EMP: 10
Web: www.ryerson.com
SIC: 5051 3316 Steel; Cold finishing of steel shapes
HQ: Joseph T. Ryerson & Son, Inc.
227 W Monroe St Fl 27
Chicago IL 60606
312 292-5000

(G-11130)
JOSHUA KALIN MD
314 E Main St Ste 302 (19711-7181)
PHONE..................302 737-6900
Joshua Kalin, *Pr*
Harriet Kalin, *VP*
EMP: 13 **EST:** 1970
SALES (est): 211.5K **Privately Held**
SIC: 8011 Opthalmologist

(G-11131)
JP MORGAN INTL FIN LTD (PA)
500 Stanton Christiana Rd (19713-2105)
PHONE..................212 270-6000
EMP: 8 **EST:** 2020
SALES (est): 549.72K
SALES (corp-wide): 549.72K **Privately Held**
SIC: 6282 Investment advice

(G-11132)
JP MORGAN TRUST COMPANY DEL
500 Stanton Christiana Rd Fl 2 (19713-2105)
PHONE..................302 634-3800
Denise Matheny, *Ex Dir*
EMP: 166 **EST:** 1911
SALES (est): 9.85MM
SALES (corp-wide): 154.79B **Publicly Held**
Web: www.jpmorgan.com
SIC: 6021 National commercial banks
PA: Jpmorgan Chase & Co.
383 Madison Ave
New York NY 10179
212 270-6000

(G-11133)
JPMORGAN CHASE & CO
500 Stanton Christiana Rd (19713-2105)
PHONE..................312 732-2801
EMP: 19
SALES (corp-wide): 154.79B **Publicly Held**
Web: www.jpmorganchase.com
SIC: 6021 National commercial banks
PA: Jpmorgan Chase & Co.
383 Madison Ave
New York NY 10179
212 270-6000

(G-11134)
JUDITH E MCCANN DMD
101 Barksdale Professional Ctr (19711-3258)
PHONE..................302 368-7463
EMP: 7 **EST:** 1997
SALES (est): 234.89K **Privately Held**
Web: www.drjudymccann.com
SIC: 8021 Dentists' office

Newark - New Castle County (G-11135) GEOGRAPHIC SECTION

(G-11135)
JULIA TEGARDEN JORDA
820 Hilltop Rd (19711-2712)
PHONE..................302 731-1901
Julia Tegarden Jorda, *Pr*
EMP: 6 **EST:** 2018
SALES (est): 22.18K **Privately Held**
SIC: 8049 Offices of health practitioner

(G-11136)
JULIANA RECYCLING CORPORATION
61 Mcmillan Way Ste A (19713-3420)
PHONE..................347 753-6584
EMP: 6 **EST:** 2017
SALES (est): 207.72K **Privately Held**
Web: juliana-recycling.business.site
SIC: 4953 Recycling, waste materials

(G-11137)
JUNIOR BD OF CHRISTIANA CARE
Glass Box, The
4755 Stanton Ogletown Rd (19718-0001)
PHONE..................302 733-1100
Noreen West, *Mgr*
EMP: 5
SALES (corp-wide): 613.93K **Privately Held**
Web: www.christianacare.org
SIC: 5047 5947 Hospital equipment and furniture; Gift shop
PA: Junior Board Of Christiana Care Inc
501 W 14th St
Wilmington DE 19801
302 428-2246

(G-11138)
JUST FOR WOMEN OB/GYN PA
875 Aaa Blvd (19713-3624)
PHONE..................302 224-9400
EMP: 13 **EST:** 2009
SALES (est): 752.8K **Privately Held**
Web: www.justforwomenobgyn.com
SIC: 8011 Gynecologist

(G-11139)
JUSTLABORMOVERS INC
7 Westerly St (19713-1647)
PHONE..................302 444-7599
Michael Denmon, *Pr*
EMP: 5 **EST:** 2011
SALES (est): 124.65K **Privately Held**
Web: www.justlabormovers.com
SIC: 4789 Cargo loading and unloading services

(G-11140)
KALIN EYE ASSOC
Also Called: Kalin, Neil S MD
314 E Main St Ste 302 (19711-7181)
PHONE..................302 292-2020
Neil Kalin, *Owner*
EMP: 5 **EST:** 1975
SALES (est): 402.84K **Privately Held**
Web: www.kalineye.com
SIC: 8011 8049 Opthalmologist; Nutrition specialist

(G-11141)
KANGO EXPRESS INC
20 Shea Way Ste 205 (19713-3447)
PHONE..................808 725-1688
Richard Williams, *Genl Mgr*
EMP: 30 **EST:** 2015
SALES (est): 2.41MM **Privately Held**
Web: www.kangoexpress.com
SIC: 4731 Freight forwarding

(G-11142)
KARINS ENGINEERING INC (PA)
Also Called: Karins & Associates
17 Polly Drummond Shpg Ctr Ste 201 (19711-4820)
PHONE..................302 369-2900
Dev Sitaram, *Pr*
Bruce Buker, *
Edward Politowski, *
Michael Szmanski, *
EMP: 27 **EST:** 1973
SALES (est): 5.38MM
SALES (corp-wide): 5.38MM **Privately Held**
Web: www.karinsengineering.com
SIC: 8711 Consulting engineer

(G-11143)
KARIZMA SPARKS LLC
28 Clarion Ct (19713-1604)
PHONE..................302 607-5445
Katrina Brison, *CEO*
EMP: 6 **EST:** 2011
SALES (est): 270.04K **Privately Held**
SIC: 7379 0181 2015 0252 Computer related consulting services; Plants, potted: growing of; Egg processing; Chicken eggs

(G-11144)
KARLI FLANAGAN DVM
Also Called: In Home Veterinary Care
18 Silverwood Blvd (19711-8306)
PHONE..................302 893-7872
Karli Flanagan, *Owner*
EMP: 6 **EST:** 2011
SALES (est): 266.38K **Privately Held**
Web: www.inhomevets.com
SIC: 0742 Animal hospital services, pets and other animal specialties

(G-11145)
KAUTEX INC
100 Lake Dr (19702-3340)
PHONE..................302 456-1455
Clarence Garnett, *Genl Mgr*
EMP: 446
SALES (corp-wide): 12.87B **Publicly Held**
Web: www.kautex.com
SIC: 3714 Motor vehicle parts and accessories
HQ: Kautex Inc.
800 Tower Dr Ste 200
Troy MI 48098
248 616-5100

(G-11146)
KBR INC
242 Chapman Rd (19702-5405)
PHONE..................302 452-9386
Michael Kaplan, *Mgr*
EMP: 6
Web: www.kbr.com
SIC: 1629 Land preparation construction
PA: Kbr, Inc.
601 Jefferson St Ste 3400
Houston TX 77002

(G-11147)
KBR ENGINEERING COMPANY LLC
Also Called: BE&k
242 Chapman Rd (19702-5405)
PHONE..................302 452-9000
Keith Reece, *Brnch Mgr*
EMP: 80
SIC: 8711 Construction and civil engineering
HQ: Kbr Engineering Company, Llc
2000 International Pk Dr
Birmingham AL 35243
205 972-6000

(G-11148)
KCI TECHNOLOGIES INC
1352 Marrows Rd (19711-5475)
PHONE..................302 731-9176
Dwight Walters, *Brnch Mgr*
EMP: 36
Web: www.kci.com
SIC: 8711 8712 Civil engineering; Architectural services
HQ: Kci Technologies, Inc.
936 Ridgebrook Rd
Sparks MD 21152
410 316-7800

(G-11149)
KEENER-SENSENIG CO
491 Gender Rd (19713-2828)
PHONE..................302 453-8584
Dana Ressler, *Pt*
Allen Ressler, *Pt*
James Ressler, *Pt*
EMP: 12 **EST:** 1970
SQ FT: 4,000
SALES (est): 443.12K **Privately Held**
SIC: 0782 Lawn care services

(G-11150)
KELLER WILLIAMS REALTY
Also Called: Keller Williams Realtors
3 Berley Ct (19702-2839)
PHONE..................302 293-8654
Lakeisha Cunningham, *Prin*
EMP: 5 **EST:** 2016
SALES (est): 89.4K **Privately Held**
Web: www.kw.com
SIC: 6531 Real estate agent, residential

(G-11151)
KELLY ROBERT & ASSOC LLC
Also Called: Liberty Tax Service
418 Suburban Dr (19711-3564)
PHONE..................302 737-7785
EMP: 10 **EST:** 2005
SALES (est): 199.04K **Privately Held**
Web: www.libertytax.com
SIC: 7291 Tax return preparation services

(G-11152)
KELLY SERVICES INC
225 Corporate Blvd (19702-3326)
PHONE..................302 366-1741
EMP: 5 **EST:** 2017
SALES (est): 59.96K **Privately Held**
Web: www.kellyservices.com
SIC: 7363 Temporary help service

(G-11153)
KENCKO FOODS INC (PA)
2035 Sunset Lake Rd Ste B2 (19702-2600)
PHONE..................616 253-6256
Tomas Froes, *CEO*
Ricardo Santos, *Chief Business Officer*
EMP: 6 **EST:** 2017
SALES (est): 4.45MM
SALES (corp-wide): 4.45MM **Privately Held**
SIC: 2037 Fruit juices

(G-11154)
KENDAL CORP PENSION PLAN
591 Collaboration Way (19713-4053)
PHONE..................610 388-7001
Sean M Kelly, *Pr*
EMP: 16 **EST:** 2014
SALES (est): 2.84MM **Privately Held**
Web: www.kendal.org
SIC: 8051 Skilled nursing care facilities

(G-11155)
KENDAL CORPORATION (PA)
591 Collaboration Way Ste 603 (19713-5500)
PHONE..................610 335-1200
EMP: 101 **EST:** 1991
SALES (est): 11.82MM **Privately Held**
Web: www.kendal.org
SIC: 6513 Retirement hotel operation

(G-11156)
KENDAL MANAGEMENT SERVICES
591 Collaboration Way (19713-5500)
PHONE..................610 388-5594
John Diffey, *Pr*
William Rogers, *Ch*
Mark Myers, *VP*
Larry Frolik, *Treas*
EMP: 25 **EST:** 1974
SALES (est): 6.61MM **Privately Held**
Web: www.kendal.org
SIC: 6513 Retirement hotel operation

(G-11157)
KENDAL OUTREACH LLC
591 Collaboration Way (19713-4053)
PHONE..................610 335-1200
Amy Harrison, *Mgr*
John Diffey, *CEO*
EMP: 10 **EST:** 2006
SQ FT: 12,137
SALES (est): 614.74K **Privately Held**
Web: www.kendaloutreach.org
SIC: 8051 Skilled nursing care facilities

(G-11158)
KERCHER GROUP INC (PA)
254 Chapman Rd Ste 202 (19702-5422)
PHONE..................302 894-1098
Alan Kercher, *Pr*
EMP: 8 **EST:** 1994
SALES (est): 1.57MM **Privately Held**
Web: www.kerchergroup.com
SIC: 8711 Consulting engineer

(G-11159)
KERRY S KIRIFIDES MD PA
Also Called: Just Kids Pediatrics
875 Aaa Blvd Ste C (19713-3624)
PHONE..................302 918-6400
Kerry Kirifides Md, *Pr*
EMP: 21 **EST:** 2007
SALES (est): 1.76MM **Privately Held**
Web: www.justkidspediatrics.com
SIC: 8011 Pediatrician

(G-11160)
KEVAL CORP
Also Called: Comfort Inn
100 Mcintosh Plz (19713-3232)
PHONE..................302 453-9100
Jack Patel, *Owner*
EMP: 10 **EST:** 2004
SALES (est): 475.5K **Privately Held**
Web: www.motel6.com
SIC: 7011 Hotels and motels

(G-11161)
KEVAL CORPORATION
Also Called: Econo Lodge Newark
100 Mcintosh Plz (19713-3232)
PHONE..................302 453-9100
R Patel, *Prin*
EMP: 20 **EST:** 2009
SALES (est): 196.55K **Privately Held**
SIC: 7011 Hotel, franchised

(G-11162)
KEVIN J MURRAY DC
179 W Chestnut Hill Rd # 1 (19713-2210)

PHONE..................302 453-4043
Kevin Murray, *Prin*
EMP: 6 **EST**: 2018
SALES (est): 89.23K **Privately Held**
SIC: **8041** Offices and clinics of chiropractors

(G-11163)
KEVIN SMITH ✪
Also Called: Golden Incorporated
200 Continental Dr # 401 (19713-4334)
PHONE..................800 878-1356
Kevin Smith, *Prin*
EMP: 50 **EST**: 2022
SALES (est): 999.9K **Privately Held**
SIC: **7349** Chemical cleaning services

(G-11164)
KEYSTONE AUTISM SERVICES
7 Firethorn Ct (19711-4900)
PHONE..................302 731-3115
John Pengsir, *Dir*
EMP: 20 **EST**: 2002
SALES (est): 440.82K **Privately Held**
Web: www.khs.org
SIC: **8361** Halfway group home, persons with social or personal problems

(G-11165)
KEYSTONE FAMILY OFFICE INC
112 Capitol Trl (19711-3716)
PHONE..................302 377-4500
EMP: 11
SALES (est): 416.96K **Privately Held**
SIC: **8721** Accounting, auditing, and bookkeeping

(G-11166)
KEYSTONE SERVICE SYSTEMS INC
300 Creek View Rd Ste 210 (19711-8546)
PHONE..................302 286-7234
Denise Cragg, *Mgr*
EMP: 114
SALES (corp-wide): 204.33MM **Privately Held**
Web: www.khs.org
SIC: **8361** Mentally handicapped home
HQ: Keystone Service Systems, Inc.
4391 Sturbridge Dr
Harrisburg PA 17260
717 232-7509

(G-11167)
KFS STRATEGIC MGT SVCS LLC
1 Innovation Way Ste 426 (19711-5463)
PHONE..................302 757-6631
Frederick Smith Junior, *CEO*
◆ **EMP**: 5 **EST**: 2006
SALES (est): 178.61K **Privately Held**
Web: www.kfssms.com
SIC: **8748** **8742** Business consulting, nec; Business management consultant

(G-11168)
KHA-NEKE INC
Also Called: RC Turner Collection
25 Hempstead Dr (19702-7713)
PHONE..................302 440-4728
Roger Turner, *Pr*
EMP: 3 **EST**: 1998
SQ FT: 1,000
SALES (est): 250.35K **Privately Held**
SIC: **2329** Shirt and slack suits: men's, youths', and boys'

(G-11169)
KHANNA ENTPS LTD A LTD PARTNR
Also Called: Country Suites By Carlson
1024 Old Churchmans Rd (19713-2102)
PHONE..................302 266-6400
Richard Carter, *Mgr*
EMP: 15
SALES (corp-wide): 4.38MM **Privately Held**
Web: www.radissonhotels.com
SIC: **7011** Hotels and motels
PA: Khanna Enterprises, Ltd., A Limited Partnership
2601 Main St Ste 320
Irvine CA 92614
949 502-7892

(G-11170)
KHMISAT LLC ✪
254 Chapman Rd (19702-5413)
PHONE..................302 533-1303
Yassine Mohdar, *Managing Member*
EMP: 2 **EST**: 2023
SALES (est): 92.41K **Privately Held**
SIC: **2844** **7389** Shampoos, rinses, conditioners: hair; Business Activities at Non-Commercial Site

(G-11171)
KIDDIE INTERNATIONAL ACADEMY
843 Salem Church Rd (19702-4015)
PHONE..................302 838-2183
EMP: 9 **EST**: 2007
SALES (est): 69.3K **Privately Held**
Web: www.kiadaycare.com
SIC: **8351** Group day care center

(G-11172)
KIDS CLUB FOUNDATION DELAWARE
111 Register Dr (19711-2287)
PHONE..................302 733-0168
Nicole M Quinn, *Asst Sec*
EMP: 5 **EST**: 2018
SALES (est): 55.35K **Privately Held**
Web: www.kidsclubfoundation.org
SIC: **8641** Civic and social associations

(G-11173)
KIDS KASTLE DAY CARE
2 Stallion Dr (19713-3570)
PHONE..................302 740-8803
Coco Thompson, *Dir*
EMP: 10 **EST**: 2018
SALES (est): 22.66K **Privately Held**
SIC: **8351** Group day care center

(G-11174)
KIDS NEST DAY CARE
24 Donaldson Dr (19713-1783)
PHONE..................302 731-7017
EMP: 5 **EST**: 2011
SALES (est): 104.08K **Privately Held**
Web: www.kidsnestdaycare.com
SIC: **8351** Preschool center

(G-11175)
KIMBERTON APARTMENTS ASSOC LP
Also Called: Carrington Way Apartments
100 Kimberton Dr (19713-1676)
PHONE..................302 368-0116
William Demarco, *Pt*
Michael Stahler, *Contrlr*
EMP: 5 **EST**: 2009
SALES (est): 129.22K **Privately Held**
SIC: **6513** Apartment building operators

(G-11176)
KINDERCARE LEARNING CTRS LLC
100 Paxson Dr (19702-4738)
PHONE..................302 834-6931
Irene Kerrigan, *Dir*
EMP: 15
SALES (corp-wide): 967.64MM **Privately Held**
Web: www.kindercare.com
SIC: **8351** **8211** Group day care center; Kindergarten
HQ: Kindercare Learning Centers, Llc
650 Ne Holladay St # 1400
Portland OR 97232

(G-11177)
KINETIC OASIS LLC ✪
254 Chapman Rd Ste 208 (19702-5422)
PHONE..................508 202-0559
Zachary Frew, *CEO*
EMP: 2 **EST**: 2023
SALES (est): 66.57K **Privately Held**
SIC: **3679** Electronic components, nec

(G-11178)
KING OF MANGOES
2 Greenwich Ct (19702-4235)
PHONE..................302 547-2500
EMP: 5 **EST**: 2019
SALES (est): 68.12K **Privately Held**
Web: www.kingofmangoes.com
SIC: **0191** General farms, primarily crop

(G-11179)
KINGS TOWING COMPANY LLC ✪
160 Scottfield Dr (19713-2458)
P.O. Box 1183 (19701-7183)
PHONE..................302 345-3134
EMP: 9 **EST**: 2022
SALES (est): 287.79K **Privately Held**
SIC: **7549** **7389** Towing service, automotive; Business services, nec

(G-11180)
KINNEYS ENTERPRISES LLC
17 Latham Ln (19713-3118)
PHONE..................302 300-2012
Joseph Mugo, *Pr*
EMP: 5 **EST**: 2018
SALES (est): 414.12K **Privately Held**
SIC: **5088** Transportation equipment and supplies

(G-11181)
KIRKS FLOWERS INC
Also Called: Kirk Flowers
7 Ash Ave (19711-5500)
PHONE..................302 737-3931
John Mayer, *Pr*
Elizabeth Mayer, *VP*
EMP: 8 **EST**: 1934
SQ FT: 6,000
SALES (est): 389.66K **Privately Held**
Web: www.kirksflowers.com
SIC: **5992** **7389** Flowers, fresh; Interior decorating

(G-11182)
KIRKWOOD ANMAL BRDING GROOMING
Also Called: V C A Kirkwood Animal Hospital
1501 Capitol Trl (19711-5715)
PHONE..................302 737-1098
Linda Simione, *Mgr*
EMP: 11 **EST**: 2000
SALES (est): 372.09K
SALES (corp-wide): 42.84B **Privately Held**
Web: www.vcahospitals.com
SIC: **0742** Animal hospital services, pets and other animal specialties
HQ: Vca Inc.
12401 W Olympic Blvd
Los Angeles CA 90064
310 571-6500

(G-11183)
KIRKWOOD DENTAL ASSOCIATES PA
1260 Peoples Plz Bldg 1200 (19702-5701)
PHONE..................302 834-7700
EMP: 8
SALES (corp-wide): 2.46MM **Privately Held**
Web: www.kirkwooddental.com
SIC: **8021** Dentists' office
PA: Kirkwood Dental Associates Pa
710 Greenbank Rd Ste A
Wilmington DE 19808
302 994-2582

(G-11184)
KIRKWOOD DENTAL ASSOCIATES PA
1200 Peoples Plz Ste 1260 (19702-5701)
PHONE..................302 834-7700
EMP: 6
SALES (corp-wide): 2.38MM **Privately Held**
Web: www.kirkwooddental.com
SIC: **8021** Dentists' office
PA: Kirkwood Dental Associates Pa
710 Greenbank Rd Ste A
Wilmington DE 19808
302 994-2582

(G-11185)
KIRKWOOD SMOKE SHOP
151 E Main St (19711-7313)
PHONE..................302 525-6718
EMP: 5 **EST**: 2010
SALES (est): 171.13K **Privately Held**
SIC: **5159** Tobacco distributors and products

(G-11186)
KIRKWOOD TIRES INC
1929 Kirkwood Hwy (19711-5773)
PHONE..................302 737-2460
TOLL FREE: 800
Clarence E Ward Junior, *Pr*
EMP: 5 **EST**: 1963
SQ FT: 4,000
SALES (est): 572.89K **Privately Held**
Web: www.admiraltire.com
SIC: **5531** **7538** Automotive tires; General automotive repair shops

(G-11187)
KISSANGEN INC
Also Called: Ksn
113 Barksdale Pro Ctr (19711-3258)
PHONE..................414 446-4182
Jeff Hunter, *COO*
Mark Hufham, *CEO*
EMP: 7 **EST**: 2013
SQ FT: 20,000
SALES (est): 128.77K **Privately Held**
SIC: **3569** **3511** **3621** Gas producers, generators, and other gas related equipment; Turbines and turbine generator sets; Storage battery chargers, motor and engine generator type

(G-11188)
KITTY JAZZY PUBLISHING
702 Cobble Creek Curv (19702-2421)
PHONE..................302 897-8842
Kevin Attaway, *Owner*
EMP: 4 **EST**: 2015
SALES (est): 59.3K **Privately Held**
SIC: **2741** Miscellaneous publishing

(G-11189)
KJOY LLC
356 E Main St (19711-7194)
PHONE..................302 588-5420
EMP: 5 **EST**: 2009
SALES (est): 121.83K **Privately Held**

Newark - New Castle County (G-11190) **GEOGRAPHIC SECTION**

SIC: 6519 Real property lessors, nec

(G-11190)
KLEINHOMERS
15 Forestal Cir (19711-2985)
PHONE..................302 234-2392
Kevin Kleinhomer, *Prin*
EMP: 5 EST: 2016
SALES (est): 86.48K **Privately Held**
SIC: 1521 Single-family housing construction

(G-11191)
KLICK INC
40 Garvey Ln (19702-6302)
PHONE..................302 292-8455
Chris Caputo, *Owner*
EMP: 12 EST: 2007
SALES (est): 431.66K **Privately Held**
Web: www.klick.com
SIC: 7389 Business Activities at Non-Commercial Site

(G-11192)
KMK PORTABLE MOVING & STOR LLC
40 Silverwood Blvd (19711-8306)
PHONE..................302 734-0410
Chris Roethel, *Owner*
EMP: 5 EST: 2006
SALES (est): 228.81K **Privately Held**
SIC: 4214 Local trucking with storage

(G-11193)
KMP MECHANICAL LLC
406 Suburban Dr # 155 (19711-3566)
PHONE..................410 392-6126
EMP: 5
Web: www.kmpmechanical.com
SIC: 1711 Mechanical contractor
PA: Kmp Mechanical Llc
45 Appleton Rd
Elkton MD 21921

(G-11194)
KMP MECHANICAL LLC
118 Sandy Dr Ste 5 (19713-1177)
PHONE..................410 392-6126
EMP: 5
Web: www.kmpmechanical.com
SIC: 1711 Mechanical contractor
PA: Kmp Mechanical Llc
45 Appleton Rd
Elkton MD 21921

(G-11195)
KNEADING TO HEEL
103 Forsythia Dr (19711-6856)
PHONE..................302 740-4647
Michelle Rutter, *Prin*
EMP: 5 EST: 2010
SALES (est): 176.06K **Privately Held**
Web: www.kneadingtoheelmassage.com
SIC: 7299 Massage parlor

(G-11196)
KNEISLEY EYE CARE PA
45 E Main St Ste 201 (19711-4600)
PHONE..................302 224-3000
Yvonne Kneisley, *Pr*
EMP: 5 EST: 2007
SALES (est): 495.52K **Privately Held**
Web: www.kneisleyeye.com
SIC: 8042 Specialized optometrists

(G-11197)
KNIGHT INSUR CONSULTING GROUP
535 Canary Dr (19702-4291)
PHONE..................973 704-1112
Wanda Knight, *Prin*
EMP: 5 EST: 2018

SALES (est): 69.86K **Privately Held**
SIC: 8748 Business consulting, nec

(G-11198)
KNOWCRUNCH INC
2035 Sunset Lake Rd (19702-2600)
PHONE..................210 300-7214
EMP: 5
SALES (est): 46.16K **Privately Held**
Web: www.knowcrunch.com
SIC: 7371 Computer software development and applications

(G-11199)
KOGUT TECH CONSULTING INC
Also Called: Ktc
24 Ohio State Dr (19713-1164)
PHONE..................302 455-0388
Spence Kogut, *Pr*
EMP: 5 EST: 2005
SALES (est): 266.05K **Privately Held**
SIC: 7379 Computer related consulting services

(G-11200)
KORN CONSULT GROUP US INC
40 E Main St Ste 2700 (19711-4639)
PHONE..................304 933-5355
Rajiv Iyengar, *Pr*
EMP: 7 EST: 2017
SALES (est): 2.1MM **Privately Held**
Web: www.korn-consult.com
SIC: 8748 Systems analysis and engineering consulting services

(G-11201)
KOZY KENNELS
303 Shisler Ct (19702-1341)
PHONE..................302 455-1152
Jefferie Silverberg, *Prin*
EMP: 5 EST: 2008
SALES (est): 82.8K **Privately Held**
SIC: 0752 Boarding services, kennels

(G-11202)
KRISTIAN EXPRESS LLC ◇
110 Rustic Dr (19713-4215)
PHONE..................302 528-7577
EMP: 5 EST: 2022
SALES (est): 245.72K **Privately Held**
SIC: 7389 Business Activities at Non-Commercial Site

(G-11203)
KRISTOL CTR FOR JEWISH LF INC
47 W Delaware Ave (19711-4635)
PHONE..................302 453-0479
EMP: 5 EST: 2010
SALES (est): 901.27K **Privately Held**
Web: www.udhillel.org
SIC: 8641 Youth organizations

(G-11204)
L & B PUBLISHING
44 Lakewood Cir (19711-2343)
PHONE..................302 743-4061
Kelly Penoyer, *Prin*
EMP: 5 EST: 2015
SALES (est): 80K **Privately Held**
SIC: 2741 Miscellaneous publishing

(G-11205)
L & L CARPET DISCOUNT CTRS INC
Also Called: Lane Carpet Company
900 Interchange Blvd Ste 901 (19711-3563)
PHONE..................302 292-3712
EMP: 6
SALES (corp-wide): 23.58MM **Privately Held**

SIC: 5023 5713 Floor coverings; Carpets
PA: L & L Carpet Discount Centers, Inc.
7459 Mason King Ct
Manassas VA 20109
703 368-5025

(G-11206)
L A MASONARY INC
125 Sun Ct (19711-3413)
P.O. Box 6272 (19804-0872)
PHONE..................302 239-6833
Leon T Ashcraft, *Pr*
Faith A Smith, *Sec*
EMP: 19 EST: 1976
SALES (est): 473.13K **Privately Held**
SIC: 1741 Masonry and other stonework

(G-11207)
L L DETAILING
995 S Chapel St (19713-3441)
PHONE..................302 453-8000
EMP: 5 EST: 2010
SALES (est): 231.02K **Privately Held**
SIC: 7542 Washing and polishing, automotive

(G-11208)
L SQUARED HEALTHCARE LLC
2600 Glasgow Ave Ste 200 (19702-4773)
PHONE..................302 289-5425
EMP: 6
SALES (est): 264.62K **Privately Held**
SIC: 8041 Offices and clinics of chiropractors

(G-11209)
L&J PAINTING
10 Myers Rd (19713-2317)
PHONE..................267 423-6040
Luis Montanez, *Prin*
EMP: 6 EST: 2019
SALES (est): 204.39K **Privately Held**
Web: www.ljpaintingde.com
SIC: 1721 Painting and paper hanging

(G-11210)
LA VIE CHOCOLAT LLC
250 Corporate Blvd (19702-3329)
PHONE..................302 750-4540
Martin Sevcik, *Prin*
EMP: 5 EST: 2020
SALES (est): 62.38K **Privately Held**
SIC: 2064 Candy and other confectionery products

(G-11211)
LABORATORY CORPORATION AMERICA
Also Called: Lab
314 E Main St Ste 105 (19711-7180)
PHONE..................302 731-0244
Dana Mc Fadden, *Prin*
EMP: 7
Web: www.labcorp.com
SIC: 8071 Pathological laboratory
HQ: Laboratory Corporation Of America
531 S Spring St
Burlington NC 27215
336 229-1127

(G-11212)
LABOURS OF LOVE INC
21 W Kyla Marie Dr (19702-5430)
PHONE..................443 593-2776
Takima White, *CEO*
EMP: 6
SALES (est): 61.07K **Privately Held**
SIC: 8699 Charitable organization

(G-11213)
LABWARE
2 Polaris Dr (19711-3015)
PHONE..................302 521-0250
EMP: 6 EST: 2018
SALES (est): 65.2K **Privately Held**
Web: www.labware.com
SIC: 7371 Computer software development

(G-11214)
LACIEAH INC
14 Creek Ln (19702-5937)
PHONE..................302 365-5585
Lorraine Green, *CEO*
EMP: 5 EST: 2009
SALES (est): 182.48K **Privately Held**
SIC: 1799 Special trade contractors, nec

(G-11215)
LAKE THERAPY CREATIONS
2271 Sunset Lake Rd (19702-2633)
PHONE..................410 920-7130
EMP: 5 EST: 2018
SALES (est): 87.85K **Privately Held**
SIC: 8093 Rehabilitation center, outpatient treatment

(G-11216)
LAMBERT KISHAYRA
Also Called: Dreamreal Events
24 Keith St (19713-1624)
PHONE..................215 287-6252
Lambert Kishayra, *Prin*
EMP: 5 EST: 2011
SALES (est): 45.43K **Privately Held**
SIC: 7299 Facility rental and party planning services

(G-11217)
LANDEX LLC (PA) ◇
254 Chapman Rd Ste 208 (19702-5422)
PHONE..................903 293-9466
Chi Hoang, *Managing Member*
EMP: 5 EST: 2023
SALES (est): 76.67K
SALES (corp-wide): 76.67K **Privately Held**
SIC: 6531 Real estate agents and managers

(G-11218)
LANDMARK ENGINEERING INC (PA)
Also Called: Landmark Science & Engineering
200 Continental Dr Ste 400 (19713-4337)
PHONE..................302 323-9377
Ted Williams, *Pr*
Joseph Charma, *
Bruce J Tease, *
Keith Kooker, *
Helen Apostolico, *
EMP: 55 EST: 1987
SQ FT: 10,000
SALES (est): 9.65MM **Privately Held**
Web: www.landmark-se.com
SIC: 8711 8713 8748 8999 Civil engineering; Surveying services; Environmental consultant; Natural resource preservation service

(G-11219)
LANDMARK ENGINEERING INC
Also Called: L E I
200 Continental Dr Ste 400 (19713-4337)
PHONE..................302 734-9597
EMP: 8
Web: www.landmark-se.com
SIC: 8711 8713 Civil engineering; Surveying services
PA: Landmark Engineering, Inc.
200 Continental Dr # 400
Newark DE 19713

GEOGRAPHIC SECTION

Newark - New Castle County (G-11250)

(G-11220)
LANG DEVELOPMENT GROUP LLC
100 Dean Dr (19711-8545)
PHONE..................302 731-1340
EMP: 5
SALES (est): 183.18K **Privately Held**
Web: www.langdevelopmentgroup.com
SIC: 6552 Subdividers and developers, nec

(G-11221)
LANG DEVELOPMENT GROUP LLC (PA)
100 Dean Dr (19711-8545)
PHONE..................302 731-1340
Jeffery Lang, *Managing Member*
EMP: 9 EST: 2002
SQ FT: 1,000
SALES (est): 12.33MM
SALES (corp-wide): 12.33MM **Privately Held**
Web: www.langdevelopmentgroup.com
SIC: 6552 Land subdividers and developers, commercial

(G-11222)
LARSON ENGINEERING INC
910 S Chapel St Ste 200 (19713-3469)
PHONE..................302 731-7434
EMP: 9 EST: 1996
SALES (est): 900.02K **Privately Held**
Web: www.larsonengineering.net
SIC: 8711 Consulting engineer

(G-11223)
LAS QUALITY TREE SERVICE LLC
12 Glezman Dr (19702-3514)
PHONE..................302 981-3243
Laura Aguirre, *Prin*
EMP: 6 EST: 2011
SALES (est): 221.97K **Privately Held**
Web: www.lasqualitytree.com
SIC: 0783 Planting, pruning, and trimming services

(G-11224)
LASEANA FORD
2033 Rivers Dr (19702-3687)
PHONE..................215 201-8070
Laseana Ford, *Owner*
EMP: 5
SALES (est): 106.48K **Privately Held**
SIC: 8399 Social services, nec

(G-11225)
LATINICIDA INC
16 Ashkirk Pl (19702-4099)
PHONE..................302 277-6645
Andrea Moreno, *Pr*
Katarina Wabrek, *VP*
Amanda Coger, *Treas*
Natalie Donis, *Dir*
Alicia Tavares, *Dir*
EMP: 6 EST: 2020
SALES (est): 86.05K **Privately Held**
Web: www.latinicidainc.org
SIC: 8699 Charitable organization

(G-11226)
LAURA D HALLEY MS CCC-SLP
56 Millwright Dr (19711-8009)
PHONE..................302 738-0692
Laura Halley, *Mgr*
EMP: 6 EST: 2011
SALES (est): 74.28K **Privately Held**
SIC: 8049 Speech pathologist

(G-11227)
LAUREL BRIDGE SOFTWARE INC
500 Creek View Rd Ste 200 (19711-8549)
PHONE..................302 453-0222
Mark M Blair, *Pr*
Mark M Blair, *Pr*
Suzan Ragean, *Mgr*
EMP: 3 EST: 1999
SALES (est): 666.07K **Privately Held**
Web: www.laurelbridge.com
SIC: 7372 Business oriented computer software

(G-11228)
LAURI BROCKSON
680 S College Ave (19713-1306)
PHONE..................302 383-0147
EMP: 6 EST: 2009
SALES (est): 97.72K **Privately Held**
Web: www.lauribrockson.com
SIC: 8742 Real estate consultant

(G-11229)
LAVANTE N DORSEY & ASSOC LLC
256 Chapman Rd Ste 203 (19702-5415)
PHONE..................302 956-9188
Lavante Dorsey, *Prin*
EMP: 10 EST: 2018
SALES (est): 117.21K **Privately Held**
Web: www.lavantedorsey.com
SIC: 8322 General counseling services

(G-11230)
LAW OFFICE OF MICHAEL BEDNASH
100 Biddle Ave Ste 104 (19702-3982)
PHONE..................302 838-9077
EMP: 5 EST: 2014
SALES (est): 140.28K **Privately Held**
Web: www.bednashlaw.com
SIC: 8111 General practice law office

(G-11231)
LAW OFFICE OF RBERT I MSTEN JR
500 Creek View Rd Ste 304 (19711-8549)
PHONE..................302 358-2044
Robert I Masten Junior, *Prin*
EMP: 5 EST: 2012
SALES (est): 141.39K **Privately Held**
Web: www.rmastenlaw.com
SIC: 8111 Bankruptcy law

(G-11232)
LAWING MUSICAL PRODUCTS LLC
416 Paper Mill Rd (19711-7512)
PHONE..................302 533-7548
Claire Lawing, *Prin*
EMP: 5 EST: 2010
SALES (est): 159.43K **Privately Held**
Web: www.lawingmusicalproducts.com
SIC: 7389 Music and broadcasting services

(G-11233)
LAWNWORKS INC
667 Dawson Dr Ste D (19713-3437)
P.O. Box 5538 (19714-5538)
PHONE..................302 368-5699
William F Hobbs Iii, *Pr*
Bonnie M Hobbs, *VP*
EMP: 10 EST: 1992
SQ FT: 1,250
SALES (est): 657.92K **Privately Held**
SIC: 0782 Lawn care services

(G-11234)
LAWRENCE KENNEDY
Also Called: Ikeno Tech Business Solutions
262 Chapman Rd Ste 107 (19702-5412)
PHONE..................302 533-5880
Lawrence Kennedy, *Owner*
EMP: 10 EST: 2018
SALES (est): 230.18K **Privately Held**
SIC: 8741 Business management

(G-11235)
LAYERCAKE LLC
Also Called: Layercake
42 Hawthorne Ave (19711-5566)
PHONE..................571 449-7538
Emmanuel T'chawi, *CEO*
EMP: 6 EST: 2016
SALES (est): 232.02K **Privately Held**
SIC: 7379 Online services technology consultants

(G-11236)
LEADERSHIP INSTITUTE INC
76 Omega Dr (19713-2064)
PHONE..................302 368-7292
James Bettle, *Pr*
Deborah A Bettle, *Sec*
EMP: 12 EST: 1980
SQ FT: 1,300
SALES (est): 77.4K **Privately Held**
Web: www.campusreform.org
SIC: 8331 Job training and related services

(G-11237)
LEANSCOUT INC
2035 Sunset Lake Rd Ste B2 (19702-2600)
PHONE..................628 236-9599
EMP: 5 EST: 2017
SALES (est): 51.29K **Privately Held**
Web: www.leanscout.com
SIC: 7371 Computer software development and applications

(G-11238)
LEARNING EXPRESS PRESCHOOL
300 Darling St (19702-3775)
PHONE..................302 737-8990
Beth Smith, *Dir*
EMP: 17 EST: 2011
SALES (est): 239.46K **Privately Held**
Web: www.learningexpresschool.org
SIC: 8351 Preschool center

(G-11239)
LEEBER LIMITED USA
Also Called: Elegance
420 Corporate Blvd (19702-3330)
PHONE..................302 733-0991
Alice Ho, *Pr*
Floyd Ho, *VP*
Willy Ho, *VP*
◆ EMP: 14 EST: 1981
SALES (est): 954.18K **Privately Held**
Web: www.leeber.com
SIC: 3914 Silverware

(G-11240)
LEEMAN ELECTRIC
102 Dawes Ct (19702-1453)
PHONE..................302 737-1753
EMP: 5 EST: 2018
SALES (est): 64.44K **Privately Held**
SIC: 1731 Electrical work

(G-11241)
LEGACY CONTRACTORS LLC
6002 Vicky Dr (19702-8122)
PHONE..................302 442-8817
Orlando Mercado, *Prin*
EMP: 5 EST: 2018
SALES (est): 102.53K **Privately Held**
SIC: 1799 Special trade contractors, nec

(G-11242)
LEGION TRANSFORMATION CENTER
130 Executive Dr Ste 5 (19702-3349)
PHONE..................302 533-6178
EMP: 7 EST: 2017
SALES (est): 55.48K **Privately Held**
Web: www.legiontransform.com
SIC: 7991 Physical fitness facilities

(G-11243)
LEGIT GLOBAL INC ✪
254 Chapman Rd Ste 208 (19702-5422)
PHONE..................661 444-9085
Jagannadha Rao Yelisetti, *CEO*
EMP: 6 EST: 2023
SALES (est): 249.97K **Privately Held**
SIC: 7371 Software programming applications

(G-11244)
LEMON FIN- VEST INC ✪
256 Chapman Rd (19702-5499)
PHONE..................905 442-8480
Olotuche Ochigbo, *Prin*
EMP: 10 EST: 2022
SALES (est): 365.81K **Privately Held**
SIC: 8741 Management services

(G-11245)
LENDING MANAGER HOLDINGS LLC
152 E Main St (19711-7308)
PHONE..................888 501-0335
Steve Grossman, *Mng Pt*
EMP: 9 EST: 2017
SALES (est): 749.92K
SALES (corp-wide): 10.5MM **Privately Held**
SIC: 6163 Loan brokers
PA: Volly
    53 Commerce Way
    Woburn MA 01801
    781 938-1175

(G-11246)
LEONARDO CHARITABLE I LLC
220 Continental Dr (19713-4311)
PHONE..................302 571-1818
EMP: 5 EST: 2014
SALES (est): 106.24K **Privately Held**
SIC: 8699 Charitable organization

(G-11247)
LETSBELEGALCOM
260 Chapman Rd Ste 201 (19702-5491)
PHONE..................302 894-4357
Mary Higgins, *Prin*
EMP: 5 EST: 2017
SALES (est): 102.41K **Privately Held**
Web: www.letsbelegal.com
SIC: 8111 General practice attorney, lawyer

(G-11248)
LEWES WALK-IN MEDICAL LLC
1103 La Grange Pkwy (19702-3836)
PHONE..................302 561-5429
Hlen Nguyen, *Asst Sec*
EMP: 6 EST: 2018
SALES (est): 107.32K **Privately Held**
SIC: 8099 Health and allied services, nec

(G-11249)
LEWIS CK CONSTRUCTION
2311 Ogletown Rd (19711-5435)
PHONE..................443 910-1598
EMP: 5 EST: 2019
SALES (est): 61.92K **Privately Held**
Web: www.chespfb.com
SIC: 1761 Roofing, siding, and sheetmetal work

(G-11250)
LEXAN GROUP LLC ✪
254 Chapman Rd Ste 208 (19702-5413)
PHONE..................704 900-0190
Xavier Alexander, *Managing Member*
EMP: 5 EST: 2023

Newark - New Castle County (G-11251) GEOGRAPHIC SECTION

SALES (est): 280.46K **Privately Held**
Web: www.lexangroupllc.com
SIC: 6531 Real estate managers

(G-11251)
LEXINGTON GREEN APARTMENTS
1201 Kingston Bldg (19702-5261)
PHONE.................................302 322-8959
Diane Grant, *Genl Mgr*
Sue Rimel, *Genl Mgr*
EMP: 7
SALES (est): 532.17K **Privately Held**
SIC: 6513 Apartment building operators

(G-11252)
LIBERTY ELEVATOR EXPERTS LLC
Also Called: Vertical Trnsp Eqp Solutions
625 Barksdale Rd Ste 113 (19711-4535)
PHONE.................................302 650-4688
Christopher Dodds, *Prin*
EMP: 23 EST: 2013
SALES (est): 2.87MM **Privately Held**
Web: www.libertyelevatorexperts.com
SIC: 5084 Elevators

(G-11253)
LIBERTY ELEVATOR EXPERTS LLC
113 Barksdale Professional Ctr (19711-3258)
PHONE.................................844 542-3538
EMP: 6 EST: 2020
SALES (est): 628.51K **Privately Held**
Web: www.libertyelevatorexperts.com
SIC: 5084 Elevators

(G-11254)
LIFE FORCE ELDERCARE CORP
1203 Plly Drummond Off Pa (19711)
PHONE.................................302 737-4400
Josephine Grands, *Dir*
EMP: 9 EST: 2007
SALES (est): 112.14K **Privately Held**
SIC: 8082 Home health care services

(G-11255)
LIFE INNOVATIONS
260 Chapman Rd Ste 203e (19702-5491)
PHONE.................................302 525-6521
EMP: 7 EST: 2014
SALES (est): 59.04K **Privately Held**
Web: www.innovatinglife.net
SIC: 8322 General counseling services

(G-11256)
LIFETOUCH PORTRAIT STUDIOS INC
Also Called: Lifetouch
606 Christiana Mall (19702)
PHONE.................................302 453-8080
Tracy Telletier, *Brnch Mgr*
EMP: 6
SALES (corp-wide): 2.47B **Privately Held**
Web: www.lifetouch.com
SIC: 7221 Photographer, still or video
HQ: Lifetouch Portrait Studios Inc.
    11000 Viking Dr
    Eden Prairie MN 55344
    952 826-4335

(G-11257)
LIGHTWAVE LOGIC INC
1 Innovation Way Ste 100 (19711-5462)
PHONE.................................302 737-6412
Thomas E Zelibor, *Brnch Mgr*
EMP: 5
Web: www.lightwavelogic.com
SIC: 8071 8731 Testing laboratories; Commercial research laboratory
PA: Lightwave Logic, Inc.
    369 Inverness Pkwy # 350
    Englewood CO 80112

(G-11258)
LIGNOLIX INC
47 Foxtail Ct (19711-4380)
PHONE.................................516 660-2558
EMP: 7 EST: 2019
SALES (est): 94.21K **Privately Held**
Web: www.lignolix.com
SIC: 2899 Chemical preparations, nec

(G-11259)
LIL EINSTEINS LEARNING ACADEMY
201 Possum Park Rd (19711-3831)
PHONE.................................302 466-3003
EMP: 13 EST: 2016
SALES (est): 83.17K **Privately Held**
Web: www.lelaonline.com
SIC: 8351 Preschool center

(G-11260)
LILLY FASTENERS & CUSTOMIZATION LLC (PA)
855 Dawson Dr (19713-3415)
P.O. Box 6005 (19714-6005)
PHONE.................................302 366-7640
EMP: 22 EST: 1967
SALES (est): 7.1MM
SALES (corp-wide): 7.1MM **Privately Held**
Web: www.kglilly.com
SIC: 5072 Hardware

(G-11261)
LIMITLESS CONSULTING MKTG LLC
207 S Gerald Dr (19713-3220)
PHONE.................................302 743-0520
EMP: 40 EST: 2017
SALES (est): 1.53MM **Privately Held**
SIC: 8742 Management consulting services

(G-11262)
LINGUATEXT LTD
103 Walker Way (19711-6119)
PHONE.................................302 453-8695
Tom Lathrop, *Pr*
EMP: 2 EST: 1974
SALES (est): 318.71K **Privately Held**
Web: www.linguatextbooks.com
SIC: 5192 2731 Books; Textbooks: publishing and printing

(G-11263)
LINNE INDUSTRIES LLC
11 Bridle Brook Ln (19711-2003)
P.O. Box 9856 (19714-4956)
PHONE.................................302 454-1439
Sandra Burton, *Prin*
Craig Burton, *Prin*
EMP: 2 EST: 2013
SALES (est): 237.12K **Privately Held**
Web: www.pondhawk.com
SIC: 3563 Air and gas compressors

(G-11264)
LION ELECTRIC MFG USA INC
2915 Ogletown Rd # 3965 (19713-1927)
PHONE.................................833 512-5466
Marc Bedard, *Pr*
Nicolas Brunet, *VP*
Francois Duquette, *Sec*
Brian Piern, *Sec*
EMP: 11 EST: 2021
SALES (est): 500.05K **Privately Held**
SIC: 3714 Motor vehicle electrical equipment

(G-11265)
LIPPSTONE LAW PLLC
1 S Fawn Dr (19711-2544)
PHONE.................................302 252-1481
Andrew H Lippstone, *Owner*
EMP: 5 EST: 2017
SALES (est): 106.84K **Privately Held**
SIC: 8111 Legal services

(G-11266)
LISA BROADBENT INSURANCE INC
Also Called: Nationwide
20 Polly Drummond Hill Rd (19711-5703)
PHONE.................................302 731-0044
EMP: 9 EST: 1987
SALES (est): 900.38K **Privately Held**
Web: www.lisabroadbentinsurance.com
SIC: 6411 Insurance agents, nec

(G-11267)
LISA BURROUGHS
500 Creek View Rd Ste 109 (19711-8549)
PHONE.................................302 454-8010
EMP: 5 EST: 2017
SALES (est): 197.28K **Privately Held**
Web: www.alliance-counseling.com
SIC: 8049 Clinical psychologist

(G-11268)
LISA R SAVAGE
260 Chapman Rd Ste 100b (19702-5410)
PHONE.................................302 353-7052
Lisa R Savage, *Ofcr*
EMP: 7 EST: 2017
SALES (est): 104.51K **Privately Held**
SIC: 8322 Social worker

(G-11269)
LIT XPRESS LLC
1914 Spearfish Ct (19702-3685)
PHONE.................................302 690-9520
EMP: 8
SALES (est): 525.44K **Privately Held**
SIC: 4215 7389 Courier services, except by air; Business services, nec

(G-11270)
LITTLE MIRACLES CHILD CARE CTR
11 Christina Woods Ct Ste B (19702-2724)
PHONE.................................302 367-4838
EMP: 6 EST: 2015
SALES (est): 77.37K **Privately Held**
SIC: 8099 Health and allied services, nec

(G-11271)
LITTLE PEOPLE BIG WORLD
11 Ashkirk Pl (19702-6000)
PHONE.................................302 310-0965
EMP: 9 EST: 2016
SALES (est): 72.87K **Privately Held**
SIC: 8351 Preschool center

(G-11272)
LITTLE SCHOLARS CTR
2050 S College Ave (19702-3302)
PHONE.................................302 368-7584
Karen Rice, *Dir*
EMP: 8 EST: 2019
SALES (est): 17.57K **Privately Held**
SIC: 8351 Preschool center

(G-11273)
LITTLE SISTERS OF THE POOR
Also Called: JEANNE JUGAN RESIDENCE
185 Salem Church Rd (19713-2997)
PHONE.................................302 368-5886
Margaret Halloran, *Pr*
Cecile Zeringue, *
EMP: 80 EST: 1903
SALES (est): 9.94MM **Privately Held**
Web: www.littlesistersofthepoordelaware.org
SIC: 8059 8361 8052 Rest home, with health care; Residential care; Intermediate care facilities

(G-11274)
LLC GAGE PARK
850 Library Ave Ste 204 (19711-7174)
PHONE.................................302 738-6680
EMP: 5 EST: 2020
SALES (est): 261.25K **Privately Held**
SIC: 7389 Business services, nec

(G-11275)
LLOYD RICHARD LLC
131 W Rutherford Dr (19713-2026)
PHONE.................................302 584-8798
Lloyd Richard, *Prin*
EMP: 5 EST: 2011
SALES (est): 87.1K **Privately Held**
SIC: 1522 Residential construction, nec

(G-11276)
LLP CONNOLLY GALLAGHER
267 E Main St (19711-7314)
PHONE.................................302 757-7300
EMP: 65
SALES (corp-wide): 9.93MM **Privately Held**
Web: www.connollygallagher.com
SIC: 8111 General practice attorney, lawyer
PA: Gallagher Connolly Llp
    1201 N Market St Ste 2000
    Wilmington DE 19801
    302 757-7300

(G-11277)
LNH INC
Also Called: Hosting.com
650 Pencader Dr (19702-3348)
PHONE.................................302 731-4948
Art Zeile, *Prin*
EMP: 16 EST: 2011
SALES (est): 1.62MM **Privately Held**
Web: www.hostmysite.com
SIC: 4813 Internet host services

(G-11278)
LOCKER CONSTRUCTION INC
314 Cox Rd (19711-3025)
PHONE.................................302 239-2859
Roy Locker, *Pr*
EMP: 5 EST: 1989
SQ FT: 1,000
SALES (est): 371.9K **Privately Held**
SIC: 8741 1521 1542 Construction management; General remodeling, single-family houses; Commercial and office building, new construction

(G-11279)
LOMBARD TRADING INTERNATIONAL
112 Capitol Trl (19711-3716)
PHONE.................................786 659-5010
EMP: 5 EST: 2019
SALES (est): 480.5K **Privately Held**
SIC: 5153 Grains

(G-11280)
LONGHORN ENTERPRISES INC
2604 Eastburn Ctr (19711-7285)
PHONE.................................302 737-7444
EMP: 7 EST: 2018
SALES (est): 397.5K **Privately Held**
Web: newark.thecleaningauthority.com
SIC: 7699 Cleaning services

(G-11281)
LOOMCRAFT TEXTILE & SUPPLY CO
Also Called: Interior Alternative, The
211 Executive Dr Ste 13 (19702-3358)
PHONE.................................302 454-3232
Victoria Moulen, *Mgr*
EMP: 10

SALES (corp-wide): 23.29MM **Privately Held**
Web: www.thefabricoutlet.com
SIC: 5131 5949 Piece goods and other fabrics; Fabric stores piece goods
PA: Loomcraft Textile & Supply Company
645 Lakeview Pkwy
Vernon Hills IL 60061
336 282-1100

(G-11282)
LOOP MISSION CORP
2915 Ogletown Rd Ste 4010 (19713-1927)
PHONE.................................514 994-7625
Julie Poitras-saulnier, *CEO*
EMP: 50 EST: 2021
SALES (est): 1.44MM **Privately Held**
Web: www.loopmission.com
SIC: 2033 Fruit juices: fresh

(G-11283)
LOPESCO INC
2 Morning Glen Ln (19711-4394)
PHONE.................................908 482-5616
Steve Lopes, *Prin*
EMP: 6 EST: 2016
SALES (est): 271.84K **Privately Held**
SIC: 1521 Single-family housing construction

(G-11284)
LOPESCO INC
Also Called: Stanley Steamers Carpet Clrs
2 Morning Glen Ln (19711-4394)
PHONE.................................732 985-7776
Stephan A Lopes, *Pr*
Doris Lopes, *
EMP: 30 EST: 1996
SALES (est): 1.98MM **Privately Held**
Web: www.stanleysteemer.com
SIC: 7217 Carpet and furniture cleaning on location

(G-11285)
LORIS HANDS INC
Also Called: Lori's Hands
100 Discovery Blvd Fl 4 (19713-1325)
PHONE.................................302 440-5454
Sarah Lafave, *CEO*
Maggie Ratnayake, *Dir*
EMP: 6 EST: 2009
SALES (est): 173.94K **Privately Held**
Web: www.lorishands.org
SIC: 8399 Community development groups

(G-11286)
LOTUS SEPARATIONS LLC
32 Belfort Loop (19702-5526)
PHONE.................................302 345-2510
Christina Kraml, *Prin*
EMP: 5 EST: 2011
SALES (est): 96.41K **Privately Held**
Web: www.lotussep.com
SIC: 7389 Business Activities at Non-Commercial Site

(G-11287)
LOUVIERS FEDERAL CREDIT UNION (PA)
185 S Main St (19711-7941)
PHONE.................................302 733-0426
EMP: 10 EST: 1968
SQ FT: 3,600
SALES (est): 7.62MM **Privately Held**
Web: www.louviers.com
SIC: 6061 Federal credit unions

(G-11288)
LOVE & HOPE RESCUE MISSION INC
101 Mederia Cir (19702-1541)
PHONE.................................302 332-3829
Erlande Rose Simon, *CEO*
Guilande Dice, *VP*
EMP: 9 EST: 2021
SALES (est): 290.16K **Privately Held**
SIC: 7389 Business Activities at Non-Commercial Site

(G-11289)
LOVE N CARE DAYCARE
215 Capitol Trl (19711-3860)
PHONE.................................302 369-8092
EMP: 6 EST: 2018
SALES (est): 15.97K **Privately Held**
SIC: 8351 Child day care services

(G-11290)
LOVETT FINANCIAL ADVISORS LLC
630 Churchmans Rd Ste 109 (19702-1943)
PHONE.................................302 250-4740
Kim W Lovett, *Prin*
EMP: 5 EST: 2013
SALES (est): 101.26K **Privately Held**
SIC: 6282 Investment advisory service

(G-11291)
LOWES HOME CENTERS LLC
Also Called: Lowe's
2000 Ogletown Rd (19711-5439)
PHONE.................................302 781-1154
Kevin Andrews, *Off Mgr*
EMP: 136
SALES (corp-wide): 97.06B **Publicly Held**
Web: www.lowes.com
SIC: 5211 5031 5722 5064 Home centers; Building materials, exterior; Household appliance stores; Electrical appliances, television and radio
HQ: Lowe's Home Centers, Llc
1000 Lowes Blvd
Mooresville NC 28117
336 658-4000

(G-11292)
LPL FINANCIAL
220 Continental Dr Ste 207 (19713-4311)
PHONE.................................302 737-6559
EMP: 12 EST: 2016
SALES (est): 126.22K **Privately Held**
Web: www.lpl.com
SIC: 8742 Financial consultant

(G-11293)
LSREF4 LIGHTHOUSE CORP ACQSTN
146 Chestnut Crossing Dr (19713-2600)
PHONE.................................302 737-8500
Annmarie Hobson, *Brnch Mgr*
EMP: 7
SIC: 6513 Apartment building operators
PA: Lsref4 Lighthouse Corporate Acquisitions, Llc
11459 Cronhill Dr
Owings Mills MD 21117

(G-11294)
LUKE DESTEFANO INC
Also Called: First State Printing
107 Albe Dr Ste B (19702-1336)
PHONE.................................302 455-0710
Luke Destefano, *Pr*
EMP: 2 EST: 1991
SQ FT: 1,000
SALES (est): 163.94K **Privately Held**
Web: www.firststateprinting.net
SIC: 2752 Offset printing

(G-11295)
LUMI CASES LLC
501 Capitol Trl Apt 201 (19711-5507)
PHONE.................................302 525-6971
EMP: 2 EST: 2013
SALES (est): 90.22K **Privately Held**
SIC: 3523 Farm machinery and equipment

(G-11296)
LUXZ AUTO TECH LLC
528 Old Barksdale Rd (19711-4534)
PHONE.................................302 305-5899
EMP: 9 EST: 2021
SALES (est): 106.22K **Privately Held**
SIC: 7538 General automotive repair shops

(G-11297)
LUZ D REYNOSO
179 W Chestnut Hill Rd Ste 6 (19713-2210)
PHONE.................................302 358-6237
Luz Del Alba Reynoso Lcsw, *Prin*
EMP: 7 EST: 2018
SALES (est): 81.56K **Privately Held**
SIC: 8322 Individual and family services

(G-11298)
LYCRA COMPANY LLC
Also Called: The Lycra Company, LLC
150 Red Mill Rd (19711-6632)
PHONE.................................302 731-6800
EMP: 288
SALES (corp-wide): 293.57K **Privately Held**
Web: www.lycra.com
SIC: 2221 Textile mills, broadwoven: silk and manmade, also glass
HQ: The Lycra Company Llc
2711 Centerville Rd # 300
Wilmington DE

(G-11299)
M & M TIRE SERVICES INC
2615 Pulaski Hwy (19702-3909)
PHONE.................................302 731-1004
EMP: 6 EST: 2020
SALES (est): 271.03K **Privately Held**
SIC: 7534 Tire repair shop

(G-11300)
M CUBED TECHNOLOGIES INC
1300 Marrows Rd (19711-5445)
PHONE.................................302 454-8600
Elmer Miller, *Brnch Mgr*
EMP: 85
SALES (corp-wide): 5.16B **Publicly Held**
Web: www.mmmt.com
SIC: 3444 Sheet metalwork
HQ: M Cubed Technologies, Inc.
31 Pecks Ln Ste 8
Newtown CT 06470
203 304-2940

(G-11301)
M DAVIS & SONS INC (PA)
24 Mcmillan Way (19713-3420)
PHONE.................................302 998-3385
TOLL FREE: 800
Margaret D Del Fabbro, *CEO*
Charles R Davis, *
John S Bonk, *
▲ EMP: 237 EST: 1900
SALES (est): 65.58MM
SALES (corp-wide): 65.58MM **Privately Held**
Web: www.mdavisinc.com
SIC: 1711 1731 1791 Plumbing contractors; General electrical contractor; Iron work, structural

(G-11302)
M DIANA METZGER MD
665 Churchmans Rd (19702-1918)
PHONE.................................302 731-0942
EMP: 10 EST: 1980
SALES (est): 357.34K **Privately Held**
SIC: 8011 General and family practice, physician/surgeon

(G-11303)
M IMRAN MD
2707 Kirkwood Hwy Ste 1 (19711-6828)
PHONE.................................302 453-7399
Mohammad Imran Md, *Owner*
EMP: 6 EST: 1984
SALES (est): 417.22K **Privately Held**
SIC: 8011 Gynecologist

(G-11304)
M R PLUMBING
136 Wren Way (19711-8330)
PHONE.................................302 738-7978
Nicholas J Maidanos, *Prin*
EMP: 5 EST: 2016
SALES (est): 106.65K **Privately Held**
Web: www.rentalsmr.com
SIC: 6799 Investors, nec

(G-11305)
M TEAM CREATIVE
6 Castlegate Ct (19702-2152)
PHONE.................................302 275-5658
EMP: 6 EST: 2017
SALES (est): 126.74K **Privately Held**
Web: www.mteamcreative.com
SIC: 8742 Marketing consulting services

(G-11306)
M&M GARAGE DOORS INC
302 Webb Rd (19711-2651)
PHONE.................................302 304-1397
Philip Stewart, *Prin*
EMP: 5 EST: 2018
SALES (est): 53.36K **Privately Held**
Web: www.mmgaragedoorsinc.com
SIC: 1751 Garage door, installation or erection

(G-11307)
M&M MASS SPEC CONSULTING LLC
Also Called: ASAP Mass Spectrometry
28 Tenby Chase Dr (19711-2441)
P.O. Box 191 (19707-0191)
PHONE.................................302 250-4488
EMP: 2 EST: 2010
SALES (est): 150.69K **Privately Held**
Web: www.asap-ms.com
SIC: 3826 Analytical instruments

(G-11308)
M3 CONTRACTING LLC
13 Garfield Way (19713-3450)
PHONE.................................302 781-3143
EMP: 30 EST: 2010
SALES (est): 4.56MM **Privately Held**
Web: www.m3contracting.net
SIC: 1742 Drywall

(G-11309)
MACAPPSTUDIO INC
Sunset Lake Rd Ste B-2 (19702)
PHONE.................................415 799-7415
EMP: 8 EST: 2017
SALES (est): 80K **Privately Held**
SIC: 7371 Computer software development and applications

(G-11310)
MAD MACS
801 S College Ave (19713-4001)
PHONE.................................302 737-4800
EMP: 9 EST: 2017
SALES (est): 594.17K **Privately Held**
Web: www.mad-macs.com

Newark - New Castle County (G-11311)

SIC: 7336 Commercial art and graphic design

(G-11311)
MAESTRIK INC
2035 Sunset Lake Rd D2 (19702-2600)
PHONE..................................312 925-3116
Mario Tobon, Pr
EMP: 32 EST: 2018
SALES (est): 787.56K Privately Held
SIC: 7371 Custom computer programming services

(G-11312)
MAIN EVENT ENTRMT WILMINGTON
2900 Fashion Center Blvd (19702-3249)
PHONE..................................302 722-9466
EMP: 7 EST: 2018
SALES (est): 20.82K Privately Held
Web: www.mainevent.com
SIC: 7933 Ten pin center

(G-11313)
MAIN STREET CLEANERS
179 E Main St (19711-7313)
PHONE..................................302 738-4385
EMP: 5 EST: 2017
SALES (est): 68.85K Privately Held
SIC: 7212 Pickup station, laundry and drycleaning

(G-11314)
MAIN STREET DENTAL
29 Center St (19711-2368)
PHONE..................................302 368-2558
EMP: 7 EST: 2020
SALES (est): 82.97K Privately Held
Web: www.mainstreetdentalnewark.com
SIC: 8021 Dentists' office

(G-11315)
MAIN STREET MOVIES 5 LLC
401 Newark Shopping Ctr (19711-7304)
PHONE..................................302 738-4555
EMP: 6 EST: 2017
SALES (est): 490.13K Privately Held
Web: www.mainstreetmovies5.com
SIC: 7832 Motion picture theaters, except drive-in

(G-11316)
MAJDELL GROUP USA INC
Also Called: Majdell Group
40 E Main St 790 (19711-4639)
PHONE..................................302 722-8223
Gary Majdell, Pr
▲ EMP: 8 EST: 2012
SALES (est): 179.19K Privately Held
Web: www.majdellgroup.com
SIC: 2329 5136 Men's and boys' sportswear and athletic clothing; Underwear, men's and boys'

(G-11317)
MAL VENTURES INC
213 Mulberry Rd (19711-5519)
PHONE..................................302 454-1170
Mark Liebal, Prin
EMP: 6 EST: 2010
SALES (est): 195.57K Privately Held
SIC: 7299 Handyman service

(G-11318)
MALLARD ADVISORS LLC (HQ)
750 Barksdale Rd Ste 3 (19711-3245)
PHONE..................................302 239-1654
EMP: 5 EST: 1996
SQ FT: 1,315
SALES (est): 2.49MM
SALES (corp-wide): 164.45MM Privately Held

Web: www.merceradvisors.com
SIC: 6282 Investment advisory service
PA: Mercer Global Advisors, Inc.
1200 17th St Ste 500
Denver CO 80202
888 885-8101

(G-11319)
MALLARD FINANCIAL PARTNERS INC
750 Barksdale Rd Ste 3 (19711-3245)
PHONE..................................302 737-4546
Paul Baumbach, Pr
EMP: 105 EST: 2013
SALES (est): 807.05K
SALES (corp-wide): 164.45MM Privately Held
Web: www.mallardfinancial.com
SIC: 6282 Investment advisory service
PA: Mercer Global Advisors, Inc.
1200 17th St Ste 500
Denver CO 80202
888 885-8101

(G-11320)
MALS SPORTS
4 Bemis Rd (19711-7605)
PHONE..................................302 598-8247
Michael Malatesta, Prin
EMP: 5 EST: 2010
SALES (est): 78.48K Privately Held
Web: mals.udel.edu
SIC: 4832 Sports

(G-11321)
MANCHESTER TRADING CO
40 E Main St (19711-4639)
PHONE..................................302 500-4010
EMP: 15 EST: 2020
SALES (est): 1.61MM Privately Held
Web: www.mtcor.com
SIC: 5031 Building materials, exterior

(G-11322)
MANDIP LLC
65 Geoffrey Dr (19713-3603)
PHONE..................................302 218-7449
EMP: 10 EST: 2011
SALES (est): 85.84K Privately Held
SIC: 7011 Inns

(G-11323)
MANUFACTURERS & TRADERS TR CO
Also Called: M&T
82 E Main St (19711-4640)
PHONE..................................302 651-1618
Amy Plant, Brnch Mgr
EMP: 5
SALES (corp-wide): 8.6B Publicly Held
Web: ir.mtb.com
SIC: 6022 State commercial banks
HQ: Manufacturers And Traders Trust Company
1 M&T Plz Fl 3
Buffalo NY 14203
716 842-4200

(G-11324)
MANUFACTURERS & TRADERS TR CO
Also Called: M&T
550 Suburban Dr (19711-1808)
PHONE..................................302 472-3335
Barbara French, Brnch Mgr
EMP: 8
SALES (corp-wide): 8.6B Publicly Held
Web: ir.mtb.com
SIC: 6022 State commercial banks

HQ: Manufacturers And Traders Trust Company
1 M&T Plz Fl 3
Buffalo NY 14203
716 842-4200

(G-11325)
MAPLE CREST LLC
1626 Old Coochs Bridge Rd (19702-2430)
PHONE..................................302 540-9937
EMP: 5 EST: 2018
SALES (est): 55.68K Privately Held
SIC: 6512 Nonresidential building operators

(G-11326)
MARA PUGLISI HOLISTIC HLTH LLC
909 Pickett Ln (19711-2641)
PHONE..................................302 368-4245
Mike Puglisi, Prin
EMP: 6 EST: 2014
SALES (est): 74.39K Privately Held
SIC: 8099 Health and allied services, nec

(G-11327)
MARA PUGLISI HOLISTIC HLTH LLC
19 Hidden Valley Dr (19711-7463)
PHONE..................................240 338-0137
Mike Puglisi, Ofcr
EMP: 7 EST: 2018
SALES (est): 38.22K Privately Held
Web: www.marapuglisihealth.com
SIC: 8099 Health and allied services, nec

(G-11328)
MARC RICHMAN PHD
2600 Glasgow Ave Ste 124 (19702-4777)
PHONE..................................302 834-3039
Marc Richman, Prin
EMP: 7 EST: 2000
SALES (est): 85.71K Privately Held
Web: www.behavioralhealthassociatesde.com
SIC: 8049 Clinical psychologist

(G-11329)
MARCUS MATERIALS CO
9 Renee Ct (19711-2759)
PHONE..................................302 731-7519
David Mcelwee, Genl Mgr
EMP: 5 EST: 1992
SALES (est): 495.67K Privately Held
Web: www.marcusmaterials.com
SIC: 5032 Ceramic construction materials, excluding refractory

(G-11330)
MARGHERITA VINCENT & ANTHONY
5 Misty Ct (19702-4726)
PHONE..................................302 834-9023
Vincent Margherita, Prin
EMP: 5 EST: 1993
SALES (est): 137.65K Privately Held
SIC: 1752 Floor laying and floor work, nec

(G-11331)
MARIAN ROSELLA FOUNDATION INC
523 Concord Bridge Pl (19702-5205)
PHONE..................................888 977-1937
Kenyesta Candies, Pr
Kasia Haughton, VP
Janice Harris D.o.s., Prin
EMP: 5 EST: 2020
SALES (est): 93.37K Privately Held
SIC: 8699 Charitable organization

(G-11332)
MARJAM SUPPLY CO INC
200 Bellevue Rd (19713-3428)
PHONE..................................302 283-1020
Jeff Benson, Brnch Mgr

EMP: 10
Web: www.fbmsales.com
SIC: 5031 5211 Building materials, exterior; Lumber and other building materials
HQ: Marjam Supply Co., Inc.
885 Conklin St
Farmingdale NY 11735
631 249-4900

(G-11333)
MARK DUPHILY TRUCKING INC
127 Bartley Dr (19702-2203)
PHONE..................................302 292-2271
Mark Duphily, Prin
EMP: 7 EST: 2015
SALES (est): 79.07K Privately Held
SIC: 4212 Local trucking, without storage

(G-11334)
MARK GLASSNER MD
324 E Main St Ste 202 (19711-7150)
PHONE..................................302 369-9002
Mark Glassner Md, Owner
EMP: 10 EST: 1999
SALES (est): 816.83K Privately Held
SIC: 8011 General and family practice, physician/surgeon

(G-11335)
MARK IV BEAUTY SALON INC
Also Called: Mark IV Hair Design
240 College Sq (19711-5489)
PHONE..................................302 737-4994
Debra Demaio, Pr
EMP: 8 EST: 1975
SQ FT: 1,500
SALES (est): 272.9K Privately Held
Web: www.markivhairdesigns.com
SIC: 7231 Hairdressers

(G-11336)
MARK JB INC
254 Chapman Rd Ste 208 (19702-5422)
PHONE..................................888 984-5845
Jasmine Bright, CEO
EMP: 5 EST: 2019
SALES (est): 338.54K Privately Held
SIC: 5999 5499 0139 8412 Alarm and safety equipment stores; Health foods; Herb or spice farm; Museums and art galleries

(G-11337)
MARK SANFORD
14 Quartz Mill Rd (19711-2326)
PHONE..................................302 593-9773
Mark Sanford, Mgr
EMP: 6 EST: 2017
SALES (est): 67.25K Privately Held
SIC: 8049 Offices of health practitioner

(G-11338)
MARSHALL KYLE
Also Called: Marshall Construction
323 Jaymar Blvd (19702-2881)
PHONE..................................302 454-7838
Kyle Marshall, Prin
EMP: 10 EST: 2009
SALES (est): 996.27K Privately Held
Web: www.marshallconstructionllc.com
SIC: 1521 New construction, single-family houses

(G-11339)
MARSHALL T WILLIAMS MD PHD
537 Stanton Christiana Rd (19713-2146)
PHONE..................................302 994-9692
Marshall Williams Md, Owner
EMP: 6 EST: 1985
SALES (est): 108.83K Privately Held

GEOGRAPHIC SECTION
Newark - New Castle County (G-11367)

SIC: 8011 Infectious disease specialist, physician/surgeon

(G-11340)
MARTA GROUP
885 Marrows Rd Apt D6 (19713-1571)
P.O. Box 1066 (19715-1066)
PHONE.................302 737-2008
Lauren Demichiel, *Pr*
EMP: 5 EST: 1987
SALES (est): 456.29K **Privately Held**
Web: www.marta-group.com
SIC: 8741 Management services

(G-11341)
MARTIN COLLISION CENTER
298 E Cleveland Ave (19711-3711)
PHONE.................302 452-2711
EMP: 5 EST: 2019
SALES (est): 51.04K **Privately Held**
SIC: 7539 Automotive repair shops, nec

(G-11342)
MARTIN CONSTRUCTION SVCS LLC
340 W Chestnut Hill Rd (19713-1101)
PHONE.................302 200-0885
Richard Martin, *Managing Member*
EMP: 18 EST: 2007
SQ FT: 1,000
SALES (est): 3.08MM **Privately Held**
Web: www.martincsllc.com
SIC: 1542 1522 Commercial and office building contractors; Residential construction, nec

(G-11343)
MARTIN DEALERSHIP
298 E Cleveland Ave (19711-3711)
PHONE.................302 738-5200
Homi Poursaied, *Prin*
EMP: 7 EST: 1995
SALES (est): 752.04K **Privately Held**
SIC: 7532 5511 Body shop, automotive; New and used car dealers

(G-11344)
MARTIN DIRECT INSURANCE
298 E Cleveland Ave (19711-3711)
PHONE.................302 452-2700
William Camp, *Asst Sec*
EMP: 5 EST: 2017
SALES (est): 50.78K **Privately Held**
SIC: 6411 Insurance agents, brokers, and service

(G-11345)
MARTIN NEWARK DEALERSHIP INC
Also Called: Martin Honda
298 E Cleveland Ave (19711-3711)
PHONE.................302 454-9300
EMP: 58 EST: 1994
SALES (est): 23.2MM **Privately Held**
Web: www.honda.com
SIC: 5511 7538 7515 7513 Automobiles, new and used; General automotive repair shops; Passenger car leasing; Truck rental and leasing, no drivers

(G-11346)
MARY KATE JOHNSTON
228 Suburban Dr (19711-3596)
PHONE.................302 388-5654
Mary Johnston, *Prin*
EMP: 5 EST: 2010
SALES (est): 138.69K **Privately Held**
SIC: 6531 Real estate agent, residential

(G-11347)
MARYRUTH L NICH
86 Omega Dr (19713-2065)
PHONE.................302 623-1929
Maryruth Nich, *Prin*
EMP: 6 EST: 2017
SALES (est): 63.56K **Privately Held**
SIC: 8049 Offices of health practitioner

(G-11348)
MASON BUILDING GROUP INC
35 Albe Dr (19702-1321)
PHONE.................302 292-0600
Christopher Mason, *Pr*
Rita Thomas, *
EMP: 150 EST: 1991
SQ FT: 11,000
SALES (est): 48.77MM **Privately Held**
Web: www.masonbuilding.com
SIC: 1542 1751 Commercial and office building, new construction; Framing contractor

(G-11349)
MASSAGE ENVY - CHRISTIANA
Also Called: Massage Envy
3148 Fashion Center Blvd (19702-3246)
PHONE.................302 266-2762
EMP: 5 EST: 2018
SALES (est): 72.48K **Privately Held**
Web: www.massageenvy.com
SIC: 7299 Massage parlor

(G-11350)
MASTER INTERIORS INC (PA)
113 Sandy Dr (19713-1148)
PHONE.................302 368-9361
Mary Humpton, *Pr*
EMP: 44 EST: 1984
SQ FT: 10,000
SALES (est): 9.86MM
SALES (corp-wide): 9.86MM **Privately Held**
Web: www.masterinteriors.com
SIC: 1742 Acoustical and ceiling work

(G-11351)
MASTER SIDLOW & ASSOCIATES PA
750 Prides Xing Ste 100 (19713-6108)
P.O. Box 4080 (19807-0080)
PHONE.................302 652-3480
Judy Scarborough, *Owner*
William H Master, *
Michael T Mccudden, *VP*
EMP: 50 EST: 1978
SALES (est): 8.85MM **Privately Held**
Web: www.mastersidlow.com
SIC: 8721 Certified public accountant

(G-11352)
MATEINA US INC
2915 Ogletown Rd (19713-1927)
PHONE.................514 443-4945
Nicolas Beaupre, *CEO*
EMP: 8
SALES (est): 402.04K **Privately Held**
SIC: 5149 Groceries and related products, nec

(G-11353)
MATERNITY GYNECOLOGY ASSOC PA
4745 Ogletown Stanton Rd Ste 207 (19713-2074)
PHONE.................302 368-9000
George Liarkos Md, *Pr*
EMP: 18 EST: 1976
SALES (est): 486.35K **Privately Held**
Web: www.maternity-gynecology.com
SIC: 8011 Obstetrician

(G-11354)
MATTHEW & MICHELE DENN
441 Coldspring Run (19711-2466)
PHONE.................302 235-0175
Matthew Denn, *Prin*
EMP: 6 EST: 2009
SALES (est): 74.86K **Privately Held**
SIC: 8049 Clinical psychologist

(G-11355)
MATTLEMAN WEINROTH & MILLER PC
200 Continental Dr Ste 215 (19713-4335)
PHONE.................302 731-8349
Adam Elgart, *Mgr*
EMP: 8
SALES (corp-wide): 8.79MM **Privately Held**
Web: www.mwm-law.com
SIC: 8111 General practice attorney, lawyer
PA: Mattleman, Weinroth & Miller, P.C.
401 Rte 70 Mrlton Pike E
Cherry Hill NJ 08034
856 429-5507

(G-11356)
MAVEN WORKFORCE LLC
200 Continental Dr Ste 401 (19713-4334)
PHONE.................551 214-8937
EMP: 6 EST: 2012
SALES (est): 247.73K **Privately Held**
Web: www.mavenworkforce.com
SIC: 8742 Business management consultant

(G-11357)
MAVERICK REALTY LLC
Also Called: Real Estate
200 Continental Dr Ste 401 (19713-4334)
PHONE.................302 373-6591
Darlene R Morton, *CEO*
Chad Morton, *Prin*
EMP: 10 EST: 2019
SALES (est): 754.84K **Privately Held**
SIC: 6531 Real estate agents and managers

(G-11358)
MAX RE ASSOCIATES INC
Also Called: Re/Max
228 Suburban Dr (19711-3596)
PHONE.................302 453-3200
Paul Saulk, *Genl Mgr*
EMP: 39
Web: www.remax.com
SIC: 6531 Real estate agent, residential
PA: Max Re Associates Inc
228 Suburban Dr
Newark DE 19711

(G-11359)
MAX RE ASSOCIATES INC (PA)
Also Called: Re/Max
228 Suburban Dr (19711-3596)
PHONE.................302 477-3900
EMP: 45 EST: 1996
SALES (est): 4.58MM **Privately Held**
Web: www.remax.com
SIC: 6531 Real estate agent, residential

(G-11360)
MAXICARE AMBULANCE SERVICES
19 Peddlers Row (19702-1525)
PHONE.................302 990-3777
EMP: 5 EST: 2019
SALES (est): 64.26K **Privately Held**
SIC: 4119 Ambulance service

(G-11361)
MAXIMUM ELECTRICAL SVCS LLC
4142 Ogletown Stanton Rd Unit 254 (19713-4169)
PHONE.................302 521-2820
Raleigh Veney, *Managing Member*
EMP: 7 EST: 2006
SALES (est): 1.2MM **Privately Held**
Web: www.maximumelectrical.com
SIC: 1731 General electrical contractor

(G-11362)
MAYSCAPES LLC
129 Phyllis Dr (19711-6605)
PHONE.................302 389-5999
Jonathon May, *Prin*
EMP: 5 EST: 2016
SALES (est): 64.92K **Privately Held**
Web: www.mayscapesde.com
SIC: 1799 Fence construction

(G-11363)
MAZZOLA SYSTEMS INC
Also Called: Mazzola Construction
560 Peoples Plz Ste 112 (19702-4798)
PHONE.................302 738-6808
Donato Mazzola, *Pr*
EMP: 8 EST: 1995
SALES (est): 275K **Privately Held**
Web: www.mazzolainc.com
SIC: 1521 1522 Single-family housing construction; Residential construction, nec

(G-11364)
MAZZPAC LLC
94 Salem Church Rd (19713-2935)
PHONE.................973 641-9159
Wolfgang Maslo, *Managing Member*
EMP: 4 EST: 2010
SALES (est): 374.52K **Privately Held**
Web: www.mazzpac.com
SIC: 3541 7389 Machine tool replacement & repair parts, metal cutting types; Business Activities at Non-Commercial Site

(G-11365)
MCBRIDE AND ZIEGLER INC
2607 Eastburn Ctr (19711-7267)
PHONE.................302 737-9138
Mark Ziegler, *Pr*
EMP: 25 EST: 1970
SALES (est): 2.25MM **Privately Held**
Web: www.mcbrideziegler.com
SIC: 8711 Civil engineering

(G-11366)
MCCALL BROOKS INSURANCE AGENCY
Also Called: Nationwide
110 Christiana Medical Ctr (19702-1697)
PHONE.................302 475-8200
Brooks M Mc Caull, *Owner*
Brooks M Mccaull, *Prin*
EMP: 7 EST: 1994
SALES (est): 785.95K **Privately Held**
Web: www.nationwide.com
SIC: 6411 Insurance agents, nec

(G-11367)
MCCORMICK TAYLOR INC
220 Continental Dr Ste 200 (19713-4312)
PHONE.................302 738-0208
EMP: 7
SALES (corp-wide): 171.01MM **Privately Held**
Web: www.mccormicktaylor.com
SIC: 8711 Consulting engineer
PA: Mccormick Taylor, Inc.
1818 Market St Fl 16
Philadelphia PA 19103
215 592-4200

Newark - New Castle County (G-11368)   GEOGRAPHIC SECTION

(G-11368)
MDS SERVICES INC
207 E Cobblefield Ct (19713-2267)
PHONE....................302 547-3861
EMP: 6 EST: 2012
SALES (est): 149.7K Privately Held
SIC: 8011 Offices and clinics of medical doctors

(G-11369)
MEADOWOOD MOBIL STATION
Also Called: Exxon
2650 Kirkwood Hwy (19711)
PHONE....................302 731-5602
Jeff Ozdmer, Owner
EMP: 5 EST: 1958
SQ FT: 2,800
SALES (est): 510.54K Privately Held
Web: corporate.exxonmobil.com
SIC: 5541 7539 Filling stations, gasoline; Brake repair, automotive

(G-11370)
MEADOWWOOD
115 Rockrose Dr (19711-6800)
PHONE....................302 286-7004
EMP: 9 EST: 2018
SALES (est): 91.32K Privately Held
Web: www.meadowwoodhospital.com
SIC: 7999 Recreation services

(G-11371)
MECHANICAL SYSTEMS INTL CORP
9 Lewis St. (19711)
PHONE....................302 453-8315
EMP: 9 EST: 1994
SALES (est): 155.6K Privately Held
SIC: 3545 Tools and accessories for machine tools

(G-11372)
MEDIA FUSION US LLC
214 W General Grey Ct (19702-3831)
PHONE....................256 532-3874
EMP: 5 EST: 2018
SALES (est): 125.2K Privately Held
SIC: 8742 General management consultant

(G-11373)
MEDIASTREET LLC
2035 Sunset Lake Rd Ste B2 (19702-2600)
PHONE....................800 308-6579
EMP: 5 EST: 2016
SALES (est): 52.9K Privately Held
SIC: 7313 Electronic media advertising representatives

(G-11374)
MEDICAL BILLING & MGT SVCS INC (PA)
111 Continental Dr Ste 315 (19713-4302)
PHONE....................610 564-5314
Tom Schovee, CEO
Cathy Sells, Pr
Tischa Roberts, COO
Lori Shore, Compliance Vice President
Jason Cavallaro, VP
EMP: 22 EST: 1986
SQ FT: 4,000
SALES (est): 4.32MM
SALES (corp-wide): 4.32MM Privately Held
Web: www.mbms.net
SIC: 8721 Billing and bookkeeping service

(G-11375)
MEDICAL MASSAGE DELAWARE LLC (PA)
254 Chapman Rd Ste 112 (19702-5413)
PHONE....................888 757-1951
Jackie Staker, Pt
Linda Ogilvie, Pt
Patricia Peterson, Pt
Zac Meiyu, Pt
EMP: 5 EST: 2008
SALES (est): 71.38K
SALES (corp-wide): 71.38K Privately Held
Web: www.medicalmassageofdelaware.com
SIC: 8049 Massage Therapist

(G-11376)
MEDICAL ONCLOGY HMTLOGY CONS P
Also Called: Delduca, Vincent Jr MD
4701 Ogletown Stanton Rd Ste 2200 (19713-2055)
PHONE....................302 366-1200
Doctor Stephen Grubbs, Pt
Michael Griliano, *
EMP: 36 EST: 1989
SALES (est): 4.58MM Privately Held
Web: www.mohcde.com
SIC: 8011 Oncologist

(G-11377)
MEDICAL SOCIETY OF DELAWARE (PA)
900 Prides Xing (19713-6100)
P.O. Box 8155 (19714-8155)
PHONE....................302 366-1400
Mark Thompson, Ex Dir
EMP: 20 EST: 1776
SQ FT: 1,500
SALES (est): 2.78MM
SALES (corp-wide): 2.78MM Privately Held
Web: www.medicalsocietyofdelaware.org
SIC: 8621 2731 Medical field-related associations; Book publishing

(G-11378)
MEDIRENTS AND SALES INC
2860 Ogletown Rd (19713-1857)
PHONE....................302 286-7999
Thomas S Petr, Pr
EMP: 7 EST: 2015
SALES (est): 33.42K Privately Held
Web: www.medirents.net
SIC: 4899 Communication services, nec

(G-11379)
MEDUSIND SOLUTIONS INC
111 Continental Dr Ste 412 (19713-4332)
PHONE....................800 250-7063
Vipul Bansal, CEO
EMP: 410
SALES (corp-wide): 4.88MM Privately Held
Web: www.medusind.com
SIC: 7389 Personal service agents, brokers, and bureaus
PA: Medusind Solutions Inc.
31103 Rancho Viejo Rd
San Juan Capistrano CA 92675
949 240-8895

(G-11380)
MEGAN COUCH
113 Country Club Dr (19711-2736)
PHONE....................302 981-0687
Megan Couch, Owner
EMP: 6 EST: 2017
SALES (est): 34.97K Privately Held
SIC: 8049 Offices of health practitioner

(G-11381)
MEGAN MC GRAW LCSW
200 Christina Pkwy # P (19713-4000)
PHONE....................302 283-0414
Megan Mcgraw, Prin
EMP: 7 EST: 2004
SALES (est): 64.22K Privately Held
SIC: 8322 Social worker

(G-11382)
MEI APP INC (PA)
2035 Sunset Lake Rd Ste B2 (19702-2600)
PHONE....................617 877-6603
Shiwen Li, CEO
EMP: 7 EST: 2017
SALES (est): 1MM
SALES (corp-wide): 1MM Privately Held
SIC: 7371 Computer software development and applications

(G-11383)
MEINEKE CARE CARE CENTER
750 E Chestnut Hill Rd (19713-1830)
PHONE....................302 368-0700
Jake Williams, Owner
EMP: 8 EST: 2016
SALES (est): 469.66K Privately Held
Web: www.meineke.com
SIC: 7539 5013 Automotive repair shops, nec; Automotive supplies

(G-11384)
MELALEUCA WELLNESS COMPANY
903 Vinings Way (19702-7613)
PHONE....................336 314-5635
Larone Smith, Prin
EMP: 7 EST: 2017
SALES (est): 88.95K Privately Held
Web: www.melaleuca.info
SIC: 8099 Health and allied services, nec

(G-11385)
MELANIN MIXX BEAUTY BRAND INC
Also Called: Melanin Mixx Beauty
7 Peddlers Row Ste B (19702-1584)
PHONE....................302 266-1010
Davon Barrett, Admn
EMP: 4 EST: 2019
SALES (est): 263.66K Privately Held
Web: www.melaninmixx.com
SIC: 5122 2844 7991 7389 Cosmetics, perfumes, and hair products; Shampoos, rinses, conditioners: hair; Spas; Interior design services

(G-11386)
MENDING COVE LLC
31 Thorn Ln Apt 11 (19711-4435)
PHONE....................856 803-9958
Melinda Taylor, Pr
EMP: 5 EST: 2021
SALES (est): 59.69K Privately Held
Web: www.mendingcove.com
SIC: 8322 General counseling services

(G-11387)
MENTAL FUEL INC
200 Continental Dr Ste 401 (19713-4334)
PHONE....................302 291-4858
EMP: 5
SALES (est): 32.92K Privately Held
Web: www.mentalfuelinc.com
SIC: 8322 General counseling services

(G-11388)
MERAKEY USA
6301 Vicky Dr (19702-8125)
PHONE....................302 836-1809
EMP: 11 EST: 2020
SALES (est): 480.1K Privately Held
Web: www.merakey.org
SIC: 8093 Mental health clinic, outpatient

(G-11389)
MERIT MECHANICAL CO INC
39 Albe Dr (19702-1321)
PHONE....................302 366-8601
John Rettig, VP
EMP: 70 EST: 1959
SALES (est): 6.64MM Privately Held
SIC: 1711 Mechanical contractor

(G-11390)
MERIT SERVICES INC
39 Albe Dr (19702-1321)
PHONE....................302 366-8601
Richard M Rettig, Pr
Virginia Rettig, *
John Travis Rettig, *
EMP: 23 EST: 1958
SQ FT: 14,000
SALES (est): 452.43K Privately Held
SIC: 1711 Mechanical contractor

(G-11391)
MERRY MAIDS
Also Called: Merry Maids
1 Washington St (19711-7140)
PHONE....................302 266-6243
EMP: 6 EST: 2014
SALES (est): 37.39K Privately Held
Web: www.merrymaids.com
SIC: 7349 Maid services, contract or fee basis

(G-11392)
MET TECHNOLOGIES LLC
40 E Main St (19711-4639)
PHONE....................302 468-5243
EMP: 8 EST: 2012
SALES (est): 209.38K Privately Held
Web: www.met-technologies.com
SIC: 8641 Civic and social associations

(G-11393)
METAMAX TECHNOLOGY INC
8 Innovation Way (19711-5443)
PHONE....................302 587-0060
Gilbert Shawn, CEO
EMP: 10
SALES (est): 348.32K Privately Held
SIC: 7371 Computer software development

(G-11394)
METROFORM GROUP INC
4639 Ogletown Stanton Rd (19713-2006)
PHONE....................302 737-1165
Marchello A Charleston, Prin
EMP: 14 EST: 2006
SALES (est): 231.31K Privately Held
SIC: 8011 Gynecologist

(G-11395)
METZ JADE ASSOCIATES
3 Aubrey Ln (19711-2478)
PHONE....................302 239-2414
EMP: 5 EST: 2017
SALES (est): 56.82K Privately Held
Web: www.metzjade.com
SIC: 5065 Electronic parts

(G-11396)
MEXICOM USA INC
2915 Ogletown Rd (19713-1927)
PHONE....................956 516-7201
EMP: 5 EST: 2019
SALES (est): 81.26K Privately Held
SIC: 4731 Freight transportation arrangement

(G-11397)
MG GLOBAL GROUP LLC ◊
254 Chapman Rd Ste 209 (19702-5413)
PHONE....................302 217-3724

GEOGRAPHIC SECTION

Newark - New Castle County (G-11424)

Walter Garcia, *Managing Member*
EMP: 5 **EST:** 2023
SALES (est): 220.38K **Privately Held**
SIC: 1731 7389 Fiber optic cable installation; Business Activities at Non-Commercial Site

(G-11398)
MI-1 LLC
3 Bobby Dr (19713-4019)
PHONE..................302 369-3447
Md Tawhedul H Khan, *Prin*
EMP: 5 **EST:** 2019
SALES (est): 170.14K **Privately Held**
SIC: 1389 Oil and gas field services, nec

(G-11399)
MI-DEE INC
Also Called: Edu-Care Preschool & Daycare
345 Polly Drummond Hill Rd # R (19711-4809)
PHONE..................302 453-7326
Helen Shih, *Pr*
Lynne Magrogan, *
Neda Horne, *
EMP: 12 **EST:** 1983
SALES (est): 333.99K **Privately Held**
Web: www.educarepreschool.com
SIC: 8351 Group day care center

(G-11400)
MICHAEL A ANDREOLI CONTRACTING
18 Reubens Cir (19702-3034)
PHONE..................302 274-8709
Jessica Phippin, *Prin*
EMP: 5 **EST:** 2018
SALES (est): 74.57K **Privately Held**
SIC: 1799 Special trade contractors, nec

(G-11401)
MICHAEL A MEKULSKI GENERA
25 Madrigal Dr (19702-4749)
PHONE..................302 834-8260
Christina Mekulski, *Prin*
EMP: 6 **EST:** 2006
SALES (est): 227.35K **Privately Held**
SIC: 1521 New construction, single-family houses

(G-11402)
MICHAEL G SUGARMAN MD
774 Christiana Rd Ste 202 (19713-4221)
PHONE..................302 366-7671
Michael Sugarman, *Ofcr*
EMP: 9 **EST:** 2018
SALES (est): 54.13K **Privately Held**
Web: www.delawareneurosurgicalgroup.com
SIC: 8011 Offices and clinics of medical doctors

(G-11403)
MICHELLE M MANASSERI PSYD LLC
774 Christiana Rd Ste 202 (19713-4221)
PHONE..................302 478-1578
Michelle Manasseri, *Prin*
EMP: 9 **EST:** 2016
SALES (est): 242.06K **Privately Held**
SIC: 8049 Clinical psychologist

(G-11404)
MICHELLE MENZER
102 W Mill Station Dr (19711-7484)
PHONE..................302 366-7456
Michelle Menzer, *Prin*
EMP: 6 **EST:** 2011
SALES (est): 113.57K **Privately Held**
SIC: 8049 Offices of health practitioner

(G-11405)
MID ATLANTIC CARDIOVASCULAR
1213 Churchmans Rd (19713-2149)
PHONE..................302 294-1044
EMP: 6 **EST:** 2019
SALES (est): 60.66K **Privately Held**
SIC: 8011 Cardiologist and cardio-vascular specialist

(G-11406)
MID ATLANTIC INDUS BELTING
15 Garfield Way (19713-3450)
P.O. Box 1518 (19707-5518)
PHONE..................302 453-7353
EMP: 4 **EST:** 1995
SQ FT: 10,000
SALES (est): 490.37K **Privately Held**
Web: www.midatlanticbelting.com
SIC: 3496 Conveyor belts

(G-11407)
MID ATLANTIC MECHANICAL INC
705 Stanton Christiana Rd (19713-2027)
P.O. Box 5904 (19808-0904)
PHONE..................302 999-9209
Larry Fox, *Pr*
EMP: 20 **EST:** 1998
SQ FT: 4,500
SALES (est): 1.59MM **Privately Held**
SIC: 1711 Mechanical contractor

(G-11408)
MID ATLANTIC RETINA
4102 Ogletown Stanton Rd (19713-4183)
PHONE..................800 331-6634
EMP: 15 **EST:** 2019
SALES (est): 209.57K **Privately Held**
Web: www.midatlanticretina.com
SIC: 8011 Opthalmologist

(G-11409)
MID ATLANTIC SPINE
100 Biddle Ave Ste 101 (19702-3982)
PHONE..................302 369-1700
Frank Falco, *Owner*
EMP: 18 **EST:** 2001
SALES (est): 2.43MM **Privately Held**
Web: www.midatlanticspine.com
SIC: 8011 Orthopedic physician

(G-11410)
MID-ATLANTIC BEHAVIORAL HEALTH
90 Blue Hen Dr (19713-3406)
PHONE..................302 224-1400
EMP: 7 **EST:** 2019
SALES (est): 235.76K **Privately Held**
Web: www.lifestance.com
SIC: 8049 Clinical psychologist

(G-11411)
MID-ATLANTIC REALTY CO INC
Also Called: Abbey Walk Apts
39 Abbey Ln (19711-6869)
PHONE..................302 737-3110
Kim Dreyer, *Mgr*
EMP: 6
SALES (corp-wide): 5.35MM **Privately Held**
Web: www.midatlanticrealtyco.com
SIC: 6531 6513 Real estate managers; Apartment building operators
PA: Mid-Atlantic Realty Co Inc
39 Abbey Ln
Newark DE 19711
302 658-7642

(G-11412)
MID-ATLANTIC REALTY CO INC (PA)
39 Abbey Ln (19711-6869)
PHONE..................302 658-7642
Edward L Davidson, *Pr*
Verino Pettinaro, *VP*
EMP: 20 **EST:** 1975
SQ FT: 1,662
SALES (est): 5.35MM
SALES (corp-wide): 5.35MM **Privately Held**
Web: www.midatlanticrealtyco.com
SIC: 6531 Condominium manager

(G-11413)
MID-ATLNTIC SLS MKTG GROUP LLC
Also Called: Sales & Marketing Bus Svcs
1 Whitehaven Ct (19713-3444)
PHONE..................215 515-6077
Steven Mason, *Pr*
EMP: 5 **EST:** 2013
SALES (est): 258.18K **Privately Held**
Web: www.midatlanticsmg.com
SIC: 8742 Marketing consulting services

(G-11414)
MID-ATLNTIC WTRPROOFING MD INC (PA)
802 Interchange Blvd (19711-3570)
PHONE..................301 206-9500
TOLL FREE: 800
Edwin D Fennell, *Pr*
Charles M Levine, *VP*
Shawn C Fennell, *Sec*
Eric Tullio, *COO*
EMP: 15 **EST:** 1995
SALES (est): 3.91MM
SALES (corp-wide): 3.91MM **Privately Held**
SIC: 1799 Waterproofing

(G-11415)
MIDATLANTIC PAIN INSTITUTE
Also Called: Midatlantic Spine
100 Biddle Ave Ste 101 (19702-3982)
PHONE..................302 369-1700
Frank Falco, *Pr*
EMP: 18 **EST:** 2005
SALES (est): 910.31K **Privately Held**
Web: www.midatlanticspine.com
SIC: 8093 Specialty outpatient clinics, nec

(G-11416)
MIDI LABS INC
225 Corporate Blvd Ste E (19702-3520)
PHONE..................302 737-4297
Myron Sasser, *Pr*
Craig Kunitsky, *Mktg Dir*
EMP: 12 **EST:** 1995
SALES (est): 1.32MM
SALES (corp-wide): 14.69MM **Privately Held**
Web: www.biolog.com
SIC: 8734 Testing laboratories
PA: Biolog, Inc.
21124 Cabot Blvd
Hayward CA 94545
510 785-2564

(G-11417)
MIH INTERNATIONAL LLC
112 Capitol Trl (19711-3716)
PHONE..................301 908-4233
EMP: 5 **EST:** 2013
SALES (est): 225K **Privately Held**
Web: www.m-brace.com
SIC: 3842 Surgical appliances and supplies

(G-11418)
MILES SCIENTIFIC CORPORATION
Also Called: Analtech
75 Blue Hen Dr (19713-3405)
P.O. Box 7558 (19714-7558)
PHONE..................302 737-6960
Steven Miles, *Pr*
◆ **EMP:** 21 **EST:** 1961
SQ FT: 10,000
SALES (est): 1.68MM **Privately Held**
Web: www.milesscientific.com
SIC: 3231 5049 3826 Laboratory glassware; Laboratory equipment, except medical or dental; Chromatographic equipment, laboratory type

(G-11419)
MILESTONE CONSTRUCTION CO INC
4 Mill Park Ct Ste A (19713-1901)
PHONE..................302 442-4252
Steven Sieja, *Pr*
EMP: 19 **EST:** 2009
SALES (est): 2.9MM **Privately Held**
Web: www.milestonede.com
SIC: 1542 Commercial and office building contractors

(G-11420)
MILITARY ORDER OF THE PURPLE
1795 Brigade Ct (19702-2481)
PHONE..................302 563-0435
EMP: 8 **EST:** 2018
SALES (est): 47.24K **Privately Held**
Web: www.purpleheart.org
SIC: 8641 Civic associations

(G-11421)
MILLAN CONTRACTORS
11 Cynthia Rd (19702-5117)
PHONE..................302 983-9365
EMP: 7
SALES (est): 293.51K **Privately Held**
SIC: 1799 Special trade contractors, nec

(G-11422)
MILLENNIAL VENTURES GROUP LLC ✿
200 Continental Dr Ste 401 (19713-4337)
PHONE..................877 533-3337
Brandi Baldwin, *Managing Member*
EMP: 10 **EST:** 2022
SALES (est): 563.44K **Privately Held**
Web: www.millennialventures.co
SIC: 8742 Marketing consulting services

(G-11423)
MILTON WORLDWIDE MEDIA LLC
220 E Delaware Ave (19711-4607)
PHONE..................302 353-4470
Romain Brabant, *Prin*
EMP: 5 **EST:** 2007
SALES (est): 118.36K **Privately Held**
SIC: 4899 Communication services, nec

(G-11424)
MINIMLLY INVSIVE SRGCAL NRSCNC
774 Christiana Rd Ste 2 (19713-4219)
PHONE..................302 738-0300
Suzanne Rodenheiser, *CEO*
Fred Hyde, *
Nicole Carrington, *
EMP: 102 **EST:** 2003
SALES (est): 4.49MM
SALES (corp-wide): 2.54B **Publicly Held**
Web: www.dedocs.com
SIC: 8011 Surgeon
PA: Surgery Partners, Inc.
340 Sven Sprng Way Ste 60
Brentwood TN 37027
615 234-5900

Newark - New Castle County (G-11425)

(G-11425)
MINKERS CONSTRUCTION INC
830 Dawson Dr (19713-3416)
PHONE.....................302 239-9239
Matt Minker, *Pr*
Mark Price, ▪
Robert Blanck, ▪
Kevin Lucas, ▪
Carol Minker, ▪
EMP: 19 EST: 1981
SQ FT: 6,000
SALES (est): 396.56K **Privately Held**
Web: www.specialtyfinishesde.com
SIC: 1521 Single-family housing construction

(G-11426)
MINUTE LOAN CENTER
2693 Pulaski Hwy (19702-3919)
PHONE.....................302 607-2202
EMP: 6 EST: 2018
SALES (est): 163.25K **Privately Held**
Web: www.minuteloancenter.com
SIC: 6141 Personal credit institutions

(G-11427)
MIOPS INC
2035 Sunset Lake Rd Ste B2 (19702-2600)
PHONE.....................302 451-9571
EMP: 6
SALES (est): 68.89K **Privately Held**
Web: www.miops.com
SIC: 7371 Computer software development

(G-11428)
MISSIONS FOR LIFE INC
165 E Green Valley Cir (19711-6792)
PHONE.....................302 981-1915
Matthew Morrison, *Pr*
Mark Cieniewicz, *VP*
Jennifer Morrison Aa, *Prin*
EMP: 5 EST: 2016
SALES (est): 77.53K **Privately Held**
Web: www.missionsforlife.net
SIC: 8399 Advocacy group

(G-11429)
MIXX ENTERTAINMENT LLC
112 Miners Ln (19713-1183)
PHONE.....................302 635-9966
EMP: 5 EST: 2018
SALES (est): 77.06K **Privately Held**
SIC: 7929 Entertainers and entertainment groups

(G-11430)
MJ WILMINGTON HOTEL ASSOC LP
Also Called: Hilton Christiana
100 Continental Dr (19713-4327)
PHONE.....................302 454-1500
EMP: 159 EST: 1996
SALES (est): 9.17MM **Privately Held**
Web: www.hiltonchristiana.com
SIC: 7011 Hotels
PA: Meyer Jabara Hotels, Llc
7 Kenosia Ave Ste 2a
Danbury CT 06810

(G-11431)
MJ WILMINGTON HOTEL ASSOC LP
Also Called: Hilton
100 Continental Dr (19713-4327)
PHONE.....................302 454-1500
Vince Difonzo, *Brnch Mgr*
EMP: 189
SALES (corp-wide): 3.02MM **Privately Held**
Web: www.hiltongrandvacations.com
SIC: 7011 Resort hotel
PA: Mj Wilmington Hotel Associates Lp
7 W Kenosia Ave
Danbury CT 06810
203 798-1099

(G-11432)
ML NEWARK LLC
Also Called: Christina Mill Apartments
100 Christina Mill Dr (19711-3572)
PHONE.....................302 737-2868
Grace Grey, *Managing Member*
EMP: 1139 EST: 2007
SALES (est): 390.59K
SALES (corp-wide): 367.25MM **Privately Held**
Web: www.christinamillapts.com
SIC: 6513 Apartment building operators
HQ: Lowe Enterprises Investment Management, Inc
11777 San Vicente Blvd
Los Angeles CA 90049

(G-11433)
ML RUIZ ENTERPRISES INC
110 Astro Shopping Ctr (19711-7254)
PHONE.....................302 894-9000
EMP: 5 EST: 2010
SALES (est): 212.98K **Privately Held**
SIC: 7389 Business services, nec

(G-11434)
MMS ENTERPRISES LLC ✪
254 Chapman Rd Ste 208 (19702-5422)
PHONE.....................888 786-9290
Jonathan Mejia, *Managing Member*
EMP: 5 EST: 2023
SALES (est): 207.81K **Privately Held**
SIC: 8742 Management consulting services

(G-11435)
MOBILE AIR LLC
200 Interchange Blvd (19711-9100)
PHONE.....................302 502-7743
EMP: 6 EST: 2020
SALES (est): 233.83K **Privately Held**
Web: www.mobileair.com
SIC: 1711 Warm air heating and air conditioning contractor

(G-11436)
MOBILE MAGIC DETAILING LLC
2840 Ogletown Rd Unit 2 (19713-1826)
PHONE.....................302 444-8644
Randall Simons, *Pr*
EMP: 5 EST: 2020
SALES (est): 44.56K **Privately Held**
Web: www.ceramicprode.com
SIC: 7542 Washing and polishing, automotive

(G-11437)
MODERN SAMURAI COMBAT FITNESS
8 Photinia Dr (19702-3921)
PHONE.....................302 229-5399
Lawrence Walther, *Prin*
EMP: 5 EST: 2017
SALES (est): 47.65K **Privately Held**
SIC: 7991 Physical fitness facilities

(G-11438)
MOMENEE AND ASSOCIATES INC (PA)
Also Called: Momenee Survey Group
17 Polly Drummond Shpg Ctr Ste 201 (19711-4820)
PHONE.....................610 527-3030
Kevin Momenee, *Pr*
EMP: 9 EST: 1986
SALES (est): 2.02MM **Privately Held**
SIC: 8711 Civil engineering

(G-11439)
MOMMIN WITH SWAG LLC
3 Cymbal Ct (19702-5342)
PHONE.....................302 373-6316
Kawana House, *Managing Member*
EMP: 5
SALES (est): 220.1K **Privately Held**
SIC: 2339 7389 Athletic clothing: women's, misses', and juniors'; Business Activities at Non-Commercial Site

(G-11440)
MONEY MAILER OF DELAWARE
Also Called: Money Mailer
5 Beacon Ln (19711-1904)
PHONE.....................302 235-7262
EMP: 10 EST: 2008
SALES (est): 532.58K **Privately Held**
Web: www.moneymailer.com
SIC: 7331 Direct mail advertising services

(G-11441)
MONEYBALL DFS LLC
200 Continental Dr # 401 (19713-4334)
PHONE.....................302 240-0051
EMP: 5 EST: 2018
SALES (est): 20.78K **Privately Held**
SIC: 7999 Amusement and recreation, nec

(G-11442)
MONGE WOODWORKING LLC
4 Barnard St (19711-4345)
PHONE.....................302 455-0175
EMP: 4 EST: 2018
SALES (est): 54.13K **Privately Held**
SIC: 2431 Millwork

(G-11443)
MONICA MEHRING DDS
179 W Chestnut Hill Rd Ste 4 (19713-2210)
PHONE.....................302 368-0054
Monica Mehring D.d.s., *Owner*
EMP: 11 EST: 1998
SALES (est): 431.36K **Privately Held**
Web: www.mehringdds.com
SIC: 8021 Dentists' office

(G-11444)
MONOFOR INC
2035 Sunset Lake Rd Ste B2 (19702-2600)
PHONE.....................415 800-4925
EMP: 7 EST: 2017
SALES (est): 61.3K **Privately Held**
Web: www.monofor.com
SIC: 7371 Computer software development

(G-11445)
MONOGRAM SPECIALTIES
701 Valley Rd (19711-2580)
PHONE.....................302 292-2424
Nancy Franklin, *Owner*
Chuck Franklin, *Prin*
EMP: 2 EST: 1990
SALES (est): 148.28K **Privately Held**
Web: www.inthedomain.com
SIC: 3999 Embroidery kits

(G-11446)
MONTEREY SW LLC
111 Continental Dr # 114 (19713-4306)
PHONE.....................302 504-4901
EMP: 10 EST: 2012
SALES (est): 531.73K **Privately Held**
SIC: 6221 Commodity contracts brokers, dealers

(G-11447)
MONTEREY SWF LLC
111 Continental Dr # 114 (19713-4306)
PHONE.....................302 504-4901
EMP: 10 EST: 2012
SALES (est): 630K **Privately Held**
SIC: 6221 Commodity contracts brokers, dealers

(G-11448)
MOON BOUNCE MANIA
5047 Ogletown Stanton Rd (19713-2014)
PHONE.....................302 588-1300
Travis Leary, *Prin*
EMP: 5 EST: 2010
SALES (est): 59.66K **Privately Held**
SIC: 7299 Party planning service

(G-11449)
MOPPERT AUTO COLLISION OF
1801 Ogletown Rd (19711-5429)
PHONE.....................302 453-2900
EMP: 6 EST: 2019
SALES (est): 236.97K **Privately Held**
Web: www.moppertautocollision.com
SIC: 7538 General automotive repair shops

(G-11450)
MORAN ENVMTL RECOVERY LLC
9 Garfield Way (19713-3450)
PHONE.....................302 322-6008
Justin Woodard, *Mgr*
EMP: 124
Web: www.moranenvironmental.com
SIC: 8999 Earth science services
HQ: Moran Environmental Recovery Llc
75 York Ave Ste D
Randolph MA 02368
781 815-1100

(G-11451)
MORE ABOUT YOU INC
220 Christiana Medical Ctr (19702-1652)
PHONE.....................302 660-8899
EMP: 9 EST: 2018
SALES (est): 444.88K **Privately Held**
Web: www.moreaboutyouinc.com
SIC: 8049 Offices of health practitioner

(G-11452)
MORE PROPERTY RECOVERY
14 Sonnet Dr (19702-4525)
PHONE.....................302 834-4788
Patrick Moore, *Prin*
EMP: 7 EST: 2016
SALES (est): 75.13K **Privately Held**
Web: www.moorepropertyrecovery.com
SIC: 6531 Real estate agents and managers

(G-11453)
MORGAN GARANTY INTL FINCL CORP (HQ)
Also Called: Morgan Guaranty
500 Stanton Christiana Rd (19713-2105)
PHONE.....................302 634-1000
Richard Mcloughlin, *Pr*
EMP: 31 EST: 1959
SALES (est): 6.4MM
SALES (corp-wide): 154.79B **Publicly Held**
SIC: 6211 Investment firm, general brokerage
PA: Jpmorgan Chase & Co.
383 Madison Ave
New York NY 10179
212 270-6000

(G-11454)
MORRIS JAMES LLP
16 Polly Drummond Hill Rd (19711-5703)
PHONE.....................302 368-4200
EMP: 15
SALES (corp-wide): 24.52MM **Privately Held**
Web: www.morrisjames.com

SIC: 8111 General practice attorney, lawyer
PA: Morris James Llp
500 Delaware Ave Ste 1500
Wilmington DE 19801
302 888-6800

(G-11455)
MOSAIC
Also Called: Marthin Luther Homes of Del
261 Chapman Rd Ste 201 (19702-5428)
PHONE.................................302 456-5995
Terry Olson, Dir
EMP: 88
SALES (corp-wide): 373.92MM **Privately Held**
Web: www.mosaicinfo.org
SIC: 8322 8741 8052 Association for the handicapped; Management services; Intermediate care facilities
PA: Mosaic
4980 S 118th St
Omaha NE 68137
402 896-3884

(G-11456)
MOSAIC
Also Called: Charlan Neighborhood Home
8 Stoddard Dr (19702-2205)
PHONE.................................302 456-5995
Terry Oflin, Dir
EMP: 80
SALES (corp-wide): 373.92MM **Privately Held**
Web: www.mosaicinfo.org
SIC: 8052 Home for the mentally retarded, with health care
PA: Mosaic
4980 S 118th St
Omaha NE 68137
402 896-3884

(G-11457)
MOSAP GLOBAL INC
1 Innovation Way Ste 300 (19711-5490)
PHONE.................................302 559-3036
Olufemi A Osinubi Ph.d., Pr
EMP: 30 EST: 2019
SALES (est): 1.31MM **Privately Held**
SIC: 6531 Real estate brokers and agents

(G-11458)
MOTHER HUBBARD CHILD CARE CTR
2050 S College Ave (19702-3302)
PHONE.................................302 368-7584
April Hubbard, Pr
EMP: 10 EST: 1980
SALES (est): 72.51K **Privately Held**
SIC: 8351 Group day care center

(G-11459)
MOTION COMPOSITES CORP
2915 Ogletown Rd # 2270 (19713-1927)
PHONE.................................302 266-8200
Eric Simoneau, Pr
EMP: 10 EST: 2014
SALES (est): 1.04MM **Privately Held**
Web: www.motioncomposites.com
SIC: 5047 Medical and hospital equipment

(G-11460)
MOVETEC FITNESS EQUIPMENT LLC (PA)
Also Called: Movetec
790 Salem Church Rd (19702-3623)
PHONE.................................302 563-4387
Robert Bob Piane Junior, Managing Member
EMP: 4 EST: 2012
SALES (est): 201.12K

SALES (corp-wide): 201.12K **Privately Held**
SIC: 3949 7389 Exercise equipment; Business services, nec

(G-11461)
MOVING ON TIME
113 Barksdale Professional Ctr (19711-3258)
PHONE.................................302 613-4066
Katie Merlini, Mgr
EMP: 6 EST: 2013
SALES (est): 116.88K **Privately Held**
Web: www.movingontime.com
SIC: 4789 Transportation services, nec

(G-11462)
MP DIVERSIFIED SERVICES LLC
38 Albe Dr Ste 1 (19702-1351)
PHONE.................................302 828-1060
Matt Pannell, Pr
EMP: 8 EST: 2017
SALES (est): 257.22K **Privately Held**
Web: www.mp-diversified.com
SIC: 1521 1522 1751 1542 Single-family housing construction; Residential construction, nec; Cabinet and finish carpentry; Commercial and office building contractors

(G-11463)
MPI PROPERTIES LLC
6 Cabot Pl (19711-2987)
PHONE.................................302 635-7143
Paul Owens, Asst Sec
EMP: 5 EST: 2017
SALES (est): 179.96K **Privately Held**
SIC: 6512 Nonresidential building operators

(G-11464)
MR ROOTER PLUMBING OF NEW
Also Called: Mr. Rooter
250 Corporate Blvd Ste D (19702-3329)
PHONE.................................302 463-5720
EMP: 8 EST: 2018
SALES (est): 368.4K **Privately Held**
Web: www.mrrooter.com
SIC: 1711 Plumbing contractors

(G-11465)
MRB GOLF LLC
300 W Main St (19711-3218)
PHONE.................................302 368-7008
EMP: 5 EST: 2016
SALES (est): 38.16K **Privately Held**
SIC: 7997 Golf club, membership

(G-11466)
MSL ASSOCIATES LLC
Also Called: Net Sports Group
2915 Ogletown Rd (19713-1927)
PHONE.................................207 391-4420
EMP: 50 EST: 2004
SALES (est): 8.7MM **Privately Held**
SIC: 1629 Athletic field construction

(G-11467)
MSTM LLC
28 Tenby Chase Dr (19711-2441)
PHONE.................................302 239-4447
Sarah Trimpin, Ltd Pt
EMP: 2 EST: 2013
SALES (est): 245.75K **Privately Held**
Web: www.mstmsolutions.com
SIC: 3826 Mass spectrometers

(G-11468)
MTC USA LLC
Also Called: M T C
411 Woodlawn Ave (19711-5535)

PHONE.................................980 999-8888
Wenyi Tiang, Managing Member
EMP: 10 EST: 2015
SQ FT: 2,000
SALES (est): 456.62K **Privately Held**
Web: cn.mtcsys.us
SIC: 5734 8742 Software, business and non-game; Marketing consulting services

(G-11469)
MTO HOSE SOLUTIONS INC (DH)
214 Interchange Blvd (19711-3551)
PHONE.................................302 266-6555
Don Malizia, Pr
▲ EMP: 8 EST: 2003
SQ FT: 10,000
SALES (est): 3.51MM **Privately Held**
Web: www.mtohose.com
SIC: 5013 3492 Motor vehicle supplies and new parts; Hose and tube fittings and assemblies, hydraulic/pneumatic
HQ: Uni Gasket Srl
Via Lombardia 16
Villongo BG 24060
035925032

(G-11470)
MTRIGGER LLC
339 Mourning Dove Dr (19711-4109)
PHONE.................................302 502-7262
Brian Pryor, Managing Member
EMP: 3 EST: 2015
SALES (est): 245.56K **Privately Held**
Web: www.mtrigger.com
SIC: 5999 3845 Medical apparatus and supplies; Electromedical equipment

(G-11471)
MULTIFMILY MGT PHLADELPHIA LLC
100 Liberty Ter (19702-5259)
PHONE.................................302 322-8953
EMP: 8 EST: 2019
SALES (est): 95.96K **Privately Held**
Web: www.mmsgroup.com
SIC: 8741 Management services

(G-11472)
MURPHY MENTAL HEALTH
1 Gristmill Ln (19711-8003)
PHONE.................................302 463-7903
EMP: 5 EST: 2017
SALES (est): 90.25K **Privately Held**
SIC: 8099 Health and allied services, nec

(G-11473)
MURPHY STEEL INC
727 Dawson Dr (19713-3495)
P.O. Box 9071 (19714-9071)
PHONE.................................302 366-8676
Nancy Baffone, Pr
Aleseo Baffone, Sec
EMP: 20 EST: 1979
SALES (est): 3.46MM **Privately Held**
Web: www.murphysteel.com
SIC: 1521 3446 3444 Single-family housing construction; Architectural metalwork; Sheet metalwork

(G-11474)
MUSEUM STUDIES PROGRAM
77 E Main St (19711-5000)
PHONE.................................302 831-1251
EMP: 5 EST: 2016
SALES (est): 31.35K **Privately Held**
Web: museumstudies.udel.edu
SIC: 8412 Museum

(G-11475)
MUSHROOM SUPPLY & SERVICES INC

1643 Pulaski Hwy (19702)
P.O. Box 1360 (19707-5360)
PHONE.................................610 268-0800
David Iaconi, Pr
▲ EMP: 6 EST: 2005
SALES (est): 297.47K **Privately Held**
Web: www.mushroomsupplyinc.com
SIC: 2033 Mushrooms: packaged in cans, jars, etc.

(G-11476)
MY COUSIN VINNYS HVAC
8 Rolling Dr (19713-2020)
PHONE.................................302 266-1888
EMP: 6 EST: 2019
SALES (est): 56.99K **Privately Held**
Web: www.mycousinvinnie.com
SIC: 1711 Heating and air conditioning contractors

(G-11477)
MY SISTERS PLACE INC
50 Currant Dr (19702-2852)
PHONE.................................302 737-5303
Robert E Young, Pr
EMP: 5 EST: 2008
SALES (est): 1.1K **Privately Held**
Web: www.mysistersplacedc.org
SIC: 8322 Social service center

(G-11478)
MYMOROCCANBAZAR INC
2035 Sunset Lake Rd (19702-2600)
PHONE.................................323 238-5747
Oualid Ben Naid, CEO
EMP: 5 EST: 2016
SALES (est): 232.46K **Privately Held**
SIC: 2389 5961 4724 Apparel and accessories, nec; Electronic shopping; Travel agencies

(G-11479)
N MALLARI GC CORP
44 Bastille Loop (19702-5528)
PHONE.................................302 516-7738
EMP: 10 EST: 2015
SALES (est): 985.43K **Privately Held**
Web: www.nmallarigc.com
SIC: 1799 Special trade contractors, nec

(G-11480)
NAB MOTEL INC
200 Nathan Ct (19711-3932)
PHONE.................................302 983-0849
EMP: 11 EST: 2019
SALES (est): 32.59K **Privately Held**
SIC: 7011 Motels

(G-11481)
NABSTAR HOSPITALITY
630 S College Ave (19713-1315)
PHONE.................................302 453-1700
Bharet Patel, Owner
EMP: 5 EST: 2009
SALES (est): 358.87K **Privately Held**
Web: www.codepluseuropeanconcepts.com
SIC: 8748 Business consulting, nec

(G-11482)
NACSTAR
Also Called: Sleep Inn
630 S College Ave (19713-1315)
PHONE.................................302 453-1700
Alice Yang, Pr
Thi-thu Yeh, Stockholder
Wei-thu Yeh, Stockholder
Thi-lin Young, Stockholder
Ching-nei Young, Stockholder
EMP: 21 EST: 1989

Newark - New Castle County (G-11483)   GEOGRAPHIC SECTION

SALES (est): 242.24K **Privately Held**
Web: www.choicehotels.com
SIC: **7011** Hotels and motels

(G-11483)
NACURH INC
310 Haines St (19717-5226)
PHONE.................................302 722-6933
EMP: 14 **EST**: 2012
SALES (est): 359.07K **Privately Held**
Web: www.nacurh.org
SIC: **8699** Charitable organization

(G-11484)
NANCY CANNONE
230 Executive Dr (19702-3338)
PHONE.................................302 368-3572
Nancy Cannone, *Prin*
EMP: 5 **EST**: 2012
SALES (est): 36.27K **Privately Held**
SIC: **0722** Crop harvesting

(G-11485)
NANCY T BROHAWN
39 Country Hills Dr (19711-2517)
PHONE.................................302 453-1866
Nancy T Brohawn, *Prin*
EMP: 6 **EST**: 2013
SALES (est): 62.17K **Privately Held**
SIC: **8049** Clinical psychologist

(G-11486)
NANOSELECT INC
15 Innovation Way (19711-5449)
PHONE.................................302 355-1795
EMP: 27 **EST**: 2019
SALES (est): 196.59K **Privately Held**
Web: www.nanoselect-sensors.com
SIC: **3624** Carbon and graphite products

(G-11487)
NAPOLEON HERNANDEZ
Also Called: Ace of Seed
528 Old Barksdale Rd (19711-4534)
PHONE.................................302 368-2237
Hernandez Napoleon, *Owner*
EMP: 6 **EST**: 2015
SALES (est): 34.4K **Privately Held**
SIC: **7241** Hair stylist, men

(G-11488)
NARINDER SINGH MD
295 E Main St Ste 100 (19711-7338)
PHONE.................................302 737-2600
Narinder Singh Md, *Owner*
EMP: 6 **EST**: 1977
SALES (est): 480.32K **Privately Held**
SIC: **8011** General and family practice, physician/surgeon

(G-11489)
NATHANIEL JON BENT DDS PA
625 Barksdale Rd Ste 117 (19711-4535)
PHONE.................................302 731-4907
Nathaniel Jon Bent, *Prin*
EMP: 13 **EST**: 2015
SALES (est): 325.36K **Privately Held**
SIC: **8021** Dentists' office

(G-11490)
NATIONAL ASSN FOR RGLTORY ADMI
910 Glen Falls Ct (19711-3452)
PHONE.................................302 234-4152
Ann Ditty, *Prin*
EMP: 5 **EST**: 2010
SALES (est): 91K **Privately Held**
SIC: **8699** Membership organizations, nec

(G-11491)
NATIONWIDE INSURANCE
Also Called: Nationwide
258 E Main St (19711-7390)
PHONE.................................302 453-9698
Debra Mcafee, *Mgr*
EMP: 7 **EST**: 2017
SALES (est): 55.85K **Privately Held**
Web: www.nationwide.com
SIC: **6411** Insurance agents, nec

(G-11492)
NATURAL DAIRY PRODUCTS CORP
Also Called: Natural By Nature
316 Markus Ct (19713-1151)
PHONE.................................302 455-1261
EMP: 7 **EST**: 1995
SQ FT: 8,000
SALES (est): 2.35MM **Privately Held**
Web: www.naturalbynaturedairy.com
SIC: **0241** Dairy farms

(G-11493)
NATURAL HOUSE INC
2515 Kirkwood Hwy (19711-7249)
PHONE.................................302 218-0338
Yoo Won Jang, *Pr*
EMP: 10 **EST**: 2004
SALES (est): 361.2K **Privately Held**
Web: www.delawareproduce.com
SIC: **8741** Business management

(G-11494)
NATURAL HYPERTENSION INST INC
207 Sutton Way (19711-3244)
PHONE.................................302 533-7704
Zelda Johnson, *Prin*
EMP: 5 **EST**: 2019
SALES (est): 88.54K **Privately Held**
SIC: **8699** 8062 Charitable organization; General medical and surgical hospitals

(G-11495)
NB RETAIL MANAGEMENT INC
1267 Churchmans Rd (19713-2149)
PHONE.................................302 230-3065
Tyler Muse, *Prin*
EMP: 6 **EST**: 2018
SALES (est): 363.16K **Privately Held**
SIC: **8741** Management services

(G-11496)
NCC COOPERATIVE EXTENSION OFF
461 Wyoming Rd (19716-5901)
PHONE.................................302 831-8965
Maria Pippidis, *Dir*
EMP: 6 **EST**: 2014
SALES (est): 48.44K **Privately Held**
SIC: **7231** Hairdressers

(G-11497)
NEAR AND DEAR HOME CARE
1002 Birchwood Dr (19713-3010)
PHONE.................................302 530-6498
Samantha Pfeifer, *Prin*
EMP: 7 **EST**: 2016
SALES (est): 67.1K **Privately Held**
SIC: **8082** Home health care services

(G-11498)
NEIL G MCANENY DDS
400 New London Rd (19711-7010)
PHONE.................................302 368-0329
Neil Mcaneny, *Ofcr*
EMP: 9 **EST**: 2018
SALES (est): 184.6K **Privately Held**
Web: www.barksdaledental.com
SIC: **8021** Dentists' office

(G-11499)
NEIL G MCANENY DDS PC
117 Barksdale Professional Ctr (19711-3258)
PHONE.................................302 731-4907
Neil Mcaneny, *Pr*
EMP: 14 **EST**: 1973
SALES (est): 127.72K **Privately Held**
Web: www.barksdaledental.com
SIC: **8021** Dentists' office

(G-11500)
NEITSCH LTD LIABILITY COMPANY
Also Called: Neitsch Group, The
254 Chapman Rd (19702-5413)
PHONE.................................708 634-8724
EMP: 5 **EST**: 2008
SALES (est): 221.62K **Privately Held**
SIC: **8742** 8748 Management consulting services; Systems analysis and engineering consulting services

(G-11501)
NEKO COLORS USA INC
Also Called: Neko Colors
2915 Ogletown Rd Ste 2668 (19713-1927)
PHONE.................................844 365-6356
Anatoli Nekhim, *CEO*
EMP: 8 **EST**: 2016
SALES (est): 509.19K **Privately Held**
SIC: **2821** Plastics materials and resins

(G-11502)
NEMOURS FOUNDATION
Also Called: Nemours Dupont Pediatrics
200 Biddle Ave Ste 100 (19702-3967)
PHONE.................................302 836-7820
Lawrence Pradell, *Brnch Mgr*
EMP: 12
SALES (corp-wide): 1.94B **Privately Held**
Web: www.nemours.org
SIC: **8011** Pediatrician
PA: Nemours Foundation
   10140 Centurion Pkwy N
   Jacksonville FL 32256
   904 697-4100

(G-11503)
NEMOURS FUNDATION PENSION PLAN
Also Called: Nemours
1400 Peoples Plz Ste 300 (19702-5708)
PHONE.................................302 836-7820
EMP: 654
SALES (corp-wide): 205.65MM **Privately Held**
Web: www.nemours.org
SIC: **8011** Pediatrician
PA: The Nemours Foundation Pension Plan
   10140 Centurion Pkwy N
   Jacksonville FL 32256
   904 697-4100

(G-11504)
NEOBEX CORP
2915 Ogletown Rd (19713-1927)
PHONE.................................833 460-2027
Philippe Beaudoin, *Pr*
EMP: 5 **EST**: 2021
SALES (est): 385.48K **Privately Held**
Web: www.neobexmedical.com
SIC: **5047** Medical equipment and supplies

(G-11505)
NEOTERIC ASCENSION LLC (PA) ◊
254 Chapman Rd Ste 20814318 (19702-5413)
PHONE.................................302 250-7243
Azeez Ellegood, *Managing Member*
EMP: 6 **EST**: 2023

SALES (est): 87.88K
SALES (corp-wide): 87.88K **Privately Held**
SIC: **5045** Computers, peripherals, and software

(G-11506)
NEPHROLOGY ASSOCIATES PA
4923 Ogletown Stanton Rd Ste 200 (19713-6005)
PHONE.................................302 225-0451
William E Miller Md, *Pr*
EMP: 34 **EST**: 1976
SALES (est): 3.94MM **Privately Held**
Web: www.delawarekidney.com
SIC: **8011** Nephrologist

(G-11507)
NETDATA INC
2035 Sunset Lake Rd Ste B2 (19702-2600)
PHONE.................................650 407-3589
Konstantinos Tsaousis, *CEO*
EMP: 45 **EST**: 2019
SALES (est): 2.31MM **Privately Held**
Web: www.netdata.cloud
SIC: **7371** Computer software development

(G-11508)
NETJECTIIVES
6 Pleasantwood Rd (19702-1017)
PHONE.................................302 998-4436
EMP: 5 **EST**: 2017
SALES (est): 61.12K **Privately Held**
SIC: **7379** Computer related consulting services

(G-11509)
NETRAGY LLC
10 Cheswold Blvd Apt 1d (19713-4121)
PHONE.................................973 846-7018
EMP: 6 **EST**: 2012
SALES (est): 260.45K **Privately Held**
SIC: **8748** Business consulting, nec

(G-11510)
NETWORKS PROGRAMS
30 Blue Hen Dr (19713-3445)
PHONE.................................302 454-2233
EMP: 23 **EST**: 2012
SALES (est): 201.26K **Privately Held**
Web: www.christinak12.org
SIC: **6531** Escrow agent, real estate

(G-11511)
NEUROLOGY ASSOCIATES PA
Also Called: Edelsohn, Lanny MD
774 Christiana Rd Ste 201 (19713-4221)
PHONE.................................302 731-3017
Lanny Edelsohn, *Pr*
Sung Ho Bae Md, *CEO*
Ted E Chronister Md, *VP*
Thomas Vates Junior Md, *Sec*
Michael J Carunchio, *Prin*
EMP: 33 **EST**: 1970
SQ FT: 2,500
SALES (est): 1.23MM **Privately Held**
Web: www.christianacare.org
SIC: **8011** General and family practice, physician/surgeon

(G-11512)
NEUROSURGERY CONSULTANTS PA
79 Omega Dr Bldg C (19713-2064)
P.O. Box 339 (19707-0339)
PHONE.................................302 738-9145
Bikash Bose Md, *Pr*
EMP: 5 **EST**: 1986
SQ FT: 3,000
SALES (est): 504.87K **Privately Held**
Web: www.bikashbose.com
SIC: **8011** Neurosurgeon

GEOGRAPHIC SECTION
Newark - New Castle County (G-11540)

(G-11513)
NEW AMERICAN FUNDING
111 Continental Dr Ste 211 (19713-4330)
PHONE.................302 200-4607
EMP: 6 **EST:** 2019
SALES (est): 87.81K **Privately Held**
Web: www.newamericanfunding.com
SIC: 6153 Working capital financing

(G-11514)
NEW BEGINNINGS CNSLNG CNST
11 Winchester Rd (19713-3120)
PHONE.................302 525-6268
EMP: 8 **EST:** 2018
SALES (est): 32.59K **Privately Held**
SIC: 7011 Hotels and motels

(G-11515)
NEW CARE SPA
33 Chestnut Hill Plz (19713-2701)
PHONE.................302 292-2067
Qian Xiuqin, *Prin*
EMP: 5 **EST:** 2013
SALES (est): 34.37K **Privately Held**
SIC: 7231 Beauty shops

(G-11516)
NEW CASTLE CONSERVATION DST
2430 Old County Rd (19702-4702)
PHONE.................302 832-3100
Larry Irelan, *District Co-ordinator*
EMP: 10 **EST:** 1945
SALES (est): 488.9K **Privately Held**
Web: www.newcastlecd.org
SIC: 8999 Natural resource preservation service

(G-11517)
NEW CASTLE COUNTY FLOORING
2923 Ogletown Rd (19713-1927)
PHONE.................302 218-0507
Eric Parsons, *Pr*
EMP: 6 **EST:** 2002
SQ FT: 3,000
SALES (est): 430.34K **Privately Held**
Web: www.nccflooringandremodeling.com
SIC: 1752 1611 Carpet laying; General contractor, highway and street construction

(G-11518)
NEW CASTLE COUNTY HEAD START (PA)
256 Chapman Rd Ste 103 (19702-5417)
PHONE.................302 452-1500
Jeff Benatti, *Ex Dir*
EMP: 13 **EST:** 1976
SALES (est): 6.15MM
SALES (corp-wide): 6.15MM **Privately Held**
Web: www.ncchs.org
SIC: 8351 Head Start center, except in conjunction with school

(G-11519)
NEW CASTLE FAMILY CARE PA
14 Magil Ct (19702-8636)
PHONE.................302 275-3428
Mike James, *Pr*
EMP: 10 **EST:** 2009
SALES (est): 122.25K **Privately Held**
SIC: 8011 Offices and clinics of medical doctors

(G-11520)
NEW CREATION LOGISTICS INC
6 Sussex Rd Apt J (19713-3119)
PHONE.................302 438-3154
Makori Danvas, *Pr*
Helen Maina, *VP*
EMP: 10 **EST:** 2007
SQ FT: 1,200
SALES (est): 622.28K **Privately Held**
SIC: 4214 4731 5531 4225 Local trucking with storage; Freight transportation arrangement; Auto and home supply stores ; General warehousing and storage

(G-11521)
NEW DIRECTION EARLY HEADSTART
321 S College Ave (19716-3366)
PHONE.................302 831-0584
Heidi Beck, *Dir*
EMP: 11 **EST:** 2003
SALES (est): 60.5K **Privately Held**
Web: ndehs.udel.edu
SIC: 8351 Head Start center, except in conjunction with school

(G-11522)
NEW FOUNDATIONS LLC
560 Peoples Plz (19702-4798)
PHONE.................302 753-3135
Ernest Beers, *Prin*
EMP: 19 **EST:** 2010
SALES (est): 469.04K **Privately Held**
Web: www.newfoundations.org
SIC: 8641 Civic and social associations

(G-11523)
NEW IMAGE INC
2401 Ogletown Rd Ste A (19711-6403)
P.O. Box 369 (19936-0369)
PHONE.................302 738-6824
TOLL FREE: 800
Nancy Quade, *CEO*
Ronald M Cox, *Pr*
EMP: 6 **EST:** 1972
SQ FT: 4,000
SALES (est): 553.86K **Privately Held**
Web: www.nuimage.com
SIC: 2759 5199 2752 Screen printing; Advertising specialties; Commercial printing, lithographic

(G-11524)
NEW LONDON VETERINARY CENTER
437 New London Rd (19711-7009)
PHONE.................302 738-5000
Mickey King, *Owner*
EMP: 8 **EST:** 1992
SALES (est): 274.07K **Privately Held**
Web: www.newlondonvet.com
SIC: 0742 Animal hospital services, pets and other animal specialties

(G-11525)
NEW STANDARD PRODUCT DIST INC
Also Called: Spitzer Lighting
702 Interchange Blvd (19711-3595)
PHONE.................844 312-4574
Alan Su, *Ch Bd*
EMP: 11 **EST:** 2018
SALES (est): 1.39MM **Privately Held**
Web: www.spitzerlighting.com
SIC: 3645 Residential lighting fixtures

(G-11526)
NEW VISION SERVICES INC
Also Called: McKie Foundation, The
812 Village Cir Apt B (19713-4907)
PHONE.................484 350-6495
Khari Mckie, *CEO*
EMP: 5 **EST:** 2013
SALES (est): 167.47K **Privately Held**
Web: www.themckiefoundation.com
SIC: 8361 7389 Residential care for children; Business Activities at Non-Commercial Site

(G-11527)
NEW VISIONS INV GROUP LLC
31 Phoenix Ave (19702-2406)
PHONE.................302 299-6234
Steven Coleman, *Managing Member*
EMP: 5 **EST:** 2016
SALES (est): 253.73K **Privately Held**
SIC: 6282 Investment advice

(G-11528)
NEW YORK BLOOD CENTER INC (PA)
Also Called: Blood Bank of Delmarva
100 Hygeia Dr (19713-2047)
PHONE.................302 737-8405
Christopher Hillyer, *CEO*
EMP: 82 **EST:** 1954
SALES (est): 29.61MM
SALES (corp-wide): 29.61MM **Privately Held**
Web: www.delmarvablood.org
SIC: 8099 Blood bank

(G-11529)
NEWARK AFRC
1001 Ogletown Rd (19711-5413)
PHONE.................302 292-1050
EMP: 7 **EST:** 2016
SALES (est): 202.66K **Privately Held**
SIC: 6552 Subdividers and developers, nec

(G-11530)
NEWARK BUILDING SERVICES LLC
9 Cartier Ct (19711-5951)
PHONE.................302 377-7687
Stephen Davis, *Managing Member*
EMP: 5 **EST:** 2019
SALES (est): 274.07K **Privately Held**
SIC: 1522 Residential construction, nec

(G-11531)
NEWARK CHRISTIAN CHILDCARE
680 S Chapel St (19713-1541)
PHONE.................302 369-3000
Clara Orlando, *Dir*
James Fulghum, *Owner*
EMP: 5 **EST:** 2004
SALES (est): 200.09K **Privately Held**
Web: www.newarkchristianchildcare.com
SIC: 8351 Preschool center

(G-11532)
NEWARK COUNTRY CLUB
300 W Main St (19711-3287)
PHONE.................302 368-7008
Ron Gardner, *Pr*
Guy Johnson, *
Todd Ladutko, *
Tom Demedio, *
EMP: 51 **EST:** 1921
SQ FT: 18,000
SALES (est): 1.89MM **Privately Held**
Web: www.newarkcc.com
SIC: 7997 5812 Country club, membership; Eating places

(G-11533)
NEWARK CTR FOR CREATIVE LRNG
401 Phillips Ave (19711-5166)
PHONE.................302 368-7772
Betty Balder, *Admn*
EMP: 19 **EST:** 1971
SALES (est): 1.16MM **Privately Held**
Web: www.ncclschool.org
SIC: 8211 8351 Private elementary school; Child day care services

(G-11534)
NEWARK DAY-NURSERY ASSOCIATION
Also Called: NEWARK DAY NURSERY AND CHILDRE
921 Barksdale Rd (19711-3205)
PHONE.................302 731-4925
William Carl, *Ex Dir*
EMP: 32 **EST:** 1960
SALES (est): 1.73MM **Privately Held**
Web: www.newarkdaynursery.org
SIC: 8351 Preschool center

(G-11535)
NEWARK DENTAL ASSOC INC
344 E Main St (19711-7187)
PHONE.................302 737-5170
Katy Brown, *Genl Mgr*
Joseph Stout D.d.s., *Pr*
Edward Stout D.d.s., *Sec*
William H Ralston D.d.s., *Treas*
EMP: 24 **EST:** 1961
SALES (est): 690.93K **Privately Held**
Web: www.newarkdental.com
SIC: 8021 Dentists' office

(G-11536)
NEWARK EMERGENCY CENTER INC
324 E Main St (19711-7169)
PHONE.................302 738-4300
Amir Mansoori, *Pr*
EMP: 22 **EST:** 1973
SQ FT: 2,300
SALES (est): 4.64MM **Privately Held**
Web: www.newarkurgentcare.org
SIC: 8011 Freestanding emergency medical center

(G-11537)
NEWARK FENCE CO
24 Briarcliffe Ct (19702-2214)
PHONE.................302 368-5329
Robert Rash, *Prin*
EMP: 6 **EST:** 1994
SALES (est): 405.23K **Privately Held**
Web: www.newarkfence.com
SIC: 1799 Fence construction

(G-11538)
NEWARK HERITAGE PARTNERS I LLC
501 S Harmony Rd (19713-3338)
PHONE.................302 283-0540
EMP: 26 **EST:** 2013
SALES (est): 1.2MM
SALES (corp-wide): 934.59MM **Privately Held**
SIC: 8051 Skilled nursing care facilities
HQ: Alerislife Inc.
255 Washington St Ste 300
Newton MA 02458

(G-11539)
NEWARK INSULATION CO INC
68 Albe Dr # A (19702-1322)
P.O. Box 1095 (19715-1095)
PHONE.................302 731-8970
Dominic J Maida Junior, *Pr*
Gail Maida, *VP*
EMP: 7 **EST:** 1979
SQ FT: 5,000
SALES (est): 436.13K **Privately Held**
Web: www.valvewraps.com
SIC: 1742 Insulation, buildings

(G-11540)
NEWARK KUBOTA INC
Also Called: Kubota Authorized Dealer
2063 Pulaski Hwy (19702-3503)
PHONE.................302 365-6000

Newark - New Castle County (G-11541)

TOLL FREE: 800
Mark Babbit, *Pr*
EMP: 10 **EST:** 1986
SALES (est): 1.37MM **Privately Held**
Web: www.burkeequipment.com
SIC: 5999 5083 Farm tractors; Farm and garden machinery

(G-11541)
NEWARK LAND GROUP INC
Also Called: Baymont Inn & Suites
630 S College Ave (19713-1315)
PHONE.................302 453-1700
Tarpan Patel, *Prin*
EMP: 15 **EST:** 2019
SALES (est): 571.74K **Privately Held**
Web: www.wyndhamhotels.com
SIC: 7011 Hotels and motels

(G-11542)
NEWARK MONTESSORI PRESCHOOL
1031 S Chapel St (19702-1305)
PHONE.................302 366-1481
Penny Escobar, *Dir*
EMP: 6 **EST:** 1980
SALES (est): 115.6K **Privately Held**
Web: www.newarkmontessori.org
SIC: 8351 Montessori child development center

(G-11543)
NEWARK NATIONAL LITTLE LEAGUE
Possum Park Rd (19711)
P.O. Box 15031 (19711-0031)
PHONE.................302 738-0881
Danny Balint, *Prin*
EMP: 11 **EST:** 2001
SALES (est): 111.23K **Privately Held**
Web: www.newarknationalll.com
SIC: 7997 Baseball club, except professional and semi-professional

(G-11544)
NEWARK PEDIATRICIAN INC
314 E Main St Ste 101 (19711-7180)
PHONE.................302 738-4800
Jay Bartley Stewart Md, *Prin*
Joann Villanarin Md, *Prin*
EMP: 10 **EST:** 1967
SALES (est): 485.41K **Privately Held**
SIC: 8011 Pediatrician

(G-11545)
NEWARK RECYCLING CENTER INC
6 Albe Dr (19702-1322)
PHONE.................302 737-7300
Carmen Micucio Junior, *Pr*
EMP: 6 **EST:** 1993
SQ FT: 10,000
SALES (est): 964.4K **Privately Held**
Web: www.newarkrecycling.com
SIC: 4953 Recycling, waste materials

(G-11546)
NEWARK SENIOR CENTER INC
200 Whitechapel Dr (19713-3811)
PHONE.................302 737-2336
Carla Grygiel, *Ex Dir*
EMP: 27 **EST:** 1966
SQ FT: 29,000
SALES (est): 1.86MM **Privately Held**
Web: www.newarkseniorcenter.com
SIC: 8322 Senior citizens' center or association

(G-11547)
NEWARK UNITED METHODIST
Also Called: United Methodist Church
69 E Main St (19711-4645)
PHONE.................302 368-8774
Pastor Bernard Keels, *Prin*
Randy Weins, *Prin*
EMP: 22 **EST:** 1799
SALES (est): 1.89MM **Privately Held**
Web: www.newark-umc.org
SIC: 8661 8351 Methodist Church; Preschool center

(G-11548)
NEWARK URGENT CARE
324 E Main St (19711-7150)
PHONE.................302 738-4300
EMP: 7 **EST:** 2020
SALES (est): 303.08K **Privately Held**
Web: www.newarkurgentcare.org
SIC: 8011 Freestanding emergency medical center

(G-11549)
NEWARK WINGS LLC
136 Astro Shopping Ctr (19711-7254)
PHONE.................302 455-9464
EMP: 29 **EST:** 2007
SALES (est): 780.06K **Privately Held**
SIC: 7389 Business Activities at Non-Commercial Site

(G-11550)
NEWMAN WATER PROOFING&MOLD
7 Gilbert Ct (19713-1613)
PHONE.................302 373-7579
Steve Newman, *Prin*
EMP: 5 **EST:** 2018
SALES (est): 184.43K **Privately Held**
SIC: 1799 Waterproofing

(G-11551)
NEWTON ONE ADVISORS
131 Continental Dr Ste 206 (19713-4333)
PHONE.................302 731-1326
H Thomas Hollinger, *Pr*
EMP: 10 **EST:** 1986
SALES (est): 1.62MM **Privately Held**
Web: www.newtonone.com
SIC: 8742 Financial consultant

(G-11552)
NEXT CENTURY MEDICAL CARE LLC
620 Stanton Christiana Rd (19713-2134)
PHONE.................302 375-6746
EMP: 6 **EST:** 2019
SALES (est): 135.31K **Privately Held**
Web: www.nextcenturymedicalcare.com
SIC: 8099 Health and allied services, nec

(G-11553)
NFLATE YOUR PARTY
211 Thorn Ln Apt 3a (19711-8118)
PHONE.................302 562-9774
Melvin Judkins, *Prin*
EMP: 5 **EST:** 2009
SALES (est): 39.77K **Privately Held**
SIC: 7299 Party planning service

(G-11554)
NIAZ M A MD
266 S College Ave (19711-5235)
PHONE.................302 368-2563
EMP: 9 **EST:** 2019
SALES (est): 164.89K **Privately Held**
Web: www.haywoodquilttrails.org
SIC: 8011 Offices and clinics of medical doctors

(G-11555)
NICHOLAS O BIASOTTO CO
620 Stanton Christiana Rd Ste 205 (19713-2130)
PHONE.................302 998-1235
N Biasotto, *Prin*
EMP: 10 **EST:** 2006
SALES (est): 738.45K **Privately Held**
SIC: 8031 Offices and clinics of osteopathic physicians

(G-11556)
NICHOLS NURSERY INC
Also Called: Nichols Excavation and Ldscp
324 Markus Ct (19713-1151)
PHONE.................302 834-2426
Stephen Nichols, *Pr*
Charlene Nichols, *
EMP: 49 **EST:** 1976
SALES (est): 8.9MM **Privately Held**
Web: www.nicholsexc.com
SIC: 0781 Landscape planning services

(G-11557)
NICKLE ELEC COMPANIES INC (PA)
125 Ruthar Dr (19711-8025)
PHONE.................302 453-4000
Steven Dignan, *Pr*
Deborah Dignan, *
Neal Donaldson, *
EMP: 120 **EST:** 1986
SQ FT: 4,000
SALES (est): 34.24MM
SALES (corp-wide): 34.24MM **Privately Held**
Web: www.nickleelectrical.com
SIC: 1731 General electrical contractor

(G-11558)
NLCDD
111 Allison Hall W (19716-3398)
PHONE.................302 831-4728
Kristen Loomis, *Prin*
EMP: 8 **EST:** 2017
SALES (est): 105.03K **Privately Held**
Web: www.natleadership.org
SIC: 8331 Job training and related services

(G-11559)
NOBELONE INC
200 Continental Dr Ste 401 (19713-4337)
PHONE.................617 283-8871
Jason Flanders, *Pr*
EMP: 9 **EST:** 2017
SALES (est): 231.23K **Privately Held**
Web: www.nobelcom.com
SIC: 4813 Telephone communications broker

(G-11560)
NOBLE HEARTS INC
200 Continental Dr Ste 401 (19713-4334)
PHONE.................215 908-6525
Salih Grevious, *Prin*
EMP: 6 **EST:** 2020
SALES (est): 34.78K **Privately Held**
Web: www.nobleheartshr.com
SIC: 8699 Charitable organization

(G-11561)
NOEL AUTO SALES LLC
1 Currant Ct (19702-2871)
PHONE.................302 286-7355
Enoel Moret, *Managing Member*
EMP: 5 **EST:** 2016
SALES (est): 433.94K **Privately Held**
SIC: 5511 7389 New and used car dealers; Business Activities at Non-Commercial Site

(G-11562)
NORAMP INC
16 Higgins Rd (19711-4361)
PHONE.................914 266-0153
Daniel Kiani, *CEO*
EMP: 8
SALES (est): 306.16K **Privately Held**
SIC: 7371 Computer software development

(G-11563)
NORTH BAY MEDICAL ASSOCIATES
313 W Main St Ste A (19711-3217)
PHONE.................302 731-4620
Gary A Beste Md, *Pr*
EMP: 11 **EST:** 1983
SALES (est): 224.13K **Privately Held**
Web: www.nbmaprimary.com
SIC: 8011 Physicians' office, including specialists

(G-11564)
NORTH EAST CONTRACTORS INC
87 Blue Hen Dr (19713-3405)
PHONE.................302 286-6324
Kevin Garber, *Pr*
Donald Smith, *VP*
EMP: 20 **EST:** 2001
SALES (est): 4.26MM **Privately Held**
Web: www.northeastcontractorsinc.com
SIC: 1542 Commercial and office building, new construction

(G-11565)
NORTH POINT BUILDERS LLC
6 Nola Ln (19702-4751)
PHONE.................843 246-1516
Andrew Nee Junior, *Prin*
EMP: 8 **EST:** 2016
SALES (est): 735.58K **Privately Held**
Web: www.northpoint-builders.com
SIC: 1521 1799 Single-family home remodeling, additions, and repairs; Kitchen and bathroom remodeling

(G-11566)
NORTH POINT MKTG & MGT LLC ○
200 Continental Dr # 401 (19713-4334)
PHONE.................855 931-4075
Mary E Pritchett, *Managing Member*
EMP: 11 **EST:** 2022
SALES (est): 489.32K **Privately Held**
SIC: 8742 Marketing consulting services

(G-11567)
NU IMAGE LANDSCAPING INC
68 Martindale Dr (19713-2537)
PHONE.................302 366-8699
EMP: 6 **EST:** 2007
SALES (est): 63.47K **Privately Held**
SIC: 7231 Beauty shops

(G-11568)
NUR SHRNERS ANCENT ARAB ORDER
120 Four Seasons Pkwy (19702-2327)
P.O. Box 10085 (19850-0085)
PHONE.................302 328-6100
EMP: 5 **EST:** 2010
SALES (est): 156K **Privately Held**
Web: www.nurshrine.org
SIC: 8641 Fraternal associations

(G-11569)
NURSERY FITNESS LLC
1007 Church Rd (19702-5101)
PHONE.................410 609-0106
EMP: 5 **EST:** 2017
SALES (est): 61.3K **Privately Held**
SIC: 7991 Physical fitness facilities

(G-11570)
NUTAX FINANCIAL SERVICES LLC
523 Capitol Trl Ste C (19711-3859)
PHONE.................302 834-9357
Adebayo Gbadebo, *CEO*
EMP: 5 **EST:** 2002
SALES (est): 229.13K **Privately Held**

GEOGRAPHIC SECTION

Newark - New Castle County (G-11599)

Web: www.nutax.com
SIC: 7389 Financial services

(G-11571)
NVR INC
Also Called: Ryan Homes
1302 Drummond Plz Bldg 1ste1032 (19711-5741)
PHONE..................................302 731-5770
EMP: 10
Web: www.ryanhomes.com
SIC: 1531 1522 1521 Operative builders; Residential construction, nec; Single-family housing construction
PA: Nvr, Inc.
    11700 Plaza America Dr # 500
    Reston VA 20190

(G-11572)
O2DIESEL FUELS INC
100 Commerce Dr Ste 301 (19713-2878)
PHONE..................................302 266-6000
Alan Rae, *CEO*
EMP: 18 EST: 2009
SALES (est): 1.46MM **Privately Held**
Web: www.o2diesel.net
SIC: 2911 Petroleum refining

(G-11573)
OASIS REALTY INV GROUP LLC
69 Bay Blvd (19702-4838)
PHONE..................................302 277-6885
EMP: 10 EST: 2020
SALES (est): 518.4K **Privately Held**
Web: www.oasisrealtyig.com
SIC: 6799 Real estate investors, except property operators

(G-11574)
OBERLE WILLIAM A JR ST REP
2 Danvers Way (19702-2700)
PHONE..................................302 738-6241
William Oberle, *Prin*
EMP: 5 EST: 2011
SALES (est): 50.35K **Privately Held**
SIC: 0752 Training services, horses (except racing horses)

(G-11575)
OCEAN CLB RSORT RSERVATION CTR
153 E Chestnut Hill Rd Ste 200 (19713-4046)
PHONE..................................302 369-1420
Laurie Uriani, *Genl Mgr*
EMP: 6 EST: 2001
SALES (est): 305.1K **Privately Held**
Web: www.dannylasoski.com
SIC: 7011 Resort hotel

(G-11576)
OCONNOR BELTING INTL INC
Also Called: Derco USA
728 Dawson Dr (19713-3414)
PHONE..................................302 452-2500
Paul O'connors Senior, *Pr*
Paul O'connors Junior, *VP*
Eric O'connors Senior, *VP*
▲ EMP: 27 EST: 2011
SQ FT: 53,000
SALES (est): 6.25MM **Privately Held**
Web: www.dercousa.com
SIC: 5085 Industrial supplies

(G-11577)
OCTOBER PHOENIX RLTY GROUP LLC
Also Called: Kimax Investments
406 Suburban Dr (19711-3566)
PHONE..................................302 722-5125

K Gadsden, *Managing Member*
EMP: 5 EST: 2009
SALES (est): 187.12K **Privately Held**
SIC: 6531 6411 Real estate brokers and agents; Pension and retirement plan consultants

(G-11578)
ODONNELL SERVICES
1228 Old Coochs Bridge Rd (19713-2330)
PHONE..................................302 252-5134
David O'donnell, *Prin*
EMP: 5 EST: 2017
SALES (est): 160.4K **Privately Held**
Web: www.odonnellservicesllc.com
SIC: 1521 General remodeling, single-family houses

(G-11579)
OEM AUTO PARTS
104 Lynch Farm Dr (19713-2813)
PHONE..................................302 983-6475
EMP: 5 EST: 2015
SALES (est): 34.18K **Privately Held**
SIC: 7538 General automotive repair shops

(G-11580)
OGLETOWN BAPTIST CHURCH
Also Called: Southern Baptist Church
316 Red Mill Rd (19713-1990)
PHONE..................................302 737-2511
Pastor Drew Landry, *Prin*
EMP: 12 EST: 1991
SALES (est): 1.54MM **Privately Held**
Web: www.ogletown.org
SIC: 8661 8351 Baptist Church; Child day care services

(G-11581)
OHS LIBERTY CLEANERS INC
69 Worthington Park Rd (19711-2819)
PHONE..................................302 454-1322
EMP: 5 EST: 2002
SALES (est): 111.9K **Privately Held**
SIC: 7216 Cleaning and dyeing, except rugs

(G-11582)
OILMINERS CBD LLC
22 Gershwin Cir (19702-3039)
PHONE..................................484 885-9417
George Lee Crampton Junior, *Managing Member*
EMP: 2 EST: 2019
SALES (est): 73.4K **Privately Held**
SIC: 2299 Hemp yarn, thread, roving, and textiles

(G-11583)
OLD HOUSE RESTORATION
23 E Cherokee Dr (19713-3921)
PHONE..................................302 737-0806
EMP: 5 EST: 2019
SALES (est): 56.76K **Privately Held**
SIC: 1799 Special trade contractors, nec

(G-11584)
OMARICHET LLC ✪
112 Capitol Trl Ste A407 (19711-3716)
PHONE..................................302 442-0812
EMP: 2 EST: 2022
SALES (est): 92.41K **Privately Held**
SIC: 3663 Space satellite communications equipment

(G-11585)
OMEGA IMAGING ASSOCIATES LLC (PA)
Also Called: Diagnostic Imaging Associates
6 Omega Dr (19713-2056)
PHONE..................................302 738-9300

Joseph R Peacock Md, *Managing Member*
EMP: 25 EST: 1984
SQ FT: 5,554
SALES (est): 10.63MM
SALES (corp-wide): 10.63MM **Privately Held**
Web: www.radnet.com
SIC: 8011 Radiologist

(G-11586)
OMNIWAY CORPORATION (PA)
Also Called: Water's Edge
2300 Waters Edge Dr (19702-6355)
PHONE..................................302 738-5076
Hugh Martin, *Pr*
Margaret Martin, *VP*
EMP: 14 EST: 1977
SQ FT: 4,460
SALES (est): 34.75K
SALES (corp-wide): 34.75K **Privately Held**
SIC: 8741 8742 7532 Construction management; Management consulting services; Antique and classic automobile restoration

(G-11587)
ON DEMAND SERVICES LLC
Also Called: On Demand Moving Services
46 Chambord Dr (19702-5548)
PHONE..................................302 388-1215
EMP: 4 EST: 2011
SALES (est): 190.67K **Privately Held**
Web: www.ondemand-services.com
SIC: 3577 Printers and plotters

(G-11588)
ON LEVEL HOME IMPROVEMENT
25 Greenridge Rd (19711-6704)
PHONE..................................302 368-7152
EMP: 5 EST: 1996
SALES (est): 147.69K **Privately Held**
SIC: 1521 Single-family home remodeling, additions, and repairs

(G-11589)
ON THE MARK LOCATORS LLC
1080 S Chapel St Ste 201 (19702-1379)
P.O. Box 918 (19701-0918)
PHONE..................................888 272-6065
Tyese Gillespie, *Managing Member*
EMP: 6 EST: 2016
SALES (est): 523K **Privately Held**
Web: www.onthemarklocators.com
SIC: 4939 Combination utilities, nec

(G-11590)
ONCOLOGY CARE HOME
267 E Main St (19711-7314)
PHONE..................................610 274-2437
EMP: 11 EST: 2018
SALES (est): 207.15K **Privately Held**
SIC: 8059 Nursing and personal care, nec

(G-11591)
ONE EASTON
1 Easton Ct (19711-7395)
PHONE..................................302 509-3900
EMP: 5 EST: 2016
SALES (est): 136.04K **Privately Held**
Web: www.oneeaston.com
SIC: 6513 Apartment building operators

(G-11592)
ONE HOUR PRINTING
122 Balmoral Way (19702-5253)
PHONE..................................302 220-1684
EMP: 4 EST: 2018
SALES (est): 83.91K **Privately Held**
SIC: 2752 Commercial printing, lithographic

(G-11593)
ONE STEP AHEAD CHILDCARE
432 Salem Church Rd (19702-2707)
PHONE..................................302 292-1162
Dawn Sheehan-reilly, *Dir*
EMP: 5 EST: 2002
SALES (est): 108.67K **Privately Held**
SIC: 7231 Beauty shops

(G-11594)
ONENESS MASSAGE THERAPY
Also Called: Oneness
10 Blue Jay Dr (19713-1210)
PHONE..................................302 893-0348
Wendy Forrest, *Prin*
EMP: 5 EST: 2011
SALES (est): 116.42K **Privately Held**
Web: www.onenessmassagetherapy.com
SIC: 8093 Rehabilitation center, outpatient treatment

(G-11595)
OPPENHEIMER GROUP INC
200 Continental Dr Ste 301 (19713-4336)
PHONE..................................302 533-0779
Brett Libke, *VP*
EMP: 31 EST: 1986
SALES (est): 7.17MM **Privately Held**
Web: www.oppy.com
SIC: 5141 Food brokers
HQ: David Oppenheimer And Company I, L.L.C
    11 Burbidge St Suite 101
    Coquitlam BC V3K 7
    604 461-6779

(G-11596)
OPTI-MAG INC
11 Peddlers Row (19702-1525)
P.O. Box 10902 (19702)
PHONE..................................302 738-2903
Clifford Krieger, *Pr*
Pamela Joyce Schein, *Stockholder*
EMP: 8 EST: 1992
SQ FT: 1,350
SALES (est): 517.63K **Privately Held**
SIC: 5045 5734 5961 Computers, peripherals, and software; Computer and software stores; Computers and peripheral equipment, mail order

(G-11597)
OPULENCE COLLECTION LLC
1 Chestnut Hill Plz 1045 (19713-2761)
PHONE..................................267 808-1781
Charnae Oliver, *CEO*
EMP: 4 EST: 2020
SALES (est): 39.69K **Privately Held**
SIC: 3999 Hair and hair-based products

(G-11598)
ORDER OF THE EASTERN STAR DEL
Also Called: General Chapter Eastern Star
134 Capitol Trl (19711-3716)
PHONE..................................302 369-0729
Verna W Garvin, *Treas*
EMP: 7 EST: 2012
SALES (est): 50.97K **Privately Held**
SIC: 8641 Civic associations

(G-11599)
ORDERHIVE INC
2035 Sunset Lake Rd Ste B2 (19702-2600)
PHONE..................................888 878-5538
EMP: 7 EST: 2018
SALES (est): 46.16K **Privately Held**
Web: www.cin7.com
SIC: 7371 Computer software development

Newark - New Castle County (G-11600)   GEOGRAPHIC SECTION

(G-11600)
ORGNOSTIC INC
2035 Sunset Lake Rd Ste B2 (19702-2600)
PHONE.....................................617 871-9987
Luka Babic, *CEO*
EMP: 34 **EST:** 2019
SALES (est): 1.03MM **Privately Held**
Web: www.orgnostic.com
SIC: 7371 Software programming applications

(G-11601)
ORTHOPEDIC PROPERTIES LLC
1096 Old Churchmans Rd (19713-2102)
PHONE.....................................302 998-2310
EMP: 19 **EST:** 2013
SALES (est): 495.74K **Privately Held**
Web: www.delortho.com
SIC: 8011 Orthopedic physician

(G-11602)
ORTHOPEDIC SPECIALISTS
Also Called: Mohammad Kamali, MD
1096 Old Churchmans Rd (19713-2102)
PHONE.....................................302 351-4848
Mohammad Kamali, *Prin*
EMP: 33 **EST:** 2001
SALES (est): 5.45MM **Privately Held**
Web: www.delortho.com
SIC: 8011 Orthopedic physician

(G-11603)
OSPREY FLIGHT SOLUTIONS INC
200 Continental Dr Ste 401 (19713-4334)
PHONE.....................................302 318-1401
David Andrew Nicholson, *Pr*
Bruce Norfolk, *Dir*
Thomas Hoppe, *Dir*
EMP: 6 **EST:** 2019
SALES (est): 316.7K
SALES (corp-wide): 7.62MM **Privately Held**
Web: www.ospreyflightsolutions.com
SIC: 7299 Miscellaneous personal service
PA: Sora Risk Solutions Limited
  Ground Floor Cromwell House
  Winchester HANTS SO23

(G-11604)
OSSANDEEP ASSOCIATES LLC
61 Mcmillan Way Unit B (19713-3420)
PHONE.....................................302 660-8545
Osiel Lugo, *Prin*
EMP: 7 **EST:** 2019
SALES (est): 415.76K **Privately Held**
Web: www.ossandeepassociates.com
SIC: 1521 Single-family housing construction

(G-11605)
OTHERWORLD CO
256 Chapman Rd (19702-5499)
PHONE.....................................424 335-5671
Artem Larin, *CEO*
EMP: 5 **EST:** 2021
SALES (est): 107.01K **Privately Held**
SIC: 7371 Computer software development and applications

(G-11606)
OUT OF ASHES LLC
2931 Ogletown Rd (19713-1927)
PHONE.....................................302 507-4623
Coley Harris, *Managing Member*
EMP: 5 **EST:** 2015
SALES (est): 65.13K **Privately Held**
Web: www.outoftheashesllc.com
SIC: 8322 Individual and family services

(G-11607)
OUTDOOR DESIGN GROUP LLC
935 Rahway Dr (19711-2687)
P.O. Box 670 (19701-0670)
PHONE.....................................302 743-2363
EMP: 10 **EST:** 2008
SALES (est): 735.2K **Privately Held**
SIC: 0782 Lawn and garden services

(G-11608)
P A ALFIERI CARDIOLOGY
2600 Glasgow Ave Ste 103 (19702-5703)
PHONE.....................................302 836-2003
Colleen Buchanan, *Brnch Mgr*
EMP: 42
Web: www.alfiericardiology.com
SIC: 8011 Cardiologist and cardio-vascular specialist
PA: P A Alfieri Cardiology
  701 Foulk Rd Ste 2b
  Wilmington DE 19803

(G-11609)
P H I PEPCO
Also Called: Delmarva Power
401 Eagle Run Rd (19702-1602)
P.O. Box 9239 (19714-9239)
PHONE.....................................302 454-4085
Joe Rigby, *CEO*
Joe Rigby, *Pr*
EMP: 39 **EST:** 2008
SALES (est): 20.39MM **Privately Held**
SIC: 4911 Distribution, electric power

(G-11610)
PACIFICO INDUSTRIAL LTD
113 Barksdale Pro Ctr (19711-3258)
PHONE.....................................213 435-1181
EMP: 12 **EST:** 2007
SALES (est): 193.47K **Privately Held**
SIC: 3089 Plastics kitchenware, tableware, and houseware

(G-11611)
PADDYS
2702 Kirkwood Hwy (19711)
PHONE.....................................302 388-3625
Pat Ferris, *Owner*
EMP: 14 **EST:** 2013
SALES (est): 950.83K **Privately Held**
Web: www.gopaddys.com
SIC: 1521 General remodeling, single-family houses

(G-11612)
PAFS AUTO LLC
11 Country Ln (19702-3739)
PHONE.....................................302 213-3881
Sanni Ibrahim, *Prin*
Judy Mcneil, *Prin*
Temi Ibrahim, *Prin*
EMP: 5 **EST:** 2014
SALES (est): 249.51K **Privately Held**
SIC: 5012 Automobiles and other motor vehicles

(G-11613)
PAIN SOLUTION CENTERS
630 Churchmans Rd Ste 109 (19702-1943)
PHONE.....................................215 750-9600
Stephen Ficchi, *Prin*
EMP: 11 **EST:** 2016
SALES (est): 227.96K **Privately Held**
SIC: 8011 Offices and clinics of medical doctors

(G-11614)
PAINTING PARTIES
77 Worthington Park Rd (19711-2821)
PHONE.....................................302 299-9355
EMP: 5 **EST:** 2014
SALES (est): 107.64K **Privately Held**
Web: www.painting-parties.com
SIC: 1721 Painting and paper hanging

(G-11615)
PALERMO FRANCIS A MD FACC PA
Also Called: Palermo, Francis A MD PA
620 Stanton Christiana Rd (19713-2133)
PHONE.....................................302 994-1100
EMP: 8 **EST:** 1995
SALES (est): 866.4K **Privately Held**
SIC: 8011 General and family practice, physician/surgeon

(G-11616)
PALLADIAN MANAGEMENT LLC
Also Called: Hunters Crossing
41 Fairway Rd Ofc 2c (19711-5660)
PHONE.....................................302 737-1971
EMP: 15
SALES (corp-wide): 2.49MM **Privately Held**
Web: www.palladianmgmt.com
SIC: 6513 Apartment building operators
PA: Palladian Management Llc
  1071 Post Rd E Ste 1a
  Westport CT 06880
  203 557-3526

(G-11617)
PAMPER PERFECT MOBILE SPA
12 Beatrice Ct Ste 1 (19702-5218)
PHONE.....................................302 482-5938
Allison Butler, *Prin*
Alison Moore, *Pt*
EMP: 6 **EST:** 2011
SALES (est): 61.1K **Privately Held**
Web: www.pamperperfectmobilespa.com
SIC: 7991 Spas

(G-11618)
PANARUM CORP ◊
112 Capitol Trl (19711-3716)
PHONE.....................................302 994-2000
EMP: 10 **EST:** 2022
SALES (est): 365.81K **Privately Held**
Web: www.panarum.com
SIC: 8731 Biotechnical research, commercial

(G-11619)
PANCO MANAGEMENT CORPORATION
Also Called: English Village
15 Fox Hall # 15 (19711-5941)
PHONE.....................................302 366-1875
Esther Lesieur, *Mgr*
EMP: 24
SALES (corp-wide): 22.96MM **Privately Held**
Web: www.pancomanagement.com
SIC: 6531 6513 Real estate managers; Apartment building operators
PA: Panco Management Corporation
  50 Main St Ste 1120
  White Plains NY 10606
  201 556-0900

(G-11620)
PAPASTVROS ASSOC MED IMGING LL (HQ)
40 Polly Drummond Hill Rd Ste 4 (19711-5703)
PHONE.....................................302 652-3016
EMP: 50 **EST:** 1958
SALES (est): 26.03MM **Publicly Held**
Web: www.papastavros.com
SIC: 8011 Radiologist
PA: Radnet, Inc.
  1510 Cotner Ave
  Los Angeles CA 90025

(G-11621)
PAPASTVROS ASSOC MED IMGING LL
Also Called: Radiology Associates
40 Polly Drummond Hill Rd # 4 (19711-5703)
PHONE.....................................302 644-2590
Lisa Daniello, *Prin*
EMP: 76
Web: www.papastavros.com
SIC: 8011 8071 Radiologist; X-ray laboratory, including dental
HQ: Papastavros' Associates Medical Imaging L.L.C.
  40 Polly Drummond Hill Rd
  Newark DE 19711
  302 652-3016

(G-11622)
PAPER STREET LLC
20 Harris Cir (19711-2459)
PHONE.....................................614 515-1259
EMP: 5 **EST:** 2016
SALES (est): 60.09K **Privately Held**
SIC: 7371 Computer software development and applications

(G-11623)
PARAGON DESIGN INC
18 Haines St (19711-4611)
PHONE.....................................302 292-1523
EMP: 15 **EST:** 2019
SALES (est): 1.07MM **Privately Held**
Web: www.paragon-design.net
SIC: 7311 Advertising consultant

(G-11624)
PARAGON SERENITY LLC ◊
702 Vinings Way (19702-7611)
PHONE.....................................302 784-4979
Quatisha Cottman, *Managing Member*
EMP: 6 **EST:** 2022
SALES (est): 64.36K **Privately Held**
SIC: 7021 7389 Rooming and boarding houses; Business services, nec

(G-11625)
PARAGS GLASS COMPANY
107 Albe Dr Ste D (19702-1300)
PHONE.....................................302 737-0101
William Parag, *Owner*
EMP: 6 **EST:** 1987
SQ FT: 2,500
SALES (est): 466.54K **Privately Held**
Web: www.paragsglass.com
SIC: 1793 7536 Glass and glazing work; Automotive glass replacement shops

(G-11626)
PARIENTS PAINTING LLC
19 Carlisle Rd (19713-2504)
PHONE.....................................302 738-6819
EMP: 5 **EST:** 2011
SALES (est): 218.65K **Privately Held**
SIC: 1721 Painting and paper hanging

(G-11627)
PARIKH MONA ASHISH MD
68 Omega Dr (19713-2063)
PHONE.....................................302 300-4246
Mona Parikh Md, *Owner*
EMP: 8 **EST:** 2018
SALES (est): 54.13K **Privately Held**
SIC: 8011 Offices and clinics of medical doctors

GEOGRAPHIC SECTION
Newark - New Castle County (G-11657)

(G-11628)
PARK HOTELS & RESORTS INC
640 S College Ave (19713-1315)
PHONE.....................703 883-1000
EMP: 13
SALES (corp-wide): 2.5B **Publicly Held**
Web: www.pkhotelsandresorts.com
SIC: 7011 Hotels and motels
PA: Park Hotels & Resorts Inc.
    1775 Tysons Blvd Fl 7
    Tysons VA 22102
    571 302-5757

(G-11629)
PARK PLACE DENTAL
210 W Park Pl (19711-4519)
PHONE.....................302 455-0333
Michael C Duffy, *Pr*
EMP: 10 EST: 2017
SALES (est): 264.28K **Privately Held**
Web: www.thedentalgroupofdelaware.com
SIC: 8021 Prosthodontist

(G-11630)
PARTNER VANTAGE POINT LLC
200 Continental Dr (19713-4334)
PHONE.....................312 927-8990
EMP: 8
SALES (est): 400.53K **Privately Held**
SIC: 5045 Computers, peripherals, and software

(G-11631)
PARTS WORLD USA LLC
200 Continental Dr # 401 (19713-4337)
PHONE.....................302 451-9920
EMP: 6 EST: 2016
SALES (est): 80.17K **Privately Held**
SIC: 5013 Automotive supplies and parts

(G-11632)
PATAFOODS INC
60 E Main St (19711-4640)
PHONE.....................267 981-6411
Jessica Spureenegger, *CEO*
EMP: 10 EST: 2013
SALES (est): 525.21K **Privately Held**
SIC: 2032 Baby foods, including meats: packaged in cans, jars, etc.

(G-11633)
PATEL ASIT
550 Stanton Christiana Rd Ste 303 (19713-2125)
PHONE.....................302 502-3181
Asit Patel, *Prin*
EMP: 8 EST: 2015
SALES (est): 139.84K **Privately Held**
SIC: 8011 Offices and clinics of medical doctors

(G-11634)
PATEL VAIDEHI
23 Moonlight Ct (19702-8606)
PHONE.....................302 295-0435
Vaidehi Patel, *Owner*
EMP: 6 EST: 2018
SALES (est): 41.29K **Privately Held**
SIC: 8049 Offices of health practitioner

(G-11635)
PATENT INFORMATION USERS GROUP
40 E Main St (19711-4639)
PHONE.....................302 660-3275
Tom Woff, *Prin*
EMP: 10 EST: 2013
SALES (est): 98.46K **Privately Held**
Web: www.piug.org
SIC: 8748 Business consulting, nec

(G-11636)
PATHS LLC
1352 Marrows Rd Ste 110 (19711-5476)
PHONE.....................302 294-1494
EMP: 19
SALES (corp-wide): 9.07MM **Privately Held**
Web: www.hcpaths.com
SIC: 8721 Billing and bookkeeping service
PA: Paths Llc
    9 Executive Campus
    Cherry Hill NJ 08002
    856 671-6000

(G-11637)
PATRICIA DISARIO DAY CARE
4 Cottonwood Ct (19702-2893)
PHONE.....................302 737-8889
James Disario, *Prin*
EMP: 5 EST: 2005
SALES (est): 77.02K **Privately Held**
SIC: 8351 Group day care center

(G-11638)
PATRICIA R WOOD
Also Called: Pace Life Coaching
15 Cottonwood Ct (19702-2893)
PHONE.....................302 737-3674
Patricia Wood, *Prin*
EMP: 7 EST: 2011
SALES (est): 52.91K **Privately Held**
SIC: 8322 General counseling services

(G-11639)
PATRIOT ICE ARENA LLC
101 John F Campbell Rd (19711-5457)
PHONE.....................302 266-0777
EMP: 10 EST: 2020
SALES (est): 273.44K **Privately Held**
Web: www.patrioticecenter.com
SIC: 7997 Membership sports and recreation clubs

(G-11640)
PATTERSON PRICE RE LLC
1101 Millstone Dr (19711-1811)
PHONE.....................302 366-0200
A John Price, *Pr*
EMP: 8
SALES (corp-wide): 950.15K **Privately Held**
Web: www.pattersonprice.com
SIC: 6531 6552 Real estate agent, residential ; Subdividers and developers, nec
PA: Patterson Price Real Estate Llc
    143 Wiggins Mill Rd
    Townsend DE 19734
    302 378-9550

(G-11641)
PATTERSON-SCHWARTZ & ASSOC INC
680 S College Ave (19713-1396)
PHONE.....................302 733-7000
Christopher Cashman, *Mgr*
EMP: 40
SALES (corp-wide): 24.38MM **Privately Held**
Web: www.pattersonschwartz.com
SIC: 6531 Real estate agent, residential
PA: Patterson-Schwartz And Associates, Inc.
    7234 Lancaster Pike
    Hockessin DE 19707
    302 234-5250

(G-11642)
PAUL A NICLE INC
14 Mill Park Ct Ste E (19713-2262)
PHONE.....................302 453-4000
Paul Sinnott, *Owner*
EMP: 5 EST: 2011
SALES (est): 167.97K **Privately Held**
SIC: 7539 Electrical services

(G-11643)
PAUL HALLER
211 Tamara Cir (19711-6947)
PHONE.....................302 737-0525
Paul Haller, *Prin*
EMP: 5 EST: 2010
SALES (est): 212.04K **Privately Held**
SIC: 0782 Lawn care services

(G-11644)
PAXELAX
40 E Main St (19711-4639)
PHONE.....................302 722-7290
EMP: 5 EST: 2012
SALES (est): 160.9K **Privately Held**
Web: www.paxelax.com
SIC: 8742 Management consulting services

(G-11645)
PAY IT 4-WARD INC
254 Chapman Rd Ste 208 (19702-5413)
PHONE.....................424 268-1127
Rebecca Cisero, *CEO*
EMP: 6
SALES (est): 119.28K **Privately Held**
SIC: 8699 Charitable organization

(G-11646)
PAYPERGIGS INC
2035 Sunset Lake Rd B2 (19702-2600)
PHONE.....................917 336-2162
Zahidul Islam Khan, *Dir*
EMP: 612 EST: 2017
SALES (est): 1.03MM **Privately Held**
SIC: 7372 Application computer software

(G-11647)
PAYROLL MANAGEMENT ASSISTANTS
409 White Clay Center Dr (19711-5468)
PHONE.....................302 456-6816
James Paoli, *Pr*
Peggy Smith, *VP*
EMP: 6 EST: 1986
SALES (est): 524.28K **Privately Held**
Web: www.pmapayroll.com
SIC: 8721 Billing and bookkeeping service

(G-11648)
PC SUPPLIES INC
1003 S Chapel St Ste A (19702-1357)
PHONE.....................302 368-4800
R Scott Martin, *Pr*
Judy Larosch, *VP*
Charlie Rudewick, *VP*
EMP: 8 EST: 1984
SQ FT: 1,400
SALES (est): 2.02MM **Privately Held**
Web: www.pcsupplies.com
SIC: 5045 7378 5734 Computer peripheral equipment; Computer and data processing equipment repair/maintenance; Computer peripheral equipment

(G-11649)
PEACE BY PIECE INC
888 Salem Church Rd (19702-4037)
PHONE.....................302 266-2556
Rebecca Bucci, *Prin*
Kelli Disabatino, *Prin*
Saad Soliman, *Prin*
EMP: 15 EST: 2017
SALES (est): 696.58K **Privately Held**
SIC: 8322 Individual and family services

(G-11650)
PEACHI INC
2035 Sunset Lake Rd B2 (19702-2600)
PHONE.....................347 907-0138
Justin Ramos, *CEO*
EMP: 5 EST: 2020
SALES (est): 131.52K **Privately Held**
SIC: 8399 Community development groups

(G-11651)
PEARCE Q FOUNDATION INC
4142 Ogletown Stanton Rd Ste 227 (19713-4169)
PHONE.....................302 753-8612
Andrew E Quesenberry, *Prin*
EMP: 5 EST: 2010
SALES (est): 115.81K **Privately Held**
Web: www.pearceqfoundation.org
SIC: 8641 Civic and social associations

(G-11652)
PECKS DRAIN CLEANING
12 Milkweed Ct (19713-1085)
PHONE.....................302 345-4101
EMP: 5 EST: 2014
SALES (est): 39.29K **Privately Held**
Web: www.pecksdraincleaning.com
SIC: 7699 Cleaning services

(G-11653)
PEDDIE JOHN
18 Photinia Dr (19702-3922)
PHONE.....................302 838-8771
John Peddie, *Prin*
EMP: 9 EST: 2009
SALES (est): 148.53K **Privately Held**
SIC: 8748 Business consulting, nec

(G-11654)
PEDIATRIC ASSOCIATES PA
4735 Ogletown Stanton Rd Ste 1116 (19713-7006)
PHONE.....................302 368-8612
Victoria A Levin, *Pr*
Neal B Cohn,   *
Joseph A Vitale,   *
Barbara L Light,   *
EMP: 20 EST: 1954
SQ FT: 4,000
SALES (est): 884.86K **Privately Held**
Web: www.pediatricassociates.org
SIC: 8011 Pediatrician

(G-11655)
PELICAN KEY LLC BRKSDALE A SRI
175 S Main St (19711-7941)
PHONE.....................302 563-9493
Harold B Prettyman Iii, *Prin*
EMP: 8 EST: 2019
SALES (est): 550.59K **Privately Held**
SIC: 1521 Single-family housing construction

(G-11656)
PELSA COMPANY INC
610 Peoples Plz (19702-5600)
PHONE.....................302 834-3771
Michael Paraskewich, *Pr*
EMP: 9 EST: 1987
SALES (est): 920.87K **Privately Held**
Web: www.thepelsacompany.com
SIC: 8711 8732 Civil engineering; Survey service: marketing, location, etc.

(G-11657)
PENACHE BEAUTY SALON
16 Polly Drummond Shpg Ctr (19711-4861)

PHONE.................302 731-5912
Ronald Wilkinson, *Owner*
EMP: 5 **EST:** 1971
SQ FT: 1,800
SALES (est): 101.59K **Privately Held**
SIC: 7231 Unisex hair salons

(G-11658)
PENCADER CONSULTING GROUP
401 Ivory Ln (19702-3666)
PHONE.................302 454-8004
Christopher Baldwin, *Prin*
EMP: 6 **EST:** 2016
SALES (est): 105.25K **Privately Held**
SIC: 8748 Business consulting, nec

(G-11659)
PENCADER GROUP LLC
273 S Dillwyn Rd (19711-5549)
PHONE.................302 366-0721
Sally Miller, *Prin*
EMP: 5 **EST:** 2019
SALES (est): 69.97K **Privately Held**
SIC: 8699 Membership organizations, nec

(G-11660)
PENCADER HERITAGE AREA ASSN
211 Executive Dr (19702-3357)
P.O. Box 7772 (19714-7772)
PHONE.................518 578-3559
EMP: 5 **EST:** 2019
SALES (est): 66.36K **Privately Held**
Web: www.pencaderheritage.org
SIC: 8699 Charitable organization

(G-11661)
PENCADER SELF STORAGE
101 Executive Dr (19702-3314)
PHONE.................302 709-3180
Shawn White, *Mgr*
EMP: 5 **EST:** 2001
SALES (est): 99.08K **Privately Held**
Web: www.reybold.com
SIC: 4225 Warehousing, self storage

(G-11662)
PENCO CORPORATION
121 Sandy Dr (19713-1148)
PHONE.................302 738-3212
TOLL FREE: 800
Rick Peterson, *Mgr*
EMP: 8
SALES (corp-wide): 24.24MM **Privately Held**
Web: www.pencocorp.com
SIC: 5074 Plumbing fittings and supplies
PA: Penco Corporation
   1503 W Stein Hwy
   Seaford DE 19973
   302 629-7911

(G-11663)
PENNONI
121 Continental Dr Ste 207 (19713-4341)
PHONE.................302 234-4600
EMP: 84 **EST:** 1975
SQ FT: 6,000
SALES (est): 904.18K **Privately Held**
Web: www.pennoni.com
SIC: 8711 Consulting engineer

(G-11664)
PENNONI ASSOCIATES INC
121 Continental Dr Ste 207 (19713-4341)
PHONE.................302 655-4451
Edward Rasiul, *Brnch Mgr*
EMP: 6
SALES (corp-wide): 225.03MM **Privately Held**
Web: www.pennoni.com

SIC: 8711 Consulting engineer
PA: Pennoni Associates Inc.
   1900 Market St Ste 300
   Philadelphia PA 19103
   215 222-3000

(G-11665)
PERFECT NAILS
210 University Plz (19702-1550)
PHONE.................302 731-1964
Larry Truong, *Owner*
Peter Bo, *Owner*
EMP: 5 **EST:** 1997
SALES (est): 173.56K **Privately Held**
Web: www.perfect-nails.com
SIC: 7231 Manicurist, pedicurist

(G-11666)
PERIOPERATIVE SERVICES LLC (PA)
111 Continental Dr Ste 412 (19713-4332)
PHONE.................302 733-0806
EMP: 52 **EST:** 1997
SQ FT: 16,000
SALES (est): 4.69MM
SALES (corp-wide): 4.69MM **Privately Held**
Web: www.periop.com
SIC: 8721 Billing and bookkeeping service

(G-11667)
PERISTALSIS PRODUCTIONS INC
6 Newside Ct (19711-4807)
PHONE.................302 366-1106
Cheryl Swift, *Prin*
EMP: 5 **EST:** 2010
SALES (est): 212.22K **Privately Held**
SIC: 7822 Motion picture and tape distribution

(G-11668)
PERRY INITIATIVE
130 Academy St (19716-3198)
PHONE.................302 319-1113
EMP: 9 **EST:** 2017
SALES (est): 173.13K **Privately Held**
Web: www.perryinitiative.org
SIC: 8641 Civic and social associations

(G-11669)
PERSONAL TAX SERVICES
22 N Valley Stream Cir (19702-2962)
PHONE.................302 562-5051
Howard Karten, *Prin*
EMP: 5 **EST:** 2017
SALES (est): 18.45K **Privately Held**
SIC: 7291 Tax return preparation services

(G-11670)
PERSONAL TOUCH CHILD CARE
201 Possum Park Rd (19711-3831)
PHONE.................302 368-2229
Dirimo Gonzalez, *Brnch Mgr*
EMP: 30
SALES (corp-wide): 1.06MM **Privately Held**
Web: www.personaltouchchildcare.com
SIC: 8351 Child day care services
PA: Personal Touch Child Care
   4828 N Broad St
   Philadelphia PA 19141
   215 457-2229

(G-11671)
PESSAGNO EQUIPMENT INC
109 Sandy Dr (19713-1148)
PHONE.................302 738-7001
Robert Pessagino, *Prin*
EMP: 4 **EST:** 1990
SALES (est): 460.42K **Privately Held**

SIC: 3799 Trailers and trailer equipment

(G-11672)
PETER M D ROCCA
537 Stanton Christiana Rd Ste 101 (19713-2145)
PHONE.................302 683-9400
Peter Rocca, *COO*
EMP: 12 **EST:** 2017
SALES (est): 480.5K **Privately Held**
SIC: 8011 Offices and clinics of medical doctors

(G-11673)
PETER M WITHERELL M D
774 Christiana Rd Ste 202 (19713-4221)
PHONE.................302 478-7001
Peter Witherell, *Ofcr*
EMP: 8 **EST:** 2018
SALES (est): 220.32K **Privately Held**
SIC: 8071 Medical laboratories

(G-11674)
PETRA INVESTMENTS LLC (PA) ◊
254 Chapman Rd Ste 208 (19702-5422)
PHONE.................312 887-1558
Rene Bendana, *CEO*
EMP: 6 **EST:** 2023
SALES (est): 71.99K
SALES (corp-wide): 71.99K **Privately Held**
SIC: 5499 5141 Beverage stores; Food brokers

(G-11675)
PETTINARO CONSTRUCTION CO INC
100 Cindy Dr (19702-8132)
PHONE.................302 832-8823
Gregory Pettinaro, *Brnch Mgr*
EMP: 35
SALES (corp-wide): 40.28MM **Privately Held**
Web: www.pettinaro.com
SIC: 6531 Real estate agent, commercial
PA: Pettinaro Construction Co Inc
   234 N James St
   Wilmington DE 19804
   302 999-0708

(G-11676)
PETTINARO MANAGEMENT LLC
100 Cindy Dr (19702-8132)
PHONE.................302 832-8823
EMP: 9 **EST:** 2014
SALES (est): 108.9K **Privately Held**
Web: www.pettinaro.com
SIC: 8741 Business management

(G-11677)
PETTITT CONSTRUCTION LLC
12 Carlisle Rd (19713-2525)
PHONE.................302 690-0831
William Pettitt, *Pt*
Blythe Pettitt, *Pt*
EMP: 5 **EST:** 1978
SQ FT: 3,000
SALES (est): 780.9K **Privately Held**
SIC: 1542 Nonresidential construction, nec

(G-11678)
PEXMALL LTD LIABILITY COMPANY
40 E Main St (19711-4639)
PHONE.................347 414-9879
Yury Kalinin, *Prin*
EMP: 7 **EST:** 2012
SALES (est): 151.34K **Privately Held**
SIC: 6351 Liability insurance

(G-11679)
PHARMERICA LONG-TERM CARE LLC

Also Called: Ltc Pharmacy
111 Ruthar Dr (19711-8025)
PHONE.................302 454-8234
Victor Manuel, *Brnch Mgr*
EMP: 32
SALES (corp-wide): 7.72B **Publicly Held**
Web: www.pharmerica.com
SIC: 5122 Pharmaceuticals
HQ: Pharmerica Long-Term Care, Llc
   3625 Queen Palm Dr
   Tampa FL 33619
   877 874-2768

(G-11680)
PHASE SNSITIVE INNOVATIONS INC (PA)
116 Sandy Dr Ste A (19713-1187)
PHONE.................302 286-5191
Dennis W Prather, *CEO*
EMP: 14 **EST:** 2007
SALES (est): 3.01MM **Privately Held**
Web: www.phasesensitiveinc.com
SIC: 8711 Engineering services

(G-11681)
PHD TECHNOLOGY SOLUTIONS LLC
111 Continental Dr Ste 309 (19713-4317)
PHONE.................410 961-7895
Donnell Friend, *Managing Member*
EMP: 30 **EST:** 2011
SALES (est): 2.44MM **Privately Held**
Web: www.phdtechsolutions.com
SIC: 7373 Office computer automation systems integration

(G-11682)
PHEONIXFIRE L L C ◊
37 Munro Rd (19711-3635)
PHONE.................302 588-8820
Zhisheng Zhong, *Pr*
EMP: 5 **EST:** 2023
SALES (est): 164.52K **Privately Held**
SIC: 7389 Business Activities at Non-Commercial Site

(G-11683)
PHI SERVICE CO
500 N Wakefield Dr (19702-5440)
P.O. Box 6066 (19714-6066)
PHONE.................302 451-5224
EMP: 8 **EST:** 2006
SALES (est): 230.62K **Privately Held**
SIC: 8641 Civic and social associations

(G-11684)
PHILIPS B ERIC DMD PA
Also Called: Omega Endodontics
Omega Prof Ctr Ste J31 (19713)
PHONE.................302 738-7303
EMP: 10 **EST:** 1993
SALES (est): 960.51K **Privately Held**
SIC: 8011 Cardiologist and cardio-vascular specialist

(G-11685)
PHILLIPS & COHEN ASSOC LTD
Also Called: PHILLIPS & COHEN ASSOCIATES, LTD.
258 Chapman Rd Ste 205 (19702-5444)
PHONE.................302 355-3500
Christy Nicholson, *Brnch Mgr*
EMP: 160
SALES (corp-wide): 25.45MM **Privately Held**
Web: www.phillips-cohen.com
SIC: 7322 Adjustment and collection services
PA: Phillips & Cohen Associates Ltd
   1002 Justison St
   Wilmington DE 19801
   609 518-9000

Newark - New Castle County (G-11714)

(G-11686)
PHOENIX REHABILITATION
210 Louviers Dr (19711-4167)
PHONE.................................302 533-5313
EMP: 5 **EST:** 2019
SALES (est): 144.29K **Privately Held**
SIC: 8322 General counseling services

(G-11687)
PHYSIATRIST
1101 Twin C Ln Ste 101 (19713-2158)
PHONE.................................302 993-0282
Daniel Clinton, *Pr*
EMP: 7 **EST:** 2018
SALES (est): 106.96K **Privately Held**
SIC: 8011 Offices and clinics of medical doctors

(G-11688)
PIENTKA MASONRY CNSTR LLC
310 Markus Ct (19713-1151)
PHONE.................................302 420-6748
EMP: 8 **EST:** 2019
SALES (est): 248.97K **Privately Held**
Web: www.pientkamasonry.com
SIC: 1521 Single-family housing construction

(G-11689)
PIERCE MULTI SOLUTIONS LLC
1 Chestnut Hill Plz Pmb 1210 (19713-2761)
PHONE.................................302 609-7000
Eric Pierce, *Pr*
EMP: 2 **EST:** 2021
SALES (est): 58.32K **Privately Held**
SIC: 3999 8742 Hair and hair-based products ; Management consulting services

(G-11690)
PIKE CREEK ANIMAL HOSPITAL
297 Polly Drummond Hill Rd (19711-4834)
PHONE.................................302 454-7780
Laura Richardson, *CEO*
Doctor Alan Mckersie, *Pr*
EMP: 10 **EST:** 1988
SALES (est): 213.19K **Privately Held**
Web: www.pikecreekanimalhospital.com
SIC: 0742 Animal hospital services, pets and other animal specialties

(G-11691)
PIKE CREEK CONSTRUCTION
1124 Mayflower Dr (19711-6823)
PHONE.................................302 453-0611
Gregory Reiter, *Prin*
EMP: 5 **EST:** 2015
SALES (est): 294.63K **Privately Held**
Web: www.pikecreekconstruction.com
SIC: 1521 Single-family housing construction

(G-11692)
PIKE CREEK MORTGAGE SERVICES (PA)
Also Called: Pike Creek Mortgage Group
2100 Drummond Plz Bldg 2 (19711-5743)
PHONE.................................302 892-2811
Wayne Moses, *Pr*
EMP: 9 **EST:** 1995
SALES (est): 4.94MM
SALES (corp-wide): 4.94MM **Privately Held**
Web: www.pikecreekloans.com
SIC: 6163 Mortgage brokers arranging for loans, using money of others

(G-11693)
PIKE CREEK PSYCHLOGICAL CTR PA (PA)
8 Polly Drummond Hill Rd (19711-5703)
PHONE.................................302 738-6859
J D Willetts, *Pr*
EMP: 8 **EST:** 1992
SALES (est): 818.62K **Privately Held**
Web: www.pikecreekpsych.com
SIC: 8322 8049 General counseling services ; Psychologist, psychotherapist and hypnotist

(G-11694)
PINTALK INC
2035 Sunset Lake Rd Ste B2 (19702-2600)
PHONE.................................844 386-0178
Antoine Berton, *Prin*
EMP: 6 **EST:** 2018
SALES (est): 46.16K **Privately Held**
SIC: 7371 Software programming applications

(G-11695)
PIONEER HOUSE
413 Salem Church Rd (19702-1452)
PHONE.................................302 286-0892
Cinthia Guy, *Dir*
EMP: 8 **EST:** 2004
SALES (est): 89.05K **Privately Held**
SIC: 8322 Social services for the handicapped

(G-11696)
PIRULOS CHILD CARE CENTER LLC
799 Salem Church Rd (19702-3612)
PHONE.................................302 836-3520
Joseph Hurst, *Mgr*
EMP: 5 **EST:** 2006
SALES (est): 193.81K **Privately Held**
Web: www.piruloschildcare.com
SIC: 8351 Group day care center

(G-11697)
PIVOT OCCUPATIONAL HEALTH LLC
15 Omega Dr Bldg K (19713-2057)
PHONE.................................302 368-5100
EMP: 14 **EST:** 2015
SALES (est): 247.94K **Privately Held**
SIC: 8099 Physical examination and testing services

(G-11698)
PLACERS INC OF DELAWARE
Also Called: Placers
850 Library Ave Ste 106 (19711-7170)
PHONE.................................302 709-0973
Chris Burkhard, *Pr*
EMP: 10 **EST:** 2011
SALES (est): 2.69MM
SALES (corp-wide): 11.51MM **Privately Held**
Web: www.myplacers.com
SIC: 7361 Employment agencies
PA: C.B.I. Group, L.L.C.
      850 Library Ave Ste 106
      Newark DE 19711
      302 266-0860

(G-11699)
PLANNED PARENTHOOD OF DELAWARE
140 E Delaware Ave (19711-4649)
PHONE.................................302 731-7801
Brenda Peirce, *Mgr*
EMP: 6
SALES (corp-wide): 4.5MM **Privately Held**
Web: www.plannedparenthood.org
SIC: 8093 Family planning clinic
PA: Planned Parenthood Of Delaware Inc
      625 N Shipley St
      Wilmington DE 19801
      302 655-7293

(G-11700)
PLATINUM LOGISTICS LLC
35 Salem Church Rd Ste 80 (19713-4927)
PHONE.................................412 708-6476
Ben Blemahdoo, *Managing Member*
EMP: 6 **EST:** 2020
SALES (est): 675K **Privately Held**
SIC: 4731 Freight forwarding

(G-11701)
PLUGILO INC
200 Continental Dr # 401 (19713-4334)
PHONE.................................628 202-4444
Michael Mohr, *Pr*
EMP: 13 **EST:** 2016
SALES (est): 515.7K **Privately Held**
SIC: 7371 Computer software development and applications

(G-11702)
PLUMBERS PPFITTERS LOCAL UN 74
201 Executive Dr (19702-3316)
PHONE.................................302 636-7400
Michael Hackendorn, *Mgr*
EMP: 5 **EST:** 1988
SALES (est): 1.59MM **Privately Held**
Web: www.ualocal74.com
SIC: 8631 Labor union

(G-11703)
PLURIBUS TECHNOLOGIES INC
3 Fairfield Dr (19711-2767)
PHONE.................................302 373-2670
Martin Duncan, *Pr*
EMP: 5 **EST:** 2016
SALES (est): 56.62K **Privately Held**
Web: www.pluribustechnologies.com
SIC: 8731 Commercial physical research

(G-11704)
PMBTEXAS ENTERPRISES LLC ✪
254 Chapman Rd Ste 208 (19702-5422)
PHONE.................................254 993-1530
Preston Brigando, *CEO*
EMP: 5 **EST:** 2023
SALES (est): 257.92K **Privately Held**
Web: www.pmbtexas-enterprises.com
SIC: 7389 Business services, nec

(G-11705)
PMC PUBLICATIONS LLC
201 Michelle Ct (19711-6769)
PHONE.................................302 268-4480
EMP: 4 **EST:** 2018
SALES (est): 73.86K **Privately Held**
SIC: 2741 Miscellaneous publishing

(G-11706)
PNC BANK NATIONAL ASSOCIATION
Also Called: PNC
4643 Ogletown Stanton Rd (19713-2006)
PHONE.................................302 733-7190
Sterling Doughty, *Mgr*
EMP: 5
SALES (corp-wide): 23.54B **Publicly Held**
Web: www.pncbank.com
SIC: 6021 National trust companies with deposits, commercial
HQ: Pnc Bank, National Association
      300 5th Ave
      Pittsburgh PA 15222
      877 762-2000

(G-11707)
POINT TO POINT TECH USA INC
503 Interchange Blvd (19711-3558)
PHONE.................................302 359-5343
Brett Haysom, *Prin*
EMP: 5 **EST:** 2018
SALES (est): 122.31K **Privately Held**
SIC: 5045 Computers, peripherals, and software

(G-11708)
POLAND & SULLIVAN INSUR INC
Also Called: Nationwide
106 Haines St (19711-5362)
P.O. Box 418 (19715-0418)
PHONE.................................302 738-3535
Andre Hoeschel, *Pr*
John Yasik, *VP*
EMP: 15 **EST:** 1965
SALES (est): 2.92MM **Privately Held**
Web: www.poland-sullivan.com
SIC: 6411 Insurance agents, nec

(G-11709)
POLARSTAR ENGINEERING & MCH
5 Garfield Way Ste B (19713-3457)
PHONE.................................302 368-4639
Stephen Hague, *Owner*
▲ **EMP:** 4 **EST:** 1996
SQ FT: 2,500
SALES (est): 581.56K **Privately Held**
Web: www.polarstarengineering.com
SIC: 3599 Machine shop, jobbing and repair

(G-11710)
POLE PRESS LLC
2035 Sunset Lake Rd Ste B2 (19702-2600)
PHONE.................................260 209-4628
EMP: 6 **EST:** 2019
SALES (est): 150.06K **Privately Held**
Web: www.polepress.com
SIC: 2741 Miscellaneous publishing

(G-11711)
POLYMER TECHNOLOGIES INC (PA)
420 Corporate Blvd (19702-3330)
PHONE.................................302 738-9001
Robert Prybutok, *CEO*
Carl Wolaver, *
Suzanne Prybutok, *
◆ **EMP:** 90 **EST:** 1989
SQ FT: 86,000
SALES (est): 26.84MM **Privately Held**
Web: www.polytechinc.com
SIC: 2821 Polyurethane resins

(G-11712)
POOL MAN INC
470 Hopkins Bridge Rd (19711-2102)
PHONE.................................302 737-8696
Bob Witmer, *Prin*
EMP: 8 **EST:** 2005
SALES (est): 248.71K **Privately Held**
Web: www.poolmaninc.com
SIC: 1799 Swimming pool construction

(G-11713)
POPSYCLE LLC
200 Continental Dr Ste 4012450 (19713-4334)
PHONE.................................202 831-0211
Jeffrey Kaplan, *Managing Member*
EMP: 8
SALES (est): 312.73K **Privately Held**
SIC: 7311 Advertising agencies

(G-11714)
PORTER NISSAN BUICK NEWARK
600 Ogletown Rd (19711-5406)
PHONE.................................302 368-6300
Douglas Cameron, *CFO*
EMP: 24 **EST:** 1988
SALES (est): 606.74K **Privately Held**
Web: www.nissanusa.com

Newark - New Castle County (G-11715) — **GEOGRAPHIC SECTION**

SIC: **5511** 5012 Automobiles, new and used; Automobiles

(G-11715)
POSEIDON ADVENTURES INC
80 Albe Dr (19702-1322)
PHONE.....................302 533-7815
R Scott, *Prin*
EMP: 6 EST: 2015
SALES (est): 67.81K **Privately Held**
Web: poseidon-adventures-myscubashop.myshopify.com
SIC: **7999** Outfitters, recreation

(G-11716)
POTTS WLDG BOILER REPR CO INC (HQ)
1901 Ogletown Rd (19711-5437)
PHONE.....................302 453-2550
Dennis Dakin, *Pr*
▼ EMP: 189 EST: 1929
SQ FT: 200,000
SALES (est): 39.64MM
SALES (corp-wide): 85.66MM **Privately Held**
Web: www.pottswelding.com
SIC: **3441** 3491 Fabricated structural metal; Industrial valves
PA: St. John Holdings, Inc.
320 King Of Prussia Rd
Radnor PA 19087
610 964-8702

(G-11717)
POURED FOUNDATIONS OF DE INC
409 Capitol Trl (19711-3864)
PHONE.....................302 234-2050
Richard Sexton, *Prin*
EMP: 10 EST: 2007
SALES (est): 492.64K **Privately Held**
Web: www.delawareconcrete.net
SIC: **1771** Concrete work

(G-11718)
POWER DELIVERY SOLUTIONS LLC
100 Commerce Dr Ste 201 (19713-2850)
PHONE.....................302 260-3114
Frank Cascino, *Pr*
Richard Conlin, *VP Opers*
Eric Pres Transmissions Whalen V, *Prin*
EMP: 30 EST: 2012
SQ FT: 10,000
SALES (est): 4.22MM **Privately Held**
Web: www.asplundhengineering.com
SIC: **8711** Consulting engineer

(G-11719)
POWERTRAIN TECHNOLOGY INC
Also Called: Benchmark Transmissions
2101 Ogletown Rd (19711-5433)
PHONE.....................302 368-4900
Dante Principe, *Pr*
EMP: 5 EST: 1989
SALES (est): 560K **Privately Held**
Web: www.benchmarkonline.biz
SIC: **7538** 7537 General automotive repair shops; Automotiv e transmission repair shops

(G-11720)
PRACTICAL SYSTEMS
106 Avignon Ct (19702-5524)
PHONE.....................302 753-8885
William Good, *Prin*
EMP: 7 EST: 2010
SALES (est): 90.16K **Privately Held**
SIC: **1711** Warm air heating and air conditioning contractor

(G-11721)
PRECIOUS KNWLDG ERLY LRNG CTR
1000 Village Cir (19713-2952)
PHONE.....................302 293-2588
Lozetta Hayden, *Prin*
EMP: 11 EST: 2011
SALES (est): 197.75K **Privately Held**
SIC: **8351** Group day care center

(G-11722)
PRECISE ALIGNMENT MCH TL CO
59 Avignon Dr (19702-5553)
PHONE.....................302 832-2922
Alfred A Lance Senior, *Owner*
EMP: 6 EST: 1999
SALES (est): 294.12K **Privately Held**
Web: www.whitecompany.us
SIC: **8711** Engineering services

(G-11723)
PRECISION AIRCONVEY CORP (PA)
465 Corporate Blvd (19702-3331)
PHONE.....................302 999-8000
Tom Embley, *CEO*
Lawrence Green, *Pr*
EMP: 18 EST: 1968
SQ FT: 10,000
SALES (est): 4.95MM **Privately Held**
Web: www.precisionairconvey.com
SIC: **3569** Filters

(G-11724)
PREDICTIVE ANALYTICS GROUP
100 Discovery Blvd Ste 802 (19713-1325)
PHONE.....................844 733-5724
EMP: 17 EST: 2017
SALES (est): 503.39K **Privately Held**
Web: www.predictiveanalyticsgroup.net
SIC: **8742** Management consulting services

(G-11725)
PRELUDE TX
550 S College Ave (19716-1304)
PHONE.....................302 273-3369
EMP: 6 EST: 2016
SALES (est): 186.64K **Privately Held**
SIC: **6531** Real estate agents and managers

(G-11726)
PREMIER DRMTLOGY CSMTC SURGERY
537 Stanton Christiana Rd Ste 107 (19713-2148)
PHONE.....................302 633-7550
EMP: 46 EST: 2019
SALES (est): 5.45MM **Privately Held**
Web: www.premierdermde.com
SIC: **8011** Dermatologist

(G-11727)
PREMIER EMPLOYEE SOLUTIONS
200 Continental Dr # 401 (19713-4334)
PHONE.....................843 421-5579
EMP: 6 EST: 2017
SALES (est): 241.01K **Privately Held**
SIC: **7361** Employment agencies

(G-11728)
PREMIER HEALTHCARE INC
Also Called: Newark Manor
254 W Main St (19711-3235)
PHONE.....................302 731-5576
David Boyer, *Admn*
Bruce Boyer, *
Gail Boyer, *
EMP: 48 EST: 1964
SQ FT: 24,000
SALES (est): 4.08MM **Privately Held**
Web: www.newarkmanor.net

SIC: **8051** Skilled nursing care facilities

(G-11729)
PREMIER PEDIATRICS LLC
2600 Glasgow Ave Ste 213 (19702-5704)
PHONE.....................302 836-4440
Bradley James Smith Md, *Prin*
EMP: 13 EST: 2013
SALES (est): 761.16K **Privately Held**
Web: www.premier4kids.com
SIC: **8011** Pediatrician

(G-11730)
PREMIER SOCCER
1237 Churchmans Rd (19713-2149)
PHONE.....................302 533-7340
EMP: 6 EST: 2015
SALES (est): 60.61K **Privately Held**
SIC: **7999** Amusement and recreation, nec

(G-11731)
PREMIER VOLLEYBALL DELAWARE
45 Anthony Dr (19702-8428)
PHONE.....................302 593-4593
EMP: 7 EST: 2017
SALES (est): 124.96K **Privately Held**
Web: www.premiervbde.com
SIC: **7997** Membership sports and recreation clubs

(G-11732)
PREMIERE PHYSICIANS PA
314 E Main St Ste 103 (19711-7180)
PHONE.....................302 584-6799
Reynold Agard, *Ex Dir*
EMP: 15 EST: 2003
SALES (est): 985.86K **Privately Held**
Web: www.gonnabuyahome.com
SIC: **8011** General and family practice, physician/surgeon

(G-11733)
PRESERVE AT DEACONS WALK
2112 Sheldon Dr (19711-4357)
P.O. Box 15080 (19711-0080)
PHONE.....................302 613-4775
Marie Alvarez, *Prin*
EMP: 5 EST: 2017
SALES (est): 118.7K **Privately Held**
Web: www.livedeaconswalk.com
SIC: **8641** Civic associations

(G-11734)
PRESTEGE LLC
16 N Bellwoode Dr (19702-3415)
P.O. Box 724 (19701-0724)
PHONE.....................302 312-8548
EMP: 7 EST: 2007
SALES (est): 167.27K **Privately Held**
SIC: **8999** Actuarial consultant

(G-11735)
PRESTIGE POWDER INC
13 Tyler Way (19713-3449)
PHONE.....................302 737-7086
Allen Boyle, *Prin*
EMP: 5 EST: 2007
SALES (est): 466.73K **Privately Held**
Web: www.americraftawning.com
SIC: **3993** 5099 5999 Signs and advertising specialties; Signs, except electric; Awnings

(G-11736)
PRESTIGE POWDER FINISHING INC
13 Tyler Way (19713-3449)
PHONE.....................302 737-7500
Allen Boyle, *Pr*
EMP: 10 EST: 1998
SQ FT: 18,500
SALES (est): 956.96K **Privately Held**

Web: www.prestigepowder.com
SIC: **3479** Painting of metal products

(G-11737)
PRICE AUTOMOTIVE GROUP
220 E Cleveland Ave (19711-3711)
PHONE.....................302 383-8669
EMP: 44 EST: 2015
SALES (est): 996.88K **Privately Held**
Web: www.priceautogroup.com
SIC: **7538** General automotive repair shops

(G-11738)
PRIDE HEATING & AIR CONDITIONG
208 Mercury Rd (19711-3036)
PHONE.....................302 234-4751
EMP: 5 EST: 2005
SALES (est): 182.54K **Privately Held**
SIC: **1711** Warm air heating and air conditioning contractor

(G-11739)
PRIDE HOME WARRANTY
200 Continental Dr Ste 401 (19713-4337)
PHONE.....................302 894-1689
EMP: 7 EST: 2019
SALES (est): 176.04K **Privately Held**
Web: www.prideac.com
SIC: **6512** Commercial and industrial building operation

(G-11740)
PRIDE OF DEL LDGE NO 349 IMPRV
57 W Cleveland Ave (19711-7004)
PHONE.....................215 453-9236
William Cornish, *Pr*
EMP: 5 EST: 1923
SQ FT: 1,400
SALES (est): 377.56K **Privately Held**
SIC: **8611** Community affairs and services

(G-11741)
PRIDES COURT APARTMENTS
Also Called: West Minister Management
6 Sussex Rd Ofc F (19713-3119)
PHONE.....................302 737-2085
Jonathan Cohen, *Mgr*
EMP: 7 EST: 1960
SALES (est): 535.22K **Privately Held**
Web: www.pridescourtapts.com
SIC: **6513** Apartment building operators

(G-11742)
PRIMARY RESIDENTIAL MRTG INC
248 E Chestnut Hill Rd Ste 4 (19713-3700)
PHONE.....................302 292-1009
EMP: 26
SALES (corp-wide): 273.11MM **Privately Held**
Web: www.delawaremortgageloans.net
SIC: **6162** Mortgage bankers and loan correspondents
PA: Primary Residential Mortgage, Inc.
1480 N 2200 W
Salt Lake City UT 84116
801 596-8707

(G-11743)
PRIME DIRECTIVE INC
503 Paisley Pl (19711-3453)
PHONE.....................302 383-5607
Daniel Siders, *Prin*
EMP: 8 EST: 2014
SALES (est): 224.22K **Privately Held**
Web: www.flynn.io
SIC: **7371** Computer software development

(G-11744)
PRIMELENDING A PLAINSCAPITAL
1450 Capitol Trl Ste 108 (19711-5700)

GEOGRAPHIC SECTION

Newark - New Castle County (G-11773)

PHONE.............................302 733-7599
EMP: 10
SALES (corp-wide): 1.42B **Publicly Held**
Web: www.primelending.com
SIC: 6162 Mortgage bankers and loan correspondents
HQ: Primelending A Plainscapital Company
18111 Preston Rd Ste 900
Dallas TX 75252
800 317-7463

(G-11745)
PRIMERICA
520 Christiana Medical Ctr (19702-1655)
PHONE.............................302 455-9460
EMP: 9 EST: 2019
SALES (est): 245.01K **Privately Held**
Web: www.primerica.com
SIC: 6282 Investment advice

(G-11746)
PRINCETON COML HOLDINGS LLC
113 Barksdale Professional Ctr (19711-3258)
PHONE.............................302 449-4836
EMP: 5 EST: 2010
SALES (est): 413.38K **Privately Held**
SIC: 8748 6531 Business consulting, nec; Real estate agents and managers

(G-11747)
PRINT ON THIS
3 Green Ct (19702-1355)
PHONE.............................302 235-9475
Ivan Meikle, *Prin*
EMP: 4 EST: 2016
SALES (est): 83.91K **Privately Held**
SIC: 2752 Commercial printing, lithographic

(G-11748)
PRINTED SOLID INC
2860 Ogletown Rd Bldg 6-8 (19713-1820)
PHONE.............................302 439-0098
David Randolph, *CEO*
▲ EMP: 13 EST: 2013
SALES (est): 1.75MM **Privately Held**
Web: www.printedsolid.com
SIC: 2752 Commercial printing, lithographic
PA: Prusa Research A.S.
Partyzanska 188/7a
Praha 7 - Holesovice 170 0

(G-11749)
PRINTS AND PRINCESSES
202 Hanover Pl (19711-2755)
PHONE.............................703 881-1057
Mary L Anest, *Owner*
EMP: 4 EST: 2017
SALES (est): 61K **Privately Held**
SIC: 2752 Commercial printing, lithographic

(G-11750)
PRIORITY RADIO INC
179 Stanton Christiana Rd (19702-1619)
P.O. Box 372 (19899-0372)
PHONE.............................302 540-5690
Steve Hare, *Prin*
EMP: 6 EST: 1994
SALES (est): 311.08K **Privately Held**
SIC: 4832 Radio broadcasting stations

(G-11751)
PRIORITY SERVICES LLC
70 Albe Dr (19702-1322)
PHONE.............................302 918-3070
EMP: 25 EST: 2002
SALES (est): 924.04K **Privately Held**
SIC: 7349 Building maintenance services, nec

(G-11752)
PRISM EVENTS INC
2035 Sunset Lake Rd Ste B2 (19702-2600)
PHONE.............................424 252-1070
Imran Ali, *Prin*
Raghib Khan, *Prin*
Faisal Abbas, *Prin*
EMP: 5 EST: 2018
SALES (est): 173.34K **Privately Held**
Web: www.prismevents.co
SIC: 8748 Business consulting, nec

(G-11753)
PRIVATE SOCIETY LLC
521 Concord Bridge Pl (19702-5205)
PHONE.............................302 319-7126
EMP: 5 EST: 2021
SALES (est): 65.26K **Privately Held**
SIC: 5611 7389 Clothing, sportswear, men's and boys'; Business Activities at Non-Commercial Site

(G-11754)
PRO CONTRACTORS
2501 Normandy Court (19713-4413)
PHONE.............................302 894-2611
EMP: 5 EST: 2017
SALES (est): 83.82K **Privately Held**
Web: www.procontractors.solutions
SIC: 1799 Special trade contractors, nec

(G-11755)
PRO RAD ONC
111 Continental Dr # 412 (19713-4306)
PHONE.............................302 709-4508
Kimberly Fell, *Prin*
EMP: 10 EST: 2014
SALES (est): 54.13K **Privately Held**
SIC: 8011 Oncologist

(G-11756)
PROAUTOMATED INC
100 Lake Dr Ste 205 (19702-3361)
PHONE.............................302 294-6121
John Webb, *CEO*
Nicholas Kruse, *
EMP: 92 EST: 2007
SALES (est): 6.31MM **Privately Held**
Web: www.proautomated.com
SIC: 8742 Automation and robotics consultant

(G-11757)
PROBLEM CONSULTING CO
254 Chapman Rd Ste 2087804 (19702-5413)
PHONE.............................347 809-3402
Tiffan Meloney, *CEO*
EMP: 7
SALES (est): 264.9K **Privately Held**
SIC: 7371 Computer software development

(G-11758)
PRODUCE FOR BTTER HLTH FNDTION
Also Called: 5 A Day Warehouse
5341 Limestone Rd (19711)
PHONE.............................302 235-2329
Steve Wilcox, *Brnch Mgr*
EMP: 5
Web: www.fruitsandveggies.org
SIC: 8099 Nutrition services
PA: Produce For Better Health Foundation
8816 Manchester Rd
Saint Louis MO 63144

(G-11759)
PROFESSIONAL TECHNICIANS INC
100 Biddle Ave Ste 200 (19702-3983)
PHONE.............................215 364-4911
EMP: 22 EST: 2017
SALES (est): 495.52K **Privately Held**
Web: www.ptihealth.com
SIC: 8011 Offices and clinics of medical doctors

(G-11760)
PROFESSIONAL WINDOW TINTING
9 Albe Dr Ste A (19702-1380)
PHONE.............................302 456-3456
Gail Bluestein, *Pr*
Steven Bluestein, *VP*
EMP: 5 EST: 2001
SALES (est): 490.96K **Privately Held**
Web: www.tintglass.com
SIC: 1799 Glass tinting, architectural or automotive

(G-11761)
PROGRESIVE DENTAL ARTS
685 E Chestnut Hill Rd (19713-1827)
PHONE.............................302 455-9569
Bruce Fay, *Pr*
EMP: 27 EST: 1989
SQ FT: 2,800
SALES (est): 1.14MM **Privately Held**
Web: www.progressivedentalartsde.com
SIC: 8021 Dentists' office

(G-11762)
PROMISE OF LIGHT INC
10 Capano Dr (19702-1844)
PHONE.............................201 471-5848
Augustus Gogoe, *CEO*
EMP: 10 EST: 2021
SALES (est): 680K **Privately Held**
SIC: 8361 Self-help group home

(G-11763)
PROMOTION ZONE LLC
Also Called: Promotion Zone
50 Albe Dr Ste A (19702-1330)
PHONE.............................302 832-8565
EMP: 5 EST: 2003
SALES (est): 398.72K **Privately Held**
Web: www.promotionzone.biz
SIC: 7336 2759 5199 2754 Commercial art and graphic design; Decals: printing, nsk; Advertising specialties; Commercial printing, gravure

(G-11764)
PROMOTIONS PLUS INC
700 Peoples Plz (19702-5601)
PHONE.............................302 836-2820
George Kaufmann, *Pr*
Sam Onessi, *VP*
EMP: 9 EST: 1984
SQ FT: 2,000
SALES (est): 804.3K **Privately Held**
Web: www.promotionsplusde.com
SIC: 7336 Silk screen design

(G-11765)
PROPERTY ADVISORY SERVICE
100 Liberty Ter (19702-5259)
PHONE.............................401 453-4455
EMP: 5 EST: 2019
SALES (est): 138.99K **Privately Held**
Web: www.propertyadvisorygroup.com
SIC: 6512 Nonresidential building operators

(G-11766)
PROTOTEK MACHINING & DEV
Also Called: Prototek Machining & Dev
307 Markus Ct (19713-1151)
PHONE.............................302 368-1226
Jeff Coffman, *Pr*
EMP: 3 EST: 1999
SALES (est): 223.62K **Privately Held**
Web: www.prototekde.com
SIC: 3599 Machine shop, jobbing and repair

(G-11767)
PROVIDE LLC
Also Called: Modern Mail
100 Pencader Dr (19702-3321)
P.O. Box 674 (19701-0674)
PHONE.............................302 391-1200
EMP: 45
Web: www.providegroup.com
SIC: 7331 Direct mail advertising services

(G-11768)
PROVISION GROUP LLC
200 Continental Dr Ste 401 (19713-4334)
PHONE.............................844 220-7200
EMP: 5
SALES (est): 114K **Privately Held**
SIC: 8071 Medical laboratories

(G-11769)
PRUDENT CAPITAL ADVISOR
260 Chapman Rd Ste 200 (19702-5491)
PHONE.............................302 569-9444
Donald E Jones, *Prin*
EMP: 5 EST: 2004
SALES (est): 172.5K **Privately Held**
Web: www.legalservicesnewark.com
SIC: 8742 Financial consultant

(G-11770)
PSYCHOTHERAPEUTIC SERVICES
5 Kensington Ln (19713-3706)
PHONE.............................302 737-1597
EMP: 42
Web: www.psychotherapeuticservices.com
SIC: 8093 Mental health clinic, outpatient
HQ: Psychotherapeutic Services Inc
870 High St Ste 2
Chestertown MD 21620
410 778-1933

(G-11771)
PULSAR360 CORP
Also Called: Pulsar360
2915 Ogletown Rd Ste 3240 (19713-1927)
PHONE.............................855 578-5727
Michael Williams, *Pr*
EMP: 20 EST: 2013
SALES (est): 4.65MM
SALES (corp-wide): 56.56MM **Privately Held**
Web: www.pulsar360.com
SIC: 4813 7389 3825 8322 Data telephone communications; Business services, nec; Network analyzers; Disaster service
HQ: Sherweb Inc.
2915 Ogletown Rd 1073
Newark DE 19713
888 567-6610

(G-11772)
PURE POWER PRESSURE WSHG LLC
8 Higgins Rd (19711-4361)
PHONE.............................302 266-9933
Tyler Kreisher, *Owner*
EMP: 5 EST: 2017
SALES (est): 47.21K **Privately Held**
Web: www.purepowerpressurewashing.com
SIC: 1799 Cleaning building exteriors, nec

(G-11773)
PURE WELLNESS LLC (PA)
Also Called: Pure Wellness Chiropractic
550 Stanton Christiana Rd Ste 302 (19713-2132)
PHONE.............................302 365-5470

Newark - New Castle County (G-11774)

Holly J Corbett, *Prin*
EMP: 10 EST: 2008
SALES (est): 2.76MM
SALES (corp-wide): 2.76MM **Privately Held**
Web: www.purewellchiro.com
SIC: 8041 Offices and clinics of chiropractors

(G-11774)
PUREBREAD
47 Beech Hill Dr (19711-2944)
PHONE...................302 528-5591
Mike Nardozzi, *Prin*
EMP: 6 EST: 2013
SALES (est): 212.94K **Privately Held**
Web: www.purebreaddeli.com
SIC: 8741 Management services

(G-11775)
PURPLE THINKERS INC
112 Capitol Trl Ste A429 (19711-3716)
PHONE...................760 349-7603
EMP: 5 EST: 2016
SALES (est): 63.12K **Privately Held**
SIC: 7371 Computer software development and applications

(G-11776)
PUSAN RE NEWARK LLC
205 Cunane Cir (19702-2070)
PHONE...................302 737-3087
Parthiban Jayaraman, *Prin*
EMP: 5 EST: 2015
SALES (est): 244.87K **Privately Held**
SIC: 6799 Investors, nec

(G-11777)
PUZS BODY SHOP INC
97 Peoples Dr (19702-1323)
PHONE...................302 368-8265
Francis Walls, *Pr*
EMP: 6 EST: 1980
SALES (est): 453.31K **Privately Held**
Web: www.puzsautobody.com
SIC: 7532 Body shop, automotive

(G-11778)
PYIR CONSTRUCTION & DESIGN
121 Britain Ct (19702-6323)
PHONE...................302 824-9015
EMP: 5 EST: 2019
SALES (est): 177.82K **Privately Held**
SIC: 1521 Single-family housing construction

(G-11779)
PYLE HLG & JUNK REMOVAL LLC
6 Sunny Bnd (19702-2324)
PHONE...................302 750-7227
Jamie Pyle, *Managing Member*
EMP: 5 EST: 2021
SALES (est): 199.4K **Privately Held**
SIC: 7389 Business Activities at Non-Commercial Site

(G-11780)
PYRAMID GROUP MGT SVCS CORP
227 E Delaware Ave (19711-4606)
PHONE...................302 737-1770
Andrew Bondy, *Pr*
EMP: 5 EST: 2001
SALES (est): 443.03K **Privately Held**
SIC: 8742 Business management consultant

(G-11781)
QBECK INSPECTION GROUP
242 Chapman Rd (19702-5405)
PHONE...................302 452-9257
Larry Macnallen, *Mgr*
EMP: 13 EST: 1992
SALES (est): 922.75K **Publicly Held**

SIC: 8711 Construction and civil engineering
HQ: Be&K, Inc.
2000 International Pk Dr
Birmingham AL 35243

(G-11782)
QBENCH INC ◇
254 Chapman Rd (19702-5413)
PHONE...................888 680-5834
Nicholas Evans, *CEO*
EMP: 21 EST: 2022
SALES (est): 1.06MM **Privately Held**
Web: www.qbench.com
SIC: 7372 Prepackaged software

(G-11783)
QOE INC
955 Dawson Dr Ste 3 (19713-5814)
P.O. Box 7717 (19714-7717)
PHONE...................302 455-1234
EMP: 6 EST: 1994
SQ FT: 5,000
SALES (est): 597.61K **Privately Held**
Web: www.qoeinc.com
SIC: 5999 7629 Business machines and equipment; Electrical repair shops

(G-11784)
QPS LLC
Also Called: Quest Pharmaceutical Services
110 Executive Dr Ste 7 (19702-3352)
PHONE...................302 369-3753
EMP: 153
Web: www.qps.com
SIC: 5122 Pharmaceuticals
PA: Qps, Llc
3 Innovation Way Ste 240
Newark DE 19711

(G-11785)
QPS HOLDINGS LLC (PA)
3 Innovation Way Ste 240 (19711-5456)
PHONE...................302 369-5601
EMP: 10 EST: 2007
SALES (est): 81.8MM **Privately Held**
Web: www.qps.com
SIC: 6719 Personal holding companies, except banks

(G-11786)
QUALITY CONTRACTOR SVCS LLC
8 W Stephen Dr (19713-1867)
PHONE...................302 502-6815
Derek Scarfo, *Prin*
EMP: 5 EST: 2017
SALES (est): 103.84K **Privately Held**
SIC: 1799 Special trade contractors, nec

(G-11787)
QUALITY HOME SERVICES INC
30 Albe Dr (19702-1352)
PHONE...................302 266-6113
EMP: 7 EST: 2017
SALES (est): 180.24K **Privately Held**
Web: www.qualityhomeservices.com
SIC: 1761 Roofing contractor

(G-11788)
QUALITY IN-HOUSE VIDEO INC
Also Called: Quality Video Service
1 N Redspire Ct (19702-3947)
PHONE...................302 834-5654
Richard Delcoglin, *Pr*
EMP: 5 EST: 1997
SALES (est): 141.64K **Privately Held**
SIC: 7841 Video tape rental

(G-11789)
QUALITY INN
Also Called: Quality Inn

48 Geoffrey Dr (19713-3603)
PHONE...................302 292-1500
Fred Acosta, *Prin*
EMP: 16 EST: 2012
SALES (est): 221.04K **Privately Held**
Web: www.choicehotels.com
SIC: 7011 Hotels and motels

(G-11790)
QUALITY INN NEWARK
Also Called: Quality Inn
65 Geoffrey Dr (19713-3603)
PHONE...................707 622-5339
EMP: 9 EST: 2018
SALES (est): 157.42K **Privately Held**
Web: www.choicehotels.com
SIC: 7011 Hotels and motels

(G-11791)
QUALITYFASTFORYOU LLC ◇
254 Chapman Rd Ste 208 # 10485 (19702-5422)
PHONE...................618 540-1209
Drew Mcintire, *Prin*
EMP: 6 EST: 2022
SALES (est): 66.07K **Privately Held**
SIC: 8742 Retail trade consultant

(G-11792)
QUANTEAM NORTH AMERICA INC
2915 Ogletown Rd (19713-1927)
PHONE...................929 262-8538
EMP: 5 EST: 2016
SALES (est): 148.34K **Privately Held**
Web: www.quanteam.fr
SIC: 8742 Business management consultant

(G-11793)
QUANTICA ELECTRONICS LLC
750 Prides Xing (19713-6104)
PHONE...................302 648-4684
EMP: 3 EST: 2021
SALES (est): 56.54K **Privately Held**
SIC: 7372 Application computer software

(G-11794)
QUANTUM CORPORATION
211 Executive Dr Ste 1 (19702-3358)
PHONE...................302 737-7012
Donald Drew, *Brnch Mgr*
EMP: 9
SALES (corp-wide): 412.75MM **Publicly Held**
Web: www.quantum.com
SIC: 3572 Computer storage devices
PA: Quantum Corporation
224 Airport Pkwy Ste 550
San Jose CA 95110
408 944-4000

(G-11795)
QUANTUM LEAP INNOVATIONS INC (PA)
3 Innovation Way Ste 100 (19711-5456)
P.O. Box 970 (19703-0970)
PHONE...................302 894-8045
Joseph B Elad, *Pr*
Joseph B Elad, *Pr*
Faith Elad, *Treas*
Frank Abbott, *VP*
Apperson Johnson, *VP*
EMP: 18 EST: 1995
SALES (est): 2.43MM
SALES (corp-wide): 2.43MM **Privately Held**
Web: www.quantumleapinnovations.com
SIC: 7371 7379 Computer software development; Computer related consulting services

(G-11796)
QUANTUM POLYMERS CORPORATION
211 Executive Dr Ste 1 (19702-3358)
PHONE...................302 737-7012
Hemant Bheda, *CEO*
EMP: 11 EST: 2008
SQ FT: 22,000
SALES (est): 2.44MM **Privately Held**
Web: www.quantum-aep.com
SIC: 3089 Stock shapes, plastics

(G-11797)
QUARTZ MILL CONTRACTING
34 Quartz Mill Rd (19711-2330)
PHONE...................302 750-6683
EMP: 5 EST: 2017
SALES (est): 110.26K **Privately Held**
SIC: 1799 Special trade contractors, nec

(G-11798)
QUERYLOOP INC
Also Called: Publica.la
2035 Sunset Lake Rd Ste B2 (19702-2600)
PHONE...................412 253-6265
Pablo Laurino, *CEO*
EMP: 2 EST: 2016
SALES (est): 56.54K **Privately Held**
Web: www.publica.la
SIC: 7372 Publisher's computer software

(G-11799)
QUESO TIME DE 3 LLC ◇
58 E Main St (19711-4667)
PHONE...................302 368-4541
EMP: 5 EST: 2022
SALES (est): 188K **Privately Held**
SIC: 5143 Cheese

(G-11800)
QUIKSTAMP LLC
Also Called: Quikstamp
140 Songsmith Dr (19702-4458)
PHONE...................302 659-7555
Andre Austin, *CEO*
EMP: 10 EST: 2015
SALES (est): 507.82K **Privately Held**
Web: www.quikstamp.com
SIC: 7389 6411 8734 2899 Notary publics; Inspection and investigation services, insurance; Testing laboratories; Drug testing kits, blood and urine

(G-11801)
QWINTRY LLC
825 Dawson Dr (19713-3438)
PHONE...................858 633-6353
Victor Prodi, *Prin*
EMP: 10 EST: 2014
SALES (est): 496.21K **Privately Held**
Web: www.qwintry.com
SIC: 4212 Delivery service, vehicular

(G-11802)
R & J TAYLOR INC
Also Called: Master Shower Doors
1712 Ogletown Rd (19711-5428)
PHONE...................302 368-7888
Jean Taylor, *Pr*
Ron Taylor, *VP*
EMP: 6 EST: 1990
SALES (est): 799.76K **Privately Held**
Web: www.mastershowerdoors.com
SIC: 1799 1751 Home/office interiors finishing, furnishing and remodeling; Window and door (prefabricated) installation

GEOGRAPHIC SECTION

Newark - New Castle County (G-11832)

(G-11803)
R & K MOTORS & MACHINE SHOP
60 Aleph Dr (19702-1319)
PHONE.............................302 737-4596
Peter Kopalovick, *Pr*
EMP: 3 **EST:** 1972
SQ FT: 2,200
SALES (est): 232.18K **Privately Held**
SIC: 7538 3599 Diesel engine repair: automotive; Machine shop, jobbing and repair

(G-11804)
R A BABA A HOLDINGS INC ✪
200 Continental Dr # 401 (19713-4334)
PHONE.............................302 533-8441
Rasheed Askia, *CEO*
EMP: 5 **EST:** 2022
SALES (est): 199.4K **Privately Held**
SIC: 7389 Brokers, contract services

(G-11805)
R A CHANCE PLUMBING INC
11 Fern Ct (19702-2886)
PHONE.............................302 292-1315
Richard A Chance, *Pr*
EMP: 9 **EST:** 1988
SQ FT: 1,600
SALES (est): 992.93K **Privately Held**
Web: www.rachance.com
SIC: 1711 Plumbing contractors

(G-11806)
R E EXCAVATION LLC
15 Prestbury Sq (19713-2608)
PHONE.............................302 273-3669
EMP: 7 **EST:** 2011
SALES (est): 462.78K **Privately Held**
Web: www.randexcavation.com
SIC: 1522 Residential construction, nec

(G-11807)
R E MICHEL COMPANY LLC
904 Interchange Blvd (19711-3563)
PHONE.............................302 368-9410
EMP: 6
SALES (corp-wide): 1.43B **Privately Held**
Web: www.remichel.com
SIC: 5075 Warm air heating equipment and supplies
PA: R. E. Michel Company, Llc
  1 Re Michel Dr
  Glen Burnie MD 21060
  410 760-4000

(G-11808)
R F BROWN INC
Also Called: Delaware Trenching
18 Albe Dr Ste H (19702-1353)
PHONE.............................302 737-1993
Ronald F Brown, *Pr*
EMP: 7 **EST:** 1975
SQ FT: 1,000
SALES (est): 1.21MM **Privately Held**
SIC: 1623 Cable television line construction

(G-11809)
R MACPHERSON DR
29 Bay Blvd (19702-4835)
PHONE.............................302 834-8308
R Macpherson, *Prin*
EMP: 8 **EST:** 2008
SALES (est): 153.54K **Privately Held**
SIC: 8011 Offices and clinics of medical doctors

(G-11810)
R SMILEY LLC
7 Metten Rd (19713-1565)
PHONE.............................302 463-5111
EMP: 5 **EST:** 2018
SALES (est): 27.27K **Privately Held**
SIC: 8072 Dental laboratories

(G-11811)
R/T DECKS
1667 Iron Hill Rd (19702-1103)
PHONE.............................302 983-4397
Charles Chambers, *Prin*
EMP: 5 **EST:** 2010
SALES (est): 96.82K **Privately Held**
SIC: 1521 Patio and deck construction and repair

(G-11812)
RAAD360 LLC
550 S College Ave Ste 107 (19713-1324)
PHONE.............................855 722-3360
Michael Loveless, *Prin*
Michael Loveless, *CEO*
Vamsi Godavarthi, *VP*
Pete Scilla, *VP*
Dieter Hotz, *VP*
EMP: 10 **EST:** 2012
SQ FT: 307
SALES (est): 302.73K **Privately Held**
Web: www.raad360.com
SIC: 7372 7374 2741 7371 Business oriented computer software; Data processing and preparation; Internet publishing and broadcasting; Computer software development and applications

(G-11813)
RAAS INFOTEK LLC
262 Chapman Rd Ste 105a (19702-5418)
PHONE.............................302 894-3184
EMP: 40 **EST:** 2010
SALES (est): 5.75MM **Privately Held**
Web: www.raasinfotek.com
SIC: 7379 7371 Computer related consulting services; Computer software development

(G-11814)
RAC NATIONAL PRODUCT SERVICE L
230 Executive Dr Ste 5 (19702-3338)
PHONE.............................972 801-1100
Mitchell E Fadel, *Prin*
EMP: 5 **EST:** 2004
SALES (est): 148.15K **Privately Held**
SIC: 8999 Artists and artists' studios

(G-11815)
RADAAR LLC
112 Capitol Trl Ste A627 (19711-3716)
PHONE.............................855 623-0723
EMP: 7 **EST:** 2020
SALES (est): 120K **Privately Held**
Web: www.radaar.io
SIC: 8742 Marketing consulting services

(G-11816)
RADER SERVICES LLC
111 Rosewood Dr (19713-4210)
PHONE.............................302 454-0373
Wendi Rader, *Prin*
EMP: 5 **EST:** 2012
SALES (est): 37.15K **Privately Held**
SIC: 7299 Massage parlor

(G-11817)
RADFERTILITY
4735 Ogletown Stanton Rd Ste 3217 (19713-2072)
PHONE.............................302 602-8822
EMP: 40 **EST:** 2019
SALES (est): 605.72K **Privately Held**
Web: www.radfertility.com
SIC: 8011 Gynecologist

(G-11818)
RADIANT TECHNOLOGIES INC
254 Chapman Rd Ste 107 (19702-5489)
PHONE.............................800 301-0980
EMP: 7 **EST:** 2019
SALES (est): 441.62K **Privately Held**
SIC: 7371 Computer software development

(G-11819)
RADIATION ONCOLOGY
4755 Stanton Ogeltown Rd (19718-0001)
P.O. Box 4460 (19807-0460)
PHONE.............................302 733-1830
Christopher Koprowski, *Pr*
EMP: 9 **EST:** 1965
SALES (est): 128.05K **Privately Held**
SIC: 8011 Radiologist

(G-11820)
RAIDEN TECH GROUP INC
119 Blue Ridge Cir (19702-2981)
PHONE.............................302 330-8514
EMP: 5
SALES (est): 203.68K **Privately Held**
SIC: 7379 7389 Computer related services, nec; Business Activities at Non-Commercial Site

(G-11821)
RAIN OF LIGHT INC
28 Tyre Ave (19711-7142)
PHONE.............................302 312-7642
EMP: 7 **EST:** 2010
SALES (est): 172.51K **Privately Held**
SIC: 8322 Individual and family services

(G-11822)
RAINBOW SEVEN SPA
610 Capitol Trl (19711-3869)
PHONE.............................302 533-6916
EMP: 5 **EST:** 2016
SALES (est): 35.74K **Privately Held**
Web: www.rainbow7spa.us
SIC: 7991 Spas

(G-11823)
RAM ELECTRIC
6 Radka Dr (19702-6824)
PHONE.............................302 379-3351
Ram Khanna, *Prin*
EMP: 5 **EST:** 2012
SALES (est): 155.16K **Privately Held**
SIC: 1731 General electrical contractor

(G-11824)
RAMUNNO RAMUNNO
201 Louviers Dr (19711-4164)
PHONE.............................302 737-6909
EMP: 5 **EST:** 2016
SALES (est): 63.66K **Privately Held**
Web: www.ramunnolaw.com
SIC: 8111 General practice attorney, lawyer

(G-11825)
RAND ACCESSORIES USA INC
2915 Ogletown Rd (19713-1927)
PHONE.............................302 266-8200
EMP: 6
SALES (est): 1.29MM
SALES (corp-wide): 15.76MM **Privately Held**
SIC: 5094 Jewelry
HQ: Rand Accessories Inc.
  1350 Rue Mazurette Bureau 212
  Montreal QC H4N 1
  514 385-3482

(G-11826)
RAO D BHASKAR MD
1 Centurian Dr Ste 307 (19713-2127)
PHONE.............................302 733-5700
D Bhaskar Rao, *Prin*
EMP: 9 **EST:** 2014
SALES (est): 76.79K **Privately Held**
SIC: 8011 Offices and clinics of medical doctors

(G-11827)
RAPE OF THE LOCKE INC
700 Barksdale Rd Ste 5 (19711-3260)
PHONE.............................302 368-5370
Susan Annone, *Pr*
EMP: 6 **EST:** 1974
SQ FT: 2,000
SALES (est): 167.22K **Privately Held**
Web: www.rapeofthelocke.com
SIC: 7231 7241 Hairdressers; Barber shops

(G-11828)
RATH INCORPORATED (DH)
Also Called: Rath Performance Fibers
100 Commerce Dr Ste 303 (19713-2878)
PHONE.............................302 294-4446
David Grube, *Managing Member*
Les Crippenton, *
Ralph T Grizzel, *
▲ **EMP:** 17 **EST:** 1990
SALES (est): 38.99MM
SALES (corp-wide): 355.83K **Privately Held**
Web: www.go-foncier.com
SIC: 5169 Manmade fibers
HQ: Chamottewaren- Und Thonofenfabrik
  Aug. Rath Jun. Gmbh
  HafnerstraBe 3
  KrummnuBbaum 3375
  275724010

(G-11829)
RAYMOND ENTRMT GROUP LLC
62 N Chapel St Ste 4 (19711-2238)
PHONE.............................302 731-2000
EMP: 5 **EST:** 2000
SQ FT: 1,200
SALES (est): 242.41K **Privately Held**
SIC: 7929 Musical entertainers

(G-11830)
RAYMOND HARNER
Also Called: Accent Coatings
317 Jaymar Blvd (19702-2881)
PHONE.............................302 737-0755
EMP: 7 **EST:** 2009
SALES (est): 165.32K **Privately Held**
SIC: 3479 Metal coating and allied services

(G-11831)
RAYMOND V FEEHERY JR DPM
Also Called: New Castle Assoc & Podiatry
620 Stanton Christiana Rd Ste 303 (19713-2135)
PHONE.............................302 999-8511
Raymond V Feehery Junior, *Owner*
EMP: 9 **EST:** 1985
SALES (est): 551.88K **Privately Held**
Web: www.delawarefootdoctor.com
SIC: 8043 Offices and clinics of podiatrists

(G-11832)
RAYMOND W PETRUNICH DDS
2444 Pulaski Hwy (19702-3906)
PHONE.............................302 836-3565
EMP: 9 **EST:** 2019
SALES (est): 136.6K **Privately Held**
SIC: 8021 Dentists' office

Newark - New Castle County (G-11833)

(G-11833)
REACKT LLC (PA)
Also Called: Reackt
2035 Sunset Lake Rd Ste B2 (19702-2600)
PHONE..................267 210-4743
Eugene Yakovlev, *CEO*
EMP: 6 **EST:** 2019
SALES (est): 71.56K
SALES (corp-wide): 71.56K **Privately Held**
SIC: 7371 Computer software development and applications

(G-11834)
REBECCA E ORR
557 Upper Pike Creek Rd (19711-4338)
PHONE..................302 521-4920
Rebecca E Orr R.n. Ibclc, *Owner*
EMP: 6 **EST:** 2017
SALES (est): 22.18K **Privately Held**
SIC: 8049 Offices of health practitioner

(G-11835)
REBECCA SMLAK-KETTLEHAKE PSY D
200 Biddle Ave (19702-3968)
PHONE..................302 261-6901
EMP: 6 **EST:** 2018
SALES (est): 164.86K **Privately Held**
SIC: 8049 Clinical psychologist

(G-11836)
REBUILDING TGTHER PHILADELPHIA
525 Judges Ct (19711-2432)
PHONE..................302 234-4417
EMP: 6 **EST:** 2017
SALES (est): 52.01K **Privately Held**
Web: www.rebuildingtogether.org
SIC: 8699 Charitable organization

(G-11837)
RECOVERY INOVATIONS INC
659 E Chestnut Hill Rd (19713-1827)
PHONE..................602 636-4608
Charles Schultz, *Prin*
EMP: 6 **EST:** 2012
SALES (est): 87.33K **Privately Held**
SIC: 8093 Mental health clinic, outpatient

(G-11838)
RED LION MEDICAL SAFETY INC
123a Sandy Dr (19713-1148)
PHONE..................302 731-8600
Jess A Mcbride, *CEO*
EMP: 6 **EST:** 1978
SALES (est): 550.33K **Privately Held**
Web: www.redlionmedical.com
SIC: 8734 Product certification, safety or performance

(G-11839)
RED RHINO LABS LLC
2035 Sunset Lake Rd B2 (19702-2600)
PHONE..................650 275-2464
Ryan Lee, *Managing Member*
EMP: 2 **EST:** 2018
SALES (est): 15K **Privately Held**
SIC: 7372 Application computer software

(G-11840)
RED ROOF INNS INC
Also Called: Red Roof Inn
415 Stanton Christiana Rd (19713-2119)
PHONE..................302 292-2870
Ben Cummins, *Brnch Mgr*
EMP: 44
Web: www.redroof.com
SIC: 7011 Hotels and motels
HQ: Red Roof Inns, Inc.
7815 Walton Pkwy
New Albany OH 43054
614 744-2600

(G-11841)
REDDY DR VEENA
537 Stanton Christiana Rd Ste 211 (19713-2148)
PHONE..................302 998-0304
Veena Reddy D.m.d., *Owner*
EMP: 8 **EST:** 2017
SALES (est): 63.14K **Privately Held**
SIC: 8011 Offices and clinics of medical doctors

(G-11842)
REDMILL AUTO REPAIR
1209 Capitol Trl (19711-3923)
PHONE..................302 292-2155
Marty Krajawski, *Owner*
EMP: 5 **EST:** 2003
SALES (est): 474.24K **Privately Held**
SIC: 7538 General automotive repair shops

(G-11843)
REGIONAL HMATOLOGY ONCOLOGY PA
Also Called: Hosford-Skapof, Martha A MD
4701 Ogletown Stanton Rd Ste 2100 (19713-2055)
PHONE..................302 731-7782
Timothy Wozniak, *Mgr*
EMP: 7
SALES (corp-wide): 2.39MM **Privately Held**
Web: rhopa.navigatingcare.com
SIC: 8011 Oncologist
PA: Regional Hematology&Oncology, Pa Inc
1010 N Bancroft Pkwy # 21
Wilmington DE 19805
302 731-7782

(G-11844)
REGIONAL PROPERTIES LLC
1096 Old Churchmans Rd (19713-2102)
PHONE..................302 740-9740
Joshua D Vaught, *Admn*
EMP: 5 **EST:** 2010
SALES (est): 166.69K **Privately Held**
SIC: 6512 Commercial and industrial building operation

(G-11845)
REHABILITATION ASSOCIATES PA
200 Biddle Ave Ste 204 (19702-3966)
PHONE..................302 293-6877
EMP: 5
SALES (est): 170.27K **Privately Held**
SIC: 8093 Specialty outpatient clinics, nec

(G-11846)
REHABILITATION ASSOCIATES PA (PA)
2600 Glasgow Ave Ste 210 (19702-5704)
PHONE..................302 832-8894
Barry Bakst, *Pr*
Craig D Sternberg, *Prin*
Arnold Glassman, *Prin*
EMP: 41 **EST:** 1986
SALES (est): 4.8MM
SALES (corp-wide): 4.8MM **Privately Held**
Web: www.delawarebackpain.com
SIC: 8011 Physical medicine, physician/surgeon

(G-11847)
REILLY SWEEPING INC
10 Albe Dr (19702-1334)
PHONE..................302 738-8961
EMP: 144

SALES (corp-wide): 536.39MM **Privately Held**
Web: www.sweepingcorp.com
SIC: 4959 Sweeping service: road, airport, parking lot, etc.
HQ: Reilly Sweeping, Inc.
10 Kresge Rd
Fairless Hills PA 19030
215 736-1556

(G-11848)
RELAX MASSAGE THERAPY
105 Louviers Dr (19711-4163)
PHONE..................302 738-7300
John Glenn, *Prin*
EMP: 9 **EST:** 2010
SALES (est): 88.42K **Privately Held**
SIC: 8093 Rehabilitation center, outpatient treatment

(G-11849)
RELIABLE PRPERTY SOLUTIONS LLC
108 W Main St (19711-3229)
PHONE..................302 753-1299
EMP: 5 **EST:** 2015
SALES (est): 428.47K **Privately Held**
SIC: 6512 Nonresidential building operators

(G-11850)
REMLINE CORP
456 Corporate Blvd (19702-3330)
PHONE..................302 737-7228
Stephanie Petrella, *Pr*
Joseph Reardon, *
▲ **EMP:** 25 **EST:** 1979
SQ FT: 22,500
SALES (est): 8.54MM **Privately Held**
Web: www.remline.com
SIC: 7311 8732 5199 8743 Advertising agencies; Market analysis or research; Advertising specialties; Promotion service

(G-11851)
RENEW INTEGRATIVE HEALTH
256 Chapman Rd (19702-5417)
PHONE..................302 444-4366
EMP: 7 **EST:** 2018
SALES (est): 224.04K **Privately Held**
Web: www.renewinthealth.org
SIC: 8099 Health and allied services, nec

(G-11852)
RENTLY SOFTWARE LLC
2035 Sunset Lake Rd (19702-2600)
PHONE..................718 502-6575
Guido Zanon, *Managing Member*
EMP: 18 **EST:** 2021
SALES (est): 583.41K **Privately Held**
SIC: 7371 Computer software development

(G-11853)
RENTOKIL NORTH AMERICA INC
Also Called: Ehrlich Pest Control
955 Dawson Dr Ste 2 (19713-5814)
PHONE..................410 882-1000
EMP: 16
SALES (corp-wide): 4.47B **Privately Held**
SIC: 7342 Disinfecting and pest control services
HQ: Rentokil North America, Inc.
1125 Berkshire Blvd # 15
Wyomissing PA 19610
470 643-3300

(G-11854)
RENTOKIL NORTH AMERICA INC
701 Dawson Dr (19713-3413)
PHONE..................302 325-2687
EMP: 33

SALES (corp-wide): 4.47B **Privately Held**
SIC: 7342 Pest control in structures
HQ: Rentokil North America, Inc.
1125 Berkshire Blvd # 15
Wyomissing PA 19610
470 643-3300

(G-11855)
RENTOKIL NORTH AMERICA INC
1712 Ogletown Rd (19711-5428)
P.O. Box 7959 (19714-7959)
PHONE..................302 733-0851
Charlie Huth, *Brnch Mgr*
EMP: 33
SALES (corp-wide): 4.47B **Privately Held**
SIC: 0782 7342 Lawn and garden services; Bird proofing
HQ: Rentokil North America, Inc.
1125 Berkshire Blvd # 15
Wyomissing PA 19610
470 643-3300

(G-11856)
RENU CHRPRCTIC WLLNESS INJURY
1352 Marrows Rd (19711-5475)
PHONE..................302 368-0124
Doris Leach, *COO*
EMP: 16 **EST:** 2013
SALES (est): 361.7K **Privately Held**
Web: www.renumedicalinjury.com
SIC: 8041 Offices and clinics of chiropractors

(G-11857)
REP
285 The Grn (19716-2517)
PHONE..................910 622-0252
EMP: 6 **EST:** 2018
SALES (est): 47.88K **Privately Held**
Web: rep.udel.edu
SIC: 7922 Legitimate live theater producers

(G-11858)
REPAIR MY PLACE LLC
25 Lynam Lookout Dr (19702-1128)
PHONE..................302 286-7721
Michael Burcham, *Prin*
EMP: 5 **EST:** 2009
SALES (est): 60K **Privately Held**
SIC: 7699 Repair services, nec

(G-11859)
REPORTING SOLUTIONS LLC
102 Cannonball Ln (19702-3097)
PHONE..................857 284-3583
Bildad St Louis, *Managing Member*
EMP: 6
SALES (corp-wide): 367.44K **Privately Held**
Web: www.readygroupkw.com
SIC: 7371 Computer software development and applications
PA: Reporting Solutions, Llc
745 Atlantic Ave
Boston MA 02111
857 284-3583

(G-11860)
REPRODUCTIVE ASSOCIATES DEL PA (PA)
Also Called: Reproductive Associates Del
4735 Ogletown Stanton Rd Ste 3217 (19713-2072)
PHONE..................302 602-8822
EMP: 10 **EST:** 1995
SALES (est): 4.69MM **Privately Held**
Web: www.radfertility.com
SIC: 8011 Gynecologist

GEOGRAPHIC SECTION
Newark - New Castle County (G-11890)

(G-11861)
RESCUE PRINTIG
17 Lynch Farm Dr (19713-2823)
PHONE....................302 286-7266
Joan Poirier, *Prin*
EMP: 5 EST: 2017
SALES (est): 115.59K **Privately Held**
SIC: 2752 Offset printing

(G-11862)
RESCUE SURGICAL SOLUTIONS LLC
1305 Whittaker Rd (19702-1024)
PHONE....................302 722-5877
Kafui Gbewonyo, *Prin*
EMP: 7 EST: 2017
SALES (est): 90.15K **Privately Held**
SIC: 8011 Medical centers

(G-11863)
RESIDENCE INN BY MARRIOTT LLC
Also Called: Residence Inn By Marriott
240 Chapman Rd (19702-5421)
PHONE....................302 453-9200
Aaron Smith, *Mgr*
EMP: 68
SALES (corp-wide): 20.77B **Publicly Held**
Web: residence-inn.marriott.com
SIC: 7011 Hotels and motels
HQ: Residence Inn By Marriott, Llc
    10400 Fernwood Rd
    Bethesda MD 20817

(G-11864)
RESIDNCE INN WLMNGTON NWRK/ CHR
240 Chapman Rd (19702-5405)
PHONE....................302 453-9200
EMP: 9 EST: 2019
SALES (est): 99.56K **Privately Held**
SIC: 7011 Inns

(G-11865)
RESISTBOT INC
2035 Sunset Lake Rd B2 (19702-2600)
PHONE....................408 599-2094
Jason Putorti, *Pr*
EMP: 5 EST: 2018
SALES (est): 83.61K **Privately Held**
SIC: 7371 Computer software development and applications

(G-11866)
RESOLUTE INDUSTRIAL
200 Interchange Blvd (19711-9100)
PHONE....................267 401-0973
EMP: 10 EST: 2016
SALES (est): 180.73K **Privately Held**
Web: www.resolute-industrial.com
SIC: 6531 Real estate agents and managers

(G-11867)
RESOURCEFUL RAE LLC (PA)
513 Shue Dr (19713-1747)
PHONE....................302 220-7704
Rachel Wells, *Managing Member*
EMP: 6 EST: 2021
SALES (est): 18.95K
SALES (corp-wide): 18.95K **Privately Held**
SIC: 7299 Miscellaneous personal service

(G-11868)
RESOURCES FOR HUMAN DEV
28 Stature Dr (19713-3562)
PHONE....................215 848-1947
Adrienne Rotella, *Prin*
EMP: 7 EST: 2019
SALES (est): 110.33K **Privately Held**
Web: www.rhd.org
SIC: 8742 Business planning and organizing services

(G-11869)
RESOURCES FOR HUMAN DEV INC
12 Montrose Dr (19713-2757)
PHONE....................302 731-5283
EMP: 15
SALES (corp-wide): 292.52MM **Privately Held**
Web: www.rhd.org
SIC: 8742 Business planning and organizing services
PA: Resources For Human Development, Inc.
    4700 Wissahickon Ave # 126
    Philadelphia PA 19144
    215 951-0300

(G-11870)
RESOURCES FOR HUMAN DEV INC
256 Chapman Rd Ste 202 (19702-5415)
PHONE....................215 951-0300
EMP: 30
SALES (corp-wide): 292.52MM **Privately Held**
Web: www.rhd.org
SIC: 8322 Individual and family services
PA: Resources For Human Development, Inc.
    4700 Wissahickon Ave # 126
    Philadelphia PA 19144
    215 951-0300

(G-11871)
RETHMERICA ACCOUNTING AND
260 Chapman Rd (19702-5490)
PHONE....................302 317-2417
EMP: 5 EST: 2019
SALES (est): 205.35K **Privately Held**
Web: www.rethmerica.com
SIC: 8621 Accounting association

(G-11872)
RETREAT AT NEWARK
74 E Main St (19711-4640)
PHONE....................302 294-6520
EMP: 5 EST: 2014
SALES (est): 120.53K **Privately Held**
SIC: 6513 Apartment building operators

(G-11873)
RETROSHEET INC
20 Sunset Rd (19711-5236)
PHONE....................302 731-1570
David Smith, *Pr*
EMP: 5 EST: 1989
SALES (est): 150.69K **Privately Held**
Web: www.retrosheet.org
SIC: 8699 Personal interest organization

(G-11874)
REVIEW
325 Academy St Rm 201 (19716-6199)
PHONE....................302 831-2771
Sandy Iverson, *Pr*
EMP: 32 EST: 1987
SALES (est): 162.63K **Privately Held**
Web: www.reviewzerz.com
SIC: 2711 2741 Newspapers, publishing and printing; Miscellaneous publishing

(G-11875)
REX AUTO BODY INC
27 North St (19711-2250)
PHONE....................302 731-4707
William R Cockerham, *Pr*
Betty Cockerham, *Sec*
Joe Cockerham, *Genl Mgr*
EMP: 9 EST: 1971
SQ FT: 3,000
SALES (est): 495.89K **Privately Held**
SIC: 7532 Body shop, automotive

(G-11876)
REYNOLDS METALS COMPANY LLC
Also Called: Alcoa
700 Pencader Dr (19702-3310)
PHONE....................302 366-0555
TOLL FREE: 800
Mike M Burk, *Genl Mgr*
EMP: 1251
SALES (corp-wide): 12.45B **Publicly Held**
SIC: 3411 Aluminum cans
HQ: Reynolds Metals Company, Llc
    390 Park Ave
    New York NY 10022
    212 518-5400

(G-11877)
RHINO CABLING GROUP INC
528 Sepia Ct (19702-3669)
PHONE....................302 312-1033
Kevin Harris, *Pr*
EMP: 10 EST: 2003
SALES (est): 698.92K **Privately Held**
Web: www.rhinocabling.com
SIC: 1731 Fiber optic cable installation

(G-11878)
RHINO LNNGS DEL AUTO STYLE INC
841 Old Baltimore Pike (19702-1317)
PHONE....................302 368-4660
EMP: 10 EST: 1995
SQ FT: 13,000
SALES (est): 1.26MM **Privately Held**
Web: www.rhinoliningsde.com
SIC: 5531 5085 Truck equipment and parts; Industrial supplies

(G-11879)
RHINO SMART PUBLICATIONS
55 Shull Dr (19711-7716)
PHONE....................302 737-3422
Weldon Burge, *Prin*
EMP: 2 EST: 2011
SALES (est): 86.19K **Privately Held**
Web: www.smartrhino.com
SIC: 2741 Miscellaneous publishing

(G-11880)
RHOYAL EXTENSIONS
37 W Kyla Marie Dr (19702-5430)
PHONE....................318 572-2549
Rhandi Turner, *Prin*
EMP: 5 EST: 2017
SALES (est): 28.73K **Privately Held**
SIC: 7231 Hairdressers

(G-11881)
RI INT
659 E Chestnut Hill Rd (19713-1827)
PHONE....................302 318-6032
EMP: 21 EST: 2016
SALES (est): 62.59K **Privately Held**
SIC: 8322 Individual and family services

(G-11882)
RICHARD DALE RODGERS
311 Laurel Ave (19711-4730)
PHONE....................814 323-0450
Richard Rodgers, *Prin*
EMP: 7 EST: 2010
SALES (est): 64.96K **Privately Held**
SIC: 8011 Offices and clinics of medical doctors

(G-11883)
RICOS CLEANING SERVICES INC
51 Fairway Rd Apt 3d (19711-5677)
PHONE....................302 357-8155
EMP: 5 EST: 2018
SALES (est): 49.45K **Privately Held**
SIC: 7699 Cleaning services

(G-11884)
RIGHT KNDA GUYS CAR SLTONS LLC ✪
35 Salem Church Rd Ste 66 (19713-4924)
PHONE....................302 772-8717
EMP: 5 EST: 2022
SALES (est): 506.69K **Privately Held**
SIC: 4731 7389 Freight transportation arrangement; Business Activities at Non-Commercial Site

(G-11885)
RIKARBON INC
550 S College Ave Ste 107 (19713-1324)
PHONE....................765 237-7649
Basudeb Saha, *Pr*
EMP: 7 EST: 2016
SALES (est): 238.38K **Privately Held**
Web: www.rikarbon.com
SIC: 7299 Miscellaneous personal service

(G-11886)
RILEY ELECTRIC
1235 Old Coochs Bridge Rd (19713-2334)
PHONE....................302 533-5918
Ron Kellett, *Prin*
EMP: 8 EST: 2009
SALES (est): 233.08K **Privately Held**
SIC: 1731 General electrical contractor

(G-11887)
RILEY ELECTRIC INC
1235 Old Coochs Bridge Rd (19713-2334)
PHONE....................302 276-3581
John Riley, *Pr*
Gene Grady, *VP*
Lisa Kellett, *Off Mgr*
EMP: 5 EST: 2005
SALES (est): 457.8K **Privately Held**
Web: rileyelectric.comcastbiz.net
SIC: 1731 Banking machine installation and service

(G-11888)
RINEHIMER BODY SHOP INC
Also Called: Rinehimer Auto Works
6 Mill Park Ct (19713-1986)
PHONE....................302 737-7350
Richie Rinehimer, *Pr*
Donna Rinehimer, *Sec*
EMP: 10 EST: 1959
SALES (est): 412.01K **Privately Held**
SIC: 7538 General automotive repair shops

(G-11889)
RISING SUNSET PUBLISHING LLC
200 Continental Dr # 401 (19713-4334)
PHONE....................877 231-5425
EMP: 5 EST: 2019
SALES (est): 150K **Privately Held**
SIC: 8699 Literary, film or cultural club

(G-11890)
RIVAS ULISES
Also Called: Rivas Ironworks
31 Albe Dr Ste 3 (19702-1360)
PHONE....................302 454-8595
Ulises Rivas, *Owner*
EMP: 3 EST: 2005
SALES (est): 230.16K **Privately Held**
Web: rivasironw859584-211191-sml-1.hibustudio.com
SIC: 3441 Fabricated structural metal

Newark - New Castle County (G-11891)

(G-11891)
RKL FINANCIAL CORPORATION (HQ)
Also Called: Sallie Mae Financial
300 Continental Dr Fl 1 (19713-4322)
P.O. Box 3409 (19804-0249)
PHONE..................302 283-8000
Joanne Jackson, *Pr*
Carol Rymal, *Sec*
Michael Yurko, *Treas*
EMP: 38 **EST:** 1998
SQ FT: 30,000
SALES (est): 6.92MM
SALES (corp-wide): 2.37B **Publicly Held**
SIC: 6111 6162 Student Loan Marketing Association; Mortgage bankers and loan correspondents
PA: Slm Corporation
300 Continental Dr
Newark DE 19713
302 451-0200

(G-11892)
RMB CLEANING SERVICES LLC
1 Chestnut Hill Plz Ste 1217 (19713-2701)
PHONE..................302 753-0622
EMP: 5
SALES (est): 62.02K **Privately Held**
SIC: 7699 Cleaning services

(G-11893)
RMM BUILDERS LLC
1 Haywood Ct (19711-7455)
PHONE..................302 983-0734
Michael Outten, *Prin*
EMP: 5 **EST:** 2017
SALES (est): 101.23K **Privately Held**
SIC: 1521 New construction, single-family houses

(G-11894)
RNH INSTALLATION
42 Albe Dr Ste E (19702-1358)
PHONE..................302 731-8900
Chris Wilberg, *Prin*
EMP: 6 **EST:** 2007
SALES (est): 383.27K **Privately Held**
SIC: 1799 Service station equipment installation, maint., and repair

(G-11895)
ROAD & RAIL SERVICES INC
502 S College Ave Ste C (19713-1302)
PHONE..................302 731-2552
Robert Arnrine, *Mgr*
EMP: 71
SALES (corp-wide): 94.24MM **Privately Held**
Web: www.roadandrail.com
SIC: 4789 4741 Railroad maintenance and repair services; Rental of railroad cars
PA: Road & Rail Services, Inc.
4233 Bardstown Rd Ste 200
Louisville KY 40218
502 495-6688

(G-11896)
ROBERT A PENNA DMD
4735 Ogletown Stanton Rd Ste 1104 (19713-2089)
PHONE..................302 623-4060
EMP: 5 **EST:** 1999
SALES (est): 220.52K **Privately Held**
Web: www.pennaortho.com
SIC: 8021 Orthodontist

(G-11897)
ROBERT DRESSLER MD
4923 Ogletown Stanton Rd Ste 200 (19713-2081)
PHONE..................302 733-6343
Robert Dressler Md, *Prin*
EMP: 10 **EST:** 2013
SALES (est): 166.31K **Privately Held**
SIC: 8011 Physicians' office, including specialists

(G-11898)
ROBERT ELGART AUTOMOTIVE
698 Pencader Dr (19702-3348)
PHONE..................800 220-7777
Robert Elgart, *Prin*
EMP: 8 **EST:** 2016
SALES (est): 194.9K **Privately Held**
SIC: 2992 Lubricating oils

(G-11899)
ROBERT S CALLAHAN MD PA
32 Omega Dr # J (19713-2058)
PHONE..................302 731-0942
Robert S Callahan, *Prin*
EMP: 10 **EST:** 2008
SALES (est): 244.26K **Privately Held**
SIC: 8031 8011 Offices and clinics of osteopathic physicians; Physicians' office, including specialists

(G-11900)
ROBERT T JONES & FOARD INC
Also Called: Foard R T & Jones Funeral Home
122 W Main St (19711-3241)
PHONE..................302 731-4627
Robert T Foard Junior, *Pr*
EMP: 6 **EST:** 1902
SQ FT: 4,500
SALES (est): 498.22K **Privately Held**
Web: www.rtfoard.com
SIC: 7261 Funeral home

(G-11901)
ROBIN J SIMPSON DO
300 Biddle Ave Ste 200 (19702-3972)
PHONE..................302 838-4750
Nancy Howard, *Prin*
EMP: 8 **EST:** 2010
SALES (est): 112.4K **Privately Held**
SIC: 8011 General and family practice, physician/surgeon

(G-11902)
ROCACCION INC
2035 Sunset Lake Rd Ste B2 (19702-2600)
PHONE..................617 902-8779
Eduardo S Aguilar-alvarez, *Ch Bd*
EMP: 6 **EST:** 2018
SALES (est): 250K **Privately Held**
SIC: 7371 Computer software development

(G-11903)
ROCKEIAS JOURNEY LLC
119 Dufferin Dr (19702-4059)
PHONE..................302 304-3055
EMP: 5 **EST:** 2021
SALES (est): 275.19K **Privately Held**
SIC: 5699 5961 7389 Sports apparel; Electronic shopping; Business Activities at Non-Commercial Site

(G-11904)
ROCKHARD GRANITE LLC
2043 Pulaski Hwy (19702-3503)
PHONE..................302 737-9300
Mike Watkins, *Pr*
EMP: 8 **EST:** 2014
SALES (est): 348.79K **Privately Held**
Web: www.rockhardgranite.net
SIC: 1799 Counter top installation

(G-11905)
ROCKWOOD APARTMENTS
100 Cindy Dr (19702-8132)
PHONE..................302 832-8823
Stephanie Woodruff, *Mgr*
EMP: 10 **EST:** 2001
SALES (est): 134.09K **Privately Held**
Web: www.pettinaro.com
SIC: 6513 Apartment building operators

(G-11906)
RODNEY TRUST CO
100 Commerce Dr Ste 305 (19713-2878)
PHONE..................302 737-1205
Gregory Belcher, *Pr*
EMP: 5 **EST:** 1999
SALES (est): 492.52K **Privately Held**
Web: www.rodneytrust.com
SIC: 6733 Trusts, nec

(G-11907)
ROHM AND HAAS EQUITY CORP (PA)
451 Bellevue Rd (19713-3431)
PHONE..................302 366-0500
EMP: 3
SALES (est): 602.05K **Privately Held**
SIC: 2821 Plastics materials and resins

(G-11908)
ROHM HAAS ELCTRNIC MTLS CMP IN (HQ)
451 Bellevue Rd (19713-3431)
EMP: 49 **EST:** 1968
SALES (est): 102.25MM
SALES (corp-wide): 13.02B **Publicly Held**
SIC: 3471 Polishing, metals or formed products
PA: Dupont De Nemours, Inc.
974 Centre Rd Bldg 730
Wilmington DE 19805
302 774-3034

(G-11909)
ROHM HAAS ELECTRONIC MTLS LLC
Also Called: Dow Electronic Materials
451 Bellevue Rd (19713-3431)
PHONE..................302 366-0500
EMP: 30
SALES (corp-wide): 13.02B **Publicly Held**
Web: www.dupont.com
SIC: 2819 2869 Industrial inorganic chemicals, nec; Industrial organic chemicals, nec
HQ: Rohm And Haas Electronic Materials Llc
455 Forest St
Marlborough MA 01752
508 481-7950

(G-11910)
ROHM HAAS ELECTRONIC MTLS LLC
Also Called: Rohm and Haas Co
231 Lake Dr (19702-3320)
PHONE..................302 366-0500
EMP: 24
SALES (corp-wide): 13.02B **Publicly Held**
Web: www.dupont.com
SIC: 2819 Industrial inorganic chemicals, nec
HQ: Rohm And Haas Electronic Materials Llc
455 Forest St
Marlborough MA 01752
508 481-7950

(G-11911)
ROHMA INC
2035 Sunset Lake Rd Ste B2 (19702-2600)
PHONE..................909 234-5381
Raymond Dai, *Pr*
Terry Giang, *Pr*
EMP: 6 **EST:** 2017
SALES (est): 204.72K **Privately Held**
SIC: 7389 Business Activities at Non-Commercial Site

(G-11912)
ROLLER SERVICE CORPORATION (PA)
Also Called: R S C
23 Mcmillan Way (19713-3400)
PHONE..................302 737-5000
James R Veacock Senior, *Pr*
John Dempsey, *
John Veacock, *
John Gentile, *
EMP: 34 **EST:** 1977
SQ FT: 12,800
SALES (est): 4.65MM
SALES (corp-wide): 4.65MM **Privately Held**
Web: www.rollerservice.com
SIC: 3555 3562 Printing trade parts and attachments; Roller bearings and parts

(G-11913)
ROMANO MASONRY INC
Also Called: Romano Masonry
322 Markus Ct Ste A (19713-1192)
PHONE..................302 368-4155
D Barry Romano, *Pr*
Greg Romano, *
EMP: 14 **EST:** 1976
SQ FT: 4,400
SALES (est): 1.45MM **Privately Held**
Web: www.romanomasonry.com
SIC: 1741 Masonry and other stonework

(G-11914)
ROMER LABS TECHNOLOGY INC
130 Sandy Dr (19713-1147)
P.O. Box 66971 (63166-6971)
PHONE..................855 337-6637
EMP: 25 **EST:** 2012
SALES (est): 5.24MM
SALES (corp-wide): 10.42B **Privately Held**
Web: www.romerlabs.com
SIC: 3823 Analyzers, industrial process type
HQ: Romer Labs Division Holding Gmbh
Erber Campus 1
Getzersdorf 3131
27828030

(G-11915)
ROSARIO FERRANTE GENERAL CONTR
25 Haileys Trl (19711-3059)
PHONE..................302 234-1911
Rosario Ferrante, *Prin*
EMP: 5 **EST:** 2013
SALES (est): 159.76K **Privately Held**
SIC: 1799 Special trade contractors, nec

(G-11916)
ROSEMARIE CIARROCCHI
4745 Ogletown Stanton Rd Ste 134 (19713-2067)
PHONE..................302 731-9225
Rosemarie Ciarrocchi, *Ofcr*
EMP: 8 **EST:** 2016
SALES (est): 31.35K **Privately Held**
Web: www.christianacare.org
SIC: 8049 Physical therapist

GEOGRAPHIC SECTION

Newark - New Castle County (G-11945)

(G-11917)
ROTO-ROOTER SERVICES COMPANY
Also Called: Roto-Rooter
1001 Dawson Dr Ste 3 (19713-5804)
PHONE..................302 659-7637
Marty Smith, *Mgr*
EMP: 9
SALES (corp-wide): 2.13B Publicly Held
Web: www.rotorooter.com
SIC: 7699 1711 7623 Sewer cleaning and rodding; Plumbing, heating, air-conditioning ; Refrigeration repair service
HQ: Roto-Rooter Services Company
255 E 5th St Ste 2500
Cincinnati OH 45202
513 762-6690

(G-11918)
ROULEAU SUZANNE LCSW
8 Blue Jay Dr (19713-1210)
PHONE..................302 479-5157
Suzanne M Rouleau, *Prin*
EMP: 7 EST: 2010
SALES (est): 49.66K Privately Held
Web: rouleau-suzanne-lcsw.hub.biz
SIC: 8322 General counseling services

(G-11919)
ROUTERABBIT INC
2035 Sunset Lake Rd Ste B2 (19702-2600)
PHONE..................508 596-8735
Bhaskar P Rao, *Prin*
EMP: 5 EST: 2017
SALES (est): 77.92K Privately Held
Web: www.routerabbit.com
SIC: 3652 Prerecorded records and tapes

(G-11920)
ROWING AND FITNESS
101 Peoples Dr (19702-1306)
PHONE..................302 722-5445
EMP: 5 EST: 2019
SALES (est): 29.54K Privately Held
Web: www.breakingbarriersde.org
SIC: 7991 Physical fitness facilities

(G-11921)
ROYAL FARMS
457 Stanton Christiana Rd (19713-2119)
PHONE..................302 409-3992
EMP: 5 EST: 2019
SALES (est): 99.15K Privately Held
Web: www.royalfarms.com
SIC: 0191 General farms, primarily crop

(G-11922)
ROYAL TECH AUTO REPAIR LLC
725 Dawson Dr (19713-3413)
PHONE..................302 737-6852
Yin Shen, *Pr*
EMP: 8 EST: 2011
SALES (est): 230.38K Privately Held
Web: www.royaltechauto.com
SIC: 7538 General automotive repair shops

(G-11923)
ROZ HEALTH LLC (PA)
2035 Sunset Lake Rd Ste B2 (19702-2600)
PHONE..................415 259-8992
Nathaniel Beyor, *CEO*
EMP: 6 EST: 2017
SALES (est): 253.54K
SALES (corp-wide): 253.54K Privately Held
SIC: 8082 7371 7389 Home health care services; Computer software development and applications; Business services, nec

(G-11924)
RS WERKS
61b Mcmillan Way (19713-3420)
PHONE..................302 740-1516
EMP: 5 EST: 2019
SALES (est): 91.37K Privately Held
Web: www.rswerks.com
SIC: 7538 General automotive repair shops

(G-11925)
RUBY ROAD LLC
249 E Main St Ste 3 (19711-7323)
PHONE..................856 887-1422
Susan White, *Prin*
EMP: 9 EST: 2017
SALES (est): 201.61K Privately Held
Web: www.rubyroad.org
SIC: 8322 General counseling services

(G-11926)
RULESWARE LLC
10 Lowe Ct (19711-2300)
PHONE..................302 293-4077
EMP: 6 EST: 2019
SALES (est): 62.27K Privately Held
Web: www.rulesware.com
SIC: 8748 Business consulting, nec

(G-11927)
RUMSEY ELECTRIC CO
501 Interchange Blvd (19711-3558)
PHONE..................302 368-9161
Charles Cannon, *Mgr*
EMP: 6 EST: 2017
SALES (est): 198.41K Privately Held
SIC: 5063 Electrical supplies, nec

(G-11928)
RUSSELL ASSOCIATES INC
Also Called: Pall Aerospace
560 Peoples Plz # 125 (19702-4798)
PHONE..................443 992-5777
Ruby R Chandy, *Prin*
EMP: 3
SALES (corp-wide): 31.47B Publicly Held
Web: www.russellassociatesinc.com
SIC: 3812 Acceleration indicators and systems components, aerospace
HQ: Russell Associates Inc
10540 Ridge Rd Ste 300
New Port Richey FL 34654
727 815-3100

(G-11929)
S T GOOD INSURANCE INC (HQ)
Also Called: Nationwide
100 Christiana Medical Ctr (19702-1697)
P.O. Box 5284 (19808-0284)
PHONE..................215 969-8385
TOLL FREE: 800
Jeffrey Good, *VP*
EMP: 18 EST: 1979
SALES (est): 3.57MM
SALES (corp-wide): 260.93MM Privately Held
Web: www.thegoodagency.com
SIC: 6411 Insurance agents, nec
PA: Relation Insurance, Inc.
1277 Treat Blvd Ste 400
Walnut Creek CA 94597
925 937-5858

(G-11930)
SAAS DIGITAL TECHNOLOGIES INC ✪
112 Capitol Trl (19711-3716)
PHONE..................302 994-2000
Mark Marinzoli, *Pr*
EMP: 2 EST: 2023
SALES (est): 87.4K Privately Held
SIC: 7372 Application computer software

(G-11931)
SABINI PAUL MD FACS
537 Stanton Christiana Rd Ste 107 (19713-2145)
PHONE..................302 998-8007
Paul Sabini, *Prin*
EMP: 11 EST: 2007
SALES (est): 161.27K Privately Held
Web: www.premiercosmeticsurgeryde.com
SIC: 8011 8031 Plastic surgeon; Offices and clinics of osteopathic physicians

(G-11932)
SAENGER PORCELAIN
18 Mimosa Dr (19711-7510)
PHONE..................302 738-5349
Peter Saenger, *Owner*
EMP: 2 EST: 1970
SALES (est): 76K Privately Held
Web: www.saengerporcelain.com
SIC: 3262 Tableware, vitreous china

(G-11933)
SAGE HOSPITALITY RESOURCES LLC
Also Called: Fairfield Inn
65 Geoffrey Dr (19713-3603)
PHONE..................302 292-1500
Danielle Brown, *Mgr*
EMP: 163
SALES (corp-wide): 286.23MM Privately Held
Web: fairfield.marriott.com
SIC: 7011 Hotels and motels
PA: Sage Hospitality Resources L.L.C.
1575 Welton St Ste 300
Denver CO 80202
303 595-7200

(G-11934)
SAIENNI STAIRS LLC
120 Sandy Dr Ste E (19713-1135)
PHONE..................302 292-2699
Michael Saienni, *Pr*
EMP: 20 EST: 1988
SQ FT: 2,000
SALES (est): 2.37MM Privately Held
Web: www.saiennistairs.com
SIC: 2431 Millwork

(G-11935)
SALLY BEAUTY SUPPLY LLC
Also Called: Cosmoprof
2665 Capitol Trl (19711-7242)
PHONE..................302 731-0285
Sherry Letnainzyn, *Mgr*
EMP: 5
Web: www.sallybeauty.com
SIC: 5087 Beauty parlor equipment and supplies
HQ: Sally Beauty Supply Llc
3001 Colorado Blvd
Denton TX 76210
940 898-7500

(G-11936)
SALLY BEAUTY SUPPLY LLC
Also Called: Sally Beauty Supply
220 College Sq (19711-5489)
PHONE..................302 737-8837
EMP: 5
Web: www.sallybeauty.com
SIC: 5087 Beauty parlor equipment and supplies
HQ: Sally Beauty Supply Llc
3001 Colorado Blvd
Denton TX 76210
940 898-7500

(G-11937)
SALON LALA MAMOUNE
43 Glencoe Dr (19702-2061)
PHONE..................302 737-5264
F Lima, *Prin*
EMP: 5 EST: 2010
SALES (est): 34.53K Privately Held
SIC: 7231 Hairdressers

(G-11938)
SALON RISPOLI INC
1115 Churchmans Rd (19713-2112)
PHONE..................302 731-9202
Mario Rispoli, *CEO*
EMP: 18 EST: 2007
SALES (est): 997.09K Privately Held
Web: www.salonrispoli.com
SIC: 7231 Hairdressers

(G-11939)
SAMMYS AUTO LLC
23 Gurnsey Dr (19713-4167)
PHONE..................302 368-5203
EMP: 6 EST: 2017
SALES (est): 226.65K Privately Held
SIC: 7538 General automotive repair shops

(G-11940)
SAMTO MEDICAL SERVICES
254 Chapman Rd Ste 103 (19702-5489)
PHONE..................302 266-4933
EMP: 5 EST: 2020
SALES (est): 219.17K Privately Held
Web: www.samtomedical.com
SIC: 8099 Health and allied services, nec

(G-11941)
SANDLER OCCPTNAL MDICINE ASSOC
168 S Main St Ste 206 (19711-7962)
PHONE..................302 369-0171
Howard Sandler, *Pr*
EMP: 9 EST: 2004
SALES (est): 200.79K Privately Held
Web: www.somaonline.com
SIC: 8748 Business consulting, nec

(G-11942)
SANDLER OCCUPATIONAL HEALTH
280 E Main St (19711-7333)
PHONE..................302 607-7365
EMP: 6 EST: 2017
SALES (est): 175.95K Privately Held
SIC: 8099 Health and allied services, nec

(G-11943)
SANTANAS ROOFING LLC
147 Council Cir (19702-4168)
PHONE..................302 887-0067
Angel E Santana, *Pr*
EMP: 5 EST: 2014
SALES (est): 224.87K Privately Held
Web: www.santanascontracting.com
SIC: 1761 Roofing contractor

(G-11944)
SANTO STUCCO
13 Metten Rd (19713-1565)
PHONE..................302 453-0901
Rayma Vreeland, *Prin*
EMP: 3 EST: 2007
SALES (est): 119.74K Privately Held
SIC: 1771 3299 Exterior concrete stucco contractor; Stucco

(G-11945)
SANTORA CPA GROUP PA
220 Continental Dr Ste 112 (19713-4304)
PHONE..................302 737-6200
TOLL FREE: 800

Newark - New Castle County (G-11946)

Bill Santora, *Dir*
EMP: 41 **EST:** 1983
SQ FT: 9,000
SALES (est): 7.5MM **Privately Held**
Web: www.santoracpagroup.com
SIC: 8721 8748 Certified public accountant; Business consulting, nec

(G-11946)
SARAH K SMITH DDS
83 Beech Hill Dr (19711-2945)
PHONE..................302 442-3233
Sarah K Smith D.d.s., *Owner*
EMP: 7 **EST:** 2018
SALES (est): 75.39K **Privately Held**
SIC: 8021 Dentists' office

(G-11947)
SARAH LOCKHEAD
113 E Main St Unit 208 (19711-7351)
PHONE..................484 941-4712
Sarah Lockhead, *Owner*
EMP: 6 **EST:** 2017
SALES (est): 24.4K **Privately Held**
SIC: 8049 Offices of health practitioner

(G-11948)
SARDO & SONS WAREHOUSING INC
401 Pencader Dr Ste A (19702-3339)
PHONE..................302 737-3000
Gary Zicarelli, *Mgr*
EMP: 6
SALES (corp-wide): 18.85MM **Privately Held**
Web: www.sswi.com
SIC: 4225 General warehousing
PA: Sardo & Sons Warehousing, Inc.
  56 W Main St Ste 208
  Christiana DE 19702
  302 369-2100

(G-11949)
SARDO & SONS WAREHOUSING INC
300 White Clay Center Dr (19711-5467)
PHONE..................302 369-0852
Dave Sardo, *Brnch Mgr*
EMP: 7
SALES (corp-wide): 18.85MM **Privately Held**
Web: www.sswi.com
SIC: 4225 General warehousing
PA: Sardo & Sons Warehousing, Inc.
  56 W Main St Ste 208
  Christiana DE 19702
  302 369-2100

(G-11950)
SAREGAMA INDIA LIMITED
Also Called: Saregama
200 Continental Dr Ste 401 (19713-4334)
PHONE..................859 490-0156
Jai Mitwa, *Dir*
EMP: 7
Web: www.saregama.com
SIC: 3652 Compact laser discs, prerecorded
HQ: Saregama India Limited
  2nd Floor, Spencer Building, 30,
  Forjett Street
  Mumbai MH 40003

(G-11951)
SAS NANOTECHNOLOGIES INC
804 Interchange Blvd (19711-3570)
PHONE..................214 235-1008
Sumedh Surwade, *CEO*
EMP: 3 **EST:** 2016
SALES (est): 387.42K **Privately Held**
Web: www.sasnanotechnologies.com
SIC: 2869 Industrial organic chemicals, nec

(G-11952)
SASSY KITTY AND LASH SPA LLC
90 Hickory Pl (19702-4008)
PHONE..................443 983-1125
EMP: 2 **EST:** 2020
SALES (est): 90.74K **Privately Held**
SIC: 2676 Feminine hygiene paper products

(G-11953)
SAVANT INTERNATIONAL HOLDINGS
2035 Sunset Lake Rd (19702-2600)
PHONE..................305 768-9395
Juan Baena, *Pr*
EMP: 50 **EST:** 2017
SIC: 6719 Holding companies, nec

(G-11954)
SAVING OUR YUTH MTTERS INCRPRT
630 Capitol Trl Apt G2 (19711-3872)
PHONE..................917 889-0086
Felicia Wilson, *Prin*
EMP: 6 **EST:** 2016
SALES (est): 67.64K **Privately Held**
SIC: 8322 Individual and family services

(G-11955)
SBS GLOBAL LLC
28 Golf View Dr Apt A6 (19702-1733)
PHONE..................302 898-2911
EMP: 2 **EST:** 2021
SALES (est): 40K **Privately Held**
SIC: 3999 7231 Hair and hair-based products; Beauty shops

(G-11956)
SCALIAS DAY CARE CENTER INC
701 Old Harmony Rd (19711-6919)
PHONE..................302 366-1430
Esther Scalia, *Pr*
EMP: 11 **EST:** 1967
SALES (est): 245.95K **Privately Held**
Web: www.scaliasdaycare.com
SIC: 8351 Group day care center

(G-11957)
SCHILLNG-DGLAS SCHL HAIR DSIGN
211 Louviers Dr (19711-4167)
PHONE..................737 510-0101
Douglas David, *Pt*
James Schilling, *Pt*
EMP: 10 **EST:** 1977
SQ FT: 4,500
SALES (est): 925.73K **Privately Held**
Web: www.schillingdouglas.edu
SIC: 7231 5999 Cosmetology school; Toiletries, cosmetics, and perfumes

(G-11958)
SCHLOSSER ASSOC MECH CNTRS INC
2047 Sunset Lake Rd (19702-2629)
P.O. Box 7984 (19714-7984)
PHONE..................302 738-7333
Paul Schlosser Junior, *Pr*
Steve Dennis, *
Joanne Schlosser, *
Paul Schlosser Senior, *Stockholder*
EMP: 25 **EST:** 1958
SQ FT: 7,000
SALES (est): 4.76MM **Privately Held**
Web: www.schlosserandassociates.com
SIC: 1711 5983 Plumbing contractors; Fuel oil dealers

(G-11959)
SCHOENBECK PA
51 W Periwinkle Ln (19711-6211)
PHONE..................302 584-4519

EMP: 6 **EST:** 2017
SALES (est): 156.01K **Privately Held**
Web: www.schoenbeck.com
SIC: 8621 Professional organizations

(G-11960)
SCHOOLS LANDSCAPING
80 Aleph Dr (19702-1319)
PHONE..................302 613-8224
Michael Schools, *Prin*
EMP: 7 **EST:** 2017
SALES (est): 28.65K **Privately Held**
SIC: 0781 Landscape services

(G-11961)
SCHOON INC
Also Called: System4 of Delaware
200 Continental Dr Ste 401 (19713-4334)
PHONE..................302 894-7574
Alex Wilson, *Pr*
Susan Canale, *Ofcr*
EMP: 9 **EST:** 2017
SALES (est): 238.81K **Privately Held**
Web: www.system4delaware.com
SIC: 7349 Cleaning service, industrial or commercial

(G-11962)
SCIGATE HOLDINGS LLC (PA)
3211 Kildoon Dr (19702-4021)
PHONE..................970 481-4949
EMP: 2 **EST:** 2014
SALES (est): 236.23K
SALES (corp-wide): 236.23K **Privately Held**
SIC: 3999 5043 3499 5112 Stereographs, photographic; Printing apparatus, photographic; Novelties and giftware, including trophies; Albums (photo) and scrapbooks

(G-11963)
SCORELOGIX LLC
1 Innovation Way Ste 300 (19711-5490)
PHONE..................302 294-6532
Vince Leusner, *Prin*
Sureh Annappindi, *CEO*
EMP: 14 **EST:** 2003
SALES (est): 418.98K **Privately Held**
Web: www.scorelogix.com
SIC: 7371 Computer software development

(G-11964)
SDIX LLC
Also Called: Sdix
111 Pencader Dr (19702-3322)
PHONE..................302 456-6789
Wei-wu He Ph.d., *Pr*
EMP: 100 **EST:** 1990
SALES (est): 21.85MM **Privately Held**
Web: www.sdix.com
SIC: 8731 Biotechnical research, commercial
PA: Origene Technologies, Inc.
  9620 Med Ctr Dr Ste 200
  Rockville MD 20850

(G-11965)
SDN ESSENTIALS LLC
40 E Main St Ste 1214 (19711-4639)
PHONE..................415 902-5702
Steve Dyer, *Dir*
Marco Alves, *Dir*
EMP: 11 **EST:** 2015
SALES (est): 82.83K **Privately Held**
Web: www.redapt.com
SIC: 8243 7372 Software training, computer; Business oriented computer software

(G-11966)
SE GAMING SERVICES INC
254 Chapman Rd Ste 208 (19702-5422)
PHONE..................303 867-8090
Krystal Yang, *CEO*
Krystal Yang, *Prin*
Destiny Ellis, *
EMP: 30 **EST:** 2019
SALES (est): 1.56MM **Privately Held**
SIC: 7372 5734 7379 Publisher's computer software; Software, computer games; Computer related consulting services

(G-11967)
SEAN THOMAS JOYNT MSPT ATC
44 Lisa Dr (19702-3755)
PHONE..................302 286-6282
Joynt Sean, *Prin*
EMP: 7 **EST:** 2012
SALES (est): 79.76K **Privately Held**
SIC: 8049 Physical therapist

(G-11968)
SEASONS HSPICE PLLTIVE CARE DE
220 Continental Dr Ste 407 (19713-4311)
PHONE..................847 692-1000
David Schlesinger, *
EMP: 23 **EST:** 2008
SALES (est): 27.61MM **Privately Held**
SIC: 8082 Home health care services

(G-11969)
SECURITY 101 PHILADLEPHIA LLC
Also Called: Security 101
14 Mill Park Ct (19713-2262)
PHONE..................484 369-7101
EMP: 12 **EST:** 2018
SALES (est): 58.83K **Privately Held**
Web: www.security101.com
SIC: 7382 Security systems services

(G-11970)
SECURITY QUALITY
930 Old Harmony Rd Ste H (19713-4161)
PHONE..................302 286-1200
G Dipasquale, *VP*
Gaetano Dipasquale, *VP*
EMP: 7 **EST:** 2006
SALES (est): 360.21K **Privately Held**
Web: www.qualitysecurity.us
SIC: 7382 Burglar alarm maintenance and monitoring

(G-11971)
SECURITY WATCH CORP
260 Chapman Rd Ste 100c (19702-5410)
PHONE..................302 286-6728
Fred Roper, *Mgr*
EMP: 7
SALES (corp-wide): 850.67K **Privately Held**
SIC: 7381 Security guard service
PA: Security Watch Corp
  1254 W Chester Pike # 206
  Havertown PA
  610 924-0110

(G-11972)
SEKOIYA INC
2035 Sunset Lake Rd Ste B2 (19702-2600)
PHONE..................323 761-9028
Kalpana David, *Pr*
EMP: 5 **EST:** 2015
SALES (est): 146.14K **Privately Held**
SIC: 5122 Cosmetics

(G-11973)
SELECT HEALTH SERVICES LLC
560 Peoples Plz (19702-4798)
PHONE..................504 737-4300

GEOGRAPHIC SECTION

Newark - New Castle County (G-12003)

EMP: 7 EST: 2008
SALES (est): 368.72K **Privately Held**
Web: www.selecthealthservices.com
SIC: 8099 Health and allied services, nec

(G-11974)
SELWOR ENTERPRISES INC
Also Called: Goddard Early Learning Center
50 Polly Drummond Hill Rd (19711-5703)
PHONE.................................302 454-9454
Edd Rolls, *Pr*
Ed Rolls, *Pr*
Cindy Rolls, *Sec*
EMP: 16 EST: 1990
SQ FT: 6,500
SALES (est): 146.28K **Privately Held**
SIC: 8351 7299 Preschool center; House and babysitting services

(G-11975)
SENDIBLE USA INC
2035 Sunset Lake Rd Ste 2 (19702-2600)
PHONE.................................646 569-9029
EMP: 6 EST: 2017
SALES (est): 33.85K **Privately Held**
Web: www.sendible.com
SIC: 7371 Computer software development

(G-11976)
SENDSAFELY LLC
40 E Main St Ste 897 (19711-4639)
PHONE.................................917 375-5891
Brian Holyfield, *Managing Member*
EMP: 10 EST: 2013
SALES (est): 500K **Privately Held**
SIC: 7379 Online services technology consultants

(G-11977)
SENIORTECH INC
630 Churchmans Rd Ste 107 (19702-1943)
PHONE.................................302 533-5988
EMP: 6 EST: 2019
SALES (est): 127.3K **Privately Held**
SIC: 8082 Home health care services

(G-11978)
SENTRYLIGHT INC
62 N Chapel St Ste 200 (19711-2238)
PHONE.................................302 420-8844
EMP: 5 EST: 2011
SALES (est): 94.74K **Privately Held**
SIC: 5063 Lighting fixtures

(G-11979)
SEPARATION METHODS TECH INC
31 Blue Hen Dr (19713-3405)
PHONE.................................302 368-0610
EMP: 14 EST: 1993
SQ FT: 10,000
SALES (est): 2.04MM **Privately Held**
Web: www.separationmethods.com
SIC: 3826 8731 Analytical instruments; Biotechnical research, commercial

(G-11980)
SEPAX TECHNOLOGIES INC
5 Innovation Way Ste 100 (19711-5459)
PHONE.................................302 366-1101
Xueying Huang, *Pr*
Helen Gu, *VP Sls*
Xueying Helen, *Prin*
▲ EMP: 13 EST: 2002
SALES (est): 9.24MM **Privately Held**
Web: www.sepax-tech.com
SIC: 5169 3829 Chemicals and allied products, nec; Measuring and controlling devices, nec

(G-11981)
SERENE MINDS LLC
80 Omega Dr Bldg C (19713-2064)
PHONE.................................302 478-6199
EMP: 7 EST: 2019
SALES (est): 218.06K **Privately Held**
Web: www.serenemindsllc.com
SIC: 8011 Psychiatrist

(G-11982)
SERRANO INC
Also Called: Rock Diamond Paving
902 Linfield Rd (19713-2411)
PHONE.................................302 607-1779
Raul Serrano, *Pr*
EMP: 6 EST: 2017
SALES (est): 490K **Privately Held**
Web: www.rockdiamondpaving.com
SIC: 2389 0782 7389 Apparel for handicapped; Lawn and garden services; Swimming pool and hot tub service and maintenance

(G-11983)
SERTIFIER INC
112 Capitol Trl Ste A (19711-3716)
PHONE.................................302 487-3193
EMP: 7 EST: 2020
SALES (est): 352.09K **Privately Held**
Web: www.sertifier.com
SIC: 7372 Prepackaged software

(G-11984)
SERVANT SUPPORT SERVICES LLC
1 Whitehaven Ct (19711-3444)
PHONE.................................215 201-5990
Steven Mason, *Pr*
EMP: 12 EST: 2021
SALES (est): 267.01K **Privately Held**
SIC: 8082 7389 Home health care services; Business services, nec

(G-11985)
SERVICEMASTER OF NEWARK
Also Called: ServiceMaster
116 Cann Rd (19702-4714)
PHONE.................................302 834-8006
George Crossland, *Pr*
Linda Crossland, *VP*
EMP: 15 EST: 2001
SALES (est): 74.92K **Privately Held**
Web: www.servicemaster.com
SIC: 7349 Building maintenance services, nec

(G-11986)
SERVPRO OF NORWALK/WILTON
Also Called: SERVPRO
173 E Main St (19711-7369)
PHONE.................................203 866-2871
EMP: 9 EST: 2018
SALES (est): 26.76K **Privately Held**
Web: www.servpro.com
SIC: 7349 Building maintenance services, nec

(G-11987)
SETH L IVINS MD LLC
620 Stanton Christiana Rd Ste 305 (19713-2135)
PHONE.................................302 824-7280
EMP: 12 EST: 2007
SALES (est): 545.68K **Privately Held**
Web: www.sethivinsmd.com
SIC: 8011 Internal medicine, physician/surgeon

(G-11988)
SGS TELEKOM INC
200 Continental Dr Ste 401 (19713-4334)
PHONE.................................774 482-2236
Radhika Rane, *VP*
EMP: 5 EST: 2021
SALES (est): 73.93K **Privately Held**
SIC: 7372 Prepackaged software

(G-11989)
SHAMMAH LLC
1 S Old Baltimore Pike Ste 201 (19702-1573)
PHONE.................................302 533-7359
EMP: 8 EST: 2019
SALES (est): 308.8K **Privately Held**
SIC: 7371 Computer software development

(G-11990)
SHAMROCK PRINTING COMPANY
261 E Main St (19711-7314)
PHONE.................................302 368-8888
Kathy Sumner, *Pr*
David O'reilly, *VP*
Michael O'reilly, *Treas*
EMP: 6 EST: 1972
SQ FT: 5,000
SALES (est): 519.82K **Privately Held**
Web: www.shamrockprint.net
SIC: 2752 Offset printing

(G-11991)
SHAWNEE 1892 LLC
850 Library Ave Ste 204 (19711-7174)
PHONE.................................302 738-6680
EMP: 5 EST: 2020
SALES (est): 244.1K **Privately Held**
SIC: 7389 Business services, nec

(G-11992)
SHAYLIN M SHORTS
260 Chapman Rd Ste 107 (19702-5410)
PHONE.................................302 494-2451
Shaylin M Shorts, *Owner*
EMP: 8 EST: 2019
SALES (est): 78.99K **Privately Held**
Web: www.vremsing.com
SIC: 8011 Offices and clinics of medical doctors

(G-11993)
SHAYONA HEALTH INC
505 S Twin Lakes Blvd (19711-1826)
PHONE.................................570 677-5509
Jay Patel, *Prin*
EMP: 8 EST: 2015
SALES (est): 269.22K **Privately Held**
SIC: 8099 Health and allied services, nec

(G-11994)
SHELDON LIMITED PARTNERSHIP
Also Called: Bluffs, The
810 Sheldon Dr (19711-4319)
PHONE.................................302 738-3048
Donna Clementoni, *Mgr*
EMP: 6
SALES (corp-wide): 1.07MM **Privately Held**
Web: www.thebluffsapartmenthomes.com
SIC: 6513 Apartment building operators
PA: Sheldon Limited Partnership
    8120 Woodmont Ave Ste 900
    Bethesda MD 20814
    301 951-0500

(G-11995)
SHELLYSONS ELECTRICAL CONTRACT
818 Pencader Dr Unit C (19702-3367)
PHONE.................................302 275-8010
EMP: 8 EST: 2018
SALES (est): 967.72K **Privately Held**
Web: www.shellysons.com
SIC: 1731 General electrical contractor

(G-11996)
SHELTER DEVELOPMENT LLC
Also Called: Vinings At Christiana
200 Vinings Way (19702-7602)
PHONE.................................302 737-4999
Anita Robinson, *Mgr*
EMP: 5
Web: www.viningsatchristiana.com
SIC: 6513 Apartment building operators
HQ: Shelter Development, Llc
    218 N Charles St Ste 220
    Baltimore MD 21201
    410 962-0595

(G-11997)
SHIPTHIS INC
200 Continental Dr Ste 401 (19713-4334)
PHONE.................................209 395-1293
Ahmed Bolwar, *CEO*
EMP: 10
SALES (est): 527.02K **Privately Held**
SIC: 7371 Computer software development and applications

(G-11998)
SHIRLEY I BLACKBURN REAL ESTAT
680 S College Ave (19713-1306)
PHONE.................................302 292-6684
Shirley Blackburn, *Prin*
EMP: 5 EST: 2004
SALES (est): 153.82K **Privately Held**
SIC: 6531 Real estate brokers and agents

(G-11999)
SHORE WELL DRILLERS INC
1168 Elkton Rd (19711-3509)
PHONE.................................302 737-7707
Robert Munyan, *Pr*
EMP: 6 EST: 2002
SALES (est): 371.31K **Privately Held**
SIC: 1781 Water well drilling

(G-12000)
SHOSHIN KARATE LLC
243 S Main St (19711-4564)
PHONE.................................302 369-9300
EMP: 6 EST: 2019
SALES (est): 180.02K **Privately Held**
Web: www.shoshinkarateacademy.com
SIC: 7999 Martial arts school, nec

(G-12001)
SHOUTDEL MAGAZINE LLC
27 Prestbury Sq (19713-2608)
PHONE.................................302 533-6070
EMP: 4 EST: 2018
SALES (est): 226.44K **Privately Held**
Web: www.shoutdel.com
SIC: 2721 Magazines: publishing only, not printed on site

(G-12002)
SHRI SWAMI NARAYAN LLC
Also Called: Howard Johnson
1119 S College Ave (19713-2307)
PHONE.................................302 738-3198
EMP: 76 EST: 1995
SALES (est): 2.42MM **Privately Held**
Web: www.wyndhamhotels.com
SIC: 7011 Hotels and motels

(G-12003)
SIEGFRIED J SCHULZE INC
Also Called: Schulze, S J
12 Mill Park Ct (19713-1986)
PHONE.................................302 737-0403
Lutz S Schulze, *Pr*

Newark - New Castle County (G-12004) GEOGRAPHIC SECTION

Mark M Mackiewicz, *VP*
Elke Mackiewicz, *Sec*
EMP: 10 **EST:** 1976
SQ FT: 1,000
SALES (est): 427.83K **Privately Held**
SIC: 1711 Plumbing contractors

(G-12004)
SIEMENS CORPORATION
100 Gbc Dr (19702-2461)
PHONE...........................302 690-2046
George Plummer, *Dir*
EMP: 21
SALES (corp-wide): 84.48B **Privately Held**
Web: new.siemens.com
SIC: 5063 Electrical apparatus and equipment
HQ: Siemens Corporation
300 New Jersey Ave Nw # 100
Washington DC 20001
202 434-4800

(G-12005)
SIEMENS HLTHCARE DGNOSTICS INC
500 Gbc Dr (19702-2466)
P.O. Box 6101 (19714-6101)
PHONE...........................302 631-7357
Cathy Knutsen, *Mgr*
EMP: 65
SALES (corp-wide): 84.48B **Privately Held**
Web: new.siemens.com
SIC: 5047 2835 Medical equipment and supplies; Diagnostic substances
HQ: Siemens Healthcare Diagnostics Inc.
511 Benedict Ave
Tarrytown NY 10591
914 631-8000

(G-12006)
SIEMENS INDUSTRY INC
500 Gbc Dr (19702-2466)
PHONE...........................302 631-8410
Alex Kobetis, *Brnch Mgr*
EMP: 2
SALES (corp-wide): 84.48B **Privately Held**
Web: new.siemens.com
SIC: 5063 3569 Electrical apparatus and equipment; Heaters, swimming pool: electric
HQ: Siemens Industry, Inc.
100 Technology Dr
Alpharetta GA 30005
847 215-1000

(G-12007)
SIGMA DATA SYSTEMS INC
197 Possum Park Rd (19711-3817)
P.O. Box 9767 (19714-9767)
PHONE...........................302 453-8812
H Dean Spears, *Pr*
Michael Poirier, *VP*
EMP: 11 **EST:** 1978
SQ FT: 5,000
SALES (est): 1.94MM **Privately Held**
Web: www.sigmadatainc.com
SIC: 7379 Computer related consulting services

(G-12008)
SIMBIOSE INC ◊
2035 Sunset Lake Rd (19702-2600)
PHONE...........................708 459-8068
Gabriel Menegat, *CEO*
EMP: 80 **EST:** 2022
SALES (est): 1.26MM **Privately Held**
SIC: 7371 Software programming applications

(G-12009)
SIMM ASSOCIATES INC
800 Pencader Dr (19702-3354)
P.O. Box 7526 (19714-7526)
PHONE...........................302 283-2800
Gregory Simendinger, *CEO*
Gregory L Simendinger, *
Jeff Simendinger, *
EMP: 170 **EST:** 1991
SQ FT: 32,000
SALES (est): 13.18MM **Privately Held**
Web: www.simmassociates.com
SIC: 7322 Collection agency, except real estate

(G-12010)
SIMON MSTR & SIDLOW ASSOC INC
750 Prides Xing Ste 100 (19713-6108)
PHONE...........................302 652-3480
Bill Master, *Pr*
EMP: 8 **EST:** 2012
SALES (est): 129.09K **Privately Held**
Web: www.mastersidlow.com
SIC: 8721 Certified public accountant

(G-12011)
SIMPLE STAYS LLC
254 Chapman Rd (19702-5413)
PHONE...........................949 290-5775
EMP: 5
SALES (est): 76.34K **Privately Held**
SIC: 6531 Real estate leasing and rentals

(G-12012)
SIMPLY CLEAN
103 Linden Tree Ln (19711-7201)
PHONE...........................302 894-1569
Danie Winterringer, *Prin*
EMP: 5 **EST:** 2015
SALES (est): 40.47K **Privately Held**
Web: www.simplycleanjanitorialservices.com
SIC: 7349 Janitorial service, contract basis

(G-12013)
SINKEEAS LOUNGE & BAR LLC
72 Alexis Dr (19702-5496)
PHONE...........................302 434-2530
Sinkeea Gibbs, *Managing Member*
EMP: 12
SALES (est): 406.37K **Privately Held**
SIC: 7389 5813 Business Activities at Non-Commercial Site; Bars and lounges

(G-12014)
SIREN GROUP USA INC
40 E Main St (19711-4639)
PHONE...........................302 298-3307
EMP: 6 **EST:** 2018
SALES (est): 241.97K **Privately Held**
SIC: 8742 Marketing consulting services

(G-12015)
SIRIUSIQ MOBILE LLC
200 Continental Dr (19713-4334)
PHONE...........................888 414-2047
EMP: 12 **EST:** 2015
SALES (est): 890.33K **Privately Held**
Web: www.siriusiq.com
SIC: 8742 7372 General management consultant; Business oriented computer software

(G-12016)
SISU FIT CLUB
119 Saint Regis Dr (19711-3822)
PHONE...........................302 562-3920
EMP: 5 **EST:** 2013
SALES (est): 52.25K **Privately Held**
SIC: 7997 Membership sports and recreation clubs

(G-12017)
SITES FITNESS OF DELAWARE LLC
201 Louviers Dr (19711-4164)
PHONE...........................302 533-6040
EMP: 5 **EST:** 2018
SALES (est): 35.74K **Privately Held**
SIC: 7991 Physical fitness facilities

(G-12018)
SIXTEENPENNY LLC
300 Vassar Dr (19711-3161)
PHONE...........................302 463-7992
Keith Petka, *Prin*
EMP: 5 **EST:** 2017
SALES (est): 62.29K **Privately Held**
SIC: 7374 Computer graphics service

(G-12019)
SKANSKA USA BUILDING INC
313 Wyoming Rd (19711-5311)
PHONE...........................215 495-8790
EMP: 35
SALES (corp-wide): 15.55B **Privately Held**
Web: usa.skanska.com
SIC: 1541 Industrial buildings and warehouses
HQ: Skanska Usa Building Inc.
389 Interpace Pkwy Ste 5
Parsippany NJ 07054
973 753-3500

(G-12020)
SKETCHES AND PIXELS LLC
2035 Sunset Lake Rd B2 (19702-2600)
PHONE...........................312 834-4402
EMP: 5 **EST:** 2018
SALES (est): 100K **Privately Held**
SIC: 7371 Computer software development and applications

(G-12021)
SKILLBIRD LLC
4 Peddlers Row (19702-1525)
PHONE...........................302 216-1811
EMP: 50
SALES (est): 694.16K **Privately Held**
SIC: 8331 Job counseling

(G-12022)
SKIN SOLUTIONS BY WENDI
3023 Mcdaniel Ln (19702-4506)
PHONE...........................302 312-1569
EMP: 5 **EST:** 2017
SALES (est): 61.8K **Privately Held**
Web: www.skinsolutionsbywendi.com
SIC: 7231 Electrolysis and epilatory services

(G-12023)
SKIPLIST INC
2035 Sunset Lake Rd B2 (19702-2600)
PHONE...........................440 855-0319
Andrew Wolfe, *CEO*
EMP: 6 **EST:** 2018
SALES (est): 328.58K **Privately Held**
SIC: 7379 Online services technology consultants

(G-12024)
SKS ENTERPRISE
200 Continental Dr (19713-4334)
PHONE...........................302 310-2511
Kenneth Walker Junior, *Prin*
EMP: 65 **EST:** 2013
SQ FT: 40,000
SALES (est): 5.15MM **Privately Held**
SIC: 6211 6531 Syndicate shares (real estate, entertainment, equip.) sales; Auction, real estate

(G-12025)
SKY TOUCH LLC
4 Washington Ct (19702-6309)
PHONE...........................302 454-7040
Wilson Cabrera, *Prin*
EMP: 5 **EST:** 2016
SALES (est): 101.15K **Privately Held**
SIC: 5087 Beauty salon and barber shop equipment and supplies

(G-12026)
SKY4VIDEO
4 Balanger Rd (19711-3806)
PHONE...........................302 377-3748
Amos Whitridge, *Prin*
EMP: 5 **EST:** 2015
SALES (est): 58.69K **Privately Held**
SIC: 7841 Video tape rental

(G-12027)
SKYGATE INC
2035 Sunset Lake Rd Ste B2 (19702-2600)
PHONE...........................310 601-4201
Chris Parjaszewski, *CEO*
EMP: 7 **EST:** 2019
SALES (est): 166.25K **Privately Held**
SIC: 7371 Software programming applications

(G-12028)
SKYLARK LABS INC
2035 Sunset Lake Rd (19702-2600)
PHONE...........................415 609-3633
Amarjot Singh, *CEO*
EMP: 6 **EST:** 2018
SALES (est): 64.74K **Privately Held**
SIC: 7382 Security systems services

(G-12029)
SKYLINE SUPPLY INC
62 Albe Dr Ste C (19702-1370)
PHONE...........................302 894-9190
Dave Malatesta, *CEO*
Dennis M Ludwig, *Treas*
EMP: 5 **EST:** 2001
SQ FT: 4,000
SALES (est): 716.59K **Privately Held**
SIC: 5085 Fasteners, industrial: nuts, bolts, screws, etc.

(G-12030)
SLEEP DISORDERS CTR-CHRISTIANA
774 Christiana Rd Ste 103 (19713-4248)
PHONE...........................302 623-0650
Mary Hancock, *Prin*
EMP: 11 **EST:** 2011
SALES (est): 196.02K **Privately Held**
Web: www.christianacare.org
SIC: 8093 Drug clinic, outpatient

(G-12031)
SLING IT LLC
523 Capitol Trl Ste C (19711-3859)
PHONE...........................302 648-5488
EMP: 5 **EST:** 2017
SALES (est): 492.23K **Privately Held**
Web: www.sling-it-llc.com
SIC: 4789 Freight car loading and unloading

(G-12032)
SLM CORPORATION (PA)
Also Called: Sallie Mae
300 Continental Dr (19713-4322)
PHONE...........................302 451-0200
Jonathan W Witter, *CEO*

Mary Carter Warren Franke, *Ch Bd*
Steven J Mcgarry, *Ex VP*
Donna F Vieira, *CCO*
Munish Pahwa, *CRO*
EMP: 492 **EST:** 1972
SQ FT: 160,000
SALES (est): 2.37B
SALES (corp-wide): 2.37B **Publicly Held**
Web: www.salliemae.com
SIC: 6111 6141 7322 Student Loan Marketing Association; Personal credit institutions; Adjustment and collection services

(G-12033)
SLR TRANSPORT LLC ✪
245 W General Grey Ct (19702-3830)
PHONE.............................302 316-3306
EMP: 2 **EST:** 2022
SALES (est): 92.41K **Privately Held**
SIC: 3537 Trucks: freight, baggage, etc.: industrial, except mining

(G-12034)
SMART ARMOR PROTECTED LLC
19 Kris Ct (19702-6843)
PHONE.............................480 823-8122
Justin Zastrow, *Managing Member*
EMP: 40 **EST:** 2016
SALES (est): 1.12MM **Privately Held**
SIC: 7379 Online services technology consultants

(G-12035)
SMART PRINTING MGT LLC
560 Peoples Plz Ste 301 (19702-4798)
PHONE.............................855 549-4900
Jane Stevens, *Prin*
EMP: 5 **EST:** 2011
SALES (est): 154.92K **Privately Held**
Web: www.smartprintmgmt.com
SIC: 8741 Management services

(G-12036)
SMB EDUCATION FUNDING LLC
300 Continental Dr (19713-4322)
PHONE.............................302 451-0537
EMP: 5 **EST:** 2016
SALES (est): 934.3K **Privately Held**
SIC: 6722 Management investment, open-end

(G-12037)
SMB LIGHTING
36 Anthony Dr (19702-8429)
PHONE.............................302 733-0664
Shawn Butcher, *Prin*
EMP: 5 **EST:** 2011
SALES (est): 62.72K **Privately Held**
SIC: 3648 Lighting equipment, nec

(G-12038)
SMB PRVATE EDCATN LN TR 2020-A
300 Continental Dr (19713-4322)
PHONE.............................302 451-0537
EMP: 5
SALES (est): 164.82K **Privately Held**
Web: www.salliemae.com
SIC: 6733 Trusts, nec

(G-12039)
SMB PRVATE EDCATN LN TR 2022-A ✪
300 Continental Dr (19713-4322)
PHONE.............................302 451-0537
EMP: 5 **EST:** 2022
SALES (est): 69.68K **Privately Held**
Web: www.salliemae.com
SIC: 6733 Trusts, nec

(G-12040)
SMILE BRITE DENTAL CARE LLC (PA)
300 Biddle Ave Ste 204 (19702-3972)
PHONE.............................302 838-8306
EMP: 6 **EST:** 2005
SALES (est): 987.26K **Privately Held**
Web: www.smilebritedelaware.com
SIC: 8021 Dentists' office

(G-12041)
SMITH BROTHERS COMMUNICATION
27 Harkfort Rd (19702-6307)
P.O. Box 2901 (19805-0901)
PHONE.............................302 293-5224
Terry Smith, *CEO*
EMP: 6 **EST:** 1992
SALES (est): 159.31K **Privately Held**
SIC: 7629 Telecommunication equipment repair (except telephones)

(G-12042)
SMP ENTERPRISES INC
208 Goodsir St (19702-3764)
PHONE.............................302 252-5331
Pat Singh, *Pr*
EMP: 5 **EST:** 2009
SALES (est): 267K **Privately Held**
SIC: 8748 Business consulting, nec

(G-12043)
SMT REAL ESTATE HOLDINGS LLC
16 Bridleshire Rd (19711-2451)
PHONE.............................302 668-3512
Scott Tucker, *Prin*
EMP: 5 **EST:** 2019
SALES (est): 231.53K **Privately Held**
SIC: 6531 Real estate brokers and agents

(G-12044)
SN & PARTNERS ✪
254 Chapman Rd Ste 208 (19702-5422)
PHONE.............................312 826-3255
Esenkul Momunkulov, *Managing Member*
EMP: 5 **EST:** 2022
SALES (est): 70.17K **Privately Held**
SIC: 7379 8299 5149 1389 Computer related services, nec; Language school; Honey; Construction, repair, and dismantling services

(G-12045)
SNMP3 SECURITY LLC
254 Chapman Rd Ste 208 Pmb 10809 (19702-5422)
PHONE.............................302 448-8501
Howard Mallard, *Managing Member*
EMP: 5 **EST:** 2005
SALES (est): 486K **Privately Held**
Web: www.snmp3.com
SIC: 7373 Computer integrated systems design

(G-12046)
SOBIESKI LIFE SAFETY
1325 Old Coochs Bridge Rd (19713-2311)
PHONE.............................800 321-1332
Walter Telford, *Prin*
EMP: 20 **EST:** 2013
SALES (est): 386.73K **Privately Held**
Web: www.sobieskiinc.com
SIC: 7382 Security systems services

(G-12047)
SOBIESKI SERVICES INC
1325 Old Coochs Bridge Rd (19713-2311)
PHONE.............................302 993-0104
EMP: 47 **EST:** 2018
SALES (est): 11.23MM **Privately Held**
Web: www.sobieskiinc.com

SIC: 1711 Plumbing contractors

(G-12048)
SOCIAL ENTERPRISES
112 Capitol Trl (19711-3716)
PHONE.............................302 526-4800
Samet Oynamis, *Prin*
EMP: 6 **EST:** 2016
SALES (est): 385.93K **Privately Held**
Web: www.delawaresirket.com
SIC: 8748 Business consulting, nec

(G-12049)
SOCIETY FOR WHOLE-BODY AUTORAD
110 Executive Dr Ste 7 (19702-3352)
PHONE.............................302 369-5240
Doctor Eric Solon, *Pr*
EMP: 6 **EST:** 1996
SALES (est): 143.92K **Privately Held**
SIC: 8621 Scientific membership association

(G-12050)
SOFTWARE BANANAS LLC
2915 Ogletown Rd Ste 2304 (19713-1927)
PHONE.............................302 348-8488
EMP: 4 **EST:** 2015
SALES (est): 68.85K **Privately Held**
Web: www.softwarebananas.com
SIC: 7372 Prepackaged software

(G-12051)
SOFTWARE RADIO SYSTEMS USA INC
2035 Sunset Lake Rd B2 (19702-2600)
PHONE.............................339 368-6321
Paul Sutton, *Dir*
Ismael Gomez, *Dir*
EMP: 13 **EST:** 2018
SALES (est): 286.28K **Privately Held**
SIC: 7372 7371 Prepackaged software; Custom computer programming services
PA: Software Radio Systems Limited
12a The Ceders Castlejane Woods
Cork

(G-12052)
SOLAR ELECTRIC POWER ASSOC
11 Bridle Brook Ln (19711-2003)
PHONE.............................302 893-1354
EMP: 6 **EST:** 2019
SALES (est): 494.04K **Privately Held**
SIC: 4911 Electric services

(G-12053)
SOLON LABS CORP ✪
Also Called: Solon Labs
254 Chapman Rd Ste 208 (19702-5422)
PHONE.............................860 876-7766
Maxwell J Lyman, *CEO*
EMP: 5 **EST:** 2022
SALES (est): 199.4K **Privately Held**
SIC: 7371 Computer software development and applications

(G-12054)
SOLVAY SPCLTY POLYMERS USA LLC
100 Interchange Blvd (19711-3549)
PHONE.............................302 452-6609
EMP: 17
SALES (corp-wide): 146.05MM **Privately Held**
Web: www.solvay.com
SIC: 2819 Industrial inorganic chemicals, nec
HQ: Solvay Specialty Polymers Usa, L.L.C.
4500 Mcginnis Ferry Rd
Alpharetta GA 30005
770 772-8200

(G-12055)
SONESTA INTL HOTELS CORP
240 Chapman Rd (19702-5405)
PHONE.............................302 453-9200
Michael Fruin, *Brnch Mgr*
EMP: 29
SALES (corp-wide): 449.18MM **Privately Held**
Web: www.sonesta.com
SIC: 7011 Hotels
PA: Sonesta International Hotels Corporation
400 Centre St Ste 100
Newton MA 02458
770 923-1775

(G-12056)
SORTD INC
2035 Sunset Lake Rd B2 (19702-2600)
PHONE.............................415 870-1075
EMP: 9 **EST:** 2019
SALES (est): 220.73K **Privately Held**
Web: www.sortd.com
SIC: 7379 7371 Computer related services, nec; Computer software development and applications

(G-12057)
SOS CALL CENTER INC
86 Albe Dr # 1e (19702-1322)
PHONE.............................302 319-5988
EMP: 6 **EST:** 2019
SALES (est): 156.58K **Privately Held**
Web: www.soscallsolutions.com
SIC: 8748 Business consulting, nec

(G-12058)
SOULSCAPE PUBLISHING LLC
108 Tanglewood Ln (19711-3120)
PHONE.............................303 834-7060
EMP: 4 **EST:** 2018
SALES (est): 89.24K **Privately Held**
Web: www.soulscapepublishing.com
SIC: 2741 Miscellaneous publishing

(G-12059)
SOUTH FORKS INC
Also Called: Party Restaurant Outlet
136 Sandy Dr (19713-1147)
PHONE.............................302 731-0344
Anthony Over, *Pr*
Tom Grant, *VP*
Elizabeth A Over, *Sec*
EMP: 6 **EST:** 1986
SALES (est): 1.93MM **Privately Held**
Web: www.profoods.net
SIC: 5046 5087 5149 5147 Restaurant equipment and supplies, nec; Janitors' supplies; Dried or canned foods; Meats, fresh

(G-12060)
SOUTH PAXON LLC
254 Chapman Rd Ste 208 (19702-5413)
PHONE.............................302 918-5226
Story Brown, *Managing Member*
EMP: 7
SALES (est): 78.16K **Privately Held**
SIC: 2326 Medical and hospital uniforms, men's

(G-12061)
SPALLCO ENTERPRISES INC
Also Called: Spallco Car & Truck Rental
915 S Chapel St (19713-3419)
PHONE.............................302 368-5950
Mike Parkowski, *Mgr*
EMP: 5
Web: www.spallcorentals.com

Newark - New Castle County (G-12062) GEOGRAPHIC SECTION

SIC: **7514** Rent-a-car service
PA: Spallco Enterprises, Inc
702 Philadelphia Pike
Wilmington DE 19809

(G-12062)
SPARKLEAN LAUNDROMAT
750 Peoples Plz (19702-5601)
PHONE...................302 838-2226
EMP: 5 EST: 2017
SALES (est): 45.74K **Privately Held**
SIC: **7215** Laundry, coin-operated

(G-12063)
SPECIAL OLYMPICS DELAWARE INC
619 S College Ave (19716)
PHONE...................302 831-4653
Ann Grunert, *Mgr*
EMP: 10 EST: 1971
SALES (est): 2.18MM **Privately Held**
Web: www.sode.org
SIC: **8322** Association for the handicapped

(G-12064)
SPECIMEN COLLECTION SVCS LLC
64 W Kyla Marie Dr (19702-5432)
PHONE...................302 465-0494
Aaron Johnson, *Owner*
EMP: 6 EST: 2019
SALES (est): 218.48K **Privately Held**
SIC: **8082** Home health care services

(G-12065)
SPECTRUM HONE & LACE LLC
310 Haines St Ste 116 (19717-5226)
PHONE...................313 268-5455
Jessica Cornwell, *Prin*
EMP: 6 EST: 2016
SALES (est): 73.98K **Privately Held**
SIC: **3291** Hones

(G-12066)
SPEEDY PUBLISHING LLC
40 E Main St # 1156 (19711-4639)
PHONE...................888 248-4521
EMP: 7 EST: 2013
SALES (est): 414.23K **Privately Held**
Web: www.speedypublishing.co
SIC: **2741** Miscellaneous publishing

(G-12067)
SPICER MULLIKIN FUNERAL HOMES
121 W Park Pl (19711-4567)
PHONE...................302 368-9500
Harvey C Smith Junior, *Pr*
EMP: 7
SALES (corp-wide): 2.27MM **Privately Held**
Web: www.spicermullikin.com
SIC: **7261** Funeral home
PA: Spicer Mullikin Funeral Homes Inc
1000 N Dupont Hwy
New Castle DE 19720
302 368-9500

(G-12068)
SPINE & ORTHOPEDIC SPECIALIST
1101 Twin C Ln Ste 203 (19713-2159)
PHONE...................302 633-1280
Julie Marley, *Prin*
EMP: 13 EST: 2009
SALES (est): 204.47K **Privately Held**
Web: www.sosptdelaware.com
SIC: **8049** Physical therapist

(G-12069)
SPINE CARE OF DELAWARE
4102b Ogletown Stanton Rd (19713-4183)
PHONE...................302 894-1900
Rachel Magner, *Mng Dir*

Bruce Rudin, *CEO*
EMP: 7 EST: 2000
SQ FT: 1,000
SALES (est): 953.41K **Privately Held**
Web: www.spinecaredelaware.com
SIC: **8011** Orthopedic physician

(G-12070)
SPM TIRE SERVICE LLC ◆
2615 Pulaski Hwy (19702-3909)
PHONE...................302 731-1004
EMP: 6 EST: 2023
SALES (est): 78.16K **Privately Held**
SIC: **3011** Tires and inner tubes

(G-12071)
SPORT CLIPS
1255 Churchmans Rd (19713-2149)
PHONE...................302 294-1774
EMP: 5 EST: 2018
SALES (est): 25.14K **Privately Held**
Web: www.sportclips.com
SIC: **7231** Unisex hair salons

(G-12072)
SPORT CLIPS
450 Peoples Plz (19702-4797)
PHONE...................302 836-9900
EMP: 5 EST: 2018
SALES (est): 80.83K **Privately Held**
Web: www.haircutmennewarkde.com
SIC: **7231** Unisex hair salons

(G-12073)
SPORT CLIPS
1 Washington St (19711-7140)
PHONE...................302 456-9900
EMP: 6 EST: 2015
SALES (est): 85.1K **Privately Held**
Web: www.sportclips.com
SIC: **7231** Beauty shops

(G-12074)
SPORT SPINE CHIROPRACTIC CTRS
4635 Ogletown Stanton Rd (19713-2006)
PHONE...................302 600-1675
EMP: 6 EST: 2019
SALES (est): 54.13K **Privately Held**
Web: www.sportandspinecenter.com
SIC: **8011** Orthopedic physician

(G-12075)
SPRINGBOARD INC
500 Creek View Rd Ste 3e (19711-8549)
PHONE...................302 607-2580
Paul Alford, *Pr*
▲ EMP: 7 EST: 2014
SALES (est): 312.81K **Privately Held**
SIC: **7311** 7371 Advertising agencies; Computer software development and applications

(G-12076)
SPRINGHILL SUITES NEWARK DOWNT
402 Ogletown Rd (19711-5402)
PHONE...................888 205-7322
EMP: 19 EST: 2019
SALES (est): 251.34K **Privately Held**
SIC: **7011** Hotels and motels

(G-12077)
SPRINGSIDE LLC
200 Biddle Ave Ste 205 (19702-3966)
PHONE...................302 838-7223
Jell Rule, *Managing Member*
EMP: 5 EST: 2000
SALES (est): 376.68K **Privately Held**
Web: www.springsideplaza.com

SIC: **6531** Real estate leasing and rentals

(G-12078)
SREEVEN INFOTECH INC
29 Berkley Dr (19702-7700)
PHONE...................302 465-2402
EMP: 5 EST: 2013
SALES (est): 118.28K **Privately Held**
SIC: **7379** Computer related consulting services

(G-12079)
SSN CHRISTIANA LLC
Also Called: Four Pnts By Shrton Nwark Chrs
56 S Old Baltimore Pike (19702-1596)
PHONE...................302 266-6600
Amanda Santare, *Managing Member*
Bryan Chiaramante, *
EMP: 36 EST: 2015
SALES (est): 2.44MM **Privately Held**
Web: sheraton.marriott.com
SIC: **7011** Hotels

(G-12080)
ST JOHNS COMMUNITY SERVICES
26 Golf View Dr (19702-1769)
PHONE...................302 292-1044
EMP: 6 EST: 2019
SALES (est): 70.12K **Privately Held**
SIC: **8011** Offices and clinics of medical doctors

(G-12081)
STACKD STUDIO LLC
Also Called: Stackdkjewelry.com
254 Chapman Rd Ste 208 (19702-5422)
PHONE...................240 304-1085
Jabbar Ford, *CEO*
EMP: 2 EST: 2021
SALES (est): 64.65K **Privately Held**
SIC: **3911** 5632 Jewelry, precious metal; Costume jewelry

(G-12082)
STALLARD CHASSIS CO
123 Sandy Dr (19713-1148)
PHONE...................302 292-1800
Mark Stallard Senior, *Pr*
EMP: 11 EST: 1981
SQ FT: 30,000
SALES (est): 424.53K **Privately Held**
SIC: **3799** Midget autos, power driven

(G-12083)
STANDARD MERGER SUB LLC
Also Called: Sdix
128 Sandy Dr (19713-1147)
PHONE...................302 456-6785
Richard C Birkmeyer, *Pr*
EMP: 30
SALES (corp-wide): 415.01MM **Publicly Held**
SIC: **3826** 2835 Analytical instruments; Diagnostic substances
HQ: Standard Merger Sub, Llc
155 Mineola Blvd
Mineola NY 11501
302 248-1100

(G-12084)
STANDARD PIPE SERVICES LLC
567 Walther Rd (19702-2903)
PHONE...................302 286-0701
Rob Tullman, *Pr*
EMP: 65 EST: 2016
SALES (est): 12.26MM
SALES (corp-wide): 1.27B **Privately Held**
Web: www.standardpipeservices.com
SIC: **1623** Underground utilities contractor
HQ: Aegion Corporation

580 Goddard Ave
Chesterfield MO 63005
636 530-8000

(G-12085)
STANTEC CONSULTING SVCS INC
121 Continental Dr Ste 308 (19713-4325)
PHONE...................302 395-1919
Rich Hubner, *Brnch Mgr*
EMP: 9
SALES (corp-wide): 4.23B **Privately Held**
Web: www.stantec.com
SIC: **8748** Environmental consultant
HQ: Stantec Consulting Services Inc.
410 17th St Ste 1400
Denver CO 80202
303 410-4000

(G-12086)
STANTON DOOR CO INC
Also Called: Stanton Door
20 Shea Way Ste 206 (19713-3447)
PHONE...................302 731-4167
EMP: 11
Web: www.stantondoor.com
SIC: **5031** 5211 Doors, nec; Door and window products

(G-12087)
STAR CAMPUS II
550 S College Ave Ste 107 (19713-1324)
PHONE...................302 514-7586
EMP: 5 EST: 2016
SALES (est): 116.14K **Privately Held**
SIC: **3711** Motor vehicles and car bodies

(G-12088)
STAR STATES LEASING CORP
Also Called: Wsfs Credit
30 Blue Hen Dr Ste 200 (19713-3445)
PHONE...................302 283-4500
Mike Muller, *VP*
John Hricik, *
EMP: 35 EST: 1974
SALES (est): 7.83MM
SALES (corp-wide): 963.95MM **Publicly Held**
SIC: **6159** 7515 Automobile finance leasing; Passenger car leasing
HQ: Wilmington Savings Fund Society
500 Delaware Ave
Wilmington DE 19801
302 792-6000

(G-12089)
STARFISH SPCLTY INSUR SVCS LLC
200 Continental Dr Ste 401 (19713-4334)
PHONE...................914 556-3200
Jeremy R Hitzig, *Managing Member*
EMP: 6 EST: 2021
SALES (est): 630.33K **Privately Held**
SIC: **6411** Advisory services, insurance

(G-12090)
STARK TRUSS COMPANY INC
10 Aleph Dr (19702-1319)
PHONE...................302 368-8566
EMP: 11
SALES (corp-wide): 144.79MM **Privately Held**
Web: www.starktruss.com
SIC: **2439** 2426 Trusses, wooden roof; Hardwood dimension and flooring mills
PA: Stark Truss Company, Inc.
109 Miles Ave Sw
Canton OH 44710
330 478-2100

GEOGRAPHIC SECTION

Newark - New Castle County (G-12121)

(G-12091)
STATE FARM JEFF GARDINER
Also Called: State Farm Insurance
1352 Marrows Rd (19711-5475)
PHONE.................302 286-7130
Rocky Billitto, *Mgr*
EMP: 5 **EST:** 2016
SALES (est): 173.29K **Privately Held**
Web: www.302agent.com
SIC: 6411 Insurance agents and brokers

(G-12092)
STATE WIDE PLUMBING INC
Also Called: Statewide Plumbing
27 Albe Dr Ste J (19702-1325)
P.O. Box 77 (19709-0077)
PHONE.................302 292-0924
Tom Pulgini, *Pr*
EMP: 11 **EST:** 1993
SQ FT: 2,000
SALES (est): 426.71K **Privately Held**
SIC: 1711 Plumbing contractors

(G-12093)
STEADY INC
70 Aleph Dr Ste C (19702-1359)
PHONE.................302 266-4144
Xuan Hou, *Pr*
EMP: 5 **EST:** 2014
SALES (est): 201.69K **Privately Held**
SIC: 6512 Nonresidential building operators

(G-12094)
STEDIM N SARTORIUS AMER INC
221 Lake Dr (19702-3320)
PHONE.................800 635-2906
EMP: 33
SALES (corp-wide): 4.34B **Privately Held**
Web: www.sartorius.us
SIC: 8731 Biological research
HQ: Sartorius Stedim North America Inc.
565 Johnson Ave
Bohemia NY 11716

(G-12095)
STEFANIE N MARSHALL DO
875 Aaa Blvd Ste B (19713-3624)
PHONE.................302 454-9800
Stefanie Marshall, *Pr*
EMP: 8 **EST:** 2018
SALES (est): 93.37K **Privately Held**
SIC: 8011 Gynecologist

(G-12096)
STEPHEN A NIEMOELLER DMD PA
523 Capitol Trl (19711-3859)
PHONE.................302 737-3320
Stephen A Niemoeller, *Owner*
EMP: 5 **EST:** 2007
SALES (est): 245.23K **Privately Held**
Web: www.nemodentistry.com
SIC: 8021 Dentists' office

(G-12097)
STEPHEN M BENECK M D
87 Omega Dr (19713-2065)
PHONE.................302 733-0980
Stephen Beneck, *Prin*
EMP: 11 **EST:** 2014
SALES (est): 177.75K **Privately Held**
Web: www.delawarebackpain.com
SIC: 8011 Orthopedic physician

(G-12098)
STEPHEN S GRUBBS M D
4701 Ogletown Stanton Rd # 2200
(19713-7000)
PHONE.................302 366-1200
Stephen Grubbs, *Pt*
EMP: 8 **EST:** 2018
SALES (est): 241.59K **Privately Held**
SIC: 8011 Oncologist

(G-12099)
STEPSHIP LLC
2401 Ogletown Rd (19711-6403)
PHONE.................773 503-2110
EMP: 5 **EST:** 2020
SALES (est): 157.63K **Privately Held**
Web: www.stepship.com
SIC: 4731 Brokers, shipping

(G-12100)
STEREOCHEMICAL INC
667 Dawson Dr Ste E (19713-3437)
PHONE.................302 266-0700
Lawrence D Kwart, *Pr*
Edward J Gaffney, *CFO*
EMP: 3 **EST:** 1996
SQ FT: 3,800
SALES (est): 233.02K **Privately Held**
Web: www.efty.com
SIC: 8731 8734 2869 Chemical laboratory, except testing; Testing laboratories; Industrial organic chemicals, nec

(G-12101)
STERN & EISENBERG PC
500 Creek View Rd Ste 304 (19711-8549)
PHONE.................302 731-7200
EMP: 8 **EST:** 2015
SALES (est): 133.92K **Privately Held**
Web: www.sterneisenberg.com
SIC: 8111 General practice attorney, lawyer

(G-12102)
STONES SOUP INC (PA)
Also Called: Japan Gourmet Pass
2035 Sunset Lake Rd B2 (19702-2600)
PHONE.................803 835-7123
Jaume Colomer, *CEO*
EMP: 5
SALES (est): 107.01K
SALES (corp-wide): 107.01K **Privately Held**
SIC: 7371 Computer software development and applications

(G-12103)
STORYBOARDS INC
2035 Sunset Lake Rd (19702-2600)
PHONE.................214 272-0222
Gavin Glick, *CEO*
EMP: 8
SALES (est): 579.99K **Privately Held**
Web: www.storyboards.io
SIC: 2273 Art squares

(G-12104)
STOVOO INC
256 Chapman Rd Ste 105-4 (19702-5499)
PHONE.................302 451-9589
Faithful Freeman, *Pr*
EMP: 5 **EST:** 2021
SALES (est): 285.37K **Privately Held**
SIC: 4212 7389 Delivery service, vehicular; Business services, nec

(G-12105)
STRATEGIC SOLUTIONS INTL INC
700 Barksdale Rd Ste 6 (19711-3260)
PHONE.................302 525-6313
Connie R Charles, *CEO*
EMP: 5 **EST:** 1990
SALES (est): 849.48K **Privately Held**
Web: www.ssizone.com
SIC: 8742 Business management consultant

(G-12106)
STRATEGY HOUSE INC
231 Executive Dr Ste 15 (19702-3324)
PHONE.................302 658-1500
Paul Bastianelli, *Pr*
EMP: 6 **EST:** 2009
SALES (est): 429.76K **Privately Held**
Web: www.strategyhouseinc.com
SIC: 8748 Business consulting, nec

(G-12107)
STRATIS VISUALS LLC
20 Tyler Way Ste 102 (19713-3465)
PHONE.................860 482-1208
EMP: 11
SALES (corp-wide): 9.85MM **Privately Held**
Web: www.mccoyprinting.com
SIC: 2752 Offset printing
PA: Stratis Visuals Llc
129 Industrial Ln
Torrington CT 06790
860 482-1208

(G-12108)
STRATUS BUILDING SOLUTIONS
625 Dawson Dr Ste D (19713-3433)
PHONE.................302 414-9749
EMP: 7 **EST:** 2017
SALES (est): 47.61K **Privately Held**
Web: www.stratusclean.com
SIC: 7349 Janitorial service, contract basis

(G-12109)
STUART JA INC
102 Albe Dr (19702-1347)
PHONE.................302 378-8299
Scott Stuart, *Prin*
EMP: 6 **EST:** 2012
SALES (est): 91.18K **Privately Held**
SIC: 1731 General electrical contractor

(G-12110)
STUDENT MEDIA GROUP
500 Creek View Rd Ste 3e (19711-8549)
PHONE.................302 607-2580
▲ **EMP:** 14 **EST:** 2009
SALES (est): 716.29K **Privately Held**
Web: www.bloomplanners.com
SIC: 2721 Magazines: publishing and printing

(G-12111)
STUDIO GREEN APARTMENTS
91 Thorn Ln (19711-4489)
PHONE.................302 544-9070
EMP: 6 **EST:** 2010
SALES (est): 129.25K **Privately Held**
Web: www.campuslivingvillages.com
SIC: 6513 Apartment building operators

(G-12112)
STYLES CELEBRITY
230 University Plz (19702-1550)
PHONE.................302 286-7825
EMP: 6 **EST:** 2014
SALES (est): 36.59K **Privately Held**
SIC: 7231 Hairdressers

(G-12113)
STYLIN IMAGE
1007 Vinings Way (19702-7615)
PHONE.................302 407-8698
Pedro Morales, *CEO*
EMP: 7 **EST:** 2005
SALES (est): 66.39K **Privately Held**
SIC: 7299 Apartment locating service

(G-12114)
STYLING HER ESTEEM
10 Swansea Ln (19702-4286)
PHONE.................302 494-1010
Marc Herring, *Prin*
EMP: 6 **EST:** 2015
SALES (est): 73.97K **Privately Held**
SIC: 7231 Hairdressers

(G-12115)
SUBER TANISHA LASHAY LPN
143 Chestnut Crossing Dr Apt H
(19713-2677)
PHONE.................215 910-8361
Tanisha Suber, *Pr*
EMP: 6 **EST:** 2016
SALES (est): 41.29K **Privately Held**
SIC: 8049 Offices of health practitioner

(G-12116)
SUBURBAN PLAZA MERCHANTS ASSN
226 Suburban Dr (19711-3596)
PHONE.................302 737-8072
John Mayer, *Prin*
EMP: 5 **EST:** 2017
SALES (est): 37.81K **Privately Held**
SIC: 8699 Charitable organization

(G-12117)
SUCCULENTS SOAP SAND SCENTS
103 Rockrose Dr (19711-6825)
PHONE.................302 757-0697
Jay Lynch, *Prin*
EMP: 4 **EST:** 2015
SALES (est): 192.28K **Privately Held**
SIC: 2844 Perfumes, cosmetics and other toilet preparations

(G-12118)
SUMMER CONSULTANTS INC
131 Continental Dr Ste 302 (19713-4323)
PHONE.................484 493-4150
Edward Kroman, *Mgr*
EMP: 10
SALES (corp-wide): 5.45MM **Privately Held**
Web: www.summerconsultants.com
SIC: 8711 Engineering services
PA: Summer Consultants Inc
7900 Westpark Dr Ste A405
Mc Lean VA 22102
703 556-8820

(G-12119)
SUMMIT BRIDGE INV PRPTS LLC
912 Westerly Ct (19702-4823)
PHONE.................410 499-1456
EMP: 5 **EST:** 2016
SQ FT: 7,200
SALES (est): 241.58K **Privately Held**
SIC: 6531 Real estate leasing and rentals

(G-12120)
SUMMIT INDUSTRIAL CORPORATION
93 Albe Dr Ste A (19702-1362)
PHONE.................302 368-2718
Sandra Patnovic, *Pr*
Robert Patnovic, *Sec*
EMP: 5 **EST:** 1970
SALES (est): 488.3K **Privately Held**
Web: www.summitindustrialcorp.com
SIC: 3599 Machine shop, jobbing and repair

(G-12121)
SUMMIT MECHANICAL INC
106 Canal Way (19702-4840)
PHONE.................302 373-1132
Edward Mendez, *Prin*
EMP: 9 **EST:** 2010

Newark - New Castle County (G-12122) — **GEOGRAPHIC SECTION**

SALES (est): 116.41K **Privately Held**
Web: www.summitmechanical.org
SIC: 1711 Mechanical contractor

(G-12122)
SUMMIT PROPERTIES INC
Also Called: Summit Pike Creek
100 Red Fox Ln Bldg 100 (19711-5999)
PHONE..................302 737-3747
Christina Hunt, *Mgr*
EMP: 8
Web: www.summitproperties.ca
SIC: 6513 Apartment building operators
HQ: Summit Properties Inc.
309 E Morehead St Ste 200
Charlotte NC 28202
704 334-3000

(G-12123)
SUNFLIXX LLC
4 Peddlers Row Unit 150 (19702-1525)
PHONE..................302 206-0859
EMP: 6
SALES (est): 311.93K **Privately Held**
SIC: 5023 Kitchen tools and utensils, nec

(G-12124)
SUNFLOWERS
503 Nottingham Rd (19711-7405)
PHONE..................302 731-3150
Marianne Barrett, *Prin*
EMP: 5 EST: 2013
SALES (est): 107.76K **Privately Held**
SIC: 7389 Business Activities at Non-Commercial Site

(G-12125)
SUNLIGHT SALON LLC
610 Plaza Dr (19702-6368)
PHONE..................302 456-1799
Ben Ho, *Pt*
EMP: 9 EST: 2004
SALES (est): 213.92K **Privately Held**
Web: www.sunlightsalon.net
SIC: 7231 Manicurist, pedicurist

(G-12126)
SUNNY GALLERY LLC
349 Matthew Flocco Dr (19713-2301)
PHONE..................302 757-3960
EMP: 5 EST: 2010
SALES (est): 62K **Privately Held**
SIC: 8412 Art gallery

(G-12127)
SUPER C INC
226 W General Grey Ct (19702-3831)
PHONE..................302 533-6024
Fei Deng, *Pr*
EMP: 9 EST: 2016
SALES (est): 123.42K **Privately Held**
Web: www.super-cone.com
SIC: 7699 Cleaning services

(G-12128)
SUPERCRITICAL FLUID TECH
Also Called: SUPERCRITICAL FLUID TECHNOLOGIES, INC
120 Sandy Dr Ste 2b (19713-1135)
PHONE..................302 738-3420
EMP: 8
Web: www.supercriticalfluids.com
SIC: 3826 Analytical instruments
PA: Supercritical Fluid Technologies, Inc.
1 Innovation Way Ste 303
Newark DE 19711

(G-12129)
SUPERCRITICAL FLUID TECH INC (PA)

Also Called: Sft
1 Innovation Way Ste 303 (19711-5490)
PHONE..................302 738-3420
Robert James, *Pr*
Kirk Chandler, *Prin*
▲ EMP: 4 EST: 1994
SQ FT: 7,000
SALES (est): 1.21MM **Privately Held**
Web: www.supercriticalfluids.com
SIC: 3826 5084 Analytical instruments; Industrial machinery and equipment

(G-12130)
SUPERIOR METALS ALLOYS USA INC
200 Continental Dr Ste 401 (19713-4334)
PHONE..................860 208-6438
Clarence Brunet, *Pr*
EMP: 7 EST: 2017
SALES (est): 782.22K **Privately Held**
Web: www.superiormetals.ca
SIC: 5051 Steel

(G-12131)
SURE GOOD FOODS USA LLC
40 E Main St Ste 1187 (19711-4639)
PHONE..................905 288-1136
Troy Warren, *Pr*
EMP: 45 EST: 2017
SALES (est): 7.32MM
SALES (corp-wide): 329.17MM **Privately Held**
SIC: 5147 Meats and meat products
PA: Sure Good Foods Ltd
2333 North Sheridan Way Suite 100
Mississauga ON L5K 1
905 286-1619

(G-12132)
SURGE NETWORKS INC
2035 Sunset Lake Rd B2 (19702-2600)
PHONE..................206 432-5047
EMP: 8 EST: 2018
SALES (est): 401.63K **Privately Held**
SIC: 7371 Computer software development and applications

(G-12133)
SURGICAL ASSOC OF NEWARK
324 E Main St (19711-7150)
PHONE..................302 737-4990
EMP: 9 EST: 2015
SALES (est): 241.49K **Privately Held**
SIC: 8011 Medical centers

(G-12134)
SURGICAL CRITICAL ASSOC
4735 Ogletown Stanton Rd # 3301 (19713-7021)
PHONE..................302 623-4370
EMP: 8 EST: 2019
SALES (est): 159.82K **Privately Held**
SIC: 8011 Surgeon

(G-12135)
SUSAN T FISCHER
Also Called: Let's Have Fun Daycare
57 Avignon Dr (19702-5553)
PHONE..................302 832-2570
Susan T Fischer, *Prin*
EMP: 9 EST: 2011
SALES (est): 55.41K **Privately Held**
SIC: 8351 Group day care center

(G-12136)
SUSSEX PROTECTION SERVICE LLC
126 Sandy Dr (19713-1147)
P.O. Box 568 (19933-0568)
PHONE..................302 832-5700
EMP: 15 EST: 1998

SQ FT: 4,000
SALES (est): 2.16MM **Privately Held**
Web: www.sussexprotection.com
SIC: 7359 5084 Work zone traffic equipment (flags, cones, barrels, etc.); Safety equipment

(G-12137)
SUZANNE S TOWNSEND
774 Christiana Rd Ste 201 (19713-4221)
PHONE..................302 593-6253
Suzanne Townsend, *Ofcr*
EMP: 6 EST: 2018
SALES (est): 96.53K **Privately Held**
SIC: 8049 Offices of health practitioner

(G-12138)
SWAROVSKI US HOLDING LIMITED
715 Christiana Mall (19702-3213)
PHONE..................302 737-4811
Alice Andree, *Brnch Mgr*
EMP: 4
SALES (corp-wide): 3.33B **Privately Held**
SIC: 3961 Costume jewelry
HQ: Swarovski U.S. Holding Limited
1 Kenney Dr
Cranston RI 02920

(G-12139)
SWEDISH BRICKYARD
2404 Sunset Lake Rd (19702-4039)
PHONE..................302 893-4143
Michael Rausch, *Prin*
EMP: 5 EST: 2015
SALES (est): 112.78K **Privately Held**
SIC: 1741 Masonry and other stonework

(G-12140)
SWEETEN COMPANIES INC
Also Called: Sweeten Solar
149 Salem Church Rd (19713-2941)
PHONE..................302 737-6161
EMP: 3
SALES (est): 481.12K **Privately Held**
Web: www.sweetencontracting.com
SIC: 5074 3448 1611 Heating equipment and panels, solar; Sunrooms, prefabricated metal; General contractor, highway and street construction

(G-12141)
SWEETS BY SAMANTHA LLC
Also Called: Sweet Luci
3 Linette Ct (19702-6815)
PHONE..................302 740-2218
Samantha Zebrowski, *Mng Pt*
Samantha Zebrowski, *Managing Member*
EMP: 7 EST: 2010
SALES (est): 250K **Privately Held**
SIC: 2051 Cakes, bakery: except frozen

(G-12142)
SWIFT POOLS INC
1123 Capitol Trl (19711-3921)
PHONE..................302 738-9800
John E Swift Senior, *Pr*
John E Swift Iv, *Treas*
Bonnie Swift, *
EMP: 32 EST: 1974
SQ FT: 3,500
SALES (est): 944.05K **Privately Held**
Web: www.swiftpools.com
SIC: 1799 5999 Swimming pool construction ; Swimming pools, hot tubs, and sauna equipment and supplies

(G-12143)
SWIIRL INC (PA) ◆
Also Called: Swiirl
254 Chapman Rd Ste 208 (19702-5422)

PHONE..................650 430-5256
Daniel Mohanrao, *CEO*
EMP: 3 EST: 2023
SALES (est): 146.44K
SALES (corp-wide): 146.44K **Privately Held**
SIC: 7372 Educational computer software

(G-12144)
SWIPETECH LIMITED INC
256 Chapman Rd Ste 105-4 (19702-5499)
PHONE..................929 293-8175
Temidayo Duada, *Prin*
Ayodeji Audu, *Prin*
Oyejide Odofin, *Prin*
EMP: 6 EST: 2021
SALES (est): 67.44K **Privately Held**
SIC: 7389 Financial services

(G-12145)
SYFT ANALYTICS INC (PA)
Also Called: Syft Analytics
200 Continental Dr Ste 401 (19713-4334)
PHONE..................862 308-0525
Vangelis Kyriazis, *CEO*
Eleftherios Kyriazis, *CPO*
EMP: 14 EST: 2018
SALES (est): 1.28MM
SALES (corp-wide): 1.28MM **Privately Held**
SIC: 7371 Computer software development and applications

(G-12146)
SYGUL INC
Also Called: Edufar
2035 Sunset Lake Rd B2 (19702-2600)
PHONE..................315 384-1848
EMP: 20 EST: 2018
SALES (est): 25K **Privately Held**
Web: www.sygul.com
SIC: 7371 Computer software development

(G-12147)
SYNERGY MEDICAL USA INC
2915 Ogletown Rd Ste 2565 (19713-1927)
PHONE..................302 444-0163
Jean Boutin, *Pr*
EMP: 10 EST: 2021
SALES (est): 863.75K **Privately Held**
SIC: 5047 Medical and hospital equipment

(G-12148)
SYSTEMS APPROACH LTD
309 Palomino Dr (19711-8310)
PHONE..................302 743-6331
Roger Voyce, *Pr*
Roger Boyce, *Pr*
EMP: 7 EST: 1983
SALES (est): 554.23K **Privately Held**
Web: www.systemsapproachltd.com
SIC: 7389 Drafting service, except temporary help

(G-12149)
SYSTEMS INC COMMUNIT
310 Valley Stream Dr (19702-2906)
PHONE..................302 294-1872
EMP: 5 EST: 2012
SALES (est): 32.92K **Privately Held**
SIC: 8322 Community center

(G-12150)
T & F LOGISTICS LLC
451 Strathaven Ct (19702-5029)
PHONE..................302 602-1285
Tyrell A Drumgo, *Pr*
EMP: 5 EST: 2016
SALES (est): 97.93K **Privately Held**

GEOGRAPHIC SECTION

Newark - New Castle County (G-12177)

SIC: 4789 Cargo loading and unloading services

(G-12151)
T AND T WIRELESS
2515 Kirkwood Hwy (19711-7249)
PHONE.................302 894-1189
Tnt Uppal, *Owner*
EMP: 7 **EST:** 2010
SALES (est): 222.61K **Privately Held**
SIC: 4812 Cellular telephone services

(G-12152)
T B PAINTING RESTORATION
162 Madison Dr (19711-4406)
PHONE.................610 283-4100
EMP: 4 **EST:** 2016
SALES (est): 68.05K **Privately Held**
SIC: 5198 2851 Paints, varnishes, and supplies; Wood fillers or sealers

(G-12153)
T-MOBILE USA INC
Also Called: T-Mobile Store 9933
164 Christiana Mall Spc 1548 (19702-3202)
PHONE.................302 366-8380
EMP: 6
SALES (corp-wide): 79.57B **Publicly Held**
Web: www.t-mobile.com
SIC: 4812 Cellular telephone services
HQ: T-Mobile Usa, Inc.
12920 Se 38th St
Bellevue WA 98006
425 378-4000

(G-12154)
TADE INFO TECH SOLUTIONS
60 Avignon Dr (19702-5518)
PHONE.................302 832-1449
Thomas Kitchen, *Pr*
EMP: 5 **EST:** 2005
SALES (est): 192.39K **Privately Held**
SIC: 8748 Business consulting, nec

(G-12155)
TAGHLEEF INDUSTRIES INC (DH)
Also Called: Aet Films
800 Prides Xing Ste 200 (19713)
PHONE.................302 326-5500
Detlef Schuhmann, *CEO*
Rashed Al Ghurair, *
Wolfgang Meyer, *
◆ **EMP:** 92 **EST:** 1986
SQ FT: 50,000
SALES (est): 275.37MM **Privately Held**
Web: www.ti-films.com
SIC: 3081 Polypropylene film and sheet
HQ: Taghleef Industries (L L C)
Near Dutco Tanant Ti Building,
Industrial Area 1, Jebel Ali
Dubai

(G-12156)
TALENTMATCH INC
256 Chapman Rd (19702-5499)
PHONE.................508 825-6171
EMP: 5 **EST:** 2021
SALES (est): 240.19K **Privately Held**
Web: www.talentmatch.net
SIC: 7371 Computer software development and applications

(G-12157)
TALLEY BROTHERS INC
210 Executive Dr Ste 7 (19702-3335)
P.O. Box 5505 (19714-5505)
PHONE.................302 224-5376
R Scott Killen, *Pr*
William West, *
EMP: 39 **EST:** 1985
SALES (est): 3.9MM **Privately Held**
Web: www.talleybrothersinc.com
SIC: 1541 1771 1542 Industrial buildings, new construction, nec; Concrete work; Commercial and office building, new construction

(G-12158)
TAMP INC
Also Called: TAMP
2035 Sunset Lake Rd Ste B2 (19702-2600)
PHONE.................302 283-9195
David Hall, *CEO*
EMP: 10 **EST:** 2019
SALES (est): 250K **Privately Held**
Web: www.theampdr.com
SIC: 8299 8011 7379 5734 Educational service, nondegree granting: continuing educ.; Offices and clinics of medical doctors ; Online services technology consultants; Software, business and non-game

(G-12159)
TANTALUM BOLT & FASTENER LLC
Also Called: Extreme Bolt & Fastener
280 E Main St Ste 107 (19711-7324)
PHONE.................888 393-4517
James Sullivan, *Pt*
EMP: 10 **EST:** 2012
SALES (est): 7MM **Privately Held**
Web: www.extreme-bolt.com
SIC: 3965 5085 5072 Fasteners; Fasteners, industrial: nuts, bolts, screws, etc.; Miscellaneous fasteners

(G-12160)
TANTINI LLC
136 S Main St (19711-7974)
PHONE.................302 444-4024
Sonya Bright, *Brnch Mgr*
EMP: 26
SALES (corp-wide): 307.68K **Privately Held**
Web: www.mytantini.com
SIC: 7299 Tanning salon
PA: Tantini, L.L.C.
172 William L Dalton Dr
Glassboro NJ 08028
856 582-0826

(G-12161)
TAPORTERELECTRIC
104 Smith Woods Ln (19711-4722)
PHONE.................302 366-0108
Todd Porter, *Prin*
EMP: 5 **EST:** 2009
SALES (est): 174.39K **Privately Held**
SIC: 4911 Electric services

(G-12162)
TASHA P BROWN
Also Called: Tpwb69
107 Durso Dr (19711-6903)
PHONE.................732 948-7591
Tasha P Brown, *Owner*
EMP: 5 **EST:** 2019
SALES (est): 116.3K **Privately Held**
SIC: 4731 Freight transportation arrangement

(G-12163)
TAYLOR MCCORMICK INC
409 Abbotsford Ln (19711-1511)
PHONE.................302 897-2171
Mitsuru Tanaka, *Engr*
EMP: 10 **EST:** 1946
SALES (est): 95.39K **Privately Held**
Web: www.mccormicktaylor.com
SIC: 8711 Consulting engineer

(G-12164)
TC CLEAN
5 Vassar Dr (19711-3157)
PHONE.................302 737-3360
EMP: 5 **EST:** 2018
SALES (est): 131.33K **Privately Held**
Web: www.tcclean.net
SIC: 7699 Cleaning services

(G-12165)
TDM PHARMACEUTICAL RES INC
100 Biddle Ave Ste 202 (19702-3983)
PHONE.................302 832-1008
Changfu Cheng, *Pr*
EMP: 5 **EST:** 2020
SALES (est): 89.56K **Privately Held**
SIC: 8748 Business consulting, nec

(G-12166)
TDM PHARMACEUTICAL RES LLC
100 Biddle Ave Ste 202 (19702-3983)
PHONE.................302 832-1008
EMP: 9 **EST:** 2008
SALES (est): 988.37K **Privately Held**
Web: www.tdmpharmaceuticalresearch.com
SIC: 8733 Noncommercial research organizations

(G-12167)
TECH BEACH RETREAT INC
2035 Sunset Lake Rd (19702-2600)
PHONE.................786 790-5922
Kyle Maloney, *Dir*
EMP: 10
SALES (est): 351.13K **Privately Held**
Web: www.techbeach.net
SIC: 7372 Prepackaged software

(G-12168)
TECHADOX INC
258 Chapman Rd Ste 202 (19702-5443)
PHONE.................302 691-9130
EMP: 12 **EST:** 2016
SALES (est): 905.35K **Privately Held**
Web: www.techadox.com
SIC: 7389 Brokers, business: buying and selling business enterprises

(G-12169)
TECHNCAL STFFING RESOURCES LLC
Also Called: Allstates Technical Services
262 Chapman Rd Ste 101 (19702-5448)
P.O. Box 8255 (19714-8255)
PHONE.................302 452-9933
Robert Pinson, *Genl Mgr*
EMP: 135
Web: www.technicalstaffingresources.com
SIC: 8711 Construction and civil engineering
HQ: Technical Staffing Resources, Llc
10 Inverness Center Pkwy
Hoover AL 35242

(G-12170)
TECHNICARE INC
39 Lakewood Cir (19711-2349)
PHONE.................302 322-7766
Denise M Cairo, *Pr*
Denise Cairo, *Pr*
Robert A Cairo, *VP*
EMP: 7 **EST:** 1988
SQ FT: 5,700
SALES (est): 808.15K **Privately Held**
SIC: 5084 1731 7378 Recycling machinery and equipment; Safety and security specialization; Computer peripheral equipment repair and maintenance

(G-12171)
TECHNOLOGY TRANSFERS INC
16 Anderson Ln (19711-3064)
PHONE.................302 234-4718
Godwin Igwe, *Pr*
EMP: 5 **EST:** 2005
SALES (est): 354.69K **Privately Held**
SIC: 8711 Consulting engineer

(G-12172)
TECHXPONENT INC
131 Arielle Dr (19702-2678)
PHONE.................410 701-0089
Muhammad Baqir, *Prin*
Mark Quinn, *Prin*
Naveed Baqir, *Prin*
Amna Latif, *Prin*
Salsabila Mouiz, *Prin*
EMP: 10 **EST:** 2014
SALES (est): 354.51K **Privately Held**
SIC: 7389 Business Activities at Non-Commercial Site

(G-12173)
TECS PLUS
261 Chapman Rd (19702-5423)
PHONE.................302 437-6890
Amanda Pokhan, *Prin*
EMP: 15 **EST:** 2016
SALES (est): 538.68K **Privately Held**
Web: www.tecsplus.com
SIC: 7379 Computer related consulting services

(G-12174)
TEK TREE LLC (PA)
1106 Drummond Plz (19711-5705)
PHONE.................302 368-2730
Raghuveer Bandi, *Managing Member*
EMP: 17 **EST:** 2005
SALES (est): 8.1MM **Privately Held**
Web: www.tektreeinc.com
SIC: 8748 Systems engineering consultant, ex. computer or professional

(G-12175)
TEKSOLV USD INC (PA)
130 Executive Dr Ste 5 (19702-3349)
PHONE.................302 738-1050
John Mouser, *President USA*
Kevin Hurd Csp, *Ex VP*
Bryan Jones, *Ex VP*
Matthew Netsch, *VP*
Adam Micun, *VP*
EMP: 18 **EST:** 2009
SALES (est): 23.45MM
SALES (corp-wide): 23.45MM **Privately Held**
Web: www.teksolv.com
SIC: 8741 Business management

(G-12176)
TEKSOLV USD INC
100 Lake Dr (19702-3340)
PHONE.................302 738-1050
Chris Bonson, *Brnch Mgr*
EMP: 6
SALES (corp-wide): 23.45MM **Privately Held**
Web: www.teksolv.com
SIC: 3531 Construction machinery
PA: Teksolv Usd, Inc.
130 Executive Dr Ste 5
Newark DE 19702
302 738-1050

(G-12177)
TEMP-AIR INC
Also Called: Tempair
200 Happy Ln (19711-8006)

Newark - New Castle County (G-12178)   GEOGRAPHIC SECTION

PHONE..................................302 369-3880
Michael Schmib, *Mgr*
EMP: 10
SALES (corp-wide): 9.67B **Privately Held**
Web: www.tempairsales.com
SIC: 7353 Heavy construction equipment rental
HQ: Temp-Air, Inc.
    3700 W Preserve Blvd
    Burnsville MN 55337
    800 836-7432

(G-12178)
TEN BEARS ENVIRONMENTAL LLC
Also Called: Ten Bears Environmental
1080 S Chapel St Ste 200 (19702-1379)
PHONE..................................302 731-8633
J Mcandrew, *Managing Member*
Joe Mcandrew, *Managing Member*
John Gurski, *Mgr*
EMP: 9 EST: 2000
SALES (est): 694.72K **Privately Held**
Web: www.tenbearsenvironmental.com
SIC: 8748 8711 Environmental consultant; Engineering services

(G-12179)
TERI LYN BUSCH MSW/LCSW
10 Wink Dr (19702-2841)
PHONE..................................302 731-9110
Teri Lyn Busch, *Prin*
EMP: 7 EST: 2012
SALES (est): 77.18K **Privately Held**
SIC: 8322 Social worker

(G-12180)
TERRY WHITE
Also Called: State Farm Insurance
200 Continental Dr Ste 109 (19713-4334)
PHONE..................................302 652-4969
Terry White, *Owner*
EMP: 6 EST: 1997
SALES (est): 968K **Privately Held**
Web: www.terrywhite.net
SIC: 6411 Insurance agents and brokers

(G-12181)
TESLA ENERGY OPERATIONS INC
231 Executive Dr Ste 1 (19702-3324)
PHONE..................................650 638-1028
EMP: 5
SALES (corp-wide): 81.46B **Publicly Held**
Web: www.solarcity.com
SIC: 1711 Solar energy contractor
HQ: Tesla Energy Operations, Inc.
    3055 Clearview Way
    San Mateo CA 94402

(G-12182)
TESTEX INC
8 Fox Ln (19711-2071)
P.O. Box 867 (19715-0867)
PHONE..................................302 731-5693
Mary Ellen Stachnik, *Pr*
Robert Stachnik, *Dir*
EMP: 6 EST: 1964
SALES (est): 492K **Privately Held**
Web: www.testextape.com
SIC: 3829 Measuring and controlling devices, nec

(G-12183)
TETRA TECH INC
240 Continental Dr Ste 200 (19713-4360)
PHONE..................................302 738-7551
Andy Mazzeo, *Mgr*
EMP: 13
SALES (corp-wide): 4.52B **Publicly Held**
Web: www.tetratech.com
SIC: 8711 Consulting engineer
PA: Tetra Tech, Inc.

3475 E Foothill Blvd
Pasadena CA 91107
626 351-4664

(G-12184)
TETRA TECH INC
Also Called: Tetra Tech Engrg & Arch Svcs
240 Continental Dr Ste 200 (19713-4360)
PHONE..................................302 738-7551
Robert Maffia, *Brnch Mgr*
EMP: 6
SALES (corp-wide): 4.52B **Publicly Held**
Web: www.tetratech.com
SIC: 8711 Consulting engineer
PA: Tetra Tech, Inc.
    3475 E Foothill Blvd
    Pasadena CA 91107
    626 351-4664

(G-12185)
TEXCEL LLC
211 Executive Dr Ste 9 (19702-3358)
PHONE..................................302 738-4313
EMP: 7 EST: 2021
SALES (est): 79.91K **Privately Held**
Web: www.texcelrubber.com
SIC: 5085 Industrial supplies

(G-12186)
THE ASCENDANT GROUP INC
2035 Sunset Lake Rd Ste B2 (19702-2600)
PHONE..................................302 450-4494
EMP: 12 EST: 2009
SQ FT: 1,100
SALES (est): 2.39MM **Privately Held**
Web: www.ascendantgroupbranding.com
SIC: 8743 Public relations services

(G-12187)
THE TONDO GROUP LLC
17 Mcmillan Way (19713-3420)
PHONE..................................302 893-8849
EMP: 6 EST: 2021
SALES (est): 512.11K **Privately Held**
SIC: 7389 Subscription fulfillment services: magazine, newspaper, etc.

(G-12188)
THEPOWERMBA INC
2035 Sunset Lake Rd Ste B2 (19702-2600)
PHONE..................................917 508-5535
John Mackey, *Prin*
Jennifer Fleiss, *Prin*
Steve Chen, *Prin*
Chris Barton, *Prin*
EMP: 9 EST: 2019
SALES (est): 251.38K **Privately Held**
Web: global.thepower.education
SIC: 8741 Business management

(G-12189)
THINKLEVER LLC
560 Peoples Plz (19702-4798)
PHONE..................................302 388-7461
Jerry Rulewicz, *Prin*
EMP: 6 EST: 2011
SALES (est): 275.35K **Privately Held**
Web: www.thinklever.com
SIC: 7379 Computer related consulting services

(G-12190)
THOMAS A COFRAN & SONS INC
203 Sunset Rd (19711-4524)
PHONE..................................302 368-5157
EMP: 6 EST: 1992
SALES (est): 477.48K **Privately Held**
SIC: 1521 General remodeling, single-family houses

(G-12191)
THOMAS B DAVIS
Also Called: Maintenance Troubleshooting
1 Arlington St (19711-4363)
PHONE..................................302 692-0871
Thomas B Davis, *Owner*
EMP: 9 EST: 1976
SQ FT: 4,000
SALES (est): 667.82K **Privately Held**
Web: www.mtroubleshooting.com
SIC: 8742 5192 5099 3829 Management consulting services; Books; Video cassettes, accessories and supplies; Measuring and controlling devices, nec

(G-12192)
THOMAS BROTHERS LLC
12 Oak Ave (19711-4728)
PHONE..................................302 366-1316
Stuart Thomas, *Managing Member*
EMP: 7 EST: 1996
SALES (est): 692.42K **Privately Held**
Web: www.thomasbrothersbuilders.com
SIC: 1522 Residential construction, nec

(G-12193)
THOMAS BUILDING GROUP INC
35 Albe Dr (19702-1321)
PHONE..................................302 283-0600
Lori Loller, *Pr*
EMP: 12 EST: 2000
SQ FT: 2,500
SALES (est): 1.08MM **Privately Held**
Web: www.truenet.com
SIC: 1795 1742 1751 5082 Demolition, buildings and other structures; Drywall; Lightweight steel framing (metal stud) installation; General construction machinery and equipment

(G-12194)
THORNLEY COMPANY INC
1 Innovation Way Ste 100 (19711-5462)
P.O. Box 269 (19428-0269)
PHONE..................................302 224-8300
H Douglas Thornley, *Pr*
▲ EMP: 8 EST: 1954
SQ FT: 2,000
SALES (est): 2.04MM **Privately Held**
Web: www.thornleycompany.com
SIC: 5169 Industrial chemicals

(G-12195)
TICKET SPORTS AND ENTRMT CORP
254 Chapman Rd Ste 209 (19702-5413)
PHONE..................................224 522-3517
Alrick Wright, *CEO*
EMP: 6
SALES (est): 314.1K **Privately Held**
SIC: 7371 Computer software development

(G-12196)
TIMTEC INC
301 Ruthar Dr Ste A (19711-8031)
P.O. Box 8941 (19714-8941)
PHONE..................................302 292-8500
Murat Niyazymbetov, *Pr*
EMP: 10 EST: 1995
SALES (est): 948.16K **Privately Held**
Web: www.timtec.net
SIC: 2819 Ammonium compounds, except fertilizers, nec

(G-12197)
TIMTEC LLC
301 Ruthar Dr Ste A (19711-8031)
P.O. Box 8941 (19714-8941)
PHONE..................................302 292-8500
Murat Niyazymbetov, *Managing Member*

EMP: 10 EST: 2005
SALES (est): 691.82K **Privately Held**
Web: www.timtec.net
SIC: 8731 8742 Biotechnical research, commercial; Management consulting services

(G-12198)
TIPTON COMMUNICATIONS GROUP
323 E Main St (19711-7152)
PHONE..................................302 454-7901
Daniel R Tipton, *Pr*
Laura B Tipton, *Sec*
EMP: 16 EST: 2006
SALES (est): 2.85MM **Privately Held**
Web: www.tiptonhealth.com
SIC: 8743 8249 8742 Public relations services; Business training services; Hospital and health services consultant

(G-12199)
TIRE 24 X 7 INC
402 Welsh Hill Rd (19702-1000)
PHONE..................................833 847-3247
Krishan Arora, *Pr*
EMP: 4
SALES (est): 87.5K **Privately Held**
SIC: 5015 3312 Tires, used: retail only; Wheels

(G-12200)
TJ CUSTOM WOODWORKS INC
4 Mistweave Ct (19711-2980)
PHONE..................................302 563-8535
Thomas Jenkins, *Prin*
EMP: 5 EST: 2015
SALES (est): 151.33K **Privately Held**
SIC: 2431 Millwork

(G-12201)
TNT WINDOW CLEANING
35 Salem Church Rd (19713-4928)
PHONE..................................302 326-2411
Tom Robinson, *Owner*
EMP: 5 EST: 2004
SALES (est): 122.2K **Privately Held**
SIC: 7349 Window cleaning

(G-12202)
TO A TEE PRINTING
2860 Ogletown Rd (19713-1857)
PHONE..................................302 525-6336
EMP: 5 EST: 2008
SALES (est): 125.88K **Privately Held**
SIC: 2759 Screen printing

(G-12203)
TODAYS KID INC (NOT INC)
10 Songsmith Dr (19702-4405)
P.O. Box 283 (19701-0283)
PHONE..................................302 834-5620
EMP: 8 EST: 1995
SALES (est): 127.8K **Privately Held**
SIC: 8351 Preschool center

(G-12204)
TOLBERT ENTERPRISE INC ◆
200 Cntnntal Dr Chrstana (19713)
PHONE..................................866 986-5237
Shamarr Tolbert, *CEO*
EMP: 5 EST: 2022
SALES (est): 250K **Privately Held**
SIC: 3537 Trucks: freight, baggage, etc.: industrial, except mining

(G-12205)
TOM CAN AND SON GENERAL CONTR
210 S Dillwyn Rd (19711-5550)
PHONE..................................302 737-5551

GEOGRAPHIC SECTION

Thomas Fredrick Cannon Junior, *Prin*
EMP: 5 **EST:** 2010
SALES (est): 162.69K **Privately Held**
SIC: 1522 Residential construction, nec

(G-12206)
TOM MCDONALD CONTRACTING
302 Mcfarland Dr (19702-3681)
PHONE...................302 219-7939
EMP: 5 **EST:** 2017
SALES (est): 96.34K **Privately Held**
Web: www.tom-mcdonald-lightning-rods.com
SIC: 1799 Special trade contractors, nec

(G-12207)
TOM WISELEY INSURANCE AGENCY
Also Called: Allstate
1400 Peoples Plz Ste 228 (19702-5708)
PHONE...................302 832-7700
Tom Wiseley, *Owner*
EMP: 8 **EST:** 1997
SALES (est): 765.76K **Privately Held**
Web: www.allstate.com
SIC: 6411 Insurance agents, brokers, and service

(G-12208)
TOMI INC
2035 Sunset Lake Rd (19702-2600)
PHONE...................650 488-3054
EMP: 5 **EST:** 2019
SALES (est): 71.79K **Privately Held**
SIC: 8742 Management consulting services

(G-12209)
TONER JEROME P SR PATRICI
111 Great Circle Rd (19711-2335)
PHONE...................302 239-7271
Jerome P Toner Senior, *Prin*
EMP: 5 **EST:** 2010
SALES (est): 84.27K **Privately Held**
SIC: 1521 Single-family housing construction

(G-12210)
TOP NOTCH HOME SERVICES
33 Donaldson Dr (19713-1784)
PHONE...................302 275-2459
Michael Cerminaro, *Owner*
EMP: 5 **EST:** 2012
SALES (est): 197.81K **Privately Held**
SIC: 1522 Residential construction, nec

(G-12211)
TOTAL CLIMATE CONTROL INC
Also Called: Honeywell Authorized Dealer
2694 Frazer Rd (19702-4503)
PHONE...................302 836-6240
Carl Chopack, *Pr*
Janet Chopack, *VP*
EMP: 5 **EST:** 1988
SQ FT: 3,000
SALES (est): 565.54K **Privately Held**
Web: www.honeywell.com
SIC: 1711 Warm air heating and air conditioning contractor

(G-12212)
TOTAL PEST SOLUTIONS
4 Mill Park Ct Ste C (19713-1901)
PHONE...................302 368-8081
Zach Fesaras, *Owner*
EMP: 10 **EST:** 2010
SALES (est): 70K **Privately Held**
Web: www.hoffmanexterminating.com
SIC: 7342 Pest control in structures

(G-12213)
TOWN HAIR SALON
106 Peoples Plz (19702-4794)
PHONE...................302 803-4535
EMP: 7 **EST:** 2017
SALES (est): 204.67K **Privately Held**
Web: www.townhair.net
SIC: 7231 Hairdressers

(G-12214)
TOWNE PLACE SUITES BY MARRIOTT
Also Called: Nab Hospitality
410 Eagle Run Rd (19702-1603)
PHONE...................302 369-6212
Joan Payne, *Genl Mgr*
EMP: 100 **EST:** 2005
SALES (est): 1.55MM **Privately Held**
Web: www.marriott.com
SIC: 7011 Hotel, franchised

(G-12215)
TRAINING CENTER
146 Brookside Blvd (19713-2624)
PHONE...................302 538-0847
Janice Powers, *Prin*
EMP: 5 **EST:** 2017
SALES (est): 48.94K **Privately Held**
Web: www.tcgym.com
SIC: 7991 Physical fitness facilities

(G-12216)
TRAINING SOLUTION
406 Suburban Dr (19711-3566)
PHONE...................302 379-3070
EMP: 5 **EST:** 2011
SALES (est): 111.77K **Privately Held**
SIC: 8742 Marketing consulting services

(G-12217)
TRANQUILITY COUNSELING INC
314 E Main St Ste 402 (19711-7182)
PHONE...................302 636-0700
Kimberley Colgan, *Prin*
EMP: 6 **EST:** 2008
SALES (est): 242.31K **Privately Held**
Web: www.tranquilitycounselinginc.com
SIC: 8322 Social worker

(G-12218)
TRANSFORMERS LLC
113 Register Dr (19711-2287)
PHONE...................302 757-3803
EMP: 6 **EST:** 2014
SALES (est): 299.41K **Privately Held**
SIC: 1521 Single-family housing construction

(G-12219)
TREXGEN NUTRASCIENCE LLC ✪
254 Chapman Rd Ste 208 (19702-5422)
PHONE...................302 520-2406
Piyushkumar Vekaria, *Managing Member*
EMP: 7 **EST:** 2023
SALES (est): 71.67K **Privately Held**
SIC: 5499 7389 Health and dietetic food stores; Business services, nec

(G-12220)
TRI STATE BTRY & AUTO ELC INC (PA)
Also Called: Tri State Battery
107 Albe Dr Ste H (19702-1300)
P.O. Box 5808 (19714-5808)
PHONE...................302 292-2330
Gary Emory Sutch Ii, *Pr*
Debbie Davis, *VP*
▲ **EMP:** 10 **EST:** 1988
SQ FT: 6,000
SALES (est): 2.41MM **Privately Held**
Web: www.tristatebattery.com
SIC: 5013 5063 Automotive batteries; Electrical supplies, nec

(G-12221)
TRI STATE TERMITE & PEST CTRL
1170 Corner Ketch Rd (19711-2324)
PHONE...................302 239-0512
Don Klenotiz, *Pr*
Lori Christina, *Sec*
EMP: 5 **EST:** 1987
SALES (est): 574.59K **Privately Held**
Web: www.tristatepestmgt.com
SIC: 7342 Pest control in structures

(G-12222)
TRI-COUNTY SECURITY
1901 Ogletown Rd (19711-5437)
PHONE...................302 709-2244
EMP: 8 **EST:** 2013
SALES (est): 73.34K **Privately Held**
Web: www.tri-countysecuritynj.com
SIC: 7381 Security guard service

(G-12223)
TRI-STATE BIRD RESCUE RES INC
170 Possum Hollow Rd (19711-3910)
PHONE...................302 737-9543
Lisa Smith, *Ex Dir*
EMP: 20 **EST:** 1977
SALES (est): 2.48MM **Privately Held**
Web: www.tristatebird.org
SIC: 0752 Shelters, animal

(G-12224)
TRI-STATE BTRY ALTERNATOR LLC
Also Called: Tri State Battery
107 Albe Dr Ste H (19702-1300)
PHONE...................320 292-2330
John Tilly, *Prin*
John Tilly, *Pr*
Emory Sutch, *
Stephanie Sutch, *
EMP: 30 **EST:** 2019
SALES (est): 2.12MM **Privately Held**
Web: www.tristatebattery.com
SIC: 5013 Automotive batteries

(G-12225)
TRI-STATE GROUTING LLC
567 Walther Rd (19702-2903)
P.O. Box 99 (19701-0099)
PHONE...................302 286-0701
EMP: 8 **EST:** 1977
SQ FT: 4,000
SALES (est): 9.43MM
SALES (corp-wide): 2.29B **Publicly Held**
Web: www.standardpipeservices.com
SIC: 1623 Underground utilities contractor
HQ: Aqua Resources, Inc.
   762 W Lancaster Ave
   Bryn Mawr PA 19010
   610 525-1400

(G-12226)
TRI-STATE POOPER SCOOPERS INC
21 Prestbury Sq (19713-2608)
P.O. Box 32 (29067-0032)
PHONE...................302 322-4522
EMP: 8 **EST:** 2018
SALES (est): 452.66K **Privately Held**
Web: www.tristatepooperscoopers.com
SIC: 0752 Animal specialty services

(G-12227)
TRI-STATE SEC & CONTRLS LLC
2860 Ogletown Rd Apt 2 (19713-1857)
PHONE...................302 299-2175
Marc Bobik, *Managing Member*
EMP: 13 **EST:** 2005
SALES (est): 1.44MM **Privately Held**
Web: www.tscinnovations.com
SIC: 1731 General electrical contractor

(G-12228)
TRICOMM SERVICES CORPORATION
604 Interchange Blvd (19711-3560)
PHONE...................302 454-2975
Joe Kirkner, *Prin*
EMP: 9 **EST:** 1981
SALES (est): 921.76K **Privately Held**
Web: www.tricommcorp.com
SIC: 1731 Cable television installation

(G-12229)
TRILOGY SALON AND DAY SPA INC
1200 Capitol Trl (19711-3924)
PHONE...................302 292-3511
Randy Richardson, *Pr*
EMP: 13 **EST:** 2002
SQ FT: 5,700
SALES (est): 436.9K **Privately Held**
Web: www.trilogysalon.com
SIC: 7231 Hairdressers

(G-12230)
TRIMBLE INC
Also Called: Eastern Percision
107c Albe Dr Ste C (19702-1336)
PHONE...................302 368-2434
Gay Carter, *Mgr*
EMP: 5
SALES (corp-wide): 3.68B **Publicly Held**
Web: www.trimble.com
SIC: 5049 Surveyor's instruments
PA: Trimble Inc.
   10368 Westmoor Dr
   Westminster CO 80021
   720 887-6100

(G-12231)
TRINITY EMS EDUCATORS STAFFING
65 S Skyward Dr (19713-2847)
PHONE...................302 373-7276
Hank Smith, *Prin*
EMP: 5 **EST:** 2014
SALES (est): 82.42K **Privately Held**
Web: www.emsdoneright.com
SIC: 7361 Employment agencies

(G-12232)
TRINITY FREIGHT LOGISTICS INC
12 Castlegate Ct (19702-2152)
PHONE...................302 543-3128
Willys Nyabiosi, *Prin*
EMP: 5 **EST:** 2013
SALES (est): 240.6K **Privately Held**
SIC: 4789 Transportation services, nec

(G-12233)
TRINITY HOME HEALTH CARE CORP (PA)
1400 Peoples Plz Ste 215 (19702-5708)
PHONE...................302 838-2710
EMP: 28 **EST:** 2010
SQ FT: 1,383
SALES (est): 2.86MM **Privately Held**
Web: www.trinityhomehealthcares.com
SIC: 8082 Home health care services

(G-12234)
TRINITY HOME HEALTH CARE LLC
1400 Peoples Plz Ste 215 (19702-5708)
PHONE...................410 620-9366
Colleen Curtis, *CEO*
EMP: 7 **EST:** 2006
SQ FT: 1,383
SALES (est): 431.62K **Privately Held**
Web: www.trinityhomehealthcares.com
SIC: 8082 Home health care services
PA: Trinity Home Health Care Corp.
   1400 Peoples Plz Ste 215
   Newark DE 19702

(PA)=Parent Co (HQ)=Headquarters
✪ = New Business established in last 2 years

Newark - New Castle County (G-12235)

(G-12235)
TRISTATE FBRCN AND MACHG
38 Albe Dr (19702-1351)
PHONE..................302 533-5877
EMP: 5 EST: 2017
SALES (est): 310.2K Privately Held
SIC: 1522 Residential construction, nec

(G-12236)
TRISTATE REMODELING CORP
625 Dawson Dr Ste F (19713-3433)
PHONE..................302 444-8314
Roland Ridgeway, Pr
EMP: 7 EST: 2013
SALES (est): 372.74K Privately Held
Web: www.tristateremodels.net
SIC: 1521 General remodeling, single-family houses

(G-12237)
TRIUMPH BIKE DETAILING
268 Whitherspoon Ln (19713-3810)
PHONE..................302 463-3606
Merrill Stanton, Prin
EMP: 5 EST: 2010
SALES (est): 38.1K Privately Held
SIC: 7542 Washing and polishing, automotive

(G-12238)
TRIUMPH WORLDWIDE INC
112 E Green Valley Cir (19711-6717)
PHONE..................302 465-6898
Shreyank Patel, CEO
EMP: 20 EST: 2020
SALES (est): 1.23MM Privately Held
SIC: 6111 Export/Import Bank

(G-12239)
TROLLEY SQUARE NUTRITION
294 Campfield Rd (19713-2444)
PHONE..................302 757-6669
EMP: 5 EST: 2014
SALES (est): 46.62K Privately Held
SIC: 8099 Nutrition services

(G-12240)
TROY GRANITE INC (PA)
711 Interchange Blvd (19711-3594)
PHONE..................302 292-1750
Mustafa Tuncer, Pr
▲ EMP: 8 EST: 2006
SALES (est): 4.7MM Privately Held
Web: www.troygranite.com
SIC: 1799 Counter top installation

(G-12241)
TRUE RELIGION APPAREL INC
132 Christiana Mall (19702-3202)
PHONE..................302 894-9425
EMP: 3
SALES (corp-wide): 1.14B Privately Held
Web: www.truereligion.com
SIC: 2325 2339 5651 Jeans: men's, youths', and boys'; Jeans: women's, misses', and juniors'; Family clothing stores
HQ: True Religion Apparel, Inc.
500 W 190th St Ste 300
Gardena CA 90248
323 266-3072

(G-12242)
TSB INC
Also Called: Tri-State Battery
107 Albe Dr Ste H (19702-1300)
PHONE..................302 292-2330
EMP: 6 EST: 2009
SALES (est): 369.84K Privately Held
SIC: 5063 Batteries

(G-12243)
TT LUXURY GROUP LLC
Also Called: Tickle Toes
46 Vansant Rd (19711-4839)
PHONE..................732 242-9795
Nicole Fiorina, Managing Member
EMP: 9 EST: 2007
SALES (est): 441.7K Privately Held
SIC: 2361 Dresses: girls', children's, and infants'

(G-12244)
TUCKER VACATION RENTALS INC
16 Bridleshire Rd (19711-2451)
PHONE..................302 668-3512
Scott Tucker, Prin
EMP: 5 EST: 2020
SALES (est): 212.6K Privately Held
SIC: 7359 Equipment rental and leasing, nec

(G-12245)
TURF PRO INC
103 Sandy Dr Ste 100 (19713-1193)
PHONE..................302 218-3530
EMP: 9 EST: 1994
SALES (est): 468.82K Privately Held
Web: www.turfproinc.net
SIC: 0782 Landscape contractors

(G-12246)
TURNING CRNRS-HAND IN HAND LLC
256 Chapman Rd Ste 105-6 (19702-5499)
PHONE..................302 689-3562
EMP: 6 EST: 2019
SALES (est): 119.53K Privately Held
SIC: 8011 Offices and clinics of medical doctors

(G-12247)
TURQUOISE AMERICA LLC
84 Munro Rd (19711-3559)
PHONE..................302 608-7008
EMP: 2
SALES (est): 92.41K Privately Held
SIC: 3949 7389 Sporting and athletic goods, nec; Business services, nec

(G-12248)
TURQUOISE SHOP INC
Also Called: Janvier Jewelers
543 Christiana Mall (19702-3209)
PHONE..................302 366-7448
Edward Janvier, Pr
Harvey Lee Janvier, VP
EMP: 11 EST: 1975
SQ FT: 960
SALES (est): 472.61K Privately Held
Web: www.janvierjewelers.com
SIC: 5944 7631 Jewelry, precious stones and precious metals; Jewelry repair services

(G-12249)
TWISTED HAIR DESIGNS
2622 Kirkwood Hwy (19711)
PHONE..................302 533-6104
Lewis Holveck Young, Owner
EMP: 5 EST: 2014
SALES (est): 50.43K Privately Held
Web: twistedhairdesigns.askforspecial.com
SIC: 7231 Hairdressers

(G-12250)
TXTHINKING INC
2035 Sunset Lake Rd Ste B-2 (19702-2600)
PHONE..................646 820-1235
EMP: 5 EST: 2020
SALES (est): 68.89K Privately Held
Web: www.txthinking.com
SIC: 7371 Computer software development

(G-12251)
TYLAUR INC
Also Called: Signs By Tomorrow
2659 Kirkwood Hwy (19711-7242)
PHONE..................302 894-9330
Sharon L Rizzo, Pr
Clement Rizzo, Sec
EMP: 5 EST: 2001
SQ FT: 1,200
SALES (est): 488.37K Privately Held
Web: www.signsbytomorrow.com
SIC: 3993 Signs and advertising specialties

(G-12252)
U A G INC
841 Old Baltimore Pike (19702-1317)
PHONE..................302 731-2747
Michael D Lattomus, Pr
EMP: 8 EST: 2008
SALES (est): 120.04K Privately Held
SIC: 7536 Automotive glass replacement shops

(G-12253)
U GOOD ENTERPRISES LLC
166 Haut Brion Ave (19702-4542)
PHONE..................302 566-8038
EMP: 16 EST: 2020
SALES (est): 647.9K Privately Held
SIC: 8711 7371 Consulting engineer; Computer software systems analysis and design, custom

(G-12254)
U S A REPAIR SHOP
444 Polly Drummond Hill Rd (19711-4341)
PHONE..................302 545-5991
Rasha Almasou, Owner
EMP: 5 EST: 2015
SALES (est): 66.17K Privately Held
SIC: 7699 Repair services, nec

(G-12255)
U-HAUL
607 Old Harmony Rd (19711-6917)
PHONE..................302 565-4423
Samuel Miller, Ofcr
EMP: 7 EST: 2018
SALES (est): 135.54K Privately Held
Web: www.uhaul.com
SIC: 7513 Truck rental and leasing, no drivers

(G-12256)
U-HAUL INTERNATIONAL
Also Called: U-Haul
50 Marrows Rd (19713-3702)
PHONE..................302 565-4056
EMP: 8 EST: 2010
SALES (est): 127.5K Privately Held
Web: www.uhaul.com
SIC: 7513 Truck rental and leasing, no drivers

(G-12257)
U-HAUL NEIGHBORHOOD DEALER
Also Called: U-Haul
660 Capitol Trl (19711-3869)
PHONE..................302 722-8016
Neil Mcfadden, CEO
EMP: 8 EST: 2014
SALES (est): 124.14K Privately Held
Web: www.uhaul.com
SIC: 7513 Truck rental and leasing, no drivers

(G-12258)
UAW-GM LEGAL SERVICES PLAN
Also Called: U A W Legal Services
4051 Ogletown Rd Ste 201 (19713-3101)
PHONE..................302 562-8212
Sandra E Messick, Mgr
EMP: 12
SALES (corp-wide): 14.65MM Privately Held
SIC: 8111 Legal aid service
PA: Uaw-Gm Legal Services Plan
1400 Woodbridge St
Detroit MI 48207
313 202-8100

(G-12259)
UD STUDENT WELLNESS HLTH PROM
231 S College Ave (19716-3500)
PHONE..................302 831-3457
EMP: 5 EST: 2018
SALES (est): 88.24K Privately Held
SIC: 8099 Health and allied services, nec

(G-12260)
UDAIRY CREAMERY PROD FCILTY
529 S College Ave (19716-1304)
PHONE..................302 831-2486
EMP: 18
SALES (est): 294.97K Privately Held
Web: www.udel.edu
SIC: 1541 Industrial buildings and warehouses

(G-12261)
UHS OF ROCKFORD LLC
Also Called: UHS
100 Rockford Dr (19713-2120)
PHONE..................302 892-4224
John Mckenna, CEO
EMP: 100 EST: 2000
SALES (est): 23.32MM
SALES (corp-wide): 13.4B Publicly Held
Web: www.rockfordcenter.com
SIC: 8062 8063 General medical and surgical hospitals; Psychiatric hospitals
PA: Universal Health Services, Inc.
367 S Gulph Rd
King Of Prussia PA 19406
610 768-3300

(G-12262)
ULTRAWORKING INC
2035 Sunset Lake Rd Ste B2 (19702-2600)
PHONE..................848 243-0008
EMP: 8 EST: 2018
SALES (est): 32.18K Privately Held
Web: www.ultraworking.com
SIC: 7379 7371 Computer related services, nec; Computer software development and applications

(G-12263)
UMBRELLA TRANSPORT GROUP INC
39 Glennwood Dr (19702-3769)
PHONE..................301 919-1623
Virginia Navarro, Pr
William Hawkins, COO
EMP: 6 EST: 2010
SALES (est): 348.15K Privately Held
SIC: 4731 Brokers, shipping

(G-12264)
UNDER WHISTLE
49 N Bellwoode Dr (19702-3409)
PHONE..................302 250-8400
EMP: 3 EST: 2010
SALES (est): 66.69K Privately Held
SIC: 3999 Whistles

GEOGRAPHIC SECTION
Newark - New Castle County (G-12289)

(G-12265)
UNION FNOSA FINCL SVCS USA LLC
850 Library Ave Ste 204f (19711-7196)
PHONE..................................302 738-6680
Donald J Puglisi, *Dir*
Gregory Lavelle, *Dir*
EMP: 10 **EST:** 2017
SALES (est): 296.77K **Privately Held**
SIC: 6282 Investment advice
PA: Naturgy Energy Group Sa.
Avenida America 38
Madrid M 28028

(G-12266)
UNITED AUTO SALES INC
209 Harris Cir (19711-2430)
PHONE..................................302 325-3000
Brian Wolf, *Pr*
EMP: 5 **EST:** 1984
SALES (est): 886.99K **Privately Held**
Web: www.unitedautosales.com
SIC: 5521 7538 Automobiles, used cars only
; General automotive repair shops

(G-12267)
UNITED AUTO WORKERS LOCAL 435
698 Old Baltimore Pike (19702-1312)
PHONE..................................302 995-6001
Dave Myers, *Pr*
Dave Myers, *Prin*
James G Brown, *Sec*
William Wosik, *Recording Secretary*
EMP: 10 **EST:** 1947
SALES (est): 360.61K **Privately Held**
SIC: 8631 Collective bargaining unit

(G-12268)
UNITED BROKERAGE PACKAGING
110 Executive Dr Ste 5 (19702-3352)
PHONE..................................302 294-6782
EMP: 8 **EST:** 2015
SALES (est): 671.29K **Privately Held**
Web: www.ubpackaging.com
SIC: 6282 Investment advisory service

(G-12269)
UNITED COCOA PROCESSOR INC
Also Called: U C P
701 Pencader Dr Ste F (19702-3360)
PHONE..................................302 731-0825
Peter Liu, *CEO*
Jonathan Liu, *
James Liu, *
◆ **EMP:** 42 **EST:** 1992
SQ FT: 93,000
SALES (est): 25.65MM **Privately Held**
Web: www.unitedcocoa.com
SIC: 2066 Chocolate
PA: Indeca Industria E Comercio De
Cacau Ltda
Av. Elias Yazbek 2678
Embu Das Artes SP 06803

(G-12270)
UNITED PARCEL SERVICE INC
Also Called: UPS
211 Lake Dr (19702-3320)
PHONE..................................302 453-7462
EMP: 54
SALES (corp-wide): 100.34B **Publicly Held**
Web: www.ups.com
SIC: 4512 Air cargo carrier, scheduled
HQ: United Parcel Service, Inc.
55 Glenlake Pkwy
Atlanta GA 30328
404 828-6000

(G-12271)
UNITED STATES POWER EQP LLC
200 Continental Dr (19713-4334)
PHONE..................................302 294-2562
EMP: 5 **EST:** 2019
SALES (est): 159.73K **Privately Held**
Web: www.uspowerequip.com
SIC: 5084 Industrial machinery and equipment

(G-12272)
UNITED TELE WKRS LOCAL 13101
Also Called: UNITED TELEPHONE WORKERS OF DE
350 Gooding Dr (19702-1906)
PHONE..................................302 737-0400
Walter Speakman, *Pr*
Sandy Taylor, *Sec*
EMP: 6
SALES (est): 20.13K **Privately Held**
Web: www.cwa13101.org
SIC: 8631 8641 Labor union; Civic and social associations

(G-12273)
UNITED WORLDWIDE EXPRESS LLC
605 Interchange Blvd (19711-3561)
PHONE..................................347 651-5111
EMP: 10 **EST:** 2015
SALES (est): 948.3K **Privately Held**
SIC: 8742 Franchising consultant

(G-12274)
UNITY GROWTH FUND LLC
200 Continental Dr Ste 401 (19713-4334)
PHONE..................................703 585-7915
Shankar Gupta Boddu, *Managing Member*
EMP: 5 **EST:** 2021
SALES (est): 219.98K **Privately Held**
Web: www.unitygrowthfund.com
SIC: 6799 Venture capital companies

(G-12275)
UNIVERSITY GARDEN ASSOCIATES
Also Called: University Garden Apts
281 Beverly Rd Apt H5 (19711-7926)
PHONE..................................302 368-3823
Ralph V Watts, *Owner*
EMP: 8 **EST:** 1976
SALES (est): 504.83K **Privately Held**
SIC: 6513 Apartment hotel operation

(G-12276)
UNIVERSITY OF DE PRINTING
222 S Chapel St Rm 124 (19702)
PHONE..................................302 831-2153
Rodney Brown, *Mgr*
EMP: 14 **EST:** 2005
SALES (est): 71.99K **Privately Held**
Web: www.udel.edu
SIC: 7389 Printing broker

(G-12277)
UNIVERSITY OF DELAWARE
Also Called: Computing & Network Service
192 S Chapel St (19716-4320)
PHONE..................................302 831-6041
Susan J Foster, *VP*
EMP: 12
SALES (corp-wide): 1.6B **Privately Held**
Web: www.udel.edu
SIC: 7379 8221 Computer related maintenance services; University
PA: University Of Delaware
210 S College Ave
Newark DE 19716
302 831-2107

(G-12278)
UNIVERSITY OF DELAWARE
Also Called: Bartol Research Institute
104 The Grn Rm 217 (19716-2593)
PHONE..................................302 831-4811
Stuart Pittel, *Dir*
EMP: 6
SALES (corp-wide): 1.6B **Privately Held**
Web: www.udel.edu
SIC: 8733 8221 Noncommercial research organizations; University
PA: University Of Delaware
210 S College Ave
Newark DE 19716
302 831-2107

(G-12279)
UNIVERSITY OF DELAWARE
Also Called: Delaware Geological Survey
257 Academy St (19716-7500)
PHONE..................................302 831-2833
David Wunsch, *Dir*
EMP: 6
SALES (corp-wide): 1.6B **Privately Held**
Web: www.udel.edu
SIC: 8733 8221 Research institute; University
PA: University Of Delaware
210 S College Ave
Newark DE 19716
302 831-2107

(G-12280)
UNIVERSITY OF DELAWARE
Also Called: Univ of Del
363 New London Rd (19711-7044)
PHONE..................................302 831-2501
Marvin Friger, *Mgr*
EMP: 5
SALES (corp-wide): 1.6B **Privately Held**
Web: www.udel.edu
SIC: 8322 8221 Multi-service center; University
PA: University Of Delaware
210 S College Ave
Newark DE 19716
302 831-2107

(G-12281)
UNIVERSITY OF DELAWARE
Also Called: Student Health Service
282 The Grn (19716-0009)
PHONE..................................302 831-2226
E F Joseph Siebold, *Prin*
EMP: 29
SALES (corp-wide): 1.6B **Privately Held**
Web: www.udel.edu
SIC: 8011 8221 Dispensary, operated by physicians; University
PA: University Of Delaware
210 S College Ave
Newark DE 19716
302 831-2107

(G-12282)
UNIVERSITY OF DELAWARE
Also Called: Protermant Services
222 S Chapel St (19716-5600)
PHONE..................................302 831-2792
George Walueff, *Brnch Mgr*
EMP: 15
SALES (corp-wide): 1.6B **Privately Held**
Web: www.udel.edu
SIC: 7299 8221 Visa procurement service; University
PA: University Of Delaware
210 S College Ave
Newark DE 19716
302 831-2107

(G-12283)
UP AND AWAY TRAVEL HEALTH
210 Hull Ave (19711-6939)
PHONE..................................302 455-8416
Candace Sandal, *Prin*
EMP: 6 **EST:** 2017
SALES (est): 163.15K **Privately Held**
SIC: 8099 Health and allied services, nec

(G-12284)
UPBOUND GROUP INC
Also Called: Rent-A-Center
19 Chestnut Hill Plz (19713-2701)
PHONE..................................302 731-7900
Ronda Rawlings, *Brnch Mgr*
EMP: 5
Web: www.rentacenter.com
SIC: 7359 Appliance rental
PA: Upbound Group, Inc.
5501 Headquarters Dr
Plano TX 75024

(G-12285)
UPLOOP TECHNOLOGIES LP
4 Peddlers Row Ste 33 (19702-1525)
PHONE..................................514 922-0399
Alexandra Giuliani, *Genl Pt*
EMP: 10
SALES (est): 351.2K **Privately Held**
SIC: 7371 Computer software development and applications

(G-12286)
UPPERSTACK INC
2035 Sunset Lake Rd B2 (19702-2600)
PHONE..................................410 925-8216
Michael Rottman, *CEO*
EMP: 5 **EST:** 2017
SALES (est): 72.38K **Privately Held**
SIC: 7299 Consumer buying service

(G-12287)
UPS SUPPLY CHAIN SOLUTIONS INC
Also Called: UPS
220 Lake Dr Ste 1 (19702-3353)
PHONE..................................302 631-5259
Addison Paul, *Brnch Mgr*
EMP: 10
SALES (corp-wide): 100.34B **Publicly Held**
Web: www.ups.com
SIC: 4731 Freight forwarding
HQ: Ups Supply Chain Solutions, Inc.
12380 Morris Rd
Alpharetta GA 30005
678 258-2000

(G-12288)
URS GROUP INC
Also Called: URS
4051 Ogletown Rd Ste 300 (19713-3101)
PHONE..................................302 731-7824
Lee Anne Simmar, *Mgr*
EMP: 202
SALES (corp-wide): 14.38B **Publicly Held**
Web: www.aecom.com
SIC: 8711 Consulting engineer
HQ: Urs Group, Inc.
300 S Grand Ave Ste 900
Los Angeles CA 90071
213 593-8000

(G-12289)
US FLEXO SOLUTIONS LLC
560 Peoples Plz Ste 410 (19702-4798)
PHONE..................................302 838-7805
EMP: 5 **EST:** 2018
SALES (est): 166.59K **Privately Held**
Web: www.usflexo.com

Newark - New Castle County (G-12290)

(G-12290)
USA ANGELALIGN TECHNOLOGY ◇
300 Creek View Rd Ste 209 (19711-8548)
PHONE..................570 573-3515
Jason Tabb, *Managing Member*
EMP: 14 EST: 2022
SALES (est): 632.96K **Privately Held**
SIC: 2752 Commercial printing, lithographic
SIC: 5047 Medical equipment and supplies

(G-12291)
UTAX 4 LESS TAX SVC
3 Farland Way (19702-5344)
PHONE..................302 743-6905
Maria Correa, *Prin*
EMP: 5 EST: 2015
SALES (est): 45.72K **Privately Held**
SIC: 7291 Tax return preparation services

(G-12292)
UTZ QUALITY FOOD INC
710 Dawson Dr (19713-3462)
PHONE..................302 266-6982
Bob Kirkwood, *Prin*
EMP: 3 EST: 2010
SALES (est): 225.63K **Privately Held**
SIC: 2096 Potato chips and similar snacks

(G-12293)
UVAX BIO LLC
100 Biddle Ave Ste 202 (19702-3983)
PHONE..................818 859-3988
Ji Li, *CEO*
EMP: 20 EST: 2018
SALES (est): 3.31MM **Privately Held**
Web: www.uvaxbio.com
SIC: 2836 Vaccines

(G-12294)
V COLBERT INC
34 Gill Dr (19713-2367)
PHONE..................302 420-5502
EMP: 5 EST: 2015
SALES (est): 46.05K **Privately Held**
Web: www.vcolbert.com
SIC: 1521 Single-family housing construction

(G-12295)
V E GUERRAZZI INC
122 Sandy Dr Ste D (19713-1188)
PHONE..................302 369-5557
Vernon Guerrazzi, *Pr*
EMP: 10 EST: 1998
SQ FT: 3,000
SALES (est): 988.24K **Privately Held**
SIC: 3444 Sheet metalwork

(G-12296)
V F W POST HOME
Also Called: VFW Post 475
100 Veterans Dr (19711-4515)
PHONE..................302 366-8438
William Schaen, *VP*
EMP: 7 EST: 1922
SQ FT: 5,500
SALES (est): 124.77K **Privately Held**
Web: www.vfwpost475.com
SIC: 8641 Veterans' organization

(G-12297)
VACUUM GROUP INC
2035 Sunset Lake Rd B2 (19702-2600)
PHONE..................212 377-2073
Emanuele Lana, *CEO*
EMP: 8 EST: 2020
SALES (est): 153.56K **Privately Held**
SIC: 7359 Home appliance, furniture, and entertainment rental services

(G-12298)
VAL-TECH INC
Also Called: V T I
24 Mcmillan Way (19713-3492)
PHONE..................302 738-0500
Roger Beam, *Pr*
Joanna Beam, *VP*
Susan Haupt, *General Vice President*
EMP: 36 EST: 1970
SQ FT: 15,000
SALES (est): 843.17K **Privately Held**
Web: www.mdavisinc.com
SIC: 3625 3679 3822 Control equipment, electric; Electronic switches; Environmental controls

(G-12299)
VALASSIS DIRECT MAIL INC
300 Mcintire Dr (19711-1800)
PHONE..................302 861-3567
Mark Wise, *Dir*
EMP: 129
Web: www.vericast.com
SIC: 7331 Mailing service
HQ: Valassis Direct Mail, Inc.
  15955 La Cantera Pkwy
  San Antonio TX 06095
  800 437-0479

(G-12300)
VALENTINA LIQUORS
430 Old Baltimore Pike (19702-8410)
PHONE..................302 368-3264
Dean Grisco, *Owner*
EMP: 8 EST: 1993
SALES (est): 968.38K **Privately Held**
Web: valentinaliquors.ambz.com
SIC: 5149 Soft drinks

(G-12301)
VALLEY STREAM TOWNHOMES
100 N Barrett Ln (19702-2927)
PHONE..................302 613-4859
EMP: 8 EST: 2016
SALES (est): 60.97K **Privately Held**
Web: www.capanoresidential.com
SIC: 8641 Condominium association

(G-12302)
VALOR CONSTRUCTION LLC
Also Called: Construction
30 Albe Dr Ste A (19702-1352)
P.O. Box 7049 (19714-7049)
PHONE..................302 455-7994
Steven Gallaher, *Pr*
Steven Gallaher, *Prin*
Ashley Gallaher, *Prin*
Linda Gallaher, *Prin*
EMP: 5 EST: 2018
SALES (est): 252K **Privately Held**
Web: www.valorconstruction.us
SIC: 1521 General remodeling, single-family houses

(G-12303)
VANCE A FUNK III
273 E Main St Ste 100 (19711-7331)
PHONE..................302 368-2561
Vance A Funk Iii, *Owner*
EMP: 6 EST: 1976
SALES (est): 483.08K **Privately Held**
Web: www.funklawoffices.com
SIC: 8111 General practice attorney, lawyer

(G-12304)
VANCE GEMS LLC
530 Peoples Plz (19702-4798)
PHONE..................954 205-3982
EMP: 5 EST: 2005
SALES (est): 228.29K **Privately Held**
SIC: 5094 Precious stones (gems), nec

(G-12305)
VANILLA INNOVATIONS INC (PA)
2035 Sunset Lake Rd Ste B2 (19702-2600)
PHONE..................305 815-7586
EMP: 7 EST: 2019
SALES (est): 46.16K
SALES (corp-wide): 46.16K **Privately Held**
Web: www.vanillainnovations.it
SIC: 7371 Computer software development and applications

(G-12306)
VASCULAR SPECIALISTS DEL PA
1 Centurian Dr Ste 307 (19713-2127)
PHONE..................302 733-5700
Rhonda Disabatino, *Prin*
EMP: 17 EST: 2012
SALES (est): 1.24MM **Privately Held**
Web: www.vascularspecialists-de.com
SIC: 8011 Cardiologist and cardio-vascular specialist

(G-12307)
VASSALLO MICHAEL ELEC CONTR
4 Mill Park Ct (19713-1901)
PHONE..................302 455-9405
Michael Vassallo, *Pr*
Roberta A Vassallo, *Sec*
EMP: 13 EST: 1985
SQ FT: 3,964
SALES (est): 1.3MM **Privately Held**
SIC: 1731 General electrical contractor

(G-12308)
VCA ANIMAL HOSPITALS INC
Also Called: VCA Kirkwood Animal Hospital
1501 Capitol Trl (19711-5715)
PHONE..................302 738-1738
Linda Simione, *Brnch Mgr*
EMP: 11
SALES (corp-wide): 42.84B **Privately Held**
Web: www.petschoice.com
SIC: 0742 Animal hospital services, pets and other animal specialties
HQ: Vca Animal Hospitals, Inc.
  12401 W Olympic Blvd
  Los Angeles CA 90064

(G-12309)
VCA PIKE CREEK ANIMAL HOSPITAL
297 Polly Drummond Hill Rd (19711-4834)
PHONE..................302 307-1077
EMP: 5 EST: 2018
SALES (est): 122,46K **Privately Held**
Web: www.vcahospitals.com
SIC: 0742 Animal hospital services, pets and other animal specialties

(G-12310)
VELO AMIS
24 Nightingale Cir (19711-3776)
PHONE..................302 757-2783
EMP: 5 EST: 2017
SALES (est): 126.72K **Privately Held**
Web: www.veloamis.org
SIC: 7997 Membership sports and recreation clubs

(G-12311)
VEMO ACU LLC ◇
254 Chapman Rd Ste 209 (19702-5413)
PHONE..................508 654-7885
Mark Kim, *Managing Member*
EMP: 5 EST: 2023
SALES (est): 118.09K **Privately Held**
SIC: 8099 Health and allied services, nec

(G-12312)
VENICE INTERNATIONAL PDTS LLC
200 Continental Dr # 401 (19713-4334)
PHONE..................630 571-7171
EMP: 5 EST: 2021
SALES (est): 255.58K **Privately Held**
SIC: 3231 Products of purchased glass

(G-12313)
VEOLIA ENVMTL SVCS N AMER LLC
131 Continental Dr (19713-4305)
PHONE..................302 444-9172
EMP: 666
Web: www.veolianorthamerica.com
SIC: 8711 Engineering services
HQ: Veolia Environmental Services North America Llc
  53 State St Ste 14
  Boston MA 02109
  617 849-6600

(G-12314)
VERITAS CONSULTANT GROUP LLC
16 Anderson Ln (19711-3064)
PHONE..................302 893-9794
C Frank Igwe, *Managing Member*
EMP: 5 EST: 2008
SALES (est): 316.33K **Privately Held**
SIC: 8748 Business consulting, nec

(G-12315)
VERIZON DELAWARE LLC
Also Called: Verizon
945 S Chapel St (19713-3463)
PHONE..................302 738-3000
Janice Porter, *Prin*
EMP: 151
SALES (corp-wide): 136.84B **Publicly Held**
Web: www.verizon.com
SIC: 4813 Telephone communication, except radio
HQ: Verizon Delaware Llc
  901 N Tatnall'St Fl 2
  Wilmington DE 19801
  302 571-1571

(G-12316)
VERIZON WIRELESS INC
Also Called: Verizon Wireless
1209 Churchmans Rd (19713-2149)
PHONE..................302 737-5028
Ramsey Moorman, *Mgr*
EMP: 5
SALES (corp-wide): 133.97B **Publicly Held**
Web: www.verizonwireless.com
SIC: 4812 4813 Cellular telephone services; Telephone communication, except radio
HQ: Verizon Wireless, Inc.
  1 Verizon Way
  Basking Ridge NJ 07920

(G-12317)
VERSATILE IMPEX INC
Also Called: American Sports
74 Albe Dr Ste 3 (19702-1350)
PHONE..................302 369-9480
▲ EMP: 5 EST: 1995
SALES (est): 593.52K **Privately Held**
SIC: 5091 Sporting and recreation goods

(G-12318)
VERSITRON INC
83 Albe Dr Ste C (19702-1374)
PHONE..................302 894-0699
Richard Tull, *Pr*
Nadine Tull, *Pr*
EMP: 75 EST: 1995
SQ FT: 7,500

SALES (est): 5.88MM **Privately Held**
Web: www.versitron.com
SIC: **3661** 3669 Fiber optics communications equipment; Visual communication systems

(G-12319)
VERYUTILS INC
2035 Sunset Lake Rd B2 (19702-2600)
PHONE..................................858 939-9928
Frank Xue, *CEO*
EMP: 5 EST: 2019
SALES (est): 100K **Privately Held**
SIC: **7371** Computer software development and applications

(G-12320)
VESTA WASH LLC
146 Woodland Rd (19702-1474)
PHONE..................................302 559-7533
Timothy Tim, *Managing Member*
EMP: 5 EST: 2013
SALES (est): 137.47K **Privately Held**
Web: www.vestawash.com
SIC: **7699** Cleaning services

(G-12321)
VETERANS OF FOREIGN WARS
100 Veterans Dr (19711-4515)
PHONE..................................302 366-8438
EMP: 5 EST: 2019
SALES (est): 198.83K **Privately Held**
Web: www.vfw3420.org
SIC: **8641** Veterans' organization

(G-12322)
VICTOR COLBERT CONSTRUCTION
723 Old Baltimore Pike (19702-1316)
PHONE..................................302 368-7270
Victor Colbert, *Owner*
EMP: 5 EST: 1971
SALES (est): 241.37K **Privately Held**
SIC: **1771** Concrete work

(G-12323)
VICTORIA MEWS GROUP INVSTORS L (PA)
13 Odaniel Ave (19711-3521)
PHONE..................................610 543-0303
Robert D Wright, *Managing Member*
EMP: 7 EST: 2022
SALES (est): 77.4K
SALES (corp-wide): 77.4K **Privately Held**
SIC: **6513** Apartment building operators

(G-12324)
VINAY HOSMANE MD
2600 Glasgow Ave Ste 103 (19702-5703)
PHONE..................................302 836-2727
Vinay Hosmane, *Ofcr*
EMP: 9 EST: 2004
SALES (est): 54.13K **Privately Held**
Web: www.hosmanecardiology.com
SIC: **8011** Cardiologist and cardio-vascular specialist

(G-12325)
VINCES SPORTS CENTER INC
14 Gender Rd (19713-2899)
PHONE..................................302 738-4859
Vince Santucci, *Pr*
EMP: 5 EST: 1960
SQ FT: 16,800
SALES (est): 482.39K **Privately Held**
Web: www.vincessports.com
SIC: **7999** 7992 Miniature golf course operation; Public golf courses

(G-12326)
VINTAGE REALTY
2612 Kirkwood Hwy (19711)
PHONE..................................302 731-1000
Barbara Helmstadter, *Owner*
EMP: 7 EST: 1989
SALES (est): 93.79K **Privately Held**
Web: www.vintagerealty.com
SIC: **6531** Real estate agent, commercial

(G-12327)
VIR CONSULTANT LLC
256 Chapman Rd (19702-5499)
PHONE..................................747 666-2169
Ranjit Raj, *Managing Member*
EMP: 30 EST: 2021
SALES (est): 867.09K **Privately Held**
Web: www.virconsultants.com
SIC: **8742** 7389 Business management consultant; Business services, nec

(G-12328)
VIRCAP LLC ✪
112 Capitol Trl Ste A (19711-3716)
PHONE..................................302 261-9892
EMP: 10 EST: 2022
SALES (est): 348.32K **Privately Held**
SIC: **7389** Financial services

(G-12329)
VIRTUAL OPLOSSING PVT LTD ✪
256 Chapman Rd Ste 105-4 (19702-5499)
PHONE..................................866 268-0333
Prabnek Singh, *CEO*
EMP: 5 EST: 2022
SALES (est): 68.89K **Privately Held**
SIC: **7371** Software programming applications

(G-12330)
VISION CAPITAL III LLC
200 Continental Dr # 401 (19713-4334)
PHONE..................................312 576-2247
EMP: 10 EST: 2021
SALES (est): 376.36K **Privately Held**
SIC: **7389** Financial services

(G-12331)
VISION CAPITAL VI LLC
200 Continental Dr # 401 (19713-4334)
PHONE..................................312 576-2247
EMP: 10 EST: 2021
SALES (est): 305.13K **Privately Held**
SIC: **7389** Financial services

(G-12332)
VITAS HEALTHCARE CORPORATION
100 Commerce Dr. Christina Corp Ctr #302 (19713)
PHONE..................................302 451-4000
Hugh Westbrook, *Brnch Mgr*
EMP: 119
SALES (corp-wide): 2.13B **Publicly Held**
Web: www.vitas.com
SIC: **8052** Personal care facility
HQ: Vitas Healthcare Corporation
201 S Biscayne Blvd # 400
Miami FL 33131
305 374-4143

(G-12333)
VLS IT CONSULTING INC
260 Chapman Rd Ste 104a (19702-5410)
PHONE..................................302 368-5656
Lilma Jagnanan, *Pr*
EMP: 10 EST: 2002
SALES (est): 272.47K **Privately Held**
Web: www.vlsitconsulting.com
SIC: **7379** Online services technology consultants

(G-12334)
VNA OF DELAWARE
Also Called: Christiana High Sch Wellness
190 Salem Church Rd (19713-2938)
PHONE..................................302 454-5422
Lynn Jones, *Dir*
EMP: 10 EST: 2000
SALES (est): 186.15K **Privately Held**
Web: www.christinak12.org
SIC: **8082** Home health care services

(G-12335)
VONEXPY SOFTECH LLC
440 Jacobsen Dr (19702-1595)
PHONE..................................512 484-8340
Ram Varma, *Prin*
EMP: 5 EST: 2019
SALES (est): 72.08K **Privately Held**
SIC: **7379** Computer related consulting services

(G-12336)
VONOGRPHY-THE PERFECT SHOT LLC
38 Bastille Loop (19702-5528)
PHONE..................................202 923-9532
EMP: 5 EST: 2021
SALES (est): 100K **Privately Held**
SIC: **7335** Commercial photography

(G-12337)
VP RACING FUELS INC
Also Called: Vp Racing Fuels
16 Brookhill Dr (19702-1301)
PHONE..................................302 368-1500
James J Kelly, *Brnch Mgr*
EMP: 8
Web: www.vpracingfuels.com
SIC: **5172** Lubricating oils and greases
HQ: Vp Racing Fuels, Inc.
10205 Oasis Dr
San Antonio TX 78216

(G-12338)
VPHO
2671 Kirkwood Highway (19711)
PHONE..................................302 369-3993
EMP: 4 EST: 2017
SALES (est): 95.4K **Privately Held**
Web: www.vpho.net
SIC: **2099** Food preparations, nec

(G-12339)
VYLO INC (PA)
256 Chapman Rd (19702-5499)
PHONE..................................310 902-9693
EMP: 7
SALES (est): 298.62K
SALES (corp-wide): 298.62K **Privately Held**
SIC: **2741** 7389 Internet publishing and broadcasting; Business Activities at Non-Commercial Site

(G-12340)
W B MASON CO INC
100 Interchange Blvd (19711-3549)
PHONE..................................888 926-2766
Sara Jester, *Pr*
EMP: 45
SALES (corp-wide): 1.01B **Privately Held**
Web: www.wbmason.com
SIC: **5712** 2752 Office furniture; Commercial printing, lithographic
PA: W. B. Mason Co., Inc.
59 Centre Street
Brockton MA 02301
508 586-3434

(G-12341)
W L GORE & ASSOCIATES INC
1901 Barksdale Rd (19711-2542)
PHONE..................................302 368-3700
EMP: 119
SALES (corp-wide): 4.5B **Privately Held**
Web: www.gore.com
SIC: **3357** 2821 5131 3841 Communication wire; Polytetrafluoroethylene resins, teflon; Synthetic fabrics, nec; Medical instruments and equipment, blood and bone work
PA: W. L. Gore & Associates, Inc.
555 Paper Mill Rd
Newark DE 19711
302 738-4880

(G-12342)
W L GORE & ASSOCIATES INC (PA)
Also Called: Sitka
555 Paper Mill Rd (19711-7513)
P.O. Box 9329 (19714-9329)
PHONE..................................302 738-4880
▲ EMP: 60 EST: 1958
SALES (est): 4.5B
SALES (corp-wide): 4.5B **Privately Held**
Web: www.gore.com
SIC: **3357** 2821 5131 3841 Aircraft wire and cable, nonferrous; Polytetrafluoroethylene resins, teflon; Synthetic fabrics, nec; Medical instruments and equipment, blood and bone work

(G-12343)
WAFFLES & WIFI LLC
254 Chapman Rd (19702-5413)
PHONE..................................267 909-0174
EMP: 3
SALES (est): 137.66K **Privately Held**
SIC: **2099** Food preparations, nec

(G-12344)
WALKERS FOR JOCELYN
5 Fairway Rd (19711-5624)
PHONE..................................302 465-7461
Judy Cash, *Prin*
EMP: 5 EST: 2010
SALES (est): 60.06K **Privately Held**
SIC: **8399** Advocacy group

(G-12345)
WALLACE MONTGOMERY & ASSOC LLP
200 Continental Dr (19713-4335)
PHONE..................................302 510-1080
Matthew Allen, *Pt*
EMP: 67
SALES (corp-wide): 20.1MM **Privately Held**
Web: www.wallacemontgomery.com
SIC: **8711** Civil engineering
PA: Wallace Montgomery & Assoc Llp
10150 York Rd Ste 200
Hunt Valley MD
410 494-9093

(G-12346)
WALNUT GROVE COOP INC
321 Laurel Ave (19711-4730)
PHONE..................................302 545-3000
EMP: 6 EST: 2018
SALES (est): 78.65K **Privately Held**
Web: www.walnutgrovecoop.com
SIC: **0173** Walnut grove

(G-12347)
WARREN G BUTT M D
4745 Ogletown Stanton Rd Ste 134 (19713-2074)
PHONE..................................302 738-5300
Warren Butt, *Mgr*

Newark - New Castle County (G-12348) GEOGRAPHIC SECTION

EMP: 9 EST: 2018
SALES (est): 59.55K **Privately Held**
Web:
www.endoscopycenterofdelaware.com
SIC: **8011** Gastronomist

(G-12348)
WATER IS LIFE KENYA INC
314 E Main St Ste 2 (19711-7195)
PHONE...................................302 894-7335
EMP: 9 EST: 2011
SALES (est): 321.44K **Privately Held**
Web: www.waterislifekenya.com
SIC: **8699** Charitable organization

(G-12349)
WAY TO GO LED LIGHTING COMPANY
702 Interchange Blvd (19711-3595)
PHONE...................................844 312-4574
Limin Su, *Pr*
▲ EMP: 10 EST: 2013
SALES (est): 945.05K **Privately Held**
SIC: **5063** Lighting fixtures

(G-12350)
WAZOPLUS LLC
4 Peddlers Row (19702-1525)
PHONE...................................302 496-0042
EMP: 2
SALES (est): 59.23K **Privately Held**
SIC: **2741** Internet publishing and broadcasting

(G-12351)
WE MANAGE YOUR SITE INC
2035 Sunset Lake Rd Ste B2 (19702-2600)
PHONE...................................916 586-7724
EMP: 8 EST: 2017
SALES (est): 158.66K **Privately Held**
Web: www.wemanageyoursite.com
SIC: **8741** Management services

(G-12352)
WEALTH ACCESS SERVICES LLC
200 Continental Dr Ste 401 (19713-4334)
PHONE...................................302 327-4174
Derrick Green, *Managing Member*
EMP: 5 EST: 2020
SALES (est): 235.68K **Privately Held**
SIC: **8742** Financial consultant

(G-12353)
WEBMOST
56 Upland Ct (19713-2817)
PHONE...................................302 345-0807
EMP: 6 EST: 2014
SALES (est): 75.81K **Privately Held**
Web: www.webmost.com
SIC: **7374** Computer graphics service

(G-12354)
WEED REAL ESTATE LLC
5 Sumac Ct (19702-2885)
PHONE...................................302 981-6388
EMP: 5 EST: 2018
SALES (est): 134.08K **Privately Held**
Web: www.longandfoster.com
SIC: **6531** Real estate brokers and agents

(G-12355)
WEGMAN BROS INC
2612 Ogletown Rd (19713-1824)
P.O. Box 7625 (19714-7625)
PHONE...................................302 738-4328
Danny Wegman, *CEO*
Chuck Wegman, *Pr*
Colleen Wegman, *Pr*
Ray Wegman, *VP*
Joyce Wegman, *Sec*

EMP: 10 EST: 1959
SALES (est): 973.92K **Privately Held**
Web: www.wegmanbrothers.com
SIC: **1711** Plumbing contractors

(G-12356)
WEITRON INC (PA)
Also Called: Weitron
801 Pencader Dr (19702-3337)
PHONE...................................800 398-3816
Deborah W Dayton, *Pr*
◆ EMP: 24 EST: 1992
SQ FT: 40,000
SALES (est): 20.9MM
SALES (corp-wide): 20.9MM **Privately Held**
Web: www.weitron.com
SIC: **7623** Refrigeration service and repair

(G-12357)
WELLNESS PLUS
212 Cloverlea Rd (19711-6806)
PHONE...................................302 368-7990
Leny Hugh, *Prin*
EMP: 5 EST: 2010
SALES (est): 59.24K **Privately Held**
SIC: **8099** Health and allied services, nec

(G-12358)
WELLS FARGO BANK NATIONAL ASSN
2624 Capitol Trl (19711-7252)
PHONE...................................302 631-1500
Phyllis Maher, *Mgr*
EMP: 8
SALES (corp-wide): 82.86B **Publicly Held**
Web: www.wellsfargo.com
SIC: **6021** National commercial banks
HQ: Wells Fargo Bank, National Association
  420 Montgomery St San
  San Francisco CA 94104
  605 575-6900

(G-12359)
WELLS FARGO CLEARING SVCS LLC
Also Called: Wells Fargo Advisors
131 Continental Dr Ste 102 (19713-4310)
P.O. Box 8096 (19714-8096)
PHONE...................................302 731-2131
Frank Alteri, *Mgr*
EMP: 8
SALES (corp-wide): 82.86B **Publicly Held**
Web: www.wellsfargoadvisors.com
SIC: **6211** Security brokers and dealers
HQ: Wells Fargo Clearing Services, Llc
  1 N Jefferson Ave Fl 7
  Saint Louis MO 63103

(G-12360)
WELLS KRYSTAL
207 Kinross Dr (19711-1531)
PHONE...................................302 738-4191
Krystal Wells, *Prin*
EMP: 5 EST: 2008
SALES (est): 108.41K **Privately Held**
SIC: **6021** National commercial banks

(G-12361)
WESTECH INDUSTRIES INC
Also Called: Westech
101 Alan Dr (19711-8028)
PHONE...................................302 453-0301
Thomas Goetz, *Pr*
▲ EMP: 8 EST: 1978
SQ FT: 20,000
SALES (est): 1.41MM **Privately Held**
Web: www.westech-industries.net
SIC: **4225** General warehousing and storage

(G-12362)
WESTOVER MANAGEMENT COMPANY LP
Also Called: Allandale Village Apartments
1 Allandale Dr (19713-3167)
PHONE...................................302 738-5775
Janet Yanneuzzi, *Mgr*
EMP: 6
SALES (corp-wide): 12.66MM **Privately Held**
Web: www.rentallandalevillage.com
SIC: **6513** Apartment hotel operation
PA: Westover Management Company, L.P.
  550 American Ave Ste 1
  King Of Prussia PA 19406
  610 494-6430

(G-12363)
WESTOVER MANAGEMENT COMPANY LP
Also Called: Glen Eagle Villaige
24 Sandalwood Dr Ofc 5 (19713-3541)
PHONE...................................302 731-1638
Michelle Carre, *Mgr*
EMP: 10
SALES (corp-wide): 12.66MM **Privately Held**
Web: www.westovercompanies.com
SIC: **6513** Apartment hotel operation
PA: Westover Management Company, L.P.
  550 American Ave Ste 1
  King Of Prussia PA 19406
  610 494-6430

(G-12364)
WESTSIDE FAMILY HEALTHCARE INC
27 Marrows Rd (19713-3701)
PHONE...................................302 455-0900
Janell Williams, *Mgr*
EMP: 35
Web: www.westsidehealth.org
SIC: **8011** 8021 Clinic, operated by physicians; Offices and clinics of dentists
PA: Westside Family Healthcare, Inc.
  300 Water St Ste 200
  Wilmington DE 19801

(G-12365)
WHET INDUSTRIES INC
560 Peoples Plz Ste 144 (19702-4798)
PHONE...................................302 236-2182
EMP: 3 EST: 2013
SALES (est): 59.71K **Privately Held**
SIC: **3999** Manufacturing industries, nec

(G-12366)
WHITE CLAY CREEK VTRINARY HOSP
Also Called: Spencer, Richard N Jr Vmd
107 Albe Dr Ste A (19702-1300)
PHONE...................................302 738-9611
Richard Spencer, *Pr*
EMP: 8 EST: 1991
SALES (est): 203.4K **Privately Held**
Web: www.whiteclaycreekvet.com
SIC: **0742** Animal hospital services, pets and other animal specialties

(G-12367)
WHITE EAGLE ELECTRIC
50 Albe Dr (19702-1330)
PHONE...................................302 533-7799
EMP: 5 EST: 2017
SALES (est): 70.14K **Privately Held**
SIC: **1731** General electrical contractor

(G-12368)
WHITE MINK BEAUTY SALON
330 College Sq (19711-5494)
PHONE...................................302 737-2081
Don Bettner, *Owner*
EMP: 5 EST: 1962
SALES (est): 98.1K **Privately Held**
SIC: **7231** Beauty shops

(G-12369)
WHITING-TURNER CONTRACTING CO
131 Continental Dr Ste 404 (19713-4358)
PHONE...................................302 292-0676
James Martini, *Sr VP*
EMP: 40
SALES (corp-wide): 8.62B **Privately Held**
Web: www.whiting-turner.com
SIC: **1541** 1542 Industrial buildings and warehouses; Nonresidential construction, nec
PA: The Whiting-Turner Contracting Company
  300 E Joppa Rd Ste 800
  Baltimore MD 21286
  410 821-1100

(G-12370)
WHITING-TURNER CONTRACTING CO
79 Amstel Ave (19716-4200)
PHONE...................................302 266-7450
EMP: 10 EST: 2018
SALES (est): 236.92K **Privately Held**
Web: www.whiting-turner.com
SIC: **1542** Commercial and office building, new construction

(G-12371)
WHY UNIFIED CORP
200 Continental Dr Ste 401 (19713-4334)
PHONE...................................302 803-5892
Robert Nikic, *CEO*
EMP: 25 EST: 2018
SALES (est): 1.08MM **Privately Held**
Web: www.whyunified.com
SIC: **8742** Marketing consulting services

(G-12372)
WIK ASSOCIATES INC
10 Donaldson Dr (19713-1783)
PHONE...................................302 322-2558
Beverly J Wik, *Pr*
Marian Young, *VP*
EMP: 7 EST: 1984
SQ FT: 12,000
SALES (est): 237.98K **Privately Held**
SIC: **8748** Environmental consultant

(G-12373)
WILLIAM B FUNK MD
665 Churchmans Rd (19702-1918)
PHONE...................................302 731-0900
William B Funk Md, *Owner*
EMP: 10 EST: 1980
SALES (est): 600.04K **Privately Held**
SIC: **8011** Physicians' office, including specialists

(G-12374)
WILLIAM B TABELING
22 Revelstone Dr (19711-2984)
PHONE...................................302 234-9401
William B Tabeling, *Prin*
EMP: 6 EST: 2010
SALES (est): 94.43K **Privately Held**
SIC: **8721** Certified public accountant

GEOGRAPHIC SECTION

Newark - New Castle County (G-12403)

(G-12375)
WILLIAM H RALSTON DDS OFFICE
344 E Main St (19711-7148)
PHONE.........................336 957-4948
EMP: 7 **EST:** 2019
SALES (est): 61.51K **Privately Held**
SIC: 8021 Dentists' office

(G-12376)
WILLIAM R ATKINS MD
550 Stanton Christiana Rd Ste 201 (19713-2125)
PHONE.........................302 633-4525
William R Atkins, *Prin*
EMP: 9 **EST:** 2010
SALES (est): 132.78K **Privately Held**
SIC: 8011 Offices and clinics of medical doctors

(G-12377)
WILLIAM REDDING AND SON
241 Smalleys Dam Rd A (19702-3007)
PHONE.........................302 562-4026
William Redding, *Prin*
EMP: 5 **EST:** 2008
SALES (est): 139.95K **Privately Held**
SIC: 1522 Residential construction, nec

(G-12378)
WILMINGTON & NEWARK DENTAL
13 Aronimink Dr (19711-3801)
PHONE.........................302 571-0526
Richard Dettro, *Pr*
Jack Leyh Cdt, *VP*
EMP: 7 **EST:** 1971
SALES (est): 493.49K **Privately Held**
SIC: 8072 Dental laboratories

(G-12379)
WILMINGTON AREA PLG COUNCIL
Also Called: Wilmapco
100 Discovery Blvd Ste 800 (19713-1325)
PHONE.........................302 737-6205
Tigist Zegeye, *Ex Dir*
Alexander Caft, *Dir*
Charls L Backer, *Asst Dir*
EMP: 10 **EST:** 1964
SALES (est): 983.7K **Privately Held**
Web: www.wilmapco.org
SIC: 8748 Urban planning and consulting services

(G-12380)
WILMINGTON CHRISTIANA COU
48 Geoffrey Dr (19713-3603)
PHONE.........................302 456-3800
Bill Holper, *Owner*
EMP: 19 **EST:** 2007
SALES (est): 236.92K **Privately Held**
SIC: 7011 Hotel, franchised

(G-12381)
WILMINGTON PHARMATECH CO LLC (PA)
2309 Sunset Lake Rd (19702-3618)
PHONE.........................302 737-9916
Hui-yin Harry Li, *Pr*
EMP: 22 **EST:** 2001
SQ FT: 4,000
SALES (est): 1.6MM
SALES (corp-wide): 1.6MM **Privately Held**
Web: www.wilmingtonpharmatech.com
SIC: 8731 Biotechnical research, commercial

(G-12382)
WILMINGTON SAVINGS FUND SOC
Also Called: University Plaza Branch
100 University Plz (19702-1551)
PHONE.........................302 456-6404
Karen Harris, *Mgr*
EMP: 10
SALES (corp-wide): 963.95MM **Publicly Held**
Web: www.wsfsbank.com
SIC: 6022 State commercial banks
HQ: Wilmington Savings Fund Society
500 Delaware Ave
Wilmington DE 19801
302 792-6000

(G-12383)
WILMINGTON TRAIL CLUB
15 Tenby Chase Dr (19711-2440)
PHONE.........................302 521-3815
EMP: 6 **EST:** 2016
SALES (est): 47.52K **Privately Held**
Web: www.wilmingtontrailclub.org
SIC: 7997 Membership sports and recreation clubs

(G-12384)
WILMINGTON TRAP ASSOCIATION
Also Called: Wta
2828 Pulaski Hwy (19702-3913)
P.O. Box 203 (19715-0203)
PHONE.........................302 834-9320
Allan Brown, *Pr*
Steve Hastings, *Sec*
William Trone, *VP*
EMP: 6 **EST:** 2002
SALES (est): 235.1K **Privately Held**
SIC: 8641 Recreation association

(G-12385)
WILMINGTON VA MEDICAL CENT
47 Oklahoma State Dr (19713-1196)
PHONE.........................302 294-6743
Mary Kozel, *Prin*
EMP: 6 **EST:** 2013
SALES (est): 90.4K **Privately Held**
SIC: 8099 Health and allied services, nec

(G-12386)
WILSON CARE WILSON CO
5 William Davis Ct (19702-1160)
PHONE.........................302 897-5059
Henry Wilson, *Prin*
EMP: 9 **EST:** 2010
SALES (est): 115.16K **Privately Held**
SIC: 8351 Child day care services

(G-12387)
WINMILL CLEANING
35 Country Ln W (19702-3723)
PHONE.........................302 731-4139
Leo Polanco, *Prin*
EMP: 5 **EST:** 2006
SALES (est): 30.36K **Privately Held**
SIC: 7699 Cleaning services

(G-12388)
WINNER FORD OF NEWARK INC
303 E Cleveland Ave (19711-3793)
PHONE.........................302 731-2415
John Hynansky, *Pr*
Mike Hynansky, *
John Hynansky, *VP*
▼ **EMP:** 10 **EST:** 1972
SQ FT: 24,000
SALES (est): 394.17K **Privately Held**
Web: www.ford.com
SIC: 5511 7515 7513 5531 Automobiles, new and used; Passenger car leasing; Truck leasing, without drivers; Auto and home supply stores

(G-12389)
WINNER GROUP INC
Also Called: Saturn
1801 Ogletown Rd (19711-5429)
PHONE.........................302 292-8200
Wayne Weir, *Mgr*
EMP: 14
SALES (corp-wide): 49.87MM **Privately Held**
Web: www.winnerauto.com
SIC: 5012 7538 7515 5531 Automobiles; General automotive repair shops; Passenger car leasing; Auto and home supply stores
PA: Winner Group, Inc
911 N Tatnall St
Wilmington DE 19801
302 764-5900

(G-12390)
WIRELESS CENTER
50 E Main St (19711-4673)
PHONE.........................302 455-7220
EMP: 5 **EST:** 2019
SALES (est): 35.32K **Privately Held**
SIC: 4812 Cellular telephone services

(G-12391)
WLG EQUITY INC (HQ)
551 Paper Mill Rd (19711-7513)
PHONE.........................302 738-4880
EMP: 42 **EST:** 2012
SALES (est): 424.85K
SALES (corp-wide): 4.5B **Privately Held**
SIC: 3999 Manufacturing industries, nec
PA: W. L. Gore & Associates, Inc.
555 Paper Mill Rd
Newark DE 19711
302 738-4880

(G-12392)
WNA INFOTECH LLC
704 Sloop Ct (19702-4826)
PHONE.........................302 668-5977
EMP: 25 **EST:** 2018
SALES (est): 1.44MM **Privately Held**
Web: www.wna-infotech.com
SIC: 2741 5961 7371 Internet publishing and broadcasting; Electronic shopping; Software programming applications
PA: Wna Infotech Private Limited
243, Vibhusha, Ghuma, Village Taluka City, Dist
Ahmedabad GJ 38005

(G-12393)
WOLFE BACKHOE SERVICE
8 Springlake Dr (19711-6742)
PHONE.........................302 737-2628
EMP: 4 **EST:** 2017
SALES (est): 60.08K **Privately Held**
SIC: 3531 Backhoes

(G-12394)
WOMEN FIRST LLC
4745 Ogletown Stanton Rd Ste 105 (19713-2070)
PHONE.........................302 368-3257
EMP: 14 **EST:** 2009
SALES (est): 1.62MM **Privately Held**
Web: www.womenfirstllc.com
SIC: 8011 Gynecologist

(G-12395)
WOMEN OF MORE
16 Birchgrove Rd (19702-3749)
PHONE.........................260 760-8083
EMP: 5 **EST:** 2016
SALES (est): 63.18K **Privately Held**
SIC: 8399 Advocacy group

(G-12396)
WOMENS HEALTHCARE CONSULTANTS
1400 Peoples Plz Ste 301 (19702-5708)
PHONE.........................443 553-1398
Joseph M Knapp, *Owner*
EMP: 5 **EST:** 2018
SALES (est): 280.62K **Privately Held**
SIC: 8748 Business consulting, nec

(G-12397)
WOMENS IMAGING CENTER DELAWARE
46 Omega Dr Ste J24 (19713-2060)
PHONE.........................302 738-9494
Steven Edell Md, *Pr*
EMP: 8 **EST:** 1986
SALES (est): 153.48K **Privately Held**
SIC: 8099 Physical examination and testing services

(G-12398)
WOMENS TENNIS CLUB OF NEW
446 Haystack Dr (19711-8316)
PHONE.........................302 731-1456
EMP: 6 **EST:** 2017
SALES (est): 51.08K **Privately Held**
Web: www.wtcncc.org
SIC: 7997 Membership sports and recreation clubs

(G-12399)
WOMENS WELLNESS CTR & MED SPA
1400 Peoples Plz Ste 301 (19702-5708)
PHONE.........................302 643-2500
J Michael Knapp D.o.s., *Owner*
EMP: 6 **EST:** 2017
SALES (est): 415.21K **Privately Held**
Web: www.womenswellnessde.com
SIC: 8011 7231 Gynecologist; Cosmetology and personal hygiene salons

(G-12400)
WONCHIN INSTITUTE
8 Mercer Dr (19713-1562)
P.O. Box 129 (19720-0129)
PHONE.........................302 602-5753
Lan Chu, *Prin*
EMP: 5 **EST:** 2010
SALES (est): 73.96K **Privately Held**
SIC: 8733 Noncommercial research organizations

(G-12401)
WOOD EXPRESSIONS INCORPORATED
2 Savoy Rd (19702-8610)
PHONE.........................302 738-6189
Patricia A Veney, *Prin*
EMP: 6 **EST:** 2008
SALES (est): 167.24K **Privately Held**
SIC: 2491 Wood products, creosoted

(G-12402)
WOODEN WHEELS SVC & REPR LLC
208 Louviers Dr (19711-4167)
PHONE.........................302 368-2453
David Ferguson, *Managing Member*
EMP: 5 **EST:** 2018
SALES (est): 147.59K **Privately Held**
Web: www.woodenwheels.bike
SIC: 7699 Bicycle repair shop

(G-12403)
WOOS FOUNDATION
5 Farmhouse Rd (19711-7458)
PHONE.........................302 366-0259
EMP: 6 **EST:** 2011
SALES (est): 46.77K **Privately Held**
SIC: 8699 Charitable organization

Newark - New Castle County (G-12404)   GEOGRAPHIC SECTION

(G-12404)
WORKATIV SFTWR SOLUTIONS LLC
2035 Sunset Lake Rd B2 (19702-2600)
PHONE..................312 375-1062
EMP: 16 EST: 2019
SALES (est): 100K Privately Held
SIC: 7371 Software programming applications

(G-12405)
WORKFORCE CLOUD TECH INC (PA)
2035 Sunset Lake Rd Ste B2 (19702-2600)
PHONE..................915 800-2362
Ajay Mallapurkar, *CEO*
EMP: 12
SALES (est): 2.24MM
SALES (corp-wide): 2.24MM Privately Held
SIC: 7371 Software programming applications

(G-12406)
WORKPRO HEALTH
4051 Ogletown Rd (19713-3101)
PHONE..................302 722-4471
EMP: 11 EST: 2015
SALES (est): 79.25K Privately Held
Web: www.ohsde.org
SIC: 8011 Clinic, operated by physicians

(G-12407)
WORKWALL INC
256 Chapman Rd Ste 105-4 (19702-5499)
PHONE..................415 800-2809
Harsh Gautam, *CEO*
EMP: 10 EST: 2021
SALES (est): 348.32K Privately Held
SIC: 7371 7389 Computer software development and applications; Business Activities at Non-Commercial Site

(G-12408)
WORLD CLASS PRODUCTS LLC
Also Called: World Class Supply
375 Wedgewood Rd (19711-2041)
PHONE..................302 737-1441
EMP: 3 EST: 2007
SALES (est): 267.57K Privately Held
Web: www.worldclasssupply.com
SIC: 3433 Room and wall heaters, including radiators

(G-12409)
WORLD TRADE SPONSOR INC
113 Barksdale Professional Ctr (19711-3258)
PHONE..................404 780-3333
EMP: 6 EST: 2008
SALES (est): 75.42K Privately Held
SIC: 8742 Retail trade consultant

(G-12410)
WORLD WIDE TRADING BROKERS
606 Benham Ct (19711-6015)
PHONE..................302 368-7041
Nader Ramadan, *Pr*
EMP: 8 EST: 1998
SALES (est): 650.51K Privately Held
SIC: 5084 5047 Industrial machinery and equipment; Medical and hospital equipment

(G-12411)
WORLDS BEST MASSAGE THERAPY
412 Capitol Trl (19711-3865)
PHONE..................302 366-8777
Carrie Nelson, *Owner*
EMP: 8 EST: 2013
SALES (est): 123.84K Privately Held
Web: www.pandaasianmassage.com

SIC: 8093 Rehabilitation center, outpatient treatment

(G-12412)
WRENCHTIME AUTO LLC (PA)
42 Albe Dr (19702-1358)
PHONE..................302 500-5558
Dwayne Lindenmuth, *Mgr*
EMP: 7 EST: 2021
SALES (est): 273.75K
SALES (corp-wide): 273.75K Privately Held
SIC: 7539 Automotive repair shops, nec

(G-12413)
WSP USA SOLUTIONS INC
254 Chapman Rd Ste 203 (19702-5413)
PHONE..................302 737-1872
Louis Berger, *Brnch Mgr*
EMP: 30
SALES (corp-wide): 8.88B Privately Held
Web: www.wsp.com
SIC: 8711 Consulting engineer
HQ: Wsp Usa Solutions Inc.
350 Mount Kemble Ave # 2
Morristown NJ 07960
973 407-1000

(G-12414)
WSWMS HVAC
1114 Janice Dr (19713-2353)
PHONE..................302 454-1987
Walter A Ruth, *Owner*
EMP: 7 EST: 2015
SALES (est): 219.94K Privately Held
SIC: 1711 Heating and air conditioning contractors

(G-12415)
WYNRIGHT CORP
28 Donegal Ct (19711-3441)
PHONE..................302 239-9796
EMP: 6 EST: 2019
SALES (est): 61.12K Privately Held
Web: www.daifukuia.com
SIC: 5084 Materials handling machinery

(G-12416)
XPRESS TRANSPORT LOGISTICS LLC
1115 Elkton Rd (19711-3508)
PHONE..................610 800-2288
Walter Nyandiba, *Pr*
EMP: 5 EST: 2015
SALES (est): 375.49K Privately Held
SIC: 4789 Transportation services, nec

(G-12417)
XROSSWATER USA LLC
40 E Main St Ste 118 (19711-4639)
PHONE..................917 310-1344
Malcolm Harrison, *Managing Member*
EMP: 2 EST: 2008
SQ FT: 5,000
SALES (est): 235.84K Privately Held
Web: www.xrosswater.com
SIC: 3625 Marine and navy auxiliary controls

(G-12418)
YCLAS INC
2035 Sunset Lake Rd B2 (19702-2600)
PHONE..................929 377-1239
EMP: 6 EST: 2019
SALES (est): 87.5K Privately Held
Web: www.yclas.com
SIC: 7371 Computer software development and applications

(G-12419)
YES U CAN CORPORATION
2504 Creekside Dr (19711-6747)
PHONE..................302 286-1399
Vickie George, *Prin*
EMP: 5 EST: 2010
SALES (est): 11.91K Privately Held
Web: www.yesucanusa.org
SIC: 8699 Charitable organization

(G-12420)
YMCA OF DELAWARE B/A SCH PGRM
Also Called: YMCA
351 George Williams Way (19702-3518)
PHONE..................302 836-9622
Karen Shearer, *Dir*
EMP: 21 EST: 2015
SALES (est): 200.74K Privately Held
Web: www.ymcade.org
SIC: 8641 Youth organizations

(G-12421)
YOGO FACTORY
2610 Kirkwood Hwy (19711-7252)
PHONE..................302 266-4506
EMP: 6 EST: 2014
SALES (est): 118.2K Privately Held
SIC: 7999 5143 Yoga instruction; Yogurt

(G-12422)
YOUNG MNS CHRSTN ASSN WLMNGTON
Also Called: YMCA
2600 Kirkwood Hwy (19711)
PHONE..................302 709-9622
Mary Young, *Dir*
EMP: 124
SALES (corp-wide): 40.98MM Privately Held
Web: www.ymcade.org
SIC: 7997 8641 7991 7999 Membership sports and recreation clubs; Civic and social associations; Physical fitness facilities ; Recreation center
PA: Young Men's Christian Association Of Delaware
100 W 10th St Ste 1100
Wilmington DE 19801
302 571-6968

(G-12423)
YOUR SUPERFOODS INC
2035 Sunset Lake Rd (19702-2600)
PHONE..................424 387-6165
EMP: 9 EST: 2019
SALES (est): 125.1K Privately Held
SIC: 7374 Computer graphics service

(G-12424)
YUMI NUTRITION INC
2035 Sunset Lake Rd Ste B2 (19702-2600)
PHONE..................917 909-2166
Adam Barker, *Ex Dir*
EMP: 3 EST: 2018
SALES (est): 150K Privately Held
Web: www.yuminutrition.com
SIC: 2023 Dietary supplements, dairy and non-dairy based

(G-12425)
YWCA DELAWARE
Also Called: Young Wns Christn Assocation
153 E Chestnut Hill Rd Ste 102 (19713-4044)
PHONE..................302 224-4060
EMP: 13
SALES (corp-wide): 3.87MM Privately Held
Web: www.ywcade.org

SIC: 8641 7991 8351 7032 Youth organizations; Physical fitness facilities; Child day care services; Youth camps
PA: Ywca Delaware
100 W 10th St Ste 515
Wilmington DE 19801
302 655-0039

(G-12426)
Z DATA INC
Also Called: Zdata Mt
40 E Main St Ste 610 (19711-4639)
PHONE..................800 676-5614
David Seybold, *CEO*
Anil Agarwal, *CFO*
EMP: 5 EST: 2007
SALES (est): 937.62K
SALES (corp-wide): 129.21MM Privately Held
Web: www.zdatainc.com
SIC: 7371 Custom computer programming services
PA: Atos Se
Immeuble River Ouest
Bezons 95870
964450614

(G-12427)
Z DATA INC
40 E Main St Ste 610 (19711-4639)
PHONE..................800 676-5614
David Seybold, *CEO*
Anil Agarwal, *CFO*
EMP: 5 EST: 2011
SALES (est): 819.66K
SALES (corp-wide): 129.21MM Privately Held
Web: www.zdatainc.com
SIC: 7371 7379 Computer software development; Computer related consulting services
HQ: Atos It Solutions And Services Inc.
5920 Wndhven Pkwy Ste 120
Plano TX 75093
682 978-8622

(G-12428)
ZABEL PLSTC&RECNSTRCTVE SURGRY
550 Stanton Christiana Rd Ste 202 (19713-2198)
PHONE..................302 996-6400
David Zabel, *Prin*
EMP: 17 EST: 2009
SALES (est): 2.41MM Privately Held
Web: www.zabelplasticsurgery.com
SIC: 8011 Surgeon

(G-12429)
ZACROS AMERICA INC
Also Called: Zacros America Hedwin Division
220 Lake Dr Ste 4 (19702-3353)
PHONE..................302 391-2200
Richard Broo, *Pr*
EMP: 200 EST: 2015
SALES (est): 53.72MM Privately Held
Web: www.zacrosamerica.com
SIC: 2671 Plastic film, coated or laminated for packaging
PA: Fujimori Kogyo Co.,Ltd.
1-1-1, Koishikawa
Bunkyo-Ku TKY 112-0

(G-12430)
ZEHNACKER RUSS CRNA PA
263 W Chestnut Hill Rd (19713-2212)
PHONE..................302 834-7523
Russell Zehnacker, *Prin*
EMP: 6 EST: 2010
SALES (est): 78.54K Privately Held

SIC: 8049 Nurses, registered and practical

(G-12431)
ZENNER INC
200 Continental Dr Ste 401 (19713-4334)
PHONE..............................302 781-9833
Elad Schaffer, *CEO*
EMP: 10 EST: 2019
SALES (est): 500K **Privately Held**
Web: www.zenner.ai
SIC: 4724 Travel agencies

(G-12432)
ZENPLI LLC
256 Chapman Rd Ste 105-4 (19702-5499)
PHONE..............................302 314-5231
Rodolfo Chiari, *Managing Member*
EMP: 10 EST: 2021
SALES (est): 348.32K **Privately Held**
SIC: 7371 7389 Custom computer programming services; Business services, nec

(G-12433)
ZENW LLC
200 Continental Dr (19713-4334)
PHONE..............................302 722-7379
EMP: 2
SALES (est): 92.41K **Privately Held**
SIC: 2834 Vitamin, nutrient, and hematinic preparations for human use

(G-12434)
ZIGGYS INC
Also Called: Ziggy's Wood Floor Mechanics
885 New London Rd (19711-2111)
PHONE..............................302 453-1285
Zigmund M Mielnikiewicz, *Pr*
Barbara Hearne, *Sec*
EMP: 8 EST: 1986
SALES (est): 747.48K **Privately Held**
Web: www.ziggyswoodfloors.com
SIC: 1752 Wood floor installation and refinishing

(G-12435)
ZIRAS TECHNOLOGIES INC
260 Chapman Rd Ste 200 (19702-5491)
PHONE..............................302 286-7303
Dharmendra Kalakota, *Prin*
Haritha Jaggabarapu, *Dir*
EMP: 10 EST: 2015
SALES (est): 831.04K **Privately Held**
Web: www.zirastech.net
SIC: 7379 Computer related consulting services

(G-12436)
ZIZO TAXI CAB LLC
69 Northfield Rd (19713-2714)
PHONE..............................302 528-5663
Mahmoud Abdou, *Prin*
EMP: 6 EST: 2008
SALES (est): 191.71K **Privately Held**
SIC: 4121 Taxicabs

(G-12437)
ZOGO INC
2035 Sunset Lake Rd (19702-2600)
PHONE..............................978 810-8895
David Neyhart, *Sec*
EMP: 5 EST: 2018
SALES (est): 212.9K **Privately Held**
SIC: 7389 Business services, nec

(G-12438)
ZZHOUSE INC
Also Called: Zzhouse Design
400 Eagle Run Rd (19702-1603)
PHONE..............................302 453-1180
Stephen Webb, *Pr*
Julie Webb, *VP*
EMP: 5 EST: 2003
SALES (est): 395.51K **Privately Held**
Web: www.zzhousedesign.com
SIC: 7336 Graphic arts and related design

Newport
New Castle County

(G-12439)
ACADEMY SOUNDS LLC
520 Copper Dr (19804-2418)
PHONE..............................302 276-5027
Dennis Ekhuya, *Pr*
EMP: 5 EST: 2016
SALES (est): 40.74K **Privately Held**
Web: www.academysoundsllc.com
SIC: 1731 7359 Sound equipment specialization; Audio-visual equipment and supply rental

(G-12440)
AIR LQIDE ADVANCED SEPARATIONS
305 Water St (19804-2410)
PHONE..............................302 225-1100
EMP: 13 EST: 2019
SALES (est): 869.6K **Privately Held**
Web: advancedseparations.airliquide.com
SIC: 2813 Industrial gases

(G-12441)
AIR LQIDE ADVANCED TECH US LLC
Also Called: Air Liquide Advanced Tech
305 Water St (19804-2410)
PHONE..............................302 225-1100
EMP: 24
SALES (corp-wide): 101.26MM **Privately Held**
SIC: 2813 Industrial gases
HQ: Air Liquide Advanced Technologies Us Llc
9807 Katy Fwy
Houston TX 77024

(G-12442)
ALLAN MYERS
102 Larch Cir Ste 203 (19804-2371)
PHONE..............................302 658-4417
Allan Myers, *Prin*
EMP: 7 EST: 2017
SALES (est): 134.78K **Privately Held**
Web: www.allanmyers.com
SIC: 1611 General contractor, highway and street construction

(G-12443)
CCDIESEL LLC
401 S Dupont Rd (19804-1623)
PHONE..............................302 353-0842
Craig Carpenter, *Prin*
EMP: 5 EST: 2017
SALES (est): 137.63K **Privately Held**
SIC: 7538 General automotive repair shops

(G-12444)
COLORS & EFFECTS USA LLC
Also Called: Sunchemical
205 S James St (19804-2424)
PHONE..............................302 996-2910
EMP: 5 EST: 2016
SALES (est): 71.62K **Privately Held**
SIC: 2893 Printing ink

(G-12445)
CUPCAKE KOUTURE BAKERY LLC
212 W Market St (19804-3152)
PHONE..............................302 602-6058
EMP: 2
SALES (est): 62.38K **Privately Held**
SIC: 2051 Cakes, bakery: except frozen

(G-12446)
CUTTING OF PRECISION CONCRETE
213 Maryland Ave (19804-3040)
PHONE..............................302 543-5833
Gary Tucker, *Pr*
EMP: 5 EST: 2011
SALES (est): 366.37K **Privately Held**
Web: www.precisionconcretellc.com
SIC: 1771 Concrete work

(G-12447)
DANIEL D RAPPA INC
302 Cedar St (19804-2246)
PHONE..............................302 994-1199
Daniel D Rappa Senior, *Pr*
Daniel D Rappa Junior, *Sec*
EMP: 9 EST: 1950
SALES (est): 240.68K **Privately Held**
SIC: 1711 Warm air heating and air conditioning contractor

(G-12448)
DELAWARE KIDS FUND
405 Marsh Ln Ste 1 (19804-2445)
PHONE..............................302 323-9300
EMP: 5 EST: 2018
SALES (est): 158.15K **Privately Held**
Web: www.dekidsfund.com
SIC: 6726 Management investment funds, closed-end

(G-12449)
DIAMOND STATE HOME AUXILIARY
Also Called: VFW Post 2863
8 S Dupont Rd (19804-1323)
PHONE..............................302 652-9331
Paul Philipps, *Pr*
Allen Lynch, *Pr*
EMP: 5 EST: 1930
SALES (est): 134.37K **Privately Held**
SIC: 8641 Veterans' organization

(G-12450)
ELECTRO SOUND SYSTEMS INC
330 Water St Ste 108 (19804-2433)
PHONE..............................302 543-2292
Thomas Manchester, *CEO*
Sara Bristol, *Prin*
EMP: 10 EST: 2017
SALES (est): 600K **Privately Held**
Web: www.electrosoundsystems.com
SIC: 7812 Video production

(G-12451)
ENDOSPACE CORPORATION
240 N James St Ste 100 (19804-3167)
PHONE..............................732 271-8700
Howard Loonan, *VP*
EMP: 3 EST: 2013
SALES (est): 233.01K **Privately Held**
Web: www.endospacecorp.com
SIC: 3841 7389 Gastroscopes, except electromedical; Business Activities at Non-Commercial Site

(G-12452)
FAMILY FIRST FUNERAL SVCS LLC (PA)
212 E Justis St (19804-2522)
PHONE..............................800 377-6949
EMP: 7
SALES (est): 58.7K
SALES (corp-wide): 58.7K **Privately Held**
Web: www.familyfirstfuneralservices.com
SIC: 7261 Funeral home

(G-12453)
GUNNING PARTNERS LLC
Also Called: Carpevita Home Care
240 N James St Ste 103 (19804-3167)
PHONE..............................302 482-4305
Robyn Mooney, *Managing Member*
EMP: 99 EST: 2017
SALES (est): 1.94MM **Privately Held**
Web: www.carpevitahomecare.com
SIC: 8082 Home health care services

(G-12454)
HARVEY HANNA & ASSOCIATES INC
405 Marsh Ln Ste 1 (19804-2445)
PHONE..............................302 323-9300
E Thomas Harvey Iii, *Pr*
Michael Kinnard, *VP*
EMP: 7 EST: 1993
SALES (est): 1.59MM **Privately Held**
Web: www.harveyhanna.com
SIC: 8742 Real estate consultant

(G-12455)
NATIONAL ASSN LTR CARRIERS
Also Called: N A L C
8 S Dupont Rd Fl 2 (19804-1323)
PHONE..............................302 652-2933
Bob Wilkerson, *Admn*
EMP: 8
SALES (corp-wide): 351.63K **Privately Held**
Web: www.nalc.org
SIC: 8631 Labor union
PA: National Association Of Letter Carriers
100 Indana Ave Nw Ste 709
Washington DC 20001
202 393-4695

(G-12456)
ROBERT B GREGG
301 S Dupont Rd (19804-1327)
PHONE..............................302 994-9300
Robert B Gregg, *Owner*
EMP: 9 EST: 1951
SALES (est): 331.23K **Privately Held**
SIC: 8721 Certified public accountant

Ocean View
Sussex County

(G-12457)
ADVANCED MASSAGE OF DELAWARE
29 Atlantic Ave Ste P (19970-9155)
P.O. Box 357 (19970-0357)
PHONE..............................443 485-7024
Michelle L Reynolds, *Prin*
EMP: 5 EST: 2016
SALES (est): 20.84K **Privately Held**
Web: www.advancedmassagede.com
SIC: 7299 Massage parlor

(G-12458)
ADVANCED PROTECTION LLC
Also Called: Signature Alert
9 Briarcliffe Ct (19970-9013)
PHONE..............................302 539-6041
Andrea Barnes, *Admn*
EMP: 7 EST: 2009
SALES (est): 207.9K **Privately Held**
Web: www.signaturealert.com
SIC: 7382 Security systems services

Ocean View - Sussex County (G-12459)   GEOGRAPHIC SECTION

(G-12459)
AMANDA COPPINGER
37139 Lord Baltimore Ln (19970-3242)
PHONE.....................................301 938-2346
Amanda Coppinger, *Pr*
EMP: 6 EST: 2017
SALES (est): 63.64K **Privately Held**
SIC: 8049 Offices of health practitioner

(G-12460)
AMERICAN HANDYMAN SERVICES
30958 Maplewood Rd (19970-3820)
PHONE.....................................302 616-2559
Gary Uzmack, *Owner*
EMP: 5 EST: 2014
SALES (est): 62.97K **Privately Held**
SIC: 7299 Handyman service

(G-12461)
AMY LINZEY
38241 Yacht Basin Rd # 9 (19970-3366)
PHONE.....................................302 541-4447
Amy Linzey, *Owner*
EMP: 6 EST: 2017
SALES (est): 62.48K **Privately Held**
SIC: 8049 Offices of health practitioner

(G-12462)
ANCHORS AWEIGH ENTRMT LLC
37959 William Chandler Blvd (19970-2818)
PHONE.....................................302 236-1587
EMP: 5 EST: 2017
SALES (est): 57.45K **Privately Held**
Web: www.precisionpaintball.net
SIC: 7929 Entertainment service

(G-12463)
ANNE POWELL LLC
10 Daisey Ave (19970-9129)
PHONE.....................................302 245-9245
EMP: 5 EST: 2012
SALES (est): 99.15K **Privately Held**
Web: www.anniepowell.com
SIC: 6531 Real estate brokers and agents

(G-12464)
ARTISAN INTERIORS GROUP LLC
Also Called: Behind Closed Doors
30089 Cedar Neck Rd (19970-2750)
PHONE.....................................302 537-4811
Paul Manna, *Mgr*
EMP: 10 EST: 2018
SALES (est): 773.91K **Privately Held**
Web: www.bcdclosets.com
SIC: 3089 Organizers for closets, drawers, etc.; plastics

(G-12465)
ASHCRAFT MASONRY INC
30171 Jump Ln (19970-2787)
PHONE.....................................302 537-4298
David S Ashcraft, *Owner*
James Ashcraft, *VP*
Regina Ashcraft, *Treas*
EMP: 10 EST: 2001
SALES (est): 965.81K **Privately Held**
Web: www.ashcraftmasonry.com
SIC: 1741 Masonry and other stonework

(G-12466)
ATLANTIC CONTRACTOR LL
207 E Orlando Ave (19970-9759)
PHONE.....................................302 537-4361
EMP: 5 EST: 2008
SALES (est): 164.41K **Privately Held**
SIC: 1799 Special trade contractors, nec

(G-12467)
BARBARA SOCHA MD
96 Atlantic Ave Ste 103 (19970-9103)
PHONE.....................................302 541-4460
Barbara Socha, *Prin*
EMP: 8 EST: 2008
SALES (est): 82.47K **Privately Held**
SIC: 8011 Physicians' office, including specialists

(G-12468)
BAY FOREST HOMEOWNERS ASSN
36115 Bay Forest Dr (19970-8017)
PHONE.....................................302 537-6580
Anise Murray, *Prin*
EMP: 5 EST: 2009
SALES (est): 399.6K **Privately Held**
Web: engage.goenumerate.com
SIC: 8641 Homeowners' association

(G-12469)
BAYBIW DEVELOPMENT LLC
Also Called: Rent Equip
123 Atlantic Ave (19967-6741)
PHONE.....................................302 537-9700
EMP: 11 EST: 1987
SQ FT: 6,000
SALES (est): 1.08MM **Privately Held**
Web: www.toolandpartyrentalsde.com
SIC: 7359 5251 Tool rental; Tools

(G-12470)
BAYSHORE INC
Also Called: Vine Creek Mobile Home Park
Rr 1 Box 252 (19970)
PHONE.....................................302 539-7200
Elmer Cox, *Pr*
Brett Cox, *Sec*
EMP: 6 EST: 1966
SALES (est): 203.4K **Privately Held**
Web: www.bayshorecampground.com
SIC: 7033 6515 5271 4493 Campsite; Mobile home site operators; Mobile home dealers; Marinas

(G-12471)
BAYSIDE AT BTHANY LKES CLBHUSE
38335 Old Mill Way (19970-3707)
PHONE.....................................302 539-4378
Nancy Lowe, *Prin*
EMP: 6 EST: 2010
SALES (est): 65.63K **Privately Held**
Web: www.vacasa.com
SIC: 7997 Membership sports and recreation clubs

(G-12472)
BAYSIDE GOLF LLC DBA BEAR TRAP
7 Clubhouse Dr (19970-3235)
P.O. Box 577 (19970-0577)
PHONE.....................................302 537-5600
Jack Stone, *Mgr*
EMP: 13 EST: 2010
SALES (est): 255.86K **Privately Held**
Web: www.beartrapdunes.com
SIC: 7992 Public golf courses

(G-12473)
BEAR TRAP PARTNERS
Also Called: Bear Trap Dunes
County Rte 84 (19970)
PHONE.....................................302 537-5600
Joshua Freeman, *Pt*
EMP: 17 EST: 1998
SALES (est): 434.5K **Privately Held**
Web: www.beartrapdunes.com
SIC: 7992 Public golf courses

(G-12474)
BEAR TRAP SALES
21 Village Green Dr Ste 101 (19970)
PHONE.....................................302 541-5454
EMP: 9 EST: 2007
SALES (est): 225.57K **Privately Held**
SIC: 7997 Golf club, membership

(G-12475)
BECK JR THOMAS D DO
88 Atlantic Ave (19970-9116)
PHONE.....................................302 541-4500
Thomas Beck, *CEO*
EMP: 8 EST: 2018
SALES (est): 123.73K **Privately Held**
SIC: 8011 Offices and clinics of medical doctors

(G-12476)
BEHAVIORAL HEALTH CENTER INC
33316 Heavenly Way (19970-3473)
PHONE.....................................808 944-6900
Melinda Kohr, *Prin*
EMP: 6 EST: 2018
SALES (est): 38.22K **Privately Held**
SIC: 8099 Health and allied services, nec

(G-12477)
BENJAMIN B SMITH BUILDERS INC
54 Central Ave (19970-9226)
P.O. Box 762 (19930-0762)
PHONE.....................................302 537-1916
Benjamin B Smith, *Pr*
EMP: 5 EST: 1987
SALES (est): 575.4K **Privately Held**
SIC: 1542 1521 Commercial and office buildings, renovation and repair; New construction, single-family houses

(G-12478)
BETHANY BEACH CLEANING LLC
29 Atlantic Ave Ste L (19970-9155)
PHONE.....................................302 858-6524
EMP: 6 EST: 2019
SALES (est): 119.34K **Privately Held**
Web: www.bethanybeachcleaners.com
SIC: 7699 Cleaning services

(G-12479)
BETHANY BLOOMS
27 Indian Hill Ln (19970-9794)
PHONE.....................................302 829-8578
Bethany Blooms, *Prin*
EMP: 5 EST: 2011
SALES (est): 77.43K **Privately Held**
SIC: 0781 Landscape services

(G-12480)
BETHANY PLUMBING AND HEATING
37949 Muddy Neck Rd (19970-2844)
P.O. Box 367 (19930-0367)
PHONE.....................................302 539-1022
EMP: 5 EST: 2020
SALES (est): 249.49K **Privately Held**
SIC: 1711 Plumbing contractors

(G-12481)
BFB HOSPITALITY LLC
30415 Cedar Neck Rd (19970-2744)
PHONE.....................................302 829-1418
EMP: 12 EST: 2016
SALES (est): 227.62K **Privately Held**
SIC: 7011 Hotels and motels

(G-12482)
BOBS MARINE SERVICE INC
Routes 17 & 26 (19970)
P.O. Box 306 (19970-0306)
PHONE.....................................302 539-3711
Helen Littleton, *Pr*
Tracy Littleton, *Mgr*
Carl Littleton, *Admn*
Robert Littleton Iii, *Admn*
EMP: 18 EST: 1962
SQ FT: 8,600
SALES (est): 2.31MM **Privately Held**
Web: www.bobsmarineservice.com
SIC: 7699 5551 Boat repair; Boat dealers

(G-12483)
BRUCE MEARS DESIGNER-BUILDER
31370 Railway Rd # 2 (19970-3443)
PHONE.....................................302 539-2355
Bruce Mears, *Pr*
EMP: 15 EST: 1985
SALES (est): 877.81K **Privately Held**
Web: www.brucemears.com
SIC: 1521 New construction, single-family houses

(G-12484)
BUILDER SUPPLY OF DEL MARVA
61 Atlantic Ave (19970-9167)
PHONE.....................................302 829-8650
EMP: 7 EST: 2015
SALES (est): 86K **Privately Held**
Web: www.bsdshowroom.com
SIC: 1799 Special trade contractors, nec

(G-12485)
CAP TITLE OF DELAWARE LLC
29 Atlantic Ave Ste E (19970-9155)
PHONE.....................................302 537-3788
EMP: 7 EST: 2006
SALES (est): 264.18K **Privately Held**
SIC: 6531 Real estate listing services

(G-12486)
CARL M FREEMAN ASSOCIATES INC
21 Village Green Dr Ste 101 (19970-3663)
PHONE.....................................302 436-3000
Josh Freeman, *Brnch Mgr*
EMP: 90
SALES (corp-wide): 42.66MM **Privately Held**
Web: www.freemancompanies.com
SIC: 1522 Residential construction, nec
PA: Carl M. Freeman Associates, Inc.
909 Rose Ave Ste 1000
Rockville MD 20852
240 453-3000

(G-12487)
CASTLES BY SEA LLC
154 Naomi Dr (19970-9785)
PHONE.....................................302 539-2508
Rose Walker, *Owner*
EMP: 5 EST: 2005
SALES (est): 144.54K **Privately Held**
Web: rosewalker1.brightmlshomes.com
SIC: 6531 Real estate brokers and agents

(G-12488)
CESN PARTNERS INC
Also Called: Charles Moon Plumbing & Htg
34541 Atlantic Ave (19970-3547)
PHONE.....................................302 537-1814
Charles Moon, *CEO*
Sheila Neff, *Pr*
Karen Neff, *Mgr*
EMP: 10 EST: 2001
SALES (est): 546.61K **Privately Held**
SIC: 1711 Plumbing contractors

(G-12489)
CLARKSVILLE AUTO SERVICE CTR (PA)
Also Called: Clarksville Parts Plus
34461 Atlantic Ave (19970-3546)
PHONE.....................................302 539-1700

GEOGRAPHIC SECTION

Ocean View - Sussex County (G-12518)

David Hamm, *Pr*
Glenn Phillips, *
Veronica Hamm, *
Kelly Phillips, *
EMP: 31 **EST:** 1984
SALES (est): 9.6MM
SALES (corp-wide): 9.6MM **Privately Held**
Web: www.oceanareatire.com
SIC: 5531 7534 5013 Automotive tires; Tire retreading and repair shops; Automotive supplies and parts

(G-12490)
CLOVER FARMS MEATS
Also Called: A & D Enterprises
15 William Ave (19970-9293)
P.O. Box 142 (18235-0142)
PHONE.................610 428-8066
Steven Jzaortis, *Pr*
Charles Aberchinski, *Pr*
Robert Ronyack, *VP*
EMP: 6 **EST:** 1950
SALES (est): 197.51K **Privately Held**
SIC: 0191 General farms, primarily crop

(G-12491)
COASTAL COTTAGE
101 Atlantic Ave (19970-9137)
PHONE.................302 539-7821
EMP: 9 **EST:** 2019
SALES (est): 138.4K **Privately Held**
Web: www.thecoastalcottageshop.com
SIC: 7011 Hotels and motels

(G-12492)
COASTAL PLANT CARE LLC
32621 Bella Via Ct (19970-3196)
PHONE.................703 994-6905
Jeremy Hager, *Prin*
EMP: 5 **EST:** 2016
SALES (est): 190.63K **Privately Held**
Web: www.coastalplantcare.com
SIC: 0782 Garden services

(G-12493)
COASTAL POINT
111 Atlantic Ave Ste 2 (19970-9166)
P.O. Box 1324 (19970-1324)
PHONE.................302 539-1788
Susan Lyons, *Pt*
EMP: 17 **EST:** 2003
SALES (est): 433.8K **Privately Held**
Web: www.coastalpoint.com
SIC: 2711 Newspapers, publishing and printing

(G-12494)
COASTAL PRINTING COMPANY
Also Called: Coastal Printing
Rte 26, Shops Of Millville (19970)
P.O. Box 1340 (19970-1340)
PHONE.................302 537-1700
Lance Fargo, *Pr*
EMP: 8 **EST:** 1988
SQ FT: 9,000
SALES (est): 929.75K **Privately Held**
Web: www.coastprint.com
SIC: 2752 Offset printing

(G-12495)
COASTAL SERVICES LLC
30430 Cedar Neck Rd (19970-4157)
PHONE.................302 616-2906
EMP: 12 **EST:** 2017
SALES (est): 920.98K **Privately Held**
Web: www.coastalservicesllc.net
SIC: 7699 General household repair services

(G-12496)
CONCIERGE HOME SERVICES
27 Atlantic Ave Fl 2 (19970-9169)
PHONE.................302 539-6178
Adam Cosgrove, *Prin*
EMP: 5 **EST:** 2017
SALES (est): 65.12K **Privately Held**
SIC: 7299 Miscellaneous personal service

(G-12497)
CONNOR MANAGEMENT LLC
31685 Edith St (19970-4509)
PHONE.................302 539-1678
EMP: 8 **EST:** 2013
SALES (est): 483.59K **Privately Held**
SIC: 8741 Management services

(G-12498)
DANDY SIGNS
37384 Club House Rd (19970-3637)
PHONE.................301 399-8746
Danny Davis, *Owner*
EMP: 7 **EST:** 1976
SALES (est): 243.01K **Privately Held**
SIC: 3993 Signs and advertising specialties

(G-12499)
DAVES BUILDERS INC
38308 Lu Lee Ct (19970-3331)
P.O. Box 1568 (19970-1568)
PHONE.................302 539-4058
Dave Okoniewski, *Owner*
EMP: 5 **EST:** 2010
SALES (est): 196.14K **Privately Held**
SIC: 1521 New construction, single-family houses

(G-12500)
DELAWARE SEASIDE RAILROAD CLUB
P.O. Box 479 (19970-0479)
PHONE.................302 682-4652
Donald Hollenbeck, *Prin*
EMP: 5 **EST:** 2010
SALES (est): 84.68K **Privately Held**
Web: www.delawareseasiderailroadclub.com
SIC: 8699 Charitable organization

(G-12501)
DELFRAMING INC
30897 Fresh Pond Dr (19970-4702)
PHONE.................302 363-2658
Moacir D Lopes, *Prin*
EMP: 7 **EST:** 2015
SALES (est): 235.71K **Privately Held**
SIC: 1751 Carpentry work

(G-12502)
DELMARVA PLUMBING LLC
17 Longview Dr (19970-9549)
PHONE.................571 274-4926
Batzorig Mogi, *Asst Sec*
EMP: 5 **EST:** 2018
SALES (est): 56.99K **Privately Held**
SIC: 1711 Plumbing contractors

(G-12503)
DELTA EPSILON TAU
31257 Bird Haven St (19970-3613)
PHONE.................302 541-0450
EMP: 6 **EST:** 2016
SALES (est): 46.76K **Privately Held**
Web: www.deths.org
SIC: 7041 Fraternities and sororities

(G-12504)
DENISE BEAM
Also Called: State Farm Insurance
112 Atlantic Ave (19970-9152)
PHONE.................302 539-1900
Denise Beam, *Owner*
EMP: 5 **EST:** 1987
SALES (est): 426.73K **Privately Held**
Web: www.denisebeam.com
SIC: 6411 Insurance agents and brokers

(G-12505)
DJLONG SERVICES
23 Longview Dr (19970-9549)
PHONE.................302 541-4884
David Long, *Prin*
EMP: 5 **EST:** 2014
SALES (est): 84.19K **Privately Held**
SIC: 1522 Residential construction, nec

(G-12506)
DODD HEALTH INNOVATION LLC
Also Called: Bdc-Healthit
31027 Scissorbill Rd (19970-8027)
PHONE.................410 598-7266
John C Dodd, *Pr*
Phillip Cooke, *COO*
EMP: 8
SALES (est): 363.94K **Privately Held**
SIC: 7372 7373 Prepackaged software; Computer integrated systems design

(G-12507)
DR STEVEN SCURNICK
30958 Scissorbill Rd (19970-8030)
PHONE.................410 442-1173
Steven Scurnick, *Prin*
EMP: 10 **EST:** 2007
SALES (est): 233.14K **Privately Held**
Web: www.dovedaledentalcare.com
SIC: 8021 Dentists' office

(G-12508)
EIVA NAILS & SPA LLC
29 Atlantic Ave Ste I (19970-9155)
PHONE.................302 537-1888
EMP: 5 **EST:** 2015
SALES (est): 19.5K **Privately Held**
SIC: 7231 Manicurist, pedicurist

(G-12509)
FAIRWAY VILLAGE
101 Augusta Dr (19970-3277)
PHONE.................302 354-1021
EMP: 5 **EST:** 2018
SALES (est): 55.91K **Privately Held**
Web: www.livefairway.com
SIC: 6513 Apartment building operators

(G-12510)
FAMILY OF ALL TRADES
31145 Whites Neck Dr (19970-3501)
PHONE.................302 334-2710
David Russell, *Pr*
EMP: 5 **EST:** 2014
SALES (est): 61.71K **Privately Held**
Web: www.familyofalltrades.com
SIC: 5199 Nondurable goods, nec

(G-12511)
FCI OF DELMARVA LLC ✪
111 Atlantic Ave Ste 8 (19970-9166)
PHONE.................443 614-1794
John Neff, *Managing Member*
EMP: 6 **EST:** 2023
SALES (est): 89.59K **Privately Held**
SIC: 8741 Management services

(G-12512)
FOSHEE PROPERTY MAINTENANCE
33403 Oak Street Ext (19970-4416)
P.O. Box 929 (19970-0929)
PHONE.................302 344-6410
Louis Foshee, *Prin*
EMP: 5 **EST:** 2016
SALES (est): 123.83K **Privately Held**
Web: www.fosheepropertymaintenance.com
SIC: 7349 Building maintenance services, nec

(G-12513)
FOSTER LONG REAL ESTATE
31045 Scissorbill Rd (19970-8028)
PHONE.................302 864-3216
EMP: 5 **EST:** 2018
SALES (est): 105.43K **Privately Held**
Web: www.longandfoster.com
SIC: 6531 Real estate brokers and agents

(G-12514)
FRATERNAL ORDER OF EAGLES BR
Also Called: FRATERNAL ORDER OF EAGLES, BRYAN AERIE 2233 OF BRYAN, OHIO
35083 Atlantic Ave (19970-3522)
P.O. Box 1074 (19970-1074)
PHONE.................302 616-2935
Francis W Culbert, *Pr*
EMP: 7
SALES (corp-wide): 4.44MM **Privately Held**
Web: mail.foe.com
SIC: 8641 Fraternal associations
PA: Mansfield, Ohio Aerie No. 336, Fraternal Order Of Eagles, Inc.
221 S Walnut St
Bryan OH 43506
419 636-7812

(G-12515)
FULTON BANK NATIONAL ASSN
Also Called: Fulton Financial Advisors
60 Atlantic Ave (19970-9170)
PHONE.................302 539-8031
Sherry Huovinen, *Brnch Mgr*
EMP: 9
SALES (corp-wide): 1.09B **Publicly Held**
Web: www.fultonbank.com
SIC: 6022 State commercial banks
HQ: Fulton Bank, National Association
1 Penn Sq
Lancaster PA 17602
717 581-3166

(G-12516)
G A HASTINGS & ASSOCIATES
102 Central Ave Ste 1 (19970-9019)
PHONE.................302 537-5760
EMP: 6 **EST:** 1988
SQ FT: 750
SALES (est): 829.8K **Privately Held**
Web: www.gahastings.com
SIC: 8712 House designer

(G-12517)
GALE FORCE CLEANING & RESTORE
14 Atlantic Ave (19970-9108)
PHONE.................302 539-6244
Leslie Gale, *Prin*
EMP: 9 **EST:** 2011
SALES (est): 504.13K **Privately Held**
Web: www.galeforceinc.com
SIC: 7349 Building maintenance services, nec

(G-12518)
GALLERY ONE
125 Atlantic Ave (19967-6741)
P.O. Box 302 (19970-0302)
PHONE.................302 537-5055
Cheryl Wisbrock, *Owner*
EMP: 6 **EST:** 2010
SALES (est): 207.31K **Privately Held**

Ocean View - Sussex County (G-12519)

Web: www.galleryonede.com
SIC: 8412 Art gallery

(G-12519)
GFRS CONSTRUCTION ONE LLC
37138 Pinewood Rd (19970-3818)
PHONE..................484 357-5218
EMP: 5 EST: 2017
SALES (est): 230.49K Privately Held
SIC: 1521 Single-family housing construction

(G-12520)
GRAND VIEW TOUR & TRAVEL
20996 Cormorant Way (19970-8130)
PHONE..................610 361-7979
Denise Hay, Prin
EMP: 5 EST: 2018
SALES (est): 198.04K Privately Held
SIC: 4725 Tours, conducted

(G-12521)
HEALTHY TO CORE
57 Golden Eagle Dr (19970-3263)
PHONE..................240 506-4202
Wendy Cope, Prin
EMP: 5 EST: 2018
SALES (est): 42.64K Privately Held
SIC: 8611 Business associations

(G-12522)
HERSHEY EXTERIORS LLC
33229 Parker House Rd (19970-3671)
PHONE..................302 278-2004
EMP: 8 EST: 2019
SALES (est): 449.75K Privately Held
Web: www.hersheyexteriors.com
SIC: 7699 General household repair services

(G-12523)
HOLISTIC HEALTH CARE DELAWARE
796 Hickman Dr (19970-9792)
PHONE..................302 545-1552
Michelle Quigley, Prin
EMP: 7 EST: 2017
SALES (est): 85.43K Privately Held
SIC: 8099 Health and allied services, nec

(G-12524)
INDIAN RIVER SOCCER CLUB
32221 Gum Rd (19970)
P.O. Box 1366 (19970-1366)
PHONE..................302 542-6397
Rebecca Mais, Pr
EMP: 5 EST: 2009
SALES (est): 153.36K Privately Held
Web: www.riversoccerclub.com
SIC: 7997 Soccer club, except professional and semi-professional

(G-12525)
INTERIORS BY KIM INC
33 Central Ave (19970-9315)
PHONE..................302 537-2480
Kim Bennett, Pr
Jeff Bennett, VP
Christine Miller, Sec
EMP: 7 EST: 1991
SQ FT: 5,000
SALES (est): 938.16K Privately Held
Web: www.interiorsbykimde.com
SIC: 5713 1799 5231 5722 Floor covering stores; Window treatment installation; Wallcoverings; Electric household appliances, major

(G-12526)
J F GOETZ ASSOCIATES LLC
40 Fairway Dr (19970-3260)
PHONE..................302 537-2485
EMP: 5 EST: 2014
SALES (est): 31.3K Privately Held
Web: www.jfgoetzassoc.com
SIC: 7381 Guard services

(G-12527)
J RILEY EATON
5 Plantation Ct (19970-3238)
PHONE..................302 539-4537
Barbara Stettner-eaton, Prin
EMP: 5 EST: 2010
SALES (est): 72.43K Privately Held
SIC: 8641 Civic and social associations

(G-12528)
JEFFERSON URIAN DANE STRNER PA
92 Atlantic Ave Ste D (19970-9178)
P.O. Box 477 (19970-0477)
PHONE..................302 539-5543
David Doane, Mgr
EMP: 10
SALES (corp-wide): 5.15MM Privately Held
Web: www.juds.com
SIC: 8721 Certified public accountant
PA: Jefferson, Urian, Doane & Sterner, P.A.
651 N Bedford St
Georgetown DE 19947
302 856-3900

(G-12529)
JENNIFER R RODGERS
98 Central Ave (19970-9715)
PHONE..................302 542-7095
Jennifer R Rodgers Lmt, Owner
EMP: 5 EST: 2018
SALES (est): 22.18K Privately Held
SIC: 8049 Offices of health practitioner

(G-12530)
K SQUARED ENTERPRISES LLC
33514 Weshampton Ln (19970-2813)
PHONE..................302 402-3082
EMP: 5 EST: 2017
SALES (est): 172.3K Privately Held
SIC: 1522 Residential construction, nec

(G-12531)
K&S HOME SERVICES LLC
37738 Balsa St (19970-3187)
PHONE..................302 604-3563
EMP: 6 EST: 2018
SALES (est): 213.87K Privately Held
SIC: 1521 Single-family housing construction

(G-12532)
KELLER WILLIAMS REALTY
Also Called: Keller Williams Realtors
37367 Main St (19970-3866)
PHONE..................302 519-1683
Susan Raymond, Prin
EMP: 5 EST: 2018
SALES (est): 75.13K Privately Held
Web: www.kw.com
SIC: 6531 Real estate agent, residential

(G-12533)
KEVIN M BIELANSKI
15 Edisto Ct (19970-3247)
PHONE..................908 752-8210
Kevin Bielanski, CEO
EMP: 6 EST: 2017
SALES (est): 88.95K Privately Held
SIC: 8049 Offices of health practitioner

(G-12534)
KIERAN PY MD
96 Atlantic Ave Ste 101 (19970-9103)
PHONE..................302 541-4460
EMP: 6 EST: 2019
SALES (est): 54.13K Privately Held
SIC: 8011 Offices and clinics of medical doctors

(G-12535)
KYLES TILE LLC
38525 Reservation Trl (19970-2704)
PHONE..................302 462-0959
EMP: 5 EST: 2015
SALES (est): 124.02K Privately Held
Web: www.kylestile.com
SIC: 1743 Tile installation, ceramic

(G-12536)
LANDTECH LLC
Also Called: Landtech Land Survey
118 Atlantic Ave (19970-9163)
PHONE..................302 539-2366
EMP: 7 EST: 1985
SALES (est): 497.41K Privately Held
SIC: 8713 Surveying services

(G-12537)
LELA CAPITAL LLC
37259 Fox Dr (19970-3845)
PHONE..................917 428-0304
EMP: 12 EST: 2017
SIC: 6719 Investment holding companies, except banks

(G-12538)
LEVEL & CLEAN LLC
57 Golden Eagle Dr (19970-3263)
PHONE..................302 616-1585
John H Cope, Asst Sec
EMP: 5 EST: 2018
SALES (est): 23.7K Privately Held
SIC: 7699 Cleaning services

(G-12539)
LIGHTHOUSE REALTY GROUP INC
5 Dove Ct (19970-9017)
PHONE..................302 864-0952
Susan Clark, Prin
EMP: 5 EST: 2010
SALES (est): 78.38K Privately Held
SIC: 6531 Real estate agent, residential

(G-12540)
LOIS JAMES DDS
17 Atlantic Ave Ste 4 (19970-9102)
PHONE..................302 537-4500
Lois James D.d.s., Owner
EMP: 7 EST: 1998
SALES (est): 496.61K Privately Held
Web: www.drloisjames.com
SIC: 8021 Dentists' office

(G-12541)
LULLA WOODWORKING LLC
1 New Castle Ct (19970-9777)
PHONE..................302 841-8800
Joel Antonioli, Prin
EMP: 5 EST: 2017
SALES (est): 93.08K Privately Held
Web: www.lullawoodworking.com
SIC: 2431 Millwork

(G-12542)
MARIE BERNIER
126f October Glory Ave (19970-4229)
PHONE..................240 731-1555
EMP: 6 EST: 2018
SALES (est): 54.13K Privately Held
Web: www.mariebernier.com
SIC: 8011 General and family practice, physician/surgeon

(G-12543)
MASTER KLEAN COMPANY
Cedar Neck Rd (19970)
P.O. Box 1198 (19930-1198)
PHONE..................302 539-4290
James G Martin, Owner
EMP: 5 EST: 1974
SALES (est): 136.08K Privately Held
Web: www.masterklean.com
SIC: 7349 5722 7629 Janitorial service, contract basis; Vacuum cleaners; Vacuum cleaner repair

(G-12544)
MAYER RACING STABLES
37223 Lord Baltimore Ln (19970-3243)
PHONE..................302 829-8673
Barbara Mayer, Prin
EMP: 5 EST: 2010
SALES (est): 48.88K Privately Held
SIC: 0752 Training services, horses (except racing horses)

(G-12545)
MERRY MAIDS OF OCEAN VIEW
Also Called: Merry Maids
38452 Resort Rv Cir (19970-4162)
PHONE..................410 729-6661
EMP: 5 EST: 2019
SALES (est): 22.81K Privately Held
Web: www.merrymaids.com
SIC: 7349 Maid services, contract or fee basis

(G-12546)
MICHAEL J HURD
17 Atlantic Ave Ste 4 (19970-9102)
P.O. Box 1554 (19970-1554)
PHONE..................302 539-5986
Michael Hurd, Prin
EMP: 6 EST: 2017
SALES (est): 65.51K Privately Held
Web: www.drhurd.com
SIC: 8322 General counseling services

(G-12547)
MILLVILLE ORGANIC CENTER
30916 Whites Neck Rd (19970-3599)
PHONE..................302 423-2601
EMP: 7 EST: 2018
SALES (est): 480.05K Privately Held
Web: www.millvilleorganiccenter.com
SIC: 4953 Recycling, waste materials

(G-12548)
MIRANDA ENTERPRISES LLC
30530 Quillen Point Rd (19970-2738)
PHONE..................302 236-0897
EMP: 8 EST: 2015
SALES (est): 235K Privately Held
SIC: 0752 Boarding services, kennels

(G-12549)
MR NATURAL BOTTLED WATER INC
31919 Christine Ln (19970-4114)
P.O. Box 490 (19970-0490)
PHONE..................302 436-7700
Rodney J Short, Pr
Eileen Short, VP
EMP: 6 EST: 1983
SALES (est): 921.14K Privately Held
SIC: 5149 Mineral or spring water bottling

(G-12550)
NALLY VENTURES CNSTR LLC
102 Central Ave Ste 3 (19970-9019)
PHONE..................302 581-9243
T Micheal Nally, Prin
Conor Nally, Prin
EMP: 5 EST: 2019

GEOGRAPHIC SECTION

Ocean View - Sussex County (G-12579)

SALES (est): 265.13K **Privately Held**
Web: www.nallyventures.com
SIC: **8748** Business consulting, nec

(G-12551)
NEW YORK LIFE INS CO
31286 Pine Pl (19970-3618)
PHONE.................................302 537-7060
EMP: **7 EST:** 2019
SALES (est): 32.06K **Privately Held**
Web: www.newyorklife.com
SIC: **6311** Life insurance

(G-12552)
NORMAN JOHNSON BUILDERS
38218 Yacht Basin Rd (19970-3360)
PHONE.................................302 670-9201
EMP: **6 EST:** 2018
SALES (est): 205.99K **Privately Held**
SIC: **1521** New construction, single-family houses

(G-12553)
NOVACARE REHABILITATION
118 Atlantic Ave Ste 302 (19970-9163)
PHONE.................................302 537-7762
EMP: **9 EST:** 2018
SALES (est): 186.93K **Privately Held**
Web: www.novacare.com
SIC: **8049** Physical therapist

(G-12554)
OCEAN PINES AUTO SVC CTR INC
Also Called: Ocean Pines Parts
34461 Atlantic Ave (19970-3546)
PHONE.................................410 641-7800
David R Hamm, *Pr*
Doctor Andreas Goldner, *VP*
Glenn R Phillips, *Sec*
EMP: **10 EST:** 1992
SALES (est): 476.94K **Privately Held**
SIC: **7538** 5531 General automotive repair shops; Automotive parts

(G-12555)
OCEAN VIEW ANIMAL HOSPITAL
118 Atlantic Ave Ste 101 (19970-9163)
PHONE.................................302 539-2273
Nathan Sheldon, *Prin*
EMP: **8 EST:** 2010
SALES (est): 474.44K **Privately Held**
Web: www.oceanviewanimalhospital.com
SIC: **0742** Animal hospital services, pets and other animal specialties

(G-12556)
OCEAN VIEW HISTORICAL SOCIETY
39 Central Ave (19970-9315)
P.O. Box 576 (19970-0576)
PHONE.................................302 258-7470
Barbara Slavin, *Pr*
David Coll, *Treas*
Kimberly Grimes, *Sec*
EMP: **6 EST:** 2019
SALES (est): 31.02K **Privately Held**
Web: www.hvov.org
SIC: **8412** Museum

(G-12557)
PARSONS & ROBINSON PA
Also Called: Law Office Parsons Robinson PA
118 Atlantic Ave Ste 401 (19970-9163)
PHONE.................................302 539-2220
EMP: **7 EST:** 1982
SALES (est): 237.35K **Privately Held**
Web: www.steve-parsons.net
SIC: **8111** General practice attorney, lawyer

(G-12558)
PARTHIAN LLC
7 West Ave (19970-9420)
PHONE.................................240 441-8301
Sousan Salimi, *Prin*
EMP: **5 EST:** 2018
SALES (est): 71.41K **Privately Held**
SIC: **1522** Residential construction, nec

(G-12559)
PIN UP GIRLS SALON LLC
29 Atlantic Ave (19970-9155)
PHONE.................................302 537-1325
EMP: **5 EST:** 2016
SALES (est): 61.94K **Privately Held**
Web: www.pinupgirlssalon.com
SIC: **7231** Hairdressers

(G-12560)
PRECIOUS PAWS ANIMAL HOSPITAL
118 Atlantic Ave Ste 101 (19970-9163)
PHONE.................................302 539-2273
John Maniatty, *Prin*
Kelly Krivitski, *Off Mgr*
EMP: **12 EST:** 2011
SALES (est): 491.97K **Privately Held**
Web: www.preciouspawsanimalhospital.com
SIC: **0742** Animal hospital services, pets and other animal specialties

(G-12561)
RELYANCE SKIM CAMP
36774 Cedar St (19970-3410)
PHONE.................................717 343-3588
EMP: **5 EST:** 2014
SALES (est): 61.75K **Privately Held**
SIC: **7032** Sporting and recreational camps

(G-12562)
RENT EQUIPMENT
Also Called: Rent Equip
9 Town Rd (19970-9132)
P.O. Box 794 (19975-0794)
PHONE.................................302 537-9797
Keith Smith, *Owner*
EMP: **7 EST:** 2015
SALES (est): 275.66K **Privately Held**
Web: www.toolandpartyrentalsde.com
SIC: **7353** 7359 Heavy construction equipment rental; Party supplies rental services

(G-12563)
RESORTQUEST
21 Village Green Dr (19970-3663)
PHONE.................................302 616-1040
EMP: **16 EST:** 2010
SALES (est): 136.56K **Privately Held**
Web: www.vacasa.com
SIC: **7011** Vacation lodges

(G-12564)
S&M SMALL ENGINE REPAIR LLC
37514 Cedar St (19970-4459)
PHONE.................................302 893-7341
Stanley Merritt, *Prin*
EMP: **5 EST:** 2016
SALES (est): 93.92K **Privately Held**
SIC: **7538** Engine repair

(G-12565)
SALON ON CENTRAL LLC
11 Woodland Ave (19970-9223)
PHONE.................................302 539-1882
EMP: **5 EST:** 2010
SALES (est): 69.87K **Privately Held**
SIC: **7231** Hairdressers

(G-12566)
SCHRIDER ENTERPRISES INC
Also Called: Fabri-Zone Cleaning Systems
327 Atlantic Ave (19967-6702)
P.O. Box 850 (19930-0850)
PHONE.................................302 539-1036
Wendy J Schrider, *Pr*
Stephen J Schrider, *VP*
William J Schrider, *VP*
Isabelle M Schrider, *Sec*
EMP: **5 EST:** 1984
SALES (est): 240.66K **Privately Held**
SIC: **7217** Carpet and furniture cleaning on location

(G-12567)
SHORELINE HOME IMPRVS LLC
509 Harbor Rd (19970-9632)
PHONE.................................302 616-1090
Larry R Marhefka, *Asst Sec*
EMP: **6 EST:** 2018
SALES (est): 447.94K **Privately Held**
Web: www.shorelinehillc.com
SIC: **1521** General remodeling, single-family houses

(G-12568)
SPWA SERVICES LLC
38841 Bayberry Ct (19970-2722)
PHONE.................................856 761-4621
Beatriz Canal, *Mgr*
EMP: **5 EST:** 2018
SALES (est): 67.24K **Privately Held**
Web: www.spwaservices.org
SIC: **8082** Home health care services

(G-12569)
STEEN WAEHLER SCHRIDER FOX LLC
92 Atlantic Ave Ste B (19970-9178)
P.O. Box 1398 (19970-1398)
PHONE.................................302 539-7900
Mary Schrider Fox, *Managing Member*
EMP: **9 EST:** 2008
SALES (est): 956.45K **Privately Held**
Web: www.swsflaw.com
SIC: **8111** General practice attorney, lawyer

(G-12570)
STEVE GEORGE PAINTING
38578 Daina Dr (19970-3176)
P.O. Box 942 (19970-0942)
PHONE.................................302 616-1456
Steve George, *Prin*
EMP: **5 EST:** 2017
SALES (est): 45.72K **Privately Held**
SIC: **1721** Painting and paper hanging

(G-12571)
STUDIO43
43 Woodland Ave (19970-9223)
PHONE.................................302 539-8577
Nancy Colella, *Prin*
EMP: **5 EST:** 2010
SALES (est): 41.69K **Privately Held**
SIC: **7299** Miscellaneous personal service

(G-12572)
SUMMER HILL CUSTOM HOME BLDR
70 Atlantic Ave (19970-9170)
PHONE.................................302 462-5853
Steve Smith, *Owner*
EMP: **6 EST:** 2008
SALES (est): 763.74K **Privately Held**
Web: www.summerhillbuilders.com
SIC: **1521** New construction, single-family houses

(G-12573)
SUMTER CONTRACTING CORP
36504 Pine Grove Ln (19970-3570)
PHONE.................................703 323-7210
George Hammond, *Pr*
Cynthia Hammond, *VP*
Anita Buroker, *VP*
EMP: **9 EST:** 1985
SALES (est): 2.04MM **Privately Held**
Web: www.sumtercontractingcorp.com
SIC: **1542** Commercial and office buildings, renovation and repair

(G-12574)
SUPERIOR SCREEN & GLASS
1 Town Rd (19970-9132)
PHONE.................................302 541-5399
Joel Antonioli, *Owner*
EMP: **8 EST:** 2001
SQ FT: 6,000
SALES (est): 491.37K **Privately Held**
Web: www.screenandwire.com
SIC: **1799** 1793 1751 Screening contractor: window, door, etc.; Glass and glazing work; Store fixture installation

(G-12575)
SWEDISH MASSAGE THERAPY
38227 Muddy Neck Rd (19970-2837)
PHONE.................................302 841-3166
Geradine Finiello, *Prin*
EMP: **8 EST:** 2018
SALES (est): 97.75K **Privately Held**
SIC: **8093** Rehabilitation center, outpatient treatment

(G-12576)
TIDEWATER PHYSCL THRPY AND REB
63 Atlantic Ave (19970-9167)
PHONE.................................302 537-7260
Dawn Belanger, *Mgr*
EMP: **5**
Web: www.tidewaterpt.com
SIC: **8049** Physical therapist
PA: Tidewater Physical Therapy And Rehabilitation Associates Pa
406 Marvel Ct
Easton MD 21601

(G-12577)
TITLE ONE & ASSOCIATES INC
6 Summerville Ct (19970-3218)
PHONE.................................410 758-1831
Steve Donovan, *Prin*
EMP: **5 EST:** 2008
SALES (est): 233.28K **Privately Held**
SIC: **8742** Management consulting services

(G-12578)
UTILITY SALES ASSOCIATES INC
47 October Glory Ave (19970-3209)
PHONE.................................410 479-0646
Michael Cutright, *VP*
EMP: **6 EST:** 2012
SALES (est): 48.81K **Privately Held**
Web: www.struxurteam.com
SIC: **7389** Design services

(G-12579)
VAN BUREN MORTGAGE LLC
37901 Island Dr (19970-3471)
PHONE.................................302 725-0723
Hayden Evans, *Brnch Mgr*
EMP: **8**
Web: www.jgwentworth.com
SIC: **6163** Mortgage brokers arranging for loans, using money of others
HQ: Van Buren Mortgage, Llc
3350 Commission Ct

Woodbridge VA 22192
888 349-3773

(G-12580)
VILLAGE SQ ACDEMY LRNG CTR LLC
30792 Whites Neck Rd (19970-3612)
PHONE..................................302 539-5000
Tecola G Hernandez, *Dir*
Tecola Gibbs-hernandez, *Dir*
EMP: 8 EST: 2015
SALES (est): 411.87K **Privately Held**
SIC: **8351** Preschool center

Odessa
New Castle County

(G-12581)
AUTOAWARDS INC
313 N Dupont Hwy (19730)
P.O. Box 5000 (19730-5000)
PHONE..................................302 696-6000
EMP: 18 EST: 2012
SALES (est): 646.56K **Privately Held**
Web: www.autoawards.com
SIC: **7371** Computer software development and applications

(G-12582)
CREATIVE MED CONSULTING LLC
111 6th St S Dupont Hwy (19730-2077)
PHONE..................................302 313-1411
EMP: 6 EST: 2005
SALES (est): 54.13K **Privately Held**
Web: www.creativemedicalde.com
SIC: **8011** Offices and clinics of medical doctors

(G-12583)
DUNKLEY ENTERPRISES LLC
Also Called: Hungry Student Athletes
139 Wallace Rd (19730-2055)
P.O. Box 222 (19730-0222)
PHONE..................................302 275-0100
Spencer Dunkley, *Managing Member*
EMP: 5 EST: 1999
SALES (est): 284.64K **Privately Held**
SIC: **4214** Furniture moving and storage, local

(G-12584)
FALCONE TRUMAN PLBG & HTG INC
3891 South Dupont Parkway (19730)
PHONE..................................302 376-7483
EMP: 20
SALES (corp-wide): 2.4MM **Privately Held**
Web: www.falconeandtruman.com
SIC: **1711 7389** Plumbing contractors; Safety inspection service
PA: Falcone And Truman Plumbing And Heating Inc.
510 Abbott Dr Ste F
Broomall PA 19008
610 328-6914

(G-12585)
NUCAR CONSULTING INC
313 N Dupont Hwy Ste 100 (19730)
P.O. Box 5000 (19730-5000)
PHONE..................................302 696-6000
Jim Capron, *Pr*
Chris Blum, *VP*
EMP: 23 EST: 1997
SALES (est): 703.79K **Privately Held**
Web: www.autoawards.com
SIC: **8748** Business consulting, nec

(G-12586)
ODESSA HISTORIC FOUNDATION
201 Main St (19730-2007)
P.O. Box 697 (19730-0697)
PHONE..................................302 378-4119
H Donnan Sharp, *Pr*
William Gotwals, *Treas*
EMP: 12 EST: 2004
SALES (est): 2.33MM **Privately Held**
Web: www.historicodessa.org
SIC: **8412** Museum

(G-12587)
SMITH HARVEY C JR FUNERAL DIRE
201 High St (19730-2029)
PHONE..................................302 376-0200
Harvey C Smith Junior, *Ofcr*
EMP: 6 EST: 2002
SALES (est): 56.11K **Privately Held**
SIC: **7261** Funeral home

Port Penn
New Castle County

(G-12588)
GJ CHALFANT WELDING LLC
119 S Congress St (19731-3105)
PHONE..................................302 983-0822
Greg Chalfant, *Prin*
EMP: 5 EST: 2019
SALES (est): 218.67K **Privately Held**
SIC: **7692** Welding repair

Rehoboth Beach
Sussex County

(G-12589)
24/7 CLUB FITNESS
18908 Rehoboth Mall Blvd Ste 5 (19971-6134)
PHONE..................................302 226-4853
Lisa Lawson, *Pr*
EMP: 7 EST: 2017
SALES (est): 59.45K **Privately Held**
SIC: **7991** Health club

(G-12590)
2520 HAIR SALON & DAY SPA
11 Sea Bright Way (19971-9695)
PHONE..................................717 845-2241
Bob Wisotzkey, *Owner*
EMP: 5 EST: 2017
SALES (est): 225.83K **Privately Held**
Web: www.2520hairsalondayspa.com
SIC: **7231** Hairdressers

(G-12591)
550 SUITES LLC
18633 Fir Drive Ext (19971-8650)
PHONE..................................508 651-8197
EMP: 5 EST: 2020
SALES (est): 288.16K **Privately Held**
Web: www.thesuites.com
SIC: **7389** Office facilities and secretarial service rental

(G-12592)
A SUCCESSFUL WOMAN
21 Robins Ln (19971-1201)
PHONE..................................234 567-8910
EMP: 3 EST: 2017
SALES (est): 59.87K **Privately Held**
SIC: **7372** Prepackaged software

(G-12593)
A V C INC
Also Called: Audio Visual Communications
20807 Coastal Hwy Ste 4 (19971-8013)
PHONE..................................302 227-2549
Joseph P Wastler, *Pr*
EMP: 7 EST: 1976
SQ FT: 600
SALES (est): 1.84MM **Publicly Held**
SIC: **5999 5065** Telephone and communication equipment; Closed circuit TV
PA: Ceco Environmental Corp.
14651 Dallas Pkwy Ste 500
Dallas TX 75254

(G-12594)
A WINDOW TO WELLNESS
19606 Coastal Hwy (19971-8596)
PHONE..................................302 567-5468
EMP: 6 EST: 2019
SALES (est): 133.71K **Privately Held**
Web: www.awindowtowellness.com
SIC: **5031** Lumber, plywood, and millwork

(G-12595)
ABSOLUTION INC
19119 Stonewood Ln Unit 48 (19971-4683)
PHONE..................................302 528-2330
Mark Mills, *Prin*
EMP: 5 EST: 2017
SALES (est): 114.77K **Privately Held**
Web: www.absolutionde.com
SIC: **1771** Concrete work

(G-12596)
ACOPIA HOME LOANS
405 Rehoboth Ave (19971-3125)
PHONE..................................302 242-6272
EMP: 5 EST: 2019
SALES (est): 117.31K **Privately Held**
Web: www.acopiahomeloans.com
SIC: **6162** Mortgage bankers and loan correspondents

(G-12597)
ADMIRAL HOTEL
2 Baltimore Ave (19971-2104)
PHONE..................................302 227-2103
Walter Brett, *Owner*
EMP: 5 EST: 1982
SQ FT: 17,500
SALES (est): 399.98K **Privately Held**
Web: www.admiralonbaltimore.com
SIC: **7011** Motels

(G-12598)
ADMIRAL ON BALTIMORE
2 Baltimore Ave (19971-2104)
PHONE..................................302 227-1300
EMP: 21 EST: 2019
SALES (est): 477.3K **Privately Held**
Web: www.admiralonbaltimore.com
SIC: **7011** Motels

(G-12599)
AJM ENTERPRISES INC
19545 Camelot Dr Ste A (19971-1197)
PHONE..................................302 212-2020
EMP: 5 EST: 2015
SALES (est): 176.66K **Privately Held**
SIC: **7389** Business services, nec

(G-12600)
ALEX AND ANI LLC
Also Called: Alex and Ani
36494 Seaside Outlet Dr Unit 1420 (19971-1232)
PHONE..................................302 227-7360
EMP: 8
SALES (corp-wide): 91.95MM **Privately Held**
Web: www.alexandani.com
SIC: **5944 3911** Jewelry, precious stones and precious metals; Jewelry, precious metal
HQ: Alex And Ani, Llc
10 Briggs Dr
East Greenwich RI 02818

(G-12601)
ALLEN JARMON ENTERPRISES INC
317 Rehoboth Ave (19971-3127)
PHONE..................................302 745-5122
Nathan Jarmon, *Prin*
EMP: 5 EST: 2012
SALES (est): 144.02K **Privately Held**
SIC: **8748** Business consulting, nec

(G-12602)
AMS OF DELAWARE
Also Called: AMS
20576 Coastal Hwy (19971-8062)
PHONE..................................302 227-1320
Michael Errico, *Prin*
EMP: 6 EST: 2011
SALES (est): 428.88K **Privately Held**
Web: www.amsdelaware.com
SIC: **8322** Alcoholism counseling, nontreatment

(G-12603)
ANCHORAGE MOTEL INC
18809 Coastal Hwy (19971-6153)
PHONE..................................302 645-8320
Cleburn Johnston, *Pr*
Cleburn Johnston Iii, *Treas*
EMP: 6 EST: 1973
SQ FT: 17,000
SALES (est): 449.06K **Privately Held**
Web: www.anchoragemotelinc.com
SIC: **7011** Motels

(G-12604)
ANDERSON FLOOR COVERINGS INC
4286 Highway One (19971)
PHONE..................................302 227-3244
Stephen Anderson, *Pr*
John Fleming, *VP*
Mark Matushik, *Sec*
EMP: 10 EST: 1976
SQ FT: 10,500
SALES (est): 927.86K **Privately Held**
SIC: **1752 5713** Floor laying and floor work, nec; Carpets

(G-12605)
ANDY STATON REAL ESTATE INC
309 Rehoboth Ave (19971-3127)
PHONE..................................302 703-9090
EMP: 5 EST: 2018
SALES (est): 163.85K **Privately Held**
Web: www.shopdelawarehomes.com
SIC: **6531** Real estate brokers and agents

(G-12606)
ANITA BARBARA PEGHINI RABER GA
49 Baltimore Ave (19971-2131)
PHONE..................................302 227-2888
EMP: 5 EST: 2018
SALES (est): 31.35K **Privately Held**
Web: www.rehobothart.com
SIC: **8412** Art gallery

(G-12607)
ANS CORPORATION (PA)
Also Called: Accent On Travel
37156 Rehoboth Avenue Ext Unit 3 (19971-3104)
PHONE..................................410 296-8330
Annette Stellhorn, *CEO*

GEOGRAPHIC SECTION

Rehoboth Beach - Sussex County (G-12635)

Richard Stellhorn, *CFO*
EMP: 5 **EST:** 1989
SQ FT: 14,000
SALES (est): 2.38MM
SALES (corp-wide): 2.38MM **Privately Held**
SIC: 4724 Tourist agency arranging transport, lodging and car rental

(G-12608)
ANYONE FITNESS
18908 Rehoboth Mall Blvd Ste 5 (19971-6134)
PHONE 302 226-4653
Michael Anthony, *Owner*
EMP: 33 **EST:** 2019
SALES (est): 83.03K **Privately Held**
Web: www.everyonefitness.com
SIC: 7991 Health club

(G-12609)
APPLE ELECTRIC INC
18854 John J Williams Hwy (19971-4402)
PHONE 302 645-5105
EMP: 25 **EST:** 1991
SQ FT: 1,500
SALES (est): 2.17MM **Privately Held**
Web: www.theappleelectric.com
SIC: 1731 General electrical contractor

(G-12610)
ARIEL C RUBIN
5 Caroline Ln (19971-2722)
PHONE 443 854-9901
Ariel Rubin, *Pr*
EMP: 6 **EST:** 2017
SALES (est): 24.4K **Privately Held**
SIC: 8049 Offices of health practitioner

(G-12611)
ARTISANS BANK INC
17211 Hood Rd (19971-4490)
PHONE 302 296-0155
Tiffany Walter, *Mgr*
EMP: 7
SALES (corp-wide): 25.62MM **Privately Held**
Web: www.artisansbank.com
SIC: 6036 State savings banks, not federally chartered
PA: Artisans Bank Inc
  2961 Centerville Rd # 101
  Wilmington DE 19808
  302 658-6881

(G-12612)
ASPEN MEADOWS
36179 Palace Ln (19971-3856)
PHONE 302 227-4266
Elizabeth Dittmar, *Mgr*
EMP: 5 **EST:** 2014
SALES (est): 135.15K **Privately Held**
Web: www.aspenmeadowsha.com
SIC: 5039 Mobile homes

(G-12613)
ATI HOLDINGS LLC
Also Called: ATI Physical Therapy
19266 Coastal Hwy Unit 9 (19971-6117)
PHONE 302 226-2230
Philip Allen, *Prin*
EMP: 15
SALES (corp-wide): 635.67MM **Publicly Held**
Web: www.atipt.com
SIC: 8049 Physical therapist
HQ: Ati Holdings, Llc
  790 Remington Blvd
  Bolingbrook IL 60440

(G-12614)
ATLANTIC MANAGEMENT
34821 Derrickson Dr (19971-6144)
PHONE 302 222-3919
Chris Burg, *Prin*
EMP: 5 **EST:** 2012
SALES (est): 468.12K **Privately Held**
Web: www.atlanticlimode.com
SIC: 8741 Management services

(G-12615)
ATLANTIC MANAGEMENT LTD
29 Midway Shopping Ctr (19971)
PHONE 302 645-9511
Richard H Derrickson, *Pr*
Norma Lee Derrickson, *Sec*
EMP: 10 **EST:** 1985
SALES (est): 372.82K **Privately Held**
SIC: 8741 6512 Hotel or motel management; Shopping center, property operation only

(G-12616)
ATLANTIC THEATERS LLC
Also Called: Movies At Midway, The
18585 Coastal Hwy Unit 1 (19971-6147)
PHONE 302 645-9511
Richard H Derrickson, *Prin*
EMP: 50 **EST:** 2021
SALES (est): 180.94K **Privately Held**
SIC: 7832 Motion picture theaters, except drive-in

(G-12617)
ATRIFICO LLC
179 Rehoboth Ave Unit 16 (19971-7901)
PHONE 302 858-0161
EMP: 5 **EST:** 2013
SALES (est): 92.36K **Privately Held**
SIC: 8742 Management consulting services

(G-12618)
AUTOMOTIVEONLY
57 Bryan Dr (19971-9732)
PHONE 302 727-1064
Lee Kabino, *Prin*
EMP: 5 **EST:** 2013
SALES (est): 53.19K **Privately Held**
SIC: 7539 Automotive repair shops, nec

(G-12619)
AVENUE DAY SPA
Also Called: Avenue Apothecary and Spa
110 Rehoboth Ave Ste A (19971-2108)
PHONE 302 227-5649
Victoria Fry, *Pr*
Tin Desilver, *VP*
EMP: 15 **EST:** 2000
SALES (est): 1.08MM **Privately Held**
Web: www.avenuedayspa.com
SIC: 7991 Spas

(G-12620)
AVIS CAR RENTAL
19563 Coastal Hwy Unit A (19971-6220)
PHONE 302 227-1507
EMP: 6 **EST:** 2018
SALES (est): 67.62K **Privately Held**
Web: www.avis.com
SIC: 7514 Rent-a-car service

(G-12621)
BAD HAIR DAY INC
20 Lake Ave (19971-2110)
PHONE 302 226-4247
EMP: 34 **EST:** 1997
SALES (est): 2.42MM **Privately Held**
Web: www.badhairday.biz
SIC: 7231 Hairdressers

(G-12622)
BANK OF DELMARVA
18578 Coastal Hwy (19971-6215)
PHONE 302 226-8900
June Betts, *Brnch Mgr*
EMP: 5
Web: www.bankofdelmarvahb.com
SIC: 6022 6029 State trust companies accepting deposits, commercial; Commercial banks, nec
PA: The Bank Of Delmarva
  2245 Northwood Dr
  Salisbury MD 21801

(G-12623)
BASIC BLOCK CORP
Also Called: H & R Block
4590 Highway One Ste 118 (19971-9790)
PHONE 302 645-2000
Ernest Deangelis Junior, *Pr*
EMP: 10 **EST:** 1982
SQ FT: 2,200
SALES (est): 152.96K **Privately Held**
Web: www.hrblock.com
SIC: 7291 Tax return preparation services

(G-12624)
BATESCAINELLI LLC
319 Byview Ave Rhboth Bch Rehoboth Beach (19971)
PHONE 202 618-2040
EMP: 2 **EST:** 2012
SALES (est): 89.55K **Privately Held**
SIC: 8748 7372 7373 7389 Systems engineering consultant, ex. computer or professional; Business oriented computer software; Office computer automation systems integration; Business services, nec

(G-12625)
BCG MANAGEMENT LLC
234 Rehoboth Ave (19971-2134)
PHONE 302 278-7677
EMP: 10 **EST:** 2017
SALES (est): 493.73K **Privately Held**
SIC: 8741 Management services

(G-12626)
BEACH ARCADE CENTRAL
101 S Boardwalk (19971-2931)
PHONE 302 227-1043
EMP: 5 **EST:** 2018
SALES (est): 40.76K **Privately Held**
Web: www.zelkys.com
SIC: 7993 Arcades

(G-12627)
BEACH BABIES CHILD CARE
Also Called: BEACH BABIES CHILD CARE
35245 Hudson Way (19971-4481)
PHONE 302 645-5010
Deborah Toner, *Brnch Mgr*
EMP: 8
SALES (corp-wide): 2.46MM **Privately Held**
Web: www.beachbabieschildcare.com
SIC: 8351 Group day care center
PA: Beach Babies Child Care At Townsend
  104 Canal View Ct
  Rehoboth Beach DE 19971
  302 644-1585

(G-12628)
BEACH BBIES CHILD CARE AT TWNS (PA)
104 Canal View Ct (19971-4168)
PHONE 302 644-1585
Deborah Toner, *Owner*
Thomas Toner, *Owner*
EMP: 24 **EST:** 1997
SALES (est): 2.46MM
SALES (corp-wide): 2.46MM **Privately Held**
Web: www.beachbabieschildcare.com
SIC: 8351 Group day care center

(G-12629)
BEACH TANS AND HAIR DESIGN
Also Called: Beach Tans & Hair Designs
23 Midway Shopping Ctr (19971)
PHONE 302 645-8267
EMP: 7 **EST:** 1987
SALES (est): 118.03K **Privately Held**
Web: www.beachtansandhairdesigns.com
SIC: 7299 Tanning salon

(G-12630)
BEACON HOSPITALITY
36619 Tanger Blvd (19971-1345)
PHONE 302 567-2213
EMP: 11 **EST:** 2017
SALES (est): 134.73K **Privately Held**
Web: www.beaconhospitality.com
SIC: 7011 Hotels and motels

(G-12631)
BEACON MEDICAL GROUP PA
18947 John J Williams Hwy Unit 303 (19971-4477)
PHONE 302 947-9767
EMP: 5 **EST:** 2010
SALES (est): 918.11K **Privately Held**
SIC: 8062 General medical and surgical hospitals

(G-12632)
BEACON PEDIATRICS LLC
18947 John J Williams Hwy Unit 212 (19971-4476)
PHONE 302 645-8212
Nancy M Gideon, *Prin*
EMP: 12 **EST:** 2011
SALES (est): 2.49MM **Privately Held**
Web: www.beaconpediatrics.net
SIC: 8011 Pediatrician

(G-12633)
BEAUTY AND BEACH HAIR BOUTIQUE
37169 Rehoboth Avenue Ext (19971-1683)
PHONE 302 260-9383
EMP: 5 **EST:** 2019
SALES (est): 77.71K **Privately Held**
Web: www.rehobothbeautyboutique.com
SIC: 7231 Hairdressers

(G-12634)
BEAVER TREE SERVICE INC
108 2nd St (19971)
PHONE 302 226-3564
James Beaver, *Brnch Mgr*
EMP: 7
SALES (corp-wide): 916.64K **Privately Held**
Web: www.beavertreeserviceinc.net
SIC: 0783 Planting, pruning, and trimming services
PA: Beaver Tree Service, Inc.
  1301 S Division St
  Salisbury MD 21804
  410 651-0779

(G-12635)
BEEBE MEDICAL CENTER INC
18947 John J Williams Hwy Unit 201 # 20 (19971-4476)
PHONE 302 645-3100
EMP: 37
SALES (corp-wide): 581.97MM **Privately Held**

Rehoboth Beach - Sussex County (G-12636)

Web: www.beebehealthcare.org
SIC: 8062 General medical and surgical hospitals
PA: Beebe Medical Center, Inc.
424 Savannah Rd
Lewes DE 19958
302 645-3300

(G-12636)
BEEBE MEDICAL CENTER INC
38149 Terrace Rd (19971-2074)
PHONE..................302 645-3289
EMP: 21
SALES (corp-wide): 581.97MM Privately Held
Web: www.beebehealthcare.org
SIC: 8062 General medical and surgical hospitals
PA: Beebe Medical Center, Inc.
424 Savannah Rd
Lewes DE 19958
302 645-3300

(G-12637)
BEEBE MEDICAL CENTER INC
Also Called: Women's Imaging Center
18941 John J Williams Hwy (19971-4404)
Rural Route 24 (19971)
PHONE..................302 645-3010
EMP: 42
SALES (corp-wide): 581.97MM Privately Held
Web: www.beebehealthcare.org
SIC: 8062 General medical and surgical hospitals
PA: Beebe Medical Center, Inc.
424 Savannah Rd
Lewes DE 19958
302 645-3300

(G-12638)
BELL ROCK CAPITAL LLC (DH)
35568 Airport Rd (19971-4620)
PHONE..................302 227-7607
Cassandra Toroian, *Managing Member*
EMP: 10 EST: 2009
SALES (est): 12.06MM
SALES (corp-wide): 963.95MM Publicly Held
Web: www.bmt.com
SIC: 6799 Investors, nec
HQ: Bryn Mawr Capital Management, Llc
5803 Kennett Pike Ste C
Wilmington DE 19807
302 429-8436

(G-12639)
BELL ROCK CAPITAL LLC
35568 Airport Rd (19971-4620)
PHONE..................302 227-7607
Jim Baurley, *Prin*
EMP: 6 EST: 2008
SALES (est): 112.24K Privately Held
Web: www.bmt.com
SIC: 6282 Investment advisory service

(G-12640)
BELLA DONNA SPA
5 S Branch Way (19971-6107)
PHONE..................703 313-7945
EMP: 5 EST: 2020
SALES (est): 85.75K Privately Held
SIC: 7991 Spas

(G-12641)
BERKSHIRE HATHAWAY HOME
37230 Rehoboth Avenue Ext (19971-3198)
PHONE..................302 227-6554
EMP: 11 EST: 2014
SALES (est): 253.41K Privately Held
Web: beachrentals.penfedrealty.com
SIC: 6531 Real estate agent, residential

(G-12642)
BEST WESTERN GOLDLEAF HT LLC
Also Called: Best Western
1400 Hwy 1 (19971)
PHONE..................302 226-1100
Maha Awayes, *Pr*
EMP: 33 EST: 1989
SALES (est): 374.06K Privately Held
Web: www.goldleafhotel.com
SIC: 7011 Motels

(G-12643)
BIG FISH WHOLESALE LLC (PA)
Also Called: Big Fish Wholesales Sea Fd Co
37369 Martin St (19971-8046)
P.O. Box 546 (19971-0546)
PHONE..................302 226-3474
Bob Moyer, *Prin*
EMP: 5 EST: 2008
SALES (est): 1.82MM
SALES (corp-wide): 1.82MM Privately Held
Web: www.bigfishrestaurantgroup.com
SIC: 5146 Seafoods

(G-12644)
BINGEBUILDER INC
18585 Coastal Hwy Unit 102006 (19971-6147)
PHONE..................415 529-8306
Andrae Washington, *CEO*
EMP: 25
SALES (est): 668.72K Privately Held
SIC: 8742 Management consulting services

(G-12645)
BLUE PLANET
159 Columbia Ave (19971-1647)
PHONE..................410 977-3426
Robert Durrell, *Prin*
EMP: 5 EST: 2017
SALES (est): 241.86K Privately Held
Web: www.bpellc.us
SIC: 8748 Environmental consultant

(G-12646)
BLUECOAST REHOBOTH
30115 Veterans Way (19971-4220)
PHONE..................302 278-7395
EMP: 6 EST: 2018
SALES (est): 20.78K Privately Held
Web: www.bluecoastrehoboth.com
SIC: 7999 Recreation services

(G-12647)
BOARDWALK BUILDERS INC
37395 Martin St (19971-8046)
PHONE..................302 227-5754
Patricia Mcdaniel, *Pr*
Patricia Mc Daniel, *Pr*
EMP: 14 EST: 1986
SALES (est): 4.3MM Privately Held
Web: www.boardwalkbuilders.com
SIC: 1521 New construction, single-family houses

(G-12648)
BOARDWALK PLAZA INCORPORATED (PA)
2 Olive Ave (19971-2806)
PHONE..................302 227-0441
TOLL FREE: 800
Jeffrey E Zerby, *CEO*
L Orme Meade, *
Ruth Ann Zerby, *
Kathryn E Meade, *
EMP: 39 EST: 1989
SALES (est): 4.86MM Privately Held
Web: www.boardwalkplaza.com
SIC: 7011 5812 Hotels; Eating places

(G-12649)
BOYS GIRLS CLUBS
19285 Holland Glade Rd (19971-4180)
PHONE..................302 260-9864
Demaris Miller, *Dir*
Millie Tronic, *Prin*
EMP: 5 EST: 2011
SALES (est): 173.37K Privately Held
Web: www.bgclubs.org
SIC: 8641 Youth organizations

(G-12650)
BRAIN LOVE NEUROTHERAPY
19633 Blue Bird Ln Unit 5 (19971-6130)
PHONE..................302 278-7828
EMP: 5 EST: 2017
SALES (est): 52.93K Privately Held
SIC: 8099 Health and allied services, nec

(G-12651)
BRANDYWINE SNIOR LVING MGT LLC
Also Called: Brandywine Senior Living
36101 Seaside Blvd (19971-6165)
PHONE..................302 226-8750
Donna Winegar, *Ex Dir*
EMP: 37
SALES (corp-wide): 95.35MM Privately Held
Web: www.brandycare.com
SIC: 8051 Skilled nursing care facilities
PA: Brandywine Senior Living Management Llc
525 Fellowship Rd Ste 360
Mount Laurel NJ 08054
856 778-6100

(G-12652)
BREAKERS ASSOCIATES
Also Called: Breakers Hotel, The
105 2nd St (19971-2283)
PHONE..................302 227-6688
Ronald Lankford, *Owner*
EMP: 20 EST: 1979
SALES (est): 977.17K Privately Held
Web: www.thebreakershotel.com
SIC: 7011 Resort hotel

(G-12653)
BRIAN COSTLEIGH LLC
1 Beach Ave (19971-2501)
PHONE..................302 645-3775
Brian Costleigh, *Prin*
EMP: 18 EST: 2012
SALES (est): 986.49K Privately Held
SIC: 8062 General medical and surgical hospitals

(G-12654)
BRIGHTON HOTELS LLC
Also Called: Brighton Suites Hotel
34 Wilmington Ave (19971-2217)
PHONE..................302 227-5780
EMP: 16 EST: 2000
SALES (est): 221.73K Privately Held
Web: www.brightonsuites.com
SIC: 7011 Motels

(G-12655)
BROADPOINT CONSTRUCTION LLC
Also Called: Broadpoint Custom Homes
37251 Rehoboth Avenue Ext (19971-3192)
PHONE..................302 567-2100
EMP: 6 EST: 2013
SALES (est): 1.51MM Privately Held
Web: www.broadpointcustomhomes.com
SIC: 1541 1542 1531 Industrial buildings, new construction, nec; Nonresidential construction, nec; Operative builders

(G-12656)
BROADPOINT CONSTRUCTION LLC
70 Rehoboth Ave (19971-2171)
PHONE..................302 228-8007
EMP: 9
SALES (est): 248.82K Privately Held
SIC: 1521 Single-family housing construction

(G-12657)
BROADWATER OYSTER COMPANY LLC
4 S Lake Ter (19971-4155)
PHONE..................610 220-7776
Ted Nowakowski, *Owner*
EMP: 5 EST: 2015
SALES (est): 72.7K Privately Held
SIC: 3732 Fishing boats: lobster, crab, oyster, etc.: small

(G-12658)
BROYDRICK & ASSOCIATES INC (PA)
102 Saint Lawrence St (19971-2268)
PHONE..................414 224-9393
Cynthia Broydrick, *Pr*
William Broydrick, *VP*
EMP: 7 EST: 1981
SALES (est): 2.2MM Privately Held
Web: www.broydrick.com
SIC: 8743 Lobbyist

(G-12659)
BRUCE PALMER LLC
20245 Bay Vista Rd (19971-8022)
PHONE..................302 654-1135
Bruce Coon, *Owner*
EMP: 6 EST: 2017
SALES (est): 364.49K Privately Held
Web: www.brucepalmerllc.com
SIC: 8748 Business consulting, nec

(G-12660)
BUDGET RENT A CAR
Also Called: Budget Rent-A-Car
19563 Coastal Hwy (19971-6220)
PHONE..................302 227-3041
Vince Iulanetti, *Owner*
EMP: 7 EST: 2015
SALES (est): 99.06K Privately Held
Web: www.budget.com
SIC: 7514 7359 Rent-a-car service; Equipment rental and leasing, nec

(G-12661)
BUDGET TRUCK RENTAL LLC
Also Called: Ryder
18744 John J Williams Hwy (19971-4400)
PHONE..................302 644-0132
EMP: 459
SALES (corp-wide): 11.99B Publicly Held
Web: www.budgettruck.com
SIC: 7514 Rent-a-car service
HQ: Budget Truck Rental Llc
6 Sylvan Way Ste 1
Parsippany NJ 07054

(G-12662)
CAMELS HUMP INC
63 Fields End (19971-1611)
PHONE..................302 227-5719
Mohammad Shihadeh, *Pr*
Marcia W Shihadeh, *Treas*
EMP: 10 EST: 1975
SQ FT: 5,000
SALES (est): 236.14K Privately Held

GEOGRAPHIC SECTION

Rehoboth Beach - Sussex County (G-12691)

SIC: 5812 5813 5141 Eating places; Bar (drinking places); Groceries, general line

(G-12663)
CAPE HENLOPEN SENIOR CENTER
11 Christian St (19971-3001)
PHONE...............................302 227-2055
Linda Vonvillle, *Admn*
EMP: 6 EST: 1966
SALES (est): 430.19K **Privately Held**
Web: www.capehenlopenseniorcenter.org
SIC: 8322 8699 Senior citizens' center or association; Charitable organization

(G-12664)
CAR PART PLANET
18585 Coastal Hwy (19971-6147)
PHONE...............................888 412-2772
EMP: 5 EST: 2021
SALES (est): 116.51K **Privately Held**
Web: www.carpartplanet.com
SIC: 7389 Business services, nec

(G-12665)
CARTINO NAIL SPA
19330 Lighthouse Plaza Blvd Unit 1a (19971-6161)
PHONE...............................302 212-2510
EMP: 5 EST: 2014
SALES (est): 159.55K **Privately Held**
SIC: 7231 Manicurist, pedicurist

(G-12666)
CENTER FOR INLAND BAYS INC
Also Called: CENTER FOR THE INLAND BAYS
39375 Inlet Rd (19971-2600)
PHONE...............................302 226-8105
EMP: 7 EST: 1999
SALES (est): 2.49MM **Privately Held**
Web: www.inlandbays.org
SIC: 8641 Environmental protection organization

(G-12667)
CENTURY 21 MANN & SONS
Also Called: Mann & Moore Associates
19606 Coastal Hwy Unit 205 (19971-8596)
PHONE...............................302 227-9477
Betty Mann, *Pr*
Bob Mcvai, *Prin*
EMP: 12 EST: 1984
SALES (est): 2.48MM **Privately Held**
Web: www.rehobothbeachvacationrentals.com
SIC: 6531 Real estate agent, residential

(G-12668)
CERTAPRO PAINTERS OF REHOBOTH
21810 D St (19971-8416)
PHONE...............................302 212-5742
EMP: 5 EST: 2016
SALES (est): 57.36K **Privately Held**
Web: www.certapro.com
SIC: 1721 Residential painting

(G-12669)
CES ENTERPRISES LLC
18585 Coastal Hwy (19971-6147)
PHONE...............................302 313-5229
EMP: 5 EST: 2016
SALES (est): 52.76K **Privately Held**
SIC: 7389 Business services, nec

(G-12670)
CHESAPEAKE BROKERAGE LLC
18766 John J Williams Hwy Ste 4395 (19971-4417)
PHONE...............................410 517-1592
Jeffrey Levy, *Managing Member*
EMP: 7 EST: 2011
SALES (est): 3.1MM **Privately Held**
Web: www.chesapeakebrokerage.com
SIC: 6311 6351 Life insurance; Credit and other financial responsibility insurance
PA: Simplicity Financial Marketing Holdings Inc.
86 Summit Ave Ste 303
Summit NJ 07901

(G-12671)
CHESAPEAKEMAINE TREY
316 Rehoboth Ave (19971-3108)
PHONE...............................302 226-3600
EMP: 7 EST: 2016
SALES (est): 126.5K **Privately Held**
Web: www.dogfish.com
SIC: 2082 Malt beverages

(G-12672)
CHOICE CONSTRUCTION CO INC
Rr 2 Box 137b (19971-9802)
PHONE...............................302 226-1732
EMP: 5 EST: 1994
SALES (est): 173.66K **Privately Held**
SIC: 1799 1521 Special trade contractors, nec; Single-family home remodeling, additions, and repairs

(G-12673)
CITY CAB OF DELWARE INC
Also Called: City Cab
164 Henlopen Ave (19971-1633)
PHONE...............................302 227-8294
Tom Antonio, *Pr*
EMP: 7
Web: www.citycabde.com
SIC: 4121 Taxicabs
PA: City Cab Of Delware Inc
1203 State College Rd
Dover DE 19904

(G-12674)
CLAYTON WEST LLC
42 Rehoboth Ave Ste 23 (19971-2122)
PHONE...............................302 530-3492
EMP: 5 EST: 2006
SALES (est): 112.09K **Privately Held**
SIC: 8748 Business consulting, nec

(G-12675)
CLEAN ENERGY USA LLC (PA)
20184 Phillips St (19971-8049)
PHONE...............................302 227-1337
Dave Preston, *Managing Member*
EMP: 8 EST: 2009
SQ FT: 3,000
SALES (est): 2.45MM **Privately Held**
Web: www.ceusa.com
SIC: 1711 Solar energy contractor

(G-12676)
CLEAN ENERGY USA LLC
37342 Martin St (19971-8042)
PHONE...............................302 227-1337
EMP: 5 EST: 2020
SALES (est): 26.07K **Privately Held**
Web: www.ceusa.com
SIC: 7699 Cleaning services

(G-12677)
CLEAN GREEN HORIZONS
18585 Coastal Hwy (19971-6147)
PHONE...............................302 258-9808
EMP: 6 EST: 2011
SALES (est): 55.01K **Privately Held**
Web: www.cleangreenhorizons.com

SIC: 7699 Cleaning services

(G-12678)
CLEANING BUSSINESS
36181 Field Ln (19971-8655)
PHONE...............................302 260-9023
Jennifer Kellogg, *Prin*
EMP: 5 EST: 2016
SALES (est): 87.5K **Privately Held**
SIC: 7699 Cleaning services

(G-12679)
CLMS LLC
21136 Laguna Dr (19971-4822)
PHONE...............................703 629-3231
Leslie Mcclintick, *Mgr*
EMP: 8 EST: 1997
SALES (est): 659.9K **Privately Held**
Web: www.clmsllc.com
SIC: 8742 7374 Management consulting services; Data processing and preparation

(G-12680)
CLUBTAC SUPPLY CRATES LTD LLC
18766 John J Williams Hwy # 4 (19971-4417)
PHONE...............................855 258-2822
EMP: 5 EST: 2017
SALES (est): 92.31K **Privately Held**
Web: www.clubtac.com
SIC: 5099 Durable goods, nec

(G-12681)
CMD INTERIORS INC
402 Rehoboth Ave (19971-3113)
PHONE...............................917 826-8867
EMP: 5 EST: 2018
SALES (est): 209.93K **Privately Held**
Web: www.cmdinterior.com
SIC: 7389 Interior designer

(G-12682)
COASTAL CUSTOM PAINTING LLC (PA)
18977 Munchy Branch Rd Ste 3g (19971-8763)
PHONE...............................302 242-6134
Kris Groszer, *Owner*
EMP: 6 EST: 2012
SALES (est): 231.92K
SALES (corp-wide): 231.92K **Privately Held**
Web: www.coastalcustompainting.com
SIC: 1721 Residential painting

(G-12683)
COASTAL IT CONSULTING
4 Tall Oaks Ct (19971-8602)
PHONE...............................302 226-9395
Norman Blackwood, *Owner*
EMP: 7 EST: 2002
SALES (est): 249.29K **Privately Held**
SIC: 7378 Computer maintenance and repair

(G-12684)
COASTAL KID WATCH
34 Club House Dr (19971-9679)
PHONE...............................302 537-0793
Paula R Nadig, *Owner*
EMP: 18 EST: 2007
SALES (est): 889.39K **Privately Held**
SIC: 8011 Pediatrician

(G-12685)
COASTAL PLAINS WOOD & TILE LLC
2 Tall Oaks Ct (19971-8602)
PHONE...............................302 670-7853
Timothy Bigman, *Prin*
EMP: 7 EST: 2017
SALES (est): 374.92K **Privately Held**

Web: www.coastalplainswoodtile.com
SIC: 1743 Tile installation, ceramic

(G-12686)
COASTAL PROPERTIES I LLC
Also Called: Bellmoor, The
6 Christian St (19971-3002)
P.O. Box 1 (19971-0001)
PHONE...............................302 227-5800
Robert H Moore, *Pr*
Robert Chadwick, *
Todd W Moore, *
Jb Moore, *VP*
Marion W Moore, *
EMP: 25 EST: 1974
SALES (est): 2.28MM **Privately Held**
Web: www.thebellmoor.com
SIC: 7011 5812 Motels; Eating places

(G-12687)
COLDWELL BANKER RESORT REALTTY
Also Called: Coldwell Banker
36462 E Estate Dr (19971-3876)
PHONE...............................302 864-0053
Edward Mantyla, *Prin*
EMP: 5 EST: 2019
SALES (est): 82.25K **Privately Held**
Web: www.coldwellbanker.com
SIC: 6531 Real estate agent, residential

(G-12688)
COLDWELL BANKER RESORT REALTY
41 Bay Reach (19971-1928)
PHONE...............................302 841-8470
William Vernon, *Pr*
EMP: 5 EST: 2020
SALES (est): 82.25K **Privately Held**
Web: www.coldwellbanker.com
SIC: 6531 Real estate agent, residential

(G-12689)
COLDWELL BANKER VILLAGE GREEN
Also Called: Coldwell Banker
317 Rehoboth Ave (19971-3127)
PHONE...............................302 227-3818
Eileen Kelly, *COO*
EMP: 6 EST: 2018
SALES (est): 189.81K **Privately Held**
Web: www.coldwellbanker.com
SIC: 6531 Real estate agent, residential

(G-12690)
COLDWELL BNKR RHBOTH RSORT RLT
Also Called: Coldwell Banker
20184 Coastal Hwy (19971-8020)
PHONE...............................302 227-5000
James J Kiernan, *Mgr*
Jeffrey Zerby, *
Veronica Kiernon, *
Ruth Ann Zerby, *
EMP: 31 EST: 1978
SQ FT: 3,500
SALES (est): 1.9MM **Privately Held**
Web: www.coldwellbanker.com
SIC: 6531 Real estate agent, residential

(G-12691)
COLLIERS TRIM SHOP INC
2206 Hwy One (19971)
PHONE...............................302 227-8398
Michael Sockriter, *Pr*
EMP: 5 EST: 1949
SALES (est): 475.6K **Privately Held**
SIC: 7641 7532 Furniture upholstery repair; Interior repair services

Rehoboth Beach - Sussex County (G-12692) GEOGRAPHIC SECTION

(G-12692)
COLONIAL EAST MANAGEMENT
18389 Olde Coach Dr (19971-6191)
PHONE..................302 644-6500
Terri Rock, *Mgr*
EMP: 5 EST: 2011
SALES (est): 126.14K **Privately Held**
SIC: 8741 Management services

(G-12693)
COLONIAL OAKS HOTEL LLC
Also Called: Residence Inn By Marriott
18964 John J Williams Hwy (19971-4403)
PHONE..................302 645-7766
EMP: 127
SALES (corp-wide): 801.02K **Privately Held**
Web: www.marriott.com
SIC: 7011 Hotels and motels
PA: Colonial Oaks Hotel, Llc
   19113 Coastal Hwy
   Rehoboth Beach DE 19971
   302 645-7766

(G-12694)
COLONIAL OAKS HOTEL LLC (PA)
Also Called: Fairfield Inn Suites Rehoboth
19113 Coastal Hwy (19971-6125)
PHONE..................302 645-7766
Christian Hudson, *Mgr*
Toni Coverdale, *Bookkpr*
EMP: 5 EST: 2014
SQ FT: 90,000
SALES (est): 801.02K
SALES (corp-wide): 801.02K **Privately Held**
Web: www.marriott.com
SIC: 7011 Motels

(G-12695)
COMMON SENSE HEALTH RESEARCH
46 Baltimore Ave (19971-2424)
PHONE..................302 260-9811
EMP: 8
SALES (est): 52.05K **Privately Held**
SIC: 8099 Health and allied services, nec

(G-12696)
COMMUNITY PRIDE
72 Glade Cir E (19971-4115)
PHONE..................302 236-6591
EMP: 5 EST: 2017
SALES (est): 51.89K **Privately Held**
SIC: 8322 Community center

(G-12697)
CONLEY & WRIGHT DDS
Also Called: Maplewood Dental Associates
18913 John J Williams Hwy (19971-4404)
PHONE..................302 645-6671
T E Conley D.d.s., *Pt*
Bruce Wright, *Pt*
Steve Wright, *Pt*
EMP: 5 EST: 1980
SALES (est): 1.01MM **Privately Held**
Web: www.rehobothbeachsmiles.com
SIC: 8021 Dentists' office

(G-12698)
COOK ROBINSON EYES SRGCAL ASSO
18791 John J Williams Hwy (19971-4487)
PHONE..................302 645-2300
David Robinson Md, *Pr*
EMP: 21 EST: 1990
SALES (est): 618.32K **Privately Held**
Web: www.delawareeye.com
SIC: 8011 Opthalmologist

(G-12699)
COOL SPRING STORAGE CENTER INC
18585 Coastal Hwy Unit 17 (19971-6147)
PHONE..................302 448-8164
EMP: 5 EST: 2018
SALES (est): 69.94K **Privately Held**
Web: www.coolspringstorage.com
SIC: 4225 Warehousing, self storage

(G-12700)
COOPER SIMPLER ASSOCIATES INC
Also Called: Beach View Motel
6 Wilmington Ave (19971-2926)
PHONE..................302 227-2999
Samuel Cooper, *Pr*
Kenneth Simpler, *Pt*
Karen Simpler, *Pt*
EMP: 9 EST: 1982
SQ FT: 12,000
SALES (est): 453K **Privately Held**
Web: www.rehobothbeachview.com
SIC: 7011 Motels

(G-12701)
COOTER BRWNS TWSTED STHERN KIT
70 Rehoboth Ave (19971-2171)
PHONE..................302 567-2132
EMP: 6 EST: 2017
SALES (est): 261.48K **Privately Held**
Web: www.cooterbrownsrehoboth.com
SIC: 8621 Bar association

(G-12702)
COUNTY BANK (PA)
19927 Shuttle Rd (19971-4215)
PHONE..................302 226-9800
EMP: 19 EST: 1990
SQ FT: 15,000
SALES (est): 25.65MM **Privately Held**
Web: www.countybankdel.com
SIC: 6022 State commercial banks

(G-12703)
CRAZY EIGHT
36508 Seaside Outlet Dr (19971-1225)
PHONE..................302 227-7429
EMP: 3 EST: 2010
SALES (est): 190.09K **Privately Held**
SIC: 3643 Outlets, electric: convenience

(G-12704)
CROSSFIT RIVERFRONT
21331 Catalina Cir (19971-4804)
PHONE..................302 462-5176
EMP: 5 EST: 2015
SALES (est): 47.41K **Privately Held**
SIC: 7991 Physical fitness facilities

(G-12705)
CROWLEY AND ASSOC RLTY INC
20250 Coastal Hwy (19971-8065)
P.O. Box 465 (19971-0465)
PHONE..................302 227-6131
Wanda M Crowley, *Prin*
EMP: 11
SALES (corp-wide): 992.23K **Privately Held**
Web: www.crowleyrealestate.com
SIC: 6531 Real estate agent, residential
PA: Crowley And Associates Realty, Inc.
   1000 N Pennsylvania Ave
   Bethany Beach DE
   302 539-4013

(G-12706)
CRX CONSULTING LLC
20245 Bay Vista Rd Unit 305 (19971-8023)
PHONE..................302 864-7377
EMP: 5 EST: 2016
SALES (est): 198.45K **Privately Held**
Web: www.crxconstruction.com
SIC: 8748 Business consulting, nec

(G-12707)
CRX CONSULTING LLC
201 Lakeview Shrs (19971-4172)
PHONE..................302 864-7377
EMP: 5 EST: 2016
SALES (est): 398.38K **Privately Held**
Web: www.crxconstruction.com
SIC: 8748 Business consulting, nec

(G-12708)
CRYPTO TRADER LLC
Also Called: McOmm Installer
19266 Coastal Hwy (19971-6117)
PHONE..................302 339-7500
Shane Myles, *CEO*
EMP: 6 EST: 2018
SALES (est): 328.69K **Privately Held**
SIC: 1623 Cable laying construction

(G-12709)
D F QUILLEN & SONS INC (PA)
Also Called: True Value
803 Rehoboth Ave Ste F (19971-1151)
PHONE..................302 227-2531
Dennard F Quillen Junior, *CEO*
Dennard F Quillen Iii, *Pr*
Christopher Quillen, *VP*
Charlotte Quillen, *Sec*
Frederick Ward, *VP*
EMP: 20 EST: 1927
SQ FT: 20,000
SALES (est): 2.76MM
SALES (corp-wide): 2.76MM **Privately Held**
Web: www.truevalue.com
SIC: 5251 5211 1521 Hardware stores; Lumber and other building materials; Single-family home remodeling, additions, and repairs

(G-12710)
DACK TRADING LLC
18585 Coastal Hwy Unit 10 (19971)
PHONE..................917 576-4432
Amr Elewa, *Managing Member*
EMP: 5 EST: 2018
SALES (est): 378.41K **Privately Held**
Web: www.dacktrading.com
SIC: 5153 5031 Grains; Pallets, wood

(G-12711)
DANIEL W CUOZZO DO
18947 John J Williams Hwy Unit 201 (19971-4476)
PHONE..................302 645-4801
Daniel Cuozzo, *Owner*
EMP: 13 EST: 2015
SALES (est): 220.41K **Privately Held**
SIC: 8062 General medical and surgical hospitals

(G-12712)
DCOR
37545 Atlantic Ave (19971-1199)
PHONE..................302 227-9341
Ed Albers, *Prin*
EMP: 5 EST: 2009
SALES (est): 499.88K **Privately Held**
Web: www.rehobothinteriors.com
SIC: 8621 Professional organizations

(G-12713)
DEBBIE REED
Also Called: Re/Max
319 Rehoboth Ave (19971-3127)
PHONE..................302 227-3818
Debbie Reed, *Owner*
EMP: 11 EST: 1988
SALES (est): 797.91K **Privately Held**
Web: www.debbiereed.com
SIC: 6531 Real estate agent, residential

(G-12714)
DEBORA REED TEAM
319 Rehoboth Ave (19971-3127)
PHONE..................302 227-3818
Debbie Reed, *Prin*
EMP: 5 EST: 2012
SALES (est): 244.89K **Privately Held**
Web: www.debbiereed.com
SIC: 6531 Real estate agent, commercial

(G-12715)
DELAWARE BEACH LIFE
37587 Bay Harbor Dr (19971-1584)
PHONE..................302 227-9499
EMP: 10 EST: 2017
SALES (est): 137.51K **Privately Held**
Web: www.delawarebeachlife.com
SIC: 2721 Magazines: publishing only, not printed on site

(G-12716)
DELAWARE EYE INSTITUTE PA
Also Called: Delaware Eye Optical
18791 John J Williams Hwy Ste 1 (19971-9435)
PHONE..................302 645-2300
EMP: 30 EST: 2010
SALES (est): 5.65MM **Privately Held**
Web: www.delawareeye.com
SIC: 8011 Opthalmologist

(G-12717)
DELAWARE EYE SURGERY CENTER
18791 John J Williams Hwy (19971-4487)
PHONE..................302 645-2300
Robert Uffelman, *Admn*
EMP: 5 EST: 2005
SALES (est): 2.2MM **Privately Held**
Web: www.delawareeye.com
SIC: 8011 Eyes, ears, nose, and throat specialist: physician/surgeon

(G-12718)
DELAWARE LANDSCAPE CNSTR LLC
30 Coventry Rd (19971-3512)
PHONE..................302 841-3010
Matthew L Blakeman, *Prin*
EMP: 5 EST: 2010
SALES (est): 247.99K **Privately Held**
SIC: 1521 Single-family housing construction

(G-12719)
DELAWARE REALTY GROUP INC
Also Called: Re/Max
317 Rehoboth Ave (19971-3127)
PHONE..................302 227-4800
Joseph Reed, *Pr*
EMP: 7 EST: 1990
SALES (est): 1.14MM **Privately Held**
Web: www.homerb.com
SIC: 6531 Real estate agent, residential

(G-12720)
DELMARVA PADDLERS RETREAT
11 Eagle Dr (19971-1437)
PHONE..................302 542-0818
Christopher Beckman, *Owner*
EMP: 5 EST: 2017
SALES (est): 48.09K **Privately Held**
SIC: 8699 Membership organizations, nec

GEOGRAPHIC SECTION

Rehoboth Beach - Sussex County (G-12751)

(G-12721)
DESIGNER CONSIGNER INC
5 N 1st St (19971-2115)
PHONE..................302 373-6318
EMP: 20
SALES (corp-wide): 473.86K **Privately Held**
Web: www.designerconsignerde.com
SIC: 7389 Design services
PA: Designer Consigner Inc
7185 Lancaster Pike
Hockessin DE 19707
302 239-4034

(G-12722)
DESTORAGE REHOBOTH LLC
19659 Blue Bird Ln (19971-8599)
PHONE..................302 231-2127
EMP: 5 EST: 2016
SALES (est): 105.91K **Privately Held**
Web: www.destorage.com
SIC: 4225 General warehousing

(G-12723)
DEWITT & ASSOCIATES LLC
55 Fields End (19971-1611)
P.O. Box 1480 (19971-5480)
PHONE..................302 226-0521
Henry K Dewitt, *Prin*
EMP: 5 EST: 2014
SALES (est): 188.91K **Privately Held**
Web: www.dewitt-assoc.com
SIC: 8742 Management consulting services

(G-12724)
DEWSON CONSTRUCTION CO
20616 Coastal Hwy (19971-8031)
PHONE..................302 227-3095
Tim Dewson, *Prin*
EMP: 22
SALES (corp-wide): 1.25MM **Privately Held**
Web: www.dewsonconstruction.com
SIC: 1542 1521 Commercial and office building contractors; Single-family housing construction
PA: Dewson Construction Co
9 Jefferson Ave
Wilmington DE 19805
302 427-2250

(G-12725)
DF QUILLEN SONS INC DBA
19897 Hebron Rd Unit F (19971-1253)
PHONE..................302 227-7368
EMP: 5 EST: 2018
SALES (est): 244.09K **Privately Held**
SIC: 1521 New construction, single-family houses

(G-12726)
DIAMOND STATE MEATS LLC
37369 Martin St (19971-8046)
PHONE..................302 270-0009
EMP: 5 EST: 2018
SALES (est): 713.05K **Privately Held**
SIC: 5147 Meats and meat products

(G-12727)
DIAZ AND COSTA HARDWOOD FLRNG
19871 Coastal Hwy (19971-6115)
PHONE..................302 212-5923
EMP: 6 EST: 2016
SALES (est): 96.66K **Privately Held**
SIC: 1752 Floor laying and floor work, nec

(G-12728)
DIGITAL SOUNDS
24 Tiffany Dr (19971-9729)
PHONE..................302 644-9187
Beverly Crowley, *Prin*
EMP: 6 EST: 2007
SALES (est): 126.61K **Privately Held**
SIC: 1731 Sound equipment specialization

(G-12729)
DINNER BELL INN
2 Christian St (19971-3002)
PHONE..................302 227-2561
EMP: 10 EST: 2017
SALES (est): 89.44K **Privately Held**
SIC: 7011 Inns

(G-12730)
DOGFISH HEAD INC
Also Called: Dogfish Head Brewings & Eats
320 Rehoboth Ave (19971-3108)
PHONE..................302 226-2739
EMP: 14 EST: 1994
SALES (est): 1.06MM **Privately Held**
Web: www.dogfish.com
SIC: 5812 2082 Seafood restaurants; Malt beverages

(G-12731)
DONOVAN PAINTING AND DRYWALL
36983 Rehoboth Avenue Ext Unit C (19971-7143)
PHONE..................302 745-6306
EMP: 8 EST: 2017
SALES (est): 428.98K **Privately Held**
Web: www.donovanspaintinganddrywall.com
SIC: 1721 Painting and paper hanging

(G-12732)
DONOVAN PAINTING LLC
85 Bryan Dr (19971-9732)
PHONE..................302 745-6306
EMP: 9 EST: 2008
SALES (est): 494.03K **Privately Held**
SIC: 1721 Painting and paper hanging

(G-12733)
DOUGLAS R BRIGGS
26 Midway Shopping Ctr (19971-6147)
PHONE..................302 645-6681
Douglas R Briggs, *Prin*
EMP: 9 EST: 2011
SALES (est): 95.86K **Privately Held**
Web: www.firststatehealth.com
SIC: 8041 Offices and clinics of chiropractors

(G-12734)
DOVER EAST LLC
19545 Camelot Dr Ste A (19971-1197)
PHONE..................302 330-3040
EMP: 11 EST: 2020
SALES (est): 463.44K
SALES (corp-wide): 10.58MM **Privately Held**
SIC: 8748 Business consulting, nec
PA: Twenty Nine Corp.
19545 Camelot Dr Ste A
Rehoboth Beach DE 19971
302 330-3040

(G-12735)
DOWNTOWN BEACH RENTALS
20 Baltimore Ave (19971-2104)
PHONE..................410 472-9480
Tom Mcglone, *Prin*
EMP: 6 EST: 2018
SALES (est): 171.26K **Privately Held**
SIC: 7359 Equipment rental and leasing, nec

(G-12736)
DUSTNTIME
36181 Field Ln (19971-8655)
PHONE..................302 858-7876
EMP: 7 EST: 2009
SALES (est): 237.88K **Privately Held**
Web: www.dustntime.com
SIC: 7699 7389 Cleaning services; Business Activities at Non-Commercial Site

(G-12737)
ECHELON INTERIORS LLC
55 Cascade Ln Ste A (19971-8528)
PHONE..................302 519-9151
Beth Remington, *Managing Member*
EMP: 5 EST: 2008
SALES (est): 926.93K **Privately Held**
SIC: 7389 Interior designer

(G-12738)
ECONO LODGE INN SUITES RESORT
Also Called: Econo Lodge
19540 Coastal Hwy (19971-6120)
PHONE..................302 227-0500
Terry Bartley, *Genl Mgr*
Sal Gallo, *Pr*
EMP: 35 EST: 1985
SQ FT: 13,500
SALES (est): 468.67K **Privately Held**
Web: www.choicehotels.com
SIC: 7011 Motels

(G-12739)
EGG
510 Rehoboth Ave (19971-2185)
PHONE..................302 227-3447
EMP: 5 EST: 2017
SALES (est): 90.89K **Privately Held**
Web: www.eggrehoboth.com
SIC: 5144 Eggs

(G-12740)
ELECTRIC FISH LLC
42 Rehoboth Ave Ste 5 (19971-2122)
PHONE..................484 804-5149
Colleen Simmons, *Prin*
EMP: 5 EST: 2018
SALES (est): 60.51K **Privately Held**
Web: electric-fish-llc.business.site
SIC: 1731 General electrical contractor

(G-12741)
ELECTRIC TIGER TATTOO
19972 Church St (19971-3193)
PHONE..................302 226-1138
Drew Winner, *Prin*
EMP: 5 EST: 2016
SALES (est): 108.5K **Privately Held**
Web: electrictigertattoo.wordpress.com
SIC: 7299 Tattoo parlor

(G-12742)
ELEVEE EVENTS
260 Sea Eagle Dr Unit 2 (19971-2751)
P.O. Box 488 (19971-0488)
PHONE..................302 212-2112
Nicole Bailey, *Prin*
EMP: 5 EST: 2014
SALES (est): 74.02K **Privately Held**
Web: www.eleveeevents.com
SIC: 7299 Party planning service

(G-12743)
ENHANCED DENTAL CARE
18947 John J Williams Hwy Unit 301 (19971-4474)
PHONE..................302 645-7200
EMP: 9 EST: 2017
SALES (est): 459.87K **Privately Held**
Web: www.enhanceddentalcare.com
SIC: 8021 Offices and clinics of dentists

(G-12744)
ENTERPRISE RENTACAR
18767 Coastal Hwy (19971-6152)
PHONE..................302 645-5005
Lance Hogsten, *Prin*
EMP: 6 EST: 2015
SALES (est): 68.97K **Privately Held**
Web: www.enterprise.com
SIC: 7514 Rent-a-car service

(G-12745)
ERIN BENDLER
8 London Cir N (19971-1456)
PHONE..................201 704-6252
Erin Bendler, *Prin*
EMP: 5 EST: 2019
SALES (est): 24.86K **Privately Held**
SIC: 8049 Offices of health practitioner

(G-12746)
ERNIE DEANGELIS (PA)
Also Called: Tomato Sunshine
19791 Coastal Hwy (19971-6157)
PHONE..................302 226-9533
Ernie Deangelis, *Owner*
EMP: 10 EST: 1990
SALES (est): 1.38MM
SALES (corp-wide): 1.38MM **Privately Held**
Web: www.tomatosunshine.com
SIC: 5148 0782 Fresh fruits and vegetables; Garden services

(G-12747)
EXODUS ESCAPE ROOMS LLC
19266 Coastal Hwy (19971-6117)
PHONE..................302 278-7679
EMP: 6 EST: 2016
SALES (est): 219.8K **Privately Held**
Web: www.axxiomnewark.com
SIC: 7929 Entertainment service

(G-12748)
EXPRESS HOTEL INC
19953 Shuttle Rd (19971-4214)
PHONE..................302 227-4030
EMP: 14 EST: 2010
SALES (est): 154.43K **Privately Held**
SIC: 7011 Hotels and motels

(G-12749)
EZTRACKIT INC
19266 Coastal Hwy Unit 4 # 6 (19971-6117)
PHONE..................800 371-5956
EMP: 8 EST: 2012
SALES (est): 307.08K **Privately Held**
Web: www.eztrackit.com
SIC: 7371 Computer software development

(G-12750)
FANNON COLOR PRINTING LLC
20 Harbor Rd (19971-1204)
PHONE..................302 227-2164
James Fannon, *Prin*
EMP: 2 EST: 2010
SALES (est): 144.13K **Privately Held**
SIC: 2752 Offset printing

(G-12751)
FAW CASSON
20245 Bay Vista Rd (19971-8023)
PHONE..................302 226-1082
EMP: 9 EST: 2019
SALES (est): 229.3K **Privately Held**
Web: www.fawcasson.com
SIC: 6512 Commercial and industrial building operation

Rehoboth Beach - Sussex County (G-12752)   GEOGRAPHIC SECTION

(G-12752)
FAW CASSON
20376 Coastal Hwy Ste 204 (19971-8015)
PHONE..................................302 226-1919
Alison Houck, *Mng Pt*
EMP: 6 **EST:** 2014
SALES (est): 185.57K **Privately Held**
Web: www.fawcasson.com
SIC: 8721 Certified public accountant

(G-12753)
FENWAY BARR LLC
107 Cotton Tail Ct S (19971-9768)
PHONE..................................302 222-1913
EMP: 6 **EST:** 2005
SALES (est): 115.57K **Privately Held**
SIC: 7389 Business Activities at Non-Commercial Site

(G-12754)
FESTIVAL OF CHEER
19406 Coastal Hwy (19971-6126)
PHONE..................................302 227-4325
EMP: 6 **EST:** 2017
SALES (est): 102.28K **Privately Held**
Web: www.festivalofcheer.org
SIC: 7999 Festival operation

(G-12755)
FIRST MEDIA RADIO LLC
9 Stockley St (19971-2921)
PHONE..................................410 253-9406
EMP: 5 **EST:** 2017
SALES (est): 181.74K **Privately Held**
SIC: 4832 Radio broadcasting stations

(G-12756)
FISHTAIL PRINT COMPANY
18585 Coastal Hwy (19971-6147)
PHONE..................................302 408-4800
EMP: 6 **EST:** 2018
SALES (est): 89.64K **Privately Held**
Web: www.fishtailprinting.com
SIC: 2752 Offset printing

(G-12757)
FISHTAIL PRINT COMPANY
36837 Winner Cir (19971-1093)
PHONE..................................302 682-3053
Connor Ghabra, *Prin*
EMP: 5 **EST:** 2018
SALES (est): 112.37K **Privately Held**
Web: www.fishtailprinting.com
SIC: 2752 Offset printing

(G-12758)
FITCH-IT
21183 K St (19971-8435)
PHONE..................................302 260-9657
Nancy Fitch, *Owner*
EMP: 5 **EST:** 2012
SALES (est): 94.42K **Privately Held**
SIC: 1522 Residential construction, nec

(G-12759)
FOSTER LONG VACATION RENTALS
527 N Boardwalk (19971-2831)
PHONE..................................302 226-2919
EMP: 7 **EST:** 2017
SALES (est): 120.53K **Privately Held**
Web: www.lfvacations.com
SIC: 7359 Equipment rental and leasing, nec

(G-12760)
FRANK COSTA CONSTR HANDYMAN
5 N 1st St (19971-2115)
PHONE..................................302 561-5792
Frank Costa, *Owner*
EMP: 5 **EST:** 2017
SALES (est): 66.22K **Privately Held**
SIC: 7299 Handyman service

(G-12761)
FREES ELECTRIC
19266 Coastal Hwy Unit 10 (19971-6117)
PHONE..................................302 752-8895
EMP: 5 **EST:** 2013
SALES (est): 83.54K **Privately Held**
Web: www.freeselectric.com
SIC: 1731 General electrical contractor

(G-12762)
FUN SPORT INC
Also Called: Midway Speedway
Rr 1 (19971)
P.O. Box 960 (19971-0960)
PHONE..................................302 644-2042
Jim Loomis, *Pr*
EMP: 6 **EST:** 1994
SALES (est): 978.16K **Privately Held**
Web: www.midwayspeedwaypark.com
SIC: 7999 Tennis services and professionals

(G-12763)
FURTADO KIM ND
35252 Hudson Way (19971-4419)
PHONE..................................302 945-2107
Kimberly Furtado, *Prin*
EMP: 6 **EST:** 2007
SALES (est): 48.06K **Privately Held**
SIC: 8049 Acupuncturist

(G-12764)
G REHOBOTH
234 Rehoboth Ave (19971-2134)
PHONE..................................302 278-7677
EMP: 40 **EST:** 2017
SALES (est): 46.41K **Privately Held**
SIC: 7999 Recreation services

(G-12765)
GALLO REALTY INC (PA)
Also Called: Prudential Gallo Realtor
37230 Rehoboth Avenue Ext (19971-3198)
PHONE..................................302 945-7368
Elizabeth D Gallo, *Pr*
EMP: 6 **EST:** 1979
SQ FT: 2,000
SALES (est): 1.72MM
SALES (corp-wide): 1.72MM **Privately Held**
Web: beachrentals.penfedrealty.com
SIC: 6531 Real estate agent, residential

(G-12766)
GARAGE
4544 Highway One (19971-6152)
PHONE..................................302 645-7288
Robert Wyatt, *Owner*
EMP: 5 **EST:** 2003
SALES (est): 536.77K **Privately Held**
SIC: 5013 7539 Radiators; Automotive repair shops, nec

(G-12767)
GEMCRAFT HOMES AT SUMMERCREST
34795 Mute Swan Ln (19971-4470)
PHONE..................................302 703-6763
EMP: 6 **EST:** 2018
SALES (est): 106.92K **Privately Held**
Web: www.gemcrafthomes.com
SIC: 1521 New construction, single-family houses

(G-12768)
GEORGE H BUNTING JR
Also Called: State Farm Insurance
19716 Sea Air Ave # 1 (19971-3800)
P.O. Box 377 (19971-0377)
PHONE..................................302 227-3891
George H Bunting Junior, *Owner*
EMP: 5 **EST:** 1974
SALES (est): 463.67K **Privately Held**
Web: www.gbunting.com
SIC: 6411 Insurance agents and brokers

(G-12769)
GEORGE METZ
Also Called: Sea Esta Motel III
713 Rehoboth Ave (19971-3191)
PHONE..................................302 227-4343
George Metz, *Owner*
EMP: 7 **EST:** 1995
SALES (est): 230K **Privately Held**
Web: www.seaesta.com
SIC: 7011 Motels

(G-12770)
GGE AMUSEMENTS
34974 Oyster House Rd (19971)
P.O. Box 622 (19971-0622)
PHONE..................................302 227-0661
Rita Falcone, *Pr*
EMP: 7 **EST:** 1969
SALES (est): 371.7K **Privately Held**
SIC: 7359 7929 Vending machine rental; Entertainment service

(G-12771)
GIF NORTH AMERICA LLC
18227 Shockley Dr (19971-1337)
PHONE..................................703 969-9243
EMP: 7 **EST:** 2009
SALES (est): 106.63K **Privately Held**
SIC: 8711 3714 Engineering services; Motor vehicle parts and accessories

(G-12772)
GOLDS GYM
3712 Highway One (19971-1749)
PHONE..................................302 226-4653
Lisa Lawson, *Pr*
EMP: 9 **EST:** 1998
SQ FT: 11,000
SALES (est): 340.17K **Privately Held**
Web: www.goldsgym.com
SIC: 7991 Physical fitness facilities

(G-12773)
GOVER COUNSELING PSYCHOLOGY
The Lndg (19971)
PHONE..................................302 226-3661
EMP: 5 **EST:** 2007
SALES (est): 80K **Privately Held**
SIC: 8049 Clinical psychologist

(G-12774)
GOVERNMENT AFFAIRS
12 Beaver Dam Reach (19971-6105)
PHONE..................................302 226-2704
Andrew Stayton, *Owner*
EMP: 5 **EST:** 2012
SALES (est): 113.83K **Privately Held**
SIC: 8748 Business consulting, nec

(G-12775)
GOVERNMENT PORTFOLIO LLC
35546 Hatteras Ct (19971-4820)
PHONE..................................301 718-9742
EMP: 10 **EST:** 2006
SQ FT: 1,000
SALES (est): 1.1MM **Privately Held**
SIC: 6722 Money market mutual funds

(G-12776)
GRACE MECHANICAL
18746 Munchy Branch Rd (19971-8755)
PHONE..................................302 542-4102
Stephen Garyantes, *Prin*
EMP: 5 **EST:** 2017
SALES (est): 135.52K **Privately Held**
SIC: 1711 Mechanical contractor

(G-12777)
GRAMONOLI ENTERPRISES INC
Also Called: Yesteryars Phtgraphic Emporium
21 Rehoboth Ave (19971-2119)
PHONE..................................302 227-1288
James Miller, *Pr*
EMP: 6 **EST:** 1981
SALES (est): 312.91K **Privately Held**
Web: www.oldtimephotosrehoboth.com
SIC: 7221 Photographer, still or video

(G-12778)
GREEN LUNAR LLC
19266 Coastal Hwy (19971-6117)
PHONE..................................650 507-9049
Tomer Nahumi, *CEO*
EMP: 6
SALES (est): 238.26K **Privately Held**
SIC: 7389 Business services, nec

(G-12779)
HABIB BOLOURCHI MD FACC
Also Called: Henlopen Cardiology
4503 Hwy 1 (19971)
PHONE..................................302 645-7672
Habib Bolourchi Md, *Owner*
EMP: 6 **EST:** 1980
SALES (est): 336.58K **Privately Held**
SIC: 8011 Offices and clinics of medical doctors

(G-12780)
HARBORSIDE DEVELOPMENT II LLC
Also Called: Inn At Canal Square, The
18826 Coastal Hwy (19971-6150)
P.O. Box 101 (19958-0101)
PHONE..................................302 644-3377
EMP: 24 **EST:** 2000
SALES (est): 219.6K **Privately Held**
SIC: 7011 Inns

(G-12781)
HARRY K FOUNDATION
313 S Boardwalk (19971-2933)
PHONE..................................301 226-0675
Harry Keswani, *Pr*
Tarrie Miller, *VP*
Laurie Harper, *Treas*
Donna Winegar, *Sec*
Laura Annan, *Ex Dir*
EMP: 15 **EST:** 2013
SALES (est): 624.03K **Privately Held**
Web: www.harrykfoundation.org
SIC: 8641 Civic and social associations

(G-12782)
HEALTHY AT HOME CARE LLC
7 Kendal Ln (19971-2721)
PHONE..................................571 228-5935
EMP: 5 **EST:** 2018
SALES (est): 62.79K **Privately Held**
SIC: 8082 Home health care services

(G-12783)
HELOPEN CONDOMINIUM COUNCIL
Also Called: Henlopen Condominiums
527 N Boardwalk (19971-2831)
PHONE..................................302 227-6409
Anthony Casale, *Pr*
Ellen Daleiao, *Pr*
EMP: 7 **EST:** 1975
SALES (est): 787.89K **Privately Held**
Web: www.henlopen.com
SIC: 8641 Condominium association

Rehoboth Beach - Sussex County

(G-12784)
HENLOPEN ACRES BEACH CLUB INC
28 Dune Way (19971)
P.O. Box 184 (19971-0184)
PHONE.................................302 227-9919
Joni Reich, *Pr*
EMP: 5 EST: 2008
SALES (est): 103.69K **Privately Held**
Web: www.henlopenacresbeachclub.com
SIC: 7997 Country club, membership

(G-12785)
HENLOPEN CARDIOLOGY PA (PA)
18959 Coastal Hwy Ste A (19971-6214)
PHONE.................................302 645-7671
Nasi Bollurchi, *Mgr*
EMP: 5 EST: 1994
SALES (est): 683.22K **Privately Held**
SIC: 8011 Cardiologist and cardio-vascular specialist

(G-12786)
HENLOPEN HOTEL INC
511 N Boardwalk (19971-2162)
PHONE.................................302 227-2551
TOLL FREE: 800
Louis J Capano, *Pr*
Steve Collins, *Genl Mgr*
EMP: 13 EST: 1973
SQ FT: 90,000
SALES (est): 438.65K **Privately Held**
Web: www.henlopenhotel.com
SIC: 7011 Resort hotel

(G-12787)
HOLIDAY INN EXPRESS
Also Called: Holiday Inn
19953 Shuttle Rd (19971-4214)
PHONE.................................302 227-4030
Sharleen Norris, *Owner*
Crystal Smith, *Mgr*
Isac Henry, *Mgr*
Gretchen Howk, *Mgr*
Stephanie Mchenry, *Mgr*
EMP: 19 EST: 1997
SALES (est): 451.6K **Privately Held**
Web: www.holidayinn.com
SIC: 7011 Hotels and motels

(G-12788)
HOMESTEAD AT REHOBOTH BB
35060 Warrington Rd (19971-2092)
PHONE.................................302 226-7625
Mary Ford, *Owner*
EMP: 9 EST: 2006
SALES (est): 116.78K **Privately Held**
Web: www.homesteadrehoboth.com
SIC: 7011 Bed and breakfast inn

(G-12789)
HOMEWARD TATTOO
37169 Rehoboth Avenue Ext Unit 10 (19971-1683)
PHONE.................................302 226-8145
EMP: 5 EST: 2016
SALES (est): 78.17K **Privately Held**
Web: www.homewardtattoo.com
SIC: 7299 Tattoo parlor

(G-12790)
HOMEWATCH CONCIERGE
75 Kings Creek Cir (19971-1059)
PHONE.................................302 542-4087
Jenny Barto, *Prin*
EMP: 5 EST: 2012
SALES (est): 140.89K **Privately Held**
Web: www.homewatch-concierge.com
SIC: 6331 Property damage insurance

(G-12791)
HOOSIER OSTEOTRONIX CORP
35669 Kiawah Path (19971-4832)
PHONE.................................410 241-7627
Austin Mault, *Pr*
EMP: 7 EST: 2016
SALES (est): 406.61K **Privately Held**
Web: www.hoosierosteotronix.com
SIC: 5999 7389 Medical apparatus and supplies; Business services, nec

(G-12792)
HUDSON JNES JAYWORK FISHER LLC
Also Called: Hudson Jones
309 Rehoboth Ave (19971-3127)
PHONE.................................302 227-9441
Bill Becker, *Mgr*
EMP: 10
SALES (corp-wide): 3.82MM **Privately Held**
Web: www.delawarelaw.com
SIC: 8111 General practice law office
PA: Hudson Jones Jaywork & Fisher Llc
225 S State St
Dover DE 19901
302 734-7401

(G-12793)
IMMANUEL SHELTER INC
19285 Holland Glade Rd (19971-4180)
PHONE.................................888 634-9992
EMP: 7 EST: 2017
SALES (est): 92.35K **Privately Held**
Web: www.immanuelshelter.org
SIC: 8322 Social service center

(G-12794)
INDIAN RVER CPTINS ASSOC WBMST
39415 Inlet Rd (19971-2600)
PHONE.................................302 227-3071
EMP: 6 EST: 2011
SALES (est): 189.82K **Privately Held**
Web: www.destateparks.com
SIC: 4493 Boat yards, storage and incidental repair

(G-12795)
INN AT REHOBOTH APARTMENTS
27 Brooklyn Ave (19971-2901)
PHONE.................................302 226-1760
EMP: 6 EST: 2018
SALES (est): 71.2K **Privately Held**
Web: www.innatrehoboth.com
SIC: 7011 Inns

(G-12796)
INNS OF REHOBOTH BEACH LLC
18826 Coastal Hwy (19971-6150)
PHONE.................................302 645-8003
Renei Thompson, *Brnch Mgr*
EMP: 37 EST: 2013
SALES (est): 497.68K **Privately Held**
SIC: 7011 Inns

(G-12797)
JACK LINGO ASSET MGT LLC
19335 Coastal Hwy (19971-6100)
PHONE.................................302 226-6645
EMP: 11 EST: 2011
SALES (est): 76.02K **Privately Held**
SIC: 6726 Management investment funds, closed-end

(G-12798)
JACK LINGO INC REALTOR (PA)
246 Rehoboth Ave (19971-2134)
P.O. Box 605 (19971-0605)
PHONE.................................302 227-3883
Jack Lingo, *Pr*
T William Lingo, *Stockholder**
John E Lingo, *Stockholder**
Bryce M Lingo, *Stockholder**
Derrick O Lingo, *Stockholder**
EMP: 37 EST: 1975
SQ FT: 2,200
SALES (est): 10.96MM
SALES (corp-wide): 10.96MM **Privately Held**
Web: www.jacklingo.com
SIC: 6531 Real estate agent, residential

(G-12799)
JACK LINGO REALTOR
97 Tidewaters Rd (19971-1617)
PHONE.................................302 344-9188
EMP: 6 EST: 2018
SALES (est): 114.64K **Privately Held**
Web: www.jacklingo.com
SIC: 6531 Real estate brokers and agents

(G-12800)
JAMES E DEAKYNE JR PA
300 Salisbury St (19971-3323)
PHONE.................................302 226-1200
James E Deakyne Junior, *Prin*
EMP: 5 EST: 2010
SALES (est): 55.67K **Privately Held**
SIC: 8111 General practice attorney, lawyer

(G-12801)
JAMES E DEAKYNE JR PA
300 Salisbury St (19971-3323)
PHONE.................................302 226-1200
James E Deakyne Junior, *Prin*
EMP: 5 EST: 2012
SALES (est): 70.97K **Privately Held**
Web: www.jamesdlaw.net
SIC: 8621 Professional organizations

(G-12802)
JBJ ENTERPRISE LLC
19361 Copper Dr N (19971-4676)
PHONE.................................302 227-6080
John A Black, *Prin*
EMP: 5 EST: 2009
SALES (est): 157.41K **Privately Held**
SIC: 7389 Business services, nec

(G-12803)
JENNIFER M D HUNG
18947 John J Williams Hwy U (19971-4474)
PHONE.................................302 644-0690
Jennifer Hung, *Mgr*
EMP: 9 EST: 2017
SALES (est): 109.63K **Privately Held**
SIC: 8011 Pediatrician

(G-12804)
JESSICA S DICERBO DDS
18947 John J Williams Hwy Unit 309 (19971-4474)
PHONE.................................302 644-4460
Jessica Dicerbo, *Prin*
EMP: 8 EST: 2018
SALES (est): 110.58K **Privately Held**
Web: www.smogpeople.com
SIC: 8021 Dentists' office

(G-12805)
JETSET TRAVEL INC
19470 Coastal Hwy Unit 7 (19971-6127)
PHONE.................................302 678-5050
Angela Armutcu, *Pr*
EMP: 5 EST: 2005
SALES (est): 447.89K **Privately Held**
Web: www.jetsettravel.biz
SIC: 4724 Tourist agency arranging transport, lodging and car rental

(G-12806)
JOE HALLOCK CONTRACTING LLC
18 Lauras Way (19971-9592)
PHONE.................................302 236-6423
Joseph Hallock, *Ofcr*
EMP: 5 EST: 2018
SALES (est): 128K **Privately Held**
SIC: 1799 Special trade contractors, nec

(G-12807)
JOE MAGGIO REALTY (PA)
37169 Rehoboth Avenue Ext Unit 11 (19971-1683)
PHONE.................................302 251-8792
EMP: 5 EST: 2018
SALES (est): 478.96K
SALES (corp-wide): 478.96K **Privately Held**
Web: www.rehobothleweshomes.com
SIC: 6531 Real estate agent, residential

(G-12808)
JOHNSON ORTHODONTICS
18947 John J Williams Hwy Unit 310 (19971-4477)
PHONE.................................302 645-5554
Jonathan Johnson, *Owner*
EMP: 5 EST: 2010
SALES (est): 331.79K **Privately Held**
Web: www.rehoborthodontics.com
SIC: 8021 Orthodontist

(G-12809)
JOSEPH SCHWARTZ PSYD
19606 Coastal Hwy Unit 102 (19971-8596)
PHONE.................................302 213-3287
EMP: 6 EST: 2018
SALES (est): 80.53K **Privately Held**
SIC: 8011 Offices and clinics of medical doctors

(G-12810)
JUDY V
39401 Inlet Rd (19971-2600)
PHONE.................................302 226-2214
EMP: 6 EST: 1964
SALES (est): 161.92K **Privately Held**
Web: www.fishjudyv.com
SIC: 7999 Fishing boats, party: operation

(G-12811)
JUICEFRESH DIMITRA YOGA
43 Rehoboth Ave (19971-2119)
PHONE.................................302 645-9100
EMP: 7 EST: 2016
SALES (est): 47.11K **Privately Held**
Web: www.dimitrayoga.com
SIC: 7999 Yoga instruction

(G-12812)
JUNGLE JIMS ADVENTURE WORLD
Also Called: Jungle Jim's
8 Country Club Rd (19971-1088)
PHONE.................................302 227-8444
William Lingo, *Pr*
EMP: 70 EST: 1977
SALES (est): 2.23MM **Privately Held**
Web: www.funatjunglejims.com
SIC: 7996 Amusement parks

(G-12813)
K-10 DOG TRAINING
1013 Scarborough Ave (19971-1864)
PHONE.................................302 236-2497
Nancy Lafontaine, *Prin*
EMP: 5 EST: 2010
SALES (est): 51.72K **Privately Held**

Rehoboth Beach - Sussex County (G-12814)   GEOGRAPHIC SECTION

Web: www.k10dogtraining.com
SIC: 0752 Training services, pet and animal specialties (not horses)

(G-12814)
KARL J ZEREN DDS
18947 John J Williams Hwy Unit 301 (19971-4474)
PHONE..................302 644-2773
Karl J Zeren, *Prin*
EMP: 8 EST: 2016
SALES (est): 115.62K **Privately Held**
Web: www.enhanceddentalcare.com
SIC: 8021 Dentists' office

(G-12815)
KATHI JENKS
19869 Sea Blossom Blvd (19971-7142)
PHONE..................302 226-7791
Kathi Jenks, *Prin*
EMP: 6 EST: 2017
SALES (est): 59.04K **Privately Held**
SIC: 8049 Offices of health practitioner

(G-12816)
KATHLEEN MCGUINESS
6 Broad Hollow St (19971-1609)
PHONE..................302 245-7355
Kathleen Mcguiness, *Prin*
EMP: 6 EST: 2016
SALES (est): 77.15K **Privately Held**
SIC: 8049 Offices of health practitioner

(G-12817)
KELLER WILLIAMS REALTY
Also Called: Keller Williams Realtors
36115 Knight St (19971-3851)
PHONE..................862 588-1342
Evita Monteagudo, *Prin*
EMP: 10 EST: 2017
SALES (est): 304.83K **Privately Held**
Web: www.kw.com
SIC: 6531 Real estate agent, residential

(G-12818)
KELLER WILLIAMS REALTY AT BCH
Also Called: Keller Williams Realtors
36765 Harness Ct (19971-1095)
PHONE..................302 360-0300
Evita Monteagudo, *Prin*
EMP: 18 EST: 2014
SALES (est): 543.22K **Privately Held**
Web: www.kw.com
SIC: 6531 Real estate agent, residential

(G-12819)
KENNY SIMPLER
Also Called: Avenue Inn
33 Wilmington Ave (19971-2218)
PHONE..................302 226-2900
Kenny Simpler, *Owner*
EMP: 7 EST: 1986
SALES (est): 382.78K **Privately Held**
Web: www.avenueinn.com
SIC: 7011 Motels

(G-12820)
KENSINGTON CROSS LTD (PA)
18585 Coastal Hwy Unit 10 (19971-6147)
PHONE..................888 999-9360
Frederick S Gnesin, *Pr*
Michael J Piazza, *VP*
EMP: 12 EST: 1986
SQ FT: 3,000
SALES (est): 1.83MM
SALES (corp-wide): 1.83MM **Privately Held**
Web: www.kensingtoncross.com
SIC: 6211 Investment bankers

(G-12821)
KEVIN SCOTT CAMERON
35645 Elk Camp Rd (19971-8716)
PHONE..................515 314-3400
Kevin Cameron, *CEO*
EMP: 6 EST: 2017
SALES (est): 48.71K **Privately Held**
SIC: 8322 Individual and family services

(G-12822)
KIDS COTTAGE LLC
35448 Wolfe Neck Rd (19971-8788)
PHONE..................302 644-7690
EMP: 20 EST: 2008
SALES (est): 807.73K **Privately Held**
Web: www.kidscottage.com
SIC: 8351 Preschool center

(G-12823)
KINGS CREEK COUNTRY CLUB INC
1 Kings Creek Cir (19971-1034)
PHONE..................302 227-8951
Stephen R Lett, *Pr*
Kenneth H Diggs, *VP*
John Hardin Young, *Sec*
Gail Petren, *Treas*
EMP: 10 EST: 1990
SALES (est): 2.13MM **Privately Held**
Web: www.kingscreekcountryclub.com
SIC: 7997 Country club, membership

(G-12824)
KODYS KIDS INC
36270 King St (19971-3875)
PHONE..................302 858-0884
EMP: 7 EST: 2019
SALES (est): 28.68K **Privately Held**
Web: www.kodyskids.org
SIC: 8351 Child day care services

(G-12825)
KOHR BROTHERS INC
Also Called: Kohr Brothers Frozen Custard
5 Rehoboth Ave (19971-2119)
PHONE..................302 227-9354
Sean Martin, *Mgr*
EMP: 42
SALES (corp-wide): 14.07MM **Privately Held**
Web: www.kohrbros.com
SIC: 5812 6794 Frozen yogurt stand; Franchises, selling or licensing
PA: Kohr Brothers, Inc.
     2151 Richmond Rd Ste 200
     Charlottesville VA 22911
     434 975-1500

(G-12826)
KWIK & CRAFTY CONTRACTING
18977 Munchy Branch Rd (19971-8763)
PHONE..................302 227-2550
EMP: 6 EST: 2009
SALES (est): 180K **Privately Held**
SIC: 5082 General construction machinery and equipment

(G-12827)
LAWSON FIRM LLC
402 Rehoboth Ave (19971-3113)
PHONE..................302 212-0655
EMP: 5 EST: 2016
SALES (est): 201.42K **Privately Held**
SIC: 8111 General practice law office

(G-12828)
LEFTYS ALLEY & EATS
75 Kings Creek Cir (19971-1059)
PHONE..................302 344-5858
EMP: 6 EST: 2016
SALES (est): 415.07K **Privately Held**
Web: www.ilovelefty s.com
SIC: 7933 Ten pin center

(G-12829)
LEGGS HANES BALI PLAYTEX OTLT
36454 Seaside Outlet Dr (19971-1222)
PHONE..................302 227-8943
Sarah Lee, *Owner*
EMP: 8 EST: 2005
SALES (est): 129.35K **Privately Held**
Web: outlets.onehanesplace.com
SIC: 3643 Outlets, electric: convenience

(G-12830)
LEGREE & FMLY INVESTMENTS LLC
19266 Cstl Hwy Unit 4-112 (19971)
PHONE..................302 245-5218
EMP: 5 EST: 2021
SALES (est): 80K **Privately Held**
SIC: 6531 Buying agent, real estate

(G-12831)
LEWES SPINE CENTER LLC
18947 John J Williams Hwy Unit 311 (19971-4477)
PHONE..................302 231-4333
EMP: 6 EST: 2018
SALES (est): 491.4K **Privately Held**
Web: www.lewesspinecenter.com
SIC: 8011 Orthopedic physician

(G-12832)
LINDA VISTA REAL ESTATE
18806 John J Williams Hwy # 2 (19971-4402)
PHONE..................302 313-1600
Jose Quinones, *Prin*
EMP: 12 EST: 2015
SALES (est): 206.52K **Privately Held**
SIC: 6531 Real estate agent, residential

(G-12833)
LITH AF GAMAL TRU LLC ◆
19266 Coastal Hwy Unit 4-109 (19971)
PHONE..................833 552-0181
Brandon Paterson, *Mgr*
EMP: 9 EST: 2023
SALES (est): 561.17K
SALES (corp-wide): 635.2K **Privately Held**
SIC: 6732 Trusts: educational, religious, etc.
HQ: First Faiths Holding Llc
     220 Adams Dr Ste 280-1036
     Weatherford TX 76086
     888 596-5660

(G-12834)
LITTLE LEAGUE BASEBALL INC
125 Beachfield Dr (19971-9674)
PHONE..................302 227-0888
EMP: 8 EST: 2016
SALES (est): 41.64K **Privately Held**
Web: www.littleleague.org
SIC: 7997 Baseball club, except professional and semi-professional

(G-12835)
LIVING RESOURCES INC
P.O. Box 1554 (19971-5554)
PHONE..................302 227-6867
Michael Hurd, *Prin*
EMP: 5 EST: 2010
SALES (est): 132.8K **Privately Held**
Web: www.drhurd.com
SIC: 8742 Business planning and organizing services

(G-12836)
LOGO MOTIVE INC
35576 Airport Rd (19971-4620)
PHONE..................302 645-2959
Jeff Vernon, *Mgr*
EMP: 3 EST: 2011
SALES (est): 412.64K **Privately Held**
Web: www.logomotivede.com
SIC: 2759 Screen printing

(G-12837)
LONG & FOSTER REAL ESTATE INC
Also Called: LONG & FOSTER REAL ESTATE INC
37156 Rehoboth Avenue Ext Unit 5 (19971-3104)
PHONE..................302 227-3821
Carol Mapderniak, *Genl Mgr*
EMP: 5
SALES (corp-wide): 302.09B **Publicly Held**
Web: www.longandfoster.com
SIC: 6531 6519 Real estate agent, residential ; Real property lessors, nec
HQ: Long & Foster Real Estate Inc
     11225 Nuckols Rd Ste A
     Glen Allen VA 23059
     804 346-4411

(G-12838)
LONGBOAT CONDOMINIUM LLC
81 Kings Creek Cir (19971-1043)
PHONE..................302 227-4785
EMP: 5 EST: 2008
SALES (est): 72.67K **Privately Held**
SIC: 8641 Condominium association

(G-12839)
LOVELY NAILS & SPA LLC
19287 Miller Rd Unit 10 (19971-6124)
PHONE..................302 260-9231
Lionel Sainsume, *Ofcr*
EMP: 5 EST: 2015
SALES (est): 59.55K **Privately Held**
SIC: 7231 Manicurist, pedicurist

(G-12840)
LOWELL SCOTT MD PA
Also Called: Scott Pediatrics
38398 Josephine St (19971-2060)
PHONE..................302 684-1119
Lowell Scott Md, *Pr*
EMP: 6 EST: 2002
SALES (est): 563.43K **Privately Held**
SIC: 8011 General and family practice, physician/surgeon

(G-12841)
LUXY STAY IMPERIAL LLC
19266 Cstl Hwy Unit 41013 (19971)
PHONE..................844 483-5383
EMP: 5 EST: 2021
SALES (est): 200.46K **Privately Held**
SIC: 6798 Real estate investment trusts

(G-12842)
M C TEK LLC
Also Called: Geekytek
19122 Coastal Hwy Unit B (19971-6136)
P.O. Box 125 (19971-0125)
PHONE..................302 644-9695
EMP: 8 EST: 2006
SALES (est): 622.73K **Privately Held**
SIC: 7373 8741 Computer integrated systems design; Business management

(G-12843)
MAGGIO/SHIELDS TEAMS
70 Rehoboth Ave Ste 101 (19971-2127)
PHONE..................302 226-3770
Betty Mann, *Prin*
EMP: 6 EST: 2004
SALES (est): 245.32K **Privately Held**

GEOGRAPHIC SECTION
Rehoboth Beach - Sussex County (G-12871)

SIC: 6531 Real estate agent, residential

(G-12844)
MAILBIZ
4590 Highway One (19971-9790)
PHONE.................302 644-9035
Thomas Kopunek, Prin
EMP: 5 EST: 2007
SALES (est): 167.6K Privately Held
Web: www.mailbizexpress.com
SIC: 7331 Mailing service

(G-12845)
MAN MAID CLEANING INC
29 Fox Creek Dr (19971-8615)
PHONE.................302 226-5050
Joe Biliski, Pr
EMP: 6 EST: 2002
SALES (est): 104.54K Privately Held
SIC: 7699 Cleaning services

(G-12846)
MANN & SONS INC
19606 Coastal Hwy Unit 104 (19971-8576)
PHONE.................302 841-0077
EMP: 16 EST: 2017
SALES (est): 265K Privately Held
Web: www.mannandsons.com
SIC: 6531 Real estate agent, residential

(G-12847)
MANUFACTURERS & TRADERS TR CO
Also Called: M&T
302 Rehoboth Ave (19971-3108)
PHONE.................302 855-2227
Patricia Hastings, Mgr
EMP: 7
SALES (corp-wide): 8.6B Publicly Held
Web: ir.mtb.com
SIC: 6022 State commercial banks
HQ: Manufacturers And Traders Trust Company
    1 M&T Plz Fl 3
    Buffalo NY 14203
    716 842-4200

(G-12848)
MARK A HORNE
Also Called: Garden Bears Landscaping
35721 Elk Camp Rd (19971-8723)
PHONE.................302 381-6672
Mark A Horne, Prin
EMP: 5 EST: 2009
SALES (est): 78.6K Privately Held
SIC: 0781 Landscape services

(G-12849)
MARK SHOWELL INTERIORS LTD
37025 Rehoboth Avenue Ext Unit L (19971-7146)
PHONE.................302 227-2272
Mark Showell, Pr
EMP: 10 EST: 1993
SALES (est): 965.2K Privately Held
Web: www.markshowellinteriors.com
SIC: 7389 Interior designer

(G-12850)
MARSHALL WAGNER & ASSOCIATES
19643 Blue Bird Ln Unit 2 (19971-6129)
PHONE.................302 227-2537
Doug Marshall, Pt
EMP: 7 EST: 2001
SALES (est): 599.03K Privately Held
Web: www.marshallwagner.com
SIC: 8721 Certified public accountant

(G-12851)
MARY COSTAS WOODWORKING
527 School Ln (19971-1807)
PHONE.................302 227-6255
Mary Costa, Prin
EMP: 2 EST: 2011
SALES (est): 176.16K Privately Held
SIC: 2431 Millwork

(G-12852)
MASSAGE ENVY LEWES
Also Called: Massage Envy
18949 Coastal Hwy Unit 104 (19971-6217)
PHONE.................302 703-4100
EMP: 5 EST: 2017
SALES (est): 55.72K Privately Held
Web: www.massageenvy.com
SIC: 7299 Massage parlor

(G-12853)
MICROCOM TECH LLC
18971 Goldfinch Cv (19971-4462)
PHONE.................858 775-5559
Hung Nguyen, CEO
EMP: 5 EST: 2017
SALES (est): 238.03K Privately Held
Web: www.microcom.us
SIC: 7371 7389 Computer software development and applications; Business services, nec

(G-12854)
MICROLOG CORPORATION MARYLAND
Also Called: Microlog
17027 Taramac Dr (19971-9644)
PHONE.................301 540-5501
Richard E Meccarielli, Pr
EMP: 8 EST: 1977
SQ FT: 25,000
SALES (est): 792.1K Privately Held
Web: www.microlog.com
SIC: 7371 Computer software development

(G-12855)
MID ATLANTIC WELLNESS GRO
8 Wood Duck Pt (19971-4135)
PHONE.................302 864-7766
EMP: 7 EST: 2019
SALES (est): 496.9K Privately Held
SIC: 8099 Health and allied services, nec

(G-12856)
MIDWAY FITNESS CENTER
Also Called: Midway Fitnes Racquetball CLB
28b Midway Shopping Ctr (19971)
PHONE.................302 645-0407
EMP: 7 EST: 1999
SALES (est): 175.53K Privately Held
Web: www.midwayfitness.com
SIC: 7991 5941 Athletic club and gymnasiums, membership; Sporting goods and bicycle shops

(G-12857)
MIDWAY REALTY CORP
34821 Derrickson Dr (19971-6144)
PHONE.................302 645-9511
Richard H Derrickson, Pr
Norma Lee Derrickson, *
Sabrina Hill, *
Tiffany Derrickson, *
Lance Derrickson, *
EMP: 45 EST: 1953
SALES (est): 2.2MM Privately Held
Web: www.midwayrealtyks.com
SIC: 6531 Real estate brokers and agents

(G-12858)
MINDBODY FITNESS
57 Sussex St Apt 3 (19971-2121)
PHONE.................302 893-6212
Jessica Bonini, Pr
EMP: 8 EST: 2018
SALES (est): 54.47K Privately Held
SIC: 7991 Physical fitness facilities

(G-12859)
MINUTE CENTER
19470 Coastal Hwy Unit 4 (19971-6127)
PHONE.................302 645-9396
EMP: 5 EST: 2018
SALES (est): 74.78K Privately Held
SIC: 8111 Legal services

(G-12860)
MOORES ENTERPRISES INC
Also Called: Oceanus Motel
6 2nd St (19971-2118)
P.O. Box 324 (19971-0324)
PHONE.................302 227-8200
Robert H Moore, Pr
EMP: 10 EST: 1965
SQ FT: 12,000
SALES (est): 464.69K Privately Held
Web: www.oceansrehoboth.com
SIC: 7011 Motels

(G-12861)
MORANS REFRIGERATION SVC INC
Also Called: Morans Heating & A/C & Plbg
146 Glade Cir W (19971-4106)
PHONE.................703 642-1200
Charles H Moran, Pr
Charles H Moran Iii, Pr
Frances Moran, Treas
Barbara Moran, Sec
EMP: 9 EST: 1971
SALES (est): 471.93K Privately Held
SIC: 1711 7623 Warm air heating and air conditioning contractor; Refrigeration repair service

(G-12862)
MORGAN STNLEY SMITH BARNEY LLC
55 Cascade Ln (19971-8528)
PHONE.................302 644-6600
Ed Duffy, Brnch Mgr
EMP: 105
SALES (corp-wide): 53.67B Publicly Held
Web: www.morganstanley.com
SIC: 6282 Investment advisory service
HQ: Morgan Stanley Smith Barney, Llc
    1585 Broadway
    New York NY 10036

(G-12863)
MORRIS JAMES LLP
19339 Coastal Hwy Unit 300 (19971-6213)
PHONE.................302 260-7290
EMP: 7
SALES (corp-wide): 24.52MM Privately Held
Web: www.morrisjamespersonalinjurylawyers.com
SIC: 8111 General practice attorney, lawyer
PA: Morris James Llp
    500 Delaware Ave Ste 1500
    Wilmington DE 19801
    302 888-6800

(G-12864)
MOSQUITO AUTHORITY
Also Called: Mosquito Authority
36837 Winner Cir (19971-1093)
PHONE.................302 228-5821
Susan Ghabra, Prin
EMP: 7 EST: 2010
SALES (est): 172.56K Privately Held
Web: www.mosquito-authority.com
SIC: 7342 Pest control services

(G-12865)
MOVENDI MOVING
30 Ocean Breeze Dr (19971-9584)
PHONE.................302 542-9346
Joel Cosbey, Prin
EMP: 5 EST: 2017
SALES (est): 128.37K Privately Held
Web: www.movendimoving.com
SIC: 4789 Transportation services, nec

(G-12866)
MR COPY INC
20200 Coastal Hwy Ste A (19971-8057)
PHONE.................302 227-4666
George Banashak, Pr
EMP: 5 EST: 1994
SQ FT: 1,800
SALES (est): 282.35K Privately Held
Web: www.nflfeatherflags.com
SIC: 7334 3993 Photocopying and duplicating services; Signs and advertising specialties

(G-12867)
MUNCIE INSURANCE & FINCL SVCS
Also Called: Nationwide Insurance
18767 Coastal Hwy (19971-6152)
PHONE.................302 645-7740
EMP: 6 EST: 2009
SALES (est): 48.37K Privately Held
Web: www.muncieinsurance.net
SIC: 7389 6411 Financial services; Insurance agents, brokers, and service

(G-12868)
MVRP FOUNDATION INC
19723 Queen St (19971-3871)
PHONE.................347 683-1974
Alison Rosen, Prin
EMP: 5 EST: 2015
SALES (est): 38.73K Privately Held
Web: www.mvrpfoundation.org
SIC: 8641 Civic and social associations

(G-12869)
NETTEL PARTNERS LLC
8 Venetian Dr (19971-1937)
PHONE.................215 290-7383
John Neff, Brnch Mgr
EMP: 18
SALES (corp-wide): 76.56K Privately Held
SIC: 7389 Telemarketing services
PA: Nettel Partners, Llc
    101 N Synnott Ave
    Wenonah NJ 08090
    215 964-9345

(G-12870)
NEW PENN FINANCIAL LLC
19269 Coastal Hwy Ste 1 (19971-6113)
PHONE.................240 475-4741
Scott Dostal, Brnch Mgr
EMP: 5 EST: 2018
SALES (est): 961.18K
SALES (corp-wide): 4.73B Publicly Held
SIC: 6162 Mortgage bankers and loan correspondents
PA: Rithm Capital Corp.
    799 Broadway
    New York NY 10003
    212 850-7770

(G-12871)
NORTHEAST CONTROLS INC (PA)
18766 John J Williams Hwy (19971-4417)

Rehoboth Beach - Sussex County (G-12872)

P.O. Box 9 (19969-0009)
PHONE..................................201 419-6111
Ronald V Yates, *Pr*
Todd Yates, *VP*
Gail Yates, *VP*
EMP: 12 EST: 1938
SQ FT: 6,000
SALES (est): 3.45MM
SALES (corp-wide): 3.45MM **Privately Held**
Web: www.nciweb.net
SIC: 5084 Controlling instruments and accessories

(G-12872)
NVR HOMES NATIONAL
31790 Carmine Dr (19971-9417)
PHONE..................................302 278-7099
EMP: 5 EST: 2016
SALES (est): 70.39K **Privately Held**
SIC: 6531 Real estate agents and managers

(G-12873)
OCEAN ATLANTIC AGENCY INC
330 Rehoboth Ave (19971-3108)
PHONE..................................302 227-6767
Ronald Lankford, *Owner*
EMP: 100 EST: 2010
SALES (est): 2.46MM **Privately Held**
Web: www.oceanatlantic.net
SIC: 6531 Real estate agent, residential

(G-12874)
OCEAN ATLANTIC ASSOCIATES LLC
Also Called: Ocean Atlantic Companies
18949 Coastal Hwy Unit 301 (19971-6219)
PHONE..................................302 227-3573
Preston Schell, *Pt*
Jennifer Nagle, *Pt*
Erin Scharp, *Pt*
EMP: 10 EST: 1998
SALES (est): 1.29MM **Privately Held**
Web: www.oacompanies.com
SIC: 6531 Real estate brokers and agents

(G-12875)
OCEAN ATLANTIC MANAGEMENT LLC
Also Called: Ocean Atlantic Companies
18949 Coastal Hwy Unit 301 (19971-6219)
PHONE..................................302 227-3573
Preston Schell, *Pr*
EMP: 8 EST: 2016
SALES (est): 682.76K **Privately Held**
Web: www.oacompanies.com
SIC: 6552 Land subdividers and developers, residential

(G-12876)
OCEAN GLASS INN
37299 Rehoboth Avenue Ext (19971-3238)
PHONE..................................302 227-2844
EMP: 12 EST: 2019
SALES (est): 180.21K **Privately Held**
Web: www.oceanglassinn.com
SIC: 7011 Motels

(G-12877)
OCEAN SUDS LAUNDRY MAT
18675 Coastal Hwy Unit 4 (19971-6146)
PHONE..................................302 703-6601
EMP: 7 EST: 2015
SALES (est): 218.89K **Privately Held**
SIC: 7215 Laundry, coin-operated

(G-12878)
OLD INLET BAIT AND TACKLE INC (PA)
Also Called: Wetsu Tackle Distributors
25012 Coastal Hwy (19971-8009)
P.O. Box 129 (19971-0129)
PHONE..................................302 227-7974
Amos Evans, *Pr*
Linda Evans, *Sec*
EMP: 11 EST: 1962
SQ FT: 3,200
SALES (est): 867.82K
SALES (corp-wide): 867.82K **Privately Held**
Web: www.oldinlet.com
SIC: 5941 5091 Bait and tackle; Fishing equipment and supplies

(G-12879)
OLDFATHER CAPITAL INC
330 Rehoboth Ave (19971-3108)
PHONE..................................302 296-6644
EMP: 6 EST: 2019
SALES (est): 295.2K **Privately Held**
Web: www.theoldfathergroup.com
SIC: 6799 Investors, nec

(G-12880)
OPERATION WATER INC
5 Fairway Dr (19971-9678)
PHONE..................................787 599-0555
Phillips-page Hylton, *Prin*
EMP: 5 EST: 2016
SALES (est): 147.2K **Privately Held**
Web: www.operationwater.org
SIC: 8399 Social services, nec

(G-12881)
OUTLET LIQUORS
19724 Coastal Hwy Unit 1 (19971-6198)
PHONE..................................302 227-7700
Sue Cassidy, *Mgr*
EMP: 5 EST: 2010
SALES (est): 501.35K **Privately Held**
Web: www.outletliquors.net
SIC: 5182 Liquor

(G-12882)
PACKEM ASSOCIATES PARTNERSHIP
Also Called: Brighton Suites Hotel, The
34 Wilmington Ave (19971-2217)
PHONE..................................302 227-5780
Joe Callahan, *Brnch Mgr*
EMP: 9
SALES (corp-wide): 2.25MM **Privately Held**
Web: www.brightonsuites.com
SIC: 7011 Hotels
PA: Packem Associates Ltd Partnership
     4750 Owings Mills Blvd
     Owings Mills MD 21117
     410 356-9900

(G-12883)
PAR 4 GOLF INC
38 Glade Cir E (19971-4140)
PHONE..................................302 227-5663
James Jones, *Owner*
EMP: 5 EST: 2015
SALES (est): 99.85K **Privately Held**
SIC: 3949 Sporting and athletic goods, nec

(G-12884)
PARK AVENUE DRY CLEANERS LLC
19470 Coastal Hwy Unit 3 (19971-6127)
PHONE..................................302 725-9430
Jeong Kim, *Prin*
EMP: 5 EST: 2014
SALES (est): 103.22K **Privately Held**
SIC: 7216 Drycleaning plants, except rugs

(G-12885)
PEN PAVE CONTRACTORS PAVE
20873 Old Landing Rd (19971-4654)
PHONE..................................302 226-7283
EMP: 5 EST: 2014
SALES (est): 152.97K **Privately Held**
SIC: 1799 Special trade contractors, nec

(G-12886)
PENCO CORPORATION
Rte 1 By The Canal (19971-9801)
PHONE..................................302 227-9188
Brad Jester, *Mgr*
EMP: 7
SALES (corp-wide): 24.24MM **Privately Held**
Web: www.pencocorp.com
SIC: 5074 Plumbing fittings and supplies
PA: Penco Corporation
     1503 W Stein Hwy
     Seaford DE 19973
     302 629-7911

(G-12887)
PENSKE TRUCK LEASING CORP
Also Called: Penske
19659 Blue Bird Ln (19971-8599)
PHONE..................................302 260-7039
EMP: 5
SALES (corp-wide): 5.16B **Privately Held**
Web: www.pensketruckrental.com
SIC: 7513 Truck rental and leasing, no drivers
HQ: Penske Truck Leasing Corporation
     2675 Morgantown Rd
     Reading PA 19607
     610 775-6000

(G-12888)
PEP-UP INC
Also Called: Pep-Up 11
18979 Coastal Hwy (19971)
PHONE..................................302 645-2600
Dawn Baldwin, *Mgr*
EMP: 5
SALES (corp-wide): 23.77MM **Privately Held**
Web: www.pepupinc.com
SIC: 5172 5984 Service station supplies, petroleum; Liquefied petroleum gas, delivered to customers' premises
PA: Pep-Up, Inc.
     24987 Dupont Blvd
     Georgetown DE 19947
     302 856-2555

(G-12889)
PERI SRIHARI MD
18947 John J Williams Hwy (19971-4474)
PHONE..................................302 645-3770
Srihari Peri, *Owner*
EMP: 10 EST: 2015
SALES (est): 214.92K **Privately Held**
Web: www.beebehealthcare.org
SIC: 8062 General medical and surgical hospitals

(G-12890)
PHIPPINS CABINETRY
20807 Coastal Hwy Apt 1 (19971-8013)
PHONE..................................302 212-2189
George Phippin, *Prin*
EMP: 6 EST: 2012
SALES (est): 160.52K **Privately Held**
Web: www.phippins.com
SIC: 2434 Wood kitchen cabinets

(G-12891)
PICCARD HOMES
21227 Catalina Cir (19971-4805)
PHONE..................................302 727-5145
EMP: 6 EST: 2018
SALES (est): 111.86K **Privately Held**
Web: www.piccardhomes.com
SIC: 1521 New construction, single-family houses

(G-12892)
PLUMMER CO INC
20184 Coastal Hwy (19971-8020)
PHONE..................................302 227-5000
James Plummer, *Prin*
EMP: 8 EST: 2010
SALES (est): 281.99K **Privately Held**
Web: www.cbanker.com
SIC: 1711 Plumbing contractors

(G-12893)
PMSA IT SERVICES LLC
36520 Harmon Bay Blvd (19971-1326)
PHONE..................................301 806-5163
Don Nachtwey, *CEO*
Eunice Beale, *Mgr*
EMP: 6 EST: 2012
SALES (est): 237.7K **Privately Held**
SIC: 7373 7371 Computer integrated systems design; Computer software writing services

(G-12894)
POINT COFFEE SHOP AND BAKERY
722 Rehoboth Ave (19971-1667)
PHONE..................................302 260-9734
Anne Tillig, *Prin*
EMP: 12 EST: 2010
SALES (est): 155.17K **Privately Held**
Web: www.thepointcoffee.com
SIC: 5812 5149 Coffee shop; Bakery products

(G-12895)
POLKAMOTION REHOBOTH
229 Rehoboth Ave (19971-2137)
PHONE..................................410 729-9697
EMP: 10 EST: 2017
SALES (est): 74.23K **Privately Held**
Web: www.polkamotion.com
SIC: 7011 Inns

(G-12896)
PORT DEL-MAR-VA INC
260 Port Delmarva (19971-9501)
PHONE..................................302 227-7409
A Richard Powell, *Pr*
William F Boyce Junior, *VP*
Samuel Duckworth, *Treas*
Charles Pierce, *Treas*
William A Cambell, *Sec*
EMP: 9 EST: 1967
SQ FT: 2,000
SALES (est): 115.2K **Privately Held**
Web: www.portdelmarva.com
SIC: 7033 Campgrounds

(G-12897)
POWERS APPRAISING LLC (PA)
324 Laurel St (19971-1857)
PHONE..................................410 337-8664
Patrick Powers, *Prin*
EMP: 5 EST: 2010
SALES (est): 238.3K
SALES (corp-wide): 238.3K **Privately Held**
Web: www.powersappraising.com
SIC: 6531 Appraiser, real estate

(G-12898)
PRECISION MARINE CONSTRUCTION
202 Woodbridge Hls (19971-4165)
PHONE..................................302 227-2711
EMP: 9 EST: 2020
SALES (est): 1.4MM **Privately Held**
Web: www.precisionmarine.us

GEOGRAPHIC SECTION

Rehoboth Beach - Sussex County (G-12927)

SIC: 1629 Marine construction

(G-12899)
PRECISION MARINE CONSTRUCTION
125 Blackpool Rd (19971-3516)
PHONE.................................302 227-2711
Charles Hopkins, *Prin*
EMP: 7 EST: 2009
SALES (est): 439.87K **Privately Held**
Web: www.precisionmarine.us
SIC: 1521 Single-family housing construction

(G-12900)
PRESICSON PAIN RHBLTATION SVCS
18958 Coastal Hwy (19971-6196)
PHONE.................................302 827-2321
Jeffrey Conly, *Prin*
EMP: 10 EST: 2010
SALES (est): 142.2K **Privately Held**
SIC: 8093 Rehabilitation center, outpatient treatment

(G-12901)
PSYCH TOTAL CARE LLC
18947 John J Williams Hwy (19971-4474)
PHONE.................................302 478-7981
David Kalkstein, *Prin*
EMP: 10 EST: 2012
SALES (est): 149.59K **Privately Held**
SIC: 8011 Offices and clinics of medical doctors

(G-12902)
QOMO FARMS LLC
19888 Church St (19971-3171)
PHONE.................................202 462-5349
Wayne Silby, *Prin*
EMP: 5 EST: 2017
SALES (est): 62.84K **Privately Held**
SIC: 0191 General farms, primarily crop

(G-12903)
QUILLENS RENT ALL INC
Also Called: Grand Rental Station
803 Rehoboth Ave Ste G (19971-1151)
PHONE.................................302 227-3151
Chris Quillen, *Pr*
EMP: 8 EST: 1987
SQ FT: 3,600
SALES (est): 1.01MM **Privately Held**
Web: www.truevalue.com
SIC: 7359 Equipment rental and leasing, nec

(G-12904)
RADIO REHOBOTH
37290 Rehoboth Avenue Ext (19971-3199)
PHONE.................................302 754-1444
EMP: 6 EST: 2019
SALES (est): 34.59K **Privately Held**
Web: www.radiorehoboth.com
SIC: 4832 Radio broadcasting stations

(G-12905)
RATTAN COMPANY INC
38131 Terrace Rd (19971-2074)
PHONE.................................302 226-2404
EMP: 3 EST: 2020
SALES (est): 46.28K **Privately Held**
SIC: 2519 Household furniture, nec

(G-12906)
RBAH INC
20259 Coastal Hwy (19971-8028)
PHONE.................................302 227-2009
Timothy Dabkowski, *Prin*
EMP: 6 EST: 2010
SALES (est): 489.05K **Privately Held**
Web: rehobothbeachvet.com
SIC: 0742 Animal hospital services, pets and other animal specialties

(G-12907)
RCK SOLIATIRE LLC
19266 Cstl Hwy Unit 4108 (19971)
PHONE.................................551 358-8400
EMP: 10 EST: 2017
SALES (est): 272.62K **Privately Held**
SIC: 3911 Jewelry, precious metal

(G-12908)
RE/MAX REALTY GROUP-RENTALS
323 Rehoboth Ave Ste A (19971-2178)
PHONE.................................302 227-4800
Tyler Fleck, *Dir*
EMP: 10 EST: 2017
SALES (est): 250.29K **Privately Held**
Web: www.remax.com
SIC: 6531 Real estate agent, residential

(G-12909)
READY SET TEXTILES INC
19266 Coastal Hwy (19971-6117)
PHONE.................................302 518-6583
Iain Scorgie, *Pr*
▲ EMP: 6 EST: 2017
SQ FT: 500
SALES (est): 1.13MM **Privately Held**
Web: www.readysettextiles.com
SIC: 5023 Sheets, textile

(G-12910)
REAL HVAC SERVICES
18389 Olde Coach Dr (19971-6191)
PHONE.................................302 727-0272
EMP: 7 EST: 2018
SALES (est): 113.9K **Privately Held**
Web: www.realhvacservices.com
SIC: 1711 Warm air heating and air conditioning contractor

(G-12911)
REGIONAL ENTERPRISES LLC
307 S Boardwalk (19971-2942)
PHONE.................................302 227-0202
Robert Wright, *Ofcr*
EMP: 5 EST: 2015
SALES (est): 78.54K **Privately Held**
SIC: 8621 Professional organizations

(G-12912)
REGIS CORPORATION
Also Called: Holiday Hair 141
19330 Coastal Hwy Unit 6 (19971-6119)
PHONE.................................302 227-9730
Mary Ann Gardheir, *Mgr*
EMP: 7
SALES (corp-wide): 233.33MM **Publicly Held**
Web: www.signaturestyle.com
SIC: 7231 Unisex hair salons
PA: Regis Corporation
     3701 Wayzata Blvd Ste 500
     Minneapolis MN 55416
     952 947-7777

(G-12913)
REHOBOTH ANIMAL HOSPITAL
20259 Coastal Hwy (19971-8028)
PHONE.................................302 227-2009
John W Boros, *Owner*
John W Boros D.v.m., *Owner*
EMP: 9 EST: 1970
SQ FT: 1,500
SALES (est): 480K **Privately Held**
Web: www.rehobothbeachvet.com
SIC: 0742 Animal hospital services, pets and other animal specialties

(G-12914)
REHOBOTH BAY SAILING ASSN
Highway One (19971)
P.O. Box 483 (19971-0483)
PHONE.................................302 227-9008
EMP: 5 EST: 2010
SALES (est): 291.66K **Privately Held**
Web: www.rbsa.org
SIC: 7997 Membership sports and recreation clubs

(G-12915)
REHOBOTH BCH DWEY BCH CHMBER C
501 Rehoboth Ave (19971-3126)
PHONE.................................302 227-2233
Carol Everhart, *Ex Dir*
EMP: 10 EST: 1984
SALES (est): 1.14MM **Privately Held**
Web: www.beach-fun.com
SIC: 8611 Chamber of Commerce

(G-12916)
REHOBOTH BCH SISTER CITES ASSN
41 Sussex St (19971-2113)
PHONE.................................302 249-7878
Pat Coluzzi, *Pr*
Mary Jane Deets, *Sec*
Francis G Markert, *Treas*
Mary Teresa Morrison, *Bd of Dir*
Karen Zakarian, *Bd of Dir*
EMP: 7 EST: 2012
SALES (est): 104.33K **Privately Held**
Web: www.rehobothsistercities.org
SIC: 8641 7389 Civic and social associations ; Business services, nec

(G-12917)
REHOBOTH BEACH
105 2nd St (19971-2283)
PHONE.................................302 245-0304
Orin Burdette, *Prin*
EMP: 7 EST: 1994
SALES (est): 215.49K **Privately Held**
Web: www.rehoboth.com
SIC: 4813 Internet connectivity services

(G-12918)
REHOBOTH BEACH COUNTRY CLUB
221 W Side Dr (19971-1308)
P.O. Box 291 (19971-0291)
PHONE.................................302 227-3811
Michael Stattler, *Pr*
EMP: 60 EST: 1925
SQ FT: 43,000
SALES (est): 6.49MM **Privately Held**
Web: www.rehobothbeachcc.com
SIC: 7997 Country club, membership

(G-12919)
REHOBOTH BEACH DANCE & COMPANY
19287 Miller Rd (19971-6124)
PHONE.................................302 245-8132
Christa Pardocchi, *Prin*
EMP: 8 EST: 2017
SALES (est): 43.8K **Privately Held**
Web: www.camprehoboth.com
SIC: 7911 Dance studio and school

(G-12920)
REHOBOTH BEACH DENT
19643 Blue Bird Ln (19971-6129)
PHONE.................................302 226-7960
Curtis Leciejewski, *Owner*
Michael Keller, *Prin*
EMP: 8 EST: 2013
SALES (est): 364.35K **Privately Held**
Web: www.rehobothbeachdental.com
SIC: 8021 Dentists' office

(G-12921)
REHOBOTH BEACH HISTORICAL SOC (PA)
Also Called: Rehoboth Beach Museum
17 Christian St (19971-3001)
PHONE.................................302 227-7310
Bill Bahan, *Pr*
Nancy Alexander, *Dir*
EMP: 14 EST: 2005
SALES (est): 339.33K
SALES (corp-wide): 339.33K **Privately Held**
Web: www.rehobothbeachmuseum.org
SIC: 8412 Museum

(G-12922)
REHOBOTH BEACH YOGA CENTR
Yoga Center (19971)
P.O. Box 5 (19971-0005)
PHONE.................................302 226-7646
Terry Gardner, *Prin*
EMP: 5 EST: 2002
SALES (est): 64.3K **Privately Held**
Web: www.rehobothbeachyoga.com
SIC: 7999 Yoga instruction

(G-12923)
REHOBOTH CAR WASH INC
37053 Rehoboth Avenue Ext (19971-7141)
PHONE.................................302 227-6177
Christopher Dispoto, *Owner*
EMP: 6 EST: 2002
SALES (est): 102.35K **Privately Held**
Web: www.mrwash.com
SIC: 7542 Washing and polishing, automotive

(G-12924)
REHOBOTH CAR WASH INC
19898 Hebron Rd (19971-1241)
PHONE.................................302 245-6839
EMP: 5 EST: 2020
SALES (est): 171.26K **Privately Held**
Web: www.rehobothcarwash.com
SIC: 7542 Washing and polishing, automotive

(G-12925)
REHOBOTH FITNESS LLC ✪
Also Called: Rise Fitness and Adventure
35770 Airport Rd (19971-4663)
PHONE.................................410 742-7990
Nicholas Taghipour, *Managing Member*
EMP: 29 EST: 2022
SALES (est): 283.27K **Privately Held**
SIC: 7991 Physical fitness clubs with training equipment

(G-12926)
REHOBOTH GOLF PARK
12 Chatham Rd (19971-3500)
PHONE.................................302 542-1295
EMP: 5 EST: 2018
SALES (est): 20.78K **Privately Held**
Web: www.rehobothgolfpark.com
SIC: 7999 Golf services and professionals

(G-12927)
REHOBOTH HOME SALES INC
19 Fairway Dr (19971-9678)
PHONE.................................609 924-7701
Christopher Chianese, *Prin*
EMP: 5 EST: 2018
SALES (est): 206.34K **Privately Held**
Web: www.rehoboth.com
SIC: 6531 Real estate brokers and agents

Rehoboth Beach - Sussex County (G-12928)

(G-12928)
REHOBOTH HOUSE OF JERKY
149 Rehoboth Ave Unit 8b (19971-2148)
PHONE..........................215 272-4217
EMP: 4 EST: 2019
SALES (est): 93.92K **Privately Held**
SIC: 2013 Snack sticks, including jerky; from purchased meat

(G-12929)
REHOBOTH INN LLC
20494 Coastal Hwy (19971-8030)
P.O. Box 737 (19971-0737)
PHONE..........................302 226-2410
EMP: 6 EST: 1997
SALES (est): 297.25K **Privately Held**
Web: www.rehobothinn.com
SIC: 7011 Motels

(G-12930)
REHOBOTH NAILS & SPA
18701 Coastal Hwy (19971-6190)
PHONE..........................302 703-6481
EMP: 6 EST: 2019
SALES (est): 20.99K **Privately Held**
Web: www.rbnailsandspa.com
SIC: 7231 Hairdressers

(G-12931)
REHOBOTH PROFESSIONAL CTR LLC
18977 Munchy Branch Rd Ste 2 (19971-8763)
PHONE..........................302 226-8334
EMP: 6 EST: 2009
SALES (est): 103.15K **Privately Held**
Web: www.rehoboth.com
SIC: 6515 Mobile home site operators

(G-12932)
REHOBOTH REAL ESTATE
246 Rehoboth Ave (19971-2134)
PHONE..........................302 226-6417
EMP: 6 EST: 2017
SALES (est): 485.78K **Privately Held**
Web: www.rehobothrealestate.com
SIC: 6531 Real estate agent, residential

(G-12933)
REHOBOTH REALTY INC
Also Called: Coldwell Banker Resort Realty
20184 Coastal Hwy (19971-8020)
PHONE..........................302 227-5000
Kathy Newcom, *Pr*
Bruce Plummer, *CEO*
Maryellen Kiernan, *Owner*
Amy Kiernan, *Owner*
Jennifer Bastian, *Owner*
EMP: 24 EST: 1978
SALES (est): 800K **Privately Held**
Web: www.cbanker.com
SIC: 6531 Real estate agent, residential

(G-12934)
RESORT HOTEL LLC
Also Called: Comfort Inn
19210 Coastal Hwy (19971-6116)
PHONE..........................302 226-1515
EMP: 20 EST: 1994
SALES (est): 815.85K **Privately Held**
Web: www.choicehotels.com
SIC: 7011 Hotels and motels

(G-12935)
RICHARD W KRICK JR
8 Fox Creek Dr (19971-8611)
PHONE..........................302 227-6974
EMP: 5 EST: 2010
SALES (est): 68.57K **Privately Held**
SIC: 1522 Residential construction, nec

(G-12936)
RIVERBEND INV MGT LLC IS A RGS
179 Rehoboth Ave Unit 165 (19971-7907)
PHONE..........................302 219-3080
John Rothe, *Pr*
EMP: 5 EST: 2006
SALES (est): 261.96K **Privately Held**
SIC: 6799 7389 Investors, nec; Business Activities at Non-Commercial Site

(G-12937)
RODEWAY INN
19604 Blue Bird Ln (19971-8597)
PHONE..........................302 227-0401
EMP: 30 EST: 1998
SALES (est): 58.73K **Privately Held**
Web: www.choicehotels.com
SIC: 7011 Hotels and motels

(G-12938)
RONALD L BARROWS
Also Called: Rehoboth Country Club
184 E Side Dr (19971-1300)
PHONE..........................302 227-3616
Ronald L Barrows, *Owner*
EMP: 9 EST: 1966
SALES (est): 146.13K **Privately Held**
SIC: 7997 Country club, membership

(G-12939)
ROOFING SPECIALIST
224 Salt Forest Ln (19971-9539)
PHONE..........................302 344-2507
EMP: 5 EST: 2011
SALES (est): 120.9K **Privately Held**
SIC: 1761 Roofing contractor

(G-12940)
ROYAL DELTA SPECIALTIES LLC
19266 Cstl Hwy Unit 4 85r (19971)
P.O. Box 2241 (76099-2241)
PHONE..........................908 410-7478
EMP: 8 EST: 2019
SALES (est): 340K **Privately Held**
SIC: 2899 Chemical preparations, nec

(G-12941)
RUTH VAN PELT BEEBE MEM SCH TR
132 E Side Dr (19971-1300)
PHONE..........................302 226-9498
EMP: 5 EST: 2010
SALES (est): 41.02K **Privately Held**
SIC: 8699 Charitable organization

(G-12942)
RYANS MINI GOLF
1 Delaware Ave (19971-2903)
PHONE..........................302 227-2667
Joseph Ryan, *Prin*
EMP: 6 EST: 2016
SALES (est): 30.43K **Privately Held**
Web: www.ryansbeachshop.com
SIC: 7999 Golf cart, power, rental

(G-12943)
SALT MARSH FOODS INC
314 Swedes St (19971-3317)
PHONE..........................302 260-9556
Melissa Ryan, *Prin*
EMP: 5 EST: 2009
SALES (est): 93.98K **Privately Held**
SIC: 1541 Food products manufacturing or packing plant construction

(G-12944)
SALTY PAWS RB LLC
Also Called: Salty Paws
43 Rehoboth Ave (19971-2119)
PHONE..........................484 667-7122
EMP: 10 EST: 2018
SALES (est): 444.27K **Privately Held**
Web: www.saltypawsicecream.com
SIC: 0752 Animal specialty services

(G-12945)
SALVATORE SEELEY
37 Baltimore Ave (19971-2131)
PHONE..........................302 270-5503
Salvatore Seeley, *Prin*
EMP: 7 EST: 2016
SALES (est): 81.05K **Privately Held**
Web: www.camprehoboth.com
SIC: 8699 Charitable organization

(G-12946)
SAMPSON INTERIORS
1 Ocean Breeze Dr (19971-9585)
PHONE..........................865 438-5097
Palmer Sampson, *Prin*
EMP: 5 EST: 2017
SALES (est): 182.41K **Privately Held**
SIC: 1522 Residential construction, nec

(G-12947)
SANDS INC
Also Called: Atlantic Sands Hotel
101 N Boardwalk (19971-2160)
PHONE..........................302 227-2511
Ronald E Lankford, *Pr*
Herbert Flickinger, *
Rick Perez, *
EMP: 65 EST: 1959
SQ FT: 80,000
SALES (est): 4.64MM **Privately Held**
Web: www.atlanticsandshotel.com
SIC: 7011 Motels

(G-12948)
SCHELL BROTHERS LLC (PA)
20184 Phillips St (19971-8049)
PHONE..........................302 226-1994
EMP: 25 EST: 2003
SALES (est): 95.97MM
SALES (corp-wide): 95.97MM **Privately Held**
Web: www.schellbrothers.com
SIC: 1521 New construction, single-family houses

(G-12949)
SEA ESTA 4
20902 Coastal Hwy (19971-8019)
P.O. Box 394 (19971-0394)
PHONE..........................302 354-1245
EMP: 8 EST: 2019
SALES (est): 116.06K **Privately Held**
Web: www.seaestamotels.com
SIC: 7011 Motels

(G-12950)
SEA SHELL SHOP INC (PA)
4405 Coastal Hwy Rte 1 (19971-9801)
PHONE..........................302 227-4323
EMP: 15 EST: 1950
SALES (est): 2.33MM
SALES (corp-wide): 2.33MM **Privately Held**
Web: www.seashellshop.com
SIC: 5947 7999 Gift shop; Miniature golf course operation

(G-12951)
SEACHANGE VACATION RENTALS
20 Baltimore Ave Ste 1 (19971-2104)
PHONE..........................302 727-5566
EMP: 6 EST: 2018
SALES (est): 196.55K **Privately Held**
Web: www.vacasa.com
SIC: 7359 Equipment rental and leasing, nec

(G-12952)
SEAGREEN BICYCLE LLP
54 Baltimore Ave (19971-2130)
PHONE..........................302 226-2323
Eric Lowe, *Pt*
EMP: 5 EST: 2014
SALES (est): 273.02K **Privately Held**
Web: www.seagreenbicycle.com
SIC: 5091 6531 7699 Bicycles; Real estate leasing and rentals; Bicycle repair shop

(G-12953)
SEASIDE AMUSEMENTS INC
Also Called: Funland
6 Delaware Ave (19971-2904)
PHONE..........................302 227-1921
Allen R Fasnacht, *Brnch Mgr*
EMP: 7
SALES (corp-wide): 957.43K **Privately Held**
Web: www.funlandrehoboth.com
SIC: 7993 Coin-operated amusement devices
PA: Seaside Amusements, Inc.
359 E Granada Ave
Hershey PA 17033
717 227-2785

(G-12954)
SEASIDE POINTE
36101 Seaside Blvd (19971-6165)
PHONE..........................302 226-8750
EMP: 10 EST: 2014
SALES (est): 236.07K **Privately Held**
Web: www.brandycare.com
SIC: 8051 Skilled nursing care facilities

(G-12955)
SHARON FARM INSURANCE
6 Sandalwood Dr (19971-9668)
PHONE..........................215 333-5544
Sharon Owens, *Owner*
EMP: 6 EST: 2001
SALES (est): 500.24K **Privately Held**
Web: www.owensagency.com
SIC: 6411 Insurance agents and brokers

(G-12956)
SHELL WE BOUNCE
20699 Coastal Hwy (19971-8064)
PHONE..........................302 727-5411
Julie Derick, *Owner*
EMP: 6 EST: 2014
SALES (est): 427.68K **Privately Held**
Web: www.shellwebounce.com
SIC: 7359 Equipment rental and leasing, nec

(G-12957)
SHORE COMMUNITY MEDICAL
18947 John J Williams Hwy Unit 215 (19971-4476)
P.O. Box 1598 (19971-5598)
PHONE..........................302 827-4365
Thomas Kelly, *Prin*
Thomas Kelly Ph.d., *Prin*
EMP: 5 EST: 2011
SALES (est): 455.58K **Privately Held**
Web: www.shorecommunitymedical.com
SIC: 8011 General and family practice, physician/surgeon

(G-12958)
SHORE TAX SERVICE INC
19725 Old Landing Rd (19971-4611)

PHONE..............................302 226-9792
Robert A Waegele, Asst Sec
EMP: 5 EST: 2012
SALES (est): 63.18K Privately Held
SIC: 7291 Tax return preparation services

(G-12959)
SILVER ELECTRIC LLC
14 Sconset Ct (19971-7701)
P.O. Box 1026 (19971-5026)
PHONE..............................302 227-1107
EMP: 5 EST: 2015
SALES (est): 143.35K Privately Held
Web: www.silverelectricllc.com
SIC: 1731 General electrical contractor

(G-12960)
SIMPLER AND SONS LLC
37139 Rehoboth Avenue Ext (19971-3194)
PHONE..............................302 296-4400
Alex Moore, CEO
Patrick Staib, COO
EMP: 16 EST: 2013
SALES (est): 242.19K Privately Held
SIC: 7011 Resort hotel

(G-12961)
SKIM USA
1904 Highway One (19971)
PHONE..............................302 227-4011
EMP: 6 EST: 2011
SALES (est): 23.57K Privately Held
Web: www.skim-usa.com
SIC: 8699 7997 Amateur sports promotion; Membership sports and recreation clubs

(G-12962)
SKINIFY LLC
Also Called: Decalgirl.com
19621 Blue Bird Ln Unit 4 (19971-8796)
PHONE..............................302 212-5689
Ryan Peters, Managing Member
EMP: 24 EST: 1997
SALES (est): 2.3MM Privately Held
Web: www.decalgirl.com
SIC: 2752 Decals, lithographed

(G-12963)
SLEEP EMPORIUM LLC
18675 Coastal Hwy Unit 2a (19971)
PHONE..............................302 313-5061
Lyron Deputy, Owner
EMP: 8 EST: 2010
SALES (est): 190.71K Privately Held
Web: www.thesleepemporium.com
SIC: 8011 Specialized medical practitioners, except internal

(G-12964)
SOCIAL SELLING LLC
18670 Coastal Hwy (19971-6148)
PHONE..............................888 384-3710
EMP: 5 EST: 2021
SALES (est): 104.37K Privately Held
SIC: 7379 Online services technology consultants

(G-12965)
SODEL CONCEPTS II LLC
220 Rehoboth Ave Unit A (19971-2134)
P.O. Box 49 (19971-0049)
PHONE..............................302 228-3786
EMP: 113 EST: 2015
SALES (est): 4.87MM Privately Held
Web: www.sodelconcepts.com
SIC: 8741 Restaurant management

(G-12966)
SOFLETE LLC
19621 Blue Bird Ln (19971-8796)

PHONE..............................773 983-4692
Aron J Woolman, COO
EMP: 6 EST: 2015
SALES (est): 230.93K Privately Held
Web: www.soflete.com
SIC: 7999 Physical fitness instruction

(G-12967)
SOLE CONTRACTING INC
4 Back Bay (19971-1948)
PHONE..............................302 420-4429
Mark Willhoite, Pr
Jason Popercer, VP
EMP: 37 EST: 2017
SALES (est): 2.38MM Privately Held
SIC: 1711 Solar energy contractor

(G-12968)
SOLUTIONS PROPERTY MANAGEMENT
38 Hannah Loop (19971-3149)
P.O. Box 594 (19930-0594)
PHONE..............................302 581-9060
Cathy Mccallister, Prin
EMP: 6 EST: 2012
SALES (est): 145.9K Privately Held
Web: www.solutionspropertymgt.org
SIC: 8641 Condominium association

(G-12969)
SOUTHERN DELAWARE SURGERY CTR
18941 John J Williams Hwy (19971-4404)
PHONE..............................302 644-6992
Susan Fausett, Managing Member
Eric Cancoski, Dir
EMP: 59 EST: 1999
SQ FT: 13,137
SALES (est): 7.37MM Privately Held
Web: www.beebehealthcare.org
SIC: 8062 General medical and surgical hospitals

(G-12970)
SPORT CLIPS HRCUTS RHBOTH BCH
18756 Coastal Hwy (19971-6155)
PHONE..............................302 291-2391
EMP: 10 EST: 2018
SALES (est): 106.48K Privately Held
Web: www.haircutmenharborsquarerehobothbeachde.com
SIC: 7231 Beauty shops

(G-12971)
SPORTSMANS HALL LLC
Also Called: Sportsmans Hall Rller Skting R
38097 West Dr Unit 738 (19971-1770)
PHONE..............................410 429-6030
Eric T Kaylor, Managing Member
EMP: 6 EST: 2002
SALES (est): 248.53K Privately Held
SIC: 1771 7999 Concrete work; Skating rink operation services

(G-12972)
STAR OF THE SEA ASSOC OF OWNRS
Also Called: Star of Sea Condominium
307 S Boardwalk Ste L2 (19971-2273)
PHONE..............................302 227-6006
Roger Applegate, Pr
Donald Alexander, Treas
EMP: 7 EST: 1985
SALES (est): 479K Privately Held
Web: www.staroftheseade.com
SIC: 8641 Condominium association

(G-12973)
STATERA HOMES
75 Lake Ave (19971-2107)
P.O. Box 605 (19958-0605)
PHONE..............................302 313-9949
EMP: 5 EST: 2016
SALES (est): 473.51K Privately Held
Web: www.staterahomes.com
SIC: 6531 Real estate agents and managers

(G-12974)
STAUFFER FAMILY LLC
Also Called: Rodney's Animal Crackers
36 Glade Cir E (19971-4140)
P.O. Box 1393 (19971-5393)
PHONE..............................302 227-5820
Rodney Stauffer, Pr
Scott Stauffer, CFO
EMP: 2 EST: 2010
SALES (est): 149.35K Privately Held
Web: www.rodneysanimalcrackers.com
SIC: 2052 7389 Cookies; Business Activities at Non-Commercial Site

(G-12975)
STITCH-STASH LLC
102 N 1st St (19971-2147)
PHONE..............................302 227-1943
EMP: 4 EST: 2018
SALES (est): 171.11K Privately Held
Web: www.stitch-stash.com
SIC: 2395 Embroidery and art needlework

(G-12976)
STONE HARBOR SQUARE LLC
42 Rehoboth Ave Ste 23 (19971-2122)
PHONE..............................302 227-5227
Clinton Bunting, Prin
EMP: 13 EST: 2015
SALES (est): 736.85K Privately Held
SIC: 8011 Offices and clinics of medical doctors

(G-12977)
STRATGIC SLAR SLTONS LTD LBLTY
2 Glade Cir E (19971-4138)
PHONE..............................703 307-6761
EMP: 8 EST: 2020
SALES (est): 265.25K Privately Held
Web: www.strategicsolarsolutions.com
SIC: 1711 Solar energy contractor

(G-12978)
STUART KINGSTON INC (PA)
19470 Coastal Hwy Unit 1 (19971-6127)
PHONE..............................302 227-2524
Joseph Stein, Pr
Diane Stein, Sec
▲ EMP: 8 EST: 1930
SALES (est): 1.56MM
SALES (corp-wide): 1.56MM Privately Held
Web: www.stuartkingston.com
SIC: 5331 5713 5999 5094 Variety stores; Carpets; Art dealers; Precious stones (gems), nec

(G-12979)
SUBURBAN FLOOR COVERINGS
35514 Copper Dr S (19971-4674)
PHONE..............................302 430-8494
EMP: 5 EST: 2018
SALES (est): 43.69K Privately Held
SIC: 5023 Floor coverings

(G-12980)
SUNNY HOSPITALITY LLC
Also Called: AmericInn
36012 Airport Rd (19971-4645)
PHONE..............................302 226-0700

EMP: 38 EST: 1995
SALES (est): 452.55K Privately Held
Web: www.americaninnde.com
SIC: 7011 Hotels and motels

(G-12981)
SUNNYWORLD LLC
19513 Manchester Dr (19971-4022)
PHONE..............................240 506-8870
EMP: 5 EST: 2017
SALES (est): 168.96K Privately Held
SIC: 1522 Residential construction, nec

(G-12982)
SUNRISE REAL ESTATE
75 Lake Ave (19971-2107)
P.O. Box 605 (19958-0605)
PHONE..............................302 313-9949
EMP: 5 EST: 2017
SALES (est): 233.98K Privately Held
Web: www.sunrisesells.com
SIC: 6531 Real estate brokers and agents

(G-12983)
SUPERCUTS
Also Called: Supercuts
18701 Coastal Hwy Unit 7 (19971-6190)
PHONE..............................302 644-4288
EMP: 5 EST: 2014
SALES (est): 53.26K Privately Held
Web: www.supercuts.com
SIC: 7231 Unisex hair salons

(G-12984)
SUSSEX FINANCIAL SERVICES INC
804 King Charles Ave (19971-2236)
P.O. Box 134 (19971-0134)
PHONE..............................302 227-7814
William V Ehrlich, Prin
EMP: 5 EST: 2009
SALES (est): 133.29K Privately Held
SIC: 7389 Financial services

(G-12985)
SUSSEX PLMNARY ENDOCRINE CNSLT
23 Patriots Way (19971-1056)
PHONE..............................302 249-9970
Vikas Barta Md, Prin
EMP: 5 EST: 2008
SALES (est): 203.03K Privately Held
SIC: 8748 Business consulting, nec

(G-12986)
SWORD PARTS LLC
19266 Coastal Hwy Unit 4-37 (19971-6117)
PHONE..............................302 246-1346
EMP: 2 EST: 2014
SALES (est): 80.75K Privately Held
SIC: 3714 Transmissions, motor vehicle

(G-12987)
T R ROOFING
2 Sea Chase Dr (19971-9558)
P.O. Box 437 (19958-0437)
PHONE..............................302 226-4510
Tom Ream, Pr
EMP: 10 EST: 1984
SALES (est): 253.06K Privately Held
Web: www.platinumroofs.com
SIC: 1761 Roofing contractor

(G-12988)
TANGER OUTLET CTR MIDWAY
35016 Ctr Outlet Dr Ste 303 (19971)
PHONE..............................302 645-2525
Lorie Web, Mgr
EMP: 8 EST: 1995
SALES (est): 879.59K Privately Held
Web: www.tanger.com

Rehoboth Beach - Sussex County (G-12989)   GEOGRAPHIC SECTION

SIC: 6512 Shopping center, property operation only

(G-12989)
TAPP NETWORKS LLC
20421 Jeb Dr Unit 44 (19971-1564)
PHONE..................................302 222-3384
EMP: 6 **EST:** 2012
SALES (est): 869.96K **Privately Held**
Web: www.tappnetwork.com
SIC: 7379 8742 7311 Online services technology consultants; Marketing consulting services; Advertising agencies

(G-12990)
TATTOO GALAXY REHOBETH BEACH
19470 Coastal Hwy (19971-6127)
PHONE..................................302 226-8118
EMP: 5 **EST:** 2017
SALES (est): 68.75K **Privately Held**
Web: www.tattoogalaxy.net
SIC: 7299 Tattoo parlor

(G-12991)
TD BANK NA
Also Called: Rehoboth Beach, De Branch
34980 Midway Outlet Dr (19971-8585)
PHONE..................................302 644-0952
EMP: 9
SALES (corp-wide): 37.35B **Privately Held**
Web: www.td.com
SIC: 6029 6021 Commercial banks, nec; National commercial banks
HQ: Td Bank, National Association
   1701 Route 70 E Ste 102
   Cherry Hill NJ 08003
   856 751-2739

(G-12992)
TEKMEN GROUP
20891 Coastal Hwy (19971-8007)
PHONE..................................302 381-0161
Rivera Tekman, *Prin*
EMP: 5 **EST:** 2009
SALES (est): 115.19K **Privately Held**
SIC: 8748 Business consulting, nec

(G-12993)
THETA VEST INC
Also Called: Rehoboth Bay Mobile Home Cmnty
21707 B St (19971-8410)
PHONE..................................302 227-3745
Craig Hudson, *Pr*
Joseph R Hudson Senior, *VP*
Caron Thompson, *Dir*
EMP: 7 **EST:** 1976
SQ FT: 3,000
SALES (est): 377.88K **Privately Held**
Web: www.thetavest.com
SIC: 6515 5271 Mobile home site operators; Mobile home dealers

(G-12994)
THREE BS PAINTING CONTRACTORS
37021 Rehoboth Avenue Ext D (19971-6159)
PHONE..................................302 227-1497
Raymond G Harp, *Pr*
William D Emmert, *Pr*
Raymond Harp, *Sec*
EMP: 5 **EST:** 1983
SQ FT: 2,000
SALES (est): 260.4K **Privately Held**
SIC: 1721 1742 Painting and paper hanging; Drywall

(G-12995)
TIFFANY PINES CONDO ASSN INC
20037 Old Landing Rd (19971-4612)
PHONE..................................302 227-0913
Christopher Quillen, *Prin*
EMP: 5 **EST:** 2009
SALES (est): 99.39K **Privately Held**
SIC: 8641 Condominium association

(G-12996)
TSE SPORTS
8 Good Hope Ct (19971-1063)
P.O. Box 1354 (19971-5354)
PHONE..................................856 889-4913
EMP: 5 **EST:** 2018
SALES (est): 72.31K **Privately Held**
Web: www.tsebaseball.net
SIC: 7997 Membership sports and recreation clubs

(G-12997)
TUNNELL CANCER CTR
18947 John J Williams Hwy (19971-4474)
PHONE..................................302 645-3770
EMP: 9 **EST:** 2020
SALES (est): 201.39K **Privately Held**
Web: www.beebehealthcare.org
SIC: 8062 General medical and surgical hospitals

(G-12998)
TURNSTONE BUILDERS LLC
37395 Oyster House Rd (19971-8058)
PHONE..................................302 227-8876
EMP: 13 **EST:** 2004
SALES (est): 2.2MM **Privately Held**
Web: www.tchde.com
SIC: 1521 New construction, single-family houses

(G-12999)
TURNSTONE HOLDINGS LLC
Also Called: Turnstone Custom Homes
37395 Oyster House Rd (19971-8058)
PHONE..................................302 227-8876
Harvey V Ryan, *CEO*
David Eppes, *Pr*
Grantland Saulsbury, *CFO*
Erin Bagnatori, *COO*
EMP: 17 **EST:** 2008
SALES (est): 1.16MM **Privately Held**
Web: www.tchde.com
SIC: 1521 New construction, single-family houses

(G-13000)
U TRANSIT INC
Also Called: Jolly Trolley
12 Hazlett St (19971-2507)
P.O. Box 311 (19971-0311)
PHONE..................................302 227-1197
EMP: 8 **EST:** 1991
SALES (est): 893.75K **Privately Held**
Web: www.jollytrolley.com
SIC: 2721 7319 4725 4111 Magazines: publishing only, not printed on site; Display advertising service; Sightseeing tour companies; Trolley operation

(G-13001)
UPPER DARBY COMMUNITY OUT
123 Landing Dr (19971-9766)
PHONE..................................610 352-7008
EMP: 10 **EST:** 2018
SALES (est): 48.04K **Privately Held**
SIC: 8322 Community center

(G-13002)
UPS STORE
18766 John J Williams Hwy Unit 4 (19971)
PHONE..................................302 360-0264
EMP: 5 **EST:** 2018
SALES (est): 190.87K **Privately Held**
Web: www.theupsstore.com
SIC: 7389 Mailbox rental and related service

(G-13003)
VICTORIAS SECRET STORES LLC
Also Called: Victoria's Secret
35000 Midway Outlet Dr (19971-8515)
PHONE..................................302 644-1035
EMP: 9
SALES (corp-wide): 6.34B **Publicly Held**
Web: www.victoriassecret.com
SIC: 5632 2341 Lingerie (outerwear); Women's and children's underwear
HQ: Victoria's Secret Stores, Llc
   4 Limited Pkwy E
   Reynoldsburg OH 43068
   800 411-5116

(G-13004)
WAGAMONS SCHELL BROTHERS
20184 Phillips St (19971-8049)
PHONE..................................302 664-1680
EMP: 7 **EST:** 2013
SALES (est): 80.21K **Privately Held**
Web: www.schellbrothers.com
SIC: 6531 Real estate brokers and agents

(G-13005)
WALTER STARK DR
4 Rolling Rd (19971-1616)
PHONE..................................302 227-4990
Walter Stark, *Prin*
EMP: 8 **EST:** 2004
SALES (est): 69.38K **Privately Held**
SIC: 8011 Internal medicine, physician/surgeon

(G-13006)
WARACHAI THAI BOXING ASSN
19818 Hebron Rd (19971-1238)
PHONE..................................302 257-9794
Rain Burgess, *Mgr*
EMP: 6 **EST:** 2014
SALES (est): 59.53K **Privately Held**
Web: www.warachaithaiboxing.com
SIC: 8699 Membership organizations, nec

(G-13007)
WARD & TAYLOR LLC
37212 Rehoboth Avenue Ext (19971-3198)
PHONE..................................302 227-1403
Ingrid Wilcox, *Brnch Mgr*
EMP: 6
Web: www.wardtaylor.com
SIC: 8111 Real estate law
PA: Ward & Taylor, Llc
   2710 Centerville Rd # 210
   Wilmington DE 19808

(G-13008)
WATERSTONE MORTGAGE CORP
330 Rehoboth Ave Ste B (19971-3108)
PHONE..................................302 227-8252
EMP: 6 **EST:** 2017
SALES (est): 89.59K **Privately Held**
Web: www.waterstonemortgage.com
SIC: 6162 Mortgage bankers and loan correspondents

(G-13009)
WATKINS CONSULTING INC (PA)
73 Blackpool Rd (19971-3515)
PHONE..................................240 479-7273
Bernard Genevish, *Pr*
EMP: 8 **EST:** 1990
SALES (est): 1.93MM **Privately Held**
Web: www.watkinsconsulting.com

SIC: 7389 Financial services

(G-13010)
WATKINS CONSULTING GROUP JV
73 Blackpool Rd (19971-3515)
PHONE..................................202 861-0200
Bernard Genevish, *Pt*
EMP: 6 **EST:** 2008
SALES (est): 471.73K **Privately Held**
SIC: 8742 Financial consultant

(G-13011)
WATKINS-DAVIS KINARD JV
73 Blackpool Rd (19971-3515)
PHONE..................................240 479-7273
Michael Block, *Pt*
EMP: 5 **EST:** 2015
SQ FT: 1,200
SALES (est): 80.88K **Privately Held**
SIC: 7291 Tax return preparation services

(G-13012)
WELLS FARGO BANK NATIONAL ASSN
4600 Hwy 1 (19971)
PHONE..................................302 644-6351
Michelle Gallagher, *Mgr*
EMP: 10
SALES (corp-wide): 82.86B **Publicly Held**
Web: www.wellsfargo.com
SIC: 6021 National commercial banks
HQ: Wells Fargo Bank, National Association
   420 Montgomery St San
   San Francisco CA 94104
   605 575-6900

(G-13013)
WELLS FARGO HOME MORTGAGE INC
Also Called: Wells Fargo
18977 Munchy Branch Rd Ste 6 (19971-8763)
PHONE..................................302 227-5700
Ed Swiatek, *Mgr*
EMP: 8
SALES (corp-wide): 82.86B **Publicly Held**
Web: www.wellsfargo.com
SIC: 6021 National commercial banks
HQ: Wells Fargo Home Mortgage Inc
   1 Home Campus
   Des Moines IA 50328
   515 324-3707

(G-13014)
WERTZ & CO
20845 Coastal Hwy (19971-8006)
PHONE..................................302 727-5643
EMP: 8 **EST:** 2019
SALES (est): 140.68K **Privately Held**
Web: www.wertzandco.com
SIC: 6512 Commercial and industrial building operation

(G-13015)
WHARTONS LANDSCAPING LLC
Also Called: Whartons Landscaping Grdn Ctr
19385 Old Landing Rd (19971-4686)
PHONE..................................302 426-4854
EMP: 18 **EST:** 2017
SALES (est): 236.87K **Privately Held**
Web: www.whartonsde.com
SIC: 0781 Landscape services

(G-13016)
WIEDMAN ENTERPRISES INC
Also Called: Matt's Auto Care
38335 Martins Ln (19971-2078)
PHONE..................................302 226-2407
Matthew Wiedman, *Pr*
EMP: 5 **EST:** 1992

GEOGRAPHIC SECTION   Seaford - Sussex County (G-13042)

SALES (est): 372.6K **Privately Held**
SIC: 7538 General automotive repair shops

(G-13017)
WILLIAM D EMMERT
317 Rehoboth Ave (19971-3127)
P.O. Box 650 (19971-0650)
PHONE.....................302 227-1433
William D Emmert, *Prin*
EMP: 5 **EST:** 2006
SALES (est): 448.89K **Privately Held**
Web: www.emmertauction.com
SIC: 7389 Auctioneers, fee basis

(G-13018)
WILLIAM GONCE
36536 Harmon Bay Blvd (19971-1326)
PHONE.....................302 235-2400
William Gonce, *Prin*
EMP: 11 **EST:** 2010
SALES (est): 228.42K **Privately Held**
Web: www.enhanceddentalcare.com
SIC: 8021 Dentists' office

(G-13019)
WILLIAMS INSURANCE AGENCY INC (PA)
20220 Coastal Hwy (19971-8021)
P.O. Box 1174 (19971-0814)
PHONE.....................302 227-2501
Joseph T Moore, *Pr*
Carol Wright, *
Susan Moore, *
Bud Clark, *
EMP: 27 **EST:** 1948
SQ FT: 4,000
SALES (est): 5.67MM
SALES (corp-wide): 5.67MM **Privately Held**
Web: www.williamsagency.com
SIC: 6411 Insurance agents, nec

(G-13020)
WOLFE NECK TREATMENT PLANT
36160 Wolfe Neck Rd (19971-8719)
PHONE.....................302 644-2761
Gordon German, *Mgr*
Kay Dewson, *Mgr*
EMP: 5 **EST:** 1995
SALES (est): 165.3K **Privately Held**
SIC: 4952 Sewerage systems

(G-13021)
WONDERFUL HOMES
29 Kent St (19971-2155)
PHONE.....................610 304-4744
EMP: 5 **EST:** 2019
SALES (est): 113.29K **Privately Held**
Web: www.wonderfulhomes.net
SIC: 1521 Single-family housing construction

(G-13022)
WORMHOLE SOFT LLC
18585 Coastal Hwy (19971-6147)
PHONE.....................302 424-4374
EMP: 6
SALES (est): 237.56K **Privately Held**
SIC: 7371 Computer software development and applications

(G-13023)
WRIGHT BRUCE B DDS OFFICE RES
15 Venetian Dr (19971-1937)
PHONE.....................302 227-3707
Bruce Wright, *Prin*
EMP: 10 **EST:** 2010
SALES (est): 66.9K **Privately Held**
SIC: 8021 Dentists' office

(G-13024)
WRIGHT STEVEN B DMD PA
18912 John J Williams Hwy (19971-4489)
PHONE.....................302 645-6671
EMP: 16 **EST:** 2015
SALES (est): 322.35K **Privately Held**
SIC: 8021 Dentists' office

(G-13025)
WRITERS RELIEF
18766 John J Williams Hwy (19971-4417)
PHONE.....................866 405-3003
EMP: 8 **EST:** 2019
SALES (est): 1.14MM **Privately Held**
Web: www.writersrelief.com
SIC: 2741 Miscellaneous publishing

(G-13026)
YACHT ANYTHING LTD
Also Called: Alarm Cmmncations Sytems Group
20913 Coastal Hwy (19971-8001)
PHONE.....................302 226-3335
William L Delle Donne, *Pr*
EMP: 5 **EST:** 1995
SALES (est): 736.27K **Privately Held**
SIC: 1623 1731 Telephone and communication line construction; Communications specialization

(G-13027)
YOUNG MNS CHRSTN ASSN WLMNGTON
Also Called: YMCA
105 Church St (19971-1111)
PHONE.....................302 296-9622
Terry Rasberry, *Dir*
EMP: 124
SALES (corp-wide): 40.98MM **Privately Held**
Web: www.ymcade.org
SIC: 7997 7991 8351 7032 Membership sports and recreation clubs; Physical fitness facilities; Child day care services; Youth camps
PA: Young Men's Christian Association Of Delaware
    100 W 10th St Ste 1100
    Wilmington DE 19801
    302 571-6968

Rockland
New Castle County

(G-13028)
BLACKSTONE BUILDING GROUP
100 S Rockland Falls Rd (19732-2917)
PHONE.....................302 660-5528
Christopher C Bell, *Prin*
EMP: 10 **EST:** 2019
SALES (est): 108.2K **Privately Held**
Web: www.blackstonebg.com
SIC: 1799 Special trade contractors, nec

(G-13029)
CANDELAY INDUSTRIES LLC
702 Rockland Rd (19732-2922)
PHONE.....................302 696-2464
EMP: 5 **EST:** 2019
SALES (est): 212.31K **Privately Held**
Web: www.valorcrafthc.com
SIC: 2023 Dietary supplements, dairy and non-dairy based

(G-13030)
DELAWARE COUNSEL GROUP LLP
100 S Rockland Falls Rd (19732-2917)
PHONE.....................302 543-4870
Ellisa Habbart, *Owner*

EMP: 28
SALES (corp-wide): 944.36K **Privately Held**
Web: www.delawarecounselgroup.com
SIC: 8111 General practice attorney, lawyer
PA: The Delaware Counsel Group Llp
    2 Mill Rd Ste 108
    Wilmington DE 19806
    302 576-9600

(G-13031)
GREENVILLE CAPITAL MANAGEMENT
100 S Rockland Falls Rd (19732-2917)
PHONE.....................302 429-9799
Charles S Cruice, *Pr*
EMP: 7 **EST:** 1988
SALES (est): 190.03K **Privately Held**
SIC: 6282 Investment advisory service

Saint Georges
New Castle County

(G-13032)
BLUE HORIZON PROMOTIONS LLC
1 Delaware St (19733-2013)
PHONE.....................302 547-0913
Lawrence Fontana, *Prin*
EMP: 5 **EST:** 2017
SALES (est): 109.03K **Privately Held**
Web: www.bluehorizonpromotions.com
SIC: 8743 Promotion service

(G-13033)
F SARTIN TYSON INC
4376 Kirkwood St Georges Rd (19733-2027)
P.O. Box 97 (19733-0097)
PHONE.....................302 834-4571
Paul Fisher, *Pr*
Ann Fisher, *Sec*
EMP: 15 **EST:** 1941
SQ FT: 5,000
SALES (est): 534.36K **Privately Held**
Web: www.tysonfsartin.com
SIC: 3272 Concrete products, nec

(G-13034)
INTEGRATED WIRG SOLUTIONS LLC
1695 S Dupont Hwy (19733-2031)
P.O. Box 65 (19733-0065)
PHONE.....................302 999-8448
EMP: 20 **EST:** 2015
SALES (est): 1.38MM **Privately Held**
Web: www.integratedwiringllc.com
SIC: 1731 General electrical contractor

(G-13035)
KENCREST SERVICES
240 Clarks Corner Rd (19733-2012)
P.O. Box 245 (19733-0245)
PHONE.....................302 834-3365
Barbara Cephas, *Brnch Mgr*
EMP: 7
Web: www.kencrest.org
SIC: 8361 Residential care
PA: Kencrest Services
    960a Harvest Dr Ste 100
    Blue Bell PA 19422

(G-13036)
KEVINS ROAD SVC
4663 Kirkwood St Georges Rd (19733-2029)
P.O. Box 94 (19733-0094)
PHONE.....................302 218-2869
Kevin Meck, *Prin*
EMP: 5 **EST:** 2017
SALES (est): 28.25K **Privately Held**

SIC: 7538 General automotive repair shops

(G-13037)
MARTOM LANDSCAPING CO INC
1699 St Georges Business Ctr (19733)
P.O. Box 6 (19733-0006)
PHONE.....................302 322-1920
Mark Thompson, *Pr*
EMP: 17 **EST:** 1986
SQ FT: 3,000
SALES (est): 443.31K **Privately Held**
SIC: 0782 Landscape contractors

(G-13038)
SAINT GEORGES CULTR & ARTS REV
1 Delaware St (19733-2013)
PHONE.....................302 836-8202
Lawrence Fontana, *Pr*
Russell Rozanski, *Dir*
Benjamin Rizzo, *Treas*
Howard Isenberg, *Bd of Dir*
EMP: 7 **EST:** 2012
SALES (est): 252.12K **Privately Held**
Web: www.arts-revival.org
SIC: 8399 Social services, nec

(G-13039)
STAPLEFORDS SALES AND SERVICE
Also Called: Stapleford's Oldsmobile
1402 S Dupont Hwy (19733-2030)
P.O. Box 68 (19733-0068)
PHONE.....................302 834-4568
Charles E Stapleford Junior, *Pr*
Richard B Stapleford, *
EMP: 9 **EST:** 1913
SQ FT: 5,000
SALES (est): 526.87K **Privately Held**
Web: www.staplefordssalesandservice.com
SIC: 5012 7539 4141 Automobiles; Automotive repair shops, nec; Local bus charter service

(G-13040)
VICTOR A MALDONADO
1 Delaware St (19733-2013)
PHONE.....................302 420-9749
Victor A Maldonado, *Prin*
EMP: 6 **EST:** 2011
SALES (est): 90.64K **Privately Held**
SIC: 8748 Business consulting, nec

Seaford
Sussex County

(G-13041)
1100 NRMAN ESKRDGE HWY OPRTONS
Also Called: Seaford Center
1100 Norman Eskridge Hwy (19973-1724)
PHONE.....................302 629-3575
D Schonbrunner, *Ex Dir*
EMP: 435
SALES (est): 45.22MM **Privately Held**
SIC: 8051 Convalescent home with continuous nursing care
HQ: Genesis Healthcare Llc
    101 E State St
    Kennett Square PA 19348

(G-13042)
1995 PROPERTY MANAGEMENT INC
25309 Church Rd (19973-8666)
P.O. Box 1295 (19973-5295)
PHONE.....................302 745-1187
Shawn Sylvia, *Prin*
EMP: 5 **EST:** 2009

Seaford - Sussex County (G-13043)   GEOGRAPHIC SECTION

SALES (est): 330.51K **Privately Held**
SIC: **8741** Management services

(G-13043)
A & B GENERAL CONTRACTING
25680 Covert St (19973-8410)
PHONE.................................302 604-9696
Belinda Savage, *Prin*
EMP: 5 EST: 2011
SALES (est): 66.05K **Privately Held**
SIC: **1799** Special trade contractors, nec

(G-13044)
A J E CONSTRUCTION LLC
24705 Rosalyn Dr (19973-7337)
PHONE.................................302 217-2268
Adan Tepox, *Prin*
EMP: 5 EST: 2017
SALES (est): 140.11K **Privately Held**
SIC: **1521** Single-family housing construction

(G-13045)
AARONS SALES & LEASING
Also Called: Aaron's F244
850 Norman Eskridge Hwy (19973-1718)
PHONE.................................302 628-8870
Jay Richards, *Owner*
EMP: 7 EST: 2004
SALES (est): 306.16K **Privately Held**
SIC: **7359** Furniture rental

(G-13046)
ACCUTRENCH CONTRACTING LLC
407 Highland Dr (19973-4832)
PHONE.................................410 829-5157
EMP: 7 EST: 2016
SALES (est): 244.83K **Privately Held**
SIC: **1799** Special trade contractors, nec

(G-13047)
ACTS RTRMNT-LIFE CMMNITIES INC
Also Called: Manor House
1001 Middleford Rd (19973-3638)
PHONE.................................302 629-4368
EMP: 208
SALES (corp-wide): 542.68MM **Privately Held**
Web: www.actsretirement.org
SIC: **6513** Retirement hotel operation
PA: Acts Retirement-Life Communities, Inc.
   420 Delaware Dr
   Fort Washington PA 19034
   215 661-8330

(G-13048)
ADAMS OIL CO INC
Pine St Extd (19973)
P.O. Box 532 (19973-0532)
PHONE.................................302 629-4531
Wayne Adams, *Pr*
Marvin Adams, *VP*
Delores Lloyd, *Sec*
EMP: 7 EST: 1969
SQ FT: 1,000
SALES (est): 883.44K **Privately Held**
SIC: **5172** Fuel oil

(G-13049)
ADDICTION MEDICAL FACILITY LLC
Also Called: Medical Facility Lls Medical
1309 Bridgeville Hwy (19973-1616)
PHONE.................................302 629-2300
EMP: 10 EST: 2017
SALES (est): 1.37MM **Privately Held**
Web: www.addictionmedicalfacility.com
SIC: **8069** Drug addiction rehabilitation hospital

(G-13050)
ADVANCE MBLITY PHYSCL THRAPY L
24488 Sussex Hwy Ste 2 (19973-8470)
PHONE.................................443 359-0132
EMP: 8 EST: 2015
SALES (est): 193.72K **Privately Held**
SIC: **8049** Physical therapist

(G-13051)
AERO-MARINE LAMINATES INC
Also Called: Aero Marine Laminates
22762 Sussex Hwy (19973-5837)
PHONE.................................302 628-3944
Remsen Haynes, *Pr*
Peter Calimano, *VP*
Troy Zelo, *Mgr*
▼ **EMP: 10 EST:** 1981
SALES (est): 746.4K **Privately Held**
Web: www.aeromarinercboats.com
SIC: **3944** 5945 Boat and ship models, toy and hobby; Models, toy and hobby

(G-13052)
ALAN PASSWATERS
Also Called: Passwaters Towing
9551 N Shore Dr (19973-7824)
PHONE.................................302 245-9114
Alan Passwaters, *Owner*
EMP: 7 EST: 2017
SALES (est): 243.68K **Privately Held**
SIC: **7549** Towing service, automotive

(G-13053)
ALFRED IDPONT HOSP FOR CHLDREN
49 Fallon Ave (19973-1577)
PHONE.................................302 629-5030
Kimberly Young-conner, *Mgr*
EMP: 500
SALES (corp-wide): 1.94B **Privately Held**
Web: www.nemours.org
SIC: **0742** Animal hospital services, pets and other animal specialties
HQ: Alfred I.Dupont Hospital For Children
   1600 Rockland Rd
   Wilmington DE 19803

(G-13054)
ALKA CONSTRUCTION LLC
10730 Serenity Cir (19973-8682)
PHONE.................................443 944-9058
EMP: 5 EST: 2019
SALES (est): 212.25K **Privately Held**
SIC: **1521** Single-family housing construction

(G-13055)
ALL CLEAR PEST CONTROL
46 Read St (19973-2106)
PHONE.................................443 359-5623
Mark White, *Prin*
EMP: 5 EST: 2016
SALES (est): 60.02K **Privately Held**
SIC: **7342** Pest control in structures

(G-13056)
ALLEN HARIM FOODS LLC
Also Called: Seaford Feed Mill
20799 Allen Rd (19973)
PHONE.................................302 629-9460
Chad Allen, *Brnch Mgr*
EMP: 75
SALES (corp-wide): 345.31MM **Privately Held**
Web: www.allenharimllc.com
SIC: **5153** Grains
HQ: Allen Harim Foods, Llc
   29984 Pinnacle Way
   Millsboro DE 19966
   302 629-9136

(G-13057)
ALLIANCE RE PROFESSIONALS
26673 Sussex Hwy (19973-8525)
PHONE.................................302 519-7735
EMP: 5 EST: 2015
SALES (est): 97.06K **Privately Held**
Web: www.are-pros.com
SIC: **6531** Real estate agent, residential

(G-13058)
ALLIANCE REAL ESTATE PROS
26673 Sussex Hwy (19973-8525)
PHONE.................................302 536-1838
EMP: 5 EST: 2015
SALES (est): 170.34K **Privately Held**
Web: www.are-pros.com
SIC: **6531** Real estate agent, residential

(G-13059)
AMBER B WOODLAND
225 High St (19973-3926)
PHONE.................................302 628-4140
Amber Woodland, *Ofcr*
EMP: 7 EST: 2018
SALES (est): 162.28K **Privately Held**
Web: www.pwwlaw.com
SIC: **8111** General practice attorney, lawyer

(G-13060)
AMBIENT MEDICAL CARE
24459 Sussex Hwy Ste 2 (19973-4433)
P.O. Box 1827 (19973-8827)
PHONE.................................302 629-3099
Robert A Henry, *Prin*
EMP: 5 EST: 2008
SALES (est): 455.62K **Privately Held**
Web: www.ambientmedicalcare.com
SIC: **8011** General and family practice, physician/surgeon

(G-13061)
AMERICAN LEGION (PA)
601 Bridgeville Hwy Ste 213 (19973-1523)
P.O. Box 930 (19973-0930)
PHONE.................................302 628-5221
Richard Santos, *Dir*
EMP: 10 EST: 2006
SALES (est): 489.16K **Privately Held**
Web: www.delegion.org
SIC: **8641** Veterans' organization

(G-13062)
AMERICAN LEGION AUX DEPT DEL
Also Called: American Legion
386 Graham Branch Rd (19973-6239)
PHONE.................................302 629-3435
EMP: 7 EST: 2011
SALES (est): 51.35K **Privately Held**
Web: www.delegion.org
SIC: **8641** Veterans' organization

(G-13063)
AMERICAN PRECAST
8506 Potts Ln (19973-5975)
PHONE.................................302 629-6688
EMP: 7 EST: 2018
SALES (est): 231.4K **Privately Held**
Web: hstrial-dmoore321.homestead.com
SIC: **3272** Concrete products, nec

(G-13064)
AMERICAN WATER WELL SYSTEM
1129 A Brickyard Rd (19973)
P.O. Box 300 (19973-0300)
PHONE.................................302 629-3796
John A Mcfarland, *Pr*
John A Mc Farland Junior, *Pr*
John A Mc Farland Senior, *Ch Bd*
EMP: 10 EST: 1986
SALES (est): 1.04MM **Privately Held**

SIC: **1781** Servicing, water wells

(G-13065)
AMISH TRADESMEN
26673 Sussex Hwy (19973-8525)
PHONE.................................302 349-5550
EMP: 6 EST: 2018
SALES (est): 464.97K **Privately Held**
Web: www.theamishtradesmen.com
SIC: **1521** General remodeling, single-family houses

(G-13066)
ANCHOR ENTERPRISES
22 W High St (19973-4147)
PHONE.................................302 629-7969
EMP: 7 EST: 2019
SALES (est): 460.56K **Privately Held**
SIC: **3441** Fabricated structural metal

(G-13067)
ANGIES SUPER CLEAN
223b N Willey St (19973-3109)
P.O. Box 56 (19973-0056)
PHONE.................................302 519-0828
Angela J Borggreen, *Owner*
EMP: 5 EST: 2015
SALES (est): 51.45K **Privately Held**
Web: www.angiessuperclean.com
SIC: **7699** Cleaning services

(G-13068)
ARBOR CARE
31 Rivers End Dr (19973-8005)
PHONE.................................302 258-8909
Thurman Ritchie, *Prin*
EMP: 11 EST: 2014
SALES (est): 573.73K **Privately Held**
Web: www.arborcarede.com
SIC: **0783** Planting, pruning, and trimming services

(G-13069)
ASA V PEUGH INC
Also Called: Anchor Enterprises
22 W High St (19973-4147)
PHONE.................................302 629-7969
Asa V Peugh, *Pr*
Michael Peugh, *Treas*
EMP: 22 EST: 1977
SQ FT: 8,000
SALES (est): 739.77K **Privately Held**
SIC: **3441** 3446 Fabricated structural metal; Ornamental metalwork

(G-13070)
ATI HOLDINGS LLC
Also Called: ATI Physical Therapy
22832 Sussex Hwy (19973-5862)
PHONE.................................302 536-5562
Ryan Kardos, *Dir*
EMP: 8
SALES (corp-wide): 635.67MM **Publicly Held**
Web: www.atipt.com
SIC: **8049** Physical therapist
HQ: Ati Holdings, Llc
   790 Remington Blvd
   Bolingbrook IL 60440

(G-13071)
ATKISON TRUCKING
40 Rivers End Dr (19973-8007)
PHONE.................................302 396-0322
Andrea Allen, *Prin*
EMP: 5 EST: 2016
SALES (est): 218.01K **Privately Held**
SIC: **4212** Local trucking, without storage

GEOGRAPHIC SECTION

Seaford - Sussex County (G-13100)

(G-13072)
ATLANTIC FINANCE
22937 Sussex Hwy (19973-5871)
PHONE.....................302 629-6266
EMP: 6 **EST:** 2019
SALES (est): 120.76K **Privately Held**
Web: www.atlanticfinanceandpawn.com
SIC: 6141 Personal credit institutions

(G-13073)
ATLANTIC REALTY MANAGEMENT
Also Called: Village of Cool Branch Homes
100 Hitch Pond Cir (19973-6221)
PHONE.....................302 629-0770
Lary Mckinly, *Pr*
EMP: 4 **EST:** 1999
SALES (est): 411.82K **Privately Held**
SIC: 2451 Mobile homes

(G-13074)
AUTO EXPRESS TRANSPORT INC
24290 Shufelt Rd (19973-6716)
P.O. Box 599 (19973-0599)
PHONE.....................302 628-4601
Kevin Thawley, *Pr*
Alan Loudon, *VP*
EMP: 10 **EST:** 1997
SALES (est): 975.04K **Privately Held**
Web: www.autoexpresstransport.org
SIC: 4213 4424 Automobiles, transport and delivery; Intercoastal transportation, freight

(G-13075)
BANK OF DELMARVA
Also Called: Bank of Delmar
910 Norman Eskridge Hwy (19973-1720)
PHONE.....................302 629-2700
Ingunn Straume, *Brnch Mgr*
EMP: 5
Web: www.bankofdelmarvahb.com
SIC: 6022 6029 State trust companies accepting deposits, commercial; Commercial banks, nec
PA: The Bank Of Delmarva
  2245 Northwood Dr
  Salisbury MD 21801

(G-13076)
BARTONS LANDSCAPING/LAWN INC
20689 Sussex Hwy (19973-5690)
PHONE.....................302 629-2213
Philip C Barton, *Pr*
Tim Conaway, *
Julie Barton, *
EMP: 35 **EST:** 1977
SQ FT: 2,225
SALES (est): 2.48MM **Privately Held**
Web: www.bartons.pro
SIC: 0782 5261 Landscape contractors; Retail nurseries and garden stores

(G-13077)
BAY AREA WILDLIFE LLC
10533 Old Furnace Rd (19973-8116)
PHONE.....................410 829-6368
William J Russell, *Admn*
EMP: 6 **EST:** 2013
SALES (est): 77.22K **Privately Held**
Web: www.bayareawildlifesolutions.com
SIC: 7342 Pest control in structures

(G-13078)
BAYNUM ENTERPRISES INC (PA)
Also Called: Pizza King
300 W Stein Hwy (19973-1335)
PHONE.....................302 629-6104
Shirley Baynum, *Pr*
Brad Baynum, *
EMP: 100 **EST:** 1978
SQ FT: 8,000
SALES (est): 9.15MM
SALES (corp-wide): 9.15MM **Privately Held**
Web: www.pizzakingde.com
SIC: 5812 6514 Pizza restaurants; Dwelling operators, except apartments

(G-13079)
BDB SERVICES
25560 Business Park (19973-4201)
PHONE.....................302 536-1410
EMP: 5 **EST:** 2012
SALES (est): 103.02K **Privately Held**
SIC: 1742 Insulation, buildings

(G-13080)
BEACH CITIES REPTILE RESCUE
10333 Airport Rd (19973-6317)
PHONE.....................949 412-6366
Anthony Rohrbaugh, *Owner*
EMP: 5 **EST:** 2013
SALES (est): 57.51K **Privately Held**
Web: www.beachcitiesreptilerescue.org
SIC: 0752 Shelters, animal

(G-13081)
BEACHBALLS COM LLC
112 S Bradford St (19973-3802)
PHONE.....................302 628-8888
David Layton, *Owner*
▲ **EMP:** 5 **EST:** 2009
SALES (est): 248.44K **Privately Held**
Web: www.beachballs.com
SIC: 3949 Balls: baseball, football, basketball, etc.

(G-13082)
BENEVLENT PRTCTIVE ORDER ELKS
Also Called: ELKS LODGE
8846 Elks Rd (19973-5647)
P.O. Box 476 (19973-0476)
PHONE.....................302 629-2458
EMP: 10 **EST:** 1972
SALES (est): 147.74K **Privately Held**
SIC: 8641 Civic associations

(G-13083)
BENSON CONCRETE CNSTR LLC
26500 Asbury Rd (19973-8205)
PHONE.....................410 382-5112
EMP: 5 **EST:** 2019
SALES (est): 200.6K **Privately Held**
Web: www.bensonconcreteconstruction.com
SIC: 1521 Single-family housing construction

(G-13084)
BEST OFFICE PROS
26082 Butler Branch Rd (19973-6971)
P.O. Box 820 (19973-0820)
PHONE.....................302 629-4561
Eva Dupont, *Pt*
Eva Dupont, *Mng Pt*
EMP: 3 **EST:** 2009
SALES (est): 139.79K **Privately Held**
Web: www.bestofficepros.com
SIC: 2759 Business forms: printing, nsk

(G-13085)
BETTER HOMES OF SEAFORD INC (PA)
101 Independence Dr (19973-1559)
PHONE.....................302 629-8048
Norman Poole, *Pr*
William Roupp, *Dir*
Jane Smack, *Sec*
EMP: 12 **EST:** 1969
SALES (est): 193.84K
SALES (corp-wide): 193.84K **Privately Held**
Web: www.oginorth.com
SIC: 6513 Apartment building operators

(G-13086)
BETTER HOMES OF SEAFORD INC
2 Chandler St (19973-2816)
PHONE.....................302 629-6522
EMP: 11
SALES (corp-wide): 193.84K **Privately Held**
Web: www.oginorth.com
SIC: 6513 Apartment building operators
PA: Better Homes Of Seaford, Inc.
  101 Independence Dr
  Seaford DE 19973
  302 629-8048

(G-13087)
BETTS AND BIDDLE EYE CARE PA
8500 Herring Run Rd (19973-5795)
PHONE.....................302 697-2151
Sonja Biddle, *Prin*
EMP: 15 **EST:** 2009
SALES (est): 408.42K **Privately Held**
Web: www.bettsandbiddleeyecare.com
SIC: 8042 Specialized optometrists

(G-13088)
BIG JIMS TRUCKING
73 Hitch Pond Cir (19973-6215)
PHONE.....................214 504-1320
James Carey, *Prin*
EMP: 5 **EST:** 2017
SALES (est): 228.55K **Privately Held**
SIC: 4212 Local trucking, without storage

(G-13089)
BIO MEDIC CORPORATION (PA)
742 Sussex Ave (19973-2057)
PHONE.....................302 628-4300
George Gabriel, *Ch Bd*
Edmond Silverberg, *VP*
Frank Marinaccio, *VP*
◆ **EMP:** 13 **EST:** 1971
SALES (est): 49.41MM
SALES (corp-wide): 49.41MM **Privately Held**
Web: www.aviditiyscience.com
SIC: 5049 3821 3496 3914 Laboratory equipment, except medical or dental; Laboratory apparatus and furniture; Cages, wire; Cutlery, nsk

(G-13090)
BLUE DIAMOND POOLS INC
5669 Galestown Reliance Rd (19973-6052)
PHONE.....................302 265-2165
Russell Smith, *Prin*
EMP: 5 **EST:** 2015
SALES (est): 121.73K **Privately Held**
SIC: 1799 Special trade contractors, nec

(G-13091)
BRADLEY DISTRIBUTING INC
2929 Woodland Ferry Rd (19973-4640)
PHONE.....................302 245-7508
Jason Bradley, *Prin*
EMP: 5 **EST:** 2016
SALES (est): 492.05K **Privately Held**
SIC: 5199 Nondurable goods, nec

(G-13092)
BRAINERD LLC
100 Industrial Park Blvd (19973-9477)
PHONE.....................918 622-1214
Mat Brainerd, *Managing Member*
EMP: 16
SALES (est): 788.17K **Privately Held**
SIC: 5169 Chemicals and allied products, nec

(G-13093)
BROAD CREEK MEDICAL SERVICE
Also Called: Broadcreek Medical Service
1601 Middleford Rd (19973-3617)
PHONE.....................302 629-0202
Tod Emeigh, *Pr*
EMP: 10 **EST:** 1979
SQ FT: 1,800
SALES (est): 846.47K **Privately Held**
SIC: 7352 5047 Medical equipment rental; Medical laboratory equipment

(G-13094)
BROKER POST
1310 Bridgeville Hwy (19973-1617)
P.O. Box 569 (19973-0569)
PHONE.....................302 628-8467
John Hannenfeld, *Pr*
John Hennenfeld, *Owner*
EMP: 5
SALES (est): 443.5K **Privately Held**
Web: www.buyatauction.com
SIC: 6531 Real estate agent, commercial

(G-13095)
BROOKESIDE STUDIO
7 Woodland Dr (19973-9500)
PHONE.....................302 629-2829
Tammy Kearney, *Prin*
EMP: 5 **EST:** 2011
SALES (est): 42.51K **Privately Held**
SIC: 7299 Miscellaneous personal service

(G-13096)
BRUCE M DOPLER MD
24488 Sussex Hwy Ste 6 (19973-8470)
PHONE.....................302 628-7730
EMP: 8 **EST:** 2018
SALES (est): 231.58K **Privately Held**
SIC: 8011 Offices and clinics of medical doctors

(G-13097)
BRUCES WELDING INC
21263 Nattell Ln (19973-6560)
PHONE.....................302 629-3891
Bruce Burtelle, *Pr*
EMP: 3 **EST:** 1979
SQ FT: 7,600
SALES (est): 339.01K **Privately Held**
SIC: 7692 Welding repair

(G-13098)
BUSYMAMA CUPCAKES
328 E Poplar St (19973-3414)
PHONE.....................302 259-9988
EMP: 3 **EST:** 2015
SALES (est): 149.86K **Privately Held**
SIC: 2051 Bread, cake, and related products

(G-13099)
C VARGAS CONSTRUCTION LLC
89 Monticello Ct (19973-1128)
PHONE.....................302 470-2004
EMP: 8 **EST:** 2020
SALES (est): 792.4K **Privately Held**
Web: www.cvargasconstruction.com
SIC: 1521 Single-family housing construction

(G-13100)
C WHITE & SONS LLC
5635 Neals School Rd (19973-6746)
PHONE.....................302 629-4848
EMP: 9 **EST:** 1999
SALES (est): 932.89K **Privately Held**
Web: www.cwhiteandsons.biz
SIC: 7699 Septic tank cleaning service

Seaford - Sussex County (G-13101)   GEOGRAPHIC SECTION

(G-13101)
CANNON SPAS
Also Called: Cannon Spas & Pools
10747 Hastings Farm Rd (19973-7000)
P.O. Box 618 (19973-0618)
PHONE..................302 628-9404
Steven C Cannon, *Owner*
EMP: 7 EST: 1989
SALES (est): 358.4K **Privately Held**
Web: www.cannonpools.net
SIC: 5999 1799 Spas and hot tubs; Swimming pool construction

(G-13102)
CAPITAL ORTHOPAEDIC
1320 Middleford Rd (19973-3649)
PHONE..................302 628-7702
Richard Du, *Pr*
EMP: 8 EST: 2017
SALES (est): 169.94K **Privately Held**
SIC: 8011 Orthopedic physician

(G-13103)
CDI INC SOFR SYSTEM LLC
Also Called: CDI
1330 Middleford Rd (19973-3648)
PHONE..................302 536-7325
Jesse Frederick-conaway, *CEO*
EMP: 5 EST: 2011
SALES (est): 75.7K **Privately Held**
SIC: 3535 Conveyors and conveying equipment

(G-13104)
CEDAR CREEK MARINE CENTER
20676 Sussex Hwy (19973-5684)
PHONE..................302 629-3581
EMP: 8 EST: 2017
SALES (est): 138.17K **Privately Held**
Web: www.cedarcreekmarina.com
SIC: 4493 Boat yards, storage and incidental repair

(G-13105)
CENTURY SEALS INC (PA)
503 Harrington St (19973-3719)
P.O. Box 720 (19973-0720)
PHONE..................302 629-0324
Terry Phillips, *Pr*
Lisa Fizer, *VP*
Donna Lauck, *VP*
EMP: 26 EST: 1999
SQ FT: 6,000
SALES (est): 5.1MM **Privately Held**
Web: www.centuryseals.com
SIC: 3053 Gaskets and sealing devices

(G-13106)
CESARS VARGAS STONE INC C
220 High St Apt A (19973-3932)
PHONE..................302 296-7881
EMP: 5 EST: 2011
SALES (est): 195.06K **Privately Held**
SIC: 1741 Masonry and other stonework

(G-13107)
CGW CORP
9585 Cedar Ln (19973-8617)
PHONE..................631 903-5700
EMP: 5 EST: 2018
SALES (est): 44.13K **Privately Held**
Web: www.cgwcorp.com
SIC: 7379 Computer related consulting services

(G-13108)
CHALLENGE AUTOMOTIVE SVCS INC
Also Called: AAMCO Transmissions
22598 Sussex Hwy (19973-5835)
PHONE..................302 629-3058
Carl Schulze, *Owner*
EMP: 11 EST: 2010
SALES (est): 236.99K **Privately Held**
Web: www.aamco.com
SIC: 7537 Automotive transmission repair shops

(G-13109)
CHAMBERS MOTORS INC
20610 Sussex Hwy (19973-5684)
P.O. Box 494 (19973-0494)
PHONE..................302 629-3553
William Chambers Junior, *Pr*
EMP: 28 EST: 1977
SQ FT: 7,000
SALES (est): 2.39MM **Privately Held**
Web: www.chambersmotorsde.com
SIC: 7549 Towing service, automotive

(G-13110)
CHANDLER HEIGHTS II LP
802 Clementine Ct (19973-2873)
PHONE..................302 629-8048
William Roupp, *Ex Dir*
EMP: 5 EST: 2014
SALES (est): 74.54K **Privately Held**
SIC: 6514 Dwelling operators, except apartments

(G-13111)
CHANEY ENTERPRISES
22223 Eskridge Rd (19973-8144)
PHONE..................302 990-5039
EMP: 11 EST: 2017
SALES (est): 186.41K **Privately Held**
Web: www.chaneyenterprises.com
SIC: 3273 Ready-mixed concrete

(G-13112)
CHAPIS DRAFTING & BLUE PRINT
8057 Hearns Pond Rd (19973-5719)
PHONE..................302 629-6373
John Chapis, *Prin*
EMP: 5 EST: 2011
SALES (est): 192.2K **Privately Held**
SIC: 2752 Commercial printing, lithographic

(G-13113)
CHARLOTTE WILSON
Also Called: Christian Recovery Spa
629 Rosemary Dr (19973-7627)
PHONE..................302 500-1440
Charlotte Wilson, *Owner*
Cordelia Hicks, *Ex Sec*
Isaac Hicks, *Asstg*
EMP: 5 EST: 2018
SALES (est): 59.45K **Privately Held**
SIC: 7231 Cosmetology and personal hygiene salons

(G-13114)
CHERRY BUILDING GROUP
26739 Sussex Hwy (19973-8527)
PHONE..................302 280-6876
EMP: 9 EST: 2019
SALES (est): 489.82K **Privately Held**
Web: www.cherrybuildinggroup.com
SIC: 1799 Special trade contractors, nec

(G-13115)
CHESAPEAKE BAY ORTHOPEDICS
1340 Middleford Rd (19973-3665)
PHONE..................302 404-5954
Michael Ward, *Owner*
EMP: 6 EST: 2017
SALES (est): 242.4K **Privately Held**
SIC: 8011 Orthopedic physician

(G-13116)
CHESAPEAKE CARRIERS INC
518 Bridgeville Hwy (19973-1522)
PHONE..................302 628-3838
H Melvin Williamson, *Pr*
Lisa Melvin, *VP*
EMP: 20 EST: 1989
SALES (est): 1.09MM **Privately Held**
SIC: 4213 Trucking, except local

(G-13117)
CHESAPEAKE HEARTH STONE CO LLC
26950 Danny Dr (19973-6384)
PHONE..................302 943-5276
EMP: 5 EST: 2020
SALES (est): 621.66K **Privately Held**
SIC: 5032 Brick, stone, and related material

(G-13118)
CHESAPEAKECAREGIVERS LLC
10105 Concord Rd (19973-8649)
PHONE..................302 841-9686
Patrick Murray, *Prin*
EMP: 7 EST: 2017
SALES (est): 102.96K **Privately Held**
SIC: 8082 Home health care services

(G-13119)
CHILDREN FMILIES FIRST DEL INC
Also Called: Seafood House, The
400 N Market Street Ext (19973-1573)
PHONE..................302 629-6996
Don Loden, *Brnch Mgr*
EMP: 57
SALES (corp-wide): 17.22MM **Privately Held**
Web: www.cffde.org
SIC: 8322 8361 Child related social services; Residential care for children
PA: Children & Families First Delaware Inc.
809 N Washington St
Wilmington DE 19801
302 658-5177

(G-13120)
CITIFINANCIAL CREDIT COMPANY
Also Called: Citifinancial
22974 Sussex Hwy (19973-5861)
PHONE..................302 628-9253
Kari Paquette, *Mgr*
EMP: 5
SALES (corp-wide): 101.08B **Publicly Held**
SIC: 6141 Consumer finance companies
HQ: Citifinancial Credit Company
300 Saint Paul Pl Fl 3
Baltimore MD 21202
410 332-3000

(G-13121)
CITY CAB INC
704 Norman Eskridge Hwy (19973-1716)
PHONE..................302 628-2588
Tom Antonio, *Owner*
EMP: 15 EST: 2001
SALES (est): 310K **Privately Held**
SIC: 4121 Taxicabs

(G-13122)
CITY OF SEAFORD
Also Called: Hooper's Landing
1019 W Locust St (19973-2124)
PHONE..................302 629-2890
EMP: 9
SALES (corp-wide): 6.96MM **Privately Held**
Web: www.seafordde.com
SIC: 7992 Public golf courses
PA: City Of Seaford
414 High St
Seaford DE 19973
302 629-9173

(G-13123)
CLARKS SWIMMING POOLS INC
22855 Sussex Hwy (19973-5851)
PHONE..................302 629-8835
Chad E Clark, *Pr*
EMP: 9 EST: 1973
SQ FT: 3,200
SALES (est): 2.46MM **Privately Held**
Web: www.clarksswimmingpools.com
SIC: 1799 5999 Swimming pool construction; Swimming pools, above ground

(G-13124)
CLEAN BEES
308 Oak Rd (19973-2030)
PHONE..................302 470-1125
Elizabeth Smith, *Prin*
EMP: 5 EST: 2018
SALES (est): 61.82K **Privately Held**
Web: www.cleanbees.com
SIC: 7699 Cleaning services

(G-13125)
CLINICAL PSTRAL CNSLING PRGRAM
54 South State St (19973)
P.O. Box 299 (19973-0299)
PHONE..................302 632-8842
EMP: 7 EST: 2010
SALES (est): 80.53K **Privately Held**
SIC: 8322 General counseling services

(G-13126)
COASTAL CABINETRY LLC
400 Megan Ave (19973-9405)
PHONE..................302 542-4155
EMP: 10 EST: 2010
SALES (est): 852.62K **Privately Held**
Web: www.coastalcabinetryllc.com
SIC: 2434 1751 Wood kitchen cabinets; Cabinet building and installation

(G-13127)
COASTAL MAINTENANCE LLC
25731 Winners Circle Dr (19973-6394)
PHONE..................302 536-1290
Mark Huffman, *Managing Member*
EMP: 25 EST: 2012
SALES (est): 2.22MM **Privately Held**
SIC: 1799 0751 Welding on site; Poultry services

(G-13128)
COLDWELL BANKER RESORT REALTY
22350 Sussex Hwy (19973-5833)
PHONE..................302 245-2145
Lee Johnson, *Prin*
EMP: 8 EST: 2016
SALES (est): 190.12K **Privately Held**
Web: www.cbanker.com
SIC: 6531 Real estate agent, residential

(G-13129)
COMCAST CORPORATION
Also Called: Comcast Cable
22992 Sussex Hwy (19973-5861)
PHONE..................302 526-0109
EMP: 5
SALES (corp-wide): 121.57B **Publicly Held**
Web: corporate.comcast.com
SIC: 4841 Cable television services
PA: Comcast Corporation
1 Comcast Ctr
Philadelphia PA 19103
215 286-1700

GEOGRAPHIC SECTION

Seaford - Sussex County (G-13158)

(G-13130)
COMCAST CORPORATION
500 High St (19973-3916)
PHONE.................302 262-8996
EMP: 5
SALES (corp-wide): 121.43B **Publicly Held**
Web: corporate.comcast.com
SIC: 4841 Cable television services
PA: Comcast Corporation
   1 Comcast Ctr
   Philadelphia PA 19103
   215 286-1700

(G-13131)
COMFORT SUITES
Also Called: Comfort Suites
23420 Sussex Hwy (19973-5867)
PHONE.................302 628-5400
Manish Patel, *Owner*
EMP: 22 **EST:** 2008
SALES (est): 428.21K **Privately Held**
Web: www.choicehotels.com
SIC: 7011 Hotel, franchised

(G-13132)
COMPLETE AUTO BODY INC
Also Called: Hertrich's Collision Center
26907 Sussex Hwy (19973-8559)
PHONE.................302 629-3955
EMP: 10 **EST:** 1978
SQ FT: 25,000
SALES (est): 435.38K **Privately Held**
SIC: 7532 Body shop, automotive

(G-13133)
CONNECTIONSCSP INC
310 Virginia Ave (19973-1516)
PHONE.................302 383-8482
EMP: 8 **EST:** 2011
SALES (est): 56.99K **Privately Held**
SIC: 8322 Social service center

(G-13134)
CONNECTONS CMNTY SPPORT PRGRAM
105 N Front St (19973-2707)
PHONE.................302 536-1952
EMP: 99
Web: coras.flywheelsites.com
SIC: 8322 8093 Social service center; Detoxification center, outpatient
PA: Connections Community Support Programs, Inc.
   590 Naamans Rd
   Claymont DE 19703

(G-13135)
CONSOLIDATED CONSTRUCTION SVCS
7450 Rivershore Dr (19973-4328)
PHONE.................302 629-6070
Chuck Harrison, *Pr*
Debra Harrison, *Sec*
EMP: 10 **EST:** 1984
SALES (est): 1.46MM **Privately Held**
Web: www.ccsflooring.com
SIC: 5032 1743 Ceramic wall and floor tile, nec; Terrazzo work

(G-13136)
CONTRACT PT LLC
10430 Gravelly Creek Ln (19973-7942)
PHONE.................302 628-0705
EMP: 5 **EST:** 2017
SALES (est): 132.07K **Privately Held**
SIC: 1799 Special trade contractors, nec

(G-13137)
COTTEN ENGINEERING LLC
10087 Concord Rd (19973-8646)
PHONE.................302 628-9164
Michael Cotten, *Prin*
EMP: 5 **EST:** 2011
SALES (est): 460.09K **Privately Held**
Web: www.cotteneng.com
SIC: 8711 Engineering services

(G-13138)
COVEYS CAR CARE INC
1300 Middleford Rd (19973-3612)
PHONE.................302 629-2746
C Kenneth Covey, *Pr*
EMP: 7 **EST:** 1964
SALES (est): 860.43K **Privately Held**
Web: www.coveyscarcare.com
SIC: 7538 5013 General automotive repair shops; Automotive supplies and parts

(G-13139)
CRAIG METZNER
22661 Atlanta Rd (19973-6625)
PHONE.................302 629-9576
Craig Metzner, *Prin*
EMP: 5 **EST:** 2011
SALES (est): 104.69K **Privately Held**
SIC: 0742 Animal hospital services, pets and other animal specialties

(G-13140)
CRAIG TECHNOLOGIES INC (PA)
103 Davis Dr (19973-9408)
P.O. Box 180 (19973-0180)
PHONE.................302 628-9900
Donald Hollenbeck, *Pr*
Robert Hollenbeck, *VP*
Paul Hollenbeck, *VP*
Leo O'hara, *Treas*
▲ **EMP:** 22 **EST:** 1959
SQ FT: 250,000
SALES (est): 9.85MM
SALES (corp-wide): 9.85MM **Privately Held**
Web: www.craigtechnologies.com
SIC: 3089 Injection molding of plastics

(G-13141)
CRYSTAL BLU SERVICES LLC
902 Heritage Dr (19973-1122)
PHONE.................302 404-5389
Jack Chambers, *Prin*
EMP: 6 **EST:** 2019
SALES (est): 240.09K **Privately Held**
Web: www.crystalbluservices.com
SIC: 7699 Cleaning services

(G-13142)
CURIOSITY SERVICE FOUNDATION
2001 Bridgeville Hwy (19973-1728)
P.O. Box 826 (19973-0826)
PHONE.................302 628-4140
Michelle Trocino-wells, *Prin*
EMP: 8 **EST:** 2008
SALES (est): 306.48K **Privately Held**
SIC: 8699 Charitable organization

(G-13143)
CUTEM UP TREE CARE DEL INC
10404 Old Furnace Rd (19973-8110)
PHONE.................302 629-4655
EMP: 5 **EST:** 1995
SALES (est): 250K **Privately Held**
Web: www.cutemuptree.com
SIC: 0783 0782 Planting, pruning, and trimming services; Landscape contractors

(G-13144)
D & S PAINTERS LLC
23415 Sussex Hwy (19973-5875)
PHONE.................302 241-7221
Salman Duray, *Asst Sec*
EMP: 5 **EST:** 2018
SALES (est): 42.66K **Privately Held**
SIC: 1721 Painting and paper hanging

(G-13145)
DANTUONO VINCENZO S MD
1350 Middleford Rd # 502 (19973-3664)
PHONE.................302 628-8300
Vincenzo D'antuono Md, *Prin*
EMP: 9 **EST:** 2017
SALES (est): 168.56K **Privately Held**
SIC: 8011 Internal medicine, physician/surgeon

(G-13146)
DAVIS LOCK AND SAFE LLC
9758 Warrens Way (19973-7948)
P.O. Box 617 (19973-0617)
PHONE.................302 628-5397
EMP: 5 **EST:** 2016
SALES (est): 57.64K **Privately Held**
SIC: 7699 Locksmith shop

(G-13147)
DAVIS WELDING SERVICE LLC
26075 River Rd (19973-5905)
PHONE.................302 465-3004
EMP: 3 **EST:** 2019
SALES (est): 82.17K **Privately Held**
SIC: 7692 Welding repair

(G-13148)
DAYS INN AND SUITES SEAFORD
Also Called: Days Inn
23450 Sussex Hwy (19973-5867)
PHONE.................302 629-4300
Shaan Christy, *Prin*
EMP: 13 **EST:** 2008
SALES (est): 225.64K **Privately Held**
Web: www.wyndhamhotels.com
SIC: 7011 Hotels and motels

(G-13149)
DEBBIE BRITTINGHAM - COLDWELL
22350 Sussex Hwy (19973-5833)
PHONE.................302 745-1886
EMP: 6 **EST:** 2017
SALES (est): 72.84K **Privately Held**
Web: www.cbanker.com
SIC: 6531 Real estate agent, residential

(G-13150)
DEL MAR ONSITE SOLUTIONS
5635 Neals School Rd (19973-6746)
PHONE.................302 629-2568
EMP: 6 **EST:** 2009
SALES (est): 60.84K **Privately Held**
SIC: 7699 Sewer cleaning and rodding

(G-13151)
DELAWARE FAMILY POLICY COUNCIL
1201 Bridgeville Hwy (19973-1613)
P.O. Box 925 (19973-0925)
PHONE.................302 296-8698
John Taylor, *Prin*
EMP: 7 **EST:** 2010
SALES (est): 92.84K **Privately Held**
Web: www.delawarefamilies.org
SIC: 8322 Individual and family services

(G-13152)
DELAWARE INJURY CARE LLC
608 N Porter St (19973-2441)
PHONE.................302 628-8008
EMP: 5 **EST:** 2020
SALES (est): 22.18K **Privately Held**
Web: www.delawareinjurycare.org
SIC: 8049 Offices of health practitioner

(G-13153)
DELAWARE TITLE LOANS INC
22994 Sussex Hwy (19973-5861)
PHONE.................302 629-8843
EMP: 11
SALES (corp-wide): 820.18K **Privately Held**
Web: www.delawaretitleloansinc.com
SIC: 6159 General and industrial loan institutions
PA: Delaware Title Loans, Inc.
   8601 Dunwoody Pl Ste 406
   Atlanta GA 30350
   770 552-9840

(G-13154)
DELMARVA ICE LLC
24483 Sussex Hwy (19973-4433)
PHONE.................302 593-7095
EMP: 9 **EST:** 2017
SALES (est): 498.14K **Privately Held**
Web: www.delmarvaice.com
SIC: 6512 Shopping center, neighborhood (30,000-100,000 sq. ft.)

(G-13155)
DELMARVA KLEANING KLUB LLC
24262 Chapel Branch Rd (19973-6929)
PHONE.................302 629-4706
EMP: 5 **EST:** 2018
SALES (est): 53.33K **Privately Held**
Web: delmarva-kleaning-klub-llc.business.site
SIC: 7699 Cleaning services

(G-13156)
DELMARVA TEEN CHALLENGE INC (PA)
Also Called: Delmarva Adult Teen Challenge
611 3rd St (19973-2723)
P.O. Box 1271 (19973-5271)
PHONE.................302 629-8824
Susan Bramble, *Ex Dir*
Robert Carey, *Ex Dir*
EMP: 5 **EST:** 2008
SALES (est): 928.67K **Privately Held**
Web: www.delmarvateenchallenge.org
SIC: 8322 Individual and family services

(G-13157)
DENISE CROTHERS
26378 Bethel Concord Rd (19973-6313)
PHONE.................302 629-7390
Denise Crothers, *Prin*
EMP: 5 **EST:** 2010
SALES (est): 163.64K **Privately Held**
SIC: 7389 Business services, nec

(G-13158)
DENT PRO INC
14470 Baker Mill Rd (19973-8251)
PHONE.................302 628-0978
David Hignutt, *Pr*
EMP: 5
SALES (corp-wide): 1.23MM **Privately Held**
Web: www.dentpro.com
SIC: 7532 Body shop, automotive
PA: Dent Pro Inc
   2205 Winchester Blvd
   Campbell CA 95008
   408 370-9500

Seaford - Sussex County (G-13159)

(G-13159)
DESANCTIS INSURANCE AGENCY LLC
26982 Crest Dr (19973-6986)
PHONE..................302 629-8841
EMP: 5 EST: 2020
SALES (est): 50.78K Privately Held
SIC: 6411 Insurance agents, nec

(G-13160)
DIANES BUS SERVICE
Rt 2 Box 79 (19973)
PHONE..................302 629-4336
EMP: 8 EST: 1981
SALES (est): 246.72K Privately Held
SIC: 4151 School buses

(G-13161)
DIGITAL MEMORIES VIDEOGRAPHY
217 N Bradford St (19973-3205)
PHONE..................302 682-9180
Kevin J Wishart, Owner
EMP: 5 EST: 2017
SALES (est): 60.75K Privately Held
SIC: 7812 Video production

(G-13162)
DITCH WITCH OF VIRGINIA
182 Kent Dr (19973-1585)
PHONE..................302 629-3602
EMP: 7 EST: 2019
SALES (est): 809.93K Privately Held
Web: www.ditchwitchva.com
SIC: 5082 General construction machinery and equipment

(G-13163)
DON-LEE MARGIN CORPORATION
25271 Figgs Rd (19973-6943)
PHONE..................302 629-7567
Denise Dickerson, Pr
EMP: 30 EST: 1966
SQ FT: 4,000
SALES (est): 2.47MM Privately Held
Web: www.don-leemargin.com
SIC: 7349 Janitorial service, contract basis

(G-13164)
DUNBAR ARMORED INC
186 Kent Dr (19973-1585)
PHONE..................302 628-5401
Harvey Sourey, Brnch Mgr
EMP: 25
SALES (corp-wide): 4.54B Publicly Held
Web: www.dunbarsecurity.com
SIC: 7381 Security guard service
HQ: Dunbar Armored, Inc.
50 Schilling Rd
Hunt Valley MD 21031
410 584-9800

(G-13165)
EAST COAST BUILDERS INC
Rte 1 Box 350 (19973)
P.O. Box 413 (19973-0413)
PHONE..................302 629-3551
Randy Pentoney, Pr
Diane Pentoney, Sec
EMP: 10 EST: 1983
SQ FT: 2,000
SALES (est): 1.1MM Privately Held
SIC: 1521 New construction, single-family houses

(G-13166)
EAST COAST HEALTH & FITNES LLC
620 W Stein Hwy (19973-1204)
PHONE..................410 213-7697
EMP: 6 EST: 2019
SALES (est): 29.54K Privately Held
Web: www.eastcoastfit.com
SIC: 7991 Physical fitness facilities

(G-13167)
EAST COAST SWAG
94 Rivers End Dr (19973-8015)
PHONE..................302 628-2674
Kelly L Glessner, Owner
EMP: 8 EST: 2017
SALES (est): 269.34K Privately Held
Web: www.buyfromecs.com
SIC: 5199 Advertising specialties

(G-13168)
EASTERN SHORE METAL DETECTORS
20380 Wesley Church Rd (19973-6557)
PHONE..................302 628-1985
John Rebman, Prin
EMP: 4 EST: 2009
SALES (est): 204.01K Privately Held
SIC: 3669 Metal detectors

(G-13169)
EASTERN SHORE METALS LLC
102 Park Ave (19973-9479)
PHONE..................302 629-6629
Chris Marvel, Pr
▲ EMP: 19 EST: 2012
SALES (est): 10.8MM Privately Held
Web: easternshoreme.wpengine.com
SIC: 5084 7389 3542 Sawmill machinery and equipment; Metal slitting and shearing; Presses: forming, stamping, punching, sizing (machine tools)

(G-13170)
EDWARD J KAYE CONSTRUCTION
22288 Coverdale Rd (19973-7036)
PHONE..................302 629-7483
Eddie Kaye, Pr
Vince Kaye, VP
EMP: 15 EST: 1981
SQ FT: 1,600
SALES (est): 490.28K Privately Held
SIC: 1794 Excavation work

(G-13171)
EFFICIENT SERVICES INC
24660 German Rd (19973-7319)
P.O. Box 858 (19973-0858)
PHONE..................302 629-2124
Phillip Grice, Pr
Vernon Grice, VP
Myra Grice, Sec
EMP: 7 EST: 1970
SALES (est): 239.69K Privately Held
SIC: 7349 5812 5962 Janitorial service, contract basis; Caterers; Merchandising machine operators

(G-13172)
ELAINE WILLEY
24979 Len St (19973-6765)
PHONE..................302 536-1286
Elaine Willey, Dir
EMP: 6 EST: 2019
SALES (est): 100.13K Privately Held
SIC: 8099 Health and allied services, nec

(G-13173)
ELITE LUBRICANTS LLC
8734 Concord Rd (19973-8423)
PHONE..................302 629-3301
EMP: 5 EST: 2019
SALES (est): 318.31K Privately Held
Web: www.elitelubricants.com
SIC: 5013 7389 Automotive supplies and parts; Business Activities at Non-Commercial Site

(G-13174)
EMMA KANE & VALERIE TAYLOR DAY
23856 Dove Rd (19973-7254)
PHONE..................302 629-4347
Emma Kane, Dir
EMP: 10 EST: 2005
SALES (est): 55.64K Privately Held
SIC: 8351 Group day care center

(G-13175)
ENT ALLERGY CENTER
8468 Herring Run Rd (19973-5763)
PHONE..................302 629-3400
Claude Dimarco, Owner
Candice Clayton, Off Mgr
EMP: 7 EST: 1992
SALES (est): 902.31K Privately Held
Web: www.entandallergy.com
SIC: 8011 Ears, nose, and throat specialist: physician/surgeon

(G-13176)
ENTERPRISE RENTACAR
26876 Sussex Hwy (19973-8599)
PHONE..................302 628-2931
EMP: 7 EST: 2015
SALES (est): 100.97K Privately Held
Web: www.enterprise.com
SIC: 7514 Rent-a-car service

(G-13177)
EPHPHATHA MED CARE SVCS LLC
1350 Middleford Rd Ste 501 (19973-3664)
PHONE..................925 222-9572
Emanie Dorival, CEO
EMP: 7 EST: 2019
SALES (est): 271.55K Privately Held
Web: www.ephphathamedical.com
SIC: 8099 Health and allied services, nec

(G-13178)
ERIC C JAMES
Also Called: Sound Improvements
26735 Asbury Meadows Ln (19973-7104)
PHONE..................302 841-0930
Eric James, Prin
EMP: 5 EST: 2010
SALES (est): 94.25K Privately Held
SIC: 1731 Sound equipment specialization

(G-13179)
EXACT CONSTRUCTION OF DE
Rr 2 Box 308a (19973)
PHONE..................302 629-0464
Dennis Mancinelli, Owner
EMP: 5 EST: 1994
SALES (est): 100K Privately Held
SIC: 1521 Single-family housing construction

(G-13180)
EXTERIOR HOMEWORKS LLC
18 E 6th St (19973-4536)
P.O. Box 823 (19973-0823)
PHONE..................302 249-0012
EMP: 5 EST: 2015
SALES (est): 122.77K Privately Held
SIC: 1522 Residential construction, nec

(G-13181)
F S D TRUCKING
14596 Concord Rd (19973-8241)
PHONE..................302 629-7498
Frank Dill, Prin
EMP: 5 EST: 2008
SALES (est): 242.81K Privately Held
SIC: 4212 Dump truck haulage

(G-13182)
FALCO INDUSTRIES INC
200 Bedford Falls Dr Unit 1 (19973-1594)
PHONE..................302 628-1170
EMP: 2 EST: 2006
SALES (est): 114.56K Privately Held
SIC: 3999 Atomizers, toiletry

(G-13183)
FANTASY BEAUTY SALON
224 High St (19973-3932)
PHONE..................302 629-6762
Sara Lee Thomas, Owner
EMP: 7 EST: 1970
SALES (est): 119.25K Privately Held
SIC: 7231 Hairdressers

(G-13184)
FEDEX GROUND PACKAGE SYS INC
Also Called: Fedex
161 Venture Dr (19973-1576)
PHONE..................800 463-3339
EMP: 6
SALES (corp-wide): 90.16B Publicly Held
Web: www.fedex.com
SIC: 4212 Delivery service, vehicular
HQ: Fedex Ground Package System, Inc.
1000 Fedex Dr
Coraopolis PA 15108
800 463-3339

(G-13185)
FIDELITY ENGINEERING
25600 Business Park (19973-4292)
PHONE..................302 536-7655
Jim Slechta, Pr
EMP: 10 EST: 2013
SALES (est): 394.78K Privately Held
Web: www.fidelitybsg.com
SIC: 8711 Engineering services

(G-13186)
FIRST STATE FABRICATION LLC
Also Called: First State Fabrication
26546 Seaford Rd (19973-5949)
P.O. Box 763 (19956-0763)
PHONE..................302 875-2417
Scott Calloway, Managing Member
EMP: 6 EST: 1999
SALES (est): 1.09MM Privately Held
Web: www.firststatefab.com
SIC: 3441 Fabricated structural metal

(G-13187)
FIRST STATE ORAL MXLLFCIAL SRG
9096 Riverside Dr (19973-3658)
PHONE..................302 883-6051
Douglas Ditty, Mgr
EMP: 9 EST: 2017
SALES (est): 236.75K Privately Held
Web: www.firststateoms.com
SIC: 8021 Dental surgeon

(G-13188)
FOGARTY LLC
5 Coty Ln (19973-8016)
PHONE..................610 731-4804
EMP: 7 EST: 2018
SALES (est): 246.46K Privately Held
SIC: 8082 Home health care services

(G-13189)
FORTALEZA FITNESS
27431 Patricks Ln (19973-8584)
PHONE..................302 448-0922
Larissa Quintero, Prin
EMP: 5 EST: 2018
SALES (est): 29.54K Privately Held
SIC: 7991 Physical fitness facilities

GEOGRAPHIC SECTION
Seaford - Sussex County (G-13218)

(G-13190)
FREEDOM RIDES AUTO
26831 Sussex Hwy (19973-8529)
P.O. Box 650 (19973-0650)
PHONE.................................302 422-4559
Kelly Gale, *Prin*
EMP: 5 **EST:** 2012
SALES (est): 1.83MM **Privately Held**
Web: www.freedomridesauto.com
SIC: 7538 General automotive repair shops

(G-13191)
FSD INC
14596 Concord Rd (19973-8241)
PHONE.................................302 629-7498
L Franklin Dill, *Prin*
EMP: 5 **EST:** 2012
SALES (est): 248.09K **Privately Held**
SIC: 7389 Business Activities at Non-Commercial Site

(G-13192)
G ALVAREZ PAINTING
12329 Concord Rd (19973-8273)
PHONE.................................443 783-2240
Guillermo Alvarez, *Prin*
EMP: 5 **EST:** 2014
SALES (est): 60.66K **Privately Held**
SIC: 1721 Painting and paper hanging

(G-13193)
G K SERVICES 238
415 Harrington St (19973-3721)
PHONE.................................302 629-6729
Pat Fridley, *Mgr*
EMP: 6 **EST:** 2008
SALES (est): 113.85K **Privately Held**
SIC: 7213 Uniform supply

(G-13194)
GAEA PROPERTY DEVELOPMENT LLC
27964 Sussex Hwy (19973-8558)
PHONE.................................302 536-7646
EMP: 5 **EST:** 2012
SALES (est): 80.18K **Privately Held**
SIC: 6512 Nonresidential building operators

(G-13195)
GARDNER INDUSTRIES INC
25938 Nanticoke Ave (19973-4012)
PHONE.................................302 448-9195
EMP: 6 **EST:** 2016
SALES (est): 74.76K **Privately Held**
Web: www.gardner-gibson.com
SIC: 3999 Manufacturing industries, nec

(G-13196)
GARDNER-GIBSON MFG INC
25938 Nanticoke Ave (19973-4012)
PHONE.................................302 628-4290
EMP: 10
SALES (corp-wide): 923.49MM **Privately Held**
Web: www.gardner-gibson.com
SIC: 2951 Asphalt paving mixtures and blocks
HQ: Gardner-Gibson Manufacturing, Inc.
4161 E 7th Ave
Tampa FL 33605
813 248-2101

(G-13197)
GEORGE MILES & BUHR LLC
Also Called: Gmb - Seaford
400 High St (19973-3914)
PHONE.................................302 628-1421
EMP: 5
SALES (corp-wide): 13.46MM **Privately Held**

Web: www.gmbnet.com
SIC: 8711 Consulting engineer
PA: George, Miles & Buhr Llc
206 W Main St
Salisbury MD 21801
410 742-3115

(G-13198)
GINA K ALDERSON MD
24488 Sussex Hwy Ste 6 (19973-8470)
PHONE.................................302 628-7730
Gina Alderson, *Ofcr*
EMP: 8 **EST:** 2017
SALES (est): 140.96K **Privately Held**
SIC: 8011 Offices and clinics of medical doctors

(G-13199)
GOVERNOR ROSS MANSION & PLNTN
203 High St (19973-3909)
PHONE.................................302 628-9500
Margaret Alexander, *Mgr*
EMP: 6 **EST:** 2014
SALES (est): 82.44K **Privately Held**
SIC: 8412 Museum

(G-13200)
GOVPLUS LLC
Also Called: GOVPLUS LLC
22870 Sussex Hwy (19973-5852)
PHONE.................................302 628-6150
Pamela Jones, *Brnch Mgr*
EMP: 10
SALES (corp-wide): 9.07B **Publicly Held**
Web: www.govplus.com
SIC: 6022 State commercial banks
HQ: Citizens Bank, National Association
1 Citizens Plz
Providence RI 02903

(G-13201)
GRIFFIN HIGGINS TEAM LLC
24994 Sussex Hwy (19973-8466)
PHONE.................................302 856-1458
EMP: 5 **EST:** 2016
SALES (est): 244.95K **Privately Held**
Web: www.griffinhigginsteam.com
SIC: 6531 Real estate agent, residential

(G-13202)
GUARDIAN ADVISORS LLC
60 Rivers End Dr (19973-8009)
PHONE.................................302 220-8729
Chris Theis, *Prin*
EMP: 5 **EST:** 2018
SALES (est): 71.3K **Privately Held**
SIC: 6282 Investment advisory service

(G-13203)
GUARDIAN GENERAL
112 S Tull Dr (19973-1182)
PHONE.................................443 205-1210
Julie Frey, *Prin*
EMP: 5 **EST:** 2018
SALES (est): 106.91K **Privately Held**
SIC: 8699 Membership organizations, nec

(G-13204)
H & H STABLES INC
26705 River Rd (19973-4341)
P.O. Box 1420 (19973-5420)
PHONE.................................302 629-5100
Charles Tribbett, *Mgr*
EMP: 7 **EST:** 2001
SALES (est): 84.79K **Privately Held**
SIC: 7999 Amusement and recreation, nec

(G-13205)
HAMILTON DISTRIBUTORS INC
6920 Robin Dr (19973-6844)
PHONE.................................302 542-7860
Clayton Hamilton, *Prin*
EMP: 5 **EST:** 2018
SALES (est): 207.68K **Privately Held**
SIC: 5199 Nondurable goods, nec

(G-13206)
HAMPTON INN SEAFORD
Also Called: Hampton By Hilton
799 N Dual Hwy (19973)
PHONE.................................302 629-4500
Theresa Horseman, *Prin*
EMP: 18 **EST:** 2009
SALES (est): 77.84K **Privately Held**
Web: www.hilton.com
SIC: 7011 Hotels and motels

(G-13207)
HARBOR HOUSE SEAFOOD INC (PA)
Also Called: Harbor House Seafood
504 Bridgeville Hwy (19973-1522)
PHONE.................................302 629-0444
Gary Colbourne, *Pr*
Mark Bryan, *
▲ **EMP:** 71 **EST:** 1987
SQ FT: 6,600
SALES (est): 26.35MM
SALES (corp-wide): 26.35MM **Privately Held**
Web: www.harborhouseseafood.com
SIC: 5146 Seafoods

(G-13208)
HARIM USA LTD (PA)
126 N Shipley St (19973-3100)
P.O. Box 1380 (19966-5380)
PHONE.................................302 629-9136
EMP: 20 **EST:** 2011
SALES (est): 345.31MM
SALES (corp-wide): 345.31MM **Privately Held**
Web: www.allenharimllc.com
SIC: 2015 Poultry, processed, nsk

(G-13209)
HARROLD & SON INC
27129 Woodland Rd (19973-6961)
PHONE.................................302 629-9504
EMP: 6 **EST:** 1981
SALES (est): 492.64K **Privately Held**
SIC: 1796 Millwright

(G-13210)
HERR FOODS INCORPORATED
22706 Sussex Hwy (19973-5837)
PHONE.................................302 628-9161
TOLL FREE: 800
Kevin Johnson, *Mgr*
EMP: 28
SALES (corp-wide): 392.21MM **Privately Held**
Web: www.herrs.com
SIC: 5145 Snack foods
PA: Herr Foods Incorporated
20 Herr Dr
Nottingham PA 19362
610 932-9330

(G-13211)
HOLLYWOOD GRILL RESTAURANT
Also Called: Hampton Inn
799 N Dual Hwy (19973)
PHONE.................................302 629-4500
Shalin Patel, *Genl Mgr*
EMP: 76
SALES (corp-wide): 8.88MM **Privately Held**

Web: www.hilton.com
SIC: 7011 Motels
PA: Hollywood Grill Restaurant Inc
3513 Concord Pike # 3300
Wilmington DE 19803
302 655-1348

(G-13212)
HOME SWEEP HOME
21 Crossgate Dr (19973-1249)
PHONE.................................302 536-7339
EMP: 6 **EST:** 2016
SALES (est): 20.74K **Privately Held**
Web: www.hshcleaning.com
SIC: 7699 Cleaning services

(G-13213)
HOME TEAM REALTY
959 Norman Eskridge Hwy (19973-1719)
PHONE.................................302 629-7711
Frank Parks, *CEO*
EMP: 11 **EST:** 2002
SALES (est): 939.4K **Privately Held**
Web: www.4htr.com
SIC: 6531 Real estate agent, residential

(G-13214)
HOMELESS CAT HELPERS INC
550 N Pine St (19973-2518)
P.O. Box 1234 (19973-5234)
PHONE.................................302 344-3015
EMP: 10 **EST:** 2010
SALES (est): 162.15K **Privately Held**
SIC: 0752 Shelters, animal

(G-13215)
HOMESTEAD FUNDING CORP
116 S Market St (19973-4130)
PHONE.................................302 628-2828
EMP: 13 **EST:** 2013
SALES (est): 133.62K **Privately Held**
Web: www.homesteadfunding.com
SIC: 6162 Mortgage bankers

(G-13216)
HOOBER INC
6367 Stein Hwy Ste A (19973-6942)
PHONE.................................302 629-3075
Allen Quillen, *Brnch Mgr*
EMP: 18
SALES (corp-wide): 24.92MM **Privately Held**
Web: www.hoober.com
SIC: 5083 Agricultural machinery and equipment
PA: Hoober, Inc.
3452 Old Phladelphia Pike
Intercourse PA 17534
717 768-8231

(G-13217)
HOPES HELPING HANDS LLC
1330 Middleford Rd Ste 303 (19973-3648)
PHONE.................................443 365-5115
Michelle Harris, *Prin*
EMP: 7 **EST:** 2018
SALES (est): 230.74K **Privately Held**
Web: www.hopeshelpinghandsllc.org
SIC: 8322 Individual and family services

(G-13218)
HYDROPAC
742 Sussex Ave (19973-2057)
PHONE.................................410 306-6345
Don Matheny, *Prin*
EMP: 5 **EST:** 2018
SALES (est): 123.1K **Privately Held**
Web: www.labproductsinc.com
SIC: 8748 Business consulting, nec

Seaford - Sussex County (G-13219)

(G-13219)
IG BURTON & COMPANY INC
24799 Sussex Hwy (19973-8463)
PHONE..........................302 629-2800
I G Burton, *Mgr*
EMP: 87
SALES (corp-wide): 51.18MM **Privately Held**
Web: www.igburton.com
SIC: 5511 5013 Automobiles, new and used; Motor vehicle supplies and new parts
PA: I.G. Burton & Company, Inc.
  793 Bay Rd
  Milford DE 19963
  302 422-3041

(G-13220)
II ALFRED COLLINS
15005 County Seat Hwy (19973-8299)
PHONE..........................302 542-7010
Alfred Collins, *Pr*
EMP: 7 **EST:** 2017
SALES (est): 24.27K **Privately Held**
SIC: 8049 Offices of health practitioner

(G-13221)
IMPACT GRAPHIX
415 Harrington St (19973-3721)
PHONE..........................302 337-7076
Thomas Weaver, *Pr*
EMP: 15 **EST:** 2015
SALES (est): 466.17K **Privately Held**
Web: www.impactgraphix302.com
SIC: 3993 Signs and advertising specialties

(G-13222)
INFECTOUS DSEASE SOLUTIONS LLC
1320 Middleford Rd Ste 202 (19973-3649)
PHONE..........................302 841-0634
Vincenzo Scotto D'antuono, *Prin*
EMP: 8 **EST:** 2010
SALES (est): 65.17K **Privately Held**
SIC: 8011 Infectious disease specialist, physician/surgeon

(G-13223)
INTEGRA ADM GROUP INC (PA)
Also Called: F & S Property Management Co
110 S Shipley St (19973-3714)
PHONE..........................800 959-3518
David Smith, *Pr*
EMP: 13 **EST:** 1971
SQ FT: 2,000
SALES (est): 4.51MM
SALES (corp-wide): 4.51MM **Privately Held**
Web: www.integratpa.com
SIC: 6411 Insurance claim processing, except medical

(G-13224)
INTEGRITY BRANDS LLC
10467 Foxtail Ct (19973-7544)
PHONE..........................302 853-0709
Brandon Tull, *Prin*
EMP: 5 **EST:** 2014
SALES (est): 222.95K **Privately Held**
SIC: 8748 Business consulting, nec

(G-13225)
IRON LION ENTERPRISES INC
22319 Dixie Ln (19973-6661)
PHONE..........................302 628-8320
EMP: 2 **EST:** 1990
SALES (est): 166.11K **Privately Held**
SIC: 3965 Fasteners, hooks and eyes

(G-13226)
J & L SERVICES INC
5670 Galestown Reliance Rd (19973-6044)
PHONE..........................410 943-3355
James A Burt, *Pr*
Hazel Burt, *Sec*
EMP: 11 **EST:** 1986
SALES (est): 485.71K **Privately Held**
SIC: 1799 1751 1521 Building site preparation; Carpentry work; Single-family housing construction

(G-13227)
J AND J DISPLAY
101 Park Ave Unit 2 (19973-5798)
P.O. Box 237 (19973-0237)
PHONE..........................302 628-4190
Robert Hemmen, *Managing Member*
▲ **EMP:** 3 **EST:** 2005
SALES (est): 258.32K **Privately Held**
Web: www.jjdisplay.com
SIC: 2542 Partitions and fixtures, except wood

(G-13228)
JACKSON HEWITT TAX SERVICE (PA)
Also Called: Jackson Hewitt Tax Service
1004 W Stein Hwy (19973-1145)
PHONE..........................302 629-4548
EMP: 6 **EST:** 1993
SQ FT: 1,800
SALES (est): 427.64K **Privately Held**
Web: www.jacksonhewitt.com
SIC: 7291 Tax return preparation services

(G-13229)
JAMES F PALMER (PA)
Also Called: Mantikote Podiaky
8857 Riverside Dr (19973-3654)
PHONE..........................302 629-6162
James F Palmer, *Owner*
EMP: 5 **EST:** 1992
SALES (est): 817.33K **Privately Held**
SIC: 8043 Offices and clinics of podiatrists

(G-13230)
JASON L TORLISH SR
9415 Cherry Tree Ln (19973-9705)
PHONE..........................302 682-3874
Jason Torlish, *Prin*
EMP: 5 **EST:** 2017
SALES (est): 25.64K **Privately Held**
SIC: 0783 Ornamental shrub and tree services

(G-13231)
JBS SOUDERTON INC
Also Called: Mopak
4957 Stein Hwy Rte 20 W (19973-6762)
PHONE..........................302 629-0725
Donnie Kerr, *Mgr*
EMP: 3
Web: www.mopac.com
SIC: 2048 Livestock feeds
HQ: Jbs Souderton, Inc.
  249 Allentown Rd
  Souderton PA 18964
  215 723-5555

(G-13232)
JCR ENTERPRISES INC
126 N Shipley St (19973-3100)
PHONE..........................302 629-9163
Pat Cawley, *Pr*
Warren R Allen Junior, *VP*
EMP: 25 **EST:** 2002
SQ FT: 80,000
SALES (est): 2.96MM **Privately Held**
SIC: 2015 Turkey processing and slaughtering

(G-13233)
JEFFREY L PREMO
310 High St (19973-3912)
PHONE..........................302 877-0468
Jeffrey L Premo, *Owner*
EMP: 5 **EST:** 2007
SALES (est): 165.66K **Privately Held**
Web: www.premohurtfinancial.com
SIC: 8721 Certified public accountant

(G-13234)
JEFFS TOTAL HEATING N AIR
324 E Poplar St (19973-3414)
P.O. Box 1721 (19973-6121)
PHONE..........................302 682-1816
Jeff Slemons, *Prin*
EMP: 6 **EST:** 2010
SALES (est): 153.63K **Privately Held**
Web: www.jeffstotalheatingandair.net
SIC: 1711 Warm air heating and air conditioning contractor

(G-13235)
JOAQUIN CABRERA MD
8472 Herring Run Rd (19973-5763)
PHONE..........................302 629-8977
Joaquin Cabrera Md, *Owner*
EMP: 7 **EST:** 1989
SALES (est): 420.07K **Privately Held**
Web: www.easternbulk.net
SIC: 8011 Obstetrician

(G-13236)
JOHN C LYNCH DDS PA
543 N Shipley St Ste E (19973-2339)
PHONE..........................302 629-7115
John Lynch D.d.s., *Pr*
EMP: 8 **EST:** 1976
SALES (est): 728.84K **Privately Held**
Web: www.lrkdental.com
SIC: 8021 Dentists' office

(G-13237)
JOHN R GUNDRY
4610 Woodland Church Rd (19973-4777)
PHONE..........................302 629-9877
John R Gundry, *Prin*
John R Gundry, *Owner*
EMP: 5 **EST:** 1956
SALES (est): 126.43K **Privately Held**
SIC: 0191 General farms, primarily crop

(G-13238)
JOHN WINGATE INSURANCE
8140 1st St (19973-5963)
PHONE..........................302 339-5185
John Wingate, *Prin*
EMP: 5 **EST:** 2011
SALES (est): 91.77K **Privately Held**
Web: www.johnwingateinsurance.com
SIC: 6411 Insurance agents, brokers, and service

(G-13239)
JRM CONSTRUCTION LLC
23748 German Rd (19973-7307)
PHONE..........................302 362-7453
EMP: 6 **EST:** 2017
SALES (est): 321.41K **Privately Held**
SIC: 1521 Single-family housing construction

(G-13240)
JULIE A CARSON PA
24459 Sussex Hwy (19973-4433)
PHONE..........................302 629-3099
Julie Carson, *Pr*
EMP: 6 **EST:** 2017
SALES (est): 68.49K **Privately Held**
SIC: 8049 Offices of health practitioner

(G-13241)
JULIE H REMENTER
900 S Arch St (19973-4553)
PHONE..........................302 628-4416
Julie Rementer, *Prin*
EMP: 6 **EST:** 2017
SALES (est): 22.18K **Privately Held**
SIC: 8049 Offices of health practitioner

(G-13242)
K SUPPLY COMPANY INC
208 Peterson Dr (19973-1276)
PHONE..........................302 629-3925
EMP: 13
SALES (corp-wide): 4.66MM **Privately Held**
Web: www.ksupplycompany.com
SIC: 5099 Brass goods
PA: K Supply Company, Inc.
  930 Nixon Chapel Rd
  Albertville AL 35950
  256 894-0034

(G-13243)
KAREN SCHREIBER
Also Called: Little Sprouts Learning Academ
425 E Stein Hwy (19973)
PHONE..........................302 628-3007
Karen Schreiber, *Owner*
EMP: 8 **EST:** 2015
SQ FT: 4,300
SALES (est): 191.26K **Privately Held**
SIC: 8351 Preschool center

(G-13244)
KATHLEEN KENNEY
1310 Middleford Rd # 101 (19973-3670)
PHONE..........................302 541-5700
Kathleen Kenney, *Pr*
EMP: 6 **EST:** 2017
SALES (est): 69.45K **Privately Held**
SIC: 8049 Offices of health practitioner

(G-13245)
KAYAVA CREATIONS LLC
109 Valley Run (19973-4836)
PHONE..........................302 430-2231
EMP: 2 **EST:** 2020
SALES (est): 20K **Privately Held**
SIC: 2396 Printing and embossing on plastics fabric articles

(G-13246)
KAYE CONSTRUCTION
22223 Eskridge Rd (19973-8144)
PHONE..........................302 628-6962
Edward J Kaye, *Owner*
Edward J Kaye, *Pr*
EMP: 6 **EST:** 2007
SALES (est): 445.88K **Privately Held**
Web: www.kayeconstruction.com
SIC: 1521 1794 4953 New construction, single-family houses; Excavation work; Recycling, waste materials

(G-13247)
KEITH A SARGENT DO
100 Rawlins Dr (19973-5881)
PHONE..........................302 990-3300
Keith Sargent, *Pr*
EMP: 11 **EST:** 2017
SALES (est): 54.13K **Privately Held**
Web: www.tidalhealth.org
SIC: 8011 Offices and clinics of medical doctors

GEOGRAPHIC SECTION

Seaford - Sussex County (G-13276)

(G-13248)
KENCO GROUP INC
Also Called: KENCO GROUP, INC.
1700 Dulany St (19973-1906)
PHONE..................302 629-4295
Donald Colburn, *Brnch Mgr*
EMP: 6
SALES (corp-wide): 1.36B Privately Held
Web: www.kencogroup.com
SIC: 4225 6512 General warehousing; Nonresidential building operators
PA: Rivermill Group, Inc.
  2001 Rverside Dr Ste 3100
  Chattanooga TN 37406
  800 758-3289

(G-13249)
KIM AND EVANS FMLY FNDTION INC
123 Village Dr (19973-8035)
PHONE..................302 629-7166
Joseph Kim, *Prin*
EMP: 5 **EST:** 2018
SALES (est): 75.66K Privately Held
Web: www.kimandevansff.org
SIC: 8641 Civic and social associations

(G-13250)
KINGS CUST CLEAN & HM SER LLC
103 Shallow Brooke Ct (19973-4825)
PHONE..................302 542-3920
EMP: 5 **EST:** 2014
SALES (est): 41.67K Privately Held
SIC: 7699 Cleaning services

(G-13251)
L & L GEOTHERMAL HVAC SVCS LLC
9592 Domenica Ct (19973-8162)
P.O. Box 403 (19956-0403)
PHONE..................302 536-7120
EMP: 5 **EST:** 2011
SALES (est): 137.29K Privately Held
Web: www.landlgeothermalheatingandair.com
SIC: 1711 Warm air heating and air conditioning contractor

(G-13252)
LA BELLA MED SPA
1350 Middleford Rd Ste 502 (19973-3664)
PHONE..................302 990-8770
Ivonne Herrara, *Prin*
EMP: 5 **EST:** 2016
SALES (est): 51.31K Privately Held
SIC: 7299 Personal appearance services

(G-13253)
LA RED HEALTH CENTER INC
300 High St (19973-3940)
PHONE..................408 533-3189
EMP: 53
SALES (corp-wide): 14.82MM Privately Held
Web: www.laredhealthcenter.org
SIC: 8099 Blood related health services
PA: La Red Health Center, Inc.
  21444 Carmean Way
  Georgetown DE 19947
  302 855-1233

(G-13254)
LA ZMX RADIO
26715 Sussex Hwy (19973-8527)
PHONE..................302 702-2952
EMP: 5 **EST:** 2017
SALES (est): 34.59K Privately Held
Web: www.lazmxradio.com
SIC: 4832 Radio broadcasting stations

(G-13255)
LAB PRODUCTS LLC
742 Sussex Ave (19973-2057)
P.O. Box 700 (21001-0700)
PHONE..................302 628-4300
John Soper, *COO*
▲ **EMP:** 11 **EST:** 1969
SQ FT: 2,000
SALES (est): 2.69MM
SALES (corp-wide): 1.9B Privately Held
Web: www.labproductsinc.com
SIC: 8734 Testing laboratories
HQ: Avidity Science, Llc
  819 Bakke Ave
  Waterford WI 53185
  262 534-5181

(G-13256)
LAMBDEN BUS SERVICE LLC
10174 Airport Rd (19973-8508)
PHONE..................302 629-4358
Beverly Lambden, *Owner*
EMP: 5 **EST:** 1970
SALES (est): 366.86K Privately Held
SIC: 4151 School buses

(G-13257)
LANK JOHNSON AND TULL
521 N Market Street Ext (19973-1574)
P.O. Box 418 (19973-0418)
PHONE..................302 629-9543
Richard Tull, *Genl Mgr*
EMP: 5
SALES (corp-wide): 2.38MM Privately Held
Web: www.ljtcpa.com
SIC: 8721 Certified public accountant
PA: Lank, Johnson And Tull
  268 Milford Harrington Hw
  Milford DE 19963
  302 422-3308

(G-13258)
LEGACY VULCAN LLC
14208 County Seat Hwy (19973-8314)
PHONE..................302 875-5733
EMP: 4
Web: www.vulcanmaterials.com
SIC: 3273 Ready-mixed concrete
HQ: Legacy Vulcan, Llc
  1200 Urban Center Dr
  Vestavia AL 35242
  205 298-3000

(G-13259)
LEWIS MILLER INC
Also Called: Miller Lewis Surveyors
8957 Middleford Rd (19973-7829)
PHONE..................302 629-9895
Don Miller, *Pr*
EMP: 8 **EST:** 1961
SALES (est): 540K Privately Held
SIC: 8713 Surveying services

(G-13260)
LIBERTY TAX SERVICE
614 W Stein Hwy (19973-1204)
PHONE..................302 404-2140
EMP: 6 **EST:** 2019
SALES (est): 111.56K Privately Held
Web: www.libertytax.com
SIC: 7291 Tax return preparation services

(G-13261)
LIL KRITTERS CHILDCARE
201 Ross St (19973-1618)
PHONE..................302 362-9047
Deketra Mstos, *Prin*
EMP: 8 **EST:** 2016
SALES (est): 63.61K Privately Held
SIC: 8351 Child day care services

(G-13262)
LISA RYAN HOBBS DPM
543 N Shipley St Ste C (19973-2339)
PHONE..................302 629-3000
Lisa Hobbs, *Prin*
EMP: 6 **EST:** 2017
SALES (est): 73.85K Privately Held
SIC: 8043 Offices and clinics of podiatrists

(G-13263)
LITTLE GYM
23 Tidewater Dr (19973-9766)
PHONE..................302 856-2310
EMP: 5 **EST:** 2018
SALES (est): 41.98K Privately Held
Web: www.thelittlegym.com
SIC: 7999 Gymnastic instruction, non-membership

(G-13264)
LON KIEFFER
10589 Wilkinson Dr (19973-7927)
PHONE..................888 466-2379
Lon Kieffer, *Prin*
EMP: 5 **EST:** 2010
SALES (est): 105.96K Privately Held
Web: www.defenderofcaregivers.com
SIC: 8999 Author

(G-13265)
LOWES HOME CENTERS LLC
Also Called: Lowe's
22880 Sussex Hwy (19973-5852)
PHONE..................302 536-4000
EMP: 92
SALES (corp-wide): 97.06B Publicly Held
Web: www.lowes.com
SIC: 5211 5031 5722 5064 Home centers; Building materials, exterior; Household appliance stores; Electrical appliances, television and radio
HQ: Lowe's Home Centers, Llc
  1000 Lowes Blvd
  Mooresville NC 28117
  336 658-4000

(G-13266)
LRK DENTAL
543 N Shipley St (19973-2339)
PHONE..................302 629-7115
EMP: 10 **EST:** 2019
SALES (est): 471.44K Privately Held
Web: www.lrkdental.com
SIC: 8021 Dentists' office

(G-13267)
LTC SERVICES LLC
125 E Locust St (19973-2503)
PHONE..................302 396-8598
Enock Jean, *Prin*
EMP: 6 **EST:** 2014
SALES (est): 166.34K Privately Held
SIC: 1542 Commercial and office building, new construction

(G-13268)
LUCKY WELLNESS CENTER INC
120 N Cannon St Unit 1 (19973-3302)
PHONE..................302 990-5441
Di Huanyao, *Asst Sec*
EMP: 6 **EST:** 2018
SALES (est): 95.06K Privately Held
SIC: 8099 Health and allied services, nec

(G-13269)
LYNN CONSTRUCTION LLC
7041 Atlanta Cir (19973-6836)
PHONE..................302 236-6596
Bartley Knox, *Pr*
EMP: 9 **EST:** 2014
SALES (est): 941.52K Privately Held
SIC: 1521 Single-family housing construction

(G-13270)
M HS LIFT OF DELAWARE INC
25560 Business Park (19973-4201)
PHONE..................302 629-4490
Robert Levin, *Pr*
EMP: 15 **EST:** 2011
SALES (est): 226.66K Privately Held
Web: www.mhslift.com
SIC: 5084 Materials handling machinery

(G-13271)
MAF INDUSTRIES
27797 Oneals Rd (19973-6301)
PHONE..................302 249-1254
Nicholas Disalvo, *Prin*
EMP: 6 **EST:** 2015
SALES (est): 208.43K Privately Held
Web: www.maf-roda.com
SIC: 3999 Manufacturing industries, nec

(G-13272)
MANICURED LAWNS
9804 Nanticoke Cir (19973-8642)
PHONE..................302 853-2222
Justin Hignutt, *Prin*
EMP: 5 **EST:** 2008
SALES (est): 80K Privately Held
SIC: 0782 Lawn care services

(G-13273)
MANUFACTURERS & TRADERS TR CO
Also Called: M&T
509 W Stein Hwy (19973-1201)
PHONE..................302 856-4470
Dennis Kinnel, *Brnch Mgr*
EMP: 7
SALES (corp-wide): 8.6B Publicly Held
Web: ir.mtb.com
SIC: 6022 State commercial banks
HQ: Manufacturers And Traders Trust Company
  1 M&T Plz Fl 3
  Buffalo NY 14203
  716 842-4200

(G-13274)
MANUFACTURING SUPPORT INDS INC
Also Called: MSI
108 Park Ave (19973-9479)
PHONE..................410 334-6140
Lee Lusby, *CEO*
Robert Correa, *Pr*
EMP: 19 **EST:** 1998
SALES (est): 4.09MM Privately Held
Web: www.mfg-support.com
SIC: 3599 Machine shop, jobbing and repair

(G-13275)
MARK EVANGELISTA MD
1501 Middleford Rd (19973-3615)
PHONE..................302 629-4569
Mark Evangelista, *Prin*
EMP: 8 **EST:** 2017
SALES (est): 107.58K Privately Held
Web: www.seafordinternalmedicine.com
SIC: 8011 Internal medicine, physician/surgeon

(G-13276)
MAVERICK TATTOO COMPANY LLC
22585 Bridgeville Hwy (19973-5822)
PHONE..................443 858-1511
Tanya Zamm, *Prin*

Seaford - Sussex County (G-13277) GEOGRAPHIC SECTION

EMP: 5 EST: 2016
SALES (est): 21.23K **Privately Held**
SIC: 7299 Tattoo parlor

(G-13277)
MC MULLEN SEPTIC SERVICE INC
22593 Bridgeville Hwy (19973-5822)
PHONE..................................302 629-6221
Mike Mcmullen, *Pr*
Brian Mcmullen, *VP*
EMP: 5 EST: 1970
SALES (est): 499.25K **Privately Held**
Web: www.mcmullenseptic.com
SIC: 7699 Septic tank cleaning service

(G-13278)
MEADE INC
22536 Sussex Hwy (19973-5835)
PHONE..................................302 262-3394
Darryl Meade, *Brnch Mgr*
EMP: 5
Web: www.meade100.com
SIC: 2759 Screen printing
PA: Meade, Inc.
    8207 Cloverleaf Dr Frnt
    Millersville MD 21108

(G-13279)
MEARS HEALTH CAMPUS
200 Rawlins Dr (19973-5812)
PHONE..................................302 628-6300
Steve Rose, *Prin*
EMP: 8 EST: 2018
SALES (est): 237.05K **Privately Held**
SIC: 8071 Medical laboratories

(G-13280)
MERNIES MARKET
4610 Woodland Church Rd (19973-4777)
PHONE..................................302 629-9877
John Gundry, *Pt*
Anthony Gundry, *Pt*
EMP: 9 EST: 1987
SALES (est): 247.54K **Privately Held**
SIC: 0161 Market garden

(G-13281)
MESSICK AND JOHNSON LLC
955 Norman Eskridge Hwy (19973-1719)
P.O. Box 505 (19973-0505)
PHONE..................................302 628-3111
EMP: 5 EST: 2006
SALES (est): 339.21K **Privately Held**
Web: www.messick-johnsonbuilders.com
SIC: 1521 New construction, single-family houses

(G-13282)
MHS LIFT OF DELAWARE INC
25560 Business Park (19973-4201)
PHONE..................................302 629-4490
Bo Dryden, *Mgr*
EMP: 16 EST: 2011
SALES (est): 189.81K **Privately Held**
Web: www.mhslift.com
SIC: 7359 Equipment rental and leasing, nec

(G-13283)
MID-ATLANTIC SERVICES A-TEAM (PA)
8558 Elks Rd (19973-5643)
P.O. Box 708 (19973-0708)
PHONE..................................302 628-3403
Rosemary Everton, *Pr*
Rosemary Everton, *Pr*
Michael R Everton, *
Mary Baker, *Stockholder**
Theresa Everton, *Stockholder**
EMP: 31 EST: 1984
SQ FT: 3,000

SALES (est): 2.47MM
SALES (corp-wide): 2.47MM **Privately Held**
Web: www.ateamcorp.com
SIC: 7349 Janitorial service, contract basis

(G-13284)
MILLER SAMUEL MD
543 N Shipley St Ste A (19973-2339)
PHONE..................................302 629-8662
Samuel Miller, *Prin*
EMP: 8 EST: 2017
SALES (est): 54.13K **Privately Held**
SIC: 8011 Offices and clinics of medical doctors

(G-13285)
MINUTE LOAN CENTER
855 Norman Eskridge Hwy (19973-1717)
PHONE..................................302 629-5366
EMP: 7 EST: 2018
SALES (est): 219.39K **Privately Held**
Web: www.minuteloancenter.com
SIC: 6141 Personal credit institutions

(G-13286)
MISTY TRAVEL
26227 Line Rd (19973-5078)
PHONE..................................302 628-1815
Barbara Stetzer, *Pr*
EMP: 5 EST: 1998
SALES (est): 124.82K **Privately Held**
Web: www.misty-travel.com
SIC: 4724 Travel agencies

(G-13287)
MITCHELL JAMISON
200 Federal St (19973-5764)
PHONE..................................302 359-4163
Mitchell Jamison, *Prin*
EMP: 8 EST: 2017
SALES (est): 22.18K **Privately Held**
SIC: 8049 Offices of health practitioner

(G-13288)
MONTGOMERY CARPET CLEANING
10554 Concord Rd (19973-6338)
P.O. Box 455 (19973-0455)
PHONE..................................302 258-6036
Harry Montgomery, *Prin*
EMP: 5 EST: 2016
SALES (est): 53.68K **Privately Held**
SIC: 7699 Cleaning services

(G-13289)
MORNING STAR PUBLICATIONS INC
Also Called: Seaford Star
951 Norman Eskridge Hwy # D (19973-1719)
P.O. Box 1000 (19973-1000)
PHONE..................................302 629-9788
Bryant Richardson, *Pr*
Carol Richardson, *Treas*
EMP: 10 EST: 1996
SALES (est): 831.62K **Privately Held**
Web: www.starpublications.online
SIC: 2711 Newspapers, publishing and printing

(G-13290)
MOTEL 6
Also Called: Motel 6
24057 Sussex Hwy (19973-5873)
PHONE..................................302 990-5291
Hetal Patel, *Prin*
EMP: 11 EST: 2015
SALES (est): 236.78K **Privately Held**
Web: www.motel6.com
SIC: 7011 Hotels and motels

(G-13291)
MOUNTAIRE FARMS INC
110 N Cannon St (19973-3302)
PHONE..................................302 404-5057
EMP: 66
SALES (corp-wide): 2.07B **Privately Held**
Web: www.mountaire.com
SIC: 0191 General farms, primarily crop
HQ: Mountaire Farms Inc.
    1901 Napa Valley Dr
    Little Rock AR 72212
    501 372-6524

(G-13292)
MOVING OUT
25631 S Parkway Rd (19973-8443)
PHONE..................................302 470-5308
Jason Pierce, *Prin*
EMP: 6 EST: 2017
SALES (est): 67.07K **Privately Held**
Web: www.hireahelper.com
SIC: 4789 Transportation services, nec

(G-13293)
MT AIRE
4933 Stein Hwy (19973-6762)
PHONE..................................302 629-8739
Gene Miller, *Prin*
EMP: 7 EST: 2010
SALES (est): 82.71K **Privately Held**
Web: www.mtaire.com
SIC: 7032 Dude ranch

(G-13294)
MULLEN THOMAS R DMD PA
8466 Herring Run Rd # D (19973-5763)
PHONE..................................302 629-3588
Thomas Mullen, *Prin*
EMP: 5 EST: 1979
SALES (est): 364.64K **Privately Held**
SIC: 8021 Dental surgeon

(G-13295)
MULTI MICHEL SERVICES
107 N Pine St (19973-3319)
PHONE..................................302 628-3288
EMP: 5 EST: 2014
SALES (est): 50.82K **Privately Held**
SIC: 7291 Tax return preparation services

(G-13296)
MUNCIE INSURANCE SERVICES (PA)
Also Called: Nationwide
1011 Norman Eskridge Hwy (19973-1721)
PHONE..................................302 629-9414
Marvin Muncie, *Owner*
EMP: 6 EST: 2002
SALES (est): 794.75K **Privately Held**
Web: www.muncieinsurance.net
SIC: 6411 Insurance agents, nec

(G-13297)
MURPHYS CONSTRUCTION
11015 Pit Rd (19973-7460)
PHONE..................................302 462-0319
Bryan Murphy, *Prin*
EMP: 5 EST: 2017
SALES (est): 153.14K **Privately Held**
SIC: 1521 Single-family housing construction

(G-13298)
MURRAY JAMES
613 High St (19973-3503)
PHONE..................................302 629-3923
Murray James, *Prin*
EMP: 8 EST: 2010
SALES (est): 130.52K **Privately Held**
SIC: 8011 Obstetrician

(G-13299)
MY EYE DR OPTOMETRISTS LLC
Also Called: Myeyedr
1301 Bridgeville Hwy (19973-1616)
PHONE..................................302 629-9197
EMP: 6
SALES (corp-wide): 100.43MM **Privately Held**
Web: www.myeyedr.com
SIC: 8042 Offices and clinics of optometrists
PA: My Eye Dr. Optometrists, Llc
    8614 Wstwd Ctr Dr Ste 900
    Vienna VA 22182
    703 847-8899

(G-13300)
NANTICOKE BARIATRIC SERVICES
8472 Herring Run Rd (19973-5763)
PHONE..................................302 536-5398
EMP: 12 EST: 2017
SALES (est): 108.05K **Privately Held**
SIC: 8011 Surgeon

(G-13301)
NANTICOKE CARDIOLOGY
200 Federal St (19973-5764)
PHONE..................................302 629-9099
Richard Simons, *Pt*
Richard Simons, *Pt*
Angel Alicea, *Pt*
EMP: 15 EST: 1998
SALES (est): 779.72K **Privately Held**
Web: www.tidalhealth.org
SIC: 8011 Cardiologist and cardio-vascular specialist

(G-13302)
NANTICOKE DBTES ENDCRNLOGY CTR
801 Middleford Rd (19973-3636)
PHONE..................................302 629-0452
EMP: 12 EST: 2016
SALES (est): 146.94K **Privately Held**
Web: www.tidalhealth.org
SIC: 8011 Endocrinologist

(G-13303)
NANTICOKE FENCE LLC
23464 Sussex Hwy (19973-5869)
P.O. Box 244 (19973-0244)
PHONE..................................302 628-7808
EMP: 5 EST: 2002
SALES (est): 272.22K **Privately Held**
Web: www.nanticokefence.com
SIC: 1799 Fence construction

(G-13304)
NANTICOKE GASTROENTEROLOGY
Also Called: Dr Mackler
924 Middleford Rd (19973-3604)
PHONE..................................302 629-2229
Bradley P Mackler, *Pr*
EMP: 8 EST: 1994
SALES (est): 878.24K **Privately Held**
Web: www.nanticokegastro.com
SIC: 8011 Gastronomist

(G-13305)
NANTICOKE HEALTH SERVICES INC (PA)
801 Middleford Rd (19973-3636)
PHONE..................................302 629-6611
EMP: 416 EST: 1985
SALES (est): 164.27MM **Privately Held**
Web: www.tidalhealth.org
SIC: 8099 Medical services organization

GEOGRAPHIC SECTION — Seaford - Sussex County (G-13333)

(G-13306)
NANTICOKE INDUSTRIES LLC
28986 Cannon Dr (19973-3025)
PHONE..................302 245-8825
Grace Whitaker, *Managing Member*
Roy Whitaker, *Managing Member*
EMP: 4 **EST:** 2015
SQ FT: 3,000
SALES (est): 292.22K **Privately Held**
Web: www.tidalhealth.org
SIC: 2499 3732 Applicators, wood; Yachts, building and repairing

(G-13307)
NANTICOKE OBGYN ASSOCIATES P A
10 Tidewater Dr (19973-9768)
PHONE..................302 629-2434
James Rupp, *Pr*
EMP: 10 **EST:** 1988
SALES (est): 663.42K **Privately Held**
Web: www.tidalhealth.org
SIC: 8011 General and family practice, physician/surgeon

(G-13308)
NANTICOKE REHAB
100 Rawlins Dr (19973-5881)
PHONE..................302 629-6224
Pelot Tres, *Mgr*
EMP: 9 **EST:** 2018
SALES (est): 147.58K **Privately Held**
Web: www.tidalhealth.org
SIC: 8049 Offices of health practitioner

(G-13309)
NANTICOKE RIVER ARTS COUNCIL
Also Called: Gallery 107
324 High St (19973-3931)
P.O. Box 6 (19973-0006)
PHONE..................302 628-2787
Tammy Kearney, *VP*
EMP: 6 **EST:** 2008
SALES (est): 121.96K **Privately Held**
Web: www.nanticokeriverartscouncil.org
SIC: 8699 5944 5999 Art council; Jewelry, precious stones and precious metals; Art dealers

(G-13310)
NANTICOKE RIVER PHYSICIANS LLC
801 Middleford Rd (19973-3636)
PHONE..................302 629-9735
EMP: 13 **EST:** 2019
SALES (est): 789.24K **Privately Held**
Web: www.tidalhealth.org
SIC: 8011 Offices and clinics of medical doctors

(G-13311)
NANTICOKE SENIOR CTR
1001 W Locust St (19973-2124)
P.O. Box 406 (19973-0406)
PHONE..................302 629-4939
Sue Franckowiak, *Ex Dir*
EMP: 18 **EST:** 2009
SALES (est): 896.85K **Privately Held**
Web: www.nanticokeseniorcenter.com
SIC: 8322 Senior citizens' center or association

(G-13312)
NANTICOKE WEIGHT LOSS & GEN
8472 Herring Run Rd (19973-5763)
PHONE..................302 536-5395
EMP: 12 **EST:** 2018
SALES (est): 156.84K **Privately Held**
Web: www.tidalhealth.org
SIC: 8011 Surgeon

(G-13313)
NATIONAL HVAC SERVICE
Also Called: Comfort Service Company
N Usa Rt 13 (19973)
P.O. Box 1500 (19973-5500)
PHONE..................570 825-2894
Joe Aurillo, *Mgr*
EMP: 7
Web: www.nationalhvacservice.com
SIC: 1711 Warm air heating and air conditioning contractor
PA: National H.V.A.C. Service, Ltd
   624 Grassmere Park Ste 8
   Nashville TN 37211

(G-13314)
NATIONWIDE INSUR - WLGUS INSUR
Also Called: Nationwide
22937 Sussex Hwy (19973-5871)
PHONE..................302 629-5140
Harry Insley Junior, *Mgr*
EMP: 8 **EST:** 2017
SALES (est): 74.34K **Privately Held**
Web: www.nationwide.com
SIC: 6411 Insurance agents, nec

(G-13315)
NEAT AS A PIN LLC
24657 German Rd (19973-7332)
PHONE..................302 519-4504
Alana Maryland, *Asst Sec*
EMP: 5 **EST:** 2018
SALES (est): 97.09K **Privately Held**
Web: neat-as-a-pin-llc.ueniweb.com
SIC: 7699 Cleaning services

(G-13316)
NEMOURS FUNDATION PENSION PLAN
49 Fallon Ave (19973-1577)
PHONE..................302 629-5030
EMP: 654
SALES (corp-wide): 205.65MM **Privately Held**
Web: www.nemours.org
SIC: 8011 Pediatrician
PA: The Nemours Foundation Pension Plan
   10140 Centurion Pkwy N
   Jacksonville FL 32256
   904 697-4100

(G-13317)
NEMOURS HLTH & PREVENTION SVCS
49 Fallon Ave (19973-1577)
PHONE..................302 628-8304
John Hollis, *Brnch Mgr*
EMP: 24
Web: www.nemours.org
SIC: 8611 Community affairs and services
PA: Nemours Health And Prevention Svcs
   252 Chapman Rd Ste 200
   Newark DE 19702

(G-13318)
NEUROLOGY CENTER SOUTH DEL
24488 Sussex Hwy Ste 6 (19973-8470)
PHONE..................443 944-9733
EMP: 11 **EST:** 2018
SALES (est): 822.39K **Privately Held**
Web: www.neurodelaware.com
SIC: 8011 Neurologist

(G-13319)
NOUVIR LIGHTING CORPORATION
Also Called: Nouvir Research
20915 Sussex Hwy (19973-5692)
PHONE..................302 628-9933
Rugh Ellen Miller, *Pr*
Jack Miller, *VP*
Bernice Miller, *Stockholder*
Matthew Miller, *VP*
EMP: 10 **EST:** 1976
SALES (est): 968.14K **Privately Held**
Web: www.nouvir.com
SIC: 3357 Fiber optic cable (insulated)

(G-13320)
NOUVIR LIGHTING CORPORATION
Also Called: Design Technology
20915 Sussex Hwy (19973-5692)
PHONE..................302 628-9888
Ruth E Miller, *Pr*
EMP: 2 **EST:** 2010
SALES (est): 123.41K **Privately Held**
Web: www.nouvir.com
SIC: 3357 3643 7389 Fiber optic cable (insulated); Lightning arrestors and coils; Design services

(G-13321)
NOVACARE REHABILITATION SEAFOR
300 Health Services Dr Unit 301 (19973)
PHONE..................302 990-2951
EMP: 5 **EST:** 2017
SALES (est): 87.08K **Privately Held**
SIC: 8093 Rehabilitation center, outpatient treatment

(G-13322)
O REILLY ELECTRIC
23442 Sussex Hwy (19973-5867)
P.O. Box 225 (19973-0225)
PHONE..................302 381-6058
Frederick Oreilly, *Owner*
EMP: 10 **EST:** 2004
SALES (est): 418.93K **Privately Held**
Web: www.oreillyelectricdemd.com
SIC: 1731 General electrical contractor

(G-13323)
OIL SPOT EXPRESS LUBE CENTER
915 Norman Eskridge Hwy (19973-1719)
PHONE..................302 628-9866
EMP: 8 **EST:** 1988
SALES (est): 234.75K **Privately Held**
SIC: 7538 General automotive repair shops

(G-13324)
ONEMAIN FINANCIAL GROUP LLC
Also Called: Onemain Financial
22974 Sussex Hwy (19973-5861)
PHONE..................302 628-9253
Linda Birch, *Mgr*
EMP: 6
SALES (corp-wide): 5.06B **Publicly Held**
Web: www.onemainfinancial.com
SIC: 6282 Investment advice
HQ: Onemain Financial Group, Llc
   100 International Dr # 23
   Baltimore MD 21202
   855 663-6246

(G-13325)
ONSITE CONSTRUCTION INC
9654 Brickyard Rd Unit 2 (19973-8434)
PHONE..................302 628-4244
Kevin Pritchett, *Pr*
Kimberly George, *CFO*
EMP: 16 **EST:** 2003
SALES (est): 960.39K **Privately Held**
Web: www.onsitecon.com
SIC: 1521 Single-family housing construction

(G-13326)
ORIENT CORPORATION OF AMERICA
Also Called: Orient Corp of America
111 Park Ave (19973-9478)
PHONE..................302 628-1300
Dave Curry, *Mgr*
EMP: 20
SQ FT: 8,000
Web: www.orient-usa.com
SIC: 2865 2899 Dyes and pigments; Chemical preparations, nec
HQ: Orient Corporation Of America
   6 Commerce Dr Ste 301
   Cranford NJ 07016
   908 298-0990

(G-13327)
ORIGINAL TUBE T SHIRT COM
24455 Lighthouse Pt (19973-7850)
PHONE..................845 291-7031
EMP: 4 **EST:** 2018
SALES (est): 182.01K **Privately Held**
SIC: 2396 Screen printing on fabric articles

(G-13328)
OWENS JR LOUIS F MD PA
701 Middleford Rd (19973-3600)
P.O. Box 1675 (19973-8975)
PHONE..................302 629-0448
EMP: 8 **EST:** 2011
SALES (est): 105.56K **Privately Held**
SIC: 8011 Offices and clinics of medical doctors

(G-13329)
OWN LANE CONSTRUCTION LLC ✺
105 Loblolly Dr (19973-9001)
PHONE..................302 579-8103
EMP: 4 **EST:** 2022
SALES (est): 74.44K **Privately Held**
SIC: 1389 Construction, repair, and dismantling services

(G-13330)
PATIENT FIRST MEDICAL LLC
1330 Middleford Rd Ste 301 (19973-3648)
PHONE..................302 536-7740
EMP: 5 **EST:** 2009
SALES (est): 380.67K **Privately Held**
Web: www.patientfirst.com
SIC: 8011 Clinic, operated by physicians

(G-13331)
PAUL H AGUILLON MD
Also Called: Sussex Medical Center
401 Concord Rd (19973-4274)
PHONE..................302 629-6664
H Paul Aguillon Md, *Owner*
EMP: 6 **EST:** 1995
SALES (est): 490.95K **Privately Held**
SIC: 8011 General and family practice, physician/surgeon

(G-13332)
PENCO CORPORATION
1503 W Stein Hwy (19973-1198)
PHONE..................302 629-7911
Steve Milligan, *Mgr*
EMP: 4
SALES (corp-wide): 26.19MM **Privately Held**
Web: www.pencocorp.com
SIC: 1541 2611 Industrial buildings and warehouses; Pulp mills
PA: Penco Corporation
   1503 W Stein Hwy
   Seaford DE 19973
   302 629-7911

(G-13333)
PENCO CORPORATION
1800 Dulany St # 6 (19973-1908)
PHONE..................302 629-3061
Steve Milligan, *Mgr*

Seaford - Sussex County (G-13334)

EMP: 5
SALES (corp-wide): 24.24MM **Privately Held**
Web: www.pencocorp.com
SIC: 4225 General warehousing and storage
PA: Penco Corporation
1503 W Stein Hwy
Seaford DE 19973
302 629-7911

(G-13334)
PENCO CORPORATION (PA)
1503 W Stein Hwy (19973-1198)
P.O. Box 690 (19973-0690)
PHONE..................302 629-7911
TOLL FREE: 800
Kent T Peterson, *Pr*
George H Sapna Ii, *Sec*
EMP: 58 EST: 1949
SQ FT: 63,000
SALES (est): 24.24MM
SALES (corp-wide): 24.24MM **Privately Held**
Web: www.pencocorp.com
SIC: 4225 5074 General warehousing; Plumbing fittings and supplies

(G-13335)
PENINSULA CHIROPRACTIC CENTER
26685 Sussex Hwy (19973-8525)
PHONE..................302 629-4344
Michael Triglia, *Pr*
EMP: 7 EST: 1979
SALES (est): 347.94K **Privately Held**
Web: www.peninsulachiropcenter.com
SIC: 8041 Offices and clinics of chiropractors

(G-13336)
PENINSULA HOME CARE LLC
8466 Herring Run Rd (19973-5763)
PHONE..................302 629-4914
Todd Wiebusch, *Prin*
EMP: 25 EST: 2004
SALES (est): 379.51K **Privately Held**
Web: www.peninsulahomecare.com
SIC: 8059 Personal care home, with health care

(G-13337)
PENINSULA HOME HEALTH CARE
514 W Stein Hwy (19973-1202)
PHONE..................302 629-5672
Chuck Kelly, *Pr*
Mark Obier, *VP*
Chris Obier, *Sec*
Karen Kelly, *Treas*
EMP: 10 EST: 1995
SQ FT: 3,200
SALES (est): 2.43MM **Privately Held**
Web: www.peninsulahomecare.com
SIC: 5047 Medical equipment and supplies

(G-13338)
PENINSULA OIL CO INC (PA)
Also Called: Peninsula Oil & Propane
40 S Market St (19973)
PHONE..................302 422-6691
Geraud Darnis, *CEO*
Virginia E Willey, *
EMP: 25 EST: 1936
SQ FT: 4,000
SALES (est): 24.98MM
SALES (corp-wide): 24.98MM **Privately Held**
Web: www.penoil.com
SIC: 5171 5411 Petroleum bulk stations; Convenience stores, independent

(G-13339)
PENINSULA UROLOGY ASSOC PA
1340 Middleford Rd Ste 402 (19973-3665)
PHONE..................302 628-4222
EMP: 6
Web: www.unitedurology.com
SIC: 8011 Urologist
PA: Peninsula Urology Associates Pa
1342 S Div St Ste 401
Salisbury MD 21804

(G-13340)
PENNEY ENTERPRISES INC
Also Called: Print Shack
9203 Brickyard Rd (19973-8468)
PHONE..................302 629-4430
William Whaley, *Pr*
Martha E Whaley, *VP*
EMP: 4 EST: 1987
SALES (est): 444.88K **Privately Held**
SIC: 2752 3993 Offset printing; Advertising novelties

(G-13341)
PENNSULA HOME CARE LLC
501 Health Services Dr (19973-5782)
PHONE..................302 629-4914
Robyn Coughenour, *Prin*
EMP: 17 EST: 2011
SALES (est): 392K **Privately Held**
Web: www.peninsulahomecare.com
SIC: 8082 Home health care services

(G-13342)
PENSKE TRUCK LEASING CORP
Also Called: Penske
24799 Sussex Hwy (19973-8463)
PHONE..................302 629-5373
Sean Mullins, *Brnch Mgr*
EMP: 5
SALES (corp-wide): 5.16B **Privately Held**
Web: www.gopenske.com
SIC: 7513 Truck rental and leasing, no drivers
HQ: Penske Truck Leasing Corporation
2675 Morgantown Rd
Reading PA 19607
610 775-6000

(G-13343)
PERDUE FARMS INCORPORATED
Also Called: Perdue Farms
1000 Nanticoke Ave (19973-4009)
PHONE..................302 629-3216
Den Bao, *Mgr*
EMP: 7
SALES (corp-wide): 1.24B **Privately Held**
Web: www.perdue.com
SIC: 2015 Poultry slaughtering and processing
PA: Perdue Farms Incorporated
31149 Old Ocean City Rd
Salisbury MD 21804
800 473-7383

(G-13344)
PERDUE-AGRIRECYCLE LLC
28338 Enviro Way (19973-5964)
PHONE..................302 628-2360
Cathy Kline, *Managing Member*
Patti Vega, *
EMP: 174 EST: 2000
SQ FT: 68,000
SALES (est): 965.98K
SALES (corp-wide): 1.24B **Privately Held**
SIC: 4953 Recycling, waste materials
PA: Perdue Farms Incorporated
31149 Old Ocean City Rd
Salisbury MD 21804
800 473-7383

(G-13345)
PERFECTION CUSTOM PAINTING LLC
26907 Lonesome Rd (19973-4675)
PHONE..................303 536-7572
Rosa Wasbers, *Prin*
EMP: 5 EST: 2017
SALES (est): 59.36K **Privately Held**
SIC: 1721 Painting and paper hanging

(G-13346)
PHILIPS PAINTING LLC
228 Stoney Br (19973-6232)
PHONE..................302 344-0535
Philip Swetz, *Prin*
EMP: 5 EST: 2015
SALES (est): 66.7K **Privately Held**
SIC: 1721 Residential painting

(G-13347)
PHILLIPS SIGNS INC
20874 Sussex Hwy (19973-5686)
PHONE..................302 629-3550
Benjamin Phillips, *Pr*
Ben Phillips, *Pr*
Robin Ruggiero, *Sec*
EMP: 17 EST: 1981
SQ FT: 2,596
SALES (est): 754.71K **Privately Held**
Web: www.phillipssigns.biz
SIC: 3993 Signs, not made in custom sign painting shops

(G-13348)
PLANET FITNESS
800 Norman Eskridge Hwy (19973-1718)
PHONE..................302 262-8676
EMP: 7 EST: 2019
SALES (est): 29.54K **Privately Held**
Web: www.planetfitness.com
SIC: 7991 Physical fitness facilities

(G-13349)
PNC BANK NATIONAL ASSOCIATION
Also Called: PNC
1200 W Stein Hwy (19973-1150)
PHONE..................302 629-5000
Paula Coulbourn, *Mgr*
EMP: 6
SALES (corp-wide): 23.54B **Publicly Held**
Web: www.pncbank.com
SIC: 6021 National commercial banks
HQ: Pnc Bank, National Association
300 5th Ave
Pittsburgh PA 15222
877 762-2000

(G-13350)
POLYTECHNIC RESOURCES INC
185 Kent Dr (19973-1585)
P.O. Box 1557 (19973-5557)
PHONE..................302 629-4221
Amitabh Sharma, *Prin*
EMP: 8 EST: 2008
SALES (est): 998.04K **Privately Held**
Web: www.polytechres.com
SIC: 3089 Injection molding of plastics

(G-13351)
POORMAN AUTO
11057 Henry Dr (19973-8658)
PHONE..................302 628-0404
Steve Murphy, *Pr*
EMP: 5 EST: 2010
SALES (est): 50.71K **Privately Held**
SIC: 7538 General automotive repair shops

(G-13352)
POWERHOUSE GYM
620 W Stein Hwy (19973-1204)
PHONE..................302 262-0262
Tony Taglipour, *Owner*
EMP: 5 EST: 2004
SALES (est): 127.39K **Privately Held**
Web: www.powerhousegym.com
SIC: 7991 Health club

(G-13353)
POWWA ELECTRIC
Also Called: Powwa Electric
10997 Pit Rd (19973-7461)
PHONE..................302 236-2649
Michele Casey, *Prin*
EMP: 5 EST: 2010
SALES (est): 80.86K **Privately Held**
SIC: 1731 General electrical contractor

(G-13354)
PREMIER SPINE AND REHAB
8470 Herring Run Rd (19973-5763)
PHONE..................302 404-5293
EMP: 6 EST: 2017
SALES (est): 82.87K **Privately Held**
SIC: 8093 Rehabilitation center, outpatient treatment

(G-13355)
PREMIER STAFFING SOLUTIONS INC
809 Norman Eskridge Hwy (19973-1717)
PHONE..................302 628-7700
EMP: 58
SALES (corp-wide): 4.06MM **Privately Held**
Web: www.premierstaffingsolutions.net
SIC: 7361 Employment agencies
PA: Premier Staffing Solutions, Inc.
123 W Market St
Georgetown DE 19947
302 344-5996

(G-13356)
PRESENTABLE PROPERTIES
3408 Woodpecker Rd (19973-4627)
PHONE..................302 853-5111
Timothy S Degroat, *Owner*
EMP: 5 EST: 2017
SALES (est): 165.51K **Privately Held**
Web: www.presentableproperties.com
SIC: 6512 Nonresidential building operators

(G-13357)
PRETTY NAILS
22986 Sussex Hwy (19973-5861)
PHONE..................302 628-3937
Hong Tom, *Owner*
EMP: 5 EST: 2001
SALES (est): 75.09K **Privately Held**
SIC: 7231 Manicurist, pedicurist

(G-13358)
PRINT SHACK INC
9203 Brickyard Rd (19973-8468)
PHONE..................302 629-4430
EMP: 5 EST: 2012
SALES (est): 215.7K **Privately Held**
Web: www.printshackde.com
SIC: 2752 Offset printing

(G-13359)
PROFESSIONAL LEASING INC
Also Called: Plp Financial
740 Sussex Ave (19973-2057)
P.O. Box 149 (19973-0149)
PHONE..................302 629-4350
George S Gabriel, *Pr*
Frank Anderson, *Sec*
EMP: 9 EST: 1982

GEOGRAPHIC SECTION

Seaford - Sussex County (G-13387)

SQ FT: 4,500
SALES (est): 1.25MM **Privately Held**
Web: www.professionalease.com
SIC: 7359 7515 Equipment rental and leasing, nec; Passenger car leasing

(G-13360)
QUALITY STAFFING SERVICES
308 E Stein Hwy (19973-1416)
PHONE.................................302 990-5623
Cecilia Seman, *Prin*
EMP: 11 EST: 2016
SALES (est): 300.67K **Privately Held**
Web: www.easternshorejobs.com
SIC: 7361 Executive placement

(G-13361)
QUICK CLEAN - QUICK FIX LLC
110 S Conwell St (19973-3906)
PHONE.................................302 245-9494
Sonja Mehaffey, *Prin*
EMP: 5 EST: 2018
SALES (est): 85.16K **Privately Held**
SIC: 7699 Cleaning services

(G-13362)
QUILLEN SIGNS LLC
20874 Sussex Hwy (19973-5686)
PHONE.................................302 684-3661
Patrick Quillen, *Pt*
Margaret Quillen, *Pt*
Theresa Townsend, *Pt*
EMP: 4 EST: 1975
SALES (est): 253.62K **Privately Held**
Web: www.phillipssigns.biz
SIC: 3993 7532 Signs, not made in custom sign painting shops; Lettering and painting services

(G-13363)
R & T HEATING & AIR
307 N Pine St (19973-2512)
PHONE.................................302 629-4011
Ray Hall, *Prin*
EMP: 6 EST: 2008
SALES (est): 194.4K **Privately Held**
SIC: 1711 Warm air heating and air conditioning contractor

(G-13364)
RAKESH N PATEL DPM
1501 Middleford Rd (19973-3615)
PHONE.................................302 629-4569
Rakesh N Patel Dpm, *Owner*
EMP: 7 EST: 2018
SALES (est): 47.44K **Privately Held**
SIC: 8043 Offices and clinics of podiatrists

(G-13365)
RAWLINS FERGUSON JONES & LEWIS
9308 N Point Cmns (19973-9600)
PHONE.................................302 337-8231
Allen Jones, *Pr*
W Allen Jones, *Pr*
EMP: 5 EST: 1906
SALES (est): 482.14K **Privately Held**
SIC: 6411 Insurance agents, nec

(G-13366)
RAYMOND M COOK
26329 Line Rd (19973-5079)
PHONE.................................302 236-0087
Raymond M Cook, *Prin*
EMP: 6 EST: 2014
SALES (est): 199.36K **Privately Held**
SIC: 4911 Electric services

(G-13367)
RAYS AND SONS MECHANICAL LLC
Also Called: Rays and Sons
307 S Winding Brooke Dr (19973-4813)
P.O. Box 288 (19980-0288)
PHONE.................................302 697-2100
Sharon Andrews, *Managing Member*
EMP: 8 EST: 2010
SALES (est): 789.16K **Privately Held**
SIC: 1711 7389 Warm air heating and air conditioning contractor; Business Activities at Non-Commercial Site

(G-13368)
RBW PROPERTIES II
25488 Green Briar Rd (19973-4609)
PHONE.................................302 236-5155
EMP: 5 EST: 2009
SALES (est): 207.92K **Privately Held**
SIC: 6512 Nonresidential building operators

(G-13369)
REGENT OPEN MRI
1350 Middleford Rd Ste 503 (19973-3664)
PHONE.................................252 430-6246
EMP: 6 EST: 2019
SALES (est): 212.64K **Privately Held**
SIC: 8011 Offices and clinics of medical doctors

(G-13370)
REGIONAL BUILDERS INC
100 Park Ave (19973-9479)
P.O. Box 769 (19973-0769)
PHONE.................................302 628-8660
Robert S Boyd, *CEO*
Joan E Neal, *Pr*
EMP: 12 EST: 1997
SQ FT: 7,700
SALES (est): 11.78K **Privately Held**
Web: www.regionalbuilders.com
SIC: 1542 3448 Commercial and office building, new construction; Prefabricated metal buildings

(G-13371)
REGIS CORPORATION
Also Called: Holiday Hair
632 N Dual Hwy (19973)
PHONE.................................302 629-2916
EMP: 7
SALES (corp-wide): 233.33MM **Publicly Held**
Web: www.signaturestyle.com
SIC: 7231 Unisex hair salons
PA: Regis Corporation
3701 Wayzata Blvd Ste 500
Minneapolis MN 55416
952 947-7777

(G-13372)
REGIS CORPORATION
22899 Sussex Hwy (19973-5851)
PHONE.................................302 628-0484
EMP: 8
SALES (corp-wide): 233.33MM **Publicly Held**
Web: www.regiscorp.com
SIC: 7231 Unisex hair salons
PA: Regis Corporation
3701 Wayzata Blvd Ste 500
Minneapolis MN 55416
952 947-7777

(G-13373)
RICHARD E WILLIAMS
8443 Cannon Rd (19973-5656)
PHONE.................................302 956-0374
Richard E Williams, *Prin*
EMP: 6 EST: 2007

SALES (est): 122.93K **Privately Held**
SIC: 7389 Business Activities at Non-Commercial Site

(G-13374)
RISING STAR COMMUNICATION
14830 Josephs Rd (19973-8231)
PHONE.................................302 462-5474
William E Webb Junior, *Prin*
EMP: 5 EST: 2010
SALES (est): 109.38K **Privately Held**
SIC: 4899 Communication services, nec

(G-13375)
RIVERVIEW MEDICAL CENTER
8534 Concord Rd (19973-8418)
PHONE.................................302 396-1204
EMP: 11 EST: 2019
SALES (est): 73.83K **Privately Held**
Web: www.hackensackmeridianhealth.org
SIC: 8011 Medical centers

(G-13376)
ROBERT F CLENDENIN
23748 German Rd (19973-7307)
P.O. Box 8 (19973-0008)
PHONE.................................302 396-7922
Robert Clendenin, *Prin*
EMP: 5 EST: 2012
SALES (est): 144.75K **Privately Held**
SIC: 4212 Local trucking, without storage

(G-13377)
ROBERTS OXYGEN COMPANY INC
Also Called: Robert Oxygen Company 33
22855 Sussex Hwy 102 (19973-5850)
PHONE.................................302 337-9666
Dave Garner, *Mgr*
EMP: 6
SALES (corp-wide): 7.74MM **Privately Held**
Web: www.robertsoxygen.com
SIC: 5085 5169 Welding supplies; Compressed gas
PA: Roberts Oxygen Company, Inc.
15830 Redland Rd
Rockville MD 20855
301 315-9090

(G-13378)
ROBINSON REALESTATE
Also Called: Robinson Insurance Agency
605 N Hall St (19973-2437)
P.O. Box 571 (19973-0571)
PHONE.................................302 629-4574
Geraldine P Thomas, *Owner*
EMP: 6 EST: 1960
SQ FT: 2,500
SALES (est): 472.7K **Privately Held**
Web: www.robinsonrealestateteam.com
SIC: 6531 Real estate agent, residential

(G-13379)
RONALD A LUNA M D
1501 Middleford Rd (19973-3615)
PHONE.................................302 629-4569
Ronald A Luna Md, *Owner*
EMP: 9 EST: 2018
SALES (est): 126.39K **Privately Held**
SIC: 8011 Offices and clinics of medical doctors

(G-13380)
RT TAXIDERMY LLC
12564 Baker Mill Rd (19973-6366)
PHONE.................................302 629-7501
Ronald Tyndall Junior, *Asst Sec*
EMP: 5 EST: 2018
SALES (est): 80.67K **Privately Held**

SIC: 7699 Taxidermists

(G-13381)
RUARK INC
325 Petunia Pl (19973-1233)
PHONE.................................302 846-2332
EMP: 5 EST: 1995
SALES (est): 170.52K **Privately Held**
SIC: 1794 Excavation work

(G-13382)
RYAN ARCHITECTURE LLC
905 Short Ln (19973-1135)
PHONE.................................302 629-6458
Patrick Ryan, *Prin*
EMP: 5 EST: 2015
SALES (est): 77.02K **Privately Held**
SIC: 8712 Architectural services

(G-13383)
SALLY BEAUTY SUPPLY LLC
Also Called: Sally Beauty Supply
22883 Sussex Hwy (19973-5851)
PHONE.................................302 629-5160
Tiffany Thomas, *Mgr*
EMP: 5
Web: www.sallybeauty.com
SIC: 5999 5122 Cosmetics; Cosmetics
HQ: Sally Beauty Supply Llc
3001 Colorado Blvd
Denton TX 76210
940 898-7500

(G-13384)
SC ENNIS INCORPORATED
Also Called: UPS Store, The
23000 Sussex Hwy (19973-5866)
PHONE.................................302 629-8771
Laura Rogers, *Pr*
EMP: 10 EST: 2010
SALES (est): 435.84K **Privately Held**
Web: www.theupsstore.com
SIC: 7389 Mailbox rental and related service

(G-13385)
SEA CARE LLC
7905 Gum Branch Rd (19973-4364)
PHONE.................................410 688-4230
EMP: 7 EST: 2018
SALES (est): 45.02K **Privately Held**
Web: www.seacarede.com
SIC: 8082 Home health care services

(G-13386)
SEAFORD ANIMAL HOSPITAL INC
22661 Atlanta Rd (19973-6625)
PHONE.................................302 629-7325
William C Wade, *Pr*
Suzanne Wade, *Sec*
EMP: 10 EST: 1997
SALES (est): 984.24K **Privately Held**
Web: www.seafordah.com
SIC: 0742 Animal hospital services, pets and other animal specialties

(G-13387)
SEAFORD APARTMENT VENTURES LLC
Also Called: Stoney Brook
23033 Meadow Wood Ct (19973-7718)
PHONE.................................302 629-0909
Jacqueline Corrado, *Prin*
EMP: 5 EST: 2012
SALES (est): 236.24K **Privately Held**
Web: www.liveatstoneybrook.com
SIC: 6513 Apartment hotel operation

Seaford - Sussex County (G-13388)　　　GEOGRAPHIC SECTION

(G-13388)
SEAFORD ENDOSCOPY CENTER
13 Fallon Ave (19973-1577)
PHONE..................302 629-7177
Bradley Mackler, Pr
EMP: 9 EST: 2007
SALES (est): 929.25K Privately Held
Web: www.seafordendo.com
SIC: 8011 Gastronomist

(G-13389)
SEAFORD MACHINE WORKS INC
1451 Middleford Rd (19973-3613)
P.O. Box 621 (19973-0621)
PHONE..................302 629-6034
John La Prad, Pr
Philip La Prad, VP
EMP: 16 EST: 1948
SQ FT: 6,000
SALES (est): 973.4K Privately Held
Web: www.seafordmachshop.com
SIC: 3599 3541 7692 Machine shop, jobbing and repair; Machine tool replacement & repair parts, metal cutting types; Welding repair

(G-13390)
SEAFORD MEDICAL SPECIALISTS
1350 Middleford Rd # 502 (19973-3664)
PHONE..................302 628-8300
Ivonne Herrera, Owner
EMP: 7 EST: 2010
SALES (est): 76.47K Privately Held
SIC: 8099 Health and allied services, nec

(G-13391)
SEAFORD MISSION INC
611 3rd St (19973-2723)
P.O. Box 1271 (19973-5271)
PHONE..................302 629-2559
EMP: 8 EST: 1996
SALES (est): 3.04MM Privately Held
SIC: 8661 8744 Methodist Church; Facilities support services

(G-13392)
SEAFORD POLICE DEPT
300 Virginia Ave (19973-1516)
PHONE..................302 629-6644
EMP: 5 EST: 1993
SALES (est): 208.46K Privately Held
SIC: 8641 Youth organizations

(G-13393)
SEAFORD PRESERVATION ASSOC LLC
Also Called: Seaford Meadows Apartments
122 Seaford Meadows Dr (19973-1633)
PHONE..................302 629-6416
EMP: 5 EST: 2011
SALES (est): 287.69K Privately Held
SIC: 6513 Apartment building operators

(G-13394)
SENIOR NANTICOKE CENTER INC
310 Virginia Ave Ste B (19973-1516)
PHONE..................302 629-4939
Susan Franckowiak, Dir
EMP: 12 EST: 1971
SALES (est): 208.58K Privately Held
Web: www.nanticokeseniorcenter.com
SIC: 8322 Senior citizens' center or association

(G-13395)
SERVICE GENERAL CORP
801 Norman Eskridge Hwy 809 (19973)
PHONE..................302 629-9701
Vamdad Bahar, Prin
EMP: 5 EST: 2016
SALES (est): 170.84K Privately Held
Web: www.servicegeneral.net
SIC: 6099 Check cashing agencies

(G-13396)
SERVICE GLASS INC
Rte 20 W (19973)
P.O. Box 373 (19973-0373)
PHONE..................302 629-9139
Bob Booth, Pr
Michelle Booth, Stockholder
EMP: 12 EST: 1988
SQ FT: 7,200
SALES (est): 2.03MM Privately Held
SIC: 1793 Glass and glazing work

(G-13397)
SERVICE TIRE TRUCK CENTER INC
24873 Sussex Hwy (19973-8464)
PHONE..................302 629-5533
Glen High, Brnch Mgr
EMP: 33
SALES (corp-wide): 109.87MM Privately Held
Web: www.sttc.com
SIC: 7534 5531 Tire recapping; Truck equipment and parts
PA: Service Tire Truck Center, Inc.
2255 Avenue A
Bethlehem PA 18017
610 954-8473

(G-13398)
SERVICEXPRESS CORPORATION
809 Norman Eskridge Hwy (19973-1717)
PHONE..................302 854-9118
Bamdad Bahar, Brnch Mgr
EMP: 546
Web: www.servicexpressworks.net
SIC: 7361 Labor contractors (employment agency)
PA: Servicexpress Corporation
120 N Ray St
Georgetown DE 19947

(G-13399)
SHAMROCK GLASS CO INC
200 N Delaware Ave (19973-2429)
P.O. Box 686 (19973-0686)
PHONE..................302 629-5500
Bunnie Gallagher, Sec
Loretta Gallagher Williams Bun nie Gallagher, Prin
Al Williams, Pr
EMP: 10 EST: 1981
SALES (est): 720.18K Privately Held
Web: www.shamrockglass.biz
SIC: 3231 Medical and laboratory glassware: made from purchased glass

(G-13400)
SHANNON A FISCH
400 N Market Street Ext (19973-1573)
PHONE..................302 536-5667
Shannon Fisch, Mgr
EMP: 7 EST: 2017
SALES (est): 72.8K Privately Held
SIC: 8322 Individual and family services

(G-13401)
SHIP SHAPE MARINE INC
15100 County Seat Hwy (19973-8222)
PHONE..................302 841-7355
Joanna Mccutchen, Prin
EMP: 6 EST: 2015
SALES (est): 46.54K Privately Held
SIC: 7349 Building maintenance services, nec

(G-13402)
SILVERMAN MCDONALD & FRIEDMAN
300 High St (19973-3940)
PHONE..................302 629-3350
EMP: 6 EST: 2018
SALES (est): 148.45K Privately Held
Web: www.smflegal.com
SIC: 8111 General practice attorney, lawyer

(G-13403)
SIR GROUT DELAWARE LLC
Also Called: Sir Grout
8811 Weeping Willow Trl (19973-5864)
PHONE..................302 401-1700
EMP: 5 EST: 2020
SALES (est): 184.09K Privately Held
Web: www.sirgroutdelaware.com
SIC: 1743 Tile installation, ceramic

(G-13404)
SKATEWORLD INC (PA)
23601 Dove Rd (19973-7263)
PHONE..................302 875-2121
Richard Slatcher, Pr
Deborah Slatcher, Sec
EMP: 8 EST: 1980
SQ FT: 12,000
SALES: 998K
SALES (corp-wide): 998K Privately Held
Web: www.skateworldlaurel.com
SIC: 7999 Roller skating rink operation

(G-13405)
SMITH FIRM LLC
8866 Riverside Dr (19973-3655)
PHONE..................302 875-5595
Mike Smith, Prin
EMP: 7 EST: 2012
SALES (est): 379.86K Privately Held
Web: www.thesmithfirm.org
SIC: 8111 General practice law office

(G-13406)
SOIL SERVICE INC
117 New St (19973-3901)
PHONE..................302 629-7054
Ralph Byron Palmer Senior, Pr
Charles E Palmer, VP
Ralph Byron Palmer Junior, Sec
EMP: 7 EST: 1934
SQ FT: 1,500
SALES (est): 1.47MM Privately Held
SIC: 5191 5261 Fertilizer and fertilizer materials; Fertilizer

(G-13407)
SOUTHERN BELLE BARN VENUE LLC
5607 Lakeshore Dr (19973-6033)
PHONE..................410 896-5408
Ashley Dryden, Prin
EMP: 5 EST: 2018
SALES (est): 199.99K Privately Held
Web: the-southern-belle-barn.business.site
SIC: 7299 Wedding consultant

(G-13408)
SOUTHERN DELAWARE FOOT
543 N Shipley St Ste C (19973-2339)
PHONE..................302 404-5915
Bradley T Lemon Dpm, Owner
EMP: 14 EST: 2013
SALES (est): 426.78K Privately Held
Web: www.sodelfootandankle.com
SIC: 8043 Offices and clinics of podiatrists

(G-13409)
SOUTHERN DENTAL LLC
703 Health Services Dr (19973-5784)
PHONE..................302 536-7589
Paul Edwin Brown, Owner
EMP: 10 EST: 2014
SALES (est): 253.22K Privately Held
Web: www.brownbardentistry.com
SIC: 8021 Dentists' office

(G-13410)
SOUTHERN STATES COOP INC
Also Called: S S C Seed Warehouse
200 Allen St (19973-2000)
PHONE..................302 629-7991
FAX: 302 629-0257
EMP: 9
SALES (corp-wide): 2.21B Privately Held
SIC: 2048 4225 Prepared feeds, nec; General warehousing and storage
PA: Southern States Cooperative, Incorporated
6606 W Broad St Ste B
Richmond VA 23230
804 281-1000

(G-13411)
STATE LINE FARMS LLC
26394 Old Carriage Rd (19973-4664)
PHONE..................302 628-4506
EMP: 5 EST: 2011
SALES (est): 212.43K Privately Held
SIC: 0251 Broiler, fryer, and roaster chickens

(G-13412)
STEPHEN M D CAREY
2 Chelsea Ct (19973-8030)
PHONE..................302 629-8662
Stephen Carey, Prin
EMP: 7 EST: 2017
SALES (est): 202.71K Privately Held
Web: www.gingerbreadlane.net
SIC: 8011 Offices and clinics of medical doctors

(G-13413)
STEPHENS ENTERPRISES INC
Also Called: Pallet Masters
26286 Seaford Rd (19973-5924)
PHONE..................302 629-0322
Todd Stephens, Pr
EMP: 8 EST: 2002
SALES (est): 980.2K Privately Held
SIC: 2448 Wood pallets and skids

(G-13414)
STEPHENS MANAGEMENT CORP
321 E Stein Hwy (19973-1415)
P.O. Box 594 (19973-0594)
PHONE..................302 629-4393
Darlene Warner, Pr
June Woodward, VP
EMP: 7 EST: 1979
SALES (est): 730.13K Privately Held
SIC: 6531 Real estate managers

(G-13415)
STYLES BY US
324 E Stein Hwy (19973-1416)
PHONE..................302 629-3244
Angie Collins, Owner
EMP: 7 EST: 1997
SALES (est): 134.03K Privately Held
Web: www.stylesbyusinc.com
SIC: 7231 Hairdressers

(G-13416)
SUNSHINE CLEANING SERVICES LLC
5138 Boyce Rd (19973-6640)

GEOGRAPHIC SECTION
Seaford - Sussex County (G-13443)

PHONE.....................302 430-8416
EMP: 7 **EST:** 2018
SALES (est): 61.27K **Privately Held**
SIC: 7349 Cleaning service, industrial or commercial

(G-13417)
SURGICAL NANTICOKE ASSOC PA
543 N Shipley St Ste A (19973-2339)
PHONE.....................302 629-8662
Steven Carey, *Pr*
Samuel Miller Md, *VP*
EMP: 7 **EST:** 1986
SALES (est): 673.99K **Privately Held**
SIC: 8011 Cardiologist and cardio-vascular specialist

(G-13418)
SUSAN J BETTS OD
8500 Herring Run Rd (19973-5795)
PHONE.....................302 629-6691
EMP: 8 **EST:** 1982
SALES (est): 338.07K **Privately Held**
Web: www.bettsandbiddleeyecare.com
SIC: 8042 Specialized optometrists

(G-13419)
SUSSEX MONTESSORI
24960 Dairy Ln (19973-6997)
PHONE.....................302 404-5367
EMP: 10 **EST:** 2019
SALES (est): 321.94K **Privately Held**
Web: www.sussexmontessoricharter.com
SIC: 8351 Montessori child development center

(G-13420)
SUSSEX PRINTING CORP
24904 Sussex Hwy (19973-8466)
P.O. Box 1210 (19973-5210)
PHONE.....................302 629-9303
Layton Ayres, *Pr*
Timothy Ayres, *
Elizabeth Ayres, *
EMP: 50 **EST:** 1957
SQ FT: 3,000
SALES (est): 6.65MM
SALES (corp-wide): 14.29MM **Privately Held**
Web: www.theguide.com
SIC: 2741 2791 2771 2759 Guides; publishing and printing; Typesetting; Greeting cards; Commercial printing, nec
PA: O'rourke Media Group, Llc
281 N Main St
Saint Albans VT 05478
802 524-9771

(G-13421)
SUSSEX PRSCHOOL ERLY CARE CTRS
Also Called: Discovery Island Preschool
126 N Shipley St (19973-3100)
P.O. Box 14 (19973-0014)
PHONE.....................302 732-7529
Margaret Clark, *Owner*
EMP: 7 **EST:** 2014
SALES (est): 250.42K **Privately Held**
Web: www.sussexpreschools.org
SIC: 8351 Preschool center

(G-13422)
SUSSEX SAND & GRAVEL INC
22223 Eskridge Rd (19973-8144)
PHONE.....................302 628-6962
EMP: 3 **EST:** 2009
SALES (est): 179.78K **Privately Held**
Web: www.sussexsandandgravel.com
SIC: 1442 Gravel mining

(G-13423)
SVN DELAWARE LLC
26673 Sussex Hwy (19973-8525)
PHONE.....................302 536-1838
Rob Harman, *Prin*
EMP: 6 **EST:** 2017
SALES (est): 458.56K **Privately Held**
SIC: 6531 Real estate agent, commercial

(G-13424)
T HARRY WHEEDLETON
26955 Line Rd (19973-4637)
PHONE.....................302 629-7414
T Harry Wheedleton, *Prin*
EMP: 5 **EST:** 2006
SALES (est): 185.27K **Privately Held**
SIC: 0119 Cash grains, nec

(G-13425)
TAP TRANSPORTATION LLC
328 N Market St (19973-2612)
PHONE.....................302 217-2729
EMP: 6 **EST:** 2020
SALES (est): 125K **Privately Held**
SIC: 4789 Transportation services, nec

(G-13426)
TEAGLE AND SONS
6 N Street Ext (19973-1510)
PHONE.....................302 682-8639
EMP: 6 **EST:** 2011
SALES (est): 78.75K **Privately Held**
SIC: 7349 Building maintenance services, nec

(G-13427)
TELAMON CORPORATION
517 Bridgeville Hwy (19973-1521)
PHONE.....................302 629-5557
Margaret Antel, *Brnch Mgr*
EMP: 8
SALES (corp-wide): 85.01MM **Privately Held**
Web: www.telamon.org
SIC: 8331 Job training services
PA: Telamon Corporation
5560 Munford Rd Ste 201
Raleigh NC 27612
919 851-7611

(G-13428)
TENDER LAWN & CARE
214 Otter Run Ct (19973-7432)
PHONE.....................410 310-6550
Frank Updike, *Prin*
EMP: 8 **EST:** 2017
SALES (est): 57.08K **Privately Held**
Web: www.mytenderlawncare.com
SIC: 0782 Lawn care services

(G-13429)
TIDALHEALTH NANTICOKE INC (HQ)
801 Middleford Rd (19973-3636)
PHONE.....................302 629-6611
EMP: 655 **EST:** 1945
SALES (est): 151.44MM **Privately Held**
Web: www.tidalhealth.org
SIC: 8062 General medical and surgical hospitals
PA: Nanticoke Health Services, Inc.
801 Middleford Rd
Seaford DE 19973

(G-13430)
TIDEMARK FEDERAL CREDIT UNION (PA)
1941 Bridgeville Hwy (19973-1614)
P.O. Box 1800 (19973-8800)
PHONE.....................302 629-0100
Richard Stoops, *Mgr*
▲ **EMP:** 18 **EST:** 1959
SALES (est): 16.58MM
SALES (corp-wide): 16.58MM **Privately Held**
Web: www.tidemarkfcu.org
SIC: 6061 Federal credit unions

(G-13431)
TIDEWATER PHYSCL THRPY AND REB
Also Called: Tidewater Electricmyology
808 Middleford Rd Ste 7 (19973-3650)
P.O. Box 1564 (21601-8932)
PHONE.....................302 629-4024
EMP: 9
Web: www.tidewaterpt.com
SIC: 8049 8093 Physical therapist; Rehabilitation center, outpatient treatment
PA: Tidewater Physical Therapy And Rehabilitation Associates Pa
406 Marvel Ct
Easton MD 21601

(G-13432)
TINAS TINY TOTS DAYCARE
8779 Concord Rd (19973-8422)
PHONE.....................302 536-7077
Christina L Mummert, *Prin*
EMP: 5 **EST:** 2010
SALES (est): 84.02K **Privately Held**
SIC: 8351 Group day care center

(G-13433)
TOWERS SIGNS LLC
22876 Sussex Hwy Unit 6 (19973-5853)
PHONE.....................302 629-7450
EMP: 3 **EST:** 1983
SQ FT: 1,400
SALES (est): 248.64K **Privately Held**
Web: www.towerssigns.net
SIC: 3993 Signs and advertising specialties

(G-13434)
TRACTOR SUPPLY COMPANY
20952 Sussex Hwy (19973-5687)
PHONE.....................302 629-3627
Richard Geddes, *Mgr*
EMP: 10
SALES (corp-wide): 14.2B **Publicly Held**
Web: www.tractorsupply.com
SIC: 5191 Farm supplies
PA: Tractor Supply Company
5401 Virginia Way
Brentwood TN 37027
615 440-4000

(G-13435)
TRINITY HEATING & AIR
9674 Tharp Rd (19973-7712)
PHONE.....................302 344-3628
Joe Morris, *Owner*
EMP: 6 **EST:** 2015
SALES (est): 75.79K **Privately Held**
SIC: 1711 Warm air heating and air conditioning contractor

(G-13436)
TRINITY LOGISTICS INC (HQ)
50 Fallon Ave (19973-1578)
P.O. Box 1620 (19973-8920)
PHONE.....................302 253-3900
Donnan R Burris, *
Donnan R Burris, *
William Banning, *
Darrel Banning, *
Doug Potvin, *
EMP: 165 **EST:** 1979
SQ FT: 50,000
SALES (est): 206.83MM
SALES (corp-wide): 1.24B **Privately Held**
Web: www.trinitylogistics.com
SIC: 4731 Truck transportation brokers
PA: Burris Logistics
501 Se 5th St
Milford DE 19963
302 839-4531

(G-13437)
U-HAUL CO
1022 W Stein Hwy (19973-1145)
PHONE.....................302 628-8197
EMP: 7 **EST:** 2018
SALES (est): 86.02K **Privately Held**
Web: www.uhaul.com
SIC: 7513 Truck rental and leasing, no drivers

(G-13438)
UPBOUND GROUP INC
Also Called: Rent-A-Center
23002 Sussex Hwy (19973-5866)
PHONE.....................302 629-8925
EMP: 5
Web: www.rentacenter.com
SIC: 7359 Appliance rental
PA: Upbound Group, Inc.
5501 Headquarters Dr
Plano TX 75024

(G-13439)
VACATION CLUB
9290 River Vista Dr (19973-8600)
P.O. Box 1396 (19973-5396)
PHONE.....................302 628-1144
EMP: 5 **EST:** 2008
SALES (est): 48.41K **Privately Held**
Web: www.vacationclubtrips.com
SIC: 7997 Membership sports and recreation clubs

(G-13440)
VERIZON DELAWARE LLC
Also Called: Verizon
8722 Concord Rd (19973-8423)
PHONE.....................302 629-4502
Gary Allison, *Mgr*
EMP: 49
SALES (corp-wide): 133.97B **Publicly Held**
Web: www.delaware.gov
SIC: 4813 Local and long distance telephone communications
HQ: Verizon Delaware Llc
901 N Tatnall St Fl 2
Wilmington DE 19801
302 571-1571

(G-13441)
VIDEO DEN
27180 Williams Ave (19973-5921)
PHONE.....................302 628-9835
James Horne, *Owner*
EMP: 5 **EST:** 1983
SQ FT: 1,600
SALES (est): 279.11K **Privately Held**
SIC: 7841 7359 5735 5731 Video disk/tape rental to the general public; Video cassette recorder and accessory rental; Video tapes, prerecorded; Tape recorders and players

(G-13442)
WAKED TAREK MD
121 S Front St (19973-3511)
PHONE.....................703 342-7744
EMP: 6 **EST:** 2018
SALES (est): 123.2K **Privately Held**
SIC: 8099 Health and allied services, nec

(G-13443)
WAKED HAMMOUD TAREK M MD
8472 Herring Run Rd (19973-5763)

Seaford - Sussex County (G-13444)

PHONE..................302 536-5395
EMP: 10 EST: 2019
SALES (est): 191.97K Privately Held
SIC: 8011 Surgeon

(G-13444)
WARREN ELECTRIC CO INC
21621 Sussex Hwy (19973)
P.O. Box 557 (19973-0557)
PHONE..................302 629-9134
David Mc Natt Junior, *Pr*
David Mc Natt Senior, *VP*
EMP: 6 EST: 1959
SALES (est): 453.82K Privately Held
SIC: 7694 5063 Electric motor repair; Motors, electric

(G-13445)
WATSON-MARLOW FLOW SMART INC
213 Nesbitt Dr (19973-9401)
PHONE..................302 536-6388
Steve Lavargna, *CEO*
▲ EMP: 45 EST: 2009
SQ FT: 27,800
SALES (est): 6MM
SALES (corp-wide): 1.94B Privately Held
Web: www.flowsmartinc.com
SIC: 3053 Gaskets and sealing devices
HQ: Watson-Marlow Limited
     Bickland Water Road
     Falmouth TR11

(G-13446)
WENTWORTH INC
Also Called: H & R Block
22946 Sussex Hwy (19973-5861)
PHONE..................302 629-6284
Elizabeth Wentworth, *Pr*
EMP: 7 EST: 2000
SALES (est): 179.14K Privately Held
Web: www.hrblock.com
SIC: 7291 Tax return preparation services

(G-13447)
WESTERN UNION
701 W Stein Hwy (19973-1242)
PHONE..................302 629-3001
EMP: 6 EST: 2017
SALES (est): 110.84K Privately Held
Web: www.westernunion.com
SIC: 7389 Finishing services

(G-13448)
WILLIAM A ODAY
Also Called: William A O'Day Ands Son
4148 Woodland Ferry Rd (19973-4651)
PHONE..................302 629-7854
William A Oday, *Managing Member*
William A Oday, *Owner*
EMP: 5 EST: 2005
SALES (est): 331.66K Privately Held
SIC: 0191 General farms, primarily crop

(G-13449)
WILLIAM H GROTON CONSTRUC
11690 Baker Mill Rd (19973-6354)
PHONE..................302 697-4744
William Groton, *Prin*
EMP: 7 EST: 2006
SALES (est): 131.37K Privately Held
SIC: 1799 Special trade contractors, nec

(G-13450)
WILLIAM H METCAFF & SONS INC
183 Kent Dr (19973-1585)
PHONE..................301 868-6330
Pat Rowan, *Mgr*
EMP: 6 EST: 2012
SALES (est): 56.99K Privately Held

SIC: 1711 Plumbing, heating, air-conditioning

(G-13451)
WILLIAMS CLIMATE CONTROL
26165 Green Briar Rd (19973-4617)
PHONE..................302 628-0440
EMP: 6 EST: 2019
SALES (est): 142.86K Privately Held
SIC: 1711 Warm air heating and air conditioning contractor

(G-13452)
WILLIN FARMS LLC
2864 Long Acre Ln (19973-5088)
PHONE..................302 629-2520
EMP: 8 EST: 2010
SQ FT: 1,200
SALES (est): 511.54K Privately Held
SIC: 0191 General farms, primarily crop

(G-13453)
WILMINGTON SAVINGS FUND SOC
22820 Sussex Hwy (19973-5862)
PHONE..................302 360-0440
Paul B Hughes, *VP*
EMP: 9
SALES (corp-wide): 963.95MM Publicly Held
Web: www.wsfsbank.com
SIC: 6022 State commercial banks
HQ: Wilmington Savings Fund Society
    500 Delaware Ave
    Wilmington DE 19801
    302 792-6000

(G-13454)
WOMENS MEDICAL CENTER INC
Also Called: Women's Medical Center PA
1301 Middleford Rd (19973-3611)
PHONE..................302 629-5409
Patrick Tierno, *Pr*
EMP: 9 EST: 1985
SALES (est): 888.33K Privately Held
SIC: 8011 Gynecologist

(G-13455)
WORMS QUALITY CARPET CARE
21729 Maple Dr (19973-5674)
PHONE..................302 629-3114
EMP: 10 EST: 2002
SALES (est): 434.27K Privately Held
Web: www.wormscarpetcare.us
SIC: 7217 Carpet and upholstery cleaning

(G-13456)
XPO LOGISTICS FREIGHT INC
104 Park Ave (19973-9479)
PHONE..................302 629-5228
EMP: 22
SALES (corp-wide): 7.74B Publicly Held
Web: www.xpo.com
SIC: 4213 Contract haulers
HQ: Xpo Logistics Freight, Inc.
    2211 Old Earhart Rd # 100
    Ann Arbor MI 48105
    800 755-2728

Selbyville
Sussex County

(G-13457)
1 ON 1 PERSONAL TRAINER LLC
38792 Wilson Ave (19975-4414)
PHONE..................717 418-2719
Bruce Casher, *Prin*
EMP: 6 EST: 2016
SALES (est): 82.75K Privately Held
SIC: 7991 Physical fitness facilities

(G-13458)
ABLE WHELLING AND MACHIENE
Also Called: Able Welding & Machine
45 Railroad Ave (19975-9675)
P.O. Box 1075 (19975-1075)
PHONE..................302 436-1929
Debra Behney, *Owner*
EMP: 4 EST: 1989
SQ FT: 2,400
SALES (est): 412.74K Privately Held
SIC: 5712 7349 3599 Mattresses; Building maintenance services, nec; Machine shop, jobbing and repair

(G-13459)
ALL CLEAN POWER WASHING
Also Called: Power Washing
36668 Hudson Rd (19975-3376)
PHONE..................877 325-3215
EMP: 10
SALES (est): 249.88K Privately Held
Web: www.allcleanpowerwashing.com
SIC: 7699 Cleaning services

(G-13460)
ALPHA GMMA RHO ALMNI ASSN OF T
37805 Crab Bay Ln (19975-3924)
PHONE..................301 490-9972
EMP: 9 EST: 2010
SALES (est): 65.31K Privately Held
SIC: 7041 Fraternities and sororities

(G-13461)
ALUTECH UNITED INC (PA)
Also Called: Alutech Awnings
117 Dixon St (19975-3022)
P.O. Box 329 (19975-0329)
PHONE..................302 436-6005
Joachim Schanz, *Pr*
George Pfaller, *VP*
Kim Stoll, *Sec*
◆ EMP: 5 EST: 1993
SQ FT: 25,000
SALES (est): 8.4MM Privately Held
Web: www.alutech.com
SIC: 3442 Shutters, door or window: metal

(G-13462)
ANIMAL HEALTH SALES INC
Also Called: Selbyville Pet and Garden Ctr
44 Rte 113 (19975)
PHONE..................302 436-8286
Donald J Lynch, *Pr*
Jean Lynch, *VP*
Kevin Lynch, *Treas*
EMP: 12 EST: 1954
SQ FT: 14,400
SALES (est): 2.16MM Privately Held
Web: www.selbyvillepetandgarden.com
SIC: 5122 5199 Animal medicines; Pet supplies

(G-13463)
ANTEBELLUM HOSPITALITY INC
118 W Church St (19975-2010)
P.O. Box 519 (19975-0519)
PHONE..................302 436-4375
Bill Shoemaker, *Pr*
Gloria Shoemaker, *VP*
EMP: 7 EST: 1987
SALES (est): 744.5K Privately Held
Web: www.ahi-services.com
SIC: 8741 Business management

(G-13464)
ANTHONY FERGUSON
37200 W White Tail Dr (19975-3540)
PHONE..................610 906-4998
Anthony Ferguson, *Prin*

EMP: 5 EST: 2011
SALES (est): 99.01K Privately Held
SIC: 1522 Residential construction, nec

(G-13465)
ATI HOLDINGS LLC
38394 Dupont Blvd Unit 1 (19975-3049)
PHONE..................302 524-5951
EMP: 7
SALES (corp-wide): 635.67MM Publicly Held
Web: www.atipt.com
SIC: 8049 Physical therapist
HQ: Ati Holdings, Llc
    790 Remington Blvd
    Bolingbrook IL 60440

(G-13466)
ATLANTIC GENERAL HOSPITAL CORP
Also Called: Atlantic General Hospital
38394 Dupont Blvd Ste H (19975-3049)
PHONE..................302 524-5007
Brandi Musselman, *Brnch Mgr*
EMP: 25
Web: www.atlanticgeneral.org
SIC: 8062 General medical and surgical hospitals
PA: Atlantic General Hospital Corporation
    9733 Healthway Dr
    Berlin MD 21811

(G-13467)
ATLANTIC INDUSTRIAL OPTICS
Also Called: A I O
38249 Bay Vista Dr Apt 1246 (19975-2857)
PHONE..................302 856-7905
Richard Vanderhook, *Pr*
EMP: 8 EST: 1980
SALES (est): 654.53K Privately Held
SIC: 3679 3299 3827 Quartz crystals, for electronic application; Tubing for electrical purposes, quartz; Optical instruments and lenses

(G-13468)
ATLANTIC PUMPING INC
10 Discovery Ln (19975-9642)
P.O. Box 395 (21813-0395)
PHONE..................302 436-5047
John Rice, *Prin*
EMP: 12 EST: 2001
SALES (est): 450.1K Privately Held
Web: www.atlanticpumping.com
SIC: 7359 7699 Portable toilet rental; Septic tank cleaning service

(G-13469)
AVALANCHE STRATEGIES LLC
Also Called: Think Fast Toys.com
144 Dixon St (19975-3053)
PHONE..................302 436-7060
William Spraul, *CEO*
Stu Eisenman, *
Cyrus Jiroir, *
Edward Timmons Junior, *Sec*
James Fishinger, *
▲ EMP: 180 EST: 2015
SQ FT: 100,000
SALES (est): 29.3MM Privately Held
Web: www.avalancheind.com
SIC: 7384 8742 Photographic services; Marketing consulting services

(G-13470)
BAYSIDE MILLWORK INC
11062 Destination Dr (19975-3719)
PHONE..................443 324-4376
EMP: 5 EST: 2014
SALES (est): 144.72K Privately Held
SIC: 5031 Millwork

GEOGRAPHIC SECTION

Selbyville - Sussex County (G-13497)

(G-13471)
BAYSIDE RESORT GOLF CLUB
Also Called: Golf Bayside
31806 Lakeview Dr (19975-3700)
PHONE.................302 436-3400
Robert C Crowther, *Dir*
EMP: 19 **EST:** 2007
SALES (est): 811.6K **Privately Held**
Web: www.golfbayside.com
SIC: 7997 7992 Golf club, membership; Public golf courses

(G-13472)
BAYSIDE SPORTS CLUB LLC
31381 Sorsyphia (19975)
PHONE.................302 436-3550
EMP: 10 **EST:** 2004
SALES (est): 218.97K **Privately Held**
SIC: 7997 Membership sports and recreation clubs

(G-13473)
BAYVILLE POSTAL SVC
37232 Lighthouse Rd (19975-3981)
PHONE.................302 436-2715
Andrew Adkins, *Managing Member*
EMP: 5 **EST:** 2010
SALES (est): 447.85K **Privately Held**
Web: www.bayvilleshoppingcenter.com
SIC: 7389 Post office contract stations

(G-13474)
BEACHSIDE CLEANING LLC
37080 Canvasback Rd (19975-3209)
PHONE.................717 875-3141
EMP: 5 **EST:** 2017
SALES (est): 76.39K **Privately Held**
SIC: 7699 Cleaning services

(G-13475)
BEGINNERS CHOICE DAY CARE CTR
38081 Community Ln (19975-3108)
PHONE.................302 436-4460
EMP: 7 **EST:** 2015
SALES (est): 249.23K **Privately Held**
SIC: 8099 Health and allied services, nec

(G-13476)
BETHANY RESORT FURN WHSE
Also Called: Bethany Resort Furnishings
145 Dixon St (19975-3022)
PHONE.................302 251-4101
Bill Timmons, *Contrlr*
▲ **EMP:** 6 **EST:** 2015
SALES (est): 161.2K **Privately Held**
Web: www.bethanyresortfurnishings.com
SIC: 2392 Household furnishings, nec

(G-13477)
BILL CANNONS GARAGE INC
Also Called: Bill Cannon's Garage
Rd 2 Box 125 A Rt 113 North (19975)
PHONE.................302 436-4200
William D Cannon, *Pr*
Becky Cannon, *VP*
EMP: 10 **EST:** 1983
SQ FT: 12,200
SALES (est): 1.05MM **Privately Held**
Web: www.awesomeengines.biz
SIC: 7538 5531 General automotive repair shops; Automotive parts

(G-13478)
BLACK SEA CONTRACTOR LLC
3 Waterford Ln (19975-9121)
PHONE.................856 558-1821
Ahmet Karaosman, *Prin*
EMP: 5 **EST:** 2017
SALES (est): 56.76K **Privately Held**
SIC: 1799 Special trade contractors, nec

(G-13479)
BODY DOUBLE SWIMWEAR
1007 Coastal Hwy (19944-4419)
PHONE.................302 537-1444
Nancy Rupert, *Owner*
EMP: 6 **EST:** 2002
SQ FT: 1,700
SALES (est): 450.98K **Privately Held**
Web: www.bodydoubleswimwear.com
SIC: 5699 2339 Bathing suits; Bathing suits: women's, misses', and juniors'

(G-13480)
BRANDON TATUM
Also Called: Vogue On 54
36666 Bluewater Run W Unit 7 (19975-4392)
PHONE.................302 564-7428
Brandon Tatum, *Owner*
EMP: 7 **EST:** 2016
SALES (est): 68.95K **Privately Held**
Web: www.vogueon54.com
SIC: 7231 Hairdressers

(G-13481)
BRANDYWINE ASSSTED LVING AT FN
Also Called: Brandywine Sr Care
21111 Arrington Dr Unit 101 (19975-3607)
PHONE.................302 436-0808
EMP: 1494 **EST:** 2007
SALES (est): 7.69MM
SALES (corp-wide): 95.35MM **Privately Held**
SIC: 8361 Aged home
PA: Brandywine Senior Living Management Llc
525 Fellowship Rd Ste 360
Mount Laurel NJ 08054
856 778-6100

(G-13482)
BRANDYWINE SENIOR CARE INC
36413 Redwood Way (19975-3603)
PHONE.................302 436-2920
EMP: 10 **EST:** 2007
SALES (est): 107.16K **Privately Held**
SIC: 8322 Senior citizens' center or association

(G-13483)
BRASURES CARPET CARE INC (PA)
35131 Lighthouse Rd (19975-4048)
P.O. Box 114 (19975-0114)
PHONE.................302 436-5652
David L Brasure, *Pr*
Peggy L Brasure, *VP*
EMP: 9 **EST:** 1983
SQ FT: 6,000
SALES (est): 788.82K
SALES (corp-wide): 788.82K **Privately Held**
Web: www.brasurescarpetcare.com
SIC: 7217 7216 5713 Carpet and furniture cleaning on location; Drapery, curtain drycleaning; Rugs

(G-13484)
BRASURES PEST CONTROL INC
38187 Dickerson Rd (19975-3527)
P.O. Box 1100 (19975-1100)
PHONE.................302 436-8140
Carroll W Brasure, *Pr*
EMP: 25 **EST:** 1971
SALES (est): 2.38MM **Privately Held**
Web: www.brasurespestcontrol.com
SIC: 5713 7342 Floor covering stores; Exterminating and fumigating

(G-13485)
BUDGET TRUCK RENTAL
Also Called: Budget Rent-A-Car
34821 W Line Rd Unit 9 (19975-4087)
PHONE.................302 436-5416
Matt Engle, *Owner*
EMP: 7 **EST:** 2010
SALES (est): 133.77K **Privately Held**
Web: www.budget.com
SIC: 7514 Rent-a-car service

(G-13486)
BUNTING & MURRAY CNSTR CORP
32996 Lighthouse Rd (19975-4024)
PHONE.................302 436-5144
Jay C Murray, *Pr*
C Coleman Bunting Junior, *Pr*
Susan Ross, *
Clifton Murray, *
Carlton Murray, *
EMP: 55 **EST:** 1983
SQ FT: 4,000
SALES (est): 10.45MM **Privately Held**
Web: www.ascentresources-store.com
SIC: 1623 1794 Water, sewer, and utility lines ; Excavation work

(G-13487)
BUNTING CONSTRUCTION CORP
32996 Lighthouse Rd (19975-4024)
PHONE.................302 436-5124
C Coleman Bunting, *Pr*
Michael Sasada, *VP*
Steven Yoder, *VP*
Donna Lynch, *Sec*
Susan W Ross, *Treas*
EMP: 18 **EST:** 1971
SQ FT: 4,000
SALES (est): 5.03MM **Privately Held**
Web: www.buntingconstruction.com
SIC: 1521 1542 New construction, single-family houses; Commercial and office building, new construction

(G-13488)
C R PAINTING
28044 Puncheon Rd (19975-3003)
PHONE.................302 519-3938
Casey Robinson, *Prin*
EMP: 5 **EST:** 2017
SALES (est): 42.66K **Privately Held**
SIC: 1721 Painting and paper hanging

(G-13489)
CABINETRY UNLIMITED LLC
7 Hosier St (19975-9300)
P.O. Box 687 (19975-0687)
PHONE.................302 436-5030
Dieter Baier, *Pr*
Joseph A Dougherty, *
Mary Ellen Dougherty, *
EMP: 30 **EST:** 1968
SQ FT: 22,000
SALES (est): 9.47MM **Privately Held**
Web: www.cabinetryunlimited.com
SIC: 5031 2541 5211 Kitchen cabinets; Table or counter tops, plastic laminated; Counter tops

(G-13490)
CARL M FREEDMAN COMMUNITIES
31822 Lakeview Dr (19975-3700)
PHONE.................302 436-4102
EMP: 6 **EST:** 2019
SALES (est): 45.3K **Privately Held**
Web: www.carlmfreemanfoundation.org
SIC: 8699 Charitable organization

(G-13491)
CARL M FREEMAN
36558 Wild Rose Cir (19975-3737)
PHONE.................302 988-1669
Carl M Freeman, *Prin*
EMP: 8 **EST:** 2018
SALES (est): 207.41K **Privately Held**
Web: www.freemancompanies.com
SIC: 1521 Single-family housing construction

(G-13492)
CARL M FREEMAN FOUNDATION INC
31255 Americana Pkwy (19975-3785)
PHONE.................302 436-6241
Patti Grimes, *Ex Dir*
Michelle D Freeman, *Dir*
EMP: 5 **EST:** 2014
SALES (est): 3.92MM **Privately Held**
Web: www.freemancompanies.com
SIC: 8699 Charitable organization

(G-13493)
CARNY CONSTRUCTION
36884 Chandler Dr (19975-4145)
PHONE.................302 436-9738
Melissa Carney, *Prin*
EMP: 5 **EST:** 2010
SALES (est): 81.69K **Privately Held**
SIC: 1521 Single-family housing construction

(G-13494)
CAROLINES SPA & GOODS LLC
46 N Main St (19975-9688)
PHONE.................302 200-2635
Hee Kim, *Prin*
EMP: 6 **EST:** 2017
SALES (est): 239.47K **Privately Held**
SIC: 7542 Carwashes

(G-13495)
CASTLE-LAMBERT SON CONTG INC
39034 Bayview W (19975-4521)
PHONE.................410 329-8192
Gary Lambert, *Pr*
EMP: 5 **EST:** 1954
SALES (est): 818.23K **Privately Held**
SIC: 1521 General remodeling, single-family houses

(G-13496)
CHARLES A KLEIN & SONS INC
Also Called: Charles A. Klein & Sons
3 Mason Dr (19975-9617)
PHONE.................410 549-6960
EMP: 8
SALES (corp-wide): 28.45MM **Privately Held**
Web: www.caklein.com
SIC: 1711 Plumbing contractors
PA: Charles A. Klein & Sons, Inc.
5220 Klee Mill Rd S
Sykesville MD 21784
410 781-4946

(G-13497)
CHARLES A ZONKO BUILDERS INC
Also Called: Zonko Builders
37116 Lighthouse Rd (19975-3909)
PHONE.................302 436-0222
Charles A Zonko, *Pr*
Bonnie Zonko, *
EMP: 11 **EST:** 1973
SQ FT: 1,500
SALES (est): 616.07K **Privately Held**
Web: www.zonkobuilders.com
SIC: 1521 New construction, single-family houses

Selbyville - Sussex County (G-13498) **GEOGRAPHIC SECTION**

(G-13498)
CHESAPEAKE SEAGLASS JEWELRY
11505 W Sand Cove Rd (19975-3796)
PHONE..............................410 778-4999
EMP: 4 EST: 2017
SALES (est): 37.59K Privately Held
SIC: 2741 Miscellaneous publishing

(G-13499)
CHRISTINA M HANNA
37680 Pine Rd (19975-3973)
PHONE..............................302 236-7280
Christina Hanna, Owner
EMP: 6 EST: 2017
SALES (est): 22.18K Privately Held
SIC: 8049 Offices of health practitioner

(G-13500)
CLATCHEY ELECTRICAL CONTR INC
36892 Wood Duck Way (19975-3855)
PHONE..............................443 845-3720
EMP: 5 EST: 2018
SALES (est): 109.64K Privately Held
SIC: 1731 Electrical work

(G-13501)
COASTAL CARE PHYSCL THRAPY INC
37197 E Stoney Run (19975-4325)
PHONE..............................480 236-3863
Maricryst Birao, Asst Sec
EMP: 10 EST: 2018
SALES (est): 194.68K Privately Held
Web: www.coastalcarept.com
SIC: 8049 Physical therapist

(G-13502)
COASTAL EDGE LANDSCAPE LLC
37252 Hudson Rd (19975-3403)
PHONE..............................443 880-6270
EMP: 7 EST: 2019
SALES (est): 495.65K Privately Held
Web: www.coastaledgelandscape.com
SIC: 0781 Landscape services

(G-13503)
COASTAL TILE AMP STONE IN
7 N Williams St (19975-7514)
PHONE..............................301 748-0754
EMP: 5 EST: 2019
SALES (est): 142.18K Privately Held
Web: www.coastaltiledelaware.com
SIC: 1743 Tile installation, ceramic

(G-13504)
COASTAL VETERINARY LLC
33053 Lighthouse Rd (19975-4017)
PHONE..............................302 524-8550
EMP: 8 EST: 2016
SALES (est): 593.34K Privately Held
Web: www.coastalveterinary.com
SIC: 0742 Animal hospital services, pets and other animal specialties

(G-13505)
CODE VANGUARD LLC
37105 Hudson Rd (19975-3370)
PHONE..............................302 463-8265
James Stephens, Prin
EMP: 5 EST: 2018
SALES (est): 78.25K Privately Held
SIC: 7372 Prepackaged software

(G-13506)
CORE FUNCTIONS LLC
21142 Arrington Dr (19975-3600)
PHONE..............................443 956-9626
Mary Grimm, Owner
Maureen Kitchelt, Owner
EMP: 5 EST: 2014

SALES (est): 140.14K Privately Held
SIC: 7389 8742 Business Activities at Non-Commercial Site; Management engineering

(G-13507)
CRAFTSMAN CBNTRY WOODWORKS INC
37357 Tree Top Ln (19975-3350)
PHONE..............................302 841-5274
Richard Jensen, Prin
EMP: 8 EST: 2013
SQ FT: 2,000
SALES (est): 484.19K Privately Held
SIC: 8741 Construction management

(G-13508)
CRAIGS WOODWORKS LLC
38208 Rock Elm Dr (19975-4377)
PHONE..............................302 998-4201
Craig T Lamey, Prin
EMP: 5 EST: 2019
SALES (est): 177.1K Privately Held
SIC: 2431 Millwork

(G-13509)
CREEKSIDE PAINTING LLC
34411 Waters Run (19975-4173)
PHONE..............................302 983-1914
James Hagan, Prin
EMP: 5 EST: 2016
SALES (est): 122.6K Privately Held
SIC: 1721 Painting and paper hanging

(G-13510)
CROOSRAODS AUTO REPAIR INC
32469 Lighthouse Rd (19975-3410)
PHONE..............................302 436-9100
Lloyd Bare, Owner
EMP: 5 EST: 2011
SALES (est): 478.39K Privately Held
Web: www.crossroadsautorepairllc.com
SIC: 7538 General automotive repair shops

(G-13511)
CROSSROADS VETERINARY CLINIC
36774 Dupont Blvd (19975-3008)
PHONE..............................302 436-5984
Christian Brandt, Prin
EMP: 6 EST: 2009
SALES (est): 442.95K Privately Held
Web: www.selbyvilleanimalhospital.com
SIC: 0742 Animal hospital services, pets and other animal specialties

(G-13512)
CRYSTAL CLEAR MECHANICAL LLC
31950 Phillips Rd (19975-3323)
PHONE..............................302 344-2531
Beverly Sweitzer, Prin
EMP: 6 EST: 2013
SALES (est): 56.99K Privately Held
SIC: 1711 Mechanical contractor

(G-13513)
CYGNET CONSTRUCTION CORP
50 Saw Mill Ln (19975)
PHONE..............................302 436-5212
Gladys Swann, Pr
James E Swann Iii, VP
Nancy Swann, Sec
EMP: 6 EST: 1949
SALES (est): 567.04K Privately Held
SIC: 1794 Excavation work

(G-13514)
D A JONES INC
Also Called: Champion Window Cleaners
37479 Leisure Dr (19975-3841)
PHONE..............................302 836-9238
David A Jones, Pr

EMP: 5 EST: 1988
SALES (est): 126.78K Privately Held
SIC: 7349 Maid services, contract or fee basis

(G-13515)
DATATECH ENTERPRISES INC (PA)
Also Called: Acolyst
36322 Sunflower Blvd (19975-3751)
PHONE..............................540 370-0010
Ellie Nazemoff, Pr
Kaveh Nazemoff, Technology Vice President
EMP: 15 EST: 1989
SALES (est): 2.13MM
SALES (corp-wide): 2.13MM Privately Held
Web: www.acolyst.com
SIC: 7379 7373 7371 7372 Computer related consulting services; Computer integrated systems design; Custom computer programming services; Prepackaged software

(G-13516)
DEAD ON CONSTRUCTION
P.O. Box 1092 (19975-1092)
PHONE..............................302 462-5023
Lazaro Agustin, Prin
EMP: 6 EST: 2010
SALES (est): 332.65K Privately Held
SIC: 1521 Single-family housing construction

(G-13517)
DEC HOME SERVICES
37116 Hudson Rd (19975-3369)
PHONE..............................240 793-4818
David Lee Efird, Owner
EMP: 5 EST: 2012
SALES (est): 194.16K Privately Held
SIC: 1522 Residential construction, nec

(G-13518)
DELMARVA SKIN PA
38394 Dupont Blvd Unit Fg (19975-3049)
PHONE..............................302 564-0001
EMP: 6 EST: 2018
SALES (est): 207.2K Privately Held
Web: www.delmarvaskin.com
SIC: 8011 Dermatologist

(G-13519)
DELMARVA WHISKEY CLUB
36414 Azalea Ave (19975-4243)
P.O. Box 1175 (19975-1175)
PHONE..............................215 815-1706
EMP: 7 EST: 2015
SALES (est): 46.04K Privately Held
Web: www.delmarvawhiskey.com
SIC: 7997 Membership sports and recreation clubs

(G-13520)
DELTA SALES CORP
5 W Church St Unit 202 (19975-2003)
P.O. Box 681 (19975-0681)
PHONE..............................302 436-6063
EMP: 10 EST: 1995
SALES (est): 371.72K Privately Held
SIC: 5051 Steel

(G-13521)
DONNAS FAMILY CUT & CURL INC
106 Bayville Shopping Ctr (19975)
PHONE..............................302 436-8999
EMP: 8 EST: 1996
SALES (est): 104.17K Privately Held
Web: donnas-family-cut-curl-inc.business.site
SIC: 7231 Hairdressers

(G-13522)
DOUBLE D RESTORATION LLC
33 W Church St (19975-2003)
P.O. Box 93 (19975-0093)
PHONE..............................302 853-2176
EMP: 5 EST: 2014
SALES (est): 82.13K Privately Held
SIC: 1799 Special trade contractors, nec

(G-13523)
DOUGLAS M HELFER
20 S Main St (19975-9663)
PHONE..............................302 988-8127
Douglas M Helfer, Prin
EMP: 5 EST: 2011
SALES (est): 197.37K Privately Held
SIC: 8111 General practice attorney, lawyer

(G-13524)
DR JAMES KRAMER
13 S Main St # 348 (19975-9664)
PHONE..............................302 436-5133
James Kenneth Kramer, Prin
EMP: 10 EST: 2008
SALES (est): 198.81K Privately Held
Web: www.drjameskramer.com
SIC: 8021 Dentists' office

(G-13525)
DUNES MANOR HOTEL
38312 Ocean Vista Dr (19975-2833)
PHONE..............................610 256-4307
Joanne Cunningham, Prin
EMP: 16 EST: 2018
SALES (est): 67.95K Privately Held
SIC: 7011 Hotels

(G-13526)
DUNWORTH MACHINES LLC ◆
34676 Horseshoe Dr (19975-4072)
P.O. Box 4191 (59604-4191)
PHONE..............................434 977-4790
EMP: 4 EST: 2022
SALES (est): 62.08K Privately Held
Web: www.dunworthmachines.com
SIC: 3732 Boatbuilding and repairing

(G-13527)
EAST COAST ELASTOMERICS INC
Also Called: Ece Weatherguard
35115 Johnson Store Rd (19975-3526)
PHONE..............................302 524-8004
Daniel Ash, Pr
EMP: 10 EST: 1993
SALES (est): 814.32K Privately Held
Web: www.kaleidoscopedesign.net
SIC: 1799 Waterproofing

(G-13528)
EASTERN SHORE PORCH PATIO INC
17 Mason Dr (19975-3057)
P.O. Box 168 (19975-0168)
PHONE..............................302 436-9520
Robert C Douglas, Pr
EMP: 20 EST: 1992
SQ FT: 9,000
SALES (est): 2.14MM Privately Held
Web: www.esvinylproducts.com
SIC: 1799 1521 5712 Fence construction; General remodeling, single-family houses; Outdoor and garden furniture

(G-13529)
EASTERN SHORE VINYL PRODU
17 Mason Dr (19975-3057)
PHONE..............................302 436-9520
EMP: 8 EST: 2019
SALES (est): 94.72K Privately Held
Web: www.esvinylproducts.com

GEOGRAPHIC SECTION

Selbyville - Sussex County (G-13558)

SIC: 7822 Motion picture and tape distribution

(G-13530)
ED HILEMAN DRYWALL INC
36722 Roxana Rd (19975-3305)
PHONE...................302 436-6277
Ed Hileman, *Pr*
EMP: 7 EST: 1994
SALES (est): 500K **Privately Held**
Web: www.edhilemandrywall.com
SIC: 1742 Drywall

(G-13531)
EDWARD M TINGLE
209 Hosier Street Ext (19975-9314)
P.O. Box 212 (19975-0212)
PHONE...................302 436-5539
Edward M Tingle, *Prin*
EMP: 5 EST: 2007
SALES (est): 244.03K **Privately Held**
SIC: 6515 Mobile home site operators

(G-13532)
ELEMENTS HVAC SERVICES LLC
38015 Sunny Winters Dr (19975-3979)
PHONE...................302 448-9641
EMP: 6 EST: 2016
SALES (est): 72.75K **Privately Held**
Web: www.elementshvacservices.com
SIC: 1711 Warm air heating and air conditioning contractor

(G-13533)
ENERGY GYM
36666 Bluewater Run W Unit 1 (19975-4392)
PHONE...................302 436-9001
Tony Hall, *Prin*
EMP: 5 EST: 2010
SALES (est): 222.98K **Privately Held**
Web: www.energygym247.com
SIC: 7991 Health club

(G-13534)
ENVIRONMENTAL RESOURCES INC
38173 Dupont Blvd (19975-3033)
P.O. Box 169 (19975-0169)
PHONE...................302 436-9637
Thomas Nobile, *Prin*
EMP: 5 EST: 2009
SALES (est): 440.51K **Privately Held**
Web: www.ericonsultants.com
SIC: 8748 Environmental consultant

(G-13535)
FERRELL COOLING & HEATING INC
32971 Lighthouse Rd (19975-4088)
P.O. Box 1070 (19975-1070)
PHONE...................302 436-2922
Sally Ferrell, *Prin*
EMP: 6 EST: 2005
SALES (est): 446.81K **Privately Held**
Web: www.ferrellcoolingandheating.com
SIC: 1711 Warm air heating and air conditioning contractor

(G-13536)
FREEMAN ARTS PAVILION INC
31255 Americana Pkwy (19975-3785)
PHONE...................302 436-6241
Michelle Freeman, *Prin*
EMP: 13 EST: 2017
SALES (est): 1.48MM **Privately Held**
Web: www.freemanarts.org
SIC: 7922 Performing arts center production

(G-13537)
GLOBAL MARKET INSIGHTS INC
4 N Main St (19975-9688)
P.O. Box 1027 (19975-1027)
PHONE...................302 470-2829
George Taube, *Pr*
Charanjeet Ailsinghani, *Sec*
Herr Gretchen, *Operations*
EMP: 6 EST: 2016
SQ FT: 1,600
SALES (est): 1.52MM **Privately Held**
Web: www.gminsights.com
SIC: 8732 Market analysis or research

(G-13538)
GOOD NEIGHBOR LLC
37524 Leisure Dr (19975-3837)
PHONE...................302 228-9910
EMP: 7 EST: 2009
SALES (est): 200.96K **Privately Held**
SIC: 1522 Residential construction, nec

(G-13539)
GPM INVESTMENTS LLC
Also Called: Shore Stop 294
36345 Lighthouse Rd Ste 301 (19975-3985)
PHONE...................302 436-6330
L Leatherbury, *Genl Mgr*
EMP: 10
SALES (corp-wide): 9.14B **Publicly Held**
Web: www.gpminvestments.com
SIC: 6799 Investors, nec
HQ: Gpm Investments, Llc
8565 Magellan Pkwy # 400
Richmond VA 23227
276 328-3669

(G-13540)
H & R BLOCK
Also Called: H & R Block
38445 Dupont Blvd Unit 3 (19975-3056)
PHONE...................302 436-0260
EMP: 7 EST: 2015
SALES (est): 18.45K **Privately Held**
Web: www.hrblock.com
SIC: 7291 Tax return preparation services

(G-13541)
HAINES FABRICATION & MCH LLC
45 Railroad Ave (19975-9675)
PHONE...................302 436-1929
Donald Haines, *Managing Member*
EMP: 15 EST: 2008
SALES (est): 1.71MM **Privately Held**
Web: haines-fabrication-machine-llc.hub.biz
SIC: 3599 Machine shop, jobbing and repair

(G-13542)
HARDY DEVELOPMENT
Also Called: Hardy's Development
32984 Lighthouse Rd (19975-4024)
PHONE...................302 436-4496
Bonnie Hardy, *Brnch Mgr*
EMP: 6
Web: www.hardysselfstorage.com
SIC: 4225 Warehousing, self storage
PA: Hardy Development
328 S Main St
Bel Air MD 21014

(G-13543)
HARFORD HEALTH SERVICES INC
37454 Woods Run Cir (19975-4098)
PHONE...................410 420-8108
Jose Torres, *Pr*
EMP: 9 EST: 2001
SALES (est): 2.04MM **Privately Held**
SIC: 5122 Pharmaceuticals

(G-13544)
HEARTLAND PAYMENT SYSTEMS LLC
37126 E White Tail Dr (19975-3537)
PHONE...................302 228-9365
Traci Stong, *Prin*
EMP: 7
SALES (corp-wide): 9.65B **Publicly Held**
Web: www.heartlandpaymentsystems.com
SIC: 7389 Credit card service
HQ: Heartland Payment Systems, Llc
3550 Lenox Rd Ne Ste 3000
Atlanta GA 30326
877 729-2968

(G-13545)
HEAVENLY HOUND HOTEL
33049 Lighthouse Rd (19975-4017)
P.O. Box 54 (19975-0054)
PHONE...................302 436-2926
Janice Baker, *Pr*
Joseph Baker, *Sec*
EMP: 5 EST: 1989
SALES (est): 243.56K **Privately Held**
Web: www.heavenlyhoundhotel.com
SIC: 0752 Boarding services, kennels

(G-13546)
HIGH TIDE NEWS
11243 Signature Blvd (19975-3703)
PHONE...................302 727-0390
Judy Layman, *Prin*
EMP: 5 EST: 2016
SALES (est): 70.48K **Privately Held**
Web: www.hightidenews.com
SIC: 2711 Newspapers

(G-13547)
HOBAN AUTO & MACHINESHOP INC
Also Called: Hoban Service Center
19 N Main St (19975-9697)
P.O. Box 43 (19975-0043)
PHONE...................302 436-8013
EMP: 6 EST: 1983
SALES (est): 496.18K **Privately Held**
SIC: 7538 General automotive repair shops

(G-13548)
HOLLAND CORP
33357 Deer Run Rd (19975-3531)
PHONE...................302 245-5645
G Shoemaker, *Pr*
EMP: 5 EST: 2010
SALES (est): 133.88K **Privately Held**
Web: www.selbyvilletractorde.com
SIC: 7389 Interior design services

(G-13549)
INSPIRATION BENNINGTON CERAMIC
11 Discovery Ln (19975-9642)
PHONE...................302 436-5544
EMP: 8 EST: 2015
SALES (est): 459.23K **Privately Held**
Web: www.benningtontilesolutions.com
SIC: 1743 Tile installation, ceramic

(G-13550)
J & J BULKHEADING
Snow Goose Lane, Unit 3c (19975)
P.O. Box 600 (19975-0600)
PHONE...................302 436-2800
Jerry Kenney, *Managing Member*
EMP: 8 EST: 2003
SALES (est): 973.13K **Privately Held**
Web: www.jandjbulkheading.com
SIC: 1629 Dock construction

(G-13551)
JOHN V REITZ
Also Called: Dr John Reitz
27148 Briny Bluff Ln (19975-4544)
PHONE...................610 320-9993
John V Reitz, *Owner*
EMP: 7 EST: 1982
SALES (est): 453.03K **Privately Held**
SIC: 8021 Dentists' office

(G-13552)
JOHNSON JR HENRY & SON FARM
37047 Johnson Rd (19975-3524)
PHONE...................302 436-8501
EMP: 7 EST: 2010
SALES (est): 932.94K **Privately Held**
SIC: 5153 Grains

(G-13553)
JOSHUA M FREEMAN FOUNDATION
31255 Americana Pkwy (19975-3785)
PHONE...................302 436-3003
EMP: 18 EST: 2007
SALES (est): 6.53MM **Privately Held**
Web: www.freemanarts.com
SIC: 7922 Performing arts center production

(G-13554)
KAMAX CONSTRUCTION LLC
37268 W White Tail Dr (19975-3540)
PHONE...................302 296-8270
EMP: 8 EST: 2016
SALES (est): 83.47K **Privately Held**
Web: www.kamax.com
SIC: 1521 Single-family housing construction

(G-13555)
KATHYS DAY CARE
32187 Lynch Rd (19975-3416)
PHONE...................302 436-4308
Kathy Collins, *Dir*
EMP: 8 EST: 2018
SALES (est): 23.52K **Privately Held**
SIC: 8351 Group day care center

(G-13556)
KB COLDIRON INC
36546 Dupont Blvd (19975-3006)
P.O. Box 297 (19945-0297)
PHONE...................302 436-4224
Kerry Coldiron, *Pr*
Ron Orash, *
EMP: 60 EST: 1973
SQ FT: 20,000
SALES (est): 8.62MM **Privately Held**
Web: www.kbcoldiron.com
SIC: 1542 Commercial and office building, new construction

(G-13557)
KEITH PROPERTIES INC
38016 Fenwick Shoals Blvd Unit 4 (19975-3986)
PHONE...................302 258-9224
Richard Keith Junior, *Prin*
EMP: 6 EST: 2004
SALES (est): 222.75K **Privately Held**
Web: www.thefrenchlaundry.net
SIC: 6512 Nonresidential building operators

(G-13558)
KELLER WILLIAMS RLTY DELMARVA
37458 Lion Dr (19975-3887)
PHONE...................410 430-2721
EMP: 5 EST: 2019
SALES (est): 133.27K **Privately Held**
Web: www.jenchughes.com
SIC: 6531 Real estate agent, residential

Selbyville - Sussex County (G-13559)

(G-13559)
KTM 2 LLC
Also Called: Arrow Safety Device Company
123 Dixon St (19975-3022)
PHONE.................302 856-2516
Travis Wyshock, *Managing Member*
EMP: 8 **EST:** 2021
SALES (est): 1MM **Privately Held**
Web: www.arrowsafetydevice.com
SIC: 4731 Freight transportation arrangement

(G-13560)
LAND TECH ASSOCIATES INC
Also Called: Landtech Associates
36308 Royal Tern Dr (19975-4164)
PHONE.................301 277-8878
EMP: 10 **EST:** 1994
SALES (est): 507.46K **Privately Held**
Web: walkershomerepair.webs.com
SIC: 8713 Photogrammetric engineering

(G-13561)
LIGHTHOUSE DANCE AND YOGA LLC
37473 Albatross Dr (19975-4156)
PHONE.................302 564-7611
EMP: 5 **EST:** 2018
SALES (est): 21.12K **Privately Held**
SIC: 7911 Dance studio and school

(G-13562)
LONG AND FOSTER
36897 Wood Duck Way (19975-3855)
PHONE.................302 858-7805
Heather Gates, *Prin*
EMP: 6 **EST:** 2018
SALES (est): 137.62K **Privately Held**
Web: www.longandfoster.com
SIC: 6531 Real estate brokers and agents

(G-13563)
M & L CONTRACTORS INC
13354 Blueberry Rd (19975)
P.O. Box 512 (19975-0512)
PHONE.................302 436-9303
Carlton Murray, *Pr*
Jay Murray, *VP*
Clifton Murray, *Sec*
EMP: 10 **EST:** 1990
SQ FT: 1,500
SALES (est): 714.47K **Privately Held**
SIC: 1741 Concrete block masonry laying

(G-13564)
MALLERD LAKES
37976 Pelican Ln (19975-4604)
PHONE.................443 783-2993
Stacey Seldy, *Admn*
EMP: 10 **EST:** 2014
SALES (est): 168.84K **Privately Held**
SIC: 8641 Condominium association

(G-13565)
MANOR CREEK CONSTRUCTION INC
213 Gumboro Rd (19975-9499)
PHONE.................302 245-2887
Richard Blitz, *Owner*
EMP: 5 **EST:** 2014
SALES (est): 105.92K **Privately Held**
SIC: 1521 Single-family housing construction

(G-13566)
MARYS LITTLE LAMBS DAYCARE
31730 Phillips Rd (19975-3321)
PHONE.................302 436-5796
Mary Atkins, *Prin*
EMP: 5 **EST:** 2009
SALES (est): 82.68K **Privately Held**
SIC: 8351 Group day care center

(G-13567)
MASTRACCI MASTRACCI
30107 Tammy Ct (19975-3561)
PHONE.................410 869-3400
Mike Mastracci, *Prin*
EMP: 5 **EST:** 2010
SALES (est): 208.37K **Privately Held**
SIC: 8111 General practice attorney, lawyer

(G-13568)
MATT CARPET GUY LLC
50 N Main St (19975-9688)
PHONE.................443 497-3281
EMP: 8 **EST:** 2010
SALES (est): 466.58K **Privately Held**
Web: www.mattthecarpetguy.com
SIC: 1771 1752 5087 5023 Flooring contractor; Carpet laying; Carpet installation equipment; Floor coverings

(G-13569)
MAXIM HAIR & NAILS LLC
31225 Americana Pkwy Unit 7 (19975-3793)
PHONE.................410 920-8656
Ramona Sterca, *Managing Member*
EMP: 5 **EST:** 2016
SALES (est): 81.66K **Privately Held**
SIC: 7231 Hairdressers

(G-13570)
MERRITT MARINE CNSTR INC
32992 Lighthouse Rd (19975-4024)
PHONE.................302 436-2881
Demmy Merritt, *Pr*
Janice Merritt, *Sec*
EMP: 6 **EST:** 1964
SALES (est): 617.16K **Privately Held**
SIC: 1629 Marine construction

(G-13571)
MICHAEL J TRUITT
Also Called: J & S Lawn Service
36261 Zion Church Rd (19975-4120)
PHONE.................302 436-4081
Michael J Truitt, *Prin*
EMP: 5 **EST:** 2011
SALES (est): 207.2K **Privately Held**
SIC: 0782 Lawn services

(G-13572)
MID-LANTIC ENTERPRISES INC
Also Called: Mid-Lantic Distributors
68 Duke Street Ext (19975-9484)
P.O. Box 70 (19975-0070)
PHONE.................302 436-2772
Bruce Hrebik, *Pr*
EMP: 9 **EST:** 1996
SALES (est): 392.34K **Privately Held**
SIC: 8741 Management services

(G-13573)
MIDCOAST GYMNSTICS DNCE STUDIO
Also Called: Mid-Coast Gymnastic Studio
15 Dukes Street Ext (19975-9319)
P.O. Box 50 (19975-0050)
PHONE.................302 436-6007
Kimberly Wickham, *Owner*
EMP: 8 **EST:** 1995
SALES (est): 218.34K **Privately Held**
Web: www.midcoastgymnastics.com
SIC: 7999 Gymnastic instruction, non-membership

(G-13574)
MIDDLESEX WATER COMPANY
36252 Lighthouse Rd (19975-3912)
PHONE.................302 436-4625
EMP: 7
SALES (corp-wide): 162.43MM **Publicly Held**
Web: www.middlesexwater.com
SIC: 4941 Water supply
PA: Middlesex Water Company
485c Route 1 S Ste 400
Iselin NJ 08830
732 634-1500

(G-13575)
MIDLANTIC MARINE CENTER INC
36624 Dupont Blvd (19975-3007)
PHONE.................302 436-2628
EMP: 10 **EST:** 2001
SALES (est): 680.91K **Privately Held**
Web: www.midlanticmarinecenter.com
SIC: 7699 4493 Boat repair; Boat yards, storage and incidental repair

(G-13576)
MIDNIGHT BLUE INC
Also Called: McGraphix Advertising Products
37091 E White Tail Dr (19975-3536)
PHONE.................302 436-9665
Steve Mcdonald, *Pr*
Al Mcdonald, *VP*
EMP: 13 **EST:** 1983
SALES (est): 460.92K **Privately Held**
Web: www.mcgraphixinc.com
SIC: 2759 7389 Screen printing; Embroidery advertising

(G-13577)
MIRANDA OBRIEN
36252 Lighthouse Rd (19975-3912)
PHONE.................302 436-6411
Miranda O'brien, *Owner*
EMP: 7 **EST:** 2017
SALES (est): 22.18K **Privately Held**
SIC: 8049 Offices of health practitioner

(G-13578)
MOLLY WILLIAMS
31556 Winterberry Pkwy (19975-3707)
PHONE.................302 436-3015
Molly Williams, *Prin*
EMP: 5 **EST:** 2014
SALES (est): 46.56K **Privately Held**
SIC: 7922 Performing arts center production

(G-13579)
MONEY MAILER TRI COUNTIES
Also Called: Money Mailer
36461 Wild Rose Cir (19975-3740)
PHONE.................240 832-1340
EMP: 6 **EST:** 2016
SALES (est): 122.4K **Privately Held**
Web: www.moneymailer.com
SIC: 7331 Direct mail advertising services

(G-13580)
MOUNTAIRE FARMS INC
Also Called: Mountaire Farms
Hoosier St (19975)
P.O. Box 710 (19975-0710)
PHONE.................302 436-8241
Mike Steele, *Brnch Mgr*
EMP: 1600
SALES (corp-wide): 2.07B **Privately Held**
Web: www.mountaire.com
SIC: 0191 General farms, primarily crop
HQ: Mountaire Farms Inc.
1901 Napa Valley Dr
Little Rock AR 72212
501 372-6524

(G-13581)
MOUNTAIRE FARMS INC
35 Railroad Ave (19975-9675)
P.O. Box 710 (19975-0710)
PHONE.................302 988-6200
Owen Phillip, *Brnch Mgr*
EMP: 397
SALES (corp-wide): 2.07B **Privately Held**
Web: www.mountaire.com
SIC: 2015 Poultry slaughtering and processing
HQ: Mountaire Farms Inc.
1901 Napa Valley Dr
Little Rock AR 72212
501 372-6524

(G-13582)
MOUNTAIRE OF DELMARVA INC
55 Hosier St (19975-9300)
P.O. Box 710 (19975-0710)
PHONE.................302 988-6207
William Reeves, *Dir*
EMP: 23 **EST:** 2007
SALES (est): 1.67MM **Privately Held**
Web: www.mountaire.com
SIC: 2015 Poultry slaughtering and processing

(G-13583)
MUMFORD SHEET METAL WORKS INC
101 Cemetery Rd (19975-9312)
P.O. Box 170 (19975-0170)
PHONE.................302 436-8251
John Mumford, *Pr*
Dale Mumford Junior, *VP*
Stewart Mumford, *VP*
EMP: 12 **EST:** 1932
SQ FT: 40,000
SALES (est): 881.22K **Privately Held**
Web: www.mumfordmetal.com
SIC: 5074 5031 5072 1761 Plumbing fittings and supplies; Lumber, plywood, and millwork; Hardware; Sheet metal work, nec

(G-13584)
MURRAY BROTHERS
Also Called: Murray Farms
8908 Ebenezer Rd (19975)
PHONE.................302 436-3639
Clifton C Murray, *Pt*
Jay Murray, *Pt*
Carlton Murray, *Pt*
EMP: 8 **EST:** 1935
SALES (est): 515.94K **Privately Held**
SIC: 0116 0115 0213 0251 Soybeans; Corn; Hogs; Broiler, fryer, and roaster chickens

(G-13585)
MURRAY BUNTING CONSTR
32924 Lighthouse Rd (19975-4024)
PHONE.................302 436-5144
EMP: 17 **EST:** 2020
SALES (est): 816.52K **Privately Held**
SIC: 1521 Single-family housing construction

(G-13586)
NORTH BAY MARINA INCORPORATED
36543 Lighthouse Rd (19975-3977)
PHONE.................302 436-4211
J Scott Mccurdy, *Pr*
Mary M Mc Curdy, *VP*
Bernadine K Mc Curdy, *Sec*
Roy F Moore, *Treas*
EMP: 21 **EST:** 1983
SQ FT: 8,500
SALES (est): 1.77MM **Privately Held**
Web: www.northbaymarina.com
SIC: 5551 4493 Motor boat dealers; Boat yards, storage and incidental repair

GEOGRAPHIC SECTION

Selbyville - Sussex County (G-13615)

(G-13587)
OCEAN AIR
32971 Lighthouse Rd (19975-4088)
PHONE.............................302 524-8003
Rob Cole, *Ofcr*
EMP: 5 **EST:** 2015
SALES (est): 77.55K **Privately Held**
SIC: 1711 Heating systems repair and maintenance

(G-13588)
OCEAN SERVICES OF DE INC
37822 Fenwick Cir (19975-4138)
PHONE.............................410 524-1518
David Dekowsky, *Prin*
EMP: 5 **EST:** 2018
SALES (est): 145.86K **Privately Held**
SIC: 1521 Single-family housing construction

(G-13589)
PAMPER ME PINK LLC
46 N Main St (19975-9688)
PHONE.............................302 200-2635
Leshell Dennis, *CEO*
EMP: 10 **EST:** 2021
SALES (est): 179.03K **Privately Held**
Web: www.pampermepinkde.com
SIC: 7231 8299 Beauty shops; Educational services

(G-13590)
PDO CONSTRUCTION LLC
1 W 1st St (19975-7518)
PHONE.............................302 542-0963
Philip Oneschuk, *Owner*
EMP: 5 **EST:** 2007
SALES (est): 150.12K **Privately Held**
SIC: 1521 Single-family housing construction

(G-13591)
PLUMBING ENTERPRISES LLC
37232 Lighthouse Rd Ste 463 (19975-3981)
PHONE.............................302 515-4620
EMP: 10 **EST:** 2018
SALES (est): 881.02K **Privately Held**
Web: www.pellcusa.com
SIC: 1711 Plumbing contractors

(G-13592)
PMB ASSOCIATES LLC
37816 Eagle Ln Unit 325 (19975-4644)
PHONE.............................302 436-0111
EMP: 2 **EST:** 2007
SALES (est): 191.38K **Privately Held**
SIC: 2732 Book printing

(G-13593)
PNC BANK NATIONAL ASSOCIATION
Also Called: PNC
31231 Americana Pkwy (19975-3785)
PHONE.............................302 436-5400
Kathy Castrovillo, *Brnch Mgr*
EMP: 9
SALES (corp-wide): 23.54B **Publicly Held**
Web: www.pnc.com
SIC: 6021 National commercial banks
HQ: Pnc Bank, National Association
300 5th Ave
Pittsburgh PA 15222
877 762-2000

(G-13594)
POOLSIDE CNSTR & RENOVATION
Route 54 (19975)
PHONE.............................302 436-9711
Julius Oairey Iii, *Pr*
EMP: 5 **EST:** 2001
SALES (est): 526.13K **Privately Held**
Web: www.poolsideconstruction.net
SIC: 1521 8111 General remodeling, single-family houses; Legal services

(G-13595)
QUINTECCENT INC
37808 Salty Way W (19975-3918)
PHONE.............................443 838-5447
Ken G Limparis, *Pr*
EMP: 2 **EST:** 2015
SALES (est): 483.49K **Privately Held**
SIC: 3663 8711 8734 8742 Radio and t.v. communications equipment; Engineering services; Testing laboratories; Management consulting services

(G-13596)
RED DOG PLUMBING AND HTG CORP
Also Called: Red Dog Associates
37058 Roxana Rd (19975-3308)
P.O. Box 1070 (19975-1070)
PHONE.............................302 436-2922
Sally Bergeron, *Pr*
EMP: 27 **EST:** 2015
SALES (est): 4MM **Privately Held**
Web: www.reddogac.com
SIC: 1711 Warm air heating and air conditioning contractor

(G-13597)
RED SUN CUSTOM APPAREL INC
1 Mason Dr (19975-9617)
PHONE.............................302 988-8230
William E Regan, *Pr*
EMP: 17 **EST:** 2000
SQ FT: 5,000
SALES (est): 458.01K **Privately Held**
Web: www.redsuncustom.com
SIC: 7389 2396 Embroidery advertising; Screen printing on fabric articles

(G-13598)
RESORT POKER LEAGUE
38291 Osprey Ct Apt 1168 (19975-2846)
PHONE.............................302 604-8706
EMP: 5 **EST:** 2011
SALES (est): 75.65K **Privately Held**
SIC: 7997 Membership sports and recreation clubs

(G-13599)
RHS REALTY
32191 Bixler Rd (19975-3339)
PHONE.............................302 436-6478
Ernest Blaser, *Owner*
EMP: 5 **EST:** 2018
SALES (est): 170.14K **Privately Held**
SIC: 6531 Real estate brokers and agents

(G-13600)
RICH HEBERT & ASSOCIATES
38027 Fenwick Shoals Blvd (19975-9102)
PHONE.............................202 255-3474
Richard Hebert, *Owner*
EMP: 5 **EST:** 2011
SALES (est): 109.55K **Privately Held**
Web: www.rthebert.com
SIC: 7832 Motion picture theaters, except drive-in

(G-13601)
ROYAL LAWN CARE & PROPERTY MAI
4 N Main St (19975-9688)
PHONE.............................302 436-9800
EMP: 5 **EST:** 2018
SALES (est): 478.7K **Privately Held**
Web: www.rlclawns.com
SIC: 0782 Lawn care services

(G-13602)
S&R PRESSURE WASHING LLC
36828 Herring Way (19975-3862)
PHONE.............................410 430-9864
Charles Griffin, *Prin*
EMP: 5 **EST:** 2015
SALES (est): 67.43K **Privately Held**
SIC: 1799 Special trade contractors, nec

(G-13603)
SEASIDE GRAPHICS CORP
1 Mason Dr (19975-9617)
PHONE.............................302 436-9460
Debbie Maxfield, *Pr*
Steven Hershey, *VP*
▼ **EMP:** 8 **EST:** 1978
SQ FT: 10,000
SALES (est): 418.95K **Privately Held**
Web: www.seasidegraphics.com
SIC: 7336 Silk screen design

(G-13604)
SELBYVILLE CLEANERS INC (PA)
Also Called: Wilgus Glamorama
68 Hosier St (19975-9308)
P.O. Box 1010 (19975-1010)
PHONE.............................302 249-3444
Jeff Wilgus, *Pr*
EMP: 45 **EST:** 1939
SQ FT: 26,000
SALES (est): 1.02MM
SALES (corp-wide): 1.02MM **Privately Held**
SIC: 7211 7213 Power laundries, family and commercial; Linen supply

(G-13605)
SMI SERVICES OF DELAWARE LLC
20 Railroad Ave (19975-9676)
PHONE.............................302 436-4410
EMP: 89
SALES (corp-wide): 9.67MM **Privately Held**
Web: www.smicompanies.net
SIC: 7349 Building maintenance services, nec
PA: Smi Services Of Delaware, Llc
5609 Dupont Pkwy
Smyrna DE 19977
302 514-9681

(G-13606)
SNEADS HEATING & AC
31555 Lighthouse Rd (19975-3461)
PHONE.............................302 524-8090
Leroy Sneads, *Owner*
EMP: 7 **EST:** 2010
SALES (est): 237.58K **Privately Held**
SIC: 1711 Warm air heating and air conditioning contractor

(G-13607)
SOUTH SHORE PROVISIONS LLC
18 Ruth St (19975-9619)
PHONE.............................443 614-2442
Debra Behney, *Managing Member*
EMP: 5 **EST:** 2015
SALES (est): 224.12K **Privately Held**
SIC: 5941 4493 Fishing equipment; Marinas

(G-13608)
SPACEPORT SUPPORT SERVICES
6 Dixon St (19975)
P.O. Box 681 (19975-0681)
PHONE.............................302 524-4020
Sep Mostaghim, *Prin*
EMP: 6 **EST:** 2008
SALES (est): 509.65K **Privately Held**
SIC: 8711 Engineering services

(G-13609)
SPRING MIX SPORT FSHING CHRTER
38403 Bayberry Ln (19975-4391)
PHONE.............................443 463-8902
Paul J Lebling, *Prin*
EMP: 6 **EST:** 2014
SALES (est): 25.62K **Privately Held**
Web: www.springmixfishing.com
SIC: 7999 Fishing lakes and piers, operation

(G-13610)
SUSSEX CENTRAL HIGH SCHOO
31 Hosier St (19975-9300)
PHONE.............................304 261-2873
EMP: 6 **EST:** 2019
SALES (est): 227.06K **Privately Held**
Web: schs.irsd.net
SIC: 8699 Membership organizations, nec

(G-13611)
T & T PRODUCE LLC
34668 W Line Rd (19975-4009)
PHONE.............................302 245-6235
Deborah Hall, *Prin*
EMP: 5 **EST:** 2019
SALES (est): 90.77K **Privately Held**
SIC: 7822 Motion picture and tape distribution

(G-13612)
TIDALHLTH PNNSULA REGIONAL INC
Also Called: Peninsula Regional Prmry Care
15 N Williams St (19975-7514)
PHONE.............................302 436-8004
Carolanne Erker, *Mgr*
EMP: 6
SALES (corp-wide): 1.18MM **Privately Held**
Web: www.tidalhealth.org
SIC: 8062 8011 General medical and surgical hospitals; Offices and clinics of medical doctors
HQ: Tidalhealth Peninsula Regional, Inc.
100 E Carroll St
Salisbury MD 21801
410 546-6400

(G-13613)
TRAVEL OFFSHORE
22 Berue Ct (19975-9465)
PHONE.............................410 246-6648
Thomas Preston, *Prin*
EMP: 5 **EST:** 2017
SALES (est): 121.71K **Privately Held**
SIC: 4724 Travel agencies

(G-13614)
UFCW LOCAL 27
3 Mason Dr (19975-9617)
PHONE.............................302 436-6105
Eric Masten, *CEO*
EMP: 7 **EST:** 2018
SALES (est): 54.45K **Privately Held**
SIC: 8631 Labor union

(G-13615)
ULTIMATE EXPRESS INC
37976 Bayview Cir E (19975-2871)
PHONE.............................443 523-0800
Nikolajs Litvinenkovs, *Pr*
EMP: 10 **EST:** 2013
SQ FT: 13,000
SALES (est): 490.17K **Privately Held**
SIC: 4213 Trucking, except local

(PA)=Parent Co (HQ)=Headquarters
✪ = New Business established in last 2 years

Selbyville - Sussex County (G-13616) GEOGRAPHIC SECTION

(G-13616)
VALLIANT HOME IMPROVEMENTS
37104 Johnson Rd (19975-3523)
PHONE................................302 363-7109
Josh Valliant, *Prin*
EMP: 5 EST: 2010
SALES (est): 118.31K **Privately Held**
SIC: 1521 Single-family housing construction

(G-13617)
WAGS TO RICHES
36735 Roxana Rd (19975-3315)
PHONE................................302 436-4766
EMP: 5 EST: 2013
SALES (est): 69.39K **Privately Held**
Web:
www.wagstorichespetgrooming.com
SIC: 0752 Grooming services, pet and animal specialties

(G-13618)
WAYNE R BONLIE M D
33195 Lighthouse Rd # 8 (19975-4071)
PHONE................................302 436-0901
Wayne R Bonlie, *Prin*
EMP: 7 EST: 2018
SALES (est): 84.15K **Privately Held**
SIC: 8011 General and family practice, physician/surgeon

(G-13619)
WEATHER OR NOT INC
38294 London Ave Unit 3 (19975-4079)
PHONE................................302 436-7533
Bryan Warner, *Brnch Mgr*
EMP: 16
SIC: 1522 Condominium construction
PA: Weather Or Not Inc
      660 S Coastal Hwy
      Bethany Beach DE 19930

(G-13620)
WRPATRICK ENTERPRISES LLC
37695 Crab Bay Ln (19975-3930)
PHONE................................302 988-1061
Warren Patrick, *Prin*
EMP: 5 EST: 2014
SALES (est): 41.08K **Privately Held**
SIC: 8748 Business consulting, nec

(G-13621)
XERIMIS INC
36414 Azalea Ave (19975-4243)
PHONE................................215 815-1706
EMP: 6 EST: 2019
SALES (est): 68.54K **Privately Held**
Web: www.xerimis.com
SIC: 8748 Business consulting, nec

(G-13622)
ZICHERHEIT LLC
38824 Wilson Ave (19975-4415)
PHONE................................302 510-3718
EMP: 5 EST: 2014
SALES (est): 205.41K **Privately Held**
SIC: 7381 7389 Security guard service; Notary publics

Smyrna
Kent County

(G-13623)
190 STADIUM LLC
Also Called: Best Western Smyrna Inn
190 Stadium St (19977-2813)
PHONE................................302 659-3635
EMP: 18 EST: 2008
SALES (est): 105.37K **Privately Held**
Web: www.bestwestern.com
SIC: 7011 Inns

(G-13624)
A DISH NETWORK
103 S Dupont Blvd (19977-1579)
PHONE................................302 223-5754
EMP: 6 EST: 2013
SALES (est): 39.12K **Privately Held**
Web: www.dish.com
SIC: 4841 Direct broadcast satellite services (DBS)

(G-13625)
A DOUGLAS CHERVENAK DO
319 N Carter Rd (19977-1282)
PHONE................................302 653-1050
A Chervenak, *Ofcr*
EMP: 11 EST: 2016
SALES (est): 445.33K **Privately Held**
SIC: 8011 Offices and clinics of medical doctors

(G-13626)
A-1 KEVINS LANDSCAPING
620 W South St (19977-1204)
PHONE................................302 270-6914
Kevin Patterson, *Prin*
EMP: 8 EST: 2019
SALES (est): 538.69K **Privately Held**
Web: www.a1kevinslandscaping.com
SIC: 0781 Landscape services

(G-13627)
A1 SANITATION SERVICE INC
27 E Chestnut St (19977-1401)
PHONE................................302 653-9591
Anthony Smertka, *Pr*
Michael Rosco, *Pr*
EMP: 9 EST: 1950
SALES (est): 187.67K **Privately Held**
SIC: 7699 5099 Septic tank cleaning service; Toilets, portable

(G-13628)
ABE JUNK REMOVAL & HOME SVCS
16 Annie Gillis Ln (19977-2217)
PHONE................................302 540-3722
Andrew Abe, *Prin*
EMP: 5 EST: 2018
SALES (est): 446.05K **Privately Held**
SIC: 4953 Garbage: collecting, destroying, and processing

(G-13629)
ACADEMY OF EARLY LEARNING
310 N Main St Bldg A (19977-1078)
PHONE................................302 659-0750
Eftihia Zerefos, *Pr*
EMP: 8 EST: 2010
SALES (est): 143.18K **Privately Held**
SIC: 8351 Group day care center

(G-13630)
ACL SERVICES
250 Ashton Ct (19977-1855)
PHONE................................302 423-0276
Albert Leskovar, *Prin*
EMP: 5 EST: 2017
SALES (est): 54.97K **Privately Held**
Web: www.acl.gov
SIC: 8322 Individual and family services

(G-13631)
ACORN BOOKS INC
Also Called: Acorn Books
727 Lexington Ave (19977-1254)
PHONE................................302 508-2219
Ginny M Jewell, *Prin*
Ginny Jewell, *Pr*
Glynda Marie Shane, *VP*
EMP: 7 EST: 2012
SALES (est): 708.52K **Privately Held**
Web: www.acornbookstore.com
SIC: 5192 Books

(G-13632)
AFRICAN VIOLET SOCIETY-AMER
36 S Main St (19977-1431)
PHONE................................302 653-6449
Quentin Schlieder, *Mgr*
EMP: 6 EST: 2017
SALES (est): 71.65K **Privately Held**
Web:
www.africanvioletsocietyofamerica.org
SIC: 8611 Business associations

(G-13633)
ALFRED MOORE
1057 Wheatleys Pond Rd (19977-3819)
PHONE................................302 653-7600
Alfred Moore, *Prin*
EMP: 5 EST: 1962
SALES (est): 250.11K **Privately Held**
SIC: 0191 General farms, primarily crop

(G-13634)
ALL IN WRIST
231 S Dupont Blvd (19977-1550)
PHONE................................302 659-1010
Reese Dorsey, *Prin*
EMP: 6 EST: 2009
SALES (est): 66.4K **Privately Held**
SIC: 7241 Barber shops

(G-13635)
ALL PETS MEDICAL CENTER
Also Called: Dover Animal Hospital
10 Artisan Dr (19977-3711)
PHONE................................302 653-2300
Patricia Woody, *Owner*
EMP: 9 EST: 1989
SALES (est): 490.05K **Privately Held**
Web: www.allpetsdelaware.com
SIC: 0742 Animal hospital services, pets and other animal specialties

(G-13636)
ALS TV SERVICE
1200 Wheatleys Pond Rd (19977-3804)
P.O. Box 188 (19936-0188)
PHONE................................302 653-3711
EMP: 7 EST: 1962
SQ FT: 2,000
SALES (est): 263.33K **Privately Held**
Web: www.dovertvrepairservice.com
SIC: 7622 Television repair shop

(G-13637)
AMBER WAVES ONE LLC
335 Ryan Rd (19977-3698)
PHONE................................302 653-4641
Dee Watson, *Owner*
EMP: 5 EST: 2018
SALES (est): 124.49K **Privately Held**
Web: www.azureconstructioninc.com
SIC: 4213 Trucking, except local

(G-13638)
AMERICAN BEAUTY LDSCPG LLC
Also Called: American Beauty Landscaping
1578 Sunnyside Rd (19977-3612)
PHONE................................302 653-6460
EMP: 7 EST: 1971
SALES (est): 220K **Privately Held**
SIC: 0781 Landscape services

(G-13639)
AMERICAN LEGION AMBULANCE
210 E North St (19977-1596)
PHONE................................302 653-3557
EMP: 6 EST: 2017
SALES (est): 186.52K **Privately Held**
Web: www.ambulance64.com
SIC: 8641 Civic and social associations

(G-13640)
AMERICAN LGION AMBLNCE STN 64
900 Smyrna Clayton Blvd (19977-2230)
P.O. Box 345 (19977-0345)
PHONE................................302 653-6465
Jeanette Havel, *
Jason Mills, *
Mark Carlson, *
EMP: 35 EST: 1924
SALES (est): 593.15K **Privately Held**
Web: www.ambulance64.org
SIC: 8641 Veterans' organization

(G-13641)
ANDERSON LANDSCAPING
95 Jump Dr (19977-4633)
PHONE................................302 423-3904
Brian Anderson, *Prin*
EMP: 11 EST: 2015
SALES (est): 410.03K **Privately Held**
SIC: 0781 Landscape services

(G-13642)
ANDREW B PRICE CUSTOM BUILDE
312 W Mount Vernon St (19977-1129)
PHONE................................302 659-5368
Andrew Price, *Prin*
EMP: 6 EST: 2008
SALES (est): 363.13K **Privately Held**
SIC: 1521 General remodeling, single-family houses

(G-13643)
ANKOR TREE SERVICE LLC ✪
316 N School Ln (19977-1046)
PHONE................................302 514-7447
Francis Taylor, *Managing Member*
EMP: 5 EST: 2023
SALES (est): 54.76K **Privately Held**
SIC: 0783 7389 Planting, pruning, and trimming services; Business Activities at Non-Commercial Site

(G-13644)
ANNALISSAS PLAYHOUSE
316 Lisa Ct (19977-9407)
PHONE................................302 653-3529
EMP: 5 EST: 2018
SALES (est): 38.67K **Privately Held**
SIC: 7922 Theatrical producers and services

(G-13645)
ANYTIME FITNESS
599 Jimmy Dr Ste 18 (19977-5811)
PHONE................................302 653-4496
Daniel Fonedless, *Prin*
EMP: 6 EST: 2009
SALES (est): 136.52K **Privately Held**
Web: www.anytimefitness.com
SIC: 7991 Physical fitness clubs with training equipment

(G-13646)
AOD SMYMA 43
222 N Dupont Blvd (19977-1511)
PHONE................................302 659-5060
Amy Fibelkorn, *Prin*
EMP: 9 EST: 2010
SALES (est): 119.26K **Privately Held**
SIC: 8093 Mental health clinic, outpatient

(G-13647)
AQUA PRO INC
Also Called: API
104 Big Woods Rd (19977-3500)

GEOGRAPHIC SECTION
Smyrna - Kent County (G-13676)

P.O. Box 329 (19734-0329)
PHONE..................................302 659-6593
Robert Metzgar, *Pr*
EMP: 8 **EST:** 1998
SALES (est): 427.19K **Privately Held**
Web: www.apicancleanit.com
SIC: 7349 1711 Cleaning service, industrial or commercial; Plumbing, heating, air-conditioning

(G-13648)
ASCENSION INDUSTRIES LLC
104 Needham Dr (19977-4472)
PHONE..................................302 659-1778
EMP: 5 **EST:** 2013
SALES (est): 237.52K **Privately Held**
SIC: 8742 7389 New products and services consultants; Business Activities at Non-Commercial Site

(G-13649)
ASHLEY N KACZOROWSKI
255 W Pembrooke Dr (19977-4016)
PHONE..................................302 430-9610
Ashley Kaczorowski, *Owner*
EMP: 7 **EST:** 2017
SALES (est): 24.4K **Privately Held**
SIC: 8049 Offices of health practitioner

(G-13650)
ASTER DRY WALL LLC
1156 Paddock Rd (19977-9612)
PHONE..................................302 757-2750
EMP: 8 **EST:** 2018
SALES (est): 222.16K **Privately Held**
Web: www.asterdrywall.com
SIC: 1742 Drywall

(G-13651)
AT EAZE MASSAGE THERAPY
311 Arctic Ln (19977-4105)
PHONE..................................302 559-3019
Bronte L Wilson, *Prin*
EMP: 6 **EST:** 2014
SALES (est): 78.33K **Privately Held**
SIC: 8093 Rehabilitation center, outpatient treatment

(G-13652)
ATD CONTRACTING LLC
93 N Fairfield Dr (19977-1516)
PHONE..................................302 535-1013
Vincent Alioa Junior, *Prin*
EMP: 5 **EST:** 2016
SALES (est): 90.84K **Privately Held**
SIC: 1799 Special trade contractors, nec

(G-13653)
ATI HOLDINGS LLC
Also Called: ATI Physical Therapy
1000 Smyrna Clayton Blvd Ste 4 (19977-2228)
PHONE..................................302 659-3102
Shawn Schlegel, *Brnch Mgr*
EMP: 7
SALES (corp-wide): 635.67MM **Publicly Held**
Web: www.atipt.com
SIC: 8049 Physical therapist
HQ: Ati Holdings, Llc
     790 Remington Blvd
     Bolingbrook IL 60440

(G-13654)
ATLANTIC REALTY MANAGEMENT LLC
14 Village Sq (19977-1852)
P.O. Box 366 (19977-0366)
PHONE..................................302 875-9571
EMP: 5 **EST:** 2013

SALES (est): 187.92K **Privately Held**
Web: www.sdcmhc.com
SIC: 8741 Management services

(G-13655)
ATTENTION TO DETAIL IN SMYRNA
5702 Dupont Pkwy (19977-9601)
PHONE..................................302 388-1267
Samuel Bane, *Prin*
EMP: 6 **EST:** 2016
SALES (est): 94.26K **Privately Held**
SIC: 7542 Washing and polishing, automotive

(G-13656)
AUTO EVRYTHING AT SLEPY HLLOW
1231 S Dupont Blvd Ste 100 (19977-1875)
PHONE..................................302 376-3010
EMP: 5 **EST:** 2015
SALES (est): 426.64K **Privately Held**
SIC: 7538 General automotive repair shops

(G-13657)
AZTECH INDUSTRIES INC (PA)
Also Called: Algiclor Liquid Chlorine
1501 S Dupont Blvd (19977-2889)
PHONE..................................302 653-1430
Steven Scarpetti, *Pr*
Marcello Valenzano, *VP*
Giuliana Valenzano, *Sec*
EMP: 4 **EST:** 1987
SALES (est): 529.58K **Privately Held**
SIC: 3089 3433 3589 2873 Plastics hardware and building products; Solar heaters and collectors; Water filters and softeners, household type; Nitrogenous fertilizers

(G-13658)
B&P TRANSIT
979 Mount Friendship Rd (19977-3879)
P.O. Box 293 (19977-0293)
PHONE..................................302 653-8466
Pearl Cole, *Pt*
Jacqueline Painter, *Pt*
EMP: 7 **EST:** 1992
SALES (est): 235.21K **Privately Held**
SIC: 4151 School buses

(G-13659)
BARKLEY HEATING & AIR LLC
931 Boxwood Dr (19977-1790)
PHONE..................................302 653-5971
Ginger Barkley, *Managing Member*
EMP: 12 **EST:** 2015
SALES (est): 879.07K **Privately Held**
Web: www.barkleyheatingandair.com
SIC: 1711 Warm air heating and air conditioning contractor

(G-13660)
BEFORE & AFTER ENTRMT LLC
486 Joseph Wick Dr (19977-4659)
PHONE..................................302 857-9659
EMP: 5 **EST:** 2008
SALES (est): 31.24K **Privately Held**
SIC: 7929 Entertainment service

(G-13661)
BILL TORBERT
347 Lake Como Cir (19977-1322)
PHONE..................................302 734-9804
Bill Torbert, *Prin*
EMP: 10 **EST:** 2004
SALES (est): 274.81K **Privately Held**
SIC: 7389 Personal service agents, brokers, and bureaus

(G-13662)
BIO REFERENCE LABORATORIES
100 S Main St (19977-1477)
PHONE..................................302 223-6896
Lillian Rogers, *Mgr*
EMP: 5 **EST:** 2009
SALES (est): 89.62K **Privately Held**
SIC: 8734 Testing laboratories

(G-13663)
BLANCA O LIM MD
38 Deak Dr (19977-1268)
PHONE..................................302 653-1669
Blanca Lim, *Owner*
EMP: 13 **EST:** 2000
SALES (est): 357.26K **Privately Held**
SIC: 8011 Internal medicine, physician/surgeon

(G-13664)
BLUE HEN DENTAL LLC
231 S Dupont Blvd (19977-1550)
PHONE..................................302 538-0448
EMP: 10 **EST:** 2015
SALES (est): 186.14K **Privately Held**
Web: www.bluehendental.com
SIC: 8021 Dental clinic

(G-13665)
BOYS & GIRLS CLUBS OF AMERICA
240 E Commerce St (19977-1506)
PHONE..................................302 659-5610
Trisha Moses, *Dir*
EMP: 10
SALES (corp-wide): 128.99MM **Privately Held**
Web: www.bgca.org
SIC: 8641 Youth organizations
PA: Boys & Girls Clubs Of America
     1275 Peachtree St Ne # 100
     Atlanta GA 30309
     404 487-5700

(G-13666)
BRAID NATION LLC
5609 Dupont Pkwy Ste 15 (19977-9211)
PHONE..................................302 508-5913
Shana Wallace, *Pr*
EMP: 5 **EST:** 2017
SALES (est): 52.52K **Privately Held**
Web: braidnation.simplybook.vip
SIC: 7231 Hairdressers

(G-13667)
BRIGHT FINISH LLC
56 Arrowood Dr (19977-4436)
PHONE..................................888 974-4747
Kosta Papanicolas, *Managing Member*
EMP: 7 **EST:** 2017
SALES (est): 380.74K **Privately Held**
Web: www.brightfinish302.com
SIC: 1799 1522 Exterior cleaning, including sandblasting; Hotel/motel and multi-family home renovation and remodeling

(G-13668)
BRITTONS WISE COMPUTERS INC
Also Called: Bwci Animal Hospital MGT Sys
777 Paddock Rd (19977-9687)
PHONE..................................302 659-0343
TOLL FREE: 800
EMP: 7 **EST:** 1993
SALES (est): 498.52K **Privately Held**
Web: www.bwci.com
SIC: 7371 7373 Computer software development; Computer integrated systems design

(G-13669)
BUCK ALGONQUIN CO
370 N Main St (19977-1011)
PHONE..................................302 659-6900
FAX: 302 659-6909
EMP: 2
SALES (est): 123K **Privately Held**
SIC: 3429 Hardware, nec

(G-13670)
BUSCEMI PRESSURE WASHING LLC
1960 Wheatleys Pond Rd (19977-3701)
PHONE..................................302 223-6295
Keith Buscemi, *Prin*
EMP: 5 **EST:** 2017
SALES (est): 183.54K **Privately Held**
SIC: 1799 Cleaning building exteriors, nec

(G-13671)
C & C TECHNOLOGIES INC
441 Pier Head Blvd (19977-8205)
P.O. Box 1081 (19938-1081)
PHONE..................................302 653-7623
David O Czetli, *Pr*
Ute Czetli, *VP*
EMP: 4 **EST:** 1995
SALES (est): 437.52K **Privately Held**
Web: www.vreeland-inc.com
SIC: 3599 Machine shop, jobbing and repair

(G-13672)
CAIMAR CORPORATION
Also Called: Di Sabatino, M P DDS
17 W Glenwood Ave (19977-1106)
PHONE..................................302 653-5011
Mario Di Sabatino D.d.s., *Pr*
Carol Di Sabatino, *VP*
EMP: 9 **EST:** 1970
SQ FT: 2,800
SALES (est): 462.7K **Privately Held**
Web: www.glenwooddentalassoc.com
SIC: 8021 Dentists' office

(G-13673)
CANDLELIGHT CLEANING
379 Lake Dr (19977-1320)
PHONE..................................302 270-1218
Christy Willis, *Pt*
Nicki Shirey, *Pt*
EMP: 6 **EST:** 2001
SALES (est): 97.73K **Privately Held**
SIC: 7699 Cleaning services

(G-13674)
CARGO ALIGEORGIA LLC
74 E Glenwood Ave Ste 5198 (19977-1002)
PHONE..................................302 899-1025
EMP: 7
SALES (est): 78.16K **Privately Held**
SIC: 3086 Packaging and shipping materials, foamed plastics

(G-13675)
CARIDAD ROSAL MA MD
Also Called: SMA Pediatrics
38 Deak Dr (19977-1268)
PHONE..................................302 653-6174
Rosal Caridad, *Owner*
EMP: 16 **EST:** 2006
SALES (est): 826.45K **Privately Held**
SIC: 8011 Pediatrician

(G-13676)
CHRISTIANA CARE HEALTH SYS INC
100 S Main St Ste 105 (19977-1478)
PHONE..................................302 659-4401
Kevin Schultz, *Mgr*
EMP: 182
SALES (corp-wide): 666.58K **Privately Held**

Smyrna - Kent County (G-13677)   GEOGRAPHIC SECTION

Web: www.christianacare.org
SIC: 8011 8031 Offices and clinics of medical doctors; Offices and clinics of osteopathic physicians
HQ: Christiana Care Health System, Inc.
200 Hygeia Dr
Newark DE 19713
302 733-1000

(G-13677)
CHRISTINA H BOVELSKY M D
320 E North St (19977-1536)
PHONE.................................302 514-3371
Christina Bovelsky, *Prin*
EMP: 8 **EST:** 2017
SALES (est): 65.48K **Privately Held**
SIC: 8011 Offices and clinics of medical doctors

(G-13678)
CIPOLLONI BROTHERS LLC
879 Black Diamond Rd (19977-9663)
PHONE.................................302 449-0960
Brande Cipolloni, *Pr*
EMP: 12 **EST:** 2015
SALES (est): 499.28K **Privately Held**
SIC: 1771 Concrete work

(G-13679)
CLASS LIMOUSINE SERVICE
1271 S Dupont Blvd (19977-2892)
PHONE.................................302 653-1166
Kevin Alexander, *Pr*
EMP: 5 **EST:** 2005
SALES (est): 151.9K **Privately Held**
SIC: 4119 Limousine rental, with driver

(G-13680)
CLAYTON LIONS CLUB
545 S Carter Rd (19977-1710)
PHONE.................................302 450-6098
EMP: 14 **EST:** 2009
SALES (est): 80K **Privately Held**
Web: www.lionsclubs.org
SIC: 8641 Civic associations

(G-13681)
CLEAN HANDS LLC
Also Called: Clean Hands
60 Markham Ct (19977-3915)
PHONE.................................215 681-1435
EMP: 10 **EST:** 2013
SALES (est): 147.98K **Privately Held**
Web: www.cleanhands.us
SIC: 7349 1721 Building and office cleaning services; Commercial painting

(G-13682)
CLEANING AUTHORITY
222 E Glenwood Ave (19977-1080)
PHONE.................................302 508-5080
EMP: 6 **EST:** 2018
SALES (est): 83.19K **Privately Held**
Web: www.thecleaningauthority.com
SIC: 7699 Cleaning services

(G-13683)
COBB TRUCKING INC
363 E Commerce St Apt 408 (19977-1598)
PHONE.................................917 561-6263
Edward Cobb, *Pr*
EMP: 6 **EST:** 2021
SALES (est): 262.95K **Privately Held**
SIC: 4213 7389 Trucking, except local; Business Activities at Non-Commercial Site

(G-13684)
COLEMANS HEALTHCR STFFNGFFING ◊
42 Liborio Ln (19977-7711)
P.O. Box 764 (19977-0764)
PHONE.................................302 423-9385
EMP: 10 **EST:** 2022
SALES (est): 224.39K **Privately Held**
Web: www.colemanshealthcarestaffing.com
SIC: 7922 Employment agency: theatrical, radio, and television

(G-13685)
COLLABRTIVE EFFORT TO RNFRCE T
699 S Carter Rd Unit 1 (19977-7754)
PHONE.................................302 731-0301
EMP: 95
SALES (corp-wide): 1.46MM **Privately Held**
Web: www.forwardjourney.org
SIC: 8051 8049 Skilled nursing care facilities ; Physical therapist
PA: Collaborative Effort To Reinforce Transition Sucess, Inc.
52 Reads Way
New Castle DE 19720
302 731-0301

(G-13686)
COLLETT AND SONS WELDING
370 N Main St (19977-1011)
P.O. Box 660 (19977-0660)
PHONE.................................302 223-6525
John V Collett, *Pr*
EMP: 25 **EST:** 2013
SALES (est): 1.46MM **Privately Held**
Web: www.collettandsonswelding.com
SIC: 7692 Welding repair

(G-13687)
CORE CONSTRUCTION LLC
115 E Glenwood Ave (19977-1424)
PHONE.................................302 449-4186
EMP: 5 **EST:** 2008
SQ FT: 1,200
SALES (est): 283.79K **Privately Held**
SIC: 8748 Business consulting, nec

(G-13688)
CREATIVE FLOORING CONTRS INC
100c E Glenwood Ave (19977-1003)
P.O. Box 350 (19977-0350)
PHONE.................................302 653-7521
Lisa M Rose, *Pr*
Lorraine M Rose, *VP*
EMP: 22 **EST:** 1983
SQ FT: 8,000
SALES (est): 778.19K **Privately Held**
Web: creative-flooring-contractors.sbcontract.com
SIC: 1752 Floor laying and floor work, nec

(G-13689)
CRUITCAST INC
285 W Pembrooke Dr (19977-4016)
PHONE.................................856 693-3869
EMP: 6 **EST:** 2019
SALES (est): 106K **Privately Held**
Web: www.cruitcast.com
SIC: 8748 Business consulting, nec

(G-13690)
CURBS ETC INC
3528 S Dupont Blvd (19977-2857)
PHONE.................................302 653-3511
Carol Ewing, *Pr*
Charles Ewing Iii, *VP*
EMP: 7 **EST:** 1989
SQ FT: 1,800
SALES (est): 609.33K **Privately Held**
Web: www.curbsetc.com
SIC: 0782 1771 Highway lawn and garden maintenance services; Concrete work

(G-13691)
D R DEAKYNE DDS
231 N New St (19977-1133)
PHONE.................................302 653-6661
David R Deakyne D.d.s., *Pr*
EMP: 8 **EST:** 1972
SQ FT: 3,458
SALES (est): 423.24K **Privately Held**
Web: www.deakynedental.com
SIC: 8021 Dentists' office

(G-13692)
DAVID L TOWNSEND CO INC
Also Called: Townsend Fitness Equipment
1041 Clayton Greenspring Rd (19977-9414)
PHONE.................................302 378-7967
David Townsend, *Pr*
Melissa Caldwell, *Sec*
Maryann Townsend, *Treas*
EMP: 8 **EST:** 1993
SALES (est): 243.25K **Privately Held**
SIC: 7991 Physical fitness facilities

(G-13693)
DE EXPRESS INC
334 W Pembrooke Dr (19977-4012)
PHONE.................................302 387-7178
Mariusz Opechowski, *Pr*
EMP: 5 **EST:** 2014
SALES (est): 391.73K **Privately Held**
SIC: 4212 Local trucking, without storage

(G-13694)
DE MEDICAL CARE
51 Deak Dr (19977-1268)
PHONE.................................302 653-1281
Islam Aljunaidi, *Pr*
EMP: 10 **EST:** 2000
SALES (est): 885.54K **Privately Held**
SIC: 8099 Health and allied services, nec

(G-13695)
DE/RE INVESTMENT GROUP
452 Greens Branch Ln (19977-1185)
P.O. Box 674 (19977-0674)
PHONE.................................302 450-6202
Priscilla Williams, *Owner*
EMP: 6 **EST:** 2011
SALES (est): 155.71K **Privately Held**
Web: pwilliams.yourdehome.com
SIC: 6799 Investors, nec

(G-13696)
DEBORAH KIRK
100 S Main St Ste 205 (19977-1479)
PHONE.................................302 653-6022
Deborah T Kirk, *Prin*
EMP: 5 **EST:** 2007
SALES (est): 474.49K **Privately Held**
Web: www.kirkfamilypractice.com
SIC: 8011 General and family practice, physician/surgeon

(G-13697)
DEL-ONE FEDERAL CREDIT UNION
201 Pharmacy Dr (19977-5813)
PHONE.................................302 739-4496
EMP: 10
Web: www.del-one.org
SIC: 6061 Federal credit unions
PA: Del-One Federal Credit Union
270 Beiser Blvd
Dover DE 19904

(G-13698)
DELAWARE DEPT HLTH SOCIAL SVCS
Also Called: Delaware Hosp For Chrnclly Ill
100 Sunnyside Rd (19977-1752)
PHONE.................................302 223-1000
Jack Askin, *Dir*
EMP: 177
SALES (corp-wide): 11.27B **Privately Held**
Web: www.delaware.gov
SIC: 8069 9431 8051 Chronic disease hospital; Administration of public health programs; Skilled nursing care facilities
HQ: Delaware Dept Of Health And Social Services
1901 N Dupont Hwy
New Castle DE 19720

(G-13699)
DELAWARE INTL AGRCLTURE ENTP L
22 Zion Dr (19977-6800)
PHONE.................................302 450-2008
Dorothy Lewis, *Pr*
EMP: 5 **EST:** 2020
SALES (est): 307.87K **Privately Held**
Web: delaware-international-agriculture.business.site
SIC: 5153 Grains

(G-13700)
DELAWARE MAGICAL WISHES ASSN
715 W South St (19977-1616)
PHONE.................................302 653-6974
James Cayz, *Prin*
EMP: 5 **EST:** 2015
SALES (est): 92.4K **Privately Held**
Web: www.delawaremagicalwishes.org
SIC: 8699 Charitable organization

(G-13701)
DELAWARE MUNICIPAL ELC CORP
Also Called: Demec
22 Artisan Dr (19977-3711)
P.O. Box 310 (19977-0310)
PHONE.................................302 659-0200
Patrick E Mccular, *Pr*
Patrick E Mccullar, *Pr*
Richard Carmean, *Ch*
Dolores Slatcher, *VP*
Frances L Patterson, *Sec*
EMP: 9 **EST:** 1979
SQ FT: 2,000
SALES (est): 153.34MM **Privately Held**
Web: www.demecinc.net
SIC: 4911 Distribution, electric power

(G-13702)
DELAWARE MUSEUM ASSOCIATION
165 Brick Store Lnding Rd (19977-9628)
PHONE.................................302 644-5005
Wade Sallings, *Prin*
EMP: 6 **EST:** 2016
SALES (est): 31.35K **Privately Held**
SIC: 8412 Museum

(G-13703)
DELAWARE ORTHOPEDIC AND SPORTS
208 N Dupont Blvd (19977-1511)
PHONE.................................302 653-8389
EMP: 22
SALES (est): 500K **Privately Held**
SIC: 8049 Physical therapist

(G-13704)
DELAWARE PHARMACIST SOCIETY
27 N Main St (19977-1111)
PHONE.................................302 659-3088

Pat Grant, *Dir*
EMP: 5 **EST:** 2001
SALES (est): 383.75K **Privately Held**
Web: www.dpsrx.org
SIC: 5122 Pharmaceuticals

(G-13705)
DELAWARE PUBLIC HEALTH LAB
30 Sunnyside Rd (19977-1707)
PHONE.................302 223-1520
EMP: 22 **EST:** 2016
SALES (est): 3.83MM **Privately Held**
SIC: 8071 Medical laboratories

(G-13706)
DELAWARE REMODELING CO
334 W Commerce St (19977-1121)
PHONE.................302 545-0075
Timothy E Conley, *Prin*
EMP: 5 **EST:** 2016
SALES (est): 243.81K **Privately Held**
Web: www.homeremodelde.com
SIC: 1521 General remodeling, single-family houses

(G-13707)
DELAWARE TITLE LOANS INC
202 N Dupont Blvd (19977-1511)
PHONE.................302 653-8315
EMP: 11
SALES (corp-wide): 820.18K **Privately Held**
Web: www.delawaretitleloansinc.com
SIC: 6141 Personal credit institutions
PA: Delaware Title Loans, Inc.
8601 Dunwoody Pl Ste 406
Atlanta GA 30350
770 552-9840

(G-13708)
DELCAPS INC
Also Called: Delaware Odyssey of The Mind
4134 Wheatleys Pond Rd (19977-3717)
PHONE.................302 242-6953
Jacquie Blevins, *Dir*
EMP: 7 **EST:** 2001
SALES (est): 52.91K **Privately Held**
Web: www.deootm.org
SIC: 8699 Charitable organization

(G-13709)
DIAMOND STANDARD PRODUCTIONS
359 E Frazier St (19977-1520)
PHONE.................302 508-2931
Wallace Diamond Junior, *Prin*
EMP: 5 **EST:** 2017
SALES (est): 60.82K **Privately Held**
SIC: 7822 Motion picture and tape distribution

(G-13710)
DIAMOND STATE DIESEL
5585 Dupont Pkwy (19977-9610)
PHONE.................864 784-6608
EMP: 5 **EST:** 2018
SALES (est): 28.25K **Privately Held**
SIC: 7538 General automotive repair shops

(G-13711)
DOMIAN INTERNATIONAL SVC LLC
22 Zion Dr (19977-6800)
PHONE.................804 837-3616
Dakaque Lewis, *Managing Member*
Hans Lewis, *Pt*
EMP: 4 **EST:** 2013
SALES (est): 75.42K **Privately Held**
SIC: 7299 7389 5199 5399 Consumer purchasing services; Personal service agents, brokers, and bureaus; General merchandise, non-durable; Army-Navy goods stores

(G-13712)
DONALD GOLDSBOROUGH
1784 Woodland Beach Rd (19977-3301)
PHONE.................302 653-1081
Donald Goldsborough, *Prin*
EMP: 5 **EST:** 2011
SALES (est): 86.74K **Privately Held**
SIC: 1522 Residential construction, nec

(G-13713)
DOUGLAS B ALLEN DO
100 S Main St Ste 101 (19977-1478)
PHONE.................302 659-4545
Douglas Allen, *Pr*
EMP: 8 **EST:** 2017
SALES (est): 100.71K **Privately Held**
SIC: 8011 Offices and clinics of medical doctors

(G-13714)
DOVER AUTOMOTIVE INC
Also Called: NAPA Auto Parts
5 E Glenwood Ave (19977-1423)
PHONE.................302 653-9234
EMP: 7
SALES (corp-wide): 2.41MM **Privately Held**
Web: www.napaonline.com
SIC: 5531 5013 Auto and truck equipment and parts; Motor vehicle supplies and new parts
PA: Dover Automotive, Inc.
29 S West St
Dover DE
302 674-0211

(G-13715)
DRAIN KINGS LLC
Also Called: First State Drain Kings
3867 Wheatleys Pond Rd (19977-3739)
P.O. Box 1135 (19938-1135)
PHONE.................302 399-8980
Stacey Ferrell, *Managing Member*
EMP: 5 **EST:** 2017
SALES (est): 459.43K **Privately Held**
SIC: 7699 Sewer cleaning and rodding

(G-13716)
DUCK CREEK ANIMAL HOSPITAL
10 Artisan Dr (19977-3711)
PHONE.................302 663-6112
EMP: 6 **EST:** 2018
SALES (est): 246.85K **Privately Held**
Web: www.duckcreekanimalhospital.com
SIC: 0742 Animal hospital services, pets and other animal specialties

(G-13717)
DUCTS UNLIMITED INC
421 Smyrna Clayton Blvd (19977-1273)
P.O. Box 242 (19977-0242)
PHONE.................302 378-4125
Cheryl Sparco, *Pr*
EMP: 28 **EST:** 2005
SALES (est): 2.39MM **Privately Held**
Web: www.ductsde.com
SIC: 1711 1761 3444 5039 Warm air heating and air conditioning contractor; Sheet metal work, nec; Ducts, sheet metal; Air ducts, sheet metal

(G-13718)
DXQUISITE HAIR FACTORY LLC
79 Buckeye Ln (19977-5244)
PHONE.................267 298-0821
EMP: 2 **EST:** 2021
SALES (est): 92.41K **Privately Held**
SIC: 3999 7389 Barber and beauty shop equipment; Business Activities at Non-Commercial Site

(G-13719)
E2 ENGINEERING LLC
106 W Commerce St (19977-1119)
P.O. Box 498 (19977-0498)
PHONE.................302 659-9090
Cheryl Ide, *Prin*
EMP: 6 **EST:** 2018
SALES (est): 440.29K **Privately Held**
Web: www.e2engllc.com
SIC: 8711 Consulting engineer

(G-13720)
EASTMOOR DIGITAL
221 N Walnut St (19977-1179)
PHONE.................302 514-7002
EMP: 5 **EST:** 2017
SALES (est): 169.67K **Privately Held**
Web: www.eastmoordigital.com
SIC: 8742 Marketing consulting services

(G-13721)
EDEN HILL EXPRESSCARE LLC
300 Jimmy Dr (19977-5844)
PHONE.................302 696-2129
Rachelle S Bailey-el, *Dir*
EMP: 7 **EST:** 2018
SALES (est): 100.11K **Privately Held**
SIC: 8011 Pediatrician

(G-13722)
ENVIRONMENTAL OUTPOST & MNTJOY
585 Big Oak Rd (19977-3580)
PHONE.................302 659-5003
EMP: 7 **EST:** 2018
SALES (est): 31.35K **Privately Held**
Web: www.dasef.org
SIC: 8412 Planetarium

(G-13723)
EP ENGINE PERFORMANCE
32 W Pembrooke Dr (19977-4010)
PHONE.................302 521-0435
Evan Potter, *Prin*
EMP: 7 **EST:** 2012
SALES (est): 445.5K **Privately Held**
Web: www.epengineperformance.com
SIC: 7538 Engine rebuilding: automotive

(G-13724)
ERICSONS GARAGE
742 Tush Rd (19977-9312)
PHONE.................302 653-5032
Christopher Ericson, *Prin*
EMP: 6 **EST:** 2011
SALES (est): 51.27K **Privately Held**
SIC: 7538 General automotive repair shops

(G-13725)
ESSENTIAL BGNNNGS BHVIOR LRNG
28 E Mount Vernon St (19977-1483)
PHONE.................302 278-0052
EMP: 10
SALES (est): 347.15K **Privately Held**
Web: www.essentialbeginnings.org
SIC: 8093 Mental health clinic, outpatient

(G-13726)
ESSENTIAL CONTRACTING LLC
142 Belmont Ave (19977-1705)
PHONE.................330 984-1971
William Falkner, *Prin*
EMP: 6
SALES (est): 84.63K **Privately Held**
SIC: 1542 Nonresidential construction, nec

(G-13727)
EVERGREEN LANDSCAPING DE
11 Ferndale Dr (19977-4532)
PHONE.................302 724-0787
Andre French, *Prin*
EMP: 5 **EST:** 2016
SALES (est): 143.28K **Privately Held**
SIC: 0781 Landscape services

(G-13728)
EXPANDING OUR KIDS WORLD
3460 S Dupont Blvd (19977-2856)
PHONE.................302 659-0293
Marlena George, *Dir*
EMP: 12 **EST:** 2005
SALES (est): 234.73K **Privately Held**
SIC: 8351 Group day care center

(G-13729)
FAIRWAYS INN
296 W Clarendon Dr (19977-4045)
PHONE.................302 653-7044
Rose Moffitt, *Owner*
EMP: 11 **EST:** 2017
SALES (est): 67.77K **Privately Held**
Web: fairways-inn.business.site
SIC: 7011 Inns

(G-13730)
FAMILY MEDICINE SMYRNA CLAYTON
679 S Carter Rd Unit 4 (19977-7755)
PHONE.................302 653-1050
A Douglas Chervenak, *Pr*
EMP: 7 **EST:** 1993
SALES (est): 609.92K **Privately Held**
SIC: 8031 Offices and clinics of osteopathic physicians

(G-13731)
FIBRENEW NORTHERN & CENTRAL DE
Also Called: Fibrenew
88 Durham Ln (19977-4454)
PHONE.................833 427-3639
EMP: 5 **EST:** 2018
SALES (est): 72.08K **Privately Held**
Web: www.fibrenew.com
SIC: 7641 Upholstery work

(G-13732)
FINE ART FABRICATION
581 Smyrna Landing Rd (19977-9604)
PHONE.................302 632-4371
EMP: 5 **EST:** 2015
SALES (est): 38.13K **Privately Held**
SIC: 8412 Art gallery

(G-13733)
FIRST CLASS HAULING LLC
304 Garnet Ln (19977-9647)
PHONE.................302 535-2338
Yvette Dupree, *Prin*
EMP: 5 **EST:** 2017
SALES (est): 233.2K **Privately Held**
SIC: 4212 Light haulage and cartage, local

(G-13734)
FIRST LINE DEFENSE LLC
885 Mount Friendship Rd (19977-3880)
PHONE.................302 287-2764
Nathaniel Johnson, *Prin*
EMP: 5 **EST:** 2016
SALES (est): 219.27K **Privately Held**
SIC: 3812 Defense systems and equipment

Smyrna - Kent County (G-13735)

(G-13735)
FIRST STATE ORTHOPAEDICS PA
100 S Main St Ste 200 (19977-1479)
PHONE..................302 653-5100
EMP: 6
SALES (corp-wide): 31.54MM **Privately Held**
Web: www.firststateortho.com
SIC: 8011 Orthopedic physician
PA: First State Orthopaedics, P.A.
4745 Ogltn Stntn Rd # 225
Newark DE 19713
302 731-2888

(G-13736)
FISHER AUTO PARTS INC
Also Called: Manlove Auto Parts
5736 Dupont Pkwy (19977-9601)
PHONE..................302 653-9241
Robert Solloway, *Brnch Mgr*
EMP: 7
SALES (corp-wide): 525.52MM **Privately Held**
Web: www.fisherautoparts.com
SIC: 5013 Automotive supplies and parts
PA: Fisher Auto Parts, Inc.
512 Greenville Ave
Staunton VA 24401
540 885-8901

(G-13737)
FLETCHER PLUMBING HTG & AC INC (PA)
18 Myrtle St (19977-1075)
PHONE..................302 653-6277
Edward Fletcher, *Pr*
Brian Fletcher, *VP*
EMP: 10 EST: 1972
SALES (est): 2.53MM **Privately Held**
Web: www.fletcherplumbingheatcool.com
SIC: 1711 Warm air heating and air conditioning contractor

(G-13738)
FREEDOM PLAZA ENTERPRISES LLC
20 York Dr (19977-4623)
PHONE..................302 653-9676
Markos Zerefos, *Prin*
EMP: 5 EST: 2016
SALES (est): 199.82K **Privately Held**
SIC: 6531 Real estate agents and managers

(G-13739)
FRIENDS OF BELMONT HALL INC
21 E Commerce St (19977-1403)
P.O. Box 345 (19977-0345)
PHONE..................302 653-9212
Macklin Hall, *Prin*
EMP: 5 EST: 2010
SALES (est): 96.74K **Privately Held**
Web: www.belmonthall.org
SIC: 8699 Membership organizations, nec

(G-13740)
FUTURE LEADERS
906 Boxwood Dr (19977-1265)
PHONE..................862 262-7312
Althea Parrish, *Prin*
EMP: 8 EST: 2017
SALES (est): 42.04K **Privately Held**
SIC: 8351 Child day care services

(G-13741)
GARRISONS LAKE GOLF CLUB INC
101 W Fairways Cir (19977-1829)
PHONE..................302 659-1206
Carol Russell Press, *Prin*
EMP: 17 EST: 1977
SALES (est): 379.19K **Privately Held**
Web: www.garrisonslakegolf.com
SIC: 7992 Public golf courses

(G-13742)
GERRY GRAY
63 White Rabbit Dr (19977-3484)
PHONE..................302 856-4101
Gerry Gray, *Prin*
EMP: 5 EST: 2010
SALES (est): 137.93K **Privately Held**
Web: www.gerrygraylaw.com
SIC: 8111 General practice attorney, lawyer

(G-13743)
GIFT LOVE EARLY LEARNING CTR
115 E North St (19977-1444)
PHONE..................302 659-1984
Mark Bell, *Pt*
EMP: 5 EST: 2013
SALES (est): 128.48K **Privately Held**
Web: www.giftofloveearlylearningcenterllc.com
SIC: 8351 Group day care center

(G-13744)
GLENWOOD DENTAL ASSOCIATES LLP
17 W Glenwood Ave (19977-1106)
PHONE..................302 653-5011
EMP: 5 EST: 2007
SALES (est): 248.76K **Privately Held**
Web: www.glenwooddentalassoc.com
SIC: 8021 Dentists' office

(G-13745)
GODDESS OF BARN
295 Black Diamond Rd (19977-9606)
PHONE..................302 363-1062
Daren Ludlam, *Prin*
EMP: 5 EST: 2015
SALES (est): 44.59K **Privately Held**
SIC: 7231 Beauty shops

(G-13746)
GOLD MEDAL GYMNASTICS INC
56 Artisan Dr Ste 1 (19977-3775)
PHONE..................302 659-5569
Brenda Luft, *Pr*
EMP: 6 EST: 2005
SALES (est): 437.15K **Privately Held**
Web: www.gmgym.com
SIC: 7999 Gymnastic instruction, non-membership

(G-13747)
GOLF COURSE AT GARRISONS LAKE
101 W Fairways Cir (19977-1829)
PHONE..................302 659-1206
EMP: 9 EST: 2010
SALES (est): 166.63K **Privately Held**
Web: www.garrisonslakegolf.com
SIC: 7992 Public golf courses

(G-13748)
GOVERNORS PLACE TOWNHOMES
17 Providence Dr (19977-1052)
PHONE..................302 653-6655
Ronald Cantor, *Owner*
EMP: 5 EST: 1988
SALES (est): 300.85K **Privately Held**
Web: www.governorsplace.net
SIC: 6513 Apartment hotel operation

(G-13749)
GOVPLUS LLC
Also Called: Citizens Bank
7 W Glenwood Ave (19977-1106)
PHONE..................302 653-9245
Sharon Wright, *Mgr*
EMP: 6
SALES (corp-wide): 9.07B **Publicly Held**
Web: www.govplus.com
SIC: 6022 State trust companies accepting deposits, commercial
HQ: Citizens Bank, National Association
1 Citizens Plz
Providence RI 02903

(G-13750)
GRANTLIN FABRICATION LLC
872 Blackbird Greenspring Rd (19977-9462)
PHONE..................302 270-3708
EMP: 5 EST: 2016
SALES (est): 211.39K **Privately Held**
SIC: 1522 Residential construction, nec

(G-13751)
GREAT CLIPS
Also Called: Great Clips
232 E Glenwood Ave (19977-1080)
PHONE..................302 514-9819
Amber Payne, *Mgr*
EMP: 6 EST: 2014
SALES (est): 52.72K **Privately Held**
Web: www.greatclips.com
SIC: 7231 Unisex hair salons

(G-13752)
GREEN VALLEY PAVILION
3034 S Dupont Blvd (19977-1898)
PHONE..................302 653-5085
Joyce Winters, *Prin*
EMP: 13 EST: 2008
SALES (est): 217.56K **Privately Held**
SIC: 8361 8059 8051 Geriatric residential care; Nursing home, except skilled and intermediate care facility; Skilled nursing care facilities

(G-13753)
GREEN VALLEY SNF LLC
3034 S Dupont Blvd (19977-1898)
PHONE..................302 653-5085
EMP: 8 EST: 2020
SALES (est): 217.92K **Privately Held**
SIC: 8361 Rest home, with health care incidental

(G-13754)
GRIME 2 SHINE LLC
105 Oak Dr (19977-1538)
PHONE..................302 264-6709
Sharon Clay, *CEO*
EMP: 5 EST: 2016
SALES (est): 64.9K **Privately Held**
SIC: 7699 Cleaning services

(G-13755)
HALPERN EYE ASSOCIATES INC
201 Stadium St (19977-2899)
PHONE..................302 653-3400
Sherri Taylor, *Mgr*
EMP: 7
SALES (corp-wide): 9.06MM **Privately Held**
Web: www.myeyedr.com
SIC: 8042 Specialized optometrists
PA: Halpern Eye Associates, Inc.
885 S Governors Ave
Dover DE 19904
302 734-5861

(G-13756)
HCS ELECTRIC
206 N Canvasback Ct (19977-9516)
PHONE..................302 824-3743
Carl Ramsey Junior, *Owner*
EMP: 8 EST: 2004
SALES (est): 448.47K **Privately Held**
SIC: 1731 Electrical work

(G-13757)
HEAVEN MAID SERVICES INC
272 Golden Plover Dr (19977-3477)
PHONE..................302 223-6086
Jacqueline O'neal, *Prin*
EMP: 5 EST: 2009
SALES (est): 68.56K **Privately Held**
SIC: 7349 Maid services, contract or fee basis

(G-13758)
HEIRLOOM CREATIONS
5899 Underwoods Corner Rd (19977-3759)
P.O. Box 471 (19938-0471)
PHONE..................302 659-1817
Deborah Perrine, *Owner*
EMP: 2 EST: 2000
SALES (est): 112.15K **Privately Held**
Web: www.heirloomcreations.com
SIC: 2521 Wood office furniture

(G-13759)
HIATUS BUSINESS SOLUTIONS INC
56 Ogden Ct (19977-3910)
PHONE..................302 883-7324
T Humphrey Gbassagee Ii, *Prin*
EMP: 5 EST: 2014
SALES (est): 85.14K **Privately Held**
SIC: 8741 Business management

(G-13760)
HIGH HORSE PERFORMANCE INC
93 Artisan Dr Ste 6 (19977-3765)
PHONE..................302 894-1115
Joshua Schwartz, *Pr*
EMP: 6 EST: 2004
SALES (est): 530.36K **Privately Held**
Web: www.highhorseperformance.com
SIC: 7538 General automotive repair shops

(G-13761)
HIGHER POWER YOGA
751 Dorchester Ct (19977-1639)
PHONE..................302 354-5826
EMP: 6 EST: 2014
SALES (est): 56.98K **Privately Held**
SIC: 7999 Yoga instruction

(G-13762)
HOLLY HILL ESTATES
271 Berry Dr (19977-2726)
PHONE..................302 653-7503
Holly Malone, *Owner*
EMP: 6 EST: 1998
SALES (est): 455.24K **Privately Held**
Web: www.hollyhillestates.com
SIC: 6515 Mobile home site operators

(G-13763)
HOLLYWOOD TANS
502 Greens Branch Ln (19977-4100)
PHONE..................302 367-5959
Veronica Rivera, *Prin*
EMP: 5 EST: 2016
SALES (est): 18.95K **Privately Held**
Web: www.hollywoodtansnj.com
SIC: 7299 Tanning salon

(G-13764)
HOME WORKS
473 Pier Head Blvd (19977-8205)
PHONE..................302 514-9974
Daryl Jester, *Dir*
EMP: 5 EST: 2014
SALES (est): 60.96K **Privately Held**

GEOGRAPHIC SECTION

Smyrna - Kent County (G-13796)

SIC: 7349 Building maintenance services, nec

(G-13765)
HOPPY LLC DBA BRICK WORKS
230 S Dupont Blvd (19977-1573)
PHONE..................302 653-8961
EMP: 12 EST: 2016
SALES (est): 231.12K **Privately Held**
Web: www.brickworksde.com
SIC: 1741 Masonry and other stonework

(G-13766)
HORNS MACHINE SHOP INC
3652 Big Woods Rd (19977-2935)
P.O. Box 810 (19938-0810)
PHONE..................302 653-6663
Ricky Nash, *Pr*
Tricia Nash, *VP*
EMP: 6 EST: 1966
SQ FT: 2,840
SALES (est): 470.03K **Privately Held**
SIC: 3599 Machine shop, jobbing and repair

(G-13767)
HOUND DOG RECOVERY LLC
2151 S Dupont Blvd (19977-2882)
P.O. Box 28 (19977-0028)
PHONE..................302 836-3806
Crystal Grelock, *Managing Member*
EMP: 7 EST: 2008
SALES (est): 488.05K **Privately Held**
Web: www.hounddogrecovery.com
SIC: 7549 Towing services

(G-13768)
HOUSE OF WRIGHT MORTUARY
48 E Commerce St (19977-1404)
P.O. Box 447 (19899-0447)
PHONE..................302 659-5517
Alan Schoenberg, *Bmch Mgr*
EMP: 7
Web: www.wrightmortuary.com
SIC: 7261 Funeral home
PA: The House Of Wright Mortuary & Cremation Service Inc
208 E 35th St
Wilmington DE 19802

(G-13769)
I3A LLC
5819 Underwoods Corner Rd (19977-3759)
PHONE..................302 659-9090
EMP: 5 EST: 2009
SALES (est): 233.54K **Privately Held**
Web: www.i3allc.com
SIC: 8711 Consulting engineer

(G-13770)
INNOVATIONS FUNDING LLC
608 Dairy Dr (19977-1782)
PHONE..................302 743-6213
EMP: 5 EST: 2020
SALES (est): 253.57K **Privately Held**
SIC: 6153 Working capital financing

(G-13771)
INNOVATIVE HOME IMPRVS LLC
401 Kates Way (19977-1636)
PHONE..................302 388-2950
Steven Leonzio, *Prin*
EMP: 5 EST: 2017
SALES (est): 248.59K **Privately Held**
SIC: 1521 Single-family housing construction

(G-13772)
INTEGRITY BILLING SPECIALIST
600 Saks St (19977-1798)
PHONE..................302 383-1704
Karen Stratton, *Prin*
EMP: 5 EST: 2016
SALES (est): 216.53K **Privately Held**
SIC: 8721 Billing and bookkeeping service

(G-13773)
INTEGRITY COMPANIONS
6 Grant Ln (19977-9648)
PHONE..................302 659-2936
Edith Watson, *Prin*
EMP: 7 EST: 2010
SALES (est): 57.98K **Privately Held**
SIC: 8322 Individual and family services

(G-13774)
INTEGRITY NURSING AND HEA
6 Grant Ln (19977-9648)
PHONE..................302 275-8838
EMP: 5 EST: 2018
SALES (est): 118.06K **Privately Held**
SIC: 8099 Health and allied services, nec

(G-13775)
INTERIM HEALTHCARE DEL LLC
Also Called: Interim Healthcare of Delaware
100 S Main St Ste 203 (19977-1479)
PHONE..................302 322-2743
EMP: 15 EST: 2011
SALES (est): 576.69K **Privately Held**
Web: www.interimde.com
SIC: 7363 8082 Temporary help service; Visiting nurse service

(G-13776)
INTERNTNAL AGRCLTURE PROD GROU
22 Zion Dr (19977-6800)
PHONE..................302 450-2008
EMP: 5 EST: 2019
SALES (est): 88.82K **Privately Held**
SIC: 2066 Cocoa and cocoa products

(G-13777)
IRON SOURCE 2
5722 Dupont Pkwy (19977-9601)
PHONE..................302 653-7562
EMP: 6 EST: 2019
SALES (est): 222.06K **Privately Held**
Web: www.ironsourcede.com
SIC: 3446 Architectural metalwork

(G-13778)
ISOLVRISK INC ✪
74 E Glenwood Ave 211 (19977-1002)
PHONE..................508 838-7708
Joseph Zaarour, *CEO*
EMP: 5 EST: 2022
SALES (est): 68.89K **Privately Held**
SIC: 7371 Custom computer programming services

(G-13779)
J A BANKS & ASSOCIATES LLC
486 Joseph Wick Dr (19977-4659)
PHONE..................914 260-2003
EMP: 10 EST: 2017
SALES (est): 383.79K **Privately Held**
SIC: 6799 6531 Investors, nec; Real estate leasing and rentals

(G-13780)
JALAL BAYAR CONTRACTING
67 Harkins Dr (19977-1593)
PHONE..................302 535-7294
Jalal B Bayar, *Prin*
EMP: 5 EST: 2015
SALES (est): 87.19K **Privately Held**
SIC: 1799 Special trade contractors, nec

(G-13781)
JLW CONSULTING LLC
396 N School Ln (19977-1022)
PHONE..................302 653-7283
Rhonda Wilson, *Prin*
EMP: 5 EST: 2010
SALES (est): 113.07K **Privately Held**
Web: www.jlwconsultingllc.com
SIC: 8748 Business consulting, nec

(G-13782)
JOURNEY2WELLNESS
1000 Smyrna Clayton Blvd (19977-2228)
PHONE..................302 399-6755
Tanya Thornton, *Prin*
EMP: 7 EST: 2014
SALES (est): 121.06K **Privately Held**
SIC: 8099 Health and allied services, nec

(G-13783)
JUST LIKE HOME
314 W Mount Vernon St (19977-1129)
PHONE..................302 653-0605
D Laub, *Prin*
EMP: 11 EST: 2004
SALES (est): 81.13K **Privately Held**
SIC: 8051 Skilled nursing care facilities

(G-13784)
JUSTIN DAVID ENNIS
2224 Big Oak Rd (19977-3043)
PHONE..................302 650-4934
Jill Ennis, *Prin*
EMP: 6 EST: 2018
SALES (est): 52.7K **Privately Held**
SIC: 7538 General automotive repair shops

(G-13785)
KC JANITORIAL SERVICES
76 E Pembrooke Dr (19977-4000)
PHONE..................302 653-5435
Kim Carter, *Prin*
EMP: 7 EST: 2015
SALES (est): 196.32K **Privately Held**
SIC: 7349 Janitorial service, contract basis

(G-13786)
KDG SOLUTIONS LLC
654 Brenford Station Rd (19977-4618)
PHONE..................302 494-4693
Karla Gubbine, *Genl Mgr*
EMP: 5 EST: 2012
SALES (est): 169.14K **Privately Held**
SIC: 5961 7389 Electronic shopping; Business Activities at Non-Commercial Site

(G-13787)
KEN DECKER DC
699 S Carter Rd Unit 5 (19977-7754)
PHONE..................302 389-8915
EMP: 5 EST: 2018
SALES (est): 78.61K **Privately Held**
Web: www.purewellchiro.com
SIC: 8041 Offices and clinics of chiropractors

(G-13788)
KENT CONSTRUCTION CO (PA)
2 Big Oak Rd (19977-3501)
PHONE..................302 653-6469
Ernest C Davison Iii, *Pr*
EMP: 39 EST: 1973
SQ FT: 7,000
SALES (est): 11.07MM
SALES (corp-wide): 11.07MM **Privately Held**
Web: www.kentconstructionco.com
SIC: 1542 1541 Commercial and office building, new construction; Industrial buildings, new construction, nec

(G-13789)
KENT COUNTY REPUBLICAN PARTY
130 Dodge Dr (19977-1879)
PHONE..................302 653-2355
Patrick Murray, *Prin*
EMP: 9 EST: 2010
SALES (est): 103.95K **Privately Held**
Web: www.kentrepublicans.com
SIC: 8651 Political action committee

(G-13790)
KENT GENERAL HOSPITAL
401 N Carter Rd (19977-1281)
PHONE..................302 653-2010
EMP: 5
Web: www.bayhealth.org
SIC: 8062 General medical and surgical hospitals
HQ: Kent General Hospital
640 S State St
Dover DE 19901
302 674-4700

(G-13791)
KEVIN M MILLER
Also Called: Millers Lawn Care
11 S Clements St (19977-1248)
PHONE..................302 514-7111
Kevin M Miller, *Owner*
EMP: 5 EST: 2011
SALES (est): 78.1K **Privately Held**
Web: www.millerslawns.com
SIC: 0782 Lawn care services

(G-13792)
KMS SERVIVES
248 E North St (19977-1534)
PHONE..................302 502-5287
Becky Crick, *Prin*
EMP: 6 EST: 2014
SALES (est): 109.91K **Privately Held**
SIC: 1522 Residential construction, nec

(G-13793)
KREAM PUFF CLEAN
49 Trala St (19977-2216)
PHONE..................251 509-1639
Thomas Bell, *Prin*
EMP: 10 EST: 2017
SALES (est): 124.89K **Privately Held**
SIC: 7699 Cleaning services

(G-13794)
LA COMMUNICATION LLC
109 Savannah Dr (19977-9641)
PHONE..................302 653-1210
Ludric Francis, *Prin*
EMP: 5 EST: 2007
SALES (est): 74.92K **Privately Held**
SIC: 4899 Communication services, nec

(G-13795)
LAN CHESTER SHEDS GAZEBOS
28 S Dupont Blvd (19977-1513)
PHONE..................302 653-7392
EMP: 5 EST: 2018
SALES (est): 195.74K **Privately Held**
Web: www.lcsheds.com
SIC: 4225 General warehousing and storage

(G-13796)
LAST TANGLE SALON AND SPA
76 E Glenwood Ave (19977-1002)
PHONE..................302 653-6638
Denise Janeka, *Pr*
EMP: 6 EST: 2011
SALES (est): 124.43K **Privately Held**
SIC: 7991 Spas

(PA)=Parent Co (HQ)=Headquarters
✪ = New Business established in last 2 years

Smyrna - Kent County (G-13797) GEOGRAPHIC SECTION

(G-13797)
LEAGER CONSTRUCTION INC
732 Smyrna Landing Rd (19977-9631)
P.O. Box 146 (19977-0146)
PHONE.....................302 653-8021
EMP: 6 EST: 1980
SALES (est): 436.32K **Privately Held**
SIC: 1771 1711 Concrete work; Septic system construction

(G-13798)
LEARNING IS FUNDAMENTAL CHILD
281 Blackbird Greenspring Rd (19977-9495)
PHONE.....................302 653-1047
Jennifer Reed, *Owner*
EMP: 9 EST: 2015
SALES (est): 26.07K **Privately Held**
SIC: 8351 Preschool center

(G-13799)
LEGACY DISTILLING LLC
106 W Commerce St (19977-1119)
PHONE.....................302 983-1269
Ron Gomes Junior, *Prin*
EMP: 11 EST: 2013
SALES (est): 476.63K **Privately Held**
Web: www.paintedstave.com
SIC: 2085 Distilled and blended liquors

(G-13800)
LEISURE HOME BUILDERS LLC
96 Century Dr (19977-4474)
PHONE.....................302 528-4873
Gary Brobst, *Prin*
EMP: 6 EST: 2009
SALES (est): 247.58K **Privately Held**
SIC: 1521 New construction, single-family houses

(G-13801)
LENAPE BUILDERS INC
671 S Carter Rd Ste 1 (19977-7756)
PHONE.....................302 376-3971
Edward Brown, *Pr*
John Richard Paiper, *Pr*
EMP: 11 EST: 1989
SQ FT: 13,000
SALES (est): 2.45MM **Privately Held**
Web: www.lenapebuilders.net
SIC: 1521 8741 New construction, single-family houses; Construction management

(G-13802)
LIBERTY TAX SERVICE
123 E Glenwood Ave (19977-1424)
PHONE.....................302 270-4135
EMP: 6 EST: 2008
SALES (est): 47.9K **Privately Held**
Web: www.libertytax.com
SIC: 7291 Tax return preparation services

(G-13803)
LINDA LAWTON DPM
1000 Smyrna Clayton Blvd Ste 3 (19977-2228)
PHONE.....................302 659-0500
Linda Lawton, *Prin*
EMP: 6 EST: 2008
SALES (est): 140K **Privately Held**
Web: www.wilmingtonfootdoc.com
SIC: 8043 Offices and clinics of podiatrists

(G-13804)
LINDA LAWTON DPM
665 S Carter Rd Unit 2 (19977-7728)
P.O. Box 515 (19977-0515)
PHONE.....................302 659-0500
Linda Lawton, *Pr*
EMP: 8 EST: 2013

SALES (est): 466.45K **Privately Held**
Web: www.wilmingtonfootdoc.com
SIC: 8043 Offices and clinics of podiatrists

(G-13805)
LISA A FAGIOLETTI DMD LLC
25 W Commerce St (19977-1463)
PHONE.....................302 514-9064
Lisa A Fagioletti, *Prin*
EMP: 5 EST: 2011
SALES (est): 254.03K **Privately Held**
Web: www.lisaafagiolettidmd.com
SIC: 8021 Dentists' office

(G-13806)
LISA TRABAUDO DAY CARE
316 Lisa Ct (19977-9407)
PHONE.....................302 653-3529
Lisa Trabaudo, *Dir*
EMP: 5 EST: 2006
SALES (est): 84.61K **Privately Held**
SIC: 8351 Child day care services

(G-13807)
LITTLE KIDS SWAGG LRNG CTR LLC
433 S Dupont Blvd (19977-1701)
PHONE.....................302 480-4404
Shakiah Davis, *Prin*
EMP: 17 EST: 2015
SALES (est): 420.3K **Privately Held**
Web: lkswaggdaycare.wixsite.com
SIC: 8351 Child day care services

(G-13808)
LIVING WELL NATURAL HEALTH
74 E Glenwood Ave (19977-1002)
PHONE.....................302 653-9748
Johnnymae N'dione, *Prin*
EMP: 7 EST: 2019
SALES (est): 285.4K **Privately Held**
Web: www.livingwellpharm.com
SIC: 8099 Health and allied services, nec

(G-13809)
LORCYS MASSAGE & BDY WORKS LLC
101 N Main St (19977-1112)
PHONE.....................302 240-3958
Anne Lorcy, *Prin*
EMP: 5 EST: 2019
SALES (est): 53.38K **Privately Held**
Web: www.massagesmyrna.com
SIC: 7299 Massage parlor

(G-13810)
LOUD & CLEAR H T SOLUTIONS LLC
509 Sequoia Dr (19977-2551)
PHONE.....................302 985-1576
Ronald Edwards, *CEO*
EMP: 5 EST: 2018
SALES (est): 104.73K **Privately Held**
SIC: 1731 Electrical work

(G-13811)
LUBE DEPOT
205 W Glenwood Ave (19977-1108)
PHONE.....................302 659-3329
Gary Register, *Owner*
EMP: 9 EST: 1996
SALES (est): 681.82K **Privately Held**
SIC: 7538 General automotive repair shops

(G-13812)
M DENIGHT LAWN CARE LLC
2209 Wheatleys Pond Rd (19977-3747)
PHONE.....................302 528-4152
Matthew Denight, *Prin*
EMP: 5 EST: 2016
SALES (est): 64.66K **Privately Held**

SIC: 0782 Lawn care services

(G-13813)
MACS AUTO SERVICES
235 1st Ave (19977-1559)
PHONE.....................302 223-6771
Tony Roberts, *Owner*
EMP: 6 EST: 2014
SALES (est): 242.16K **Privately Held**
SIC: 7538 General automotive repair shops

(G-13814)
MAHMOOD B OMAID
61 Wicksfield Blvd (19977-4069)
PHONE.....................302 399-7849
Mahmood B Omaid, *Prin*
EMP: 5 EST: 2010
SALES (est): 62.04K **Privately Held**
SIC: 7349 Maid services, contract or fee basis

(G-13815)
MARKETING MOMMA
568 Owens Brooke Dr (19977-1625)
PHONE.....................302 259-1644
EMP: 5 EST: 2017
SALES (est): 88.12K **Privately Held**
Web: www.themarketingmomma.com
SIC: 6512 Commercial and industrial building operation

(G-13816)
MARY HAZLETT
82 Monrovia Ave (19977-1530)
PHONE.....................302 653-8823
Mary Hazlett, *Prin*
EMP: 9 EST: 2012
SALES (est): 86.02K **Privately Held**
Web: www.hesterscreativeschools.com
SIC: 8011 Offices and clinics of medical doctors

(G-13817)
MASON MECHANICAL LLC
345 Southern View Dr (19977-4088)
PHONE.....................302 653-4022
EMP: 6 EST: 2014
SALES (est): 237.9K **Privately Held**
SIC: 1711 Warm air heating and air conditioning contractor

(G-13818)
MASTEN ELECTRIC INC
405 W Commerce St (19977-1216)
PHONE.....................302 653-4300
William V Masten Junior, *Pr*
EMP: 10 EST: 1994
SQ FT: 1,650
SALES (est): 830.05K **Privately Held**
SIC: 1731 General electrical contractor

(G-13819)
MATT BASILE STATE FARM INSUR
28 N Dupont Blvd (19977-1509)
PHONE.....................302 659-9000
Matt Basile, *Pr*
EMP: 6 EST: 2017
SALES (est): 166.02K **Privately Held**
Web: www.mattbasile.com
SIC: 6411 Insurance agents and brokers

(G-13820)
MATTHEWS TOWING & RECOVERY
710 Black Diamond Rd (19977-9672)
PHONE.....................302 463-1108
Lucas Matthews, *Pr*
EMP: 10 EST: 2015
SALES (est): 480.59K **Privately Held**
Web: www.matthewstow.com

SIC: 7549 Towing service, automotive

(G-13821)
MCJ SEAL & LINE STRIPING LLC
40 Loder Dr (19977-6814)
PHONE.....................302 416-1326
EMP: 8 EST: 2018
SALES (est): 928.82K **Privately Held**
Web: www.mcjseallinestriping.com
SIC: 1611 Surfacing and paving

(G-13822)
METRO BY T-MOBILE
70 E Glenwood Ave (19977-1002)
PHONE.....................302 508-5123
EMP: 5 EST: 2019
SALES (est): 117.03K **Privately Held**
SIC: 4812 Cellular telephone services

(G-13823)
MICHAEL H MCGRATH
650 Johns Rd (19977-1608)
PHONE.....................302 242-3849
Michael H Mcgrath, *Prin*
EMP: 7 EST: 2013
SALES (est): 44.41K **Privately Held**
SIC: 8322 Substance abuse counseling

(G-13824)
MIDDLETOWN COUNSELING
268 Brenford Station Rd (19977-4612)
PHONE.....................302 540-9003
Megan Sartin, *Prin*
EMP: 6 EST: 2010
SALES (est): 58.46K **Privately Held**
Web: www.middletowncounseling.com
SIC: 8322 Family counseling services

(G-13825)
MIH ENTERPRISES
57 Pier Head Blvd Ste 2 (19977-8223)
PHONE.....................302 480-4443
EMP: 5 EST: 2019
SALES (est): 40.81K **Privately Held**
SIC: 7929 Entertainers and entertainment groups

(G-13826)
MISSION BRACELETS LLC
1201 Woodland Beach Rd (19977-3456)
PHONE.....................302 528-5065
Katie Brobst, *Prin*
EMP: 5 EST: 2018
SALES (est): 102.7K **Privately Held**
SIC: 3961 Bracelets, except precious metal

(G-13827)
MORRIS CT TRUCKING INC
803 Masseys Church Rd (19977-9451)
PHONE.....................302 653-2396
Carol Morris, *Pr*
EMP: 5 EST: 1979
SALES (est): 431.78K **Privately Held**
SIC: 4212 Local trucking, without storage

(G-13828)
MOSIAC OF DELAWARE
4966 Dupont Pkwy (19977-9658)
PHONE.....................302 653-8889
Onome Kuyebi, *Mgr*
EMP: 8 EST: 2010
SALES (est): 83.3K **Privately Held**
SIC: 8011 Medical centers

(G-13829)
MRS RITA FISHER
564 Dairy Dr (19977-1755)
PHONE.....................215 500-6280
Rita Fisher, *Prin*
EMP: 6 EST: 2019

GEOGRAPHIC SECTION
Smyrna - Kent County (G-13859)

SALES (est): 36.89K **Privately Held**
SIC: **8322** Social worker

(G-13830)
MURRY TRUCKING LLC
568 Blackbird Greenspring Rd (19977-9476)
PHONE.....................302 653-4811
John Joseph Murry, *Managing Member*
EMP: 12 EST: 2011
SALES (est): 1.2MM **Privately Held**
SIC: **4212 7389** Local trucking, without storage; Business Activities at Non-Commercial Site

(G-13831)
MY EYE DR OPTOMETRISTS LLC
Also Called: Myeyedr
201 Stadium St (19977-2899)
PHONE.....................302 653-3400
EMP: 6
SALES (corp-wide): 100.43MM **Privately Held**
Web: www.myeyedr.com
SIC: **8042** Offices and clinics of optometrists
PA: My Eye Dr. Optometrists, Llc
8614 Wstwd Ctr Dr Ste 900
Vienna VA 22182
703 847-8899

(G-13832)
N BIGGS PROFESSIONAL SVCS LLC
382 N High Street Extended (19977-1183)
P.O. Box 473 (19977-0473)
PHONE.....................302 632-7598
Neda Biggs, *Prin*
EMP: 5 EST: 2015
SALES (est): 72.64K **Privately Held**
SIC: **8621** Professional organizations

(G-13833)
NATIONAL AUTO MOVERS LLC
46 Bluegrass Blvd (19977-3938)
PHONE.....................302 229-9256
EMP: 6 EST: 2013
SALES (est): 285.3K **Privately Held**
Web: www.nationalautomovers.net
SIC: **4789** Cargo loading and unloading services

(G-13834)
NEXT STEP QUALITY HM CARE LLC
121 E Glenwood Ave (19977-1424)
PHONE.....................888 367-5722
Timothy Mcdonald, *Managing Member*
EMP: 10 EST: 2020
SALES (est): 293.48K **Privately Held**
SIC: **8082** Home health care services

(G-13835)
NKS DISTRIBUTORS INC (PA)
205 Big Woods Rd (19977-3565)
P.O. Box 810 (19977-0810)
PHONE.....................302 322-1811
James V Tigani Senior, *Ch Bd*
Robert Tigani, *
▲ EMP: 88 EST: 1946
SQ FT: 50,000
SALES (est): 24.65MM
SALES (corp-wide): 24.65MM **Privately Held**
Web: www.nksdistributors.com
SIC: **5181 5182** Beer and other fermented malt liquors; Wine

(G-13836)
NOVACARE REHABILITATION
208 N Dupont Blvd (19977-1511)
PHONE.....................302 653-8359
EMP: 11 EST: 1998
SALES (est): 82.71K **Privately Held**
Web: www.novacare.com
SIC: **8049** Physical therapist

(G-13837)
NU BEGINNING CENTER LLC
229 N Main St Ste 203 (19977-1113)
PHONE.....................302 276-8483
Elsa Smith, *Prin*
EMP: 6 EST: 2019
SALES (est): 73.36K **Privately Held**
Web: www.nubeginningcenter.com
SIC: **8093** Specialty outpatient clinics, nec

(G-13838)
NURSES N KIDS
25 Ramunno Dr (19977-1786)
PHONE.....................302 528-6902
EMP: 12 EST: 2018
SALES (est): 46.21K **Privately Held**
Web: www.nursesnkids.com
SIC: **8011** Pediatrician

(G-13839)
NY CONSTRUCTION
19 Grayton Dr (19977-4458)
PHONE.....................302 377-1846
Marc Creamer, *Prin*
EMP: 5 EST: 2016
SALES (est): 137.36K **Privately Held**
SIC: **1521** Single-family housing construction

(G-13840)
OAK FOREST PARK LLC
P.O. Box 452 (19977-0452)
PHONE.....................302 947-9328
Tim Johnson, *Prin*
EMP: 7 EST: 2004
SALES (est): 100K **Privately Held**
SIC: **7033** Campgrounds

(G-13841)
OERIGO CONSULTING LLC
Also Called: Oerigo Consulting
82 E Cayhill Ln (19977-3923)
PHONE.....................302 353-4719
Regis L Williams, *Owner*
EMP: 5 EST: 2007
SALES (est): 86.78K **Privately Held**
Web: www.kuwaitchurches.com
SIC: **7231 7389** Beauty shops; Business services, nec

(G-13842)
OLYMPUS CONSULTING LLC ✪
219 Alyssa Way (19977-5285)
PHONE.....................302 353-7329
Jezerie Blango, *CEO*
EMP: 5 EST: 2023
SALES (est): 248.05K **Privately Held**
Web: www.olympusconsult.com
SIC: **8748 7389** Business consulting, nec; Business services, nec

(G-13843)
ORTHO ON SILVER LAKE
446 Fletcher Dr (19977-2818)
PHONE.....................302 653-5636
EMP: 7 EST: 2018
SALES (est): 87.89K **Privately Held**
SIC: **8021** Orthodontist

(G-13844)
PAGE PRECISION CUTS
203 N High St (19977-1225)
PHONE.....................302 272-2380
EMP: 6 EST: 2014
SALES (est): 249.17K **Privately Held**
SIC: **0781** Landscape services

(G-13845)
PENINSULA ACOUSTICAL CO INC
441 Pier Head Blvd (19977-8205)
PHONE.....................302 653-3551
Dana Stonesifer, *Pr*
EMP: 7 EST: 1954
SALES (est): 818.27K **Privately Held**
Web: peninsulaacoustical.thebluebook.com
SIC: **1742 1743** Acoustical and ceiling work; Tile installation, ceramic

(G-13846)
PERSANTE SLEEP CENTER
100 S Main St Ste 201 (19977-1479)
PHONE.....................302 508-2130
EMP: 14 EST: 2015
SALES (est): 78.53K **Privately Held**
Web: www.persante.com
SIC: **8011** Offices and clinics of medical doctors

(G-13847)
PINNACLE RHBILITATION HLTH CTR
3034 S Dupont Blvd (19977-1898)
PHONE.....................302 653-5085
Karen Hickman, *Dir*
EMP: 51 EST: 2009
SALES (est): 16.38MM **Privately Held**
Web: www.glenbrookrhc.com
SIC: **8051** Convalescent home with continuous nursing care

(G-13848)
PLATINUM SALON LLC
Also Called: Allure Salon
599 Jimmy Dr Ste 15 (19977-5811)
PHONE.....................302 653-6125
Shannon Mcgalillard, *Owner*
EMP: 8 EST: 2006
SALES (est): 123.12K **Privately Held**
Web: www.allurehairsmyrna.com
SIC: **7231** Hairdressers

(G-13849)
PLEASANT HILL AUTO SVC LLC
34 Spruce Ct (19977-2706)
PHONE.....................302 376-6712
Joy Krupka, *Owner*
EMP: 5 EST: 2018
SALES (est): 88.95K **Privately Held**
Web: pleasanthillautoservicellc.vpweb.com
SIC: **7538** General automotive repair shops

(G-13850)
PNC BANK NATIONAL ASSOCIATION
Also Called: PNC
7 S Main St (19977-1430)
PHONE.....................302 653-2475
Rose Mary Mast, *Mgr*
EMP: 6
SALES (corp-wide): 23.54B **Publicly Held**
Web: www.pnc.com
SIC: **6021** National commercial banks
HQ: Pnc Bank, National Association
300 5th Ave
Pittsburgh PA 15222
877 762-2000

(G-13851)
PREMIER PHYSICAL THERAPY &
100 S Main St Ste 300 (19977-1495)
PHONE.....................302 389-7855
Richard Binstein, *Prin*
EMP: 22 EST: 2018
SALES (est): 392.65K **Publicly Held**
Web: www.premierptsp.com
SIC: **8049** Physical therapist
PA: U. S. Physical Therapy, Inc.
1300 W Sam Houston Pkwy S # 300
Houston TX 77042

(G-13852)
PREPAID LEGAL SERVICE
956 Shorts Landing Rd (19977-3362)
PHONE.....................302 376-1952
EMP: 5 EST: 2018
SALES (est): 102.65K **Privately Held**
SIC: **8111** Legal services

(G-13853)
PRESTIGIOUS SOLUTION LLC ✪
34 Dozer Ct (19977-1900)
PHONE.....................800 392-2103
EMP: 5 EST: 2022
SALES (est): 260.34K **Privately Held**
SIC: **8742** Marketing consulting services

(G-13854)
PRESTWICK HOUSE INC
58 Artisan Dr (19977-3711)
P.O. Box 658 (19938-0658)
PHONE.....................302 659-2070
James Scott, *Pr*
Patricia Scott, *
Kendra Scott, *
EMP: 30 EST: 1983
SQ FT: 15,000
SALES (est): 6MM **Privately Held**
Web: www.prestwickhouse.com
SIC: **2741 5942** Miscellaneous publishing; Book stores

(G-13855)
PRO 2 RESPIRATORY SERVICES
56 Artisan Dr Ste 5 (19977-3775)
PHONE.....................302 514-9843
EMP: 5 EST: 2019
SALES (est): 61.12K **Privately Held**
SIC: **8082** Home health care services

(G-13856)
PROFESSIONAL IMAGING
97 Nita Dr (19977-4838)
PHONE.....................302 653-3522
EMP: 6 EST: 2011
SALES (est): 76.74K **Privately Held**
SIC: **8071** Medical laboratories

(G-13857)
PROGNSTIC HLTHCARE RSURCES LLC
540 Groundhog Ln (19977-3487)
PHONE.....................762 217-6323
Rolnique Lewis-ned, *Managing Member*
EMP: 5
SALES (est): 114K **Privately Held**
SIC: **8059 7389** Nursing and personal care, nec; Business services, nec

(G-13858)
PROPERTY MAINTENANCE MGT
3807 Wheatleys Pond Rd (19977-3739)
PHONE.....................302 883-1441
Joseph Daniels, *Prin*
EMP: 5 EST: 2017
SALES (est): 121.3K **Privately Held**
SIC: **8741** Management services

(G-13859)
PURE WELLNESS LLC
699 S Carter Rd Unit 5 (19977-7754)
PHONE.....................302 389-8915
EMP: 7
SALES (corp-wide): 2.76MM **Privately Held**
Web: www.purewellchiro.com

(PA)=Parent Co (HQ)=Headquarters
✪ = New Business established in last 2 years

Smyrna - Kent County (G-13860)

SIC: 8099 Childbirth preparation clinic
PA: Pure Wellness, Llc
550 Stanton Christn Rd # 302
Newark DE 19713
302 365-5470

(G-13860)
QUALITY INN
190 Stadium St (19977-2813)
PHONE.................302 659-3635
EMP: 9 EST: 2019
SALES (est): 32.59K **Privately Held**
Web: www.choicehotels.com
SIC: 7011 Hotels and motels

(G-13861)
RAINBOW XPRESS LRNG ACDEMY LLC ✪
310 N Main St (19977-1078)
PHONE.................302 659-0750
EMP: 6 EST: 2022
SALES (est): 125.69K **Privately Held**
SIC: 8351 7389 Child day care services; Business Activities at Non-Commercial Site

(G-13862)
RALPH CAHALL & SON PAVING
2284 Bryn Zion Rd (19977-3895)
PHONE.................302 653-4220
R Steven Cahall, *Pr*
Diane Cahall, *
EMP: 19 EST: 1987
SALES (est): 531.44K **Privately Held**
SIC: 1794 1611 1771 Excavation work; Surfacing and paving; Concrete work

(G-13863)
READ CONSTRUCTION INC
100 N Canvasback Ct (19977-9500)
PHONE.................302 659-1144
John Read, *Prin*
EMP: 5 EST: 2014
SALES (est): 190.76K **Privately Held**
SIC: 1521 Single-family housing construction

(G-13864)
RECORDS - GEBHART AGENCY INC
Also Called: Records-Gebhart Insurance
2 N Market St (19977-1115)
PHONE.................302 653-9211
Kyle Gebhart, *Pr*
EMP: 6 EST: 1959
SQ FT: 2,100
SALES (est): 673.74K **Privately Held**
Web: www.recordsgebhart.com
SIC: 6411 Insurance agents, nec

(G-13865)
REHRIG PENN LOGISTICS INC
171 Hemlock Way (19977-2729)
PHONE.................302 659-3337
Terry Fenwick, *Prin*
EMP: 64
Web: www.rehrigpacific.com
SIC: 5031 Pallets, wood
HQ: Rehrig Penn Logistics, Inc.
7800 100th St
Pleasant Prairie WI 53158

(G-13866)
RICHARDS INVESTMENT GROUP CORP
381 Grayton Dr (19977-4461)
PHONE.................302 399-0450
Sean Richards, *Ofcr*
EMP: 6 EST: 2015
SALES (est): 78.68K **Privately Held**
Web: www.richardsinvestmentgroup.com
SIC: 7699 Industrial equipment cleaning

(G-13867)
ROBERT DONLICK MD
16 Garrisons Cir (19977-2858)
PHONE.................302 653-8916
Robert Donlick Md, *Owner*
EMP: 6 EST: 1969
SQ FT: 1,516
SALES (est): 476.29K **Privately Held**
SIC: 8011 General and family practice, physician/surgeon

(G-13868)
ROBIN R PRATOLA
100 S Main St Ste 101 (19977-1478)
PHONE.................302 653-5100
Robin Pratola, *Pr*
EMP: 6 EST: 2017
SALES (est): 81.6K **Privately Held**
SIC: 8049 Offices of health practitioner

(G-13869)
ROMMEL CYCLES LLC (PA)
Also Called: Harley-Davidson
450 Stadium St (19977-2839)
PHONE.................302 658-8800
EMP: 30 EST: 1998
SALES (est): 8.16MM
SALES (corp-wide): 8.16MM **Privately Held**
Web: www.harley-davidson.com
SIC: 7699 5571 Motorcycle repair service; Motorcycle parts and accessories

(G-13870)
ROOFING GRIFFITH
1728 Marcy Dr (19977-9403)
PHONE.................302 762-1241
EMP: 5 EST: 2010
SALES (est): 135.49K **Privately Held**
SIC: 1761 Roof repair

(G-13871)
RPJ WASTE SERVICES INC (PA)
453 Pier Head Blvd (19977-8205)
PHONE.................302 653-9999
Julie E Davidson, *Pr*
Earnest Davidson, *VP*
James Davidson, *VP*
EMP: 7 EST: 2004
SQ FT: 6,000
SALES (est): 10.46MM
SALES (corp-wide): 10.46MM **Privately Held**
Web: www.rpjwaste.com
SIC: 1795 Demolition, buildings and other structures

(G-13872)
RUFF & RUFF LLC
28 White Rabbit Dr (19977-3482)
PHONE.................267 243-3906
Jenetta Ruff, *Managing Member*
EMP: 5 EST: 2020
SALES (est): 241.57K **Privately Held**
Web: www.ruffllc.com
SIC: 8111 General practice attorney, lawyer

(G-13873)
RUSH REALTY LLC
395 Southern View Dr (19977-4088)
PHONE.................302 219-6707
EMP: 6 EST: 2016
SALES (est): 256K **Privately Held**
SIC: 6531 Real estate brokers and agents

(G-13874)
RWM EMBROIDERY & MORE LLC
19 Village Sq (19977-1852)
P.O. Box 352 (19938-0352)
PHONE.................302 653-8384
Bob Mcginnis, *Owner*
EMP: 8 EST: 2014
SALES (est): 390.72K **Privately Held**
Web: www.promotewithrwm.com
SIC: 2395 Embroidery products, except Schiffli machine

(G-13875)
SA RYAN LLC
5 Ferndale Dr (19977-4532)
PHONE.................302 757-6440
EMP: 6 EST: 2012
SALES (est): 50K **Privately Held**
Web: www.ryan.com
SIC: 8748 Business consulting, nec

(G-13876)
SAGGIO MANAGEMENT GROUP INC
350 N High Street Extended (19977-1183)
PHONE.................302 659-6560
Ralph Estep, *Prin*
EMP: 5 EST: 2010
SALES (est): 217.7K **Privately Held**
Web: www.saggioaccounting.com
SIC: 8741 Management services

(G-13877)
SAGGIO MANAGEMENT GROUP INC
665 S Carter Rd Unit 2 (19977-7728)
PHONE.................302 659-6560
Ralph Estep, *Prin*
EMP: 5 EST: 2010
SALES (est): 168.5K **Privately Held**
Web: www.saggioaccounting.com
SIC: 6282 Investment advice

(G-13878)
SARAH CRAIG LMT
5609 Dupont Pkwy Ste 7 (19977-9211)
PHONE.................302 480-4792
Sarah Craig Lmt, *Owner*
EMP: 5 EST: 2014
SALES (est): 63.9K **Privately Held**
Web: www.smyrnamassageandwellness.com
SIC: 8049 Massage Therapist

(G-13879)
SAVING OUR SLVES PRPRTY INVSTO
34 Dozer Ct (19977-1900)
PHONE.................267 879-0464
Sajdah Kelly, *CEO*
EMP: 7 EST: 2020
SALES (est): 155K **Privately Held**
SIC: 6799 Real estate investors, except property operators

(G-13880)
SCHREPPLER CHROPRACTIC OFFS PA
892 S Dupont Blvd (19977-1723)
PHONE.................302 653-5525
George Schreppler D.c., *Pr*
EMP: 5 EST: 1983
SALES (est): 246.91K **Privately Held**
Web: www.smyrnadchiro.com
SIC: 8041 Offices and clinics of chiropractors

(G-13881)
SCHUSTER MANAGEMENT CORP
Also Called: SCHUSTER MANAGEMENT CORP
200 Goldsborough Way (19977-2505)
PHONE.................302 653-1235
Patsy Robbins, *Mgr*
EMP: 5
SALES (corp-wide): 1.47MM **Privately Held**
SIC: 6513 Apartment building operators
PA: Schuster Management Corp
836 Littlestown Pike
Westminster MD 21157
410 833-5484

(G-13882)
SERVICEVET TECHNOLOGIES LLC
777 Paddock Rd (19977-9687)
PHONE.................302 659-0343
EMP: 6 EST: 2017
SALES (est): 91.74K **Privately Held**
Web: www.servicevet.vet
SIC: 7371 Computer software development

(G-13883)
SHARLAY COMPUTER SYSTEMS
15 Delhi Ct (19977-4854)
PHONE.................302 588-3170
Al Ballard, *Pr*
Sylvia Snow-ballard, *Sec*
EMP: 5 EST: 2002
SALES (est): 178.78K **Privately Held**
SIC: 7373 Systems engineering, computer related

(G-13884)
SHORE SMOKE SEASONINGS LLC
13 Borealis Ct (19977-3962)
PHONE.................302 943-4675
EMP: 2
SALES (est): 62.38K **Privately Held**
Web: www.shoresmokeseasonings.com
SIC: 2099 7389 Seasonings and spices; Business Activities at Non-Commercial Site

(G-13885)
SHURE-LINE ELECTRICAL INC
100 Artisan Dr (19977-3711)
PHONE.................302 389-1114
Edgar L Hitch Junior, *Pr*
EMP: 60 EST: 2008
SALES (est): 12.03MM **Privately Held**
Web: www.shurelineelectrical.com
SIC: 1731 General electrical contractor

(G-13886)
SIMAR FUEL INC
126 S Dupont Blvd (19977-1514)
PHONE.................302 304-1969
EMP: 6 EST: 2011
SALES (est): 169.05K **Privately Held**
SIC: 2869 Fuels

(G-13887)
SINGER EQUIPMENT CO INC
135 W Cook Ave (19977-1700)
PHONE.................484 332-3386
EMP: 6 EST: 2019
SALES (est): 108.88K **Privately Held**
Web: www.singerequipment.com
SIC: 5046 Restaurant equipment and supplies, nec

(G-13888)
SKAGGS ELECTRIC LLC
74 Alley Corner Rd (19977-3771)
PHONE.................302 653-0576
EMP: 8 EST: 2018
SALES (est): 414.77K **Privately Held**
SIC: 1731 Electrical work

(G-13889)
SMI SERVICES OF DELAWARE LLC (PA)
5609 Dupont Pkwy (19977-9211)
P.O. Box 187 (19955-0187)
PHONE.................302 514-9681
EMP: 7 EST: 2017
SALES (est): 9.67MM

GEOGRAPHIC SECTION

Smyrna - Kent County (G-13921)

SALES (corp-wide): 9.67MM **Privately Held**
Web: www.smicompanies.net
SIC: 1542 Commercial and office building contractors

(G-13890)
SMILE PLACE
17 N Main St (19977-1111)
P.O. Box 659 (19977-0659)
PHONE..................................302 514-6200
Lewis Yu, *Prin*
EMP: 10 EST: 2016
SALES (est): 468.6K **Privately Held**
Web: www.thesmileplacede.com
SIC: 8021 Dentists' office

(G-13891)
SMYRNA CLAYTON LITTLE LEAGUE I
Duck Creek Rd (19977)
PHONE..................................302 653-7550
EMP: 14 EST: 2001
SALES (est): 80.91K **Privately Held**
Web: www.scllbaseball.com
SIC: 7997 Baseball club, except professional and semi-professional

(G-13892)
SMYRNA CLYTON LDGE 2046 ORDER
2035 S Dupont Blvd (19977-2883)
P.O. Box 475 (19977-0475)
PHONE..................................302 653-2046
EMP: 6 EST: 2010
SALES (est): 246.25K **Privately Held**
SIC: 8641 Civic associations

(G-13893)
SMYRNA DE
1271 S Dupont Blvd (19977-2892)
PHONE..................................302 653-1166
EMP: 5 EST: 2017
SALES (est): 49.6K **Privately Held**
Web: smyrna.delaware.gov
SIC: 8641 Condominium association

(G-13894)
SMYRNA DENTAL CENTER PA
679 S Carter Rd Unit 5 (19977-7755)
PHONE..................................302 223-6194
Rama Lakshmi Yerneni, *Pr*
EMP: 9 EST: 2008
SALES (est): 220.23K **Privately Held**
Web: www.smyrnadental.com
SIC: 8021 Dentists' office

(G-13895)
SMYRNA MEDICAL AID UNIT
100 S Main St Ste 101 (19977-1478)
PHONE..................................302 659-4444
EMP: 7 EST: 2019
SALES (est): 246.91K **Privately Held**
SIC: 8099 Health and allied services, nec

(G-13896)
SMYRNA MEDICAL ASSOCIATES PA
38 Deak Dr (19977-1268)
PHONE..................................302 653-6174
Rufino V Rosal Md, *Prin*
EMP: 14 EST: 2000
SQ FT: 3,908
SALES (est): 168.25K **Privately Held**
SIC: 8011 Internal medicine, physician/surgeon

(G-13897)
SMYRNA SCHOOL DISTRICT
Also Called: Special Services Center
80 Monrovia Ave (19977-1530)
PHONE..................................302 653-3135
Donald Bates, *Dir*
EMP: 53
SALES (corp-wide): 72.88MM **Privately Held**
Web: www.smyrna.k12.de.us
SIC: 8211 8351 Public elementary and secondary schools; Child day care services
PA: Smyrna School District
    82 Monrovia Ave
    Smyrna DE 19977
    302 653-8585

(G-13898)
SNOW FARMS INC
249 Raymond Neck Rd (19977-2928)
PHONE..................................302 653-7534
Bruce Snow, *Pr*
EMP: 5 EST: 1965
SALES (est): 441.78K **Privately Held**
SIC: 0191 General farms, primarily crop

(G-13899)
SOUTHERN DEL PHYSCL THERAPY
207 Stadium St (19977-2899)
PHONE..................................302 659-0173
Julie Moyerknowles, *CEO*
EMP: 5
SIC: 8049 Physical therapist
PA: Southern Delaware Physical Therapy Inc
    701 Savannah Rd Ste A
    Lewes DE 19958

(G-13900)
STATE OF DE
118 S Delaware St (19977-1447)
P.O. Box 97 (19977-0097)
PHONE..................................302 653-0593
EMP: 5 EST: 2018
SALES (est): 48.11K **Privately Held**
SIC: 4789 Transportation services, nec

(G-13901)
STERLING NURSERY INC
1575 Vandyke Greenspring Rd (19977-9489)
PHONE..................................302 653-7060
Richard W Sterling, *Pr*
EMP: 5 EST: 1976
SALES (est): 397.43K **Privately Held**
Web: www.thesterlingnursery.com
SIC: 0181 5193 Nursery stock, growing of; Nursery stock

(G-13902)
STL & ASSOCIATES LLC
198 Greens Branch Ln (19977-1097)
P.O. Box 126 (19977-0126)
PHONE..................................302 359-2801
EMP: 8 EST: 2007
SALES (est): 245.14K **Privately Held**
Web: www.yourjanitorialservices.com
SIC: 7349 7389 Janitorial service, contract basis; Business services, nec

(G-13903)
STOVER CONSTRUCTION LLC
5625 Dupont Pkwy (19977-9203)
PHONE..................................302 653-6195
EMP: 6 EST: 2020
SALES (est): 246.3K **Privately Held**
Web: www.stoverconstruction.com
SIC: 1521 Single-family housing construction

(G-13904)
STYLES DIVINE UNLIMITED
310 N Main St Bldg C (19977-1078)
PHONE..................................302 409-4612
Glenice Jernigan-wescott, *Prin*
EMP: 5 EST: 2018
SALES (est): 55.36K **Privately Held**
SIC: 7231 Hairdressers

(G-13905)
SURPLUS & EXCESS LINE LTD
4 Village Sq Ste 900 (19977-1852)
PHONE..................................302 653-5016
Howell Wallace, *Pr*
Mike Mercer, *VP*
Teresa Boole, *Sec*
EMP: 5 EST: 1971
SQ FT: 1,500
SALES (est): 380.07K **Privately Held**
Web: www.surplus-excesslines.com
SIC: 6411 Insurance brokers, nec

(G-13906)
SYMACK CAPITAL MGT US CORP
231 Stadium St Unit 240 (19977-2891)
PHONE..................................469 607-6092
Nick Khamis, *Managing Member*
EMP: 15
SALES (est): 580.9K **Privately Held**
SIC: 6726 Management investment funds, closed-end

(G-13907)
SYMACK CAPITAL US CORP
231 Stadium St (19977-2891)
PHONE..................................469 607-6092
EMP: 15
SALES (est): 580.9K **Privately Held**
SIC: 6799 Investors, nec

(G-13908)
SYMACK PROF SVCS US CORP
231 Stadium St Unit 240 (19977-2891)
PHONE..................................469 607-6092
EMP: 15
SALES (est): 515.3K **Privately Held**
SIC: 8742 Management consulting services

(G-13909)
SYMACK US CORP
231 Stadium St Unit 240 (19977-2891)
PHONE..................................469 607-6092
EMP: 15
SIC: 6719 Holding companies, nec

(G-13910)
T A H FIRST INC
571 Kates Way (19977-1623)
P.O. Box 432 (19977-0432)
PHONE..................................302 653-6114
Harold Horan Iii, *Pr*
EMP: 5 EST: 1990
SALES (est): 386.35K **Privately Held**
SIC: 4213 Automobiles, transport and delivery

(G-13911)
TAMI S CREECH
462 Fletcher Dr (19977-2818)
PHONE..................................302 670-7798
Tami Creech, *Prin*
EMP: 10 EST: 2004
SQ FT: 2,575
SALES (est): 213.28K **Privately Held**
SIC: 8011 Plastic surgeon

(G-13912)
TEAM DEMARCO FITNESS LLC
59 Oriole Ln (19977-4066)
PHONE..................................347 743-3170
Demarco Rivera, *Prin*
EMP: 5 EST: 2014
SALES (est): 29.54K **Privately Held**
SIC: 7991 Physical fitness facilities

(G-13913)
TINY TOKEN TRCKG & TRNSP LLC
17 Maria Ln (19977-7701)
PHONE..................................929 602-5512
EMP: 5 EST: 2020
SALES (est): 211.28K **Privately Held**
SIC: 7389 Business Activities at Non-Commercial Site

(G-13914)
TO THE MOON AND BACK CHILDCARE
307 Kent Way (19977-1317)
PHONE..................................302 508-2749
EMP: 6 EST: 2017
SALES (est): 17.47K **Privately Held**
SIC: 8351 Child day care services

(G-13915)
TORRENGINEERING LLC
26 E Commerce St Ste 1 (19977-1404)
PHONE..................................302 367-8365
EMP: 10 EST: 2019
SALES (est): 557.25K **Privately Held**
Web: www.torrellc.com
SIC: 8711 Engineering services

(G-13916)
TOYS STORY LLC
75 Oriole Ln (19977-4066)
PHONE..................................267 334-9822
EMP: 5 EST: 2021
SALES (est): 106.48K **Privately Held**
SIC: 8351 Child day care services

(G-13917)
TRACTOR SUPPLY COMPANY
1300 S Dupont Blvd (19977-1804)
PHONE..................................302 659-3333
EMP: 17
SALES (corp-wide): 14.2B **Publicly Held**
Web: www.tractorsupply.com
SIC: 5191 Farm supplies
PA: Tractor Supply Company
    5401 Virginia Way
    Brentwood TN 37027
    615 440-4000

(G-13918)
TRI STATE CONSTRUCTION INC
13 Buckeye Ln (19977-5244)
PHONE..................................609 980-1000
EMP: 7 EST: 2018
SALES (est): 305.68K **Privately Held**
SIC: 1521 Single-family housing construction

(G-13919)
TRU GRIT LLC
525 Black Diamond Rd (19977-9669)
PHONE..................................302 593-4700
EMP: 15 EST: 2020
SALES (est): 949.12K **Privately Held**
Web: www.trugritllc.com
SIC: 1794 Excavation work

(G-13920)
TRUDY L HASTINGS
365 N Main St (19977-1010)
PHONE..................................302 653-3145
Trudy L A Hastings, *Prin*
EMP: 9 EST: 2011
SALES (est): 79.34K **Privately Held**
SIC: 8011 Offices and clinics of medical doctors

(G-13921)
TRUE STREET AUTOMOTIVE LLC
899 S Dupont Blvd (19977-1759)
PHONE..................................302 480-4119
Schuyler Wisniewski, *Prin*

Smyrna - Kent County (G-13922)

EMP: 6 EST: 2017
SALES (est): 246.92K **Privately Held**
SIC: 7538 General automotive repair shops

(G-13922)
TURN OF WRENCH
100 S Canvasback Ct (19977-9520)
PHONE..................302 584-1824
EMP: 5 EST: 2013
SALES (est): 184.6K **Privately Held**
Web: www.turnofthewrench.com
SIC: 7538 General automotive repair shops

(G-13923)
U-HAUL
5786 Dupont Pkwy (19977-9601)
PHONE..................302 514-0034
Sandy Humbertson, *Owner*
EMP: 5 EST: 2018
SALES (est): 46.21K **Privately Held**
Web: www.uhaul.com
SIC: 7513 Truck rental and leasing, no drivers

(G-13924)
UNREAL VAPORS
81 Ramunno Dr (19977-1786)
PHONE..................302 750-6213
Kevin Christensen, *CEO*
EMP: 5 EST: 2014
SALES (est): 143.84K **Privately Held**
SIC: 5194 Smokeless tobacco

(G-13925)
UPBOUND GROUP INC
Also Called: Rent-A-Center
120 E Glenwood Ave (19977-1003)
PHONE..................302 653-3701
Selix Wilson, *Mgr*
EMP: 5
Web: www.rentacenter.com
SIC: 7359 Appliance rental
PA: Upbound Group, Inc.
5501 Headquarters Dr
Plano TX 75024

(G-13926)
UPPAL UMSA
66 E Glenwood Ave (19977-1002)
PHONE..................302 897-7434
Umsa Uppal, *Owner*
EMP: 6 EST: 2018
SALES (est): 78.46K **Privately Held**
SIC: 8049 Offices of health practitioner

(G-13927)
V A TRUCK & TRAILER REPAIR LLC
304 Garnet Ln (19977-9647)
PHONE..................302 653-7936
EMP: 7 EST: 2011
SALES (est): 303.27K **Privately Held**
SIC: 7539 Trailer repair

(G-13928)
VALOUR ARABIANS
1950 Vandyke Greenspring Rd (19977-9448)
PHONE..................302 653-4066
Margo Wallace, *Owner*
EMP: 8 EST: 1981
SALES (est): 292.82K **Privately Held**
Web: www.valourarabians.com
SIC: 0272 Horse farm

(G-13929)
VERIZON AUTHORIZED RET TCC
239 N Dupont Blvd (19977-1546)
PHONE..................302 653-8183
EMP: 6 EST: 2019
SALES (est): 33.14K **Privately Held**
Web: locations.tccrocks.com
SIC: 4812 Cellular telephone services

(G-13930)
VETERANS OF FOREIGN WARS NEWMN
Also Called: Veterans Fgn Wars Nwman L-Urba
4941 Wheatleys Pond Rd (19977-3731)
PHONE..................302 653-8801
EMP: 6 EST: 1984
SALES (est): 130.51K **Privately Held**
SIC: 8641 Veterans' organization

(G-13931)
VICTOROUS KNGDOM CTZENS NTWRK
541 Sequoia Dr (19977-2551)
PHONE..................302 409-0701
Tyrence Junior, *Ch Bd*
EMP: 5
SALES (est): 46.17K **Privately Held**
Web: www.vkcitizensnetwork.com
SIC: 8661 7389 Religious organizations; Business services, nec

(G-13932)
W D PRESSLEY INC
5779 Dupont Pkwy (19977-9635)
P.O. Box 477 (19977-0477)
PHONE..................302 653-4381
William Pressley Senior, *CEO*
Brenda Pressley, *VP*
EMP: 8 EST: 1988
SALES (est): 1.17MM **Privately Held**
Web: www.wdpressley.com
SIC: 1521 1542 General remodeling, single-family houses; Commercial and office buildings, renovation and repair

(G-13933)
WEEKFISH LLC
196 York Dr (19977-4624)
PHONE..................800 979-5501
Michael Dove, *Prin*
EMP: 5 EST: 2017
SALES (est): 91.82K **Privately Held**
Web: www.weekfish.com
SIC: 8732 Commercial nonphysical research

(G-13934)
WELLSPRING COUNSELING SERVICES
115 E Glenwood Ave (19977-1424)
PHONE..................302 373-8904
Michael M Bryson, *Owner*
EMP: 9 EST: 2018
SALES (est): 125.89K **Privately Held**
SIC: 8322 General counseling services

(G-13935)
WENTZEL TRANSPORTATION
33 Brenford Station Rd (19977-4600)
PHONE..................302 355-9465
Maryjane Wentzel, *Prin*
EMP: 6 EST: 2007
SALES (est): 850K **Privately Held**
Web: wentzel.us.com
SIC: 4731 Freight transportation arrangement

(G-13936)
WER WIRELESS OF SMYRNA INC
Also Called: Veze Wireless of Smyrna Inc
239 N Dupont Blvd (19977-1546)
PHONE..................302 653-8183
Ricky Singh, *Pr*
EMP: 10 EST: 2007
SALES (est): 172.98K **Privately Held**
SIC: 5999 4812 Mobile telephones and equipment; Cellular telephone services
PA: We R Wireless Inc.
520 Fellowship Rd E508
Mount Laurel NJ 08054

(G-13937)
WHITNER HOUSE PUBLISHING LLC
5 S Howard St (19977-1229)
PHONE..................267 338-9741
Marshieta Walker, *Managing Member*
EMP: 2 EST: 2021
SALES (est): 72.72K **Privately Held**
SIC: 2711 Job printing and newspaper publishing combined

(G-13938)
WILLIAM H RDFORD NURSERIES INC
Also Called: William H Radford Ldscp Contrs
853 Black Diamond Rd (19977-9663)
PHONE..................302 659-3130
Bill Radford, *Pr*
Karla Radford, *VP*
EMP: 20 EST: 2005
SALES (est): 1.11MM **Privately Held**
SIC: 0782 Landscape contractors

(G-13939)
WILLIS FORD INC
Also Called: Quick Lane
15 N Dupont Blvd (19977-1544)
PHONE..................302 653-5900
William H Willis Junior, *Pr*
William H Willis Junior, *Pr*
Harry D Willis, *
EMP: 25 EST: 1994
SALES (est): 14.57MM **Privately Held**
Web: www.willisford.com
SIC: 5511 5531 7538 7532 Automobiles, new and used; Automotive parts; General automotive repair shops; Top and body repair and paint shops

(G-13940)
WILLOW COUNSELING SERVICES
19 Ormonde Cir (19977-4024)
PHONE..................814 779-9653
Alisha Mccanney, *Prin*
EMP: 6 EST: 2019
SALES (est): 47.22K **Privately Held**
Web: www.willowcounselingservicesde.com
SIC: 8322 General counseling services

(G-13941)
YOUNG MUSIC LLC
2358 Dutch Neck Rd (19977-3048)
PHONE..................302 307-1997
EMP: 9 EST: 2017
SALES (est): 313.5K **Privately Held**
Web: www.prodigies.com
SIC: 7371 8299 Computer software development and applications; Music and drama schools

(G-13942)
YOUNITY LOUNGE LLC
74 Pristine Crt (19977)
PHONE..................302 359-5609
Robert Taylor, *Managing Member*
EMP: 6
SALES (est): 58.79K **Privately Held**
SIC: 7929 Entertainment service

(G-13943)
ZOOMIN & GROOMIN
259 Rons Way (19977-2513)
PHONE..................302 985-3963
Kathryn Jester, *Prin*
EMP: 6 EST: 2018
SALES (est): 89.98K **Privately Held**
Web: www.zoomingroomin.com
SIC: 0752 Grooming services, pet and animal specialties

Talleyville
New Castle County

(G-13944)
ABBOTT DYNAMICS LLC
330 Delaware Ave 210-A (19803-2581)
PHONE..................951 923-5996
Dannia Verges Simmons, *Pr*
EMP: 3 EST: 2020
SALES (est): 100K **Privately Held**
SIC: 2262 Printing, manmade fiber and silk broadwoven fabrics

(G-13945)
PERFORMANCE BASED RESULTS
Also Called: P B R
400 Delaware Ave (19803-5232)
PHONE..................302 478-4443
Paul Cherry, *Owner*
EMP: 8 EST: 1996
SALES (est): 602.1K **Privately Held**
Web: www.pbresults.com
SIC: 8742 Training and development consultant

(G-13946)
SILVERSIDE CLUB INC
418 Brandywine Blvd (19803-1806)
P.O. Box 7206 (19803-0206)
PHONE..................302 478-4568
Alfred Burke Junior, *Prin*
EMP: 8 EST: 2010
SALES (est): 61.46K **Privately Held**
Web: www.silversideswimclub.com
SIC: 7997 Golf club, membership

(G-13947)
STEVEN SACHS APPRAISAL ACCESS
19 Brandywine Blvd (19803-1838)
PHONE..................302 477-9676
Steven Sachs, *Owner*
EMP: 5 EST: 2001
SALES (est): 241.19K **Privately Held**
Web: www.stevensachsappraisal.com
SIC: 6531 Appraiser, real estate

Townsend
New Castle County

(G-13948)
360 PAINTING
310 Androssan Pl (19734-2861)
PHONE..................302 373-4867
EMP: 5
SALES (est): 75.07K **Privately Held**
Web: www.360painting.com
SIC: 1721 Residential painting

(G-13949)
3E CLEANING SERVICES
401 Bassett Ct (19734-9049)
PHONE..................215 359-8323
Steven Ashby, *Prin*
EMP: 5 EST: 2016
SALES (est): 43.52K **Privately Held**
SIC: 7699 Cleaning services

(G-13950)
A B W SERVICES LLC
281 Camerton Ln (19734-2873)
PHONE..................856 449-1329

Angela Bakerware, *Managing Member*
EMP: 6
SALES (est): 64.36K **Privately Held**
SIC: 8322 7389 Individual and family services; Notary publics

(G-13951)
ADVANCED BIZZ INNOVATIONS LLC
405 South St (19734-3017)
P.O. Box 122 (19709-0122)
PHONE.................................302 397-1162
EMP: 5 EST: 2011
SALES (est): 110.68K **Privately Held**
SIC: 7349 Janitorial service, contract basis

(G-13952)
ADVANCED TECHNOLOGY SALES
556 Stonehaven Dr (19734-3812)
PHONE.................................732 446-9681
Kathleen Tarantino, *Pr*
EMP: 5 EST: 2017
SALES (est): 32.18K **Privately Held**
SIC: 7379 Computer related consulting services

(G-13953)
AERO ENTERPRISES INC
1270 Caldwell Corner Rd (19734-9255)
PHONE.................................302 378-1396
EMP: 6 EST: 1995
SALES (est): 485.33K **Privately Held**
Web: www.aeroenterprises.com
SIC: 4581 Aircraft maintenance and repair services

(G-13954)
AG & G SHEET METAL INC
470 Oak Hill School Rd (19734-9204)
PHONE.................................302 653-4111
Ronald Grantland, *Pr*
EMP: 9 EST: 1983
SALES (est): 946K **Privately Held**
SIC: 3444 Sheet metalwork

(G-13955)
AIR QUALITY REMEDIATION LLC
1274 Caldwell Corner Rd (19734-9255)
P.O. Box 337 (19734-0337)
PHONE.................................302 464-1050
David Brenton, *Managing Member*
Connie Haymond, *Managing Member*
EMP: 10 EST: 2004
SALES (est): 878.45K **Privately Held**
Web: www.aqracure.biz
SIC: 7342 Disinfecting services

(G-13956)
ALL ABOUT HOUSING LLC
126 Tweedsmere Dr (19734-2815)
P.O. Box 1196 (19709-7196)
PHONE.................................302 465-3246
EMP: 6 EST: 2016
SALES (est): 474.88K **Privately Held**
SIC: 6531 Real estate agents and managers

(G-13957)
ALL CLEAN SERVICES
859 Union Church Rd (19734-9121)
PHONE.................................302 378-7376
Frank Lorusso, *Owner*
EMP: 7 EST: 1996
SALES (est): 151.97K **Privately Held**
SIC: 7349 Janitorial service, contract basis

(G-13958)
ALPHA TECH CONSULTING LLC
1405 Gibraltar Ct (19734-2887)
PHONE.................................302 898-2862
Olajide Balogun, *Managing Member*
EMP: 15 EST: 2018

SALES (est): 895.44K **Privately Held**
SIC: 7361 Placement agencies

(G-13959)
AMERICAN LEGION
3 Owensby Dr (19734-9783)
PHONE.................................302 378-4882
Raymond Abbott, *Prin*
EMP: 7 EST: 2010
SALES (est): 57.55K **Privately Held**
Web: www.legion.org
SIC: 8641 Veterans' organization

(G-13960)
ANGEL PIZZARO
1760 Harvey Straughn Rd (19734-9292)
PHONE.................................302 653-4844
Angel Pizarro, *Prin*
EMP: 5 EST: 2010
SALES (est): 32.62K **Privately Held**
SIC: 7699 Cleaning services

(G-13961)
ATTIC AWAY FROM HOME
893 Noxontown Rd (19734-9363)
PHONE.................................302 378-2600
Don Mckeown, *Owner*
EMP: 13 EST: 1999
SALES (est): 98.39K **Privately Held**
SIC: 8351 Child day care services

(G-13962)
BEACH BBIES CHILD CARE AT TWNS
6020 Summit Bridge Rd (19734-9614)
PHONE.................................302 378-4778
Deborah Toner, *Brnch Mgr*
EMP: 8
SALES (corp-wide): 2.46MM **Privately Held**
Web: www.beachbabieschildcare.com
SIC: 8351 Group day care center
PA: Beach Babies Child Care At Townsend
104 Canal View Ct
Rehoboth Beach DE 19971
302 644-1585

(G-13963)
BESHORE LAWN SERVICE LLC
Also Called: Releaf Property Services
251 Union Church Rd (19734-9115)
PHONE.................................302 313-6924
Timothy Beshore, *Brnch Mgr*
EMP: 8
SALES (corp-wide): 453.5K **Privately Held**
Web: www.releafpropertyservices.com
SIC: 6512 Nonresidential building operators
PA: Beshore Lawn Service Llc
251 Union Church Rd
Townsend DE 19734
717 991-9468

(G-13964)
BLACKBIRD COMMUNITY ASSN INC
120 Blackbird Forest Rd (19734-9618)
PHONE.................................302 598-7447
EMP: 7 EST: 1950
SALES (est): 79.68K **Privately Held**
SIC: 8641 Community membership club

(G-13965)
BRANDX HEIRLOOM TOMATOES
103 Ashley Ann Ct (19734-2030)
PHONE.................................302 287-1782
Xiomara Lozano, *Prin*
EMP: 6 EST: 2017
SALES (est): 80.68K **Privately Held**
SIC: 8099 Health and allied services, nec

(G-13966)
BREEZE CONSTRUCTION LLC
39 Basalt St (19734-2013)
PHONE.................................302 522-9201
Sommer Flynn, *Managing Member*
EMP: 5 EST: 2019
SALES (est): 386.02K **Privately Held**
SIC: 1542 1522 1521 Commercial and office building contractors; Multi-family dwellings, new construction; New construction, single-family houses

(G-13967)
BRIGHT STARS DAYCARE
24 Dornoch Way (19734-2863)
PHONE.................................302 449-9198
Patel Ankita, *Prin*
EMP: 8 EST: 2015
SALES (est): 53.56K **Privately Held**
SIC: 8351 Group day care center

(G-13968)
BROBST HOME IMPROVEMENT LLC
5909 Summit Bridge Rd (19734-9613)
PHONE.................................302 376-1656
EMP: 6 EST: 2004
SALES (est): 407.46K **Privately Held**
Web: www.brobsthomeimprovements.com
SIC: 1522 Residential construction, nec

(G-13969)
BUBBA GAME CALLS
158 Blackbird Station Rd (19734-9506)
PHONE.................................302 332-2004
Timothy Seward, *Prin*
EMP: 5 EST: 2018
SALES (est): 47.08K **Privately Held**
SIC: 3949 Game calls

(G-13970)
CC DRYWALL CONTRACTORS NO
553 Money Rd (19734-9343)
PHONE.................................302 307-6400
EMP: 7 EST: 2018
SALES (est): 424.76K **Privately Held**
SIC: 1742 Drywall

(G-13971)
CHRISTIANA CARE HEALTH SYSTEM
606 Union Church Rd (19734-9112)
PHONE.................................302 674-1390
Gary Ferguson, *CIO*
EMP: 12 EST: 2017
SALES (est): 54.13K **Privately Held**
Web: www.christianacare.org
SIC: 8011 Offices and clinics of medical doctors

(G-13972)
CLEANING BEES
1342 Caldwell Corner Rd (19734-9626)
PHONE.................................302 723-2421
Heather Sweetman, *Prin*
EMP: 5 EST: 2017
SALES (est): 54.56K **Privately Held**
SIC: 7699 Cleaning services

(G-13973)
COBALT PACIFIC LLC
642 Courtly Rd (19734-2895)
PHONE.................................302 437-4761
EMP: 2 EST: 2021
SALES (est): 49.23K **Privately Held**
SIC: 1389 5085 8711 Oil and gas field services, nec; Pipeline wrappings, anti-corrosive; Engineering services

(G-13974)
COLETTE W BLEISTINE PAYING IT
537 Stonehaven Dr (19734-3810)
PHONE.................................609 217-1925
Rqxanne Phillips, *VP*
EMP: 5 EST: 2017
SALES (est): 53.28K **Privately Held**
SIC: 8641 Civic and social associations

(G-13975)
COLLETT & SON WELDING INC
550 Green Giant Rd (19734-9322)
P.O. Box 660 (19977-0660)
PHONE.................................302 376-1830
John V Collett, *Pr*
Kimberly J Collet, *Sec*
Margaret Bowman, *Sec*
EMP: 9 EST: 1984
SALES (est): 1.79MM **Privately Held**
Web: www.collettandsonswelding.com
SIC: 1799 Welding on site

(G-13976)
CORRIN TREE & LANDSCAPE CO
Also Called: Corrin Expert Tree Care
299 Saw Mill Rd (19734-9640)
PHONE.................................302 753-8733
Kenneth M Corrin, *Pr*
EMP: 5 EST: 2011
SALES (est): 321.82K **Privately Held**
Web: www.corrintree.com
SIC: 0781 Landscape services

(G-13977)
COUNTRY KIDS HOME DAY CARE
1069 Vndyke Grenspring Rd (19734-9231)
PHONE.................................302 653-4134
Dawn Carden, *Prin*
EMP: 5 EST: 2010
SALES (est): 56.23K **Privately Held**
SIC: 8351 Group day care center

(G-13978)
CREATIVE MINDS DAYCARE
2 Mica St (19734-2027)
PHONE.................................302 378-0741
Michelle Craig, *Prin*
EMP: 5 EST: 2009
SALES (est): 89.73K **Privately Held**
SIC: 8351 Group day care center

(G-13979)
CROKER OARS USA INC
212 Karins Blvd (19734-3029)
PHONE.................................302 897-6705
EMP: 2 EST: 2008
SALES (est): 160.9K **Privately Held**
Web: www.crokerusa.com
SIC: 3732 Boatbuilding and repairing

(G-13980)
CROSSFIT 1ST STATE
36 Dornoch Way (19734-2863)
PHONE.................................302 382-0603
Dean Jud, *Pr*
EMP: 6 EST: 2014
SALES (est): 52.76K **Privately Held**
SIC: 7991 Health club

(G-13981)
CUSTOM PORCELAIN INC
1245 Caldwell Corner Rd (19734-9255)
PHONE.................................302 659-6590
Patricia Wyatt, *Pr*
EMP: 5 EST: 1984
SALES (est): 403.14K **Privately Held**
Web: www.customceramic.com
SIC: 1799 Bathtub refinishing

Townsend - New Castle County (G-13982)   **GEOGRAPHIC SECTION**

(G-13982)
D & G INC
4195 Dupont Pkwy (19734-9728)
PHONE...................302 378-4877
Fredrick Drake, Pr
EMP: 10 EST: 1994
SALES (est): 391.65K Privately Held
SIC: 7549 7371 Towing services; Computer software development and applications

(G-13983)
DAGERS WATERFOWL HUNTING
Also Called: Guide Svcs
166 Gardner Rd (19734-9028)
PHONE...................302 659-1766
EMP: 5 EST: 2011
SALES (est): 50.79K Privately Held
SIC: 7999 Tour and guide services

(G-13984)
DAN PRINSLOO
217 Olivine Cir (19734-2009)
PHONE...................302 373-8891
Dan Prinsloo, Prin
EMP: 5 EST: 2017
SALES (est): 88.9K Privately Held
SIC: 1522 Residential construction, nec

(G-13985)
DAVID R DANIELS
375 Vandyke Maryland Line Rd (19734-9637)
PHONE...................410 275-8141
David Daniels, Prin
EMP: 5 EST: 2002
SALES (est): 215.1K Privately Held
SIC: 0119 Cash grains, nec

(G-13986)
DD&K LOGISTICS LLC
318 Sunnyside Ln (19734-9044)
PHONE...................301 523-5984
Derick Harris, Managing Member
EMP: 2 EST: 2021
SALES (est): 70.94K Privately Held
SIC: 3537 7389 Trucks: freight, baggage, etc.: industrial, except mining; Business Activities at Non-Commercial Site

(G-13987)
DELAWARE HOMES INC (PA)
401 Main St (19734-9022)
P.O. Box 38 (19734-0038)
PHONE...................302 378-9510
Michael C Selvaggio, Pr
EMP: 10 EST: 1986
SALES (est): 2.25MM
SALES (corp-wide): 2.25MM Privately Held
Web: www.yourdehome.com
SIC: 1521 New construction, single-family houses

(G-13988)
DELAWARE PATIO & LANDSCPG INC
176 Olivine Cir (19734-2005)
PHONE...................302 218-3738
EMP: 6 EST: 2012
SALES (est): 249.9K Privately Held
Web: www.delawarepatio.com
SIC: 0781 Landscape services

(G-13989)
DELAWARE PEDIATRICS PA (PA)
3920 Dupont Pkwy Ste A (19734-9000)
PHONE...................302 762-6222
EMP: 5 EST: 1990
SALES (est): 2.92MM Privately Held
Web: www.depediatrics.com
SIC: 8011 Pediatrician

(G-13990)
DELCARM LLC (PA)
1482 Levels Rd (19734)
PHONE...................610 345-9001
EMP: 10 EST: 2007
SALES (est): 2.5MM Privately Held
SIC: 0721 Crop spraying services

(G-13991)
DEPRO-SERICAL USA INC
Also Called: Depro Serical
4676 Dupont Pkwy (19734-9100)
PHONE...................302 368-8040
Guenter Lehming, Ch
Ute Lehming, Pr
EMP: 6 EST: 1984
SQ FT: 20,000
SALES (est): 520.09K Privately Held
SIC: 5032 2752 Brick, stone, and related material; Commercial printing, lithographic

(G-13992)
DIBIASOS CLG RSTRATION SVC INC
690 Blackbird Station Rd (19734-9304)
P.O. Box 43 (19734-0043)
PHONE...................302 376-7111
EMP: 7 EST: 1995
SALES (est): 376.98K Privately Held
Web: www.dibiasos.com
SIC: 7217 7389 8744 Carpet and upholstery cleaning; Water softener service; Environmental remediation

(G-13993)
DONNAS GARDEN GOODIES
1412 Dexter Corner Rd (19734-9238)
PHONE...................302 399-3691
Donna Draper, Prin
EMP: 4 EST: 2016
SALES (est): 46.57K Privately Held
SIC: 2741 Miscellaneous publishing

(G-13994)
DUCOS REALTY INC
217 Karins Blvd (19734-3028)
PHONE...................302 563-6902
Grisette Ducos, VP
EMP: 5 EST: 2017
SALES (est): 210.7K Privately Held
SIC: 6531 Real estate brokers and agents

(G-13995)
DW HEATING AND COOLING SVCS
306 Androssan Pl (19734-2861)
PHONE...................302 373-7786
David Werts, Prin
EMP: 7 EST: 2017
SALES (est): 237.78K Privately Held
SIC: 1711 Warm air heating and air conditioning contractor

(G-13996)
E LAWRENCE JESTER
747 Green Giant Rd (19734-9631)
PHONE...................302 378-8970
Lawernce E Jester, Prin
EMP: 7 EST: 2007
SALES (est): 478.97K Privately Held
SIC: 0191 General farms, primarily crop

(G-13997)
EDWARD L BALLARD
Also Called: Ballard Business Services
157 Wiggins Mill Rd (19734-9537)
PHONE...................302 363-4302
EMP: 5 EST: 2009
SALES (est): 184.7K Privately Held
SIC: 4141 Local bus charter service

(G-13998)
ESTEPP CONSTRUCTION CO INC
1047 Dexter Corner Rd (19734-9242)
PHONE...................302 378-4958
James T Estepp Junior, Pr
Phyliss Estepp, VP
EMP: 5 EST: 1983
SALES (est): 581.47K Privately Held
SIC: 1521 1741 Single-family housing construction; Masonry and other stonework

(G-13999)
EVERGREEN LED
29 Dornoch Way (19734-2863)
PHONE...................302 218-7819
Sam Scherwitz, Prin
Bob Aellis, VP
EMP: 6 EST: 2009
SALES (est): 313.81K Privately Held
SIC: 3648 Lighting equipment, nec

(G-14000)
EZ DECK LLC
Also Called: American Quality Construction
107 Ashley Ann Ct (19734-2030)
PHONE...................302 444-2268
Jonathon Pechickjian, Pr
EMP: 7 EST: 2013
SALES (est): 905.13K Privately Held
Web: www.mylocaldeckpro.com
SIC: 1521 Single-family housing construction

(G-14001)
F AND M EQUIPMENT LTD
3272 Dupont Pkwy (19734-9414)
PHONE...................302 449-2850
EMP: 16
SIC: 5082 General construction machinery and equipment
HQ: F And M Equipment, Ltd.
2240 Bethlehem Pike
Hatfield PA 19440

(G-14002)
FISH LAWN AND TREE LLC
912 Dexter Corner Rd (19734-9234)
PHONE...................302 383-4202
EMP: 11 EST: 2018
SALES (est): 619.94K Privately Held
Web: www.fishlawnandtree.com
SIC: 0782 Lawn care services

(G-14003)
FRED DRAKE AUTOMOTIVE INC
Also Called: Fred Drake Salvage
4195 Dupont Pkwy (19734-9728)
PHONE...................302 378-4877
Fred Drake Junior, Pr
Bob Hill, Clerk
EMP: 7 EST: 1980
SQ FT: 2,500
SALES (est): 692.25K Privately Held
Web: www.freddrakeauto.com
SIC: 7549 5015 5932 Towing service, automotive; Motor vehicle parts, used; Used merchandise stores

(G-14004)
FRESH COAT PAINTERS OF MOT
413 Prestwick Pl (19734-2838)
PHONE...................302 313-6124
EMP: 7 EST: 2018
SALES (est): 42.66K Privately Held
Web: www.freshcoatpainters.com
SIC: 1721 Painting and paper hanging

(G-14005)
GEARS GARAGE LLC
282 Deer Run Rd (19734-9711)
PHONE...................302 653-3684
EMP: 5 EST: 2017
SALES (est): 77K Privately Held
Web: www.gearsgarageautomotive.com
SIC: 7538 General automotive repair shops

(G-14006)
GENERATION ELECTRICAL SVCS LLC
128 Edgar Rd (19734-2411)
PHONE...................302 298-1868
Brent Greenfield, Prin
EMP: 6 EST: 2016
SALES (est): 556.26K Privately Held
Web: www.generationelectricalservices.com
SIC: 1731 General electrical contractor

(G-14007)
GEORGE J MARTINO
Also Called: G & D Lawn Service
440 Dogtown Rd (19734-9694)
PHONE...................302 376-5162
George J Martino, Owner
EMP: 5 EST: 2002
SALES (est): 70.23K Privately Held
SIC: 0782 Lawn care services

(G-14008)
GLORY CONTRACTING
231 Ratledge Rd (19734-9547)
PHONE...................302 275-5430
Daniel Moody, Owner
EMP: 5 EST: 2013
SALES (est): 220.88K Privately Held
SIC: 2491 Wood preserving

(G-14009)
GONE HUNTING INC
112 Deer Run Rd (19734-9155)
PHONE...................302 659-5010
John Gonce, Prin
EMP: 6 EST: 2011
SALES (est): 92.25K Privately Held
SIC: 5091 Hunting equipment and supplies

(G-14010)
GRACE LOGISTICS LLC
328 Camerton Ln (19734-2872)
PHONE...................302 287-4838
Felix Fokuo, Pr
EMP: 5 EST: 2016
SALES (est): 283.92K Privately Held
SIC: 4789 Transportation services, nec

(G-14011)
GREGG & SONS MECHANICAL LLC
256 Gum Bush Rd (19734-9769)
PHONE...................302 223-8145
Gregg Uhde, Managing Member
Myriam Uhde, Managing Member
Beverly Bartlett, Prin
EMP: 5 EST: 2005
SALES (est): 444.43K Privately Held
Web: www.greggandsons.com
SIC: 1799 1711 Food service equipment installation; Refrigeration contractor

(G-14012)
H&S CLEANING SERVICE INC
684 Southerness Dr (19734-3802)
PHONE...................302 449-2928
Sheila Ramsey, Pr
Henry Ramsey, *
EMP: 6 EST: 1986
SQ FT: 10,000
SALES (est): 186.35K Privately Held
SIC: 7349 Building cleaning service

GEOGRAPHIC SECTION

Townsend - New Castle County (G-14043)

(G-14013)
HAMPTON ENTERPRISES INC
Also Called: Hampton Enterprises Delaware
413 Prestwick Pl (19734-2838)
PHONE.....................302 378-7365
Lamont Hampton, *CEO*
EMP: 7 **EST:** 1997
SALES (est): 479.48K **Privately Held**
Web: www.hampton-enterprises.com
SIC: 7217 1721 1799 2842 Carpet and upholstery cleaning; Painting and paper hanging; Paint and wallpaper stripping; Paint and wallpaper cleaners

(G-14014)
HB&T AUTOMOTIVE LLC
3171 Dupont Pkwy (19734-9780)
P.O. Box 1442 (19701-7442)
PHONE.....................302 378-3333
EMP: 6 **EST:** 2018
SALES (est): 370.77K **Privately Held**
Web: hbt-automotive.business.site
SIC: 7538 General automotive repair shops

(G-14015)
INC CHIMES
409 Zamora Ct (19734-3054)
PHONE.....................302 449-1926
EMP: 6 **EST:** 2011
SALES (est): 81.78K **Privately Held**
SIC: 3699 Chimes, electric

(G-14016)
INDEPENDENT DISPOSAL SERVICES
604 Cannery Ln (19734-9409)
P.O. Box 490 (19734-0490)
PHONE.....................302 378-5400
Bruce Georgov, *Owner*
EMP: 5 **EST:** 1996
SALES (est): 293.02K **Privately Held**
SIC: 4953 Recycling, waste materials

(G-14017)
INFORMED TUCH MSSAGE THRAPY LL
905 Ibiza Ct (19734-3052)
PHONE.....................302 229-8239
Jodi Collins, *Prin*
EMP: 7 **EST:** 2017
SALES (est): 87.42K **Privately Held**
SIC: 8093 Rehabilitation center, outpatient treatment

(G-14018)
INSIGHT ENGINEERING SOLUTIONS
Also Called: Ies
640 Ravenglass Dr (19734-2829)
PHONE.....................302 378-4842
Devanand M Prasad, *CEO*
Michael Robertson, *VP*
EMP: 9 **EST:** 2009
SALES (est): 717K **Privately Held**
SIC: 7376 8748 7371 7373 Computer facilities management; Systems engineering consultant, ex. computer or professional; Computer software systems analysis and design, custom; Local area network (LAN) systems integrator

(G-14019)
JAMIES AUTO REPAIR SOUTH
98 Main St (19734-9047)
PHONE.....................302 378-7933
EMP: 7 **EST:** 2017
SALES (est): 305.78K **Privately Held**
Web: www.jamiesautodelaware.com
SIC: 7538 General automotive repair shops

(G-14020)
JANETTE REDROW LTD
Also Called: Jr
635 Cannery Ln (19734-9420)
P.O. Box 296 (19734-0296)
PHONE.....................302 659-3534
Janette H Redrow, *Pr*
▲ **EMP:** 5 **EST:** 1992
SALES (est): 822.55K **Privately Held**
Web: www.fmclain.com
SIC: 5088 1629 1541 Transportation equipment and supplies; Drainage system construction; Steel building construction

(G-14021)
KALEO INC
2 Feldspar Way (19734-2018)
PHONE.....................302 376-0327
EMP: 5 **EST:** 2019
SALES (est): 48.82K **Privately Held**
Web: www.kaleo.com
SIC: 8748 Business consulting, nec

(G-14022)
KEE BUILDERS
730 Union Church Rd (19734-9725)
PHONE.....................302 376-9858
Steve Kee, *Owner*
EMP: 5 **EST:** 2004
SALES (est): 203.77K **Privately Held**
SIC: 1521 New construction, single-family houses

(G-14023)
KNIGHTS GOLF INC
113 Esch St (19734-3044)
PHONE.....................484 553-1119
EMP: 5 **EST:** 2016
SALES (est): 27.07K **Privately Held**
SIC: 7999 Golf professionals

(G-14024)
KW CONTRACTING INC
207 Ratledge Rd (19734-9547)
PHONE.....................302 420-0159
Kim Weismiller, *Pr*
EMP: 7 **EST:** 2016
SALES (est): 248.6K **Privately Held**
SIC: 1799 Antenna installation

(G-14025)
LATHAM LOGISTICS
101 Edgar Rd (19734-2415)
PHONE.....................215 760-4724
Michael Latham, *CEO*
EMP: 5 **EST:** 2021
SALES (est): 115K **Privately Held**
SIC: 4789 7389 Transportation services, nec ; Business Activities at Non-Commercial Site

(G-14026)
LC HOMES
1002 Bilboa Ct (19734-3055)
PHONE.....................302 376-7004
EMP: 5 **EST:** 2012
SALES (est): 76.41K **Privately Held**
Web: www.lchomesde.com
SIC: 1521 New construction, single-family houses

(G-14027)
LIFEHUSE ERLY CHLDHOOD CTR LLC
101 Karins Blvd (19734)
PHONE.....................302 464-1105
Jeff Sareyka, *Managing Member*
EMP: 25 **EST:** 2020
SALES (est): 256.67K **Privately Held**
Web: www.lifehouseecc.com
SIC: 8351 7389 Child day care services; Business Activities at Non-Commercial Site

(G-14028)
LOYALTY SOAP AND CANDLE CO LLC
304 Helen Dr (19734-2404)
PHONE.....................302 373-5854
EMP: 4 **EST:** 2018
SALES (est): 43.66K **Privately Held**
SIC: 3999 Candles

(G-14029)
MAKK-O INDUSTRIES INC
4640 Dupont Pkwy (19734-9100)
PHONE.....................302 376-0160
Vincent Passalacqua, *Pr*
EMP: 5 **EST:** 1981
SQ FT: 5,000
SALES (est): 599.04K **Privately Held**
Web: www.makk-o.com
SIC: 5085 Fasteners, industrial: nuts, bolts, screws, etc.

(G-14030)
MARCELLE L PASCHALL DSC
419 South St (19734-3018)
PHONE.....................302 376-1768
Marcelle L Paschall, *Prin*
EMP: 8 **EST:** 2011
SALES (est): 89.35K **Privately Held**
SIC: 8011 Offices and clinics of medical doctors

(G-14031)
MARKEL AND ASSOCIATES LLC
412 Sitka Spruce Ln (19734-9442)
PHONE.....................302 898-5684
EMP: 5
SALES (est): 264.79K **Privately Held**
Web: www.markel.com
SIC: 8742 Management consulting services

(G-14032)
MATT MATIASET
212 Karins Blvd (19734-3029)
PHONE.....................302 376-3042
Mary Doyle, *Prin*
EMP: 5 **EST:** 2010
SALES (est): 42.65K **Privately Held**
SIC: 7299 Handyman service

(G-14033)
MEGHAN ZGLER HLTH WELLNESS LLC
126 Wedge Ct (19734-2842)
PHONE.....................302 379-9967
Meghan Zeigler, *Prin*
EMP: 6 **EST:** 2016
SALES (est): 71.1K **Privately Held**
SIC: 8099 Health and allied services, nec

(G-14034)
MELISSA M DAMIANO DO
3920 Dupont Pkwy (19734-9000)
PHONE.....................302 449-2570
Melissa Damiano, *Mgr*
EMP: 10 **EST:** 2018
SALES (est): 172.99K **Privately Held**
SIC: 8011 Offices and clinics of medical doctors

(G-14035)
MICHAEL A BEECHER
Also Called: Swamp Machine Shop
1122 Dexter Corner Rd (19734-9671)
PHONE.....................302 285-3357
Michael Beecher, *Prin*
EMP: 4 **EST:** 2011
SALES (est): 212.3K **Privately Held**
Web: www.swampmachineshop.com
SIC: 3599 Machine shop, jobbing and repair

(G-14036)
MICHAEL LO SAPIO
900 Grears Corner Rd (19734-9672)
PHONE.....................201 919-2643
Michael Lo Sapio, *Prin*
EMP: 6 **EST:** 2011
SALES (est): 94.98K **Privately Held**
SIC: 7997 Membership sports and recreation clubs

(G-14037)
MIDDLETOWN TOWING
4008 Dupont Pkwy (19734-9392)
PHONE.....................302 357-6484
EMP: 6 **EST:** 2008
SALES (est): 128.11K **Privately Held**
Web: www.middletowntowingde.com
SIC: 7549 Towing service, automotive

(G-14038)
ML WHITEMAN AND SONS INC
261 Gum Bush Rd (19734-9768)
P.O. Box 34 (19734-0034)
PHONE.....................302 659-1001
EMP: 6 **EST:** 2012
SALES (est): 514.98K **Privately Held**
SIC: 1521 Single-family housing construction

(G-14039)
MOUNTAIRE FARMS DELAWARE INC
Also Called: Peavey
402 Main St (19734-9021)
P.O. Box 36 (19734-0036)
PHONE.....................302 378-2271
Marshall Ellsworth, *Mgr*
EMP: 5
SALES (corp-wide): 2.07B **Privately Held**
Web: www.mountaire.com
SIC: 5153 Grain elevators
HQ: Mountaire Farms Of Delaware, Inc.
  1901 Napa Valley Dr
  Little Rock AR 72212
  501 372-6524

(G-14040)
MRS KLEEN INC
1047 Dexter Corner Rd (19734-9242)
PHONE.....................302 530-7330
Phyllis Estepp, *Prin*
EMP: 5 **EST:** 2017
SALES (est): 41.55K **Privately Held**
SIC: 7699 Cleaning services

(G-14041)
MWM CONSTRUCTION
6210 Summit Bridge Rd (19734-9376)
PHONE.....................302 218-5222
Michael Montgomery, *Asstg*
EMP: 5 **EST:** 2000
SALES (est): 231.49K **Privately Held**
SIC: 1521 Single-family housing construction

(G-14042)
NANCY DUFRESNE
Also Called: Guap International Enterprise
4 Denny Lynn Dr (19734-2022)
PHONE.....................302 378-7236
Nancy Dufresne, *Prin*
EMP: 5 **EST:** 2017
SALES (est): 104.73K **Privately Held**
Web: www.dufresneministries.org
SIC: 7389 Business Activities at Non-Commercial Site

(G-14043)
NEXTMOVE INC
401 Main St (19734-9022)

Townsend - New Castle County (G-14044)　　　　　　　　　　　　　　　　　　　　　　　　　　　　　　　**GEOGRAPHIC SECTION**

P.O. Box 38 (19734-0038)
PHONE..................302 593-7830
EMP: 5 EST: 2011
SALES (est): 83.97K **Privately Held**
SIC: **1522** Hotel/motel and multi-family home construction

(G-14044)
ODESSA EARLY EDUCATION CENTER
27 Mailly Dr (19734-2207)
PHONE..................302 376-5254
Cristine Aguilar, *Owner*
EMP: 8 EST: 2000
SALES (est): 81.69K **Privately Held**
SIC: **8351** Nursery school

(G-14045)
ODESSA NATIONAL CIVIC ASSN
293 Camerton Ln (19734-2873)
PHONE..................302 530-1804
EMP: 6 EST: 2015
SALES (est): 34.78K **Privately Held**
Web: www.odessanationalgolfclub.com
SIC: **8699** Membership organizations, nec

(G-14046)
ODESSA NATIONAL GOLF CRSE LLC
1131 Fieldsboro Rd (19734-9188)
PHONE..................302 464-1007
Dale Loeslein, *Mgr*
EMP: 8 EST: 2008
SALES (est): 238.07K **Privately Held**
Web: www.odessanationalgolfclub.com
SIC: **7992** Public golf courses

(G-14047)
P&H REALTY LLC
5668 Summit Bridge Rd (19734-9364)
PHONE..................302 378-3484
Jean Hitch, *Prin*
EMP: 5 EST: 2005
SALES (est): 233.42K **Privately Held**
SIC: **6531** Real estate brokers and agents

(G-14048)
PARKWAY LAW LLC
3171 Dupont Pkwy (19734-9780)
P.O. Box 1016 (19709-7016)
PHONE..................302 449-0400
Dominic Dalascio, *Managing Member*
EMP: 8 EST: 2012
SALES (est): 966.9K **Privately Held**
Web: www.parkway-law.com
SIC: **8111** General practice law office

(G-14049)
PASSAVANT MEMORIAL HOMES
202 Buckingham Ct (19734-9676)
PHONE..................302 449-2202
EMP: 6 EST: 2017
SALES (est): 92.59K **Privately Held**
Web: www.pmhfos.org
SIC: **6531** Real estate agents and managers

(G-14050)
PATTERSON PRICE RE LLC (PA)
143 Wiggins Mill Rd (19734-9537)
PHONE..................302 378-9550
EMP: 8 EST: 1953
SALES (est): 950.15K
SALES (corp-wide): 950.15K **Privately Held**
Web: www.pattersonprice.com
SIC: **6531** **6552** Real estate agent, residential ; Subdividers and developers, nec

(G-14051)
PAUL OJEWOYE
241 Avonbridge Dr (19734-2868)
PHONE..................443 844-1345
Grace Ojewoye, *Prin*
EMP: 6 EST: 2017
SALES (est): 24.4K **Privately Held**
SIC: **8049** Offices of health practitioner

(G-14052)
PIPE PROS JETTING & PLBG LLC
479 Blackbird Landing Rd (19734-9144)
PHONE..................302 562-0522
Kelly Albanese, *Prin*
EMP: 11 EST: 2015
SALES (est): 915.11K **Privately Held**
Web: www.pipeprosjettingde.com
SIC: **1711** Plumbing contractors

(G-14053)
POWELL LIFE SKILLS INC
209 Glenshee Dr (19734-3814)
P.O. Box 338 (19734-0338)
PHONE..................302 378-2706
Rita Powell, *Pr*
EMP: 9 EST: 2012
SALES (est): 158.59K **Privately Held**
SIC: **8399** Council for social agency

(G-14054)
PREMIER COMFORT SERVICES
306 Androssan Pl (19734-2861)
PHONE..................302 740-0712
David V Werts, *Prin*
EMP: 5 EST: 2016
SALES (est): 52.08K **Privately Held**
SIC: **1711** Warm air heating and air conditioning contractor

(G-14055)
RE BATH OF NORTHERN DE
Also Called: Re-Bath
135 Lynemore Dr (19734-2837)
PHONE..................302 414-9751
EMP: 5 EST: 2019
SALES (est): 97.54K **Privately Held**
Web: www.rebath.com
SIC: **1799** Kitchen and bathroom remodeling

(G-14056)
REETZ FAMILY PRACTICE LLC
116 Tweedsmere Dr (19734-2815)
PHONE..................215 806-0318
EMP: 8 EST: 2019
SALES (est): 54.13K **Privately Held**
SIC: **8011** General and family practice, physician/surgeon

(G-14057)
RENTZS SIGN SERVICE
4676 Dupont Pkwy (19734-9100)
PHONE..................302 378-9607
Robert Rentz, *Prin*
EMP: 4 EST: 2017
SALES (est): 46.08K **Privately Held**
SIC: **3993** Signs and advertising specialties

(G-14058)
RETIRED-N-FIT
Also Called: Beyond Fifty
138 Wye Oak Dr (19734-9422)
PHONE..................302 478-4191
EMP: 10 EST: 2015
SALES (est): 164.55K **Privately Held**
Web: www.beyondfiftyde.com
SIC: **7991** Physical fitness facilities

(G-14059)
REVA STAYS LLC
353 Mingo Way (19734-9441)
PHONE..................347 599-8599
EMP: 6
SALES (est): 64.36K **Privately Held**
SIC: **7021** Rooming and boarding houses

(G-14060)
REVOLVE TECHNOLOGIES LLC
266 Camerton Lane (19734-2871)
PHONE..................302 528-2647
EMP: 5 EST: 2016
SALES (est): 57.88K **Privately Held**
SIC: **7371** Computer software development

(G-14061)
ROBERT MICHAEL CORP
436 Caledonia Way (19734-3801)
PHONE..................302 378-4164
Michael Young, *Prin*
EMP: 5 EST: 2015
SALES (est): 120.87K **Privately Held**
SIC: **1521** Single-family home remodeling, additions, and repairs

(G-14062)
RSHORT ROOFING LLC
6091 Summit Bridge Rd (19734-9377)
PHONE..................302 276-9531
Ralph Short Junior, *Prin*
EMP: 8 EST: 2016
SALES (est): 859.69K **Privately Held**
Web: www.rshortroofing.com
SIC: **1761** Roofing contractor

(G-14063)
RYNO IRON
17 Spring Creek Dr (19734-9048)
PHONE..................302 464-2973
John Priem, *Prin*
EMP: 6 EST: 2012
SALES (est): 141.64K **Privately Held**
SIC: **5064** Irons

(G-14064)
SKYYLIMIT LLC
146 Abbigail Xing (19734-2891)
PHONE..................302 256-3212
Kwame Asante, *Pr*
EMP: 6 EST: 2015
SALES (est): 459.83K **Privately Held**
SIC: **4789** Transportation services, nec

(G-14065)
SMT HTG AND AIR COND LLC
4361 Dupont Pkwy (19734-9397)
PHONE..................302 285-9219
Dwayne Burns, *Owner*
EMP: 5 EST: 2015
SALES (est): 32.06K **Privately Held**
SIC: **7623** Refrigeration service and repair

(G-14066)
SOUL PURPOSE
282 Camerton Ln (19734-2871)
PHONE..................302 420-1254
Lisa Brown, *Prin*
EMP: 5 EST: 2010
SALES (est): 81.46K **Privately Held**
SIC: **6324** Hospital and medical service plans

(G-14067)
SOUTH DELAWARE MASONRY INC
319 Main St (19734-7703)
P.O. Box 72 (19734-0072)
PHONE..................302 378-1998
Joseph Mandes, *Pr*
EMP: 9 EST: 1969
SQ FT: 2,760

SALES (est): 785.14K **Privately Held**
SIC: **1741** Masonry and other stonework

(G-14068)
SPARE PARTS LLC
218 Avonbridge Dr (19734-2869)
PHONE..................302 333-2683
EMP: 5 EST: 2013
SALES (est): 46.23K **Privately Held**
SIC: **7933** Ten pin center

(G-14069)
SPEECH LADDER INC
1210 Glen Mohr Ct (19734-2888)
PHONE..................770 355-0719
Alyce Rouse, *Managing Member*
EMP: 6 EST: 2006
SALES (est): 198.54K **Privately Held**
SIC: **8741** Business management

(G-14070)
SPRIG
169 Pine Tree Rd (19734-9784)
P.O. Box 429 (19734-0429)
PHONE..................302 753-6859
Ashley Dimichele, *Prin*
EMP: 7 EST: 2018
SALES (est): 588.82K **Privately Held**
Web: www.spriginc.net
SIC: **1623** Underground utilities contractor

(G-14071)
STADA FITNESS CONCEPT LLC
1004 W Founds St (19734-3005)
PHONE..................215 589-0914
Stacy Whitehead, *Prin*
EMP: 5 EST: 2016
SALES (est): 56.76K **Privately Held**
SIC: **7991** Physical fitness facilities

(G-14072)
STANLEY J LEPOWSKI JR
Also Called: Handymen USA
125 Gum Bush Rd (19734-9737)
PHONE..................302 378-7284
Stanley J Lepowski Junior, *Prin*
EMP: 5 EST: 2009
SALES (est): 43.6K **Privately Held**
SIC: **7299** Handyman service

(G-14073)
STATEWIDE MECHANICAL INC
3295 Harris Rd (19734-9735)
P.O. Box 170 (19731-0170)
PHONE..................302 376-6117
Paige Stewart, *Pr*
Robert Stewart, *VP*
EMP: 6 EST: 1999
SALES (est): 812.41K **Privately Held**
SIC: **1711** Mechanical contractor

(G-14074)
SUMMIT HEATING AND AC LLC (PA)
4361 Dupont Pkwy (19734-9397)
PHONE..................302 378-1203
Jeanette Burns, *Prin*
EMP: 7 EST: 2010
SALES (est): 472.44K
SALES (corp-wide): 472.44K **Privately Held**
Web: www.summitcomfort.com
SIC: **1711** Heating systems repair and maintenance

(G-14075)
SUPERIOR LAWNCARE LLC ✪
180 Black Stallion Rd (19734-9653)
PHONE..................302 373-3289
EMP: 7 EST: 2023
SALES (est): 54.76K **Privately Held**

GEOGRAPHIC SECTION   Wilmington - New Castle County (G-14105)

SIC: 0782 Lawn services

(G-14076)
T&G CONSTRUCTION LLC
635 Cannery Ln Ste E (19734-9420)
PHONE.................................302 922-1674
Lauren Green, *Managing Member*
EMP: 4 EST: 2018
SALES (est): 60K **Privately Held**
SIC: 1389 Construction, repair, and dismantling services

(G-14077)
TANNER OPERATIONS INC
39 Anchor Inn Rd (19734-9733)
PHONE.................................302 464-2194
EMP: 10 EST: 2010
SALES (est): 534.36K **Privately Held**
SIC: 5064 Electrical appliances, television and radio

(G-14078)
TC DENTAL EQUIPMENT SERVICES
262 Dogtown Rd (19734-9632)
PHONE.................................302 740-9049
EMP: 4 EST: 2014
SALES (est): 104.31K **Privately Held**
SIC: 3843 Dental equipment

(G-14079)
THOMAS FENIMORE
311 Blackbird Station Rd (19734-9261)
PHONE.................................302 464-2633
Sharon Fenimore, *Prin*
EMP: 5 EST: 2014
SALES (est): 119.33K **Privately Held**
SIC: 6732 Trusts: educational, religious, etc.

(G-14080)
TIKANA MOTORSPORTS
282 Deer Run Rd (19734-9711)
PHONE.................................302 290-0869
Mike Geier, *Prin*
EMP: 5 EST: 2013
SALES (est): 241.88K **Privately Held**
SIC: 7549 High performance auto repair and service

(G-14081)
TIM 2 MY BRO AWRNESS BLNCE FND ✪
316 Putter St (19734-2851)
PHONE.................................302 278-2191
Norman Green, *Prin*
EMP: 5 EST: 2022
SALES (est): 64.36K **Privately Held**
SIC: 8399 Social services, nec

(G-14082)
TOMS SEALING & STRIPING CO
986 Caldwell Corner Rd (19734-9625)
PHONE.................................302 531-7039
Tom Loughry, *Owner*
EMP: 6 EST: 2011
SALES (est): 142.53K **Privately Held**
SIC: 7521 Parking garage

(G-14083)
TOTAL BATH TRANSFORMATIONS
402 Union Church Rd (19734-9110)
PHONE.................................302 985-7649
Charlotte Conover, *Pr*
EMP: 7 EST: 2014
SALES (est): 417.65K **Privately Held**
Web: www.transformmybath.com
SIC: 1799 Kitchen and bathroom remodeling

(G-14084)
TRI-STATE UNDERGROUND INC
4369 Dupont Pkwy (19734-9397)
PHONE.................................302 836-8030
Rick Hess, *Pr*
EMP: 11 EST: 2015
SALES (est): 1.86MM **Privately Held**
Web: www.tristateug.com
SIC: 1623 Underground utilities contractor

(G-14085)
TRIO ENTERPRISES LLC
202 Loft St (19734-2845)
PHONE.................................302 832-5575
Sue A Elentrio, *Prin*
EMP: 5 EST: 2009
SALES (est): 247.27K **Privately Held**
Web: www.trioenterprises.com
SIC: 8748 Business consulting, nec

(G-14086)
TRU CONSTRUCTION LLC
1028 W Founds St (19734-3006)
PHONE.................................302 740-9691
Tru Nguyen, *Asst Sec*
EMP: 5 EST: 2017
SALES (est): 277.86K **Privately Held**
Web: www.truconstructionde.com
SIC: 1521 General remodeling, single-family houses

(G-14087)
UNITED GARAGE DOORS
51 Spring Creek Dr (19734-9048)
PHONE.................................302 414-9220
EMP: 6 EST: 2019
SALES (est): 53.36K **Privately Held**
Web: www.unitedgaragedoors247.com
SIC: 1751 Garage door, installation or erection

(G-14088)
VIRTUALLY FORTIFIED STAFFING
1470 Caldwell Corner Rd (19734-9257)
PHONE.................................302 547-9065
Lisa Holt, *Owner*
EMP: 5 EST: 2013
SALES (est): 243.91K **Privately Held**
Web: www.vfstaffing.com
SIC: 7363 Help supply services

(G-14089)
VOLLEYBALL
142 Tweedsmere Dr (19734-2815)
PHONE.................................302 593-4414
Randy Day, *Prin*
EMP: 5 EST: 2017
SALES (est): 42.43K **Privately Held**
SIC: 7941 Sports clubs, managers, and promoters

(G-14090)
WEIGHTED WITH LOVE LLC
117 Oliver Guessford Rd (19734-9297)
PHONE.................................302 378-2041
Della Danz, *Pr*
EMP: 7 EST: 2017
SALES (est): 81.33K **Privately Held**
Web: www.weightedwithlove.net
SIC: 8093 Rehabilitation center, outpatient treatment

(G-14091)
WILLEY FARMS INC
Also Called: Willey Farms
4092 Dupont Pkwy (19734-9392)
PHONE.................................302 378-8441
Christopher Willey, *Pr*
Sarah Willey, *
Irene Willey, *

EMP: 65 EST: 1975
SQ FT: 30,000
SALES (est): 10.89MM **Privately Held**
Web: www.willeyfarmsde.com
SIC: 5148 5431 5261 5023 Fruits; Fruit and vegetable markets; Nursery stock, seeds and bulbs; Home furnishings, wicker, rattan or reed

---

Viola
Kent County

(G-14092)
CENTRAL DEL SCHL OF THE ARTS F
8 Ruritan Ln (19979-1251)
PHONE.................................302 943-2274
EMP: 6 EST: 2017
SALES (est): 50.11K **Privately Held**
SIC: 8351 Child day care services

(G-14093)
CHAMBERS BUS SERVICE INC
8964 S Dupont Hwy (19979)
P.O. Box 47 (19979-0047)
PHONE.................................302 284-9655
Betty Chambers, *Pr*
William Chambers Junior, *VP*
EMP: 8 EST: 1999
SALES (est): 313.77K **Privately Held**
SIC: 4131 Intercity bus line

(G-14094)
ERIC HOBBS TRUCKING INC
3292 Turkey Point Rd (19979-2009)
P.O. Box 60 (19979-0060)
PHONE.................................302 697-2090
EMP: 26 EST: 1992
SQ FT: 1,500
SALES (est): 1.45MM **Privately Held**
SIC: 4213 Trucking, except local

(G-14095)
GSM SYSTEMS INC (PA)
215 E Evens Rd (19979-9700)
PHONE.................................302 284-8304
Patricia A Mayer, *Pr*
EMP: 10 EST: 1992
SALES (est): 700K
SALES (corp-wide): 700K **Privately Held**
Web: www.gsmsystems.com
SIC: 7363 7389 Engineering help service; Business Activities at Non-Commercial Site

(G-14096)
HOBBS ENTERPRISES INC
4398 Turkey Point Rd (19979-9712)
PHONE.................................302 697-2090
Greg N Hobbs, *Prin*
EMP: 5 EST: 2008
SALES (est): 352.83K **Privately Held**
SIC: 4213 Trucking, except local

(G-14097)
WALTERS AUCTIONEERING
139 Princess Ann Ave (19979-9747)
PHONE.................................302 284-0914
Sam Walters, *Prin*
EMP: 5 EST: 2010
SALES (est): 73K **Privately Held**
SIC: 7389 Auction, appraisal, and exchange services

(G-14098)
WILLIAM CHAMBERS AND SON
8964 S Dupont Hwy (19979)
P.O. Box 47 (19979-0047)
PHONE.................................302 284-9655
William Chambers Junior, *Pr*
Betty L Chambers, *Sec*

EMP: 6 EST: 1915
SQ FT: 7,000
SALES (est): 946.3K **Privately Held**
Web: www.wmchambersandson.com
SIC: 1799 7538 Welding on site; Truck engine repair, except industrial

---

Wilmington
New Castle County

(G-14099)
1 RIGHTER LLC
2 Righter Pkwy (19803-1532)
PHONE.................................302 479-9257
EMP: 5 EST: 2015
SALES (est): 469.86K **Privately Held**
SIC: 6722 Management investment, open-end

(G-14100)
10-4 SAFETY LLC (PA)
3411 Silverside Rd Ttnallb (19810-4812)
PHONE.................................847 997-5515
Patrick Burke, *Managing Member*
EMP: 6 EST: 2020
SALES (est): 494.09K
SALES (corp-wide): 494.09K **Privately Held**
SIC: 8748 Safety training service

(G-14101)
1000 DEGREES PIZZERIA
Also Called: 1000 Degrees Pizzeria
4500 New Linden Rd (19808)
PHONE.................................609 382-3022
EMP: 11 EST: 2015
SALES (est): 122.6K **Privately Held**
Web: www.1000degreespizza.com
SIC: 5812 6794 Pizza restaurants; Franchises, selling or licensing

(G-14102)
103 WHOLESALE&DISTRIBUTION LLC
2154 Grafton Dr (19808-5904)
PHONE.................................302 344-2093
EMP: 2 EST: 2020
SALES (est): 77.45K **Privately Held**
SIC: 3086 Packaging and shipping materials, foamed plastics

(G-14103)
1102 WEST STREET LTD PARTNR
Also Called: Courtyard By Marriott
1102 N West St (19801-1006)
PHONE.................................302 429-7600
Christina Vanzandt, *Pt*
EMP: 68 EST: 1991
SALES (est): 449.35K **Privately Held**
Web: courtyard.marriott.com
SIC: 7011 Hotels and motels

(G-14104)
1110 ON PARKWAY NEDI SPA
1110 N Bancroft Pkwy Ste 2 (19805-2669)
PHONE.................................302 576-1110
EMP: 7 EST: 2013
SALES (est): 237.64K **Privately Held**
Web: www.1110ontheparkway.com
SIC: 7991 Spas

(G-14105)
1212 CORPORATION
2700 N Washington St (19802-3536)
PHONE.................................302 764-4048
Steven Burns, *CEO*
William J Harrison, *Pr*
EMP: 6 EST: 1982
SALES (est): 246.39K **Privately Held**

Wilmington - New Castle County (G-14106)

GEOGRAPHIC SECTION

SIC: 8069 Alcoholism rehabilitation hospital

(G-14106)
1300 PUBLISHING COMPANY LLC
1306 W 6th St (19805-3216)
PHONE.................................302 268-2684
EMP: 4 EST: 2017
SALES (est): 57.11K **Privately Held**
SIC: 2741 Miscellaneous publishing

(G-14107)
1313 INNOVATION
1313 N Market St Ste 1150nw
(19801-6101)
PHONE.................................302 407-0420
Paul Mcconnell, *Pr*
EMP: 7 EST: 2017
SALES (est): 236.53K **Privately Held**
Web: www.1313innovation.com
SIC: 7389 Office facilities and secretarial service rental

(G-14108)
1313 OWNER LLC
1201 N Market St Ste 400 (19801-1164)
PHONE.................................302 225-7896
Shawn Thipman, *Acctnt*
EMP: 9 EST: 2017
SALES (est): 849.52K **Privately Held**
SIC: 8641 Dwelling-related associations

(G-14109)
1320 CBW LLC
1320 Clifford Brown Walk (19801-3147)
PHONE.................................302 656-5599
EMP: 5 EST: 2017
SALES (est): 103.25K **Privately Held**
SIC: 6519 Real property lessors, nec

(G-14110)
1401 CONDOMINIUM ASSOCIATION
1401 Pennsylvania Ave (19806-4125)
PHONE.................................302 656-8171
Chris Bell, *Pr*
Stephen Sfida, *Mgr*
EMP: 11 EST: 1980
SALES (est): 480K **Privately Held**
SIC: 8641 Condominium association

(G-14111)
15 DIVISION LLC
2810 N Church St (19802-4447)
PHONE.................................667 334-0861
Jeremy Jackson, *Managing Member*
EMP: 5
SALES (est): 220.71K **Privately Held**
SIC: 4214 Household goods moving and storage, local

(G-14112)
15 RENWICK STREET LLC
1925 Lovering Ave (19806-2157)
PHONE.................................302 652-2900
Sinead Rossi, *Prin*
EMP: 5 EST: 2017
SALES (est): 92.36K **Privately Held**
Web: www.15renwick.com
SIC: 6513 Apartment building operators

(G-14113)
18 POMEGRANETS INC
501 Silverside Rd (19809-1374)
PHONE.................................800 839-1754
EMP: 5 EST: 2010
SALES (est): 89.24K **Privately Held**
Web: www.pomegranads.us
SIC: 8699 Charitable organization

(G-14114)
1SOURCE SAFETY HEALTH
200 Powder Mill Rd 361 (19803-2907)
PHONE.................................302 470-2001
EMP: 7 EST: 2018
SALES (est): 92.89K **Privately Held**
SIC: 8099 Health and allied services, nec

(G-14115)
1ST ENGINEERING SOLUTIONS LLC
1000 N West St Ste 1200 (19801-1058)
PHONE.................................302 966-9439
Manny Belmar, *Owner*
EMP: 6 EST: 2014
SALES (est): 145.22K **Privately Held**
Web: www.1stengineeringsolutions.com
SIC: 5049 Scientific and engineering equipment and supplies

(G-14116)
1ST STATE REAL ESTATE LLC (PA)
175 Fairhill Dr (19808-4312)
PHONE.................................302 319-4051
Joann L Wacksman, *Prin*
EMP: 10 EST: 2013
SALES (est): 189.22K
SALES (corp-wide): 189.22K **Privately Held**
SIC: 6531 Real estate brokers and agents

(G-14117)
1ST-RECRUIT LLC
3 Germay Dr Unit 4-2031 (19804-1127)
PHONE.................................732 666-4106
Umesh Kumar, *CEO*
Umesh Kumar, *Managing Member*
EMP: 10 EST: 2021
SALES (est): 484.7K **Privately Held**
Web: www.1st-recruit.com
SIC: 8742 7361 7379 Management consulting services; Employment agencies; Computer related consulting services

(G-14118)
2 DAYS BATH LLC
6603 Governor Printz Blvd (19809-2027)
PHONE.................................302 798-0103
EMP: 12 EST: 2002
SQ FT: 3,606
SALES (est): 499.4K **Privately Held**
Web: www.bathsurvey.com
SIC: 1799 Kitchen and bathroom remodeling

(G-14119)
20 MONT LLC
234 N James St (19804-3132)
PHONE.................................302 999-0708
Gregory Pettinaro, *Mgr*
EMP: 5 EST: 2015
SALES (est): 351.24K **Privately Held**
SIC: 6512 Commercial and industrial building operation

(G-14120)
21ST CENTURY INSURANCE GROUP
3 Beaver Valley Rd (19803-1124)
PHONE.................................302 478-3109
EMP: 21 EST: 2003
SALES (est): 1.04MM **Privately Held**
Web: www.21st.com
SIC: 6411 Insurance agents, brokers, and service

(G-14121)
21ST CENTURY N AMER INSUR CO (DH)
Also Called: 21st Century Insurance
3 Beaver Valley Rd (19803-1124)
PHONE.................................877 310-5687
Bruce W Marlow, *Pr*
Michael J Cassanego, *
Richard A Andre, *Senior Vice President Human Resources**
John M Lorentz, *
EMP: 1500 EST: 1956
SQ FT: 406,000
SALES (est): 860.33MM
SALES (corp-wide): 71.15B **Privately Held**
Web: www.21st.com
SIC: 6411 Property and casualty insurance agent
HQ: Farmers Group, Inc.
6301 Owensmouth Ave # 300
Woodland Hills CA 91367
323 932-3200

(G-14122)
22D LLC
24a Trolley Sq Ste 2234 (19806-3334)
PHONE.................................347 857-8807
N Steven Larsen, *Managing Member*
EMP: 6 EST: 2020
SALES (est): 200K **Privately Held**
SIC: 7373 Value-added resellers, computer systems

(G-14123)
2NDQUADRANT INC
1000 Nw St Ste 1200 (19801-1058)
PHONE.................................650 378-1218
Faiz S Husain, *Pr*
EMP: 24 EST: 2016
SALES (est): 1.33MM **Privately Held**
Web: www.enterprisedb.com
SIC: 7379 Computer related consulting services

(G-14124)
302 SPORTS
116 Winston Ave (19804-1755)
PHONE.................................302 650-8479
Nicholas Halliday, *Owner*
EMP: 6 EST: 2012
SALES (est): 137.62K **Privately Held**
Web: www.302sports.com
SIC: 4832 Sports

(G-14125)
360 DC RENTALS LLC
401 Justison St (19801-5199)
PHONE.................................202 432-3655
EMP: 3
SALES (est): 121.77K **Privately Held**
SIC: 3861 Photographic equipment and supplies

(G-14126)
360 WELLNESS LLC
5519 E Timberview Ct (19808-3627)
PHONE.................................302 286-0118
Sharon Steele, *Prin*
EMP: 6 EST: 2015
SALES (est): 81.82K **Privately Held**
Web: www.wellness360.co
SIC: 8099 Health and allied services, nec

(G-14127)
3E MARKETING SOLUTIONS
9 Kathlyn Ct (19808-3817)
PHONE.................................302 383-4325
EMP: 5 EST: 2012
SALES (est): 144.05K **Privately Held**
Web: www.3emarketingsolutions.com
SIC: 8732 Market analysis, business, and economic research

(G-14128)
3H AGENT SERVICES INC
1201 N Orange St Ste 710 (19801-1186)
PHONE.................................518 583-0639
EMP: 10 EST: 2019
SALES (est): 182.06K **Privately Held**
Web: www.3hcs.com
SIC: 7299 Miscellaneous personal service

(G-14129)
3IMACHINECOM INC
1209 N Orange St (19801-1120)
PHONE.................................301 233-7562
Joe Callanan, *Pr*
EMP: 3 EST: 2020
SALES (est): 123.86K **Privately Held**
SIC: 3089 Thermoformed finished plastics products, nec

(G-14130)
3PHASE EXCEL ELEVATOR LLC
300 B And O Ln (19804-1448)
PHONE.................................508 350-9900
EMP: 5 EST: 2019
SALES (est): 109.45K **Privately Held**
SIC: 7699 Elevators: inspection, service, and repair

(G-14131)
3RD STATE WELDING SUPPLY LLC
32 Germay Dr Ste C (19804-1118)
PHONE.................................302 777-1088
Joe Belahanty, *Prin*
EMP: 3 EST: 2010
SALES (est): 165.11K **Privately Held**
SIC: 7692 Welding repair

(G-14132)
3W3D INC ◆
1201 N Orange St (19801-1155)
PHONE.................................858 263-5883
EMP: 10 EST: 2022
SALES (est): 406.52K **Privately Held**
SIC: 1799 Special trade contractors, nec

(G-14133)
4 YOUTH PRODUCTIONS INC
1900 Superfine Ln Ste 9 (19802-4920)
P.O. Box 3932 (19807-0932)
PHONE.................................347 338-8243
EMP: 6 EST: 2018
SALES (est): 67.11K **Privately Held**
SIC: 7819 Developing and laboratory services, motion picture

(G-14134)
409 FITNESS
1701 Concord Pike (19803-3603)
PHONE.................................302 354-7011
EMP: 5 EST: 2018
SALES (est): 41.55K **Privately Held**
Web: www.409fitness.com
SIC: 7991 Physical fitness facilities

(G-14135)
44 NEW ENGLAND MANAGEMENT CO
Also Called: Courtyard By Marriott
320 Rocky Run Pkwy (19803-1515)
PHONE.................................302 477-9500
Laura Farrell, *Mgr*
EMP: 51
SALES (corp-wide): 142.01MM **Privately Held**
Web: courtyard.marriott.com
SIC: 7011 Hotels and motels
HQ: 44 New England Management Co
450 Friendship Rd
Harrisburg PA 17111
717 412-5500

GEOGRAPHIC SECTION　　　　　　　　　　　　　　　　　　　　　　　　　　　Wilmington - New Castle County (G-14165)

(G-14136)
44 NEW ENGLAND MANAGEMENT CO
Also Called: Inn At Wilmington
300 Rocky Run Pkwy (19803-1515)
PHONE..................................302 479-7900
Christine Campanella, *Brnch Mgr*
EMP: 24
SALES (corp-wide): 142.01MM **Privately Held**
SIC: 7011 Hotels
HQ: 44 New England Management Co
450 Friendship Rd
Harrisburg PA 17111
717 412-5500

(G-14137)
4SIGHT GROUP LLC
4023 Kennett Pike (19807)
PHONE..................................800 490-2131
Linda M Dickey, *Pt*
EMP: 5 **EST:** 2003
SALES (est): 478.43K **Privately Held**
Web: www.4sightgroup.com
SIC: 7379 Online services technology consultants

(G-14138)
4TH PHASE THECHNOLOGIES INC
501 Silverside Rd Ste 98 (19809-1376)
PHONE..................................610 420-5765
EMP: 10 **EST:** 2017
SALES (est): 650.86K **Privately Held**
SIC: 3761 Guided missiles and space vehicles

(G-14139)
4TH STREET CHIRO PAIN MGMT
318 N Market St (19801-2530)
PHONE..................................302 656-5009
EMP: 5 **EST:** 2018
SALES (est): 37.19K **Privately Held**
SIC: 8041 Offices and clinics of chiropractors

(G-14140)
4YOUTHPRODUCTIONS
308 Campbell Rd (19807-2010)
PHONE..................................302 690-5602
Theresa Emmett, *Prin*
Raphael Dahan, *Bd of Dir*
EMP: 5 **EST:** 2013
SALES (est): 89.76K **Privately Held**
Web: www.4youthproductions.org
SIC: 8399 Community development groups

(G-14141)
5-STAR CLEANING SERVICES
218 S Maryland Ave (19804-1344)
PHONE..................................302 476-9604
EMP: 9 **EST:** 2019
SALES (est): 365.88K **Privately Held**
Web: www.5starcleaningservicesllc.com
SIC: 7699 Cleaning services

(G-14142)
5N1-MC COSMETICS LLC
1007 N Orange St (19801-1239)
PHONE..................................866 561-6226
EMP: 2 **EST:** 2020
SALES (est): 48K **Privately Held**
Web: www.5n1mc.com
SIC: 2844 Cosmetic preparations

(G-14143)
613 FOUNDATION
501 Silverside Rd (19809-1374)
PHONE..................................800 839-1754
EMP: 6 **EST:** 2010
SALES (est): 82.21K **Privately Held**
SIC: 8699 Charitable organization

(G-14144)
629 MARKET RETAIL LLC
1000 N West St Ste 1000 # 1000 (19801-1000)
PHONE..................................302 691-2100
Barbara Neuse, *CFO*
EMP: 8 **EST:** 2017
SALES (est): 360.52K **Privately Held**
SIC: 2086 Carbonated beverages, nonalcoholic: pkged. in cans, bottles

(G-14145)
6AM RUN
108 Talleyrand Dr (19810-3948)
P.O. Box 5561 (19808-8561)
PHONE..................................302 521-0023
EMP: 6 **EST:** 2019
SALES (est): 207.95K **Privately Held**
Web: www.6amrun.com
SIC: 7991 Physical fitness facilities

(G-14146)
700 NRTH KING ST WLMINGTON LLC
Also Called: Doubletree Downtown Wilmington
700 N King St (19801-3504)
PHONE..................................302 655-0400
Alan Filer, *Genl Mgr*
EMP: 110 **EST:** 2013
SALES (est): 7.81MM
SALES (corp-wide): 370.56MM **Privately Held**
SIC: 7011 Hotels and motels
PA: Crestline Hotels & Resorts, Llc
3950 University Dr # 301
Fairfax VA 22030
571 529-6100

(G-14147)
77 LEGACY LLC
1209 N Orange St (19801-1120)
PHONE..................................404 576-7265
EMP: 4 **EST:** 2021
SALES (est): 111.3K **Privately Held**
SIC: 1442 Construction sand and gravel

(G-14148)
786 CELLULAR AND ACCESSORY
702 Wilmington Ave (19805-5111)
PHONE..................................302 482-3024
Aisha Uppal, *Prin*
EMP: 6 **EST:** 2012
SALES (est): 80.38K **Privately Held**
SIC: 4812 Cellular telephone services

(G-14149)
7CHAKRAS SPA LOUNGE
508 E 6th St (19801-4402)
PHONE..................................302 584-7793
Keisha Nesbitt-cohen, *Prin*
EMP: 6 **EST:** 2010
SALES (est): 38.47K **Privately Held**
SIC: 7991 Spas

(G-14150)
7TH HEAVEN INC (PA) ✪
910 Foulk Rd Ste 201 (19803-3159)
PHONE..................................201 282-1925
Daniel Bareket, *CEO*
EMP: 8 **EST:** 2022
SALES (est): 702.28K
SALES (corp-wide): 702.28K **Privately Held**
SIC: 2066 Chocolate and cocoa products

(G-14151)
8FIG GROWTH LLC (PA)
1007 N Orange St (19801-1239)
PHONE..................................442 888-4303
Yaron Shapira, *Managing Member*
EMP: 50 **EST:** 2021
SALES (est): 3.66MM
SALES (corp-wide): 3.66MM **Privately Held**
Web: www.8fig.co
SIC: 7389 Financial services

(G-14152)
8FIGURES INC ✪
251 Little Falls Dr (19808-1674)
PHONE..................................484 291-8881
Andrey Izyumov, *CEO*
EMP: 5 **EST:** 2022
SALES (est): 209.21K **Privately Held**
SIC: 7372 7389 Application computer software; Business services, nec

(G-14153)
8TH & MARKET SPINAL CENTER
207 N Market St (19801-2527)
PHONE..................................302 652-6000
EMP: 6 **EST:** 2015
SALES (est): 82.57K **Privately Held**
Web: www.marketspinalpaincenter.com
SIC: 8011 Offices and clinics of medical doctors

(G-14154)
900 F STREET OWNER LLC
251 Little Falls Dr (19808-1674)
PHONE..................................212 355-1500
Wendy Mosler, *Pr*
Billy Cohen, *VP*
Len Goldberg, *VP*
Peter Allen, *VP*
EMP: 55 **EST:** 2017
SALES (est): 899.6K **Privately Held**
SIC: 7011 Hotels

(G-14155)
9ROUND
1812 Marsh Rd Ste 405 (19810-4522)
PHONE..................................302 543-2545
EMP: 7 **EST:** 2018
SALES (est): 33.09K **Privately Held**
Web: www.9round.com
SIC: 7991 Physical fitness facilities

(G-14156)
9ROUND
4565 Linden Hill Rd (19808)
PHONE..................................302 525-6045
EMP: 6 **EST:** 2018
SALES (est): 74.67K **Privately Held**
Web: www.9round.com
SIC: 7991 Physical fitness facilities

(G-14157)
A & R BAIL BONDS LLC
1710 Philadelphia Pike (19809-1543)
PHONE..................................302 357-1221
Rodney Burns, *Owner*
EMP: 5 **EST:** 2016
SALES (est): 180.48K **Privately Held**
Web: www.aandrbailbonds.net
SIC: 6351 Surety insurance

(G-14158)
A BALANCED LIFE MASSAGE
1 Murphy Rd # 2 (19803-3044)
PHONE..................................302 543-4004
Jermaine Cannon, *Prin*
EMP: 7 **EST:** 2015
SALES (est): 245.33K **Privately Held**
Web: www.demassages.com
SIC: 7299 Massage parlor

(G-14159)
A C EMSLEY & ASSOCIATES
12 S Union St (19805-3828)
PHONE..................................302 429-9191
Allen C Emsley, *Pt*
EMP: 8 **EST:** 1994
SALES (est): 572.01K **Privately Held**
SIC: 6531 Real estate agent, residential

(G-14160)
A CARING DOCTOR MINNESOTA PA
Also Called: Banfield Pet Hospital 1103
3010 Brandywine Pkwy (19803-1498)
P.O. Box 7138 (19803-0138)
PHONE..................................302 478-3910
S Tyson, *Brnch Mgr*
EMP: 16
SALES (corp-wide): 42.84B **Privately Held**
SIC: 0742 Animal hospital services, pets and other animal specialties
HQ: A Caring Doctor Minnesota Pa
8000 Ne Tillamook St
Portland OR 97213
503 922-5000

(G-14161)
A D ALPINE DMD
Also Called: Rafetto, Ray S DMD
4901 Limestone Rd (19808-1271)
PHONE..................................302 239-4600
A D Alpine D.m.d., *Pt*
EMP: 18 **EST:** 1989
SALES (est): 724.66K **Privately Held**
Web: www.beachbraces.com
SIC: 8021 Orthodontist

(G-14162)
A E G CONTRACTING LLC
400 Valley Rd (19804-1355)
PHONE..................................302 250-5438
EMP: 5 **EST:** 2017
SALES (est): 131.67K **Privately Held**
Web: www.aeg4windows.com
SIC: 1799 Special trade contractors, nec

(G-14163)
A GENTLEMANS TOUCH INC
Also Called: Wibsc
1321 Lancaster Ave Ste A (19805-3901)
PHONE..................................302 585-5805
Theo Rollins, *Managing Member*
R Scott Rollins Senior, *Pr*
Tiny L Lewis, *VP*
Theo A Rollins, *Asst Mgr*
EMP: 10 **EST:** 1991
SALES (est): 65K **Privately Held**
SIC: 8231 7241 7231 Documentation center; Barber shops; Beauty shops

(G-14164)
A J DAUPHIN & SON INC
3313 Elizabeth Ave (19808-6106)
PHONE..................................302 994-1454
Daniel J Dauphin, *Pr*
A John Dauphin Iii, *VP*
Karen Dauphin, *VP*
EMP: 9 **EST:** 1939
SQ FT: 3,000
SALES (est): 769.74K **Privately Held**
Web: www.ajdauphinandson.com
SIC: 1711 Plumbing contractors

(G-14165)
A KLEENSWEEP
910 Marion Ave (19809-2639)
PHONE..................................302 764-7964
Linda Williams, *Admn*
EMP: 2 **EST:** 2002
SALES (est): 152.05K **Privately Held**

Wilmington - New Castle County (G-14166)   GEOGRAPHIC SECTION

SIC: 2842 Specialty cleaning

(G-14166)
A L MERCED GENERAL CONTRACTORS
322 6th Ave (19805-4716)
PHONE.................................302 658-1618
Angelo Merced, *Prin*
EMP: 6 EST: 2014
SALES (est): 89.72K **Privately Held**
SIC: 1799 Special trade contractors, nec

(G-14167)
A LEAP OF FAITH INC
Also Called: A Leap Faith Child Dev Ctr
1715 W 4th St (19805-3547)
PHONE.................................302 543-6256
Melanie T Price, *Ex Dir*
EMP: 10 EST: 2003
SQ FT: 12,000
SALES (est): 671.69K **Privately Held**
Web: www.aleapoffaithcdc.com
SIC: 8351 Preschool center

(G-14168)
A MAGCAL ESCAPE THRPTIC BDYWRK
2502 Silverside Rd Ste 9 (19810-3740)
PHONE.................................302 375-6533
Renee Underwood, *Prin*
EMP: 5 EST: 2018
SALES (est): 100.17K **Privately Held**
Web: www.amescape.com
SIC: 7299 Massage parlor

(G-14169)
A MINOR TUNE UP LLC
1704 N Scott St (19806-2316)
PHONE.................................302 658-1587
Chris Cromer, *Prin*
EMP: 5 EST: 2009
SALES (est): 271.39K **Privately Held**
Web: www.aminortuneup.com
SIC: 7539 Tune-up service, automotive

(G-14170)
A R MYERS CORPORATION
Also Called: A R Myers Auto Body
1300 E 18th St (19801)
PHONE.................................302 652-3164
Aubrey R Myers, *Pr*
Donna Myers, *VP*
EMP: 11 EST: 1960
SQ FT: 20,000
SALES (est): 375.52K **Privately Held**
Web: www.armyersglass.com
SIC: 7532 7536 Paint shop, automotive; Automotive glass replacement shops

(G-14171)
A SEED HOPE COUNSELING CTR LLC
1601 Milltown Rd Ste 1 (19808-4047)
PHONE.................................302 605-6702
Kelly Hatton, *Prin*
EMP: 6 EST: 2017
SALES (est): 493.74K **Privately Held**
Web: www.aseedofhopecounselingcenter.com
SIC: 8322 General counseling services

(G-14172)
A SHARED SPACE LLC
Also Called: Shared Space
3640 Concord Pike Unit 1136 (19803-5022)
PHONE.................................240 727-9917
EMP: 5 EST: 2021
SALES (est): 199.4K **Privately Held**
SIC: 7371 Computer software development and applications

(G-14173)
A T I FUNDING CORPORATION (HQ)
Also Called: ATI Funding
801 N West St 2nd Fl (19801-1525)
PHONE.................................302 656-8937
Kenneth J Kubacki, *Treas*
Mary W Snyder, *Pr*
Peter C Fulweilber, *VP*
Dale Reid, *Prin*
EMP: 15 EST: 1988
SALES (est): 3.59B **Publicly Held**
SIC: 3462 Iron and steel forgings
PA: Ati Inc.
2021 Mckinney Ave # 1100
Dallas TX 75201

(G-14174)
A V RESOURCES INC
240 N James St Ste B2 (19804-3172)
P.O. Box 5602 (19808-0602)
PHONE.................................302 994-1488
Kathleen Yacucci, *Pr*
Rob Yacucci, *VP*
EMP: 5 EST: 1991
SQ FT: 3,000
SALES (est): 359.97K **Privately Held**
Web: www.trustavr.com
SIC: 5999 7359 Audio-visual equipment and supplies; Audio-visual equipment and supply rental

(G-14175)
A+ PRINTING
501 Birmingham Ave (19804-1907)
PHONE.................................302 273-3147
EMP: 4 EST: 2018
SALES (est): 65.5K **Privately Held**
SIC: 2752 Offset printing

(G-14176)
A1 EXPRESS TRUCKING INC
3200 Kirkwood Hwy Ste 1068 (19808-6153)
PHONE.................................302 544-9273
Glenard Boone, *CEO*
Christina Hinojosa, *CFO*
Robert Deloatch, *Sec*
EMP: 10 EST: 2021
SALES (est): 531.59K **Privately Held**
Web: www.a1express.us
SIC: 4213 Trucking, except local

(G-14177)
A1 NATIONWIDE LLC
1201 N Orange St Ste 7037 (19801-1189)
PHONE.................................302 327-9302
EMP: 9 EST: 2010
SALES (est): 237.02K **Privately Held**
SIC: 7389 Repossession service

(G-14178)
A1G0 LLC
2055 Limestone Rd Ste 200c (19808-5536)
PHONE.................................855 661-0101
Abayomi Tejumola, *Managing Member*
EMP: 25 EST: 2021
SALES (est): 2.07MM **Privately Held**
SIC: 8742 Marketing consulting services

(G-14179)
A2B AUTO GROUP
1211 E 15th St (19802-5214)
P.O. Box 9526 (19809-0526)
PHONE.................................302 786-2331
EMP: 6 EST: 2013
SALES (est): 90.89K **Privately Held**
Web: www.a2bautogroup.com
SIC: 7538 General automotive repair shops

(G-14180)
A66 INC
2711 Centerville Rd Ste 400 (19808-1660)
P.O. Box 65913 (50265-0913)
PHONE.................................800 444-0446
George Davey, *Pr*
Michael Pieper, *VP*
EMP: 2 EST: 2005
SALES (est): 223.32K **Privately Held**
Web: www.a66.com
SIC: 8733 2834 5122 Noncommercial research organizations; Pharmaceutical preparations; Pharmaceuticals

(G-14181)
AAA CLUB ALLIANCE INC (PA)
Also Called: AAA Keystone
1 River Pl (19801-5125)
PHONE.................................302 299-4700
Thomas C Wiedemann, *CEO*
Allen J Dewalle, *
EMP: 300 EST: 2007
SQ FT: 160,000
SALES: 485.77MM
SALES (corp-wide): 485.77MM **Privately Held**
Web: mwg.aaa.com
SIC: 4724 6331 6351 6512 Travel agencies; Property damage insurance; Liability insurance; Commercial and industrial building operation

(G-14182)
AAA MID-ATLANTIC
1 River Pl (19801-5125)
PHONE.................................302 299-4230
EMP: 45 EST: 2018
SALES (est): 13.29MM **Privately Held**
Web: cluballiance.aaa.com
SIC: 6411 Insurance agents, nec

(G-14183)
AAA WASHINGTON
Also Called: AAA
1 River Pl (19801-5125)
PHONE.................................860 371-9783
EMP: 23 EST: 2019
SALES (est): 1.89MM **Privately Held**
Web: cluballiance.aaa.com
SIC: 4724 Travel agencies

(G-14184)
AAERT INC
2900 Fairhope Rd (19810-1624)
P.O. Box 9826 (19809-0826)
PHONE.................................302 765-3510
EMP: 5 EST: 2013
SALES (est): 82.99K **Privately Held**
SIC: 8611 Trade associations

(G-14185)
AAQUAONE INC
1226 N King St Ste 128 (19801-3232)
PHONE.................................949 331-5405
Bo Wu, *Ch Bd*
EMP: 6 EST: 2020
SALES (est): 336.3K **Privately Held**
SIC: 5023 Homefurnishings

(G-14186)
AARON ALFANO
3608 Lancaster Pike (19805-1509)
PHONE.................................302 995-9600
Aaron Alfano, *Mgr*
EMP: 7 EST: 2016
SALES (est): 253.35K **Privately Held**
Web: www.delawarefamilycenter.com
SIC: 8049 Clinical psychologist

(G-14187)
AARON AND SONS ELECTRIC LLC
200 W 38th St (19802-2108)
PHONE.................................302 764-5610
Aaron Reeves, *Managing Member*
EMP: 5 EST: 2019
SALES (est): 250.45K **Privately Held**
Web: www.aaronsonselectricllc.com
SIC: 1731 7389 General electrical contractor ; Business services, nec

(G-14188)
AARP
Also Called: AARP Delaware
222 Delaware Ave Ste 1610 (19801-1675)
PHONE.................................202 434-2277
John Barnes, *Ex Dir*
EMP: 10
SALES (corp-wide): 1.64B **Privately Held**
Web: www.aarp.org
SIC: 8399 Health systems agency
PA: Aarp
601 E St Nw
Washington DC 20049
202 434-2277

(G-14189)
AB BROWN REAL ESTATE INC
4808 Plum Run Ct (19808-1721)
PHONE.................................302 731-1031
Diane A Brown, *Owner*
EMP: 5 EST: 2011
SALES (est): 134.35K **Privately Held**
SIC: 6531 Real estate brokers and agents

(G-14190)
AB CREATIVE PUBLISHING LLC
1104 Philadelphia Pike (19809-2031)
PHONE.................................202 802-6909
EMP: 9 EST: 2019
SALES (est): 92.03K **Privately Held**
SIC: 2721 Magazines: publishing and printing

(G-14191)
ABA2DAY BEHAVIOR SERVICES
1526 Villa Rd (19809-2273)
PHONE.................................302 494-4303
EMP: 9 EST: 2018
SALES (est): 179.11K **Privately Held**
Web: www.hhfamily.com
SIC: 8093 Mental health clinic, outpatient

(G-14192)
ABACUS TAX SERVICE
2604 Kirkwood Hwy (19805-4931)
PHONE.................................302 543-5619
Kunbi Alabi, *Prin*
EMP: 6 EST: 2011
SALES (est): 66.05K **Privately Held**
SIC: 7291 Tax return preparation services

(G-14193)
ABAD & SALAMEDA PA
Also Called: Brandy Bine Medical Associates
1508 Penns Ave Ste 1c (19806-4347)
PHONE.................................302 652-4705
Aileen Abad, *Pr*
Remedios Abad Md, *Prin*
Lolita Salameda Md, *Prin*
EMP: 6 EST: 1994
SALES (est): 272.72K **Privately Held**
SIC: 8011 General and family practice, physician/surgeon

(G-14194)
ABBY PUBUSKY
1805 Foulk Rd Ste A (19810-3700)
PHONE.................................302 897-8932
EMP: 5 EST: 2019
SALES (est): 231.46K **Privately Held**

GEOGRAPHIC SECTION
Wilmington - New Castle County (G-14223)

Web: www.covermeabby.com
SIC: 6411 Insurance agents and brokers

(G-14195)
ABBY PUBUSKY INSURANCE
1601 Concord Pike Ste 88 (19803-3623)
PHONE...................302 434-3333
Abby Pubusky, *Owner*
EMP: 5 EST: 2017
SALES (est): 160.34K Privately Held
Web: www.covermeabby.com
SIC: 6411 Insurance agents and brokers

(G-14196)
ABC SALES & SERVICE INC
2520 W 6th St (19805-2909)
PHONE...................302 652-3683
George Skomorucha, *Pr*
Joan Skomorucha, *Sec*
Matthew Skomorucha, *VP*
Stephen Skomorucha, *VP*
EMP: 14 EST: 1949
SALES (est): 1.32MM Privately Held
Web: www.abcsalesandservice.com
SIC: 5722 7629 5064 Electric household appliances, major; Electrical household appliance repair; Electrical appliances, major

(G-14197)
ABC TREE SVC
2204 Rodman Rd (19805-4132)
PHONE...................302 737-8733
Robert Gallo, *Pr*
EMP: 6 EST: 2014
SALES (est): 205.99K Privately Held
SIC: 0783 Planting, pruning, and trimming services

(G-14198)
ABCFOC A BTTER CHNCE FOR OUR C
1307 Philadelphia Pike (19809-1821)
PHONE...................302 746-7265
Daniel P Edgar, *Pr*
EMP: 12 EST: 2017
SALES (est): 1.6MM Privately Held
Web: www.abcfoc.org
SIC: 8399 Advocacy group

(G-14199)
ABEKS FINANCIAL CONSULTING LLC
3501 Silverside Rd # 206 (19810-4910)
PHONE...................302 351-5910
EMP: 6 EST: 2005
SALES (est): 29.08K Privately Held
SIC: 8742 Financial consultant

(G-14200)
ABEL CENTER FOR OCULOFACIAL
1941 Limestone Rd Ste 201 (19808-5400)
PHONE...................302 998-3220
Ari Abel, *Pr*
EMP: 5 EST: 2010
SALES (est): 438.31K Privately Held
Web: www.abelcenter.com
SIC: 8011 Plastic surgeon

(G-14201)
ABHA ARCHITECTS INC
1621 N Lincoln St (19806-2521)
PHONE...................302 658-6426
Chandra Nilekani, *VP*
Chandra Nilekani, *Pr*
Michael Deptula, *
EMP: 25 EST: 1949
SQ FT: 4,000
SALES (est): 3.38MM Privately Held
Web: www.abha.com

SIC: 8712 7389 Architectural engineering; Interior design services

(G-14202)
ABIGAIL E MARTIN M D
1600 Rockland Rd (19803-3607)
PHONE...................302 651-4000
Abigail Martin, *Ofcr*
EMP: 15 EST: 2017
SALES (est): 235.8K Privately Held
Web: www.nemours.org
SIC: 8011 Pediatrician

(G-14203)
ABILITY NETWORK OF DELAWARE
100 W 10th St Ste 103 (19801-1632)
PHONE...................302 622-9177
EMP: 9 EST: 2019
SALES (est): 162.44K Privately Held
Web: www.abilitynetworkde.org
SIC: 8322 Social service center

(G-14204)
ABITECHNO INC
3 Germay Dr (19804-1127)
PHONE...................302 213-6700
Albert Tonetto, *CEO*
EMP: 6
SALES (est): 81.29K Privately Held
SIC: 6221 Commodity contracts brokers, dealers

(G-14205)
ABM JANITORIAL SERVICES INC
2110 Duncan Rd (19808-4602)
PHONE...................302 571-9900
Polly Shweiger, *Mgr*
EMP: 41
SALES (corp-wide): 8.1B Publicly Held
Web: www.abm.com
SIC: 7349 7217 Janitorial service, contract basis; Carpet and upholstery cleaning
HQ: Abm Janitorial Services, Inc.
    1111 Fannin St Ste 1500
    Houston TX 77002
    866 624-1520

(G-14206)
ABM SECURITY SERVICES INC
2110 Duncan Rd (19808-4602)
PHONE...................302 992-9733
Danielle Carter, *Prin*
EMP: 62
SALES (corp-wide): 8.1B Publicly Held
SIC: 7382 Security systems services
HQ: Abm Security Services, Inc.
    3800 Buffalo Spdwy Ste 32
    Houston TX 77098
    713 928-5344

(G-14207)
ABOVE AND BEYOND COVERAGE LLC
3616 Kirkwood Hwy (19808-5124)
PHONE...................201 417-5189
EMP: 50 EST: 2018
SALES (est): 1.18MM Privately Held
SIC: 8742 Management consulting services

(G-14208)
ABRAMS & BAYLISS LLP
20 Montchanin Rd Ste 200 (19807-2174)
PHONE...................302 778-1000
Kevin G Abrams, *Pt*
Thompson Bayliss, *Pt*
John M Seaman, *Pt*
EMP: 14 EST: 2005
SALES (est): 2.72MM Privately Held
Web: www.abramsbayliss.com

SIC: 8111 General practice attorney, lawyer

(G-14209)
ABSALOM JONES SENIOR CENTER
310 Kiamensi Rd Ste B (19804-2958)
PHONE...................302 998-0363
Joan Budrow, *Dir*
Diana Zanning, *Dir*
Lynn Balfour, *Dir*
EMP: 5 EST: 1976
SALES (est): 240K Privately Held
SIC: 8322 Senior citizens' center or association

(G-14210)
ABUNDANT NATURAL HEALTH INC
1925 Lovering Ave (19806-2157)
PHONE...................302 652-2900
EMP: 7 EST: 2020
SALES (est): 61.22K Privately Held
Web: www.abundantnaturalhealth.com.au
SIC: 8099 Health and allied services, nec

(G-14211)
AC GROUP INC
Also Called: Accelcomm
3422 Old Capitol Trl 163 (19808-6124)
PHONE...................201 840-5566
James Kontolios, *Mng Pt*
EMP: 3 EST: 2005
SALES (est): 191.92K Privately Held
Web: www.acgroup.org
SIC: 8711 8748 3679 3825 Electrical or electronic engineering; Systems analysis and engineering consulting services; Microwave components; Digital test equipment, electronic and electrical circuits

(G-14212)
AC HOME SOLUTIONS
1205 Lorrain Ave (19808-5719)
PHONE...................302 442-2516
Anthony Ciabattoni, *Prin*
EMP: 6 EST: 2011
SALES (est): 155.19K Privately Held
SIC: 1711 Warm air heating and air conditioning contractor

(G-14213)
ACA MORTGAGE CO INC
3202 Kirkwood Hwy Ste 205 (19808-6154)
PHONE...................302 225-1390
Clare Crossan, *Pr*
EMP: 9 EST: 1997
SALES (est): 840.58K Privately Held
SIC: 6163 Mortgage brokers arranging for loans, using money of others

(G-14214)
ACADEMY BUSINESS MCH & PRTG CO
Also Called: Academy Printing
12 S Maryland Ave (19804-1340)
PHONE...................302 654-3200
Edward Purzycki, *Pr*
EMP: 6 EST: 1977
SQ FT: 3,000
SALES (est): 472.84K Privately Held
Web: www.academyprinting.com
SIC: 2752 Offset printing

(G-14215)
ACADEMY MORTGAGE
4758 Limestone Rd (19808-4389)
PHONE...................484 680-8092
Jim Bromwell, *Prin*
EMP: 7 EST: 2018
SALES (est): 117.31K Privately Held

SIC: 6162 Mortgage bankers and loan correspondents

(G-14216)
ACBUSA INC
24a Trolley Sq (19806-3334)
PHONE...................302 985-9395
Jesse Daniels, *CEO*
EMP: 23 EST: 2020
SALES (est): 490K Privately Held
SIC: 7379 Online services technology consultants

(G-14217)
ACCELERATED INTELLIGENCE INC
Also Called: Xium
717 N Union St Ste 150 (19805-3031)
PHONE...................800 765-3628
Gary L Willoughby, *CEO*
▲ EMP: 8 EST: 2011
SALES (est): 154.54K Privately Held
Web: www.acceleratedintelligence.org
SIC: 2834 Vitamin preparations

(G-14218)
ACCENTURE
501 Carr Rd Ste 200 (19809-2866)
PHONE...................302 830-5800
EMP: 63 EST: 2019
SALES (est): 944.29K Privately Held
Web: www.accenture.com
SIC: 8742 Business management consultant

(G-14219)
ACCERA DIGITAL LLC
1201 N Market St (19801-1147)
PHONE...................877 855-2501
Tony Monaco, *Mgr*
EMP: 10 EST: 2019
SALES (est): 341.86K Privately Held
SIC: 7311 Advertising agencies

(G-14220)
ACCESS FUNDING 2010-A LLC
5500 Brandywine Pkwy (19803-1444)
PHONE...................484 653-3300
EMP: 10 EST: 2014
SALES (est): 146.77K Privately Held
SIC: 6153 Working capital financing

(G-14221)
ACCESS FUNDING 2013-1 LLC ✪
5500 Brandywine Pkwy (19803-1444)
PHONE...................302 477-4071
EMP: 7 EST: 2022
SALES (est): 81.29K Privately Held
SIC: 6153 Working capital financing

(G-14222)
ACCESSHEAT INC
913 N Market St Ste 200 (19801-3097)
PHONE...................302 373-9524
Jack Harrison, *Ch*
Ruth Berenstein, *Managing Member*
Hunter Jones Industry, *Advisor*
Kregg Wiggins Industry, *Advisor*
Jeff Cullman Industry, *Advisor*
EMP: 25 EST: 2020
SALES (est): 5MM Privately Held
Web: www.access-heat.com
SIC: 6211 1731 3822 1711 Investment firm, general brokerage; Environmental system control installation; Environmental controls; Plumbing, heating, air-conditioning

(G-14223)
ACCESSQUINT LLC
300 Delaware Ave Ste 200 (19801-6601)
PHONE...................302 351-4064
EMP: 10 EST: 2018

(PA)=Parent Co (HQ)=Headquarters
✪ = New Business established in last 2 years

2024 Harris Directory of Delaware Businesses

Wilmington - New Castle County (G-14224)

GEOGRAPHIC SECTION

SALES: (est): 507.35K **Privately Held**
Web: www.accessquint.com
SIC: **7372** Prepackaged software

(G-14224)
ACCLAIM ACADEMY LLC
1521 Concord Pike Ste 301 (19803-3644)
PHONE..........................215 848-7827
EMP: 19 EST: 2013
SALES (est): 921.73K **Privately Held**
Web: www.acclaimacademy.org
SIC: **8351** Preschool center

(G-14225)
ACCOLADE GLOBAL INC
Also Called: Accolade Global
4023 Kennett Pike Ste 1000 (19807-2018)
PHONE..........................209 645-0225
EMP: 8 EST: 2012
SQ FT: 3,000
SALES (est): 130K **Privately Held**
Web: www.accoladeglobal.com
SIC: **6799** Venture capital companies

(G-14226)
ACCOMMODATING NURSES LLC
1521 Concord Pike Ste 301 (19803-3644)
PHONE..........................302 390-8065
Lakeia Wiles, *Prin*
EMP: 5 EST: 2017
SALES (est): 110.32K **Privately Held**
SIC: **7389** Business Activities at Non-Commercial Site

(G-14227)
ACCU PERSONNEL INC
1707 Concord Pike (19803-3603)
PHONE..........................302 384-8777
EMP: 18
SALES (corp-wide): 11.99MM **Privately Held**
Web: www.accustaffing.com
SIC: **7361** Employment agencies
PA: Accu Personnel Inc.
  911 Kings Hwy N Ste 100
  Cherry Hill NJ 08034
  856 482-2222

(G-14228)
ACCURATE METAL SOLUTIONS LLC
1209 N Orange St (19801-1120)
EMP: 525
SIC: **3444** Sheet metal specialties, not stamped

(G-14229)
ACENTIUM INC
251 Little Falls Dr (19808-1674)
P.O. Box 231177 (02123-1177)
PHONE..........................617 938-3938
Amine Hamdi, *CEO*
EMP: 10 EST: 2015
SALES (est): 302.82K **Privately Held**
SIC: **7389** Business services, nec

(G-14230)
ACER SYNERGY TECH AMERICA CORP
251 Little Falls Dr (19808-1674)
PHONE..........................267 901-4569
EMP: 5 EST: 2021
SALES (est): 880.57K **Privately Held**
SIC: **8742** Business management consultant
HQ: Acer Synergy Tech Corp.
  7f-10, No. 8, Ziqiang S. Rd.,
  Zhubei City HSI 30244

(G-14231)
ACHIEVE LGSTC SYSTEMS TRNSP L
510 A St (19801-5328)
PHONE..........................302 654-4701
Darral Mosley, *Managing Member*
EMP: 11 EST: 2016
SALES (est): 1.18MM **Privately Held**
Web: www.achievelogistic.com
SIC: **4731** 4151 Freight transportation arrangement; School buses

(G-14232)
ACHIEVERS HOLDINGS INC
1209 N Orange St (19801-1120)
PHONE..........................647 265-9032
Zaheer Bagha, *Pr*
EMP: 400 EST: 2020
SALES (est): 70MM **Privately Held**
SIC: **7389** Business Activities at Non-Commercial Site

(G-14233)
ACI ENERGY INC
1105 N Market St Ste 650 (19801-1216)
PHONE..........................302 588-3024
EMP: 69 EST: 1984
SALES (est): 21.97MM **Privately Held**
Web: www.aciinc.net
SIC: **4911** Electric services

(G-14234)
ACIA FREIGHT & LOGISTICS LLC
2711 Centerville Rd Ste 400 (19808-1660)
PHONE..........................800 362-8837
EMP: 8 EST: 2016
SALES (est): 283.72K **Privately Held**
SIC: **4789** Transportation services, nec

(G-14235)
ACMEGRC LIMITED ◊
251 Little Falls Dr (19808-1674)
PHONE..........................401 626-7684
Abraham Bloom, *Prin*
EMP: 3 EST: 2023
SALES (est): 128.34K **Privately Held**
SIC: **7372** Prepackaged software

(G-14236)
ACN CLEANING LLC
1916 W 7th St (19805-3040)
P.O. Box 3324 (19804-4324)
PHONE..........................302 588-7485
Eric Nordin, *Prin*
EMP: 5 EST: 2015
SALES (est): 58.52K **Privately Held**
SIC: **7699** Cleaning services

(G-14237)
ACORN ENERGY INC (PA)
Also Called: Acorn
1000 N West St Ste 1200 (19801-1058)
PHONE..........................410 654-3315
Jan H Loeb, *Pr*
Tracy Clifford, *CFO*
EMP: 2 EST: 1986
SALES (est): 7MM **Publicly Held**
Web: www.acornenergy.com
SIC: **8711** 3823 7372 Engineering services; Industrial process control instruments; Prepackaged software

(G-14238)
ACOUSTIC AUDIO TEK LLC
1000 N West St Ste 1200 (19801-1058)
PHONE..........................302 685-2113
EMP: 3 EST: 2014
SALES (est): 222.82K **Privately Held**
SIC: **3651** Household audio and video equipment

(G-14239)
ACP SERVICES LLC
1 River Pl (19801-5125)
PHONE..........................302 299-4225
EMP: 5 EST: 2012
SALES (est): 107.72K **Privately Held**
SIC: **1521** Single-family housing construction

(G-14240)
ACTION AUTOMOTIVE INC
Also Called: Brandywine Auto Parts
2200 Rodman Rd (19805-4132)
PHONE..........................302 429-0643
Bruce Hansel, *Genl Mgr*
EMP: 5
SALES (corp-wide): 4.54MM **Privately Held**
Web: www.brandywine-ap.com
SIC: **5013** 5531 Automotive supplies and parts; Automotive parts
PA: Action Automotive, Inc.
  8 E 9th St
  Chester PA 19013
  610 876-7271

(G-14241)
ACTION ENVIRONMENTAL SERVICE
501 Silverside Rd Ste 114 (19809-1376)
PHONE..........................302 798-3100
Charlotte Baldwin, *Pr*
William C Baldwin, *Mgr*
EMP: 7 EST: 1986
SQ FT: 400
SALES (est): 556.22K **Privately Held**
Web: www.actionenv.com
SIC: **8748** Environmental consultant

(G-14242)
ACTIVATING CHANGE INC
919 N Market St Ste 950 (19801-3036)
PHONE..........................646 457-8067
Nancy Smith, *Prin*
EMP: 13 EST: 2021
SALES (est): 509.39K **Privately Held**
Web: www.activatingchange.org
SIC: **8399** Advocacy group

(G-14243)
ACTIVE CRANE RENTALS INC
103 Water St (19804-2492)
PHONE..........................302 998-1000
Steven Schmeusser, *Pr*
Rebecca Kendall, *VP*
Karen Schmeusser, *Sec*
EMP: 20 EST: 1968
SQ FT: 5,000
SALES (est): 3.1MM **Privately Held**
Web: www.activecrane.com
SIC: **7353** Cranes and aerial lift equipment, rental or leasing

(G-14244)
ACTIVE HOPE
19 W 39th St (19802-2203)
PHONE..........................302 545-2494
Leonila Capron, *Owner*
EMP: 5 EST: 2017
SALES (est): 61.53K **Privately Held**
SIC: **8322** General counseling services

(G-14245)
ACTS RTRMNT-LIFE CMMNITIES INC
Also Called: Country House
4830 Kennett Pike (19807-1866)
PHONE..........................302 654-5101
Marylou Dellafera, *Brnch Mgr*
EMP: 478
SALES (corp-wide): 542.68MM **Privately Held**
Web: www.actsretirement.org

SIC: **8082** Home health care services
PA: Acts Retirement-Life Communities, Inc.
  420 Delaware Dr
  Fort Washington PA 19034
  215 661-8330

(G-14246)
ACUITIVE INC
4001 Kennett Pike Ste 134 (19807-2000)
PHONE..........................214 738-1099
Mark Hoover, *Pr*
John M Jaeger, *Ex VP*
Thomas C Garland, *VP*
David E Danielson, *Ex VP*
Judith H Boyle, *Sec*
EMP: 5 EST: 1996
SALES (est): 379.35K **Privately Held**
SIC: **8748** Business consulting, nec

(G-14247)
ACUITY SPCIALTY PDTS GROUP INC
2711 Keswick Ct (19808-3632)
PHONE..........................302 369-6949
Geoffrey Jones, *Prin*
EMP: 5 EST: 2008
SALES (est): 208.97K **Privately Held**
SIC: **5072** Hardware

(G-14248)
ACUMEN HEALTH TECHNOLOGIES LLC
2207 Concord Pike 224 (19803-2908)
PHONE..........................800 941-0356
EMP: 10 EST: 2009
SALES (est): 487.4K **Privately Held**
SIC: **7372** Educational computer software

(G-14249)
ADAM KLEINMEULMAN
3522 Silverside Rd (19810-4916)
PHONE..........................302 757-4517
Adam Kleinmeulman, *Prin*
EMP: 8 EST: 2012
SALES (est): 144.54K **Privately Held**
SIC: **8322** General counseling services

(G-14250)
ADAMS AUTO PARTS LLC (HQ)
Also Called: Adams Auto Parts
1601 Northeast Blvd (19802-5119)
PHONE..........................302 655-9693
William King, *Pr*
Jeffrey A Adams, *VP*
EMP: 15 EST: 1945
SQ FT: 7,100
SALES (est): 4.25MM
SALES (corp-wide): 22.1B **Publicly Held**
Web: www.napaonline.com
SIC: **5013** 5531 Automotive supplies and parts; Auto and truck equipment and parts
PA: Genuine Parts Company
  2999 Wildwood Pkwy
  Atlanta GA 30339
  678 934-5000

(G-14251)
ADAPEX LLC
3422 Old Capitol Trl (19808-6124)
PHONE..........................718 618-9982
Debra Fleenor, *Managing Member*
EMP: 28 EST: 2013
SALES (est): 956.75K **Privately Held**
SIC: **7311** Advertising consultant

(G-14252)
ADASH INC
1740 W 4th St (19805-3548)
PHONE..........................302 654-3977
EMP: 6 EST: 2009
SALES (est): 101.41K **Privately Held**

GEOGRAPHIC SECTION
Wilmington - New Castle County (G-14279)

Web: www.adash.com
SIC: 5084 Industrial machinery and equipment

(G-14253)
ADDLESTONE LLC
1511 New London Rd (19807-1919)
P.O. Box 4561 (19807-4561)
PHONE.....................302 373-1598
EMP: 7 EST: 2010
SALES (est): 234.24K Privately Held
Web: www.addlestone.us
SIC: 7382 Security systems services

(G-14254)
ADDUS HEALTHCARE INC
3521 Silverside Rd (19810-4900)
PHONE.....................302 995-9010
Sheila Zwook, Mgr
EMP: 6
Web: www.addus.com
SIC: 8082 Home health care services
HQ: Addus Healthcare, Inc.
  2300 Warrenville Rd
  Downers Grove IL 60515
  630 296-3400

(G-14255)
ADEPT CONSULTING
407 Eastlawn Ave (19802-2823)
PHONE.....................267 398-7449
EMP: 6 EST: 2015
SALES (est): 112.09K Privately Held
Web: www.adeptusa.com
SIC: 8748 Business consulting, nec

(G-14256)
ADKINS & ASSOC CPA
Also Called: Adkins & Associates CPA
2615 E Riding Dr (19808-3640)
PHONE.....................302 737-2390
EMP: 5 EST: 1964
SALES (est): 110.9K Privately Held
SIC: 7291 Tax return preparation services

(G-14257)
ADMIRAL WEST INC
Also Called: Admiral Motel
726 Greenwood Rd (19807-2986)
PHONE.....................609 729-0031
Margaret C Hill, Pr
EMP: 23 EST: 1966
SQ FT: 140,000
SALES (est): 242.51K Privately Held
Web: www.admiral-west.com
SIC: 7011 Motels

(G-14258)
ADOPTION HOUSE INC
3411 Silverside Rd # 101 (19810-4806)
PHONE.....................302 477-0944
Harlan Tenenbaum, Dir
EMP: 7 EST: 1999
SALES (est): 430K Privately Held
SIC: 8322 Adoption services

(G-14259)
ADP CAPITAL MANAGEMENT INC
800 Delaware Ave Ste 601 (19801-1365)
PHONE.....................302 657-4060
John Daly, Dir Fin
EMP: 5 EST: 1996
SALES (est): 1.2MM
SALES (corp-wide): 18.01B Publicly Held
Web: www.adp.com
SIC: 6722 Management investment, open-end
PA: Automatic Data Processing, Inc.
  1 Adp Blvd Ste 1 # 1
  Roseland NJ 07068
  973 974-5000

(G-14260)
ADP PACIFIC INC
800 Delaware Ave Ste 601 (19801-1365)
PHONE.....................302 657-4060
Carlos A Rodriguez, CEO
Steve J Anenen, Pr
Mark D Benjamin, Pr
John C Ayala, VP
Michael A Bonarti, VP
EMP: 47 EST: 1989
SALES (est): 486.6K
SALES (corp-wide): 18.01B Publicly Held
SIC: 8742 Human resource consulting services
PA: Automatic Data Processing, Inc.
  1 Adp Blvd Ste 1 # 1
  Roseland NJ 07068
  973 974-5000

(G-14261)
ADPESE LLC
3616 Kirkwood Hwy Ste A-1011 (19808-5124)
PHONE.....................302 223-5411
Davida Harris, CEO
Allene Harris, Pr
Araina Moon, Sec
EMP: 7 EST: 2017
SALES (est): 290.2K Privately Held
SIC: 7299 Personal document and information services

(G-14262)
ADR INVESTMENTS LLC
2711 Centerville Rd # 400 (19808-1660)
PHONE.....................800 710-6184
EMP: 6 EST: 2014
SALES (est): 340.48K Privately Held
SIC: 6159 Small business investment companies

(G-14263)
ADVACARE LLC
3601 Old Capitol Trl Unit A5a6 (19808-6042)
PHONE.....................302 448-5045
David Botha, Managing Member
EMP: 4 EST: 2017
SALES (est): 242.43K Privately Held
Web: www.advacare.co.za
SIC: 2389 5023 Apparel for handicapped; Blankets

(G-14264)
ADVANCE CENTRAL SERVICES INC (PA)
1313 N Mkt St Fl 10 (19801-6107)
PHONE.....................302 830-9732
Jeff Hively, Pr
Erich Walburn, *
EMP: 14 EST: 2003
SQ FT: 100,000
SALES (est): 11.23MM
SALES (corp-wide): 11.23MM Privately Held
Web: www.advancelocal.com
SIC: 8741 Administrative management

(G-14265)
ADVANCE CONSTRUCTION TECHNIQUE
1000 N West St Ste 1200 (19801-1058)
PHONE.....................270 257-0377
EMP: 8 EST: 2015
SALES (est): 874.82K Privately Held
SIC: 1629 1521 Heavy construction, nec; Single-family housing construction

(G-14266)
ADVANCE FORWARD LLC
222 Hawthorne Ln (19803-4025)
PHONE.....................302 762-1615
EMP: 6 EST: 2011
SALES (est): 99.65K Privately Held
SIC: 8049 Physical therapist

(G-14267)
ADVANCE MAGAZINE PUBLS INC
Also Called: Advance Magazine Group
1201 N Market St Ste 600 (19801-1160)
PHONE.....................302 830-4630
Bill Cauffman, Mgr
EMP: 3
SALES (corp-wide): 2.88B Privately Held
Web: www.condenast.com
SIC: 2721 Magazines: publishing and printing
HQ: Advance Magazine Publishers Inc.
  1 World Trade Ctr
  New York NY 10007

(G-14268)
ADVANCE MARINE LLC
900 Smiths Bridge Rd (19807-1330)
PHONE.....................302 656-2111
▲ EMP: 3 EST: 2011
SALES (est): 400K Privately Held
Web: www.advamar.com
SIC: 0919 3531 5084 4491 Whale fishing and whale products; Construction machinery; Industrial machinery and equipment; Marine cargo handling

(G-14269)
ADVANCE PHYSICAL THERAPY LLC
1021 Gilpin Ave (19806-3270)
PHONE.....................302 407-3592
EMP: 7 EST: 2014
SALES (est): 98K Privately Held
SIC: 8049 8011 Physical therapist; Offices and clinics of medical doctors

(G-14270)
ADVANCED ANESTHESIOLOGY & PAIN
5307 Limestone Rd Ste 103 (19808-1275)
PHONE.....................302 283-3300
Paul Hannan, Prin
EMP: 9 EST: 2012
SALES (est): 103.3K Privately Held
SIC: 8011 Anesthesiologist

(G-14271)
ADVANCED CARE OBGYN
1941 Limestone Rd Ste 217 (19808-5400)
PHONE.....................302 633-9083
Emmanuel Baka, Owner
EMP: 7 EST: 2018
SALES (est): 234.15K Privately Held
Web: www.obgyndelaware.com
SIC: 8011 Gynecologist

(G-14272)
ADVANCED CARE OBSTTRICS GYNCLO
1941 Limestone Rd Ste 217 (19808-5400)
PHONE.....................302 275-2202
Emmanuel J Esaka, Prin
EMP: 10 EST: 2010
SALES (est): 273.29K Privately Held
Web: www.obgyndelaware.com
SIC: 8011 Gynecologist

(G-14273)
ADVANCED DEFENSE TECHNOLOGY
Also Called: Decoded USA
3422 Old Capitol Trl Ste 200 (19808-6124)
PHONE.....................888 298-5775
Karim Boumajdi, Pr
EMP: 127 EST: 2011
SQ FT: 7,000
SALES (est): 7.85MM Privately Held
SIC: 3694 3812 3842 Automotive electrical equipment, nec; Defense systems and equipment; Personal safety equipment

(G-14274)
ADVANCED GLOBAL NETWORKS INC
108 W 13th St (19801)
PHONE.....................302 308-6460
Steven Marusich, Pr
EMP: 6 EST: 2003
SALES (est): 434.09K Privately Held
SIC: 7373 Local area network (LAN) systems integrator

(G-14275)
ADVANCED MATERIALS TECHNOLOGY
3521 Silverside Rd Ste 1k (19810-4900)
PHONE.....................302 477-2510
Joseph Destefano, Pr
Timothy Langlois, VP
Joseph Jack Kirkland A B, VP
Timothy J Langlois B.sc., VP
John P Larmann, VP
EMP: 5 EST: 2005
SQ FT: 2,000
SALES (est): 1.57MM Privately Held
Web: www.halocolumns.com
SIC: 8731 Biotechnical research, commercial

(G-14276)
ADVANCED NETWORKING INC
1316 Philadelphia Pike (19809-1855)
PHONE.....................302 442-6199
Richard B Raphael, Pr
Lori A Raphael, VP
EMP: 12 EST: 1987
SQ FT: 1,500
SALES (est): 1.35MM Privately Held
Web: www.advnetwork.com
SIC: 1731 Telephone and telephone equipment installation

(G-14277)
ADVANCED PARTICLE SENSORS LLC
2409 Raven Rd (19810-3538)
PHONE.....................302 695-4883
David Scott, Prin
EMP: 5 EST: 2018
SALES (est): 74.45K Privately Held
Web: www.particlesci.com
SIC: 3826 Analytical instruments

(G-14278)
ADVANCED PRTTYPING SLTIONV LLC ✪
Also Called: Advanced Prototyping Solutions
6517 Governor Printz Blvd (19809-2037)
PHONE.....................302 375-6048
Tamas Cserei, Pr
Tamas Cserei, Managing Member
EMP: 2 EST: 2022
SALES (est): 78.16K Privately Held
SIC: 3599 3451 3999 3452 Machine shop, jobbing and repair; Screw machine products ; Barber and beauty shop equipment; Bolts, nuts, rivets, and washers

(G-14279)
ADVANCED RCVABLE SOLUTIONS INC
1300 First State Blvd Ste A (19804)
PHONE.....................302 225-6001
Jeff Kucharski, CEO
Thomas Nusspickle, *

Wilmington - New Castle County (G-14280) GEOGRAPHIC SECTION

EMP: 6 EST: 2004
SALES (est): 88.56K **Privately Held**
SIC: 7322 Collection agency, except real estate

(G-14280)
ADVANCED REAL ESTATE INC
903 Newgate Ln (19808-1527)
PHONE..................302 994-7424
Wheeler K Neff, *Prin*
EMP: 5 EST: 2007
SALES (est): 148.12K **Privately Held**
SIC: 6531 Real estate agent, residential

(G-14281)
ADVANCED STUDENT TRNSP INC
1400 First State Blvd (19804-3563)
PHONE..................302 998-6726
Blake Krapf, *CEO*
EMP: 180 EST: 2002
SALES (est): 5.18MM **Privately Held**
Web: www.krapfbus.com
SIC: 4151 School buses

(G-14282)
ADVANCED SURGICAL SPECIALISTS
1401 Foulk Rd Ste 207 (19803-2764)
PHONE..................302 475-4900
Katherine A Sahm, *Prin*
EMP: 10 EST: 2010
SALES (est): 220.39K **Privately Held**
Web: www.advsurgicalassociates.com
SIC: 8011 Surgeon

(G-14283)
ADVANTAGE ASSETS II INC
1000 N West St Ste 1200 (19801-1058)
PHONE..................877 858-3855
EMP: 13 EST: 2015
SALES (est): 275.35K **Privately Held**
SIC: 7322 Adjustment and collection services

(G-14284)
ADVANTAGE CORP
3213 Emerald Pl (19810-2234)
PHONE..................302 478-7977
Laurie Conslato, *Prin*
EMP: 5 EST: 2016
SALES (est): 45.96K **Privately Held**
Web: www.advantage-de.com
SIC: 7291 Tax return preparation services

(G-14285)
ADVANTAGE DELAWARE LLC
3524 Silverside Rd (19810-4929)
PHONE..................302 479-7764
EMP: 5 EST: 2015
SALES (est): 128.2K **Privately Held**
Web: www.advantage-de.com
SIC: 7291 Tax return preparation services

(G-14286)
ADVANTAGE SECURITY INC
802 First State Blvd (19804-3573)
PHONE..................302 652-3060
Carl Ottosen, *Prin*
Joseph Allen, *Prin*
EMP: 10 EST: 1999
SALES (est): 767.41K
SALES (corp-wide): 1.64MM **Privately Held**
Web: www.advantagesecurity.com
SIC: 7382 Security systems services
PA: Sonitrol Security Of Delaware Valley
802 First State Blvd
Wilmington DE 19804
302 652-3060

(G-14287)
ADVENT CAD LLC
5017 The Pines Blvd (19808-1032)
PHONE..................302 569-1793
EMP: 5 EST: 2018
SALES (est): 211.94K **Privately Held**
Web: www.advent-cad.com
SIC: 7379 Computer related services, nec

(G-14288)
ADVENTUM LLC
2701 Centerville Rd (19808-1607)
PHONE..................518 620-1441
Nils Henderik, *Mgr*
EMP: 5 EST: 2021
SALES (est): 259.97K **Privately Held**
SIC: 5199 Advertising specialties

(G-14289)
ADVERTISED MEDIA INC ◊
3411 Silverside Rd Ste 104 (19810-4812)
PHONE..................415 967-8100
Nicolas Zagarzazu, *Pr*
EMP: 5 EST: 2022
SALES (est): 199.4K **Privately Held**
SIC: 7371 Software programming applications

(G-14290)
ADVERTISING IS SIMPLE
14 Ashley Pl (19804-1314)
PHONE..................302 407-0431
EMP: 6 EST: 2017
SALES (est): 210.79K **Privately Held**
Web: www.advertisingissimple.com
SIC: 6512 Commercial and industrial building operation

(G-14291)
ADVISORY TRUST CO OF DELAWARE
2710 Centerville Rd Ste 101 (19808-1696)
PHONE..................302 636-8500
Jeffrey Lauterbach, *CEO*
EMP: 12 EST: 2017
SALES (est): 989.01K **Privately Held**
Web: www.wilmingtontrust.com
SIC: 6021 National commercial banks

(G-14292)
ADVOSERV INC
750 Shipyard Dr Ste 213 (19801-5160)
PHONE..................302 365-8050
Kelly Mccrann, *CEO*
Judith Favell, *CCO*
Kathy Shea, *CFO*
Robert Bacon, *COO*
EMP: 73 EST: 1996
SALES (est): 3.41MM **Privately Held**
Web: www.castlefamilyhealth.org
SIC: 8011 Medical centers

(G-14293)
AECOM GLOBAL LLC (HQ)
Corporation Trust Company 1209 Orange St (19801)
PHONE..................213 593-8100
EMP: 32
SALES (est): 5.46MM
SALES (corp-wide): 14.38B **Publicly Held**
SIC: 8711 Engineering services
PA: Aecom
13355 Noel Rd Ste 400
Dallas TX 75240
972 788-1000

(G-14294)
AEGIS NETWORKS LLC
251 Little Falls Dr (19808-1674)
PHONE..................917 378-7524

Simon Lee, *Managing Member*
EMP: 6
SALES (est): 265.67K **Privately Held**
SIC: 8748 Telecommunications consultant

(G-14295)
AEGIS PM GROUP INC
4023 Kennett Pike (19807-2018)
PHONE..................302 456-0402
EMP: 5 EST: 2015
SALES (est): 83.8K **Privately Held**
SIC: 8748 Business consulting, nec

(G-14296)
AERO TAXI INC
1315 Chadwick Rd (19803-4115)
PHONE..................302 328-3430
Dirk Dinkeloo, *Pr*
Erin Jacob, *VP*
EMP: 9 EST: 1960
SALES (est): 235.55K **Privately Held**
Web: www.aerotaxi.com
SIC: 4522 Flying charter service

(G-14297)
AESIR CAPITAL MANAGEMENT LP
1105 N Market St (19801-1216)
PHONE..................302 656-9161
EMP: 5 EST: 2012
SALES (est): 102.06K **Privately Held**
SIC: 8748 Business consulting, nec

(G-14298)
AESTHTIC PLSTIC SURGERY DEL PA
1600 Pennsylvania Ave Ste A (19806-4048)
PHONE..................302 656-0214
Ian Lonergan, *Pr*
EMP: 10 EST: 1972
SALES (est): 986.12K **Privately Held**
Web: www.facesandfigures.com
SIC: 8011 Surgeon

(G-14299)
AESTHTIC SPECIAL CARE ASSOC PA
2323 Pennsylvania Ave Ste Ll (19806-1332)
PHONE..................302 482-4444
Chane Poum, *Prin*
EMP: 27 EST: 2005
SALES (est): 1.09MM **Privately Held**
SIC: 8021 Dentists' office

(G-14300)
AETOLIA CAPTIAL LLC
3828 Kennett Pike (19807-2320)
PHONE..................302 397-8238
EMP: 5 EST: 2017
SALES (est): 182.38K **Privately Held**
Web: www.aetoliacapital.com
SIC: 6799 Investors, nec

(G-14301)
AEZI ELECTRICAL SERVICES LLC
302 Robinson Ln (19805-4686)
PHONE..................302 279-8344
EMP: 5 EST: 2014
SALES (est): 486.74K **Privately Held**
Web: www.aezielectrical.com
SIC: 1731 Electrical work

(G-14302)
AFFILATE MARKS INVESTMENTS INC
3411 Silverside Rd Ste 205bc (19810-4812)
PHONE..................302 478-7451
David Apostiloco, *Pr*
EMP: 5 EST: 2001
SALES (est): 1.66MM

SALES (corp-wide): 121.57B **Publicly Held**
SIC: 6794 Patent buying, licensing, leasing
HQ: Comcast Holdings Corporation
1 Comcast Ctr
Philadelphia PA 19103

(G-14303)
AFFILIATE INVESTMENT INC
3411 Silverside Rd Ste 205a (19810)
PHONE..................302 478-7451
EMP: 235 EST: 1999
SALES (est): 471.71K **Publicly Held**
SIC: 6799 Investors, nec
HQ: Qvc, Inc.
1200 Wilson Dr
West Chester PA 19380
484 701-1000

(G-14304)
AFFILIATE VENTURE GROUP
2419 Kirkwood Hwy (19805-4906)
PHONE..................302 379-6961
EMP: 2 EST: 2008
SALES (est): 73.17K **Privately Held**
SIC: 3944 Banks, toy

(G-14305)
AFFINITY RESEARCH CHEMICALS (PA)
406 Meco Dr (19804-1112)
PHONE..................302 525-4060
Peng Wei, *Pr*
Yaxi Shen, *VP*
Peipei Li, *Treas*
Yuanyuan Huang, *Sec*
EMP: 4 EST: 2012
SQ FT: 3,300
SALES (est): 1.18MM
SALES (corp-wide): 1.18MM **Privately Held**
Web: www.affinitychem.com
SIC: 2819 Industrial inorganic chemicals, nec

(G-14306)
AFFINITY WEALTH MANAGEMENT
2961 Centerville Rd Ste 310 (19808-1666)
PHONE..................302 652-6767
Donald Kalil, *Pr*
James Kalil Senior, *Ch*
James Kalil Junior, *VP*
EMP: 25 EST: 1969
SALES (est): 3.91MM **Privately Held**
Web: www.affinitywealth.com
SIC: 8742 Financial consultant

(G-14307)
AFFLAIR EVENTS
1 Paschall Ct (19803-4923)
PHONE..................302 762-5765
Kameron Mcconnell, *Prin*
EMP: 5 EST: 2010
SALES (est): 55.01K **Privately Held**
Web: www.afflairevents.com
SIC: 7299 Party planning service

(G-14308)
AFGCEAA CORPORATION
1521 Concord Pike Ste 303 (19803-3644)
PHONE..................617 314-0814
Nnaemeka Osakwe, *Pr*
Ruby Opara, *Sec*
EMP: 8 EST: 2014
SQ FT: 500
SALES (est): 50.25K **Privately Held**
SIC: 8699 Charitable organization

(G-14309)
AFINCLIC FINANCIAL TECH INC ◊
1209 N Orange St (19801-1120)

GEOGRAPHIC SECTION

Wilmington - New Castle County (G-14339)

PHONE..............................646 946-1687
Jaaziel Muoz, *Prin*
EMP: 3 **EST:** 2023
SALES (est): 128.34K **Privately Held**
SIC: 7372 Prepackaged software

(G-14310)
AFMENSAH LLC
1521 Concord Pike Ste 301 (19803-3644)
PHONE..............................302 777-0538
EMP: 5 **EST:** 2012
SALES (est): 116.67K **Privately Held**
SIC: 7389 Business Activities at Non-Commercial Site

(G-14311)
AGAINST GRAIN LLC
403 Grandview Ave (19809-3042)
PHONE..............................302 388-1667
EMP: 5 **EST:** 2015
SALES (est): 53.16K **Privately Held**
SIC: 5153 Grains

(G-14312)
AGENTS AND CORPORATIONS INC (PA)
1201 N Orange St Ste 600 (19801-1171)
P.O. Box 511 (19899-0511)
PHONE..............................302 575-0877
David N Williams, *Pr*
EMP: 8 **EST:** 1976
SALES (est): 1.92MM
SALES (corp-wide): 1.92MM **Privately Held**
Web: www.incnow.com
SIC: 8742 Corporation organizing consultant

(G-14313)
AGGREKO HOLDINGS INC
1105 N Market St (19801-1216)
PHONE..............................302 652-4076
Phil Harrower, *Pr*
Terrel P Dressel Junior, *Sec*
◆ **EMP:** 806 **EST:** 1981
SALES (est): 28.89MM
SALES (corp-wide): 2.14B **Privately Held**
SIC: 7359 Equipment rental and leasing, nec
HQ: Aggreko Limited
    Stirling Road
    Dumbarton

(G-14314)
AGH PARENT LLC
1209 N Orange St (19801-1120)
PHONE..............................919 298-2267
Greg Lindberg, *Managing Member*
EMP: 5000 **EST:** 2016
SALES (est): 11.83MM **Privately Held**
SIC: 8399 Advocacy group

(G-14315)
AGILE 1
Also Called: Act One
1013 Centre Rd Ste 200 (19805-1265)
PHONE..............................302 791-6900
Kristina Williams, *Dir*
EMP: 14 **EST:** 2006
SALES (est): 969.79K **Privately Held**
Web: www.agile-one.com
SIC: 8741 Management services

(G-14316)
AGILE WASTE LLC
1209 N Orange St (19801-1120)
PHONE..............................302 772-4882
John Gilham, *Managing Member*
EMP: 6
SALES (est): 78.96K **Privately Held**
SIC: 4953 Recycling, waste materials

(G-14317)
AGILEBITS USA INC
1000 N West St Ste 1200 (19801-1058)
PHONE..............................416 371-3328
EMP: 8 **EST:** 2020
SALES (est): 355.88K **Privately Held**
SIC: 7379 Computer related services, nec

(G-14318)
AGILENT TECHNOLOGIES INC
300 Century Blvd (19808-6270)
PHONE..............................408 345-8886
Linda Johnson, *Brnch Mgr*
EMP: 55
SALES (corp-wide): 6.83B **Publicly Held**
Web: www.agilent.com
SIC: 3825 Instruments to measure electricity
PA: Agilent Technologies, Inc.
    5301 Stevens Creek Blvd
    Santa Clara CA 95051
    800 227-9770

(G-14319)
AGILENT TECHNOLOGIES INC
2850 Centerville Rd (19808-1610)
PHONE..............................877 424-4536
Jeff Langan, *Prin*
EMP: 1500
SALES (corp-wide): 6.83B **Publicly Held**
Web: www.agilent.com
SIC: 3825 Instruments to measure electricity
PA: Agilent Technologies, Inc.
    5301 Stevens Creek Blvd
    Santa Clara CA 95051
    800 227-9770

(G-14320)
AGILITE SYSTEMS INCORPORATED
2711 Centerville Rd (19808-1660)
PHONE..............................870 298-4152
Elie Isaacson, *CEO*
Benjamin Legziel, *COO*
EMP: 2 **EST:** 2012
SALES (est): 57.88K **Privately Held**
SIC: 3949 Sporting and athletic goods, nec

(G-14321)
AGMAF INC
300 Delaware Ave Ste 210 (19801-6601)
PHONE..............................302 508-6991
Houston Bolton, *CEO*
EMP: 39 **EST:** 2020
SALES (est): 1.07MM **Privately Held**
SIC: 8741 Construction management

(G-14322)
AGUILERA TAX PREPARATION
1800 Philadelphia Pike (19809-1553)
PHONE..............................302 746-7253
EMP: 5 **EST:** 2013
SALES (est): 70.27K **Privately Held**
SIC: 7291 Tax return preparation services

(G-14323)
AGVENTURE INC
974 Centre Rd (19805-1269)
P.O. Box 2915 (19805-0915)
PHONE..............................302 992-5940
EMP: 7 **EST:** 2016
SALES (est): 318.61K **Privately Held**
Web: www.agventure.com
SIC: 2099 Food preparations, nec

(G-14324)
AH THERAPY SERVICES LLC
725 Halstead Rd (19803-2227)
PHONE..............................302 379-0528
EMP: 5 **EST:** 2015
SALES (est): 81.09K **Privately Held**

SIC: 8093 Rehabilitation center, outpatient treatment

(G-14325)
AI ATHENA LLC
2711 Centerville Rd # 400 (19808-1660)
PHONE..............................212 247-6400
EMP: 6 **EST:** 2013
SALES (est): 130K **Privately Held**
SIC: 7371 Computer software development and applications

(G-14326)
AI DUPONT
2200 Concord Pike (19803-2909)
PHONE..............................302 528-6520
Ai Dupont, *Prin*
EMP: 6 **EST:** 2017
SALES (est): 94.45K **Privately Held**
SIC: 2879 Agricultural chemicals, nec

(G-14327)
AI DUPONT HOSP FOR CHILDREN
1600 Rockland Rd (19803-3607)
PHONE..............................302 651-4620
David Bailey Md, *Pr*
Steven R Sparks, *
Gina Altieri, *
Debbie I Chang, *
R Jay Cummings, *
EMP: 4000 **EST:** 1940
SALES (est): 26.74MM **Privately Held**
Web: www.nemours.org
SIC: 8062 General medical and surgical hospitals

(G-14328)
AIDS CARE GROUP
209 Murphy Rd (19803-3128)
PHONE..............................610 220-8058
EMP: 5 **EST:** 2018
SALES (est): 94.8K **Privately Held**
SIC: 8322 Social service center

(G-14329)
AIDS DELAWARE INC (PA)
100 W 10th St Ste 315 (19801-1642)
PHONE..............................302 652-6776
EMP: 22 **EST:** 1984
SQ FT: 55,000
SALES (est): 7.01MM **Privately Held**
Web: www.aidsdelaware.org
SIC: 8322 7389 Aid to Families with Dependent Children (AFDC); Fund raising organizations

(G-14330)
AIEC
21 Oxford Way (19807-2577)
PHONE..............................302 993-0931
Julianne Lin, *Pr*
EMP: 10 **EST:** 2010
SALES (est): 131.43K **Privately Held**
Web: www.aiec.coop
SIC: 8011 General and family practice, physician/surgeon

(G-14331)
AIG GLOBAL REAL ESTATE INC
600 N King St (19801-3776)
PHONE..............................302 655-2141
EMP: 6 **EST:** 2015
SALES (est): 296.63K **Privately Held**
Web: www.aig.com
SIC: 6531 Real estate brokers and agents

(G-14332)
AIHS THEATER
50 Hillside Rd (19807-2263)
PHONE..............................302 651-2626

EMP: 6 **EST:** 2017
SALES (est): 38.67K **Privately Held**
SIC: 7922 Legitimate live theater producers

(G-14333)
AIM METALS & ALLOYS USA INC (PA)
1209 N Orange St (19801-1120)
PHONE..............................212 450-4519
Elaine Hegler, *Mgr*
EMP: 2 **EST:** 2013
SALES (est): 406.66K
SALES (corp-wide): 406.66K **Privately Held**
SIC: 1389 Oil and gas field services, nec

(G-14334)
AION OAKWOOD VENTURE LLC
2711 Centerville Rd (19808-1660)
PHONE..............................212 849-9200
EMP: 5 **EST:** 2015
SALES (est): 34.22K **Privately Held**
SIC: 7342 Disinfecting and pest control services

(G-14335)
AIR MASTERS HVAC INC
218 W Pembrey Dr (19803-2008)
PHONE..............................267 292-2204
EMP: 7 **EST:** 2018
SALES (est): 52.89K **Privately Held**
Web: www.airemaster.com
SIC: 7342 Disinfecting and deodorizing

(G-14336)
AIRBNB INC
2711 Centerville Rd (19808-1660)
PHONE..............................415 800-5959
EMP: 14
SALES (corp-wide): 8.4B **Publicly Held**
Web: www.airbnb.com
SIC: 7041 Membership-basis organization hotels
PA: Airbnb, Inc.
    888 Brannan St Fl 4
    San Francisco CA 94103
    415 510-4027

(G-14337)
AIRCRAFTERS INC
320 Cornell Dr (19801-5783)
PHONE..............................302 777-5000
EMP: 9
SALES (est): 137.91K **Privately Held**
Web: www.aircrafters.com
SIC: 4581 Aircraft maintenance and repair services

(G-14338)
AIRGAS INC
Also Called: Airgas
1521 Concord Pike Ste 101 (19803-3614)
PHONE..............................302 575-1822
Boyce Fagioli, *Pr*
EMP: 5
SALES (corp-wide): 101.26MM **Privately Held**
Web: www.airgas.com
SIC: 5084 Welding machinery and equipment
HQ: Airgas, Inc.
    259 N Radnor Chester Rd # 100
    Radnor PA 19087
    610 687-5253

(G-14339)
AIS
2625 Grubb Rd (19810-2407)
PHONE..............................302 407-0430
EMP: 5 **EST:** 2019
SALES (est): 80.06K **Privately Held**

Wilmington - New Castle County (G-14340)

(G-14340)
AJJ TRADES AND INVESTMENT LLC
1207 Delaware Ave Ste 3314 (19806-4743)
PHONE...................302 403-7165
Akintoye Johnson, *Managing Member*
EMP: 6
SALES (est): 76.37K **Privately Held**
SIC: 6799 Real estate investors, except property operators

(G-14341)
AJKO GENERAL CONTRACTOR
906 Shipley Rd (19803-4928)
PHONE...................302 373-4030
Angel Cielo, *Prin*
EMP: 6 EST: 2014
SALES (est): 142.2K **Privately Held**
SIC: 1799 Special trade contractors, nec

(G-14342)
AJP FINANCIAL SERVICES LLC
506 Woodside Ave (19809-1637)
P.O. Box 7136 (19803-0136)
PHONE...................302 798-7582
Anthony Passerini, *Prin*
EMP: 5 EST: 2017
SALES (est): 192.09K **Privately Held**
SIC: 7389 Financial services

(G-14343)
AK MULTINATIONAL LLC
300 Delaware Ave Ste 210 (19801-6601)
PHONE...................845 542-8155
Kripa Shroff, *Managing Member*
Aniket Shroff, *Managing Member*
EMP: 45 EST: 2020
SALES (est): 4MM **Privately Held**
Web: www.akmultinational.com
SIC: 5045 Computer peripheral equipment

(G-14344)
ALAN L FRANK LAW ASSOCIATES PA
521 N West St (19801-2139)
PHONE...................302 502-2702
Alan L Frank, *Pr*
EMP: 8 EST: 2015
SALES (est): 92.3K **Privately Held**
SIC: 8111 General practice law office

(G-14345)
ALAN M BILLINGSLEY JR
Also Called: B & B Contracting
2502 Tigani Dr (19808-2519)
PHONE...................302 998-7907
Alan M Billingsley Junior, *Prin*
EMP: 6 EST: 2009
SALES (est): 497.13K **Privately Held**
Web: www.bb4contracting.com
SIC: 1799 Kitchen and bathroom remodeling

(G-14346)
ALAN R LEVINE DDS
Also Called: Sirkin Levine Dental Assoc
2018 Naamans Rd Ste A2 (19810-2660)
PHONE...................302 475-3743
Alan R Levine D.d.s., *Owner*
EMP: 7 EST: 1960
SALES (est): 216K **Privately Held**
Web: www.levinevaughandental.com
SIC: 8021 Dentists' office

(G-14347)
ALANTYS TECHNOLOGY
1201 N Orange St Ste 700 (19801-1186)
PHONE...................302 573-2312
EMP: 8 EST: 2013
SALES (est): 127.75K **Privately Held**
Web: www.alantys.com
SIC: 8731 Commercial physical research

(G-14348)
ALBAN ASSOCIATES
Also Called: Canby Park Apartments
1600 Bonwood Rd (19805-4634)
P.O. Box 10723 (19850-0723)
PHONE...................302 656-1827
Paul Boerger, *Owner*
EMP: 7 EST: 1960
SALES (est): 378.25K **Privately Held**
SIC: 6513 Apartment building operators

(G-14349)
ALBERT J ROOP
8 E 13th St (19801-3202)
PHONE...................302 655-4600
Albert Roop, *Pr*
EMP: 5 EST: 2015
SALES (est): 244.15K **Privately Held**
Web: www.collinslawdelaware.com
SIC: 8111 General practice attorney, lawyer

(G-14350)
ALBERTINI LANDSCAPING
1 Glover Cir (19804-3201)
PHONE...................302 998-7593
EMP: 5 EST: 2011
SALES (est): 41K **Privately Held**
SIC: 0781 Landscape services

(G-14351)
ALCHEMY SOFTWARE SOLUTIONS LLC
1000 N West St Ste 1200 (19801-1058)
PHONE...................201 627-0638
Shilpi Sarkar, *Mgr*
EMP: 50 EST: 2014
SALES (est): 1.75MM **Privately Held**
SIC: 7371 Computer software development

(G-14352)
ALERISLIFE INC
Also Called: Foulk Manor North
1212 Foulk Rd Ste 1 (19803-2765)
PHONE...................302 478-4296
Virginia Gray, *Mgr*
EMP: 47
SALES (corp-wide): 934.59MM **Privately Held**
Web: www.foulkmanornorth.com
SIC: 8361 Aged home
HQ: Alerislife Inc.
255 Washington St Ste 300
Newton MA 02458

(G-14353)
ALERT SECURITY & TECHNOLOGIES
704 N King St (19801-3583)
P.O. Box 12443 (19850-2443)
PHONE...................302 294-9100
EMP: 6 EST: 2018
SALES (est): 352.11K **Privately Held**
Web: www.alertsecurityandtechnologies.com
SIC: 7381 Guard services

(G-14354)
ALEXIS WIRT
Also Called: Petal Pushers Flowers
610 Harrington St (19805-3723)
PHONE...................302 654-4236
Alexis Wirt, *Prin*
EMP: 2 EST: 2010
SALES (est): 158.7K **Privately Held**
Web: www.petalpushersdel.com
SIC: 3545 Pushers

(G-14355)
ALFRED I DUPONT HOSPITAL
Also Called: Dupont Children's Rehab
1600 Rockland Rd (19803-3607)
P.O. Box 269 (19899-0269)
PHONE...................302 651-4000
Jane Crowley, *Dir*
EMP: 61 EST: 1987
SALES (est): 1.37MM **Privately Held**
Web: www.nemours.org
SIC: 8049 Clinical psychologist

(G-14356)
ALFRED IDPONT HOSP FOR CHLDREN (HQ)
Also Called: A I Dupont Hosp For Children
1600 Rockland Rd (19803-3607)
P.O. Box 269 (19899-0269)
PHONE...................302 651-4000
Thomas Ferry, *CEO*
Stephen T Lawless, *
William Britton, *
EMP: 2568 EST: 1995
SALES (est): 630.09MM
SALES (corp-wide): 1.94B **Privately Held**
Web: www.nemours.org
SIC: 8062 General medical and surgical hospitals
PA: Nemours Foundation
10140 Centurion Pkwy N
Jacksonville FL 32256
904 697-4100

(G-14357)
ALICE R OBRIEN MS LPCMH
130 Downs Dr (19807-2556)
PHONE...................302 521-3859
Alice O'brien, *Prin*
EMP: 7 EST: 2016
SALES (est): 96.04K **Privately Held**
SIC: 8011 Offices and clinics of medical doctors

(G-14358)
ALIVE WITH MEDIA
18 Hemlock Pl (19810-1920)
PHONE...................302 746-7831
EMP: 5 EST: 2014
SALES (est): 71.2K **Privately Held**
SIC: 4899 Communication services, nec

(G-14359)
ALIXPARTNERS LLP
3711 Kennett Pike Ste 130 (19807-2156)
PHONE...................302 824-7139
Jim Bucknam, *Brnch Mgr*
EMP: 10
SALES (corp-wide): 255.56MM **Privately Held**
Web: www.alixpartners.com
SIC: 7389 Personal service agents, brokers, and bureaus
PA: Alixpartners, Llp
909 3rd Ave Fl 30
New York NY 10022
212 490-2500

(G-14360)
ALL ABOUT LAWNS LANDSCAPING
414 W Summit Ave (19804-1812)
PHONE...................302 530-1868
Erik Duricek, *Owner*
EMP: 6 EST: 2014
SALES (est): 231.75K **Privately Held**
Web: www.allaboutlawnslandscaping.com
SIC: 0781 Landscape services

(G-14361)
ALL ABOUT WOMEN
4600 Linden Hill Rd Ste 202 (19808-2953)
PHONE...................302 995-7073
EMP: 9 EST: 2017
SALES (est): 213.63K **Privately Held**
SIC: 8011 Gynecologist

(G-14362)
ALL AMERICAN TRUCK BROKERS
2205 E Huntington Dr (19808-4952)
PHONE...................302 654-6101
Joseph B Walther, *Pr*
William Patterson, *VP*
EMP: 5 EST: 1986
SQ FT: 14,000
SALES (est): 250K **Privately Held**
SIC: 4212 5013 7538 Dump truck haulage; Truck parts and accessories; General truck repair

(G-14363)
ALL AROUND MOVERZ
314 W 35th St (19802-2639)
PHONE...................302 494-9925
EMP: 6 EST: 2010
SALES (est): 500.5K **Privately Held**
Web: www.allaroundmoverz.com
SIC: 4212 Moving services

(G-14364)
ALL FLATS ROOFING
410 Junction St (19805-5117)
PHONE...................302 383-6762
EMP: 5 EST: 2009
SALES (est): 139.61K **Privately Held**
SIC: 1761 Roofing contractor

(G-14365)
ALL IN ONE TRANSPORTATION LLC
32 Brookside Dr (19894-9000)
PHONE...................302 482-3222
EMP: 65 EST: 2012
SALES (est): 4.67MM **Privately Held**
Web: www.alln1transport.com
SIC: 4789 Cargo loading and unloading services

(G-14366)
ALL METALS FABRICATORS INC
Also Called: AMF
6 Hadco Rd (19804-1014)
PHONE...................302 691-8805
EMP: 18 EST: 1974
SALES (est): 2.45MM **Privately Held**
Web: www.goamf.com
SIC: 3599 Machine shop, jobbing and repair

(G-14367)
ALL MY CHILDREN INC
Also Called: All My Children Elsmere
8 Walnut Ave (19805-1144)
PHONE...................302 995-9191
Nichole Tarentino, *Owner*
EMP: 7 EST: 1992
SALES (est): 80.47K **Privately Held**
Web: www.allmychildreninc.org
SIC: 8351 Group day care center

(G-14368)
ALL STAR LINEN AND UNIFORM CO
3217 Heathwood Rd (19810-3427)
PHONE...................302 897-9003
EMP: 5 EST: 2010
SALES (est): 232.64K **Privately Held**
Web: www.allstarlinen.com
SIC: 7213 Linen supply

GEOGRAPHIC SECTION   Wilmington - New Castle County (G-14399)

(G-14369)
ALL TUNE & LUBE
Also Called: All Tune & Lube
3 W Salisbury Dr (19809-3415)
PHONE..................................302 367-6369
EMP: 5 **EST:** 2016
SALES (est): 63.01K **Privately Held**
Web: www.alltuneandlube.com
SIC: 7538 General automotive repair shops

(G-14370)
ALLAN C GOLDFEDER DMD
2415 Milltown Rd (19808-3903)
PHONE..................................302 994-1782
Allan C Goldfeder Md, *Owner*
EMP: 8 **EST:** 1983
SALES (est): 292.28K **Privately Held**
Web: www.drgoldfeder.com
SIC: 8021 Dentists' office

(G-14371)
ALLAN HUGHES EXP INC (PA)
701 Bennett St (19801-4305)
PHONE..................................302 230-6666
EMP: 6 **EST:** 2018
SALES (est): 99.52K
SALES (corp-wide): 99.52K **Privately Held**
SIC: 4212 Local trucking, without storage

(G-14372)
ALLCAP DEVELOPMENT GROUP LLC
105 Foulk Rd Fl 2 (19803-3740)
PHONE..................................302 429-8700
Louis J Capano Junior, *Prin*
EMP: 7 **EST:** 2008
SALES (est): 254.76K **Privately Held**
SIC: 6552 Subdividers and developers, nec

(G-14373)
ALLEN & ASSOCIATES
4250 Lancaster Pike # 230 (19805-1520)
PHONE..................................302 234-8600
Michele Allen, *Prin*
EMP: 10 **EST:** 2019
SALES (est): 218.33K **Privately Held**
Web: www.allenlaborlaw.com
SIC: 8111 General practice attorney, lawyer

(G-14374)
ALLEN INSURANCE GROUP (PA)
Also Called: Smith & Allen Insurance
410 Delaware Ave (19801-1508)
PHONE..................................302 654-8823
W Bradley Allen, *Pr*
Jacklyn Allen, *VP*
EMP: 9 **EST:** 1930
SALES (est): 2.04MM
SALES (corp-wide): 2.04MM **Privately Held**
Web: www.alleninsurance.com
SIC: 6411 Insurance agents, nec

(G-14375)
ALLERGY ASSOCIATES PA
1403 Silverside Rd Ste 4b (19810-4434)
PHONE..................................302 570-0865
EMP: 9 **EST:** 2018
SALES (est): 243.53K **Privately Held**
Web: www.wilmingtonallergist.com
SIC: 8011 Allergist

(G-14376)
ALLERGY ASSOCIATES PA INC
1400 Philadelphia Pike Ste A6
(19809-1856)
PHONE..................................302 798-8070
Michael Wydila, *Pr*
EMP: 11 **EST:** 1973
SQ FT: 1,000
SALES (est): 717.34K **Privately Held**
Web: www.wilmington-allergist.com
SIC: 8011 Allergist

(G-14377)
ALLIANCE CHEMICALS GLOBAL LLC (PA) ✪
3524 Silverside Rd Ste 35b (19810-4929)
PHONE..................................507 202-6872
Akin Jekami, *Admn*
Olu Akanmu, *Managing Member*
EMP: 16 **EST:** 2022
SALES (est): 5.3MM
SALES (corp-wide): 5.3MM **Privately Held**
SIC: 5169 Industrial chemicals

(G-14378)
ALLIANCE DATA
2 Righter Pkwy Ste 310 (19803-1551)
PHONE..................................302 256-0853
EMP: 9 **EST:** 2017
SALES (est): 123.8K **Privately Held**
SIC: 8748 Business consulting, nec

(G-14379)
ALLIANCE TOTAL CARE
1851 Marsh Rd (19810-4505)
PHONE..................................302 225-9000
EMP: 7 **EST:** 2019
SALES (est): 492.6K **Privately Held**
SIC: 8082 Home health care services

(G-14380)
ALLIED ELEC SOLUTIONS LTD
4661 Malden Dr (19803-4817)
PHONE..................................302 893-0257
EMP: 8 **EST:** 2009
SALES (est): 160.8K **Privately Held**
Web: www.aesltdonline.com
SIC: 1731 1711 General electrical contractor ; Solar energy contractor

(G-14381)
ALLIED LOCK & SAFE COMPANY
709 N Shipley St (19801-1728)
PHONE..................................302 658-3172
Joseph Blansfield, *Pt*
Donna Blansfield, *Pt*
EMP: 8 **EST:** 1958
SQ FT: 6,000
SALES (est): 1.58MM **Privately Held**
Web: www.allied-lock.com
SIC: 5072 5251 7699 Security devices, locks ; Door locks and lock sets; Locksmith shop

(G-14382)
ALLIED PROPERTIES
Also Called: Allied Retail Properties
4737 Concord Pike (19803-1442)
P.O. Box 7189 (19803-0189)
PHONE..................................302 479-8314
Jim Oeste, *VP*
EMP: 10 **EST:** 1991
SALES (est): 429.92K **Privately Held**
Web: www.alliedretailprop.com
SIC: 6531 Condominium manager

(G-14383)
ALLIEDBARTON SECURITY SVCS LLC
Also Called: Allied Barton Security Svcs
824 N Market St Ste 102 (19801-4937)
PHONE..................................302 498-0450
Gordon Sebree, *Mgr*
EMP: 6
SALES (corp-wide): 8.78B **Privately Held**
Web: www.aus.com
SIC: 7381 Security guard service
HQ: Alliedbarton Security Services Llc
8 Tower Brdge 161 Wash St
Conshohocken PA 19428

(G-14384)
ALLISON R RANDALL
1307 Philadelphia Pike (19809-1821)
PHONE..................................302 893-3817
Allison R Randall, *Prin*
EMP: 6 **EST:** 2016
SALES (est): 49.45K **Privately Held**
SIC: 8049 Offices of health practitioner

(G-14385)
ALLSTATE INSRNCE BOB SBRACCIA
5307 Limestone Rd Ste 101 (19808-1275)
PHONE..................................302 300-4500
Bob Sbraccia, *Mgr*
EMP: 5 **EST:** 2015
SALES (est): 61.44K **Privately Held**
SIC: 6411 Insurance agents, brokers, and service

(G-14386)
ALLY AUTO ASSETS LLC
1209 N Orange St (19801-1120)
PHONE..................................313 656-5500
EMP: 5 **EST:** 2014
SALES (est): 538.52K **Privately Held**
SIC: 6159 Equipment and vehicle finance leasing companies

(G-14387)
ALLY AUTO RCEIVABLES TR 2017-1
1209 N Orange St (19801-1120)
PHONE..................................313 656-5500
EMP: 5 **EST:** 2017
SALES (est): 514.47K **Privately Held**
SIC: 6733 Trusts, nec

(G-14388)
ALLY AUTO RCEIVABLES TR 2019-1
1209 N Orange St (19801-1120)
PHONE..................................313 656-5500
EMP: 11 **EST:** 2018
SALES (est): 176.5K **Privately Held**
SIC: 6733 Trusts, nec

(G-14389)
ALOHA MOVERS
4306 Miller Rd (19802-1949)
PHONE..................................302 559-4310
Fadi Takla, *Prin*
EMP: 10 **EST:** 2012
SALES (est): 390.31K **Privately Held**
SIC: 4789 Cargo loading and unloading services

(G-14390)
ALOYSIUS BUTLR CLARK ASSOC INC
Also Called: AB&c
600 N King St (19801-1595)
PHONE..................................302 655-1552
Michael Gallagher, *Prin*
Thomas Mcgivney, *Prin*
Paul Pomeroy, *
EMP: 75 **EST:** 1972
SALES (est): 12.38MM **Privately Held**
Web: www.abccreative.com
SIC: 7311 8743 Advertising consultant; Public relations services

(G-14391)
ALPHA TECHNOLOGIES INC
704 N King St Fl 4 (19801-3593)
PHONE..................................917 412-9211
EMP: 15 **EST:** 2016
SALES (est): 1.05MM **Privately Held**
Web: www.alphait.us
SIC: 7379 Computer related consulting services

(G-14392)
ALPHA TECHNOLOGIES USA INC
Also Called: Alpha Technologies
704 N King St Fl 4 (19801-3593)
PHONE..................................302 510-8205
Jamie Cruz, *Pr*
Harbans Virk, *
EMP: 72 **EST:** 1997
SALES (est): 9.47MM **Privately Held**
Web: www.alphait.us
SIC: 7371 7376 7379 Computer software development; Computer facilities management; Computer related consulting services

(G-14393)
ALPHAFORCE TECH SOLUTIONS INC
108 W 13th St (19801-1145)
PHONE..................................917 231-3796
David Krick, *Prin*
EMP: 9 **EST:** 2019
SALES (est): 373.72K **Privately Held**
SIC: 7379 Computer related consulting services

(G-14394)
ALPHAGRAPHICS FRANCHISING INC
Also Called: AlphaGraphics
248 Weldin Ridge Rd (19803-3974)
PHONE..................................302 559-8369
EMP: 6 **EST:** 2019
SALES (est): 87.97K **Privately Held**
Web: www.alphagraphics.com
SIC: 2752 Commercial printing, lithographic

(G-14395)
ALPHATARAXIA QUICKSILVER LLC
1209 N Orange St (19801-1120)
PHONE..................................571 367-7133
Peter Zhang, *Managing Member*
EMP: 5 **EST:** 2021
SALES (est): 21.57K **Privately Held**
SIC: 8731 Energy research

(G-14396)
ALPINE RAFETTO ORTHODONTICS
4901 Limestone Rd Ste 4 (19808-1271)
PHONE..................................302 239-2304
Vickie Dobroski, *Prin*
EMP: 13 **EST:** 2016
SALES (est): 837.39K **Privately Held**
Web: www.beachbraces.com
SIC: 8021 Orthodontist

(G-14397)
ALSTON ASSOCIATES COUNSELING
1232 N King St Ste 305 (19801-3226)
PHONE..................................302 223-4797
Sonya Boggs-alston, *Prin*
EMP: 8 **EST:** 2017
SALES (est): 46.31K **Privately Held**
Web: www.alston-systems.com
SIC: 8322 General counseling services

(G-14398)
ALTRA CARGO INC
4004 N Market St (19802-2220)
PHONE..................................302 256-0748
Sampson Opoku, *Pr*
EMP: 6 **EST:** 2014
SALES (est): 443.19K **Privately Held**
Web: www.altracargo.com
SIC: 4789 Cargo loading and unloading services

(G-14399)
ALU-REX USA INC
108 W 13th St (19801-1145)
PHONE..................................418 832-7632

(PA)=Parent Co (HQ)=Headquarters
✪ = New Business established in last 2 years

2024 Harris Directory of Delaware Businesses

Wilmington - New Castle County (G-14400) GEOGRAPHIC SECTION

Nicolas Aube, *Pr*
EMP: 30 **EST:** 2018
SALES (est): 3.46MM
SALES (corp-wide): 5.07MM **Privately Held**
SIC: 3444 Gutters, sheet metal
PA: Alu-Rex Inc
  2180 Av De La Rotonde
  Levis QC G6X 2
  418 832-7632

(G-14400)
ALVARENGA CLEANER
123 Lorewood Ave (19804-1525)
PHONE...................302 427-2308
Jose Alvarenga, *Prin*
EMP: 5 **EST:** 2015
SALES (est): 74.12K **Privately Held**
SIC: 7699 Cleaning services

(G-14401)
ALVAREZ PAINTING
29 2nd Ave (19808-4966)
PHONE...................302 287-1457
Teodoro Alvarez, *Prin*
EMP: 5 **EST:** 2018
SALES (est): 42.66K **Privately Held**
Web:
alvarez-painting-painting-service.business.site
SIC: 1721 Painting and paper hanging

(G-14402)
ALVATEK ELECTRONICS LLC
1200 Pennsylvania Ave Ste 101 (19806-4350)
P.O. Box 7847 (19803-0847)
PHONE...................302 655-5870
▲ **EMP:** 10 **EST:** 2006
SQ FT: 1,600
SALES (est): 2.02MM **Privately Held**
Web: www.alvatek.com
SIC: 5065 Electronic parts

(G-14403)
ALVINI & ASSOC FINCL PLANNERS
29 Bancroft Mills Rd (19806-2039)
PHONE...................302 397-8135
Michael J Alvini C.p.a., *Prin*
EMP: 6 **EST:** 2016
SALES (est): 487.56K **Privately Held**
Web: www.alviniassociates.com
SIC: 8742 6311 6282 Financial consultant; Life insurance; Investment advice

(G-14404)
ALWAYS DUWELL CLEAN
2809 Landon Dr (19810-2212)
PHONE...................610 905-0779
EMP: 5 **EST:** 2013
SALES (est): 34.09K **Privately Held**
SIC: 7699 Cleaning services

(G-14405)
ALYCE E DUFFY
Also Called: Whiskazz & Pawzz Specialty
1880 Superfine Ln Apt 40 (19802-4919)
PHONE...................302 383-5921
Alyce E Duffy, *Prin*
EMP: 5 **EST:** 2011
SALES (est): 145.7K **Privately Held**
SIC: 0752 Animal specialty services

(G-14406)
ALZHEIMERS ASSN DEL CHAPTER
2306 Kirkwood Hwy (19805-4927)
PHONE...................302 633-4420
Edna Ellett, *Dir*
EMP: 9 **EST:** 1986
SALES (est): 123.99K **Privately Held**
SIC: 8322 Individual and family services

(G-14407)
AMA RESOURCE LLC
6 Lombardy Dr (19803-3961)
P.O. Box 9796 (19809-0796)
PHONE...................410 977-5101
EMP: 7 **EST:** 2009
SQ FT: 12,000
SALES (est): 954.2K **Privately Held**
Web: www.amawasterecycling.com
SIC: 1795 Demolition, buildings and other structures

(G-14408)
AMAIRA NTRAL SKNCARE SLTONS IN
2711 Centerville Rd Ste 400 (19808-1660)
PHONE...................424 330-5231
Joel Smith, *CEO*
EMP: 5 **EST:** 2021
SALES (est): 425.62K **Privately Held**
Web: www.amairaskincare.com
SIC: 5122 Cosmetics

(G-14409)
AMALGAM RX INC (PA)
206 Alapocas Dr (19803-4505)
PHONE...................302 983-0001
Ryan Sysko, *CEO*
Chris Bergstrom, *Pr*
EMP: 14 **EST:** 2016
SALES (est): 4.78MM
SALES (corp-wide): 4.78MM **Privately Held**
Web: www.amalgamrx.com
SIC: 8082 Home health care services

(G-14410)
AMANDA L PORTER
5307 Limestone Rd Ste 101 (19808-1275)
PHONE...................302 234-2026
Amanda Porter, *Prin*
EMP: 9 **EST:** 2012
SALES (est): 99.51K **Privately Held**
SIC: 8011 Physical medicine, physician/surgeon

(G-14411)
AMANI BIRTH
1401 Pennsylvania Ave (19806-4124)
PHONE...................302 668-7506
Aisha Al Hajjar, *CEO*
EMP: 12 **EST:** 2012
SALES (est): 263.82K **Privately Held**
Web: www.amanibirth.com
SIC: 8621 8299 Education and teacher association; Educational service, nondegree granting: continuing educ.

(G-14412)
AMANI FAMILY FOUNDATION
501 Silverside Rd (19809-1374)
PHONE...................800 839-1754
EMP: 5
SALES (est): 168.23K **Privately Held**
SIC: 8699 Charitable organization

(G-14413)
AMANTYA TECHNOLOGIES INC
1201 N Market St Ste 111 (19801-1156)
PHONE...................302 439-6030
Anuradha Gupta, *CEO*
Saurabh Gupta, *Dir*
Vinod Tiwari, *Research & Development*
EMP: 9 **EST:** 2019
SALES (est): 383.5K **Privately Held**
Web: www.amantyatech.com
SIC: 7822 Motion picture and tape distribution

(G-14414)
AMAZAND THETA LLC
3316 Cross Country Dr (19810-3311)
PHONE...................302 285-9586
EMP: 6
SALES (est): 81.29K **Privately Held**
SIC: 6282 Investment advice

(G-14415)
AMAZINGDOC INC
251 Little Falls Dr (19808-1674)
PHONE...................847 909-0409
EMP: 5 **EST:** 2020
SALES (est): 46.16K **Privately Held**
Web: www.amazingdoc.com
SIC: 7371 Computer software development and applications

(G-14416)
AMBIENCE INC
3701 Oak Ridge Rd (19808-1338)
PHONE...................302 239-4822
EMP: 20 **EST:** 2018
SALES (est): 1.02MM **Privately Held**
Web: www.ambience239hvac.com
SIC: 1711 Warm air heating and air conditioning contractor

(G-14417)
AMBROGI INTEGRATIVE HLTH SERVI
2000 Pennsylvania Ave (19806-2450)
PHONE...................610 368-1006
Joanne Ambrogi, *Owner*
EMP: 8 **EST:** 2014
SALES (est): 160.4K **Privately Held**
SIC: 8099 Health and allied services, nec

(G-14418)
AMBRUX HOSPITALITY LLC
4409 Kennett Pike (19807-1805)
PHONE...................302 521-2492
EMP: 8 **EST:** 2012
SALES (est): 56.85K **Privately Held**
SIC: 7011 Hotels and motels

(G-14419)
AMBULATORYS SURGERY CTR
1941 Limestone Rd Ste 113 (19808-5436)
P.O. Box 5030 (19808-0030)
PHONE...................302 633-9416
Thomas Mulharn, *Prin*
EMP: 8 **EST:** 2010
SALES (est): 103.95K **Privately Held**
SIC: 8011 Surgeon

(G-14420)
AMEENAHKO LLC
Also Called: Aameenah Ali Muhammad
201 Woodlawn Ave Apt B (19805-3338)
P.O. Box 2929 (19805-0929)
PHONE...................302 601-3720
Lacrecia Muse-jones, *Managing Member*
EMP: 5 **EST:** 2019
SALES (est): 305.11K **Privately Held**
SIC: 4731 Freight transportation arrangement

(G-14421)
AMER INC
Also Called: Sir Speedy
1010 N Union St Ste D (19805-2731)
PHONE...................302 654-2498
Dan Nester, *Pr*
Karen Marshall, *Prin*
◆ **EMP:** 7 **EST:** 1986
SQ FT: 5,000
SALES (est): 986.87K **Privately Held**
Web: www.sirspeedy.com
SIC: 2759 7334 2791 2789 Commercial printing, nec; Photocopying and duplicating services; Typesetting; Bookbinding and related work

(G-14422)
AMER INDUSTRIAL TECH INC
Also Called: A I T
100 Amer Rd Ste 200 (19809-3564)
P.O. Box 293 (19736-0293)
PHONE...................302 765-3318
Ahmad E Amer, *Pr*
Ralph Lecky,
EMP: 37 **EST:** 1977
SQ FT: 200,000
SALES (est): 974.72K **Privately Held**
SIC: 3443 Industrial vessels, tanks, and containers

(G-14423)
AMERICA GROUP
2036 Foulk Rd Ste 104 (19810-3649)
PHONE...................302 529-1320
Ken Rudzinski, *Owner*
EMP: 6 **EST:** 1987
SALES (est): 476.15K **Privately Held**
SIC: 8742 Financial consultant

(G-14424)
AMERICAN AIR LEASE FINANCE LLC
Also Called: Philly Air Show
605 N Market St Fl 2 (19801-3167)
PHONE...................646 643-6303
Jacques Pope, *CEO*
EMP: 5 **EST:** 2012
SALES (est): 370K **Privately Held**
SIC: 6159 6282 8742 Equipment and vehicle finance leasing companies; Investment advisory service; Business management consultant

(G-14425)
AMERICAN BIRDING ASSOCIATION
20 Murphy Rd (19803-3045)
PHONE...................610 864-0370
EMP: 6 **EST:** 2017
SALES (est): 65.05K **Privately Held**
Web: www.aba.org
SIC: 8699 Membership organizations, nec

(G-14426)
AMERICAN CENTENNIAL INSUR CO
1415 Foulk Rd Ste 202 (19803-2748)
PHONE...................302 479-2100
Shaker A Youssef, *Pr*
EMP: 8 **EST:** 1970
SALES (est): 1.66MM
SALES (corp-wide): 6.02MM **Privately Held**
SIC: 6331 Property damage insurance
PA: White Mountains Services Holdings, Inc.
  80 S Main St
  Hanover NH 03755
  603 643-1567

(G-14427)
AMERICAN CHIROPRACTIC CENTER
1324 N King St (19801-3220)
P.O. Box 727 (19950-0727)
PHONE...................302 407-3046
EMP: 5 **EST:** 2017
SALES (est): 40.91K **Privately Held**
SIC: 8041 Offices and clinics of chiropractors

(G-14428)
AMERICAN CHMBER CMMRCE IN UKRI (PA)
1209 N Orange St (19801-1120)
PHONE...................352 505-9709

EMP: 45
SALES (est): 1.13MM
SALES (corp-wide): 1.13MM Privately Held
SIC: 7389

(G-14429)
AMERICAN CHMBER CMMRCE IN UZBK
1209 N Orange St (19801-1120)
PHONE..................202 590-9294
Hugo Minderhoud, Pr
EMP: 6 EST: 1996
SALES (est): 37.88K Privately Held
SIC: 8611 Chamber of Commerce

(G-14430)
AMERICAN CLLGE OF PHYSICIANS
2 Richards Dr (19810-3901)
PHONE..................540 631-0426
EMP: 6 EST: 2018
SALES (est): 60.66K Privately Held
SIC: 8011 Offices and clinics of medical doctors

(G-14431)
AMERICAN INCOME LF - RYAN BSAN
300 Delaware Ave Ste 210 (19801-6601)
PHONE..................484 442-8148
EMP: 6 EST: 2019
SALES (est): 193.54K Privately Held
Web: www.bisanzorganization.com
SIC: 8111 Legal services

(G-14432)
AMERICAN INCORPORATORS LTD
Also Called: REGISTERED AGENTS
1013 Centre Rd Ste 403a (19805-1270)
PHONE..................302 421-5752
EMP: 23 EST: 1991
SALES (est): 267.64K Privately Held
Web: www.ailcorp.com
SIC: 8111 Legal services

(G-14433)
AMERICAN INSERT FLANGE CO INC
1603 Jessup St Ste 6 (19802-4255)
P.O. Box 7187 (19803-0187)
PHONE..................302 777-7464
William Yanchulis, VP
Candia Yanchulis, Pr
EMP: 5 EST: 2006
SALES (est): 754.05K Privately Held
Web: www.americaninsertflange.com
SIC: 5085 Valves and fittings

(G-14434)
AMERICAN KARATE STUDIO
1812 Marsh Rd Ste 421 (19810-4522)
PHONE..................302 529-7800
Pat Caputo, Owner
EMP: 10 EST: 1970
SALES (est): 232.56K Privately Held
Web: www.delawarekarate.com
SIC: 7999 Karate instruction

(G-14435)
AMERICAN LIFE INSURANCE CO (HQ)
Also Called: MetLife
1 Alico Plz 600 King St (19801-3784)
P.O. Box 2226 (19899-2226)
PHONE..................302 594-2000
Marlene Debel, CEO
EMP: 100 EST: 1921
SALES (est): 491.21MM
SALES (corp-wide): 69.9B Publicly Held
Web: www.metlife.com

SIC: 6411 6321 6324 Insurance agents, nec; Accident and health insurance; Group hospitalization plans
PA: Metlife, Inc.
   200 Park Ave Fl 1200
   New York NY 10166
   212 578-9500

(G-14436)
AMERICAN MARKETING AGENCY INC
3524 Silverside Rd 35b (19810-4929)
PHONE..................484 424-9683
Anne Kwong, CEO
EMP: 10 EST: 2015
SALES (est): 200K Privately Held
SIC: 8742 Marketing consulting services

(G-14437)
AMERICAN METER HOLDINGS CORP
1105 N Market St Ste 1300 (19801-1241)
PHONE..................302 477-0208
Frederick Janssen, Pr
Michael W Cunningham, *
▲ EMP: 1400 EST: 1978
SALES (est): 86.24MM
SALES (corp-wide): 35.47B Publicly Held
SIC: 3824 3823 Gasmeters, domestic and large capacity: industrial; On-stream gas/liquid analysis instruments, industrial
HQ: Elster Gmbh
   Steinern Str. 19-21
   Mainz-Kastel HE 55252
   61346050

(G-14438)
AMERICAN NATIONAL RED CROSS
Also Called: Red Cross
5329 Concord Pike (19803-1418)
PHONE..................215 451-4372
Patricia Reid, Quality
EMP: 6
SALES (corp-wide): 3.18B Privately Held
Web: www.redcross.org
SIC: 8322 Social service center
PA: The American National Red Cross
   431 18th St Nw
   Washington DC 20006
   202 737-8300

(G-14439)
AMERICAN NUTRA GROUP LLC ✪
1000 N West St Ste 1200 (19801-1058)
PHONE..................305 610-9448
Michael Wojnicki, Managing Member
EMP: 5 EST: 2023
SALES (est): 258.29K Privately Held
SIC: 5122 Drugs, proprietaries, and sundries

(G-14440)
AMERICAN PUBLIC GARDENS ASSN
Also Called: Apga
1207 Delaware Ave (19806-4736)
PHONE..................610 708-3010
Daniel Stark, Ex Dir
EMP: 9 EST: 1940
SALES (est): 2.25MM Privately Held
Web: www.publicgardens.org
SIC: 8611 Growers' associations

(G-14441)
AMERICAN RESTORATION CARP
Also Called: American Restoration Services
412 Greenwood Dr (19808-1963)
PHONE..................302 993-7900
EMP: 9 EST: 2018
SALES (est): 104.75K Privately Held
Web: www.americanrestoration.com
SIC: 1799 Special trade contractors, nec

(G-14442)
AMERICAN SEABOARD EXTERIORS
14 Ashley Pl (19804-1314)
PHONE..................302 571-9896
Brian Blair, CEO
Adam Hamby, *
Michael Gallo, *
Howard J Cresswell Junior, Sec
Jerry Creswell, Ex VP
EMP: 50 EST: 1975
SQ FT: 5,000
SALES (est): 4.15MM Privately Held
Web: www.amsb.net
SIC: 1799 Cleaning building exteriors, nec

(G-14443)
AMERICAN SOC CYTOPATHOLOGY INC
Also Called: A S C
100 W 10th St Ste 605 (19801-6604)
PHONE..................302 543-6583
Elizabeth Jenkins, Ex Dir
Andrew Renshaw, Pr
EMP: 5 EST: 1951
SALES (est): 1.61MM Privately Held
Web: www.cytopathology.org
SIC: 8641 Civic and social associations

(G-14444)
AMERICAN SPORTS LICENSING INC (PA)
1011 Ctr Rd Ste 310 (19805-1266)
PHONE..................302 288-0122
Michael Hines, Pr
EMP: 14 EST: 1995
SALES (est): 2.09MM
SALES (corp-wide): 2.09MM Privately Held
SIC: 7997 Membership sports and recreation clubs

(G-14445)
AMERICAN-EURASIAN EXCH CO LLC
Also Called: Aeec
4023 Kennett Pike 267 (19807-2018)
PHONE..................202 701-4009
EMP: 5 EST: 2011
SALES (est): 164.39K Privately Held
SIC: 7389 Personal service agents, brokers, and bureaus

(G-14446)
AMERICO INC
117 Bunche Blvd (19801-5759)
PHONE..................302 981-9410
Robert Edwards, Prin
EMP: 10 EST: 2021
SALES (est): 1.02MM Privately Held
Web: www.americo.org
SIC: 1521 Single-family housing construction

(G-14447)
AMERIHALTH INTEGRATED BENEFITS (DH)
919 N Market, Ste 1200 (19801-3062)
PHONE..................302 777-6400
G Fred Di Bona Junior Esq, Pr
Patricia R Hatler Esq, Sec
EMP: 45 EST: 1985
SQ FT: 12,000
SALES (est): 91.8MM
SALES (corp-wide): 7.47B Privately Held
SIC: 8748 6324 Employee programs administration; Hospital and medical service plans
HQ: Amerihealth, Inc.
   1901 Market St Fl 32
   Philadelphia PA 19103
   215 241-3019

(G-14448)
AMERIPRISE FINANCIAL SERVICES
2 Righter Pkwy (19803-1532)
PHONE..................302 476-8000
James Miller, Mgr
EMP: 5 EST: 2015
SALES (est): 289.69K Privately Held
Web: www.ameripriseadvisors.com
SIC: 6282 Investment advice

(G-14449)
AMERIPRISE FINANCIAL SVCS INC
Also Called: AMERIPRISE FINANCIAL SERVICES, INC.
5195 W Woodmill Dr 27 (19808-4067)
PHONE..................302 543-5784
Robert Allen, Brnch Mgr
EMP: 10
SALES (corp-wide): 14.27B Publicly Held
Web: www.ameripriseadvisors.com
SIC: 6282 Investment advice
HQ: Ameriprise Financial Services, Llc
   707 2nd Ave S
   Minneapolis MN 55402
   612 671-3131

(G-14450)
AMERIPRISE FINANCIAL SVCS INC
Also Called: Ameriprise Financial Services
1805 Foulk Rd Ste A (19810-3700)
PHONE..................302 475-5105
Harry Orth, Brnch Mgr
EMP: 10
SALES (corp-wide): 14.27B Publicly Held
Web: www.ameripriseadvisors.com
SIC: 6282 Investment advice
HQ: Ameriprise Financial Services, Llc
   707 2nd Ave S
   Minneapolis MN 55402
   612 671-3131

(G-14451)
AMERIPRISE FINANCIAL SVCS INC
Also Called: AMERIPRISE FINANCIAL SERVICES, INC.
1011 Centre Rd Ste 100 (19805-1270)
PHONE..................302 468-8200
Jason Salinsky, Mgr
EMP: 15
SALES (corp-wide): 14.27B Publicly Held
Web: www.ameripriseadvisors.com
SIC: 6282 Investment advisory service
HQ: Ameriprise Financial Services, Llc
   707 2nd Ave S
   Minneapolis MN 55402
   612 671-3131

(G-14452)
AMERIPRISE FINANCIAL SVCS LLC
Also Called: Ameriprise Financial Services
2106 Silverside Rd Ste 201 (19810-4164)
PHONE..................302 475-2357
EMP: 10
SALES (corp-wide): 14.27B Publicly Held
Web: www.ameripriseadvisors.com
SIC: 6282 Investment advice
HQ: Ameriprise Financial Services, Llc
   707 2nd Ave S
   Minneapolis MN 55402
   612 671-3131

(G-14453)
AMERIRPISE
1 Righter Pkwy Ste 250 (19803-1555)
PHONE..................302 656-7773
EMP: 5 EST: 2008
SALES (est): 151.92K Privately Held
SIC: 6282 Investment advice

Wilmington - New Castle County (G-14454)

GEOGRAPHIC SECTION

(G-14454)
AMERISOURCE HERITAGE CORP
1403 Foulk Rd Ste 106 (19803-2788)
P.O. Box 8985 (19899-8985)
PHONE..................800 829-3132
Daniel Hirst, *VP*
EMP: 8 EST: 2000
SALES (corp-wide): 262.17B **Publicly Held**
SIC: 6719 Investment holding companies, except banks
PA: Cencora, Inc.
  1 W 1st Ave
  Conshohocken PA 19428
  610 727-7000

(G-14455)
AMES ENGINEERING CORP
805 E 13th St (19802-5000)
PHONE..................302 658-6945
Steve Ames, *Pr*
Richard Gotwals, *VP Engg*
Spencer Beckett, *Genl Mgr*
EMP: 10 EST: 1981
SQ FT: 32,000
SALES (est): 181.2K **Privately Held**
Web: www.amesengineering.com
SIC: 8711 3565 Electrical or electronic engineering; Packaging machinery

(G-14456)
AMF BOWLING CENTERS INC
Also Called: AMF
3215 Kirkwood Hwy (19808-6129)
PHONE..................302 998-5316
Kevin Sass, *Mgr*
EMP: 21
SALES (corp-wide): 1.06B **Publicly Held**
Web: www.amf.com
SIC: 7933 Ten pin center
HQ: Amf Bowling Centers, Inc.
  7313 Bell Creek Rd
  Mechanicsville VA 23111

(G-14457)
AMICK MART J MD
3105 Limestone Rd Ste 301 (19808-2156)
PHONE..................302 633-1700
Doctor Mart J Amick Md, *Owner*
EMP: 13 EST: 1993
SALES (est): 147.37K **Privately Held**
SIC: 8011 Pulmonary specialist, physician/surgeon

(G-14458)
AMITRA VITTA INCORPORATED
831 N Tatnall St Ste M148 (19801)
PHONE..................267 905-3766
Lucinda Porter, *CEO*
EMP: 50 EST: 2019
SALES (est): 1.07MM **Privately Held**
SIC: 6799 Real estate investors, except property operators

(G-14459)
AMITY LODGES LTD
251 Little Falls Dr (19808-1674)
P.O. Box 1861 (76048-8861)
PHONE..................833 462-6489
Christopher A Brewer, *Managing Member*
EMP: 23 EST: 2018
SALES (est): 1.08MM **Privately Held**
SIC: 8741 Hotel or motel management

(G-14460)
AMP MANUFACTURING LLC
6 Hadco Rd (19804-1014)
PHONE..................302 691-8883
EMP: 7 EST: 2016
SALES (est): 112.7K **Privately Held**

SIC: 3312 Ammonia and liquor, from chemical recovery coke ovens

(G-14461)
AMPACET OHIO LLC
300 Delaware Ave Ste 210 (19801-6601)
PHONE..................914 631-6600
EMP: 41 EST: 1999
SALES (est): 6.1MM
SALES (corp-wide): 455.35MM **Privately Held**
Web: www.ampacet.com
SIC: 2816 Color pigments
PA: Ampacet Corporation
  660 White Plns Rd Ste 36
  Tarrytown NY 10591
  914 631-6600

(G-14462)
AMPLE BUSINESS SOLUTIONS INC
501 Silverside Rd (19809-1374)
PHONE..................302 752-4270
Anil Rajasekhar Chunduru, *Dir*
▼ EMP: 16 EST: 2012
SQ FT: 1,000
SALES (est): 464.01K **Privately Held**
Web: www.amplesoln.com
SIC: 7374 Data processing and preparation

(G-14463)
AMSOFT CORP
4023 Kennett Pike (19807-2018)
PHONE..................859 351-7688
EMP: 5 EST: 2017
SALES (est): 106.78K **Privately Held**
SIC: 8748 Business consulting, nec

(G-14464)
AMSTEL BARBER SHOP
1319 Mckennans Church Rd (19808-2132)
PHONE..................302 543-4515
EMP: 7 EST: 2013
SALES (est): 36.29K **Privately Held**
Web: www.amstelbarbershop.com
SIC: 7241 Hair stylist, men

(G-14465)
AMWAL TECH INC
2055 Limestone Rd (19808-5536)
PHONE..................650 391-5496
Mohammed Zaghoo, *CEO*
EMP: 10
SALES (est): 354.58K **Privately Held**
SIC: 7389 Financial services

(G-14466)
AMYLIN PHARMACEUTICALS LLC
1800 Concord Pike (19897-0001)
P.O. Box 4000 (08543-4000)
PHONE..................858 552-2200
▲ EMP: 1300
SIC: 2834 8731 Pharmaceutical preparations ; Medical research, commercial

(G-14467)
ANALYTTICA DATALAB INC (PA)
1007 N Orange St Fl 4 (19801-1242)
PHONE..................917 300-3325
Rajiv Baphna, *CEO*
Shilpi Jain, *
Rupal Baphna, *CAO**
EMP: 45 EST: 2014
SALES (est): 1.06MM
SALES (corp-wide): 1.06MM **Privately Held**
Web: www.analyttica.com
SIC: 7374 7372 8299 5999 Data processing and preparation; Educational computer software; Educational services; Training materials, electronic

(G-14468)
ANCAR ENTERPRISES LLC (PA)
Also Called: AlphaGraphics
3411 Silverside Rd # 103 (19810-4812)
PHONE..................302 477-1884
Atul Chugh, *Pr*
EMP: 3 EST: 2015
SALES (est): 1.2MM
SALES (corp-wide): 1.2MM **Privately Held**
Web: www.alphagraphics.com
SIC: 2752 2754 Commercial printing, lithographic; Labels: gravure printing

(G-14469)
ANCATT
9 Germay Dr (19804-1155)
PHONE..................302 513-9392
EMP: 7 EST: 2017
SALES (est): 81.48K **Privately Held**
Web: www.ancatt.com
SIC: 3479 Coating of metals and formed products

(G-14470)
ANCIENT ORDER HBERNIANS LADIES
401 Jackson Ave (19804-2115)
PHONE..................302 633-0810
EMP: 6 EST: 2017
SALES (est): 75.34K **Privately Held**
Web: www.aohwilmingtonnc.com
SIC: 8641 Civic associations

(G-14471)
ANDERSON CATANIA SURETLY SVC
Also Called: Nationwide
707 Philadelphia Pike (19809-2539)
PHONE..................302 762-7599
Thomas Donovan, *Admn*
EMP: 10 EST: 2019
SALES (est): 1.52MM **Privately Held**
Web: www.acsurety.com
SIC: 6351 Surety insurance

(G-14472)
ANDERSON GROUP INC
3411 Silverside Rd Ste 103 (19810-4812)
PHONE..................302 478-6160
Herbert F Gerhard, *Pr*
Howard L Nelson, *
George P Warren Junior, *Sec*
Mark F Fornari, *
◆ EMP: 805 EST: 1991
SALES (est): 89.03MM
SALES (corp-wide): 1.56B **Publicly Held**
SIC: 5047 5063 5099 7699 Industrial safety devices: first aid kits and masks; Electrical apparatus and equipment; Lifesaving and survival equipment (non-medical); Hydraulic equipment repair
HQ: Charter Consolidated Limited
  Warlies Park House
  Waltham Abbey EN9 3

(G-14473)
ANDERSON RNEE CHARLES ANDERSON
101 Maplewood Ln (19810-2748)
PHONE..................302 529-7845
Renee Anderson, *Prin*
EMP: 5 EST: 2009
SALES (est): 94.98K **Privately Held**
SIC: 8748 Business consulting, nec

(G-14474)
ANDREW BOBICH
1316 N Union St (19806-2534)
PHONE..................312 384-9323
Andrew Bobich, *Prin*
EMP: 5 EST: 2017

SALES (est): 93.93K **Privately Held**
SIC: 6411 Insurance agents, brokers, and service

(G-14475)
ANDREW E QUESENBERRY CARPENTRY
1012 Stanton Rd (19808-5831)
P.O. Box 632 (19715-0632)
PHONE..................302 994-0700
Andrew Quesenberry, *Owner*
EMP: 6 EST: 2010
SALES (est): 228.44K **Privately Held**
Web: www.aeqcarpentry.com
SIC: 1751 Cabinet and finish carpentry

(G-14476)
ANDREW J GLICK MD
2000 Foulk Rd Ste F (19810-3642)
PHONE..................302 652-8990
Andrew Glick Md, *Pt*
Doctor Bruce Benge, *Pt*
Michael Lovis, *Pt*
EMP: 24 EST: 1991
SALES (est): 204.28K **Privately Held**
Web: www.brandywineuc.com
SIC: 8011 Urologist

(G-14477)
ANDREW SIMOFF HORSE TRNSP
3719 Old Capitol Trl (19808-6001)
PHONE..................302 994-1433
Andrew Simoff, *Pr*
EMP: 5 EST: 1981
SQ FT: 1,500
SALES (est): 500K **Privately Held**
Web: www.simoffhorsetransport.com
SIC: 4213 Trucking, except local

(G-14478)
ANDREW T PATTERSON CPA
503 Carr Rd Ste 120 (19809-2863)
PHONE..................302 652-4194
Andrew Patterson, *Prin*
EMP: 5 EST: 2018
SALES (est): 26.39K **Privately Held**
Web: www.horty.com
SIC: 8721 Certified public accountant

(G-14479)
ANDREW W DONOHUE DO
1906 Maryland Ave (19805-4605)
PHONE..................302 235-3725
Andrew Donohue, *Pr*
EMP: 6 EST: 2018
SALES (est): 81.44K **Privately Held**
SIC: 8099 8011 Health and allied services, nec; Offices and clinics of medical doctors

(G-14480)
ANDREW WEINSTEIN MD INC
Also Called: Asthma Allergy Care Delaware
111 Walnut Ridge Rd (19807-1635)
P.O. Box 247 (19732-0247)
PHONE..................302 428-1675
Andrew G Weinstein, *Pr*
EMP: 7 EST: 1986
SALES (est): 262.03K **Privately Held**
SIC: 8011 Ears, nose, and throat specialist; physician/surgeon

(G-14481)
ANDREWS & SPRINGER LLC
4001 Kennett Pike Ste 250 (19807-2029)
PHONE..................302 504-4957
Peter B Andrews, *Prin*
EMP: 11 EST: 2014
SALES (est): 887.77K **Privately Held**
Web: www.andrewsspringer.com

GEOGRAPHIC SECTION
Wilmington - New Castle County (G-14511)

SIC: 8111 General practice law office

(G-14482)
ANGELA SALDARRIAGA
5578 Kirkwood Hwy (19808-5002)
PHONE.....................302 633-1182
Angela Saldarriaga, *Owner*
EMP: 7 EST: 2005
SALES (est): 470.26K **Privately Held**
Web:
www.childsupportcollectionspecialists.com
SIC: 8011 Offices and clinics of medical doctors

(G-14483)
ANGELS VISITING
3101 Limestone Rd Ste E (19808-2148)
PHONE.....................302 691-8700
Justin Smith, *Mgr*
EMP: 97 EST: 2012
SALES (est): 224.52K **Privately Held**
Web: www.visitingangels.com
SIC: 8082 Home health care services

(G-14484)
ANGLIN CNSULTING SOLUTIONS LLC
1201 N Market St (19801-1147)
PHONE.....................302 406-0233
Donna Anglin, *Managing Member*
EMP: 12
SALES (est): 406.37K **Privately Held**
SIC: 8748 Business consulting, nec

(G-14485)
ANIP ACQUISITION COMPANY
2003 Kentmere Pkwy (19806-2036)
PHONE.....................302 652-2021
Charlotte C Arnold, *Owner*
EMP: 2 EST: 2013
SALES (est): 250.06K **Publicly Held**
SIC: 2834 Pharmaceutical preparations
PA: Ani Pharmaceuticals, Inc.
210 W Main St
Baudette MN 56623

(G-14486)
ANKLE AND FOOT SURGICAL ASSOC
Also Called: Advanced Foot & Ankle Center
701 N Clayton St Fl 4 (19805-3165)
PHONE.....................302 425-5720
EMP: 8 EST: 1996
SALES (est): 80.02K **Privately Held**
Web: www.ankleandfootsurgical.com
SIC: 8043 Offices and clinics of podiatrists

(G-14487)
ANLATAN LLC
2055 Limestone Rd Ste 200c (19808-5536)
PHONE.....................618 318-5334
Eren Dogan, *Managing Member*
EMP: 7 EST: 2021
SALES (est): 129.38K **Privately Held**
SIC: 7929 Entertainment service

(G-14488)
ANNA J BLOMMER
1010 W 4th St (19805-3602)
PHONE.....................302 576-4136
Anna Blommer, *Mgr*
EMP: 8 EST: 2017
SALES (est): 48.17K **Privately Held**
SIC: 8322 Individual and family services

(G-14489)
ANNA MARIE MAZOCH DDS PA
2601 Annand Dr Ste 18 (19808-3719)
PHONE.....................302 998-9594
Anna Marie Mazoch, *Prin*
EMP: 5 EST: 2008
SALES (est): 132.82K **Privately Held**
Web: www.drmazoch.com
SIC: 8021 Dentists' office

(G-14490)
ANNA VASSALLO PIERA
1812 Marsh Rd Ste 423 (19810-4522)
PHONE.....................302 529-2607
Vernon Vassallo, *Prin*
EMP: 5 EST: 2010
SALES (est): 100.42K **Privately Held**
SIC: 7241 Barber shops

(G-14491)
ANNADALE OLADIMEJI (PA) ✪
Also Called: Andels Home Care
501 Silverside Rd Ste 28 (19809-1375)
PHONE.....................267 357-9718
Annadale Oladimeji, *Owner*
EMP: 6 EST: 2023
SALES (est): 365.1K
SALES (corp-wide): 365.1K **Privately Held**
SIC: 8082 7389 Home health care services; Business services, nec

(G-14492)
ANNE ANSTASI CHRTBLE FUNDATION
501 Silverside Rd (19809-1374)
PHONE.....................800 839-1754
EMP: 5
SALES (est): 125.21K **Privately Held**
SIC: 8699 Charitable organization

(G-14493)
ANNIEJWELS ERLY CHILD DEV CTR
118 Bunche Blvd (19801-5723)
PHONE.....................302 981-1904
Aisha M Copeland, *Prin*
EMP: 9 EST: 2017
SALES (est): 72.83K **Privately Held**
SIC: 8351 Child day care services

(G-14494)
ANNIEMAC HOME MORTGAGE LLC
4839 Limestone Rd (19808-1902)
PHONE.....................302 234-2956
Vincent Ingui, *Pr*
EMP: 118
SALES (corp-wide): 41.64MM **Privately Held**
Web: www.annie-mac.com
SIC: 6162 Mortgage bankers
PA: Anniemac Home Mortgage Llc
700 E Gate Dr Ste 400
Mount Laurel NJ 08054
856 252-1506

(G-14495)
ANSEL HEALTH INC
1209 N Orange St (19801-1120)
PHONE.....................844 987-1070
Travis Knight, *Prin*
EMP: 19
SALES (est): 424.88K **Privately Held**
Web: www.joinbrella.com
SIC: 6411 Insurance agents, brokers, and service

(G-14496)
ANUTIO INC
704 N King St Ste 500 (19801-3583)
PHONE.....................647 607-8378
Ehi Agbonlahor, *CEO*
EMP: 10
SALES (est): 365.44K **Privately Held**
SIC: 7372 Educational computer software

(G-14497)
ANYBODIES INC
2810 N Church St (19802-4447)
PHONE.....................646 699-8781
Elli Gouveia, *CEO*
EMP: 15
SALES (est): 627.46K **Privately Held**
SIC: 7389 Design services

(G-14498)
ANYTIME FITNESS
1851 Marsh Rd (19810-4505)
PHONE.....................302 475-2404
Valesta Tejan-kamara, *Owner*
EMP: 14 EST: 2008
SALES (est): 170.2K **Privately Held**
Web: www.anytimefitness.com
SIC: 7991 Physical fitness clubs with training equipment

(G-14499)
AOLA INC (PA) ✪
Also Called: Aola
919 N Market St Ste 950 (19801-3036)
PHONE.....................610 245-8231
Oleg Tumanov, *CEO*
EMP: 8 EST: 2022
SALES (est): 368.58K
SALES (corp-wide): 368.58K **Privately Held**
SIC: 7371 Computer software development and applications

(G-14500)
AON3D INC
1209 N Orange St (19801-1120)
PHONE.....................650 410-3120
EMP: 6 EST: 2016
SALES (est): 71.62K **Privately Held**
Web: www.aon3d.com
SIC: 3555 Printing trades machinery

(G-14501)
AOREL TECH INVESTMENTS LLC
3 Germay Dr Ste 4 (19804-1127)
PHONE.....................610 674-1516
EMP: 5 EST: 2016
SALES (est): 64.94K **Privately Held**
SIC: 5045 Computer software

(G-14502)
APACHE SOFTWARE FOUNDATION
1000 Nw St Ste 1200 (19801-1058)
PHONE.....................302 295-4884
James Jagielski, *Pr*
Sander Striker, *Ch Bd*
Mark Thomas, *OF BRAND MGT*
EMP: 9 EST: 1999
SALES (est): 1.77MM **Privately Held**
Web: www.apache.org
SIC: 8699 Charitable organization

(G-14503)
APARTMENT COMMUNITIES CORP
Also Called: Town Court Apartments
402 Foulk Rd Apt 1a9 (19803-3813)
P.O. Box 7189 (19803-0189)
PHONE.....................302 656-7781
Frank E Acierno, *Pr*
Patty Fredricks, *
EMP: 8 EST: 1968
SALES (est): 351.76K **Privately Held**
Web: www.brandywine100.com
SIC: 6513 8741 Apartment hotel operation; Management services

(G-14504)
APARTMENTS SDK
3120 Naamans Rd (19810-2139)
PHONE.....................302 478-1215
EMP: 6 EST: 2013
SALES (est): 187.13K **Privately Held**
Web: www.sdkstratford.com
SIC: 6513 Apartment hotel operation

(G-14505)
APEX ENGINEERING INC
27 W Market St (19804-3138)
PHONE.....................302 994-1900
EMP: 22 EST: 1995
SALES (est): 1.61MM **Privately Held**
Web: www.apexengineeringinc.com
SIC: 8711 Consulting engineer

(G-14506)
APEX PIPING SYSTEMS INC (PA)
302 Falco Dr (19804-2401)
PHONE.....................302 995-6136
Pat Oakes, *Pr*
Mathew J Hicken, *
John L Stevens, *
Steve Onley, *
EMP: 77 EST: 1967
SQ FT: 35,000
SALES (est): 20.89MM
SALES (corp-wide): 20.89MM **Privately Held**
Web: www.apexpiping.com
SIC: 3498 3443 3317 3312 Piping systems for pulp, paper, and chemical industries; Process vessels, industrial: metal plate; Welded pipe and tubes; Pipes and tubes

(G-14507)
APL LGSTICS TRNSP MGT SVCS LTD
200 Powder Mill Rd Bldg 402 (19803-2907)
PHONE.....................302 230-2656
Don Gray, *Genl Mgr*
EMP: 29
Web: www.apllogistics.com
SIC: 4731 Freight forwarding
HQ: Apl Logistics Transportation Management Services, Ltd.
17600 N Perimeter Dr # 150
Scottsdale AZ 85255
602 357-9100

(G-14508)
APOLLO HEALTH & WELLNESS LLC
5503 Kirkwood Hwy (19808-5001)
PHONE.....................302 994-2273
EMP: 7 EST: 2018
SALES (est): 227.02K **Privately Held**
SIC: 8099 Health and allied services, nec

(G-14509)
APPCANO LLC ✪
2810 N Church St # 42197 (19802-4447)
PHONE.....................951 285-3632
Taylor Martinez, *Managing Member*
EMP: 2 EST: 2022
SALES (est): 49.23K **Privately Held**
SIC: 7389 7372 Business Activities at Non-Commercial Site; Application computer software

(G-14510)
APPLETREE ANSWERING SERVICES INC
1521 Concord Pike Ste 202 (19803-3645)
PHONE.....................302 227-9015
EMP: 260
Web: www.appletreeanswers.com
SIC: 7389 Telephone answering service

(G-14511)
APPLIED BANK (PA)
2200 Concord Pike Ste 102 (19803-2978)
P.O. Box P.O Box 15060 (19885-0001)
PHONE.....................302 326-4200

Wilmington - New Castle County (G-14512) GEOGRAPHIC SECTION

EMP: 20 EST: 1996
SQ FT: 10,000
SALES (est): 10.33MM **Privately Held**
Web: www.appliedbank.com
SIC: 6021 National commercial banks

(G-14512)
APPLIED CARD HOLDINGS INC
601 Delaware Ave Ste 100 (19801-1463)
P.O. Box 17125 (19850-7125)
PHONE..................302 326-4200
Rocco A Abessinio, *Ch Bd*
EMP: 10 EST: 1999
SALES (est): 925.31K **Privately Held**
SIC: 7389 Credit card service

(G-14513)
APPMOTION INC
1000 N West St Ste 1200 (19801-1058)
PHONE..................347 513-6333
Mhd-ammar Aboulnasr, *Dir*
EMP: 3 EST: 2014
SQ FT: 100
SALES (est): 230.99K **Privately Held**
SIC: 7372 Publisher's computer software

(G-14514)
APPTRIUM INC
Also Called: Invent.us
1000 N West St Ste 1200 (19801-1058)
PHONE..................800 888-0706
Oleg Tishkevich, *CEO*
EMP: 80 EST: 2017
SALES (est): 1.96MM **Privately Held**
SIC: 7371 Computer software development and applications

(G-14515)
APRIORIT LLC
3524 Silverside Rd Ste 35b (19810-4929)
PHONE..................202 780-9339
Dennis Turpitka, *CEO*
EMP: 250 EST: 2017
SALES (est): 19.77MM **Privately Held**
Web: www.apriorit.com
SIC: 7371 Computer software development and applications

(G-14516)
APTUSTECH LLC
1209 Ornge St Corp Tr Ctr (19801)
PHONE..................347 254-5619
EMP: 3 EST: 2009
SALES (est): 127.06K **Privately Held**
SIC: 2323 7389 Men's and boy's neckwear; Business services, nec

(G-14517)
AQORN INC
427 N Tatnall St (19801-2230)
PHONE..................916 123-4567
EMP: 6 EST: 2016
SALES (est): 140.45K **Privately Held**
Web: www.aqorn.com
SIC: 7299 Miscellaneous personal service

(G-14518)
AQUASOLI
3422 Old Capitol Trl (19808-6124)
PHONE..................704 696-8400
EMP: 5 EST: 2017
SALES (est): 125.15K **Privately Held**
Web: www.aquasoli.com
SIC: 8711 Consulting engineer

(G-14519)
AQUATIC MANAGEMENT
4905 Mermaid Blvd (19808-1004)
PHONE..................302 235-1818
Michael Ramon, *Owner*
EMP: 5 EST: 2007
SALES (est): 273.74K **Privately Held**
Web: www.amspools.com
SIC: 7389 Swimming pool and hot tub service and maintenance

(G-14520)
AR PRO INC
2055 Limestone Rd Ste 200c (19808-5536)
PHONE..................323 677-0503
Ashwin Appalasami, *CEO*
Shie Whan Hor, *COO*
EMP: 10 EST: 2021
SALES (est): 1.1MM **Privately Held**
SIC: 5169 5047 Food additives and preservatives; Medical equipment and supplies

(G-14521)
ARAB THERAPY INC
108 W 13th St (19801-1145)
PHONE..................310 956-4252
Tariq Dalbah, *CEO*
EMP: 20 EST: 2021
SALES (est): 220K **Privately Held**
SIC: 8099 Medical services organization

(G-14522)
ARACENT HEALTHCARE LLC
3411 Silverside Rd Ste 202 (19810-4810)
PHONE..................302 478-8865
EMP: 6 EST: 2004
SQ FT: 2,000
SALES (est): 2.19MM **Privately Held**
Web: www.aracent.com
SIC: 5047 Medical equipment and supplies
PA: Ritchie Sawyer Corporation
2502 Pin Oak Dr
Wilmington DE 19810

(G-14523)
ARBITEXCH LLC ◊
500 N King St (19801-3703)
PHONE..................302 490-0111
Gilbert Tonetto, *CEO*
EMP: 5 EST: 2022
SALES (est): 68.89K **Privately Held**
Web: www.arbitexch.com
SIC: 7371 Computer software development and applications

(G-14524)
ARBOR MANAGEMENT LLC (PA)
4 Denny Rd Ste 1 (19809-3445)
PHONE..................302 764-6450
Kevin P Kelly, *Pr*
EMP: 169 EST: 2004
SALES (est): 9.99MM
SALES (corp-wide): 9.99MM **Privately Held**
Web: www.lnwa.com
SIC: 6531 Real estate managers

(G-14525)
ARBORVINE LANDSCAPING LLC
114 Chatham Pl (19810-4404)
PHONE..................302 502-5605
Greg Chakar, *Prin*
EMP: 10 EST: 2019
SALES (est): 884.27K **Privately Held**
Web: www.arborvinelandscaping.com
SIC: 0781 Landscape services

(G-14526)
ARC FALCON I INC (PA)
251 Little Falls Dr (19808-1674)
PHONE..................302 636-5401
EMP: 6 EST: 2021
SALES (est): 72.36K
SALES (corp-wide): 72.36K **Privately Held**
SIC: 7389 Personal service agents, brokers, and bureaus

(G-14527)
ARC FINANCE LTD
251 Little Falls Dr (19808-1674)
PHONE..................914 478-3851
EMP: 5 EST: 2010
SALES (est): 301.8K **Privately Held**
Web: www.arcfinance.org
SIC: 8399 Advocacy group

(G-14528)
ARC HUD I INC
2 S Augustine St (19804-2504)
PHONE..................302 996-9400
Patricia Kelleher, *Admn*
Vanessa Corbin, *Acctg Mgr*
EMP: 7 EST: 2012
SALES (est): 354.38K **Privately Held**
SIC: 8748 Urban planning and consulting services

(G-14529)
ARC HUD II INC
2 S Augustine St (19804-2504)
PHONE..................302 996-9400
Patricia Kelleher, *Admn*
EMP: 7 EST: 2012
SALES (est): 115.56K **Privately Held**
Web: www.thearcofdelaware.org
SIC: 8322 Individual and family services

(G-14530)
ARC HUD VII INC
2 S Augustine St (19804-2504)
PHONE..................302 996-9400
Vanessa Corbin, *Acctg Mgr*
Terry Olson, *Prin*
EMP: 7 EST: 2012
SALES (est): 363.06K **Privately Held**
SIC: 8748 City planning

(G-14531)
ARC OF DELAWARE
2 S Augustine St Ste B (19804-2504)
PHONE..................302 996-9400
Elizabeth Harris, *Admn*
EMP: 13 EST: 1953
SALES (est): 45.3K **Privately Held**
Web: www.thearcofdelaware.org
SIC: 8699 Charitable organization

(G-14532)
ARC OF DELAWARE
2 S Augustine St Ste B (19804-2504)
PHONE..................302 996-9400
EMP: 20 EST: 2010
SALES (est): 291K **Privately Held**
Web: www.thearcofdelaware.org
SIC: 8322 Social services for the handicapped

(G-14533)
ARC OFFSHORE INVESTMENTS INC
3511 Silverside Rd # 105 (19810-4902)
PHONE..................561 670-9938
Lawrence Pirritino, *Prin*
EMP: 2
SALES (est): 118.7K **Privately Held**
SIC: 1389 Oil consultants

(G-14534)
ARC RESIN CORP
2112 Lindell Blvd (19808-4044)
PHONE..................859 230-7063
EMP: 6 EST: 2019
SALES (est): 88.97K **Privately Held**
SIC: 2821 Plastics materials and resins

(G-14535)
ARC STUDIO LABS INC ◊
2810 N Church St Pmb 65228 (19802-4447)
PHONE..................323 990-8787
EMP: 6 EST: 2022
SALES (est): 46.16K **Privately Held**
Web: www.arcstudiopro.com
SIC: 7371 Computer software development and applications

(G-14536)
ARC WILMINGTON
100 W 10th St (19801-6603)
PHONE..................302 656-6620
EMP: 10 EST: 1996
SALES (est): 218.62K **Privately Held**
SIC: 8322 Social service center

(G-14537)
ARCADIA THERAPEUTIC MASSAGE
918 Wilson Rd (19803-4018)
PHONE..................302 438-3251
Helen Baker, *Prin*
EMP: 5 EST: 2010
SALES (est): 56.68K **Privately Held**
SIC: 7299 Massage parlor

(G-14538)
ARCADIS US INC
1007 N Orange St Fl 1 (19801-1267)
PHONE..................302 658-1718
Robert Daoust, *Mgr*
EMP: 10
SALES (corp-wide): 3.14B **Privately Held**
Web: www.arcadis.com
SIC: 8711 Consulting engineer
HQ: Arcadis U.S., Inc.
630 Plaza Dr Ste 200
Highlands Ranch CO 80129
720 344-3500

(G-14539)
ARCANGEL INC
Also Called: Catherine Deane
1013 Centre Rd Ste 403 (19805-1270)
PHONE..................347 771-0789
Catherine Deane, *CEO*
EMP: 2 EST: 2013
SALES (est): 819.45K
SALES (corp-wide): 294.19K **Privately Held**
Web: www.catherinedeane.com
SIC: 2335 Wedding gowns and dresses
HQ: Atelier Arcangel Limited
Office 4
Chester

(G-14540)
ARCASOFT LLC
1201 N Orange St Ste 7306 (19801-1155)
PHONE..................402 575-1234
EMP: 5
SALES (est): 68.89K **Privately Held**
SIC: 7371 Computer software development and applications

(G-14541)
ARCHER & GREINER A PROF CORP
300 Delaware Ave Ste 1100 (19801-1670)
PHONE..................302 777-4350
L Peter, *Prin*
EMP: 5
SALES (corp-wide): 44.8MM **Privately Held**
Web: www.archerlaw.com
SIC: 8111 General practice law office
PA: Archer & Greiner, A Professional Corporation
1025 Laurel Oak Rd

GEOGRAPHIC SECTION

Wilmington - New Castle County (G-14569)

Voorhees NJ 08043
856 795-2121

(G-14542)
ARCHITECT ENGINEER INS CO RISK
Also Called: Architects Engineers Loss Ctrl
4001 Kennett Pike Ste 318 (19807-2039)
PHONE...................302 658-2342
Harold A Dombeck, *Pr*
Mitch Sellett, *VP*
C Roy Vince, *VP*
George X Cannon, *Pr*
David R Wahrlich, *Sec*
EMP: 7 **EST:** 1987
SQ FT: 1,800
SALES (est): 902.12K **Privately Held**
Web: insurance.delaware.gov
SIC: 6321 Reinsurance carriers, accident and health

(G-14543)
ARCHITECTURE PLUS PA
234 N James St (19804-3132)
PHONE...................302 999-1614
Mark Hitchcock, *Pr*
EMP: 6 **EST:** 1994
SALES (est): 442.87K **Privately Held**
SIC: 8712 Architectural engineering

(G-14544)
ARCPOINT LABS
222 Philadelphia Pike Ste 5 (19809-3166)
P.O. Box 9534 (19809-0534)
PHONE...................302 268-6560
EMP: 7 **EST:** 2016
SALES (est): 144.15K **Privately Held**
Web: www.arcpointlabs.com
SIC: 8734 Testing laboratories

(G-14545)
ARDEN COURTS OF WILMINGTON
700 1/2 Foulk Rd (19803-3739)
PHONE...................302 762-7800
EMP: 9 **EST:** 2020
SALES (est): 225.28K **Privately Held**
Web: www.arden-courts.org
SIC: 8051 Convalescent home with continuous nursing care

(G-14546)
ARDEN COURTS WILMINGTON DE LLC ✪
Also Called: Arden Courts of Wilmington
700 One Half Foulk Rd (19803)
PHONE...................302 764-0181
EMP: 13 **EST:** 2022
SALES (est): 3.47MM **Privately Held**
SIC: 8051 Convalescent home with continuous nursing care

(G-14547)
ARDEN MEDIA RESOURCES
1302 N West St (19801-1028)
PHONE...................256 656-8631
John Williams, *Prin*
EMP: 5 **EST:** 2017
SALES (est): 26.91K **Privately Held**
Web: www.ardenmediaresources.com
SIC: 7812 Motion picture and video production

(G-14548)
AREA 51 AUTOMOTIVE
8 Hadco Rd (19804-1003)
PHONE...................302 993-9114
David Mitchell, *Pr*
EMP: 6 **EST:** 2012
SALES (est): 64.93K **Privately Held**
SIC: 7538 General automotive repair shops

(G-14549)
ARGO US FEEDER FUND LP
251 Little Falls Dr (19808-1674)
PHONE...................345 769-4154
EMP: 5 **EST:** 2020
SALES (est): 186.81K **Privately Held**
SIC: 7389 Business services, nec

(G-14550)
ARIANNA & ANGELINA ENTPS LLC
Also Called: A & A Enterprises
2801 Centerville Rd (19808-1609)
PHONE...................484 574-8119
EMP: 22 **EST:** 2006
SALES (est): 4.96MM **Privately Held**
Web: www.ricksequipmentsales.com
SIC: 3531 Excavators: cable, clamshell, crane, derrick, dragline, etc.

(G-14551)
ARIES SECURITY LLC
1226 N King St (19801-3232)
PHONE...................302 365-0026
Brian Markus, *CEO*
Orv Varner, *CFO*
EMP: 6 **EST:** 2008
SALES (est): 1.02MM **Privately Held**
Web: www.ariessecurity.com
SIC: 5045 8711 8731 7371 Computers, peripherals, and software; Consulting engineer; Computer (hardware) development; Computer software systems analysis and design, custom

(G-14552)
ARM CHAIR SCOUTS LLC
427 N Tatnall St 24852 (19801-2230)
PHONE...................315 360-8692
Aaron Sanford, *Pr*
EMP: 10 **EST:** 2017
SALES (est): 434.25K **Privately Held**
SIC: 8742 Management consulting services

(G-14553)
ARMAND DE MD SANCTIC
2101 Foulk Rd (19810-4710)
PHONE...................302 475-2535
Armand De Sanctic Md, *Owner*
EMP: 10 **EST:** 1979
SALES (est): 680.96K **Privately Held**
SIC: 8011 Offices and clinics of medical doctors

(G-14554)
ARMEHTECH SOLUTIONS LLC ✪
919 N Market St Ste 950 (19801-3036)
PHONE...................302 309-9645
EMP: 95 **EST:** 2022
SALES (est): 1.27MM **Privately Held**
Web: www.armehtech.com
SIC: 8742 Human resource consulting services

(G-14555)
ARMODIAS LLC
4023 Kennett Pike # 273 (19807-2018)
PHONE...................302 384-9794
EMP: 5 **EST:** 2011
SALES (est): 233.72K **Privately Held**
SIC: 8748 Business consulting, nec

(G-14556)
ARMSTRONG CORK FINANCE LLC
818 N Washington St (19801-1510)
PHONE...................302 652-1520
George A Lorch, *Pr*
William J Wimer, *Ex VP*
Robert A Sills, *VP*
Louis L Davenport, *VP*
EMP: 44 **EST:** 1974
SALES (est): 874.53K
SALES (corp-wide): 1.23B **Publicly Held**
SIC: 6153 Short-term business credit institutions, except agricultural
PA: Armstrong World Industries, Inc.
    2500 Columbia Ave
    Lancaster PA 17603
    717 397-0611

(G-14557)
AROS DESIGN STUDIO LLC
2604 Whittier Pl (19808-3714)
PHONE...................505 560-0603
Ketevan Arevadze, *CEO*
EMP: 8
SALES (est): 306.16K **Privately Held**
SIC: 7371 Computer software development

(G-14558)
AROUND AGAIN AND AGAIN BKS LLC
1400 Philadelphia Pike (19809-1856)
PHONE...................302 439-3847
EMP: 5 **EST:** 2018
SALES (est): 197.36K **Privately Held**
Web: www.aroundagainandagainbooks.com
SIC: 5192 Books

(G-14559)
ARRIM LLC (PA)
919 N Market St Ste 950 (19801-3036)
PHONE...................617 697-7914
EMP: 2 **EST:** 2018
SALES (est): 338.74K
SALES (corp-wide): 338.74K **Privately Held**
SIC: 3829 7389 Measuring and controlling devices, nec; Business services, nec

(G-14560)
ART FLOOR INC
9 Jefferson Ave (19805-1322)
P.O. Box 1299 (19707-5299)
PHONE...................302 636-9201
William Bartoshesky, *Pr*
Cynthia Bartoshesky, *
EMP: 10 **EST:** 1949
SALES (est): 1.28MM **Privately Held**
Web: www.artfloorinc.com
SIC: 5023 5713 Floor coverings; Floor covering stores

(G-14561)
ARTCRAFT UPHOISTERY LLC
116 Center Ct (19810-2523)
PHONE...................302 764-2067
Richard Leach, *Prin*
EMP: 5 **EST:** 2012
SALES (est): 52.77K **Privately Held**
SIC: 7641 Upholstery work

(G-14562)
ARTEAGA PROPERTIES LLC
2711 Centerville Rd # 200 (19808-1660)
PHONE...................808 339-6906
EMP: 5 **EST:** 2016
SQ FT: 5,000
SALES (est): 124.68K **Privately Held**
SIC: 7699 5088 Aircraft and heavy equipment repair services; Aircraft engines and engine parts

(G-14563)
ARTEMUNDI LLC
3411 Silverside Rd Ste 104 (19810-4812)
PHONE...................302 988-5002
Javier Lumbreras, *CEO*
EMP: 10 **EST:** 2016
SALES (est): 574.76K **Privately Held**
Web: www.artemundi.com
SIC: 8748 Business consulting, nec

(G-14564)
ARTEVET LLC
Also Called: Artevet
1000 N West St Ste 1200 (19801-1058)
PHONE...................443 255-0016
Aniket Parikh, *Managing Member*
EMP: 5 **EST:** 2014
SALES (est): 928.65K **Privately Held**
Web: www.artevet.com
SIC: 2836 Veterinary biological products

(G-14565)
ARTHOUSE USA INCORPORATED
1209 N Orange St (19801-1120)
PHONE...................800 677-3394
Paul Mullan, *CEO*
EMP: 5 **EST:** 2017
SALES (est): 250K **Privately Held**
SIC: 5198 Wallcoverings

(G-14566)
ARTIFICIAL BRAIN TECH INC (PA) ✪
1209 N Orange St (19801-1120)
PHONE...................302 601-7201
Jitesh Lalwani, *CEO*
EMP: 6 **EST:** 2022
SALES (est): 87.5K
SALES (corp-wide): 87.5K **Privately Held**
SIC: 5045 Computer software

(G-14567)
ARTISANS BANK INC
223 W 9th St (19801-1631)
PHONE...................302 656-8188
Katie Wroten, *COO*
EMP: 7
SALES (corp-wide): 25.62MM **Privately Held**
Web: www.artisansbank.com
SIC: 6036 State savings banks, not federally chartered
PA: Artisans Bank Inc
    2961 Centerville Rd # 101
    Wilmington DE 19808
    302 658-6881

(G-14568)
ARTISANS BANK INC (PA)
Also Called: ARTISANS BANK
2961 Centerville Rd Ste 101 (19808-1672)
PHONE...................302 658-6881
Stephen C Nelson, *Pr*
James Flanders, *Sr VP*
Charles Brown, *Sr VP*
Mark E Huntley, *Pr*
Steve C Lyons, *CFO*
EMP: 100 **EST:** 1861
SQ FT: 15,000
SALES (est): 25.62MM
SALES (corp-wide): 25.62MM **Privately Held**
Web: www.artisansbank.com
SIC: 6036 State savings banks, not federally chartered

(G-14569)
ARTISANS BANK INC
3631 Silverside Rd (19810-5101)
PHONE...................302 479-2553
Janice Zebley, *Mgr*
EMP: 6
SALES (corp-wide): 25.62MM **Privately Held**
Web: www.artisansbank.com
SIC: 6036 State savings banks, not federally chartered
PA: Artisans Bank Inc
    2961 Centerville Rd # 101

Wilmington - New Castle County (G-14570) GEOGRAPHIC SECTION

Wilmington DE 19808
302 658-6881

(G-14570)
ARTISANS BANK INC
1706 Marsh Rd (19810-4606)
PHONE..................................302 479-2550
Florence Miller, *Mgr*
EMP: 5
SALES (corp-wide): 25.62MM **Privately Held**
Web: www.artisansbank.com
SIC: 6036 State savings banks, not federally chartered
PA: Artisans Bank Inc
  2961 Centerville Rd # 101
  Wilmington DE 19808
  302 658-6881

(G-14571)
ARTISANS BANK INC
Also Called: Aritisans Wilmington Bank
4901 Kirkwood Hwy (19808-5011)
PHONE..................................302 993-8220
Maira Carillo, *Mgr*
EMP: 8
SALES (corp-wide): 25.62MM **Privately Held**
Web: www.artisansbank.com
SIC: 6036 State savings banks, not federally chartered
PA: Artisans Bank Inc
  2961 Centerville Rd # 101
  Wilmington DE 19808
  302 658-6881

(G-14572)
ARTISANS BANK INC
4551 Linden Hill Rd (19808)
PHONE..................................302 738-3744
Ken Beaudean, *Mgr*
EMP: 7
SALES (corp-wide): 25.62MM **Privately Held**
Web: www.artisansbank.com
SIC: 6036 8231 6029 State savings banks, not federally chartered; Libraries; Commercial banks, nec
PA: Artisans Bank Inc
  2961 Centerville Rd # 101
  Wilmington DE 19808
  302 658-6881

(G-14573)
ARUGIE ENTERPRISES CORP
Also Called: Arg Communications
612 S Colonial Ave Ste A (19805-1956)
PHONE..................................302 225-2000
Joseph Ruggieri, *Pr*
EMP: 7 **EST:** 2003
SALES (est): 965.92K **Privately Held**
Web: www.whyarg.com
SIC: 1731 Telephone and telephone equipment installation

(G-14574)
ARUN JAIN ADVICOACH
2 Camp David Rd (19810-3260)
PHONE..................................302 442-0053
EMP: 7 **EST:** 2017
SALES (est): 76.27K **Privately Held**
SIC: 8011 Offices and clinics of medical doctors

(G-14575)
ARVI VR INC
108 W 13th St (19801-1145)
PHONE..................................844 615-8194
Michael Dementii, *CEO*
EMP: 6 **EST:** 2019
SALES (est): 314.98K **Privately Held**

SIC: 7389 Business Activities at Non-Commercial Site

(G-14576)
ASBURY CARBONS INC
103 Foulk Rd Ste 202 (19803-3742)
PHONE..................................302 652-0266
Michael Ball, *Brnch Mgr*
EMP: 10
SALES (corp-wide): 135.5MM **Privately Held**
Web: www.asbury.com
SIC: 1499 Gemstone and industrial diamond mining
HQ: Asbury Carbons, Inc.
  405 Old Main St
  Asbury NJ 08802
  908 537-2155

(G-14577)
ASFERIK LLC
717 W Oakmeade Dr (19810-1455)
PHONE..................................302 981-6519
EMP: 3 **EST:** 2015
SALES (est): 88.58K **Privately Held**
SIC: 3949 Sporting and athletic goods, nec

(G-14578)
ASHANTI PRODUCE INTERNATIONAL
Also Called: Agriculture /Chemicals
1000 N West St Ste 1200 (19801-1058)
PHONE..................................800 295-9790
Michael A Griffin, *CEO*
EMP: 10 **EST:** 1995
SALES (est): 1.14MM **Privately Held**
Web: www.ashantiproduce.com
SIC: 2879 8748 0182 Agricultural chemicals, nec; Agricultural consultant; Fruits, grown under cover

(G-14579)
ASHBY & GEDDES
500 Delaware Ave Ste 8 (19801-7400)
P.O. Box 1150 (19899-1150)
PHONE..................................302 654-1888
James Mc C Geddes, *Pr*
Lawrence C Ashby Attorney, *Prin*
EMP: 40 **EST:** 1979
SALES (est): 6.34MM **Privately Held**
Web: www.ashbygeddes.com
SIC: 8111 General practice attorney, lawyer

(G-14580)
ASHFORD CAPITAL MANAGEMENT
1 Walkers Mill Rd (19807-2134)
P.O. Box 4172 (19807-0172)
PHONE..................................302 655-1750
Theodore H Ashford, *Pr*
Gregory Falcon, *VP*
EMP: 10 **EST:** 1979
SALES (est): 2.48MM **Privately Held**
Web: www.ashfordcapital.com
SIC: 6282 Investment advisory service

(G-14581)
ASHFORD CONSULTING GROUP INC
2 Righter Pkwy Ste 105 (19803-1528)
PHONE..................................302 691-0228
EMP: 5 **EST:** 2014
SALES (est): 169.61K **Privately Held**
SIC: 6282 Investment advisory service

(G-14582)
ASHLAND CHEMCO INC
Also Called: Ashland Credit Union
500 Hercules Rd (19808-1513)
PHONE..................................302 995-4180
John Hoffman, *Mgr*
EMP: 32

SALES (corp-wide): 2.19B **Publicly Held**
Web: www.ashland.com
SIC: 5169 Alkalines and chlorine
HQ: Ashland Chemco Inc.
  5475 Rings Rd Ste 500
  Dublin OH 43017
  859 815-3333

(G-14583)
ASHLAND INC (PA)
Also Called: Ashland
8145 Blazer Dr (19808)
PHONE..................................302 995-3000
Guillermo Novo, *Ch Bd*
J Kevin Willis, *Sr VP*
Osama M Musa, *Sr VP*
Eileen M Drury, *Chief Human Resources Officer*
Robin E Lampkin, *Sr VP*
EMP: 112 **EST:** 1936
SALES (est): 2.19B
SALES (corp-wide): 2.19B **Publicly Held**
Web: www.ashland.com
SIC: 5169 Chemicals and allied products, nec

(G-14584)
ASHLAND SPCALTY INGREDIENTS GP (DH)
8145 Blazer Dr (19808)
PHONE..................................302 594-5000
Guillermo Novo, *Ch Bd*
◆ **EMP:** 120 **EST:** 2008
SALES (est): 438.29MM
SALES (corp-wide): 2.19B **Publicly Held**
Web: www.ashland.com
SIC: 2869 Industrial organic chemicals, nec
HQ: Ashland Chemco Inc.
  5475 Rings Rd Ste 500
  Dublin OH 43017
  859 815-3333

(G-14585)
ASHLEY LNTTI HOLISTIC HLTH LLC
2207 Brookline Rd (19803-5221)
PHONE..................................804 347-2641
EMP: 5 **EST:** 2017
SALES (est): 71.16K **Privately Held**
SIC: 8099 Health and allied services, nec

(G-14586)
ASHLEY LYNN KONTRA
3521 Silverside Rd Ste 2j (19810-4900)
PHONE..................................302 543-5454
EMP: 6 **EST:** 2017
SALES (est): 22.18K **Privately Held**
SIC: 8049 Offices of health practitioner

(G-14587)
ASHLEY WIPER
204 Milltown Rd (19808-3112)
PHONE..................................302 994-6838
EMP: 5 **EST:** 2009
SALES (est): 110K **Privately Held**
SIC: 1711 Warm air heating and air conditioning contractor

(G-14588)
ASOMBRO EXTREMO LLC
3411 Silverside Rd Ste A (19810-4813)
PHONE..................................305 495-1471
EMP: 8 **EST:** 2019
SALES (est): 800K **Privately Held**
Web: www.somosasombro.com
SIC: 7311 Advertising agencies

(G-14589)
ASPHALT KINGDOM LLC
Also Called: Asphalt Kingdom
1209 N Orange St (19801-1120)

PHONE..................................866 399-5562
Amienna Colquhoun, *Managing Member*
EMP: 7 **EST:** 2020
SALES (est): 225.48K **Privately Held**
SIC: 2951 7371 Asphalt paving mixtures and blocks; Computer software development and applications

(G-14590)
ASPIRE + BUILD LLC
427 N Tatnall St # 57021 (19801-2230)
PHONE..................................617 602-7400
Jo Saint-surin, *Prin*
Derick Saint-surin, *Prin*
Caleb Saint-surin, *Prin*
EMP: 71 **EST:** 2020
SALES (est): 1.61MM **Privately Held**
SIC: 1799 Special trade contractors, nec

(G-14591)
ASSET MANAGEMENT ALLIANCE
222 Delaware Ave Ste 109 (19801-1681)
PHONE..................................302 656-5238
Dave Casey, *Pt*
EMP: 14 **EST:** 1987
SALES (est): 1.77MM **Privately Held**
Web: www.assetmanagementalliance.com
SIC: 6531 Real estate managers

(G-14592)
ASSOCIATES INTERNATIONAL INC
100 Rogers Rd (19801-5704)
PHONE..................................302 656-4500
Lammot Copeland, *CEO*
Charles Copeland, *
Bryan Taylor, *
William Englehart, *
Joe Farley Junior, *COO*
▲ **EMP:** 60 **EST:** 1973
SQ FT: 29,214
SALES (est): 11.03MM **Privately Held**
Web: www.associatesinternational.com
SIC: 2752 2791 2741 Commercial printing, lithographic; Typesetting; Miscellaneous publishing

(G-14593)
ASSOCIATION EDUCTIONAL PUBLR
300 Martin Luther King Blvd (19801-2437)
PHONE..................................302 295-8350
Charlene Gaynor, *CEO*
EMP: 10 **EST:** 1895
SALES (est): 175.34K **Privately Held**
Web: www.bingoviews.com
SIC: 8699 Charitable organization

(G-14594)
ASSOCTES HMTLOGY ONCLOGY GROUP
701 N Clayton St Ste 502 (19805-3165)
PHONE..................................302 421-4860
EMP: 9 **EST:** 2014
SALES (est): 94.03K **Privately Held**
SIC: 8011 Oncologist

(G-14595)
ASSOCTES IN HLTH PSYCHLOGY LLC (PA)
Also Called: AHP
1521 Concord Pike Ste 103 (19803-3614)
PHONE..................................302 428-0205
EMP: 12 **EST:** 1996
SALES (est): 528.03K **Privately Held**
Web: www.ahpdelaware.com
SIC: 8049 Clinical psychologist

(G-14596)
ASSOCTION BRDS THLGCAL EDUCATN

GEOGRAPHIC SECTION
Wilmington - New Castle County (G-14621)

Also Called: IN TRUST
1100 W 10th St Ste 703 (19801-6605)
PHONE..................302 654-7770
Anne Anderson, *Ch*
Reverend Dr Richard Bliese, *Pr*
EMP: 8 **EST:** 2015
SALES (est): 608.14K **Privately Held**
Web: www.intrust.org
SIC: 8748 Business consulting, nec

(G-14597)
ASSOCTION FOR THE RGHTS CTZENS (PA)
Also Called: ARC OF DELAWARE
1016 Centre Rd Ste 1 (19805-1234)
PHONE..................302 996-9400
Eliane Raign, *Prin*
EMP: 12 **EST:** 1953
SALES (est): 505.48K **Privately Held**
SIC: 8621 Professional organizations

(G-14598)
ASSOCTION PATHOLOGY CHAIRS INC
100 W. 10th St Ste 603 (19801-6604)
PHONE..................302 660-4940
Kenneth Endicott, *Ex Dir*
Fred Becker, *Pr*
EMP: 7 **EST:** 1975
SQ FT: 400
SALES (est): 986.73K **Privately Held**
Web: apc.memberclicks.net
SIC: 8621 8011 Medical field-related associations; Pathologist

(G-14599)
ASSURANCE MEDIA LLC
590 Century Blvd Ste B (19808-6272)
P.O. Box 5087 (19808-0087)
PHONE..................302 892-3540
Jennifer Mckenzie, *Pr*
Mark Stellini, *Prin*
Tom Diorrio, *Prin*
Chris Honeycutt, *Prin*
James Bowe, *Prin*
EMP: 20 **EST:** 2009
SQ FT: 20,000
SALES (est): 9.53MM **Privately Held**
Web: www.assurancemedia.com
SIC: 1731 Computer installation

(G-14600)
ASSURANCE PARTNERS INTL
1201 N Market St Ste 1600 (19801-1147)
P.O. Box 7316 (19803-0316)
PHONE..................302 478-0173
EMP: 10 **EST:** 1990
SALES (est): 985.22K **Privately Held**
SIC: 6411 6211 Insurance agents, nec; Investment firm, general brokerage

(G-14601)
AST SPORTS INTERNACIONAL LLC
2711 Centerville Rd (19808-1660)
PHONE..................786 445-8081
EMP: 5 **EST:** 2018
SALES (est): 112.22K **Privately Held**
SIC: 8748 Business consulting, nec

(G-14602)
ASTERLAB ADVISORS LLC
1000 N West St Ste 1200 (19801-1058)
PHONE..................302 295-4888
EMP: 6
SALES (est): 202.3K **Privately Held**
Web: www.asterlabllc.com
SIC: 8611 Growers' marketing advisory service

(G-14603)
ASTHMA AND ALLERGY CARE DEL (PA)
1941 Limestone Rd Ste 209 (19808-5400)
PHONE..................302 995-2952
Richard Kim, *Pt*
EMP: 5 **EST:** 2001
SALES (est): 1.08MM
SALES (corp-wide): 1.08MM **Privately Held**
Web: www.entad.org
SIC: 8011 Ears, nose, and throat specialist: physician/surgeon

(G-14604)
ASTON HOME HEALTH
1021 Gilpin Ave Ste 100 (19806-3271)
PHONE..................302 421-3686
Maria Consuelo Singson V, *Prin*
EMP: 12 **EST:** 2007
SALES (est): 924.3K **Privately Held**
Web: www.essexlad.com
SIC: 8049 Nurses and other medical assistants

(G-14605)
ASTORIA BUILDERS LLC
96 Wayland Rd (19807-2584)
PHONE..................302 993-7951
Cynthia Light, *Prin*
EMP: 6 **EST:** 2010
SALES (est): 188.6K **Privately Held**
Web: www.astoriabuildersllc.com
SIC: 1521 New construction, single-family houses

(G-14606)
ASTRAZENECA LLC (HQ)
1800 Concord Pike (19803-2910)
PHONE..................800 236-9933
Ruud Dobber, *Pr*
Jamie Freedman, *Pr*
Christie Bloomquist, *VP*
Tosh Butt, *VP*
Marc Howells, *VP*
EMP: 93 **EST:** 2014
SALES (est): 56.21MM
SALES (corp-wide): 44.35B **Privately Held**
Web: careers.astrazeneca.com
SIC: 5122 Pharmaceuticals
PA: Astrazeneca Plc
1 Francis Crick Avenue
Cambridge CAMBS CB2 0
203 749-5000

(G-14607)
ASTRAZENECA FINANCE LLC
1209 N Orange St (19801-1120)
PHONE..................800 677-3394
EMP: 5 **EST:** 2021
SALES (est): 297.33K **Privately Held**
SIC: 7389 Financial services

(G-14608)
ASTRAZENECA FOUNDATION
1800 Concord Pike (19850)
P.O. Box 15437 (19850-5437)
PHONE..................302 886-3000
EMP: 8 **EST:** 2010
SALES (est): 167.01K **Privately Held**
SIC: 8699 Charitable organization

(G-14609)
ASTRAZENECA LP (DH)
Also Called: Astrazeneca
1800 Concord Pike (19803-2910)
P.O. Box 15437 (19850-5437)
PHONE..................302 886-3000
Antony Zook, *CEO*
James Reid, *Treas*
Cecilia White, *Sec*
Trudy Tan, *Prin*
▲ **EMP:** 2500 **EST:** 1997
SQ FT: 1,200,000
SALES (est): 1.64B
SALES (corp-wide): 44.35B **Privately Held**
Web: careers.astrazeneca.com
SIC: 2834 Pharmaceutical preparations
HQ: Astrazeneca Pharmaceuticals Lp
1800 Concord Pike
Wilmington DE 19850

(G-14610)
ASTRAZENECA PHARMACEUTICALS LP (HQ)
1800 Concord Pike (19850)
P.O. Box 15437 (19803)
PHONE..................800 456-3669
◆ **EMP:** 4000 **EST:** 1997
SQ FT: 1,200,000
SALES (est): 2.07B
SALES (corp-wide): 44.35B **Privately Held**
Web: www.astrazeneca.com
SIC: 5122 2834 Pharmaceuticals; Pharmaceutical preparations
PA: Astrazeneca Plc
1 Francis Crick Avenue
Cambridge CAMBS CB2 0
203 749-5000

(G-14611)
ASTRAZNECA CLLBRTION VNTRES LL
Also Called: Astrazeneca
1800 Concord Pike (19897-0001)
PHONE..................302 886-3000
Ruud Dobber, *Ex VP*
EMP: 23 **EST:** 2012
SALES (est): 488.28K
SALES (corp-wide): 44.35B **Privately Held**
SIC: 6799 Venture capital companies
PA: Astrazeneca Plc
1 Francis Crick Avenue
Cambridge CAMBS CB2 0
203 749-5000

(G-14612)
AT SYSTEMS ATLANTIC INC
4200 Governor Printz Blvd (19802-2315)
PHONE..................302 762-5444
Marvin Woods, *Pr*
EMP: 7 **EST:** 2000
SALES (est): 215.76K **Privately Held**
SIC: 7389 Personal service agents, brokers, and bureaus

(G-14613)
AT THE G SPOT LLC
Also Called: G Spot Tattoos, The
2302 W Newport Pike (19804-3847)
PHONE..................302 998-5010
EMP: 5 **EST:** 2004
SALES (est): 104.66K **Privately Held**
Web: www.thegspottattoos.com
SIC: 7299 Tattoo parlor

(G-14614)
AT WILMINGTON
1 Middleton Dr (19808-4320)
PHONE..................302 235-2554
EMP: 6 **EST:** 2017
SALES (est): 130.69K **Privately Held**
Web: www.visitwilmingtonde.com
SIC: 7389 Convention and show services

(G-14615)
AT-BAY INSURANCE SERVICES LLC
1013 Centre Rd Ste 403s (19805-1270)
PHONE..................888 338-9522
EMP: 6 **EST:** 2017
SALES (est): 70.63K **Privately Held**
SIC: 6411 Professional standards services, insurance

(G-14616)
ATA TECHNOLOGY INC (PA)
1500 Shallcross Ave 2a-6 (19806-3037)
PHONE..................862 233-0007
Jamar Jackson, *CEO*
EMP: 5 **EST:** 2018
SALES (est): 231.58K
SALES (corp-wide): 231.58K **Privately Held**
SIC: 7379 Computer related consulting services

(G-14617)
ATECHNOLOGIE LLC
1521 Concord Pike Ste 301 (19803-3644)
PHONE..................781 325-5230
Tony Harb, *Pr*
EMP: 8 **EST:** 2010
SALES (est): 1.96MM **Privately Held**
Web: www.aatechnologie.com
SIC: 5065 1799 Electronic parts; Antenna installation

(G-14618)
ATHENA CHIROPRACTIC
222 Philadelphia Pike (19809-3166)
P.O. Box 7338 (19803-0338)
PHONE..................302 543-4227
Karen C Feeney D.c., *Owner*
EMP: 7 **EST:** 2014
SALES (est): 448.83K **Privately Held**
Web: www.athenachiropractic.com
SIC: 8041 Offices and clinics of chiropractors

(G-14619)
ATI HOLDINGS LLC
Also Called: ATI Physical Therapy
1208 Kirkwood Hwy (19805-2120)
PHONE..................302 993-1450
Timothy Mchugh, *Brnch Mgr*
EMP: 7
SALES (corp-wide): 635.67MM **Publicly Held**
Web: www.atipt.com
SIC: 8049 Physical therapist
HQ: Ati Holdings, Llc
790 Remington Blvd
Bolingbrook IL 60440

(G-14620)
ATI HOLDINGS LLC
Also Called: ATI Physical Therapy
100 Valley Center Rd (19808-2950)
PHONE..................302 994-1200
Brian Larue, *Brnch Mgr*
EMP: 7
SALES (corp-wide): 635.67MM **Publicly Held**
Web: www.atipt.com
SIC: 8049 Physical therapist
HQ: Ati Holdings, Llc
790 Remington Blvd
Bolingbrook IL 60440

(G-14621)
ATI HOLDINGS LLC
Also Called: North Orthopedic and Hand Ctr
1812 Marsh Rd Ste 505 (19810-4515)
PHONE..................302 475-7500
EMP: 8
SALES (corp-wide): 635.67MM **Publicly Held**
Web: www.atipt.com
SIC: 8049 Physical therapist
HQ: Ati Holdings, Llc
790 Remington Blvd
Bolingbrook IL 60440

Wilmington - New Castle County (G-14622)   GEOGRAPHIC SECTION

(G-14622)
ATI HOLDINGS LLC
Also Called: ATI Physical Therapy
914 Justison St (19801-5150)
PHONE.................302 351-0302
EMP: 8
SALES (corp-wide): 635.67MM **Publicly Held**
Web: www.atipt.com
SIC: 8049 Physical therapist
HQ: Ati Holdings, Llc
    790 Remington Blvd
    Bolingbrook IL 60440

(G-14623)
ATI HOLDINGS LLC
Also Called: ATI Physical Therapy
1600 N Washington St (19802-4722)
PHONE.................302 656-2521
Edward R Miersch, *Owner*
EMP: 10
SALES (corp-wide): 635.67MM **Publicly Held**
Web: www.atipt.com
SIC: 8049 Physical therapist
HQ: Ati Holdings, Llc
    790 Remington Blvd
    Bolingbrook IL 60440

(G-14624)
ATI HOLDINGS LLC
Also Called: ATI Physical Therapy
213 Greenhill Ave Ste C (19805-1800)
PHONE.................302 658-7800
Jason Mafabolta, *Dir*
EMP: 10
SALES (corp-wide): 635.67MM **Publicly Held**
Web: www.atipt.com
SIC: 8049 Physical therapist
HQ: Ati Holdings, Llc
    790 Remington Blvd
    Bolingbrook IL 60440

(G-14625)
ATI PHYSICAL THERAPY
3620 Concord Pike (19803-5022)
PHONE.................302 281-3072
EMP: 8 EST: 2018
SALES (est): 126.13K **Privately Held**
Web: locations.atipt.com
SIC: 8049 Physical therapist

(G-14626)
ATLAN INC
Also Called: Atlan
1000 N West St Ste 1281 Pmb M171 (19801-1050)
PHONE.................650 288-6722
Prukalpa Sankar, *Pr*
EMP: 6 EST: 2020
SALES (est): 506.95K **Privately Held**
Web: www.atlan.com
SIC: 7371 Software programming applications

(G-14627)
ATLANTIC CITY ELECTRIC CO
800 N King St Ste 400 (19895-1100)
PHONE.................302 429-3200
David Velazquez, *CEO*
EMP: 8 EST: 2017
SALES (est): 2.05MM **Privately Held**
SIC: 4911 Distribution, electric power

(G-14628)
ATLANTIC CITY ELECTRIC CO
630 Martin Luther King Blvd (19801-2306)
PHONE.................302 588-6675
EMP: 6 EST: 2019

SALES (est): 294.11K **Privately Held**
SIC: 4911 Distribution, electric power

(G-14629)
ATLANTIC LANDSCAPE CO
800 A St (19801-5334)
PHONE.................302 661-1950
Bill Gioffre, *Pr*
EMP: 8 EST: 1988
SALES (est): 868.9K **Privately Held**
Web: www.alcde.com
SIC: 0781 Landscape services

(G-14630)
ATLAS MANAGEMENT INC (DH)
103 Foulk Rd (19803-3742)
PHONE.................302 576-2749
Brian J Duffy, *Pr*
Andrew Panaccione, *VP*
Timothy Gifford, *Sec*
EMP: 24 EST: 1994
SALES (est): 441.43MM
SALES (corp-wide): 9.24B **Privately Held**
SIC: 6726 Management investment funds, closed-end
HQ: Skf Usa Inc.
    890 Forty Foot Rd
    Lansdale PA 19446
    267 436-6000

(G-14631)
ATLAS SOLAR III LLC
1209 N Orange St (19801-1120)
PHONE.................949 677-1308
EMP: 5 EST: 2020
SALES (est): 56.99K **Privately Held**
SIC: 1711 Solar energy contractor

(G-14632)
ATLAS SP PARTNERS LP ◆
Also Called: Atlas Scuritized Pdts Partners
251 Little Falls Dr (19808-1674)
PHONE.................212 325-2777
EMP: 6 EST: 2022
SALES (est): 70.26K **Privately Held**
SIC: 7389 Business services, nec

(G-14633)
ATOM ALLOYS LLC
Also Called: Atom Solutions United States
3411 Silverside Rd Ste 104 (19810-4812)
PHONE.................786 975-3771
John Fillmon, *Ex VP*
EMP: 10 EST: 2011
SALES (est): 699.71K **Privately Held**
Web: www.atomalloys.com
SIC: 3443 Fuel tanks (oil, gas, etc.), metal plate

(G-14634)
ATOMIC GARAGE
462 B And O Ln (19804-1452)
PHONE.................302 898-1380
Gabriel Padilla, *Prin*
EMP: 5 EST: 2018
SALES (est): 28.25K **Privately Held**
SIC: 7538 General automotive repair shops

(G-14635)
ATR ELECTRICAL SERVICES INC
529 W Champlain Ave (19804-2007)
PHONE.................302 384-7044
Sean Mccarron, *Owner*
EMP: 5 EST: 2015
SALES (est): 77.41K **Privately Held**
SIC: 1731 General electrical contractor

(G-14636)
ATTABOTICS (US) CORP
3 Germay Dr Ste 4 (19804-1127)

PHONE.................403 454-0995
Scott Gravelle, *CEO*
EMP: 36 EST: 2020
SALES (est): 2.43MM **Privately Held**
SIC: 8742 Automation and robotics consultant

(G-14637)
ATTACK ADDICTION
2615 Crossgate Dr (19808-2310)
PHONE.................302 994-1550
Joyce White, *Prin*
EMP: 5 EST: 2015
SALES (est): 57.7K **Privately Held**
Web: www.attackaddiction.org
SIC: 8641 Civic and social associations

(G-14638)
ATTENTION TO DTILS STRTGIES LL
2207 Concord Pike Ste 399 (19803-2908)
PHONE.................877 870-2837
EMP: 5 EST: 2014
SALES (est): 109.97K **Privately Held**
Web: www.atdstrategies.com
SIC: 4213 Trucking, except local

(G-14639)
ATWORK PERSONNEL SERVICES
1021 Kent Rd (19807-2819)
PHONE.................302 660-1062
Caleb Brokaw, *Prin*
EMP: 7 EST: 2018
SALES (est): 68.44K **Privately Held**
Web: www.atwork.com
SIC: 7361 Employment agencies

(G-14640)
AUGUSTIN STABLE
3801 Kennett Pike (19807-2321)
PHONE.................302 571-8322
Augustin Stable, *Prin*
EMP: 5 EST: 2010
SALES (est): 102.32K **Privately Held**
SIC: 0752 Training services, horses (except racing horses)

(G-14641)
AUM LLC
Also Called: Leadsrain
20c Trolley Sq (19806-3355)
PHONE.................302 385-6767
EMP: 10 EST: 2013
SALES (est): 991.24K **Privately Held**
Web: www.leadsrain.com
SIC: 7371 Computer software development

(G-14642)
AURA SMART AIR INC
Also Called: Aura Air
1007 N Orange St Fl 10 (19801-1277)
PHONE.................847 909-5822
Roei Friedberg, *CEO*
Ofer Bluemenfeld, *Prin*
Luca Doan, *Prin*
Oren Milgram, *Prin*
EMP: 4 EST: 2018
SALES (est): 432.47K **Privately Held**
Web: www.auraair.io
SIC: 3564 7389 Air purification equipment; Business Activities at Non-Commercial Site

(G-14643)
AURAGIN LLC
427 N Tatnall St (19801-2230)
PHONE.................800 383-5109
EMP: 2 EST: 2016
SALES (est): 436.66K **Privately Held**
Web: www.auraginhealth.com
SIC: 2834 Pharmaceutical preparations

(G-14644)
AURIC JETS LLC
251 Little Falls Dr (19808-1674)
PHONE.................866 887-5414
Stan Kisselev, *Managing Member*
EMP: 5 EST: 2018
SALES (est): 251.58K **Privately Held**
SIC: 5088 Aircraft and parts, nec

(G-14645)
AURORA CORPORATION (PA)
3422 Old Capitol Trl (19808-6124)
PHONE.................302 656-6717
Larry A Distefano, *Pr*
J Leslie Di Stefano, *VP*
▲ EMP: 6 EST: 1992
SQ FT: 1,000
SALES (est): 2.5MM **Privately Held**
Web: www.auroracorporation.com
SIC: 4959 Sanitary services, nec

(G-14646)
AURORA REIKI LLC
506 N Union St (19805-3028)
PHONE.................443 553-3233
Reiki Aurora, *Prin*
EMP: 6 EST: 2017
SALES (est): 51.3K **Privately Held**
SIC: 8049 Massage Therapist

(G-14647)
AUSTIN ALLIANCE ELECTRIC INC
300 Delaware Ave Ste 210a (19801-6601)
PHONE.................843 297-8078
Cristina Davenport, *Mgr*
EMP: 42
SALES (corp-wide): 7.25MM **Privately Held**
SIC: 8742 Construction project management consultant
PA: Austin Alliance Electric, Inc.
    1807 Unit 104 Capitl Blvd
    Raleigh NC 27604
    843 297-8078

(G-14648)
AUTHENTIC TAILORING SERVICE
3207 Miller Rd (19802-2544)
PHONE.................302 740-1185
Mckinley Womack Junior, *Prin*
EMP: 5 EST: 2018
SALES (est): 183.38K **Privately Held**
SIC: 7219 Garment alteration and repair shop

(G-14649)
AUTHENTIK CHICK
1412 Kynlyn Dr (19809-2423)
PHONE.................267 815-4132
Nakesha Ross, *Pr*
EMP: 3 EST: 2017
SALES (est): 25K **Privately Held**
SIC: 2211 Apparel and outerwear fabrics, cotton

(G-14650)
AUTO CHEAP QUOTES INS-WLMGTN
813 E Newport Pike (19804-1920)
PHONE.................302 992-9736
Mark Coney, *Owner*
EMP: 5 EST: 2007
SALES (est): 68.84K **Privately Held**
SIC: 6411 Insurance agents, nec

(G-14651)
AUTOLAB INC
Also Called: Auto-Lab
1201 N Orange St Ste 600 (19801-1171)
PHONE.................416 820-1636
EMP: 25 EST: 2020

GEOGRAPHIC SECTION   Wilmington - New Castle County (G-14681)

SALES (est): 307.39K **Privately Held**
Web: www.autolabusa.com
SIC: 7538   General automotive repair shops

(G-14652)
AUTOMATION INC
408 Harvey Dr (19804-2493)
P.O. Box 3016 (19804-0016)
PHONE.................................302 999-0971
Donald Sheldrake Junior, *Pr*
Mary J Sheldrake, *VP*
EMP: 19 EST: 1970
SQ FT: 20,000
SALES (est): 1.89MM **Privately Held**
Web: www.automationinc.net
SIC: 3599 3625   Machine shop, jobbing and repair; Relays and industrial controls

(G-14653)
AUTOMATION PARTNERSHIP
Also Called: Tap
502 First State Blvd (19804-3746)
PHONE.................................302 478-9060
Richard Archer, *CEO*
EMP: 5 EST: 1997
SALES (est): 764.03K **Privately Held**
SIC: 5084   Robots, industrial

(G-14654)
AUTOMATION SOLUTIONS INC
20 Montchanin Rd Ste 200 (19807-2174)
PHONE.................................302 478-9060
Andrew Parrott, *Mgr*
EMP: 6
SALES (corp-wide): 8.8MM **Privately Held**
Web: www.automationsolutionsinc.com
SIC: 5021   Office and public building furniture
PA: Automation Solutions, Inc.
        38 3rd Ave Ste 100w
        Boston MA 02129
        617 681-6700

(G-14655)
AUTOMIZY INC
3422 Old Capitol Trl Ste 700 (19808-6124)
PHONE.................................361 253-8238
EMP: 6 EST: 2014
SALES (est): 46.16K **Privately Held**
Web: www.automizy.com
SIC: 7371   Computer software development

(G-14656)
AUTOMOTIVE SERVICES INC
Also Called: Northeast Body Shop
2510 Northeast Blvd (19802-4511)
PHONE.................................302 762-0100
Charles A Allen, *Pr*
Bonnie Allen, *Sec*
EMP: 14 EST: 1959
SQ FT: 5,000
SALES (est): 996.05K **Privately Held**
Web: www.northeastbodyshop.com
SIC: 7532 5521   Body shop, automotive; Automobiles, used cars only

(G-14657)
AUTOWEB TECHNOLOGIES INC
2801 Centerville Rd (19808)
PHONE.................................443 485-4200
Ben Vaughn, *CEO*
EMP: 5 EST: 2011
SALES (est): 310.96K **Privately Held**
Web: www.autowebtech.com
SIC: 7371   Computer software development

(G-14658)
AUTUMN HILL PATIO & LANDSCAPE
242 Barberry Dr (19808-1950)
PHONE.................................302 293-1183
Ryan Coyne, *Owner*

EMP: 8 EST: 2009
SALES (est): 488.88K **Privately Held**
Web: www.autumnhillpatio.com
SIC: 0781   Landscape services

(G-14659)
AUXO RAIL HOLDINGS LLC
251 Little Falls Dr (19808-1674)
PHONE.................................304 325-7245
Jeff Helminski, *Managing Member*
EMP: 75 EST: 2021
SALES (est): 1.47MM **Privately Held**
SIC: 4789   Railroad maintenance and repair services

(G-14660)
AV AUTO WORX LLC
124 Middleboro Rd (19804-1660)
PHONE.................................302 384-7646
EMP: 10 EST: 2014
SALES (est): 789.35K **Privately Held**
Web: www.avautoworx.com
SIC: 7538   General automotive repair shops

(G-14661)
AVACORE LLC
Also Called: Avacore
3524 Silverside Rd Ste 35b (19810-4929)
PHONE.................................302 327-8830
Kenneth Douglas, *Managing Member*
EMP: 5 EST: 2019
SALES (est): 671.24K **Privately Held**
Web: www.avacore.aero
SIC: 3728 5599   Aircraft body assemblies and parts; Aircraft dealers

(G-14662)
AVALANCHE CANYON FOUNDATION
501 Silverside Rd (19809-1374)
PHONE.................................800 839-1754
EMP: 5 EST: 2010
SALES (est): 75.22K **Privately Held**
SIC: 8699   Charitable organization

(G-14663)
AVALON DENTAL
34 Kiamensi Rd (19804-2908)
PHONE.................................302 999-8822
Parham Farhi, *Pr*
EMP: 13 EST: 2008
SALES (est): 224.12K **Privately Held**
Web: www.avalondentalde.com
SIC: 8021   Dentists' office

(G-14664)
AVALON DENTAL OF NEWPORT
6 Larch Ave Ste 402 (19804-2366)
PHONE.................................267 312-3184
EMP: 6 EST: 2019
SALES (est): 169.01K **Privately Held**
Web: www.avalondentalde.com
SIC: 8021   Dentists' office

(G-14665)
AVANTI HOMES LLC
4023 Kennett Pike (19807-2018)
PHONE.................................302 374-0999
EMP: 5 EST: 2018
SALES (est): 237K **Privately Held**
Web: www.avantihomesllc.com
SIC: 6531   Real estate agents and managers

(G-14666)
AVENUE CUTS INC
1700 N Scott St Lowr (19806-2356)
PHONE.................................302 655-1718
Kelly Hughes, *Pr*
EMP: 7 EST: 1990
SALES (est): 103.7K **Privately Held**
SIC: 7231   Hairdressers

(G-14667)
AVENUE MONTAIGNE INC
919 N Market St Ste 950 (19801-3036)
PHONE.................................310 926-6678
Erin Mihok, *CEO*
EMP: 10 EST: 2020
SALES (est): 432.82K **Privately Held**
Web: www.avenuemontaigne.com
SIC: 8742   Management consulting services

(G-14668)
AVERY INSTITUTE
3 Germay Dr Ste 4 (19804-1127)
PHONE.................................302 803-6784
EMP: 8 EST: 2019
SALES (est): 196.32K **Privately Held**
Web: www.averyinstitute.us
SIC: 8011   Offices and clinics of medical doctors

(G-14669)
AVIMAN MANAGEMENT LLC
3411 Silverside Rd Ste 101 (19810-4806)
PHONE.................................302 377-5788
EMP: 26 EST: 2003
SALES (est): 9.25MM **Privately Held**
Web: www.avimanmanagement.com
SIC: 1542 1622 7389   Commercial and office building contractors; Bridge, tunnel, and elevated highway construction; Business Activities at Non-Commercial Site

(G-14670)
AVIRM INC ✪
1201 N Orange St Ste 600one (19801-1155)
PHONE.................................626 603-1000
Bradley Mantha, *Pr*
Daniel Peragine, *
Bernard Cheng, *
Tyler Schelfhaut, *
EMP: 53 EST: 2022
SALES (est): 5.41MM **Privately Held**
SIC: 5065 7389   Electronic parts; Business services, nec

(G-14671)
AVIS CAR RENTAL
100 French St (19801-5016)
PHONE.................................302 654-8044
EMP: 7 EST: 2018
SALES (est): 62.7K **Privately Held**
Web: www.avis.com
SIC: 7514   Rent-a-car service

(G-14672)
AVIS CAR RENTAL
702 Philadelphia Pike (19809-2540)
PHONE.................................302 762-3825
EMP: 6 EST: 2018
SALES (est): 53.46K **Privately Held**
Web: www.avis.com
SIC: 7514   Rent-a-car service

(G-14673)
AVKIN INC
103 S James St (19804-2518)
PHONE.................................302 562-7468
Amy Cowperthwait, *CEO*
Mike Patterson, *COO*
Amy Bucha, *CSO*
EMP: 12 EST: 2015
SALES (est): 1.3MM **Privately Held**
Web: www.avkin.com
SIC: 5999 8299 3999   Education aids, devices and supplies; Educational services; Education aids, devices and supplies

(G-14674)
AVONTRO INC
251 Little Falls Dr (19808-1674)
PHONE.................................510 766-2803
Irfan Mohammed, *CEO*
EMP: 5 EST: 2018
SALES (est): 124.81K **Privately Held**
SIC: 8742   Human resource consulting services

(G-14675)
AVT PAINTS LLC
501 Silverside Rd Ste 105 (19809-1376)
PHONE.................................800 476-1634
◆ EMP: 5 EST: 2008
SALES (est): 214.94K **Privately Held**
SIC: 5198   Paints

(G-14676)
AWARENESS & THERAPEUTIC ATTACH
309 Walden Rd (19803-2423)
PHONE.................................302 655-6555
Beth Dovovan, *Prin*
EMP: 6 EST: 2016
SALES (est): 26.84K **Privately Held**
SIC: 8049   Offices of health practitioner

(G-14677)
AWAS LEASING ONE LLC
200 Bellevue Pkwy Ste 210 (19809-3709)
PHONE.................................425 440-6000
EMP: 10 EST: 2007
SALES (est): 327.41K **Privately Held**
SIC: 7359   Equipment rental and leasing, nec

(G-14678)
AXALTA COATING SYSTEMS LLC
1007 Market St (19898-1100)
PHONE.................................925 838-9876
EMP: 9
SALES (corp-wide): 4.88B **Publicly Held**
Web: www.axalta.com
SIC: 7389   Personal service agents, brokers, and bureaus
HQ: Axalta Coating Systems, Llc
        50 Applied Bank Blvd # 300
        Glen Mills PA 19342
        855 547-1461

(G-14679)
AXCHEM HOLDING COMPANY (PA)
1209 N Orange St (19801-1120)
PHONE.................................336 632-0500
Catherine T Hawkins, *Sec*
EMP: 6 EST: 2000
SALES (est): 8.14MM
SALES (corp-wide): 8.14MM **Privately Held**
Web: www.axchemgroup.com
SIC: 8748   Business consulting, nec

(G-14680)
AXENCIS INC
1201 N Orange St Ste 7160 (19801-1197)
PHONE.................................302 888-9002
Ralph Schoenfelder, *CEO*
EMP: 30 EST: 2020
SALES (est): 510.94K **Privately Held**
SIC: 8111   Patent, trademark and copyright law

(G-14681)
AXES GLOBAL INC
Also Called: Axes
2055 Limestone Rd Ste 200c (19808-5536)
PHONE.................................415 602-4049
Khaleel Musleh, *CEO*
EMP: 10 EST: 2021
SALES (est): 348.32K **Privately Held**

Wilmington - New Castle County (G-14682)

SIC: 7371 Computer software development and applications

(G-14682)
AXIOM DIST & FULFILLMENT ◊
1007 N Orange St Fl 4 (19801-1242)
PHONE..................................519 620-2000
Joe Sferrazza, *CEO*
EMP: 2 EST: 2022
SALES (est): 233.27K **Privately Held**
SIC: 3442 Metal doors, sash, and trim

(G-14683)
AXITECH INC
3411 Silverside Rd (19810-4812)
PHONE..................................248 318-9067
Matt Hodges, *CEO*
EMP: 7 EST: 2018
SALES (est): 32.18K **Privately Held**
SIC: 7379 Online services technology consultants

(G-14684)
AXMOS TECHNOLOGIES INC ◊
2810 N Church St (19802-4447)
PHONE..................................650 229-9094
Manuel E Torres Carmona, *CEO*
EMP: 30 EST: 2023
SALES (est): 788.31K **Privately Held**
SIC: 7371 Custom computer programming services

(G-14685)
AYALA PAINTING LLC
3706 Old Capitol Trl (19808-6036)
PHONE..................................208 777-2654
EMP: 9 EST: 2009
SALES (est): 860.14K **Privately Held**
Web: www.ayalapainting.com
SIC: 1721 Residential painting

(G-14686)
AYEA LLC
Also Called: Delaware Limo
2305 Pyle St (19805-3335)
PHONE..................................302 319-3329
Elorm Ahiamadjie, *Managing Member*
EMP: 5 EST: 2018
SALES (est): 428.27K **Privately Held**
SIC: 4119 Limousine rental, with driver

(G-14687)
AYON LANDSCAPING
313 Orinda Dr (19804-1115)
P.O. Box 30312 (19805-7312)
PHONE..................................302 275-0205
Bill Ayon, *Owner*
EMP: 5 EST: 2012
SALES (est): 59.33K **Privately Held**
Web: www.ayonlandscaping.com
SIC: 0781 Landscape services

(G-14688)
AZTEC COPIES LLC
Also Called: Aztec Printing and Design
3636 Silverside Rd (19810-5191)
PHONE..................................302 575-1993
Jeffrey Durham, *Pr*
Edward Dwornik, *VP*
EMP: 14 EST: 1998
SQ FT: 7,500
SALES (est): 2.48MM **Privately Held**
Web: www.aztecprintingand design.com
SIC: 2752 Offset printing

(G-14689)
AZUR GCS INC
1201 N Orange St Ste 7293 (19801-1271)
PHONE..................................302 884-6713
Andrew Thompson, *CEO*
EMP: 6 EST: 2008
SALES (est): 333.15K **Privately Held**
Web: www.azurgcs.com
SIC: 4813 Telephone communication, except radio

(G-14690)
B & B INDUSTRIES INC
1507 A St (19801-5411)
P.O. Box 2662 (19805-0662)
PHONE..................................302 655-6156
Michael A Bloom, *Pr*
David Bloom, *Sec*
Daniel Bloom, *VP*
EMP: 10 EST: 1985
SQ FT: 55,000
SALES (est): 1.06MM **Privately Held**
Web: www.iconde.com
SIC: 5051 Steel

(G-14691)
B & F CERAMICS
2644 Boxwood Dr (19810-1608)
PHONE..................................302 475-4721
EMP: 3 EST: 2013
SALES (est): 44.85K **Privately Held**
SIC: 3269 Pottery products, nec

(G-14692)
B & M MEATS INC
21 Commerce St (19801-5425)
P.O. Box 491 (19899-0491)
PHONE..................................302 655-5521
Yossi Baruch, *Pr*
Annette Baruch, *Sec*
EMP: 12 EST: 1950
SQ FT: 3,000
SALES (est): 9.8MM **Privately Held**
Web: www.bmphillysteaks.com
SIC: 5147 Meats, fresh
PA: Wonder Meats, Inc.
20 Broad St Ste 1
Carlstadt NJ 07072

(G-14693)
B AND B AUTOMOTIVE
305 Commercial Dr (19805-1906)
PHONE..................................302 559-2087
William Bryant Junior, *Prin*
EMP: 6 EST: 2016
SALES (est): 220.17K **Privately Held**
SIC: 7538 General automotive repair shops

(G-14694)
B AND D DETAILING
2800 Governor Printz Blvd (19802-3734)
PHONE..................................302 543-6221
Daywon Hunter, *Owner*
EMP: 6 EST: 2014
SALES (est): 58.9K **Privately Held**
Web: www.autodetailingwilmington.com
SIC: 7542 Washing and polishing, automotive

(G-14695)
B BOONE PAINTING
2029 Wildwood Dr (19805-1060)
PHONE..................................302 740-2576
Victoria Boone, *Prin*
EMP: 5 EST: 2009
SALES (est): 75.04K **Privately Held**
SIC: 1721 Painting and paper hanging

(G-14696)
B C CONSULTING
1521 Concord Pike Ste 202 (19803-3645)
PHONE..................................215 534-3805
Brian Criscuolo, *Prin*
EMP: 5 EST: 2008
SALES (est): 104.9K **Privately Held**

SIC: 8748 Business consulting, nec

(G-14697)
B DOHERTY INC
5301 Limestone Rd Ste 100 (19808-1251)
P.O. Box 7543 (19714-7543)
PHONE..................................302 239-3500
Bernard Doherty, *Pr*
EMP: 7 EST: 1999
SALES (est): 1.02MM **Privately Held**
Web: www.dohertyandassociates.com
SIC: 1522 1542 Residential construction, nec
; Commercial and office building contractors

(G-14698)
B F P SOTHEBYS INTL REALTY
5701 Kennett Pike (19807-1311)
PHONE..................................302 545-5266
Debbie Portale, *Mgr*
EMP: 7 EST: 2018
SALES (est): 212.52K **Privately Held**
Web: www.bfpsir.com
SIC: 6531 Real estate brokers and agents

(G-14699)
B F P TRADING LLC
214 E Lea Blvd (19802-2301)
PHONE..................................347 927-0535
Mordechai Rosenfeld, *Managing Member*
EMP: 10 EST: 2020
SALES (est): 731.28K **Privately Held**
SIC: 5065 Electronic parts and equipment, nec

(G-14700)
B F SHIN OF SALISBURY INC
1715 Lovering Ave (19806-2119)
PHONE..................................302 652-3521
James Shinn, *Pr*
EMP: 7 EST: 1994
SALES (est): 1.02MM **Privately Held**
SIC: 5198 Paints

(G-14701)
B FRANK SHINN PAINT CO (PA)
1715 Lovering Ave (19806-2119)
PHONE..................................302 652-3521
EMP: 12 EST: 1903
SALES (est): 1.51MM
SALES (corp-wide): 1.51MM **Privately Held**
Web: www.shinnpaint.com
SIC: 5231 5198 Paint; Paints

(G-14702)
B LAWRENCE HOMES LLC
1907 Dorcas Ln (19806-1163)
PHONE..................................302 559-1779
EMP: 6 EST: 2004
SALES (est): 110.43K **Privately Held**
Web: www.blawrencehomes.com
SIC: 1521 7389 General remodeling, single-family houses; Business Activities at Non-Commercial Site

(G-14703)
B SAFE INC (PA)
Also Called: Honeywell Authorized Dealer
109 Baltimore Ave (19805-2554)
PHONE..................................302 633-1833
Philip H Gardner, *Pr*
Joseph Gallagher, *
EMP: 26 EST: 1978
SALES (est): 9.72MM
SALES (corp-wide): 9.72MM **Privately Held**
Web: www.bsafealarms.com
SIC: 7382 Burglar alarm maintenance and monitoring

(G-14704)
B WILLIAMS HOLDING CORP (HQ)
1011 Centre Rd Ste 319 (19805-1266)
PHONE..................................302 656-8596
Kenneth Kubacki, *Pr*
EMP: 17 EST: 1995
SALES (est): 18.8MM
SALES (corp-wide): 3.54B **Publicly Held**
SIC: 3579 3661 3861 7359 Mailing machines
; Facsimile equipment; Photocopy machines
; Business machine and electronic equipment rental services
PA: Pitney Bowes Inc.
3001 Summer St
Stamford CT 06905
203 356-5000

(G-14705)
B&F DRYWALL
2896 Shipley Rd (19810-3213)
PHONE..................................302 218-2467
Mark Barbato, *Prin*
EMP: 7 EST: 2017
SALES (est): 55.51K **Privately Held**
SIC: 1742 Drywall

(G-14706)
B2W2 INC
809 N Washington St (19801-1509)
P.O. Box 1637 (19899-1637)
PHONE..................................302 658-5177
EMP: 9 EST: 2010
SALES (est): 295.43K **Privately Held**
SIC: 8322 Individual and family services

(G-14707)
BA CREDIT CARD TRUST
1100 N King St (19884-0011)
PHONE..................................704 386-5681
EMP: 20 EST: 2001
SALES (est): 968.72K
SALES (corp-wide): 94.95B **Publicly Held**
SIC: 6733 Trusts, nec
PA: Bank Of America Corporation
100 N Tryon St Ste 2650
Charlotte NC 28202
704 386-5681

(G-14708)
BAABAO INC
300 Delaware Ave Ste 210a (19801-6601)
PHONE..................................415 990-6767
Jennifer Chao, *CEO*
Pei-pei Ni, *Pr*
EMP: 2 EST: 2016
SALES (est): 68.41K **Privately Held**
SIC: 7372 Application computer software

(G-14709)
BABBLE PLATFORMS INC
1007 N Orange St (19801-1239)
PHONE..................................416 825-0602
Cecilia Rozario, *CEO*
EMP: 4
SALES (est): 73.93K **Privately Held**
SIC: 7372 Application computer software

(G-14710)
BABE STYLING STUDIO INC
213 N Market St (19801-2527)
PHONE..................................302 543-7738
Ebon Flagg, *Pr*
EMP: 8 EST: 2009
SALES (est): 45.02K **Privately Held**
Web: www.babestylingstudios.com
SIC: 7231 Hairdressers

(G-14711)
BABES ON SQUARE
1413 Foulk Rd Ste 100 (19803-2760)

GEOGRAPHIC SECTION

Wilmington - New Castle County (G-14737)

PHONE..................302 477-9190
Andrea Keating, *Owner*
EMP: 6 **EST:** 1996
SALES (est): 429.95K **Privately Held**
Web: www.babesonthesquare.com
SIC: 8351 Group day care center

(G-14712)
BACK CLINIC INC
5550 Kirkwood Hwy (19808-5000)
PHONE..................302 995-2100
Ellen H Levine, *Dir*
EMP: 18 **EST:** 1983
SALES (est): 417.46K **Privately Held**
Web: www.backclinicinc.com
SIC: 8049 Physical therapist

(G-14713)
BACK TO BLANCE HEALING THERAPY
2844 Kennedy Rd (19810-3430)
PHONE..................302 478-6470
Gail Pineault, *Prin*
EMP: 7 **EST:** 2014
SALES (est): 66.88K **Privately Held**
SIC: 8093 Rehabilitation center, outpatient treatment

(G-14714)
BADGES SPORTS BAR
300 N Union St (19805-3455)
PHONE..................302 256-0202
EMP: 5 **EST:** 2013
SALES (est): 117.69K **Privately Held**
SIC: 5199 Badges

(G-14715)
BAIL ENFORCEMENT AGENT
1601 Milltown Rd (19808-4027)
PHONE..................302 543-6305
Lionel Sainsume, *Ofcr*
EMP: 5 **EST:** 2015
SALES (est): 174.68K **Privately Held**
SIC: 6351 Surety insurance

(G-14716)
BAIZ NANCY MILLER-
3711 Kennett Pike Ste 130 (19807-2156)
PHONE..................302 576-6821
Nancy Miller-baiz, *Prin*
EMP: 5 **EST:** 2005
SALES (est): 131.06K **Privately Held**
SIC: 6531 Real estate brokers and agents

(G-14717)
BAKER JAMES CCJR DDS
1304 N Broom St Uppr (19806-4239)
PHONE..................302 658-9511
James C Baker Junior D.d.s., *Owner*
EMP: 6 **EST:** 1941
SALES (est): 233.06K **Privately Held**
SIC: 8021 Dentists' office

(G-14718)
BALANCECO2 INC
103 Ascension Dr (19808-7901)
PHONE..................302 494-9476
Natarajan Kumaresan, *CEO*
Selva Kumar, *Ex Dir*
EMP: 7 **EST:** 2009
SALES (est): 83.46K **Privately Held**
Web: www.balanceco2.ca
SIC: 4931 Electric and other services combined

(G-14719)
BALANCED AUDIO TECHNOLOGY
26 Beethoven Dr (19807-1923)
PHONE..................302 996-9496
Victor Khomenko, *Owner*

EMP: 6 **EST:** 1997
SALES (est): 69.03K **Privately Held**
Web: www.balanced.com
SIC: 3651 Household audio and video equipment

(G-14720)
BALANCED BODY INC
903 Shipley Rd (19803-4927)
PHONE..................302 373-3463
Nicole Stoessel, *Prin*
EMP: 6 **EST:** 2012
SALES (est): 81.8K **Privately Held**
SIC: 7532 Body shop, automotive

(G-14721)
BALFOUR BEATTY LLC (HQ)
1011 Centre Rd Ste 322 (19805-1266)
PHONE..................302 573-3873
Peter Zinkin, *VP*
Leslie Cohn, *VP*
Joanne Bonfiglio, *Asst VP*
Barry Crozier, *Treas*
Christine Schiltz, *Sec*
◆ **EMP:** 5 **EST:** 1979
SALES (est): 5.21B
SALES (corp-wide): 9.19B **Privately Held**
Web: www.balfourbeattyus.com
SIC: 1542 8712 8741 Commercial and office building, new construction; Architectural engineering; Management services
PA: Balfour Beatty Plc
5 Churchill Place Canary Wharf
London E14 5
207 216-6800

(G-14722)
BALICK & BALICK PLLC
711 N King St (19801-3503)
PHONE..................302 658-4265
Adam Balick, *Pt*
Autum Schneider, *Sec*
EMP: 7 **EST:** 1977
SQ FT: 2,000
SALES (est): 845.79K **Privately Held**
Web: www.balick.com
SIC: 8111 General practice attorney, lawyer

(G-14723)
BALLARD SPAHR LLP
919 N Market St Ste 1201 (19801-3062)
PHONE..................302 252-4465
Tobby Daluz Mng Ptrn, *Brnch Mgr*
EMP: 7
SALES (corp-wide): 224.22MM **Privately Held**
Web: www.ballardspahr.com
SIC: 8111 General practice attorney, lawyer
PA: Ballard Spahr Llp
1735 Market St Fl 51
Philadelphia PA 19103
215 665-8500

(G-14724)
BALLISTICS TECHNOLOGY INTL LTD (PA)
2207 Concord Pike # 657 (19803-2908)
PHONE..................877 291-1111
James Sigurdson, *Pr*
▲ **EMP:** 2 **EST:** 1996
SQ FT: 13,000
SALES (est): 831.17K
SALES (corp-wide): 831.17K **Privately Held**
SIC: 3272 Concrete products, nec

(G-14725)
BALLY HOLDING COMPANY DELAWARE (HQ)
3411 Silverside Rd Ste 100 (19810-4812)

PHONE..................610 845-7511
John J Dau, *Ch*
John J Dau, *Ch Bd*
James P Reichart, *Pr*
Ann D Conway, *VP*
Carol L Beadencup, *Treas*
EMP: 7 **EST:** 1981
SALES (est): 15.37MM
SALES (corp-wide): 15.37MM **Privately Held**
SIC: 2499 Kitchen, bathroom, and household ware: wood
PA: Bally Holding Company Of Pennsylvania
30 S 7th St
Bally PA 19503
610 845-7511

(G-14726)
BALU GANESH R MD
390 Mitch Rd (19804-3943)
PHONE..................302 992-9191
Ganesh Balu, *Prin*
EMP: 6 **EST:** 2017
SALES (est): 107.03K **Privately Held**
Web: www.painrehab.net
SIC: 8011 Offices and clinics of medical doctors

(G-14727)
BANACOM SIGNS INC
3201 Miller Rd Ste A (19802-2542)
PHONE..................302 429-6243
Hector Delfabro, *Pr*
Gabriel Delfabro, *Treas*
EMP: 4 **EST:** 1985
SALES (est): 235.24K **Privately Held**
SIC: 3993 Signs and advertising specialties

(G-14728)
BANANA SPOT CO (PA) ✪
1201 N Orange St Ste 600 (19801-1171)
PHONE..................916 342-9519
Eric Chandler, *CEO*
EMP: 10 **EST:** 2023
SALES (est): 394.7K
SALES (corp-wide): 394.7K **Privately Held**
SIC: 8399 Social services, nec

(G-14729)
BANCORP INC (PA)
409 Silverside Rd Ste 105 (19809-1771)
PHONE..................302 385-5000
Damian M Kozlowski, *CEO*
Daniel G Cohen, *Ch Bd*
Paul Frenkiel, *Ex VP*
Gregor Garry, *Ex VP*
Mark Connolly, *CCO*
EMP: 97 **EST:** 1999
SQ FT: 70,968
SALES (est): 413.98MM
SALES (corp-wide): 413.98MM **Publicly Held**
Web: www.thebancorp.com
SIC: 6021 National commercial banks

(G-14730)
BANCORP BANK NATIONAL ASSN (HQ)
Also Called: Bancorp Bank, The
409 Silverside Rd Ste 105 (19809-1771)
PHONE..................302 385-5000
Betsy Z Cohen, *CEO*
Daniel G Cohen, *Ch Bd*
Frank M Mastrangelo, *Pr*
Marty Egan, *CFO*
Gregor Garry, *Ex VP*
EMP: 40 **EST:** 2000
SALES (est): 326.56MM
SALES (corp-wide): 413.98MM **Publicly Held**

Web: thebancorp.mybankingservices.com
SIC: 6029 Commercial banks, nec
PA: The Bancorp Inc
409 Silverside Rd Ste 105
Wilmington DE 19809
302 385-5000

(G-14731)
BANCORP COML MRTG 2018-CRE4 TR
409 Silverside Rd (19809-1770)
PHONE..................302 385-5000
EMP: 9
SALES (est): 210.51K **Privately Held**
Web: www.thebancorp.com
SIC: 6733 Trusts, nec

(G-14732)
BANCORP COML MRTG 2019-CRE6 TR
409 Silverside Rd (19809-1770)
PHONE..................302 385-5000
EMP: 6
SALES (est): 639.79K **Privately Held**
Web: www.thebancorp.com
SIC: 6733 Trusts, nec

(G-14733)
BANCROFT
904 N Broom St (19806-4528)
PHONE..................302 654-1408
EMP: 8 **EST:** 2018
SALES (est): 48.67K **Privately Held**
Web: www.bancroftconstruction.com
SIC: 1542 Commercial and office building, new construction

(G-14734)
BANCROFT BEHAVIORAL HEALTH
1601 Milltown Rd Ste 12 (19808-4084)
PHONE..................302 273-2319
EMP: 6
SALES (est): 108.08K **Privately Held**
Web: www.bancrofthealth.com
SIC: 8049 Clinical psychologist

(G-14735)
BANCROFT BEHAVIORAL HEALTH
1601 Milltown Rd (19808-4027)
PHONE..................302 690-0626
Erica Why, *Prin*
EMP: 6 **EST:** 2016
SALES (est): 155.34K **Privately Held**
Web: www.bancrofthealth.com
SIC: 8099 Health and allied services, nec

(G-14736)
BANCROFT BEHAVIORAL HEALTH INC
1601 Milltown Rd Ste 12 (19808-4084)
PHONE..................302 502-3255
EMP: 5 **EST:** 2019
SALES (est): 240.88K **Privately Held**
Web: www.bancrofthealth.com
SIC: 8093 Mental health clinic, outpatient

(G-14737)
BANCROFT CARPENTRY COMPANY (HQ)
44 Bancroft Mills Rd (19806-2028)
PHONE..................302 655-3434
Stephen M Mockbee, *Pr*
Nash Childs, *VP*
John Barr, *Treas*
EMP: 4 **EST:** 1981
SQ FT: 4,000
SALES (est): 3.19MM
SALES (corp-wide): 125.83MM **Privately Held**

Wilmington - New Castle County (G-14738)   GEOGRAPHIC SECTION

SIC: **2431** 2434 Millwork; Wood kitchen cabinets
PA: Bancroft Construction Company
1300 N Grant Ave Ste 101
Wilmington DE 19806
302 655-3434

(G-14738)
BANCROFT CONSTRUCTION COMPANY (PA)
1300 N Grant Ave Ste 101 (19806-2456)
PHONE..................................302 655-3434
Greg Sawka, *CEO*
Jack Barr, *
John Barr, *
Casey Mccabe, *CFO*
▲ **EMP:** 101 **EST:** 1975
SALES (est): 125.83M
SALES (corp-wide): 125.83MM **Privately Held**
Web: www.bancroftconstruction.com
SIC: **1542** 1541 Commercial and office building, new construction; Industrial buildings and warehouses

(G-14739)
BANCROFT HOMES INC
1300 N Grant Ave Ste 204 (19806-2456)
PHONE..................................302 655-5461
Steven Mockbee, *Pr*
EMP: 8 **EST:** 1982
SALES (est): 2.34MM **Privately Held**
Web: www.bancrofthomes.com
SIC: **1521** New construction, single-family houses

(G-14740)
BANCROFT NEUROHEALTH
Also Called: BANCROFT NEUROHEALTH, A NEW JERSEY NONPROFIT CORPORATION
321 E 11th St (19801-3422)
PHONE..................................302 691-8531
Carol Chapin, *Ex Dir*
EMP: 53
Web: www.bancroft.org
SIC: **8099** Blood related health services
HQ: Bancroft, A New Jersey Nonprofit Corporation
1255 Caldwell Rd
Cherry Hill NJ 08034
844 234-8387

(G-14741)
BANCROFT VLANT JOINT VENTR LLC
1300 N Grant Ave Ste 101 (19806-2456)
PHONE..................................717 553-0165
Robert Judge Mbe, *Prin*
EMP: 5 **EST:** 2021
SALES (est): 122.74K **Privately Held**
SIC: **8741** Management services

(G-14742)
BANK AMERICA NATIONAL ASSN
Also Called: Bank of America
1100 N King St (19884-0011)
PHONE..................................302 765-2108
Jason Donovan, *Prin*
EMP: 19
SALES (corp-wide): 94.95B **Publicly Held**
Web: www.bankofamerica.com
SIC: **6021** National commercial banks
HQ: Bank Of America, National Association
100 N Tryon St
Charlotte NC 28202
704 386-5681

(G-14743)
BANK AMERICA NATIONAL ASSN
Also Called: Bank of America
5215 Concord Pike (19803-1416)
PHONE..................................302 478-1005
EMP: 9
SALES (corp-wide): 94.95B **Publicly Held**
Web: www.bankofamerica.com
SIC: **6021** National commercial banks
HQ: Bank Of America, National Association
100 N Tryon St
Charlotte NC 28202
704 386-5681

(G-14744)
BANK AMERICA NATIONAL ASSN
Also Called: Bank of America
3816 Kennett Pike (19807-2302)
PHONE..................................302 656-5399
EMP: 9
SALES (corp-wide): 94.95B **Publicly Held**
Web: www.bankofamerica.com
SIC: **6021** National commercial banks
HQ: Bank Of America, National Association
100 N Tryon St
Charlotte NC 28202
704 386-5681

(G-14745)
BANK AMERICA NATIONAL ASSN
Also Called: Bank of America, N.a
5215 Concord Pike (19803-1416)
PHONE..................................704 386-8539
EMP: 7
SALES (corp-wide): 93.85B **Publicly Held**
Web: www.bankofamerica.com
SIC: **6021** National commercial banks
HQ: Bank Of America, National Association
100 N Tryon St
Charlotte NC 28202
704 386-5681

(G-14746)
BANK AMERICA NATIONAL ASSN
1020 N French St (19884-0009)
PHONE..................................704 386-8539
EMP: 7
SALES (corp-wide): 93.85B **Publicly Held**
Web: www.bankofamerica.com
SIC: **6021** National commercial banks
HQ: Bank Of America, National Association
100 N Tryon St
Charlotte NC 28202
704 386-5681

(G-14747)
BANK FILLERS ENTERTAINMENT LLC
Also Called: Bfe
831 N Tatnall St Ste M (19801-1717)
PHONE..................................302 930-0262
EMP: 10 **EST:** 2020
SALES (est): 100K **Privately Held**
SIC: **7929** Entertainers and entertainment groups

(G-14748)
BANK OF NEW YORK MELLON CORP
4005 Kennett Pike (19807-2018)
PHONE..................................302 421-2207
Gregg Landis, *Brnch Mgr*
EMP: 8
SALES (corp-wide): 19.99B **Publicly Held**
Web: www.bnymellon.com
SIC: **6722** Money market mutual funds
PA: The Bank Of New York Mellon Corporation
240 E Greenwich St
New York NY 10007
212 495-1784

(G-14749)
BANKER STEEL CO LLC
1209 N Orange St (19801-1120)
PHONE..................................708 478-0111
EMP: 7 **EST:** 2015
SALES (est): 281.07K **Privately Held**
Web: www.bankersteel.com
SIC: **4212** Local trucking, without storage

(G-14750)
BANKRUPTCY ANYWHERE
922 New Rd (19805-5199)
PHONE..................................302 426-4777
Mark Billion, *Prin*
EMP: 5 **EST:** 2017
SALES (est): 93.69K **Privately Held**
SIC: **8111** Bankruptcy law

(G-14751)
BANRIS CONSTRUCTION LLC
347 Mitchell Dr (19808-1362)
PHONE..................................302 722-0958
Ricardo Banarez, *Prin*
EMP: 5 **EST:** 2018
SALES (est): 244.65K **Privately Held**
Web: www.banrisconstruction.com
SIC: **1521** Single-family housing construction

(G-14752)
BAR & ASSOCIATES LTD
Also Called: Bar & Associates Intr Design
3410 Old Capitol Trl Ste 2 (19808-6152)
PHONE..................................302 999-9233
Humberto Humes, *Pr*
EMP: 7 **EST:** 1987
SALES (est): 569.78K **Privately Held**
SIC: **7389** Interior design services

(G-14753)
BARAMI DE INC
735 S Market St Ste A (19801-5246)
PHONE..................................201 993-9678
Elya Barami Dze, *Pr*
EMP: 8 **EST:** 2014
SALES (est): 438.91K **Privately Held**
Web: www.barami.us
SIC: **4225** General warehousing and storage

(G-14754)
BARBACANE THORNTON & COMPANY
3411 Silverside Rd Ste 202 (19810-4812)
PHONE..................................302 478-8940
Robert M Barbacane, *Pt*
Pamela Baker, *Pt*
Frank Defroda, *Pt*
Al Pisanelli, *Pt*
EMP: 25 **EST:** 1978
SALES (est): 2.46MM **Privately Held**
Web: www.btcpa.com
SIC: **8721** Certified public accountant

(G-14755)
BARBARA GRAPHICS INC
Also Called: Signs Now
506 First State Blvd (19804-3746)
PHONE..................................302 636-9040
Barbara Carlson, *Pr*
Mark Carlson, *VP*
EMP: 3 **EST:** 1999
SALES (est): 208.08K **Privately Held**
Web: www.signsnow.com
SIC: **3993** Signs and advertising specialties

(G-14756)
BARBARA MOORE FINE ART
1514 Ridge Rd (19809-1832)
P.O. Box 179 (19317-0179)
PHONE..................................610 357-6100
EMP: 5 **EST:** 2018
SALES (est): 31.35K **Privately Held**
Web: www.barbaramoorefineart.com
SIC: **8412** Art gallery

(G-14757)
BARBIZON OF DELAWARE INC
Also Called: Barbizon School of Modeling
17 Trolley Sq Ste B (19806)
PHONE..................................302 658-6666
Joan S Bernard, *Pr*
EMP: 22 **EST:** 1980
SALES (est): 1.51MM **Privately Held**
Web: www.barbizonchique.com
SIC: **8299** 7361 Finishing school, charm and modeling; Model registry

(G-14758)
BARCLAY & ASSOCIATES PC
2401 Kentmere Pkwy (19806-2026)
PHONE..................................515 292-3023
Gregory P Barclay, *Prin*
EMP: 6 **EST:** 2017
SALES (est): 86.15K **Privately Held**
Web: www.drbarclay.com
SIC: **8049** Offices of health practitioner

(G-14759)
BARCLAYS BANK DELAWARE (DH)
Also Called: BARCLAYCARD US
100 S West St (19801-5015)
P.O. Box 8801 (19899-8801)
PHONE..................................302 255-8000
Barry Rodrigues, *CEO*
James Stewart, *
EMP: 260 **EST:** 2000
SALES (est): 3.97B
SALES (corp-wide): 44.49B **Privately Held**
Web: cards.barclaycardus.com
SIC: **6035** Federal savings banks
HQ: Barclays Financial Corporation
125 S West St
Wilmington DE 19801
302 622-8990

(G-14760)
BARCLAYS FINANCIAL CORPORATION
100 S West St (19801-5015)
PHONE..................................302 652-6201
EMP: 750
SALES (corp-wide): 44.49B **Privately Held**
Web: cards.barclaycardus.com
SIC: **6282** Investment advice
HQ: Barclays Financial Corporation
125 S West St
Wilmington DE 19801
302 622-8990

(G-14761)
BARDELL VIDEO PRODUCTIONS
212 Potomac Rd (19803-3121)
PHONE..................................302 377-9936
Ralph Bardell, *Prin*
EMP: 5 **EST:** 2009
SALES (est): 100K **Privately Held**
SIC: **7812** Video production

(G-14762)
BARGAIN TIRE
3018 Governor Printz Blvd (19802-2829)
PHONE..................................302 764-8900
EMP: 5 **EST:** 2019
SALES (est): 316.31K **Privately Held**
Web: www.bargaintireandservice.com
SIC: **7539** Automotive repair shops, nec

(G-14763)
BARGAIN TIRE & SERVICE INC
3415 N Market St Ste 17 (19802-2731)
PHONE..................................302 764-8900

▲ = Import ▼ = Export
◆ = Import/Export

Mario Ferroni, *Pr*
Christopher Russ, *Mgr*
EMP: 10 **EST:** 1961
SQ FT: 5,000
SALES (est): 1.3MM **Privately Held**
SIC: 5531 5014 7539 Automotive tires; Tires and tubes; Shock absorber replacement

(G-14764)
BARI CONCRETE CNSTR CORP
202 New Rd (19805-4140)
P.O. Box 2540 (19805-0540)
PHONE..................................302 384-7093
EMP: 8 **EST:** 2013
SALES (est): 449.5K **Privately Held**
Web: www.bariconcretecorp.com
SIC: 5032 1521 Concrete and cinder building products; Single-family housing construction

(G-14765)
BARI CONCRETE CONTRACTORS
1805 W 8th St (19805-3033)
PHONE..................................302 757-9512
Louis Delloso, *Prin*
EMP: 9 **EST:** 2017
SALES (est): 467.15K **Privately Held**
Web: www.bariconcretecorp.com
SIC: 1771 Concrete work

(G-14766)
BARLOWS UPHOLSTERY INC
Also Called: Barlow Upholstery
1002 W 28th St (19802-2999)
PHONE..................................302 655-3955
David Barlow, *Pr*
Jay Barlow, *VP*
Barbara Pfarner, *Sec*
EMP: 4 **EST:** 1958
SQ FT: 16,000
SALES (est): 272.94K **Privately Held**
Web: www.barlowupholstery.com
SIC: 2512 7641 2391 Upholstered household furniture; Reupholstery; Draperies, plastic and textile: from purchased materials

(G-14767)
BARONSKY PATRICK & ASSOCIATES
2643 Bellows Dr (19810-1013)
PHONE..................................302 529-7585
EMP: 6 **EST:** 2017
SALES (est): 59.57K **Privately Held**
Web: www.pbassociates.us
SIC: 7389 Building inspection service

(G-14768)
BARROJA VENTURES LLC
Also Called: Barroja
1709 Delaware Ave (19806-2329)
PHONE..................................302 256-0883
EMP: 5 **EST:** 2019
SALES (est): 468.28K **Privately Held**
SIC: 8621 Bar association

(G-14769)
BARRY MANAGEMENT GROUP DE LLC
1715 Montgomery Rd (19805-1248)
PHONE..................................302 480-0519
EMP: 3 **EST:** 2020
SALES (est): 500K **Privately Held**
SIC: 1389 Construction, repair, and dismantling services

(G-14770)
BARSHAY STEPHANIE LPLMH
Also Called: Stephanie Barshay Lplmh
1200 N Van Buren St (19806-4313)
PHONE..................................302 312-6466

Stephanie Kim Barshay, *Prin*
EMP: 8 **EST:** 2011
SALES (est): 70.76K **Privately Held**
SIC: 8322 Social worker

(G-14771)
BASE CARRIERS LLC
Also Called: Base Carriers
501 Garasches Ln (19801-5524)
P.O. Box 2048 (19899-2048)
PHONE..................................215 559-1132
EMP: 6 **EST:** 2017
SALES (est): 255.56K **Privately Held**
SIC: 8742 Transportation consultant

(G-14772)
BASELL CAPITAL CORPORATION
2 Righter Pkwy Ste 300 (19803-1551)
PHONE..................................302 683-8000
EMP: 14 **EST:** 2009
SALES (est): 1.43MM **Privately Held**
SIC: 2869 Industrial organic chemicals, nec

(G-14773)
BASEMENT GURUS LLC
244 W Champlain Ave (19804-1838)
PHONE..................................800 834-6584
Daniel Kelly, *Managing Member*
EMP: 20 **EST:** 2019
SALES (est): 1.29MM **Privately Held**
Web: www.basementwaterproofinggurus.com
SIC: 1799 Waterproofing

(G-14774)
BASF CORPORATION
Also Called: Coating Effects Div
205 S James St (19804-2424)
PHONE..................................302 992-5600
EMP: 200
SALES (corp-wide): 90.7B **Privately Held**
Web: www.basf.com
SIC: 2869 2865 Industrial organic chemicals, nec; Cyclic crudes and intermediates
HQ: Basf Corporation
100 Park Ave
Florham Park NJ 07932
800 962-7831

(G-14775)
BASF UK FINANCE LLC (PA)
1209 N Orange St (19801-1120)
PHONE..................................973 245-6000
EMP: 6 **EST:** 2016
SALES (est): 1.02MM
SALES (corp-wide): 1.02MM **Privately Held**
SIC: 6153 Direct working capital financing

(G-14776)
BAT CAPITAL CORPORATION
103 Foulk Rd Ste 120 (19803-3747)
PHONE..................................302 691-6323
Carl L Schoenbachler, *Pr*
Carl L Schoenbachler, *VP*
Susan Ivey, *CEO*
EMP: 21 **EST:** 1981
SALES (est): 945.49K **Privately Held**
SIC: 5194 Cigarettes
HQ: B.A.T Industries P.L.C.
Globe House
London WC2R
207 845-1000

(G-14777)
BAT ELECTRONICS INC
Also Called: Balanced Audio Technology
1300 First State Blvd Ste A (19804)
PHONE..................................302 999-8855
James Davis, *Pr*

EMP: 6 **EST:** 2012
SALES (est): 895.44K **Privately Held**
Web: www.balanced.com
SIC: 3651 Audio electronic systems
PA: Audiophile Music Direct Inc.
1811 W Bryn Mawr Ave
Chicago IL 60660

(G-14778)
BATTA RAMESH C ASSOCIATES PA (PA)
4600 Linden Hill Rd Ste 102 (19808)
PHONE..................................302 998-9463
Ramesh C Batta, *Pr*
Mary Batta, *
Michelle Batta, *
EMP: 25 **EST:** 1978
SQ FT: 2,400
SALES (est): 2.4MM
SALES (corp-wide): 2.4MM **Privately Held**
Web: www.rcbatta.com
SIC: 8711 8713 Civil engineering; Surveying services

(G-14779)
BATTAGLIA JOSEPH A & DIAMOND
900 Foulk Rd Ste 200 (19803-3155)
PHONE..................................302 655-8868
Steven Diamond, *Owner*
EMP: 5 **EST:** 1997
SALES (est): 242.35K **Privately Held**
SIC: 8031 Offices and clinics of osteopathic physicians

(G-14780)
BAUER FAMILY FOUNDATION INC
501 Silverside Rd (19809-1374)
PHONE..................................800 639-1754
EMP: 5
SALES (est): 1.03MM **Privately Held**
SIC: 8699 Charitable organization

(G-14781)
BAUMANN INDUSTRIES INC
2412 W Heather Rd Ste 200 (19803-2720)
PHONE..................................302 593-1049
Bruce Ritterson, *Prin*
EMP: 3 **EST:** 2005
SALES (est): 185.34K **Privately Held**
Web: www.baumannindustries.com
SIC: 3999 Barber and beauty shop equipment

(G-14782)
BAXET GROUP INC
919 N Market St Ste 950 (19801-3036)
PHONE..................................917 938-7088
EMP: 5 **EST:** 2019
SALES (est): 46.16K **Privately Held**
SIC: 7371 Computer software development and applications

(G-14783)
BAY AREA INFLATABLES LLC (PA)
28 Whitekirk Dr (19808-1347)
PHONE..................................302 379-2821
EMP: 7 **EST:** 2018
SALES (est): 127.19K
SALES (corp-wide): 127.19K **Privately Held**
Web: www.bayarea-inflatables.com
SIC: 7359 Party supplies rental services

(G-14784)
BAYADA HOME HEALTH CARE INC
Also Called: Delaware Assistive Care
4250 Lancaster Pike Ste 310 (19805-1520)
PHONE..................................302 351-1244
EMP: 60
SALES (corp-wide): 694.21MM **Privately Held**

Web: www.bayada.com
SIC: 8082 Visiting nurse service
PA: Bayada Home Health Care, Inc.
1 W Main St
Moorestown NJ 08057
856 231-1000

(G-14785)
BAYADA HOME HEALTH CARE INC
4250 Lancaster Pike Ste 308 (19805-1520)
PHONE..................................302 351-3633
EMP: 60
SALES (corp-wide): 694.21MM **Privately Held**
Web: www.bayada.com
SIC: 8082 Visiting nurse service
PA: Bayada Home Health Care, Inc.
1 W Main St
Moorestown NJ 08057
856 231-1000

(G-14786)
BAYADA HOME HEALTH CARE INC
4250 Lancaster Pike Ste 300 (19805-1520)
PHONE..................................302 658-3000
EMP: 60
SALES (corp-wide): 694.21MM **Privately Held**
Web: www.bayada.com
SIC: 8082 Visiting nurse service
PA: Bayada Home Health Care, Inc.
1 W Main St
Moorestown NJ 08057
856 231-1000

(G-14787)
BAYADA HOME HEALTH CARE INC
Also Called: Delaware Nursing Adult
4250 Lancaster Pike Ste 312 (19805-1520)
PHONE..................................302 351-3636
EMP: 59
SALES (corp-wide): 694.21MM **Privately Held**
Web: www.bayada.com
SIC: 8082 Visiting nurse service
PA: Bayada Home Health Care, Inc.
1 W Main St
Moorestown NJ 08057
856 231-1000

(G-14788)
BAYESIAN HEALTH INC
251 Little Falls Dr (19808-1674)
PHONE..................................408 205-8035
Suchi Saria, *CEO*
EMP: 8 **EST:** 2016
SALES (est): 802.41K **Privately Held**
SIC: 7372 Utility computer software

(G-14789)
BAYNARD HOUSE CONDOMINIUMS
2400 Baynard Blvd (19802-3948)
PHONE..................................302 319-3740
Morgan Conner, *Pr*
Brian Lamborn, *VP*
William Donnelly, *Treas*
Stephen Crary, *Sec*
EMP: 7 **EST:** 1979
SALES (est): 130.39K **Privately Held**
Web: www.baynard.house
SIC: 8641 Condominium association

(G-14790)
BAYNARD PROPERTY MGT LLC
2710 Centerville Rd Ste 200 (19808-1644)
PHONE..................................302 225-3350
EMP: 5 **EST:** 2018
SALES (est): 157.31K **Privately Held**
SIC: 8741 Management services

Wilmington - New Castle County (G-14791)

GEOGRAPHIC SECTION

(G-14791)
BAYTOWN SYSTEMS INC
2711 Centerville Rd # 400 (19808-1660)
PHONE.................................302 689-3421
Alit Suryadi, *Mgr*
EMP: 5 **EST:** 2013
SQ FT: 500
SALES (est): 363.09K **Privately Held**
SIC: 5045 Printers, computer

(G-14792)
BB TECHNOLOGIES INC
801 N West St 2nd Fl (19801-1525)
PHONE.................................302 652-2300
EMP: 7 **EST:** 1991
SALES (est): 2.27MM **Privately Held**
SIC: 5045 Computer peripheral equipment
HQ: Black Box Corporation Of Pennsylvania
1000 Park Dr
Lawrence PA 15055
724 746-5500

(G-14793)
BBA USA HOLDINGS INC (PA)
2801 Centerville Rd (19808-1609)
PHONE.................................450 464-2111
Colette Rainville, *Prin*
EMP: 7 **EST:** 2018
SALES (est): 494.86K
SALES (corp-wide): 494.86K **Privately Held**
SIC: 8711 Engineering services

(G-14794)
BCA MENTAL HEALTH COUNSELING
900 Philadelphia Pike (19809-2280)
PHONE.................................302 513-9565
EMP: 6 **EST:** 2016
SALES (est): 104.88K **Privately Held**
SIC: 8099 Health and allied services, nec

(G-14795)
BCG HOLDING CORP (HQ)
1209 N Orange St (19801-1120)
PHONE.................................617 850-3700
John R Frantz, *Pr*
EMP: 39 **EST:** 1988
SALES (est): 5.51MM
SALES (corp-wide): 1.52B **Privately Held**
Web: www.bcg.com
SIC: 8742 Business management consultant
PA: The Boston Consulting Group Inc
200 Pier 4 Blvd Ste 1000
Boston MA 02210
617 973-1200

(G-14796)
BCP FINANCE CORP A DEL CORP
2711 Centerville Rd # 400 (19808-1660)
PHONE.................................225 673-6121
Mark J Schneider, *Pr*
EMP: 8 **EST:** 2001
SALES (est): 145.25K **Privately Held**
SIC: 6153 Working capital financing

(G-14797)
BDB LLC
1201 N Orange St Ste 600 (19801-1171)
PHONE.................................469 288-7672
EMP: 6 **EST:** 2015
SALES (est): 62.38K **Privately Held**
SIC: 2095 Roasted coffee

(G-14798)
BDO USA LLP
Also Called: BDO USA, LLP
4250 Lancaster Pike Ste 120 (19805-1520)
P.O. Box 3566 (19807-0566)
PHONE.................................302 656-5500
James Doyle, *Mng Pt*
EMP: 72
Web: www.bdo.com
SIC: 8721 Certified public accountant
HQ: Bdo Usa, P.A.
330 N Wabash Ave Ste 3200
Chicago IL 60611
312 240-1236

(G-14799)
BE BEAUTIFUL BOSSY
1207 D St Ste 2035 (19801-5627)
PHONE.................................888 558-9047
Ashley Williams, *Managing Member*
EMP: 6 **EST:** 2020
SALES (est): 56.98K **Privately Held**
SIC: 8741 Management services

(G-14800)
BEACON HOPE CHRISTIAN MINISTRY
Also Called: Beacon of Hope Daycare Center
4001 N Market St (19802-2219)
PHONE.................................302 764-7162
Jessica Harris, *Dir*
EMP: 5
SALES (corp-wide): 58.75K **Privately Held**
SIC: 8351 Group day care center
PA: Beacon Of Hope Christian Ministry
4001 N Market St
Wilmington DE 19802
302 764-7162

(G-14801)
BEACON WEALTH MANAGEMENT LLC
1018 Crestover Rd (19803-3307)
PHONE.................................302 383-2671
Monnarae Fraim, *Prin*
EMP: 5 **EST:** 2017
SALES (est): 129.42K **Privately Held**
SIC: 8741 Management services

(G-14802)
BEAMM TECHNOLOGIES INC
3 Germay Dr Unit 41563 (19804-1127)
PHONE.................................302 402-5551
Charles Beuthin, *Ex Dir*
EMP: 7 **EST:** 2020
SALES (est): 254.53K **Privately Held**
SIC: 7371 Custom computer programming services

(G-14803)
BEANE ASSOC INC
614 Haverhill Rd (19803-2435)
PHONE.................................302 559-1452
EMP: 6 **EST:** 2017
SALES (est): 52.65K **Privately Held**
Web: www.beaneassociates.com
SIC: 8742 Management consulting services

(G-14804)
BEANSTOCK MEDIA INC (PA)
300 Delaware Ave Ste 1100 (19801-1670)
PHONE.................................415 912-1530
James Waltz, *CEO*
Jim Waltz, *
Audrey Agustine-kirk, *VP Fin*
Joe Lyons, *CRO*
Ryan Maynard, *
EMP: 24 **EST:** 2010
SALES (est): 2.09MM
SALES (corp-wide): 2.09MM **Privately Held**
SIC: 7311 Advertising consultant

(G-14805)
BEAR ALIGNMENT CENTER
1317 N Scott St (19806-4023)
PHONE.................................302 655-9219
Robert Gregg, *Owner*
EMP: 5 **EST:** 1948
SALES (est): 297.53K **Privately Held**
Web: www.bearalignmentde.com
SIC: 7538 General automotive repair shops

(G-14806)
BEASLEY FM ACQUISITION CORP
812 Philadelphia Pike (19809-2372)
PHONE.................................302 765-1160
EMP: 10 **EST:** 1988
SALES (est): 284.71K **Privately Held**
SIC: 4832 Radio broadcasting stations

(G-14807)
BEAU BDEN FNDTION FOR THE PRTC
4601 Concord Pike (19803-1406)
PHONE.................................302 598-1885
EMP: 12 **EST:** 2015
SALES (est): 941.87K **Privately Held**
Web: www.beaubidenfoundation.org
SIC: 8641 Civic and social associations

(G-14808)
BEAUTFUL GATE OUTREACH CTR INC
604 N Walnut St (19801-3808)
PHONE.................................302 472-3002
Janet Bivins, *Pr*
Renee Beaman, *Ex Dir*
EMP: 14 **EST:** 2000
SQ FT: 3,000
SALES (est): 325.14K **Privately Held**
Web: www.bgate.org
SIC: 8322 Social service center

(G-14809)
BEAUTIFUL SMILES DELAWARE LLC
4901 Limestone Rd Ste 1 (19808-1271)
PHONE.................................302 656-0558
Victor Venturena, *Prin*
EMP: 12 **EST:** 2014
SALES (est): 234.07K **Privately Held**
Web: www.pikecreekdental.com
SIC: 8021 Dentists' office

(G-14810)
BEC CAPITAL LLC
3422 Old Capitol Trl Ste 438 (19808-6124)
PHONE.................................917 658-5867
Nir Ronen, *Managing Member*
EMP: 5 **EST:** 2013
SALES (est): 95.93K **Privately Held**
Web: www.bec-capital.com
SIC: 8741 Financial management for business

(G-14811)
BECKERS CHIMNEY AND ROOFG LLC
209 Main St (19804-3904)
PHONE.................................302 463-8294
EMP: 25 **EST:** 2013
SALES (est): 2.35MM **Privately Held**
Web: www.beckerschimneyandroofing.com
SIC: 1761 Roofing contractor

(G-14812)
BEFORESUNSET INC
24a Trolley Sq (19806-3334)
PHONE.................................812 341-0038
Begm Gt, *CEO*
EMP: 12
SALES (est): 406.37K **Privately Held**
SIC: 7371 Computer software development

(G-14813)
BEKART HOLDING LLC
1201 N Orange St Ste 7524 (19801-1298)
PHONE.................................302 600-7000
EMP: 10 **EST:** 2019
SALES (est): 810.88K **Privately Held**
Web: www.primedoc.com
SIC: 1522 6798 Hotel/motel and multi-family home construction; Real estate investment trusts

(G-14814)
BELCHIM CROP PRTECTION US CORP (HQ)
2751 Centerville Rd Ste 100 (19808-1627)
P.O. Box 1347 (19899-1347)
PHONE.................................302 407-3590
Thomas Wood, *Pr*
EMP: 12 **EST:** 2016
SQ FT: 5,000
SALES (est): 5.03MM
SALES (corp-wide): 334.33MM **Privately Held**
Web: www.belchimusa.com
SIC: 6719 2879 Investment holding companies, except banks; Agricultural chemicals, nec
PA: Certis Belchim
Technoogielaan 7
Londerzeel 1840
52300906

(G-14815)
BELCO INC
909 Delaware Ave (19806-4701)
P.O. Box 1909 (19899-1909)
PHONE.................................302 655-1561
James D Carota, *VP*
Arthur A Carota Junior, *VP*
Larry Gehrke, *VP*
Robert Logue, *Contrlr*
Carl Cantera, *Dir*
EMP: 9 **EST:** 1986
SQ FT: 15,000
SALES (est): 705.78K **Privately Held**
SIC: 6512 Commercial and industrial building operation

(G-14816)
BELFINT LYONS & SHUMAN PA
1011 Ctr Rd Ste 310 (19805-1266)
PHONE.................................302 225-0600
Norman J Shuman, *Pr*
EMP: 60 **EST:** 1923
SALES (est): 9.44MM **Privately Held**
Web: www.belfint.com
SIC: 8721 Accounting services, except auditing

(G-14817)
BELL FUNERAL HOME
909 Clifford Brown Walk (19801-3600)
PHONE.................................302 658-1555
EMP: 5 **EST:** 2019
SALES (est): 58.44K **Privately Held**
Web: www.bellfh.com
SIC: 7261 Funeral home

(G-14818)
BELL INFO SOLUTIONS LLC
3522 Silverside Rd Ste 30 (19810-4915)
PHONE.................................302 541-1200
EMP: 6 **EST:** 2020
SALES (est): 212K **Privately Held**
SIC: 7379 Computer related consulting services

(G-14819)
BELLAA BOMB LLC
3911 Concord Pike Unit 8030 (19803-1736)

PHONE..................800 409-2521
EMP: 3 EST: 2019
SALES (est): 90K **Privately Held**
SIC: 3229 Optical glass

(G-14820)
BELLEVUE COMMUNITY CENTER
500 Duncan Rd Ofc A (19809-2369)
PHONE..................302 762-1391
EMP: 16 EST: 2017
SALES (est): 527.49K **Privately Held**
Web: www.bellevuecc.org
SIC: 8322 Community center

(G-14821)
BELLEVUE CONTRACTORS LLC
909 Delaware Ave (19806-4701)
P.O. Box 8909 (19899-8909)
PHONE..................302 655-1522
EMP: 15 EST: 2004
SQ FT: 8,000
SALES (est): 2.66MM **Privately Held**
Web: www.bellevuecontractors.com
SIC: 1521 Single-family housing construction

(G-14822)
BELLEVUE HEART GROUP LLC
1508 Pennsylvania Ave Ste 2a (19806-4339)
PHONE..................302 468-4500
Hamid Deliri, *Managing Member*
EMP: 9 EST: 2014
SALES (est): 466.18K **Privately Held**
Web: www.bellevueheartgroup.com
SIC: 8011 Cardiologist and cardio-vascular specialist

(G-14823)
BELLEVUE REALTY CO
909 Delaware Ave (19806-4701)
P.O. Box 1909 (19899-1909)
PHONE..................302 655-1818
EMP: 10 EST: 1987
SALES (est): 1.64MM **Privately Held**
Web: www.bellevuerealtyco.com
SIC: 6531 Real estate brokers and agents

(G-14824)
BELLUNO MANAGER LLC
251 Little Falls Dr (19808-1674)
PHONE..................650 395-8185
EMP: 5 EST: 2017
SALES (est): 356.28K **Privately Held**
Web: www.bellunoholdings.com
SIC: 8748 Environmental consultant

(G-14825)
BELLWETHER BEHAVIORAL HEALTH
750 Shipyard Dr Ste 213 (19801-5160)
PHONE..................856 769-2042
Katina Saunders, *Prin*
EMP: 9 EST: 2016
SALES (est): 158.9K **Privately Held**
SIC: 8093 Mental health clinic, outpatient

(G-14826)
BENCH WALK ADVISORS LLC (PA)
123 S Justison St 7th Fl (19801-5360)
PHONE..................302 426-2100
EMP: 8 EST: 2016
SALES (est): 63.66K
SALES (corp-wide): 63.66K **Privately Held**
Web: www.benchwalk.com
SIC: 8111 Specialized legal services

(G-14827)
BENCHMARK BUILDERS INC (PA)
818 First State Blvd (19804-3573)
P.O. Box 3246 (19804-0346)
PHONE..................302 995-6945

Matt Egan, *Pr*
Francis Julian, *
Richard Julian, *
EMP: 26 EST: 1988
SQ FT: 7,500
SALES (est): 20.66MM
SALES (corp-wide): 20.66MM **Privately Held**
Web: www.benchmarkbuilders.com
SIC: 1521 New construction, single-family houses

(G-14828)
BENCHMARK TRANSMISSIONS INC
1301 Centerville Rd (19808-6219)
PHONE..................302 999-9400
Joseph Principe, *Mgr*
EMP: 5 EST: 1982
SALES (est): 247.88K **Privately Held**
SIC: 7537 Automotive transmission repair shops

(G-14829)
BENCO
1914 Julian Rd (19803-3145)
PHONE..................302 650-0053
EMP: 7 EST: 2017
SALES (est): 50.68K **Privately Held**
Web: www.benco.com
SIC: 5047 Dental equipment and supplies

(G-14830)
BENE MARKET LLC
1201 N Market St (19801-1156)
PHONE..................717 357-4117
EMP: 5 EST: 2019
SALES (est): 241.7K **Privately Held**
SIC: 8742 Marketing consulting services

(G-14831)
BENEFICIAL CONSUMER DISC CO (DH)
Also Called: Beneficial
301 N Walnut St (19801-4050)
PHONE..................302 425-2500
Elizabeth A Dawson, *VP*
Daniel E Rosequist, *Pr*
Ross Longfield, *Ex VP*
Janice Lewis, *VP*
Bradford Harrison, *VP*
EMP: 5 EST: 1976
SALES (est): 88.37MM
SALES (corp-wide): 93.79B **Privately Held**
SIC: 6141 Consumer finance companies
HQ: Hsbc Finance Corporation
1421 W Shure Dr Ste 100
Arlington Heights IL 60004
224 880-7000

(G-14832)
BENEFICIAL OKLAHOMA INC (DH)
Also Called: Beneficial
301 N Walnut St (19801-4050)
PHONE..................302 529-8701
David Greenwood, *Prin*
EMP: 15 EST: 1941
SALES (est): 88.37MM
SALES (corp-wide): 93.79B **Privately Held**
SIC: 6035 Federal savings and loan associations
HQ: Hsbc Finance Corporation
1421 W Shure Dr Ste 100
Arlington Heights IL 60004
224 880-7000

(G-14833)
BENEFIT SERVICES UNLIMITED
2500 Grubb Rd Ste 140 (19810-4711)
PHONE..................302 479-5696
EMP: 10 EST: 1987
SQ FT: 11,000

SALES (est): 226.96K **Privately Held**
SIC: 6371 Pension funds

(G-14834)
BENESCH ATTORNEYS AT LAW
222 Delaware Ave (19801-1621)
PHONE..................302 442-7005
EMP: 13 EST: 2011
SALES (est): 495.4K **Privately Held**
Web: www.beneschlaw.com
SIC: 8111 General practice attorney, lawyer

(G-14835)
BENESCH FRDLNDER CPLAN ARNOFF
Also Called: Attorney Rymond H Lemischs Off
1313 N Market St Fl 12 (19801-1151)
PHONE..................216 363-4500
Raymond H Lemisch, *Mgr*
EMP: 10
SALES (corp-wide): 48.78MM **Privately Held**
Web: www.beneschlaw.com
SIC: 8111 General practice attorney, lawyer
PA: Benesch, Friedlander, Coplan & Aronoff Llp
200 Public Sq Ste 2300
Cleveland OH 44114
216 363-4500

(G-14836)
BENJAMIN M D COOPER
410 Foulk Rd Ste 203 (19803-3802)
PHONE..................302 652-3331
Benjamin Cooper, *Prin*
EMP: 9 EST: 2018
SALES (est): 240.34K **Privately Held**
SIC: 8011 Offices and clinics of medical doctors

(G-14837)
BENJAMIN W KEENAN
500 Delaware Ave Ste 800 (19801-7408)
PHONE..................302 654-1888
Benjamin Benjamin, *Owner*
EMP: 5 EST: 2018
SALES (est): 63.66K **Privately Held**
Web: www.ashbygeddes.com
SIC: 8111 General practice attorney, lawyer

(G-14838)
BENNETT SERVICES INC
Also Called: Havc & Heating
412 Rogers Rd (19801-5749)
PHONE..................302 656-4107
Jimmy Bennett, *Prin*
EMP: 6 EST: 2010
SALES (est): 141.97K **Privately Held**
SIC: 1711 Plumbing, heating, air-conditioning

(G-14839)
BENOIT HOME IMPROVEMENTS LLC
103 Westgate Dr (19808-1427)
PHONE..................302 633-9284
EMP: 5 EST: 2016
SALES (est): 252.01K **Privately Held**
Web: www.benoithomeimprovements.com
SIC: 1521 General remodeling, single-family houses

(G-14840)
BENTLEY MILLS INC
2711 Centerville Rd Ste 400 (19808-1660)
PHONE..................800 423-4709
EMP: 2
SALES (corp-wide): 127.73MM **Privately Held**
Web: www.bentleymills.com

SIC: 2273 Carpets, textile fiber
PA: Bentley Mills, Inc.
14641 Don Julian Rd
City Of Industry CA 91746
626 333-4585

(G-14841)
BEOX LLC
501 Silverside Rd Ste 105 (19809-1376)
PHONE..................
EMP: 14 EST: 2008
SALES (est): 171.26K **Privately Held**
Web: www.beox.com
SIC: 4812 Radiotelephone communication

(G-14842)
BERKANA DEFENSE SECURITY LLC
2711 Centerville Rd (19808-1660)
PHONE..................302 504-4455
EMP: 7 EST: 2016
SALES (est): 154.16K **Privately Held**
SIC: 7381 Guard services

(G-14843)
BERKSHIRE AT LIMESTONE
1526 Braken Ave (19808-4388)
PHONE..................302 635-7495
Jean Simpson, *Off Mgr*
EMP: 5 EST: 2012
SALES (est): 131.17K **Privately Held**
SIC: 5032 Limestone

(G-14844)
BERKSHIRE HATHAWAY GLOBAL
Also Called: Bhhs Fox & Roach Brandywine
2200 Concord Pike Fl 1 (19803-2978)
PHONE..................302 477-5500
EMP: 25 EST: 2015
SALES (est): 600.77K **Privately Held**
SIC: 6531 Real estate agent, residential

(G-14845)
BERLEY SECURITY SYSTEMS INC
6701 Governor Printz Blvd (19809-1809)
PHONE..................302 791-9056
EMP: 10 EST: 1993
SALES (est): 885.29K **Privately Held**
Web: www.berleysecurity.com
SIC: 7382 Burglar alarm maintenance and monitoring

(G-14846)
BERMAN LOREN MD
1600 Rockland Rd (19803-3607)
PHONE..................302 651-4000
Loren Berman, *Pr*
EMP: 12 EST: 2018
SALES (est): 249.49K **Privately Held**
Web: www.nemours.org
SIC: 8011 Pediatrician

(G-14847)
BERNARD RUTH SGEL JWISH CMNTY
101 Garden Of Eden Rd Ste 102 (19803-1511)
PHONE..................302 478-5660
EMP: 100 EST: 1901
SALES (est): 7.89MM **Privately Held**
Web: www.siegeljcc.org
SIC: 8322 Community center

(G-14848)
BERNARDON LLC
123 S Justison St Ste 101 (19801-5364)
PHONE..................302 622-9550
William E Halloway, *Pr*
EMP: 10
SALES (corp-wide): 9MM **Privately Held**
Web: www.bernardon.com

Wilmington - New Castle County (G-14849)   GEOGRAPHIC SECTION

SIC: 8712 0781 7389 Architectural engineering; Landscape planning services; Interior decorating
PA: Bernardon, Llc
10 N High St Ste 310
West Chester PA 19380
610 444-2900

(G-14849)
BERNICES EDCTL SCHL AGE CTR IN
2516 W 4th St (19805-3308)
PHONE..................................302 651-0286
Bernice Thomas, *Pr*
EMP: 5 EST: 1999
SALES (est): 165.45K **Privately Held**
Web: www.besacinc.com
SIC: 8351 Group day care center

(G-14850)
BERNIES FOUNDATION INC
1523 W 6th St (19805-3105)
PHONE..................................302 750-7117
Shamla Mclaurin, *Ex Dir*
EMP: 5
SALES (est): 65.81K **Privately Held**
SIC: 8322 Individual and family services

(G-14851)
BESSEMER TRUST COMPANY DEL NA (PA)
20 Montchanin Rd Ste 1500 (19807-2160)
PHONE..................................212 708-9182
EMP: 20 EST: 2015
SALES (est): 1.88MM
SALES (corp-wide): 1.88MM **Privately Held**
Web: www.bessemertrust.com
SIC: 6021 National commercial banks

(G-14852)
BEST BUDDIES INTERNATIONAL INC
1401 Pennsylvania Ave Ste 104 (19806-4125)
PHONE..................................302 691-3187
EMP: 6
Web: www.bestbuddies.org
SIC: 8641 Civic and social associations
PA: Best Buddies International, Inc.
100 Se 2nd St Ste 2200
Miami FL 33131

(G-14853)
BEST EGG TECHNOLOGIES LLC
Also Called: Best Egg
3419 Silverside Rd (19810-4801)
PHONE..................................302 358-2730
Brian Conneen, *Managing Member*
EMP: 99 EST: 2019
SALES (est): 3.56MM **Privately Held**
SIC: 6153 Credit card services, central agency collection

(G-14854)
BEST HOLDING LLC
103 Foulk Rd (19803-3742)
PHONE..................................302 691-6023
EMP: 5 EST: 2014
SALES (est): 124.6K **Privately Held**
SIC: 6799 Investors, nec

(G-14855)
BEST PLANET SCIENCE LLC
1209 N Orange St (19801-1120)
PHONE..................................754 200-1913
EMP: 5
SALES (est): 209.42K **Privately Held**
SIC: 8731 Biotechnical research, commercial

(G-14856)
BEST PROCESSING SOLUTIONS LLC
1013 Centre Rd Ste 40 (19805-1265)
PHONE..................................212 739-7845
Michael Balyasnyy, *Managing Member*
EMP: 8 EST: 2013
SALES (est): 151.59K **Privately Held**
SIC: 7389 Financial services

(G-14857)
BEST STONEWORKS INC
3015 Bellevue Ave (19802-2401)
PHONE..................................302 765-3497
Howard Garfinkel, *Pr*
EMP: 8 EST: 1999
SALES (est): 1.15MM **Privately Held**
Web: www.beststoneworks.com
SIC: 3272 Building stone, artificial; concrete

(G-14858)
BESTFIELD ASSOCIATES INC
Also Called: Bestfield Homes
200 Mary Ella Dr (19805-1542)
PHONE..................................302 633-6361
Anthony Di Egidio Senior, *Pr*
EMP: 16 EST: 1987
SQ FT: 1,500
SALES (est): 913.05K **Privately Held**
Web: www.bestfieldhomes.com
SIC: 1521 New construction, single-family houses

(G-14859)
BESTFIELD PROPERTIES LLC
1424 N Clayton St (19806-4006)
PHONE..................................302 658-1000
Stacy Young, *Mgr*
EMP: 7 EST: 2006
SALES (est): 125.28K **Privately Held**
Web: www.bestfieldproperties.com
SIC: 6512 Nonresidential building operators

(G-14860)
BETH STEWART VO LLC
127 Alders Dr (19803-5301)
PHONE..................................302 540-7782
Elizabeth Stewart, *Prin*
EMP: 7 EST: 2014
SALES (est): 139.98K **Privately Held**
Web: www.bethstewartvo.com
SIC: 7389 Recording studio, noncommercial records

(G-14861)
BETHEL MULTIMEDIA DEPT
306 S Connell St (19805-3963)
PHONE..................................302 563-0918
Bryan Hart, *Prin*
EMP: 5 EST: 2010
SALES (est): 43.31K **Privately Held**
SIC: 4899 Communication services, nec

(G-14862)
BETHEL VILLA ASSOCIATES LP
Also Called: Bethel Villa
506 E 5th St Fl 2 (19801-4706)
PHONE..................................302 426-9688
Alfred Good, *Mgr*
EMP: 43
SIC: 6513 Apartment building operators
HQ: Villa Associates Bethel L P
832 Germantown Pike Ste 5
Plymouth Meeting PA 19462

(G-14863)
BETTER SEARCH CORPORATION ◊
251 Little Falls Dr (19808-1674)
PHONE..................................415 610-4825
Jamshidbek Mirzakhalov, *CEO*
Axhens Mara, *COO*
EMP: 5 EST: 2022
SALES (est): 209.21K **Privately Held**
SIC: 7372 Educational computer software

(G-14864)
BETTS INC
3002 Fairhope Rd (19810-1626)
PHONE..................................302 475-3754
Brian Betts, *Prin*
EMP: 9 EST: 2012
SALES (est): 140.55K **Privately Held**
Web: www.betts1868.com
SIC: 3493 Steel springs, except wire

(G-14865)
BETZ&BETZ ENTERPRISES LLC
528 W 3rd St (19801-2320)
PHONE..................................302 602-0613
EMP: 2
SALES (est): 90.74K **Privately Held**
SIC: 2676 7389 Towels, napkins, and tissue paper products; Business services, nec

(G-14866)
BEVERAGE INFOSYSTEMS LTD LBLTY
Also Called: Beverage Trade Network
501 Silverside Rd Ste 77 (19809-1394)
PHONE..................................732 762-5299
Sehul Patel, *Prin*
EMP: 31 EST: 2011
SALES (est): 644.55K **Privately Held**
Web: www.beveragetradenetwork.com
SIC: 7373 Systems software development services

(G-14867)
BEVERLY L BOVE PA
Also Called: Beverly Bove Attorney At Law
1020 W 18th St Ste 2 (19802-3892)
P.O. Box 1607 (19899-1607)
PHONE..................................302 777-3500
Beverly L Bove Pa, *Owner*
EMP: 8 EST: 1996
SALES (est): 890.48K **Privately Held**
Web: www.bevbovelaw.com
SIC: 8111 General practice attorney, lawyer

(G-14868)
BEVERLYS HELPING HANDS
400 W 9th St Ste 100 (19801-1504)
PHONE..................................302 651-9304
EMP: 5 EST: 2018
SALES (est): 71.28K **Privately Held**
SIC: 8322 Adult day care center

(G-14869)
BEW PRODUCTIONS
Also Called: Entertainment Production Svcs
1004 Berkeley Rd (19807-2814)
P.O. Box 708 (19720-0708)
PHONE..................................302 547-8661
Robert Hendry, *Prin*
EMP: 5 EST: 2016
SALES (est): 220.98K **Privately Held**
Web: www.bewproductions.com
SIC: 7822 Motion picture and tape distribution

(G-14870)
BEYOND GUTTERS INC
2002 Wildwood Dr (19805-1061)
PHONE..................................302 999-1422
Patricia Armato, *Owner*
EMP: 5 EST: 2011
SALES (est): 86.71K **Privately Held**
SIC: 1761 Gutter and downspout contractor

(G-14871)
BFC INVESTORS TRUST
1100 N Market St (19890-1100)
PHONE..................................302 636-6466
EMP: 6 EST: 2015
SALES (est): 111.74K **Privately Held**
Web: www.wilmingtontrust.com
SIC: 6733 Trusts, nec

(G-14872)
BGP PUBLICITY INC
Also Called: Gillespiehall
3106 Centerville Rd (19807-2502)
PHONE..................................302 234-9500
Bridget Paverd, *Pr*
EMP: 12 EST: 1996
SALES (est): 2.37MM **Privately Held**
Web: www.slicecommunications.com
SIC: 8743 Public relations and publicity

(G-14873)
BHAPI INC
2810 N Church St (19802-4447)
PHONE..................................859 475-1924
Michael Esber, *CEO*
EMP: 5 EST: 2021
SALES (est): 107.01K **Privately Held**
SIC: 7371 Software programming applications

(G-14874)
BI SOLUTIONS GROUP LLC
1000 N West St (19801-1050)
PHONE..................................253 366-5173
Kindra Lockett, *Managing Member*
EMP: 28 EST: 2021
SALES (est): 350K **Privately Held**
SIC: 8744 Facilities support services

(G-14875)
BIA SEPARATIONS INC
1000 N West St Ste 1200 (19801-1058)
PHONE..................................510 740-4045
Darryl G Glover, *CEO*
EMP: 3 EST: 2008
SALES (est): 450.29K **Privately Held**
Web: www.biaseparations.com
SIC: 3826 Analytical instruments

(G-14876)
BID 4 LEASE CORP
3616 Kirkwood Hwy Ste A # 1285 (19808-5124)
PHONE..................................302 244-9943
Dennis Krasilshchikov, *CEO*
EMP: 8 EST: 2018
SALES (est): 366.6K **Privately Held**
SIC: 7371 Computer software development and applications

(G-14877)
BIDEN FOR AG INC
4 E 8th St (19801-3553)
PHONE..................................302 295-8340
Biden Hunter, *Prin*
EMP: 6 EST: 2010
SALES (est): 157.89K **Privately Held**
SIC: 8111 General practice attorney, lawyer

(G-14878)
BIDR TV LLC ◊
3411 Silverside Rd 104b (19810-4812)
PHONE..................................561 569-0931
Jake Galvin, *Prin*
EMP: 6 EST: 2022
SALES (est): 237.56K **Privately Held**
SIC: 7371 Custom computer programming services

GEOGRAPHIC SECTION
Wilmington - New Castle County (G-14908)

(G-14879)
BIELLI & KLAUDER LLC
1204 N King St (19801-3218)
PHONE..................................302 803-4600
EMP: 7 EST: 2016
SALES (est): 177.98K Privately Held
Web: www.bk-legal.com
SIC: 8111 General practice law office

(G-14880)
BIFFERATO GENTILOTTI LLC (PA)
4250 Lancaster Pike Ste 130 (19805)
P.O. Box 2165 (19899-2165)
PHONE..................................302 429-1900
EMP: 5 EST: 1996
SALES (est): 3.59MM
SALES (corp-wide): 3.59MM Privately Held
Web: www.bglawde.com
SIC: 8111 General practice attorney, lawyer

(G-14881)
BIG PLAN INC (PA)
108 W 13th St (19801-1145)
PHONE..................................910 556-9311
Fang Fang, CEO
EMP: 5 EST: 2018
SALES (est): 322.21K
SALES (corp-wide): 322.21K Privately Held
SIC: 7371 Computer software development and applications

(G-14882)
BIG SPRINGS INC
1209 N Orange St (19801-1120)
PHONE..................................443 570-3003
EMP: 6 EST: 2020
SALES (est): 88.66K Privately Held
SIC: 7389 Business services, nec

(G-14883)
BIG TOMORROW LLC
800 Delaware Ave (19801-1322)
PHONE..................................650 714-3912
EMP: 10 EST: 2013
SALES (est): 380K Privately Held
SIC: 8742 7389 Management consulting services; Business services, nec

(G-14884)
BIG TOY CUSTOM CAR CARE INC
1806 Tulip St (19805-3824)
PHONE..................................302 668-6729
Chevy L Anderson Senior, Prin
EMP: 5 EST: 2016
SALES (est): 215.14K Privately Held
SIC: 7542 Carwashes

(G-14885)
BIGBEN1613 LLC
Also Called: Corner Stone Group
1400 Vandever Ave (19802-4631)
PHONE..................................305 926-3872
Benjamin Winkler, Managing Member
EMP: 25 EST: 2008
SQ FT: 4,000
SALES (est): 15.91MM Privately Held
SIC: 5045 Computers and accessories, personal and home entertainment

(G-14886)
BIGCENTRIC APPLIANCE
151 Edgemoor Rd (19809-3153)
PHONE..................................302 691-8510
Jae Rhee, Pr
EMP: 5 EST: 2012
SALES (est): 100.11K Privately Held
Web: www.bigcentric.com
SIC: 7629 Electrical household appliance repair

(G-14887)
BIGCENTRIC INC ✪
151 Edgemoor Rd (19809-3153)
PHONE..................................410 456-1968
EMP: 5 EST: 2022
SALES (est): 59.87K Privately Held
Web: www.bigcentric.com
SIC: 7629 Electrical household appliance repair

(G-14888)
BIGGS & BATTAGLIA
921 N Orange St (19801-1603)
P.O. Box 1489 (19899-1489)
PHONE..................................302 655-9677
Victor F Battaglia, Pt
John Biggs Iii, Pt
Philip Bartoshesky, Pt
Robert K Beste Junior, Pt
Robert D Goldberg, Pt
EMP: 14 EST: 1956
SALES (est): 495.13K Privately Held
SIC: 8111 General practice law office

(G-14889)
BIJAN K SOROURI MD
4014 Kennett Pike (19807-2019)
PHONE..................................302 652-1218
Bijan K Sorouri, Prin
EMP: 9 EST: 2010
SALES (est): 154.02K Privately Held
SIC: 8011 Physicians' office, including specialists

(G-14890)
BIJIN
31 Sharons Way (19808-5231)
PHONE..................................302 777-4040
Judy Stellini, Owner
EMP: 5 EST: 2007
SALES (est): 199.65K Privately Held
Web: www.bijindelaware.com
SIC: 7299 Miscellaneous personal service

(G-14891)
BIJOTI INC
1808 N Washington St (19802-4730)
PHONE..................................908 916-7764
Joshua Marpet, CEO
EMP: 10 EST: 2014
SQ FT: 9,300
SALES (est): 277.47K Privately Held
SIC: 7372 Application computer software

(G-14892)
BILLOWS ELECTRIC SUPPLY CO INC
480 First State Blvd (19804-3745)
PHONE..................................302 996-9133
Jeff Billows, CEO
EMP: 8
SALES (corp-wide): 12.53MM Privately Held
Web: www.billows.com
SIC: 5063 Electrical supplies, nec
HQ: Billows Electric Supply Company, Inc.
1813 Underwood Blvd
Delran NJ 08075

(G-14893)
BING RCHEL ZHANG FMLY FNDATION
314 Oracle Rd (19808-1561)
PHONE..................................302 294-1859
Bing Zhang, Asst Sec
EMP: 5 EST: 2018
SALES (est): 178.58K Privately Held
SIC: 8641 Civic and social associations

(G-14894)
BIO-DIVERSIFIED VENTURES INC
910 Foulk Rd Ste 201 (19803-3159)
PHONE..................................720 680-9418
Torin Kline, CEO
EMP: 10 EST: 2021
SALES (est): 705.81K Privately Held
SIC: 1541 Food products manufacturing or packing plant construction

(G-14895)
BIOMATIK USA LLC
105 Silverside Rd 501 (19809-1727)
PHONE..................................800 836-8089
EMP: 8 EST: 2010
SALES (est): 98.57K Privately Held
Web: www.biomatik.com
SIC: 8731 Biotechnical research, commercial

(G-14896)
BIRCH POINTE CONDO ASSC
3411 Haley Ct (19808-2825)
PHONE..................................302 685-4310
EMP: 6 EST: 2015
SALES (est): 54.63K Privately Held
Web: www.birchpointe.net
SIC: 8641 Condominium association

(G-14897)
BISHOP ENTERPRISES CORPORATION
2207 Concord Pike Ste 412 (19803-2908)
PHONE..................................302 379-2884
EMP: 8 EST: 2010
SALES (est): 118.58K Privately Held
Web: www.bishopenterprises.com
SIC: 8748 Business consulting, nec

(G-14898)
BITCARTER INC
925 N Orange St (19801-1548)
PHONE..................................518 512-9238
Faithful Freeman, CEO
EMP: 15
SALES (est): 650.61K Privately Held
SIC: 5045 Computer software

(G-14899)
BIZDATA INC
3422 Old Capitol Trl Ste 45 (19808-6124)
PHONE..................................650 283-1644
EMP: 7 EST: 2018
SALES (est): 229.58K Privately Held
Web: www.bizdata360.com
SIC: 7371 Computer software development

(G-14900)
BK TEMP HOME CARE
2101 N Tatnall St (19802-4109)
PHONE..................................302 575-1400
EMP: 10 EST: 2014
SALES (est): 834.73K Privately Held
SIC: 8059 Personal care home, with health care

(G-14901)
BLACK FEATHER ENTRMT LLC ✪
3911 Concord Pike # 803 (19803-1736)
Rural Route 1621 Yale Pl (20850)
PHONE..................................248 787-8060
Winter Qiu, Managing Member
EMP: 3 EST: 2022
SALES (est): 128.34K Privately Held
SIC: 7372 Application computer software

(G-14902)
BLACKHOUSE CAMPAIGN LLC
804 W 24th St (19802-3336)
PHONE..................................302 465-0980
EMP: 5 EST: 2011
SALES (est): 65.71K Privately Held
SIC: 7929 Entertainment service

(G-14903)
BLACKROCK 2022 GLOBL INCOME OP
100 Bellevue Pkwy (19809-3716)
PHONE..................................212 754-5560
John M Perlowski, Pr
Jonathan Diorio, VP
Trent Walker, CFO
EMP: 8 EST: 2016
SALES (est): 12.87MM Privately Held
Web: www.blackrock.com
SIC: 6726 Management investment funds, closed-end

(G-14904)
BLACKROCK ADVNTAGE ESG EMRGING
100 Bellevue Pkwy (19809-3716)
PHONE..................................302 797-2000
EMP: 5
SALES (est): 168.03K Privately Held
SIC: 6722 Money market mutual funds

(G-14905)
BLACKROCK BOND FUND INC
100 Bellevue Pkwy (19809-3716)
PHONE..................................800 441-7762
EMP: 9 EST: 2021
SALES (est): 477.83K Privately Held
SIC: 6722 Management investment, open-end

(G-14906)
BLACKROCK CAL MNICPL INCOME TR
Also Called: Mutual Fund Department
100 Bellevue Pkwy (19809-3716)
PHONE..................................800 882-0052
John M Perlowski, Pr
R Glenn Hubbard, Ch Bd
W Carl Kester, V Ch Bd
Trent Walker, CFO
Aaron Wasserman, CCO
EMP: 8 EST: 2001
SALES (est): 1.3MM Privately Held
SIC: 6726 6722 Management investment funds, closed-end; Money market mutual funds

(G-14907)
BLACKROCK CAPITL ALLOCATION TR
100 Bellevue Pkwy (19809-3716)
PHONE..................................800 882-0052
John M Perlowski, Pr
R Glenn Hubbard, Ch Bd
W Carl Kester, V Ch Bd
Trent Walker, CFO
Charles Park, CCO
EMP: 8 EST: 2020
SALES (est): 98.24MM Privately Held
SIC: 6726 Management investment funds, closed-end

(G-14908)
BLACKROCK CORE BOND TRUST
100 Bellevue Pkwy (19809-3716)
PHONE..................................800 882-0052
John M Perlowski, Pr
R Glenn Hubbard, Ch Bd
W Carl Kester, V Ch Bd
Trent Walker, CFO

Wilmington - New Castle County (G-14909)

Charles Park, *CCO*
EMP: 8 **EST:** 2001
SALES (est): 46.11MM **Privately Held**
SIC: 6726 Management investment funds, closed-end

(G-14909)
BLACKROCK CORP HIGH YELD FUND
100 Bellevue Pkwy (19809-3716)
PHONE..................800 441-7762
EMP: 199 **EST:** 2014
SALES (est): 20.09MM **Publicly Held**
Web: www.blackrock.com
SIC: 6722 Money market mutual funds
HQ: Blackrock Advisors, Llc
800 Scudders Mill Rd
Plainsboro NJ 08536

(G-14910)
BLACKROCK CPITL INV ADVSORS LL
100 Bellevue Pkwy (19809-3716)
PHONE..................800 882-0052
EMP: 5 **EST:** 2017
SALES (est): 1.82MM **Publicly Held**
SIC: 6722 Money market mutual funds
PA: Blackrock, Inc.
50 Hudson Yards
New York NY 10001

(G-14911)
BLACKROCK EMRGING MKTS LNG/SHO
100 Bellevue Pkwy (19809-3716)
PHONE..................302 797-2000
EMP: 5 **EST:** 2015
SALES (est): 461.02K **Privately Held**
Web: www.blackrock.com
SIC: 6722 Money market mutual funds

(G-14912)
BLACKROCK ENHNCED GLOBL DVDEND
100 Bellevue Pkwy (19809-3716)
PHONE..................800 882-0052
John M Perlowski, *Pr*
R Glenn Hubbard, *Ch Bd*
W Carl Kester, *V Ch Bd*
Jonathan Diorio, *VP*
Trent Walker, *CFO*
EMP: 8 **EST:** 2005
SALES (est): 29.14MM **Privately Held**
Web: www.blackrock.com
SIC: 6733 Trusts, nec

(G-14913)
BLACKROCK FINCL INSTITUTIONS S
100 Bellevue Pkwy (19809-3716)
PHONE..................800 441-7762
EMP: 7 **EST:** 1987
SALES (est): 343.87K **Privately Held**
Web: www.blackrock.com
SIC: 6722 Money market mutual funds

(G-14914)
BLACKROCK FUNDS IV
100 Bellevue Pkwy (19809-3716)
PHONE..................800 441-7762
EMP: 9 **EST:** 2018
SALES (est): 360.89K **Privately Held**
SIC: 6733 Trusts, nec

(G-14915)
BLACKROCK FUNDS V
100 Bellevue Pkwy (19809-3716)
PHONE..................302 797-2000
EMP: 9 **EST:** 2021
SALES (est): 1.01MM **Privately Held**
Web: www.blackrock.com
SIC: 6722 Money market mutual funds

(G-14916)
BLACKROCK FUTURE US THEMES ETF
100 Bellevue Pkwy (19809-3716)
PHONE..................302 797-2000
EMP: 5 **EST:** 2021
SALES (est): 106.48K **Privately Held**
SIC: 6722 Money market mutual funds

(G-14917)
BLACKROCK GLOBL SMLLCAP FUND I
100 Bellevue Pkwy (19809-3716)
PHONE..................800 441-7762
EMP: 10 **EST:** 2014
SALES (est): 257.66K **Privately Held**
Web: www.blackrock.com
SIC: 6722 Money market mutual funds

(G-14918)
BLACKROCK HEALTH SCIENCES TR
100 Bellevue Pkwy (19809-3716)
PHONE..................800 882-0052
John M Perlowski, *Pr*
R Glenn Hubbard, *Ch Bd*
W Carl Kester, *V Ch Bd*
Trent Walker, *CFO*
Charles Park, *CCO*
EMP: 8 **EST:** 2005
SALES (est): 6.4MM **Privately Held**
Web: www.blackrock.com
SIC: 6726 Management investment funds, closed-end

(G-14919)
BLACKROCK HLTH SCIENCES TR II
100 Bellevue Pkwy (19809-3716)
PHONE..................800 882-0052
EMP: 6
SALES (est): 278.96K **Privately Held**
SIC: 6733 Trusts, nec

(G-14920)
BLACKROCK INCOME TRUST INC
100 Bellevue Pkwy (19809-3716)
PHONE..................800 441-7762
John M Perlowski, *Pr*
Neal J Andrews, *CFO*
Charles Park, *CCO*
EMP: 8 **EST:** 1988
SALES (est): 1.89MM **Privately Held**
Web: www.blackrock.com
SIC: 6726 Management investment funds, closed-end

(G-14921)
BLACKROCK INSTNL MGT CORP
Also Called: Pimc
100 Bellevue Pkwy (19809-3716)
PHONE..................302 797-2000
Ralph L Schlosstein, *Prin*
Susan L Wagner, *
EMP: 42 **EST:** 1977
SQ FT: 10,000
SALES (est): 13.51MM **Publicly Held**
Web: www.blackrock.com
SIC: 6722 Money market mutual funds
HQ: Blackrock Holdco 2, Inc.
50 Hudson Yards
New York NY 10001
212 754-5300

(G-14922)
BLACKROCK LNG-HRZON EQITY FUND
100 Bellevue Pkwy (19809-3716)
PHONE..................800 441-7762
EMP: 16 **EST:** 2005
SALES (est): 1.98MM **Publicly Held**
Web: www.blackrock.com
SIC: 6722 Money market mutual funds
PA: Blackrock, Inc.
50 Hudson Yards
New York NY 10001

(G-14923)
BLACKROCK LRGE CAP GRWTH VI FU
100 Bellevue Pkwy (19809-3716)
PHONE..................302 797-2000
EMP: 62 **EST:** 2014
SALES (est): 1.65MM **Publicly Held**
SIC: 6722 Money market mutual funds
HQ: Blackrock Advisors, Llc
800 Scudders Mill Rd
Plainsboro NJ 08536

(G-14924)
BLACKROCK MACRO THEMES FUND
100 Bellevue Pkwy (19809-3716)
PHONE..................302 797-2000
EMP: 62 **EST:** 2014
SALES (est): 1.05MM **Publicly Held**
SIC: 6722 Money market mutual funds
HQ: Blackrock Advisors, Llc
800 Scudders Mill Rd
Plainsboro NJ 08536

(G-14925)
BLACKROCK MIDCAP INDEX FUND
100 Bellevue Pkwy (19809-3716)
PHONE..................302 797-2000
EMP: 62 **EST:** 2015
SALES (est): 1.72MM **Publicly Held**
SIC: 6722 Money market mutual funds
HQ: Blackrock Advisors, Llc
800 Scudders Mill Rd
Plainsboro NJ 08536

(G-14926)
BLACKROCK MLT-SECTOR INCOME TR
100 Bellevue Pkwy (19809-3716)
PHONE..................800 882-0052
EMP: 10 **EST:** 2019
SALES (est): 979.97K **Privately Held**
SIC: 6722 Money market mutual funds

(G-14927)
BLACKROCK MNCPL 2030 TRGET TER
100 Bellevue Pkwy (19809-3716)
PHONE..................800 882-0052
John M Perlowski, *Pr*
R Glenn Hubbard, *Ch Bd*
W Carl Kester, *V Ch Bd*
Trent Walker, *CFO*
Aaron Wasserman, *CCO*
EMP: 8 **EST:** 2012
SALES (est): 2.26MM **Privately Held**
SIC: 6726 Management investment funds, closed-end

(G-14928)
BLACKROCK MNCPL INCOME INV QLT
100 Bellevue Pkwy (19809-3716)
PHONE..................800 441-7762
John M Perlowski, *Pr*
Neal J Andrews, *CFO*
Charles Park, *CCO*
EMP: 8 **EST:** 2002
SALES (est): 9.38MM **Privately Held**
Web: www.blackrock.com
SIC: 6722 Money market mutual funds

(G-14929)
BLACKROCK MNHLDNGS CAL QLTY FU
100 Bellevue Pkwy (19809-3716)
PHONE..................800 882-0052
John M Perlowski, *Pr*
R Glenn Hubbard, *Ch Bd*
W Carl Kester, *V Ch Bd*
Trent Walker, *CFO*
Aaron Wasserman, *CCO*
EMP: 8 **EST:** 1997
SALES (est): 2.2MM **Privately Held**
SIC: 6726 Management investment funds, closed-end

(G-14930)
BLACKROCK MNHLDNGS NJ QLTY FUN
100 Bellevue Pkwy (19809-3716)
PHONE..................800 882-0052
John M Perlowski, *Pr*
R Glenn Hubbard, *Ch Bd*
W Carl Kester, *V Ch Bd*
Trent Walker, *CFO*
Charles Park, *CCO*
EMP: 8 **EST:** 1998
SALES (est): 33.43MM **Privately Held**
SIC: 6726 Management investment funds, closed-end

(G-14931)
BLACKROCK MNYELD CAL QLTY FUND
Also Called: MCA
100 Bellevue Pkwy (19809-3716)
PHONE..................800 882-0052
John M Perlowski, *Pr*
Trent Walker, *CFO*
Charles Park, *CCO*
EMP: 8 **EST:** 1992
SALES (est): 31.36MM **Privately Held**
SIC: 6726 Management investment funds, closed-end

(G-14932)
BLACKROCK MUNIASSETS FUND INC
100 Bellevue Pkwy (19809-3716)
PHONE..................302 797-2000
EMP: 8 **EST:** 2006
SALES (est): 128.81K **Privately Held**
Web: www.blackrock.com
SIC: 6722 Money market mutual funds

(G-14933)
BLACKROCK MUNICIPAL BOND TRUST
100 Bellevue Pkwy (19809-3716)
PHONE..................888 825-2257
Maureen Henman, *Prin*
EMP: 12 **EST:** 2007
SALES (est): 662K **Privately Held**
Web: www.blackrock.com
SIC: 6722 Money market mutual funds

(G-14934)
BLACKROCK MUNICIPAL INCOME TR
100 Bellevue Pkwy (19809-3716)
PHONE..................888 882-0052
John M Perlowski, *Pr*
W Carl Kester, *V Ch Bd*
Trent Walker, *CFO*
Charles Park, *CCO*
EMP: 8 **EST:** 2001
SALES (est): 37.95MM **Privately Held**
Web: www.blackrock.com
SIC: 6726 6722 Management investment funds, closed-end; Money market mutual funds

GEOGRAPHIC SECTION

Wilmington - New Castle County (G-14964)

(G-14935)
BLACKROCK MUNICPL INCOME TR II
100 Bellevue Pkwy (19809-3716)
PHONE....................302 797-2000
EMP: 6 EST: 2009
SALES (est): 383.54K Privately Held
Web: www.blackrock.com
SIC: 6722 Money market mutual funds

(G-14936)
BLACKROCK MUNIYIELD FUND INC
100 Bellevue Pkwy (19809-3716)
PHONE....................800 441-7762
EMP: 6
SALES (est): 631.52K Privately Held
SIC: 6726 Management investment funds, closed-end

(G-14937)
BLACKROCK NATURAL RESOURCES TR
100 Bellevue Pkwy (19809-3716)
PHONE....................212 810-5300
Robert C Doll, CEO
EMP: 10 EST: 2010
SALES (est): 271.14K Privately Held
Web: www.blackrock.com
SIC: 6722 Money market mutual funds

(G-14938)
BLACKROCK NY MNCPL INCOME QLTY
100 Bellevue Pkwy (19809-3716)
PHONE....................800 441-7762
John M Perlowski, Pr
Neal J Andrews, CFO
Charles Park, CCO
EMP: 8 EST: 2002
SALES (est): 5.87MM Privately Held
SIC: 6726 Management investment funds, closed-end

(G-14939)
BLACKROCK NY MNCPL INCOME TR I
100 Bellevue Pkwy (19809-3716)
PHONE....................800 441-7762
John M Perlowski, Pr
Neal J Andrews, CFO
Charles Park, CCO
EMP: 8 EST: 2002
SALES (est): 5.18MM Privately Held
SIC: 6733 Trusts, nec

(G-14940)
BLACKROCK NY MUNICPL INCOME TR
100 Bellevue Pkwy (19809-3716)
PHONE....................800 882-0052
John M Perlowski, Pr
R Glenn Hubbard, Ch Bd
W Carl Kester, V Ch Bd
Trent Walker, CFO
Aaron Wasserman, CCO
EMP: 8 EST: 2001
SALES (est): 970.8K Privately Held
SIC: 6726 6722 Management investment funds, closed-end; Money market mutual funds

(G-14941)
BLACKROCK SCIENCE & TECH TR
100 Bellevue Pkwy (19809-3716)
PHONE....................302 797-2000
John M Perlowski, CEO
EMP: 7 EST: 2014
SALES (est): 261.25K Privately Held
Web: www.blackrock.com
SIC: 6722 Money market mutual funds

(G-14942)
BLACKROCK SMALL CAP GRO
100 Bellevue Pkwy (19809-3716)
PHONE....................302 797-2000
Travis Cooke, Mgr
EMP: 6 EST: 2014
SALES (est): 275.81K Privately Held
SIC: 6722 Money market mutual funds

(G-14943)
BLACKROCK SMALL CAP GRWTH FUND
100 Bellevue Pkwy (19809-3716)
PHONE....................212 810-5300
EMP: 5 EST: 2009
SALES (est): 193.71K Privately Held
Web: www.blackrock.com
SIC: 6722 Money market mutual funds

(G-14944)
BLACKROCK SMD-CAP GRWTH EQITY ✪
100 Bellevue Pkwy (19809-3716)
PHONE....................302 797-2000
EMP: 5 EST: 2022
SALES (est): 106.48K Privately Held
SIC: 6722 Money market mutual funds

(G-14945)
BLACKROCK SSTNBLE BLNCED PRTFL ✪
100 Bellevue Pkwy (19809-3716)
PHONE....................800 537-4942
EMP: 5 EST: 2022
SALES (est): 106.48K Privately Held
SIC: 6722 Money market mutual funds

(G-14946)
BLACKROCK US GVRNMENT BOND VI
100 Bellevue Pkwy (19809-3716)
PHONE....................302 797-2000
EMP: 62 EST: 2014
SALES (est): 1.14MM Publicly Held
SIC: 6722 Money market mutual funds
HQ: Blackrock Advisors, Llc
    800 Scudders Mill Rd
    Plainsboro NJ 08536

(G-14947)
BLACKROCK VLUE OPPRTNTIES VI F
100 Bellevue Pkwy (19809-3716)
PHONE....................302 797-2000
Robin Elise Baum, VP
EMP: 5 EST: 2014
SALES (est): 179.76K Privately Held
Web: www.blackrock.com
SIC: 6722 Money market mutual funds

(G-14948)
BLACKSTONE BUILDING GROUP LLC
1705 Lovering Ave (19806-2119)
PHONE....................302 824-4632
Benjamin Bell, Managing Member
EMP: 20 EST: 2017
SALES (est): 4.49MM Privately Held
Web: www.blackstonebg.com
SIC: 1542 Nonresidential construction, nec

(G-14949)
BLACKWELL HR SOLUTIONS
1601 Concord Pike Ste 78 (19803-3630)
PHONE....................202 246-0084
Michelle Ray, CEO
EMP: 6 EST: 2018
SALES (est): 250K Privately Held
Web: www.blackwellhr.com
SIC: 8742 Human resource consulting services

(G-14950)
BLAIR MATERIALS INC
6 Denny Rd Ste 200 (19809-3444)
PHONE....................815 278-0999
EMP: 9
SALES (est): 932.64K Privately Held
SIC: 4212 Local trucking, without storage

(G-14951)
BLAKE AND VAUGHAN ENGRG INC
800 Woodlawn Ave (19805-2815)
PHONE....................302 888-1780
Daniel Blake, Managing Member
Daniel Blake, Pr
Jeff Vaughan, Prin
EMP: 20 EST: 2003
SQ FT: 3,000
SALES (est): 963.42K Privately Held
Web: www.blakevaughan.com
SIC: 8711 Heating and ventilation engineering

(G-14952)
BLANK ROME LLP
1201 N Market St Ste 800 (19801-1807)
PHONE....................302 425-6400
EMP: 6
SALES (corp-wide): 177.04MM Privately Held
Web: www.blankrome.com
SIC: 8111 General practice attorney, lawyer
PA: Blank Rome Llp
    1 Logan Sq
    Philadelphia PA 19103
    215 569-5500

(G-14953)
BLB SERVICES LLC
251 Little Falls Dr (19808-1674)
PHONE....................678 989-7908
Brian Mcguire, Managing Member
EMP: 13
SALES (est): 445.76K Privately Held
SIC: 7371 Computer software development and applications

(G-14954)
BLEEKS LLC
3575 Silverside Rd # 101 (19810-4939)
PHONE....................443 990-0496
Arie Mangrum Iv, Mgr
EMP: 8 EST: 2020
SALES (est): 321.87K Privately Held
SIC: 7371 Computer software development and applications

(G-14955)
BLESS YA HART CNSLTING GROUP L
300 Delaware Ave Ste 210 (19801-1607)
PHONE....................844 748-9017
Ryan Smart, Managing Member
EMP: 12
SALES (est): 423.5K Privately Held
SIC: 8742 Management consulting services

(G-14956)
BLEU SAFE INC
300 Delaware Ave Ste 210a (19801-6601)
PHONE....................619 416-6166
Zara Geol, CEO
EMP: 3 EST: 2020
SALES (est): 500K Privately Held
SIC: 3999 Manufacturing industries, nec

(G-14957)
BLINDSIGHT DELAWARE LLC
2915 Newport Gap Pike (19808-2376)
PHONE....................302 998-5913
L Hrper-brown, Ex Dir
Loretta Harper-brown, Ex Dir
EMP: 30 EST: 2015
SALES (est): 120.18K Privately Held
Web: www.blindsightdelaware.org
SIC: 8699 Charitable organization

(G-14958)
BLINQIO INC ✪
1007 N Orange St (19801-1239)
PHONE....................718 710-4529
Tal Barmeir, CEO
EMP: 12 EST: 2023
SALES (est): 406.37K Privately Held
SIC: 7371 Computer software development and applications

(G-14959)
BLISS STONE MASONRY
106 S Marshall St (19804-2533)
PHONE....................302 293-9194
Jeff Bliss, Owner
EMP: 7 EST: 2009
SALES (est): 334.57K Privately Held
SIC: 1741 Stone masonry

(G-14960)
BLOCKSITE LP
1007 N Orange St (19801-1239)
PHONE....................302 449-4227
Avi Israel, Pt
EMP: 6 EST: 2020
SALES (est): 32.18K Privately Held
Web: www.blocksite.co
SIC: 7379 Online services technology consultants

(G-14961)
BLOOM CONSULTING
2812 Landon Dr (19810-2213)
PHONE....................302 584-1592
Seth Bloom, Pr
EMP: 6 EST: 2003
SALES (est): 444.28K Privately Held
Web: www.digitalcountryindex.com
SIC: 8742 Financial consultant

(G-14962)
BLOOMING SPEECH
12 Peirce Rd (19803-3726)
PHONE....................302 528-6663
EMP: 7 EST: 2014
SALES (est): 81.44K Privately Held
Web: www.blooming-speech.com
SIC: 8093 Rehabilitation center, outpatient treatment

(G-14963)
BLUE DIAMOND DENTAL PA
Also Called: Vincent J Daniels DMD
2300 Pennsylvania Ave Ste 2c (19806-1379)
PHONE....................302 655-8387
Vincent Daniels D.m.d., Pr
Vincent J Daniels D.m.d., Pr
Melanie Daniels, Stockholder
EMP: 9 EST: 1999
SQ FT: 4,000
SALES (est): 814.77K Privately Held
Web: www.bluediamonddental.com
SIC: 8021 Dentists' office

(G-14964)
BLUE DIAMOND RPS & SVCS LLC (PA) ✪
1500-1506 N Hills (19802)

Wilmington - New Castle County (G-14965)

PHONE.....................856 242-0480
Nola Krivda, *Managing Member*
EMP: 5 **EST:** 2022
SALES (est): 240.77K
SALES (corp-wide): 240.77K **Privately Held**
SIC: 7299 7389 Home improvement and renovation contractor agency; Business services, nec

(G-14965)
BLUE DMND HLDG INVESTMENTS LLC
501 N Spruce St (19801-4436)
PHONE.....................302 588-8946
EMP: 7 **EST:** 2017
SALES (est): 279.61K **Privately Held**
SIC: 8742 Management consulting services

(G-14966)
BLUE FIN SERVICES LLC
103 Water St (19804-2406)
PHONE.....................302 633-3354
Kenneth Halfen, *Pr*
EMP: 5 **EST:** 2015
SALES (est): 207.04K **Privately Held**
SIC: 7389 Financial services

(G-14967)
BLUE HEN CC LLC
234 N James St (19804-3132)
PHONE.....................302 999-0708
EMP: 7 **EST:** 2010
SALES (est): 758.36K **Privately Held**
Web: www.pettinaro.com
SIC: 6531 Real estate agent, commercial

(G-14968)
BLUE HEN HOSPITALITY LLC (PA)
Also Called: Crossroad Restaurant
4579 Kirkwood Hwy (19808-5117)
PHONE.....................302 530-5066
John Schulte, *Managing Member*
EMP: 12 **EST:** 2020
SALES (est): 1.88MM
SALES (corp-wide): 1.88MM **Privately Held**
SIC: 5812 7371 Eating places; Computer software development and applications

(G-14969)
BLUE MARBLE LOGISTICS LLC (PA)
800 N King St Ste 102 (19801-3544)
P.O. Box 147 (19899-0147)
PHONE.....................302 661-4390
Dan Boylan, *Pr*
Jeff Berryman, *VP*
Andrew Thompson, *VP*
Dennis Schofield, *VP*
EMP: 9 **EST:** 2003
SQ FT: 3,000
SALES (est): 2.84MM
SALES (corp-wide): 2.84MM **Privately Held**
Web: bluemarbledd.homestead.co
SIC: 5044 Copying equipment

(G-14970)
BLUE PHOENIX LOGISTICS LLC
407 E Ayre St Ste 1071 (19804-2512)
PHONE.....................347 424-7491
EMP: 6
SALES (est): 76.63K **Privately Held**
SIC: 4215 Courier services, except by air

(G-14971)
BLUE PROFIT CLEANING LLC
10 Tamarack Ave (19805-5028)
PHONE.....................302 377-3286
Shawn Marshall, *Prin*

EMP: 6 **EST:** 2017
SALES (est): 78.18K **Privately Held**
SIC: 7699 Cleaning services

(G-14972)
BLUE RIVER RESOURCES LLC
1000 S Heald St (19801-5735)
PHONE.....................302 652-3150
Herb Northrop, *Pt*
EMP: 35 **EST:** 2011
SALES (est): 1.61MM **Privately Held**
SIC: 8742 Business planning and organizing services

(G-14973)
BLUE ROCK LANDSCAPING
103 Farm Ave (19810-2926)
PHONE.....................302 229-8861
EMP: 6 **EST:** 2019
SALES (est): 435.99K **Privately Held**
Web: www.bluerocklandscaping.com
SIC: 0781 Landscape services

(G-14974)
BLUE ROCK LANDSCAPING
502 Beaver Valley Rd (19803-1106)
PHONE.....................302 408-0626
Nick Coppola, *Prin*
EMP: 5 **EST:** 2017
SALES (est): 149.08K **Privately Held**
SIC: 0781 Landscape services

(G-14975)
BLUE SKY CLEAN
293 Carlow Dr (19808-3683)
PHONE.....................302 584-5800
Gary Ventresca, *Prin*
EMP: 2 **EST:** 2002
SALES (est): 155.47K **Privately Held**
Web: www.blueskyclean.net
SIC: 7699 2899 5087 Cleaning services; Chemical supplies for foundries; Laundry equipment and supplies

(G-14976)
BLUE SKY STONES INC (PA) ◆
1013 Centre Rd Ste 403b (19805-1270)
PHONE.....................201 359-1368
Mayank Jhanjhri, *Pr*
EMP: 6 **EST:** 2022
SALES (est): 962.57K
SALES (corp-wide): 962.57K **Privately Held**
SIC: 5032 Brick, stone, and related material

(G-14977)
BLUE SWAN CLEANERS INC (PA)
Also Called: Swan Cleaners
2001 Delaware Ave (19806-2207)
P.O. Box 3722 (19807-0722)
PHONE.....................302 652-7607
Ronald Olivere, *Pr*
Ronald Olivere, *VP*
Kathleen Dent, *Sec*
EMP: 16 **EST:** 1960
SQ FT: 3,500
SALES (est): 647.01K
SALES (corp-wide): 647.01K **Privately Held**
SIC: 7216 7212 Drycleaning plants, except rugs; Garment pressing

(G-14978)
BLUEBALLROOM DANCE STUDIO
206 Weldin Ln (19809-2823)
PHONE.....................302 765-3511
EMP: 6 **EST:** 2018
SALES (est): 27.88K **Privately Held**
Web: www.blueballroom.net

SIC: 7911 Dance studio and school

(G-14979)
BLUEBERRY STAFFING LLC
3 Germay Dr Ste 4 (19804-1127)
PHONE.....................302 445-6300
EMP: 5 **EST:** 2021
SALES (est): 331.04K **Privately Held**
Web: www.blueberrystaffing.com
SIC: 7361 Employment agencies

(G-14980)
BLUEFIN LLC
191 Edgemoor Rd (19809-3153)
PHONE.....................302 731-5770
EMP: 5 **EST:** 2019
SALES (est): 85.91K **Privately Held**
SIC: 1761 Roofing contractor

(G-14981)
BLUEPRINT MOTORSPORT
112 A St (19801-5219)
PHONE.....................302 333-2746
John Tamar, *Prin*
EMP: 5 **EST:** 2017
SALES (est): 110.48K **Privately Held**
SIC: 7549 High performance auto repair and service

(G-14982)
BLUESTONE COMMUNICATIONS INC (DH)
3600 Silverside Rd (19810-5100)
PHONE.....................302 478-4200
Richard E Gibbons Junior, *Pr*
Michael C Goeller, *VP*
Gerard J Herr, *VP*
Philip Lavallee, *VP*
EMP: 5 **EST:** 2005
SQ FT: 10,000
SALES (est): 67.06MM
SALES (corp-wide): 362.45MM **Privately Held**
Web: www.bluestonecomm.com
SIC: 8748 Telecommunications consultant
HQ: Hatzel And Buehler, Inc.
3600 Silverside Rd Ste A
Wilmington DE 19810
302 478-4200

(G-14983)
BLUEVAULT LLC
Also Called: CMS
1300 N Broom St (19806-4206)
P.O. Box 288 (19899-0288)
PHONE.....................302 425-4367
Joe Grieco, *CFO*
EMP: 24 **EST:** 2003
SQ FT: 2,400
SALES (est): 4.24MM **Privately Held**
Web: www.bluevault.com
SIC: 7372 Business oriented computer software

(G-14984)
BLUJIN CORP ◆
251 Little Falls Dr (19808-1674)
PHONE.....................973 219-2638
Jeffrey Kevelson, *Prin*
EMP: 7 **EST:** 2023
SALES (est): 355.22K **Privately Held**
SIC: 5045 Computers, peripherals, and software

(G-14985)
BLW ENTERPRISE INC
1701 Newport Gap Pike (19808-6119)
PHONE.....................302 384-7459
Seth Weaver, *CEO*
EMP: 5

SALES (est): 711.37K **Privately Held**
SIC: 5014 Tires, used

(G-14986)
BMO DELAWARE TRUST COMPANY
20 Montchanin Rd Ste 240 (19807-2174)
PHONE.....................302 652-1660
Douglas Lundblad, *Admn*
EMP: 5 **EST:** 2012
SALES (est): 376.69K **Privately Held**
Web: uswealth.bmo.com
SIC: 6022 State trust companies accepting deposits, commercial

(G-14987)
BNI
6 Oaknoll Rd (19808-3114)
PHONE.....................302 668-9467
EMP: 6 **EST:** 2018
SALES (est): 165.96K **Privately Held**
Web: www.bnidvr.com
SIC: 8621 Professional organizations

(G-14988)
BNY INVESTMENT MGT SVCS LLC
103 Bellevue Pkwy (19809-3701)
PHONE.....................212 495-1784
EMP: 107
SALES (corp-wide): 19.99B **Publicly Held**
SIC: 6022 State commercial banks
HQ: Bny Investment Management Services Llc
1 Wall St
New York NY 10005
212 495-1784

(G-14989)
BOB DAVIS INC
7 Georgetown Ave (19809-1213)
PHONE.....................302 798-2561
Karleen Davis, *Prin*
EMP: 6 **EST:** 2010
SALES (est): 155.22K **Privately Held**
SIC: 1711 Plumbing contractors

(G-14990)
BOB LAFAZIA
Also Called: Bob's Custom Clubs
2635 Grendon Dr (19808-3828)
PHONE.....................302 633-1456
Bob Lafazia, *Prin*
EMP: 6 **EST:** 2009
SALES (est): 79.19K **Privately Held**
Web: www.bobscustomclubs.com
SIC: 7997 Membership sports and recreation clubs

(G-14991)
BOB MOBLEY
4007 Kennett Pike Ste D (19807-2043)
P.O. Box 4574 (19807-4574)
PHONE.....................302 652-2005
Bob Mobley, *Mgr*
EMP: 6 **EST:** 2010
SALES (est): 86.39K **Privately Held**
Web: www.bobmobley.com
SIC: 6411 Insurance agents, nec

(G-14992)
BODELL BOVE LLC
1225 N King St Ste 1000 (19801-3250)
PHONE.....................302 655-6749
Joseph Bodell Junior, *Pt*
EMP: 9
Web: www.bodellbove.com
SIC: 8111 General practice attorney, lawyer
PA: Bodell Bove, Llc
1845 Walnut St Ste 1100
Philadelphia PA 19103

GEOGRAPHIC SECTION
Wilmington - New Castle County (G-15023)

(G-14993)
BODY ELECTRIC LLC
5700 Kirkwood Hwy Ste 205 (19808-4884)
PHONE.................302 559-5577
EMP: 5 EST: 2018
SALES (est): 98.21K Privately Held
Web: the-body-electric-llc.business.site
SIC: 1731 Electrical work

(G-14994)
BODY IMAGES TANNING
2900 Concord Pike Ste E (19803-5097)
PHONE.................302 622-8267
Eileen Morris, Prin
EMP: 6 EST: 2005
SALES (est): 101.28K Privately Held
Web: www.bodyimagesspa.com
SIC: 7299 Tanning salon

(G-14995)
BODY SCLPTING PRFESSIONALS LLC ✪
919 N Market St Ste 950 (19801-3036)
PHONE.................986 999-8238
Kodiak Brown, VP
EMP: 5 EST: 2023
SALES (est): 101.79K Privately Held
SIC: 7991 Physical fitness facilities

(G-14996)
BOERO USA INC
1209 N Orange St (19801-1120)
PHONE.................800 935-6596
Ed Mattingly, Pr
EMP: 6 EST: 2018
SALES (est): 246K Privately Held
Web: www.boerousa.com
SIC: 5198 Paints

(G-14997)
BOMBSHELL BEAUTY INC
331 Rockmeade Dr (19810-1423)
PHONE.................302 559-3011
Suzanne Martinelli, CEO
EMP: 5 EST: 2011
SQ FT: 2,500
SALES (est): 274.88K Privately Held
SIC: 3999 Hair, dressing of, for the trade

(G-14998)
BOND APP LLC
1207 Delaware Ave (19806-4743)
PHONE.................415 418-4017
Chloe Samaha, Managing Member
EMP: 2
SALES (est): 87.4K Privately Held
SIC: 7372 Prepackaged software

(G-14999)
BONDED BUSINESS SERVICES
6 Colony Boulevard Apt 208 (19802-1479)
PHONE.................302 438-6007
Caleeb Watson, Prin
EMP: 8 EST: 2017
SALES (est): 52.35K Privately Held
Web: www.bbsltdcollects.com
SIC: 7322 Collection agency, except real estate

(G-15000)
BONNA-AGELA TECHNOLOGIES INC (PA)
2038a Telegraph Rd (19808-5230)
PHONE.................302 438-8798
▲ EMP: 22 EST: 2011
SALES (est): 4.32MM Privately Held
Web: www.agela.com
SIC: 3826 Analytical instruments

(G-15001)
BOOKE AI INC
919 N Market St (19801-3023)
PHONE.................650 540-1316
EMP: 6
SALES (est): 68.89K Privately Held
SIC: 7371 Computer software development

(G-15002)
BOOKME AI INC
2810 N Church St (19802-4447)
PHONE.................650 436-9210
Jonathan Olvera, CEO
EMP: 6
SALES (est): 305.19K Privately Held
SIC: 7371 Computer software development and applications

(G-15003)
BOOKS & TOBACCOS INC
4555 Kirkwood Hwy (19808-5117)
PHONE.................302 994-3156
Andy Summer, Pr
Donna R Summer, VP
EMP: 7 EST: 1991
SALES (est): 533.69K Privately Held
SIC: 5192 7999 5199 Books, periodicals, and newspapers; Lottery tickets, sale of; Lighters, cigarette and cigar

(G-15004)
BOOMSET INC
Also Called: Boomset
2810 N Church St (19802-4447)
PHONE.................860 266-6738
Kerem Baran, CEO
Cem Kozinoglu, CEO
Ahmet Can, COO
Johnny Boufarhat, CEO
EMP: 19 EST: 2009
SALES (est): 2.39MM Privately Held
Web: www.boomset.com
SIC: 7371 5045 Computer software development; Computers, peripherals, and software

(G-15005)
BOOST LEARNING LLC
721 Ambleside Dr (19808-1502)
PHONE.................302 691-5821
Eric Randolph, Prin
EMP: 10 EST: 2013
SALES (est): 242.11K Privately Held
Web: www.boostlearningonline.com
SIC: 8351 Preschool center

(G-15006)
BOOST MOBILE
1200 Northeast Blvd (19802-5183)
PHONE.................302 482-1193
EMP: 8 EST: 2017
SALES (est): 88.67K Privately Held
Web: my.boostmobile.com
SIC: 4812 Cellular telephone services

(G-15007)
BOOST MOBILE BY INFINITY WIREL
206 W Market St (19804-3152)
PHONE.................856 691-7800
EMP: 5 EST: 2017
SALES (est): 35.32K Privately Held
SIC: 4812 Cellular telephone services

(G-15008)
BORSELLO IRRIGATION INC
2001 Monroe Pl (19802-3923)
PHONE.................302 652-6717
EMP: 5 EST: 2019
SALES (est): 35.16K Privately Held
Web: www.borselloinc.com
SIC: 4971 Irrigation systems

(G-15009)
BOSTON LAND CO MGT SVCS INC
Also Called: Quaker Hill Place Co
200 N Washington St Ofc 1 (19801-2300)
PHONE.................302 571-0100
Judith Vansice, Prin
EMP: 9
SALES (corp-wide): 8.55MM Privately Held
Web: www.bostonland.com
SIC: 6531 6513 Real estate managers; Apartment building operators
PA: The Boston Land Company Management Services Inc
411 Waverly Oaks Rd # 31
Waltham MA 02452
781 547-4280

(G-15010)
BOUDART & MENSINGER LLP
2710 Centerville Rd Ste 101 (19808-1644)
PHONE.................302 428-0100
Thomas Jenkins, Prin
EMP: 6 EST: 2007
SALES (est): 936.52K Privately Held
Web: www.pmcelaw.com
SIC: 8111 General practice attorney, lawyer

(G-15011)
BOUDREAUX ILENE LEFKOWITZ MD
3521 Silverside Rd Ste 1f (19810-4900)
PHONE.................302 479-5505
Ilene Boudreaux, Owner
EMP: 12 EST: 2008
SALES (est): 82.26K Privately Held
SIC: 8011 Pediatrician

(G-15012)
BOULARES INNOVATIONS LLC
300 Delaware Ave (19801-1607)
PHONE.................504 575-2386
EMP: 5
SALES (est): 57.44K Privately Held
SIC: 7381 Private investigator

(G-15013)
BOULDEN BUSES INC
32 Honeysuckle Ln (19804-3992)
PHONE.................302 998-5463
Kenneth Darsney, Pr
Charlene Fanny, *
EMP: 13 EST: 1933
SALES (est): 517.41K Privately Held
SIC: 4151 School buses

(G-15014)
BOUNCE BACK PHYSICAL THERAPY
106 Dale Rd (19810-4302)
PHONE.................484 582-0660
Charan Chadha, Prin
EMP: 6 EST: 2017
SALES (est): 70.61K Privately Held
SIC: 8049 Physical therapist

(G-15015)
BOUNDLESS ENTERPRISES INC
1207 Delaware Ave (19806-4743)
PHONE.................628 201-9286
Noel Chenu, CEO
EMP: 3
SALES (est): 128.34K Privately Held
SIC: 7372 Application computer software

(G-15016)
BOVE PSYCHOLOGICAL SVCS LLC
108 Peirce Rd (19803-3728)
PHONE.................302 299-5193
EMP: 6 EST: 2017
SALES (est): 68.17K Privately Held
SIC: 8059 Personal care home, with health care

(G-15017)
BOWIE REFINED COAL LLC
2711 Centerville Rd # 400 (19808-1660)
PHONE.................302 636-5401
EMP: 7 EST: 2012
SALES (est): 200K Privately Held
SIC: 5052 Coal

(G-15018)
BOWLES CONSTRUCTION LLC
1 Queens Ct (19808-1816)
PHONE.................302 332-5641
EMP: 5 EST: 2015
SALES (est): 139.22K Privately Held
Web: www.bowlesconstructionde.com
SIC: 1521 General remodeling, single-family houses

(G-15019)
BOYER & BOYER (PA)
Also Called: BOPyer& Boyer CPA
2392 Limestone Rd (19808-4127)
PHONE.................302 998-3700
Donald L Boyer, Owner
Janet Edwards, Mgr
EMP: 6 EST: 1975
SQ FT: 3,500
SALES (est): 907.87K Privately Held
Web: www.boyercpa.net
SIC: 8721 Certified public accountant

(G-15020)
BOYS & GIRLS CLUBS DEL INC (PA)
669 S Union St (19805-3852)
PHONE.................302 658-1870
Stuart Sharkey, Ch Bd
George Krupanski Junior, Pr
James C Logullo, *
Christopher Basher, *
Ellen Mclean, VP
EMP: 305 EST: 1930
SQ FT: 10,000
SALES (est): 33.26MM
SALES (corp-wide): 33.26MM Privately Held
Web: www.bgclubs.org
SIC: 8641 Youth organizations

(G-15021)
BP STAFFING INC
Also Called: Bernard Personnel
5187 W Woodmill Dr Ste 1 (19808-4067)
PHONE.................302 999-7213
Al Collins, Pr
EMP: 10 EST: 2005
SALES (est): 363.8K Privately Held
Web: www.bernardstaff.com
SIC: 7363 8742 Help supply services; Personnel management consultant

(G-15022)
BPG JUSTISON P4 B1 LLC
340 S Madison St (19801-7100)
PHONE.................302 652-1876
EMP: 5 EST: 2009
SALES (est): 134.89K Privately Held
SIC: 6519 Farm land leasing

(G-15023)
BPG OFFICE
233 N King St (19801-2545)
PHONE.................302 654-8535
EMP: 13 EST: 2010
SALES (est): 268.13K Privately Held
Web: www.bpgroup.net

(PA)=Parent Co (HQ)=Headquarters
✪ = New Business established in last 2 years

Wilmington - New Castle County (G-15024) — GEOGRAPHIC SECTION

SIC: 6519 Real property lessors, nec

(G-15024)
BPG OFFICE INVSTORS III/IV LLC
Also Called: Bpg
1000 N West St Ste 900 (19801-1000)
PHONE..................302 691-2100
C F Buccini, *Managing Member*
Christopher F Buccini, *Managing Member*
EMP: 10 EST: 2003
SQ FT: 4,000
SALES (est): 1.09MM **Privately Held**
SIC: 6531 Real estate agent, commercial

(G-15025)
BPG OFFICE PARTNERS VIII LLC
1000 N West St Ste 900 (19801-1000)
PHONE..................302 250-3065
Christopher Buccini, *Prin*
EMP: 50 EST: 2007
SALES (est): 4.52MM **Privately Held**
Web: bpg-office-partners-viii.hub.biz
SIC: 6798 Real estate investment trusts

(G-15026)
BPG REAL ESTATE SERVICES LLC
3505 Silverside Rd Ste 105 (19810-4905)
PHONE..................302 478-1190
Chris Derasmo, *Prin*
EMP: 6
SALES (corp-wide): 4.94MM **Privately Held**
Web: www.bpgroup.net
SIC: 6531 Real estate agent, commercial
PA: Bpg Real Estate Services Llc
1000 N West St Ste 1000 # 1000
Wilmington DE 19801
302 777-2000

(G-15027)
BPG REAL ESTATE SERVICES LLC (PA)
Also Called: Bpg
1000 N West St Ste 1000 (19801-1000)
PHONE..................302 777-2000
EMP: 19 EST: 2001
SALES (est): 4.94MM
SALES (corp-wide): 4.94MM **Privately Held**
Web: www.bpgroup.net
SIC: 6531 Real estate leasing and rentals

(G-15028)
BPG RSDENTIAL PARTNERS III LLC
22 A St Ste 300 (19801-5217)
PHONE..................302 691-2100
EMP: 8 EST: 2004
SALES (est): 135.04K **Privately Held**
SIC: 6531 Real estate agent, commercial

(G-15029)
BPGS CONSTRUCTION LLC
1000 N West St (19801-1050)
PHONE..................302 691-2111
EMP: 55 EST: 1999
SALES (est): 10.97MM **Privately Held**
Web: www.bpgsconstruction.com
SIC: 8741 Construction management

(G-15030)
BPPN LLC
707 N Union St (19805-3031)
PHONE..................302 384-5119
EMP: 9 EST: 2017
SALES (est): 76.21K **Privately Held**
Web: www.bppn.org
SIC: 8322 Individual and family services

(G-15031)
BQT INC
3613 Kirkwood Hwy Ste F (19808-5132)
PHONE..................347 443-8911
Damian Archer, *COO*
Blanca Gonzlez, *Dir*
Donald R Rice, *Prin*
EMP: 6 EST: 2012
SALES (est): 226.92K **Privately Held**
Web: www.bqtglobal.com
SIC: 7389 Translation services

(G-15032)
BRADLEY J SANDELLA DO
1401 Foulk Rd Ste 100 (19803-2764)
PHONE..................302 477-3300
Bradley Sandella, *CEO*
EMP: 8 EST: 2018
SALES (est): 168.69K **Privately Held**
SIC: 8011 General and family practice, physician/surgeon

(G-15033)
BRADSWORTH DIGITAL SOLUTIONS
251 Little Falls Dr (19808-1674)
PHONE..................630 200-2251
Arthur Taulbee, *CEO*
Arthur R Taulbee, *CEO*
EMP: 6 EST: 2016
SALES (est): 345.4K **Privately Held**
Web: www.bradsworth.com
SIC: 8742 Management consulting services

(G-15034)
BRADY LAW FIRM PA
240 N James St (19804-3169)
PHONE..................302 482-4124
EMP: 5 EST: 2018
SALES (est): 221.98K **Privately Held**
Web: www.bradylawde.com
SIC: 8111 General practice law office

(G-15035)
BRAE CORP
103 Foulk Rd (19803-3742)
PHONE..................302 691-6043
EMP: 5 EST: 2004
SALES (est): 24.5K **Privately Held**
SIC: 8721 Certified public accountant

(G-15036)
BRAINCX INC (PA) ◆
300 Dlware Ave Ste 210 (19801)
PHONE..................954 892-9101
Tariq Alinur, *CEO*
Rose Jim Flores Alinur, *CEO*
EMP: 10 EST: 2022
SALES (est): 355.79K
SALES (corp-wide): 355.79K **Privately Held**
SIC: 7374 7389 Computer processing services; Patent brokers

(G-15037)
BRAINIAC BRANDS USA INC
919 N Market St Ste 950 (19801-3036)
PHONE..................778 869-4099
Yuriy Rubin, *Ex Dir*
EMP: 5 EST: 2018
SALES (est): 800K **Privately Held**
SIC: 2023 Dietary supplements, dairy and non-dairy based

(G-15038)
BRAINSTORM FORCE US LLC
300 Delaware Ave Ste 210a (19801-6601)
PHONE..................302 330-8557
Sujay Pawar, *Prin*
EMP: 6 EST: 2019
SALES (est): 64.74K **Privately Held**
SIC: 7374 Data processing and preparation

(G-15039)
BRAND BUILDER SOLUTIONS LLC
232 Steeplechase Cir (19808-1977)
PHONE..................302 234-4239
Joseph Jerome, *Mgr*
EMP: 6 EST: 2020
SALES (est): 232.1K **Privately Held**
Web: www.brandbuildersolutions.com
SIC: 1521 Single-family housing construction

(G-15040)
BRAND DESIGN CO INC
Also Called: House Industries
2927 Faulkland Rd (19808-2513)
PHONE..................302 234-2356
EMP: 8 EST: 1993
SALES (est): 971.1K **Privately Held**
SIC: 7336 Graphic arts and related design

(G-15041)
BRANDI WINE PEDIATRIC INC
Also Called: Disanto, Joseph MD
3521 Silverside Rd Ste 1f (19810-4900)
PHONE..................302 478-7805
Rob Walter, *Pr*
Joseph Di Santo, *
EMP: 25 EST: 1972
SALES (est): 4.99MM **Privately Held**
SIC: 8011 Pediatrician

(G-15042)
BRANDYWINE APARTMENT ASSOC LP
2702 Jacqueline Dr Apt H19 (19810-2032)
PHONE..................302 475-8600
Paul Gravenhorst, *Pt*
EMP: 9 EST: 1984
SQ FT: 3,000
SALES (est): 492.45K **Privately Held**
Web: www.brandywineapartmentsdelaware.com
SIC: 6513 Apartment hotel operation

(G-15043)
BRANDYWINE ARTS FESTIVAL
1302 W 9th St (19806-4621)
PHONE..................302 363-5955
EMP: 8 EST: 2011
SALES (est): 44.4K **Privately Held**
Web: www.brandywinearts.com
SIC: 7999 Festival operation

(G-15044)
BRANDYWINE BODY SHOP INC
1325 Newport Gap Pike (19804-2845)
PHONE..................302 998-0424
Gary Louth, *CEO*
Lisa Louth, *VP*
EMP: 9 EST: 1983
SQ FT: 10,000
SALES (est): 814.49K **Privately Held**
Web: www.brandywinebodyshop.com
SIC: 7532 Body shop, automotive

(G-15045)
BRANDYWINE BODYWORKS
1400 Philadelphia Pike (19809-1856)
PHONE..................302 798-0801
EMP: 5 EST: 2019
SALES (est): 112.99K **Privately Held**
Web: www.brandywinebodywork.com
SIC: 7532 Body shop, automotive

(G-15046)
BRANDYWINE BOTANICALS LLC
318 Tindall Rd (19805-1305)
PHONE..................302 354-4650
Robin Kielkowski, *Prin*
EMP: 4 EST: 2017
SALES (est): 160.71K **Privately Held**
SIC: 2844 Perfumes, cosmetics and other toilet preparations

(G-15047)
BRANDYWINE CAD DESIGN INC
3204 Concord Pike (19803-5015)
PHONE..................302 478-8334
Donald Lloyd, *Pr*
Patricia Lloyd, *
EMP: 24 EST: 1987
SQ FT: 7,000
SALES (est): 3.22MM **Privately Held**
Web: www.bcad.com
SIC: 7374 8711 8712 Data processing and preparation; Engineering services; Architectural services

(G-15048)
BRANDYWINE CARE L L C
Also Called: Charles E Hill MD
1300 Delaware Ave Ste 1 (19806-4727)
PHONE..................302 658-5822
EMP: 10 EST: 1992
SALES (est): 277.03K **Privately Held**
Web: www.brandywinemed.com
SIC: 8011 General and family practice, physician/surgeon

(G-15049)
BRANDYWINE CENTER FOR AUTISM
510 Philadelphia Pike Fl 2 (19809-2169)
PHONE..................302 762-2636
Marcus A Henry, *CEO*
EMP: 52 EST: 2015
SALES (est): 353.81K **Privately Held**
Web: www.brandywinecenterforautism.com
SIC: 8322 Social service center

(G-15050)
BRANDYWINE CHRYSLER JEEP DODGE (PA)
Also Called: Brandywine Chrysler Jeep
3807 Kirkwood Hwy (19808-5107)
P.O. Box 5923 (19808-0923)
PHONE..................302 998-0458
Robert T Jones Junior, *Pr*
Francine Young, *Pr*
EMP: 70 EST: 1968
SQ FT: 20,000
SALES (est): 23.52MM
SALES (corp-wide): 23.52MM **Privately Held**
Web: www.wilmingtoncdjr.com
SIC: 5511 7539 Automobiles, new and used; Automotive repair shops, nec

(G-15051)
BRANDYWINE CNSLING CMNTY SVCS (PA)
2713 Lancaster Ave (19805-5220)
PHONE..................302 655-9880
Lynn M Fahey, *Ex Dir*
EMP: 60 EST: 1984
SALES (est): 16.65MM
SALES (corp-wide): 16.65MM **Privately Held**
Web: www.brandywinecounseling.com
SIC: 8322 General counseling services

(G-15052)
BRANDYWINE COUNSELING
500 Duncan Rd Ofc 1 (19809-2369)
PHONE..................302 762-7120
Lynn M Fahey, *Mgr*
EMP: 29
SALES (corp-wide): 16.65MM **Privately Held**
Web: www.brandywinecounseling.com

GEOGRAPHIC SECTION

Wilmington - New Castle County (G-15080)

SIC: 8322 General counseling services
PA: Brandywine Counseling & Community Services, Inc.
2713 Lancaster Ave
Wilmington DE 19805
302 655-9880

(G-15053)
BRANDYWINE COUNTRY CLUB
302 River Rd Apt D2 (19809-2749)
PHONE.................................302 478-4604
Ronald Rottmann, *Ex Dir*
EMP: 39 **EST:** 1945
SQ FT: 3,500
SALES (est): 2.81MM **Privately Held**
Web: www.brandywinecountryclub.net
SIC: 7997 Golf club, membership

(G-15054)
BRANDYWINE CTR FOR DNCE THE PR
1812 Marsh Rd Ste 419 (19810-4522)
PHONE.................................302 416-6959
EMP: 6 **EST:** 2018
SALES (est): 21.12K **Privately Held**
Web: www.brandywinecenterfordance.com
SIC: 7911 Dance studio and school

(G-15055)
BRANDYWINE ELEVATOR CO INC (PA)
300 B And O Ln (19804-1448)
PHONE.................................866 636-0102
Michael Sanfrancesco, *Pr*
EMP: 9 **EST:** 2009
SQ FT: 1,800
SALES (est): 2.69MM
SALES (corp-wide): 2.69MM **Privately Held**
Web: www.3phaseelevator.com
SIC: 5084 1796 Elevators; Elevator installation and conversion

(G-15056)
BRANDYWINE EXTERIORS CORP
221 Valley Rd (19804-1356)
PHONE.................................302 746-7134
Joshua Boesen, *Pr*
EMP: 25 **EST:** 2012
SALES (est): 2.23MM **Privately Held**
Web: www.brandywineexteriors.com
SIC: 1761 Roofing contractor

(G-15057)
BRANDYWINE FINE PROPERTIES
5701 Kennett Pike (19807-1311)
PHONE.................................302 691-3052
George Hobbs, *Owner*
EMP: 10 **EST:** 2006
SALES (est): 975.03K **Privately Held**
Web: www.bfpsir.com
SIC: 6531 Real estate brokers and agents

(G-15058)
BRANDYWINE FOOD SERVICES LLC
800 N King St Ste 303 (19801-3549)
PHONE.................................302 276-5165
John V Work, *Prin*
EMP: 5 **EST:** 2016
SALES (est): 155.11K **Privately Held**
SIC: 5141 Groceries, general line

(G-15059)
BRANDYWINE FOOT CARE
2106 Silverside Rd Ste 102 (19810-4163)
PHONE.................................302 478-8099
EMP: 6 **EST:** 2020
SALES (est): 175.28K **Privately Held**

SIC: 8043 Offices and clinics of podiatrists

(G-15060)
BRANDYWINE FUND INC
Also Called: Brandywine
3711 Kennett Pike Ste 100 (19807-2156)
P.O. Box 4166 (19807-0166)
PHONE.................................302 656-3017
Bill D Alonzo, *Pr*
EMP: 10 **EST:** 2006
SALES (est): 242.61K **Privately Held**
Web: www.friess.com
SIC: 6722 Money market mutual funds

(G-15061)
BRANDYWINE GLOBAL INVESTEMENT
4005 Kennett Pike Ste 250 (19807-2018)
PHONE.................................610 380-2110
EMP: 5 **EST:** 2014
SALES (est): 149.89K **Privately Held**
SIC: 6722 Money market mutual funds

(G-15062)
BRANDYWINE GRAPHICS INC
Also Called: CNW Enterprise
500 S Colonial Ave (19805-1900)
PHONE.................................302 655-7571
Robert R Shaw Senior, *Pr*
Aida Shaw, *Pr*
Robert R Shaw Junior, *VP Sls*
Craig Shaw, *VP Fin*
EMP: 7 **EST:** 1969
SQ FT: 18,500
SALES (est): 926.83K **Privately Held**
Web: www.brandywinegraphicsinc.com
SIC: 2761 2752 5112 Strip forms (manifold business forms); Offset printing; Business forms

(G-15063)
BRANDYWINE HEATING & AIR LLC
216 S Maryland Ave (19804-1344)
P.O. Box 30078 (19805-7078)
PHONE.................................302 299-0180
Averill Peak, *Prin*
EMP: 7 **EST:** 2018
SALES (est): 271.76K **Privately Held**
Web: www.brandywineheatingandair.com
SIC: 1711 Warm air heating and air conditioning contractor

(G-15064)
BRANDYWINE HILLS APARTMENTS
Also Called: Evergreen Reallty
4310 Miller Rd Apt 106 (19802-1919)
PHONE.................................302 764-3242
Steven Woolfgang, *Owner*
EMP: 7 **EST:** 1965
SALES (est): 154.5K **Privately Held**
Web: www.videoapt.com
SIC: 6513 Apartment building operators

(G-15065)
BRANDYWINE HNDRED VTRNARY HOSP
806 Silverside Rd (19809-1324)
PHONE.................................302 792-2777
Steven Hardy, *Owner*
EMP: 10 **EST:** 1974
SALES (est): 469.49K **Privately Held**
Web: www.brandywinehundredvets.com
SIC: 0742 Animal hospital services, pets and other animal specialties

(G-15066)
BRANDYWINE HUNDRED FAMILY MDCN
1401 Foulk Rd Ste 202 (19803-2764)
PHONE.................................302 478-5650

Pat Thomson, *Off Mgr*
EMP: 13 **EST:** 2018
SALES (est): 573.14K **Privately Held**
Web: www.bhfmde.com
SIC: 8011 General and family practice, physician/surgeon

(G-15067)
BRANDYWINE HUNDRED FIRE CO 1
Also Called: BRANDYWINE HUNDRED FIRE CO NO
1006 Brandywine Blvd (19809-2530)
PHONE.................................302 764-4901
Thomas Finlechiro, *Chief*
EMP: 80 **EST:** 1924
SQ FT: 9,900
SALES (est): 2.45MM **Privately Held**
Web: www.bhfc11.com
SIC: 7389 8322 Fire protection service other than forestry or public; Emergency shelters

(G-15068)
BRANDYWINE I & 2 APTS
2702 Jacqueline Dr H19 (19810-2093)
PHONE.................................302 475-8600
Wanda Hirchy, *Owner*
EMP: 10 **EST:** 1986
SALES (est): 413.57K **Privately Held**
SIC: 6513 Apartment building operators

(G-15069)
BRANDYWINE LACROSSE CLUB
2403 W Heather Rd (19803-2719)
PHONE.................................302 249-1840
Kenneth Rittenhouse, *Prin*
EMP: 6 **EST:** 2017
SALES (est): 90.25K **Privately Held**
Web: www.brandywinelacrosse.com
SIC: 7997 Membership sports and recreation clubs

(G-15070)
BRANDYWINE LIGHTING GALLERY
4723 Concord Pike Ste F (19803-1446)
PHONE.................................302 543-6939
Tom Vari, *Prin*
EMP: 8 **EST:** 2015
SALES (est): 244.9K **Privately Held**
Web: www.brandywinelightinggallery.com
SIC: 8412 Historical society

(G-15071)
BRANDYWINE MARKETING SERVICES
17 Stone Crop Rd (19810-1315)
PHONE.................................302 761-9755
Gerald R Ansul, *Pr*
Harriet B Ansul, *
EMP: 33 **EST:** 1986
SALES (est): 929.15K **Privately Held**
SIC: 7389 Telemarketing services

(G-15072)
BRANDYWINE MASTER CARPENTRY
2824 W Oakland Dr (19808-2409)
PHONE.................................302 463-9773
Michael Durkee, *Prin*
EMP: 5 **EST:** 2016
SALES (est): 71.03K **Privately Held**
SIC: 1751 Carpentry work

(G-15073)
BRANDYWINE MILL WORK
1907 N Market St (19802-4812)
PHONE.................................302 652-3008
EMP: 2
SALES (est): 171.15K **Privately Held**
SIC: 2431 Millwork

(G-15074)
BRANDYWINE NRSING RHBLTTION CT
505 Greenbank Rd (19808-3164)
PHONE.................................302 683-0444
Harry Tractman, *Pr*
Fred Dibartolo, *
EMP: 45 **EST:** 1975
SQ FT: 22,000
SALES (est): 4.27MM **Privately Held**
SIC: 8051 Convalescent home with continuous nursing care

(G-15075)
BRANDYWINE NURSERIES INC
4 James Ct (19801-5250)
P.O. Box 9333 (19809-0333)
PHONE.................................302 429-0865
Brien H Jamison, *Pr*
Joseph F Jamison Junior, *VP*
EMP: 48 **EST:** 1946
SQ FT: 5,000
SALES (est): 2MM **Privately Held**
Web: www.brandywinenurseries.com
SIC: 0781 0782 Landscape planning services ; Landscape contractors

(G-15076)
BRANDYWINE OB GYN
3520 Silverside Rd Ste 2l1 (19810-4933)
PHONE.................................302 477-1375
Joseph Espinosa, *Mgr*
EMP: 5 **EST:** 2010
SALES (est): 399.39K **Privately Held**
SIC: 8011 Gynecologist

(G-15077)
BRANDYWINE OCCPATIONAL THERAPY
800 Carr Rd (19809-2163)
PHONE.................................302 740-4798
Lauren Janusz, *Prin*
EMP: 10 **EST:** 2010
SALES (est): 182.96K **Privately Held**
Web: www.brandywineot.com
SIC: 8093 Rehabilitation center, outpatient treatment

(G-15078)
BRANDYWINE PAIN CENTER
4512 Kirkwood Hwy Ste 200 (19808-5122)
PHONE.................................302 998-2585
Emmanuel Devotta, *Prin*
EMP: 12 **EST:** 1997
SALES (est): 757.8K **Privately Held**
Web: www.painmanagementdelaware.com
SIC: 8011 Orthopedic physician

(G-15079)
BRANDYWINE PARK CONDOS
Also Called: Brandywine Park Condominiums
1704 N Park Dr Apt 115 (19806-2167)
PHONE.................................302 655-2262
Thomas Kraph, *Pt*
Ann Lemay, *Pt*
Louis Capano, *Pt*
EMP: 5 **EST:** 1985
SALES (est): 509.42K **Privately Held**
SIC: 8641 Condominium association

(G-15080)
BRANDYWINE PDT GROUP INTL INC
Also Called: Bpg International
3 Mill Rd Ste 202 (19806-2147)
PHONE.................................302 472-1463
Rob Heflin, *Pr*
Frank Lesniak, *
▲ **EMP:** 46 **EST:** 2004
SALES (est): 9.26MM **Privately Held**

Wilmington - New Castle County (G-15081) GEOGRAPHIC SECTION

SIC: 3999 Atomizers, toiletry

(G-15081)
BRANDYWINE PROCESS SERVERS
2500 Delaware Ave (19806-1220)
P.O. Box 1360 (19899-1360)
PHONE..................................302 475-2600
Kevin Dunn, Pr
EMP: 5 EST: 1983
SALES (est): 395.91K Privately Held
Web:
www.1daydelawareprocessservers.com
SIC: 7389 Process serving service

(G-15082)
BRANDYWINE REALTY MANAGEMENT
Also Called: Brandywine Management
3200 Lancaster Ave (19805-1463)
PHONE..................................302 656-1058
Harold F Thomas, Pr
Deborah Brumbaugh, VP
Bud Thomas, Pr
EMP: 9 EST: 1985
SALES (est): 421.95K Privately Held
Web: www.renthome.org
SIC: 6531 Real estate managers

(G-15083)
BRANDYWINE RESURFACING
2213 Brookline Rd (19803-5221)
PHONE..................................302 654-8744
Joe Ross, Prin
EMP: 5 EST: 2005
SALES (est): 226.27K Privately Held
Web: www.brandywineresurfacing.com
SIC: 1799 Exterior cleaning, including sandblasting

(G-15084)
BRANDYWINE RUBBER MILLS LLC
1704 N Park Dr Apt 508 (19806-2171)
PHONE..................................267 499-3993
EMP: 5 EST: 2017
SALES (est): 83.48K Privately Held
SIC: 3069 Fabricated rubber products, nec

(G-15085)
BRANDYWINE RVER REPRESENTATIVE
122 Brook Valley Rd (19807-2004)
PHONE..................................302 984-2861
Andy Molter, Prin
EMP: 7 EST: 2011
SALES (est): 437.06K Privately Held
Web: www.brreps.com
SIC: 5199 Nondurable goods, nec

(G-15086)
BRANDYWINE TOTAL HEALTH CARE
3214 Naamans Rd (19810-1004)
PHONE..................................302 478-3028
Donald F Feeney, Pr
EMP: 5 EST: 1971
SALES (est): 392.09K Privately Held
Web: www.bwtotalhealth.com
SIC: 8041 Offices and clinics of chiropractors

(G-15087)
BRANDYWINE TREE AND SHRUB LLC
214 Alders Dr (19803-5304)
PHONE..................................302 475-7594
John Florentino, Managing Member
EMP: 8 EST: 2008
SALES (est): 917.96K Privately Held
Web: www.brandywinetree.net
SIC: 0783 Planting, pruning, and trimming services

(G-15088)
BRANDYWINE UROLOGY CONS PA (PA)
2000 Foulk Rd Ste F (19810-3642)
PHONE..................................302 652-8990
David J Cozzolino, Pt
EMP: 15 EST: 2000
SALES (est): 3.3MM
SALES (corp-wide): 3.3MM Privately Held
Web: www.brandywineuc.com
SIC: 8011 Urologist

(G-15089)
BRANDYWINE VALLEY PROPERTIES
1806 Breen Ln (19810-4507)
P.O. Box 7368 (19803-0368)
PHONE..................................302 475-7660
David L Sibert, Pr
EMP: 6 EST: 1994
SALES (est): 460.34K Privately Held
Web: www.bvprops.com
SIC: 6531 Condominium manager

(G-15090)
BRANDYWINE VALLEY SPCA
1110 Graylyn Rd (19803-3335)
PHONE..................................302 475-9294
EMP: 7 EST: 2019
SALES (est): 53.59K Privately Held
Web: www.bvspca.org
SIC: 8699 Animal humane society

(G-15091)
BRANDYWINE VALLEY WOODWORKING
1212 Bruce Rd (19803-4202)
PHONE..................................302 743-5640
Richard Blaylock, Owner
EMP: 2 EST: 1998
SQ FT: 1,200
SALES (est): 98K Privately Held
Web: www.bvwinc.com
SIC: 2511 Children's wood furniture

(G-15092)
BRANDYWINE VOLLEYBALL CLUB
3023 Maple Shade Ln (19810-3423)
PHONE..................................302 898-6452
Gina Trinsey, Dir
EMP: 7 EST: 2011
SALES (est): 123.19K Privately Held
Web: www.brandywinevbc.com
SIC: 7997 Membership sports and recreation clubs

(G-15093)
BRANDYWINE WATERPROOFING DEL
2407 Saint Francis St (19808-4049)
PHONE..................................302 482-4368
Edward S Purzycki, Pr
EMP: 5 EST: 2010
SALES (est): 117.28K Privately Held
SIC: 1799 Waterproofing

(G-15094)
BRANDYWINE ZOO
1001 N Park Dr (19802-3801)
PHONE..................................302 571-7747
Mark Shafer, Ex Dir
Larry Gurrkie,
Nancy Salscolaski,
EMP: 28 EST: 2000
SALES (est): 623.62K Privately Held
Web: www.brandywinezoo.com
SIC: 8422 Botanical and zoological gardens

(G-15095)
BRANTNGHAM CRROLL HOLDINGS INC (PA)
1209 N Orange St (19801-1120)
PHONE..................................724 266-0400
Mathew Carroll, Prin
EMP: 5 EST: 2018
SALES (est): 123.24K
SALES (corp-wide): 123.24K Privately Held
SIC: 8741 Management services

(G-15096)
BRAUN AGENCY INC
Also Called: Nationwide
1906 Newport Gap Pike (19808-6136)
PHONE..................................302 998-1412
EMP: 6 EST: 2019
SALES (est): 55.85K Privately Held
Web: www.nationwide.com
SIC: 6411 Insurance agents, nec

(G-15097)
BREAKOUT TRADING GROUP LLC ◊
2810 N Church St Pmb 544583 (19802-4447)
PHONE..................................302 365-0947
Alex Miningham, Managing Member
EMP: 3 EST: 2023
SALES (est): 128.34K Privately Held
SIC: 7372 Prepackaged software

(G-15098)
BREAKWTER ACCNTING ADVSORY GRO
1601 Concord Pike Ste 100 (19803-3600)
PHONE..................................302 543-4564
Lee Podolsky, Prin
Lee Podolsky, CEO
EMP: 44 EST: 2000
SALES (est): 4.73MM Privately Held
Web: www.breakwatercorp.com
SIC: 8721 Certified public accountant

(G-15099)
BRECKSTONE GROUP INC
Also Called: Breckstone Architecture
2417 Lancaster Ave (19805-3736)
P.O. Box 65 (19710-0065)
PHONE..................................302 654-3646
EMP: 8 EST: 1993
SQ FT: 2,500
SALES (est): 946.31K Privately Held
Web: www.breckstonearchitecture.com
SIC: 8712 Architectural engineering

(G-15100)
BREEDING & DAY INC (PA)
3316 Silverside Rd (19810-3307)
PHONE..................................302 478-4585
Clifford Breeding, Pr
EMP: 20 EST: 1977
SQ FT: 1,500
SALES (est): 2.36MM
SALES (corp-wide): 2.36MM Privately Held
Web: www.chaddsfordclimatecontrol.com
SIC: 1711 Warm air heating and air conditioning contractor

(G-15101)
BREES HOME DAY CARE
915 E 26th St (19802-4433)
PHONE..................................302 762-0876
Brenda Villanueva, Prin
EMP: 5 EST: 2010
SALES (est): 60.35K Privately Held
SIC: 8351 Child day care services

(G-15102)
BREEZLE LLC
1201 N Orange St Ste 6001 (19801-1155)
PHONE..................................774 435-1566
EMP: 6 EST: 2011
SALES (est): 65.65K Privately Held
SIC: 7371 Custom computer programming services

(G-15103)
BREWSTER PRODUCTS INC
3607 Downing Dr Ste E (19802-2409)
PHONE..................................302 764-4463
EMP: 5 EST: 1970
SQ FT: 2,000
SALES (est): 383.8K Privately Held
Web: www.brewsterproducts.com
SIC: 5046 Restaurant equipment and supplies, nec

(G-15104)
BRIAN J GALINAT M D
1941 Limestone Rd Ste 101 (19808-5413)
PHONE..................................302 633-3555
Brian J Galinat, Prin
EMP: 8 EST: 2018
SALES (est): 65.5K Privately Held
Web: www.delortho.com
SIC: 8011 Orthopedic physician

(G-15105)
BRIAN T PHILLIPS
3 Main Ave (19804-1828)
PHONE..................................302 593-3815
Brian Phillips, Owner
EMP: 5 EST: 2016
SALES (est): 68.52K Privately Held
Web: www.briantphillips.com
SIC: 1721 Painting and paper hanging

(G-15106)
BRIDGE ENTERPRISES LLC
113 Marsh Rd (19809-3137)
PHONE..................................302 750-0828
EMP: 50
SALES (est): 2.1MM Privately Held
Web: www.gobridgeenterprises.com
SIC: 8741 Management services

(G-15107)
BRIDGESOFT INFOSEC LLC (HQ)
1000 N West St Ste 1200 (19801-1058)
PHONE..................................270 799-4779
EMP: 10 EST: 2018
SALES (est): 3.61MM Privately Held
Web: www.bridgesoft.com
SIC: 7372 Prepackaged software
PA: Bridge Soft Solutions Private Limited D No 48-8-1, 2nd Floor, Somayaji Building
Visakhapatnam AP 53001

(G-15108)
BRIDGESTONE RET OPERATIONS LLC
Also Called: Firestone
3301 Old Capitol Trl (19808-6209)
PHONE..................................302 995-2487
Britton Merritt, Mgr
EMP: 8
Web: www.bridgestoneamericas.com
SIC: 5531 7534 Automotive tires; Rebuilding and retreading tires
HQ: Bridgestone Retail Operations, Llc
333 E Lake St Ste 300
Bloomingdale IL 60108
630 259-9000

GEOGRAPHIC SECTION
Wilmington - New Castle County (G-15135)

(G-15109)
BRIGHT HORIZONS CHLD CTRS LLC
Also Called: Eagle's Nest
201 N Walnut St (19801-2920)
PHONE..................302 282-6378
Jen Solwik, *Dir*
EMP: 8
SALES (corp-wide): 2.02B **Publicly Held**
Web: www.brighthorizons.com
SIC: 8351 Group day care center
HQ: Bright Horizons Children's Centers Llc
2 Wells Ave Ste 1
Newton MA 02459
617 673-8000

(G-15110)
BRIGHT HORIZONS CHLD CTRS LLC
3511 Silverside Rd (19810-4902)
PHONE..................302 475-6780
EMP: 7
SALES (corp-wide): 2.02B **Publicly Held**
Web: child-care-preschool.brighthorizons.com
SIC: 8351 Group day care center
HQ: Bright Horizons Children's Centers Llc
2 Wells Ave Ste 1
Newton MA 02459
617 673-8000

(G-15111)
BRIGHT HORIZONS CHLD CTRS LLC
Also Called: Bright Horizons Child Care Ctr
3515 Silverside Rd Ste 102 (19810-4906)
PHONE..................302 477-1023
Meg Panner, *Dir*
EMP: 12
SALES (corp-wide): 2.02B **Publicly Held**
Web: www.brighthorizons.com
SIC: 8351 Group day care center
HQ: Bright Horizons Children's Centers Llc
2 Wells Ave Ste 1
Newton MA 02459
617 673-8000

(G-15112)
BRIGHT NEW BEGINNINGS
8 W Holly Oak Rd (19809-1343)
PHONE..................610 637-9809
Beverly Gray, *Prin*
EMP: 9 **EST:** 2011
SALES (est): 74.78K **Privately Held**
Web: www.newbeginnings1de.org
SIC: 8351 Child day care services

(G-15113)
BRIGHTFIELDS INC (PA)
801 Industrial St (19801-4368)
PHONE..................302 656-9600
Marian Young, *Pr*
Marian Young, *Pr*
Mark Lannan, *
EMP: 41 **EST:** 2003
SQ FT: 5,000
SALES (est): 10.18MM
SALES (corp-wide): 10.18MM **Privately Held**
Web: www.brightfieldsinc.com
SIC: 8748 8711 8999 8744 Environmental consultant; Engineering services; Earth science services; Facilities support services

(G-15114)
BRIGHTMINDS SOCIAL INC
3422 Old Capitol Trl # 558 (19808-6124)
PHONE..................424 333-8879
Doctor Terrance Bell, *CEO*
EMP: 16 **EST:** 2020
SALES (est): 560.78K **Privately Held**
SIC: 7379 7372 Online services technology consultants; Application computer software

(G-15115)
BRIK LABS INC
1007 N Orange St Fl 4 (19801-1239)
PHONE..................302 499-4423
Alexander Sharkov, *CEO*
EMP: 10
SALES (est): 348.32K **Privately Held**
SIC: 7389 7379 Business Activities at Non-Commercial Site; Online services technology consultants

(G-15116)
BRILLIANCE LIVING CORPORATION
Also Called: Brillnce Asssted Lving Edgwter
2711 Centerville Rd # 400 (19808-1660)
PHONE..................386 690-1709
EMP: 8 **EST:** 2017
SALES (est): 81.32K **Privately Held**
SIC: 8051 Skilled nursing care facilities

(G-15117)
BRIM PRTNERS CNSLTING GROUP IN (PA)
3911 Concord Pike # 8030 (19803-1736)
PHONE..................657 234-7424
F Sanchez Brim, *CEO*
EMP: 9 **EST:** 2020
SALES (est): 695.63K
SALES (corp-wide): 695.63K **Privately Held**
SIC: 8742 Management consulting services

(G-15118)
BRISBIE LLC
103 Foulk Rd Ste 202 (19803-3742)
PHONE..................650 690-1433
EMP: 11 **EST:** 2018
SALES (est): 1.49MM
SALES (corp-wide): 134.9B **Publicly Held**
SIC: 8741 Management services
PA: Meta Platforms, Inc.
1 Meta Way
Menlo Park CA 94025
650 543-4800

(G-15119)
BRISTOL-MYERS SQUIBB COMPANY
Also Called: Bristol-Myers Squibb
1209 N Orange St (19801-1120)
PHONE..................800 321-1335
James M Cornelius, *Ch*
EMP: 4
SALES (corp-wide): 45.01B **Publicly Held**
Web: www.bms.com
SIC: 2834 Pharmaceutical preparations
PA: Bristol-Myers Squibb Company
430 E 29th St Fl 14
New York NY 10016
212 546-4000

(G-15120)
BRITTINGHAM INC
5809 Kennett Pike (19807-1115)
PHONE..................302 656-8173
William A Wolhar, *Pr*
George Herman, *Pr*
Lavelle Arnold, *VP*
Baird C Brittingham, *Ex VP*
EMP: 5 **EST:** 1951
SQ FT: 2,500
SALES (est): 574.19K **Privately Held**
Web: www.bryanandbrittingham.com
SIC: 6211 Stock brokers and dealers

(G-15121)
BROADBERRY DATA SYSTEMS LLC
1308 Delaware Ave (19806-4740)
PHONE..................302 295-1086
Mark Ray, *Brnch Mgr*
EMP: 41
Web: www.broadberry.com
SIC: 3571 5045 Electronic computers; Computer peripheral equipment
PA: Broadberry Data Systems Llc
501 Silverside Rd Ste 119
Wilmington DE 19809

(G-15122)
BROADBERRY DATA SYSTEMS LLC (PA)
501 Silverside Rd Ste 119 (19809-1376)
PHONE..................800 496-9918
Mark Ray, *Pr*
EMP: 7 **EST:** 2006
SALES (est): 320.38K **Privately Held**
Web: www.broadberry.com
SIC: 3571 5045 Electronic computers; Computer peripheral equipment

(G-15123)
BROCCWORTH HOUSING FIRM LLC ✪
1207 Delaware Ave (19806-4743)
PHONE..................860 937-6308
Lawanza Holder, *Managing Member*
EMP: 5 **EST:** 2022
SALES (est): 246.73K **Privately Held**
SIC: 6514 7389 Residential building, four or fewer units: operation; Business Activities at Non-Commercial Site

(G-15124)
BROKERS REALTY NETWORK
3203 Concord Pike Ste 3 (19803-5036)
PHONE..................302 593-3998
John Linehan, *Admn*
EMP: 6 **EST:** 2013
SALES (est): 228.4K **Privately Held**
Web: www.brokersrealtygroup.com
SIC: 6531 Real estate agent, residential

(G-15125)
BROMWELL CONSTRUCTION CO LLC
1800 Newport Gap Pike (19808-6122)
PHONE..................302 598-7072
Francis Bromwell, *Managing Member*
EMP: 12 **EST:** 2018
SALES (est): 1.03MM **Privately Held**
Web: www.bromwellconstruction.com
SIC: 1521 General remodeling, single-family houses

(G-15126)
BROOKS COURIER SERVICE INC
831 E 28th St (19802-3606)
P.O. Box 9560 (19809-0560)
PHONE..................302 762-4661
William F Brooks, *Pr*
EMP: 140 **EST:** 1951
SQ FT: 22,000
SALES (est): 7.79MM **Privately Held**
Web: www.brookscourier.com
SIC: 7389 4215 Courier or messenger service; Courier services, except by air

(G-15127)
BROOKVIEW TOWNHOMES REDEV LLC
300 Water St (19801-5037)
PHONE..................302 472-7200
Brock Vinton, *Pr*
EMP: 8 **EST:** 2009
SALES (est): 286.13K **Privately Held**
SIC: 8641 Condominium association

(G-15128)
BROWN ADVISORY INCORPORATED
5701 Kennett Pike # 100 (19807-1311)
PHONE..................302 351-7600
EMP: 6
Web: www.brownadvisory.com
SIC: 6282 Investment advisory service
PA: Brown Advisory Incorporated
901 S Bond St Ste 400
Baltimore MD 21231

(G-15129)
BROWN STONE NIMEROFF LLC
901 N Market St (19801-3022)
PHONE..................302 428-8142
Robert Munsell, *Brnch Mgr*
EMP: 33
Web: www.bsnlawyers.com
SIC: 8111 Administrative and government law
PA: Brown Stone Nimeroff Llc
1500 John F Kennedy Blvd
Philadelphia PA 19102

(G-15130)
BROWNE CONSULTING
3704 Wild Cherry Ln (19808-4612)
PHONE..................302 482-1410
EMP: 5 **EST:** 2014
SALES (est): 89.47K **Privately Held**
SIC: 8748 Environmental consultant

(G-15131)
BROWNS UNLIMITED 4U LLC ✪
1303 Delaware Ave Apt 405 (19806-3419)
PHONE..................800 940-5880
Jared Brown, *CEO*
EMP: 8 **EST:** 2023
SALES (est): 319.06K **Privately Held**
SIC: 8742 7389 Management consulting services; Business services, nec

(G-15132)
BROWSE CONTACTS
3524 Silverside Rd 35b (19810-4929)
PHONE..................302 261-9495
EMP: 5 **EST:** 2019
SALES (est): 177.05K **Privately Held**
SIC: 4822 Telegraph and other communications

(G-15133)
BRUCE E MATTHEWS DDS PA (PA)
1403 Silverside Rd Ste A (19810-4434)
PHONE..................302 475-9220
Bruce Matthews D.d.s., *Owner*
EMP: 5 **EST:** 1983
SALES (est): 994.93K
SALES (corp-wide): 994.93K **Privately Held**
Web: www.drmatthewswilmington.com
SIC: 8021 Dentists' office

(G-15134)
BRUCE G & MARY A ROBERT FML FD
501 W 9th St (19801-1401)
PHONE..................302 598-1609
EMP: 5 **EST:** 2009
SALES (est): 53.79K **Privately Held**
SIC: 8641 Civic and social associations

(G-15135)
BRUCE G FAY DMD PA
900 Foulk Rd Ste 203 (19803-3155)
PHONE..................302 778-3822
Bruce Fay, *Pr*
EMP: 7 **EST:** 1994
SALES (est): 763.8K **Privately Held**
Web: www.newconceptdental.com
SIC: 8021 Dentists' office

Wilmington - New Castle County (G-15136) GEOGRAPHIC SECTION

(G-15136)
BRUCKE INC
1201 N Orange St (19801-1155)
PHONE..................302 319-9614
EMP: 7 EST: 2015
SALES (est): 230.36K Privately Held
Web: www.bruckeinc.com
SIC: 8611 Trade associations

(G-15137)
BRYN MAWR CAPITAL MGT LLC (HQ)
5803 Kennett Pike Ste C (19807-1195)
PHONE..................302 429-8436
Robert J Schneider, *Pr*
EMP: 9 EST: 2016
SALES (est): 12.06MM
SALES (corp-wide): 963.95MM Publicly Held
Web: www.wsfsbank.com
SIC: 6021 National commercial banks
PA: Wsfs Financial Corporation
    500 Delaware Ave
    Wilmington DE 19801
    302 792-6000

(G-15138)
BRYSK INC
108 W 13th St (19801-1145)
PHONE..................224 508-9542
Ankur Sharma, *CEO*
EMP: 16
SALES (est): 575.1K Privately Held
SIC: 5961 7371 Electronic shopping; Computer software development and applications

(G-15139)
BUCCINI/POLLIN GROUP INC (PA)
Also Called: Bpg
1000 N West St Ste 1000 (19801-1000)
PHONE..................302 691-2100
EMP: 46 EST: 1994
SQ FT: 5,000
SALES (est): 35.17MM Privately Held
Web: www.bpgroup.net
SIC: 7011 Hotels and motels

(G-15140)
BUCK ROAD EAST ASSOCIATION
1 River Pl (19801-5125)
P.O. Box 3630 (19807-0630)
PHONE..................302 658-2400
EMP: 15 EST: 2010
SALES (est): 174.81K Privately Held
Web: www.hagley.org
SIC: 8699 Membership organizations, nec

(G-15141)
BUCK SIMPERS ARCHT + ASSOC INC
954 Justison St (19801-5149)
PHONE..................302 658-9300
Buck Simpers, *Pr*
EMP: 10 EST: 1982
SALES (est): 1.41MM Privately Held
Web: www.simpers.com
SIC: 8712 8741 7389 Architectural engineering; Construction management; Interior design services

(G-15142)
BUCKLEYS INC
Also Called: Buckley's Autocare
1604 E Newport Pike (19804-2529)
PHONE..................302 999-8285
Greg Buckley, *Pr*
EMP: 8 EST: 1966
SQ FT: 5,500
SALES (est): 1MM Privately Held
Web: www.buckleysautocare.com
SIC: 7538 General automotive repair shops

(G-15143)
BUDGET RENT A CAR
Also Called: Budget Rent-A-Car
702 Philadelphia Pike (19809-2540)
PHONE..................302 762-4824
EMP: 6 EST: 2019
SALES (est): 86.82K Privately Held
Web: www.budget.com
SIC: 7514 Rent-a-car service

(G-15144)
BUDGET RENT A CAR SYSTEM INC
Also Called: Budget Rent-A-Car
100 S Front St (19801)
PHONE..................302 652-0629
Lisa Spano, *Mgr*
EMP: 5
SALES (corp-wide): 11.99B Publicly Held
Web: www.budget.com
SIC: 7514 Rent-a-car service
HQ: Budget Rent A Car System, Inc.
    6 Sylvan Way Ste 1
    Parsippany NJ 07054
    973 496-3500

(G-15145)
BUG EYED WEASEL PRODUCTIONS LL
1004 Berkeley Rd (19807-2814)
P.O. Box 708 (19720-0708)
PHONE..................302 547-8661
Robert Hendry, *Prin*
EMP: 6 EST: 2008
SALES (est): 218.09K Privately Held
SIC: 7822 Motion picture and tape distribution

(G-15146)
BUILDING SYSTEMS AND SVCS INC
1504 Kirkwood Hwy (19805-4916)
PHONE..................302 996-0900
Kevin D Haskins, *Pr*
▲ EMP: 22 EST: 1986
SQ FT: 5,000
SALES (est): 10.51MM Privately Held
Web: www.bssinc.net
SIC: 5075 Warm air heating and air conditioning

(G-15147)
BULK MRO INDUSTRIAL SUPPLY INC (PA)
1013 Centre Rd Ste 403b (19805-1270)
PHONE..................646 713-1060
Devang Shah, *Pr*
Gaurang Shah, *Prin*
EMP: 6 EST: 2016
SALES (est): 8.53MM
SALES (corp-wide): 8.53MM Privately Held
Web: www.bulkmro.com
SIC: 5085 Industrial supplies

(G-15148)
BULK SOLUTIONS LLC
704 N King St (19801-3583)
PHONE..................310 906-0901
EMP: 5 EST: 2012
SALES (est): 370.65K Privately Held
Web: www.bulkvs.com
SIC: 8748 Telecommunications consultant

(G-15149)
BULLIONCOM LLC ◆
800 N King St Ste 304 (19801-3549)
PHONE..................833 629-3927
EMP: 3 EST: 2023
SALES (est): 128.34K Privately Held
SIC: 7372 Prepackaged software

(G-15150)
BULLSEYE PRODUCTS LLC
717 N Union St (19805-3031)
PHONE..................302 468-5086
EMP: 6 EST: 2017
SALES (est): 122.72K Privately Held
Web: www.bullseyeproductsusa.com
SIC: 7822 Motion picture and tape distribution

(G-15151)
BUMPERS & COMPANY PROF ASSN
1104 Philadelphia Pike (19809-2031)
PHONE..................302 798-3300
John Mager, *Owner*
EMP: 18 EST: 1995
SALES (est): 4.59MM Privately Held
Web: www.bumpersco.com
SIC: 8721 Accounting services, except auditing

(G-15152)
BURGEON IT SERVICES LLC
1601 Concord Pike Ste 36e (19803-3635)
PHONE..................302 613-0999
Nandakishore Umar Lakakuna, *Managing Member*
EMP: 14 EST: 2010
SALES (est): 1.48MM Privately Held
Web: www.burgeonits.com
SIC: 7379 Computer related consulting services

(G-15153)
BURLINGTON MNOR PRSRVTION ASSO
4 Denny Rd (19809-3445)
PHONE..................302 761-7306
EMP: 5
SALES (est): 221.96K Privately Held
SIC: 6519 Real property lessors, nec

(G-15154)
BURR & FORMAN LLP
1201 N Market St Ste 140 (19801-1163)
PHONE..................302 425-6400
EMP: 15
Web: www.burr.com
SIC: 8111 General practice attorney, lawyer
PA: Burr & Forman Llp
    420 20th St N Ste 3400
    Birmingham AL 35203

(G-15155)
BUSABILITY CORPORATION
1013 Centre Rd Ste 403s (19805-1270)
PHONE..................845 821-4609
Terence Talerman, *CFO*
EMP: 7 EST: 2019
SALES (est): 375.1K Privately Held
SIC: 7371 Computer software development and applications

(G-15156)
BUSINESS FUNDING PRO
913 N Market St Ste 100 (19801-3097)
PHONE..................888 705-8278
EMP: 5 EST: 2017
SALES (est): 229.57K Privately Held
Web: www.businessfundingpro.com
SIC: 6153 Working capital financing

(G-15157)
BUSINESS HISTORY CONFERENCE
298 Buck Rd (19807-2106)
P.O. Box 3630 (19807-0630)
PHONE..................302 658-2400
EMP: 2 EST: 2010
SALES (est): 225.93K Privately Held
Web: www.thebhc.org
SIC: 2721 Periodicals

(G-15158)
BUSINESS INCORPORATORS
1019 Cypress Rd (19810-1905)
PHONE..................302 475-6596
George Jones, *Pr*
EMP: 5 EST: 2007
SALES (est): 101.56K Privately Held
Web: www.worldwideincorporators.com
SIC: 8111 Legal services

(G-15159)
BUSINESS INTRFACE WRKFRCE SVCS
800 N King St Ste 101 (19801-3550)
PHONE..................302 660-7123
Rodney Carroll, *CEO*
EMP: 28 EST: 2006
SALES (est): 2.34MM Privately Held
Web: www.bfacellc.com
SIC: 8748 Business consulting, nec

(G-15160)
BUTAMAX ADVANCED BIOFUELS LLC (PA)
Route 141 & Henry Clay (19880)
PHONE..................302 695-6787
EMP: 4 EST: 2009
SALES (est): 20.32MM Privately Held
Web: www.butamax.com
SIC: 2869 Industrial organic chemicals, nec

(G-15161)
BUTLER HOSPITALITY LLC
1204 N King St (19801-3218)
PHONE..................888 288-5846
EMP: 96 EST: 2008
SALES (est): 855.39K Privately Held
SIC: 7011 5812 Hotels; Caterers

(G-15162)
BUYGOODS INC
1201 N Orange St Ste 7223 (19801-1219)
PHONE..................302 573-2500
EMP: 7 EST: 2018
SALES (est): 263.74K Privately Held
Web: www.buygoods.com
SIC: 5045 Computers, peripherals, and software

(G-15163)
BW DRILLING CO
100 W 10th St (19801-6603)
PHONE..................302 658-0410
S H Livesay, *Pt*
EMP: 7 EST: 2008
SALES (est): 114.75K Privately Held
SIC: 1781 Water well drilling

(G-15164)
BY MAIL ERIC GRAHAM INTL
427 N Tatnall St (19801-2230)
PHONE..................816 368-1641
EMP: 5 EST: 2015
SALES (est): 43.82K Privately Held
SIC: 8748 Business consulting, nec

(G-15165)
BYRDS NEST LLC
2627 Point Breeze Dr (19810-1115)
PHONE..................302 475-4949
James Byrd, *Prin*
EMP: 5 EST: 2016
SALES (est): 160.84K Privately Held
SIC: 1711 Plumbing contractors

GEOGRAPHIC SECTION　　　　　　　　　　　　　　　　　　　　　　　　　　　　Wilmington - New Castle County (G-15195)

(G-15166)
BYRON & DAVIS CCCC
601 Philadelphia Pike (19809-2549)
P.O. Box 9049 (19809-0049)
PHONE..................................302 792-2334
Glenn Davis, Pr
EMP: 9 **EST:** 1969
SALES (est): 443.49K **Privately Held**
SIC: 7322 8742 Collection agency, except real estate; Financial consultant

(G-15167)
BZ CONSTRUCTION SERVICES INC
120 E Ayre St (19804-2507)
PHONE..................................302 999-7505
Brian Zych, Pr
EMP: 9 **EST:** 2004
SALES (est): 1.53MM **Privately Held**
Web: www.bzconstructionservices.com
SIC: 1521 Single-family housing construction

(G-15168)
C & A MANAGEMENT INC
919 Market Street Flr 2 (19801-3023)
PHONE..................................302 888-2786
Sanjay Kumar, Pr
Charles Mcwade, VP
Peter Schwartz, VP
EMP: 3 **EST:** 1988
SALES (est): 657.32K
SALES (corp-wide): 35.82B **Publicly Held**
SIC: 7372 Prepackaged software
HQ: Ca Investment, Inc.
　　100 Baylis Rd Ste 250
　　Melville NY 11747

(G-15169)
C & B INTERNET SERVICES LLC
704 N King St Ste 500 (19801-3584)
PHONE..................................302 384-9804
EMP: 5 **EST:** 2012
SALES (est): 231.54K **Privately Held**
SIC: 4813 Internet connectivity services

(G-15170)
C & C AUTOBROKERS
601 A St (19801-5329)
PHONE..................................302 442-5464
EMP: 6 **EST:** 2018
SALES (est): 28.25K **Privately Held**
SIC: 7538 General automotive repair shops

(G-15171)
C & D CONTRACTORS INC
734 Hertford Rd (19803-1618)
P.O. Box 9236 (19809-0236)
PHONE..................................302 764-2020
Kathy Ryan, Pr
William Mc Mahon, *
EMP: 11 **EST:** 1967
SALES (est): 574.5K **Privately Held**
SIC: 1711 Mechanical contractor

(G-15172)
C & S BATTERY INC
12 Penarth Dr (19803-2012)
PHONE..................................610 459-2227
Joan Colby, Pr
William Colby, VP
Leonard Colby, Sec
EMP: 8 **EST:** 1983
SALES (est): 478.61K **Privately Held**
SIC: 7699 5063 Battery service and repair; Storage batteries, industrial

(G-15173)
C AND C MANAGEMENT GROUP LLC
Also Called: Real Estate Invstmnt/Asset MGT
1201 N Market St Ste 111 (19801-1156)
PHONE..................................302 946-4179
Craig Williams, Managing Member
EMP: 7 **EST:** 2018
SALES (est): 597.46K **Privately Held**
SIC: 6531 Real estate managers

(G-15174)
C AND L BRADFORD AND ASSOC
1604 Trevalley Rd (19810-4330)
PHONE..................................302 529-8566
Carol B Holt, Pr
Laura Durojaiye, VP
EMP: 9 **EST:** 1999
SALES (est): 445.61K **Privately Held**
SIC: 8741 8748 Management services; Business consulting, nec

(G-15175)
C P M INDUSTRIES INC
3511 Silverside Rd Ste 210 (19810-4902)
P.O. Box 6006 (19804-0606)
PHONE..................................302 478-8200
Leonard L Yowell, Pr
▲ **EMP:** 7 **EST:** 1982
SQ FT: 2,500
SALES (est): 730.07K **Privately Held**
Web: www.cpmindustries.com
SIC: 2851 Paints and allied products

(G-15176)
C S C CORPORATION TEXAS INC
Also Called: C S C
2711 Centerville Rd Ste 400 (19808-1660)
PHONE..................................302 636-5440
John Fortunado, CFO
EMP: 12 **EST:** 1950
SALES (est): 2.46MM **Privately Held**
SIC: 8611 Business associations

(G-15177)
C V INTERNATIONAL INC
603 Christiana Ave (19801-5834)
PHONE..................................302 427-0440
EMP: 8
SALES (corp-wide): 13.12MM **Privately Held**
Web: www.cvinternational.com
SIC: 4731 Brokers, shipping
PA: C V International, Inc.
　　1128 W Olney Rd
　　Norfolk VA 23507
　　757 466-1170

(G-15178)
C&S MECHANICAL SERVICES INC
202 S Van Buren St (19805-4021)
PHONE..................................302 377-2343
Raymond Costanzo, Prin
EMP: 5 **EST:** 2017
SALES (est): 56.99K **Privately Held**
SIC: 1711 Mechanical contractor

(G-15179)
C-STACKS INC
1313 N Market St Ste 5100 (19801-6111)
PHONE..................................617 480-2555
Elnor Rozenrot, CEO
EMP: 5 **EST:** 2015
SALES (est): 267.02K **Privately Held**
SIC: 8742 Management consulting services

(G-15180)
C2 CONSTRUCTION LLC
2913 N Van Buren St (19802-2955)
PHONE..................................302 438-3901
EMP: 7 **EST:** 2009
SALES (est): 72.15K **Privately Held**
Web: www.c2construction.net
SIC: 1521 Single-family housing construction

(G-15181)
CA ALL WRLD EX US EQITY CEF FU ✪
4005 Kennett Pike Ste 250 (19807-2018)
PHONE..................................610 380-2110
EMP: 5 **EST:** 2022
SALES (est): 76.37K **Privately Held**
SIC: 6722 Money market mutual funds

(G-15182)
CA BRIGGS CONTRACTING
307 3rd Ave (19804-2232)
PHONE..................................302 250-8858
Charles Briggs, Prin
EMP: 9 **EST:** 2010
SALES (est): 170.15K **Privately Held**
SIC: 1799 Special trade contractors, nec

(G-15183)
CABICASH SOLUTIONS INC
Also Called: Ualett
1000 N West St Ste 1200 (19801-1058)
PHONE..................................315 961-2005
Wilfredo Vidal, CEO
Carlos Michel Presbot, *
EMP: 40 **EST:** 2018
SALES (est): 4.16MM **Privately Held**
SIC: 6153 Factoring services

(G-15184)
CACTUS ANNIES RESTAURANT & BAR
211 W 9th St (19801-1619)
PHONE..................................302 655-9004
Ann Ackerson, Owner
EMP: 10 **EST:** 1998
SALES (est): 558.86K **Privately Held**
SIC: 8741 Restaurant management

(G-15185)
CADIA RHABILITATION PIKE CREEK
3540 Three Little Bakers Blvd (19808-1754)
PHONE..................................302 455-0808
Karen Litwa, Prin
EMP: 28 **EST:** 2009
SALES (est): 17.35MM **Privately Held**
Web: www.cadiahealthcare.com
SIC: 8051 Mental retardation hospital

(G-15186)
CADIA RHABILITATION SILVERSIDE
3322 Silverside Rd (19810-3307)
PHONE..................................302 478-8889
EMP: 19 **EST:** 2013
SALES (est): 906.97K **Privately Held**
Web: www.cadiahealthcare.com
SIC: 8322 Rehabilitation services

(G-15187)
CADIA RVERSIDE HEALTHCARE SVCS
3540 Three Little Bakers Blvd (19808-1754)
PHONE..................................302 455-0808
EMP: 19 **EST:** 2010
SALES (est): 497.43K **Privately Held**
Web: www.cadiahealthcare.com
SIC: 8051 Skilled nursing care facilities

(G-15188)
CADRENDER INC
716 N Tatnall St (19801-1716)
PHONE..................................302 657-0700
Andrew Burkert, Managing Member
EMP: 7 **EST:** 1992
SALES (est): 583.35K **Privately Held**
Web: www.cadrender.com
SIC: 7374 8712 Computer graphics service; Architectural services

(G-15189)
CAE(US) INC (HQ)
1011 Ct Rd Ste 322 (19805)
PHONE..................................813 885-7481
Stephane Lefebvre, Pr
Darrel Lane, Finance Treasurer
Hartland Paterson, Sec
◆ **EMP:** 2 **EST:** 1988
SALES (est): 980.97MM
SALES (corp-wide): 3.1B **Privately Held**
SIC: 3559 Cryogenic machinery, industrial
PA: Cae Inc
　　8585 Ch De La Cote-De-Liesse
　　Saint-Laurent QC H4T 1
　　514 341-6780

(G-15190)
CAFE MANAGEMENT ASSOCIATES
1428 N Clayton St (19806-4006)
PHONE..................................302 655-4959
Jonas Miller, Mgr
EMP: 5 **EST:** 2013
SALES (est): 225.05K **Privately Held**
SIC: 8741 Management services

(G-15191)
CALCOM INC
251 Little Falls Dr (19808-1674)
PHONE..................................442 227-3200
Peer Richelsen, CEO
Alexis Ohanian, Bd of Dir
EMP: 21 **EST:** 2021
SALES (est): 600.56K **Privately Held**
SIC: 7371 Custom computer programming services

(G-15192)
CALCULUS BUS SOLUTIONS INC
1521 Concord Pike Ste 301 (19803-3644)
PHONE..................................302 676-2162
Michael J Mahoney, CEO
Sooraj Vasudevan, *
Fahad Ahmad Siddiqui, *
EMP: 33 **EST:** 2021
SALES (est): 1.01MM **Privately Held**
SIC: 8748 Telecommunications consultant

(G-15193)
CALFO & HAIGHT INC
21 Glover Cir (19804-3201)
PHONE..................................302 998-3852
Augustine J Calfo, Pr
Geraldine Calfo, Sec
Nick Calfo, VP
EMP: 14 **EST:** 1967
SQ FT: 2,500
SALES (est): 434.26K **Privately Held**
SIC: 1711 Plumbing contractors

(G-15194)
CALIFORNIA EXPLOSION LLC (PA)
300 Delaware Ave Ste 210a (19801-6601)
PHONE..................................516 404-9892
Colby Eisenberg, Managing Member
EMP: 7 **EST:** 2016
SALES (est): 91.5K
SALES (corp-wide): 91.5K **Privately Held**
SIC: 7812 Motion picture and video production

(G-15195)
CALIFORNIA VIDEO 2
Also Called: California Video
1716 Marsh Rd (19810-4606)
PHONE..................................302 477-6944
Jeff Stalter, Owner
EMP: 8 **EST:** 1996
SALES (est): 169.86K **Privately Held**
SIC: 7841 Video tape rental

Wilmington - New Castle County (G-15196)

(G-15196)
CALIMA GROUP LLC
704 N King St Ste 500 (19801-3584)
PHONE.................................443 742-2134
Andrew Uribe, *Managing Member*
EMP: 2
SALES (est): 126.92K **Privately Held**
SIC: **2035** Pickles, sauces, and salad dressings

(G-15197)
CALL CARE 24 INC
1201 N Orange St Ste 6001 (19801-1155)
PHONE.................................832 217-0864
Badruddin Pitter, *Pr*
EMP: 14 EST: 2020
SALES (est): 321.17K **Privately Held**
SIC: **8011** Group health association

(G-15198)
CALLSYNETWORK LLC
2055 Limestone Rd 200c (19808-5536)
PHONE.................................785 241-7841
EMP: 5 EST: 2021
SALES (est): 33.14K **Privately Held**
SIC: **4813** Internet connectivity services

(G-15199)
CALLVU INC
1000 N West St Ste 1501 (19801-1001)
PHONE.................................646 506-4915
EMP: 6 EST: 2017
SALES (est): 61.3K **Privately Held**
SIC: **7371** Computer software development

(G-15200)
CALM MEDICAL MASSAGE EXPRT INC
1994 Carol Dr (19808-4885)
PHONE.................................443 566-0655
Cheryl Williams, *Asst Sec*
EMP: 6 EST: 2018
SALES (est): 41.23K **Privately Held**
SIC: **8099** Health and allied services, nec

(G-15201)
CALMET
717 N Union St Ste 100 (19805-3031)
PHONE.................................714 505-6765
Anupam Thakur, *Pr*
◆ EMP: 10 EST: 1993
SQ FT: 500
SALES (est): 1.42MM **Privately Held**
Web: www.calmet.com
SIC: **5051** Steel

(G-15202)
CALVERT MECHANICAL SYSTEMS INC
Also Called: Calvert Comfort Cooling & Htg
410 Meco Dr (19804-1112)
PHONE.................................302 998-0460
Christopher Lenhard, *Pr*
David Murray, *
EMP: 30 EST: 1991
SQ FT: 9,200
SALES (est): 6.43MM **Privately Held**
Web: www.calvertcomfort.com
SIC: **1711** Warm air heating and air conditioning contractor

(G-15203)
CAMBRIDGE INSURANCE GROUP INC
1740 Lancaster Ave (19805-3927)
PHONE.................................302 888-2440
EMP: 8 EST: 2006
SALES (est): 62.92K **Privately Held**
SIC: **6411** Insurance agents, nec

(G-15204)
CAMECK PUBLISHING
3306 Coachman Rd (19803-1946)
PHONE.................................302 598-4799
Jessica Sinarski, *Prin*
EMP: 5 EST: 2017
SALES (est): 89.86K **Privately Held**
SIC: **2741** Miscellaneous publishing

(G-15205)
CAMELO LLC
2055 Limestone Rd Ste 200c (19808-5536)
PHONE.................................302 574-6556
Tien Le, *Prin*
EMP: 5 EST: 2021
SALES (est): 20K **Privately Held**
Web: www.camelohq.com
SIC: **7371** Computer software development

(G-15206)
CAMERAS ETC INC (PA)
Also Called: Cameras Etc T V & Video
2303 Baynard Blvd (19802-3943)
PHONE.................................302 764-9400
James F Cycyk, *Pr*
Paul Beacher, *VP*
Susan A Cycyk, *Sec*
EMP: 10 EST: 1977
SQ FT: 3,500
SALES (est): 864.44K
SALES (corp-wide): 864.44K **Privately Held**
Web: www.camerasetc.net
SIC: **5946** 5043 5731 Cameras; Photographic cameras, projectors, equipment and supplies; Video cameras, recorders, and accessories

(G-15207)
CAMMOCK BOYS AUTO
2103 Carter St (19802-4217)
PHONE.................................302 409-0645
Garfield Cammock, *Prin*
EMP: 5 EST: 2016
SALES (est): 31.07K **Privately Held**
SIC: **7538** General automotive repair shops

(G-15208)
CAMP ARROWHEAD BUSINE
913 Wilson Rd (19803-4012)
PHONE.................................302 448-6919
Walt Lafontaine, *Dir*
EMP: 13 EST: 2013
SALES (est): 167.59K **Privately Held**
Web: www.camparrowhead.net
SIC: **7032** Sporting and recreational camps

(G-15209)
CAMP POSSIBILITIES FOUNDATION
P.O. Box 331 (21078-0331)
PHONE.................................302 563-9460
EMP: 5 EST: 2010
SALES (est): 143.88K **Privately Held**
SIC: **8641** Civic and social associations

(G-15210)
CAMPBELL & LEVINE LLC
222 Delaware Ave Ste 1600 (19801-1659)
PHONE.................................302 426-1900
Stanley Levine, *Brnch Mgr*
EMP: 5
SALES (corp-wide): 2.14MM **Privately Held**
Web: www.camlev.com
SIC: **8111** General practice attorney, lawyer
PA: Campbell & Levine, Llc
   310 Grant St Ste 1700
   Pittsburgh PA 15219
   412 261-0310

(G-15211)
CAMPBELL FINCL SOLUTIONS LLC
1201 N Market St Ste 111 (19801-1147)
PHONE.................................302 202-9029
Rasheeda Campbell, *Managing Member*
EMP: 5
SALES (est): 82.38K **Privately Held**
Web: www.campbellfinancialsolutions.com
SIC: **6282** Investment advisory service

(G-15212)
CANANWILL CORP
Also Called: Cananwill Premium Funding Co
300 Delaware Ave (19801-1607)
PHONE.................................302 576-3499
Mildred J Young, *Prin*
Vaughn Hooks, *Prin*
EMP: 9 EST: 2003
SALES (est): 136.52K **Privately Held**
SIC: **6211** Security brokers and dealers

(G-15213)
CANCER SUPPORT CMNTY DEL INC
4810 Lancaster Pike (19807-2516)
PHONE.................................302 995-2850
Nicole Pickles, *Ex Dir*
Cynthia Dwyer, *Ex Dir*
EMP: 7 EST: 1996
SALES (est): 773.68K **Privately Held**
Web: www.cancersupportdelaware.org
SIC: **8322** Social service center

(G-15214)
CANDLESTICK PUBLISHING INC
4023 Kennett Pike (19807-2018)
PHONE.................................817 939-1306
Gareth Evan Glaser, *CEO*
EMP: 8 EST: 2021
SALES (est): 347.13K **Privately Held**
SIC: **2759** Promotional printing

(G-15215)
CANINE CREATIONS
5903 Orchard Ave (19808-4513)
PHONE.................................302 593-2684
Jennifer Vawter, *Owner*
EMP: 5 EST: 2013
SALES (est): 69.91K **Privately Held**
SIC: **0752** Grooming services, pet and animal specialties

(G-15216)
CANN-ERIKSON BINDERY INC
Also Called: Cann-Erikson
1 Meco Cir (19804-1108)
P.O. Box 3171 (19804-0171)
PHONE.................................302 995-6636
Joseph Vanloon, *Pr*
Joseph Van Loon, *VP*
Steve Lillard, *Sec*
EMP: 17 EST: 1935
SQ FT: 10,000
SALES (est): 1.15MM **Privately Held**
Web: www.cann-erikson.com
SIC: **2675** 2782 Die-cut paper and board; Looseleaf binders and devices

(G-15217)
CANNA CARE DOCS DELAWARE LLC
9 Germay Dr (19804-1155)
PHONE.................................302 594-0630
EMP: 6 EST: 2015
SALES (est): 239.06K **Privately Held**
Web: www.cannacaredocs.com
SIC: **8099** Health and allied services, nec

(G-15218)
CANON SOLUTIONS AMERICA INC
300 Bellevue Pkwy Ste 135 (19809-3704)
PHONE.................................302 792-8700
Jeff Van Tiem, *Brnch Mgr*
EMP: 27
Web: csa.canon.com
SIC: **5044** Photocopy machines
HQ: Canon Solutions America, Inc.
   1 Canon Park
   Melville NY 11747
   631 330-5000

(G-15219)
CANSURROUND PBC
1815 W 13th St Ste 5 (19806-4054)
PHONE.................................302 540-2270
Margaret Maley, *CEO*
Jill Teixeira, *VP*
EMP: 3 EST: 2013
SALES (est): 210.12K **Privately Held**
Web: www.cansurround.com
SIC: **7372** Application computer software

(G-15220)
CAPADE LLC ✪
1222 Crestover Rd (19803-3311)
PHONE.................................302 786-5775
Gia Hoang, *Mgr*
EMP: 5 EST: 2024
SALES (est): 164.52K **Privately Held**
SIC: **7389** Business Activities at Non-Commercial Site

(G-15221)
CAPANO HOMES INC
Also Called: Capano Management
4420 Limestone Rd Ste 202a (19808-2005)
PHONE.................................302 384-7980
Louis Capano, *Pr*
Joe Capano, *
EMP: 25 EST: 1990
SALES (est): 8.54MM **Privately Held**
Web: www.capanoresidential.com
SIC: **1521** Single-family housing construction

(G-15222)
CAPE MAY LEWES FERRY
820 N French St (19801-3509)
PHONE.................................302 577-2011
EMP: 7 EST: 2010
SALES (est): 100.06K **Privately Held**
Web: www.cmlf.com
SIC: **4789** Transportation services, nec

(G-15223)
CAPGEMINI AMERICA INC
405 N King St (19801-3773)
PHONE.................................302 656-7491
Matthew Bernardini, *Brnch Mgr*
EMP: 14
SALES (corp-wide): 415.14MM **Privately Held**
Web: www.capgemini.com
SIC: **7379** Computer related consulting services
HQ: Capgemini America, Inc.
   79 5th Ave Fl 3
   New York NY 10003
   212 314-8000

(G-15224)
CAPICHE EVENT PLANNING LLC
520 Milton Dr (19802-1115)
PHONE.................................302 743-1522
Erica Razze, *Prin*
EMP: 5 EST: 2017
SALES (est): 32.64K **Privately Held**
Web: www.capicheplanning.com

SIC: 7299 Party planning service

(G-15225)
CAPITAL AND WORTH
1202 Foulk Rd (19803-2796)
PHONE.................................302 477-0660
John J Hartnett Junior C.p.a., *Pr*
EMP: 6 **EST:** 2017
SALES (est): 444.36K **Privately Held**
Web: www.capitalandworth.com
SIC: 6799 Investors, nec

(G-15226)
CAPITAL AUTO RCVBLES ASSET TR
1209 N Orange St (19801-1120)
PHONE.................................212 250-6864
EMP: 5 **EST:** 2014
SALES (est): 415.71K **Privately Held**
SIC: 6799 Investors, nec

(G-15227)
CAPITAL AUTO RECEIVABLES
301 Bellevue Pkwy Fl 3 (19809-3705)
PHONE.................................313 656-6304
EMP: 11 **EST:** 2018
SALES (est): 269.5K **Privately Held**
SIC: 6733 Trusts, nec

(G-15228)
CAPITAL COMMERCIAL REALTY LLC
5307 Limestone Rd Ste 102 (19808-1275)
P.O. Box 5856 (19808-0856)
PHONE.................................302 734-4400
EMP: 5 **EST:** 2008
SALES (est): 378.57K **Privately Held**
Web: www.capcomrealty.com
SIC: 6531 Real estate agent, commercial

(G-15229)
CAPITAL MARKETS IQ LLC
427 N Tatnall St Ste 52811 (19801)
PHONE.................................310 882-6380
EMP: 8 **EST:** 2015
SALES (est): 568.68K **Privately Held**
Web: www.capitalmarketsiq.com
SIC: 6799 Investors, nec

(G-15230)
CAPITAL ONE NATIONAL ASSN
802 Delaware Ave Fl 1 (19801-1377)
PHONE.................................877 383-4802
EMP: 11 **EST:** 2019
SALES (est): 495.59K **Privately Held**
SIC: 6021 National commercial banks

(G-15231)
CAPITAL ONE NATIONAL ASSN
1 S Orange St (19801-5006)
PHONE.................................302 658-3302
EMP: 293
SIC: 6021 National trust companies with deposits, commercial
HQ: Capital One, National Association
1680 Capital One Dr
Mc Lean VA 22102
800 655-2265

(G-15232)
CAPITOL BROADBAND DEV CO LLC
Also Called: Connexion Technologies
1000 N West St Fl 10 (19801-1059)
EMP: 27 **EST:** 2002
SALES (est): 1.43MM **Privately Held**
SIC: 4813 Online service providers

(G-15233)
CAPITOL LITTLE LEAGUE INC
2148 Elder Dr (19808-4742)
PHONE.................................302 999-1184
Michelle Pyle, *Pr*
Tom Eoppolo, *Treas*
EMP: 12 **EST:** 1972
SALES (est): 125.53K **Privately Held**
SIC: 7997 Outdoor field clubs

(G-15234)
CAPITOL TITLE LOANS
101 N Union St (19805-3427)
PHONE.................................302 652-3591
EMP: 6 **EST:** 2018
SALES (est): 178.29K **Privately Held**
Web: www.capitoltitleloans.com
SIC: 6512 Commercial and industrial building operation

(G-15235)
CAPTON LLC
1007 N Orange St Fl 4 (19801-1242)
PHONE.................................510 766-2803
EMP: 5 **EST:** 2021
SALES (est): 259.87K **Privately Held**
Web: www.captoninc.com
SIC: 7371 Computer software development

(G-15236)
CAR SHOPPE LLC
2205 Mitch Rd (19804-3917)
PHONE.................................302 992-9669
William Calloway, *Prin*
EMP: 7 **EST:** 2010
SALES (est): 238.4K **Privately Held**
SIC: 7533 Muffler shop, sale or repair and installation

(G-15237)
CAR WASH OF PRICES CORNER
Also Called: Prices Corner Car Wash
3213 Kirkwood Hwy (19804-6129)
PHONE.................................302 994-9274
John Medek, *Pr*
Sharon Medek, *Sec*
William Kincaid, *Mgr*
EMP: 10 **EST:** 1991
SALES (est): 492.44K **Privately Held**
Web: www.pricescornercarwash.com
SIC: 7542 Washing and polishing, automotive

(G-15238)
CARA GUITARS MANUFACTURING
112 Water St (19804-2407)
PHONE.................................302 521-0119
Jim Cara, *Pr*
EMP: 7 **EST:** 2010
SALES (est): 140.9K **Privately Held**
SIC: 3931 Guitars and parts, electric and nonelectric

(G-15239)
CARA PLASTICS INC
1201 N Market St Ste 2100 (19801-1165)
PHONE.................................302 622-7070
Richard Wool, *CEO*
EMP: 3 **EST:** 2004
SALES (est): 165.16K **Privately Held**
SIC: 3089 Carafes, plastics

(G-15240)
CARE AT HOME OF DELAWARE LLC ✪
20 Montchanin Rd Ste 50 (19807-2179)
PHONE.................................302 502-7138
Morris Peterzell, *Pr*
EMP: 6 **EST:** 2023
SALES (est): 128.85K **Privately Held**
SIC: 8059 Nursing and personal care, nec

(G-15241)
CARE MENTOR AI LLC
910 Foulk Rd Ste 201 (19803-3159)
PHONE.................................302 830-3700
EMP: 22 **EST:** 2018
SALES (est): 689.13K **Privately Held**
Web: www.carementor.me
SIC: 7373 Systems software development services

(G-15242)
CAREERMINDS
1601 Concord Pike Ste 82 (19803-3630)
PHONE.................................302 352-0511
EMP: 30 **EST:** 2019
SALES (est): 956.05K **Privately Held**
Web: www.careerminds.com
SIC: 7361 Executive placement

(G-15243)
CARELON RESEARCH INC (HQ)
123 S Justison St Ste 200 (19801-5365)
PHONE.................................302 230-2000
EMP: 10 **EST:** 1995
SALES (est): 37.78MM
SALES (corp-wide): 156.59B **Publicly Held**
Web: www.carelonresearch.com
SIC: 8733 Noncommercial biological research organization
PA: Elevance Health, Inc.
220 Virginia Ave
Indianapolis IN 46204
800 331-1476

(G-15244)
CAREPORTMD LLC
4365 Kirkwood Hwy (19808-5113)
PHONE.................................302 202-3020
EMP: 7
SALES (corp-wide): 5K **Privately Held**
Web: www.careforcemd.com
SIC: 8082 Home health care services
PA: Careportmd, Llc
1 Innovation Way Ste 400
Newark DE 19711
302 283-9001

(G-15245)
CAREWALLET INC (PA) ✪
Also Called: Carewallet
1013 Ctr Rd Ste 403s (19805-1270)
PHONE.................................732 477-4149
Evan Smith, *CEO*
EMP: 9 **EST:** 2023
SALES (est): 368.58K
SALES (corp-wide): 368.58K **Privately Held**
SIC: 7371 Computer software development and applications

(G-15246)
CARGILL MEAT SOLUTIONS CORP
1209 N Orange St (19801-1120)
PHONE.................................305 826-3699
Brian Sikes, *Pr*
EMP: 22 **EST:** 1974
SALES (est): 4.32MM
SALES (corp-wide): 176.74B **Privately Held**
SIC: 2099 Food preparations, nec
PA: Cargill, Incorporated
15407 Mcginty Rd W
Wayzata MN 55391
800 227-4455

(G-15247)
CARGO CUBE LICENSING LLC
2711 Centerville Rd # 400 (19808-1660)
PHONE.................................844 200-2823

EMP: 5 **EST:** 2014
SALES (est): 216.09K **Privately Held**
SIC: 7389 Business services, nec

(G-15248)
CARIBB TRANSPORT INC
Also Called: Caribb Moto Cars
2800 Governor Printz Blvd Ste 3 (19802-3734)
PHONE.................................302 274-2112
Garfield G Cammock, *Pr*
Laressia Ann Wright, *Stockholder*
EMP: 5 **EST:** 2017
SALES (est): 233.46K **Privately Held**
SIC: 7538 General automotive repair shops

(G-15249)
CARING HNDS PHLBOTOMY SVCS LLC
301 6th Ave (19805-4715)
P.O. Box 30938 (19805-7938)
PHONE.................................302 559-5539
Denara Charles, *Managing Member*
EMP: 6 **EST:** 2020
SALES (est): 104K **Privately Held**
Web: www.caringhandsphleb.com
SIC: 8059 Rest home, with health care

(G-15250)
CARING MINDS MEDICAL CTR LLC
5223 W Woodmill Dr Ste 41 (19808-4068)
PHONE.................................302 516-7936
EMP: 5 **EST:** 2016
SALES (est): 254.83K **Privately Held**
Web: www.caringmindsmedicalcenter.com
SIC: 8011 Medical centers

(G-15251)
CARISMA TELECOM INC
Also Called: Carisma Tel
501 Silverside Rd Ste 105 (19809-1376)
PHONE.................................302 357-3650
Errol Samuel, *Pr*
EMP: 7 **EST:** 2009
SALES (est): 140K **Privately Held**
SIC: 4813 Internet host services

(G-15252)
CARLETON COURT ASSOCIATES LP
Also Called: Carleton Court Apartments
4 Denny Rd (19809-3445)
PHONE.................................302 454-1800
William Demarco, *VP*
Leon Weiner, *Owner*
Lori Miller, *Mgr*
EMP: 12 **EST:** 1979
SALES (est): 676.33K **Privately Held**
Web: www.lnwa.com
SIC: 6513 Apartment building operators

(G-15253)
CARLISLE GROUP
Also Called: Winterset Farms
2801 Ebright Rd (19810-1130)
PHONE.................................302 475-3010
Mary Ellen Brooks, *Mgr*
EMP: 7 **EST:** 1971
SALES (est): 583.37K **Privately Held**
Web: www.wintersetfarms.com
SIC: 6515 0752 Mobile home site operators; Training services, horses (except racing horses)

(G-15254)
CARMEDIS INC
1207 Delaware Ave (19806-4743)
PHONE.................................725 712-2559
EMP: 5
SALES (est): 257.92K **Privately Held**

Wilmington - New Castle County (G-15255)

GEOGRAPHIC SECTION

SIC: 7371 Computer software development and applications

(G-15255)
CARMELLA P KEENER ATTY
919 N Market St (19801-3023)
PHONE..................................302 656-4333
Carmella Keener, *Owner*
EMP: 5 **EST:** 2017
SALES (est): 204.76K **Privately Held**
SIC: 8111 General practice attorney, lawyer

(G-15256)
CARMINE POTTER & ASSOCIATES (PA)
1719 Delaware Ave (19806-2353)
P.O. Box 30409 (19805-7409)
PHONE..................................302 658-8940
Stephen B Potter, *Pt*
Kenneth Carmine, *Pt*
EMP: 6 **EST:** 1978
SALES (est): 1.03MM
SALES (corp-wide): 1.03MM **Privately Held**
Web: www.pottercarmine.com
SIC: 8111 General practice attorney, lawyer

(G-15257)
CAROLINE M WIESNER
Also Called: Family Benefit Home Care
3322 Englewood Rd (19810-3302)
PHONE..................................877 220-9755
Caroline M Wiesner, *Prin*
EMP: 6 **EST:** 2010
SALES (est): 241.83K **Privately Held**
Web: www.familybenefithomecare.com
SIC: 8082 Home health care services

(G-15258)
CARRIAGE HOUSE ASSOC
1100 N Grant Ave (19805-2671)
PHONE..................................302 225-2040
EMP: 5 **EST:** 1994
SALES (est): 115.86K **Privately Held**
SIC: 6513 Apartment building operators

(G-15259)
CARROLL M CARPENTER
600 Center Mill Rd (19807-1502)
PHONE..................................302 654-7558
EMP: 5 **EST:** 2016
SALES (est): 58.7K **Privately Held**
SIC: 1751 Carpentry work

(G-15260)
CARSPECKEN-SCOTT INC
Also Called: Fcw
3007 Rosemont Ave (19802-2423)
PHONE..................................302 762-7955
EMP: 2
SALES (corp-wide): 452.39K **Privately Held**
Web: www.carspeckenscott.com
SIC: 2499 Picture and mirror frames, wood
PA: Carspecken-Scott Inc
1707 N Lincoln St
Wilmington DE 19806
302 655-7173

(G-15261)
CARSPECKEN-SCOTT INC (PA)
1707 N Lincoln St (19806-2309)
PHONE..................................302 655-7173
Frederick J Carspecken, *Pr*
Don Strabley, *Mgr*
Laura Cristy, *Mgr*
EMP: 5 **EST:** 1973
SQ FT: 2,000
SALES (est): 452.39K
SALES (corp-wide): 452.39K **Privately Held**
Web: www.carspeckenscott.com
SIC: 7699 Picture framing, custom

(G-15262)
CASALE MARBLE IMPORTS INC
Also Called: Distribution Headquarters
3518 Silverside Rd Ste 22 (19810-4907)
PHONE..................................561 404-4213
◆ **EMP:** 25 **EST:** 1993
SQ FT: 67,000
SALES (est): 838.33K **Privately Held**
SIC: 1743 5211 5032 Terrazzo, tile, marble and mosaic work; Masonry materials and supplies; Granite building stone

(G-15263)
CASARINO CHRSTMAN SHALK RNSOM
1007 N Orange St (19801-1239)
P.O. Box 1276 (19899-1276)
PHONE..................................302 594-4500
Beth H Christman, *Prin*
EMP: 21 **EST:** 1999
SALES (est): 11.81MM **Privately Held**
Web: www.casarino.com
SIC: 8111 General practice attorney, lawyer

(G-15264)
CASE MANAGEMENT SERVICES
234 Philadelphia Pike Ste 6 (19809-3126)
P.O. Box 9548 (19809-0548)
PHONE..................................302 354-3711
Cheri L Pfeiffer, *Prin*
EMP: 5 **EST:** 2007
SALES (est): 242.23K **Privately Held**
SIC: 8741 Business management

(G-15265)
CASTANEDA LANDSCAPING & PATIOS
1000 Stanton Rd (19808-5831)
PHONE..................................302 377-1674
Ortiz Juan Castaneda, *Owner*
EMP: 5 **EST:** 2017
SALES (est): 105.14K **Privately Held**
Web: www.castanedalandscapingco.com
SIC: 0781 Landscape services

(G-15266)
CASTLE BAG COMPANY
115 Valley Rd (19804-1310)
PHONE..................................302 656-1001
Christine Ditzler, *Pr*
Harry B Russell, *Pr*
Christine Russell Ditzler, *VP*
EMP: 2 **EST:** 1969
SQ FT: 6,000
SALES (est): 331.74K **Privately Held**
Web: www.castlebag.com
SIC: 2673 Plastic bags: made from purchased materials

(G-15267)
CASTLE HL TTAL RETURN FUND LLC
2711 Centerville Rd # 400 (19808-1660)
PHONE..................................626 844-4862
EMP: 6 **EST:** 2014
SALES (est): 110K **Privately Held**
SIC: 6722 Money market mutual funds

(G-15268)
CASTLE SERVICES INC
3 Germay Dr Ste 4 # 1095 (19804-1127)
PHONE..................................302 481-6633
Robert Straughn, *Pr*
EMP: 5 **EST:** 2008
SALES (est): 406.9K **Privately Held**

(G-15269)
CASTOR RESEARCH INC
Also Called: Castor Edc
1209 N Orange St (19801-1120)
PHONE..................................415 484-5347
Nicola Collier, *CEO*
EMP: 15 **EST:** 2018
SALES (est): 639.35K **Privately Held**
SIC: 7371 Computer software development

(G-15270)
CASTOS INC
1209 N Orange St (19801-1120)
PHONE..................................800 677-3394
Hewitt Craig, *CEO*
EMP: 6 **EST:** 2021
SALES (est): 127.86K **Privately Held**
SIC: 2741 Internet publishing and broadcasting

(G-15271)
CASTRO JOSE MD
2055 Limestone Rd Ste 111 (19808-5536)
PHONE..................................302 999-8169
Jose Castro, *Prin*
EMP: 8 **EST:** 2018
SALES (est): 93.54K **Privately Held**
SIC: 8011 Offices and clinics of medical doctors

(G-15272)
CASUAL COLORS INC ◯
1013 Centre Rd Ste 403s (19805-1270)
PHONE..................................302 298-0523
Kelly A Farley, *CFO*
EMP: 5 **EST:** 2023
SALES (est): 296.09K **Privately Held**
SIC: 7389 5947 Decoration service for special events; Souvenirs

(G-15273)
CATALYST FOUNDRY LLC (PA)
1209 N Orange St (19801-1120)
PHONE..................................917 471-0947
Devin Blong, *Managing Member*
EMP: 13 **EST:** 2016
SALES (est): 2.38MM
SALES (corp-wide): 2.38MM **Privately Held**
SIC: 7371 Computer software development and applications

(G-15274)
CATHERINES CSAC INC
1105 N Market St Ste 1300 (19801-1241)
PHONE..................................302 478-6160
EMP: 241 **EST:** 2009
SALES (est): 1.75MM **Privately Held**
SIC: 8111 General practice attorney, lawyer
HQ: Charming Shoppes, Inc.
8323 Walton Pkwy
New Albany OH 43054

(G-15275)
CATHOLIC CEMETARIES INC (PA)
Also Called: Cathedral Cemetary
2400 Lancaster Ave (19805-3737)
PHONE..................................302 254-4701
Mark Christian, *Dir*
Joseph F Redman, *Dir*
EMP: 10 **EST:** 1876
SALES (est): 1.06MM
SALES (corp-wide): 1.06MM **Privately Held**
Web: www.cdow.org
SIC: 6553 Cemeteries, real estate operation

(G-15276)
CATHOLIC CEMETARIES INC
Also Called: Saints Cemetary
6001 Kirkwood Hwy (19808-4816)
PHONE..................................302 737-2524
Tom Kane, *Superintnt*
EMP: 7
SALES (corp-wide): 1.06MM **Privately Held**
Web: www.cdow.org
SIC: 6553 Cemeteries, real estate operation
PA: Catholic Cemetaries Inc
2400 Lancaster Ave
Wilmington DE 19805
302 254-4701

(G-15277)
CATHOLIC CHARITIES INC (PA)
Also Called: Catholic Charities
2601 W 4th St (19805-3309)
PHONE..................................302 655-9624
Richelle Vible, *Ex Dir*
EMP: 50 **EST:** 1830
SQ FT: 20,000
SALES (est): 8.08MM
SALES (corp-wide): 8.08MM **Privately Held**
Web: www.ccwilm.org
SIC: 8322 Social service center

(G-15278)
CATHY BROWN LBW NCTMB
Veale Rd Ardencroft (19801)
PHONE..................................302 475-1477
Cathy Brown, *Prin*
EMP: 6 **EST:** 2007
SALES (est): 60.61K **Privately Held**
SIC: 8049 Physical therapist

(G-15279)
CATLEZA LLC
1521 Concord Pike Ste 301 (19803-3644)
PHONE..................................415 812-2676
Nicky Nguyen, *Dir*
Viet Hien Nguyen, *Prin*
EMP: 8 **EST:** 2021
SALES (est): 363.44K **Privately Held**
Web: www.catleza.com
SIC: 7389 Design services

(G-15280)
CAVALIER GROUP (PA)
Also Called: Cavalier Apartments
105 Foulk Rd (19803-3740)
PHONE..................................302 429-8700
Louis J Capano Junior, *Genl Pt*
Joseph M Capano, *Genl Pt*
EMP: 6 **EST:** 1971
SQ FT: 1,000
SALES (est): 4.45MM
SALES (corp-wide): 4.45MM **Privately Held**
Web: www.capanomanagement.com
SIC: 6513 Apartment building operators

(G-15281)
CAVAN INC
713 Ashford Rd (19803-2221)
PHONE..................................302 598-4176
EMP: 5 **EST:** 2013
SALES (est): 85.94K **Privately Held**
SIC: 1521 Single-family housing construction

(G-15282)
CAVEGGO INC (PA) ◯
108 W 13th St (19801-1145)
PHONE..................................201 213-4630
Felix Belferman, *Prin*

GEOGRAPHIC SECTION
Wilmington - New Castle County (G-15309)

EMP: 3 **EST:** 2022
SALES (est): 135.7K
SALES (corp-wide): 135.7K **Privately Held**
SIC: 2091 Caviar, preserved

(G-15283)
CAWSL ENTERPRISES INC (HQ)
3411 Silverside Rd (19810-4812)
PHONE..........................302 478-6160
Thomas L Sandor, *Pr*
William G Warden Iii, *VP*
William G Warden Iv, *VP*
John A Sanders, *Sec*
▲ **EMP:** 6 **EST:** 1984
SALES (est): 408.98MM
SALES (corp-wide): 408.98MM **Privately Held**
SIC: 6211 Investment firm, general brokerage
PA: Superior Group, Inc.
  100 Front St Ste 525
  Conshohocken PA 19428
  610 397-2040

(G-15284)
CBBC OPCO LLC (PA)
200 Bellevue Pkwy Ste 210 (19809-3709)
PHONE..........................863 967-0636
EMP: 6 **EST:** 2017
SALES (est): 372.14K
SALES (corp-wide): 372.14K **Privately Held**
SIC: 2011 Boxed beef, from meat slaughtered on site

(G-15285)
CBC HOLDING INC
1201 N Market St 9th Fl (19801-1147)
PHONE..........................302 254-2000
Richard J Nolan Junior, *Ex VP*
Peter F Tobin, *
Matthew J Trachtenberg, *
David S Barrell, *Deputy Controller*
EMP: 13824 **EST:** 1982
SQ FT: 180,000
SALES (corp-wide): 154.79B **Publicly Held**
SIC: 6712 6022 Bank holding companies; State commercial banks
PA: Jpmorgan Chase & Co.
  383 Madison Ave
  New York NY 10179
  212 270-6000

(G-15286)
CBHI INC
3423 N Rockfield Dr (19810-3237)
PHONE..........................484 751-7752
EMP: 10 **EST:** 2019
SALES (est): 39.43K **Privately Held**
Web: www.italianhome.org
SIC: 8322 Social service center

(G-15287)
CBRE INC
3711 Kennett Pike (19807-2161)
PHONE..........................302 661-6700
Robert Walters, *Mgr*
EMP: 9
Web: www.cbre.com
SIC: 6531 Real estate agent, commercial
HQ: Cbre, Inc.
  2100 Mckinney Ave # 1250
  Dallas TX 75201
  866 225-3099

(G-15288)
CCGSR INC
2711 Centerville Rd # 400 (19808-1660)
PHONE..........................800 927-9800
EMP: 6 **EST:** 2016
SALES (est): 312.54K **Privately Held**
SIC: 6411 Insurance agents, brokers, and service

(G-15289)
CCS PAINTING LLC
7 Sharons Way (19808-5237)
PHONE..........................302 438-4398
Chris Steele, *Prin*
EMP: 5 **EST:** 2015
SALES (est): 65.29K **Privately Held**
SIC: 1721 Painting and paper hanging

(G-15290)
CDA ENGINEERING INC
6 Larch Ave Ste 401 (19804-2366)
PHONE..........................302 998-9202
Colmcille Deascanis, *Owner*
EMP: 5 **EST:** 2006
SALES (est): 488.03K **Privately Held**
Web: www.cdaengineering.com
SIC: 8711 Civil engineering

(G-15291)
CDI GRANITE & MBL FABRICATION
811 Kiamensi Rd (19804-3419)
PHONE..........................302 235-7010
EMP: 5 **EST:** 2019
SALES (est): 186.34K **Privately Held**
SIC: 1799 Counter top installation

(G-15292)
CDM INSTITUE
3707 N Market St (19802-2213)
PHONE..........................302 482-3234
EMP: 6 **EST:** 2010
SALES (est): 71.53K **Privately Held**
SIC: 8611 Business associations

(G-15293)
CECIL VAULT & MEMORIAL CO INC
5701 Kirkwood Hwy (19808-4810)
PHONE..........................302 994-3806
TOLL FREE: 877
Dan Cecil, *Pr*
Constance Cecil, *VP*
EMP: 8 **EST:** 1920
SQ FT: 7,000
SALES (est): 710.21K **Privately Held**
Web: www.sabayetinc.org
SIC: 3272 5999 Burial vaults, concrete or precast terrazzo; Tombstones

(G-15294)
CECON GROUP LLC
242 N James St Ste 202 (19804-3168)
P.O. Box 4322 (19807-0322)
PHONE..........................302 994-8000
Michael C Fisher, *Pr*
Stanley Tocker, *Ex VP*
EMP: 7 **EST:** 1985
SQ FT: 1,600
SALES (est): 971.23K
SALES (corp-wide): 42.27MM **Privately Held**
Web: www.cecon.com
SIC: 8711 8748 Consulting engineer; Business consulting, nec
PA: Becht Engineering Co. Inc.
  22 Church St
  Liberty Corner NJ 07938
  908 580-1119

(G-15295)
CEDAR HAMILTON INSUR SVCS LLC
1201 N Market St Ste 1100 (19801-1807)
PHONE..........................302 573-3000
EMP: 8 **EST:** 2021
SALES (est): 268.29K **Privately Held**
SIC: 6411 Insurance agents, brokers, and service

(G-15296)
CEGIS CYBER INC ✪
251 Little Falls Dr (19808-1674)
PHONE..........................800 809-2599
Leamon Crooms, *CEO*
Hank Hu, *COO*
EMP: 3 **EST:** 2022
SALES (est): 61.94K **Privately Held**
Web: www.cegiscyber.com
SIC: 7372 Prepackaged software

(G-15297)
CEI CAPITAL LLC
1105 N Market St Ste 1300 (19801-1241)
PHONE..........................302 573-3875
EMP: 6 **EST:** 2011
SALES (est): 235.69K **Privately Held**
Web: www.ceimaine.org
SIC: 6799 Investors, nec

(G-15298)
CELANESE INTERNATIONAL CORP
Silverside Rd Rodney 34 (19810)
PHONE..........................972 443-4000
EMP: 77 **EST:** 1995
SALES (est): 2.8MM
SALES (corp-wide): 9.67B **Publicly Held**
SIC: 2819 2821 2869 Industrial inorganic chemicals, nec; Polyethylene resins; Acetates: amyl, butyl, and ethyl
PA: Celanese Corporation
  222 Las Colinas Blvd W
  Irving TX 75039
  877 295-0004

(G-15299)
CELANESE POLYMER PRODUCTS LLC (HQ)
Also Called: Dupont
200 Powder Mill Rd Bldg 304 (19803-2907)
PHONE..........................302 774-1000
Edward Breen, *CEO*
EMP: 66 **EST:** 2021
SALES (est): 105.15MM
SALES (corp-wide): 9.67B **Publicly Held**
Web: www.dupont.com
SIC: 2821 Plastics materials and resins
PA: Celanese Corporation
  222 Las Colinas Blvd W
  Irving TX 75039
  877 295-0004

(G-15300)
CELERI HEALTH INC
1815 W 13th St Ste 5 (19806-4054)
PHONE..........................302 438-0766
EMP: 18 **EST:** 2018
SALES (est): 262.18K **Privately Held**
Web: www.celerihealth.com
SIC: 8099 Health and allied services, nec

(G-15301)
CELLCO PARTNERSHIP
Also Called: Verizon
4407 Concord Pike (19803-1489)
PHONE..........................302 530-4620
Chuck Linsdrom, *Brnch Mgr*
EMP: 8
SALES (corp-wide): 133.97B **Publicly Held**
Web: www.verizonwireless.com
SIC: 4812 Cellular telephone services
HQ: Cellco Partnership
  1 Verizon Way
  Basking Ridge NJ 07920

(G-15302)
CELLCO PARTNERSHIP
Also Called: Verizon
844 N King St (19801-3519)
PHONE..........................814 946-5596
EMP: 25
SALES (corp-wide): 133.97B **Publicly Held**
Web: www.verizonwireless.com
SIC: 4812 Cellular telephone services
HQ: Cellco Partnership
  1 Verizon Way
  Basking Ridge NJ 07920

(G-15303)
CENTER FOR INTEGRATIVE CHANGE
607 W 22nd St (19802-3926)
PHONE..........................302 230-1962
Nicholas Kotchision, *Prin*
EMP: 5 **EST:** 2010
SALES (est): 55.34K **Privately Held**
SIC: 8399 Advocacy group

(G-15304)
CENTER FOR SPINE SURGERY LLC
1219 Jefferson St (19801-1033)
PHONE..........................302 366-7671
Pawan Rastogi, *Managing Member*
EMP: 11 **EST:** 2020
SALES (est): 1.14MM **Privately Held**
SIC: 8062 General medical and surgical hospitals

(G-15305)
CENTER MEETING ASSOCIATES LLC
300 Water St Ste 300 (19801-5046)
PHONE..........................302 740-9700
EMP: 6 **EST:** 2016
SALES (est): 154.97K **Privately Held**
SIC: 8611 Trade associations

(G-15306)
CENTERVILLE VETERINARY HOSP
5804 Kennett Pike (19807-1197)
PHONE..........................302 655-3315
Don Coats, *Mgr*
EMP: 13 **EST:** 1958
SALES (est): 223.69K **Privately Held**
Web: www.centrevilleveterinary.com
SIC: 0742 Animal hospital services, pets and other animal specialties

(G-15307)
CENTRAL AMERICAN TRADE CO LLC
1209 N Orange St (19801-1120)
PHONE..........................305 440-0420
EMP: 5 **EST:** 2020
SALES (est): 1.1MM **Privately Held**
SIC: 4731 Freight transportation arrangement

(G-15308)
CENTRAL FIRM LLC
1201 N Orange St Ste 7016 (19801-1188)
PHONE..........................610 470-9836
Margaret Loftus, *CEO*
A Robert Gallagher, *Pr*
EMP: 2 **EST:** 2016
SQ FT: 138
SALES (est): 88.38K **Privately Held**
SIC: 3661 4841 7373 8111 Telephone central office equipment, dial or manual; Direct broadcast satellite services (DBS); Value-added resellers, computer systems; Specialized legal services

(G-15309)
CENTRAL KANSAS AROSPC MFG LLC
251 Little Falls Dr (19808-1674)
PHONE..........................314 406-6550
Patrick Leffel, *CEO*

Wilmington - New Castle County (G-15310)

GEOGRAPHIC SECTION

EMP: 200 **EST:** 2021
SALES (est): 24.96MM
SALES (corp-wide): 77.79B **Publicly Held**
SIC: 3721 Aircraft
PA: The Boeing Company
929 Long Bridge Dr
Arlington VA 22202
703 414-6338

(G-15310)
CENTRALLO CORPORATION (HQ)
1201 N Orange St Ste 600 (19801-1171)
PHONE..................212 355-0880
Michael Sher, *CEO*
EMP: 5 **EST:** 2013
SALES (est): 3.29MM
SALES (corp-wide): 4.07MM **Privately Held**
Web: www.infiniteblue.com
SIC: 7371 Computer software development and applications
PA: Infinite Blue Applications, Llc
2500 Monroe Blvd
Norristown PA 19403
267 341-9610

(G-15311)
CENTRIX HR
213 W 4th St (19801-2204)
PHONE..................302 777-7818
Bill Black, *Owner*
EMP: 5 **EST:** 2002
SALES (est): 316.96K **Privately Held**
Web: www.centrixstaffing.com
SIC: 7361 Employment agencies

(G-15312)
CENTRIX WEB SERVICES LLC
831 N Tatnall St Ste M217 (19801-1717)
PHONE..................302 319-5122
EMP: 6 **EST:** 2016
SALES (est): 65.37K **Privately Held**
SIC: 4813 Data telephone communications

(G-15313)
CERAMIC TILE SUPPLY CO (PA)
Also Called: Bath, Kitchen & Tile Center
103 Greenbank Rd (19808-4721)
P.O. Box 2680 (19805-0680)
PHONE..................302 992-9200
EMP: 73 **EST:** 1967
SALES (est): 28.9MM
SALES (corp-wide): 28.9MM **Privately Held**
Web: www.bathkitchenandtile.com
SIC: 5031 Building materials, interior

(G-15314)
CEROBRAND LLC
2810 N Church St (19802-4447)
PHONE..................740 971-2576
Santiago Tejeda, *Managing Member*
EMP: 6
SALES (est): 86.31K **Privately Held**
SIC: 5122 Toiletries

(G-15315)
CERTIFIED ASSETS MGT INTL LLC
100 Todds Ln (19802-3212)
PHONE..................302 765-3352
Alberto Washington, *Mgr*
EMP: 9 **EST:** 2012
SALES (est): 549.06K **Privately Held**
SIC: 5094 Coins

(G-15316)
CERTIFIED LOCK & ACCESS LLC
3 Germay Dr Ste 7 (19804-1127)
PHONE..................302 383-7507
Stephen Miller, *VP*
EMP: 5 **EST:** 2009
SALES (est): 496.83K **Privately Held**
Web: www.certifiedlockandaccess.com
SIC: 7699 1731 Locksmith shop; Access control systems specialization

(G-15317)
CERTIFIED MECHANICAL CONTRS
117 David Rd (19804-2648)
PHONE..................302 559-3727
Kenneth R Silva, *Owner*
EMP: 6 **EST:** 2011
SALES (est): 484.6K **Privately Held**
Web: www.cmcde.com
SIC: 1711 Mechanical contractor

(G-15318)
CERTINAL INC
919 N Market St Ste 950 (19801-3036)
PHONE..................609 799-5664
EMP: 2 **EST:** 2021
SALES (est): 891.27K **Privately Held**
Web: www.certinal.com
SIC: 7372 Application computer software
HQ: Zycus Inc.
103 Carnegie Ctr Ste 300
Princeton NJ 08540
609 799-5664

(G-15319)
CFG LAB INC
1521 Concord Pike Ste 301 (19803-3644)
PHONE..................302 261-3403
Aleksandr Goldshtadt, *Prin*
EMP: 6 **EST:** 2013
SALES (est): 190.68K **Privately Held**
SIC: 5169 2869 Chemicals and allied products, nec; Laboratory chemicals, organic

(G-15320)
CFG PROPERTIES
113 Thissell Ln (19807-1221)
PHONE..................302 993-1260
EMP: 5 **EST:** 2008
SALES (est): 149.64K **Privately Held**
SIC: 6512 Nonresidential building operators

(G-15321)
CG GLOBAL MGT SOLUTIONS LLC
501 Silverside Rd Ste 10 (19809-1375)
PHONE..................215 735-3745
EMP: 10 **EST:** 2009
SQ FT: 100
SALES (est): 775.15K **Privately Held**
Web: www.cggmanagement.com
SIC: 8742 1731 7371 8748 Marketing consulting services; Energy management controls; Computer software development; Energy conservation consultant

(G-15322)
CG JCF CORP
1209 N Orange St (19801-1120)
PHONE..................302 658-7581
EMP: 5 **EST:** 2010
SALES (est): 130K **Privately Held**
SIC: 6211 Security brokers and dealers

(G-15323)
CGC CONSULTING LLC
5400 Limestone Rd Ste 200 (19808-1232)
PHONE..................302 489-2280
EMP: 6 **EST:** 2010
SQ FT: 20,000
SALES (est): 497.11K **Privately Held**
Web: www.cgcconsult.com
SIC: 8711 Civil engineering

(G-15324)
CGS INFOTECH INC
501 Silverside Rd Ste 105 (19809-1376)
PHONE..................302 351-2434
Ami Shah, *Dir*
EMP: 25 **EST:** 2004
SALES (est): 1.14MM **Privately Held**
Web: www.cgsinfotech.com
SIC: 7374 Computer graphics service

(G-15325)
CH WILMINGTON LLC
1300 N Market St (19801-1136)
PHONE..................302 655-1641
EMP: 16 **EST:** 2015
SALES (est): 279.11K **Privately Held**
SIC: 8111 General practice attorney, lawyer

(G-15326)
CHAD WISWALL AGENCY
520 Philadelphia Pike (19809-2155)
PHONE..................302 791-7600
Charles A Neal, *Owner*
EMP: 5 **EST:** 2010
SALES (est): 184.52K **Privately Held**
Web: www.wiswall-insurance.com
SIC: 6411 Insurance agents, nec

(G-15327)
CHALLENGE PROGRAM
1124 E 7th St (19801-4502)
PHONE..................302 655-0945
Andrew Mcknight, *Pr*
EMP: 8 **EST:** 1992
SALES (est): 2.23MM **Privately Held**
Web: www.challengeprogram.org
SIC: 8699 Charitable organization

(G-15328)
CHAMPIONS + LEGENDS CORP
251 Little Falls Dr (19808-1674)
PHONE..................702 605-2522
Shahin Mottahed, *CEO*
EMP: 8 **EST:** 2019
SALES (est): 217.6K **Privately Held**
Web: www.championsandlegends.com
SIC: 2834 Tinctures, pharmaceutical

(G-15329)
CHANCERY COURT REPORTERS
500 N King St Ste 11400 (19801-3768)
PHONE..................302 255-0515
Lorraine Marino, *Prin*
EMP: 5 **EST:** 1996
SALES (est): 240.04K **Privately Held**
SIC: 7338 Court reporting service

(G-15330)
CHANDLER NICHOL & SLOAN PA
3510 Silverside Rd Ste 4 (19810-4937)
PHONE..................302 478-9800
Jay Chandler, *Prin*
Ed Lynch, *Pt*
EMP: 7 **EST:** 1992
SALES (est): 240.73K **Privately Held**
Web: www.thechandlercpas.com
SIC: 8721 Accounting, auditing, and bookkeeping

(G-15331)
CHANGING PLACE
848 N Madison St (19801-1438)
PHONE..................302 397-8731
EMP: 6 **EST:** 2018
SALES (est): 32.92K **Privately Held**
SIC: 8322 Individual and family services

(G-15332)
CHANGING PLACE INC
809 Morrow St (19801-1340)
PHONE..................302 357-6107
Anthony Boone, *Prin*
EMP: 11 **EST:** 2016
SALES (est): 57.94K **Privately Held**
SIC: 7011 Hotels and motels

(G-15333)
CHANNELAPE INC
2810 N Church St Pmb 82108 (19802-4447)
PHONE..................570 351-9335
Michael Averto, *CEO*
EMP: 25 **EST:** 2017
SALES (est): 1.04MM **Privately Held**
Web: www.channelape.com
SIC: 7371 Computer software development

(G-15334)
CHARAE LANDSCAPING INC
3201 Miller Rd (19802-2542)
PHONE..................302 792-9411
EMP: 9 **EST:** 2007
SALES (est): 304.31K **Privately Held**
Web: www.charae.org
SIC: 0782 Lawn care services

(G-15335)
CHARLES H HUTSON III
221 Westmoreland Ave (19804-1843)
PHONE..................302 378-9001
Charles H Hutson Iii, *Prin*
EMP: 6 **EST:** 2009
SALES (est): 86.52K **Privately Held**
Web: pwisdo.seacoastrealty.com
SIC: 7991 Physical fitness facilities

(G-15336)
CHARLES J VEITH DMD
2300 Pennsylvania Ave Ste 5c (19806-1305)
PHONE..................302 658-7354
EMP: 6 **EST:** 1995
SALES (est): 229.4K **Privately Held**
SIC: 8021 Offices and clinics of dentists

(G-15337)
CHARLES L HOBBS DPM
1706 N Park Dr Apt 9 (19806-2136)
PHONE..................302 655-7735
EMP: 7 **EST:** 2018
SALES (est): 78.17K **Privately Held**
SIC: 8011 Offices and clinics of medical doctors

(G-15338)
CHARLES M WALLACE
1906 Newport Gap Pike (19808-6136)
PHONE..................302 998-1412
Charles Wallace, *Owner*
EMP: 8 **EST:** 1974
SALES (est): 488.13K **Privately Held**
SIC: 6411 Insurance agents, nec

(G-15339)
CHARLES S RESKOVITZ INC
1018 Liberty Rd (19804-2857)
P.O. Box 5068 (19808-0068)
PHONE..................302 999-9455
Charles Stephan, *Pr*
Joanne Stephan, *Sec*
Daniel Stephan, *VP*
EMP: 9 **EST:** 1921
SQ FT: 2,400
SALES (est): 908.91K **Privately Held**
Web: www.reskovitz.com
SIC: 1711 Plumbing contractors

GEOGRAPHIC SECTION
Wilmington - New Castle County (G-15366)

(G-15340)
CHARLES SCHWAB & CO INC
Also Called: Charles Schwab
4021 Kennett Pike Ste A (19807-2040)
PHONE.................................800 435-4000
Rich Hepp, *Brnch Mgr*
EMP: 13
SALES (corp-wide): 20.76B **Publicly Held**
Web: www.schwab.com
SIC: 6211 Brokers, security
HQ: Charles Schwab & Co., Inc.
3000 Schwab Way
Westlake TX 76262
415 636-7000

(G-15341)
CHARLES WANG MD PA
1700 Wawaset St Ste 200 (19806-2142)
PHONE.................................302 655-1500
Charles Wang, *Owner*
EMP: 6 **EST:** 1978
SALES (est): 457.18K **Privately Held**
SIC: 8011 Opthalmologist

(G-15342)
CHARLES WILLIAMS
Also Called: Lytehouse Automotive
1202 E 16th St (19802-5217)
PHONE.................................302 274-2996
Charles Williams, *Owner*
EMP: 15 **EST:** 2021
SALES (est): 551.99K **Privately Held**
Web: www.charlesedwardwilliams.com
SIC: 3089 Automotive parts, plastic

(G-15343)
CHARLIE SQUARE CLEANERS LLC
2001 Delaware Ave (19806-2207)
PHONE.................................302 778-3807
EMP: 5 **EST:** 2018
SALES (est): 107.98K **Privately Held**
SIC: 7699 Cleaning services

(G-15344)
CHARTER DYNAMICS LLC
Also Called: Enteraxion
427 N Tatnall St Ste 70775 (19802)
PHONE.................................888 260-4579
Julian Brinkley, *Managing Member*
Nathalie Brinkley, *CFO*
EMP: 4 **EST:** 2015
SALES (est): 245.29K **Privately Held**
SIC: 7372 Prepackaged software

(G-15345)
CHASE CENTER ON RIVER
815 Justison St Ste B (19801-5156)
PHONE.................................302 655-2187
Richard Encao, *Pr*
EMP: 6 **EST:** 2009
SALES (est): 1.01MM **Privately Held**
Web: www.centerontheriverfront.com
SIC: 8322 Geriatric social service

(G-15346)
CHASE FIELDHOUSE
401 Garasches Ln (19801-5522)
PHONE.................................610 996-0425
EMP: 6 **EST:** 2016
SALES (est): 63.12K **Privately Held**
Web: www.thechasefieldhouse.com
SIC: 7941 Basketball club

(G-15347)
CHATAM INTERNATIONAL INCORPORATED
1105 N Market St Ste 1300 (19801-1241)
PHONE.................................302 478-6185
◆ **EMP:** 200
SIC: 2085 2084 Rye whiskey; Wines

(G-15348)
CHATHAM FINANCIAL CORPORATION
1105 N Market St (19801-1216)
PHONE.................................570 510-0490
EMP: 8 **EST:** 2014
SALES (est): 523.26K **Privately Held**
Web: www.chathamfinancial.com
SIC: 6282 Investment advice

(G-15349)
CHECK PLUS CLEANING LLC
503 W 30th St (19802-3063)
PHONE.................................302 837-7308
EMP: 5 **EST:** 2011
SALES (est): 43.79K **Privately Held**
SIC: 7699 Cleaning services

(G-15350)
CHECK-IT ELECTRIC LLC
40 Harlech Dr (19807-2508)
PHONE.................................302 650-1921
EMP: 5 **EST:** 2018
SALES (est): 245.18K **Privately Held**
Web: www.checkitelectric.com
SIC: 4911 Electric services

(G-15351)
CHELSEA CREEK CAPITAL CO LLC
251 Little Falls Dr (19808-1674)
PHONE.................................312 977-4583
EMP: 6 **EST:** 1997
SALES (est): 287.67K **Privately Held**
SIC: 6799 Investors, nec

(G-15352)
CHELTEN APARTMENTS ASSOC LP
Also Called: Chelten Apartments
4 Denny Rd (19809-3445)
PHONE.................................302 322-6323
EMP: 9 **EST:** 2011
SALES (est): 718.41K **Privately Held**
Web: www.arbormanagement.com
SIC: 6513 Apartment hotel operation

(G-15353)
CHEM TECH INC
6725 Governor Printz Blvd (19809-1800)
P.O. Box 9658 (19809-0658)
PHONE.................................302 798-9675
C R Donovan Junior, *Pr*
EMP: 3 **EST:** 1963
SQ FT: 4,000
SALES (est): 255.08K **Privately Held**
SIC: 2992 2842 Lubricating oils and greases ; Cleaning or polishing preparations, nec

(G-15354)
CHEMFIRST INC (HQ)
1007 Market St (19898-1100)
P.O. Box 7005 (39568-7005)
PHONE.................................302 774-1000
Jeff Coe, *Pr*
Chet Webb, *
Daniel P Anderson, *
Max P Bowman, *
Kenneth Porter, *
◆ **EMP:** 59 **EST:** 1983
SALES (est): 40.24MM
SALES (corp-wide): 6.79B **Publicly Held**
Web: www.chemours.com
SIC: 2865 3567 3312 Cyclic crudes and intermediates; Incinerators, metal: domestic or commercial; Ingots, steel
PA: The Chemours Company
1007 Market St
Wilmington DE 19898
302 773-1000

(G-15355)
CHEMOURS CO FC LLC
200 Powder Mill Rd (19803-2907)
PHONE.................................302 353-5003
EMP: 19 **EST:** 2019
SALES (est): 7.15MM
SALES (corp-wide): 6.79B **Publicly Held**
Web: www.chemours.com
SIC: 2899 Chemical preparations, nec
PA: The Chemours Company
1007 Market St
Wilmington DE 19898
302 773-1000

(G-15356)
CHEMOURS COMPANY (PA)
Also Called: Chemours
1007 Market St (19898-1100)
P.O. Box 2047 (19899-2047)
PHONE.................................302 773-1000
Mark E Newman, *Pr*
Alvenia Scarborough Senior, *Chief Business Officer*
Jonathan S Lock, *Sr VP*
Susan M Kelliher, *Senior Vice President Human Resources*
Matthew Abbott, *ENTRPRSE TRNSFRMTN*
▲ **EMP:** 498 **EST:** 2014
SALES (est): 6.79B
SALES (corp-wide): 6.79B **Publicly Held**
Web: www.chemours.com
SIC: 2899 Chemical preparations, nec

(G-15357)
CHEMOURS COMPANY FC LLC
Also Called: Surface Protection
1007 Market St (19898-1100)
PHONE.................................302 545-0072
Thomas Band, *Mgr*
EMP: 129
SALES (corp-wide): 6.79B **Publicly Held**
Web: www.chemours.com
SIC: 2819 Industrial inorganic chemicals, nec
HQ: The Chemours Company Fc Llc
1007 Market St
Wilmington DE 19898
302 773-1000

(G-15358)
CHEMOURS COMPANY FC LLC (HQ)
Also Called: Chemours
1007 Market St (19898-1100)
P.O. Box 2047 (19899-2047)
PHONE.................................302 773-1000
Mark Newman, *Pr*
Jonathan S Lock, *
◆ **EMP:** 31 **EST:** 2014
SALES (est): 1.29B
SALES (corp-wide): 6.79B **Publicly Held**
Web: www.chemours.com
SIC: 2879 2816 2899 Agricultural chemicals, nec; Titanium dioxide, anatase or rutile (pigments); Chemical preparations, nec
PA: The Chemours Company
1007 Market St
Wilmington DE 19898
302 773-1000

(G-15359)
CHEMOURS COMPANY FC LLC
Animal Health Solutions
4301 Lancaster Pike (19805)
PHONE.................................678 427-1530
Gabriel Pardo, *Mgr*
EMP: 147
SALES (corp-wide): 6.79B **Publicly Held**
Web: www.chemours.com
SIC: 2879 Agricultural chemicals, nec
HQ: The Chemours Company Fc Llc
1007 Market St
Wilmington DE 19898
302 773-1000

(G-15360)
CHEMOURS COMPANY FC LLC
Also Called: Fluoroproducts
Chestnut Run (19880)
PHONE.................................302 540-5423
Simone Genna, *Mgr*
EMP: 64
SALES (corp-wide): 6.79B **Publicly Held**
Web: www.chemours.com
SIC: 2899 Chemical preparations, nec
HQ: The Chemours Company Fc Llc
1007 Market St
Wilmington DE 19898
302 773-1000

(G-15361)
CHEMOURS COMPANY FC LLC
Also Called: Performance Lubricants
1007 Market St (19898-1100)
PHONE.................................302 773-1267
Mark Gullo, *Mgr*
EMP: 75
SALES (corp-wide): 6.79B **Publicly Held**
Web: www.chemours.com
SIC: 5172 Lubricating oils and greases
HQ: The Chemours Company Fc Llc
1007 Market St
Wilmington DE 19898
302 773-1000

(G-15362)
CHEMRING NORTH AMER GROUP INC (DH)
1105 N Market St (19801-1216)
PHONE.................................302 658-5687
Daniel Mckenrick, *Pr*
EMP: 4 **EST:** 2008
SALES (est): 2.09MM
SALES (corp-wide): 573MM **Privately Held**
SIC: 3479 Coating of metals and formed products
HQ: Chemring Holdings Limited
Roke Manor
Romsey HANTS SO51

(G-15363)
CHERRINGTON SERVICE CORP
106 Haywood Rd (19807-1114)
PHONE.................................302 777-4064
Lee L Alexander, *Prin*
EMP: 5 **EST:** 2010
SALES (est): 35.75K **Privately Held**
SIC: 8611 Trade associations

(G-15364)
CHERRY ISLAND RNWBLE ENRGY LLC
1706 E 12th St (19809-3562)
PHONE.................................302 379-0722
EMP: 5
SALES (est): 46.16K **Privately Held**
SIC: 7371 Computer software development and applications

(G-15365)
CHERYL CANTRELL
1701 Augustine Cut Off Ste 100 (19803-4415)
PHONE.................................610 793-9202
Cheryl K Cantrell Md, *Owner*
EMP: 8 **EST:** 2018
SALES (est): 105.49K **Privately Held**
SIC: 8011 Offices and clinics of medical doctors

(G-15366)
CHESAPAKE CNFRNCE SVNTH-DAY AD
Also Called: Wilmington Junior Academy

3003 Mill Creek Rd (19808-1335)
PHONE.................................302 998-3961
Mike Marinkovic, Prin
EMP: 9
SALES (corp-wide): 171.65MM Privately Held
Web: www.wjachildcareandpreschool.com
SIC: 8351 8211 Preschool center; Academy
HQ: Chesapeake Conference Of Seventh-Day Adventists
6600 Martin Rd
Columbia MD 21044
301 596-5600

(G-15367)
CHESAPEAKE NEUROLOGY SERVICE
12 Stable Ln (19803-1935)
PHONE.................................302 563-7253
EMP: 8 EST: 2010
SALES (est): 177.12K Privately Held
SIC: 8011 Neurologist

(G-15368)
CHESTER BTHEL UNTD MTHDST PRE
Also Called: Chester Bethel Preschool
2619 Foulk Rd (19810-1421)
PHONE.................................302 475-3549
Vicky Anignani, Dir
Diane Anonaratl, Dir
EMP: 14 EST: 1776
SQ FT: 130,000
SALES (est): 362.9K Privately Held
Web: www.chesterbethel.org
SIC: 8661 8351 Methodist Church; Child day care services

(G-15369)
CHESTNUT RUN FEDERAL CR UN (PA)
974 Centre Rd (19805-1269)
P.O. Box 5037 (19808-0037)
PHONE.................................302 999-2967
Cheryl Chilcutt, Mgr
Cheryl Chilcutt, Prin
John G Ingram, Prin
Peter Sonne, Prin
John Poore, Prin
EMP: 14 EST: 1959
SQ FT: 4,100
SALES (est): 2.56MM
SALES (corp-wide): 2.56MM Privately Held
Web: www.chestnutrunfcu.org
SIC: 6061 Federal credit unions

(G-15370)
CHICKSX LLC ◊
2055 Limestone Rd Ste 200 Pmb C (19808-5536)
PHONE.................................518 727-1890
Alladin Alof, CEO
Austin Shav, CFO
EMP: 20 EST: 2022
SALES (est): 849.13K Privately Held
SIC: 6282 7389 Investment counselors; Business services, nec

(G-15371)
CHICOS CROWS NEST TTTOO STUDIO
2204 Grubb Rd (19810-2857)
PHONE.................................302 475-6805
Mike Everly, Owner
EMP: 9 EST: 2007
SALES (est): 139.29K Privately Held
Web: www.crowsnesttattoo.com

SIC: 7299 Personal appearance services

(G-15372)
CHILD INC (PA)
507 Philadelphia Pike (19809-2177)
PHONE.................................302 762-8989
Martha V Dupont Bd, Pr
Tim Brandau, *
EMP: 30 EST: 1963
SQ FT: 6,000
SALES (est): 5.53MM
SALES (corp-wide): 5.53MM Privately Held
Web: www.childinc.com
SIC: 8322 8699 Outreach program; Charitable organization

(G-15373)
CHILD CARE CTR
221 N Jackson St (19805-3649)
PHONE.................................302 652-8992
Ronald Giannone, Prin
EMP: 8 EST: 2017
SALES (est): 17.57K Privately Held
SIC: 8351 Child day care services

(G-15374)
CHILDREN YOUTH & THEIR FAM
321 E 11th St Fl 1 (19801-3417)
PHONE.................................302 577-6011
EMP: 6
SALES (corp-wide): 11.27B Privately Held
Web: kids.delaware.gov
SIC: 8322 9441 Child related social services; Administration of social and manpower programs, State government
HQ: Children, Youth & Their Families, Delaware Dept Of Services For
1825 Faulkland Rd
Wilmington DE 19805

(G-15375)
CHILDREN FMILIES FIRST DEL INC (PA)
809 N Washington St (19801-1509)
P.O. Box 1637 (19899-1637)
PHONE.................................302 658-5177
Jennifer B Jonach, Ch
Katy Connolly, *
Barbara Ridgeley, *
Jessica Bain, *
Peter Hazen, *
EMP: 54 EST: 1919
SALES (est): 17.22MM
SALES (corp-wide): 17.22MM Privately Held
Web: www.cffde.org
SIC: 8322 Child related social services

(G-15376)
CHILDREN FMLIES FRST ENDOWMENT
809 N Washington St (19801-1509)
PHONE.................................302 658-5177
EMP: 6 EST: 2011
SALES (est): 103.73K Privately Held
SIC: 8322 Multi-service center

(G-15377)
CHILDREN YUTH THEIR FMLIES DEL
Division Child Mntal Hlth Svcs
1825 Faulkland Rd (19805-1121)
PHONE.................................302 633-2600
Darbar Gorezowerk, Sec
EMP: 8
SALES (corp-wide): 11.27B Privately Held
Web: kids.delaware.gov
SIC: 8011 9431 Occupational and industrial specialist, physician/surgeon; Administration of public health programs

HQ: Children, Youth & Their Families, Delaware Dept Of Services For
1825 Faulkland Rd
Wilmington DE 19805

(G-15378)
CHILDRENS ADVOCACY CENTER
P.O. Box 269 (19899-0269)
PHONE.................................302 651-4567
EMP: 7 EST: 2000
SALES (est): 68.61K Privately Held
Web: www.cacofde.org
SIC: 8322 Child related social services

(G-15379)
CHILDRENS ADVOCACY CTR OF DEL
1600 Rockland Rd Rm 3f-27 (19803-3607)
PHONE.................................302 651-4615
Randall Williams, Ex Dir
EMP: 5
SALES (corp-wide): 1.75MM Privately Held
Web: www.cacofde.org
SIC: 8322 Child related social services
PA: Children's Advocacy Center Of Delaware Inc
611 S Dupont Hwy Ste 201
Dover DE 19901
302 741-2123

(G-15380)
CHILDRENS BEACH HOUSE INC (PA)
100 W 10th St Ste 411 (19801-1643)
PHONE.................................302 655-4288
Richard Garrett, Ex Dir
Thomas Sturgis, Pr
Charles Sterner, Treas
EMP: 22 EST: 1936
SALES (est): 3.09MM
SALES (corp-wide): 3.09MM Privately Held
Web: www.cbhinc.org
SIC: 8322 Childrens' aid society

(G-15381)
CHILDRENS DNTL HLTH WLMNGTON W
3301 Lancaster Pike (19805-1436)
PHONE.................................302 803-6560
EMP: 10 EST: 2019
SALES (est): 426.75K Privately Held
Web: www.childrensdentalhealth.com
SIC: 8021 Dentists' office

(G-15382)
CHIME INC
Also Called: Wave
1013 Centre Rd Ste 403 (19805-1270)
PHONE.................................978 844-1162
Drew Durbin, CEO
EMP: 65 EST: 2011
SALES (est): 3.62MM Privately Held
Web: www.sendwave.com
SIC: 7389 Design services

(G-15383)
CHIMICLES SCHWRTZ KRNER DNLDSN
2711 Centerville Rd Ste 201 (19808-1660)
PHONE.................................302 656-2500
Randolph Dan, Brnch Mgr
EMP: 15
SALES (corp-wide): 5.3MM Privately Held
Web: www.chimicles.com
SIC: 8111 General practice attorney, lawyer
PA: Chimicles Schwartz Kriner & Donaldson-Smith Llp
361 W Lancaster Ave
Haverford PA 19041
610 642-8500

(G-15384)
CHIP DIAGNOSTICS INC (PA)
1105 N Market St Ste 1800 (19801-1272)
PHONE.................................302 752-1064
Kathryn Spruance, Adm/Asst
David Issadore, COO
EMP: 5 EST: 2015
SALES (est): 152.93K
SALES (corp-wide): 152.93K Privately Held
SIC: 8731 Biotechnical research, commercial

(G-15385)
CHIQUITA BRANDS LLC
Also Called: Chiquita
101 River Rd (19801-5886)
PHONE.................................302 571-9781
Phil Colgate, Mgr
EMP: 11
SALES (corp-wide): 3.64B Privately Held
Web: www.chiquita.com
SIC: 5148 Fruits
HQ: Chiquita Brands L.L.C.
1855 Griffin Rd Ste C436
Dania FL 33004
954 924-5801

(G-15386)
CHIRO MED CHIROPRACTIC LLC
213 W 4th St (19801-2204)
PHONE.................................302 256-0363
EMP: 10 EST: 2019
SALES (est): 470.6K Privately Held
Web: www.chiromedchi.com
SIC: 8041 Offices and clinics of chiropractors

(G-15387)
CHIROFUSION LLC
3411 Silverside Rd Ste 106 (19810-4810)
PHONE.................................877 210-3230
EMP: 6 EST: 2019
SALES (est): 111.51K Privately Held
Web: www.chirofusionsoftware.com
SIC: 7372 Prepackaged software

(G-15388)
CHIROSTAFF LLC
903 Shipley Rd (19803-4927)
PHONE.................................302 332-3312
EMP: 5 EST: 2017
SALES (est): 72.53K Privately Held
SIC: 8041 Offices and clinics of chiropractors

(G-15389)
CHISEL CREEK GOLF CLUB
2602 Belaire Dr (19808-3810)
PHONE.................................302 379-6011
EMP: 5 EST: 2017
SALES (est): 47.84K Privately Held
SIC: 7997 Membership sports and recreation clubs

(G-15390)
CHOI EUNHWA
30 Weilers Bnd (19810-4156)
PHONE.................................302 559-3771
Eunhwa Choi, Pr
EMP: 7 EST: 2017
SALES (est): 96.69K Privately Held
SIC: 8049 Offices of health practitioner

(G-15391)
CHOPIN IMPORTS LTD
3422 Old Capitol Trl (19808-6124)
PHONE.................................612 226-9875
Tadeusz Dorda, Pr
Douglas Andersen, Prin
EMP: 19 EST: 2010
SALES (est): 1.6MM Privately Held
Web: www.chopinimports.com

SIC: 8742 Food and beverage consultant

(G-15392)
CHOTCUT INC
2055 Limestone Rd Ste 200c (19808-5536)
PHONE..................................706 437-7890
Deji Jimi, Mng Pt
EMP: 5
SALES (est): 46.16K Privately Held
Web: www.chotcut.com
SIC: 7371 Computer software development and applications

(G-15393)
CHPTER HOLDINGS INC ✪
2810 N Church St (19802-4447)
PHONE..................................650 223-1786
Kevin Muiruri, Prin
EMP: 10 EST: 2022
SALES (est): 510.11K Privately Held
SIC: 5961 7371 Electronic shopping; Computer software development and applications

(G-15394)
CHRIS AND TRACEY HAVERKAMP FAM
501 Silverside Rd Ste 123 (19809-1377)
PHONE..................................800 839-1754
EMP: 5 EST: 2011
SALES (est): 79.95K Privately Held
SIC: 8699 Charitable organization

(G-15395)
CHRISSINGER AND BAUMBERGER
Also Called: Liberty Mutual
3 Mill Rd Ste 301 (19806-2164)
PHONE..................................302 777-0100
Ted Kelley, Owner
EMP: 7 EST: 2003
SALES (est): 468.46K Privately Held
Web: www.libertymutualgroup.com
SIC: 6331 Automobile insurance

(G-15396)
CHRIST CH EPISCPAL PRESCHOOL
505 E Buck Rd (19807-2167)
P.O. Box 3510 (19807-0510)
PHONE..................................302 472-0021
EMP: 10 EST: 2011
SALES (est): 385.85K Privately Held
Web: www.ccepde.org
SIC: 8661 8351 Episcopal Church; Preschool center

(G-15397)
CHRISTANA CARE HM HLTH CMNTY S
Also Called: Evergreen Ctr Alzhmer Day Trtm
3000 Newport Gap Pike (19808-2378)
PHONE..................................302 995-8448
Lynn Williams-spencer, Mgr
EMP: 280
SALES (corp-wide): 666.58K Privately Held
Web: www.christianacare.org
SIC: 8082 8322 Visiting nurse service; Adult day care center
HQ: Christiana Care Home Health And Community Services Inc
     1 Reads Way Ste 100
     New Castle DE 19720
     302 327-5583

(G-15398)
CHRISTENSEN EVERT J PLUMBING &
Dartmouth Woods St (19810)
PHONE..................................302 475-9249
Evert J Christensen, Prin
EMP: 6 EST: 2002
SALES (est): 177.77K Privately Held
SIC: 1711 Plumbing contractors

(G-15399)
CHRISTIANA BODY SHOP INC
96 Germay Dr (19804-1105)
PHONE..................................302 655-1085
Christine D Cox, Pr
Ernie Cox, VP
Megan Cox, Off Mgr
EMP: 7 EST: 1962
SALES (est): 612.05K Privately Held
Web: www.christianabody.com
SIC: 7532 Body shop, automotive

(G-15400)
CHRISTIANA CARE HEALTH SYS INC
Also Called: Cardiac Diagnostic Center
3521 Silverside Rd Ste 1a (19810-4900)
PHONE..................................302 477-6500
EMP: 8
SALES (corp-wide): 666.58K Privately Held
Web: www.christianacare.org
SIC: 8011 8734 Cardiologist and cardiovascular specialist; Testing laboratories
HQ: Christiana Care Health System, Inc.
     200 Hygeia Dr
     Newark DE 19713
     302 733-1000

(G-15401)
CHRISTIANA CARE HEALTH SYS INC
Also Called: Asari, Julie Y MD
4512 Kirkwood Hwy Ste 300 (19808-5129)
PHONE..................................302 623-7500
James E Damour Md, Pr
EMP: 272
SALES (corp-wide): 666.58K Privately Held
Web: www.christianacare.org
SIC: 8062 General medical and surgical hospitals
HQ: Christiana Care Health System, Inc.
     200 Hygeia Dr
     Newark DE 19713
     302 733-1000

(G-15402)
CHRISTIANA CARE HEALTH SYS INC
4000 Nexus Dr (19803-3000)
PHONE..................................302 428-6219
EMP: 205
SALES (corp-wide): 666.58K Privately Held
Web: www.christianacare.org
SIC: 8062 General medical and surgical hospitals
HQ: Christiana Care Health System, Inc.
     200 Hygeia Dr
     Newark DE 19713
     302 733-1000

(G-15403)
CHRISTIANA CARE HEALTH SYS INC
3506 Kennett Pike (19807-3019)
PHONE..................................302 623-1929
EMP: 228
SALES (corp-wide): 666.58K Privately Held
Web: www.christianacare.org
SIC: 8062 General medical and surgical hospitals
HQ: Christiana Care Health System, Inc.
     200 Hygeia Dr
     Newark DE 19713
     302 733-1000

(G-15404)
CHRISTIANA CARE HEALTH SYS INC
Also Called: Center For Rehabilitation
501 W 14th St (19801-1013)
PHONE..................................302 733-1000
Charles Smith, Pr
EMP: 228
SALES (corp-wide): 666.58K Privately Held
Web: www.christianacare.org
SIC: 8741 8062 Hospital management; General medical and surgical hospitals
HQ: Christiana Care Health System, Inc.
     200 Hygeia Dr
     Newark DE 19713
     302 733-1000

(G-15405)
CHRISTIANA CARE HEALTH SYSTEM
100 N Dupont Rd (19807-3106)
PHONE..................................302 992-5545
Thomal L Corrigan, Prin
EMP: 11 EST: 2018
SALES (est): 188.58K Privately Held
Web: www.christianacare.org
SIC: 8099 8062 Health and allied services, nec; General medical and surgical hospitals

(G-15406)
CHRISTIANA CARE HLTH SVCS INC
Also Called: Alan B Evantash
2302 W 16th St (19806-1307)
PHONE..................................302 733-1805
EMP: 6
SALES (corp-wide): 666.58K Privately Held
Web: www.christianacare.org
SIC: 8062 General medical and surgical hospitals
PA: Christiana Care Health Services, Inc.
     4755 Ogletown Stanton Rd
     Newark DE 19718
     302 733-1000

(G-15407)
CHRISTIANA CARE HLTH SVCS INC
Also Called: Christiana Physcl Therapy Plus
1401 Foulk Rd Ste 100 (19803-2764)
PHONE..................................302 477-3300
Paul Schweizer, Pr
EMP: 10
SALES (corp-wide): 666.58K Privately Held
Web: www.christianacare.org
SIC: 8049 Physical therapist
PA: Christiana Care Health Services, Inc.
     4755 Ogletown Stanton Rd
     Newark DE 19718
     302 733-1000

(G-15408)
CHRISTIANA CARE HLTH SVCS INC
Also Called: Wellness Centers
2501 Ebright Rd (19810-1125)
PHONE..................................302 477-3960
Jody Pezzner, Dir
EMP: 7
SALES (corp-wide): 666.58K Privately Held
Web: www.christianacare.org
SIC: 8011 Primary care medical clinic
PA: Christiana Care Health Services, Inc.
     4755 Ogletown Stanton Rd
     Newark DE 19718
     302 733-1000

(G-15409)
CHRISTIANA COUNSELING
Also Called: Christiana Counseling
5235 W Woodmill Dr Ste 47& (19808-4068)
PHONE..................................302 995-1680
Robert Blaine Morris, Pr
Adam Morris, VP
Robert Blaine Morris Iii, VP
Kris Fowler, Sec
EMP: 5 EST: 1986
SALES (est): 888.53K Privately Held
Web: www.christianacounseling.com
SIC: 8011 Psychiatrists and psychoanalysts

(G-15410)
CHRISTIANA INCORPORATORS INC
508 Main St (19804-3911)
PHONE..................................302 998-2008
Ralph V Estep, Pr
EMP: 7 EST: 1972
SALES (est): 458.48K Privately Held
Web: www.deincorporate.com
SIC: 8721 Certified public accountant

(G-15411)
CHRISTIANA MATERIALS INC
305 W Newport Pike (19804-3154)
PHONE..................................302 633-5600
EMP: 12 EST: 1995
SALES (est): 2.23MM Privately Held
Web: www.harmonyconst.com
SIC: 2951 5032 Asphalt paving mixtures and blocks; Building stone

(G-15412)
CHRISTIANA PHYS THERPY & SPINE
5307 Limestone Rd Ste 101 (19808-1275)
PHONE..................................302 731-2660
Dennis Whitesel, Prin
EMP: 8 EST: 2008
SALES (est): 183.11K Privately Held
SIC: 8049 8011 Physical therapist; Physicians' office, including specialists

(G-15413)
CHRISTINA CARE VNA
4000 Nexus Dr (19803-3000)
PHONE..................................302 327-5212
Steven Rombach, Owner
EMP: 18 EST: 2001
SALES (est): 2.4MM Privately Held
Web: www.christianacare.org
SIC: 8093 Respiratory therapy clinic

(G-15414)
CHRISTINA CRESCENT
125 S West St (19801-5014)
PHONE..................................302 528-9182
EMP: 5 EST: 2018
SALES (est): 101.5K Privately Held
SIC: 6531 Real estate agent, commercial

(G-15415)
CHRISTINA CULTURAL ARTS CENTER
Also Called: EARLY CHILDHOOD EDUCATION ARTS
705 N Market St (19801-3008)
PHONE..................................302 652-0101
H Ray Jones Avery, Dir
Steven Werbey,
Ivory Brock, *
EMP: 41 EST: 1946
SQ FT: 170
SALES (est): 1.45MM Privately Held
Web: www.ccacde.org
SIC: 8699 Art council

(G-15416)
CHRISTINA RIVER EXCHANGE LLC
1000 N West St Ste 800 (19801-1059)
PHONE..................................302 691-2139
EMP: 8 EST: 2017
SALES (est): 376.89K Privately Held
Web: www.christinariverexchange.com

Wilmington - New Castle County (G-15417)   GEOGRAPHIC SECTION

SIC: **8742** Business planning and organizing services

(G-15417)
CHRISTINE DIPAOLO
1600 Rockland Rd (19803-3607)
PHONE.....................302 651-4000
Christine Dipaolo, *Prin*
EMP: **6** EST: 2014
SALES (est): 98.65K **Privately Held**
SIC: **8049** Offices of health practitioner

(G-15418)
CHRISTINE W MAYNARD MD
4600 New Lndn Hll Rd 20 (19808)
PHONE.....................302 995-7073
Christine Maynard Md, *Owner*
EMP: **7** EST: 1989
SALES (est): 149.56K **Privately Held**
SIC: **8049** Offices of health practitioner

(G-15419)
CHRISTNCARE CTR FOR CMPRHNSIVE
205 W 14th St (19801-1114)
PHONE.....................302 320-9108
EMP: **57** EST: 2020
SALES (est): 510.1K **Privately Held**
Web: www.christianacare.org
SIC: **8011** Medical centers

(G-15420)
CHRISTNCARE PRMRY CARE AT LNDE
100 S Riding Blvd (19808-3692)
PHONE.....................302 623-2850
EMP: **8** EST: 2020
SALES (est): 440.82K **Privately Held**
Web: www.christianacare.org
SIC: **8062** General medical and surgical hospitals

(G-15421)
CHRISTNCARE PRMRY CARE FMLY MD
1401 Foulk Rd (19803-2763)
PHONE.....................302 477-3300
EMP: **17** EST: 2020
SALES (est): 702.68K **Privately Held**
Web: www.christianacare.org
SIC: **8011** Medical centers

(G-15422)
CHRISTNCARE RHBLTTION SVCS AT
5311 Limestone Rd (19808-1246)
PHONE.....................302 623-1500
EMP: **7** EST: 2020
SALES (est): 32.92K **Privately Held**
Web: www.christianacare.org
SIC: **8322** Rehabilitation services

(G-15423)
CHRISTOPHER BARAN DDS
1601 Milltown Rd Ste 19 (19808-4084)
PHONE.....................903 968-7467
Christopher Baran, *Prin*
EMP: **10** EST: 2019
SALES (est): 219.89K **Privately Held**
Web: www.brownbarandentistry.com
SIC: **8021** Dentists' office

(G-15424)
CHRISTOPHER MCGLINN PHD
1415 Foulk Rd Ste 104 (19803-2748)
PHONE.....................302 478-1450
Christopher Mcglinn, *Pr*
EMP: **6** EST: 2018
SALES (est): 24.4K **Privately Held**

SIC: **8049** Clinical psychologist

(G-15425)
CHUBB REALTY GROUP
505 Falkirk Rd (19803-2445)
PHONE.....................302 388-8699
Billie Chubb, *Prin*
EMP: **5** EST: 2015
SALES (est): 109.1K **Privately Held**
SIC: **6531** Real estate agent, residential

(G-15426)
CHUBB US HOLDINGS INC
Also Called: Ace Global Solution
1 Beaver Valley Rd # 4e (19803-1115)
PHONE.....................215 640-1000
Usha Ravinath, *Brnch Mgr*
EMP: **126**
Web: www.chubb.com
SIC: **6411** Property and casualty insurance agent
HQ: Chubb Us Holdings Inc.
    1601 Chestnut St
    Philadelphia PA 19192

(G-15427)
CHUCK GEORGE INC
Also Called: Delaware Metals
400 Water St (19804-2421)
PHONE.....................302 994-7444
Chuck George, *Pr*
Karen George, *
EMP: **30** EST: 1953
SQ FT: **16,000**
SALES (est): 4.54MM **Privately Held**
Web: www.delawaremetals.com
SIC: **7692** 3599 Welding repair; Machine shop, jobbing and repair

(G-15428)
CHUCK LAGER LLC
Also Called: Chuck Lager
4500 Linden Hill Rd (19808-2905)
PHONE.....................302 482-1773
Chuck Lager, *Owner*
EMP: **77** EST: 2019
SALES (est): 1.14MM
SALES (corp-wide): 1.47MM **Privately Held**
Web: www.chucklager.com
SIC: **5812** 6794 American restaurant; Franchises, selling or licensing
PA: Fabio Viviani Hospitality, Llc
    4714 Elderberry Ave
    Moorpark CA 93021
    805 813-1622

(G-15429)
CHURCHFUNERALS DIRECT INC
1000 N West St Ste 1200 (19801-1058)
PHONE.....................800 308-3590
EMP: **6** EST: 2019
SALES (est): 233.18K **Privately Held**
Web: www.churchfuneralsdirect.com
SIC: **6099** Check cashing agencies

(G-15430)
CI DE CORP (PA)
39 Brookside Dr (19804-1101)
PHONE.....................302 998-3944
Guy Devito, *Pr*
EMP: **9** EST: 1968
SALES (est): 5.63MM
SALES (corp-wide): 5.63MM **Privately Held**
SIC: **1771** 1541 Foundation and footing contractor; Industrial buildings, new construction, nec

(G-15431)
CIANCON GLOBAL LLC
Also Called: Castle Consultants
501 Silverside Rd Ste 105 (19809-1376)
PHONE.....................302 365-0956
EMP: **10** EST: 2009
SQ FT: **1,200**
SALES (est): 479.96K **Privately Held**
SIC: **4953** Recycling, waste materials

(G-15432)
CIBA SPECIALTY CHEM N AMER
205 S James St (19804-2424)
PHONE.....................302 992-5600
John Shaphly, *Prin*
EMP: **9** EST: 2014
SALES (est): 412.61K **Privately Held**
SIC: **5169** Chemicals and allied products, nec

(G-15433)
CIBC PRIVATE WEALTH GROUPS LLC
Also Called: Cibc ATL Tr Private Wealth MGT
1 Righter Pkwy Ste 180 (19803-1550)
PHONE.....................302 478-4050
EMP: **5**
SALES (corp-wide): 15.86B **Privately Held**
Web: private-wealth.us.cibc.com
SIC: **6282** Investment counselors
HQ: Cibc Private Wealth Groups Llc
    3290 Northside Pkwy Nw # 7
    Atlanta GA 30327
    404 881-3400

(G-15434)
CICONTE WASSERMAN & SCERBA LLC
1300 N King St (19801-3220)
PHONE.....................302 658-7101
Edward Ciconte, *Prin*
EMP: **10** EST: 2015
SALES (est): 760.64K **Privately Held**
Web: www.cskdelaw.com
SIC: **8111** General practice attorney, lawyer

(G-15435)
CIELO SALON & SPA INC
600 Delaware Ave (19801-1430)
PHONE.....................302 575-0400
Laron Thomas, *Pr*
EMP: **11** EST: 2004
SALES (est): 164.71K **Privately Held**
Web: www.cielosalonspa.com
SIC: **7231** Hairdressers

(G-15436)
CIGNA REAL ESTATE INC (DH)
Also Called: Cigna
1 Beaver Valley Rd (19803-1115)
P.O. Box 15050 (19850-5050)
PHONE.....................302 476-3337
William C Hartman, *Pr*
EMP: **6** EST: 1983
SALES (est): 5.49MM **Privately Held**
Web: www.cignaglobal.com
SIC: **6531** 6512 6799 6519 Real estate agents and managers; Nonresidential building operators; Investors, nec; Real property lessors, nec
HQ: Ace Property And Casualty Insurance Company
    2 Librty Pl 1601 Chstnut 2 Liberty Place
    Philadelphia PA 19102

(G-15437)
CIGNITIX GLOBAL LLC
2055 Limestone Rd Ste 200c (19808-5536)
PHONE.....................408 638-9350
EMP: **5**

SALES (est): 107.01K **Privately Held**
Web: www.cignitix.com
SIC: **7371** Computer software development

(G-15438)
CINDY L TUCKER PHD
2500 Grubb Rd Ste 240 (19810-4796)
PHONE.....................302 743-5775
Cindy Tucker, *Prin*
EMP: **7** EST: 2007
SALES (est): 72.05K **Privately Held**
SIC: **8049** Clinical psychologist

(G-15439)
CINEMARK USA INC
Also Called: Cinemark Movies 10
1796 W Newport Pike (19804-3540)
PHONE.....................302 994-7280
Ron Landry, *Brnch Mgr*
EMP: **6**
Web: www.cinemark.com
SIC: **7832** Motion picture theaters, except drive-in
HQ: Cinemark Usa, Inc.
    3900 Dallas Pkwy Ste 500
    Plano TX 75093
    972 665-1000

(G-15440)
CINNAIRE REGISTERED INVESTMENT
100 W 10th St Ste 302 (19801-1642)
PHONE.....................302 655-1420
James Peffley, *Prin*
EMP: **16** EST: 2016
SALES (est): 713.65K **Privately Held**
Web: www.cinnaire.com
SIC: **6799** Investors, nec

(G-15441)
CINTAS CORPORATION NO 2
Also Called: Cintas J98
2925 Governor Printz Blvd (19802-3705)
PHONE.....................302 765-6460
EMP: **8**
SALES (corp-wide): 8.82B **Publicly Held**
Web: www.cintas.com
SIC: **5084** Safety equipment
HQ: Cintas Corporation No. 2
    6800 Cintas Blvd
    Mason OH 45040

(G-15442)
CIO STORY LLC
19c Trolley Sq (19806-3355)
PHONE.....................408 915-5559
Vijay Karthik Udayakumar, *Prin*
EMP: **4** EST: 2015
SALES (est): 84.05K **Privately Held**
SIC: **2721** Magazines: publishing and printing

(G-15443)
CIRCLE TIME LEARNING CENTER
1002 S Grant Ave (19805-4110)
PHONE.....................302 384-7193
Serritta Jeffers, *Prin*
EMP: **5** EST: 2010
SALES (est): 88.95K **Privately Held**
SIC: **8351** Group day care center

(G-15444)
CIRCLE VETERINARY CLINIC
Also Called: McCracken M Jill
1212 E Newport Pike (19804-1941)
PHONE.....................302 652-6587
David Wilkins, *Pr*
EMP: **15** EST: 1958
SQ FT: **1,350**
SALES (est): 984.65K **Privately Held**
Web: www.circlevet.com

SIC: 0742 Animal hospital services, pets and other animal specialties

(G-15445)
CIRRUS ENTERPRISES
19c Trolley Sq (19806-3355)
PHONE...............................302 650-1648
Andrew Fairbanks, *Pr*
EMP: 5 **EST:** 2017
SALES (est): 137.24K **Privately Held**
SIC: 4213 Trucking, except local

(G-15446)
CIRRUS NEXUS CORP
300 Delaware Ave (19801-1607)
PHONE...............................302 492-2700
Chris Noble, *CEO*
EMP: 25 **EST:** 2021
SALES (est): 750.74K **Privately Held**
Web: www.cirrus-nexus.com
SIC: 7379 Online services technology consultants

(G-15447)
CITED INC
2711 Centerville Rd (19808-1660)
PHONE...............................302 384-9810
EMP: 6 **EST:** 2016
SALES (est): 86.23K **Privately Held**
Web: www.citedcorp.com
SIC: 7373 7371 Systems engineering, computer related; Computer software development and applications

(G-15448)
CITIFINANCIAL CREDIT COMPANY
Also Called: Citifinancial
4500 Linden Hill Rd 3rd Fl (19808-2922)
PHONE...............................302 683-4917
Frank Garcia, *Sr VP*
EMP: 11
SALES (corp-wide): 101.08B **Publicly Held**
Web: www.citigroup.com
SIC: 6141 Consumer finance companies
HQ: Citifinancial Credit Company
  300 Saint Paul Pl Fl 3
  Baltimore MD 21202
  410 332-3000

(G-15449)
CITIGROUP GLOBL MKTS FNCL PDTS
1209 N Orange St (19801-1120)
PHONE...............................212 559-1000
EMP: 10 **EST:** 1997
SALES (est): 524.96K **Privately Held**
SIC: 6211 Security brokers and dealers

(G-15450)
CITROSUCO NORTH AMERICA INC
1000 Ferry Rd (19801-5862)
PHONE...............................302 652-8763
Phill Spears, *Brnch Mgr*
EMP: 10
SALES (corp-wide): 851.9MM **Privately Held**
Web: www.citrosuco.com
SIC: 4222 Warehousing, cold storage or refrigerated
HQ: Citrosuco North America, Inc.
  5937 State Road 60 E
  Lake Wales FL 33898
  863 696-7400

(G-15451)
CITY ELECTRIC CONTRACTING CO
204 Channel Rd (19809-3595)
PHONE...............................302 764-0775
Dan Mitchell, *VP*

Albina Baraba, *Sec*
Denise Widdoes, *Pr*
EMP: 10 **EST:** 1953
SQ FT: 4,800
SALES (est): 893.62K **Privately Held**
Web: www.cityelectriccontracting.com
SIC: 1731 General electrical contractor

(G-15452)
CITY ELECTRIC SUPPLY COMPANY
6 Medori Blvd (19801-5781)
PHONE...............................302 777-5300
Jimmy Resh, *Brnch Mgr*
EMP: 5
SALES (corp-wide): 2.39B **Privately Held**
Web: www.cityelectricsupply.com
SIC: 5063 Electrical supplies, nec
HQ: City Electric Supply Company
  400 S Record St Ste 1500
  Dallas TX 75202
  214 865-6801

(G-15453)
CITY FARE
1703 W 10th St (19805-2709)
PHONE...............................302 421-3734
EMP: 7 **EST:** 2017
SALES (est): 76.74K **Privately Held**
Web: www.cityfare.org
SIC: 8699 Charitable organization

(G-15454)
CITY OF WILMINGTON
Also Called: Utility Billing
800 N French St (19801-3537)
PHONE...............................302 576-2584
Mike Marinelli, *Mgr*
EMP: 14
Web: www.wilmingtonde.gov
SIC: 4941 Water supply
PA: City Of Wilmington
  800 N French St Fl 5
  Wilmington DE 19801
  302 576-2415

(G-15455)
CITY ONE HOUR CLEANERS
615 N King St (19801-3775)
PHONE...............................302 658-0001
Yong H Cha, *Owner*
EMP: 6 **EST:** 1952
SQ FT: 1,000
SALES (est): 283.79K **Privately Held**
SIC: 7216 Cleaning and dyeing, except rugs

(G-15456)
CITY WINDOW CLEANING OF DEL
130b Middleboro Rd (19804-1621)
P.O. Box 53 (19899-0053)
PHONE...............................302 633-0633
H Herbert Hirzel, *Pr*
EMP: 25 **EST:** 1910
SQ FT: 3,200
SALES (est): 2.37MM **Privately Held**
Web: www.citywindowcleaning.com
SIC: 7349 Window cleaning

(G-15457)
CITYWIDE TRANSPORTATION INC
6705 Governor Printz Blvd (19809-1800)
PHONE...............................302 792-0159
Vincent Strmel, *Pr*
EMP: 9 **EST:** 2003
SALES (est): 445.21K **Privately Held**
Web: www.cwlimo.com
SIC: 4119 Limousine rental, with driver

(G-15458)
CK SKIN & MAKEUP LLC
1035 N Lincoln St (19805-2738)

PHONE...............................302 317-2367
EMP: 5 **EST:** 2017
SALES (est): 19.4K **Privately Held**
SIC: 7231 Cosmetology and personal hygiene salons

(G-15459)
CL WALTON ENTERPRISES LLC
300 Delaware Ave Ste 210a (19801-6601)
PHONE...............................443 360-1120
EMP: 12 **EST:** 2019
SALES (est): 233.66K **Privately Held**
SIC: 8748 Business consulting, nec

(G-15460)
CLAIRVYANT TECHNOSOLUTIONS INC
Also Called: Mentoris
5700 Kirkwood Hwy Ste 107 (19808-4883)
PHONE...............................302 999-7172
Sundar Seth, *CEO*
Aho Bilam, *
EMP: 19 **EST:** 2003
SQ FT: 1,700
SALES (est): 848.43K **Privately Held**
SIC: 7372 Business oriented computer software

(G-15461)
CLAREMONT SCHOOL LLC
1501 Marsh Rd (19803-3546)
PHONE...............................302 478-4531
Stephani Richardson, *Prin*
Victoria Boone, *Pr*
Mark Boone, *VP*
EMP: 5 **EST:** 1977
SQ FT: 3,000
SALES (est): 239.91K **Privately Held**
Web: www.theclaremontschool.com
SIC: 8351 Montessori child development center

(G-15462)
CLARIFI
710 N Lincoln St (19805-3016)
PHONE...............................267 546-0430
EMP: 7 **EST:** 2018
SALES (est): 48.04K **Privately Held**
Web: www.clarifi.org
SIC: 8322 Individual and family services

(G-15463)
CLARIP INC
20 Montchanin Rd Ste 20 (19807-2160)
PHONE...............................888 252-5653
EMP: 5 **EST:** 2015
SALES (est): 144.74K **Privately Held**
SIC: 7389 Business services, nec

(G-15464)
CLARK & SONS INC (PA)
314 E Ayre St (19804-2587)
PHONE...............................302 998-7552
Paul T Clark Senior, *Pr*
William W Clark, *
Clifford H Clark, *
James K Clark, *
EMP: 25 **EST:** 1963
SQ FT: 21,000
SALES (est): 8.99MM
SALES (corp-wide): 8.99MM **Privately Held**
Web: www.clarkandsonsdoors.com
SIC: 1751 Garage door, installation or erection

(G-15465)
CLARK & SONS OVERHEAD DOORS
314 E Ayre St (19804-2587)
PHONE...............................302 998-7552

James Clark, *Pr*
EMP: 13 **EST:** 1976
SALES (est): 125.37K **Privately Held**
Web: www.clarkandsonsdoors.com
SIC: 1751 5072 Garage door, installation or erection; Hardware

(G-15466)
CLASSIC AUTO BODY INC
Also Called: Classic Auto Body Wilmington
103 Brookside Dr (19804-1103)
PHONE...............................302 655-4044
Earl V Nichols Junior, *Pr*
Cathryne D Nichols, *VP*
EMP: 5 **EST:** 1982
SALES (est): 339.15K **Privately Held**
Web: www.classicautobodyde.com
SIC: 7532 Body shop, automotive

(G-15467)
CLASSIC COOKIES OF DOWINGTOWN
2628 Longwood Dr (19810-3704)
PHONE...............................302 494-9662
Jeffrey A Schoch, *Prin*
EMP: 5 **EST:** 2003
SALES (est): 429.65K **Privately Held**
Web: www.schochappraisals.com
SIC: 5149 Cookies

(G-15468)
CLAYMORE SENIOR CENTER INC
504 S Clayton St (19805-4211)
PHONE...............................302 428-3170
Donna Mcpoland, *Ex Dir*
Beverly Mccool, *Program Coordinator*
EMP: 5 **EST:** 1974
SQ FT: 20,000
SALES (est): 295.01K **Privately Held**
Web: www.claymoresc.org
SIC: 8322 Senior citizens' center or association

(G-15469)
CLEAMOL LLC
330 Water St Ste 105 (19804-2433)
PHONE...............................513 885-3462
Rongyu Yuan, *Ch*
EMP: 4 **EST:** 2015
SALES (est): 262.77K **Privately Held**
SIC: 2836 Biological products, except diagnostic

(G-15470)
CLEAN CONNECT INC
501 Silverside Rd Ste 201 (19809-1374)
PHONE...............................331 330-5662
EMP: 28 **EST:** 2019
SALES (est): 78.31K **Privately Held**
SIC: 7371 Computer software development and applications

(G-15471)
CLEAN COOKING AFRICA CORP ✪
1201 N Orange St (19801-1155)
PHONE...............................706 691-9813
Yang Lee, *Pr*
EMP: 6 **EST:** 2022
SALES (est): 81.29K **Privately Held**
SIC: 6111 Commodity Credit Corporation

(G-15472)
CLEAN-A-TANK INC
207 S Ogle Ave (19805-1422)
P.O. Box 329 (19468-0329)
PHONE...............................302 250-4229
EMP: 5 **EST:** 2010
SALES (est): 199.01K **Privately Held**
Web: www.cleanatank.com

Wilmington - New Castle County (G-15473)

GEOGRAPHIC SECTION

SIC: 0279 Animal specialties, nec

(G-15473)
CLEANBAY RENEWABLES LLC (PA)
1209 N Orange St (19801-1120)
PHONE..................................866 691-1519
EMP: 7 EST: 2019
SALES (est): 1.97MM
SALES (corp-wide): 1.97MM **Privately Held**
Web: www.cleanbayrenewables.com
SIC: 4911 Electric services

(G-15474)
CLEANING BY DIANA
3115 Acacia St (19804-3935)
PHONE..................................302 345-8904
Diana Myers, *Owner*
EMP: 5 EST: 2016
SALES (est): 43.95K **Privately Held**
Web: www.cleaningbydiana.com
SIC: 7699 Cleaning services

(G-15475)
CLEANING FAIRIES
615 Curtis Ave (19804-2107)
PHONE..................................302 753-3617
Tara Thompson, *Prin*
EMP: 5 EST: 2015
SALES (est): 37.95K **Privately Held**
SIC: 7699 Cleaning services

(G-15476)
CLEAR CHANNEL OUTDOOR LLC
24 Germay Dr (19804-1105)
PHONE..................................302 658-5520
EMP: 20
Web: www.clearchanneloutdoor.com
SIC: 7312 3993 Billboard advertising; Signs and advertising specialties
HQ: Clear Channel Outdoor, Llc
4830 N Loop 160 W Ste 111
San Antonio TX 78249

(G-15477)
CLEARVUE SOLUTIONS ✪
300 Delaware Ave Ste 210 (19801-6601)
PHONE..................................301 213-3358
Clearvue Solutions, *CEO*
EMP: 5 EST: 2023
SALES (est): 164.52K **Privately Held**
SIC: 7389 Business Activities at Non-Commercial Site

(G-15478)
CLEMENT OGUNWANDE DO
1800 N Broom St Ste 109 (19802-3809)
PHONE..................................302 762-4545
EMP: 8 EST: 2018
SALES (est): 84.07K **Privately Held**
Web: www.pronetdirect.com
SIC: 8011 Offices and clinics of medical doctors

(G-15479)
CLEVER ME INC
1209 N Orange St (19801-1120)
PHONE..................................832 866-8866
Tuan La, *Admn*
EMP: 5
SALES (est): 233.11K **Privately Held**
SIC: 8742 Marketing consulting services

(G-15480)
CLEW MEDICAL INC
1313 N Market St Ste 5100 (19801-6111)
PHONE..................................623 414-9009
Gal Salomon, *Prin*
EMP: 5 EST: 2014
SALES (est): 281.62K **Privately Held**

Web: www.clewmed.com
SIC: 7371 Computer software development

(G-15481)
CLIFFORD L ANZILOTTI DDS PC (PA)
2101 Foulk Rd (19810-4710)
PHONE..................................302 475-2050
Clifford L Anzilotti D.d.s., *Pr*
Dea Zufelt, *Mgr*
EMP: 10 EST: 1970
SQ FT: 2,000
SALES (est): 1.08MM
SALES (corp-wide): 1.08MM **Privately Held**
Web: www.anzilottiortho.com
SIC: 8021 Orthodontist

(G-15482)
CLIFFORD O SMITH
3 Woodbrook Cir (19810-4119)
PHONE..................................302 995-9600
Clifford O Smith, *Prin*
EMP: 6 EST: 2018
SALES (est): 62.77K **Privately Held**
SIC: 8049 Clinical psychologist

(G-15483)
CLIMATE ACTION SYSTEMS INC
251 Little Falls Dr (19808-1674)
PHONE..................................802 356-6541
EMP: 5 EST: 2019
SALES (est): 46.16K **Privately Held**
SIC: 7371 Computer software development and applications

(G-15484)
CLIMATE SOLUTIONS SERVICE
3605 Old Capitol Trl (19808-6043)
PHONE..................................302 824-2293
EMP: 7 EST: 2018
SALES (est): 416.24K **Privately Held**
SIC: 3585 Parts for heating, cooling, and refrigerating equipment

(G-15485)
CLIMATE SOLUTIONS SERVICES
2426 Calf Run Dr (19804-4265)
PHONE..................................302 275-9919
EMP: 6 EST: 2014
SALES (est): 242.02K **Privately Held**
Web: www.cssihvac.com
SIC: 1711 Warm air heating and air conditioning contractor

(G-15486)
CLINICAL BREAST IMAGING
2401 Pennsylvania Ave Ste 115 (19806-1432)
PHONE..................................302 658-4800
EMP: 7 EST: 1990
SALES (est): 217.09K **Privately Held**
SIC: 8071 X-ray laboratory, including dental

(G-15487)
CLINPHARMA CLINICAL RES LLC
1000 N West St Ste 1200 (19801-1058)
PHONE..................................646 961-3437
Mike Xie, *Mgr*
EMP: 20 EST: 2007
SALES (est): 2.22MM **Privately Held**
SIC: 8071 7371 Medical laboratories; Computer software development and applications

(G-15488)
CLOUD BIG DATA TECH LLC
3524 Silverside Rd Ste 35b (19810-4929)
PHONE..................................573 201-5937
Tyler Warner, *Prin*
EMP: 63 EST: 2016

SALES (est): 1.29MM **Privately Held**
Web: www.cloudbigd.com
SIC: 7379 Computer related consulting services

(G-15489)
CLOUD FINANCIAL CORPORATION
919 N Market St Ste 950 (19801-3036)
PHONE..................................845 729-5513
Wesley Powell, *CEO*
Indrani Pal-chaudhury, *Prin*
EMP: 9 EST: 2018
SALES (est): 729.64K **Privately Held**
Web: www.cloudfinancial.com
SIC: 6282 8742 7363 Investment advice; Management consulting services; Office help supply service

(G-15490)
CLOUD KINGS RC CLUB
119 Kirkwood Sq (19808-4859)
PHONE..................................717 284-0164
EMP: 6 EST: 2017
SALES (est): 48.27K **Privately Held**
Web: www.cloudkingsrc.org
SIC: 7997 Membership sports and recreation clubs

(G-15491)
CLOUD SERVICES SOLUTIONS INC (PA)
1521 Concord Pike Ste 301 (19803-3644)
PHONE..................................888 335-3132
Stephen Roche, *CEO*
EMP: 26 EST: 2017
SALES (est): 2.37MM
SALES (corp-wide): 2.37MM **Privately Held**
Web: www.csserp.com
SIC: 8741 8742 Business management; Management consulting services

(G-15492)
CLOUD SOFTWARE DEVELOPMENT LLC
3411 Silverside Rd # 104 (19810-4812)
PHONE..................................703 957-9847
Tom Parker, *CEO*
Shawn Duffy, *Pr*
EMP: 5 EST: 2017
SALES (est): 194.08K **Privately Held**
SIC: 7371 Custom computer programming services

(G-15493)
CLOUDARMEE LTD
251 Little Falls Dr (19808-1674)
PHONE..................................714 673-8104
Rajesh Marar, *CEO*
EMP: 10
SALES (est): 348.32K **Privately Held**
SIC: 7371 Software programming applications

(G-15494)
CLOUDINFO INC
1000 N West St Ste 1263 (19801-1050)
PHONE..................................302 314-5748
EMP: 6 EST: 2019
SALES (est): 50.19K **Privately Held**
Web: www.cloudinfoinc.com
SIC: 7389 Business services, nec

(G-15495)
CLOUDOKYO TECHNOLOGIES INC
251 Little Falls Dr (19808-1674)
PHONE..................................845 551-8627
James Qiu, *CEO*
Jackson Zhu, *Prin*
EMP: 5 EST: 2021

SALES (est): 105.38K **Privately Held**
SIC: 7379 Computer related consulting services

(G-15496)
CLOUGH HEALTH AND WELLNESS LLC
115 Norris Rd (19803-4516)
PHONE..................................443 414-3764
EMP: 6 EST: 2017
SALES (est): 117.94K **Privately Held**
SIC: 8099 Health and allied services, nec

(G-15497)
CLOVYR CO
251 Little Falls Dr (19808-1674)
PHONE..................................302 636-5401
EMP: 6 EST: 2018
SALES (est): 67.74K **Privately Held**
SIC: 7372 Application computer software

(G-15498)
CLR MARKETING SERVICES LLC
1201 N Market St (19801-1147)
PHONE..................................302 688-9059
EMP: 10 EST: 2021
SALES (est): 2.5MM **Privately Held**
SIC: 8742 Marketing consulting services

(G-15499)
CLUB WASHINGTON LLC
143 Carpenters Row (19807-2136)
PHONE..................................215 594-1332
Xinyan Zhang, *Prin*
EMP: 6 EST: 2017
SALES (est): 47.42K **Privately Held**
SIC: 7997 Membership sports and recreation clubs

(G-15500)
CMC STEEL HOLDING COMPANY (HQ)
Also Called: C M C
802 N West St Ste 302 (19801-1526)
PHONE..................................302 691-6200
◆ EMP: 3 EST: 1988
SALES (est): 665.37M
SALES (corp-wide): 8.8B **Publicly Held**
SIC: 3441 3312 Fabricated structural metal; Primary finished or semifinished shapes
PA: Commercial Metals Company
6565 N Macarthur Blvd # 800
Irving TX 75039
214 689-4300

(G-15501)
CMPLIFY LLC
1201 N Orange St Ste 600 (19801-1171)
PHONE..................................248 716-5136
EMP: 2 EST: 2019
SALES (est): 100K **Privately Held**
SIC: 7372 Application computer software

(G-15502)
CMS LOGISTICS
1521 Concord Pike (19803-3642)
PHONE..................................302 409-3138
Jeff Miller, *Mgr*
EMP: 11 EST: 2015
SALES (est): 555.46K **Privately Held**
SIC: 4789 Transportation services, nec

(G-15503)
CMV AUDIO LLC (PA)
1000 N West St Ste 1501 (19801-1001)
PHONE..................................929 229-9926
Daniel Amaral Santana Reis, *CEO*
EMP: 34 EST: 2017
SALES (est): 1.95MM
SALES (corp-wide): 1.95MM **Privately Held**

GEOGRAPHIC SECTION

Wilmington - New Castle County (G-15531)

SIC: 5099 Video and audio equipment

(G-15504)
CNH CPTAL OPRTING LASE EQP RCV
1209 N Orange St (19801-1120)
PHONE...................262 636-6011
EMP: 2879
SALES (est): 3.62MM **Privately Held**
SIC: 3523 3531 Tractors, farm; Tractors, construction
HQ: Case Construction Equipment, Inc.
700 State St
Racine WI 53404

(G-15505)
CNOOC FINANCE 2015 USA LLC
2711 Centerville Rd (19808-1660)
PHONE...................302 636-5400
EMP: 10 **EST:** 2015
SALES (est): 673.75K **Privately Held**
SIC: 7389 Financial services
HQ: Cnooc Uk Limited
Prospect House
Uxbridge MIDDX UB8 1
189 523-7700

(G-15506)
COACHHUB INC
1209 N Orange St (19801-1120)
PHONE...................929 930-1450
Yannis Niebelchutz, *Pr*
Alberto Mujica, *VP*
EMP: 7 **EST:** 2020
SALES (est): 33.14K **Privately Held**
Web: www.coachhub.com
SIC: 4813 Proprietary online service networks

(G-15507)
COALITION TO SAVE LIVES
1510 Bondridge Rd (19805-1230)
PHONE...................267 579-2875
Michael Kingsley, *Prin*
EMP: 5 **EST:** 2017
SALES (est): 52.44K **Privately Held**
SIC: 8399 Advocacy group

(G-15508)
COASTAL
1201 N Orange St Ste 700 (19801-1186)
PHONE...................302 319-4061
Margaret Greene, *Admn*
EMP: 40 **EST:** 2016
SALES (est): 702.68K **Privately Held**
Web: www.coastal-one.com
SIC: 6282 Investment advice

(G-15509)
COASTAL EQUITIES INC
1201 N Orange St (19801-1155)
PHONE...................302 543-2784
EMP: 63 **EST:** 2019
SALES (est): 9.75MM **Privately Held**
Web: www.coastal-one.com
SIC: 6411 Insurance agents, brokers, and service

(G-15510)
COASTAL MECHANICAL
Also Called: Tristate Mechanical
1 Carsdale Ct (19808-2141)
PHONE...................302 994-9100
Damian A Nardo, *Pr*
EMP: 18 **EST:** 1968
SALES (est): 448.83K **Privately Held**
SIC: 1711 Warm air heating and air conditioning contractor

(G-15511)
COBI GROUP INC
3424 Old Capitol Trl (19808-6124)
PHONE...................302 407-3085
Anne Jacobi, *Pr*
EMP: 10 **EST:** 2015
SALES (est): 967.64K **Privately Held**
Web: www.thecobigroup.net
SIC: 1542 Commercial and office building, new construction

(G-15512)
COBRA INVESTMENTS MGT INC
103 Foulk Rd (19803-3742)
PHONE...................302 691-6333
EMP: 41 **EST:** 2003
SALES (est): 7.05MM **Privately Held**
SIC: 6282 8741 Investment advisory service; Business management
HQ: Pmc Group International, Inc.
1288 Route 73 Ste 401
Mount Laurel NJ 08054
856 533-1866

(G-15513)
COBRA RAZORS
4007 Montchanin Rd (19807-1342)
PHONE...................302 540-0464
EMP: 3 **EST:** 2015
SALES (est): 121.91K **Privately Held**
SIC: 3421 Razor blades and razors

(G-15514)
CODE GUIDE LLC
1521 Concord Pike Ste 301 (19803-3644)
PHONE...................530 424-8919
Kathlene Faith Manalo, *Managing Member*
EMP: 5 **EST:** 2021
SALES (est): 500K **Privately Held**
SIC: 8742 Programmed instruction service

(G-15515)
CODEISCODE MKTG CONSULTING LLC
427 N Tatnall St (19801-2230)
PHONE...................415 202-5303
EMP: 6 **EST:** 2011
SALES (est): 88.24K **Privately Held**
SIC: 8748 Business consulting, nec

(G-15516)
CODY A BOWERS DPM
1601 Milltown Rd Ste 24 (19808-4084)
PHONE...................302 998-0178
Cody Bowers, *Prin*
EMP: 6 **EST:** 2017
SALES (est): 47.44K **Privately Held**
SIC: 8043 Offices and clinics of podiatrists

(G-15517)
COGENTRIX DELAWARE HOLDINGS (DH)
1105 N Market St Ste 1108 (19801-1216)
PHONE...................847 908-2800
EMP: 392 **EST:** 1993
SALES (est): 240.44MM
SALES (corp-wide): 4.44B **Publicly Held**
SIC: 4911 Generation, electric power
HQ: Cogentrix Energy Power Management Llc
13860 Balntyn Corp Pl
Charlotte NC 28277
704 525-3800

(G-15518)
COGHAN-HAES LLC
101 S Mary St (19804-3112)
PHONE...................302 325-4210
Coghan Richard Junior, *Managing Member*
Richard Coghan Junior, *Managing Member*
EMP: 9 **EST:** 2013
SALES (est): 821.47K **Privately Held**
SIC: 1761 Gutter and downspout contractor

(G-15519)
COGNITIVE TECH SOLUTIONS INC
1000 N West St Ste 1200 (19801-1058)
PHONE...................302 207-1824
EMP: 6 **EST:** 2019
SALES (est): 297.11K **Privately Held**
Web: www.cognitiveincorp.com
SIC: 5084 Industrial machinery and equipment

(G-15520)
COHESIVE STRATEGIES INC
Also Called: Archer Group, The
600 N King St Ste 2 (19801-3776)
PHONE...................302 429-9120
Todd Miller, *Pr*
Patrick Callahan, *
Michael Derins, *
EMP: 35 **EST:** 2003
SALES (est): 6.65MM **Privately Held**
SIC: 7311 Advertising consultant

(G-15521)
COIFFURE LTD
4031 Kennett Pike (19807-2047)
PHONE...................302 652-3463
Sam Terranova, *Brnch Mgr*
EMP: 5
SALES (corp-wide): 377.53K **Privately Held**
SIC: 7231 Hairdressers
PA: Coiffure Ltd
2401 Penns Ave Ste 104
Wilmington DE 19806
302 652-3443

(G-15522)
COINBASE GLOBAL INC (PA)
Also Called: COINBASE
1209 N Orange St (19801-1120)
PHONE...................302 777-0200
Brian Armstrong, *Ch Bd*
Emilie Choi, *Pr*
Alesia J Haas, *CFO*
Paul Grewal, *CLO*
Surojit Chatterjee, *CPO*
EMP: 56 **EST:** 2012
SALES (est): 3.19B
SALES (corp-wide): 3.19B **Publicly Held**
SIC: 7389 6099 Financial services; Foreign currency exchange

(G-15523)
COKO PRINTS
3 Doe Run Ct Apt 1b (19808-2046)
PHONE...................302 507-1683
Oscar O Dominguez, *Prin*
EMP: 4 **EST:** 2016
SALES (est): 69.12K **Privately Held**
SIC: 2752 Commercial printing, lithographic

(G-15524)
COLDWELL BNKR COML AMATO ASSOC
Also Called: Coldwell Banker
413 Larch Cir (19804-2370)
PHONE...................302 224-7700
Susan Amato, *Prin*
EMP: 5 **EST:** 2008
SALES (est): 983.06K **Privately Held**
Web: www.coldwellbanker.com
SIC: 6531 6519 Real estate agent, residential ; Real property lessors, nec

(G-15525)
COLE REALTY INC
Also Called: ERA
705 Philadelphia Pike (19809-2539)
PHONE...................302 764-4700
Margaret Cole, *Pr*
EMP: 8 **EST:** 1969
SALES (est): 353.34K **Privately Held**
Web: www.colerealtyhomes.com
SIC: 6531 Real estate agent, residential

(G-15526)
COLE SCHOTZ PC
500 Delaware Ave Ste 1410 (19801-1496)
PHONE...................302 984-9541
Marion M Quirk, *Mgr*
EMP: 5
SALES (corp-wide): 17.89MM **Privately Held**
Web: www.coleschotz.com
SIC: 8111 General practice attorney, lawyer
PA: Cole Schotz P.C.
25 Main St Ste 300
Hackensack NJ 07601
201 489-3000

(G-15527)
COLGATE-PALMOLIVE COMPANY
Also Called: Colgate-Palmolive
1105 N Market St Ste 1300 (19801-1241)
PHONE...................302 428-1554
Shanahan William, *Mgr*
EMP: 4
SALES (corp-wide): 17.97B **Publicly Held**
Web: www.colgatepalmolive.com
SIC: 2834 Pharmaceutical preparations
PA: Colgate-Palmolive Company
300 Park Ave Fl 8
New York NY 10022
212 310-2000

(G-15528)
COLLABRTING FOR NVEL SLTONS LL
2711 Centerville Rd Ste 300 (19808-1660)
PHONE...................619 252-6060
EMP: 7 **EST:** 2016
SALES (est): 20K **Privately Held**
SIC: 8011 Offices and clinics of medical doctors

(G-15529)
COLLECT AFRICA INC
256 Chapman Rd Ste 105-4 (19808)
PHONE...................657 204-4749
Abraham Ojes, *CEO*
EMP: 9
SALES (est): 232.51K **Privately Held**
SIC: 7389 Financial services

(G-15530)
COLLEGE AVE STDNT LN 2021-B LL
1105 N Market St 20th Fl (19801-1216)
PHONE...................302 497-0701
EMP: 6
SALES (est): 69.68K **Privately Held**
Web: www.salliemae.com
SIC: 6733 Trusts, nec

(G-15531)
COLLEGE AVENUE STUDENT LN LLC
Also Called: College Ave Student Loans
233 N King St Ste 400 (19801-2545)
PHONE...................302 684-6070
Joseph A Depaulo, *CEO*
Timothy Staley, *
James Keller, *
Lisa Strauch Eggers, *
Angela Colatriano, *CMO**

Wilmington - New Castle County (G-15532) — GEOGRAPHIC SECTION

EMP: 56 EST: 2014
SALES (est): 16.42MM **Privately Held**
Web: www.collegeavestudentloans.com
SIC: 6141 Licensed loan companies, small

(G-15532)
COLLEGE HUNKS HAULING JUNK MVG
12 Hadco Rd (19804-1014)
PHONE..............................302 232-6200
Brian Gonyo, *Prin*
EMP: 9 EST: 2017
SALES (est): 622.38K **Privately Held**
Web: www.collegehunkshaulingjunk.com
SIC: 4212 4213 Furniture moving, local; without storage; Contract haulers

(G-15533)
COLLEGIATE NETWORK INC
3901 Centerville Rd (19807-1938)
PHONE..............................302 652-4600
EMP: 5 EST: 2010
SALES (est): 780.35K **Privately Held**
Web: www.isi.org
SIC: 8699 Charitable organization

(G-15534)
COLONIAL CLEANING SERVICES INC
126b Middleboro Rd (19804-1621)
P.O. Box 6546 (19804-0546)
PHONE..............................302 660-2067
Bobby Friant, *Pr*
EMP: 5 EST: 2014
SALES (est): 66.03K **Privately Held**
SIC: 7217 7349 Carpet and upholstery cleaning; Air duct cleaning

(G-15535)
COLONIAL CONSTRUCTION COMPANY
Also Called: Colonial Cleaning
126 Middleboro Rd (19804-1621)
PHONE..............................302 994-5705
Joseph L Fragomele, *CEO*
EMP: 19 EST: 1955
SQ FT: 10,000
SALES (est): 2.43MM **Privately Held**
Web: www.colonialconstructionde.com
SIC: 1521 1541 1542 General remodeling, single-family houses; Prefabricated building erection, industrial; Commercial and office buildings, renovation and repair

(G-15536)
COLONIAL PARKING INC (HQ)
715 N Orange St (19801-1755)
PHONE..............................302 651-3600
John Hatfield, *Pr*
Richard G Hatfield, *Ch*
Chris Hankins, *VP Opers*
Joseph Nadel, *VP Fin*
EMP: 20 EST: 1965
SQ FT: 10,000
SALES (est): 6.8MM
SALES (corp-wide): 106.78MM **Privately Held**
Web: www.colonialparking.com
SIC: 7521 Parking garage
PA: Forge Company
1050 Thmas Jfferson St Nw
Washington DC 20007
202 295-8100

(G-15537)
COLONY NORTH APARTMENTS
319 E Lea Blvd (19802-2353)
PHONE..............................302 762-0405
Ralph Paul, *Pt*
Roslaie Paul, *Pt*
Douglas Paul, *Pt*
EMP: 10 EST: 1967
SQ FT: 750,000
SALES (est): 1.57MM **Privately Held**
Web: www.colonynorthapartments.com
SIC: 6513 Apartment building operators

(G-15538)
COLOR GURU LLC
Also Called: Color Guru
1605 Sunset Ln (19810-4128)
PHONE..............................267 972-4447
Jeannie Stith, *Managing Member*
EMP: 5 EST: 2019
SALES (est): 257.87K **Privately Held**
SIC: 7372 Prepackaged software

(G-15539)
COLOR STREET
911 Lovering Ave (19806-3224)
PHONE..............................302 574-0409
Meredith Hyman, *Prin*
EMP: 6 EST: 2018
SALES (est): 74.55K **Privately Held**
Web: www.colorstreet.com
SIC: 8111 General practice attorney, lawyer

(G-15540)
COLOURWORKS PHOTOGRAPHIC SVCS
1902 Superfine Ln (19802-4922)
PHONE..............................302 428-0222
Eric Russell, *Pr*
Gerard E Piotrowski, *Sec*
EMP: 8 EST: 1989
SQ FT: 5,000
SALES (est): 458.25K **Privately Held**
Web: www.colourworks.com
SIC: 7384 7335 Film processing and finishing laboratory; Photographic studio, commercial

(G-15541)
COLUMBUS INN MANAGEMENT I
105 Foulk Rd (19803-3740)
PHONE..............................302 429-8700
Joseph Capano, *Prin*
EMP: 5 EST: 2010
SALES (est): 360K **Privately Held**
SIC: 8741 Management services

(G-15542)
COMCAST CLFRN/CLRD/LLNS/NDN/TX
Also Called: Comcast
1201 N Market St Ste 1000 (19801-1807)
PHONE..............................248 233-4724
Jeff Ossowski, *Pr*
EMP: 100 EST: 2006
SALES (est): 24.86MM
SALES (corp-wide): 121.57B **Publicly Held**
SIC: 4813 4841 Telephone communications broker; Cable and other pay television services
PA: Comcast Corporation
1 Comcast Ctr
Philadelphia PA 19103
215 286-1700

(G-15543)
COMCAST MO INVESTMENTS LLC
1201 N Market St Ste 1000 (19801-1807)
PHONE..............................302 594-8705
Mark Mossman, *Prin*
EMP: 9 EST: 2014
SALES (est): 1.72MM
SALES (corp-wide): 121.43B **Publicly Held**
SIC: 4841 Cable television services
PA: Comcast Corporation
1 Comcast Ctr
Philadelphia PA 19103
215 286-1700

(G-15544)
COMEET TECHNOLOGIES INC
1313 N Market St Ste 5100 (19801-6111)
PHONE..............................650 433-9027
Omer Tadjer, *CEO*
EMP: 6 EST: 2013
SQ FT: 400
SALES (est): 105.23K **Privately Held**
SIC: 7371 Computer software development

(G-15545)
COMMERCE GLOBAL INC
2419 Dorval Rd (19810-3528)
PHONE..............................302 478-0853
Thomas Boettcher, *Pr*
EMP: 5 EST: 1991
SALES (est): 303.9K **Privately Held**
SIC: 8711 Consulting engineer

(G-15546)
COMMERCIAL CLEANING SERVICES
814 Philadelphia Pike Ste A (19809-2357)
P.O. Box 3318 (19804-4318)
PHONE..............................302 764-3424
Diane Arthur, *Prin*
EMP: 5 EST: 2001
SALES (est): 242.55K **Privately Held**
Web: www.commercialcleaningccs.com
SIC: 7699 Cleaning services

(G-15547)
COMMERCIAL EQUIPMENT SERVICE
2645 Longwood Dr (19810-3714)
P.O. Box 428 (19703-0428)
PHONE..............................302 475-6682
James Valentine, *Pr*
Nancy Valentine, *Sec*
EMP: 5 EST: 1985
SALES (est): 427.79K **Privately Held**
Web: www.commercialequipmentserviceinc.com
SIC: 7623 Air conditioning repair

(G-15548)
COMMERCIAL EQUIPMENT SVC
6603 Governor Printz Blvd (19809-2027)
PHONE..............................302 475-6682
Jim Valentine, *Mgr*
EMP: 6 EST: 2005
SALES (est): 31.82K **Privately Held**
Web: www.commercialequipmentserviceinc.com
SIC: 7629 Electrical household appliance repair

(G-15549)
COMMITTED HEARTS FOUNDATION
106 Country Club Dr (19803-2918)
PHONE..............................402 850-4644
Kathleen Kammer, *Prin*
EMP: 5 EST: 2016
SALES (est): 38.73K **Privately Held**
SIC: 8641 Civic and social associations

(G-15550)
COMMON COOPERATIVE COMPANY
Also Called: Common
919 N Market St Ste 950 (19801-3036)
PHONE..............................504 333-0731
EMP: 7
SALES (est): 196.11K **Privately Held**
SIC: 8093 Specialty outpatient clinics, nec

(G-15551)
COMMONWEALTH CONSTRUCTION
2317 Pennsylvania Ave (19806-1318)
P.O. Box 918 (19899-0918)
PHONE..............................302 654-6611
Benjamin Vinton Iii, *Pr*
EMP: 10 EST: 2010
SALES (est): 2.27MM **Privately Held**
Web: www.itscommonwealth.com
SIC: 1521 New construction, single-family houses

(G-15552)
COMMONWEALTH CONTRUCTION CO
2317 Pennsylvania Ave (19806-1318)
P.O. Box 918 (19899-0918)
PHONE..............................302 654-6611
Benjamin Vinton Iii, *Pr*
EMP: 24 EST: 1983
SQ FT: 3,000
SALES (est): 3.29MM **Privately Held**
Web: www.itscommonwealth.com
SIC: 1542 1521 Commercial and office building, new construction; New construction, single-family houses

(G-15553)
COMMONWEALTH GROUP LLC (PA)
300 Water St Ste 300 (19801-5046)
PHONE..............................302 472-7200
Brock J Vinton, *Pr*
EMP: 24 EST: 1972
SALES (est): 2.97MM
SALES (corp-wide): 2.97MM **Privately Held**
Web: www.commonwealthltd.net
SIC: 6531 6552 Real estate managers; Land subdividers and developers, commercial

(G-15554)
COMMONWEALTH MOTOR INC
1126 Lodge St (19802-5134)
PHONE..............................302 505-5555
Xiao Fu, *CEO*
EMP: 5
SALES (corp-wide): 10MM **Privately Held**
Web: www.comm-motor.com
SIC: 5521 5571 7532 3711 Used car dealers ; Motorcycle dealers; Collision shops, automotive; Chassis, motor vehicle
PA: Commonwealth Motor Inc
159 Old Belmont Ave
Bala Cynwyd PA 19004
302 505-5555

(G-15555)
COMMONWEALTH PARTNERS MGT LLC
717 N Union St # 45 (19805-3031)
PHONE..............................302 223-5941
EMP: 10 EST: 2019
SALES (est): 491.9K **Privately Held**
SIC: 8741 Management services

(G-15556)
COMMONWEALTH TRUST CO
29 Bancroft Mills Rd (19806-2039)
P.O. Box 350 (19899-0350)
PHONE..............................302 658-7214
Peter A Horty, *Ch*
Caroline Horty Dickerson, *CEO*
Cynthia D M Brown, *Pr*
James A Horty, *VP*
EMP: 10 EST: 1936
SQ FT: 6,500
SALES (est): 5.02MM **Privately Held**
Web: www.commonwealth-trust.com
SIC: 6733 6531 Trusts, nec; Real estate agents and managers

GEOGRAPHIC SECTION
Wilmington - New Castle County (G-15584)

(G-15557)
COMMUNICATION CONCEPTS LLC
300 Delaware Ave Ste 210a (19801-6601)
PHONE..................302 658-9800
Shane Austin, *Mgr*
EMP: 8 **EST:** 2017
SALES (est): 566K **Privately Held**
SIC: 7389 Design services

(G-15558)
COMMUNITIES IN SCHOOLS DEL
522 S Walnut St (19801-5230)
PHONE..................704 724-3737
EMP: 21 **EST:** 2012
SALES (est): 133.77K **Privately Held**
Web: www.cisdelaware.org
SIC: 8322 Community center

(G-15559)
COMMUNITY ATHC SOLUTIONS LLC
913 N Market St Ste 200 (19801-3097)
PHONE..................302 468-5493
EMP: 5 **EST:** 2017
SALES (est): 43.08K **Privately Held**
Web: www.communityathleticsolutions.com
SIC: 7997 Membership sports and recreation clubs

(G-15560)
COMMUNITY DAY
1501 Barley Mill Rd (19807-2231)
PHONE..................302 757-3700
Richard Sternberg, *Supervisor*
EMP: 6 **EST:** 2017
SALES (est): 38.16K **Privately Held**
SIC: 8322 Community center

(G-15561)
COMMUNITY HOUSING INC (PA)
613 N Washington St (19801-2135)
PHONE..................302 652-3991
Gary Pollio, *Dir*
EMP: 6 **EST:** 1969
SQ FT: 5,000
SALES (est): 2.16MM
SALES (corp-wide): 2.16MM **Privately Held**
Web: www.ichde.org
SIC: 6513 Apartment building operators

(G-15562)
COMMUNITY INTERACTIONS INC
Also Called: COMMUNITY INTERACTIONS, INC
625 W Newport Pike (19804-3259)
PHONE..................302 993-7846
Tonya Richardson, *Brnch Mgr*
EMP: 58
SALES (corp-wide): 30.17MM **Privately Held**
Web: www.ciinc.org
SIC: 8322 Social service center
PA: Community Interactions, Inc.
740 S Chester Rd Ste A
Swarthmore PA 19081
610 328-9008

(G-15563)
COMMUNITY LEGAL AID SOCIETY (PA)
Also Called: Legal Aid
100 W 10th St Ste 801 (19801-6605)
PHONE..................302 757-7001
William Dunn, *Dir*
Dan Atkins, *
EMP: 80 **EST:** 1946
SALES (est): 5.71MM
SALES (corp-wide): 5.71MM **Privately Held**

Web: www.declasi.org
SIC: 8111 Legal aid service

(G-15564)
COMMUNITY SOLUTIONS INC
1421 Marsh Rd (19802-5305)
PHONE..................302 660-8691
EMP: 8 **EST:** 2018
SALES (est): 48.04K **Privately Held**
SIC: 8322 Social service center

(G-15565)
COMMUNITY TWERED FEDERAL CR UN
3670 Kirkwood Hwy (19808-5104)
PHONE..................302 994-3617
Carl Bliey, *Brnch Mgr*
EMP: 9
SALES (corp-wide): 3.46MM **Privately Held**
Web: www.cpwrfcu.org
SIC: 6061 Federal credit unions
PA: Community Towered Federal Credit Union
401 Eagle Run Rd
Newark DE 19702
302 368-2396

(G-15566)
COMPANY CORPORATION (HQ)
Also Called: CSC
251 Little Falls Dr (19808-1674)
PHONE..................302 636-5440
Bruce Wynn, *CEO*
Brett Davis, *
▲ **EMP:** 37 **EST:** 1973
SALES (est): 22.29MM
SALES (corp-wide): 661.37MM **Privately Held**
Web: www.incorporate.com
SIC: 8742 Corporation organizing consultant
PA: Corporation Service Company
251 Little Falls Dr
Wilmington DE 19808
302 636-5400

(G-15567)
COMPASSIONATE CARE TRNSPT LLC
510 Howard St (19804-1222)
PHONE..................215 847-9836
EMP: 5 **EST:** 2018
SALES (est): 204.79K **Privately Held**
SIC: 4789 Transportation services, nec

(G-15568)
COMPASSRED INC
112 S French St # 4 (19801-5035)
PHONE..................302 383-2856
Patrick Callahan, *CEO*
Greg Farrell, *CFO*
EMP: 5 **EST:** 2015
SALES (est): 739.91K **Privately Held**
Web: www.compassred.com
SIC: 7371 Custom computer programming services

(G-15569)
COMPETE HR INC
1007 N Orange St (19801-1239)
PHONE..................310 989-9857
Amit Rapaport, *Mgr*
EMP: 25 **EST:** 2020
SALES (est): 641.67K **Privately Held**
Web: www.competewith.com
SIC: 7389 8742 Business Activities at Non-Commercial Site; Human resource consulting services

(G-15570)
COMPETITION GAME CALLS
208 Brookland Ave (19805-1113)
PHONE..................302 345-7463
EMP: 3 **EST:** 2017
SALES (est): 57.04K **Privately Held**
SIC: 3949 Game calls

(G-15571)
COMPLETE FAMILY CARE INC
534 Greenhill Ave (19805-1851)
PHONE..................302 482-3347
Mayda Melendez, *Prin*
EMP: 5 **EST:** 2009
SALES (est): 470.84K **Privately Held**
SIC: 8011 Primary care medical clinic

(G-15572)
COMPLETE FAMILY CARE INC
2500 W 4th St Ste 6 (19805-3352)
PHONE..................302 232-5002
EMP: 11 **EST:** 2020
SALES (est): 953.47K **Privately Held**
Web: www.completefamilyrede.com
SIC: 8062 8049 8011 7231 General medical and surgical hospitals; Offices of health practitioner; Offices and clinics of medical doctors; Beauty shops

(G-15573)
COMPLETE HEMP LLC
4023 Kennett Pike Ste 622 (19807-2018)
PHONE..................888 901-6150
EMP: 50 **EST:** 2018
SALES (est): 1.21MM **Privately Held**
SIC: 5159

(G-15574)
COMPTON PK PRSRVTION ASSOC LLC
Also Called: Compton Apartments
650 N Walnut St (19801-3807)
PHONE..................302 654-4369
Fern Moore, *Mgr*
EMP: 6 **EST:** 1995
SALES (est): 437.36K **Privately Held**
SIC: 6513 Apartment building operators

(G-15575)
COMPTON TWNE PRSRVTION ASSOC L
Also Called: Compton Townehouse Apartments
831a Towne Ct (19801-3630)
PHONE..................302 764-6450
Glen Brooks, *Prin*
Marykate Kearney, *Prin*
EMP: 8 **EST:** 2019
SALES (est): 495.05K **Privately Held**
Web: www.arbormanagement.com
SIC: 6552 Land subdividers and developers, commercial

(G-15576)
COMPUTERSHARE INC
919 N Market St Ste 1600 (19801-3046)
PHONE..................781 575-2000
EMP: 992
Web: www.computershare.com
SIC: 6733 Trusts, nec
HQ: Computershare Inc.
150 Royall St Ste 205
Canton MA 02021

(G-15577)
CONCI LLC
1013 Centre Rd (19805-1265)
PHONE..................847 665-9285
David Persiko, *Managing Member*
EMP: 55 **EST:** 2017

SALES (est): 1.19MM **Privately Held**
SIC: 7371 Custom computer programming services

(G-15578)
CONCORD AGENCY INC
3520 Silverside Rd Ste 28 (19810-4933)
PHONE..................302 478-4000
Donald Balick, *Pr*
Loretta Rivera, *VP*
Jean Balick, *Sec*
EMP: 5 **EST:** 1970
SQ FT: 3,800
SALES (est): 469.62K **Privately Held**
Web: www.concordagency.com
SIC: 6411 Insurance agents, nec

(G-15579)
CONCORD CORPORATE SERVICES INC (DH)
1100 Carr Rd (19809-1610)
PHONE..................302 791-8200
Edward T Haslam, *Pr*
EMP: 500 **EST:** 1992
SQ FT: 110,000
SALES (est): 139.17MM
SALES (corp-wide): 17.74B **Publicly Held**
SIC: 6099 Electronic funds transfer network, including switching
HQ: Concord Efs, Inc
7000 Goodlett Frm Pkwy
Cordova TN 38016
901 371-8000

(G-15580)
CONCORD DENTAL
2304 Concord Pike (19803-2912)
PHONE..................302 836-3750
EMP: 12 **EST:** 2018
SALES (est): 471.24K **Privately Held**
Web: www.concorddentalde.com
SIC: 8021 Dentists' office

(G-15581)
CONCORD HIGH SCHOOL BASEBALL
2629 Epping Rd (19810-1166)
PHONE..................302 475-2537
Timothy P Hamberger, *Prin*
EMP: 6 **EST:** 2014
SALES (est): 98.86K **Privately Held**
SIC: 7997 Baseball club, except professional and semi-professional

(G-15582)
CONCORD MALL LLC
4737 Concord Pike 3rd Fl (19803-1442)
P.O. Box 7189 (19803-0189)
PHONE..................302 478-9271
EMP: 30 **EST:** 1998
SQ FT: 900,000
SALES (est): 2.49MM **Privately Held**
Web: www.concordmall.com
SIC: 6512 Shopping center, regional (300,000-1,000,000) sq. ft.)

(G-15583)
CONCORD MED SPINE & PAIN CTR
6 Sharpley Rd (19803-2941)
PHONE..................302 652-1107
Trent Ryan D.c., *Prin*
EMP: 13 **EST:** 2014
SALES (est): 607.29K **Privately Held**
SIC: 8011 8041 Medical centers; Offices and clinics of chiropractors

(G-15584)
CONCORD PRESCHOOL CHILDCA
1243 Lakewood Dr (19803-3505)
PHONE..................302 750-7082

Wilmington - New Castle County (G-15585) GEOGRAPHIC SECTION

EMP: 9 EST: 2018
SALES (est): 94.48K Privately Held
Web: www.concordpreschoolandchildcare.com
SIC: 8351 Preschool center

(G-15585)
CONCORD SOCCER ASSOCIATION
2 Onyx Ct (19810-2227)
P.O. Box 7063 (19803-0063)
PHONE..................302 479-5030
Mike Finizio, Prin
EMP: 17 EST: 2008
SALES (est): 348.58K Privately Held
Web: www.concordsoccer.com
SIC: 8611 Merchants' association

(G-15586)
CONCRETE CO INC
101 Brookside Dr (19804-1103)
PHONE..................302 652-1101
Eugene F Gentile, Pr
Dennis Gerace, VP
Judy Gerace, Sec
EMP: 6 EST: 1971
SQ FT: 2,500
SALES (est): 739.17K Privately Held
Web: www.theconcretecompanyde.com
SIC: 3273 Ready-mixed concrete

(G-15587)
CONDE NAST INTERNATIONAL INC
Also Called: Cond Nast's
1313 N Market St Fl 11 (19801-1151)
PHONE..................515 243-3273
Charles H Townsend, Ch
Robert A Sauerberg Junior, CEO
Edward Menicheschi, Pr
Fred Santarpia, Ex VP
John Bellando, CFO
EMP: 239 EST: 2006
SALES (est): 9.83MM
SALES (corp-wide): 2.88B Privately Held
Web: www.condenast.com
SIC: 2721 Magazines: publishing and printing
PA: Advance Publications, Inc.
1 World Trade Ctr Fl 43
New York NY 10007
718 981-1234

(G-15588)
CONDUCERENT INCORPORATED
1011 Centre Rd Ste 104 (19805-1266)
P.O. Box 237 (19732-0237)
PHONE..................302 543-8525
Magdalena Keenan, Pr
Kim Paternoster, Ch Bd
Angela Foley, Sr VP
EMP: 5 EST: 2017
SALES (est): 230.04K Privately Held
SIC: 8742 7389 7361 Management consulting services; Business services, nec; Executive placement

(G-15589)
CONECMI LLC
3616 Kirkwood Hwy A117 (19808-5124)
PHONE..................302 740-9261
Homairah Baqi, Managing Member
EMP: 6 EST: 2020
SALES (est): 200K Privately Held
SIC: 2741 Internet publishing and broadcasting

(G-15590)
CONECTIV LLC
630 Martin Luther King Blvd (19801-2306)
PHONE..................800 375-7117
Vonda Ellerbe, Prin
EMP: 10
SALES (corp-wide): 19.08B Publicly Held

Web: www.conectiv.com
SIC: 4911 Generation, electric power
HQ: Conectiv, Llc
500 N Wkfeld Drv Mlsto
Newark DE 19702
202 872-2680

(G-15591)
CONEXIAM SOLUTIONS INC
1201 N Orange St Ste 700 (19801-1186)
PHONE..................302 884-6746
EMP: 7 EST: 2015
SALES (est): 72.21K Privately Held
Web: www.conexiam.com
SIC: 7373 Computer integrated systems design

(G-15592)
CONFAB INC
1216 D St (19801-5628)
P.O. Box 574 (19703-0574)
PHONE..................302 429-0140
EMP: 2 EST: 1994
SALES (est): 247.67K Privately Held
Web: www.confab.com
SIC: 3449 Bars, concrete reinforcing: fabricated steel

(G-15593)
CONGO CAPITAL MANAGEMENT LLC (HQ)
Also Called: Congo Capital Management
3911 Concord Pike (19803-1736)
PHONE..................732 337-6643
Dale A Congo, Pr
EMP: 11 EST: 2010
SQ FT: 2,500
SALES (est): 1.77MM
SALES (corp-wide): 1.77MM Privately Held
Web: www.congocapitalmanagement.com
SIC: 1711 8999 Solar energy contractor; Weather related services
PA: Congo Industries, Inc.
3911 Concord Pike
Wilmington DE 19803
732 337-6643

(G-15594)
CONGO FUNERAL HOME (PA)
2317 N Market St (19802-4297)
P.O. Box 2593 (19805-0593)
PHONE..................302 652-6640
Ernest M Congo, Pr
Cheris D Congo, VP
EMP: 10 EST: 1975
SQ FT: 2,500
SALES (est): 1.76MM
SALES (corp-wide): 1.76MM Privately Held
Web: www.congofuneralhome.com
SIC: 7261 Funeral home

(G-15595)
CONGO FUNERAL HOME
201 N Gray Ave (19805-1838)
PHONE..................302 652-8887
EMP: 7
SALES (corp-wide): 1.76MM Privately Held
Web: www.congofuneralhome.com
SIC: 7261 Funeral home
PA: Congo Funeral Home
2317 N Market St
Wilmington DE 19802
302 652-6640

(G-15596)
CONGO INDUSTRIES INC (PA)
3911 Concord Pike (19803-1736)
PHONE..................732 337-6643
Dale Congo, Pr
EMP: 6 EST: 2010
SALES (est): 1.77MM
SALES (corp-wide): 1.77MM Privately Held
Web: www.congocapitalmanagement.com
SIC: 1711 8999 Solar energy contractor; Weather related services

(G-15597)
CONLIN CORPORATION
Also Called: Delaware Tool Cleaning
737 Ambleside Dr (19808-1541)
PHONE..................302 633-9174
Douglas C Conlin, Pr
Joann Christian, VP
EMP: 9 EST: 1991
SALES (est): 109.21K Privately Held
SIC: 2241 Rubber thread and yarns, fabric covered

(G-15598)
CONMAC SECURITY SYSTEMS INC
205 Beau Tree Dr (19810-1177)
PHONE..................302 529-9286
Michael Connelly, Pr
EMP: 8 EST: 2002
SQ FT: 800
SALES (est): 158.14K Privately Held
SIC: 7381 Security guard service

(G-15599)
CONNECTING GENERATIONS INC
100 W 10th St Ste 102 (19801-6606)
PHONE..................302 656-2122
Donna Thomas, Prin
EMP: 10 EST: 1989
SALES (est): 460.03K Privately Held
Web: www.connecting-generations.org
SIC: 8742 Human resource consulting services

(G-15600)
CONNECTIONS CSP
507 W 9th St (19801-1401)
PHONE..................302 384-8140
EMP: 5 EST: 2018
SALES (est): 222.4K Privately Held
Web: coras.flywheelsites.com
SIC: 6512 Commercial and industrial building operation

(G-15601)
CONNECTIONS DEVELOPMENT CORP (PA)
3821 Lancaster Pike (19805-1512)
PHONE..................302 984-3380
EMP: 14 EST: 2011
SALES (est): 983.18K Privately Held
SIC: 8011 General and family practice, physician/surgeon

(G-15602)
CONNECTNOW VRTUAL CALL CTR LLC
3 Germay Dr Ste 42743 (19804-1127)
PHONE..................888 226-4130
Danica Brown, Managing Member
EMP: 50
SALES (est): 1.19MM Privately Held
SIC: 8742 Management consulting services

(G-15603)
CONNIE F CICORELLI DDS PA
1401 Silverside Rd Ste 2a (19810-4400)
PHONE..................302 798-5797
Connie F Cicorelli D.d.s., Pr
EMP: 5 EST: 1990
SALES (est): 438.79K Privately Held
Web: www.cicorellidental.com
SIC: 8021 Dentists' office

(G-15604)
CONNOLLY BOVE LODGE & HUTZ LLP
1007 N Orange St Ste 800 (19801-1280)
PHONE..................302 658-9141
Zhun Lu, Pt
Frank S Stransky, CFO
EMP: 9 EST: 2002
SALES (est): 457.06K Privately Held
Web: www.connollygallagher.com
SIC: 8111 Specialized law offices, attorneys

(G-15605)
CONNOLLY FLOORING INC
315 Water St (19804-2410)
PHONE..................302 996-9470
Mike Connolly, Pr
Wendy Connolly, *
EMP: 30 EST: 1982
SALES (est): 189.69K Privately Held
Web: www.connollyflooring.com
SIC: 1752 5713 Carpet laying; Floor covering stores

(G-15606)
CONQUEST TECH SOLUTIONS INC
300 Delaware Ave Ste 210 (19801-6601)
PHONE..................302 356-1423
Ameer Mohammed, Pr
EMP: 6 EST: 2013
SQ FT: 300
SALES (est): 6.55MM Privately Held
Web: www.conq-tech.com
SIC: 7371 7379 7373 Custom computer programming services; Computer related maintenance services; Computer systems analysis and design

(G-15607)
CONSERVE PROPERTY GROUP
4302 Marlowe Rd (19802-1315)
PHONE..................302 275-8616
Michael Lewis, Prin
EMP: 5 EST: 2018
SALES (est): 232.35K Privately Held
SIC: 6512 Nonresidential building operators

(G-15608)
CONSOLDTED FABRICATION CONSTRS
1216 D St (19801-5628)
PHONE..................302 654-9001
Tor Larson, Mgr
EMP: 114
SALES (corp-wide): 81.39MM Privately Held
Web: www.consfab.com
SIC: 3324 Steel investment foundries
PA: Consolidated Fabrication And Constructors Inc
3851 Ellsworth St
Gary IN 46408
219 884-6150

(G-15609)
CONSOLIDATED LLC
1216 D St (19801-5600)
PHONE..................302 654-9001
Tor Larson, Managing Member
EMP: 28 EST: 2004

GEOGRAPHIC SECTION

Wilmington - New Castle County (G-15637)

SALES (est): 23.4MM **Privately Held**
Web: www.consfab.com
SIC: 1542 Nonresidential construction, nec

(G-15610)
CONSTELLATION PUMPS CORP
2711 Centerville Rd Ste 400 (19808-1660)
PHONE.................................301 323-9000
EMP: 12 EST: 2017
SALES (est): 839.7K
SALES (corp-wide): 1.56B **Publicly Held**
SIC: 3561 Pumps and pumping equipment
PA: Enovis Corporation
      2711 Centerville Rd # 400
      Wilmington DE 19808
      301 252-9160

(G-15611)
CONSTRUCT APP INC
2711 Centerville Rd # 400 (19808-1660)
PHONE.................................415 702-0634
Patrick Albert, *Engg Mgr*
Drew Beaurline, *CEO*
EMP: 6 EST: 2016
SALES (est): 84.64K **Privately Held**
SIC: 7371 Computer software development and applications

(G-15612)
CONSTRUCTION MGT SVCS INC (PA)
3600 Silverside Rd (19810-5100)
P.O. Box 7499 (19803-0499)
PHONE.................................302 478-4200
William A Goeller, *Pr*
Michael C Goeller, *
Gerard J Herr, *
EMP: 650 EST: 1984
SQ FT: 10,000
SALES (est): 362.45MM
SALES (corp-wide): 362.45MM **Privately Held**
Web: www.bluestonecomm.com
SIC: 1731 8741 General electrical contractor ; Construction management

(G-15613)
CONSULT DYNAMICS INC (PA)
Also Called: D C A Net
1016 Delaware Ave (19806-4704)
PHONE.................................302 654-1019
Keith Duncan, *Pr*
J David Duncan, *
Irwin Duncan, *
EMP: 24 EST: 1990
SQ FT: 3,300
SALES (est): 4.35MM **Privately Held**
Web: www.dca.net
SIC: 7373 4813 Value-added resellers, computer systems; Telephone communication, except radio

(G-15614)
CONSULTING GROUP CPITL MKTS FN
222 Delaware Ave (19801-1621)
PHONE.................................302 888-4104
Paul Magnuson, *Prin*
EMP: 17 EST: 1993
SALES (est): 558.38K **Privately Held**
SIC: 6722 Money market mutual funds

(G-15615)
CONTACTLIFELINE INC (PA)
314 Brandywine Blvd (19809-3242)
P.O. Box 9525 (19809-0525)
PHONE.................................302 761-9800
Patricia Tedford, *Ex Dir*
EMP: 8 EST: 1982
SALES (est): 648.67K
SALES (corp-wide): 648.67K **Privately Held**

Web: www.contactlifeline.org
SIC: 8322 Crisis intervention center

(G-15616)
CONTI ELECTRIC OF N J INC
2633 Skylark Rd (19808-1633)
PHONE.................................302 996-3905
John Conti, *Pr*
EMP: 6 EST: 2002
SALES (est): 89.41K **Privately Held**
SIC: 1731 General electrical contractor

(G-15617)
CONTINENTAL CNSTR & RMDLG
2508 Dorval Rd (19810-2222)
PHONE.................................302 332-6367
Richard H Knight Junior, *Prin*
EMP: 5 EST: 2016
SALES (est): 78.37K **Privately Held**
SIC: 1521 General remodeling, single-family houses

(G-15618)
CONTINENTAL FINANCE CO LLC (PA)
4550 Linden Hill Rd Ste 400 (19808-2952)
P.O. Box 8099 (19714-8099)
PHONE.................................302 456-1930
Steve Mcsorley, *Managing Member*
EMP: 18 EST: 2005
SALES (est): 12.7MM **Privately Held**
Web: www.continentalfinance.net
SIC: 7389 Credit card service

(G-15619)
CONTINENTAL FUNDING LLC
4550 Linden Hill Rd Ste 400 (19808-2930)
PHONE.................................302 456-1930
Steve Mcsorley, *Managing Member*
EMP: 5 EST: 2017
SALES (est): 931.52K **Privately Held**
SIC: 7389 Credit card service
PA: Continental Finance Company, Llc
      4550 Linden Hill Rd # 400
      Wilmington DE 19808

(G-15620)
CONTINENTAL JEWELERS INC
2209 Silverside Rd (19810-4501)
PHONE.................................302 475-2000
Paul Cohen, *Owner*
Chrysa Cohen, *Owner*
EMP: 9 EST: 1955
SQ FT: 2,500
SALES (est): 752.11K **Privately Held**
Web: www.continentaljewelersinc.com
SIC: 5944 7631 Jewelry, precious stones and precious metals; Jewelry repair services

(G-15621)
CONTINENTAL MORTGAGE CORP
3422 Old Capitol Trl (19808-6124)
PHONE.................................302 996-5807
Russell Murray, *Pr*
EMP: 6 EST: 1990
SQ FT: 168
SALES (est): 1.03MM **Privately Held**
SIC: 6162 Mortgage brokers, using own money

(G-15622)
CONTRACT ENVIRONMENTS INC
2055 Limestone Rd Ste 302 (19808-5536)
PHONE.................................302 658-0668
Beverly Thomes, *Pr*
EMP: 6 EST: 1982
SALES (est): 977.69K **Privately Held**
Web: www.contractenvironments.us
SIC: 7389 Interior designer

(G-15623)
CONTRACTOR RASHMI & PENNY
1980 Superfine Ln Apt 804 (19802-4927)
PHONE.................................302 778-5771
Charles Paschall, *Prin*
EMP: 5 EST: 2007
SALES (est): 67.12K **Privately Held**
SIC: 1799 Fence construction

(G-15624)
CONTRACTORS MATERIALS LLC
925 S Heald St (19801-5732)
PHONE.................................302 656-6066
Bonnie Tipton, *Prin*
EMP: 10 EST: 2016
SALES (est): 213.41K **Privately Held**
Web: www.cmcmmi.com
SIC: 1429 Crushed and broken stone, nec

(G-15625)
CONVERGENCE GROUP INC
1011 Centre Rd Ste 104 (19805-1266)
PHONE.................................302 234-7400
Kevin Foley, *Pr*
EMP: 10 EST: 1997
SALES (est): 1.26MM
SALES (corp-wide): 5.78MM **Privately Held**
Web: www.convergencegroup.com
SIC: 8742 Marketing consulting services
PA: De Novo Corporation
      1011 Centre Rd Ste 104
      Wilmington DE 19805
      302 234-7407

(G-15626)
CONVIDA WIRELESS LLC
200 Bellevue Pkwy Ste 300 (19809-3727)
PHONE.................................302 281-3707
Alan Proithis, *Managing Member*
Matteo Sabattini, *CLO*
EMP: 5 EST: 2012
SALES (est): 206.84K **Privately Held**
SIC: 8732 Business research service

(G-15627)
COOCH AND TAYLOR A PROF ASSN (PA)
Also Called: Cooch and Taylor Attys At Law
1007 N Orange St Ste 1120 (19801-1236)
P.O. Box 1680 (19899-1680)
PHONE.................................302 984-3800
Thomas Shellenberger, *Pr*
Donald C Taylor, *
H Alfred Tarrant Junior, *Dir*
Robert W Crowe, *
Bonnie H Sheer, *
EMP: 45 EST: 1960
SALES (est): 10.52MM
SALES (corp-wide): 10.52MM **Privately Held**
Web: www.coochtaylor.com
SIC: 8111 General practice attorney, lawyer

(G-15628)
COOK & COOK LTD PARTNERSHIP
304 Centennial Cir (19807-2130)
PHONE.................................302 428-0109
G Leigh Cook, *Pt*
EMP: 13 EST: 2004
SALES (est): 86.98K **Privately Held**
SIC: 8021 Dentists' office

(G-15629)
COOL NERDS MARKETING INC
300 N Market St Ste 208 (19801-2530)
PHONE.................................302 304-3440
Bruce Gunacti, *CEO*
EMP: 15 EST: 2014
SQ FT: 3,000

SALES (est): 1.45MM **Privately Held**
Web: www.coolnerdsmarketing.com
SIC: 7311 Advertising agencies

(G-15630)
COOLAUTOMATION INC
919 N Market St Ste 950 (19801-3036)
PHONE.................................941 587-2287
Ron Zauderer, *Ch*
Yaron Benvenisti, *CEO*
Igor Mitbarg, *VP*
EMP: 9 EST: 2020
SALES (est): 219.49K **Privately Held**
Web: www.coolautomation.com
SIC: 7371 Computer software development

(G-15631)
COOLPOP NATION
2418 Rambler Rd (19810-3828)
PHONE.................................302 584-8833
EMP: 4 EST: 2014
SALES (est): 107.5K **Privately Held**
SIC: 2211 7389 Sheets, bedding and table cloths: cotton; Business Activities at Non-Commercial Site

(G-15632)
COOLTRADE INC
1013 Centre Rd Ste 403b (19805-1270)
PHONE.................................844 356-2952
Evgenii Dubovoii, *CEO*
EMP: 25 EST: 2017
SALES (est): 2.78MM **Privately Held**
SIC: 5064 Air conditioning room units, self-contained

(G-15633)
COOPERSON ASSOCIATES LLC
1504 N French St (19801-3118)
PHONE.................................302 655-1105
Jay Cooperson, *Managing Member*
EMP: 9 EST: 2009
SALES (est): 931.5K **Privately Held**
Web: www.coopersonassoc.com
SIC: 8712 Architectural engineering

(G-15634)
COOSCO AUTO TECH LLC
1201 N Market St Ste 111 (19801-1156)
PHONE.................................302 391-6043
EMP: 9 EST: 2021
SALES (est): 230.86K **Privately Held**
SIC: 7549 Automotive services, nec

(G-15635)
COPIRI INC
4023 Kennett Pike (19807-2018)
PHONE.................................703 863-4304
Jeremy Barnes, *CEO*
EMP: 7 EST: 2016
SALES (est): 315.29K **Privately Held**
Web: www.copiri.com
SIC: 7371 Custom computer programming services

(G-15636)
CORA SYSTEMS US INC
2801 Centerville Rd Fl 1 (19808-1609)
PHONE.................................833 269-5756
John Fitzgerald, *Prin*
EMP: 11 EST: 2016
SALES (est): 1.18MM **Privately Held**
Web: www.corasystems.com
SIC: 7371 Computer software development

(G-15637)
CORBLOCKS INC
1201 N Orange St Ste 600 (19801-1171)
PHONE.................................832 217-0864
Badruddin Pitter, *Pr*

Wilmington - New Castle County (G-15638)   GEOGRAPHIC SECTION

EMP: 8 EST: 2020
SALES (est): 379.07K **Privately Held**
Web: www.corblocks.com
SIC: 7371 Computer software systems analysis and design, custom

(G-15638)
CORCORAN & ASSOCIATES PA CPA
Also Called: Corcoran & Company PA CPA
3801 Kennett Pike Ste C100 # 100 (19807-2321)
PHONE..................302 478-9515
Thomas J Corcoran, *Pr*
EMP: 5 EST: 1977
SALES (est): 241K **Privately Held**
SIC: 8721 Certified public accountant

(G-15639)
CORE PURCHASE LLC
910 Foulk Rd Ste 201 (19803-3159)
PHONE..................616 328-5715
EMP: 5 EST: 2016
SALES (est): 66.23K **Privately Held**
SIC: 7372 Publisher's computer software

(G-15640)
CORE RESULTS INC (PA)
1209 N Orange St (19801-1120)
PHONE..................805 552-6624
Eddie Ross, *Pr*
EMP: 6 EST: 2016
SALES (est): 228.98K
SALES (corp-wide): 228.98K **Privately Held**
SIC: 7371 Computer software development and applications

(G-15641)
CORE VALUE GLOBAL LLC
1209 N Orange St (19801-1120)
PHONE..................908 312-4070
EMP: 5 EST: 2018
SALES (est): 286.82K **Privately Held**
SIC: 8742 Management consulting services

(G-15642)
CORNERSTONE HEALTH PARTNERS
2303 Woods Rd (19808-2520)
PHONE..................302 561-4080
Adrian Mccullough, *Prin*
EMP: 6 EST: 2018
SALES (est): 342.84K **Privately Held**
Web: www.mychp.org
SIC: 8099 Health and allied services, nec

(G-15643)
CORPORATE ARCFT TECHNICAL SVCS
415 Riblett Ln (19808-1303)
PHONE..................302 383-9400
Gary Fender, *Pr*
Terry Fender, *VP*
EMP: 7 EST: 2002
SQ FT: 1,200
SALES (est): 138.43K **Privately Held**
SIC: 7622 8711 Aircraft radio equipment repair; Structural engineering

(G-15644)
CORPORATION SERVICE COMPANY (PA)
Also Called: C S C
251 Little Falls Dr (19808-1674)
PHONE..................302 636-5400
Rodman Ward Iii, *CEO*
Ian Mcconnel, *CRO CCO*
▲ EMP: 450 EST: 1920
SALES (est): 661.37MM
SALES (corp-wide): 661.37MM **Privately Held**

Web: www.cscglobal.com
SIC: 8111 Specialized law offices, attorneys

(G-15645)
CORRIN TREE LANDSCAPE
1307 N Rodney St (19806-4226)
PHONE..................302 521-8333
Philip A Cornell, *Prin*
EMP: 9 EST: 2010
SALES (est): 679.78K **Privately Held**
Web: www.corrintree.com
SIC: 0781 Landscape planning services

(G-15646)
CORTEVA (CHINA) LLC (HQ)
974 Centre Rd Bldg 735 (19805-1269)
PHONE..................833 267-8382
EMP: 26
SALES (est): 11.41MM
SALES (corp-wide): 17.23B **Publicly Held**
SIC: 2879 Agricultural chemicals, nec
PA: Corteva, Inc.
9330 Zionsville Rd
Indianapolis IN 46268
833 267-8382

(G-15647)
CORTEVA AGRISCIENCE LLC
974 Centre Rd Chestnut Run Plz 735 (19805)
P.O. Box 80735 (19805)
PHONE..................302 485-3000
EMP: 24
SALES (corp-wide): 17.23B **Publicly Held**
Web: www.corteva.com
SIC: 2879 Agricultural chemicals, nec
HQ: Corteva Agriscience Llc
9330 Zionsville Rd
Indianapolis IN 46268

(G-15648)
COSMIC STRANDS LLC
1201 N Market St Ste 111 (19801-1156)
PHONE..................302 660-3268
Ashrant Malhotra, *Managing Member*
EMP: 22 EST: 2014
SALES (est): 907.96K **Privately Held**
SIC: 2731 Book publishing

(G-15649)
COSTA AND RIHL INC
3518 Silverside Rd Ste 22 (19810-4907)
PHONE..................856 534-7325
EMP: 140 EST: 1969
SALES (est): 7.17MM **Privately Held**
SIC: 1711 3444 Mechanical contractor; Ducts, sheet metal

(G-15650)
COTALKER INC
251 Little Falls Dr (19808-1674)
PHONE..................954 643-1497
Nicolas Steinman, *CEO*
EMP: 45
SALES (est): 1.18MM **Privately Held**
Web: www.cotalker.com
SIC: 7371 Computer software development and applications

(G-15651)
COUNCIL OF DEVON
2401 Pennsylvania Ave Apt 606 (19806-1409)
PHONE..................302 658-5366
Lawernce O'brien, *Mgr*
EMP: 7 EST: 1985
SALES (est): 422.75K **Privately Held**
SIC: 8641 Condominium association

(G-15652)
COUNCIL ON HLTH RES FOR DEV US
1 Wood Rd (19806-2021)
PHONE..................202 255-5300
Carolus Ijsselmuiden, *Pr*
Jonathon Moore, *Sec*
EMP: 5 EST: 2007
SALES (est): 162.29K **Privately Held**
Web: www.cohred-usa.org
SIC: 8399 Social services, nec

(G-15653)
COUNSELING SERVICES INC
116 David Rd (19804-2665)
PHONE..................302 894-1477
Ron Wolskee, *Pr*
EMP: 9 EST: 1998
SALES (est): 174.19K **Privately Held**
SIC: 8322 General counseling services

(G-15654)
COUNTERFEIT COMBAT TECHNOLOGY
251 Little Falls Dr (19808-1674)
PHONE..................614 874-7414
Bruce R Winn, *Dir*
EMP: 6 EST: 2016
SALES (est): 46.16K **Privately Held**
SIC: 7371 Computer software development and applications

(G-15655)
COUNTERPOINT SOFTWARE INC
1901 N Lincoln St (19806-2313)
PHONE..................302 426-6500
Alan Yandziak, *Pr*
Scott Vanosten, *Mgr*
Athena Vekkos, *Treas*
EMP: 6 EST: 1986
SALES (est): 800.91K **Privately Held**
Web: www.counterpointsoftwareinc.com
SIC: 7372 Prepackaged software

(G-15656)
COUNTERTOP SHOP LLC
45 Germay Dr Ste B (19804-1126)
PHONE..................302 654-0700
Thomas Donnelly, *Managing Member*
EMP: 3 EST: 2016
SALES (est): 132.09K **Privately Held**
Web: www.thecountertopshopofde.com
SIC: 2434 Wood kitchen cabinets

(G-15657)
COURAGE CAPITAL MANAGEMENT
1105 N Market St Ste 1300 (19801-1241)
PHONE..................302 658-2459
EMP: 6 EST: 2007
SALES (est): 509.25K **Privately Held**
SIC: 6282 Investment advice

(G-15658)
COURT RECORD & DATA MGT SVCS
Also Called: Crds
1300 First State Blvd Ste H (19804)
PHONE..................302 476-8976
Antoinette Ruocchio, *CEO*
EMP: 10 EST: 2013
SQ FT: 2,000
SALES (est): 508.5K **Privately Held**
Web: www.crds-inc.com
SIC: 7374 Optical scanning data service

(G-15659)
COURTNEY CONSTRUCTION
7 Park Ln (19809-2011)
PHONE..................302 798-2393
EMP: 5 EST: 2018
SALES (est): 83.62K **Privately Held**

SIC: 1521 Single-family housing construction

(G-15660)
COURTNEY CONSTRUCTION INC
23 Selborne Dr (19807-1215)
PHONE..................302 521-5865
Courtney Thomas, *Prin*
EMP: 5 EST: 2009
SALES (est): 102.69K **Privately Held**
SIC: 1521 Single-family housing construction

(G-15661)
COURTYARD MANAGEMENT CORP
Also Called: Marriott
1102 N West St (19801-1006)
PHONE..................302 429-7600
Barbara Dell, *Brnch Mgr*
EMP: 27
SALES (corp-wide): 20.77B **Publicly Held**
Web: www.marriott.com
SIC: 7011 Hotels and motels
HQ: Courtyard Management Llc
7750 Wisconsin Ave
Bethesda MD 20814

(G-15662)
COVENANT PRESCHOOL
503 Duncan Rd (19809-2333)
PHONE..................302 764-8503
EMP: 12 EST: 1974
SALES (est): 233.41K **Privately Held**
Web: www.covenantps.org
SIC: 8351 Preschool center

(G-15663)
COVENANT PROPERTIES I
15 Middleton Dr (19808-4320)
PHONE..................302 234-5655
EMP: 5 EST: 2008
SALES (est): 169.77K **Privately Held**
Web: www.covenantwealthstrategies.com
SIC: 6512 Nonresidential building operators

(G-15664)
COVENANT WEALTH STRATEGIES
11 Middleton Dr (19808-4320)
PHONE..................302 234-5655
EMP: 17 EST: 2017
SALES (est): 884.29K **Privately Held**
Web: www.covenantwealthstrategies.com
SIC: 6512 Commercial and industrial building operation

(G-15665)
COVER & ROSSITER PA
2711 Centerville Rd Ste 100 (19808-1660)
PHONE..................302 656-6632
Geoff Langdon, *Pr*
Diane Burke, *
EMP: 30 EST: 1978
SALES (est): 4.4MM **Privately Held**
Web: www.coverrossiter.com
SIC: 8721 Certified public accountant

(G-15666)
COVERAGEX LLC ◆
919 N Market St Ste 950 (19801-3036)
PHONE..................310 854-2677
Vajira Samararatne, *Managing Member*
EMP: 5 EST: 2023
SALES (est): 385.29K **Privately Held**
SIC: 6399 Warranty insurance, automobile

(G-15667)
COVERDECK SYSTEMS INC
408 Meco Dr # A (19804-1112)
PHONE..................302 427-7578
▲ EMP: 15 EST: 1994

GEOGRAPHIC SECTION

Wilmington - New Castle County (G-15697)

SALES (est): 2MM **Privately Held**
Web: www.coverdeck.com
SIC: 1521 Patio and deck construction and repair

(G-15668)
COVR FINANCIAL TECH INC
1209 N Orange St (19801-1120)
PHONE................................800 377-6344
EMP: 15 **EST:** 2016
SALES (est): 359.92K **Privately Held**
Web: www.covrtech.com
SIC: 6282 Investment advice

(G-15669)
COWAN CHIROPRACTIC REHAB PA
2500 W 4th St Ste 3 (19805-3352)
PHONE................................302 559-5261
William Cowan, *Prin*
EMP: 6 **EST:** 2016
SALES (est): 238.95K **Privately Held**
Web: www.cowanchiro.com
SIC: 8041 Offices and clinics of chiropractors

(G-15670)
COWAN SYSTEMS LLC
603 Christiana Ave (19801-5834)
PHONE................................302 656-1403
EMP: 129
SIC: 4213 Trucking, except local
PA: Cowan Systems, Llc
    4555 Hollins Ferry Rd
    Baltimore MD 21227

(G-15671)
COWCHOK TF INC
2615 Kimbrough Dr (19810-1404)
PHONE................................302 475-4510
T F Cowchok, *Prin*
EMP: 6 **EST:** 1970
SALES (est): 134.19K **Privately Held**
SIC: 6331 Fire, marine and casualty insurance and carriers

(G-15672)
COWIE TECHNOLOGY CORP
510 First State Blvd (19804)
PHONE................................302 998-7037
Goerge Cowie, *Owner*
EMP: 9 **EST:** 2005
SALES (est): 519.59K **Privately Held**
Web: www.cowie.com
SIC: 8731 Commercial physical research

(G-15673)
COZEN OCONNOR
1201 N Market St Ste 1001 (19801-1166)
PHONE................................302 295-2000
Joe Lepo, *Mgr*
EMP: 14
SALES (corp-wide): 1.51MM **Privately Held**
Web: www.cozen.com
SIC: 8111 General practice attorney, lawyer
PA: Cozen O'connor
    1650 Market St Ste 2800
    Philadelphia PA 19103
    215 665-2053

(G-15674)
COZTEL LLC
300 Delaware Ave Ste 210233 (19801)
PHONE................................832 224-5638
Muhammad Sajjad, *Managing Member*
EMP: 5 **EST:** 2019
SALES (est): 65.1K **Privately Held**
Web: www.coztel.com
SIC: 8999 Communication services

(G-15675)
CP FITNESS WILMINGTON LLC
Also Called: Club Pilates
5610 Concord Pike (19803-1425)
PHONE................................302 797-1400
Kathy Mckay, *Managing Member*
EMP: 10 **EST:** 2021
SALES (est): 157.03K **Privately Held**
Web: www.clubpilates.com
SIC: 7991 Physical fitness facilities

(G-15676)
CPEX PHARMACEUTICALS INC
1105 N Market St Ste 1300 (19801-1241)
PHONE................................302 651-8300
John A Sedor, *Pr*
Lance Berman, *Chief Medical Officer*
Nils Bergenhem, *VP*
Robert P Hebert, *VP*
EMP: 12 **EST:** 2008
SQ FT: 15,700
SALES (est): 3.18MM
SALES (corp-wide): 3.18MM **Privately Held**
Web: www.cpexpharmaceuticals.com
SIC: 2834 Drugs acting on the cardiovascular system, except diagnostic
HQ: I Fcb Holdings Inc
    933 Macarthur Blvd
    Mahwah NJ 07430

(G-15677)
CPF CKD LLC
1209 N Orange St (19801-1120)
PHONE................................855 386-2799
Nathan Goldstein, *CEO*
Nathan Goldstein, *Managing Member*
Meaghan Jones, *
EMP: 30 **EST:** 2021
SALES (est): 1.02MM **Privately Held**
SIC: 7389 Business Activities at Non-Commercial Site

(G-15678)
CR24 INC
1605 E Ayre St Ste 24 (19804-2514)
PHONE................................888 427-9357
EMP: 8 **EST:** 2014
SALES (est): 184.3K **Privately Held**
Web: www.cr24usa.com
SIC: 7371 Computer software development

(G-15679)
CRADLEAPPS LLC
251 Little Falls Dr (19808-1674)
PHONE................................202 492-7953
EMP: 5 **EST:** 2019
SALES (est): 96.95K **Privately Held**
Web: www.cradle.app
SIC: 7371 Computer software development and applications

(G-15680)
CRAFTS REPORT PUBLISHING CO
100 Rogers Rd (19801-5704)
P.O. Box 1992 (19899-1992)
PHONE................................302 656-2209
EMP: 7 **EST:** 1975
SQ FT: 10,000
SALES (est): 165.23K **Privately Held**
SIC: 2721 Magazines: publishing and printing

(G-15681)
CRAIG AND COMPANY LLC
28 Sharons Way (19808-5236)
PHONE................................609 221-9959
EMP: 5 **EST:** 2012
SALES (est): 40.59K **Privately Held**
SIC: 7929 Disc jockey service

(G-15682)
CRAIG WEINER
209 N Pembrey Dr (19803-2005)
PHONE................................267 226-8511
Craig Weiner, *Owner*
EMP: 6 **EST:** 2017
SALES (est): 228.58K **Privately Held**
SIC: 7291 Tax return preparation services

(G-15683)
CRAMER & DIMICHELE PA
1801 W Newport Pike (19804-3529)
PHONE................................302 293-1230
EMP: 6 **EST:** 2010
SALES (est): 131.7K **Privately Held**
Web: www.derealestatelaw.com
SIC: 8621 Professional organizations

(G-15684)
CRAMER DIMICHELE
5305 Limestone Rd Ste 200 (19808-1247)
PHONE................................302 235-8561
EMP: 5 **EST:** 2017
SALES (est): 226.52K **Privately Held**
Web: www.derealestatelaw.com
SIC: 8111 General practice attorney, lawyer

(G-15685)
CRANSTON HALL APARTMENTS
3314 Old Capitol Trl Ofc 2 (19808-6276)
PHONE................................302 999-7001
Donald Mc Kay, *Pr*
Steve Lendz, *Superintnt*
EMP: 9 **EST:** 1950
SQ FT: 1,500
SALES (est): 785.69K **Privately Held**
Web: www.mckayapartments.com
SIC: 6513 Apartment hotel operation

(G-15686)
CRE8TIVE MINDS ENT LLC
5803 Highland Ct (19802-1732)
PHONE................................302 293-3461
Charles Purnell, *Prin*
EMP: 5 **EST:** 2007
SALES (est): 30.3K **Privately Held**
Web: www.cre8tivemindsllc.com
SIC: 7929 Entertainers and entertainment groups

(G-15687)
CREATED LIFE COACHING
442 S Bancroft Pkwy (19805-3708)
PHONE................................302 584-7112
Betsy Conlan, *Prin*
EMP: 5 **EST:** 2017
SALES (est): 36.21K **Privately Held**
Web: www.getlifecoaching.com
SIC: 8322 General counseling services

(G-15688)
CREATEYOURSCHOLARSHIPORG
2810 N Church St Ste 41193 (19802-4447)
PHONE................................415 822-8266
Peter Ross, *Dir*
Gary Roth, *Dir*
Czashka Ross, *Dir*
EMP: 5 **EST:** 2021
SALES (est): 77.06K **Privately Held**
Web: www.createyourscholarship.org
SIC: 8699 Charitable organization

(G-15689)
CREATIONS BY MAE ENTPS LLC
427 S Rodney St (19805-3958)
PHONE................................302 985-5797
Donyiell Adams, *Managing Member*
EMP: 5 **EST:** 2020
SALES (est): 119.77K **Privately Held**

SIC: 7389 Business Activities at Non-Commercial Site

(G-15690)
CREATIVE BEGINNINGS
3 Paoletti Dr (19808-2243)
PHONE................................302 633-4575
Michele Griffiths, *Prin*
EMP: 9 **EST:** 2017
SALES (est): 44.4K **Privately Held**
Web: www.cblckids.com
SIC: 8351 Preschool center

(G-15691)
CREATIVE EMBROIDERY INC
47 Germay Dr Ste C (19804-1125)
PHONE................................302 661-7313
Joseph A Santillo Junior, *Pr*
Joseph A Santillo Iii, *VP*
EMP: 4 **EST:** 2003
SALES (est): 373.64K **Privately Held**
Web: www.cespde.com
SIC: 2395 Embroidery and art needlework

(G-15692)
CREATIVE LAND CARE
520 Robinson Ln (19805-4616)
PHONE................................302 482-1944
EMP: 9 **EST:** 2018
SALES (est): 455.02K **Privately Held**
Web: www.creativelandcare.net
SIC: 8351 Child day care services

(G-15693)
CREATIVE LEARNING CHILD CARE
1220 Apple St (19801-5414)
PHONE................................302 691-3167
Tina Flowers, *Owner*
EMP: 5 **EST:** 2011
SALES (est): 81.19K **Privately Held**
SIC: 8351 Group day care center

(G-15694)
CREATIVE MARKETING CONCEPTS
2419 W Newport Pike (19804-3846)
PHONE................................302 367-7100
EMP: 7 **EST:** 2010
SALES (est): 74.9K **Privately Held**
Web: www.redicarpet.com
SIC: 7389 Design services

(G-15695)
CREATIVE XCHANGE INC
919 N Market St Ste 950 (19801-3036)
PHONE................................888 502-5618
Sarthak Patnaik, *Pr*
Ramon Mendez, *Sec*
EMP: 7 **EST:** 2017
SALES (est): 41.04K **Privately Held**
Web: www.creativexchangeinc.com
SIC: 7371 Computer software development and applications

(G-15696)
CREDIT ACCPTNCE AUTO LN TR 201
300 Delaware Ave Fl 9 (19801-1607)
PHONE................................302 576-3706
EMP: 6 **EST:** 2014
SALES (est): 456.68K **Privately Held**
SIC: 6733 Trusts, nec

(G-15697)
CREDIT CONCIERGE LLC
427 N Ttnall St Unit 6571 (19801)
PHONE................................877 860-9877
EMP: 25 **EST:** 2015
SALES (est): 701.22K **Privately Held**
SIC: 8741 Management services

(G-15698)
CREEKSIDE CARPENTRY LLC
400 N Augustine St (19804-2735)
PHONE..................302 218-4434
Daniel Connell, *Prin*
EMP: 5 **EST:** 2018
SALES (est): 109.73K **Privately Held**
SIC: 1751 Carpentry work

(G-15699)
CRESCENT BUSINESS CENTER LLC
4708 Kirkwood Hwy (19808-5022)
PHONE..................302 683-0300
James Comis Iii, *VP*
EMP: 7 **EST:** 2008
SALES (est): 939.13K **Privately Held**
SIC: 6513 Apartment building operators

(G-15700)
CRESCENT MANAGEMENT INC
4708 Kirkwood Hwy Ste C (19808-5022)
P.O. Box 4544 (19807-4544)
PHONE..................302 449-4560
Sami Khan, *Pr*
EMP: 8 **EST:** 1988
SALES (est): 456.26K **Privately Held**
Web: www.fairfieldapartmentsde.com
SIC: 8741 Management services

(G-15701)
CRESTVIEW MEDICAL CENTER
1800 N Broom St Ste 109 (19802-3809)
PHONE..................302 762-4545
EMP: 7 **EST:** 2019
SALES (est): 242.33K **Privately Held**
Web: www.crestviewmedicalcenter.com
SIC: 8011 Medical centers

(G-15702)
CRH INVESTMENTS INC
1105 N Market St (19801-1216)
PHONE..................302 427-0924
John Edwards, *Mgr*
EMP: 7 **EST:** 2015
SALES (est): 498.27K **Privately Held**
SIC: 6211 Security brokers and dealers

(G-15703)
CRICKET
1012 Wilmington Ave Ste A (19805-1560)
PHONE..................302 482-3658
EMP: 5 **EST:** 2017
SALES (est): 57.98K **Privately Held**
SIC: 4812 Cellular telephone services

(G-15704)
CRISWELL HOUSE
724 N Madison St (19801-1414)
PHONE..................302 498-5174
EMP: 5 **EST:** 2016
SALES (est): 92.36K **Privately Held**
Web: criswell-house.hub.biz
SIC: 8361 Aged home

(G-15705)
CRITERIUM JAGIASI ENGINEERS
1500 Shallcross Ave (19806-3037)
PHONE..................302 498-5600
Janis Edwards, *Prin*
EMP: 5 **EST:** 2006
SALES (est): 494.79K **Privately Held**
Web: www.criterium-jagiasi.com
SIC: 8711 Consulting engineer

(G-15706)
CRITICAL BS HOLDINGS LLC
1201 N Market St Ste 111 (19801-1147)
PHONE..................833 479-5375
EMP: 5
SALES (est): 199.4K **Privately Held**
SIC: 8748 Business consulting, nec

(G-15707)
CRITICAL DESIGN AND CNSTR CORP
1525 Barley Mill Rd (19807-2231)
PHONE..................302 588-4406
Scott Capaldi, *Pr*
EMP: 7 **EST:** 2015
SALES (est): 366.39K **Privately Held**
SIC: 1521 Single-family housing construction

(G-15708)
CROCHET CREATIONS BY DEBBIE
1219 Mckennans Church Rd (19808-2130)
PHONE..................302 287-2462
Debra Tomchick, *Prin*
EMP: 4 **EST:** 2016
SALES (est): 44.01K **Privately Held**
SIC: 2399 Hand woven and crocheted products

(G-15709)
CROESUS INC
1007 N Orange St (19801-1239)
PHONE..................302 472-9260
EMP: 14 **EST:** 2005
SALES (est): 430.97K **Privately Held**
Web: www.croesus.us
SIC: 3599 Industrial machinery, nec

(G-15710)
CROPSOFT SOLUTIONS LLC ✪
3524 Silverside Rd Ste 35b (19810-4929)
PHONE..................201 284-1535
Andrii Svyrydov, *Managing Member*
EMP: 35 **EST:** 2022
SALES (est): 1.08MM **Privately Held**
SIC: 7372 Prepackaged software

(G-15711)
CROSS & SIMON LLC
913 N Market St Ste 1100 (19801-3029)
P.O. Box 1380 (19899-1380)
PHONE..................302 777-4200
Richard H Cross Junior, *Managing Member*
EMP: 15 **EST:** 2002
SALES (est): 3.9MM **Privately Held**
Web: www.crosslaw.com
SIC: 8111 Specialized law offices, attorneys

(G-15712)
CROSS FIT API
4905 Mermaid Blvd (19808-1004)
PHONE..................302 235-8763
Joe Deascanis, *Prin*
EMP: 5 **EST:** 2014
SALES (est): 84.48K **Privately Held**
Web: www.crossfitapi.com
SIC: 7991 Health club

(G-15713)
CROSSFIT DIAMOND STATE LLC
1801 Lincoln Ave (19809-1428)
PHONE..................201 803-1159
EMP: 6 **EST:** 2013
SALES (est): 133.57K **Privately Held**
Web: www.diamondstatefitness.com
SIC: 7991 Health club

(G-15714)
CROSSFIT RIVERFRONT
512 Justison St (19801-5142)
PHONE..................302 745-2348
EMP: 6 **EST:** 2018
SALES (est): 64.06K **Privately Held**
Web: www.rivathletics.com
SIC: 7991 Physical fitness facilities

(G-15715)
CROSSROADS WIRELESS HOLDG LLC
Also Called: Crossroads Wireless
919 N Market St Ste 600 (19801-3037)
PHONE..................405 946-1200
EMP: 11 **EST:** 2006
SQ FT: 6,000
SALES (est): 521.09K **Privately Held**
SIC: 4812 5999 Cellular telephone services; Mobile telephones and equipment

(G-15716)
CROWN CORK SEAL RCVBLES DE COR (HQ)
Also Called: Crown Cork Seal Receivables De
5301 Limestone Rd Ste 221 (19808-1265)
PHONE..................215 698-5100
Timothy J Donahue, *Pr*
Thomas Kelly, *CFO*
Kevin Clothier, *VP*
▼ **EMP:** 4 **EST:** 1997
SALES (est): 4.55MM
SALES (corp-wide): 12.94B **Publicly Held**
SIC: 3411 Metal cans
PA: Crown Holdings Inc.
  770 Township Line Rd # 100
  Yardley PA 19067
  215 698-5100

(G-15717)
CROWNING GLORY STYLING SALON
3808 Old Capitol Trl (19808-5824)
PHONE..................302 999-8237
Bai May, *Prin*
EMP: 5 **EST:** 2010
SALES (est): 90.13K **Privately Held**
SIC: 7231 Hairdressers

(G-15718)
CRRRAW HOLDINGS LLC
2810 N Church St Unit 765891 (19802-4447)
PHONE..................832 917-9442
EMP: 5
SALES (est): 199.4K **Privately Held**
SIC: 7371 Computer software development and applications

(G-15719)
CRYPTOMARKET INC (PA)
Also Called: Cryptomkt
1209 N Orange St (19801-1120)
PHONE..................860 222-0318
Martin Jofre, *CEO*
EMP: 9 **EST:** 2018
SALES (est): 2.18MM
SALES (corp-wide): 2.18MM **Privately Held**
SIC: 7372 Application computer software

(G-15720)
CRYSTAL HOLDINGS INC (PA)
110 S Poplar St Ste 400 (19801-5044)
PHONE..................302 421-5700
Brian Disabatino, *Pr*
EMP: 55 **EST:** 1980
SQ FT: 17,000
SALES (est): 30.73MM
SALES (corp-wide): 30.73MM **Privately Held**
Web: www.ediscompany.com
SIC: 8741 6531 1541 1542 Administrative management; Real estate managers; Industrial buildings, new construction, nec; Commercial and office building, new construction

(G-15721)
CS ASSOCIATES LLC (PA) ✪
3911 Concord Pike Unit 8030 (19803-1736)
PHONE..................909 827-2335
Caleb Sykes, *Managing Member*
EMP: 5 **EST:** 2022
SALES (est): 281.2K
SALES (corp-wide): 281.2K **Privately Held**
SIC: 4213 Trucking, except local

(G-15722)
CSC CORPORATE DOMAINS INC (HQ)
Also Called: CSC
251 Little Falls Dr (19808-1674)
PHONE..................866 403-5272
Mark Calandra, *Sr VP*
EMP: 93 **EST:** 1997
SALES (est): 135.66MM
SALES (corp-wide): 661.37MM **Privately Held**
Web: www.cscglobal.com
SIC: 8111 Legal services
PA: Corporation Service Company
  251 Little Falls Dr
  Wilmington DE 19808
  302 636-5400

(G-15723)
CSC DOMAINS LLC (HQ)
Also Called: CSC
2711 Centerville Rd Ste 400 (19808-1660)
PHONE..................302 636-5400
Bruce R Winn, *Managing Member*
EMP: 45 **EST:** 2006
SALES (est): 24.3MM
SALES (corp-wide): 661.37MM **Privately Held**
Web: www.cscglobal.com
SIC: 8111 Legal services
PA: Corporation Service Company
  251 Little Falls Dr
  Wilmington DE 19808
  302 636-5400

(G-15724)
CSC NETWORKS INC
251 Little Falls Dr (19808-1674)
PHONE..................302 636-5401
EMP: 7 **EST:** 2018
SALES (est): 218.93K **Privately Held**
Web: www.cscglobal.com
SIC: 7389 Financial services

(G-15725)
CSRJ CONTRACTING
2007 Baird Ave (19808-5201)
PHONE..................302 290-6208
Carmen Dicriscio, *Prin*
EMP: 5 **EST:** 2017
SALES (est): 57.79K **Privately Held**
Web: www.csrjcontracting.com
SIC: 1799 Special trade contractors, nec

(G-15726)
CSX TRANSPORTATION INC
Also Called: CSX
1155 Centerville Rd (19804-2005)
PHONE..................302 998-8613
EMP: 5
SALES (corp-wide): 14.85B **Publicly Held**
Web: www.csx.com
SIC: 4011 Railroads, line-haul operating
HQ: Csx Transportation, Inc.
  500 Water St 15
  Jacksonville FL 32202
  904 359-3100

(G-15727)
CT CORPORATION SYSTEM (PA)
1209 N Orange St (19801-1120)
PHONE..............................302 658-4968
Ct Raynes, *Prin*
EMP: 9 **EST:** 2012
SALES (est): 2.16MM
SALES (corp-wide): 2.16MM **Privately Held**
SIC: 7372 Business oriented computer software

(G-15728)
CT PARTNERS LLC
4001 Kennett Pike Ste 242 (19807-2029)
PHONE..............................302 766-4176
EMP: 6 **EST:** 2018
SALES (est): 38.93K **Privately Held**
SIC: 8099 Health and allied services, nec

(G-15729)
CUBE MEDIA LLC
501 Silverside Rd 345 (19809-1374)
PHONE..............................716 239-2789
EMP: 7 **EST:** 2018
SALES (est): 37.91K **Privately Held**
SIC: 7929 Entertainment service

(G-15730)
CUBIC LOGICS INC
Twenty Four A Trolley Square #4058 (19806)
PHONE..............................480 382-8242
EMP: 6 **EST:** 2014
SALES (est): 65.65K **Privately Held**
SIC: 7371 Custom computer programming services

(G-15731)
CUBIC PRODUCTS LLC
2711 Centerville Rd (19808-1660)
PHONE..............................781 990-3886
Nicola Sloan, *Managing Member*
EMP: 7 **EST:** 2014
SALES (est): 150.2K **Privately Held**
SIC: 2599 Cabinets, factory

(G-15732)
CULIQUIP LLC
20 Germay Dr (19804-1105)
PHONE..............................302 654-4974
Angelo Bizzarro, *Prin*
EMP: 42 **EST:** 2008
SALES (est): 437.64K
SALES (corp-wide): 12.37MM **Privately Held**
Web: www.culiquip.com
SIC: 2434 Wood kitchen cabinets
PA: Fsph, Inc.
2301 E Evesham Rd Ste 210
Voorhees NJ 08043
301 349-2001

(G-15733)
CUMMINS POWER GENERATION INC
Also Called: Cummins
1706 E 12th St (19809-3562)
PHONE..............................302 762-2027
Dave Santarosa, *Mgr*
EMP: 29
SALES (corp-wide): 34.06B **Publicly Held**
SIC: 3621 3519 Generators and sets, electric; Internal combustion engines, nec
HQ: Cummins Power Generation Inc.
1400 73rd Ave Ne
Minneapolis MN 55432
763 574-5000

(G-15734)
CURRENCY TECHNICS METRICS INC
4200 Governor Printz Blvd (19802-2315)
P.O. Box 9560 (19809-0560)
PHONE..............................302 482-4846
Bill Brooks, *Pr*
Robert Dickerson, *VP*
EMP: 42 **EST:** 2003
SQ FT: 8,000
SALES (est): 6.41MM **Privately Held**
Web: www.ctm.com
SIC: 3695 Computer software tape and disks: blank, rigid, and floppy

(G-15735)
CURRIE HAIR SKIN NAILSS
Also Called: CURRIE HAIR SKIN NAILSS
317 Justison St (19801-5164)
PHONE..............................302 777-7755
Randy Currie, *Prin*
EMP: 9
SALES (corp-wide): 5.57MM **Privately Held**
Web: www.curriedayspa.com
SIC: 7231 Manicurist, pedicurist
PA: Currie Hair Skin And Nails Of Wayne, Llc
605 Lancaster Ave
Wayne PA 19087
610 558-4247

(G-15736)
CURTIS D FROEHLICH M D
1600 Rockland Rd (19803-3607)
PHONE..............................302 651-4000
Curtis Froehlich, *Mgr*
EMP: 15 **EST:** 2018
SALES (est): 252.01K **Privately Held**
Web: www.nemours.org
SIC: 8011 Pediatrician

(G-15737)
CURZON CORP
Also Called: Seymour's Cleaners
900 N Union St (19805-5326)
PHONE..............................302 655-5551
Andrew Berger, *Owner*
Sally Berger, *Sec*
EMP: 10 **EST:** 1910
SQ FT: 4,500
SALES (est): 217.3K **Privately Held**
Web: www.seymoursdrycleaners.com
SIC: 7216 7219 7251 Cleaning and dyeing, except rugs; Garment making, alteration, and repair; Shoe repair shop

(G-15738)
CUSTOM AMERICA
173 Edgemoor Rd (19809-9001)
PHONE..............................856 516-1103
▲ **EMP:** 8 **EST:** 2015
SALES (est): 244.21K **Privately Held**
Web: www.custom.biz
SIC: 3089 Injection molding of plastics

(G-15739)
CUSTOM CREATIONS BY DESIGN
1 Murphy Rd (19803-3044)
PHONE..............................302 482-2267
Scott Gillespie, *Owner*
EMP: 5 **EST:** 2010
SALES (est): 168.58K **Privately Held**
Web: www.customcreations-bydesign.com
SIC: 7389 Design services

(G-15740)
CUSTOM DESIGN CONTRACTING LLC
16 E Salisbury Dr (19809-3414)
PHONE..............................302 333-0547
Mackenzie Cheeseman, *Asst Sec*
EMP: 5 **EST:** 2019
SALES (est): 62.44K **Privately Held**
SIC: 1799 Special trade contractors, nec

(G-15741)
CUSTOM IRON SHOP INC
735 S Market St Ste A (19801-5246)
P.O. Box 2633 (19805-0633)
PHONE..............................302 654-5201
Joseph R Swarter, *Pr*
Charles G Swarter, *Treas*
Frederick J Swarter, *VP*
EMP: 9 **EST:** 1951
SQ FT: 6,500
SALES (est): 1MM **Privately Held**
Web: www.customironshopde.com
SIC: 1799 1791 Ornamental metal work; Structural steel erection

(G-15742)
CUSTOM LAWN SERVICES INC
4023 Kennett Pike Ste 258 (19807-2018)
PHONE..............................302 540-4180
Dave D Di Donato, *Owner*
EMP: 5 **EST:** 2014
SALES (est): 69.18K **Privately Held**
Web: www.firststatetree.com
SIC: 0782 Lawn care services

(G-15743)
CUSTOM METAL WORKS INC
530 Ruxton Dr (19809-2830)
PHONE..............................302 765-2653
Jacek Sroczynski, *Prin*
EMP: 5 **EST:** 2015
SALES (est): 63.57K **Privately Held**
SIC: 1761 Sheet metal work, nec

(G-15744)
CUSTOM SHEET METAL OF DELAWARE
464 E Ayre St (19804-2513)
PHONE..............................302 998-6865
Bill Wilson, *Pr*
EMP: 5 **EST:** 1981
SALES (est): 458.71K **Privately Held**
Web: www.customsheetmetalde.com
SIC: 3599 3444 Machine shop, jobbing and repair; Sheet metalwork

(G-15745)
CUSTOMS BENEFITS
501 Silverside Rd Ste 120 (19809-1377)
PHONE..............................302 798-2884
Leon Champagne, *Owner*
Leon Champagne, *Pr*
James W Kelly, *Sec*
EMP: 5 **EST:** 1978
SQ FT: 1,000
SALES (est): 305.29K **Privately Held**
SIC: 7389 Packaging and labeling services

(G-15746)
CUTLER INDUSTRIES INC
2711 Centerville Rd # 400 (19808-1660)
PHONE..............................302 689-3779
Alit Suryadi, *Mgr*
EMP: 5 **EST:** 2005
SQ FT: 500
SALES (est): 440K **Privately Held**
SIC: 5045 Printers, computer

(G-15747)
CUTTING EDGE OF DELAWARE INC
511 E 5th St (19801-4705)
P.O. Box 104 (19731-0104)
PHONE..............................302 834-8723
Sean P Johnston, *Pr*
EMP: 11 **EST:** 2000
SALES (est): 228.3K **Privately Held**
Web: www.thecuttingedgeofde.com
SIC: 7241 0782 0781 Barber shops; Landscape contractors; Landscape planning services

(G-15748)
CWP ENERGY SOLUTION INC ✪
Also Called: Cwp Energy Solution
1209 N Orange St (19801-1120)
PHONE..............................514 360-0270
Alain Brisebois, *Pr*
Philippe Boisclair, *VP*
Christian Labb, *Sec*
EMP: 6 **EST:** 2022
SALES (est): 1.5MM
SALES (corp-wide): 286.49MM **Privately Held**
SIC: 4911 Electric services
HQ: Energie Cwp Inc
407 Rue Mcgill Bureau 315
Montreal QC H2Y 2
514 871-2090

(G-15749)
CWS BALLANTYNE II 99 LLC
251 Little Falls Dr (19808-1674)
PHONE..............................302 636-5401
Gary Carmell, *Managing Member*
EMP: 6 **EST:** 2004
SALES (est): 116.76K **Privately Held**
SIC: 7389 Business Activities at Non-Commercial Site

(G-15750)
CYBELE SOFTWARE INC
3422 Old Capitol Trl Ste 1125 (19808-6124)
PHONE..............................302 892-9625
Gustavo Ricardi, *Pr*
EMP: 39 **EST:** 2002
SALES (est): 2.5MM **Privately Held**
Web: www.cybelesoft.com
SIC: 7372 Prepackaged software

(G-15751)
CYBERCORE HOLDING INC
1209 N Orange St (19801-1120)
PHONE..............................410 560-7177
EMP: 99 **EST:** 2011
SALES (est): 1.8MM **Privately Held**
SIC: 8711 Engineering services

(G-15752)
CYNASH INC
1 Righter Pkwy Ste 260 (19803-1555)
PHONE..............................415 850-7842
Richard Robinson, *CEO*
EMP: 5 **EST:** 2017
SALES (est): 293.41K **Privately Held**
SIC: 8748 Business consulting, nec

(G-15753)
CYNTHIA A MUMMA DDS
1 Zachary Ct (19803-3967)
PHONE..............................302 652-2451
EMP: 7 **EST:** 2007
SALES (est): 482.58K **Privately Held**
Web: www.dentalhealthde.com
SIC: 8021 Dentists' office

(G-15754)
CYNTHIA CROSSER DC FIAMA
3101 Limestone Rd Ste B (19808-2148)
PHONE..............................302 239-5014
EMP: 6 **EST:** 2018
SALES (est): 385.6K **Privately Held**
Web: www.crossernaturalhealth.com
SIC: 8062 General medical and surgical hospitals

Wilmington - New Castle County (G-15755)   GEOGRAPHIC SECTION

(G-15755)
CYPRESS SUPPORT LLC
1202 Faun Rd (19803-3317)
PHONE..............................410 937-2511
Karissa Desiderio, *Prin*
EMP: 6 **EST:** 2016
SALES (est): 51.5K **Privately Held**
SIC: 8322 Individual and family services

(G-15756)
CYTEC INDUSTRIES INC
3 Weldin Park Dr (19803-4708)
PHONE..............................302 530-7665
Bryant Ries, *Prin*
EMP: 28
SALES (corp-wide): 146.05MM **Privately Held**
Web: www.syensqo.com
SIC: 2899 Chemical preparations, nec
HQ: Cytec Industries Inc.
    504 Carnegie Ctr
    Princeton NJ 08540

(G-15757)
D & H AUTOMOTIVE & TOWING INC
4016th Ave Ste B (19805)
PHONE..............................302 655-7611
Dave Hudson, *Pr*
EMP: 7 **EST:** 1978
SQ FT: 1,500
SALES (est): 443.27K **Privately Held**
SIC: 7539 7549 Automotive repair shops, nec ; Towing service, automotive

(G-15758)
D B NIBOUAR DDS
5317 Limestone Rd (19808-1252)
PHONE..............................302 239-0502
D B Nibouar D.d.s., *Owner*
EMP: 10 **EST:** 1985
SALES (est): 226.25K **Privately Held**
Web: www.limestonedental.com
SIC: 8021 Dentists' office

(G-15759)
D C MITCHELL LLC
8 Hadco Rd Ste B (19804-1003)
PHONE..............................302 998-1181
Dave Mitchell, *Managing Member*
EMP: 2 **EST:** 1980
SQ FT: 3,000
SALES (est): 181.5K **Privately Held**
Web: www.dcmitchell.org
SIC: 3429 Hardware, nec

(G-15760)
D F DISTRIBUTION INC
Also Called: Cloudbrst Lawn Sprnklr Systems
6603 Governor Printz Blvd Ste A (19809-2027)
P.O. Box 24 (19703-0024)
PHONE..............................302 798-5999
Brett Forrest, *Pr*
EMP: 22 **EST:** 1984
SALES (est): 2.34MM **Privately Held**
Web: www.cloudburstsprinkler.com
SIC: 1711 Irrigation sprinkler system installation

(G-15761)
D M IANNONE INC
103 S Augustine St (19804-2505)
PHONE..............................302 999-0893
David M Iannone III, *Pr*
David M Iannone Iii, *Pr*
David M Iannone Junior, *VP*
Christine Iannone, *Sec*
EMP: 7 **EST:** 1951
SALES (est): 250K **Privately Held**
Web: www.dmisheetmetal.com
SIC: 3444 7692 Sheet metal specialties, not stamped; Welding repair

(G-15762)
D SHINN INC
1409 Haines Ave (19809-2716)
PHONE..............................302 792-2033
Don Shinn, *Pr*
EMP: 22 **EST:** 1980
SALES (est): 2.36MM **Privately Held**
Web: www.dshinninc.com
SIC: 1761 Roofing contractor

(G-15763)
D&C CONCEPTS LLC
919 N Market St Ste 950 (19801-3036)
PHONE..............................770 335-2503
Dain Pool, *CEO*
EMP: 11 **EST:** 2020
SALES (est): 321.21K **Privately Held**
SIC: 5812 7371 Fast food restaurants and stands; Computer software development and applications

(G-15764)
D1 SPORTS BASKETBALL TRAINING
919 N Market St Ste 425 (19801-3014)
PHONE..............................317 985-5125
Shawn Teague, *Pr*
EMP: 6 **EST:** 2018
SALES (est): 101.03K **Privately Held**
SIC: 7941 Basketball club

(G-15765)
DAABO INC
2055 Limestone Rd (19808-5536)
PHONE..............................816 559-4169
Igiebor David, *CEO*
EMP: 18
SALES (est): 583.41K **Privately Held**
Web: www.getdaabo.com.ng
SIC: 7371 Computer software development and applications

(G-15766)
DABVASAN INC
Also Called: Pak Mail
1812 Marsh Rd Ste 6 (19810-4533)
PHONE..............................302 529-1100
Carol Holt, *Pr*
EMP: 9 **EST:** 1992
SALES (est): 606K **Privately Held**
Web: www.pakmail.com
SIC: 7389 Mailbox rental and related service

(G-15767)
DAILEY RESOURCES
2302 Riddle Ave (19806-2179)
PHONE..............................302 655-1811
Patricia Gilroy, *Prin*
EMP: 5 **EST:** 2010
SALES (est): 141.14K **Privately Held**
Web: www.daileyresources.com
SIC: 8742 Business planning and organizing services

(G-15768)
DAISY CONSTRUCTION COMPANY
102 Larch Cir Ste 301 (19804-2371)
PHONE..............................302 658-4417
Leonard Iacono, *Pr*
Verino Pettinaro, *
EMP: 100 **EST:** 1973
SQ FT: 10,000
SALES (est): 9.11MM **Privately Held**
Web: www.daisyconstruction.com
SIC: 1771 1611 Concrete work; Surfacing and paving

(G-15769)
DALCO CONSTRUCTION CO
1112 Marsh Rd (19803-4342)
PHONE..............................302 475-2099
EMP: 5 **EST:** 1994
SALES (est): 120K **Privately Held**
SIC: 1521 Single-family housing construction

(G-15770)
DALE HAWKINS
Also Called: Hawkins Reporting Service
715 N King St Ste 200 (19801-3551)
PHONE..............................302 658-6697
Dale C Hawkins, *Owner*
EMP: 8 **EST:** 1976
SQ FT: 1,200
SALES (est): 306.01K **Privately Held**
Web: www.hawkinsreporting.com
SIC: 7338 Court reporting service

(G-15771)
DALOU PROPERTY MANAGEMENT
3 Germay Dr (19804-1127)
PHONE..............................866 575-9387
Louis Morse, *CEO*
EMP: 15 **EST:** 2001
SALES (est): 723.32K **Privately Held**
SIC: 6531 8741 Real estate managers; Management services

(G-15772)
DALSTRONG AMERICA INC
3411 Silverside Rd Ste 104 (19810-4812)
PHONE..............................716 380-4998
Gizem Gulec, *CFO*
EMP: 2 **EST:** 2019
SALES (est): 88.88K **Privately Held**
SIC: 3421 Knife blades and blanks

(G-15773)
DALTON & ASSOCIATES PA
1106 W 10th St (19806-4522)
PHONE..............................302 652-2050
Bartholomew Dalton, *Pr*
EMP: 9 **EST:** 2000
SALES (est): 1.04MM **Privately Held**
Web: www.dalton.law
SIC: 8111 General practice attorney, lawyer

(G-15774)
DALY CONCEPTS
1607 W 13th St Apt 2 (19806-4074)
PHONE..............................215 266-0866
Frank Daly, *Prin*
EMP: 5 **EST:** 2015
SALES (est): 69.45K **Privately Held**
SIC: 7538 General automotive repair shops

(G-15775)
DAMIONS SOLAR SHADES
2800 Kirkwood Hwy (19805-4914)
PHONE..............................302 661-1500
EMP: 6 **EST:** 2013
SALES (est): 241.49K **Privately Held**
Web: www.damionsolarshades.com
SIC: 7542 Washing and polishing, automotive

(G-15776)
DANA CONTAINER INC
Also Called: Dana Railcare
1280 Railcar Ave (19802-4614)
PHONE..............................302 652-8550
Ron Dana, *Pr*
EMP: 18
SALES (corp-wide): 27.55MM **Privately Held**
Web: www.danacompanies.com
SIC: 4741 Railroad car cleaning, icing, ventilating, and heating
PA: Dana Container, Inc.
    210 Essex Ave E
    Avenel NJ 07001
    732 750-9100

(G-15777)
DANA RAILCARE INC
1280 Railcar Ave (19802-4614)
PHONE..............................302 652-8550
Golden Workman, *VP*
EMP: 23 **EST:** 1980
SALES (est): 1.96MM **Privately Held**
Web: www.danacompanies.com
SIC: 4789 4741 Railroad car repair; Railroad car cleaning, icing, ventilating, and heating

(G-15778)
DANCEDELAWARE
2005 Concord Pike Ste 204 (19803-2982)
PHONE..............................302 998-1222
Valerie Smith Byron, *Owner*
EMP: 5 **EST:** 2009
SALES (est): 130.18K **Privately Held**
Web: www.dancedelaware.com
SIC: 7911 Dance studio and school

(G-15779)
DANE & CASH ENTERPRISE LLC
300 Delaware Ave Fl 10 (19801-1658)
PHONE..............................302 281-4031
EMP: 10 **EST:** 2021
SALES (est): 200K **Privately Held**
SIC: 8742 Management consulting services

(G-15780)
DANFOSS POWER SOLUTIONS US CO
251 Little Falls Dr (19808-1674)
PHONE..............................515 956-5185
Jess Herrin, *Pr*
EMP: 49
SALES (corp-wide): 10.68B **Privately Held**
Web: www.danfoss.com
SIC: 3511 Hydraulic turbine generator set units, complete
HQ: Danfoss Power Solutions (Us) Company
    2800 E 13th St
    Ames IA 50010
    515 239-6000

(G-15781)
DANIEL G WNDA K ODELL FMLY FND
501 Silverside Rd (19809-1374)
PHONE..............................800 839-1754
EMP: 5 **EST:** 2010
SALES (est): 570.27K **Privately Held**
SIC: 8699 Charitable organization

(G-15782)
DANIEL KAREN BERMAN FOUNDATION
501 Silverside Rd Ste 123 (19809-1377)
PHONE..............................800 839-1754
EMP: 6 **EST:** 2010
SALES (est): 41.49K **Privately Held**
SIC: 8699 Charitable organization

(G-15783)
DANIEL MITSDARFER T A DAN
1413 Oak Hill Dr (19805-1353)
PHONE..............................302 998-1295
Dan Mitsdarfer, *Prin*
EMP: 6 **EST:** 2010
SALES (est): 184.37K **Privately Held**
SIC: 7389 Business Activities at Non-Commercial Site

GEOGRAPHIC SECTION
Wilmington - New Castle County (G-15814)

(G-15784)
DANIEL P MCCOLLOM
222 Delaware Ave (19801-1621)
PHONE..............................302 888-6865
Admiral Chuck Harvath, *Admn*
EMP: 13 **EST:** 1932
SALES (est): 200K **Privately Held**
Web: www.mdsulaw.com
SIC: 8111 General practice attorney, lawyer

(G-15785)
DANIELS CUSTOM FINISHES LLC
9 W 26th St (19802-3501)
PHONE..............................302 357-5806
EMP: 5 **EST:** 2017
SALES (est): 244.75K **Privately Held**
Web: www.danielscustomfinishing.com
SIC: 1521 Single-family housing construction

(G-15786)
DANIELS LAWN AND TREE LLC
3210 Wilson Ave (19808-6212)
PHONE..............................302 218-0173
Daniel Davis, *Prin*
EMP: 10 **EST:** 2010
SALES (est): 829.71K **Privately Held**
Web: www.danielslawnandtree.com
SIC: 0781 0782 Landscape services; Landscape contractors

(G-15787)
DANISCO EUROPEAN HOLDING INC
974 Centre Rd (19805-1269)
PHONE..............................302 999-4083
EMP: 10 **EST:** 2017
SALES (est): 2.39MM
SALES (corp-wide): 13.02B **Publicly Held**
SIC: 0721 Crop planting and protection
PA: Dupont De Nemours, Inc.
974 Centre Rd Bldg 730
Wilmington DE 19805
302 774-3034

(G-15788)
DANISCO USA INC
Also Called: Danisco USA
974 Centre Rd Crp735 (19805)
PHONE..............................866 583-2583
Michele Fite, *Pr*
EMP: 70
SALES (corp-wide): 12.44B **Publicly Held**
Web: www.iff.com
SIC: 2099 Food preparations, nec
HQ: Danisco Usa Inc.
4 New Century Pkwy
New Century KS 66031
913 764-8100

(G-15789)
DANN J GLADNICK DMD PA
1104 N Broom St (19806-4315)
PHONE..............................302 654-7243
Dann J Gladnick, *Prin*
EMP: 5 **EST:** 2009
SALES (est): 321.52K **Privately Held**
SIC: 8021 Dental surgeon

(G-15790)
DANNEMAN FIRM LLC
3411 Silverside Rd Ste 108wb (19810-4891)
PHONE..............................302 793-9660
George J Danneman, *Owner*
EMP: 10 **EST:** 2010
SALES (est): 689.94K **Privately Held**
Web: www.dannemanfirm.com
SIC: 8111 General practice law office

(G-15791)
DANNEMANN & DANNEMAN LLC
3411 Silverside Rd Ste 108wb (19810-4891)
PHONE..............................302 368-4685
Gene Danneman, *Prin*
EMP: 6 **EST:** 2012
SALES (est): 253.18K **Privately Held**
SIC: 6512 Nonresidential building operators

(G-15792)
DANYO PLASTIC SURGERY
4001 Kennett Pike Ste 234 (19807-2029)
PHONE..............................302 753-6424
EMP: 12 **EST:** 2018
SALES (est): 846.87K **Privately Held**
Web: www.danyoplasticsurgery.com
SIC: 8011 Surgeon

(G-15793)
DARBY LEASING LLC
3411 Silverside Rd Ste 104 (19810-4812)
PHONE..............................302 477-0500
EMP: 5 **EST:** 2008
SALES (est): 305.5K **Privately Held**
SIC: 7359 Equipment rental and leasing, nec

(G-15794)
DARK KNIGHT SERVICES INC
3 Germay Dr Ste 4-2158 (19804-1127)
PHONE..............................302 468-6237
Jerel Brown, *Pr*
EMP: 11 **EST:** 2021
SALES (est): 337.56K **Privately Held**
SIC: 7389 Design services

(G-15795)
DASTOR LLC (PA)
1201 N Market St Ste 201 (19801-1160)
PHONE..............................610 337-5560
Kevin Mulqueen, *CEO*
EMP: 29 **EST:** 2021
SALES (est): 2.65MM
SALES (corp-wide): 2.65MM **Privately Held**
Web: www.dastorllc.com
SIC: 7374 Data processing service

(G-15796)
DATA CLOUD PARTNERS LLC
1209 N Orange St (19801-1120)
PHONE..............................805 729-1088
EMP: 5 **EST:** 2018
SALES (est): 23.63K **Privately Held**
SIC: 7374 Data processing and preparation

(G-15797)
DATA SYSTEMS & SOLUTIONS LLC
1013 Centre Rd (19805-1265)
PHONE..............................858 826-5995
Joseph Schmitt, *Brnch Mgr*
EMP: 32
SALES (corp-wide): 16.28B **Privately Held**
SIC: 8742 Corporate objectives and policies consultant
HQ: Data Systems & Solutions Llc
6725 Odyssey Dr Nw
Huntsville AL 35806
256 971-6758

(G-15798)
DATA-BI LLC
601 Entwisle Ct (19808-1512)
PHONE..............................302 290-3138
EMP: 5 **EST:** 2015
SALES (est): 266.33K **Privately Held**
SIC: 7371 7373 7374 7379 Computer software development; Systems integration services; Data processing and preparation; Data processing consultant

(G-15799)
DATASCOPE SOLUTIONS CORP
251 Little Falls Dr (19808-1674)
PHONE..............................562 373-0209
Nicolas Serrano, *CEO*
EMP: 5
SALES (est): 46.16K **Privately Held**
SIC: 7371 Computer software development and applications

(G-15800)
DATASPINDLE LLC
2207 Concord Pike Ste 425 (19803-2908)
PHONE..............................302 448-4988
EMP: 6 **EST:** 2012
SALES (est): 117.72K **Privately Held**
Web: www.dataspindle.com
SIC: 7382 Security systems services

(G-15801)
DAVID A DOREY ESQ
1201 N Market St Ste 800 (19801-1807)
PHONE..............................302 425-6400
EMP: 5 **EST:** 2011
SALES (est): 190.64K **Privately Held**
Web: www.brossfrankel.com
SIC: 8111 General practice attorney, lawyer

(G-15802)
DAVID A KING DDS
2601 Annand Dr Ste 10 (19808-3719)
PHONE..............................302 998-0331
David A King, *Prin*
EMP: 9 **EST:** 2018
SALES (est): 74.03K **Privately Held**
SIC: 8021 Dentists' office

(G-15803)
DAVID BROWN GEAR SYSTEMS USA I (PA)
300 Delaware Ave Ste 1370 (19801-1658)
P.O. Box 5040 (23058-5040)
PHONE..............................540 416-2062
Marcelo Zatatero, *Pr*
◆ **EMP:** 9 **EST:** 2012
SQ FT: 1,600
SALES (est): 2.62MM
SALES (corp-wide): 2.62MM **Privately Held**
SIC: 3566 Gears, power transmission, except auto

(G-15804)
DAVID D FINOCCHIARO ATTORNEY
916 Cranbrook Dr (19803-4804)
PHONE..............................302 764-7113
David D Finocchiaro, *Prin*
EMP: 5 **EST:** 2012
SALES (est): 124.54K **Privately Held**
SIC: 8111 General practice attorney, lawyer

(G-15805)
DAVID D SCHEID M D
3105 Limestone Rd Ste 301 (19808-2156)
PHONE..............................302 633-1700
David D Scheid, *Prin*
EMP: 9 **EST:** 2018
SALES (est): 152.55K **Privately Held**
SIC: 8011 Offices and clinics of medical doctors

(G-15806)
DAVID L ISAACS DDS
707 Foulk Rd Ste 103 (19803-3737)
PHONE..............................302 654-2904
David L Isaacs D.d.s., *Pr*
EMP: 19 **EST:** 2002
SALES (est): 260.54K **Privately Held**
Web: www.isaacsdent.com
SIC: 8021 Dentists' office

(G-15807)
DAVID M PRESSEL M D
1600 Rockland Rd (19803-3607)
PHONE..............................302 651-4000
EMP: 12
SALES (est): 246.82K **Privately Held**
Web: www.nemours.org
SIC: 8011 Pediatrician

(G-15808)
DAVID RAPPAPORT
1600 Rockland Rd (19803-3607)
PHONE..............................302 651-6040
EMP: 13 **EST:** 2017
SALES (est): 268.97K **Privately Held**
Web: www.nemours.org
SIC: 8011 Pediatrician

(G-15809)
DAVID ROBINSON
2300 Naamans Rd (19810-1233)
PHONE..............................302 324-3253
David Robinson, *Prin*
EMP: 5 **EST:** 2016
SALES (est): 50.27K **Privately Held**
SIC: 7699 Cleaning services

(G-15810)
DAVID ROCKWELL & ASSOCIATES
208 W Pembrey Dr (19803-2008)
PHONE..............................302 478-9900
David Rockwell, *Pr*
EMP: 7 **EST:** 1992
SALES (est): 168.42K **Privately Held**
SIC: 0782 Landscape contractors

(G-15811)
DAVID S JEZYK M D
4515 Griffin Dr (19808-4254)
PHONE..............................302 261-6343
David Jezyk, *Owner*
EMP: 5 **EST:** 2018
SALES (est): 82.11K **Privately Held**
Web: www.nhfm.org
SIC: 8011 Offices and clinics of medical doctors

(G-15812)
DAVID SAUNDERS GENERAL CONTRS
1204 E Willow Run Dr (19805-1254)
PHONE..............................302 998-0056
Dave Saunders, *Pr*
Mike Pirk, *Mgr*
EMP: 5 **EST:** 1998
SALES (est): 341.06K **Privately Held**
SIC: 1761 Roofing contractor

(G-15813)
DAVID T SPRINGER MD
1228 Gilbert Ave (19808-5718)
PHONE..............................302 477-1830
David T Springer, *Prin*
EMP: 8 **EST:** 2010
SALES (est): 75.99K **Privately Held**
Web: www.davidtspringermd.com
SIC: 8011 General and family practice, physician/surgeon

(G-15814)
DAVID W WEST M D
1701 Rockland Rd (19803-3631)
PHONE..............................302 651-4317
David West, *Prin*
EMP: 9 **EST:** 2014
SALES (est): 95.22K **Privately Held**
SIC: 8011 Offices and clinics of medical doctors

Wilmington - New Castle County (G-15815)

(G-15815)
DAVIS INDEX INC
919 N Market St Ste 950 (19801-3036)
PHONE.................................732 659-0456
Sean Davidson, *CEO*
EMP: 40 **EST:** 2019
SALES (est): 918.17K **Privately Held**
Web: www.davisindex.com
SIC: 8732 Market analysis, business, and economic research

(G-15816)
DAVIS SAMUEL F JR GEN CONTR
2100 Brandywood Dr (19810-2402)
PHONE.................................302 475-2607
Samuel Davis, *Prin*
EMP: 5 **EST:** 2010
SALES (est): 192.93K **Privately Held**
SIC: 1521 Single-family housing construction

(G-15817)
DAWN RUNS WITH SCISSORS
1600 Delaware Ave (19806-3304)
PHONE.................................302 293-4517
EMP: 5 **EST:** 2013
SALES (est): 39.34K **Privately Held**
SIC: 7231 Beauty shops

(G-15818)
DAWN US HOLDINGS LLC
Also Called: Evoque
251 Little Falls Dr (19808-1674)
PHONE.................................619 322-2799
EMP: 14 **EST:** 2018
SALES (est): 441.04K **Privately Held**
SIC: 7375 Information retrieval services

(G-15819)
DAY 1 MOTEL
5029 Governor Printz Blvd (19809-2703)
PHONE.................................302 397-8412
Sam Patel, *Owner*
EMP: 10 **EST:** 2016
SALES (est): 35.85K **Privately Held**
Web: www.blacksunarchives.com
SIC: 7011 Motels

(G-15820)
DAY BY DAY CALENDARS
4737 Concord Pike (19803-1442)
PHONE.................................302 477-1763
EMP: 7 **EST:** 2009
SALES (est): 58K **Privately Held**
Web: www.goretailgroup.com
SIC: 5199 Calendars

(G-15821)
DAYPAINTERS LLC
214 S Ford Ave (19805-5214)
PHONE.................................302 415-3365
Samuel Diaz, *Prin*
EMP: 5 **EST:** 2017
SALES (est): 46.01K **Privately Held**
SIC: 1721 Painting and paper hanging

(G-15822)
DAYSTAR SILLS INC
330 Water St Ste 1 (19804-2433)
PHONE.................................302 633-1421
EMP: 75 **EST:** 1991
SALES (est): 10.3MM **Privately Held**
Web: www.daystarsills.com
SIC: 1542 1541 Commercial and office building, new construction; Industrial buildings and warehouses

(G-15823)
DBEAVER CORPORATION
1000 N West St Ste 1200 (19801-1058)
PHONE.................................347 809-3202
Dion Cornett, *Pr*
Tatiana Krupenya, *Prin*
Serge Rider, *Prin*
EMP: 30 **EST:** 2018
SALES (est): 1.5MM **Privately Held**
SIC: 7379 Computer related consulting services

(G-15824)
DC CONSULTING SERVICE LLC
3422 Old Capitol Trl Ste 700 (19808-6124)
PHONE.................................617 594-9780
EMP: 10 **EST:** 2010
SALES (est): 1MM **Privately Held**
Web: www.dcconsulting.com
SIC: 7371 7389 Computer software development and applications; Business Activities at Non-Commercial Site

(G-15825)
DC MAC
1 Ave Of The Arts (19801-5047)
PHONE.................................302 660-3350
EMP: 11 **EST:** 2013
SALES (est): 255.8K **Privately Held**
SIC: 8041 Offices and clinics of chiropractors

(G-15826)
DC PRINTING INC
2305 Pennsylvania Ave (19806-1318)
PHONE.................................302 545-6666
EMP: 2 **EST:** 2011
SALES (est): 116.36K **Privately Held**
SIC: 2752 Commercial printing, lithographic

(G-15827)
DCC DESIGN GROUP LLC
2 Mill Rd Ste 103 (19806-2175)
PHONE.................................302 777-2100
EMP: 6 **EST:** 2015
SALES (est): 676.44K **Privately Held**
Web: www.dccdesigngroup.com
SIC: 7389 Interior design services

(G-15828)
DCC INC
2639 Grendon Dr (19808-3828)
PHONE.................................302 750-1207
EMP: 11 **EST:** 2012
SALES (est): 178.54K **Privately Held**
SIC: 8351 Group day care center

(G-15829)
DCODER INC
251 Little Falls Dr (19808-1674)
PHONE.................................716 638-0426
EMP: 5 **EST:** 2019
SALES (est): 101.56K **Privately Held**
SIC: 7389 Business services, nec

(G-15830)
DCRAC
600 S Harrison St (19805-4306)
PHONE.................................302 298-3289
Lillian Harrison, *Prin*
EMP: 7 **EST:** 2014
SALES (est): 135.02K **Privately Held**
Web: www.dcrac.org
SIC: 8699 Charitable organization

(G-15831)
DD & E INVESTMENT GROUP INC
1000 N. Street (19801)
PHONE.................................302 319-2780
David Davis, *Pr*
EMP: 5 **EST:** 2011
SALES (est): 263.84K **Privately Held**
SIC: 6799 Investors, nec

(G-15832)
DD SNACKS LLC
230 Alban Dr (19805-4630)
PHONE.................................302 652-3850
Donald Downs, *Prin*
EMP: 8 **EST:** 2017
SALES (est): 88.28K **Privately Held**
SIC: 8021 Offices and clinics of dentists

(G-15833)
DDESK LLC
501 Silverside Rd Ste 105 (19809-1376)
PHONE.................................302 407-1558
EMP: 6 **EST:** 2011
SALES (est): 106.31K **Privately Held**
SIC: 8741 Management services

(G-15834)
DDK
3825 Lancaster Pike (19805-1559)
PHONE.................................302 999-1132
EMP: 8 **EST:** 2010
SALES (est): 158.52K **Privately Held**
Web: www.ddk.com
SIC: 3545 Diamond cutting tools for turning, boring, burnishing, etc.

(G-15835)
DDP SPCLTY ELCTRNIC MTLS US 9 (DH)
974 Centre Rd (19805-1269)
PHONE.................................302 774-1000
Mark A Bachman, *Pr*
EMP: 8 **EST:** 2017
SQ FT: 9,000
SALES (est): 96.66MM
SALES (corp-wide): 13.02B **Publicly Held**
SIC: 2869 Silicones
HQ: Rohm And Haas Electronic Materials Cmp Inc.
451 Bellevue Rd
Newark DE 19713

(G-15836)
DDX3X FOUNDATION
322 A St Ste 300 (19801-5354)
PHONE.................................917 796-3514
EMP: 6 **EST:** 2018
SALES (est): 582.89K **Privately Held**
Web: www.ddx3x.org
SIC: 8641 Civic and social associations

(G-15837)
DE CATERING INC
Also Called: Sherm's Catering
913 Brandywine Blvd (19809-2545)
P.O. Box 11983 (19850-1983)
PHONE.................................302 607-7200
Michael Porter, *Pr*
EMP: 25 **EST:** 2015
SALES (est): 1.1MM **Privately Held**
Web: www.shermscatering.com
SIC: 5812 8742 Contract food services; Restaurant and food services consultants

(G-15838)
DE NEUROLOGY GROUP
708 Greenbank Rd (19808-3168)
PHONE.................................302 893-5301
EMP: 7 **EST:** 2018
SALES (est): 159.52K **Privately Held**
SIC: 8011 Neurologist

(G-15839)
DE NOVO CORPORATION (PA)
Also Called: Creative Solutions Intl
1011 Centre Rd Ste 104 (19805-1266)
PHONE.................................302 234-7407
Kevin Foley, *Pr*
William Keenan, *Pr*
Kim Paternoster, *Ex VP*
Kevin Foley, *Ex VP*
EMP: 20 **EST:** 1996
SALES (est): 5.78MM
SALES (corp-wide): 5.78MM **Privately Held**
Web: www.denovocorp.com
SIC: 7336 8748 Creative services to advertisers, except writers; Business consulting, nec

(G-15840)
DE VAL STRUCTUREZ
3329 Coachman Rd Unit B (19803-1904)
PHONE.................................302 575-9090
EMP: 5 **EST:** 2013
SALES (est): 186.07K **Privately Held**
Web: www.delvalstructures.com
SIC: 1521 Single-family housing construction

(G-15841)
DE WILD CHEER AND TUMBLE LLC
416 E Ayre St (19804-2513)
PHONE.................................302 438-7740
EMP: 6 **EST:** 2016
SALES (est): 33.09K **Privately Held**
Web: www.flyhighcheerandtumble.com
SIC: 7999 Gymnastic instruction, non-membership

(G-15842)
DE-INFNTY ALL STAR CHEER TMBLE
6 N Clifton Ave (19805-2262)
PHONE.................................302 383-0945
EMP: 5 **EST:** 2018
SALES (est): 21.12K **Privately Held**
SIC: 7911 Dance studio and school

(G-15843)
DEACT MEDICAL SOLUTIONS INC
827 Jasmine Dr (19808-1947)
PHONE.................................302 354-6575
Trevor Brown, *Prin*
EMP: 6 **EST:** 2017
SALES (est): 38.22K **Privately Held**
SIC: 8099 Health and allied services, nec

(G-15844)
DEALER AUTOMATION SERVICES LLC
1007 N Market St (19801-1227)
P.O. Box 140519 (33114-0519)
PHONE.................................305 803-3201
EMP: 19
SALES (est): 583.41K **Privately Held**
SIC: 7371 Computer software development and applications

(G-15845)
DEALS ON WHEELS INC (PA)
Also Called: Deals On Wheels Used Cars
1220 Centerville Rd (19808-6237)
PHONE.................................302 999-9955
Vincent Avallone, *Pr*
EMP: 31 **EST:** 1981
SALES (est): 2.17MM
SALES (corp-wide): 2.17MM **Privately Held**
Web: www.dealsonwheelsde.com
SIC: 7538 5521 General automotive repair shops; Automobiles, used cars only

(G-15846)
DEAN DIGITAL IMAGING INC
2 S Poplar St Ste B (19801-5052)
PHONE.................................302 655-6992
Floyd Dean, *Pr*
Vicky Yelton, *Sec*
EMP: 7 **EST:** 1993
SALES (est): 488.05K **Privately Held**

Wilmington - New Castle County (G-15875)

Web: www.deandigital.com
SIC: 7335 Commercial photography

(G-15847)
DEAVEN DEVELOPMENT CORP
1615 E Ayre St (19804-2514)
PHONE..............................302 994-5793
Donald F Deaven, *Pr*
Lori Deaven, *Treas*
EMP: 2 EST: 1991
SQ FT: 2,000
SALES (est): 180K Privately Held
SIC: 3441 1791 3446 Fabricated structural metal; Structural steel erection; Ornamental metalwork

(G-15848)
DECK MASTERS LLC
123 S Clifton Ave (19805-2306)
PHONE..............................302 563-4459
EMP: 8 EST: 2018
SALES (est): 435.28K Privately Held
Web: www.deckmastersde.com
SIC: 1521 Single-family housing construction

(G-15849)
DECKROBOT INC
300 Delaware Ave Ste 210 (19801-6601)
PHONE..............................617 765-7494
Tony Urban, *CEO*
EMP: 12 EST: 2017
SALES (est): 454.36K Privately Held
Web: www.deckrobot.com
SIC: 7371 Computer software development and applications

(G-15850)
DECO ENGINEERING CORP
1201 N Orange St (19801-1155)
PHONE..............................302 576-6564
EMP: 6 EST: 2016
SALES (est): 51.69K Privately Held
SIC: 8711 Engineering services

(G-15851)
DECORYOUCRAZY
Also Called: Ursewcrazy
220 W 35th St (19802-2613)
PHONE..............................302 357-8175
Tiaa Stanford, *Pt*
Derek Stanford, *Pt*
EMP: 10 EST: 2021
SALES (est): 386.39K Privately Held
SIC: 7389 Business services, nec

(G-15852)
DEDICTED FIBR CMMNICATIONS LLC
913 N Market St Ste 200 (19801-3097)
PHONE..............................302 416-3088
EMP: 6 EST: 2014
SALES (est): 66.62K Privately Held
SIC: 4813 Internet connectivity services

(G-15853)
DEEP MUSCLE THERAPY CENTER DEL
Also Called: Deeps On Massage
5700 Kirkwood Hwy Ste 206 (19808-4884)
PHONE..............................302 397-8073
Debbi Jedlicka, *Pr*
EMP: 6 EST: 1991
SALES (est): 191.06K Privately Held
Web: www.dmtcmassage.com
SIC: 7299 Massage parlor

(G-15854)
DEFA INC ✪
108 W 13th St (19801-1145)
PHONE..............................302 219-5994

Yongfeng Gao, *Dir*
EMP: 20 EST: 2022
SALES (est): 588.11K Privately Held
SIC: 7371 Computer software development and applications

(G-15855)
DEFENDANT DATA SOLUTIONS LLC
1007 N Orange St Fl 4 (19801-1242)
PHONE..............................302 440-3042
EMP: 5 EST: 2017
SALES (est): 95.22K Privately Held
SIC: 8742 Management consulting services

(G-15856)
DEFY TECHNOLOGIES INC
251 Little Falls Dr (19808-1674)
PHONE..............................732 213-7165
EMP: 7 EST: 2020
SALES (est): 103.88K Privately Held
SIC: 7999 Amusement and recreation, nec

(G-15857)
DEFY THERAPY SERVICES LLC
2213 Beaumont Rd (19803-3016)
PHONE..............................302 290-9562
Mary Mccormick, *Prin*
EMP: 7 EST: 2018
SALES (est): 239.39K Privately Held
Web: www.defytherapyservices.com
SIC: 8093 Rehabilitation center, outpatient treatment

(G-15858)
DEHUMIDIFICATION TECH LP
1 Limousine Dr (19803-4363)
PHONE..............................317 228-2000
EMP: 9 EST: 2018
SALES (est): 21.57K Privately Held
Web: www.rentdh.com
SIC: 8731 Commercial physical research

(G-15859)
DEL CAMPO PLUMBING & HEATING
2429 Hartley Pl (19804-4258)
PHONE..............................302 998-3648
Michael A Delcampo, *Pr*
EMP: 5 EST: 1976
SALES (est): 420K Privately Held
Web: www.delcampoplumbing.com
SIC: 1711 Plumbing contractors

(G-15860)
DEL-ONE FEDERAL CREDIT UNION
Also Called: Delaware Fedral Credit Union
824 N Market St Ste 104 (19801-4937)
PHONE..............................302 577-2667
EMP: 5
Web: www.del-one.org
SIC: 6061 Federal credit unions
PA: Del-One Federal Credit Union
270 Beiser Blvd
Dover DE 19904

(G-15861)
DELAWARE 4 SNIORS HOMECARE LLC
1000 N West St Ste 1200 (19801-1058)
PHONE..............................302 386-8080
EMP: 10 EST: 2020
SALES (est): 335.17K Privately Held
SIC: 8082 Home health care services

(G-15862)
DELAWARE ALL-STATE THEATRE
2208 Van Buren Pl (19802-3931)
PHONE..............................302 559-6667
EMP: 7 EST: 2012
SALES (est): 89.68K Privately Held
Web: www.jalexanderproductions.com

SIC: 6411 Insurance agents and brokers

(G-15863)
DELAWARE ALNCE AGNST SXUAL VLN
405 Foulk Rd (19803-3809)
PHONE..............................302 468-7731
Ariana Langford, *Prin*
Alisa Drew, *Prin*
Stephanie Hamilton, *Prin*
Javonne Rich, *Prin*
Amy Hopkins, *Prin*
EMP: 5 EST: 2019
SALES (est): 257.02K Privately Held
SIC: 8111 Legal services

(G-15864)
DELAWARE AMERICAN LF INSUR CO
600 N King St (19801-3776)
PHONE..............................302 594-2871
Michael Enwright, *COO*
EMP: 51 EST: 2017
SALES (est): 30.11MM
SALES (corp-wide): 69.9B Publicly Held
Web: www.metlife.com
SIC: 6311 Life insurance
PA: Metlife, Inc.
200 Park Ave Fl 1200
New York NY 10166
212 578-9500

(G-15865)
DELAWARE APARTMENT ASSOCIATION
240 N James St Ste 208 (19804-3171)
P.O. Box 1610 (19701-7610)
PHONE..............................617 680-3463
Michelle Garibian, *Pr*
EMP: 6 EST: 2017
SALES (est): 212.1K Privately Held
Web: www.mvzllc.com
SIC: 8699 Membership organizations, nec

(G-15866)
DELAWARE ART MUSEUM INC
2301 Kentmere Pkwy (19806-2019)
PHONE..............................302 571-9590
Danielle Rice, *Pr*
EMP: 45 EST: 1912
SQ FT: 100,000
SALES (est): 5.14MM Privately Held
Web: www.delart.org
SIC: 8412 Museum

(G-15867)
DELAWARE ASSN FOR THE EDCATN Y
2004 Foulk Rd Ste 6 (19810-3641)
PHONE..............................302 764-1500
John Rendle, *Prin*
EMP: 9 EST: 2009
SALES (est): 1.94MM Privately Held
Web: www.deaeyc.org
SIC: 8621 Professional organizations

(G-15868)
DELAWARE ASSOCIATION FOR BLIND (PA)
2915 Newport Gap Pike (19808-2376)
PHONE..............................302 998-5913
Linda S Lauria, *Dir*
Sharon Sutlic, *Prin*
Janet Berry, *Dir*
EMP: 41 EST: 1948
SALES (est): 344.75K
SALES (corp-wide): 344.75K Privately Held
Web: www.dabdel.org

SIC: 8322 Social service center

(G-15869)
DELAWARE AUTO SALVAGE INC
155 Hay Rd (19809-3508)
PHONE..............................302 322-2328
TOLL FREE: 800
Johnnie Sue Russell, *Pr*
EMP: 5 EST: 1974
SALES (est): 2.36MM Privately Held
Web: www.delawareautosalvageinc.com
SIC: 5015 5093 Automotive parts and supplies, used; Automotive wrecking for scrap

(G-15870)
DELAWARE AVE WEALTH PLANNERS
1831 Delaware Ave (19806-2357)
PHONE..............................302 254-2400
EMP: 7 EST: 2019
SALES (est): 703.28K Privately Held
Web: www.whcompany.com
SIC: 6282 Investment advice

(G-15871)
DELAWARE BD TRADE HOLDINGS INC
Also Called: Dbot
1313 N Market St Fl 8 (19801-6107)
PHONE..............................302 298-0600
John F Wallace, *CEO*
Joseph L Valenza, *CRO*
Joseph Jennings, *CFO*
Dennis J Boylan, *COO*
Thomas C Hack, *Chief Compliance Officer*
EMP: 15 EST: 2013
SQ FT: 11,000
SALES (est): 2.68MM Publicly Held
SIC: 6231 Security and commodity exchanges
PA: Ideanomics, Inc.
1441 Broadway Ste 5116
New York NY 10018

(G-15872)
DELAWARE BEHAVIORAL HEALTH
240 N James St (19804-3169)
PHONE..............................302 397-8958
Erica Lyn Benedict, *Mgr*
EMP: 9 EST: 2014
SALES (est): 239.08K Privately Held
Web: www.delawarebehavioralhealth.org
SIC: 8049 8031 8011 Speech specialist; Offices and clinics of osteopathic physicians ; Offices and clinics of medical doctors

(G-15873)
DELAWARE BIOSCIENCE ASSN
2110 Concord Pike (19803-3609)
PHONE..............................302 635-0445
EMP: 7 EST: 2019
SALES (est): 204.51K Privately Held
Web: www.delawarebio.org
SIC: 8699 Membership organizations, nec

(G-15874)
DELAWARE BOOTS ON GROUND
P.O. Box 5894 (19808-0894)
PHONE..............................302 326-7789
EMP: 5 EST: 2011
SALES (est): 72.73K Privately Held
Web: www.debotg.org
SIC: 8699 Charitable organization

(G-15875)
DELAWARE BRAST CNCER CLTION IN (PA)
100 W 10th St Ste 209 (19801-1641)
PHONE..............................302 778-1102

Wilmington - New Castle County (G-15876)   GEOGRAPHIC SECTION

Victoria Cooke, *Ex Dir*
Victoria Cooke, *Dir*
EMP: 9 **EST:** 1991
SALES (est): 504.93K **Privately Held**
Web: www.debreastcancer.org
SIC: 8322 Social service center

(G-15876)
DELAWARE BRICK COMPANY (PA)
Also Called: Delaware Brick Co
1114 Centerville Rd (19804-2097)
PHONE.............................302 994-0948
Margaret Hinton, *Pr*
Frank Schauber, *
Charles Schauber, *
Sean C Callaghan, *
Kenneth B Barnes Junior, *Prin*
EMP: 26 **EST:** 1946
SQ FT: 3,500
SALES (est): 10.59MM
SALES (corp-wide): 10.59MM **Privately Held**
Web: www.delawarebrick.com
SIC: 5211 5032 Brick; Brick, except refractory

(G-15877)
DELAWARE BUS INCORPORATORS INC
3422 Old Capitol Trl Ste 700 (19808-6124)
P.O. Box 5722 (19808-0722)
PHONE.............................302 996-5819
Douglas Murray, *Pr*
EMP: 5 **EST:** 1986
SQ FT: 3,000
SALES (est): 1.09MM **Privately Held**
Web: www.delawarebusinessincorporators.com
SIC: 8111 Specialized legal services

(G-15878)
DELAWARE CAPITAL FORMATION INC (HQ)
501 Silverside Rd Ste 5 (19809-1375)
PHONE.............................302 793-4921
Alfred Suesser, *VP*
Jeremiah Mulligan, *VP*
Lloyd Martin, *VP*
Robert Whoriskey, *Asst Tr*
EMP: 7 **EST:** 1985
SALES (est): 1.04B
SALES (corp-wide): 8.51B **Publicly Held**
Web: www.doversourcing.com
SIC: 5084 3463 3542 3823 Food product manufacturing machinery; Bearing and bearing race forgings, nonferrous; Machine tools, metal forming type; Flow instruments, industrial process type
PA: Dover Corporation
3005 Highland Pkwy # 200
Downers Grove IL 60515
630 541-1540

(G-15879)
DELAWARE CAPITAL HOLDINGS INC (DH)
501 Silverside Rd Ste 5 (19809-1375)
PHONE.............................302 793-4921
John F Mc Niff, *Pr*
Robert Kuhbach, *Sec*
Alfred Suesser, *VP*
◆ **EMP:** 6 **EST:** 1985
SALES (est): 1.04B
SALES (corp-wide): 8.51B **Publicly Held**
SIC: 5084 3533 7699 Food product manufacturing machinery; Oil field machinery and equipment; Elevators: inspection, service, and repair
HQ: Delaware Capital Formation, Inc.
501 Silverside Rd Ste 5
Wilmington DE 19809
302 793-4921

(G-15880)
DELAWARE CAR COMPANY
Second & Lombard St (19801)
P.O. Box 233 (19899-0233)
PHONE.............................302 655-6665
Harry E Hill, *Mng Pt*
Thomas J Crowley, *Genl Pt*
EMP: 50 **EST:** 1983
SQ FT: 133,000
SALES (est): 7.97MM **Privately Held**
Web: www.delawarecarcompany.com
SIC: 4789 3743 Railroad car repair; Railroad equipment

(G-15881)
DELAWARE CARE COLLABORATION
701 N Clayton St (19805-3165)
PHONE.............................302 575-8371
EMP: 12 **EST:** 2017
SALES (est): 397.67K **Privately Held**
Web: www.trinityhealthma.org
SIC: 8099 Health and allied services, nec

(G-15882)
DELAWARE CENTER FOR JUSTICE
100 W 10th St Ste 905 (19801-6605)
PHONE.............................302 658-7174
Janet A Leban, *Ex Dir*
EMP: 38 **EST:** 1920
SALES (est): 2.07MM **Privately Held**
Web: www.dcjustice.org
SIC: 8399 Community development groups

(G-15883)
DELAWARE CHEMICAL CORPORATION
1105 N Market St Ste 1300 (19801-1241)
P.O. Box 8985 (19899-8985)
PHONE.............................302 427-8752
Edward J Jones, *Pr*
Mary Irons, *VP*
EMP: 31 **EST:** 1971
SALES (est): 1.26MM
SALES (corp-wide): 125.67MM **Privately Held**
SIC: 2819 Industrial inorganic chemicals, nec
PA: Arkema
420 Rue D Estienne D Orves
Colombes 92700
149008080

(G-15884)
DELAWARE CLAIMS PROC FCILTY
1007 N Orange St Fl 1 (19801-1239)
PHONE.............................302 427-8913
John Mekus, *Ex Dir*
EMP: 79 **EST:** 1998
SALES (est): 9.73MM **Privately Held**
Web: www.delcpf.com
SIC: 6733 Trusts, nec

(G-15885)
DELAWARE CLTION AGNST DOM VLNC
100 W 10th St Ste 903 (19801-6605)
PHONE.............................302 658-2958
Carol Post, *Dir*
EMP: 6 **EST:** 1994
SALES (est): 1.98MM **Privately Held**
Web: www.dcadv.org
SIC: 8322 Social service center

(G-15886)
DELAWARE CMNTY RNVSTMENT ACTIO
600 S Harrison St (19805-4306)
PHONE.............................302 298-3250
Rashmi Rangan, *Mgr*
Carol Davis, *Ch Bd*
EMP: 7 **EST:** 1987
SALES (est): 1.42MM **Privately Held**
Web: www.dcrac.org
SIC: 8611 8699 Business associations; Charitable organization

(G-15887)
DELAWARE COLLEGE SCHOLARS INC
4 E 8th St (19801-3553)
P.O. Box 392 (19899-0392)
PHONE.............................302 437-6144
EMP: 10 **EST:** 2018
SALES (est): 1.08MM **Privately Held**
Web: www.delawarecollegescholars.com
SIC: 8641 Civic and social associations

(G-15888)
DELAWARE COLON HYDROTHERAPY
6 Larch Ave (19804-2300)
PHONE.............................302 543-5717
Cheryl Tyler, *Prin*
EMP: 7 **EST:** 2017
SALES (est): 115.42K **Privately Held**
SIC: 8099 Health and allied services, nec

(G-15889)
DELAWARE COLOR LAB
Also Called: Foschi Fine Photography
2107 Naamans Rd (19810-1326)
PHONE.............................302 529-1339
Rudy Foschi, *Pt*
Ted Foschi, *Pt*
EMP: 7 **EST:** 1982
SALES (est): 372.13K **Privately Held**
Web: www.photographybyfoschi.com
SIC: 7221 Photographer, still or video

(G-15890)
DELAWARE COMMUNITY FOUNDATION (PA)
100 W 10th St Ste 115 (19801-1660)
PHONE.............................302 571-8004
Fred Spears, *Pr*
EMP: 9 **EST:** 1986
SALES (est): 24.02MM **Privately Held**
Web: www.delcf.org
SIC: 6732 8733 Charitable trust management; Noncommercial research organizations

(G-15891)
DELAWARE COMMUNITY INV CORP
100 W 10th St Ste 303 (19801-1642)
PHONE.............................302 655-1420
Doris Schnider, *Pr*
Dee Johnson, *CFO*
Christina Stanley, *VP*
EMP: 6 **EST:** 1993
SALES (est): 1.09MM **Privately Held**
SIC: 6162 Mortgage bankers and loan correspondents

(G-15892)
DELAWARE CORPORATE CENTER
2 Righter Pkwy (19803-1532)
PHONE.............................302 690-3789
EMP: 5 **EST:** 2017
SALES (est): 190.72K **Privately Held**
SIC: 6512 Commercial and industrial building operation

(G-15893)
DELAWARE CORPORATE REGISTRY
15 Center Meeting Rd (19807-1301)
PHONE.............................302 655-6500
EMP: 5 **EST:** 2018
SALES (est): 121.57K **Privately Held**
Web: www.delawarecorporateregistry.com
SIC: 8111 Legal services

(G-15894)
DELAWARE COUNSEL GROUP LLP (PA)
Also Called: Decg
2 Mill Rd Ste 108 (19806-2175)
P.O. Box 348 (19732-0348)
PHONE.............................302 576-9600
Ellisa Opstbaum Habbart, *Pt*
EMP: 8 **EST:** 2004
SALES (est): 944.36K
SALES (corp-wide): 944.36K **Privately Held**
Web: www.delawarecounselgroup.com
SIC: 8111 General practice law office

(G-15895)
DELAWARE CTR FOR CNTMPRARY ART
Also Called: DCCA
200 S Madison St (19801-5110)
PHONE.............................302 656-6466
Jay Miller, *Pr*
EMP: 17 **EST:** 1979
SALES (est): 858.69K **Privately Held**
Web: www.decontemporary.org
SIC: 8412 Museum

(G-15896)
DELAWARE CTR FOR HMLESS VTRANS
Also Called: Dchv
10 Birch Knoll Rd (19810-1302)
PHONE.............................302 384-2350
David Mosley, *Pr*
EMP: 35 **EST:** 2010
SALES (est): 701.15K **Privately Held**
Web: www.dchv.org
SIC: 8322 Social service center

(G-15897)
DELAWARE CTR FOR HMLESS VTRANS
1405 Veale Rd (19810-4331)
PHONE.............................302 898-2647
EMP: 9 **EST:** 2011
SALES (est): 396.61K **Privately Held**
Web: www.dchv.org
SIC: 8322 Social service center

(G-15898)
DELAWARE CTR FOR HRTCLTURE INC
Also Called: DCH
1810 N Dupont St (19806-3308)
PHONE.............................302 658-6262
Pamela Sapko, *Ex Dir*
Pamela Sapko, *Pr*
EMP: 25 **EST:** 1977
SQ FT: 12,000
SALES (est): 1.31MM **Privately Held**
Web: www.thedch.org
SIC: 8699 Personal interest organization

(G-15899)
DELAWARE CURATIVE WORKSHOP (PA)
Also Called: Delaware Curative
1600 N Washington St (19802-4722)
P.O. Box 4453 (19807-0453)
PHONE.............................302 656-2521
Mike Walls, *Dir*
EMP: 88 **EST:** 1944
SQ FT: 40,000
SALES (est): 360.82K
SALES (corp-wide): 360.82K **Privately Held**
SIC: 8093 8049 Rehabilitation center, outpatient treatment; Physical therapist

GEOGRAPHIC SECTION
Wilmington - New Castle County (G-15926)

(G-15900)
DELAWARE DANCE CENTER INC
4751 Shopp Of Lindenhill Rd (19808)
PHONE.................302 454-1440
Jane Griffin, *Pr*
EMP: 9 **EST:** 1975
SALES (est): 151.15K **Privately Held**
Web: www.delawaredancecenter.com
SIC: 7911 Dance studio and school

(G-15901)
DELAWARE DENTAL STUDIO LLC
2500 Grubb Rd (19810-4799)
PHONE.................302 475-0600
EMP: 9 **EST:** 2018
SALES (est): 474.02K **Privately Held**
Web: www.delawaredentalstudio.com
SIC: 8021 Dentists' office

(G-15902)
DELAWARE DEPARTMENT TRNSP
Also Called: Delaware Transit
119 Lower Beech St Ste 100 (19805)
PHONE.................302 658-8960
EMP: 5
SALES (corp-wide): 11.27B **Privately Held**
Web: www.deldot.gov
SIC: 4141 9621 Local bus charter service; Regulation, administration of transportation
HQ: Delaware Department Of Transportation
800 S Bay Rd Ste 1
Dover DE 19901

(G-15903)
DELAWARE DEPOSITORY SVC CO LLC
3601 N Market St (19802-2736)
PHONE.................302 762-2635
EMP: 8 **EST:** 1999
SQ FT: 20,000
SALES (est): 3.5MM
SALES (corp-wide): 10.54MM **Privately Held**
Web: www.delawaredepository.com
SIC: 6099 Safe deposit companies
PA: Fidelitrade Incorporated
3601 N Market St
Wilmington DE 19802
302 762-6200

(G-15904)
DELAWARE DERMATOLOGIC
14 Alders Ln (19807-3050)
PHONE.................302 593-8625
Ben Bansal, *Prin*
EMP: 8 **EST:** 2008
SALES (est): 129.88K **Privately Held**
SIC: 2834 Dermatologicals

(G-15905)
DELAWARE DIAGNOSTIC GROUP LLC
2060 Limestone Rd (19808-5500)
PHONE.................302 472-5555
Muhammad Haq, *Prin*
EMP: 10 **EST:** 2010
SALES (est): 163.7K **Privately Held**
Web: www.radnet.com
SIC: 8011 Radiologist

(G-15906)
DELAWARE DIAMOND KNIVES INC
3825 Lancaster Pike Ste 200 (19805-1559)
PHONE.................302 999-7476
Joseph Tabeling, *Pr*
Linda Tabeling, *
EMP: 25 **EST:** 1984
SALES (est): 3.69MM **Privately Held**
Web: www.ddk.com
SIC: 3421 Knife blades and blanks

(G-15907)
DELAWARE DIGITAL VIDEO FACC
1709 Concord Pike (19803-3603)
PHONE.................302 888-2737
Henry Black, *Prin*
EMP: 5 **EST:** 2007
SALES (est): 96.63K **Privately Held**
Web: www.ddvf.com
SIC: 7812 Video production

(G-15908)
DELAWARE DIRECT INC
220 Valley Rd (19804-1312)
PHONE.................302 658-8223
Jeffrey Gooding, *Pr*
EMP: 7 **EST:** 1990
SQ FT: 7,600
SALES (est): 973.3K **Privately Held**
Web: www.dedirect.net
SIC: 4226 Special warehousing and storage, nec

(G-15909)
DELAWARE DIV PARKS RECREATION
Also Called: Brandywine Zoo
1001 N Park Dr (19802-3801)
PHONE.................302 571-7788
Nancy Falasco, *Dir*
EMP: 10
SALES (corp-wide): 11.27B **Privately Held**
Web: www.destateparks.com
SIC: 7999 9512 Zoological garden, commercial; Land, mineral, and wildlife conservation
HQ: Delaware Division Of Parks & Recreation
89 Kings Hwy
Dover DE 19901
302 739-9220

(G-15910)
DELAWARE DIV PARKS RECREATION
Also Called: Bellevue State Park
800 Carr Rd (19809-2163)
PHONE.................302 761-6963
Paul Nicholson, *Supervisor*
EMP: 14
SALES (corp-wide): 11.27B **Privately Held**
Web: www.destateparks.com
SIC: 8611 9512 Business associations; Land, mineral, and wildlife conservation
HQ: Delaware Division Of Parks & Recreation
89 Kings Hwy
Dover DE 19901
302 739-9220

(G-15911)
DELAWARE DNCE EDCATN ORGNZTION
208 Oakwood Rd (19803-3133)
PHONE.................302 897-6245
Lynnette Overby, *Pr*
Kim Schroeder, *VP*
Theresa Emmons, *Ofcr*
At Moffett, *Sec*
Marion Hammermesh, *Treas*
EMP: 8 **EST:** 2018
SALES (est): 102.41K **Privately Held**
SIC: 8641 Civic and social associations

(G-15912)
DELAWARE ECUMENICAL COUNCIL
2629 W 19th St (19806-1116)
PHONE.................302 225-1040
EMP: 9 **EST:** 1987
SALES (est): 188.58K **Privately Held**
Web: www.deccf.org
SIC: 8322 Social service center

(G-15913)
DELAWARE ELDER LAW CENTER
3711 Kennett Pike (19807-2155)
PHONE.................302 300-4390
EMP: 5 **EST:** 2018
SALES (est): 211.29K **Privately Held**
Web: www.delawareelderlawcenter.com
SIC: 8111 General practice law office

(G-15914)
DELAWARE EQUITY FUND IV
Also Called: Cynwyd Club Apartments
100 W 10th St Ste 303 (19801-1642)
PHONE.................302 655-1420
Doris Schnider, *Pt*
EMP: 6 **EST:** 2000
SALES (est): 462.73K **Privately Held**
SIC: 6513 Apartment building operators

(G-15915)
DELAWARE EXPRESS GAR DOOR SVC
56 Lakeview Ct (19810-1909)
PHONE.................302 562-5080
EMP: 5 **EST:** 2018
SALES (est): 200.52K **Privately Held**
Web: www.degaragedoors.com
SIC: 1751 Garage door, installation or erection

(G-15916)
DELAWARE EYE SURGEONS
2710 Centerville Rd Ste 102 (19808-1652)
PHONE.................302 956-0285
S Gregory Smith Md, *Owner*
Amanda Fichter D.o.s., *Prin*
EMP: 8 **EST:** 1984
SALES (est): 758.66K **Privately Held**
Web: www.deeyesurgeons.com
SIC: 8011 Opthalmologist

(G-15917)
DELAWARE FAMILY VOICES INC
Also Called: FAMILY TO FAMILY
3301 Englewood Rd (19810-3323)
PHONE.................302 588-4908
EMP: 10 **EST:** 2010
SALES (est): 470.59K **Privately Held**
Web: www.delawarefamilytofamily.org
SIC: 8748 Urban planning and consulting services

(G-15918)
DELAWARE FAMILY VOICES INC
222 Philadelphia Pike Ste 11 (19809-3166)
PHONE.................302 669-3030
Ann Phillips, *Prin*
EMP: 6 **EST:** 2016
SALES (est): 159.25K **Privately Held**
Web: www.delawarefamilytofamily.org
SIC: 8322 Social service center

(G-15919)
DELAWARE FIRST FEDERAL CR UN (PA)
1815 Newport Gap Pike Ste A (19808)
PHONE.................302 998-0665
Sharon Shaper, *Pr*
James Brown, *Treas*
Michael Matweychuk, *Corporate Secretary*
EMP: 10 **EST:** 1962
SQ FT: 3,000
SALES (est): 670.05K
SALES (corp-wide): 670.05K **Privately Held**
Web: www.cpwrfcu.org
SIC: 6061 6163 Federal credit unions; Loan brokers

(G-15920)
DELAWARE FOSTER CARE
2003 N Jefferson St Fl 1 (19802-4015)
PHONE.................302 656-2655
EMP: 6 **EST:** 2010
SALES (est): 46.24K **Privately Held**
Web: www.delawarefostercareresources.org
SIC: 8099 Health and allied services, nec

(G-15921)
DELAWARE GDNCE SVCS FOR CHLDRE (PA)
1213 Delaware Ave (19806-4707)
PHONE.................302 652-3948
Steve Walczak, *Pr*
Bruce Kelsey, *Ex Dir*
Robert Miller, *Dir*
EMP: 15 **EST:** 1952
SALES (est): 7.01MM
SALES (corp-wide): 7.01MM **Privately Held**
Web: www.delawareguidance.org
SIC: 8322 Family counseling services

(G-15922)
DELAWARE HARDSCAPE SUPPLY LLC
401 B And O Ln (19804-1450)
PHONE.................302 996-6464
EMP: 6 **EST:** 2020
SALES (est): 227.17K **Privately Held**
Web: www.dehardscapesupply.com
SIC: 0781 Landscape services

(G-15923)
DELAWARE HARDSCAPE SUPPLY LLC
4701 B And O Ln (19804)
PHONE.................302 996-6464
EMP: 6 **EST:** 2011
SALES (est): 574.64K **Privately Held**
Web: www.dehardscapesupply.com
SIC: 5261 5083 Lawn and garden equipment; Landscaping equipment

(G-15924)
DELAWARE HEALTH CORP
2801 W 6th St (19805-1828)
PHONE.................302 655-0955
Karen Litwa, *Contrlr*
EMP: 30 **EST:** 2010
SALES (est): 421.77K **Privately Held**
Web: www.delaware.gov
SIC: 8099 Health and allied services, nec

(G-15925)
DELAWARE HEALTH NET INC
601 New Castle Ave (19801-5821)
PHONE.................410 788-9715
Craig Law, *CEO*
EMP: 6 **EST:** 2008
SALES (est): 837.87K **Privately Held**
Web: www.delawarehealth.net
SIC: 8099 Medical services organization

(G-15926)
DELAWARE HISTORY MUSEUM
504 N Market St (19801-3005)
PHONE.................302 656-0637
EMP: 8 **EST:** 2019
SALES (est): 34.3K **Privately Held**
Web: www.hsd.org
SIC: 8412 Museum

Wilmington - New Castle County (G-15927)

GEOGRAPHIC SECTION

(G-15927)
DELAWARE HIV SERVICES INC
100 W 10th St Ste 415 (19801-1643)
PHONE....................302 654-5471
Peter Houle, *Dir*
Robert Raup, *Contrlr*
EMP: 42 EST: 1994
SQ FT: 3,000
SALES (est): 3.84MM **Privately Held**
Web: www.delawarehiv.org
SIC: 8322 Social service center

(G-15928)
DELAWARE HMANITIES COUNCIL INC
Also Called: DELAWARE HUMANITIES
100 W 10th St Ste 509 (19801-6612)
PHONE....................302 657-0650
Michele Anstine, *Ex Dir*
EMP: 5 EST: 1976
SALES (est): 911.67K **Privately Held**
Web: www.dehumanities.org
SIC: 8399 Council for social agency

(G-15929)
DELAWARE HOMES PERFORMANCE
1603 Jessup St Ste 4 (19802-4255)
PHONE....................302 233-3917
Mike Roth, *Pr*
EMP: 5 EST: 2017
SALES (est): 45.36K **Privately Held**
SIC: 8611 Business associations

(G-15930)
DELAWARE INCORPORATION SVCS
704 N King St Ste 500 (19801-3584)
P.O. Box 1031 (19899-1031)
PHONE....................302 658-1733
Paul Cotrell, *Pr*
EMP: 10 EST: 1998
SALES (est): 620.32K **Privately Held**
Web: www.delaware-incorporation.com
SIC: 8742 Financial consultant

(G-15931)
DELAWARE INJURY ASSOCIATES PA
707 Foulk Rd Ste 102 (19803-3737)
PHONE....................302 332-1932
Kurt Ross, *Pr*
EMP: 10 EST: 2013
SALES (est): 164.79K **Privately Held**
Web: www.whenyourehurtcallkurt.com
SIC: 8041 Offices and clinics of chiropractors

(G-15932)
DELAWARE INJURY CARE
4023 Kennett Pike (19807-2018)
PHONE....................914 960-1145
Edwin Juste, *Prin*
EMP: 5 EST: 2019
SALES (est): 234.99K **Privately Held**
Web: www.delawareinjurycare.org
SIC: 8041 Offices and clinics of chiropractors

(G-15933)
DELAWARE INNOVATION SPACE INC
200 Powder Mill Rd E500 (19803-2907)
PHONE....................302 695-2201
William Provine, *CEO*
Charles Riordan, *Ch Bd*
Jeff Bullock, *Treas*
Alexa Dembek, *Sec*
EMP: 8 EST: 2017
SQ FT: 100,000
SALES (est): 6.03MM **Privately Held**
Web: www.innovationspace.org
SIC: 8748 7389 8741 8731 Business consulting, nec; Management services; Biological research

(G-15934)
DELAWARE INTERCORP INC
3511 Silverside Rd Ste 105 (19810-4902)
PHONE....................302 266-9367
Russell P Rozanski, *Pr*
EMP: 8 EST: 1996
SQ FT: 2,500
SALES (est): 1.31MM **Privately Held**
Web: www.wolterskluwer.com
SIC: 8742 Corporation organizing consultant

(G-15935)
DELAWARE KIDS DENTAL CENTER
708 Foulk Rd (19803-3734)
PHONE....................302 764-7714
EMP: 8 EST: 2019
SALES (est): 125.93K **Privately Held**
SIC: 8021 Dentists' office

(G-15936)
DELAWARE LABOR RESOURCES INC
6 Coffee Run Ln (19808-1510)
PHONE....................302 377-5752
Kristen Lantz, *Prin*
EMP: 6 EST: 2019
SALES (est): 232.19K **Privately Held**
Web: www.delaborresources.com
SIC: 8742 Business planning and organizing services

(G-15937)
DELAWARE LACROSSE FOUNDATION
P.O. Box 5066 (19808-0066)
PHONE....................302 831-8661
Robert F Shillinglaw, *Pr*
EMP: 5 EST: 1993
SQ FT: 2,207
SALES (est): 14.87K **Privately Held**
SIC: 8699 7997 Charitable organization; Membership sports and recreation clubs

(G-15938)
DELAWARE LAWN CREW LLC
1001 Garasches Ln (19801-5534)
PHONE....................302 368-3344
EMP: 5 EST: 2019
SALES (est): 456.75K **Privately Held**
Web: www.delawarelawncrew.com
SIC: 0782 Lawn care services

(G-15939)
DELAWARE MARKETING PARTNERS
Also Called: Delaware Marketing Group
3801 Kennett Pike Ste D301 (19807-2328)
PHONE....................302 575-1610
Kenneth Scott, *Pr*
Susan Hanway Scott, *VP*
EMP: 7 EST: 1993
SQ FT: 1,000
SALES (est): 1.84MM **Privately Held**
Web: www.dmgdmg.com
SIC: 8742 Financial consultant

(G-15940)
DELAWARE MATERIAL RECOVERY & R
1000 S Heald St (19801-5735)
PHONE....................302 652-3150
EMP: 11 EST: 2015
SALES (est): 37.76K **Privately Held**
SIC: 4953 Recycling, waste materials

(G-15941)
DELAWARE MEAT COMPANY LLC
Also Called: Lab
28 Brookside Dr (19804-1102)
PHONE....................302 438-0252
Terri Sorantino, *Managing Member*
EMP: 2 EST: 2015
SALES (est): 80.06K **Privately Held**
Web: www.liquidalchemybeverages.com
SIC: 2084 Wines

(G-15942)
DELAWARE MEDICAL ASSOCIATES PA
Also Called: Dr. Armand Neal Dsanctis Jr MD
2101 Foulk Rd Ste 2 (19810-4710)
PHONE....................302 475-2535
Armand N Desanctis, *Prin*
EMP: 18 EST: 2009
SALES (est): 932.03K **Privately Held**
SIC: 8011 Orthopedic physician

(G-15943)
DELAWARE MEDICAL CARE INC
Also Called: Delaware Family Care Assoc
2700 Silverside Rd Ste 2 (19810-3724)
PHONE....................302 225-6868
Nancy Chambers, *Mgr*
EMP: 24 EST: 1977
SQ FT: 32,000
SALES (est): 4.76MM **Privately Held**
Web: www.delawarefamilycare.com
SIC: 8011 General and family practice, physician/surgeon

(G-15944)
DELAWARE MERCHANT SERVICES
Also Called: Metro Merchant Services
510 Century Blvd (19808-6272)
PHONE....................302 838-9100
Mark S Landis, *Pr*
Karen Landis, *VP*
EMP: 6 EST: 1998
SALES (est): 1.56MM **Privately Held**
Web: www.metropaytech.com
SIC: 7389 Credit card service

(G-15945)
DELAWARE MOTOR SALES INC (PA)
Also Called: Autoteam Delaware
1606 Pennsylvania Ave (19806-4089)
PHONE....................302 656-3100
Michael Uffner, *Pr*
Marilyn Uffner, *
EMP: 65 EST: 1982
SQ FT: 39,000
SALES (est): 48.76MM
SALES (corp-wide): 48.76MM **Privately Held**
Web: www.delawarecadillac.com
SIC: 5511 7515 Automobiles, new and used; Passenger car leasing

(G-15946)
DELAWARE MSEUM NTRAL HSTORY IN
4840 Kennett Pike (19807-1827)
P.O. Box 3937 (19807-0937)
PHONE....................302 658-9111
W Halsey Spruance, *
William D Zantzinger, *
Gregory A Inskip, *
John J Kirby, *
Kurt M Heyman, *
EMP: 26 EST: 1957
SQ FT: 66,000
SALES (est): 2.53MM **Privately Held**
Web: www.delmns.org
SIC: 8412 Museum

(G-15947)
DELAWARE OFFICES LLC (PA)
4828 Kennett Pike (19807-1814)
PHONE....................302 295-1215
EMP: 5 EST: 2009
SALES (est): 483.19K
SALES (corp-wide): 483.19K **Privately Held**
Web: www.delawareoffices.com
SIC: 8111 General practice law office

(G-15948)
DELAWARE OFFICES LLC
219 W 9th St Ste 200 (19801-1619)
PHONE....................302 295-1214
EMP: 6
SALES (corp-wide): 483.19K **Privately Held**
Web: www.delawareoffices.com
SIC: 8111 General practice law office
PA: Delaware Offices Llc
4828 Kennett Pike
Wilmington DE 19807
302 295-1215

(G-15949)
DELAWARE OPHTHALMOLOGY CONS PA (PA)
Also Called: Delaware Ophthalmology Cons
3501 Silverside Rd (19810-4910)
PHONE....................302 479-3937
Robert Abel Junior Md, *Pr*
Edward F Becker Md, *VP*
Harry A Lebowitz Md, *VP*
Gordon A Bussard Md, *VP*
EMP: 50 EST: 1977
SQ FT: 12,086
SALES (est): 9.49MM
SALES (corp-wide): 9.49MM **Privately Held**
Web: www.delawareeyes.com
SIC: 8011 Opthalmologist

(G-15950)
DELAWARE ORCHID SOCIETY
9 Carriage Rd (19807-2237)
PHONE....................302 654-8883
EMP: 6 EST: 2013
SALES (est): 51.43K **Privately Held**
Web: www.delawareorchidsociety.com
SIC: 8412 Historical society

(G-15951)
DELAWARE ORTHOPAEDIC SPECIALIS
1941 Limestone Rd Ste 101 (19808-5413)
PHONE....................302 633-3555
Joshua D Vaught, *Prin*
EMP: 55 EST: 2010
SALES (est): 16.89MM **Privately Held**
Web: www.delortho.com
SIC: 8011 Orthopedic physician

(G-15952)
DELAWARE PARK RACING LLC
777 Delaware Park Blvd (19804-4122)
PHONE....................302 994-6700
James Hashimoto, *Prin*
EMP: 12 EST: 2005
SALES (est): 175.86K **Privately Held**
Web: www.delawarepark.com
SIC: 7992 Public golf courses

(G-15953)
DELAWARE PERIODONTICS
1110 N Bancroft Pkwy Ste 1 (19805-2669)
PHONE....................302 658-7871
Bradford Klassman, *Prin*
Bradford L Klassman, *Prin*
EMP: 7 EST: 2011
SALES (est): 707.51K **Privately Held**
Web: www.delawareperiodontics.com
SIC: 8021 Periodontist

Wilmington - New Castle County (G-15980)

(G-15954)
DELAWARE PROFESSIONAL SQUASH
4825 Kennett Pike (19807-1813)
PHONE.................................302 655-6171
EMP: 5 EST: 2019
SALES (est): 49.38K Privately Held
Web: delaware.ussquash.com
SIC: 7941 Professional and semi-professional sports clubs

(G-15955)
DELAWARE PSYCHIATRY LLC
5700 Kirkwood Hwy (19808-4857)
PHONE.................................302 397-8516
Nana Berkashvilli, Owner
EMP: 9 EST: 2016
SALES (est): 238.59K Privately Held
Web: www.delawarepsychllc.com
SIC: 8011 Psychiatrist

(G-15956)
DELAWARE RACING ASSOCIATION (PA)
Also Called: Delaware Park
777 Delaware Park Blvd (19804-4122)
PHONE.................................302 994-2521
William M Rickman Junior, CEO
William Fasy, *
▲ EMP: 1000 EST: 1937
SQ FT: 580,000
SALES (est): 53.41MM
SALES (corp-wide): 53.41MM Privately Held
Web: www.delawarepark.com
SIC: 7948 7993 Horse race track operation; Slot machine

(G-15957)
DELAWARE RE ADVISORS LLC
Also Called: Integra Realty Resources
1013 Centre Rd Ste 201 (19805-1265)
PHONE.................................302 998-4030
EMP: 5 EST: 2006
SALES (est): 390.16K Privately Held
Web: www.derealestategirl.com
SIC: 6531 Real estate agent, commercial

(G-15958)
DELAWARE RE ANSWERS LLC
Also Called: Fine Remodeling
2516 W 3rd St (19805-3305)
PHONE.................................302 635-0375
EMP: 5 EST: 2011
SALES (est): 528.89K Privately Held
Web: www.derealestateanswers.com
SIC: 1521 General remodeling, single-family houses

(G-15959)
DELAWARE REGISTRY LTD
3511 Silverside Rd Ste 105 (19810-4902)
PHONE.................................302 477-9800
EMP: 8 EST: 1982
SALES (est): 1.88MM
SALES (corp-wide): 44.28MM Privately Held
Web: www.wolterskluwer.com
SIC: 7361 Registries
HQ: Yacht Delaware Registry, Ltd
3511 Silverside Rd # 105
Wilmington DE 19810
302 477-9800

(G-15960)
DELAWARE RETIRED SCHL PRSNL
100 Galewood Ct (19803-3977)
P.O. Box 7262 (19803-0262)
PHONE.................................302 674-8252
Everett Toomey, Pr

Wayne Emsley, Ex Dir
EMP: 20 EST: 1998
SALES (est): 134.15K Privately Held
Web: www.drspa.org
SIC: 8641 7389 Civic and social associations; Business Activities at Non-Commercial Site

(G-15961)
DELAWARE RIDERS BASBAL CLB INC
2214 Nassau Dr (19810-2831)
PHONE.................................302 475-1915
EMP: 6 EST: 2010
SALES (est): 61.43K Privately Held
SIC: 7997 Membership sports and recreation clubs

(G-15962)
DELAWARE RIVER STEVEDORES INC
1 Hausel Rd Ste 115 (19801-5876)
PHONE.................................302 657-0472
Robert Palaima, Pr
EMP: 9
SALES (corp-wide): 12.77MM Privately Held
Web: www.d-r-s.com
SIC: 4491 Stevedoring
PA: Delaware River Stevedores Inc
2 International Plz # 635
Philadelphia PA 19113
215 440-4100

(G-15963)
DELAWARE RUG CO INC
5 Forrest Ave (19805-5016)
PHONE.................................302 998-8881
Nick Michael, Pr
Maria V Michael, VP
EMP: 5 EST: 1951
SQ FT: 5,000
SALES (est): 602.78K Privately Held
Web: www.delawarerugcompany.com
SIC: 5713 7217 Carpets; Carpet and furniture cleaning on location

(G-15964)
DELAWARE SCHOOL NUTRITION ASSN
4 Mount Lebanon Rd (19803-1714)
PHONE.................................302 323-2743
Melissa Sayers, Pr
EMP: 5 EST: 2017
SALES (est): 85.52K Privately Held
Web: www.deschoolnutrition.org
SIC: 8699 Membership organizations, nec

(G-15965)
DELAWARE SEAMSTRESS
2413 W 2nd St (19805-3316)
PHONE.................................302 286-8210
Diana Klenk, Prin
EMP: 5 EST: 2016
SALES (est): 18.27K Privately Held
SIC: 7219 Seamstress

(G-15966)
DELAWARE SOLID WASTE AUTHORITY
Also Called: Cherry Island Landfill
1706 E 12th St (19809-3562)
PHONE.................................302 764-2732
Robin Roddie, Mgr
EMP: 5
SALES (corp-wide): 47.22MM Privately Held
Web: www.dswa.org
SIC: 4953 Sanitary landfill operation
PA: Delaware Solid Waste Authority

1128 S Bradford St
Dover DE 19904
302 739-5361

(G-15967)
DELAWARE SPORTS LEAGUE INC
4 E 8th St Ste 300a (19801-3559)
PHONE.................................302 654-8787
Robert Downing, Prin
EMP: 11 EST: 2016
SALES (est): 66.31K Privately Held
Web: www.heydayathletic.com
SIC: 7997 Membership sports and recreation clubs

(G-15968)
DELAWARE STAR DENTAL
5507 Kirkwood Hwy (19808-5001)
PHONE.................................302 994-3093
Syed Shetar, Pr
EMP: 11 EST: 2016
SALES (est): 323.41K Privately Held
Web: www.delawarestardental.com
SIC: 8021 Offices and clinics of dentists

(G-15969)
DELAWARE STATE AFLCIO
3304 Old Capitol Trl (19808-6902)
PHONE.................................302 256-0310
EMP: 6 EST: 2017
SALES (est): 150.94K Privately Held
Web: www.council81.org
SIC: 8631 Labor union

(G-15970)
DELAWARE STATE BAR ASSOCIATION
405 N King St Ste 100 (19801-3700)
PHONE.................................302 658-5279
Rina Marks, Ex Dir
EMP: 6 EST: 1923
SALES (est): 2MM Privately Held
Web: www.dsba.org
SIC: 8621 Bar association

(G-15971)
DELAWARE STATE CHMBER CMMRCE I
Also Called: DELAWARE STATE CHAMBER OF COMM
1201 N Orange St Ste 200 (19801-1167)
P.O. Box 671 (19899-0671)
PHONE.................................302 655-7221
Joan Verplanck, Pr
Jeanne Mell, Ex VP
A Richard Heffron, Sr VP
Marianae Antonini, Sr VP
James Wolfe, Pr
EMP: 15 EST: 1836
SALES (est): 1.76MM Privately Held
Web: www.dscc.com
SIC: 8611 Chamber of Commerce

(G-15972)
DELAWARE STATE GRANGE INC
4201 Limestone Rd (19808-2008)
PHONE.................................302 994-0295
Barbara Narvel, Prin
EMP: 6 EST: 2011
SALES (est): 80.13K Privately Held
SIC: 8641 Fraternal associations

(G-15973)
DELAWARE SURGICAL GROUP PA (PA)
1941 Limestone Rd Ste 213 (19808-5434)
PHONE.................................302 892-2100
Michael K Conway Md, Pr
EMP: 6 EST: 1995
SALES (est): 1.07MM

SALES (corp-wide): 1.07MM Privately Held
Web: www.delawaresurgeons.com
SIC: 8011 Surgeon

(G-15974)
DELAWARE SWIM & FITNESS CENTER
4905 Mermaid Blvd (19808-1004)
PHONE.................................302 234-8500
Suzanne D Di Carlo, Prin
EMP: 10 EST: 2008
SALES (est): 195.75K Privately Held
Web: www.delswimfit.com
SIC: 7991 Health club

(G-15975)
DELAWARE THEATRE COMPANY
200 Water St (19801-5030)
PHONE.................................302 594-1100
Amery Camerido, Dir
EMP: 31 EST: 1978
SALES (est): 1.53MM Privately Held
Web: www.delawaretheatre.org
SIC: 7922 Theatrical companies

(G-15976)
DELAWARE TITLE LOANS INC
3300 Concord Pike Ste 2 (19803-5038)
PHONE.................................302 478-8505
Patricia Lewis, Mgr
EMP: 11
SALES (corp-wide): 820.18K Privately Held
Web: www.delawaretitleloansinc.com
SIC: 6163 Loan brokers
PA: Delaware Title Loans, Inc.
8601 Dunwoody Pl Ste 406
Atlanta GA 30350
770 552-9840

(G-15977)
DELAWARE TRUST COMPANY
251 Little Falls Dr (19808-1674)
PHONE.................................302 636-5404
EMP: 36 EST: 2018
SALES (est): 24.18MM
SALES (corp-wide): 661.37MM Privately Held
Web: www.delawaretrust.com
SIC: 7389 Financial services
PA: Corporation Service Company
251 Little Falls Dr
Wilmington DE 19808
302 636-5400

(G-15978)
DELAWARE VALLEY BROKERAGE INC
1415 Foulk Rd Ste 103 (19803-2748)
PHONE.................................302 477-9700
Frank Kesselman, Pr
EMP: 9 EST: 1997
SALES (est): 1.32MM Privately Held
Web: www.dvblife.com
SIC: 6211 Investment firm, general brokerage

(G-15979)
DELAWARE VALLEY DEV GROUP LLC
5718 Kennett Pike (19807-1312)
PHONE.................................302 235-2500
George Beer, Owner
EMP: 6 EST: 2013
SALES (est): 493.36K Privately Held
SIC: 6531 Real estate agents and managers

(G-15980)
DELAWARE VALLEY DEV LLC
5718 Kennett Pike (19807-1312)

Wilmington - New Castle County (G-15981)   GEOGRAPHIC SECTION

PHONE..................302 235-2500
EMP: 10 EST: 1999
SALES (est): 2.01MM **Privately Held**
Web: www.dvdc.com
SIC: 6552 Subdividers and developers, nec

(G-15981)
DELAWARE VALLEY FIELD SVCS LLC
321 Robinson Ln (19805-4690)
PHONE..................302 384-8617
EMP: 6 EST: 2010
SALES (est): 235.32K **Privately Held**
Web: www.delawarevalleyfieldservices.com
SIC: 7389 Interior decorating

(G-15982)
DELAWARE VALLEY GROUP LLC
Also Called: Dynamic Recycling Enterprise
1720 Gilpin Ave (19806-2304)
PHONE..................302 777-7007
EMP: 5 EST: 2004
SALES (est): 433.99K **Privately Held**
Web: www.delvalleygroup.com
SIC: 7361 Employment agencies

(G-15983)
DELAWARE VALLEY RE SOLUTIONS
502 Beaver Valley Rd (19803-1106)
PHONE..................302 668-1694
EMP: 5 EST: 2013
SALES (est): 105.11K **Privately Held**
SIC: 6531 Real estate brokers and agents

(G-15984)
DELAWARE VASCULAR & VEIN CENTE
701 N Clayton St (19805-3165)
PHONE..................302 354-4671
EMP: 10 EST: 2020
SALES (est): 788.7K **Privately Held**
Web: www.delawareadvancedveincenter.com
SIC: 8011 Cardiologist and cardio-vascular specialist

(G-15985)
DELAWARE ZOOLOGICAL SOC INC
1001 N Park Dr (19802-3801)
PHONE..................302 571-7747
Mark Shafer, *Ex Dir*
EMP: 6 EST: 1979
SALES (est): 293.81K **Privately Held**
Web: www.brandywinezoo.org
SIC: 0752 Animal specialty services

(G-15986)
DELAWRSCHOOLOFMASSAGE BODYWORK
1601 Milltown Rd Ste 15 (19808-4084)
PHONE..................302 407-5986
EMP: 5 EST: 2017
SALES (est): 22.18K **Privately Held**
SIC: 8049 Massage Therapist

(G-15987)
DELCASTE GOLF COURSE
3601 Miller Rd (19802-2523)
PHONE..................302 225-9821
EMP: 10 EST: 2017
SALES (est): 20.78K **Privately Held**
Web: www.delcastlegc.com
SIC: 7999 7992 Golf professionals; Public golf courses

(G-15988)
DELCASTLE GOLF CLUB MANAGEMENT
Also Called: Delcastle Golf Club
3800 Valley Brook Dr (19808-1345)
PHONE..................302 998-9505
William Hackett, *Pr*
Darrell Mc Cabe, *
Margaret Hackett, *
EMP: 16 EST: 1985
SALES (est): 476.96K **Privately Held**
Web: www.delcastlegc.com
SIC: 7992 7299 5812 5813 Public golf courses; Banquet hall facilities; Eating places; Drinking places

(G-15989)
DELCASTLE GOLF MANAGEMENT LLC
801 Mckennans Church Rd (19808-2124)
PHONE..................302 998-9505
EMP: 13 EST: 2019
SALES (est): 403.99K **Privately Held**
Web: www.delcastlegc.com
SIC: 7992 Public golf courses

(G-15990)
DELCHEM INC
1318 E 12th St Ste 1 (19802-5301)
P.O. Box 10703 (19850-0703)
PHONE..................302 426-1800
Richard Fagioli, *Pr*
EMP: 24 EST: 1980
SQ FT: 35,000
SALES (est): 2.39MM **Privately Held**
Web: www.delchem.com
SIC: 2891 Sealants

(G-15991)
DELCOLLO SECURITY TECH INC
226 Brookside Dr (19804-1319)
PHONE..................302 994-5400
Daniel Delcollo, *Prin*
EMP: 12 EST: 2005
SALES (est): 488.97K **Privately Held**
Web: www.delcollo.com
SIC: 1731 General electrical contractor

(G-15992)
DELFIS CLEAN LLC
3879 Evelyn Dr (19808-4644)
PHONE..................302 740-0989
Aida Perez, *Prin*
EMP: 5 EST: 2015
SALES (est): 34.7K **Privately Held**
SIC: 7699 Cleaning services

(G-15993)
DELICA INC
251 Little Falls Dr (19808-1674)
PHONE..................917 566-7308
Andrew Pendrill, *CEO*
EMP: 7 EST: 2020
SALES (est): 309.05K **Privately Held**
SIC: 7379 Online services technology consultants

(G-15994)
DELIRI HAMID
1016 Delaware Ave (19806-4704)
PHONE..................302 468-4500
Hamid Deliri, *Owner*
EMP: 10 EST: 2015
SALES (est): 198.77K **Privately Held**
SIC: 8011 General and family practice, physician/surgeon

(G-15995)
DELL PUMP COMPANY
1507 A St (19801-5411)
PHONE..................302 655-2436
EMP: 6 EST: 2018
SALES (est): 409.65K **Privately Held**
Web: www.dellpump.com
SIC: 1522 Residential construction, nec

(G-15996)
DELMAR TERMITE & PEST CONTROL
700 Cornell Dr (19801-5762)
P.O. Box 3836 (19807-0836)
PHONE..................302 658-5010
Darnell Drummond, *Prin*
EMP: 6 EST: 2007
SALES (est): 490.18K **Privately Held**
Web: www.delmarpestcontrol.com
SIC: 7342 Pest control in structures

(G-15997)
DELMARVA POWER & LIGHT COMPANY
800 Delmarva Lane (19801)
PHONE..................302 668-3809
Enid Wallace-simms, *Brnch Mgr*
EMP: 14
SALES (corp-wide): 19.08B **Publicly Held**
Web: www.delmarva.com
SIC: 4911 Distribution, electric power
HQ: Delmarva Power & Light Company
500 N Wakefield Dr Fl 2
Newark DE 19702
302 454-0300

(G-15998)
DELMARVA POWER FINANCING I
800 N King St Ste 400 (19801-3543)
PHONE..................202 872-2000
EMP: 5
SALES (est): 246.26K **Privately Held**
SIC: 4931 Electric and other services combined

(G-15999)
DELONG ZHOU
2115 Concord Pike (19803-2972)
PHONE..................302 256-0124
Delong Zhou, *Prin*
EMP: 5 EST: 2014
SALES (est): 232.56K **Privately Held**
Web: www.delongzhoucpa.com
SIC: 8721 Certified public accountant

(G-16000)
DELPHI FINANCIAL GROUP INC (HQ)
Also Called: Delphi
1105 N Market St Ste 1230 (19801-1216)
P.O. Box 8985 (19899-8985)
PHONE..................302 478-5142
Robert Rosenkranz, *CEO*
Donald A Sherman, *Pr*
Harold F Ilg, *Ex VP*
Chad W Coulter, *Sr VP*
Thomas W Burghart, *Sr VP*
EMP: 218 EST: 1987
SALES (est): 870.25MM **Privately Held**
Web: www.delphifin.com
SIC: 6321 Disability health insurance
PA: Tokio Marine Holdings, Inc.
2-6-4, Otemachi
Chiyoda-Ku TKY 100-0

(G-16001)
DELRIN USA LLC ◊
Also Called: Derlin USA
Building 308 Experimental Station 200 Power Mill Rd (19803)
PHONE..................302 295-5900
Brian Ammons, *Pr*
Angad Singh Kalsi, *VP*
Michael P Heffernan, *Sr VP*
EMP: 19 EST: 2022
SALES (est): 3.17MM **Privately Held**
SIC: 2821 5162 Plastics materials and resins; Plastics materials and basic shapes

(G-16002)
DELTA CENTRIC LLC
251 Little Falls Dr (19808-1674)
PHONE..................302 268-9359
Vincentas Grinius, *Managing Member*
EMP: 15 EST: 2015
SALES (est): 8.12MM
SALES (corp-wide): 112.44K **Privately Held**
SIC: 4813 8731 Internet host services; Computer (hardware) development
HQ: Ipxo Uk Limited
207 Regent Street
London W1B 3
870 820-0222

(G-16003)
DELTA FORMS INC
5 Germay Dr (19804-1104)
PHONE..................302 652-3266
David Disabatino, *Pr*
EMP: 11 EST: 1970
SALES (est): 2.17MM **Privately Held**
Web: www.deltaforms.com
SIC: 2752 Color lithography

(G-16004)
DELTA GAMMA LLC
300 Delaware Ave Ste 210a (19801-6601)
P.O. Box 761 (10008-0761)
PHONE..................347 387-6956
EMP: 6 EST: 2018
SALES (est): 124.94K **Privately Held**
Web: www.deltagamma.org
SIC: 8641 University club

(G-16005)
DELVERDE CORPORATION
103 Foulk Rd Ste 202 (19803-3742)
PHONE..................302 656-1950
Peter Nolan, *VP*
EMP: 8 EST: 1991
SALES (est): 340.55K **Privately Held**
SIC: 7389 Financial services

(G-16006)
DELWARE INJURY CARE LLC
4901 Limestone Rd (19808-1271)
PHONE..................302 235-1111
EMP: 6 EST: 2018
SALES (est): 56.66K **Privately Held**
Web: www.delawareinjurycare.org
SIC: 8041 Offices and clinics of chiropractors

(G-16007)
DENCO INC
501 Silverside Rd Ste 132 (19809-1386)
PHONE..................302 798-4200
Dudley Spencer Ph.d., *Pr*
EMP: 7 EST: 1985
SQ FT: 7,000
SALES (est): 491.79K **Privately Held**
SIC: 3841 Surgical and medical instruments

(G-16008)
DENISE A CUNHA PHD
1020 W 18th St (19802-3892)
PHONE..................302 652-7733
Denise Cunha, *Prin*
EMP: 8 EST: 2001
SALES (est): 180.45K **Privately Held**
Web: www.behavioralhealthassociatesde.com
SIC: 8049 Clinical psychologist

Wilmington - New Castle County

(G-16009)
DENISE MILLER DAY CARE CE
2904 N West St (19802-3117)
PHONE.................302 482-9347
EMP: 6 EST: 2018
SALES (est): 64.89K Privately Held
SIC: 8351 Child day care services

(G-16010)
DENMARK SCHOOL
215 W 23rd St (19802-4125)
PHONE.................302 416-6180
Clifford I Johnson, Pr
EMP: 7 EST: 2014
SALES (est): 104.5K Privately Held
SIC: 8099 Health and allied services, nec

(G-16011)
DENOVIX INC
Also Called: Denovix
3411 Silverside Rd Ste 101hb (19810-4879)
PHONE.................302 442-6911
Fernando Kielhorn, CEO
Kevin Kelley, *
◆ EMP: 25 EST: 2012
SQ FT: 5,400
SALES (est): 3.2MM Privately Held
Web: www.denovix.com
SIC: 3826 Spectroscopic and other optical properties measuring equip.

(G-16012)
DENTAL ASSOCIATES PA
2300 Pennsylvania Ave Ste 6cd (19806-1392)
PHONE.................302 571-0878
Daniel Truono, Pr
EMP: 7 EST: 1973
SALES (est): 481.23K Privately Held
Web: www.dentalassociatespa.com
SIC: 8021 Dentists' office

(G-16013)
DENTAL ASSOCIATES DELAWARE PA (PA)
Also Called: Group Investments Associates
1415 Foulk Rd Ste 200 (19803-2748)
PHONE.................302 477-4900
William A Friz D.d.s., Pr
K F Anziotti D.d.s., Treas
EMP: 40 EST: 1977
SQ FT: 5,000
SALES (est): 7.65MM
SALES (corp-wide): 7.65MM Privately Held
Web:
www.dentalassociatesofdelaware.com
SIC: 8021 Dentists' office

(G-16014)
DENTAL ASSOCIATES HOCKESSIN
1415 Foulk Rd Ste 201 (19803-2748)
PHONE.................302 239-5917
Richard D Bond, Prin
EMP: 15 EST: 2015
SALES (est): 466.93K Privately Held
Web:
www.dentalassociatesofdelaware.com
SIC: 8021 Dentists' office

(G-16015)
DENTAL HEALTH CENTER DEL-TECH
333 N Shipley St (19801-2412)
PHONE.................302 657-5176
Stephanie Clark, Prin
Stephanie Clark, Coordtr
EMP: 8 EST: 2009
SALES (est): 126.71K Privately Held
SIC: 8099 8699 Health and allied services, nec; Charitable organization

(G-16016)
DENTAL SLEEP SOLUTION
4901 Limestone Rd (19808-1271)
PHONE.................302 235-8249
EMP: 8 EST: 2017
SALES (est): 85.32K Privately Held
SIC: 8021 8299 Offices and clinics of dentists; Meditation therapy

(G-16017)
DENTISTRY FOR CHILDREN
2036 Foulk Rd Ste 200 (19810-3650)
PHONE.................302 475-7640
Rachel Maher, Off Mgr
EMP: 10
SALES (corp-wide): 955.78K Privately Held
Web: www.dentistryforchildrende.com
SIC: 8021 Dentists' office
PA: Dentistry For Children
1450 E Chestnut Ave 6c
Vineland NJ 08361
856 696-5400

(G-16018)
DEPOSITORY TRUST CO DEL LLC
3601 N Market St (19802-2736)
PHONE.................302 762-2635
EMP: 40 EST: 2010
SALES (est): 5.54MM
SALES (corp-wide): 10.54MM Privately Held
Web: www.fidelitrade.com
SIC: 6091 Nondeposit trust facilities
PA: Fidelitrade Incorporated
3601 N Market St
Wilmington DE 19802
302 762-6200

(G-16019)
DERIVED DATA LLC
2801 Centerville Rd (19808-1609)
PHONE.................845 300-1805
EMP: 5
SALES (est): 492.75K Privately Held
Web: www.ivolatility.com
SIC: 7371 Computer software development

(G-16020)
DERIVED DATA LLC
Also Called: Ivolatility.com
2801 Centerville Rd Pmb 610 (19808)
PHONE.................201 275-1111
Gena Ioffe, CEO
Oleg Doina, CFO
EMP: 5 EST: 2019
SQ FT: 1,000
SALES (est): 298.38K Privately Held
Web: www.ivolatility.com
SIC: 7375 Data base information retrieval

(G-16021)
DERPROSA SPCALTY FILMS USA LLC
2751 Centerville Rd Ste 400 (19808-1627)
PHONE.................856 845-7524
Filip Sarky, Managing Member
EMP: 9 EST: 2013
SALES (est): 250.09K Privately Held
Web: www.derprosa.com
SIC: 2671 Plastic film, coated or laminated for packaging

(G-16022)
DESALITECH INC
974 Centre Rd (19805-1269)
P.O. Box 734974 (60673-4974)
PHONE.................508 981-7950
Thomas Lebeau, CEO
Nadav Efraty, *
Francesco Fragasso, *
EMP: 40 EST: 2012
SQ FT: 8,000
SALES (est): 10.16MM
SALES (corp-wide): 17.23B Publicly Held
Web: www.dupont.com
SIC: 1629 Waste water and sewage treatment plant construction
HQ: Eidp, Inc.
9330 Zionsville Rd
Indianapolis IN 46268
833 267-8382

(G-16023)
DESIGN LLC
2711 Centerville Rd # 120 (19808-1660)
PHONE.................888 520-7070
EMP: 7 EST: 2010
SALES (est): 256.83K Privately Held
SIC: 7389 Design services

(G-16024)
DESIGN COLLABORATIVE INC
Also Called: D C I
1211 Delaware Ave Ste Dc1 (19806-4719)
PHONE.................302 652-4221
Lee Sparks Iv, Pr
Joseph Chickadel, VP
Lee Sparks, Pr
EMP: 10 EST: 1979
SQ FT: 2,200
SALES (est): 956.51K Privately Held
Web: www.dciarchitects.com
SIC: 8712 Architectural engineering

(G-16025)
DESIGN CONTRACTING INC
1000 N Heald St (19802-5237)
P.O. Box 25125 (19899-5125)
PHONE.................302 429-6900
Andrew Diffley, Pr
EMP: 5 EST: 1986
SQ FT: 6,200
SALES (est): 882.72K Privately Held
Web: www.designcontracting.com
SIC: 1795 Demolition, buildings and other structures

(G-16026)
DESIGN SPECIFIC US INC
501 Silverside Rd Ste 105 (19809-1376)
PHONE.................650 318-6473
Richard Fletcher, Pr
▲ EMP: 2 EST: 2007
SALES (est): 789.86K
SALES (corp-wide): 1.05MM Privately Held
Web: designspecific.us.com
SIC: 3999 2515 Wheelchair lifts; Foundations and platforms
PA: Design Specific Limited
Unit 1-5
Lewes E SUSSEX BN8 6
127 381-3904

(G-16027)
DESIGN TRIBE REPUBLIC LLC
300 Delaware Ave Ste 210a (19801-6601)
PHONE.................302 918-5279
EMP: 10 EST: 2017
SALES (est): 658.91K Privately Held
SIC: 8742 8748 8299 Marketing consulting services; Business consulting, nec; Educational services

(G-16028)
DESKZONE LLC
4023 Kennett Pike (19807-2018)
PHONE.................212 608-7081
EMP: 5 EST: 2014
SALES (est): 127.56K Privately Held
SIC: 0971 Game services

(G-16029)
DESTINY WAY LOGISTICS LLC
1007 N Orange St (19801-1239)
PHONE.................866 526-4900
EMP: 10 EST: 2017
SALES (est): 1.14MM Privately Held
SIC: 4731 Truck transportation brokers

(G-16030)
DETAILING GOOD BROTHERS ✪
1600 N Locust St (19802-5132)
PHONE.................302 482-3348
Dijon Hunter, CEO
EMP: 5 EST: 2023
SALES (est): 103.98K Privately Held
SIC: 7542 Washing and polishing, automotive

(G-16031)
DEUTSCHE BANK TR CO AMERICAS
1011 Centre Rd Ste 200 (19805-1266)
PHONE.................302 636-3301
Edward Reznick, Pr
EMP: 21
SALES (corp-wide): 23B Privately Held
Web: www.db.com
SIC: 6021 6211 National commercial banks; Security brokers and dealers
HQ: Deutsche Bank Trust Company Americas
60 Wall St
New York NY 10005
212 250-2500

(G-16032)
DEUTSCHE BANK TRUST CO DEL
1011 Centre Rd Ste 200 (19805-1266)
PHONE.................302 636-3300
Donna Mitchell, Pr
Edward A Reznick, *
James T Byrne Junior, Sec
Stefan Krause, *
Henry Ritchotte, *
EMP: 151 EST: 1985
SQ FT: 43,000
SALES (est): 13.62MM
SALES (corp-wide): 23B Privately Held
SIC: 6021 National commercial banks
HQ: Deutsche Bank Trust Corporation
60 Wall St Bsmt
New York NY 10005
212 250-2500

(G-16033)
DEVADASI
4904 Old Hill Rd (19807-2522)
PHONE.................302 229-7216
Dinah Kirby, Prin
EMP: 5 EST: 2010
SALES (est): 53.68K Privately Held
Web: www.devadasibellydance.com
SIC: 7911 Dance instructor

(G-16034)
DEVAL PATEL-LENNON ESQ PA INC
5153 W Woodmill Dr # 18 (19808-4067)
PHONE.................302 998-2000
EMP: 5 EST: 2009
SALES (est): 155.76K Privately Held
Web: www.dplesquire.com
SIC: 8111 General practice attorney, lawyer

Wilmington - New Castle County (G-16035)   GEOGRAPHIC SECTION

(G-16035)
DEVELOPING MINDS PRESCHOOL
2106 Saint James Church Rd (19808-5225)
PHONE................................302 995-9611
EMP: 8 **EST:** 1996
SALES (est): 137.88K **Privately Held**
Web: www.developingmindspreschool.com
SIC: 8351 Preschool center

(G-16036)
DEVLIN LAW FIRM LLC
1526 Gilpin Ave (19806-3016)
PHONE................................302 449-9010
Timothy Devlin, *Mng Pt*
EMP: 37 **EST:** 2014
SALES (est): 5.89MM **Privately Held**
Web: www.devlinlawfirm.com
SIC: 8111 General practice law office

(G-16037)
DEWBERRY INSURANCE AGENCY INC
5700 Kirkwood Hwy Ste 103 (19808-4871)
P.O. Box 5286 (19808-0286)
PHONE................................302 995-9550
Steve Dewberry, *Pr*
EMP: 6 **EST:** 1973
SALES (est): 771.72K **Privately Held**
Web: www.dewberryinsurance.com
SIC: 6411 Insurance agents, nec

(G-16038)
DEWSON CONSTRUCTION CO (PA)
9 Jefferson Ave (19805-1322)
PHONE................................302 427-2250
EMP: 9 **EST:** 2020
SALES (est): 1.25MM
SALES (corp-wide): 1.25MM **Privately Held**
Web: www.dewsonconstruction.com
SIC: 1521 New construction, single-family houses

(G-16039)
DEWSON CONSTRUCTION COMPANY (PA)
7 S Lincoln St (19805-3809)
PHONE................................302 427-2250
Timothy J Dewson, *Pr*
EMP: 36 **EST:** 1991
SQ FT: 1,000
SALES (est): 7.76MM **Privately Held**
Web: www.dewsonconstruction.com
SIC: 1521 New construction, single-family houses

(G-16040)
DEXSTA FEDERAL CREDIT UNION
300 Foulk Rd Ste 100 (19803-3819)
PHONE................................302 996-4893
Ben Patterson, *Mgr*
EMP: 8
SALES (corp-wide): 11.52MM **Privately Held**
Web: www.dexsta.com
SIC: 6061 Federal credit unions
PA: Dexsta Federal Credit Union
1310 Centerville Rd
Wilmington DE 19808
302 996-4893

(G-16041)
DEXSTA FEDERAL CREDIT UNION (PA)
1310 Centerville Rd (19808-6220)
PHONE................................302 996-4893
Christine M Kaczmarczyk, *Pr*
Keith Parsons, *Ex VP*
Jerry King, *VP Fin*
EMP: 21 **EST:** 1937
SALES (est): 11.52MM
SALES (corp-wide): 11.52MM **Privately Held**
Web: www.dexsta.com
SIC: 6061 Federal credit unions

(G-16042)
DEXSTA FEDERAL CREDIT UNION
E 444-108 (19880)
PHONE................................302 695-3888
Keith Parsons, *Mgr*
EMP: 10
SALES (corp-wide): 11.52MM **Privately Held**
Web: www.dexsta.com
SIC: 6061 6062 Federal credit unions; State credit unions
PA: Dexsta Federal Credit Union
1310 Centerville Rd
Wilmington DE 19808
302 996-4893

(G-16043)
DEZINS UNLIMITED INC
323 Clubhouse Ln (19810-2263)
PHONE................................302 652-4545
Ellen Sarafian, *Owner*
EMP: 6 **EST:** 2008
SALES (est): 250.74K **Privately Held**
Web: www.dezinsunlimited.com
SIC: 1799 Window treatment installation

(G-16044)
DH TECH WILMINGTON DE
1 Limousine Dr (19803-4363)
PHONE................................215 680-9194
Timothy Lillard, *Prin*
EMP: 2 **EST:** 2011
SALES (est): 118.34K **Privately Held**
Web: www.rentdh.com
SIC: 1389 Construction, repair, and dismantling services

(G-16045)
DHM WILMINGTON LLC
Also Called: Doubletree Hotel Wilmington
700 N King St (19801-3504)
PHONE................................302 656-8952
Eric Jolikko, *Managing Member*
Andrew Jarrett, *Prin*
EMP: 49 **EST:** 2008
SALES (est): 1.72MM **Privately Held**
Web: www.hilton.com
SIC: 7011 Hotels

(G-16046)
DIABLO WORKS LLC
1521 Concord Pike Ste 301 (19803-3644)
PHONE................................302 559-2118
Todd Davis, *Managing Member*
EMP: 20 **EST:** 2021
SALES (est): 2.5MM **Privately Held**
SIC: 8742 Management consulting services

(G-16047)
DIABUDDIES
4023 Greenmount Dr (19810-3303)
PHONE................................302 893-0311
Jeremy Hartnett, *Prin*
EMP: 8 **EST:** 2016
SALES (est): 56.87K **Privately Held**
Web: www.mydiabuddies.com
SIC: 8699 Charitable organization

(G-16048)
DIALOG NEWS PAPER INC
1925 Delaware Ave Fl 3 (19806-2301)
P.O. Box 2208 (19899-2208)
PHONE................................302 573-3109
Jim Grant, *Genl Mgr*
EMP: 8 **EST:** 1965
SALES (est): 487.96K
SALES (corp-wide): 46.59MM **Privately Held**
Web: www.thedialog.org
SIC: 8999 Editorial service
PA: Catholic Diocese Of Wilmington, Inc.
1925 Delaware Ave
Wilmington DE 19806
302 573-3100

(G-16049)
DIAMOND CHEMICAL & SUPPLY CO
Also Called: Airwick/Delaware
524 S Walnut St Ste B (19801-5243)
PHONE................................302 656-7786
Richard L Ventresca Senior, *Pr*
Richard G Ventresca, *
EMP: 25 **EST:** 1923
SQ FT: 24,040
SALES (est): 9.56MM **Privately Held**
Web: www.diamondchemical.com
SIC: 5087 5113 5169 7359 Janitors' supplies ; Paper, wrapping or coarse, and products; Industrial chemicals; Equipment rental and leasing, nec

(G-16050)
DIAMOND CHIROPRACTIC
2100 Baynard Blvd Ste B (19802-3900)
PHONE................................302 300-4242
EMP: 10 **EST:** 2013
SALES (est): 185.34K **Privately Held**
Web: www.diamondspineclinic.com
SIC: 8041 Offices and clinics of chiropractors

(G-16051)
DIAMOND MATERIALS LLC
242 N James St Ste 102 (19804-3183)
PHONE................................302 658-6524
EMP: 100 **EST:** 1995
SALES (est): 44.66MM **Privately Held**
Web: www.diamondmaterials.com
SIC: 2951 Paving mixtures

(G-16052)
DIAMOND PEST CONTROL
6 Weldin Park Dr (19803-4708)
PHONE................................302 654-2300
Frank Krzanowski, *Owner*
EMP: 6 **EST:** 1954
SALES (est): 441.47K **Privately Held**
Web: www.diamondpest.net
SIC: 7342 Pest control in structures

(G-16053)
DIAMOND STANDARD LLC
3 Germay Dr (19804-1127)
PHONE................................917 676-6312
EMP: 6 **EST:** 2019
SALES (est): 49.23K **Privately Held**
Web: www.diamondstandard.co
SIC: 7389 Business services, nec

(G-16054)
DIAMOND STATE GHOST INVSTGTORS
37 Longspur Dr (19808-1972)
PHONE................................302 463-4589
EMP: 6 **EST:** 2018
SALES (est): 106.09K **Privately Held**
Web: www.diamondstateghostinvestigators.com
SIC: 7381 Private investigator

(G-16055)
DIAMOND STATE PORT CORPORATION
Also Called: Port of Wilmington
1 Hausel Rd Lbby (19801-5882)
PHONE................................302 472-7678
Jeffrey Bullock, *Ch*
Richard Geisenberger, *Vice Chairman*
EMP: 105 **EST:** 1995
SALES (est): 9.73MM **Privately Held**
Web: www.portwilmington.com
SIC: 4491 Waterfront terminal operation

(G-16056)
DIAMOND STATE PROMOTIONS
3211 Dunlap Dr (19808-2413)
PHONE................................302 999-1900
EMP: 5 **EST:** 1994
SALES (est): 602.35K **Privately Held**
Web: www.diamondstatepromotions.com
SIC: 5199 Advertising specialties

(G-16057)
DIAMOND STATE PTY RENTL & SLS
53 Germay Dr (19804-1104)
PHONE................................302 777-6677
Mary Beth Jones, *Pr*
Susanne Jones, *VP*
Anne Cecilia Jones, *Treas*
EMP: 9 **EST:** 1984
SQ FT: 18,000
SALES (est): 371.03K **Privately Held**
Web: www.diamondstatepartyrentals.com
SIC: 7359 5812 Party supplies rental services; Eating places

(G-16058)
DIAMOND STATE RECYCLING CORP
1600 Bowers St (19802-4699)
P.O. Box 9798 (19809-0798)
PHONE................................302 655-1501
Scott Sherr, *CEO*
EMP: 22 **EST:** 1990
SQ FT: 22,000
SALES (est): 4.49MM **Privately Held**
Web: www.diamondstaterecycling.com
SIC: 5093 4953 3341 Metal scrap and waste materials; Recycling, waste materials; Secondary nonferrous metals

(G-16059)
DIAMOND STATE TELE COML UN
Also Called: Local 13100 Cwa
1819 Newport Rd Ste A (19808-6039)
PHONE................................302 999-1100
Diana Markowski, *Pr*
Rosemary Delong, *Sec*
Patrice Swift, *VP*
Debrah Wright, *Treas*
EMP: 6 **EST:** 1951
SALES (est): 54.32K **Privately Held**
SIC: 8631 Labor union

(G-16060)
DIAMOND TECHNOLOGIES INC
4001 Miller Rd Ste 3 (19802-1961)
PHONE................................302 421-8252
EMP: 50 **EST:** 1996
SQ FT: 10,000
SALES (est): 9.99MM **Privately Held**
Web: www.diamondtechnologies.com
SIC: 7379 Computer related consulting services

(G-16061)
DIANE NEWMAN
204 Milltown Rd (19808-3112)
PHONE................................302 994-6838
Diane Newman, *Prin*
EMP: 5 **EST:** 2010
SALES (est): 41.44K **Privately Held**
SIC: 8049 Naturopath

GEOGRAPHIC SECTION
Wilmington - New Castle County (G-16091)

(G-16062)
DIFF CONSULTING LLC
919 N Market St Ste 725 (19801-3065)
PHONE.....................................302 689-3979
EMP: 5 EST: 2020
SALES (est): 110.63K **Privately Held**
SIC: 8748 Business consulting, nec

(G-16063)
DIGITAL ARC LLC
1723a Marsh Rd Ste 117 (19810-4607)
PHONE.....................................855 275-2770
John Murphy, *Managing Member*
EMP: 15 EST: 2020
SALES (est): 504.84K **Privately Held**
Web: www.wearc.com
SIC: 7371 Computer software development

(G-16064)
DIGITAL BROADCAST CORPORATION
2207 Concord Pike # 619 (19803-2908)
PHONE.....................................215 285-0912
EMP: 10 EST: 1995
SQ FT: 2,500
SALES (est): 630.01K **Privately Held**
Web: www.digitalbcast.com
SIC: 7389 Music and broadcasting services

(G-16065)
DIGITAL INK SCIENCES LLC
3 Germay Dr Ste 4 (19804-1127)
PHONE.....................................951 757-0027
Scott Colman, *Managing Member*
EMP: 3 EST: 2016
SQ FT: 2,500
SALES (est): 431.19K **Privately Held**
SIC: 2893 Printing ink

(G-16066)
DIGITAL INTERXION HOLDING LLC (DH)
1209 N Orange St (19801-1120)
PHONE.....................................737 281-0101
EMP: 13 EST: 2018
SALES (est): 187.11K
SALES (corp-wide): 4.69B **Privately Held**
SIC: 7389 Personal service agents, brokers, and bureaus
HQ: Digital Realty Trust, L.P.
    5707 Sw Pkwy Bldg 1
    Austin TX 78735
    737 281-0101

(G-16067)
DIGITAL PEAK INC
3422 Old Capitol Trl Ste 368 (19808-6124)
PHONE.....................................214 215-9054
EMP: 5 EST: 2018
SALES (est): 37.86K **Privately Held**
SIC: 7812 Motion picture and video production

(G-16068)
DIGITAL TECHNICA LLC
1201 N Orange St Ste 7167 (19801-1186)
PHONE.....................................416 829-8400
Zameer Mulla, *CEO*
EMP: 10 EST: 2017
SALES (est): 361.92K **Privately Held**
SIC: 7379 Computer related services, nec

(G-16069)
DIGITALAI SOFTWARE INC
4023 Kennett Pike Unit 50128 (19807-2018)
PHONE.....................................678 268-3340
Stephen Elop, *CEO*
Jeff Moloughney, *CMO*
Bruce Chesebrough, *CRO*
Prasenjit Dasgupta, *CFO*
John Allessio, *CCO*
EMP: 10 EST: 1999
SALES (est): 57.8K **Privately Held**
Web: www.digital.ai
SIC: 7373 Systems software development services

(G-16070)
DIGITALXC INC
1013 Centre Rd Ste 403s (19805-1270)
PHONE.....................................650 319-7249
N Srirama Muralidharanc, *CEO*
EMP: 14 EST: 2018
SALES (est): 150K **Privately Held**
Web: www.digitalxc.com
SIC: 7372 Business oriented computer software

(G-16071)
DILIGENT DETAIL
2203 Mitch Rd (19804-3917)
PHONE.....................................302 482-2836
Doug Breakiron, *Owner*
EMP: 2 EST: 2009
SALES (est): 167.5K **Privately Held**
Web: www.combscissorsbs.com
SIC: 2842 Automobile polish

(G-16072)
DIMA II INC
2400 W 4th St (19805-3306)
PHONE.....................................302 427-0787
EMP: 13 EST: 2010
SALES (est): 63.01K **Privately Held**
SIC: 8093 Mental health clinic, outpatient

(G-16073)
DIMA IX INC
2400 W 4th St (19805-3306)
PHONE.....................................302 427-0787
Burley Melton, *Pr*
Merton Briggs, *Dir*
EMP: 8 EST: 1999
SALES (est): 63.23K **Privately Held**
SIC: 8322 Individual and family services

(G-16074)
DINO DICRISCIO
610 Foulk Rd (19803-3741)
PHONE.....................................302 762-0610
EMP: 6 EST: 2009
SALES (est): 80.59K **Privately Held**
SIC: 1751 Carpentry work

(G-16075)
DIOCESAN COUNCIL INC
Also Called: St David's Episcopal Day Sch
2320 Grubb Rd (19810-2702)
PHONE.....................................302 475-4688
Janet Leishman, *Dir*
EMP: 19
SALES (corp-wide): 4.63MM **Privately Held**
Web: www.stdavidsde.church
SIC: 8661 8351 Episcopal Church; Child day care services
PA: The Council Diocesan Inc
    913 Wilson Rd
    Wilmington DE 19803
    302 256-0374

(G-16076)
DIPNA INC
Also Called: Days Inn Wilmington
5209 Concord Pike (19803-1416)
PHONE.....................................302 478-0300
Dipak Shah, *Pr*
Pragna Shah, *
Pierson Carter, *
EMP: 102 EST: 1984
SQ FT: 35,000
SALES (est): 896.6K **Privately Held**
Web: www.wyndhamhotels.com
SIC: 7011 Hotels and motels

(G-16077)
DIRECT CREMATION SERVICES DEL
1900 Delaware Ave (19806-2302)
PHONE.....................................302 656-6873
EMP: 10 EST: 1996
SALES (est): 201.57K **Privately Held**
Web: www.dohertyfh.com
SIC: 7261 Funeral home

(G-16078)
DIRECT MEDICAL LLC
1000n N West St Ste 1501 (19801)
PHONE.....................................781 640-7474
Michael Golinder, *Managing Member*
EMP: 4 EST: 2020
SALES (est): 172.96K **Privately Held**
SIC: 3841 Medical instruments and equipment, blood and bone work

(G-16079)
DIRECT MOBILE TRANSIT INC
Also Called: Direct Mobile Transit
2110 Duncan Rd # 3 (19808-4602)
PHONE.....................................302 218-5106
Michael Dana Bantum, *Pr*
EMP: 10 EST: 2016
SALES (est): 2.33MM **Privately Held**
Web: www.directmobiletransit.com
SIC: 4111 Local and suburban transit

(G-16080)
DIRECT TRENDS USA LLC ✪
2055 Limestone Rd (19808-5536)
PHONE.....................................347 354-2899
EMP: 8 EST: 2022
SALES (est): 544.34K **Privately Held**
SIC: 5199 General merchandise, non-durable

(G-16081)
DIRECTV
4901 Limestone Rd (19808-1271)
PHONE.....................................302 203-9162
EMP: 7 EST: 2018
SALES (est): 35.32K **Privately Held**
Web: www.directv.com
SIC: 4841 Cable and other pay television services

(G-16082)
DIS DAYCARE
1725 W 7th St (19805-3168)
PHONE.....................................302 888-0350
Diane R Fitzgerald, *Prin*
EMP: 14 EST: 2010
SALES (est): 407.67K **Privately Held**
SIC: 8351 Group day care center

(G-16083)
DIS MANAGEMENT
713 Greenbank Rd (19808-3167)
PHONE.....................................302 543-4481
Brent Applebaum, *Prin*
EMP: 5 EST: 2008
SALES (est): 249.93K **Privately Held**
SIC: 8741 Business management

(G-16084)
DISABATINO CONSTRUCTION CO
1 S Cleveland Ave (19805-1400)
PHONE.....................................302 652-3838
Lawrence Disabatino, *Pr*
Lawrence J Disabatino, *
Michael Di Sabatino, *
EMP: 80 EST: 1980
SQ FT: 11,000
SALES (est): 32.75MM **Privately Held**
Web: www.disabatino.com
SIC: 1541 1522 1521 1542 Industrial buildings and warehouses; Residential construction, nec; Single-family housing construction; Commercial and office building, new construction

(G-16085)
DISABATINO ENTERPRISES LLC
1 S Cleveland Ave (19805-1400)
PHONE.....................................302 652-3838
Lawrence Disabatino, *Managing Member*
EMP: 75 EST: 2001
SALES (est): 5.32MM **Privately Held**
Web: www.disabatino.com
SIC: 1611 General contractor, highway and street construction

(G-16086)
DISABATINO LANDSCAPING INC
471 B And O Ln (19804-1450)
PHONE.....................................302 764-0408
Chris Disabatino, *CEO*
EMP: 100 EST: 2015
SALES (est): 5.03MM **Privately Held**
Web: www.disabatinoinc.com
SIC: 0781 Landscape services

(G-16087)
DISABATINO LDSCPG TREE SVC INC
471 B And O Ln (19804-1450)
PHONE.....................................302 764-0408
Christopher Disabatino, *Pr*
Thomas W Wiechecki, *VP*
EMP: 10 EST: 1995
SQ FT: 4,000
SALES (est): 1.01MM **Privately Held**
Web: www.disabatinoinc.com
SIC: 0781 Landscape services

(G-16088)
DISPLAYPLAN INC ✪
1013 Centre Rd Ste 403a (19805-1270)
P.O. Box 5031 Pmb 49708 (60204-5031)
PHONE.....................................502 767-1946
Neil Campbell, *Pr*
EMP: 6 EST: 2022
SALES (est): 88.9K **Privately Held**
SIC: 8742 Marketing consulting services

(G-16089)
DISTRIBUTION MARKETING OF DEL
818 S Heald St Ste A (19801-5790)
PHONE.....................................302 658-6397
Robert Rebock, *Pr*
Herb Stant, *Sec*
Stanley Budner, *Stockholder*
EMP: 6 EST: 1979
SALES (est): 885.4K **Privately Held**
SIC: 5192 Newspapers

(G-16090)
DITO VENTURES INC
3 Germay Dr Unit 41736 (19804-1127)
PHONE.....................................305 424-9877
EMP: 5
SALES (est): 46.16K **Privately Held**
Web: www.ditoventures.com
SIC: 7371 Computer software development and applications

(G-16091)
DIVAS INN
223 E 35th St (19802-2811)
PHONE.....................................302 753-2170
Nay Bernard, *Prin*
EMP: 13 EST: 2010
SALES (est): 89K **Privately Held**

Wilmington - New Castle County (G-16092)   GEOGRAPHIC SECTION

SIC: **7011** Inns

(G-16092)
DIVERGENT LLC
Also Called: Divergent Real Estate & Inv
405 W 34th St (19802-2634)
PHONE..................302 275-7019
Barbara Smith, *CEO*
Wayne C Smith, *COO*
EMP: **7** EST: 2010
SALES (est): 119.34K **Privately Held**
Web: www.divergentmusic.net
SIC: **1521** 1522 6798 Single-family housing construction; Residential construction, nec; Realty investment trusts

(G-16093)
DIVERSFIED ENTPS WORLDWIDE LLC
1000 N West St Ste 1200 (19801-1050)
PHONE..................888 230-3703
EMP: **5**
SALES (est): 251.1K **Privately Held**
SIC: **8711** Building construction consultant

(G-16094)
DIVERSIFIED LLC
2200 Concord Pike Ste 104 (19803-2978)
PHONE..................302 765-3500
David Levy, *Managing Member*
Andrew Rosen, *
Michael Fisher, *
Michael Horwath, *
EMP: **35** EST: 1975
SALES (est): 15MM **Privately Held**
Web: www.diversifiedllc.com
SIC: **6282** 8721 Investment advisory service; Accounting, auditing, and bookkeeping

(G-16095)
DIVERSIFIED CHEMICAL PDTS INC
60 Germay Dr (19804-1105)
PHONE..................302 656-5293
James Longo Junior, *Pr*
David Longo, *VP*
EMP: **9** EST: 1974
SQ FT: 4,000
SALES (est): 982.18K **Privately Held**
Web: www.diversifiedchemical.com
SIC: **8731** 2899 Commercial research laboratory; Chemical preparations, nec

(G-16096)
DIVERSIFIED LIGHTING ASSOC INC
Also Called: DIVERSIFIED LIGHTING ASSOCIATES, INC.
5466 Fairmont Dr (19808-3432)
PHONE..................302 286-6370
Bob Minutella, *Prin*
EMP: **6**
SALES (corp-wide): 19.02MM **Privately Held**
SIC: **5063** Lighting fixtures
PA: I2c Synergy, Inc.
    1 Ivybrook Blvd Ste 100
    Warminster PA 18974
    215 442-0700

(G-16097)
DIVERSITY IN BEAUTY INC
919 N Market St Ste 950 (19801-3036)
PHONE..................323 840-8801
Tia Tappan, *CEO*
EMP: **4** EST: 2019
SALES (est): 130.49K **Privately Held**
SIC: **2721** Periodicals, publishing and printing

(G-16098)
DIVINE PROFILES INC
2606 Kirkwood Hwy (19805-4910)
PHONE..................302 633-3400
James Gibson, *Owner*
EMP: **6** EST: 2011
SALES (est): 99.89K **Privately Held**
SIC: **7231** Hairdressers

(G-16099)
DIVISION ONE BASKETBALL LLC
1201 N Orange St Ste 7193 (19801-1155)
PHONE..................302 573-2528
EMP: **10**
SALES (est): 57.06K **Privately Held**
SIC: **7032** 7929 Sporting camps; Entertainment service

(G-16100)
DIXON BROTHERS LLC
601 A St (19801-5329)
PHONE..................302 377-8289
Vincent Dixon, *CEO*
EMP: **60** EST: 2018
SALES (est): 2.07MM **Privately Held**
SIC: **4789** Transportation services, nec

(G-16101)
DJANGO STARS LTD LIABILITY CO
2711 Centerville Rd Ste 400 (19808-1660)
PHONE..................415 996-8054
EMP: **12** EST: 2016
SALES (est): 295.98K **Privately Held**
Web: www.djangostars.com
SIC: **7371** Computer software development

(G-16102)
DJT OPERATIONS LLC
3 Germay Dr Ste 2475 (19804-1127)
PHONE..................302 498-9070
David Thompson, *Managing Member*
EMP: **6** EST: 2021
SALES (est): 253.45K **Privately Held**
SIC: **8742** Management consulting services

(G-16103)
DKMRBH INC
704 N King St Ste 500 (19801-3584)
PHONE..................302 250-4428
Akhilesh Kandhari, *Pr*
EMP: **19** EST: 2012
SALES (est): 555.03K **Privately Held**
Web: www.dkmrbh.com
SIC: **7361** Employment agencies

(G-16104)
DLA PIPER LLP (US)
919 N Market St (19801-3023)
PHONE..................302 654-3025
Lee I Miller, *Brnch Mgr*
EMP: **37**
Web: www.dlapiper.com
SIC: **8111** Corporate, partnership and business law
HQ: Dla Piper Llp (Us)
    650 S Exeter St
    Baltimore MD 21202
    410 580-3000

(G-16105)
DLS DISCOVERY LLC
Also Called: Digital Legal
1007 N Orange St Ste 510 (19801-1248)
PHONE..................302 888-2060
Edward Carp, *Pt*
▲ EMP: **22** EST: 1995
SALES (est): 6.06MM **Privately Held**
Web: www.dlsdiscovery.net
SIC: **7389** 8111 Document embossing; Legal services

(G-16106)
DLT FEDERAL BUS SYST CORP
1000 N West St Ste 1200 (19801-1058)
PHONE..................302 358-2229
Michael Johnson, *Prin*
EMP: **5** EST: 2016
SALES (est): 189.13K **Privately Held**
SIC: **7371** Computer software development

(G-16107)
DMD BUSINESS FORMS & PRTG CO
204 S Maryland Ave (19804-1344)
PHONE..................302 998-8200
EMP: **4** EST: 1995
SQ FT: 800
SALES (est): 386.87K **Privately Held**
Web: www.dmdprinting.com
SIC: **2752** Offset printing

(G-16108)
DMG MARKETING INC
5722 Kennett Pike (19807-1312)
PHONE..................302 575-1610
Ken Scott, *Pr*
EMP: **13** EST: 1993
SALES (est): 99.02K **Privately Held**
SIC: **8742** Marketing consulting services

(G-16109)
DMM INTERNATIONAL GROUP INC
1007 N Orange St (19801-1239)
PHONE..................214 233-6898
Michael Orizu, *CEO*
EMP: **10**
SALES (est): 405.78K **Privately Held**
SIC: **6799** Commodity contract trading companies

(G-16110)
DMP SECURITY AGENCY LLC
706 N West St (19801-1524)
PHONE..................302 384-3745
EMP: **10** EST: 2016
SALES (est): 392.29K **Privately Held**
Web: www.dmpsecurityservices.com
SIC: **7381** Security guard service

(G-16111)
DND LIMOUSINE SERVICE
104c S John St (19804-3109)
PHONE..................302 998-5856
Dan Merry, *Pr*
EMP: **7** EST: 1987
SALES (est): 231.13K **Privately Held**
Web: www.expiredwixdomain.com
SIC: **4119** Limousine rental, with driver

(G-16112)
DOCKLANDS RIVERFRONT
110 S West St (19801-5015)
PHONE..................302 658-6626
EMP: **7** EST: 2019
SALES (est): 18.95K **Privately Held**
Web: www.docklandsriverfront.com
SIC: **7299** Facility rental and party planning services

(G-16113)
DOCULOGICA CORP
104 David Rd (19804-2649)
PHONE..................302 753-5944
Krista Pilichowski, *Pr*
Eric Elfman, *Sec*
EMP: **2** EST: 2019
SALES (est): 60.4K **Privately Held**
Web: doculogica.business.site
SIC: **7338** 7389 4226 7374 Formal writing services; Mailing and messenger services; Special warehousing and storage, nec; Data processing and preparation

(G-16114)
DOCUMO INC
919 N Market St Ste 950 (19801-3036)
PHONE..................858 299-5295
Matthew Herrera, *Prin*
Matthew Schultz, *Prin*
EMP: **38**
SALES (est): 646.99K **Privately Held**
Web: www.documo.com
SIC: **7389** Document storage service

(G-16115)
DOE LEGAL LLC
1200 Philadelphia Pike Ste 1 (19809-2040)
PHONE..................302 798-7500
Thomas J Russo, *Managing Member*
Thomas J Russo, *Pr*
John C Russo, *
Joe Timlin, *
EMP: **45** EST: 1971
SQ FT: 10,000
SALES (est): 6.45MM **Privately Held**
Web: www.doelegal.com
SIC: **5045** Computers, peripherals, and software

(G-16116)
DOE TECHNOLOGIES INC
Also Called: DOE Legal
1200 Philadelphia Pike Ste 1 (19809-2040)
PHONE..................302 792-1285
Thomas J Russo, *Pr*
John Russo, *
Joe Timlin, *
EMP: **42** EST: 2002
SQ FT: 30,000
SALES (est): 4MM **Privately Held**
Web: www.doelegal.com
SIC: **7371** 7389 Computer software development; Recording studio, noncommercial records

(G-16117)
DOG STOP
101 Greenbank Rd (19808-4721)
PHONE..................302 416-4646
EMP: **7** EST: 2015
SALES (est): 31.26K **Privately Held**
Web: www.thedogstop.com
SIC: **0752** Grooming services, pet and animal specialties

(G-16118)
DOGWATCH OF DELAWARE
1417 Spruce Ave (19805-1337)
PHONE..................302 268-3434
John Kennish, *Prin*
EMP: **5** EST: 2019
SALES (est): 122.72K **Privately Held**
Web: www.dogwatchdelaware.com
SIC: **1799** Fence construction

(G-16119)
DOHERTY & ASSOCIATES INC
4550 Linden Hill Rd Ste 130 (19808-2930)
PHONE..................302 239-3500
Debria Doherty, *Pr*
EMP: **10** EST: 2001
SALES (est): 829.88K **Privately Held**
Web: www.dohertyandassociates.com
SIC: **8721** Billing and bookkeeping service

(G-16120)
DOHERY FUNERAL HOMES INC
3200 Limestone Rd (19808-2199)
PHONE..................302 999-8277
James Mullin, *Pr*
EMP: **9** EST: 1999
SALES (est): 214.96K **Privately Held**
Web: www.dohertyfh.com

GEOGRAPHIC SECTION
Wilmington - New Castle County (G-16149)

SIC: 7261 Funeral director

(G-16121)
DOJUPA LLC
Also Called: Dxl
5586 Kirkwood Hwy (19808-5002)
PHONE..................302 300-2009
Jean Paul Libert, CEO
Emmanuel Galichon, CFO
EMP: 5 EST: 2011
SALES (est): 296.45K Privately Held
SIC: 8742 Marketing consulting services

(G-16122)
DOLE FOOD COMPANY INC
Also Called: Dole Food
Port Of Wilmington Lbr Rd (19899)
P.O. Box 725 (19720-0725)
PHONE..................302 652-6060
Sean Clancy, Mgr
EMP: 115
SQ FT: 200
Web: www.dole.com
SIC: 0161 Vegetables and melons
HQ: Dole Food Company, Inc.
 200 S Tryon St Ste 600
 Charlotte NC 28202
 818 874-4000

(G-16123)
DOLE FRESH FRUIT COMPANY
Also Called: Dole
70 Gist Rd (19801-5880)
PHONE..................302 652-6484
EMP: 11
Web: dolecareers.silkroad.com
SIC: 5148 Fruits, fresh
HQ: Dole Fresh Fruit Company
 200 S Tryon St Ste 600
 Charlotte NC 28202
 818 874-4000

(G-16124)
DOLE FRESH FRUIT COMPANY
Also Called: Dole
1 Hausel Rd (19801-5800)
PHONE..................302 652-2215
EMP: 10
Web: dolecareers.silkroad.com
SIC: 5148 Fruits, fresh
HQ: Dole Fresh Fruit Company
 200 S Tryon St Ste 600
 Charlotte NC 28202
 818 874-4000

(G-16125)
DOLPHIN BEACH LLC
2400 W 11th St (19805-2608)
PHONE..................302 654-3543
Kent Smith, Asst Sec
EMP: 11 EST: 2018
SALES (est): 102.18K Privately Held
SIC: 7011 Resort hotel

(G-16126)
DOMENIC DI DONATO PLBG HTG INC
128 Shrewsbury Dr (19810-1410)
PHONE..................856 207-4919
Domenic Didonato, Pr
EMP: 8 EST: 1997
SALES (est): 693.21K Privately Held
Web: domenic-didonato-plumbing-heating-inc.business.site
SIC: 1711 Plumbing contractors

(G-16127)
DOMESTIC MARKETING SVCS LLC
2711 Centerville Rd # 400 (19808-1660)
PHONE..................646 361-9827
EMP: 6 EST: 2017
SALES (est): 80.17K Privately Held
SIC: 5092 Toys and hobby goods and supplies

(G-16128)
DOMINIC A DI FEBO & SONS
812 Rose St (19805-2818)
PHONE..................302 425-5054
Dominic A Di Febo, Pr
Joseph Di Febo, VP
John Di Febo, Treas
Angela Crowl, Sec
EMP: 8 EST: 1936
SALES (est): 226.9K Privately Held
SIC: 1752 Wood floor installation and refinishing

(G-16129)
DOMINIC GIOFFRE DDS PA
4901 Limestone Rd (19808-1271)
PHONE..................302 239-0410
Dominic Gioffre D.d.s., Pr
EMP: 22 EST: 1971
SALES (est): 256.01K Privately Held
Web: www.pikecreekdental.com
SIC: 8021 Dentists' office

(G-16130)
DON A BESKRONE
500 Delaware Ave Ste 800 (19801-7408)
PHONE..................302 654-1888
Don Beskrone, Prin
EMP: 5 EST: 2017
SALES (est): 63.66K Privately Held
Web: www.ashbygeddes.com
SIC: 8111 General practice attorney, lawyer

(G-16131)
DON D CORP
1615 E Ayre St (19804-2514)
PHONE..................302 994-5793
Don Deaven, Pr
Lori Deaven, Sec
EMP: 9 EST: 1971
SQ FT: 2,000
SALES (est): 408.34K Privately Held
SIC: 7353 Cranes and aerial lift equipment, rental or leasing

(G-16132)
DON ROGERS INC (PA)
242 N James St Ste 102 (19804-3183)
PHONE..................302 658-6524
Don Rogers, Prin
Dennis Robinson, Prin
EMP: 18 EST: 1953
SQ FT: 10,000
SALES (est): 2.75MM
SALES (corp-wide): 2.75MM Privately Held
Web: www.donrogersincnj.com
SIC: 1611 1794 Highway and street paving contractor; Excavation and grading, building construction

(G-16133)
DONAHUE JULIE ANN LPC LPCMH
7 Pinecrest Dr (19810-1414)
PHONE..................610 764-8652
Matthew Donahue, Prin
EMP: 6 EST: 2020
SALES (est): 32.92K Privately Held
SIC: 8322 Individual and family services

(G-16134)
DONALD A GIRARD MD
2601 Annand Dr Ste 19 (19808-3719)
P.O. Box 5338 (08857-5338)
PHONE..................302 633-5755
Donald Girard Md, Owner
EMP: 7 EST: 1999
SALES (est): 235.57K Privately Held
Web: www.girardgastro.com
SIC: 8011 Gastronomist

(G-16135)
DONALD F DEAVEN INC
1615 E Ayre St (19804-2514)
PHONE..................302 994-5793
Donald D Deaven, Pr
Lori Deaven, Treas
Lisa Deaven, Sec
EMP: 42 EST: 1965
SQ FT: 2,000
SALES (est): 3.6MM Privately Held
SIC: 3441 1791 3446 Fabricated structural metal; Structural steel erection; Ornamental metalwork

(G-16136)
DONALD LAMBERT III
1900 Newport Gap Pike (19808-6136)
PHONE..................302 421-1081
Donald Lambert, Owner
EMP: 7 EST: 2018
SALES (est): 110.74K Privately Held
SIC: 8049 Offices of health practitioner

(G-16137)
DONALD M BROWN
2402 W 2nd St (19805-3317)
PHONE..................302 777-1840
Donald Brown, Prin
EMP: 6 EST: 2002
SALES (est): 76.19K Privately Held
Web: www.dhhlawfirm.com
SIC: 8111 General practice attorney, lawyer

(G-16138)
DONALDSON ELECTRIC INC
124 Middleboro Rd Ste A (19804-1660)
PHONE..................302 660-7534
Kimberly Donaldson, Pr
Michael Donaldson, VP
Kimberly Ann Donaldon, Pr
EMP: 20 EST: 2000
SALES (est): 1.8MM Privately Held
Web: www.donaldson-electric.com
SIC: 1731 General electrical contractor

(G-16139)
DONE RIGHT TODAY INC
313 Goodley Rd (19803-2321)
PHONE..................302 528-4294
EMP: 8 EST: 2018
SALES (est): 499.94K Privately Held
SIC: 1711 Plumbing contractors

(G-16140)
DONGJIN USA INC
Also Called: Big Centric
175 Edgemoor Rd (19809-9002)
PHONE..................302 691-8510
Jay Rehee, Pr
Stephan Rhee, Pr
EMP: 10 EST: 2012
SALES (est): 224.2K Privately Held
Web: www.phillyappliances.com
SIC: 3089 Coloring and finishing of plastics products

(G-16141)
DONORWARE FOUNDATION
110 W 9th St Pmb 602 (19801-1618)
PHONE..................302 230-7171
EMP: 7 EST: 2010
SALES (est): 87.33K Privately Held
SIC: 8641 Civic and social associations

(G-16142)
DONR LLC
251 Little Falls Dr (19808-1674)
PHONE..................857 400-8679
EMP: 2 EST: 2017
SQ FT: 990
SALES (est): 101.82K Privately Held
SIC: 7372 Business oriented computer software

(G-16143)
DONRIGHT SERVICES LLC
11 Deville Cir (19808-4532)
PHONE..................302 685-7540
Armani Hawkins, Managing Member
EMP: 6
SALES (est): 86.27K Privately Held
SIC: 5511 7389 New and used car dealers; Business services, nec

(G-16144)
DOPPLE LABS INC ✪
251 Little Falls Dr (19808-1674)
PHONE..................754 216-8175
Tristan Chaudhry, Pt
Isaac Nakash, Pt
EMP: 8 EST: 2023
SALES (est): 306.16K Privately Held
SIC: 7371 Computer software development and applications

(G-16145)
DORILYN ENGLISH PHD
18c Trolley Sq (19806-3355)
PHONE..................302 655-6506
Dorilyn English, Ofcr
EMP: 6 EST: 2017
SALES (est): 105.71K Privately Held
Web: www.dorilynenglishphd.com
SIC: 8049 Clinical psychologist

(G-16146)
DORILYN ENGLISH PHD
1020 W 18th St (19802-3892)
PHONE..................302 652-7733
Dorilyn English, Prin
EMP: 7 EST: 2001
SALES (est): 104.42K Privately Held
SIC: 8049 Clinical psychologist

(G-16147)
DORLEEON LLC
1007 N Orange St Fl 4 (19801-1239)
PHONE..................302 415-3106
EMP: 5
SALES (est): 68.89K Privately Held
Web: www.dorleeon.com
SIC: 7371 Computer software development and applications

(G-16148)
DORMAKABA US HOLDING LTD
1201 N Market St Ste 1347 (19801-1163)
PHONE..................252 200-5414
Summer Dickinson, Ofcr
EMP: 400 EST: 2013
SIC: 6719 Personal holding companies, except banks
PA: Dormakaba Holding Ag
 Hofwisenstrasse 24
 RUmlang ZH 8153

(G-16149)
DOROSHOW PSQALE KRWITZ SGEL BH (PA)
Also Called: Doroshow Pasquale Law Offices
1202 Kirkwood Hwy (19805-2120)
PHONE..................302 998-2397
Robert Pasquale, Pt
Eric M Doroshow, Pt

Wilmington - New Castle County (G-16150)   GEOGRAPHIC SECTION

Arthur Krawitz, *Pt*
Shaku Bhaya, *Pt*
EMP: 45 **EST:** 1977
SQ FT: 1,500
SALES (est): 9.95MM
SALES (corp-wide): 9.95MM **Privately Held**
Web: www.dplaw.com
SIC: 8111   General practice attorney, lawyer

(G-16150)
DOROSHOW PSQALE KRWITZ SGEL BH
1208 Kirkwood Hwy (19805-2120)
PHONE.................................302 998-0100
EMP: 15
SALES (corp-wide): 9.95MM **Privately Held**
Web: www.dplaw.com
SIC: 8111   General practice attorney, lawyer
PA: Doroshow Pasquale Krawitz Siegel Bhaya
1202 Kirkwood Hwy
Wilmington DE 19805
302 998-2397

(G-16151)
DORSEY & WHITNEY LLP
1105 N Market St Ste 1600 (19801-1201)
PHONE.................................302 383-1011
EMP: 5 **EST:** 2018
SALES (est): 184.44K **Privately Held**
Web: www.dorsey.com
SIC: 8111   General practice attorney, lawyer

(G-16152)
DOT AND LINE INC
221 W 9th St (19801-1619)
PHONE.................................650 391-4837
Maheen Adamjee, *CEO*
EMP: 25
SALES (est): 888.88K **Privately Held**
SIC: 7372   Prepackaged software

(G-16153)
DOT POP INC
Also Called: Sign and Graphics
1010 N Union St Ste D (19805-2731)
PHONE.................................302 691-3160
Dan Nestor, *Prin*
EMP: 5 **EST:** 2014
SALES (est): 257.66K **Privately Held**
Web: www.popdotsigns.com
SIC: 3993   Electric signs

(G-16154)
DOUG GREEN WOODWORKING
330 N Maryland Ave (19804-1302)
PHONE.................................302 652-6522
Douglas G Green, *Owner*
EMP: 3 **EST:** 2010
SALES (est): 224.35K **Privately Held**
Web: www.douggreenwoodworking.com
SIC: 2431   Millwork

(G-16155)
DOUGHERTY DENTAL SOLUTIONS LLC
1805 Foulk Rd Ste D (19810-3700)
PHONE.................................302 475-3270
EMP: 11 **EST:** 2019
SALES (est): 856.41K **Privately Held**
Web: www.doughertydentalsolutions.com
SIC: 8021   Dentists' office

(G-16156)
DOUGLAS MORROW
Also Called: Emergency Medical Mgmnt
211 Beau Tree Dr Ste 100 (19810-1177)
PHONE.................................302 750-9161
Douglas Morrow, *Prin*
EMP: 5 **EST:** 2011
SALES (est): 148.93K **Privately Held**
SIC: 8099   Health and allied services, nec

(G-16157)
DOYJUL APARTMENTS
Also Called: Doyjul Center
3403 Lancaster Pike (19805-5533)
PHONE.................................302 998-0088
Harry A Simeone, *Owner*
EMP: 10 **EST:** 1965
SALES (est): 762.53K **Privately Held**
Web: www.dorjulapartments.com
SIC: 6513 6512   Apartment building operators ; Shopping center, property operation only

(G-16158)
DOZR LTD (PA)
3411 Silverside Rd Ste 104 (19810-4812)
PHONE.................................844 218-3697
Kevin Forestell, *CEO*
EMP: 10 **EST:** 2016
SALES (est): 2.76MM
SALES (corp-wide): 2.76MM **Privately Held**
SIC: 7353   Heavy construction equipment rental

(G-16159)
DP FIRE & SAFETY INC
411 Orinda Dr (19804-1113)
PHONE.................................302 998-5430
Deborah C Pruitt, *Pr*
David Pruitt, *Sec*
EMP: 10 **EST:** 1984
SALES (est): 734.09K **Privately Held**
Web: www.dpfire.com
SIC: 5999 3699   Fire extinguishers; Fire control or bombing equipment, electronic

(G-16160)
DPSG - DLGTION PYMNT SYSTEMS G
2711 Centerville Rd Ste 400 (19808-1660)
PHONE.................................201 755-0912
Erez Moscovich, *CEO*
EMP: 10 **EST:** 2013
SQ FT: 1,200
SALES (est): 373.16K **Privately Held**
Web: www.thumzap.com
SIC: 7371   Software programming applications

(G-16161)
DR ALVIN L TURNER
222 Philadelphia Pike (19809-3166)
PHONE.................................302 777-3202
Alvin L Turner, *Prin*
EMP: 7 **EST:** 2010
SALES (est): 117.92K **Privately Held**
SIC: 8049   Clinical psychologist

(G-16162)
DR AZARCON & ASSOC
3411 Silverside Rd Ste 107r (19810-4812)
PHONE.................................302 478-2969
EMP: 5 **EST:** 2007
SALES (est): 446.99K **Privately Held**
Web: www.drazarcon.com
SIC: 8011   Physicians' office, including specialists

(G-16163)
DR CASEY MAE FOUSE DC
3910 Concord Pike (19803-1716)
PHONE.................................302 472-4878
EMP: 5 **EST:** 2018
SALES (est): 80.42K **Privately Held**
SIC: 8041   Offices and clinics of chiropractors

(G-16164)
DR DOUGLAS BRIGGS
910 N Union St (19805-5334)
PHONE.................................302 654-4001
Jessica Evans, *Mgr*
EMP: 8 **EST:** 2014
SALES (est): 100K **Privately Held**
Web: www.firststatehealth.com
SIC: 8041   Offices and clinics of chiropractors

(G-16165)
DR GS WEIGHTLOSS
3801 Kennett Pike Ste E-126 (19807-2321)
PHONE.................................302 232-5153
EMP: 5 **EST:** 2018
SALES (est): 185.22K **Privately Held**
Web: www.drgsweightloss.com
SIC: 8093   Weight loss clinic, with medical staff

(G-16166)
DR JEFFREY E FELZER DMD PC
3105 Limestone Rd Ste 203 (19808-2151)
PHONE.................................302 995-6979
Jeffrey Felzer, *Prin*
EMP: 11 **EST:** 2011
SALES (est): 485.21K **Privately Held**
Web: www.pikecreekperio.com
SIC: 8021   Dentists' office

(G-16167)
DR JILLIAN G STEVENS DO
812 Bezel Rd (19803-4824)
PHONE.................................302 762-7332
Jillian G Stevens, *Prin*
EMP: 8 **EST:** 2011
SALES (est): 80.13K **Privately Held**
SIC: 8031   Offices and clinics of osteopathic physicians

(G-16168)
DR ROBERT M COLLINS
5500 Skyline Dr Ste 3 (19808-1772)
PHONE.................................302 239-3655
Robert M Collins, *Prin*
EMP: 7 **EST:** 2006
SALES (est): 469.4K **Privately Held**
Web: www.delawarechildrensdentist.com
SIC: 8021   Dentists' office

(G-16169)
DR SHEFALI PANDYA
707 Foulk Rd (19803-3737)
PHONE.................................302 421-9960
Shefali Pandya, *Prin*
EMP: 11 **EST:** 2010
SALES (est): 473.54K **Privately Held**
Web: www.mywilmingtondentist.com
SIC: 8021   Dentists' office

(G-16170)
DR TIMOTHY G COOK DO
131 Parrish Ln (19810-3457)
PHONE.................................215 823-5800
Timothy G Cook, *Prin*
EMP: 7 **EST:** 2011
SALES (est): 80.27K **Privately Held**
SIC: 8031   Offices and clinics of osteopathic physicians

(G-16171)
DRAGON CLOUD INC
1 Cmmrce Ctr 1201 Ste 6 (19899)
PHONE.................................702 508-2676
Srinu Gedela, *Dir*
EMP: 6 **EST:** 2014
SALES (est): 166.34K **Privately Held**
SIC: 2731   Books, publishing and printing

(G-16172)
DRAVO BAY LLC
1 Ave Of The Arts Ste A (19801-5047)
PHONE.................................302 660-3350
Todd A Roselle, *Asst Sec*
EMP: 5 **EST:** 2018
SALES (est): 233.92K **Privately Held**
Web: www.bluerockfg.com
SIC: 6282   Investment advice

(G-16173)
DRAYTON ELECTRIC LLC
Also Called: Drayton Electric
8 N Clifton Ave (19805-2262)
PHONE.................................302 893-0884
EMP: 5 **EST:** 2015
SALES (est): 163.66K **Privately Held**
SIC: 1731   Electrical work

(G-16174)
DREAM CHASERS GYMNASTICS
21 Lloyd St (19804-2819)
PHONE.................................302 559-5561
Myron Horsey, *Prin*
EMP: 6 **EST:** 2017
SALES (est): 60.41K **Privately Held**
SIC: 7999   Gymnastic instruction, non-membership

(G-16175)
DREAM CONCEPTION LLC
108 W 13th St (19801)
PHONE.................................302 319-9822
EMP: 7 **EST:** 2012
SALES (est): 73.67K **Privately Held**
Web: www.dreamconception.com
SIC: 7371   Computer software development and applications

(G-16176)
DREAM SPA
1408 N King St (19801-3122)
PHONE.................................646 717-5397
EMP: 5 **EST:** 2018
SALES (est): 63.17K **Privately Held**
SIC: 7991   Spas

(G-16177)
DREAM WEAVER LLC
1521 Concord Pike Ste 301 (19803-3644)
PHONE.................................302 352-9473
Trinanjan Gupta, *Managing Member*
Manish Gupta, *Mgr*
EMP: 7 **EST:** 2012
SALES (est): 422.04K **Privately Held**
Web: www.goldenbustours.com
SIC: 7371 7372   Custom computer programming services; Business oriented computer software

(G-16178)
DREAMS CHILDCARE LLC
725 N Union St (19805-3031)
PHONE.................................302 652-1085
EMP: 9 **EST:** 2017
SALES (est): 202.15K **Privately Held**
SIC: 8351   Child day care services

(G-16179)
DRIFTWOOD HOSPITALITY MGT LLC
Also Called: Double Tree By Hilton
700 N King St (19801-3504)
PHONE.................................302 655-0400
Alan Filer, *Prin*
EMP: 20 **EST:** 2010
SALES (est): 2.23MM
SALES (corp-wide): 119.88MM **Privately Held**

GEOGRAPHIC SECTION
Wilmington - New Castle County (G-16205)

Web: www.hilton.com
SIC: 7011 Hotels and motels
PA: Driftwood Hospitality Management Llc
   11770 Us Highway 1 # 202
   North Palm Beach FL 33408
   561 207-2700

(G-16180)
DRY CLEANING HOME SERVICE INC
2402 Shellpot Dr (19803-2548)
PHONE.............................302 777-7444
Glenn Merchant, *Prin*
EMP: 7 EST: 2006
SALES (est): 55.48K **Privately Held**
Web: www.seymoursdrycleaners.com
SIC: 7216 Cleaning and dyeing, except rugs

(G-16181)
DS SUPPLY LLC
3605 Old Capitol Trl Unit C4 (19808-6043)
PHONE.............................302 377-3974
Shmuel Kahanov, *Pt*
EMP: 5
SALES (corp-wide): 259.42K **Privately Held**
SIC: 5122 Cosmetics, perfumes, and hair products
PA: Ds Supply Llc
   3601 Old Capitol Trl
   Wilmington DE 19808
   602 946-9817

(G-16182)
DSD APP LLC (PA)
1209 N Orange St (19801-1120)
PHONE.............................302 465-6606
EMP: 6 EST: 2017
SALES (est): 667.65K
SALES (corp-wide): 667.65K **Privately Held**
SIC: 8021 Dentists' office

(G-16183)
DSM COMMERCIAL
3304 Old Capitol Trl (19808-6902)
PHONE.............................302 842-2450
EMP: 22 EST: 2019
SALES (est): 1.93MM **Privately Held**
Web: www.dsmre.com
SIC: 1521 Single-family housing construction

(G-16184)
DSS SSTNABLE SOLUTIONS USA INC
4023 Kennett Pike Pmb 282 (19807-2018)
PHONE.............................800 532-7233
Davide Vassallo, *CEO*
Tina Scaran, *
EMP: 40 EST: 2019
SALES (est): 3.17MM **Privately Held**
Web: www.consultdss.com
SIC: 8742 Management consulting services

(G-16185)
DT INVESTMENT PARTNERS LLC
1013 Centre Rd (19805-1265)
PHONE.............................302 442-6203
Jonathan Smith, *Brnch Mgr*
EMP: 19
Web: www.dtinvestmentpartners.com
SIC: 6799 Investors, nec
PA: Dt Investment Partners Llc
   1 Dickinson Dr Ste 103
   Chadds Ford PA 19317

(G-16186)
DTI DIRECT INC
251 Little Falls Dr (19808-1674)
PHONE.............................855 374-3836
EMP: 6 EST: 2017

SALES (est): 71.62K **Privately Held**
SIC: 3944 Games, toys, and children's vehicles

(G-16187)
DU PONT LYNNE M MD
910 Foulk Rd (19803-3158)
PHONE.............................302 777-7966
Margaret L Dupont, *Prin*
EMP: 11 EST: 2002
SALES (est): 183.12K **Privately Held**
SIC: 8011 Pediatrician

(G-16188)
DU PONT CHEM ENRGY OPRTONS INC (DH)
Also Called: Dupont
974 Centre Rd (19805-1269)
PHONE.............................302 774-1000
Charles Holiday, *CEO*
Edgar Woolard, *VP*
▼ EMP: 185 EST: 1988
SALES (est): 746.78MM
SALES (corp-wide): 17.23B **Publicly Held**
Web: www.dupont.com
SIC: 2819 3482 Industrial inorganic chemicals, nec; Small arms ammunition
HQ: Eidp, Inc.
   9330 Zionsville Rd
   Indianapolis IN 46268
   833 267-8382

(G-16189)
DU PONT DELAWARE INC (DH)
Also Called: Dupont
974 Centre Rd Chestnut Run Plaza Bldg 730 (19805)
P.O. Box 2915 (19805-0915)
PHONE.............................302 774-1000
Ellen Kullman, *Ch Bd*
Chad Holliday, *Ch Bd*
Catsey Kiley, *Sec*
▼ EMP: 66 EST: 1986
SALES (est): 104.99MM
SALES (corp-wide): 17.23B **Publicly Held**
Web: www.dupont.com
SIC: 8999 Actuarial consultant
HQ: Eidp, Inc.
   9330 Zionsville Rd
   Indianapolis IN 46268
   833 267-8382

(G-16190)
DU PONT ELASTOMERS LP
974 Centre Rd (19805-1269)
PHONE.............................302 774-1000
EMP: 46 EST: 1996
SALES (est): 38.98MM
SALES (corp-wide): 17.23B **Publicly Held**
Web: www.dupont.com
SIC: 5171 Petroleum bulk stations and terminals
HQ: Eidp, Inc.
   9330 Zionsville Rd
   Indianapolis IN 46268
   833 267-8382

(G-16191)
DU PONT FOREIGN SALES CORP
974 Centre Rd (19805-1269)
PHONE.............................302 774-1000
Charles Holliday, *CEO*
EMP: 38 EST: 1995
SALES (est): 1.54MM
SALES (corp-wide): 17.23B **Publicly Held**
Web: www.dupont.com
SIC: 7389 Personal service agents, brokers, and bureaus
HQ: Eidp, Inc.
   9330 Zionsville Rd
   Indianapolis IN 46268
   833 267-8382

(G-16192)
DU WIRELESS
9 Courtyard Ln (19802-1470)
PHONE.............................302 407-5532
EMP: 5 EST: 2014
SALES (est): 73.58K **Privately Held**
SIC: 4812 Cellular telephone services

(G-16193)
DUALITYBIO INC
3524 Silverside Rd 35b (19810-4929)
PHONE.............................201 486-7858
John Zhu, *CEO*
Joyce Pei, *Chief Business Officer*
Wei Zhu, *CMO*
EMP: 20 EST: 2021
SALES (est): 608.03K **Privately Held**
SIC: 8731 Biological research

(G-16194)
DUCT CLEANING CORP
3 Germay Dr Ste 4 (19804-1127)
P.O. Box 9265 (19809-0265)
PHONE.............................302 310-4060
EMP: 6 EST: 2019
SALES (est): 98.84K **Privately Held**
SIC: 7699 Cleaning services

(G-16195)
DUFFIELD ASSOCIATES LLC (HQ)
Also Called: Duffield
5400 Limestone Rd (19808-1284)
PHONE.............................302 239-6634
Gerry Salontai, *CEO*
Stacy Ziegler, *
Guy Marcozzi, *
Deirdre Smith, *
EMP: 47 EST: 1976
SQ FT: 20,000
SALES (est): 23.08MM
SALES (corp-wide): 163.8MM **Privately Held**
Web: www.verdantas.com
SIC: 8711 Consulting engineer
PA: Verdantas Llc
   6397 Emerald Pkwy Ste 200
   Dublin OH 43016
   614 793-8777

(G-16196)
DUGAN DT ROOFING INC
Also Called: Dugan, Dt Roofing Co
20 S Woodward Ave (19805-2355)
PHONE.............................302 636-9300
Dan T Dugan, *Owner*
EMP: 6 EST: 1980
SQ FT: 3,000
SALES (est): 472.13K **Privately Held**
SIC: 1521 Single-family home remodeling, additions, and repairs

(G-16197)
DUHA LOGISTICS INC
3 Germay Dr Ste 4 # 2159 (19804-1127)
PHONE.............................888 493-5999
Kenneth Taylor, *Pr*
EMP: 12 EST: 2021
SALES (est): 584.91K **Privately Held**
SIC: 4731 Freight forwarding

(G-16198)
DULY NOTED LLC
427 N Tatnall St (19801-2230)
PHONE.............................302 353-4585
Oleh Hereliuk, *CEO*
EMP: 5 EST: 2021
SALES (est): 351.19K **Privately Held**
Web: www.dulynoted.co.uk
SIC: 8111 Legal services

(G-16199)
DUN RITE CLEANERS
132 Concord Ave (19802-4108)
PHONE.............................302 654-3958
Jai Choi, *Owner*
EMP: 5 EST: 1946
SALES (est): 209.73K **Privately Held**
Web: www.dunritede.com
SIC: 7216 Cleaning and dyeing, except rugs

(G-16200)
DUNBAR ARMORED INC
320 Water St Ste A (19804-2434)
PHONE.............................302 892-4950
Kris Nonnenmacher, *Mgr*
EMP: 38
SALES (corp-wide): 4.54B **Publicly Held**
Web: www.dunbarsecurity.com
SIC: 7381 Security guard service
HQ: Dunbar Armored, Inc.
   50 Schilling Rd
   Hunt Valley MD 21031
   410 584-9800

(G-16201)
DUNS INVESTING CORPORATION
801 N West St Fl 2 (19801-1525)
PHONE.............................302 651-2050
EMP: 5
SIC: 6719 Investment holding companies, except banks

(G-16202)
DUPONT ATHNTCATION SYSTEMS LLC
4417 Lancaster Pike (19805-1523)
PHONE.............................800 345-9999
EMP: 10 EST: 2001
SALES (est): 230.86K **Privately Held**
SIC: 2819 Industrial inorganic chemicals, nec

(G-16203)
DUPONT CAPITAL MANAGEMENT CORP
974 Centre Rd (19805-1269)
PHONE.............................302 477-6000
Valerie J Sill, *CIO*
EMP: 7 EST: 1993
SALES (est): 9.98MM
SALES (corp-wide): 17.23B **Publicly Held**
Web: www.dupontcapital.com
SIC: 6722 Money market mutual funds
HQ: Eidp, Inc.
   9330 Zionsville Rd
   Indianapolis IN 46268
   833 267-8382

(G-16204)
DUPONT CAPITAL MGT GEM TR
974 Centre Rd (19805-1269)
PHONE.............................302 477-6000
Andrea Alvarado, *Prin*
EMP: 6 EST: 2008
SALES (est): 212.88K **Privately Held**
Web: www.dupontcapital.com
SIC: 6733 Trusts, nec

(G-16205)
DUPONT DE NEMOURS INC (PA)
974 Centre Rd Bldg 730 (19805-1269)
PHONE.............................302 774-3034
Edward D Breen, *Ex Ch Bd*
Lori D Koch, *Ex VP*
Christopher Raia, *Chief Human Resource Officer*
Erik T Hoover, *Sr VP*
Steve Larrabee, *CIO*
EMP: 5000 EST: 1802
SALES (est): 13.02B
SALES (corp-wide): 13.02B **Publicly Held**

Wilmington - New Castle County (G-16206)
GEOGRAPHIC SECTION

Web: www.dupont.com
SIC: 2821 3081 3086 3674 Thermoplastic materials; Plastics film and sheet; Plastics foam products; Solar cells

(G-16206)
DUPONT DISPLAYS INC (DH)
974 Centre Rd (19805-1269)
PHONE..................805 562-9293
Ellen J Kullman, *CEO*
Johns S Richard, *
Steve Quindlen, *
Steve Gallow, *
EMP: 35 EST: 1990
SALES (est): 24.21MM
SALES (corp-wide): 17.23B **Publicly Held**
Web: www.dupont.com
SIC: 3674 8731 Light emitting diodes; Commercial research laboratory
HQ: Eidp, Inc.
    9330 Zionsville Rd
    Indianapolis IN 46268
    833 267-8382

(G-16207)
DUPONT ELECTRONICS HOLDING LLC
974 Centre Rd (19805-1269)
PHONE..................302 999-4083
EMP: 7 EST: 2018
SALES (est): 966.1K
SALES (corp-wide): 12.44B **Publicly Held**
Web: www.dupont.com
SIC: 0721 Crop planting and protection
PA: International Flavors & Fragrances Inc.
    521 W 57th St
    New York NY 10019
    212 765-5500

(G-16208)
DUPONT ESL SECURITY
200 Powder Mill Rd (19803-2907)
PHONE..................302 695-1657
EMP: 7 EST: 2010
SALES (est): 197.05K **Privately Held**
Web: www.dupont.com
SIC: 7381 Guard services

(G-16209)
DUPONT FLAMENTS - AMERICAS LLC
974 Centre Rd Chestnut Run Plaza Bldg 730 (19805)
P.O. Box 80022 (19880-0022)
PHONE..................302 774-1000
John Locklear, *Managing Member*
◆ EMP: 48 EST: 2004
SALES (est): 914.64K
SALES (corp-wide): 9.67B **Publicly Held**
Web: www.dupont.com
SIC: 3991 Brushes, household or industrial
PA: Celanese Corporation
    222 Las Colinas Blvd W
    Irving TX 75039
    877 295-0004

(G-16210)
DUPONT INDUS BSCIENCES USA LLC (HQ)
974 Centre Rd (19805-1269)
PHONE..................302 774-1000
EMP: 31 EST: 2017
SALES (est): 13.54MM
SALES (corp-wide): 13.02B **Publicly Held**
Web: www.dupont.com
SIC: 2879 2824 2865 2821 Agricultural chemicals, nec; Nylon fibers; Dyes and pigments; Thermoplastic materials
PA: Dupont De Nemours, Inc.
    974 Centre Rd Bldg 730
    Wilmington DE 19805
    302 774-3034

(G-16211)
DUPONT JOHN GARDNER
2002 Woodlawn Ave (19806-2234)
PHONE..................302 777-3730
John Dupont, *Prin*
EMP: 7 EST: 2010
SALES (est): 51.85K **Privately Held**
Web: www.dupont.com
SIC: 2819 Industrial inorganic chemicals, nec

(G-16212)
DUPONT OPERATIONS INC
974 Centre Rd (19805-1269)
PHONE..................302 992-5940
EMP: 27 EST: 1998
SALES (est): 1.23MM
SALES (corp-wide): 17.45B **Publicly Held**
Web: www.dupont.com
SIC: 8999 Actuarial consultant
HQ: Eidp, Inc.
    9330 Zionsville Rd
    Indianapolis IN 46268
    833 267-8382

(G-16213)
DUPONT PRFMCE COATINGS INC
Also Called: Dupont
4417 Lancaster Pike (19805)
PHONE..................302 892-1064
Ellen Kullman, *CEO*
EMP: 81 EST: 1998
SALES (est): 13.23MM **Privately Held**
Web: www.dupont.com
SIC: 2819 Industrial inorganic chemicals, nec

(G-16214)
DUPONT PRFMCE ELASTOMERS LLC (DH)
4417 Lancaster Pike Bldg 728 (19805-1523)
◆ EMP: 450 EST: 1996
SALES (est): 191.41MM
SALES (corp-wide): 17.23B **Publicly Held**
Web: www.dupont.com
SIC: 2821 Plastics materials and resins
HQ: Eidp, Inc.
    9330 Zionsville Rd
    Indianapolis IN 46268
    833 267-8382

(G-16215)
DUPONT S&C HOLDING LLC
974 Centre Rd (19805-1269)
PHONE..................302 999-4083
EMP: 6 EST: 2018
SALES (est): 812.25K
SALES (corp-wide): 12.44B **Publicly Held**
Web: www.dupont.com
SIC: 0721 Crop planting and protection
PA: International Flavors & Fragrances Inc.
    521 W 57th St
    New York NY 10019
    212 765-5500

(G-16216)
DUPONT SPECIALTY PDTS USA LLC (HQ)
974 Centre Rd (19805-1269)
PHONE..................302 992-2941
Edward Breen, *CEO*
EMP: 32 EST: 2017
SALES (est): 505.49MM
SALES (corp-wide): 13.02B **Publicly Held**
Web: www.dupont.com
SIC: 2821 3081 3086 3674 Thermoplastic materials; Plastics film and sheet; Plastics foam products; Solar cells
PA: Dupont De Nemours, Inc.
    974 Centre Rd Bldg 730
    Wilmington DE 19805
    302 774-3034

(G-16217)
DUPONT TATE LYLE BIO PDTS LLC
1007 Market St Fl 2 (19898-1100)
P.O. Box 1039 (19899-1039)
PHONE..................865 408-1962
EMP: 2 EST: 2000
SALES (est): 399.7K **Privately Held**
Web: www.covationbiopdo.com
SIC: 2869 Polyhydric alcohol esters, aminos, etc.

(G-16218)
DUPONT TXTLES INTRIORS DEL INC
974 Centre Rd (19805-1269)
PHONE..................302 774-1000
Ellen Kullman, *Pr*
Richard Goodmanson, *Ex VP*
Linda West, *VP*
Michael Walker, *VP*
Jeff Keefer, *CFO*
▼ EMP: 42 EST: 2002
SALES (est): 3.72MM
SALES (corp-wide): 17.23B **Publicly Held**
Web: www.dupont.com
SIC: 2789 Bookbinding and related work
HQ: Eidp, Inc.
    9330 Zionsville Rd
    Indianapolis IN 46268
    833 267-8382

(G-16219)
DUPONT US HOLDING LLC
974 Centre Rd (19805-1269)
PHONE..................302 999-4083
EMP: 11 EST: 2018
SALES (est): 4.68MM
SALES (corp-wide): 12.44B **Publicly Held**
Web: www.dupont.com
SIC: 0721 Crop planting and protection
PA: International Flavors & Fragrances Inc.
    521 W 57th St
    New York NY 10019
    212 765-5500

(G-16220)
DURAFIBER TECH DFT ENTPS INC (HQ)
Also Called: Durafiber Technologies
300 Delaware Ave Ste 1100 (19801-1670)
PHONE..................704 912-3770
Frank Papa, *CEO*
Frank Papa, *Pr*
Rick Spurlock, *
Erwin Bette, *
David Ascher, *Legal**
◆ EMP: 75 EST: 2004
SALES (est): 337.25MM
SALES (corp-wide): 3.46B **Privately Held**
SIC: 2824 Nylon fibers
PA: Sun Capital Partners, Inc.
    5200 Town Center Cir # 450
    Boca Raton FL 33486
    561 394-0550

(G-16221)
DURATION MEDIA LLC
1209 N Orange St (19801-1120)
PHONE..................917 283-5971
Andrew Batkin, *CEO*
EMP: 9 EST: 2018
SALES (est): 771.71K **Privately Held**
SIC: 7311 7389 Advertising agencies; Business services, nec

(G-16222)
DUST AWAY CLEANING SVCS INC
700 Cornell Dr Ste E1 (19801-5762)
P.O. Box 346 (19899-0346)
PHONE..................302 658-8803
Carrie Myer, *Pr*
EMP: 10 EST: 2003
SQ FT: 1,500
SALES (est): 196.37K **Privately Held**
SIC: 7349 Janitorial service, contract basis

(G-16223)
DUX TECHNOLOGIES INC ○
251 Little Falls Dr (19808-1674)
PHONE..................507 312-9687
Or Latovitz, *CEO*
EMP: 5 EST: 2023
SALES (est): 209.21K **Privately Held**
SIC: 7372 Prepackaged software

(G-16224)
DVD AND GAME EXCHANGE DE
2707 Pecksniff Rd (19808-2177)
PHONE..................302 530-1199
Tony Dipacco, *Prin*
EMP: 5 EST: 2010
SALES (est): 55.33K **Privately Held**
SIC: 7841 Video tape rental

(G-16225)
DVHD INC
Also Called: Delaware Valley Housing Dev
1716 Shallcross Ave Ste 02 (19806-2322)
P.O. Box 9083 (19809-0083)
PHONE..................302 584-3547
Junius Nichols, *Ch Bd*
Allexea Blackwell, *CEO*
Junius Nichols, *Ex Dir*
EMP: 5 EST: 2004
SALES (est): 274.15K **Privately Held**
SIC: 8748 Urban planning and consulting services

(G-16226)
DYATECH LLC
1000 N West St Ste 1200 (19801-1058)
PHONE..................845 666-0786
Arsalan Khan, *Managing Member*
Louis Graham, *Dir*
EMP: 15 EST: 2018
SALES (est): 1.02MM **Privately Held**
Web: www.dyatechs.com
SIC: 7371 Computer software systems analysis and design, custom

(G-16227)
DYNAMIC DENTAL SOLUTIONS LLC
1007 N Orange St (19801-1239)
PHONE..................888 908-8225
Nina Bond, *Managing Member*
EMP: 15 EST: 2018
SALES (est): 712.32K **Privately Held**
Web: www.dynamicdentalsolutions.net
SIC: 8621 Dental association

(G-16228)
DYNAMIC DEVICES LLC
8 Lewis Cir (19804-1618)
PHONE..................302 994-2401
EMP: 10 EST: 1999
SALES (est): 1.66MM **Privately Held**
Web: www.dynamicdevices.com
SIC: 8742 Management consulting services

(G-16229)
DYNAMIC PHYSICAL THERAPY
2701 Kirkwood Hwy (19805-4911)
PHONE..................302 668-1768
Derek Schiller, *Prin*
EMP: 15 EST: 2016
SALES (est): 200.63K **Privately Held**
Web: www.pivotphysicaltherapy.com
SIC: 8049 Physical therapist

(G-16230)
DYNAMIC SUPPORT SERVICES INC
1209 N Orange St (19801-1120)

GEOGRAPHIC SECTION
Wilmington - New Castle County (G-16258)

PHONE.................202 820-3113
Sifatullah Muradi, *Prin*
Salim Shirzai, *Prin*
Nathan Ertel, *Prin*
EMP: 5 EST: 2017
SALES (est): 104.73K **Privately Held**
SIC: 8748 Business consulting, nec

(G-16231)
DYNAMIC TRNSP & LOGISTICS LLC
1201 N Market St (19801-1147)
PHONE.................302 991-1005
Ryan Larsen, *CEO*
EMP: 5 EST: 2017
SALES (est): 340.45K **Privately Held**
SIC: 4731 Brokers, shipping

(G-16232)
DYNASEP INC
4023 Kennett Pike Ste 278 (19807-2018)
PHONE.................302 268-6464
Brian Waibel, *Pr*
Joy Waibel, *VP*
EMP: 4 EST: 2011
SALES (est): 492.47K **Privately Held**
Web: www.dynasep.com
SIC: 3559 Refinery, chemical processing, and similar machinery

(G-16233)
DYSIS MEDICAL
920 N King St Lbby 2 (19801-3319)
PHONE.................813 997-8979
EMP: 9 EST: 2018
SALES (est): 190.85K **Privately Held**
Web: www.dysismedical.com
SIC: 8099 Health and allied services, nec

(G-16234)
E B D MANAGEMENT INC
Also Called: Edward B De Seta & Associates
4001 Kennett Pike Ste 10 (19807-2000)
P.O. Box 20516 (29413-0516)
PHONE.................302 428-1313
Edward B De Seta, *Pr*
EMP: 7 EST: 1970
SALES (est): 806.63K **Privately Held**
SIC: 6531 Real estate managers

(G-16235)
E BAUMANN CONTRACTING
317 Marsh Rd (19809-3139)
PHONE.................302 824-3765
EMP: 5 EST: 2017
SALES (est): 229.18K **Privately Held**
Web: www.ebaumanncontracting.com
SIC: 1799 Special trade contractors, nec

(G-16236)
E BUSINESS PAGES LLC
1201 N Orange St Ste 600 (19801-1171)
PHONE.................302 504-4403
Enrico Saunders, *Mgr*
EMP: 5 EST: 2014
SALES (est): 225.35K **Privately Held**
Web: www.ebusinesspages.com
SIC: 7311 Advertising agencies

(G-16237)
E E ROSSER INC
5109 Governor Printz Blvd (19809-2743)
PHONE.................302 762-9643
Gary Rosser, *Pr*
EMP: 6 EST: 1964
SALES (est): 1.1MM **Privately Held**
SIC: 5084 5169 Welding machinery and equipment; Compressed gas

(G-16238)
E EARLE DOWNING INC
1221 Bowers St Ste 5 (19802-4637)
P.O. Box 1151 (19899-1151)
PHONE.................302 656-9908
Bruce Downing, *Pr*
Mary Anne Downing, *VP*
EMP: 20 EST: 1938
SQ FT: 2,000
SALES (est): 1.06MM **Privately Held**
Web: www.downingpaving.com
SIC: 1611 Highway and street paving contractor

(G-16239)
E I DU PONT DE NEMOURS & CO
1 Righter Pkwy (19803-1534)
PHONE.................843 335-5934
Valerie J Sill Cfa, *CEO*
EMP: 20 EST: 2016
SALES (est): 1.13MM **Privately Held**
Web: www.dupontcapital.com
SIC: 2899 Chemical preparations, nec

(G-16240)
E M C PROCESS COMPANY INC
1663 E Ayre St (19804-2514)
P.O. Box 3035 (19804-0035)
PHONE.................302 999-9204
George F Baumeister, *Pr*
EMP: 5 EST: 1977
SQ FT: 4,000
SALES (est): 492.04K **Privately Held**
Web: www.emcprocess.com
SIC: 3479 Coating of metals and formed products

(G-16241)
E W BROWN INC
1202 E 16th St (19802-5217)
P.O. Box 1680 (19707-5680)
PHONE.................302 652-6612
Charles E Brown, *Pr*
Charles E Brown Junior, *VP*
EMP: 4 EST: 1928
SQ FT: 3,400
SALES (est): 254.32K **Privately Held**
Web: www.ewbrown.com
SIC: 2394 1799 Awnings, fabric: made from purchased materials; Awning installation

(G-16242)
E-CUBE
143 Carpenters Row (19807-2136)
PHONE.................302 290-7413
Lake Silver, *Prin*
EMP: 7 EST: 2017
SALES (est): 90.77K **Privately Held**
SIC: 6799 Investors, nec

(G-16243)
E-INDUSTRIAL SUPPLIERS LLC
2207 Concord Pike Ste 648 (19803-2908)
PHONE.................302 251-6210
EMP: 7 EST: 2007
SALES (est): 500.8K **Privately Held**
Web: www.eindustrialsuppliers.com
SIC: 5085 5082 Industrial supplies; General construction machinery and equipment

(G-16244)
E-VOLVE FITNESS STUDIO
3680 Kirkwood Hwy (19808-5104)
PHONE.................302 513-9641
EMP: 5 EST: 2018
SALES (est): 29.54K **Privately Held**
Web: www.e-volvefitnessstudio.com
SIC: 7991 Exercise facilities

(G-16245)
EAGAN US HOLDCO LLC ✪
Also Called: Elite
401 Old Kennett Rd (19807-1731)
PHONE.................414 339-8275
Mark Dorman, *CEO*
Zain Kaj, *CFO*
EMP: 610 EST: 2023
SALES (est): 51.51MM
SALES (corp-wide): 2.96B **Publicly Held**
SIC: 7371 7372 Computer software development and applications; Business oriented computer software
HQ: Tpg Inc.
    301 Commerce St Ste 3300
    Fort Worth TX 76102
    817 871-4000

(G-16246)
EAGLE PLAZA ASSOCIATES INC
234 N James St (19804-3132)
PHONE.................302 999-0708
Verino Pettinaro, *Pr*
Gregory Pettinaro, *Pt*
Tracy Crowley, *Pt*
Cindy Pettinaro, *Pt*
Victoria Pettinaro, *Pt*
EMP: 6 EST: 1981
SQ FT: 2,000
SALES (est): 192.32K **Privately Held**
SIC: 6512 Shopping center, property operation only

(G-16247)
EAMO HEALTH LLC
1201 N Market St Ste 1404 (19801-1163)
PHONE.................302 565-7528
EMP: 5 EST: 2021
SALES (est): 267.86K **Privately Held**
Web: www.eamohealthacademy.education
SIC: 8742 Hospital and health services consultant

(G-16248)
EARLY FOUNDATIONS THERAPEUTIC
Also Called: Early Foundation Preschool
2814 W 2nd St (19805-1807)
PHONE.................302 384-6905
Joan D Fletcher, *Prin*
EMP: 5 EST: 2012
SALES (est): 80.58K **Privately Held**
Web: www.earlyfoundationcenter.com
SIC: 8641 Civic and social associations

(G-16249)
EARLY LEARNING CENTER
1218 B St (19801-5844)
PHONE.................302 831-0584
Heidi Beck, *Prin*
EMP: 10 EST: 2015
SALES (est): 157.43K **Privately Held**
SIC: 8351 Preschool center

(G-16250)
EAST COAST CLEANING CO LLC
528 Ruxton Dr (19809-2830)
P.O. Box 7588 (19803-0588)
PHONE.................302 762-6820
Curtis Jackson, *Owner*
Michelle Jackson, *Pt*
EMP: 5 EST: 1998
SALES (est): 201.42K **Privately Held**
Web: www.eastcoastcleaningco.com
SIC: 5087 Cleaning and maintenance equipment and supplies

(G-16251)
EAST COAST ELECTRIC INC
824 Kiamensi Rd (19804-3420)
PHONE.................302 998-1577
Robert C Race, *Pr*
EMP: 10 EST: 1971
SALES (est): 900.87K **Privately Held**
Web: www.eastcoastelectric.net
SIC: 1731 General electrical contractor

(G-16252)
EAST COAST MINORITY SUPPLIER
610 W 8th St (19801-1450)
PHONE.................302 656-3337
Rock Brown, *Pr*
EMP: 5 EST: 2000
SALES (est): 171.57K **Privately Held**
SIC: 5231 5211 1522 1541 Wallpaper; Lumber and other building materials; Residential construction, nec; Industrial buildings and warehouses

(G-16253)
EAST COAST PROPERTY MGT INC
200 N Poplar St (19801-3926)
PHONE.................302 654-2196
Renee Robinson, *Brnch Mgr*
EMP: 8
SALES (corp-wide): 10.61MM **Privately Held**
Web: www.eastcoastmgt.com
SIC: 7299 Apartment locating service
HQ: East Coast Property Management, Inc.
    977 E Masten Cir
    Milford DE 19963

(G-16254)
EAST COAST SALES & LEASE LLC
3623 Kirkwood Hwy (19808-5103)
PHONE.................302 995-7505
EMP: 5 EST: 2011
SALES (est): 376.95K **Privately Held**
SIC: 6519 Real property lessors, nec

(G-16255)
EASTERN BRNDYWINE HNDRED CRDNT
1212 Haines Ave (19809-2713)
PHONE.................302 764-2476
Terrence K Wright, *Prin*
EMP: 5 EST: 2012
SALES (est): 12.85K **Privately Held**
SIC: 8641 Civic and social associations

(G-16256)
EASTERN CHRISTIAN MANAGEMENT
330 Water St (19804-2433)
PHONE.................302 633-1421
Matthew Haney, *Admn*
EMP: 5 EST: 2012
SALES (est): 114.51K **Privately Held**
SIC: 8741 Management services

(G-16257)
EASTERN HEALTH CARE CTR
813 N Market St (19801-3010)
PHONE.................302 543-4998
Ji Zhe, *Prin*
EMP: 6 EST: 2016
SALES (est): 105.5K **Privately Held**
SIC: 8049 Acupuncturist

(G-16258)
EASTERN HOME IMPROVEMENTS INC (PA)
Also Called: Four Seasons Sunrooms
3112 Lancaster Ave (19805-1461)
PHONE.................302 655-9920
Ken Quinn, *Pr*

(PA)=Parent Co (HQ)=Headquarters
✪ = New Business established in last 2 years

Wilmington - New Castle County (G-16259)

Eric Quinn, *VP*
EMP: 8 **EST:** 1982
SQ FT: 2,200
SALES (est): 1.1MM
SALES (corp-wide): 1.1MM **Privately Held**
Web: www.fourseasonssunrooms.com
SIC: 1521 1793 1542 General remodeling, single-family houses; Glass and glazing work; Commercial and office buildings, renovation and repair

(G-16259)
EASTERN HWY SPECIALISTS INC
3604 Downing Dr (19802-2406)
P.O. Box 129 (19710-0129)
PHONE.................................302 777-7673
Robert Field, *Pr*
Clairemarie Field, *Stockholder*
EMP: 52 **EST:** 2003
SQ FT: 800
SALES (est): 9.5MM **Privately Held**
Web: www.easternhighwayspecialists.com
SIC: 1622 Bridge construction

(G-16260)
EASTERN PROPERTY ASSOC INC
715 Dorcaster Dr (19808-2213)
P.O. Box 5951 (19808-0951)
PHONE.................................302 998-0962
Ron Yanacek, *Pr*
EMP: 5 **EST:** 1983
SALES (est): 640K **Privately Held**
SIC: 1531 Operative builders

(G-16261)
EASTERN PROPERTY GROUP INC
Also Called: Pebble Hill Apartments
3408 Miller Rd Apt C7 (19802-2529)
PHONE.................................302 764-7112
Marene Riser, *Brnch Mgr*
EMP: 5
SALES (corp-wide): 2.29MM **Privately Held**
Web: www.easternpropertygroup.com
SIC: 6513 Apartment building operators
PA: Eastern Property Group, Inc.
  28 S Waterloo Rd Ste 201
  Devon PA 19333
  610 293-1400

(G-16262)
EASTERN PROSPERITY GROUP
Also Called: Pebble Hill Assoc A Partnr
3408 Miller Rd (19802-2529)
PHONE.................................302 764-7112
Nancy Huston, *Mgr*
EMP: 5
SQ FT: 125,000
SALES (est): 326.19K **Privately Held**
Web: www.easternstatesgroup.com
SIC: 6513 Apartment building operators

(G-16263)
EASTERN SPECIALTY FINANCE INC
Also Called: Check 'n Go 2801
800 W 4th St Ste 401 (19801-2045)
PHONE.................................302 658-5431
EMP: 10
SALES (corp-wide): 696.24MM **Privately Held**
SIC: 6141 Personal credit institutions
HQ: Eastern Specialty Finance, Inc.
  7755 Montgomery Rd # 400
  Cincinnati OH

(G-16264)
EASTERN STATES CNSTR SVC INC
702 First State Blvd (19804-3558)
PHONE.................................302 995-2259
Richard J Julian, *Prin*
Richard J Julian, *Pr*
Eugene Julian,
Terence T Gleason,
Patricia M Falgowski,
EMP: 80 **EST:** 1983
SQ FT: 6,500
SALES (est): 15.72MM **Privately Held**
Web: www.eastern-states.net
SIC: 1799 1623 1611 Building site preparation; Underground utilities contractor ; General contractor, highway and street construction

(G-16265)
EASTERN STATES DEVELPMENT INC
702 First State Blvd (19804-3558)
PHONE.................................302 998-0683
Eugene M Julian, *Pr*
Richard J Julian, *VP*
Francis R Julian, *VP*
EMP: 5 **EST:** 1958
SQ FT: 1,000
SALES (est): 1.32MM **Privately Held**
Web: www.eastern-states.net
SIC: 6552 Land subdividers and developers, commercial

(G-16266)
EASTSIDE BLUPRT CMNTY DEV CORP
121 N Poplar St (19801-3955)
PHONE.................................302 384-2350
David Mosley, *Ex Dir*
EMP: 10 **EST:** 2008
SALES (est): 124.98K **Privately Held**
SIC: 8399 Community development groups

(G-16267)
EASY ANALYTIC SOFTWARE INC
Also Called: Easy Analytic Software Inc
21 Paladin Dr (19802-1701)
PHONE.................................302 762-4271
Gregory Gergen, *Brnch Mgr*
EMP: 2
Web: www.easidemographics.com
SIC: 7372 Prepackaged software
PA: Easy Analytic Software Inc
  131 Four Seasons Dr
  Caldwell NJ 07006

(G-16268)
EASY LIVING SERVICE
2301 W Newport Pike (19804-3848)
PHONE.................................302 633-4849
Peter Tran, *Prin*
EMP: 6 **EST:** 2001
SALES (est): 128.38K **Privately Held**
SIC: 1799 Special trade contractors, nec

(G-16269)
EASY MONEY EMG
2501 Concord Pike (19803-5002)
PHONE.................................302 421-3610
Taminka Bryant, *Mgr*
EMP: 6 **EST:** 2010
SALES (est): 136.34K **Privately Held**
Web: www.easymoneynow.com
SIC: 6099 Check cashing agencies

(G-16270)
EASY SALES SOLUTIONS INC
2055 Limestone Rd (19808-5536)
PHONE.................................929 273-0505
Faisal Qarni, *Prin*
EMP: 5
SALES (est): 104.37K **Privately Held**
SIC: 7379 Online services technology consultants

(G-16271)
EASY SEND INC
103 Center Ct Ste 403 (19810-2523)
PHONE.................................610 389-0622
Tal Daskal, *CEO*
EMP: 18 **EST:** 2019
SALES (est): 462.62K **Privately Held**
SIC: 7371 Computer software development and applications
PA: Easysend Ltd
  18 Caro Yosef
  Tel Aviv-Jaffa

(G-16272)
EAT CLEAN JUICE BAR LLC
225 N Market St (19801-2527)
PHONE.................................856 397-9112
EMP: 10 **EST:** 2018
SALES (est): 286.19K **Privately Held**
Web: www.eatcleande.com
SIC: 7699 Cleaning services

(G-16273)
EBC CARPET SERVICES CORP
1300 First State Blvd Ste I (19804)
PHONE.................................302 995-7461
Christopher Rankin, *Pr*
Christine Rankin,
Gerald Denhof,
EMP: 30 **EST:** 1998
SALES (est): 2.62MM **Privately Held**
Web: www.millicare.com
SIC: 7217 Carpet and rug cleaning and repairing plant

(G-16274)
EBC NATIONAL INC
1300 First State Blvd (19804-3548)
PHONE.................................302 995-7461
EMP: 16 **EST:** 2008
SALES (est): 425.17K **Privately Held**
SIC: 7217 Carpet and upholstery cleaning

(G-16275)
EBC SYSTEMS LLC
1 Ave Of The Arts (19801-5047)
PHONE.................................302 472-1896
EMP: 8 **EST:** 2010
SALES (est): 398.35K **Privately Held**
Web: www.millicare.com
SIC: 7373 Systems integration services

(G-16276)
EBRIGHT FOUNDATION LL
607 W 18th St (19802-4707)
PHONE.................................215 370-2821
Matthew Ditty, *Dir*
EMP: 7 **EST:** 2016
SALES (est): 201.56K **Privately Held**
Web: www.ebrightcollaborative.com
SIC: 8641 Civic and social associations

(G-16277)
EC INNOVATIONS USA INC
501 Silverside Rd Ste 105 (19809-1376)
PHONE.................................312 863-1966
Michael Asquith, *Pr*
EMP: 23 **EST:** 2017
SALES (est): 606.31K **Privately Held**
Web: www.ecinnovations.com
SIC: 7389 Translation services

(G-16278)
ECIRCULAR LLC ◇
2810 N Church St Ste 624369 (19802-4447)
PHONE.................................713 514-4675
Tim Aubrey, *Managing Member*
EMP: 10 **EST:** 2023
SALES (est): 355.79K **Privately Held**
SIC: 7374 Computer processing services

(G-16279)
ECLIPES ERECTION INC
330 Water St (19804-2433)
PHONE.................................302 633-1421
EMP: 9 **EST:** 1994
SALES (est): 529.98K **Privately Held**
SIC: 1799 Erection and dismantling of forms for poured concrete

(G-16280)
ECLIPSE SOFTWARE INC
908 Greenhill Ave (19805-2640)
PHONE.................................212 727-1136
Andrew Weigel, *Pr*
EMP: 5 **EST:** 2010
SALES (est): 68.13K **Privately Held**
Web: www.eclipsesoftware.biz
SIC: 7372 Business oriented computer software

(G-16281)
ECM CARPENTRY LLC
12 1st Ave (19808-4909)
PHONE.................................302 494-8995
Erick Cortes, *Prin*
EMP: 6 **EST:** 2016
SALES (est): 87.48K **Privately Held**
Web: www.ecmcarpentry.com
SIC: 1751 Finish and trim carpentry

(G-16282)
ECO PLASTIC PRODUCTS DEL INC
18 Germay Dr (19804-1105)
PHONE.................................302 575-9227
Jim Kelley, *CEO*
EMP: 10 **EST:** 2015
SALES (est): 226.28K **Privately Held**
Web: www.ecoplasticproducts.org
SIC: 2611 Pulp manufactured from waste or recycled paper

(G-16283)
ED DURYNSKI
130 Landis Way N (19803-6403)
PHONE.................................302 994-6642
Ed Durynski, *Prin*
EMP: 5 **EST:** 2009
SALES (est): 228.68K **Privately Held**
SIC: 1522 Residential construction, nec

(G-16284)
ED TURULSKI CUSTOM WOODWORKING
1020 Liberty Rd (19804-2857)
P.O. Box 5935 (19808-0935)
PHONE.................................302 658-2221
EMP: 9 **EST:** 1994
SALES (est): 979.3K **Privately Held**
SIC: 1751 Cabinet building and installation

(G-16285)
EDAURA INC
1209 N Orange St (19801-1120)
PHONE.................................707 330-9836
Nidal Khalifeh, *CEO*
EMP: 8 **EST:** 2015
SALES (est): 374.77K **Privately Held**
SIC: 7372 Educational computer software

(G-16286)
EDEN LAND CARE
202 New Rd Unit 7 (19805-4141)
P.O. Box 1581 (19707-5581)
PHONE.................................302 379-2405
EMP: 11 **EST:** 2014
SALES (est): 197.11K **Privately Held**
Web: www.edenlandcare.com

GEOGRAPHIC SECTION
Wilmington - New Castle County (G-16314)

SIC: 8351 Child day care services

(G-16287)
EDEN ROCK
2210 Swiss Ln (19810-4241)
PHONE..................302 475-9400
Mark Roth, *Pr*
EMP: 23 **EST:** 1999
SALES (est): 1.1MM **Privately Held**
Web: www.edenrockgroup.com
SIC: 6513 Retirement hotel operation

(G-16288)
EDGE CONSTRUCTION CORP
300 Martin Luther King Blvd Ste 300 (19801)
PHONE..................302 778-5200
Dan Bachtle, *CEO*
EMP: 6 **EST:** 1988
SALES (est): 978.55K **Privately Held**
Web: www.edgeconstructioncorp.com
SIC: 1521 1542 New construction, single-family houses; Commercial and office building, new construction

(G-16289)
EDGEMOOR COMMUNITY CENTER INC
500 Duncan Rd Ofc A (19809-2360)
PHONE..................302 762-1391
Scott Borino, *Ex Dir*
EMP: 56 **EST:** 1978
SQ FT: 48,000
SALES (est): 2.77MM **Privately Held**
SIC: 8351 Child day care services

(G-16290)
EDGEMOOR MATERIALS INC
1230 Railcar Ave (19802-4614)
PHONE..................302 655-1510
EMP: 13
Web: www.edgemoormaterials.com
SIC: 5032 Aggregate

(G-16291)
EDGEMOOR RVTALIZATION COOP INC
Also Called: ERC
41 S Cannon Dr (19809-3311)
P.O. Box 9563 (19809-0563)
PHONE..................302 293-3944
Cheri Whitney, *Prin*
EMP: 6 **EST:** 2009
SALES (est): 71.11K **Privately Held**
Web: www.edgemooronline.org
SIC: 8322 8399 Youth center; Community action agency

(G-16292)
EDIFY INC
1007 N Orange St Fl 4 (19801-1239)
PHONE..................302 520-2403
David Ogbonna-eze, *CEO*
EMP: 2
SALES (est): 65.58K **Privately Held**
SIC: 7812 7372 Motion picture and video production; Prepackaged software

(G-16293)
EDIS BUILDING SYSTEMS INC
110 S Poplar St (19801-5053)
PHONE..................302 421-5700
E Andrew Disabatino, *Pr*
Richard P Di Sabatino Junior, *VP*
Michael Miller, *Treas*
Frances F Williams, *Sec*
EMP: 5 **EST:** 1981
SQ FT: 17,000
SALES (est): 1.98MM
SALES (corp-wide): 30.73MM **Privately Held**
Web: www.ediscompany.com
SIC: 5039 Prefabricated buildings
PA: Crystal Holdings, Inc.
110 S Poplar St Ste 400
Wilmington DE 19801
302 421-5700

(G-16294)
EDIS COMPANY
110 S Poplar St Ste 400 (19801-5053)
P.O. Box 2697 (19805-0697)
PHONE..................302 421-5700
A Andrew Di Sabatino Junior, *Pr*
Richard P Di Sabatino Junior, *VP*
Frances F Williams, *
EMP: 45 **EST:** 1908
SQ FT: 17,000
SALES (est): 28.75MM
SALES (corp-wide): 30.73MM **Privately Held**
Web: www.ediscompany.com
SIC: 1541 1542 Industrial buildings, new construction, nec; Commercial and office building, new construction
PA: Crystal Holdings, Inc.
110 S Poplar St Ste 400
Wilmington DE 19801
302 421-5700

(G-16295)
EDIT INC
1026 Sedwick Dr (19803-3331)
PHONE..................302 478-7069
Richard B Tippett, *Pr*
Judith Tippett, *VP*
EMP: 2 **EST:** 1969
SALES (est): 141.29K **Privately Held**
Web: www.epic-edit.com
SIC: 2741 Business service newsletters: publishing and printing

(G-16296)
EDS AUTO REPAIR
4601 Governor Printz Blvd (19809-3443)
PHONE..................302 468-0955
EMP: 6 **EST:** 2017
SALES (est): 227.1K **Privately Held**
SIC: 7538 General automotive repair shops

(G-16297)
EDTECH CONSULTING LLC
1201 N Orange St (19801-1155)
PHONE..................661 644-2990
EMP: 6
SALES (est): 277.49K **Privately Held**
Web: www.edtech-consult.com
SIC: 7372 7389 Educational computer software; Business services, nec

(G-16298)
EDUCATION SVCS UNLIMITED LLC
Also Called: Lifespan Development Centers
610 Westmont Dr (19808-1537)
PHONE..................302 650-4210
EMP: 10 **EST:** 2014
SALES (est): 196.34K **Privately Held**
Web: www.tldcenters.org
SIC: 8351 Preschool center

(G-16299)
EDUCATION VOICES INC
1510 W 5th St (19805-3157)
PHONE..................302 559-7889
Devon Hynson, *Prin*
EMP: 5 **EST:** 2013
SALES (est): 61.83K **Privately Held**
SIC: 8699 Charitable organization

(G-16300)
EDUCATIONAL ENRICHMENT CENTER
Also Called: Eec
730 Halstead Rd (19803-2228)
PHONE..................302 478-8697
Nancy Mcconnell, *Pr*
EMP: 30 **EST:** 1979
SALES (est): 1.03MM **Privately Held**
Web: www.eecde.org
SIC: 8351 Group day care center

(G-16301)
EDWARD B DE SETA & ASSOCIATES
Also Called: Dbd Maangment
4001 Kennett Pike Ste 10 (19807-2000)
P.O. Box 4549 (19807-4549)
PHONE..................302 428-1313
Edward B De Seta, *Pr*
Wanda L De Seta, *VP*
EMP: 5 **EST:** 1970
SALES (est): 500K **Privately Held**
SIC: 6552 Subdividers and developers, nec

(G-16302)
EDWARD J DESETA CO INC
322 A St Ste 200 (19801-5355)
PHONE..................302 420-0900
Lisa Mckewen, *Finance*
EMP: 11 **EST:** 2018
SALES (est): 2.2MM **Privately Held**
Web: www.ejdeseta.com
SIC: 1711 Mechanical contractor

(G-16303)
EDWARD S YALISOVE DDS PA
1111 N Franklin St (19806-4327)
PHONE..................302 658-4124
Edward Yalisove D.d.s., *Owner*
EMP: 5 **EST:** 1975
SALES (est): 237.44K **Privately Held**
Web: www.gorgeoussmilesofdelaware.com
SIC: 8021 Dentists' office

(G-16304)
EDWARDS MTHER EARTH FOUNDATION
501 Silverside Rd Ste 123 (19809-1377)
PHONE..................800 839-1754
EMP: 6
SALES (est): 1.83MM **Privately Held**
Web: www.edwardsmotherearth.org
SIC: 8699 Charitable organization

(G-16305)
EDWIN S KUIPERS DDS
300 Foulk Rd Ste 101 (19803-3819)
PHONE..................302 652-3775
Edwin Kuipers, *Ofcr*
EMP: 9 **EST:** 2015
SALES (est): 97.21K **Privately Held**
Web: www.thedentalgroupofdelaware.com
SIC: 8021 Dentists' office

(G-16306)
EEA LIFE SETTLEMENTS INC
1007 N Orange St Ste 1461 (19801-1239)
PHONE..................302 472-7429
EMP: 5 **EST:** 2009
SALES (est): 117.61K **Privately Held**
SIC: 6311 Life insurance

(G-16307)
EEC INCUBATOR
920 Justison St (19801-5150)
PHONE..................302 737-4343
EMP: 6 **EST:** 2019
SALES (est): 67.88K **Privately Held**
Web: www.ncccc.com
SIC: 8611 Chamber of Commerce

(G-16308)
EFECTIBO LLC
Also Called: Efectibo
251 Little Falls Dr (19808-1674)
PHONE..................305 498-8630
Francisco Diaz, *Managing Member*
EMP: 5 **EST:** 2010
SALES (est): 289.85K **Privately Held**
SIC: 7371 Computer software development and applications

(G-16309)
EFFLORESCENCE SKIN CARE
1207 Oak St (19805-4338)
PHONE..................302 250-3232
Nancy Decrease, *Prin*
EMP: 5 **EST:** 2010
SALES (est): 50.2K **Privately Held**
SIC: 7231 Facial salons

(G-16310)
EGS FINANCIAL CARE INC
P.O. Box 15110 (19850-5110)
PHONE..................800 227-4000
EMP: 7
SALES (corp-wide): 845.12MM **Privately Held**
SIC: 6282 Investment advice
HQ: Egs Financial Care, Inc.
5 Park Plz Ste 1100
Irvine CA 92614
877 217-4423

(G-16311)
EHG MECHANICAL
115 Fallon Ave (19804-1916)
PHONE..................302 530-4438
EMP: 5 **EST:** 2009
SALES (est): 143.72K **Privately Held**
SIC: 1711 Mechanical contractor

(G-16312)
EHS LLC
901 Merribrook Rd (19810-3103)
PHONE..................302 332-4247
James Simmons, *Prin*
EMP: 6 **EST:** 2016
SALES (est): 58.19K **Privately Held**
SIC: 7032 Sporting and recreational camps

(G-16313)
EIA INSURERS GROUP LLC
Also Called: Nationwide
1601 Concord Pike (19803-3637)
PHONE..................302 543-4572
Courtney Piccioni, *Mgr*
EMP: 8 **EST:** 2013
SALES (est): 223.92K **Privately Held**
Web: www.nationwide.com
SIC: 6411 Insurance agents, nec

(G-16314)
EIDP INC
Also Called: Dupont
16237 Brandywine Bldg (19898-0001)
PHONE..................302 774-1000
John Breckenridge, *Bmch Mgr*
EMP: 50
SALES (corp-wide): 17.45B **Publicly Held**
Web: www.dupont.com
SIC: 2819 5169 Industrial inorganic chemicals, nec; Chemicals and allied products, nec
HQ: Eidp, Inc.
9330 Zionsville Rd
Indianapolis IN 46268
833 267-8382

Wilmington - New Castle County (G-16315)

(G-16315)
EIDP INC
Dupont
30 Barley Mill Dr (19807-2218)
PHONE..................302 992-2012
EMP: 3
SALES (corp-wide): 17.23B **Publicly Held**
Web: www.dupont.com
SIC: 2752 Commercial printing, lithographic
HQ: Eidp, Inc.
    9330 Zionsville Rd
    Indianapolis IN 46268
    833 267-8382

(G-16316)
EIDP INC
Also Called: Dupont
702 Canter Rd (19810-1026)
PHONE..................302 999-3301
Donald Dunn, *Mgr*
EMP: 24
SALES (corp-wide): 17.23B **Publicly Held**
Web: www.dupont.com
SIC: 2819 Industrial inorganic chemicals, nec
HQ: Eidp, Inc.
    9330 Zionsville Rd
    Indianapolis IN 46268
    833 267-8382

(G-16317)
EIDP INC
Also Called: Dupont
4417 Lancaster Pike (19805-1523)
PHONE..................302 892-8832
John Little, *Dir*
EMP: 410
SALES (corp-wide): 17.23B **Publicly Held**
Web: www.dupont.com
SIC: 2819 Industrial inorganic chemicals, nec
HQ: Eidp, Inc.
    9330 Zionsville Rd
    Indianapolis IN 46268
    833 267-8382

(G-16318)
EIDP INC
Also Called: Dupont Corp Remediation Group
974 Centre Rd (19805-1269)
PHONE..................302 999-2874
Sheryl Telford, *Dir*
EMP: 4
SALES (corp-wide): 17.45B **Publicly Held**
Web: www.dupont.com
SIC: 2819 Industrial inorganic chemicals, nec
HQ: Eidp, Inc.
    9330 Zionsville Rd
    Indianapolis IN 46268
    833 267-8382

(G-16319)
EIDP INC
Also Called: Dupont Building Innovations
4417 Lancaster Pike (19805-1523)
PHONE..................302 892-8832
EMP: 6
SALES (corp-wide): 17.45B **Publicly Held**
Web: www.dupont.com
SIC: 2819 Industrial inorganic chemicals, nec
HQ: Eidp, Inc.
    9330 Zionsville Rd
    Indianapolis IN 46268
    833 267-8382

(G-16320)
EIDP INC
Also Called: Dupont Industrial Biosciences
200 Powder Mill Rd (19803)
PHONE..................302 695-7228
EMP: 18
SALES (corp-wide): 17.45B **Publicly Held**
Web: www.dupont.com
SIC: 2819 Industrial inorganic chemicals, nec
HQ: Eidp, Inc.
    9330 Zionsville Rd
    Indianapolis IN 46268
    833 267-8382

(G-16321)
EIDP INC
Also Called: Dupont
Chestnut Run Plz 708 Rm 141 (19805)
PHONE..................302 999-4356
Galum Hatter, *Brnch Mgr*
EMP: 6
SALES (corp-wide): 17.45B **Publicly Held**
Web: www.dupont.com
SIC: 2819 Industrial inorganic chemicals, nec
HQ: Eidp, Inc.
    9330 Zionsville Rd
    Indianapolis IN 46268
    833 267-8382

(G-16322)
EIDP INC
Also Called: Dupont
300 Delaware Ave (19801-1607)
PHONE..................302 792-4371
H L Kelley, *Prin*
EMP: 47
SALES (corp-wide): 17.23B **Publicly Held**
Web: www.dupont.com
SIC: 2819 Industrial inorganic chemicals, nec
HQ: Eidp, Inc.
    9330 Zionsville Rd
    Indianapolis IN 46268
    833 267-8382

(G-16323)
EIDP INC
Dupont
15305 Brandywine Bldg B (19898-0001)
PHONE..................302 774-2102
Jim Sinex, *Brnch Mgr*
EMP: 50
SALES (corp-wide): 17.23B **Publicly Held**
Web: www.dupont.com
SIC: 2819 Industrial inorganic chemicals, nec
HQ: Eidp, Inc.
    9330 Zionsville Rd
    Indianapolis IN 46268
    833 267-8382

(G-16324)
EIDP INC
Also Called: Dupont
Barley Mill Plz (19898-0001)
PHONE..................302 774-1000
Carol Kugelman, *Mgr*
EMP: 4
SALES (corp-wide): 17.23B **Publicly Held**
Web: www.dupont.com
SIC: 2819 Industrial inorganic chemicals, nec
HQ: Eidp, Inc.
    9330 Zionsville Rd
    Indianapolis IN 46268
    833 267-8382

(G-16325)
EIDP INC
Also Called: Playhouse On Rodney Square
901 Market (19801-3022)
PHONE..................302 888-0200
John Gardner, *Mgr*
EMP: 3
SALES (corp-wide): 17.23B **Publicly Held**
Web: www.dupont.com
SIC: 2819 Industrial inorganic chemicals, nec
HQ: Eidp, Inc.
    9330 Zionsville Rd
    Indianapolis IN 46268
    833 267-8382

(G-16326)
EIDP INC
Also Called: Dupont
22 Barley Mill (19807-2218)
PHONE..................302 668-8644
EMP: 10
SALES (corp-wide): 17.23B **Publicly Held**
Web: www.dupont.com
SIC: 2819 Industrial inorganic chemicals, nec
HQ: Eidp, Inc.
    9330 Zionsville Rd
    Indianapolis IN 46268
    833 267-8382

(G-16327)
EIDP INC
Also Called: Dupont
6235 Brandywine Building (19898-0001)
PHONE..................302 773-6287
V Johnson, *Brnch Mgr*
EMP: 4
SALES (corp-wide): 17.23B **Publicly Held**
Web: www.dupont.com
SIC: 2298 Fishing lines, nets, seines: made in cordage or twine mills
HQ: Eidp, Inc.
    9330 Zionsville Rd
    Indianapolis IN 46268
    833 267-8382

(G-16328)
EIDP INC
Also Called: Dupont
Faulkland Rd & Centre Rd (19808)
PHONE..................302 999-4329
Frank Stillburn, *Prin*
EMP: 3
SALES (corp-wide): 17.23B **Publicly Held**
Web: www.dupont.com
SIC: 2819 Industrial inorganic chemicals, nec
HQ: Eidp, Inc.
    9330 Zionsville Rd
    Indianapolis IN 46268
    833 267-8382

(G-16329)
EIDP INC
Also Called: Dupont
1 Little Leaf Ct (19810-3702)
PHONE..................302 999-2533
Wil Ambrose, *Brnch Mgr*
EMP: 7
SALES (corp-wide): 17.23B **Publicly Held**
Web: www.dupont.com
SIC: 2819 Industrial inorganic chemicals, nec
HQ: Eidp, Inc.
    9330 Zionsville Rd
    Indianapolis IN 46268
    833 267-8382

(G-16330)
EIDP INC
Also Called: Dupont Experimental Station
200 Powder Mill Rd (19803-2907)
PHONE..................302 695-3742
Robert Scott, *Brnch Mgr*
EMP: 51
SALES (corp-wide): 17.23B **Publicly Held**
Web: www.dupont.com
SIC: 2819 Industrial inorganic chemicals, nec
HQ: Eidp, Inc.
    9330 Zionsville Rd
    Indianapolis IN 46268
    833 267-8382

(G-16331)
EIDP INC
Also Called: Nonwovens Indus & Active Packg
4417 Lancaster Pike (19805-1523)
P.O. Box 2915 (19805-0915)
PHONE..................302 999-5072
Otto Fernandez, *Mktg Mgr*
EMP: 5
SALES (corp-wide): 17.23B **Publicly Held**
Web: www.dupont.com
SIC: 2819 Industrial inorganic chemicals, nec
HQ: Eidp, Inc.
    9330 Zionsville Rd
    Indianapolis IN 46268
    833 267-8382

(G-16332)
EIDP INC
Also Called: Dupont
Laurel Run Building (19880)
PHONE..................302 999-4321
Steve Lewis, *Prin*
EMP: 37
SALES (corp-wide): 17.23B **Publicly Held**
Web: www.dupont.com
SIC: 2819 Industrial inorganic chemicals, nec
HQ: Eidp, Inc.
    9330 Zionsville Rd
    Indianapolis IN 46268
    833 267-8382

(G-16333)
EIDP INC
Also Called: Dupont
N-9541 Nemours Bldg (19898-0001)
PHONE..................302 774-1000
EMP: 5
SALES (corp-wide): 17.23B **Publicly Held**
Web: www.dupont.com
SIC: 2819 Industrial inorganic chemicals, nec
HQ: Eidp, Inc.
    9330 Zionsville Rd
    Indianapolis IN 46268
    833 267-8382

(G-16334)
EIDP INC
Also Called: Dupont
5537 Nemours Bldg (19898-0001)
PHONE..................302 774-1000
EMP: 3
SALES (corp-wide): 17.23B **Publicly Held**
Web: www.dupont.com
SIC: 2819 Industrial inorganic chemicals, nec
HQ: Eidp, Inc.
    9330 Zionsville Rd
    Indianapolis IN 46268
    833 267-8382

(G-16335)
EIDP INC
Dupont Qualicon
Experimental Station Bldg 400 Box 80400 (19880)
PHONE..................302 695-5300
EMP: 4
SALES (corp-wide): 17.23B **Publicly Held**
Web: www.dupont.com
SIC: 2819 3556 2835 Industrial inorganic chemicals, nec; Food products machinery; Diagnostic substances
HQ: Eidp, Inc.
    9330 Zionsville Rd
    Indianapolis IN 46268
    833 267-8382

(G-16336)
EIDP INC
Also Called: Dupont
1011 Centre Rd Ste 200 (19805-1266)
PHONE..................302 654-8198
Elliott Golinkoff, *Ex VP*
EMP: 4
SALES (corp-wide): 17.45B **Publicly Held**
Web: www.dupont.com

GEOGRAPHIC SECTION   Wilmington - New Castle County (G-16363)

SIC: 2821 Thermoplastic materials
HQ: Eidp, Inc.
   9330 Zionsville Rd
   Indianapolis IN 46268
   833 267-8382

(G-16337)
EIDP INC
Also Called: Dupont
Bldg B14232 (19898-0001)
PHONE..................................302 656-9626
EMP: 50
SALES (corp-wide): 17.23B **Publicly Held**
Web: www.dupont.com
SIC: 2865 2869 Dyes and pigments; Industrial organic chemicals, nec
HQ: Eidp, Inc.
   9330 Zionsville Rd
   Indianapolis IN 46268
   833 267-8382

(G-16338)
EIDP INC
Also Called: Dupont
Centre Rd (19805)
PHONE..................................302 992-2065
Jim Davis, *Prin*
EMP: 150
SALES (corp-wide): 17.45B **Publicly Held**
Web: www.dupont.com
SIC: 2879 Agricultural chemicals, nec
HQ: Eidp, Inc.
   9330 Zionsville Rd
   Indianapolis IN 46268
   833 267-8382

(G-16339)
EIDP INC
Also Called: Dupont
974 Centre Rd Bldg 730 (19805-1269)
PHONE..................................302 999-2826
EMP: 6
SALES (corp-wide): 17.45B **Publicly Held**
Web: www.dupont.com
SIC: 2879 2865 2821 Agricultural chemicals, nec; Dyes and pigments; Thermoplastic materials
HQ: Eidp, Inc.
   9330 Zionsville Rd
   Indianapolis IN 46268
   833 267-8382

(G-16340)
EIDP INC
Also Called: Dupont
1007 Market St (19898-1100)
PHONE..................................844 773-2436
EMP: 27
SALES (corp-wide): 17.45B **Publicly Held**
Web: www.dupont.com
SIC: 2879 Agricultural chemicals, nec
HQ: Eidp, Inc.
   9330 Zionsville Rd
   Indianapolis IN 46268
   833 267-8382

(G-16341)
EIDP INC
Also Called: Dupont
Rte 41 & 48 (19880)
PHONE..................................615 847-6920
EMP: 31
SALES (corp-wide): 17.45B **Publicly Held**
Web: www.dupont.com
SIC: 2911 Petroleum refining
HQ: Eidp, Inc.
   9330 Zionsville Rd
   Indianapolis IN 46268
   833 267-8382

(G-16342)
EIDP INC
Also Called: Dupont
Barley Mill Plaza, Bldg 21 (19880)
PHONE..................................302 774-1000
Chad Holliday Vp Electronics, *Brnch Mgr*
EMP: 200
SALES (corp-wide): 17.23B **Publicly Held**
Web: www.dupont.com
SIC: 3679 Electronic circuits
HQ: Eidp, Inc.
   9330 Zionsville Rd
   Indianapolis IN 46268
   833 267-8382

(G-16343)
EIDP INC
Also Called: Dupont
Barley Mill Plz Bldg 24 (19898-0001)
PHONE..................................302 996-4000
Barry Day, *Prin*
EMP: 9
SALES (corp-wide): 17.23B **Publicly Held**
Web: www.dupont.com
SIC: 3844 3841 X-ray apparatus and tubes; Surgical and medical instruments
HQ: Eidp, Inc.
   9330 Zionsville Rd
   Indianapolis IN 46268
   833 267-8382

(G-16344)
EIDP INC
Packaging and Indus Polymrers
4417 Lancaster Pike (19805-1523)
PHONE..................................302 992-2458
EMP: 6
SALES (corp-wide): 17.23B **Publicly Held**
Web: www.dupont.com
SIC: 3081 Unsupported plastics film and sheet
HQ: Eidp, Inc.
   9330 Zionsville Rd
   Indianapolis IN 46268
   833 267-8382

(G-16345)
EIKON INT INC
300 Delaware Ave Ste 200 (19801-6601)
PHONE..................................312 550-2648
Cale Swanson, *Pr*
EMP: 5 EST: 2019
SALES (est): 337.07K **Privately Held**
SIC: 4731 Freight forwarding

(G-16346)
EITV USA INC
501 Silverside Rd Ste 105 (19809-1376)
PHONE..................................305 517-7715
Rodrigo Araujo, *CEO*
Rodrigo Araugo, *CEO*
EMP: 3 EST: 2011
SALES (est): 173.22K **Privately Held**
Web: www.eitv.com.br
SIC: 7372 Application computer software

(G-16347)
EL BLUEBIRD LLC
1000 N West St Ste 1200 (19801-1050)
PHONE..................................775 773-3255
Jd Zelaya, *Managing Member*
EMP: 5
SALES (est): 258.29K **Privately Held**
SIC: 5141 Food brokers

(G-16348)
EL DIABLO
837 N Market St (19801-3010)
PHONE..................................302 691-3081
EMP: 5 EST: 2019

SALES (est): 125.82K **Privately Held**
Web: www.eldiabloburritos.com
SIC: 8742 Marketing consulting services

(G-16349)
ELDERLY COMFORT CORPORATION
800 N West St Ste 301 (19801-1565)
P.O. Box 1570 (19899-1570)
PHONE..................................302 530-6680
Tina Larose, *Ch*
EMP: 9 EST: 2011
SALES (est): 95.64K **Privately Held**
SIC: 8052 Personal care facility

(G-16350)
ELDERTRUST
2711 Centerville Rd Ste 108 (19808-1668)
PHONE..................................302 993-1022
Michael R Walker, *Ch Bd*
EMP: 7 EST: 1998
SALES (est): 58.87MM
SALES (corp-wide): 4.13B **Publicly Held**
SIC: 6798 6531 Real estate investment trusts; Real estate agents and managers
PA: Ventas, Inc.
   353 N Clark St Ste 3300
   Chicago IL 60654
   877 483-6827

(G-16351)
ELECTRIC LADY STUDIOS LLC ELEC
20 Montchanin Rd Ste 250 (19807-2181)
PHONE..................................212 677-4700
EMP: 6 EST: 2018
SALES (est): 197.42K **Privately Held**
SIC: 7929 Entertainers and entertainment groups

(G-16352)
ELECTRO SOUND SYSTEMS
2310 Henlopen Ave (19804-3810)
PHONE..................................302 367-9840
Tom Manchester, *Prin*
EMP: 6 EST: 2017
SALES (est): 231.75K **Privately Held**
SIC: 1731 Sound equipment specialization

(G-16353)
ELEMENT MTLS TECH WLMNGTON INC
Also Called: S L Pharma Labs, Inc.
1300 First State Blvd Ste C (19804-3548)
PHONE..................................302 636-0202
Waheed Sheikh, *Pr*
EMP: 14 EST: 1997
SALES (est): 4.59MM **Privately Held**
Web: www.slpharmalabs.com
SIC: 8734 Water testing laboratory
HQ: Exova Group Limited
   Lochend Industrial Estate Queen Anne Drive
   Newbridge EH28

(G-16354)
ELEUTHERIAN TRUST CO
1105 N Market St Ste 900 (19801-1216)
PHONE..................................302 294-0821
EMP: 6 EST: 2019
SALES (est): 229.14K **Privately Held**
SIC: 6733 Trusts, nec

(G-16355)
ELEUTHRIAN MLLS-HGLEY FNDTION
Also Called: HAGLEY MUSEUM AND LIBRARY
200 Hawley St (19807)
P.O. Box 3630 (19807-0630)
PHONE..................................302 658-2400
Jeanne Belk, *Treas*
Marjorie Kelly, *

EMP: 160 EST: 1952
SQ FT: 53,500
SALES (est): 13.82MM **Privately Held**
Web: www.hagley.org
SIC: 8412 Museum

(G-16356)
ELEVATE DVM INC
3 Penny Lane Ct (19803-4023)
PHONE..................................302 761-9650
Kathy Gloyd D.v.m., *Prin*
EMP: 5 EST: 2015
SALES (est): 240.37K **Privately Held**
Web: www.elevatedvm.com
SIC: 0742 Veterinary services, specialties

(G-16357)
ELEVATE RCM CONSULTING ✪
300 Delaware Ave (19801-1607)
PHONE..................................484 655-8733
Sheonte Stevens, *CEO*
EMP: 5 EST: 2024
SALES (est): 164.52K **Privately Held**
SIC: 8748 7389 Business consulting, nec; Business Activities at Non-Commercial Site

(G-16358)
ELEVATED STUDIOS HQ
34a Trolley Sq (19806-3334)
PHONE..................................302 407-3229
EMP: 6 EST: 2015
SALES (est): 111.02K **Privately Held**
Web: www.elevatedstudiosmartialarts.com
SIC: 7999 Martial arts school, nec

(G-16359)
ELEVATION OFFICE FURN LLC
2509 Duncan Rd (19808-4609)
PHONE..................................267 261-0124
Joseph Cutler, *Prin*
EMP: 10 EST: 2016
SALES (est): 242.44K **Privately Held**
SIC: 2521 Wood office desks and tables

(G-16360)
ELEVATIONS IN ECOM LLC
501 Silverside Rd Ste 516 (19809-1374)
PHONE..................................302 797-1709
EMP: 4 EST: 2020
SALES (est): 460K **Privately Held**
SIC: 3231 Products of purchased glass

(G-16361)
ELEVATOR ORGANIZATION INC ✪
2055 Limestone Rd Ste 200c (19808-5536)
PHONE..................................847 431-2927
EMP: 6 EST: 2022
SALES (est): 59.87K **Privately Held**
SIC: 5084 Elevators

(G-16362)
ELITE AUTO WORKS LLC
2501 W 3rd St (19805-3348)
PHONE..................................302 252-1045
Bryan Alston, *Prin*
EMP: 5 EST: 2016
SALES (est): 123.63K **Privately Held**
SIC: 7538 General automotive repair shops

(G-16363)
ELITE CLEANING COMPANY INC
Also Called: Elite Building Services
2200 Concord Pike (19803-2909)
PHONE..................................302 439-4430
Cheryl Ecton, *Pr*
EMP: 620 EST: 1989
SALES (est): 12MM **Privately Held**
SIC: 7349 Janitorial service, contract basis

Wilmington - New Castle County (G-16364)   GEOGRAPHIC SECTION

(G-16364)
ELITE LANDSCAPE
108 Boxwood Rd (19804-1823)
PHONE...................................302 543-7305
Carl Berny, *Owner*
EMP: 9 **EST:** 2009
SALES (est): 212.04K **Privately Held**
Web: www.elitelandscapede.com
SIC: 0781 Landscape services

(G-16365)
ELITE MEETINGS INTERNATIONAL
100 Greenhill Ave Ste C (19805-1863)
PHONE...................................302 516-7997
EMP: 6 **EST:** 2019
SALES (est): 28.2K **Privately Held**
SIC: 7539 Automotive repair shops, nec

(G-16366)
ELITE TAX SERVICES LLC
30b Trolley Sq (19806-3352)
PHONE...................................302 256-0401
EMP: 5 **EST:** 2013
SALES (est): 181.47K **Privately Held**
SIC: 7291 8721 Tax return preparation services; Accounting, auditing, and bookkeeping

(G-16367)
ELITE TRNSPT & LOGISTICS INC
300 Delaware Ave Ste 210 (19801-6601)
PHONE...................................302 348-8480
Amanda Perez, *Prin*
Shaun Shells, *Prin*
EMP: 5 **EST:** 2014
SALES (est): 535.63K **Privately Held**
SIC: 4789 Freight car loading and unloading

(G-16368)
ELIZABETH A HUSSEY
401 E 12th St (19801-3403)
PHONE...................................302 577-5400
Elizabeth A Hussey Lcsw, *Owner*
EMP: 5 **EST:** 2018
SALES (est): 78.02K **Privately Held**
SIC: 8322 Social worker

(G-16369)
ELIZABETH L THOMAS-BAUER
1320 Philadelphia Pike Ste 101 (19809-1818)
PHONE...................................302 798-0666
Elizabeth Thomas-bauer, *Prin*
EMP: 6 **EST:** 2012
SALES (est): 62.96K **Privately Held**
SIC: 8049 Psychologist, psychotherapist and hypnotist

(G-16370)
ELIZABETH SUTTON MACE PSYD
501 Silverside Rd Ste 145 (19809-1372)
PHONE...................................302 293-4920
EMP: 6 **EST:** 2012
SALES (est): 61.98K **Privately Held**
SIC: 8049 Clinical psychologist

(G-16371)
ELLA HEALTH INC
4600 Linden Hill Rd (19808)
PHONE...................................302 543-4396
Ella Burton, *Prin*
EMP: 7 **EST:** 2014
SALES (est): 109.29K **Privately Held**
SIC: 8099 Health screening service

(G-16372)
ELLEN A SPURRIER M D
1600 Rockland Rd (19803-3607)
PHONE...................................302 651-6660
Ellen Spurrier, *Owner*
EMP: 11 **EST:** 2018
SALES (est): 506.38K **Privately Held**
Web: www.nemours.org
SIC: 8011 Pediatrician

(G-16373)
ELLIS CONTRACTING LLC
238 Barberry Dr (19808-1950)
PHONE...................................302 559-5105
Stephen Ellis, *Pr*
EMP: 5 **EST:** 2015
SALES (est): 104.96K **Privately Held**
SIC: 1799 Special trade contractors, nec

(G-16374)
ELLMORE AUTO COLLISION
Also Called: Frank Smths Twing Atobody Repr
4921 Governor Printz Blvd (19809-3501)
PHONE...................................302 762-2301
Frank Smith, *CEO*
EMP: 7 **EST:** 1954
SQ FT: 3,000
SALES (est): 548.11K **Privately Held**
Web: www.ellmoreautocollisionllc.com
SIC: 7549 7532 Towing service, automotive; Body shop, automotive

(G-16375)
ELM PROPERTIES INC
301 Old Dupont Rd Ste G (19804-1084)
PHONE...................................302 762-3757
Evette Morrow, *CEO*
EMP: 5 **EST:** 2013
SALES (est): 965K **Privately Held**
Web: www.elmproperties.net
SIC: 8741 Management services

(G-16376)
ELMER SCHULTZ SERVICES INC
Also Called: Commercial Food Equipment Repr
36 Belmont Ave (19804-1538)
PHONE...................................302 655-8900
Roger Mcguire, *Brnch Mgr*
EMP: 7
SALES (corp-wide): 9.01MM **Privately Held**
Web: www.elmerschultz.com
SIC: 5046 Restaurant equipment and supplies, nec
PA: Elmer Schultz Services, Inc.
540 N 3rd St
Philadelphia PA 19123
215 627-5400

(G-16377)
ELOIM ENTERPRISES LLC
2711 Centerville Rd # 400 (19808-1660)
PHONE...................................510 209-3670
EMP: 10 **EST:** 2021
SALES (est): 500K **Privately Held**
SIC: 6799 Real estate investors, except property operators

(G-16378)
ELSMERE FIRE CO 1 INC
1107 Kirkwood Hwy (19805-2117)
PHONE...................................302 999-0183
Warren F Jones, *Pr*
Jack Parisi, *VP*
Mike Shall, *Treas*
Dennis Codack, *Sec*
EMP: 5 **EST:** 1921
SQ FT: 6,000
SALES (est): 2.38MM **Privately Held**
Web: www.elsmerefc.com
SIC: 7389 Fire protection service other than forestry or public

(G-16379)
ELSMERE INSURANCE AGENCY LLC
1000 N West St Ste 1220 (19801-1058)
PHONE...................................317 574-2861
EMP: 13 **EST:** 2015
SALES (est): 282.16K **Privately Held**
SIC: 6411 Insurance agents, nec

(G-16380)
ELSMERE NUTRITION
15 Sanders Rd (19805-5406)
PHONE...................................302 502-2061
EMP: 5 **EST:** 2019
SALES (est): 43.62K **Privately Held**
SIC: 8099 Nutrition services

(G-16381)
ELSMERE PRESBYTERIAN CHURCH
Also Called: Presbyterian Church USA
606 New Rd (19805-5125)
PHONE...................................302 998-6365
Pastor Tom Stouk, *Prin*
EMP: 10 **EST:** 1974
SALES (est): 261.22K **Privately Held**
Web: www.elsmerepres.org
SIC: 8661 8351 Presbyterian Church; Child day care services

(G-16382)
ELWYN PENNSYLVANIA AND DEL
Also Called: Delaware Elwyn
321 E 11th St Fl 1 (19801-3417)
PHONE...................................302 658-8860
Sandy Hanley, *Dir*
EMP: 83
SALES (corp-wide): 236.28MM **Privately Held**
Web: www.elwyn.org
SIC: 8093 8331 2441 2396 Rehabilitation center, outpatient treatment; Job counseling ; Nailed wood boxes and shook; Automotive and apparel trimmings
PA: Elwyn Of Pennsylvania And Delaware
111 Elwyn Rd
Media PA 19063
610 891-2000

(G-16383)
ELZUFON ASTIN RRDON TRLOV MNDE (PA)
300 Delaware Ave Ste 1700 (19801-1612)
P.O. Box 1630 (19899-1630)
PHONE...................................302 428-3181
John Elzufon, *Pt*
EMP: 38 **EST:** 1997
SALES (est): 4.51MM
SALES (corp-wide): 4.51MM **Privately Held**
Web: www.elzufon.com
SIC: 8111 General practice attorney, lawyer

(G-16384)
EMA CORP (HQ)
1105 N Market St (19801-1216)
PHONE...................................302 479-9434
Abraham Gosman, *Pr*
EMP: 30 **EST:** 1986
SALES (est): 25.63MM
SALES (corp-wide): 6.15B **Publicly Held**
SIC: 6726 6719 7389 Investment offices, nec ; Investment holding companies, except banks; Financial services
PA: Ametek, Inc.
1100 Cassatt Rd
Berwyn PA 19312
610 647-2121

(G-16385)
EMAEP LLC
Also Called: Amphitrades

1201 N Orange St (19801-1155)
PHONE...................................202 836-7886
Renato Perez, *Pr*
EMP: 32 **EST:** 2019
SALES (est): 1.43MM **Privately Held**
SIC: 6221 Commodity traders, contracts

(G-16386)
EMAGINATION STORE USA INC
1201 N Orange St Ste 7291 (19801-1271)
PHONE...................................302 884-6746
EMP: 6 **EST:** 2021
SALES (est): 233.89K **Privately Held**
SIC: 7313 Printed media advertising representatives

(G-16387)
EMBARCDERO ARCFT SCRTZATION TR
1100 N Market St (19801-1243)
PHONE...................................302 651-1000
Pete Feiblitz, *Bd of Dir*
James Bryan Junior, *Bd of Dir*
Gregory Dolbin, *Bd of Dir*
EMP: 7 **EST:** 2000
SALES (est): 584.45K **Privately Held**
SIC: 6733 Trusts, nec

(G-16388)
EMBRACE HOME LOANS INC
5341 Limestone Rd Ste 101 (19808-1222)
PHONE...................................302 635-7998
Joseph Beacher, *Brnch Mgr*
EMP: 9
SALES (corp-wide): 109.03MM **Privately Held**
Web: www.embracehomeloans.com
SIC: 6162 Mortgage bankers and loan correspondents
PA: Embrace Home Loans, Inc.
25 Enterprise Ctr
Middletown RI 02842
401 846-3100

(G-16389)
EMENDO BIO INC
1811 Silverside Rd (19810-4345)
PHONE...................................516 595-1849
Todd Wider, *Prin*
David Baram, *Prin*
Julie Amar, *Prin*
EMP: 5 **EST:** 2019
SALES (est): 104.73K **Privately Held**
Web: www.emendobio.com
SIC: 7389 Business Activities at Non-Commercial Site

(G-16390)
EMERA US FINANCE LP
2711 Centerville Rd Ste 400 (19808-1660)
PHONE...................................302 636-5400
EMP: 9 **EST:** 2018
SALES (est): 295.74K **Privately Held**
SIC: 4911 Electric services

(G-16391)
EMERGENT FREST FIN ACCLRTOR IN
251 Little Falls Dr (19808-1674)
PHONE...................................347 796-4450
EMP: 13 **EST:** 2019
SALES (est): 766.27K **Privately Held**
SIC: 8742 Banking and finance consultant

(G-16392)
EMERGING TRAVEL INC (PA)
Also Called: Emerging Travel Group
1000 N West St Ste 1200 (19801-1058)
PHONE...................................302 295-3838
Felix Shpilman, *Pr*

GEOGRAPHIC SECTION
Wilmington - New Castle County (G-16422)

EMP: 5 EST: 2010
SALES (est): 2.51MM
SALES (corp-wide): 2.51MM **Privately Held**
Web: www.emergingtravel.com
SIC: 4725 Tour operators

(G-16393)
EMERGNCY RESPONSE PROTOCOL LLC
101 W Ayre St (19804-3103)
PHONE..................302 994-2600
Angela Tiberi, *CEO*
Al Abuasi, *VP*
Dave Tiberi, *Pr*
EMP: 8 EST: 2017
SALES (est): 496.84K **Privately Held**
Web: www.erpsafety.com
SIC: 7382 1731 Protective devices, security; Fiber optic cable installation

(G-16394)
EMILY CRAWFORD PHD
3608 Lancaster Pike (19805-1509)
PHONE..................302 995-9600
Emily Crawford, *Owner*
EMP: 8 EST: 2015
SALES (est): 143.48K **Privately Held**
Web: www.delawarefamilycenter.com
SIC: 8322 General counseling services

(G-16395)
EMMA JEFFERIES DAY CARE
603 W 39th St (19802-2034)
PHONE..................302 762-3235
Lewis V Jefferies, *Prin*
EMP: 5 EST: 2005
SALES (est): 76.7K **Privately Held**
SIC: 8351 Group day care center

(G-16396)
EMMA SYSTEMS INC ✪
1013 Centre Rd Ste 403b (19805-1270)
PHONE..................407 773-8536
Wissam Costandi, *CEO*
EMP: 2 EST: 2023
SALES (est): 88.67K **Privately Held**
SIC: 7372 Prepackaged software

(G-16397)
EMMANUEL TROUMOUHIS
735 Philadelphia Pike (19809-2544)
PHONE..................302 762-3200
EMP: 5 EST: 2017
SALES (est): 65.66K **Privately Held**
SIC: 7699 Repair services, nec

(G-16398)
EMMENT A OAT CONTRACTOR INC
501 W Newport Pike (19804-3233)
PHONE..................302 999-1567
Robert E Oat, *Pr*
Emment A Oat, *VP*
Donna R Oat, *Sec*
EMP: 5 EST: 1958
SALES (est): 500K **Privately Held**
SIC: 1541 Renovation, remodeling and repairs: industrial buildings

(G-16399)
EMPIRE FLIPPERS LLC
427 N Tatnall St # 34425 (19801-2230)
PHONE..................323 638-0348
EMP: 42 EST: 2015
SALES (est): 1.7MM **Privately Held**
Web: www.empireflippers.com
SIC: 7389 Brokers, business: buying and selling business enterprises

(G-16400)
EMPIRICAL CRE HOLDINGS CORP (PA)
108 W 13th St (19801)
PHONE..................816 582-8041
EMP: 7 EST: 2018
SALES (est): 397.13K
SALES (corp-wide): 397.13K **Privately Held**
SIC: 7371 Computer software systems analysis and design, custom

(G-16401)
EMPOWERED YOGA
2000 Pennsylvania Ave Apt 208 (19806-2460)
PHONE..................302 654-9642
John Gillespie, *Owner*
EMP: 15 EST: 2014
SALES (est): 77.83K **Privately Held**
Web: www.empoweredwellnessstudio.com
SIC: 7999 Yoga instruction

(G-16402)
EMPOWERED YOGA
20 Montchanin Rd Ste 60 (19807-2179)
PHONE..................302 409-0192
Deb Dandrea, *Prin*
EMP: 6 EST: 2017
SALES (est): 22.86K **Privately Held**
Web: www.empoweredwellnessstudio.com
SIC: 7999 Yoga instruction

(G-16403)
ENABLD TECHNOLOGIES INC (PA)
3524 Silverside Rd Ste 35b (19810-4929)
PHONE..................917 340-1606
Calin Calancea, *CEO*
EMP: 13 EST: 2021
SALES (est): 1.12MM
SALES (corp-wide): 1.12MM **Privately Held**
Web: www.enabld.tech
SIC: 8741 Management services

(G-16404)
ENCENTIV ENERGY LLC
801 W Newport Pike Ste 202 (19804)
PHONE..................302 504-8506
EMP: 11
Web: www.allfacilities.com
SIC: 1731 Energy management controls
PA: Encentiv Energy, Llc
  1501 Ardmore Blvd Ste 102
  Pittsburgh PA 15221

(G-16405)
ENCOMPASS ACCOUNTING INC
2607 Belaire Dr (19808-3809)
PHONE..................302 229-3572
EMP: 5 EST: 2015
SALES (est): 31.93K **Privately Held**
Web: www.encompassde.com
SIC: 8721 Accounting services, except auditing

(G-16406)
ENCOMPASS CORPORATION US INC
1209 N Orange St (19801-1120)
PHONE..................212 523-0340
Wayne Johnston, *CEO*
EMP: 5 EST: 2020
SALES (est): 234.53K **Privately Held**
SIC: 7371 Software programming applications

(G-16407)
ENCROSS LLC
1521 Concord Pike Ste 301 (19803-3644)
PHONE..................302 351-2593
Randall Hirt, *Prin*
EMP: 10 EST: 2009
SALES (est): 154.78K **Privately Held**
Web: www.encrosscorp.com
SIC: 7373 7379 7371 8748 Systems software development services; Computer related consulting services; Computer software systems analysis and design, custom; Business consulting, nec

(G-16408)
END OF LIFE DOULA
2511 Lori Ln N (19810-3445)
PHONE..................302 478-6958
Janey Layman, *Prin*
EMP: 6 EST: 2017
SALES (est): 48.18K **Privately Held**
Web: www.doulagivers.com
SIC: 8322 Individual and family services

(G-16409)
ENDEVOR LLC
Also Called: Endevor
3844 Kennett Pike Ste 210 (19807-2305)
PHONE..................302 543-5055
Timothy Johnson, *Managing Member*
EMP: 6 EST: 2012
SQ FT: 1,300
SALES (est): 4.71MM **Privately Held**
Web: www.endevorllc.com
SIC: 7371 Computer software development

(G-16410)
ENDLESS OS FOUNDATION LLC
24a Trolley Sq # 2319 (19806-3334)
PHONE..................415 413-4159
EMP: 3 EST: 2020
SALES (est): 56.54K **Privately Held**
Web: www.endlessos.org
SIC: 7372 Operating systems computer software

(G-16411)
ENDOSCOPY SUITE PARTNERS LLC
2207 Concord Pike Ste 167 (19803-2908)
PHONE..................267 243-3850
EMP: 5 EST: 2009
SALES (est): 183.41K **Privately Held**
SIC: 8011 Offices and clinics of medical doctors

(G-16412)
ENDURE TO CURE FOUNDATION
1201 N Orange St Ste 7089 (19801-1192)
PHONE..................866 400-2121
Jason Sissel, *Prin*
EMP: 7 EST: 2011
SALES (est): 133.07K **Privately Held**
Web: www.enduretocure.org
SIC: 8641 Civic and social associations

(G-16413)
ENDURE WALLS ✪
3704 Kennett Pike (19807-2172)
PHONE..................302 479-7614
EMP: 6 EST: 2022
SALES (est): 63.4K **Privately Held**
Web: www.endurewalls.com
SIC: 7389 Design services

(G-16414)
ENDURNCE REINSURANCE CORP AMER
1209 N Orange St (19801-1120)
PHONE..................973 898-9575
Perry Roderick, *Prin*

EMP: 25 EST: 2008
SALES (est): 602.08K **Privately Held**
SIC: 6411 Insurance brokers, nec

(G-16415)
ENER-G GROUP INC
3422 Old Capitol Trl (19808-6124)
PHONE..................917 281-0020
Samina Sadiq, *Prin*
EMP: 10 EST: 2010
SALES (est): 677.05K **Privately Held**
SIC: 8731 Energy research

(G-16416)
ENERCON
3411 Silverside Rd Ste 100 (19810-4812)
PHONE..................302 407-3179
EMP: 18 EST: 2014
SALES (est): 186.99K **Privately Held**
Web: www.enercon.com
SIC: 8711 Consulting engineer

(G-16417)
ENERGY HEALING PATHWAYS LLC
5 Stones Throw Rd (19803-2617)
PHONE..................302 478-6383
EMP: 5 EST: 2012
SALES (est): 58.28K **Privately Held**
SIC: 8049 Offices of health practitioner

(G-16418)
ENERGY TECH HOLDINGS LLC (PA)
1209 N Orange St (19801-1120)
PHONE..................212 356-6130
Frank Bokaemper, *Managing Member*
EMP: 22 EST: 2020
SALES (est): 1.57B
SALES (corp-wide): 1.57B **Privately Held**
SIC: 3356 Battery metal

(G-16419)
ENERSOURCE ELECTRICAL SVC LLC
831 N Tatnall St (19801-1717)
PHONE..................302 842-8714
EMP: 6 EST: 2019
SALES (est): 714.23K **Privately Held**
Web: www.enersourcellc.com
SIC: 4911 Electric services

(G-16420)
ENG JERALD MD
3521 Silverside Rd Ste 1f (19810-4900)
PHONE..................302 478-4845
Jerald Eng, *Pr*
EMP: 10 EST: 2018
SALES (est): 176.19K **Privately Held**
SIC: 8011 Pediatrician

(G-16421)
ENGAGE XR LLC
251 Little Falls Dr (19808-1674)
PHONE..................302 877-2028
EMP: 5
SALES (est): 199.4K **Privately Held**
SIC: 7371 Custom computer programming services

(G-16422)
ENGATI TECHNOLOGIES INC
919 N Market St Ste 950 (19801-3036)
PHONE..................215 368-3551
Deepak Moolchand Nachnani, *Prin*
EMP: 6 EST: 2020
SALES (est): 46.16K **Privately Held**
Web: www.engati.com
SIC: 7371 Software programming applications

Wilmington - New Castle County (G-16423)

(G-16423)
ENGINEERED SYSTEMS & DESIGNS
Also Called: Esd
3 S Tatnall St (19801-2457)
PHONE..................302 456-0446
Robert Spring, *Pr*
William Spring, *VP*
EMP: 4 **EST:** 1975
SQ FT: 5,000
SALES (est): 435.52K **Privately Held**
Web: www.esdinc.com
SIC: 3823 3825 Water quality monitoring and control systems; Instruments to measure electricity

(G-16424)
ENGINEERING INCORPORATED
6 Lewis Cir (19804-1618)
PHONE..................302 995-6862
Karl M Mruz, *Pr*
EMP: 7 **EST:** 1962
SQ FT: 9,000
SALES (est): 852.7K **Privately Held**
Web: www.apexengineeringinc.com
SIC: 3441 Joists, open web steel: long-span series

(G-16425)
ENGLISH REALTY LLC ✪
1000 N West St Ste 1200 (19801-1050)
PHONE..................302 295-4845
Maurrell English, *Pr*
EMP: 23 **EST:** 2024
SALES (est): 667.02K **Privately Held**
Web: www.englishrealty.co
SIC: 6531 Real estate brokers and agents

(G-16426)
ENOU LABS LLC
2055 Limestone Rd Ste 200c (19808-5536)
PHONE..................321 343-4362
EMP: 11
SALES (est): 397.02K **Privately Held**
Web: www.enou.co
SIC: 7371 Computer software development and applications

(G-16427)
ENOVANTE LLC
2055 Limestone Rd Ste 200c (19808-5536)
PHONE..................917 960-8384
Malinda Dharmasiri, *CEO*
EMP: 15 **EST:** 2021
SALES (est): 505.06K **Privately Held**
SIC: 7379 Computer related consulting services

(G-16428)
ENOVIS CORPORATION (PA)
2711 Centerville Rd Ste 400 (19808-1660)
PHONE..................301 252-9160
Matthew Trerotola, *CEO*
Mitchell P Rales, *Ch Bd*
Brady R Shirley, *Pr*
Christopher Hix, *Ex VP*
Bradley J Tandy, *Corporate Secretary*
EMP: 207 **EST:** 1860
SALES (est): 1.56B
SALES (corp-wide): 1.56B **Publicly Held**
Web: www.enovis.com
SIC: 3842 3841 5047 Surgical appliances and supplies; Surgical and medical instruments; Medical equipment and supplies

(G-16429)
ENPASS TECHNOLOGIES INC (PA)
1201 N Market St Ste 111 (19801-1156)
PHONE..................415 671-5123
EMP: 6 **EST:** 2019
SALES (est): 403.61K
SALES (corp-wide): 403.61K **Privately Held**
Web: www.enpass.io
SIC: 7371 Computer software development

(G-16430)
ENSYN RENEWABLES INC
1521 Concord Pike Ste 205 (19803-3645)
PHONE..................302 425-3740
Robert Doherty, *CFO*
EMP: 18 **EST:** 1997
SALES (est): 334.95K **Privately Held**
Web: www.ensyn.com
SIC: 2869 Industrial organic chemicals, nec

(G-16431)
ENT AND ALLERGY DELAWARE LLC
1941 Limestone Rd (19808-5408)
PHONE..................302 998-0300
Kieran Connolly, *Owner*
EMP: 15
SALES (corp-wide): 5.07MM **Privately Held**
Web: www.entad.org
SIC: 8011 Ears, nose, and throat specialist: physician/surgeon
PA: Ent And Allergy Of Delaware, Llc
700 Prides Xing Ste 200
Newark DE 19713
302 478-8467

(G-16432)
ENTEK MANUFACTURING INC
300 Delaware Ave Ste 800 (19801-1697)
PHONE..................302 576-5860
EMP: 9 **EST:** 2005
SALES (est): 85.57K **Privately Held**
SIC: 1711 Heating and air conditioning contractors

(G-16433)
ENTERPRISE FLASHER CO INC
4 Hadco Rd (19804-1085)
PHONE..................302 999-0856
Anne Builderback, *Pr*
Courtney Roehm, *VP*
EMP: 23 **EST:** 1975
SQ FT: 8,000
SALES (est): 1.72MM **Privately Held**
Web: www.enterpriseflasher.com
SIC: 7359 5999 Work zone traffic equipment (flags, cones, barrels, etc.); Safety supplies and equipment

(G-16434)
ENTERPRISE LEARNING SOLUTIONS
236 Weldin Ridge Rd (19803-3974)
PHONE..................302 762-6595
EMP: 8 **EST:** 2017
SALES (est): 57.78K **Privately Held**
SIC: 8351 Child day care services

(G-16435)
ENTERPRISE LSG PHLADELPHIA LLC
Also Called: Alamo
100 S French St Unit 115a (19801-5019)
PHONE..................302 425-4404
EMP: 6
SALES (corp-wide): 7.04B **Privately Held**
Web: www.enterprise.com
SIC: 7514 Rent-a-car service
HQ: Enterprise Leasing Company Of Philadelphia, Llc
2434 W Main St 2436
Norristown PA 19403

(G-16436)
ENTERPRISE LSG PHILADELPHIA LLC
Also Called: Enterprise Rent-A-Car
4727 Concord Pike (19803-1408)
PHONE..................302 479-7829
EMP: 6
SALES (corp-wide): 7.04B **Privately Held**
Web: www.enterprise.com
SIC: 7514 Rent-a-car service
HQ: Enterprise Leasing Company Of Philadelphia, Llc
2434 W Main St 2436
Norristown PA 19403

(G-16437)
ENTERPRISE LSG PHILADELPHIA LLC
Also Called: Enterprise Rent-A-Car
100 Philadelphia Pike (19809-3180)
PHONE..................302 761-4545
EMP: 6
SALES (corp-wide): 7.04B **Privately Held**
Web: www.enterprise.com
SIC: 7514 Rent-a-car service
HQ: Enterprise Leasing Company Of Philadelphia, Llc
2434 W Main St 2436
Norristown PA 19403

(G-16438)
ENTERPRISE MASONRY CORPORATION
3010 Bellevue Ave (19802-2402)
PHONE..................302 764-6858
EMP: 45 **EST:** 1993
SQ FT: 12,500
SALES (est): 5.19MM **Privately Held**
Web: www.emcbrick.com
SIC: 1741 Masonry and other stonework

(G-16439)
ENTERPRISE RENT A CAR
1602 E Newport Pike (19804-2529)
PHONE..................302 636-0660
Matt Conn, *Mgr*
EMP: 6 **EST:** 2015
SALES (est): 76.81K **Privately Held**
Web: www.enterprise.com
SIC: 7514 Rent-a-car service

(G-16440)
ENTERPRISE RENT-A-CAR
Also Called: Enterprise Rent-A-Car
4616 Kirkwood Hwy (19808-5006)
PHONE..................717 968-1966
EMP: 6 **EST:** 2019
SALES (est): 231.98K **Privately Held**
Web: www.enterprise.com
SIC: 7514 Rent-a-car service

(G-16441)
ENTERTECH INC
1521 Concord Pike Ste 301 (19803-3644)
PHONE..................415 840-0204
EMP: 5 **EST:** 2020
SALES (est): 46.16K **Privately Held**
SIC: 7371 Computer software development and applications

(G-16442)
ENTRILIA INC (PA)
919 N Market St Ste 950 (19801-3036)
PHONE..................954 372-1715
EMP: 15 **EST:** 2021
SALES (est): 518.76K
SALES (corp-wide): 518.76K **Privately Held**
SIC: 7372 Prepackaged software

(G-16443)
ENVIRONMENTAL ALLIANCE INC (HQ)
5341 Limestone Rd (19808-1222)
PHONE..................302 234-4400
William Smith, *Pr*
Paul C Miller, *
Laurie Mason, *
EMP: 29 **EST:** 1991
SQ FT: 8,500
SALES (est): 6.75MM
SALES (corp-wide): 544.42MM **Publicly Held**
Web: www.envalliance.com
SIC: 8748 Environmental consultant
PA: Montrose Environmental Group, Inc.
5120 Northshore Dr
North Little Rock AR 72118
501 900-6400

(G-16444)
ENVISION CONSULTING LLC
2008 Woodlawn Ave (19806-2234)
PHONE..................302 658-9027
Sally C Coonin, *Prin*
EMP: 5 **EST:** 2009
SALES (est): 194K **Privately Held**
SIC: 8748 Business consulting, nec

(G-16445)
ENZ PARTY RENTAL
Also Called: E&Z Party Rental
2700 Lancaster Ave (19805-5298)
PHONE..................302 287-5995
Janell Nichols, *Prin*
EMP: 5 **EST:** 2011
SALES (est): 225.01K **Privately Held**
Web: www.enzpartyrental.com
SIC: 7359 Party supplies rental services

(G-16446)
ENZIGMA LLC
1201 N Orange St Ste 7403 (19801-1286)
PHONE..................415 830-3694
EMP: 6 **EST:** 2019
SALES (est): 82.5K **Privately Held**
Web: www.enzigma.com
SIC: 7371 Computer software development

(G-16447)
ENZYMETRICS BIOSCIENCE INC
1 Righter Pkwy Ste 260 (19803-1555)
PHONE..................302 763-3658
Althea Stillman, *CEO*
EMP: 3 **EST:** 2020
SALES (est): 288.41K **Privately Held**
SIC: 2835 In vitro diagnostics

(G-16448)
EON MIST LLC
427 N Tatnall St 85923 (19801-2230)
PHONE..................310 500-2140
Austin Hurst, *Managing Member*
EMP: 6 **EST:** 2020
SALES (est): 510.23K **Privately Held**
Web: www.eonmist.com
SIC: 2842 Disinfectants, household or industrial plant

(G-16449)
EPB ASSOCIATES INC
107 W Sutton Pl (19810-4115)
P.O. Box 7397 (19803-0397)
PHONE..................302 475-7301
Frank A Bush Junior, *Pr*
Edwin Bush, *VP*
Lydia White, *Sec*
EMP: 15 **EST:** 1986
SALES (est): 847.9K **Privately Held**

GEOGRAPHIC SECTION
Wilmington - New Castle County (G-16476)

SIC: **1629** 1623 Earthmoving contractor; Sewer line construction

(G-16450)
EPIC RESEARCH LLC
1105 N Market St Ste 1600 (19801-1201)
PHONE..................................302 510-1338
Jim Stewart, *Managing Member*
Paul Ricci, *Managing Member*
Ben Brake, *Managing Member*
Megan Basilio, *Managing Member*
EMP: 20 EST: 2007
SALES (est): 2.32MM **Privately Held**
Web: www.epicresearch.net
SIC: **8733** Research institute

(G-16451)
EPOTEC INC
62 Rockford Rd (19806-1047)
PHONE..................................302 654-3090
J Hayes Batson, *Pr*
Catherine Gross, *CIO*
Richard D Flanagan Ph.d., *CCO*
EMP: 8 EST: 1997
SALES (est): 224.53K **Privately Held**
Web: www.joaniefit.com
SIC: **7371** Computer software development

(G-16452)
EPRINTIT USA INC
1000 N West St (19801-1050)
PHONE..................................613 299-7105
Tony Gagliano, *Pr*
Mark Patenaude, *VP*
EMP: 10 EST: 2012
SQ FT: 1,200
SALES (est): 2.07MM
SALES (corp-wide): 387.55MM **Privately Held**
Web: www.eprintit.com
SIC: **8741** Management services
HQ: 1772887 Ontario Limited
15 Benton Rd
North York ON M6M 3
416 248-4868

(G-16453)
EQUITY PLUS INC
Also Called: Equity Plus Mortgage Company
500 Philadelphia Pike C (19809-2174)
PHONE..................................302 762-3122
William Rawheiser, *Pr*
EMP: 10 EST: 1996
SALES (est): 680K **Privately Held**
SIC: **6162** 6163 Mortgage bankers; Loan brokers

(G-16454)
ERBAN MNDSET LFSTYLE SLTONS IN
Also Called: Er
1412 Fresno Rd (19803-5122)
PHONE..................................407 608-0134
Anthony Robinson, *CEO*
EMP: 10 EST: 2019
SALES (est): 517.25K **Privately Held**
SIC: **8742** Management consulting services

(G-16455)
ERCO CEILINGS & INTERIORS INC (HQ)
Also Called: Erco
2 S Dupont Rd (19805-1446)
PHONE..................................302 994-6200
Richard Sykora, *Pr*
EMP: 15 EST: 1998
SALES (est): 4.31MM
SALES (corp-wide): 23.8MM **Privately Held**
Web: www.ercoonline.com

SIC: **1742** 5211 Acoustical and ceiling work; Lumber and other building materials
PA: Erco Ceilings, Inc.
32 Delsea Dr N
Glassboro NJ 08028
856 881-4200

(G-16456)
ERI INVESTMENTS INC
801 N West St Fl 2 (19801-1525)
PHONE..................................302 656-8089
EMP: 10 EST: 1995
SALES (corp-wide): 7.5B **Publicly Held**
SIC: **6719** Investment holding companies, except banks
PA: Eqt Corporation
625 Liberty Ave Ste 1700
Pittsburgh PA 15222
412 553-5700

(G-16457)
ERIK A UNDERHILL MD
1806 N Van Buren St Ste 200 (19802-3851)
PHONE..................................302 652-3772
Erik Underhill, *Prin*
EMP: 7 EST: 2016
SALES (est): 73.39K **Privately Held**
SIC: **8011** Offices and clinics of medical doctors

(G-16458)
ERIK LEMUS
7 Claire Pl (19808-4613)
PHONE..................................302 293-5178
Erik Lemus, *Prin*
EMP: 5 EST: 2016
SALES (est): 259.51K **Privately Held**
SIC: **4789** Transportation services, nec

(G-16459)
ERIK S BRADLEY DDS
1415 Foulk Rd Ste 200 (19803-2748)
PHONE..................................302 239-5917
EMP: 9 EST: 2018
SALES (est): 179.25K **Privately Held**
Web: www.dentalassociatesofdelaware.com
SIC: **8021** Dentists' office

(G-16460)
ERM EMERALD US INC
1150 N Market St Ste 1300 (19801)
PHONE..................................302 651-8300
John C Stipa, *Pr*
Mark R B Pearson, *
Joanne Della Valle, *
Roy A Burrows, *
William K Langan, *
EMP: 1580 EST: 2011
SALES (est): 31.8MM
SALES (corp-wide): 439.17MM **Privately Held**
SIC: **8748** Environmental consultant
HQ: Eagle 4 Limited
2nd Floor Exchequer Court
London EC3A

(G-16461)
ERM-DELAWARE INC (HQ)
1105 N Market St Ste 1300 (19801-1241)
PHONE..................................302 651-8300
John Stipa, *Pr*
David Mcarthur, *Ex VP*
Joanne Dellavalle, *
Mark Pearson, *
EMP: 305 EST: 1998
SALES (est): 1.3MM
SALES (corp-wide): 673.68MM **Privately Held**
SIC: **6719** Investment holding companies, except banks

PA: Erm-Na Holdings Corp.
75 Valley Stream Pkwy
Malvern PA 19355
484 913-0300

(G-16462)
ESAFETY LIGHTS LLC
Also Called: Eco Safety Lights
251 Little Falls Dr (19808-1674)
PHONE..................................800 236-8621
Robert Chowaniec, *Pr*
EMP: 5 EST: 2014
SALES (est): 862.91K **Privately Held**
Web: www.esafetylights.com
SIC: **3648** 3647 Strobe lighting systems; Locomotive and railroad car lights

(G-16463)
ESCAPE YACHTS INC
3511 Silverside Rd # 105 (19810-4902)
PHONE..................................302 691-9070
EMP: 4 EST: 2006
SALES (est): 310.55K **Privately Held**
SIC: **3732** Motorized boat, building and repairing

(G-16464)
ESIS INC
P.O. Box 15054 (19850-5054)
PHONE..................................215 640-1000
Joe Vasquez, *CEO*
EMP: 6
Web: www.esis.com
SIC: **6411** Insurance agents, nec
HQ: Esis, Inc.
436 Walnut St
Philadelphia PA 19106
215 640-1000

(G-16465)
ESPOSITO MANSORY LLC
471 B And O Ln (19804-1450)
PHONE..................................302 996-4961
EMP: 10 EST: 2005
SALES (est): 649.28K **Privately Held**
Web: www.disabatinoinc.com
SIC: **1741** Concrete block masonry laying

(G-16466)
ESSENTIALS RECOVERY DELAWARE
3700 Lancaster Pike (19805-1511)
PHONE..................................302 256-0454
EMP: 16 EST: 2019
SALES (est): 1.65MM **Privately Held**
Web: www.essentialsrecovery.com
SIC: **8093** Substance abuse clinics (outpatient)

(G-16467)
ESSILOR AMERICA HOLDING CO INC (HQ)
1209 N Orange St (19801-1120)
PHONE..................................214 496-4000
EMP: 218 EST: 1996
SALES (est): 113.39MM
SALES (corp-wide): 2.55MM **Privately Held**
SIC: **3851** 5048 Ophthalmic goods; Ophthalmic goods
PA: Essilorluxottica
147 Rue De Paris
Charenton Le Pont 94220
149774224

(G-16468)
ESTATE PLANNING COUNCIL OF DEL
2751 Centerville Rd Ste 310 (19808-1627)
PHONE..................................610 581-4748

EMP: 6 EST: 2010
SALES (est): 69.28K **Privately Held**
Web: www.epcdelaware.org
SIC: **6531** Real estate brokers and agents

(G-16469)
ESTEP RALPH V EA PA
508 Main St Fl 1 (19804-3911)
PHONE..................................302 998-2008
Ralph Estep, *Prin*
EMP: 6 EST: 2011
SALES (est): 214.54K **Privately Held**
Web: www.taxesbyestep.com
SIC: **8721** Certified public accountant

(G-16470)
ESTIMATORS CORP ✪
Also Called: Estimators
1007 N Orange St Fl 777 (19801-1239)
PHONE..................................760 492-6405
Gor Samsonyan, *CEO*
EMP: 5 EST: 2022
SALES (est): 219.93K **Privately Held**
SIC: **7371** Custom computer programming services

(G-16471)
ESTU INC ✪
Also Called: Estu Life
1209 N Orange St (19801-1120)
P.O. Box 771547 (34777-1547)
PHONE..................................407 881-6177
Raul Loeb Wald, *Pr*
Marcos Pereira, *COO*
EMP: 20 EST: 2023
SALES (est): 588.11K **Privately Held**
SIC: **7389** Financial services

(G-16472)
ESUPPLY LLC
1000 N West St Ste 1200 (19801-1058)
PHONE..................................415 315-9963
EMP: 5 EST: 2016
SALES (est): 1.53MM **Privately Held**
SIC: **5045** 5044 Computers, peripherals, and software; Office equipment

(G-16473)
ETERNAL HEALTH LLC
5231 W Woodmill Dr (19808-4068)
PHONE..................................302 635-7421
Megan E Richardson, *Pr*
EMP: 7 EST: 2016
SALES (est): 232.57K **Privately Held**
SIC: **8099** Health and allied services, nec

(G-16474)
ETHEREAL TECH US CORP
1013 Centre Rd Ste 403s (19805-1265)
PHONE..................................567 694-8888
Liang Lu, *CEO*
EMP: 20
SALES (est): 588.11K **Privately Held**
SIC: **7371** Computer software development

(G-16475)
ETLGR LLC
913 N Market St Ste 200 (19801-3097)
PHONE..................................302 204-0596
EMP: 5 EST: 2020
SALES (est): 100K **Privately Held**
Web: www.etlgr.com
SIC: **7371** Software programming applications

(G-16476)
EUROPEAN PERFORMANCE INC
806 Wilmington Ave (19805-5113)
PHONE..................................302 633-1122
John Lengyel, *Pr*

Wilmington - New Castle County (G-16477)

Laura Lengyel, *VP*
Susan Wiley, *Sec*
EMP: 8 **EST:** 1987
SALES (est): 985.87K **Privately Held**
Web: www.europeanperformancede.com
SIC: 7538   Engine rebuilding: automotive

(G-16477)
EUROSOFT TECH INC
910 Foulk Rd (19803-3158)
PHONE.............................737 263-0307
Imranullah Khan, *CEO*
EMP: 4
SALES (est): 171.34K **Privately Held**
SIC: 7372   Prepackaged software

(G-16478)
EVAN DAVID FOUNDATION
7 Barley Mill Dr (19807-2217)
P.O. Box 4156 (19807-0156)
PHONE.............................302 778-4546
Kathleen Ittel, *Ex Dir*
EMP: 6 **EST:** 2011
SALES (est): 87.4K **Privately Held**
Web: www.evandavidfdn.org
SIC: 8641   Civic and social associations

(G-16479)
EVANS
203 Lauren Dr (19804-1612)
PHONE.............................302 998-3356
EMP: 5 **EST:** 2007
SALES (est): 68.99K **Privately Held**
SIC: 8111   Specialized law offices, attorneys

(G-16480)
EVANS ACT INC
501 Silverside Rd (19809-1374)
PHONE.............................302 792-0355
Bob Domains, *Mgr*
EMP: 5 **EST:** 2004
SALES (est): 36.11K **Privately Held**
SIC: 8748   Business consulting, nec

(G-16481)
EVC INC
Also Called: Corbett & Associates
230 N Market St (19801-2528)
P.O. Box 25085 (19899-5085)
PHONE.............................302 571-0510
Ellen C Hannum, *Pr*
EMP: 12 **EST:** 1975
SQ FT: 3,600
SALES (est): 730K **Privately Held**
SIC: 7338   Court reporting service

(G-16482)
EVEN & ODD MINDS LLC (PA)
1521 Concord Pike Ste 301 (19803-3644)
PHONE.............................619 663-7284
Ravi Goel, *Managing Member*
EMP: 15 **EST:** 2012
SQ FT: 1,000
SALES (est): 2.44MM
SALES (corp-wide): 2.44MM **Privately Held**
Web: www.eominds.com
SIC: 8742 7379   Human resource consulting services; Computer related consulting services

(G-16483)
EVENT ENHANCERS
2115 Exton Dr (19810-2315)
PHONE.............................267 217-3868
Chris Brower, *Prin*
EMP: 5 **EST:** 2016
SALES (est): 61.83K **Privately Held**
Web: www.eventenhancers.com
SIC: 7929   Disc jockey service

(G-16484)
EVEREST FOODS ENTERPRISES INC
4603 Laura Dr (19804-4103)
Rural Route 3100sw117 (33330)
PHONE.............................215 896-8902
Glenn Harmon, *Pr*
EMP: 10 **EST:** 2017
SALES (est): 544.75K **Privately Held**
Web: www.everestfoodsenterprises.com
SIC: 5141 7389   Food brokers; Business Activities at Non-Commercial Site

(G-16485)
EVERGREEN HARDSCAPING INC
21 W Ayre St (19804-3101)
PHONE.............................302 633-4045
Richard Piendak, *Pr*
EMP: 5 **EST:** 2018
SALES (est): 172.44K **Privately Held**
Web: www.evergreenhardscaping.com
SIC: 0781   Landscape services

(G-16486)
EVERGREEN REALTY
Also Called: Newport Terrace Apartments
100 Ethan Ct Apt H (19804-3163)
PHONE.............................302 999-8805
EMP: 10 **EST:** 1995
SALES (est): 466.96K **Privately Held**
Web: www.evergreenapartments.com
SIC: 6513   Apartment building operators

(G-16487)
EVERGREEN REALTY INC
Also Called: Driftwood Club Apartments
125 Greenbank Rd Apt A4 (19808-4746)
PHONE.............................302 998-0354
Kevin Wolfegang, *Pr*
EMP: 5 **EST:** 1966
SALES (est): 389.29K **Privately Held**
Web: www.evergreenapartments.com
SIC: 6513   Apartment building operators

(G-16488)
EVERGREEN RESOURCES GROUP LLC
2 Righter Pkwy Ste 120 (19803-1528)
PHONE.............................302 477-0189
Scott Cullinan, *Pr*
EMP: 7
SALES (est): 499.51K **Publicly Held**
SIC: 8999   Earth science services
HQ: Etp Legacy Lp
   8111 Westchester Dr # 600
   Dallas TX 75225
   214 981-0700

(G-16489)
EVERSTAGE INC
3524 Silverside Rd Ste 35b (19810-4929)
PHONE.............................518 882-3489
Siva Rajamani, *CEO*
EMP: 5 **EST:** 2020
SALES (est): 40.64K **Privately Held**
SIC: 7372   Business oriented computer software

(G-16490)
EVERVAULT INC
1209 N Orange St (19801-1120)
PHONE.............................213 527-8608
Shane Curran, *CEO*
EMP: 15 **EST:** 2020
SALES (est): 639.35K **Privately Held**
Web: www.evervault.com
SIC: 7371   Software programming applications

(G-16491)
EVERYONE CAN ACHIEVE LLC
405 S Claymont St (19801-5805)
PHONE.............................404 317-1228
Earl Cooper, *Pr*
EMP: 45 **EST:** 2014
SALES (est): 2.31MM **Privately Held**
Web: www.ecamot.com
SIC: 1721 1542 1522 1611   Painting and paper hanging; Commercial and office buildings, renovation and repair; Remodeling, multi-family dwellings; Concrete construction: roads, highways, sidewalks, etc.

(G-16492)
EVIDENCE MANAGEMENT CENTER
3 Lewis Cir (19804-1618)
PHONE.............................302 691-8944
EMP: 9 **EST:** 2018
SALES (est): 478.47K **Privately Held**
Web: www.emcevidence.com
SIC: 8741   Management services

(G-16493)
EVOLUTION ENERGY PARTNERS LLC
2312 Ridgeway Rd (19805-2629)
PHONE.............................302 425-5008
Michael Steiner, *Owner*
EMP: 6 **EST:** 2015
SALES (est): 291.34K **Privately Held**
Web: www.evolutionsg.com
SIC: 4911   Electric services

(G-16494)
EVONSYS LLC (PA)
4550 Linden Hill Rd Ste 104 (19808)
PHONE.............................302 544-2156
Arunkumar M Subramanian, *CEO*
EMP: 8 **EST:** 2015
SQ FT: 2,000
SALES (est): 1.4MM
SALES (corp-wide): 1.4MM **Privately Held**
Web: www.evonsys.com
SIC: 7379   Online services technology consultants

(G-16495)
EVS LAWN SERVICE INC
2609 Ebright Rd (19810-1146)
PHONE.............................302 475-9222
Christopher Evens, *Pr*
EMP: 5 **EST:** 1990
SALES (est): 120.73K **Privately Held**
SIC: 0782   Lawn care services

(G-16496)
EWASTE EXPRESS
6 Rosetree Ct (19810-3209)
PHONE.............................302 691-8052
Rebecca Deshetler, *Pr*
EMP: 5 **EST:** 2013
SQ FT: 7,000
SALES (est): 252.23K **Privately Held**
SIC: 5093   Scrap and waste materials

(G-16497)
EWEBVALET CO INC
22 Center Meeting Rd (19807-1302)
PHONE.............................302 893-0903
Charles Beattie, *Pr*
EMP: 6 **EST:** 1999
SALES (est): 328.76K **Privately Held**
SIC: 4813   Internet connectivity services

(G-16498)
EXCAPE ENTERTAINMENT US LTD
704 N King St Ste 500 (19801-3584)
PHONE.............................949 943-9219

James Fiorillo Ortega, *CEO*
Steven Teear, *COO*
EMP: 7 **EST:** 2015
SALES (est): 479.79K **Privately Held**
SIC: 7359   3699   Home entertainment equipment rental; Automotive driving simulators (training aids), electronic

(G-16499)
EXCELLENT CHOICE LLC
1013 Centre Rd Ste 403s (19805-1270)
PHONE.............................818 322-6376
EMP: 7 **EST:** 2013
SALES (est): 65.65K **Privately Held**
SIC: 8043   Offices and clinics of podiatrists

(G-16500)
EXCEPTIONAL DENTISTRY DELAWARE
900 Foulk Rd Ste 203 (19803-3155)
PHONE.............................302 797-1212
EMP: 8 **EST:** 2020
SALES (est): 224.26K **Privately Held**
Web: www.exceptionaldentistryde.com
SIC: 8021   Dentists' office

(G-16501)
EXCLUSIVE GROUP LLC
108 W 13 St (19801)
PHONE.............................917 207-7299
EMP: 10
SIC: 5065 7389   Telephone equipment; Business Activities at Non-Commercial Site

(G-16502)
EXCO INC (HQ)
1007 N Orange St (19801-1239)
PHONE.............................905 477-3065
Brian Robbins, *CEO*
Paul Riganelli, *
Drew Knight, *
EMP: 100 **EST:** 1983
SALES (est): 224.74MM
SALES (corp-wide): 375.75MM **Privately Held**
SIC: 6719   3111   Public utility holding companies; Industrial leather products
PA: Exco Technologies Limited
   130 Spy Crt Fl 2
   Markham ON L3R 5
   905 477-3065

(G-16503)
EXECUTIVE AUTO REPAIRS INC
480 B And O Ln (19804-1452)
PHONE.............................302 995-6220
Michael Groome, *Pr*
Vincent Colasante, *VP*
Diane Groome, *Treas*
EMP: 6 **EST:** 1986
SQ FT: 6,000
SALES (est): 677.53K **Privately Held**
Web: www.yourbodyman.com
SIC: 7532   Body shop, automotive

(G-16504)
EXODUS ESCAPE ROOMS
1708 Marsh Rd (19810-4606)
PHONE.............................302 407-5362
EMP: 6 **EST:** 2016
SALES (est): 290.86K **Privately Held**
Web: www.axxiomwilmington.com
SIC: 7929   Entertainment service

(G-16505)
EXP GROWTH LLC
3 Germay Dr (19804-1127)
PHONE.............................804 855-8910
EMP: 6
SALES (est): 71.67K **Privately Held**

GEOGRAPHIC SECTION
Wilmington - New Castle County (G-16535)

SIC: 4111 Local and suburban transit

(G-16506)
EXPLORATION SYSTEMS & TECH
Also Called: Est
1209 N Orange St (19801-1120)
PHONE..............................302 335-3911
Robert Poisson, *Owner*
Lynn Rollins, *Prin*
▼ EMP: 6 EST: 2007
SALES (est): 467.23K **Privately Held**
SIC: 3728 Aircraft parts and equipment, nec

(G-16507)
EXPLORER NEW BUILD LLC
2711 Centerville Rd Ste 400 (19808-1660)
PHONE..............................305 436-4000
EMP: 8 EST: 2013
SALES (est): 836.56K
SALES (corp-wide): 4.84B **Publicly Held**
SIC: 4731 Brokers, shipping
PA: Norwegian Cruise Line Holdings Ltd.
7665 Corp Ctr Dr
Miami FL 33126
305 436-4000

(G-16508)
EXPLOSIVE TATTOO NORTHSIDE
722 Philadelphia Pike (19809-2541)
PHONE..............................302 762-1650
EMP: 6 EST: 2004
SALES (est): 98.32K **Privately Held**
Web: www.northsidetattoos.com
SIC: 7299 Tattoo parlor

(G-16509)
EXPRESS LEGAL DOCUMENTS LLC
(HQ)
Also Called: Eld
1201 N Orange St (19801-1155)
PHONE..............................212 710-1374
EMP: 9 EST: 2004
SALES (est): 2.32MM
SALES (corp-wide): 23.85MM **Privately Held**
SIC: 8742 8111 Industry specialist consultants; Specialized legal services
PA: Hunte Corporate Enterprise, Llc
1201 N Orange St Ste 7777
Wilmington DE 19801
212 710-1341

(G-16510)
EXTENSHIP LLC
520 Robinson Ln Unit 4 (19805-4616)
PHONE..............................302 400-5480
EMP: 5 EST: 2018
SALES (est): 120K **Privately Held**
SIC: 7371 Software programming applications

(G-16511)
EYE CONSULTANTS LLC
1941 Limestone Rd Ste 200 (19808-5400)
PHONE..............................302 998-2333
Heather L Dealy, *Prin*
EMP: 6 EST: 2009
SALES (est): 1.24MM **Privately Held**
Web: www.eyeconsultantsde.com
SIC: 8011 Opthalmologist

(G-16512)
EYE PHYSICIANS AND SURGEONS PA
Also Called: Wahl, John MD
1207 N Scott St Ste 1 (19806-4059)
PHONE..............................302 225-1018
S H Franklin Md, *Pr*
Dennis Mirra O.d., *Prin*
EMP: 42 EST: 1970

SALES (est): 4.89MM **Privately Held**
Web: www.eyephysicians.com
SIC: 8011 Opthalmologist

(G-16513)
EYETOWER LLC
2711 Centerville Rd Ste 300 (19808-1660)
PHONE..............................302 298-0944
Todd Carpenter, *Mgr*
EMP: 5 EST: 2016
SALES (est): 133.64K **Privately Held**
SIC: 1521 Single-family housing construction

(G-16514)
EYLIDEN HOMELIFE INC
1226 N King St 208 (19801-3232)
PHONE..............................858 336-9471
Tao Jiang, *Pr*
EMP: 16 EST: 2019
SALES (est): 597.68K **Privately Held**
SIC: 5092 Arts and crafts equipment and supplies

(G-16515)
EZ SIPS CORPORATION
501 Silverside Rd Ste 105 (19809-1376)
PHONE..............................888 747-7488
Richard Lewin, *Pr*
EMP: 6 EST: 2016
SALES (est): 772.2K **Privately Held**
Web: www.structuralinsulatedpanels.com
SIC: 5039 Prefabricated structures

(G-16516)
EZ WAY TRANSPORT LLC
9 Durborow Rd (19810-4101)
PHONE..............................302 367-5272
EMP: 6 EST: 2017
SALES (est): 1.06MM **Privately Held**
SIC: 4731 Freight forwarding

(G-16517)
EZDORMS INC ✪
300 Dlware Ave Ste 210-52 (19801)
PHONE..............................202 599-2953
Mark Travis, *Pr*
EMP: 18 EST: 2023
SALES (est): 441.65K **Privately Held**
SIC: 7389 7021 5734 Business Activities at Non-Commercial Site; Dormitory, commercially operated; Software, business and non-game

(G-16518)
EZION FAIR COMMUNITY ACADEMY
1400 B St (19801-5837)
PHONE..............................302 652-9114
Christopher Curry, *Dir*
Doctor Christopher Curry, *Pastor*
EMP: 10 EST: 2012
SALES (est): 385.23K **Privately Held**
Web: www.myezionfair.org
SIC: 8351 Child day care services

(G-16519)
F & G CONSTRUCTION CO INC
25 Maple Ave, B & O Ln (19804-1434)
PHONE..............................302 994-1406
Anthony Fontana, *Pr*
EMP: 5 EST: 1971
SQ FT: 2,400
SALES (est): 625.25K **Privately Held**
SIC: 1611 Concrete construction: roads, highways, sidewalks, etc.

(G-16520)
F & S TAX SOLUTIONS INC
2504 Tigani Dr (19808-2519)
PHONE..............................302 477-4357

Walter L Gifford, *Prin*
EMP: 5 EST: 2010
SALES (est): 65.95K **Privately Held**
SIC: 7291 Tax return preparation services

(G-16521)
F P T & W MEDICAL ASSOCIATES
1508 Penns Ave Ste 2b (19806-4339)
PHONE..............................800 421-2368
Doctor Dennis L Farr, *Pt*
Doctor Patricia H Purcell, *Pt*
Doctor Carl E Turner, *Pt*
Doctor Marc A Woolley, *Pt*
EMP: 18 EST: 1982
SQ FT: 1,500
SALES (est): 336.75K **Privately Held**
SIC: 8071 X-ray laboratory, including dental

(G-16522)
FABBY INC
1013 Centre Rd Ste 403b (19805-1270)
PHONE..............................408 891-7991
Andrei Kulik, *CEO*
EMP: 10 EST: 2016
SALES (est): 451.3K **Privately Held**
SIC: 7371 Computer software development and applications

(G-16523)
FABIT CORP
1201 N Orange St Ste 775 (19801-1173)
PHONE..............................832 217-0864
Badruddin Pitter, *Sec*
EMP: 5 EST: 2010
SALES (est): 417.93K **Privately Held**
Web: www.fabitcorp.com
SIC: 7371 Computer software systems analysis and design, custom

(G-16524)
FABRICS AND TEXTILES LLC
2711 Centerville Rd # 400 (19808-1660)
PHONE..............................507 369-2641
EMP: 5 EST: 2003
SALES (est): 110.83K **Privately Held**
SIC: 8742 Management consulting services

(G-16525)
FACILITY SERVICES GROUP INC
300 Cornell Dr Ste A1 (19801-5768)
PHONE..............................302 317-3029
Albert Grimes, *Pr*
▲ EMP: 5 EST: 2012
SALES (est): 571.55K **Privately Held**
Web: www.fsgmaintenance.com
SIC: 1752 Carpet laying

(G-16526)
FACTORI INC
1207 Delaware Ave (19806-4743)
PHONE..............................682 392-3913
Ajaie Albert, *Prin*
EMP: 6
SALES (est): 251.16K **Privately Held**
SIC: 8742 Management consulting services

(G-16527)
FACTORY UNIVERSE CO
1201 N Market St (19801-1147)
PHONE..............................302 216-2025
Jeremy Oliver, *CEO*
EMP: 15
SALES (est): 515.28K **Privately Held**
SIC: 7371 Computer software development and applications

(G-16528)
FAEGRE DRNKER BIDDLE REATH LLP
222 Delaware Ave Ste 1400 (19801-1633)

PHONE..............................302 467-4200
Beth Coyder, *Brnch Mgr*
EMP: 10
SALES (corp-wide): 733.12K **Privately Held**
Web: www.faegredrinker.com
SIC: 8111 General practice law office
PA: Faegre Drinker Biddle & Reath Llp
1 Logan Sq Ste 2000
Philadelphia PA 19103
215 988-2700

(G-16529)
FAIR SQUARE FINANCIAL LLC
1000 N West St Ste 1100 (19801-1050)
PHONE..............................571 205-0305
Rob Habgood, *CEO*
EMP: 86 EST: 2016
SALES (est): 8.17MM
SALES (corp-wide): 10.78B **Publicly Held**
Web: www.ollocard.com
SIC: 8742 Financial consultant
PA: Ally Financial Inc.
500 Woodward Ave Fl 10
Detroit MI 48226
866 710-4623

(G-16530)
FAIRWOOD CORPORATION
1201 N Orange St Ste 7901 (19801-1155)
PHONE..............................302 884-6749
John B Sganga, *Ex VP*
EMP: 3190 EST: 1988
SALES (est): 24MM **Privately Held**
SIC: 2512 2511 Upholstered household furniture; Wood household furniture

(G-16531)
FALCON CONSTRUCTION LLC
104 Boxwood Rd (19804-1823)
PHONE..............................302 668-6874
EMP: 5 EST: 2017
SALES (est): 71.29K **Privately Held**
SIC: 1521 Single-family housing construction

(G-16532)
FALCON CREST INV INTL INC
1201 N Orange St Ste 600 (19801-1171)
PHONE..............................240 701-1746
EMP: 5 EST: 2010
SALES (est): 314.91K **Privately Held**
SIC: 1522 Residential construction, nec

(G-16533)
FALCON STEEL CO
Also Called: Falcon Steel
811 S Market St (19801-5223)
PHONE..............................302 571-0890
William E Obrien, *Pr*
John O'brien, *VP*
Helen O'brien, *Sec*
▲ EMP: 48 EST: 1965
SQ FT: 10,000
SALES (est): 2.17MM **Privately Held**
SIC: 1791 Structural steel erection

(G-16534)
FAMILY CHIROPRACTIC OFFICE PA
3105 Limestone Rd Ste 303 (19808-2156)
PHONE..............................302 993-9113
Tim Ciolkosz, *Owner*
EMP: 5 EST: 1998
SALES (est): 385.51K **Privately Held**
SIC: 8041 Offices and clinics of chiropractors

(G-16535)
FAMILY CNSLING CTR ST PULS INC
Also Called: AMANECER COUNSELING & RESOURCE
301 N Van Buren St (19805-3615)

Wilmington - New Castle County (G-16536)

GEOGRAPHIC SECTION

P.O. Box 3803 (19807-0803)
PHONE..................302 576-4136
EMP: 11 EST: 2010
SALES (est): 847.39K Privately Held
Web: www.amanecerde.org
SIC: 8322 General counseling services

(G-16536)
FAMILY DENTAL CARE
1601 Milltown Rd Ste 19 (19808-4084)
PHONE..................302 999-7600
Alfred B Brown D.d.s., Mng Pt
Mark Brown, Prin
EMP: 9 EST: 1980
SALES (est): 575.48K Privately Held
Web: www.brownbarandentistry.com
SIC: 8021 Dentists' office

(G-16537)
FAMILY DENTAL CENTER
1 Winston Ave (19804-1760)
PHONE..................302 656-8266
Donald Jones, Owner
EMP: 85 EST: 1968
SALES (est): 1.54MM Privately Held
Web: www.myfamilydentalcenter.com
SIC: 8021 Dentists' office

(G-16538)
FAMILY DENTISTRY WILMINGTON
1708 Lovering Ave Ste 101 (19806-2141)
PHONE..................302 656-2434
Stacy Slocomb, Prin
EMP: 9 EST: 2017
SALES (est): 90.98K Privately Held
Web: www.wahlfamilydentistry.com
SIC: 8021 Dentists' office

(G-16539)
FAMILY EAR NOSE THROAT PHYSCAN
1941 Limestone Rd Ste 210 (19808-5400)
PHONE..................302 998-0300
EMP: 21 EST: 1983
SALES (est): 908.25K Privately Held
SIC: 8011 Ears, nose, and throat specialist; physician/surgeon

(G-16540)
FAMILY ENT PHYSICIANS INC (PA)
1941 Limestone Rd Ste 210 (19808-5400)
PHONE..................302 998-0300
Timoteo R Gabriel, Pr
Kuwon Suh, *
EMP: 24 EST: 1983
SALES (est): 2.42MM
SALES (corp-wide): 2.42MM Privately Held
SIC: 8011 Ears, nose, and throat specialist; physician/surgeon

(G-16541)
FAMILY LEGACY LLCCOM
1616 Bonwood Rd Apt P2 (19805-4650)
PHONE..................302 256-1406
EMP: 30 EST: 2021
SALES (est): 1.13MM Privately Held
SIC: 4449 7389 Transportation (freight) on bays and sounds of the ocean; Business services, nec

(G-16542)
FAMILY MEDICAL ASSOC DELAWARE
2300 Pennsylvania Ave Ste 1a (19806-1333)
PHONE..................302 655-0355
EMP: 9 EST: 2021
SALES (est): 385.15K Privately Held
Web: www.fmadelaware.com

SIC: 8011 General and family practice, physician/surgeon

(G-16543)
FAMILY MEDICINE AT GREENVILLE
213 Greenhill Ave Ste B (19805-1800)
PHONE..................302 429-5870
Stephanie Malleus, Pr
EMP: 10 EST: 2001
SALES (est): 864.81K Privately Held
Web: www.fmagreenhill.com
SIC: 8011 General and family practice, physician/surgeon

(G-16544)
FAMILY OFFICE SOLUTIONS L
3801 Kennett Pike Ste C30 (19807-2321)
P.O. Box 4079 (19807-4079)
PHONE..................610 255-0623
EMP: 7 EST: 2017
SALES (est): 171.02K Privately Held
Web: www.jmfos.com
SIC: 8721 Certified public accountant

(G-16545)
FAMILY PRACTICE ASSOCIATION PA
1100 S Broom St Ste 1 (19805-4599)
PHONE..................302 656-5416
Edward Sobel, Pr
John Moore Md, VP
EMP: 46 EST: 1949
SALES (est): 1.53MM Privately Held
SIC: 8011 Neurologist

(G-16546)
FAMILY PRMISE NTHRN NEW CSTLE
2104 Saint James Church Rd (19808-5225)
PHONE..................302 998-2222
Patrick V Downes, Prin
Denison Hatch, Pr
Carolyn Gordon, Ex Dir
EMP: 6 EST: 2009
SALES (est): 1.67MM Privately Held
Web: www.familypromisede.org
SIC: 8322 Social service center

(G-16547)
FAMILY SERVICES DIV
119 Lower Beech St Ste 100 (19805)
PHONE..................302 577-3824
Nancy Jackson, Prin
EMP: 7 EST: 2004
SALES (est): 59.98K Privately Held
SIC: 8322 General counseling services

(G-16548)
FAMILY WRKPLACE CONNECTION INC (PA)
2005 Baynard Blvd (19802-3917)
PHONE..................302 479-1660
Ralph Klesius, Ex Dir
EMP: 46 EST: 1986
SQ FT: 10,000
SALES (est): 1.67MM Privately Held
SIC: 8322 8351 Child related social services; Child day care services

(G-16549)
FAN PAYMENT SOLUTIONS LLC (PA)
Also Called: Fandom Pay
108 W 13th St (19801-1145)
PHONE..................617 901-3970
EMP: 14 EST: 2019
SALES (est): 322.96K
SALES (corp-wide): 322.96K Privately Held
SIC: 8641 7371 Social club, membership; Computer software development and applications

(G-16550)
FANTASYTHRONE LLC (PA)
300 Delaware Ave Ste 210a (19801-6601)
PHONE..................512 431-8658
Connor Gibson, Pr
EMP: 5 EST: 2018
SALES (est): 404.71K
SALES (corp-wide): 404.71K Privately Held
SIC: 7371 Computer software development and applications

(G-16551)
FANTICIPATE INC
251 Little Falls Dr (19808-1674)
PHONE..................763 777-4232
Edward Blach, CEO
EMP: 5 EST: 2020
SALES (est): 104.73K Privately Held
Web: www.fanticipate.com
SIC: 7389 Auctioneers, fee basis

(G-16552)
FARAZAD INVESTMENTS INC
1201 N Orange St (19801-1155)
PHONE..................302 573-2320
Korosh Farazad, CEO
EMP: 8 EST: 2008
SALES (est): 158.16K Privately Held
Web: www.farazadinvest.com
SIC: 6799 Investors, nec

(G-16553)
FAREMART INC (PA)
3524 Silverside Rd Ste 35b (19810-4929)
PHONE..................800 965-5819
EMP: 7 EST: 2016
SALES (est): 219.26K
SALES (corp-wide): 219.26K Privately Held
Web: www.faremart.com
SIC: 4724 Travel agencies

(G-16554)
FARMERS MUTL FIRE INSUR SLEM C (PA)
Also Called: Farmers Insurance
1 Ave Of The Arts (19801-5047)
P.O. Box 263 (08079-0263)
PHONE..................856 935-1851
William Decinque, Ch Bd
William C Hancock, *
William C Decinque, *
Kent W Jones, *
Patricia Hendrickson, *
EMP: 43 EST: 1851
SQ FT: 12,000
SALES (est): 23.11MM
SALES (corp-wide): 23.11MM Privately Held
Web: www.farmersofsalem.com
SIC: 6411 Insurance agents, brokers, and service

(G-16555)
FARUQI & FARUQI LLP
3828 Kennett Pike Ste 201 (19807-2331)
PHONE..................302 482-3182
James C Strum, Pt
EMP: 5
Web: www.faruqilaw.com
SIC: 8111 General practice law office
PA: Faruqi & Faruqi, Llp
685 3rd Ave Fl 26
New York NY 10017

(G-16556)
FAST BAILBONDS LLC
Also Called: Fast Bailbonds
1224 N King St (19801-3232)
PHONE..................302 778-4400
EMP: 6 EST: 2007
SALES (est): 373.57K Privately Held
SIC: 7389 Bail bonding

(G-16557)
FAST FCE INC
Also Called: Web Fce
2207 Concord Pike Ste 446 (19803-2908)
PHONE..................833 327-8323
Carl Contino, Pr
Steven Stanko, CEO
EMP: 5 EST: 2017
SALES (est): 180K Privately Held
SIC: 7371 Computer software development and applications

(G-16558)
FAST PAY RX LLC
108 W 13th St (19801-1145)
PHONE..................833 511-9500
EMP: 5 EST: 2017
SALES (est): 108.14K Privately Held
SIC: 8082 Home health care services

(G-16559)
FASTCOLD LLC
221 W 9th St (19801-1619)
PHONE..................302 240-4402
EMP: 5
SALES (est): 81.26K Privately Held
SIC: 4731 Freight forwarding

(G-16560)
FASTTRAK
1500 Eastlawn Ave (19802-2403)
PHONE..................302 761-5454
Charles Mcclure, Pr
EMP: 18 EST: 1991
SALES (est): 247.66K Privately Held
Web: www.fasttrakcoatingsco.com
SIC: 1752 Floor laying and floor work, nec

(G-16561)
FASTTRAK COATINGS CO
Also Called: Neotrak
1500 Eastlawn Ave (19802-2403)
PHONE..................302 761-5454
James P Mccarthy, Pr
Glenda Mccarthy, Sec
EMP: 15 EST: 1991
SQ FT: 30,000
SALES (est): 576.49K Privately Held
Web: www.fasttrakcoatingsco.com
SIC: 1771 Concrete work

(G-16562)
FATHERS DAY GALA INC
436 S Buttonwood St (19801-5306)
PHONE..................302 981-4117
Karen Y Burton, CEO
EMP: 5 EST: 2006
SALES (est): 108.79K Privately Held
SIC: 8399 Social services, nec

(G-16563)
FBH BUSINESS CONSULTING LLC
24a Trolley Sq Ste 1162 (19806-3334)
PHONE..................267 266-8149
Jorrell Lawton, Managing Member
EMP: 8
SALES (est): 323.68K Privately Held
SIC: 8742 8748 Management consulting services; Business consulting, nec

(G-16564)
FBK GRAPHICO INC
2207 Concord Pike (19803-2908)
PHONE..................302 743-4784
Jim Fagan, Pr

GEOGRAPHIC SECTION   Wilmington - New Castle County (G-16592)

EMP: 2 EST: 2005
SALES (est): 96.19K **Privately Held**
SIC: 2759 Screen printing

(G-16565)
FEATLY INC
2055 Limestone Rd (19808-5536)
PHONE.............................505 305-6844
Dmitry Lazarev, *CFO*
EMP: 8
SALES (est): 306.16K **Privately Held**
SIC: 7371 Computer software development and applications

(G-16566)
FEBYS FISHERY INC
3701 Lancaster Pike (19805-1510)
PHONE.............................302 998-9501
Phillip Di Febo, *Pr*
Mary Di Febo, *
EMP: 29 EST: 1974
SQ FT: 7,000
SALES (est): 1.14MM **Privately Held**
Web: www.febysfishery.com
SIC: 5812 5421 5146 Seafood restaurants; Seafood markets; Seafoods

(G-16567)
FEDERAL BUSINESS SYSTEMS CORPORATION GOVERNMENT DIVISION
Also Called: Federal Business Systems
1000 N West St Ste 1200 (19801-1058)
PHONE.............................877 489-2111
EMP: 72
Web: fbscgov.us.com
SIC: 7389 Personal service agents, brokers, and bureaus

(G-16568)
FEDERAL COURT REPORTERS
844 N King St Unit 24 (19801-3519)
PHONE.............................302 573-6195
Leonard Dibbs, *Owner*
EMP: 7 EST: 1974
SALES (est): 292.17K **Privately Held**
SIC: 7338 Court reporting service

(G-16569)
FEDERAL ENERGY INF
251 Little Falls Dr (19808-1674)
PHONE.............................858 521-3300
EMP: 10 EST: 2018
SALES (est): 455.92K **Privately Held**
SIC: 1731 Energy management controls

(G-16570)
FEDERAL EXPRESS CORPORATION
Also Called: Fedex
1209 N Orange St (19801-1120)
PHONE.............................800 463-3339
EMP: 5
SALES (corp-wide): 90.16B **Publicly Held**
Web: www.fedex.com
SIC: 4513 Air courier services
HQ: Federal Express Corporation
    3610 Hacks Cross Rd
    Memphis TN 38125
    901 369-3600

(G-16571)
FEDERAL HOME LOAN ADM INC
1201 N Orange St Ste 600 (19801-1171)
P.O. Box 11141 (92658-5020)
PHONE.............................855 345-2669
Nicholas Krakana, *CEO*
EMP: 7 EST: 2013
SQ FT: 4,500
SALES (est): 235.61K **Privately Held**
SIC: 6162 Bond and mortgage companies

(G-16572)
FEDEX OFFICE & PRINT SVCS INC
Also Called: Fedex
1201 N Market St Ste 1200 (19801-1163)
PHONE.............................302 652-2151
EMP: 5
SALES (corp-wide): 90.16B **Publicly Held**
Web: www.fedex.com
SIC: 7334 Photocopying and duplicating services
HQ: Fedex Office And Print Services, Inc.
    3 Gallria Twr 13155 Noel 3 Galleria Tower
    Dallas TX 75240
    800 463-3339

(G-16573)
FEDEX OFFICE & PRINT SVCS INC
Also Called: Fedex
4721a Kirkwood Hwy (19808-5007)
PHONE.............................302 996-0264
EMP: 4
SALES (corp-wide): 90.16B **Publicly Held**
Web: www.fedex.com
SIC: 7334 2759 5099 Photocopying and duplicating services; Commercial printing, nec; Signs, except electric
HQ: Fedex Office And Print Services, Inc.
    3 Gallria Twr 13155 Noel 3 Galleria Tower
    Dallas TX 75240
    800 463-3339

(G-16574)
FEDI INC (PA) ✪
251 Little Falls Dr (19808-1674)
PHONE.............................797 372-0606
EMP: 5 EST: 2022
SALES (est): 72.36K
SALES (corp-wide): 72.36K **Privately Held**
SIC: 7371 Computer software development and applications

(G-16575)
FEDMET RESOURCES CORPORATION (PA)
1000 N West St Ste 1200 # 889 (19801-1058)
PHONE.............................514 931-5711
◆ EMP: 20 EST: 1983
SALES (est): 9.71MM **Privately Held**
Web: www.frcglobal.com
SIC: 5032 Ceramic construction materials, excluding refractory

(G-16576)
FEELZ LLC
704 N King St Ste 500 (19801-3584)
PHONE.............................347 860-5813
EMP: 4 EST: 2020
SALES (est): 50K **Privately Held**
SIC: 2051 Bakery: wholesale or wholesale/retail combined

(G-16577)
FELIX C VERGARA M D
2601 Annand Dr Ste 14 (19808-3719)
PHONE.............................856 624-4312
Felix Vergara, *Ofcr*
EMP: 7 EST: 2018
SALES (est): 59.55K **Privately Held**
Web: www.ob-and-gyn.com
SIC: 8011 Gynecologist

(G-16578)
FEMISPACE CO ✪
2055 Limestone Rd Ste 200c (19808-5536)
PHONE.............................917 764-9943
EMP: 17 EST: 2022
SALES (est): 68.89K **Privately Held**
Web: www.femispace.com
SIC: 7371 Computer software development and applications

(G-16579)
FENG WANG
808 First State Blvd (19804-3573)
PHONE.............................315 677-1685
EMP: 5 EST: 2017
SALES (est): 85.44K **Privately Held**
SIC: 8011 General and family practice, physician/surgeon

(G-16580)
FENWAY AVIATION LLC
108 W 13th St (19801-1145)
PHONE.............................800 981-7183
EMP: 8 EST: 2013
SALES (est): 391.53K **Privately Held**
SIC: 7363 Pilot service, aviation

(G-16581)
FERGUSON ENTERPRISES LLC
2000 Maryland Ave (19805-4606)
PHONE.............................302 656-4421
Brad Smith, *Brnch Mgr*
EMP: 12
SALES (corp-wide): 2.67MM **Privately Held**
Web: www.ferguson.com
SIC: 5074 Plumbing fittings and supplies
HQ: Ferguson Enterprises, Llc
    751 Lakefront Cmns
    Newport News VA 23606
    757 969-4011

(G-16582)
FERGUSON ENTERPRISES LLC
Also Called: Ferguson Enterprises 1861
1000 First State Blvd (19804-3575)
PHONE.............................302 429-5850
EMP: 6
SALES (corp-wide): 2.67MM **Privately Held**
Web: www.ferguson.com
SIC: 5074 Plumbing fittings and supplies
HQ: Ferguson Enterprises, Llc
    751 Lakefront Cmns
    Newport News VA 23606
    757 969-4011

(G-16583)
FERGUSON ENTERPRISES LLC
919 S Heald St (19801-5732)
PHONE.............................302 225-4082
EMP: 7
SALES (corp-wide): 2.67MM **Privately Held**
Web: www.ferguson.com
SIC: 5074 Plumbing fittings and supplies
HQ: Ferguson Enterprises, Llc
    751 Lakefront Cmns
    Newport News VA 23606
    757 969-4011

(G-16584)
FERM DEVELOPMENT LLC
501 Silverside Rd (19809-1374)
PHONE.............................302 792-1102
EMP: 15 EST: 2000
SALES (est): 1.69MM **Privately Held**
Web: www.fermassociates.com
SIC: 6552 Subdividers and developers, nec

(G-16585)
FERRARA ASSET MANAGEMENT INC
2711 Centerville Rd Ste 400 (19808-1660)
PHONE.............................401 286-8464
William Ferrara, *CEO*
EMP: 7 EST: 2014
SALES (est): 628.57K **Privately Held**
SIC: 6722 7389
; Business services, nec

(G-16586)
FERRARA HALEY & BEVIS
1716 Wawaset St (19806-2131)
PHONE.............................302 656-7247
Louis Ferrara, *Owner*
EMP: 7 EST: 1991
SALES (est): 236.12K **Privately Held**
Web: www.glfsite.com
SIC: 8111 General practice attorney, lawyer

(G-16587)
FERRARI HAIR STUDIO LTD
4559 Linden Hill Rd (19808)
PHONE.............................302 731-7505
Angelo J Ferrari, *Pr*
Ronald F Ferrari, *VP*
EMP: 9 EST: 1984
SQ FT: 2,000
SALES (est): 215.98K **Privately Held**
Web: www.ferrarihs.com
SIC: 7231 Hairdressers

(G-16588)
FERRIS HOME IMPROVEMENTS
325 Oracle Rd (19808-1562)
PHONE.............................302 377-8003
Kelley Ferris, *Prin*
EMP: 7 EST: 2019
SALES (est): 129.21K **Privately Held**
Web: www.ferrishomeimprovements.com
SIC: 1521 General remodeling, single-family houses

(G-16589)
FERRIS PROPERTIES INC
818 S Broom St Apt 1a (19805-4262)
PHONE.............................302 472-0875
Christina Ferris, *Pr*
EMP: 7 EST: 1999
SALES (est): 620K **Privately Held**
Web: www.ferrisproperties.com
SIC: 6512 Nonresidential building operators

(G-16590)
FERRY JOSEPH & PEARCE PA (PA)
1521 Concord Pike Ste 202 (19803-3645)
P.O. Box 1351 (19899-1351)
PHONE.............................302 575-1555
David J Ferry Junior, *Pr*
Michael B Joseph, *VP*
EMP: 14 EST: 1990
SALES (est): 3.84MM **Privately Held**
Web: www.ferryjoseph.com
SIC: 8111 General practice attorney, lawyer

(G-16591)
FETCH SOCIAL INC
251 Little Falls Dr (19808-1674)
PHONE.............................813 858-5774
Christian Mcwilliams, *CEO*
EMP: 2 EST: 2018
SALES (est): 62.19K **Privately Held**
SIC: 7372 7389 Application computer software; Business Activities at Non-Commercial Site

(G-16592)
FFI GENERAL CONTRACTOR IN
13 Perth Dr (19803-2612)
PHONE.............................302 420-1242
Hope Townsend, *Mgr*
EMP: 5 EST: 2000
SALES (est): 686.47K **Privately Held**

Wilmington - New Castle County (G-16593) GEOGRAPHIC SECTION

Web: www.healthynailinstitute.com
SIC: 1611 General contractor, highway and street construction

(G-16593)
FIA CARD SERVICES NAT ASSN
11 King St (19884-0001)
PHONE..................302 457-0517
Richard Proctor, *Brnch Mgr*
EMP: 710
SALES (corp-wide): 94.95B **Publicly Held**
SIC: 7389 Credit card service
HQ: Fia Card Services, National Association
1100 N King St
Wilmington DE 19884
800 362-6255

(G-16594)
FIA CARD SERVICES NAT ASSN (HQ)
1100 N King St (19884-0011)
PHONE..................800 362-6255
Brian T Moynihan, *Pr*
Mogensen Lauren A, *
Linsz Mark D, *
▲ EMP: 39 EST: 2013
SALES (est): 23.55MM
SALES (corp-wide): 94.95B **Publicly Held**
SIC: 7389 Credit card service
PA: Bank Of America Corporation
100 N Tryon St Ste 2650
Charlotte NC 28202
704 386-5681

(G-16595)
FIA CARD SERVICES NAT ASSN
655 Paper Mill Rd (19884-1510)
PHONE..................302 458-0365
Gary Morris, *Brnch Mgr*
EMP: 255
SALES (corp-wide): 94.95B **Publicly Held**
SIC: 7389 Credit card service
HQ: Fia Card Services, National Association
1100 N King St
Wilmington DE 19884
800 362-6255

(G-16596)
FIA CARD SERVICES NAT ASSN
1200 N French St (19884-0012)
PHONE..................302 432-1573
Ceil Sculthorpe, *Mgr*
EMP: 289
SALES (corp-wide): 94.95B **Publicly Held**
SIC: 7389 Credit card service
HQ: Fia Card Services, National Association
1100 N King St
Wilmington DE 19884
800 362-6255

(G-16597)
FIBRE PROCESSING CORPORATION
701 Garasches Ln (19801-5528)
PHONE..................302 654-3659
Anthony J Di Ottavio, *Pr*
Jacquelyne Di Ottavio, *
◆ EMP: 68 EST: 1887
SQ FT: 100,000
SALES (est): 7.77MM **Privately Held**
Web: www.fibrep.com
SIC: 2299 Batting, wadding, padding and fillings

(G-16598)
FIDELITRADE INCORPORATED (PA)
3601 N Market St (19802-2736)
PHONE..................302 762-6200
Jonathan E Potts, *Pr*
Simon Schatz, *VP*
EMP: 10 EST: 1997
SQ FT: 20,404
SALES (est): 10.54MM

SALES (corp-wide): 10.54MM **Privately Held**
Web: www.fidelitrade.com
SIC: 4226 Special warehousing and storage, nec

(G-16599)
FIDELITY NATIONAL INFO SVCS (PA)
Also Called: Fidelity National
600 N King St Fl 10 (19801-3783)
PHONE..................302 658-2102
Christina Gray, *Pr*
Dean M Lusky, *Pr*
EMP: 17 EST: 1986
SALES (est): 2.43MM
SALES (corp-wide): 2.43MM **Privately Held**
Web: www.fisglobal.com
SIC: 6411 Insurance agents, nec

(G-16600)
FIDELITY OXFORD STREET TRUST
1201 N Market St (19801-1147)
PHONE..................214 281-6351
Richard Durben, *Prin*
EMP: 8 EST: 2006
SALES (est): 467.42K **Privately Held**
SIC: 6722 Money market mutual funds

(G-16601)
FIDUKS INDUSTRIAL SERVICES INC (PA)
7 Meco Cir (19804-1193)
PHONE..................302 994-2534
Gerald H Wybranski, *Pr*
Harold J Kuhn, *Prin*
EMP: 17 EST: 1963
SQ FT: 10,000
SALES (est): 2.06MM
SALES (corp-wide): 2.06MM **Privately Held**
Web: www.fiduks.com
SIC: 7699 5084 Industrial machinery and equipment repair; Machine tools and accessories

(G-16602)
FIDUKS INDUSTRIAL SERVICES INC
7 Meco Cir (19804-1193)
PHONE..................302 994-2534
Karen Kershaw, *Brnch Mgr*
EMP: 10
SALES (corp-wide): 2.06MM **Privately Held**
Web: www.fiduks.com
SIC: 5084 Hydraulic systems equipment and supplies
PA: Fiduk's Industrial Services, Inc.
7 Meco Cir
Wilmington DE 19804
302 994-2534

(G-16603)
FIELDSTONE GOLF CLUB LP
1000 Dean Rd (19807-1648)
PHONE..................302 254-4569
Mike Sanders, *Genl Mgr*
▲ EMP: 75 EST: 1999
SALES (est): 4.54MM **Privately Held**
Web: www.fieldstonegolf.com
SIC: 7992 Public golf courses

(G-16604)
FIGUEROA T ERNESTO MD
1600 Rockland Rd (19803-3607)
PHONE..................302 651-5980
T Figueroa, *Prin*
EMP: 12 EST: 2018
SALES (est): 387.87K **Privately Held**
Web: www.nemours.org
SIC: 8011 Pediatrician

(G-16605)
FILMUSTAGE INC
2810 N Church St Pmb 68039 (19802-4447)
PHONE..................260 225-3050
Egor Dubrovsky, *CEO*
EMP: 10 EST: 2020
SALES (est): 321.66K **Privately Held**
SIC: 7371 Computer software development and applications

(G-16606)
FINAL FINISHES INC
708 Woodtop Rd (19804-2628)
PHONE..................302 995-1850
Wayne Gravell, *Pr*
Mickey Gravell, *Sec*
EMP: 5 EST: 1995
SALES (est): 409.03K **Privately Held**
Web: www.finalfinishes.net
SIC: 1721 Interior residential painting contractor

(G-16607)
FINANCE BUSINESS SOLUTIONS LLC
3616 Kirkwood Hwy (19808-5124)
PHONE..................646 707-1290
Geoffrey Cavey, *Managing Member*
EMP: 5 EST: 2016
SALES (est): 103.94K **Privately Held**
SIC: 8742 Financial consultant

(G-16608)
FINANCIAL HOUSE INC
5818 Kennett Pike (19807-1116)
PHONE..................302 654-5451
Joseph E Biloon C.f.p, *Pt*
Joseph D Joe Blair C.f.p, *Prin*
Mary Ann Blair, *Pt*
Robert D Griesemer Clu Chfc, *Prin*
Robert S Pennartz C.f.p, *Prin*
EMP: 30 EST: 1983
SQ FT: 4,500
SALES (est): 1.72MM **Privately Held**
Web: www.financialhouse.com
SIC: 8742 Financial consultant

(G-16609)
FINANCIAL SERVICES
Also Called: Rmch
1000 N West St Ste 1200 (19801-1058)
P.O. Box 132 (19736-0132)
PHONE..................302 478-4707
Randi Dorante, *CEO*
R Natashi, *CFO*
Jim Chu, *V Ch Bd*
Randy Vaughn, *Vice Chairman*
EMP: 29 EST: 2005
SQ FT: 500
SALES (est): 1.32MM **Privately Held**
Web: www.equityfinancialservices.net
SIC: 8742 Management consulting services

(G-16610)
FINEMAN KREKSTEIN & HARRIS PC
1300 N King St (19801-3220)
PHONE..................312 655-0800
EMP: 6
SALES (corp-wide): 5.18MM **Privately Held**
Web: www.finemanlawfirm.com
SIC: 8111 General practice law office
PA: Fineman Krekstein & Harris, P.C.
1801 Market St Fl 11
Philadelphia PA 19103
215 893-9300

(G-16611)
FIREBIRD ENERGY II LLC ✪
251 Little Falls Dr (19808-1674)
PHONE..................817 857-7800
Steven Loh, *Managing Member*
EMP: 32 EST: 2023
SALES (est): 610.95K **Privately Held**
SIC: 1311 Crude petroleum and natural gas production

(G-16612)
FIREBOLT ANALYTICS INC (PA)
1007 N Orange St (19801-1239)
PHONE..................302 314-3135
Eldad Farkash, *CEO*
Itay Link, *VP Fin*
EMP: 14 EST: 2018
SALES (est): 100K
SALES (corp-wide): 100K **Privately Held**
Web: www.firebolt.io
SIC: 5045 Computer software

(G-16613)
FIREBRICK WIND LLC
251 Little Falls Dr (19808-1674)
PHONE..................647 352-9533
EMP: 6 EST: 2020
SALES (est): 109.34K **Privately Held**
Web: www.cordeliopower.com
SIC: 1796 Power generating equipment installation

(G-16614)
FIRST ADVANCE LOAN CENTER INC
2100 Naamans Rd (19810-1327)
PHONE..................302 482-7294
Natalie Marrero, *Pr*
EMP: 5 EST: 2019
SALES (est): 120.76K **Privately Held**
SIC: 6141 Licensed loan companies, small

(G-16615)
FIRST AMERICAN TITLE INSUR CO
704 N King St (19801-3583)
PHONE..................302 421-9440
Donna Penge, *Mgr*
EMP: 5
Web: www.firstam.com
SIC: 6541 Title and trust companies
HQ: First American Title Insurance Company
1 First American Way
Santa Ana CA 92707
800 854-3643

(G-16616)
FIRST CLASS LAWNCARE
4009 Greenmount Dr (19810-3303)
PHONE..................302 753-0761
Andrew Ogden, *Prin*
EMP: 11 EST: 2016
SALES (est): 955.98K **Privately Held**
Web: www.firstclasslawncarellc.com
SIC: 0782 Lawn care services

(G-16617)
FIRST DATA
Also Called: First Data
101 Bellevue Pkwy (19809-3726)
PHONE..................302 793-5945
EMP: 6 EST: 2020
SALES (est): 456.94K **Privately Held**
Web: merchants.fiserv.com
SIC: 6512 Commercial and industrial building operation

(G-16618)
FIRST HALTHCARE COMPLIANCE LLC
3903 Centerville Rd (19807-1938)

PHONE..............................302 416-4329
Julie Sheppard, *Pr*
Sheba Vine, *VP*
EMP: 10 **EST:** 2013
SALES (est): 913.49K **Privately Held**
Web: www.1sthcc.com
SIC: 8099 7389 7372 Health and allied services, nec; Educational computer software

(G-16619)
FIRST LINCOLN HOLDINGS INC
1219 N West St (19801-1044)
P.O. Box 249 (19899-0249)
PHONE..............................302 429-4900
Martin Oliner, *Ch Bd*
Martin Oliner, *Ch Bd*
Dave Taylor, *Treas*
EMP: 13 **EST:** 1969
SALES (est): 327.45K **Privately Held**
SIC: 6311 Life insurance carriers

(G-16620)
FIRST PERSON ARTS
1010 W 8th St (19806-4604)
PHONE..............................267 402-2055
Vicki Solot, *Pr*
Jamie Brunson, *Ex Dir*
EMP: 5 **EST:** 1999
SALES (est): 167.54K **Privately Held**
Web: www.firstpersonarts.org
SIC: 8699 Charitable organization

(G-16621)
FIRST POWER LLC
22 Peirce Rd (19803-3726)
PHONE..............................610 247-5750
Jeffrey Macel, *Managing Member*
EMP: 9
SALES (est): 389.93K **Privately Held**
SIC: 6552 Subdividers and developers, nec

(G-16622)
FIRST STATE AUTO GLASS
605 Curtis Ave (19804-2107)
PHONE..............................302 559-8902
Erik Klapcuniak, *Prin*
EMP: 6 **EST:** 2015
SALES (est): 41.36K **Privately Held**
SIC: 7538 General automotive repair shops

(G-16623)
FIRST STATE BALLET THEATRE INC
818 N Market St (19801-3087)
PHONE..............................302 658-7897
Kristina Kambalov, *Ex Dir*
Robert Grenfell, *Pr*
EMP: 7 **EST:** 1999
SALES (est): 569.45K **Privately Held**
Web: www.firststateballet.org
SIC: 7922 7911 Ballet production; Dance studio and school

(G-16624)
FIRST STATE BANCORP INC (HQ)
1105 N Market St Ste 1300 (19801-1241)
P.O. Box 10 (76241-0010)
PHONE..............................302 427-3637
Frank Morris, *Ch Bd*
Ben Hatcher, *Pr*
Lloyd Martin, *VP*
Mike Paulson, *Sec*
EMP: 9 **EST:** 1989
SALES (est): 69.98MM **Privately Held**
Web: www.firststate.bank
SIC: 6712 Bank holding companies
PA: Red River Bancorp, Inc.
   801 E California St
   Gainesville TX 76240

(G-16625)
FIRST STATE BOWLING CENTER
Also Called: First State Lanes
4601 Bedford Blvd (19803-3901)
PHONE..............................302 762-3883
Rita Justice, *CEO*
Rita Justice, *Pr*
Kim Justice-bowers, *Prin*
EMP: 7 **EST:** 1958
SALES (est): 199.15K **Privately Held**
Web: www.firststatelanes.com
SIC: 7933 5813 5812 Ten pin center; Bars and lounges; Snack bar

(G-16626)
FIRST STATE CONTROLS INC
2207 Concord Pike 220 (19803-2908)
PHONE..............................302 559-7822
EMP: 9 **EST:** 2010
SQ FT: 1,500
SALES (est): 87.86K **Privately Held**
SIC: 3357 Communication wire

(G-16627)
FIRST STATE DISTRIBUTORS INC
222a 7th Ave (19805-4762)
PHONE..............................302 655-8266
Mike Catts, *Pr*
Dan Mumford, *VP*
EMP: 7 **EST:** 1990
SALES (est): 956.98K **Privately Held**
SIC: 5084 5198 Safety equipment; Paints

(G-16628)
FIRST STATE DRVWAY SEALCOATING
211 Waverly Rd (19803-3134)
PHONE..............................302 478-2266
EMP: 5 **EST:** 2010
SALES (est): 121.81K **Privately Held**
SIC: 1611 Surfacing and paving

(G-16629)
FIRST STATE HOOD & DUCT LLC
23 S Clayton St (19805-3968)
PHONE..............................888 866-7389
EMP: 5 **EST:** 2020
SALES (est): 80.15K **Privately Held**
Web: www.hoodcleaningphiladelphia.com
SIC: 7342 Disinfecting and pest control services

(G-16630)
FIRST STATE MEDICAL ASSOC LLC
2055 Limestone Rd Ste 111 (19808-5536)
PHONE..............................302 999-8169
EMP: 7 **EST:** 2007
SQ FT: 1,900
SALES (est): 790.24K **Privately Held**
SIC: 8011 Clinic, operated by physicians

(G-16631)
FIRST STATE NUTRITION
910 N Union St (19805-5334)
PHONE..............................302 384-7104
EMP: 7 **EST:** 2017
SALES (est): 139.75K **Privately Held**
Web: www.firststatehealth.com
SIC: 8099 Nutrition services

(G-16632)
FIRST STATE PODIATRY LLC
390 Mitch Rd (19804-3943)
PHONE..............................302 678-4612
EMP: 9 **EST:** 2007
SALES (est): 219.86K **Privately Held**
SIC: 8043 Offices and clinics of podiatrists

(G-16633)
FIRST STATE REHAB HOME LLC
111 Oxford Pl (19803-4517)
PHONE..............................302 304-9729
Anthony Gangemi, *Prin*
EMP: 8 **EST:** 2016
SALES (est): 203.94K **Privately Held**
Web: www.firststaterehabathome.com
SIC: 8049 Physical therapist

(G-16634)
FIRST STATE SPINE AND PAIN CTR
5311 Limestone Rd Ste 204 (19808-1258)
PHONE..............................302 439-3063
EMP: 8 **EST:** 2012
SALES (est): 125.78K **Privately Held**
SIC: 8011 Orthopedic physician

(G-16635)
FIRST STATE SQUASH INC
501 W 11th St (19801-6406)
PHONE..............................312 919-6767
Serena A Carbonell, *Prin*
EMP: 5 **EST:** 2017
SALES (est): 220.69K **Privately Held**
Web: www.firststatesquash.org
SIC: 8399 Social services, nec

(G-16636)
FIRST STATE STFFING SLTION LLC
112 S French St (19801-5035)
PHONE..............................302 285-9044
Gary Carter, *CEO*
Gary Carter, *Prin*
EMP: 25 **EST:** 2015
SALES (est): 1.29MM **Privately Held**
Web: www.1ststatestaffingsolutions.com
SIC: 7363 7361 Temporary help service; Employment agencies

(G-16637)
FIRST STATE TRUST COMPANY
1 Righter Pkwy Ste 120 (19803-1533)
PHONE..............................302 573-5967
Marianne Quinn, *Pr*
Richard J Gelinas, *CFO*
EMP: 41 **EST:** 1982
SALES (est): 200 **Privately Held**
Web: www.fs-trust.com
SIC: 6091 Nondeposit trust facilities

(G-16638)
FIRST STATE VEIN AND LASER CTR
1300 N Franklin St (19806-4212)
PHONE..............................302 294-0700
Lynn Shapira, *Pr*
EMP: 12 **EST:** 2011
SALES (est): 1.28MM **Privately Held**
Web: www.firststatemedspa.com
SIC: 8011 Dermatologist

(G-16639)
FIRST STATE WAX LLC
Also Called: European Wax Center
5603 Concord Pike (19803-1428)
PHONE..............................302 529-8888
EMP: 5 **EST:** 2013
SALES (est): 197.85K **Privately Held**
Web: www.waxcenter.com
SIC: 7231 Beauty shops

(G-16640)
FIRST TECH
700 Cornell Dr Ste E5 (19801-5762)
PHONE..............................302 421-3650
Bill Florio, *Pr*
EMP: 13 **EST:** 2003
SALES (est): 470.39K **Privately Held**
SIC: 7378 Computer maintenance and repair

(G-16641)
FIRST TEE OF DELAWARE
800 N Dupont Rd (19807-2920)
PHONE..............................302 593-2062
EMP: 9 **EST:** 2015
SALES (est): 195.25K **Privately Held**
Web: www.thefirstteedelaware.org
SIC: 8641 Youth organizations

(G-16642)
FIRSTBASE INC (PA)
251 Little Falls Drive (19808-1674)
PHONE..............................917 331-6863
Christopher Herd, *CEO*
EMP: 10 **EST:** 2020
SALES (est): 250K
SALES (corp-wide): 250K **Privately Held**
Web: www.firstbase.com
SIC: 1731 Computer installation

(G-16643)
FIS INVESTMENT VENTURES LLC (HQ)
Also Called: Sungard
1105 N Market St Ste 1412 (19801-1216)
PHONE..............................484 582-2000
EMP: 30 **EST:** 2005
SALES (est): 8.76MM
SALES (corp-wide): 14.53B **Publicly Held**
SIC: 7374 Data processing and preparation
PA: Fidelity National Information Services, Inc.
   347 Riverside Ave
   Jacksonville FL 32202
   904 438-6000

(G-16644)
FISERV WRLDWIDE SLTIONS II LLC (HQ)
251 Little Falls Dr (19808-1674)
PHONE..............................800 872-7882
EMP: 11 **EST:** 1998
SALES (est): 4.71MM
SALES (corp-wide): 17.74B **Publicly Held**
SIC: 7374 Data processing service
PA: Fiserv, Inc.
   255 Fiserv Dr
   Brookfield WI 53045
   262 879-5000

(G-16645)
FISH & MONKEY PRODUCTIONS LLC
1612 W 16th St (19806-4026)
PHONE..............................302 897-4318
Dan Healy, *Prin*
EMP: 5 **EST:** 2010
SALES (est): 205.8K **Privately Held**
SIC: 7822 Motion picture and tape distribution

(G-16646)
FISH & RICHARDSON PC
222 Delaware Ave Fl 17 (19801-1621)
P.O. Box 1114 (19899-1114)
PHONE..............................302 652-5070
William J Marsden Junior, *Prin*
EMP: 112
SALES (corp-wide): 132.63MM **Privately Held**
Web: www.fr.com
SIC: 8111 Patent solicitor
PA: Fish & Richardson P.C.
   1 Marina Park Dr Ste 1700
   Boston MA 02210
   617 542-5070

(G-16647)
FISH AND SON SERVICES
307 Brighton Ave (19805-2407)
PHONE..............................302 383-4202

Wilmington - New Castle County (G-16648) GEOGRAPHIC SECTION

Jeff Fish, *Prin*
EMP: 5 EST: 2012
SALES (est): 49.01K **Privately Held**
Web: www.fishandsonservices.com
SIC: 0783 Ornamental shrub and tree services

(G-16648)
FISHER AUTO PARTS INC
Also Called: Manlove Auto Parts
1600 E Newport Pike Ste C (19804-2541)
PHONE...................................302 998-3111
Bradley Eaton, *Bmch Mgr*
EMP: 9
SALES (corp-wide): 525.52MM **Privately Held**
Web: www.fisherautoparts.com
SIC: 5013 5531 Automotive supplies and parts; Automotive parts
PA: Fisher Auto Parts, Inc.
   512 Greenville Ave
   Staunton VA 24401
   540 885-8901

(G-16649)
FITBODY PERSONAL TRAINING
727 N Market St (19801-4935)
PHONE...................................302 442-3685
EMP: 5 EST: 2016
SALES (est): 304.93K **Privately Held**
Web: www.myfitbodytraining.com
SIC: 7991 Physical fitness facilities

(G-16650)
FITE LLC
3464 Naamans Rd (19810-1066)
PHONE...................................302 478-1002
EMP: 9 EST: 2015
SALES (est): 68.15K **Privately Held**
Web: www.fiteplumbing.com
SIC: 7241 Hair stylist, men

(G-16651)
FIVE FRIENDS AUTO
199 Philadelphia Pike (19809-3161)
PHONE...................................302 407-6326
Jasmin Watkins, *Prin*
EMP: 8 EST: 2017
SALES (est): 279.21K **Privately Held**
SIC: 7538 General automotive repair shops

(G-16652)
FIVE POINT CHINESE LAUNDRY
Also Called: 5 Point Gloria Laundry & Clr
118 N Maryland Ave (19804-1336)
PHONE...................................302 656-6051
Hyun K Chunt, *Owner*
EMP: 5 EST: 1995
SALES (est): 62.61K **Privately Held**
SIC: 7211 Power laundries, family and commercial

(G-16653)
FIVE SIXTY ENTERPRISE LLC
501 Silverside Rd Ste 505 (19809-1374)
PHONE...................................302 268-6530
Steven Johnson, *Managing Member*
EMP: 20 EST: 2018
SALES (est): 1.13MM **Privately Held**
SIC: 8742 Management consulting services

(G-16654)
FIVE STAR FRANCHISING LLC (HQ)
Also Called: Five-Star Basketball
1209 N Orange St (19801-1120)
PHONE...................................646 838-3992
EMP: 5 EST: 2014
SALES (est): 672.12K
SALES (corp-wide): 672.12K **Privately Held**

Web: www.5starglobal.com
SIC: 7941 Sports clubs, managers, and promoters
PA: Five-Star Basketball Group Llc
   1091 Boston Post Rd
   Rye NY

(G-16655)
FIVE STAR SENIOR LIVING INC
Also Called: Foulk Manor South
407 Foulk Rd (19803-3809)
PHONE...................................302 655-6249
Mike Salitsky, *Bmch Mgr*
EMP: 63
SALES (corp-wide): 934.59MM **Privately Held**
Web: www.foulkmanorsouth.com
SIC: 8051 Skilled nursing care facilities
HQ: Alerislife Inc.
   255 Washington St Ste 300
   Newton MA 02458

(G-16656)
FIVE-STAR CLEANING SERVICES
3207 Crystal Ct (19810-2256)
P.O. Box 303 (19703-0303)
PHONE...................................302 746-7178
EMP: 5 EST: 2014
SALES (est): 198.29K **Privately Held**
Web: www.5starcleaningservicesllc.com
SIC: 7699 Cleaning services

(G-16657) ✪
FIXCOM INC
Also Called: Fix.com
251 Little Falls Dr (19808-1674)
PHONE...................................916 534-8872
Ben Graham, *CEO*
EMP: 7 EST: 2022
SALES (est): 264.9K **Privately Held**
SIC: 7371 Computer software development and applications

(G-16658)
FJS CAPITAL MANAGEMENT INC
300 Delaware Ave Ste 210 (19801-6601)
PHONE...................................267 850-1123
EMP: 5 EST: 2018
SALES (est): 487.93K **Privately Held**
SIC: 6211 Security brokers and dealers

(G-16659)
FLAG RIDE LLC (PA)
942 Bennett St Fl 2nf (19801-4310)
PHONE...................................202 390-4850
EMP: 6 EST: 2015
SALES (est): 79.35K
SALES (corp-wide): 79.35K **Privately Held**
SIC: 4119 Local passenger transportation, nec

(G-16660)
FLEDGLING FUND
501 Silverside Rd Ste 123 (19809-1377)
PHONE...................................800 839-1754
EMP: 5
SALES (est): 109.49K **Privately Held**
Web: www.thefledglingfund.org
SIC: 8699 Charitable organization

(G-16661)
FLIGHT CENTRE TRAVEL GROUP USA
4737 Concord Pike Ste 835 (19803-1494)
PHONE...................................302 479-7581
EMP: 7
Web: www.libertytravel.com
SIC: 4724 Tourist agency arranging transport, lodging and car rental
HQ: Flight Centre Travel Group (Usa) Inc

5 Paragon Dr Ste 200
Montvale NJ 07645
201 934-3500

(G-16662)
FLO HEALTH INC (PA)
1013 Centre Rd Ste 403b (19805-1270)
PHONE...................................302 498-8369
Yury Hurski, *CEO*
Yakov Moldavskiy, *Sec*
Maxim Scrobov, *CFO*
EMP: 21 EST: 2016
SALES (est): 6.29MM
SALES (corp-wide): 6.29MM **Privately Held**
Web: www.flo.health
SIC: 7371 Computer software development and applications

(G-16663)
FLO MECHANICAL LLC
1017 W 25th St (19802-3311)
PHONE...................................302 543-5462
Larry Shub, *Managing Member*
EMP: 14 EST: 2015
SALES (est): 250.2K **Privately Held**
Web: www.flomechanical.com
SIC: 1711 Mechanical contractor

(G-16664)
FLORA F PETILLO
1600 N Washington St (19802-4722)
PHONE...................................302 658-8191
Flora Petillo, *Pr*
EMP: 7 EST: 2017
SALES (est): 22.18K **Privately Held**
SIC: 8049 Offices of health practitioner

(G-16665)
FLORES DESIGN AND CONSTRUCTION
2417 Lancaster Ave (19805-3736)
PHONE...................................302 635-7345
EMP: 6 EST: 2018
SALES (est): 160.61K **Privately Held**
Web: www.floresdesignandconstruction.com
SIC: 1521 General remodeling, single-family houses

(G-16666)
FLORES ENTERPRISES LLC
3902 Newport Gap Pike (19808-1414)
PHONE...................................484 880-5134
EMP: 5 EST: 2014
SALES (est): 305.01K **Privately Held**
SIC: 1522 Residential construction, nec

(G-16667)
FLORIENT CONTRACTING FIRM LLC
1201 N Market St (19801-1147)
PHONE...................................888 250-1915
Kelvin Wallace Simo, *CEO*
EMP: 5 EST: 2020
SALES (est): 237.06K **Privately Held**
SIC: 7379 Computer related consulting services

(G-16668)
FLOWERS REAL ESTATE LLC
406 Robinson Dr (19801-5745)
PHONE...................................302 383-8955
EMP: 5 EST: 2020
SALES (est): 450K **Privately Held**
SIC: 6361 Real estate title insurance

(G-16669)
FLOWLINE TECHNOLOGIES INC
1201 N Orange St Ste 600 (19801-1171)
PHONE...................................302 256-5825

Kim Lavery, *Pr*
Christopher Larson, *Mgr*
Mister R Matarajan, *Mgr*
EMP: 7 EST: 2012
SALES (est): 500.59K **Privately Held**
SIC: 8711 Industrial engineers

(G-16670)
FLOWPAY CORPORATION
221 W 9th St Ste 300 (19801-1619)
PHONE...................................720 425-3244
EMP: 2 EST: 2011
SQ FT: 4,000
SALES (est): 132.63K **Privately Held**
Web: www.flowpaycorp.com
SIC: 7372 7371 Business oriented computer software; Computer software development and applications

(G-16671)
FLOYD ALLAN GREGORY
Also Called: Whizbang Productions
707 W 21st St Lower Level (19802-3816)
PHONE...................................302 658-0295
Floyd Gregory, *Prin*
EMP: 5 EST: 2011
SALES (est): 77.94K **Privately Held**
Web: www.whizbangproductions.com
SIC: 7812 Motion picture and video production

(G-16672)
FLOYD DEAN INC
2 S Poplar St Ste B (19801-5052)
PHONE...................................302 655-7193
Floyd Dean, *Pr*
Victoria M Yelton, *VP*
EMP: 8 EST: 1986
SQ FT: 4,500
SALES (est): 540.59K **Privately Held**
Web: www.floyddean.com
SIC: 7335 Photographic studio, commercial

(G-16673)
FLUENTAAI INC
1209 N Orange St (19801-1120)
PHONE...................................323 739-5417
EMP: 5 EST: 2021
SALES (est): 63.4K **Privately Held**
SIC: 7371 Computer software development and applications

(G-16674)
FLUOROGISTX LLC
Also Called: Delaware Specialty Dist
3704 Kennett Pike Ste 100 (19807-2173)
PHONE...................................302 479-7614
David Jones, *Pr*
EMP: 32 EST: 1993
SALES (est): 22.33MM **Privately Held**
Web: www.fluorogistx.com
SIC: 3086 Plastics foam products

(G-16675)
FLUOROGISTX CT LLC (PA)
3704 Kennett Pike Ste 100 (19807-2172)
PHONE...................................800 373-7811
Robert Smith, *Pr*
Todd Fredette, *COO*
EMP: 14 EST: 2017
SALES (est): 4.88MM
SALES (corp-wide): 4.88MM **Privately Held**
SIC: 5162 Plastics materials and basic shapes

(G-16676)
FLUTE PRO SHOP INC
4023 Kennett Pike Ste 30 (19807-2018)
P.O. Box 4023 (19807-0023)

PHONE..................302 479-5000
EMP: 5 EST: 2010
SALES (est): 494K **Privately Held**
Web: www.fluteproshop.com
SIC: 5736 7699 7389 Pianos; Musical instrument repair services; Business Activities at Non-Commercial Site

(G-16677)
FLYOGI LLC
605 N Market St Fl 2 (19801)
PHONE..................302 298-0926
Jason Aviles, *Prin*
EMP: 5 EST: 2014
SALES (est): 68.58K **Privately Held**
Web: www.flyogi.co
SIC: 7999 Yoga instruction

(G-16678)
FNX TECHNOLOGIES LTD (PA)
251 Little Falls Dr (19808-1674)
PHONE..................844 969-0070
EMP: 8 EST: 2019
SALES (est): 142.18K
SALES (corp-wide): 142.18K **Privately Held**
SIC: 7371 Computer software development and applications

(G-16679)
FOCUS BEHAVIORAL HEALTH
410 Foulk Rd Ste 105 (19803-3835)
P.O. Box 552 (19943-0552)
PHONE..................302 762-2285
Diane Carrado, *Prin*
EMP: 8 EST: 2015
SALES (est): 184.69K **Privately Held**
Web: www.focusbehavioralhealth.com
SIC: 8093 Mental health clinic, outpatient

(G-16680)
FOLDFAST GOALS LLC
1211 Stony Run Dr (19803-3539)
PHONE..................302 478-7881
▲ EMP: 2 EST: 2006
SQ FT: 3,500
SALES (est): 170K **Privately Held**
SIC: 3949 Lacrosse equipment and supplies, general

(G-16681)
FOOD AND BEV INNOVATIONS LLC
300 Delaware Ave (19801-1607)
PHONE..................302 722-8058
EMP: 4
SALES (est): 180.26K **Privately Held**
SIC: 2086 Bottled and canned soft drinks

(G-16682)
FOOD EQUIPMENT SERVICE INC
3316a Old Capitol Trl (19808-6210)
P.O. Box 5281 (19808-0281)
PHONE..................302 996-9363
George Fox, *Pr*
EMP: 9 EST: 1992
SALES (est): 919.73K **Privately Held**
Web: www.foodequipmentservice.com
SIC: 7389 7629 Industrial and commercial equipment inspection service; Electrical equipment repair services

(G-16683)
FOODSTR INC
251 Little Falls Dr (19808-1674)
PHONE..................707 500-0599
Mykhailo Minov, *CEO*
EMP: 3
SALES (est): 71.13K **Privately Held**
SIC: 7372 Prepackaged software

(G-16684)
FOOS CONSTRUCTION INC
230 Philadelphia Pike (19809-3125)
PHONE..................302 753-3667
EMP: 6 EST: 2019
SALES (est): 254.66K **Privately Held**
SIC: 7389

(G-16685)
FOOT AND ANKLE ASSOCIATES LLC
3801 Kennett Pike Ste A102 (19807-2307)
PHONE..................302 652-5767
EMP: 10
Web: www.footandanklellp.com
SIC: 8043 Offices and clinics of podiatrists
PA: Foot And Ankle Associates, Llc
692 Unionville Rd
Kennett Square PA 19348

(G-16686)
FOOT CARE GROUP INC (PA)
Also Called: Haley, David
1601 Milltown Rd Ste 24 (19808-4084)
PHONE..................302 998-0178
Doctor David Haley, *Owner*
▲ EMP: 20 EST: 1995
SALES (est): 955.95K **Privately Held**
Web: www.footcaregroup.org
SIC: 8043 Offices and clinics of podiatrists

(G-16687)
FORBES MRKTPLACE OPRATIONS INC
251 Little Falls Dr (19808-1674)
PHONE..................973 393-0073
Achir Kalra, *Dir*
EMP: 30 EST: 2020
SALES (est): 2.47MM **Privately Held**
SIC: 6794 Performance rights, publishing and licensing

(G-16688)
FORCEBEYOND INC
Also Called: Wholesale
1521 Concord Pike Ste 301 (19803-3644)
PHONE..................302 995-6588
Steve Bai, *Pr*
Nicholas Lintner, *
Sunny Chen, *
▲ EMP: 35 EST: 2006
SALES (est): 6.21MM **Privately Held**
Web: www.forcebeyond.com
SIC: 3324 3089 3544 3069 Commercial investment castings, ferrous; Injection molding of plastics; Dies and die holders for metal cutting, forming, die casting; Rubber automotive products

(G-16689)
FORD INTERNATIONAL FIN CORP
1209 N Orange St (19801-1120)
PHONE..................313 845-5712
EMP: 51 EST: 1973
SALES (est): 675.78K **Privately Held**
Web: www.ford.com
SIC: 3711 Motor vehicles and car bodies

(G-16690)
FORENSIC ASSOCIATES DEL LLC
2055 Limestone Rd (19808-5536)
PHONE..................302 415-4944
Laura Cooney-koss, *Managing Member*
EMP: 7 EST: 2014
SALES (est): 47.09K **Privately Held**
Web: www.forensicassociatesde.com
SIC: 8049 Clinical psychologist

(G-16691)
FOREST PARK APARTMENTS
5501 Limeric Cir Ofc 33 (19808-3431)
PHONE..................302 737-6151
Doug Kelley, *Dir*
EMP: 7 EST: 1975
SALES (est): 434.35K **Privately Held**
Web: www.rentfairwayparkapts.com
SIC: 6513 Apartment building operators

(G-16692)
FOREVER INC (PA)
Also Called: Fulton Paper & Party Supply
1006 W 27th St (19802-2946)
PHONE..................302 594-0400
Michael D Gavetti, *Pr*
Dorothy L Quigley, *VP*
EMP: 15 EST: 1997
SQ FT: 30,000
SALES (est): 2.26MM
SALES (corp-wide): 2.26MM **Privately Held**
Web: www.fultonparty.com
SIC: 5947 5199 5113 Balloon shops; Party favors, balloons, hats, etc.; Bags, paper and disposable plastic

(G-16693)
FORGOTTEN FEW FOUNDATION INC
1927 W 4th St (19805-3421)
PHONE..................302 494-6212
Brunilda Luna-mercado, *Ex Dir*
EMP: 8
SQ FT: 1,500
SALES (est): 62.67K **Privately Held**
SIC: 8322 Emergency social services

(G-16694)
FORIS SOLUTIONS LLC
330 Water St Ste 109 (19804-2433)
PHONE..................302 343-6396
EMP: 5 EST: 2019
SALES (est): 160.7K **Privately Held**
Web: www.forissolutions.com
SIC: 8748 Business consulting, nec

(G-16695)
FORMCLICK LLC ✪
1007 N Orange St Fl 4 (19801-1242)
PHONE..................302 212-0311
R Anwaarul Haque, *Managing Member*
EMP: 4 EST: 2022
SALES (est): 171.34K **Privately Held**
SIC: 7372 Prepackaged software

(G-16696)
FORT HILL COMPANY INC
1104 Philadelphia Pike (19809-2031)
P.O. Box 192 (19710-0192)
PHONE..................302 651-9223
Cal Wick, *Ch Bd*
EMP: 10 EST: 1999
SALES (est): 819.97K **Privately Held**
Web: www.forthillcompany.com
SIC: 8742 Business management consultant

(G-16697)
FORUM TO ADVNCE MNRTIES IN ENG
Also Called: Fame
2005 Baynard Blvd (19802-3917)
PHONE..................302 777-3254
Don Baker, *Ex Dir*
William Brazel, *Prin*
EMP: 40 EST: 1975
SQ FT: 900
SALES (est): 2.24MM **Privately Held**
Web: www.famedelaware.org
SIC: 7389 Personal service agents, brokers, and bureaus

(G-16698)
FORWOOD CHIROPRACTIC CENTER
6 Sharpley Rd (19803-2941)
PHONE..................302 652-0411
Wellington Whitlock, *Pt*
EMP: 7 EST: 2015
SALES (est): 85.82K **Privately Held**
SIC: 8041 8031 8011 Offices and clinics of chiropractors; Offices and clinics of osteopathic physicians; Offices and clinics of medical doctors

(G-16699)
FOSS-BROWN INC (PA)
3411 Silverside Rd Ste 100wb (19810-4812)
PHONE..................610 940-6040
Lance Charen, *Pr*
EMP: 6 EST: 1958
SQ FT: 2,200
SALES (est): 1.97MM
SALES (corp-wide): 1.97MM **Privately Held**
SIC: 5072 Builders' hardware, nec

(G-16700)
FOTOMASTER LLC
1013 Centre Rd Ste 403b (19805-1270)
PHONE..................646 233-3371
Boaz Telem, *CEO*
EMP: 5 EST: 2019
SALES (est): 306.46K **Privately Held**
Web: www.fotomaster.com
SIC: 7371 Computer software development and applications

(G-16701)
FOULK LAWN & EQUIPMENT CO INC
Also Called: John Deere Authorized Dealer
2018 Foulk Rd (19810-3624)
PHONE..................302 475-3233
Anthony J Socorso Senior, *Pr*
A Joseph Socorso Junior, *Sec*
EMP: 5 EST: 1954
SQ FT: 3,000
SALES (est): 672.75K **Privately Held**
Web: www.foulklawn.com
SIC: 5261 7699 5082 Lawnmowers and tractors; Lawn mower repair shop; Construction and mining machinery

(G-16702)
FOULK PR-SCHOOL DAY CARE CTR I (PA)
2 Tenby Dr (19803-2619)
PHONE..................302 478-3047
Benjamin S Crawford, *Pr*
Judith J Crawford, *VP*
Keith Crawford, *Sec*
EMP: 9 EST: 1964
SQ FT: 3,000
SALES (est): 627.42K
SALES (corp-wide): 627.42K **Privately Held**
Web: www.foulkpreschool.com
SIC: 8351 Preschool center

(G-16703)
FOULK PRE-SCHL & DAY CRE CNTR
2711 Carpenter Station Rd (19810-2057)
PHONE..................302 529-1580
Judy Crawford, *Dir*
EMP: 6
SALES (corp-wide): 627.42K **Privately Held**
Web: www.foulkpreschool.com
SIC: 8351 Preschool center
PA: Foulk Pre-School And Day Care Center Incorporated
2 Tenby Dr
Wilmington DE 19803
302 478-3047

Wilmington - New Castle County (G-16704)

GEOGRAPHIC SECTION

(G-16704)
FOULK ROAD DENTAL & ASSOCIATES
300 Foulk Rd Ste 101 (19803-3819)
PHONE.................302 652-3775
John Russo, *Dir*
Nicholas J Russo, *Dir*
Andrea Boffa, *Mgr*
EMP: 14 **EST:** 1997
SALES (est): 528.11K **Privately Held**
Web: www.thedentalgroupofdelaware.com
SIC: 8021 Dentists' office

(G-16705)
FOUNDATION OF HEALTH
112 South Rd (19809-3033)
PHONE.................302 762-5973
Claudia Robbins, *Prin*
EMP: 10 **EST:** 2017
SALES (est): 140.18K **Privately Held**
Web: www.nemours.org
SIC: 8099 Health and allied services, nec

(G-16706)
FOUNDATION SOURCE CHAR FDN INC
501 Silverside Rd Ste 123 (19809-1377)
PHONE.................800 839-1754
EMP: 5 **EST:** 2010
SALES (est): 84.37K **Privately Held**
SIC: 8699 Charitable organization

(G-16707)
FOUNDATION SOURCE PHILANTHROPI
501 Silverside Rd (19809-1374)
PHONE.................800 839-1754
EMP: 64
SALES (corp-wide): 43.1MM **Privately Held**
Web: www.foundationsource.com
SIC: 8699 Charitable organization
PA: Foundation Source Philanthropic Services Inc.
55 Walls Dr
Fairfield CT 06824
203 319-3700

(G-16708)
FOUR BROTHERS AUTO SERVICE
101 N Union St (19805-3427)
PHONE.................302 482-2932
Wilfredo Rosa, *Owner*
EMP: 10 **EST:** 2014
SALES (est): 508.01K **Privately Held**
Web: www.4brothersauto.com
SIC: 7538 General automotive repair shops

(G-16709)
FOUR C HEALTH SOLUTIONS
3903 Centerville Rd (19807-1938)
PHONE.................804 601-2628
Julie Sheppard, *Prin*
EMP: 21 **EST:** 2016
SALES (est): 104.38K **Privately Held**
Web: www.ctxgroup.com
SIC: 8099 Health and allied services, nec

(G-16710)
FOURTH FLOOR
1205 N Orange St (19801-1120)
PHONE.................302 472-8416
Patrick Ashley, *Mgr*
EMP: 6 **EST:** 1980
SALES (est): 482.92K **Privately Held**
Web: www.e-4thfloor.com
SIC: 7389 Financial services

(G-16711)
FOWLER FAMILY CHARITABLE FOUN
501 Silverside Rd Ste 123 (19809-1377)
PHONE.................800 839-1754
EMP: 5 **EST:** 2010
SALES (est): 112.77K **Privately Held**
SIC: 8699 Charitable organization

(G-16712)
FOX LOGISTICS LLC
601 Cornell Dr Ste G10 (19801-5792)
PHONE.................302 444-4750
EMP: 5 **EST:** 2016
SALES (est): 82.29K **Privately Held**
SIC: 8742 Business management consultant

(G-16713)
FOX LOGISTICS LLC
700 Cornell Dr Ste E16 (19801-5776)
PHONE.................302 444-4750
EMP: 6 **EST:** 2017
SQ FT: 1,500
SALES (est): 256.92K **Privately Held**
SIC: 4789 Transportation services, nec

(G-16714)
FOX POINT PROGRAMS INC
706 Philadelphia Pike Ste 2 (19809-2546)
PHONE.................302 765-6018
Glenn W Clark, *Pr*
EMP: 6 **EST:** 2008
SALES (est): 109.89K **Privately Held**
SIC: 6411 Insurance agents, nec

(G-16715)
FOX ROTHSCHILD LLP
919 N Market St (19801-3023)
P.O. Box 2323 (19899-2323)
PHONE.................302 654-7444
Neal Levitsky, *Prin*
Michael Isaacs, *Pt*
EMP: 73 **EST:** 1980
SALES (est): 2.53MM **Privately Held**
Web: www.foxrothschild.com
SIC: 8111 General practice attorney, lawyer

(G-16716)
FPL ENERGY AMERICAN WIND LLC
3801 Kennett Pike Ste C200 (19807-2321)
PHONE.................302 655-0632
EMP: 16 **EST:** 2007
SALES (est): 2.42MM
SALES (corp-wide): 20.96B **Publicly Held**
SIC: 4911 Generation, electric power
HQ: Nextera Energy Resources, Llc
700 Universe Blvd
Juno Beach FL 33408
561 691-7171

(G-16717)
FPL ENERGY AMERICAN WIND LLC
201 W 29th St (19802-3125)
PHONE.................302 655-0632
EMP: 4 **EST:** 2007
SALES (est): 68.09K **Privately Held**
SIC: 3494 Plumbing and heating valves

(G-16718)
FRAIM MONNARAE
814 Philadelphia Pike (19809-2357)
PHONE.................302 761-1313
Monnarae Fraim, *Ofcr*
EMP: 5 **EST:** 2017
SALES (est): 50.78K **Privately Held**
SIC: 6411 Insurance agents, brokers, and service

(G-16719)
FRAMEMAKERS SHOP
4416 Kirkwood Hwy (19808-5116)
PHONE.................302 999-9968
George Dunmire, *Mgr*
EMP: 5 **EST:** 2007
SALES (est): 98.27K **Privately Held**
Web: www.framemakeronline.com
SIC: 7699 Picture framing, custom

(G-16720)
FRANCIS KELLY SONS INC
8 Meco Cir (19804-1109)
PHONE.................302 999-7400
Daniel K Kelly, *Pr*
Daniel J Kelly, *Pr*
EMP: 9 **EST:** 1956
SQ FT: 2,000
SALES (est): 500K **Privately Held**
Web: www.franciskellysonsconcrete.com
SIC: 1771 Concrete work

(G-16721)
FRANCIS MASE MD PA
209 Sulky Cir (19810-2268)
PHONE.................302 762-5656
EMP: 5 **EST:** 2019
SALES (est): 158.66K **Privately Held**
SIC: 8011 Offices and clinics of medical doctors

(G-16722)
FRANCIS MASE PEDIATRICS
700 W Lea Blvd Ste 209 (19802-2545)
PHONE.................302 762-5656
EMP: 10 **EST:** 2009
SALES (est): 490.31K **Privately Held**
SIC: 8011 Pediatrician

(G-16723)
FRANCIS POLLINGER & SON INC
57 Germay Dr (19804-1104)
PHONE.................302 655-8097
Francis Pollinger Senior, *Pr*
Francis Pollinger Junior, *VP*
Kay Pollinger, *Sec*
Colleen Pollinger, *Sec*
EMP: 25 **EST:** 1964
SQ FT: 4,800
SALES (est): 2.9MM **Privately Held**
Web: www.francispollingerandson.com
SIC: 1761 1751 1521 Roofing contractor; Window and door installation and erection; General remodeling, single-family houses

(G-16724)
FRANCIS X NORTON CENTER
917 N Madison St (19801-1439)
PHONE.................302 594-9455
EMP: 11 **EST:** 2013
SALES (est): 71.12K **Privately Held**
Web: www.ministryofcaring.org
SIC: 8699 Charitable organization

(G-16725)
FRANK & YETTA CHAIKEN FOU
4002 Lakeview Dr (19807-2250)
PHONE.................302 737-7427
Yetta Chaiken, *Prin*
EMP: 5 **EST:** 2001
SALES (est): 98.98K **Privately Held**
SIC: 8641 Civic and social associations

(G-16726)
FRANKEL ENTERPRISES INC
Also Called: Mayfair Apartments
1300 N Harrison St Ofc A100 (19806-3267)
PHONE.................302 652-6364
Kathleen S Mcmanus, *Mgr*
EMP: 6
SALES (corp-wide): 2.44MM **Privately Held**
Web: www.frankelenterprises.com
SIC: 6513 Apartment building operators
PA: Frankel Enterprises Inc
1845 Walnut St Ste 1610
Philadelphia PA 19103
215 751-0900

(G-16727)
FRANKLIN & PROKOPIK
300 Delaware Ave Ste 1340 (19801-1658)
PHONE.................302 594-9780
EMP: 8 **EST:** 2019
SALES (est): 140.43K **Privately Held**
Web: www.fandpnet.com
SIC: 8111 General practice attorney, lawyer

(G-16728)
FRANKLIN FIBRE-LAMITEX CORP
903 E 13th St (19802-5102)
P.O. Box 1768 (19899-1768)
PHONE.................302 652-3621
TOLL FREE: 800
James E Vachris Junior, *Pr*
Virginia Carr, *
▲ **EMP:** 26 **EST:** 1931
SQ FT: 56,000
SALES (est): 9.94MM **Privately Held**
Web: www.franklinfibre.com
SIC: 3083 Laminated plastics plate and sheet

(G-16729)
FRANKLIN KENNET LLC
1113 N Franklin St (19806-4301)
PHONE.................302 655-6536
Tom H Delporte, *Pt*
EMP: 5 **EST:** 1998
SALES (est): 99.72K **Privately Held**
SIC: 8742 Human resource consulting services

(G-16730)
FRANKLIN RUBBER STAMP CO INC
301 W 8th St Frnt (19801-1553)
PHONE.................302 654-8841
Tom Tanzilli, *Pr*
Susan Stoltz, *VP*
EMP: 5 **EST:** 1930
SALES (est): 298.89K **Privately Held**
Web: www.franklinstamps.com
SIC: 3953 Marking devices

(G-16731)
FRANKLIN TMPLTON COMPANIES LLC
919 N Market St Ste 600 (19801-3037)
PHONE.................800 632-2301
EMP: 9 **EST:** 2019
SALES (est): 2.16MM
SALES (corp-wide): 7.85B **Publicly Held**
SIC: 6722 Money market mutual funds
PA: Franklin Resources, Inc.
1 Franklin Pkwy
San Mateo CA 94403
650 312-2000

(G-16732)
FRC GLOBAL INC
Also Called: Diamond Graphite
1000 N West St Ste 3008 (19801-1050)
PHONE.................800 609-5711
Julianne Lord, *Pr*
Mark Mattar, *CSO*
James Conrad, *OF GLOBAL Sales & Marketing*
EMP: 60 **EST:** 2020
SALES (est): 6MM **Privately Held**
Web: www.frcglobal.com
SIC: 3255 Clay refractories

GEOGRAPHIC SECTION
Wilmington - New Castle County (G-16763)

(G-16733)
FREAKIN FRESH SALSA INC
2 Biltmore Ct (19808-1378)
P.O. Box 863 (19707-0863)
PHONE..................302 750-9789
Cecilia Andrzejewski, *Pr*
Michael Andrzejewski, *VP*
EMP: 2 EST: 2009
SALES (est): 251.06K **Privately Held**
SIC: 5149 2032 Condiments; Mexican foods, nec: packaged in cans, jars, etc.

(G-16734)
FRED L WRIGHT DDS
5309 Limestone Rd (19808-1222)
PHONE..................302 239-1641
Fred Wright D.d.s., *Owner*
EMP: 7 EST: 1992
SALES (est): 179.89K **Privately Held**
SIC: 8021 Dentists' office

(G-16735)
FRED S FINK ORTHODONTIST
23 The Commons (19810-4907)
PHONE..................302 478-6930
Fred Fink, *Ofcr*
EMP: 13 EST: 1987
SALES (est): 208.28K **Privately Held**
SIC: 8021 Orthodontist

(G-16736)
FRED S SMALLS INSURANCE (PA)
Also Called: Nationwide
5227 W Woodmill Dr Ste 43 (19808-4068)
PHONE..................302 633-1980
Fred Small, *Owner*
EMP: 12 EST: 1979
SQ FT: 3,200
SALES (est): 2.11MM
SALES (corp-wide): 2.11MM **Privately Held**
Web: www.smallsinsuranceagency.com
SIC: 6411 Insurance brokers, nec

(G-16737)
FREDERICK ENTERPRISES INC
Also Called: Joseph Frederick & Sons
810 Stanton Rd (19804-3640)
PHONE..................302 994-5786
Brian Frederick, *Pr*
John Ratcliffe, *
EMP: 39 EST: 2003
SQ FT: 8,800
SALES (est): 6.57MM **Privately Held**
Web: www.jfrederickandsons.com
SIC: 1711 Boiler and furnace contractors

(G-16738)
FREDERICK L COTTRELL
920 N King St Lbby 1 (19801-3319)
PHONE..................302 651-7686
Frederick L Cottrell, *Prin*
EMP: 5 EST: 2010
SALES (est): 156.38K **Privately Held**
SIC: 8111 General practice attorney, lawyer

(G-16739)
FREE HOSTING LLC
Suite 606-1220 N.Market St (19801-3022)
PHONE..................302 421-5750
EMP: 5 EST: 2002
SALES (est): 73.43K **Privately Held**
SIC: 4813 Internet host services

(G-16740)
FREEDOM AT HOME
609 Ohio Ave (19805-1022)
PHONE..................302 740-7054
Erica Gillespie, *Prin*
EMP: 7 EST: 2010
SALES (est): 90.64K **Privately Held**
Web: www.melaleuca.com
SIC: 1521 Single-family housing construction

(G-16741)
FREEDOM CENTRAL HOLDINGS LLC ✪
1209 N Orange St (19801-1120)
PHONE..................803 567-6400
EMP: 6 EST: 2022
SALES (est): 290.51K **Privately Held**
SIC: 6726 Investment offices, nec

(G-16742)
FREEDOM OUTREACH
2506 N Market St (19802-4234)
PHONE..................302 655-2724
EMP: 6 EST: 2011
SALES (est): 36.89K **Privately Held**
Web: www.freedom-outreach.org
SIC: 8322 Outreach program

(G-16743)
FREEMAN COURIER EXPRESS
123 Governor House Cir (19809-2446)
PHONE..................610 803-3933
Quinton Freeman, *Owner*
EMP: 5 EST: 2021
SALES (est): 136.96K **Privately Held**
SIC: 4215 7389 Courier services, except by air; Business Activities at Non-Commercial Site

(G-16744)
FREEMARKETS INVESTMENT CO INC
1105 N Market St Ste 1300 (19801-1241)
PHONE..................302 427-2089
Sean Breiner, *Dir*
EMP: 6 EST: 1999
SALES (est): 789.48K **Privately Held**
SIC: 6211 Security brokers and dealers

(G-16745)
FREESTYLES LTD
4905 Mermaid Blvd (19808-1004)
PHONE..................302 584-8601
EMP: 5 EST: 2010
SALES (est): 452.82K **Privately Held**
Web: www.fusionfreestyle.com
SIC: 7999 Martial arts school, nec

(G-16746)
FREIBOTT LAW FIRM
1711 E Newport Pike (19804-2530)
P.O. Box 6168 (19804-0768)
PHONE..................302 633-9000
Frederick Freibott, *Owner*
EMP: 11 EST: 2001
SALES (est): 795.06K **Privately Held**
Web: www.freibottlaw.com
SIC: 8111 General practice attorney, lawyer

(G-16747)
FRENIUS MEDICAL CARE
7 S Clayton St (19805-3948)
PHONE..................302 421-9177
Betty Babb, *Mgr*
EMP: 11 EST: 2015
SALES (est): 262.5K **Privately Held**
SIC: 8062 General medical and surgical hospitals

(G-16748)
FRENSENIUS MEDICAL CTR
4000 N Washington St (19802-2136)
PHONE..................302 762-2903
Alica Vogleson, *Off Mgr*
EMP: 11 EST: 2018
SALES (est): 122.03K **Privately Held**
SIC: 8011 Medical centers

(G-16749)
FRESENIUS MEDICAL CARE N AMER
Also Called: FRESENIUS MEDICAL CARE NORTH AMERICA
605 W Newport Pike (19804-3235)
PHONE..................302 633-6228
EMP: 5
SALES (corp-wide): 20.15B **Privately Held**
Web: www.fmcna.com
SIC: 8092 Kidney dialysis centers
HQ: Fresenius Usa Manufacturing, Inc.
920 Winter St
Waltham MA 02451

(G-16750)
FRESHBOOKS USA INC
2801 Centerville Rd (19808-1609)
PHONE..................416 525-5384
Levi Cooperman, *Ch Bd*
EMP: 2 EST: 2008
SALES (est): 204.88K **Privately Held**
Web: www.freshbooks.com
SIC: 7372 7389 Business oriented computer software; Business services, nec

(G-16751)
FRESHPAC LLC
1 Hausel Rd (19801-5800)
PHONE..................559 648-2210
EMP: 10 EST: 2016
SALES (est): 191.34K **Privately Held**
SIC: 7389 Packaging and labeling services

(G-16752)
FRIEDLANDER AND GORRIS
1201 N Market St Ste 2200 (19801-1165)
PHONE..................302 573-3500
Joel Friedlander, *Prin*
Jeffrey Gorris, *Prin*
EMP: 7 EST: 2001
SALES (est): 1.04MM **Privately Held**
Web: www.friedlandergorris.com
SIC: 8111 Corporate, partnership and business law

(G-16753)
FRIENDS INC
3209 Miller Rd (19802-2507)
PHONE..................302 764-4488
EMP: 5 EST: 2019
SALES (est): 336.76K **Privately Held**
SIC: 8699 Membership organizations, nec

(G-16754)
FRIENDS OF DLWRES GMBRNUS STTU
2313 W 16th St (19806-1306)
PHONE..................302 981-5972
John Medkeff, *Prin*
EMP: 5 EST: 2017
SALES (est): 34.78K **Privately Held**
Web: www.restoretheking.com
SIC: 8699 Charitable organization

(G-16755)
FRIENDS OF JAMES SPADOLA
1504 N Broom St Ste 18 (19806-3048)
PHONE..................302 383-3798
James Spadola, *Prin*
EMP: 5 EST: 2016
SALES (est): 48.03K **Privately Held**
Web: www.jamesspadola.com
SIC: 8699 Charitable organization

(G-16756)
FRIENDS OF NEW CTIES FUNDATION
1209 N Orange St (19801-1120)
PHONE..................718 896-8900
EMP: 8 EST: 2017
SALES (est): 100.44K **Privately Held**
SIC: 8641 Civic and social associations

(G-16757)
FRIENDS OF STB
38 E Mccaulley Ct (19801-4041)
PHONE..................302 765-2566
Stephanie Bolden, *Prin*
EMP: 5 EST: 2010
SALES (est): 91K **Privately Held**
SIC: 8699 Membership organizations, nec

(G-16758)
FRIENDS OF THE GOOD SAMARIT
13 Lombardy Dr (19803-3961)
PHONE..................302 762-4937
Mary Ann Wozniak, *Prin*
EMP: 9 EST: 2010
SALES (est): 66.58K **Privately Held**
Web: www.friendsofgoodsamaritan.org
SIC: 8361 Orphanage

(G-16759)
FRIENDSHIP HOUSE INCORPORATED
720 N Orange St (19801-1708)
PHONE..................302 652-8033
Marcy Perkins, *Brnch Mgr*
EMP: 10
Web: www.friendshiphousede.org
SIC: 8322 Social service center
PA: Friendship House Incorporated
1503 W 13th St
Wilmington DE 19806

(G-16760)
FRIENDSHIP HOUSE INCORPORATED (PA)
1503 W 13th St (19806-4255)
P.O. Box 1517 (19899-1517)
PHONE..................302 652-8133
Kim Eppelheimer, *CEO*
Curt Johnson, *Pr*
Donald Drane, *Pr*
EMP: 14 EST: 1987
SQ FT: 10,000
SALES (est): 1.79MM **Privately Held**
Web: www.friendshiphousede.org
SIC: 8322 Social service center

(G-16761)
FROM HARPS TO HALOS
6 N Clifton Ave (19805-2262)
PHONE..................302 932-0956
James Booker, *Mgr*
EMP: 5 EST: 2017
SALES (est): 55.95K **Privately Held**
Web: www.harps2halos.com
SIC: 7929 Entertainers and entertainment groups

(G-16762)
FRONT ROW ENTERPRISES LLC
Also Called: Island Gigs
901 N Market St Ste 705 (19801-3098)
PHONE..................646 862-6380
EMP: 7 EST: 2010
SALES (est): 233.83K **Privately Held**
Web: www.islandgigs.com
SIC: 4724 Travel agencies

(G-16763)
FRONTIER EMERGING MARKETS FUND
4005 Kennett Pike Ste 250 (19807-2018)
PHONE..................610 380-2110
EMP: 5 EST: 2005
SALES (est): 109.2K **Privately Held**

Wilmington - New Castle County (G-16764)

SIC: 6722 Money market mutual funds

(G-16764)
FRONTIER SGS 360 LLC
1521 Concord Pike Ste 302 (19803-3645)
PHONE............................609 919-1133
Srini Vengad, *Managing Member*
EMP: 6 EST: 2017
SALES (est): 208.17K **Privately Held**
SIC: 7363 Temporary help service

(G-16765)
FRONZA MEDIA LLC
1833 W 8th St (19805-3033)
PHONE............................856 693-0975
Anthony Fronza, *Prin*
EMP: 5 EST: 2017
SALES (est): 63.26K **Privately Held**
Web: www.fronzamedia.com
SIC: 4899 Communication services, nec

(G-16766)
FTC ENERGY LTD LLC
1201 N Orange St Ste 600 (19801-1171)
P.O. Box 5712 (73083-5712)
PHONE............................405 410-9040
Rickey Vick, *Managing Member*
EMP: 6 EST: 2018
SALES (est): 463.11K **Privately Held**
Web: www.ftcenergyltd.com
SIC: 6211 7389 Mineral, oil, and gas leasing and royalty dealers; Business services, nec

(G-16767)
FUEL LABS INC
Also Called: Telefuel.com
501 Silverside Rd Ste 105 (19809-1376)
PHONE............................302 364-0442
Matthew Nguyen, *Prin*
EMP: 5 EST: 2019
SALES (est): 46.16K **Privately Held**
SIC: 7371 Computer software development

(G-16768)
FULCRUM PHARMACY MGT INC
Also Called: Fulcrum Pharmacy
501 N Shipley St (19801-2226)
P.O. Box 2695 (19805-0695)
PHONE............................302 658-8020
Cristy Crkvenac, *Owner*
EMP: 4 EST: 2002
SALES (est): 994.17K **Privately Held**
Web: www.fulcrumrx.com
SIC: 5122 2834 Pharmaceuticals; Pharmaceutical preparations

(G-16769)
FULTON BANK NATIONAL ASSN
Also Called: Fulton Financial Advisors
800 Foulk Rd (19803-3109)
PHONE............................302 407-3291
Sara Defrancis, *Brnch Mgr*
EMP: 9
SALES (corp-wide): 1.09B **Publicly Held**
Web: www.fultonbank.com
SIC: 6022 State commercial banks
HQ: Fulton Bank, National Association
    1 Penn Sq
    Lancaster PA 17602
    717 581-3166

(G-16770)
FULTON PAPER COMPANY
Also Called: Fulton Paper Co
1006 W 27th St (19802-2990)
PHONE............................302 594-0400
Michael D Gavetti, *Pr*
Dorothy L Quigley, *Sec*
EMP: 17 EST: 1934
SQ FT: 30,000

SALES (est): 729.78K **Privately Held**
Web: www.fultonparty.com
SIC: 5943 5947 5113 Stationery stores; Party favors; Bags, paper and disposable plastic

(G-16771)
FUNDOMUNDO ✪
1401 Pennsylvania Ave (19806-4124)
PHONE............................617 606-1650
Emre Ekmekci, *Ch Bd*
EMP: 5 EST: 2022
SALES (est): 199.4K **Privately Held**
SIC: 7389 Business Activities at Non-Commercial Site

(G-16772)
FUR BABY TRACKER LLC
302 Taft Ave (19805-1303)
PHONE............................610 563-3294
Amanda Hoffmeyer, *Prin*
EMP: 5 EST: 2018
SALES (est): 104.73K **Privately Held**
Web: www.furbabytracker.com
SIC: 0752 Animal specialty services

(G-16773)
FUSION
3444 Naamans Rd 1st Fl (19810-1064)
PHONE............................302 479-9444
Lorri Czarnota, *Owner*
EMP: 8 EST: 1993
SALES (est): 185.6K **Privately Held**
Web: www.fusionsalonde.com
SIC: 7231 Beauty shops

(G-16774)
FUSURA LLC
800 Delaware Ave Ste 500 (19801-1366)
P.O. Box 70 (19710-0070)
PHONE............................302 397-2200
EMP: 65 EST: 2000
SALES (est): 6.27MM **Privately Held**
SIC: 6411 Insurance agents, nec

(G-16775)
FUTURE DEV LRNG ACDEMY FDLA LL
500 Maryland Ave (19805-4427)
PHONE............................302 652-7500
Haneefah Allen, *Pr*
Yusuf Allen, *CFO*
EMP: 5 EST: 2007
SALES (est): 437.21K **Privately Held**
SIC: 8351 Group day care center

(G-16776)
FUTURE FORD SALES INC (PA)
Also Called: Sheridan Ford Sales
4001 Kirkwood Hwy (19808-5111)
PHONE............................302 999-0261
Joseph E Sheridan, *Pr*
Roy Chapman, *
Steve Boyd Gem, *Mgr*
EMP: 85 EST: 1963
SQ FT: 33,000
SALES (est): 45.23MM
SALES (corp-wide): 45.23MM **Privately Held**
Web: www.sheridanford.com
SIC: 7515 5511 5013 5521 Passenger car leasing; Automobiles, new and used; Automotive supplies and parts; Used car dealers

(G-16777)
FUTURE GOLD TECHNOLOGY INC
865 Powder Mill Rd (19803)
PHONE............................302 786-1388
Wyatt Tanase, *CEO*

EMP: 10
SALES (est): 348.32K **Privately Held**
SIC: 8748 Business consulting, nec

(G-16778)
FUTURE PROMISES FOUNDATION INC
807 N Union St (19805-5323)
P.O. Box 843 (19701-0843)
PHONE............................302 689-3392
EMP: 6 EST: 2018
SALES (est): 38.73K **Privately Held**
Web: www.futurepromises.org
SIC: 8641 Civic and social associations

(G-16779)
FUTUREADVISOR INC
400 Bellevue Pkwy (19809-3723)
PHONE............................302 797-2000
EMP: 16 EST: 2010
SALES (est): 1.63MM **Publicly Held**
SIC: 6282 Investment advice
PA: Blackrock, Inc.
    50 Hudson Yards
    New York NY 10001

(G-16780)
FUZEBITS INC
1201 N Orange St Ste 7452 (19801-1155)
PHONE............................302 533-8623
Vitaliy Hoy, *Ex Dir*
EMP: 4
SALES (est): 171.34K **Privately Held**
SIC: 7372 Application computer software

(G-16781)
FWC2026 US INC
251 Little Falls Dr (19808-1674)
PHONE............................469 505-2635
EMP: 33 EST: 2021
SALES (est): 1.11MM **Privately Held**
SIC: 7941 Soccer club
PA: Federation Internationale De Football Association (Fifa)
    Fifa-Strasse 20
    ZUrich ZH 8044

(G-16782)
FWD CONTRACTING ENTPS LLC
1705 Talley Rd (19803-3915)
PHONE............................302 377-3459
Ford Downes, *Prin*
EMP: 5 EST: 2010
SALES (est): 120.19K **Privately Held**
SIC: 1799 Special trade contractors, nec

(G-16783)
G & D COLLECTION GROUP INC
234 Philadelphia Pike Ste 9 (19809-3126)
PHONE............................302 482-2512
Edward J Gavin, *CEO*
Brian Dunphy, *Pr*
EMP: 10 EST: 2007
SQ FT: 2,000
SALES (est): 394.78K **Privately Held**
SIC: 7322 Collection agency, except real estate

(G-16784)
G B LYONS DDS
100 W Rockwind Rd (19801)
P.O. Box 295 (19710-0295)
PHONE............................302 654-1765
Garett B Lyons D.d.s., *Owner*
G B Lyons Junior D.d.s., *Owner*
EMP: 8 EST: 1958
SALES (est): 176.31K **Privately Held**
Web: www.garrettblyonsdds.com
SIC: 8021 Maxillofacial specialist

(G-16785)
G FEDALE ROOFING AND SIDING
101 S Mary St (19804-3112)
PHONE............................302 225-7663
Glen Fedale, *Owner*
EMP: 11 EST: 2014
SALES (est): 4.54MM **Privately Held**
Web: www.gfedale.com
SIC: 1761 Roofing contractor

(G-16786)
G W KELLER DDS
1110 N Bancroft Pkwy Ste 2 (19805-2669)
PHONE............................302 652-3586
EMP: 20 EST: 1996
SALES (est): 404.31K **Privately Held**
Web: www.kellerperio.com
SIC: 8021 Periodontist

(G-16787)
G2 PERFORMANCE BAND ACC
2207 Concord Pike Ste 220 (19803-2908)
PHONE............................800 554-8523
EMP: 5 EST: 2018
SALES (est): 133.19K **Privately Held**
SIC: 2389 Band uniforms

(G-16788)
GA TELESIS LLC
251 Little Falls Dr (19808-1674)
PHONE............................845 356-8390
EMP: 11 EST: 2019
SALES (est): 3.47MM **Privately Held**
Web: www.gatelesis.com
SIC: 5088 Aircraft and parts, nec

(G-16789)
GABRIEL JR TIMOTEO R MD
Also Called: Family Ear Nose Throat Physcn
1941 Limestone Rd Ste 210 (19808-5400)
PHONE............................302 998-0300
Timoteo R Gabriel Junior, *Pr*
EMP: 5 EST: 1983
SALES (est): 299.01K **Privately Held**
SIC: 8011 Eyes, ears, nose, and throat specialist: physician/surgeon

(G-16790)
GADDE & CHIRRA INC
4524 Kirkwood Hwy (19808-5118)
P.O. Box 5670 (19808-5670)
PHONE............................302 384-6384
Chaitanya R Gadde, *Prin*
EMP: 13 EST: 2010
SALES (est): 571.06K **Privately Held**
SIC: 8011 Medical centers

(G-16791)
GAGL SALES LLC
847 Cranbrook Dr (19803-4801)
PHONE............................302 299-0084
EMP: 5 EST: 2015
SALES (est): 230.57K **Privately Held**
SIC: 4812 Cellular telephone services

(G-16792)
GAIL S LEVINSON
1303 Delaware Ave Ste 103 (19806-3421)
PHONE............................302 764-0474
Gail Levinson, *Prin*
EMP: 7 EST: 2017
SALES (est): 38.53K **Privately Held**
SIC: 8322 Social worker

(G-16793)
GAINOR AWNINGS INC
1 Elm Ave (19805-1199)
PHONE............................302 998-8611
Woodward Eastburn, *Pr*
EMP: 8 EST: 1929

SQ FT: 2,400
SALES (est): 442.76K **Privately Held**
SIC: 2394 1799 Awnings, fabric: made from purchased materials; Awning installation

(G-16794)
GALAXY SIGN & LIGHTING
2117 Armour Dr (19808-5303)
PHONE...................302 757-5349
David Gail, *Prin*
EMP: 4 EST: 2018
SALES (est): 46.08K **Privately Held**
SIC: 3993 Signs and advertising specialties

(G-16795)
GALLAGHER & ASSOCIATES PA
5500 Skyline Dr Ste 6 (19808-1772)
PHONE...................302 239-5501
Michael Gallagher, *Pr*
EMP: 5 EST: 1988
SALES (est): 216.57K **Privately Held**
SIC: 8721 Certified public accountant

(G-16796)
GALLIUM US HOLDINGS INC
1209 N Orange St (19801-1120)
PHONE...................713 213-0644
Mario De Carvalho, *Pr*
Anthony Childers, *Sec*
EMP: 6 EST: 2007
SIC: 6719 Personal holding companies, except banks

(G-16797)
GALTOGETHER GROUP ✪
187 Odyssey Dr (19808-1568)
PHONE...................302 562-9170
Qin Liang, *CEO*
EMP: 6 EST: 2023
SALES (est): 76.37K **Privately Held**
SIC: 6732 7389 Trusts: educational, religious, etc.; Business services, nec

(G-16798)
GAME GENIUS INNOVATIONS LLC ✪
1007 N Orange St Fl 4 (19801-1242)
PHONE...................321 588-7798
Faye Terante, *Managing Member*
EMP: 10 EST: 2023
SALES (est): 365.44K **Privately Held**
SIC: 7372 Prepackaged software

(G-16799)
GAME LABS INC
1000 N West St Ste 1200 (19801-1058)
PHONE...................385 444-5639
Maksim Zasov, *CEO*
EMP: 30 EST: 2021
SALES (est): 1.13MM **Privately Held**
SIC: 7372 Prepackaged software

(G-16800)
GAMUT COLOR INC
1600 N Scott St (19806-2528)
PHONE...................302 652-7171
Shawn Mc Clafferty, *Pr*
EMP: 9 EST: 1991
SQ FT: 500
SALES (est): 642.6K **Privately Held**
SIC: 8748 Publishing consultant

(G-16801)
GANVIX INC
1 Righter Pkwy (19803-1534)
PHONE...................508 904-3345
EMP: 5
SALES (est): 78.16K **Privately Held**
SIC: 3674 Semiconductors and related devices

(G-16802)
GARCIA PODIATRY GROUP
Also Called: Garcia, Luis M Jr DPM
1941 Limestone Rd Ste 208 (19808-5432)
PHONE...................302 994-5956
Luis Garcia, *Owner*
EMP: 5 EST: 1986
SALES (est): 341.17K **Privately Held**
SIC: 8043 Offices and clinics of podiatrists

(G-16803)
GARDA CL ATLANTIC INC (HQ)
Also Called: Gcl A
4200 Governor Printz Blvd (19802-2315)
PHONE...................302 762-5444
Stephan Cretier, *Pr*
Chris W Jamroz, *
Patrick Prince, *
Vicki Benoit, *
EMP: 35 EST: 1951
SALES (est): 25.37MM
SALES (corp-wide): 437.24MM **Privately Held**
Web: www.garda.com
SIC: 7381 Armored car services
PA: Gardaworld Cash Services, Inc.
2000 Nw Corporate Blvd
Boca Raton FL 33431
561 939-7000

(G-16804)
GARG MANISH MD
2006 Limestone Rd Ste 7 (19808-5553)
PHONE...................302 355-2383
Manish Garg, *Pr*
EMP: 7 EST: 2017
SALES (est): 73.34K **Privately Held**
Web: www.nephrologydelaware.com
SIC: 8011 Offices and clinics of medical doctors

(G-16805)
GARLAND THOMPSON AGENCY
4 E 8th St Ste 200 (19801-3553)
PHONE...................302 407-6260
Garland Thompson, *Mgr*
EMP: 5 EST: 2014
SALES (est): 117.23K **Privately Held**
Web: www.garlandthompsoninsurance.com
SIC: 6411 Insurance agents and brokers

(G-16806)
GARLAND THOMPSON AGENCY
1211 N King St (19801-3217)
PHONE...................302 407-6262
EMP: 5 EST: 2018
SALES (est): 244.18K **Privately Held**
Web: www.garlandthompsoninsurance.com
SIC: 6411 Insurance agents and brokers

(G-16807)
GARRETT MOTION INC (DH)
251 Little Falls Dr (19808-1674)
PHONE...................973 867-7017
Olivier Rabiller, *CEO*
EMP: 12 EST: 2018
SALES (est): 3.6B
SALES (corp-wide): 3.99MM **Privately Held**
Web: www.garrettmotion.com
SIC: 3511 Turbines and turbine generator sets
HQ: Garrett Motion Sarl
Zone D'activites La Piece 16
Rolle VD 1180

(G-16808)
GARY GERACE
205 W 14th St (19801-1114)
P.O. Box 1668 (19899-1668)
PHONE...................302 320-2100
Gary Gerace, *Owner*
EMP: 7 EST: 2015
SALES (est): 85.84K **Privately Held**
SIC: 8049 Clinical psychologist

(G-16809)
GARY L WAITE DMD
5500 Skyline Dr Ste 2 (19808-1772)
PHONE...................302 239-8586
Gary Waite D.m.d., *Owner*
Gary Waite, *Owner*
EMP: 5 EST: 1983
SALES (est): 239.24K **Privately Held**
Web: www.drgarywaite.com
SIC: 8021 Dentists' office

(G-16810)
GARY R COLLINS DDS
5500 Skyline Dr Ste 1 (19808-1772)
PHONE...................302 239-3531
Gary R Collins, *Prin*
EMP: 5 EST: 1984
SALES (est): 170.78K **Privately Held**
Web: www.delawarechildrensdentist.com
SIC: 8021 Dentists' office

(G-16811)
GASTROMIND INC
1401 Pennsylvania Ave Ste 105 (19806-4125)
PHONE...................302 252-8401
EMP: 6 EST: 2012
SALES (est): 70.43K **Privately Held**
SIC: 7372 Prepackaged software

(G-16812)
GATEKEEPER SYSTEMS USA INC
221 Valley Rd (19804-1356)
PHONE...................434 477-6596
EMP: 9 EST: 2019
SALES (est): 49.23K **Privately Held**
Web: www.gatekeeper-systems.com
SIC: 7382 Security systems services

(G-16813)
GATES AND COMPANY LLC
Also Called: Gates and Company
4914 Threadneedle Rd (19807-2528)
PHONE...................302 428-1338
David Gates, *Managing Member*
EMP: 10 EST: 1999
SALES (est): 964.18K **Privately Held**
Web: www.gatesandcompany.com
SIC: 6211 Security brokers and dealers

(G-16814)
GATESAIR INC
2711 Centerville Rd (19808-1660)
PHONE...................513 459-3400
EMP: 46
SALES (corp-wide): 1.81B **Privately Held**
Web: www.gatesair.com
SIC: 1731 3663 7371 Communications specialization; Radio and t.v. communications equipment; Computer software development and applications
HQ: Gatesair, Inc.
5300 Kings Island Dr # 1
Mason OH 45040
513 459-3400

(G-16815)
GATEWAY HOUSE INC
121 N Poplar St Apt A11 (19801-3955)
PHONE...................302 571-8885
Sherrie Johnson, *Ex Dir*
Lottie Lee, *Pr*
EMP: 14 EST: 1996
SQ FT: 2,500
SALES (est): 259.24K **Privately Held**
Web: www.gatewayhouserecovery.org
SIC: 8361 Residential care

(G-16816)
GATX TRMNALS OVRSEAS HLDG CORP
251 Little Falls Dr (19808-1674)
PHONE...................302 636-5400
Brian A Kenney, *Ch Bd*
EMP: 14 EST: 1999
SALES (est): 2.21MM
SALES (corp-wide): 1.27B **Publicly Held**
SIC: 4731 Freight forwarding
PA: Gatx Corporation
233 S Wacker Dr
Chicago IL 60606
312 621-6200

(G-16817)
GAUDENZIA INC
Also Called: Gaudenzia Fresh Start
604 W 10th St (19801-1424)
PHONE...................302 421-9945
Macolm Ennel, *Prin*
EMP: 5 EST: 2006
SALES (est): 226.47K **Privately Held**
Web: www.gaudenzia.org
SIC: 8361 Rehabilitation center, residential: health care incidental

(G-16818)
GAUGE GIRL TRAINING LLC
41 Ross Rd (19810-1143)
PHONE...................267 471-7104
EMP: 6 EST: 2019
SALES (est): 303.81K **Privately Held**
Web: www.gaugegirltraining.com
SIC: 7299 Miscellaneous personal service

(G-16819)
GAVINSOLMONESE
919 N Market St (19801-3023)
PHONE...................302 655-8997
Joe Solmonese, *Dir*
EMP: 10 EST: 2013
SALES (est): 2.23MM **Privately Held**
Web: www.gavinsolmonese.com
SIC: 8742 Business management consultant

(G-16820)
GAWTHROP GREENWOOD PC
3711 Kennett Pike Ste 100 (19807-2156)
PHONE...................302 351-1273
Gawthrop Greenwood, *Prin*
EMP: 8 EST: 2018
SALES (est): 156K **Privately Held**
Web: www.gawthrop.com
SIC: 8111 General practice attorney, lawyer

(G-16821)
GB HOME IMPROVEMENT
100 Greenhill Ave Ste F # G (19805-1863)
PHONE...................302 654-5411
Kenneth Moses, *Prin*
EMP: 6 EST: 2008
SALES (est): 130.43K **Privately Held**
Web: www.gbatyourservice.com
SIC: 7299 Home improvement and renovation contractor agency

(G-16822)
GBANA ENTERTAINMENT LLC
28b Trolley Sq (19806-3352)
PHONE...................302 307-1695
Kofa Freeman, *Managing Member*

Wilmington - New Castle County (G-16823) GEOGRAPHIC SECTION

EMP: 5 EST: 2020
SALES (est): 139.24K **Privately Held**
SIC: 7922 7929 Concert management service; Entertainers and entertainment groups

(G-16823)
GBC BUSINESS GROUP LLC
2055 Limestone Rd Ste 200c (19808-5536)
PHONE..................................970 644-6319
Mohsin Ahmad, *Mgr*
EMP: 9 EST: 2021
SALES (est): 329.78K **Privately Held**
Web: www.gbc.edu
SIC: 7371 Software programming applications

(G-16824)
GBC INTERNATIONAL CORP (PA)
Also Called: Smart Shoppers
2711 Centerville Rd Ste 400 (19808-1660)
PHONE..................................404 860-2533
Benjamin Lau, *CEO*
EMP: 5 EST: 1998
SALES (est): 3.71MM
SALES (corp-wide): 3.71MM **Privately Held**
Web: www.gbc.edu
SIC: 8732 Market analysis, business, and economic research

(G-16825)
GCORA CORP
3616 Kirkwood Hwy Ste A (19808-5124)
PHONE..................................302 310-1000
Charles Graham, *CEO*
Tim Graham, *VP*
EMP: 7 EST: 2003
SALES (est): 483.42K **Privately Held**
SIC: 8711 Engineering services

(G-16826)
GEM GROUP LP
501 Carr Rd (19809-2866)
PHONE..................................302 762-2008
Scott Ernsberger, *Brnch Mgr*
EMP: 11
SALES (corp-wide): 372.42MM **Privately Held**
Web: gemgroup.zenith-american.com
SIC: 6399 Deposit insurance
HQ: The Gem Group L P
3 Gateway Ctr 401 Lbrty Av 3 Gateway Ctr
Pittsburgh PA 15222
412 471-2885

(G-16827)
GEMINI BUILDING SYSTEMS LLC
Also Called: Janitorial Services and Sups
1607 E Newport Pike (19804-2528)
P.O. Box 6444 (19804-0444)
PHONE..................................302 654-5310
EMP: 18 EST: 1998
SQ FT: 10,000
SALES (est): 694.73K **Privately Held**
Web: www.geminillc.net
SIC: 1799 7349 Construction site cleanup; Building and office cleaning services

(G-16828)
GEMINI HAIR DESIGNS
2207 Baynard Blvd (19802-3938)
PHONE..................................302 654-9371
Erna Bollock, *Owner*
EMP: 7 EST: 1977
SALES (est): 142.64K **Privately Held**
SIC: 7231 Manicurist, pedicurist

(G-16829)
GEN DIGITAL INC
Also Called: Symantec
1209 N Orange St (19801-1120)
PHONE..................................650 527-8000
EMP: 3
SALES (corp-wide): 3.34B **Publicly Held**
Web: www.nortonlifelock.com
SIC: 3674 Semiconductors and related devices
PA: Gen Digital Inc.
60 E Rio Salado Pkwy # 1
Tempe AZ 85281
650 527-8000

(G-16830)
GENE TFFIN A RAY FMLY FNDATION
501 Silverside Rd Ste 123 (19809-1377)
PHONE..................................800 839-1754
EMP: 5 EST: 2010
SALES (est): 30.63K **Privately Held**
SIC: 8699 Charitable organization

(G-16831)
GENERAL CONTRACTOR
4306 Miller Rd Apt 109 (19802-1925)
PHONE..................................302 241-8285
Perry Herbert, *Prin*
EMP: 7 EST: 2017
SALES (est): 112.03K **Privately Held**
Web: www.generalcontractors.org
SIC: 1799 Special trade contractors, nec

(G-16832)
GENERATE NB FUEL CELLS LLC ◆
251 Little Falls Dr (19808-1674)
PHONE..................................415 360-3063
Scott Jacobs, *Managing Member*
EMP: 6 EST: 2022
SALES (est): 68.89K **Privately Held**
SIC: 8748 Energy conservation consultant

(G-16833)
GENERATION GLORY MINISTRIES
302 W Matson Run Pkwy (19802-2111)
PHONE..................................302 438-4335
Alex White Senior, *Pastor*
EMP: 6 EST: 2016
SALES (est): 54.34K **Privately Held**
SIC: 8661 7371 Religious organizations; Computer software development and applications

(G-16834)
GENERATIONS HOME CARE INC
5211 W Woodmill Dr (19808-4068)
PHONE..................................302 322-3100
Paulette Austin, *Prin*
EMP: 21 EST: 2006
SALES (est): 3.9MM **Privately Held**
Web: www.ghcde.org
SIC: 8082 Home health care services

(G-16835)
GENERATIONS HOME CARE INC
5211 W Woodmill Dr # 36 (19808-4068)
PHONE..................................302 856-7774
Debbie Ferrero, *Dir*
EMP: 103
SALES (corp-wide): 8.36MM **Privately Held**
SIC: 8082 Home health care services
PA: Generations Home Care, Inc
103 Rogers Rd
Wilmington DE

(G-16836)
GENESIS HLTHCARE CTRS HLDNGS I
Also Called: Genesis
103 Foulk Rd Ste 202 (19803-3742)
PHONE..................................302 652-4720
Michael R Walker, *Ch Bd*
Richard R Howard, *Pr*
David C Barr, *Ex VP*
Lewis Hoch, *Corporate Counsel*
George V Hager, *Sr VP*
EMP: 64 EST: 1990
SALES (est): 21.62MM
SALES (corp-wide): 5.86B **Publicly Held**
SIC: 8051 Convalescent home with continuous nursing care
HQ: Genesis Hc Llc
101 E State St
Kennett Square PA 19348
610 444-6350

(G-16837)
GENESIS LABORATORIES INC (PA)
11 Middleton Dr (19808-4320)
PHONE..................................832 217-8585
Fabian Maclaren, *CEO*
EMP: 5 EST: 2014
SQ FT: 17,000
SALES (est): 515.98K
SALES (corp-wide): 515.98K **Privately Held**
SIC: 2834 Pharmaceutical preparations

(G-16838)
GENEVA HOTEL LLC
251 Little Falls Dr (19808-1674)
PHONE..................................440 901-2030
EMP: 5 EST: 2020
SALES (est): 74.09K **Privately Held**
SIC: 1522 Hotel/motel, new construction

(G-16839)
GENKI FOREST (AMERICA) INC
108 W 13th St (19801-1145)
PHONE..................................626 456-2664
Liu Zhen, *CEO*
EMP: 10 EST: 2020
SALES (est): 585.21K **Privately Held**
SIC: 2086 Carbonated soft drinks, bottled and canned

(G-16840)
GENSOURCE FINCL ASRN CO LLC
Also Called: Gensource
3422 Old Capitol Trl (19808-6124)
PHONE..................................302 415-3030
EMP: 10 EST: 2013
SQ FT: 20,000
SALES (est): 383.34K **Privately Held**
SIC: 7389 Financial services

(G-16841)
GENSPEC MATERIALS INC
1201 N Orange St Ste 700 (19801-1186)
PHONE..................................302 777-1100
Frank Russo, *Pr*
EMP: 6 EST: 2019
SALES (est): 124.27K **Privately Held**
Web: www.genspecmaterials.com
SIC: 1541 Food products manufacturing or packing plant construction

(G-16842)
GENTLE TOUCH DENTISTRY
303 E Lea Blvd (19802-2353)
PHONE..................................302 765-3373
EMP: 9 EST: 2019
SALES (est): 219.55K **Privately Held**
Web: www.gentletouchsmiles.com
SIC: 8021 Dentists' office

(G-16843)
GENUN GAMES INC ◆
1013 Centre Rd Ste 403b (19805-1270)
PHONE..................................425 344-4883
Michael Yagi, *Pr*
Christopher Jung, *CEO*
EMP: 7 EST: 2022
SALES (est): 355.22K **Privately Held**
SIC: 5092 Video games

(G-16844)
GEORGE E FRATTALI DDS
1801 Rockland Rd Ste 100 (19803-3650)
PHONE..................................302 651-4408
George Frattali, *Owner*
EMP: 5 EST: 2018
SALES (est): 67.67K **Privately Held**
SIC: 8021 Dentists' office

(G-16845)
GEORGE H BURNS INC
Also Called: Honeywell Authorized Dealer
200 N Ford Ave (19805-1834)
P.O. Box 2524 (19805-0524)
PHONE..................................302 658-0752
Philip Burns, *Pr*
Norman Williamson Senior, *VP*
Norman Williamson Junior, *Sec*
Allan Koch, *Treas*
EMP: 20 EST: 1964
SQ FT: 5,000
SALES (est): 2.22MM **Privately Held**
Web: www.georgehburnshvac.com
SIC: 1711 Warm air heating and air conditioning contractor

(G-16846)
GEORGE J WEINER ASSOCIATES
2711 Centerville Rd (19808-1660)
PHONE..................................302 658-0218
Terrence L Wolf, *Pr*
Donald T Fulton, *Treas*
Xavier F Decaire, *VP*
Karen Skipicki, *Sec*
EMP: 11 EST: 1972
SALES (est): 397.74K **Privately Held**
SIC: 6411 Insurance agents, nec

(G-16847)
GEORGE MARCUS SALON INC
3629 Silverside Rd Ste 1 (19810-5106)
PHONE..................................302 475-7530
EMP: 5 EST: 1996
SALES (est): 54.43K **Privately Held**
Web: www.spicedelaware.com
SIC: 7231 Hairdressers

(G-16848)
GEOSYNTEC HOLDINGS LLC ◆
251 Little Falls Dr (19808-1674)
PHONE..................................561 995-0900
Peter Zeeb, *Managing Member*
EMP: 8 EST: 2022
SALES (est): 500MM
SALES (corp-wide): 436.97MM **Privately Held**
SIC: 8711 8748 1799 4959 Engineering services; Environmental consultant; Decontamination services; Environmental cleanup services
PA: Geosyntec Consultants, Inc.
900 Broken Sound Pkwy Nw
Boca Raton FL 33487
561 995-0900

(G-16849)
GEOTECH LLC
1600 Newport Gap Pike (19808-6208)
PHONE..................................302 353-9769
Victoria Esposito, *Managing Member*
EMP: 9 EST: 2012
SALES (est): 889.28K **Privately Held**
Web: www.gogeotech.com

GEOGRAPHIC SECTION   Wilmington - New Castle County (G-16878)

SIC: 1795 1799 4212 Wrecking and demolition work; Building site preparation; Dump truck haulage

(G-16850)
GERIATRIC & PALLIATIVE SVCS
104 Jade Dr (19810-2251)
PHONE...................302 438-5440
EMP: 5 EST: 2017
SALES (est): 83.6K Privately Held
SIC: 8322 Geriatric social service

(G-16851)
GERM NETWORK INC ✪
2810 N Church St Pmb 57729 (19802-4447)
PHONE...................773 965-7004
Tessa Brown, CEO
EMP: 3 EST: 2022
SALES (est): 147.32K Privately Held
SIC: 7372 Prepackaged software

(G-16852)
GERMANTOWN MEDICAL ASSOCIATES
420 Derby Way (19810-2266)
PHONE...................484 431-5226
Dawn Mccoy, Prin
EMP: 6 EST: 2018
SALES (est): 131.96K Privately Held
SIC: 8099 Health and allied services, nec

(G-16853)
GESSO LABS INC
2810 N Church St (19802-4447)
PHONE...................888 206-4024
Tara Fung, CEO
EMP: 14
SALES (est): 481.04K Privately Held
SIC: 7371 Computer software development

(G-16854)
GETRESPONSE INC
1011 Centre Rd Ste 322 (19805-1266)
PHONE...................302 573-3895
EMP: 33
SALES (corp-wide): 1.53MM Privately Held
SIC: 7371 Computer software development and applications
PA: Getresponse Inc.
    71 Summer St Fl 5
    Boston MA 02110
    617 778-2422

(G-16855)
GETTIER STAFFING SERVICES INC
2 Centerville Rd (19808-4708)
P.O. Box 1095 (19709-7095)
PHONE...................302 478-0911
James Gettier, CEO
Louis Manerchia, Pr
Ronald Phillips, Sr VP
EMP: 9 EST: 2010
SALES (est): 217.18K Privately Held
SIC: 1541 1542 Industrial buildings, new construction, nec; Nonresidential construction, nec

(G-16856)
GFP CEMENT CONTRACTORS LLC
14 Hadco Rd (19804-1014)
PHONE...................302 998-7687
EMP: 15 EST: 2012
SALES (est): 8.94MM Privately Held
Web: www.gfpcement.com
SIC: 1541 Industrial buildings, new construction, nec

(G-16857)
GFP MOBILE MIX SUPPLY LLC
14 Hadco Rd (19804-1014)
PHONE...................302 998-7687
EMP: 11 EST: 2018
SALES (est): 1.97MM Privately Held
Web: www.gfpmobilemix.com
SIC: 3273 Ready-mixed concrete

(G-16858)
GIERD INC
Also Called: Digital Marketing & Sales
2810 N Church St Ste 24479 (19802-4447)
PHONE...................206 289-0011
Jon Pederson, CEO
EMP: 20 EST: 2019
SALES (est): 630.51K Privately Held
Web: www.gierd.com
SIC: 8742 7373 7379 8748 Management consulting services; Systems integration services; Data processing consultant; Business consulting, nec

(G-16859)
GIGIS LAUNDRY ROOM
3612 Miller Rd (19802-2524)
PHONE...................302 764-7777
EMP: 5 EST: 2017
SALES (est): 27.18K Privately Held
Web: gigis-laundry-room.business.site
SIC: 7215 Laundry, coin-operated

(G-16860)
GILDEA ENTERPRISES INC
2100 Willow Way (19810-4154)
PHONE...................302 420-8900
Robert Gildea Junior, Pr
Susan Gildea, Sec
EMP: 5 EST: 1989
SALES (est): 270K Privately Held
SIC: 0782 Landscape contractors

(G-16861)
GILLIAM & GARCA RE INV CO LLC
700 W 32nd St (19802-2660)
PHONE...................302 377-5764
Toni Garcia, Managing Member
EMP: 6
SALES (est): 76.37K Privately Held
SIC: 6799 Real estate investors, except property operators

(G-16862)
GILPIN AVENUE FITNESS INC
1406 Gilpin Ave (19806-3014)
PHONE...................302 654-6385
Laura Johnson, Owner
EMP: 5 EST: 2011
SALES (est): 131.55K Privately Held
SIC: 7991 Physical fitness facilities

(G-16863)
GILPIN MEDICAL CENTER
1021 Gilpin Ave Ste 100 (19806-3271)
PHONE...................302 623-4250
EMP: 7 EST: 2010
SALES (est): 160K Privately Held
SIC: 8011 Medical centers

(G-16864)
GILPIN MORTGAGE
1400 N Dupont St (19806-4030)
PHONE...................302 656-5400
Anne Riley, Owner
EMP: 5 EST: 2010
SALES (est): 150.58K Privately Held
Web: www.gilpin.com
SIC: 6162 Mortgage bankers

(G-16865)
GINA M FREEMAN DPM
1800 N Broom St Ste 109b (19802-3809)
PHONE...................302 765-2505
Gina Freeman, Mgr
EMP: 6 EST: 2017
SALES (est): 47.44K Privately Held
SIC: 8043 Offices and clinics of podiatrists

(G-16866)
GIORDANO DELCOLLO & WERB LLC
Also Called: Giordano, Delcollo Werb Gdw
5315 Limestone Rd (19808-1222)
PHONE...................302 234-6855
EMP: 6 EST: 2012
SALES (est): 2.44MM Privately Held
Web: www.gdwlawfirm.com
SIC: 8111 General practice attorney, lawyer

(G-16867)
GIORGI KITCHENS INC
4 Meco Cir (19804-1109)
PHONE...................302 762-1121
EMP: 10
SALES (corp-wide): 1.88MM Privately Held
Web: www.giorgikitchens.com
SIC: 1799 Kitchen and bathroom remodeling
PA: Giorgi Kitchens Inc
    218 Philadelphia Pike
    Wilmington DE
    302 762-1121

(G-16868)
GIRASOL PAYMENT SOLUTIONS LLC ✪
1209 N Orange St (19801-1120)
PHONE...................561 866-4343
EMP: 5 EST: 2023
SALES (est): 199.4K Privately Held
SIC: 7371 Custom computer programming services

(G-16869)
GIRLS INCORPORATE OF DELAWARE (PA)
1019 Brown St (19805-4812)
PHONE...................302 575-1041
Suzzette Schultz, Pr
EMP: 8 EST: 1955
SALES (est): 342.59K
SALES (corp-wide): 342.59K Privately Held
Web: www.girlsincde.org
SIC: 8641 Youth organizations

(G-16870)
GIRLS INCORPORATE OF DELAWARE
Also Called: Girls Incorporated of Delaware
1501 N Market St Ste 100 (19801)
PHONE...................302 575-1041
Myles Henry, Mgr
EMP: 12
SALES (corp-wide): 342.59K Privately Held
Web: www.girlsincde.org
SIC: 8641 Youth organizations
PA: Girls Incorporate Of Delaware
    1019 Brown St
    Wilmington DE 19805
    302 575-1041

(G-16871)
GIRLS ON RUN
615 W 18th St (19802-4707)
PHONE...................302 668-1720
EMP: 6 EST: 2012
SALES (est): 151.55K Privately Held

Web: www.gotrde.org
SIC: 8641 Youth organizations

(G-16872)
GKG CONSULTING LLC (PA)
517 Marsh Rd (19809-2120)
PHONE...................888 918-0718
Arthur Kirksey, Prin
EMP: 53 EST: 2020
SALES (est): 1.47MM
SALES (corp-wide): 1.47MM Privately Held
SIC: 8748 Business consulting, nec

(G-16873)
GKUA INC
1000 N West St Ste 1200 (19801-1058)
PHONE...................415 971-5341
Beau Golob, Prin
EMP: 12 EST: 2017
SALES (est): 760.63K Privately Held
SIC: 7319 8742 Advertising, nec; Marketing consulting services

(G-16874)
GL ROBINS CO INC
Also Called: Supercuts
2504 Foulk Rd (19810-1420)
PHONE...................302 475-5001
Ester Dougherty, Brnch Mgr
EMP: 9
SALES (corp-wide): 2.49MM Privately Held
Web: www.supercuts.com
SIC: 7231 Unisex hair salons
PA: Gl Robins Co Inc
    4919 Township Line Rd # 250
    Drexel Hill PA 19026
    610 399-4400

(G-16875)
GL ROBINS CO INC
Also Called: Supercuts
1406 N Dupont St (19806)
PHONE...................302 654-4477
EMP: 8
SALES (corp-wide): 2.49MM Privately Held
Web: www.supercuts.com
SIC: 7231 Unisex hair salons
PA: Gl Robins Co Inc
    4919 Township Line Rd # 250
    Drexel Hill PA 19026
    610 399-4400

(G-16876)
GLA COMPANY LTD
5615 Kirkwood Hwy (19808-5003)
PHONE...................502 267-7522
Mike Voight, Managing Member
EMP: 17 EST: 2003
SALES (est): 1.1MM Privately Held
SIC: 8748 Business consulting, nec

(G-16877)
GLACIER AUTOS
111 N Union St (19805-3427)
PHONE...................302 510-6771
EMP: 6 EST: 2018
SALES (est): 179.13K Privately Held
SIC: 7538 General automotive repair shops

(G-16878)
GLACIERPOINT ENTERPRISES INC (PA)
251 Little Falls Dr (19808-1674)
PHONE...................302 636-5401
Jim Schubauer, CEO
EMP: 24 EST: 2021
SALES (est): 402.87MM

(PA)=Parent Co (HQ)=Headquarters
✪ = New Business established in last 2 years

SALES (corp-wide): 402.87MM **Privately Held**
SIC: 5143 Dairy products, except dried or canned

(G-16879)
GLADYS WALKER
Also Called: Braid Babe
937 N Lombard St Apt 2 (19801-4049)
PHONE.....................302 480-0713
Gladys Walker, *Owner*
EMP: 3 EST: 2021
SALES (est): 73.2K **Privately Held**
SIC: 2844 Hair preparations, including shampoos

(G-16880)
GLANBIA INC
3411 Silverside Rd Ste 104 (19810-4812)
PHONE.....................208 733-7555
EMP: 6 EST: 2019
SALES (est): 218.83K **Privately Held**
Web: www.glanbia.com
SIC: 2834 Pharmaceutical preparations

(G-16881)
GLAXOSMITHKLINE CAPITAL INC
1105 N Market St Ste 622 (19801-1216)
P.O. Box 8985 (19899-8985)
PHONE.....................302 656-5280
William K Langan, *Sec*
EMP: 46 EST: 2007
SALES (est): 905.07K
SALES (corp-wide): 35.31B **Privately Held**
SIC: 2834 Pharmaceutical preparations
PA: Gsk Plc
 G S K House
 Brentford MIDDX TW8 9
 208 047-5000

(G-16882)
GLAXOSMTHKLINE HLDNGS AMRCAS I (DH)
Also Called: Glaxosmithkline Svcs Unlimited
1105 N Market St Ste 622 (19801-1216)
P.O. Box 8985 (19899-8985)
PHONE.....................302 984-6932
Deirdre Connelly, *Pr*
Julian S Heslop, *CFO*
◆ EMP: 250 EST: 1830
SQ FT: 500,000
SALES (est): 1.16B
SALES (corp-wide): 35.31B **Privately Held**
Web: www.gsk.com
SIC: 2834 2836 2833 2844 Cough medicines ; Vaccines and other immunizing products; Antibiotics; Face creams or lotions
HQ: Glaxosmithkline Finance Plc
 G S K House
 Brentford MIDDX TW8 9
 208 047-5000

(G-16883)
GLEAM MDRN PARENTING SOLUTIONS ✪
108 W 13th St Ste 100 (19801-1145)
PHONE.....................302 416-6460
Yoav Kolodner, *CEO*
EMP: 2 EST: 2023
SALES (est): 87.4K **Privately Held**
SIC: 7372 Application computer software

(G-16884)
GLENMEDE TRUST CO NAT ASSN
1201 N Market St Ste 1501 (19801-1163)
PHONE.....................302 661-2900
Jeffrey Rogers, *Prin*
EMP: 5
Web: www.glenmede.com

SIC: 6282 Investment advisory service
HQ: The Glenmede Trust Company National Association
 1650 Market St Ste 1200
 Philadelphia PA 19103
 215 419-6000

(G-16885)
GLOBAL BRANDS USA INC
251 Little Falls Dr (19808-1674)
PHONE.....................314 401-2477
Steve Perez, *CEO*
EMP: 5 EST: 2020
SALES (est): 286.93K **Privately Held**
SIC: 2086 Bottled and canned soft drinks

(G-16886)
GLOBAL CURRENTS INV MGT LLC
2 Righter Pkwy (19803-1528)
PHONE.....................302 476-3800
EMP: 22 EST: 2007
SALES (est): 728.2K
SALES (corp-wide): 7.85B **Publicly Held**
SIC: 6722 Money market mutual funds
HQ: Legg Mason Inc
 100 International Dr
 Baltimore MD 21202
 410 539-0000

(G-16887)
GLOBAL DEV PARTNERS INC
2711 Centerville Rd # 400 (19808-1660)
PHONE.....................480 330-7931
Faisal Naveed, *CEO*
EMP: 5 EST: 2016
SALES (est): 110.63K **Privately Held**
SIC: 8748 Business consulting, nec

(G-16888)
GLOBAL ENTP WORLDWIDE LLC (PA)
1201 N Orange St Ste 700 # 7140 (19801-1186)
PHONE.....................713 260-9687
▼ EMP: 11 EST: 2010
SQ FT: 20,000
SALES (est): 3.91MM **Privately Held**
Web: www.tektraglobal.com
SIC: 5099 Wood chips

(G-16889)
GLOBAL ESSENTIALS INC
30b Trolley Sq (19806-3352)
PHONE.....................703 483-9544
EMP: 5 EST: 2018
SALES (est): 152.12K **Privately Held**
Web: www.globalessentials.us
SIC: 7371 Custom computer programming services

(G-16890)
GLOBAL GAMING BUSINESS
2413 Horace Dr (19808-3356)
PHONE.....................302 994-3898
Roger Gros, *Prin*
EMP: 2 EST: 2010
SALES (est): 92.15K **Privately Held**
Web: www.enkabaptist.org
SIC: 7372 Publisher's computer software

(G-16891)
GLOBAL LAW CENTERS
1403 N Rodney St (19806-4218)
PHONE.....................302 654-4800
Pecos T Olurin, *Prin*
EMP: 6 EST: 2010
SALES (est): 207.17K **Privately Held**
Web: www.olurin.com
SIC: 8111 Legal services

(G-16892)
GLOBAL NETWORK EXECUTIVE INC
Also Called: G E N
702 N West St Ste 101 (19801-1524)
PHONE.....................302 251-8940
Martin Hegi, *Pr*
EMP: 10 EST: 2012
SALES (est): 1.62MM **Privately Held**
Web: www.theglobalexecutivenetwork.com
SIC: 7361 Executive placement

(G-16893)
GLOBAL PARTNER LLC (PA)
501 Silverside Rd Ste 105 (19809-1376)
PHONE.....................646 630-9128
EMP: 7 EST: 2019
SALES (est): 246.41K
SALES (corp-wide): 246.41K **Privately Held**
SIC: 8748 Business consulting, nec

(G-16894)
GLOBAL PROTECTION MGT LLC
1105 N Market St Ste 400 (19801-1389)
PHONE.....................302 425-4190
Anthony Gentile, *Pr*
EMP: 355 EST: 2012
SALES (est): 936.61K
SALES (corp-wide): 8.78B **Privately Held**
Web: www.glprotect.com
SIC: 7381 Protective services, guard
HQ: Sos Security Llc
 1915 Us Highway 46
 Parsippany NJ 07054
 973 402-6600

(G-16895)
GLOBAL TELECOM GROUP LLC
1201 N Orange St Ste 6001 (19801-1155)
PHONE.....................302 295-2883
EMP: 5 EST: 2015
SALES (est): 46.16K **Privately Held**
SIC: 7371 Custom computer programming services

(G-16896)
GLOBAL WIRELESS ACCESORIES LLC
21 W Market St (19804-3138)
PHONE.....................302 753-7337
EMP: 5 EST: 2013
SALES (est): 152.28K **Privately Held**
SIC: 4812 Cellular telephone services

(G-16897)
GLOBALTEC NETWORKS INC
1013 Centre Rd (19805-1265)
PHONE.....................646 321-8627
Graeme Savill, *Dir*
Barry Chalmers, *Dir*
EMP: 5 EST: 2014
SALES (est): 260K **Privately Held**
Web: www.globaltecnetworks.co.uk
SIC: 4813 Telephone communications broker

(G-16898)
GLOSSGIRL INC
1320 N Union St (19806-2534)
PHONE.....................302 888-4520
EMP: 7
SALES (corp-wide): 466.39K **Privately Held**
Web: www.salondelaware.com
SIC: 7231 Hairdressers
PA: Glossgirl, Inc.
 77 E Main St Ste 2
 Newark DE 19711
 302 737-8080

(G-16899)
GMG SOLUTIONS LLC
Also Called: Mysherpa
4550 Linden Hill Rd Ste 301 (19808-2930)
PHONE.....................302 781-3008
EMP: 20 EST: 2002
SQ FT: 3,500
SALES (est): 3MM **Privately Held**
Web: www.mysherpa.com
SIC: 7379 Computer related consulting services

(G-16900)
GO MARKETPLACE LLC (PA) ✪
1007 N Market St Ste G20 (19801-1235)
PHONE.....................630 624-9079
Eric Vassilatos, *Managing Member*
EMP: 6 EST: 2023
SALES (est): 72.36K
SALES (corp-wide): 72.36K **Privately Held**
SIC: 7389 Brokers, business: buying and selling business enterprises

(G-16901)
GO4SPIN CORPORATION
251 Little Falls Dr (19808-1674)
PHONE.....................310 400-2588
Mikhail Khrushch, *CEO*
EMP: 5 EST: 2018
SALES (est): 165.56K **Privately Held**
Web: www.go4spin.com
SIC: 7514 Passenger car rental

(G-16902)
GOAL CAPITAL FUNDING TR 2010-1
1100 N Market St (19890-1100)
PHONE.....................302 636-6188
Jean Oller, *VP*
EMP: 5 EST: 2013
SALES (est): 566.47K **Privately Held**
SIC: 6733 Trusts, nec

(G-16903)
GOAT FINANCIAL LLC
1521 Concord Pike Ste 102 (19803-3614)
PHONE.....................800 843-4608
EMP: 9 EST: 2019
SALES (est): 934.14K **Privately Held**
SIC: 6282 Investment advice

(G-16904)
GODDARD SYSTEMS INC
111 S West St (19801-5014)
PHONE.....................302 651-7995
EMP: 19 EST: 2008
SALES (est): 215.96K **Privately Held**
Web: www.goddardschool.com
SIC: 8351 Preschool center

(G-16905)
GODFREY PLUMBING SERVICES
2606 Longwood Dr (19810-3704)
P.O. Box 8338 (19803-8338)
PHONE.....................302 985-1593
EMP: 6 EST: 2018
SALES (est): 234.52K **Privately Held**
SIC: 1711 Plumbing contractors

(G-16906)
GODSPEED TRANSPORT LLC
307 Pennsylvania Ave (19804-3042)
PHONE.....................302 803-2929
EMP: 5 EST: 2019
SALES (est): 150K **Privately Held**
SIC: 4213 Contract haulers

(G-16907)
GODWITS LLC ✪
1207 Delaware Ave 1006 (19806-4743)
PHONE.....................424 242-4462

GEOGRAPHIC SECTION

Wilmington - New Castle County (G-16936)

Song Wu, *Dir*
EMP: 5 **EST:** 2023
SALES (est): 78.16K **Privately Held**
SIC: 2099 Yeast

(G-16908)
GOKART TRANSPORTATION LLC ✪
1201 N Market St Ste 111 (19801-1156)
PHONE...............................302 202-9171
Anthony Hoskin, *Managing Member*
EMP: 6 **EST:** 2022
SALES (est): 320.39K **Privately Held**
Web: www.gokarttransport.com
SIC: 4121 Taxicabs

(G-16909)
GOLD MEDAL ENVMTL DE LLC
1000 S Heald St (19801-5735)
PHONE...............................302 652-3150
EMP: 5 **EST:** 2018
SALES (est): 142.6K **Privately Held**
SIC: 4953 Recycling, waste materials

(G-16910)
GOLDBERRY LLC
919 N Market St (19801-3023)
PHONE...............................800 268-4956
EMP: 6 **EST:** 2016
SALES (est): 308.35K **Privately Held**
Web: www.goldberryllc.com
SIC: 7389 Business Activities at Non-Commercial Site

(G-16911)
GOLDEN APPLE SPA
2601 Carpenter Station Rd (19810-2056)
PHONE...............................302 375-6505
EMP: 7 **EST:** 2019
SALES (est): 56.28K **Privately Held**
SIC: 7991 Spas

(G-16912)
GOLDEN GLOBE INTL SVCS LTD
913 N Market St Ste 200 (19801-3097)
PHONE...............................302 487-0022
Mehbub Manji, *Prin*
Sukaina Manji, *Pr*
EMP: 130 **EST:** 2017
SALES (est): 3.2MM **Privately Held**
SIC: 7389

(G-16913)
GOLDEN JEWELRY
1902 Maryland Ave (19805-4605)
PHONE...............................302 777-2121
Elizabeth So, *Owner*
EMP: 5 **EST:** 2007
SALES (est): 86.43K **Privately Held**
SIC: 5621 5944 7389 7631 Bridal shops; Jewelry stores; Flea market; Jewelry repair services

(G-16914)
GOLDIS HOLDINGS INC (HQ)
Also Called: I K O Productions
6 Denny Rd Ste 200 (19809-3444)
PHONE...............................302 764-3100
Sarena Koschitzky, *Pr*
EMP: 66 **EST:** 1992
SALES (est): 73.01MM
SALES (corp-wide): 1.26B **Privately Held**
SIC: 2952 5033 Roofing materials; Roofing and siding materials
PA: Iko Industries Ltd
   71 Orenda Rd
   Brampton ON L6W 3
   905 457-2880

(G-16915)
GOLDMAN SACHS TR CO NAT ASSN
Also Called: Goldman Sachs
200 Bellevue Pkwy Ste 250 (19809-3727)
PHONE...............................302 793-3276
EMP: 23 **EST:** 2019
SALES (est): 594.16K
SALES (corp-wide): 68.71B **Publicly Held**
SIC: 6733 Trusts, nec
PA: The Goldman Sachs Group Inc
   200 West St Bldg 200 # 200
   New York NY 10282
   212 902-1000

(G-16916)
GOLDSTONE & ASSOCIATES LLC
1521 Concord Pike Ste 303 (19803-3644)
PHONE...............................302 857-0051
EMP: 5 **EST:** 2018
SALES (est): 129.48K **Privately Held**
Web: www.davidgoldstone.com
SIC: 8748 Business consulting, nec

(G-16917)
GOLFCLUB LLC
Also Called: Golfclub
1209 Orange St Wilmington (19801)
PHONE...............................908 770-7892
Christopher Silano, *CEO*
George Taskos, *Engr*
EMP: 2 **EST:** 2017
SALES (est): 113.61K **Privately Held**
SIC: 3949 Driving ranges, golf, electronic

(G-16918)
GOLIATHS HAVEN INC
4023 Kennett Pike Ste 50142 (19807-2018)
PHONE...............................888 793-9311
Travis Westry, *Pr*
EMP: 11 **EST:** 2017
SALES (est): 780K **Privately Held**
SIC: 6719 Holding companies, nec

(G-16919)
GONSER AND GONSER P A
3411 Silverside Rd Ste 203hg (19810-4811)
PHONE...............................302 478-4445
Andrew Gonser, *Pr*
EMP: 8 **EST:** 2010
SALES (est): 2.1MM **Privately Held**
Web: www.gonserandgonserlaw.com
SIC: 8111 Divorce and family law

(G-16920)
GOOBERS GARAGE
3 Mill Rd Ste 102 (19806-2146)
PHONE...............................443 309-0328
EMP: 5 **EST:** 2020
SALES (est): 117.74K **Privately Held**
SIC: 7538 General automotive repair shops

(G-16921)
GOOD HOME SOLUTIONS LLC
20 North Ave (19804-1842)
PHONE...............................302 540-3190
Nancy Good, *Prin*
EMP: 5 **EST:** 2011
SALES (est): 194.89K **Privately Held**
SIC: 8748 Business consulting, nec

(G-16922)
GOOD LIFE GROUP LLC
1201 N Orange St (19801-1155)
PHONE...............................720 759-9089
EMP: 5 **EST:** 2018
SALES (est): 178.92K **Privately Held**
SIC: 6799 Investors, nec

(G-16923)
GOOD RPUTATION INVESTMENTS LLC
3 Germay Dr Ste 4 (19804-1127)
PHONE...............................888 382-1552
Sabrina Hawkins Little, *Managing Member*
EMP: 5 **EST:** 2019
SALES (est): 220.47K **Privately Held**
SIC: 6799 Investors, nec

(G-16924)
GOODEALS INC
537 Main St (19804-3910)
PHONE...............................302 999-1737
John Baker, *Prin*
EMP: 5 **EST:** 2005
SALES (est): 472.05K **Privately Held**
SIC: 4953 5932 Refuse collection and disposal services; Furniture, secondhand

(G-16925)
GOODSIZE INC
251 Little Falls Dr (19808-1674)
PHONE...............................415 481-7330
EMP: 5
SALES (est): 46.16K **Privately Held**
Web: www.in3d.io
SIC: 7371 Computer software development and applications

(G-16926)
GOODTYMES INC
Also Called: Sully Fl
132 School Rd (19803-4523)
PHONE...............................302 598-6673
EMP: 5 **EST:** 2008
SALES (est): 161.51K **Privately Held**
SIC: 6282 Investment advice

(G-16927)
GOODWILL INDS DEL DEL CNTY INC (PA)
Also Called: GOODWILL CENTER
300 E Lea Blvd (19802-2354)
PHONE...............................302 761-4640
Ted Van Name, *Pr*
Chris Quintanilla, *
EMP: 40 **EST:** 1921
SALES (est): 57.65MM **Privately Held**
Web: www.goodwillde.org
SIC: 5932 8331 Used merchandise stores; Vocational training agency

(G-16928)
GOODWORLD INC
2711 Centerville Rd Ste 400 (19808-1660)
PHONE...............................845 325-2232
John Gossart, *CEO*
EMP: 6
SALES (est): 252.53K **Privately Held**
Web: www.goodworldnow.com
SIC: 7379 7389 Online services technology consultants; Business services, nec

(G-16929)
GOODYEAR TIRE & RUBBER COMPANY
Goodyear
3217 Kirkwood Hwy (19808-6129)
PHONE...............................302 998-0428
Partick Leach, *Mgr*
EMP: 8
SALES (corp-wide): 20.8B **Publicly Held**
Web: www.goodyear.com
SIC: 5531 5014 Automotive tires; Automobile tires and tubes
PA: The Goodyear Tire & Rubber Company
   200 E Innovation Way
   Akron OH 44316
   330 796-2121

(G-16930)
GORDON FOURNARIS MAMMARELLA PA
1925 Lovering Ave (19806-2157)
PHONE...............................302 652-2900
EMP: 28 **EST:** 1994
SALES (est): 5.72MM **Privately Held**
Web: www.gfmlaw.com
SIC: 8111 General practice law office

(G-16931)
GORDONS DAYCARE HOME
2240 N Pine St (19802-5012)
PHONE...............................302 658-7854
Frances Gordon, *Prin*
EMP: 8 **EST:** 2016
SALES (est): 58.97K **Privately Held**
SIC: 8351 Child day care services

(G-16932)
GOTHAM INDEX 500 PLUS FUND
301 Bellevue Pkwy (19809-3705)
P.O. Box 534445 (15253-4445)
PHONE...............................877 974-6852
EMP: 7 **EST:** 2015
SALES (est): 252.4K **Privately Held**
SIC: 6722 Money market mutual funds

(G-16933)
GOVPLUS LLC
Also Called: Citizens Bank
4435 Kirkwood Hwy (19808-5115)
PHONE...............................302 633-4503
Dennis Eaton, *Mgr*
EMP: 6
SALES (corp-wide): 9.07B **Publicly Held**
Web: www.govplus.com
SIC: 6022 State commercial banks
HQ: Citizens Bank, National Association
   1 Citizens Plz
   Providence RI 02903

(G-16934)
GOVPLUS LLC
Also Called: GOVPLUS LLC
1422 N Dupont St (19806-4030)
PHONE...............................302 421-2248
EMP: 31
SALES (corp-wide): 9.07B **Publicly Held**
Web: www.govplus.com
SIC: 6022 State commercial banks
HQ: Citizens Bank, National Association
   1 Citizens Plz
   Providence RI 02903

(G-16935)
GOVPLUS LLC
Also Called: Citizens Bank
4720 Limestone Rd (19808-1928)
PHONE...............................302 633-3080
Stephanie Quill, *Brnch Mgr*
EMP: 10
SALES (corp-wide): 9.07B **Publicly Held**
Web: www.govplus.com
SIC: 6022 State commercial banks
HQ: Citizens Bank, National Association
   1 Citizens Plz
   Providence RI 02903

(G-16936)
GOVPLUS LLC
Also Called: Citizens Bank
2084 Naamans Rd (19810-2655)
PHONE...............................302 529-6100
Tom Minto, *Mgr*
EMP: 5
SALES (corp-wide): 9.07B **Publicly Held**
Web: www.govplus.com
SIC: 6022 State commercial banks
HQ: Citizens Bank, National Association

Wilmington - New Castle County (G-16937) GEOGRAPHIC SECTION

1 Citizens Plz
Providence RI 02903

(G-16937)
GOVPLUS LLC
Also Called: GOVPLUS LLC
919 N Market St Ste 200 (19801-3068)
PHONE..................302 421-2229
Warner S Waters Junior, *Brnch Mgr*
EMP: 44
SALES (corp-wide): 9.07B **Publicly Held**
Web: www.govplus.com
SIC: 6022 State commercial banks
HQ: Citizens Bank, National Association
1 Citizens Plz
Providence RI 02903

(G-16938)
GOVPLUS LLC
Also Called: Citizens Bank
1620 Marsh Rd (19803-3549)
PHONE..................302 477-1205
Mary A Gallagher, *Mgr*
EMP: 5
SALES (corp-wide): 9.07B **Publicly Held**
Web: www.govplus.com
SIC: 6022 State trust companies accepting deposits, commercial
HQ: Citizens Bank, National Association
1 Citizens Plz
Providence RI 02903

(G-16939)
GR LOUDON LLC
2210 Swiss Ln (19810-4241)
PHONE..................302 475-9400
Joyce Winters, *Prin*
EMP: 7 **EST:** 2016
SALES (est): 36.07K **Privately Held**
SIC: 8361 Residential care

(G-16940)
GRAB-UR-BITE INC
251 Little Falls Dr (19808-1674)
PHONE..................415 568-1717
Olawale Lasisi, *CEO*
EMP: 10 **EST:** 2019
SALES (est): 376.93K **Privately Held**
SIC: 4212 Delivery service, vehicular

(G-16941)
GRABOWSKI SPRANO VNCLETTE CPAS
Also Called: Sparano, Joseph C CPA
1814 Newport Gap Pike (19808-6148)
PHONE..................302 999-7300
C J Vincelette, *Pt*
EMP: 6 **EST:** 1988
SALES (est): 969.22K **Privately Held**
Web: www.svvcpa.com
SIC: 8721 Certified public accountant

(G-16942)
GRACE MIRACLE HOME CARE
3604 Miller Rd (19802-2524)
PHONE..................302 257-1079
Victoria Lamptey, *Owner*
Victoria Lamptey, *Prin*
EMP: 9 **EST:** 2017
SALES (est): 468.11K **Privately Held**
Web: www.gracemiraclehc.org
SIC: 8082 Home health care services

(G-16943)
GRACEFUL YOGA
3315 Elizabeth Ave (19808-6106)
PHONE..................302 994-3114
Gail Gerace, *Prin*
EMP: 5 **EST:** 2015
SALES (est): 44.21K **Privately Held**

SIC: 7999 Yoga instruction

(G-16944)
GRAFTON REEVES MD
Dupont Hosp For Children (19801)
PHONE..................302 651-5965
Grafton Reeves Md, *Prin*
EMP: 9 **EST:** 2001
SALES (est): 98.22K **Privately Held**
SIC: 8049 Offices of health practitioner

(G-16945)
GRAHAM GLOBAL CORPORATION
3616 Kirkwood Hwy Ste A (19808-5124)
PHONE..................302 839-3000
Charles E Graham, *CEO*
◆ **EMP:** 17 **EST:** 1968
SQ FT: 5,000
SALES (est): 2.25MM **Privately Held**
SIC: 3699 5082 5084 Electrical equipment and supplies, nec; Construction and mining machinery; Industrial machinery and equipment

(G-16946)
GRAND OPERA HOUSE INC
Also Called: GRAND OPERA HOUSE
818 N Market St Fl 2 (19801-3087)
PHONE..................302 652-5577
Kenneth Wesler, *Pr*
Robert V A Harra Junior, *Ch*
EMP: 50 **EST:** 1972
SQ FT: 200,000
SALES (est): 4.64MM **Privately Held**
Web: www.thegrandwilmington.org
SIC: 7922 Legitimate live theater producers

(G-16947)
GRANFORD INC
Also Called: Nimbus 9
1000 N West St Ste 1200 (19801-1058)
P.O. Box 187 (01090-0187)
PHONE..................413 474-6919
Thien Dao, *CEO*
EMP: 100 **EST:** 2014
SQ FT: 4,000
SALES (est): 10.07MM **Privately Held**
Web: www.granford.com
SIC: 5047 5065 Medical equipment and supplies; Mobile telephone equipment

(G-16948)
GRANT & EISENHOFER PA (PA)
123 S Justison St Ste 700 (19801-5366)
P.O. Box 752 (19899-0752)
PHONE..................302 622-7000
Jay W Eisenhofer, *Pr*
Adam J Levitt, *Dir*
Geoffrey C Jarvis, *Dir*
EMP: 58 **EST:** 1997
SALES (est): 12.55MM
SALES (corp-wide): 12.55MM **Privately Held**
Web: www.gelaw.com
SIC: 8111 General practice attorney, lawyer

(G-16949)
GRANT TANI BARASH & ALTMAN MAN
1100 N Mkt St Rodney Sq (19890-0001)
PHONE..................302 651-7700
Warren Grant, *Prin*
EMP: 7 **EST:** 2004
SALES (est): 293.5K **Privately Held**
SIC: 8111 Legal services

(G-16950)
GRAPEFRUIT USA INC (PA)
1000 N West St (19801-1050)
PHONE..................310 575-1175

EMP: 9 **EST:** 2017
SALES (est): 588.96K **Publicly Held**
SIC: 3999 5159

(G-16951)
GRAYDIE WELDING LLC
42 W Reamer Ave (19804-1716)
PHONE..................302 753-0695
Harry B Bachman, *Prin*
EMP: 5 **EST:** 2008
SALES (est): 68.45K **Privately Held**
Web: www.graydiewelding.com
SIC: 7692 Welding repair

(G-16952)
GRAYDON HURST & SON INC
2901 Baynard Blvd Ste 4 (19802-2973)
PHONE..................302 762-2444
Walter A Belczyk Junior, *Pr*
Cathy Belczyk, *Sec*
EMP: 6 **EST:** 1932
SALES (est): 526.41K **Privately Held**
Web: www.graydonhurst.com
SIC: 1771 1711 Concrete work; Plumbing contractors

(G-16953)
GRAYLYN CREST III SWIM CLUB
2015 Kynwyd Rd (19810-3843)
PHONE..................302 547-5809
EMP: 6 **EST:** 2011
SALES (est): 114.78K **Privately Held**
Web: www.graylyngators.com
SIC: 7997 Swimming club, membership

(G-16954)
GRAYLYN DENTAL
2205 Silverside Rd Ste 2 (19810-4534)
PHONE..................302 475-5555
Joseph Kelly, *Pr*
EMP: 7 **EST:** 1984
SALES (est): 731.26K **Privately Held**
Web: www.graylyndental.com
SIC: 8021 Dentists' office

(G-16955)
GRAYSON HOME IMPROVEMENTS LLC
911 E 27th St (19802-4435)
PHONE..................302 685-1848
EMP: 7
SALES (est): 141.03K **Privately Held**
SIC: 7299 7389 Home improvement and renovation contractor agency; Business services, nec

(G-16956)
GREANEX
1209 N Orange St (19801-1120)
PHONE..................606 477-9768
EMP: 5 **EST:** 2018
SALES (est): 161.27K **Privately Held**
Web: www.greanex.energy
SIC: 8748 Business consulting, nec

(G-16957)
GREASE CITY INC ○
900 N Madison St Apt 2 (19801-1473)
PHONE..................302 661-5675
Gregory Carter, *Prin*
EMP: 7 **EST:** 2022
SALES (est): 78.16K **Privately Held**
SIC: 3161 7389 Clothing and apparel carrying cases; Business Activities at Non-Commercial Site

(G-16958)
GREAT CLIPS
4705 Kirkwood Hwy (19808-5007)
PHONE..................302 995-2887

EMP: 6 **EST:** 2018
SALES (est): 62.77K **Privately Held**
Web: www.greatclips.com
SIC: 7231 Unisex hair salons

(G-16959)
GREAT SPIRIT VENTURES LLC
1011 Centre Rd Ste 310 (19805-1266)
PHONE..................302 573-3820
Vickie Sizemore, *Prin*
EMP: 5 **EST:** 2005
SALES (est): 64K **Privately Held**
SIC: 7389 Business services, nec

(G-16960)
GREAT VALLEY ADVISOR GROUP
1200 Pennsylvania Ave Ste 202 (19806-4350)
PHONE..................302 483-7200
EMP: 17 **EST:** 2016
SALES (est): 818.56K **Privately Held**
Web: www.greatvalleyadvisors.com
SIC: 6282 Investment advisory service

(G-16961)
GREATFUL LIVES FOUNDATION
1007 N Orange St Ste 1450 (19801-1273)
PHONE..................404 965-9300
Jonathan C Burrell, *Prin*
EMP: 5 **EST:** 2017
SALES (est): 44.48K **Privately Held**
SIC: 8641 Civic and social associations

(G-16962)
GREELEY & NISTA ORTHODONTICS
1405 Silverside Rd Ste A (19810-4445)
PHONE..................302 475-4102
John M Nista, *Pt*
M C Greeley, *Pt*
EMP: 24 **EST:** 1980
SALES (est): 619.73K **Privately Held**
Web: www.firststatesmiles.com
SIC: 8021 Orthodontist

(G-16963)
GREEN CONSTRUCTION SERVICES
3120 Naamans Rd Apt P2 (19810-2178)
PHONE..................610 675-6337
EMP: 8 **EST:** 2016
SALES (est): 98.82K **Privately Held**
SIC: 1629 Heavy construction, nec

(G-16964)
GREEN EARTH TECH GROUP LLC
1000 N West St (19801-1050)
PHONE..................302 257-5617
EMP: 14 **EST:** 2013
SALES (est): 486.68K **Privately Held**
Web: www.getgrp.com
SIC: 1795 Wrecking and demolition work

(G-16965)
GREEN OAK REAL ESTATE LP
1209 N Orange St (19801-1120)
PHONE..................212 359-7800
Andrew Yoon, *COO*
EMP: 100 **EST:** 2010
SQ FT: 10,000
SALES (est): 7.23MM **Privately Held**
SIC: 6531 Real estate brokers and agents

(G-16966)
GREEN ROOM RESTAURANT
Also Called: Hotel Dupont Company
100 W 11th St (19801)
PHONE..................302 594-3100
Jacques Amblard, *Prin*
EMP: 30 **EST:** 1912
SALES (est): 3.15MM **Privately Held**
Web: www.hoteldupont.com

GEOGRAPHIC SECTION
Wilmington - New Castle County (G-16994)

SIC: 7011 Hotels

(G-16967)
GREEN SIDE UP LAWN & LANDSCAPE
406 1/2 Hillside Ave (19805-1010)
PHONE..................302 999-7151
Bill Mellen, *Prin*
EMP: 6 EST: 2005
SALES (est): 218.94K **Privately Held**
Web: www.gsulandscape.com
SIC: 0782 Landscape contractors

(G-16968)
GREEN TEAM MOVING & DESIGN LLC
1201 N Market St Ste 111 (19801-1156)
PHONE..................252 406-7001
EMP: 3 EST: 2015
SALES (est): 75K **Privately Held**
SIC: 3537 Trucks, tractors, loaders, carriers, and similar equipment

(G-16969)
GREENBERG PRAURIG LLC
1007 N Orange St Ste 1200 (19801-1236)
PHONE..................302 661-7000
EMP: 5 EST: 2007
SALES (est): 245.82K **Privately Held**
SIC: 8111 Specialized law offices, attorneys

(G-16970)
GREENBERG SUPPLY CO INC
809 E 5th St (19801-4899)
P.O. Box 9248 (19809-0248)
PHONE..................302 656-4496
TOLL FREE: 800
Gary W Greenberg, *Pr*
Alvin Hall Junior, *VP*
Pat Beckman, *
EMP: 35 EST: 1946
SQ FT: 45,000
SALES (est): 13.42MM **Privately Held**
Web: www.greenbergsupply.com
SIC: 5075 5074 5085 5078 Air conditioning and ventilation equipment and supplies; Plumbing and hydronic heating supplies; Industrial supplies; Refrigeration equipment and supplies

(G-16971)
GREENE TWEED OF DELAWARE INC
1105 N Market St Ste 1300 (19801-1241)
PHONE..................302 888-2560
William P Maher, *Prin*
EMP: 33 EST: 2000
SALES (est): 770.08K
SALES (corp-wide): 284.93MM **Privately Held**
Web: www.gtweed.com
SIC: 3053 Gaskets and sealing devices
PA: Greene, Tweed & Co., Inc.
1684 S Broad St
Lansdale PA 19446
215 256-9521

(G-16972)
GREENLEAF LANDSCAPES LLC
301 Weldin Rd (19803-4935)
PHONE..................302 762-5027
Joseph Winemiller, *Prin*
EMP: 5 EST: 2011
SALES (est): 83.11K **Privately Held**
Web: www.greenleaf-landscapes.com
SIC: 0781 Landscape services

(G-16973)
GREENVILLE COUNTRY CLUB INC
201 Owls Nest Rd (19807-1129)
P.O. Box 3920 (19807-0920)
PHONE..................302 652-3255
Eric Holloway, *Pr*
Donald Taylor, *
Steven Griffin, *
EMP: 50 EST: 1959
SALES (est): 1.33MM **Privately Held**
Web: www.greenvillecc.com
SIC: 7997 5812 Country club, membership; Eating places

(G-16974)
GREENVILLE TOWERS LLC
220 Presidential Dr (19807-3324)
PHONE..................302 397-8016
Gregory Pettinaro, *Mgr*
EMP: 8 EST: 2017
SALES (est): 149.34K **Privately Held**
Web: www.pettinaro.com
SIC: 6513 Apartment building operators

(G-16975)
GREENVLLE RETIREMENT CMNTY LLC
Also Called: Stonegates
4031 Kennett Pike (19807-2047)
PHONE..................302 658-6200
EMP: 125 EST: 1983
SALES (est): 10.05MM **Privately Held**
Web: www.stonegates.com
SIC: 8051 Convalescent home with continuous nursing care

(G-16976)
GREGORY FOR WILMINGTON
401 W 22nd St (19802-4007)
PHONE..................302 562-3117
Gregory Theo, *Prin*
EMP: 5 EST: 2016
SALES (est): 51.32K **Privately Held**
SIC: 8399 Advocacy group

(G-16977)
GREY MATTER INC
2701 Centerville Rd (19808-1607)
PHONE..................302 764-5900
Warren Samolsky, *Pr*
EMP: 7 EST: 2015
SALES (est): 74.08K **Privately Held**
Web: www.greymatter.com
SIC: 2741 Miscellaneous publishing

(G-16978)
GRIFFEN CORPORATE SERVICES
300 Delaware Ave Fl 9 (19801-1607)
PHONE..................302 576-2890
EMP: 15
SIC: 6719 Investment holding companies, except banks

(G-16979)
GRIFFS SIGNS LLC
101 Westmoreland Ave (19804-1752)
PHONE..................302 784-5596
Matt Griffith, *Prin*
EMP: 4 EST: 2018
SALES (est): 46.08K **Privately Held**
SIC: 3993 Signs and advertising specialties

(G-16980)
GRIND KENNELS LLC (PA) ✪
24a Trolley Sq Unit 1259 (19806-3334)
PHONE..................302 442-5599
EMP: 5 EST: 2023
SALES (est): 57.47K
SALES (corp-wide): 57.47K **Privately Held**
SIC: 0752 Animal specialty services

(G-16981)
GRIND OR STARVE LLC
608 W Lea Blvd Apt C4 (19802-2049)
PHONE..................302 322-1679
EMP: 5 EST: 2015
SALES (est): 258.29K **Privately Held**
SIC: 7311 8742 Advertising consultant; Marketing consulting services

(G-16982)
GRISWOLD HOME CARE
115 Christina Landing Dr Apt 708 (19801-5401)
PHONE..................302 750-4564
Anne Eidschun, *Prin*
EMP: 12 EST: 2015
SALES (est): 276.64K **Privately Held**
Web: www.griswoldhomecare.com
SIC: 8082 Home health care services

(G-16983)
GRIZ INC
2305 Pennsylvania Ave (19806-1318)
PHONE..................302 655-1344
EMP: 6 EST: 2020
SALES (est): 108.67K **Privately Held**
SIC: 7299 Miscellaneous personal service

(G-16984)
GRM PRO IMAGING LLC
Also Called: Speed Pro Imiging
401 Marsh Ln Ste 3 (19804-2491)
PHONE..................302 999-8162
Gary Meltz, *Managing Member*
EMP: 2 EST: 2012
SQ FT: 3,000
SALES (est): 189.66K **Privately Held**
Web: www.speedpro.com
SIC: 2752 Offset printing

(G-16985)
GROOMING BAR LLC
701 S Union St Ste 4 (19805-4101)
PHONE..................302 803-8304
Joel Payne, *Managing Member*
EMP: 5 EST: 2020
SALES (est): 30.01K **Privately Held**
SIC: 7241 Barber shops

(G-16986)
GROOVVX INC
4 Guyenne Rd (19807-1414)
PHONE..................828 399-1549
Ifeanyi Umejei, *CEO*
Shuying Liu, *Finance*
Chiemelie Umenyiora, *COO*
Felix Ekwueme, *Prin*
EMP: 5 EST: 2021
SALES (est): 107.01K **Privately Held**
SIC: 7371 Computer software development and applications

(G-16987)
GROUND/WATER TRTMNT & TECH LLC
1204 E 12th St Ste 4c (19802-5317)
PHONE..................302 654-0206
Ken Kaufman, *Brnch Mgr*
EMP: 13
SALES (corp-wide): 57.52MM **Privately Held**
Web: www.gwttllc.com
SIC: 8748 Environmental consultant
HQ: Ground/Water Treatment & Technology, Llc
627 Mount Hope Rd
Wharton NJ 07885
973 983-0901

(G-16988)
GROUP THREE INC (PA)
Also Called: Gti Millwork
1100 Duncan St Ste A (19805-4782)
PHONE..................302 658-4158
Jeff Moore, *Pr*
Elliott Colton, *Sec*
EMP: 5 EST: 1989
SQ FT: 10,000
SALES (est): 956.36K **Privately Held**
Web: www.gtimillwork.com
SIC: 2511 5712 2431 Wood household furniture; Customized furniture and cabinets ; Millwork

(G-16989)
GROWING EDGES COUNSELING
5149 W Woodmill Dr Ste 20 (19808-4067)
PHONE..................484 883-6523
Stephanie Wharton, *Prin*
EMP: 7 EST: 2018
SALES (est): 50.16K **Privately Held**
SIC: 8322 General counseling services

(G-16990)
GROWTH RIVER USA LLC
1201 N Orange St Ste 600 (19801-1171)
PHONE..................617 905-5156
Robert Voss, *VP*
EMP: 6 EST: 2020
SALES (est): 468.43K **Privately Held**
Web: www.growthriver.com
SIC: 8742 Business management consultant

(G-16991)
GRUB-BUSTERS GRUB BUS LLC
1201 N Market St (19801-1147)
PHONE..................610 931-9406
EMP: 2
SALES (est): 92.41K **Privately Held**
SIC: 2099 Food preparations, nec

(G-16992)
GRUBB LUMBER COMPANY INC
200 A St (19801-5221)
P.O. Box 627 (19899-0627)
PHONE..................302 652-2800
EMP: 45 EST: 1979
SQ FT: 65,000
SALES (est): 77.88MM **Privately Held**
Web: www.grubblumber.com
SIC: 2431 5031 2426 2421 Millwork; Lumber: rough, dressed, and finished; Hardwood dimension and flooring mills; Sawmills and planing mills, general

(G-16993)
GRUPO ACOSTA ECUADOR LIMITED
501 Silverside Rd 105-3 (19809-1374)
PHONE..................302 231-2981
Jang F Acosta, *Pr*
Jang Acosta, *Pr*
Paolo Morocho, *VP*
Daniel Peters, *CFO*
EMP: 219 EST: 2011
SALES (est): 8.83MM **Privately Held**
SIC: 5199 General merchandise, non-durable

(G-16994)
GSB&B LLC
Also Called: Gellert Scali Busenkell Brown
1201 N Orange St Ste 300 (19801-1167)
PHONE..................302 425-5800
Angie Poulin, *Off Mgr*
EMP: 8 EST: 2013
SALES (est): 1.17MM **Privately Held**
Web: www.gsbblaw.com
SIC: 8111 General practice attorney, lawyer

Wilmington - New Castle County (G-16995)

(G-16995)
GSI EXPRESS LOGISTICS INC
430 E Ayre St (19804-2513)
PHONE..................201 345-3532
Min Ha Suh, *Asst Sec*
EMP: 5 EST: 2018
SALES (est): 189.24K **Privately Held**
Web: www.gsiexpress.com
SIC: 4789 Transportation services, nec

(G-16996)
GT COMMODITIES LLC
3511 Silverside Rd Ste 10 (19810-4902)
PHONE..................203 609-8300
EMP: 55
SALES (corp-wide): 387.31MM **Privately Held**
SIC: 6221 Commodity contracts brokers, dealers
HQ: Gt Commodities Llc
750 Washington Blvd Fl 5
Stamford CT 06901
203 609-8300

(G-16997)
GT DIRECTIONAL LLC
3524 Silverside Rd Ste 35b (19810-4929)
PHONE..................714 417-2826
Gabrielle Yacoob, *Managing Member*
EMP: 5 EST: 2021
SALES (est): 180K **Privately Held**
SIC: 1623 Underground utilities contractor

(G-16998)
GTS TECHNICAL LLC ◆
122 Middleboro Rd (19804-1621)
PHONE..................302 778-1362
Derrick Yant, *Managing Member*
EMP: 15 EST: 2023
SALES (est): 1.36MM **Privately Held**
SIC: 5085 Valves and fittings

(G-16999)
GUARDIAN ANGEL CHILD CARE
1000 Wilson St (19801-3432)
PHONE..................302 428-3620
Janet Chandler, *Dir*
Janet Chandler, *Mgr*
EMP: 5 EST: 2005
SALES (est): 105.19K **Privately Held**
SIC: 8351 Preschool center

(G-17000)
GUARDIAN COMPANIES INC (PA)
101 Rogers Rd Ste 101 (19801-5778)
PHONE..................302 834-1000
Nona J Cunane, *Ch Bd*
Joseph Cunane Junior, *CEO*
Bradley C P Leto, *Ex VP*
EMP: 23 EST: 1987
SQ FT: 38,000
SALES (est): 40.96MM **Privately Held**
Web: www.guardianco.com
SIC: 1623 1794 Underground utilities contractor; Excavation and grading, building construction

(G-17001)
GUARDIAN CONSTRUCTION CO INC
100 Rogers Rd (19801-5704)
PHONE..................302 656-1986
Jeffrey Boonin, *Prin*
EMP: 9 EST: 2010
SALES (est): 88K **Privately Held**
Web: www.guardianco.com
SIC: 1521 Single-family housing construction

(G-17002)
GUEDON CO
Also Called: Guco
1106 Cypress Rd (19810-1908)
PHONE..................302 375-6151
Rudolph J Ovecka Junior, *Owner*
EMP: 3 EST: 1967
SALES (est): 71.25K **Privately Held**
Web: www.alvaplastics.com
SIC: 3993 Signs and advertising specialties

(G-17003)
GUIDED FOOTSTEPS
2820 W 3rd St (19805-1813)
PHONE..................302 494-6680
Crystal G Riley, *Owner*
EMP: 5 EST: 2017
SALES (est): 46.7K **Privately Held**
SIC: 7999 Tour and guide services

(G-17004)
GUINEVERE ASSOCIATES INC
2 Nob Hill Rd (19808-1206)
PHONE..................302 635-7798
David Jonocha, *Pr*
EMP: 7 EST: 1998
SALES (est): 926.52K **Privately Held**
SIC: 5199 Gifts and novelties

(G-17005)
GULF DEVELOPMENT PARTNERS LLC (PA)
910 Foulk Rd Ste 201 (19803-3159)
PHONE..................646 334-1245
EMP: 5 EST: 2003
SALES (est): 657.23K
SALES (corp-wide): 657.23K **Privately Held**
SIC: 8742 Management consulting services

(G-17006)
GUND SECURITIES CORPORATION
1105 N Market St Ste 1300 (19801-1241)
P.O. Box 8985 (19899-8985)
PHONE..................302 479-9210
Hilton Young, *CEO*
EMP: 10 EST: 1998
SALES (est): 281.66K **Privately Held**
SIC: 6211 Security brokers and dealers

(G-17007)
GUNNIP & COMPANY
Also Called: Gunnip Employment Services
2751 Centerville Rd Ste 300 (19808-1627)
PHONE..................302 225-5000
Charles L Robertson, *Pt*
Terri Tipping, *Pt*
William Brower, *Pt*
Clifford Hunter, *Pt*
Robert D Mosch, *Pt*
EMP: 104 EST: 1948
SQ FT: 16,000
SALES (est): 11.9MM **Privately Held**
Web: www.gunnip.com
SIC: 8721 Certified public accountant

(G-17008)
GUSHER
405 N King St (19801-3773)
PHONE..................302 803-5900
EMP: 7 EST: 2019
SALES (est): 158.77K **Privately Held**
Web: www.gusher.co
SIC: 8748 Business consulting, nec

(G-17009)
GUTTER CLEANING
2328 Thomas Ln (19810-2339)
PHONE..................302 293-8461
Kevin Konitzer, *Prin*
EMP: 5 EST: 2014
SALES (est): 46.97K **Privately Held**
SIC: 7699 Cleaning services

(G-17010)
GUYS GUTTER
2406 W Newport Pike (19804-3849)
P.O. Box 6586 (19804-0586)
PHONE..................302 325-4210
Antecedents Are Undetermined, *Prin*
EMP: 11 EST: 2002
SALES (est): 231.34K **Privately Held**
Web: www.thegutterguys.com
SIC: 1761 Gutter and downspout contractor

(G-17011)
GW CONSULTING INC
4200 Governor Printz Blvd (19802-2315)
PHONE..................302 294-2114
EMP: 445
SALES (corp-wide): 175.11MM **Privately Held**
SIC: 7381 Detective services
HQ: Gw Consulting Inc.
1700 N Moore St
Arlington VA 22209
703 253-8080

(G-17012)
H & R BLOCK
Also Called: H & R Block
2407 Kirkwood Hwy (19805-4906)
PHONE..................302 999-8100
Archie Lord, *Mgr*
EMP: 9 EST: 2015
SALES (est): 114.85K **Privately Held**
Web: www.hrblock.ca
SIC: 7291 Tax return preparation services

(G-17013)
H & R BLOCK INC
Also Called: H & R Block
4711 Kirkwood Hwy (19808-5007)
PHONE..................302 999-7488
John Rudick, *Mgr*
EMP: 5
SALES (corp-wide): 3.47B **Publicly Held**
Web: www.hrblock.com
SIC: 7291 8721 Tax return preparation services; Accounting, auditing, and bookkeeping
PA: H & R Block, Inc.
1 H And R Block Way
Kansas City MO 64105
816 854-3000

(G-17014)
H & R BLOCK INC
Also Called: H & R Block
1720 Marsh Rd (19810-4606)
PHONE..................302 478-9140
EMP: 10
SALES (corp-wide): 3.47B **Publicly Held**
Web: www.hrblock.com
SIC: 7291 Tax return preparation services
PA: H & R Block, Inc.
1 H And R Block Way
Kansas City MO 64105
816 854-3000

(G-17015)
H & R BLOCK INC
Also Called: H & R Block
3629b Silverside Rd (19810-5101)
PHONE..................302 478-6300
EMP: 5
SALES (corp-wide): 3.47B **Publicly Held**
Web: www.hrblock.com
SIC: 7291 Tax return preparation services
PA: H & R Block, Inc.
1 H And R Block Way
Kansas City MO 64105
816 854-3000

(G-17016)
H CLEMONS CONSULTING INC
Also Called: Hcnrg Solutions
1000 N West St Ste 1200 (19801-1058)
PHONE..................302 295-5097
Deborah L Hunt-clemons, *Pr*
EMP: 9 EST: 2002
SQ FT: 1,600
SALES (est): 202.7K **Privately Held**
SIC: 8748 Business consulting, nec

(G-17017)
H D C INC
Also Called: Harvey Development Company
405 Marsh Ln Ste 1 (19804-2445)
PHONE..................302 323-9300
Thomas Harvey, *Pr*
EMP: 9 EST: 1989
SQ FT: 3,000
SALES (est): 958.43K **Privately Held**
SIC: 6531 Appraiser, real estate

(G-17018)
H D LEE COMPANY INC (HQ)
3411 Silverside Rd Ste 201 (19810-4817)
PHONE..................302 477-3930
Laura Meagher, *Pr*
Helen L Winslow, *VP*
Christopher M Turk, *Sec*
Jacquelyn A Pellegrino, *Sec*
EMP: 9 EST: 1889
SQ FT: 47,000
SALES (est): 1.91MM
SALES (corp-wide): 2.63B **Publicly Held**
SIC: 2211 5136 5137 Jean fabrics; Men's and boy's clothing; Women's and children's clothing
PA: Kontoor Brands, Inc.
400 N Elm St
Greensboro NC 27401
336 332-3400

(G-17019)
H DEAN MCSPADDEN DDS
Also Called: Rockland Dental Associates
11 Old Barley Mill Rd (19807-3000)
PHONE..................302 571-0680
H Dean Mc Spadden D.d.s., *Owner*
EMP: 7 EST: 1985
SALES (est): 121.79K **Privately Held**
SIC: 8021 Dentists' office

(G-17020)
H PRIVATE FOUNDATION
501 Silverside Rd Ste 123 (19809-1377)
PHONE..................800 839-1754
EMP: 5
SALES (est): 7.47K **Privately Held**
SIC: 8699 Charitable organization

(G-17021)
H S B C OVERSEAS CORP DE
300 Delaware Ave Ste 1400 (19801-1650)
PHONE..................302 657-8400
Richard Leigh, *Pr*
EMP: 68 EST: 1987
SALES (est): 3.26MM
SALES (corp-wide): 93.79B **Privately Held**
Web: www.hsbc.com
SIC: 6722 Mutual fund sales, on own account
HQ: Hsbc Usa, Inc.
452 5th Ave Frnt 1
New York NY 10018
212 525-5000

(G-17022)
H&H TRADING INTERNATIONAL LLC
1201 N Orange St Ste 600 (19801-1171)
PHONE..................480 580-3911
◆ EMP: 5 EST: 2011

GEOGRAPHIC SECTION
Wilmington - New Castle County (G-17052)

SALES (est): 275.08K **Privately Held**
SIC: 2038 7389 Ethnic foods, nec, frozen; Business services, nec

(G-17023)
H&R BLOCK EASTERN ENTERPRES
106 S Union St (19805-3829)
PHONE..................302 656-7212
EMP: 6 EST: 2010
SALES (est): 120K **Privately Held**
Web: www.hrblock.com
SIC: 8742 8721 7291 Financial consultant; Accounting, auditing, and bookkeeping; Tax return preparation services

(G-17024)
H-V TECHNICAL SERVICES INC
300 Delaware Ave Ste 525 (19801-1607)
PHONE..................302 427-5801
EMP: 5 EST: 2001
SIC: 6719 Investment holding companies, except banks

(G-17025)
H2OG FOGGER INC ✪
3200 Kirkwood Hwy (19808-6153)
PHONE..................414 333-7024
EMP: 6 EST: 2022
SALES (est): 78.16K **Privately Held**
SIC: 2899 Chemical preparations, nec

(G-17026)
HABASH COMMERCIAL REALTY LLC
205 Philadelphia Pike (19809-3159)
PHONE..................302 218-3025
Mitri Habash, *Prin*
EMP: 5 EST: 2014
SALES (est): 90.91K **Privately Held**
Web: www.habashcommercial.com
SIC: 6531 Real estate agent, commercial

(G-17027)
HABITAT FOR HMNITY NEW CSTLE C (PA)
1920 Hutton St (19802-4905)
PHONE..................302 652-0365
Kevin Smith, *CEO*
EMP: 10 EST: 1986
SQ FT: 13,000
SALES (est): 7.05MM
SALES (corp-wide): 7.05MM **Privately Held**
Web: www.habitatncc.org
SIC: 1521 8322 Single-family housing construction; Individual and family services

(G-17028)
HACK VC MANAGEMENT COMPANY LLC
1209 N Orange St (19801-1120)
PHONE..................650 575-4613
Alexander Pack, *Managing Member*
EMP: 7 EST: 2021
SALES (est): 298.45K **Privately Held**
SIC: 6799 Venture capital companies

(G-17029)
HACKETT INDUSTRIES LLC
Also Called: General Freight
701 S Franklin St (19805-4330)
PHONE..................302 516-0836
Ismaa'eel H Hackett, *CEO*
EMP: 6 EST: 2019
SALES (est): 291.17K **Privately Held**
SIC: 4213 Trucking, except local

(G-17030)
HAGERTY DRIVERS CLUB LLC
2711 Centerville Rd Ste 400 (19808-1660)
PHONE..................302 504-6086
Brian Clymer, *Prin*
EMP: 10 EST: 2018
SALES (est): 103.19K **Privately Held**
Web: www.hagerty.com
SIC: 7997 Membership sports and recreation clubs

(G-17031)
HAGERTYS ROOFING
102 Cambridge Dr (19803-2606)
PHONE..................302 650-3474
Matthew Hagerty, *Prin*
EMP: 5 EST: 2017
SALES (est): 160.17K **Privately Held**
Web: www.dehagertysroofing.com
SIC: 1761 Roofing contractor

(G-17032)
HAIR BY ASHLEIGHMONAI LLC
804 E 28th St (19802-3607)
PHONE..................215 201-6874
Ashleigh Hood, *CEO*
EMP: 4 EST: 2020
SALES (est): 125.12K **Privately Held**
SIC: 3999 Hair and hair-based products

(G-17033)
HAIR GALLERIE
2747 Shipley Rd (19810-3210)
PHONE..................302 373-4774
Sandi Paul, *Prin*
EMP: 5 EST: 2010
SALES (est): 56.49K **Privately Held**
SIC: 7231 Hairdressers

(G-17034)
HAIRWORKS INC
1601 Concord Pike Ste 21 (19803-3613)
PHONE..................302 656-0566
Patricia M Palandrani, *Pr*
Janet Milam, *Owner*
Teresa Koval, *Owner*
EMP: 7 EST: 1977
SQ FT: 1,350
SALES (est): 216.03K **Privately Held**
Web: www.hairworks.us
SIC: 7231 Unisex hair salons

(G-17035)
HAJIRS TOUCH LLC
704 W 9th St (19801-1307)
PHONE..................302 543-2302
EMP: 5 EST: 2007
SALES (est): 42.95K **Privately Held**
SIC: 8999 Personal services

(G-17036)
HAJOCA CORPORATION
Also Called: Weinstein Supply Div
303 E 30th St (19802-3201)
PHONE..................302 764-6000
Donald Elliott, *Mgr*
EMP: 10
SALES (corp-wide): 2.01B **Privately Held**
Web: www.hajoca.com
SIC: 5074 Plumbing fittings and supplies
PA: Hajoca Corporation
    2001 Joshua Rd
    Lafayette Hill PA 19444
    610 649-1430

(G-17037)
HALEN TECHNOLOGIES INC
Also Called: Halen
1007 N Market St (19801-1227)
PHONE..................302 290-3075
Edward Mbeche, *CEO*
EMP: 15 EST: 2021
SALES (est): 631.61K **Privately Held**

SIC: 4212 4789 Delivery service, vehicular; Transportation services, nec

(G-17038)
HALL BURKE VFW POST 5447 INC
Also Called: VFW Post 5447
1605 Philadelphia Pike (19809-1540)
PHONE..................302 798-2052
Edward Edwards, *Pr*
EMP: 10 EST: 1946
SQ FT: 10,000
SALES (est): 509.81K **Privately Held**
Web: www.hall-burkevfwpost5447.org
SIC: 8641 Veterans' organization

(G-17039)
HALLORAN FARKAS + KITTILA LLP
5801 Kennett Pike Ste C (19807-1123)
PHONE..................302 257-2011
EMP: 13 EST: 2019
SALES (est): 909.36K **Privately Held**
Web: www.hfk.law
SIC: 8111 General practice attorney, lawyer

(G-17040)
HALOSIL INTERNATIONAL INC
1500 Eastlawn Ave (19802-2403)
PHONE..................302 543-8095
▼ EMP: 7 EST: 2015
SALES (est): 909.58K **Privately Held**
Web: www.halosil.com
SIC: 2842 Disinfectants, household or industrial plant

(G-17041)
HALPERN EYE ASSOCIATES-MIDWAY
4605 Kirkwood Hwy (19808-5005)
PHONE..................302 993-7861
Shannon Moger, *Prin*
EMP: 7 EST: 2013
SALES (est): 99.31K **Privately Held**
SIC: 8042 Offices and clinics of optometrists

(G-17042)
HALTIA INC ✪
2810 N Church St Pmb 29349 (19802-4447)
PHONE..................302 244-7425
Arto Bendiken, *Pr*
EMP: 29 EST: 2023
SALES (est): 1.05MM **Privately Held**
SIC: 7371 Computer software development and applications

(G-17043)
HAMILTON HOUSE CONDOMINIUM
1403 Shallcross Ave Apt 304 (19806-3034)
PHONE..................302 658-7787
Louis Wiley, *Pr*
Ralph Gilby, *Treas*
EMP: 5 EST: 1973
SALES (est): 314.64K **Privately Held**
SIC: 8641 Condominium association

(G-17044)
HAND & SPA
3654 Concord Pike (19803-5022)
PHONE..................302 478-1700
Jerry Le Reux, *Owner*
EMP: 5 EST: 2014
SALES (est): 100.36K **Privately Held**
Web: www.handandstonebrandywine.com
SIC: 7991 Spas

(G-17045)
HAND AND STONE
301 Alders Dr (19803-5305)
PHONE..................302 373-6608

EMP: 6 EST: 2014
SALES (est): 39.01K **Privately Held**
Web: www.handandstone.com
SIC: 7299 Massage parlor

(G-17046)
HANDLER BUILDERS INC
Also Called: Deerborne Woods Sales Center
5169 W Woodmill Dr (19808-4067)
PHONE..................302 999-9200
Mark Handler, *Pr*
EMP: 10 EST: 1999
SALES (est): 733.77K **Privately Held**
Web: www.handlerhomes.com
SIC: 1521 New construction, single-family houses

(G-17047)
HANDLER CORPORATION
5169 W Woodmill Dr Ste 10 (19808-4015)
PHONE..................302 999-9200
Mark Handler, *Pr*
Paul Handler, *
Ruth Handler, *
EMP: 34 EST: 1975
SQ FT: 4,000
SALES (est): 7.53MM **Privately Held**
Web: www.handlerhomes.com
SIC: 1521 New construction, single-family houses

(G-17048)
HANDYMAN BILL
407 Cleveland Ave (19804-3020)
PHONE..................302 588-5887
Bill Frank, *Prin*
EMP: 5 EST: 2010
SALES (est): 44.81K **Privately Held**
SIC: 7299 Handyman service

(G-17049)
HANDYMAN MTTERS NRTHRN-DLAWARE
Also Called: Handyman Matters
4722 Mermaid Blvd (19808-1804)
PHONE..................302 540-8263
Keith Orr, *CEO*
EMP: 5 EST: 2015
SALES (est): 30.38K **Privately Held**
Web: www.acehandymanservices.com
SIC: 7299 Handyman service

(G-17050)
HANNAS PHRM SUP CO INC
2505 W 6th St (19805-2908)
PHONE..................302 571-8761
Mark Hanna, *Pr*
Matthew Hanna, *VP*
EMP: 13 EST: 1967
SQ FT: 7,600
SALES (est): 4.08MM **Privately Held**
Web: www.hannapharm.com
SIC: 5047 5122 Medical equipment and supplies; Pharmaceuticals

(G-17051)
HANSO HOME INC ✪
1007 N Orange St Fl 4401 (19801-1239)
PHONE..................760 437-2621
EMP: 7 EST: 2022
SALES (est): 107.82K **Privately Held**
SIC: 1521 Patio and deck construction and repair

(G-17052)
HANTHEJ HULIO
Also Called: Nail Expo
4011 Concord Pike Ste A (19803-1740)
PHONE..................302 478-3080
Hulio Hanthej, *Prin*

Wilmington - New Castle County (G-17053)   GEOGRAPHIC SECTION

EMP: 5 EST: 2006
SALES (est): 55.72K **Privately Held**
SIC: 7231 Manicurist, pedicurist

(G-17053)
HAPPILY ACTIVE LLC ✪
2055 Limestone Rd (19808-5536)
PHONE.....................307 317-7277
EMP: 5 EST: 2023
SALES (est): 220.07K **Privately Held**
SIC: 5999 7389 Miscellaneous retail stores, nec; Business Activities at Non-Commercial Site

(G-17054)
HARBORCHASE WILMINGTON LLC
2004 Shipley Rd (19803-5248)
PHONE.....................302 273-8630
Robert Greer, *Ex Dir*
EMP: 8 EST: 2016
SALES (est): 853.31K **Privately Held**
Web: www.harborchase.com
SIC: 8361 Aged home

(G-17055)
HARD HATTERS ROOFG & CNSTR LLC
1512 Lower Greenbriar Rd (19810-4440)
PHONE.....................302 766-3611
EMP: 7 EST: 2017
SALES (est): 205.43K **Privately Held**
Web: www.hardhattersroofing.com
SIC: 1761 Roofing contractor

(G-17056)
HARD HATTERS ROOFG CONSTRUCTI
2300 Inglewood Rd Apt B (19803-3061)
PHONE.....................302 507-4459
EMP: 5 EST: 2013
SALES (est): 69.68K **Privately Held**
Web: www.hardhattersroofing.com
SIC: 1761 Roofing contractor

(G-17057)
HARD SCIENCE INCUBATOR CORP
3411 Silverside Rd (19810-4812)
PHONE.....................302 752-1055
Michael Burychka, *Pr*
EMP: 5 EST: 2020
SALES (est): 22.47K **Privately Held**
SIC: 8733 Scientific research agency

(G-17058)
HARDWICK TACTICAL CORPORATION
251 Little Falls Dr (19808-1674)
PHONE.....................787 466-6728
EMP: 10 EST: 2019
SALES (est): 315.67K **Privately Held**
SIC: 7389 Business services, nec

(G-17059)
HARMONIOUS MIND LLC
5189 W Woodmill Dr Ste 30a (19808-4009)
PHONE.....................302 668-1059
Manisha Wadhwa, *Mgr*
EMP: 9 EST: 2005
SALES (est): 873.52K **Privately Held**
Web: www.harmoniousmind.com
SIC: 8011 Psychiatrist

(G-17060)
HARMONY TRUCKING INC
305 W Newport Pike (19804-3154)
PHONE.....................302 633-5600
EMP: 9 EST: 1995
SQ FT: 10,000
SALES (est): 1MM **Privately Held**
Web: www.harmonyconst.com

SIC: 4212 Light haulage and cartage, local

(G-17061)
HARRIET TUBMAN SAFE HOUSE INC
914 E 7th St (19801-4415)
P.O. Box 4551 (19807-4551)
PHONE.....................302 351-4434
Earl W Woodlen Junior, *Pr*
EMP: 7 EST: 2003
SQ FT: 1,200
SALES (est): 450.58K **Privately Held**
SIC: 7389 Bail bonding

(G-17062)
HARRIS BERGER LLC (PA)
1105 N Market St Ste 1100 (19801-1209)
PHONE.....................302 665-1140
EMP: 5 EST: 2009
SALES (est): 1.2MM **Privately Held**
Web: www.bergerharris.com
SIC: 8111 General practice law office

(G-17063)
HARRIS PROPERTY MANAGEMENT LLC
415 E 10th St Ofc 1c (19801-3603)
PHONE.....................302 588-8601
EMP: 10 EST: 2020
SALES (est): 200K **Privately Held**
SIC: 6531 Real estate agents and managers

(G-17064)
HARRY J LAWALL & SON INC
Also Called: Lawall Prosthetics & Orthotics
1822 Augustine Cut Off (19803-4405)
PHONE.....................302 429-7630
Ed Moran, *Brnch Mgr*
EMP: 2
SALES (corp-wide): 9.98MM **Privately Held**
Web: www.lawall.com
SIC: 3842 Limbs, artificial
PA: Harry J. Lawall & Son, Inc.
3000 Cabot Blvd W Ste 100
Langhorne PA 19047
215 338-6611

(G-17065)
HARRY MOORE PAINTING ETC
4514 Hendry Ave (19808-5606)
PHONE.....................302 803-1087
Harry Moore, *Prin*
EMP: 5 EST: 2016
SALES (est): 63.81K **Privately Held**
SIC: 1721 Painting and paper hanging

(G-17066)
HARRYS HEATING & COOLING
1 Lynbrook Rd (19804-2669)
PHONE.....................302 438-5853
Harry Marker, *Prin*
EMP: 6 EST: 2018
SALES (est): 202.3K **Privately Held**
Web: www.harryshvac.com
SIC: 1711 Warm air heating and air conditioning contractor

(G-17067)
HART HOME IMPROVEMENTS LLC
2418 Calf Run Dr (19808-4265)
PHONE.....................302 415-4764
EMP: 6 EST: 2019
SALES (est): 412.68K **Privately Held**
Web: hart-home-improvements-llc.business.site
SIC: 1521 General remodeling, single-family houses

(G-17068)
HARTING GRAPHICS LTD
305 Brandywine Blvd (19809-3241)
PHONE.....................302 762-6397
Theodore Harting, *Pr*
Helen Rolph, *Mgr*
EMP: 9 EST: 1979
SQ FT: 9,500
SALES (est): 571.39K **Privately Held**
SIC: 7336 3993 Silk screen design; Signs and advertising specialties

(G-17069)
HARTNETT PHYSICAL THERAPY
800 Woodlawn Ave (19805-2815)
PHONE.....................302 428-9420
EMP: 5 EST: 2017
SALES (est): 22.18K **Privately Held**
Web: www.hartnettpt.com
SIC: 8049 Physical therapist

(G-17070)
HARVEST MEDIA LLC
19c Trolley Sq (19806-3355)
PHONE.....................415 712-9702
EMP: 5 EST: 2018
SALES (est): 75.77K **Privately Held**
Web: www.harvest-mobile.com
SIC: 4899 Communication services, nec

(G-17071)
HARVEY ROAD AUTOMOTIVE INC
1004 W 25th St (19802-3312)
PHONE.....................302 654-7500
Joe Scanlon, *Pr*
EMP: 6 EST: 1988
SALES (est): 708.85K **Privately Held**
Web: www.harveyroadautomotive.com
SIC: 7538 General automotive repair shops

(G-17072)
HATCH CONSULTING
2100 Kentmere Pkwy (19806-2016)
PHONE.....................302 658-4380
Denison Hatch, *Owner*
EMP: 8 EST: 2010
SALES (est): 192.01K **Privately Held**
Web: www.hatch.com
SIC: 8748 Business consulting, nec

(G-17073)
HATHWORTH INC
913 N Market St Ste 200 (19801-3097)
PHONE.....................302 884-7616
EMP: 8 EST: 2017
SALES (est): 1.1MM **Privately Held**
SIC: 5031 Lumber, plywood, and millwork

(G-17074)
HATZEL AND BUEHLER INC (HQ)
3600 Silverside Rd (19810-5116)
P.O. Box 7499 (19803-0499)
PHONE.....................302 478-4200
William Goeller, *CEO*
Michael C Goeller, ✱
Gerard J Herr, ✱
Wes Howell Junior, *VP*
EMP: 44 EST: 1917
SQ FT: 10,000
SALES (est): 374.31MM
SALES (corp-wide): 362.45MM **Privately Held**
Web: www.hatzelandbuehler.com
SIC: 1731 General electrical contractor
PA: Construction Management Services, Inc.
3600 Silverside Rd
Wilmington DE 19810
302 478-4200

(G-17075)
HATZEL AND BUEHLER INC
1 Righter Pkwy Ste 110 (19803-1510)
P.O. Box 610 (19703-0610)
PHONE.....................302 798-5422
Philip Rybak, *VP*
EMP: 150
SALES (corp-wide): 362.45MM **Privately Held**
Web: www.hatzelandbuehler.com
SIC: 1731 General electrical contractor
HQ: Hatzel And Buehler, Inc.
3600 Silverside Rd Ste A
Wilmington DE 19810
302 478-4200

(G-17076)
HAUS OF LACQUER LLC (PA)
300 N Market St (19801-2530)
PHONE.....................302 690-0309
Natasha Redden, *Managing Member*
EMP: 35 EST: 2012
SQ FT: 1,800
SALES (est): 885.98K
SALES (corp-wide): 885.98K **Privately Held**
Web: www.thehausoflacquer.com
SIC: 7991 Spas

(G-17077)
HAWA AFRICAN HAIR BRAIDING
6 E 7th St (19801-3714)
PHONE.....................302 654-9456
Hawa Dieng, *Prin*
EMP: 5 EST: 2018
SALES (est): 111.92K **Privately Held**
Web: hawaafricanhairbraiding.business.site
SIC: 7231 Hairdressers

(G-17078)
HAWKINS & SONS INC
314 New Rd (19805-1914)
PHONE.....................302 426-9290
Edward Hawkins, *Brnch Mgr*
EMP: 7
SALES (corp-wide): 2.21MM **Privately Held**
Web: www.hawkinsandsons.com
SIC: 5722 7699 Electric household appliances, major; Household appliance repair services
PA: Hawkins & Sons, Inc
400 New Rd
Wilmington DE 19805
302 998-1010

(G-17079)
HAWKINS COUNSEL GROUP
521 N West St (19801-2139)
PHONE.....................302 660-0858
EMP: 6 EST: 2016
SALES (est): 112.07K **Privately Held**
Web: www.wilmingtondelawgroup.com
SIC: 8322 General counseling services

(G-17080)
HAWKSBILL SYSTEMS LLC
3411 Silverside Rd Bynardb (19810-4812)
PHONE.....................302 494-1678
Mike Barnes, *Managing Member*
EMP: 3 EST: 2018
SALES (est): 3.2MM **Privately Held**
SIC: 7372 7389 Application computer software; Business Activities at Non-Commercial Site

(G-17081)
HAYES SEWING MACHINE CO INC
4425 Concord Pike (19803-1489)

Wilmington - New Castle County (G-17110)

PHONE..................302 764-9033
Trevor D Hayes, *Pr*
Phyllis Mary Hayes, *Sec*
EMP: 8 **EST:** 1969
SQ FT: 5,000
SALES (est): 459.71K **Privately Held**
Web: www.trevhayes.com
SIC: 5722 7699 5949 Sewing machines; Gas appliance repair service; Sewing, needlework, and piece goods

(G-17082)
HB DUPONT PLAZA
422 Delaware Ave (19801-1508)
PHONE..................302 998-7271
EMP: 5 **EST:** 2017
SALES (est): 152.2K **Privately Held**
SIC: 2879 Agricultural chemicals, nec

(G-17083)
HB FITNESS CONCORD INC
Also Called: Retro Fitness
4737 Concord Pike (19803-1442)
PHONE..................302 478-9692
EMP: 12 **EST:** 2010
SALES (est): 72.4K **Privately Held**
Web: www.retrofitness.com
SIC: 7991 Physical fitness facilities

(G-17084)
HB FITNESS DELAWARE INC
Also Called: Retro Fitness
5810 Kirkwood Hwy Ste B (19808-4868)
PHONE..................302 384-7245
Bryant Aivalotis, *Prin*
EMP: 15 **EST:** 2008
SALES (est): 212.64K **Privately Held**
Web: www.retrofitness.com
SIC: 7991 Physical fitness facilities

(G-17085)
HBCU WEEK FOUNDATION INC
1022 Coleman St (19805-4825)
PHONE..................302 544-0799
Ashley Christopher, *CEO*
Brandon Purnsley, *CFO*
Clint Saunders, *COO*
EMP: 8 **EST:** 2020
SALES (est): 418.29K **Privately Held**
Web: www.hbcuweek.org
SIC: 6732 Trusts: educational, religious, etc.

(G-17086)
HC SALON HOLDINGS INC
Also Called: Hair Cuttery
3218 Kirkwood Hwy (19808-6130)
PHONE..................302 999-7724
Shelly Russell, *Brnch Mgr*
EMP: 9
SALES (corp-wide): 95.49MM **Privately Held**
Web: www.haircuttery.com
SIC: 7231 Unisex hair salons
PA: Hc Salon Holdings, Inc.
   1640 Boro Pl Fl 4
   Mc Lean VA 22102
   917 751-8869

(G-17087)
HC SALON HOLDINGS INC
Also Called: Hair Cuttery
5607 Concord Pike (19803-1428)
PHONE..................302 478-9978
EMP: 10
SALES (corp-wide): 95.49MM **Privately Held**
Web: www.haircuttery.com
SIC: 7231 Unisex hair salons
PA: Hc Salon Holdings, Inc.
   1640 Boro Pl Fl 4
   Mc Lean VA 22102
   917 751-8869

(G-17088)
HDAY SPA
1900 Newport Gap Pike (19808-6136)
PHONE..................302 482-1041
EMP: 5 **EST:** 2016
SALES (est): 42.04K **Privately Held**
SIC: 7991 Spas

(G-17089)
HEADLAND LABS LLC
427 N Tatnall St (19801-2230)
PHONE..................415 425-1997
Michael Daugherty, *Prin*
EMP: 5 **EST:** 2018
SALES (est): 80.02K **Privately Held**
SIC: 8734 Testing laboratories

(G-17090)
HEADSTREAM INC
5301 Limestone Rd Ste 204 (19808-1265)
PHONE..................302 356-0156
Prathapagirhi Aravind, *Pr*
EMP: 19 **EST:** 2006
SQ FT: 2,000
SALES (est): 2.14MM **Privately Held**
Web: www.hpe.io
SIC: 7379 Computer related consulting services

(G-17091)
HEADTOTOE MHEALTH INC
1007 N Orange St (19801-1239)
PHONE..................438 867-1908
Galia Sthwartz, *CEO*
EMP: 5
SALES (est): 253.13K **Privately Held**
SIC: 7371 Computer software development

(G-17092)
HEALEX SYSTEMS LTD
11 Middleton Dr (19808-4320)
PHONE..................302 235-5750
EMP: 16 **EST:** 1992
SALES (est): 644.74K **Privately Held**
SIC: 7371 Computer software development

(G-17093)
HEALING GODDESS INTERPRISES
1201 Philadelphia Pike Ste 2 (19809-2042)
PHONE..................301 751-0695
Vicky Primer, *Prin*
EMP: 6 **EST:** 2016
SALES (est): 56.9K **Privately Held**
Web: www.vickyprimer.com
SIC: 8322 Social worker

(G-17094)
HEALTH CARE CONSULTANTS INC
Also Called: New Behavorial Network
240 N James St Ste 111 (19804-3167)
PHONE..................302 892-9210
Linda Bagley, *Brnch Mgr*
EMP: 72
SIC: 8082 Visiting nurse service
PA: Health Care Consultants, Inc
   2 Pin Oak Ln Ste 250
   Cherry Hill NJ 08003

(G-17095)
HEALTH CARE CONSULTANTS INC
Also Called: New Behavioral Network
240 N James St Ste 209 (19804-3171)
PHONE..................302 883-9462
Janine Coleman, *Brnch Mgr*
EMP: 72
SIC: 8082 Visiting nurse service
PA: Health Care Consultants, Inc
   2 Pin Oak Ln Ste 250
   Cherry Hill NJ 08003

(G-17096)
HEALTH CARE PRACTICE MGT
1602 Newport Gap Pike (19808-6208)
P.O. Box 5110 (19808-0110)
PHONE..................302 633-5840
Cindy Groux, *Pr*
Robert Groux, *VP*
EMP: 20 **EST:** 1992
SALES (est): 2.17MM **Privately Held**
Web: www.hcpm.net
SIC: 8742 8721 7322 Hospital and health services consultant; Billing and bookkeeping service; Adjustment and collection services

(G-17097)
HEALTH SUPPORT SERVICES
732 E 11th St (19801-4118)
PHONE..................302 287-4952
Sandra Jackson, *Prin*
EMP: 6 **EST:** 2015
SALES (est): 74.47K **Privately Held**
SIC: 8099 Health and allied services, nec

(G-17098)
HEALTHSHIELD LLC
1601 Milltown Rd Ste 3 (19808-4047)
PHONE..................302 352-0517
EMP: 7 **EST:** 2013
SALES (est): 485.82K **Privately Held**
Web: www.hshield.com
SIC: 8621 Professional organizations

(G-17099)
HEALTHSOURCE OF WILMINGTON
1305 Kirkwood Hwy (19805-2121)
PHONE..................302 319-4623
EMP: 5 **EST:** 2013
SALES (est): 68.92K **Privately Held**
Web: www.healthsourceofwilmingtonsouth.com
SIC: 8041 Offices and clinics of chiropractors

(G-17100)
HEALTHY HOMES DE INC
3925 Kirkwood Hwy (19808-5109)
PHONE..................302 998-1001
Tom Walsh, *Pr*
EMP: 8 **EST:** 2007
SALES (est): 788.25K **Privately Held**
SIC: 3635 Household vacuum cleaners

(G-17101)
HEALTHYLONGEVITYCAFE INC
2055 Limestone Rd Ste 200c (19808-5536)
PHONE..................408 599-6369
Peter Sramek, *CEO*
EMP: 5 **EST:** 2021
SALES (est): 46.16K **Privately Held**
SIC: 7371 Computer software development and applications

(G-17102)
HEALY LONG & JEVIN INC
2000 Rodman Rd (19805-4135)
P.O. Box 30278 (19805-7278)
PHONE..................302 654-8039
John E Healy Iii, *CEO*
Michael A Jevin, *Pr*
John E Healy Iv, *Sec*
EMP: 10 **EST:** 2001
SQ FT: 7,000
SALES (est): 29.91K **Privately Held**
Web: www.healylongjevin.com
SIC: 1771 Exterior concrete stucco contractor
PA: Healy & Long Holdings, Inc.
   2000 Rodman Rd
   Wilmington DE 19805

(G-17103)
HEARST MEDIA SERVICES CONN LLC
1209 N Orange St (19801-1120)
PHONE..................203 330-6231
EMP: 50 **EST:** 2007
SALES (est): 2.02MM **Privately Held**
SIC: 2711 Newspapers, publishing and printing

(G-17104)
HEART IN GAME FOUNDATION INC
3535 Silverside Rd (19810-4955)
PHONE..................302 494-3133
Thomas Firestone, *Prin*
EMP: 5 **EST:** 2014
SALES (est): 38.73K **Privately Held**
SIC: 8641 Civic and social associations

(G-17105)
HEART START ER TRAINING INC
2724 Jacqueline Dr M33 (19810-2043)
PHONE..................302 420-1917
Clarence Pearsall Iii, *Prin*
EMP: 5 **EST:** 2010
SALES (est): 87.94K **Privately Held**
SIC: 8351 Head Start center, except in conjunction with school

(G-17106)
HEART VSCLAR CLINIC WILMINGTON
410 Foulk Rd Ste 101 (19803-3835)
PHONE..................302 518-6200
EMP: 12 **EST:** 2017
SALES (est): 241.86K **Privately Held**
Web: www.heartandvascularclinic.com
SIC: 8011 Cardiologist and cardio-vascular specialist

(G-17107)
HEARTFELT BOOKS PUBLISHING
1000 N West St Ste 1200 (19801-1058)
PHONE..................866 557-6522
Regina Lee, *CEO*
EMP: 5 **EST:** 2012
SALES (est): 230.29K **Privately Held**
Web: www.heartfeltbooks.com
SIC: 2731 Books, publishing and printing

(G-17108)
HEARTS INTERNATIONAL INC
222 Delaware Ave Fl 9 (19801-1621)
PHONE..................215 585-5597
EMP: 5 **EST:** 2014
SALES (est): 129.71K **Privately Held**
SIC: 8621 Professional organizations

(G-17109)
HEATED WEAR LLC
427 N Tatnall St Ste 16278 (19801)
PHONE..................347 510-7965
EMP: 8 **EST:** 2016
SALES (est): 288.13K **Privately Held**
Web: www.gerbing.com
SIC: 2252 2329 Socks; Hunting coats and vests, men's

(G-17110)
HEATHER L DEALY M D
1941 Limestone Rd Ste 200 (19808-5400)
PHONE..................302 998-2333
Heather L Dealy Md, *Owner*
EMP: 6 **EST:** 2018
SALES (est): 109.81K **Privately Held**
Web: www.eyeconsultantsde.com
SIC: 8011 Opthalmologist

Wilmington - New Castle County (G-17111)   GEOGRAPHIC SECTION

(G-17111)
HEAVEN & HEALTH MASSAGE T
8 S Dupont Rd (19805-1445)
PHONE..................302 999-9565
Helen Berryman, *Prin*
EMP: 5 EST: 2006
SALES (est): 132.77K **Privately Held**
SIC: 7299 Massage parlor

(G-17112)
HEAVENS TREASURES THRIFT AND
1423 N Grant Ave (19806-2437)
PHONE..................267 387-0030
EMP: 5 EST: 2017
SALES (est): 74.77K **Privately Held**
Web: www.impactthriftstores.org
SIC: 4225 General warehousing and storage

(G-17113)
HECKLER & FRABIZZIO PA
800 Delaware Ave Ste 200 (19801-1367)
P.O. Box 128 (19899-0128)
PHONE..................302 573-4800
George B Heckler Junior, *Pr*
EMP: 12 EST: 1983
SALES (est): 2.76MM **Privately Held**
Web: www.hfddel.com
SIC: 8111 General practice attorney, lawyer

(G-17114)
HEIMAN GOUGE & KAUFMAN LLP
800 N King St Ste 303 (19801-3549)
PHONE..................302 658-1800
Henry Heiman, *Pt*
Susan Kaufman, *Pt*
Donald Gouge, *Pt*
EMP: 5 EST: 2003
SALES (est): 428.29K **Privately Held**
SIC: 8111 General practice attorney, lawyer

(G-17115)
HEIMAN ABER GOLDLUST & BAKER
Also Called: Heiman, Henry A
800 N King St Ste 303 (19801-3549)
P.O. Box 1675 (19899-1675)
PHONE..................302 658-1800
Henry A Heiman, *Pt*
Gary Aber, *Pt*
Perry F Goldlust, *Pt*
Darrell Baker, *Pt*
EMP: 9 EST: 1980
SQ FT: 7,000
SALES (est): 281.67K **Privately Held**
SIC: 8111 General practice law office

(G-17116)
HELENA SCHROYER MD
Also Called: Bancroft Family Care
1010 N Bancroft Pkwy Ste L2 (19805-2690)
PHONE..................302 429-5870
Helena Schroyer, *Prin*
EMP: 10 EST: 2001
SALES (est): 216.77K **Privately Held**
Web: www.allakidzaam.com
SIC: 8011 General and family practice, physician/surgeon

(G-17117)
HELLENIC UNIV CLB WILMINGTON
1407 Foulk Rd Ste 100 (19803-2700)
PHONE..................302 479-8811
EMP: 7 EST: 2011
SALES (est): 84.51K **Privately Held**
Web: www.hucwilmington.org
SIC: 7997 Membership sports and recreation clubs

(G-17118)
HELMARK STEEL INC
813 S Market St (19801-5223)
P.O. Box 487 (19899-0487)
EMP: 150
Web: www.helmarksteel.com
SIC: 3441 Fabricated structural metal

(G-17119)
HELPINGHANDS
8 Colony Blvd Apt 325 (19802-1428)
PHONE..................302 290-1146
Joseph Frantone, *Prin*
EMP: 9 EST: 2018
SALES (est): 91.01K **Privately Held**
SIC: 8322 Individual and family services

(G-17120)
HENDRICKSON HOUSE MUSEUM
606 N Church St (19801-4421)
PHONE..................302 652-5629
EMP: 6 EST: 2019
SALES (est): 79.84K **Privately Held**
Web: www.oldswedes.org
SIC: 8412 Museum

(G-17121)
HENRIETTA JOHNSON MEDICAL
601 New Castle Ave (19801-5821)
PHONE..................302 761-4610
Ada Velez, *Mgr*
EMP: 20 EST: 2010
SALES (est): 242.36K **Privately Held**
Web: www.hjmc.org
SIC: 8011 Clinic, operated by physicians

(G-17122)
HENRY BOX BROWN LLC
412 N Monroe St (19801-2029)
PHONE..................917 749-3746
EMP: 15 EST: 2017
SALES (est): 200K **Privately Held**
SIC: 7922 Performing arts center production

(G-17123)
HENRY BROS AUTOBODY & PNT SP
Also Called: Henry Bros
2013 W Newport Pike (19804-3793)
PHONE..................302 994-4438
James J Henry Junior, *Pr*
James J Henry Senior, *Pt*
Robert J Henry Senior, *Pt*
EMP: 9 EST: 1955
SQ FT: 16,500
SALES (est): 285.91K **Privately Held**
Web: www.abraauto.com
SIC: 7532 Body shop, automotive

(G-17124)
HENRY YEE PLUMBING INC
300 Delaware Ave (19801-1607)
PHONE..................914 980-2188
EMP: 7 EST: 2018
SALES (est): 492.82K **Privately Held**
SIC: 1711 Plumbing contractors

(G-17125)
HENRYS CAR CARE INC
2207 Saint James Dr (19808-5218)
PHONE..................302 994-5766
Henry J Donato Junior, *Pr*
Garett Vallone, *VP*
EMP: 8 EST: 1946
SQ FT: 1,800
SALES (est): 850K **Privately Held**
Web: www.henryscarcare.com
SIC: 7538 General automotive repair shops

(G-17126)
HENTKOWSKI INC
Also Called: Honeywell Authorized Dealer
3420 Old Capitol Trl (19808-6199)
PHONE..................302 998-2257
Barbara Hentkowski-roberts, *Pr*
EMP: 17 EST: 1968
SQ FT: 10,500
SALES (est): 2.43MM **Privately Held**
Web: www.hentkowski.com
SIC: 1711 Warm air heating and air conditioning contractor

(G-17127)
HERBERT STUDIOS
Also Called: Advertsing Archtctural Photogr
219 N Market St (19801-2527)
PHONE..................302 229-7108
Jeff Herbert, *Pr*
EMP: 5 EST: 1987
SQ FT: 3,160
SALES (est): 307.09K **Privately Held**
Web: www.herbiz.net
SIC: 7335 Photographic studio, commercial

(G-17128)
HERCULES LLC (DH)
1313 N Market St Hercules Plz (19894-0001)
PHONE..................302 594-5000
Craig A Rogerson, *Pr*
Allen A Spizzo, *
◆ EMP: 41 EST: 1912
SQ FT: 679,000
SALES (est): 306.34MM
SALES (corp-wide): 2.19B **Publicly Held**
Web: www.hercules.com
SIC: 2869 2891 Olefins; Adhesives
HQ: Ashland Chemco Inc.
5475 Rings Rd Ste 500
Dublin OH 43017
859 815-3333

(G-17129)
HERDEG DUPONT DALLE PAZZE LLP
15 Center Meeting Rd (19807-1301)
PHONE..................302 655-6500
John A Herdeg, *Pt*
William B Dupont Junior, *Pt*
James P Dalle Pazze, *Pt*
EMP: 5 EST: 1986
SALES (est): 561.94K **Privately Held**
Web: www.dcr2.com
SIC: 8111 General practice attorney, lawyer

(G-17130)
HERITAGE MACHINE SHOP LLC
2 James Ct (19801-5250)
PHONE..................302 656-3313
Gary Allanson, *Managing Member*
EMP: 7 EST: 2005
SQ FT: 3,000
SALES (est): 757.38K **Privately Held**
Web: www.heritagemachineshop.com
SIC: 3599 Machine shop, jobbing and repair

(G-17131)
HERITAGE MEDICAL ASSOCIATES PA
2601 Annand Dr Ste 4 (19808-3719)
PHONE..................302 998-3334
EMP: 23 EST: 2007
SALES (est): 3.38MM **Privately Held**
Web: www.heritagemedical.com
SIC: 8011 General and family practice, physician/surgeon

(G-17132)
HERO FAMILY COLLECTION LLC ◆
1201 N Market St Ste 111-G25 (19801-1147)
PHONE..................833 732-3432
Jay Stewart, *CEO*
Jay Stewart, *Managing Member*
EMP: 5 EST: 2022
SALES (est): 203.58K **Privately Held**
SIC: 2731 Books, publishing and printing

(G-17133)
HERSTORY ENSEMBLE
111 W 13th St # A (19801-1104)
PHONE..................216 288-8759
Deborah Gilbert White, *Prin*
EMP: 5 EST: 2015
SALES (est): 68.39K **Privately Held**
Web: www.herstoryensemble.com
SIC: 7922 Theatrical producers and services

(G-17134)
HERTZ CORPORATION
Also Called: Hertz
100 S French St Ste D (19801-5016)
PHONE..................302 654-8312
John Moore, *Brnch Mgr*
EMP: 6
SALES (corp-wide): 9.37B **Publicly Held**
Web: www.hertz.co.uk
SIC: 7514 Rent-a-car service
HQ: The Hertz Corporation
8501 Williams Rd
Estero FL 33928
239 301-7000

(G-17135)
HES SIGN SERVICES INC
Also Called: Yesco Sign Ltg Southeastern PA
200 Hadco Rd (19804-1074)
PHONE..................302 257-5150
William Eyler, *Pr*
Michael Hewitt, *
EMP: 50 EST: 2012
SALES (est): 5.05MM **Privately Held**
Web: www.yesco.com
SIC: 3993 Electric signs

(G-17136)
HEYMAN ENERIO GATTUSO & HIRZEL
300 Delaware Ave (19801-1607)
PHONE..................302 472-7300
EMP: 10 EST: 2018
SALES (est): 2.48MM **Privately Held**
Web: www.hegh.law
SIC: 8111 General practice attorney, lawyer

(G-17137)
HF ADMINISTRATORS LTD
1201 N Orange St Ste 7004 (19801-1188)
PHONE..................302 884-6723
EMP: 5 EST: 2010
SALES (est): 110K **Privately Held**
SIC: 6282 Manager of mutual funds, contract or fee basis

(G-17138)
HI LINE AUTO DETAILING
1618 Newport Gap Pike (19808-6208)
PHONE..................302 420-5368
Colette Barbour, *Prin*
EMP: 6 EST: 2009
SALES (est): 72.09K **Privately Held**
SIC: 7542 Washing and polishing, automotive

(G-17139)
HIFU SERVICES INC
3411 Silverside Rd Ste 104 (19810-4812)
PHONE..................650 867-4972
Iggy Zhang, *CEO*
EMP: 9 EST: 2013
SALES (est): 400.3K **Privately Held**
Web: www.edap-tms.com
SIC: 8011 Offices and clinics of medical doctors

GEOGRAPHIC SECTION
Wilmington - New Castle County (G-17168)

(G-17140)
HIGH CONFECTIONARY COMPANY
251 Little Falls Dr (19808-1674)
PHONE....................213 807-6218
Jenna Goldring, *CEO*
EMP: 9 **EST:** 2021
SALES (est): 78.16K **Privately Held**
SIC: 3999

(G-17141)
HIGH POINT PREFERRED INSUR CO
Also Called: 21st Century Insurance
3 Beaver Valley Rd (19803-1124)
PHONE....................800 245-2425
EMP: 60
Web: www.plymouthrock.com
SIC: 6411 Insurance agents, nec
PA: High Point Preferred Insurance
  Company
  331 Newman Springs Rd 3
  Red Bank NJ 07701

(G-17142)
HIGH-TECH MACHINE COMPANY INC
Also Called: Htm Management
10 Lewis Cir (19804-1618)
PHONE....................302 636-0267
Neal Crosley, *Pr*
Don Piegalski, *VP*
EMP: 14 **EST:** 1993
SQ FT: 6,500
SALES (est): 2.46MM **Privately Held**
Web: www.hightechmachineinc.com
SIC: 3599 Machine shop, jobbing and repair

(G-17143)
HIGHLAND WEST CIVIC ASSOC
213 Whitekirk Dr (19808-1350)
PHONE....................302 415-5435
EMP: 5 **EST:** 2018
SALES (est): 64.1K **Privately Held**
Web: www.highlandwest.us
SIC: 8699 Membership organizations, nec

(G-17144)
HIGHMARKS INC (PA)
Also Called: Highmark Blue Cross Blue Sheld
800 Delaware Ave Ste 900 (19801-1368)
P.O. Box 1991 (19899-1991)
PHONE....................302 421-3000
Timothy J Constantine, *Pr*
William E Kirk Iii, *Sec*
Phillip A Carter, *RISK MANAGEMENT**
Dianne Coates, *
EMP: 370 **EST:** 1935
SQ FT: 30,000
SALES (est): 294.32MM
SALES (corp-wide): 294.32MM **Privately Held**
Web: www.bcbsde.com
SIC: 6321 Health insurance carriers

(G-17145)
HIGHMARKS INC
Also Called: Blue Cross
800 Delaware Ave (19809-1132)
P.O. Box 8868 (19899-8868)
PHONE....................302 421-3000
Tim Constantine, *Mgr*
EMP: 8
SALES (corp-wide): 294.32MM **Privately Held**
Web: www.bcbsde.com
SIC: 6324 6311 6331 6351 Dental insurance
; Life insurance; Fire, marine, and casualty insurance; Liability insurance
PA: Highmarks, Inc.
  800 Delaware Ave Ste 900
  Wilmington DE 19801
  302 421-3000

(G-17146)
HILL LUTH DAY CARE CENTER
1018 W 6th St (19805-3210)
PHONE....................302 656-3224
Jea Street, *Owner*
EMP: 9 **EST:** 2012
SALES (est): 104.75K **Privately Held**
Web: www.hilltoplnc.org
SIC: 8351 Child day care services

(G-17147)
HILLSIDE CENTER
Also Called: GENESIS HEALTH CARE
810 S Broom St (19805-4245)
PHONE....................302 652-1181
Kathleen Duca, *Admn*
EMP: 27 **EST:** 2009
SALES (est): 3.41MM **Privately Held**
SIC: 8322 8059 8051 8049 Rehabilitation services; Nursing home, except skilled and intermediate care facility; Skilled nursing care facilities; Physical therapist

(G-17148)
HILLTOP LTHRAN NGHBRHOOD CTR I
Also Called: EARLY CHILDHOOD ASSISTANCE PRO
1018 W 6th St (19805-3210)
PHONE....................302 656-3224
Jea Street, *Ex Dir*
Matthew Johnson, *Youth Services**
EMP: 50 **EST:** 1972
SQ FT: 2,500
SALES (est): 1.97MM **Privately Held**
Web: www.hilltoplnc.org
SIC: 8351 8661 Group day care center; Lutheran Church

(G-17149)
HILYARDS INC (PA)
Also Called: Hilyard's Business Solutions
1616 Newport Gap Pike (19808-6294)
PHONE....................302 995-2201
TOLL FREE: 800
Robert H Hilyard, *CEO*
Susan Hilyard, *
Gregory Altemus, *
EMP: 35 **EST:** 1959
SQ FT: 18,100
SALES (est): 12.7MM
SALES (corp-wide): 12.7MM **Privately Held**
Web: www.hilyards.com
SIC: 5044 Copying equipment

(G-17150)
HIMANI J PATEL DC
4837 Limestone Rd (19808-1902)
PHONE....................302 635-7421
Himani Patel, *Prin*
EMP: 6 **EST:** 2017
SALES (est): 102.16K **Privately Held**
SIC: 8041 Offices and clinics of chiropractors

(G-17151)
HINES SHEKELIA
1072 Justison St (19801-5162)
PHONE....................302 575-8255
Shekelia Hines, *Prin*
EMP: 6 **EST:** 2017
SALES (est): 22.18K **Privately Held**
SIC: 8049 Offices of health practitioner

(G-17152)
HINKLE HUSBANDS LLC
418 Geddes St (19805-3717)
PHONE....................302 827-8202
EMP: 8 **EST:** 2013
SALES (est): 166.51K **Privately Held**
SIC: 1721 Painting and paper hanging

(G-17153)
HINT AMERICA INC
112 S French St Ste 105 (19801-5035)
PHONE....................646 845-1895
Roman Taranov, *CEO*
EMP: 16
SALES (est): 1.08MM **Privately Held**
SIC: 7371 Computer software development

(G-17154)
HIROTEC INC
1209 N Orange St (19801-1120)
PHONE....................248 836-5100
Ademola Adesina, *CEO*
EMP: 6 **EST:** 2021
SALES (est): 579.59K **Privately Held**
Web: www.hirotecamerica.com
SIC: 3674 Solar cells

(G-17155)
HISTORICAL SOCIETY OF DELAWARE (PA)
505 N Market St (19801-3091)
PHONE....................302 655-7161
Daniel F Wolcott Junior, *Treas*
Joan Reynolds Hoge, *
Richard Poole, *
◆ **EMP:** 26 **EST:** 1864
SALES (est): 2.63MM
SALES (corp-wide): 2.63MM **Privately Held**
Web: www.dehistory.org
SIC: 8412 8231 5331 Historical society; Public library; Variety stores

(G-17156)
HK PAPER
2706 Alexander Dr (19810-1104)
PHONE....................302 475-3699
Robert Zembower, *Prin*
EMP: 5 **EST:** 2017
SALES (est): 101.83K **Privately Held**
Web: www.hkpaper.us
SIC: 5085 Industrial supplies

(G-17157)
HLH CONSTRUCTION MGT SVCS INC
2000 Rodman Rd (19805-4135)
P.O. Box 30288 (19805-7288)
PHONE....................302 654-7508
John E Healy Iii, *Prin*
EMP: 10 **EST:** 2008
SALES (est): 421.29K **Privately Held**
SIC: 8741 Management services

(G-17158)
HMA CONCRETE LLC
Also Called: Heritage Concrete
270 Presidential Dr # 200 (19807-3302)
PHONE....................302 777-1235
Derek S Vanderslice, *Managing Member*
EMP: 17 **EST:** 2012
SALES (est): 3.57MM **Privately Held**
Web: www.heritageconcrete.net
SIC: 3273 Ready-mixed concrete

(G-17159)
HOARD INCORPORATED
251 Little Falls Dr (19808-1674)
PHONE....................980 333-1703
Jason Davis, *CEO*
EMP: 15 **EST:** 2017
SALES (est): 532.06K **Privately Held**
SIC: 7372 Application computer software

(G-17160)
HOBE SOUND LLC
2 Sunset Ct (19810-4137)
PHONE....................302 529-7096
David Mukoda, *Mgr*
EMP: 9 **EST:** 2015
SALES (est): 102.54K **Privately Held**
SIC: 1731 Sound equipment specialization

(G-17161)
HOCHMAN C MICHAEL ATTY
1201 N Orange St Ste 400 (19801-1167)
PHONE....................302 656-8162
C Hochman Attorney, *Prin*
EMP: 5 **EST:** 2014
SALES (est): 120K **Privately Held**
SIC: 8111 General practice attorney, lawyer

(G-17162)
HOCKESSIN DAY SPA
1900 Newport Gap Pike (19808-6136)
PHONE....................302 234-7573
Jean Boland, *Prin*
EMP: 6 **EST:** 2006
SALES (est): 198.58K **Privately Held**
SIC: 7991 7231 Spas; Beauty shops

(G-17163)
HOERNER INC
602 Elizabeth Ave (19809-2666)
PHONE....................302 762-4406
Kristopher Hoerner, *Owner*
EMP: 10 **EST:** 2013
SALES (est): 502.1K **Privately Held**
SIC: 0781 Landscape counseling and planning

(G-17164)
HOFA GALLERY USA INC
Also Called: Hofa Gllery - Hse Fine Art - L
2810 N Church St (19802-4447)
PHONE....................213 270-1972
EMP: 6 **EST:** 2019
SALES (est): 52.45K **Privately Held**
Web: www.thehouseoffineart.com
SIC: 8412 Art gallery

(G-17165)
HOLIDAY INN
700 N King St (19801-3504)
PHONE....................302 655-0400
EMP: 12 **EST:** 2019
SALES (est): 32.59K **Privately Held**
Web: www.holidayinn.com
SIC: 7011 Hotels and motels

(G-17166)
HOLLAND MULCH INC
135 Hay Rd (19809-3508)
PHONE....................302 765-3100
EMP: 10 **EST:** 1996
SQ FT: 1,200
SALES (est): 2.04MM **Privately Held**
Web: www.hollandmulch.com
SIC: 4953 Recycling, waste materials

(G-17167)
HOLLAND PROPERTIES
1515 Spring Ln (19809-2240)
PHONE....................201 965-9272
Shane Hillam, *Prin*
EMP: 8 **EST:** 2014
SALES (est): 455.77K **Privately Held**
SIC: 6512 Nonresidential building operators

(G-17168)
HOLLY JORDYN ANN
5201 W Woodmill Dr (19808-4068)
PHONE....................443 945-0615
Jordyn A Holly Lcsw, *Owner*

Wilmington - New Castle County (G-17169)   GEOGRAPHIC SECTION

EMP: 7 EST: 2019
SALES (est): 38.95K **Privately Held**
Web: www.journeys-counseling.com
SIC: 8322 Social worker

(G-17169)
HOLLY OAK TOWING AND SERVICE
Also Called: Alycia
6521 Governor Printz Blvd (19809-2037)
PHONE..................................302 792-1500
Craig Mummert, *Pr*
EMP: 8 EST: 1966
SQ FT: 2,000
SALES (est): 955.7K **Privately Held**
Web: www.hollyoaktowing.com
SIC: 7538 General automotive repair shops

(G-17170)
HOLLYWELL LOGISTICS LLC
Also Called: Railway Logistics
802 Nw St Ste 105 (19801-1526)
PHONE..................................267 901-4272
Bob Kurban, *
EMP: 10 EST: 2013
SALES (est): 466.44K **Privately Held**
SIC: 4731 Freight forwarding

(G-17171)
HOLLYWOOD GRILL RESTAURANT (PA)
Also Called: Homewood Suites
3513 Concord Pike Ste 3300 (19803-5037)
PHONE..................................302 655-1348
Phil Haslett, *Stockholder*
EMP: 70 EST: 1955
SALES (est): 8.88MM
SALES (corp-wide): 8.88MM **Privately Held**
Web: www.hollywoodgrilldelaware.com
SIC: 7011 5812 5813 6531 Hotels and motels; Restaurant, family; independent; Drinking places; Real estate agents and managers

(G-17172)
HOLLYWOOD GRILL RESTAURANT
Also Called: Homewood Suites
350 Rocky Run Pkwy (19803-1515)
PHONE..................................302 479-2000
Denis Dowse, *Mgr*
EMP: 77
SALES (corp-wide): 8.88MM **Privately Held**
Web: homewoodsuites3.hilton.com
SIC: 7011 Hotels and motels
PA: Hollywood Grill Restaurant Inc
   3513 Concord Pike # 3300
   Wilmington DE 19803
   302 655-1348

(G-17173)
HOLLYWOOD NAILS
3100 Naamans Rd Ste 7 (19810-2100)
PHONE..................................302 477-4849
Eric Dao, *Owner*
EMP: 5 EST: 2007
SALES (est): 30.16K **Privately Held**
SIC: 7231 Manicurist, pedicurist

(G-17174)
HOLLYWOOD NAILS & SPA
4101 N Market St (19802-2221)
PHONE..................................302 762-1800
Vinh Ngo, *Pr*
EMP: 5 EST: 2010
SALES (est): 51.03K **Privately Held**
SIC: 7231 Manicurist, pedicurist

(G-17175)
HOLLYWOOD TANS
3100 Naamans Rd Ste 34 (19810-2100)
PHONE..................................302 478-8267
Renee Milner, *Owner*
EMP: 7 EST: 2000
SALES (est): 165.71K **Privately Held**
Web: www.hollywoodtans.com
SIC: 7299 Tanning salon

(G-17176)
HOME COURSE CREATORS LLC
206 Steeplechase Cir (19808-1977)
PHONE..................................302 419-6305
EMP: 5 EST: 2017
SALES (est): 116.55K **Privately Held**
SIC: 7992 Public golf courses

(G-17177)
HOME FINDERS REAL ESTATE CO
Also Called: Home Finders Real Estate
31 Trolley Sq Ste C (19806)
PHONE..................................302 655-8091
EMP: 5 EST: 1986
SALES (est): 356.47K **Privately Held**
Web: www.exclusivebuyer.com
SIC: 6531 Real estate agent, residential

(G-17178)
HOME FOR AGED WMN-MNQUADALE HM
Also Called: GILPIN HALL
1101 Gilpin Ave (19806-3214)
PHONE..................................302 654-1810
Linda Schwind, *Ex Dir*
Harvey Smith, *
EMP: 170 EST: 1824
SQ FT: 90,000
SALES (est): 12.11MM **Privately Held**
Web: www.gilpinhall.org
SIC: 8361 8322 8051 Aged home; Individual and family services; Skilled nursing care facilities

(G-17179)
HOME HEALTH HEARTFEL
5179 W Woodmill Dr (19808-4067)
PHONE..................................302 660-2686
Michelle Fiore, *Pr*
EMP: 9 EST: 2015
SALES (est): 232.28K **Privately Held**
SIC: 8082 Home health care services

(G-17180)
HOME HEALTH SERVICES BY TLC
287 Christiana Ave Ste 24 (19801-5445)
PHONE..................................302 322-5510
Ruel G Harriott, *Pr*
Louise Harriott, *VP*
EMP: 10 EST: 1997
SALES (est): 444.19K **Privately Held**
SIC: 8082 Home health care services

(G-17181)
HOME INTEGRATED
325 Robinson Ln (19805-4690)
PHONE..................................302 656-1624
EMP: 6 EST: 2017
SALES (est): 482.95K **Privately Held**
Web: www.ihomellc.com
SIC: 1521 Single-family housing construction

(G-17182)
HOME OF DIVINE PROVIDENCE INC
Also Called: Bayard House
300 Bayard Ave (19805-3345)
PHONE..................................302 654-1184
Shavenne Hines, *Dir*
EMP: 6 EST: 1979
SALES (est): 298.09K **Privately Held**
Web: www.ccwilm.org
SIC: 8069 Maternity hospital

(G-17183)
HOME OF MERCIFUL REST SOCIETY
Also Called: KENTMERE NURSING CARE CENTER
1900 Lovering Ave (19806-2123)
PHONE..................................302 652-3311
Eileen Mahler, *Ex Dir*
Mark Meister, *
EMP: 120 EST: 1901
SALES (est): 13.85MM **Privately Held**
Web: www.kentmererehab.com
SIC: 8051 8052 Convalescent home with continuous nursing care; Intermediate care facilities

(G-17184)
HOME SECURITY WILMINGTON
709 N Madison St (19801-1413)
PHONE..................................302 231-1142
Mandy Heffernan, *Mgr*
EMP: 5 EST: 2014
SALES (est): 38.17K **Privately Held**
SIC: 7381 Guard services

(G-17185)
HOME SERVICES LLC
3410 Old Capitol Trl (19808-6152)
PHONE..................................302 510-4580
Wayne Salvadori, *Owner*
EMP: 6 EST: 2015
SALES (est): 329.54K **Privately Held**
Web: www.homeservicesde.com
SIC: 1521 General remodeling, single-family houses

(G-17186)
HOMELAND SEC VERIFICATION LLC
Also Called: I9 Directcom
4001 Kennett Pike (19807-2315)
PHONE..................................888 791-4614
EMP: 5 EST: 2008
SALES (est): 296.37K **Privately Held**
SIC: 7375 Information retrieval services

(G-17187)
HOMER FOUNDATION
501 Silverside Rd (19809-1374)
PHONE..................................800 839-1754
EMP: 6 EST: 2010
SALES (est): 134.22K **Privately Held**
Web: www.homerfoundation.org
SIC: 8699 Charitable organization

(G-17188)
HOMERIES LLC
919 N Market St Ste 950 (19801-3023)
PHONE..................................570 575-8008
EMP: 18
SALES (est): 595.93K **Privately Held**
SIC: 7379 Online services technology consultants

(G-17189)
HOMES FOR LIFE FOUNDATION
1106 Berkeley Rd (19807-2816)
PHONE..................................302 571-1217
Lanny Edelsohn, *Pr*
EMP: 8 EST: 1999
SALES (est): 176.12K **Privately Held**
Web: www.homesforlife.org
SIC: 8399 Fund raising organization, non-fee basis

(G-17190)
HOMESTAR REMODELING LLC
405 Silverside Rd Ste 250 (19809-1773)
PHONE..................................302 528-5898
EMP: 37 EST: 2015
SALES (est): 5.52MM **Privately Held**
Web: www.homestarremodeling.com
SIC: 1521 General remodeling, single-family houses

(G-17191)
HOMEWOOD STES BY HLTON WLMNGTO
Also Called: Homewood Suites
820 Justison St (19801-5152)
PHONE..................................302 565-2100
Loren Forland, *Genl Mgr*
EMP: 30 EST: 2016
SALES (est): 986.86K **Privately Held**
Web: homewoodsuites3.hilton.com
SIC: 7011 Hotels and motels

(G-17192)
HOMSEY ARCHITECTS INC
2003 N Scott St (19806-2191)
PHONE..................................302 656-4491
Eldon Homsey, *Pr*
Charles Ryan, *VP*
EMP: 10 EST: 1935
SQ FT: 1,300
SALES (est): 993.09K **Privately Held**
Web: www.homsey.com
SIC: 8712 Architectural engineering

(G-17193)
HONESTLY SERVICE LLC
1201 N Market St Ste 111 (19801-1156)
PHONE..................................302 844-2214
Angela Scerni, *CEO*
Angela Scerni, *Pr*
EMP: 12 EST: 2019
SALES (est): 512.52K **Privately Held**
SIC: 4215 Package delivery, vehicular

(G-17194)
HONEYWELL SAFETY PDTS USA INC (HQ)
2711 Centerville Rd Ste 400 (19808-1660)
PHONE..................................302 636-5401
David M Cote, *CEO*
Tim Mahoney, *Pr*
Roger Fradin, *Pr*
Terrence Hahn, *Chief Executive Officer Transport Systems*
Andreas Kramvis, *FOR PERFORMANCE MATERIALS Technology*
▼ EMP: 26 EST: 2002
SALES (est): 710.5MM
SALES (corp-wide): 35.47B **Publicly Held**
Web: www.honeywell.com
SIC: 5099 Lifesaving and survival equipment (non-medical)
PA: Honeywell International Inc.
   855 S Mint St
   Charlotte NC 28202
   704 627-6200

(G-17195)
HOOVER COMPUTER SERVICES INC
4611 Bedford Blvd (19803-3901)
PHONE..................................302 529-7050
John Hoover, *Pr*
Susan Hoover, *VP*
EMP: 6 EST: 1984
SALES (est): 504.87K **Privately Held**
Web: www.hoovercs.com
SIC: 7371 7379 5045 Custom computer programming services; Computer related consulting services; Computer peripheral equipment

(G-17196)
HOPE HANKS INC
1706 Pennrock Rd (19809-1368)
PHONE..................................302 562-9309
Anne Mathay, *Prin*
EMP: 7 EST: 2015

GEOGRAPHIC SECTION

Wilmington - New Castle County (G-17224)

SALES (est): 85.77K **Privately Held**
SIC: 8322 General counseling services

(G-17197)
HOPE HOUSE DAYCARE
2814 W 2nd St (19805-1807)
PHONE..................................302 407-3404
Eden Coleman, *Owner*
EMP: 8 EST: 2014
SALES (est): 220.07K **Privately Held**
Web:
www.hopehouseknowledgecenter.org
SIC: 8351 7032 Preschool center; Summer camp, except day and sports instructional

(G-17198)
HOPE PRESBYTERIAN CHURCH
Also Called: Faith Day Care and Preschool
720 Marsh Rd (19803-4334)
PHONE..................................302 764-8615
James O Brown Junior, *Pastor*
Reverend James O Brown Junior, *Pastor*
Nancy Rowels, *Treas*
Pauline Jennings, *Sec*
Cindy Naylor, *Sec*
EMP: 10 EST: 1936
SALES (est): 436.18K **Privately Held**
Web: www.faithwilmington.com
SIC: 8661 8351 Presbyterian Church; Child day care services

(G-17199)
HOPE REIGNS LLC
1201 N Market St Ste 111 (19801-1156)
PHONE..................................302 406-0827
EMP: 10 EST: 2014
SALES (est): 659.54K **Privately Held**
SIC: 1521 Single-family home remodeling, additions, and repairs

(G-17200)
HOPES CARAMELS INC
36 Carpenter Plz (19810-2049)
PHONE..................................302 290-7506
Hope Shuert, *Pr*
EMP: 2 EST: 2020
SALES (est): 201K **Privately Held**
Web: www.hopescaramels.com
SIC: 2064 Candy and other confectionery products

(G-17201)
HOPEWELL PHARMA VENTURES INC
1201 N Orange St Ste 717 (19801-1186)
PHONE..................................203 273-1350
Jonathan Embleton, *CEO*
EMP: 3 EST: 2021
SALES (est): 500K **Privately Held**
Web: www.hpharmaventures.com
SIC: 2834 Pharmaceutical preparations

(G-17202)
HOPIN US INC
2810 N Church St (19802-4447)
PHONE..................................250 896-8450
Johnny Boufarhat, *CEO*
EMP: 22 EST: 2020
SALES (est): 4.51MM
SALES (corp-wide): 18.51MM **Privately Held**
Web: mp.hopin.com
SIC: 7372 Application computer software
PA: Hopin Ltd
C/O Corporation Service Company (Uk) Limited
London E14 5
756 621-0326

(G-17203)
HOPKINS AND ASSOCIATES LLC
5143 W Woodmill Dr (19808-4067)
PHONE..................................302 660-8476
EMP: 5 EST: 2015
SALES (est): 243.13K **Privately Held**
Web: www.marinerwealthadvisors.com
SIC: 7291 Tax return preparation services

(G-17204)
HORIZON AERONAUTICS INC
300 Delaware Ave Ste 300 (19801-1607)
PHONE..................................409 504-2645
Thomas Wright, *CEO*
EMP: 4 EST: 2016
SALES (est): 154.26K **Privately Held**
SIC: 2752 Schedules, transportation: lithographed

(G-17205)
HORIZON HOUSE DELAWARE
911 N Franklin St (19806-4529)
PHONE..................................302 577-3220
Scott Davis, *Mgr*
EMP: 7 EST: 2014
SALES (est): 32.92K **Privately Held**
SIC: 8322 Individual and family services

(G-17206)
HORIZON HOUSE OF DELAWARE INC
1902 Maryland Ave (19805-4605)
PHONE..................................302 658-2392
Wayne Chiodo, *Pr*
EMP: 29 EST: 1987
SQ FT: 5,000
SALES (est): 485.26K **Privately Held**
Web: www.hhinc.org
SIC: 8322 Social services for the handicapped

(G-17207)
HORIZON INTL HOLDINGS LLC
251 Little Falls Dr (19808-1674)
PHONE..................................302 636-5401
EMP: 185 EST: 2015
SALES (est): 8.95MM
SALES (corp-wide): 8.02B **Privately Held**
SIC: 3714 Trailer hitches, motor vehicle
HQ: Horizon Global Americas Inc.
47912 Halyard Dr Ste 100
Plymouth MI 48170

(G-17208)
HORIZON RENDERING CO INC
5802 Stone Pine Rd (19808-1014)
PHONE..................................302 239-4950
EMP: 2
SALES (est): 96.12K **Privately Held**
SIC: 2077 Tallow rendering, inedible

(G-17209)
HORIZON SERVICES INC (PA)
320 Century Blvd (19808-6270)
PHONE..................................302 762-1200
David Geiger, *Pr*
EMP: 187 EST: 1997
SQ FT: 8,000
SALES (est): 174.62MM **Privately Held**
Web: www.horizonservices.com
SIC: 1711 Plumbing contractors

(G-17210)
HORIZONS FAMILY PRACTICE PA
Also Called: Julio Navarro Md, Faafp
3105 Limestone Rd Ste 301 (19808-2156)
PHONE..................................302 918-6300
Julio Navarro, *Prin*
EMP: 14 EST: 2008
SALES (est): 1.92MM **Privately Held**

SIC: 8011 General and family practice, physician/surgeon

(G-17211)
HORNBERGER MANAGEMENT COMPANY (PA)
1 Commerce Center Fl 7 (19801)
PHONE..................................302 573-2541
Frederick Hornberger Cpc, *Pr*
EMP: 6 EST: 1982
SQ FT: 1,000
SALES (est): 953.67K **Privately Held**
Web: www.hornbergerusa.com
SIC: 7361 Executive placement

(G-17212)
HORNING BROS CUSTOM PAINTING
2408 Lanside Dr (19810-4511)
P.O. Box 4534 (19807-4534)
PHONE..................................302 384-7675
Jacob Horning, *Prin*
EMP: 5 EST: 2016
SALES (est): 51.62K **Privately Held**
SIC: 1721 Painting and paper hanging

(G-17213)
HORTY & HORTY PA (PA)
Also Called: Horty
503 Carr Rd Ste 120 (19809-2863)
PHONE..................................302 652-4194
Douglas Philips, *Pr*
EMP: 27 EST: 1970
SQ FT: 15,000
SALES (est): 2.4MM
SALES (corp-wide): 2.4MM **Privately Held**
Web: www.horty.com
SIC: 8721 Certified public accountant

(G-17214)
HOSMANE CARDIOLOGY
5515 Kirkwood Hwy (19808-5001)
PHONE..................................302 588-1646
EMP: 9 EST: 2019
SALES (est): 911.09K **Privately Held**
Web: www.hosmanecardiology.com
SIC: 8011 Cardiologist and cardio-vascular specialist

(G-17215)
HOSTGPO INC
108 W 13th St (19801-1145)
PHONE..................................424 422-0486
Jeffrey Iloulian, *CEO*
Heather Bulloch, *Contrlr*
EMP: 18 EST: 2019
SALES (est): 523.21K **Privately Held**
SIC: 8611 Trade associations

(G-17216)
HOUSE OF WRIGHT MORTUARY (PA)
208 E 35th St (19802-2812)
P.O. Box 447 (19899-0447)
PHONE..................................302 762-8448
Robert O Wright, *Pr*
Justin A Wribht, *VP*
Robert O Wright Ii, *Treas*
Justin A Wright, *VP*
EMP: 9 EST: 1988
SALES (est): 2.05MM **Privately Held**
Web: www.wrightmortuary.com
SIC: 7261 Funeral home

(G-17217)
HOUSEVENTURE INC ✪
251 Little Falls Dr (19808-1674)
PHONE..................................786 481-7390
Mike Chang, *CEO*
Adrian Delgado, *Pr*
EMP: 2 EST: 2023
SALES (est): 87.4K **Privately Held**

SIC: 7372 Application computer software

(G-17218)
HOUSING ALLIANCE DELAWARE INC
100 W 10th St Ste 611 (19801-6604)
PHONE..................................302 654-0126
Sara Weimer, *VP*
Jim Peffley, *Ch Bd*
Christina Showalter, *Ex Dir*
EMP: 11 EST: 2003
SALES (est): 1.3MM **Privately Held**
Web: www.hpcdelaware.org
SIC: 8322 Social service center

(G-17219)
HOWARD W ZUCKER D D S P A
205 Hoyer Ct (19803-2360)
PHONE..................................302 475-8174
Howard Zucker, *Prin*
EMP: 10 EST: 2010
SALES (est): 190K **Privately Held**
SIC: 8021 Offices and clinics of dentists

(G-17220)
HOWMEDICA OSTEONICS CORP
Also Called: Stryker Chiropractic
2118 Kirkwood Hwy Ste A (19805-4933)
PHONE..................................302 655-3239
Robert Stryker, *Brnch Mgr*
EMP: 4
SALES (corp-wide): 18.45B **Publicly Held**
SIC: 3842 Surgical appliances and supplies
HQ: Howmedica Osteonics Corp.
325 Corporate Dr
Mahwah NJ 07430
201 831-5000

(G-17221)
HQ GLOBAL WORKPLACES INC
1000 N West St Ste 1200 (19801-1058)
PHONE..................................302 295-4800
EMP: 5
SALES (corp-wide): 3.31B **Privately Held**
Web: www.hq.com
SIC: 7389 Office facilities and secretarial service rental
HQ: Hq Global Workplaces, Inc.
15305 Dallas Pkwy Ste 400
Addison TX 75001
972 361-8100

(G-17222)
HS CAPITAL LLC
300 Delaware Ave Ste 1370 (19801-1658)
PHONE..................................302 317-3614
EMP: 5 EST: 2016
SALES (est): 463.51K **Privately Held**
SIC: 6799 Investors, nec

(G-17223)
HS CAPITAL LLC
Also Called: Bay Area Market Place
300 Delaware Ave Ste 1370 (19801-1658)
PHONE..................................302 598-2961
Paul Stortini, *Managing Member*
EMP: 5 EST: 2016
SALES (est): 909.01K **Privately Held**
SIC: 5411 4731 Cooperative food stores; Agents, shipping

(G-17224)
HSBC BANK USA (DH)
Also Called: Hsbc Bank
300 Delaware Ave Ste 1400 (19801-1650)
PHONE..................................302 778-0169
Irene Dorner, *Pr*
Martin J G Glynn, *Prin*
Vincent J Mancuso, *Sr VP*
◆ EMP: 1079 EST: 1850
SALES (est): 843.96MM

Wilmington - New Castle County (G-17225)

GEOGRAPHIC SECTION

SALES (corp-wide): 93.79B **Privately Held**
Web: us.hsbc.com
SIC: **6021** National commercial banks
HQ: Hsbc Usa, Inc.
452 5th Ave Frnt 1
New York NY 10018
212 525-5000

(G-17225)
HSBC NORTH AMERICA INC
1105 N Market St Fl 1 (19801-1237)
PHONE...................302 652-4673
Louis Clay, *Mgr*
EMP: 10
SALES (corp-wide): 93.79B **Privately Held**
Web: www.hsbc.com
SIC: **6029** Commercial banks, nec
HQ: Hsbc North America Inc.
1 Hsbc Ctr
Buffalo NY 14203
716 841-2424

(G-17226)
HUANG FAMILY FOUNDATION
501 Silverside Rd Ste 123 (19809-1377)
PHONE...................800 839-1754
EMP: 6 EST: 2010
SALES (est): 91.36K **Privately Held**
SIC: **8699** Charitable organization

(G-17227)
HUANG LAW LLC
3513 Concord Pike Ste 3100 (19803-5037)
PHONE...................302 248-5138
Xiaojuan Carrie Huang Esq, *Prin*
EMP: 6 EST: 2011
SALES (est): 173.21K **Privately Held**
Web: www.xhlegal.com
SIC: **8111** General practice law office

(G-17228)
HUBGETS INC
4250 Lancaster Pike Ste 120 (19805-1520)
PHONE...................239 206-2995
Bogdan Carstoiu, *CEO*
EMP: 5 EST: 2014
SALES (est): 257.97K **Privately Held**
Web: www.hubgets.com
SIC: **7371** Computer software development

(G-17229)
HUBIOID INC
1000 N West St Ste 1200 (19801-1058)
PHONE...................312 912-1515
Tural Babayev, *CEO*
EMP: 12 EST: 2021
SALES (est): 406.37K **Privately Held**
SIC: **7371** Computer software development and applications

(G-17230)
HUMAN RESOURCES
1626 N Union St (19806-2540)
PHONE...................302 573-3126
S Donovan, *Religious Leader*
EMP: 9 EST: 2015
SALES (est): 104.82K **Privately Held**
SIC: **8742** Business planning and organizing services

(G-17231)
HUMANE ANIMAL PARTNERS INC
Also Called: HUMANE ANIMAL PARTNERS
701 A St (19801-5231)
PHONE...................302 571-0111
Kevin Usilton, *Ex Dir*
Robert Kalik, *Treas*
Debra Grandizio, *VP*
Calvin Stewart, *Pr*
Patricia Magee, *Sec*
EMP: 24 EST: 1957
SQ FT: 3,000
SALES (est): 2.73MM **Privately Held**
Web: www.humaneanimalpartners.org
SIC: **8699** Animal humane society

(G-17232)
HUMPHREY JONES SHERRY H PHD
3214 Charing Cross (19808-4369)
PHONE...................302 239-1076
Sherry Jones, *Prin*
EMP: 7 EST: 2012
SALES (est): 49.5K **Privately Held**
SIC: **8322** Social worker

(G-17233)
HUNT VICMEAD CLUB
Also Called: Bidermann Golf Course
601 Adams Dam Rd (19807-1410)
PHONE...................302 655-3336
Christopher Patterson, *Brnch Mgr*
EMP: 20
SALES (corp-wide): 5.92MM **Privately Held**
Web: www.vicmead.com
SIC: **7997** Golf club, membership
PA: Hunt Vicmead Club
903 Owls Nest Rd
Wilmington DE 19807
302 655-9601

(G-17234)
HUNT VICMEAD CLUB (PA)
Also Called: BIDERMAN GOLF CLUB
903 Owls Nest Rd (19807-1613)
P.O. Box 3501 (19807-0501)
PHONE...................302 655-9601
Christopher Patterson, *Ch*
Rodney Scott, *
Richard Cairns, *
EMP: 25 EST: 1924
SALES (est): 5.92MM
SALES (corp-wide): 5.92MM **Privately Held**
Web: www.vicmead.com
SIC: **7997** Golf club, membership

(G-17235)
HUNTE CORPORATE ENTERPRISE LLC (PA)
Also Called: Hce
1201 N Orange St Ste 7377 (19801-1283)
PHONE...................212 710-1341
EMP: 9 EST: 2004
SALES (est): 23.85MM
SALES (corp-wide): 23.85MM **Privately Held**
SIC: **6719** Personal holding companies, except banks

(G-17236)
HUNTS FAMILY CONTRACTING
522 Centerville Rd (19808-4718)
PHONE...................302 510-5585
Kevin Hunt, *Owner*
EMP: 5 EST: 2016
SALES (est): 68.21K **Privately Held**
SIC: **1799** Special trade contractors, nec

(G-17237)
HURLOCK ROOFING COMPANY
26 Brookside Dr (19804-1189)
PHONE...................302 654-2783
Alfred J Bud Hurlock Iii, *Pr*
John D Speakman Junior, *VP*
Marie V Speakman, *Sec*
EMP: 15 EST: 1951
SQ FT: 6,200
SALES (est): 483.61K **Privately Held**
Web: www.hurlockroofing.com
SIC: **1761** Roofing contractor

(G-17238)
HUTZPAH KITCHEN LLC
2055 Limestone Rd 200c (19808-5536)
PHONE...................202 641-2916
EMP: 5 EST: 2021
SALES (est): 62.38K **Privately Held**
SIC: **2099** Food preparations, nec

(G-17239)
HV SUNRISE LLC (PA) ◊
919 N Market St Ste 950 (19801-3036)
PHONE...................612 961-5783
EMP: 11 EST: 2022
SALES (est): 5.2MM
SALES (corp-wide): 5.2MM **Privately Held**
SIC: **4911** Generation, electric power

(G-17240)
HY-POINT DAIRY FARMS INC
425 Beaver Valley Rd (19803-1103)
PHONE...................302 478-1414
William Meany, *Pr*
William Meany, *VP*
James L Meany, *Stockholder**
John A Meany Stlkdr, *Prin*
EMP: 105 EST: 1919
SQ FT: 200,000
SALES (est): 38.93MM **Privately Held**
Web: www.hypointequipment.com
SIC: **5143** 2026 Ice cream and ices; Milk and cream, except fermented, cultured, and flavored

(G-17241)
HY-POINT EQUIPMENT CO
425 Beaver Valley Rd (19803-1103)
PHONE...................302 478-0388
TOLL FREE: 800
Robert Meany, *VP*
John C Meany, *Pr*
Rosemarie Lee, *Sec*
EMP: 10 EST: 1976
SQ FT: 25,000
SALES (est): 2.29MM **Privately Held**
Web: www.hypointequipment.com
SIC: **5046** Restaurant equipment and supplies, nec

(G-17242)
HYAS US INC
251 Little Falls Dr (19808-1674)
PHONE...................877 572-6446
David Ratner, *CEO*
EMP: 8 EST: 2019
SALES (est): 103K **Privately Held**
SIC: **8741** Administrative management

(G-17243)
HYBRID PROPERTY LLC
Also Called: Hybrid Property Group
300 Delaware Ave Ste 210-252 (19801)
PHONE...................302 289-6226
Glornette Henry, *CEO*
EMP: 10 EST: 2016
SALES (est): 661.98K **Privately Held**
SIC: **8742** 6531 Real estate consultant; Real estate leasing and rentals

(G-17244)
HYSIOTHERAPY ASSOCIATES INC
Also Called: Chester Cnty Orthpd Spt Physcl
3411 Silverside Rd # 105 (19810-4812)
PHONE...................610 444-1270
Roger Collins, *Dir*
EMP: 8 EST: 1981
SALES (est): 420.21K **Privately Held**

SIC: **5047** 8093 Therapy equipment; Rehabilitation center, outpatient treatment

(G-17245)
HYWATTS INC ◊
919 N Market St Ste 950 (19801-3036)
PHONE...................650 460-4488
Aleksei Ivanenko, *CEO*
EMP: 3 EST: 2023
SALES (est): 135.7K **Privately Held**
SIC: **3629** Electronic generation equipment

(G-17246)
I DO IT RIGHT 100 LLC
1502 E Ayre St (19804-2308)
PHONE...................302 304-4467
EMP: 4 EST: 2021
SALES (est): 100.05K **Privately Held**
SIC: **1389** Construction, repair, and dismantling services

(G-17247)
I HAVE A DREAM CHILD CARE
713 Vandever Ave (19802-5023)
PHONE...................302 507-2310
Tamirah Coleman, *Prin*
EMP: 8 EST: 2016
SALES (est): 15.97K **Privately Held**
SIC: **8351** Child day care services

(G-17248)
I LOVE MYSELF LLC ◊
2201 Carlton Ln (19810-3917)
PHONE...................470 474-3347
Umar Clark, *Managing Member*
EMP: 3 EST: 2022
SALES (est): 135.7K **Privately Held**
SIC: **3069** 7389 Clothing, vulcanized rubber or rubberized fabric; Business services, nec

(G-17249)
I NEED IT I WANT IT LLC
1201 N Market St Ste 111 (19801-1156)
PHONE...................888 299-1341
Gregory Hawkes Ii, *CEO*
Gregory Hawkes, *Managing Member*
EMP: 5 EST: 2019
SALES (est): 260K **Privately Held**
SIC: **8742** Management consulting services

(G-17250)
I-PULSE INC (PA)
2711 Centerville Rd Ste 400 (19808-1660)
PHONE...................604 689-8765
Robert Friedland, *Ch*
Laurent Frescaline, *CEO*
Hirofumi Katase, *Ex VP*
Philippe Boisseau, *Dir*
Ian Cockerill, *Dir*
EMP: 4 EST: 2007
SALES (est): 399.53K
SALES (corp-wide): 399.53K **Privately Held**
Web: www.ipulse-group.com
SIC: **1382** 1731 1311 Oil and gas exploration services; General electrical contractor; Crude petroleum and natural gas

(G-17251)
IAABO
118 Belmont Dr (19808-4329)
PHONE...................302 737-4396
Layne Drexel, *Prin*
EMP: 10 EST: 2018
SALES (est): 48.18K **Privately Held**
Web: www.phillyref.com
SIC: **8699** Membership organizations, nec

GEOGRAPHIC SECTION

Wilmington - New Castle County (G-17280)

(G-17252)
IACONO - SUMMER CHASE
Also Called: Village of Canterbury
102 Robino Ct Ste 101 (19804-2360)
PHONE.............................302 994-2505
Leonard Iacono, *Genl Pt*
Paul Robino, *Ltd Pt*
Michael Stortini, *Ltd Pt*
Charles Robino, *Ltd Pt*
EMP: 10 EST: 2009
SALES (est): 883.8K **Privately Held**
SIC: 6513 Apartment building operators

(G-17253)
IAMAG INC
2810 N Church St Pmb 99673
(19802-4447)
PHONE.............................317 487-9338
EMP: 6 EST: 2020
SALES (est): 23.63K **Privately Held**
Web: www.iamag.co
SIC: 7374 Computer graphics service

(G-17254)
IAP HOLDING LLC ✪
3 Germay Dr Ste 42324 (19804-1127)
PHONE.............................302 394-9795
EMP: 5 EST: 2022
SALES (est): 71.67K **Privately Held**
SIC: 4491 Marine cargo handling

(G-17255)
IBI GROUP (US) INC (DH)
501 Silverside Rd Unit 307 (19809-1374)
PHONE.............................949 833-5588
Scott Stewart, *CEO*
EMP: 119 EST: 2004
SALES (est): 133.11MM
SALES (corp-wide): 3.14B **Privately Held**
Web: www.ibigroup.com
SIC: 8711 Civil engineering
HQ: Ibi Group Inc
55 St Clair Ave W 7th Fl
Toronto ON M4V 2
416 596-1930

(G-17256)
IBR LNDSCPING LAWN CARE SVCS L ✪
1413 N Franklin St (19806-3123)
PHONE.............................610 818-7127
Awolu Ibrahim, *Managing Member*
EMP: 15 EST: 2022
SALES (est): 250.76K **Privately Held**
SIC: 0781 Landscape services

(G-17257)
ICONIC SKUS LLC
4023 Kennett Pike Ste 226 (19807-2018)
PHONE.............................302 722-4547
EMP: 5 EST: 2011
SALES (est): 237.35K **Privately Held**
SIC: 8742 Marketing consulting services

(G-17258)
ICS - WORLDWIDE INC
251 Little Falls Dr (19808-1674)
PHONE.............................800 266-5254
Effi Oren, *CEO*
EMP: 60 EST: 2020
SALES (est): 2.41MM **Privately Held**
SIC: 7363 Chauffeur service

(G-17259)
ICS AMERICA INC
1209 N Orange St (19801-1120)
PHONE.............................215 979-1320
Scott Key, *Pr*
EMP: 10 EST: 2000
SALES (est): 502.61K **Privately Held**

SIC: 7389 Personal service agents, brokers, and bureaus

(G-17260)
ICT ENTERPRISES INC
300 Delaware Ave (19801-1607)
PHONE.............................302 576-2840
EMP: 14 EST: 2008
SALES (est): 1.63MM
SALES (corp-wide): 2.67MM **Privately Held**
SIC: 7389 Telemarketing services
HQ: Foundever Operating Corporation
600 Brickell Ave Ste 3200
Miami FL 33131
813 274-1000

(G-17261)
ICTCLEAN INC (PA)
3911 Concord Pike (19803-1736)
PHONE.............................315 216-5121
Ronald Harms, *CEO*
EMP: 11 EST: 2020
SALES (est): 4.5MM
SALES (corp-wide): 4.5MM **Privately Held**
Web: www.ictclean.com
SIC: 2451 Mobile classrooms

(G-17262)
ID GRIFFITH INC
735 S Market St Frnt (19801-5246)
PHONE.............................302 656-8253
David L Zarrilli, *Pr*
Michael H Treml, *
Richard A Murphy, *
Christine M Loncki, *
EMP: 85 EST: 1945
SQ FT: 10,000
SALES (est): 22.41MM **Privately Held**
Web: www.idgriffith.com
SIC: 1711 Mechanical contractor

(G-17263)
IDEAL VENUE LLC
2409 Lancaster Ave (19805-3736)
PHONE.............................302 250-9208
EMP: 10 EST: 2021
SALES (est): 153.57K **Privately Held**
SIC: 7922 Entertainment promotion

(G-17264)
IDEATREE INC
24a Trolley Sq Pmb 1232 (19806-3334)
PHONE.............................310 844-7447
Akash Op Aurora, *CEO*
EMP: 11 EST: 2015
SQ FT: 1,250
SALES (est): 506.12K **Privately Held**
Web: www.ideatree.com
SIC: 7371 6799 Computer software development and applications; Venture capital companies

(G-17265)
IDF CONNECT INC
2207 Concord Pike # 359 (19803-2908)
PHONE.............................888 765-1611
Richard Sand, *CEO*
EMP: 7 EST: 2012
SALES (est): 139.8K **Privately Held**
Web: www.idfconnect.com
SIC: 7372 Application computer software

(G-17266)
IDREAMS HUB INC
2810 N Church St (19802-4447)
PHONE.............................740 990-2232
Johnson Okorie, *CEO*
EMP: 5
SALES (est): 257.92K **Privately Held**

SIC: 7371 Computer software development and applications

(G-17267)
IEH AUTO PARTS LLC
3315 Old Capitol Trl (19808-6209)
PHONE.............................302 994-7171
Greg Price, *Brnch Mgr*
EMP: 36
Web: autoplus1.cypresstg.com
SIC: 5013 Automotive supplies and parts
HQ: Ieh Auto Parts Llc
112 Townpark Dr Nw # 300
Kennesaw GA 30144
770 701-5000

(G-17268)
IH TECHNOLOGIES (IHT) LLC
251 Little Falls Dr (19808-1674)
PHONE.............................718 679-2613
Marco Fiorese, *Managing Member*
EMP: 3 EST: 2018
SALES (est): 123.32K **Privately Held**
SIC: 7372 7999 Application computer software; Physical fitness instruction

(G-17269)
IHANDY LLC
1007 N Orange St (19801-1239)
PHONE.............................708 239-1234
Adeniji Olalekan, *Managing Member*
EMP: 10
SALES (est): 365.44K **Privately Held**
SIC: 7372 Prepackaged software

(G-17270)
II USA CORPORATION
Also Called: Dapple
4a Trolley Sq #2138 (19806-3334)
PHONE.............................310 570-2928
Robert Phillips, *CEO*
EMP: 26 EST: 2021
SALES (est): 680.64K **Privately Held**
SIC: 7371 Computer software development and applications

(G-17271)
IJI INC
2711 Centerville Rd Ste 400 (19808-1660)
PHONE.............................732 485-9427
Vin Foresta, *Pr*
EMP: 20 EST: 2017
SALES (est): 524.29K **Privately Held**
Web: www.getsterr.com
SIC: 7379 Online services technology consultants

(G-17272)
IKENROCK ENTERTAINMENT LLC
121 W 37th St (19802-2712)
PHONE.............................302 981-8532
Kenneth Brown Junior, *Prin*
EMP: 5 EST: 2015
SALES (est): 78.3K **Privately Held**
SIC: 7929 Entertainers and entertainment groups

(G-17273)
IKO PRODUCTION INC
6 Denny Rd Ste 200 (19809-3444)
PHONE.............................302 764-3100
EMP: 20
SALES (corp-wide): 1.26B **Privately Held**
SIC: 2952 Roofing materials
HQ: Iko Production, Inc.
6 Denny Rd Ste 200
Wilmington DE 19809

(G-17274)
IKO PRODUCTION INC (DH)
Also Called: Iko Manufacturing
6 Denny Rd Ste 200 (19809-3444)
PHONE.............................302 764-3100
David Koschitzky, *Pr*
▲ EMP: 87 EST: 1992
SALES (est): 70.75MM
SALES (corp-wide): 1.26B **Privately Held**
SIC: 2952 Roofing materials
HQ: Goldis Holdings, Inc
6 Denny Rd Ste 200
Wilmington DE 19809

(G-17275)
IKO SALES INC
6 Denny Rd Ste 200 (19809-3444)
PHONE.............................360 988-9103
EMP: 12 EST: 2019
SALES (est): 1.42MM **Privately Held**
Web: www.iko.com
SIC: 7822 Motion picture and tape distribution

(G-17276)
IKO SALES INC
Also Called: Iko Productions
6 Denny Rd Ste 200 (19809-3444)
PHONE.............................302 764-3100
David Koschitzky, *Pr*
Michael X Pinder, *Sec*
Henry Fear, *VP*
EMP: 20 EST: 1992
SALES (est): 3.47MM **Privately Held**
SIC: 5033 Roofing and siding materials

(G-17277)
IKO SOUTHEAST INC (DH)
6 Denny Rd Ste 200 (19809-3444)
PHONE.............................302 764-3100
David Koschitzky, *Pr*
EMP: 30 EST: 2010
SALES (est): 22.4MM
SALES (corp-wide): 1.26B **Privately Held**
Web: www.iko.com
SIC: 3295 Roofing granules
HQ: Goldis Enterprises, Inc.
120 Hay Rd
Wilmington DE 19809
302 764-3100

(G-17278)
ILARA HEALTH INC (PA)
251 Little Falls Dr (19808-1674)
PHONE.............................646 322-7452
EMP: 6 EST: 2019
SALES (est): 392.93K
SALES (corp-wide): 392.93K **Privately Held**
Web: www.ilarahealth.com
SIC: 8099 Health and allied services, nec

(G-17279)
ILE LLC
1201 N Market St Ste 111 (19801-1156)
PHONE.............................302 389-7911
EMP: 6 EST: 2020
SALES (est): 692.56K **Privately Held**
SIC: 1381 Directional drilling oil and gas wells

(G-17280)
ILLUMINA CORPORATE FOUNDATION
501 Silverside Rd (19809-1374)
PHONE.............................516 870-7722
Charles Dadswell, *Prin*
EMP: 11 EST: 2016
SALES (est): 113.28K **Privately Held**

Wilmington - New Castle County (G-17281)

GEOGRAPHIC SECTION

SIC: 8641 Civic and social associations

(G-17281)
IMAGING GROUP DELAWARE PA
St. Francis Hospital Department Of
Radiology 7th & Clayton Sts (19805)
PHONE..................................302 421-4300
EMP: 10 EST: 2017
SALES (est): 72.52K **Privately Held**
Web: www.4rai.com
SIC: 8011 Radiologist

(G-17282)
IMAGING GROUP OF DELAWARE INC
701 N Clayton St (19805-3165)
PHONE..................................302 888-2303
Donald Ostrum, Pr
EMP: 14 EST: 2001
SALES (est): 1.07MM **Privately Held**
Web: www.4rai.com
SIC: 8011 Radiologist

(G-17283)
IMG UNIVERSE LLC
251 Little Falls Dr (19808-1674)
PHONE..................................212 774-6704
EMP: 5 EST: 2015
SALES (est): 65.78K **Privately Held**
SIC: 8742 Management consulting services

(G-17284)
IMMENSITY LOGISTICS LLC ◆
1207 Delaware Ave (19806-4743)
PHONE..................................501 500-6667
Abi Singh, Managing Member
EMP: 5 EST: 2022
SALES (est): 520.32K **Privately Held**
SIC: 4731 Truck transportation brokers

(G-17285)
IMPACT CARE INC
1209 N Orange St (19801-1120)
PHONE..................................610 628-2004
Shreya Kangovi, Prin
EMP: 14
SALES (est): 504.69K **Privately Held**
SIC: 7372 Prepackaged software

(G-17286)
IMPACT IRRGATION SOLUTIONS INC
3213 Heathwood Rd (19810-3427)
PHONE..................................484 723-3600
EMP: 6 EST: 2014
SALES (est): 108.17K **Privately Held**
Web: www.impactirrigationsolutions.com
SIC: 4971 Irrigation systems

(G-17287)
IMPACT IRRIGATION
3213 Heathwood Rd (19810-3427)
PHONE..................................484 723-3600
EMP: 5 EST: 2019
SALES (est): 35.16K **Privately Held**
Web: www.impactirrigationsolutions.com
SIC: 4971 Irrigation systems

(G-17288)
IMPACT SHARES TRUST I
1209 N Orange St (19801)
PHONE..................................469 442-8424
EMP: 5 EST: 2018
SALES (est): 69.68K **Privately Held**
Web: www.impactetfs.org
SIC: 6733 Trusts, nec

(G-17289)
IMPACTFUL TECHNOLOGY LLC
24a Trolley Sq Ste 1608 (19806-3334)
PHONE..................................646 374-9004
EMP: 6

SALES (est): 68.89K **Privately Held**
SIC: 7371 Computer software development and applications

(G-17290)
IMPERIAL DYNSTY ARTS PRGRAM IN
1 Windsor Rd (19809-2144)
PHONE..................................302 521-8551
Devin Fletcher, Pr
Tyree Miller, VP
EMP: 10 EST: 2013
SALES (est): 775.11K **Privately Held**
Web: www.imperialdynasty.org
SIC: 3931 Percussion instruments and parts

(G-17291)
IMPERIAL GUNITE
4612 Simon Rd (19803-3928)
PHONE..................................631 244-0073
EMP: 7 EST: 2017
SALES (est): 135.91K **Privately Held**
Web: www.imperialgunite.com
SIC: 1799 Swimming pool construction

(G-17292)
IMS SOFTWARE SERVICES LTD (HQ)
1209 N Orange St (19801-1120)
PHONE..................................302 472-9100
Robert Steinfeld, Prin
Richard Derr, Prin
EMP: 19 EST: 1988
SALES (est): 2.07MM **Publicly Held**
Web: www.ims-software.com
SIC: 8732 Market analysis or research
PA: Iqvia Holdings Inc.
2400 Ellis Rd
Durham NC 27703

(G-17293)
IN VISION EYE CARE
Also Called: Fairfax Eye Works
2205 Concord Pike (19803-2908)
PHONE..................................302 655-1952
Roger Ammon, Pr
EMP: 9 EST: 1948
SALES (est): 477.28K **Privately Held**
Web: eyeworks.optometry.net
SIC: 8042 Specialized optometrists

(G-17294)
IN WILMINGTON MKTG GROUP INC
1007 N Orange St Fl 4 (19801-1242)
PHONE..................................302 495-9456
EMP: 5 EST: 2015
SALES (est): 194.86K **Privately Held**
SIC: 8742 Management consulting services

(G-17295)
INA ACQUISITION CORP (DH)
1007 N Orange St Ste 1410 (19801-1242)
PHONE..................................302 472-9258
Edward Kim, Pr
EMP: 13 EST: 1992
SALES (est): 127.87MM
SALES (corp-wide): 1.27B **Privately Held**
SIC: 1623 Pipeline construction, nsk
HQ: Aegion Corporation
580 Goddard Ave
Chesterfield MO 63005
636 530-8000

(G-17296)
INACCEL LLC
24a Trolley Sq # 1397 (19806-3334)
PHONE..................................408 915-5548
EMP: 5 EST: 2018
SALES (est): 63.38K **Privately Held**
Web: www.inaccel.com

SIC: 7371 Computer software systems analysis and design, custom

(G-17297)
INC PLAN (USA)
Also Called: Plan USA
26c Trolley Sq (19806-3356)
PHONE..................................302 428-1200
EMP: 6 EST: 1991
SALES (est): 513.02K **Privately Held**
Web: www.incplan.net
SIC: 7389 Authors' agents and brokers

(G-17298)
INC PLAN USA
20c Trolley Sq (19806-3355)
PHONE..................................302 428-1200
Caroline Quigley, VP
EMP: 5 EST: 2015
SALES (est): 229.71K **Privately Held**
SIC: 8732 Business research service

(G-17299)
INCAPP INC
3411 Silverside Rd # 104 (19810-4812)
P.O. Box 860 (71221-0860)
PHONE..................................318 880-7622
Raktim Baruah, Dir
EMP: 5 EST: 2013
SALES (est): 147.25K **Privately Held**
SIC: 7371 7389 Computer software development and applications; Business services, nec

(G-17300)
INCITE SOLUTIONS INC
5714 Kennett Pike Ofc 3 (19807-1331)
PHONE..................................302 655-8952
Thomas Scott, Pr
EMP: 6 EST: 2000
SALES (est): 318.24K **Privately Held**
Web: www.incitesolutions.com
SIC: 7371 Computer software development

(G-17301)
INCOLOR INC
1401 Todds Ln (19802-2417)
PHONE..................................302 984-2695
Bob Mcclean, Pr
EMP: 5 EST: 1994
SALES (est): 474.97K **Privately Held**
Web: www.gopcgnow.com
SIC: 3993 Signs and advertising specialties

(G-17302)
INCOME & EST PLG PARTNERS PA
2706 Kirkwood Hwy Unit 5 (19805-4912)
PHONE..................................302 722-6000
EMP: 9 EST: 2016
SALES (est): 194.58K **Privately Held**
SIC: 8621 Professional organizations

(G-17303)
INCORPORATORS USA LLC
Also Called: American Incorporators
1013 Centre Rd Ste 403a (19805-1270)
PHONE..................................800 441-5940
EMP: 9 EST: 1998
SALES (est): 187.75K **Privately Held**
Web: www.incusa.com
SIC: 8748 Business consulting, nec

(G-17304)
INCOUNTRY INC (PA)
4023 Kennett Pike Ste 50376 (19807-2018)
PHONE..................................415 323-0322
EMP: 7 EST: 2019
SALES (est): 213.73K
SALES (corp-wide): 213.73K **Privately Held**

SIC: 7372 Application computer software

(G-17305)
INCREDIBLE CARE INC
1224 N King St (19801-3232)
PHONE..................................302 428-6093
EMP: 5 EST: 2016
SALES (est): 240.68K **Privately Held**
Web: www.incrediblehomecare.com
SIC: 6531 Real estate brokers and agents

(G-17306)
INCYTE CORPORATION (PA)
1801 Augustine Cut Off (19803-4404)
PHONE..................................302 498-6700
Herve Hoppenot, Ch Bd
Christiana Stamoulis, Ex VP
Dashyant Dhanak, CSO
Steven Stein, CMO
Maria E Pasquale, Ex VP
EMP: 652 EST: 1991
SQ FT: 544,000
SALES (est): 3.7B **Publicly Held**
Web: www.incyte.com
SIC: 8731 Commercial physical research

(G-17307)
INCYTE HOLDINGS CORPORATION (HQ)
1801 Augustine Cut Off (19803-4404)
PHONE..................................302 498-6700
EMP: 29 EST: 2014
SALES (est): 5.75MM **Publicly Held**
SIC: 2834 Pharmaceutical preparations
PA: Incyte Corporation
1801 Augustine Cut Off
Wilmington DE 19803

(G-17308)
INDEPENDENCE CONTRACTORS INC
302 Jackson Blvd (19803-3721)
PHONE..................................302 530-3022
EMP: 9 EST: 2010
SALES (est): 492.08K **Privately Held**
SIC: 1799 Special trade contractors, nec

(G-17309)
INDEPENDENT RESOURCES INC (PA)
6 Denny Rd Ste 101 (19809-3444)
PHONE..................................302 765-0191
Larry D Henderson, Ex Dir
Phyllis Ferrer, Dir
Joseph Derex, Prin
▲ EMP: 9 EST: 1994
SQ FT: 1,600
SALES (est): 993.18K
SALES (corp-wide): 993.18K **Privately Held**
Web: www.iri-delaware.org
SIC: 8322 Social service center

(G-17310)
INDEPENDENT SCHOOL MGT INC (PA)
1 Righter Pkwy Ste 140 (19803-1533)
PHONE..................................302 656-4944
Roxanne Higgins, CEO
W Rodman Snelling, *
Roxanne Higgins, Pr
EMP: 39 EST: 1977
SQ FT: 6,500
SALES (est): 10.52MM
SALES (corp-wide): 10.52MM **Privately Held**
Web: www.isminc.com
SIC: 6411 8742 2741 Insurance agents, brokers, and service; Management consulting services; Miscellaneous publishing

GEOGRAPHIC SECTION   Wilmington - New Castle County (G-17337)

(G-17311)
INDIGO TELECOM USA LLC
1209 N Orange St (19801-1120)
PHONE..............................727 537-0142
Peter Welch, *Managing Member*
EMP: 40 **EST:** 2021
SALES (est): 1.42MM **Privately Held**
SIC: 8748 Telecommunications consultant

(G-17312)
INDO AMINES AMERICAS LLC
5301 Limestone Rd Ste 100 (19808-1251)
PHONE..............................301 466-9902
Vijay Bhalchandra Palkar, *CEO*
EMP: 11 **EST:** 2014
SALES (est): 887.67K **Privately Held**
Web: www.iaallc.us
SIC: 2819 Chemicals, high purity: refined from technical grade

(G-17313)
INDUS INSIGHTS US INC
1000 N West St Ste 1200 (19801-1058)
PHONE..............................312 238-9815
EMP: 5 **EST:** 2018
SALES (est): 66.05K **Privately Held**
Web: www.indusinsights.com
SIC: 8742 Management consulting services

(G-17314)
INDUSTRAPLATE CORP
5 James Ct (19801-5251)
P.O. Box 10812 (19850-0812)
PHONE..............................302 654-5210
Stephen Orr, *Pr*
David Orr Junior, *VP*
Joann Glanden, *Sec*
EMP: 10 **EST:** 1961
SALES (est): 995.64K **Privately Held**
Web: www.industraplate.com
SIC: 3471 Electroplating of metals or formed products

(G-17315)
INDUSTRIAL METAL TREATING CORP
Also Called: Atlantic Heat Treat
402 E Front St (19801-3956)
PHONE..............................302 656-1677
Chris Schopfer, *Pr*
Rich Cooper, *Manager*
David Skinner, *Off Mgr*
EMP: 10 **EST:** 1964
SQ FT: 42,000
SALES (est): 1.1MM **Privately Held**
Web: www.treatmetal.com
SIC: 3398 3471 Metal heat treating; Sand blasting of metal parts

(G-17316)
INDUSTRIAL RESOURCE NETWRK INC
Also Called: Irn
707 S Church St (19801-5540)
PHONE..............................302 888-2905
William J Ries, *Pr*
EMP: 11 **EST:** 1988
SQ FT: 22,000
SALES (est): 655.25K **Privately Held**
Web: www.industrialresource.net
SIC: 7699 5085 5162 Industrial equipment services; Drums, new or reconditioned; Plastics products, nec

(G-17317)
INDUSTRIAL SLS FACTORING CORP
1200 N Orange St Ste 700 (19801-1121)
PHONE..............................302 573-2500
Richard Stat, *Pr*
Lewis Stat, *VP*
Daniel K Stat, *VP*
Mildred Stat, *Sec*
EMP: 7 **EST:** 1965
SQ FT: 1,000
SALES (est): 520K **Privately Held**
SIC: 2821 Plastics materials and resins

(G-17318)
INDUSTRY ARC
251 Little Falls Dr (19808-1674)
PHONE..............................614 588-8538
EMP: 10 **EST:** 2016
SALES (est): 552.94K **Privately Held**
Web: www.industryarc.com
SIC: 8748 Business consulting, nec

(G-17319)
INFANT SOLUTIONS
3524 Silverside Rd Ste 35b (19810-4929)
PHONE..............................302 250-4336
Robinson Vishal, *Prin*
EMP: 49 **EST:** 2018
SALES (est): 986.46K **Privately Held**
Web: www.infantsolutions.net
SIC: 8748 Business consulting, nec

(G-17320)
INFIGAGE LLC
919 N Market St (19801-3023)
PHONE..............................302 207-2148
Ashish Nair, *Managing Member*
EMP: 5
SALES (est): 203.68K **Privately Held**
SIC: 7361 Employment agencies

(G-17321)
INFINITE IMPROBABILITIES INC ✪
1209 N Orange St (19801-1120)
PHONE..............................763 516-5825
Grandville Ricks, *Ex Dir*
EMP: 6 **EST:** 2022
SALES (est): 237.56K **Privately Held**
SIC: 7371 Computer software development

(G-17322)
INFINITE SOLUTIONS LLC
531 Chariot Ct (19808-1555)
PHONE..............................302 438-5310
Nimish Rustagi, *Pr*
Nimish Rustagi, *Pt*
EMP: 10 **EST:** 2005
SALES (est): 524.55K **Privately Held**
Web: www.infinite.mn
SIC: 7373 7389 Systems software development services; Business Activities at Non-Commercial Site

(G-17323)
INFINITY HEALTH & WELLNESS DEL
6 Larch Ave Ste 397 (19804-2356)
PHONE..............................302 543-5717
EMP: 5 **EST:** 2019
SALES (est): 126.34K **Privately Held**
SIC: 8099 Health and allied services, nec

(G-17324)
INFINITY INTELLECTUALS INC
3511 Silverside Rd Ste 105 (19810-4902)
PHONE..............................302 565-4830
S Shiva Kumar, *CEO*
S Sandeep Kumar, *Pr*
M Soma Shekar, *Ch*
Sapna Savant, *CFO*
Bruce Wayne, *Opers Mgr*
EMP: 40 **EST:** 2009
SQ FT: 4,000
SALES (est): 1.08MM **Privately Held**
Web: www.infinity-intellectual.com
SIC: 8742 Marketing consulting services

(G-17325)
INFLECTION ASSOCIATES INC
251 Little Falls Dr (19808-1674)
PHONE..............................484 678-7915
Colin Kelly, *Ch Bd*
EMP: 7
SALES (est): 270.58K **Privately Held**
SIC: 7311 Advertising agencies

(G-17326)
INFO SOLUTIONS LLC
920 Justison St (19801-5150)
PHONE..............................302 793-9200
EMP: 27 **EST:** 2019
SALES (est): 3.66MM **Privately Held**
Web: www.infosolutionsllc.com
SIC: 7379 Computer related consulting services

(G-17327)
INFO SOLUTIONS NORTH AMER LLC
920 Justison St (19801-5150)
P.O. Box 5968 (19808-0968)
PHONE..............................302 793-9200
EMP: 13 **EST:** 2007
SALES (est): 4.96MM **Privately Held**
Web: www.infosolutionsllc.com
SIC: 7379 Online services technology consultants

(G-17328)
INFO SYSTEMS LLC (DH)
Also Called: ISI Connect
590 Century Blvd (19808-6273)
PHONE..............................302 633-9800
EMP: 125 **EST:** 1982
SQ FT: 18,000
SALES (est): 48.28MM
SALES (corp-wide): 440.24MM **Privately Held**
SIC: 5045 7373 Computers, nec; Computer integrated systems design
HQ: Mtm Technologies, Inc.
      507 N State Rd
      Briarcliff Manor NY 10510
      866 383-2867

(G-17329)
INFOBASE HOLDINGS INC (HQ)
Also Called: Learn360
1000 N West St Ste 1281-230 (19801-1050)
PHONE..............................212 967-8800
Mark D Mcdonnell, *Pr*
James Housley, *
▲ **EMP:** 30 **EST:** 1940
SALES (est): 55.39MM
SALES (corp-wide): 55.39MM **Privately Held**
Web: www.infobase.com
SIC: 2731 7372 Books, publishing only; Prepackaged software
PA: Infobase Publishing Company
      132 W 31st St Fl 17
      New York NY 10001
      212 967-8800

(G-17330)
INFUSION CARE DELAWARE HOME
9 N Hampshire Ct (19807-2535)
PHONE..............................302 423-2511
Sharon Burtonyoung, *Prin*
EMP: 10 **EST:** 2013
SALES (est): 237.63K **Privately Held**
SIC: 8059 Nursing and personal care, nec

(G-17331)
ING BANK FSB
Also Called: Ing Direct Wilmington Cafe
802 Delaware Ave Fl 1 (19801-1300)
PHONE..............................302 255-3750
Bryan Nook, *Mgr*
EMP: 81
SIC: 4813 Internet connectivity services
HQ: Ing Bank Fsb
      802 Delaware Ave
      Wilmington DE 19801

(G-17332)
ING BANK FSB (HQ)
Also Called: Ing Direct
802 Delaware Ave (19801-1377)
PHONE..............................302 658-2200
EMP: 71 **EST:** 2000
SQ FT: 39,000
SALES (est): 3.39MM **Publicly Held**
SIC: 6035 6211 Federal savings institutions; Security brokers and dealers
PA: Capital One Financial Corporation
      1680 Capital One Dr
      Mc Lean VA 22102

(G-17333)
ING USA HOLDING CORP
1 S Orange St (19801-5006)
PHONE..............................302 658-2200
▲ **EMP:** 1171
SIC: 6035 Federal savings institutions

(G-17334)
INGENIOUS INVENTIONS AG LLC
Also Called: Trash Smell Buster
1201 N Orange St Ste 7400 (19801-1286)
PHONE..............................818 578-8266
EMP: 3 **EST:** 2021
SALES (est): 83.48K **Privately Held**
SIC: 2673 Trash bags (plastic film): made from purchased materials

(G-17335)
INGLESIDE HOMES INC (PA)
Also Called: INGLESIDE RETIREMENT APARTMENT
1005 N Franklin St (19806-4553)
PHONE..............................302 575-0250
Lawrence R Cessna, *Pr*
EMP: 85 **EST:** 1971
SQ FT: 25,000
SALES (est): 7.34MM
SALES (corp-wide): 7.34MM **Privately Held**
Web: www.inglesidehomes.org
SIC: 8082 8322 8361 Home health care services; Geriatric social service; Geriatric residential care

(G-17336)
INGLESIDE HOMES INC
Also Called: Ingleside Assisted Living
1605 N Broom St (19806-3009)
PHONE..............................302 984-0950
Keith Ropka, *Prin*
EMP: 35
SALES (corp-wide): 7.34MM **Privately Held**
Web: www.inglesidehomes.org
SIC: 8051 8052 6513 Skilled nursing care facilities; Intermediate care facilities; Retirement hotel operation
PA: Ingleside Homes, Inc.
      1005 N Franklin St
      Wilmington DE 19806
      302 575-0250

(G-17337)
INGLESIDE RTRMENT APRTMNTS LLC
1005 N Franklin St (19806-4553)
PHONE..............................302 575-0250
EMP: 13 **EST:** 2006
SALES (est): 532.15K **Privately Held**

Wilmington - New Castle County (G-17338) — GEOGRAPHIC SECTION

Web: www.inglesidehomes.org
SIC: 6513 Retirement hotel operation

(G-17338)
INGRID S JACKOWAY
2502 Silverside Rd Ste 4 (19810-3740)
PHONE...................302 478-3702
Ingrid S Jackoway Otr, *Owner*
EMP: 6 EST: 2018
SALES (est): 22.18K **Privately Held**
SIC: 8049 Offices of health practitioner

(G-17339)
INHERITNOW INC
1002 Justison St (19801-5148)
PHONE...................877 846-4374
EMP: 6 EST: 2021
SALES (est): 513.82K **Privately Held**
Web: www.inheritnow.com
SIC: 6799 Investors, nec

(G-17340)
INIIWI LLC
1201 N Market St Ste 111 (19801-1156)
PHONE...................866 312-4536
Shacree Dorsey, *Admn*
EMP: 5 EST: 2021
SALES (est): 260K **Privately Held**
SIC: 8741 Management services

(G-17341)
INITIALLY YOURS INC
1412 Kirkwood Hwy (19805-2124)
PHONE...................302 999-0562
Therese Moore, *Pr*
Mary Ruoff, *Sec*
EMP: 4 EST: 1985
SQ FT: 1,400
SALES (est): 479.55K **Privately Held**
Web: www.iyinconline.com
SIC: 2395 7336 Emblems, embroidered; Silk screen design

(G-17342)
INKIT INC (PA)
919 N Market St Ste 725 (19801-3065)
PHONE...................612 712-1245
Michael Mccarthy, *CEO*
EMP: 10 EST: 2018
SALES (est): 1MM
SALES (corp-wide): 1MM **Privately Held**
Web: www.inkit.com
SIC: 7371 Computer software development

(G-17343)
INKLNK
717 N Union St Ste 32 (19805-3031)
PHONE...................323 854-9549
EMP: 5 EST: 2018
SALES (est): 110.12K **Privately Held**
Web: www.inklnk.com
SIC: 7299 Tattoo parlor

(G-17344)
INKWHY INC
3616 Kirkwood Hwy Ste A # 1286 (19808-5124)
PHONE...................267 243-8498
Janice Dru, *Pr*
Steve Kuntz, *Sec*
EMP: 5 EST: 2011
SALES (est): 86.1K **Privately Held**
Web: www.inkwhy.com
SIC: 8742 Marketing consulting services

(G-17345)
INLAND SALEM SQUARE LLC
1007 N Orange St (19801-1239)
PHONE...................302 472-9250
EMP: 11 EST: 2008

SALES (est): 749.48K
SALES (corp-wide): 216.41MM **Privately Held**
SIC: 1521 New construction, single-family houses
HQ: Irc Retail Centers Llc
814 Commerce Dr Ste 300
Oak Brook IL 60523
877 206-5656

(G-17346)
INN AT WILMINGTON
300 Rocky Run Pkwy (19803-1515)
PHONE...................302 479-7900
Colleen Owens, *Pr*
EMP: 17 EST: 2007
SALES (est): 197.4K **Privately Held**
Web: www.innatwilmington.com
SIC: 7011 Inns

(G-17347)
INNOVATIVE CONCEPTS MGT LLC
24a Trolley Sq (19806-3334)
PHONE...................866 952-7066
Jorrell Lawton, *Managing Member*
EMP: 10 EST: 2021
SALES (est): 414.8K **Privately Held**
SIC: 7389

(G-17348)
INNOVATIVE DERMATOLOGY
1202 Foulk Rd Ste A (19803-2796)
PHONE...................610 789-7546
EMP: 8 EST: 2019
SALES (est): 231.38K **Privately Held**
Web: www.789skin.com
SIC: 8011 Dermatologist

(G-17349)
INNOVENTIC INC
19c Trolley Sq (19806-3355)
PHONE...................302 476-2396
EMP: 5 EST: 2016
SALES (est): 91.3K **Privately Held**
SIC: 7371 Computer software development and applications

(G-17350)
INOVEN SOLUTIONS LLC ◆
3422 Old Capitol Trl (19808-6124)
PHONE...................302 273-0177
Matthew Hemingway, *Dir*
EMP: 25 EST: 2023
SALES (est): 975.99K **Privately Held**
SIC: 4924 Natural gas distribution

(G-17351)
INS REGULATORY INSURANCE SVCS
919 N Market St Ste 2600 (19801-3023)
PHONE...................302 256-0455
EMP: 6 EST: 2019
SALES (est): 240.99K **Privately Held**
Web: www.insris.com
SIC: 6411 Insurance agents, brokers, and service

(G-17352)
INSIGNIA GLOBAL CORPORATION
913 N Market St Ste 200 (19801-3097)
PHONE...................302 310-4107
Simon Borgawkar, *Pr*
EMP: 5 EST: 2019
SALES (est): 100K **Privately Held**
Web: www.insigniaglobalcorp.com
SIC: 7361 Executive placement

(G-17353)
INSITE CONSTRUCTORS INC
3201 Tanya Dr (19803-1936)
PHONE...................302 479-5555
EMP: 5 EST: 1995
SQ FT: 1,800
SALES (est): 709.38K **Privately Held**
SIC: 1542 Commercial and office building, new construction

(G-17354)
INSLEY JR HARRY AGT
901 N Market St Ste 100 (19801-3064)
PHONE...................302 656-1800
Harry Insley, *Prin*
EMP: 5 EST: 2017
SALES (est): 101.84K **Privately Held**
SIC: 6411 Insurance agents, brokers, and service

(G-17355)
INSPECTWARE
123 E Ayre St (19804-2506)
PHONE...................302 999-9601
EMP: 6 EST: 1999
SQ FT: 2,347
SALES (est): 354.69K **Privately Held**
SIC: 7372 Business oriented computer software

(G-17356)
INSPIRE AFRICAN SAFARIS LLC
2055 Limestone Rd Ste 200c (19808-5536)
PHONE...................302 250-5763
Richard Davids, *Managing Member*
EMP: 10
SALES (est): 552.11K **Privately Held**
SIC: 4724 7371 Travel agencies; Computer software development and applications

(G-17357)
INSPIUN TECH SOLUTIONS LLC
913 N Market St Ste 200 (19801-3097)
PHONE...................302 304-3949
EMP: 6 EST: 2014
SALES (est): 102.79K **Privately Held**
Web: www.ecampaignhawk.com
SIC: 7389

(G-17358)
INSTACALL LLC (PA)
2055 Limestone Rd 200c (19808-5536)
PHONE...................302 496-1166
EMP: 10 EST: 2021
SALES (est): 385.96K
SALES (corp-wide): 385.96K **Privately Held**
SIC: 4813 Voice telephone communications

(G-17359)
INSTELLARS GLOBL CNSULTING INC (PA)
919 N Market St Ste 705 (19801-3023)
PHONE...................302 613-4379
EMP: 6 EST: 2019
SALES (est): 990.95K
SALES (corp-wide): 990.95K **Privately Held**
Web: www.instellars.com
SIC: 8742 Management consulting services

(G-17360)
INSTITUTE OF MSSAGE HLING ARTS
222 Philadelphia Pike (19809-3166)
PHONE...................610 357-2925
EMP: 5 EST: 2015
SALES (est): 115.55K **Privately Held**
SIC: 8733 Noncommercial research organizations

(G-17361)
INSURANCE ADMINISTRATORS INC
2100 Braken Ave (19808-4427)
PHONE...................302 239-1688
Lori Thomas, *Pr*
EMP: 5 EST: 2012
SALES (est): 114.26K **Privately Held**
Web: www.insuranceadministratorsinc.com
SIC: 6411 Insurance agents, nec

(G-17362)
INSURANCE NETWORKS ALIANCE LLC
3411 Silverside Rd Ste 100 (19810-4812)
PHONE...................302 268-1010
EMP: 5 EST: 2017
SALES (est): 150K **Privately Held**
Web: www.networksalliance.com
SIC: 8611 Trade associations

(G-17363)
INSURANCE OFFICE AMERICA INC
Also Called: Nationwide
900 Philadelphia Pike (19809-2280)
PHONE...................302 764-1000
Diana Handy, *Prin*
EMP: 7
SALES (corp-wide): 499.98MM **Privately Held**
Web: www.ioausa.com
SIC: 6411 Insurance agents, nec
HQ: Insurance Office Of America, Inc.
1855 W State Road 434
Longwood FL 32750
407 314-6190

(G-17364)
INSURANCE TOOLKITS LLC
426 Ohio Ave (19805-1019)
PHONE...................302 272-5488
Joseph Wahl, *Pr*
EMP: 7 EST: 2019
SALES (est): 518.71K **Privately Held**
Web: www.insurancetoolkits.com
SIC: 7371 Computer software development and applications

(G-17365)
INT PAY LLC
3513 Concord Pike Ste 3100 (19803-5027)
PHONE...................347 698-8159
Junwen Jiang, *Prin*
EMP: 5 EST: 2015
SALES (est): 121.18K **Privately Held**
SIC: 4812 Cellular telephone services

(G-17366)
INTEGRAL ENTERPRISE LLC
3434 Old Capitol Trl Unit 5432 (19808-7100)
PHONE...................302 722-0827
EMP: 3
SALES (est): 135.7K **Privately Held**
SIC: 3715 Semitrailers for missile transportation

(G-17367)
INTEGRATED CASH LOGISTICS LLC
4200 Governor Printz Blvd (19802-2315)
P.O. Box 1223 (19899-1223)
PHONE...................302 652-9193
EMP: 35 EST: 2011
SALES (est): 1.05MM **Privately Held**
SIC: 6141 Personal finance licensed loan companies, small

(G-17368)
INTEGRATED DATA CORP (PA)
1000 N West St Ste 1200 (19801-1058)

PHONE..................302 295-5057
David C Bryan, *Pr*
Stuart W Settle Junior, *Sec*
Walter T Bristow Iii, *VP*
▲ **EMP:** 7 **EST:** 1968
SQ FT: 5,000
SALES (est): 535.13K
SALES (corp-wide): 535.13K **Privately Held**
Web: www.integrateddatacorp.com
SIC: 3663 Pagers (one-way)

(G-17369)
INTEGRATED MECHANICAL AND FIRE
1807 Montclair Ave (19808-6117)
PHONE..................302 420-0617
Allison Marcum, *Pr*
EMP: 5 **EST:** 2013
SALES (est): 71.38K **Privately Held**
SIC: 1711 Mechanical contractor

(G-17370)
INTEGRATED RESTORATIVE MASSAGE
1601 Concord Pike Ste 2 (19803-3638)
PHONE..................302 391-4692
Alana Smith, *Prin*
EMP: 5 **EST:** 2018
SALES (est): 213.06K **Privately Held**
Web: www.integratedmassagellc.com
SIC: 7299 Massage parlor

(G-17371)
INTEGRATED SOLUTIONS GATE INC
427 N Tatnall St No 90821 (19801-2230)
PHONE..................302 404-6080
Hossam Eldin Elsayed, *Dir*
EMP: 5 **EST:** 2017
SALES (est): 46.16K **Privately Held**
Web: www.ibsgate.com
SIC: 7371 Computer software development

(G-17372)
INTELLIGENT SIGNAGE INC (PA)
4006 Coleridge Rd (19802-1906)
PHONE..................302 762-4100
EMP: 5 **EST:** 1995
SALES (est): 750K **Privately Held**
Web: www.intelligentsignage.net
SIC: 8748 Business consulting, nec

(G-17373)
INTELLO GROUP INC
500 Delaware Ave Unit 1 # 1960 (19899)
PHONE..................832 827-3779
EMP: 16 **EST:** 2019
SALES (est): 940.54K **Privately Held**
Web: www.intellogroup.com
SIC: 7361 Executive placement

(G-17374)
INTERACTIVE TECH HOLDINGS LLC
3411 Silverside Rd Ste 103hg (19810-4812)
PHONE..................302 478-9356
EMP: 2092 **EST:** 2006
SALES (est): 55.8K
SALES (corp-wide): 121.57B **Publicly Held**
SIC: 6211 Security brokers and dealers
HQ: Comcast Holdings Corporation
   1 Comcast Ctr
   Philadelphia PA 19103

(G-17375)
INTERCOASTAL TITLE AGENCY INC
10 Cohee Cir (19803-1114)
PHONE..................302 478-7752
Charlotte E Wick, *Mgr*
EMP: 5 **EST:** 1990
SALES (est): 376.84K **Privately Held**
SIC: 6361 Title insurance

(G-17376)
INTERCOLLEGIATE STUDIES INST
3901 Centerville Rd (19807-1938)
P.O. Box 4431 (19807-0431)
PHONE..................302 656-3292
Christopher Long, *Pr*
Elaine Pinder, *
EMP: 65 **EST:** 1953
SALES (est): 7.08MM **Privately Held**
Web: www.isi.org
SIC: 8641 Educator's association

(G-17377)
INTERCONTINENTAL CHEM SVCS INC
Also Called: I C S
1020 Christiana Ave Ste B (19801-5884)
PHONE..................302 654-6800
Rick Ryan, *CEO*
John Vitale, *Pr*
John C Foreman, *VP*
EMP: 20 **EST:** 1976
SQ FT: 270,000
SALES (est): 2.53MM **Privately Held**
Web: www.icsdelaware.com
SIC: 4225 General warehousing

(G-17378)
INTERCONTINENTAL MARKETING
Also Called: Global Institute, The
807 Essex Rd (19807-2931)
PHONE..................302 429-7555
William T Grubb, *Dir*
Terry Schuster, *Pr*
Ron Davis, *CFO*
Frank Hewitt, *Admn*
EMP: 7 **EST:** 1990
SALES (est): 297.43K **Privately Held**
SIC: 8742 Financial consultant

(G-17379)
INTERDGITAL COMMUNICATIONS INC (DH)
Also Called: Interdigital
200 Bellevue Pkwy Ste 300 (19809-3727)
PHONE..................610 878-7800
William J Merritt, *Pr*
Steven T Clontz, *
Brian G Kiernan, *Executive Standards Vice President**
Richard J Brezski, *CAO**
Edward Kamins, *
EMP: 80 **EST:** 2007
SQ FT: 52,000
SALES (est): 73.25MM
SALES (corp-wide): 457.79MM **Publicly Held**
SIC: 3663 5999 Mobile communication equipment; Mobile telephones and equipment
HQ: Interdigital Wireless, Inc.
   200 Bellevue Pkwy Ste 300
   Wilmington DE 19809

(G-17380)
INTERDIGITAL INC (PA)
Also Called: Interdigital
200 Bellevue Pkwy Ste 300 (19809-3727)
PHONE..................302 281-3600
William J Merritt, *Pr*
S Douglas Hutcheson, *Ch Bd*
Kai Oistamo, *COO*
Richard J Brezski, *CFO*
Jannie K Lau, *CLO*
EMP: 26 **EST:** 1972
SQ FT: 36,200
SALES (est): 457.79MM
SALES (corp-wide): 457.79MM **Publicly Held**
SIC: 3663 5999 Mobile communication equipment; Mobile telephones and equipment

(G-17381)
INTERDIGITAL WIRELESS INC (HQ)
Also Called: INTERDIGITAL
200 Bellevue Pkwy Ste 300 (19809-3727)
PHONE..................302 281-3600
William J Merritt, *Pr*
S Douglas Hutcheson, *Ch Bd*
Kai Oistamo, *COO*
Richard J Brezski, *CFO*
Jannie K Lau, *CLO*
EMP: 24 **EST:** 1972
SQ FT: 36,200
SALES (est): 457.79MM
SALES (corp-wide): 457.79MM **Publicly Held**
Web: www.interdigital.com
SIC: 3663 5999 Mobile communication equipment; Mobile telephones and equipment
PA: Interdigital, Inc.
   200 Bellevue Pkwy Ste 300
   Wilmington DE 19809
   302 281-3600

(G-17382)
INTERFACING BUS SOLUTIONS INC
919 N Market St Ste 950 (19801-3036)
PHONE..................514 962-1344
EMP: 5 **EST:** 2021
SALES (est): 71.79K **Privately Held**
SIC: 8742 Management consulting services

(G-17383)
INTERFAITH CMNTY HSING OF DEL
Also Called: ICHDE
613 N Washington St (19801-2135)
PHONE..................302 652-3991
Gary Pollio, *Pr*
Bpb Rawlinson, *CFO*
EMP: 19 **EST:** 1986
SALES (est): 1.89MM **Privately Held**
Web: www.ichde.org
SIC: 6552 1521 6514 Land subdividers and developers, residential; Single-family housing construction; Dwelling operators, except apartments

(G-17384)
INTERJET WEST INC
1013 Centre Rd Ste 403a (19805-1270)
PHONE..................209 848-0290
Justin Barnes, *VP*
EMP: 5 **EST:** 2015
SALES (est): 120.63K **Privately Held**
Web: www.interjetwest.com
SIC: 4522 Air transportation, nonscheduled

(G-17385)
INTERLACE GLOBAL INC
251 Little Falls Dr (19808-1674)
PHONE..................917 719-6811
Aditya Mehta, *CEO*
EMP: 9
SALES (est): 313.29K **Privately Held**
SIC: 7371 Computer software development

(G-17386)
INTERNAL MEDICINE ASSOCIATES
3105 Limestone Rd Ste 301 (19808-2179)
PHONE..................302 633-1700
Ana Rutkowski, *Off Mgr*
Mart Amick, *Prin*
Robert Kopecki, *Prin*
EMP: 13 **EST:** 1989
SALES (est): 2.49MM **Privately Held**
SIC: 8011 Internal medicine, physician/surgeon

(G-17387)
INTERNATIONAL BRTHD 2271 LOCAL
912 Haines Ave (19809-3246)
PHONE..................302 559-9167
Pierce Kerr, *Pr*
EMP: 5 **EST:** 2017
SALES (est): 59.8K **Privately Held**
SIC: 8631 Labor union

(G-17388)
INTERNATIONAL ESL SERVICES LLC
2207 Concord Pike 508 (19803-2908)
PHONE..................305 934-3769
Andres Moreno, *Managing Member*
EMP: 6 **EST:** 2012
SALES (est): 67.06K **Privately Held**
SIC: 7361 Teachers' agency

(G-17389)
INTERNATIONAL LOGISTIKS LLC
Also Called: International Logistiks
4023 Kennett Pike 404 (19807-2018)
PHONE..................302 521-6338
Harry Umbrage, *Pr*
John Arnone, *INTL SALES*
Andrew Thompson, *Sales Officer*
EMP: 8 **EST:** 2008
SALES (est): 318.25K **Privately Held**
SIC: 4731 Freight forwarding

(G-17390)
INTERNATIONAL SPINE PAIN
3411 Silverside Rd Ste 103r (19810-4812)
PHONE..................302 478-7001
Peter M Witherell, *Prin*
EMP: 9 **EST:** 2006
SALES (est): 108.81K **Privately Held**
SIC: 8011 8031 8748 Orthopedic physician; Offices and clinics of osteopathic physicians ; Business consulting, nec

(G-17391)
INTERNATIONAL STD ELC CORP (DH)
1105 N Market St Ste 1217 (19801-1216)
PHONE..................302 427-3769
Marvin R Sambur, *Prin*
Daniel P Weadock, *Ch Bd*
Brenda J Furlong, *Ex VP*
Louis J Giuliani, *Ex VP*
Bertil T Nilsson, *Ex VP*
EMP: 11 **EST:** 1918
SALES (est): 49.6MM
SALES (corp-wide): 3.28B **Publicly Held**
SIC: 3711 Motor vehicles and car bodies
HQ: Itt Llc
   1133 Westchester Ave N-100
   White Plains NY 10604
   914 641-2000

(G-17392)
INTERNATIONAL TRAVEL NETWORK
Also Called: ASAP Tickets
1000 N West St Ste 1200 (19801-1058)
PHONE..................415 840-0207
Peter Vazan, *CEO*
Alex Weinstein, *Pr*
EMP: 9 **EST:** 2004
SALES (est): 2.82MM **Privately Held**
Web: www.itncorp.com
SIC: 4724 Travel agencies

(G-17393)
INTERNET ACTIVISM INC ✪
Also Called: Internet Activism
1209 N Orange St (19801-1120)

Wilmington - New Castle County (G-17394)

GEOGRAPHIC SECTION

P.O. Box 612 (94104-0612)
PHONE..................................206 861-5106
Avi Schissmann, *Pr*
EMP: 5 **EST:** 2022
SALES (est): 104.08K **Privately Held**
SIC: 8641 7389 Youth organizations; Business services, nec

(G-17394)
INTERNET VIKINGS EAST LLC
251 Little Falls Dr (19808-1674)
PHONE..................................347 879-1452
Rickard Vikstrom, *Managing Member*
EMP: 6
SALES (est): 63.67K **Privately Held**
SIC: 8999 Personal services

(G-17395)
INTERNTNAL FNDING SLUTIONS LLC
2711 Centerville Rd # 400 (19808-1660)
PHONE..................................212 765-4349
Richard Tretler, *Sec*
EMP: 7 **EST:** 2017
SALES (est): 165.37K **Privately Held**
SIC: 6153 Factoring services

(G-17396)
INTERNTNAL SOC FOR HYLRNAN SCN
605 Geddes St (19805-3718)
PHONE..................................212 992-5971
Paull Deangelis, *Prin*
EMP: 5 **EST:** 2017
SALES (est): 72 **Privately Held**
Web: www.ishas.org
SIC: 7261 Funeral service and crematories

(G-17397)
INTERPRES SECURITY INC
251 Little Falls Dr (19808-1674)
PHONE..................................570 971-9876
Nick Lantuh, *CEO*
Michael Jenks, *Prin*
Ian Roth, *Prin*
EMP: 15 **EST:** 2020
SALES (est): 506.54K **Privately Held**
SIC: 7371 Computer software development

(G-17398)
INTERSTATE HOTELS LLC (PA)
1209 N Orange St (19801-1120)
PHONE..................................302 658-7581
EMP: 6
SALES (est): 230.72K
SALES (corp-wide): 230.72K **Privately Held**
SIC: 7011 Hotels

(G-17399)
INTERSTELLAR CMNTY LIVING LLC
3524 Silverside Rd 35b (19810-4929)
PHONE..................................787 607-3939
EMP: 5 **EST:** 2018
SALES (est): 74.09K **Privately Held**
SIC: 1522 Residential construction, nec

(G-17400)
INTERSTLLAR CMNTY LVING MGT CO
3524 Silverside Rd Ste 35b (19810-4929)
PHONE..................................787 607-3939
Cecilia La Luz Diaz, *CEO*
EMP: 5 **EST:** 2018
SALES (est): 74.09K **Privately Held**
SIC: 1522 Residential construction, nec

(G-17401)
INTRINSIC PARTNERS LLC
Also Called: Intrinsic
4001 Kennett Pike Ste 134 (19807-2000)
PHONE..................................610 388-0853
Dennis Sheehy, *Managing Member*
EMP: 10 **EST:** 2006
SALES (est): 265.44K **Privately Held**
Web: www.intrins.net
SIC: 7379 8742 Computer related consulting services; Management consulting services

(G-17402)
INTUITIVE CARE THERAPY
501 Silverside Rd Ste 8 (19809-1375)
PHONE..................................302 200-6123
EMP: 7 **EST:** 2019
SALES (est): 73.36K **Privately Held**
Web: www.intuitivecaretherapy.com
SIC: 8093 Rehabilitation center, outpatient treatment

(G-17403)
INTUS SMARTCITIES INC
501 Silverside Rd # 411 (19809-1374)
PHONE..................................403 542-8879
Dimitris Agouridis, *Prin*
Jonathan Tseelon, *Prin*
Tsvi Guy, *Prin*
A C Kostis, *Prin*
Chuck Guy, *Prin*
EMP: 15 **EST:** 2018
SALES (est): 541.06K **Privately Held**
Web: www.intussmartcities.com
SIC: 8748 Business consulting, nec

(G-17404)
INVENSIS INC
1000 N West St Ste 1200 (19801-1058)
PHONE..................................470 260-0084
Vara Prasad Rongala, *Pr*
Samanth Srikantan, *
EMP: 200 **EST:** 2010
SALES (est): 21.15MM **Privately Held**
Web: www.invensis.net
SIC: 7374 Data processing and preparation
PA: Invensis Technologies Private Limited
1321, Sarakki Extension, 15th Cross
Bengaluru KA 56007

(G-17405)
INVENTIA SCIENTIFIC CORP
200 Powder Mill Rd (19803-2907)
PHONE..................................888 201-0798
Dwayne Dexter, *Managing Member*
EMP: 6 **EST:** 2020
SALES (est): 253.1K **Privately Held**
SIC: 8731 Commercial physical research

(G-17406)
INVESTMENT PROPERTY SERVICES L
102 Robino Ct Ste 101 (19804-2360)
PHONE..................................302 994-3907
Leonard Iacono, *Prin*
EMP: 7 **EST:** 2008
SALES (est): 894.68K **Privately Held**
SIC: 6282 Investment advisory service

(G-17407)
INVESTOR CASH MGT HOLDINGS INC
1201 N Market St Ste 500 (19801-1160)
P.O. Box 3516 (19807-3516)
PHONE..................................312 736-7700
Frederick Paul Phillips Iv, *CEO*
Carolina Esswein, *Prin*
EMP: 21 **EST:** 2018
SALES (est): 2.69MM **Privately Held**
Web: www.investorcashmanagement.com
SIC: 7379 Online services technology consultants

(G-17408)
INVISIBLE HAND LABS LLC
2711 Centerville Rd Ste 400 (19808-1660)
PHONE..................................434 989-9642
EMP: 3 **EST:** 2013
SALES (est): 163.02K **Privately Held**
SIC: 3999 Manufacturing industries, nec

(G-17409)
INVISTA CAPITAL MANAGEMENT LLC (HQ)
2801 Centerville Rd (19801-1609)
PHONE..................................302 683-3000
▲ **EMP:** 8 **EST:** 1930
SALES (est): 1.9B
SALES (corp-wide): 36.93B **Privately Held**
Web: www.invista.com
SIC: 2821 Plastics materials and resins
PA: Koch Industries, Inc.
4111 E 37th St N
Wichita KS 67220
316 828-5500

(G-17410)
INVISTA CAPITAL MANAGEMENT LLC
4417 Lancaster Pike (19805-1523)
PHONE..................................877 446-8478
Steve R Mccracken, *Mgr*
EMP: 140
SALES (corp-wide): 36.93B **Privately Held**
Web: www.invista.com
SIC: 2821 Plastics materials and resins
HQ: Invista Capital Management, Llc
2801 Centerville Rd
Wilmington DE 19808
302 683-3000

(G-17411)
IO PROJECTS INC
112 S French St (19801-5035)
PHONE..................................302 416-5776
EMP: 6 **EST:** 2017
SALES (est): 80.82K **Privately Held**
Web: www.i-o-projects.com
SIC: 7371 Computer software development and applications

(G-17412)
IOGEN BMTHANE SUP CHAIN III LL ✪
251 Little Falls Dr (19808-1674)
PHONE..................................613 218-2045
Brian Foody, *CEO*
Patrick J Foody, *Ex VP*
Claire Dumville, *VP*
EMP: 6 **EST:** 2023
SALES (est): 262.22K **Privately Held**
SIC: 2869 Fuels

(G-17413)
IONE GROUP LLC
1601 Concord Pike Ste 30 (19803-3637)
PHONE..................................302 584-8377
Gary Zhou, *Prin*
EMP: 5 **EST:** 2011
SALES (est): 98.76K **Privately Held**
SIC: 8748 Business consulting, nec

(G-17414)
IOVATE HEALTH SCIENCES USA INC (HQ)
1100 N Market St Ste 4 (19801-1299)
PHONE..................................888 334-4448
Paul Gardiner, *Pr*
Norm Vanderee, *CFO*
◆ **EMP:** 6 **EST:** 2003
SALES (est): 97.71MM
SALES (corp-wide): 109.65MM **Privately Held**
Web: www.iovate.com
SIC: 4225 General warehousing and storage
PA: Kerr Investment Holding Corp
381 North Service Rd W
Oakville ON L6M 0
905 678-3119

(G-17415)
IP CAMERA WAREHOUSE LLC
Also Called: National Supply Contractors
3422 Old Capitol Trl (19808-6124)
PHONE..................................302 358-2690
EMP: 5
SALES (est): 211.27K **Privately Held**
SIC: 7382 Confinement surveillance systems maintenance and monitoring

(G-17416)
IPC HEALTHCARE INC
701 N Clayton St (19805-3165)
PHONE..................................302 368-2630
Adam Singer, *Brnch Mgr*
EMP: 8
SALES (corp-wide): 3.6B **Privately Held**
SIC: 8011 Primary care medical clinic
HQ: Ipc Healthcare, Inc.
4605 Lankershim Blvd # 617
North Hollywood CA 91602
888 447-2362

(G-17417)
IPR INTERNATIONAL LLC (PA)
1201 N Market St Ste 201 (19801-1160)
PHONE..................................302 304-8774
Charles Taylor, *Ch Bd*
Michael J Emmi, *Ch Bd*
Tami Fratis, *CEO*
Robert J Bray Junior, *Ex VP*
John P Meenan, *CFO*
EMP: 34 **EST:** 2002
SQ FT: 8,800
SALES (est): 10.11MM
SALES (corp-wide): 10.11MM **Privately Held**
Web: www.iprsecure.com
SIC: 7374 7375 7376 Service bureau, computer; Information retrieval services; Computer facilities management

(G-17418)
IPS DEVELOPMENT LLC (PA)
108 W 13th St (19801)
PHONE..................................800 981-7183
EMP: 7 **EST:** 2019
SALES (est): 9.42MM
SALES (corp-wide): 9.42MM **Privately Held**
SIC: 1731 Electric power systems contractors

(G-17419)
IPTL GLOBAL INC ✪
405 N King St Fl 3 (19801-3773)
PHONE..................................408 306-8888
Steve Chiu, *CEO*
Todd Stofka, *CMO*
EMP: 10 **EST:** 2023
SALES (est): 153.57K **Privately Held**
SIC: 7999 Tennis services and professionals

(G-17420)
IQARUS AMERICAS INC
1209 N Orange St (19801-1120)
PHONE..................................407 222-5726
Jetlir Bajrami, *CFO*
EMP: 37
SALES (est): 11MM **Privately Held**

▲ = Import ▼ = Export
◆ = Import/Export

GEOGRAPHIC SECTION

Wilmington - New Castle County (G-17449)

SIC: **8062** General medical and surgical hospitals

(G-17421)
IQURE PHARMA INC
Also Called: Iqure
251 Little Falls Dr (19808-1674)
PHONE...................................908 294-1212
Pawel Zolnierczyk, *Prin*
Anna Rzewuska, *Prin*
Hendrik De Wilde, *Prin*
Peter Schiemann, *Prin*
EMP: **12 EST:** 2019
SALES (est): 1.63MM **Privately Held**
Web: www.iqurepharma.com
SIC: **2834** Pharmaceutical preparations

(G-17422)
IRONDT CORP
3411 Silverside Rd (19810-4812)
PHONE...................................347 539-6471
Sergii Tkachenko, *Dir*
EMP: **5 EST:** 2017
SALES (est): 374.74K **Privately Held**
Web: www.irondt.com
SIC: **5013** Automotive supplies and parts

(G-17423)
IROQUOIS NEW ENGLAND INC
251 Little Falls Dr (19808-1674)
PHONE...................................716 373-5511
EMP: **14 EST:** 2016
SALES (est): 387.77K **Privately Held**
SIC: **6411** Insurance agents, nec

(G-17424)
ISA PROFESSIONAL LTD
919 N Market St Ste 425 (19801-3014)
PHONE...................................647 869-1552
Alexander Caban, *Pr*
EMP: **5 EST:** 2016
SALES (est): 494.12K **Privately Held**
Web: www.isa-professional.com
SIC: **3999** Barber and beauty shop equipment

(G-17425)
ISAACS ISAACS FMLY DENTISTRY PA
707 Foulk Rd Ste 103 (19803-3737)
PHONE...................................302 654-1328
David Isaac, *Pt*
EMP: **27 EST:** 1957
SQ FT: 1,700
SALES (est): 697.49K **Privately Held**
Web: www.isaacsdent.com
SIC: **8021** Dentists' office

(G-17426)
ISHARES US SCRTZED BOND INDEX ✪
100 Bellevue Pkwy (19809-3700)
PHONE...................................800 441-7762
EMP: **5 EST:** 2022
SALES (est): 106.48K **Privately Held**
SIC: **6722** Money market mutual funds

(G-17427)
ISLAND GENIUS LLC
1201 N Market St Ste 2300 (19801-1165)
PHONE...................................888 529-5506
EMP: **3 EST:** 2018
SALES (est): 83.91K **Privately Held**
SIC: **3999** Manufacturing industries, nec

(G-17428)
ISM
15 Sharpley Rd (19803-2940)
PHONE...................................302 656-2376
EMP: **17 EST:** 2014
SALES (est): 263.92K **Privately Held**

Web: www.isminc.com
SIC: **5149** Canned goods: fruit, vegetables, seafood, meats, etc.

(G-17429)
ISP INTERNATIONAL CORP
8145 Blazer Drive (19808)
PHONE...................................302 594-5000
EMP: 5
SALES (corp-wide): 2.19B **Publicly Held**
Web: www.ashland.com
SIC: **5169** Chemicals and allied products, nec
HQ: Isp International Corp.
1361 Alps Rd
Wayne NJ 07470

(G-17430)
ISWICH LLC
28 Austin Rd (19810-2203)
PHONE...................................302 528-0229
EMP: **5 EST:** 2014
SALES (est): 434.36K **Privately Held**
SIC: **7389** Design services

(G-17431)
ITANGO INC
1201 N Orange St Ste 600 (19801-1171)
PHONE...................................302 648-2646
Adrian Le Pera, *Prin*
EMP: **2 EST:** 2015
SALES (est): 120K **Privately Held**
SIC: **7371 7372** Custom computer programming services; Application computer software

(G-17432)
ITEL RAIL HOLDINGS CORPORATION
200 W 9th St (19801-1806)
PHONE...................................302 656-5476
EMP: **63 EST:** 1981
SALES (est): 1.58MM **Publicly Held**
SIC: **4011** Railroads, line-haul operating
PA: Wesco International, Inc.
225 W Station Square Dr # 700
Pittsburgh PA 15219

(G-17433)
ITG CLOUD SOFTWARE LLC
1013 Centre Rd Ste 403s (19805-1270)
PHONE...................................786 708-6560
EMP: **30 EST:** 2020
SALES (est): 692.31K **Privately Held**
SIC: **7371** Software programming applications

(G-17434)
ITIYAM LLC
1000 N West St Ste 1200 (19801-1058)
PHONE...................................703 291-1600
EMP: **10 EST:** 2011
SALES (est): 729K **Privately Held**
Web: www.itiyam.com
SIC: **7373** Computer integrated systems design

(G-17435)
ITL (USA) LIMITED
103 Foulk Rd Ste 202 (19803-3742)
PHONE...................................302 691-6158
Denis Faucher, *Pr*
EMP: **5 EST:** 1977
SALES (est): 111.45K **Privately Held**
SIC: **7389** Business Activities at Non-Commercial Site

(G-17436)
ITUMP INC
Also Called: Itump
501 Silverside Rd Ste 520 (19809-1374)
PHONE...................................302 985-9406
Jesse Daniels, *CEO*
EMP: **23 EST:** 2017
SALES (est): 568K **Privately Held**
Web: www.itump.com
SIC: **7379** Online services technology consultants

(G-17437)
IVANHOE ELECTRIC INC
251 Little Falls Dr (19808-1674)
PHONE...................................720 933-1150
EMP: 70
SALES (corp-wide): 8.44MM **Privately Held**
Web: www.ivanhoeelectric.com
SIC: **1081** Metal mining services
PA: Ivanhoe Electric Inc
606-999 Canada Pl
Vancouver BC V6C 3
604 689-8765

(G-17438)
IVY BOY AUTO WORKS
1401 Northeast Blvd (19802-5115)
PHONE...................................302 669-8842
EMP: **6 EST:** 2019
SALES (est): 139.54K **Privately Held**
SIC: **7538** General automotive repair shops

(G-17439)
IVY GABLES LLC
2210 Swiss Ln (19810-4241)
PHONE...................................302 475-9400
Tammy Loudon, *Owner*
Rebecca White, *Ex Dir*
EMP: **18 EST:** 2014
SALES (est): 2.18MM **Privately Held**
Web: www.ivygablesseniorliving.com
SIC: **8051** Skilled nursing care facilities

(G-17440)
IWEEKENDER INC ✪
251 Little Falls Dr (19808-1674)
PHONE...................................347 696-1010
Igor Alekhin, *CEO*
EMP: **7 EST:** 2022
SALES (est): 360.89K **Privately Held**
SIC: **4724** Travel agencies

(G-17441)
IYPER LLC ✪
221 W 9th St (19801-1619)
PHONE...................................929 269-5699
Bhanu Pidikiti, *Pr*
EMP: **20 EST:** 2022
SALES (est): 588.11K **Privately Held**
SIC: **7371** Computer software systems analysis and design, custom

(G-17442)
IZZYS LAWN SERVICE INC
1936 Seneca Rd (19805-4129)
PHONE...................................302 293-9221
Ismael Romero, *Owner*
EMP: **6 EST:** 2011
SALES (est): 246.04K **Privately Held**
Web: www.izzyslawnservicesinc.com
SIC: **0782** Lawn care services

(G-17443)
J & F HOME IMPROVEMENT LLC
2120 Oak St (19808-4833)
PHONE...................................302 407-6845
EMP: **5 EST:** 2019
SALES (est): 140.69K **Privately Held**

SIC: **1521** General remodeling, single-family houses

(G-17444)
J & J SNACK FOODS CORP PA
919 N Market St Ste 200 (19801-3068)
PHONE...................................302 571-0884
Kathleen Agnes, *Mgr*
EMP: 5
SALES (corp-wide): 1.56B **Publicly Held**
Web: www.jjsnack.com
SIC: **5145** Pretzels
HQ: J & J Snack Foods Corp Of Pennsylvania
6000 Central Hwy
Pennsauken NJ 08109
856 665-9533

(G-17445)
J & M INDUSTRIES INC
1014 S Market St (19801-5228)
PHONE...................................302 575-0200
James Maddox, *Pr*
Nancy Maddox, *VP*
EMP: **5 EST:** 1973
SQ FT: 5,000
SALES (est): 512.56K **Privately Held**
Web: www.jm-industries.com
SIC: **1794** Excavation work

(G-17446)
J & R PAINTING AND WALLPAPER
409 Marshfield Rd (19803-3533)
PHONE...................................302 438-9718
EMP: **5 EST:** 2014
SALES (est): 149.65K **Privately Held**
Web: www.jandrpaintpaper.com
SIC: **1721** Painting and paper hanging

(G-17447)
J & S GENERAL CONTRACTORS
1815 Williamson St (19806-2327)
PHONE...................................302 658-4499
John W Piazza Senior, *Owner*
EMP: **5 EST:** 1979
SQ FT: 3,000
SALES (est): 467.31K **Privately Held**
SIC: **1521 1542 6513 6514** Single-family home remodeling, additions, and repairs; Commercial and office buildings, renovation and repair; Apartment building operators; Dwelling operators, except apartments

(G-17448)
J A E SEAFOOD
403 Philadelphia Pike Ste 1 (19809-2170)
PHONE...................................302 765-2546
Jay Lee, *Owner*
EMP: **5 EST:** 2006
SALES (est): 367.94K **Privately Held**
SIC: **5146** Seafoods

(G-17449)
J A MOORE & SONS INC
Also Called: Moore, J A Construction Co
3201 Miller Rd (19802-2542)
PHONE...................................302 765-0110
Tom Cekine, *Mgr*
EMP: 6
SALES (corp-wide): 896.67K **Privately Held**
Web: www.jamooredevelopment.com
SIC: **1542** Nonresidential construction, nec
PA: J A Moore & Sons Inc
20408 Silver Lake Dr A
Rehoboth Beach DE 19971
302 226-8080

Wilmington - New Castle County (G-17450)

GEOGRAPHIC SECTION

(G-17450)
J A PYNE JR DDS PA
4925 Old Capitol Trl (19808-5211)
PHONE..................302 994-7730
J A Pyne Junior D.d.s., Pr
EMP: 7 EST: 1975
SALES (est): 230.49K **Privately Held**
SIC: 8021 Dentists' office

(G-17451)
J ALEXANDER PRODUCTIONS LLC
2208 Van Buren Pl (19802-3931)
PHONE..................302 559-6667
J Alexander, Prin
EMP: 5 EST: 2007
SALES (est): 205.4K **Privately Held**
Web: www.jalexanderproductions.com
SIC: 7822 Motion picture and tape distribution

(G-17452)
J AMOAKO OPERATION LLC
913 N Market St Ste 200 (19801-3097)
PHONE..................302 246-1346
Jason Amoako, Owner
EMP: 5 EST: 2017
SALES (est): 123.77K **Privately Held**
SIC: 8741 Business management

(G-17453)
J CLAYTON ATHEY
1310 N King St (19801-3220)
PHONE..................302 888-6507
John Small, Dir
EMP: 5 EST: 2010
SALES (est): 136.69K **Privately Held**
Web: www.prickett.com
SIC: 8111 General practice attorney, lawyer

(G-17454)
J E PELLEGRINO & ASSOCIATES
301 Robinson Ln Bldg 1 (19805-4673)
PHONE..................302 655-2565
James E Pellegrino, Pr
Jean L Pellegrino, VP
EMP: 8 EST: 1976
SQ FT: 2,500
SALES (est): 741.73K **Privately Held**
SIC: 1711 Warm air heating and air conditioning contractor

(G-17455)
J E RISPOLI CONTRACTOR INC
402 Hillside Ave (19805-1010)
PHONE..................302 999-1310
Joseph A Rispoli, Pr
Joann Medori, *
EMP: 8 EST: 1964
SQ FT: 5,000
SALES (est): 173.64K **Privately Held**
SIC: 1771 Curb and sidewalk contractors

(G-17456)
J F SOBIESKI MECH CONTRS INC (PA)
Also Called: Sobieski J F Mechanical Contrs
14 Hadco Rd (19804-1014)
PHONE..................302 993-0103
John F Sobieski Iii, CEO
Robert Sobieski, *
Richard H Steele, *
EMP: 105 EST: 1987
SQ FT: 25,000
SALES (est): 43.62MM
SALES (corp-wide): 43.62MM **Privately Held**
Web: www.sobieskiinc.com
SIC: 1711 Mechanical contractor

(G-17457)
J HENRY EDWARD & SONS INC
Also Called: Henry Auto Body Shop
2300 W 4th St (19805-3325)
PHONE..................302 658-4324
Zach Dillard, Pr
Charles D Thomas, VP
Ann Marie Henry-thomas, Treas
Catherine H May, Sec
EMP: 16 EST: 1943
SQ FT: 18,900
SALES (est): 839.42K **Privately Held**
Web: www.henryautobody.com
SIC: 7532 Body shop, automotive

(G-17458)
J M AJA TRANSPORTATION LLC
524 W Holly Oak Rd (19809-1306)
PHONE..................302 562-6028
Mutasem Ajaj, Pr
EMP: 9 EST: 2014
SALES (est): 222.96K **Privately Held**
SIC: 4789 Pipeline terminal facilities, independently operated

(G-17459)
J MICHAEL FAY DDS PA
3105 Limestone Rd Ste 304 (19808-2156)
PHONE..................302 998-2244
Robert G Hahn, Prin
EMP: 19 EST: 1973
SALES (est): 900.12K **Privately Held**
Web: www.dentistinwilmingtonde.com
SIC: 8021 Dentists' office

(G-17460)
J N GRILLO & SONS CO
1000 E 12th St (19802-5122)
PHONE..................302 658-7020
Anthony Grillo, Pr
Joseph Grillo Junior, VP
Joseph Grillo Senior, Ch Bd
Vincent Grillo, Sec
EMP: 9 EST: 1957
SQ FT: 30,000
SALES (est): 1.01MM **Privately Held**
SIC: 5013 Automotive supplies and parts

(G-17461)
J RIHL INC
Also Called: Costa and Rihl Mech Contrs
3518 Silverside Rd Ste 22 (19810-4907)
PHONE..................856 778-5899
EMP: 14 EST: 2002
SALES (est): 336.21K **Privately Held**
SIC: 1711 Plumbing, heating, air-conditioning

(G-17462)
J S & ASSOC
1510 Brandywine Blvd (19809-2212)
PHONE..................302 765-2300
Antoinett Malatesta, Pr
EMP: 5 EST: 2008
SALES (est): 75.28K **Privately Held**
Web: www.ceojsastaffing.com
SIC: 7361 Employment agencies

(G-17463)
J S MCKELVEY DDS
Also Called: Dental Health Assoc Pike Creek
4901 Limestone Rd (19808-1271)
PHONE..................302 239-0303
J S Mckelvey D.d.s., Owner
EMP: 15 EST: 1989
SALES (est): 1.17MM **Privately Held**
Web: www.pikecreekdental.com
SIC: 8021 Dentists' office

(G-17464)
J STACHON PLUMBING LLC
Also Called: Plumbing
1311 Hillside Blvd (19803-4234)
PHONE..................302 998-0938
EMP: 7 EST: 2011
SALES (est): 470.86K **Privately Held**
Web: theplumbco.wix.com
SIC: 1711 Plumbing contractors

(G-17465)
J STANLEY SALON LLC
204 N Union St (19805-3430)
PHONE..................302 778-1885
Jerome Stanley, Managing Member
EMP: 9 EST: 2005
SALES (est): 161.36K **Privately Held**
Web: www.jstanleysalon.com
SIC: 7231 7299 Hairdressers; Miscellaneous personal service

(G-17466)
J V AUTO SERVICE INC
1500 W Newport Pike (19804-3546)
PHONE..................302 999-0786
Joseph Van Sant, Pr
Cheryl Vansant, Sec
EMP: 10 EST: 1967
SQ FT: 1,600
SALES (est): 905.36K **Privately Held**
Web: www.jvautoservice.net
SIC: 7538 General automotive repair shops

(G-17467)
J&J CLEANING
300 S Ford Ave (19805-1920)
PHONE..................302 507-5082
Armando Pastrana-jimenez, Prin
EMP: 5 EST: 2014
SALES (est): 171.58K **Privately Held**
Web: www.jandjcleaningllc.com
SIC: 7699 Cleaning services

(G-17468)
J&L LOGISTIC GROUP LLC
408 W 24th St (19802-3403)
PHONE..................917 499-0019
Luis Maria, Managing Member
EMP: 6
SALES (est): 270.3K **Privately Held**
SIC: 3799 Transportation equipment, nec

(G-17469)
JAB CONTRACTING LLC
2 Biltmore Ct (19808-1378)
PHONE..................302 559-1905
Cecilia Andrzejewski, Prin
EMP: 8 EST: 2019
SALES (est): 285.34K **Privately Held**
SIC: 1799 Special trade contractors, nec

(G-17470)
JABEZ CORP
Also Called: Haldas Brothers
2201 Silverside Rd (19810-4501)
PHONE..................302 475-7600
John Eleutheriou, Pr
EMP: 12 EST: 1959
SQ FT: 2,000
SALES (est): 1.51MM **Privately Held**
Web: www.haldasmarket.com
SIC: 5421 5144 Meat markets, including freezer provisioners; Poultry and poultry products

(G-17471)
JACKSON HEWITT TAX SERVICE
3209 Miller Rd (19802-2507)
PHONE..................302 761-9626
EMP: 6 EST: 2018
SALES (est): 18.45K **Privately Held**
Web: www.jacksonhewitt.com
SIC: 7291 Tax return preparation services

(G-17472)
JACKSON MASONRY
325 Olga Rd (19805-2131)
PHONE..................302 397-4202
Eric Jackson, Prin
EMP: 5 EST: 2017
SALES (est): 83.57K **Privately Held**
Web: www.jacksonmasonryde.com
SIC: 1741 Masonry and other stonework

(G-17473)
JACOBS & CRUMPLAR PA
750 Shipyard Dr Ste 200 (19801-5160)
PHONE..................302 656-5445
Robert Jacobs, Pr
Thomas C Crumplar, VP
EMP: 29 EST: 1981
SQ FT: 1,000
SALES (est): 4.09MM **Privately Held**
Web: www.jcdelaw.com
SIC: 8111 General practice attorney, lawyer

(G-17474)
JAMAICAN MI HUNGRY
2202 Kirkwood Hwy (19805-4904)
PHONE..................302 287-3337
EMP: 6 EST: 2016
SALES (est): 78.41K **Privately Held**
SIC: 7999 Recreation services

(G-17475)
JAMAIKA
1908 W 2nd St (19805-3404)
PHONE..................302 521-4842
EMP: 5
SALES (est): 113.32K **Privately Held**
SIC: 8999 7389 Services, nec; Business services, nec

(G-17476)
JAMARK ENTERPRISES INC
Also Called: Natural Lawn of America
40 Germay Dr (19804-1105)
PHONE..................302 652-2000
Katherine Yates, Pr
Rick Yates, *
EMP: 25 EST: 1991
SALES (est): 957.58K **Privately Held**
Web: www.naturalawn.com
SIC: 0782 Lawn care services

(G-17477)
JAMEIL AKEEM CNGO CRES FNDTION
2205 Lamotte St (19802-4347)
PHONE..................302 409-0791
Tynietta Congo-wright, Ex Dir
Donte Congo, Pr
Lisa Mb Johnson, Sec
Tomeko Hadley, Treas
EMP: 6 EST: 2019
SALES (est): 120.88K **Privately Held**
SIC: 8093 Specialty outpatient clinics, nec

(G-17478)
JAMES & JESSES BARBR & BUTY SP
Also Called: James Jesses Barbr Maudes Buty
931 Bennett St Ste 933 (19801-4309)
PHONE..................302 658-9617
Jesse Dandy, Owner
Jesse Dandy, Pt
EMP: 5 EST: 1962
SQ FT: 1,500
SALES (est): 131.56K **Privately Held**

GEOGRAPHIC SECTION
Wilmington - New Castle County (G-17510)

SIC: 7231 Cosmetologist

(G-17479)
JAMES B CRISSMAN
2311 Empire Dr (19810-2706)
PHONE.................302 475-1365
James B Crissman, *Prin*
EMP: 7 EST: 2010
SALES (est): 55.35K **Privately Held**
SIC: 7261 Funeral home

(G-17480)
JAMES B SALVA MD
1805 Foulk Rd Ste F (19810-3700)
PHONE.................302 762-2283
James Salva, *Prin*
EMP: 9 EST: 2007
SALES (est): 169.44K **Privately Held**
SIC: 8011 8043 Physicians' office, including specialists; Offices and clinics of podiatrists

(G-17481)
JAMES FIERRO DO PA
1805 Foulk Rd Ste F (19810-3700)
PHONE.................302 529-2255
James D Fierro, *Pr*
EMP: 5 EST: 1991
SALES (est): 864.85K **Privately Held**
Web: www.drjamesfierro.com
SIC: 8011 General and family practice, physician/surgeon

(G-17482)
JAMES L HOLZMAN
Also Called: Prickett Jones & Elliott
1310 N King St (19801-3220)
P.O. Box 1328 (19899-1328)
PHONE.................302 888-6500
James Holzman, *Pt*
EMP: 15 EST: 1973
SALES (est): 776.5K **Privately Held**
Web: www.prickett.com
SIC: 8111 General practice attorney, lawyer

(G-17483)
JAMES N WALSH JR
1013 Centre Rd Ste 402 (19805-1265)
PHONE.................302 235-7777
James Walsh, *Mgr*
EMP: 5 EST: 2016
SALES (est): 125.17K **Privately Held**
SIC: 6411 Insurance agents and brokers

(G-17484)
JAMES ROBERT KLINE
110 Harding Ave (19804-3304)
PHONE.................302 633-3926
M E Lutz, *Prin*
EMP: 5 EST: 2013
SALES (est): 89.01K **Privately Held**
SIC: 1522 Residential construction, nec

(G-17485)
JAMES S REILLY M D
1600 Rockland Rd (19803-3607)
PHONE.................302 651-4200
EMP: 11 EST: 2017
SALES (est): 368.26K **Privately Held**
Web: www.nemours.org
SIC: 8011 Pediatrician

(G-17486)
JAMES STEWART ROSTOCKI
14 Westover Cir (19807-2975)
PHONE.................302 250-5541
Jennifer M Murphy, *CEO*
EMP: 5 EST: 2012
SALES (est): 104.92K **Privately Held**
SIC: 7389 Business Activities at Non-Commercial Site

(G-17487)
JAMES T CHANDLER & SON INC (PA)
Also Called: Chandler Funeral Homes
2506 Concord Pike (19803-5003)
PHONE.................302 478-7100
James T Chandler Iv, *Pr*
Chad H Chandler, *VP*
EMP: 9 EST: 1892
SQ FT: 7,500
SALES (est): 989.64K
SALES (corp-wide): 989.64K **Privately Held**
Web: www.chandlerfuneralhome.com
SIC: 7261 Funeral home

(G-17488)
JAMES TIGANI III DDS
1021 Gilpin Ave Ste 205 (19806-3272)
PHONE.................302 571-8740
James Tigani Iii D.m.d., *Owner*
EMP: 14 EST: 1975
SALES (est): 257.35K **Privately Held**
Web: www.tiganidentistry.com
SIC: 8021 Dentists' office

(G-17489)
JAMIE H KESKENY
1600 Rockland Rd (19803-3607)
PHONE.................302 651-6060
Jamie Heather Keskeny, *Prin*
EMP: 10 EST: 2013
SALES (est): 124.36K **Privately Held**
SIC: 8069 Eye, ear, nose, and throat hospital

(G-17490)
JAMLAND STUDIO
2326 Empire Dr (19810-2707)
PHONE.................302 475-0204
Earl Wilt, *Prin*
EMP: 5 EST: 2007
SALES (est): 116.38K **Privately Held**
Web: www.jamlandstudio.com
SIC: 8999 Music arranging and composing

(G-17491)
JAN STERN EQINE ASSSTED THRAPY
112 Shinn Cir (19808-1114)
PHONE.................302 234-9835
James Stern, *Prin*
EMP: 8 EST: 2009
SALES (est): 110.79K **Privately Held**
SIC: 8093 Rehabilitation center, outpatient treatment

(G-17492)
JANE A IERARDI M D
1600 Rockland Rd (19803-3607)
PHONE.................302 651-4000
Jane Ierardi, *Owner*
EMP: 12 EST: 2017
SALES (est): 255.04K **Privately Held**
Web: www.nemours.org
SIC: 8011 Pediatrician

(G-17493)
JANELLE G EVANS LLC
27 Tamarack Ave (19805-5049)
PHONE.................302 562-6504
EMP: 7 EST: 2017
SALES (est): 153.72K **Privately Held**
SIC: 8093 Specialty outpatient clinics, nec

(G-17494)
JANET SUE WINNER
100 Odessa Ave (19809-1435)
PHONE.................302 798-3731
Janet Winner, *Prin*
EMP: 5 EST: 2009
SALES (est): 36.57K **Privately Held**

SIC: 7299 Pet sitting, in-home

(G-17495)
JANIS DICRISTOFARO DAY CARE
1104 Arundel Dr (19808-2135)
PHONE.................302 998-6630
Janis Dichristofaro, *Prin*
EMP: 5 EST: 2006
SALES (est): 66.06K **Privately Held**
SIC: 8351 Group day care center

(G-17496)
JANS HANDS MASSAGE THERAPY
2421 Newell Dr (19808-3327)
PHONE.................302 753-3962
Julia Spock, *Prin*
EMP: 7 EST: 2013
SALES (est): 66.46K **Privately Held**
SIC: 8093 Rehabilitation center, outpatient treatment

(G-17497)
JANUS HNDRSON BLNCED CLLCTIVE
1100 N Market St (19890-1100)
PHONE.................800 724-2440
EMP: 5 EST: 2021
SALES (est): 106.48K **Privately Held**
SIC: 6722 Money market mutual funds

(G-17498)
JASMINE L HEATH MS
1602 Walnut St (19809-1547)
PHONE.................215 391-3553
Jasmine L Heath, *Prin*
EMP: 5 EST: 2019
SALES (est): 65.81K **Privately Held**
SIC: 8049 Offices of health practitioner

(G-17499)
JAY D LUFTY MD
2300 Pennsylvania Ave Ste 2a (19806-1379)
PHONE.................302 658-0404
Jay Lufty, *Prin*
William Medford, *Pt*
EMP: 10 EST: 2001
SALES (est): 351.03K **Privately Held**
SIC: 8011 Ears, nose, and throat specialist: physician/surgeon

(G-17500)
JAY GUNDEL AND ASSOCIATES INC
2502 Silverside Rd Ste 8 (19810-3740)
PHONE.................302 658-1674
Jay Gundel, *Pr*
Susan Gundel, *Treas*
EMP: 5 EST: 1978
SALES (est): 492.85K **Privately Held**
SIC: 7311 Advertising consultant

(G-17501)
JAY KATZ LMM TAXATION LLC
922 New Rd Ste 3 (19805-5199)
PHONE.................302 894-9446
EMP: 5 EST: 2003
SALES (est): 140K **Privately Held**
SIC: 7291 Tax return preparation services

(G-17502)
JAYSONS LLC
Also Called: Surestay
1807 Concord Pike (19803-2901)
PHONE.................302 656-9436
Mary Taylor, *Genl Mgr*
EMP: 34 EST: 2006
SQ FT: 44,400
SALES (est): 470.26K **Privately Held**
Web: www.brandywineinn.com

SIC: 7011 Hotels and motels

(G-17503)
JAZMINERENAE
3 Germay Dr Ste 4 (19804-1127)
P.O. Box 3 (19899-0003)
PHONE.................302 784-4710
Jazmine Frisby, *Pr*
EMP: 11 EST: 2020
SALES (est): 910.13K **Privately Held**
Web: www.jazminerenae.com
SIC: 8742 8741 Marketing consulting services; Business management

(G-17504)
JAZZERCISE
Also Called: Jazzercise
4900 Concord Pike (19803-1412)
PHONE.................610 485-9044
EMP: 5 EST: 2018
SALES (est): 70.33K **Privately Held**
Web: www.jazzercise.com
SIC: 7991 Aerobic dance and exercise classes

(G-17505)
JBIZA ENTERPRISES LLC
106 W 36th St (19802-2711)
PHONE.................302 764-3389
Jeffery Beard, *Prin*
EMP: 5 EST: 2009
SALES (est): 128.18K **Privately Held**
SIC: 8748 Business consulting, nec

(G-17506)
JBS CONTRACTING
2211 Bradmoor Rd (19803-3018)
PHONE.................302 543-7264
EMP: 5 EST: 2013
SALES (est): 240K **Privately Held**
SIC: 1799 Special trade contractors, nec

(G-17507)
JBS TECHNOLOGIES INC
1201 N Orange St Ste 7460 (19801-1293)
PHONE.................302 683-1098
EMP: 18 EST: 2015
SALES (est): 350.48K **Privately Held**
Web: www.jbstinc.com
SIC: 7361 Executive placement

(G-17508)
JC GENERAL CONSTRUCTION INC
232 W Ayre St (19804-3106)
PHONE.................302 383-3152
Jose Castendada, *Prin*
EMP: 7 EST: 2014
SALES (est): 218.18K **Privately Held**
SIC: 1542 Nonresidential construction, nec

(G-17509)
JC WEIGHT LOSS CENTRES INC
Also Called: Jenny Craig
4447 Concord Pike (19803-1489)
PHONE.................302 477-9202
Camille Nuccio, *Dir*
EMP: 5
Web: www.jennycraig.com
SIC: 7299 Diet center, without medical staff
PA: Jc Weight Loss Centres, Inc.
5770 Fleet St
Carlsbad CA 92008

(G-17510)
JDH CONSTRUCTION INC
Also Called: Thermal Seal Experts
1104 Kirkwood Hwy Frnt (19805-2108)
PHONE.................302 993-0720
John D Husband Junior, *Pr*
EMP: 6 EST: 1993

Wilmington - New Castle County (G-17511) GEOGRAPHIC SECTION

SALES (est): 482.18K **Privately Held**
Web: www.thermalsealexperts.com
SIC: 1742 Insulation, buildings

(G-17511)
JEAN L BINKLEY
2906 Newport Gap Pike (19808-2377)
PHONE..................302 598-5582
Jean Binkley, Ofcr
EMP: 6 EST: 2014
SALES (est): 59.83K **Privately Held**
SIC: 8049 Offices of health practitioner

(G-17512)
JEANETTE Y SON DENTIST
2601 Annand Dr Ste 8 (19808-3719)
PHONE..................302 998-8283
EMP: 5 EST: 1992
SALES (est): 257.38K **Privately Held**
Web: www.drjeanetteson.com
SIC: 8021 Dentists' office

(G-17513)
JEB PLASTICS INC
Also Called: Jeb Plastics
4550 Linden Hill Rd Ste 105 (19808-2909)
PHONE..................302 479-9223
Robert Rosini, Pr
Kathryn Rosini, Treas
EMP: 3 EST: 1992
SALES (est): 268.93K **Privately Held**
Web: www.jebplastics.com
SIC: 2673 2759 Bags: plastic, laminated, and coated; Bags, plastic: printing, nsk

(G-17514)
JEENA M JOLLY DDS
217 W 9th St (19801-1619)
PHONE..................302 655-2626
Jeena Jolly, Prin
EMP: 9 EST: 2014
SALES (est): 84.94K **Privately Held**
SIC: 8021 Dentists' office

(G-17515)
JEFF TETRICK
31 Paxon Dr (19803-2001)
PHONE..................302 478-7185
Jeff Tetrick, Prin
EMP: 5 EST: 2010
SALES (est): 179.43K **Privately Held**
SIC: 1522 Residential construction, nec

(G-17516)
JEFF WARNOCK CARPENTRY PAINTNG
1102 Talley Rd (19809-2524)
PHONE..................484 995-4812
Jeffrey Warnock, Prin
EMP: 5 EST: 2016
SALES (est): 45.66K **Privately Held**
SIC: 1721 Painting and paper hanging

(G-17517)
JEFFERSON GROUP LLC
4615 Sylvanus Dr (19803-4813)
PHONE..................302 764-1550
EMP: 5 EST: 2008
SALES (est): 95.96K **Privately Held**
SIC: 7389 Design services

(G-17518)
JEFFREY D KARRON LLC
21 Emsley Dr (19810-3263)
PHONE..................302 494-3724
Jeffrey Karron, Prin
EMP: 5 EST: 2011
SALES (est): 75.68K **Privately Held**
Web: www.karronlab.com

SIC: 8621 Professional standards review board

(G-17519)
JEFFREY GOLDSTEIN DR
4 Curry Ct (19810-3312)
PHONE..................302 478-5433
Jeffrey Goldstein, Prin
EMP: 8 EST: 2009
SALES (est): 95.62K **Privately Held**
SIC: 8011 Physicians' office, including specialists

(G-17520)
JEFFREY L WHITTERS JR LLC
131 Scarborough Park Dr (19804-1067)
PHONE..................800 563-6006
EMP: 5 EST: 2021
SALES (est): 94.01K **Privately Held**
SIC: 4119 Local passenger transportation, nec

(G-17521)
JEFFREY SCHLERF ATTY
919 N Market St (19801-3023)
PHONE..................302 622-4212
Jeffrey Schlerf, Prin
EMP: 5 EST: 2009
SALES (est): 108.43K **Privately Held**
SIC: 8111 General practice attorney, lawyer

(G-17522)
JEFFRIE J SILVERBERG PHD
2401 Pennsylvania Ave Apt 511 (19806-1407)
PHONE..................302 507-3039
Jeffrie J Silverberg, Prin
EMP: 9 EST: 2010
SALES (est): 112.7K **Privately Held**
SIC: 8322 Family counseling services

(G-17523)
JENNER ENTERPRISES INC (PA)
Also Called: Fastsigns
1300 First State Blvd Ste G (19804)
P.O. Box 5471 (19808-0471)
PHONE..................302 998-6755
Michael P Levitsky, Pr
Michael Levitsky, Pr
Janet Levitsky, Sec
EMP: 17 EST: 1989
SQ FT: 1,500
SALES (est): 2.51MM **Privately Held**
Web: www.fastsigns.com
SIC: 3993 Signs and advertising specialties

(G-17524)
JENNER ENTERPRISES INC
Also Called: Fastsigns
3203 Concord Pike (19803-5036)
PHONE..................302 479-5686
EMP: 2
Web: www.fastsigns.com
SIC: 3993 Signs and advertising specialties
PA: Jenner Enterprises Inc
1300 Frst State Blvd Ste
Wilmington DE 19804

(G-17525)
JENNIFER L JOSEPH DDS
5317 Limestone Rd Ste 2 (19808-1252)
PHONE..................302 239-6677
Jennifer Joseph, Ofcr
EMP: 10 EST: 2015
SALES (est): 92.49K **Privately Held**
SIC: 8021 Dentists' office

(G-17526)
JENNIFER L KOPAZNA
3 Harding Ave (19804-3301)

PHONE..................215 868-1466
Jennifer L Kopazna Lcsw, Prin
EMP: 6 EST: 2019
SALES (est): 80.29K **Privately Held**
SIC: 8049 Offices of health practitioner

(G-17527)
JENNIFER M DRAGONE
411 Northwood Rd (19803-3537)
PHONE..................302 353-7133
Jennifer Dragone, Owner
EMP: 6 EST: 2018
SALES (est): 69.93K **Privately Held**
SIC: 8049 Offices of health practitioner

(G-17528)
JENNS TAIL WAGGERS
8 Carpenter Plz (19810-2049)
PHONE..................302 475-9621
Jenn Schmidt, Owner
EMP: 10 EST: 2005
SALES (est): 672.75K **Privately Held**
SIC: 0752 Grooming services, pet and animal specialties

(G-17529)
JENNY CRAIG HOLDINGS INC
4447 Concord Pike (19803-1489)
PHONE..................302 477-9202
EMP: 1382 EST: 2011
SALES (est): 386.95K
SALES (corp-wide): 46.8MM **Privately Held**
Web: www.jennycraig.com
SIC: 7299 Diet center, without medical staff
PA: North Castle Partners, L.L.C.
183 E Putnam Ave
Greenwich CT 06830
203 485-0216

(G-17530)
JENRIN DISCOVERY LLC
2515 Lori Ln N (19810-3445)
PHONE..................302 379-1679
John F Mcelroy, Brnch Mgr
EMP: 5
SALES (corp-wide): 197.31K **Privately Held**
Web: www.jenrindiscovery.com
SIC: 8731 Biotechnical research, commercial
PA: Jenrin Discovery, Llc
1193 Killarney Ln
West Chester PA 19382
302 379-1679

(G-17531)
JEREMY SHEIKER
2119 Shipley Rd (19803-2303)
PHONE..................302 540-3741
Debbi Sheiker, Prin
EMP: 5 EST: 2010
SALES (est): 182.15K **Privately Held**
SIC: 1521 Single-family housing construction

(G-17532)
JERRY P GLUCKMAN M D
4830 Kennett Pike # 8000 (19807-1866)
PHONE..................302 426-8012
Jerry Gluckman, Ofcr
EMP: 7 EST: 2015
SALES (est): 71.05K **Privately Held**
SIC: 8011 Offices and clinics of medical doctors

(G-17533)
JESSICA A WHISLER MRS
3519 Silverside Rd (19810-4909)
PHONE..................302 438-3720
Jessica A Whisler Lcsw, Owner
EMP: 6 EST: 2018

SALES (est): 47.49K **Privately Held**
SIC: 8049 Offices of health practitioner

(G-17534)
JESSICA YANG INC
251 Little Falls Dr (19808-1674)
PHONE..................612 217-0220
Jessica Yang, Pr
EMP: 6 EST: 2018
SALES (est): 65K **Privately Held**
SIC: 6411 Insurance agents, brokers, and service

(G-17535)
JET PHYNX FILMS LLC
204 Birch Ave (19805-2504)
PHONE..................302 803-0109
Jet Phynx, Prin
EMP: 5 EST: 2018
SALES (est): 27.48K **Privately Held**
Web: www.jetphynxfilms.com
SIC: 7819 Services allied to motion pictures

(G-17536)
JET PRODUCTS LLC (PA)
2207 Concord Pike 640 (19803-2908)
PHONE..................877 453-8868
▲ EMP: 5 EST: 2005
SQ FT: 25,000
SALES (est): 2.5MM
SALES (corp-wide): 2.5MM **Privately Held**
SIC: 5032 Cement

(G-17537)
JET SETTING TOURS LLC
808 W 24th St (19802-3336)
PHONE..................707 217-6967
EMP: 6
SALES (est): 81.26K **Privately Held**
SIC: 4725 Tour operators

(G-17538)
JEWISH COMMUNITY CENTER INC
Also Called: J C C Fitness Center
101 Garden Of Eden Rd Ste 102 (19803-1511)
PHONE..................302 478-5660
Connie Sugarman, Pr
Amy Levtion, *
Nan Lipstein, *
Robert Davis, *
Martin Lubaroff, *
EMP: 48 EST: 1902
SQ FT: 15,000
SALES (est): 4.66MM **Privately Held**
Web: www.siegeljcc.org
SIC: 8322 Community center

(G-17539)
JEWISH FAMILY SERVICES OF DEL (PA)
Also Called: J F S
99 Passmore Dr (19803-1548)
PHONE..................302 478-9411
Dory Zatuchni, Dir
Valerie C Middlebrooks, Pr
EMP: 15 EST: 1899
SQ FT: 6,000
SALES (est): 5.03MM
SALES (corp-wide): 5.03MM **Privately Held**
Web: www.jfsdelaware.org
SIC: 8322 Social service center

(G-17540)
JEWISH FEDERATION OF DELAWARE
101 Garden Of Eden Rd (19803-1511)
PHONE..................302 478-5660
Barry Kayne, Pr

GEOGRAPHIC SECTION
Wilmington - New Castle County (G-17570)

Sam Asher, *VP*
EMP: 13 **EST:** 1936
SALES (est): 6.1MM **Privately Held**
Web: www.shalomdelaware.org
SIC: 8399 8661 Advocacy group; Religious organizations

(G-17541)
JG PLASTICS
1601 Concord Pike Ste 36d (19803-3635)
PHONE..............................302 545-4888
EMP: 7 **EST:** 2018
SALES (est): 198.82K **Privately Held**
SIC: 3089 Injection molding of plastics

(G-17542)
JGCOUNSELING
733 Ambleside Dr (19808-1541)
PHONE..............................302 354-0074
Jill Gaumer, *Prin*
EMP: 6 **EST:** 2019
SALES (est): 61.4K **Privately Held**
SIC: 8322 General counseling services

(G-17543)
JI DCI JOINT VENTURE 1
1211 Delaware Ave (19806-4716)
PHONE..............................302 652-4221
Paul Johnstone, *Prin*
EMP: 8 **EST:** 2013
SALES (est): 337.18K **Privately Held**
SIC: 8712 Architectural engineering

(G-17544)
JI DCI JV-II
1211 Delaware Ave (19806-4716)
PHONE..............................302 652-4221
Leigh P Johnstone, *Prin*
Paul Johnstone, *Mng Pt*
EMP: 6 **EST:** 2015
SALES (est): 83.4K **Privately Held**
Web: www.dciarchitects.com
SIC: 8712 8711 0781 7389 Architectural engineering; Engineering services; Landscape counseling and planning; Building inspection service

(G-17545)
JIA FINANCE INC
3524 Silverside Rd Ste 35b (19810-4929)
PHONE..............................202 341-0311
EMP: 5 **EST:** 2020
SALES (est): 580.5K **Privately Held**
Web: i.jiafinance.com
SIC: 6162 7371 Mortgage bankers and loan correspondents; Computer software development and applications

(G-17546)
JIFFYSHIRTSCOM (US) LP
1000 Nw St Ste 1280 (19801-1050)
PHONE..............................302 319-2063
John Murdoch, *Pt*
Christopher Serflek, *Pt*
EMP: 10 **EST:** 2008
SALES (est): 2.43MM **Privately Held**
Web: www.jiffyshirts.com
SIC: 5961 5137 Electronic shopping; Women's and children's clothing

(G-17547)
JILL GARRIDO DDS
2000 Foulk Rd Ste C (19810-3642)
PHONE..............................302 475-3110
Jill Garrido, *Prin*
EMP: 8 **EST:** 2018
SALES (est): 74.43K **Privately Held**
SIC: 8021 Dentists' office

(G-17548)
JILLANN I HOUNSELL DDS
2300 Pennsylvania Ave Ste 6a (19806-1301)
PHONE..............................302 691-3000
Jillann Hounsell, *Ofcr*
EMP: 8 **EST:** 2017
SALES (est): 67.67K **Privately Held**
Web: www.hounselldental.com
SIC: 8021 Dentists' office

(G-17549)
JIM KNNAS OPTMTRSTS OPTCANS IN (PA)
501 Silverside Rd Ste 105-3708 (19809-1374)
PHONE..............................302 722-6197
Jim Kounnas, *Pr*
EMP: 7 **EST:** 2001
SQ FT: 2,500
SALES (est): 2.3MM
SALES (corp-wide): 2.3MM **Privately Held**
Web: www.kuonopt.com
SIC: 3851 5995 5048 Frames, lenses, and parts, eyeglass and spectacle; Eyeglasses, prescription; Frames, ophthalmic

(G-17550)
JING JIN MD PHD
101 Shrewsbury Dr (19810-1400)
PHONE..............................302 651-5040
Jing Md, *Prin*
EMP: 13 **EST:** 2007
SALES (est): 89.48K **Privately Held**
SIC: 8011 8031 8062 Opthalmologist; Offices and clinics of osteopathic physicians; General medical and surgical hospitals

(G-17551)
JIVOSITE INC
1013 Centre Rd Ste 403b (19805-1270)
PHONE..............................408 604-0183
EMP: 9 **EST:** 2013
SALES (est): 333.41K **Privately Held**
SIC: 7379 Online services technology consultants

(G-17552)
JJC INDEPENDENT CONTRACTOR LLC
9 Nina Ct (19810-1512)
PHONE..............................302 388-5499
EMP: 9 **EST:** 2008
SALES (est): 106K **Privately Held**
Web: www.jjc.edu
SIC: 1799 Special trade contractors, nec

(G-17553)
JJS INDUSTRIES LP
2424 E Parris Dr (19808-4508)
PHONE..............................302 690-2957
EMP: 3 **EST:** 2019
SALES (est): 110.81K **Privately Held**
SIC: 3999 Manufacturing industries, nec

(G-17554)
JLD AUTO REPAIR AND TRANSM
3607 Downing Dr (19802-2409)
PHONE..............................302 650-8613
EMP: 6 **EST:** 2016
SALES (est): 82.9K **Privately Held**
SIC: 7537 Automotive e transmission repair shops

(G-17555)
JLE INC
20 Germay Dr (19804-1105)
PHONE..............................302 656-3590
TOLL FREE: 800
EMP: 22

SIC: 5046 Restaurant equipment and supplies, nec

(G-17556)
JMB GLAMSQUAD LLC
251 Little Falls Dr (19808-1674)
PHONE..............................844 695-4526
Vikas Tandon, *Managing Member*
EMP: 10 **EST:** 2021
SALES (est): 48.72K **Privately Held**
SIC: 7231 Beauty shops

(G-17557)
JMK BEHAVIOR LLC
1601 Milltown Rd (19808-4084)
PHONE..............................302 384-7354
EMP: 6 **EST:** 2019
SALES (est): 213.21K **Privately Held**
Web: www.jmkbehavior.com
SIC: 8099 Health and allied services, nec

(G-17558)
JMT SERVICES INC (PA)
520 Robinson Ln (19805-4616)
PHONE..............................302 407-5978
EMP: 7 **EST:** 2018
SALES (est): 536.21K
SALES (corp-wide): 536.21K **Privately Held**
Web: www.jmt.com
SIC: 8748 Business consulting, nec

(G-17559)
JNI CCC JV1 LLP
2317 Pennsylvania Ave (19806-1318)
P.O. Box 918 (19899-0918)
PHONE..............................302 654-6611
EMP: 13 **EST:** 2010
SALES (est): 942.3K **Privately Held**
SIC: 1542 Commercial and office building, new construction

(G-17560)
JOANN M SCHNEIDMAN
13 Dansfield Dr (19803-4805)
PHONE..............................302 761-9119
Joann Schneidman, *Prin*
EMP: 7 **EST:** 2017
SALES (est): 48.11K **Privately Held**
SIC: 8322 General counseling services

(G-17561)
JOEL GONZALEZ
Also Called: Custom Ceramics
4104 Lancaster Pike (19805-1518)
PHONE..............................302 562-6878
Gina Gonzalez, *Prin*
EMP: 5 **EST:** 2011
SALES (est): 78.1K **Privately Held**
SIC: 3269 Pottery products, nec

(G-17562)
JOHN F YASIK FUNERAL SERVICES
1900 Delaware Ave (19806-2302)
PHONE..............................302 428-9986
EMP: 5 **EST:** 2017
SALES (est): 87.53K **Privately Held**
Web: www.yasikfuneralhome.com
SIC: 7261 Funeral home

(G-17563)
JOHN FENICE MD
2601 Annand Dr Ste 4 (19808-3719)
PHONE..............................302 998-3334
John Fenice, *Prin*
EMP: 10 **EST:** 2012
SALES (est): 238.53K **Privately Held**
Web: www.amifasintl.org
SIC: 8011 Physicians' office, including specialists

(G-17564)
JOHN H WILLIAMS JR ATTY
1225 N King St Ste 700 (19801-3246)
PHONE..............................302 571-4780
John H Williams Junior, *Prin*
EMP: 10 **EST:** 2007
SALES (est): 227.57K
SALES (corp-wide): 223.19MM **Privately Held**
SIC: 8111 General practice attorney, lawyer
PA: Ikb Deutsche Industriebank Ag
Wilhelm-Botzkes-Str. 1
Dusseldorf NW 40474
21182210

(G-17565)
JOHN J BUCKLEY ASSOCIATES INC
105 Farm Ave (19810-2926)
PHONE..............................302 475-5443
John J Buckley, *Pr*
Sheila B Buckley, *Sec*
EMP: 2 **EST:** 1979
SALES (est): 200.65K **Privately Held**
SIC: 2819 5084 Industrial inorganic chemicals, nec; Cleaning equipment, high pressure, sand or steam

(G-17566)
JOHN JOHNSON DR
325 S Dupont St (19805-3916)
PHONE..............................302 999-7104
John Johnson, *Prin*
EMP: 9 **EST:** 2007
SALES (est): 95.05K **Privately Held**
SIC: 8011 8049 Physicians' office, including specialists; Offices of health practitioner

(G-17567)
JOHN N RUSSO DDS
300 Foulk Rd Ste 101 (19803-3819)
PHONE..............................302 652-3775
John Russo D.d.s., *Owner*
John Russo, *Pt*
EMP: 8 **EST:** 1971
SALES (est): 129.83K **Privately Held**
SIC: 8021 Dentists' office

(G-17568)
JOHNNY FITNESS LLC
2000 Penns Ave Apt 208 (19806-2460)
PHONE..............................302 654-9642
▲ **EMP:** 8 **EST:** 2000
SALES (est): 129.21K **Privately Held**
SIC: 7999 Yoga instruction

(G-17569)
JOHNS SALLY H LCSW
1601 Milltown Rd Ste 8g (19808-4073)
PHONE..............................302 547-7710
Sally H Johns, *Prin*
EMP: 7 **EST:** 2010
SALES (est): 55.62K **Privately Held**
SIC: 8322 Family counseling services

(G-17570)
JOHNSON & JOHNSON
Also Called: Johnson & Johnson
500 Swedes Landing Rd (19801-4417)
PHONE..............................302 652-3840
EMP: 48
SALES (corp-wide): 94.94B **Publicly Held**
Web: www.jnj.com
SIC: 3842 Dressings, surgical
PA: Johnson & Johnson
1 Johnson And Johnson Plz
New Brunswick NJ 08933
732 524-0400

Wilmington - New Castle County (G-17571)   GEOGRAPHIC SECTION

(G-17571)
JOLLYLOOK INC
251 Little Falls Dr (19808-1674)
PHONE.....................754 267-1885
Yevhenii Ivanov, *CEO*
EMP: 12
SALES (est): 906.38K **Privately Held**
SIC: 3861 Cameras, microfilm

(G-17572)
JONATHAN P CONTOMPASIS DPM
3801 Kennett Pike Ste A102 (19807-2321)
P.O. Box 3772 (19807-0772)
PHONE.....................302 983-8366
Jonathan Contompasis, *Ofcr*
EMP: 6 **EST:** 2016
SALES (est): 123.23K **Privately Held**
SIC: 8043 Offices and clinics of podiatrists

(G-17573)
JONATHON GORDON
Also Called: Terrareef
2818 Mill Creek Rd (19808-1361)
PHONE.....................302 690-0614
Jonathon Gordon, *Prin*
EMP: 5 **EST:** 2011
SALES (est): 96.31K **Privately Held**
Web: www.terrareef.com
SIC: 7389 Swimming pool and hot tub service and maintenance

(G-17574)
JONES ENTERPRISES INCORPORATED
1521 Concord Pike Ste 301 (19803-3644)
PHONE.....................888 639-1194
Joe Jones, *CEO*
EMP: 6 **EST:** 2014
SALES (est): 344.89K **Privately Held**
SIC: 6531 Real estate brokers and agents

(G-17575)
JONES PROPERTY COMPANY
Also Called: Jones Company
1308 Lancaster Ave (19805-3902)
PHONE.....................302 213-2695
Necia Jones, *CEO*
EMP: 5 **EST:** 2017
SALES (est): 267.15K **Privately Held**
SIC: 8742 7389 Real estate consultant; Notary publics

(G-17576)
JOSEPH A HURLEY PA
1215 N King St (19801-3285)
PHONE.....................302 658-8980
Joseph Hurley, *Owner*
EMP: 7 **EST:** 2002
SALES (est): 528.99K **Privately Held**
SIC: 8111 General practice attorney, lawyer

(G-17577)
JOSEPH A KUHN MD LLC
102 Haywood Rd (19807-1114)
PHONE.....................302 656-3801
Joseph A Kuhn Md, *Owner*
EMP: 8 **EST:** 2015
SALES (est): 92.57K **Privately Held**
SIC: 8011 Offices and clinics of medical doctors

(G-17578)
JOSEPH A SANTILLO INC
2403 E Parris Dr (19808-4507)
PHONE.....................302 661-7313
Carmilla R Santillo, *Pr*
Joseph A Santillo, *VP*
Carmella S Santillo, *Pr*
EMP: 6 **EST:** 1990
SALES (est): 979.75K **Privately Held**

SIC: 1542 Commercial and office buildings, renovation and repair

(G-17579)
JOSEPH C KELLY DDS
2205 Silverside Rd Ste 2 (19810-4534)
PHONE.....................302 475-5555
Joe Creazzo, *Mgr*
EMP: 10 **EST:** 2017
SALES (est): 221.05K **Privately Held**
SIC: 8021 Dentists' office

(G-17580)
JOSEPH CARTWRIGHT JR
Also Called: Jtc Towing
14 Colonial Ave (19805-5202)
PHONE.....................302 658-9487
Joseph Cartwright Junior, *Prin*
EMP: 6 **EST:** 2012
SALES (est): 163.36K **Privately Held**
SIC: 7549 Towing services

(G-17581)
JOSEPH G GOLDBERG OD
801 E Newport Pike (19804-1920)
PHONE.....................302 999-1286
Joseph G Goldberg O.d., *Owner*
EMP: 7 **EST:** 1993
SALES (est): 415.43K **Privately Held**
Web: www.wilmingtonfamilyeyecare.com
SIC: 8011 8042 Offices and clinics of medical doctors; Offices and clinics of optometrists

(G-17582)
JOSEPH H PIATT MD
1600 Rockland Rd (19803-3607)
PHONE.....................302 651-4000
Joseph Piatt, *Ofcr*
EMP: 12 **EST:** 2017
SALES (est): 249.5K **Privately Held**
Web: www.nemours.org
SIC: 8011 Pediatrician

(G-17583)
JOSEPH NAPOLI MD
1600 Rockland Rd (19803-3607)
PHONE.....................302 651-5981
Joseph Napoli, *Prin*
EMP: 16 **EST:** 2014
SALES (est): 258.52K **Privately Held**
Web: www.nemours.org
SIC: 8011 Pediatrician

(G-17584)
JOSEPH R KASOWSKI
Also Called: Partners Gen Cont
2503 Maple Ave (19808-3224)
PHONE.....................302 379-0523
Joseph R Kasowski, *Prin*
EMP: 5 **EST:** 2012
SALES (est): 153.71K **Privately Held**
SIC: 1522 Residential construction, nec

(G-17585)
JOSEPH TRUONO
1 Riverside Dr (19809-2644)
PHONE.....................302 762-6822
Joseph Truono, *Prin*
EMP: 5 **EST:** 2011
SALES (est): 115.99K **Privately Held**
SIC: 1521 Single-family housing construction

(G-17586)
JOSEPH V BAKANAS DPM
306 Odessa Ave (19809-1439)
PHONE.....................302 898-3783
Joseph Bakanas, *Prin*
EMP: 6 **EST:** 2011
SALES (est): 61.63K **Privately Held**

SIC: 8043 Offices and clinics of podiatrists

(G-17587)
JOSEPH W BENSON PA
1701 N Market St (19802-4808)
P.O. Box 248 (19899-0248)
PHONE.....................302 656-8811
Joseph W Benson, *Pr*
EMP: 7 **EST:** 1971
SALES (est): 723.21K **Privately Held**
SIC: 8111 General practice attorney, lawyer

(G-17588)
JOSEPH W SMALL ASSOCIATES INC
Also Called: Small Associates
2003 Marsh Rd (19810-3911)
EMP: 15 **EST:** 1964
SALES (est): 1.4MM **Privately Held**
Web: www.smallprinting.com
SIC: 2752 5199 Offset printing; Advertising specialties

(G-17589)
JOSES LANDSCAPING
4931 Old Capitol Trl (19808-5211)
PHONE.....................302 584-2656
Jose Ayllon, *Prin*
EMP: 5 **EST:** 2014
SALES (est): 41.82K **Privately Held**
SIC: 0781 Landscape services

(G-17590)
JOSH N SCHMIDT
Also Called: Into The Light Life Coaching
3219 Whiteman Rd (19808-2724)
PHONE.....................302 668-1304
Josh N Schmidt, *Prin*
EMP: 7 **EST:** 2012
SALES (est): 60.63K **Privately Held**
SIC: 8322 General counseling services

(G-17591)
JOSUE BARBER SHOP
509 Maryland Ave (19805-4426)
PHONE.....................302 650-5362
Josue Barber, *Ofcr*
EMP: 5 **EST:** 2015
SALES (est): 20.5K **Privately Held**
SIC: 7241 Barber shops

(G-17592)
JOURNEYS LLC
5201 W Woodmill Dr Ste 31 (19808-4068)
PHONE.....................302 384-7843
Rebecca Trent, *CEO*
EMP: 27 **EST:** 2017
SALES (est): 1.14MM **Privately Held**
SIC: 8093 Mental health clinic, outpatient

(G-17593)
JOY CLEANERS INC
301 Greenhill Ave (19805-1846)
PHONE.....................302 656-3537
Harry Amey, *Pr*
EMP: 8 **EST:** 1962
SALES (est): 346.6K **Privately Held**
SIC: 7216 7219 Cleaning and dyeing, except rugs; Fur garment cleaning, repairing, and storage

(G-17594)
JOY-HOPE FOUNDATION
215 Beau Tree Dr (19810-1177)
PHONE.....................302 379-1209
Amy Benton, *Prin*
EMP: 5 **EST:** 2010
SALES (est): 54.93K **Privately Held**
Web: www.joyhopefoundation.com
SIC: 8699 Charitable organization

(G-17595)
JOYN EXPERIENCES INC
1013 Centre Rd Ste 403b (19805-1270)
PHONE.....................214 437-8349
Bharath Varma, *CEO*
Sreevani Penumatcha, *Dir*
EMP: 5 **EST:** 2020
SALES (est): 46.16K **Privately Held**
SIC: 7371 Software programming applications

(G-17596)
JP MORGAN MULTI-MANAGER ALTERN
880 Powder Mill Rd (19803-2966)
PHONE.....................866 541-2724
EMP: 19 **EST:** 2017
SALES (est): 202.57K **Privately Held**
SIC: 6722 Management investment, open-end

(G-17597)
JPL M&R
11 Derickson Dr (19808-1901)
PHONE.....................302 883-9534
Stanley Lyons, *Prin*
John Lyons, *Prin*
EMP: 5 **EST:** 2013
SALES (est): 176.78K **Privately Held**
SIC: 1522 Residential construction, nec

(G-17598)
JPMORGAN CHASE BANK NAT ASSN
Also Called: Jpmc Card Services
201 N Walnut St (19801-2920)
PHONE.....................302 282-9000
EMP: 7
SALES (corp-wide): 154.79B **Publicly Held**
Web: www.jpmorgan.com
SIC: 6021 National commercial banks
HQ: Jpmorgan Chase Bank, National Association
1111 Polaris Pkwy
Columbus OH 43240
614 436-3055

(G-17599)
JPV TAX SERVICES
1719 Newport Gap Pike (19808-6119)
PHONE.....................302 740-6383
Juan Vasquez, *Prin*
EMP: 5 **EST:** 2016
SALES (est): 89.14K **Privately Held**
SIC: 7291 Tax return preparation services

(G-17600)
JR GETTIER & ASSOCIATES INC
Also Called: Gettier Security
2 Centerville Rd (19808-4708)
P.O. Box 1095 (19709-7095)
PHONE.....................302 478-0911
Jim Gettier, *CEO*
Lou Manerchia, *
EMP: 44 **EST:** 1987
SQ FT: 4,500
SALES (est): 6.32MM **Privately Held**
Web: www.gettier.com
SIC: 7381 8748 Private investigator; Business consulting, nec

(G-17601)
JR WALKER ROOFING INC
234 Philadelphia Pike Ste 11 (19809-3126)
PHONE.....................302 761-3744
Jessie Walker, *Pr*
EMP: 8 **EST:** 2011
SALES (est): 220.07K **Privately Held**
Web: www.jrwalkerroofing.com

GEOGRAPHIC SECTION
Wilmington - New Castle County (G-17632)

SIC: **1761** Roofing contractor

(G-17602)
JS LIQUORS
900 N Dupont St (19805-5311)
PHONE.....................302 656-4066
Paul Coen, *Prin*
EMP: 5 **EST:** 2010
SALES (est): 160.05K **Privately Held**
SIC: **5182** Liquor

(G-17603)
JS SHEDS LLC
9 Saint John Dr (19808-4629)
PHONE.....................484 918-0633
Joseph Speciale, *Managing Member*
EMP: 10 **EST:** 2021
SALES (est): 484.4K **Privately Held**
SIC: **3531 7389** Construction machinery; Business services, nec

(G-17604)
JS TIRE CORPORATION
3724 Kirkwood Hwy (19808-5106)
PHONE.....................302 558-2320
EMP: 8 **EST:** 1989
SALES (est): 117.11K **Privately Held**
SIC: **3011** Tires and inner tubes

(G-17605)
JSF CONSTRUCTION CO INC
316 Main St (19804-3907)
PHONE.....................302 999-9573
James Fulghum, *Pr*
Morine Fulghum, *VP*
EMP: 6 **EST:** 1981
SQ FT: 1,500
SALES (est): 1.07MM **Privately Held**
Web: www.jsfconstruction.org
SIC: **1521 1761 1731 1711** New construction, single-family houses; Roofing contractor; General electrical contractor; Warm air heating and air conditioning contractor

(G-17606)
JTHAN LLC
7 Meco Cir (19804-1108)
PHONE.....................302 994-2534
EMP: 9 **EST:** 2017
SALES (est): 654.5K **Privately Held**
SIC: **7389** Business services, nec

(G-17607)
JUBE MEDICAL SPA LLC
3521 Silverside Rd (19810-4900)
PHONE.....................302 478-4020
Isaias Irgau, *Prin*
EMP: 8 **EST:** 2008
SALES (est): 108.63K **Privately Held**
SIC: **7991** Spas

(G-17608)
JUDIE AI INC
2810 N Church St (19802-4447)
PHONE.....................407 401-4421
Alex Hassan, *CEO*
EMP: 12
SALES (est): 540.76K **Privately Held**
SIC: **7372** Educational computer software

(G-17609)
JULIAN H NICOL
Also Called: Jhn
706 Maple Ave (19809-3009)
PHONE.....................484 390-1980
Julian H Nicol, *Owner*
EMP: 6 **EST:** 2007
SALES (est): 116.3K **Privately Held**

SIC: **4731** Freight transportation arrangement

(G-17610)
JULIET THORBURN
1300 Pennsylvania Ave (19806-4311)
PHONE.....................302 598-1841
EMP: 5 **EST:** 2015
SALES (est): 116.98K **Privately Held**
Web: www.julietthorburn.com
SIC: **8412** Art gallery

(G-17611)
JUMPIN JACKS
508 E 35th St (19802-2818)
PHONE.....................302 762-7604
Jackie Bowers, *Owner*
Jackie Locket, *Owner*
EMP: 9 **EST:** 2000
SALES (est): 78.51K **Privately Held**
Web: www.jumpinjacksmonroe.com
SIC: **8351** Child day care services

(G-17612)
JUNEBUGS LITTLE RUBIES LLC
1104 D St 1106 (19801)
PHONE.....................302 494-7552
EMP: 7 **EST:** 2017
SALES (est): 49.82K **Privately Held**
SIC: **8351** Child day care services

(G-17613)
JUNG B KIM DDS
1815 W 13th St Ste 7 (19806-4054)
PHONE.....................302 652-3556
EMP: 8 **EST:** 2018
SALES (est): 67.67K **Privately Held**
SIC: **8021** Offices and clinics of dentists

(G-17614)
JUNI HOLDINGS INC
251 Little Falls Dr (19808-1674)
PHONE.....................415 949-4860
Robert Lamptey, *Prin*
EMP: 12 **EST:** 2018
SALES (est): 200K **Privately Held**
SIC: **6099 7371** Money order issuance; Computer software development and applications

(G-17615)
JUNIPER BANK
100 S West St (19801-5015)
PHONE.....................302 255-8000
Erik Toivonen, *Prin*
EMP: 19 **EST:** 2007
SALES (est): 3.72MM **Privately Held**
Web: cards.barclaycardus.com
SIC: **6099** Functions related to deposit banking

(G-17616)
JUNO INSURANCE SERVICES LLC
3 Germay Dr Ste 4 (19804-1127)
PHONE.....................650 380-8449
EMP: 6 **EST:** 2021
SALES (est): 508.51K **Privately Held**
Web: www.junokids.com
SIC: **6411** Insurance agents, brokers, and service

(G-17617)
JUST HOMES LLC
5560 Kirkwood Hwy (19808-5002)
P.O. Box 1701 (19701-7701)
PHONE.....................302 322-2233
Melinda Proctor, *Prin*
EMP: 6 **EST:** 2010
SALES (est): 232.48K **Privately Held**
SIC: **1521** Single-family housing construction

(G-17618)
JUST WALLET INC
3422 Old Capitol Trl 2002 (19808-6124)
PHONE.....................770 925-5098
Ryan Johnson, *CEO*
EMP: 5 **EST:** 2018
SALES (est): 104.73K **Privately Held**
Web: www.justwallet.com
SIC: **7389** Financial services

(G-17619)
JUSTIN BRIAN SALON LLC
1600 Kirkwood Hwy (19805-4918)
PHONE.....................302 597-8945
Vjustin Ditter, *Prin*
EMP: 5 **EST:** 2017
SALES (est): 44.77K **Privately Held**
Web: justinbriansalon.business.site
SIC: **7231** Hairdressers

(G-17620)
JUSTIN R CONNOR M D
1600 Rockland Rd (19803-3607)
PHONE.....................302 651-4200
Justin Connor, *Pr*
EMP: 11 **EST:** 2018
SALES (est): 246.45K **Privately Held**
Web: www.nemours.org
SIC: **8011** Pediatrician

(G-17621)
JUSTISON APTS LLC
1000 N West St (19801-1050)
PHONE.....................302 691-2100
Robert E Buccini, *Prin*
EMP: 6 **EST:** 2012
SALES (est): 538.98K **Privately Held**
SIC: **6513** Apartment building operators

(G-17622)
JUSTISON INVESTORS LLC
1000 N West St Ste 900 (19801-1050)
PHONE.....................302 691-2100
Robert E Buccini, *Prin*
EMP: 5 **EST:** 2012
SALES (est): 82.73K **Privately Held**
SIC: **6513** Apartment hotel operation

(G-17623)
JUSTTAI
1013 Centre Rd Ste 403 (19805-1270)
PHONE.....................781 771-0329
Ofir Tahor, *CEO*
EMP: 5 **EST:** 2021
SALES (est): 690.11K **Privately Held**
SIC: **6231** Security and commodity exchanges

(G-17624)
JUSTYCE BARBER & BEAUTY SALON
634 S Maryland Ave (19804-1632)
PHONE.....................302 998-7788
Devon Grasse, *Prin*
EMP: 5 **EST:** 2006
SALES (est): 59.16K **Privately Held**
SIC: **7231** Unisex hair salons

(G-17625)
JW TULL CONTRACTING SVCS LLC
1203 Philadelphia Pike (19809-2032)
PHONE.....................302 494-8179
Jason Tull, *Pr*
Stephanie Tull, *VP*
Richard Chiu, *Mgr*
EMP: 10 **EST:** 2014
SALES (est): 1.34MM **Privately Held**
Web: www.jwtull.com

SIC: **1799 1761 1542** Antenna installation; Roofing, siding, and sheetmetal work; Commercial and office buildings, renovation and repair

(G-17626)
K 1 NG LOGISTICS LLC
2203 Alister Dr (19808-3301)
PHONE.....................516 459-3316
Von-andrez Bhoorasingh, *Managing Member*
EMP: 3
SALES (est): 135.7K **Privately Held**
SIC: **3537** Trucks, tractors, loaders, carriers, and similar equipment

(G-17627)
K AND L GATES
600 N King St Ste 901 (19801-3777)
P.O. Box 2899 (25402-2899)
PHONE.....................302 416-7000
Steven L Caponi, *Pt*
Eric N Feldman, *Pt*
Nicholas L Froio, *Pt*
Andrew Skouvakis, *Pt*
Lisa R Stark, *Pt*
EMP: 58 **EST:** 2017
SALES (est): 422.46K **Privately Held**
Web: www.klgates.com
SIC: **8742 8111** Corporate objectives and policies consultant; Corporate, partnership and business law

(G-17628)
K CONTE
305 Sharpley Rd (19803-2441)
PHONE.....................302 283-9613
Kevin Conte, *Prin*
EMP: 5 **EST:** 2000
SALES (est): 104.08K **Privately Held**
SIC: **5044** Office equipment

(G-17629)
K DIAMOND DELIVERY INC
23 E Dale Rd (19810-4303)
PHONE.....................215 882-2585
Greg Ketter, *Pr*
EMP: 12
SALES (est): 528.7K **Privately Held**
SIC: **4215** Package delivery, vehicular

(G-17630)
K F DUNN & ASSOCIATES
819 N Washington St (19801-1509)
PHONE.....................302 328-3347
Kathleen F Dunn, *Pr*
EMP: 10 **EST:** 1988
SALES (est): 307.63K **Privately Held**
SIC: **7311** Advertising consultant

(G-17631)
K&B INVESTORS LLC
Also Called: Lawfully Yours
1908 Oak Lane Rd (19803-5215)
P.O. Box 7346 (19803-0346)
PHONE.....................302 357-9723
K'june Evans-harris, *Mgr*
K'june Evans-harris, *Managing Member*
Brian K Harris, *Co-Managing Member*
EMP: 2 **EST:** 2008
SALES (est): 185.68K **Privately Held**
SIC: **6798 2679 7929** Real estate investment trusts; Gift wrap and novelties, paper; Entertainment service

(G-17632)
K-TRON TECHNOLOGIES INC
300 Delaware Ave Ste 900 (19801-1671)
PHONE.....................302 421-7361
Alan R Sukoneck, *Pr*

Wilmington - New Castle County (G-17633)   GEOGRAPHIC SECTION

EMP: 100 EST: 1994
SALES (est): 43.86MM **Publicly Held**
SIC: 3532 Feeders, ore and aggregate
HQ: K-Tron International, Inc.
590 Woodbury Glassboro Rd
Sewell NJ 08080
856 589-0500

(G-17633)
K9 NATURAL FOODS USA LLC
108 W 13th St (19801)
PHONE.....................855 596-2887
EMP: 27 EST: 2018
SALES (est): 1.52MM **Privately Held**
SIC: 3999 Pet supplies

(G-17634)
KAHL COMPANY INC
3526 Silverside Rd Ste 38 (19810-4901)
PHONE.....................302 478-8450
Louis R Kahl, *Pr*
EMP: 6 EST: 1966
SQ FT: 2,000
SALES (est): 993.18K **Privately Held**
Web: www.kahlco.com
SIC: 5084 Chemical process equipment

(G-17635)
KAISER TIME INC
Also Called: Kaiser, Steven
623 Haverhill Rd (19803-2402)
PHONE.....................646 473-1640
Steven Kaiser, *Pr*
▲ EMP: 7 EST: 2000
SALES (est): 530.9K **Privately Held**
SIC: 8748 Business consulting, nec

(G-17636)
KALANAAI LLC
3 Germay Dr Ste 41648 (19804-1127)
PHONE.....................516 701-3977
EMP: 5 EST: 2020
SALES (est): 107.01K **Privately Held**
SIC: 7371 Software programming applications

(G-17637)
KALEIDO HEALTH SOLUTIONS INC
2810 N Church St (19802-4447)
P.O. Box 21789 (29413-1789)
PHONE.....................843 303-9168
Joe Bachana, *CEO*
Susan Collins Vp Customer Succ ess, *Prin*
Michelle Pae, *Product Management Vice-President*
Vanessa Johnson, *Dir Opers*
EMP: 5 EST: 2017
SALES (est): 1.25MM **Privately Held**
Web: www.kaleido-health.com
SIC: 7371 Computer software development and applications

(G-17638)
KALISIGN USA
2801 Centerville Rd Fl 1 (19808-1609)
PHONE.....................302 268-6946
EMP: 7 EST: 2017
SALES (est): 109.98K **Privately Held**
Web: usa.kalisign.com
SIC: 3993 Signs and advertising specialties

(G-17639)
KALMAR INVESTMENTS INC
3701 Kennett Pike Ste 100 (19807-2163)
P.O. Box 4157 (19807-0157)
PHONE.....................302 658-7575
Ford B Draper Junior, *Pr*
Brian D Draper, *
EMP: 17 EST: 1981
SQ FT: 5,000

SALES (est): 1.47MM **Privately Held**
Web: www.kalmarinvestments.com
SIC: 6282 Investment advisory service

(G-17640)
KALMAR NYCKEL FOUNDATION
1124 E 7th St (19801-4509)
PHONE.....................302 429-7447
C Parsells, *Ex Dir*
Georgeanna L Windley, *Sec*
George C Hering Iii, *Ch*
Richard Julian, *Pr*
Martin B Mcdonough, *Treas*
EMP: 6 EST: 1986
SALES (est): 1.42MM **Privately Held**
Web: www.kalmarnyckel.org
SIC: 8412 Museums and art galleries

(G-17641)
KAM ELECTRIC INC
845 Kiamensi Rd (19804-3449)
PHONE.....................302 998-5262
EMP: 8 EST: 2019
SALES (est): 238.42K **Privately Held**
Web: www.kamelectricinc.com
SIC: 1731 Electrical work

(G-17642)
KAM MARKETING HOLDINGS INC
128 Saint Moritz Dr (19807-1060)
PHONE.....................302 658-7778
EMP: 8 EST: 2019
SALES (est): 301.38K **Privately Held**
Web: www.kammarketing.com
SIC: 8742 Marketing consulting services

(G-17643)
KAMARA LLC
831 N Tatnall St (19801-1717)
PHONE.....................302 220-9570
EMP: 5 EST: 2017
SALES (est): 181.88K **Privately Held**
SIC: 7389 Business Activities at Non-Commercial Site

(G-17644)
KAMINA LLC ◊
3411 Silverside Rd Bldg 104 (19810-4812)
PHONE.....................347 200-0935
Jens Thobocarlsen, *CEO*
Carlos Emanuel, *Dir*
EMP: 9 EST: 2023
SALES (est): 313.29K **Privately Held**
SIC: 7389 Financial services

(G-17645)
KAN TRUCKING LLC
919 N Market St Ste 950 (19801-3036)
PHONE.....................413 358-7832
EMP: 5 EST: 2021
SALES (est): 400K **Privately Held**
SIC: 4231 Trucking terminal facilities

(G-17646)
KANACI TECHNOLOGIES INC (PA)
1209 N Orange St (19801)
PHONE.....................302 658-7581
Thomas E Bray, *CEO*
EMP: 15 EST: 2021
SALES (est): 23.24MM
SALES (corp-wide): 23.24MM **Privately Held**
SIC: 7549 Emissions testing without repairs, automotive

(G-17647)
KANGSTERS INC (PA) ◊
1007 N Orange St Ste 1382 (19801-1267)
PHONE.....................716 563-8225
Kang Kim, *CEO*

EMP: 3 EST: 2023
SALES (est): 104.82K
SALES (corp-wide): 104.82K **Privately Held**
SIC: 3999 Manufacturing industries, nec

(G-17648)
KANU INC
251 Little Falls Dr (19808-1674)
PHONE.....................401 533-6112
Andrew Bikash, *CEO*
EMP: 2 EST: 2018
SALES (est): 46.16K **Privately Held**
Web: www.kanu.us
SIC: 7372 7371 Educational computer software; Computer software development and applications

(G-17649)
KAPPA ALPHA FDN FOR LEAD SERV
1015 Linda Rd (19810-3009)
PHONE.....................302 475-4917
EMP: 5 EST: 2011
SALES (est): 71.25K **Privately Held**
SIC: 8641 University club

(G-17650)
KAPUR NEERAJ MD
2601 Annand Dr (19808-3719)
PHONE.....................302 789-0545
Neeraj Kapur, *Owner*
EMP: 9 EST: 2015
SALES (est): 65.5K **Privately Held**
SIC: 8011 Offices and clinics of medical doctors

(G-17651)
KARCHER MUNICIPAL NORTH AMER
3411 Silverside Rd # 104 (19810-4812)
PHONE.....................401 230-3296
Michael Hausermann, *CEO*
Robert Aranbitskiy, *
Stefanie Pollman, *
EMP: 24 EST: 2016
SALES (est): 1.19MM **Privately Held**
SIC: 5084 Industrial machinery and equipment

(G-17652)
KARDMASTER BROCHURES INC
24 Colony Blvd (19802-1402)
PHONE.....................610 434-5262
William Snyder, *Pr*
EMP: 6 EST: 1947
SQ FT: 1,200
SALES (est): 170.43K **Privately Held**
SIC: 2741 2731 2752 Miscellaneous publishing; Pamphlets: publishing only, not printed on site; Commercial printing, lithographic

(G-17653)
KAREN KIM ZOGHEIB LCSW
2110 Dunhill Dr (19810-4702)
PHONE.....................786 897-3022
Karen Kim Zogheib, *Prin*
EMP: 8 EST: 2011
SALES (est): 152.92K **Privately Held**
SIC: 8322 Social worker

(G-17654)
KARL W MCINTOSH M D
1300 Pennsylvania Ave (19806-4311)
PHONE.....................302 594-9000
Karl Mcintosh, *Mgr*
EMP: 8 EST: 2018
SALES (est): 101.38K **Privately Held**
SIC: 8011 Offices and clinics of medical doctors

(G-17655)
KARO HEALTHCARE INC ◊
1209 N Orange St (19801-1120)
PHONE.....................973 975-8306
Richard Edstrom, *CFO*
EMP: 5 EST: 2023
SALES (est): 116.57K **Privately Held**
SIC: 8099 Health screening service

(G-17656)
KASPAR KARRS
1027 W 25th St (19802-3372)
PHONE.....................302 660-2256
Kaspar Karrs, *Prin*
EMP: 6 EST: 2013
SALES (est): 74.85K **Privately Held**
SIC: 7538 General automotive repair shops

(G-17657)
KAT GERALIS HOME TEAM
1521 Concord Pike Ste 102 (19803-3614)
PHONE.....................302 383-5412
EMP: 22 EST: 2017
SALES (est): 251.89K **Privately Held**
Web: www.kghometeam.com
SIC: 6531 Real estate agent, residential

(G-17658)
KATABAT LLC (HQ)
112 S French St Ste 500 (19801-5035)
PHONE.....................302 830-9262
Ray Peloso, *CEO*
EMP: 37 EST: 2016
SALES (est): 10.91MM
SALES (corp-wide): 42.18MM **Privately Held**
Web: www.katabat.com
SIC: 7371 Computer software development
PA: Ontario Systems, Llc
1150 W Kilgore Ave
Muncie IN 47305
765 751-7000

(G-17659)
KATALIST LLC
501 Silverside Rd Ste 105 (19809-1376)
PHONE.....................302 502-0091
EMP: 6 EST: 2021
SALES (est): 318.23K **Privately Held**
Web: www.katalist-international.com
SIC: 8741 Business management

(G-17660)
KATHARINE L MAYER ATTY
Also Called: McCarter English
919 N Market St (19801-3023)
PHONE.....................302 984-6312
EMP: 6 EST: 2008
SALES (est): 251.07K **Privately Held**
SIC: 8111 General practice attorney, lawyer

(G-17661)
KATHERINE LAFFEY
Also Called: Family Mediation Services
1509 Gilpin Ave (19806-3015)
PHONE.....................302 651-7999
EMP: 5 EST: 1988
SALES (est): 487.76K **Privately Held**
SIC: 8111 General practice attorney, lawyer

(G-17662)
KATHERINE NWMAN DSIGN INTL LLC
2711 Centerville Rd (19808-1660)
PHONE.....................416 922-5806
EMP: 5 EST: 2005
SALES (est): 58.53K **Privately Held**
Web: www.katherinenewmandesign.com
SIC: 7389 Design services

GEOGRAPHIC SECTION   Wilmington - New Castle County (G-17692)

(G-17663)
KATHERINE T SAMWORTH
742 Westcliff Rd (19803-1712)
PHONE.................302 478-7485
Katherine T Samworth, *Prin*
EMP: 6 **EST:** 2009
SALES (est): 67.56K **Privately Held**
SIC: 8049 Clinical psychologist

(G-17664)
KATHLEEN LOONEY
4659 Malden Dr (19803-4817)
PHONE.................302 762-0106
Kathleen Looney, *Prin*
EMP: 5 **EST:** 2010
SALES (est): 163.36K **Privately Held**
SIC: 7361 Nurses' registry

(G-17665)
KATHLEEN M CRONAN MD
Also Called: Emergency Room
1600 Rockland Rd (19803-3607)
P.O. Box 269 (19899-0269)
PHONE.................302 651-5860
Kathleen Cronan Md, *Dir*
EMP: 18 **EST:** 2000
SALES (est): 524.35K **Privately Held**
Web: www.nemours.org
SIC: 8011 Pediatrician

(G-17666)
KATIE BUTERA
4404 Sandy Dr (19808-5630)
PHONE.................815 979-5129
Katie Butera, *Pr*
EMP: 6 **EST:** 2017
SALES (est): 55.25K **Privately Held**
SIC: 8049 Offices of health practitioner

(G-17667)
KATU SOFTWARE GLOBAL LLC
3 Germay Dr Ste 4 (19804)
PHONE.................302 803-5330
Hector Tolmo Tores, *Managing Member*
EMP: 10 **EST:** 2021
SALES (est): 348.32K **Privately Held**
Web: www.katusoftware.com
SIC: 7371 8742 Custom computer programming services; Management consulting services

(G-17668)
KATY E CROWE MD
3105 Limestone Rd Ste 301 (19808-2156)
PHONE.................302 230-4965
EMP: 7 **EST:** 2019
SALES (est): 120.12K **Privately Held**
SIC: 8011 Offices and clinics of medical doctors

(G-17669)
KB ELECTRICAL SERVICES
1 S Clayton St (19805-3948)
PHONE.................302 276-5733
EMP: 7 **EST:** 2018
SALES (est): 768.17K **Privately Held**
Web: www.kbelectricalservices.net
SIC: 4911 Electric services

(G-17670)
KC & ASSOCIATES INC
155 Oldbury Dr (19808-1433)
PHONE.................302 633-3300
Carolyn Warawa, *Pr*
EMP: 8 **EST:** 1992
SALES (est): 980.38K **Privately Held**
Web: www.kcassociatesinc.com
SIC: 8742 8732 Marketing consulting services; Market analysis or research

(G-17671)
KDI SOLUTIONS LLC ✪
1201 N Market St Ste 111 (19801-1156)
PHONE.................302 406-0224
EMP: 5 **EST:** 2022
SALES (est): 81.26K **Privately Held**
Web: www.kdi-inc.com
SIC: 4731 Freight transportation arrangement

(G-17672)
KEBLE INC ✪
2055 Limestone Rd Ste 200c (19808-5536)
PHONE.................810 893-3352
Oballa Emmanuel, *Pr*
EMP: 6 **EST:** 2022
SALES (est): 251.16K **Privately Held**
SIC: 7371 Computer software development and applications

(G-17673)
KEE JR RAYVANN
1401 Foulk Rd Ste 100 (19803-2764)
PHONE.................267 975-2199
EMP: 6 **EST:** 2017
SALES (est): 74.23K **Privately Held**
SIC: 8049 Offices of health practitioner

(G-17674)
KEEN COMPRESSED GAS CO (PA)
Also Called: Keen Compressed Gas
101 Rogers Rd Ste 200 (19801-5797)
P.O. Box 15146 (19850-5146)
PHONE.................302 594-4545
Bryan Keen, *Pr*
J Merrill Keen, *CEO*
Will Keen, *VP*
Jon Keen, *VP*
David Haas, *VP*
EMP: 11 **EST:** 1919
SQ FT: 30,000
SALES (est): 38.14MM
SALES (corp-wide): 38.14MM **Privately Held**
Web: www.keengas.com
SIC: 5169 5085 2813 5084 Gases, compressed and liquefied; Welding supplies ; Industrial gases; Welding machinery and equipment

(G-17675)
KEEP IN TOUCH SYSTEMS INC
19c Trolley Sq (19806-3355)
PHONE.................510 868-8088
EMP: 5 **EST:** 2008
SALES (est): 498.83K **Privately Held**
Web: www.kit-systems.com
SIC: 4813 Internet host services

(G-17676)
KEEPGO USA INC
1013 Centre Rd Ste 403a (19805-1270)
PHONE.................832 998-8753
EMP: 6 **EST:** 2018
SALES (est): 65.37K **Privately Held**
SIC: 4813 Internet connectivity services

(G-17677)
KEITH D STOLTZ FOUNDATION
20 Montchanin Rd Ste 250 (19807-2181)
PHONE.................302 654-3600
EMP: 8 **EST:** 2011
SALES (est): 431.21K **Privately Held**
SIC: 8699 Charitable organization

(G-17678)
KELF LLC
Also Called: Styles II
2353 Carpenter Station Rd (19810-3145)
PHONE.................302 229-2195
EMP: 5 **EST:** 2015
SALES (est): 106.13K **Privately Held**
SIC: 7231 Unisex hair salons

(G-17679)
KELLY & ASSOC INSUR GROUP INC
Also Called: Kelly Benefit Strategy
1201 N Orange St Ste 1100 (19801-1191)
PHONE.................302 661-6324
Jason Danner, *Brnch Mgr*
EMP: 8
SALES (corp-wide): 96.99MM **Privately Held**
Web: www.kellybenefits.com
SIC: 6411 Insurance brokers, nec
PA: Kelly & Associates Insurance Group, Inc.
1 Kelly Way
Sparks MD 21152
410 527-3400

(G-17680)
KELLY ANN HATTON
1601 Milltown Rd Ste 1 (19808-4047)
PHONE.................484 571-5369
EMP: 8 **EST:** 2017
SALES (est): 85.3K **Privately Held**
SIC: 8021 Offices and clinics of dentists

(G-17681)
KELMAR ASSOCIATES LLC
2200 Concord Pike # 12 (19803-2978)
PHONE.................781 213-6926
EMP: 60
SALES (corp-wide): 30.76MM **Privately Held**
Web: www.kelmarassoc.com
SIC: 8742 Management consulting services
PA: Kelmar Associates, Llc
500 Edgewater Dr Ste 525
Wakefield MA 01880
781 224-7310

(G-17682)
KELMON CONSTRUCTION
42 Iowa Rd (19808-5417)
PHONE.................302 357-4391
Kelly Montes, *Prin*
EMP: 5 **EST:** 2010
SALES (est): 107.63K **Privately Held**
SIC: 1521 Single-family housing construction

(G-17683)
KEN-DEL PRODUCTIONS INC
Also Called: Delaware Film & Tape Vault Co
1500 First State Blvd (19804-3596)
PHONE.................302 999-1111
H Edwin Kennedy, *Pr*
Marjorie L Kennedy, *VP*
Shirley Lotz, *Sec*
EMP: 7 **EST:** 1950
SQ FT: 25,000
SALES (est): 229.88K **Privately Held**
Web: www.ken-del.com
SIC: 7812 Video production

(G-17684)
KENDALL G RITZ M D
20 Montchanin Rd Ste 60 (19807-2179)
PHONE.................302 652-3586
Kendall Ritz, *Owner*
EMP: 8 **EST:** 2017
SALES (est): 98.73K **Privately Held**
SIC: 8011 Offices and clinics of medical doctors

(G-17685)
KENNEDY HEATHER ANN MD
500 Justison St (19801-5142)
PHONE.................302 655-7108
Heather Kennedy, *Prin*

EMP: 13 **EST:** 2000
SALES (est): 82.51K **Privately Held**
SIC: 8011 General and family practice, physician/surgeon

(G-17686)
KENNEDY HEALTH PAIN RELIEF AND
6 Sharpley Rd (19803-2941)
PHONE.................302 691-0110
Steven Bojarski Md, *Prin*
EMP: 8 **EST:** 2017
SALES (est): 657.28K **Privately Held**
Web: www.kennedyhealthcenter.org
SIC: 8099 Health and allied services, nec

(G-17687)
KENNETH DE GROUT DC
1401 Silverside Rd Ste 1 (19810-4400)
PHONE.................302 475-5600
Kenneth De Grout, *Pr*
EMP: 7 **EST:** 1983
SALES (est): 323.52K **Privately Held**
SIC: 8041 Offices and clinics of chiropractors

(G-17688)
KENNETH SSAN KING FNDATION INC
501 Silverside Rd Ste 123 (19809-1377)
PHONE.................800 839-1754
EMP: 5 **EST:** 2010
SALES (est): 719 **Privately Held**
SIC: 8699 Charitable organization

(G-17689)
KENNIS CAPITAL (USA) LLC
251 Little Falls Dr (19808-1674)
PHONE.................302 605-6228
Dean Bryan, *Managing Member*
EMP: 5
SALES (est): 219.98K **Privately Held**
SIC: 6798 Real estate investment trusts

(G-17690)
KENS LAWN SERVICE INC
732 Westcliff Rd (19803-1712)
PHONE.................302 478-2714
Ken Takvorian, *Pr*
EMP: 8 **EST:** 1993
SQ FT: 4,000
SALES (est): 502.78K **Privately Held**
Web: www.kenslawninc.com
SIC: 0782 Lawn care services

(G-17691)
KENSINGTON TOURS LTD
Also Called: Horizon and Co
2207 Concord Pike # 645 (19803-2908)
PHONE.................888 903-2001
Jeff Willner, *CEO*
EMP: 49 **EST:** 2005
SQ FT: 17,000
SALES (est): 3.12MM **Privately Held**
Web: www.kensingtontours.com
SIC: 7999 Tour and guide services

(G-17692)
KENT COUNTY PAINTING INC
1700 First State Blvd (19804-3566)
P.O. Box 3042 (19804-0042)
PHONE.................302 994-9628
Anthony Maccari, *Pr*
EMP: 35 **EST:** 1976
SQ FT: 18,000
SALES (est): 440.74K
SALES (corp-wide): 4.96MM **Privately Held**
SIC: 1721 Commercial painting
PA: Maccari Companies, Inc.
1700 First State Blvd

Wilmington - New Castle County (G-17693)   GEOGRAPHIC SECTION

Wilmington DE 19804
302 994-9628

(G-17693)
KENTMERE HLTHCARE CNSLTING COR
3511 Silverside Rd Ste 202 (19810-4902)
PHONE..................................302 478-7600
Jeffrey Petrizzi, *Prin*
Russel E Kaufman, *CMO*
EMP: 14 **EST:** 2007
SALES (est): 955.98K **Privately Held**
Web: www.kentmerehealth.com
SIC: 8011 Clinic, operated by physicians

(G-17694)
KENTMERE RHBLTTION HLTHCARE CT
1900 Lovering Ave (19806-2123)
PHONE..................................302 652-3311
EMP: 24 **EST:** 1901
SALES (est): 472.29K **Privately Held**
Web: www.kentmererehab.com
SIC: 8322 Rehabilitation services

(G-17695)
KERAHEALTH FRANCE LLC
5301 Limestone Rd Ste 100 (19808-1251)
PHONE..................................302 351-3377
EMP: 6 **EST:** 2016
SALES (est): 565.5K **Privately Held**
Web: www.kerahealth.com
SIC: 5122 Vitamins and minerals

(G-17696)
KERLINK INC
1209 N Orange St (19801-1120)
PHONE..................................805 407-9208
William Gouesbet, *Pr*
EMP: 6 **EST:** 2017
SALES (est): 34.23K **Privately Held**
Web: www.kerlink.com
SIC: 8748 Telecommunications consultant

(G-17697)
KERRY & G INC
1621 Willow Ave (19804-3531)
PHONE..................................302 999-0022
Kerry Elliot, *Mgr*
EMP: 5 **EST:** 2000
SALES (est): 68.38K **Privately Held**
SIC: 8351 Child day care services

(G-17698)
KERRY HARRISON PHOTOGRAPHY
2423 Nicholby Dr (19808-4236)
PHONE..................................302 494-4141
EMP: 5 **EST:** 2016
SALES (est): 83.1K **Privately Held**
Web: www.kerryharrison.net
SIC: 7221 Photographer, still or video

(G-17699)
KEVIN A JOHNSON
Also Called: Kaj Home Improvements
406 W 35th St (19802-2641)
PHONE..................................302 762-7671
Kevin A Johnson, *Prin*
EMP: 5 **EST:** 2010
SALES (est): 129.02K **Privately Held**
SIC: 1521 Single-family housing construction

(G-17700)
KEVIN KEOUGH DR
215 S Bancroft Pkwy (19805-3705)
PHONE..................................302 384-8173
Kevin Keough, *Prin*
EMP: 9 **EST:** 2008
SALES (est): 75.62K **Privately Held**

SIC: 8011 Offices and clinics of medical doctors

(G-17701)
KEWMARS E DADMARZ MD
7 Stabler Cir (19807-2554)
PHONE..................................302 691-5179
EMP: 6 **EST:** 2017
SALES (est): 76.51K **Privately Held**
SIC: 8011 General and family practice, physician/surgeon

(G-17702)
KEY-TEL COMMUNICATIONS INC
2642 Foulk Rd (19810-1422)
PHONE..................................302 475-3066
Kenneth Donahoe, *Pr*
Lawrence Donahoe, *VP*
EMP: 5 **EST:** 1983
SALES (est): 373.32K **Privately Held**
SIC: 4813 5999 Telephone communication, except radio; Telephone equipment and systems

(G-17703)
KEYLENT INC
1000 N West St Ste 1200 (19801-1058)
PHONE..................................401 864-6498
Ravi Mudunuri, *Pr*
EMP: 100 **EST:** 2010
SQ FT: 700
SALES (est): 5.01MM **Privately Held**
Web: app.netlify.com
SIC: 7371 Computer software development and applications

(G-17704)
KEYNOVA GROUP LLC
251 Little Falls Dr (19808-1674)
P.O. Box 2131 (01240-5131)
PHONE..................................410 785-6257
Elizabeth Robertson, *Managing Member*
Susan Foulds, *Managing Member*
EMP: 12 **EST:** 2019
SALES (est): 497.89K **Privately Held**
SIC: 8732 Market analysis or research

(G-17705)
KEYROCK LLC
3524 Silverside Rd Ste 35b (19810-4929)
PHONE..................................818 605-7772
EMP: 5 **EST:** 2019
SALES (est): 100K **Privately Held**
SIC: 1389 Construction, repair, and dismantling services

(G-17706)
KEYSTATE CORPORATE MGT LLC
824 N Market St Ste 210 (19801-4909)
PHONE..................................302 425-5158
Monte Miller, *CEO*
Joshua Miller, *Pr*
EMP: 19 **EST:** 2003
SALES (est): 387.1K **Privately Held**
Web: www.key-state.com
SIC: 8741 Business management

(G-17707)
KEYSTONE FINISHING INC
1800 Lovering Ave (19806-2122)
PHONE..................................925 825-2498
Patrick Keen, *Pr*
EMP: 12 **EST:** 2016
SALES (est): 490.68K **Privately Held**
Web: www.keystonefinishing.com
SIC: 1721 Painting and paper hanging

(G-17708)
KEYSTONE FLASHING COMPANY
8 Lombardy Dr (19803-3961)

PHONE..................................215 329-8500
Thomas N Spink Junior, *Pr*
Michael Spink, *VP*
EMP: 7 **EST:** 1938
SALES (est): 991.35K **Privately Held**
Web: www.keystoneflashing.com
SIC: 3444 5051 Sheet metalwork; Metals service centers and offices

(G-17709)
KEYSTONE HUMAN SERVICES
20 Rockford Rd (19806-1004)
PHONE..................................302 502-2158
EMP: 10 **EST:** 2017
SALES (est): 92.11K **Privately Held**
Web: www.khs.org
SIC: 8322 Social service center

(G-17710)
KGC ENTERPRISES INC
Also Called: Kc Sign Wilmington
3617 Kirkwood Hwy (19808-5103)
PHONE..................................302 668-1835
Eric Watkins, *Brnch Mgr*
EMP: 4
Web: www.kcsignco.com
SIC: 1799 3993 Sign installation and maintenance; Signs and advertising specialties
PA: Kgc Enterprises, Inc.
  142 Conchester Hwy
  Aston PA 19014

(G-17711)
KHAN FAMILY FOUNDATION INC
501 Silverside Rd (19809-1374)
PHONE..................................800 839-1754
EMP: 7 **EST:** 2010
SALES (est): 2.04MM **Privately Held**
SIC: 8699 Charitable organization

(G-17712)
KHAOS BEAUTY LLC
1313 N Market St Fl 2 (19801-6104)
PHONE..................................302 427-0119
Toshio Hoshino, *Pr*
Louis A Hoeweler, *
EMP: 1500 **EST:** 1986
SALES (est): 27.67MM **Privately Held**
SIC: 2844 3695 2899 Perfumes, cosmetics and other toilet preparations; Computer software tape and disks: blank, rigid, and floppy; Chemical preparations, nec
PA: Kao Corporation
  1-14-10, Nihombashikayabacho
  Chuo-Ku TKY 103-0

(G-17713)
KIDBERRY INC
251 Little Falls Dr (19808-1674)
PHONE..................................857 559-3043
Raman Hlushchuk, *Pr*
EMP: 5 **EST:** 2019
SALES (est): 101.23K **Privately Held**
SIC: 7371 Computer software development and applications

(G-17714)
KIDDOCS
4600 New Linden Hl 204 (19808)
PHONE..................................302 892-3300
EMP: 5 **EST:** 1995
SALES (est): 347.93K **Privately Held**
SIC: 8011 Pediatrician

(G-17715)
KIDS KINGDOM ELC LLC
205 W 7th St (19801-2238)
PHONE..................................302 377-1698
EMP: 6 **EST:** 2019

SALES (est): 420.33K **Privately Held**
SIC: 4911 Electric services

(G-17716)
KIDS KORNER DAY CARE
706 W Newport Pike (19804-3238)
PHONE..................................302 998-4606
Karen Ness, *Dir*
Joan Lameeth, *Dir*
EMP: 5 **EST:** 1990
SALES (est): 186.35K **Privately Held**
Web: www.kidskornerfamilydaycare.com
SIC: 8351 Group day care center

(G-17717)
KIDYA PRSCHOOL LRNG GMES FOR T
900 Foulk Rd Ste 201 (19803-3155)
PHONE..................................302 483-7778
Daniel Sonnenfeld, *Managing Member*
EMP: 10
SALES (est): 359.73K **Privately Held**
SIC: 7372 Educational computer software

(G-17718)
KIDZ KLUB
200 N Union St (19805-3457)
PHONE..................................302 652-5439
Mona Sampson, *Owner*
EMP: 8 **EST:** 2017
SALES (est): 97.39K **Privately Held**
SIC: 8351 Child day care services

(G-17719)
KILLHFFER CHRITABLE FOUNDATION
2204 Gilpin Ave (19806-2218)
PHONE..................................302 994-4762
Theodore Killheffer, *Dir*
EMP: 5 **EST:** 2013
SALES (est): 856 **Privately Held**
SIC: 8699 Charitable organization

(G-17720)
KIMBERLY N GINSBERG DR
7 Chaville Way (19807-1422)
PHONE..................................215 760-0751
Kimberly N Ginsberg Au D, *Prin*
EMP: 5 **EST:** 2019
SALES (est): 82.6K **Privately Held**
SIC: 8049 Offices of health practitioner

(G-17721)
KIND MIND KIDS
111 Lands End Rd (19807-2519)
P.O. Box 3682 (19807-0682)
PHONE..................................302 545-0380
Valerie Martin, *Prin*
EMP: 9 **EST:** 2010
SALES (est): 133.79K **Privately Held**
Web: www.kindmindkids.com
SIC: 8351 Preschool center

(G-17722)
KINDERCARE LEARNING CTRS LLC
Also Called: Kindercare Center 1006
2018 Naamans Rd C (19810-2659)
PHONE..................................302 475-2212
Michelle France, *Dir*
EMP: 17
SALES (corp-wide): 967.64MM **Privately Held**
Web: www.kindercare.com
SIC: 8351 Group day care center
HQ: Kindercare Learning Centers, Llc
  650 Ne Holladay St # 1400
  Portland OR 97232

GEOGRAPHIC SECTION
Wilmington - New Castle County (G-17752)

(G-17723)
KINDERCARE LEARNING CTRS LLC
Also Called: Kindercare Center 45
3449 Hillock Ln (19808-1711)
PHONE..................302 731-7138
Kimberly Dahlberg, *Dir*
EMP: 15
SALES (corp-wide): 967.64MM **Privately Held**
Web: www.kindercare.com
SIC: 8351 Group day care center
HQ: Kindercare Learning Centers, Llc
   650 Ne Holladay St # 1400
   Portland OR 97232

(G-17724)
KINDRED COUNSELING
3411 Silverside Rd # 105 (19810-4821)
PHONE..................302 478-8888
EMP: 6 **EST:** 2016
SALES (est): 39.83K **Privately Held**
SIC: 8322 General counseling services

(G-17725)
KINDWELL INC
1007 N Orange St Fl 4 (19801-1242)
P.O. Box 9647 (19714-9647)
PHONE..................302 588-2895
Ken Hu, *CEO*
EMP: 5 **EST:** 2020
SALES (est): 500K **Privately Held**
Web: www.kindwell.io
SIC: 3826 Environmental testing equipment

(G-17726)
KINETIC SKATEBOARDING
5319 Concord Pike (19803-1418)
PHONE..................856 375-2236
EMP: 5 **EST:** 2011
SALES (est): 110.41K **Privately Held**
Web: www.kineticskateboarding.com
SIC: 3949 Skateboards

(G-17727)
KING AND MINSK PA
1805 Foulk Rd Ste D (19810-3700)
PHONE..................302 475-3270
EMP: 9 **EST:** 2020
SALES (est): 80.11K **Privately Held**
Web: www.kingandminskdental.com
SIC: 8021 Offices and clinics of dentists

(G-17728)
KING CREATIVE LLC
727 N Market St (19801-4935)
PHONE..................302 593-1595
Christopher Bruce, *Prin*
EMP: 9 **EST:** 2019
SALES (est): 537.87K **Privately Held**
Web: www.kingcreative.com
SIC: 7812 Video production

(G-17729)
KINTYRE SOLUTIONS INC
Also Called: Kintyre
2817 Kennedy Rd (19810-3447)
PHONE..................888 636-0010
Brian Kennedy, *Pr*
EMP: 9 **EST:** 2015
SALES (est): 1.04MM **Privately Held**
Web: kintyre.squarespace.com
SIC: 8742 7389 5961 Management information systems consultant; Business Activities at Non-Commercial Site; Computer software, mail order
PA: Computer Design & Integration Llc
   500 5th Ave Ste 1500
   New York NY 10111

(G-17730)
KIRK FAMILY PRACTICE
5 Courtney Rd (19807-2505)
PHONE..................302 423-2049
EMP: 8 **EST:** 2018
SALES (est): 148.05K **Privately Held**
SIC: 8011 General and family practice, physician/surgeon

(G-17731)
KIRKWOOD DENTAL ASSOCIATES PA (PA)
710 Greenbank Rd (19808-3196)
PHONE..................302 994-2582
Arthur Young, *Pr*
Eric Esbitt, *Treas*
Nicholas Punturieri, *Sec*
EMP: 19 **EST:** 1956
SALES (est): 2.38MM
SALES (corp-wide): 2.38MM **Privately Held**
Web: www.kirkwooddental.com
SIC: 8021 Dentists' office

(G-17732)
KIRKWOOD FTNES RACQUETBALL CLB (PA)
1800 Naamans Rd (19810-2600)
PHONE..................302 529-1865
Steven Qualls, *Pr*
EMP: 13 **EST:** 1970
SALES (est): 515.85K
SALES (corp-wide): 515.85K **Privately Held**
SIC: 7997 7991 Racquetball club, membership; Physical fitness clubs with training equipment

(G-17733)
KIRKWOOD PROPERTY
4700 Kirkwood Hwy (19808-5008)
P.O. Box 1891 (19899-1891)
PHONE..................302 981-0966
Rhonda Sullivan, *Prin*
EMP: 5 **EST:** 2011
SALES (est): 161.22K **Privately Held**
SIC: 6512 Nonresidential building operators

(G-17734)
KIRWA FOUNDATION
2711 Centerville Rd # 400 (19808-1660)
PHONE..................347 932-4911
EMP: 13 **EST:** 2015
SALES (est): 155.16K **Privately Held**
Web: www.kirwafoundation.org
SIC: 8399 Social services, nec

(G-17735)
KISSFLOW INC
Also Called: Kissflow
1000 N West St Ste 1200 (19801-1058)
PHONE..................650 396-7692
Suresh Sambandam, *Pr*
EMP: 200 **EST:** 2012
SALES (est): 21.39MM **Privately Held**
Web: www.kissflow.com
SIC: 7372 Prepackaged software

(G-17736)
KIT INTERNATIONAL INC
2711 Cntrvlle Rd Ste 7263 (19808)
PHONE..................201 342-7753
EMP: 7 **EST:** 2011
SALES (est): 116.26K **Privately Held**
SIC: 5147 Meats and meat products

(G-17737)
KITCHEN GALLERY INC
201 Greenhill Ave (19805-1844)
PHONE..................302 655-7214
Oskar Muenz, *Pr*
Caroline Muenz, *VP*
EMP: 5 **EST:** 1991
SQ FT: 2,200
SALES (est): 409.88K **Privately Held**
Web: www.kitchengalleryofdelaware.com
SIC: 1799 Kitchen and bathroom remodeling

(G-17738)
KJP LLC
1601 Concord Pike Ste 35 (19803-3613)
PHONE..................302 765-0134
EMP: 5 **EST:** 2010
SALES (est): 64.86K **Privately Held**
SIC: 7231 Beauty shops

(G-17739)
KJS DETAILING LLC
4615 Sylvanus Dr (19803-4813)
PHONE..................302 420-9132
EMP: 6 **EST:** 2013
SALES (est): 239.04K **Privately Held**
Web: www.kjsdetailing.com
SIC: 7542 Washing and polishing, automotive

(G-17740)
KLEAN TEAM OF WILMINGTON
301 Tyrone Ave (19804-1930)
PHONE..................302 298-5558
EMP: 5 **EST:** 2018
SALES (est): 140.25K **Privately Held**
SIC: 7699 Cleaning services

(G-17741)
KLH PROPERTIES LTD LBLTY CO
718 E 7th St (19801-4411)
PHONE..................352 208-8964
Keshialee Hill, *CEO*
EMP: 5 **EST:** 2020
SALES (est): 104.73K **Privately Held**
SIC: 7389 Business Activities at Non-Commercial Site

(G-17742)
KM KLACKO & ASSOCIATE
509 Redfern Ave (19807-3121)
PHONE..................302 652-1482
Kathrene Klacko, *Owner*
EMP: 5 **EST:** 2004
SALES (est): 71.94K **Privately Held**
SIC: 7299 Party planning service

(G-17743)
KMC MANAGEMENT LLC
1201 N Market St Ste 111 (19801-1147)
PHONE..................866 943-2205
EMP: 5
SALES (est): 199.4K **Privately Held**
SIC: 8748 Business consulting, nec

(G-17744)
KNOTTS CONSTRUCTION INC
1504 Upsan Downs Ln (19810-4444)
PHONE..................302 475-7074
Wayne Knotts, *Pr*
EMP: 7 **EST:** 1981
SALES (est): 801.55K **Privately Held**
Web: www.knottsconstruction.com
SIC: 1521 Single-family housing construction

(G-17745)
KNUS INC ✪
1000 N West St Ste 1281-268 (19801-1050)
PHONE..................855 935-5687
Charles Harris, *Prin*
EMP: 89 **EST:** 2023
SALES (est): 956.59K **Privately Held**
SIC: 8093 Specialty outpatient clinics, nec

(G-17746)
KONCORDIA GROUP LLC
1201 N Market St Ste 401 (19801-1160)
PHONE..................302 427-1350
EMP: 23 **EST:** 1997
SALES (est): 463.48K **Privately Held**
Web: www.koncordiagroup.com
SIC: 7311 Advertising consultant

(G-17747)
KOREAN MARTIAL ARTS INSTITUTE (PA)
2419 W Newport Pike (19804-3846)
PHONE..................302 992-7999
John L Godwin, *Pr*
Michele Godwin, *VP*
EMP: 6 **EST:** 1986
SALES (est): 667.07K **Privately Held**
Web: www.kmaiweb.com
SIC: 7999 Karate instruction

(G-17748)
KORSGY TECHNOLOGIES LLC
3411 Silverside Rd 235 (19810-4812)
PHONE..................302 504-6201
Kevin Harrison Grubb, *Ex Dir*
EMP: 5 **EST:** 2021
SALES (est): 211.51K **Privately Held**
Web: www.korsgy.com
SIC: 7389 8742 7379 7371 Business Activities at Non-Commercial Site; Management information systems consultant; Online services technology consultants; Software programming applications

(G-17749)
KPSS GOVERNMENT SOLUTIONS INC
1100 First State Blvd (19804-3550)
PHONE..................302 992-7950
EMP: 86
SIC: 5063 Burglar alarm systems

(G-17750)
KRAMER GROUP LLC
2116 Peachtree Dr (19805-1050)
PHONE..................717 368-2117
EMP: 8 **EST:** 2012
SALES (est): 457.43K **Privately Held**
SIC: 8748 Business consulting, nec

(G-17751)
KRAPFS COACHES INC
Also Called: Gregg Bus Service
1400 First State Blvd (19804-3563)
PHONE..................302 993-7855
Bradley Krapf, *Bmch Mgr*
EMP: 32
SALES (corp-wide): 49.08MM **Privately Held**
Web: www.krapfbus.com
SIC: 4142 4141 Bus charter service, except local; Local bus charter service
PA: Krapf's Coaches, Inc.
   1060 Saunders Ln
   West Chester PA 19380
   610 431-1500

(G-17752)
KRAVE LIKE LLC
7 Deer Run Dr (19807-2403)
PHONE..................302 482-4550
Nicholas D'alonzo, *Managing Member*
EMP: 5 **EST:** 2009
SALES (est): 217.51K **Privately Held**
SIC: 2086 Soft drinks: packaged in cans, bottles, etc.

Wilmington - New Castle County (G-17753) GEOGRAPHIC SECTION

(G-17753)
KRAYO INC
1013 Centre Rd Ste 403b (19805-1270)
PHONE..............................415 851-6250
Rohit Agarwal, *CEO*
EMP: 6 **EST:** 2021
SALES (est): 237.56K **Privately Held**
SIC: 7371 Software programming applications

(G-17754)
KREMER EYE CENTER
2060 Limestone Rd Ste 205 (19808-5530)
PHONE..............................866 206-4322
EMP: 21 **EST:** 2019
SALES (est): 243.79K **Privately Held**
Web: www.oomc.com
SIC: 8011 Opthalmologist

(G-17755)
KRENEE LLC
3200 Kirkwood Hwy (19808-6153)
PHONE..............................302 200-1025
Karma Pace, *Managing Member*
EMP: 5 **EST:** 2012
SALES (est): 79.53K **Privately Held**
SIC: 8748 Business consulting, nec

(G-17756)
KRIS WINDOW TINT LLC
804 N Lincoln St (19805-5320)
PHONE..............................302 384-6185
Kristhian Caraballo, *Prin*
EMP: 5 **EST:** 2016
SALES (est): 181.97K **Privately Held**
SIC: 5031 Windows

(G-17757)
KRISHNA WHITE MD
1600 Rockland Rd (19803-3607)
PHONE..............................302 651-6040
Krishna White, *Prin*
EMP: 14 **EST:** 2015
SALES (est): 185.16K **Privately Held**
Web: www.nemours.org
SIC: 8011 Pediatrician

(G-17758)
KRN ARCHITECTURE LLC
2207 Concord Pike 145 (19803-2908)
PHONE..............................302 536-8576
Karen Anderson, *Prin*
EMP: 5 **EST:** 2009
SALES (est): 138.53K **Privately Held**
Web: www.krnarchitecture.com
SIC: 8712 Architectural services

(G-17759)
KST LAND DESIGN INC
2627 Skylark Rd (19808-1633)
P.O. Box 169 (19720-0169)
PHONE..............................302 328-1879
Kevin S Thomas, *Pr*
EMP: 7 **EST:** 1978
SALES (est): 222.32K **Privately Held**
SIC: 0782 Lawn care services

(G-17760)
KTF ENTERPRISE LLC
224 W 29th St (19802-3109)
PHONE..............................302 932-6039
EMP: 5 **EST:** 2018
SALES (est): 331.85K **Privately Held**
SIC: 4212 Local trucking, without storage

(G-17761)
KUBASKO MCKEE GROUP RE
3711 Kennett Pike Ste 220 (19807-2161)
PHONE..............................877 302-7747
EMP: 5 **EST:** 2017
SALES (est): 96.95K **Privately Held**
SIC: 6531 Real estate agent, residential

(G-17762)
KUBERA GLOBAL SOLUTIONS LLC
1521 Concord Pike Ste 301 (19803-3644)
PHONE..............................480 241-5124
Robert Hilton, *Pr*
EMP: 6 **EST:** 2012
SALES (est): 109.5K **Privately Held**
SIC: 8741 Financial management for business

(G-17763)
KUNKUN AUTO GROUP LLC
408 W 24th St (19802-3403)
PHONE..............................917 499-0019
Luis Maria, *Prin*
EMP: 6 **EST:** 2014
SALES (est): 31.07K **Privately Held**
SIC: 7538 General automotive repair shops

(G-17764)
KUPFERMAN & ASSOCIATES LLC
1701 Shallcross Ave Ste D (19806-2347)
PHONE..............................302 656-7566
Ira Kupferman, *Managing Member*
EMP: 6 **EST:** 1970
SALES (est): 1.28MM **Privately Held**
Web: aka.cpa
SIC: 8721 Certified public accountant

(G-17765)
KURB SYSTEMS INC
300 Delaware Ave (19801-1607)
PHONE..............................732 490-1741
EMP: 4 **EST:** 2020
SALES (est): 117.34K **Privately Held**
Web: www.supportallyear.com
SIC: 7372 Prepackaged software

(G-17766)
KURT F GWYNNE
1201 N Market St Ste 1500 (19801-1163)
PHONE..............................302 778-7550
Kurt Gwynne, *Prin*
EMP: 5 **EST:** 2018
SALES (est): 70.03K **Privately Held**
SIC: 8111 General practice attorney, lawyer

(G-17767)
KURTZ COLLECTION
1010 N Union St (19805-2731)
PHONE..............................302 654-0442
EMP: 7 **EST:** 2011
SALES (est): 490.17K **Privately Held**
Web: www.kurtzcollection.com
SIC: 2273 Carpets and rugs

(G-17768)
KUSHIM INC (PA)
2711 Centerville Rd Ste 400 (19808-1660)
PHONE..............................609 919-9889
Clement Ajlietta, *CEO*
EMP: 5 **EST:** 2017
SALES (est): 494K
SALES (corp-wide): 494K **Privately Held**
Web: www.edda.co
SIC: 7371 Computer software development and applications

(G-17769)
KUSTOM ADDITIONS LLC ◊
1207 Delaware Ave (19806-4743)
PHONE..............................302 468-6865
Alisha Mason, *Managing Member*
EMP: 2 **EST:** 2022
SALES (est): 72.72K **Privately Held**

SIC: 2491 7336 2499 7359 Wood products, creosoted; Silk screen design; Wood products, nec; Party supplies rental services

(G-17770)
KVM DEPOT INC
1007 N Orange St (19801-1239)
PHONE..............................302 472-9190
David Miller, *Pr*
EMP: 7 **EST:** 2006
SALES (est): 130.54K **Privately Held**
Web: www.kvmdepot.com
SIC: 5045 Computers, peripherals, and software

(G-17771)
KWA ANALYTICS US LLC
1209 N Orange St (19801-1120)
PHONE..............................914 629-6744
EMP: 33 **EST:** 2017
SALES (est): 13.89MM **Privately Held**
SIC: 7379 Computer related consulting services

(G-17772)
KYBER CORP
112 S French St Ste 105 (19801-5035)
PHONE..............................609 203-1413
Jonathan Lear, *CEO*
EMP: 10 **EST:** 2021
SALES (est): 365.44K **Privately Held**
SIC: 7372 Prepackaged software

(G-17773)
L & M SERVICES INC
617 Lafayette Blvd (19801-2365)
P.O. Box 30661 (19805-7661)
PHONE..............................302 658-3735
Delores R Lake, *Pr*
Anthony V Mason, *VP*
Lonnie Lake, *Sec*
EMP: 5 **EST:** 1998
SALES (est): 47.41K **Privately Held**
SIC: 7217 7349 Carpet and upholstery cleaning on customer premises; Floor waxing

(G-17774)
L COR INC
201 N Walnut St Ste 906 (19801-2920)
PHONE..............................302 428-3929
Alfred Guaraldo, *Prin*
EMP: 17 **EST:** 2011
SALES (est): 73.51K **Privately Held**
SIC: 8721 Certified public accountant

(G-17775)
L E STANSELL INC
Also Called: Craft Bookbinding Co
2525 Ebright Rd (19810-1125)
PHONE..............................302 475-1534
L Edward Stansell, *Pr*
Sandra L Stansell, *Sec*
EMP: 2 **EST:** 1952
SALES (est): 147.26K **Privately Held**
Web: www.bookrestoration.net
SIC: 2789 2782 5112 Bookbinding and related work; Looseleaf binders and devices ; Looseleaf binders

(G-17776)
L E YORK LAW LLC
182 Belmont Dr (19808-4329)
PHONE..............................302 234-8338
Lydia York, *Prin*
EMP: 5 **EST:** 2014
SALES (est): 95.74K **Privately Held**
SIC: 2711 Newspapers, publishing and printing

(G-17777)
L F CONLIN DDS
1202 Foulk Rd (19803-2796)
PHONE..............................302 764-0930
L F Conlin Junior, *Owner*
EMP: 5 **EST:** 1989
SALES (est): 309.71K **Privately Held**
Web: www.dentistinwilmingtonde.com
SIC: 8021 Dentists' office

(G-17778)
L&L LOGISTICS INC ◊
1013 Centre Rd Ste 403s (19805-1270)
PHONE..............................720 232-5637
Jeff Bellamy, *Pr*
EMP: 10 **EST:** 2022
SALES (est): 647.42K **Privately Held**
SIC: 4731 7389 Freight transportation arrangement; Business services, nec

(G-17779)
LA BELLA NAILS INC
1716 Naamans Rd (19810-2610)
PHONE..............................302 475-6216
Tran Huynh, *Asst Sec*
EMP: 5 **EST:** 2017
SALES (est): 17.73K **Privately Held**
SIC: 7231 Manicurist, pedicurist

(G-17780)
LA BELLE ARTISTRY LLC
Also Called: La Belle Studio
1300 Pennsylvania Ave (19806-4311)
PHONE..............................302 656-0555
Tiffani Mitchell, *Managing Member*
EMP: 18 **EST:** 2014
SALES (est): 1.4MM **Privately Held**
Web: www.labelle-artistry.com
SIC: 7231 Cosmetology and personal hygiene salons

(G-17781)
LA FLORESTA PERDIDA INC (PA)
3411 Silverside Rd Ste 101 (19810-4870)
PHONE..............................302 478-8900
Phillip G Rust Junior, *Pr*
Richard C Rust, *VP*
Joseph Harrison, *Sec*
EMP: 10 **EST:** 1935
SALES (est): 1.86MM
SALES (corp-wide): 1.86MM **Privately Held**
SIC: 5031 Lumber, plywood, and millwork

(G-17782)
LABATON SUCHAROW LLP
Also Called: LABATON SUCHAROW LLP
222 Delaware Ave Ste 1500 (19801-1682)
PHONE..............................302 573-6938
Christine Azar, *Pt*
EMP: 32
SALES (corp-wide): 27.13MM **Privately Held**
Web: www.labaton.com
SIC: 8111 General practice law office
PA: Labaton Keller Sucharow Llp
140 Broadway Ste 2300
New York NY 10005
212 907-0700

(G-17783)
LABEL YOUR DATA
1521 Concord Pike (19803-3642)
PHONE..............................844 935-2538
Karyna Naminas, *CEO*
EMP: 5 **EST:** 2021
SALES (est): 23.63K **Privately Held**
Web: www.labelyourdata.com
SIC: 7374 Data processing service

GEOGRAPHIC SECTION
Wilmington - New Castle County (G-17812)

(G-17784)
LABWARE INC
400 Burnt Mill Rd (19807-1010)
PHONE..............................302 658-8444
EMP: 50
Web: www.labware.com
SIC: 7372 Prepackaged software
HQ: Labware, Inc.
    3 Mill Rd Ste 102
    Wilmington DE 19806

(G-17785)
LABWARE INC (HQ)
3 Mill Rd Ste 102 (19806-2154)
PHONE..............................302 658-8444
Vance Kershner, *Pr*
John Carlisle Peet, *
EMP: 50 **EST:** 2007
SQ FT: 14,000
SALES (est): 36.59MM **Privately Held**
Web: www.labware.com
SIC: 7371 Computer software development
PA: Labware Holdings, Inc.
    3 Mill Rd Ste 102
    Wilmington DE 19806

(G-17786)
LABWARE GLOBAL SERVICES INC
3 Mill Rd Ste 102 (19806-2154)
PHONE..............................302 658-8444
EMP: 14 **EST:** 2009
SALES (est): 2.81MM **Privately Held**
Web: www.labware.com
SIC: 7371 7372 6719 Computer software development and applications; Business oriented computer software; Personal holding companies, except banks
PA: Labware Holdings, Inc.
    3 Mill Rd Ste 102
    Wilmington DE 19806

(G-17787)
LABWARE HOLDINGS INC (PA)
3 Mill Rd Ste 102 (19806-2154)
PHONE..............................302 658-8444
Vance Kershner, *Pr*
John Carlisle Peet, *
David Nixon, *
EMP: 32 **EST:** 1988
SQ FT: 14,000
SALES (est): 41.71MM **Privately Held**
Web: www.labware.com
SIC: 7371 7372 6719 Computer software development; Business oriented computer software; Personal holding companies, except banks

(G-17788)
LAFAZIA CONSTRUCTION
149 Belmont Dr (19808-4330)
PHONE..............................302 234-1300
EMP: 8 **EST:** 1981
SALES (est): 692.15K **Privately Held**
Web: www.lafaziaconstruction.com
SIC: 1771 Concrete work

(G-17789)
LAKPURA LLC
1201 N Orange St Ste 7160 (19801-1197)
PHONE..............................302 786-0908
Amila Tennakoon, *CEO*
EMP: 15 **EST:** 2016
SALES (est): 1.09MM **Privately Held**
Web: us.lakpura.com
SIC: 6082 Foreign trade and international banks

(G-17790)
LAKSH CYBERSECURITY & DEF LLC
1201 N Orange St Cmmrc (19801-1155)
PHONE..............................224 258-6564
EMP: 6 **EST:** 2018
SALES (est): 233.16K **Privately Held**
SIC: 7382 7389 Security systems services; Business Activities at Non-Commercial Site

(G-17791)
LAMBDATEST INC
919 N Market St Ste 950 (19801-3036)
PHONE..............................678 701-3618
Pravin Kamble, *Ex Dir*
EMP: 60 **EST:** 2019
SALES (est): 1.14MM **Privately Held**
Web: www.lambdatest.com
SIC: 7371 Software programming applications

(G-17792)
LAMBRO TECHNOLOGIES LLC
206 Kirk Ave (19803-4920)
PHONE..............................302 351-2559
Shannon Watson, *Dir*
Byron Burpulis, *Dir*
John Jurewicz, *Dir*
EMP: 8 **EST:** 2003
SALES (est): 423.91K **Privately Held**
SIC: 7379 Computer related consulting services

(G-17793)
LAMBS OF ZION DAYCARE
20 Harrow Pl (19805-1241)
PHONE..............................302 252-6440
Norami Perez, *Prin*
EMP: 11 **EST:** 2015
SALES (est): 239.41K **Privately Held**
SIC: 8351 Preschool center

(G-17794)
LAMER GROUP LLC (PA)
3422 Old Capitol Trl Ste 79 (19808-6124)
PHONE..............................302 893-0500
Mohamed Amer, *Managing Member*
EMP: 7 **EST:** 2019
SALES (est): 180.01K
SALES (corp-wide): 180.01K **Privately Held**
SIC: 5047 5961 Medical equipment and supplies; Electronic shopping

(G-17795)
LAMONT JOSEY LCSW
219 Edgewood Dr (19809-3254)
PHONE..............................302 559-6654
Lamont Josey, *Prin*
EMP: 7 **EST:** 2012
SALES (est): 55.69K **Privately Held**
SIC: 8322 Social worker

(G-17796)
LANCE TECHNOLOGIES LLC
1007 N Orange St Ste 1382 (19801-1239)
PHONE..............................404 934-4730
Yewande Odumosu, *Prin*
EMP: 6
SALES (est): 68.89K **Privately Held**
SIC: 7371 Custom computer programming services

(G-17797)
LANDIS LTD
420 B And O Ln (19804-1451)
PHONE..............................302 656-9024
Timothy S Skirvin, *Pr*
▲ **EMP:** 5 **EST:** 1975
SQ FT: 20,000
SALES (est): 883.87K **Privately Held**
SIC: 5032 Marble building stone

(G-17798)
LANDIS RATH & COBB LLP
919 N Market St Ste 1800 (19801-3033)
PHONE..............................302 467-4400
Adam Landis, *Pt*
Daniel Rath, *Pt*
Richard Cobb, *Pt*
EMP: 20 **EST:** 2007
SALES (est): 5.97MM **Privately Held**
Web: www.lrclaw.com
SIC: 8111 General practice law office

(G-17799)
LANDMARK PARKING INC (DH)
1205 N Orange St (19801-1120)
PHONE..............................302 651-3610
Richard G Hatfield, *Pr*
John Lyon, *VP*
Gregory S Hatfield, *VP*
EMP: 5 **EST:** 1988
SQ FT: 10,000
SALES (est): 968.48K
SALES (corp-wide): 106.78MM **Privately Held**
SIC: 7521 Parking garage
HQ: Colonial Parking Inc
    715 N Orange St Fl 1
    Wilmington DE 19801
    302 651-3600

(G-17800)
LANDSCAPING
4627 Muggleton Rd (19808-4101)
PHONE..............................302 438-3471
J Heyser, *Prin*
EMP: 5 **EST:** 2011
SALES (est): 48.75K **Privately Held**
Web: www.naturescalllandscaping.com
SIC: 0781 Landscape services

(G-17801)
LANE GROUP V LLC
Also Called: Lane Roofing & Exteriors
119 Quintynnes Dr (19807-1435)
PHONE..............................302 652-7663
EMP: 7 **EST:** 2008
SALES (est): 80.37K **Privately Held**
SIC: 1761 Roofing contractor

(G-17802)
LANE HOME SERVICES INC
Also Called: Lane Roofing
119 Quintynnes Dr (19807-1435)
PHONE..............................302 652-7663
Christopher Lane, *Pr*
EMP: 11 **EST:** 1994
SALES (est): 928.31K **Privately Held**
Web: www.laneroofing.com
SIC: 1761 Roofing contractor

(G-17803)
LANE SIGN INC
2632 Bellows Dr (19810-1014)
PHONE..............................610 558-2630
Edward Protesto, *Pr*
EMP: 2 **EST:** 2001
SALES (est): 76.46K **Privately Held**
Web: www.lanesign.com
SIC: 3993 Signs and advertising specialties

(G-17804)
LANGUAGE LIAISONS LLC
9 Wellington Rd (19803-4129)
PHONE..............................302 545-4257
Bridget Zaro, *Prin*
EMP: 11 **EST:** 2011
SALES (est): 141.58K **Privately Held**
Web: www.languageliaisons.com
SIC: 7389 Translation services

(G-17805)
LANNING WOODWORKS
2404 Overlook Dr (19810-2533)
PHONE..............................302 353-4726
Harry Lanning, *Prin*
EMP: 4 **EST:** 2018
SALES (est): 54.13K **Privately Held**
Web: www.lanningwoodworks.com
SIC: 2431 Millwork

(G-17806)
LANXESS CORPORATION
200 Powder Mill Rd (19803-2907)
PHONE..............................267 205-1969
EMP: 2
SALES (corp-wide): 8.4B **Privately Held**
Web: www.lanxess.com
SIC: 2821 2822 2816 2819 Plastics materials and resins; Synthetic rubber; Inorganic pigments; Industrial inorganic chemicals, nec
HQ: Lanxess Corporation
    111 Ridc Park West Dr
    Pittsburgh PA 15275
    412 809-1000

(G-17807)
LANZA SILVANO MD
104 Stone Tower Ln (19803-4539)
PHONE..............................302 656-3305
Silvano Lanza, *Prin*
EMP: 8 **EST:** 2007
SALES (est): 92.87K **Privately Held**
SIC: 8011 Physicians' office, including specialists

(G-17808)
LARDEAR ANNE OTR/L
2602 Deepwood Dr (19810-3502)
PHONE..............................302 478-7022
Anne Lardear, *Prin*
EMP: 6 **EST:** 2012
SALES (est): 85K **Privately Held**
SIC: 8049 Offices of health practitioner

(G-17809)
LAROSA & ASSOCIATES
1225 N King St Ste 802 (19801-3246)
PHONE..............................302 250-4283
EMP: 7 **EST:** 2017
SALES (est): 126.38K **Privately Held**
Web: www.larosalaw.com
SIC: 8111 General practice law office

(G-17810)
LARRY R GLAZERMAN M D
625 N Shipley St (19801-2228)
PHONE..............................302 655-7296
Larry Glazerman, *Owner*
EMP: 9 **EST:** 2017
SALES (est): 138.07K **Privately Held**
SIC: 8011 Offices and clinics of medical doctors

(G-17811)
LARSEN LANDIS
2520 Silverside Rd (19810-3708)
PHONE..............................302 475-3175
Larsen Landis, *Prin*
EMP: 8 **EST:** 2013
SALES (est): 106.6K **Privately Held**
Web: www.larsenlandis.com
SIC: 8711 Structural engineering

(G-17812)
LASER MARKING WORKS LLC
3511 Silverside Rd # 105 (19810-4902)
PHONE..............................786 307-6203
Jose R Vigil, *Sec*
EMP: 3

SQ FT: 1,400
SALES (est): 217.44K **Privately Held**
SIC: 3555 Engraving machinery and equipment, except plates

(G-17813)
LASERS EDGE INC
3505 Silverside Rd 201c (19804-4905)
PHONE.................302 479-5997
EMP: 5 EST: 1990
SALES (est): 188.16K **Privately Held**
SIC: 7338 Secretarial and typing service

(G-17814)
LAST CHANCE RANCH
20 Montchanin Rd (19807-2160)
PHONE.................518 369-9451
EMP: 5 EST: 2016
SALES (est): 173.99K **Privately Held**
Web: www.lastchanceranch.org
SIC: 0291 General farms, primarily animals

(G-17815)
LASTING IMPRESSION INC A
504 Philadelphia Pike (19809-2155)
P.O. Box 397 (19732-0397)
PHONE.................302 762-9200
EMP: 4 EST: 1993
SQ FT: 1,700
SALES (est): 498.63K **Privately Held**
Web: www.alastingimpressioninc.com
SIC: 2759 2396 Screen printing; Screen printing on fabric articles

(G-17816)
LATIN AMERICAN CMNTY CTR CORP
Also Called: LATIN AMERICAN COMMUNITY CENTE
403 N Van Buren St (19805-3243)
PHONE.................302 655-7338
Maria Matos, *Ex Dir*
EMP: 70 EST: 1969
SQ FT: 28,000
SALES (est): 5.07MM **Privately Held**
Web: www.thelatincenter.org
SIC: 8322 Community center

(G-17817)
LATITUDE SH LLC
Also Called: Maxihost
3 Germay Dr Ste 4 # 4438 (19804-1127)
PHONE.................712 481-2400
Guilherme Soubihe, *CEO*
Lais Boffy, *Finance*
EMP: 50 EST: 2013
SALES (est): 9.59MM **Privately Held**
Web: www.latitude.sh
SIC: 4813 Internet host services

(G-17818)
LATTANZIO ELECTRICAL CNTRCTNG
3234 Brookline Rd (19808-2630)
PHONE.................302 685-0711
Stephen Lattanzio, *Owner*
EMP: 5 EST: 2017
SALES (est): 59.33K **Privately Held**
Web: www.lattanzioelectric.com
SIC: 1731 General electrical contractor

(G-17819)
LATTICE INDUSTRIES INC
1212 N King St (19801-3218)
PHONE.................708 702-4664
EMP: 9 EST: 2018
SALES (est): 410.49K **Privately Held**
Web: www.latticeindustries.com
SIC: 7371 Computer software development

(G-17820)
LATTICE SOCIAL LLC
1201 N Orange St Ste 600 (19801-1171)
PHONE.................916 580-9951
Ryan Salatti, *CEO*
EMP: 3 EST: 2020
SALES (est): 71.13K **Privately Held**
SIC: 7372 Application computer software

(G-17821)
LAU & ASSOC LTD
20 Montchanin Rd Ste 110 (19807-2160)
PHONE.................302 792-5955
Judith Lau, *Pr*
EMP: 23 EST: 1985
SALES (est): 925.87K **Privately Held**
Web: www.bmt.com
SIC: 8741 Financial management for business

(G-17822)
LAUNDRY LOVE SERVICES LLC
24a Trolley Sq (19806-3334)
PHONE.................302 367-7075
EMP: 2
SALES (est): 244.95K **Privately Held**
SIC: 3633 Laundry dryers, household or coin-operated

(G-17823)
LAURA J MANFIELD DO
4512 Kirkwood Hwy (19808-5123)
PHONE.................302 999-0137
Laura Manfield, *Prin*
EMP: 8 EST: 2013
SALES (est): 77.87K **Privately Held**
SIC: 8011 Physicians' office, including specialists

(G-17824)
LAUREL OAK CAPITL PARTNERS LLC
Corportion Trust Ctr 1209 R Ation Trust Ct (19801)
PHONE.................302 658-7581
Rena Clark, *Mng Pt*
EMP: 5 EST: 2016
SALES (est): 102.52K **Privately Held**
SIC: 6211 Investment firm, general brokerage

(G-17825)
LAURIE B JACOBS
708 Foulk Rd Ste 2 (19803-3734)
PHONE.................302 764-7714
Laurie B Jacobs, *Prin*
EMP: 9 EST: 2010
SALES (est): 153.76K **Privately Held**
SIC: 8011 Pediatrician

(G-17826)
LAVISH NAIL SPA LLC
2068 Naamans Rd (19810-2655)
PHONE.................302 829-3008
Vuong T Pham, *Prin*
EMP: 6 EST: 2019
SALES (est): 241.24K **Privately Held**
Web: www.lavishnailspade.com
SIC: 7231 Manicurist, pedicurist

(G-17827)
LAVOND MACKEY
Also Called: Mackeys Complete Cnstr Co
2808 N Jefferson St Apt 1 (19802-3020)
PHONE.................484 466-8055
Lavond Mackey, *Owner*
EMP: 7 EST: 2005
SALES (est): 194.67K **Privately Held**
SIC: 1629 Heavy construction, nec

(G-17828)
LAW FIRM
702 N King St Ste 600 (19801-3535)
P.O. Box 1675 (19899-1675)
PHONE.................302 472-4900
Gary Aber, *Owner*
EMP: 17 EST: 2003
SALES (est): 1.03MM **Privately Held**
Web: www.garyaberlaw.com
SIC: 8111 General practice attorney, lawyer

(G-17829)
LAW OFFICE DANIEL C HERR LLC
1225 N King St Ste 1000 (19801-3250)
PHONE.................302 595-9084
Daniel C Herr Esq, *Prin*
EMP: 6 EST: 2016
SALES (est): 102.81K **Privately Held**
Web: www.danielcherr.com
SIC: 8111 General practice attorney, lawyer

(G-17830)
LAW OFFICE JNNFER KATE M ARNSO
8 E 13th St (19801-3202)
PHONE.................302 655-4600
Jennifer Aaronson, *Prin*
EMP: 5 EST: 2007
SALES (est): 149.24K **Privately Held**
SIC: 8111 General practice attorney, lawyer

(G-17831)
LAW OFFICE OF EJ FORNIAS PA
615 W 18th St (19802-4707)
PHONE.................302 656-2829
E J Fornias, *Owner*
EMP: 7 EST: 2013
SALES (est): 339.51K **Privately Held**
Web: www.ejforniaslaw.com
SIC: 8111 Criminal law

(G-17832)
LAW OFFICE OF ROBERT VALIHURA
5 Serenity Ln (19802-1300)
PHONE.................302 426-1313
Robert Valihura, *Prin*
EMP: 5 EST: 2017
SALES (est): 70.03K **Privately Held**
Web: www.mvzllc.com
SIC: 8111 Specialized law offices, attorneys

(G-17833)
LAW OFFICE OF SHAUNA T HAGAN
1907 Delaware Ave (19806-2301)
PHONE.................302 651-7999
Shauna Hagan, *Prin*
EMP: 5 EST: 2015
SALES (est): 232.86K **Privately Held**
Web: www.haganfamilylaw.com
SIC: 8111 General practice law office

(G-17834)
LAWALL PRSTHTICS - ORTHTICS IN (PA)
1822 Augustine Cut Off (19803-4405)
PHONE.................302 427-3668
EMP: 10 EST: 1984
SALES (est): 6.03MM **Privately Held**
Web: www.lawall.com
SIC: 8011 5999 Specialized medical practitioners, except internal; Orthopedic and prosthesis applications

(G-17835)
LAWRENCE AGENCIES INC
113 Kirkwood Sq (19808-4859)
PHONE.................302 995-6936
Abdul Salaam Lawrence, *Pr*
EMP: 6 EST: 2012
SALES (est): 625.73K **Privately Held**
SIC: 6411 Insurance agents, nec

(G-17836)
LAWYERLAND
1209 N Orange St (19801-1120)
PHONE.................757 805-6817
EMP: 7 EST: 2016
SALES (est): 73.88K **Privately Held**
Web: www.lawyerland.com
SIC: 8111 General practice law office

(G-17837)
LAZ PARKING
101 N French St (19801-2505)
PHONE.................302 654-7730
EMP: 17 EST: 2013
SALES (est): 143.16K **Privately Held**
Web: www.lazparking.com
SIC: 7521 Parking lots

(G-17838)
LC CONSTRUCTION FLORIDA INC
105 North Rd (19809-3018)
PHONE.................302 429-8700
Cohen Steve, *Prin*
EMP: 10 EST: 2014
SALES (est): 2.35MM **Privately Held**
Web: www.lcconstructionde.com
SIC: 1521 Single-family housing construction

(G-17839)
LC HOMES INC
105 Foulk Rd (19803-3740)
PHONE.................302 429-8700
Louis Capano, *Prin*
EMP: 5 EST: 1947
SALES (est): 2.38MM **Privately Held**
Web: www.lchomesde.com
SIC: 6531 Real estate brokers and agents

(G-17840)
LC RANCH LLC
20 Montchanin Rd Ste 250 (19807-2181)
P.O. Box 731 (19710-0731)
PHONE.................302 654-3600
EMP: 5 EST: 2018
SALES (est): 44.17K **Privately Held**
Web: www.lcconstructionde.com
SIC: 0291 General farms, primarily animals

(G-17841)
LCSW CEAP LLC
1803 Breen Ln (19810-4503)
PHONE.................302 824-0290
Michael Sherman, *Prin*
EMP: 7 EST: 2010
SALES (est): 49.5K **Privately Held**
SIC: 8322 Social worker

(G-17842)
LE HERBE LLC (PA)
1209 N Orange St (19801-1120)
PHONE.................949 317-1100
Jay Grillo, *Managing Member*
EMP: 4 EST: 2019
SQ FT: 1,200
SALES (est): 960.3K
SALES (corp-wide): 960.3K **Privately Held**
Web: www.leherbe.com
SIC: 2087 Powders, drink

(G-17843)
LE LUXE NUIT ✪
300 Delaware Ave Lbby (19801-1651)
PHONE.................855 535-8935
Nailah Fisher, *CEO*
Nailah Fisher, *Managing Member*
EMP: 20 EST: 2022
SALES (est): 675.03K **Privately Held**

GEOGRAPHIC SECTION

SIC: 4212 Delivery service, vehicular

(G-17844)
LE-GEN MEDICAL LLC
915 Westover Rd (19807-2980)
PHONE..............................216 496-7113
EMP: 6 **EST:** 2018
SALES (est): 86.78K **Privately Held**
SIC: 8011 Offices and clinics of medical doctors

(G-17845)
LEAGUE OF WMEN VTERS NEW CSTLE
2400 W 17th St Rm 1 (19806-1343)
PHONE..............................302 571-8948
Marjorie Johnson, *Pr*
Anita Puglisi, *Dir*
Christine L Stillson, *Pr*
EMP: 9 **EST:** 1962
SALES (est): 138.64K **Privately Held**
Web: my.lwv.org
SIC: 8641 Civic associations

(G-17846)
LEAH & ALAIN LEBEC FOUNDATION
501 Silverside Rd (19809-1374)
PHONE..............................800 839-1754
EMP: 5 **EST:** 2010
SALES (est): 404.84K **Privately Held**
SIC: 8641 Civic and social associations

(G-17847)
LEALLURE LLC
15b Trolley Sq (19806-3343)
PHONE..............................302 386-8886
EMP: 6 **EST:** 2020
SALES (est): 150K **Privately Held**
SIC: 3161 Clothing and apparel carrying cases

(G-17848)
LEARNING CTR AT MADISON ST LLC
Also Called: Learning Center At Madison St
600 N Madison St (19801-2023)
PHONE..............................302 543-7588
Joseph Kirueya, *Prin*
EMP: 10 **EST:** 2016
SALES (est): 144.62K **Privately Held**
SIC: 8351 Preschool center

(G-17849)
LEARNING4 LRNG PROFESSIONALS
317 E Christian St (19804-2213)
P.O. Box 6431 (19804-0431)
PHONE..............................302 994-0451
Catherine Lombardozzi, *Prin*
EMP: 5 **EST:** 2012
SALES (est): 75.33K **Privately Held**
SIC: 8351 Child day care services

(G-17850)
LED COMPANY INTL LLC
Also Called: Led Company, The
3801 Kennett Pike D204 (19807-2321)
PHONE..............................302 668-8370
Robert Das, *Managing Member*
EMP: 12 **EST:** 2009
SQ FT: 5,000
SALES (est): 1.14MM **Privately Held**
SIC: 5063 5719 Lighting fixtures; Lighting fixtures

(G-17851)
LED SIGN CITY LLC
3422 Old Capitol Trl (19808-6124)
PHONE..............................866 343-4011
EMP: 7 **EST:** 2019
SALES (est): 584.91K **Privately Held**
Web: www.ledsigncity.com

SIC: 3993 Signs and advertising specialties

(G-17852)
LEDTOLIGHT (PA)
Trolley Sq Ste 20c (19806)
PHONE..............................941 323-6664
Allai Boicoune, *Pr*
EMP: 3 **EST:** 2012
SQ FT: 350
SALES (est): 602.3K
SALES (corp-wide): 602.3K **Privately Held**
SIC: 5063 3648 Lighting fittings and accessories; Lighting equipment, nec

(G-17853)
LEE BELL INC (HQ)
3411 Silverside Rd Ste 200 (19810-4812)
PHONE..............................302 477-3930
Helen Winslow, *VP*
EMP: 15 **EST:** 1988
SALES (est): 9.69MM
SALES (corp-wide): 11.61B **Publicly Held**
Web: www.leebell.com
SIC: 2325 2321 2329 2339 Jeans: men's, youths', and boys'; Men's and boys' dress shirts; Jackets (suede, leatherette, etc.), sport: men's and boys'; Jeans: women's, misses', and juniors'
PA: V.F. Corporation
1551 Wewatta St
Denver CO 80202
720 778-4000

(G-17854)
LEE MC NEILL ASSOCIATES
1302 Grinnell Rd (19803-5106)
P.O. Box 7022 (19803-0022)
PHONE..............................302 593-6172
Lee H Mcneill, *Owner*
EMP: 5 **EST:** 1978
SALES (est): 149K **Privately Held**
SIC: 7513 5012 5511 Truck leasing, without drivers; Trucks, commercial; Pickups, new and used

(G-17855)
LEE SELLS HOUSES TEAM
5700 Kirkwood Hwy Ste 101 (19808-4883)
P.O. Box 9663 (19714-9663)
PHONE..............................302 516-7674
EMP: 5 **EST:** 2017
SALES (est): 93.82K **Privately Held**
Web: www.viewdelawarevalleyhomes.com
SIC: 6531 Real estate brokers and agents

(G-17856)
LEFRAK TRUST COMPANY
1105 N Market St Ste 801 (19801-1202)
PHONE..............................302 656-2390
Harrison T Lefrak, *Pr*
EMP: 7 **EST:** 2000
SALES (est): 164 **Privately Held**
SIC: 6733 Trusts, nec

(G-17857)
LEGACY FOODS LLC
915 S Heald St (19801-5732)
PHONE..............................302 656-5540
EMP: 29
SALES (corp-wide): 4.47MM **Privately Held**
SIC: 5149 Groceries and related products, nec
PA: Legacy Foods, Llc
1501 Perryman Rd Ste 150
Aberdeen MD 21001
410 671-9005

(G-17858)
LEGACY LABS INC
300 Delaware Ave Ste 210275 (19801-1607)
PHONE..............................302 550-9966
EMP: 9
SALES (est): 313.29K **Privately Held**
SIC: 7371 Computer software development and applications

(G-17859)
LEGACY TATTOO
1504 E Newport Pike (19804-2338)
PHONE..............................302 502-2163
Zacharie Fawcett, *Prin*
EMP: 5 **EST:** 2017
SALES (est): 64.83K **Privately Held**
SIC: 7299 Tattoo parlor

(G-17860)
LEGACY TRUST COMPANY NA
919 N Market St Ste 740a (19801-3065)
PHONE..............................302 252-9991
EMP: 6 **EST:** 2011
SALES (est): 102.06K **Privately Held**
Web: www.legacytrust.com
SIC: 6733 Trusts, nec

(G-17861)
LEGAL SERVICES CORP DELAWARE
100 W 10th St (19801-1632)
PHONE..............................302 575-0408
EMP: 10 **EST:** 2010
SALES (est): 3MM **Privately Held**
Web: www.lscd.com
SIC: 8111 Legal aid service

(G-17862)
LEGAL SERVICES OF DELAWARE (PA)
100 W 10th St Ste 203 (19801-1632)
PHONE..............................302 575-0408
Douglas B Canfield, *Ex Dir*
EMP: 10 **EST:** 1996
SQ FT: 4,200
SALES (est): 1.18MM
SALES (corp-wide): 1.18MM **Privately Held**
Web: www.lscd.com
SIC: 8111 General practice attorney, lawyer

(G-17863)
LEGALEDGE SOFTWARE
1218 Hillside Blvd (19803-4212)
PHONE..............................302 761-9304
EMP: 6 **EST:** 2019
SALES (est): 70.34K **Privately Held**
SIC: 7371 Computer software development

(G-17864)
LEGION SPORTS PERFORMANCE
109 Rogers Rd Ste 1 (19801-5779)
PHONE..............................302 543-4922
Bob Thompson, *Owner*
EMP: 7 **EST:** 2015
SALES (est): 51.02K **Privately Held**
SIC: 7991 Physical fitness facilities

(G-17865)
LEGION TRANSFORMATION CTR LLC
97 Galewood Rd (19803-3962)
PHONE..............................302 543-4922
Robert Thompson, *Prin*
EMP: 7 **EST:** 2016
SALES (est): 55.58K **Privately Held**
Web: www.legiontransform.com
SIC: 7991 Physical fitness facilities

(G-17866)
LEGION TRNSFRMTION CTR WLMNGTO
109 Rogers Rd (19801-5707)
PHONE..............................302 543-4922
EMP: 7 **EST:** 2019
SALES (est): 36.58K **Privately Held**
Web: www.legiontransform.com
SIC: 7991 Physical fitness facilities

(G-17867)
LEGIST MEDIA LTD
605 N Market St Fl 2 (19801-3167)
P.O. Box 26098 (19899-6098)
PHONE..............................302 655-2730
Sharon Bradley, *VP*
EMP: 5 **EST:** 2014
SALES (est): 181.07K **Privately Held**
SIC: 4899 Communication services, nec

(G-17868)
LEGIT MARKETPLACE INTL LLC
2055 Limestone Rd (19808-5536)
PHONE..............................929 273-0505
EMP: 6
SALES (est): 123.52K **Privately Held**
SIC: 7371 Computer software development and applications

(G-17869)
LEIGHTON COMMUNICATIONS
235 Beau Tree Dr (19810-1177)
PHONE..............................610 513-6930
EMP: 5 **EST:** 2019
SALES (est): 210.44K **Privately Held**
Web: www.leightonpr.com
SIC: 4899 Communication services, nec

(G-17870)
LEILUNA LLC
4023 Kennett Pike Ste 58301 (19807-2018)
PHONE..............................813 512-2213
Aaron Samia, *Dir*
EMP: 10 **EST:** 2015
SALES (est): 728.99K **Privately Held**
Web: www.purisure.com
SIC: 2834 Vitamin, nutrient, and hematinic preparations for human use

(G-17871)
LEINY SNACKS
3 Germay Dr Ste 7 (19804-1127)
PHONE..............................302 494-2499
Marleny Poline, *Mgr*
Marleny Poline, *Prin*
EMP: 10 **EST:** 2005
SALES (est): 948.95K **Privately Held**
SIC: 2064 Candy and other confectionery products

(G-17872)
LEL WEALTH MGT & TECH SVC LLC
4 Ascension Dr (19808-7905)
PHONE..............................804 243-0009
Lynn Wang, *Managing Member*
EMP: 7 **EST:** 2018
SALES (est): 2.8MM **Privately Held**
SIC: 7379 7389 Online services technology consultants; Business Activities at Non-Commercial Site

(G-17873)
LENAPE PROPERTIES MGT INC
903 N French St Ste 106 (19801-3355)
PHONE..............................302 426-0200
Louis Ramunno, *Pr*
EMP: 6 **EST:** 2002
SALES (est): 702.5K **Privately Held**
SIC: 6531 Real estate managers

Wilmington - New Castle County (G-17874)

GEOGRAPHIC SECTION

(G-17874)
LEND HELPING HAND CHILD C
1010 E 24th St (19802-4634)
PHONE..................302 521-5298
EMP: 5 EST: 2018
SALES (est): 32.92K Privately Held
SIC: 8322 Individual and family services

(G-17875)
LENGTH WEAVE BAR
429 S Walnut St (19801-5288)
PHONE..................302 502-3171
EMP: 5 EST: 2019
SALES (est): 126.92K Privately Held
SIC: 8621 Bar association

(G-17876)
LENNIHAN RICHARD JR MD OFFICE
3317 Heritage Dr (19808-1545)
PHONE..................302 994-7821
Richard Lennihan, Prin
EMP: 8 EST: 2010
SALES (est): 68.64K Privately Held
SIC: 8011 Physicians' office, including specialists

(G-17877)
LEON N WEINER & ASSOCIATES INC (PA)
One Fox Point Ctr 4 Denny Rd (19809)
PHONE..................302 656-1354
Kevin P Kelly, Pr
David Curtis, *
Glenn Brooks, *
William Demarco, *
John Gorlich, *
EMP: 75 EST: 1961
SQ FT: 14,000
SALES (est): 73.09K
SALES (corp-wide): 73.09K Privately Held
Web: www.lnwa.com
SIC: 6552 1521 1542 Land subdividers and developers, commercial; New construction, single-family houses; Nonresidential construction, nec

(G-17878)
LEONARD H SELTZER M D
1309 Veale Rd Ste 11 (19810-4609)
PHONE..................302 229-8506
Leonard Seltzer, Prin
EMP: 10 EST: 2014
SALES (est): 235.08K Privately Held
SIC: 8011 Physical medicine, physician/surgeon

(G-17879)
LEONARD M ELZBETH T TNNNBAUM F
501 Silverside Rd (19809-1374)
PHONE..................302 793-4917
EMP: 5 EST: 2011
SALES (est): 813.38K Privately Held
SIC: 8699 Charitable organization

(G-17880)
LEONS GARDEN WORLD INC
5900 Kirkwood Hwy (19808-4815)
PHONE..................302 999-9055
Leon Silicki, Owner
EMP: 25
Web: www.leonsgardenworld.com
SIC: 0781 5261 Landscape architects; Retail nurseries
PA: Leon's Garden World Inc.
137 S Dupont Hwy
New Castle DE 19720

(G-17881)
LEOTECH LLC
1201 N Market St Ste 111 (19801-1156)
PHONE..................908 829-3813
EMP: 5 EST: 2015
SALES (est): 74.69K Privately Held
SIC: 5191 Pesticides

(G-17882)
LEOUNES CATERED AFFAIRS
511 Saint George Dr (19809-2831)
PHONE..................302 547-3233
Leslie Noji, Prin
EMP: 6 EST: 1987
SALES (est): 330.25K Privately Held
SIC: 0782 5812 Landscape contractors; Caterers

(G-17883)
LEROY A TICE ESQUIRE PA
1203 N Orange St (19801-1120)
PHONE..................302 658-6901
Leroy A Tice, Prin
EMP: 7 EST: 2012
SALES (est): 600.86K Privately Held
Web: www.teamticede.com
SIC: 8111 General practice attorney, lawyer

(G-17884)
LESLIE CONNOR
3411 Silverside Rd # 100 (19810-4811)
PHONE..................302 479-5568
Leslie Connor, Prin
EMP: 5 EST: 2016
SALES (est): 137.55K Privately Held
SIC: 8049 Clinical psychologist

(G-17885)
LESSONS LRNED DAY CARE PRSCHOO
207 N Union St (19805-3429)
PHONE..................302 777-2200
Dayna Moore, Owner
EMP: 12 EST: 1998
SALES (est): 175.78K Privately Held
SIC: 8351 Group day care center

(G-17886)
LET US LIFT IT INC
Also Called: Bafundo & Associates
802 W 20th St (19802-3815)
PHONE..................302 654-2221
Leonard Bafundo, CEO
Jamie Bafundo, Pr
EMP: 6 EST: 1989
SALES (est): 586.66K Privately Held
Web: www.bafundoroofing.com
SIC: 1761 Roofing contractor

(G-17887)
LETS GET GREEN
849 Kiamensi Rd (19804-3449)
PHONE..................302 633-4733
EMP: 5 EST: 2015
SALES (est): 67.02K Privately Held
Web: www.letsgetgreen.com
SIC: 0782 Lawn care services

(G-17888)
LEUCINE INC
1013 Centre Rd Ste 403b (19805-1270)
PHONE..................650 534-2101
EMP: 6 EST: 2021
SALES (est): 387.78K Privately Held
Web: cancerandmetabolism.biomedcentral.com
SIC: 8731 Biotechnical research, commercial
PA: Leucine Medtech Private Limited
Pc-11, Punjabi City
Sriganganagar RJ 33500

(G-17889)
LEXISNEXIS RISK ASSETS INC (DH)
Also Called: Choicepoint
1105 N Market St Ste 501 (19801-1253)
PHONE..................800 458-9410
Derek V Smith, Ch Bd
Douglas C Curling, *
David E Trine, *
David T Lee, Chief Business Officer*
Steven W Surbaugh, CAO*
EMP: 700 EST: 1997
SQ FT: 206,000
SALES (est): 1.83B
SALES (corp-wide): 10.3B Privately Held
SIC: 6411 7375 8721 7323 Information bureaus, insurance; Information retrieval services; Accounting, auditing, and bookkeeping; Credit reporting services
HQ: Reed Elsevier Us Holdings, Inc.
1105 N Market St Ste 501
Wilmington DE 19801
302 427-2672

(G-17890)
LHR-FINE ARTS STUDIOS
505 Marsh Rd (19809-2120)
PHONE..................302 981-8553
Linda H Reynolds, Prin
EMP: 5 EST: 2018
SALES (est): 50.64K Privately Held
SIC: 7999 Art gallery, commercial

(G-17891)
LIBERTY DALYSIS-WILMINGTON LLC (HQ)
Also Called: USRC
913 Delaware Ave (19806-4701)
PHONE..................302 429-0142
EMP: 11 EST: 2016
SALES (est): 3.13MM Privately Held
SIC: 8092 Kidney dialysis centers
PA: U.S. Renal Care, Inc.
5851 Legacy Cir Ste 900
Plano TX 75024

(G-17892)
LIBERTY TAX
4538 Kirkwood Hwy (19808-5118)
PHONE..................302 543-8840
EMP: 6 EST: 2018
SALES (est): 22.1K Privately Held
Web: www.libertytax.com
SIC: 7291 Tax return preparation services

(G-17893)
LIBERTY TAX
818 Maryland Ave (19805-4835)
PHONE..................302 304-8714
EMP: 6 EST: 2018
SALES (est): 20.68K Privately Held
Web: www.libertytax.com
SIC: 7291 Tax return preparation services

(G-17894)
LIBERTY TAX SERVICE
2005 N Market St (19802-4814)
PHONE..................302 691-9279
EMP: 6 EST: 2018
SALES (est): 18.45K Privately Held
Web: www.libertytax.com
SIC: 7291 Tax return preparation services

(G-17895)
LIBERTY TITLE SERVICES
919 N Market St (19801-3023)
PHONE..................302 559-4500
EMP: 5 EST: 2018
SALES (est): 49.35K Privately Held
SIC: 6541 Title and trust companies

(G-17896)
LIBERTY UNIVERSAL TECH INC
2055 Limestone Rd Ste 200c (19808-5536)
PHONE..................404 719-4728
Habeeb Bombata, CEO
EMP: 8
SALES (est): 321.21K Privately Held
SIC: 7372 Prepackaged software

(G-17897)
LIBLAB INC
251 Little Falls Dr (19808-1674)
PHONE..................302 415-3344
EMP: 8 EST: 2019
SALES (est): 74.1K Privately Held
SIC: 7371 Computer software development and applications

(G-17898)
LIBORIO-LOUVIERS LLC
903 N French St (19801-3371)
PHONE..................302 656-9400
EMP: 7 EST: 2015
SALES (est): 449.73K Privately Held
SIC: 6531 Real estate agents and managers

(G-17899)
LIFE AT ST FRNCIS HLTHCARE INC
Also Called: ST. FRANCIS LIFE
1072 Justison St (19801-5162)
PHONE..................302 660-3297
Amy L Milligan, Admn
EMP: 5 EST: 2012
SALES (est): 30.4MM Privately Held
SIC: 8099 Health and allied services, nec

(G-17900)
LIFE FNDTION LOVE IS FOR EVR ◆
12 Deville Cir (19808-4530)
PHONE..................302 660-1792
Jamel Kelley, Prin
EMP: 6 EST: 2023
SALES (est): 119.28K Privately Held
SIC: 8699 Charitable organization

(G-17901)
LIFE SCIENCES INTL LLC
1209 N Orange St (19801-1120)
PHONE..................603 436-9444
Seth Hoogasian, Pr
Ken Apicerno, Treas
Maura Spellman, Asst Tr
EMP: 3 EST: 2006
SALES (est): 2.01MM
SALES (corp-wide): 44.91B Publicly Held
SIC: 3821 Laboratory apparatus and furniture
HQ: Helmet Securities Limited
93-96 Chadwick Road
Runcorn WA7 1

(G-17902)
LIFE SOLUTIONS INC
1210 N King St (19801-3218)
P.O. Box 1507 (19899-1507)
PHONE..................302 622-8292
Mary Ferry, Owner
EMP: 9 EST: 1999
SALES (est): 235.46K Privately Held
Web: www.lifesolutions.com
SIC: 8361 Residential care

(G-17903)
LIFERITHMS INC
251 Little Falls Dr (19808-1674)
PHONE..................770 885-6565
Olumuyiwa Ogunlela, CEO
EMP: 10 EST: 2019
SALES (est): 416.65K Privately Held
SIC: 7371 Software programming applications

GEOGRAPHIC SECTION   Wilmington - New Castle County (G-17934)

(G-17904)
LIFESPAN HEALTH SCIENCE LLC
251 Little Falls Dr (19808-1674)
PHONE..................203 273-4037
Seth Flowerman, *Managing Member*
EMP: 3 EST: 2020
SALES (est): 91.38K **Privately Held**
SIC: **2023** Dietary supplements, dairy and non-dairy based

(G-17905)
LIFESTYLE FITNESS
1319 Mckennans Church Rd (19808-2132)
PHONE..................302 998-2942
EMP: 6 EST: 2019
SALES (est): 77.17K **Privately Held**
SIC: **7991** Physical fitness facilities

(G-17906)
LIFETOUR SOLUTIONS LLC
300 Delaware Ave Ste 210 (19801-6601)
P.O. Box 9401 (19809-0401)
PHONE..................215 964-5000
EMP: 10 EST: 2017
SALES (est): 544.4K **Privately Held**
SIC: **8741 7311 8742** Business management; Advertising consultant; Marketing consulting services

(G-17907)
LIG ENERGY SOLUTIONS LLC
1207 Delaware Ave Ste 1944 (19801-5627)
PHONE..................646 918-8232
EMP: 141 EST: 2015
SALES (est): 12.42MM **Privately Held**
SIC: **1711 8748** Plumbing, heating, air-conditioning; Business consulting, nec

(G-17908)
LIGHT ACTION INC
1145 E 7th St (19801-4501)
PHONE..................302 328-7800
Scott Humphrey, *Pr*
EMP: 13 EST: 1981
SALES (est): 5.96MM **Privately Held**
Web: www.lightactioninc.com
SIC: **7922 1731 5719** Lighting, theatrical; Lighting contractor; Lighting fixtures

(G-17909)
LIGHTRUN INC
1209 N Orange St (19801-1120)
PHONE..................646 453-6616
Ilan Peleg, *CEO*
EMP: 33 EST: 2020
SALES (est): 1.01MM **Privately Held**
Web: www.lightrun.com
SIC: **7371 7389** Software programming applications; Business services, nec

(G-17910)
LIGHTSCAPES INC
Also Called: Cloudburst Sprinkler Systems
6603a Governor Printz Blvd (19809-2027)
PHONE..................302 798-5451
Brett Forest, *Pr*
EMP: 8 EST: 1984
SALES (est): 660.44K **Privately Held**
SIC: **5087 1731** Sprinkler systems; Lighting contractor

(G-17911)
LIII CONSTRUCTION CO
105 Foulk Rd (19803-3740)
PHONE..................302 429-8700
Louis J Capano, *Prin*
EMP: 10 EST: 2007
SALES (est): 1.31MM **Privately Held**
SIC: **1521** Single-family housing construction

(G-17912)
LILIAN USA LLC
Also Called: Sharetea
1201 N Orange St Ste 600 (19801-1171)
PHONE..................800 246-2677
Daiby Hua, *Prin*
EMP: 11 EST: 2016
SALES (est): 81.22K **Privately Held**
Web: www.1992sharetea.com
SIC: **5812 6794** Coffee shop; Franchises, selling or licensing

(G-17913)
LIMEN HOUSE INC
600 W 10th St (19801-1424)
P.O. Box 1306 (19899-1306)
PHONE..................302 652-7969
Reginald Irby, *Dir*
EMP: 6 EST: 1969
SALES (est): 982.12K **Privately Held**
Web: www.limende.org
SIC: **8361** Rehabilitation center, residential: health care incidental

(G-17914)
LIMESTONE ACRES MAINTENANCE
2407 Darnay Ln (19808-4111)
P.O. Box 5042 (19808-0042)
PHONE..................302 222-8457
Charlie Tucci, *Prin*
EMP: 5 EST: 2010
SALES (est): 111.42K **Privately Held**
SIC: **5032** Limestone

(G-17915)
LIMESTONE MEDICAL CENTER INC
Also Called: Limestone Medical Aid Unit
1941 Limestone Rd Ste 113 (19808-5413)
P.O. Box 5040 (19808-0040)
PHONE..................302 992-0500
Tom Mulhern, *Dir*
EMP: 80 EST: 1983
SQ FT: 76,000
SALES (est): 9.92MM **Privately Held**
Web: www.limestonemed.com
SIC: **8062** General medical and surgical hospitals

(G-17916)
LIMESTONE NUTRITION
4569 Kirkwood Hwy (19808-5117)
PHONE..................302 397-8705
Byron Hobson, *Owner*
EMP: 6 EST: 2015
SALES (est): 93.25K **Privately Held**
SIC: **8049** Offices of health practitioner

(G-17917)
LIMESTONE OPEN MRI LLC (PA)
2060 Limestone Rd (19808-5500)
PHONE..................302 246-2001
EMP: 7 EST: 2008
SALES (est): 1.51MM
SALES (corp-wide): 1.51MM **Privately Held**
Web: www.delawaremriandimaging.com
SIC: **8011** Radiologist

(G-17918)
LIMITLESS FLAMES LLC
3 Germay Dr Ste 4 (19804-1127)
PHONE..................302 559-8712
Ansha Brown, *Managing Member*
EMP: 2 EST: 2021
SALES (est): 62.54K **Privately Held**
SIC: **3999** Candles

(G-17919)
LINDA CELESTIAN ART STUDIO
1808 Harvey Rd (19810-4008)
PHONE..................302 364-0278
EMP: 5 EST: 2017
SALES (est): 54.34K **Privately Held**
SIC: **7999** Art gallery, commercial

(G-17920)
LINDA DUFFY
1600 Rockland Rd (19803-3607)
PHONE..................302 651-4000
Linda Duffy, *Prin*
EMP: 6 EST: 2014
SALES (est): 99.09K **Privately Held**
SIC: **8049** Offices of health practitioner

(G-17921)
LINDA L SILVIS
5700 Kirkwood Hwy Ste 206 (19808-4884)
PHONE..................302 559-5577
Linda L Silvis Lmt, *Owner*
EMP: 6 EST: 2018
SALES (est): 22.18K **Privately Held**
SIC: **8049** Offices of health practitioner

(G-17922)
LINDA MCCORMICK
Also Called: Locust Cnstr & Contg Svcs
200 Tyrone Ave (19804-1929)
PHONE..................443 987-2099
Linda Mccormick, *Owner*
EMP: 6 EST: 2006
SALES (est): 529.01K **Privately Held**
SIC: **1542 5047 8742 1799** Commercial and office building contractors; Medical equipment and supplies; Management consulting services; Home/office interiors finishing, furnishing and remodeling

(G-17923)
LINDE GAS & EQUIPMENT INC
Also Called: Praxair
2 Medori Blvd (19805-5781)
PHONE..................302 654-8755
David Stroble, *Prin*
EMP: 8
Web: www.lindeus.com
SIC: **5084** Welding machinery and equipment
HQ: Linde Gas & Equipment Inc.
10 Riverview Dr
Danbury CT 06810
844 445-4633

(G-17924)
LINDELL PARTNERS LLC
300 Delaware Ave Ste 210a (19801-6601)
PHONE..................773 269-0837
EMP: 5 EST: 2017
SALES (est): 91.27K **Privately Held**
SIC: **8742** Management consulting services

(G-17925)
LINDEN BUILDING
625 N Orange St (19801-2296)
PHONE..................302 573-3705
EMP: 6 EST: 2011
SALES (est): 48.38K **Privately Held**
SIC: **8641** Condominium association

(G-17926)
LINDEN HILL CLEANERS INC
4561 Linden Hill Rd (19808)
PHONE..................302 368-9795
Won Lee, *Pr*
Yount Lee, *VP*
EMP: 7 EST: 1993
SALES (est): 180.19K **Privately Held**
Web: www.drycleanerslist.com
SIC: **7216** Cleaning and dyeing, except rugs

(G-17927)
LINDEN HILL ELEMENTARY PTA
3415 Skyline Dr (19808-1701)
PHONE..................302 454-3406
EMP: 6 EST: 2010
SALES (est): 65.8K **Privately Held**
SIC: **8641** Parent-teachers' association

(G-17928)
LINDEN NAILS & SPA
4500 Linden Hill Rd (19808-2905)
PHONE..................302 510-4794
EMP: 5 EST: 2019
SALES (est): 169.53K **Privately Held**
SIC: **7231** Manicurist, pedicurist

(G-17929)
LINDENBERG FINANCIAL
5301 Limestone Rd Ste 226 (19808-1265)
PHONE..................302 235-8672
EMP: 11 EST: 2017
SALES (est): 400.2K **Privately Held**
Web: www.lindenbergfinancial.com
SIC: **6282** Investment advice

(G-17930)
LINKMEUP INC ✪
1007 N Orange St Fl 4 (19801-1242)
PHONE..................302 440-3393
Emmanuel Chinonso Godfrey, *CEO*
EMP: 12 EST: 2023
SALES (est): 406.37K **Privately Held**
SIC: **7371** Computer software development and applications

(G-17931)
LION TOTALCARE INC
9 Germay Dr Ste 200a (19804-1143)
PHONE..................610 444-1700
Jeff Boles, *Pr*
EMP: 9 EST: 2007
SALES (est): 235.94K
SALES (corp-wide): 13.99MM **Privately Held**
SIC: **7699** Repair services, nec
HQ: Lion Apparel, Inc.
7200 Poe Ave Ste 400
Dayton OH 45414
937 898-1949

(G-17932)
LISSNER & ASSOCIATES LLC
310 High Ridge Rd (19807-1510)
PHONE..................302 777-4620
EMP: 5 EST: 2011
SALES (est): 77.7K **Privately Held**
Web: www.lissnerlawfirm.com
SIC: **8742** Management consulting services

(G-17933)
LISTONBURG SOLAR LLC
1209 N Orange St (19801-1120)
PHONE..................412 979-6872
EMP: 6 EST: 2020
SALES (est): 76.51K **Privately Held**
SIC: **1711** Solar energy contractor

(G-17934)
LITCHARTS LLC
2711 Centerville Rd Ste 400 (19808-1660)
P.O. Box 1162 (07940-8162)
PHONE..................646 481-4807
Justin Kestler, *Managing Member*
EMP: 2 EST: 2013
SALES (est): 97K **Privately Held**
Web: www.litcharts.com
SIC: **2741 7389** Miscellaneous publishing; Business Activities at Non-Commercial Site

(PA)=Parent Co (HQ)=Headquarters
✪ = New Business established in last 2 years

2024 Harris Directory of Delaware Businesses

Wilmington - New Castle County (G-17935)

(G-17935)
LITTLE BLESSINGS DAY CARE
1 E 31st St (19802-3207)
PHONE..................................302 762-3600
Malcom Dawson, *Owner*
EMP: 6 **EST:** 2018
SALES (est): 17.57K **Privately Held**
SIC: 8351 Group day care center

(G-17936)
LITTLE BLESSINGS DAYCARE
2010 N Market St (19802-4815)
PHONE..................................302 655-8962
Malcholm Dawson, *Pr*
EMP: 10 **EST:** 1982
SALES (est): 289.53K **Privately Held**
SIC: 8351 Group day care center

(G-17937)
LITTLE FOLKS TOO DAY CARE
1318 N Market St (19801-1133)
PHONE..................................302 652-3420
Heike Parodi, *Mgr*
EMP: 6
SALES (corp-wide): 927.55K **Privately Held**
Web: www.littlefolkstoo.com
SIC: 8351 Group day care center
PA: Little Folks Too Day Care
1320 N Market St
Wilmington DE 19801
302 652-1238

(G-17938)
LITTLE FOLKS TOO DAY CARE (PA)
1320 N Market St (19801-1179)
PHONE..................................302 652-1238
Cleonice Decherney, *Pr*
EMP: 38 **EST:** 1983
SQ FT: 5,000
SALES (est): 927.55K
SALES (corp-wide): 927.55K **Privately Held**
Web: www.littlefolkstoo.com
SIC: 8351 Group day care center

(G-17939)
LITTLE GYM OF NCC
Also Called: Little Gym, The
4758 Limestone Rd Ste A (19808-4389)
PHONE..................................302 543-5524
EMP: 6 **EST:** 1996
SALES (est): 152.88K **Privately Held**
Web: www.thelittlegym.com
SIC: 7999 Gymnastic instruction, non-membership

(G-17940)
LITTLE HEARTS CHILD CARE LLC
111 W 22nd St (19802-4103)
PHONE..................................302 442-5746
Valerie Chinn, *Managing Member*
Josette Jackson, *Pt*
EMP: 20 **EST:** 2015
SALES (est): 800K **Privately Held**
SIC: 8351 Group day care center

(G-17941)
LITTLE PEOPLES COLLEGE
3507 Old Capitol Trl (19808-6125)
PHONE..................................302 998-4929
Ann Ebaugh, *Dir*
EMP: 10 **EST:** 2011
SALES (est): 151.51K **Privately Held**
Web: www.littlepeoplecollege.com
SIC: 8351 Child day care services

(G-17942)
LITTLE SCHOLARS LEARNING CTR
2511 W 4th St Ste A (19805-3350)
P.O. Box 2807 (19805-0807)
PHONE..................................302 656-8785
Lisa Mosley, *Owner*
EMP: 9 **EST:** 2005
SALES (est): 198.94K **Privately Held**
SIC: 8351 Preschool center

(G-17943)
LITTLE STAR INC
5702 Kirkwood Hwy (19808-4811)
PHONE..................................302 995-2920
Elizabeth Cahill, *Pr*
EMP: 10 **EST:** 1992
SALES (est): 255.06K **Privately Held**
Web: www.littlestarsinc.com
SIC: 8351 Group day care center

(G-17944)
LITTLE STEPS DAYCARE
212 W 21st St (19802-4006)
PHONE..................................302 654-4867
Julia Woulard, *Prin*
EMP: 5 **EST:** 2010
SALES (est): 99.21K **Privately Held**
SIC: 8351 Group day care center

(G-17945)
LITTLJOHN BLCKSTON HLDINGS LLC
Also Called: L&B Holdings
717 N Union St Unit 74 (19805-3031)
PHONE..................................302 468-6680
EMP: 5 **EST:** 2017
SALES (est): 119.02K **Privately Held**
Web: littlejohn-blackston-holdings-llc.business.site
SIC: 6531 Real estate agent, residential

(G-17946)
LITUATION CREATIVE DESIGNS INC
3201 N Jefferson St (19802-2614)
PHONE..................................302 494-4399
Xavier Cole, *Pr*
EMP: 15 **EST:** 2019
SALES (est): 72.14K **Privately Held**
SIC: 8699 Charitable organization

(G-17947)
LITUATION ENTERTAINMENT
5205 W Woodmill Dr (19808-4068)
PHONE..................................302 543-6424
EMP: 5 **EST:** 2018
SALES (est): 54.76K **Privately Held**
SIC: 7929 Entertainers and entertainment groups

(G-17948)
LITYX LLC
1000 N West St Ste 1200 (19801-1058)
PHONE..................................888 548-9947
Paul Maiste, *Pr*
Gary Robinson, *COO*
EMP: 9 **EST:** 2006
SALES (est): 2.2MM **Privately Held**
Web: www.lityx.com
SIC: 8748 7372 Business consulting, nec; Business oriented computer software

(G-17949)
LIVE TYPING INC
1521 Concord Pike Ste 303 (19803-3644)
PHONE..................................415 670-9601
Vladislav Korobov, *CEO*
EMP: 6 **EST:** 2013
SALES (est): 78.5K **Privately Held**
SIC: 7371 7389 Computer software development; Business services, nec

(G-17950)
LIVING WATER COUNSELING LLC
3522 Silverside Rd Ste 32 (19810-4915)
PHONE..................................443 553-7317
Evelyn Cunliffe, *Prin*
EMP: 7 **EST:** 2015
SALES (est): 177.77K **Privately Held**
SIC: 8322 General counseling services

(G-17951)
LIVING WELL WITH DEMENTIA LLC
120 Churchill Ln (19808-4319)
PHONE..................................302 753-9725
Cathy Ciolek, *Prin*
EMP: 9 **EST:** 2018
SALES (est): 219.34K **Privately Held**
Web: www.livingwellwithdementiallc.com
SIC: 8051 Skilled nursing care facilities

(G-17952)
LK REJOICE CHILD CARE CENTER
725 N Union St (19805-3031)
PHONE..................................302 543-4621
EMP: 6 **EST:** 2016
SALES (est): 103.06K **Privately Held**
SIC: 8099 Health and allied services, nec

(G-17953)
LLB ACQUISITION LLC
1209 N Orange St (19801-1120)
PHONE..................................212 750-8300
Joseph Henderson, *Prin*
EMP: 16 **EST:** 2007
SALES (est): 591.13K **Privately Held**
SIC: 6799 Investors, nec

(G-17954)
LLC CASTLE LAW
2 Mill Rd Ste 202 (19806-2184)
PHONE..................................302 428-8800
Colleen Lawhorn, *Prin*
EMP: 8 **EST:** 2014
SALES (est): 440.34K **Privately Held**
Web: www.hcilaw.com
SIC: 8111 General practice law office

(G-17955)
LLC FOREVER MEDIA OF DE
2727 Shipley Rd Ste 406 (19810-3210)
PHONE..................................412 221-1629
Lynn A Deppen, *Prin*
EMP: 60 **EST:** 2019
SALES (est): 2.35MM **Privately Held**
Web: www.foreverdigitalmedia.com
SIC: 4899 Communication services, nec

(G-17956)
LLC QUICK SHIELD
1209 N Orange St (19801-1120)
PHONE..................................514 730-8040
EMP: 4 **EST:** 2021
SALES (est): 284.2K **Privately Held**
SIC: 2023 Dietary supplements, dairy and non-dairy based

(G-17957)
LLC SALES INC
1209 N Orange St (19801-1120)
PHONE..................................416 996-1856
Niharish Patel, *Acctg Mgr*
EMP: 5 **EST:** 2018
SALES (est): 420.48K **Privately Held**
SIC: 5063 Electrical supplies, nec

(G-17958)
LLOYDS WLDG & FABRICATION LLC
1101 E 8th St (19801-4356)
PHONE..................................302 384-7662
EMP: 5 **EST:** 2016
SALES (est): 131.69K **Privately Held**
SIC: 7692 Welding repair

(G-17959)
LLP CONNOLLY GALLAGHER (PA)
1201 N Market St Ste 2000 (19801-1165)
PHONE..................................302 757-7300
Matthew F Boyer, *Pt*
Chris Adamopoulos, *Pt*
Mary I Akhimien, *Pt*
Arthur G Connolly Iii, *Pt*
Charles J Durante, *Pt*
EMP: 18 **EST:** 2012
SALES (est): 9.93MM
SALES (corp-wide): 9.93MM **Privately Held**
Web: www.connollygallagher.com
SIC: 8111 General practice attorney, lawyer

(G-17960)
LLP SHAW KELLER
1105 N Market St Fl 1 (19801-1237)
PHONE..................................302 298-0700
EMP: 7 **EST:** 2019
SALES (est): 328.99K **Privately Held**
Web: www.shawkeller.com
SIC: 8111 General practice attorney, lawyer

(G-17961)
LMG ASSOCIATES IN EYE CARE
21 Oxford Way (19807-2577)
PHONE..................................302 993-0931
EMP: 6 **EST:** 2019
SALES (est): 155.67K **Privately Held**
SIC: 8042 Offices and clinics of optometrists

(G-17962)
LMS IRONWORKS
125 Saint John Dr (19808-4630)
PHONE..................................302 300-7719
Lisa Sykes, *Prin*
EMP: 5 **EST:** 2016
SALES (est): 75.55K **Privately Held**
SIC: 1791 Iron work, structural

(G-17963)
LNE POWER LLC
2711 Centerville Rd # 400 (19808-1660)
PHONE..................................913 777-7552
Rusty Smith, *Mgr*
EMP: 5 **EST:** 2017
SALES (est): 76.71K **Privately Held**
SIC: 7389 Business services, nec

(G-17964)
LNW & A CONSTRUCTION CORP
31 E Mccaulley Ct (19801-4041)
PHONE..................................302 764-9430
EMP: 12 **EST:** 1981
SALES (est): 156.01K **Privately Held**
Web: www.lnwa.com
SIC: 1522 Residential construction, nec

(G-17965)
LNZ CONSULTING LLC
1601 Concord Pike Ste 50 (19803-3630)
P.O. Box 8028 (19803-8028)
PHONE..................................302 543-6296
Lani Zlupko, *Ofcr*
EMP: 5 **EST:** 2014
SALES (est): 104.02K **Privately Held**
Web: www.lnzconsulting.com
SIC: 8322 Individual and family services

(G-17966)
LOADBALANCERORGINC
4550 Linden Hill Rd Ste 201 (19808-2930)
P.O. Box 3569 (19807-0569)
PHONE..................................888 867-9504
Malcolm Turnbull, *Pr*
Jake Borman, *Prin*

GEOGRAPHIC SECTION
Wilmington - New Castle County (G-17997)

EMP: 2 EST: 2003
SALES (est): 367.75K Privately Held
Web: www.loadbalancer.org
SIC: 7372 5961 Prepackaged software; Computer equipment and electronics, mail order

(G-17967)
LOAN SIMPLE INC
5506 Kirkwood Hwy (19808-5002)
PHONE..................302 510-4808
EMP: 6 EST: 2017
SALES (est): 168.16K Privately Held
Web: www.loansimple.com
SIC: 6141 Personal credit institutions

(G-17968)
LOAN TIL PAYDAY
1935 W 4th St (19805-3459)
PHONE..................302 428-3925
EMP: 5 EST: 2010
SALES (est): 95.7K Privately Held
SIC: 6099 Check clearing services

(G-17969)
LOBSTER MADE EASY CORP
3422 Old Capitol Trl (19808-6124)
PHONE..................902 818-9358
Mark Lowe, Pr
EMP: 5 EST: 2021
SALES (est): 358.78K Privately Held
SIC: 2092 Seafoods, frozen: prepared

(G-17970)
LOCAL AD NINJA INC
1521 Concord Pike Ste 301 (19803-3642)
PHONE..................877 894-1502
Anthony Reyna, Pr
EMP: 12 EST: 2020
SALES (est): 423.5K Privately Held
SIC: 8742 Marketing consulting services

(G-17971)
LOCALSPIN LLC
1521 Concord Pike Ste 301 (19803-3644)
P.O. Box 754 (07417-0754)
PHONE..................917 232-7203
EMP: 2 EST: 2012
SALES (est): 135.17K Privately Held
SIC: 7372 Application computer software

(G-17972)
LODES CHIROPRACTIC CENTER PA
3411 Silverside Rd Ste 102hb (19810-4879)
PHONE..................302 477-1565
Michael R Lodes, Pr
EMP: 5 EST: 1991
SALES (est): 294.06K Privately Held
Web: www.lodeschiropractic.com
SIC: 8041 Offices and clinics of chiropractors

(G-17973)
LODGE LANE ASSISTED LIVING
1221 Lodge Ln (19809-2766)
PHONE..................302 757-8100
EMP: 13
SALES (est): 916.68K Privately Held
Web: www.kutzseniorliving.org
SIC: 8059 8699 Nursing and personal care, nec; Charitable organization

(G-17974)
LODGE LANE ASSISTED LIVING
704 River Rd (19809-2746)
PHONE..................302 764-3000
EMP: 13 EST: 2019
SALES (est): 1.8MM Privately Held
Web: www.kutzseniorliving.org
SIC: 8361 Aged home

(G-17975)
LOFTS 2ND AND LOMA
211 N Market St (19801-2527)
PHONE..................302 300-1498
EMP: 7 EST: 2017
SALES (est): 176.9K Privately Held
Web: www.2ndandloma.com
SIC: 1542 Garage and service station contractors

(G-17976)
LOGUE BROTHERS INC
Also Called: Texaco
3507 Miller Rd (19802-2521)
PHONE..................302 762-1896
Robert C Logue, Pr
EMP: 10 EST: 1986
SQ FT: 22,500
SALES (est): 1.11MM Privately Held
Web: www.texaco.com
SIC: 5541 7542 Filling stations, gasoline; Carwash, automatic

(G-17977)
LOHMANN STEEL LLC
2810 N Church St (19802-4447)
PHONE..................844 488-1790
Gunnar Lohmann-huette, Managing Member
EMP: 4
SALES (est): 216.22K Privately Held
SIC: 5199 3312 General merchandise, non-durable; Plate, steel

(G-17978)
LOIZIDES & ASSOCIATES PC
1225 N King St Ste 800 (19801-3246)
PHONE..................302 654-0248
Chris Loizides, Pr
EMP: 8 EST: 2002
SQ FT: 800
SALES (est): 671.95K Privately Held
Web: www.loizides.com
SIC: 8111 General practice attorney, lawyer

(G-17979)
LOKBLOK INC
3524 Silverside Rd Ste 35b (19810-4929)
PHONE..................408 640-8644
Sue Pontius, CEO
Adrian Mccullagh, Sec
EMP: 11 EST: 2021
SALES (est): 492.03K Privately Held
Web: www.lokblok.co
SIC: 7382 7371 7374 Security systems services; Custom computer programming services; Data processing and preparation

(G-17980)
LONG & TANN & D ONOFRIO INC (PA)
3906 Concord Pike Ste F (19803-1733)
PHONE..................302 477-1970
Peter D' Onofrio, Pr
Richard Tann, Prin
EMP: 5 EST: 1965
SQ FT: 1,250
SALES (est): 746.95K
SALES (corp-wide): 746.95K Privately Held
SIC: 8711 Structural engineering

(G-17981)
LONG AND FOSTER
5301 Limestone Rd Ste 225 (19808-1250)
PHONE..................302 239-2636
EMP: 5 EST: 2014
SALES (est): 243.5K Privately Held
Web: www.homesinnewcastlede.com

SIC: 6531 Real estate agent, residential

(G-17982)
LONG RD AHEAD SHIPG LGSTIC LLC
3 Germay Dr Unit 42083 (19804-1127)
PHONE..................480 702-6438
Ashley Morgan, Managing Member
Jonathan Boone, *
EMP: 30 EST: 2021
SALES (est): 1.94MM Privately Held
SIC: 4731 Freight forwarding

(G-17983)
LONGBOTTOM DRINKS USA INC
108 W 13th St (19801-1145)
PHONE..................302 966-9177
Daniel Jones, CFO
EMP: 5
SALES (est): 220.1K Privately Held
SIC: 2033 Vegetable juices: packaged in cans, jars, etc.

(G-17984)
LONGEVITY HEALTH CORP
1209 N Orange St (19801-1120)
PHONE..................619 288-3922
Sean O'keefe, Pr
EMP: 10 EST: 2018
SALES (est): 633.62K Privately Held
SIC: 3571 Computers, digital, analog or hybrid

(G-17985)
LONGO AND ASSOCIATES LLP
2010 Limestone Rd (19808-5506)
PHONE..................302 477-7500
Carolyn Gillespie, Pt
EMP: 9 EST: 2014
SALES (est): 957.01K Privately Held
Web: www.longolawoffice.com
SIC: 8742 Management consulting services

(G-17986)
LONGOBARDI & BOYLE LLC
1700 Augustine Cut Off (19803-4403)
PHONE..................302 575-1502
EMP: 5 EST: 2015
SALES (est): 162.11K Privately Held
Web: www.longobardilaw.com
SIC: 8111 General practice attorney, lawyer

(G-17987)
LONGVIEW CAPITAL MGT LLC
2 Mill Rd Ste 105 (19806-2175)
PHONE..................302 353-4720
Christian Wagner, CEO
EMP: 10 EST: 2010
SALES (est): 275.81K Privately Held
Web: www.longviewcptl.com
SIC: 7389 Financial services
HQ: Penn Community Bank
219 S 9th St
Perkasie PA 18944
215 257-5035

(G-17988)
LONGVIEW FARMS CIVIC ASSN
1107 S Overhill Ct (19810-3109)
PHONE..................302 475-6684
EMP: 5 EST: 1965
SALES (est): 77.35K Privately Held
SIC: 8641 Dwelling-related associations

(G-17989)
LOOK GREAT MD CENTERS
3801 Kennett Pike Ste E126 (19807-2321)
PHONE..................302 658-1232
EMP: 6 EST: 2018
SALES (est): 106.53K Privately Held

Web: www.lookgreatmd.com
SIC: 8011 Dermatologist

(G-17990)
LOOKBACK APP CO
251 Little Falls Dr (19808-1674)
PHONE..................508 735-1903
EMP: 5
SALES (est): 27.98K Privately Held
SIC: 7371 Computer software development and applications

(G-17991)
LOOKSIEBIN LLC
4708 Weatherhill Dr (19808-1995)
PHONE..................410 869-2192
Christopher Wells, Prin
Nicholas Goble, Prin
EMP: 5 EST: 2017
SALES (est): 165.7K Privately Held
SIC: 7389 Business Activities at Non-Commercial Site

(G-17992)
LOOM NETWORK INC
427 N Tatnall St 38768 (19801-2230)
PHONE..................404 939-1294
Matthew Campbell, CEO
EMP: 11 EST: 2017
SALES (est): 378.47K Privately Held
SIC: 7371 Computer software development and applications

(G-17993)
LOPEZ GELASIO
2110 Kirkwood Hwy Apt B (19805-4902)
PHONE..................302 377-2591
EMP: 6 EST: 2008
SALES (est): 168.64K Privately Held
SIC: 1611 Surfacing and paving

(G-17994)
LORD PRINTING LLC
Also Called: Minuteman Press
1812 Marsh Rd Ste 411 (19810-4522)
PHONE..................302 439-3253
James Lord, Prin
Thomas Lord, Prin
EMP: 4 EST: 2008
SQ FT: 1,364
SALES (est): 485.67K Privately Held
Web: www.minuteman.com
SIC: 2752 Commercial printing, lithographic

(G-17995)
LORELTON
Also Called: The Lorelton
2200 W 4th St Apt 229 (19805-3359)
PHONE..................302 573-3580
Kenneth Carson, Ex Dir
Michael Comegys, Ex Dir
EMP: 31 EST: 1983
SALES (est): 2.82MM Privately Held
Web: www.lorelton.com
SIC: 6513 Retirement hotel operation

(G-17996)
LORELTON FOUNDATION
1201 N Orange St Ste 700 (19801-1186)
PHONE..................302 573-2500
EMP: 7 EST: 2010
SALES (est): 4.13MM Privately Held
Web: www.lorelton.com
SIC: 8641 Civic and social associations

(G-17997)
LORNA LEE PC
2111 Willow Way (19810-4151)
PHONE..................302 761-9191
Lorna Lee, Prin

Wilmington - New Castle County (G-17998) GEOGRAPHIC SECTION

EMP: 9 EST: 2010
SALES (est): 117.75K **Privately Held**
SIC: 8011 Pediatrician

(G-17998)
LOS JARDINES INC
1000 W 5th St (19805-3271)
PHONE..................................302 652-6390
EMP: 5 EST: 2010
SALES (est): 303.29K **Privately Held**
SIC: 6531 Rental agent, real estate

(G-17999)
LOS VERDOR LLC (PA) ◆
251 Little Falls Dr (19808-1674)
PHONE..................................971 344-0173
Sravan Kumar Matlapudi, *Managing Member*
EMP: 5 EST: 2022
SALES (est): 69.25K
SALES (corp-wide): 69.25K **Privately Held**
SIC: 0762 Farm management services

(G-18000)
LOSCO AND MARCONI PA
1926 Zebley Rd (19810-1504)
P.O. Box 1677 (19899-1677)
PHONE..................................302 656-7776
Daniel R Losco, *Pr*
EMP: 9 EST: 1995
SALES (est): 951.04K **Privately Held**
SIC: 8111 Specialized law offices, attorneys

(G-18001)
LOTUS LEASE HOSPITALITY
619 Amberley Rd (19803-2434)
PHONE..................................302 357-4699
EMP: 5 EST: 2019
SALES (est): 448K **Privately Held**
SIC: 7359 Equipment rental and leasing, nec

(G-18002)
LOTUS LOGISTICS LLC
Also Called: Discount Central
3524 Silverside Rd Ste 35b (19810-4929)
PHONE..................................573 240-4154
EMP: 30 EST: 2019
SALES (est): 2.82MM **Privately Held**
Web: www.lotuslgx.com
SIC: 4212 Local trucking, without storage

(G-18003)
LOTUS RCVERY CTR PRCES CRNR LL
1812 Newport Gap Pike (19808-6179)
PHONE..................................302 999-8900
EMP: 26 EST: 2020
SALES (est): 298.15K **Privately Held**
Web: www.lotusrecoverycenters.com
SIC: 8093 Substance abuse clinics (outpatient)

(G-18004)
LOUGHRAN MEDICAL GROUP PA
3411 Silverside Rd Ste 103wb (19810-4848)
P.O. Box 1599 (19971-5599)
PHONE..................................302 479-8464
Joseph Loughran Md, *Pr*
James Loughran Md, *VP*
Timothy Hennesy, *Pt*
EMP: 7 EST: 1990
SALES (est): 820.94K **Privately Held**
Web: www.loughranmedicalgroup.com
SIC: 8011 Internal medicine, physician/surgeon

(G-18005)
LOUIE UNCLE FOODS
15 Gale Ln (19807-2264)
PHONE..................................302 750-0117
Dea Zufelt, *Prin*
EMP: 5 EST: 2013
SALES (est): 197.82K **Privately Held**
SIC: 1541 Food products manufacturing or packing plant construction

(G-18006)
LOUIS K RAFETTO DMD
3512 Silverside Rd Ste 12 (19810-4913)
PHONE..................................302 477-1800
Louis K Rafetto D.m.d., *Owner*
EMP: 5 EST: 1980
SALES (est): 433.61K **Privately Held**
Web: www.drrafetto.com
SIC: 8021 Dental surgeon

(G-18007)
LOUIS L RDDING CTY/COUNTY BLDG
800 N French St Fl 9 (19801-3594)
PHONE..................................302 576-2100
EMP: 5 EST: 2018
SALES (est): 56.76K **Privately Held**
SIC: 1799 Special trade contractors, nec

(G-18008)
LOUIS P MARTIN DDS
1941 Limestone Rd Ste 105 (19808-5413)
PHONE..................................302 994-4900
Louis P Martin D.d.s., *Prin*
EMP: 7 EST: 1984
SALES (est): 235.97K **Privately Held**
SIC: 8021 Dentists' office

(G-18009)
LOUISE M FLYNN
1600 Rockland Rd (19803-3607)
PHONE..................................302 651-4000
Louise Flynn, *Prin*
EMP: 12 EST: 2014
SALES (est): 30.53K **Privately Held**
Web: www.nemours.org
SIC: 8049 Offices of health practitioner

(G-18010)
LOUVIERS FEDERAL CREDIT UNION
1007 N Market St (19801-1227)
PHONE..................................302 571-9513
EMP: 30
Web: www.louviers.com
SIC: 6061 Federal credit unions
PA: Louviers Federal Credit Union
185 S Main St
Newark DE 19711

(G-18011)
LOUVIERS MORTGAGE CORPORATION
4839 Limestone Rd (19808-1902)
PHONE..................................302 234-4129
Vincent Ingui, *Pr*
EMP: 6 EST: 2003
SALES (est): 239.7K **Privately Held**
SIC: 6163 Mortgage brokers arranging for loans, using money of others

(G-18012)
LOWES AIRPORT (FA77)
1900 Prior Rd (19809-1316)
PHONE..................................813 366-7655
Judy Smith, *Mgr*
EMP: 5 EST: 2016
SALES (est): 79.73K **Privately Held**
SIC: 4581 Airports, flying fields, and services

(G-18013)
LOWES HOME CENTERS LLC
Also Called: Lowe's
3100 Brandywine Pkwy Fl 1 (19803-1496)
PHONE..................................302 479-7799
Frank Ancos, *Mgr*
EMP: 117
SALES (corp-wide): 97.06B **Publicly Held**
Web: www.lowes.com
SIC: 5211 5031 5722 5064 Home centers; Building materials, exterior; Household appliance stores; Electrical appliances, television and radio
HQ: Lowe's Home Centers, Llc
1000 Lowes Blvd
Mooresville NC 28117
336 658-4000

(G-18014)
LOYAL ORDER MOSE CLYMONT LODGE
5101 Governor Printz Blvd (19809)
PHONE..................................302 764-9765
EMP: 6 EST: 2011
SALES (est): 55.6K **Privately Held**
SIC: 8641 Civic associations

(G-18015)
LOYALTY IS EARNED INC (PA)
Also Called: Lie
3 Germay Dr Ste 1740 (19804-1127)
PHONE..................................347 606-6383
Reginald A Brown Junior, *Pr*
EMP: 5 EST: 2015
SALES (est): 163.91K
SALES (corp-wide): 163.91K **Privately Held**
SIC: 7549 3999 Towing services; Advertising display products

(G-18016)
LP SMOKED LLC
20 Montchanin Rd Ste 250 (19807-2181)
P.O. Box 1266 (19899-1266)
PHONE..................................302 379-3059
EMP: 6 EST: 2012
SALES (est): 100.01K **Privately Held**
SIC: 4493 Marinas

(G-18017)
LPL FINANCIAL
1303 Delaware Ave Ste 112 (19806-3421)
PHONE..................................617 423-3644
EMP: 9 EST: 2019
SALES (est): 231.71K **Privately Held**
Web: www.lpl.com
SIC: 8742 Financial consultant

(G-18018)
LRC NORTH AMERICA INC
1105 N Market St (19801-1216)
PHONE..................................302 427-2845
Andrew Slater, *Pr*
Robert Kaiser, *VP*
◆ EMP: 39 EST: 1963
SALES (est): 2.43MM
SALES (corp-wide): 17.4B **Privately Held**
SIC: 2834 3069 3421 Proprietary drug products; Medical sundries, rubber; Clippers, fingernail and toenail
HQ: London International Group Limited
35 New Bridge Street
London
207 580-4242

(G-18019)
LS ANDERSON REPRODUCTIONS INC
2900 Faulkland Rd (19808-2514)
PHONE..................................302 999-9940
Larry Anderson, *Prin*
EMP: 5 EST: 2006
SALES (est): 115.52K **Privately Held**
SIC: 7822 Motion picture and tape distribution

(G-18020)
LS AUTO EXPERIENCE LLC (PA)
701 N Claymont St (19801-4369)
PHONE..................................302 983-9668
Larry Jackson, *Managing Member*
EMP: 7 EST: 2021
SALES (est): 126.03K
SALES (corp-wide): 126.03K **Privately Held**
SIC: 7532 Body shop, automotive

(G-18021)
LSF NETWORKS LLC
300 Delaware Ave Ste 210a (19801-6601)
PHONE..................................213 537-2402
EMP: 3 EST: 2017
SALES (est): 86.51K **Privately Held**
SIC: 2741 Internet publishing and broadcasting

(G-18022)
LTR PRIVATE FOUNDATION
206 Haystack Ln (19807-1122)
PHONE..................................610 745-5000
EMP: 6 EST: 2014
SALES (est): 67.69K **Privately Held**
SIC: 8641 Civic and social associations

(G-18023)
LUBILL PROPERTIES LLC
1201 N Market St Ste 111 (19801-1156)
PHONE..................................302 946-4188
Dewayne Phillips, *CEO*
EMP: 5 EST: 2020
SALES (est): 498.18K **Privately Held**
SIC: 6799 Real estate investors, except property operators

(G-18024)
LUCID COLLOIDS AMER
2213 Jones Ln (19810-2710)
PHONE..................................302 475-2393
EMP: 3 EST: 2017
SALES (est): 48.05K **Privately Held**
Web: www.lucidcolloids.com
SIC: 1382 Oil and gas exploration services

(G-18025)
LUMBER INDUSTRIES INC
5809 Kennett Pike (19807-1115)
PHONE..................................302 655-9651
Baird Brittingham, *Ch*
George D Herman, *Pr*
Steve Sweeny, *VP*
Robert Brittingham, *Sec*
John Brittingham, *Treas*
EMP: 7 EST: 1923
SQ FT: 1,000
SALES (est): 948.26K **Privately Held**
SIC: 7389 Financial services

(G-18026)
LUMENTY TECHNOLOGIES INC
Also Called: Lumenty
3411 Silverside Rd # 104 (19810-4812)
PHONE..................................971 331-3113
Andrey Veremeev, *Mktg Mgr*
▲ EMP: 14 EST: 2018
SALES (est): 1.06MM **Privately Held**
SIC: 5065 Mobile telephone equipment

(G-18027)
LUMHAA LLC
108 W 13th St (19801-1145)

GEOGRAPHIC SECTION　　　　　　　　　　　　　　　　　　　　　　　　　Wilmington - New Castle County (G-18055)

PHONE..................916 517-9972
EMP: 7 EST: 2018
SALES (est): 193.91K Privately Held
Web: www.lumhaa.com
SIC: 2741 Internet publishing and broadcasting

(G-18028)
LUNDGREN CHAIZHUNUSSOV LTD LLC ✪
824 N Market St Ste 220 (19801-3024)
PHONE..................508 828-0058
Julien Lundgren, *Managing Member*
EMP: 2 EST: 2022
SALES (est): 87.4K Privately Held
SIC: 7372 Prepackaged software

(G-18029)
LUNE ROUGE ENTRMT USA INC
251 Little Falls Dr (19808-1674)
PHONE..................514 556-2101
Stphane Mongeau, *Pr*
EMP: 25 EST: 2018
SALES (est): 206.47K Privately Held
SIC: 7929 Entertainment service

(G-18030)
LUPUS FOUNDTN OF AMER PHILA TR
100 W 10th St (19801-6603)
PHONE..................302 622-8700
Annette Myrick, *CEO*
EMP: 13 EST: 2010
SALES (est): 83.49K Privately Held
SIC: 8641 Recreation association

(G-18031)
LUTHERAN COMMUNITY SERVICES
2809 Baynard Blvd (19802-2967)
PHONE..................302 654-8886
Jean Warren, *Dir*
EMP: 6 EST: 1959
SALES (est): 1.65MM Privately Held
Web: www.lcsde.org
SIC: 8322 8741 Social service center; Financial management for business

(G-18032)
LUTHERAN SENIOR SERVICES INC
Also Called: Luther Towers II
1420 N Franklin St Ste 1 (19806-3122)
PHONE..................302 654-4490
EMP: 5
SALES (corp-wide): 4.42MM Privately Held
Web: www.luthertowers.com
SIC: 6513 Retirement hotel operation
PA: Lutheran Senior Services, Inc.
 1201 N Harrison St # 1204
 Wilmington DE 19806
 302 654-4490

(G-18033)
LUTHERAN SENIOR SERVICES INC (PA)
1201 N Harrison St Apt 1204 (19806-3534)
PHONE..................302 654-4490
John Teoli, *Ex Dir*
Linda Dugan, *Building Manager*
EMP: 60 EST: 1967
SALES (est): 4.42MM
SALES (corp-wide): 4.42MM Privately Held
Web: www.luthertowers.com
SIC: 8052 Intermediate care facilities

(G-18034)
LUTWIN-KAWALEC MALGORZATA MD
1600 Rockland Rd (19803-3607)

PHONE..................302 651-4000
Malgorzata Lutwin Kawalec, *Pr*
EMP: 15 EST: 2017
SALES (est): 59.55K Privately Held
Web: www.nemours.org
SIC: 8011 Pediatrician

(G-18035)
LUUT TECHNOLOGIES INC
1209 N Orange St (19801-1120)
PHONE..................302 658-7581
Anthony Lacavera, *Prin*
EMP: 5
SALES (est): 129.73K Privately Held
SIC: 7373 Computer systems analysis and design

(G-18036)
LUX PARADISE PROPERTIES LLC (PA) ✪
3911 Concord Pike # 8030 (19803-1736)
PHONE..................502 631-2008
Timothy Juback, *Managing Member*
EMP: 5 EST: 2022
SALES (est): 229.84K
SALES (corp-wide): 229.84K Privately Held
SIC: 6514 Dwelling operators, except apartments

(G-18037)
LUXCORE LLC
300 Delaware Ave Ste 210a (19801-6601)
PHONE..................302 777-0538
EMP: 19 EST: 2018
SALES (est): 658.7K Privately Held
SIC: 7379 Computer related consulting services

(G-18038)
LUXIASUITES LLC
Also Called: Residences At City Center
1007 N Orange St (19801-1239)
PHONE..................302 778-3000
Dan Jasinski, *Mgr*
EMP: 16
SALES (corp-wide): 865.99K Privately Held
Web: www.luxiasuites.com
SIC: 7299 Apartment locating service
PA: Luxiasuites Llc
 322 A St Ste 300
 Wilmington DE 19801
 302 778-2900

(G-18039)
LUXIASUITES LLC
Also Called: Justison Landing
331 Justison St (19801-5181)
PHONE..................302 654-8527
EMP: 16
SALES (corp-wide): 865.99K Privately Held
Web: www.residencesatjustisonlanding.com
SIC: 6513 Apartment building operators
PA: Luxiasuites Llc
 322 A St Ste 300
 Wilmington DE 19801
 302 778-2900

(G-18040)
LUXIASUITES LLC (PA)
322 A St Ste 300 (19801-5354)
PHONE..................302 778-2900
Robert E Buccini, *Managing Member*
EMP: 7 EST: 2013
SALES (est): 865.99K
SALES (corp-wide): 865.99K Privately Held
Web: www.luxiasuites.com

SIC: 7011 Hotels

(G-18041)
LUXIASUITES LLC
Also Called: Christina Landing
115 Christina Landing Dr (19801-5401)
PHONE..................302 426-1200
EMP: 16
SALES (corp-wide): 865.99K Privately Held
Web: www.residencesatchristinalanding.com
SIC: 7011 Hotels
PA: Luxiasuites Llc
 322 A St Ste 300
 Wilmington DE 19801
 302 778-2900

(G-18042)
LUXURY RESIDENCE LLC
1201 N Market St Ste 11 (19801-1147)
PHONE..................302 216-2102
EMP: 15 EST: 2021
SALES (est): 580.9K Privately Held
Web: www.residencesatharlanflats.com
SIC: 6799 Real estate investors, except property operators

(G-18043)
LYCRA COMPANY LLC
1209 N Orange St (19801-1120)
PHONE..................540 949-2972
EMP: 6
SALES (est): 539.78K Privately Held
Web: www.lycra.com
SIC: 5137 Women's and children's clothing

(G-18044)
LYFT INC (PA)
1209 N Orange St (19801-1120)
PHONE..................302 747-0124
EMP: 6 EST: 2019
SALES (est): 127.11K
SALES (corp-wide): 127.11K Privately Held
Web: www.lyft.com
SIC: 4121 Taxicabs

(G-18045)
LYME YARNBOMBS INC
7 Denbeigh Ct (19808-1538)
PHONE..................302 547-1340
Marian Eastman, *Prin*
EMP: 6 EST: 2017
SALES (est): 62.39K Privately Held
SIC: 8399 Social services, nec

(G-18046)
LYNCH JIM HEATHER E
1104 Grandview Ave (19809-2316)
PHONE..................302 562-6336
Heather Elaine Lynch-james, *Prin*
EMP: 9 EST: 2011
SALES (est): 70.87K Privately Held
SIC: 8011 General and family practice, physician/surgeon

(G-18047)
LYNDA D ARAI M D
1600 Rockland Rd (19803-3607)
PHONE..................302 651-5350
Lynda Arai, *Pr*
EMP: 15 EST: 2017
SALES (est): 64.64K Privately Held
Web: www.nemours.org
SIC: 8011 Pediatrician

(G-18048)
LYNEER STAFFING SOLUTIONS
639 W Newport Pike (19804-3259)

PHONE..................302 892-9494
EMP: 12 EST: 2014
SALES (est): 109.15K Privately Held
Web: www.lyneer.com
SIC: 7361 Employment agencies

(G-18049)
LYNKMAX LLC
1201 N Orange St Ste 7107 (19801-1194)
PHONE..................302 573-3568
EMP: 6 EST: 2017
SALES (est): 200K Privately Held
Web: www.lynkmax.com
SIC: 8742 Management information systems consultant

(G-18050)
LYNN M FUCHS M D
1600 Rockland Rd (19803-3607)
PHONE..................302 651-4000
Lynn Fuchs, *Ofcr*
EMP: 12 EST: 2017
SALES (est): 269.27K Privately Held
Web: www.nemours.org
SIC: 8011 Pediatrician

(G-18051)
LYNNANNE KASARDA MD
1802 W 4th St (19805-3420)
PHONE..................302 655-5822
Lynnanne Kasarda, *Prin*
EMP: 10 EST: 2017
SALES (est): 132.52K Privately Held
SIC: 8011 Offices and clinics of medical doctors

(G-18052)
LYONS COMPANIES LLC
501 Carr Rd (19809-2866)
PHONE..................302 658-5508
EMP: 89 EST: 2017
SALES (est): 3.6MM Privately Held
Web: www.lyonsinsurance.com
SIC: 6411 Insurance agents, brokers, and service

(G-18053)
LYONS DAVID J LAW OFFICE
1526 Gilpin Ave (19806-3016)
PHONE..................302 777-5698
David J Lyons, *Owner*
EMP: 5 EST: 2000
SALES (est): 577.15K Privately Held
Web: www.lyonslaw1.com
SIC: 8111 General practice attorney, lawyer

(G-18054)
LYONS INSURANCE AGENCY INC (PA)
Also Called: Nationwide
501 Carr Rd Ste 301 (19809-2866)
PHONE..................302 227-7100
David Lyons, *Pr*
EMP: 64 EST: 1984
SALES (est): 10.87MM
SALES (corp-wide): 10.87MM Privately Held
Web: www.lyonsinsurance.com
SIC: 6411 Insurance agents, nec

(G-18055)
M & F FINANCIAL CORP
300 Delaware Ave Ste 1704 (19801-1612)
PHONE..................302 427-5755
Bruce Wighs, *Pr*
Vernon Bryant, *VP*
Charles Cox, *Sec*
EMP: 11 EST: 1990
SALES (est): 2.38MM
SALES (corp-wide): 25.96MM Privately Held

Wilmington - New Castle County (G-18056) GEOGRAPHIC SECTION

SIC: **6022** 6162 State commercial banks; Mortgage bankers
PA: Texasbanc Holding Co
  102 N Main St
  Weatherford TX
  817 598-2265

(G-18056)
M & M DETAIL WRAP AND TINT LLC ✪
2001 N West St Ste 79 (19802-4827)
P.O. Box 9720 (19809-0720)
PHONE.................................302 260-8988
Geoffrey X Gilbert, *Managing Member*
EMP: 6 **EST:** 2022
SALES (est): 62.38K **Privately Held**
SIC: **7549** 7389 Automotive customizing services, nonfactory basis; Business services, nec

(G-18057)
M AUGER ENTERPRISE INC
Also Called: Badger Electric
101 Cassidy Dr (19804)
PHONE.................................302 992-9922
◆ **EMP:** 18 **EST:** 2010
SALES (est): 1.23MM **Privately Held**
Web: www.badgerde.com
SIC: **1731** General electrical contractor

(G-18058)
M DAVIS & SONS INC
200 Hadco Rd (19804-1074)
PHONE.................................302 998-3385
Charles Davis, *Prin*
EMP: 6
SALES (corp-wide): 65.58MM **Privately Held**
Web: www.mdavisinc.com
SIC: **1711** Mechanical contractor
PA: M. Davis & Sons, Inc.
  24 Mcmillan Way
  Newark DE 19713
  302 998-3385

(G-18059)
M MICHELLE MILLIGAN LCSW
5235 W Woodmill Dr Ste 47 (19808-4068)
PHONE.................................302 540-9136
M Milligan, *Owner*
EMP: 5 **EST:** 2015
SALES (est): 32.92K **Privately Held**
Web: www.journeytwoserenity.net
SIC: **8322** Social worker

(G-18060)
M O T H E R S INC
212 W 21st St (19802-4006)
PHONE.................................302 275-4163
Merna Suber, *Pr*
EMP: 10 **EST:** 2010
SALES (est): 94.27K **Privately Held**
SIC: **8351** Child day care services

(G-18061)
M T INVESTMENT GROUP
501 Silverside Rd Ste 6 (19809-1375)
PHONE.................................302 793-4917
Paul Longua, *Pr*
EMP: 5 **EST:** 2018
SALES (est): 18.95K **Privately Held**
SIC: **7299** Miscellaneous personal service

(G-18062)
MA ADAS LLC
1201 N Market St Ste 111e-91 (19801-1147)
PHONE.................................302 420-8158
EMP: 5
SALES (est): 199.4K **Privately Held**
SIC: **7389** Business Activities at Non-Commercial Site

(G-18063)
MAACO COLLISION REPR AUTO PNTG
2400 Northeast Blvd (19802-4509)
PHONE.................................610 628-3867
Craig Schlott, *Owner*
EMP: 7 **EST:** 2015
SALES (est): 378.87K **Privately Held**
Web: www.maaco-wilmington.com
SIC: **7542** 7532 Carwash, automatic; Body shop, automotive

(G-18064)
MACCARI COMPANIES INC (PA)
1700 First State Blvd (19804-3566)
P.O. Box 6468 (19804-0468)
PHONE.................................302 994-9628
Anthony Maccari, *Pr*
Jean M Maccan, *Sec*
EMP: 17 **EST:** 1986
SQ FT: 20,000
SALES (est): 4.96MM
SALES (corp-wide): 4.96MM **Privately Held**
SIC: **1721** 1799 Industrial painting; Sandblasting of building exteriors

(G-18065)
MACCARI MOTORS
1202 First State Blvd (19804-3561)
PHONE.................................302 563-3361
Nicholas Maccari, *Prin*
EMP: 6 **EST:** 2012
SALES (est): 180K **Privately Held**
SIC: **1541** Truck and automobile assembly plant construction

(G-18066)
MACDONALD CONTRACTING LLC
10 Germay Dr Ste A (19804-1141)
PHONE.................................302 668-2022
Robert Macdonald, *Prin*
EMP: 5 **EST:** 2010
SALES (est): 135.14K **Privately Held**
SIC: **1799** Special trade contractors, nec

(G-18067)
MACELREE & HARVEY LTD
5721 Kennett Pike (19807-1311)
PHONE.................................302 654-4454
Felice Glennon Kerr, *Prin*
EMP: 24 **EST:** 2010
SALES (est): 1.13MM **Privately Held**
Web: www.macelree.com
SIC: **8111** General practice attorney, lawyer

(G-18068)
MACFARLANE A RADFORD MD PA
Also Called: Millcreek Pediatrics
203 W Pembrey Dr (19803-2008)
PHONE.................................302 633-6338
A Radford Macfarland, *Pr*
EMP: 10 **EST:** 1999
SALES (est): 941.25K **Privately Held**
Web: www.millcreekpediatrics.com
SIC: **8011** Pediatrician

(G-18069)
MACIELS IMPORTS LLC
300 Delaware Ave Ste 210a (19801-6601)
PHONE.................................562 295-6773
EMP: 5 **EST:** 2016
SALES (est): 120.85K **Privately Held**
SIC: **7389**

(G-18070)
MACINTOSH ENGINEERING INC
2 Mill Rd Ste 100 (19806-2175)
PHONE.................................302 252-9200
Robert Macintosh, *Pr*
EMP: 17 **EST:** 1998
SALES (est): 2.43MM **Privately Held**
Web: www.macintosheng.com
SIC: **8711** Civil engineering

(G-18071)
MACKLYN HOME CARE
5179 W Woodmill Dr (19808-4067)
PHONE.................................302 690-9397
Krista Gaul, *Owner*
Donna Durnan, *Dir*
EMP: 8 **EST:** 2015
SALES (est): 1.3MM **Privately Held**
Web: www.macklynhomecare.net
SIC: **8082** 4119 Home health care services; Local passenger transportation, nec

(G-18072)
MACRO POLYMERS NA LLC
501 Silverside Rd Ste 600 (19809-1374)
PHONE.................................302 660-6926
EMP: 5 **EST:** 2018
SALES (est): 222.7K **Privately Held**
SIC: **2821** Plastics materials and resins
PA: Macro Polymers Private Limited
  165, Maha Gujarat Industrial Estate
  Ahmedabad GJ 38221

(G-18073)
MADDIX OWENS LILLIAN
Also Called: Lisa Owens Child Care
114 W 25th St (19802-4114)
PHONE.................................302 897-1997
EMP: 8 **EST:** 2011
SALES (est): 33.44K **Privately Held**
SIC: **8351** Child day care services

(G-18074)
MADISON REAL ESTATE INC
112 S French St (19801-5035)
PHONE.................................718 947-6350
Traci Madison, *Pr*
EMP: 5 **EST:** 2016
SALES (est): 247.15K **Privately Held**
Web: www.madisonrealestateinc.com
SIC: **6531** Real estate agent, residential

(G-18075)
MADO CREATIVE AGENCY INC
300 Delaware Ave Ste 210 (19801-6601)
PHONE.................................302 223-9532
Linda Watson, *CEO*
EMP: 5 **EST:** 2020
SALES (est): 30K **Privately Held**
SIC: **8742** Marketing consulting services

(G-18076)
MAELYS COSMETICS USA INC
251 Little Falls Dr (19808-1674)
PHONE.................................312 888-5007
Daniel De Castro, *Prin*
Yaniv Dagan, *Prin*
EMP: 11 **EST:** 2018
SALES (est): 6.16MM **Privately Held**
Web: www.maelyscosmetics.com
SIC: **5122** Cosmetics

(G-18077)
MAGAN FORMAN
325 Oracle Rd (19808-1562)
PHONE.................................443 394-9534
Magan Forman, *Prin*
EMP: 9 **EST:** 2010
SALES (est): 54.13K **Privately Held**

SIC: **8011** Orthopedic physician

(G-18078)
MAGELLAN MIDSTREAM PARTNERS LP
Also Called: Megellan Terminal
1050 Christiana Ave Ste A (19801-5867)
PHONE.................................302 654-3717
John Weaver, *Mgr*
EMP: 12
SALES (corp-wide): 22.39B **Publicly Held**
Web: www.magellanlp.com
SIC: **4612** Crude petroleum pipelines
HQ: Magellan Midstream Partners, Lp
  1 Williams Ctr Bsmt 2
  Tulsa OK 74172
  918 574-7000

(G-18079)
MAGIC CAR WASH II INC
4917 Kirkwood Hwy (19808-5011)
PHONE.................................302 660-8066
EMP: 8 **EST:** 2016
SALES (est): 282.97K **Privately Held**
Web: www.magiccarwashinc.com
SIC: **7542** Washing and polishing, automotive

(G-18080)
MAGIC CAR WASH INC
3221 Naamans Rd (19810-1003)
PHONE.................................302 479-5911
Dave Emerson, *Pr*
Eve Emerson, *
EMP: 10 **EST:** 1999
SALES (est): 696.33K **Privately Held**
Web: www.magiccarwashinc.com
SIC: **7542** Washing and polishing, automotive

(G-18081)
MAGIC CLEANING
58 Holly St (19808-4937)
PHONE.................................302 723-4328
Graciela Rivas, *Prin*
EMP: 5 **EST:** 2017
SALES (est): 23.7K **Privately Held**
SIC: **7699** Cleaning services

(G-18082)
MAGIC INC
2810 N Church St (19802-4447)
PHONE.................................415 319-6331
EMP: 11 **EST:** 2018
SALES (est): 634.11K **Privately Held**
Web: www.magicinc.org
SIC: **8641** Civic and social associations

(G-18083)
MAGIPOP INC
1007 N Orange St Fl 4 (19801-1239)
PHONE.................................217 898-3115
Chenxiao Li, *CEO*
EMP: 7
SALES (est): 264.9K **Privately Held**
SIC: **7371** Computer software development

(G-18084)
MAGNIFASKIN MEDSPA
3901 Concord Pike (19803-1715)
PHONE.................................302 516-7287
EMP: 9 **EST:** 2018
SALES (est): 173.18K **Privately Held**
Web: www.magnifaskinmedspa.com
SIC: **8011** Dermatologist

(G-18085)
MAGUIRE & SONS INC
Also Called: Maguire Pest Control
1035 Philadelphia Pike Ste C (19809-2039)

▲ = Import ▼ = Export
◆ = Import/Export

P.O. Box 684 (19703-0684)
PHONE..................302 798-1200
Allan Maguire, Pr
EMP: 8 **EST:** 1991
SALES (est): 429.21K **Privately Held**
Web: www.maguirepestde.com
SIC: 7342 Pest control in structures

(G-18086)
MAHAVIR LLC
Also Called: Goddard School, The
111 S West St (19801-5014)
PHONE..................302 651-7995
EMP: 35 **EST:** 2017
SALES (est): 2.35MM **Privately Held**
Web: www.goddardschool.com
SIC: 8351 Preschool center

(G-18087)
MAHLE INDUSTRIAL THERMAL SYSTE
1209 N Orange St (19801-1120)
PHONE..................915 612-1611
EMP: 5 **EST:** 2016
SALES (est): 390.45K **Privately Held**
SIC: 8741 Management services

(G-18088)
MAIN GATE LAUNDRY
123 Kirkwood Sq (19808-4859)
PHONE..................302 998-9949
Linda Burns, Owner
EMP: 5 **EST:** 1988
SALES (est): 139.41K **Privately Held**
SIC: 7216 7211 Drycleaning plants, except rugs; Power laundries, family and commercial

(G-18089)
MAIN LIGHT INDUSTRIES INC
1614 Newport Gap Pike (19808-6208)
P.O. Box 1352 (19899-1352)
PHONE..................302 998-8017
Aidas Gimbutas, Pr
EMP: 119 **EST:** 1986
SQ FT: 16,000
SALES (est): 10.97MM **Privately Held**
Web: www.mainlight.com
SIC: 3648 5049 7922 Stage lighting equipment; Theatrical equipment and supplies; Equipment rental, theatrical

(G-18090)
MAIN SOCIAL MEDIA
1201 N Orange St (19801-1155)
PHONE..................302 268-6979
EMP: 13 **EST:** 2018
SALES (est): 267.27K **Privately Held**
Web: www.mainsocialmedia.com
SIC: 4899 Communication services, nec

(G-18091)
MAINTENANCE TROUBLESHOOTI
2917 Cheshire Rd (19810-3202)
PHONE..................302 477-1045
Thomas B Davis, Prin
EMP: 7 **EST:** 2010
SALES (est): 212.63K **Privately Held**
SIC: 7349 Building maintenance services, nec

(G-18092)
MAJOR MAHH LEVELS LLC
2404 Jacqueline Dr Apt A7 (19810-2006)
PHONE..................973 494-4767
EMP: 7 **EST:** 2019
SALES (est): 225.57K **Privately Held**
SIC: 3651 Music distribution apparatus

(G-18093)
MAKE PRODUCTIONS
1511 2nd Ave (19805-5002)
PHONE..................302 593-1595
David Pierce, Prin
EMP: 6 **EST:** 2017
SALES (est): 47.2K **Privately Held**
Web: www.makeproductionsllc.com
SIC: 7819 Developing and laboratory services, motion picture

(G-18094)
MAKUA INC ✪
Also Called: Makua
251 Little Falls Dr (19808-1674)
PHONE..................310 923-8549
Amy Dugan, CEO
EMP: 7 **EST:** 2022
SALES (est): 132.62K **Privately Held**
Web: www.halemakua.org
SIC: 8082 Home health care services

(G-18095)
MALONE CEMENT CONSTRUCTION INC
Also Called: Malone Concrete Cnstr Co
11 Rosecroft Ct (19808-4334)
PHONE..................302 239-9399
John I Malone, Pr
Mario Malone, VP
EMP: 12 **EST:** 1957
SALES (est): 745.93K **Privately Held**
SIC: 1771 Concrete work

(G-18096)
MALONG LLC
1013 Centre Rd Ste 4035 (19805-1265)
PHONE..................516 336-9992
EMP: 50
SALES (est): 1.06MM **Privately Held**
SIC: 7371 Custom computer programming services

(G-18097)
MAMMELES INC
Also Called: Mammele's Paint Stores
2300 Kirkwood Hwy (19805-4905)
P.O. Box 4458 (19807-0458)
PHONE..................302 998-0541
Robert Alan Peoples, Pr
John E Peoples, VP
Andrew M Peoples, VP
EMP: 14 **EST:** 1897
SQ FT: 12,000
SALES (est): 2.18MM **Privately Held**
Web: www.mammeles.com
SIC: 5198 5231 Paints; Paint

(G-18098)
MANAGEMENT ASSOCIATES INC
Also Called: Interfaith Community Housing
613 N Washington St (19801-2135)
PHONE..................302 652-3991
Gary Polil, Pr
EMP: 16 **EST:** 1974
SALES (est): 2.16MM
SALES (corp-wide): 2.16MM **Privately Held**
Web: www.ichde.org
SIC: 6513 Apartment building operators
PA: Community Housing Inc
613 N Washington St
Wilmington DE 19801
302 652-3991

(G-18099)
MANAGEMENT PAIN LLC
5231 W Woodmill Dr Ste 45 (19808-4068)
PHONE..................302 543-5180
Liana Lera Ayotte, Prin
EMP: 6 **EST:** 2011
SALES (est): 286.29K **Privately Held**
Web: www.delpain.com
SIC: 8093 Specialty outpatient clinics, nec

(G-18100)
MANAGEMENT PL INVESTME
20 Montchanin Rd (19807-2160)
PHONE..................888 654-5449
Howard C Richardson, Prin
EMP: 5 **EST:** 2011
SALES (est): 194.99K **Privately Held**
Web: www.imandp.com
SIC: 6282 Investment advisory service

(G-18101)
MANCOMTEC LLC
2055 Limestone Rd Ste 200c (19808-5536)
PHONE..................234 243-4256
EMP: 5 **EST:** 2021
SALES (est): 33.14K **Privately Held**
Web: www.mancomtec.com
SIC: 4813 Data telephone communications

(G-18102)
MANCOR US INC
1011 Centre Rd Ste 322 (19805-1266)
PHONE..................302 573-3858
Mike Andrews, CEO
EMP: 51 **EST:** 2000
SALES (est): 1.57MM
SALES (corp-wide): 156.64MM **Privately Held**
SIC: 3441 Building components, structural steel
PA: Mancor Canada Inc
2485 Speers Rd
Oakville ON L6L 2
905 827-3737

(G-18103)
MANETO INC (HQ)
103 Foulk Rd (19803-3742)
PHONE..................302 656-4285
EMP: 21 **EST:** 1985
SALES (est): 5.27MM
SALES (corp-wide): 686.34MM **Privately Held**
SIC: 3996 3253 2273 2435 Hard surface floor coverings, nec; Wall tile, ceramic; Rugs, tufted; Veneer stock, hardwood
PA: Mannington Mills Inc.
75 Mannington Mills Rd
Salem NJ 08079
800 356-6787

(G-18104)
MANIFESTA
135 Devonshire Rd (19803-3026)
PHONE..................610 883-0202
EMP: 6 **EST:** 2014
SALES (est): 47.98K **Privately Held**
Web: www.manifesta.org
SIC: 8412 Museum

(G-18105)
MANLEY HVAC INC
3705 Wild Cherry Ln (19808-4611)
PHONE..................302 998-4654
EMP: 5 **EST:** 1997
SALES (est): 430K **Privately Held**
SIC: 1711 Heating and air conditioning contractors

(G-18106)
MANNING GROSS + MASSENBURG LLP
1007 N Orange St Apt 1051 (19801-1250)
PHONE..................302 657-2100
Harry L Manion, Brnch Mgr
EMP: 13
SALES (corp-wide): 23.99MM **Privately Held**
Web: www.mgmlaw.com
SIC: 8111 General practice law office
PA: Manning Gross + Massenburg Llp
125 High St Ste 630
Boston MA 02110
617 670-8800

(G-18107)
MANTIS FARMS
2 Winston Pl (19804-1848)
PHONE..................302 507-4851
EMP: 6 **EST:** 2018
SALES (est): 63.98K **Privately Held**
Web: www.mantis.com
SIC: 0191 General farms, primarily crop

(G-18108)
MANUFACTURERS & TRADERS TR CO
Also Called: M&T
3801 Kennett Pike (19807-2321)
PHONE..................302 651-8738
Patricia Clark, Brnch Mgr
EMP: 7
SALES (corp-wide): 8.6B **Publicly Held**
Web: www.wilmingtontrust.com
SIC: 6022 State commercial banks
HQ: Manufacturers And Traders Trust Company
1 M&T Plz Fl 3
Buffalo NY 14203
716 842-4200

(G-18109)
MANUFACTURERS & TRADERS TR CO
Also Called: M&T
15 W Lea Blvd (19802-1324)
PHONE..................302 472-3161
Jane Smith, Mgr
EMP: 5
SALES (corp-wide): 8.6B **Publicly Held**
Web: ir.mtb.com
SIC: 6022 State commercial banks
HQ: Manufacturers And Traders Trust Company
1 M&T Plz Fl 3
Buffalo NY 14203
716 842-4200

(G-18110)
MANUFACTURERS & TRADERS TR CO
Also Called: M&T
1100 N Market St (19801-1243)
PHONE..................302 636-6000
EMP: 10
SALES (corp-wide): 8.6B **Publicly Held**
Web: www.wilmingtontrust.com
SIC: 6022 State commercial banks
HQ: Manufacturers And Traders Trust Company
1 M&T Plz Fl 3
Buffalo NY 14203
716 842-4200

(G-18111)
MANUFACTURERS & TRADERS TR CO
Also Called: M&T
4899 Limestone Rd Stoney Creek Plaza (19808-1902)
PHONE..................302 472-3309
Jim Whittaker, Mgr
EMP: 5
SALES (corp-wide): 8.6B **Publicly Held**
Web: ir.mtb.com

Wilmington - New Castle County (G-18112)

GEOGRAPHIC SECTION

SIC: **6022** State commercial banks
HQ: Manufacturers And Traders Trust Company
1 M&T Plz Fl 3
Buffalo NY 14203
716 842-4200

(G-18112)
MANUFACTURERS & TRADERS TR CO
Also Called: M&T
2301 Concord Pike (19803-2911)
PHONE..................302 472-3233
Charles Emory, *Brnch Mgr*
EMP: 9
SALES (corp-wide): **8.6B Publicly Held**
Web: ir.mtb.com
SIC: **6022** State trust companies accepting deposits, commercial
HQ: Manufacturers And Traders Trust Company
1 M&T Plz Fl 3
Buffalo NY 14203
716 842-4200

(G-18113)
MANUFACTURERS & TRADERS TR CO
Also Called: M&T
2371 Limestone Rd (19808-4103)
PHONE..................302 651-1757
Porche Johnson, *Mgr*
EMP: 6
SALES (corp-wide): **8.6B Publicly Held**
Web: ir.mtb.com
SIC: **6022** State trust companies accepting deposits, commercial
HQ: Manufacturers And Traders Trust Company
1 M&T Plz Fl 3
Buffalo NY 14203
716 842-4200

(G-18114)
MANUFACTURERS & TRADERS TR CO
Also Called: M&T
1812 Marsh Rd (19810-4581)
PHONE..................302 651-1803
Kendrall Elder, *Brnch Mgr*
EMP: 10
SALES (corp-wide): **8.6B Publicly Held**
Web: ir.mtb.com
SIC: **6022** State trust companies accepting deposits, commercial
HQ: Manufacturers And Traders Trust Company
1 M&T Plz Fl 3
Buffalo NY 14203
716 842-4200

(G-18115)
MANUFACTURERS & TRADERS TR CO
Also Called: M&T
100 N James St (19804-3123)
PHONE..................302 651-1544
Dianne Franehitti, *Mgr*
EMP: 6
SALES (corp-wide): **8.6B Publicly Held**
Web: ir.mtb.com
SIC: **6022** State trust companies accepting deposits, commercial
HQ: Manufacturers And Traders Trust Company
1 M&T Plz Fl 3
Buffalo NY 14203
716 842-4200

(G-18116)
MANUFACTURERS & TRADERS TR CO
Also Called: M&T
1207 N Union St (19806-2531)
PHONE..................302 656-1260
Shirley Hawk, *Mgr*
EMP: 10
SALES (corp-wide): **8.6B Publicly Held**
Web: ir.mtb.com
SIC: **6022** State trust companies accepting deposits, commercial
HQ: Manufacturers And Traders Trust Company
1 M&T Plz Fl 3
Buffalo NY 14203
716 842-4200

(G-18117)
MARA LABS INC (PA)
1013 Ctr Rd Ste 403-B (19805-1270)
PHONE..................650 564-4971
Nishith Rastogi, *CEO*
EMP: 39 EST: 2015
SALES (est): 2.26MM
SALES (corp-wide): **2.26MM Privately Held**
Web: www.locus.sh
SIC: **7371** Computer software development

(G-18118)
MARBLE CITY SOFTWARE INC
1900 Gilpin Ave (19806-2308)
PHONE..................302 658-2583
EMP: 2 EST: 1990
SALES (est): **106.04K Privately Held**
SIC: **7372** Prepackaged software

(G-18119)
MARC V FELIZZI
4402 Limestone Rd (19808-1904)
PHONE..................302 897-4942
Marc Felizzi, *Prin*
EMP: 6 EST: 2017
SALES (est): **63.19K Privately Held**
SIC: **8322** Social worker

(G-18120)
MARC WSBURG LPCMH MNTAL HLTH C
1201 Philadelphia Pike (19809-2042)
PHONE..................302 798-4400
EMP: 8 EST: 2019
SALES (est): **224.6K Privately Held**
Web: www.marcweisburg.com
SIC: **8093** Mental health clinic, outpatient

(G-18121)
MARCH OF DIMES INC
Also Called: Delaware Chapter
236 N James St Ste C (19804-3165)
PHONE..................302 225-1020
Leslie Kosck, *Ex Dir*
EMP: 6
SALES (corp-wide): **212.94MM Privately Held**
Web: www.marchofdimes.org
SIC: **8399** Fund raising organization, non-fee basis
PA: March Of Dimes Inc.
1550 Crystal Dr Ste 1300
Arlington VA 22202
571 257-2324

(G-18122)
MARCON JOHN SOLUTIONS INC
1000 N West St Ste 1200 (19801-1058)
PHONE..................302 295-4806
Vir Mary Gaile Reyes, *CEO*
EMP: 6 EST: 2016
SALES (est): **63.12K Privately Held**
SIC: **8748** Business consulting, nec

(G-18123)
MARCONE
228 W Market St (19804-3152)
PHONE..................800 482-6022
EMP: 7 EST: 2015
SALES (est): **54.85K Privately Held**
Web: www.marcone.com
SIC: **5099** Durable goods, nec

(G-18124)
MARGARET HARRIS-NEMTUDA
3513 Concord Pike # 1000 (19803-5027)
PHONE..................302 477-5500
Walter Keiper, *Owner*
EMP: 5 EST: 2013
SALES (est): **86.55K Privately Held**
SIC: **6531** Real estate agents and managers

(G-18125)
MARGO LEWIS-JAH LEONA
237 Dumont Rd (19804-1001)
PHONE..................610 800-9524
Margo Lewis, *Prin*
EMP: 6 EST: 2018
SALES (est): **32.92K Privately Held**
SIC: **8322** Individual and family services

(G-18126)
MARIA RUBINO WATKINS
125 Montchan Dr (19807-2125)
PHONE..................405 532-4023
Maria Rubino Watkins, *Prin*
EMP: 10 EST: 2010
SALES (est): **128.81K Privately Held**
SIC: **8011** General and family practice, physician/surgeon

(G-18127)
MARIANNA J MCSWEENEY PT
174 Belmont Dr (19808-4329)
PHONE..................302 234-1803
Marianna Mcsweeney, *Mgr*
EMP: 6 EST: 2017
SALES (est): **67.44K Privately Held**
SIC: **8049** Offices of health practitioner

(G-18128)
MARIANO LOZANO
121 Alders Dr (19803-5301)
PHONE..................302 478-6710
Mariano Lozano, *Prin*
EMP: 5 EST: 2006
SALES (est): **130K Privately Held**
SIC: **7389** Business Activities at Non-Commercial Site

(G-18129)
MARIN BAYARD
521 N West St (19801-2139)
PHONE..................302 658-4200
Bayard Marin, *Owner*
EMP: 5 EST: 1997
SALES (est): **444.9K Privately Held**
Web: www.bayardmarinlaw.com
SIC: **8111** Malpractice and negligence law

(G-18130)
MARINE & ENERGY TRADING CORP
Also Called: M&E Trading
1201 N Orange St (19801-1155)
PHONE..................857 207-7999
Chukwudi Ifedinma, *Pr*
EMP: 32 EST: 2019
SALES (est): **1.67MM Privately Held**
Web: www.marine-energycorp.com
SIC: **8711** Marine engineering

(G-18131)
MARINE LUBRICANTS INC
1130 E 7th St (19801-4502)
P.O. Box 389 (19720-0389)
PHONE..................302 429-7570
Joseph K Mc Cammon, *Pr*
H Hickman Rowland, *Sec*
EMP: 8 EST: 1983
SQ FT: 15,000
SALES (est): **893.04K Privately Held**
Web: www.marinelubricants.us
SIC: **4213** Liquid petroleum transport, non-local

(G-18132)
MARIO F MEDORI INC
20 Millside Dr (19801-5542)
PHONE..................302 239-4550
Mark Medori, *Pr*
Mario F Medori, *VP*
Mary A Medori, *Sec*
EMP: 8 EST: 1962
SALES (est): **959.69K Privately Held**
SIC: **1741** 1541 Stone masonry; Industrial buildings and warehouses

(G-18133)
MARIO MEDORI INC
20 Millside Dr (19801-5542)
PHONE..................302 656-8432
Mario Medori, *CEO*
EMP: 10 EST: 1964
SALES (est): **311.69K Privately Held**
SIC: **1741** Masonry and other stonework

(G-18134)
MARITIME LOGISTICS CORP LLC
1130 E 7th St (19801-4502)
PHONE..................302 420-3007
Ken Beatty, *Mgr*
EMP: 6
SALES (corp-wide): **127.16K Privately Held**
SIC: **4225** Warehousing, self storage
PA: Maritime Logistics Corporation, Llc
27706 Valley Run Dr
Wilmington DE 19810
302 420-3007

(G-18135)
MARITIME LOGISTICS CORP LLC (PA)
27706 Valley Run Dr (19810-1944)
P.O. Box 374 (08094-0374)
PHONE..................302 420-3007
EMP: 7 EST: 2020
SALES (est): 127.16K
SALES (corp-wide): **127.16K Privately Held**
SIC: **4424** Deep sea domestic transportation of freight

(G-18136)
MARK A FORTUNATO
1415 Foulk Rd (19803-2748)
PHONE..................302 477-4900
Mark A Fortunato, *Prin*
EMP: 50 EST: 2010
SALES (est): **748.84K Privately Held**
Web: www.dentalassociatesofdelaware.com
SIC: **8021** Dentists' office

(G-18137)
MARK ADCOCK
5560 Kirkwood Hwy (19808-5002)
PHONE..................302 660-0909
Mark Adcock, *Prin*
EMP: 5 EST: 2016
SALES (est): **94.19K Privately Held**

Web: www.realestateagentwilmington.com
SIC: 6531 Real estate agent, residential

(G-18138)
MARK C GLADNICK DDS
5513 Kirkwood Hwy (19808-5001)
PHONE..................................302 994-2660
Mark Gladnick D.d.s., *Owner*
Mark C Gladnick D.d.s., *Owner*
EMP: 7 EST: 1979
SALES (est): 397.74K **Privately Held**
Web: www.dedental.com
SIC: 8021 Dentists' office

(G-18139)
MARK MATHEW MAURAGAS DC
134 Belmont Dr (19808-4329)
PHONE..................................302 750-8084
Mark Mathew Mauragas, *Prin*
EMP: 7 EST: 2011
SALES (est): 59.16K **Privately Held**
SIC: 8041 Offices and clinics of chiropractors

(G-18140)
MARK W ECKARD
1201 N Market St Ste 1500 (19801-1163)
PHONE..................................302 778-7518
Mark Eckard, *Prin*
▲ EMP: 5 EST: 2008
SALES (est): 140.62K **Privately Held**
SIC: 8111 Criminal law

(G-18141)
MARK WANNER
4017 Greenmount Dr (19810-3303)
PHONE..................................302 478-6878
Mark Wanner, *Prin*
EMP: 5 EST: 2009
SALES (est): 209.79K **Privately Held**
SIC: 1522 Residential construction, nec

(G-18142)
MARKATOS SERVICES INC
Also Called: Markatos Cleaning Services
1411 Philadelphia Pike Ste B (19809-1823)
PHONE..................................302 792-0606
Harry Markatos, *Pr*
Susan Markatos, *VP*
EMP: 18 EST: 2006
SQ FT: 4,000
SALES (est): 704.01K **Privately Held**
Web: www.markatosservices.com
SIC: 7699 Cleaning services

(G-18143)
MARKES INTERNATIONAL INC
270 Presidential Dr (19807-3302)
PHONE..................................302 656-5500
Charles H Elter, *Prin*
EMP: 7 EST: 2011
SALES (est): 237.98K **Privately Held**
SIC: 3826 Analytical instruments

(G-18144)
MARKET EDGE LLC (PA)
1003 Park Pl (19806-4304)
PHONE..................................302 442-6800
Paul Drees, *Pr*
EMP: 8 EST: 2000
SALES (est): 2.34MM
SALES (corp-wide): 2.34MM **Privately Held**
Web: www.mkt-edge.com
SIC: 8742 Marketing consulting services

(G-18145)
MARKET ST CHRPRCTIC RHBLTTION
727 N Market St Ste 1 (19801-4935)
P.O. Box 26336 (19899-6336)
PHONE..................................302 652-6000
Todd Watson, *Prin*
EMP: 7 EST: 2011
SALES (est): 228K **Privately Held**
SIC: 8041 Offices and clinics of chiropractors

(G-18146)
MARKETING CREATORS INC
802 N West St (19801-1526)
PHONE..................................302 409-0344
Paul Dukes, *Pr*
EMP: 6 EST: 2009
SALES (est): 449.47K **Privately Held**
SIC: 8742 Marketing consulting services

(G-18147)
MARKING SERVICES INC
3505 Silverside Rd Ste 101 (19810-4905)
PHONE..................................302 478-0381
Jeff Dickinson, *Pr*
EMP: 6 EST: 2004
SALES (est): 416.11K **Privately Held**
Web: www.markserv.com
SIC: 3531 Line markers, self-propelled

(G-18148)
MARKIZON PRINTING
111 Nevada Ave (19803-3231)
PHONE..................................610 715-7989
EMP: 3 EST: 2018
SALES (est): 89.43K **Privately Held**
SIC: 2752 Commercial printing, lithographic

(G-18149)
MARKLAND AFFILIATES LLC
2126 W Nwport Pike Ste 20 (19804)
PHONE..................................302 633-9134
EMP: 5 EST: 2001
SALES (est): 117.56K **Privately Held**
SIC: 7389 8742 Financial services; Financial consultant

(G-18150)
MARKS ONILL OBRIEN DHRTY KLLY
300 Delaware Ave Ste 900 (19801-1671)
PHONE..................................302 658-6538
K Simmons, *Prin*
EMP: 7
Web: www.moodklaw.com
SIC: 8111 General practice attorney, lawyer
PA: Marks, O'neill, O'brien, Doherty & Kelly, P.C.
1617 John F Kennedy Blvd
Philadelphia PA 19103

(G-18151)
MARKVELL DELARIE GILMORE TRUST
24a Trolley Sq Ste 1372 (19806-3334)
PHONE..................................772 742-1499
Alribu Ttee, *Admn*
EMP: 6
SALES (est): 81.29K **Privately Held**
SIC: 6211 Security brokers and dealers

(G-18152)
MARLETTE SERVICES INC
3419 Silverside Rd (19810-4801)
PHONE..................................302 358-2730
EMP: 8 EST: 2018
SALES (est): 389.37K **Privately Held**
SIC: 8742 Management consulting services

(G-18153)
MARLINGS INC
Also Called: Marlings Emrgncy Wtr Rmval Crp
41 Germay Dr Ste D (19804-1100)
PHONE..................................302 325-1759
John Marling, *Pr*
EMP: 14 EST: 1990
SALES (est): 867.35K **Privately Held**
Web: www.marlings.us
SIC: 7349 1799 7217 Building maintenance services, nec; Post disaster renovations; Carpet and upholstery cleaning

(G-18154)
MARON MRVEL BRDLEY ANDERSON PA (PA)
1201 N Market St Ste 900 (19801-1100)
P.O. Box 288 (19899-0288)
PHONE..................................302 425-5177
EMP: 51 EST: 1996
SALES (est): 12.01MM **Privately Held**
Web: www.maronmarvel.com
SIC: 8111 General practice attorney, lawyer

(G-18155)
MARQUEZ MISAEL MD
2601 Annand Dr Ste 13 (19808-3719)
PHONE..................................302 995-6192
Misael Marquez, *Prin*
EMP: 8 EST: 2017
SALES (est): 104.39K **Privately Held**
SIC: 8011 Offices and clinics of medical doctors

(G-18156)
MARRA LANDING LLC
6 W Clivden Dr (19807-2538)
PHONE..................................302 530-5800
EMP: 5 EST: 2010
SALES (est): 209.19K **Privately Held**
Web: www.marrahomes.com
SIC: 1521 Single-family housing construction

(G-18157)
MARRIOTT VCTONS WRLDWIDE OWNER
1220 N Market St Ste 202 (19801-2535)
PHONE..................................302 636-6128
EMP: 9 EST: 2013
SALES (est): 1.22MM **Publicly Held**
SIC: 6733 Trusts, nec
PA: Marriott Vacations Worldwide Corporation
7812 Palm Pkwy
Orlando FL 32836

(G-18158)
MARSHALL DNNHEY WRNER CLMAN GG
1007 N Orange St Ste 600 (19801-1266)
PHONE..................................302 504-3341
EMP: 37
SALES (corp-wide): 129.68MM **Privately Held**
Web: www.marshalldennehey.com
SIC: 8111 General practice law office
PA: Marshall Dennehey Warner Coleman & Goggin P.C.
2000 Market St Ste 2300
Philadelphia PA 19103
215 575-2600

(G-18159)
MARSHALL DNNHEY WRNER CLMAN GG
1220 N Market St Ste 201 (19801-2540)
PHONE..................................302 552-4300
EMP: 31
SALES (corp-wide): 129.68MM **Privately Held**
Web: www.marshalldennehey.com
SIC: 8111 General practice law office
PA: Marshall Dennehey Warner Coleman & Goggin P.C.
2000 Market St Ste 2300
Philadelphia PA 19103
215 575-2600

(G-18160)
MARSHALL SERVICES INC
2202 Fairfield Pl (19805-2646)
PHONE..................................302 655-0076
Gary C Marshall, *Prin*
EMP: 5 EST: 2012
SALES (est): 94.38K **Privately Held**
SIC: 1522 Residential construction, nec

(G-18161)
MARSICO & WEINSTIEN DDS
Also Called: Marsico Weinstien
2390 Limestone Rd (19808-4104)
PHONE..................................302 998-8474
Edward Weinstien D.d.s., *Pt*
EMP: 7 EST: 1964
SALES (est): 765.44K **Privately Held**
Web: www.edweinsteindds.com
SIC: 8021 Dentists' office

(G-18162)
MARTA BISKUP DDS
3522 Silverside Rd (19810-4916)
PHONE..................................302 478-0000
EMP: 9 EST: 2017
SALES (est): 258.77K **Privately Held**
Web: www.blackhurstdentalpa.com
SIC: 8021 Dentists' office

(G-18163)
MARTA BLACKHURST DMD
3522 Silverside Rd (19810-4916)
PHONE..................................302 478-1504
Marta Blackhurst D.m.d., *Prin*
EMP: 17 EST: 2005
SALES (est): 371.54K **Privately Held**
Web: www.blackhurstdentalpa.com
SIC: 8021 Dentists' office

(G-18164)
MARTELLO RE HOLDINGS LTD LLC
251 Little Falls Dr (19808-1674)
PHONE..................................302 636-5401
Dennis Ho, *CEO*
EMP: 7 EST: 2021
SALES (est): 391.8K **Privately Held**
Web: www.martellore.com
SIC: 6351 Liability insurance

(G-18165)
MARTIN & CALLOWAY
3601 Old Capitol Trl Unit A3 (19808-6042)
PHONE..................................302 268-6655
EMP: 5 EST: 2019
SALES (est): 139.99K **Privately Held**
Web: www.martincalloway.com
SIC: 7699 General household repair services

(G-18166)
MARTIN & CALLOWAY LLC
1224 Mckennans Church Rd (19808-2149)
PHONE..................................302 482-1180
EMP: 5 EST: 2010
SALES (est): 112.86K **Privately Held**
Web: www.martincalloway.com
SIC: 1751 Carpentry work

(G-18167)
MARTIN D HVRLY ATTORNEY AT LAW
2500 Grubb Rd Ste 240b (19810-4796)
PHONE..................................302 529-0121
Martin Haverly, *Pr*
EMP: 7 EST: 2017
SALES (est): 63.66K **Privately Held**
Web: www.haverlylaw.com
SIC: 8111 General practice attorney, lawyer

Wilmington - New Castle County (G-18168)

GEOGRAPHIC SECTION

(G-18168)
MARTIN DANIEL D & ASSOC LLC
1301 N Harrison St (19806-3128)
PHONE..................302 658-2884
EMP: 6 EST: 2005
SALES (est): 457.86K **Privately Held**
Web: www.danielmartinlaw.com
SIC: 8111 General practice law office

(G-18169)
MARTIN ZUKOFF CPA
2523 Bona Rd (19810-2219)
PHONE..................302 478-4734
Martin Zukoff, *Prin*
EMP: 5 EST: 1997
SALES (est): 80.09K **Privately Held**
SIC: 8721 Certified public accountant

(G-18170)
MARTINELLI HOLDINGS LLC (PA)
Also Called: Today Media
1000 N West St (19801-1050)
PHONE..................302 656-1809
EMP: 18 EST: 2010
SALES (est): 15.56MM
SALES (corp-wide): 15.56MM **Privately Held**
Web: site.todaymediainc.com
SIC: 2721 Magazines: publishing only, not printed on site

(G-18171)
MARTINREA INTERNATIONAL US INC
1209 N Orange St (19801-1120)
PHONE..................615 212-0586
EMP: 6 EST: 2019
SALES (est): 71.92K **Privately Held**
SIC: 3714 Motor vehicle parts and accessories

(G-18172)
MARTINS HOME IMPROVEMENTS
405 Milton Dr (19802-1221)
PHONE..................302 367-4789
Martin Jodko, *Owner*
EMP: 9 EST: 2009
SALES (est): 936.93K **Privately Held**
Web: www.martinshomeimprovements.com
SIC: 1521 General remodeling, single-family houses

(G-18173)
MARVI CLEANERS LIMITED INC
309 Philadelphia Pike (19809-2150)
PHONE..................302 764-3077
Mario Marconi, *Pr*
Christine Marconi, *VP*
EMP: 7 EST: 1959
SQ FT: 1,250
SALES (est): 180.97K **Privately Held**
Web: www.marvi-cleaners.com
SIC: 7216 7212 7219 Cleaning and dyeing, except rugs; Garment pressing; Garment alteration and repair shop

(G-18174)
MARVIN & PALMER ASSOCIATES
200 Bellevue Pkwy Ste 220 (19809-3727)
PHONE..................302 573-3570
Dave Marvin, *Ch*
Stan Palmer, *Vice Chairman**
Karen Buckley, *
EMP: 23 EST: 1986
SQ FT: 12,000
SALES (est): 4.99MM **Privately Held**
Web: www.marvinandpalmer.com
SIC: 6282 Investment counselors

(G-18175)
MARVIN & PALMER US EQUITY LP
200 Bellevue Pkwy Ste 220 (19809-3727)
PHONE..................302 573-3570
EMP: 6 EST: 1988
SALES (est): 175.94K **Privately Held**
SIC: 6722 Money market mutual funds

(G-18176)
MARVIN PALMER GLOBL EQUITY LP
200 Bellevue Pkwy Ste 220 (19809-3727)
PHONE..................302 573-3570
EMP: 9 EST: 1986
SALES (est): 87.17K **Privately Held**
SIC: 8742 Financial consultant

(G-18177)
MARY CAMPBELL CENTER INC
4641 Weldin Rd (19803-4829)
PHONE..................302 762-6025
Jerrold P Spilecki, *Ex Dir*
EMP: 170 EST: 1976
SQ FT: 60,000
SALES (est): 23.72MM **Privately Held**
Web: www.marycampbellcenter.org
SIC: 8052 8361 Intermediate care facilities; Children's home

(G-18178)
MARY E HERRING DAYCARE CENTER
Also Called: Mary E. Herring Day Care
2450 N Market St Ste 1 (19802-4200)
PHONE..................302 652-5978
Juanita P Matthews, *Dir*
Juanita Lyles, *Dir*
EMP: 6 EST: 1969
SALES (est): 145.57K **Privately Held**
SIC: 8351 Group day care center

(G-18179)
MARY HUFF
1500 Shallcross Ave Ste 1a (19806-3037)
PHONE..................302 650-2460
Mary Huff, *Owner*
EMP: 5 EST: 2017
SALES (est): 78.16K **Privately Held**
SIC: 8049 Offices of health practitioner

(G-18180)
MARY L KREIDER
Also Called: Medical Billing Associates
2001 Woodbrook Dr (19810-4343)
PHONE..................302 375-6232
Mary L Kreider, *Prin*
EMP: 7 EST: 2011
SALES (est): 71.63K **Privately Held**
SIC: 8099 Health and allied services, nec

(G-18181)
MARY MOTHER HOPE HOUSE 1
Also Called: Ministry of Caring
1103 W 8th St (19806-4605)
PHONE..................302 652-8532
Anne Mountain, *Dir*
EMP: 15 EST: 2014
SALES (est): 81.89K **Privately Held**
Web: www.ministryofcaring.org
SIC: 8322 Emergency shelters

(G-18182)
MARY SWEENEY-LEHR
3209 Coachman Rd (19803-1902)
PHONE..................302 764-0589
Mary Sweeney-lehr, *Prin*
EMP: 11 EST: 2010
SALES (est): 210K **Privately Held**
SIC: 8021 Offices and clinics of dentists

(G-18183)
MASLEY ENTERPRISES INC
1601 Jessup St (19802-4209)
PHONE..................302 427-9885
Francis J Masley, *CEO*
Donna Masley, *
EMP: 50 EST: 2000
SQ FT: 20,000
SALES (est): 3.78MM **Privately Held**
Web: www.militarygloves.com
SIC: 2381 3151 5199 3949 Fabric dress and work gloves; Welders' gloves; Leather goods, except footwear, gloves, luggage, belting; Mitts and gloves, baseball

(G-18184)
MASS FOR THE HOMELESS INC
2817 Ambler Ct (19808-2802)
PHONE..................302 368-1030
Wilson G Somers, *Prin*
Susan Booker, *Pr*
EMP: 6 EST: 2010
SALES (est): 108.23K **Privately Held**
Web: www.musicwithamission.org
SIC: 8699 Charitable organization

(G-18185)
MASTER EXTNDED MKT INDEX SRIES
100 Bellevue Pkwy (19809-3700)
PHONE..................800 441-7762
EMP: 7
SALES (est): 357.8K **Privately Held**
SIC: 6722 Money market mutual funds

(G-18186)
MASTER FOCUS GROWTH LLC
100 Bellevue Pkwy (19809-3700)
PHONE..................800 441-7762
Alice Pellegrino, *Prin*
EMP: 6 EST: 2013
SALES (est): 186.54K **Privately Held**
SIC: 6722 Money market mutual funds

(G-18187)
MASTER G ENTERTAINMENT
1427 Athens Rd (19803-5111)
PHONE..................302 547-9367
EMP: 5 EST: 2013
SALES (est): 27.55K **Privately Held**
SIC: 7929 Musical entertainers

(G-18188)
MASTER-HALCO INC
P.O. Box 1791 (19899-1791)
PHONE..................302 475-6714
EMP: 6
Web: www.masterhalco.com
SIC: 5039 Wire fence, gates, and accessories
HQ: Master-Halco, Inc.
3010 Lyndon B Johnson Fwy
Dallas TX 75234
972 714-7300

(G-18189)
MAT SITE MANAGEMENT LLC
3828 Kennett Pike Ste 201 (19807-2331)
PHONE..................302 397-8561
Michael Mckenna, *Prin*
EMP: 7 EST: 2015
SALES (est): 204.58K **Privately Held**
Web: www.matmanagement.com
SIC: 8741 Business management

(G-18190)
MATER ELLIS LLC
919 N Market St (19801-3023)
PHONE..................302 508-0938
EMP: 5 EST: 2019
SIC: 6719 Investment holding companies, except banks

(G-18191)
MATERIAL SUPPLY INC
924 S Heald St (19801-5733)
PHONE..................302 658-6524
Quentin Saienni, *Pr*
EMP: 24 EST: 1971
SALES (est): 781.85K **Privately Held**
Web: www.diamondmaterials.com
SIC: 1611 2951 General contractor, highway and street construction; Asphalt paving mixtures and blocks

(G-18192)
MATERNITY WOMENS HEALTH
2601 Annand Dr Ste 14 (19808-3719)
PHONE..................302 994-0979
EMP: 8 EST: 2019
SALES (est): 450.76K **Privately Held**
Web: www.ob-and-gyn.com
SIC: 8011 Gynecologist

(G-18193)
MATRICA LABS INC
1209 N Orange St (19801-1120)
PHONE..................818 573-7394
Dushan Perera, *CEO*
EMP: 15
SALES (est): 528.73K **Privately Held**
SIC: 7371 Computer software development

(G-18194)
MATTER MUSIC INC
427 N Tatnall St # 25426 (19801-2230)
PHONE..................650 793-7749
Paul Meed, *CEO*
EMP: 15
SALES (est): 305.24K **Privately Held**
Web: www.matter.online
SIC: 7372 7389 Prepackaged software; Business services, nec

(G-18195)
MATTHEW B LUNN
1000 N West St (19801-1050)
PHONE..................302 571-6646
Matthew Lunn, *Prin*
EMP: 5 EST: 2008
SALES (est): 92.67K **Privately Held**
Web: www.youngconaway.com
SIC: 8111 General practice attorney, lawyer

(G-18196)
MATTHEW EICHERBAUM
1941 Limestone Rd (19808-5408)
PHONE..................302 655-9494
Matthew Eicherbaum, *Prin*
EMP: 10 EST: 2011
SALES (est): 138.5K **Privately Held**
SIC: 8011 Orthopedic physician

(G-18197)
MATTHEW J MCILRATH DC
1201 Philadelphia Pike (19809-2042)
PHONE..................302 798-7033
Matthew J Mc Ilrath D.c., *Owner*
EMP: 5 EST: 1997
SALES (est): 117.14K **Privately Held**
Web: www.healthonepa.com
SIC: 8041 Offices and clinics of chiropractors

(G-18198)
MATTHEW KIRBY
113 Dickinson Ln (19807-3139)
PHONE..................302 427-0911
Matthew Kirby, *Prin*
EMP: 6 EST: 2009
SALES (est): 174.26K **Privately Held**

SIC: 1771   Concrete work

(G-18199)
MATTHEW W LAWRENCE DO
1500 Shallcross Ave (19806-3037)
PHONE...................................302 652-6050
Matthew Lawrence, *Owner*
EMP: 10 EST: 2013
SALES (est): 312.55K **Privately Held**
SIC: 8011   Surgeon

(G-18200)
MATYKOS BEAUTY LLC
200 Brandywine Blvd (19809-3240)
PHONE...................................302 213-6879
EMP: 7
SALES (est): 606.37K **Privately Held**
SIC: 2844   Face creams or lotions

(G-18201)
MAUREEN FREEBERY
Also Called: Maureens Beauty Salon
4801 Limestone Rd (19808-1902)
PHONE...................................302 234-7800
Maureen Freebery, *Owner*
EMP: 5 EST: 1968
SALES (est): 93.25K **Privately Held**
SIC: 7231   Hairdressers

(G-18202)
MAURTEN US CORPORATION
1000 N West St Ste 1200 (19801-1058)
PHONE...................................302 669-9085
Olof Skold, *CEO*
EMP: 2 EST: 2016
SALES (est): 1.22MM
SALES (corp-wide): 13.22MM **Privately Held**
Web: www.maurten.com
SIC: 2086   Carbonated beverages, nonalcoholic: pkged. in cans, bottles
HQ: Maurten Ab
  Gibraltargatan 1a
  GOteborg 411 3
  707918335

(G-18203)
MAWI INC ✪
919 N Market St Ste 950 (19801-3023)
PHONE...................................888 937-6868
Andrew Klymenko, *CEO*
EMP: 5 EST: 2022
SALES (est): 72.16K **Privately Held**
SIC: 8011   Cardiologist and cardio-vascular specialist

(G-18204)
MAX VALUE SOFTWARE LLC
1209 N Orange St (19801-1120)
PHONE...................................630 254-8044
EMP: 10 EST: 2017
SALES (est): 326.28K **Privately Held**
Web: www.holdemmanager.com
SIC: 7372   Prepackaged software

(G-18205)
MAXIM HEALTHCARE SERVICES INC
Also Called: De Homecare
1523 Concord Pike Ste 100 (19803-3653)
PHONE...................................302 478-3434
Bryan Wade, *Brnch Mgr*
EMP: 339
Web: www.maximhealthcare.com
SIC: 7363   Medical help service
PA: Maxim Healthcare Services, Inc.
  7227 Lee Deforest Dr
  Columbia MD 21046

(G-18206)
MAXINES DAYCARE
1027 Lancaster Ave (19805-4006)
PHONE...................................302 652-7242
Maxine Williams, *Prin*
EMP: 5 EST: 2010
SALES (est): 108.43K **Privately Held**
Web: www.maxinescenter.com
SIC: 8351   Group day care center

(G-18207)
MAXWEB INC
1201 N Orange St Ste 7266 (19801-1268)
PHONE...................................302 208-8361
EMP: 6 EST: 2016
SALES (est): 63.12K **Privately Held**
SIC: 7389   Business Activities at Non-Commercial Site

(G-18208)
MAXWELL FINANCIAL FIRM LLC
303 Waverly Rd (19803-3136)
PHONE...................................302 332-3454
Yao-tian Pao-huang, *Prin*
EMP: 20 EST: 2018
SALES (est): 885.72K **Privately Held**
Web: www.maxwellfinancial.org
SIC: 6282   Investment advice

(G-18209)
MAYFLOWER HEALTHCARE LLC ✪
108 W 13th St Ste 100 (19801-1145)
PHONE...................................908 414-8026
Zev Schwartz, *Managing Member*
EMP: 6 EST: 2023
SALES (est): 70.57K **Privately Held**
SIC: 8011   Offices and clinics of medical doctors

(G-18210)
MAYPLE LTD
2810 N Church St Pmb 15700 (19802-4447)
PHONE...................................917 558-0698
Ammar Poonawala, *CEO*
EMP: 5 EST: 2020
SALES (est): 216.13K **Privately Held**
SIC: 8742   Marketing consulting services

(G-18211)
MB STORE LLC ✪
1207 Delaware Ave (19806-4743)
PHONE...................................425 310-2574
Nikolai Avardi, *COO*
Nikolai Avardo, *COO*
EMP: 15 EST: 2022
SALES (est): 639.35K **Privately Held**
SIC: 8748   Business consulting, nec

(G-18212)
MBNA CONSUMER SERVICES INC
1100 N King St (19884-0011)
PHONE...................................302 453-9930
Bruce Hammonds, *Ch Bd*
John J Hewes, *
Vernon Wright, *
EMP: 3009 EST: 1992
SALES (est): 335.59MM
SALES (corp-wide): 94.95B **Publicly Held**
SIC: 6211   Mortgages, buying and selling
PA: Bank Of America Corporation
  100 N Tryon St Ste 2650
  Charlotte NC 28202
  704 386-5681

(G-18213)
MBNA MARKETING SYSTEMS INC
Also Called: MBNA
1100 N King St (19884-0011)
PHONE...................................302 456-8588
Bruce Hammonds, *CEO*
John R Cochran, *Vice Chairman*
Vernon Wright, *
John Scheflen, *
EMP: 1484 EST: 1990
SALES (est): 12.35MM
SALES (corp-wide): 94.95B **Publicly Held**
SIC: 7389   Telemarketing services
HQ: Fia Card Services, National Association
  1100 N King St
  Wilmington DE 19884
  800 362-6255

(G-18214)
MCB LANDSCAPING LLC
1020 Darley Rd (19810-2910)
P.O. Box 354 (19078-0354)
PHONE...................................215 421-1083
Sabrina Rumpeltin, *Prin*
Jared Rumpeltin, *Prin*
EMP: 5 EST: 2016
SALES (est): 134.08K **Privately Held**
SIC: 0781   Landscape services

(G-18215)
MCC FOUNDATION INC
Also Called: MARY CAMPBELL CENTER
4641 Weldin Rd (19803-4829)
PHONE...................................302 762-6025
EMP: 19 EST: 1987
SALES (est): 442.42K **Privately Held**
Web: www.marycampbellcenter.org
SIC: 8322   Individual and family services

(G-18216)
MCCABE WEISBERG CONWAY PC
1407 Foulk Rd Ste 100 (19803-2700)
PHONE...................................302 409-3520
Jackson Phillips, *Prin*
EMP: 12 EST: 2017
SALES (est): 457.07K **Privately Held**
Web: www.mwc-law.com
SIC: 8111   General practice law office

(G-18217)
MCCAR AUTO GROUP LLC
2527 Eaton Rd (19810-3556)
PHONE...................................302 478-3049
Paul Mccarthy, *Prin*
EMP: 6 EST: 2014
SALES (est): 93.19K **Privately Held**
SIC: 7538   General automotive repair shops

(G-18218)
MCCARTER & ENGLISH LLP
405 N King St Ste 800 (19801-3715)
PHONE...................................302 984-6300
Bobbi Mortimer, *Brnch Mgr*
EMP: 20
SALES (corp-wide): 81.16MM **Privately Held**
Web: www.mccarter.com
SIC: 8111   General practice attorney, lawyer
PA: Mccarter & English Llp
  4 Gatway Ctr 100 Mlbrry S 4 Gateway Ctr
  Newark NJ 07102
  973 622-4444

(G-18219)
MCCARTHY CATE
1409 Foulk Rd Ste 204 (19803-2755)
PHONE...................................302 477-0708
C R Mccarthy Ph.d., *Owner*
EMP: 6 EST: 2018
SALES (est): 93.29K **Privately Held**
SIC: 8322   General counseling services

(G-18220)
MCCLAFFERTY PRINTING COMPANY
1600 N Scott St (19806-2599)
PHONE...................................302 652-8112
Mary Beth Mcclafferty, *Pr*
EMP: 46 EST: 1948
SQ FT: 12,500
SALES (est): 9.17MM **Privately Held**
Web: www.mcclaffertyprinting.com
SIC: 2752   Offset printing

(G-18221)
MCCLOSKEY BARBARA LCSW
114 Hitching Post Dr (19803-1913)
PHONE...................................302 479-5916
Mccloskey Barbara Lcsw, *Prin*
EMP: 7 EST: 2012
SALES (est): 54.23K **Privately Held**
SIC: 8322   Social worker

(G-18222)
MCCOLLOM DMLIO SMITH UBLER LLC
2751 Centerville Rd Ste 400 (19808-1627)
PHONE...................................302 468-5960
EMP: 19 EST: 2019
SALES (est): 3.53MM **Privately Held**
Web: www.mdsulaw.com
SIC: 8111   General practice law office

(G-18223)
MCCONNELL BROS INC
400 E Ayre St (19804-2513)
PHONE...................................302 218-4240
Dan Mc Connell, *Pr*
EMP: 6 EST: 1997
SALES (est): 472.3K **Privately Held**
Web: www.mcconnellbros.ie
SIC: 1761 7389   Roofing contractor; Building inspection service

(G-18224)
MCCONNELL JOHNSON RE CO LLC
1201 N Market St Ste 1605 (19801-1164)
PHONE...................................302 421-2000
Scott Johnson, *Managing Member*
EMP: 22 EST: 2000
SALES (est): 2.05MM **Privately Held**
Web: www.mcconnelldevelopment.com
SIC: 6531   Real estate agent, commercial

(G-18225)
MCCRERY FUNERAL HOMES INC
3924 Concord Pike (19803-1782)
PHONE...................................302 478-2204
Albert J Mccrery Iii, *CEO*
Dorothy Mccrery, *Treas*
EMP: 8 EST: 1912
SQ FT: 4,000
SALES (est): 899.03K **Privately Held**
Web: www.mccreryandharra.com
SIC: 7261   Funeral home

(G-18226)
MCCULLOUGH & ASSOCIATES INC
2303 Woods Rd (19808-2520)
PHONE...................................302 250-7679
EMP: 5 EST: 2012
SALES (est): 160.65K **Privately Held**
SIC: 8742   Management consulting services

(G-18227)
MCDONALD SAFETY EQUIPMENT INC
Also Called: Brandywine Vly Fire Safety Div
581 Copper Dr (19804-2409)
P.O. Box 6008 (19804-0608)
PHONE...................................302 999-0151
Brian Mc Donald, *Pr*
Brian Mcdonald, *Pr*

Bernadette Krajewski, *VP*
Thomas Jones, *VP*
Denise Jones, *Stockholder*
EMP: 32 **EST:** 1978
SALES (est): 9.47MM **Privately Held**
Web: www.mcdonaldsafety.com
SIC: 5099 Safety equipment and supplies

(G-18228)
MCELROY & SON INC
15 E Redmont Rd (19804)
PHONE.................................302 995-2623
Sandra Mcelroy, *Pr*
James Mc Elroy Junior, *VP*
Christopher Mc Elroy, *Sec*
EMP: 6 **EST:** 1994
SALES (est): 241.07K **Privately Held**
SIC: 1721 Painting and paper hanging

(G-18229)
MCGIVNEY KLUGER & COOK PC
1201 N Orange St Ste 504 (19801-1119)
PHONE.................................302 656-1200
Paul Sunshine, *Brnch Mgr*
EMP: 6
Web: www.mcgivneyandkluger.com
SIC: 8111 General practice attorney, lawyer
PA: Mcgivney, Kluger & Cook, P.C.
18 Columbia Tpke Fl 3
Florham Park NJ 07932

(G-18230)
MCI COMMUNICATIONS CORPORATION
Also Called: Verizon Business
200 Bellevue Pkwy Ste 500 (19809-3741)
PHONE.................................302 791-4900
EMP: 10
SALES (corp-wide): 133.97B **Publicly Held**
SIC: 4813 Local and long distance telephone communications
HQ: Mci Communications Corporation
22001 Loudoun County Pkwy
Ashburn VA 20147
703 886-5600

(G-18231)
MCJ SEAL & LINE STRIPING LLC
35 Indiana Rd (19808-5446)
PHONE.................................302 691-3255
Manuel Carbajal, *Prin*
EMP: 6 **EST:** 2014
SALES (est): 135.43K **Privately Held**
Web: www.mcjseallinestriping.com
SIC: 1611 Surfacing and paving

(G-18232)
MCKELVEY HIRES DRY CLEANING
Also Called: 1 Hour Martinizing
808 First State Blvd (19804-3573)
PHONE.................................302 998-9191
Barbara Hires, *Pr*
Connie Mckelvey, *Sec*
EMP: 10 **EST:** 1985
SQ FT: 2,500
SALES (est): 151.14K **Privately Held**
SIC: 7212 7216 Pickup station, laundry and drycleaning; Cleaning and dyeing, except rugs

(G-18233)
MCLAUGHLIN GORDON L LAW OFFICE
1203 N Orange St (19801-1120)
PHONE.................................302 651-7979
EMP: 5 **EST:** 1989
SALES (est): 328.67K **Privately Held**
SIC: 8111 General practice attorney, lawyer

(G-18234)
MCLAUGHLIN MORTON HOLDG CO LLC
1203 N Orange St Fl 2 (19801-1120)
PHONE.................................302 426-1313
EMP: 10 **EST:** 1998
SALES (est): 527.06K **Privately Held**
SIC: 8111 General practice attorney, lawyer

(G-18235)
MCLEEN PROPERTIES
240n Janes St Ste 100c (19804-3167)
P.O. Box 7289 (19803-0289)
PHONE.................................302 482-1486
EMP: 7 **EST:** 2013
SALES (est): 711.97K **Privately Held**
Web: mcleenproperties.managebuilding.com
SIC: 6512 Nonresidential building operators

(G-18236)
MCNEIL AND FMLY MGT GROUP LLC
2 White Oak Rd (19809-3265)
PHONE.................................302 830-3267
EMP: 10 **EST:** 2018
SALES (est): 481.81K **Privately Held**
SIC: 8741 Management services

(G-18237)
MCNICHOLAS PAINTING
202 Redwood Ave (19804-3824)
PHONE.................................302 995-0964
Michael Mcnicholas, *Prin*
EMP: 5 **EST:** 2016
SALES (est): 53.67K **Privately Held**
SIC: 1721 Residential painting

(G-18238)
MD22 LIONS LOW VISION REHAB
1400 Forrest Rd (19810-4314)
PHONE.................................410 737-2671
Alfred K Chew, *Prin*
EMP: 5 **EST:** 2017
SALES (est): 42.22K **Privately Held**
SIC: 8641 Civic and social associations

(G-18239)
MDM MCHNCAL INSTLLTION USA LLC
1201 N Orange St Ste 700 (19801-1186)
PHONE.................................617 938-9634
Cezary Sadlinski, *Admn*
EMP: 5 **EST:** 2014
SALES (est): 224.57K **Privately Held**
SIC: 1711 Mechanical contractor

(G-18240)
MDS INTERPRETING LLC
116 Churchill Ln (19808-4319)
P.O. Box 5453 (19808-0453)
PHONE.................................302 507-2393
EMP: 6 **EST:** 2012
SALES (est): 81.11K **Privately Held**
Web: www.mdsinterpreting.com
SIC: 8011 Offices and clinics of medical doctors

(G-18241)
ME GEEK SQUAD LLC
727 Maryland Ave (19805-4852)
PHONE.................................302 990-8092
EMP: 9
SALES (est): 842.63K **Privately Held**
SIC: 7378 Computer maintenance and repair

(G-18242)
MEADOWBROOK GOLF GROUP INC
Also Called: Ed Oliver Golf Club
800 N Dupont Rd (19807-2920)
PHONE.................................302 571-9041

Chris Bloss, *Brnch Mgr*
EMP: 41
Web: www.edolivergolfclub.com
SIC: 7992 Public golf courses
PA: Meadowbrook Golf Group, Inc.
5385 Gateway Blvd Ste 12
Lakeland FL 33811

(G-18243)
MEBRO INC
Also Called: SERVPRO
225 N James St (19804-3124)
PHONE.................................302 992-0104
Drew Mehan Senior, *CEO*
Linda Mehan, *VP*
Tara Brown, *Treas*
EMP: 20 **EST:** 1990
SQ FT: 50,000
SALES (est): 1.73MM **Privately Held**
Web: www.servprohockessinelsmere.com
SIC: 7349 1521 1799 1542 Building maintenance services, nec; Repairing fire damage, single-family houses; Construction site cleanup; Commercial and office buildings, renovation and repair

(G-18244)
MED TECH EQUIPMENT INC
2207 Concord Pike Ste 135 (19803-2908)
PHONE.................................800 322-2609
David J Gentile, *Pr*
EMP: 4 **EST:** 1992
SALES (est): 242.99K **Privately Held**
Web: www.buymedtech.com
SIC: 7699 5047 3841 Hospital equipment repair services; Therapy equipment; Surgical and medical instruments

(G-18245)
MEDAL LP
Also Called: Air Liquide
305 Water St (19804-2410)
PHONE.................................302 225-1100
EMP: 53 **EST:** 1991
SALES (est): 9.11MM **Privately Held**
Web: advancedseparations.airliquide.com
SIC: 3569 Gas separators (machinery)

(G-18246)
MEDEXPRESS
2722 Concord Pike (19803-5007)
PHONE.................................302 477-1406
Tim Bugin, *VP*
EMP: 70 **EST:** 2012
SALES (est): 429.44K **Privately Held**
Web: www.medexpress.com
SIC: 8011 Freestanding emergency medical center

(G-18247)
MEDIASURFER INC
Also Called: Mediasurfer
1232 N King St Ste 1028 (19801-3226)
PHONE.................................814 300-8335
Jing Li, *CEO*
EMP: 15 **EST:** 2018
SALES (est): 489.67K **Privately Held**
SIC: 7311 Advertising agencies

(G-18248)
MEDICAL BILLING MANAGEMENT
5301 Limestone Rd Ste 100 (19808-1251)
P.O. Box 5869 (19714-5869)
PHONE.................................302 239-2235
Michelle Bullock, *Prin*
EMP: 7 **EST:** 2017
SALES (est): 163.87K **Privately Held**
Web: www.medbillinginc.com

SIC: 8741 Management services

(G-18249)
MEDICAL JOYWORKS LLC
4023 Kennett Pike # 55630 (19807-2018)
PHONE.................................310 919-4287
Sandaruwan Gunathilake, *Prin*
EMP: 10 **EST:** 2015
SALES (est): 83.01K **Privately Held**
Web: www.medicaljoyworks.com
SIC: 8099 Health and allied services, nec

(G-18250)
MEDICAL TOURISM AGENCY LLC
427 N Tatnall St (19801-2230)
PHONE.................................855 753-3833
EMP: 8 **EST:** 2017
SALES (est): 54.13K **Privately Held**
Web: www.medicaltourismagency.com
SIC: 8011 Offices and clinics of medical doctors

(G-18251)
MEDICI VENTURES INC
1209 N Orange St (19801-1120)
PHONE.................................801 319-7029
Jonathan Johnson, *Pr*
Steve Hopkins, *COO*
EMP: 35 **EST:** 2016
SALES (est): 2.87MM
SALES (corp-wide): 1.93B **Publicly Held**
SIC: 7371 6799 Computer software development and applications; Venture capital companies
PA: Beyond, Inc.
799 W Coliseum Way
Midvale UT 84047
801 947-3100

(G-18252)
MEDICTEK INC
902 N Market St Apt 805 (19801-3051)
PHONE.................................302 351-4924
G B Hendrickson, *Pr*
EMP: 6 **EST:** 2014
SQ FT: 1,500
SALES (est): 58.91K **Privately Held**
Web: www.medictek.com
SIC: 7373 Office computer automation systems integration

(G-18253)
MEDIGUIDE INTERNATIONAL LLC (PA)
4550 Linden Hill Rd Ste 103 (19808-2909)
PHONE.................................302 425-5900
Susan Kelley, *Managing Member*
EMP: 70 **EST:** 1999
SALES (est): 8.38MM
SALES (corp-wide): 8.38MM **Privately Held**
Web: www.mediguide.com
SIC: 8062 General medical and surgical hospitals

(G-18254)
MEDIMAPS GROUP USA LLC
913 N Market St Ste 200n (19801-3097)
PHONE.................................302 416-3063
EMP: 8 **EST:** 2017
SALES (est): 534.04K **Privately Held**
Web: www.medimapsgroup.com
SIC: 8099 Health and allied services, nec

(G-18255)
MEDIMMUNE LLC
1800 Concord Pike (19897-0001)
PHONE.................................301 398-1200
EMP: 4
SALES (corp-wide): 44.35B **Privately Held**

GEOGRAPHIC SECTION

Wilmington - New Castle County (G-18282)

Web: www.astrazeneca.com
SIC: 2834 Pharmaceutical preparations
HQ: Medimmune, Llc
1 Medimmune Way
Gaithersburg MD 20878
301 398-0000

(G-18256)
MEDLANTA INC
1000 N West St Ste 1200 (19801-1058)
PHONE..................610 991-2929
Joseph Ruffin, CEO
Calvin Roberts, COO
EMP: 5 EST: 2020
SALES (est): 88.23K Privately Held
SIC: 7213 Coat supply

(G-18257)
MEDREP INC
903 Berkeley Rd (19807-2811)
PHONE..................302 571-0263
Robert M Sommerlatte, Pr
EMP: 5 EST: 1992
SALES (est): 399.5K Privately Held
Web: www.medrepinc.com
SIC: 5047 Medical equipment and supplies

(G-18258)
MEDSHIFTS INC
Also Called: Medshift Cyber
1201 N Orange St Ste 600 (19801-1171)
P.O. Box 684 (08043-0684)
PHONE..................856 834-0074
Albert Paramito, Pr
EMP: 5 EST: 2016
SALES (est): 360.56K Privately Held
Web: www.medshiftcyber.com
SIC: 7371 6552 Computer software development; Subdividers and developers, nec

(G-18259)
MEETRECORD INC ✪
1013 Centre Rd Ste 403b (19805-1270)
PHONE..................281 407-7338
Snehal Nimje, CEO
EMP: 6 EST: 2022
SALES (est): 237.56K Privately Held
SIC: 7371 Computer software development

(G-18260)
MEFTA LLC
Also Called: Middle East Free Trade Assoc
1220 N Market St (19801-2535)
PHONE..................804 433-3566
EMP: 12
SQ FT: 1,200
SALES (est): 950K Privately Held
Web: www.mefta.com
SIC: 8748 6221 Business consulting, nec; Commodity traders, contracts

(G-18261)
MEG A FRIZZOLA DO
1600 Rockland Rd (19803-3607)
PHONE..................302 651-4000
Meg Frizzola, Ofcr
EMP: 12 EST: 2017
SALES (est): 238.69K Privately Held
Web: www.nemours.org
SIC: 8011 Pediatrician

(G-18262)
MELANATED MINDS FOUNDATION LLC
4004 N Shipley St (19802-2230)
PHONE..................302 312-5303
Akaycia Curry, Prin
EMP: 5 EST: 2020
SALES (est): 104.73K Privately Held

SIC: 7389 Business Activities at Non-Commercial Site

(G-18263)
MELISSAS CHILDCARE
24 Overlook Ave (19808-5828)
PHONE..................302 547-6722
EMP: 6 EST: 2018
SALES (est): 66.77K Privately Held
SIC: 8351 Child day care services

(G-18264)
MELLO FINANCIAL INC
251 Middle Falls Dr (19808)
PHONE..................801 877-7787
Dexter Tan, CEO
EMP: 6
SALES (est): 237.56K Privately Held
SIC: 7389 7371 Financial services; Computer software development and applications

(G-18265)
MELLON PRIVATE WEALTH MGT
4005 Kennett Pike (19807-2018)
PHONE..................302 421-2306
EMP: 6 EST: 2007
SALES (est): 1.72MM
SALES (corp-wide): 19.99B Publicly Held
SIC: 6722 Money market mutual funds
PA: The Bank Of New York Mellon Corporation
240 E Greenwich St
New York NY 10007
212 495-1784

(G-18266)
MELODIC MVMNTS PRFRMG ARTS PRG
Also Called: Melodic Movements
28 W 38th St (19802-2210)
PHONE..................302 543-5257
Melody Dale, CEO
EMP: 10 EST: 2018
SALES (est): 183.96K Privately Held
Web: www.melodicmovements.org
SIC: 7941 Sports clubs, managers, and promoters

(G-18267)
MELODY ENTERTAINMENT USA INC
Also Called: Melody Entertainment
717 N Union St Apt 68 (19805-3031)
PHONE..................305 505-7659
EMP: 6 EST: 2010
SALES (est): 93.17K Privately Held
SIC: 7812 2741 7313 Television film production; Music book and sheet music publishing; Radio, television, publisher representatives

(G-18268)
MELTRONE INC
Also Called: Captain's Catch
5828 Kirkwood Hwy (19808-4813)
PHONE..................302 998-3457
Richard S Melson, Pr
Barbara Melson, VP
EMP: 10 EST: 1977
SALES (est): 487.04K Privately Held
SIC: 5421 5146 Seafood markets; Seafoods

(G-18269)
MEMORIAL HALL OF TLLYVLLE FIRE
3919 Concord Pike (19803-1715)
PHONE..................302 478-1110
Daniel R Kiley, Owner
EMP: 10 EST: 2001
SALES (est): 132.08K Privately Held
Web: www.talleyvillefireco.org

SIC: 6512 Auditorium and hall operation

(G-18270)
MEMORIAL SLOAN KTTRING CNCER C
400 Foulk Rd (19803-3804)
PHONE..................302 384-7588
EMP: 40 EST: 2013
SALES (est): 337.74K Privately Held
Web: www.mskcc.org
SIC: 8069 Cancer hospital

(G-18271)
MENCHACA BUILDING CORP
4 Lloyd Pl (19810-1325)
PHONE..................302 475-4581
Richard Menchaca, Pr
EMP: 6 EST: 1978
SALES (est): 360.96K Privately Held
SIC: 1751 Framing contractor

(G-18272)
MENTAL HEALTH ASSN IN DEL
100 W 10th St Ste 600 (19801-6604)
PHONE..................302 654-6833
James Lafferty, Ex Dir
Amy Milligan, Pr
EMP: 8 EST: 1932
SQ FT: 2,500
SALES (est): 1.72MM Privately Held
Web: www.mhainde.org
SIC: 8093 Mental health clinic, outpatient

(G-18273)
MENTOR CONSULTANTS INC
3200 Concord Pike (19803-5015)
P.O. Box 489 (19331-0489)
PHONE..................610 566-4004
Sheldon D Barnett, Pr
Sue Barnett, Sec
EMP: 6 EST: 1980
SALES (est): 466.87K Privately Held
Web: www.mentormail.com
SIC: 8748 7371 8742 Systems analysis or design; Computer software development; Management information systems consultant

(G-18274)
MERCANTILE PRESS INC
3007 Bellevue Ave (19802-2428)
PHONE..................302 764-6884
Coleman E Bye Iii, Pr
Coleman E Bye Junior, Ch
Jane S Bye, Sec
EMP: 18 EST: 1884
SQ FT: 20,000
SALES (est): 2.32MM Privately Held
Web: www.mercantilepress.com
SIC: 2752 2671 2672 Offset printing; Paper, coated and laminated packaging; Paper, coated and laminated, nec

(G-18275)
MERCATANTE BEATRICE AN
4600 New Lndn Hill Rd 2 (19808)
PHONE..................302 995-7073
EMP: 6 EST: 2012
SALES (est): 22.18K Privately Held
SIC: 8049 Nurses, registered and practical

(G-18276)
MERCURI INC (PA)
1209 N Orange St (19801-1120)
PHONE..................425 395-5238
Thomas Lapham, Prin
EMP: 8 EST: 2020
SALES (est): 223.47K
SALES (corp-wide): 223.47K Privately Held

SIC: 7379 7389 Online services technology consultants; Business services, nec

(G-18277)
MERCURY FINANCIAL LLC
123 S Justison St Ste 602 (19801-5360)
PHONE..................302 588-0107
Kathleen Leonik, Mgr
EMP: 10
SALES (corp-wide): 9.15MM Privately Held
Web: www.mercuryfinancial.com
SIC: 6163 Loan agents
PA: Mercury Financial Llc
11401 Century Oaks Ter # 470
Austin TX 78758
800 317-9240

(G-18278)
MERCURYSEND LLC
1220 N Market St (19801-2535)
PHONE..................917 267-8627
EMP: 5 EST: 2017
SALES (est): 81.54K Privately Held
Web: www.mercurysend.com
SIC: 7371 Computer software development and applications

(G-18279)
MERESTONE CONSULTANTS INC (PA)
5215 W Woodmill Dr Ste 38 (19808-4068)
PHONE..................302 992-7900
Michael Early, Pr
EMP: 5 EST: 1996
SALES (est): 2.14MM
SALES (corp-wide): 2.14MM Privately Held
Web: www.merestoneconsultants.com
SIC: 8713 8711 Surveying services; Construction and civil engineering

(G-18280)
MERGERS ACQSTONS STRTEGIES LLC (PA)
Also Called: Rls Associates
5183 W Woodmill Dr Ste 3 (19808-4067)
PHONE..................302 992-0400
David Bernstein, Managing Member
EMP: 5 EST: 1986
SQ FT: 1,600
SALES (est): 2.14MM Privately Held
Web: www.rlsassociates.com
SIC: 7389 Brokers, business: buying and selling business enterprises

(G-18281)
MERIDIAN BANK
5301 Limestone Rd Ste 224 (19808-1265)
PHONE..................302 635-7500
EMP: 15
Web: www.meridianbanker.com
SIC: 6162 Mortgage bankers and loan correspondents
PA: Meridian Bank
9 Old Lincoln Hwy Ste 101
Malvern PA 19355

(G-18282)
MERIDIAN BANK
1601 Concord Pike Ste 45 (19803-3634)
PHONE..................302 477-9449
EMP: 25
Web: www.meridianbanker.com
SIC: 6021 National commercial banks
PA: Meridian Bank
9 Old Lincoln Hwy Ste 101
Malvern PA 19355

(PA)=Parent Co (HQ)=Headquarters
✪ = New Business established in last 2 years

2024 Harris Directory of Delaware Businesses

Wilmington - New Castle County (G-18283)   GEOGRAPHIC SECTION

(G-18283)
MERIT CNSTR ENGINEERS INC
5700 Kirkwood Hwy Ste 201 (19808-4884)
PHONE....................302 992-9810
Ronald Dills, *Pr*
EMP: 13 EST: 2009
SALES (est): 849.87K **Privately Held**
Web: www.mce85.com
SIC: 8711 Civil engineering

(G-18284)
MERIT CONSTRUCTION ENGINEERS
1605 E Ayre St (19804-2514)
P.O. Box 651 (19720-0651)
PHONE....................302 992-9810
Ron Dills, *Pr*
Matt Ballintyn, *VP*
EMP: 19 EST: 1985
SQ FT: 650
SALES (est): 453.15K **Privately Held**
Web: www.mce85.com
SIC: 1794 1623 1771 Excavation and grading, building construction; Water main construction; Concrete work

(G-18285)
MERIT INC
207 S Market St (19801-5202)
PHONE....................302 778-4732
EMP: 7 EST: 2009
SALES (est): 121.46K **Privately Held**
Web: www.mce85.com
SIC: 5171 Petroleum bulk stations

(G-18286)
MERMAN MANAGEMENT INC
5145 W Woodmill Dr # 22 (19808-4067)
PHONE....................302 456-9904
Maryanne Murray, *Prin*
EMP: 5 EST: 2008
SALES (est): 100.92K **Privately Held**
SIC: 8741 Management services

(G-18287)
MERRILL LYNCH PRCE FNNER SMITH
Also Called: Merrill Lynch
1201 N Market St Ste 2000 (19801-1165)
P.O. Box 10922 (19850-0922)
PHONE....................302 571-5100
Lisa Primack, *Dir*
EMP: 10
SALES (corp-wide): 94.95B **Publicly Held**
Web: www.ml.com
SIC: 6211 6726 Security brokers and dealers ; Investment offices, nec
HQ: Merrill Lynch, Pierce, Fenner & Smith Incorporated
111 8th Ave
New York NY 10011
800 637-7455

(G-18288)
MERYLS
2500 Grubb Rd Ste 240 (19810-4796)
PHONE....................302 475-7555
EMP: 6 EST: 2016
SALES (est): 63.4K **Privately Held**
Web: www.merylbrownstein.com
SIC: 8322 General counseling services

(G-18289)
METAQUOTES SOFTWARE CORP
602 Rockwood Rd (19802-1121)
PHONE....................657 859-6918
Marcus Moore, *Prin*
EMP: 50 EST: 2014
SALES (est): 5MM **Privately Held**
SIC: 7371 7389 Computer software development and applications; Business services, nec

(G-18290)
METAWORK CORPORATION
2810 N Church St (19802-4447)
PHONE....................347 756-1222
Margaret Henry, *Admn*
Margaret Henry, *CFO*
EMP: 8 EST: 2020
SALES (est): 469.46K **Privately Held**
SIC: 7372 7389 Application computer software; Business services, nec

(G-18291)
METL TECHNOLOGY INC
1209 Norange Ste (19801)
PHONE....................954 309-4589
Anna Vladi, *CEO*
EMP: 10 EST: 2020
SALES (est): 510.93K **Privately Held**
SIC: 6211 Security brokers and dealers

(G-18292)
METLIFE INC
Also Called: MetLife
600 N King St Fl 7 (19801-3776)
PHONE....................302 594-2085
EMP: 35
SALES (corp-wide): 69.9B **Publicly Held**
Web: www.metlife.com
SIC: 6411 Insurance agents and brokers
PA: Metlife, Inc.
200 Park Ave Fl 1200
New York NY 10166
212 578-9500

(G-18293)
METRO BY T-MOBILE
107 N Maryland Ave (19804-1391)
PHONE....................302 384-7158
EMP: 5 EST: 2019
SALES (est): 33.14K **Privately Held**
SIC: 4812 Cellular telephone services

(G-18294)
METROPOLITAN WEALTH MGT LLC
2711 Centerville Rd # 300 (19808-1665)
PHONE....................212 607-2488
EMP: 7 EST: 2015
SALES (est): 436.77K **Privately Held**
SIC: 6211 Security brokers and dealers

(G-18295)
MEYER & MEYER INC
Also Called: Meyer & Meyer Reatly
2706 Kirkwood Hwy (19805-4912)
PHONE....................302 994-9600
Peter Meyers, *Pr*
Justin Meyer, *VP*
EMP: 12 EST: 1997
SQ FT: 4,000
SALES (est): 968.32K **Privately Held**
Web: www.meyer2realty.com
SIC: 6531 Real estate agent, residential

(G-18296)
MEYER PROPERTIES LLC
2102 Kirkwood Hwy (19805-4902)
PHONE....................302 278-4100
EMP: 5 EST: 2017
SALES (est): 244.56K **Privately Held**
SIC: 6512 Nonresidential building operators

(G-18297)
MFF OILFIELD SOLUTIONS LLC
1 Commerce St # 1201 (19801)
PHONE....................603 795-0617
EMP: 7 EST: 2014
SALES (est): 27.98K **Privately Held**
Web: www.mff-oilfield.com
SIC: 1389 Oil field services, nec

(G-18298)
MFR MANUFACTURING CORP INC
251 Little Falls Dr (19808-1674)
PHONE....................815 552-3333
EMP: 9 EST: 2018
SALES (est): 2.68MM **Privately Held**
SIC: 5084 Elevators

(G-18299)
MGJ ENTERPRISES INC
Also Called: Irg
4023 Kennett Pike # 624 (19807-2018)
PHONE....................866 525-8529
Michael Luzio, *Pr*
EMP: 29
SALES (corp-wide): 969.44MM **Privately Held**
Web: www.vectorsecurity.com
SIC: 4813 Internet connectivity services
HQ: Mgj Enterprises, Inc.
2000 Ericsson Dr
Warrendale PA 15086
866 525-8529

(G-18300)
MGTS GLOBAL INC
704 N King St Ste 600 (19801-3583)
PHONE....................302 385-6636
EMP: 6 EST: 2018
SALES (est): 153.56K **Privately Held**
Web: www.milltechfx.com
SIC: 7389 Financial services

(G-18301)
MH-TEQ LLC
101 W 10th St Ste 408 (19801-1676)
PHONE....................302 897-2182
EMP: 5 EST: 2018
SALES (est): 275K **Privately Held**
SIC: 7371 7379 8243 Software programming applications; Online services technology consultants; Software training, computer

(G-18302)
MICHAEL A KELCZEWSKI
5701 Kennett Pike (19807-1311)
PHONE....................302 654-6500
EMP: 5 EST: 2018
SALES (est): 75.13K **Privately Held**
Web: www.michaelkelczewski.com
SIC: 6531 Real estate brokers and agents

(G-18303)
MICHAEL A MADANAT
2617 Bardell Dr (19808-3023)
PHONE....................302 998-6613
Michael A Madanat, *Prin*
EMP: 5 EST: 2011
SALES (est): 177.68K **Privately Held**
SIC: 1522 Residential construction, nec

(G-18304)
MICHAEL A MEALEY & SONS INC (PA)
Also Called: Mealey Funeral Homes
703 N Broom St (19805-3117)
P.O. Box 2866 (19805-0866)
PHONE....................302 652-5913
Charles F Mealey Junior, *Pr*
EMP: 12 EST: 1912
SALES (est): 957.05K
SALES (corp-wide): 957.05K **Privately Held**
Web: www.mealeyfuneralhomes.com
SIC: 7261 Funeral home

(G-18305)
MICHAEL A MEALEY & SONS INC
Also Called: Mealey Fnrl Homes & Crematory
2509 Limestone Rd (19808-4107)
P.O. Box 2866 (19805-0866)
PHONE....................302 654-3005
Laura Mealey, *Mgr*
EMP: 17
SALES (corp-wide): 957.05K **Privately Held**
Web: www.mealeyfuneralhomes.com
SIC: 7261 Funeral home
PA: Michael A Mealey & Sons Inc
703 N Broom St
Wilmington DE 19805
302 652-5913

(G-18306)
MICHAEL A OBRIEN & SONS
405 E Ayre St (19804-2512)
PHONE....................302 994-2894
Michael A O'brien Senior, *Owner*
EMP: 2 EST: 1963
SALES (est): 203.86K **Privately Held**
SIC: 2541 2434 1751 Table or counter tops, plastic laminated; Wood kitchen cabinets; Cabinet building and installation

(G-18307)
MICHAEL A POLECK DDS PA
5501 Kirkwood Hwy (19808-5001)
P.O. Box 13 (19736-0013)
PHONE....................302 994-7730
Michael A Poleck D.d.s., *Pr*
EMP: 8 EST: 1979
SALES (est): 450.12K **Privately Held**
Web: www.nathanpoleckdmd.com
SIC: 8021 Dentists' office

(G-18308)
MICHAEL B TUMAS
1313 N Market St (19801-6101)
PHONE....................302 984-6029
Michael Tumas, *Prin*
EMP: 8 EST: 2018
SALES (est): 57.87K **Privately Held**
Web: www.potteranderson.com
SIC: 8111 General practice attorney, lawyer

(G-18309)
MICHAEL BOBER MD
P.O. Box 269 (19899-0269)
PHONE....................302 651-5916
Michael Bober, *Prin*
EMP: 9 EST: 2002
SALES (est): 109.5K **Privately Held**
SIC: 8011 Offices and clinics of medical doctors

(G-18310)
MICHAEL D MERRILL
1601 Kirkwood Hwy (19805-4917)
PHONE....................302 994-2511
Michael Douglas Merrill, *Prin*
EMP: 9 EST: 2013
SALES (est): 137.32K **Privately Held**
SIC: 8011 Offices and clinics of medical doctors

(G-18311)
MICHAEL ELLER INCOME TAX SVC
724 N Union St (19805-3068)
PHONE....................302 652-5916
Michael Eller, *Pr*
EMP: 5 EST: 1991
SALES (est): 188.26K **Privately Held**
SIC: 7291 Tax return preparation services

Wilmington - New Castle County (G-18341)

(G-18312)
MICHAEL ERCKA HYNNSKY FMLY FND
1300 N Union St (19806-2534)
PHONE.................................302 545-4600
EMP: 5 EST: 2018
SALES (est): 532K **Privately Held**
SIC: 8641 Civic and social associations

(G-18313)
MICHAEL G SCHWRTZ MEM FNDATION
5520 E Timberview Ct (19808-3628)
P.O. Box 5972 (19808-0972)
PHONE.................................302 453-9233
Shirley A Schwartz, *Prin*
EMP: 5 EST: 2010
SALES (est): 29.41K **Privately Held**
SIC: 8641 Civic and social associations

(G-18314)
MICHAEL J DI SALVO
5610 Kirkwood Hwy (19808-5004)
PHONE.................................302 636-0169
Michael Di Salvo, *Mgr*
EMP: 7 EST: 2017
SALES (est): 32.92K **Privately Held**
SIC: 8322 Individual and family services

(G-18315)
MICHAEL K ROSENTHAL
2300 Pennsylvania Ave Ste 3c (19806-1379)
PHONE.................................302 652-3469
Michael Rosenthal, *Prin*
EMP: 11 EST: 2015
SALES (est): 496.74K **Privately Held**
SIC: 8011 Dermatologist

(G-18316)
MICHAEL L BERMAN
1000 N West St Ste 1500 (19801-1054)
PHONE.................................302 300-3450
Michael Berman, *CEO*
EMP: 5 EST: 2017
SALES (est): 57.87K **Privately Held**
SIC: 8111 Legal services

(G-18317)
MICHAEL L SARUK MD
3411 Silverside Rd Ste 107 (19810-4812)
PHONE.................................302 478-8532
EMP: 11 EST: 2018
SALES (est): 235.18K **Privately Held**
Web: www.delawarevalleyderm.com
SIC: 8011 Dermatologist

(G-18318)
MICHAEL M WYDILA M D
1403 Silverside Rd Ste B (19810-4434)
PHONE.................................302 798-8070
Michael M Wydila, *Prin*
EMP: 9 EST: 2018
SALES (est): 239.22K **Privately Held**
SIC: 8011 Offices and clinics of medical doctors

(G-18319)
MICHAEL MARINO INC
112 Hoiland Dr (19803-3228)
PHONE.................................302 764-5319
Elizabeth Marino, *Prin*
EMP: 5 EST: 2012
SALES (est): 176.69K **Privately Held**
SIC: 1522 Residential construction, nec

(G-18320)
MICHAEL MATTHIAS
3801 Kennett Pike Ste E207 (19807-2340)
PHONE.................................302 575-0100
Michael Matthias, *Owner*
EMP: 5 EST: 2006
SALES (est): 220.58K **Privately Held**
Web: www.yourdentistrytoday.com
SIC: 8011 8021 Offices and clinics of medical doctors; Offices and clinics of dentists

(G-18321)
MICHAEL P MORTON PA
3704 Kennett Pike Ste 200 (19807-2173)
PHONE.................................302 426-1313
EMP: 9 EST: 1996
SALES (est): 613.69K **Privately Held**
Web: www.mvzllc.com
SIC: 8111 General practice attorney, lawyer

(G-18322)
MICHAEL P ROSENTHAL MD
1400 N Washington St (19801-1024)
PHONE.................................302 255-1300
Michael Rosenthal, *Prin*
EMP: 10 EST: 2014
SALES (est): 75.74K **Privately Held**
SIC: 8011 Physicians' office, including specialists

(G-18323)
MICHAEL S WIROSLOFF DMD
5185 W Woodmill Dr Ste 2 (19808-4067)
PHONE.................................302 998-8588
Michael Wirosloff, *Owner*
EMP: 5 EST: 1993
SALES (est): 171.68K **Privately Held**
Web: www.delawaregentledentist.com
SIC: 8021 Orthodontist

(G-18324)
MICHAEL SCHWARTZ
Also Called: A B C Ticket Co
1400 Philadelphia Pike (19809-1856)
PHONE.................................302 791-9999
EMP: 17
SQ FT: 2,000
SALES (est): 202.12K **Privately Held**
SIC: 7922 7999 Ticket agency, theatrical; Ticket sales office for sporting events, contract

(G-18325)
MICHAEL SPRADLEY (PA)
Also Called: K Y Property Management
45 E Reamer Ave (19804-1374)
PHONE.................................404 475-2647
Michael Spradley, *Owner*
EMP: 7 EST: 2018
SALES (est): 495.06K
SALES (corp-wide): 495.06K **Privately Held**
SIC: 8741 Management services

(G-18326)
MICHELET FINANCE INC
1105 N Market St Ste 1300 (19801-1241)
PHONE.................................302 427-8751
EMP: 22 EST: 1989
SALES (est): 867.45K
SALES (corp-wide): 125.67MM **Privately Held**
SIC: 5044 Office equipment
PA: Arkema
420 Rue D Estienne D Orves
Colombes 92700
149008080

(G-18327)
MICHELLE C JOHNSON LCSW
504 S Clayton St (19805-4211)
PHONE.................................302 893-9235
Michelle C Johnson, *Prin*
EMP: 9 EST: 2012
SALES (est): 59.14K **Privately Held**
SIC: 8322 Social worker

(G-18328)
MICHELLE E PAPA DO
1100 S Broom St Ste 1 (19805-4585)
PHONE.................................302 656-5424
Michelle E Papa, *Prin*
EMP: 8 EST: 2019
SALES (est): 78.53K **Privately Held**
SIC: 8011 Offices and clinics of medical doctors

(G-18329)
MICROHM INC
1000 N West St (19801-1050)
PHONE.................................302 543-2178
EMP: 9 EST: 2011
SALES (est): 90.04K **Privately Held**
Web: www.microhm.net
SIC: 3675 Electronic capacitors

(G-18330)
MICRON INCORPORATED
Also Called: Micron
3815 Lancaster Pike (19805-1599)
PHONE.................................302 998-1184
James F Ficca Junior, *Pr*
James M Ficca, *VP*
Katherine Melody, *VP*
EMP: 7 EST: 1966
SQ FT: 12,000
SALES (est): 874.57K **Privately Held**
Web: www.micronanalytical.com
SIC: 8734 Testing laboratories

(G-18331)
MICROTELECOM SYSTEMS LLC
Also Called: Microtelecom
1000 N West St Ste 1200 (19801-1058)
PHONE.................................718 707-0012
Yonathan Shechter, *CEO*
Jonathan Shechter, *
EMP: 74 EST: 2008
SQ FT: 5,000
SALES (est): 2.99MM **Privately Held**
Web: www.microtelecom.com
SIC: 7371 7373 7372 Computer software development; Systems software development services; Application computer software

(G-18332)
MID ATLANTIC CARE LLC (PA)
520 Robinson Ln (19805-4616)
P.O. Box 6511 (19804-0511)
PHONE.................................302 266-8306
Yousif Omer, *Managing Member*
EMP: 5 EST: 2011
SALES (est): 965.99K
SALES (corp-wide): 965.99K **Privately Held**
Web: www.midatlanticcare.com
SIC: 4119 Ambulance service

(G-18333)
MID ATLANTIC SURGICAL LLC
1500 Shallcross Ave Ste 1 (19806-3037)
PHONE.................................302 652-6050
Nora Truscello, *Mgr*
EMP: 8 EST: 2018
SALES (est): 246.19K **Privately Held**
SIC: 8011 Offices and clinics of medical doctors

(G-18334)
MID ATLANTIC SURGICAL PRACTICE
701 N Clayton St (19805-3165)
PHONE.................................302 652-6050
Nora Truscello, *Mgr*
EMP: 8 EST: 2007
SALES (est): 483.69K **Privately Held**
Web: www.surgicaldocs.com
SIC: 8011 Surgeon

(G-18335)
MID ATLANTIC WARRANTY
10 8th Ave (19805-4773)
PHONE.................................302 893-4220
Felix Coreano, *Prin*
EMP: 5 EST: 2011
SALES (est): 127.74K **Privately Held**
SIC: 6399 Warranty insurance, automobile

(G-18336)
MID STATES SALES & MARKETING
3411 Silverside Rd Ste 104 (19810-4812)
PHONE.................................302 888-2475
EMP: 15 EST: 1990
SALES (est): 1.44MM **Privately Held**
Web: www.midstatesales.com
SIC: 5122 8742 Toiletries; Management consulting services

(G-18337)
MID-ATLANTIC SERVICES A-TEAM
700 Cornell Dr (19801-5762)
PHONE.................................302 984-9559
Rosemary Everton, *Brnch Mgr*
EMP: 88
SALES (corp-wide): 2.47MM **Privately Held**
Web: www.ateamcorp.com
SIC: 7349 Janitorial service, contract basis
PA: Mid-Atlantic Services A-Team Corp
8558 Elks Rd
Seaford DE 19973
302 628-3403

(G-18338)
MID-ATLNTIC REG COMM ON HGHER
Also Called: MIDDLE STATES COMMISSION ON HI
1007 N Orange St Fl 4 Pmb 166 (19801-1242)
PHONE.................................267 284-5024
Heather Perfetti, *Pr*
Kathie Jeffries, *
EMP: 37 EST: 1919
SALES (est): 12.04MM **Privately Held**
Web: www.msche.org
SIC: 8621 Education and teacher association

(G-18339)
MID-COUNTY INC
1st Regiment Rd S Pk Ii (19808)
PHONE.................................302 995-6555
EMP: 6
SALES (est): 394.61K **Privately Held**
Web: www.midcountyseniorcenter.org
SIC: 8322 Senior citizens' center or association

(G-18340)
MID-TOWN MASSAGE LLC
213 W 4th St (19801-2204)
PHONE.................................302 256-0363
EMP: 10
SALES (est): 210.71K **Privately Held**
SIC: 8041 Offices and clinics of chiropractors

(G-18341)
MIDCOAST COMMUNITY BANK
2901 Concord Pike (19803-5010)
PHONE.................................302 482-4250
EMP: 11 EST: 2018
SALES (est): 116.69K **Privately Held**

Wilmington - New Castle County (G-18342) GEOGRAPHIC SECTION

SIC: **6036** Savings institutions, except federal

(G-18342)
MIDDLE RUN CHRTABLE FOUNDATION
5803 Kennett Pike (19807-1195)
PHONE.............................302 658-7796
EMP: **5** EST: 2017
SALES (est): 648.46K **Privately Held**
Web: www.middlerunfoundation.com
SIC: **8699** Charitable organization

(G-18343)
MIDDLEWARE INC
1000 N West St Ste 1200 (19801-1058)
PHONE.............................415 213-2625
Oleksandr Vityaz, *Pr*
Erina Serbina, *
EMP: **50** EST: 2014
SQ FT: 1,000
SALES (est): 5.5MM **Privately Held**
SIC: **7371** Computer software development and applications

(G-18344)
MIDLANTIC BLDG RSTORATIONS INC
2201 Orleans Rd (19810-4042)
PHONE.............................302 475-8084
EMP: **5** EST: 2017
SALES (est): 239.03K **Privately Held**
SIC: **1799** Special trade contractors, nec

(G-18345)
MIDWAY TOWING INC
1122 Wagoner Dr (19805-1119)
PHONE.............................302 323-4850
Steven Mullins, *Mgr*
Roger Crannell, *Mgr*
EMP: **7** EST: 1998
SALES (est): 463.55K **Privately Held**
Web: www.midwaytowing.net
SIC: **7549** Towing service, automotive

(G-18346)
MIDWINTER CO LLC
303 Hawthorne Dr (19802-1213)
PHONE.............................302 463-9578
Samantha Bird, *Prin*
EMP: **6** EST: 2013
SALES (est): 249.27K **Privately Held**
Web: www.midwinter.co
SIC: **8049** Midwife

(G-18347)
MIG CONSULTING LLC (PA)
1624 Newport Gap Pike (19808-6208)
PHONE.............................302 999-1888
Inderpreet Singh, *Managing Member*
EMP: **9** EST: 2013
SALES (est): 1.01MM
SALES (corp-wide): 1.01MM **Privately Held**
Web: www.migconsulting.net
SIC: **8711** Engineering services

(G-18348)
MIGHTY ACORN DIGITAL INC ○
24a Trolley Sq (19806-3334)
PHONE.............................877 277-8085
Robert Bayliss, *Pr*
EMP: **5** EST: 2023
SALES (est): 199.4K **Privately Held**
SIC: **7371** Custom computer programming services

(G-18349)
MIGUEL ESPARZA
27 Weer Cir (19808-5700)
PHONE.............................302 518-7873
Andy Esparza, *Prin*
EMP: **6** EST: 2016
SALES (est): 221.8K **Privately Held**
SIC: **0781** Landscape services

(G-18350)
MIKE DIFONZO
1708 Marsh Rd (19810-4606)
PHONE.............................302 764-0100
Mike Difonzo, *Prin*
EMP: **5** EST: 2001
SALES (est): 141.04K **Privately Held**
Web: www.mikedifonzo.com
SIC: **6531** Real estate agent, residential

(G-18351)
MIKE MOLITOR
Also Called: Mike Molitor Contractor
101 Scarborough Park Dr Apt 5 (19804-1061)
PHONE.............................302 528-6300
Mike Molitor, *Prin*
EMP: **5** EST: 2010
SALES (est): 66.25K **Privately Held**
Web: www.mikemolitorcontractor.com
SIC: **1799** Special trade contractors, nec

(G-18352)
MIL INTERNATIONAL LLC
203 Alisons Way (19807-1759)
PHONE.............................302 234-7501
Mohan Iyer, *Pr*
▲ EMP: **6** EST: 1993
SQ FT: 800
SALES (est): 1.03MM **Privately Held**
Web: www.milinternational.com
SIC: **5169** Chemical additives

(G-18353)
MILES PER HOUR INC ○
Also Called: Mph.com
1007 N Orange St Ste 1382 (19801-1239)
PHONE.............................800 370-3050
Chase Zimmerman, *Prin*
EMP: **6** EST: 2023
SALES (est): 78.16K **Privately Held**
SIC: **3711** Motor vehicles and car bodies

(G-18354)
MILES1 INC
Also Called: Milespa
1409 Coleman St (19805-4750)
PHONE.............................267 506-0004
Devon Logan, *CEO*
Shandy Perez, *COO*
EMP: **5** EST: 2018
SALES (est): 112.95K **Privately Held**
SIC: **4119** 7372 Local rental transportation; Application computer software

(G-18355)
MILEWSKI STEPHAN
824 N Market St (19801-3024)
PHONE.............................302 467-4502
Milewski Stephan, *Prin*
EMP: **5** EST: 2010
SALES (est): 84.31K **Privately Held**
SIC: **8111** General practice attorney, lawyer

(G-18356)
MILIEUX LLC ○
1007 N Orange St Fl 4 (19801-1242)
PHONE.............................302 770-5868
Shaina Mosley, *CEO*
EMP: **3** EST: 2022
SALES (est): 60.47K **Privately Held**
Web: www.milieuxandco.com
SIC: **8748** 8742 3572 Business consulting, nec; Management information systems consultant; Computer storage devices

(G-18357)
MILL CREEK SELECT
2006 Limestone Rd (19808-5553)
PHONE.............................302 995-2090
EMP: **6** EST: 2018
SALES (est): 217.3K **Privately Held**
Web: www.millcreekselect.com
SIC: **8021** Offices and clinics of dentists

(G-18358)
MILL WILMINGTON LLC
1007 N Orange St Ste 400 (19801-1239)
PHONE.............................302 218-7527
EMP: **8** EST: 2016
SALES (est): 224.68K **Privately Held**
Web: www.themillspace.com
SIC: **8748** Business consulting, nec

(G-18359)
MILLCREEK MOBILE HM PK LAND CO
Also Called: Murray Manor
5600 Old Capitol Trl (19808-4951)
PHONE.............................302 998-3045
Lee Murray, *Pr*
Bernice Murray, *VP*
Bill Ferguson, *Mgr*
EMP: **6** EST: 1948
SALES (est): 359.36K **Privately Held**
SIC: **6515** Mobile home site operators

(G-18360)
MILLCREEK TEXACO STATION
Also Called: Millcreek Texaco
109 Bellant Cir (19807-2219)
PHONE.............................302 571-8489
John Lamgrell, *Owner*
EMP: **8** EST: 1966
SQ FT: 1,500
SALES (est): 568.99K **Privately Held**
SIC: **5541** 7538 Filling stations, gasoline; General automotive repair shops

(G-18361)
MILLCREEKINVESTMENTS
452 E Ayre St (19804-2513)
PHONE.............................302 407-5034
Dan Parncutt, *Owner*
EMP: **5** EST: 2017
SALES (est): 50.01K **Privately Held**
SIC: **1799** Special trade contractors, nec

(G-18362)
MILLENIUM LOAN FUND LLC
4600 Linden Hill Rd (19808)
PHONE.............................302 996-4811
Gary Farrar, *Mgr*
EMP: **6** EST: 2010
SALES (est): 264.55K **Privately Held**
SIC: **7389** Fund raising organizations

(G-18363)
MILLENNIUM INV GROUP LLC
300 Delaware Ave (19801-1607)
PHONE.............................703 586-7968
Najeeb Salahuddin, *Managing Member*
EMP: **5** EST: 2007
SALES (est): 69.68K **Privately Held**
SIC: **6733** Personal investment trust management

(G-18364)
MILLER & ASSOCIATES PA
Also Called: Miller & Associates Cpas
5500 Skyline Dr Ste 5 (19808-1717)
PHONE.............................302 234-0678
David M Miller, *Pr*
EMP: **6** EST: 1986
SALES (est): 529.41K **Privately Held**
Web: www.millercpa.net

SIC: **8721** 7291 Certified public accountant; Tax return preparation services

(G-18365)
MILLER DR ELINOR M D
721 Blackshire Rd (19805-2837)
PHONE.............................302 654-8291
Elinor Miller Md, *Owner*
EMP: **7** EST: 2018
SALES (est): 74.5K **Privately Held**
SIC: **8011** General and family practice, physician/surgeon

(G-18366)
MILLER-MAURO GROUP INC
3512 Silverside Rd Ste 9 (19810-4941)
PHONE.............................302 426-6565
Joseph Mauro, *CEO*
EMP: **5** EST: 1984
SQ FT: 1,635
SALES (est): 752.08K **Privately Held**
Web: www.millermauro.com
SIC: **7311** Advertising consultant

(G-18367)
MILLWRIGHT COMPANY LLC
919 N Market St Ste 950 (19801-3036)
PHONE.............................302 274-9590
Eric Magana, *Managing Member*
EMP: **10** EST: 2017
SALES (est): 300K **Privately Held**
SIC: **1796** Millwright

(G-18368)
MILLWRIGHTS LOCAL UNION 1548
1013 Centre Rd Ste 201 (19805-1265)
PHONE.............................410 355-0011
Jack L Johns, *Pr*
Patrick Williams, *VP*
Robert Lipscomb, *Recording Secretary*
David Morris, *Treas*
Michael Schmidt, *Sec*
EMP: **10** EST: 1971
SALES (est): 115.49K **Privately Held**
SIC: **8631** Labor union

(G-18369)
MILPA NATIVA INC ○
1007 N Orange St Fl 4 (19801-1242)
PHONE.............................512 668-9033
Alex Luhrman, *Pr*
EMP: **3** EST: 2023
SALES (est): 135.7K **Privately Held**
SIC: **2046** 7389 Corn milling by-products; Business Activities at Non-Commercial Site

(G-18370)
MILTON & HATTIE KUTZ FOUNDATON
101 Garden Of Eden Rd (19803-1511)
PHONE.............................302 427-2100
EMP: **7** EST: 2011
SALES (est): 94.7K **Privately Held**
Web: www.shalomdelaware.org
SIC: **6732** Charitable trust management

(G-18371)
MILTON & HATTIE KUTZ HOME INC
Also Called: KUTZ HOME
704 River Rd (19809-2746)
PHONE.............................302 764-7000
Karen Friedman, *Dir*
Karen Freeman, *
Dave Bacher, *
Karen Friedman, *Ex Dir*
EMP: **140** EST: 1913
SQ FT: 49,500
SALES (est): 14.95MM **Privately Held**
Web: www.kutzseniorliving.org

SIC: **8051** 8052 Convalescent home with continuous nursing care; Personal care facility

(G-18372)
MINIMUM CORPORATION (PA)
251 Little Falls Dr (19808-1674)
PHONE.................................857 928-0317
Freddie Evans, *CEO*
Freddie Green, *COO*
EMP: 15 **EST:** 2020
SALES (est): 108K
SALES (corp-wide): 108K **Privately Held**
Web: www.incnow.com
SIC: **7371** Computer software development

(G-18373)
MINISTRY OF CARING INC (PA)
115 E 14th St (19801-3209)
PHONE.................................302 428-3702
Ronald Giannone, *Ex Dir*
EMP: 7 **EST:** 1977
SQ FT: 4,500
SALES (est): 11.84MM
SALES (corp-wide): 11.84MM **Privately Held**
Web: www.ministryofcaring.org
SIC: **8699** 8661 Charitable organization; Nonchurch religious organizations

(G-18374)
MINISTRY OF CARING INC
Also Called: House of Joseph
1328 W 3rd St (19805-3662)
PHONE.................................302 652-0904
Willy Newfon, *Dir*
EMP: 6
SALES (corp-wide): 11.84MM **Privately Held**
Web: www.ministryofcaring.org
SIC: **8322** 7021 Temporary relief service; Rooming and boarding houses
PA: Ministry Of Caring, Inc
115 E 14th St
Wilmington DE 19801
302 428-3702

(G-18375)
MINISTRY OF CARING INC
830 N Spruce St Lowr (19801-4239)
PHONE.................................302 652-8947
Doctor Gary Isaacs, *Dir*
EMP: 155
SALES (corp-wide): 11.84MM **Privately Held**
Web: www.ministryofcaring.org
SIC: **8399** Health and welfare council
PA: Ministry Of Caring, Inc
115 E 14th St
Wilmington DE 19801
302 428-3702

(G-18376)
MINISTRY OF CARING INC
Also Called: Mary Mother of Hope House III
515 N Broom St (19805-3114)
PHONE.................................302 652-0970
EMP: 7
SALES (corp-wide): 11.84MM **Privately Held**
Web: www.ministryofcaring.org
SIC: **8322** Social service center
PA: Ministry Of Caring, Inc
115 E 14th St
Wilmington DE 19801
302 428-3702

(G-18377)
MINISTRY OF CARING INC
Also Called: Ministry Caring Distribution
1410 N Claymont St (19802-5227)
PHONE.................................302 652-0969
EMP: 9
SALES (corp-wide): 11.84MM **Privately Held**
Web: www.ministryofcaring.org
SIC: **8322** Social service center
PA: Ministry Of Caring, Inc
115 E 14th St
Wilmington DE 19801
302 428-3702

(G-18378)
MINISTRY OF CARING INC
Also Called: Emmanuel Diningroom
121 N Jackson St (19805-3670)
PHONE.................................302 658-6123
Brother Miguel Ramirez, *Dir*
EMP: 8
SALES (corp-wide): 11.84MM **Privately Held**
Web: www.ministryofcaring.org
SIC: **8322** Meal delivery program
PA: Ministry Of Caring, Inc
115 E 14th St
Wilmington DE 19801
302 428-3702

(G-18379)
MINKLIST DIGITAL INC
251 Little Falls Dr (19808-1674)
PHONE.................................917 364-8868
Nk Vos, *CEO*
EMP: 5 **EST:** 2020
SALES (est): 33.14K **Privately Held**
SIC: **4813** Web search portals

(G-18380)
MINOR LEAGUE BASEBALL
801 Shipyard Dr (19801-5154)
PHONE.................................302 658-6336
EMP: 6 **EST:** 2019
SALES (est): 43.67K **Privately Held**
Web: www.bluerocks.com
SIC: **8699** Athletic organizations

(G-18381)
MINTFLINT INC
251 Little Falls Dr (19808-1674)
PHONE.................................236 991-3735
Sambhav Ratnakar, *CEO*
EMP: 7 **EST:** 2020
SALES (est): 104.03K **Privately Held**
SIC: **7371** Software programming applications

(G-18382)
MINTZER SAROWITZ ZERIS LEOVAR
919 N Market St Ste 200 (19801-3068)
PHONE.................................302 655-2181
Daniel Bennett, *Prin*
EMP: 5 **EST:** 2010
SALES (est): 249.94K **Privately Held**
Web: www.defensecounsel.com
SIC: **8111** General practice attorney, lawyer

(G-18383)
MINUTE LOAN CENTER
3301 Lancaster Pike Ste 1a (19805-1436)
PHONE.................................302 427-8041
EMP: 6 **EST:** 2018
SALES (est): 154.75K **Privately Held**
Web: www.minuteloancenter.com
SIC: **6141** Personal credit institutions

(G-18384)
MINUTE LOAN CENTER
3210 Kirkwood Hwy (19808-6130)
PHONE.................................302 994-6588
EMP: 7 **EST:** 2017
SALES (est): 207.6K **Privately Held**
Web: www.minuteloancenter.com
SIC: **6141** Personal credit institutions

(G-18385)
MIRACLE MOO LLC ✪
1209 N Orange St (19801-1120)
PHONE.................................321 948-4678
EMP: 6 **EST:** 2023
SALES (est): 78.16K **Privately Held**
SIC: **2023** Dietary supplements, dairy and non-dairy based

(G-18386)
MIT SHAH LLC
100 E Lea Blvd (19802-2358)
PHONE.................................469 307-6571
EMP: 6 **EST:** 2009
SALES (est): 80.5K **Privately Held**
SIC: **4213** Household goods transport

(G-18387)
MITCHELL ASSOCIATES INC
15 James Ct (19801-5251)
PHONE.................................302 594-9415
Lou Rosenberg, *Pr*
EMP: 13
SALES (corp-wide): 5.44MM **Privately Held**
Web: www.mitchellai.com
SIC: **1751** Carpentry work
PA: Mitchell Associates, Inc.
100 W Cmmons Blvd Ste 300
New Castle DE 19720
302 594-9400

(G-18388)
MITSDARFER BROS TREE SERVICE
21 Whitekirk Dr (19808-1358)
PHONE.................................302 540-6029
EMP: 10 **EST:** 2013
SALES (est): 523.84K **Privately Held**
Web: www.mitsdarferbrotherstree.com
SIC: **0783** Planting, pruning, and trimming services

(G-18389)
MIZZEN EDUCATION INC ✪
3411 Silverside Rd # 104 (19810-4812)
PHONE.................................213 262-6196
Janine Krause, *Opers Mgr*
EMP: 7 **EST:** 2022
SALES (est): 277.92K **Privately Held**
SIC: **7372** Prepackaged software

(G-18390)
MJM FABRICATIONS INC
506 Crest Rd (19803-4322)
PHONE.................................302 764-0163
Michael Molder, *Pr*
EMP: 6 **EST:** 2007
SALES (est): 410.55K **Privately Held**
SIC: **3441** Fabricated structural metal

(G-18391)
MK MANAGEMENT GROUP LLC
214 Bromley Dr (19808-1374)
PHONE.................................302 543-4414
Min Day, *Prin*
EMP: 5 **EST:** 2013
SALES (est): 85.22K **Privately Held**
SIC: **8741** Management services

(G-18392)
MMR INDUSTRIES INC
7 Dartmouth Rd (19808-4633)
PHONE.................................302 999-9561
Michael S Brenner, *Prin*
EMP: 2 **EST:** 2010
SALES (est): 101.65K **Privately Held**
SIC: **3999** Manufacturing industries, nec

(G-18393)
MMT CONSTRUCTION SERVICES INC
2201 Duncan Rd (19808-4603)
PHONE.................................302 357-8506
EMP: 5 **EST:** 2016
SALES (est): 246.52K **Privately Held**
SIC: **1521** Single-family housing construction

(G-18394)
MOBILE MUZIC INC
2517 Nicholby Dr (19808-4212)
PHONE.................................302 998-5951
Tony Lewis, *Pr*
EMP: 6 **EST:** 1977
SALES (est): 77.93K **Privately Held**
SIC: **7929** Disc jockey service

(G-18395)
MOBILELINK
456 S Market St (19801-5207)
PHONE.................................302 502-3062
EMP: 8 **EST:** 2017
SALES (est): 59.2K **Privately Held**
Web: www.mobilelinkusa.com
SIC: **4812** Cellular telephone services

(G-18396)
MOBILEN COMMUNICATIONS INC
3422 Old Capitol Trl Ste 700 (19808-6124)
PHONE.................................844 580-7233
Christopher Stojcev, *CEO*
EMP: 6 **EST:** 2021
SALES (est): 332.32K **Privately Held**
SIC: **8748** Telecommunications consultant

(G-18397)
MOBIUS NEW MEDIA INC
818 N Market St Fl 2r (19801-3087)
PHONE.................................302 475-9880
Matt Urban, *Pr*
Barry Crell, *Treas*
Joe Del Tufo, *Sec*
EMP: 8 **EST:** 1996
SALES (est): 499.69K **Privately Held**
Web: www.nupointmarketing.com
SIC: **7374** Computer graphics service

(G-18398)
MODERNTHINK LLC
2 Mill Rd Ste 102 (19806-2175)
PHONE.................................302 764-4477
EMP: 10 **EST:** 2004
SALES (est): 905.15K **Privately Held**
Web: www.modernthink.com
SIC: **8742** Business management consultant

(G-18399)
MODIFIED THERMOSET RESINS INC
Also Called: Ppc Coatings
2 Pixie Rd (19810-1314)
PHONE.................................302 235-3710
EMP: 9 **EST:** 2006
SQ FT: 1,000
SALES (est): 512.57K **Privately Held**
Web: www.ppccoatings.com
SIC: **2851** Paints and allied products

(G-18400)
MOECO IOT INC
221 W 9th St Ste 574 (19801-1619)
PHONE.................................626 869-7140
EMP: 6 **EST:** 2018
SALES (est): 46.16K **Privately Held**
Web: www.moeco.io
SIC: **7371** Computer software development

Wilmington - New Castle County (G-18401)

(G-18401)
MOHAWK TILE MBL DISTRS OF DEL
2700 W 3rd St Greenhill Ave (19805-1811)
PHONE..................302 655-7164
Robert M Klinges, *Pr*
Edward F Klinges, *Sec*
Micheal J Klinges, *Treas*
EMP: 5 **EST:** 1968
SQ FT: 7,000
SALES (est): 382.93K **Privately Held**
Web: www.mohawktile.com
SIC: 1743 Tile installation, ceramic

(G-18402)
MOJIO
901 N Market St (19801-3022)
PHONE..................831 747-5141
EMP: 6 **EST:** 2019
SALES (est): 174.53K **Privately Held**
Web: www.moj.io
SIC: 7371 Computer software development

(G-18403)
MOKKA LLC
1007 N Orange St Ste 1382 (19801-1239)
PHONE..................646 388-2449
EMP: 5
SALES (est): 270.14K **Privately Held**
SIC: 7372 Prepackaged software

(G-18404)
MOLDED COMPONENTS INC
3817 Katherine Ave (19808-4638)
PHONE..................302 588-2240
Ryan Rebecca Carpenter, *Prin*
EMP: 6 **EST:** 2013
SALES (est): 89.21K **Privately Held**
SIC: 3089 Molding primary plastics

(G-18405)
MOLTEX ENERGY USA LLC
301 N Market St Ste 1414 (19801-2529)
PHONE..................775 346-7520
EMP: 9 **EST:** 2018
SALES (est): 404.22K **Privately Held**
Web: www.moltexenergy.com
SIC: 4911 Electric services

(G-18406)
MOMENTUM MANAGEMENT GROUP INC
Also Called: Corexcel
3411 Silverside Rd Ste 201w (19810-4806)
PHONE..................302 477-9730
Susan Bowlby, *Pr*
EMP: 6 **EST:** 1997
SQ FT: 1,500
SALES (est): 1.26MM **Privately Held**
Web: www.corexcel.com
SIC: 8742 Training and development consultant

(G-18407)
MOMS CLEANING SERVICE INC
5517 E Timberview Ct (19808-3627)
PHONE..................302 547-5729
EMP: 5 **EST:** 2014
SALES (est): 41.09K **Privately Held**
SIC: 7699 Cleaning services

(G-18408)
MONADA INC ◆
1209 N Orange St (19801-1120)
PHONE..................302 253-7382
Elad Ben-sadeh, *CEO*
EMP: 15 **EST:** 2022
SALES (est): 639.35K **Privately Held**
SIC: 7371 Computer software development

(G-18409)
MONARCH NASCENT INC
427 N Tatnall St (19801-2230)
PHONE..................310 601-4702
EMP: 14
SALES (est): 501.3K **Privately Held**
SIC: 7371 Computer software development and applications

(G-18410)
MONDRIAN FOCUSED GLOBAL
1105 N Market St (19801-1216)
PHONE..................302 428-3839
EMP: 6 **EST:** 2011
SALES (est): 417.44K **Privately Held**
SIC: 6722 Money market mutual funds

(G-18411)
MONDRIAN INTERNATIONAL SMALL
1105 N Market St Ste 118 (19801-1216)
PHONE..................302 428-3839
EMP: 5 **EST:** 2009
SALES (est): 183.4K **Privately Held**
SIC: 6722 Money market mutual funds

(G-18412)
MONET INTERMEDIATE LLC
251 Little Falls Dr (19808-1674)
PHONE..................929 559-5423
Leonardo Devincenzi, *Pr*
Miguel Londono Gomez, *
Andres Londono Botero, *
EMP: 35 **EST:** 2021
SALES (est): 1.03MM **Privately Held**
SIC: 7374 Data processing and preparation

(G-18413)
MONEY NEVER SLEEPS ENTRMT LLC
1000 N West St (19801-1050)
PHONE..................646 234-7285
Wan Junior, *Managing Member*
EMP: 5
SALES (est): 104.08K **Privately Held**
SIC: 7929 Entertainment service

(G-18414)
MONEYKEY - TX INC
3422 Old Capitol Trl Ste 1613 (19808-6124)
PHONE..................866 255-1668
Clive Kinross, *Pr*
EMP: 48 **EST:** 2012
SALES (est): 763.82K **Privately Held**
Web: www.moneykey.com
SIC: 6141 Personal credit institutions

(G-18415)
MONEYKEY-MO INC
3422 Old Capitol Trl Ste 1613 (19808-6124)
PHONE..................866 255-1668
Clive Kinross, *Pr*
EMP: 14 **EST:** 2017
SALES (est): 858.09K **Privately Held**
SIC: 6153 Short-term business credit institutions, except agricultural

(G-18416)
MONICA KHAN
1416 Lancaster Ave (19805-3905)
PHONE..................302 652-1994
Monica Khan, *Prin*
EMP: 6 **EST:** 2018
SALES (est): 105.44K **Privately Held**
SIC: 8049 Offices of health practitioner

(G-18417)
MONOPY INTERNATIONAL INC
108 W 13th St (19801-1145)
PHONE..................312 339-8751
Rain Feng, *Pr*
EMP: 5 **EST:** 2019
SALES (est): 812.17K **Privately Held**
SIC: 3263 3253 Kitchen articles, semivitreous earthenware; Ceramic wall and floor tile
PA: Tangshan Monopy Ceramic Co., Ltd.
     Dongjiantuo, Xige Town, Fengnan District
     Tangshan HE 06331

(G-18418)
MONROE ENTERPRISING SVCS LLC
5410 Old Capitol Trl (19808-4947)
PHONE..................302 345-1527
EMP: 5
SALES (est): 123.37K **Privately Held**
SIC: 1389 Construction, repair, and dismantling services

(G-18419)
MONROE IKO INC
120 Hay Rd (19809-3509)
PHONE..................302 764-3100
Henry Koschitzky, *Pr*
EMP: 16 **EST:** 1997
SALES (est): 316K **Privately Held**
SIC: 2952 Roofing materials

(G-18420)
MONTCHANIN BUILDERS
300 Water St Ste 300 (19801-5046)
PHONE..................302 472-7213
Anthony Ruggio, *Pr*
EMP: 14 **EST:** 2010
SALES (est): 2.45MM **Privately Held**
Web: www.montchaninbuilders.net
SIC: 1521 New construction, single-family houses

(G-18421)
MONTCHANIN DESIGN GROUP INC
1907 N Market St (19802-4812)
PHONE..................302 652-3008
Michael Looney, *Pr*
Zachary Davis, *VP*
EMP: 22 **EST:** 1985
SQ FT: 2,500
SALES (est): 2.5MM **Privately Held**
Web: www.montchanindesign.com
SIC: 8712 8741 Architectural engineering; Construction management

(G-18422)
MONTESINO ASSOCIATES
1719 Delaware Ave # 3 (19806-2362)
PHONE..................302 888-2355
Peter J Schmitt, *Owner*
EMP: 9 **EST:** 1996
SALES (est): 408.64K **Privately Held**
SIC: 8742 Marketing consulting services

(G-18423)
MONTESINO TECHNOLOGIES INC
1719 Delaware Ave # 3 (19806-2362)
PHONE..................302 888-2355
Peter Schmitt, *Pr*
EMP: 5 **EST:** 1999
SALES (est): 390K **Privately Held**
Web: www.montesino.com
SIC: 7389 Packaging and labeling services

(G-18424)
MONTESSORI LEARNING CENTER LLC
2313 Concord Pike (19803-2911)
PHONE..................302 478-2575
Vienna Broadbelt, *Owner*
Vienna Boroadbelt, *Owner*
EMP: 9 **EST:** 1974
SQ FT: 2,100
SALES (est): 266.17K **Privately Held**
Web: www.montessorilc.com
SIC: 8351 Montessori child development center

(G-18425)
MONTGMERY MCCRCKEN WLKER RHADS
300 Delaware Ave Ste 750 (19801-6600)
PHONE..................302 504-7800
John M Bloxom Iv, *Brnch Mgr*
EMP: 17
SALES (corp-wide): 29.88MM **Privately Held**
Web: www.mmwr.com
SIC: 8111 General practice attorney, lawyer
PA: Montgomery, Mccracken, Walker & Rhoads, Llp
     123 S Broad St Fl 26
     Philadelphia PA 19109
     215 772-1500

(G-18426)
MONTGOMERY KENNETH JOHN
610 Ohio Ave (19805-1023)
PHONE..................302 992-0484
Kenneth J Montgomery, *Owner*
EMP: 6 **EST:** 1997
SALES (est): 392.19K **Privately Held**
SIC: 4213 Trucking, except local

(G-18427)
MONZACK MRSKY MCLGHLIN BRWDER
1201 N Orange St Ste 400 (19801-1167)
P.O. Box 2031 (19899-2031)
PHONE..................302 656-8162
Melvin Monzack, *Pt*
Melvin Monzack, *Prin*
Francis Monaco Junior, *Prin*
EMP: 28 **EST:** 1972
SALES (est): 2.78MM **Privately Held**
Web: www.monlaw.com
SIC: 8111 General practice attorney, lawyer

(G-18428)
MOODY LAWN CARE & RENOVATIONS
1000 N West St Ste 1200 (19801-1058)
PHONE..................302 685-2338
Rhian Ward, *Owner*
EMP: 5 **EST:** 2015
SALES (est): 89.59K **Privately Held**
SIC: 0782 Lawn care services

(G-18429)
MOON BUYER INC (PA)
251 Little Falls Dr (19808-1674)
PHONE..................302 636-5401
EMP: 15 **EST:** 2021
SALES (est): 37.9MM
SALES (corp-wide): 37.9MM **Privately Held**
SIC: 7371 Computer software development

(G-18430)
MOON DEVICES INC
919 N Market St Ste 725 (19801-3065)
PHONE..................650 206-8011
EMP: 5 **EST:** 2020
SALES (est): 46.16K **Privately Held**
SIC: 7371 Computer software development and applications

▲ = Import ▼ = Export
◆ = Import/Export

Wilmington - New Castle County (G-18456)

(G-18431)
MOONLOOP PHOTOGRAPHY LLC
1704 Green Ln (19810-4004)
PHONE..............................484 748-0812
EMP: 5 **EST:** 2015
SALES (est): 204.9K **Privately Held**
Web: www.moonloopphoto.com
SIC: 7221 Photographer, still or video

(G-18432)
MOONSWORTH LLC
Also Called: Moonsworth
1201 N Market St Ste 111 (19801-1156)
PHONE..............................302 439-6039
Francisco Saldanha, *Prin*
EMP: 5 **EST:** 2019
SALES (est): 138.27K **Privately Held**
SIC: 7371 Computer software development and applications

(G-18433)
MOOR INSTRUMENTS INC
501 Silverside Rd Ste 66 (19809-1394)
PHONE..............................302 798-7470
David Boggett, *Pr*
Hazel Boggett, *Sec*
EMP: 2 **EST:** 1994
SQ FT: 220
SALES (est): 266.11K **Privately Held**
Web: www.moor.co.uk
SIC: 3841 Surgical and medical instruments

(G-18434)
MOORE INSURANCE & FINANCIAL
1702 Kirkwood Hwy Ste 101 (19805-4939)
PHONE..............................302 999-9101
Darren Moore, *Mgr*
Darren Moore, *Prin*
EMP: 6 **EST:** 1990
SALES (est): 495.87K **Privately Held**
Web: www.darrenmooregroup.com
SIC: 6411 Insurance agents and brokers

(G-18435)
MOORE LTD
222 Delaware Ave Ste 1436 (19801-1621)
PHONE..............................302 427-5760
Tom Moore, *Pr*
EMP: 5 **EST:** 1977
SALES (est): 434.77K
SALES (corp-wide): 81.32MM **Privately Held**
SIC: 2258 Fabric finishing, warp knit
PA: The Moore Company
36 Beach St
Westerly RI 02891
401 596-2816

(G-18436)
MOORE PHYSCIAL THERAPY
1806 N Van Buren St Ste 200 (19802-3851)
PHONE..............................302 654-8142
Robert Altschuler, *Prin*
EMP: 7 **EST:** 2010
SALES (est): 92.88K **Privately Held**
SIC: 8093 Rehabilitation center, outpatient treatment

(G-18437)
MOORE SERVICES
1723 Chestnut St (19805-3909)
P.O. Box 2811 (19805-0811)
PHONE..............................302 588-3984
T J Moore, *Prin*
EMP: 5 **EST:** 2018
SALES (est): 183.21K **Privately Held**
SIC: 1522 Residential construction, nec

(G-18438)
MOORE SHAUN PT
3317 Tunison Dr (19810-3225)
PHONE..............................302 477-3998
Shaun Moore, *Prin*
EMP: 5 **EST:** 2009
SALES (est): 71.99K **Privately Held**
SIC: 8049 Physical therapist

(G-18439)
MOORWAY PAINTING MANAGEMENT
1 Hayden Ave (19804-1742)
PHONE..............................302 764-5002
Rahim El, *Owner*
Kamira El, *Mgr*
EMP: 8 **EST:** 2004
SALES (est): 655.64K **Privately Held**
Web: www.moorwaymanagement.com
SIC: 8741 5231 Business management; Paint and painting supplies

(G-18440)
MORALES GTO EMPIRE LLC
6 Kathlyn Ct (19808-3818)
PHONE..............................302 824-4315
Oscar Morales, *Prin*
EMP: 5 **EST:** 2018
SALES (est): 125.58K **Privately Held**
SIC: 1521 Single-family housing construction

(G-18441)
MORE THAN FITNESS INC
718 Grandview Ave (19809-2627)
PHONE..............................302 690-5655
Jeremy Moore, *Prin*
Brett Wu, *Prin*
Stacey Richardson, *Prin*
Brandon Pratta, *Prin*
Robyn Howton, *Prin*
EMP: 6 **EST:** 2018
SALES (est): 65.45K **Privately Held**
Web: www.morethan.fitness
SIC: 7991 Physical fitness facilities

(G-18442)
MORE THAN SHY INC
2810 N Church St (19802-4447)
PHONE..............................603 918-1612
Rebecca Martel, *CEO*
EMP: 2
SALES (est): 87.4K **Privately Held**
SIC: 7372 Application computer software

(G-18443)
MORGAN KALMAN CLINIC PA
2501 Silverside Rd Ste 1 (19810-3726)
PHONE..............................302 529-5500
Craig D Morgan Md, *Pt*
Victor R Kalman, *Pt*
EMP: 25 **EST:** 1998
SQ FT: 3,000
SALES (est): 1.92MM **Privately Held**
Web: www.morgankalman.com
SIC: 8011 Orthopedic physician

(G-18444)
MORGAN BUILDERS INC
403 Tatum Ave (19805-1360)
PHONE..............................302 575-9943
Jillynn French, *Prin*
EMP: 7 **EST:** 2018
SALES (est): 121.86K **Privately Held**
SIC: 1521 New construction, single-family houses

(G-18445)
MORGAN KALMAN CLINIC
2701 Kirkwood Hwy (19805-4911)
PHONE..............................610 869-5757
Morgan Kalman, *Brnch Mgr*
EMP: 15
Web: www.morgankalman.com
SIC: 8011 Clinic, operated by physicians
PA: Kalman Morgan Clinic
900 W Baltimore Pike # 103
West Grove PA 19390

(G-18446)
MORGAN LEWIS INTERNATIONAL LLC (PA)
1007 N Orange St Ste 501 (19801-1254)
PHONE..............................302 574-3000
EMP: 6 **EST:** 2010
SALES (est): 190.8K
SALES (corp-wide): 190.8K **Privately Held**
SIC: 8111 General practice attorney, lawyer

(G-18447)
MORGAN STANLEY & CO LLC
Also Called: Morgan Stanley
2751 Centerville Rd Ste 104 (19808-1600)
PHONE..............................302 573-4000
Donald Didoeato, *Mgr*
EMP: 8
SALES (corp-wide): 53.67B **Publicly Held**
Web: www.morganstanley.com
SIC: 6282 Investment advisory service
HQ: Morgan Stanley & Co. Llc
1585 Broadway
New York NY 10036
212 761-4000

(G-18448)
MORGAN STNLEY INTL HLDINGS INC
2751 Centerville Rd Ste 104 (19808-1627)
PHONE..............................302 657-2000
Sean Farrell, *Mgr*
EMP: 100
SALES (corp-wide): 53.67B **Publicly Held**
Web: www.morganstanley.com
SIC: 6719 Investment holding companies, except banks
HQ: Stanley Morgan International Holdings Inc
1585 Broadway
New York NY 10036

(G-18449)
MORGAN STNLEY SMITH BARNEY LLC
2751 Centerville Rd Ste 104 (19808-1600)
PHONE..............................302 636-5500
Gerald Laudicina, *Brnch Mgr*
EMP: 105
SALES (corp-wide): 53.67B **Publicly Held**
Web: www.morganstanley.com
SIC: 6211 Security brokers and dealers
HQ: Morgan Stanley Smith Barney, Llc
1585 Broadway
New York NY 10036

(G-18450)
MORI AMERICA LLC (PA) ✪
Also Called: Mt D.C. One
251 Little Falls Dr (19808-1674)
PHONE..............................703 918-4663
William Newman, *Managing Member*
EMP: 5 **EST:** 2023
SALES (est): 320.8K
SALES (corp-wide): 320.8K **Privately Held**
SIC: 6519 Real property lessors, nec

(G-18451)
MORNING HORNET LLC
103 Foulk Rd Ste 202 (19803-3742)
PHONE..............................650 543-4800
EMP: 12 **EST:** 2017
SALES (est): 1.89MM
SALES (corp-wide): 134.9B **Publicly Held**
SIC: 7374 Data processing and preparation
PA: Meta Platforms, Inc.
1 Meta Way
Menlo Park CA 94025
650 543-4800

(G-18452)
MORNINGSTAR PROPERTY GROUP LLC
Also Called: Morningstar City Group
214 W 7th St Apt 1 (19801-2265)
PHONE..............................302 543-4093
EMP: 5 **EST:** 2011
SALES (est): 406.19K **Privately Held**
Web: www.apartmentsbymorningstar.com
SIC: 6512 Nonresidential building operators

(G-18453)
MORRIS JAMES LLP
803 N Broom St (19806-4624)
PHONE..............................302 655-2599
Francis J Jones Junior, *Brnch Mgr*
EMP: 15
SALES (corp-wide): 24.52MM **Privately Held**
Web: www.morrisjamespersonalinjurylawyers.com
SIC: 8111 General practice attorney, lawyer
PA: Morris James Llp
500 Delaware Ave Ste 1500
Wilmington DE 19801
302 888-6800

(G-18454)
MORRIS JAMES LLP (PA)
Also Called: Mars James Hitchens & Williams
500 Delaware Ave Ste 1500 (19801-1494)
P.O. Box 2306 (19899-2306)
PHONE..............................302 888-6800
Noris P Wright, *Genl Pt*
Richard Gallperin, *Pt*
Edward M Mcnally, *Pt*
D P Mucollough, *Pt*
David H Williams, *Pt*
EMP: 97 **EST:** 1932
SALES (est): 24.52MM
SALES (corp-wide): 24.52MM **Privately Held**
Web: www.morrisjamespersonalinjurylawyers.com
SIC: 8111 General practice attorney, lawyer

(G-18455)
MORRIS NCHOLS ARSHT TNNELL LLP
1201 N Market St Ste 1800 (19801-1147)
P.O. Box 1347 (19899-1347)
PHONE..............................302 658-9200
Walter C Tuthill, *Pt*
A Gilchrist Sparks, *Pt*
Jack Blumenfeld, *Pt*
Andrew Johnston, *Pt*
Alan Stone, *Pt*
EMP: 200 **EST:** 1932
SQ FT: 67,000
SALES (est): 40.49MM **Privately Held**
Web: www.morrisnichols.com
SIC: 8111 General practice attorney, lawyer

(G-18456)
MORTGAGE AMERICA INC
5315 Limestone Rd (19808-1222)
PHONE..............................302 239-0600
Damian Gallagher, *Mgr*
EMP: 7
Web: www.mymortgageamerica.com
SIC: 6162 Mortgage bankers
PA: Mortgage America, Inc.
1425 Grape St
Whitehall PA 18052

Wilmington - New Castle County (G-18457)

(G-18457)
MORTGAGE NETWORK SOLUTIONS LLC (PA)
2036 Foulk Rd Ste 102 (19810-3649)
PHONE..................................302 252-0100
EMP: 31 EST: 2008
SALES (est): 9.51MM **Privately Held**
Web: www.mortgagens.com
SIC: 6162 Mortgage bankers and loan correspondents

(G-18458)
MORTGAGE NETWORK SOLUTIONS LLC
223 Pine Cliff Dr (19810-1312)
PHONE..................................302 252-0100
EMP: 15
Web: www.mortgagens.com
SIC: 6162 Mortgage bankers
PA: Mortgage Network Solutions, Llc
    2036 Foulk Rd Ste 102
    Wilmington DE 19810

(G-18459)
MORTON VALIHURA & ZERBATO LLC
3704 Kennett Pike Ste 200 (19807-2173)
PHONE..................................302 426-1313
EMP: 6 EST: 2020
SALES (est): 434.88K **Privately Held**
Web: www.mvzllc.com
SIC: 8111 General practice attorney, lawyer

(G-18460)
MOSCOVA ENTERPRISES INC
300 Delaware Ave Ste 210 (19801-6601)
PHONE..................................347 973-2522
Vickens Moscova, *CEO*
EMP: 10 EST: 2014
SQ FT: 1,000
SALES (est): 890.3K **Privately Held**
Web: www.moscovaenterprises.com
SIC: 8742 2741 7311 Management consulting services; Internet publishing and broadcasting; Advertising consultant

(G-18461)
MOSCOVA SVRIGN IRRVCBLE PRVATE
300 Delaware Ave (19801-1607)
PHONE..................................347 973-2522
Vickens Moscova, *CEO*
EMP: 5
SALES (est): 199.4K **Privately Held**
SIC: 7389 Business Activities at Non-Commercial Site

(G-18462)
MOT FAMILY CHIRO-WILMINGTON
2005 Concord Pike Ste 202 (19803-2982)
PHONE..................................302 593-0031
EMP: 6 EST: 2019
SALES (est): 37.19K **Privately Held**
SIC: 8041 Offices and clinics of chiropractors

(G-18463)
MOTHER TERESA HOUSE INC
115 E 14th St (19801-3209)
PHONE..................................302 652-5523
EMP: 5 EST: 2018
SALES (est): 65.13K **Privately Held**
SIC: 8361 Residential care

(G-18464)
MOTHERS IN UNITY
1227 W 4th St (19805-3605)
PHONE..................................302 442-1904
Natalie Matthews, *Pr*
EMP: 6 EST: 2016
SALES (est): 87.87K **Privately Held**
SIC: 8399 Advocacy group

(G-18465)
MOTORFYX INC ◆
1207 Delaware Ave Ste 125 (19806-4743)
PHONE..................................858 500-6677
Cameron Khoroushi, *CEO*
EMP: 2 EST: 2023
SALES (est): 83.48K **Privately Held**
SIC: 7372 Prepackaged software

(G-18466)
MOUNTAIN W INSUR FNCL SVCS LLC
1209 N Orange St (19801-1120)
PHONE..................................970 824-8185
EMP: 13 EST: 2017
SALES (est): 288.5K **Privately Held**
Web: www.mtnwst.com
SIC: 6411 Insurance agents, brokers, and service

(G-18467)
MOVING SCIENCES LLC
1201 N Orange St Ste 600 (19801-1171)
PHONE..................................617 871-9892
Yz Lee, *CEO*
EMP: 2 EST: 2009
SALES (est): 117.39K **Privately Held**
SIC: 7372 7371 7389 Application computer software; Computer software development; Business services, nec

(G-18468)
MOXIE APPAREL INC
Also Called: Moxie Scrubs
300 Delaware Ave Ste 210 (19801-6601)
PHONE..................................844 894-1435
Alicia Tuless, *CEO*
EMP: 10 EST: 2019
SALES (est): 395.76K **Privately Held**
SIC: 2339 Women's and misses' outerwear, nec

(G-18469)
MOYER PEST CONTROL
23 Brookside Dr (19804-1101)
PHONE..................................302 353-4404
EMP: 8 EST: 2018
SALES (est): 37.65K **Privately Held**
Web: www.emoyer.com
SIC: 7342 Pest control in structures

(G-18470)
MPE GLOBAL INCORPORATED ◆
1401 Pennsylvania Ave Ste 105 (19806-4125)
PHONE..................................856 376-0434
Damien Payne, *CEO*
EMP: 5 EST: 2023
SALES (est): 152.07K **Privately Held**
SIC: 8742 Marketing consulting services

(G-18471)
MPHASIS CORPORATION
1220 N Market St Ste 806 (19801-2595)
PHONE..................................212 686-6655
Nitin Rakesh, *CEO*
EMP: 12 EST: 1998
SALES (est): 2.43MM **Privately Held**
Web: www.mphasis.com
SIC: 7371 Computer software development
HQ: Mphasis Limited
    Bagmane World Technology Center,
    Marathahalli Outer Ring Road,
    Bengaluru KA 56004

(G-18472)
MRESOURCE LLC (PA)
1220 N Market St Ste 808 (19801-2595)
P.O. Box 5370 (60680-5370)
PHONE..................................312 608-4789
EMP: 4 EST: 2009
SALES (est): 180.42K
SALES (corp-wide): 180.42K **Privately Held**
Web: www.mresourceglobal.com
SIC: 7372 Application computer software

(G-18473)
MRM LANDSCAPING LLC
914 Maple Ave (19809-3013)
P.O. Box 9635 (19809-0635)
PHONE..................................302 602-1203
EMP: 7 EST: 2012
SALES (est): 118.51K **Privately Held**
Web: www.mrmlandscaping.com
SIC: 0781 Landscape services

(G-18474)
MS FINANCING LLC
Also Called: Morgan Stanley
1209 N Orange St (19801-1120)
PHONE..................................212 276-1206
Ethan Schiffman, *Mgr*
EMP: 100 EST: 1986
SALES (est): 8.87MM
SALES (corp-wide): 53.67B **Publicly Held**
SIC: 6282 Investment advice
PA: Morgan Stanley
    1585 Broadway
    New York NY 10036
    212 761-4000

(G-18475)
MS HATHERS LRNG CTR CHILDCARE
205 Brookland Ave (19805-1112)
PHONE..................................302 994-2448
Heather Wiktorwizz, *Owner*
EMP: 9 EST: 2012
SALES (est): 101.08K **Privately Held**
SIC: 8351 Child day care services

(G-18476)
MSM FOODS LLC
3100 Naamans Rd Ste 1 (19810-2100)
PHONE..................................302 524-4470
EMP: 6 EST: 2021
SALES (est): 134.03K **Privately Held**
SIC: 7371 Computer software development

(G-18477)
MSRCOSMOS LLC (HQ)
1000 N West St Ste 1200 (19801-1058)
PHONE..................................925 218-6919
Saijyothsnadevi Kondapi, *CEO*
Sivagopal Madadugula, *CSO*
EMP: 18 EST: 2008
SQ FT: 650
SALES (est): 11.34MM **Privately Held**
Web: www.msrcosmos.com
SIC: 7379 Computer related consulting services
PA: M S R Cosmos It Llp
    D No 1-90/7/B/29/C, Msr Business
    Park, Phase-Ii 3rd Line
    Hyderabad TG 50008

(G-18478)
MSS ENERGY HOLDINGS LLC
Also Called: Calibrant Energy
251 Little Falls Dr (19808-1674)
PHONE..................................212 231-2505
EMP: 7 EST: 2020
SALES (est): 694.68K **Privately Held**
SIC: 8748 Business consulting, nec

(G-18479)
MT FOREIGN HOLDINGS INC (HQ)
2711 Centerville Rd Ste 400 (19808-1660)
PHONE..................................301 252-9160
EMP: 65
SALES (est): 14.57MM
SALES (corp-wide): 1.56B **Publicly Held**
SIC: 3842 Surgical appliances and supplies
PA: Enovis Corporation
    2711 Centerville Rd # 400
    Wilmington DE 19808
    301 252-9160

(G-18480)
MTB ARTISANS LLC
2205 Kentmere Pkwy (19806-2017)
PHONE..................................303 475-9024
Chris Squier, *Mgr*
EMP: 3 EST: 2017
SALES (est): 99.49K **Privately Held**
Web: www.mtbartisans.com
SIC: 2511 Wood household furniture

(G-18481)
MUJIB R OBEIDY
1401 Silverside Rd Ste A (19810-4400)
PHONE..................................302 478-5900
Mujib R Obeidy, *Owner*
EMP: 8 EST: 2016
SALES (est): 186.21K **Privately Held**
SIC: 8031 8011 Offices and clinics of osteopathic physicians; Offices and clinics of medical doctors

(G-18482)
MULLICO GENERAL CONSTRUCTION
510 Foulkstone Rd (19803-2414)
PHONE..................................302 475-4400
Eugene D Mulligan Iii, *Pr*
Rosalie A Mulligan, *Sec*
Dennis W Mulligan, *Treas*
EMP: 10 EST: 1977
SALES (est): 1.68MM **Privately Held**
Web: www.mullicoconstruction.com
SIC: 1521 General remodeling, single-family houses

(G-18483)
MULTISPECIALTY HEALTHCARE
1010 Concord Ave (19802-3367)
PHONE..................................302 575-9794
EMP: 8 EST: 2018
SALES (est): 193.86K **Privately Held**
Web: www.excelsiainjurycare.com
SIC: 8093 Specialty outpatient clinics, nec

(G-18484)
MULTIWAVE INVESTMENT INC
1201 N Market St Ste 1707 (19801-1147)
PHONE..................................302 658-9200
Lue Marclni, *Pr*
EMP: 40 EST: 1990
SALES (est): 1.32MM **Publicly Held**
SIC: 7291 Tax return preparation services
PA: Ciena Corporation
    7035 Ridge Rd
    Hanover MD 21076

(G-18485)
MUMFORD-BJORKMAN ASSOC INC
Also Called: M B A
222a 7th Ave (19805-4762)
P.O. Box 733 (19720-0733)
PHONE..................................302 655-8234
Mike Catts, *Pr*
Daniel Mumford, *Pr*
Linda Mumford, *Sec*

Michael Catts, *VP*
Andrew Mumford, *VP*
EMP: 15 **EST:** 1986
SQ FT: 800
SALES (est): 956.73K **Privately Held**
Web: www.mbatanks.com
SIC: 7389 Inspection and testing services

(G-18486)
MUNCIE INS & FNCL SVCS INC
Also Called: Nationwide
4400 N Market St (19802-1308)
PHONE.................................302 761-9611
EMP: 8 **EST:** 2012
SALES (est): 97.31K **Privately Held**
Web: www.nationwide.com
SIC: 6411 Insurance agents, nec

(G-18487)
MUNI TECH LLC
605 N Market St (19801-3166)
PHONE.................................302 383-1487
EMP: 5 **EST:** 2019
SALES (est): 276.32K **Privately Held**
Web: www.munillc.com
SIC: 7371 Custom computer programming services

(G-18488)
MURPHY & LANDON PC
Also Called: Murphy Spadaro & Landon
1011 Centre Rd Ste 210 (19805-1266)
PHONE.................................302 472-8100
Frank Murphy, *Pr*
Roger Landon, *VP*
Phillip Edwards, *Pt*
Jonathan Parshall, *Pt*
EMP: 19 **EST:** 1992
SQ FT: 11,000
SALES (est): 4.06MM **Privately Held**
Web: www.msllaw.com
SIC: 8111 General practice attorney, lawyer

(G-18489)
MURPHY MARINE SERVICES INC
701 Christiana Ave (19801-5842)
PHONE.................................302 571-4700
John Coulahan, *Pr*
Mark Murphy, *
EMP: 300 **EST:** 1994
SALES (est): 7.41MM **Privately Held**
Web: www.murphymarine.com
SIC: 4491 Stevedoring

(G-18490)
MURRAY MNOR HMWNERS ASSCTON LL
27 2nd Ave (19808-4966)
PHONE.................................302 298-5997
Charles Millis, *Prin*
EMP: 5 **EST:** 2017
SALES (est): 57.69K **Privately Held**
SIC: 8641 Homeowners' association

(G-18491)
MUSE MARKETING & CREATIVE LLC
2214 Buckingham Rd (19810-4107)
PHONE.................................856 823-1601
EMP: 6 **EST:** 2017
SALES (est): 154.08K **Privately Held**
Web: www.musemc.com
SIC: 8742 Marketing consulting services

(G-18492)
MUSHU INC
251 Little Falls Dr (19808-1674)
PHONE.................................650 862-3863
David Elsonbaty, *Prin*
EMP: 5 **EST:** 2021
SALES (est): 117.25K **Privately Held**

SIC: 7372 Application computer software

(G-18493)
MUSI COMMERCIAL PROPERTIES INC
5700 Kennett Pike (19807-1312)
PHONE.................................302 594-1000
Ken J Musi, *Pr*
EMP: 6 **EST:** 2004
SQ FT: 2,000
SALES (est): 493.8K **Privately Held**
Web: www.musicommercial.com
SIC: 6531 Real estate agent, commercial

(G-18494)
MUST APP CORP
1013 Centre Rd Ste 403b (19805-1270)
PHONE.................................905 537-5522
Evgeny Muravjev, *CEO*
EMP: 10 **EST:** 2016
SALES (est): 425.62K **Privately Held**
SIC: 7371 Computer software development and applications

(G-18495)
MUVERS INC
427 N Tatnall St Ste 14582 (19801-2230)
PHONE.................................888 508-4849
Mark Daniels, *Pr*
EMP: 7 **EST:** 2018
SQ FT: 920
SALES (est): 1.2MM **Privately Held**
SIC: 4212 Moving services

(G-18496)
MV CRUISE PARTNERS LLC
251 Little Falls Dr (19808-1674)
PHONE.................................561 329-3209
EMP: 7 **EST:** 2019
SALES (est): 360.16K **Privately Held**
SIC: 3731 Commercial passenger ships, building and repairing

(G-18497)
MV FARINOLA INC
4023 Kennett Pike Ste 219 (19807-2018)
PHONE.................................302 545-8492
Michael V Farinola, *Pr*
Veronica Farinola, *VP*
EMP: 2 **EST:** 1992
SALES (est): 156.98K **Privately Held**
SIC: 8742 3534 Administrative services consultant; Elevators and equipment

(G-18498)
MVL STRUCTURES GROUP LLC
1000 N West St Ste 1501 (19801-1001)
PHONE.................................302 652-7580
Jamil Oudeif, *Prin*
EMP: 35 **EST:** 2017
SALES (est): 1.25MM **Privately Held**
SIC: 8711 1542 Building construction consultant; Commercial and office building, new construction

(G-18499)
MVL-AL OTHMAN AL ZAMEL JV LLC
1000 N West St Ste 1501 (19801-1001)
PHONE.................................832 302-2757
Ibrahim Musa, *Mgr*
Marty Muller, *Proj Mgr*
EMP: 50
SALES (est): 2.4MM **Privately Held**
SIC: 1542 Commercial and office building, new construction

(G-18500)
MVL-SAQA JV LLC
1000 N West St Ste 1501 (19801-1001)
PHONE.................................832 302-2757

Ibrahim Musa, *Mgr*
Marty Muller, *Proj Mgr*
EMP: 50
SALES (est): 2.47MM **Privately Held**
SIC: 1542 Commercial and office building, new construction

(G-18501)
MWIDM INC (PA)
1201 N Market St Ste 111 (19801-1156)
PHONE.................................302 298-0101
Amrinder Romana, *Pr*
EMP: 46 **EST:** 2014
SALES (est): 45.24MM
SALES (corp-wide): 45.24MM **Privately Held**
Web: www.mwidm.com
SIC: 8742 7372 7361 Management consulting services; Prepackaged software; Executive placement

(G-18502)
MY 3 SONS
612 Fallon Ave (19804-2112)
PHONE.................................302 559-7252
Nancy Glynn, *Owner*
EMP: 5 **EST:** 2015
SALES (est): 163.81K **Privately Held**
SIC: 1522 Residential construction, nec

(G-18503)
MY BENEFIT ADVISOR LLC
2207 Concord Pike Ste 152 (19803-2908)
PHONE.................................302 588-7242
EMP: 7 **EST:** 2008
SQ FT: 1,800
SALES (est): 351.31K **Privately Held**
Web: www.mybenefitadvisor.com
SIC: 8748 Business consulting, nec

(G-18504)
MY DIGITAL SHIELD
300 Delaware Ave Ste 210 (19801-6601)
PHONE.................................423 310-8977
Zhanna Brown, *Prin*
EMP: 7 **EST:** 2015
SALES (est): 476.24K **Privately Held**
Web: www.omninet.io
SIC: 7379 Computer related consulting services

(G-18505)
MY EYE DR OPTOMETRISTS LLC
4605 Kirkwood Hwy (19808-5005)
PHONE.................................302 999-7171
EMP: 6
SALES (corp-wide): 100.43MM **Privately Held**
Web: www.myeyedr.com
SIC: 8042 Specialized optometrists
PA: My Eye Dr. Optometrists, Llc
8614 Wstwd Ctr Dr Ste 900
Vienna VA 22182
703 847-8899

(G-18506)
MY INSTALL PRO LTD LBLTY CO
300 Delaware Ave Ste 210a (19801-6601)
PHONE.................................803 486-3831
Tyrone Frazier, *Managing Member*
EMP: 30 **EST:** 2020
SALES (est): 2.02MM **Privately Held**
SIC: 4212 Delivery service, vehicular

(G-18507)
MY LIVE LIFE WORLD CORP ✪
501 Silverside Rd Ste 102 (19809-1376)
PHONE.................................347 560-5425
Hanna Bohinskaya, *Prin*
EMP: 2 **EST:** 2023

SALES (est): 87.4K **Privately Held**
SIC: 7372 Prepackaged software

(G-18508)
MY QME INC
1000 Kirk Ave Ste 1000 # 1000 (19806-4633)
PHONE.................................302 218-8730
Bentley Charlemagne, *CEO*
Fred Barnett, *VP*
Tom Bergey, *VP*
EMP: 4 **EST:** 2013
SALES (est): 104.42K **Privately Held**
SIC: 8742 3555 7374 Marketing consulting services; Printing trades machinery; Computer graphics service

(G-18509)
MY RED TEA LLC
4023 Kennett Pike (19807-2018)
PHONE.................................415 259-4166
Robert Koen, *Prin*
EMP: 4 **EST:** 2016
SALES (est): 207.88K **Privately Held**
Web: www.myredtea.com
SIC: 2099 5149 Food preparations, nec; Tea

(G-18510)
MY SALON SUITES
3620 Kirkwood Hwy (19808-5104)
PHONE.................................302 575-9035
EMP: 9 **EST:** 2015
SALES (est): 32.59K **Privately Held**
Web: www.mysalonsuite.com
SIC: 7011 Hotels and motels

(G-18511)
MY WORLD TRAVEL INC
501 Silverside Rd Ste 41 (19809-1388)
PHONE.................................610 358-3744
John M Maiorano, *Pr*
EMP: 10 **EST:** 1981
SALES (est): 971.42K **Privately Held**
Web: www.uniglobredcarpettravel.com
SIC: 4724 Tourist agency arranging transport, lodging and car rental

(G-18512)
MYBITE HOLDINGS LLC ✪
108 W 13th St Ste 100 (19801-1145)
PHONE.................................647 225-1385
Sender Shamiss, *Managing Member*
EMP: 7 **EST:** 2023
SALES (est): 277.92K **Privately Held**
SIC: 7372 Prepackaged software

(G-18513)
MYSTASH INC
Also Called: Mystash
2055 Limestone Rd 200c (19808-5536)
PHONE.................................202 867-8874
Adebowale Oparinu, *Pr*
EMP: 10 **EST:** 2021
SALES (est): 319.94K **Privately Held**
SIC: 7389 Financial services

(G-18514)
N BARTON ASSOC
849 Kiamensi Rd (19804-3449)
PHONE.................................302 575-9882
N Barton, *Ofcr*
EMP: 5 **EST:** 2015
SALES (est): 66.6K **Privately Held**
SIC: 1761 Roofing contractor

(G-18515)
N J JACKSON REALESTATE INV LLC
431 Homestead Rd Ste 2 (19805-6404)
P.O. Box 7810 (19714-7810)
PHONE.................................602 783-4064

Wilmington - New Castle County (G-18516) GEOGRAPHIC SECTION

EMP: 12 **EST:** 2021
SALES (est): 433.95K **Privately Held**
SIC: 7389 Business Activities at Non-Commercial Site

(G-18516)
NA INSTITUTE CHRISTIA
3521 Silverside Rd (19810-4900)
PHONE................................302 478-4020
EMP: 6 **EST:** 2011
SALES (est): 162.35K **Privately Held**
Web: www.chrias.com
SIC: 8733 Noncommercial research organizations

(G-18517)
NAAMANS CREEK WATERSHED
2204 Hillside Rd (19810-4018)
PHONE................................302 475-3037
Maryann Cinaglia, *Pr*
EMP: 7 **EST:** 1997
SALES (est): 508.08K **Privately Held**
Web: www.theardens.com
SIC: 4941 Water supply

(G-18518)
NAB MOTEL INC
Also Called: Fairview Inn
1051 S Market St (19801-5227)
PHONE................................302 656-9431
Bob Patel, *Pr*
Nalini Patel, *Sec*
EMP: 10 **EST:** 1985
SALES (est): 463.98K **Privately Held**
Web: www.fairviewde.com
SIC: 7011 Motel, franchised

(G-18519)
NAGENGAST JANET DAY CARE
602 Ashford Rd (19803-2406)
PHONE................................302 656-6898
Janet Nagengast, *Dir*
EMP: 9 **EST:** 2005
SALES (est): 70.84K **Privately Held**
SIC: 8351 Child day care services

(G-18520)
NAGIN C PATEL
Also Called: Swami Contractor
1716 Lovering Ave (19806-2120)
PHONE................................302 559-4357
Nagin C Patel, *Prin*
EMP: 6 **EST:** 2011
SALES (est): 102.56K **Privately Held**
SIC: 1799 Special trade contractors, nec

(G-18521)
NAIL ART
3234 Kirkwood Hwy Ste B (19808-6156)
PHONE................................302 999-7807
EMP: 5 **EST:** 2009
SALES (est): 21.34K **Privately Held**
SIC: 7231 Manicurist, pedicurist

(G-18522)
NAKED AND THRIVING INC
251 Little Falls Dr (19808-1674)
PHONE................................855 943-0521
EMP: 5 **EST:** 2020
SALES (est): 307.25K **Privately Held**
Web: www.nakedandthriving.com
SIC: 2844 Face creams or lotions

(G-18523)
NAKED FEET KITCHEN LLC (PA) ◊
3200 Kirkwood Hwy 1131 (19806-6153)
PHONE................................404 576-4426
Camille Burney, *Managing Member*
EMP: 6 **EST:** 2023
SALES (est): 77.13K

SALES (corp-wide): 77.13K **Privately Held**
SIC: 1731 Voice, data, and video wiring contractor

(G-18524)
NANAS BUTTER LLC
212 E 35th St (19802-2812)
PHONE................................302 510-3937
EMP: 7 **EST:** 2020
SALES (est): 39.68K **Privately Held**
SIC: 7231 Beauty shops

(G-18525)
NANCY M BALL
Also Called: Nancy M Ball Lcsw
1500 Shallcross Ave Ste 2b (19806-3037)
PHONE................................302 655-8101
EMP: 5 **EST:** 2012
SALES (est): 45.2K **Privately Held**
SIC: 8322 General counseling services

(G-18526)
NANNAS HAINES & SCHIAVO PA
Also Called: Nannas & Schiavo
1407 Foulk Rd Ste 100 (19803-2700)
PHONE................................302 479-8800
Theodore Nannas, *Pr*
Charles A Schiavo, *Sec*
David Haines, *Treas*
EMP: 20 **EST:** 1947
SQ FT: 2,700
SALES (est): 3.66MM **Privately Held**
SIC: 8721 Accounting services, except auditing

(G-18527)
NANO MAGNETICS
2801 Centerville Rd (19808-1609)
PHONE................................888 629-6266
EMP: 5 **EST:** 2016
SALES (est): 216.72K **Privately Held**
SIC: 5065 Electronic parts and equipment, nec

(G-18528)
NANO MAGNETICS USA INC
2801 Centerville Rd (19808-1609)
PHONE................................888 629-6266
Timothy Jing Yin Szeto, *Prin*
EMP: 9 **EST:** 2009
SALES (est): 499.37K **Privately Held**
SIC: 5065 Electronic parts and equipment, nec

(G-18529)
NANO WALLET COMPANY LLC (PA)
1209 N Orange St (19801-1120)
PHONE................................443 610-3402
EMP: 5 **EST:** 2018
SALES (est): 194.82K
SALES (corp-wide): 194.82K **Privately Held**
SIC: 7371 7389 Custom computer programming services; Business services, nec

(G-18530)
NANODROP TECHNOLOGIES LLC
3411 Silverside Rd Ste 100bc (19810-4812)
PHONE................................302 479-7707
Chris Petty, *Mgr*
EMP: 39 **EST:** 2000
SALES (est): 2.42MM
SALES (corp-wide): 44.91B **Publicly Held**
Web: www.thermofisher.com
SIC: 3826 Analytical instruments
PA: Thermo Fisher Scientific Inc.
168 3rd Ave
Waltham MA 02451
781 622-1000

(G-18531)
NANOSHEL LLC
3422 Old Capitol Trl Ste 1305 (19808-6124)
PHONE................................302 268-6163
EMP: 11 **EST:** 2009
SALES (est): 86.23K **Privately Held**
Web: www.nanoshel.com
SIC: 1081 Metal mining services

(G-18532)
NAPIGEN INC
200 Powder Mill Rd (19803-2907)
PHONE................................302 644-5464
Hajime Sakai, *CEO*
Byung Chun Yoo, *Dir*
EMP: 7 **EST:** 2020
SALES (est): 527.67K **Privately Held**
Web: www.napigen.com
SIC: 8731 Biotechnical research, commercial

(G-18533)
NAQEEBI TRANSPORT INC
2528 Jacqueline Dr Apt E43 (19810-2022)
PHONE................................267 246-9321
Akhtar Nawaiz, *Prin*
EMP: 5 **EST:** 2015
SALES (est): 89.02K **Privately Held**
SIC: 4789 Transportation services, nec

(G-18534)
NARISSA BUILDING COMPANY LLC
501 S Broom St (19805-4209)
PHONE................................908 619-6419
Assiran Dass, *VP*
EMP: 9 **EST:** 2014
SALES (est): 490.34K **Privately Held**
Web: www.narissabldgco.com
SIC: 1799 Special trade contractors, nec

(G-18535)
NASH OMNISCAPING LLC
118 Valley Rd (19804-1300)
P.O. Box 40 (19710-0040)
PHONE................................302 654-4000
Michael Nash, *Managing Member*
EMP: 7 **EST:** 2006
SALES (est): 444.53K **Privately Held**
Web: www.omniscaping.com
SIC: 0782 Landscape contractors

(G-18536)
NASHCO ENTERPRISES LTD
3511 Silverside Rd (19810-4902)
PHONE................................403 590-0846
Theresa Stainsby, *Owner*
EMP: 6 **EST:** 2008
SALES (est): 169.01K **Privately Held**
SIC: 8748 Business consulting, nec

(G-18537)
NASON CONSTRUCTION INC
3411 Silverside Rd Ste 200 (19810-4812)
PHONE................................302 529-2510
EMP: 44 **EST:** 2000
SQ FT: 6,500
SALES (est): 22.68MM **Privately Held**
Web: www.nasonconstruction.com
SIC: 1542 1541 Commercial and office building, new construction; Industrial buildings and warehouses

(G-18538)
NATIONAL ALNCE ON MNTAL ILLNES
2400 W 4th St (19805-3306)
PHONE................................302 427-0787
J Thomas-acker, *Ex Dir*
Josh Thomas-acker, *Ex Dir*
EMP: 25 **EST:** 1983

SQ FT: 1,700
SALES (est): 877.87K **Privately Held**
Web: www.namidelaware.org
SIC: 8093 Mental health clinic, outpatient

(G-18539)
NATIONAL CLLGATE RGBY ORGNZTIO
300 Delaware Ave Ste 210 (19801-6601)
PHONE................................603 748-1947
Rafael Zahralddin, *Pr*
Jayme Pendergast, *VP*
Kyle Smith, *Treas*
Brett Akner, *Sec*
Jeremy Treece, *CEO*
EMP: 26 **EST:** 2020
SALES (est): 287.56K **Privately Held**
Web: ncr.rugby
SIC: 7997 Membership sports and recreation clubs

(G-18540)
NATIONAL HOLDING INVESTMENT CO (HQ)
1011 Centre Rd (19805-1267)
PHONE................................302 573-3887
Steve Moores, *Prin*
▲ **EMP:** 68 **EST:** 1979
SALES (est): 8.37MM
SALES (corp-wide): 321.62MM **Publicly Held**
SIC: 6726 Investment offices, nec
PA: National Presto Industries, Inc.
3925 N Hastings Way
Eau Claire WI 54703
715 839-2121

(G-18541)
NATIONAL HOME RENTALS LP
251 Little Falls Dr (19808-1674)
PHONE................................302 636-5401
EMP: 5
SALES (est): 46.16K **Privately Held**
Web: www.nationalhomerentals.com
SIC: 7371 Computer software development and applications

(G-18542)
NATIONAL INCOME TAX SERVICE
2 Vandever Ave (19802-4220)
PHONE................................302 777-1040
EMP: 5 **EST:** 2018
SALES (est): 65.69K **Privately Held**
Web: www.newcastlecountytaxservices.com
SIC: 7291 Tax return preparation services

(G-18543)
NATIONAL INDUSTRIAL LLC
1614 E Ayre St (19804-2515)
PHONE................................302 407-6233
EMP: 7 **EST:** 2016
SALES (est): 148.45K **Privately Held**
Web: www.natindllc.com
SIC: 5085 Industrial supplies

(G-18544)
NATIONAL INDUSTRIES FOR THE BL
3314 Tunison Dr (19810-3230)
PHONE................................302 477-0860
EMP: 5 **EST:** 2017
SALES (est): 84.27K **Privately Held**
SIC: 3999 Manufacturing industries, nec

(G-18545)
NATIONAL METERING SERVICE INC
303 E Ayre St (19804-2510)
PHONE................................302 516-7418
EMP: 8 **EST:** 2015
SALES (est): 108.51K **Privately Held**

Web: www.nmsnj.com
SIC: 5084 Industrial machinery and equipment

(G-18546)
NATIONAL SIGNING SOURCE LLC
1521 Concord Pike Ste 300 (19803-3645)
PHONE..................................773 885-3285
Kristine Castillo, *Prin*
Kim Davis, *Prin*
EMP: 5 EST: 2014
SALES (est): 63.12K **Privately Held**
SIC: 7389

(G-18547)
NATIONAL SOCIETY INC
Also Called: Delaware Soc Rdlgy Profession
1538 Cleland Crse (19805-4517)
PHONE..................................302 656-9572
Carla Lafferty, *Pr*
EMP: 5 EST: 1999
SALES (est): 146.69K **Privately Held**
SIC: 8621 Health association

(G-18548)
NATIONAL STRESS CLINIC LLC
1201 N Orange St Ste 600 (19801-1171)
PHONE..................................646 571-8627
EMP: 7 EST: 2011
SALES (est): 242.87K **Privately Held**
SIC: 8093 Rehabilitation center, outpatient treatment

(G-18549)
NATIONAL TAPE DUPLICATORS
1500 First State Blvd (19804-3564)
PHONE..................................302 999-1110
Bill Burges, *Off Mgr*
EMP: 3 EST: 2001
SALES (est): 110.19K **Privately Held**
Web: www.ken-del.com
SIC: 3695 Optical disks and tape, blank

(G-18550)
NATIONWIDE INSRNCE WSWALL AGCY
Also Called: Nationwide
1035 N Lincoln St Ste 300 (19805-2726)
PHONE..................................302 791-7600
EMP: 5 EST: 2020
SALES (est): 74.34K **Privately Held**
Web: www.wiswall-insurance.com
SIC: 6411 Insurance agents, nec

(G-18551)
NATIONWIDE MUTUAL INSURANCE CO
200 Bellevue Pkwy Ste 250 (19809-3747)
PHONE..................................434 426-9410
EMP: 7 EST: 2018
SALES (est): 161.24K **Privately Held**
Web: www.nationwide.com
SIC: 6411 Insurance agents, nec

(G-18552)
NATIXIS GLOBL ASSET MGT HLDNGS
1209 N Orange St (19801-1120)
PHONE..................................617 449-2100
EMP: 8 EST: 2001
SALES (est): 2.33MM
SALES (corp-wide): 41.09MM **Privately Held**
SIC: 6282 Investment advisory service
HQ: Natixis Investment Managers, Llc
888 Boylston St Ste 800
Boston MA 02199
617 449-2100

(G-18553)
NATURAL HAIR CONSORTIUM LLC ✿
2055 Limestone Rd 200c (19808-5536)
PHONE..................................240 508-1494
Joy Harley Holland, *Managing Member*
EMP: 5 EST: 2022
SALES (est): 113.46K **Privately Held**
SIC: 7231 Unisex hair salons

(G-18554)
NATURAL HEALING TRADITIONS
2321 Fells Ln (19808-2405)
PHONE..................................302 994-6838
Ashley Wienberg, *Prin*
EMP: 6 EST: 1998
SALES (est): 34.87K **Privately Held**
SIC: 8049 Offices of health practitioner

(G-18555)
NATURAL NAIL STUDIO
1707 Marsh Rd (19810-4605)
PHONE..................................302 478-0077
EMP: 6 EST: 2018
SALES (est): 77.51K **Privately Held**
Web: www.naturalnailstudiode.com
SIC: 7231 Manicurist, pedicurist

(G-18556)
NATURALAWN OF AMERICA INC
40 Germay Dr (19804-1105)
PHONE..................................302 652-2000
EMP: 10
SALES (corp-wide): 12.54MM **Privately Held**
Web: www.naturalawn.com
SIC: 0782 Lawn care services
PA: Naturalawn Of America, Inc.
1 E Church St
Frederick MD 21701
301 694-5440

(G-18557)
NATURE IMPACT INC
2055 Limestone Rd Ste 200c (19808-5536)
PHONE..................................650 241-8301
Osman Ugur Kaya, *CEO*
EMP: 6 EST: 2021
SALES (est): 78.16K **Privately Held**
Web: www.nature.org
SIC: 3999 Pet supplies

(G-18558)
NATURES CALL LLC
601 Philadelphia Pike (19809-2549)
PHONE..................................302 777-7767
EMP: 5 EST: 2005
SQ FT: 10,000
SALES (est): 488.67K **Privately Held**
Web: www.naturescalllandscaping.com
SIC: 0781 Landscape architects

(G-18559)
NATURES RULE LLC
1013 Centre Rd Ste 403 (19805-1270)
PHONE..................................518 961-5196
EMP: 9 EST: 2014
SALES (est): 483.48K **Privately Held**
Web: www.naturesrule.com
SIC: 2048 Feed supplements

(G-18560)
NAVA ✿
Also Called: Mj Global
1207 Delaware Ave Ste 347 (19806-4743)
PHONE..................................515 495-4577
Elvin Soe, *Prin*
EMP: 4 EST: 2022
SALES (est): 69.69K **Privately Held**

SIC: 7389 3911 Styling of fashions, apparel, furniture, textiles, etc.; Jewelry apparel

(G-18561)
NAVIENT PRVATE EDCATN LN TR 20
1011 Centre Rd Ste 200 (19805-1266)
PHONE..................................302 636-3300
EMP: 7 EST: 2014
SALES (est): 593.01K **Privately Held**
Web: www.navient.com
SIC: 6111 Student Loan Marketing Association

(G-18562)
NAVIENT SOLUTIONS LLC (HQ)
123 S Justison St Ste 300 (19801-5363)
PHONE..................................703 810-3000
Jon Mello, *COO*
Ameri Christian, *VP*
Chris Lown, *CFO*
EMP: 200 EST: 1972
SQ FT: 200,000
SALES (est): 1.17B
SALES (corp-wide): 3.84B **Publicly Held**
Web: www.navient.com
SIC: 6111 Student Loan Marketing Association
PA: Navient Corporation
13865 Sunrise Valley Dr # 110
Herndon VA 20171
703 810-3000

(G-18563)
NAVIGINE CORPORATION (PA)
1013 Centre Rd Ste 403b (19805-1270)
PHONE..................................339 234-0827
Alexey Panyov, *CEO*
EMP: 8 EST: 2014
SALES (est): 990.39K
SALES (corp-wide): 990.39K **Privately Held**
Web: www.navigine.com
SIC: 7371 Computer software development

(G-18564)
NAVIPOINT HEALTH INC
1209 N Orange St (19801-1120)
PHONE..................................888 902-3998
Dave Utpal, *Prin*
EMP: 6 EST: 2020
SALES (est): 61.22K **Privately Held**
Web: www.navipointhealth.com
SIC: 8099 Health and allied services, nec

(G-18565)
NAVY LEAGUE OF UNITED STATES
2205 Glen Avon Rd (19808-5209)
PHONE..................................302 456-4410
Matthew Mccartney, *Brnch Mgr*
EMP: 6
SALES (corp-wide): 7.84MM **Privately Held**
Web: www.navyleague.org
SIC: 8621 Education and teacher association
PA: Navy League Of The United States
2300 Wilson Blvd Ste 200
Arlington VA 22201
703 528-1775

(G-18566)
NAYACHI INC
2055 Limestone Rd (19808-5536)
PHONE..................................302 400-0072
EMP: 6 EST: 2021
SALES (est): 123.52K **Privately Held**
SIC: 7371 Computer software development and applications

(G-18567)
NE CARE MANAGEMENT SERVICE LLC
3616 Kirkwood Hwy (19808-5124)
PHONE..................................302 501-6449
EMP: 5 EST: 2016
SALES (est): 379.45K **Privately Held**
Web: www.necaremanagementservices.com
SIC: 8741 Management services

(G-18568)
NECESSARY LUXURY
Also Called: Necessary Lxury Mssage Therapy
806 Woodsdale Rd (19809-2245)
PHONE..................................302 764-4032
Susan Rissolo, *Prin*
EMP: 6 EST: 2010
SALES (est): 112.54K **Privately Held**
SIC: 8093 Rehabilitation center, outpatient treatment

(G-18569)
NECTAR LIFESCIENCES USA LLC
508 Main St (19804-3911)
PHONE..................................518 229-8228
EMP: 7 EST: 2014
SALES (est): 464.93K **Privately Held**
Web: www.neclife.com
SIC: 5149 Groceries and related products, nec

(G-18570)
NEHEMIAH GTWY CMNTY DEV CORP
201 W 23rd St (19802-4125)
PHONE..................................302 655-0803
Victor Valentine, *CEO*
Joan Chandler, *Dir*
Carol Davis, *Dir*
EMP: 8 EST: 2000
SALES (est): 504.68K **Privately Held**
Web: www.nehemiahgateway.org
SIC: 8699 8322 Charitable organization; Individual and family services

(G-18571)
NEIGHBORHOOD HOUSE INC (PA)
1218 B St (19801-5898)
PHONE..................................302 658-5404
Alison Windle, *Ex Dir*
Judy Morton, *Sec*
EMP: 13 EST: 1974
SALES (est): 1.21MM
SALES (corp-wide): 1.21MM **Privately Held**
Web: www.neighborhoodhse.org
SIC: 8322 1521 8299 8351 Community center; Single-family housing construction; Tutoring school; Child day care services

(G-18572)
NEIGHBORLY HOME CARE
2101 W 2nd St (19805-3322)
PHONE..................................610 420-1868
Rod Rhen, *Prin*
EMP: 12 EST: 2013
SALES (est): 551.8K **Privately Held**
Web: www.neighborlyhomecare.com
SIC: 8082 Home health care services

(G-18573)
NEIGHBORS TO NICARAGUA INC
2605 Marhill Dr (19810-2403)
PHONE..................................302 362-2642
EMP: 6 EST: 2015
SALES (est): 201K **Privately Held**
Web: www.neighborstonicaragua.com
SIC: 8699 Charitable organization

Wilmington - New Castle County (G-18574) — GEOGRAPHIC SECTION

(G-18574)
NEIL SERVICES INC
1201 N Market St Ste 1100 (19801-1807)
PHONE..................................302 573-2265
EMP: 9 EST: 2018
SALES (est): 222.87K Privately Held
SIC: 7389 Inspection and testing services

(G-18575)
NEILSON ASSOCIATES INC
4023 Kennett Pike Ste 119 (19807-2018)
PHONE..................................610 793-2271
Brenda Nealson Hansen, *Pr*
Sandra Neilson, *Sec*
Arthur Neilson, *VP*
EMP: 10 EST: 1978
SQ FT: 2,500
SALES (est): 624.78K Privately Held
Web: www.neilsonassociates.com
SIC: 8742 Management consulting services

(G-18576)
NEMOURS CHILDRENS HEALTH SYS
2200 Concord Pike Fl 6 (19803-2978)
PHONE..................................610 642-4040
David J Bailey Md, *CEO*
EMP: 18 EST: 2016
SALES (est): 1.16MM Privately Held
Web: www.nemours.org
SIC: 8011 Pediatrician

(G-18577)
NEMOURS ENERGY (PA)
400 W 9th St Ste 200 (19801-1504)
P.O. Box 4488 (19807-0488)
PHONE..................................302 655-4838
J S Dean Junior, *Pt*
EMP: 3 EST: 1984
SALES (est): 1.21MM
SALES (corp-wide): 1.21MM Privately Held
Web: www.nemours.org
SIC: 1311 Crude petroleum production

(G-18578)
NEMOURS FOUNDATION
Also Called: Nemours Ctr For Pdtric Clncal
1600 Rockland Rd (19803-3607)
PHONE..................................302 651-6811
William Higginbotham, *Mgr*
EMP: 40
SALES (corp-wide): 1.94B Privately Held
Web: www.nemours.org
SIC: 8011 Pediatrician
PA: Nemours Foundation
10140 Centurion Pkwy N
Jacksonville FL 32256
904 697-4100

(G-18579)
NEMOURS FOUNDATION
Also Called: Nemours Dpont Pdiatrics Jessup
1602 Jessup St (19802-4210)
PHONE..................................302 576-5050
Hal Byck Md, *Brnch Mgr*
EMP: 11
SALES (corp-wide): 1.94B Privately Held
Web: www.nemours.org
SIC: 8011 Pediatrician
PA: Nemours Foundation
10140 Centurion Pkwy N
Jacksonville FL 32256
904 697-4100

(G-18580)
NEMOURS FOUNDATION
Also Called: Nemours Senior Care Wilmington
1801 Rockland Rd (19803-3648)
PHONE..................................302 651-4400
EMP: 13
SALES (corp-wide): 1.94B Privately Held
Web: www.nemours.org
SIC: 8011 Pediatrician
PA: Nemours Foundation
10140 Centurion Pkwy N
Jacksonville FL 32256
904 697-4100

(G-18581)
NEMOURS FOUNDATION
Alfred I Dpont Hosp For Chldre
1600 Rockland Rd (19803-3607)
P.O. Box 269 (19899-0269)
PHONE..................................302 651-4000
Thomas Ferry Ph.d., *Admn*
EMP: 1800
SALES (corp-wide): 1.94B Privately Held
Web: www.nemours.org
SIC: 8069 8062 Specialty hospitals, except psychiatric; General medical and surgical hospitals
PA: Nemours Foundation
10140 Centurion Pkwy N
Jacksonville FL 32256
904 697-4100

(G-18582)
NEOCOMM DE
2715 N Market St (19802-3611)
PHONE..................................302 762-6678
EMP: 5 EST: 2017
SALES (est): 75.41K Privately Held
SIC: 4812 Cellular telephone services

(G-18583)
NEOFITHUB INC
2810 N Church St (19802-4447)
PHONE..................................408 365-4156
Roman Zakyan, *CEO*
EMP: 10
SALES (est): 348.32K Privately Held
SIC: 7371 Computer software development and applications

(G-18584)
NEPI CONTRACTING INC
709 Cheltenham Rd (19808-1506)
PHONE..................................302 250-6820
Lauren Nepi, *Prin*
EMP: 5 EST: 2011
SALES (est): 63.82K Privately Held
SIC: 1799 Special trade contractors, nec

(G-18585)
NEPTUNE GLOBAL HOLDINGS LLC
717 N Union St Ste 103 (19805-3031)
PHONE..................................302 256-5080
EMP: 6 EST: 2020
SALES (est): 98.64K Privately Held
Web: www.neptuneglobal.com
SIC: 6211 Security brokers and dealers

(G-18586)
NERDIT FOUNDATION
1614 W Newport Pike (19804-3500)
PHONE..................................302 482-5979
Markevis Gideon, *Prin*
Jasmine Morton-thompson, *Prin*
Jabari Jones, *Prin*
EMP: 5 EST: 2018
SALES (est): 199.81K Privately Held
Web: www.nerditcares.org
SIC: 8621 Professional organizations

(G-18587)
NERDIT NOW LLC
3030 Bowers St (19802-2405)
PHONE..................................302 482-5979
Markevis Gideon, *Pr*
EMP: 17 EST: 2015
SALES (est): 2.19MM Privately Held
Web: www.nerditnow.com
SIC: 5999 5734 3577 5084 Mobile telephones and equipment; Computer and software stores; Computer peripheral equipment, nec; Recycling machinery and equipment

(G-18588)
NESTAL MDSPHERE CONSULTING LLC
1201 N Orange St Ste 7209 (19801-1219)
PHONE..................................302 404-6506
EMP: 3 EST: 2019
SALES (est): 118.51K Privately Held
SIC: 8748 5047 5049 3842 Systems analysis and engineering consulting services; Medical and hospital equipment; Professional equipment, nec; Surgical appliances and supplies

(G-18589)
NESTL HOLDINGS INC
1209 N Orange St (19801-1120)
PHONE..................................203 629-7482
Paul Grimwood, *CEO*
Steve Presley, *CFO*
Jonathan Jackman, *Sec*
EMP: 6 EST: 2015
SALES (est): 130.44K Privately Held
SIC: 6799 6719 Investment clubs; Investment holding companies, except banks

(G-18590)
NET 2 APPS LLC
251 Little Falls Dr (19808-1674)
PHONE..................................214 810-2592
Muhammad Boghani, *Managing Member*
EMP: 6
SALES (est): 65.1K Privately Held
SIC: 8999 Services, nec

(G-18591)
NETATMO LLC
1209 N Orange St (19801-1120)
PHONE..................................302 703-7680
EMP: 6 EST: 2011
SALES (est): 77.17K Privately Held
SIC: 5065 5961 Closed circuit TV; Electronic shopping

(G-18592)
NETFOUNDRY INC
251 Little Falls Drive (19808-1674)
PHONE..................................855 284-2007
Galeal Zino, *CEO*
James W Clardy, *
Troy Reynolds, *
EMP: 65 EST: 2019
SALES (est): 10.61MM Privately Held
Web: www.netfoundry.io
SIC: 7371 Computer software development
PA: Tata Communications Limited
Plot No. C21 & C36, G' Block,
Mumbai MH 40009

(G-18593)
NETINSTINCTS INC
501 Silverside Rd Ste 105 (19809-1376)
PHONE..................................302 521-9478
Kiran Chepyala, *CEO*
EMP: 5 EST: 2007
SQ FT: 2,000
SALES (est): 110.28K Privately Held
SIC: 8748 Telecommunications consultant

(G-18594)
NETWERX LLC
69 Westhampton Dr (19808-1355)
P.O. Box 715 (07728-0715)
PHONE..................................732 245-8521
Haisheng Wang, *Pr*
EMP: 5 EST: 2005
SALES (est): 496.71K Privately Held
Web: www.netwerxinc.com
SIC: 8748 Business consulting, nec

(G-18595)
NETWORK CONNECT INC
1200 N French St (19801-3239)
PHONE..................................302 300-1222
Erin Hutt, *CEO*
EMP: 15 EST: 2019
SALES (est): 75K Privately Held
Web: www.networkconnect.org
SIC: 8641 Youth organizations

(G-18596)
NETWORK DESIGN TECHNOLOGIES
Also Called: NDT
1000 N West St Ste 1200 (19801-1058)
P.O. Box 332 (19004-0332)
PHONE..................................610 991-2929
Joseph Ruffin, *CEO*
Joseph D Ruffin Junior, *CEO*
EMP: 20 EST: 2006
SALES (est): 1.8MM Privately Held
Web: www.networkdesigntechnologies.com
SIC: 7379 8742 1731 8748 Computer related consulting services; Management consulting services; Electric power systems contractors; Telecommunications consultant

(G-18597)
NETWORK MAPPING INC
1013 Centre Rd Ste 403a (19805-1270)
PHONE..................................310 560-4142
EMP: 5 EST: 2010
SALES (est): 1.07MM
SALES (corp-wide): 3.68B Publicly Held
SIC: 8711 Engineering services
PA: Trimble Inc.
10368 Westmoor Dr
Westminster CO 80021
720 887-6100

(G-18598)
NETWORK SCRAP METAL CORP (PA)
Also Called: Nsmc
1000 Nw St Ste 1501 (19801-1001)
PHONE..................................702 354-0600
Samuel Miller, *Ch Bd*
Miles Kath, *VP*
EMP: 7 EST: 2013
SALES (est): 1.64MM
SALES (corp-wide): 1.64MM Privately Held
Web: www.networkscrapmetal.com
SIC: 5052 5093 Iron ore; Metal scrap and waste materials

(G-18599)
NEUBERGER & BERMAN TRUST CO
919 N Market St Ste 506 (19801-3065)
PHONE..................................302 658-8522
Albert C Bellas, *Ch Bd*
Stephen Brent Wells, *Pr*
John Mac, *VP*
EMP: 5 EST: 1996
SALES (est): 9.96MM Privately Held
SIC: 6733 Trusts, nec

(G-18600)
NEUBERGER BERMAN TR CO DEL NA
919 N Market St Ste 506 (19801-3065)
PHONE..................................302 830-4340
EMP: 5 EST: 2015
SALES (est): 73K Privately Held

GEOGRAPHIC SECTION
Wilmington - New Castle County

SIC: 6733 Trusts, nec

(G-18601)
NEURACON BIOTECH INC
1313 N Market St Ste 5100 (19801-6111)
PHONE...................813 966-3129
EMP: 5
SALES (est): 339.21K Privately Held
SIC: 2834 Pharmaceutical preparations

(G-18602)
NEURALIGHT INC (PA)
Also Called: Neuralight
1209 N Orange St (19801-1120)
PHONE...................203 615-1333
EMP: 11
SALES (est): 1.75MM
SALES (corp-wide): 1.75MM Privately Held
Web: www.neuralight.ai
SIC: 7371 Computer software development and applications

(G-18603)
NEURO FITNESS THERAPY
3300 Concord Pike Ste 4 (19803-5038)
PHONE...................302 753-2700
EMP: 6 EST: 2017
SALES (est): 87.45K Privately Held
Web: www.neurofitnesstherapy.com
SIC: 7991 Physical fitness facilities

(G-18604)
NEURORX INC
1201 N Market St Ste 111 (19801-1156)
PHONE...................202 340-1352
Jonathan Javitt, CEO
James Lawrence, Dir
Chaim Hurvitz, Dir
Daniel Javitt, Dir
EMP: 10 EST: 2015
SALES (est): 2.36MM Publicly Held
Web: www.nrxpharma.com
SIC: 8731 Biotechnical research, commercial
PA: Nrx Pharmaceuticals, Inc.
1201 N Orange St Ste 600
Wilmington DE 19801
484 254-6134

(G-18605)
NEUWING RENEWABLE ENERGY LLC
913 N Market St Ste 1001 (19801-4927)
PHONE...................267 319-1144
Chad Gottesman, Prin
EMP: 6 EST: 2016
SALES (est): 109.55K Privately Held
Web: www.neuwingenergy.com
SIC: 1711 Plumbing, heating, air-conditioning

(G-18606)
NEVRON SOFTWARE LLC
501 Silverside Rd Ste 105 (19809-1376)
PHONE...................855 370-5511
▼ EMP: 10 EST: 2007
SQ FT: 150
SALES (est): 512.45K Privately Held
Web: www.nevron.com
SIC: 7372 Prepackaged software

(G-18607)
NEW B & M MEATS INC
21 Commerce St (19801-5425)
P.O. Box 491 (19899-0491)
PHONE...................302 655-5331
Yossi Baruch, Pr
EMP: 16 EST: 2016
SALES (est): 1.05MM Privately Held
SIC: 2013 2015 Prepared beef products, from purchased beef; Chicken, processed: frozen

(G-18608)
NEW CASTLE CNTY BD OF REALTORS
Also Called: NEW CASTLE COUNTY BOARD OF REA
3615 Miller Rd (19802-2523)
PHONE...................302 762-4800
Susan Helm, Ex VP
EMP: 7 EST: 1924
SALES (est): 1.06MM Privately Held
Web: www.nccbor.com
SIC: 6531 Real estate brokers and agents

(G-18609)
NEW CASTLE HOT MIX INC
Also Called: Minquadale Plant
925 S Heald St (19801-5732)
PHONE...................302 655-2119
EMP: 5 EST: 1997
SALES (est): 547.47K
SALES (corp-wide): 6.84MM Privately Held
SIC: 1771 Blacktop (asphalt) work
PA: Bear Materials Llc
4048 New Castle Ave
New Castle DE 19720
302 658-5241

(G-18610)
NEW CINGULAR WIRELESS SVCS INC
Also Called: AT&T Wireless
3401 Kirkwood Hwy (19808-6133)
PHONE...................302 999-0055
Mai Storey, Brnch Mgr
EMP: 10
SALES (corp-wide): 120.74B Publicly Held
SIC: 4812 Cellular telephone services
HQ: New Cingular Wireless Services, Inc.
7277 164th Ave Ne
Redmond WA 98052
425 827-4500

(G-18611)
NEW CNDLELIGHT PRODUCTIONS INC
2208 Millers Rd (19810-4000)
PHONE...................302 475-2313
Maureen T Cotellese, Mgr
EMP: 11 EST: 2009
SALES (est): 1.38MM Privately Held
Web: www.candlelighttheatredelaware.org
SIC: 7822 Motion picture and tape distribution

(G-18612)
NEW COLONY NORTH ENTERPRISES
319 E Lea Blvd (19802-2353)
PHONE...................302 762-0405
Ralph Paul, Owner
Douglas Paul, Off Mgr
EMP: 8 EST: 1967
SALES (est): 613.26K Privately Held
SIC: 6513 Apartment building operators

(G-18613)
NEW CONCEPT DENTAL
2004 Foulk Rd Ste 1 (19810-3641)
PHONE...................302 778-3822
Kristie Kaufman, Mgr
EMP: 5 EST: 2002
SALES (est): 471.76K Privately Held
Web: www.newconceptdental.com
SIC: 8021 Dental clinic

(G-18614)
NEW CONCEPT TECHNOLOGIES LLC
3422 Old Capitol Trl Ste 948 (19808-6124)
PHONE...................518 533-5367
EMP: 8 EST: 2013
SALES (est): 118.8K Privately Held
Web: www.newconcepttechnologies.com
SIC: 7371 4813 Computer software development and applications; Online service providers

(G-18615)
NEW CSTLE CNTY CHLD HSE MNTSSO
Also Called: CHILDREN'S HOUSE MONTESSORI SC
2848 Grubb Rd (19810-2353)
PHONE...................302 529-9259
Cathy L Cooling, CEO
Bill Deely, Pr
EMP: 19 EST: 1975
SQ FT: 5,700
SALES (est): 1.44MM Privately Held
Web: www.childrenshouse-de.org
SIC: 8351 Montessori child development center

(G-18616)
NEW CSTLE CNTY CHMBER COMMERCE
920 Justison St (19801-5150)
PHONE...................302 737-4343
Ron Walker, Pr
EMP: 22 EST: 1922
SQ FT: 5,000
SALES (est): 1.17MM Privately Held
Web: www.ncccc.com
SIC: 8611 Chamber of Commerce

(G-18617)
NEW DAY MONTESSORI
1 Middleton Dr (19808-4320)
PHONE...................302 235-2554
Kim Mccolgan, Dir
EMP: 10 EST: 2006
SALES (est): 223.75K Privately Held
SIC: 8351 Montessori child development center

(G-18618)
NEW HOPE FAMILY MEDICINE LLC
4515 Griffin Dr (19808-4254)
PHONE...................302 388-9304
EMP: 7 EST: 2017
SALES (est): 246.22K Privately Held
Web: www.nhfm.org
SIC: 8099 Health and allied services, nec

(G-18619)
NEW HOPE VEHICLE EXPORTS LLC
1000 S Market St (19801-5244)
PHONE...................302 275-6482
EMP: 6 EST: 2012
SALES (est): 480.35K Privately Held
SIC: 4731 4412 Freight forwarding; Deep sea foreign transportation of freight

(G-18620)
NEW LIFE FURNITURE SYSTEMS
1675 E Ayre St (19804-2514)
PHONE...................302 994-9054
Scott Alexander, Owner
EMP: 8 EST: 2001
SALES (est): 246.87K Privately Held
Web: www.newlifefurnituresystems.com
SIC: 7641 Furniture refinishing

(G-18621)
NEW LIFE INTL CMNTY DEV CORP
2207 Concord Pike (19803-2908)
PHONE...................302 529-1997
EMP: 7 EST: 2007
SALES (est): 198.57K Privately Held
Web: www.newlifeinternationalcdc.com
SIC: 8399 Advocacy group

(G-18622)
NEW LOOK HOME INC
100 Bestfield Rd (19804-2722)
PHONE...................302 994-4397
George L Callahan, Pr
EMP: 2 EST: 2009
SALES (est): 84.81K Privately Held
SIC: 2431 Millwork

(G-18623)
NEW ORLEANS HOTEL EQUITY LLC
1000 N West St Ste 1400 (19801-1054)
PHONE...................302 757-7300
EMP: 8 EST: 2017
SALES (est): 375.87K Privately Held
SIC: 7011 Hotels

(G-18624)
NEW PENDULUM CORPORATION (PA)
1100 N Market St Fl 4 (19890-1100)
PHONE...................302 478-6160
Bernard E Stapelfeld, Ch Bd
Constance A Penn, Sec
EMP: 11 EST: 1983
SALES (est): 23.53MM
SALES (corp-wide): 23.53MM Privately Held
Web: www.newpendulumcorp.com
SIC: 2842 Polishes and sanitation goods

(G-18625)
NEW PERSPECTIVES INC
2055 Limestone Rd Ste 109 (19808-5536)
PHONE...................302 489-0220
Dennis Karridan, Pr
EMP: 7 EST: 1996
SALES (est): 493.16K Privately Held
Web: www.newperspectivesinc.com
SIC: 8999 8049 Psychological consultant; Clinical psychologist

(G-18626)
NEW TREND HAIR SALON
4569 Kirkwood Hwy (19808-5117)
PHONE...................302 998-3331
Mike Keaten, Prin
EMP: 5 EST: 2008
SALES (est): 288.97K Privately Held
Web: www.newtrendhairsalon.com
SIC: 7231 Hairdressers

(G-18627)
NEW U NUTRITION INC
2801 Lancaster Ave (19805-5232)
PHONE...................302 543-4555
Romeo Riley, Prin
EMP: 5 EST: 2011
SALES (est): 190.54K Privately Held
Web: www.newunutritionclub.com
SIC: 8099 Nutrition services

(G-18628)
NEW WNDSOR APARTMENTS ASSOC LP
Also Called: Windsor Apartments
500 N Walnut St Ste 1 (19801-3801)
PHONE...................302 656-1354
William Demarco, Dir
Kevin Kelly, Pt
Mike Stahler, Contrlr

Wilmington - New Castle County (G-18629)

EMP: 5 EST: 1984
SALES (est): 725.49K Privately Held
SIC: 6513 Apartment building operators

(G-18629)
NEW YORK BLOOD CTR INC D/B/A B
Also Called: NEW YORK BLOOD CENTER, INC. D/B/A BLOOD BANK OF DELMARVA
913 N Market St Ste 905 (19801-4926)
PHONE..................................302 737-8400
Helen Graham, Dir
EMP: 8
SALES (corp-wide): 29.61MM Privately Held
Web: www.delmarvablood.org
SIC: 8099 Blood bank
PA: New York Blood Center, Inc.
100 Hygeia Dr
Newark DE 19713
302 737-8405

(G-18630)
NEWARC WELDING & FABRICATING
30 Commerce St (19801-5426)
PHONE..................................302 658-5214
Bruce Blair, Pr
Tracy Blair, Stockholder
EMP: 9 EST: 1949
SQ FT: 22,000
SALES (est): 1.01MM Privately Held
Web: www.newarcwelding.com
SIC: 3441 Fabricated structural metal

(G-18631)
NEWPORT
22 W Market St (19804-3139)
PHONE..................................302 995-2840
Richars Wojcik, Prin
EMP: 17 EST: 2015
SALES (est): 178.4K Privately Held
Web: newport.delaware.gov
SIC: 3648 Lighting equipment, nec

(G-18632)
NEWPORT BUILDERS & WINDOWLAND
2 E Ayre St (19804-2537)
PHONE..................................302 994-3537
Marshall Lombardi Junior, Pr
Judy Lombardi, VP
EMP: 13 EST: 1963
SQ FT: 15,000
SALES (est): 439.34K Privately Held
Web: www.newportbuildersde.com
SIC: 5211 1751 1799 Windows, storm: wood or metal; Window and door installation and erection; Screening contractor: window, door, etc.

(G-18633)
NEWSPAPER ARCHIVE INC
4023 Kennett Pike # 50005 (19807-2018)
PHONE..................................612 590-3401
Greg Garnier, Prin
EMP: 50 EST: 1994
SALES (est): 1.39MM Privately Held
Web: www.newspaperarchive.com
SIC: 2741 Miscellaneous publishing

(G-18634)
NEXT GNRATION LRNG ACADEMY LLC
4011 N Market St (19802-2219)
PHONE..................................302 691-5223
Rhonda Charles, Managing Member
EMP: 7 EST: 2021
SALES (est): 15.97K Privately Held
SIC: 8351 Preschool center

(G-18635)
NEXT TRUCKING INC
1209 N Orange St (19801-1120)
PHONE..................................213 568-0388
Hanbing Yan, Pr
Kwong Chi Chung, Stockholder
EMP: 50 EST: 2016
SALES (est): 1.84MM Privately Held
Web: www.nexttrucking.com
SIC: 4213 Trucking, except local

(G-18636)
NEXTEL COMMUNICATIONS INC
Also Called: Nextel
3200 Kirkwood Hwy (19808-6153)
PHONE..................................302 633-4330
Thomas Dezielak, Mgr
EMP: 7
SALES (corp-wide): 78.56B Publicly Held
Web: www.sprint.com
SIC: 4812 Cellular telephone services
HQ: Nextel Communications, Inc.
12502 Sunrise Valley Dr
Reston VA 20191
833 639-8353

(G-18637)
NEXTEL COMMUNICATIONS INC
Also Called: Nextel
32 Germay Dr (19804-1118)
PHONE..................................302 652-1301
EMP: 7
SALES (corp-wide): 78.56B Publicly Held
Web: www.sprint.com
SIC: 4812 Cellular telephone services
HQ: Nextel Communications, Inc.
12502 Sunrise Valley Dr
Reston VA 20191
833 639-8353

(G-18638)
NEXUS SERVICES AMERICA LLC (PA)
2711 Centerville Rd Ste 400 (19808-1660)
PHONE..................................800 946-4626
EMP: 5 EST: 2012
SALES (est): 2.45MM
SALES (corp-wide): 2.45MM Privately Held
SIC: 4789 Space flight operations, except government

(G-18639)
NFINITY INC ✪
1013 Centre Rd Ste 403s (19805-1270)
PHONE..................................852 642-9800
EMP: 10 EST: 2022
SALES (est): 426.86K Privately Held
SIC: 6099 7389 Foreign currency exchange; Business Activities at Non-Commercial Site

(G-18640)
NGK NORTH AMERICA INC (HQ)
1105 N Market St Ste 1300 (19801-1241)
P.O. Box 8985 (19899-8985)
PHONE..................................302 654-1344
Susumu Sakabe, Pr
◆ EMP: 8 EST: 1986
SALES (est): 221.76MM Privately Held
SIC: 3714 5013 3264 5063 Motor vehicle parts and accessories; Automotive supplies and parts; Insulators, electrical: porcelain; Insulators, electrical
PA: Ngk Insulators, Ltd.
2-56, Sudacho, Mizuho-Ku
Nagoya AIC 467-0

(G-18641)
NICE VISION LLC
18 W 41st St (19802-2208)
PHONE..................................267 259-8705
Daryus Gipson, Prin
EMP: 7 EST: 2017
SALES (est): 53.51K Privately Held
SIC: 8042 Offices and clinics of optometrists

(G-18642)
NICHINO AMERICA INC
4550 Linden Hill Rd Ste 501 (19808-2951)
PHONE..................................302 636-9001
Jeffrey Johnson, Pr
Francis Winslow, *
▲ EMP: 54 EST: 1997
SQ FT: 11,000
SALES (est): 11.74MM Privately Held
Web: www.nichino.net
SIC: 8731 Agricultural research
HQ: Nihon Nohyaku Co., Ltd.
1-19-8, Kyobashi
Chuo-Ku TKY 104-0

(G-18643)
NICKLE INSURANCE
Also Called: Nationwide
3920 Kennett Pike (19807-2304)
PHONE..................................302 654-0347
Henry Nickle, Owner
EMP: 8 EST: 1960
SALES (est): 482.48K Privately Held
Web: www.nationwide.com
SIC: 6411 Insurance agents, nec

(G-18644)
NICKS WELDING REPAIR LLC
3705 Oak Ridge Rd (19808-1338)
PHONE..................................302 545-1494
Nicholas Pisklak, Prin
Camila Pisklak, Prin
Stephen Pisklak, Prin
EMP: 3 EST: 2017
SALES (est): 62.91K Privately Held
SIC: 7692 Welding repair

(G-18645)
NICOLE SESTITO PHD
500 River Rd (19809-2733)
PHONE..................................610 465-7312
Nicole Sestito, Pr
EMP: 6 EST: 2018
SALES (est): 29.52K Privately Held
SIC: 8049 Clinical psychologist

(G-18646)
NICOLE SMITH
530 Harlan Blvd Unit N817 (19801-5168)
PHONE..................................302 383-8233
Nicole R Smith Lpcmh, Owner
EMP: 8 EST: 2014
SALES (est): 67.33K Privately Held
SIC: 8011 Offices and clinics of medical doctors

(G-18647)
NIEBEX INTERNATIONAL INC
24a Trolley Sq (19806-3334)
PHONE..................................415 735-4718
Michael Cox, Pr
EMP: 12
SALES (est): 406.37K Privately Held
SIC: 7371 Software programming applications

(G-18648)
NIGHTHAWK AIRCRAFT LLC ✪
704 N King St Ste 500 (19801-3584)
P.O. Box 1031 (19899-1031)
PHONE..................................703 994-0523
Andrew Schaaf, Managing Member
EMP: 8 EST: 2022
SALES (est): 531.76K Privately Held
SIC: 3728 Aircraft body assemblies and parts

(G-18649)
NIKANG THERAPEUTICS INC
200 Powder Mill Rd Bldg E500 (19803-2907)
PHONE..................................302 415-5127
Zhenhai Gao, Pr
Zhenhai Gao, Pr
Ally Cha, Operations*
Kelsey Chen, *
Joanne Lager, Chief Medical Officer*
EMP: 29 EST: 2017
SALES (est): 2.45MM Privately Held
Web: www.nikangtx.com
SIC: 8731 2834 Industrial laboratory, except testing; Pharmaceutical preparations

(G-18650)
NITERRA (USA) HOLDING INC (HQ)
1011 Centre Rd Ste 322 (19805-1266)
PHONE..................................302 288-0131
Shin Odo, Pr
◆ EMP: 174 EST: 1995
SALES (est): 117.63MM Privately Held
SIC: 3643 3264 Current-carrying wiring services; Porcelain parts for electrical devices, molded
PA: Niterra Co., Ltd.
1-1-1, Higashisakura, Higashi-Ku
Nagoya AIC 461-0

(G-18651)
NITRILITY INC
2055 Limestone Rd (19808-5536)
PHONE..................................848 702-6091
Avi Patel, CEO
EMP: 14
SALES (est): 481.04K Privately Held
SIC: 7371 Computer software development and applications

(G-18652)
NITRO IMPACT INC
3422 Old Capitol Trl # 68 (19808-6124)
PHONE..................................347 694-7000
Mark Louie Apao, Ch Bd
Louis Uretsky, Cnslt
EMP: 10 EST: 2013
SALES (est): 569.83K Privately Held
Web: www.nitroofficesupplies.com
SIC: 5112 Stationery and office supplies

(G-18653)
NIXOPE INC
2810 N Church St (19802-4447)
PHONE..................................888 991-1606
Assem Afify, CEO
EMP: 5
SALES (est): 199.4K Privately Held
SIC: 7371 Computer software development and applications

(G-18654)
NJL PRODUCTIONS
11 Stoney Run Rd (19809-2036)
PHONE..................................302 898-9187
Michele Cetola, Prin
EMP: 5 EST: 2011
SALES (est): 50.95K Privately Held
SIC: 7822 Motion picture and tape distribution

(G-18655)
NKOTB LLC
1314 N King St (19801-3220)
P.O. Box 15203 (19850-5203)
PHONE..................................302 286-5243
Donald Wahlberg, Managing Member
EMP: 5 EST: 2010

SALES (est): 107.29K **Privately Held**
Web: www.nkotb.com
SIC: 7929 Entertainers and entertainment groups

(G-18656)
NLS MACHINERY INC
1201 N Market St (19801-1156)
PHONE..................................302 416-3077
Emad Iprahim, *Mgr*
EMP: 5 EST: 2017
SALES (est): 26.07K **Privately Held**
Web: www.nlsmachineryinc.com
SIC: 7699 Industrial machinery and equipment repair

(G-18657)
NM CONSTRUCTION INC
125 Florence Ave (19803-2337)
PHONE..................................302 478-6494
Celestino Mainardi, *Prin*
EMP: 5 EST: 2005
SALES (est): 150K **Privately Held**
SIC: 1521 Single-family housing construction

(G-18658)
NNN 824 NORTH MARKET ST LLC
824 Market St Ste 111 (19801-3024)
PHONE..................................302 652-8013
Anthony W Thompson, *CEO*
EMP: 5 EST: 1998
SALES (est): 216K **Privately Held**
SIC: 6531 Real estate agent, commercial

(G-18659)
NO 3 ELINE PWERS FGURE SALONS
100 W 10th St (19801-6603)
PHONE..................................302 256-5015
B J Consono, *Prin*
EMP: 5 EST: 2010
SALES (est): 62.22K **Privately Held**
SIC: 7231 Beauty shops

(G-18660)
NO EVI-DENTS INC
2118 Jackson Ave (19808-5818)
PHONE..................................302 363-7788
Steve Camperson, *Prin*
EMP: 5 EST: 2016
SALES (est): 68.77K **Privately Held**
Web: www.noevi-dents.com
SIC: 7532 Body shop, automotive

(G-18661)
NO MORE SCRETS-MIND BDY SPIRIT
9 Mullin Rd (19809-1875)
PHONE..................................215 485-7881
EMP: 6 EST: 2018
SALES (est): 59.77K **Privately Held**
Web: www.nomoresecretsmbs.org
SIC: 7829 Motion picture distribution services

(G-18662)
NOCHE AZUL SPA
1733 Marsh Rd (19810-4607)
PHONE..................................302 345-0070
Elizabeth Martin, *Prin*
EMP: 5 EST: 2015
SALES (est): 123.22K **Privately Held**
Web: www.nocheazulspa.com
SIC: 7231 Cosmetology and personal hygiene salons

(G-18663)
NOLE-SEC INC
1007 N Orange St (19801-1239)
PHONE..................................561 693-9934
Dvir Salomon, *CEO*
EMP: 12 EST: 2020
SALES (est): 449.63K **Privately Held**
SIC: 7371 Software programming applications

(G-18664)
NOLTE & BRODOWAY PA
1013 Centre Rd (19805-1265)
PHONE..................................302 777-1700
Stokes Nolte, *Pt*
Barbara Brodoway, *Pt*
EMP: 6 EST: 1995
SALES (est): 488.81K **Privately Held**
Web: www.rmh-law.com
SIC: 8111 General practice attorney, lawyer

(G-18665)
NOMADIC CAPITAL LLC
2055 Limestone Rd Ste 200c (19808-5536)
PHONE..................................650 441-5796
EMP: 5
SALES (est): 107.01K **Privately Held**
SIC: 7371 Software programming applications

(G-18666)
NOMOD LLC
Also Called: Nomod
4023 Kennett Pike Ste 50181 (19807-2018)
PHONE..................................917 480-7432
Omar Kassim, *CEO*
EMP: 5 EST: 2014
SALES (est): 46.16K **Privately Held**
SIC: 7371 Computer software development and applications

(G-18667)
NON STOP TOWING LLC
199 Philadelphia Pike (19809-3161)
PHONE..................................302 647-1399
EMP: 11
SALES (est): 317.48K **Privately Held**
SIC: 7549 Towing services

(G-18668)
NONPROFIT BUS SOLUTIONS LLC
2701 Centerville Rd (19808-1607)
PHONE..................................302 353-4606
EMP: 13 EST: 2007
SQ FT: 2,300
SALES (est): 1.69MM **Privately Held**
Web: www.consultnbs.com
SIC: 8621 Professional organizations

(G-18669)
NOONY MEDIA LLC
1201 N Orange St Ste 600 (19801-1171)
PHONE..................................856 834-0074
EMP: 10 EST: 2019
SALES (est): 410.12K **Privately Held**
Web: www.noony.us
SIC: 7319 Media buying service

(G-18670)
NORAMCO INC (PA)
500 Swedes Landing Rd (19801-4596)
P.O. Box 41372 (93384-1372)
PHONE..................................302 652-3840
Matthew Martin, *CEO*
EMP: 5 EST: 2016
SALES (est): 2.51MM **Privately Held**
Web: www.noramco.com
SIC: 2834 Pharmaceutical preparations

(G-18671)
NORAMCO LLC
500 Swedes Landing Rd (19801-4596)
PHONE..................................302 761-2923
Allen Majewski, *Managing Member*
EMP: 50
Web: www.noramco.com
SIC: 2834 Pharmaceutical preparations
HQ: Noramco, Llc
1550 Olympic Dr
Athens GA 30601
706 286-8247

(G-18672)
NORAMCO OF DELAWARE INC
500 Swedes Landing Rd (19801-4596)
PHONE..................................302 761-2900
EMP: 175 EST: 1981
SALES (est): 18.09MM **Privately Held**
Web: www.noramco.com
SIC: 5169 Industrial chemicals

(G-18673)
NORDIC PROJEKT CO
2055 Limestone Rd Ste 200c (19808-5536)
PHONE..................................302 208-7296
Andreas Roxe, *CEO*
Ingrid Fawcett, *Dir*
EMP: 3 EST: 2021
SALES (est): 121.77K **Privately Held**
Web: www.nordicprojekt.com
SIC: 3851 Eyeglasses, lenses and frames

(G-18674)
NORMOPHARM INC
1000 N West St Ste 1200 (19801-1058)
PHONE..................................954 210-4812
Viacheslav Rastashanskiy, *CEO*
EMP: 9
SALES (est): 631.87K **Privately Held**
SIC: 5122 Vitamins and minerals

(G-18675)
NORTAL LLC
5301 Limestone Rd Ste 100 (19808-1251)
PHONE..................................425 233-0164
EMP: 6 EST: 2019
SALES (est): 127.99K **Privately Held**
Web: www.nortal.com
SIC: 7371 Computer software development

(G-18676)
NORTH AMERICAN BRANDS INC
501 Silverside Rd (19809-1374)
PHONE..................................519 680-0385
Michael Crowley, *CEO*
Devon Park, *
▲ EMP: 28 EST: 2016
SQ FT: 5,000
SALES (est): 8.69MM
SALES (corp-wide): 6.26MM **Privately Held**
SIC: 3699 Electrical equipment and supplies, nec
PA: North American Brands Inc
3 Buchanan Crt
London ON N5Z 4
519 680-1550

(G-18677)
NORTH AMERICAN HARDWOODS LTD
2711 Centerville Rd (19808-1660)
PHONE..................................516 848-7729
EMP: 7 EST: 2010
SALES (est): 326.93K **Privately Held**
SIC: 5031 Pallets, wood

(G-18678)
NORTH AMERICAN SPINE AND PAIN
1600 Pennsylvania Ave (19806-4047)
PHONE..................................302 482-3637
EMP: 9 EST: 2015
SALES (est): 200.04K **Privately Held**
Web: www.naspacmd.com
SIC: 8041 Offices and clinics of chiropractors

(G-18679)
NORTH EAST OPEN MRI INC
6 W Clivden Dr (19807-2538)
PHONE..................................610 259-3200
EMP: 8 EST: 2019
SALES (est): 855.16K **Privately Held**
SIC: 8011 Radiologist

(G-18680)
NORTH HILLS CLEANERS INC
1601 Brandywine Blvd (19809-3198)
PHONE..................................302 764-1234
Mark Peters, *Pr*
Amy L Peters, *VP*
EMP: 7 EST: 1947
SALES (est): 240.15K **Privately Held**
Web: www.northhillscleaners.com
SIC: 7216 7219 Cleaning and dyeing, except rugs; Laundry, except power and coin-operated

(G-18681)
NORTH WILMINGTON WOMENS CENTER
2002 Foulk Rd Ste A (19810-3643)
PHONE..................................302 529-7900
James Cosgrove, *Prin*
EMP: 6 EST: 2000
SALES (est): 303.47K **Privately Held**
SIC: 8062 General medical and surgical hospitals

(G-18682)
NORTHEAST MISSOURI WIND LLC
251 Little Falls Dr (19808-1674)
PHONE..................................647 352-9533
EMP: 6 EST: 2020
SALES (est): 142.06K **Privately Held**
SIC: 1796 Power generating equipment installation

(G-18683)
NORTHEAST TREATMENT CTRS INC
Also Called: Kirkwood Detox
3315 Kirkwood Hwy (19808-6131)
PHONE..................................302 691-0140
Mark Kraus, *Brnch Mgr*
EMP: 94
SALES (corp-wide): 43.64MM **Privately Held**
Web: www.netcenters.org
SIC: 8093 Mental health clinic, outpatient
PA: Northeast Treatment Centers, Inc.
499 N 5th St Ste A
Philadelphia PA 19123
215 451-7000

(G-18684)
NORTHERN CROSS INVESTMENTS
919 N Market St (19801-3023)
PHONE..................................302 655-9074
Kim Frank, *Prin*
EMP: 5 EST: 2001
SALES (est): 142.01K **Privately Held**
SIC: 6282 Investment advisory service

(G-18685)
NORTHERN ROOF TILES US INC
4023 Kennett Pike Ste 856 (19807-2018)
PHONE..................................888 678-6866
Stuart Matthews, *CEO*
Adam Matthews, *Managing Member*
▲ EMP: 2 EST: 1991
SALES (est): 146.67K **Privately Held**
Web: www.northernrooftiles.com
SIC: 3259 Roofing tile, clay

Wilmington - New Castle County (G-18686)

GEOGRAPHIC SECTION

(G-18686)
NORTHERNSIGS MFG LLC
809 Taylor St (19801-4335)
PHONE...........................302 383-9270
EMP: 4 EST: 2018
SALES (est): 59.77K **Privately Held**
SIC: 3999 Manufacturing industries, nec

(G-18687)
NORTHPOINT ENGRG SVCS LLC
102 Robino Ct Ste 203 (19804-2360)
PHONE...........................302 994-3907
EMP: 9 EST: 2008
SALES (est): 277.75K **Privately Held**
SIC: 8711 Civil engineering

(G-18688)
NORTHSTERN COATING SYSTEMS INC
140 Belmont Dr (19808-4329)
PHONE...........................302 328-6545
Vincent Falconi, Prin
EMP: 5 EST: 2011
SALES (est): 383.7K **Privately Held**
SIC: 1752 Wood floor installation and refinishing

(G-18689)
NORTHWESTERN HUMAN SERVICES
211 Harding Ave (19804-3305)
PHONE...........................302 996-4858
EMP: 7 EST: 2014
SALES (est): 82.8K **Privately Held**
SIC: 8093 Mental health clinic, outpatient

(G-18690)
NOTARY LTD
4419 Sandy Dr (19808-5636)
PHONE...........................302 635-1176
Patty Nieves, Prin
EMP: 5 EST: 2015
SALES (est): 108.45K **Privately Held**
Web: www.notaryofficial.com
SIC: 7389 Notary publics

(G-18691)
NOVACARE REHABILITATION
2401 Pennsylvania Ave Ste 112 (19806-1432)
PHONE...........................302 655-5877
EMP: 13 EST: 2011
SALES (est): 54.13K **Privately Held**
Web: www.novacare.com
SIC: 8049 Physical therapist

(G-18692)
NOVAEO LLC
4023 Kennett Pike Ste 58235 (19807-2018)
PHONE...........................832 643-2153
EMP: 20 EST: 2016
SALES (est): 1.16MM **Privately Held**
Web: www.novaeo.co
SIC: 2834 Vitamin, nutrient, and hematinic preparations for human use

(G-18693)
NOVAK DRUCE CNNLLY BV+QIGG LLP (PA)
1007 N Orange St Ste 800 (19801-1239)
PHONE...........................302 252-9922
Rudolph E Hutz, Pt
Rudolf Hutz, Pt
Frank Stransky, CFO
Jeffrey Bove, Pt
Hutz R Eric, Pt
EMP: 130 EST: 1940
SQ FT: 100,000
SALES (est): 11.23MM
SALES (corp-wide): 11.23MM **Privately Held**
Web: www.connollygallagher.com
SIC: 8111 General practice attorney, lawyer

(G-18694)
NOVARTIS CORPORATION
205 S James St (19804-2424)
PHONE...........................302 992-5610
Phil King, Mgr
EMP: 4
Web: www.novartis.com
SIC: 2834 Pharmaceutical preparations
HQ: Novartis Corporation
1 Health Plz
East Hanover NJ 07936
212 307-1122

(G-18695)
NOVASEP LLC
200 Powder Mill Rd (19803-2907)
PHONE...........................610 494-2052
Andrew Brennan, CEO
▲ EMP: 23 EST: 1997
SALES (est): 12.65MM
SALES (corp-wide): 1.24MM **Privately Held**
Web: www.axplora.com
SIC: 8731 Biological research
HQ: Novasep Process
Site Eiffel
Pompey 54340

(G-18696)
NOVIN LLC
919 N Market St Ste 425 (19801-3014)
PHONE...........................315 670-7979
Agshin Rzayev, Pr
EMP: 5 EST: 2016
SALES (est): 914.91K **Privately Held**
Web: www.novin.ltd
SIC: 6799 Commodity contract trading companies

(G-18697)
NOVITEX INTERMEDIATE LLC
251 Little Falls Dr (19808-1674)
PHONE...........................302 278-0867
Robert Rooney, Ex VP
Theresa Mohan, *
EMP: 711 EST: 2013
SALES (est): 57MM
SALES (corp-wide): 1.08B **Publicly Held**
SIC: 8748 Business consulting, nec
HQ: Novitex Holdings, Inc.
300 Stamford Pl Ste 200
Stamford CT 06902
203 487-5300

(G-18698)
NOVLT LLC ✪
2810 N Church St Pmb 226551 (19802-4447)
PHONE...........................925 332-6379
Madeline Calvert, Managing Member
EMP: 3 EST: 2023
SALES (est): 128.34K **Privately Held**
SIC: 7372 Prepackaged software

(G-18699)
NOVO INSURANCE LLC
1209 N Orange St (19801-1120)
PHONE...........................408 245-3800
Steve Debenham, Mgr
EMP: 13
SALES (est): 573.33K **Privately Held**
Web: www.novo.us
SIC: 6411 Insurance brokers, nec

(G-18700)
NOVO NORDISK PHARMACEUTICALS
107 Duncan Ave (19803-2317)
PHONE...........................302 345-0229
EMP: 7 EST: 2017
SALES (est): 81.88K **Privately Held**
SIC: 2834 Pharmaceutical preparations

(G-18701)
NOVO NRDISK US COML HLDNGS INC
103 Foulk Rd Ste 282 (19803-3742)
PHONE...........................302 691-6181
Ulrich Otte, Pr
Ulrich Otte, Pr
Craig Bleifer, Sec
EMP: 99 EST: 2019
SALES (est): 385.44K
SALES (corp-wide): 24.71B **Privately Held**
SIC: 2834 Pharmaceutical preparations
HQ: Novo Nordisk Us Holdings, Inc.
103 Foulk Rd Ste 282
Wilmington DE 19803
302 691-6181

(G-18702)
NOVOQUAD INC
2711 Centerville Rd # 120 (19808-1660)
P.O. Box 478 (08840-0478)
PHONE...........................800 916-6486
Donald Hines, Pr
Wei Xiang, Pr
EMP: 10 EST: 2009
SALES (est): 181.86K **Privately Held**
SIC: 7382 Security systems services

(G-18703)
NOWCARE LLC (PA)
1010 Concord Ave (19802-3367)
PHONE...........................302 777-5551
EMP: 5 EST: 2011
SALES (est): 426.04K
SALES (corp-wide): 426.04K **Privately Held**
Web: www.nowcarepainrelief.com
SIC: 8041 Offices and clinics of chiropractors

(G-18704)
NS 360 INC
Also Called: Natural Stacks
1209 N Orange St (19801-1120)
PHONE...........................855 678-2257
EMP: 6 EST: 2018
SALES (est): 378.28K **Privately Held**
Web: www.360local.com
SIC: 8742 Marketing consulting services

(G-18705)
NS AIR LEASING LLC
3422 Old Capitol Trl Ste 1530 (19808-6124)
PHONE...........................302 396-6546
EMP: 5 EST: 2019
SALES (est): 361.74K **Privately Held**
SIC: 7359 Equipment rental and leasing, nec

(G-18706)
NT MARINE APPS LLC
251 Little Falls Dr (19808-1674)
PHONE...........................561 329-3209
EMP: 5 EST: 2018
SALES (est): 233.53K **Privately Held**
SIC: 8748 Business consulting, nec

(G-18707)
NT PHILADELPHIA LLC
3705 Concord Pike Ste 2 (19803-5071)
PHONE...........................302 384-8967
Brent Applebaum, Brnch Mgr
EMP: 80
Web: www.coldwellbanker.com
SIC: 6531 Real estate agent, residential
HQ: Nt Philadelphia Llc
1207 Fayette St
Conshohocken PA 19428
610 828-9558

(G-18708)
NTL (TRIANGLE) LLC
2711 Centerville Rd (19808-1660)
PHONE...........................302 525-0027
Robert Mackenzie, Pr
EMP: 25 EST: 1999
SALES (est): 4.93MM
SALES (corp-wide): 7.19B **Privately Held**
SIC: 4841 Cable television services
HQ: Virgin Media Limited
500 Brook Drive
Reading BERKS RG2 6

(G-18709)
NUCHIDO INC
1209 N Orange St (19801-1120)
PHONE...........................314 260-7874
Nichola Conlon, CEO
EMP: 2 EST: 2021
SALES (est): 62.38K **Privately Held**
Web: www.nuchido.com
SIC: 2023 Dietary supplements, dairy and non-dairy based

(G-18710)
NUCLEAR ELECTRIC INSURANCE LTD (PA)
Also Called: Neil
1 Righter Pkwy # 210 (19803-1510)
PHONE...........................302 888-3000
Bruce A Sassi, Pr
Kenneth C Manne, *
Gregory J Blackburn, *
Michael W Kolodner, *
R Benjamin Mays, *
EMP: 52 EST: 1973
SALES (est): 61.78MM **Privately Held**
Web: www.myneil.com
SIC: 6331 Property damage insurance

(G-18711)
NUCLEAR SERVICE ORGANIZATION (PA)
Also Called: Nucelectric Insurance Limited
1201 N Market St Ste 1100 (19801-1807)
PHONE...........................302 888-3000
Gregory G Wilks, Pr
EMP: 7 EST: 2000
SALES (est): 478.72K
SALES (corp-wide): 478.72K **Privately Held**
Web: www.myneil.com
SIC: 4911 Nuclear electric power generation

(G-18712)
NUCURAL INC (PA) ✪
1201 N Orange St Ste 7322j (19801-1274)
PHONE...........................408 625-7047
Sreekanth Puram, CEO
EMP: 6 EST: 2023
SALES (est): 61.45K
SALES (corp-wide): 61.45K **Privately Held**
SIC: 7371 Custom computer programming services

(G-18713)
NUEVE CEROS LLC
2810 N Church St (19802-4447)
PHONE...........................415 513-0332
Mahammad Orujov, Managing Member
EMP: 9
SALES (est): 313.29K **Privately Held**
SIC: 7371 Computer software development and applications

▲ = Import ▼ = Export
◆ = Import/Export

GEOGRAPHIC SECTION

(G-18714)
NUIX NORTH AMERICA INC
408 Lee Ter (19803-1813)
PHONE.................................302 584-7542
EMP: 6 **EST:** 2019
SALES (est): 64.05K **Privately Held**
Web: www.nuix.com
SIC: 7371 Computer software development

(G-18715)
NUMBERBOX INC
1000 N West St Ste 1200 (19801-1050)
PHONE.................................302 830-8800
Edward Mance, *CEO*
EMP: 6
SALES (est): 253.63K **Privately Held**
Web: www.numberbox.com
SIC: 8742 Marketing consulting services

(G-18716)
NURAXI HOLDINGS INC
251 Little Falls Dr (19808-1674)
PHONE.................................571 213-2519
EMP: 11
SALES (est): 217.72K **Privately Held**
SIC: 8099 Health and allied services, nec

(G-18717)
NURSE MAGGIE NURSING ASSIST IN
102 Larch Ave (19804-2304)
PHONE.................................302 660-7100
EMP: 5 **EST:** 2017
SALES (est): 22.18K **Privately Held**
Web: www.nursemaggie.com
SIC: 8049 Nurses, registered and practical

(G-18718)
NURSECAREAI INC
1006 Overbrook Rd (19807-2236)
PHONE.................................717 439-0314
Mike Lang, *CEO*
EMP: 15 **EST:** 2020
SALES (est): 658.64K **Privately Held**
SIC: 7371 Software programming applications

(G-18719)
NURSES CONNECTION
1021 Gilpin Ave (19806-3270)
PHONE.................................302 421-3687
Marylou Singson, *Pr*
EMP: 5 **EST:** 2003
SALES (est): 302K **Privately Held**
SIC: 7361 Nurses' registry

(G-18720)
NUTRADRILL LLC
2055 Limestone Rd Ste 200c (19808-5536)
PHONE.................................772 277-2201
EMP: 5 **EST:** 2021
SALES (est): 293.68K **Privately Held**
Web: www.nutradrill.com
SIC: 2833 Vitamins, natural or synthetic: bulk, uncompounded

(G-18721)
NUTRITION & BIOSCIENCES INC
974 Centre Rd (19805-1269)
PHONE.................................212 765-5500
Edward D Breen, *Pr*
EMP: 1000 **EST:** 2019
SALES (est): 407.63MM
SALES (corp-wide): 12.44B **Publicly Held**
Web: www.dupont.com
SIC: 2869 Industrial organic chemicals, nec
PA: International Flavors & Fragrances Inc.
521 W 57th St
New York NY 10019
212 765-5500

(G-18722)
NVCOMPUTERS INC
300 Delaware Ave Ste 210 (19801-6601)
PHONE.................................860 878-0525
Nathan Varghese, *CEO*
EMP: 5 **EST:** 2013
SALES (est): 230.86K **Privately Held**
Web: www.nvcomputers.com
SIC: 7371 7389 Computer software development and applications; Business Activities at Non-Commercial Site

(G-18723)
O KELLY ERNST BELLI WALLEN LLC
901 N Market St Ste 1000 (19801-3070)
PHONE.................................302 778-4001
Sean T Okelly, *Prin*
EMP: 7 **EST:** 2011
SALES (est): 263.17K **Privately Held**
SIC: 8111 General practice attorney, lawyer

(G-18724)
O&G KNWLDGE SHRING PLTFORM LLC
Also Called: O&G Knwldge Sharing Consortium
808 W Boxborough Dr (19810-1457)
PHONE.................................303 872-0533
Mohammad Mian, *Managing Member*
EMP: 3 **EST:** 2016
SQ FT: 100
SALES (est): 237.18K **Privately Held**
Web: www.ogknowledgeshare.com
SIC: 1389 Oil consultants

(G-18725)
OAK GROVE SENIOR CENTER INC
484 Century Blvd (19808-6271)
PHONE.................................302 998-3319
Kathleen Gland, *Ex Dir*
EMP: 6 **EST:** 1979
SALES (est): 233.63K **Privately Held**
SIC: 8322 Senior citizens' center or association

(G-18726)
OAK LANE COURT ASSOCIATES LP
4 Denny Rd (19809-3445)
PHONE.................................302 764-6450
Leon N Weiner, *Prin*
EMP: 10 **EST:** 2010
SALES (est): 727.12K **Privately Held**
Web: www.lnwa.com
SIC: 7389 Personal service agents, brokers, and bureaus

(G-18727)
OAKFORD ACQUISITIONS LLC
1201 N Market St (19801-1147)
PHONE.................................302 406-1535
Jameka Jackson, *Managing Member*
EMP: 5
SALES (est): 209.42K **Privately Held**
SIC: 8741 Business management

(G-18728)
OAKS LAB ACADEMY LLC (PA)
251 Little Falls Dr (19808-1674)
PHONE.................................509 481-5630
Theodore Dluhy-smith, *Ex Dir*
EMP: 6 **EST:** 2017
SALES (est): 150K
SALES (corp-wide): 150K **Privately Held**
SIC: 7379 7371 7389 Computer related consulting services; Computer software development and applications; Business Activities at Non-Commercial Site

(G-18729)
OAKVILLE INDUSTRIES LLC
919 N Market St Ste 950 (19801-3036)
PHONE.................................513 436-5007
Isaac Livne, *Managing Member*
EMP: 19 **EST:** 2019
SALES (est): 3.15MM **Privately Held**
SIC: 5082 3462 Mining machinery and equipment, except petroleum; Nuclear power plant forgings, ferrous

(G-18730)
OAKWOOD FUNDING CORPORATION
913 N Market St Ste 410 (19801-3019)
PHONE.................................336 855-2400
EMP: 6
SALES (est): 291.71K
SALES (corp-wide): 225.38B **Publicly Held**
SIC: 6162 Mortgage bankers and loan correspondents
HQ: Vanderbilt Mortgage And Finance, Inc.
500 Alcoa Trl
Maryville TN 37804
865 380-3000

(G-18731)
OASIS CHILDCARE
800 N Madison St (19801-1438)
PHONE.................................302 312-5255
EMP: 6 **EST:** 2019
SALES (est): 74.49K **Privately Held**
SIC: 8351 Child day care services

(G-18732)
OASIS HOME INC ✪
1232 N King St Num 206 (19801-3226)
PHONE.................................949 331-5405
Chestorc Cheng, *CEO*
EMP: 10 **EST:** 2023
SALES (est): 454.47K **Privately Held**
SIC: 5031 7389 Lumber, plywood, and millwork; Business Activities at Non-Commercial Site

(G-18733)
OASIS SECURITY INC ✪
1007 N Orange St (19801-1239)
PHONE.................................332 867-8141
Dany Brikman, *CEO*
Amit Zimeman, *CPO*
EMP: 5 **EST:** 2023
SALES (est): 199.4K **Privately Held**
SIC: 7371 7389 Custom computer programming services; Business services, nec
PA: Oasis Security Ltd
21 Ahad Haam
Tel Aviv-Jaffa 65151

(G-18734)
OATES CONSULTANTS LLC
234 Philadelphia Pike Ste 9 (19809-3126)
PHONE.................................302 477-0109
Phadrea Oates, *Prin*
EMP: 5 **EST:** 1996
SALES (est): 100.63K **Privately Held**
SIC: 7291 Tax return preparation services

(G-18735)
OBEROD ESTATES LLC
3 Mill Rd (19806-2146)
PHONE.................................302 521-0250
EMP: 7 **EST:** 2017
SALES (est): 205.86K **Privately Held**
Web: www.labware.com
SIC: 6531 Real estate agents and managers

(G-18736)
OBJECTIVE ZERO FOUNDATION
919 N Market St Ste 425 (19801-3014)
PHONE.................................202 573-9660
Blake Bassett, *Ex Dir*
Kayla Bailey, *Prin*
EMP: 17 **EST:** 2016
SALES (est): 211.39K **Privately Held**
Web: www.objectivezero.org
SIC: 8641 Civic and social associations

(G-18737)
OBJECTS WORLDWIDE INC
Also Called: Owi
910 Foulk Rd Ste 201 (19803-3159)
P.O. Box 642 (22116-0642)
PHONE.................................703 623-7861
Tamilmaran Arulmozhidurai, *Pr*
Arunachalam S Babu, *VP*
EMP: 7 **EST:** 1995
SALES (est): 658.51K **Privately Held**
SIC: 7371 7389 Computer software development and applications; Business Activities at Non-Commercial Site

(G-18738)
OBRIEN FIRM
901 N Tatnall St (19801-1605)
PHONE.................................302 654-1515
William O'brien, *Pr*
EMP: 5 **EST:** 2015
SALES (est): 113.89K **Privately Held**
Web: www.obfirm.com
SIC: 8111 Specialized law offices, attorneys

(G-18739)
OCCIDENTAL L TRANSAMERICA
Also Called: Estate Planning Delaware Vly
1415 Foulk Rd Ste 103 (19803-2748)
PHONE.................................302 477-9700
Frank Kesselman, *CEO*
EMP: 17 **EST:** 1972
SQ FT: 2,000
SALES (est): 411.72K **Privately Held**
SIC: 6411 Insurance agents, nec

(G-18740)
OCCUPATIONAL THERAPY
3429 Faulkland Rd (19808-2361)
PHONE.................................302 994-4566
Deborah Schulte, *Prin*
EMP: 9 **EST:** 2014
SALES (est): 288.4K **Privately Held**
Web: www.brandywineot.com
SIC: 8093 Rehabilitation center, outpatient treatment

(G-18741)
OCEAN FIRST ENTERPRISES LLC
501 Silverside Rd Ste 507 (19809-1374)
PHONE.................................302 232-8547
Roger Davis, *Managing Member*
EMP: 20 **EST:** 2019
SALES (est): 938.43K **Privately Held**
SIC: 8742 Management consulting services

(G-18742)
OCI MELAMINE AMERICAS INC (DH)
1209 N Orange St (19801-1120)
PHONE.................................800 615-8284
Tim Scheerhoorn, *Pr*
▲ **EMP:** 6 **EST:** 1986
SALES (est): 2.13MM **Privately Held**
SIC: 2821 Melamine resins, melamine-formaldehyde
HQ: Oci Nitrogen B.V.
Poststraat 1
Sittard LI

Wilmington - New Castle County (G-18743)   GEOGRAPHIC SECTION

(G-18743)
OCONNELL SPEEDY PRINTING INC
Also Called: American Speedy Printing
715 N King St (19801-3540)
PHONE..................302 656-1475
Ellen Oconnell, Pr
David Oconnell, VP
EMP: 5 EST: 1984
SALES (est): 336.58K Privately Held
Web: www.americanspeedy.com
SIC: 2752 Offset printing

(G-18744)
OCULUS NETWORKS INC
1013 Centre Rd (19805-1265)
PHONE..................732 841-1624
Neil Mirchandani, CEO
EMP: 10 EST: 2021
SALES (est): 385.96K Privately Held
SIC: 4813 Internet connectivity services

(G-18745)
ODDPORIUM LLC
2115 Marsh Rd (19810-3913)
PHONE..................302 757-9544
Elizabeth Busch, Prin
EMP: 6 EST: 2015
SALES (est): 70.53K Privately Held
SIC: 8412 Art gallery

(G-18746)
ODELIAS EARLY LRNG ACADEMY ELA
3000 N Market St (19802-3151)
PHONE..................302 482-3249
EMP: 10 EST: 2016
SALES (est): 90.35K Privately Held
SIC: 8351 Preschool center

(G-18747)
ODESS PRODUCTS INC
1226 N King St Ste 128 (19801-3232)
PHONE..................253 394-0442
Chunhui Wei, Prin
EMP: 9 EST: 2020
SALES (est): 350K Privately Held
SIC: 5091 Sporting and recreation goods

(G-18748)
OFFICE MAGIC
628 Black Gates Rd (19803-2240)
PHONE..................302 229-9520
EMP: 5 EST: 2018
SALES (est): 38.6K Privately Held
Web: www.officemagic.com
SIC: 7812 Motion picture and video production

(G-18749)
OFFICE PRTNERS XIV BLLVUE PK L
1000 N West St (19801-1050)
PHONE..................302 691-2100
Robert E Buccini, Managing Member
EMP: 7 EST: 2014
SALES (est): 711.14K Privately Held
SIC: 8748 Business consulting, nec

(G-18750)
OFFIT KURMAN PA
1201 N Orange St Ste 7257 (19801-1268)
PHONE..................302 351-0900
EMP: 82 EST: 2018
SALES (est): 413.75K Privately Held
Web: www.offitkurman.com
SIC: 8111 General practice law office

(G-18751)
OK VIDEO
406 Philadelphia Pike (19809-2153)
PHONE..................302 762-2333
David Klein, Pt
Susan Olvenburg, Pt
EMP: 8 EST: 1982
SALES (est): 243.74K Privately Held
Web: www.okvideode.com
SIC: 7812 Video tape production

(G-18752)
OL BABIES LLC
4023 Kennett Pike (19807-2018)
PHONE..................302 570-0205
EMP: 9 EST: 2016
SALES (est): 21.98K Privately Held
SIC: 8351 Child day care services

(G-18753)
OLD AYALA INC
1007 N Orange St Fl 4 (19801-1242)
PHONE..................857 444-0553
Kenneth Berlin, CEO
Igor Gitelman, CFO
Andres Gutierrez, CMO
EMP: 10 EST: 2017
SALES (est): 692K
SALES (corp-wide): 250K Publicly Held
Web: www.ayalapharma.com
SIC: 8731 Biological research
PA: Ayala Pharmaceuticals, Inc.
9 Deerpark Dr Ste K1
Monmouth Junction NJ 08852
609 452-9813

(G-18754)
OLD COUNTRY GARDEN CENTER INC
414 Wilson Rd (19803-3950)
PHONE..................302 652-3317
Stephen Keulman, Pr
Erika Keulman, *
Chris Keulman, *
EMP: 18 EST: 1970
SQ FT: 3,000
SALES (est): 437.77K Privately Held
Web: www.oldcountrygardens.com
SIC: 0181 5947 5261 0782 Nursery stock, growing of; Gift shop; Retail nurseries and garden stores; Landscape contractors

(G-18755)
OLD REPUBLIC NAT TITLE INSUR
Also Called: Old Republic
600 N King St # 100 (19801-3776)
PHONE..................302 661-1997
Renee Grajewski, Dir
EMP: 11
SALES (corp-wide): 8.08B Publicly Held
Web: www.oldrepublictitle.com
SIC: 6361 Real estate title insurance
HQ: Old Republic National Title Insurance Company
11055 Wayzata Blvd # 250
Hopkins MN 55305
612 371-1111

(G-18756)
OLD REPUBLIC TITLE COMPANY
Also Called: Old Republic
600 N King St Ste 100 (19801-3776)
PHONE..................302 661-1997
Kate Blake, Brnch Mgr
EMP: 24
SALES (corp-wide): 8.08B Publicly Held
Web: www.ortconline.com
SIC: 6361 Real estate title insurance
HQ: Old Republic Title Company
275 Battery St Ste 1500
San Francisco CA 94111
415 421-3500

(G-18757)
OLD WORLD TILE WORKS
2602 Grendon Dr (19808-3806)
PHONE..................302 407-5552
EMP: 6 EST: 2014
SALES (est): 245.73K Privately Held
Web: www.oldworldtileworks.com
SIC: 1743 Tile installation, ceramic

(G-18758)
OLGA YATZUS LPCMH
5700 Kirkwood Hwy (19808-4857)
PHONE..................302 407-3743
EMP: 6 EST: 2017
SALES (est): 150.12K Privately Held
Web: olga-yatzus.business.site
SIC: 8322 General counseling services

(G-18759)
OLGAM LIFE LLC
1209 N Orange St (19801-1120)
PHONE..................917 635-1989
Rose Rosenfeld, Managing Member
EMP: 10 EST: 2020
SALES (est): 699.38K Privately Held
SIC: 5122 Blood plasma

(G-18760)
OLLANG INC
1209 N Orange St (19801)
PHONE..................212 706-1883
EMP: 5 EST: 2019
SALES (est): 46.16K Privately Held
SIC: 7371 Computer software development and applications

(G-18761)
OLUV C JOYNOR FOUNDATION
601 Delaware Ave Fl 2 (19801-1462)
PHONE..................302 793-3277
W Scott Evensen Iii, Pr
EMP: 5 EST: 2015
SALES (est): 47.24K Privately Held
Web: www.ocjoynor.org
SIC: 8641 Civic and social associations

(G-18762)
OMAR A KHAN M D
1309 Veale Rd Ste 11 (19810-4609)
PHONE..................302 478-7160
Omar Khan, Ofcr
EMP: 8 EST: 2017
SALES (est): 100.92K Privately Held
SIC: 8011 Offices and clinics of medical doctors

(G-18763)
OMAR AUTO REPAIR LLC
1027 W 25th St Ste A (19802-3372)
PHONE..................302 502-3204
EMP: 5 EST: 2016
SALES (est): 231.53K Privately Held
SIC: 7538 General automotive repair shops

(G-18764)
OMAR KAH
Also Called: Kahen Remodeling
1910 W 4th St (19805-3422)
PHONE..................718 552-6008
Omar Kah, Mgr
EMP: 5 EST: 2012
SALES (est): 168.14K Privately Held
Web: www.kahenremodeling.com
SIC: 1521 General remodeling, single-family houses

(G-18765)
OMEGA PROJECT PT LLC
1806 N Van Buren St Ste 100 (19802-3851)
PHONE..................845 323-8739
EMP: 5 EST: 2018
SALES (est): 233.76K Privately Held
Web: www.omegaprojectpt.com
SIC: 8049 Physical therapist

(G-18766)
OMG MGMT LLC
3524 Silverside Rd Ste 35b (19810-4929)
PHONE..................609 221-4572
EMP: 5 EST: 2018
SALES (est): 469.02K Privately Held
SIC: 8741 Management services

(G-18767)
OMNI INTERACTIVE HOLDING LLC
1013 Centre Rd Ste 403s (19805-1265)
PHONE..................779 612-8747
Cai Xinyi, Managing Member
EMP: 5
SALES (est): 164.52K Privately Held
SIC: 7371 Computer software development

(G-18768)
OMNI OUTREACH INC
300 Delaware Ave Ste 210 (19801-1607)
PHONE..................888 291-8952
Anthony Reyna, Pr
EMP: 11 EST: 2020
SALES (est): 397.56K Privately Held
SIC: 8742 Marketing consulting services

(G-18769)
OMNINET INTERNATIONAL INC (PA)
427 N Tatnall St (19801-2230)
PHONE..................208 246-5022
Jose Lopez, Pr
EMP: 27 EST: 2003
SQ FT: 1,000
SALES (est): 2.14MM Privately Held
Web: www.omninetglobal.com
SIC: 8742 7371 Management consulting services; Computer software development

(G-18770)
OMNIPTNTIAL ENRGY PARTNERS LLC
2207 Concord Pike # 128 (19803-2908)
PHONE..................888 429-6664
EMP: 5 EST: 2019
SALES (est): 76.04K Privately Held
Web: www.omnipotential.com
SIC: 4911 Electric services

(G-18771)
OMNIX LABS INC (HQ)
919 N Market St Ste 950 (19801-3036)
PHONE..................917 640-4949
Anoop Kanthan, CEO
EMP: 7 EST: 2017
SALES (est): 2.43MM
SALES (corp-wide): 7.66MM Privately Held
SIC: 7371 Computer software development and applications
PA: Flow Capital Corp
1 Adelaide St E Suite 3002
Toronto ON M5C 2
416 777-0383

(G-18772)
OMPAI & CO LLC (PA) ◊
24a Trolley Sq Num 1748 (19806-3334)
PHONE..................302 632-4077
EMP: 8 EST: 2022
SALES (est): 78.16K
SALES (corp-wide): 78.16K Privately Held
SIC: 3581 Automatic vending machines

Wilmington - New Castle County

(G-18773)
ON DEMAND OIL CHANGE LLC
2138 Grafton Dr (19808-5908)
PHONE..........................855 959-1599
EMP: 5 EST: 2020
SALES (est): 247.21K Privately Held
Web: www.ondemandoc.com
SIC: 7549 Automotive services, nec

(G-18774)
ON MY MIND DESIGNS
2507 Baynard Blvd Fl 2 (19802-2961)
PHONE..........................302 494-8622
Nema Bass, CEO
EMP: 10 EST: 2015
SALES (est): 35K Privately Held
SIC: 8999 Personal services

(G-18775)
ON POINT PARTNERS LLC
18 Germay Dr # 2a (19804-1105)
PHONE..........................302 655-5606
EMP: 6 EST: 2011
SALES (est): 527.11K Privately Held
Web: www.onpoint-partners.com
SIC: 8748 Business consulting, nec

(G-18776)
ON-SITE DETAILING INC
10 Meadows Ln (19807-1208)
PHONE..........................302 540-9680
Maryann Mccrow, Prin
EMP: 5 EST: 2009
SALES (est): 275.5K Privately Held
Web: www.onsitedetailing.net
SIC: 7542 Washing and polishing, automotive

(G-18777)
ONE AT A TIME FOUNDATION
501 Silverside Rd (19809-1374)
PHONE..........................800 839-1754
EMP: 6 EST: 2010
SALES (est): 117.06K Privately Held
Web: www.wagsandmenace.org
SIC: 8699 Charitable organization

(G-18778)
ONE CODEX INC ✪
2810 N Church St (19802-4447)
PHONE..........................226 406-8524
Nicholas Greenfield, Pr
EMP: 7 EST: 2022
SALES (est): 264.9K Privately Held
SIC: 7371 7389 Computer software systems analysis and design, custom; Business services, nec

(G-18779)
ONE COMMERCE CTR CONDO COUNCIL
1 Commerce St Ste 700 (19801)
PHONE..........................302 573-2513
Richard Stat, Pr
EMP: 6 EST: 1989
SALES (est): 236.42K Privately Held
SIC: 8641 Condominium association

(G-18780)
ONE EDM LLC
3524 Silverside Rd (19810-4929)
PHONE..........................908 399-0536
EMP: 30 EST: 2017
SALES (est): 1.19MM Privately Held
SIC: 2836 Culture media

(G-18781)
ONE HOUR HEATING AIR COND
410 Meco Dr (19804-1112)
PHONE..........................302 998-0460
EMP: 6 EST: 2019
SALES (est): 245.32K Privately Held
Web: www.onehourheatandair.com
SIC: 1711 Warm air heating and air conditioning contractor

(G-18782)
ONE HUNDRED WEST TENTH ST
1100 N Market St (19899)
P.O. Box 628 (19899-0628)
PHONE..........................302 651-1469
Bob Hara, Pr
EMP: 5 EST: 2001
SALES (est): 136.1K Privately Held
SIC: 6531 6733 Real estate managers; Trusts, nec

(G-18783)
ONE SOURCE CONTRACTING
2601 W 6th St (19805-2910)
PHONE..........................302 893-3753
EMP: 6 EST: 2012
SALES (est): 212.46K Privately Held
SIC: 1799 Special trade contractors, nec

(G-18784)
ONE SYSTEM INCORPORATED
4023 Kennett Pike Ste 645 (19807-2018)
PHONE..........................888 311-1110
Stan Mccade, CEO
EMP: 18 EST: 1994
SALES (est): 767.97K Privately Held
Web: www.onesystem.com
SIC: 7371 8743 Software programming applications; Public relations services

(G-18785)
ONE VILLAGE ALLIANCE INC
1401 A St (19801-5409)
P.O. Box 662 (19899-0662)
PHONE..........................302 275-1715
Chandra Pitts, Ex Dir
EMP: 7 EST: 2010
SALES (est): 304.46K Privately Held
Web: www.iamthevillage.org
SIC: 8322 9532 Outreach program; Urban and community development

(G-18786)
ONE WAY SOURCE LLC
1818 N Tatnall St (19802-4817)
PHONE..........................302 894-8359
David Gachie, Managing Member
EMP: 6
SALES (est): 65.76K Privately Held
SIC: 7699 Cleaning services

(G-18787)
ONEBOX TECHNOLOGIES INC
2055 Limestone Rd (19808-5536)
PHONE..........................415 799-8830
Kumar Vikramaditya, Prin
EMP: 6
SALES (est): 237.56K Privately Held
SIC: 7371 Computer software development and applications

(G-18788)
ONEMAIN
1011 Centre Rd Ste 402 (19805-1266)
PHONE..........................812 492-2156
Courtney Beeker, Prin
EMP: 5 EST: 2018
SALES (est): 61.8K Privately Held
SIC: 6282 Investment advice

(G-18789)
ONEX GLOBAL INC
1622 E Ayre St (19804-2542)
PHONE..........................801 413-6375
EMP: 6 EST: 2018
SALES (est): 226.88K Privately Held
Web: www.onex.ru
SIC: 3661 Telephone and telegraph apparatus

(G-18790)
ONI ACQUISITION CORP
2711 Centerville Rd (19808-1660)
PHONE..........................212 271-3800
Calvin Shintani, Sec
EMP: 6 EST: 2010
SIC: 6719 Investment holding companies, except banks

(G-18791)
ONIX SILVERSIDE LLC
3322 Silverside Rd (19810-3307)
PHONE..........................484 731-2500
Ronald Schafer, Mgr
EMP: 17 EST: 2012
SALES (est): 953.96K Privately Held
Web: www.cadiahealthcare.com
SIC: 8051 Skilled nursing care facilities

(G-18792)
ONLINE PUBLISHERS LLC
2701 Centerville Rd (19808-1607)
PHONE..........................786 617-8896
Saade Makhlouf, Managing Member
EMP: 50 EST: 2019
SALES (est): 1.23MM Privately Held
Web: www.theonlinepublishers.com
SIC: 7379 Online services technology consultants

(G-18793)
ONYX BUSINESS ALLIANCE LLC
1201 N Market St Ste 111c (19801-1147)
PHONE..........................888 368-0402
Stacey Robinson, CEO
EMP: 5 EST: 2021
SALES (est): 254.28K Privately Held
SIC: 8742 Business management consultant

(G-18794)
OPALWIRE
Also Called: Cricket Wireless
1100 Maryland Ave (19805-4838)
PHONE..........................302 502-2407
Nevina Kumari, Genl Mgr
EMP: 6 EST: 2015
SALES (est): 135.88K Privately Held
Web: www.cricketwireless.com
SIC: 4812 Cellular telephone services

(G-18795)
OPEN LANES-SOLUTIONS LLC ✪
1201 N Market St Ste 111 (19801-1156)
PHONE..........................888 410-4207
David Cesar, CEO
EMP: 15 EST: 2022
SALES (est): 342 Privately Held
Web: www.openlanes-solutions.com
SIC: 8742 8741 8999 Management consulting services; Administrative management; Scientific consulting

(G-18796)
OPEN MRI AT TROLLEY SQUARE LLC
1010 N Bancroft Pkwy (19805-2690)
PHONE..........................302 472-5555
David Schluck, Managing Member
Kristin Mills, Prin
EMP: 10 EST: 2004
SALES (est): 493.76K Privately Held
SIC: 8011 Radiologist

(G-18797)
OPEN SYSTEMS HEALTHCARE
3 Mill Rd Ste 303 (19806-2164)
PHONE..........................302 298-3260
EMP: 21 EST: 2014
SALES (est): 211.03K Privately Held
Web: www.opensystemshealthcare.com
SIC: 8099 Health and allied services, nec

(G-18798)
OPEN TEXT INC (HQ)
251 Little Falls Dr (19808-1674)
PHONE..........................248 986-6927
Mark J Barrenechea, CEO
EMP: 29 EST: 2010
SALES (est): 3.4MM
SALES (corp-wide): 832.31MM Privately Held
Web: www.opentext.com
SIC: 7371 Computer software development
PA: Open Text Corporation
275 Frank Tompa Dr
Waterloo ON N2L 0
519 888-7111

(G-18799)
OPENEYES INSUR HOLDINGS INC (PA)
1007 N Orange St Fl 4 (19801-1242)
PHONE..........................737 222-9132
Yoav Oron, Pr
EMP: 6 EST: 2020
SALES (est): 1.33MM
SALES (corp-wide): 1.33MM Privately Held
Web: insurance.delaware.gov
SIC: 6311 Life insurance carriers

(G-18800)
OPENGRID TECHNOLOGIES CO
1007 N Orange St Ste 1923 (19801-1239)
PHONE..........................202 677-2794
Nanbo Liu, CEO
EMP: 3
SALES (est): 135.7K Privately Held
SIC: 3621 Generators for gas-electric or oil-electric vehicles

(G-18801)
OPENTACT INC
3524 Silverside Rd (19810-4929)
PHONE..........................484 424-9683
Anne Kwong, CEO
EMP: 10
SALES (est): 355.79K Privately Held
SIC: 7379 Online services technology consultants

(G-18802)
OPERA PRODUCTS LLC
1000 N West St Ste 1200 (19801-1058)
PHONE..........................413 331-3669
Thien Cong Dao, CEO
EMP: 20 EST: 2018
SALES (est): 2.53MM Privately Held
Web: www.granford.com
SIC: 5047 Medical equipment and supplies

(G-18803)
OPERADELAWARE INC
Also Called: Opera Studios
4 S Poplar St (19801-5009)
PHONE..........................302 658-8063
TOLL FREE: 800
Brendan Cooke, Dir
Brendan Cooke, Mng Dir
EMP: 6 EST: 1945
SALES (est): 863.31K Privately Held
Web: www.operade.org

Wilmington - New Castle County (G-18804) GEOGRAPHIC SECTION

SIC: 7922 Performing arts center production

(G-18804)
OPINR INC (PA)
Also Called: Vetted
24a Trolley Sq Pmb 1635 (19806-3334)
PHONE..........................646 207-3000
Jagmeet Lamba, CEO
Dudley Brundige, *
Jared Ezzell, CCO*
EMP: 60 EST: 2013
SALES (est): 5.23MM
SALES (corp-wide): 5.23MM **Privately Held**
Web: www.getcerta.com
SIC: 7371 8742 Computer software systems analysis and design, custom; Management consulting services

(G-18805)
OPPORTUNITY INVESTMENTS
2528 Blackwood Rd (19810-3638)
PHONE..........................302 887-3082
EMP: 5 EST: 2008
SALES (est): 117.79K **Privately Held**
SIC: 6799 Investors, nec

(G-18806)
OPT THERAPY SVC
2502 Silverside Rd Ste 4 (19810-3740)
PHONE..........................302 478-3702
Debra Bleakney, Owner
EMP: 5 EST: 2020
SALES (est): 29.52K **Privately Held**
SIC: 8049 Physical therapist

(G-18807)
OPTIMA CLEANING SYSTEMS INC
110 Valley Rd (19804-1311)
P.O. Box 3117 (19804-0117)
PHONE..........................302 652-3979
Thomas Delle Donne, Pr
EMP: 32 EST: 1988
SALES (est): 823.94K **Privately Held**
Web: www.optimacleaning.com
SIC: 7349 Cleaning service, industrial or commercial

(G-18808)
OPUS DESIGN BUILD LLC
Also Called: Opus
1000 N West St Fl 10 (19801-1059)
PHONE..........................952 656-4444
EMP: 95 EST: 2009
SALES (est): 12.58MM **Privately Held**
Web: www.opus-group.com
SIC: 1542 Commercial and office building, new construction

(G-18809)
OPUS FINANCIAL SVCS USA INC
19c Trolley Sq (19806-3355)
PHONE..........................646 435-5616
Fred Davis, CEO
EMP: 5 EST: 2015
SALES (est): 307.22K **Privately Held**
SIC: 7361 Employment agencies

(G-18810)
ORACLE ENTERPRISES LLC (PA) ◇
14 S Union St Ste 107a (19805-3865)
PHONE..........................407 900-2828
EMP: 5 EST: 2022
SALES (est): 215.18K
SALES (corp-wide): 215.18K **Privately Held**
SIC: 8742 7389 Management consulting services; Business Activities at Non-Commercial Site

(G-18811)
ORAL & MAXILLOFACIAL SURGERY
2601 Annand Dr Ste 10 (19808-3719)
PHONE..........................302 998-0331
Judy Norcross, Mgr
EMP: 10 EST: 2017
SALES (est): 181.9K **Privately Held**
Web: www.deomfs.net
SIC: 8021 Dental surgeon

(G-18812)
ORAL MXLLFCIAL SRGERY ASSOC PA
1304 N Broom St (19806-4266)
PHONE..........................302 655-6183
James Goodwill, Pr
Michael Kremer, Mgr
EMP: 10 EST: 1976
SALES (est): 908.5K **Privately Held**
Web: www.deomfs.net
SIC: 8021 Maxillofacial specialist

(G-18813)
ORANGE POWER ELECTRIC INC
300 Delaware Ave Ste 210new (19801-1607)
PHONE..........................205 886-5815
Ishan Jaithwa, Pt
Lynette Horton, Pr
Shuhui Li, VP
EMP: 6
SALES (est): 251.52K **Privately Held**
SIC: 3629 Inverters, nonrotating: electrical

(G-18814)
ORANGETHEORY FITNESS PIKE
Also Called: Orangetheory Fitness
4754 Limestone Rd (19808-1928)
PHONE..........................302 426-2030
EMP: 6 EST: 2018
SALES (est): 91.63K **Privately Held**
Web: www.orangetheory.com
SIC: 7991 Physical fitness facilities

(G-18815)
ORBIT RESEARCH LLC (PA)
3422 Old Capitol Trl Ste 25 (19808-6124)
PHONE..........................302 683-1063
EMP: 9 EST: 1998
SALES (est): 449.76K **Privately Held**
Web: www.orbitresearch.com
SIC: 7993 Coin-operated amusement devices

(G-18816)
ORCHARD MORTGAGE LLC ◇
251 Little Falls Dr (19808-1674)
PHONE..........................888 627-0677
Gregory Botto, Managing Member
EMP: 18 EST: 2022
SALES (est): 842.35K **Privately Held**
SIC: 6162 Mortgage bankers and loan correspondents

(G-18817)
OREOMATIC MINING INC ◇
1020 N French St Ste 480-550 (19884-0009)
PHONE..........................725 255-8895
Kristin Oloso, CEO
EMP: 26 EST: 2022
SALES (est): 536.61K **Privately Held**
SIC: 1241 8711 1011 2819 Mine preparation services; Mining engineer; Iron ore mining; Alkali metals: lithium, cesium, francium, rubidium

(G-18818)
ORGANIC INTELLIGENCE LLC (PA)
251 Little Falls Dr (19808-1674)
PHONE..........................949 423-3665
EMP: 6 EST: 2019
SALES (est): 180.88K
SALES (corp-wide): 180.88K **Privately Held**
Web: www.organicintelligence.org
SIC: 7371 7389 Computer software development and applications; Business services, nec

(G-18819)
ORGANIZED FOR LIFE
109 Smyrna Ave (19809-1234)
PHONE..........................302 792-1663
Patricia Depalma, Prin
EMP: 5 EST: 2015
SALES (est): 118.97K **Privately Held**
Web: www.organizedforlifedelaware.com
SIC: 1799 Closet organizers, installation and design

(G-18820)
ORGANOX INC ◇
2810 N Church St Ste 56894 (19802-4447)
PHONE..........................216 243-2202
EMP: 7 EST: 2022
SALES (est): 365.25K **Privately Held**
SIC: 8731 Commercial physical research

(G-18821)
ORION GROUP LLC
2801 Centerville Rd (19808-1609)
PHONE..........................302 357-9137
Seth Spiller, Pr
EMP: 6 EST: 2015
SALES (est): 330.96K **Privately Held**
Web: www.orion--group.com
SIC: 8741 Business management

(G-18822)
ORJAM LTD
3602 Squirrel Hill Ct (19808-3116)
PHONE..........................302 482-5016
Damian J Davis, Pr
EMP: 10 EST: 2013
SALES (est): 773.09K **Privately Held**
Web: www.orjamconstruction.com
SIC: 1521 Single-family housing construction

(G-18823)
ORLANDO J CAMP & ASSOCIATES
1808 Pan Rd (19803-3343)
PHONE..........................302 478-3720
Orlando J Camp, Pr
EMP: 6 EST: 1996
SQ FT: 18,000
SALES (est): 590.85K **Privately Held**
SIC: 5113 Towels, paper

(G-18824)
OROS COMMUNICATIONS LLC
2711 Centerville Rd Ste 400 (19808-1660)
PHONE..........................954 228-7399
EMP: 2 EST: 2016
SALES (est): 133.6K **Privately Held**
SIC: 3663 Space satellite communications equipment

(G-18825)
ORPHAGENIX INC
300 Water St (19801-5037)
PHONE..........................267 334-5153
Michael Herr, CEO
EMP: 2 EST: 2005
SALES (est): 130K **Privately Held**
Web: www.orphagenix.com
SIC: 2836 Biological products, except diagnostic

(G-18826)
ORTHOPAEDIC & SPORTS PHYS
617 W Newport Pike (19804-3235)
PHONE..........................302 683-0782
Nalini Advani, Prin
EMP: 5 EST: 2006
SALES (est): 245.81K **Privately Held**
Web: www.osphysio.com
SIC: 8049 Physical therapist

(G-18827)
ORTHOPAEDIC SPECIALISTS PA
7 S Clayton St Ste 600 (19805-3948)
PHONE..........................302 655-9494
Errol Ger, Pt
Andrew J Gelman, Pt
EMP: 10 EST: 1995
SALES (est): 316.74K **Privately Held**
Web: www.delortho.com
SIC: 8011 Orthopedic physician

(G-18828)
OSFS WLMNGTN-PHLDLPHIA PRVNCE
2200 Kentmere Pkwy (19806-2018)
PHONE..........................302 656-8529
William Guerin, Prin
EMP: 7 EST: 2010
SALES (est): 213.95K **Privately Held**
SIC: 6733 Trusts, nec

(G-18829)
OSSUM INC
300 Delaware Ave Ste 210a (19801-6601)
PHONE..........................516 851-4607
Anthonydas Anthonyswamy, Pr
EMP: 5 EST: 2017
SALES (est): 64.94K **Privately Held**
SIC: 5045 Computer software

(G-18830)
OSTERMAN & COMPANY INC
2711 Centerville Rd (19808-1660)
PHONE..........................203 272-2233
John Dwyer, Pr
EMP: 7
SALES (corp-wide): 130.85MM **Privately Held**
Web: www.osterman-co.com
SIC: 5162 Plastics materials, nec
PA: Osterman & Company, Inc.
726 S Main St
Cheshire CT 06410
203 272-2233

(G-18831)
OSX FITNESS TRAINING CENTER
28 W Ayre St (19804-9002)
PHONE..........................302 256-0667
Steve Oldham, Owner
EMP: 7 EST: 2008
SALES (est): 67.17K **Privately Held**
SIC: 7991 Physical fitness facilities

(G-18832)
OTTO CLIPS COMPANY
725 Taunton Rd (19803-1709)
PHONE..........................267 918-9985
EMP: 7 EST: 2011
SALES (est): 247.65K **Privately Held**
SIC: 7231 Unisex hair salons

(G-18833)
OUR FUTURE CHILD CARE CTR LLC
405 Edgemoor Rd (19809-3270)
PHONE..........................302 762-8645
EMP: 8 EST: 2009
SALES (est): 110.82K **Privately Held**
SIC: 8351 Child day care services

GEOGRAPHIC SECTION — Wilmington - New Castle County (G-18863)

(G-18834)
OUR FUTURE CHRISTIAN CHLD CARE
800 E 7th St (19801-4413)
PHONE..................................302 287-4442
Jacqeline Harris, *Owner*
EMP: 10 **EST:** 2016
SALES (est): 21.26K **Privately Held**
SIC: 8351 Child day care services

(G-18835)
OUR SERVICES - TRAVELERS Q
1224 N King St (19801-3232)
PHONE..................................302 660-3680
EMP: 6 **EST:** 2018
SALES (est): 167.95K **Privately Held**
Web: www.travelersq.com
SIC: 4724 Travel agencies

(G-18836)
OUR YOUTH INC
1213 B St (19801-5605)
PHONE..................................302 655-8250
EMP: 8
SALES (est): 698.22K **Privately Held**
Web: www.ouryouthinc.org
SIC: 8322 Individual and family services

(G-18837)
OUT OF GALAXY INC
913 N Market St (19801-3019)
PHONE..................................814 441-8058
EMP: 7 **EST:** 2017
SALES (est): 362.87K **Privately Held**
Web: www.h2opal.com
SIC: 7371 Computer software development and applications

(G-18838)
OUTBURST AI LIMITED ✪
Also Called: Outburst Ai
1224 N King St (19801-3232)
PHONE..................................516 303-2097
Sarah Cheng, *Prin*
EMP: 11 **EST:** 2023
SALES (est): 513.47K **Privately Held**
SIC: 7371 Computer software development

(G-18839)
OUTPATENT ANSTHSIA SPCLISTS PA
2006 Limestone Rd Ste 5 (19808-5553)
PHONE..................................302 995-1860
David Blumberg, *Pr*
EMP: 10 **EST:** 2001
SALES (est): 1.86MM **Privately Held**
SIC: 8011 Anesthesiologist

(G-18840)
OUTSIDE SERVICES LLC
2117 Oak St (19808-4832)
P.O. Box 165 (19707-0165)
PHONE..................................302 250-3317
Richard Donaghue, *Prin*
EMP: 9 **EST:** 2016
SALES (est): 797.47K **Privately Held**
SIC: 0781 Landscape services

(G-18841)
OVERSIGHT BOARD LLC
1013 Centre Rd Ste 101 (19805-1265)
PHONE..................................302 898-2599
EMP: 5
SALES (est): 280.91K **Privately Held**
SIC: 8748 Business consulting, nec

(G-18842)
OVERTONE COLOR LLC ✪
2810 N Church St (19802-4447)
PHONE..................................520 448-3305
Ashley Sorensen, *Pr*
EMP: 9 **EST:** 2022
SALES (est): 1.91MM **Privately Held**
SIC: 2844 Hair coloring preparations

(G-18843)
OWL JUMPSTART LLC
1000 N West St Ste 1200 (19801-1058)
PHONE..................................302 467-2061
EMP: 10 **EST:** 2020
SALES (est): 120K **Privately Held**
Web: www.harmonicaland.com
SIC: 8742 Administrative services consultant

(G-18844)
OWNLEASE INC ✪
1207 Delaware Ave Ste 190 (19806-4743)
PHONE..................................855 447-4921
Zack Vandenburg, *Dir*
EMP: 6 **EST:** 2022
SALES (est): 288.23K **Privately Held**
SIC: 7359 Home appliance, furniture, and entertainment rental services

(G-18845)
OXFORD PLASTIC SYSTEMS LLC
1011 Ctr Rd Ste 312 (19805-1266)
PHONE..................................800 567-9182
EMP: 7 **EST:** 2017
SALES (est): 1.03MM
SALES (corp-wide): 29.87MM **Privately Held**
Web: www.oxfordplastics.com
SIC: 3089 Fences, gates, and accessories: plastics
HQ: Oxford Plastic Systems International Limited
Unit T2 Enstone Airfield
Chipping Norton OXON OX7 4
160 867-8888

(G-18846)
OYSTER HR AMERICAS INC
3411 Silverside Rd Ttnallb (19810-4812)
PHONE..................................912 219-2356
Tony Jamous, *CEO*
EMP: 114 **EST:** 2021
SALES (est): 5.28MM
SALES (corp-wide): 55.85MM **Privately Held**
SIC: 7371 8742 Computer software systems analysis and design, custom; Human resource consulting services
PA: Oyster Hr, Inc.
3411 Silverside Rd
Wilmington DE 19810
912 219-2356

(G-18847)
OYSTER HR INC (PA)
3411 Silverside Rd (19810-4812)
PHONE..................................912 219-2356
Tony Jamous, *CEO*
EMP: 323 **EST:** 2019
SALES (est): 55.85MM
SALES (corp-wide): 55.85MM **Privately Held**
Web: www.oysterhr.com
SIC: 7371 8742 Computer software systems analysis and design, custom; Human resource consulting services

(G-18848)
P A ALFIERI CARDIOLOGY (PA)
701 Foulk Rd (19803-3733)
PHONE..................................302 731-0001
Anthony D Alfieri, *Prin*
EMP: 10 **EST:** 2006
SALES (est): 7.51MM **Privately Held**
Web: www.alfiericardiology.com
SIC: 8011 Cardiologist and cardio-vascular specialist

(G-18849)
P A BAYARD
600 N King St Ste 400 (19801-3779)
P.O. Box 25130 (19899-5130)
PHONE..................................302 429-4212
Charlene Davis, *Dir*
Evan T Miller, *
EMP: 54 **EST:** 1966
SALES (est): 8.45MM **Privately Held**
Web: www.bayardlaw.com
SIC: 8111 General practice law office

(G-18850)
P A BRANDYWINE PEDIATRICS
3521 Silverside Rd Ste 1f (19810-4900)
PHONE..................................302 479-9610
Kate Chaplinski, *Prin*
EMP: 17 **EST:** 2012
SALES (est): 2MM **Privately Held**
Web: www.brandywinepediatrics.com
SIC: 8011 Pediatrician

(G-18851)
P C FLASTER/GREENBERG
913 N Market St Ste 1010 (19801-4927)
PHONE..................................302 351-1910
Taurig Greenberg, *Brnch Mgr*
EMP: 5
Web: www.flastergreenberg.com
SIC: 8111 General practice attorney, lawyer
PA: Flaster/Greenberg P.C.
1810 Chapel Ave W Ste 340
Cherry Hill NJ 08002

(G-18852)
P D SUPPLY INC
Also Called: Pleasant Distributors
307 Commercial Dr (19805-1906)
PHONE..................................302 655-3358
Jeff Rushie, *Pr*
EMP: 6 **EST:** 1947
SQ FT: 10,400
SALES (est): 992.16K **Privately Held**
SIC: 5031 5211 Building materials, interior; Lumber and other building materials

(G-18853)
P R C MANAGEMENT CO INC
2601 Carpenter Station Rd (19810-2050)
PHONE..................................302 475-7643
EMP: 9 **EST:** 1999
SALES (est): 673.62K **Privately Held**
SIC: 6531 Real estate managers

(G-18854)
P&L TRANSPORTATION INC (PA)
Also Called: Paducah & Louisville Railway
301 N Market St Ste 1414 (19801-2529)
PHONE..................................800 444-2580
Anthony V Reck, *Prin*
Anthony V Reck, *Ch*
J Thomas Garrett, *Pr*
Thomas A Greene, *VP*
EMP: 8 **EST:** 1995
SQ FT: 22,000
SALES (est): 50.09MM **Privately Held**
SIC: 6719 Public utility holding companies

(G-18855)
P-KS WHOLESALE GROCER INC
Also Called: Pks Food
915 S Heald St (19801-5732)
PHONE..................................302 656-5540
Pete Kirtses, *Pr*
Athy Kirtses, *Treas*
EMP: 10 **EST:** 1980
SQ FT: 15,000
SALES (est): 2.22MM **Privately Held**
SIC: 5149 Groceries and related products, nec

(G-18856)
PABIAN VENTURES LLC
101 N Maryland Ave (19804-1335)
PHONE..................................302 762-1992
Edward N Pabian, *Managing Member*
EMP: 6 **EST:** 2009
SALES (est): 987.07K **Privately Held**
Web: www.pabianproperties.com
SIC: 8742 Real estate consultant

(G-18857)
PACE ENTERPRISES LLC
1405 Silverside Rd Ste B (19810-4445)
PHONE..................................302 529-2500
Debra J Pace, *Prin*
EMP: 5 **EST:** 2000
SALES (est): 242.41K **Privately Held**
Web: www.paceendo.com
SIC: 8021 Endodontist

(G-18858)
PACE INC
5171 W Woodmill Dr Ste 9 (19808-4067)
PHONE..................................302 999-9812
EMP: 18 **EST:** 1987
SALES (est): 972.86K **Privately Held**
Web: www.paceinconline.com
SIC: 8093 Substance abuse clinics (outpatient)

(G-18859)
PACIFIC GLOBAL INC
1013 Centre Rd Ste 4035 (19805-1270)
PHONE..................................510 870-0248
Kumar Shwetabh, *CEO*
Sanjay Drabu, *Pr*
Mayur Tyagi, *Assistant Vice President Operations*
Brian Lichtlin, *VP Sls*
EMP: 7 **EST:** 2009
SALES (est): 150.73K **Privately Held**
SIC: 8399 Health systems agency

(G-18860)
PACK USA INC
300 Delaware Ave Ste 210 (19801-6601)
PHONE..................................443 655-8927
Katia Rudolf, *CEO*
EMP: 8 **EST:** 2021
SALES (est): 463.73K **Privately Held**
SIC: 4783 Packing goods for shipping

(G-18861)
PADILLA KONSTRUCTION LLC
1210 Flint Hill Rd (19808-1914)
PHONE..................................302 276-6678
Edwin Padilla, *Managing Member*
EMP: 4
SALES (est): 101.86K **Privately Held**
SIC: 1389 Construction, repair, and dismantling services

(G-18862)
PAIGE KING DMD
1805 Foulk Rd Ste D (19810-3700)
PHONE..................................302 475-3270
Paige King, *Mgr*
EMP: 9 **EST:** 2016
SALES (est): 76.13K **Privately Held**
SIC: 8021 Dentists' office

(G-18863)
PAIN & SLEEP THERAPY CENTER
4901 Limestone Rd (19808-1271)
PHONE..................................302 314-1409
EMP: 10 **EST:** 2019

Wilmington - New Castle County (G-18864)

SALES (est): 478.67K **Privately Held**
Web: www.painandsleepcenter.com
SIC: **8093** Rehabilitation center, outpatient treatment

(G-18864)
PAINLESS HOSTING LLC
3 Germay Dr Unit 4-1198 (19804-1127)
PHONE.................................703 688-2828
EMP: **10 EST:** 2020
SALES (est): 288.07K **Privately Held**
SIC: **4813** Internet host services

(G-18865)
PALA TILE & CARPET CONTRS INC
600 S Colonial Ave (19805-1956)
PHONE.................................302 652-4500
Richard Zambanini, *Pr*
William N Pala Senior, *VP*
EMP: **20 EST:** 1974
SALES (est): 2.38MM **Privately Held**
Web: www.palaflooring.com
SIC: **5713** 1743 Floor tile; Tile installation, ceramic

(G-18866)
PALADIN SPORTS CLUB INC
Also Called: Paladin Sports & Social Club
500 Paladin Dr (19802-1745)
PHONE.................................302 764-5335
EMP: **10 EST:** 1994
SALES (est): 229.52K **Privately Held**
Web: www.pcmapaladinclub.com
SIC: **7991** 7997 Athletic club and gymnasiums, membership; Indoor/outdoor court clubs

(G-18867)
PALDOR INC
2304 Newport Gap Pike (19808-3171)
PHONE.................................302 999-9691
Paul Disabatino, *Pr*
EMP: **6 EST:** 1996
SALES (est): 760K **Privately Held**
SIC: **1521** 1542 Single-family housing construction; Nonresidential construction, nec

(G-18868)
PALMETTO MGT & ENGRG LLC
4550 New Lnden Hl Rd Ste (19808)
PHONE.................................302 993-2766
EMP: **12 EST:** 2003
SALES (est): 333.08K **Privately Held**
SIC: **8741** Construction management

(G-18869)
PAMPERED PARTIES LLC
1201 N Market St Ste 111a (19801-1147)
PHONE.................................302 216-2362
Wassetta Brooks, *Managing Member*
EMP: **5 EST:** 2021
SALES (est): 40K **Privately Held**
SIC: **7299** Party planning service

(G-18870)
PANCO MANAGEMENT CORPORATION
Also Called: Cynwood Apartments
1302 Cynwyd Club Dr (19808-3047)
PHONE.................................302 995-6152
Chris Elswick, *Mgr*
EMP: 9
SALES (corp-wide): 22.96MM **Privately Held**
Web: www.pancomanagement.com
SIC: **6531** 6513 Real estate managers; Apartment building operators
PA: Panco Management Corporation
50 Main St Ste 1120
White Plains NY 10606
201 556-0900

(G-18871)
PANCO MANAGEMENT CORPORATION
Also Called: Cedar Tree Apartments
2512 Cedar Tree Dr Ofc 2d (19810-1437)
PHONE.................................302 475-9337
Gina Giovenella, *Mgr*
EMP: 9
SALES (corp-wide): 22.96MM **Privately Held**
Web: www.rentcedartreevillage.com
SIC: **6531** 6513 Real estate managers; Apartment building operators
PA: Panco Management Corporation
50 Main St Ste 1120
White Plains NY 10606
201 556-0900

(G-18872)
PANDIA PRESS INC
210 North Rd (19809-3021)
PHONE.................................352 789-8156
EMP: **10 EST:** 2019
SALES (est): 797.48K **Privately Held**
Web: www.pandiapress.com
SIC: **2741** Miscellaneous publishing

(G-18873)
PANDOL BROS INC
Christiana Ctr (19884-0001)
PHONE.................................302 571-8923
Joe Rull, *Mgr*
EMP: 24
SALES (corp-wide): 168.93MM **Privately Held**
Web: www.pandol.com
SIC: **5148** Fruits, fresh
PA: Pandol Bros., Inc.
33150 Pond Rd
Delano CA 93215
661 725-3755

(G-18874)
PANGO FINANCIAL LLC
1011 Centre Rd (19805-1267)
PHONE.................................855 949-7264
EMP: 7
SALES (est): 313.21K **Privately Held**
Web: www.pangofinancial.com
SIC: **7389** Financial services

(G-18875)
PANGRO DEVELOPMENT LLC
2600 N Broom St (19802-2911)
PHONE.................................302 351-3575
EMP: **5 EST:** 2007
SALES (est): 196.18K **Privately Held**
Web: www.pangro.net
SIC: **6552** Subdividers and developers, nec

(G-18876)
PANITCH SCHWARZE BELISARIO
2200 Concord Pike (19803-2978)
PHONE.................................302 394-6030
EMP: **9 EST:** 2017
SALES (est): 174.45K **Privately Held**
Web: www.panitchlaw.com
SIC: **8111** General practice law office

(G-18877)
PANO DEVELOPMENT INC
1701 Augustine Cut Off Ste 15 (19803-4494)
PHONE.................................302 428-1062
Mario B Capano, *Pr*
Frank Capano, *Sec*
EMP: **9 EST:** 2003
SQ FT: 17,000
SALES (est): 744.05K **Privately Held**
SIC: **1521** Single-family housing construction

(G-18878)
PAOLI SERVICES INC
400 B And O Ln (19804-1458)
PHONE.................................302 998-7031
Domenick Paoli, *Junior President*
EMP: **19 EST:** 1996
SQ FT: 8,700
SALES (est): 820.11K **Privately Held**
SIC: **1521** Single-family housing construction

(G-18879)
PAPALEO ROSEN & CHELF PA
1523 Concord Pike Ste 401 (19803-3655)
PHONE.................................302 482-3283
EMP: **6 EST:** 2019
SALES (est): 144.87K **Privately Held**
Web: www.prccpa.com
SIC: **6512** Commercial and industrial building operation

(G-18880)
PAPILLA LLC ◊
1209 N Orange St (19801-1120)
PHONE.................................302 558-7581
EMP: **6 EST:** 2023
SALES (est): 78.16K **Privately Held**
SIC: **3641** Lamps, incandescent filament, electric

(G-18881)
PAQUES ENVIRONMENTAL TECH INC
1209 N Orange St (19801-1120)
PHONE.................................412 932-3540
James W Redmond, *Admn*
EMP: **6 EST:** 2013
SALES (est): 36.79K **Privately Held**
Web: www.paques-inc.com
SIC: **8999** Earth science services

(G-18882)
PARA SCIENTIFIC CO
600 N King St Ste 800 (19801-3778)
PHONE.................................215 736-0225
Hiram Reinhart, *Pr*
EMP: **9 EST:** 1956
SALES (est): 1.22MM **Privately Held**
SIC: **5047** Diagnostic equipment, medical

(G-18883)
PARADIGM HEALTHCARE ASSOC INC
18 Kelso Ct (19808-4307)
PHONE.................................302 352-0517
Michael Balzarini, *Prin*
EMP: **10 EST:** 2016
SALES (est): 65.99K **Privately Held**
SIC: **8099** Health and allied services, nec

(G-18884)
PARADISE LANDSCAPING
717 Mount Lebanon Rd (19803-1609)
PHONE.................................302 654-4030
EMP: **7 EST:** 2011
SALES (est): 483.81K **Privately Held**
Web: www.paradise-landscaping.net
SIC: **0781** Landscape services

(G-18885)
PARADISO SOLUTIONS LLC
2810 N Church St (19802-4447)
PHONE.................................800 513-5902
EMP: **55 EST:** 2011
SALES (est): 5.38MM **Privately Held**
Web: www.paradisosolutions.com
SIC: **7371** Computer software development

(G-18886)
PARAGON ENGINEERING CORP
708 Philadelphia Pike Ste 1 (19809-2500)
PHONE.................................302 762-6010
Dave Bobiak, *Pr*
Stephen W Bobiak Junior, *Sr VP*
Lawrence Ellis, *
EMP: **20 EST:** 1985
SALES (est): 2.28MM **Privately Held**
Web: www.paragon-eng.com
SIC: **8711** Consulting engineer

(G-18887)
PARAGON MASONRY CORPORATION
501 Silverside Rd Ste 1 (19809-1375)
PHONE.................................302 798-7314
EMP: **8 EST:** 1995
SQ FT: 350
SALES (est): 259.13K **Privately Held**
SIC: **1741** Concrete block masonry laying

(G-18888)
PARCEL TECH INC (PA) ◊
919 N Market St Ste 950 (19801-3036)
PHONE.................................720 663-0558
Anubhav Girdhar, *CEO*
EMP: **7 EST:** 2022
SALES (est): 146.32K
SALES (corp-wide): 146.32K **Privately Held**
SIC: **7389** Financial services

(G-18889)
PARCELS INC (PA)
Also Called: Delaware Document Retrieval
230 N Market St (19801-2528)
P.O. Box 646 (19720-0646)
PHONE.................................302 888-1718
James Johnson, *Pr*
Maureen C Johnson, *
James A Johnson, *
EMP: **135 EST:** 1980
SQ FT: 35,000
SALES (est): 12.95MM
SALES (corp-wide): 12.95MM **Privately Held**
Web: www.parcelsinc.com
SIC: **4215** 8111 Package delivery, vehicular; Specialized legal services

(G-18890)
PARGOE FLR PREP LVLG SLTONS LL
Also Called: Pfp Leveling Solutions LLC
6 Hadco Rd (19804-1014)
PHONE.................................302 530-9450
Colin Pargoe, *CEO*
William Pargoe, *VP*
EMP: **5 EST:** 2021
SALES (est): 267.88K **Privately Held**
SIC: **1771** Concrete work

(G-18891)
PARIS CORPORATION
300 Delaware Ave (19801-1607)
PHONE.................................302 427-5985
EMP: **13 EST:** 1988
SALES (est): 405.99K **Privately Held**
SIC: **1799** Waterproofing

(G-18892)
PARK PLACE DENTAL
300 Foulk Rd (19803-3886)
PHONE.................................302 652-3775
EMP: **9 EST:** 2017
SALES (est): 254.86K **Privately Held**

GEOGRAPHIC SECTION
Wilmington - New Castle County (G-18922)

Web:
www.thedentalgroupofdelaware.com
SIC: 8021 Dentists' office

(G-18893)
PARK PLAZA CONDO ASSOCIATION
Also Called: Park Plaza Condominiums
1100 Lovering Ave Ste 15 (19806-3265)
PHONE..............................302 658-3526
Charles Griffith, *Pr*
EMP: 6 EST: 1984
SQ FT: 4,000
SALES (est): 483.27K **Privately Held**
SIC: 8641 Condominium association

(G-18894)
PARK VIEW
1800 N Broom St (19802-3809)
PHONE..............................302 429-7288
Denise Miller, *Prin*
EMP: 5 EST: 2004
SALES (est): 404.96K **Privately Held**
Web: www.parkviewfilm.com
SIC: 6513 Apartment building operators

(G-18895)
PARKVIEW COVALESCENT CENTER
2801 W 6th St (19805-1828)
PHONE..............................302 655-6135
EMP: 17 EST: 2010
SALES (est): 144.31K **Privately Held**
SIC: 8051 Convalescent home with continuous nursing care

(G-18896)
PARKVIEW DE SNF MANAGEMENT LLC
Also Called: PARKVIEW NURSING & REHABILITAT
2801 W 6th St (19805-1828)
PHONE..............................302 655-6135
EMP: 99
SALES (est): 10.81MM **Privately Held**
Web: www.parkviewnursingcare.com
SIC: 8051 8052 8059 8322 Convalescent home with continuous nursing care; Personal care facility; Nursing home, except skilled and intermediate care facility; Rehabilitation services

(G-18897)
PARKWOOD TRUST COMPANY
919 N Market St Ste 429 (19801-3014)
PHONE..............................302 426-1220
Morton L Mandel, *Ch Bd*
EMP: 5 EST: 1998
SQ FT: 1,100
SALES (est): 995.9K **Privately Held**
Web: www.parkwoodcorp.com
SIC: 6282 Investment advisory service
PA: Parkwood Corporation
1000 Lakeside Ave E
Cleveland OH 44114

(G-18898)
PARQ AT SQUARE WEBSIT
1303 Delaware Ave (19806-3419)
PHONE..............................302 656-8543
EMP: 5 EST: 2018
SALES (est): 228.37K **Privately Held**
Web: www.liveparqnow.com
SIC: 6513 Apartment building operators

(G-18899)
PARTNERSHIP FOR DELAW
110 S Poplar St (19801-5050)
PHONE..............................800 445-4935
EMP: 11 EST: 2018
SALES (est): 2.65MM **Privately Held**
Web: www.delawareestuary.org

SIC: 8399 Advocacy group

(G-18900)
PARTNRSHIP FOR DEL ESTUARY INC
110 S Poplar St Ste 202 (19801-5034)
PHONE..............................302 655-4990
Kathy Klein, *Ex Dir*
EMP: 6 EST: 1997
SALES (est): 3.35MM **Privately Held**
Web: www.delawareestuary.org
SIC: 8731 Commercial physical research

(G-18901)
PARTYTICKETS INC ✪
2055 Limestone Rd 200c (19808-5536)
PHONE..............................718 395-9590
EMP: 5 EST: 2022
SALES (est): 46.16K **Privately Held**
SIC: 7371 Computer software development and applications

(G-18902)
PASQUALE FUCCI MD
1508 Pennsylvania Ave Ste 1c (19806-4347)
PHONE..............................302 652-4705
EMP: 8 EST: 2017
SALES (est): 88.48K **Privately Held**
Web: www.brandywinemed.com
SIC: 8011 General and family practice, physician/surgeon

(G-18903)
PATEL SONIYA
701 Foulk Rd Ste 2a (19803-3733)
PHONE..............................803 524-4547
Soniya Patel, *Prin*
EMP: 7 EST: 2017
SALES (est): 23.28K **Privately Held**
SIC: 8049 Offices of health practitioner

(G-18904)
PATHSCALE INC
20c Trolley Sq (19806-3355)
PHONE..............................408 384-9948
Christopher Bergstrom, *Admn*
EMP: 7 EST: 2001
SQ FT: 16,500
SALES (est): 457.49K **Privately Held**
Web: www.pathscale.com
SIC: 7371 7379 Computer software development; Computer related consulting services

(G-18905)
PATIBANDA SUGUNA M D
2719 Pickering Rd (19808-3636)
PHONE..............................302 453-1550
Suguna Patibanda Md, *Owner*
EMP: 7 EST: 2018
SALES (est): 83.45K **Privately Held**
SIC: 8011 Offices and clinics of medical doctors

(G-18906)
PATRICIA AYERS
1003 N Lincoln St (19805-2741)
PHONE..............................609 335-8923
Patricia Ayers, *Prin*
EMP: 6 EST: 2017
SALES (est): 44.18K **Privately Held**
SIC: 8322 Social worker

(G-18907)
PATRICIA H PURCELL MD
601 Cheltenham Rd (19808-1504)
PHONE..............................302 428-1142
Patricia Purcell Md, *Owner*
EMP: 7 EST: 1978

SALES (est): 460.05K **Privately Held**
SIC: 8011 General and family practice, physician/surgeon

(G-18908)
PATRICIA HEINEMANN MD
1100 N Grant Ave (19805-2671)
PHONE..............................302 778-2229
EMP: 7 EST: 2019
SALES (est): 54.13K **Privately Held**
SIC: 8011 Offices and clinics of medical doctors

(G-18909)
PATRICIA J AVERY ARTIST
55 Indian Field Rd (19810-2914)
PHONE..............................941 223-5546
Patricia Avery, *Prin*
EMP: 5 EST: 2006
SALES (est): 61.81K **Privately Held**
SIC: 7299 Massage parlor

(G-18910)
PATRIOT GOVERNMENT SVCS INC
44 Bancroft Mills Rd (19806-2028)
PHONE..............................302 655-3434
Stephen Mockbee, *Pr*
EMP: 5 EST: 2008
SQ FT: 5,000
SALES (est): 470K **Privately Held**
Web: www.patriotgs.com
SIC: 1521 Single-family housing construction

(G-18911)
PATRIOT SELF DEFENSE
713 Greenbank Rd (19808-3167)
PHONE..............................302 420-3403
EMP: 7 EST: 2012
SALES (est): 53.84K **Privately Held**
SIC: 7999 Karate instruction

(G-18912)
PATRIOT SYSTEMS INC
1204 First State Blvd (19804-3561)
PHONE..............................302 472-9727
Peter M Harmon, *Pr*
EMP: 8 EST: 2006
SALES (est): 715.37K **Privately Held**
Web: www.patriotsystemsinc.com
SIC: 7389 Fire protection service other than forestry or public

(G-18913)
PATTERN LABS TECH INC ✪
108 W 13th St Ste 100 (19801-1145)
PHONE..............................516 340-3369
Dan Lahav, *CEO*
Shiri Nalki, *CFO*
EMP: 5 EST: 2023
SALES (est): 199.4K **Privately Held**
SIC: 7371 Computer software development

(G-18914)
PATTERSON PRICE
5 E Green St (19801)
PHONE..............................302 378-9852
Price Patterson, *Pt*
EMP: 5 EST: 2010
SALES (est): 101.22K **Privately Held**
Web: www.pattersonprice.com
SIC: 6531 Real estate managers

(G-18915)
PATTERSON-SCHWARTZ & ASSOC INC
Also Called: Patterson Schwartz Real Estate
3705 Kennett Pike (19807-2135)
PHONE..............................302 429-4500
Ann Belmonte, *Brnch Mgr*
EMP: 88

SALES (corp-wide): 24.38MM **Privately Held**
Web: www.pattersonschwartz.com
SIC: 6531 Real estate agent, residential
PA: Patterson-Schwartz And Associates, Inc.
7234 Lancaster Pike
Hockessin DE 19707
302 234-5250

(G-18916)
PATTERSON-SCHWARTZ REAL ESTATE
405 Bennington Rd (19804-3012)
PHONE..............................302 690-7746
Dan Logan, *Prin*
EMP: 9 EST: 2010
SALES (est): 120K **Privately Held**
Web: www.pattersonschwartz.com
SIC: 6531 Real estate agent, residential

(G-18917)
PAUL F CAMPANELLA INC
Also Called: Paul F Campanella Auto Service
2379 Limestone Rd (19808-4103)
PHONE..............................302 777-7170
Paul F Campanella, *Pr*
EMP: 10 EST: 1986
SALES (est): 952.18K **Privately Held**
Web: www.campanellas.com
SIC: 7538 General automotive repair shops

(G-18918)
PAUL F CAMPANELLA INC
1015 W 28th St (19802-2905)
PHONE..............................302 218-5374
EMP: 10 EST: 2019
SALES (est): 398.91K **Privately Held**
Web: www.campanellas.com
SIC: 7538 General automotive repair shops

(G-18919)
PAUL IMBER DO
2700 Silverside Rd Ste 3a (19810-3724)
PHONE..............................302 478-5647
Paul Imber D.o.s., *Owner*
EMP: 7 EST: 1997
SALES (est): 400.14K **Privately Held**
SIC: 8031 8011 Offices and clinics of osteopathic physicians; Ears, nose, and throat specialist: physician/surgeon

(G-18920)
PAUL RENZI
Also Called: Paul J Renzi Masonary
6 Brookside Dr (19804-1102)
PHONE..............................302 478-3166
Paul Renzi, *Prin*
EMP: 10 EST: 2010
SALES (est): 173.69K **Privately Held**
Web: www.renzimasonry.com
SIC: 8071 Medical laboratories

(G-18921)
PAUL ROSEN MD
1600 Rockland Rd (19803-3607)
PHONE..............................302 651-4000
EMP: 11 EST: 2018
SALES (est): 330.12K **Privately Held**
Web: www.nemours.org
SIC: 8011 Pediatrician

(G-18922)
PAUL SORVINO FOODS INC
4001 Kennett Pike Ste 134 (19807-2000)
PHONE..............................302 547-1977
Paul Sorvino, *Pr*
Ronnie Robinson, *VP*
EMP: 7 EST: 2008
SALES (est): 631.76K **Privately Held**

Wilmington - New Castle County (G-18923)

SIC: 5146 Seafoods

(G-18923)
PAULS HOUSE INC
1405 Veale Rd (19810-4331)
PHONE..................................302 384-2350
EMP: 8 EST: 2010
SALES (est): 64K **Privately Held**
SIC: 8322 Individual and family services

(G-18924)
PAWS LOVE LLC
1013 Centre Rd Ste 403s (19805-1270)
PHONE..................................267 770-0777
EMP: 5 EST: 2021
SALES (est): 86.31K **Privately Held**
SIC: 0752 Grooming services, pet and animal specialties

(G-18925)
PAXFUL INC (PA)
3422 Old Capitol Trl Pmb 989 (19808-6124)
PHONE..................................917 609-3850
Ray Youssef, *CEO*
EMP: 31 EST: 2015
SQ FT: 500
SALES (est): 13.08MM
SALES (corp-wide): 13.08MM **Privately Held**
Web: www.paxful.com
SIC: 7299 Personal financial services

(G-18926)
PAXO ASSIST LLC
2810 N Church St (19802-4447)
PHONE..................................786 351-0114
EMP: 3
SALES (est): 128.34K **Privately Held**
SIC: 7372 Prepackaged software

(G-18927)
PAY IT FRWARD NTWRKING GROUP C
1308 Lancaster Ave (19805-3902)
PHONE..................................302 213-2695
Necia Jones, *Pr*
EMP: 7
SALES (est): 65.81K **Privately Held**
SIC: 8399 Community development groups

(G-18928)
PAYMENEX INC
501 Silverside Rd Ste 105 (19809-1376)
PHONE..................................302 504-6044
Kingsley Aguoru, *Pr*
Jennifer Aguoru, *Dir*
▲ EMP: 10 EST: 2008
SQ FT: 72
SALES (est): 57.31K **Privately Held**
SIC: 7379 Online services technology consultants

(G-18929)
PAYOURSE TECHNOLOGIES INC
1007 N Orange St (19801-1239)
PHONE..................................206 922-8971
Bashir Aninu, *CEO*
EMP: 16
SALES (est): 543.62K **Privately Held**
SIC: 7389 Financial services

(G-18930)
PBE COMPANIES LLC
Also Called: Rhomboid Properties
2711 Centerville Rd Ste 400 (19808-1660)
PHONE..................................617 346-7459
EMP: 94 EST: 2011
SALES (est): 1.96MM **Privately Held**
SIC: 6512 Nonresidential building operators
HQ: Santander Holdings Usa, Inc.
75 State St
Boston MA 02109
617 346-7200

(G-18931)
PBTV GLOBAL INC
2105a W Newport Pike (19804-3719)
PHONE..................................302 292-1400
Et Jackson, *CEO*
Mark Johnson, *VP*
EMP: 10 EST: 2014
SALES (est): 512.31K **Privately Held**
SIC: 3679 7372 Electronic components, nec; Application computer software

(G-18932)
PCA ACQUISITIONS V LLC
Also Called: Invenio Financial
1002 Justison St (19801-5148)
PHONE..................................302 355-3500
Howard A Enders, *Prin*
EMP: 14 EST: 2008
SALES (est): 645.93K **Privately Held**
Web: www.inveniofinancial.com
SIC: 6799 Investors, nec

(G-18933)
PCD SOLUTIONS LLC
806 W 28th St (19802-2902)
PHONE..................................877 723-7552
EMP: 5 EST: 2019
SALES (est): 38.14K **Privately Held**
SIC: 8742 7389 Financial consultant; Business services, nec

(G-18934)
PCI OF VIRGINIA LLC (HQ)
1 Hausel Rd (19801-5800)
PHONE..................................302 655-7300
EMP: 11 EST: 2009
SALES (est): 2.21MM
SALES (corp-wide): 20.21MM **Privately Held**
Web: www.portcontractors.com
SIC: 4789 Freight car loading and unloading
PA: Port Contractors, Inc.
1 Hausel Rd
Wilmington DE 19801
302 655-7300

(G-18935)
PCMB LLC
Also Called: Primary Care Medical Billing
5201 W Woodmill Dr (19808-4068)
PHONE..................................302 482-1360
EMP: 6 EST: 2015
SALES (est): 258.75K **Privately Held**
SIC: 8741 8721 Management services; Billing and bookkeeping service

(G-18936)
PCO-TECH INC
1000 N West St Ste 1200 (19801-1058)
PHONE..................................248 276-8820
Emil Ott, *Ch*
Murad Karmali, *VP*
▼ EMP: 15 EST: 1986
SALES (est): 4.74MM
SALES (corp-wide): 5.81MM **Privately Held**
Web: www.pco-tech.com
SIC: 5049 5084 Scientific instruments; Measuring and testing equipment, electrical
PA: Optikon Corporation Ltd, The
1099 Guelph St
Kitchener ON N2B 2
519 745-4115

(G-18937)
PDE I LLC
Also Called: Sheraton
422 Delaware Ave (19801-1508)
PHONE..................................302 654-8300
Elizabeth Procaccianti, *Mgr*
Admiral Michelle Joyal, *Prin*
EMP: 92 EST: 1992
SQ FT: 199,000
SALES (est): 4.62MM **Privately Held**
Web: four-points.marriott.com
SIC: 7011 Hotels

(G-18938)
PDM INCORPORATED
Also Called: Pine Derivatives Marketing
3411 Silverside Rd Ste 104wb (19810-4851)
PHONE..................................302 478-0768
Walter L Cleaver, *Pr*
Walter L Cleaver Junior, *Pr*
▲ EMP: 5 EST: 1974
SQ FT: 2,000
SALES (est): 897.81K **Privately Held**
SIC: 5169 Chemicals and allied products, nec

(G-18939)
PEACE AND BLESSINGS CHILD CARE
22 W 30th St (19802-3127)
PHONE..................................302 543-4762
EMP: 7 EST: 2018
SALES (est): 15.97K **Privately Held**
SIC: 8351 Child day care services

(G-18940)
PEACH WIRELESS LLC
3422 Old Capitol Trl (19808-6124)
PHONE..................................646 941-4391
EMP: 5 EST: 2014
SALES (est): 42.74K **Privately Held**
SIC: 4812 Cellular telephone services

(G-18941)
PEAK CRYOTHERAPY
5507 E Timberview Ct (19808-3627)
PHONE..................................302 502-3160
EMP: 5 EST: 2016
SALES (est): 232.97K **Privately Held**
Web: www.peakcryotherapy.net
SIC: 8049 Physical therapist

(G-18942)
PEAK UPTIME SOLUTIONS LLC
2115 Exton Dr (19810-2315)
PHONE..................................856 243-5838
Christopher Brower, *Owner*
EMP: 7 EST: 2015
SALES (est): 69.26K **Privately Held**
SIC: 7371 Computer software development

(G-18943)
PEARCE RUPERTUS KATHLEEN M
501 Silverside Rd Ste 145 (19809-1372)
PHONE..................................302 388-7515
K Marie Rupertus-pearce, *Prin*
EMP: 8 EST: 2011
SALES (est): 104.06K **Privately Held**
SIC: 8011 General and family practice, physician/surgeon

(G-18944)
PEBBLES INC ◆
1013 Centre Rd Ste 403b (19805-1270)
PHONE..................................408 600-8953
Michael Hetkin, *CEO*
Thomas Taylor, *CFO*
Darrian Munroe, *CIO*
EMP: 10 EST: 2022
SALES (est): 454.47K **Privately Held**
SIC: 5045 Computer software

(G-18945)
PEERY FOUNDATION
501 Silverside Rd Ste 123 (19809-1377)
PHONE..................................650 644-4660
David Peery, *Dir*
EMP: 7 EST: 2011
SALES (est): 108.02K **Privately Held**
Web: www.peeryfoundation.org
SIC: 8699 Charitable organization

(G-18946)
PELICAN SEVEN STUDIOS
13 Saddle Ln (19803-3935)
PHONE..................................302 764-6684
Matthew Mccall, *Prin*
EMP: 5 EST: 2008
SALES (est): 55.5K **Privately Held**
Web: www.katonahartcenter.com
SIC: 7299 Apartment locating service

(G-18947)
PEMCO LIGHTING PRODUCTS LLC
150 Pemco Way (19804-3542)
PHONE..................................302 892-9000
John W Bowers, *Pr*
EMP: 15 EST: 2017
SALES (est): 1.15MM **Privately Held**
Web: www.pemcolighting.com
SIC: 3646 Commercial lighting fixtures

(G-18948)
PENFLEX III LLC
702 First State Blvd (19804-3572)
PHONE..................................302 998-0683
EMP: 5 EST: 2004
SALES (est): 462.88K **Privately Held**
SIC: 6531 Real estate leasing and rentals

(G-18949)
PENINSULA UNTD MTHDST HMES INC
Also Called: Country House, The
4830 Kennett Pike (19807-1866)
PHONE..................................302 654-5101
TOLL FREE: 800
Perri White, *Ex Dir*
EMP: 256
SALES (corp-wide): 24.28MM **Privately Held**
SIC: 8361 8051 Aged home; Convalescent home with continuous nursing care
PA: Peninsula United Methodist Homes, Inc.
726 Loveville Rd Ste 3000
Hockessin DE 19707
302 235-6800

(G-18950)
PENN CINEMA RIVERFRONT LLC (PA)
401 S Madison St (19801-5197)
PHONE..................................717 438-4800
Jonathan Byler, *Managing Member*
Bruce Darkes, *CFO*
Drew Schaffer, *Prin*
Penn Ketchum, *Prin*
EMP: 6 EST: 2010
SALES (est): 5MM
SALES (corp-wide): 5MM **Privately Held**
Web: www.penncinema.com
SIC: 7832 Motion picture theaters, except drive-in

(G-18951)
PENN DELCO EDUCATION ASSN
1216 Prospect Dr (19809-2425)
PHONE..................................610 800-8218

Elizabeth Hazlett, *Pr*
EMP: 5 **EST:** 2017
SALES (est): 38.26K **Privately Held**
SIC: 8699 Membership organizations, nec

(G-18952)
PENN LABS INC
Also Called: Glaxosmithkline Company
2711 Centerville Rd Ste 400 (19808-1660)
PHONE.................................215 751-4000
Christopher Gent, *Ch*
EMP: 48 **EST:** 1989
SALES (est): 7.44MM
SALES (corp-wide): 35.31B **Privately Held**
SIC: 2834 Pharmaceutical preparations
HQ: Glaxosmithkline Llc
  2929 Walnut St Ste 1700
  Philadelphia PA 19104
  888 825-5249

(G-18953)
PENNA ORTHODONTICS
2710 Centerville Rd (19808-1644)
PHONE.................................302 998-8783
Robert Penna, *Prin*
EMP: 7 **EST:** 2009
SALES (est): 649.2K **Privately Held**
Web: www.pennaortho.com
SIC: 8021 Orthodontist

(G-18954)
PENNENGINEERING HOLDINGS LLC
103 Foulk Rd Ste 108 (19803-3742)
PHONE.................................302 576-2746
William M Shockley, *Pr*
Joseph R Coluzzi, *VP*
Richard F Davies, *Treas*
Scott Kelley, *Sec*
EMP: 135 **EST:** 2001
SALES (est): 809.93K **Privately Held**
SIC: 3429 3549 Metal fasteners;
  Metalworking machinery, nec
HQ: Penn Engineering & Manufacturing
  Corp.
  5190 Old Easton Rd
  Danboro PA 18916
  800 237-4736

(G-18955)
PENNIE MGMT LLC ✪
251 Little Falls Dr (19808-1674)
PHONE.................................847 682-1644
Geoffrey Harris, *Managing Member*
EMP: 6 **EST:** 2023
SALES (est): 268.13K **Privately Held**
SIC: 7389 Financial services

(G-18956)
PENNMUNI-TIAA US RE FUND LLC
251 Little Falls Dr (19808-1674)
PHONE.................................302 636-5401
EMP: 7 **EST:** 2007
SALES (est): 89.53K **Privately Held**
SIC: 6361 Real estate title insurance

(G-18957)
PENNY HILL EYE CENTER
230 Philadelphia Pike (19809-3125)
PHONE.................................302 764-4613
Doctor Jane G Schweitz, *Prin*
EMP: 7 **EST:** 2013
SALES (est): 115.75K **Privately Held**
SIC: 8042 Offices and clinics of optometrists

(G-18958)
PENNY HILL LAWN & LANDSCAPING
602 Elizabeth Ave (19809-2666)
PHONE.................................302 762-4406
Christopher Hoerner, *Owner*
EMP: 6 **EST:** 2007

SALES (est): 227.28K **Privately Held**
Web: www.pennyhilllawn.com
SIC: 0781 Landscape services

(G-18959)
PENSKE PERFORMANCE INC (HQ)
Also Called: Penske
1105 N Market St (19801-1216)
PHONE.................................302 656-2082
Roger Penske, *Pr*
Walter Czarnecki, *
Richard J Peters, *
Lawrence Bluth, *
Soloman Cohen, *
EMP: 60 **EST:** 1989
SALES (est): 17.75MM
SALES (corp-wide): 5.16B **Privately Held**
Web: www.pensketruckrental.com
SIC: 3711 7513 Automobile assembly,
  including specialty automobiles; Truck
  rental and leasing, no drivers
PA: Penske Corporation
  2555 S Telegraph Rd
  Bloomfield Hills MI 48302
  248 648-2000

(G-18960)
PENSKE TRUCK LEASING CO LP
Also Called: Penske
3625 Kirkwood Hwy (19808-5103)
PHONE.................................302 994-7899
Henry Kuratle, *Brnch Mgr*
EMP: 5
SALES (corp-wide): 2.11B **Privately Held**
Web: www.pensketruckrental.com
SIC: 7513 Truck rental and leasing, no
  drivers
PA: Penske Truck Leasing Co., L.P.
  2675 Morgantown Rd
  Reading PA 19607
  610 775-6000

(G-18961)
PENSKE TRUCK LEASING CORP
Also Called: Penske
4709 Ferris Dr (19808-1103)
PHONE.................................302 658-3255
Henry Kuratle, *Brnch Mgr*
EMP: 5
SALES (corp-wide): 5.16B **Privately Held**
Web: www.pensketruckrental.com
SIC: 7513 Truck rental and leasing, no
  drivers
HQ: Penske Truck Leasing Corporation
  2675 Morgantown Rd
  Reading PA 19607
  610 775-6000

(G-18962)
PENTECO LLC
301 N Market St # 1414 (19801-2529)
PHONE.................................302 472-9105
EMP: 7 **EST:** 2019
SALES (est): 284.31K **Privately Held**
Web: www.penteco.com
SIC: 6411 Insurance agents, nec

(G-18963)
PENTIUS INC
1201 N Orange St Ste 7382 (19801-1286)
PHONE.................................855 825-3778
Theodore Hissey Iv, *Pr*
EMP: 45 **EST:** 2012
SQ FT: 2,200
SALES (est): 5.86MM **Privately Held**
Web: www.pentius.com
SIC: 7373 Systems software development
  services

(G-18964)
PEOPLES STTLMENT ASSN WLMNGTON
Also Called: PEOPLE'S SETTLEMENT DAY CARE
408 E 8th St (19801-3608)
PHONE.................................302 658-4133
Keith Lake, *Ex Dir*
Enid Wallace-simms, *Pr*
Barbara Crowell, *
Dimberu Merriam, *
Terry Toliver, *
EMP: 25 **EST:** 1901
SALES (est): 252.96K **Privately Held**
Web: www.peoplessettlementassociation.org
SIC: 8351 8322 Child day care services;
  Individual and family services

(G-18965)
PEPCO HOLDINGS LLC
630 Martin Luther King Blvd (19801-2306)
P.O. Box 231 (19899-0231)
PHONE.................................202 872-2000
EMP: 14
SALES (corp-wide): 19.08B **Publicly Held**
Web: www.exeloncorp.com
SIC: 4911 4924 Generation, electric power;
  Natural gas distribution
HQ: Pepco Holdings Llc
  701 9th St Nw Ste 3
  Washington DC 20001
  202 872-2000

(G-18966)
PEPSI-COLA BTLG OF WILMINGTON
Also Called: Pepsi-Cola
3501 Governor Printz Blvd (19802-2804)
PHONE.................................302 761-4848
Mark W Robinson, *CFO*
EMP: 110 **EST:** 1935
SQ FT: 90,000
SALES (est): 10.26MM
SALES (corp-wide): 86.39B **Publicly Held**
Web: www.pepsico.com
SIC: 2086 5149 Carbonated soft drinks,
  bottled and canned; Soft drinks
PA: Pepsico, Inc.
  700 Anderson Hill Rd
  Purchase NY 10577
  914 253-2000

(G-18967)
PERASTIC LLC
1704 N Park Dr Apt 508 (19806-2171)
PHONE.................................917 592-4219
John Gicker, *Prin*
Gregory Whitman Field, *Pr*
EMP: 5 **EST:** 2008
SALES (est): 385.88K **Privately Held**
Web: www.perastic.com
SIC: 8748 Business consulting, nec

(G-18968)
PERCH ACQUISITION CO 17 LLC
112 S French St Ste 105-19 (19801-5035)
PHONE.................................617 206-3761
Chris Bell, *Managing Member*
EMP: 5 **EST:** 2021
SALES (est): 429.73K **Privately Held**
SIC: 5199 General merchandise, non-durable

(G-18969)
PERCH FOREIGN ACQUISITION CORP
112 S French St Ste 105-56 (19801-5035)
PHONE.................................617 206-3761
Chris Bell, *Pr*
EMP: 5 **EST:** 2020
SALES (est): 86.31K **Privately Held**

SIC: 5199 General merchandise, non-durable

(G-18970)
PERELLA WEINBERG PARTNERS LLC
405 Campbell Rd (19807-2011)
PHONE.................................267 746-0569
EMP: 5 **EST:** 2019
SALES (est): 71.99K **Privately Held**
Web: www.pwpartners.com
SIC: 6282 Investment advisory service

(G-18971)
PERENNIAL DEV & CNSTR CORP ✪
1320 Philadelphia Pike Ste 202
(19809-1818)
PHONE.................................855 625-0046
William Small, *CEO*
Cheyenne Simms, *
EMP: 26 **EST:** 2022
SALES (est): 1.66MM **Privately Held**
SIC: 8742 Construction project management
  consultant

(G-18972)
PERFECT GRAND LODGE STDAVID
1511 N Claymont St (19802-5228)
PHONE.................................302 689-3579
Michael Deloatch, *Prin*
EMP: 11 **EST:** 2016
SALES (est): 49K **Privately Held**
SIC: 7011 Vacation lodges

(G-18973)
PERFECT PLUMBING PARTNERS INC
117 Median Dr (19803-5318)
PHONE.................................610 521-6654
EMP: 5 **EST:** 2013
SALES (est): 151.61K **Privately Held**
SIC: 1711 Plumbing contractors

(G-18974)
PERFECT TEN NAIL SALON DA
713 Woodsdale Rd (19809-2242)
PHONE.................................302 545-3001
Gena Marsilii, *Prin*
EMP: 5 **EST:** 2010
SALES (est): 39.96K **Privately Held**
SIC: 7231 Cosmetology and personal
  hygiene salons

(G-18975)
PERFICIENT INC
3327 Skyline Dr (19808-2712)
PHONE.................................302 690-2087
EMP: 7
SALES (corp-wide): 905.06MM **Publicly Held**
Web: www.perficient.com
SIC: 7371 Computer software development
PA: Perficient, Inc.
  555 Mryvlle Univ Dr Ste 6
  Saint Louis MO 63141
  314 930-2900

(G-18976)
PERFORMANCE MATERIALS INTL LLC
974 Centre Rd (19805-1269)
PHONE.................................302 999-4083
EMP: 6 **EST:** 2018
SALES (est): 624.81K
SALES (corp-wide): 13.02B **Publicly Held**
SIC: 0721 Crop planting and protection
PA: Dupont De Nemours, Inc.
  974 Centre Rd Bldg 730
  Wilmington DE 19805
  302 774-3034

Wilmington - New Castle County (G-18977)

(G-18977)
PERFORMANCE MATERIALS NA INC
Chestnut Run Plz 974 Ctr Rd (19805)
PHONE...................302 892-7009
Eliezer Maldonado, *Pr*
EMP: 5000 EST: 2017
SALES (est): 32.98MM
SALES (corp-wide): 44.62B **Publicly Held**
SIC: 8748 Business consulting, nec
PA: Dow Inc.
2211 H H Dow Way
Midland MI 48642
989 636-1000

(G-18978)
PERFORMING SYSTEMS INC
101 E 36th St (19802-2317)
PHONE...................302 275-5409
Billy Parton, *Prin*
EMP: 5 EST: 2010
SALES (est): 48.8K **Privately Held**
SIC: 7922 Performing arts center production

(G-18979)
PERFORMNCE SOLUTIONS HOLDG INC (DH)
200 Powder Mill Rd Bldg 304 (19803-2907)
PHONE...................302 774-1000
EMP: 6 EST: 2021
SALES (est): 2.84MM
SALES (corp-wide): 13.02B **Publicly Held**
SIC: 2821 Plastics materials and resins
HQ: Sp Holding Dps, Inc.
2030 Dow Ctr
Midland MI

(G-18980)
PERFORMNCE SPCALTY PDTS NA LLC
974 Centre Rd (19805-1269)
PHONE...................302 774-3034
Edward D Breen, *Ex Ch Bd*
EMP: 16 EST: 2017
SALES (est): 2.26MM
SALES (corp-wide): 13.02B **Publicly Held**
SIC: 0721 Crop planting and protection
PA: Dupont De Nemours, Inc.
974 Centre Rd Bldg 730
Wilmington DE 19805
302 774-3034

(G-18981)
PERKS EXPRESS INC
106 Belmont Dr (19808-4329)
PHONE...................855 924-7424
Tom Scott, *Prin*
EMP: 7 EST: 2016
SALES (est): 86.05K **Privately Held**
Web: www.perksexpress.com
SIC: 7371 Computer software development and applications

(G-18982)
PERPETUAL INVSTMENTS GROUP LLC
Also Called: Www.prptInvestmentsgroupllccom
251 Little Falls Dr (19808-1674)
PHONE...................718 795-3394
EMP: 10 EST: 2019
SALES (est): 500K **Privately Held**
Web: www.perpetual.com.au
SIC: 6799 6798 6531 Real estate investors, except property operators; Real estate investment trusts; Real estate managers

(G-18983)
PERRY & ASSOC
6 Larch Ave Ste 397 (19804-2356)
PHONE...................302 472-8701
EMP: 9 EST: 2006
SALES (est): 198.23K **Privately Held**
SIC: 8082 Home health care services

(G-18984)
PERRY AND ASSOCIATES SERVICES
300 Delaware Ave Ste 210 (19801-6601)
PHONE...................302 581-3092
Perry Veney Senior, *Prin*
Dakeisha Watson, *Prin*
EMP: 5 EST: 2011
SALES (est): 728.4K **Privately Held**
SIC: 6411 Insurance claim adjusters, not employed by insurance company

(G-18985)
PERRY ANTHONY SALON SPA NETWRK
5331 Limestone Rd (19808-1222)
PHONE...................302 239-6161
Perry Anthony Scarfo, *Owner*
Terry Scarfo, *Owner*
EMP: 7 EST: 1990
SALES (est): 185.44K **Privately Held**
Web: www.perryanthony.com
SIC: 7231 Hairdressers

(G-18986)
PERSEPHONE JONES MD
1600 Rockland Rd (19803-3607)
PHONE...................302 651-4000
Persephone Jones, *Ofcr*
EMP: 11 EST: 2017
SALES (est): 251.69K **Privately Held**
Web: www.nemours.org
SIC: 8011 Pediatrician

(G-18987)
PERSONAL HEALTH PDT DEV LLC
Also Called: Phresh Products
4023 Kennett Pike Ste 622 (19807-2018)
PHONE...................888 901-6150
EMP: 20 EST: 2010
SQ FT: 2,000
SALES (est): 2.24MM **Privately Held**
Web: www.phreshproducts.com
SIC: 2833 5047 Medicinals and botanicals; Medical equipment and supplies

(G-18988)
PERSONAL TOUCH MEMORIES
3351 Altamont Dr (19810-2101)
PHONE...................302 598-3987
Joe Euculano, *Prin*
EMP: 5 EST: 2007
SALES (est): 123.17K **Privately Held**
SIC: 7361 Employment agencies

(G-18989)
PERSONALIZED LUGGAGE INC
3411 Silverside Rd Ste 104 (19810-4812)
PHONE...................786 431-3118
Stephen Isaacs, *CEO*
EMP: 4 EST: 2019
SALES (est): 210.08K **Privately Held**
Web: www.personalizedluggage.com
SIC: 2759 Promotional printing

(G-18990)
PERSONAS INC
2711 Centerville Rd (19808-1660)
PHONE...................416 815-7000
Mark Itwaru, *CEO*
EMP: 6 EST: 2011
SALES (est): 46.16K **Privately Held**
Web: www.personasigns.com
SIC: 7371 Computer software development and applications

(G-18991)
PERTEH
1800 Naamans Rd (19810-2600)
PHONE...................302 200-0912
EMP: 4 EST: 2019
SALES (est): 188.23K **Privately Held**
Web: www.perteh.com
SIC: 2341 Women's and children's underwear

(G-18992)
PETER D FURNESS ELC CO INC
1604 Todds Ln (19802-2422)
P.O. Box 1186 (19899-1186)
PHONE...................302 764-6030
Dan Hahn, *Pr*
Tom Hoffman, *Purchasing**
Lisa Barker, *
James Paraskewich, *Estimator**
Daniel J Hahn Senior, *Ex VP*
EMP: 150 EST: 1945
SQ FT: 12,000
SALES (est): 36.02MM **Privately Held**
Web: www.furnesselectric.com
SIC: 1731 General electrical contractor

(G-18993)
PETER F SUBACH
Also Called: Giordano, Lawrence S
1601 Milltown Rd Ste 17 (19808-4084)
PHONE...................302 995-1870
Lawrence S Giordano D.d.s., *Pr*
Peter Subach, *VP*
EMP: 9 EST: 1970
SALES (est): 480.36K **Privately Held**
SIC: 8021 Maxillofacial specialist

(G-18994)
PETER F TOWNSEND MD
3519 Silverside Rd # 101 (19810-4909)
PHONE...................302 633-3555
Jana Siwek Md, *Mgr*
EMP: 10 EST: 2001
SALES (est): 88.41K **Privately Held**
SIC: 8011 Orthopedic physician

(G-18995)
PETER R COGGINS MD (PA)
Also Called: Aesthetic Surgical Associates
5811 Kennett Pike (19807-1137)
PHONE...................302 655-1115
Peter R Coggins Md, *Owner*
EMP: 7 EST: 1997
SALES (est): 472.11K **Privately Held**
Web: www.drcoggins.com
SIC: 8011 Plastic surgeon

(G-18996)
PETERS ALAN E PETERS & ASSOC
1200 Pennsylvania Ave Ste 202 (19806-4350)
PHONE...................302 656-1007
Alan E Peters, *Pr*
EMP: 5 EST: 1986
SALES (est): 549.47K **Privately Held**
Web: www.petersfinancialplanning.com
SIC: 6211 Investment firm, general brokerage

(G-18997)
PETERSON JOSHA
1100 S Broom St (19805-4585)
PHONE...................302 656-5416
Peterson Josha, *Prin*
EMP: 9 EST: 2014
SALES (est): 64.83K **Privately Held**
SIC: 8011 Primary care medical clinic

(G-18998)
PETITE PLUME LLC
Also Called: Petite Plume
605 Geddes St (19805-3718)
PHONE...................800 298-1381
Emily Hikade, *CEO*
EMP: 16 EST: 2014
SALES (est): 1.48MM **Privately Held**
Web: www.petite-plume.com
SIC: 5137 Nightwear: women's, children's, and infants'

(G-18999)
PETITE YOGI
2305 W 18th St (19806-1203)
PHONE...................570 840-5999
EMP: 5 EST: 2017
SALES (est): 34.26K **Privately Held**
SIC: 7999 Yoga instruction

(G-19000)
PETRO INTERNATIONAL CORP
1201 N Orange St Ste 708 (19801-1186)
P.O. Box 7322 (19803-0322)
PHONE...................302 884-6755
Peter Paliyenko, *Pr*
Peter B Paliyenko, *Pr*
▲ EMP: 7 EST: 2003
SQ FT: 10,000
SALES (est): 904.94K **Privately Held**
SIC: 3674 Silicon wafers, chemically doped

(G-19001)
PETTINARO CONSTRUCTION CO INC (PA)
Also Called: Pettinaro
234 N James St (19804-3197)
PHONE...................302 999-0708
Gregory Pettinaro, *CEO*
Verino Pettinaro, *
Robert Anderson, *
Katherine Pettinaro, *
Michael R Walsh, *
EMP: 92 EST: 1965
SQ FT: 25,000
SALES (est): 40.28MM
SALES (corp-wide): 40.28MM **Privately Held**
Web: www.pettinaro.com
SIC: 1541 1542 6531 6519 Industrial buildings, new construction, nec; Commercial and office building, new construction; Real estate agents and managers; Real property lessors, nec

(G-19002)
PETTINARO ENTERPRISES LLC
234 N James St (19804-3132)
PHONE...................302 999-0708
Gregory Pettinaro, *
Tracey Crowley, *
Cindy Pettinaro, *
Victoria Pettinaro, *
EMP: 30 EST: 1987
SQ FT: 25,000
SALES (est): 2.4MM **Privately Held**
Web: www.pettinaro.com
SIC: 6513 Apartment building operators

(G-19003)
PETTINARO RESIDENTIAL LLC
234 N James St (19804-3132)
PHONE...................302 999-0708
Gregory Pettinaro, *CEO*
Michael R Walsh, *COO*
Jim Buck, *CFO*
EMP: 16 EST: 2005
SALES (est): 441.53K **Privately Held**
Web: www.pettinaroresidential.com
SIC: 7389 Relocation service

GEOGRAPHIC SECTION

Wilmington - New Castle County (G-19031)

(G-19004)
PFPC TRUST COMPANY
301 Bellevue Pkwy 4th Fl (19809-3705)
PHONE..................................302 791-2000
Rudolph Bayer, *Prin*
EMP: 252 **EST:** 2006
SALES (est): 219.98K
SALES (corp-wide): 23.54B **Publicly Held**
SIC: 6091 Nondeposit trust facilities
HQ: Pfpc Worldwide Inc
  301 Bellevue Pkwy
  Wilmington DE 19809
  302 791-1700

(G-19005)
PFPC WORLDWIDE INC (DH)
301 Bellevue Pkwy (19809-3705)
PHONE..................................302 791-1700
Timothy G Shack, *Ch*
Stephen M Wynne, *Pr*
Nancy B Wolcott, *VP*
John Fulgoney, *VP*
EMP: 11 **EST:** 1998
SALES (est): 6.68MM
SALES (corp-wide): 23.54B **Publicly Held**
SIC: 6099 8721 6282 7372 Electronic funds transfer network, including switching; Accounting services, except auditing; Investment advice; Application computer software
HQ: Pnc Holding Llc
  300 Delaware Ave Ste 304
  Wilmington DE 19801

(G-19006)
PGI COMMERCIAL LLC
2711 Centerville Rd Ste 4 (19808-1660)
PHONE..................................800 686-8134
EMP: 5 **EST:** 2019
SALES (est): 387.25K **Privately Held**
SIC: 8742 General management consultant

(G-19007)
PGIM FOREIGN INVESTMENTS INC
300 Delaware Ave Ste 820 (19801-1697)
PHONE..................................302 427-9530
John A Oscar Junior, *VP*
EMP: 25 **EST:** 2000
SALES (est): 327.05K
SALES (corp-wide): 60.05B **Publicly Held**
SIC: 6799 Investors, nec
PA: Prudential Financial, Inc.
  751 Broad St
  Newark NJ 07102
  973 802-6000

(G-19008)
PHACTION INC
251 Little Falls Dr (19808-1674)
PHONE..................................240 459-5198
Brandon Wallerson, *CEO*
EMP: 3
SALES (est): 135.7K **Privately Held**
SIC: 2741 Internet publishing and broadcasting

(G-19009)
PHARMUNION LLC
3524 Silverside Rd Ste 35b (19810-4929)
PHONE..................................415 307-5128
Richard Zakchia, *CEO*
EMP: 9 **EST:** 2014
SALES (est): 1.02MM **Privately Held**
Web: www.p-h-u.com
SIC: 2834 Pharmaceutical preparations

(G-19010)
PHASE FLATS II L P
601 N Union St (19805-3029)
PHONE..................................717 291-1911
Rodney Lambert, *Pr*
Stephanie Brown, *Mgr*
EMP: 5
SALES (est): 255.31K **Privately Held**
SIC: 6513 Apartment building operators

(G-19011)
PHASE I FLATS L P
401 N Union St 535 (19805)
PHONE..................................717 291-1911
Rodney Lambert, *Pt*
Stephanie Brown, *Mgr*
EMP: 5 **EST:** 2014
SALES (est): 335.82K **Privately Held**
SIC: 6513 Apartment building operators

(G-19012)
PHAT HOLDINGS INC
251 Little Falls Dr (19808-1674)
PHONE..................................775 438-7428
EMP: 10 **EST:** 2021
SIC: 6719 Holding companies, nec

(G-19013)
PHAZEBREAK COATINGS LLC
1105 N Market St Ste 1300 (19801-1241)
PHONE..................................844 467-4293
EMP: 5 **EST:** 2015
SALES (est): 126.72K **Privately Held**
Web: www.phazebreak.com
SIC: 7389 Business Activities at Non-Commercial Site

(G-19014)
PHILADELPHIA PLUMBING
1707 Foulk Rd (19803-2770)
PHONE..................................302 468-5460
EMP: 5 **EST:** 2016
SALES (est): 56.99K **Privately Held**
SIC: 1711 Plumbing contractors

(G-19015)
PHILADLPHIA SLAR FOR RNWBLE EN ✪
251 Little Falls Dr (19808-1674)
PHONE..................................412 297-4866
Ahmad Shehadeh, *Managing Member*
EMP: 6 **EST:** 2023
SALES (est): 87.5K **Privately Held**
SIC: 5074 Heating equipment and panels, solar

(G-19016)
PHILANTHROPY DELAWARE INC
100 W 10th St (19801-6603)
PHONE..................................302 588-1342
EMP: 7 **EST:** 2018
SALES (est): 152.84K **Privately Held**
Web: www.philanthropydelaware.org
SIC: 8699 Charitable organization

(G-19017)
PHILLIP FULTON
Also Called: Fulton Mechanical
2832 W Oakland Dr (19808-2409)
PHONE..................................302 995-6412
Phillip Fulton, *Prin*
EMP: 5 **EST:** 2011
SALES (est): 93.47K **Privately Held**
SIC: 1711 Mechanical contractor

(G-19018)
PHILLIPS & COHEN ASSOCIATES (PA)
Also Called: Phillips & Cohen Associates
1002 Justison St (19801-5148)
PHONE..................................609 518-9000
Matthew M Phillips, *CEO*
Adam S Cohen, *
Howard Enders, *
John Miller, *
EMP: 80 **EST:** 1997
SQ FT: 10,000
SALES (est): 25.45MM
SALES (corp-wide): 25.45MM **Privately Held**
Web: www.phillips-cohen.com
SIC: 7322 Adjustment and collection services

(G-19019)
PHILLIPS GLDMAN MCLGHLIN HALL
1200 N Broom St (19806-4204)
PHONE..................................302 655-4200
John Phillips Junior, *Pr*
Robert S Goldman, *VP*
Stephen W Spence, *Sec*
EMP: 33 **EST:** 1990
SQ FT: 7,000
SALES (est): 2.24MM **Privately Held**
Web: www.pmhdelaw.com
SIC: 8111 General practice attorney, lawyer

(G-19020)
PHILLIPS INSULATION INC
8 Brookside Dr (19804-1102)
PHONE..................................302 655-6523
Michael D Phillips, *Pr*
Ruth Anne Phillips, *VP*
EMP: 7 **EST:** 1977
SQ FT: 1,600
SALES (est): 685.23K **Privately Held**
Web: www.phillipsinsulation.com
SIC: 1742 Insulation, buildings

(G-19021)
PHLUFFY RIDES LLC
320 Compton Ct (19801-3616)
PHONE..................................302 521-0092
Cicely Adams, *Asst Sec*
EMP: 5 **EST:** 2017
SALES (est): 49.8K **Privately Held**
SIC: 7999 Amusement ride

(G-19022)
PHLY LLC
500 Delaware Ave Unit 1 (19899-7101)
P.O. Box 1960 (19899-1960)
PHONE..................................778 882-2391
Adel Elmouassarani, *CEO*
Adam Verity, *Chief Commercial Officer*
EMP: 8 **EST:** 2018
SALES (est): 394.01K **Privately Held**
SIC: 6411 Insurance agents, brokers, and service

(G-19023)
PHM SPRINGBOARD BIDCO INC
251 Little Falls Dr (19808-1674)
PHONE..................................919 678-7700
Simon Medley, *CEO*
EMP: 5 **EST:** 2019
SALES (est): 337MM **Privately Held**
SIC: 3999 Manufacturing industries, nec

(G-19024)
PHOENIX CTR FOR HLTH WLLNESS L
222 Philadelphia Pike Ste 12 (19809-3166)
PHONE..................................302 543-5321
EMP: 5 **EST:** 2017
SALES (est): 175.39K **Privately Held**
SIC: 8093 Substance abuse clinics (outpatient)

(G-19025)
PHOENIX HOME THEATER INC
Also Called: Phoenix Restoration
403 Marsh Ln # 3 (19804-2402)
PHONE..................................302 295-1390
Brian Potts, *Pr*
EMP: 15 **EST:** 2006
SQ FT: 12,500
SALES (est): 950.8K **Privately Held**
Web: www.phoenixrestores.com
SIC: 7349 Building maintenance services, nec

(G-19026)
PHOENIX NIGHTINGALE
1702 Kirkwood Hwy Ste 2b (19805-4939)
PHONE..................................302 377-6876
Anastacia Mongelluzzo, *Prin*
EMP: 6 **EST:** 2018
SALES (est): 59.3K **Privately Held**
SIC: 8099 Health and allied services, nec

(G-19027)
PHOENIX TRNSP & LOGISTICS INC (HQ)
1000 N West St Ste 1200 (19801-1058)
PHONE..................................302 348-8814
Joel Brown, *Pr*
Chloe G Ayala, *Prin*
Tameka Y Brown, *Prin*
Lisa A Johnson, *Prin*
EMP: 18 **EST:** 2018
SALES (est): 5MM **Privately Held**
Web: www.phoenixtransportus.com
SIC: 4213 Trucking, except local
PA: Phoenix Transportation Services, Llc
  335 E Yusen Way
  Georgetown KY 40324

(G-19028)
PHREESIA INC
1521 Concord Pike Ste 301-221 (19803-3644)
PHONE..................................651 983-0426
Balaji Gandhi, *CFO*
EMP: 60
SALES (est): 12.42MM **Privately Held**
SIC: 8742 Management consulting services

(G-19029)
PHS CORPORATE SERVICES INC
1313 N Market St (19801-6101)
P.O. Box 1709 (19899-1709)
PHONE..................................302 571-1128
Richard Eckman, *Pr*
Benjamin Strauss, *VP*
Andrew Logan, *VP*
EMP: 5 **EST:** 1993
SALES (est): 577.21K **Privately Held**
SIC: 8742 Corporation organizing consultant

(G-19030)
PHYSICIAN DSPNSNG SOLUTIONS
390 Mitch Rd (19804-3943)
PHONE..................................302 734-7246
Ganesh R Balu, *Prin*
EMP: 20 **EST:** 2010
SALES (est): 860.47K **Privately Held**
SIC: 8011 General and family practice, physician/surgeon

(G-19031)
PHYSIOTHERAPY ASSOCIATES INC
2401 Pennsylvania Ave Ste 112 (19806-1432)
PHONE..................................302 655-8989
Kenneth Dill, *Brnch Mgr*
EMP: 6
Web: www.selectphysicaltherapy.com
SIC: 8049 Physical therapist
HQ: Physiotherapy Associates, Inc.
  680 American Ave Ste 200
  King Of Prussia PA 19406
  610 644-7824

Wilmington - New Castle County (G-19032) GEOGRAPHIC SECTION

(G-19032)
PHYSIOTHERAPY ASSOCIATES INC
Also Called: Physio Therapy Association
3411 Silverside Rd Ste 105 (19810-4812)
PHONE................610 444-1270
Phil Donnely, *Pr*
EMP: 8
Web: www.selectphysicaltherapy.com
SIC: 8049 Physical therapist
HQ: Physiotherapy Associates, Inc.
  680 American Ave Ste 200
  King Of Prussia PA 19406
  610 644-7824

(G-19033)
PICENO
1100 Lovering Ave Apt 908 (19806-3289)
PHONE................302 545-6406
EMP: 5 **EST:** 2017
SALES (est): 48.83K **Privately Held**
Web: www.picenowines.com
SIC: 2084 Wines

(G-19034)
PICO LARGO LLC (PA) ◆
1000 N West St Ste 1501 (19801-1001)
PHONE................915 710-2375
Julio Gonzalez, *Managing Member*
EMP: 6 **EST:** 2023
SALES (est): 83.38K
SALES (corp-wide): 83.38K **Privately Held**
SIC: 2034 Dried and dehydrated fruits

(G-19035)
PIERSON RE CONSTRUCTION
101 Rogers Rd (19801-5778)
PHONE................302 407-3308
EMP: 11 **EST:** 2017
SALES (est): 173.28K **Privately Held**
Web: www.repierson.com
SIC: 1629 1521 Heavy construction, nec; Single-family housing construction

(G-19036)
PIKE CREEK ASSOC IN WNS CARE (PA)
Also Called: Pike Creek Assoc In Wmncare PA
4600 Linden Hill Rd Ste 102 (19808)
PHONE................302 995-7062
Susan Gorondy Md, *Owner*
EMP: 14 **EST:** 1995
SALES (est): 1.15MM
SALES (corp-wide): 1.15MM **Privately Held**
SIC: 8011 Gynecologist

(G-19037)
PIKE CREEK AUTOMOTIVE INC
2379 Limestone Rd (19808-4103)
PHONE................302 998-2234
Paul Campanella, *Pr*
EMP: 11 **EST:** 2015
SALES (est): 1.06MM **Privately Held**
Web: www.campanellas.com
SIC: 7538 General automotive repair shops

(G-19038)
PIKE CREEK BIKE LINE INC
4768 Limestone Rd (19808-1928)
PHONE................610 747-1200
John Waddell, *Prin*
John Waddell, *Pr*
Thomas Casadevall, *Ch Bd*
Mary Lou Keller, *Sec*
EMP: 5 **EST:** 1985
SALES (est): 292.96K **Privately Held**
SIC: 5941 7699 Bicycle and bicycle parts; Bicycle repair shop

(G-19039)
PIKE CREEK COMPUTER COMPANY
Also Called: Pike Creek Software
2206 Milltown Rd (19808-4019)
PHONE................302 239-5113
John Knupp, *Pr*
Gloria Knupp, *VP*
Ellen Kelley, *Sec*
Steve Knupp, *Treas*
EMP: 13 **EST:** 1979
SALES (est): 381.69K **Privately Held**
SIC: 7371 Computer software systems analysis and design, custom

(G-19040)
PIKE CREEK COUNSELING
5618 Kirkwood Hwy Ste 3 (19808-5004)
PHONE................302 898-9229
Mitchell Ruoff, *Prin*
EMP: 8 **EST:** 2014
SALES (est): 104.42K **Privately Held**
SIC: 8322 General counseling services

(G-19041)
PIKE CREEK COURT CLUB INC
Also Called: Pike Creek Fitness Club
4905 Mermaid Blvd Ste B (19808-1004)
PHONE................302 239-6688
Ruly Carpenter, *Pr*
David H C Carpenter, *
EMP: 11 **EST:** 1981
SQ FT: 36,000
SALES (est): 116.92K **Privately Held**
Web: www.cinemavilla.org
SIC: 7997 7991 Membership sports and recreation clubs; Physical fitness facilities

(G-19042)
PIKE CREEK PEDIATRIC ASSOC
Also Called: Feick, Judith MD
100 S Riding Blvd (19808-3692)
PHONE................302 239-7755
Cynthia Gabrielli, *VP*
Marilyn K Lynam Md, *Pt*
EMP: 19 **EST:** 1975
SALES (est): 1.16MM **Privately Held**
Web: www.nemours.org
SIC: 8011 Pediatrician

(G-19043)
PIKS COMPANY
919 N Market St Ste 950 (19801-3036)
PHONE................310 372-5770
EMP: 5 **EST:** 2021
SALES (est): 56.54K **Privately Held**
SIC: 7372 Prepackaged software

(G-19044)
PILEPRO INC
300 Delaware Ave Ste 1100 (19801-1670)
PHONE................866 666-7453
Richard Heindl, *VP*
EMP: 10 **EST:** 2009
SALES (est): 184.72K **Privately Held**
SIC: 3444 Sheet metalwork

(G-19045)
PILLAR WEALTH ADVISORS LLC
2711 Centerville Rd Ste 110 (19808-1660)
PHONE................302 409-3502
Michael C Bree C.f.p, *Pr*
EMP: 5 **EST:** 2015
SALES (est): 489.3K **Privately Held**
Web: www.pillarwealthadvisors.com
SIC: 6799 Investors, nec

(G-19046)
PINCKNEY WDNGER URBAN JYCE LLC
2 Mill Rd Ste 204 (19806-2184)
PHONE................302 504-1497
EMP: 6 **EST:** 2009
SALES (est): 889.79K **Privately Held**
Web: www.pwujlaw.com
SIC: 8111 Corporate, partnership and business law

(G-19047)
PINK APE LOGISTICS INC
1911 Concord Pike # 803 (19803-2903)
PHONE................210 570-1033
Kendrick White, *CEO*
EMP: 5 **EST:** 2021
SALES (est): 213.03K **Privately Held**
SIC: 4213 Household goods transport

(G-19048)
PINK APP LLC
251 Little Falls Dr (19808-1674)
PHONE................408 654-4636
EMP: 23 **EST:** 2020
SALES (est): 200K **Privately Held**
SIC: 8999 Communication services

(G-19049)
PINKERTON FOUNDATION
501 Silverside Rd (19809-1374)
PHONE................800 839-1754
EMP: 8
SALES (est): 119.47K **Privately Held**
Web: www.thepinkertonfoundation.org
SIC: 8699 Charitable organization

(G-19050)
PINNACLE RESTORATION CORP
14 Murphy Rd (19803-3045)
PHONE................302 650-0520
EMP: 5 **EST:** 2010
SALES (est): 101.16K **Privately Held**
SIC: 1799 Special trade contractors, nec

(G-19051)
PINTER LAW LLC
5586 Kirkwood Hwy (19808-5002)
PHONE................302 409-0089
EMP: 5 **EST:** 2014
SALES (est): 112.48K **Privately Held**
Web: www.pinterlawonline.com
SIC: 8111 General practice law office

(G-19052)
PIONEER FENCE CO INC
109 S John St (19804-3157)
PHONE................302 998-2892
H Robert Chambers Junior, *Pr*
Richard Chambers, *VP*
Scott Chambers, *VP*
EMP: 15 **EST:** 1939
SQ FT: 4,500
SALES (est): 948.09K **Privately Held**
Web: www.pioneerfencedelaware.com
SIC: 1799 Fence construction

(G-19053)
PIONEER NATURAL RESOURCES CO
1209 N Orange St (19801-1120)
PHONE................972 444-9001
EMP: 10 **EST:** 2012
SALES (est): 836.79K **Privately Held**
SIC: 8742 Business management consultant

(G-19054)
PIPELINE FUNDING COMPANY LLC
2 Greenville Crossing (19807-2321)
PHONE................302 421-2287
Bqarbara M Morris, *Pr*
EMP: 167 **EST:** 2007
SALES (est): 680.98K
SALES (corp-wide): 20.96B **Publicly Held**
SIC: 6799 Investors, nec
HQ: Nextera Energy Capital Holdings, Inc.
  700 Universe Blvd
  Juno Beach FL 33408
  561 691-7171

(G-19055)
PITCH BLACK SEALCOATING LLC
12 Toby Ct (19808-3019)
PHONE................302 824-8135
EMP: 5 **EST:** 2018
SALES (est): 190.72K **Privately Held**
SIC: 1611 Surfacing and paving

(G-19056)
PIVOT PHYSICAL THERAPY
4512 Kirkwood Hwy (19808-5123)
PHONE................302 504-6195
EMP: 9 **EST:** 2019
SALES (est): 151.34K **Privately Held**
Web: www.pivotphysicaltherapy.com
SIC: 8049 Physical therapist

(G-19057)
PIXEL NINJA STUDIOS LLC ◆
1007 N Orange St Fl 4 (19801-1242)
PHONE................218 398-1374
Argie Cerico, *Managing Member*
EMP: 7 **EST:** 2023
SALES (est): 277.92K **Privately Held**
SIC: 7372 Prepackaged software

(G-19058)
PIXORIZE INC
Also Called: Pixorize
251 Little Falls Dr (19808-1674)
P.O. Box 1190 (10021-0037)
PHONE................737 529-4404
Nathan Liu, *COO*
David Westfall, *CEO*
EMP: 2 **EST:** 2018
SALES (est): 90K **Privately Held**
Web: www.pixorize.com
SIC: 2741 Miscellaneous publishing

(G-19059)
PIXSTAR INC
913 N Market St Ste 200 (19801-3097)
EMP: 25 **EST:** 1998
SALES (est): 1.46MM **Privately Held**
Web: www.pixstar.com
SIC: 7379 7371 Computer related consulting services; Custom computer programming services

(G-19060)
PIZAZZ BEAUTY STUDIO
4001 N Market St (19802-2219)
PHONE................302 761-9820
Beverly Monroe, *Pr*
EMP: 5 **EST:** 1984
SALES (est): 95.1K **Privately Held**
SIC: 7231 Hairdressers

(G-19061)
PK & ASSOCIATES GROUP INC ◆
28b Trolley Sq (19806-3352)
PHONE................302 394-9052
Kofa Freeman Junior, *CEO*
Ezra Ngafua, *CFO*
Sonia Warsaw, *COO*
EMP: 5 **EST:** 2022
SALES (est): 150K **Privately Held**
SIC: 7389 8742 Legal and tax services; Marketing consulting services

(G-19062)
PKG LLC
251 Little Falls Dr (19808-1674)
PHONE................269 651-8640
EMP: 2 **EST:** 2014

SALES (est): 186.13K **Privately Held**
SIC: 3423 Tools or equipment for use with sporting arms

(G-19063)
PLAIN & FANCY INC
Also Called: Plain & Fancy Interiors
5716 Kennett Pike Ste E (19807-1328)
PHONE....................302 656-9901
Molly Wiley, *Pr*
EMP: 5 **EST:** 1959
SQ FT: 1,500
SALES (est): 326.98K **Privately Held**
Web: www.plainandfancyinteriors.com
SIC: 7389 Interior designer

(G-19064)
PLANET FITNESS
900 N Madison St (19801-1473)
PHONE....................302 543-5604
EMP: 7 **EST:** 2009
SALES (est): 67K **Privately Held**
Web: www.planetfitness.com
SIC: 7991 Physical fitness facilities

(G-19065)
PLANET FITNESS INC
2201 Farrand Dr (19808-5763)
PHONE....................302 483-7740
EMP: 5
Web: www.planetfitness.com
SIC: 7991 Physical fitness clubs with training equipment
PA: Planet Fitness, Inc.
  4 Liberty Ln W
  Hampton NH 03842

(G-19066)
PLANET X SKATEBOARDS
2400 Shellpot Dr (19803-2548)
PHONE....................484 886-9287
Angel Acevedo, *Prin*
EMP: 5 **EST:** 2014
SALES (est): 126.03K **Privately Held**
SIC: 3949 Skateboards

(G-19067)
PLANIVERSITY LLC
919 N Market St Ste 425 (19801-3014)
PHONE....................315 498-0986
Erik Allen, *Prin*
EMP: 5 **EST:** 2016
SALES (est): 590.29K **Privately Held**
Web: www.planiversity.com
SIC: 4724 Travel agencies

(G-19068)
PLANKE APP LLC (PA)
1300 Del Ave Ste 210a (19806)
PHONE....................607 287-0794
EMP: 6
SALES (est): 46.41K
SALES (corp-wide): 46.41K **Privately Held**
SIC: 7999 Physical fitness instruction

(G-19069)
PLANNED PARENTHOOD OF DELAWARE (PA)
625 N Shipley St (19801-2249)
PHONE....................302 655-7293
Nanci Hoffman, *Pr*
Linda Scott, *CFO*
EMP: 20 **EST:** 1932
SQ FT: 10,000
SALES (est): 4.5MM
SALES (corp-wide): 4.5MM **Privately Held**
Web: www.plannedparenthood.org
SIC: 8093 Family planning clinic

(G-19070)
PLASTIC FREE DELAWARE INC
404 Snuff Mill Rd (19807-1028)
PHONE....................302 981-1950
Dee Durham, *Prin*
EMP: 5 **EST:** 2021
SALES (est): 60.74K **Privately Held**
Web: www.plasticfreedelaware.org
SIC: 8399 Advocacy group

(G-19071)
PLATFORM GALLERY LLC
1201 N Market St Ste 111 (19801-1156)
PHONE....................844 244-2940
Denilia Francis, *Managing Member*
EMP: 8 **EST:** 2018
SALES (est): 584.42K **Privately Held**
SIC: 6531 Real estate agent, residential

(G-19072)
PLATINUM (US) ACQUISITION LLC (DH)
1209 N Orange St (19801-1120)
PHONE....................404 414-7768
Dave Towers, *Mgr*
EMP: 9 **EST:** 2016
SALES (est): 10.81MM
SALES (corp-wide): 7.26MM **Privately Held**
SIC: 6519 Landholding office
HQ: Platinum Midco Limited
  14 Floral Street Covent Garden
  London WC2E

(G-19073)
PLATINUM US DISTRIBUTION INC
Also Called: Wellnx Life Sciences USA
1201 N Orange St Ste 741 (19801-1175)
PHONE....................905 364-8713
Dana Johnson, *Pr*
Brad Woodgate, *Prin*
EMP: 5 **EST:** 2005
SQ FT: 7,000
SALES (est): 1.53MM
SALES (corp-wide): 5.75MM **Privately Held**
SIC: 2834 Pharmaceutical preparations
PA: Global Health Technologies Inc
  6335 Edwards Blvd
  Mississauga ON
  905 364-8690

(G-19074)
PLAY BY PLAY LLC
24a Trolley Sq Ste 1389 (19806-3334)
PHONE....................302 703-7670
Charles Ricketts Junior, *Managing Member*
EMP: 6 **EST:** 2020
SALES (est): 127.7K **Privately Held**
SIC: 8748 Business consulting, nec

(G-19075)
PLAY FOR GOOD INC
3411 Silverside Rd 104r (19810-4812)
PHONE....................312 520-9788
Amee Kamdar, *Prin*
Janet Moehring, *Prin*
EMP: 6
SALES (est): 190K **Privately Held**
SIC: 6732 Charitable trust management

(G-19076)
PLAZA FUEL
2213 Concord Pike (19803-2908)
PHONE....................302 275-6242
Steven Henck, *Prin*
EMP: 9 **EST:** 2008
SALES (est): 163.31K **Privately Held**
Web: www.plazamarinegroup.com
SIC: 2869 Fuels

(G-19077)
PLEASANT HILL LANES INC
Also Called: Pleasant Hill Bowling Alley
1001 W Newport Pike (19804-3335)
PHONE....................302 998-8811
Cheryl Woodward, *Pr*
EMP: 16 **EST:** 1962
SALES (est): 413.1K **Privately Held**
Web: www.bowlphl.com
SIC: 7933 5941 Ten pin center; Bowling equipment and supplies

(G-19078)
PLEXUS FITNESS
20 Montchanin Rd Ste 60 (19807-2179)
PHONE....................302 654-9642
Jennifer Collison, *Prin*
EMP: 15 **EST:** 2012
SALES (est): 791.05K **Privately Held**
Web: www.empoweredwellnessstudio.com
SIC: 7991 Physical fitness facilities

(G-19079)
PLLAL INTERNATIONAL LLC
251 Little Falls Dr (19808-1674)
PHONE....................786 235-7800
Antonio Lepiane, *Dir*
EMP: 45 **EST:** 2008
SQ FT: 500
SALES (est): 2.41MM **Privately Held**
SIC: 8742 Management consulting services
PA: Datatec Ltd
  3rd Floor Sandown Chambers
  Sandown, 81 Maude St Gauteng
  Sandton GP 2031

(G-19080)
PLOENERS AUTOMOTIVE PDTS CO
510 S Market St (19801-5209)
P.O. Box 1408 (19899-1408)
PHONE....................302 655-4418
TOLL FREE: 800
Mark Ploener, *Pr*
Randall Ploener, *Sec*
EMP: 9 **EST:** 1947
SQ FT: 3,000
SALES (est): 943.45K **Privately Held**
Web: www.ploenersapco.com
SIC: 5013 5063 Truck parts and accessories; Storage batteries, industrial

(G-19081)
PLOTLY (US) INC
2801 Cntrvlle Rd Fl 1pmb Flr 1 (19808)
PHONE....................781 974-4062
Rob Williams, *Admn*
Gary Young, *
EMP: 60 **EST:** 2015
SALES (est): 3MM **Privately Held**
SIC: 7372 Prepackaged software

(G-19082)
PLUSHBEDS INC (PA)
1201 N Orange St Ste 7058 (19801-1190)
PHONE....................888 758-7423
Michael Hughes, *Prin*
EMP: 8 **EST:** 2010
SALES (est): 407.33K
SALES (corp-wide): 407.33K **Privately Held**
Web: www.plushbeds.com
SIC: 5712 2515 Mattresses; Mattresses and bedsprings

(G-19083)
PLUSPOINT INC
2810 N Church St (19802-4447)
PHONE....................305 901-2676
Sergii Shanin, *CEO*

EMP: 8
SALES (est): 321.21K **Privately Held**
SIC: 7372 Business oriented computer software

(G-19084)
PLY FASHION INC
055 Limestone Rd Ste 200-C (19808)
PHONE....................323 723-5337
Vladimir Shlygin, *CEO*
Tatiana Oreshkova, *Prin*
Kirill Rostovskiy, *Prin*
EMP: 5 **EST:** 2021
SALES (est): 107.01K **Privately Held**
SIC: 7371 Computer software development and applications

(G-19085)
PM CHINA INC
974 Centre Rd (19805-1269)
PHONE....................302 999-4083
EMP: 12 **EST:** 2016
SALES (est): 455.19K
SALES (corp-wide): 9.67B **Publicly Held**
SIC: 0721 Crop planting and protection
PA: Celanese Corporation
  222 Las Colinas Blvd W
  Irving TX 75039
  877 295-0004

(G-19086)
PM TAIWAN INC (HQ)
974 Centre Rd (19805-1269)
PHONE....................302 999-4083
EMP: 27 **EST:** 2016
SALES (est): 882.13K
SALES (corp-wide): 12.44B **Publicly Held**
Web: www.dupont.com
SIC: 0721 Crop planting and protection
PA: International Flavors & Fragrances Inc.
  521 W 57th St
  New York NY 10019
  212 765-5500

(G-19087)
PNA TITLE SERVICES LLC
5602 Kirkwood Hwy (19808-5004)
PHONE....................302 294-6219
EMP: 9 **EST:** 2017
SALES (est): 228.32K **Privately Held**
Web: www.pnatitleservicesllc.com
SIC: 6541 Title and trust companies

(G-19088)
PNC BANCORP INC (HQ)
Also Called: PNC
300 Delaware Ave (19801-1607)
PHONE....................302 427-5896
James E Rohr, *Ch Bd*
Maria Schaffer, *Ex VP*
Debra Falkowski, *Sec*
EMP: 163 **EST:** 1990
SQ FT: 650,000
SALES (est): 16.04B
SALES (corp-wide): 23.54B **Publicly Held**
SIC: 6021 National trust companies with deposits, commercial
PA: The Pnc Financial Services Group Inc
  300 5th Ave
  Pittsburgh PA 15222
  888 762-2265

(G-19089)
PNC BANK NATIONAL ASSOCIATION
Also Called: PNC
5325 Limestone Rd (19808-1222)
PHONE....................302 235-4010
Karen Pingley, *Mgr*
EMP: 6
SALES (corp-wide): 23.54B **Publicly Held**

Wilmington - New Castle County (G-19090)

Web: www.pncbank.com
SIC: 6021 National trust companies with deposits, commercial
HQ: Pnc Bank, National Association
300 5th Ave
Pittsburgh PA 15222
877 762-2000

(G-19090)
PNC BANK NATIONAL ASSOCIATION
Also Called: PNC
2203 Kirkwood Hwy (19805-4903)
PHONE................302 993-3000
Shirley Dowdy, Brnch Mgr
EMP: 6
SALES (corp-wide): 23.54B Publicly Held
Web: www.pnc.com
SIC: 6021 National trust companies with deposits, commercial
HQ: Pnc Bank, National Association
300 5th Ave
Pittsburgh PA 15222
877 762-2000

(G-19091)
PNC BANK NATIONAL ASSOCIATION
Also Called: PNC
2751 Centerville Rd Ste 101 (19808-1600)
PHONE................302 994-6337
EMP: 9
SALES (corp-wide): 23.54B Publicly Held
Web: www.pnc.com
SIC: 6021 National commercial banks
HQ: Pnc Bank, National Association
300 5th Ave
Pittsburgh PA 15222
877 762-2000

(G-19092)
PNC BANK NATIONAL ASSOCIATION
Also Called: PNC
222 Delaware Ave (19801-1637)
PHONE................302 429-2266
EMP: 6
SALES (corp-wide): 23.54B Publicly Held
Web: www.pnc.com
SIC: 6021 6162 National commercial banks; Mortgage bankers and loan correspondents
HQ: Pnc Bank, National Association
300 5th Ave
Pittsburgh PA 15222
877 762-2000

(G-19093)
PNC BANK NATIONAL ASSOCIATION
Also Called: PNC
1704 Marsh Rd (19810-4606)
PHONE................302 479-4529
Alice Belcher, Mgr
EMP: 10
SALES (corp-wide): 23.54B Publicly Held
Web: www.pnc.com
SIC: 6021 National commercial banks
HQ: Pnc Bank, National Association
300 5th Ave
Pittsburgh PA 15222
877 762-2000

(G-19094)
PNC BANK NATIONAL ASSOCIATION
Also Called: PNC
4111 Concord Pike (19803-1401)
PHONE................302 479-4520
Mark Digiacomo, Mgr
EMP: 10

SALES (corp-wide): 23.54B Publicly Held
Web: www.pnc.com
SIC: 6021 National commercial banks
HQ: Pnc Bank, National Association
300 5th Ave
Pittsburgh PA 15222
877 762-2000

(G-19095)
PNC BANK NATIONAL ASSOCIATION
Also Called: PNC
4725 Kirkwood Hwy (19808-5097)
PHONE................302 993-3013
Pamela Jamison, Brnch Mgr
EMP: 5
SALES (corp-wide): 23.54B Publicly Held
Web: www.pnc.com
SIC: 6021 National commercial banks
HQ: Pnc Bank, National Association
300 5th Ave
Pittsburgh PA 15222
877 762-2000

(G-19096)
PNC BANK DELAWARE
Also Called: PNC
222 Delaware Ave Lbby (19801-1637)
P.O. Box 791 (19899-0791)
PHONE................302 655-7221
EMP: 826
SIC: 6022 State trust companies accepting deposits, commercial

(G-19097)
PNC FINANCIAL SVCS GROUP INC
Also Called: PNC Financial
300 Delaware Ave Ste 1600 (19801-1607)
PHONE................302 429-1364
Morgan Calvert, Ch
EMP: 10
SALES (corp-wide): 23.54B Publicly Held
Web: www.pnc.com
SIC: 6021 National commercial banks
PA: The Pnc Financial Services Group Inc
300 5th Ave
Pittsburgh PA 15222
888 762-2265

(G-19098)
PNC HOLDING LLC (HQ)
Also Called: PNC
300 Delaware Ave Ste 304 (19801-1607)
PHONE................302 427-5897
EMP: 5 EST: 1991
SQ FT: 650,000
SALES (est): 46.86MM
SALES (corp-wide): 23.54B Publicly Held
SIC: 6712 Bank holding companies
PA: The Pnc Financial Services Group Inc
300 5th Ave
Pittsburgh PA 15222
888 762-2265

(G-19099)
PNC NATIONAL BANK OF DELAWARE (DH)
Also Called: PNC
300 Bellevue Pkwy Ste 200 (19809-3704)
PHONE................302 479-4529
EMP: 90 EST: 1996
SALES (est): 94.6MM
SALES (corp-wide): 23.54B Publicly Held
SIC: 6022 State commercial banks
HQ: Pnc Bank, National Association
300 5th Ave
Pittsburgh PA 15222
877 762-2000

(G-19100)
POINT EGHT THIRD PRDCTIONS LLC (PA)
1201 N Market St Ste 111 (19801-1156)
PHONE................302 317-9419
Gary Bogan, Managing Member
EMP: 6 EST: 2017
SQ FT: 600
SALES (est): 513.47K
SALES (corp-wide): 513.47K Privately Held
SIC: 7812 Motion picture and video production

(G-19101)
POINTE CONDOMINIUMS
1702 N Park Dr (19806-2151)
PHONE................302 656-2018
EMP: 7 EST: 2011
SALES (est): 77.33K Privately Held
SIC: 8641 Condominium association

(G-19102)
POINTE SNAPS
1000 Marsh Rd (19803-4340)
PHONE................260 602-0898
EMP: 4 EST: 2010
SALES (est): 56.41K Privately Held
Web: www.pointesnaps.com
SIC: 2211 Shoe fabrics

(G-19103)
POLICE ATHC LEAG WLMINGTON INC
3707 N Market St (19802-2213)
PHONE................302 764-6170
Wilbert Miller, Ex Dir
EMP: 8 EST: 1998
SALES (est): 2.7MM Privately Held
Web: www.palw.org
SIC: 8699 Athletic organizations

(G-19104)
POLICE ATHLETIC LEAGUE OF DE
4 S Cliffe Dr (19809-1622)
PHONE................302 792-0930
Scott Phillips, Owner
EMP: 7 EST: 2015
SALES (est): 53.95K Privately Held
Web: www.palw.org
SIC: 8641 Youth organizations

(G-19105)
POLIQUICKS LLC
2810 N Church St (19802-4447)
PHONE................512 915-7919
Vienna Mott, CEO
EMP: 5
SALES (est): 199.4K Privately Held
SIC: 7371 Computer software development

(G-19106)
POLISH AMERICAN CIVIC ASSN
618 S Franklin St (19805-4302)
PHONE................302 652-9324
Bob Wilson, Owner
Joseph Kaminski, Pr
Bob Wilson, Prin
EMP: 5 EST: 1930
SALES (est): 94.26K Privately Held
SIC: 7997 Membership sports and recreation clubs

(G-19107)
POLISH LIBRARY ASSOCIATION
433 S Van Buren St (19805-4065)
PHONE................302 652-9555
John Lafferty, Dir
Tom Olexsky, Pr
John Bartkowski, Treas

Walter Przybylek, Sec
EMP: 5 EST: 1899
SALES (est): 127.45K Privately Held
SIC: 8641 Bars and restaurants, members only

(G-19108)
POLISH NAT ALIANCE OF THE US
100 6th Ave (19805-4712)
PHONE................302 658-3324
Wieslaua Podsiad, Prin
EMP: 5 EST: 2010
SALES (est): 49.26K Privately Held
SIC: 8641 Veterans' organization

(G-19109)
POLLINTION CAPITL PARTNERS LLC ◆
251 Little Falls Dr (19808-1674)
PHONE................872 201-1168
Tony O'sullivan, Managing Member
EMP: 8 EST: 2022
SALES (est): 385K Privately Held
SIC: 6282 Investment advisory service

(G-19110)
POLONIEX LLC
1013 Centre Rd Ste 403b (19805-1270)
PHONE................302 518-6536
EMP: 8 EST: 2016
SALES (est): 210.56K Privately Held
Web: www.poloniex.com
SIC: 8742 Foreign trade consultant

(G-19111)
POLSINELLI SHALTON FLANNI
222 Delaware Ave (19801-1621)
PHONE................302 654-2984
EMP: 5 EST: 2008
SALES (est): 190.58K Privately Held
SIC: 8111 General practice law office

(G-19112)
POLYCOM INC
101 Watford Rd (19808-1423)
PHONE................302 420-8618
EMP: 6 EST: 2019
SALES (est): 121.93K Privately Held
Web: www.hp.com
SIC: 3661 Telephone and telegraph apparatus

(G-19113)
POLYDEL CORPORATION
820 N Buttonwood St (19801-4328)
P.O. Box 7234 (19803-0234)
PHONE................302 655-8200
Claude Beaudoin, Pr
Gregory Beaudoin, VP
▲ EMP: 14 EST: 1984
SQ FT: 24,000
SALES (est): 449.45K Privately Held
SIC: 2899 Chemical preparations, nec

(G-19114)
POLYJOHN ACQUISITION LLC ◆
251 Little Falls Dr (19808-1674)
PHONE................800 292-1305
EMP: 5 EST: 2022
SALES (est): 124.73K
SALES (corp-wide): 23.32MM Privately Held
SIC: 7389 Personal service agents, brokers, and bureaus
PA: Polyjohn Enterprises Corporation
2500 Gaspar Ave
Whiting IN 46394
219 659-1152

(G-19115)
POP POP MAGIC CLOWN
1511 Governor House Cir (19809-2481)
PHONE...................................302 764-5494
EMP: 5 **EST:** 2017
SALES (est): 47.41K **Privately Held**
Web: www.poppopthemagicclown.com
SIC: 7929 Entertainers

(G-19116)
POP-A-DOCS ALL NTRAL HRBAL SPP
318 New Castle Ave (19801-5440)
PHONE...................................302 622-5788
Sherrod Williams, *CEO*
Keyana Williams, *Prin*
Rahmir Williams, *Prin*
Isaiah Williams, *Prin*
Noah Williams, *Prin*
EMP: 5
SALES (est): 104.73K **Privately Held**
SIC: 7389 Business Activities at Non-Commercial Site

(G-19117)
POP-A-LOCK WILMINGTON
16 Lehigh Rd (19808-3106)
PHONE...................................866 866-6368
EMP: 7 **EST:** 2018
SALES (est): 107.48K **Privately Held**
Web: www.popalock.com
SIC: 7699 Locksmith shop

(G-19118)
PORRO REALTY GROUP
1301 N Scott St (19806-4023)
PHONE...................................302 384-6056
Mike Porro, *Prin*
EMP: 5 **EST:** 2017
SALES (est): 231.42K **Privately Held**
SIC: 6531 Real estate brokers and agents

(G-19119)
PORT CONTRACTORS INC (PA)
1 Hausel Rd (19801-5800)
PHONE...................................302 655-7300
Mary Anna Thomas, *VP*
Tom Mason, *
Bernard Parisot, *
Jean Luc Decaux, *
Paul Ryan, *
▼ **EMP:** 31 **EST:** 1981
SALES (est): 20.21MM
SALES (corp-wide): 20.21MM **Privately Held**
Web: www.portcontractors.com
SIC: 4789 Freight car loading and unloading

(G-19120)
PORTRAIT INNOVATIONS INC
5601 Concord Pike Ste D (19803-6421)
PHONE...................................302 477-1696
EMP: 8
Web: www.portraitinnovations.com
SIC: 7221 Photographer, still or video
HQ: Portrait Innovations, Inc.
2016 Ayrsley Town Blvd # 200
Charlotte NC 28273
704 499-9200

(G-19121)
POS & MERCHANT SERVICES LLC
2233 Inwood Rd (19810-2841)
PHONE...................................302 356-3030
Anthony Spennato, *Prin*
EMP: 5 **EST:** 2019
SALES (est): 180.64K **Privately Held**
Web: www.your-pos.net
SIC: 8611 Merchants' association

(G-19122)
POSH SALON
41 Harlech Dr (19807-2507)
PHONE...................................302 655-7000
Michelle Ziegler, *Pt*
Christa Rich, *Prin*
EMP: 8 **EST:** 2002
SALES (est): 205.75K **Privately Held**
Web: www.poshsalonde.com
SIC: 7231 Hairdressers

(G-19123)
POSIDON ADVENTURE INC
3301 Lancaster Pike Ste 5a (19805-1436)
PHONE...................................302 543-5024
Scott Jenkins, *Pr*
Sandra Jenkins, *VP*
Scott Jenkins, *Treas*
EMP: 10 **EST:** 1987
SALES (est): 959.24K **Privately Held**
Web: poseidon-adventures-myscubashop.myshopify.com
SIC: 5091 7999 4725 Diving equipment and supplies; Diving instruction, underwater; Tours, conducted

(G-19124)
POSITIONEERING LLC
19c Trolley Sq (19806-3355)
PHONE...................................302 415-3200
EMP: 5 **EST:** 2010
SALES (est): 258.79K **Privately Held**
SIC: 8742 7389 Business management consultant; Business services, nec

(G-19125)
POSITIVE DIRECTIONS II LLC
240 N James St (19804-3171)
PHONE...................................302 654-9444
EMP: 10 **EST:** 2010
SALES (est): 219.39K **Privately Held**
Web: www.positivedirectionsadmin.com
SIC: 8322 General counseling services

(G-19126)
POSITIVE RESULTS CLEANING INC
338 B And O Ln (19804-1448)
PHONE...................................302 575-1146
Daniel Rodriguez, *Owner*
EMP: 7 **EST:** 2002
SALES (est): 287.41K **Privately Held**
Web: www.prccarpetcleaning.com
SIC: 7217 Carpet and upholstery cleaning

(G-19127)
POSITIVE VIBES ONLY BRAND
2 Colony Blvd Apt 115 (19802-1412)
PHONE...................................302 500-1369
Williams Kareem, *Prin*
EMP: 5 **EST:** 2016
SALES (est): 35.11K **Privately Held**
SIC: 7549 Automotive services, nec

(G-19128)
POSITRON ACCESS SOLUTIONS INC
2801 Centerville Rd Fl 1 Pmb 638 (19808)
PHONE...................................888 577-5254
Reginald Weiser, *CEO*
Pierre Trudeau, *Pr*
Claude Samson, *CFO*
Alan W Pritchard, *VP Sls*
EMP: 10 **EST:** 2009
SALES (est): 2.23MM
SALES (corp-wide): 54.83MM **Privately Held**
Web: www.positronaccess.com
SIC: 3663 4899 Mobile communication equipment; Data communication services
HQ: Corporation Positron Solutions D'acces
5101 Rue Buchan Bureau 220
Montreal QC H4P 2
514 345-2220

(G-19129)
POST MEDIA INC
Also Called: Post
4023 Kennett Pike Pmb 50314 (19807-2018)
PHONE...................................203 244-8424
Noam Bardin, *CEO*
Lucy Liu, *CFO*
EMP: 20 **EST:** 2020
SALES (est): 1.32MM **Privately Held**
SIC: 7375 Information retrieval services

(G-19130)
POST RDGE PRSRVATION ASSOC LLC
4 Denny Rd (19809-3445)
PHONE...................................302 761-7303
EMP: 5 **EST:** 2018
SALES (est): 77.06K **Privately Held**
Web: www.arbormanagement.com
SIC: 6552 Land subdividers and developers, commercial

(G-19131)
POSTIMPRESSIONS INCORPORATED
1400 Maryland Ave (19805-4700)
P.O. Box 25 (19710-0025)
PHONE...................................302 656-2271
John P Grabowski, *Pr*
Pam Grabowski, *VP*
EMP: 5 **EST:** 1985
SQ FT: 10,000
SALES (est): 417.61K **Privately Held**
Web: www.postimpressionsinc.net
SIC: 2741 Miscellaneous publishing

(G-19132)
POTOMAC CHESAPEAKE ASSN FOR C
4701 Limestone Rd (19808-1927)
PHONE...................................302 225-6248
Junius Clark, *Prin*
EMP: 6 **EST:** 2014
SALES (est): 42.67K **Privately Held**
SIC: 8699 Membership organizations, nec

(G-19133)
POTTER ANDERSON & CORROON
1313 N Market St Fl 6 (19801-6108)
PHONE...................................302 984-6078
EMP: 9
SALES (est): 150K **Privately Held**
Web: www.potteranderson.com
SIC: 8111 Legal services

(G-19134)
POTTER ANDERSON & CORROON LLP
1313 N Market St (19801-6108)
P.O. Box 951 (19899-0951)
PHONE...................................302 984-6000
Donald J Wolfe Junior, *Mng Pt*
EMP: 176 **EST:** 1826
SQ FT: 7,500
SALES (est): 8.69MM **Privately Held**
Web: www.potteranderson.com
SIC: 8111 General practice attorney, lawyer

(G-19135)
POWELLS GENERAL SERVICES
706 W 38th St (19802-2033)
PHONE...................................302 384-7817
Gardner S Powell, *Prin*
EMP: 5 **EST:** 2012
SALES (est): 92.75K **Privately Held**
SIC: 1522 Residential construction, nec

(G-19136)
POWER CONTROL TECHNOLOGIES INC
42 Butternut Ct (19810-6002)
PHONE...................................203 560-2806
EMP: 5 **EST:** 2017
SALES (est): 109.84K **Privately Held**
SIC: 1731 General electrical contractor

(G-19137)
POWER FINANCIAL WELLNESS INC (PA) ✪
1209 N Orange St (19801-1120)
PHONE...................................313 413-2345
Brian Dempsey, *CEO*
EMP: 6 **EST:** 2023
SALES (est): 68.89K
SALES (corp-wide): 68.89K **Privately Held**
SIC: 7371 Software programming applications

(G-19138)
POWERCOMM LLC
6 Hadco Rd Unit 1 (19804-1014)
PHONE...................................302 235-8922
Brian Mcanulla, *Pr*
EMP: 20 **EST:** 2017
SALES (est): 1.19MM **Privately Held**
Web: www.powercommllc.com
SIC: 1731 General electrical contractor

(G-19139)
PP OF DE
625 N Shipley St (19801-2228)
PHONE...................................252 393-3691
EMP: 5 **EST:** 2019
SALES (est): 55.38K **Privately Held**
SIC: 8611 Business associations

(G-19140)
PPG ARCHITECTURAL FINISHES INC
Also Called: Glidden Professional Paint Ctr
3613 Kirkwood Hwy Ste A (19808-5132)
PHONE...................................302 454-9091
Edward Strickland, *Brnch Mgr*
EMP: 6
SQ FT: 5,000
SALES (corp-wide): 17.65B **Publicly Held**
Web: www.silvercanyonrc.com
SIC: 2851 Paints and allied products
HQ: Ppg Architectural Finishes, Inc.
1 Ppg Pl
Pittsburgh PA 15272
412 434-3131

(G-19141)
PPG ARCHITECTURAL FINISHES INC
Also Called: Glidden Professional Paint Ctr
516 Philadelphia Pike (19809-2155)
PHONE...................................302 762-0555
William Dale, *Mgr*
EMP: 4
SALES (corp-wide): 17.65B **Publicly Held**
Web: www.silvercanyonrc.com
SIC: 2851 Paints and allied products
HQ: Ppg Architectural Finishes, Inc.
1 Ppg Pl
Pittsburgh PA 15272
412 434-3131

(G-19142)
PQ HOLDING INC
3411 Silverside Rd (19810-4812)
P.O. Box 840 (19482-0840)
PHONE...................................302 478-6160
Neal Murphy, *Prin*
EMP: 20 **EST:** 1981
SALES (est): 1.31MM

Wilmington - New Castle County (G-19143)

SALES (corp-wide): 745MM **Privately Held**
SIC: 5085 Industrial supplies
PA: Pq Llc
300 Lindenwood Dr
Malvern PA 19355
610 651-4200

(G-19143)
PRACTICE WITHOUT PRESSURE
3105 Limestone Rd (19808-2147)
PHONE..................302 635-7837
EMP: 7 EST: 2018
SALES (est): 294.93K **Privately Held**
Web: www.pwppikecreek.com
SIC: 8021 Offices and clinics of dentists

(G-19144)
PRAKTIKAAI CO
919 N Market St (19801-3023)
PHONE..................959 300-0719
Adam Turaekz, *CEO*
EMP: 12
SALES (est): 251.15K **Privately Held**
Web: www.praktika.ai
SIC: 7371 Computer software development and applications

(G-19145)
PRANA BODYWORKS
112 South Rd (19809-3033)
PHONE..................302 229-3880
EMP: 5 EST: 2018
SALES (est): 22.18K **Privately Held**
SIC: 8049 Massage Therapist

(G-19146)
PRATCHER KRAYER LLC
1000 N West St Fl 10 (19801-1059)
P.O. Box 591 (19899-0591)
PHONE..................302 803-5291
EMP: 6 EST: 2017
SALES (est): 536.22K **Privately Held**
Web: www.pkinjury.com
SIC: 8111 Specialized law offices, attorneys

(G-19147)
PRAVAL TECHNOLOGIES LLC
1000 N West St Ste 1200 (19801-1050)
PHONE..................206 693-2443
Sashi Pagadal, *Managing Member*
EMP: 80
SALES (est): 1.26MM **Privately Held**
SIC: 7371 Custom computer programming services

(G-19148)
PRECIOUS LITTLE HANDS CHILDCAR
702b Wilmington Ave (19805-5111)
PHONE..................302 298-5027
Tazeema Bourne, *Prin*
Derrick Loatman, *Prin*
EMP: 8 EST: 2016
SQ FT: 3,000
SALES (est): 483K **Privately Held**
SIC: 8351 Child day care services

(G-19149)
PRECIOUS LTTLE HNDS CHLDCARE C
111 S Lincoln St (19805-3810)
PHONE..................302 256-0194
EMP: 5 EST: 2021
SALES (est): 37.32K **Privately Held**
SIC: 8351 Child day care services

(G-19150)
PRECIOUS LTTLE LAMBS CHILDCARE
509 N Dupont St (19805-3148)
PHONE..................302 723-1403
Philnise Johnson, *Prin*
EMP: 8 EST: 2016
SALES (est): 27.63K **Privately Held**
SIC: 8351 Child day care services

(G-19151)
PRECISION AUTO LLC
802 Maryland Ave (19805-4835)
PHONE..................302 384-6169
Yusuf Muflihi, *Asst Sec*
EMP: 7 EST: 2018
SALES (est): 231.92K **Privately Held**
Web: www.precisionautotires.com
SIC: 7538 General automotive repair shops

(G-19152)
PRECISION COLOR GRAPHICS LLC
1401 Todds Ln (19802-2417)
PHONE..................302 661-2595
EMP: 6 EST: 2008
SALES (est): 920.04K **Privately Held**
Web: www.gopcgnow.com
SIC: 7336 Graphic arts and related design

(G-19153)
PRECISION CON CUTNG OF DEL MD
Also Called: Precision Concrete Cutting
215 Middleboro Rd (19804-1603)
PHONE..................855 832-9876
EMP: 8 EST: 2019
SALES (est): 162.16K **Privately Held**
Web: www.precisionconcretellc.com
SIC: 1771 Concrete work

(G-19154)
PRECISION DOOR SERVICE
330 Water St Ste 109 (19804-2433)
PHONE..................302 343-6394
Dean Wilkinson, *Pr*
EMP: 8 EST: 2012
SALES (est): 234.67K **Privately Held**
Web: www.precisiondoor.net
SIC: 7699 5211 Garage door repair; Garage doors, sale and installation

(G-19155)
PRECISION HMES RMDLG GROUP LLC
500 N Augustine St (19804-2602)
PHONE..................302 293-0244
EMP: 5 EST: 2017
SALES (est): 126.55K **Privately Held**
Web: www.precisionremodelingsolutions.com
SIC: 1521 New construction, single-family houses

(G-19156)
PRECISION LANDSCAPING INC
318 7th Ave (19805-4764)
PHONE..................302 658-3855
EMP: 49
SALES (corp-wide): 335.27K **Privately Held**
SIC: 0781 Landscape services
PA: Precision Landscaping Inc
8 Maryland Ave
Newark DE 19711
302 369-6043

(G-19157)
PRECISION LANDSCAPING SVCS LLC ◊
318 7th Ave (19805-4764)
PHONE..................302 528-2935
Jesus Rosado, *CEO*
EMP: 5 EST: 2023
SALES (est): 97.1K **Privately Held**
SIC: 0781 Landscape services

(G-19158)
PRECISION SYSTEMS INDS LLC
2711 Centerville Rd # 400 (19808-1660)
PHONE..................224 388-9837
George Hines, *Mng Pt*
EMP: 5 EST: 2009
SALES (est): 422.67K **Privately Held**
SIC: 3699 Electrical equipment and supplies, nec

(G-19159)
PRECISION TECHNIC DEFENCE INC ◊
251 Little Falls Dr (19808-1674)
PHONE..................801 404-4626
Mark Anderton, *Prin*
EMP: 3 EST: 2022
SALES (est): 296.51K **Privately Held**
SIC: 3812 Defense systems and equipment

(G-19160)
PRECISIONCURE LLC
2207 Concord Pike 301 (19803-2908)
PHONE..................302 622-9119
EMP: 8 EST: 2008
SALES (est): 355.1K **Privately Held**
SIC: 7371 Computer software development and applications

(G-19161)
PREFERED TAX SERVICE INC
Also Called: Preferred Business Services
2201 N Market St Ste A (19802-4227)
PHONE..................302 654-4388
Ann Swan, *Pr*
Eddie Swan, *VP*
EMP: 6 EST: 1989
SALES (est): 247.48K **Privately Held**
Web: www.preferredtax.com
SIC: 7291 Tax return preparation services

(G-19162)
PREFERRED CONTRACTORS INC
204 S Park Dr (19809-1362)
PHONE..................302 798-5457
Michael Feil, *Pr*
Robin Feil, *VP*
Michael Feil, *Pr*
EMP: 7 EST: 1989
SQ FT: 200
SALES (est): 704.42K **Privately Held**
SIC: 1521 Single-family home remodeling, additions, and repairs

(G-19163)
PREFERRED FIRE PROTECTION
4321 Miller Rd (19802-1901)
PHONE..................302 256-0607
Earl Hood, *Prin*
EMP: 11 EST: 2012
SALES (est): 787.38K **Privately Held**
Web: www.preferred-fire.com
SIC: 1711 Fire sprinkler system installation

(G-19164)
PREFERRED MECHANICAL
1722 Newport Gap Pike (19808-6120)
PHONE..................302 668-1151
John Veasey, *Prin*
EMP: 14 EST: 2013
SALES (est): 625.72K **Privately Held**
Web: www.preferredmechanical.net
SIC: 1711 Mechanical contractor

(G-19165)
PREFERRED TERM SECURITIES XXVI
920 N King St Lbby 10 (19801-3319)
PHONE..................302 651-7642
EMP: 6 EST: 2007
SALES (est): 150K **Privately Held**
SIC: 6211 Security brokers and dealers

(G-19166)
PRELUDE THERAPEUTICS INC
175 Innovation Blvd (19805-1592)
PHONE..................302 467-1280
Kris Vaddi, *CEO*
Paul A Friedman, *
Brian Piper, *CFO*
David Mauro, *CMO*
Peggy A Scherle, *CSO*
EMP: 68 EST: 2016
SQ FT: 11,000
Web: www.preludetx.com
SIC: 2834 Pharmaceutical preparations

(G-19167)
PREMIER BUILDERS INC
2601 Annand Dr Ste 21 (19808-3719)
PHONE..................302 999-8500
Ken Ralsten, *Pr*
EMP: 5 EST: 2004
SALES (est): 727.81K **Privately Held**
Web: www.premierbuildersde.com
SIC: 1521 New construction, single-family houses

(G-19168)
PREMIER CHIROPRACTIC
701 N Market St (19801-3008)
P.O. Box 686 (19899-0686)
PHONE..................302 384-7145
Alexander Zilberman, *Prin*
EMP: 7 EST: 2014
SALES (est): 75.12K **Privately Held**
SIC: 8041 Offices and clinics of chiropractors

(G-19169)
PREMIER IL VOLO LLC
1209 N Orange St (19801-1120)
PHONE..................847 201-1760
EMP: 6 EST: 2021
SALES (est): 65.81K **Privately Held**
SIC: 8351 Child day care services

(G-19170)
PREMIER SALONS INTL INC
Also Called: Premier Salon 22920
4737 Concord Pike (19803-1442)
PHONE..................302 477-3459
EMP: 7
SALES (corp-wide): 161.45MM **Privately Held**
SIC: 7231 Hairdressers
HQ: Premier Salons International, Inc.
8341 10th Ave N
Minneapolis MN 55427

(G-19171)
PREMIERE ORAL AND FACIAL SURG
1202 Foulk Rd (19803-2796)
PHONE..................302 273-8300
David H Dieu D.m.d. Md, *Prin*
EMP: 11 EST: 2016
SALES (est): 234.85K **Privately Held**
SIC: 8011 Surgeon

(G-19172)
PREMIUM AQUATICS LLC
1209 Pecksniff Rd (19808-2117)
PHONE..................302 994-7742
Charlie Fawcett, *Owner*
EMP: 7 EST: 2007

GEOGRAPHIC SECTION
Wilmington - New Castle County (G-19203)

SALES (est): 77.92K **Privately Held**
Web: www.delawarefishstore.com
SIC: 8422 Aquarium

(G-19173)
PREMIUM DIESEL PARTS LLC
3 Germay Dr Ste 4 (19804-1127)
PHONE...................................205 723-1510
EMP: 2
SALES (est): 92.41K **Privately Held**
Web: www.premiumdieselparts.com
SIC: 3714 Motor vehicle engines and parts

(G-19174)
PREMO TECHNOLOGIES INC
1013 Centre Rd Ste 403b (19805-1270)
PHONE...................................951 514-6993
Dallas Hutchinson, *Prin*
EMP: 5 EST: 2016
SALES (est): 76.09K **Privately Held**
SIC: 7371 Computer software development and applications

(G-19175)
PRENTICE-HALL CORP SYSTEM INC (PA)
Also Called: Prentice Hall Legal Fincl Svcs
2711 Centerville Rd Ste 400 (19808-1660)
PHONE...................................302 636-5440
Daniel R Butler, *Pr*
William H Freeborn Junior, *VP*
Bruce R Winn, *Pr*
Mark A Rosser, *VP*
EMP: 85 EST: 1913
SALES (est): 2.39MM **Privately Held**
SIC: 8111 Legal services

(G-19176)
PREPARED LLC
4023 Kennett Pike # 50307 (19807-2018)
PHONE...................................650 825-5996
John Ramey, *Mng Pt*
EMP: 5
SALES (est): 92.85K **Privately Held**
Web: www.theprepared.org
SIC: 2741 Internet publishing and broadcasting

(G-19177)
PRESCIENCE CORPORATION
1201 N Orange St Ste 600 (19801-1171)
PHONE...................................208 599-3441
EMP: 23
SALES (corp-wide): 235.73K **Privately Held**
Web: www.prescience.online
SIC: 7371 Custom computer programming services
PA: Prescience Corporation
  325 N Saint Paul St # 3100
  Dallas TX 75201
  208 599-3441

(G-19178)
PRESCOTECH INC
1313 N Market St (19801-6114)
PHONE...................................502 585-5866
Rick Fransen, *Pr*
Matt Schoen, *
EMP: 80 EST: 1986
SALES (est): 3.88MM **Privately Held**
SIC: 4783 5199 2675 Packing and crating; Packaging materials; Paper die-cutting

(G-19179)
PRESSAIR INTERNATIONAL
3501 Silverside Rd (19810-4910)
PHONE...................................302 636-5440
Karl-heinz Trondle, *Prin*
EMP: 14 EST: 2005

SALES (est): 171.79K **Privately Held**
Web: www.pressair.com
SIC: 3714 Motor vehicle parts and accessories

(G-19180)
PRESTIGE AUTO
1027 W 25th St (19802-3372)
PHONE...................................302 898-5486
EMP: 5 EST: 2018
SALES (est): 89.37K **Privately Held**
SIC: 7538 General automotive repair shops

(G-19181)
PRESTIGE CONTRACTORS INC
2615 N Tatnall St (19802-3525)
P.O. Box 14 (19899-0014)
PHONE...................................302 722-1032
Zachary Jackson, *CEO*
EMP: 6 EST: 2009
SALES (est): 506.35K **Privately Held**
SIC: 1542 1522 Nonresidential construction, nec; Residential construction, nec

(G-19182)
PRESTIGE FROG CLEANING SVCS
316 N Market St (19801-2530)
P.O. Box 2677 (19805-0677)
PHONE...................................302 654-8459
Serena Smith, *Prin*
EMP: 5 EST: 2014
SALES (est): 50.97K **Privately Held**
SIC: 7699 Cleaning services

(G-19183)
PRETTY DAMN QUICK INC ✪
1007 N Orange St Fl 10 (19801-1277)
PHONE...................................201 613-2296
EMP: 5 EST: 2022
SALES (est): 76.63K **Privately Held**
SIC: 4225 General warehousing and storage

(G-19184)
PRETTY GIRL PRESS ✪
1910 N Washington St (19802-4717)
PHONE...................................484 668-0770
Jimia K Redden, *Pr*
EMP: 3 EST: 2023
SALES (est): 135.7K **Privately Held**
SIC: 2741 7389 Miscellaneous publishing; Business services, nec

(G-19185)
PREVAIL TRIAL CONSULTANTS LLC
1007 N Orange St Ste 510 (19801-1248)
PHONE...................................302 442-7836
Richard Hobbs, *Prin*
Kevin Kelly, *Prin*
Edward Carp, *Prin*
EMP: 10 EST: 2016
SALES (est): 500.53K **Privately Held**
Web: www.prevailtrial.com
SIC: 8748 Business consulting, nec

(G-19186)
PREVENT CHILD ABUSE DELAWARE
100 W 10th St Ste 715 (19801-6605)
PHONE...................................302 425-7490
Brooke Balan, *Dir*
Karen Derasmo, *Dir*
EMP: 8 EST: 1976
SALES (est): 671.44K **Privately Held**
Web: www.pcadelaware.org
SIC: 8322 Social service center

(G-19187)
PRICE EDWARD A/GNRAL CONTRACTR
10 Belmont Ave (19804-1508)
PHONE...................................302 571-9281

Edward Price, *Prin*
EMP: 5 EST: 2009
SALES (est): 84.97K **Privately Held**
SIC: 1522 Residential construction, nec

(G-19188)
PRICE IS RIGHT CONTRACTING LLC
919 N Market St Ste 950 (19801-3036)
PHONE...................................215 760-1416
EMP: 10 EST: 2012
SALES (est): 972.1K **Privately Held**
Web: www.pirremediation.com
SIC: 1799 Special trade contractors, nec

(G-19189)
PRICETWEAKERS LLC
1201 N Orange St Ste 7204 (19801-1219)
PHONE...................................424 325-0597
EMP: 9 EST: 2020
SALES (est): 56.54K **Privately Held**
Web: www.pricetweakers.net
SIC: 7372 Application computer software

(G-19190)
PRIDE INTERNATIONAL LLC (DH)
1209 N Orange St (19801-1120)
PHONE...................................713 789-1400
David A Armour, *Pr*
EMP: 10 EST: 2001
SALES (est): 288.98MM
SALES (corp-wide): 1.41B **Privately Held**
SIC: 1381 1389 8711 Drilling oil and gas wells; Servicing oil and gas wells; Petroleum, mining, and chemical engineers
HQ: Ensco United Incorporated
  1209 N Orange St
  Wilmington DE

(G-19191)
PRIME ONE GLOBAL LLC
2055 Limestone Rd (19808-5536)
PHONE...................................831 215-5123
EMP: 53 EST: 2021
SALES (est): 940K **Privately Held**
Web: www.primeone.global
SIC: 8742 Marketing consulting services

(G-19192)
PRIME PRODUCTS USA INC
118 Valley Rd (19804-1300)
PHONE...................................302 528-3866
Stewart Modell, *Pr*
▲ EMP: 9 EST: 2008
SALES (est): 934.89K **Privately Held**
Web: www.primeproductsreligiousitems.com
SIC: 2911 Oils, fuel

(G-19193)
PRIMERICA
1210 N King St (19801-3218)
PHONE...................................302 439-0206
George Earley, *COO*
EMP: 5 EST: 2019
SALES (est): 213.46K **Privately Held**
Web: www.primerica.com
SIC: 6282 Investment advice

(G-19194)
PRINCETONIAN MHC LLC
251 Little Falls Dr (19808-1674)
PHONE...................................800 927-9800
EMP: 5 EST: 2015
SALES (est): 283.69K **Privately Held**
SIC: 1521 Single-family housing construction

(G-19195)
PRINCIPAL LF GLOBL FUNDING II
1100 N Market St (19890-1100)
PHONE...................................302 636-6392

EMP: 6 EST: 2011
SALES (est): 723.79K **Privately Held**
SIC: 6722 Management investment, open-end

(G-19196)
PRINT-N-PRESS INC
300 Cassidy Dr Ste 301 (19804-2442)
PHONE...................................302 994-6665
Thomas Mc Cartney, *Pr*
EMP: 7 EST: 1982
SQ FT: 2,700
SALES (est): 469.44K **Privately Held**
Web: www.printnpress.net
SIC: 2752 Offset printing

(G-19197)
PRINTIFY INC
108 W 13th St (19801)
PHONE...................................415 978-6351
EMP: 9 EST: 2013
SALES (est): 443.95K **Privately Held**
Web: www.printify.com
SIC: 2211 Print cloths, cotton

(G-19198)
PRINTIFY LLC (PA)
108 W 13th St (19801-1145)
PHONE...................................415 968-6351
EMP: 8 EST: 2018
SALES (est): 4.77MM
SALES (corp-wide): 4.77MM **Privately Held**
Web: www.printify.com
SIC: 8742 Business management consultant

(G-19199)
PRISMA HOLDING INC (PA)
Also Called: Prisma Retail
1209 N Orange St (19801-1120)
PHONE...................................903 480-4880
Lucas Gorganchian, *CEO*
EMP: 30 EST: 2019
SALES (est): 764.29K
SALES (corp-wide): 764.29K **Privately Held**
SIC: 7371 Software programming applications

(G-19200)
PRITHVI TECHNOLOGIES LLC
2055 Limestone Rd Ste 200c (19808-5536)
PHONE...................................302 313-9273
EMP: 25
SALES (est): 655.43K **Privately Held**
SIC: 7379 Online services technology consultants

(G-19201)
PRO PEST MANAGEMENT OF DE INC
200 Cassidy Dr Ste 201 (19804-2441)
P.O. Box 3038 (19804-0038)
PHONE...................................302 994-2847
Jack Vickers, *Prin*
EMP: 7 EST: 2011
SALES (est): 223.9K **Privately Held**
SIC: 8741 Business management

(G-19202)
PRO PHYSICAL THERAPY
100 Valley Rd (19804-1311)
PHONE...................................610 368-1006
EMP: 5 EST: 2020
SALES (est): 101.02K **Privately Held**
Web: www.atipt.com
SIC: 8049 Physical therapist

(G-19203)
PRO PHYSL THERAPY FTNS ACCT
Also Called: Pro Physical Therapy

(PA)=Parent Co (HQ)=Headquarters
✪ = New Business established in last 2 years

Wilmington - New Castle County (G-19204)

GEOGRAPHIC SECTION

1812 Marsh Rd Ste 505 (19810-4515)
PHONE...................302 658-7800
Franklin Rooks, *Owner*
EMP: 8 **EST:** 2006
SALES (est): 220.69K **Privately Held**
SIC: 8049 Physical therapist

(G-19204)
PRO REHAB AND CHIROPRACTIC
2101 Foulk Rd (19810-4710)
PHONE...................302 268-6129
EMP: 9 **EST:** 2017
SALES (est): 37.19K **Privately Held**
Web: www.prorehabchiro.com
SIC: 8041 Offices and clinics of chiropractors

(G-19205)
PRO REHAB CHIROPRACTORS
215 Peirce Rd (19803-3729)
PHONE...................302 652-2225
EMP: 6 **EST:** 2014
SALES (est): 79.46K **Privately Held**
Web: www.prorehabchiro.com
SIC: 8041 Offices and clinics of chiropractors

(G-19206)
PRO RHAB CHRPRCTIC RHBLITATION
1708 Lovering Ave Ste 102-3 (19806-2141)
PHONE...................302 332-3312
EMP: 7 **EST:** 2019
SALES (est): 111.42K **Privately Held**
Web: www.prorehabchiro.com
SIC: 8041 Offices and clinics of chiropractors

(G-19207)
PROCESS ACADEMY LLC
4023 Kennett Pike Ste 56762 (19807-2018)
PHONE...................302 415-3104
EMP: 7 **EST:** 2014
SALES (est): 488.58K **Privately Held**
SIC: 7372 8243 7389 Business oriented computer software; Operator training, computer; Business services, nec

(G-19208)
PROCESSFLO INC
1212 First State Blvd (19804-3561)
PHONE...................302 633-4200
Sean Sweeney, *Brnch Mgr*
EMP: 7
SALES (corp-wide): 4.7MM **Privately Held**
Web: www.processflo.com
SIC: 5084 Pumps and pumping equipment, nec
PA: Processflo, Inc.
115 Hilton St
Easton PA 18042
610 400-8625

(G-19209)
PRODUCE SPOT LLC
2400 Northeast Blvd (19802-4509)
PHONE...................267 864-1232
EMP: 10 **EST:** 2020
SALES (est): 549.34K **Privately Held**
SIC: 2033 5142 Fruits and fruit products, in cans, jars, etc.; Fruits, frozen

(G-19210)
PROFESSIONAL HANDYMAN SVCS INC
28 Club Ln (19810-3309)
PHONE...................302 478-1237
Herbert J Gillespie, *Pr*
EMP: 7 **EST:** 2009
SALES (est): 60.2K **Privately Held**
SIC: 7299 Handyman service

(G-19211)
PROFESSIONAL PEST MGT DE
476 E Ayre St (19804-2513)
PHONE...................302 738-1036
Jack Vickers, *Owner*
EMP: 5 **EST:** 2017
SALES (est): 67.56K **Privately Held**
SIC: 7342 Pest control in structures

(G-19212)
PROFESSIONAL RECRUITING CONS
Also Called: PRC
3617a Silverside Rd (19810-5101)
PHONE...................302 479-9550
Roger Malatesta, *Pr*
EMP: 5 **EST:** 1985
SQ FT: 1,200
SALES (est): 820.01K **Privately Held**
Web: www.prcstaffing.com
SIC: 7361 Executive placement

(G-19213)
PROFESSIONAL SELECTION INC
1209 N Orange St (19801-1120)
PHONE...................905 392-7313
EMP: 12 **EST:** 2013
SALES (est): 95.69K
SALES (corp-wide): 7.77MM **Privately Held**
Web: www.professionalselection.com
SIC: 7361 Executive placement
PA: Professional Selection Inc
357 Bay St
Toronto ON M5H 2
647 725-5330

(G-19214)
PROFESSIONAL THERAPEUTICS
1407 Saint Elizabeth St (19805-4570)
PHONE...................302 438-5859
Melissa Shaw, *Prin*
EMP: 6 **EST:** 2015
SALES (est): 60.33K **Privately Held**
SIC: 8049 Physical therapist

(G-19215)
PROFESSIONALS
3812 Governor Printz Blvd (19802-2306)
PHONE...................302 764-5501
George Leach, *Pt*
Brandon Mayfield, *Pt*
EMP: 6 **EST:** 1998
SALES (est): 97.71K **Privately Held**
SIC: 7241 Barber shops

(G-19216)
PROFESSIONALS AUTO SALON
2507 W 6th St (19805-2908)
PHONE...................302 420-5691
Priest Cephas, *Prin*
EMP: 7 **EST:** 2015
SALES (est): 269.16K **Privately Held**
SIC: 7538 General automotive repair shops

(G-19217)
PROFESSIONALS LLC
Also Called: Professional Bytes
1000 N West St Ste 1283 (19801-1050)
PHONE...................302 295-2330
Shoban Pattam, *Pr*
Hari Pattam, *Ofcr*
EMP: 6 **EST:** 2005
SALES (est): 363.09K **Privately Held**
Web: www.professionalsllc.com
SIC: 7371 Computer software systems analysis and design, custom

(G-19218)
PROGRESSIVE DENTAL ARTS
5301 Limestone Rd Ste 212 (19808-1265)
PHONE...................302 234-2222
EMP: 9 **EST:** 2015
SALES (est): 99.07K **Privately Held**
Web: www.progressivedentalartspikecreek.com
SIC: 8021 Dentists' office

(G-19219)
PROGRESSIVE INVESTMENT CO INC
801 N West St Fl 2 (19801-1525)
PHONE...................302 656-8597
S Patricia Griffith, *CEO*
Susan Patricia Griffith, *CEO*
EMP: 10 **EST:** 1982
SQ FT: 75,000
SALES (est): 3.47MM
SALES (corp-wide): 49.61B **Publicly Held**
Web: www.progressiveinvestment.com
SIC: 6799 Investors, nec
PA: The Progressive Corporation
6300 Wilson Mills Rd
Mayfield Village OH 44143
440 461-5000

(G-19220)
PROGRESSIVE SERVICES INC
300 Commercial Dr (19805-1907)
PHONE...................302 658-7260
Michael Hirst, *Pr*
EMP: 50 **EST:** 1998
SQ FT: 7,000
SALES (est): 7.91MM **Privately Held**
Web: www.psielectric.com
SIC: 1731 General electrical contractor

(G-19221)
PROGRESSIVE SOFTWARE CMPT INC
2 Righter Pkwy (19803-1528)
PHONE...................302 479-9700
EMP: 125 **EST:** 1992
SALES (est): 9.95MM **Privately Held**
Web: www.psci.com
SIC: 7373 7371 Computer integrated systems design; Custom computer programming services

(G-19222)
PROGRESSIVE TELECOM LLC
3422 Old Capitol Trl Ste 1483 (19808-6124)
PHONE...................302 883-8883
EMP: 25 **EST:** 2010
SQ FT: 1,500
SALES (est): 2.45MM **Privately Held**
Web: www.progressivetele.com
SIC: 4813 Voice telephone communications

(G-19223)
PROJECT ASSISTANTS INC
1521 Concord Pike Ste 301 (19803-3644)
PHONE...................302 477-9711
EMP: 38 **EST:** 1996
SQ FT: 6,000
SALES (est): 4.44MM **Privately Held**
Web: www.wiserwulff.com
SIC: 7371 Computer software development

(G-19224)
PROJECT OF PROVIDENCE LLC
1007 Park Pl Apt A (19806-4304)
PHONE...................302 438-8970
Tamara Williams, *Prin*
EMP: 5 **EST:** 2016
SALES (est): 77.91K **Privately Held**
SIC: 8244 8742 Business college or school; Marketing consulting services

(G-19225)
PROJECT OTR LLC
1209 N Orange St (19801-1120)
PHONE...................404 964-2244
Vang Wong, *CEO*
EMP: 9 **EST:** 2019
SALES (est): 410.6K **Privately Held**
SIC: 8742 Marketing consulting services

(G-19226)
PROJECT WIDGETS INC
501 Silverside Rd Ste 29 (19809-1388)
PHONE...................302 439-3414
Ira Brown, *Pr*
EMP: 6 **EST:** 2006
SALES (est): 661.48K **Privately Held**
Web: www.projectwidgets.com
SIC: 8748 Business consulting, nec

(G-19227)
PROKSY RESEARCH LLC ◆
2055 Limestone Rd 200p (19808-5536)
PHONE...................737 238-0104
Rameez Jamal, *Managing Member*
EMP: 15 **EST:** 2022
SALES (est): 50K **Privately Held**
SIC: 8732 7389 Market analysis or research; Business services, nec

(G-19228)
PROMINENT INSURANCE SVCS INC
1201 N Orange St Ste 700 (19801-1186)
PHONE...................302 351-3368
EMP: 5 **EST:** 2011
SALES (est): 587.26K **Privately Held**
Web: www.prominentagency.com
SIC: 6411 Insurance agents, nec

(G-19229)
PROMIXCO USA CORP (PA) ◆
108 W 13th St (19801-1145)
PHONE...................814 810-3643
Samantha Islam, *Pr*
Mousumi Islam, *Dir*
Boris Davidoff, *Dir*
Masudul Hassan, *Dir*
EMP: 6 **EST:** 2022
SALES (est): 83.38K
SALES (corp-wide): 83.38K **Privately Held**
SIC: 3841 Surgical and medical instruments

(G-19230)
PROMOTE YOUR LOC BUS PWRED BY
31 Van Dyke Dr (19809-3423)
PHONE...................302 764-5588
Mark Wise, *Prin*
EMP: 5 **EST:** 2011
SALES (est): 184.04K **Privately Held**
SIC: 8631 Labor organizations

(G-19231)
PROPEL BIKES LLC (PA)
22 Germay Dr (19804-1105)
PHONE...................631 678-1946
Chris Nolte, *CEO*
EMP: 6 **EST:** 2020
SALES (est): 84.59K
SALES (corp-wide): 84.59K **Privately Held**
SIC: 3751 Bicycles and related parts

(G-19232)
PRORANK BUSINESS SOLUTIONS LLC
1201 N Orange St (19801-1155)
P.O. Box 30287 (19805-7287)
PHONE...................302 256-0642
Kyron Robinson, *CEO*
EMP: 10 **EST:** 2012
SALES (est): 554.05K **Privately Held**

GEOGRAPHIC SECTION
Wilmington - New Castle County (G-19263)

Web: www.prorankllc.com
SIC: 8741 Business management

(G-19233)
PROTEAM LLC
3521 Silverside Rd Ste 2f2 (19810-4900)
PHONE.............................847 707-1074
Purnima Yalamanchali, *Mgr*
EMP: 7 EST: 2002
SALES (est): 85.82K **Privately Held**
Web: www.proteaminc.com
SIC: 7379 Computer related consulting services

(G-19234)
PROTECT INTL RISK SFETY SVCS C
3 Germay Dr Ste 4-470 (19804-1127)
PHONE.............................877 736-0805
Stephen Hart, *Dir*
EMP: 5
SALES (est): 63.12K **Privately Held**
SIC: 8748 Business consulting, nec

(G-19235)
PROTOCOL LABS INC (PA)
427 N Tatnall St # 51207 (19801-2230)
PHONE.............................302 703-7194
Juan Batiz-benet, *CEO*
Jesse Clayburgh, *VP*
Rohit Goel, *Treas*
EMP: 240 EST: 2014
SALES (est): 23.92MM
SALES (corp-wide): 23.92MM **Privately Held**
Web: www.protocol.ai
SIC: 7371 Computer software development and applications

(G-19236)
PROVADA ENTERPRISE
4391 Kirkwood Hwy (19808-5113)
PHONE.............................302 999-7553
EMP: 6 EST: 2019
SALES (est): 555.19K **Privately Held**
SIC: 7514 Rent-a-car service

(G-19237)
PROVIDENCIAS CLEANING
319 7th Ave (19805-4763)
PHONE.............................302 507-7931
Pineda Antonio Castillo, *Prin*
EMP: 5 EST: 2016
SALES (est): 28.68K **Privately Held**
SIC: 7699 Cleaning services

(G-19238)
PROVIDGE CONSULTING LLC
2207 Concord Pike (19803-2908)
PHONE.............................888 927-6583
Gregory R Bishop, *Admn*
EMP: 24 EST: 2016
SALES (est): 1.39MM **Privately Held**
Web: www.providge.com
SIC: 8748 Business consulting, nec

(G-19239)
PRUDENT ENDODONTICS
2036 Foulk Rd (19810-3648)
PHONE.............................302 475-3803
Rinku Parmar, *Prin*
EMP: 8 EST: 2013
SALES (est): 491.55K **Privately Held**
Web: www.prudentendo.com
SIC: 8021 Endodontist

(G-19240)
PRUDENTIAL INTL INVSTMNTS CORP (HQ)
913 Market St (19801-3019)
PHONE.............................302 778-1729
EMP: 5 EST: 2001
SALES (est): 1.96MM
SALES (corp-wide): 60.05B **Publicly Held**
SIC: 6282 Investment advice
PA: Prudential Financial, Inc.
751 Broad St
Newark NJ 07102
973 802-6000

(G-19241)
PS3G INC
913 N Market St (19801-3019)
PHONE.............................302 298-0270
Ankit Goyal, *CEO*
Atma Ram, *Sr VP*
EMP: 10 EST: 2015
SALES (est): 425.01K **Privately Held**
Web: www.ps3g.com
SIC: 7371 Computer software development

(G-19242)
PSCI
1 Righter Pkwy Ste 180 (19803-1550)
PHONE.............................302 479-9700
EMP: 50 EST: 2019
SALES (est): 3.14MM **Privately Held**
Web: www.psci.com
SIC: 6021 National commercial banks

(G-19243)
PSI ZETA CHAPTER OF OMEGA PSI
P.O. Box 86 (19899-0086)
PHONE.............................302 367-8216
EMP: 5 EST: 2011
SALES (est): 86.13K **Privately Held**
Web: psizeta.weebly.com
SIC: 8641 University club

(G-19244)
PSP CORP
203 Churchill Dr (19803-4203)
P.O. Box 608 (19720-0608)
PHONE.............................302 764-7730
Philip Penrose, *Pr*
Jay Penrose, *VP*
Fran Brousseau, *Treas*
Linda Chamblee, *Sec*
Wayne Hawkins, *Mgr*
EMP: 3 EST: 1989
SALES (est): 262.81K **Privately Held**
SIC: 3317 3699 3229 Steel pipe and tubes; Security devices; Glass fiber products

(G-19245)
PSYCH WARD GENIUS
4309 Ruskin Rd (19802-1318)
PHONE.............................267 237-4528
Auston Pratt, *Prin*
EMP: 4 EST: 2017
SALES (est): 49.54K **Privately Held**
SIC: 2741 Miscellaneous publishing

(G-19246)
PSYCHEDELIC WATER INC
251 Little Falls Dr (19808-1674)
PHONE.............................855 337-7924
Pankaj Gogia, *CEO*
EMP: 4
SALES (est): 265.11K **Privately Held**
Web: www.psychedelicwater.com
SIC: 2087 Beverage bases

(G-19247)
PSYCHIATRY DELAWARE
1415 Foulk Rd Ste 104 (19803-2748)
PHONE.............................302 478-1450
Andrew W Donohue, *Owner*
EMP: 10 EST: 2017
SALES (est): 489.57K **Privately Held**
Web: www.psychiatrydelaware.com
SIC: 8011 Psychiatrist

(G-19248)
PSYCHOLOGICAL C HOCKESSIN
825 N Washington St (19801-1509)
PHONE.............................610 388-8585
EMP: 5 EST: 2017
SALES (est): 39.39K **Privately Held**
SIC: 8049 Psychologist, psychotherapist and hypnotist

(G-19249)
PSYCHOLOGICAL SERVICES
422 Woodstock Ln (19808-4413)
PHONE.............................302 489-0213
Maria Ana, *Prin*
EMP: 6 EST: 2016
SALES (est): 57.26K **Privately Held**
SIC: 8049 Clinical psychologist

(G-19250)
PTA DELAWARE CONGRESS
Also Called: National Cngress Prnts Tachers
2815 Highlands Ln (19808-3629)
PHONE.............................302 454-3424
EMP: 14 EST: 2018
SALES (est): 75.17K **Privately Held**
Web: www.pto.org
SIC: 8641 Parent-teachers' association

(G-19251)
PTA DELAWARE MILITARY ACADEMY
12 Middleboro Rd (19804)
PHONE.............................302 998-0745
EMP: 6 EST: 2011
SALES (est): 55.82K **Privately Held**
SIC: 8641 Parent-teachers' association

(G-19252)
PUBLIC ASSETS RECOVERY SERVICE
120 Vineyards Ct (19810-3955)
PHONE.............................267 767-0452
EMP: 5 EST: 2018
SALES (est): 251.88K **Privately Held**
SIC: 7322 Collection agency, except real estate

(G-19253)
PULLABLE INC
1007 N Orange St (19801-1239)
PHONE.............................302 574-6379
Nguyen Loi, *CEO*
EMP: 10
SALES (est): 348.32K **Privately Held**
SIC: 7371 Software programming applications

(G-19254)
PULMONARY ASSOCIATES PA (PA)
7 S Clayton St # 500 (19805-3948)
PHONE.............................302 656-2213
Joseph F Kestner Junior Md, *Pr*
EMP: 7 EST: 1977
SALES (est): 1.27MM
SALES (corp-wide): 1.27MM **Privately Held**
Web: www.christianacare.org
SIC: 8011 Pulmonary specialist, physician/surgeon

(G-19255)
PULSE AND PIXEL CORP ✪
1007 N Orange St Fl 4 (19801-1242)
PHONE.............................845 366-1219
EMP: 10 EST: 2023
SALES (est): 348.32K **Privately Held**
SIC: 7371 Custom computer programming services

(G-19256)
PUMA ENERGY US INC
Also Called: Texas Puma Energy US
1209 N Orange St (19801-1120)
PHONE.............................787 966-7929
Jonathan Pegler, *Pr*
EMP: 5 EST: 2015
SALES (est): 214.08K **Privately Held**
SIC: 8748 Business consulting, nec

(G-19257)
PUPPIES AND MORE RESCUE INC
3422 Old Capitol Trl (19808-6124)
PHONE.............................856 753-6538
EMP: 5
SALES (est): 144.8K **Privately Held**
Web: www.puppiesandmorerescue.org
SIC: 0752 Shelters, animal

(G-19258)
PURE AIR HOLDINGS CORP (HQ)
1105 N Market St Ste 1300 (19801-1241)
PHONE.............................302 655-7130
EMP: 5 EST: 1990
SALES (est): 23.28MM
SALES (corp-wide): 12.6B **Publicly Held**
SIC: 2813 Industrial gases
PA: Air Products And Chemicals, Inc.
1940 Air Products Blvd
Allentown PA 18106
610 481-4911

(G-19259)
PURE BARRE
3801 Kennett Pike (19807-2321)
PHONE.............................302 691-3618
EMP: 5 EST: 2018
SALES (est): 205.57K **Privately Held**
Web: www.purebarre.com
SIC: 7991 Physical fitness facilities

(G-19260)
PURE CLEANING SERVICES INC
1017 Dettling Rd (19805-1028)
PHONE.............................302 494-2693
Churica Reyes, *Prin*
EMP: 5 EST: 2017
SALES (est): 64.76K **Privately Held**
SIC: 7699 Cleaning services

(G-19261)
PURE SHAKA LLC (PA)
2207 Concord Pike Unit 114 (19803-2908)
PHONE.............................302 438-7105
Alex Whilby Nastatos, *Managing Member*
EMP: 5 EST: 2019
SALES (est): 395.66K
SALES (corp-wide): 395.66K **Privately Held**
Web: www.pureshaka.com
SIC: 5993 2833 Cannabis store; Drugs and herbs: grading, grinding, and milling

(G-19262)
PURE STORAGE INC (PA)
5 Honeysuckle Ct (19810-3422)
PHONE.............................302 383-2492
Mario Scalora, *Prin*
EMP: 5 EST: 2015
SALES (est): 714.2K
SALES (corp-wide): 714.2K **Privately Held**
SIC: 4225 General warehousing and storage

(G-19263)
PURE WELLNESS LLC
1010 N Bancroft Pkwy Ste 102 (19805-2690)
PHONE.............................302 543-5679
Holly J Corbett, *Brnch Mgr*
EMP: 7

Wilmington - New Castle County (G-19264)

GEOGRAPHIC SECTION

SALES (corp-wide): 2.76MM **Privately Held**
Web: www.purewellchiro.com
SIC: 8041 Offices and clinics of chiropractors
PA: Pure Wellness, Llc
550 Stanton Christn Rd # 302
Newark DE 19713
302 365-5470

(G-19264)
PURELIFE THERAPEUTIC MASSAGE
49 Ivy Rd (19806-2011)
PHONE..................302 379-5547
Valerie Kunicky, Prin
EMP: 5 EST: 2010
SALES (est): 78K **Privately Held**
SIC: 7299 Massage parlor

(G-19265)
PURITY HOME IMPROVEMENT INC
811 W 22nd St (19802-3301)
PHONE..................302 753-5454
E Gibson, Owner
EMP: 5 EST: 2009
SALES (est): 84.34K **Privately Held**
SIC: 1521 Single-family housing construction

(G-19266)
PURPLE WIFI INC
1013 Centre Rd (19805-1265)
PHONE..................216 292-5760
Gavin Wheelon, CEO
EMP: 8 EST: 2014
SALES (est): 391.93K **Privately Held**
SIC: 4813 Internet host services

(G-19267)
PUSH YOGA
212 W 14th St Apt 1 (19801-1134)
PHONE..................302 547-4807
Adrienne Parker, Prin
EMP: 5 EST: 2016
SALES (est): 37.69K **Privately Held**
SIC: 7999 Yoga instruction

(G-19268)
PUZZLE INVESTMENTS LLC ◆
919 N Market St Ste 950 (19801-3036)
PHONE..................774 516-6447
Andy Smith, Managing Member
EMP: 14 EST: 2024
SALES (est): 481.04K **Privately Held**
SIC: 7371 Computer software development

(G-19269)
PUZZLES LF RNTRY PRGRAM FOR WM
831 N Market St (19801-4931)
PHONE..................302 339-0327
EMP: 5
SALES (est): 85.13K **Privately Held**
SIC: 8322 Rehabilitation services

(G-19270)
PW CONSTRUCTION LLC
213 Lauren Dr (19804-1641)
PHONE..................443 309-4082
EMP: 6 EST: 2017
SALES (est): 510.13K **Privately Held**
SIC: 1521 Single-family housing construction

(G-19271)
PWP PIKE CREEK LLC
5317 Limestone Rd Ste 2 (19808-1252)
PHONE..................302 635-7837
Diane Chalfant, Prin
EMP: 7 EST: 2016
SALES (est): 167.99K **Privately Held**
Web: www.pwppikecreek.com

SIC: 7542 Washing and polishing, automotive

(G-19272)
Q VANDENBERG & SONS INC
Also Called: Totalgreen Holland
3422 Old Capitol Trl Pmb 451 (19808-6124)
PHONE..................800 242-2852
▲ EMP: 20 EST: 2010
SALES (est): 9.27MM **Privately Held**
SIC: 5191 Garden supplies
HQ: Q. Van Den Berg En Zonen N.V.
Bennebroekerdijk 150
Zwaanshoek NH 2136
235484848

(G-19273)
QARE INC
24a Trolley Sq 2134 (19806-3334)
PHONE..................408 475-7569
EMP: 3 EST: 2021
SALES (est): 56.54K **Privately Held**
SIC: 7372 Prepackaged software

(G-19274)
QASE INC
1007 N Orange St (19801-1239)
PHONE..................650 459-1800
Nikita Fedorov, CEO
EMP: 30 EST: 2019
SALES (est): 780.68K **Privately Held**
SIC: 7379 Computer related maintenance services

(G-19275)
QBR TELECOM INC
913 N Market St Ste 200 (19801-3097)
PHONE..................302 510-1155
EMP: 10 EST: 2016
SALES (est): 225.72K **Privately Held**
Web: www.qbrtelecom.com
SIC: 8999 Communication services

(G-19276)
QBS BEAUTY SALON
3207 Miller Rd (19802-2544)
PHONE..................302 691-3449
Jeffrey L Lewis, Prin
EMP: 5 EST: 2015
SALES (est): 23.6K **Privately Held**
SIC: 7231 Beauty shops

(G-19277)
QSPARK LLC
3422 Old Capitol Trl Ste 415 (19808-6124)
PHONE..................646 504-4975
Erez Shermer, Managing Member
EMP: 8 EST: 2013
SALES (est): 559.69K **Privately Held**
SIC: 8742 Marketing consulting services

(G-19278)
QSR GROUP LLC
913 N Market St Ste 200 (19801-3097)
PHONE..................302 268-6909
Jamil Ahmed Quazi, CEO
EMP: 5 EST: 2014
SQ FT: 900
SALES (est): 96.17K **Privately Held**
Web: www.qsr-group.com
SIC: 7371 4813 8748 Computer software development and applications; Telephone communication, except radio; Telecommunications consultant

(G-19279)
QUADROTECH SOLUTIONS INC
Also Called: Quadrotech It
802 N West St Ste 105 (19801-1526)

PHONE..................302 660-0166
Thomas Madsen, CEO
EMP: 105
SALES (corp-wide): 9.1MM **Privately Held**
SIC: 7371 Computer software development
PA: Quadrotech Solutions Inc.
20 Enterprise
Aliso Viejo CA 92656
949 754-8000

(G-19280)
QUAESTOR GLOBAL HOLDINGS INC
1521 Concord Pike Ste 301 (19803-3644)
PHONE..................610 745-3115
Eldon Shomber, Prin
EMP: 15 EST: 2019
SALES (est): 466.55K **Privately Held**
Web: www.quaestorglobal.com
SIC: 7389 Financial services

(G-19281)
QUAKER CHEMICAL CORPORATION
818 N Washington St (19801-1510)
PHONE..................302 791-9171
EMP: 30 EST: 1981
SALES (est): 2.4MM
SALES (corp-wide): 1.94B **Publicly Held**
Web: home.quakerhoughton.com
SIC: 5169 Chemicals and allied products, nec
PA: Quaker Chemical Corporation
901 E Hector St
Conshohocken PA 19428
610 832-4000

(G-19282)
QUALDENT LLC
1015 Cloister Rd Apt D (19809-1045)
PHONE..................856 642-4078
EMP: 5 EST: 2008
SALES (est): 87.9K **Privately Held**
SIC: 8999 7389 8748 7342 Services, nec; Safety inspection service; Business consulting, nec; Disinfecting services

(G-19283)
QUALITY DISTRIBUTORS INC
244 Steeplechase Cir (19808-1977)
PHONE..................917 335-6662
Sahir Saiyad, Pr
EMP: 5 EST: 2009
SALES (est): 486.34K **Privately Held**
Web: www.makemoneymakemoneymakemoney.com
SIC: 5065 7389 Sound equipment, electronic; Business Activities at Non-Commercial Site

(G-19284)
QUALITY HTG AR-CNDITIONING INC
Also Called: QH&a
31 Brookside Dr (19804-1101)
PHONE..................302 654-5247
Horace A Wahl Junior, Pr
Horace A Wahl Iii, Sr VP
Janice Wahl, *
EMP: 49 EST: 1965
SQ FT: 13,040
SALES (est): 4.86MM **Privately Held**
Web: www.qhainc.com
SIC: 1711 3444 1761 Warm air heating and air conditioning contractor; Sheet metalwork; Roofing, siding, and sheetmetal work

(G-19285)
QUALITY UNIT LLC
3 Germay Dr (19804-1127)
PHONE..................888 257-8754
EMP: 15 EST: 2011
SALES (est): 314.37K **Privately Held**

Web: www.qualityunit.com
SIC: 7371 Software programming applications
PA: Quality Unit, S. R. O.
Vajnorska 100/A
Bratislava - Mestska Cast Nove Mesto 831 0

(G-19286)
QUANDARY INC
Also Called: Nitelites of Delaware
5550 Kirkwood Hwy (19808-5002)
PHONE..................302 757-6300
Steve Levine, Pr
EMP: 13 EST: 2010
SALES (est): 372.69K **Privately Held**
Web: www.tollbrothers.com
SIC: 1731 Lighting contractor

(G-19287)
QUANTUM LEAP TECHNOLOGY INC
3616 Kirkwood Hwy Ste A # 1324 (19808-5124)
PHONE..................614 254-1698
Amadou Balde, Pr
EMP: 6 EST: 2017
SALES (est): 332.28K **Privately Held**
SIC: 5045 Computer software

(G-19288)
QUANTUM SATIS ENGENEERING LLC
1201 N Orange St Ste 7160 (19801-1155)
PHONE..................302 485-5448
EMP: 10
SALES (est): 369.28K **Privately Held**
Web: www.nanofulleron.com
SIC: 8711 Engineering services

(G-19289)
QUANTUS INNOVATIONS LLC
136 Fairhill Dr (19808-4309)
PHONE..................302 356-1661
EMP: 2 EST: 2010
SALES (est): 177.35K **Privately Held**
SIC: 7372 Business oriented computer software

(G-19290)
QUARRY MILL CRAFTSMEN LLC
808 W 21st St (19802-3819)
PHONE..................302 388-6289
EMP: 5 EST: 2014
SALES (est): 182.3K **Privately Held**
SIC: 1522 Residential construction, nec

(G-19291)
QUAVO INC
Also Called: Quavo,
1201 N Orange St Ste 7115 (19801-1194)
PHONE..................484 257-9846
Richard Jefferson, CEO
Daniel Penne, *
Kevin Mayes, *
David Chmielewski, *
EMP: 62 EST: 2015
SALES (est): 7.77MM **Privately Held**
Web: www.quavo.com
SIC: 7372 7371 Business oriented computer software; Software programming applications

(G-19292)
QUEEN THEATER
500 N Market St (19801-3005)
PHONE..................608 359-5507
EMP: 7 EST: 2017
SALES (est): 200.15K **Privately Held**
Web: www.thequeenwilmington.com

▲ = Import ▼ = Export
◆ = Import/Export

SIC: 7922 Theatrical companies

(G-19293)
QUEST GLOBAL DIGITAL INC
Also Called: Mobilia Technology
1220 N Market St Ste 806 (19801-2595)
PHONE.................................650 267-1334
Radhakrishnan Kupathil, *CEO*
Sanjay Khaosla, *
Eremila Radhakrishnan, *
EMP: 310 **EST:** 2012
SQ FT: 2,400
SALES (est): 23.42MM **Privately Held**
SIC: 7371 Computer software development
HQ: Quest Global Services-Na, Inc.
 175 Addison Rd
 Windsor CT 06095

(G-19294)
QUETEXT SOFTWARE LLC
251 Little Falls Dr (19808-1674)
PHONE.................................800 403-9067
Matt Anderson, *Managing Member*
EMP: 40
SALES (est): 1.07MM **Privately Held**
SIC: 7371 Computer software development

(G-19295)
QUINN DATA CORPORATION
922 New Rd Ste 1 (19805-5199)
PHONE.................................302 429-7450
Michael Quinn, *Pr*
Catherine Hazzard, *VP*
EMP: 6 **EST:** 1992
SQ FT: 1,500
SALES (est): 828.39K **Privately Held**
Web: www.quinndata.com
SIC: 5734 5045 Personal computers; Computers, nec

(G-19296)
QUINN-MILLER GROUP INC
Also Called: Wonder Medical Supply
34 Germay Dr (19804-1105)
PHONE.................................302 738-9742
Robert Quinn, *Pr*
Nancy Quinn, *Dir*
EMP: 10 **EST:** 1996
SALES (est): 1.01MM **Privately Held**
Web: www.medcaresupply.us
SIC: 7352 5047 5999 8399 Medical equipment rental; Medical equipment and supplies; Medical apparatus and supplies; Health systems agency

(G-19297)
QUIP LABORATORIES INCORPORATED
1500 Eastlawn Ave (19802-2403)
PHONE.................................302 761-2600
Tim Hidell, *Pr*
EMP: 30 **EST:** 1981
SQ FT: 30,000
SALES (est): 8.6MM **Privately Held**
Web: www.quiplabs.com
SIC: 2842 Cleaning or polishing preparations, nec

(G-19298)
QUIVER FINANCE INC
251 Little Falls Dr (19808-1674)
PHONE.................................302 803-6006
Omololu Bamisile, *CEO*
EMP: 5 **EST:** 2021
SALES (est): 199.4K **Privately Held**
SIC: 7371 Software programming applications

(G-19299)
QUORETECH LLC (PA)
200 Bellevue Pkwy Ste 210 (19809-3709)
PHONE.................................206 627-0030
EMP: 5 **EST:** 2017
SALES (est): 65.82K
SALES (corp-wide): 65.82K **Privately Held**
SIC: 8099 Health and allied services, nec

(G-19300)
R & A CONTRACTING
821 N Jefferson St (19801-1431)
PHONE.................................302 669-7144
Jimmie Wilkerson, *Prin*
EMP: 5 **EST:** 2010
SALES (est): 84.91K **Privately Held**
SIC: 1799 Special trade contractors, nec

(G-19301)
R & W TRANSPORTATION CORP
201 N Walnut St (19801-2920)
PHONE.................................703 670-5483
Rebecca J Brown, *Pr*
James M West, *Pr*
EMP: 9 **EST:** 1995
SALES (est): 561.08K **Privately Held**
SIC: 4212 Local trucking, without storage

(G-19302)
R AND L UNIFIED FOUNDATION
2901 Danby St (19802-3613)
PHONE.................................302 244-1777
Ruble Harris, *Sec*
EMP: 5 **EST:** 2019
SALES (est): 94.27K **Privately Held**
SIC: 8699 Charitable organization

(G-19303)
R C FABRICATORS INC
824 N Locust St (19801-4352)
PHONE.................................302 573-8989
Rebecca Suppe, *CEO*
Rebecca Suppe, *CEO*
Danny Reatter, *
Robert C Suppe, *
EMP: 89 **EST:** 1981
SQ FT: 50,000
SALES (est): 9.18MM **Privately Held**
Web: www.rcfabricators.com
SIC: 3441 1791 1799 7692 Fabricated structural metal; Structural steel erection; Welding on site; Welding repair

(G-19304)
R E WLLLAMS PROF ACCTG FRM TAX
3628 Silverside Rd (19810-5190)
P.O. Box 7448 (19803-0448)
PHONE.................................302 598-7171
Ronnie E Williams, *Prin*
Ronnie E Williams, *Pr*
EMP: 5 **EST:** 2009
SALES (est): 107.48K **Privately Held**
SIC: 7291 Tax return preparation services

(G-19305)
R H D BRANDYWINE HILLS
710 W Matson Run Pkwy (19802-1912)
PHONE.................................302 764-3660
Cynthia Guy, *Mgr*
EMP: 10 **EST:** 2005
SALES (est): 246.47K **Privately Held**
SIC: 8093 Mental health clinic, outpatient

(G-19306)
R S WIDDOES & SON INC
204 Channel Rd (19809-3505)
PHONE.................................302 764-7455
Michael J Widdoes, *Pr*
Richard S Widdoes, *Pr*
Mike Widdoes, *VP*
EMP: 13 **EST:** 1980
SQ FT: 1,500
SALES (est): 1.93MM **Privately Held**
Web: www.rswiddoes.com
SIC: 1611 1771 General contractor, highway and street construction; Concrete work

(G-19307)
R W HARMON CARPENTRY SVCS LLC
202 Florence Ave (19803-2340)
PHONE.................................302 477-1319
Ronald W Harmon, *Prin*
EMP: 7 **EST:** 2015
SALES (est): 185.86K **Privately Held**
SIC: 1751 Carpentry work

(G-19308)
R&R HOMECARE
100 Beauregard Ct (19810-1181)
PHONE.................................302 478-3448
Robbert Rebman, *Prin*
EMP: 8 **EST:** 2011
SALES (est): 172.71K **Privately Held**
SIC: 8082 Home health care services

(G-19309)
RAAFAT Z ABDEL-MISIH MD
1021 Gilpin Ave Ste 203 (19806-3272)
PHONE.................................302 658-7533
Raafat Z Abdel-misih, *Owner*
EMP: 8 **EST:** 1997
SALES (est): 4.37K **Privately Held**
SIC: 8011 General and family practice, physician/surgeon

(G-19310)
RAC ACCEPTANCE
3300 Brandywine Pkwy (19803-1463)
PHONE.................................302 477-1513
EMP: 6 **EST:** 2014
SALES (est): 73.97K **Privately Held**
Web: www.acceptancenow.com
SIC: 7359 Furniture rental

(G-19311)
RACKDOG LLC
1013 Centre Rd Ste 403a (19805-1270)
PHONE.................................224 803-4912
EMP: 5 **EST:** 2020
SALES (est): 177.29K **Privately Held**
SIC: 7371 Custom computer programming services

(G-19312)
RADIOGENIC SHIELDING SYSTEMS
1201 N Orange St Ste 600 (19801-1171)
PHONE.................................302 288-0644
Edgar Caballero, *Prin*
EMP: 6 **EST:** 2018
SALES (est): 30.77K **Privately Held**
Web: www.radiogenics.com
SIC: 8734 Testing laboratories

(G-19313)
RADIOLOGY ASSOCIATES INC (PA)
1701 Augustine Cut Off Ste 100 (19803-4425)
PHONE.................................302 832-5590
Magid Mansoory Md, *Pr*
Thomas Fiss Md, *VP*
Garth Koniver Md, *Treas*
EMP: 50 **EST:** 1965
SQ FT: 3,000
SALES (est): 7.13MM
SALES (corp-wide): 7.13MM **Privately Held**
SIC: 8011 Radiologist

(G-19314)
RADIUS RX DIRECT INC
501 Nrth Shpley St Unit 2 (19801-2226)
P.O. Box 1159 (19899-1159)
PHONE.................................302 658-9196
Christy Crkvenac, *Pr*
Todd Crkvenac, *VP*
EMP: 9 **EST:** 2008
SALES (est): 2.36MM **Privately Held**
Web: www.radiusrxdirect.com
SIC: 5122 Pharmaceuticals

(G-19315)
RADIUS SERVICES LLC (PA)
Also Called: Radius Services
16 Hadco Rd (19804-1014)
PHONE.................................302 993-0600
Ben Biggs, *
Sonny Telford, *
EMP: 57 **EST:** 1998
SQ FT: 30,000
SALES (est): 5.43MM
SALES (corp-wide): 5.43MM **Privately Held**
SIC: 1711 Fire sprinkler system installation

(G-19316)
RAGAMAN SERVICES INC
2810 N Church St Ste 98887 (19802-4447)
PHONE.................................339 221-6757
Joseph Eagan, *Pr*
EMP: 16
SALES (est): 1.3MM **Privately Held**
SIC: 6282 7371 Investment advisory service; Computer software development and applications

(G-19317)
RAGE WORLD LLC
1207 Delaware Ave (19806-4743)
PHONE.................................302 397-4400
Aaron Gibson, *Managing Member*
EMP: 5
SALES (est): 58.79K **Privately Held**
SIC: 7999 Amusement and recreation, nec

(G-19318)
RAHAIM & SAINTS ATTYS AT LAW (PA)
2055 Limestone Rd Ste 211 (19808-5536)
PHONE.................................302 892-9200
EMP: 12 **EST:** 1994
SALES (est): 2.13MM **Privately Held**
Web: www.dplaw.com
SIC: 8111 General practice attorney, lawyer

(G-19319)
RAINBOW CHORALE OF DEL INC
1401 Windybush Rd (19810-4419)
P.O. Box 1467 (19899-1467)
PHONE.................................302 803-4440
EMP: 10 **EST:** 1999
SALES (est): 62.63K **Privately Held**
Web: www.therainbowchorale.org
SIC: 7929 Orchestras or bands, nec

(G-19320)
RAINMAKER SOFTWARE GROUP LLC
1925 Lovering Ave (19806-2157)
PHONE.................................800 616-6701
EMP: 5 **EST:** 2013
SALES (est): 286.14K **Privately Held**
Web: www.rainmakersoftware.com
SIC: 7371 Computer software development

(G-19321)
RAL GROUP
1013 Centre Rd Ste 403a (19805-1270)
PHONE.................................302 427-6970

Wilmington - New Castle County (G-19322) — GEOGRAPHIC SECTION

EMP: 5 EST: 2016
SALES (est): 491.93K **Privately Held**
SIC: 6799 Investors, nec

(G-19322)
RALLYPOINT SOLUTIONS LLC
3411 Silverside,Weldin,Ste107
(19810-4810)
PHONE..................302 543-8087
EMP: 15 EST: 2011
SALES (est): 650.52K **Privately Held**
Web: rallypoint.us.com
SIC: 8748 Business consulting, nec

(G-19323)
RALPH G DEGLI OBIZZI & SONS
3 Colonial Ave (19805-5201)
PHONE..................302 658-5127
EMP: 5 EST: 2019
SALES (est): 56.99K **Privately Held**
Web: www.degli.com
SIC: 1711 Plumbing contractors

(G-19324)
RALPH G DEGLI OBIZZI & SONS INC
Also Called: Rgd & Sons
400 Robinson Ln (19805-4614)
P.O. Box 30200 (19805-7200)
PHONE..................302 652-3593
EMP: 50 EST: 1969
SALES (est): 10.32MM **Privately Held**
Web: www.degli.com
SIC: 1711 Mechanical contractor

(G-19325)
RALPH PAUL INC
319 E Lea Blvd (19802-2353)
PHONE..................302 764-9162
Ralph Paul, *Prin*
EMP: 7 EST: 1962
SALES (est): 112.9K **Privately Held**
SIC: 7389 Business services, nec

(G-19326)
RALPH TOMASES DDS PA
Also Called: Safian, Gary D DDS
707 Foulk Rd Ste 203 (19803-3737)
PHONE..................302 652-8656
Gary D Safan D.d.s., *Pr*
Doctor Ralph Tomases, *VP*
EMP: 5 EST: 1947
SALES (est): 452.14K **Privately Held**
SIC: 8021 Dentists' office

(G-19327)
RAMONES LANDSCAPING
4905 Mermaid Blvd (19808-1004)
PHONE..................302 268-8023
Michael Ramone, *Prin*
EMP: 8 EST: 2015
SALES (est): 871.29K **Privately Held**
Web: www.ramoneslandscaping.com
SIC: 0781 Landscape services

(G-19328)
RAMUNNO & RAMUNNO & SCERBA PA
903 N French St Ste 106 (19801-3355)
PHONE..................302 656-9400
L Vincent Ramunno, *Pr*
Lawrence Ramunno, *VP*
Vincent Ramunno, *Pr*
EMP: 10 EST: 1969
SALES (est): 734.9K **Privately Held**
Web: www.ramunnolaw.com
SIC: 8111 General practice law office

(G-19329)
RANCO CONSTRUCTION
4023 Kennett Pike Ste 218 (19807-2018)
P.O. Box 12462 (19850-2462)
PHONE..................302 322-3000
EMP: 6 EST: 2017
SALES (est): 251.44K **Privately Held**
SIC: 1521 Single-family housing construction

(G-19330)
RANDSTAD PROFESSIONALS US LLC
Also Called: Randstad Finance & Accounting
2 Mill Rd Ste 200 (19806-2184)
PHONE..................302 658-6181
EMP: 10
SALES (corp-wide): 24.5B **Privately Held**
Web: www.randstadusa.com
SIC: 7361 Executive placement
HQ: Randstad Professionals Us, Llc
150 Presidential Way Fl 4
Woburn MA 01801

(G-19331)
RANDY L CHRISTOFFERSON
4004 Springfield Ln (19807-2252)
PHONE..................302 540-2006
Randy L Christofferson, *Prin*
EMP: 6 EST: 2013
SALES (est): 101.91K **Privately Held**
Web: www.christoffersoncoaching.com
SIC: 8322 General counseling services

(G-19332)
RANGASWAMY LEELA MD
4031 Kennett Pike Apt 117 (19807-2035)
PHONE..................267 256-0721
EMP: 7 EST: 2018
SALES (est): 56.81K **Privately Held**
SIC: 8011 Offices and clinics of medical doctors

(G-19333)
RANGE INC
Also Called: Range Telecom
919 N Market St Ste 950 (19801-3036)
PHONE..................201 350-7636
Chris Rubini, *CEO*
EMP: 5 EST: 2016
SALES (est): 439.04K **Privately Held**
Web: www.rangetelecom.com
SIC: 8748 Telecommunications consultant

(G-19334)
RAPPORT IT SERVICES LLC
300 Delaware Ave Ste 210 (19801-6601)
PHONE..................302 304-8729
EMP: 31 EST: 2015
SALES (est): 1.3MM **Privately Held**
Web: www.rapportit.com
SIC: 7361 Executive placement

(G-19335)
RAS ADDIS & ASSOCIATES INC
460 Robinson Dr (19801-5745)
PHONE..................302 571-1683
Sylvia Scott, *Pr*
Richard Scott, *VP*
Crystal L Scott, *VP*
Andrew T Scott, *VP*
EMP: 7 EST: 1988
SALES (est): 242.25K **Privately Held**
SIC: 0781 7349 Landscape services; Janitorial service, contract basis

(G-19336)
RASKOB FNDTION FOR CTHLIC ACTV
10 Montchanin Rd (19807-2166)
PHONE..................302 655-4440
Frederick Perella, *Ex VP*
EMP: 10 EST: 1945
SQ FT: 30,000
SALES (est): 10.38MM **Privately Held**
Web: www.rfca.org
SIC: 8641 Civic and social associations

(G-19337)
RATIONALSTAT LLC
2055 Limestone Rd Ste 200c (19808-5536)
PHONE..................302 803-5429
Kamlesh Sharma, *Managing Member*
EMP: 15
SALES (est): 501.83K **Privately Held**
Web: www.rationalstat.com
SIC: 8732 Market analysis or research

(G-19338)
RATNER & PRESTIA PC
1007 N Orange St Ste 205 (19801-1255)
P.O. Box 1596 (19899-1596)
PHONE..................302 778-2500
Costas S Krikelis, *Mgr*
EMP: 17
SALES (corp-wide): 9.74MM **Privately Held**
Web: www.bipc.com
SIC: 8111 Patent, trademark and copyright law
PA: Ratner & Prestia, P.C.
2200 Renaissance Blvd # 350
King Of Prussia PA 19406
610 407-0700

(G-19339)
RAUMA SURVIVORS FOUNDATION
2055 Limestone Rd Ste 109 (19808-5536)
PHONE..................302 275-9705
Dennis Carradin, *Pr*
EMP: 6 EST: 2013
SALES (est): 228.01K **Privately Held**
Web: www.thetraumasurvivorsfoundation.com
SIC: 8322 Social service center

(G-19340)
RAVNUR INC
3422 Old Capitol Trl (19808-6124)
PHONE..................239 963-4404
EMP: 5 EST: 2018
SALES (est): 152.81K **Privately Held**
Web: www.ravnur.com
SIC: 7371 Computer software development

(G-19341)
RAW ESSENTIAL JUICE BAR
5335 Limestone Rd Unit B (19808-1222)
PHONE..................302 235-8019
EMP: 7 EST: 2017
SALES (est): 356.93K **Privately Held**
Web: www.dailyveg.com
SIC: 5149 Juices

(G-19342)
RAW TENNIS INC
1001 Rockland Rd (19803-2923)
PHONE..................302 421-2012
Larry Hampton, *Prin*
EMP: 7 EST: 2016
SALES (est): 109.07K **Privately Held**
Web: www.rawtennisandfitness.com
SIC: 7999 Tennis services and professionals

(G-19343)
RAYDA INC (PA) ◆
1007 N Orange St Fl 4 (19801-1242)
PHONE..................302 261-5184
EMP: 6 EST: 2022
SALES (est): 68.89K
SALES (corp-wide): 68.89K **Privately Held**
SIC: 7371 Computer software development and applications

(G-19344)
RAYMOND BABIARZ AGT
1013 Centre Rd Ste 100 (19805-1265)
PHONE..................302 993-8047
EMP: 5 EST: 2017
SALES (est): 50.78K **Privately Held**
SIC: 6411 Insurance agents, brokers, and service

(G-19345)
RAYMOND CHUNG INDUSTRIES CORP
12 Sharons Way (19808-5236)
PHONE..................302 384-9796
Raymond Chung, *Prin*
EMP: 2 EST: 2011
SALES (est): 189.13K **Privately Held**
Web: www.raystruction.com
SIC: 3999 Barber and beauty shop equipment

(G-19346)
RAYMOND JAMES & ASSOCIATES INC
Also Called: Raymond James
20 Montchanin Rd Ste 280 (19807-2174)
PHONE..................302 656-1534
EMP: 5
SALES (corp-wide): 12.99B **Publicly Held**
Web: www.raymondjames.com
SIC: 6211 Brokers, security
HQ: Raymond James & Associates Inc
880 Carillon Pkwy
Saint Petersburg FL 33716
727 567-1000

(G-19347)
RAYMOND JAMES FINANCIAL
Also Called: Raymond James
1 Trolley Square (19806)
PHONE..................302 384-8446
EMP: 12 EST: 2018
SALES (est): 220.15K **Privately Held**
Web: www.raymondjames.com
SIC: 6211 Brokers, security

(G-19348)
RAYMOND JAMES FINANCIAL SVC
Also Called: Raymon James Financial Service
900 Foulk Rd Ste 201 (19803-3155)
PHONE..................302 778-2170
EMP: 7 EST: 1997
SALES (est): 453.27K **Privately Held**
Web: www.raymondjames.com
SIC: 8742 Financial consultant

(G-19349)
RAYMOND JAMES FINCL SVCS INC
Also Called: Raymond James
20 Montchanin Rd Ste 280 (19807-2174)
PHONE..................302 656-1534
EMP: 5
SALES (corp-wide): 12.99B **Publicly Held**
Web: www.raymondjames.com
SIC: 8742 Financial consultant
HQ: Raymond James Financial Services, Inc.
880 Carillon Pkwy
Saint Petersburg FL 33716
727 567-1000

(G-19350)
RBC
2751 Centerville Rd Ste 212 (19808-1627)
PHONE..................302 892-5901
Rob Jones, *Ofcr*
EMP: 20 EST: 2014

GEOGRAPHIC SECTION

Wilmington - New Castle County (G-19379)

SALES (est): 1.02MM **Privately Held**
Web: www.rbc.com
SIC: 6211 Security brokers and dealers

(G-19351)
RBC INSURANCE HOLDINGS USA INC
1105 N Market St Ste 1300 (19801-1241)
PHONE..................................302 651-8356
EMP: 4198 EST: 2000
SALES (est): 393.61MM
SALES (corp-wide): 41.52B **Privately Held**
Web: www.rbc.com
SIC: 6311 6321 Life insurance carriers; Accident insurance carriers
HQ: Rbc Insurance Holdings Inc.
6880 Financial Dr Suite 200
Mississauga ON L5N 7
905 949-3663

(G-19352)
RBC TRUST COMPANY DELAWARE LTD
4550 Linden Hill Rd Ste 200 (19808)
PHONE..................................302 892-6900
Michael Reed, *Pr*
Edward D Deverell, *Sr VP*
Catherine E Milner, *VP*
Linda E Durso, *CFO*
EMP: 40 EST: 1914
SALES (est): 4.39MM
SALES (corp-wide): 41.52B **Privately Held**
Web: www.rbctrust.com
SIC: 6733 Trusts, nec
PA: Royal Bank Of Canada
200 Bay St Main Fl
Toronto ON M5J 2
416 974-3940

(G-19353)
RBCMNEUSA LLC (PA) ✪
1201 N Orange St Ste 600 (19801-1171)
PHONE..................................607 316-5355
Tanner Schunk, *Managing Member*
EMP: 5 EST: 2023
SALES (est): 287.99K
SALES (corp-wide): 287.99K **Privately Held**
SIC: 6531 Real estate leasing and rentals

(G-19354)
RCT STUDIO INC
251 Little Falls Dr (19808-1674)
PHONE..................................669 255-1562
Cheng Lyu, *CEO*
EMP: 7 EST: 2018
SALES (est): 352.41K **Privately Held**
SIC: 7371 Computer software development and applications

(G-19355)
RD INNOVATIVE PLANNING
608 N Market St Apt 203 (19801-3171)
PHONE..................................302 635-0767
EMP: 8 EST: 2018
SALES (est): 134.24K **Privately Held**
SIC: 8322 Individual and family services

(G-19356)
RD TRANSPORT & LOGISTICS LLC
300 Delaware Ave Ste 210 (19801-6601)
PHONE..................................302 893-8568
EMP: 10 EST: 2021
SALES (est): 100K **Privately Held**
SIC: 3799 Transportation equipment, nec

(G-19357)
RE AUTO REPAIR
1 S Claymont St (19801-5450)
PHONE..................................302 384-6508
EMP: 5 EST: 2010
SALES (est): 139.93K **Privately Held**
SIC: 7538 General automotive repair shops

(G-19358)
RE MAX OF WILMINGTON (PA)
Also Called: Re/Max
5307 Limestone Rd Ste 100 (19808-1282)
PHONE..................................302 234-2500
Jim Pettit, *Mgr*
Bruce White, *
EMP: 40 EST: 1993
SQ FT: 3,000
SALES (est): 4.05MM **Privately Held**
Web: www.remaxeliterealestate.com
SIC: 6531 Real estate agent, residential

(G-19359)
RE MAX OF WILMINGTON
Also Called: Re/Max
2323 Pennsylvania Ave (19806-1332)
PHONE..................................302 657-8000
EMP: 20
Web: www.remaxeliterealestate.com
SIC: 6531 Real estate agent, residential
PA: Re Max Of Wilmington
5307 Limestone Rd Ste 100
Wilmington DE 19808

(G-19360)
RE-UP APP INC (PA)
8603 Park Ct (19802-7702)
PHONE..................................267 972-1183
Opeyemi Oyekanmi, *CEO*
EMP: 3 EST: 2017
SALES (est): 169.33K
SALES (corp-wide): 169.33K **Privately Held**
Web: www.re-upapp.com
SIC: 7372 Prepackaged software

(G-19361)
REACH RIVERSIDE DEV CORP
Also Called: REACH RIVERSIDE
1121 Thatcher St (19802-5135)
PHONE..................................302 232-6612
Kenyetta Mccurdy-byrd, *Prin*
David Ford, *Prin*
EMP: 8 EST: 2019
SALES (est): 1.46MM **Privately Held**
Web: www.reachriverside.org
SIC: 8322 Individual and family services

(G-19362)
READING ASSIST INSTITUTE (PA)
100 W 10th St Ste 910 (19801-6605)
PHONE..................................302 425-4080
Rebecca Combs, *Ex Dir*
Kathleen Traskos, *Pr*
Aaron Hamburger, *Sec*
Heath Kahrs, *Treas*
EMP: 9 EST: 1989
SALES (est): 1.64MM **Privately Held**
Web: www.readingassist.org
SIC: 8299 8748 Reading school, including speed reading; Business consulting, nec

(G-19363)
READY ALLIANCE GROUP INC
251 Little Falls Dr (19808-1674)
P.O. Box 1709 (83864-0901)
PHONE..................................866 229-0927
EMP: 6 EST: 2020
SALES (est): 875.39K **Privately Held**
SIC: 8742 Business management consultant

(G-19364)
REAL CH INC (PA)
Also Called: Single Origin Food Co, The
2055 Limestone Rd Ste 200e (19808-5536)
PHONE..................................347 433-8945
Belal Elbanna, *CEO*
Muhammad Elkateb, *Chief Commercial Officer*
▲ EMP: 7 EST: 2014
SALES (est): 1.41MM
SALES (corp-wide): 1.41MM **Privately Held**
SIC: 5149 Groceries and related products, nec

(G-19365)
REAL DEALS LLC ✪
3 Germay Dr Ste 4 Pmb 1460 (19804-1127)
PHONE..................................484 470-8582
Jordan Davis, *Managing Member*
EMP: 25 EST: 2023
SALES (est): 707.19K **Privately Held**
SIC: 8742 Management consulting services

(G-19366)
REAL ENTREPRENEUR INC
2810 N Church St (19802-4447)
PHONE..................................989 300-0975
Brian Walsh, *Pr*
EMP: 22
SALES (est): 585.56K **Privately Held**
Web: www.realsuccess.net
SIC: 7311 Advertising agencies

(G-19367)
REAL ESTATE PARTNERS LLC
Also Called: Bill Luke Team
2800 Lancaster Ave Ste 8 (19805-5200)
PHONE..................................302 656-0251
William Luke, *Genl Mgr*
EMP: 7 EST: 1997
SALES (est): 800.14K **Privately Held**
Web: www.hometopic.com
SIC: 6531 Real estate agent, residential

(G-19368)
REAL MESSENGER INC (PA)
4001 Kennett Pike Ste 302 (19807-2039)
PHONE..................................657 237-5918
Kwai Hoi Ma, *CEO*
EMP: 15 EST: 2021
SALES (est): 794.44K
SALES (corp-wide): 794.44K **Privately Held**
SIC: 7371 Computer software development and applications

(G-19369)
REAL ONES INC (PA)
251 Little Falls Dr (19808-1674)
PHONE..................................408 857-0262
Sang Min Kim, *CEO*
EMP: 6 EST: 2021
SALES (est): 216.99K
SALES (corp-wide): 216.99K **Privately Held**
SIC: 7371 Software programming applications

(G-19370)
REAL PRO HOLDINGS INC
1209 N Orange St (19801-1120)
PHONE..................................541 743-8500
Brent Lysander, *Prin*
EMP: 5 EST: 2014
SALES (est): 117.55K **Privately Held**
SIC: 6531 Real estate brokers and agents

(G-19371)
REAL WORLD ENDO
2114 Silverside Rd (19810-4165)
PHONE..................................302 477-0960
EMP: 7 EST: 2003
SALES (est): 92.84K **Privately Held**
Web: www.realworldendo.com
SIC: 8742 Management consulting services

(G-19372)
REALCOLD MANAGER LLC (PA) ✪
251 Little Falls Dr (19808-1674)
PHONE..................................332 264-7077
Keith Goldsmith, *Managing Member*
EMP: 6 EST: 2022
SALES (est): 273.28K
SALES (corp-wide): 273.28K **Privately Held**
SIC: 4222 Refrigerated warehousing and storage

(G-19373)
REBECCA JAFFEE MD
Also Called: Desai, Parul MD
3105 Limestone Rd Ste 301 (19808-2156)
PHONE..................................302 992-0200
Rebecca Jaffee Md, *Owner*
EMP: 11 EST: 1989
SALES (est): 366.72K **Privately Held**
SIC: 8011 General and family practice, physician/surgeon

(G-19374)
RECADIA CAPITAL LLC ✪
1521 Concord Pike Ste 301 (19803-3644)
PHONE..................................866 671-1280
Gregory Vartanian, *Managing Member*
EMP: 5 EST: 2023
SALES (est): 219.98K **Privately Held**
SIC: 6798 Real estate investment trusts

(G-19375)
RECADIA CORP LLC
1521 Concord Pike Ste 301 (19803-3644)
PHONE..................................866 671-1280
Gregory Vartanian, *CEO*
EMP: 5 EST: 2012
SALES (est): 418.88K **Privately Held**
Web: www.recadia.com
SIC: 8748 6799 Business consulting, nec; Real estate investors, except property operators

(G-19376)
RECENTIA USA INC
251 Little Falls Dr (19808-1674)
PHONE..................................847 977-7571
EMP: 8 EST: 2018
SALES (est): 54.77K **Privately Held**
SIC: 8999 Personal services

(G-19377)
RECIPERO INC
2801 Centerville Rd Pmb 21 (19808-1609)
PHONE..................................888 551-1159
Mark Harman, *CEO*
EMP: 20 EST: 2014
SALES (est): 1.38MM **Privately Held**
Web: www.recipero.com
SIC: 7372 Prepackaged software

(G-19378)
RECIPROCITY HEALTH LLC
406 Hillside Rd (19807-2248)
PHONE..................................302 530-5244
EMP: 8
SALES (est): 641.91K **Privately Held**
Web: www.reciprocityhealth.com
SIC: 8099 7389 Health and allied services, nec; Business Activities at Non-Commercial Site

(G-19379)
RECOVERY INNOVATIONS INC
2508 Belford Dr (19808-4506)
PHONE..................................302 660-7560

Wilmington - New Castle County (G-19380)

EMP: 5
Web: www.riinternational.com
SIC: 8093 Mental health clinic, outpatient
PA: Recovery Innovations, Inc.
2701 N 16th St Ste 316
Phoenix AZ 85006

(G-19380)
RECREATE INC ◊
800 N King St Ste 304 (19801-3549)
PHONE..............................404 625-3387
Linear Lovett Iii, CEO
EMP: 5 EST: 2023
SALES (est): 251.22K Privately Held
Web: www.gorecreate.ai
SIC: 7389 Business services, nec

(G-19381)
RECTICEL US INC
1105 N Market St Ste 1300 (19801-1241)
PHONE..............................248 393-2100
EMP: 565 EST: 1986
SALES (est): 58.69MM
SALES (corp-wide): 200.11MM Privately Held
SIC: 5169 Chemicals and allied products, nec
PA: Recticel
Avenue Du Bourget 42
Brussel 1130
27751882

(G-19382)
RED BRICK REALTY LLC
2102 Kirkwood Hwy (19805-4902)
PHONE..............................302 540-1128
Janet Glackin, Prin
EMP: 5 EST: 2017
SALES (est): 169.9K Privately Held
SIC: 6531 Real estate brokers and agents

(G-19383)
RED CARPET TRAVEL AGENCY INC (PA)
Also Called: Uniglobe
501 Silverside Rd Ste 41 (19809-1388)
PHONE..............................302 475-1220
Mark Rachko, Pr
Steven Rachko, VP
Helen S Whitson, Sec
EMP: 17 EST: 1970
SALES (est): 3.15MM
SALES (corp-wide): 3.15MM Privately Held
Web: www.uniglobedcarpettravel.com
SIC: 4724 Tourist agency arranging transport, lodging and car rental

(G-19384)
RED EFT PAINTING
104 W Reamer Ave (19804-1718)
PHONE..............................302 636-9463
Michael E Windsor, Owner
EMP: 5 EST: 1991
SALES (est): 280.38K Privately Held
SIC: 1721 Exterior residential painting contractor

(G-19385)
RED LADDER PRODUCTIONS LLC
1209 N Orange St (19801-1120)
PHONE..............................781 970-6124
Scott E Landers, CEO
EMP: 5 EST: 2018
SALES (est): 251.84K Privately Held
SIC: 7819 Developing and laboratory services, motion picture

(G-19386)
RED LION LLC
2207 Concord Pike # 117 (19803-2908)
PHONE..............................202 559-9365
EMP: 6 EST: 2013
SALES (est): 77.01K Privately Held
Web: www.redlion.io
SIC: 8742 Management consulting services

(G-19387)
REDGAIT 2530 LLC
3 Kenleigh Ct (19808-1919)
PHONE..............................302 683-0978
William R Seward, Prin
EMP: 5 EST: 2008
SALES (est): 153.91K Privately Held
SIC: 7389 Design services

(G-19388)
REDGATE TECH INC
4023 Kennett Pike Ste 50558 (19807-2018)
PHONE..............................302 377-6563
Milind Kanani, CEO
EMP: 5
SALES (est): 220.07K Privately Held
SIC: 5999 7371 Pet supplies; Computer software development and applications

(G-19389)
REDLAND MILLS CO
1201 N Market St Ste 111 (19801-1147)
PHONE..............................706 288-6003
Patrick Fields, CEO
EMP: 5
SALES (est): 207.81K Privately Held
SIC: 8742 Marketing consulting services

(G-19390)
REDLEO SOFTWARE INC
1201 N Orange St Ste 7495 (19801-1298)
PHONE..............................302 691-9072
Love Kumar, Pr
EMP: 15 EST: 2018
SALES (est): 1MM Privately Held
Web: www.redleosoft.com
SIC: 8742 7361 Management consulting services; Employment agencies

(G-19391)
REED ELSEVIER CAPITAL INC
1105 N Market St Ste 501 (19801-1253)
PHONE..............................302 427-9299
Renee Simonton, Pr
EMP: 24 EST: 2009
SALES (est): 525.48K
SALES (corp-wide): 10.3B Privately Held
SIC: 2741 Miscellaneous publishing
HQ: Relx Group Plc
Grand Buildings
London WC2N
207 166-5500

(G-19392)
REED SMITH LLP
1201 N Market St Ste 1500 (19801-1163)
PHONE..............................302 778-7500
Kurt Gwynne, Office Managing Partner
EMP: 17
SALES (corp-wide): 488.93MM Privately Held
Web: www.reedsmith.com
SIC: 8111 General practice attorney, lawyer
PA: Reed Smith Llp
225 5th Ave Ste 1200
Pittsburgh PA 15222
412 288-3131

(G-19393)
REEDS REFUGE CENTER INC
1601 N Pine St (19802-5007)
PHONE..............................302 428-1830
EMP: 6 EST: 2008
SALES (est): 266.76K Privately Held
Web: www.reedsrefugecenter.org
SIC: 8322 Social service center

(G-19394)
REEVOY CORPORATION
919 N Market St Ste 950 (19801-3036)
PHONE..............................631 769-6681
Abhilash Sabapaty, VP
Mohit Agrwal, CFO
Ishan Dadhich, CFO
Ankur Khetan, CFO
EMP: 10 EST: 2020
SALES (est): 654.61K Privately Held
Web: www.reevooy.com
SIC: 6141 Consumer finance companies

(G-19395)
REFERMATE LLC
427 N Tatnall St (19801-2230)
PHONE..............................951 892-8159
EMP: 5
SALES (est): 63.12K Privately Held
SIC: 7371 Computer software development and applications

(G-19396)
REFLECTION BIOTECHNOLOGIES INC
1013 Centre Rd Ste 403b (19805-1270)
PHONE..............................212 765-2200
Juliana Xu, Pr
EMP: 2 EST: 2015
SALES (est): 306.37K Privately Held
SIC: 2836 Biological products, except diagnostic

(G-19397)
REGAL CINEMAS INC
Also Called: Brandywine Town Center 16
3300 Brandywine Pkwy (19803-1463)
PHONE..............................302 479-0753
EMP: 30
Web: www.regmovies.com
SIC: 7832 Motion picture theaters, except drive-in
HQ: Regal Cinemas, Inc.
101 E Blount Ave
Knoxville TN 37920

(G-19398)
REGAL PAINTING & DECORATING
209 S Woodward Ave (19805-2358)
P.O. Box 2509 (19805-0509)
PHONE..............................302 994-8943
Ronald Ciafre, Pr
Robert Jeffery, VP
Debra Jeffery, Sec
EMP: 7 EST: 1977
SQ FT: 1,500
SALES (est): 244.93K Privately Held
Web: www.regalpaintingdelaware.com
SIC: 1721 7389 Residential painting; Interior decorating

(G-19399)
REGEN III (USGC) CORPORATION
1209 N Orange St (19801-1120)
PHONE..............................604 806-5275
Gregory M Clarkes, CEO
Larry Van Hatten, Pr
Ricky Low, CFO
EMP: 3 EST: 2021
SALES (est): 706.55K Privately Held
SIC: 1381 Redrilling oil and gas wells
PA: Regen Iii Corp
400 Burrard St Suite 1750
Vancouver BC V6C 3
604 806-5275

(G-19400)
REGENCY HLTHCARE REHAB CTR LLC
Also Called: ST. FRANCIS CARE CENTER AT WIL
801 N Broom St (19806-4624)
PHONE..............................302 654-8400
EMP: 110 EST: 2007
SALES (est): 11.29MM Privately Held
Web: www.regencyhcr.com
SIC: 8051 Convalescent home with continuous nursing care

(G-19401)
REGER RIZZO & DARNALL LLP
1001 N Jefferson St Ste 202 (19801-1435)
PHONE..............................302 652-3611
Louis Rizzo, Brnch Mgr
EMP: 8
Web: www.regerlaw.com
SIC: 8111 General practice attorney, lawyer
PA: Reger Rizzo & Darnall Llp
2929 Arch St Ste 1300
Philadelphia PA 19104

(G-19402)
REGINA COLEMAN
Also Called: Creative Children
2720 Chinchilla Dr (19810-1509)
PHONE..............................215 476-4682
Regina Coleman, Owner
EMP: 6 EST: 1982
SQ FT: 27,000
SALES (est): 83.54K Privately Held
SIC: 8351 Group day care center

(G-19403)
REGINA MCLARNON
3 Beaver Valley Rd (19803-1124)
PHONE..............................800 903-8114
Regina Mclarnon, Prin
EMP: 6 EST: 2014
SALES (est): 291.82K Privately Held
SIC: 6411 Insurance agents, brokers, and service

(G-19404)
REGIONAL HMATOLOGY ONCOLOGY PA (PA)
1010 N Bancroft Pkwy Ste 21 (19805-2690)
PHONE..............................302 731-7782
Timothy Wozniak Md, Pr
Martha Hosfordskapof, Sec
EMP: 9 EST: 1982
SALES (est): 2.39MM
SALES (corp-wide): 2.39MM Privately Held
Web: rhopa.navigatingcare.com
SIC: 8011 Oncologist

(G-19405)
REGIONAL MEDICAL GROUP LLC
4512 Kirkwood Hwy Ste 202 (19808-5123)
P.O. Box 5930 (19808-0930)
PHONE..............................302 993-7890
Susan A Cassidy, Admn
EMP: 5 EST: 2013
SALES (est): 445.98K Privately Held
Web: www.regionalmedicalgroup.org
SIC: 8099 Health and allied services, nec

(G-19406)
REGIONAL ORTHOPAEDIC ASSOC (PA)
1941 Limestone Rd Ste 101 (19808-5413)
PHONE..............................302 633-3555
David L Axon Md, Pt
Brian J Galinat Md, Pt
Paul C Lupcha Md, Pt
Peter F Townsend Md, Pt

GEOGRAPHIC SECTION　　　　　　　　　　　　　　　　　　　　　　　　Wilmington - New Castle County (G-19434)

EMP: 14 EST: 1965
SALES (est): 2.26MM
SALES (corp-wide): 2.26MM Privately Held
SIC: 8011 Orthopedic physician

(G-19407)
REGISTERED AGENTS LTD
Also Called: Registered Agents Limited
1013 Centre Rd Ste 403a (19805-1270)
PHONE..................302 421-5750
H Murray Sawyer, Pr
Sid S Garnett, VP
Laura Bryda, VP
EMP: 15 EST: 1979
SALES (est): 423.25K Privately Held
Web: www.inclegal.com
SIC: 7389 Automobile recovery service

(G-19408)
REGISTRATION LLC
1013 Centre Rd (19805-1265)
PHONE..................877 955-7111
EMP: 9 EST: 2021
SALES (est): 326.49K Privately Held
Web: www.legalregistration.com
SIC: 8742 Management consulting services

(G-19409)
REGISTRED AGNTS LEGAL SVCS LLC
1013 Centre Rd Ste 403s (19805-1270)
PHONE..................302 427-6970
Michael Ashley, Managing Member
Murray Sawyer, Managing Member
EMP: 5 EST: 1999
SALES (est): 453.45K Privately Held
Web: www.inclegal.com
SIC: 8741 7389 Business management

(G-19410)
REGULATION HOLDCO LLC (HQ)
251 Little Falls Dr (19808-1674)
PHONE..................800 521-1114
EMP: 14 EST: 2018
SALES (est): 11.48MM
SALES (corp-wide): 179.25MM Privately Held
SIC: 6799 Investors, nec
PA: Dresser Utility Solutions, Llc
16240 Port Nw Ste 100
Houston TX 77041
203 661-6601

(G-19411)
REGULATORY DATACORP INC
1007 N Orange St Fl 4 (19801-1242)
PHONE..................302 299-2284
EMP: 5 EST: 2019
SALES (est): 129.91K Privately Held
SIC: 7261 Funeral service and crematories

(G-19412)
REHABILITATION CONSULTANTS INC
2401 Pennsylvania Ave Ste 112 (19806-1432)
PHONE..................302 655-5877
Michelle Woodbridge, Mgr
EMP: 7 EST: 2014
SALES (est): 51.89K Privately Held
SIC: 8049 Physical therapist

(G-19413)
REHABILITATION CONSULTANTS INC
Also Called: Novacare Rehabilitation
3411 Silverside Rd Ste 105 (19810-4867)
PHONE..................302 478-5240
Robert Catalano, Pr
EMP: 9 EST: 1970
SALES (est): 251.41K Privately Held
Web: www.rehabconsultantsinc.com
SIC: 8049 Physiotherapist
HQ: Physiotherapy Associates, Inc.
680 American Ave Ste 200
King Of Prussia PA 19406
610 644-7824

(G-19414)
REHABILITATION CONSULTANTS
3411 Silverside Rd Ste 105 (19810-4812)
PHONE..................302 478-2131
Robert M Catalano, Owner
EMP: 7 EST: 1970
SALES (est): 183.66K Privately Held
SIC: 8093 Rehabilitation center, outpatient treatment

(G-19415)
REIKI WITH REBECCA
102 David Rd (19804-2649)
PHONE..................302 528-0582
Rebecca Dehghan, Prin
EMP: 6 EST: 2015
SALES (est): 54.7K Privately Held
SIC: 8049 Massage Therapist

(G-19416)
REILLY JANICZEK & MCDEVITT PC
1013 Centre Rd Ste 210 (19805-1265)
PHONE..................302 777-1700
R Stokes Nolte, Pt
EMP: 19
SALES (corp-wide): 6.75MM Privately Held
Web: www.rmh-law.com
SIC: 8111 General practice law office
PA: Reilly Janiczek & Mcdevitt P.C.
2500 Mcclellan Ave # 240
Pennsauken NJ 08109
856 317-7180

(G-19417)
REINCARNATIO INC
251 Little Falls Dr (19808-1674)
PHONE..................703 479-1337
EMP: 7 EST: 2018
SALES (est): 163.16K Privately Held
SIC: 7538 General automotive repair shops

(G-19418)
REINVEX LLC
3801 Kennett Pike (19807-2321)
P.O. Box 4732 (19807-4732)
PHONE..................484 259-7889
Tolga Solen, Prin
EMP: 5 EST: 2017
SALES (est): 100.13K Privately Held
SIC: 1522 Residential construction, nec

(G-19419)
REIVER HYMAN & CO INC
4104 N Market St (19802-2222)
PHONE..................302 764-2040
Alan T Reiver, Pr
EMP: 5 EST: 1914
SQ FT: 5,000
SALES (est): 537.81K Privately Held
Web: www.hymanreiver.com
SIC: 5713 5023 Carpets; Floor coverings

(G-19420)
REKINDLE FAMILY MEDICINE
5590 Kirkwood Hwy (19808-5002)
PHONE..................302 565-4799
Kimberly Nalda, Prin
EMP: 8 EST: 2015
SALES (est): 222.28K Privately Held
Web: www.rekindlefamilymedicine.com
SIC: 8099 Health and allied services, nec

(G-19421)
RELATED RE FUND III LP
251 Little Falls Dr (19808-1674)
PHONE..................212 801-1013
EMP: 10 EST: 2019
SALES (est): 371.99K Privately Held
SIC: 6722 Management investment, open-end

(G-19422)
RELIABLE COPY SERVICE INC
1007 N Orange St Ste 110 (19801-1256)
PHONE..................302 654-8080
David Hernan, Genl Mgr
EMP: 95
SALES (corp-wide): 24.59MM Privately Held
Web: www.reliable-co.com
SIC: 7334 Blueprinting service
PA: Reliable Copy Service Inc.
1650 Arch St Ste 2210
Philadelphia PA 19103
215 563-3363

(G-19423)
RELIABLE HOME INSPECTION (PA)
100 Old Kennett Rd (19807-1726)
PHONE..................302 455-1200
John Kerrigan, Pr
Tammy Kerrigan, VP
EMP: 5 EST: 1993
SALES (est): 987.77K
SALES (corp-wide): 987.77K Privately Held
Web: www.reliablehomeinspectionservice.com
SIC: 7389 Building inspection service

(G-19424)
RELIANCE COMMUNICATIONS INC
2711 Centerville Rd Ste 400 (19808-1660)
P.O. Box 4444 (10163-4444)
PHONE..................888 673-5426
Michael Saur, Pr
EMP: 12 EST: 1992
SQ FT: 3,000
SALES (est): 4.67MM Privately Held
SIC: 4813 Local and long distance telephone communications
PA: Reliance Communications Limited
H Block, 1st Floor, Dhirubhai Ambani Knowledge City,
Navi Mumbai MH 40071

(G-19425)
RELIANCE EGLEFORD UPSTREAM LLC
1007 N Orange St (19801-1239)
PHONE..................302 472-7437
EMP: 8 EST: 2013
SALES (est): 331.25K Privately Held
SIC: 1481 2911 Mine exploration, nonmetallic minerals; Petroleum refining
PA: Reliance Industries Limited
3rd Floor, Maker Chamber Iv,
Mumbai MH 40002

(G-19426)
RELIANCE TRUST COMPANY LLC
200 Bellevue Pkwy (19809-3727)
PHONE..................302 246-5400
Christopher M Teevan, Prin
EMP: 6 EST: 2011
SALES (est): 352.25K Privately Held
SIC: 6021 National commercial banks

(G-19427)
RELOCATION PETTINAR
220 Presidential Dr (19807-3324)
PHONE..................302 777-5240

Matt Hepworth, Prin
EMP: 6 EST: 2013
SALES (est): 88.94K Privately Held
SIC: 1522 Remodeling, multi-family dwellings

(G-19428)
REMAX SUNVEST REALTY
5560 Kirkwood Hwy (19808-5002)
PHONE..................302 995-1589
Carl Chen, Prin
EMP: 19 EST: 2007
SALES (est): 511.05K Privately Held
Web: www.remax.com
SIC: 6531 Real estate agent, residential

(G-19429)
REMAX SUNVEST REALTY CORP (PA)
Also Called: Re/Max
2103 W Newport Pike A (19804-3719)
PHONE..................302 995-1589
Carl Chen, Pr
Kenneth Mayhew, *
Pauline Chin, *
EMP: 40 EST: 1987
SALES (est): 2.16MM Privately Held
Web: www.remax.com
SIC: 6531 Real estate agent, residential

(G-19430)
RENAISSANCE SECURITY LP
1 Mill Rd (19806-2113)
PHONE..................302 588-5975
EMP: 5 EST: 2019
SALES (est): 103.95K Privately Held
SIC: 1731 Safety and security specialization

(G-19431)
RENTWELL LEASEMANAGEMAINTAIN
3203 Concord Pike Ste E (19803-5036)
PHONE..................302 256-5356
Robert Coldwell, Prin
EMP: 5 EST: 2016
SALES (est): 197.24K Privately Held
Web: www.rentwell.com
SIC: 6512 Nonresidential building operators

(G-19432)
RENU ME PROPERTY SOLUTIONS
913 N Market St Ste 200 (19801-3097)
PHONE..................267 440-6863
EMP: 5 EST: 2019
SQ FT: 1,000
SALES (est): 432.13K Privately Held
SIC: 6512 Nonresidential building operators

(G-19433)
REOLINK INNOVATION INC ✪
251 Little Falls Dr (19808-1674)
PHONE..................833 424-0499
Liu Xiaoyu, CEO
EMP: 6 EST: 2022
SALES (est): 70.36K Privately Held
Web: reolinkdigitaltechnologycoltd894.newswire.com
SIC: 7382 Security systems services

(G-19434)
REPUBLIC SERVICES INC
1420 New York Ave (19801-5826)
PHONE..................302 658-4097
Bob Ziegler, Mgr
EMP: 6
SALES (corp-wide): 13.51B Publicly Held
Web: www.republicservices.com
SIC: 4953 Refuse collection and disposal services
PA: Republic Services, Inc.

Wilmington - New Castle County (G-19435)

18500 N Allied Way # 100
Phoenix AZ 85054
480 627-2700

(G-19435)
REPURPOSE GLOBAL INC (PA)
1209 N Orange St (19801-1120)
PHONE.................732 322-3839
EMP: 5 EST: 2017
SALES (est): 95.64K
SALES (corp-wide): 95.64K Privately Held
Web: www.repurpose.global
SIC: 8742 Business management consultant

(G-19436)
RESCUE FOR MISUNDERSTOOD INC
6002 Old Capitol Trl (19808-4839)
PHONE.................302 650-8123
Caitlyn Reynolds, *Prin*
EMP: 5 EST: 2010
SALES (est): 56.21K Privately Held
SIC: 8399 Advocacy group

(G-19437)
RESIDENCE INN
Also Called: Residence Inn By Marriott
1300 N Market St (19801-1136)
PHONE.................302 777-7373
EMP: 21 EST: 2018
SALES (est): 665.68K Privately Held
Web: www.marriott.com
SIC: 7011 Hotels and motels

(G-19438)
RESISTANCE ENERGY FUND LP ◇
1209 N Orange St (19801-1120)
PHONE.................514 871-2120
Richard Mak, *Pt*
EMP: 10 EST: 2023
SALES (est): 697.31K Privately Held
SIC: 6722 Management investment, open-end

(G-19439)
RESOURCE MORTGAGE CORP
3301 Lancaster Pike Ste 10 (19805-1436)
PHONE.................302 657-0181
Michelle Slack, *Pr*
Joe Beacher, *VP*
EMP: 10 EST: 1997
SALES (est): 760K Privately Held
SIC: 6163 Mortgage brokers arranging for loans, using money of others

(G-19440)
RESOURCES FOR HUMAN DEV
1800 N Jefferson St (19802-4710)
PHONE.................215 951-0300
Marco Giordano, *Prin*
EMP: 9 EST: 2019
SALES (est): 239.8K Privately Held
SIC: 8742 Business planning and organizing services

(G-19441)
RESOURCES FOR HUMAN DEV INC
2804 Grubb Rd (19810-2319)
PHONE.................302 691-7574
EMP: 12
SALES (corp-wide): 292.52MM Privately Held
Web: www.rhd.org
SIC: 8742 Business planning and organizing services
PA: Resources For Human Development, Inc.
4700 Wissahickon Ave # 126
Philadelphia PA 19144
215 951-0300

(G-19442)
RESPONSIBLE PUBLISHING
301 Snuff Mill Rd (19807-1025)
PHONE.................609 412-9621
Brooke Mufferi, *Prin*
EMP: 5 EST: 2016
SALES (est): 66.8K Privately Held
SIC: 2741 Miscellaneous publishing

(G-19443)
RESTORE INCORPORATED
3411 Silverside Rd Ste 104 (19810-4837)
PHONE.................302 655-6257
EMP: 16
SALES (corp-wide): 2.38MM Privately Held
Web: www.restorationchamp.com
SIC: 2992 Lubricating oils and greases
PA: Restore Incorporated
3000 Ne 30th Pl Ste 201
Fort Lauderdale FL 33306
954 563-7001

(G-19444)
RESULTICKS SOLUTION INC
1013 Centre Rd Ste 403s (19805-1270)
PHONE.................347 416-7673
Mani Gopalaratnam, *CEO*
Redickaa Subrammanian, *
Dakshen Ram, *CIO*
EMP: 25 EST: 2021
SALES (est): 470.63K Privately Held
Web: www.resulticks.com
SIC: 7371 7374 7379 Computer software development and applications; Data processing service; Data processing consultant

(G-19445)
RESUME WRITER DIRECT
427 N Tatnall St (19801-2230)
PHONE.................866 706-0973
EMP: 5 EST: 2016
SALES (est): 117.23K Privately Held
Web: www.resumewriterdirect.com
SIC: 7338 Resume writing service

(G-19446)
RETROTEKUSA INC ◇
251 Little Falls Dr (19808-1674)
PHONE.................469 619-0899
Joe Turley, *CEO*
EMP: 7 EST: 2022
SALES (est): 78.16K Privately Held
SIC: 3823 7389 Process control instruments; Business services, nec

(G-19447)
REUSE EVERYTHING INSTITUTE INC
2711 Centerville Rd Ste 400 (19808-1660)
PHONE.................607 351-1770
David Saiia, *CEO*
Vananh Le, *Ex Dir*
Christian Saiia, *VP*
EMP: 6
SALES (est): 121.91K Privately Held
Web: www.reuseeverything.org
SIC: 8732 Commercial sociological and educational research

(G-19448)
REVOLVE TRAINING STAFFING LLC
1521 Concord Pike Ste 301 (19803-3644)
PHONE.................833 973-8658
Ron Hargrove, *Managing Member*
EMP: 8 EST: 2021
SALES (est): 503.86K Privately Held
SIC: 7389 Business Activities at Non-Commercial Site

(G-19449)
REYNOLDS SERVICES LTD
251 Little Falls Dr (19808-1674)
PHONE.................877 404-2179
Dakota Davis, *Prin*
EMP: 6 EST: 1982
SALES (est): 74.73K Privately Held
SIC: 8111 General practice attorney, lawyer

(G-19450)
RFPMART LLC
3511 Silverside Rd Ste 105 (19810-4902)
PHONE.................315 627-3333
EMP: 15 EST: 2016
SALES (est): 215.29K Privately Held
Web: www.rfpmart.com
SIC: 8741 7371 4813 Office management; Computer software writing services; Web search portals

(G-19451)
RG3 TEXAS HOLDINGS LLC ◇
1209 N Orange St (19801-1120)
PHONE.................778 891-7569
Gregory M Clarkes, *CEO*
Ricky Low, *CFO*
EMP: 3 EST: 2022
SALES (est): 253.93K Privately Held
SIC: 2911 Oils, partly refined: sold for rerunning

(G-19452)
RG3 TEXAS LLC ◇
1209 N Orange St (19801-1120)
PHONE.................778 891-7569
Gregory Clarkes, *Managing Member*
Ricky Low, *CFO*
EMP: 4 EST: 2022
SALES (est): 386.81K Privately Held
SIC: 2899 Oil treating compounds

(G-19453)
RGP HOLDING INC (PA)
1105 N Market St (19801-1216)
PHONE.................302 661-0117
Raymond G Perelman, *Pr*
◆ EMP: 17 EST: 1992
SALES (est): 71.31MM Privately Held
SIC: 3255 1499 1741 Firebrick, clay; Diatomaceous earth mining; Refractory or acid brick masonry

(G-19454)
RGS TECHNOLOGY GROUP LLC
300 Delaware Ave Ste 210a (19801-6601)
PHONE.................302 397-3169
EMP: 5 EST: 2016
SALES (est): 348.67K Privately Held
SIC: 8748 8711 Telecommunications consultant; Engineering services

(G-19455)
RHEUMATOLOGY CENTER-DELAWARE
4512 Kirkwood Hwy Ste 301 (19808-5129)
PHONE.................302 994-2345
Maged Hosny, *Prin*
EMP: 7 EST: 2018
SALES (est): 236.71K Privately Held
Web: www.rheumatologyde.com
SIC: 8011 Internal medicine, physician/surgeon

(G-19456)
RHEWUM AMERICA INC
1000 N West St Ste 1200 (19801-1058)
PHONE.................215 804-7977
Sigurd Schuetz, *Pr*
Sean Koontz, *Prin*
EMP: 2 EST: 2021
SALES (est): 235.87K Privately Held
Web: www.rhewum.com
SIC: 3569 Sifting and screening machines

(G-19457)
RHI REFRACTORIES HOLDING COMPANY
1105 N Market St Ste 1300 (19801-1241)
PHONE.................302 655-6497
◆ EMP: 4500
SIC: 3255 1459 3546 3272 Clay refractories; Magnesite mining; Power-driven handtools; Solid containing units, concrete

(G-19458)
RHOADES & MORROW LLC
1225 N King St Ste 1200 (19801-3254)
P.O. Box 874 (19899-0874)
PHONE.................302 427-9500
Joseph J Rhoades, *Owner*
EMP: 14 EST: 1990
SQ FT: 1,300
SALES (est): 715K Privately Held
Web: www.rhoadeslegal.com
SIC: 8111 General practice attorney, lawyer

(G-19459)
RHODESIDE INCORPORATED
322 Compton Ct (19801-3616)
PHONE.................505 261-4568
Ronald Rhodes, *Pr*
Sherkiera Rhodes, *Prin*
Tyshawn Moreland, *Prin*
EMP: 5 EST: 2008
SALES (est): 106.07K Privately Held
SIC: 7922 Entertainment promotion

(G-19460)
RHODUNDA & WILLIAMS LLC
1521 Concord Pike Ste 205 (19803-3645)
PHONE.................302 576-2000
W Rhodunda, *Prin*
EMP: 6 EST: 2016
SALES (est): 633.77K Privately Held
Web: www.rawlaw.com
SIC: 8111 General practice attorney, lawyer

(G-19461)
RHONDIUM CORPORATION
Also Called: Triodent
35a The Commons (19810-4929)
PHONE.................800 771-4364
EMP: 10 EST: 2009
SALES (est): 891.4K Privately Held
SIC: 5047 Dentists' professional supplies

(G-19462)
RHYTHM AND HEAT LLC ◇
900 N Washington St Ste 13 (19801-1512)
PHONE.................302 897-5259
Lance Williams, *Managing Member*
EMP: 7 EST: 2022
SALES (est): 78.16K Privately Held
SIC: 2035 Seasonings and sauces, except tomato and dry

(G-19463)
RHYZE SOLUTIONS LLC ◇
1313 N Market St Ste 5100 (19801-6111)
PHONE.................850 376-4201
Syd Libsack, *CEO*
EMP: 6 EST: 2023
SALES (est): 309.27K Privately Held
SIC: 7371 Custom computer programming services

(G-19464)
RIBODYNAMICS LLC
2711 Centerville Rd # 400 (19808-1660)
PHONE.................518 339-6605

GEOGRAPHIC SECTION

Wilmington - New Castle County (G-19494)

EMP: 2
SALES (est): 136.58K **Privately Held**
SIC: 3826 8999 Analytical instruments; Scientific consulting

(G-19465)
RIC INVESTMENTS LLC
1403 Foulk Rd Ste 200 (19803-2788)
PHONE..............................302 656-8996
EMP: 5 **EST:** 2010
SALES (est): 501.71K
SALES (corp-wide): 18.51B **Privately Held**
SIC: 3842 Surgical appliances and supplies
HQ: Philips Rs North America Llc
6501 Living Pl
Pittsburgh PA 15206
800 263-3342

(G-19466)
RICHARD A & JAMES F CORROON FD
2305 W 11th St (19805-2605)
PHONE..............................302 425-4841
EMP: 5 **EST:** 2011
SALES (est): 62.66K **Privately Held**
SIC: 8699 Charitable organization

(G-19467)
RICHARD E CHODROFF DMD
3105 Limestone Rd Ste 203 (19808-2151)
PHONE..............................302 995-6979
Richard Chodroff, *Owner*
EMP: 5 **EST:** 1980
SALES (est): 192.11K **Privately Held**
SIC: 8021 Dentists' office

(G-19468)
RICHARD EARL FISHER
820 Kiamensi Rd (19804-3420)
PHONE..............................302 598-1957
Richard E Fisher, *Owner*
EMP: 4 **EST:** 1993
SALES (est): 69.69K **Privately Held**
SIC: 2673 2843 3089 2844 Bags: plastic, laminated, and coated; Oils and greases; Blister or bubble formed packaging, plastics; Suntan lotions and oils

(G-19469)
RICHARD HRRMANN STRBILDERS INC
500 Robinson Ln (19805-4616)
PHONE..............................302 654-4329
Richard Herrmann Junior, *Pr*
Keith Herrmann, *VP*
EMP: 5 **EST:** 1956
SQ FT: 6,000
SALES (est): 481.61K **Privately Held**
Web: www.herrmannstairs.net
SIC: 2431 Staircases and stairs, wood

(G-19470)
RICHARD KREN LFRAK CHRTBLE FND
1007 N Orange St (19801-1239)
PHONE..............................302 656-2390
EMP: 6 **EST:** 2011
SALES (est): 3.65MM **Privately Held**
SIC: 8699 Charitable organization

(G-19471)
RICHARD L SHERRY MD (PA)
Also Called: Brandywine Eye Center
2500 Grubb Rd Ste 234 (19810-4796)
PHONE..............................302 475-1880
Richard L Sherry Md, *Owner*
EMP: 10 **EST:** 1991
SALES (est): 2.18MM **Privately Held**
Web: www.brandywineeye.com
SIC: 8011 General and family practice, physician/surgeon

(G-19472)
RICHARD M GOLD DC
5175 W Woodmill Dr (19808-4067)
PHONE..............................302 998-1424
Richard Gold, *Ofcr*
EMP: 7 **EST:** 2005
SALES (est): 40.91K **Privately Held**
Web: www.richardgoldchiropractic.com
SIC: 8041 Offices and clinics of chiropractors

(G-19473)
RICHARD P HORGAN INSURANCE
1301 N Harrison St # 808 (19806-3128)
PHONE..............................302 934-9494
Richard Horgan, *Owner*
EMP: 5 **EST:** 2010
SALES (est): 73.67K **Privately Held**
SIC: 6411 Insurance agents, nec

(G-19474)
RICHARD S COBB ESQUIRE
919 N Market St Ste 600 (19801-3037)
P.O. Box 2087 (19899-2087)
PHONE..............................302 467-4430
Richard S Cobb, *Pt*
Adam Landis, *Pt*
Daniel Rath, *Pt*
EMP: 7 **EST:** 2003
SALES (est): 238.65K **Privately Held**
SIC: 8111 Bankruptcy law

(G-19475)
RICHARDS LAYTON & FINGER P A
Uknown (19801)
P.O. Box 551 (19899-0551)
PHONE..............................302 651-7700
Monica Ayres, *Prin*
EMP: 43 **EST:** 1978
SALES (est): 2.63MM **Privately Held**
Web: www.rlf.com
SIC: 8111 General practice attorney, lawyer

(G-19476)
RICHARDS LAYTON & FINGER P A
1 Rodney Sq 920 N King St (19801)
PHONE..............................302 651-7700
William J Wade, *Pr*
C Stephen Bigler, *
Wayne Stanford, *
Crystal Carter, *
Robert J Krapf Prev, *Prin*
EMP: 320 **EST:** 1900
SQ FT: 100,000
SALES (est): 37.5MM **Privately Held**
Web: www.rlf.com
SIC: 8111 General practice attorney, lawyer

(G-19477)
RICHARDS LAYTON & FINGER P A
920 N King St Ste 200 (19801-3300)
PHONE..............................302 651-7700
EMP: 248 **EST:** 1978
SALES (est): 13.99MM **Privately Held**
Web: www.rlf.com
SIC: 8111 General practice attorney, lawyer

(G-19478)
RIDDLE INC
3524 Silverside Rd Ste 35b (19810-4929)
PHONE..............................724 901-1810
Boris Pfeiffer, *Prin*
EMP: 5 **EST:** 2017
SALES (est): 150.57K **Privately Held**
Web: www.riddle.com
SIC: 7371 Computer software development

(G-19479)
RIDERS APP INC
1 Commerce St 1 # 1 (19801)
PHONE..............................347 484-4344
Igor Debantur, *CEO*
Anatoly Chernyakov, *VP*
EMP: 7 **EST:** 2014
SQ FT: 500
SALES (est): 284.01K **Privately Held**
SIC: 7373 Systems software development services

(G-19480)
RIDGEWOOD ELECTRIC PWR TR III
1314 N King St (19801-3220)
PHONE..............................302 888-7444
Kathleen P Mcsherry, *Prin*
EMP: 6 **EST:** 2010
SALES (est): 566.06K **Privately Held**
SIC: 4911 Electric services

(G-19481)
RIDRODSKY & LONG PA (PA)
300 Delaware Ave Ste L (19801-1634)
PHONE..............................302 691-8822
EMP: 8 **EST:** 2007
SALES (est): 1.08MM **Privately Held**
Web: www.rl-legal.com
SIC: 8111 General practice attorney, lawyer

(G-19482)
RIEMEL OF DELAWARE LLC
460 B And O Ln (19804-1452)
PHONE..............................302 998-5806
Giacomo Stella, *Pr*
EMP: 6 **EST:** 1999
SQ FT: 3,200
SALES (est): 715.67K **Privately Held**
SIC: 3599 Machine shop, jobbing and repair

(G-19483)
RIKO INC
2810 N Church St (19802-4447)
PHONE..............................216 810-5083
Nicolas Ibarra, *CEO*
EMP: 5 **EST:** 2020
SALES (est): 56.54K **Privately Held**
SIC: 7372 Application computer software

(G-19484)
RIPE TECH CORP
919 N Market St Ste 950 (19801-3023)
PHONE..............................786 633-2228
Sergey Golovko, *CEO*
EMP: 6
SALES (est): 76.37K **Privately Held**
SIC: 6794 Music licensing and royalties

(G-19485)
RIPPL LABS INC (PA)
2711 Centerville Rd # 400 (19808-1645)
PHONE..............................551 427-1997
EMP: 8 **EST:** 2015
SALES (est): 641.56K
SALES (corp-wide): 641.56K **Privately Held**
SIC: 4813 Web search portals

(G-19486)
RISING STARS CHILD CARE INC
Also Called: Rising Star Preschool
415 Milmar Rd (19804-1129)
PHONE..............................302 998-7682
Kathleen Hughes, *Pr*
EMP: 10 **EST:** 2003
SALES (est): 58.58K **Privately Held**
SIC: 8351 Group day care center

(G-19487)
RISQ TRADING CORP
1209 N Orange St (19801-1120)
PHONE..............................332 877-9934
EMP: 5
SALES (est): 76.37K **Privately Held**
SIC: 6799 Commodity contract trading companies

(G-19488)
RITCHIE SAWYER CORPORATION (PA)
2502 Pin Oak Dr (19810-1635)
P.O. Box 30558 (19805-7558)
PHONE..............................302 475-1971
EMP: 10 **EST:** 1994
SALES (est): 2.19MM **Privately Held**
SIC: 8721 7371 Certified public accountant; Computer software development

(G-19489)
RIV ATHLETICS
512 Justison St (19801-5142)
PHONE..............................610 229-9092
EMP: 6 **EST:** 2019
SALES (est): 70.58K **Privately Held**
Web: www.rivathletics.com
SIC: 7991 Physical fitness facilities

(G-19490)
RIVER RIDGE HOMEOWNERS ASSN
1538 Seton Villa Ln (19809-2269)
PHONE..............................302 761-9592
Ronald Smith, *Prin*
EMP: 5 **EST:** 2010
SALES (est): 67.03K **Privately Held**
SIC: 8641 Homeowners' association

(G-19491)
RIVER TOWER VENTURES LLC
322 A St Ste 300 (19801-5354)
PHONE..............................302 691-2100
Robert E Buccini, *Prin*
EMP: 6 **EST:** 2009
SALES (est): 261.26K **Privately Held**
SIC: 7389 Business services, nec

(G-19492)
RIVEREDGE III LLC
300 Water St (19801-5037)
PHONE..............................302 656-3631
EMP: 6 **EST:** 2009
SALES (est): 629.62K **Privately Held**
SIC: 6519 Real property lessors, nec

(G-19493)
RIVERFRONT DEV CORP DEL
Also Called: Riverfront Development
815 Justison St Ste D (19801-5156)
PHONE..............................302 425-4890
Megan Mcgoinchey, *Ex Dir*
Michael S Purzycki, *Ex Dir*
EMP: 15 **EST:** 1996
SQ FT: 125,000
SALES (est): 2.39MM **Privately Held**
Web: www.riverfrontwilm.com
SIC: 6552 Land subdividers and developers, commercial

(G-19494)
RIVERFRONT DEVELOPMENT CORP
815 Justison St Ste D (19801-5156)
PHONE..............................302 425-4890
EMP: 21
Web: www.riverfrontwilm.com
SIC: 6552 Subdividers and developers, nec

Wilmington - New Castle County (G-19495)

(G-19495)
RIVERFRONT HOTEL LLC
Also Called: Hyatt Pl Wilmington Riverfront
760 Justison St (19801-5141)
PHONE..................302 803-5888
Stephen Silver, *Managing Member*
EMP: 40 **EST:** 2019
SALES (est): 1.41MM **Privately Held**
Web: www.hyatt.com
SIC: 7011 Hotels

(G-19496)
RIVERFRONT PETS
311 Justison St (19801-5164)
PHONE..................302 428-9777
EMP: 5 **EST:** 2018
SALES (est): 194.45K **Privately Held**
Web: www.riverfrontpets.com
SIC: 0752 Grooming services, pet and animal specialties

(G-19497)
RIVERS FAMILY FOUNDATION INC
501 Silverside Rd Ste 123 (19809-1377)
PHONE..................800 839-1754
EMP: 5
SALES (est): 196.96K **Privately Held**
Web: www.threeriversfoundation.org
SIC: 8699 Charitable organization

(G-19498)
RIVERSEDGE
1 Ave Of The Arts (19801)
PHONE..................267 342-6984
EMP: 7
SALES (est): 2.35MM **Privately Held**
Web: www.riversedgeadvisors.com
SIC: 6282 Investment advisory service

(G-19499)
RIVERSEDGE ADVISORS LLC ◊
600 N King St Ste 200 (19801-3780)
PHONE..................302 573-6864
EMP: 17 **EST:** 2023
SALES (est): 68.89K **Privately Held**
SIC: 7371 Computer software development and applications

(G-19500)
RIVERWALK MINI GOLF
550 Justison St (19801-5142)
PHONE..................302 425-4890
EMP: 5 **EST:** 2020
SALES (est): 48.35K **Privately Held**
Web: www.riverwalkminigolf.com
SIC: 7999 Golf professionals

(G-19501)
RKJ CONSTRUCTION INC
2252 Saint James Dr (19808-5219)
PHONE..................302 690-0959
Kirti Joshi, *Pr*
EMP: 5 **EST:** 2014
SALES (est): 529.64K **Privately Held**
Web: www.gencodentalcare.com
SIC: 1521 Single-family housing construction

(G-19502)
RLK PRESS INC
3511 Silverside Rd (19810-4902)
PHONE..................267 565-5138
Davey Dunn, *Pr*
EMP: 5 **EST:** 2017
SALES (est): 61.14K **Privately Held**
SIC: 2741 Miscellaneous publishing

(G-19503)
RM INDUSTRIAL WELDING
1212 E 15th St (19802-5215)
PHONE..................302 407-6685
EMP: 4 **EST:** 2019
SALES (est): 36.62K **Privately Held**
Web: rm-industrial-welding.business.site
SIC: 7692 Welding repair

(G-19504)
ROADRUNNER EXPRESS INC
21 Millside Dr (19801-5541)
PHONE..................302 426-9551
EMP: 7 **EST:** 1992
SALES (est): 235.01K **Privately Held**
Web: www.roadrunnerexp.com
SIC: 4119 Limousine rental, with driver

(G-19505)
ROB WATSON
5307 Limestone Rd Ste 100 (19808-1275)
PHONE..................302 234-8877
Rob Watson, *Owner*
EMP: 5 **EST:** 2015
SALES (est): 127.39K **Privately Held**
SIC: 6531 Real estate brokers and agents

(G-19506)
ROBERT A HEINLE M D
1600 Rockland Rd (19803-3607)
PHONE..................302 651-6400
Robert Heinle, *Owner*
EMP: 12 **EST:** 2017
SALES (est): 248.78K **Privately Held**
Web: www.nemours.org
SIC: 8011 Pediatrician

(G-19507)
ROBERT A STEELE M D
1401 Foulk Rd Ste 101 (19803-2764)
PHONE..................302 478-5500
EMP: 8 **EST:** 2018
SALES (est): 109.73K **Privately Held**
SIC: 8011 Orthopedic physician

(G-19508)
ROBERT BIRD
Also Called: Home Instead Senior Care
1701 Shallcross Ave Ste A (19806-2347)
PHONE..................302 654-4003
Robert Bird, *Owner*
EMP: 22 **EST:** 2009
SALES (est): 899.72K **Privately Held**
Web: www.homeinstead.com
SIC: 8082 Home health care services

(G-19509)
ROBERT E MEASLEY MD PC
616 Kilburn Rd (19803-1705)
PHONE..................302 543-4233
Robert E Measley, *Prin*
EMP: 7 **EST:** 2005
SALES (est): 63.25K **Privately Held**
SIC: 8011 General and family practice, physician/surgeon

(G-19510)
ROBERT FRY ECONOMICS LLC
11 Pheasants Rdg N (19807-1541)
PHONE..................302 743-8553
Robert Fry, *Prin*
EMP: 5 **EST:** 2018
SALES (est): 90.45K **Privately Held**
Web: www.robertfryeconomics.com
SIC: 8748 Economic consultant

(G-19511)
ROBERT G BURKE PAINTING CO
1614 E Ayre St (19804-2515)
PHONE..................302 998-2200
Robert G Burke, *Pr*
EMP: 10 **EST:** 1980
SALES (est): 658.61K **Privately Held**
SIC: 1721 Painting and paper hanging

(G-19512)
ROBERT GOLEBIOWSKI
4 Hayloft Ct (19808-1934)
PHONE..................302 234-6583
Robert Golebiowski, *Prin*
EMP: 5 **EST:** 2009
SALES (est): 164.54K **Privately Held**
SIC: 1522 Residential construction, nec

(G-19513)
ROBERT HALF INTERNATIONAL INC
Also Called: Accountemps
2 Righter Pkwy Ste 310 (19803-1551)
PHONE..................302 252-3162
EMP: 5
SALES (corp-wide): 7.24B **Publicly Held**
Web: www.roberthalf.com
SIC: 7361 Placement agencies
PA: Robert Half Inc.
2884 Sand Hill Rd Ste 200
Menlo Park CA 94025
650 234-6000

(G-19514)
ROBERT J KRINER JR
920 N King St Ste 500 (19801-3340)
PHONE..................302 656-2500
A Naylor Attorney, *Prin*
EMP: 7 **EST:** 2018
SALES (est): 63.66K **Privately Held**
Web: www.chimicles.com
SIC: 8111 General practice attorney, lawyer

(G-19515)
ROBERT J PEOPLES INC
1 Westmoreland Ave Apt A (19804-1763)
P.O. Box 65 (19720-0065)
PHONE..................302 322-0595
Steve Pedrick, *Pr*
Sandra Pedrick, *Sec*
EMP: 10 **EST:** 1920
SQ FT: 3,000
SALES (est): 626.77K **Privately Held**
SIC: 1721 Exterior commercial painting contractor

(G-19516)
ROBERT K BESTE JR
1007 N Orange St Ste 1130 (19801-1236)
PHONE..................302 425-5089
Robert Beste, *Owner*
EMP: 6 **EST:** 2018
SALES (est): 63.66K **Privately Held**
Web: www.skjlaw.com
SIC: 8111 General practice attorney, lawyer

(G-19517)
ROBERT KOPECKI DO
3105 Limestone Rd Ste 301 (19808-2156)
PHONE..................302 230-4955
Robert Kopecki, *Ofcr*
EMP: 9 **EST:** 2018
SALES (est): 224.61K **Privately Held**
SIC: 8011 Offices and clinics of medical doctors

(G-19518)
ROBERT L THOMAS (PA)
1000 N West St (19801-1050)
PHONE..................302 571-6602
Robert Thomas, *Prin*
EMP: 5 **EST:** 2010
SALES (est): 145.24K
SALES (corp-wide): 145.24K **Privately Held**
SIC: 8111 General practice attorney, lawyer

(G-19519)
ROBERT M PANZER
Also Called: Down To Earth Wines
2000 Delaware Ave (19806-2295)
PHONE..................302 571-0717
Robert M Panzer, *Prin*
EMP: 5 **EST:** 2012
SALES (est): 181.09K **Privately Held**
SIC: 5182 Wine

(G-19520)
ROBERT S BRADY
1000 N West St (19801-1050)
PHONE..................302 571-6690
Robert Brady, *Prin*
EMP: 5 **EST:** 2010
SALES (est): 215.39K **Privately Held**
Web: www.youngconaway.com
SIC: 5072 Brads

(G-19521)
ROBIN SESAN
2500 Grubb Rd Ste 234 (19810-4796)
PHONE..................302 475-1880
Robin Sesan, *Owner*
EMP: 5 **EST:** 2018
SALES (est): 114.41K **Privately Held**
Web: www.thebrandywinecenter.com
SIC: 8049 Clinical psychologist

(G-19522)
ROBINO MANAGEMENT GROUP INC
5189 W Woodmill Dr Ste 30a (19808-4009)
PHONE..................302 633-6001
Paul A Robino, *Pr*
EMP: 38 **EST:** 1992
SQ FT: 2,300
SALES (est): 2.87MM **Privately Held**
Web: www.robino.com
SIC: 6531 Real estate managers

(G-19523)
ROBINS HAIR & TANNING
2716 Naamans Rd (19810-1139)
PHONE..................302 529-9000
Robin Bilone, *Owner*
EMP: 5 **EST:** 2001
SALES (est): 117.98K **Privately Held**
Web: www.robinshairandtanning.com
SIC: 7231 7299 Hairdressers; Tanning salon

(G-19524)
ROBINSON GRAYSON AND WARD PA
Also Called: Robinson and Grayson
910 Foulk Rd Ste 200 (19803-3159)
PHONE..................302 655-6262
Stephen Robinson, *Pt*
EMP: 5 **EST:** 1985
SALES (est): 489.01K **Privately Held**
SIC: 8111 General practice attorney, lawyer

(G-19525)
ROCA FAMILY DAYCARE
205 S Ogle Ave (19805-1422)
PHONE..................302 656-8356
EMP: 6 **EST:** 2016
SALES (est): 17.57K **Privately Held**
SIC: 8351 Group day care center

(G-19526)
ROCCOS AUTOMOTIVE SERVICE
Also Called: Rocco Automotive
2379 Limestone Rd (19808-8010)
PHONE..................302 998-2234
Tony Rocco, *Pr*
Barbara A Rocco, *VP*
Suzan J Langston, *Sec*
EMP: 9 **EST:** 1984
SQ FT: 11,000

SALES (est): 330.23K **Privately Held**
Web: www.roccoautomotive.com
SIC: 7538 Engine repair

(G-19527)
ROCK CITY CONSULTING CORP
1207 Delaware Ave (19806-4743)
PHONE..............................302 551-6844
Antonio Hennis, *Pr*
EMP: 9
SALES (est): 373.09K **Privately Held**
SIC: 4731 7389 Freight transportation arrangement; Business services, nec

(G-19528)
ROCK MAINTENANCE SERVICES LLC
11 Eastlawn Ave (19802-2828)
PHONE..............................607 624-2341
Joseph King, *Prin*
EMP: 7 **EST**: 2017
SALES (est): 219.38K **Privately Held**
Web: www.rockmaintenanceservices.com
SIC: 7349 Janitorial service, contract basis

(G-19529)
ROCK MANOR GOLF COURSE
1319 Carruthers Ln (19803-4601)
PHONE..............................302 295-1400
Kyle Dalton, *Genl Mgr*
EMP: 5 **EST**: 2011
SALES (est): 423.4K **Privately Held**
Web: www.rockmanorgolf.com
SIC: 7992 Public golf courses

(G-19530)
ROCK OF AGES TATTOOS
12 Carpenter Plz (19810-2049)
PHONE..............................302 475-8050
EMP: 6 **EST**: 2018
SALES (est): 195.38K **Privately Held**
SIC: 7299 Tattoo parlor

(G-19531)
ROCK RIVER REAL ESTATE INC
20 Montchanin Rd Ste 250 (19807-2181)
P.O. Box 731 (19710-0731)
PHONE..............................302 778-1000
Kevin Abrams, *Prin*
EMP: 5 **EST**: 2010
SALES (est): 117.72K **Privately Held**
SIC: 6531 Real estate brokers and agents

(G-19532)
ROCK SPRINGS CAPITAL LLC
1209 N Orange St (19801-1120)
PHONE..............................415 669-4545
Jonathan Rinaldo, *Pr*
EMP: 7 **EST**: 2013
SALES (est): 423.39K **Privately Held**
SIC: 6799 Investors, nec

(G-19533)
ROCKETCHAT TECHNOLOGIES CORP
251 Little Falls Dr (19808-1674)
PHONE..............................213 725-2428
Gabriel Engel, *CEO*
Marcelo Schmidt, *
Caio Bolognesi, *
Bruno Weiblen, *
Antoine Colao, *
EMP: 130 **EST**: 2016
SALES (est): 10.25MM **Privately Held**
Web: www.rocket.chat
SIC: 7371 7372 7374 Custom computer programming services; Prepackaged software; Data processing and preparation

(G-19534)
ROCKFIELD COLLISION LLC
2300 W 4th St (19805-3325)
PHONE..............................302 658-4324
EMP: 8 **EST**: 2018
SALES (est): 318.24K **Privately Held**
Web: www.henryautobody.com
SIC: 7532 Exterior repair services

(G-19535)
ROCKFORD CAPITAL PARTNERS
219 W 9th St Ste 230 (19801-1619)
PHONE..............................302 220-4786
EMP: 7 **EST**: 2011
SALES (est): 95K **Privately Held**
Web: www.rockfordcp.com
SIC: 6799 Investors, nec

(G-19536)
ROCKFORD MAP GALLERY LLC
1800 Lovering Ave (19806-2122)
PHONE..............................302 740-1851
EMP: 4 **EST**: 2005
SALES (est): 353.55K **Privately Held**
Web: www.rockfordpublishing.com
SIC: 2741 Miscellaneous publishing

(G-19537)
ROCKFORD PARK CONDOMINIUM HOME
Also Called: Rockford Park Condominium
2302 Riddle Ave Ofc (19806-2139)
PHONE..............................302 658-7842
Barbara Worrell, *Mgr*
EMP: 5 **EST**: 1971
SQ FT: 5,000
SALES (est): 221.01K **Privately Held**
Web: www.rpcawilmington.net
SIC: 8641 Condominium association

(G-19538)
ROCKFORD RE FUND IV LP
219 W 9th St Ste 230 (19801-1619)
PHONE..............................302 220-4786
EMP: 5 **EST**: 2018
SALES (est): 195.84K **Privately Held**
SIC: 6722 Money market mutual funds

(G-19539)
ROCKLAND BUILDERS INC
1605 E Ayre St (19804-2514)
PHONE..............................302 995-6800
David T Heaney, *Pr*
EMP: 10 **EST**: 2003
SALES (est): 499.74K **Privately Held**
SIC: 1521 New construction, single-family houses

(G-19540)
ROCKLAND PLACE
1519 Rockland Rd (19803-3611)
PHONE..............................302 777-3099
EMP: 10 **EST**: 2008
SALES (est): 520.68K **Privately Held**
Web: www.watermarkcommunities.com
SIC: 6513 Retirement hotel operation

(G-19541)
ROCKLAND SPORTS LLC
Also Called: Dupont Country Club
1001 Rockland Rd (19803-2923)
PHONE..............................302 654-4435
Robert Wirth, *CEO*
EMP: 55 **EST**: 2018
SALES (est): 5.14MM **Privately Held**
Web: www.dupontcountryclub.com
SIC: 7997 Country club, membership

(G-19542)
ROCKLAND SURGERY CENTER LP
Also Called: Center For Advnced Srgcal Arts
2710 Centerville Rd Ste 100 (19808-1652)
PHONE..............................302 999-0200
Stewart G Smith, *Dir*
EMP: 20 **EST**: 2004
SQ FT: 8,100
SALES (est): 2.42MM **Privately Held**
SIC: 8011 Surgeon

(G-19543)
ROCKLEDGE GLOBAL PARTNERS LTD
1000 N West St Ste 1200 (19801-1058)
PHONE..............................800 659-1102
Manuel Celaya, *Dir*
EMP: 5 **EST**: 2006
SALES (est): 127.03K **Privately Held**
SIC: 8748 Business consulting, nec

(G-19544)
ROCKWELL ASSOCIATES
2711 Centerville Rd Ste 105 (19808-1660)
PHONE..............................302 655-7151
Barbara Methven, *VP*
EMP: 8 **EST**: 1966
SALES (est): 70.35K **Privately Held**
Web: www.rockwellassoc.com
SIC: 8721 Accounting, auditing, and bookkeeping

(G-19545)
ROCKWOOD CONFERENCE CENTER
610 N Shipley St (19801-2229)
PHONE..............................302 761-4342
Regina Marini, *Mgr*
EMP: 5 **EST**: 2007
SALES (est): 21K **Privately Held**
SIC: 7299 7389 Banquet hall facilities; Advertising, promotional, and trade show services

(G-19546)
ROCKWOOD MUSEUM
610 Shipley Rd (19809-3609)
PHONE..............................302 761-4340
Phillip Nord, *Dir*
Michael Clark, *Pr*
EMP: 6 **EST**: 2002
SALES (est): 89.51K **Privately Held**
Web: www.newcastlede.gov
SIC: 8412 Museum

(G-19547)
ROCKWOOD SPECIALTIES INC
4001 Miller Road (19802-1961)
PHONE..............................302 765-6012
EMP: 24 **EST**: 1979
SALES (est): 2.43MM **Publicly Held**
SIC: 5169 Chemicals and allied products, nec
HQ: Rockwood Specialties Group, Inc.
100 Overlook Ctr Ste 101
Princeton NJ 08540
609 514-0300

(G-19548)
ROD-AES SURVERYORS CO
Also Called: AES Surveyors
3913 Old Capitol Trl (19808-5723)
PHONE..............................302 993-1059
EMP: 5 **EST**: 1994
SQ FT: 900
SALES (est): 489.57K **Privately Held**
Web: www.aessurveyors.com
SIC: 8713 Photogrammetric engineering

(G-19549)
RODNEY RBNSN LDSCP ARCHTS INC
30 Hill Rd (19806-2034)
PHONE..............................302 888-1544
EMP: 7 **EST**: 1995
SQ FT: 1,000
SALES (est): 320.91K **Privately Held**
SIC: 0781 Landscape architects

(G-19550)
RODNEY SQUARE ASSOCIATES
1 Rodney Sq (19801)
PHONE..............................302 652-1536
Barbara Paxson, *Mgr*
EMP: 6
SALES (corp-wide): 2MM **Privately Held**
Web: www.rodneysquare.org
SIC: 6512 Commercial and industrial building operation
PA: Rodney Square Associates
2005 Market St Ste 4100
Philadelphia PA 19103
215 563-3558

(G-19551)
RODNEY SQUARE SERVICES INC
100 A St (19801-5219)
PHONE..............................302 652-5891
Gabriel Fieni, *Pr*
EMP: 20 **EST**: 1986
SQ FT: 10,000
SALES (est): 1.79MM **Privately Held**
SIC: 1799 Caulking (construction)

(G-19552)
RODNEY STREET TENNIS
500 W 8th St (19801-1408)
PHONE..............................302 384-7498
Harry Shur, *Ex Dir*
EMP: 10 **EST**: 2007
SALES (est): 92.06K **Privately Held**
Web: www.rodneystreettennis.org
SIC: 7999 Games, instruction

(G-19553)
RODRIGUEZ MARIEVE O DMD PA
Also Called: Gentle Care Family Dentistry
1407 Foulk Rd (19803-2762)
PHONE..............................302 655-5862
Marieve O Rodriguez, *Prin*
EMP: 5 **EST**: 2007
SALES (est): 430.47K **Privately Held**
Web: www.drmarieverodriguez.com
SIC: 8021 Dentists' office

(G-19554)
ROEBERG MOORE & ASSOCIATES PA
Also Called: Moore, William X Jr
62 Rockford Rd (19806-1047)
PHONE..............................302 658-4757
David Roeberg, *Pt*
William Moore, *VP*
EMP: 10 **EST**: 1968
SALES (est): 1.32MM **Privately Held**
Web: www.roebergmooreandfriedman.com
SIC: 8111 General practice attorney, lawyer

(G-19555)
ROGER D ANDERSON
Also Called: Smith, Katzenscein and Jenkins
800 Delaware Ave Ste 1000 (19801-1354)
P.O. Box 410 (19899-0410)
PHONE..............................302 652-8400
Roger Anderson, *Pt*
EMP: 9 **EST**: 2002
SALES (est): 1.4MM **Privately Held**
Web: www.skjlaw.com

Wilmington - New Castle County (G-19556)

SIC: 8111 General practice attorney, lawyer

(G-19556)
ROIZMAN & ASSOCIATES INC
Also Called: Bethel Villa Apartments
506 E 5th St (19801-4706)
PHONE..................................302 426-9688
EMP: 5
SIC: 6513 6552 Apartment building operators; Subdividers and developers, nec
PA: Roizman & Associates, Inc.
832 Germantown Pike Ste 5
Plymouth Meeting PA 19462

(G-19557)
ROLLINS LEASING LLC (HQ)
2200 Concord Pike (19803-2978)
P.O. Box 563 (19603-0563)
PHONE..................................302 426-2700
David Burr, Ch Bd
I Larry Brown, *
Neil Vonnahme, *
Jim Mc Caughan, *
Carlisle Peet, *
▲ EMP: 214 EST: 1969
SQ FT: 65,000
SALES (est): 89.88MM
SALES (corp-wide): 2.11B Privately Held
Web: www.penoketruckrental.com
SIC: 7513 Truck rental, without drivers
PA: Penske Truck Leasing Co., L.P.
2675 Morgantown Rd
Reading PA 19607
610 775-6000

(G-19558)
ROMANOS ORIGINAL LLC
3 Woodland Dr (19809-2836)
PHONE..................................215 796-3271
Pete J Romano R, Prin
EMP: 5 EST: 2016
SALES (est): 67.15K Privately Held
SIC: 1799 Special trade contractors, nec

(G-19559)
ROME SOLUTIONS LLC
300 Delaware Ave Ste 210 (19801-6601)
PHONE..................................302 261-3794
EMP: 5 EST: 2020
SALES (est): 519.21K Privately Held
Web: www.rome-solutions.com
SIC: 5072 Hardware

(G-19560)
RONALD MCDONALD HOUSE DELAWARE
1901 Rockland Rd (19803-3629)
PHONE..................................302 428-5299
Pam Cornforth, Dir
EMP: 11 EST: 1986
SQ FT: 60,000
SALES (est): 3MM Privately Held
Web: www.rmhcdelaware.org
SIC: 8322 Social service center

(G-19561)
RONALD N BROWN
1106 Piper Rd (19803-3329)
PHONE..................................302 478-1108
Ronald Brown, Owner
EMP: 8 EST: 2017
SALES (est): 54.13K Privately Held
Web: www.telenko.com
SIC: 8011 Offices and clinics of medical doctors

(G-19562)
RONALD W PEACOCK INC
110 Matthes Ave (19804-1534)
PHONE..................................302 571-9313
Ronald W Peacock, Pr
Michelle Peacock, Prin
EMP: 14 EST: 1990
SQ FT: 1,200
SALES (est): 495.93K Privately Held
SIC: 1721 Painting and paper hanging

(G-19563)
RONNIE FREEMAN
515 E 3rd St (19801-3911)
PHONE..................................302 762-3252
Ronnie Freeman, Prin
EMP: 6 EST: 2010
SALES (est): 117.2K Privately Held
SIC: 1711 Plumbing contractors

(G-19564)
ROOFERS INC
Also Called: Tri State Roofers
404 Meco Dr (19804-1112)
PHONE..................................302 995-7027
Francis Nick Sanna, Pr
Charles High, *
Ron Sanna, *
Janice Sanna, *
EMP: 35 EST: 1966
SQ FT: 12,000
SALES (est): 2.41MM Privately Held
Web: www.tristatetheroofers.com
SIC: 1761 Roofing contractor

(G-19565)
ROOM2ROOM CLEANING LLC
1201 N Market St Ste 111-D77 (19801-1147)
PHONE..................................302 202-9140
EMP: 8 EST: 2018
SALES (est): 221.3K Privately Held
Web: www.room2roomcleaning.com
SIC: 7349 Janitorial service, contract basis

(G-19566)
ROPE-IT GOLF LLC
3 River Rd (19809-3205)
PHONE..................................305 767-3481
EMP: 3 EST: 2009
SALES (est): 152.35K Privately Held
Web: www.theropeit.com
SIC: 3949 Golf equipment

(G-19567)
ROSANNE TRAY INC
2211 Van Buren Pl (19802-3930)
PHONE..................................302 656-5776
Rosanne Tray, Prin
EMP: 6 EST: 2010
SALES (est): 71.4K Privately Held
SIC: 8049 Offices of health practitioner

(G-19568)
ROSE STRAB
208 School House Ln (19809-2351)
PHONE..................................302 584-2074
EMP: 6 EST: 2015
SALES (est): 89.22K Privately Held
SIC: 8011 Offices and clinics of medical doctors

(G-19569)
ROSENBERGER USA CORP (DH)
1209 N Orange St (19801-1120)
PHONE..................................717 859-8900
Andreas Ruzic, CEO
EMP: 9 EST: 2002
SQ FT: 94,145
SALES (est): 100.01MM
SALES (corp-wide): 1.72B Privately Held
SIC: 5065 Electronic parts and equipment, nec
HQ: Rosenberger Hochfrequenztechnik Gmbh & Co. Kg
Hauptstr. 1
Fridolfing BY 83413
8684180

(G-19570)
ROSENTHAL MONHAIT GODDESS PA
919 N Market St Ste 1401 (19801-3046)
P.O. Box 1070 (19899-1070)
PHONE..................................302 656-4433
Joseph Rosenthal, Mng Pt
Jeffrey Goddess, Managing Member
Carmella Kenne, Mng Pt
EMP: 11 EST: 1960
SALES (est): 444.13K Privately Held
Web: www.rmgglaw.com
SIC: 8111 General practice law office

(G-19571)
ROSS ARONSTAM & MORITZ LLP
1313 N Market St Fl 10 (19801-6107)
PHONE..................................302 576-1600
Bradley R Aronstam, Pt
Garrett B Moritz, Pt
David E Ross, Pt
Collins J Seitz Junior, Pt
EMP: 18 EST: 2011
SALES (est): 2.56MM Privately Held
Web: www.ramllp.com
SIC: 8111 General practice attorney, lawyer

(G-19572)
ROSS GET HEALTHY CHIROPRACTIC
5239 W Woodmill Dr (19808-4068)
PHONE..................................302 407-5571
Jacob Ross, Prin
EMP: 6 EST: 2014
SALES (est): 220.26K Privately Held
Web: www.gethealthychiropractic.com
SIC: 8041 Offices and clinics of chiropractors

(G-19573)
ROTO-ROOTER PLBG & WTR CLEANUP
Also Called: Roto-Rooter
900 Philadelphia Pike Ste D (19809-2280)
PHONE..................................302 256-5022
EMP: 11 EST: 1935
SALES (est): 81.21K Privately Held
Web: www.rotorooter.com
SIC: 7699 Sewer cleaning and rodding

(G-19574)
ROXLOR LLC
1013 Centre Rd Ste 106 (19805-1265)
PHONE..................................302 778-4166
▲ EMP: 5 EST: 1998
SALES (est): 610.87K Privately Held
Web: www.roxlor.com
SIC: 2023 Dietary supplements, dairy and non-dairy based

(G-19575)
ROYAL BANK AMERICA LEASING LLC
Also Called: ROYAL BANK AMERICA LEASING, LLC
20 Montchanin Rd Ste 100 (19807-2179)
PHONE..................................302 798-1790
Robert W Eaddy, Pr
EMP: 12
SALES (corp-wide): 963.95MM Publicly Held
SIC: 6022 State commercial banks
HQ: Royal Bank Amercia Leasing, Llc
915 Montgomery Ave # 401
Penn Valley PA 19072
610 668-4700

(G-19576)
ROYAL CLEANERS
3914 Concord Pike (19803-1716)
PHONE..................................302 478-0955
Steve Kim, Owner
EMP: 8 EST: 1960
SALES (est): 298.23K Privately Held
SIC: 7215 Laundry, coin-operated

(G-19577)
ROYALHALO LLC
1000 N West St Ste 1200 (19801-1058)
PHONE..................................888 418-7692
Ricardo Hernandez, Managing Member
EMP: 18 EST: 2014
SALES (est): 974.44K Privately Held
Web: www.royalhalo.com
SIC: 0723 Fruit (fresh) packing services

(G-19578)
RP VENTURES AND HOLDINGS INC (PA)
1700 Shipley Rd (19803-3269)
PHONE..................................410 398-3000
Richard Piendak, Pr
EMP: 34 EST: 1973
SALES (est): 4.38MM
SALES (corp-wide): 4.38MM Privately Held
SIC: 1771 1611 Blacktop (asphalt) work; Highway and street construction

(G-19579)
RS MARKS INC
3411 Silverside Rd (19810-4812)
PHONE..................................302 478-4371
Robert Clever, Mgr
EMP: 8 EST: 2012
SALES (est): 3.94MM Publicly Held
SIC: 4841 5961 Cable and other pay television services; Television, home shopping
PA: Qurate Retail, Inc.
12300 Liberty Blvd
Englewood CO 80112

(G-19580)
RSF MANAGED SERVICES LLC
2045 Longcome Dr (19810-3873)
PHONE..................................302 345-7162
EMP: 5 EST: 2010
SALES (est): 71.73K Privately Held
Web: www.imspros.com
SIC: 7374 7379 Data processing and preparation; Data processing consultant

(G-19581)
RSL INVESTORS INC
1105 N Market St Ste 1230 (19899)
P.O. Box 8985 (19899-8985)
PHONE..................................302 478-5142
Robert Rosekranz, Pr
EMP: 555 EST: 1987
SALES (est): 440.11K Privately Held
SIC: 6211 Investment bankers
HQ: Delphi Financial Group, Inc.
1105 N Market St Ste 1230
Wilmington DE 19801
302 478-5142

(G-19582)
RSL LOGISTICS LLC ◆
4611 Griffin Dr (19808-4113)
PHONE..................................302 521-3299
Ryan Larsen, Managing Member
EMP: 5 EST: 2023
SALES (est): 298.13K Privately Held
SIC: 4731 Transportation agents and brokers

GEOGRAPHIC SECTION

Wilmington - New Castle County (G-19612)

(G-19583)
RSM DIAGNOSTICS LAB LLC
2500 Grubb Rd Ste 120 (19810-4711)
PHONE............................302 592-4106
EMP: 6 **EST:** 2021
SALES (est): 601.49K **Privately Held**
SIC: 8071 Medical laboratories

(G-19584)
RSS LLC
3511 Silverside Rd Ste 105 (19810-4902)
PHONE............................866 801-0692
EMP: 5
SALES (est): 87.56K **Privately Held**
SIC: 4789 Transportation services, nec

(G-19585)
RUBY DIGITAL AGENCY INC
3911 Concord Pike Ste 8030 Smb Ste 50502 (19803-1736)
PHONE............................801 971-1681
Lance Allison, *CEO*
EMP: 5
SALES (est): 261.66K **Privately Held**
SIC: 7371 Custom computer programming services

(G-19586)
RUDLYN INC
Also Called: Rudy Auto Body
3900 Governor Printz Blvd (19802-2308)
PHONE............................302 764-5677
Rudy Di Bonaventura, *Pr*
Linda Di Bonaventura, *VP*
EMP: 11 **EST:** 1978
SQ FT: 17,000
SALES (est): 384.87K **Privately Held**
SIC: 7532 Body shop, automotive

(G-19587)
RUFFIN TELLIE
2005 Baynard Blvd (19802-3917)
PHONE............................302 650-3151
EMP: 7 **EST:** 2017
SALES (est): 32.92K **Privately Held**
SIC: 8322 Individual and family services

(G-19588)
RUIZ FLOORING
3405 Cranston Ave (19808-6103)
PHONE............................302 999-9350
EMP: 5 **EST:** 2007
SALES (est): 249.48K **Privately Held**
SIC: 1743 1752 5211 Tile installation, ceramic; Carpet laying; Tile, ceramic

(G-19589)
RUKKET LLC
Also Called: Rukket Sports
4023 Kennett Pike # 123 (19807-2018)
P.O. Box 4020 (19807-4020)
PHONE............................855 478-5538
Jana Skrabalkova, *Managing Member*
◆ **EMP:** 15 **EST:** 2012
SALES (est): 898.83K **Privately Held**
Web: www.rukket.com
SIC: 5941 3949 Sporting goods and bicycle shops; Sporting and athletic goods, nec

(G-19590)
RUMMEL KLEPPER & KAHL LLP
Also Called: RK&k
750 Shipyard Dr (19801-5111)
PHONE............................302 468-4880
Mark M Dumler, *Brnch Mgr*
EMP: 22
SALES (corp-wide): 206.65MM **Privately Held**
Web: www.rkk.com
SIC: 8711 Civil engineering

PA: Rummel, Klepper & Kahl, Llp
700 E Pratt St Ste 500
Baltimore MD 21202
410 728-2900

(G-19591)
RUMZ INC
2055 Limestone Rd (19808-5536)
PHONE............................571 733-0693
Adrian Paun, *Prin*
EMP: 6
SALES (est): 68.89K **Privately Held**
SIC: 7371 Computer software development and applications

(G-19592)
RUSS OTR HARDESTY
2319 Jamaica Dr (19810-2708)
PHONE............................302 598-0824
Russell Hardesty, *Prin*
EMP: 5 **EST:** 2006
SALES (est): 111.39K **Privately Held**
SIC: 8049 Offices of health practitioner

(G-19593)
RUSSELL A PAULUS & SON INC
193 Christina Landing Dr (19801-5253)
PHONE............................302 998-4494
Russell Paulus, *Pr*
Donna Paulus, *VP*
EMP: 9 **EST:** 1988
SALES (est): 693.87K **Privately Held**
SIC: 1761 Sheet metal work, nec

(G-19594)
RUSSELL J TIBBETTS DDS PA
Also Called: Thomas, Irving O DDS
3516 Silverside Rd Ste 17 (19810-4932)
PHONE............................302 479-5959
Doctor Russell J Tibbetts, *Owner*
Russell J Tibbetts, *Prin*
EMP: 7 **EST:** 1965
SQ FT: 2,000
SALES (est): 248.9K **Privately Held**
Web: www.tibbettsdental.com
SIC: 8021 Dentists' office

(G-19595)
RUSSELL PLYWOOD INC
1000 S Heald St (19801-5735)
PHONE............................302 689-0137
EMP: 12
SALES (corp-wide): 10.3MM **Privately Held**
Web: www.russellplywood.com
SIC: 5031 Plywood
PA: Russell Plywood, Inc.
401 Old Wyomissing Rd
Reading PA 19611
610 374-3206

(G-19596)
RUTMAN ENTERPRISES
3221 Swarthmore Rd (19807-3125)
PHONE............................302 777-5298
Wayne Rutman, *Prin*
EMP: 5 **EST:** 2010
SALES (est): 174.54K **Privately Held**
SIC: 8748 Business consulting, nec

(G-19597)
RW GREER INC
2109 Swinnen Dr (19810-4117)
PHONE............................302 764-0376
David Greer, *Pr*
Erin Daniels, *Sec*
EMP: 9 **EST:** 1973
SALES (est): 844.83K **Privately Held**
Web: www.robertsonsign.com

SIC: 1711 Plumbing contractors

(G-19598)
RWAZI INC
2055 Limestone Rd (19808-5536)
PHONE............................800 597-5871
EMP: 16 **EST:** 2021
SALES (est): 283.7K **Privately Held**
Web: www.rwazi.com
SIC: 7371 Computer software development

(G-19599)
RWK VENTURES LLC
3911 Concord Pike # 8030 (19803-1736)
PHONE............................305 494-4011
Kevin Lawson, *Managing Member*
EMP: 5 **EST:** 2017
SALES (est): 64.29K **Privately Held**
SIC: 2741 Internet publishing and broadcasting

(G-19600)
RYAN R DAVIES M D
1600 Rockland Rd (19803-3607)
PHONE............................302 651-6660
Deborah Rabinowitz, *Owner*
EMP: 7 **EST:** 2018
SALES (est): 162.82K **Privately Held**
Web: www.nemours.org
SIC: 8011 Pediatrician

(G-19601)
RYDER TRUCK RENTAL INC
Also Called: Ryder
6605 Governor Printz Blvd (19809-2027)
PHONE............................302 798-1472
EMP: 5
SALES (corp-wide): 12.01B **Publicly Held**
Web: www.ryder.com
SIC: 7513 7359 Truck rental, without drivers; Equipment rental and leasing, nec
HQ: Ryder Truck Rental, Inc.
11690 Nw 105th St
Medley FL 33178
305 500-3726

(G-19602)
RYERSON GERALYN
1601 Milltown Rd Ste 8 (19808-4073)
PHONE............................302 547-3060
Geralyn Ryerson, *Pr*
EMP: 7 **EST:** 2018
SALES (est): 302.93K **Privately Held**
Web: www.ryerson.com
SIC: 5051 Steel

(G-19603)
S & A HOLDING ASSOCIATES INC
4737 Concord Pike Ste 261 (19803-1477)
P.O. Box 7189 (19803-0189)
PHONE............................302 479-8314
Franch Aciero, *VP*
EMP: 5 **EST:** 1981
SALES (est): 280.41K **Privately Held**
SIC: 6512 Shopping center, property operation only

(G-19604)
S & C PROPERTIES LTD
Also Called: Cushing Construction
805 Kiamensi Rd (19804-3419)
PHONE............................302 995-1537
EMP: 7 **EST:** 1979
SALES (est): 444.24K **Privately Held**
SIC: 6512 Nonresidential building operators

(G-19605)
S & H ENTERPRISES INC
Also Called: S&H Investigative Services
112 Water St (19804-2407)

P.O. Box 12245 (19850-2245)
PHONE............................302 999-9911
John Slogowski, *Pr*
Caryn Gloyd, *VP*
EMP: 10 **EST:** 1972
SALES (est): 239.66K **Privately Held**
SIC: 7381 Private investigator

(G-19606)
S A ATRAMCO
251 Little Falls Dr (19808-1674)
PHONE............................302 310-3350
EMP: 5 **EST:** 2001
SALES (est): 206.45K **Privately Held**
SIC: 8741 Management services

(G-19607)
S G WILLIAMS & BROS CO (PA)
301 N Tatnall St (19801-2446)
PHONE............................302 656-8167
John D Griffith, *Pr*
Helen Griffith, *Sec*
EMP: 15 **EST:** 1910
SQ FT: 15,000
SALES (est): 6.88MM
SALES (corp-wide): 6.88MM **Privately Held**
Web: www.sgwilliamssupply.com
SIC: 5082 5051 1761 3444 General construction machinery and equipment; Aluminum bars, rods, ingots, sheets, pipes, plates, etc.; Roofing, siding, and sheetmetal work; Gutters, sheet metal

(G-19608)
S GREGORY SMITH MD & ASSOC PA
2710 Centerville Rd Ste 102 (19808-1652)
PHONE............................302 993-1900
EMP: 8 **EST:** 2018
SALES (est): 93.12K **Privately Held**
Web: www.deeyesurgeons.com
SIC: 8011 Opthalmologist

(G-19609)
S J DESMOND INC
22 Lloyd Pl (19810-1325)
P.O. Box 9511 (19809-0511)
PHONE............................302 475-6520
Stephen J Desmond, *Pr*
Susan Desmond, *Sec*
▲ **EMP:** 6 **EST:** 1997
SALES (est): 250K **Privately Held**
SIC: 1731 Electrical work

(G-19610)
S J DESMOND INC
120 E Ayre St (19804-2507)
PHONE............................302 256-0801
EMP: 10 **EST:** 2017
SALES (est): 267.15K **Privately Held**
Web: www.desmondelectrical.com
SIC: 1731 General electrical contractor

(G-19611)
S M COMMERCIAL ROOFING INC
412 Meco Dr (19804-1112)
PHONE............................302 478-3130
EMP: 7 **EST:** 2019
SALES (est): 454.58K **Privately Held**
Web: www.smcommercialroofing.com
SIC: 1761 Roofing contractor

(G-19612)
S P S INTERNATIONAL INV CO (DH)
1105 N Market St Ste 1300 (19801-1241)
PHONE............................302 478-9055
EMP: 7 **EST:** 1996
SALES (est): 49.73MM
SALES (corp-wide): 302.09B **Publicly Held**

Wilmington - New Castle County (G-19613)

SIC: 3324 Steel investment foundries
HQ: Sps Technologies, Llc
301 Highland Ave
Jenkintown PA 19046
215 572-3000

(G-19613)
S WALLACE HOLDINGS LLC
251 Little Falls Dr (19808-1674)
PHONE..................917 304-1164
EMP: 5 EST: 2018
SALES (est): 100K Privately Held
SIC: 7323 Credit reporting services

(G-19614)
S&D INDUSTRIES LLC
2711 Centerville Rd Ste 400 (19808-1660)
PHONE..................703 801-3643
Robert Shaver, Prin
EMP: 5 EST: 2018
SALES (est): 150.7K Privately Held
SIC: 3999 Manufacturing industries, nec

(G-19615)
S2 GROUPE LLC
300 Delaware Ave Ste 210a (19801-6601)
PHONE..................917 512-1971
EMP: 5 EST: 2018
SALES (est): 27.12K Privately Held
Web: www.selenasoo.com
SIC: 4899 Communication services, nec

(G-19616)
SA ASSOCIATES LLC
180 Gregg Dr (19808-4324)
PHONE..................302 275-7359
EMP: 6 EST: 2008
SALES (est): 77.22K Privately Held
SIC: 8742 Management consulting services

(G-19617)
SABCON CONSTRUCTION COMPANY
2500 W 5th St (19805-2905)
PHONE..................302 420-0467
EMP: 5 EST: 2018
SALES (est): 89.38K Privately Held
SIC: 1521 Single-family housing construction

(G-19618)
SABION SOUND REINFORCEMENT CO
15 W Reamer Ave (19804-1715)
PHONE..................302 427-0551
Guy D Cartelli, Owner
EMP: 2 EST: 1997
SALES (est): 130.65K Privately Held
Web: www.sabion.com
SIC: 3993 Signs and advertising specialties

(G-19619)
SABRE ASSOCIATES LLC
1202 Kirkwood Hwy (19805-2120)
PHONE..................302 998-0100
Robert Pasquale, Prin
EMP: 6 EST: 2013
SALES (est): 456.44K Privately Held
Web: www.lesabrellc.com
SIC: 8742 Management consulting services

(G-19620)
SABRE INTERNATIONAL NEWCO INC
1209 N Orange St (19801-1120)
PHONE..................682 605-6223
Douglas Barnett, Prin
EMP: 10 EST: 2007
SALES (est): 365.64K
SALES (corp-wide): 2.67MM Privately Held
SIC: 8742 Business management consultant
PA: Sabre Holdings (Luxembourg) S.a R.L.

Rue Eugene Ruppert 6
Luxembourg 2453

(G-19621)
SACHER
15 N Cliffe Dr (19809-1623)
PHONE..................302 792-0281
J Sacher, Prin
EMP: 5 EST: 2008
SALES (est): 67.11K Privately Held
Web: www.sacher.com.mx
SIC: 4731 Freight forwarding

(G-19622)
SACRED HEART VILLAGE I INC
920 N Monroe St (19801-1383)
PHONE..................302 428-0801
Ronald Giannone, Dir
Christa Rowe, Admn
EMP: 14 EST: 2004
SALES (est): 1.12MM Privately Held
Web: www.sacredheartvillage.org
SIC: 8361 Aged home

(G-19623)
SACRED HEART VILLAGE II INC
625 E 10th St (19801-4039)
PHONE..................302 428-3702
Ronald Giannone, Dir
Jean Forlano, Acctnt
EMP: 6 EST: 2012
SALES (est): 365.54K Privately Held
Web: www.sacredheartvillage.org
SIC: 8361 Aged home

(G-19624)
SAFE HOME CONTROL
Also Called: Homepay
300 Delaware Ave Ste 210a (19801-6601)
PHONE..................302 401-4379
Michael Birchall, CEO
Michael D Birchall, Pr
EMP: 11 EST: 2014
SALES (est): 454.78K Privately Held
SIC: 7299 5961 Home improvement and renovation contractor agency; Computer equipment and electronics, mail order

(G-19625)
SAFE SPACE DELAWARE INC
500 W 2nd St (19801-2312)
PHONE..................302 691-7946
Allen Conover, CEO
EMP: 19 EST: 2010
SALES (est): 901.08K Privately Held
SIC: 8093 Mental health clinic, outpatient

(G-19626)
SAFEGUARD DX LABORATORY
110 S Poplar St Ste 200 (19801-5034)
PHONE..................888 919-8275
John Distefano, Prin
EMP: 6 EST: 2019
SALES (est): 102.21K Privately Held
Web: www.safegdx.com
SIC: 3821 Clinical laboratory instruments, except medical and dental

(G-19627)
SAFEGUARD SYSTEMS INC (HQ)
1313 N Market St (19801-6101)
PHONE..................609 822-6111
Nathen Wenograd, Pr
EMP: 6 EST: 1994
SALES (est): 1.25MM
SALES (corp-wide): 1.25MM Privately Held
Web: www.safeguardconcepts.com
SIC: 5112 Business forms
PA: Softboss Corp.

1735 Market St Ste A459
Philadelphia PA 19103
215 563-7488

(G-19628)
SAFELITE GLASS CORP
Also Called: Safelite Autoglass
109 Rogers Rd Ste 4 (19801-5779)
PHONE..................302 656-4640
EMP: 20
SALES (corp-wide): 3.16B Privately Held
Web: www.safelite.com
SIC: 7536 5013 Automotive glass replacement shops; Automobile glass
HQ: Safelite Glass Corp.
7400 Safelite Way
Columbus OH 43235
614 210-9000

(G-19629)
SAFRA INC
108 W 13th St (19801-1145)
PHONE..................302 305-0755
Thaer Samara, CEO
EMP: 5 EST: 2017
SALES (est): 191.6K Privately Held
SIC: 7389 Accommodation locating services

(G-19630)
SAFS INTERNATIONAL GROUP LLC
108 W 13th St (19801-1145)
PHONE..................954 707-4627
EMP: 9 EST: 2001
SALES (est): 138.7K Privately Held
Web: www.safsgroup.com
SIC: 8748 Business consulting, nec

(G-19631)
SAGACIOUS WORKS
2713 Point Breeze Dr (19810-1150)
PHONE..................609 251-9265
Tashika Moore, Prin
EMP: 10 EST: 2017
SALES (est): 67.75K Privately Held
SIC: 8748 Business consulting, nec

(G-19632)
SAHAJ CONTRACTOR LLC
1300 Quincy Dr (19803-5132)
PHONE..................302 559-4357
EMP: 5 EST: 2018
SALES (est): 269.91K Privately Held
SIC: 1799 Special trade contractors, nec

(G-19633)
SAIN COSMOS LLC
3524 Silverside Rd Ste 35b (19810-4929)
PHONE..................936 244-7017
EMP: 10 EST: 2019
SALES (est): 499.16K Privately Held
Web: www.saincosmos.com
SIC: 7371 Computer software systems analysis and design, custom

(G-19634)
SAINT JAMES HOLDG & INV CO TR
300 Delaware Ave Ste 210 (19801-6601)
PHONE..................877 690-9052
Jeffre Saint James, Prin
EMP: 10 EST: 2017
SALES (est): 831.89K Privately Held
SIC: 6726 Unit investment trusts

(G-19635)
SAKEMPIRE DISTRIBUTION LLC
Also Called: Sakempire Distribution
300 Delaware Ave Ste 210 (19801-6601)
PHONE..................800 838-0615
Quyen Vu, CEO
EMP: 10 EST: 2021

SALES (est): 371.12K Privately Held
SIC: 7389 Business Activities at Non-Commercial Site

(G-19636)
SALEM COUNTY AMATEUR RADIO CLB
2015 Bentwood Ct (19804-3937)
PHONE..................302 689-8127
Robert Slippey, Prin
EMP: 5 EST: 2015
SALES (est): 43.76K Privately Held
SIC: 7997 Membership sports and recreation clubs

(G-19637)
SALES DOCUMENTS INC ◎
251 Little Falls Dr Ste 8088 (19808-1674)
PHONE..................302 867-9957
Mauricio Kigiela, CEO
EMP: 11 EST: 2022
SALES (est): 496.64K Privately Held
SIC: 7371 Computer software development and applications

(G-19638)
SALESBOX LLC (PA)
Also Called: Salesbox Ai
1521 Concord Pike Ste 301 (19803-3644)
PHONE..................415 361-4080
EMP: 5 EST: 2015
SALES (est): 75.1K
SALES (corp-wide): 75.1K Privately Held
SIC: 7372 Prepackaged software

(G-19639)
SALESINUSA INC
Also Called: Sales In US
620 A St (19801-5330)
PHONE..................973 771-4420
Svetlana Postnikova, Prin
EMP: 5 EST: 2018
SALES (est): 232.44K Privately Held
Web: www.salesinusa.com
SIC: 4225 General warehousing and storage

(G-19640)
SALS AUTO SERVICES INC
Also Called: Mobil
3000 Lancaster Ave (19805-1459)
PHONE..................302 654-1168
Sal Panarello, Pr
EMP: 5 EST: 1959
SQ FT: 2,500
SALES (est): 928.02K Privately Held
SIC: 5541 7549 Filling stations, gasoline; Do-it-yourself garages

(G-19641)
SALS GARAGE INC
705 N Lincoln St Ste 1 (19805-3043)
PHONE..................302 655-4981
Salvatore Vassallo, Pr
John Vassallo, VP
EMP: 5 EST: 1973
SQ FT: 5,000
SALES (est): 322.46K Privately Held
Web: www.salsgaragede.com
SIC: 7538 General automotive repair shops

(G-19642)
SALTVERK INC
251 Little Falls Dr (19808-1674)
PHONE..................412 413-9193
Bjorn Jonsson, CEO
EMP: 14
SALES (est): 629.04K Privately Held
SIC: 2899 Salt

GEOGRAPHIC SECTION
Wilmington - New Castle County (G-19671)

(G-19643)
SALVATION ARMY
Also Called: Salvation Army
610 S Walnut St (19801-5235)
PHONE..................................302 654-8808
John Swires, Admn
EMP: 32
SALES (corp-wide): 2.41B **Privately Held**
Web: www.salvationarmyusa.org
SIC: 8399 8641 Advocacy group; Civic and social associations
HQ: The Salvation Army
440 W Nyack Rd Ofc
West Nyack NY 10994
845 620-7200

(G-19644)
SALVATION ARMY
Also Called: Salvation Army
2 S Augustine St (19804-2504)
PHONE..................................302 996-9400
Terry Reilly, Pr
EMP: 14
SALES (corp-wide): 2.41B **Privately Held**
Web: www.saconnects.org
SIC: 8322 Individual and family services
HQ: The Salvation Army
440 W Nyack Rd Ofc
West Nyack NY 10994
845 620-7200

(G-19645)
SALVATION ARMY
Also Called: Salvation Army
400 N Orange St (19801-2219)
P.O. Box 308 (19899-0308)
PHONE..................................302 656-1696
Tim Duperree, Mgr
EMP: 34
SALES (corp-wide): 2.41B **Privately Held**
Web: www.salvationarmyusa.org
SIC: 8322 8351 Senior citizens' center or association; Child day care services
HQ: The Salvation Army
440 W Nyack Rd Ofc
West Nyack NY 10994
845 620-7200

(G-19646)
SAM WALTS & ASSOCIATES
Also Called: Sam Waltz & Associates Counsel
11 Downs Dr (19807-2555)
P.O. Box 3798 (19807-0798)
PHONE..................................302 777-2211
Sam Waltz, Owner
EMP: 7 EST: 1994
SQ FT: 3,000
SALES (est): 473.31K **Privately Held**
Web: www.samwaltz.com
SIC: 8742 Marketing consulting services

(G-19647)
SAM YOUR TAXES LLC
1716 W Gilpin Dr (19805-1201)
PHONE..................................302 482-9601
EMP: 5 EST: 2020
SALES (est): 136.87K **Privately Held**
Web: www.samyourtaxes.com
SIC: 7291 Tax return preparation services

(G-19648)
SAMARITAN OUTREACH
1410 N Claymont St (19802-5227)
PHONE..................................302 594-9476
Karen Lienau, Prin
EMP: 6 EST: 1995
SALES (est): 111.72K **Privately Held**
Web: www.ministryofcaring.org
SIC: 8322 Outreach program

(G-19649)
SAMS CONSTRUCTION LLC
1405 Haines Ave (19809-2716)
P.O. Box 9827 (19809-0827)
PHONE..................................302 654-6542
EMP: 13 EST: 1992
SALES (est): 808.55K **Privately Held**
SIC: 1521 Single-family housing construction

(G-19650)
SAMS CONSTRUCTION LLC
1227 E 15th St (19802-5214)
P.O. Box 9827 (19809-0827)
PHONE..................................302 654-6542
EMP: 12 EST: 2001
SQ FT: 5,000
SALES (est): 489.91K **Privately Held**
SIC: 1611 Highway and street construction

(G-19651)
SAMUEL BLUMBERG PHD
2300 Pennsylvania Ave (19806-1392)
PHONE..................................302 652-7733
Samuel Blumberg, Prin
EMP: 5 EST: 2009
SALES (est): 158.57K **Privately Held**
Web: www.samuelblumberg.com
SIC: 8049 Clinical psychologist

(G-19652)
SANARE TODAY LLC
1401 Silverside Rd (19810-4400)
PHONE..................................610 344-9600
EMP: 45 EST: 2015
SALES (est): 5.95MM **Privately Held**
Web: www.sanaretoday.com
SIC: 8322 General counseling services

(G-19653)
SANATTEST LLC
15 Center Meeting Rd (19807-1301)
PHONE..................................623 337-7849
Dorothy Anderson, CFO
EMP: 2 EST: 2020
SALES (est): 56.54K **Privately Held**
SIC: 7372 Prepackaged software

(G-19654)
SANCHASEGROUP
2100 Northeast Blvd (19802-4503)
PHONE..................................302 516-7373
EMP: 5 EST: 2016
SALES (est): 122.36K **Privately Held**
SIC: 7549 Towing services

(G-19655)
SANCO CONSTRUCTION CO INC
24 Brookside Dr (19804-1102)
PHONE..................................302 633-4156
Christopher Marcozzi, Pr
Ralph Marcozzi, Sec
EMP: 9 EST: 1984
SQ FT: 1,200
SALES (est): 1.46MM **Privately Held**
SIC: 1611 1771 Highway and street paving contractor; Parking lot construction

(G-19656)
SANCTUARY SPA AND SALOON
1847 Marsh Rd (19810-4505)
PHONE..................................302 475-1469
Joan Grave, Pt
Barbara Hafner, Mgr
EMP: 10 EST: 2003
SALES (est): 237.06K **Privately Held**
Web: www.mysanctuaryspasalon.com
SIC: 7299 7991 Massage parlor and steam bath services; Spas

(G-19657)
SANDEBBARNANRICWAY CORP
Also Called: Lewis Educational Games
2221 Inwood Rd (19810-2807)
PHONE..................................302 475-2705
Richard W Lewis, Pr
EMP: 2 EST: 1992
SALES (est): 105.25K **Privately Held**
SIC: 3999 3944 Education aids, devices and supplies; Games, toys, and children's vehicles

(G-19658)
SANDERSON ALBIDRESS AGENCY
Also Called: Nationwide
1211b Milltown Rd (19808-3003)
PHONE..................................302 368-3010
Albidress Sanderson, Owner
EMP: 5 EST: 1977
SALES (est): 353.63K **Privately Held**
Web: www.nationwide.com
SIC: 6411 Insurance agents, nec

(G-19659)
SANDRA JACKSON
23 W 37th St (19802-2225)
PHONE..................................302 510-3576
EMP: 5 EST: 2019
SALES (est): 56.81K **Privately Held**
SIC: 8011 Offices and clinics of medical doctors

(G-19660)
SANDRA L KORINES
809 N Washington St (19801-1509)
PHONE..................................201 245-2003
Sandra L Korines Lcsw, Owner
EMP: 7 EST: 2018
SALES (est): 32.92K **Privately Held**
SIC: 8322 Individual and family services

(G-19661)
SANDRA SUE RETZKY DO
146 Marcella Rd (19803-3451)
PHONE..................................302 540-3463
Sandra Sue Retzky, Prin
EMP: 6 EST: 2012
SALES (est): 71.12K **Privately Held**
SIC: 8011 Offices and clinics of medical doctors

(G-19662)
SANDS HEALTH SPA LLC
214 N Maryland Ave (19804-1364)
PHONE..................................302 543-8385
EMP: 5 EST: 2015
SALES (est): 46.24K **Privately Held**
SIC: 8099 Health and allied services, nec

(G-19663)
SANDY BRAE LABORATORIES
3 S Tatnall St (19801-2457)
PHONE..................................302 456-0446
Robert Spring, Pr
EMP: 5 EST: 2015
SALES (est): 232.02K **Privately Held**
Web: www.sandybrae.com
SIC: 5172 Lubricating oils and greases

(G-19664)
SANGITA SCIENTIFIC LLC ✿
1013 Centre Rd Ste 403b (19805-1270)
PHONE..................................866 272-6432
EMP: 2 EST: 2022
SALES (est): 266.71K **Privately Held**
SIC: 2834 Pharmaceutical preparations

(G-19665)
SANJABAN CORP
4023 Kennett Pike # 701 (19807-2018)
PHONE..................................612 805-5971
Mashfiqul Alam, Pr
EMP: 5 EST: 2012
SALES (est): 183.72K **Privately Held**
SIC: 7379 Computer related consulting services

(G-19666)
SANKHYA VENTURES LLC
2810 N Church St Ste 40809 (19802-4447)
PHONE..................................415 905-0887
Shaunak Sayta, Managing Member
EMP: 5 EST: 2018
SALES (est): 79.42K **Privately Held**
SIC: 5142 Packaged frozen goods

(G-19667)
SANOSIL INTERNATIONAL LLC
Also Called: Sanosil International
1500 Eastlawn Ave (19802-2403)
PHONE..................................302 454-8102
Christopher Ungermann, CEO
EMP: 7 EST: 2008
SALES (est): 345.16K **Privately Held**
Web: www.sanosilinternational.com
SIC: 8732 2842 3589 Market analysis or research; Ammonia, household; Water treatment equipment, industrial

(G-19668)
SANTANDER BANK NA
824 N Market St Ste 100 (19801-4937)
PHONE..................................302 654-5182
Marie Sherlock, Brnch Mgr
EMP: 10
Web: www.santanderbank.com
SIC: 6022 State commercial banks
HQ: Santander Bank, N.A.
75 State St
Boston MA 02109
617 757-3410

(G-19669)
SAP INVESTMENTS INC
300 Delaware Ave (19801-1607)
PHONE..................................302 427-7889
EMP: 11
SALES (est): 1.76MM
SALES (corp-wide): 32.06B **Privately Held**
SIC: 6211 6799 Securities flotation companies; Investors, nec
PA: Sap Se
Dietmar-Hopp-Allee 16
Walldorf BW 69190
622 774-7474

(G-19670)
SAPHIC INNOVATIONS INC
1232 N King St Ste 128 (19801-3226)
PHONE..................................820 888-0099
Huijie Jiang, Admn
EMP: 7 EST: 2020
SALES (est): 750K **Privately Held**
SIC: 5021 Outdoor and lawn furniture, nec

(G-19671)
SARAHS ART SCENE
7 Orchard Ln (19809-1719)
PHONE..................................302 792-2631
Sarah Baptist, Prin
EMP: 5 EST: 2014
SALES (est): 76.9K **Privately Held**
Web: www.sarahbaptistart.com
SIC: 7999 Art gallery, commercial

Wilmington - New Castle County (G-19672)

(G-19672)
SARGENT & LUNDY LLC
500 Delaware Ave Ste 400 (19801-7404)
PHONE..................302 622-7200
David Miller, *Mgr*
EMP: 9
SALES (corp-wide): 480.29MM **Privately Held**
Web: www.sargentlundy.com
SIC: 8711 Consulting engineer
PA: Sargent & Lundy, L.L.C.
  55 E Monroe St Ste 2700
  Chicago IL 60603
  312 269-2000

(G-19673)
SARKANA PHARMA INC
1000 Nw St Ste 1200 (19801-1058)
PHONE..................649 332-4417
Mark Cipriano, *Prin*
EMP: 8 EST: 2020
SALES (est): 185.78K **Privately Held**
SIC: 2834 Pharmaceutical preparations

(G-19674)
SASQUATCH CREATIVE LLC
1700 N Rodney St Fl 2 (19806-3022)
PHONE..................302 502-3105
Randall Neil, *Prin*
EMP: 6 EST: 2016
SALES (est): 139K **Privately Held**
Web: www.squatch.us
SIC: 7311 Advertising agencies

(G-19675)
SASSY SPA
3600 Lancaster Pike (19805-1509)
PHONE..................302 668-8008
James E Walls, *Owner*
EMP: 5 EST: 2017
SALES (est): 34.53K **Privately Held**
SIC: 7231 Cosmetology and personal hygiene salons

(G-19676)
SATELLITE CONNECTION INC
4001 Kennett Pike Ste 134 (19807-2000)
PHONE..................302 328-2462
Neeshard Ahamad, *Prin*
EMP: 8 EST: 1996
SALES (est): 215.8K **Privately Held**
SIC: 4841 Direct broadcast satellite services (DBS)

(G-19677)
SATODESIGN LLC
3 Germay Dr (19804-1127)
PHONE..................989 710-2029
Joaquin Moreno, *Managing Member*
EMP: 5
SALES (est): 26.91K **Privately Held**
SIC: 7812 7371 Video production; Computer software development and applications

(G-19678)
SATTAR A SYED DMD PA
5507 Kirkwood Hwy (19808-5001)
PHONE..................302 994-3093
Sattar A Syed, *Prin*
EMP: 7 EST: 2007
SALES (est): 473.7K **Privately Held**
Web: www.delawarestardental.com
SIC: 8021 Dentists' office

(G-19679)
SAUER HOLDINGS INC
1403 Foulk Rd Ste 200 (19803-2788)
PHONE..................302 656-8989
William N Steitz, *Pr*
Kenneth Kubacki, *
EMP: 43 EST: 1989
SALES (est): 469.39K
SALES (corp-wide): 2.48MM **Privately Held**
SIC: 8711 Civil engineering
PA: Sauer Industries, Inc.
  30 51st St
  Pittsburgh PA 15201
  412 687-4100

(G-19680)
SAUNDRA WRIGHT
1521 Concord Pike Ste 102 (19803-3614)
PHONE..................302 298-0324
Saundra Wright, *Prin*
EMP: 5 EST: 2016
SALES (est): 80.21K **Privately Held**
SIC: 6531 Real estate leasing and rentals

(G-19681)
SAVANTIS GROUP
200 Bellevue Pkwy Ste 215 (19809-3711)
PHONE..................415 297-6926
Roel Deuss, *Pr*
EMP: 7 EST: 2006
SALES (est): 901.77K
SALES (corp-wide): 5.08MM **Privately Held**
Web: www.savantis.com
SIC: 7371 Computer software development
PA: Savantis Solutions, Llc
  200 Bellevue Pkwy Ste 215
  Wilmington DE 19809
  732 906-3200

(G-19682)
SAVANTIS SOLUTIONS LLC (PA)
200 Bellevue Pkwy Ste 215 (19809-3711)
PHONE..................732 906-3200
Nick Sharma, *Managing Member*
EMP: 373 EST: 2015
SALES (est): 5.08MM
SALES (corp-wide): 5.08MM **Privately Held**
Web: www.savantis.com
SIC: 7371 7379 Computer software development; Computer data escrow service

(G-19683)
SAVERD LLC
24a Trolley Sq (19806-3334)
PHONE..................347 565-5586
EMP: 5
SALES (est): 68.89K **Privately Held**
SIC: 7371 Computer software development and applications

(G-19684)
SAVIMBO INC
300 Delaware Ave (19801-1607)
PHONE..................650 387-6648
Andrea Burbank, *CEO*
EMP: 30
SALES (est): 342.84K **Privately Held**
SIC: 8641 Environmental protection organization

(G-19685)
SAVOY ASSOCIATES
15 Ashley Pl Ste 3b (19804-1397)
PHONE..................302 658-8770
John Lynam, *Owner*
EMP: 7 EST: 2016
SALES (est): 55.85K **Privately Held**
Web: www.savoyassociates.com
SIC: 6411 Insurance brokers, nec

(G-19686)
SAWAI LLC ◆
3 Germay Dr (19804-1127)
PHONE..................800 625-3680
EMP: 25 EST: 2022
SALES (est): 715.79K **Privately Held**
SIC: 8742 Marketing consulting services

(G-19687)
SAXTON JACK 3 CONSTRUCTION
1903 N Lincoln St (19806-2313)
PHONE..................302 654-4553
Jack Saxton Iii, *Owner*
EMP: 5 EST: 2006
SALES (est): 262.55K **Privately Held**
Web: www.webstergroup.com
SIC: 1521 Single-family housing construction

(G-19688)
SB ELECTRIC LLC
2209 Patwynn Rd (19810-2749)
PHONE..................610 721-5361
EMP: 6 EST: 2011
SALES (est): 223.42K **Privately Held**
SIC: 7539 Electrical services

(G-19689)
SB GLOBAL ADVISERS (US) INC ◆
251 Little Falls Dr (19808-1674)
PHONE..................650 562-8100
Stephen Lam, *Dir*
EMP: 100 EST: 2022
SALES (est): 5.36MM **Privately Held**
SIC: 6799 Venture capital companies

(G-19690)
SB LOGISTICS LLC
607 Brier Ave (19805-1964)
PHONE..................302 494-9756
EMP: 5 EST: 2021
SALES (est): 85.85K **Privately Held**
SIC: 4789 Transportation services, nec

(G-19691)
SBH GROUP PROPERTIES LLC
4023 Kennett Pike # 256 (19807-2018)
PHONE..................302 588-1656
Long Sybounheuang, *Managing Member*
EMP: 5 EST: 2013
SALES (est): 133.28K **Privately Held**
SIC: 6512 Nonresidential building operators

(G-19692)
SBM LANDOWNER INC
110 N Poplar St (19801-3924)
PHONE..................302 652-8314
EMP: 5 EST: 2011
SALES (est): 24 **Privately Held**
SIC: 8641 Dwelling-related associations

(G-19693)
SC FOSTER LLC
43 Stonewold Way (19807-2566)
PHONE..................302 383-0201
Scott Foster, *Managing Member*
EMP: 21 EST: 1999
SQ FT: 5,000
SALES (est): 569.36K **Privately Held**
Web: www.scfoster.com
SIC: 7379 Computer related consulting services

(G-19694)
SC MARKETING US INC
2711 Centerville Rd Ste 400 (19808-1660)
PHONE..................714 352-4992
Peer Dohrn, *Ch Bd*
EMP: 5 EST: 2011
SQ FT: 250
SALES (est): 483.79K **Privately Held**
SIC: 8743 Sales promotion

(G-19695)
SC&A CONSTRUCTION INC
3411 Silverside Rd Ste 200 (19810-4803)
P.O. Box 7202 (19803-0202)
PHONE..................302 478-6030
C David Murtagh, *CEO*
Lee Weersing, *
Thomas L Cover, *
Tamara Curran, *
EMP: 26 EST: 1973
SQ FT: 4,500
SALES (est): 9.01MM **Privately Held**
Web: www.scaconstructs.com
SIC: 1542 1521 Commercial and office building, new construction; New construction, single-family houses

(G-19696)
SCANPOINT INC
5700 Kirkwood Hwy Ste 202 (19808-4884)
PHONE..................603 429-0777
Bill Cross, *Pr*
EMP: 8 EST: 2001
SALES (est): 664.96K **Privately Held**
Web: www.scanpointusa.com
SIC: 7371 Software programming applications

(G-19697)
SCHNADER HRRSON SGAL LEWIS LLP
824 N Market St Ste 800 (19801-4939)
PHONE..................302 888-4554
Joan Kluger, *Mng Pt*
EMP: 17
SALES (corp-wide): 48.55MM **Privately Held**
Web: www.schnader.com
SIC: 8111 General practice attorney, lawyer
PA: Schnader Harrison Segal & Lewis L.L.P.
  1600 Market St Ste 3600
  Philadelphia PA 19103
  215 751-2000

(G-19698)
SCHROEDL COMPANY
Also Called: Schroedl Cleaning Svcs Sup Co
422 B And O Ln (19804-1445)
PHONE..................410 358-5500
John P Gallon, *Pr*
EMP: 58 EST: 1861
SQ FT: 6,500
SALES (est): 2.19MM **Privately Held**
Web: www.drycleanbaltimore.com
SIC: 7216 Drapery, curtain drycleaning

(G-19699)
SCHULTZ CORINNA L MD
1600 Rockland Rd (19803-3607)
PHONE..................302 651-4000
Corinna Schultz, *Pr*
EMP: 14 EST: 2018
SALES (est): 264.35K **Privately Held**
Web: www.nemours.org
SIC: 8011 Pediatrician

(G-19700)
SCHUSTER JACHETTI LLP
3407 Lancaster Pike Ste A (19805-5543)
PHONE..................302 984-1000
EMP: 6
SALES (corp-wide): 249.25K **Privately Held**
Web: www.mydelawarelawyer.com
SIC: 8111 General practice attorney, lawyer
PA: Schuster Jachetti Llp
  20632 Dupont Blvd
  Georgetown DE 19947
  302 856-2400

GEOGRAPHIC SECTION
Wilmington - New Castle County (G-19728)

(G-19701)
SCHWARTZ SCHWARTZ ATTYS AT LAW
1525 Delaware Ave (19806-3074)
PHONE..................................302 998-1500
EMP: 7 **EST:** 2015
SALES (est): 210.44K **Privately Held**
Web: www.schwartzandschwartz.com
SIC: 8111 General practice attorney, lawyer

(G-19702)
SCHWEIZER CLEANING SERVICE
317 Brookside Dr (19804-1358)
PHONE..................................302 995-2816
Oscar Schweizer, *Owner*
EMP: 6 **EST:** 1990
SALES (est): 93.49K **Privately Held**
SIC: 7349 Cleaning service, industrial or commercial

(G-19703)
SCIENCE HOUSE FOUNDATION
501 Silverside Rd Ste 123 (19809-1377)
PHONE..................................800 839-1754
EMP: 6
SALES (est): 70K **Privately Held**
Web: www.dfsme.org
SIC: 8699 Charitable organization

(G-19704)
SCIENTIFIC CHEMICAL SOLUTIONS
19c Trolley Sq (19806-3355)
PHONE..................................208 490-2125
EMP: 5 **EST:** 2018
SALES (est): 106.84K **Privately Held**
Web: www.wtlireland.com
SIC: 8748 Environmental consultant

(G-19705)
SCIENTIFIC HOLDINGS CORP
2751 Centerville Rd Ste 358 (19808-1627)
PHONE..................................302 225-5065
George R Ritter, *Treas*
Deborah A Corr, *Sec*
EMP: 7 **EST:** 1991
SALES (est): 1.22MM
SALES (corp-wide): 6.97B **Publicly Held**
SIC: 5049 Laboratory equipment, except medical or dental
HQ: Vwr International, Llc
   100 W Matsonford Rd Ste 1
   Radnor PA 19087
   610 386-1700

(G-19706)
SCIENTIFIC SYSTEMS CORP
901 N Tatnall St (19801-1605)
PHONE..................................302 655-5500
EMP: 7 **EST:** 2009
SALES (est): 50K **Privately Held**
SIC: 3826 Analytical instruments

(G-19707)
SCIENTIFIC USA INC
2711 Centerville Rd (19808-1660)
PHONE..................................425 681-9462
Michael Sweaney, *CEO*
EMP: 5 **EST:** 2011
SALES (est): 326.2K **Privately Held**
Web: www.scientificliterature.org
SIC: 7389 Cosmetic kits, assembling and packaging

(G-19708)
SCINORX TECHNOLOGIES INC
1521 Concord Pike Ste 301 (19803-3652)
PHONE..................................302 268-3447
Khushbu Agrawal, *Pr*
EMP: 5 **EST:** 2017
SALES (est): 257.12K **Privately Held**
Web: www.scinorx.com
SIC: 7379 Online services technology consultants

(G-19709)
SCITUATE SOLAR I LLC
2711 Centerville Rd Ste 400 (19808-1660)
PHONE..................................212 419-4843
Richard Turnure, *Mng Pt*
EMP: 8 **EST:** 2012
SALES (est): 2.01MM
SALES (corp-wide): 12.62B **Publicly Held**
SIC: 4911 Generation, electric power
PA: The Aes Corporation
   4300 Wilson Blvd Ste 1100
   Arlington VA 22203
   703 522-1315

(G-19710)
SCOR GLOBL LF AMRCAS RNSURANCE
251 Little Falls Dr (19808-1674)
PHONE..................................704 344-2700
EMP: 241 **EST:** 2011
SALES (est): 64.54MM
SALES (corp-wide): 241.86MM **Privately Held**
Web: www.scorgloballifeamericas.com
SIC: 6411 Insurance claim adjusters, not employed by insurance company
PA: Scor Se
   Scor Immeuble Scor
   Paris 75116
   158447000

(G-19711)
SCORPION OFFSHORE INC
1209 Orange St Corporation Trust Ctr (19801)
◆ **EMP:** 400 **EST:** 2005
SQ FT: 20,000
SALES (est): 15.33MM **Privately Held**
SIC: 1381 Drilling oil and gas wells
PA: Seadrill Jack Up Holding Ltd
   C/O: Frontline Ltd
   Hamilton

(G-19712)
SCOTTS CO
100 W 10th St Lbby (19801-1647)
PHONE..................................302 777-4779
Scott Hines, *Pr*
EMP: 5 **EST:** 2005
SALES (est): 448.81K **Privately Held**
SIC: 5149 Sandwiches

(G-19713)
SCOTTS-SIERRA INVESTMENTS LLC (HQ)
Also Called: Scotts-Sierra Investments Inc
1105 N Market St Ste 1300 (19801-1241)
PHONE..................................302 622-9269
Susan Dubb, *Pr*
Mark Whens, *Sec*
EMP: 9 **EST:** 1995
SALES (est): 1.66MM
SALES (corp-wide): 3.55B **Publicly Held**
SIC: 8748 Test development and evaluation service
PA: The Scotts Miracle-Gro Company
   14111 Scottslawn Rd
   Marysville OH 43040
   937 644-0011

(G-19714)
SCOV3 LLC
501 Silverside Rd (19809-1374)
PHONE..................................973 387-9771
EMP: 2 **EST:** 2020
SALES (est): 74.42K **Privately Held**
Web: www.scovrx.com
SIC: 2834 Pharmaceutical preparations

(G-19715)
SCOV3 LLC (PA)
1201 N Orange St Ste 712 (19801-1186)
PHONE..................................973 387-9771
EMP: 2 **EST:** 2020
SALES (est): 244.62K
SALES (corp-wide): 244.62K **Privately Held**
Web: www.scovrx.com
SIC: 2834 Pharmaceutical preparations

(G-19716)
SCRUBMONEY INC
251 Little Falls Dr (19808-1674)
PHONE..................................240 671-5379
Bruce A Harms, *CEO*
EMP: 6 **EST:** 2021
SALES (est): 238.88K **Privately Held**
SIC: 7371 Software programming applications

(G-19717)
SD&L BAIL BONDS LLC
1202 W 4th St (19805-3606)
PHONE..................................302 407-6591
Lisa Doran, *Prin*
EMP: 6 **EST:** 2020
SALES (est): 51.56K **Privately Held**
Web: www.sdlbailbonds.com
SIC: 7299 Miscellaneous personal service

(G-19718)
SD&L ENTERPRISES LLC
1202 W 4th St (19805-3606)
PHONE..................................302 407-6591
EMP: 6 **EST:** 2018
SALES (est): 210.47K **Privately Held**
SIC: 8748 Business consulting, nec

(G-19719)
SEA TRANSPORT CORPORATION LLC
19c Trolley Sq (19806-3355)
PHONE..................................786 208-2433
Ross Ballatynes, *CEO*
Stephanie Dawson, *CFO*
Stuart Ballantyne, *Dir*
Jorge Rassi, *Mgr*
EMP: 30
SALES (est): 1.05MM **Privately Held**
SIC: 3731 Shipbuilding and repairing

(G-19720)
SEAL CYBRSCURITY SOLUTIONS INC ✪
Also Called: Seal Security
251 Little Falls Dr (19808-1674)
PHONE..................................302 636-5401
Itamar Sher, *CEO*
Alon Navon, *CPO*
EMP: 10 **EST:** 2023
SALES (est): 348.32K **Privately Held**
SIC: 7371 Custom computer programming services

(G-19721)
SEAL PRO PAVING AND SEAL
2001 W 6th St (19805-2902)
PHONE..................................302 379-8267
EMP: 6 **EST:** 2017
SALES (est): 148.88K **Privately Held**
Web: www.sealpropaving.com
SIC: 1611 Surfacing and paving

(G-19722)
SEAMENS CENTER WILMINGTON INC
1 Container Rd (19801-5873)
P.O. Box 405 (19899-0405)
PHONE..................................302 575-1300
Christine Lassiter, *Ex Dir*
Joan Lyons, *Dir*
EMP: 6 **EST:** 1985
SALES (est): 382.66K **Privately Held**
Web: www.scwde.org
SIC: 8621 Professional organizations

(G-19723)
SEAN E REILLY
310 N West St (19801-2453)
PHONE..................................302 690-9487
Sean E Reilly, *Prin*
EMP: 7 **EST:** 2011
SALES (est): 235.1K **Privately Held**
Web: www.reillyrecruiting.com
SIC: 7361 Executive placement

(G-19724)
SEARCH OPTICS LLC (PA)
2751 Centerville Rd Ste 109 (19808-1600)
PHONE..................................858 678-0707
David Ponn, *CEO*
Troy Smith, *
Christian Fuller, *
Jason Stesney, *
EMP: 60 **EST:** 2006
SALES (est): 3.76MM
SALES (corp-wide): 3.76MM **Privately Held**
Web: www.searchoptics.com
SIC: 7374 Computer graphics service

(G-19725)
SEARS ROEBUCK ACCEPTANCE CORP
3711 Kennett Pike Ste 120 (19807-2156)
PHONE..................................302 434-3100
EMP: 6 **EST:** 2019
SALES (est): 296.62K **Privately Held**
SIC: 6141 Personal credit institutions

(G-19726)
SECOND CHANCE SOLUTIONS LLC
1201 N Market St Ste 111 (19801-1156)
PHONE..................................302 204-0551
EMP: 7 **EST:** 2019
SALES (est): 360.87K **Privately Held**
SIC: 8742 Management consulting services

(G-19727)
SECOND FOUNDATION US TRDG LLC ✪
1209 N Orange St (19801-1120)
PHONE..................................253 777-4400
Pavol Krasnovsky, *CEO*
EMP: 10 **EST:** 2022
SALES (est): 768.07K **Privately Held**
SIC: 6799 Commodity contract trading companies

(G-19728)
SECOND FRONT SYSTEMS INC (PA)
Also Called: Second Front
1207 Delaware Ave Ste 800 (19806-4743)
PHONE..................................301 744-7318
Chrissy Mcgarry, *CEO*
Chrissy Mcgarry, *COO*
Peter Dixon, *
Patrick Ryan, *
Kristi Marquez, *
EMP: 54 **EST:** 2014
SALES (est): 4.33MM
SALES (corp-wide): 4.33MM **Privately Held**

(PA)=Parent Co (HQ)=Headquarters
✪ = New Business established in last 2 years

Web: www.secondfront.com
SIC: 7373 Systems integration services

(G-19729)
SECONDSTAX INC
251 Little Falls Dr (19808-1674)
PHONE.................................862 368-0413
Eugene Tawiah, *CEO*
EMP: 22 EST: 2020
SALES (est): 1.45MM **Privately Held**
SIC: 6211 Investment firm, general brokerage

(G-19730)
SECURE SCHOOLS ALLIANCE INC
2207 Concord Pike (19803-2908)
PHONE.................................302 333-1416
Maria P Tamburri Board, *Ch*
EMP: 7 EST: 2016
SALES (est): 142.55K **Privately Held**
Web: www.securitysalesrecruiters.com
SIC: 8641 Civic and social associations

(G-19731)
SECURITAS TECHNOLOGY CORP
1100 First State Blvd (19804-3550)
PHONE.................................302 992-7950
Dave Shakespeare, *Brnch Mgr*
EMP: 27
SALES (corp-wide): 12.7B **Privately Held**
Web: www.securitases.com
SIC: 7382 Security systems services
HQ: Securitas Technology Corporation
3800 Tabs Dr
Uniontown OH 44685
800 548-4478

(G-19732)
SECURITECH INC
205 N Marshall St (19804-2713)
PHONE.................................302 996-9230
M Scott Wilson, *Pr*
EMP: 10 EST: 1983
SALES (est): 1.15MM **Privately Held**
Web: www.securitech.net
SIC: 3699 5065 Security control equipment and systems; Security control equipment and systems

(G-19733)
SECURITY INSTRUMENT CORP DEL (PA)
Also Called: SECURITY INSTRUMENT
309 W Newport Pike (19804-3148)
PHONE.................................302 998-2261
Arthur Mattei Senior, *Pr*
Arthur Mattei Junior, *VP*
Gary Mattei, *
EMP: 77 EST: 1962
SQ FT: 5,000
SALES (est): 52.15K
SALES (corp-wide): 52.15K **Privately Held**
Web: www.securityinstrument.com
SIC: 1731 7382 Fire detection and burglar alarm systems specialization; Burglar alarm maintenance and monitoring

(G-19734)
SEDGWICK
Also Called: Sedgwick
2040 Clark St (19805-3713)
PHONE.................................302 691-8871
EMP: 11 EST: 2017
SALES (est): 683.49K **Privately Held**
Web: www.sedgwick.com
SIC: 6411 Insurance claim adjusters, not employed by insurance company

(G-19735)
SEDRAK WAGDY MD
1600 Rockland Rd (19803-3607)
PHONE.................................302 651-6386
Wagdy Sedrak, *Prin*
EMP: 9 EST: 2014
SALES (est): 67.8K **Privately Held**
SIC: 8011 Pediatrician

(G-19736)
SEECUBIC INC (PA)
1732a Marsh Rd Ste 124 (19810-4606)
PHONE.................................267 400-1565
Krzysztof Kabacinski, *CEO*
Franklin Rodgers, *VP*
EMP: 30 EST: 2020
SALES (est): 2.44MM
SALES (corp-wide): 2.44MM **Privately Held**
SIC: 7371 Computer software development and applications

(G-19737)
SEEDS OF JESUS DAY CARE LLC
12 Mary Ella Dr (19805-1548)
PHONE.................................302 494-6568
Sarah Reyes, *Prin*
EMP: 5 EST: 2012
SALES (est): 279.78K **Privately Held**
Web: sarahreyesonline.vpweb.com
SIC: 8351 Preschool center

(G-19738)
SEEMETRICS INC
1007 N Orange St (19801-1239)
PHONE.................................818 533-9806
Mike Admon, *Prin*
EMP: 15
SALES (est): 535.04K **Privately Held**
Web: www.seemetrics.co
SIC: 7371 Custom computer programming services

(G-19739)
SEIFF JENNA L MD
4512 Kirkwood Hwy Ste 201 (19808-5100)
PHONE.................................302 633-6859
Jenna Seiff, *Ofcr*
EMP: 9 EST: 2018
SALES (est): 176.84K **Privately Held**
SIC: 8011 Offices and clinics of medical doctors

(G-19740)
SEITZ VANOGTROP & GREEN
222 Delaware Ave Ste 1500 (19801-1682)
P.O. Box 68 (19899-0068)
PHONE.................................302 888-0600
Bernard Vanogtrop, *Pt*
Bernard Vanogtrop, *Prin*
George Seitz, *Prin*
James S Green, *Prin*
EMP: 12 EST: 1999
SALES (est): 1.19MM **Privately Held**
Web: www.svglaw.com
SIC: 8111 General practice attorney, lawyer

(G-19741)
SELECT MEDICAL CORPORATION
Also Called: Select Spclty Hsptal- Wlmngton
701 N Clayton St (19805-3165)
PHONE.................................302 421-4545
Marsha Edwards, *Brnch Mgr*
EMP: 20
SALES (corp-wide): 5.53B **Publicly Held**
Web: www.selectmedical.com
SIC: 8062 General medical and surgical hospitals
HQ: Select Medical Corporation
4714 Gettysburg Rd
Mechanicsburg PA 17055
717 972-1100

(G-19742)
SELECT SPECIALTY HOSPITAL
501 W 14th St (19801-1013)
PHONE.................................302 421-4590
Carol Charisman, *CEO*
EMP: 638 EST: 2002
SALES (est): 43.51MM
SALES (corp-wide): 5.53B **Publicly Held**
Web: www.selectspecialtyhospitals.com
SIC: 8062 General medical and surgical hospitals
HQ: Select Medical Corporation
4714 Gettysburg Rd
Mechanicsburg PA 17055
717 972-1100

(G-19743)
SELECTION SOLUTIONS INC ◎
3 Germay Dr Ste 4 (19804-1127)
PHONE.................................800 600-6605
Charles Asuen, *CEO*
EMP: 5 EST: 2022
SALES (est): 347.01K **Privately Held**
Web: www.siteselectionsolutions.com
SIC: 8742 Management information systems consultant

(G-19744)
SELF CARE HOLISTIC LLC
14 S Union St (19805-3865)
PHONE.................................302 407-2456
Charine Russell, *CEO*
Charine Russel, *Managing Member*
EMP: 6 EST: 2017
SALES (est): 486.3K **Privately Held**
Web: www.selfcareholistic.com
SIC: 5992 5199 5947 0139 Plants, potted; Gifts and novelties; Gift, novelty, and souvenir shop; Herb or spice farm

(G-19745)
SELFX INNOVATIONS INC
919 N Market St Ste 950 (19801-3036)
PHONE.................................551 277-9665
Pawan Gupta, *CEO*
EMP: 84
SALES (corp-wide): 39.26MM **Privately Held**
SIC: 2211 Apparel and outerwear fabrics, cotton
PA: Selfx Innovations Inc.
500 W 37th St
New York NY 10018
551 277-9665

(G-19746)
SELLERS SENIOR CENTER INC
2800 Silverside Rd (19810-3710)
PHONE.................................302 762-2050
Linda Murphy, *Pr*
Caroyln Ciccarona, *Dir*
EMP: 5 EST: 1980
SQ FT: 10,000
SALES (est): 193.19K **Privately Held**
Web: www.sellersseniorcenter.org
SIC: 8322 Senior citizens' center or association

(G-19747)
SELLING DREAMS LLC
3202 Kirkwood Hwy Ste 207 (19808-6154)
PHONE.................................302 746-7999
Clif D'mello, *Owner*
EMP: 6 EST: 2014
SALES (est): 677.69K **Privately Held**
Web: www.sellingdreamsllc.com
SIC: 5023 Decorative home furnishings and supplies

(G-19748)
SEM REVIVAL LLC
2810 N Church St (19802-4447)
PHONE.................................302 600-1497
Waheed Ahmad, *Managing Member*
EMP: 10
SALES (est): 527.93K **Privately Held**
SIC: 7311 Advertising agencies

(G-19749)
SEN TOM CARPER (D-D)
301 N Walnut St Ste 102l-1 (19801-3974)
PHONE.................................302 573-6291
Laura Wisler, *Ofcr*
EMP: 6 EST: 2004
SALES (est): 183.35K **Privately Held**
Web: carper.senate.gov
SIC: 6021 National commercial banks

(G-19750)
SENDCHAMP INC
2055 Limestone Rd Ste 200c (19808-5536)
PHONE.................................510 423-3457
EMP: 5 EST: 2021
SALES (est): 46.16K **Privately Held**
Web: www.sendchamp.com
SIC: 7371 Computer software development and applications

(G-19751)
SENSEDIA LLC (PA)
2711 Centerville Rd (19808-1660)
PHONE.................................631 764-4544
Ken Ballou, *Pr*
EMP: 6 EST: 2021
SALES (est): 68.89K
SALES (corp-wide): 68.89K **Privately Held**
SIC: 7371 Computer software development

(G-19752)
SENSIBO INC
1313 N Market St (19801-6101)
PHONE.................................302 572-2572
EMP: 6
SALES (est): 70.43K **Privately Held**
SIC: 7372 Prepackaged software

(G-19753)
SENTINEL TRANSPORTATION LLC (HQ)
3521 Silverside Rd Ste 2a (19810-4914)
PHONE.................................302 477-1640
EMP: 14 EST: 1996
SQ FT: 3,100
SALES (est): 94.25MM
SALES (corp-wide): 175.7B **Publicly Held**
Web: www.sentineltrans.com
SIC: 4212 Local trucking, without storage
PA: Phillips 66
2331 Citywest Blvd
Houston TX 77042
832 765-3010

(G-19754)
SENTINEL-SG LLC
919 N Market St Ste 425 (19801-3014)
PHONE.................................580 458-9184
Dean E Young, *Managing Member*
EMP: 5 EST: 2016
SALES (est): 371.85K **Privately Held**
SIC: 8748 Business consulting, nec

(G-19755)
SERENA JOY LLC
1805 N Washington St # 3 (19802-4763)
PHONE.................................302 312-3318
EMP: 6 EST: 2021
SALES (est): 65.19K **Privately Held**
SIC: 8299 7929 Educational services; Entertainment service

GEOGRAPHIC SECTION
Wilmington - New Castle County (G-19785)

(G-19756)
SERENE MINDS
410 Foulk Rd Ste 102 (19803-3835)
PHONE.................................302 478-6199
Christine Maccord, *Prin*
EMP: 10 **EST:** 2016
SALES (est): 454.76K **Privately Held**
Web: www.serenemindsllc.com
SIC: 8011 Psychiatrist

(G-19757)
SERENITY SPA
214 7th Ave (19805-4762)
PHONE.................................302 668-9534
Eva Torres, *Prin*
EMP: 5 **EST:** 2017
SALES (est): 44.83K **Privately Held**
Web: www.serenityspaclaymont.com
SIC: 7991 Spas

(G-19758)
SERGIOS POOL SERVICE INC
901 N Tatnall St (19801-1605)
PHONE.................................302 655-1972
Mariluz Mendez, *Mgr*
EMP: 5 **EST:** 2013
SALES (est): 44.39K **Privately Held**
Web: sergios-pool-service-inc-de.hub.biz
SIC: 7389 Swimming pool and hot tub service and maintenance

(G-19759)
SERPE & SONS INC
Also Called: Serpe & Sons Bakery
1411 Kirkwood Hwy (19805-2123)
PHONE.................................302 994-1868
Dominick Serpe Junior, *Pr*
Anthony J Serpe, *VP*
Thomas Serpe, *Sec*
Nicole Wilson, *Off Mgr*
EMP: 12 **EST:** 1952
SQ FT: 5,000
SALES (est): 940K **Privately Held**
Web: www.serpesbakery.com
SIC: 2051 Bread, all types (white, wheat, rye, etc); fresh or frozen

(G-19760)
SERVICE DISPOSAL OF DELAWARE
924 S Heald St (19801-5733)
PHONE.................................302 326-9155
Richard E Pierson, *Pr*
Kevin J Killeen, *VP*
EMP: 9 **EST:** 1999
SALES (est): 999.5K **Privately Held**
SIC: 4953 Refuse systems

(G-19761)
SERVICE MASTER OF NEWARK
Also Called: ServiceMaster
310 Cornell Dr Ste B1 (19801-5769)
PHONE.................................302 654-8145
EMP: 5 **EST:** 2019
SALES (est): 104.31K **Privately Held**
Web: www.servicemaster.com
SIC: 7349 Building maintenance services, nec

(G-19762)
SERVICE RSOURCE GROUP INTL LLC
1007 N Orange St (19801-1239)
PHONE.................................832 646-8756
Christopher Pillott, *Prin*
Michael Thurner, *Prin*
EMP: 5 **EST:** 2017
SALES (est): 124.66K **Privately Held**
SIC: 8748 Business consulting, nec

(G-19763)
SERVO2GOCOM LTD
4023 Kennett Pike Ste 583 (19807-2018)
PHONE.................................877 378-0240
Warren Osak, *Pr*
▼ **EMP:** 6 **EST:** 2007
SALES (est): 215.81K **Privately Held**
Web: www.electromate.com
SIC: 5065 Electronic parts and equipment, nec

(G-19764)
SERYALDA LLC
2810 N Church St (19802-4447)
PHONE.................................914 861-5974
Rolly Villacacan, *Managing Member*
EMP: 6
SALES (est): 78.16K **Privately Held**
SIC: 3672 Printed circuit boards

(G-19765)
SESIMI LLC
1209 N Orange St (19801-1120)
PHONE.................................302 574-6280
EMP: 5 **EST:** 2021
SALES (est): 46.16K **Privately Held**
SIC: 7371 Computer software development

(G-19766)
SESSIONS TECHNOLOGIES INC
103 Foulk Rd Ste 202 (19803-3742)
PHONE.................................302 202-0551
Radu Negulescu, *Prin*
EMP: 5 **EST:** 2020
SALES (est): 68.89K **Privately Held**
SIC: 7371 Custom computer programming services

(G-19767)
SET FA LIFE LLC
2600 N Market St (19802-4243)
PHONE.................................302 407-6773
EMP: 5 **EST:** 2018
SALES (est): 81.5K **Privately Held**
Web: set-fa-life-llc.business.site
SIC: 1522 Hotel/motel and multi-family home renovation and remodeling

(G-19768)
SEVEN SHIPPING INC
Also Called: 7 Shipping
3 Germay Dr Ste 4 (19804-1127)
PHONE.................................302 516-7150
EMP: 7 **EST:** 1998
SALES (est): 751.19K **Privately Held**
Web: www.sevenshipping.com
SIC: 4731 Freight forwarding

(G-19769)
SEVENSHOPPER INC
2020 Duncan Rd (19808-5932)
PHONE.................................302 407-6905
Lin Shou, *CEO*
EMP: 30 **EST:** 2014
SALES (est): 4.54MM **Privately Held**
Web: www.sevenshopper.com
SIC: 5063 Electrical apparatus and equipment

(G-19770)
SEVENSHOPPER LLC
3616 Kirkwood Hwy (19808-5124)
PHONE.................................302 516-7150
EMP: 8 **EST:** 2014
SALES (est): 426.47K **Privately Held**
Web: www.sevenshopper.com
SIC: 7311 Advertising agencies

(G-19771)
SEVERN TRENT INC (DH)
1011 Centre Rd (19805-1266)
PHONE.................................302 427-5990
Ken Kelly, *CEO*
Leonard F Graziano, *Pr*
David L Chester, *VP*
Peter Winnington, *Treas*
Adele A Stevens, *Sec*
◆ **EMP:** 10 **EST:** 1990
SALES (est): 52.37MM
SALES (corp-wide): 2.6B **Privately Held**
SIC: 3589 7371 8741 Water treatment equipment, industrial; Computer software writing services; Management services
HQ: Severn Trent Overseas Holdings Limited
2 St. Johns Street
Coventry W MIDLANDS CV1 2

(G-19772)
SFA AMERICA INC
2 Germay Dr Unit 42341 (19804-1105)
PHONE.................................206 265-3148
Kuo Feng William Chin, *Pr*
Gavin Hesse, *Ex VP*
EMP: 8 **EST:** 2021
SALES (est): 161.02K **Privately Held**
SIC: 3751 Motorcycles and related parts
PA: Shun On Electronic Co., Limited
2f, No. 19, Lane 146, Xinhu 2nd Rd.
Taipei City TAP 11494

(G-19773)
SFIN 3 INC
1007 N Orange St (19801-1239)
PHONE.................................302 472-9276
EMP: 9 **EST:** 2004
SALES (est): 225.66K **Privately Held**
SIC: 8742 Business management consultant

(G-19774)
SGODDE INC
2100 Northeast Blvd (19802-4503)
PHONE.................................858 336-9471
Zihui Li, *Pr*
EMP: 14 **EST:** 2020
SALES (est): 581.83K **Privately Held**
SIC: 5091 Sporting and recreation goods

(G-19775)
SGS PROPERTIES LLC
4517 Verona Dr (19808-5623)
P.O. Box 5514 (19808-0514)
PHONE.................................302 588-4010
EMP: 5 **EST:** 2018
SALES (est): 147.85K **Privately Held**
Web: www.sgsproperties.com
SIC: 6512 Nonresidential building operators

(G-19776)
SHAH & ASSOCIATES PA
503 Kirkwood Hwy (19805-5102)
PHONE.................................302 999-0420
EMP: 7 **EST:** 2015
SALES (est): 293.09K **Privately Held**
SIC: 8721 Certified public accountant

(G-19777)
SHAKER REVOLUTION LLC
Also Called: Fuelshaker
501 Silverside Rd (19809-1374)
PHONE.................................302 219-4838
▲ **EMP:** 5
SALES (est): 174.3K **Privately Held**
SIC: 3085 2389 Plastics bottles; Cummerbunds

(G-19778)
SHALLCROSS MORTGAGE CO INC (PA)
410 Century Blvd (19808-6271)
PHONE.................................302 999-9800
Jay Pierce Junior, *Pr*
Jay Pierce Senior, *Ch Bd*
Beatrice White, *Sec*
Eleanor Pierce, *Treas*
EMP: 7 **EST:** 1990
SQ FT: 3,500
SALES (est): 1.25MM **Privately Held**
SIC: 6162 Mortgage brokers, using own money

(G-19779)
SHANKIAS BEST BRAIDS
500 W 25th St (19802-3421)
PHONE.................................302 507-9891
Shankia Ramos, *Prin*
EMP: 5 **EST:** 2012
SALES (est): 46.87K **Privately Held**
SIC: 7231 Beauty shops

(G-19780)
SHANLEY ASSOC
2751 Centerville Rd Ste 401 (19808-1627)
P.O. Box 5070 (19808-0070)
PHONE.................................302 691-6838
Peter Shanley, *Prin*
EMP: 5 **EST:** 2018
SALES (est): 247.44K **Privately Held**
SIC: 8111 General practice attorney, lawyer

(G-19781)
SHARIYFA A FIELDS
1624 Jessup St (19802-4210)
PHONE.................................302 552-3574
Shariyfa A Fields Lcsw, *Owner*
EMP: 11 **EST:** 2017
SALES (est): 77.64K **Privately Held**
SIC: 8011 Offices and clinics of medical doctors

(G-19782)
SHARON BOYD M ED LPCMH
2304 Patwynn Rd (19810-2731)
PHONE.................................302 529-0220
Sharonw Boyd, *Prin*
EMP: 5 **EST:** 2015
SALES (est): 50.3K **Privately Held**
SIC: 8621 Professional organizations

(G-19783)
SHARON M ZIEG
1000 N West St (19801-1050)
P.O. Box 391 (19899-0391)
PHONE.................................302 571-6655
Sharon M Zieg, *Prin*
EMP: 5 **EST:** 2010
SALES (est): 115.42K **Privately Held**
SIC: 8111 General practice attorney, lawyer

(G-19784)
SHAYONA HEALTH INC
2511 W 4th St Ste F (19805-3350)
PHONE.................................302 660-8847
EMP: 8 **EST:** 2018
SALES (est): 497.5K **Privately Held**
SIC: 8099 Health and allied services, nec

(G-19785)
SHE PODCASTS
602 Mount Lebanon Rd (19803-1708)
PHONE.................................302 588-2317
Jessica Kupferman, *CEO*
EMP: 3 **EST:** 2014
SALES (est): 46.16K **Privately Held**
Web: www.shepodcasts.com

Wilmington - New Castle County (G-19786)   GEOGRAPHIC SECTION

SIC: 8299 2741 Educational services; Internet publishing and broadcasting

(G-19786)
SHEAR COLLECTION SALON BY MEL
2016 N Market St (19802-4815)
PHONE..................302 543-6854
EMP: 5 EST: 2012
SALES (est): 67.59K **Privately Held**
Web: www.shearcollectionsalon.biz
SIC: 7231 Hairdressers

(G-19787)
SHEEHAN CHIROPRACTIC LTD
829 N Harrison St (19806-4628)
PHONE..................302 545-7441
James Sheehan, *Prin*
EMP: 8 EST: 2016
SALES (est): 129.33K **Privately Held**
SIC: 8041 Offices and clinics of chiropractors

(G-19788)
SHEET METAL INDUSTRY ADVANCEME
P.O. Box 6520 (19804-0520)
PHONE..................302 994-7442
EMP: 5 EST: 2010
SALES (est): 124.61K **Privately Held**
SIC: 1761 Sheet metal work, nec

(G-19789)
SHEET METAL WORKERS LOCAL 19
911 New Rd (19805-5130)
P.O. Box 7018 (19803-0018)
PHONE..................302 999-0573
Robert Wood, *Dir*
EMP: 11 EST: 1985
SALES (est): 173.81K **Privately Held**
Web: www.smartlu19.org
SIC: 8631 Labor union

(G-19790)
SHEKINAH GLORY SIGN COMPANY
2608 Kirkwood Hwy (19805-4910)
PHONE..................302 256-0426
EMP: 4 EST: 2019
SALES (est): 81.08K **Privately Held**
Web: shekinah-glory-sign-company-llc.business.site
SIC: 3993 Signs and advertising specialties

(G-19791)
SHELIAS CHILDCARE CENTER
2200 Baynard Blvd (19802-3939)
PHONE..................302 472-9648
Mary Guy, *Prin*
EMP: 5 EST: 2006
SALES (est): 67.24K **Privately Held**
SIC: 8351 Group day care center

(G-19792)
SHELLCREST SWIM CLUB
916 Wilson Rd (19803-4018)
PHONE..................302 529-1464
EMP: 7 EST: 2018
SALES (est): 104.79K **Privately Held**
Web: www.shellcrestpool.com
SIC: 7997 Swimming club, membership

(G-19793)
SHELLHORN & HILL INC
3016 Edgemoor Ave (19802-2408)
P.O. Box 2569 (19805-0569)
PHONE..................302 654-4200
TOLL FREE: 800
Michael D Hill, *Pr*
Larry Dugan, *
Wayne Peace, *
EMP: 62 EST: 1931
SALES (est): 22.95MM **Privately Held**
Web: www.shellhornandhill.com
SIC: 5172 5983 5541 Petroleum products, nec; Fuel oil dealers; Gasoline service stations

(G-19794)
SHELLYS OF DELAWARE INC
Also Called: Shelly's We Do Everything
610 W 8th St (19801-1450)
PHONE..................302 656-3337
R W Rock Brown, *Pr*
Sarah Johnson, *Sec*
EMP: 8 EST: 1967
SQ FT: 3,780
SALES (est): 502.4K **Privately Held**
SIC: 1542 1521 1541 Commercial and office building, new construction; New construction, single-family houses; Industrial buildings, new construction, nec

(G-19795)
SHEPHERD STFFING CNSULTING LLC
402 Owls Nest Rd (19807-1626)
PHONE..................302 652-0899
Debbie Fincher, *Prin*
EMP: 5 EST: 2008
SALES (est): 76.72K **Privately Held**
SIC: 8999 Scientific consulting

(G-19796)
SHERRYS CHILDCARE
1514 W 6th St (19805-3158)
PHONE..................302 654-4982
EMP: 6 EST: 2018
SALES (est): 15.97K **Privately Held**
SIC: 8351 Child day care services

(G-19797)
SHERWOOD PARK CIVIC ASSN
2618 E Robino Dr (19808-2245)
PHONE..................302 994-6604
William G Matt, *Pr*
EMP: 5 EST: 2017
SALES (est): 64.47K **Privately Held**
SIC: 8699 Membership organizations, nec

(G-19798)
SHIATSU BODYWORK
1506 Evergreen Ln (19810-4432)
PHONE..................302 529-7882
Ronni Yaskin, *Prin*
EMP: 5 EST: 2017
SALES (est): 203.87K **Privately Held**
Web: www.peopleandpetmassage.com
SIC: 8049 Massage Therapist

(G-19799)
SHINGLE EXPRESS INC
125 Falcon Ln (19808-1937)
PHONE..................302 397-3773
Michael Glackin, *Prin*
EMP: 5 EST: 2016
SALES (est): 93.91K **Privately Held**
Web: www.shingleexpress.com
SIC: 1761 Roofing contractor

(G-19800)
SHINLAZA INC
2055 Limestone Rd (19808-5536)
PHONE..................800 206-0051
Ronni Shino, *Pr*
EMP: 4
SALES (est): 292.8K **Privately Held**
Web: www.shinlaza.com
SIC: 2834 Pharmaceutical preparations

(G-19801)
SHINY AGENCY LLC
1800 Wawaset St (19806-2133)
PHONE..................302 384-6494
Katherine Thorbahn, *Mng Pt*
EMP: 5 EST: 2015
SALES (est): 606.29K **Privately Held**
Web: www.shiny.agency
SIC: 7311 Advertising consultant

(G-19802)
SHIPPING CENTER LLC
3209 Miller Rd (19802-2507)
PHONE..................302 543-4968
Ai Yan, *Prin*
EMP: 5 EST: 2016
SALES (est): 116.3K **Privately Held**
Web: www.sevenshipping.com
SIC: 4731 Freight transportation arrangement

(G-19803)
SHIPYARD CENTER LLC
234 N James St (19804-3132)
PHONE..................302 999-0708
EMP: 5 EST: 2010
SALES (est): 399.46K **Privately Held**
Web: www.pettinaro.com
SIC: 6519 Real property lessors, nec

(G-19804)
SHIRE NORTH AMERICAN GROUP INC (HQ)
103 Foulk Rd Ste 202 (19803-3742)
PHONE..................484 595-8800
Christophe Weber, *CEO*
EMP: 85 EST: 2011
SALES (est): 102.08MM **Privately Held**
SIC: 2834 Pharmaceutical preparations
PA: Takeda Pharmaceutical Company Limited
2-1-1, Nihonbashihoncho
Chuo-Ku TKY 103-0

(G-19805)
SHIRLEYS LITTLE FRIENDS LLC
1818 Delaware Ave (19806-2334)
PHONE..................302 981-9991
Maureen Andrews, *Prin*
EMP: 7 EST: 2018
SALES (est): 221.12K **Privately Held**
Web: www.shirleyslittlefriendz.com
SIC: 8099 Health and allied services, nec

(G-19806)
SHOCKWAVES AQUATIC CLUB LLC
3516 Silverside Rd (19810-4932)
PHONE..................302 478-8800
Charles S Knothe, *Prin*
EMP: 8 EST: 2008
SALES (est): 70.47K **Privately Held**
SIC: 7997 Membership sports and recreation clubs

(G-19807)
SHOOSHOOS LLC
19c Trolley Sq (19806-3355)
PHONE..................302 256-5355
EMP: 7 EST: 2014
SALES (est): 100K **Privately Held**
SIC: 3149 Children's footwear, except athletic

(G-19808)
SHOP CLUB USA NETWORK HOLDING
300 Delaware Ave (19801-1607)
PHONE..................858 304-0044
EMP: 5 EST: 2017
SALES (est): 107.65K **Privately Held**
Web: www.scusanetwork.com

SIC: 7371 Custom computer programming services

(G-19809)
SHOR ASSOCIATES INC
240 Philadelphia Pike (19809-3125)
P.O. Box 9708 (19809-0708)
PHONE..................302 764-1701
Craig Shor, *Pr*
Catherine Lynch, *VP*
EMP: 5 EST: 1993
SQ FT: 600
SALES (est): 493.43K **Privately Held**
Web: www.shorandassociates.com
SIC: 7311 Advertising consultant

(G-19810)
SHORT ORDER PRODUCTION HOUSE
625 N Orange St Fl 1 (19801-2250)
PHONE..................302 656-1638
EMP: 8 EST: 2020
SALES (est): 372.79K **Privately Held**
Web: www.shortorder.co
SIC: 7822 Motion picture and tape distribution

(G-19811)
SHOWTIME REAL ESTATE
713 Greenbank Rd (19808-3167)
PHONE..................302 377-1292
Dan Shainsky, *Prin*
EMP: 5 EST: 2013
SALES (est): 149.09K **Privately Held**
Web: www.showtimere.com
SIC: 6531 Real estate brokers and agents

(G-19812)
SHUMMI US LLC
919 N Market St Ste 950 (19801-3036)
PHONE..................847 987-1686
Catherine Li, *CEO*
EMP: 7 EST: 2020
SALES (est): 534.08K **Privately Held**
SIC: 3841 Surgical and medical instruments

(G-19813)
SIDITECH LLC
2511 Cedar Tree Dr (19810-1431)
PHONE..................302 384-5088
Abdulkarim Sidibay, *Managing Member*
EMP: 7
SALES (est): 221.54K **Privately Held**
SIC: 7371 Computer software development

(G-19814)
SIEGFRIED GROUP LLP (PA)
Also Called: Siegfried Resources
1201 N Market St Ste 700 (19801-1153)
PHONE..................302 984-1800
Robert L Siegfried Junior, *Pt*
George A Siegfried, *Sr Pt*
Joan Davidson, *Pr*
EMP: 150 EST: 1988
SALES (est): 45.65MM
SALES (corp-wide): 45.65MM **Privately Held**
Web: www.siegfriedgroup.com
SIC: 8721 Certified public accountant

(G-19815)
SIEMENS
4001 Vandever Ave (19802-4609)
PHONE..................302 220-1544
EMP: 46 EST: 2017
SALES (est): 660.23K **Privately Held**
Web: www.siemens.com
SIC: 3661 Telephones and telephone apparatus

▲ = Import ▼ = Export
◆ = Import/Export

GEOGRAPHIC SECTION

(G-19816)
SIERENTZ ADVISORS LLC
2711 Centerville Rd Ste 400 (19808-1660)
PHONE..................423 665-9444
Helen Lovely, *Mgr*
EMP: 6 EST: 2012
SALES (est): 135.39K **Privately Held**
SIC: 6411 Advisory services, insurance

(G-19817)
SIERRA TMSHARE CNDUIT RCVBLES
3411 Silverside Rd Ste 104 (19810-4812)
PHONE..................702 562-8316
EMP: 18 EST: 2008
SALES (est): 4.5MM **Publicly Held**
SIC: 6722 Management investment, open-end
PA: Travel + Leisure Co.
6277 Sea Harbor Dr
Orlando FL 32821

(G-19818)
SIGMA TELECOM LLC
Also Called: Sigma Telecom
501 Silverside Rd Ste 105 (19809-1376)
PHONE..................347 741-8397
Musa Rad, *Managing Member*
EMP: 19 EST: 2015
SALES (est): 2.31MM **Privately Held**
Web: www.sigmatelecom.com
SIC: 4813 Long distance telephone communications
PA: Sigma Isletim Ve Ulastirma Sanayi Ve Ticaret Limited Sirketi
A Blok, No:2e/9 Ataturk Mahallesi
Istanbul (Anatolia) 34758

(G-19819)
SIGMASAT USA INC
501 Silverside Rd Ste 105 (19809-1376)
PHONE..................561 488-8048
EMP: 6 EST: 2006
SALES (est): 37.15K **Privately Held**
SIC: 7389

(G-19820)
SIGN EXPRESS
Also Called: Dmi
103 S Augustine St (19804-2505)
PHONE..................302 999-0893
Chris Iannone, *Owner*
EMP: 7 EST: 1999
SALES (est): 420K **Privately Held**
Web: www.signexpressdelaware.com
SIC: 3993 Signs and advertising specialties

(G-19821)
SIGNATURE INTL FOODS LLC
1209 N Orange St (19801-1120)
PHONE..................833 463-0004
EMP: 5 EST: 2020
SALES (est): 700K **Privately Held**
SIC: 2051 Bread, all types (white, wheat, rye, etc); fresh or frozen

(G-19822)
SIGNATURE PAINTING CONTRACTORS
209 W Champlain Ave (19804-1837)
PHONE..................267 571-6595
Jose Santillan, *Prin*
EMP: 5 EST: 2019
SALES (est): 42.66K **Privately Held**
SIC: 1721 Painting and paper hanging

(G-19823)
SIGNIN SOFT INC
1007 N Orange St (19801-1239)
PHONE..................315 966-6599

Surendra Kanagala, *Prin*
EMP: 10
SALES (est): 348.32K **Privately Held**
SIC: 7371 7389 Custom computer programming services; Business Activities at Non-Commercial Site

(G-19824)
SIGNSCAPE DESIGNS & SIGNS
1709 Philadelphia Pike (19809-1560)
P.O. Box 125 (19933-0125)
PHONE..................302 798-2926
Robert Lesperance, *Pt*
Mildred Winslow, *Pt*
EMP: 2 EST: 1998
SQ FT: 1,050
SALES (est): 221.33K **Privately Held**
Web: www.19703.com
SIC: 3993 Signs and advertising specialties

(G-19825)
SILLY MONKEY STUDIOS LLC
Also Called: Kanopi Studios
1000 N West St Ste 1200 (19801-1058)
PHONE..................415 517-0830
Anne Stefanyk, *Prin*
EMP: 27 EST: 2016
SALES (est): 979.56K **Privately Held**
SIC: 7371 Custom computer programming services

(G-19826)
SILVER BAY INTERNATIONAL LLC
300 Delaware Ave Ste 210a (19801-6601)
PHONE..................302 213-3006
EMP: 6 EST: 2019
SALES (est): 1.19MM **Privately Held**
Web: www.silverbayinternational.com
SIC: 5139 Footwear

(G-19827)
SILVER BRIDGE CAPITAL MGMT LLC
3701 Kennett Pike Ste 100 (19807-2163)
PHONE..................302 575-9215
Allison Taff, *Dir*
EMP: 5 EST: 2018
SALES (est): 102.76K **Privately Held**
Web: www.silverbridgeadv.com
SIC: 7389 6282 Finishing services; Investment advice

(G-19828)
SILVER LINING SOLUTIONS LLC
49 Bancroft Mills Rd P5 (19806-2032)
PHONE..................302 691-7100
Toni Beltz, *Pr*
Mark Beltz, *VP*
EMP: 5 EST: 2009
SALES (est): 296.94K **Privately Held**
SIC: 6512 Nonresidential building operators

(G-19829)
SILVERBROOK CEMETERY CO
3300 Lancaster Pike (19805-1435)
PHONE..................302 658-0953
Paul L White Junior, *Pr*
Ronald Fox, *Sec*
Brenda White, *Treas*
EMP: 6 EST: 1895
SQ FT: 3,000
SALES (est): 500K **Privately Held**
Web: www.silverbrookcemetery.com
SIC: 6553 Cemeteries, real estate operation

(G-19830)
SILVERSIDE CONTRACTING INC
2801 N Broom St (19802-2913)
PHONE..................302 798-1907
Richard W Hartnett, *Pr*
Daniel J Hartnett, *VP*

EMP: 6 EST: 1965
SALES (est): 782.59K **Privately Held**
SIC: 1521 1542 General remodeling, single-family houses; Commercial and office building, new construction

(G-19831)
SILVERSIDE OPEN MRI IMAGING
2501 Silverside Rd Ste A (19810-3722)
PHONE..................302 246-2000
Edward White, *Prin*
EMP: 5 EST: 2007
SALES (est): 193.29K **Privately Held**
SIC: 8011 3845 Radiologist; Magnetic resonance imaging device, nuclear

(G-19832)
SIMON EYE ASSOCIATES
2625 Concord Pike Ste A (19803-5033)
PHONE..................302 239-1933
Charles J Simon, *CEO*
EMP: 22 EST: 2006
SALES (est): 2.58MM **Privately Held**
Web: www.simoneye.com
SIC: 8042 Offices and clinics of optometrists

(G-19833)
SIMON EYE ASSOCIATES PA
Also Called: Simon Eye Associates
912 N Union St (19805-5326)
PHONE..................302 655-8180
Carey Mcneill, *Brnch Mgr*
EMP: 5
Web: www.simoneye.com
SIC: 8042 Specialized optometrists
PA: Simon Eye Associates, P.A.
5301 Limestone Rd Ste 128
Wilmington DE 19808

(G-19834)
SIMON EYE ASSOCIATES PA (PA)
5301 Limestone Rd Ste 128 (19808-1253)
PHONE..................302 239-1389
Charles Simon O.d., *Pr*
EMP: 10 EST: 1994
SALES (est): 5.28MM **Privately Held**
Web: www.simoneye.com
SIC: 8042 Specialized optometrists

(G-19835)
SIMPLE SPACE LLC
300 Delaware Ave Ste 210a (19801-6601)
PHONE..................801 520-3680
EMP: 5 EST: 2018
SALES (est): 169.43K **Privately Held**
SIC: 7389 Business Activities at Non-Commercial Site

(G-19836)
SIMPLER LOGISTICS LLC
300 Delaware Ave Ste 210 (19801-6601)
PHONE..................800 619-8321
EMP: 5 EST: 2018
SALES (est): 140K **Privately Held**
SIC: 8742 Transportation consultant

(G-19837)
SIMPLICA CORPORATION
Also Called: Simplica
1701 Shallcross Ave Ste B (19806-2347)
PHONE..................302 594-9899
Marcus E Rabil, *CEO*
EMP: 10 EST: 1999
SALES (est): 861.88K **Privately Held**
Web: www.simplica.com
SIC: 4813 7379 Internet host services; Online services technology consultants

(G-19838)
SIMPLY GRAND LLC
105 Christina Landing Dr (19801-5200)
PHONE..................480 278-0367
Joan W Paynter, *Prin*
EMP: 5 EST: 2016
SALES (est): 60.56K **Privately Held**
SIC: 0782 Lawn care services

(G-19839)
SIMPLY GREEN
216 S Maryland Ave (19804-1344)
PHONE..................302 256-0822
EMP: 10 EST: 2012
SALES (est): 813.79K **Privately Held**
Web: www.simplygreengrass.com
SIC: 0782 Lawn care services

(G-19840)
SIMPLY STYLNG-SCHL OF CSMTLGY
204 N Union St (19805-3430)
PHONE..................302 778-1885
Jerome Stanley, *CEO*
EMP: 3 EST: 1997
SALES (est): 367.96K **Privately Held**
SIC: 5087 6732 2721 Beauty salon and barber shop equipment and supplies; Educational trust management; Magazines: publishing only, not printed on site

(G-19841)
SIMPLYMIDDLE LLC
901 N Market St Ste 719 (19801-3098)
PHONE..................302 217-3460
Akinyemi Famakinwa, *Managing Member*
Sanni Ibrahim, *Prin*
EMP: 6 EST: 2015
SQ FT: 508
SALES (est): 101.94K **Privately Held**
SIC: 8399 7311 Social service information exchange; Advertising agencies

(G-19842)
SINOMINE RESOURCES (US) INC
1209 N Orange St (19801-1120)
PHONE..................204 340-6696
Zhiwei Wang, *CEO*
Gordon Matlock, *Mgr*
EMP: 2 EST: 1996
SALES (est): 11MM **Privately Held**
SIC: 2819 Industrial inorganic chemicals, nec
HQ: Sinomine (Hong Kong) Rare Metals Resources Co., Limited
54/F Hopewell Ctr
Wan Chai HK

(G-19843)
SINUSWARS LLC
501 Silverside Rd Ste 105 (19809-1376)
PHONE..................212 901-0805
▼ EMP: 10 EST: 2005
SALES (est): 1.46MM **Privately Held**
Web: www.sinuswars.com
SIC: 5122 Patent medicines

(G-19844)
SISTER CITIES WILMINGTON INC
2414 W 18th St (19806-1206)
PHONE..................302 383-0968
Primus Poppiti, *Pr*
Dennis Sheer, *Ch Bd*
Constance Smith, *Sec*
Catherine Coin, *Treas*
Mary Mccoy, *VP*
EMP: 8 EST: 1975
SALES (est): 102.41K **Privately Held**
Web: www.scowde.org
SIC: 8699 Charitable organization

Wilmington - New Castle County (G-19845)

(G-19845)
SIVIL TECHNOLOGIES INC
Also Called: Sivil
251 Little Falls Dr (19808-1674)
PHONE.................................214 893-9797
EMP: 6 EST: 2020
SALES (est): 135.97K Privately Held
Web: www.sivilco.com
SIC: 7371 Computer software development

(G-19846)
SIX ANGELS DEVELOPMENT INC
7 Medori Blvd (19801-5781)
PHONE.................................302 218-1548
Michael Miles, *Pr*
EMP: 8 EST: 2008
SALES (est): 482.79K Privately Held
SIC: 8748 7389 Environmental consultant; Business Activities at Non-Commercial Site

(G-19847)
SIX DAYS INC
2810 N Church St Pmb 96630
(19802-4447)
PHONE.................................888 463-5898
Wanxin Chen, *Pr*
EMP: 25 EST: 2014
SALES (est): 1.41MM Privately Held
Web: www.trustwallet.com
SIC: 7371 7389 Computer software development; Business services, nec

(G-19848)
SIX PLUS INC
4300 Kennett Pike (19807-2025)
PHONE.................................302 652-3296
George A Weymouth, *Pr*
Cary Lambert, *Sec*
EMP: 7 EST: 1968
SALES (est): 597.07K Privately Held
SIC: 8741 Management services

(G-19849)
SIX SIGMA TELECOM LLC
2711 Centerville Rd (19808-1660)
PHONE.................................302 636-5440
EMP: 7 EST: 2004
SALES (est): 79.85K Privately Held
Web: www.sigmatelecom.com
SIC: 7389 Telephone services

(G-19850)
SK CHIROPRACTIC LLC
3411 Silverside Rd Ste 106 (19810-4810)
PHONE.................................302 482-3410
EMP: 24 EST: 2017
SALES (est): 211.84K Privately Held
Web: www.skchiro.com
SIC: 8041 Offices and clinics of chiropractors

(G-19851)
SKADDEN ARPS SLATE MGHER FLOM
1 Rodney Sq (19801)
P.O. Box 636 (19899-0636)
PHONE.................................302 651-3000
Edward P Welch, *Pt*
EMP: 155
Web: www.skadden.com
SIC: 8111 General practice attorney, lawyer
HQ: Skadden, Arps, Slate, Meagher & Flom Llp
One Mnhttan W 395 9th Ave
New York NY 10001
212 735-3000

(G-19852)
SKAJAQUODA CAPITAL LLC
Also Called: Skajaquoda
717 N Union St Ste 5 (19805-3031)
PHONE.................................302 504-4448
EMP: 9 EST: 2008
SALES (est): 176.5K Privately Held
SIC: 6211 Investment bankers

(G-19853)
SKATING CLUB OF WILMINGTON INC
Also Called: Skating Club of Wilmington
1301 Carruthers Ln (19803-4601)
PHONE.................................302 656-5005
Peter A Bilous, *Pr*
EMP: 17 EST: 1961
SQ FT: 35,000
SALES (est): 804.1K Privately Held
Web: www.skatewilm.com
SIC: 7999 Ice skating rink operation

(G-19854)
SKIN CARE SCHOOL & CTR
3700 Lancaster Pike (19805-1511)
PHONE.................................302 328-0611
Debbie Fraser, *Mgr*
EMP: 7 EST: 2014
SALES (est): 73.67K Privately Held
SIC: 8099 Health and allied services, nec

(G-19855)
SKITTLE INC
Also Called: Skittleme.com
427 N Tatnall St 63204 (19801-2230)
PHONE.................................855 575-4885
EMP: 10 EST: 2017
SALES (est): 239.34K Privately Held
SIC: 7371 Computer software development and applications

(G-19856)
SKORUZ HOLDING CORPORATION
Also Called: Skoruz
1007 N Orange St (19801-1239)
PHONE.................................510 766-2803
Saminathan Susaimanickam, *CEO*
Irfan Mohammed, *VP*
EMP: 5 EST: 2021
SALES (est): 77.06K Privately Held
Web: www.skoruz.com
SIC: 7371 Computer software development

(G-19857)
SKYLINE SWIM CLUB
2901 Skyline Dr (19808-2811)
PHONE.................................302 737-4696
Mike Walsh, *Mgr*
EMP: 6 EST: 2018
SALES (est): 165.16K Privately Held
Web: www.skylineswimclubde.com
SIC: 8641 Civic and social associations

(G-19858)
SKYNETHOSTINGNET INC
501 Silverside Rd (19809-1374)
PHONE.................................302 384-1784
EMP: 15 EST: 2019
SALES (est): 615.96K Privately Held
SIC: 4813 Online service providers

(G-19859)
SKYPHER INC
1007 N Orange St (19801-1239)
PHONE.................................510 570-5843
Gaspard Vaubois, *CEO*
EMP: 10
SALES (est): 355.79K Privately Held
SIC: 7382 Security systems services

(G-19860)
SKYWORLD TRAVELER INC
1013 Centre Rd Ste 403s (19805-1270)
PHONE.................................844 591-9060
Antonio Parker, *Owner*
EMP: 10 EST: 2018
SALES (est): 608.57K Privately Held
Web: sky-world-traveler.business.site
SIC: 4724 Travel agencies

(G-19861)
SLATER FIREPLACES INC
Also Called: The Basement Shirt Co.
1726 Newport Gap Pike (19808-6120)
PHONE.................................302 999-1200
Kenneth R Slater, *Pr*
Christine Lashley, *VP*
Steven Slater, *Stockholder*
Colleen Slater, *Treas*
EMP: 7 EST: 1973
SALES (est): 963.31K Privately Held
Web: www.fireplaceshoppede.com
SIC: 5719 7349 5699 Fireplace equipment and accessories; Janitorial service, contract basis; T-shirts, custom printed

(G-19862)
SLAYBELLES LLC ◆
4737 Concord Pike (19803-1442)
PHONE.................................302 304-1027
EMP: 7 EST: 2022
SALES (est): 307.81K Privately Held
SIC: 3161 7389 Clothing and apparel carrying cases; Business Activities at Non-Commercial Site

(G-19863)
SLEEPY COACH INC
919 N Market St (19801-3023)
PHONE.................................310 372-5770
Artem Zhuravlev, *Pr*
EMP: 7 EST: 2021
SALES (est): 264.9K Privately Held
SIC: 7371 Computer software development and applications

(G-19864)
SLICE COMMUNICATIONS LLC
112 S French St (19801-5035)
PHONE.................................215 600-0050
Cassandra Bailey, *CEO*
EMP: 10 EST: 2010
SALES (est): 4.87MM Privately Held
Web: www.slicecommunications.com
SIC: 8743 Public relations and publicity
HQ: Metro Corp.
170 S Indpdnc Mall W # 201
Philadelphia PA 19106
215 564-7700

(G-19865)
SLICE GLOBAL INC (PA)
251 Little Falls Dr (19808-1674)
PHONE.................................415 801-6537
Maor Levran, *CEO*
EMP: 5
SALES (est): 283.06K
SALES (corp-wide): 283.06K Privately Held
SIC: 7379 Online services technology consultants

(G-19866)
SLIMSTIM INC
1209 N Orange St (19801-1120)
PHONE.................................310 560-4950
Jeff Brennan, *Pr*
EMP: 3 EST: 2008
SALES (est): 275.28K Privately Held
SIC: 3845 Electromedical equipment

(G-19867)
SLURRY PAVEMENT SYSTEMS
700 Cornell Dr Ste E17 (19801-5798)
PHONE.................................609 500-3828
EMP: 8 EST: 2016
SALES (est): 337.03K Privately Held
Web: www.fixasphalt.com
SIC: 1611 Surfacing and paving

(G-19868)
SM SNACKS LLC
205 Woodrow Ave (19803-2563)
PHONE.................................973 229-2845
Steven Miller, *Prin*
EMP: 5 EST: 2019
SALES (est): 365.89K Privately Held
SIC: 5199 Nondurable goods, nec

(G-19869)
SM TECHNOMINE INC
19c Trolley Sq (19806-3355)
PHONE.................................312 492-4386
Dave Pise, *Mgr*
EMP: 10
SALES (corp-wide): 5.53MM Privately Held
Web: www.smtechnomine.com
SIC: 7389 Telemarketing services
PA: Sm Technomine Inc.
802 N West St
Wilmington DE 19801
312 492-4386

(G-19870)
SM TECHNOMINE INC (PA)
802 N West St (19801-1526)
PHONE.................................312 492-4386
Sanket Modi, *CEO*
EMP: 10 EST: 2011
SALES (est): 5.53MM
SALES (corp-wide): 5.53MM Privately Held
Web: www.smtechnomine.com
SIC: 8732 7389 7371 7379 Market analysis or research; Telemarketing services; Software programming applications; Online services technology consultants

(G-19871)
SMAKKFITNESS LLC
410 N Market St (19801-3003)
PHONE.................................800 417-2558
La'marqus Collins, *Managing Member*
EMP: 5 EST: 2018
SALES (est): 111K Privately Held
SIC: 7991 Physical fitness facilities

(G-19872)
SMALL WONDER DAY CARE INC
100 Greenhill Ave Ste A (19805-1863)
PHONE.................................302 654-2269
Kim Markooni, *Dir*
EMP: 11 EST: 1989
SALES (est): 117.51K Privately Held
Web: www.smallwonderdaycareinc.com
SIC: 8351 Group day care center

(G-19873)
SMALLS REAL ESTATE COMPANY
5227 W Woodmill Dr Ste 42 (19808-4068)
PHONE.................................302 633-1985
EMP: 10 EST: 1995
SALES (est): 625.38K Privately Held
SIC: 6531 Real estate brokers and agents

(G-19874)
SMALLS STEPPING STONE
1408 Clifford Brown Walk (19801-3128)
PHONE.................................302 652-3011
Clara Smalls, *Owner*
EMP: 10 EST: 1988
SQ FT: 5,300
SALES (est): 458.63K Privately Held
Web: www.steppingstonedaycare.nl

Wilmington - New Castle County (G-19902)

SIC: 8351 Preschool center

(G-19875)
SMART 360 CO
Also Called: Smart 360 Biz
3 Germay Dr Ste 4 (19804-1127)
PHONE..................................617 657-4360
Karsten Voges, *CEO*
EMP: 2 EST: 2013
SALES (est): 149.47K **Privately Held**
Web: www.smart360.biz
SIC: 7372 Business oriented computer software

(G-19876)
SMART CHOICE HV/AC SVCS LLC
31 Dartmouth Rd (19808-4633)
PHONE..................................302 250-5762
Evan Girtain, *Prin*
EMP: 5 EST: 2017
SALES (est): 113.61K **Privately Held**
SIC: 1711 Mechanical contractor

(G-19877)
SMART HOSPITALITY & MGT LLC
Also Called: Smart
3411 Silverside Rd (19810-4812)
PHONE..................................212 444-1989
David Friedland, *Pr*
EMP: 7 EST: 2013
SQ FT: 1,100
SALES (est): 153.68K **Privately Held**
SIC: 7389 Hotel and motel reservation service

(G-19878)
SMART INVEST YAM LLC
1521 Concord Pike Ste 301 (19803-3644)
PHONE..................................302 721-5278
Cris Daniel Dubon, *Mgr*
EMP: 6 EST: 2021
SALES (est): 123.52K **Privately Held**
SIC: 7371 Software programming applications

(G-19879)
SMART START
100 Greenhill Ave (19805-1861)
PHONE..................................302 256-5104
EMP: 13 EST: 2019
SALES (est): 22.91K **Privately Held**
Web: www.newhanoverkids.org
SIC: 8351 Child day care services

(G-19880)
SMART TAX FREE RTRMENT HM OF I
205 Philadelphia Pike (19809-3159)
PHONE..................................302 472-4897
EMP: 5 EST: 2018
SALES (est): 18.45K **Privately Held**
Web: www.smarttaxfreeretirement.com
SIC: 7291 Tax return preparation services

(G-19881)
SMARTCARD MKTG SYSTEMS INC
20c Trolley Sq (19806-3355)
PHONE..................................844 843-7296
Massimo Barone, *Prin*
EMP: 9 EST: 2006
SALES (est): 521.08K **Privately Held**
SIC: 7372 Prepackaged software

(G-19882)
SMARTCOOKIEWIFI INC
2055 Limestone Rd 200c (19808-5536)
PHONE..................................424 205-4350
Adrien Laurent, *CEO*
Maxime Laurent, *COO*
EMP: 2 EST: 2021
SALES (est): 56.54K **Privately Held**

(G-19883)
SME MASONRY CONTRS LTD LBLTY
1205 Bruce Rd (19803-4201)
PHONE..................................302 743-7338
EMP: 10 EST: 2012
SALES (est): 449.73K **Privately Held**
Web: www.smecontractors.com
SIC: 1741 1611 7389 Masonry and other stonework; Concrete construction: roads, highways, sidewalks, etc.; Business Activities at Non-Commercial Site

(G-19884)
SMILE SOLUTIONS BY EMMI DENTAL
1601 Milltown Rd Ste 25 (19808-4084)
PHONE..................................302 999-8113
Jeffrey Emmi, *Prin*
EMP: 7 EST: 2010
SALES (est): 911.2K **Privately Held**
Web: www.smilesolutionsbyemmidental.com
SIC: 8021 Dentists' office

(G-19885)
SMILEBACK LLC
427 N Tatnall St Ste 64120 (19801)
PHONE..................................646 401-0024
Brad Benner, *Managing Member*
EMP: 10 EST: 2014
SALES (est): 822.52K
SALES (corp-wide): 105.88MM **Privately Held**
Web: www.smileback.com
SIC: 7372 Prepackaged software
PA: Connectwise Intermediate Holdings Ii, Inc.
400 N Tampa St Ste 130
Tampa FL 33602
813 463-4700

(G-19886)
SMITH & NEPHEW HOLDINGS INC (DH)
1201 N Orange St Ste 788 (19801-1173)
PHONE..................................302 884-6720
Cliff Lomax, *Pr*
▲ EMP: 25 EST: 1996
SALES (est): 701.36MM
SALES (corp-wide): 5.21B **Privately Held**
SIC: 5047 3841 Medical equipment and supplies; Surgical and medical instruments
HQ: Smith & Nephew (Overseas) Limited
15 Adam Street
London WC2N

(G-19887)
SMITH BILL CONCRETE MASNRY LLC
200 Belmont Ave (19804-1407)
PHONE..................................302 250-4312
EMP: 5 EST: 2012
SALES (est): 144.85K **Privately Held**
SIC: 1771 Concrete work

(G-19888)
SMITH HEALTH & LIFE LLC
4023 Kennett Pike Ste 106 (19807-2018)
PHONE..................................302 596-0641
Sylvia Redic, *Managing Member*
EMP: 6
SALES (est): 75.63K **Privately Held**
SIC: 6411 Life insurance agents

(G-19889)
SMITH HOME IMPROVEMENTS
2239 E Huntington Dr (19808-4952)
PHONE..................................302 998-8294
Richard Smith, *Prin*

EMP: 5 EST: 2011
SALES (est): 161.19K **Privately Held**
SIC: 1521 Single-family housing construction

(G-19890)
SMITH KATZENSTEIN & FURLOW LLP
1000 N West St Ste 1500 (19801-1054)
P.O. Box 410 (19899-0410)
PHONE..................................302 652-8400
Craig B Smith, *Pt*
Robert J Katzenstein, *Pt*
Clark W Furlow, *Pt*
David A Jenkins, *Pt*
Susan L Parker, *Pt*
EMP: 35 EST: 1984
SALES (est): 5.19MM **Privately Held**
Web: www.skjlaw.com
SIC: 8111 General practice attorney, lawyer

(G-19891)
SMITH-JONES SOCIETY ✪
1207 Delaware Ave Ste 636 (19806-4743)
PHONE..................................302 203-9702
Mitchellie Verzonilla, *Sec*
EMP: 5 EST: 2022
SALES (est): 529K **Privately Held**
SIC: 6732 Trusts: educational, religious, etc.

(G-19892)
SMITHKLINE BCHAM PHRMCEUTICALS
Also Called: Glaxo Smithkline Beecham
1403 Foulk Rd Ste 102 (19803-2788)
PHONE..................................302 984-6932
Kenneth Kerms, *CEO*
EMP: 15 EST: 1984
SALES (corp-wide): 35.31B **Privately Held**
SIC: 6719 Investment holding companies, except banks
PA: Gsk Plc
G S K House
Brentford MIDDX TW8 9
208 047-5000

(G-19893)
SMITHKLINE BEECHAM INTL CO
1403 Foulk Rd Ste 106 (19803-2788)
PHONE..................................302 479-5804
Kenneth Kermes, *Pr*
EMP: 23 EST: 1997
SALES (est): 1.73MM
SALES (corp-wide): 35.31B **Privately Held**
SIC: 2834 Pharmaceutical preparations
HQ: Glaxosmithkline Llc
2929 Walnut St Ste 1700
Philadelphia PA 19104
888 825-5249

(G-19894)
SMITHS GARAGE DOORS EXPERT
3600 Miller Rd (19802-2524)
PHONE..................................302 803-5337
Steve Roberts, *Owner*
EMP: 6 EST: 2017
SALES (est): 87.92K **Privately Held**
Web: box6168.bluehost.com
SIC: 1751 Garage door, installation or erection

(G-19895)
SMITHS JACK TOWING & SVC CTR
Also Called: Jack Smith Towing
1806 Philadelphia Pike (19809-1545)
PHONE..................................302 798-6667
Thomas Smith, *Pr*
Jim Smith, *VP*
EMP: 7 EST: 1927
SQ FT: 1,500
SALES (est): 926.59K **Privately Held**

Web: www.jacksmithstowingandservice.com
SIC: 7538 7549 General automotive repair shops; Towing services

(G-19896)
SMOGARD & ASSOCIATES LLC
310 Falco Dr Ste G (19804-2447)
PHONE..................................302 353-4717
EMP: 5 EST: 2010
SALES (est): 147.53K **Privately Held**
SIC: 1742 Drywall

(G-19897)
SMOOTH MVES ELITE MVG SVCS LLC
413 Mccabe Ave (19802-4048)
PHONE..................................302 521-0973
EMP: 8 EST: 2018
SALES (est): 339.82K **Privately Held**
SIC: 4212 Moving services

(G-19898)
SMS CONTRACTING
1221 Ipswich Dr (19808-3031)
PHONE..................................610 721-9943
Kristyn Dangelo Smith, *Prin*
EMP: 10 EST: 2012
SALES (est): 114.13K **Privately Held**
Web: www.smscontracting.com
SIC: 1799 Special trade contractors, nec

(G-19899)
SNAPIFY CORP
300 Delaware Ave Fl 3 (19801-1699)
PHONE..................................646 814-6388
Ran Ceo, *CEO*
EMP: 10
SALES (est): 348.32K **Privately Held**
SIC: 7371 Computer software development

(G-19900)
SNIPER LABS INC ✪
2055 Limestone Rd Ste 200c (19808-5536)
PHONE..................................925 321-0931
EMP: 10 EST: 2022
SALES (est): 348.32K **Privately Held**
Web: www.sniper.xyz
SIC: 7371 Software programming applications

(G-19901)
SNOW & ASSOC GEN CNSTR CO LLC ✪
510 Milton Dr (19802-1115)
PHONE..................................302 420-0564
EMP: 10 EST: 2022
SALES (est): 406.52K **Privately Held**
SIC: 1741 7389 Marble masonry, exterior construction; Business Activities at Non-Commercial Site

(G-19902)
SNTC HOLDING INC (DH)
919 N Market St Ste 200 (19801-3068)
PHONE..................................302 777-5261
Martin J Wygod, *Prin*
EMP: 14 EST: 2001
SALES (est): 90.24MM
SALES (corp-wide): 995.07MM **Privately Held**
SIC: 6371 Union welfare, benefit, and health funds
HQ: Webmd Health Corp.
395 Hudson St Fl 3
New York NY 10014

Wilmington - New Castle County (G-19903)

(G-19903)
SNYDER & COMPANY PA
Also Called: Dennis H Snyder Assoc
1405 Silverside Rd (19810-4445)
P.O. Box 9506 (19809-0506)
PHONE..................302 475-1600
EMP: 10 **EST:** 1982
SALES (est): 962.91K **Privately Held**
Web: www.snydercpa.com
SIC: 8721 Certified public accountant

(G-19904)
SNYDER ASSOCIATES PA
Also Called: Snyder & Associates
300 Delaware Ave Ste 1014 (19801-1671)
P.O. Box 90 (19899-0090)
PHONE..................302 657-8300
EMP: 5 **EST:** 1996
SALES (est): 340.85K **Privately Held**
Web: www.snyderlaw.pro
SIC: 8111 General practice law office

(G-19905)
SO HAIR AND BEAUTY SUPPLY
304 N Union St (19805-3432)
PHONE..................302 407-3381
Tia Parks, *Prin*
EMP: 5 **EST:** 2014
SALES (est): 122.67K **Privately Held**
SIC: 5122 Cosmetics, perfumes, and hair products

(G-19906)
SOBIESKI FIRE PROTECTION LLC
16 Hadco Rd (19804-1014)
PHONE..................302 993-0600
John F Sobieski Iii, *CEO*
EMP: 180 **EST:** 2012
SALES (est): 244.69K
SALES (corp-wide): 43.62MM **Privately Held**
Web: www.sobieskiinc.com
SIC: 1731 Fire detection and burglar alarm systems specialization
PA: J F Sobieski Mechanical Contractors, Inc.
14 Hadco Rd
Wilmington DE 19804
302 993-0103

(G-19907)
SOCIAL CONTRACT LLC
1313 N Market St (19801-6101)
PHONE..................302 357-5193
EMP: 30 **EST:** 2018
SALES (est): 5.84MM **Privately Held**
Web: www.socialcontract.org
SIC: 1799 Special trade contractors, nec

(G-19908)
SOCIAL WONDER INC
1007 N Orange St Fl 10 (19801-1239)
PHONE..................646 419-8009
Dan Bendler, *Pr*
EMP: 10
SALES (est): 498.83K **Privately Held**
Web: www.social-wonder.com
SIC: 7371 7389 Software programming applications; Business Activities at Non-Commercial Site

(G-19909)
SOCIALCASH INC
1209 N Orange St (19801-1120)
PHONE..................310 293-6072
Paul Taylor, *CEO*
EMP: 10 **EST:** 2017
SALES (est): 334.68K **Privately Held**
SIC: 7389 Financial services

(G-19910)
SOCRATICLAW CO INC
3900 Centerville Rd (19807-1939)
PHONE..................302 654-9191
Wade Scott, *Pr*
Shrew Dury, *Prin*
EMP: 2 **EST:** 2000
SALES (est): 59.38K **Privately Held**
SIC: 2741 Miscellaneous publishing

(G-19911)
SODAT - DELAWARE INC (PA)
625 N Orange St Fl 2 (19801-2296)
PHONE..................302 656-2810
Aron Shapiro, *Pr*
Eric Saul, *Ex Dir*
EMP: 13 **EST:** 1971
SALES (est): 555.67K
SALES (corp-wide): 555.67K **Privately Held**
Web: www.sodatdelaware.com
SIC: 8093 Alcohol clinic, outpatient

(G-19912)
SODRA CELL USA INC
1209 N Orange St (19801-1120)
PHONE..................503 855-3032
Bob Jank, *Pr*
EMP: 3 **EST:** 2021
SALES (est): 216.48K **Privately Held**
SIC: 2611 Pulp mills

(G-19913)
SOFT LIFE BEAUTY SUITE LLC ○
2801 Lancaster Ave (19805-5232)
PHONE..................267 496-7655
Janelle Brown, *Managing Member*
EMP: 2 **EST:** 2023
SALES (est): 92.41K **Privately Held**
SIC: 3999 Hair and hair-based products

(G-19914)
SOFTLINN LLC
251 Little Falls Dr (19808-1674)
PHONE..................718 926-2170
Mesut Duman, *Mgr*
EMP: 5 **EST:** 2021
SALES (est): 107.01K **Privately Held**
Web: www.softlinn.com
SIC: 7371 Computer software development

(G-19915)
SOFTWARE SERVICES OF DE INC (PA)
Also Called: Ssd Technology Partners
1024 Justison St (19801-5148)
PHONE..................302 654-3172
Barbara Hines, *Pr*
Nancy Froome, *VP*
EMP: 37 **EST:** 1983
SQ FT: 10,000
SALES (est): 23.37MM
SALES (corp-wide): 23.37MM **Privately Held**
Web: www.sourcepass.com
SIC: 5734 7378 7371 Modems, monitors, terminals, and disk drives: computers; Computer maintenance and repair; Custom computer programming services

(G-19916)
SOIREE FACTORY
404 Rogers Rd (19801-5749)
PHONE..................302 275-6576
Chimere Bowe, *Prin*
EMP: 5 **EST:** 2016
SALES (est): 39.77K **Privately Held**
Web: www.soireefactory.com
SIC: 7299 Party planning service

(G-19917)
SOJOURNERS PLACE INC
Also Called: SOJOURNERS' PLACE
2901 Governor Printz Blvd (19802-3705)
P.O. Box 2845 (19805-0845)
PHONE..................302 764-4592
Eric Harris, *Ex Dir*
Pat Kennerly, *Bookkpr*
EMP: 9 **EST:** 1991
SALES (est): 533.58K **Privately Held**
Web: www.sojournersplace.org
SIC: 8322 Emergency shelters

(G-19918)
SOLA SALON STUDIOS
5321 Brandywine Pkwy (19803-1471)
PHONE..................302 283-9216
EMP: 5 **EST:** 2017
SALES (est): 80.28K **Privately Held**
Web: www.solasalonstudios.com
SIC: 7231 Hairdressers

(G-19919)
SOLARI COMMERCIAL PRPTS LLC
3 Valmy Ln (19807-2255)
PHONE..................302 757-2956
EMP: 5 **EST:** 2016
SALES (est): 204.28K **Privately Held**
SIC: 6512 Nonresidential building operators

(G-19920)
SOLENIS HOLDINGS 1 LLC (PA)
3 Beaver Valley Rd Ste 500 (19803-1124)
PHONE..................866 337-1533
EMP: 16 **EST:** 2014
SALES (est): 79.96MM
SALES (corp-wide): 79.96MM **Privately Held**
Web: www.solenis.com
SIC: 2899 Sizes

(G-19921)
SOLENIS HOLDINGS 3 LLC
3 Beaver Valley Rd Ste 500 (19803-1124)
PHONE..................866 337-1533
EMP: 3766 **EST:** 2014
SALES (est): 77.68MM
SALES (corp-wide): 79.96MM **Privately Held**
Web: www.solenis.com
SIC: 5169 Chemicals and allied products, nec
PA: Solenis Holdings 1 Llc
3 Beaver Valley Rd # 500
Wilmington DE 19803
866 337-1533

(G-19922)
SOLENIS LLC (PA)
Also Called: Solenis
2475 Pinnacle Dr (19803-3700)
PHONE..................866 337-1533
John Panichella, *CEO*
Philip M Patterson Junior, *Sr VP*
Robert P Baird, *
▼ **EMP:** 350 **EST:** 2014
SQ FT: 40,000
SALES (est): 1.15B
SALES (corp-wide): 1.15B **Privately Held**
Web: www.solenis.com
SIC: 5169 Chemicals and allied products, nec

(G-19923)
SOLENIS LLC
Also Called: Ashland Water Technologies
500 Hercules Rd (19808-1513)
PHONE..................302 594-5000
EMP: 498
SALES (corp-wide): 1.15B **Privately Held**
Web: www.solenis.com
SIC: 5169 Chemicals and allied products, nec
PA: Solenis Llc
2475 Pinnacle Dr
Wilmington DE 19803
866 337-1533

(G-19924)
SOLO GLOBAL INC ○
2810 N Church St Ste 78363 (19802-4447)
PHONE..................302 307-1673
EMP: 6 **EST:** 2022
SALES (est): 261.63K **Privately Held**
Web: us.solo.global
SIC: 7371 Computer software development and applications

(G-19925)
SOLUFY CORP
1201 N Orange St Ste 7228 (19801-1233)
PHONE..................877 476-5839
Mario Boileau, *Prin*
Gerry Lamarche, *Prin*
Matthew Midas, *Prin*
EMP: 26 **EST:** 2017
SALES (est): 886.45K **Privately Held**
SIC: 7372 Prepackaged software

(G-19926)
SOLUTION SEEKER CONS LLC
14 S Union St Ste 109 (19805-3865)
PHONE..................347 230-8558
Kerroll Barnes, *Managing Member*
EMP: 5
SALES (est): 252K **Privately Held**
SIC: 8742 7389 Marketing consulting services; Business services, nec

(G-19927)
SOLVETECH INC
1711 Philadelphia Pike (19809-1568)
P.O. Box 9245 (19809-0245)
PHONE..................302 798-5400
Douglas C Lawrence, *Pr*
EMP: 9 **EST:** 1981
SQ FT: 2,000
SALES (est): 983.73K **Privately Held**
Web: www.gauging.com
SIC: 3829 Gauging instruments, thickness ultrasonic

(G-19928)
SOMA BREATH INC
1013 Centre Rd Ste 403b (19805-1270)
PHONE..................415 633-5359
Niraj Naik, *Pr*
EMP: 26 **EST:** 2019
SALES (est): 467.45K **Privately Held**
SIC: 8082 Home health care services

(G-19929)
SOPRANO DESIGN LIMITED
Also Called: Soprano Design Ltd
510 Silverside Rd (19809-1318)
P.O. Box 3161 (98083-3161)
PHONE..................206 446-4401
Mohamed Odah, *Admn*
Mohamed Odah, *Prin*
EMP: 10 **EST:** 2010
SALES (est): 1.14MM **Privately Held**
Web: www.sopranodesign.com
SIC: 4822 Telegraph and other communications
PA: Soprano Design Pty Ltd
L 15 132 Arthur St
North Sydney NSW 2060

GEOGRAPHIC SECTION
Wilmington - New Castle County (G-19956)

(G-19930)
SOS SECURITY INCORPORATED
1000 N West St Ste 200 (19801-1052)
PHONE..............................302 425-4755
Michael Wieland, *Mgr*
EMP: 8
SALES (corp-wide): 51.62MM **Privately Held**
Web: www.sossecurity.com
SIC: 7381 Security guard service
PA: Sos Security Incorporated
1915 Us Highway 46 Ste 1
Parsippany NJ 07054
973 402-6600

(G-19931)
SOSA ELOY
Also Called: E S Tile
1331 Greenleaf Rd (19805-1318)
PHONE..............................302 275-3792
EMP: 5 **EST:** 2009
SALES (est): 233.15K **Privately Held**
SIC: 1743 Tile installation, ceramic

(G-19932)
SOUND BODY PRODUCTS LLC
5 Coachman Ct (19803-1901)
PHONE..............................302 660-2296
Heather D Marshall, *Prin*
EMP: 5 **EST:** 2017
SALES (est): 96.15K **Privately Held**
SIC: 1731 Sound equipment specialization

(G-19933)
SOUND MASTER DJ
2508 Nicholby Dr (19808-4213)
PHONE..............................302 998-8235
Thomas Boone, *Prin*
EMP: 5 **EST:** 2010
SALES (est): 83.02K **Privately Held**
SIC: 1731 Sound equipment specialization

(G-19934)
SOUND SOLUTIONS
1000 N West St Ste 1200 (19801-1058)
PHONE..............................302 650-0950
EMP: 5 **EST:** 2012
SALES (est): 246.09K **Privately Held**
SIC: 1731 Sound equipment specialization

(G-19935)
SOUNDBOKS INC (PA)
2711 Centerville Rd Ste 400 (19808-1660)
PHONE..............................213 436-5888
Jesper Theil Thomsen, *CEO*
Hjalte Wieth, *Dir*
Christoffer Nyvold, *COO*
EMP: 5 **EST:** 2015
SQ FT: 300
SALES (est): 1.22MM
SALES (corp-wide): 1.22MM **Privately Held**
Web: www.soundboks.com
SIC: 3651 Speaker systems

(G-19936)
SOUNDINGBOARD PROJECT
4023 Kennett Pike (19807-2018)
PHONE..............................302 956-1112
EMP: 6 **EST:** 2018
SALES (est): 76.47K **Privately Held**
SIC: 8093 Specialty outpatient clinics, nec

(G-19937)
SOUTHBRDGE MED ADVSORY COUNCIL (PA)
Also Called: HENRIETTA JOHNSON MEDICAL CENT
601 New Castle Ave (19801-5821)
PHONE..............................302 655-6187
Rosa Rivera-prado, *CEO*
Allie Sethman, *CFO*
EMP: 23 **EST:** 1970
SQ FT: 15,000
SALES (est): 5.48MM
SALES (corp-wide): 5.48MM **Privately Held**
Web: www.hjmc.org
SIC: 8011 Primary care medical clinic

(G-19938)
SOUTHCO
2207 Coventry Dr (19810-3921)
PHONE..............................302 475-2140
EMP: 7 **EST:** 2018
SALES (est): 63.78K **Privately Held**
Web: www.southco.com
SIC: 5072 Hardware

(G-19939)
SOUTHERN CRAB COMPANY
2831 Kennedy Rd (19810-3446)
PHONE..............................302 478-0181
Barry Lamb, *Pt*
Vincent Mai, *Treas*
Patrick O'sullivan, *VP*
EMP: 6 **EST:** 1995
SQ FT: 200,000
SALES (est): 236.65K **Privately Held**
SIC: 5146 Seafoods

(G-19940)
SOUTHWEST AMERICAN CORP
Also Called: Sun West Homes
2200 N Grant Ave (19806-2240)
PHONE..............................302 652-7003
Edward Bauer, *Pr*
EMP: 6 **EST:** 2000
SALES (est): 411.04K **Privately Held**
SIC: 6798 Real estate investment trusts

(G-19941)
SOUTHWORKS LLC ✪
200 Bellevue Pkwy (19809-3727)
PHONE..............................302 295-5008
Martin Cacciola, *Managing Member*
EMP: 5 **EST:** 2023
SALES (est): 62.08K **Privately Held**
SIC: 7379 Computer related services, nec

(G-19942)
SOVEREIGN DEALER FINANCE INC
103 Foulk Rd (19803-3742)
PHONE..............................302 691-6139
EMP: 5 **EST:** 2007
SALES (est): 84K **Privately Held**
SIC: 7389 Personal service agents, brokers, and bureaus

(G-19943)
SOVEREIGN PROPERTY MGT LLC
Also Called: Arbor Pointe Rental Co
102 Larch Cir Ste 301 (19804-2371)
PHONE..............................302 994-2505
Christopher Sipe, *Brnch Mgr*
EMP: 45
SALES (corp-wide): 4.71MM **Privately Held**
Web: www.sovproperties.com
SIC: 6512 Nonresidential building operators
PA: Sovereign Property Management, Llc
102 Robino Ct Ste 101
Wilmington DE 19804
302 994-2505

(G-19944)
SOVEREIGN PROPERTY MGT LLC (PA)
102 Robino Ct Ste 101 (19804-2360)
PHONE..............................302 994-2505
Mary L Cornelius, *Managing Member*
EMP: 6 **EST:** 2009
SALES (est): 7.36MM
SALES (corp-wide): 7.36MM **Privately Held**
Web: www.sovproperties.com
SIC: 8741 Business management

(G-19945)
SOVEREIGNTACTICAL LLC
3 Germay Dr Ste 4 (19804-1127)
PHONE..............................858 336-9471
EMP: 6 **EST:** 2020
SALES (est): 344.69K **Privately Held**
SIC: 3281 Household articles, except furniture: cut stone

(G-19946)
SP HOLDING DPS INC (HQ)
974 Centre Rd (19805-1269)
PHONE..............................302 999-2806
EMP: 9 **EST:** 2017
SALES (est): 1.01MM
SALES (corp-wide): 13.02B **Publicly Held**
SIC: 7389
PA: Dupont De Nemours, Inc.
974 Centre Rd Bldg 730
Wilmington DE 19805
302 774-3034

(G-19947)
SP HOLDING ET LLC (HQ)
974 Centre Rd (19805-1269)
PHONE..............................302 999-4083
EMP: 7 **EST:** 2017
SALES (est): 667.98K
SALES (corp-wide): 13.02B **Publicly Held**
SIC: 0721 Crop planting and protection
PA: Dupont De Nemours, Inc.
974 Centre Rd Bldg 730
Wilmington DE 19805
302 774-3034

(G-19948)
SP HOLDING IB INC (HQ)
974 Centre Rd (19805-1269)
PHONE..............................302 999-4083
EMP: 7 **EST:** 2017
SALES (est): 790.17K
SALES (corp-wide): 13.02B **Publicly Held**
SIC: 0721 Crop planting and protection
PA: Dupont De Nemours, Inc.
974 Centre Rd Bldg 730
Wilmington DE 19805
302 774-3034

(G-19949)
SP PLUS CORPORATION
111 W 11th St Lowr (19801-1225)
PHONE..............................302 652-1410
Tim Meyer, *Mgr*
EMP: 6
SALES (corp-wide): 1.55B **Publicly Held**
Web: www.spplus.com
SIC: 7521 Parking lots
PA: Sp Plus Corporation
8037 Collection Center Dr
Chicago IL 60693
312 274-2000

(G-19950)
SPACE HAPPENS GAME
2003 Grant Ave (19809-1418)
PHONE..............................302 563-1949
Daniel Bandekow, *Prin*
EMP: 5 **EST:** 2016
SALES (est): 20.78K **Privately Held**
SIC: 7999 Amusement and recreation, nec

(G-19951)
SPARKIA INC
2711 Centerville Rd # 400 (19808-1660)
PHONE..............................302 636-5440
Pablo Martinez, *CEO*
Karlo Rodriguez, *Prin*
EMP: 5 **EST:** 2014
SALES (est): 168.21K **Privately Held**
SIC: 8732 Business analysis

(G-19952)
SPEAK BIZ CONSULTING LLC
3 Germay Dr Ste 4 (19804-1127)
PHONE..............................302 272-9294
Jazmine Frisby, *Pr*
EMP: 10 **EST:** 2021
SALES (est): 700K **Privately Held**
SIC: 8742 Management consulting services

(G-19953)
SPECIAL CARE INC
Also Called: Griswold Special Care
5145 W Woodmill Dr # 22 (19808-4067)
PHONE..............................302 456-9904
Mary Ann Murray, *Brnch Mgr*
EMP: 7
SALES (corp-wide): 22.56MM **Privately Held**
Web: www.griswoldsa.com
SIC: 8082 Home health care services
PA: Special Care, Inc.
800 Bethlehem Pike
Glenside PA 19038
215 402-0200

(G-19954)
SPECIALTY PRODUCTS N&H INC (HQ)
974 Centre Rd (19805-1269)
PHONE..............................302 774-1000
Micheal P Heffernan, *Pr*
Michael P Heffernan, *Pr*
Andrew R Girardi, *VP*
James P Donaghey, *VP*
Calissa W Brown, *Asst VP*
EMP: 109 **EST:** 2017
SALES (est): 23.2MM
SALES (corp-wide): 12.44B **Publicly Held**
Web: www.dupont.com
SIC: 2879 2824 Agricultural chemicals, nec; Nylon fibers
PA: International Flavors & Fragrances Inc.
521 W 57th St
New York NY 10019
212 765-5500

(G-19955)
SPECIALTY PRODUCTS US LLC
974 Centre Rd (19805-1269)
PHONE..............................302 774-1000
Mark A Bachman, *Pr*
EMP: 21 **EST:** 2018
SALES (est): 4.75MM
SALES (corp-wide): 12.44B **Publicly Held**
SIC: 2821 2869 Plastics materials and resins; Industrial organic chemicals, nec
PA: International Flavors & Fragrances Inc.
521 W 57th St
New York NY 10019
212 765-5500

(G-19956)
SPECIALTY PRODUCTS US LLC
1209 S Orange St (19801)
PHONE..............................212 765-5500
EMP: 5 **EST:** 2018
SALES (est): 141.24K **Privately Held**
SIC: 7389 Business services, nec

(PA)=Parent Co (HQ)=Headquarters
✪ = New Business established in last 2 years

Wilmington - New Castle County (G-19957)

(G-19957)
SPEDAG AMERICAS INC
2711 Centerville Rd (19808-1660)
PHONE.................................201 857-3471
Kurt Diener, *Prin*
EMP: 5 EST: 2015
SALES (est): 244.44K **Privately Held**
Web: www.mrspedag.com
SIC: 4731 Freight forwarding

(G-19958)
SPEECH & LANGUAGE FOR KIDS LLC
1910 Dorcas Ln (19806-1164)
PHONE.................................847 852-0928
Jennifer Less, *Prin*
EMP: 5 EST: 2018
SALES (est): 142.98K **Privately Held**
Web: www.speechlanguagekids.com
SIC: 8641 Youth organizations

(G-19959)
SPEECH CLINIC
5147 W Woodmill Dr Ste 21 (19808-4067)
PHONE.................................302 999-0702
John Azzara, *Dir*
EMP: 14 EST: 1986
SALES (est): 959.24K **Privately Held**
Web: www.speechclinicinc.com
SIC: 8049 Speech pathologist

(G-19960)
SPENCE HOLDING
300 Martin Luther King Blvd Ste 200 (19801-2437)
PHONE.................................973 392-1218
Lanesa Spence, *Pr*
EMP: 12 EST: 2017
SALES (est): 573.25K **Privately Held**
SIC: 8748 Business consulting, nec

(G-19961)
SPI HOLDING COMPANY
Also Called: SPI Pharma
503 Carr Rd Ste 210 (19809-2864)
PHONE.................................800 789-9755
EMP: 43 EST: 1994
SALES (est): 7.27MM
SALES (corp-wide): 24.92B **Privately Held**
Web: www.spipharma.com
SIC: 2869 Sweeteners, synthetic
PA: Associated British Foods Plc
    10 Grosvenor Street
    London W1K 4
    792 607-9543

(G-19962)
SPI PHARMA INC (HQ)
Also Called: SPI Pharma
503 Carr Rd Ste 210 (19809-2864)
PHONE.................................800 789-9755
Scott Thomson, *CEO*
▼ EMP: 50 EST: 1964
SALES (est): 126.09MM
SALES (corp-wide): 24.92B **Privately Held**
Web: www.spipharma.com
SIC: 5122 Pharmaceuticals
PA: Associated British Foods Plc
    10 Grosvenor Street
    London W1K 4
    792 607-9543

(G-19963)
SPINAL HEALTH & WELLNESS
3105 Limestone Road Ste 303 (19808-2156)
PHONE.................................302 993-9113
Timothy J Ciolkosz, *Owner*
EMP: 6 EST: 2016
SALES (est): 240.63K **Privately Held**
Web: www.famchirode.com
SIC: 8099 Health and allied services, nec

(G-19964)
SPINE GROUP LLC
1426 N Clayton St (19806-4006)
PHONE.................................302 595-3030
Damon Cary, *Managing Member*
EMP: 9 EST: 2012
SALES (est): 559.87K **Privately Held**
Web: www.thespinegroupdelaware.com
SIC: 8748 8011 Business consulting, nec; Offices and clinics of medical doctors

(G-19965)
SPINWIZARDS DJS
434 E 35th St (19802-2816)
PHONE.................................302 252-1727
Kevin Mason, *Prin*
EMP: 5 EST: 2017
SALES (est): 59.02K **Privately Held**
SIC: 7929 Entertainers and entertainment groups

(G-19966)
SPIRE INNOVATIONS INC
Also Called: Spire Tech Sltions Private Ltd
1013 Centre Rd Ste 4038 (19805-1265)
PHONE.................................646 583-1839
Saurabh Jain, *CEO*
EMP: 55 EST: 2014
SQ FT: 5,500
SALES (est): 4.51MM **Privately Held**
SIC: 7371 Computer software development
PA: Spire Technologies And Solutions Private Limited
    Umiya Business Bay, Tower-1
    Bengaluru KA 56003

(G-19967)
SPIRELIO INC
831 N Tatnall St Ste M # 109 (19801)
PHONE.................................302 467-3444
Alexander Mifsud Bonici, *CEO*
EMP: 5 EST: 2020
SALES (est): 114.11K **Privately Held**
Web: www.spirelio.com
SIC: 7389 Financial services

(G-19968)
SPIRITS PATH TO WELLNESS LLC
1405 Greenhill Ave (19806-1124)
PHONE.................................302 998-0074
Diana Bozzo, *Prin*
EMP: 6 EST: 2015
SALES (est): 83.6K **Privately Held**
SIC: 8099 Health and allied services, nec

(G-19969)
SPORTS CAR SERVICE INC
5 E 41st St (19802-2338)
PHONE.................................302 764-7439
John W Jacobson, *Owner*
EMP: 6 EST: 1957
SALES (est): 285.57K **Privately Held**
Web: www.sportscarservice.com
SIC: 7538 5521 General automotive repair shops; Automobiles, used cars only

(G-19970)
SPORTS CAR TIRE INC
1203 E 13th St (19802-5210)
P.O. Box 9295 (19809-0295)
PHONE.................................302 571-8473
Tom Cresswell, *Pr*
Les Tronzo, *VP*
EMP: 21 EST: 1992
SQ FT: 17,000
SALES (est): 5.13MM **Privately Held**
Web: www.sportscartire.com
SIC: 5531 5013 Automotive tires; Wheels, motor vehicle

(G-19971)
SPOTLIGHT PUBLICATIONS LLC
3301 Lancaster Pike Ste 5c (19805-1436)
PHONE.................................302 504-1329
Angelo Martinelli, *Prin*
EMP: 8 EST: 2008
SALES (est): 319.44K **Privately Held**
SIC: 2741 Miscellaneous publishing

(G-19972)
SPOTTERS INC
251 Little Falls Dr (19808-1674)
PHONE.................................646 662-6025
Patrick Smith, *Managing Member*
EMP: 6 EST: 2020
SALES (est): 56.54K **Privately Held**
Web: www.agencyspotter.com
SIC: 7372 Application computer software

(G-19973)
SPRATLEY PUBLISHING
Also Called: Spratley Publishing Co
1203 Apple St (19801-5413)
PHONE.................................267 779-7353
EMP: 2 EST: 2010
SALES (est): 65.53K **Privately Held**
SIC: 3555 Printing trades machinery

(G-19974)
SPRING LEAGUE LLC
3524 Silverside Rd Ste 35b (19810-4929)
PHONE.................................917 257-5801
Tony Titus, *Managing Member*
EMP: 9 EST: 2016
SALES (est): 313.19K **Privately Held**
SIC: 7941 Football club

(G-19975)
SPRING-GREEN LAWN CARE
200 Woodland Dr (19809-2842)
PHONE.................................302 762-1499
Louis Weiner, *Prin*
EMP: 5 EST: 2008
SALES (est): 59.7K **Privately Held**
Web: www.spring-green.com
SIC: 0782 Lawn care services

(G-19976)
SPRINGBOARD COLLABORATIVE INC
112 S French St (19801-5035)
PHONE.................................302 864-5220
Judson Malone, *Ex Dir*
Jeff Ronald, *Dir*
Randall Hughes, *Pr*
EMP: 10 EST: 2020
SALES (est): 57.88K **Privately Held**
Web: www.the-springboard.org
SIC: 8322 Settlement house

(G-19977)
SPRINGHAUS LLC
251 Little Falls Dr (19808-1674)
PHONE.................................302 397-5261
Jorge Huck, *Prin*
EMP: 15 EST: 2016
SALES (est): 7.14MM **Privately Held**
Web: www.springhausagro.com
SIC: 2048 Feed premixes

(G-19978)
SPRINGLEAF FINCL HOLDINGS LLC
1 Righter Pkwy (19803-1534)
PHONE.................................302 543-6767
EMP: 376
SALES (corp-wide): 1.89B **Privately Held**
Web: www.onemainfinancial.com
SIC: 7389 Financial services
PA: Springleaf Financial Holdings, Llc
    601 Nw 2nd St Ste 300
    Evansville IN 47708
    800 961-5577

(G-19979)
SPRINGS RHBLTTION AT BRNDYWINE
Also Called: Coral Sprng Rhab Hlthcare Ctr
505 Greenbank Rd (19808-3164)
PHONE.................................302 998-0101
EMP: 99 EST: 2021
SALES (est): 4.61MM **Privately Held**
Web: www.coralspringsrhc.com
SIC: 8322 Rehabilitation services

(G-19980)
SPRINT QUALITY PRINTING INC
3609 Silverside Rd (19810-5109)
P.O. Box 7121 (19803-0121)
PHONE.................................302 478-0720
Carson Dempsey, *Pr*
Kathleen Dempsey, *VP*
EMP: 5 EST: 1982
SQ FT: 3,700
SALES (est): 487.91K **Privately Held**
Web: www.sprintqp.com
SIC: 2752 Offset printing

(G-19981)
SPRINT SPECTRUM LP
Also Called: Sprint
4511 Kirkwood Hwy (19808-5117)
PHONE.................................302 993-3700
Mark Kline, *Brnch Mgr*
EMP: 11
SALES (corp-wide): 78.56B **Publicly Held**
SIC: 4812 Cellular telephone services
HQ: Sprint Spectrum L.P.
    6800 Sprint Pkwy
    Overland Park KS 66251

(G-19982)
SPROCKET LLC
251 Little Falls Dr (19808-1674)
PHONE.................................678 231-3165
EMP: 5 EST: 2021
SALES (est): 515.47K **Privately Held**
SIC: 8711 Consulting engineer

(G-19983)
SQELLA TECHNOLOGIES CORP ✪
1007 N Orange St Ste 1382 (19801-1239)
PHONE.................................302 592-6747
Mohammed Al-mayahi, *Prin*
EMP: 2 EST: 2023
SALES (est): 87.4K **Privately Held**
SIC: 7372 Prepackaged software

(G-19984)
SQS GLOBAL SOLUTIONS LLC
1201 N Orange St Ste 7383 (19801-1286)
PHONE.................................302 691-9682
EMP: 10 EST: 2017
SALES (est): 488.67K **Privately Held**
SIC: 5961 6799 8748 Electronic shopping; Commodity contract trading companies; Business consulting, nec

(G-19985)
SQUADCAST STUDIOS INC
1209 N Orange St (19801-1120)
PHONE.................................916 320-7761
Josef Rockwell Felder, *CEO*
EMP: 6 EST: 2020
SALES (est): 525.86K **Privately Held**
Web: www.squadcast.fm
SIC: 7371 Software programming applications

(G-19986)
SQUARE PROMOTE
1102 Crestover Rd (19803-3309)
PHONE.................................302 478-0736
Cory Kramer, *Prin*
EMP: 5 **EST:** 2014
SALES (est): 63.08K **Privately Held**
SIC: 8743 Promotion service

(G-19987)
SRSL AND TRANSPORTATION LLC
2711 Centerville Rd Ste 120 (19808-1660)
PHONE.................................302 295-3599
Cheryl Long Richardson, *Prin*
EMP: 5 **EST:** 2010
SALES (est): 258.08K **Privately Held**
SIC: 4789 Transportation services, nec

(G-19988)
SSBV LLC
1209 N Orange St (19801-1120)
PHONE.................................844 585-0656
EMP: 10 **EST:** 2020
SALES (est): 636.34K **Privately Held**
SIC: 6163 Loan brokers

(G-19989)
SSM INDUSTRIES INC
Ssm Industries
322 A St Ste 100 (19801-5355)
PHONE.................................856 345-2525
Ron Schnell, *Brnch Mgr*
EMP: 27
Web: www.ssmi.biz
SIC: 1711 Mechanical contractor
PA: Ssm Industries, Inc.
  3401 Grand Ave Ste C
  Pittsburgh PA 15225

(G-19990)
ST ANTHONYS COMMUNITY CENTER
1703 W 10th St (19805-2709)
PHONE.................................302 421-3721
Debra A Wirt, *Ex Dir*
Reverend Roberto Balducelli, *VP*
Richard Bacon, *
Herschel Quillen, *
Steven Mockbee, *
EMP: 12 **EST:** 1976
SQ FT: 18,000
SALES (est): 5.68MM **Privately Held**
Web: www.stanthonycenter.org
SIC: 8322 Social service center

(G-19991)
ST ANTHONYS HOUSING MGT CORP
1701 W 10th St Ste 200 (19805-2700)
PHONE.................................302 421-3756
Tori Adams, *Mgr*
Domenick Peronti, *Dir*
EMP: 6 **EST:** 1979
SALES (est): 174.04K **Privately Held**
Web: www.stanthonycenter.org
SIC: 8741 Management services

(G-19992)
ST FRANCIS HEALTH SERVICES CORPORATION
Also Called: St Francis Hospital
7th N Clayton St (19805)
P.O. Box 2500 (19805-0500)
PHONE.................................302 575-8301
EMP: 1200 **EST:** 1982
SALES (est): 88.78MM
SALES (corp-wide): 2.49B **Privately Held**
SIC: 8062 General medical and surgical hospitals
PA: Trinity Health Corporation
  20555 Victor Pkwy Ste 100
  Livonia MI 48152
  734 343-1000

(G-19993)
ST FRANCIS HOSPITAL INC
Also Called: CATHOLIC HEALTH EAST
701 N Clayton St (19805-3155)
P.O. Box 7007 (48007-7007)
PHONE.................................616 685-3538
Brian Dietz, *CEO*
Bernard Citerone, *
Dennis Gagliardo, *
EMP: 1000 **EST:** 1923
SQ FT: 400,000
SALES (est): 164.05MM
SALES (corp-wide): 2.49B **Privately Held**
Web: www.trinityhealthma.org
SIC: 8062 General medical and surgical hospitals
PA: Trinity Health Corporation
  20555 Victor Pkwy Ste 100
  Livonia MI 48152
  734 343-1000

(G-19994)
ST HELENAS EARLY LEARNING
2314 Andys Ln (19810-2314)
PHONE.................................302 561-4044
EMP: 6 **EST:** 2018
SALES (est): 56.71K **Privately Held**
SIC: 8351 Child day care services

(G-19995)
ST HELENAS EARLY LEARNING CTR
1600 Rockland Rd (19803-3607)
PHONE.................................610 497-0435
EMP: 6 **EST:** 2018
SALES (est): 104.92K **Privately Held**
Web: www.perfectdomain.com
SIC: 8351 Child day care services

(G-19996)
ST JOHN BELOVED
1100 Wynnbrook Rd (19809-2526)
PHONE.................................302 562-9129
Gregory Boulden, *Prin*
EMP: 8 **EST:** 2010
SALES (est): 88.77K **Privately Held**
Web: www.sjbkofcde.org
SIC: 8049 Offices of health practitioner

(G-19997)
ST LAWRENCE GRANT AVE TRUST
2010 Pennsylvania Ave (19806-2430)
PHONE.................................302 652-7978
James Stein, *Pt*
Joseph Stein, *Pt*
Richard Stein, *Pt*
EMP: 5 **EST:** 1981
SQ FT: 7,000
SALES (est): 555.79K **Privately Held**
SIC: 6798 Real estate investment trusts

(G-19998)
ST LOGISTICS 360 INC
300 Delaware Ave Ste 210 (19801-6601)
PHONE.................................302 607-8666
Sergio Mason, *Prin*
EMP: 5 **EST:** 2020
SALES (est): 332.94K **Privately Held**
SIC: 4789 Transportation services, nec

(G-19999)
ST MARKS UNITED METHODIST CH
Also Called: St Mark's Pre-School
1700 Limestone Rd (19804-4100)
PHONE.................................302 994-0400
Nancy Mayhew, *Ex Dir*
EMP: 10 **EST:** 1877
SALES (est): 450.65K **Privately Held**
Web: www.stmarksumcde.org
SIC: 8661 8351 Methodist Church; Preschool center

(G-20000)
ST MICHAELS SCHOOL AND NURSERY
700 N Walnut St (19801-3514)
PHONE.................................302 353-6717
EMP: 20 **EST:** 2017
SALES (est): 3.61MM **Privately Held**
Web: www.stmichaelsde.org
SIC: 8351 Preschool center

(G-20001)
ST MICHAELS SCHOOL INC
305 E 7th St (19801-3800)
PHONE.................................302 656-3389
Helen Raleigh, *Dir*
EMP: 26 **EST:** 1890
SALES (est): 948.74K **Privately Held**
Web: www.stmichaelsde.org
SIC: 8351 Preschool center

(G-20002)
ST PATRICKS CENTER INC
Also Called: SAINT PATRICK'S CENTER
107 E 14th St (19801-3209)
PHONE.................................302 652-6219
Joseph Hickey, *Pr*
EMP: 8 **EST:** 1971
SALES (est): 1.01MM **Privately Held**
Web: www.stpatrickscenter.org
SIC: 8322 Social service center

(G-20003)
STABLE APP LLC
1007 N Orange St (19801-1239)
PHONE.................................310 767-7832
Camilo Ovalle, *Managing Member*
EMP: 7
SALES (est): 264.9K **Privately Held**
SIC: 7371 Computer software development and applications

(G-20004)
STAIKOS ASSOCIATES ARCHITECTS (PA)
502 Dell Hill Rd (19809)
PHONE.................................302 764-1678
Nicholas Staikos, *Owner*
EMP: 7 **EST:** 1986
SALES (est): 952.46K **Privately Held**
Web: www.staikos.com
SIC: 8712 7389 Architectural engineering; Business Activities at Non-Commercial Site

(G-20005)
STAINLESS ALLOYS INC
103 Foulk Rd Ste 202 (19803-3742)
PHONE.................................800 499-7833
Cristobal Fuentes, *Pr*
Miguel Ferrandis, *VP*
Mary J Riley, *Sec*
EMP: 52 **EST:** 1995
SALES (est): 1.51MM **Privately Held**
SIC: 3316 Cold finishing of steel shapes
HQ: North American Stainless, Inc.
  6870 Us Highway 42 E
  Ghent KY 41045
  502 347-6000

(G-20006)
STAINLESS STEEL INVEST INC
103 Foulk Rd Ste 202 (19803-3742)
PHONE.................................800 499-7833
Cristobal Fuentes, *Pr*
Anil Yadav, *Manufacturing Operations Vice President*
Mary Jean Riley, *VP Fin*
Pat Feeley V Press Commercial, *Prin*
EMP: 78 **EST:** 1990
SALES (est): 2.19MM **Privately Held**
SIC: 3316 3312 Cold finishing of steel shapes; Blast furnaces and steel mills
HQ: North American Stainless, Inc.
  6870 Us Highway 42 E
  Ghent KY 41045
  502 347-6000

(G-20007)
STALEY HOLDINGS INC
501 Silverside Rd Ste 55 (19809-1388)
PHONE.................................302 793-0289
◆ **EMP:** 2100
SIC: 2046 Wet corn milling

(G-20008)
STAMFORD SCREEN PRINTING INC
3801 Kennett Pike Ste C107 (19807-2326)
PHONE.................................302 654-2442
Cynthia A Prendergast, *Pr*
EMP: 5 **EST:** 1993
SQ FT: 1,500
SALES (est): 987.29K **Privately Held**
Web: www.verycoolproducts.com
SIC: 5199 2759 2395 Advertising specialties; Screen printing; Embroidery products, except Schiffli machine

(G-20009)
STAMPEDE BTQ & VINTAGE LLC
1236 Prospect Dr (19809-2425)
PHONE.................................215 668-5714
EMP: 6
SALES (est): 210.84K **Privately Held**
SIC: 7389 Business Activities at Non-Commercial Site

(G-20010)
STAN PERKOSKIS PLUMBING & HTG
1818 Marsh Rd (19810-4539)
PHONE.................................302 529-1220
EMP: 29 **EST:** 1996
SALES (est): 5.18MM **Privately Held**
Web: www.leaksnheat.com
SIC: 1711 Plumbing contractors

(G-20011)
STANDARD & POORS INTL LLC (HQ)
2711 Centerville Rd (19808-1660)
PHONE.................................212 512-2000
Robert B Dimmitt, *Prin*
EMP: 9 **EST:** 2000
SALES (est): 1.85MM
SALES (corp-wide): 11.18B **Publicly Held**
Web: www.spglobal.com
SIC: 7323 6282 Credit reporting services; Investment advisory service
PA: S&P Global Inc.
  55 Water St
  New York NY 10041
  212 438-1000

(G-20012)
STANDARD DIRECT LLC
1207 Delaware Ave (19806-4743)
PHONE.................................855 550-0606
EMP: 5
SALES (est): 261.83K **Privately Held**
SIC: 5084 7389 Industrial machinery and equipment; Business Activities at Non-Commercial Site

(G-20013)
STANDARD INDUSTRIAL SUPPLY CO
1625 N Heald St (19802-5146)
P.O. Box 98 (19710-0098)
PHONE.................................302 656-1631
Andrew Gold, *Pr*
EMP: 5 **EST:** 1949
SQ FT: 10,000
SALES (est): 827.42K **Privately Held**

Wilmington - New Castle County (G-20014) — GEOGRAPHIC SECTION

Web: www.standardindustrialsupplyco.com
SIC: 5085 5072 Industrial supplies; Hardware

(G-20014)
STANDARD MAGIC CORPORATION ✪
2810 N Church St Pmb 59881 (19802-4447)
PHONE..................347 756-1222
Margaret Henry, CEO
EMP: 2 EST: 2023
SALES (est): 87.4K **Privately Held**
SIC: 7372 Application computer software

(G-20015)
STANDARD TECHNOLOGIES & MACHINE CO
3709 Old Capitol Trl (19808-6001)
PHONE..................302 994-0229
EMP: 19 EST: 1950
SALES (est): 431.95K **Privately Held**
Web: www.stmde.com
SIC: 3599 Machine shop, jobbing and repair

(G-20016)
STANDARDS SITE INC
251 Little Falls Dr (19808-1674)
PHONE..................917 449-4078
Hamish Smyth, CEO
EMP: 5
SALES (est): 203.68K **Privately Held**
SIC: 7379 Computer related services, nec

(G-20017)
STANGA GAMES INC
1000 N West St Ste 1200 (19801-1058)
PHONE..................415 549-6537
Anthony Copus, Pr
EMP: 6 EST: 2014
SQ FT: 100
SALES (est): 185.53K **Privately Held**
SIC: 7371 Computer software development

(G-20018)
STANLEY GOLDEN
Also Called: Grays Fine Printing
841 N Tatnall St (19801-1717)
P.O. Box 365 (19899-0365)
PHONE..................302 652-5626
Stanley Golden, Owner
EMP: 3 EST: 1893
SALES (est): 231.12K **Privately Held**
SIC: 2752 2759 2791 Offset printing; Letterpress printing; Typesetting

(G-20019)
STANLEY H GOLOSKOV DDS PA
2500 Grubb Rd Ste 130 (19810-4711)
PHONE..................302 475-0600
Stanley H Goloskov, Prin
Stanley H Goloskov D.d.s., Pr
Stanley H Goloskov, Pr
EMP: 9 EST: 1981
SALES (est): 432.61K **Privately Held**
Web: www.wilmington-cosmetic-dentist.com
SIC: 8021 Dentists' office

(G-20020)
STAPLEFORD ELECTRIC LLC
3847 Evelyn Dr (19808-4618)
PHONE..................302 300-1377
Michael Stapleford, Prin
EMP: 5 EST: 2016
SALES (est): 158.18K **Privately Held**
Web: www.staplefordelectric.net
SIC: 1731 General electrical contractor

(G-20021)
STAPLER ATHLETIC ASSOCIATION
1900 N Scott St (19806-2320)
PHONE..................302 652-9769
Frank Farren, Pr
EMP: 6 EST: 1961
SALES (est): 48.71K **Privately Held**
SIC: 8611 Merchants' association

(G-20022)
STAR ENRG
5700 Kirkwood Hwy Ste 106 (19808-4883)
PHONE..................302 743-6751
David Stokes, Prin
EMP: 9 EST: 2018
SALES (est): 494.57K **Privately Held**
Web: www.starenrg.com
SIC: 1711 Solar energy contractor

(G-20023)
STAR ENRG CS LLC
5700 Kirkwood Hwy 106a (19808-4857)
PHONE..................302 660-2187
David Stokes, Ex Dir
EMP: 14 EST: 2020
SALES (est): 649.22K **Privately Held**
SIC: 1731 1711 3621 1761 Electric power systems contractors; Solar energy contractor; Generators for gas-electric or oil-electric vehicles; Roofing, siding, and sheetmetal work

(G-20024)
STAR GAS & DIESEL
3927 Kirkwood Hwy (19808-5119)
PHONE..................302 998-2002
EMP: 5 EST: 2016
SALES (est): 28.25K **Privately Held**
SIC: 7538 General automotive repair shops

(G-20025)
STAR SOUND TECHNOLOGIES LLC
100 Fallon Ave (19804-1917)
PHONE..................330 260-6767
Robert Maicks, Prin
EMP: 8 EST: 2018
SALES (est): 236.59K **Privately Held**
Web: www.starsoundaudio.com
SIC: 1731 Sound equipment specialization

(G-20026)
STARBELT LLC
103 Foulk Rd Ste 202 (19803-3742)
PHONE..................256 724-9200
EMP: 9 EST: 2017
SALES (est): 2.29MM
SALES (corp-wide): 134.9B **Publicly Held**
SIC: 7374 Data processing and preparation
PA: Meta Platforms, Inc.
1 Meta Way
Menlo Park CA 94025
650 543-4800

(G-20027)
STARKS FUNERAL SERVICE LLC
2810 N Church St (19802-4447)
PHONE..................202 361-0603
Kevin Junior, Managing Member
EMP: 5
SALES (est): 113.46K **Privately Held**
SIC: 7261 Funeral service and crematories

(G-20028)
STARR WRIGHT INSUR AGCY INC
Also Called: Starr Wright USA
405 Silverside Rd Ste 102b (19809-1724)
PHONE..................302 483-0190
Bryan Lewis, Pr
Walter Wilson, *
EMP: 43 EST: 1965
SQ FT: 10,000
SALES (est): 2.46MM
SALES (corp-wide): 239.3MM **Privately Held**
Web: www.wrightusa.com
SIC: 6411 Insurance agents, nec
PA: Special Agents Mutual Benefit Association Inc
11301 Old Georgetown Rd
Rockville MD 20852
301 984-1440

(G-20029)
STARTUP AFRICA INC
818 N Market St (19801-3087)
PHONE..................302 894-8971
Erastus Mongare, Prin
EMP: 8 EST: 2011
SALES (est): 143.31K **Privately Held**
Web: www.startupafrica.org
SIC: 8699 Charitable organization

(G-20030)
STAT OFFICE SOLUTIONS
1201 N Orange St Ste 700 (19801-1186)
PHONE..................302 884-6746
Linda Grund, Prin
EMP: 5 EST: 2016
SALES (est): 216.48K **Privately Held**
Web: www.statofficesolutions.com
SIC: 6512 Nonresidential building operators

(G-20031)
STATE FARM
Also Called: State Farm Insurance
4758 Limestone Rd Ste C (19808-4389)
PHONE..................302 344-3514
EMP: 9 EST: 2018
SALES (est): 451.28K **Privately Held**
Web: www.statefarm.com
SIC: 6411 Insurance agents and brokers

(G-20032)
STATE FARM INSURANCE
4015 Newport Gap Pike (19808-1415)
PHONE..................302 547-7478
EMP: 7 EST: 2019
SALES (est): 200.52K **Privately Held**
Web: www.statefarm.com
SIC: 6411 Insurance agents and brokers

(G-20033)
STATE FARM INSURANCE
1813 Marsh Rd Ste G (19810-4544)
PHONE..................302 353-6636
John Campion, Mgr
EMP: 9 EST: 1990
SALES (est): 108.98K **Privately Held**
Web: www.statefarm.com
SIC: 6411 Insurance agents and brokers

(G-20034)
STATE FARM INSURANCE CO
Also Called: State Farm Insurance
167 Steven Ln (19808-1135)
PHONE..................302 547-4117
EMP: 6 EST: 2018
SALES (est): 55.85K **Privately Held**
Web: www.statefarm.com
SIC: 6411 Insurance agents and brokers

(G-20035)
STATE LINE MACHINE INC
200 State Line Rd (19803-1439)
P.O. Box 7617 (19803-0617)
PHONE..................302 478-0285
Fulton S Owensby Senior, Pr
Pam Owensby, Sec
EMP: 12 EST: 1966
SQ FT: 7,000
SALES (est): 2.18MM **Privately Held**
Web: www.statelinemachine.com
SIC: 7699 5085 Construction equipment repair; Industrial supplies

(G-20036)
STATEWISE ENERGY OHIO LLC
2711 Centerville Rd # 400 (19808-1660)
PHONE..................855 862-1185
Michael Gerald Haggarty, Pr
EMP: 10 EST: 2016
SQ FT: 1,000
SALES (est): 2.2MM **Privately Held**
SIC: 4911 4924 Distribution, electric power; Natural gas distribution

(G-20037)
STATUS INTL LLC DBA STTUS BRND
704 N King St Ste 500 (19801-3584)
PHONE..................202 290-6387
Timothy Robertson, CEO
EMP: 5 EST: 2018
SALES (est): 90K **Privately Held**
SIC: 8742 7311 Marketing consulting services; Advertising agencies

(G-20038)
STATWHIZ VENTURES LLC
1201 N Orange St Ste 600 (19801-1171)
PHONE..................310 819-5427
Siva Moturi, Pt
EMP: 6 EST: 2013
SALES (est): 98.07K **Privately Held**
SIC: 7372 7389 Application computer software; Business services, nec

(G-20039)
STAY PRIME INC
Also Called: Prime
1201 N Orange St Ste 600 (19801-1171)
PHONE..................612 770-6753
Tyler Hayes, CEO
Owen Imholte, CFO
Will Imholte, COO
EMP: 3 EST: 2013
SALES (est): 222.46K **Privately Held**
SIC: 7372 Application computer software

(G-20040)
STAYBRIDGE SUITES
204 Sulky Cir (19810-2268)
PHONE..................302 738-3400
EMP: 15 EST: 2019
SALES (est): 281.5K **Privately Held**
Web: www.staybridgesuites.com
SIC: 7011 Hotels and motels

(G-20041)
STAYSAF 3 LLC
1201 N Market St Ste 111 (19801-1147)
PHONE..................305 699-1454
Tristan Martinez, Managing Member
EMP: 5
SALES (est): 203.68K **Privately Held**
SIC: 7313 Electronic media advertising representatives

(G-20042)
STB CONTRACTING LLC
303 Winston Ave (19804-1733)
PHONE..................302 992-0570
Thomas Blackiston, Prin
EMP: 6 EST: 2007
SALES (est): 70.61K **Privately Held**
SIC: 1799 Athletic and recreation facilities construction

(G-20043)
STEEL SUPPLIERS INC
Also Called: Steel Suppliers Erectors

701 E Front St (19801-5040)
P.O. Box 2662 (19805-0662)
PHONE..............................302 654-5243
Michael A Bloom, *Pr*
David Bloom, *
EMP: 110 EST: 1945
SQ FT: 75,000
SALES (est): 23.5MM **Privately Held**
Web: www.steelsuppliserserectors.com
SIC: 5051 1791 3441 Steel; Building front installation, metal; Building components, structural steel

(G-20044)
STEEL SUPPLIERS ERECTORS INC
701 E Front St (19801-5040)
P.O. Box 2662 (19805-0662)
PHONE..............................302 654-5243
Michael Bloom, *Pr*
EMP: 70 EST: 1997
SALES (est): 10.61MM **Privately Held**
SIC: 5051 Metals service centers and offices

(G-20045)
STEELE INSURANCE GROUP LLC
1035 N Lincoln St Ste 600 (19805-2726)
PHONE..............................302 898-6797
Brandon White, *Prin*
EMP: 7 EST: 2017
SALES (est): 190.03K **Privately Held**
Web: www.steeleinsurance.com
SIC: 6411 Insurance agents, nec

(G-20046)
STEERING COMMITTEE
100 E Market St (19804-2543)
PHONE..............................302 994-7533
Jamie Kegerise, *Prin*
EMP: 6 EST: 2010
SALES (est): 159.28K **Privately Held**
SIC: 5032 Brick, stone, and related material

(G-20047)
STEIN TREE SERVICE INC
17 Austin Rd (19810-2202)
P.O. Box 367 (19732-0367)
PHONE..............................302 478-3511
Jeff Stein, *Pr*
EMP: 9 EST: 1983
SALES (est): 241.56K **Privately Held**
Web: www.steintree.com
SIC: 0783 Planting, pruning, and trimming services

(G-20048)
STELLAR LABS INC
251 Little Falls Dr (19808-1674)
PHONE..............................650 868-6796
Stephanie Whaley, *Pr*
EMP: 12 EST: 2016
SALES (est): 878.26K **Privately Held**
SIC: 8734 Testing laboratories

(G-20049)
STEMS LABS INC ✪
1209 N Orange St (19801-1120)
PHONE..............................708 834-3706
Haitham El Menegad, *CEO*
EMP: 10 EST: 2022
SALES (est): 348.32K **Privately Held**
SIC: 7389 Music distribution systems

(G-20050)
STENERAL CONSULTING INC
1007 N Orange St (19801-1239)
PHONE..............................302 721-6124
Srajan Dubey, *CEO*
EMP: 50
SALES (est): 1.19MM **Privately Held**
Web: www.steneral.com

SIC: 8742 Human resource consulting services

(G-20051)
STENTA APPRAISAL PORTIONS
9 Lynthwaite Farm Ln (19803-1541)
PHONE..............................302 477-9562
Anthony Stenta, *Prin*
EMP: 5 EST: 2011
SALES (est): 124.69K **Privately Held**
Web: www.stentaappraisal.com
SIC: 6531 Appraiser, real estate

(G-20052)
STEP UP DAYCARE
Also Called: Step-Up Daycare
2715 N Tatnall St (19802-3527)
PHONE..............................302 762-3183
Janice Brooks, *Prin*
EMP: 5 EST: 2010
SALES (est): 75.46K **Privately Held**
SIC: 8351 Group day care center

(G-20053)
STEPHANIE GALBRAITH
Also Called: Healthy Kneads
1429 Stapler Pl (19806-2529)
PHONE..............................302 290-2235
EMP: 5 EST: 2009
SALES (est): 215.8K **Privately Held**
Web: www.healthykneadsde.com
SIC: 7299 Massage parlor

(G-20054)
STEPHANIE ORR LCSW LLC
12 Austin Rd (19810-2203)
PHONE..............................302 478-4373
Stephanie Orr, *Prin*
EMP: 5 EST: 2013
SALES (est): 80.02K **Privately Held**
Web: www.stephanieorrlcsw.com
SIC: 8322 Social worker

(G-20055)
STEPHANIE SAROUKOS
2419 Lancaster Ave (19805-3736)
PHONE..............................302 654-1614
Stephanie Saroukos, *Prin*
EMP: 5 EST: 2016
SALES (est): 19.5K **Privately Held**
Web: www.saroukoshairco.com
SIC: 7231 Hairdressers

(G-20056)
STEPHANO SLACK LLC
1700 W 14th St (19806-4012)
PHONE..............................302 777-7400
EMP: 6
SALES (corp-wide): 12.02MM **Privately Held**
Web: www.stephanoslack.com
SIC: 8721 Certified public accountant
PA: Stephano Slack, Llc
125 Strafford Ave Ste 200
Wayne PA 19087
610 687-1600

(G-20057)
STEPHEN A COVEY
2406 Allendale Rd (19803-5226)
PHONE..............................302 478-0215
Stephen Covey, *Prin*
EMP: 6 EST: 2010
SALES (est): 159.78K **Privately Held**
SIC: 8742 Training and development consultant

(G-20058)
STEPHEN E JENKINS
1100 N Market St (19801-1243)

PHONE..............................302 654-1888
Stephen E Jenkins, *Prin*
EMP: 8 EST: 2014
SALES (est): 348.19K **Privately Held**
Web: www.ashbygeddes.com
SIC: 8111 General practice attorney, lawyer

(G-20059)
STEPHEN J CRIFASI REAL ESTATE
2300 N Grant Ave (19806-2006)
PHONE..............................302 658-9572
Stephen Crifasi, *Prin*
EMP: 5 EST: 2008
SALES (est): 244.01K **Privately Held**
SIC: 6531 Real estate brokers and agents

(G-20060)
STEPHEN JANKOVIC CHIROPRACTOR
1309 Beale Rd Ste 12 (19810)
PHONE..............................302 384-8540
Stephen Jankovic, *Owner*
EMP: 6 EST: 2011
SALES (est): 138.09K **Privately Held**
SIC: 8041 Offices and clinics of chiropractors

(G-20061)
STEPPING STONES COLLEGE
118 Bunche Blvd (19801-5723)
PHONE..............................302 983-1437
Aisha Copeland, *Prin*
EMP: 9 EST: 2016
SALES (est): 16.45K **Privately Held**
SIC: 8351 Child day care services

(G-20062)
STEPR INC ✪
300 Delaware Ave (19801-1607)
PHONE..............................866 861-1281
Daniel Alenaddaf, *Pr*
EMP: 5 EST: 2023
SALES (est): 520.9K **Privately Held**
SIC: 5091 Fitness equipment and supplies

(G-20063)
STEVE STYLES
2914 Lancaster Ave (19805-5227)
PHONE..............................302 540-4965
Steve Styles, *Pr*
EMP: 5 EST: 2016
SALES (est): 21.46K **Privately Held**
SIC: 7231 Beauty shops

(G-20064)
STEVEN BROWN & ASSOCIATES INC
9 S Cleveland Ave (19805-1426)
PHONE..............................302 652-4722
Steven D Brown, *Pr*
EMP: 5 EST: 2000
SQ FT: 2,200
SALES (est): 2.17MM **Privately Held**
Web: www.stevenbrownassociates.com
SIC: 5087 5084 1711 Sprinkler systems; Pumps and pumping equipment, nec; Fire sprinkler system installation

(G-20065)
STEVEN E DIAMOND M D
900 Foulk Rd Ste 200 (19803-3155)
PHONE..............................302 655-8868
Steven Diamond, *Owner*
EMP: 6 EST: 2018
SALES (est): 195.8K **Privately Held**
SIC: 8051 Skilled nursing care facilities

(G-20066)
STEVEN M DELLOSE
1941 Limestone Rd (19808-5408)
PHONE..............................302 655-9494
Steven M Dellose, *Prin*

EMP: 12 EST: 2011
SALES (est): 217.29K **Privately Held**
Web: www.delortho.com
SIC: 8011 General and family practice, physician/surgeon

(G-20067)
STEVEN SOULE
7 Colony Blvd Apt 212 (19802-1433)
PHONE..............................302 690-3052
EMP: 5 EST: 2009
SALES (est): 146.7K **Privately Held**
SIC: 1521 Single-family housing construction

(G-20068)
STEVENS & LEE PC
919 N Market St Ste 1300 (19801-3092)
PHONE..............................302 654-5180
Walter Mcevilly, *Pt*
EMP: 15
SALES (corp-wide): 42.45MM **Privately Held**
Web: www.stevenslee.com
SIC: 8111 General practice attorney, lawyer
PA: Stevens & Lee, P.C.
111 N 6th St
Reading PA 19601
610 478-2000

(G-20069)
STEWART BROS TURF LLC
1314 Birch Ln (19809-2467)
PHONE..............................302 333-3707
Craig Stewart, *Pr*
EMP: 5 EST: 2012
SALES (est): 224.89K **Privately Held**
Web: www.sbturf.com
SIC: 0782 Lawn care services

(G-20070)
STEWART LAW FIRM
Also Called: Stewart and Martin
301 N Market St (19801-2529)
PHONE..............................302 652-5200
Gordon Stewart, *Pr*
Dawn Kilcreasc, *
Tanya Murray, *
Leanne C Mcgrory, *Dir*
EMP: 18 EST: 1995
SALES (est): 4.05MM **Privately Held**
Web: www.delawarecorporatelaw.com
SIC: 8111 6719 Specialized law offices, attorneys; Investment holding companies, except banks

(G-20071)
STEWART LENDER SERVICES INC
2200 Concord Pike Ste 300 (19803-2909)
PHONE..............................302 433-8047
Deann Stigliano, *Opers Mgr*
EMP: 8
SALES (corp-wide): 3.07B **Publicly Held**
Web: www.stewartlenderservices.com
SIC: 6541 Title and trust companies
HQ: Stewart Lender Services, Inc.
1360 Post Oak Blvd Ste 10
Houston TX 77056

(G-20072)
STEWART VALUATION SERVICES LLC
2200 Concord Pike Ste 300 (19803-2978)
PHONE..............................888 751-9234
Beth Fowler, *CEO*
EMP: 29 EST: 2007
SALES (est): 12.53MM
SALES (corp-wide): 3.07B **Publicly Held**
Web: slsvendors.stewart.com
SIC: 6531 Real estate agent, commercial

Wilmington - New Castle County (G-20073)

PA: Stewart Information Services
Corporation
1360 Post Oak Blvd Ste 10
Houston TX 77056
713 625-8100

(G-20073)
STICK IT GYMNASTICS
12 Crawford Cir (19805-2656)
PHONE..................302 678-8780
Steve Miller, *Prin*
EMP: 8 EST: 2017
SALES (est): 62.15K **Privately Held**
Web: www.stickitgymnastics.com
SIC: 7999 Gymnastic instruction, non-membership

(G-20074)
STIFEL TRUST CO DEL NAT ASSN
100 S West St 1st Fl (19801-5015)
PHONE..................302 351-8900
Jennie Pfeifer, *Prin*
EMP: 9 EST: 2010
SALES (est): 9.86MM **Privately Held**
SIC: 6021 National commercial banks

(G-20075)
STOKES GARAGE INC
101 Old Dupont Rd (19805)
PHONE..................302 994-0613
Andrei Cratty, *Pr*
Robert Stokes Junior, *Pr*
EMP: 5 EST: 1946
SALES (est): 490.38K **Privately Held**
Web: www.stokesgarage1946.com
SIC: 7538 7532 General truck repair; Body shop, trucks

(G-20076)
STOLTZ REAL ESTATE PARTNERS
20 Montchanin Rd Ste 250 (19807-2181)
P.O. Box 731 (19710-0731)
PHONE..................302 654-3600
Lorriane Parker, *Mgr*
EMP: 6 EST: 2017
SALES (est): 225K **Privately Held**
SIC: 6531 Real estate brokers and agents

(G-20077)
STOLTZ REALTY CO (PA)
Also Called: Stoltz Management
3704 Kennett Pike Ste 200 (19807-2173)
PHONE..................302 656-2852
Jack Stoltz, *Pr*
Morris L Stoltz, *Ch Bd*
EMP: 8 EST: 1957
SQ FT: 9,000
SALES (est): 2.49MM
SALES (corp-wide): 2.49MM **Privately Held**
SIC: 6531 Real estate brokers and agents

(G-20078)
STOLTZ REALTY CO
Also Called: Plaza Apartments
1303 Delaware Ave Ste 101 (19806-3416)
PHONE..................302 656-8543
Diana Hamel, *Mgr*
EMP: 66
SALES (corp-wide): 2.49MM **Privately Held**
SIC: 6531 6513 Real estate agent, commercial; Apartment building operators
PA: Stoltz Realty Co
3704 Kennett Pike Ste 200
Wilmington DE 19807
302 656-2852

(G-20079)
STONE POWERHOUSE TRAINING
2518 W 4th St (19805-3308)
PHONE..................302 658-5077
Rory Koonce Junior, *Prin*
EMP: 5 EST: 2016
SALES (est): 55.79K **Privately Held**
Web: www.thestonepowerhouse.com
SIC: 7991 Physical fitness facilities

(G-20080)
STONEY BTTER FMLY MDCINE ASSOC
5311 Limestone Rd Ste 201 (19808-1258)
PHONE..................302 234-9109
Hal Kramer, *Pr*
EMP: 30 EST: 1992
SALES (est): 4.44MM **Privately Held**
Web: www.stoneybatterfamilymedicine.com
SIC: 8011 General and family practice, physician/surgeon

(G-20081)
STONEYBROOK ASSOCIATES LP
Also Called: Stoneybrook Apartments
4 Denny Rd (19809-3445)
PHONE..................302 764-6450
EMP: 5 EST: 2011
SALES (est): 329.13K **Privately Held**
SIC: 6513 Retirement hotel operation

(G-20082)
STOP VLNCE PRYER CHAIN FNDTION
506 N Church St (19801-4812)
PHONE..................302 513-9520
Margaret Dy, *Pr*
EMP: 5 EST: 2014
SALES (est): 58.19K **Privately Held**
Web: www.prayerchainfoundation.org
SIC: 8699 Charitable organization

(G-20083)
STORA CENTRAL LLC ◆
2055 Limestone Rd 200c (19808-5536)
PHONE..................929 273-0505
Bilguun Turboli, *Managing Member*
EMP: 20 EST: 2022
SALES (est): 588.11K **Privately Held**
SIC: 7389 Personal service agents, brokers, and bureaus

(G-20084)
STORAGE RENTALS OF AMERICA
2523 Lamotte St (19802-4358)
PHONE..................302 786-0792
EMP: 9 EST: 2018
SALES (est): 166.44K **Privately Held**
Web: www.sroa.com
SIC: 7359 Equipment rental and leasing, nec

(G-20085)
STORAGE RENTALS OF AMERICA
50 Dodson Ave (19804-2021)
PHONE..................302 313-1430
EMP: 5 EST: 2018
SALES (est): 53.46K **Privately Held**
SIC: 4225 Warehousing, self storage

(G-20086)
STORAGEOS INC (DH)
910 Foulk Rd Ste 201 (19803-3159)
PHONE..................617 971-8470
EMP: 6 EST: 2018
SALES (est): 784.52K
SALES (corp-wide): 222.8K **Privately Held**
SIC: 4225 General warehousing and storage
HQ: Storageos Ltd
20 Farringdon St (Hubhub)
London EC4A
203 983-4311

(G-20087)
STORK ELECTRIC ASSOCIATES LLC
530 Copper Dr (19804-2418)
PHONE..................302 654-9427
EMP: 6 EST: 2020
SALES (est): 799.43K **Privately Held**
SIC: 4911 Electric services

(G-20088)
STORM ENERGIA INC ◆
251 Little Falls Dr (19808-1674)
PHONE..................404 550-4862
Mj Chandilya, *Pr*
EMP: 25 EST: 2022
SALES (est): 1.64MM **Privately Held**
SIC: 3691 Storage batteries

(G-20089)
STORYIQ INC
251 Little Falls Dr (19808-1674)
PHONE..................718 801-8556
Isaac Reyes, *CEO*
EMP: 10 EST: 2021
SALES (est): 363K **Privately Held**
SIC: 8742 Training and development consultant

(G-20090)
STOUDMIRE MEDIA GROUP LLC
2103 N Church St (19802-4423)
PHONE..................302 689-3151
Dale L Stoudmire, *Prin*
EMP: 5 EST: 2015
SALES (est): 38.39K **Privately Held**
SIC: 4899 Communication services, nec

(G-20091)
STRATEGIC FUND RAISING INC (PA)
300 Delaware Ave Ste 1370 (19801-1658)
PHONE..................651 649-0404
Michael Bills, *CEO*
EMP: 20 EST: 1991
SALES (est): 8.9MM **Privately Held**
SIC: 7389 Telemarketing services

(G-20092)
STRATOS HOLDINGS INC
251 Little Falls Dr (19808-1674)
PHONE..................800 927-9800
Travis Skweres, *CEO*
EMP: 12
SIC: 6719 Holding companies, nec

(G-20093)
STREAM APP LLC
Also Called: Stream
1500 Lancaster Ave (19805-3995)
PHONE..................610 420-5864
David Polykoff, *CEO*
EMP: 7 EST: 2015
SALES (est): 374.33K **Privately Held**
SIC: 7372 7389 Prepackaged software; Business Activities at Non-Commercial Site

(G-20094)
STREAMLINE TECHNOLOGIES INC
3516 Silverside Rd Ste 20 (19810-4932)
PHONE..................302 383-3146
EMP: 11 EST: 2009
SALES (est): 321.27K **Privately Held**
Web: www.streamlinetechnologiesinc.com
SIC: 8731 Commercial physical research

(G-20095)
STREAMLNERS MGT CONSULTING LLC
1201 N Orange St Ste 7088 (19801-1192)
PHONE..................864 884-5064
EMP: 6 EST: 2020
SALES (est): 124.72K **Privately Held**
SIC: 8742 Management consulting services

(G-20096)
STREET KNOWLEDGE BOOK CTR LLC
1902b Maryland Ave (19805-4605)
PHONE..................888 401-1114
Joseph Jones, *CEO*
EMP: 3 EST: 2016
SALES (est): 190.35K **Privately Held**
Web: www.skpublishing.co
SIC: 2741 Miscellaneous publishing

(G-20097)
STRENGTH FOR JURNEY COUNSELING
99 Paladin Dr (19802-1784)
PHONE..................302 367-4266
Robert Peterson, *Prin*
EMP: 7 EST: 2010
SALES (est): 59.45K **Privately Held**
Web: www.kuumbaenterprises.com
SIC: 8322 General counseling services

(G-20098)
STRETCH 1 LLC (PA) ◆
4120 Concord Pike Ste B (19803-5401)
PHONE..................253 255-7345
EMP: 5 EST: 2022
SALES (est): 282.25K
SALES (corp-wide): 282.25K **Privately Held**
SIC: 7991 Physical fitness facilities

(G-20099)
STRIDE SERVICES INC
200 Powder Mill Rd (19803-2907)
PHONE..................302 540-4713
Debora Massouda, *CEO*
James Dinnage, *Sec*
EMP: 16 EST: 2016
SALES (est): 996.37K **Privately Held**
SIC: 8731 8999 Commercial physical research; Scientific consulting

(G-20100)
STRIDE-360 INCORPORATED (PA)
1013 Centre Rd Ste 403a (19805-1270)
PHONE..................302 421-5752
EMP: 6
SALES (est): 136.04K
SALES (corp-wide): 136.04K **Privately Held**
SIC: 7389 Business services, nec

(G-20101)
STRIPE-A-LOT INC
Also Called: Advance Paving Services
55 Germay Dr (19804-1104)
PHONE..................302 654-9175
Rick Romero, *Pr*
EMP: 20 EST: 1986
SQ FT: 1,500
SALES (est): 3.5MM **Privately Held**
Web: www.advancedpavingservices.com
SIC: 1611 Surfacing and paving

(G-20102)
STROBERT TREE SERVICES
1506 A St (19801-5412)
PHONE..................302 633-3478
Jon Auer, *Dir*
EMP: 9 EST: 2010

SALES (est): 938.46K **Privately Held**
Web: www.buymulch.com
SIC: 0783 Planting, pruning, and trimming services

(G-20103)
STROBERT TREE SERVICES INC
1806 Zebley Rd (19810-1502)
PHONE..............................302 475-7089
Andrew Strobert, *Pr*
Sam Strobert, *
▲ EMP: 45 EST: 2001
SALES (est): 4.96MM **Privately Held**
Web: www.stroberttree.com
SIC: 0783 Planting, pruning, and trimming services

(G-20104)
STUART KINGSTON GALLERIES INC
Also Called: Stuart Kingston Jewelers
3704 Kennett Pike (19807-2175)
PHONE..............................302 652-7978
Joseph Stein, *Pr*
James Stein, *VP*
EMP: 9 EST: 1930
SQ FT: 7,000
SALES (est): 490.58K **Privately Held**
Web: www.stuartkingstonjewelers.com
SIC: 5963 5947 5944 7389 Furnishings, including furniture, house-to-house; Gift shop; Jewelry, precious stones and precious metals; Interior design services

(G-20105)
STUDIO 11
2301 Penns Ave Apt D (19806-1341)
PHONE..............................302 622-9959
Carolann Leone, *Prin*
EMP: 6 EST: 2004
SALES (est): 119.7K **Privately Held**
SIC: 7997 Membership sports and recreation clubs

(G-20106)
STUDIO GROUPS INC
Also Called: ART GROUP
1305 N Franklin St (19806-4211)
PHONE..............................302 998-7895
EMP: 10
SALES (est): 41.54K **Privately Held**
Web: www.howardpylestudio.org
SIC: 8641 Civic and social associations

(G-20107)
STUDIUM INC
251 Little Falls Dr (19808-1674)
PHONE..............................614 402-0359
Chris Asman, *CEO*
EMP: 3
SALES (est): 131.48K **Privately Held**
SIC: 7372 Prepackaged software

(G-20108)
STYLE 2 FITNESS
2353 Carpenter Station Rd (19810-3145)
PHONE..............................215 254-0221
EMP: 5 EST: 2016
SALES (est): 76.36K **Privately Held**
SIC: 7991 Physical fitness facilities

(G-20109)
SUBARU INVESTMENT INC
301 N Market St (19801-2529)
PHONE..............................302 472-9266
EMP: 7 EST: 1998
SALES (est): 116.39K **Privately Held**
SIC: 6282 Investment advisory service

(G-20110)
SUBCODEVS INC
919 N Market St (19801-3023)
PHONE..............................704 234-6780
Subodh Srivastava, *CEO*
EMP: 6 EST: 2016
SALES (est): 371.16K **Privately Held**
Web: www.subcodevs.com
SIC: 7371 Computer software development

(G-20111)
SUBMIX HOLDINGS INC
1007 N Orange St (19801-1239)
PHONE..............................858 336-6467
Chris Galvin, *CEO*
EMP: 2 EST: 2019
SALES (est): 100K **Privately Held**
SIC: 7372 Educational computer software

(G-20112)
SUBURBAN INTRNAL MEDCNE ASSOCS
1403 N Rodney St (19806-4218)
PHONE..............................302 654-4800
EMP: 10 EST: 2018
SALES (est): 89.01K **Privately Held**
Web: www.nextgen.com
SIC: 8099 Health and allied services, nec

(G-20113)
SUBURBAN LAWN & EQUIPMENT INC (PA)
1601 Naamans Rd (19810-3020)
PHONE..............................302 475-4300
Anthony J Petruccelli, *Pr*
Mike J Petruccelli, *Sec*
EMP: 9 EST: 1973
SQ FT: 2,600
SALES (est): 2.28MM
SALES (corp-wide): 2.28MM **Privately Held**
Web: www.sublawneq.com
SIC: 5261 5251 7699 Lawnmowers and tractors; Chainsaws; Lawn mower repair shop

(G-20114)
SUBURBAN MARKETING ASSOCIATES (PA)
3301 Lancaster Pike 5c (19805-1436)
PHONE..............................302 656-8440
Robert F Martinelli, *Pr*
EMP: 40 EST: 1988
SQ FT: 8,000
SALES (est): 8.58MM
SALES (corp-wide): 8.58MM **Privately Held**
SIC: 5192 Magazines

(G-20115)
SUBURBAN PSYCHIATRIC SVCS LLC
5177 W Woodmill Dr Ste 6 (19808-4067)
PHONE..............................302 999-9834
Inderpreet Singh, *Prin*
EMP: 12 EST: 2017
SALES (est): 367.16K **Privately Held**
Web: www.suburbanpsychservices.com
SIC: 8322 General counseling services

(G-20116)
SUBURBAN PUBLISHING INC (PA)
Also Called: Mainline Today
3301 Lancaster Pike Ste 5c (19805-1436)
PHONE..............................302 656-1809
Robert F Martinelli, *Pr*
Angelo Martinelli, *
EMP: 44 EST: 1962
SQ FT: 10,000
SALES (est): 4.5MM
SALES (corp-wide): 4.5MM **Privately Held**
SIC: 2721 Magazines: publishing only, not printed on site

(G-20117)
SUBURBAN WASTE SERVICES INC
120 Dock St (19801-5400)
P.O. Box 1004 (19701-7004)
PHONE..............................302 661-0161
Evan Moxham, *Pr*
Tina Bizzari, *CFO*
Louis Bizzari, *VP*
Frances Moxham, *Sec*
EMP: 8 EST: 2007
SALES (est): 760K **Privately Held**
SIC: 8748 Business consulting, nec

(G-20118)
SUCCESS WONT WAIT INC
1729 Marsh Rd (19810-4607)
PHONE..............................302 388-9669
Susan E Mcneill, *Pr*
EMP: 7 EST: 2010
SALES (est): 54.91K **Privately Held**
Web: www.successwontwait.org
SIC: 8641 Civic and social associations

(G-20119)
SUEZ WATER DELAWARE INC
2000 First State Blvd (19804-3569)
P.O. Box 6508 (19804-0508)
PHONE..............................302 633-5900
David Stanton, *Pr*
EMP: 68 EST: 1930
SQ FT: 8,000
SALES (est): 11.25MM **Privately Held**
SIC: 4941 Water supply
HQ: Suez North America Inc.
461 From Rd Ste 400
Paramus NJ 07652
201 767-9300

(G-20120)
SUG BIOSCIENCES LLC ✪
251 Little Falls Dr (19808-1674)
PHONE..............................305 735-7009
EMP: 5 EST: 2022
SALES (est): 209.42K **Privately Held**
SIC: 8731 Biological research

(G-20121)
SUGARHILL INTERNATIONAL
4111 Claremont Ct (19808-2932)
PHONE..............................302 275-9257
Donnell Hill, *Prin*
EMP: 5 EST: 2012
SALES (est): 56.77K **Privately Held**
Web: www.sugarhillinc.com
SIC: 7221 Photographer, still or video

(G-20122)
SUM-R-FUN POOL PRODUCTS INC (PA)
5815 Kirkwood Hwy (19808-4873)
PHONE..............................302 998-9288
Sidney A Parry, *Pr*
Rick Parry, *
EMP: 40 EST: 1970
SQ FT: 1,800
SALES (est): 4.52MM
SALES (corp-wide): 4.52MM **Privately Held**
Web: www.sum-r-fun-pools.com
SIC: 1799 Swimming pool construction

(G-20123)
SUMMER LRNG COLLABORATIVE INC
1200 N French St (19801-3239)
PHONE..............................302 757-3940
Catherine Lindroth, *Ex Dir*
EMP: 25 EST: 2015
SALES (est): 574.12K **Privately Held**
Web: www.summercollab.org
SIC: 8699 Charitable organization

(G-20124)
SUMMIT FITNESS 180
1013 Woodstream Dr (19810-1933)
PHONE..............................610 574-3587
Phil Nicolaou, *Prin*
EMP: 6 EST: 2016
SALES (est): 53.6K **Privately Held**
Web: www.summitfitness180.com
SIC: 7991 Physical fitness facilities

(G-20125)
SUN COAL & COKE LLC
2401 Penns Ave Ste 111 (19806-1432)
PHONE..............................630 824-1000
Frederick Henderson, *CEO*
Michael Thomson, *
Denise Cade, *
Mark Newman, *
EMP: 749 EST: 1983
SALES (est): 41.37MM **Publicly Held**
SIC: 8731 Energy research
PA: Suncoke Energy, Inc.
1011 Warrenville Rd # 600
Lisle IL 60532

(G-20126)
SUN EAST FEDERAL CREDIT UNION
3630 Concord Pike (19803-5022)
PHONE..............................610 485-2960
EMP: 5 EST: 2019
SALES (est): 247.53K **Privately Held**
Web: www.suneast.org
SIC: 6061 Federal credit unions

(G-20127)
SUN-IN-ONE INC
500 Philadelphia Pike Ste 1 (19809-2146)
PHONE..............................302 762-3100
William Rawheiser, *Cnslt*
EMP: 10 EST: 2012
SQ FT: 2,000
SALES (est): 647.48K **Privately Held**
Web: www.suninone.com
SIC: 5074 3648 4911 Heating equipment and panels, solar; Outdoor lighting equipment

(G-20128)
SUN-RAY VALLEY INVESTMENTS LLC ✪
1201 N Market St Ste 111 (19801-1147)
PHONE..............................302 406-1078
Craig Williams, *Managing Member*
EMP: 8 EST: 2023
SALES (est): 319.06K **Privately Held**
SIC: 8742 Management consulting services

(G-20129)
SUNDAY BREAKFAST MISSION
600 E 5th St Apt C1 (19801-4712)
P.O. Box 342 (19899-0342)
PHONE..............................302 656-8542
Thomas Laymon, *Ex Dir*
Gerald A Foster, *Commsnr*
EMP: 10 EST: 1893
SALES (est): 6.22MM **Privately Held**
Web: www.sundaybreakfastmission.org
SIC: 8322 Social service center

(G-20130)
SUNDEW PAINTING INC
500 S Colonial Ave (19805-1900)
PHONE..............................302 994-7004
Nicholas J Nardo Senior, *Pr*
Joseph Dino Nardo, *VP*

Wilmington - New Castle County (G-20131) — GEOGRAPHIC SECTION

Shirley Nardo, *Sec*
EMP: 25 **EST:** 1962
SQ FT: 5,000
SALES (est): 2.08MM **Privately Held**
SIC: 1721 Exterior residential painting contractor

(G-20131)
SUNLIFE LLC
3 Germay Dr Unit 4-1478 (19804-1127)
PHONE..................................833 478-6669
EMP: 25 **EST:** 2020
SALES (est): 941.41K **Privately Held**
Web: www.sunlifenow.com
SIC: 1711 Solar energy contractor

(G-20132)
SUNLIGHT INSUR HOLDINGS LLC
1209 N Orange St (19801-1120)
PHONE..................................952 808-6312
EMP: 55
SALES (est): 1.18MM **Privately Held**
SIC: 7371 Software programming applications

(G-20133)
SUNNYMAC LLC
Also Called: Sunnymac Solar
413 8th Ave (19805-4745)
PHONE..................................844 786-6962
Andie Coulter, *Managing Member*
EMP: 30 **EST:** 2009
SALES (est): 5.39MM **Privately Held**
Web: www.sunnymacsolar.com
SIC: 1711 Solar energy contractor

(G-20134)
SUNRISE SENIOR LIVING LLC
Also Called: Sunrise of Wilmington
2215 Shipley Rd (19803-2305)
PHONE..................................302 475-9163
Michael Friedel, *Mgr*
EMP: 52
SALES (corp-wide): 2.92B **Privately Held**
Web: www.sunriseseniorliving.com
SIC: 8051 8361 Skilled nursing care facilities ; Residential care
HQ: Sunrise Senior Living, Llc
 7902 Westpark Dr
 Mc Lean VA 22102

(G-20135)
SUNSET PROPERTY MANAGEMENT
23 S Woodward Ave (19805-2354)
PHONE..................................410 202-1679
John Kozloski, *Prin*
EMP: 7 **EST:** 2018
SALES (est): 198.83K **Privately Held**
Web: www.sunsetspm.com
SIC: 8741 Management services

(G-20136)
SUNSHINE HEALTH
411 Rochelle Ave (19804-2117)
PHONE..................................302 463-7600
EMP: 11 **EST:** 2018
SALES (est): 303.19K **Privately Held**
Web: www.sunshinehealth.com
SIC: 8099 Health and allied services, nec

(G-20137)
SUNSHINE VENDING MACHINES LLC ◆
1207 Delaware Ave Ste 775 (19806-4743)
P.O. Box 92 (08085-0092)
PHONE..................................800 670-6557
Christine Wilcher, *Managing Member*
EMP: 2 **EST:** 2023
SALES (est): 71.19K **Privately Held**
SIC: 3581 7359 5963 Automatic vending machines; Vending machine rental; Snacks, direct sales

(G-20138)
SUNTRUST DELAWARE TRUST CO
1011 Centre Rd Ste 205 (19805-1266)
PHONE..................................302 892-9930
Barbara Odonnell, *Prin*
EMP: 29 **EST:** 2008
SALES (est): 2.14MM
SALES (corp-wide): 25.36B **Publicly Held**
SIC: 6021 National commercial banks
PA: Truist Financial Corporation
 214 N Tryon St Ste 3900
 Charlotte NC 28202
 336 733-2000

(G-20139)
SUPER WASH
1952 Maryland Ave (19805-4605)
PHONE..................................302 384-6111
EMP: 8 **EST:** 2018
SALES (est): 98.24K **Privately Held**
Web: www.superwash.com
SIC: 7542 Carwashes

(G-20140)
SUPERIOR ELECTRIC SERVICE CO
36 Germay Dr (19804-1105)
PHONE..................................302 658-5949
Jane Fitzsimmons, *Pr*
James Fitzsimmons, *
Sindy Reeves, *Mgr*
John Mckee, *Proj Mgr*
Joelle Cordrey, *Off Mgr*
EMP: 50 **EST:** 1985
SQ FT: 27,000
SALES (est): 9.91MM **Privately Held**
Web: www.superiorelectric.biz
SIC: 1731 General electrical contractor

(G-20141)
SUPERIOR EQUIPMENT RENTAL CO
36 Germay Dr (19804-1105)
PHONE..................................302 658-6193
EMP: 10 **EST:** 2019
SALES (est): 964.73K **Privately Held**
Web: www.superiorequipmentrental.com
SIC: 7359 Equipment rental and leasing, nec

(G-20142)
SUPERIOR LUXE LLC
Also Called: Seattle Luxe
1501 Concord Pike Ste 303 (19803-3601)
PHONE..................................800 325-6262
Aaron Flohr, *Owner*
EMP: 4 **EST:** 2015
SALES (est): 242.95K **Privately Held**
SIC: 2599 Boards: planning, display, notice

(G-20143)
SUPERIOR SERVICES GROUP LLC
2207 Concord Pike Unit 147 (19803-2908)
PHONE..................................888 683-8288
EMP: 7 **EST:** 2020
SALES (est): 150K **Privately Held**
SIC: 3589 Commercial cleaning equipment

(G-20144)
SUPERLATIVE IMAGE LLC
4023 Kennett Pike (19807-2018)
PHONE..................................714 369-5412
Jack Pham, *Prin*
EMP: 5 **EST:** 2017
SALES (est): 36.15K **Privately Held**
SIC: 7335 Photographic studio, commercial

(G-20145)
SUPERLODGE
1213 N West St (19801-1044)
PHONE..................................302 654-5544
Anup Patel, *Prin*
EMP: 15 **EST:** 2004
SALES (est): 107.31K **Privately Held**
Web: www.newcastlesuperlodge.net
SIC: 7011 Motels

(G-20146)
SUPERMARKET ASSOCIATES INC
4001 Kennett Pike (19807-2315)
PHONE..................................302 547-1977
Ronnie Robinson, *Pr*
Kristin Robinson, *VP*
EMP: 7 **EST:** 1996
SALES (est): 1.43MM **Privately Held**
Web: www.sbarrowines.com
SIC: 5141 Food brokers

(G-20147)
SUPERPOWER ENTERTAINMENT LLC (PA)
251 Little Falls Dr (19808-1674)
PHONE..................................650 667-0266
EMP: 7 **EST:** 2018
SALES (est): 156.25K
SALES (corp-wide): 156.25K **Privately Held**
SIC: 7371 Computer software development and applications

(G-20148)
SUPPER SOLUTIONS LLC
3619 Silverside Rd (19810-5101)
PHONE..................................302 478-5935
Cathy Hagan, *Managing Member*
EMP: 6 **EST:** 2007
SALES (est): 277.57K **Privately Held**
SIC: 2052 Bakery products, dry

(G-20149)
SUPPLY CHAIN CONSULTANTS INC
Also Called: Arkieva
5460 Fairmont Dr (19808-3432)
PHONE..................................302 738-9215
Bibi I Singh, *Pr*
Harpal Singh, *
▼ **EMP:** 40 **EST:** 1993
SQ FT: 14,160
SALES (est): 7.81MM **Privately Held**
Web: www.arkieva.com
SIC: 8742 7371 Business management consultant; Computer software development

(G-20150)
SUPPLY CHAIN MGMT INC
3524 Silverside Rd (19810-4929)
PHONE..................................302 467-2014
Pavlo Kobzar, *Pr*
EMP: 30 **EST:** 2019
SALES (est): 1.27MM **Privately Held**
SIC: 8741 Management services

(G-20151)
SUPPORTCOM INC (HQ)
Also Called: Support.com
1521 Concord Pike Ste 301 (19803-3644)
PHONE..................................650 556-9440
Lance Rosenzweig, *Pr*
Joshua E Schechter, *Ch Bd*
Christine Kowalczyk, *COO*
Caroline Rook, *CFO*
EMP: 88 **EST:** 1997
SALES (est): 43.86MM
SALES (corp-wide): 74.63MM **Privately Held**
Web: www.support.com
SIC: 7374 7372 Data processing and preparation; Business oriented computer software
PA: Realdefense Llc
 150 S Los Robles Ave # 4
 Pasadena CA 91101
 801 895-7907

(G-20152)
SUPPORTIVE ACCOUNTABILITY HUB
1209 N Orange St (19801-1120)
PHONE..................................615 579-3533
Rebecca Ackerman, *Pr*
EMP: 10 **EST:** 2020
SALES (est): 1.76MM **Privately Held**
SIC: 7389 Business Activities at Non-Commercial Site

(G-20153)
SUPPORTIVE CARE SOLUTIONS LLC
1606 Newport Gap Pike (19808-6208)
P.O. Box 5463 (19808-0463)
PHONE..................................302 598-4797
David Simkins, *Prin*
EMP: 5 **EST:** 2015
SALES (est): 104.32K **Privately Held**
Web: www.supportcares.com
SIC: 8399 Advocacy group

(G-20154)
SUPPORTYOURAPP INC
1007 N Orange St Ste 122 (19801-1242)
PHONE..................................888 959-3556
Dan Engel, *Bd of Dir*
Daria Leshchenko, *CEO*
Ann Kuss, *COO*
EMP: 25 **EST:** 2014
SALES (est): 2.22MM **Privately Held**
Web: www.supportyourapp.com
SIC: 7376 7379 7372 Computer facilities management; Computer hardware requirements analysis; Office computer automation systems integration

(G-20155)
SUPREME COURT UNITED STATES
Also Called: US Probation Pretrial
824 N Market St (19801-3024)
PHONE..................................302 252-2950
John Mcdonough, *Brnch Mgr*
EMP: 11
Web: www.supremecourt.gov
SIC: 8322 9211 Probation office; Courts
HQ: Supreme Court, United States
 1 1st St Ne
 Washington DC 20543
 202 479-3000

(G-20156)
SUPREME LEGACY INC
2705 N Madison St (19802-3069)
PHONE..................................973 567-3115
Arthur Benson, *Prin*
EMP: 5 **EST:** 2010
SALES (est): 47.61K **Privately Held**
SIC: 7699 Cleaning services

(G-20157)
SUPREME LENDING
2710 Centerville Rd (19808-1644)
PHONE..................................302 268-6244
EMP: 6 **EST:** 2019
SALES (est): 247.98K **Privately Held**
SIC: 6162 Mortgage bankers and loan correspondents

(G-20158)
SUPREME SERVICEZ LLC ◆
Also Called: Supreme Cleanerz

2212 Kirkwood Hwy (19805-4904)
PHONE..................................302 932-5724
Lashawn M Buckham, *Managing Member*
EMP: 5 **EST:** 2022
SALES (est): 108K **Privately Held**
SIC: 7349 6531 Cleaning service, industrial or commercial; Real estate agents and managers

(G-20159)
SUPREME TRADING LLC
3524 Silverside Rd Ste 35 B (19810-4929)
PHONE..................................302 415-3188
Jay Sharma, *Mgr*
▲ **EMP:** 5 **EST:** 2019
SALES (est): 264.75K **Privately Held**
Web: www.supremetradingus.com
SIC: 2099 Seasonings and spices

(G-20160)
SURESRCE CMMDTIES LLC - ORGNIC
1201 N Market St Ste 111 (19801-1156)
PHONE..................................866 697-5960
Barbara Mcgillivray, *Pr*
EMP: 11 **EST:** 2021
SALES (est): 3.82MM
SALES (corp-wide): 3.82MM **Privately Held**
SIC: 5153 Grains
PA: Suresource Commodities, Llc
1201 N Market St Ste 111
Wilmington DE 19801
866 697-5960

(G-20161)
SURETRONIX SOLUTIONS LLC
111 Brookside Dr (19804-1103)
PHONE..................................302 407-3146
Maged Zamzam, *Mgr*
EMP: 3 **EST:** 2016
SALES (est): 142.06K **Privately Held**
SIC: 8711 3825 3679 3672 Electrical or electronic engineering; Digital test equipment, electronic and electrical circuits; Electronic circuits; Printed circuit boards

(G-20162)
SURVIVORS ABUSE IN RCOVERY INC
Also Called: S.O.A.R
405 Foulk Rd (19803-3809)
PHONE..................................302 651-0181
Stephen R Brodt, *Pr*
EMP: 5 **EST:** 1992
SALES (est): 1.1MM **Privately Held**
Web: www.survivorsofabuse.org
SIC: 8322 Social service center

(G-20163)
SUSAN L BARTON
405 Foulk Rd (19803-3809)
PHONE..................................302 655-3953
Susan L Barton, *Prin*
EMP: 8 **EST:** 2014
SALES (est): 54.44K **Privately Held**
SIC: 8322 Individual and family services

(G-20164)
SUSAN MCCLAIN
2401 Pennsylvania Ave (19806-1401)
PHONE..................................302 655-5877
Susan Mcclain, *Owner*
EMP: 7 **EST:** 2014
SALES (est): 46.27K **Privately Held**
SIC: 8049 Offices of health practitioner

(G-20165)
SUSTAINABLE-GENERATION LLC
Also Called: Sustainable Generation
110 S Poplar St Ste 400 (19801-5044)
PHONE..................................917 678-6947
Scott Woods, *CEO*
Straud Ben Fredregill, *Prin*
Ben Fredregill, *VP*
EMP: 10 **EST:** 2012
SALES (est): 974.63K **Privately Held**
Web: www.sustainable-generation.com
SIC: 8748 Environmental consultant

(G-20166)
SUTTON BUS & TRUCK CO INC
5609 Old Capitol Trl Frnt (19808-4932)
PHONE..................................302 995-7444
Ronald Sutton, *Pr*
David Sutton, *
EMP: 24 **EST:** 1963
SQ FT: 1,500
SALES (est): 920.17K **Privately Held**
Web: www.farmingtonpt.com
SIC: 4151 4212 School buses; Dump truck haulage

(G-20167)
SUZANNE ISENBERG
103a Rogers Rd (19801-5767)
PHONE..................................302 470-1166
Suzanne Isenberg, *Prin*
EMP: 6 **EST:** 2017
SALES (est): 59.13K **Privately Held**
SIC: 8322 Individual and family services

(G-20168)
SWAMI ENTERPRISES INC
Also Called: Dunkin' Donuts
1702 Faulkland Rd (19805-1160)
PHONE..................................302 999-8077
Nick Baden, *Pr*
EMP: 5 **EST:** 2001
SALES (est): 352.51K **Privately Held**
Web: www.dunkindonuts.com
SIC: 5461 5812 7389 Doughnuts; Eating places; Business services, nec

(G-20169)
SWANK MEMORY CARE CENTER
205 W 14th St (19801-1114)
PHONE..................................302 320-2620
EMP: 10 **EST:** 2019
SALES (est): 171.13K **Privately Held**
SIC: 8099 Health and allied services, nec

(G-20170)
SWARTER SERVICES LLC
600 E Front St (19801-5026)
PHONE..................................302 575-9943
Jill French, *Prin*
EMP: 5 **EST:** 2019
SALES (est): 227.65K **Privately Held**
SIC: 1522 Residential construction, nec

(G-20171)
SWAVE LLC
187 Odyssey Dr (19808-1568)
PHONE..................................302 766-3125
EMP: 10 **EST:** 2019
SALES (est): 306.2K **Privately Held**
SIC: 7389 Business services, nec

(G-20172)
SWEET DREAMS DAYCARE
733 S Harrison St (19805-4334)
PHONE..................................302 425-0844
Rosa Rodriguez, *Owner*
EMP: 8 **EST:** 2018
SALES (est): 19.32K **Privately Held**
SIC: 8351 Group day care center

(G-20173)
SWEET VENOM EFFECT LLC
1004 Kirkwood St Ste 1 (19801-4024)
PHONE..................................302 674-5831
EMP: 25 **EST:** 2019
SALES (est): 591.13K **Privately Held**
SIC: 2051 Bakery: wholesale or wholesale/ retail combined

(G-20174)
SWIATOWICZ DENTAL ASSOCIATES
1211 Milltown Rd (19808-3003)
PHONE..................................302 476-8185
Andrew Swiatowicz, *Prin*
EMP: 13 **EST:** 2016
SALES (est): 1.74MM **Privately Held**
Web: www.detoothdr.com
SIC: 8021 Dentists' office

(G-20175)
SWIFT FINANCIAL LLC (HQ)
Also Called: Swift Capital
3505 Silverside Rd (19810-4905)
PHONE..................................302 374-7019
Ed Harycki, *CEO*
Doug Bland, *Pr*
Jay Lee, *PROD*
Paul Sveen, *CFO*
EMP: 59 **EST:** 2006
SALES (est): 43.69MM
SALES (corp-wide): 29.77B **Publicly Held**
Web: www.swiftfinancial.com
SIC: 6153 7389 Working capital financing; Financial services
PA: Paypal Holdings, Inc.
2211 N 1st St
San Jose CA 95131
408 967-1000

(G-20176)
SWOOP PAYMENT PROCESSING INC
Also Called: Swoop
4550 Linden Hill Rd Ste 103 (19808-2930)
PHONE..................................479 586-2952
Perry Turnbull, *Prin*
EMP: 37 **EST:** 2017
SALES (est): 125.73K **Privately Held**
Web: www.swoopbusinesssolutions.com
SIC: 7389 Credit card service

(G-20177)
SWORDFISH SECURITY USA INC
20c Trolley Sq (19806)
PHONE..................................302 327-8580
Aleksander Pinaev, *CEO*
EMP: 10 **EST:** 2013
SALES (est): 457.75K **Privately Held**
Web: www.swordfish-security.com
SIC: 7371 Software programming applications

(G-20178)
SYF INDUSTRIES
1410 Prospect Dr (19809-2429)
PHONE..................................302 384-6214
EMP: 3 **EST:** 2016
SALES (est): 63.72K **Privately Held**
SIC: 3999 Manufacturing industries, nec

(G-20179)
SYKES ORNA & CSTM IR WORKS INC
315 Bradford St (19801-5415)
PHONE..................................302 757-2103
EMP: 6 **EST:** 2018
SALES (est): 259.14K **Privately Held**
Web: sykes-ornamental-iron-and-custom-metal-works.business.site
SIC: 1791 Iron work, structural

(G-20180)
SYLVIA SAIENNA
Also Called: Majo Hair Studio
100 Westgate Dr (19808-1428)
PHONE..................................302 683-9082
Sylvia Saienna, *Owner*
EMP: 5 **EST:** 1980
SQ FT: 2,400
SALES (est): 195.35K **Privately Held**
SIC: 7231 Unisex hair salons

(G-20181)
SYMBIOSYS CONSULTING LLC
Also Called: Belsham Technologies
920 Justison St (19801-5150)
PHONE..................................302 507-7649
EMP: 10 **EST:** 2002
SALES (est): 904.94K **Privately Held**
Web: www.belsham.tech
SIC: 7379 Computer related maintenance services

(G-20182)
SYMEND US INC
251 Little Falls Dr (19808-1674)
PHONE..................................855 579-6363
EMP: 42 **EST:** 2019
SALES (est): 2.57MM **Privately Held**
Web: www.symend.com
SIC: 7371 Custom computer programming services

(G-20183)
SYMMETRY DATA SOLUTIONS INC
251 Little Falls Dr (19808-1674)
PHONE..................................805 708-4506
Casen Hunger, *CEO*
EMP: 21 **EST:** 2020
SALES (est): 598.21K **Privately Held**
SIC: 7374 Data processing service

(G-20184)
SYNCHRGNIX INFO STRATEGIES LLC (DH)
2 Righter Pkwy Ste 205 (19803-1529)
PHONE..................................302 892-4800
Kelley Kendle, *CEO*
Frank Garafalo, *
EMP: 33 **EST:** 1986
SALES (est): 12.04MM
SALES (corp-wide): 335.64M **Publicly Held**
Web: www.certara.com
SIC: 8731 Commercial physical research
HQ: Certara Usa, Inc.
100 Overlook Ctr Ste 101
Princeton NJ 08540

(G-20185)
SYNCRETIC PRESS LLC
1137 Webster Dr (19803-3459)
PHONE..................................443 723-8355
Enrique Moras, *Prin*
EMP: 5 **EST:** 2017
SALES (est): 172.1K **Privately Held**
Web: www.syncreticpress.com
SIC: 2741 Miscellaneous publishing

(G-20186)
SYNCRETIC SOFTWARE INC
1415 Foulk Rd (19803-2748)
PHONE..................................302 762-2600
Seth Rosenberg, *Pr*
Timothy Brennan, *VP*
EMP: 13 **EST:** 1997
SALES (est): 2.22MM **Privately Held**
Web: www.syncretic.com

Wilmington - New Castle County (G-20187)   GEOGRAPHIC SECTION

SIC: 7379 7371 Computer related consulting services; Software programming applications

(G-20187)
SYNERGY INTEGRATED MEDICAL CTR
1702 Kirkwood Hwy Ste 101 (19805-4939)
PHONE..................................302 777-0778
Mary Schuler, *Ofcr*
EMP: 10 EST: 2017
SALES (est): 471.34K Privately Held
Web: www.synergydelaware.com
SIC: 8041 Offices and clinics of chiropractors

(G-20188)
SYNETICS CORPORATION
2400 W 4th St (19805-3306)
PHONE..................................302 427-0787
Van Velsor Frazier, *Prin*
EMP: 8 EST: 2008
SALES (est): 520.16K Privately Held
Web: www.namidelaware.org
SIC: 8711 Consulting engineer

(G-20189)
SYNGENTA CORPORATION (DH)
3411 Silverside Rd Ste 100 (19810-4811)
PHONE..................................302 425-2000
Jason Fogden, *VP*
Henry P Graef, *
Cheryl Quain, *
◆ EMP: 25 EST: 2000
SALES (est): 1.47B Privately Held
Web: www.syngenta-us.com
SIC: 2879 5191 8741 Agricultural chemicals, nec; Seeds: field, garden, and flower; Management services
HQ: Syngenta Ag
Rosentalstrasse 67
Basel BS 4058

(G-20190)
SYNNEFA INC
2055 Limestone Rd Ste 200c (19808-5536)
PHONE..................................302 565-4405
Taita Ngetich, *CEO*
EMP: 7 EST: 2021
SALES (est): 264.9K Privately Held
Web: www.synnefa.io
SIC: 7371 Computer software development and applications

(G-20191)
SYNTEC CORPORATION (PA)
109 Rogers Rd Ste 5 (19801-5779)
PHONE..................................302 421-8393
Robert Di Stefano, *Pr*
EMP: 15 EST: 1973
SQ FT: 13,000
SALES (est): 4.41MM
SALES (corp-wide): 4.41MM Privately Held
Web: www.syntec.com
SIC: 5169 2869 Chemicals, industrial and heavy; Industrial organic chemicals, nec

(G-20192)
SYNTHEZAI CORP
919 N Market St Ste 950 (19801-3036)
PHONE..................................415 980-9792
Maksym Prasolov, *CEO*
EMP: 5 EST: 2021
SALES (est): 117.25K Privately Held
SIC: 7372 Application computer software

(G-20193)
SYNUP
1521 Concord Pike (19803-3642)
PHONE..................................844 228-2852

EMP: 24 EST: 2017
SALES (est): 2.04MM Privately Held
Web: www.synup.com
SIC: 7371 Computer software development and applications

(G-20194)
SYSTEMS CORPORATION
251 Little Falls Dr (19808-1674)
PHONE..................................323 984-7401
Aleksandr Khairullaev, *CEO*
EMP: 8 EST: 2019
SALES (est): 680.32K Privately Held
Web: www.systems-x.com
SIC: 5199 Variety store merchandise

(G-20195)
SYSTIMA INC
2055 Limestone Rd (19808-5536)
PHONE..................................929 551-4849
EMP: 10
SALES (est): 348.32K Privately Held
SIC: 7371 Computer software development and applications

(G-20196)
SZEWCZYK COMPANY P A
Also Called: Szewczyk and Company
3403 Lancaster Pike Ste 4 (19805-5533)
PHONE..................................302 998-1117
Joseph Szewczyk, *Pr*
EMP: 5 EST: 1980
SALES (est): 243.34K Privately Held
SIC: 8721 Certified public accountant

(G-20197)
T & H BAIL BONDS AGENCY LLC
625 N King St Frnt (19801-3751)
PHONE..................................302 777-7982
EMP: 6 EST: 2018
SALES (est): 542.34K Privately Held
Web: www.thbailbondagency.com
SIC: 7389 Bail bonding

(G-20198)
T & L CONSULTING SERVICES LLC
222 Philadelphia Pike Ste 4 (19809-3166)
PHONE..................................302 573-1585
EMP: 8 EST: 2017
SALES (est): 61.12K Privately Held
SIC: 8082 Home health care services

(G-20199)
T S N PUBLISHING CO INC
Also Called: Out & About
307 A St Ste C (19801-5345)
PHONE..................................302 655-6483
Gerald Duphily, *Pr*
EMP: 7 EST: 1988
SALES (est): 654.54K Privately Held
SIC: 2721 2741 Magazines: publishing only, not printed on site; Newsletter publishing

(G-20200)
T-MOBILE
Also Called: T-Mobile Preferred Retailer
724 N Market St (19801-3009)
PHONE..................................302 652-7738
Dave Chung, *Pr*
EMP: 5 EST: 2011
SALES (est): 421.77K Privately Held
Web: www.t-mobile.com
SIC: 4812 Cellular telephone services

(G-20201)
T-MOBILE USA INC
4735 Concord Pike (19803-1408)
PHONE..................................302 479-9691
Amy Loubna, *Mgr*
EMP: 6

SALES (corp-wide): 78.56B Publicly Held
Web: www.t-mobile.com
SIC: 4812 Cellular telephone services
HQ: T-Mobile Usa, Inc.
12920 Se 38th St
Bellevue WA 98006
425 378-4000

(G-20202)
T-MOBILE USA INC
3630 Kirkwood Hwy (19808-5104)
PHONE..................................302 998-0112
Alicia Griffin, *Mgr*
EMP: 5
SALES (corp-wide): 78.56B Publicly Held
Web: www.t-mobile.com
SIC: 4812 Cellular telephone services
HQ: T-Mobile Usa, Inc.
12920 Se 38th St
Bellevue WA 98006
425 378-4000

(G-20203)
TA AUSTIN PLUMBING INC
24 Duvall Ct (19808-2143)
PHONE..................................302 995-2282
EMP: 11 EST: 2020
SALES (est): 226.31K Privately Held
Web: www.taaustinplumbing.com
SIC: 1711 Plumbing contractors

(G-20204)
TA RIETDORF & SONS INC
735 S Market St Ste D (19801-5246)
P.O. Box 1528 (19899-1528)
PHONE..................................302 429-0341
Timothy Rietdorf, *Pr*
Karl Rietdorf, *VP*
June Rietdorf, *Sec*
EMP: 6 EST: 1977
SQ FT: 1,000
SALES (est): 633.54K Privately Held
SIC: 1731 General electrical contractor

(G-20205)
TABELING & CO CPA
3825 Lancaster Pike Ste 200 (19805-1559)
PHONE..................................302 999-8020
Linda Tabeling, *Prin*
EMP: 5 EST: 2006
SALES (est): 152.26K Privately Held
Web: www.tabelingcpa.com
SIC: 8721 Certified public accountant

(G-20206)
TAC FINANCIAL CORP
103 Foulk Rd Ste 202 (19803-3742)
PHONE..................................302 691-6014
Marc Stefanski, *Prin*
EMP: 8 EST: 2001
SALES (est): 263.96K Privately Held
SIC: 7299 Debt counseling or adjustment service, individuals

(G-20207)
TAG WATER RESTORATION & CNSTR
2214 N Market St (19802-4259)
PHONE..................................877 558-6646
EMP: 8 EST: 2005
SALES (est): 191.54K Privately Held
Web: www.tagwaterrestoration.com
SIC: 1521 Single-family housing construction

(G-20208)
TAIGA EXPRESS LLC
427 N Tatnall St Ste 74587 (19801-2230)
PHONE..................................718 577-2028
EMP: 5
SALES (est): 46.16K Privately Held

SIC: 7371 Computer software development and applications

(G-20209)
TAKE-A-BREAK INC
413 8th Ave (19805-4745)
P.O. Box 376 (19936-0376)
PHONE..................................302 658-8571
TOLL FREE: 800
Alan Blum, *Pr*
EMP: 22 EST: 1966
SQ FT: 18,000
SALES (est): 494.43K Privately Held
Web: www.takeabreakinc.com
SIC: 5962 7389 5963 Merchandising machine operators; Coffee service; Bottled water delivery

(G-20210)
TALE INNOVATIONS INC ✧
251 Little Falls Dr (19808-1674)
PHONE..................................301 887-7587
Josiah Faison, *CEO*
Conrad Niedzielski, *CMO*
EMP: 4 EST: 2023
SALES (est): 171.34K Privately Held
SIC: 7372 Prepackaged software

(G-20211)
TALENT HIRE CONSULTING INC
427 N Tatnall St Ste 34574 (19801)
PHONE..................................302 414-8235
Ripan Bhattacharjee, *Prin*
Amrita Bhattacharjee, *
EMP: 30 EST: 2017
SALES (est): 2.35MM Privately Held
Web: www.talenthireconsulting.com
SIC: 7361 Executive placement

(G-20212)
TALENT4HEALTH LLC
1000 N West St (19801-1050)
PHONE..................................302 314-1677
EMP: 65 EST: 2019
SALES (est): 2.95MM Privately Held
Web: www.talent4health.com
SIC: 7363 Temporary help service

(G-20213)
TALITHA DITALIA OD
3105 Limestone Rd Ste 102 (19808-2147)
PHONE..................................302 998-1395
Talitha D'italia, *Prin*
EMP: 6 EST: 2016
SALES (est): 67.9K Privately Held
SIC: 8042 Offices and clinics of optometrists

(G-20214)
TALLEYS GARAGE INC
416 Roseanna Ave (19803-1831)
PHONE..................................302 652-0463
James Talley Senior, *Pr*
James Talley Junior, *VP*
Leonard N Talley, *Treas*
EMP: 5 EST: 1922
SALES (est): 502.25K Privately Held
SIC: 5261 7699 Garden supplies and tools, nec; Lawn mower repair shop

(G-20215)
TALLEYVILLE TOWNE SHOPPES
4015 Concord Pike (19803-1717)
PHONE..................................302 478-1969
EMP: 6 EST: 2018
SALES (est): 96.26K Privately Held
Web: www.concordpikeliquors.net
SIC: 6512 Shopping center, property operation only

Wilmington - New Castle County (G-20244)

(G-20216)
TALLYVILLE ANIMAL HOSPITAL
3001 Concord Pike (19803-5012)
PHONE.............................302 478-1194
Kathryn Stoltzfus, Mgr
EMP: 7 EST: 2015
SALES (est): 224.25K Privately Held
Web: www.talleyvilleveterinary.com
SIC: 0742 Animal hospital services, pets and other animal specialties

(G-20217)
TALMO JOHN
2709 Tanager Dr (19808-1621)
PHONE.............................302 547-9657
John Talmo, Prin
EMP: 7 EST: 2010
SALES (est): 217.56K Privately Held
SIC: 1794 Excavation work

(G-20218)
TANGENT CABLE SYSTEMS INC
3700 Washington Ave (19808-6034)
PHONE.............................302 994-4104
Lee A Burkey, Pr
Susan E Burkey, *
Ray Burton, *
Cary Johnson, *
Suellen Burkey, *
EMP: 30 EST: 1996
SQ FT: 780
SALES (est): 5.29MM Privately Held
Web: www.tangentcable.com
SIC: 1731 General electrical contractor

(G-20219)
TANGTRING SEATING TECH USA LLC ✪
1013 Centre Rd Ste 403a (19805-1270)
PHONE.............................269 365-4030
EMP: 6 EST: 2022
SALES (est): 78.16K Privately Held
SIC: 2531 Public building and related furniture

(G-20220)
TAPLISTIC LLC
3422 Old Capitol Trl (19808-6124)
PHONE.............................516 362-1890
Bobby Greenfeld, Managing Member
EMP: 15
SALES (est): 650.61K Privately Held
SIC: 5045 Computer software

(G-20221)
TAPPIT TECHNOLOGIES (US) INC
251 Little Falls Dr (19808-1674)
PHONE.............................570 898-1399
Lauren Hackenburg, Cobra Vice President
EMP: 5
SALES (corp-wide): 122.01K Privately Held
SIC: 7371 Custom computer programming services
PA: Tappit Technologies (Us), Inc.
511 E John Carpenter Fwy
Irving TX 75062
570 898-1399

(G-20222)
TARAK N PATEL DC
390 Mitch Rd (19804-3943)
PHONE.............................856 904-3061
Tarak Patel, Owner
EMP: 7 EST: 2017
SALES (est): 37.19K Privately Held
SIC: 8041 Offices and clinics of chiropractors

(G-20223)
TARBURTON LANDSCAPE
2722 Duncan Rd (19808-3125)
PHONE.............................302 932-1814
Kenneth R Tarburton, Prin
EMP: 7 EST: 2011
SALES (est): 430.24K Privately Held
Web: www.tarburtonstree.com
SIC: 0783 Planting, pruning, and trimming services

(G-20224)
TARGET MARKETS LLC
3411 Silverside Rd Ste 100 (19810-4812)
PHONE.............................302 268-1010
Kate Boyle, OF MARKE
EMP: 25 EST: 2001
SALES (est): 1.18MM
SALES (corp-wide): 11.17B Publicly Held
Web: www.targetmkts.com
SIC: 7311 Advertising agencies
PA: W. R. Berkley Corporation
475 Steamboat Rd Fl 1
Greenwich CT 06830
203 629-3000

(G-20225)
TASK ANALYTICS INC
251 Little Falls Dr (19808-1674)
PHONE.............................631 388-3120
EMP: 5 EST: 2019
SALES (est): 164.18K Privately Held
SIC: 7371 Computer software development

(G-20226)
TATA COMMUNICATIONS AMER INC (HQ)
Also Called: Teleglobe Vsnl International
251 Little Falls Dr (19808-1674)
PHONE.............................703 547-5900
Troy Reynolds, Pr
Matthew Xiaobing Ma, VP
Hunter Payne, Tax Officer
EMP: 29 EST: 2002
SALES (est): 261.45MM Privately Held
Web: www.tatacommunications.com
SIC: 4813 Internet host services
PA: Tata Communications Limited
Plot No. C21 & C36, G' Block,
Mumbai MH 40009

(G-20227)
TATNALL TECHNOLOGY LLC
117 W 13th St (19801-1104)
P.O. Box 4200 (19807-0200)
PHONE.............................302 212-0959
EMP: 5 EST: 2018
SALES (est): 103.91K Privately Held
Web: www.tatnalltech.com
SIC: 7379 Computer related consulting services

(G-20228)
TATSAPOD-AAME
1112 Newport Gap Pike (19804-2865)
PHONE.............................302 897-8963
EMP: 5 EST: 2010
SALES (est): 55.46K Privately Held
SIC: 8322 Individual and family services

(G-20229)
TAWKIFY INC
3 Germay Dr Ste 4 (19804-1127)
PHONE.............................415 549-1928
Kellie Ammerman, Managing Member
EMP: 9 EST: 2012
SALES (est): 982.4K Privately Held
Web: www.tawkify.com
SIC: 8742 Management consulting services

(G-20230)
TAX AUTHORITY INC
3610 Kirkwood Hwy (19808-5104)
PHONE.............................302 633-0777
EMP: 5 EST: 2012
SALES (est): 33.24K Privately Held
SIC: 7291 Tax return preparation services

(G-20231)
TAX TAKE LLC (PA)
3422 Old Capitol Trl Ste 1945 (19808-6124)
PHONE.............................302 760-9758
EMP: 7 EST: 2015
SALES (est): 117.39K
SALES (corp-wide): 117.39K Privately Held
Web: www.taxtake.com
SIC: 7389 8721 Legal and tax services; Certified public accountant

(G-20232)
TAXDONE
106 Brookside Ave (19805-2437)
PHONE.............................302 388-5796
David B Smith, Prin
EMP: 5 EST: 2009
SALES (est): 26.16K Privately Held
SIC: 7291 Tax return preparation services

(G-20233)
TAYLOR COPELAND LLC
3801 Kennett Pike Ste D300 (19807-2327)
PHONE.............................302 598-4412
EMP: 5 EST: 2019
SALES (est): 228.91K Privately Held
Web: www.copelandtaylor.com
SIC: 8111 General practice attorney, lawyer

(G-20234)
TAYLOR MADE WATERS INC
Also Called: Taylor Hydrate
1521 Concord Pike Ste 302 (19803-3645)
PHONE.............................302 352-9979
Shavonn Jackson, CEO
Jun Kawakubo, CEO
Shavonn Jackson, Prin
EMP: 17 EST: 2016
SALES (est): 586.73K Privately Held
SIC: 2086 Bottled and canned soft drinks

(G-20235)
TAYLOR PROFESSIONAL INSURANCE
1000 N West St Fl 10 (19801-1059)
PHONE.............................302 660-3685
EMP: 5 EST: 2017
SALES (est): 223.15K Privately Held
Web: www.taylorprofessionalinsurance.com
SIC: 6411 Insurance agents, nec

(G-20236)
TC ELECTRIC COMPANY INC
6701 Governor Printz Blvd (19809-1809)
PHONE.............................302 791-0378
Thomas Curley, Pr
EMP: 30 EST: 1974
SALES (est): 4.86MM Privately Held
Web: www.tcelectric.biz
SIC: 1731 General electrical contractor

(G-20237)
TC NUTRITION CORP ✪
1000 N West St Ste 1200 (19801-1058)
PHONE.............................306 290-7457
Tony Tomas, CEO
EMP: 3 EST: 2023
SALES (est): 135.7K Privately Held
SIC: 2023 Dietary supplements, dairy and non-dairy based

(G-20238)
TCG HIGH YELD INV HOLDINGS LLC
103 Foulk Rd Ste 101 (19803-3742)
PHONE.............................302 421-7361
EMP: 10 EST: 2014
SALES (est): 24.94MM
SALES (corp-wide): 4.44B Publicly Held
SIC: 6799 Investors, nec
PA: The Carlyle Group Inc
1001 Pennsylvania Ave Nw 220s
Washington DC 20004
202 729-5626

(G-20239)
TCIM SERVICES INC
1013 Centre Rd Ste 400 (19805-1265)
PHONE.............................302 633-3000
EMP: 3200
Web: www.tcim.com
SIC: 8742 Marketing consulting services

(G-20240)
TD BANK NA
Also Called: TD BANK, N.A.
300 Delaware Ave Ste 110 (19801-1638)
PHONE.............................302 655-5031
Donna Stone, Mgr
EMP: 9
SALES (corp-wide): 37.35B Privately Held
Web: www.td.com
SIC: 6021 National commercial banks
HQ: Td Bank, National Association
1701 Route 70 E Ste 102
Cherry Hill NJ 08003
856 751-2739

(G-20241)
TD BANK NA
Also Called: Banknorth Massachusetts
2035 Limestone Rd (19808-5529)
PHONE.............................508 793-4188
Kevin Haley, Brnch Mgr
EMP: 8
SALES (corp-wide): 37.35B Privately Held
Web: www.td.com
SIC: 6021 National commercial banks
HQ: Td Bank, National Association
1701 Route 70 E Ste 102
Cherry Hill NJ 08003
856 751-2739

(G-20242)
TDY HOLDINGS LLC (DH)
1011 Centre Rd Ste 329 (19805-1203)
PHONE.............................302 254-4172
Ken Kubacki, Prin
EMP: 29 EST: 1999
SALES (est): 1.61B Publicly Held
SIC: 3462 Iron and steel forgings
HQ: Ati Operating Holdings, Llc
1000 Six Ppg Pl
Pittsburgh PA 15222
412 394-2800

(G-20243)
TE CONNECTIVITY CORPORATION
4550 Linden Hill Rd Ste 140 (19808)
PHONE.............................800 522-6752
Driscoll A Nina, VP
EMP: 13 EST: 2013
SALES (est): 268.64K Privately Held
Web: www.te.com
SIC: 3229 Fiber optics strands

(G-20244)
TEAMBRELLA INC
4023 Kennett Pike # 5001 (19807-2018)

Wilmington - New Castle County (G-20245)

PHONE.....................347 630-0528
Aleksandr Paperno, *CEO*
EMP: 5 **EST:** 2016
SALES (est): 106.33K **Privately Held**
SIC: 7389 Financial services

(G-20245)
TEAMLOGIC IT
5584 Kirkwood Hwy (19808-5002)
PHONE.....................302 446-4100
EMP: 7 **EST:** 2019
SALES (est): 62.55K **Privately Held**
Web: www.teamlogicit.com
SIC: 7378 Computer maintenance and repair

(G-20246)
TECH CENTRAL LLC
501 Silverside Rd Ste 110 (19809-1376)
P.O. Box 307 (24126-0307)
PHONE.....................717 273-3301
Douglas Fava, *Managing Member*
EMP: 8 **EST:** 2007
SALES (est): 232.65K **Privately Held**
Web: www.techcentralsales.com
SIC: 7371 Computer software development

(G-20247)
TECH CRAFT SOLUTIONS LLC ◆
1007 N Orange St Fl 4 (19801-1242)
PHONE.....................607 761-0376
Rujeet Vergavera, *Managing Member*
EMP: 8 **EST:** 2023
SALES (est): 306.16K **Privately Held**
SIC: 7389 Business services, nec

(G-20248)
TECH IMPACT
100 W 10th St Ste 915 (19801-1652)
PHONE.....................302 256-5015
Patrick Callihan, *Ex Dir*
EMP: 15 **EST:** 2013
SALES (est): 151.44K **Privately Held**
Web: www.techimpact.org
SIC: 7378 Computer maintenance and repair

(G-20249)
TECH INTERNATIONAL CORP (PA)
Also Called: Tech International
3411 Silverside Rd Ste 102w (19810-4806)
P.O. Box 417 (19899-0417)
PHONE.....................302 478-2301
Chux Amobi, *Pr*
Eugene J Amobi, *Sr VP*
EMP: 5 **EST:** 1999
SALES (est): 1.26MM
SALES (corp-wide): 1.26MM **Privately Held**
Web: www.techinternationalcorp.com
SIC: 7379 8711 Computer related consulting services; Engineering services

(G-20250)
TECH LEARN LLC
1521 Concord Pike Ste 301 (19803-3644)
PHONE.....................305 600-0775
Monirul Islam, *Managing Member*
EMP: 5 **EST:** 2021
SALES (est): 199.4K **Privately Held**
SIC: 7371 Computer software development and applications

(G-20251)
TECH NOW MOBILE LLC
219 W 8th St (19801-1735)
PHONE.....................484 480-0648
Wendell Smallwood, *Managing Member*
EMP: 5 **EST:** 2021
SALES (est): 50K **Privately Held**
SIC: 5045 7378 Computer software; Computer maintenance and repair

(G-20252)
TECHMAP INTEGRATED INC
1013 Centre Rd Ste 4035 (19805-1265)
PHONE.....................770 800-3561
Matthew Bolofinde, *Managing Member*
EMP: 5 **EST:** 2020
SALES (est): 50K **Privately Held**
SIC: 7379 Online services technology consultants

(G-20253)
TECHNEPLUS AMERICAS LLC (PA)
19c Trolley Sq (19806-3355)
PHONE.....................678 200-4052
EMP: 5 **EST:** 2020
SALES (est): 563.13K
SALES (corp-wide): 563.13K **Privately Held**
SIC: 8742 Management consulting services

(G-20254)
TECHNICAL WRITERS INC
3511 Silverside Rd Ste 201 (19810-4902)
PHONE.....................302 477-1972
Janice Tate, *Pr*
John Tate, *VP*
EMP: 10 **EST:** 1979
SALES (est): 225.76K **Privately Held**
Web: www.technicalwriters.com
SIC: 8999 Technical writing

(G-20255)
TECHNO RELIEF LIMITED
3511 Silverside Rd # 105 (19810-4902)
PHONE.....................416 453-9393
EMP: 8 **EST:** 2010
SALES (est): 209.02K **Privately Held**
SIC: 8322 Temporary relief service

(G-20256)
TECHNOLOGY EXTREME LLC ◆
919 N Market St Ste 725 (19801-3065)
PHONE.....................213 325-5455
Evan Rees, *Managing Member*
EMP: 14 **EST:** 2023
SALES (est): 635.34K **Privately Held**
SIC: 7379 Computer related consulting services

(G-20257)
TECHSOLUTIONS INC
5630 Kirkwood Hwy (19808-5004)
PHONE.....................302 656-8324
Richard Monnig, *Pr*
Richard Kenney, *VP*
Tricia Monnig, *Sec*
EMP: 24 **EST:** 1999
SALES (est): 3.57MM **Privately Held**
Web: www.techsolutionsinc.com
SIC: 7379 Computer related consulting services

(G-20258)
TECNIPLAST USA INC
1903 N Franklin St (19802-3830)
PHONE.....................484 716-2145
EMP: 5 **EST:** 2019
SALES (est): 60.52K **Privately Held**
Web: www.tecniplast.it
SIC: 8734 Testing laboratories

(G-20259)
TECNOLOGIKA USA INC
Also Called: Tecnologika USA
501 Silverside Rd (19809-1374)
PHONE.....................302 597-7611
Joseph Castle, *Dir*
EMP: 8 **EST:** 2013
SALES (est): 1.29MM
SALES (corp-wide): 159.48K **Privately Held**
Web: www.tecnologika.com
SIC: 8742 Marketing consulting services
HQ: Tecnologika Limited
91 Brick Lane
London E1 6Q
203 432-5120

(G-20260)
TECPRESSO INC
1007 N Orange St Fl 4 (19801-1242)
PHONE.....................302 240-0025
Tatsunari Sakanoue, *Pr*
EMP: 6 **EST:** 2017
SALES (est): 23.63K **Privately Held**
Web: www.tecpresso.co.jp
SIC: 7374 Computer graphics service

(G-20261)
TEDRON INC
2022 Harwyn Rd (19810-3840)
PHONE.....................302 529-1838
Ron Tedron, *Pr*
EMP: 6 **EST:** 1999
SALES (est): 428.45K **Privately Held**
SIC: 7363 Employee leasing service

(G-20262)
TEE PEES FROM RATTLESNKS
2001 Rockford Rd (19806-1241)
PHONE.....................302 654-0709
Linda Vinton, *Owner*
EMP: 2 **EST:** 1994
SALES (est): 60.09K **Privately Held**
SIC: 2394 5999 Tents: made from purchased materials; Tents

(G-20263)
TEJ STUDIO LLC
1201 N Orange St (19801-1155)
PHONE.....................302 205-3224
Dhanpreet Bevli, *Managing Member*
EMP: 5
SALES (est): 199.4K **Privately Held**
SIC: 7371 Computer software development and applications

(G-20264)
TEKSTROM INC
1301 Milltown Rd (19808-3005)
PHONE.....................302 709-5900
Charanjeet Minhas, *Pr*
EMP: 51 **EST:** 1999
SQ FT: 2,000
SALES (est): 4.61MM **Privately Held**
Web: www.tekstrom.com
SIC: 7379 Online services technology consultants

(G-20265)
TELEDUCTION ASSOCIATES INC
Also Called: Teleduction
1 Weldin Park Dr (19803-4708)
PHONE.....................302 429-0303
Sharon Baker, *CEO*
Franklin Baker, *VP*
EMP: 6 **EST:** 1976
SALES (est): 249.42K **Privately Held**
Web: www.teleduction.com
SIC: 7812 Video production

(G-20266)
TELESONIC PC INC
1330 E 12th St (19802-5316)
PHONE.....................302 658-6945
Etta Eckrich, *Asstg*
EMP: 2
SALES (corp-wide): 759.18K **Privately Held**
Web: www.telesoniconline.com
SIC: 3565 Packaging machinery
PA: Telesonic Pc Inc.
260 Milford Dr
Middletown DE 19709
302 658-6945

(G-20267)
TELGIAN CORPORATION
4001 Kennett Pike Ste 308 (19807-2039)
PHONE.....................480 753-5444
John Sannin, *Ex VP*
EMP: 32
Web: www.telgian.com
SIC: 1711 8711 1731 8748 Fire sprinkler system installation; Fire protection engineering; Fire detection and burglar alarm systems specialization; Systems analysis and engineering consulting services
PA: Telgian Corporation
10230 S 50th Pl Ste 100
Phoenix AZ 85044

(G-20268)
TELGIAN ENGRG & CONSULTING LLC
4001 Kennett Pike Ste 308 (19807-2039)
PHONE.....................480 282-5392
Drew Gerard, *Brnch Mgr*
EMP: 16
SALES (corp-wide): 10.72MM **Privately Held**
Web: www.telgian.com
SIC: 8711 Engineering services
PA: Telgian Engineering & Consulting, Llc
10230 S 50th Pl Ste 100
Phoenix AZ 85044
480 753-5444

(G-20269)
TELIVITY INC
3 Germay Dr Ste 41193 (19804-1127)
PHONE.....................312 585-8485
Dusan Milicevic, *CEO*
EMP: 11 **EST:** 2020
SALES (est): 403.19K **Privately Held**
SIC: 7371 Software programming applications

(G-20270)
TELUS INTL HOLDG USA CORP
2711 Centerville Rd Ste 400 (19808-1660)
PHONE.....................720 726-0677
EMP: 8 **EST:** 2016
SALES (est): 65.78K **Privately Held**
SIC: 8742 Human resource consulting services

(G-20271)
TEN BLADE ENTERPRISES LLC
800 Industrial St (19801-4367)
PHONE.....................484 843-4811
EMP: 7 **EST:** 2017
SALES (est): 173.91K **Privately Held**
SIC: 8059 Personal care home, with health care

(G-20272)
TENDER HEARTS
5301 Limestone Rd (19808-1251)
PHONE.....................302 234-1017
Debbie Doherty, *Pr*
EMP: 9 **EST:** 2016
SALES (est): 12.73K **Privately Held**
Web: www.tenderheartsde.org
SIC: 8351 Child day care services

(G-20273)
TENMAT INC
500 Water St (19804-2423)

GEOGRAPHIC SECTION Wilmington - New Castle County (G-20302)

PHONE..................................302 633-6600
Roberto Casini, *Genl Mgr*
Roberto Casini, *Mgr*
◆ **EMP:** 5 **EST:** 1990
SALES (est): 2.69MM **Privately Held**
Web: www.tenmausa.com
SIC: 5169 Chemicals and allied products, nec

(G-20274)
TENNR INC
1013 Centre Rd Ste 403b (19805-1265)
PHONE..................................650 288-8264
Trey Holterman, *CEO*
EMP: 8
SALES (est): 306.16K **Privately Held**
SIC: 7371 Software programming applications

(G-20275)
TERRAIN AND TACTICAL LLC
5071 E Woodmill Dr (19808-4082)
PHONE..................................302 521-9290
EMP: 2
SALES (est): 92.41K **Privately Held**
SIC: 3949 7389 Camping equipment and supplies; Business Activities at Non-Commercial Site

(G-20276)
TERRIE M WLLIAMS EXPANSION INC
438 Morehouse Dr (19801-5741)
PHONE..................................302 214-0685
Terrie M Williams, *CEO*
EMP: 5 **EST:** 2020
SALES (est): 77.06K **Privately Held**
SIC: 8699 Charitable organization

(G-20277)
TERRY A GRAY
2422 Graydon Rd (19803-2716)
PHONE..................................302 478-2042
Terry A Gray, *Prin*
EMP: 5 **EST:** 2010
SALES (est): 47.32K **Privately Held**
SIC: 7299 Handyman service

(G-20278)
TERRY WHITE-STATE FARM INS
1813 Marsh Rd Ste G (19810-4544)
PHONE..................................302 353-6636
Terry White, *Admn*
EMP: 6 **EST:** 2019
SALES (est): 113.58K **Privately Held**
Web: www.statefarm.com
SIC: 6411 Insurance agents and brokers

(G-20279)
TESS AFRCAN HAIR BRDING BUTY S
5910 Kirkwood Hwy (19808-4815)
PHONE..................................302 384-6439
Teresa Akumiah, *Owner*
EMP: 5 **EST:** 2013
SALES (est): 129.32K **Privately Held**
Web: www.tesshairbraidingandbeauty.com
SIC: 7231 Hairdressers

(G-20280)
TETRIS COMPANY LLC
103 Foulk Rd Ste 202 (19803-3742)
PHONE..................................302 656-1950
EMP: 8 **EST:** 1996
SALES (est): 51.58K **Privately Held**
Web: www.tetris.com
SIC: 3944 Board games, children's and adults'

(G-20281)
TEVEBAUGH ASSOCIATES INC (PA)
2 Mill Rd Ste 210 (19806-2184)
PHONE..................................302 984-1400
James Tevebaugh, *Pr*
Richard Stratford, *VP*
Robert J Reid, *Prin*
EMP: 10 **EST:** 1987
SALES (est): 3.3MM
SALES (corp-wide): 3.3MM **Privately Held**
Web: www.tevebaugh.com
SIC: 8712 Architectural services

(G-20282)
TEXAS LAWN CARE SVC
2516 Faulkland Rd (19808-2506)
PHONE..................................302 547-5829
Shawn Brlinge, *Prin*
EMP: 5 **EST:** 2016
SALES (est): 219.7K **Privately Held**
SIC: 0782 Lawn care services

(G-20283)
TEXAVINO LLC
3422 Old Capitol Trl Ste 1444 (19808-6124)
PHONE..................................302 295-0829
EMP: 3 **EST:** 2010
SALES (est): 61.69K **Privately Held**
Web: www.texavino.com
SIC: 2084 Wines

(G-20284)
TEXNIKOS INC
915 S Heald St (19801-5732)
PHONE..................................302 656-8088
Petros Kirtses, *Brnch Mgr*
EMP: 8
SALES (corp-wide): 146.43K **Privately Held**
SIC: 4899 Communication signal enhancement network services
PA: Texnikos, Inc.
    913 S Heald St
    Wilmington DE
    302 656-8088

(G-20285)
TEXTRONICS INC
3825 Lancaster Pike (19805-1559)
PHONE..................................302 351-2109
Stacey Burr, *CEO*
EMP: 24 **EST:** 2004
SALES (est): 2.47MM
SALES (corp-wide): 23.38B **Privately Held**
SIC: 8011 Health maintenance organization
HQ: Adidas North America, Inc.
    3449 N Anchor St Ste 500
    Portland OR 97217
    971 234-2300

(G-20286)
TG ADVISERS INC
4550 Linden Hill Rd Ste 152 (19808)
PHONE..................................302 691-3330
Stephen R Reid, *Pr*
EMP: 9 **EST:** 2004
SALES (est): 1.18MM **Privately Held**
Web: www.tgadvisers.com
SIC: 8711 Consulting engineer

(G-20287)
TGFMX INC ✪
1007 N Orange St Fl 4 (19801-1242)
PHONE..................................302 613-0128
Ricardo Hernandez, *Prin*
EMP: 5 **EST:** 2022
SALES (est): 551.47K **Privately Held**
SIC: 5148 Fresh fruits and vegetables

(G-20288)
TGI REBATE CENTER
1405 Foulk Rd Ste 200 (19803-2769)
PHONE..................................866 433-3009
EMP: 5 **EST:** 2017
SALES (est): 56.96K **Privately Held**
SIC: 8099 Health and allied services, nec

(G-20289)
TGX HOLDINGS LLC
1201 N Market St (19801-1147)
PHONE..................................212 260-6300
Yehuda Fulda, *Managing Member*
EMP: 150 **EST:** 2009
SQ FT: 8,500
SALES (est): 2.55MM **Privately Held**
Web: www.tgxna.com
SIC: 8741 Management services

(G-20290)
TH KING US LLC
Also Called: Venture Capital
600 N King St Ste 800 (19801-3778)
PHONE..................................617 903-7472
David Thomas, *CEO*
David Anderson, *VP*
Vincet Jones, *COO*
Cara Hogue, *VP*
EMP: 15 **EST:** 2018
SALES (est): 646.56K **Privately Held**
SIC: 6211 Flotation companies

(G-20291)
THE CROWELL CORPORATION
1 Crowell Rd (19804-3556)
P.O. Box 3227 (19804-0227)
PHONE..................................302 998-0558
▲ **EMP:** 100
Web: www.itape.com
SIC: 2672 Tape, pressure sensitive: made from purchased materials

(G-20292)
THE REAL ESTABLISHED INC ✪
1007 N Orange St Fl 1620 (19801-1242)
PHONE..................................917 843-8580
Scott Keeney, *CEO*
EMP: 12 **EST:** 2023
SALES (est): 406.37K **Privately Held**
SIC: 7389 Business Activities at Non-Commercial Site

(G-20293)
THE-DIRT-SQUAD
1017 Euclid Ave (19809-2623)
PHONE..................................302 723-5916
Neil Shea, *Prin*
EMP: 5 **EST:** 2015
SALES (est): 68.14K **Privately Held**
SIC: 7699 Cleaning services

(G-20294)
THEATRE N AT NEMOURS
1007 N Orange St (19801-1239)
PHONE..................................302 600-1923
EMP: 6 **EST:** 2003
SALES (est): 91.6K **Privately Held**
Web: www.theatren.com
SIC: 7832 Motion picture theaters, except drive-in

(G-20295)
THEDIGITALSUPPORT LLC
5301 Limestone Rd Ste 100 (19808-1251)
PHONE..................................347 305-4006
Joaquin Burgos, *Prin*
EMP: 7 **EST:** 2016
SALES (est): 188.49K **Privately Held**
Web: www.thedigital.support
SIC: 8399 Advocacy group

(G-20296)
THERAPEUTIC MOORE SERVICES LLC
Also Called: Moore Physical Therapy
701 Foulk Rd Ste 2d (19803-3733)
PHONE..................................302 654-8142
Shaun Moore, *Prin*
EMP: 5 **EST:** 2004
SALES (est): 80.44K **Privately Held**
SIC: 8049 Physical therapist

(G-20297)
THERMAL PIPE SYSTEMS INC (PA)
5205 W Woodmill Dr Ste 33 (19808-4068)
PHONE..................................302 999-1588
Samuel A Cousins, *Pr*
Elizabeth G Korrell, *VP*
Judith F Cousins, *Sec*
▼ **EMP:** 5 **EST:** 1980
SQ FT: 2,200
SALES (est): 3.94MM
SALES (corp-wide): 3.94MM **Privately Held**
Web: www.thermalpipesystems.com
SIC: 3498 Fabricated pipe and fittings

(G-20298)
THERMO FISHER SCIENTIFIC INC
3411 Silverside Rd Ste 100t (19810-4806)
PHONE..................................302 479-7707
EMP: 5
SALES (corp-wide): 44.91B **Publicly Held**
Web: www.thermofisher.com
SIC: 3826 Analytical instruments
PA: Thermo Fisher Scientific Inc.
    168 3rd Ave
    Waltham MA 02451
    781 622-1000

(G-20299)
THERMOELECTRICS UNLIMITED INC
5109 Governor Printz Blvd (19809-2743)
PHONE..................................302 764-6618
Jean P Paris, *Pr*
Albert Fonda, *VP*
EMP: 6 **EST:** 1964
SQ FT: 2,400
SALES (est): 511.72K **Privately Held**
Web: www.stir-kool.com
SIC: 3674 Thermoelectric devices, solid state

(G-20300)
THINK66 LLC
300 Delaware Ave Ste 210a (19801-6601)
PHONE..................................949 326-8188
EMP: 5 **EST:** 2017
SALES (est): 247.41K **Privately Held**
SIC: 3999 Manufacturing industries, nec

(G-20301)
THINKHAT SOFTWARE INC (HQ)
Also Called: Enliv
1000 N West St Ste 1200 (19801-1058)
PHONE..................................917 379-2638
Ravi Lam, *Pr*
Bharathi Nelanuthala, *
Magnus Fleming, *
EMP: 16 **EST:** 1996
SALES (est): 18.2MM **Privately Held**
Web: www.pwc.com
SIC: 7371 Computer software development
PA: Thinkhat Software Do Brasil Ltda
    Rua Visconde De Piraja 414
    Rio De Janeiro RJ

(G-20302)
THIRD SIGMA INVESTMENT ADVISOR
700 N Clayton St Ste 100 (19805-3185)
PHONE..................................302 656-1111

Wilmington - New Castle County (G-20303)

EMP: 5 EST: 2018
SALES (est): 231.56K Privately Held
Web: www.thirdsigmaadvisors.com
SIC: 6799 Investors, nec

(G-20303)
THIRST 2 LEARN LLC
802 Naamans Rd (19810-2005)
PHONE..................302 475-7080
EMP: 6 EST: 2005
SALES (est): 133.91K Privately Held
Web: www.t2leducates.org
SIC: 8351 Preschool center

(G-20304)
THIRTY BIRDS INC ⊘
251 Little Falls Dr (19808-1674)
PHONE..................351 910-5520
Ruslan Zaydullin, CEO
Anatoly Marin, CFO
Ninel Chitadze, Sec
EMP: 8 EST: 2022
SALES (est): 306.16K Privately Held
SIC: 7371 Computer software development

(G-20305)
THOMAS D LAW SHEL
1601 Milltown Rd (19808-4027)
PHONE..................302 887-9116
Thomas Shellenberger, Prin
EMP: 5 EST: 2016
SALES (est): 247.99K Privately Held
SIC: 8111 Divorce and family law

(G-20306)
THOMAS DOUGHERTY DDS
5317 Limestone Rd Ste 5 (19808-1252)
PHONE..................302 239-2500
Thomas Dougherty D.d.s., Pr
EMP: 9 EST: 1982
SALES (est): 618.38K Privately Held
SIC: 8021 Dental surgeon

(G-20307)
THOMAS F CAVANAUGH
Also Called: On Time Construction
123 Hawthorne Ave (19805-2327)
PHONE..................302 995-2859
Karen Cavanaugh, Prin
EMP: 5 EST: 2011
SALES (est): 241.84K Privately Held
SIC: 1521 Single-family housing construction

(G-20308)
THOMAS FRANCISCONI
24 Duvall Ct (19808-2143)
PHONE..................302 995-2282
Thomas Francisconi, Pr
EMP: 6 EST: 2016
SALES (est): 65.09K Privately Held
SIC: 1711 Plumbing contractors

(G-20309)
THOMAS J MCWILLIAMS
1000 N West St Ste 1500 (19801-1054)
PHONE..................312 287-5148
Charlise Williams, Mgr
EMP: 5 EST: 2017
SALES (est): 69.57K Privately Held
SIC: 8111 General practice law office

(G-20310)
THOMAS JENKINS DMD
Also Called: Aesthetis Special Care Assoc
2323 Pennsylvania Ave Ste Ll (19806-1332)
PHONE..................302 426-0526
EMP: 11 EST: 1992
SALES (est): 477.17K Privately Held
SIC: 8021 Dental surgeon

(G-20311)
THOMAS KARMANSKI
Also Called: Tom's Autobody
108 S Marshall St (19804-2533)
PHONE..................302 438-1458
Thomas Karmanski, Prin
EMP: 5 EST: 2012
SALES (est): 64K Privately Held
Web: www.computeroom.net
SIC: 7532 Body shop, automotive

(G-20312)
THOMAS WEISENFELS
1201 N Market St Ste 2000 (19801-1165)
PHONE..................302 571-5244
Thomas Weisenfels, Admn
EMP: 5 EST: 2018
SALES (est): 117.92K Privately Held
SIC: 6411 Insurance agents, brokers, and service

(G-20313)
THOMPSON CLEANERS
4746 Limestone Rd Ste A (19808-1928)
PHONE..................302 998-0935
Oscar Son, Owner
EMP: 5 EST: 1980
SALES (est): 117.83K Privately Held
SIC: 7211 Power laundries, family and commercial

(G-20314)
THOMSON REUTERS (GRC) INC
2711 Centerville Rd Ste 400 (19808-1660)
PHONE..................212 227-7357
Thomson Reuters, Prin
EMP: 9 EST: 2012
SALES (est): 155.44K Privately Held
SIC: 7291 8111 8721 8733 Tax return preparation services; Legal services; Accounting services, except auditing; Research institute

(G-20315)
THREE FIELDS CAPITAL LP
2711 Centerville Rd # 400 (19808-1660)
PHONE..................302 636-5401
EMP: 8 EST: 2010
SALES (est): 277.83K Privately Held
SIC: 6799 Investors, nec

(G-20316)
THREE JS DISC TIRE & AUTO SVC
Also Called: J Star
3724 Kirkwood Hwy (19808-5106)
PHONE..................302 995-6141
EMP: 7 EST: 1993
SALES (est): 330.79K Privately Held
SIC: 7538 General automotive repair shops

(G-20317)
THREE LITTLE BIRD PRPTS LLC
1814 Floral Dr (19810-4504)
PHONE..................302 475-2981
Joseph B Mchugh Junior, Prin
EMP: 5 EST: 2016
SALES (est): 172.56K Privately Held
SIC: 6512 Nonresidential building operators

(G-20318)
TIEDEMANN TRUST COMPANY (PA)
200 Bellevue Pkwy Ste 525 (19809-3739)
PHONE..................302 656-5644
Carl Tiedemann, Pr
EMP: 5 EST: 2001
SALES (est): 3.91MM
SALES (corp-wide): 3.91MM Privately Held
Web: www.tiedemannadvisors.com
SIC: 6733 Trusts, nec

(G-20319)
TIERS INC
1201 N Orange St Ste 7586 (19801-1155)
PHONE..................302 298-3338
EMP: 9
SALES (est): 313.29K Privately Held
SIC: 7371 Computer software development

(G-20320)
TIFFANY KISTLER BENEFITS
Also Called: KISTLER TIFFANY BENEFITS
2 Mill Rd Ste 206 (19806-2184)
PHONE..................302 425-5010
Kevin Conners, Mgr
EMP: 67
SALES (corp-wide): 422MM Privately Held
Web: www.ktbrokers.com
SIC: 6411 Insurance agents, nec
HQ: Kt Holdco Inc.
    400 Berwyn Park Ste 200
    Berwyn PA 19312

(G-20321)
TIFFGOYOGAFLOW
2420 Marilyn Dr (19810-3018)
PHONE..................302 793-9455
Tiffany Goins, Prin
EMP: 6 EST: 2016
SALES (est): 27.07K Privately Held
SIC: 7999 Yoga instruction

(G-20322)
TIGANI FAMILY DENTISTRY PA
4600 Linden Hill Rd (19808-2954)
PHONE..................302 571-8740
EMP: 14 EST: 2018
SALES (est): 909.88K Privately Held
Web: www.tiganidentistry.com
SIC: 8021 Dentists' office

(G-20323)
TIGHE AND COTTRELL PA (PA)
704 N King St Ste 500 (19801-3583)
P.O. Box 1031 (19899-1031)
PHONE..................302 658-6400
Paul Cottrell, Pt
EMP: 6 EST: 1993
SALES (est): 871.04K
SALES (corp-wide): 871.04K Privately Held
Web: www.tighecottrell.com
SIC: 8111 General practice attorney, lawyer

(G-20324)
TIGHTEN UP CLEANING SERVICES
312 Cedar Ave (19804-2902)
PHONE..................302 482-9970
Kalimah Matthews, Prin
EMP: 5 EST: 2018
SALES (est): 45.9K Privately Held
SIC: 7699 Cleaning services

(G-20325)
TILE MARKET OF DELAWARE LLC (HQ)
Also Called: Stone Shop, The
405 Marsh Ln Ste 3 (19804-2445)
PHONE..................302 777-4663
◆ EMP: 30 EST: 1996
SQ FT: 50,000
SALES (est): 11.72MM
SALES (corp-wide): 42.97MM Privately Held
Web: www.tilemarketofde.com
SIC: 1743 Tile installation, ceramic
PA: Nemo Tile Co. Llc
    121 E 24th St Fl 2
    New York NY 10010
    212 477-1425

(G-20326)
TILE SHOP LLC
1200 Rocky Run Pkwy (19803-1456)
PHONE..................302 250-4889
EMP: 41
SALES (corp-wide): 394.7MM Publicly Held
Web: www.tileshop.com
SIC: 1743 Tile installation, ceramic
HQ: The Tile Shop Llc
    14000 Carlson Pkwy
    Plymouth MN 55441
    763 541-1444

(G-20327)
TIM LATHAM
Also Called: Latham Building Group
112 N Woodward Ave (19805-1146)
PHONE..................302 530-4002
Tim Latham, Prin
EMP: 5 EST: 2009
SALES (est): 126.85K Privately Held
SIC: 6552 Subdividers and developers, nec

(G-20328)
TIME4MACHINE INC
3422 Old Capitol Trl (19808-6124)
PHONE..................302 999-7604
Denys Okhymenko, CEO
EMP: 50 EST: 2016
SALES (est): 1.41MM Privately Held
SIC: 3944 Electronic toys

(G-20329)
TIMET FINANCE MANAGEMENT CO
1007 N Orange St (19801-1239)
PHONE..................302 472-9277
EMP: 19 EST: 1997
SALES (est): 3.78MM
SALES (corp-wide): 302.09B Publicly Held
Web: www.timet.com
SIC: 8741 Business management
HQ: Titanium Metals Corporation
    4832 Richmond Rd Ste 100
    Warrenside Heights OH 44128
    740 537-5600

(G-20330)
TIMEZEST INC
2810 N Church St (19802-4447)
PHONE..................702 582-6850
Jamison West, CEO
EMP: 10
SALES (est): 752.27K Privately Held
SIC: 5045 Computer software

(G-20331)
TIMOTHY D HUMPHREYS
1831 Delaware Ave (19806-2357)
PHONE..................302 225-3000
Timothy Humphreys, Prin
EMP: 14 EST: 2004
SALES (est): 438.78K Privately Held
Web: www.whcompany.com
SIC: 8721 Certified public accountant

(G-20332)
TIMOTHY J MEYERS INC
1004 Elizabeth Ave (19809-2616)
PHONE..................302 438-3709
Timothy Meyers, Mgr
EMP: 5 EST: 2015
SALES (est): 184.08K Privately Held
SIC: 7261 Funeral home

(G-20333)
TINT WORLD
400 N Maryland Ave (19804-1303)
PHONE..................302 595-9100

EMP: 7 **EST:** 2018
SALES (est): 451.24K **Privately Held**
Web: www.tintworld.com
SIC: 1799 Glass tinting, architectural or automotive

(G-20334)
TINY TOTS CHILDCARE AND LEARNI
1014 W 24th St (19802-3308)
PHONE..................................302 651-9060
EMP: 5 **EST:** 2009
SALES (est): 323.35K **Privately Held**
Web: www.tinytotschildcarelearningcenter.com
SIC: 8351 Group day care center

(G-20335)
TIRE SALES & SERVICE INC
Also Called: Tire Sales & Service
600 First State Blvd (19804-3559)
PHONE..................................302 658-8955
Eugene M Julian, *Pr*
Frank Julian, *VP*
Thomas Jarrell, *VP*
Joseph R Julian, *Asst VP*
Richard Julian, *Sec*
EMP: 13 **EST:** 1970
SQ FT: 7,000
SALES (est): 2.49MM **Privately Held**
SIC: 5014 5531 Truck tires and tubes; Automotive tires

(G-20336)
TITAN SPIRITS LLC
2810 N Church St (19802-4447)
PHONE..................................205 568-3338
Lee Wynn, *Managing Member*
EMP: 7
SALES (est): 78.16K **Privately Held**
SIC: 2085 Distilled and blended liquors

(G-20337)
TJM FINANCIAL GROUP LLC
1944 Maryland Ave (19805-4605)
PHONE..................................302 674-7033
EMP: 7 **EST:** 2012
SALES (est): 202.81K **Privately Held**
Web: www.tjmfinancialgroupde.com
SIC: 6282 Investment advice

(G-20338)
TLC HOME CARE
2055 Melson Rd (19808-5933)
PHONE..................................302 983-5720
Harold Bozeman, *Prin*
EMP: 9 **EST:** 2008
SALES (est): 98.56K **Privately Held**
SIC: 8082 Home health care services

(G-20339)
TM MANAGEMENT LLC
30 Hill Rd (19806-2034)
PHONE..................................302 654-4940
Tracie Farnan, *Prin*
EMP: 8 **EST:** 2004
SALES (est): 379.29K **Privately Held**
Web: www.morningrage.com
SIC: 8741 Business management

(G-20340)
TMPAA INSTITUTE INC
3411 Silverside Rd (19810-4812)
PHONE..................................302 268-1010
Raymond T Scotto, *Prin*
EMP: 8 **EST:** 2017
SALES (est): 4.5K **Privately Held**
Web: www.targetmkts.com
SIC: 8733 Noncommercial research organizations

(G-20341)
TODD ROWEN DMD
25 Milltown Rd Ste A (19803-3107)
PHONE..................................302 994-5887
Todd Rowen, *Owner*
EMP: 8 **EST:** 1987
SALES (est): 361.38K **Privately Held**
Web: www.toddrowendmd.com
SIC: 8021 Dentists' office

(G-20342)
TODDLERS TECH INC
2704 W 4th St (19805-1817)
PHONE..................................302 655-4487
Alice Carter, *Dir*
Carlton Carter, *VP*
EMP: 16 **EST:** 1986
SQ FT: 3,000
SALES (est): 234.38K **Privately Held**
Web: www.toddlerstechinc.com
SIC: 8351 Group day care center

(G-20343)
TODDS
1601 Concord Pike Ste 49 (19803-3623)
PHONE..................................302 658-0387
Todd Appleton, *Owner*
EMP: 10 **EST:** 1975
SALES (est): 244.72K **Privately Held**
Web: www.toddshairsalon.com
SIC: 7231 Hairdressers

(G-20344)
TODDYS TOTS
2308 N Madison St (19802-3436)
PHONE..................................302 661-1912
Natashia Simpson, *Prin*
EMP: 8 **EST:** 2018
SALES (est): 71.85K **Privately Held**
SIC: 8351 Child day care services

(G-20345)
TOGETHERALL
1209 N Orange St (19801-1120)
PHONE..................................315 434-0911
EMP: 10
SALES (est): 375.64K **Privately Held**
Web: www.togetherall.com
SIC: 8322 Individual and family services

(G-20346)
TOIVOTEK INC ✪
1207 Delaware Ave Ste 2244 (19801-5627)
PHONE..................................224 805-9554
EMP: 3 **EST:** 2023
SALES (est): 128.34K **Privately Held**
SIC: 7372 Application computer software

(G-20347)
TOKEN SECURITY INC ✪
1007 N Orange St Fl 10 (19801-1277)
PHONE..................................972 546-9803
EMP: 6 **EST:** 2023
SALES (est): 237.56K **Privately Held**
SIC: 7389 Business Activities at Non-Commercial Site

(G-20348)
TOLL NJX 4 CORP
1010 Maple St (19805-4308)
PHONE..................................302 652-3252
EMP: 10
SALES (est): 908.96K
SALES (corp-wide): 9.99B **Publicly Held**
SIC: 1521 New construction, single-family houses
PA: Toll Brothers, Inc.
1140 Virginia Dr
Fort Washington PA 19034
215 938-8000

(G-20349)
TOMKAT
308 Potomac Rd (19803-3123)
PHONE..................................302 598-8823
Katrina Rispoli, *Prin*
EMP: 5 **EST:** 2017
SALES (est): 96.58K **Privately Held**
SIC: 1771 Concrete work

(G-20350)
TOMS BARBER SHOP
3317 Old Capitol Trl Ste A (19808-6239)
PHONE..................................302 992-9635
Jerry Gouge, *Owner*
EMP: 5 **EST:** 1992
SALES (est): 84.88K **Privately Held**
Web: www.tomsbarbershop.net
SIC: 7241 Hair stylist, men

(G-20351)
TONIC HEALTH LLC (PA)
Also Called: Tonic Health
1209 N Orange St (19801-1120)
PHONE..................................510 386-2530
Anya Alisova, *Managing Member*
EMP: 10 **EST:** 2021
SALES (est): 510K
SALES (corp-wide): 510K **Privately Held**
SIC: 7371 Software programming applications

(G-20352)
TOP DOG BEST GAMES LLC
3422 Old Capitol Trl Ste 528 (19808-6124)
PHONE..................................949 859-8869
EMP: 4 **EST:** 2014
SQ FT: 5,000
SALES (est): 254.14K **Privately Held**
SIC: 3944 Electronic games and toys

(G-20353)
TOP OF HLLBRNDYWINE APARTMENTS
Also Called: Top of The Hill-Brandwine Apts
2101 Prior Rd (19809-1127)
PHONE..................................302 482-8544
Susan Carson, *Mgr*
EMP: 9 **EST:** 1999
SALES (est): 715.3K **Privately Held**
SIC: 6513 Apartment building operators

(G-20354)
TOP QALITY INDUS FINISHERS INC
1204 E 12th St Ste 1 (19802-5317)
P.O. Box 9625 (19809-0625)
PHONE..................................302 778-5005
Edward Camacho, *Pr*
EMP: 6 **EST:** 1999
SALES (est): 502.18K **Privately Held**
SIC: 1721 3479 Residential painting; Hot dip coating of metals or formed products

(G-20355)
TOP RATED MEDIA INC
1000 N West St Ste 1200 (19801-1058)
PHONE..................................888 550-9273
Steve Simons, *CFO*
EMP: 7 **EST:** 2014
SQ FT: 5,000
SALES (est): 144.52K **Privately Held**
Web: www.topratedmediainc.com
SIC: 7311 Advertising agencies

(G-20356)
TOP TIER REMODELING
1031 Liberty Rd Ste 101 (19804-2860)
PHONE..................................302 250-4845
Hugo Lopez, *CEO*
EMP: 12 **EST:** 2017
SALES (est): 1.16MM **Privately Held**

SIC: 1521 7389 General remodeling, single-family houses; Business services, nec

(G-20357)
TOPAZ & ASSOCIATES LLC
1201 N Market St (19801-1147)
PHONE..................................302 448-8914
EMP: 10 **EST:** 2018
SALES (est): 759.81K **Privately Held**
SIC: 6531 Real estate agents and managers

(G-20358)
TOPIARY TECH LLC
2711 Centerville Rd # 400 (19808-1660)
PHONE..................................302 636-5440
EMP: 5 **EST:** 2012
SALES (est): 243.2K **Privately Held**
SIC: 7372 Application computer software

(G-20359)
TOPKIS FINANCIAL ADVISORS LLC
910 Foulk Rd Ste 200 (19803-3159)
PHONE..................................302 654-4444
William Topkis, *Mgr*
EMP: 9 **EST:** 2005
SALES (est): 581.67K **Privately Held**
Web: www.ericgrayson.com
SIC: 6282 Investment advisory service

(G-20360)
TOPMAC LLC
413 8th Ave (19805-4745)
PHONE..................................609 517-0585
EMP: 6 **EST:** 2019
SALES (est): 330K **Privately Held**
SIC: 1761 Roofing contractor

(G-20361)
TOPS INTERNATIONAL CORP
3801 Old Capitol Trl (19808-5823)
PHONE..................................302 738-8889
Jean Shih, *Pr*
EMP: 5 **EST:** 2015
SALES (est): 283.51K **Privately Held**
SIC: 5045 5159 4225 Computers and accessories, personal and home entertainment; Cotton merchants; General warehousing and storage

(G-20362)
TOPTAL LLC (PA)
2810 N Church St Ste 36879 (19802-4447)
P.O. Box 1299 (94302-1299)
PHONE..................................414 550-3054
Taso Du Val, *CEO*
Brenda Kurz, *CAO*
Andrew Good, *CFO*
Sean Middleton, *CRO*
Michelle Labbe, *CPO*
EMP: 93 **EST:** 2010
SALES (est): 25.88MM
SALES (corp-wide): 25.88MM **Privately Held**
Web: www.toptal.com
SIC: 7379 Computer related consulting services

(G-20363)
TOPTRACKER LLC
2810 N Church St Ste 36879 (19802-4447)
PHONE..................................415 230-0131
EMP: 500 **EST:** 2015
SQ FT: 150
SALES (est): 8.83MM **Privately Held**
Web: www.toptal.com
SIC: 7371 Computer software development and applications

Wilmington - New Castle County (G-20364)

(G-20364)
TORNADO II JANITORIAL SVC LLC
510 A St (19801-5328)
PHONE..................302 898-1370
EMP: 10 EST: 2009
SALES (est): 439.07K **Privately Held**
Web: www.tornado2janitorial.com
SIC: 7349 Janitorial service, contract basis

(G-20365)
TORREGIANI SETH DDO PA
2502 Silverside Rd Ste 5 (19810-3740)
PHONE..................302 407-5412
EMP: 7 EST: 2019
SALES (est): 91.63K **Privately Held**
SIC: 8011 Offices and clinics of medical doctors

(G-20366)
TOTAL BASEMENT CARE
304 Concord Ave (19802-4036)
PHONE..................302 367-4789
Martin Jodko, *Owner*
EMP: 5 EST: 2014
SALES (est): 61.43K **Privately Held**
Web: www.totalbasementcare.com
SIC: 1799 Waterproofing

(G-20367)
TOTAL BEAUTY SUPPLY INC
2320 Sconset Rd (19810-4237)
PHONE..................302 798-4647
Robert Custer, *Pr*
Vicki Schwam, *Sec*
EMP: 5 EST: 1985
SALES (est): 587.82K **Privately Held**
Web: www.total-beauty.com
SIC: 5087 5999 Beauty parlor equipment and supplies; Hair care products

(G-20368)
TOTAL CARE PHYSICIANS
2601 Annand Dr Ste 4 (19808-3719)
PHONE..................302 998-2977
Constantin Michell, *Prin*
EMP: 48
SALES (corp-wide): 7.34MM **Privately Held**
Web: www.totalcarephysicians.com
SIC: 8011 General and family practice, physician/surgeon
PA: Total Care Physicians
  405 Silverside Rd Ste 111
  Wilmington DE 19809
  302 798-0666

(G-20369)
TOTAL CARE PHYSICIANS (PA)
405 Silverside Rd Ste 111 (19809-1768)
PHONE..................302 798-0666
Theodore Michell Md, *Pr*
EMP: 30 EST: 1999
SALES (est): 7.34MM
SALES (corp-wide): 7.34MM **Privately Held**
Web: www.totalcarephysicians.com
SIC: 8011 General and family practice, physician/surgeon

(G-20370)
TOTAL HEALTH & REHABILITATION
Also Called: Total Health Rehab
1303 Veale Rd (19810-4601)
P.O. Box 9291 (19809-0291)
PHONE..................302 477-0800
EMP: 13 EST: 1995
SALES (est): 984.88K **Privately Held**
Web: www.thrpt.com
SIC: 8049 Physical therapist

(G-20371)
TOTAL HEALTH & REHABILITATION
2060 Limestone Rd Ste 202 (19808-5500)
PHONE..................302 999-9202
Craig Filippone, *Prin*
EMP: 9 EST: 2010
SALES (est): 242.69K **Privately Held**
Web: www.thrpt.com
SIC: 8093 8049 8011 Rehabilitation center, outpatient treatment; Physical therapist; Physical medicine, physician/surgeon

(G-20372)
TOTAL RESISTANCE LLC
5105 Diana Dr (19808-2820)
PHONE..................302 384-3077
Joseph Todd, *Prin*
EMP: 6 EST: 2017
SALES (est): 191.81K **Privately Held**
Web: www.thetotalresistance.com
SIC: 7371 Computer software development and applications

(G-20373)
TOTAL SERVICES INC
31 Germay Dr (19804-1104)
PHONE..................302 575-1132
Timothy M Cairo, *Prin*
EMP: 5 EST: 2012
SALES (est): 862.58K **Privately Held**
Web: www.totalservicesinc.com
SIC: 5112 Office supplies, nec

(G-20374)
TOTAL WELLNESS INNOVATIONS INC
251 Little Falls Dr (19808-1674)
PHONE..................404 543-9061
Jared Rhode, *CEO*
EMP: 8
SALES (est): 306.16K **Privately Held**
SIC: 7371 Computer software development

(G-20375)
TOUBASAM INC
710 N Market St Ste 2b (19801-4922)
P.O. Box 692 (19899-0692)
PHONE..................302 299-2954
Madior Khoussa, *Opers Mgr*
EMP: 5 EST: 2016
SALES (est): 121.94K **Privately Held**
SIC: 0711 Fertilizer application services

(G-20376)
TOUCHMAGIX INC
3524 Silverside Rd Ste 35b (19810-4929)
PHONE..................310 230-5083
EMP: 8 EST: 2018
SALES (est): 46.15K **Privately Held**
Web: www.touchmagix.com
SIC: 7993 Amusement arcade

(G-20377)
TOW PLUS
1732 Marsh Rd (19810-4606)
PHONE..................302 468-5987
EMP: 5 EST: 2016
SALES (est): 70.12K **Privately Held**
SIC: 7549 Automotive services, nec

(G-20378)
TOWLE INSTITUTE
4210 Limestone Rd (19808-2009)
PHONE..................302 993-1408
Sylvia Shows, *Brnch Mgr*
EMP: 8
Web: www.towleinstitute.com
SIC: 8733 Noncommercial research organizations
PA: Towle Institute
  505 Schoolhouse Rd
  Hockessin DE 19707

(G-20379)
TOYO FIBRE USA INC
2706 Alexander Dr (19810-1104)
PHONE..................302 475-3699
Minoru Sano, *Pr*
EMP: 2 EST: 2006
SALES (est): 138.28K **Privately Held**
Web: www.hkpaper.us
SIC: 2673 Bags: plastic, laminated, and coated

(G-20380)
TPF TECHNOLOGIES LLC
1201 N Orange St Ste 600 (19801-1171)
PHONE..................703 665-4588
EMP: 6 EST: 2012
SALES (est): 69.04K **Privately Held**
SIC: 7373 Systems software development services

(G-20381)
TRACTION WHOLESALE CENTER INC
600 S Heald St (19801-5636)
PHONE..................302 743-8473
Lance Elwood, *Mgr*
EMP: 6
SALES (corp-wide): 20.99MM **Privately Held**
Web: www.tractiontire.com
SIC: 5014 5084 Automobile tires and tubes; Tractors, industrial
PA: Traction Wholesale Center, Inc.
  3100 Marwin Rd
  Bensalem PA 19020
  215 642-3170

(G-20382)
TRACY HALTERMAN
1708 Lovering Ave Ste 201 (19806-2141)
PHONE..................302 545-9930
Tracy Halterman, *Owner*
EMP: 5 EST: 2017
SALES (est): 53.97K **Privately Held**
SIC: 7299 Miscellaneous personal service

(G-20383)
TRADE & CONSULTING GROUP CORP (DH)
3511 Silverside Rd Ste 105 (19810-4902)
PHONE..................302 477-9800
Daniel Stargatt, *VP*
EMP: 171 EST: 1994
SALES (est): 904.46K
SALES (corp-wide): 44.28MM **Privately Held**
SIC: 8748 Business consulting, nec
HQ: Yacht Delaware Registry, Ltd
  3511 Silverside Rd # 105
  Wilmington DE 19810
  302 477-9800

(G-20384)
TRADE CAFE USA INC
Also Called: Trade Cafe
2801 Cntrvlle Rd Ste 8003 (19808)
PHONE..................647 694-2656
EMP: 10 EST: 2020
SALES (est): 594.43K **Privately Held**
SIC: 6221 Commodity contracts brokers, dealers

(G-20385)
TRADE NEWS INC
427 N Tatnall St Ste 9465 (19801-2230)
PHONE..................212 884-8089
EMP: 8
SALES (corp-wide): 480.71K **Privately Held**
Web: www.tradethenews.com
SIC: 4832 News
PA: Trade The News, Inc.
  228 Park Ave S Ste 9465
  New York NY 10003
  212 884-8080

(G-20386)
TRADEMARK SIGNS
2621 Boxwood Dr (19810-1607)
PHONE..................484 832-5770
EMP: 4 EST: 2018
SALES (est): 74.73K **Privately Held**
SIC: 3993 Signs and advertising specialties

(G-20387)
TRAFFIC SIGN SOLUTIONS INC (PA)
1000 N West St Ste 1200 (19801-1058)
PHONE..................302 295-4836
EMP: 4 EST: 2007
SALES (est): 196.52K **Privately Held**
SIC: 3993 Signs and advertising specialties

(G-20388)
TRAIN HARD WIN BIG INC
100 Philadelphia Pike (19809-3180)
PHONE..................302 993-6189
Carol Swanson, *Owner*
EMP: 9 EST: 2011
SALES (est): 166.96K **Privately Held**
Web: www.trainhardwinbig.com
SIC: 7991 Physical fitness facilities

(G-20389)
TRAITEL TELECOM CORP
3422 Old Capitol Trl (19808-6124)
P.O. Box 26065 (92196-0065)
PHONE..................619 331-1913
Eli Traitel, *CEO*
EMP: 23 EST: 2011
SQ FT: 2,000
SALES (est): 1.55MM **Privately Held**
SIC: 4813 Telephone communication, except radio

(G-20390)
TRAMAINE & SONS LAWN CARE LLC
500 S Buttonwood St (19801-5308)
PHONE..................302 897-0524
Tramaine Smith, *Managing Member*
EMP: 5 EST: 2021
SALES (est): 100K **Privately Held**
SIC: 0782 Lawn care services

(G-20391)
TRANQUIL ROOTS COUNSELING
4867 Plum Run Ct (19808-1715)
PHONE..................301 275-0225
Karla Cooper, *Prin*
EMP: 6 EST: 2018
SALES (est): 82.8K **Privately Held**
Web: dr-karla-bailey-cooper-tranquil-roots-counseling.business.site
SIC: 8322 General counseling services

(G-20392)
TRANQUILITY BY TARA COLAZO
5700 Kirkwood Hwy Ste 206 (19808-4884)
PHONE..................302 668-4032
Tara Colazo, *Prin*
EMP: 5 EST: 2018
SALES (est): 46.82K **Privately Held**
SIC: 7991 Spas

(G-20393)
TRANS LOGISTICS LLC
4000 N Market St (19802-2220)

PHONE..................267 244-6550
Lawrence Amankwah, *Prin*
EMP: 12 EST: 2018
SALES (est): 482.37K **Privately Held**
SIC: 4789 Transportation services, nec

(G-20394)
TRANS UN STTLMENT SLUTIONS INC (DH)
5300 Brandywine Pkwy 100 (19803-1470)
PHONE..................800 916-8800
Rick Lynch, *Pr*
EMP: 100 EST: 1980
SALES (est): 23.92MM
SALES (corp-wide): 3.71B **Publicly Held**
SIC: 6531 6541 Real estate brokers and agents; Title abstract offices
HQ: Trans Union Llc
    555 W Adams St Fl 1
    Chicago IL 60661
    312 985-2000

(G-20395)
TRANSACTIONAL WEB INC
8 W 13th St (19801)
PHONE..................908 216-5054
Earle West, *CEO*
EMP: 5 EST: 2001
SALES (est): 259.18K **Privately Held**
Web: web.dscc.com
SIC: 7371 Computer software development

(G-20396)
TRANSCONTINENTAL AIRWAYS CORP
1000 N West St Ste 1200 (19801-1058)
PHONE..................202 817-2020
Hiwa Merani, *Dir*
Andrew Blong, *Ch*
EMP: 5 EST: 2011
SALES (est): 114.56K **Privately Held**
SIC: 4522 Air passenger carriers, nonscheduled

(G-20397)
TRANSFLO TERMINAL SERVICES INC
1205 Centerville Rd (19808-6217)
PHONE..................302 994-3853
Neil Brown, *Mgr*
EMP: 10
SALES (corp-wide): 14.85B **Publicly Held**
Web: www.transflo.net
SIC: 4011 Railroads, line-haul operating
HQ: Transflo Terminal Services, Inc.
    500 Water St J975
    Jacksonville FL 32202

(G-20398)
TRANSFORMING LIVES INC
Also Called: Tli
5614 Kirkwood Hwy (19808-5004)
PHONE..................302 379-1043
Malik Muhammad, *CEO*
Jonathan Mcallister, *Dir Opers*
EMP: 67 EST: 2015
SALES (est): 1.07MM **Privately Held**
Web: www.tliservices.org
SIC: 8399 Advocacy group

(G-20399)
TRANSMED SYSTEMS INC
1000 N West St Ste 1000 (19801-1000)
PHONE..................650 584-3316
EMP: 7 EST: 2010
SALES (est): 602.56K **Privately Held**
Web: www.inteliquet.com
SIC: 7372 Application computer software

(G-20400)
TRANSPARENCY MARKET RES INC (PA) ✪
1000 N West St Ste 1200 (19801-1058)
PHONE..................518 618-1030
EMP: 6 EST: 2022
SALES (est): 168.01K
SALES (corp-wide): 168.01K **Privately Held**
SIC: 8732 Market analysis, business, and economic research

(G-20401)
TRANSPORT WKRS UN AMER INTL UN
Also Called: TRANSPORT WORKERS UNION O LOCA
1524 Bonwood Rd (19805-4632)
PHONE..................302 652-1503
James Riley, *Pr*
John Carlton, *VP*
EMP: 7 EST: 1962
SALES (est): 132.77K **Privately Held**
SIC: 8631 Labor union

(G-20402)
TRASH PORTERS LLC ✪
112 S French St (19801-5035)
PHONE..................302 709-1550
Christopher Boozer, *Managing Member*
EMP: 5 EST: 2023
SALES (est): 261.83K **Privately Held**
SIC: 5093 Junk and scrap

(G-20403)
TRAUMA REHABILITATION PA
11b Trolley Sq (19806-3342)
PHONE..................302 777-7723
EMP: 5 EST: 2017
SALES (est): 88.07K **Privately Held**
SIC: 8093 Rehabilitation center, outpatient treatment

(G-20404)
TRAVELAPP INC
Also Called: Travelapp
300 Delaware Ave Ste 210 (19801-6601)
PHONE..................617 580-7978
Omar Bayat, *CEO*
EMP: 8 EST: 2019
SALES (est): 397.81K **Privately Held**
Web: www.travelapp.co
SIC: 7371 Computer software development and applications

(G-20405)
TRAVELERS JOY INC
11 S Hampshire Ct (19807-2582)
PHONE..................888 878-5569
Anthony Alexander, *Owner*
EMP: 5 EST: 2001
SALES (est): 48.85K **Privately Held**
Web: www.travelersjoy.com
SIC: 4724 Travel agencies

(G-20406)
TRAVELPAD RENTALS LLC (PA)
2055 Limestone Rd 200c (19808-5536)
PHONE..................203 751-1569
EMP: 7 EST: 2021
SALES (est): 53.21K
SALES (corp-wide): 53.21K **Privately Held**
SIC: 6531 Real estate leasing and rentals

(G-20407)
TREEHOUSE WELLNESS CENTER LLC
1004 N Monroe St (19801-1339)
P.O. Box 25171 (19899-5171)
PHONE..................302 893-1001
Diane Moss, *CEO*
EMP: 8 EST: 1999
SALES (est): 191.47K **Privately Held**
Web: www.treehousecafe.net
SIC: 8249 8748 Business training services; Business consulting, nec

(G-20408)
TRELLIST INC
Also Called: Forthright Consulting
2317 Macdonough Rd Ste 100 (19805-2620)
PHONE..................302 593-1432
David Atadan, *CEO*
EMP: 12
SALES (corp-wide): 9.04MM **Privately Held**
Web: www.trellist.com
SIC: 8748 Business consulting, nec
PA: Trellist, Inc.
    44 W Gay St Ste 202
    West Chester PA 19380
    302 778-1300

(G-20409)
TRETEK LLC
2055 Limestone Rd Ste 200c (19808-5536)
PHONE..................888 407-9737
Lirim Sulejmani, *Managing Member*
EMP: 5
SALES (est): 107.01K **Privately Held**
SIC: 7371 Computer software development and applications

(G-20410)
TRI STATE WASTE SOLUTIONS
P.O. Box 987 (19720-0987)
PHONE..................302 323-0200
Kevin Shegog, *Owner*
EMP: 7 EST: 2010
SALES (est): 228.32K **Privately Held**
Web: www.tswaste.com
SIC: 8748 Environmental consultant

(G-20411)
TRI VALLEY AGENCY INC
63 Standiford Ct (19804-2936)
PHONE..................302 482-3802
Joseph Lanciano, *Prin*
EMP: 6 EST: 2011
SALES (est): 76.95K **Privately Held**
SIC: 6411 Insurance agents, nec

(G-20412)
TRI-STATE CARPET MAINT INC
2 S Poplar St Fl 1 (19801-5054)
PHONE..................302 654-8193
EMP: 8 EST: 1998
SALES (est): 30.77K **Privately Held**
Web: www.tristatecpt.com
SIC: 7349 Building maintenance services, nec

(G-20413)
TRI-STATE INTEGRATIVE HLTH LLC
34b Trolley Sq (19806-3352)
PHONE..................302 743-2328
Brian Mowll, *Mgr*
EMP: 7 EST: 2018
SALES (est): 158.08K **Privately Held**
SIC: 8099 Health and allied services, nec

(G-20414)
TRI-STATE LIFT TRUCK LTD
70b Germay Dr (19804-1105)
P.O. Box 3176 (19804-0176)
PHONE..................302 427-2800
Marijo Camp, *Pr*
EMP: 5 EST: 1989
SQ FT: 2,960
SALES (est): 996.8K **Privately Held**
Web: www.tristatelifttruck.com
SIC: 5084 Materials handling machinery

(G-20415)
TRI-STATE TECHNOLOGIES INC
701 Cornell Dr Ste 13 (19801-5782)
PHONE..................302 658-5400
Edward Mendez, *Pr*
Connie Mendez, *
EMP: 15 EST: 1984
SQ FT: 4,000
SALES (est): 452.73K **Privately Held**
SIC: 1711 1731 Mechanical contractor; General electrical contractor

(G-20416)
TRI-TEK CORPORATION
1 Medori Blvd Ste B (19801-5777)
PHONE..................302 239-1638
EMP: 7 EST: 2016
SALES (est): 460.58K **Privately Held**
Web: www.tritek.com
SIC: 3599 Machine shop, jobbing and repair

(G-20417)
TRIAL TRANSPORT LOGISTICS
400 Wyoming Ave (19809-1304)
PHONE..................302 383-5907
Patricia A Schierbaum, *Pr*
EMP: 5 EST: 2010
SALES (est): 480.97K **Privately Held**
Web: www.trialtransportlogistics.com
SIC: 4789 Transportation services, nec

(G-20418)
TRIALOGICS LLC
2 Mill Rd Ste 110 (19806-2175)
PHONE..................302 313-9000
Christopher Gropp, *CEO*
John A Moore, *Ch*
EMP: 15 EST: 2016
SQ FT: 2,500
SALES (est): 922.73K **Privately Held**
Web: www.trialogics.com
SIC: 7371 Computer software development

(G-20419)
TRIBUTE INTERACTIVE INC
251 Little Falls Dr (19808-1674)
PHONE..................302 803-5432
Olesya Dyachyshyn, *Pr*
EMP: 5 EST: 2020
SALES (est): 107.01K **Privately Held**
SIC: 7371 Software programming applications

(G-20420)
TRICKLESTAR INC
251 Little Falls Dr (19808-1674)
PHONE..................888 700-1098
Bernard Emby, *CEO*
EMP: 10 EST: 2009
SALES (est): 231.78K **Privately Held**
Web: www.tricklestar.com
SIC: 3625 Switches, electronic applications

(G-20421)
TRILOGY SALON & SPA
312 Southern Rd (19804-1026)
PHONE..................302 388-1210
EMP: 5 EST: 2013
SALES (est): 68.12K **Privately Held**
Web: www.trilogysalon.com
SIC: 7991 Spas

(G-20422)
TRIMARK ENTERPRISES INC
2406 W Newport Pike (19804-3849)
PHONE..................302 683-9065

Wilmington - New Castle County (G-20423)

EMP: 5 EST: 2020
SALES (est): 462.17K **Privately Held**
SIC: 1521 General remodeling, single-family houses

(G-20423)
TRINET CONSULTANTS INC (HQ)
1106 Elderon Dr (19808-1908)
PHONE..............................302 633-9348
EMP: 10 EST: 1990
SQ FT: 3,000
SALES (est): 2.46MM **Privately Held**
SIC: 8748 Telecommunications consultant
PA: Mcnichol Enterprises Inc
    1106 Elderon Dr
    Wilmington DE 19808

(G-20424)
TRINIIITY GROUP LLC ◇
24a Trolley Sq (19806-3334)
PHONE..............................302 402-1726
Akiesha Little, *CEO*
EMP: 9 EST: 2022
SALES (est): 227.09K **Privately Held**
SIC: 7349 Janitorial service, contract basis

(G-20425)
TRINITY CLOUD COMPANY
Also Called: Trinity Cloud
1013 Centre Rd Ste 403s (19805-1270)
PHONE..............................973 494-8190
Ansela Joseph Peter, *Pr*
EMP: 50 EST: 2012
SQ FT: 1,500
SALES (est): 5.04MM **Privately Held**
Web: www.trinitycloud.com
SIC: 7361 Employment agencies

(G-20426)
TRINITY GOLD CONSULTING LLC
703 N Jackson St (19805-3242)
P.O. Box 30551 (19805-7551)
PHONE..............................302 498-9063
John Word, *CEO*
EMP: 7 EST: 2014
SALES (est): 408.88K **Privately Held**
SIC: 8748 Business consulting, nec

(G-20427)
TRINITY SUBSURFACE LLC
14 Hadco Rd Ste 103 (19804-1014)
P.O. Box 161 (19710-0161)
PHONE..............................855 387-4648
EMP: 23 EST: 2018
SALES (est): 4.3MM **Privately Held**
Web: www.trinitysubsurface.com
SIC: 8711 Engineering services

(G-20428)
TRIO ACADEMY LLC
1013 Centre Rd Ste 403b (19805-1270)
PHONE..............................646 330-9211
EMP: 7 EST: 2019
SALES (est): 46.16K **Privately Held**
Web: www.trioacademywi.com
SIC: 7371 Computer software development and applications

(G-20429)
TRISCO FOODS LLC
2711 Centerville Rd Ste 400 (19808-1660)
PHONE..............................719 352-3218
EMP: 65 EST: 2016
SALES (est): 4.44MM **Privately Held**
SIC: 2033 2087 2099 Barbecue sauce: packaged in cans, jars, etc.; Beverage bases, concentrates, syrups, powders and mixes; Dessert mixes and fillings

(G-20430)
TRISTATE COURIER & CARRIAGE
1001 N Jefferson St Ste 100 (19801-1435)
PHONE..............................302 654-3345
EMP: 6 EST: 1993
SQ FT: 3,000
SALES (est): 95.12K **Privately Held**
Web: www.tristatecourier.com
SIC: 7389 Courier or messenger service

(G-20431)
TRITEK TECHNOLOGIES INC
1 Medori Blvd Ste B (19801-5777)
PHONE..............................302 573-5096
James Malatesta, *Brnch Mgr*
EMP: 5
SALES (corp-wide): 1.27MM **Privately Held**
Web: www.tritek.com
SIC: 3579 Mailing, letter handling, and addressing machines
PA: Tritek Technologies, Inc.
    103 E Bridle Path
    Hockessin DE 19707
    302 239-1638

(G-20432)
TRIVETT CONTRACTING
4601 Governor Printz Blvd Unit F (19809-3443)
PHONE..............................302 275-6452
EMP: 6 EST: 2019
SALES (est): 607.59K **Privately Held**
Web: www.trivettcontractinginc.com
SIC: 1799 Special trade contractors, nec

(G-20433)
TROI LLC
28 Austin Rd (19810-2203)
PHONE..............................302 528-0229
EMP: 5 EST: 2011
SALES (est): 243.19K **Privately Held**
SIC: 6519 Real property lessors, nec

(G-20434)
TROLLEY LAUNDRY
Also Called: Zucchini Brothers
33a Trolley Sq (19806-3371)
PHONE..............................302 654-3538
Tom Guidl, *Pr*
EMP: 5 EST: 1980
SQ FT: 1,000
SALES (est): 224.04K **Privately Held**
Web: www.trolleylaundry.com
SIC: 7215 Laundry, coin-operated

(G-20435)
TROLLEY SQ OPN MRI & IMGNG CTR
Also Called: Bancroft Pkwy Open Mri & Imgng
1010 N Bancroft Pkwy Ste 101 (19805-2690)
PHONE..............................302 472-5555
John W Rollins, *Managing Member*
EMP: 10 EST: 2007
SALES (est): 536.6K **Privately Held**
SIC: 8011 Radiologist

(G-20436)
TROLLEY SQUARE INVESTORS LLC
2711 Centerville Rd Ste 400 (19808-1660)
PHONE..............................302 658-1000
Elizabeth Martelli, *Prin*
EMP: 5 EST: 2013
SALES (est): 391.23K **Privately Held**
Web: www.trolleysquareaptrentals.com
SIC: 6799 Investors, nec

(G-20437)
TROLLEY WEB
4611 Bedford Blvd (19803-3901)
PHONE..............................302 468-7247
EMP: 5 EST: 2014
SALES (est): 64.1K **Privately Held**
Web: www.trolleyweb.com
SIC: 7374 Computer graphics service

(G-20438)
TROPHY SHOP
303 W 8th St (19801-1730)
PHONE..............................302 656-4438
Thomas Tanzilli, *Pr*
EMP: 9 EST: 1980
SQ FT: 18,000
SALES (est): 352.42K **Privately Held**
Web: www.trophyus.com
SIC: 3993 Signs and advertising specialties

(G-20439)
TROU AUTO
735 Philadelphia Pike (19809-2544)
PHONE..............................302 762-3200
EMP: 5 EST: 2019
SALES (est): 177.74K **Privately Held**
SIC: 7538 General automotive repair shops

(G-20440)
TROUTMAN PPPER HMLTON SNDERS L
1313 N Market St Ste 5100 (19801-6111)
P.O. Box 1709 (19899-1709)
PHONE..............................302 777-6500
David Straton, *Mng Pt*
EMP: 25
SALES (corp-wide): 161.17MM **Privately Held**
Web: www.troutman.com
SIC: 8111 General practice attorney, lawyer
PA: Troutman Pepper Hamilton Sanders Llp
    600 Peachtree St Ne # 300
    Atlanta GA 30308
    404 885-3000

(G-20441)
TRU GENERAL CONTRACTOR INC
3307 Faulkland Rd (19808-2428)
PHONE..............................302 354-0553
Mustafa Kilincarslan, *Pr*
Onur Zaim, *VP*
Lisa Celik-kilincarslan, *Sec*
EMP: 5 EST: 2008
SALES (est): 289.01K **Privately Held**
SIC: 1521 New construction, single-family houses

(G-20442)
TRUE ACCESS CAPITAL CORP
100 W 10th St Ste 300 (19801-1642)
PHONE..............................302 652-6774
EMP: 10 EST: 1993
SQ FT: 4,000
SALES (est): 2.17MM **Privately Held**
Web: www.trueaccesscapital.org
SIC: 6162 Loan correspondents

(G-20443)
TRUE RIVAL FITNESS
501 Silverside Rd Ste 150 (19809-1372)
PHONE..............................302 570-0530
EMP: 5 EST: 2016
SALES (est): 50.3K **Privately Held**
SIC: 7991 Physical fitness facilities

(G-20444)
TRUE SPIRIT BEVERAGE COMPANY
3411 Silverside Rd Ste 104 (19810-4812)
PHONE..............................520 356-4730
Rodolfo Aldana, *CEO*
Ila Byrne, *CMO*
EMP: 6 EST: 2020
SALES (est): 262.22K **Privately Held**
SIC: 2086 Soft drinks: packaged in cans, bottles, etc.

(G-20445)
TRUGREEN LIMITED PARTNERSHIP
Also Called: Tru Green-Chemlawn
1350 First State Blvd (19804-3562)
P.O. Box 6209 (19804-0809)
PHONE..............................302 724-6620
Mike Matejik, *Mgr*
EMP: 21
SALES (corp-wide): 910.28MM **Privately Held**
Web: www.trugreen.com
SIC: 0782 Lawn care services
HQ: Trugreen Limited Partnership
    1790 Kirby Pkwy
    Memphis TN 38138

(G-20446)
TRUITTS HLPING HNDS CHLDCR/PRS
2915 Lancaster Ave (19805-5226)
PHONE..............................302 426-6436
EMP: 9 EST: 2019
SALES (est): 94.1K **Privately Held**
SIC: 8351 Preschool center

(G-20447)
TRUMPET LLC
919 N Market St Ste 950 (19801-3036)
PHONE..............................303 910-7444
EMP: 7 EST: 2020
SALES (est): 56.54K **Privately Held**
SIC: 7372 Application computer software

(G-20448)
TRUNK TEL LLC
2055 Limestone Rd 200c (19808-5536)
PHONE..............................302 476-2370
EMP: 5 EST: 2021
SALES (est): 71.34K **Privately Held**
SIC: 4813 Voice telephone communications

(G-20449)
TRUSTEES OF ARDENTOWN
2308 E Mall St (19810-4226)
PHONE..............................302 475-8193
EMP: 5 EST: 2010
SALES (est): 56.31K **Privately Held**
Web: ardentown.delaware.gov
SIC: 8641 Social associations

(G-20450)
TRUVERIS INC
3 Beaver Valley Rd Ste 100 (19803-1125)
PHONE..............................800 430-1430
EMP: 130 EST: 2009
SALES (est): 24.47MM **Privately Held**
Web: www.truveris.com
SIC: 7374 Data processing and preparation

(G-20451)
TRUVISION LLC
733 W 4th St (19801-2003)
PHONE..............................267 349-4550
Kimberly Hayman, *Prin*
EMP: 7 EST: 2017
SALES (est): 100.34K **Privately Held**
SIC: 8711 Engineering services

(G-20452)
TSF INCORPORATED
3204 Romilly Rd (19810-3436)
PHONE..............................518 879-6571
Kathleen Buckley, *Prin*
EMP: 5 EST: 2015
SALES (est): 26.97K **Privately Held**
SIC: 8399 Social services, nec

GEOGRAPHIC SECTION

Wilmington - New Castle County (G-20481)

(G-20453)
TSIONAS MANAGEMENT CO INC
2000 Pennsylvania Ave (19806-2457)
PHONE......................302 369-8895
EMP: 15 EST: 2002
SALES (est): 5.16MM Privately Held
Web: www.tsionasinc.com
SIC: 6513 Apartment building operators

(G-20454)
TSUDA TAKESHI MD
1600 Rockland Rd (19803-3607)
PHONE......................302 651-6660
Takeshi Tsuda, Owner
EMP: 14 EST: 2018
SALES (est): 246.45K Privately Held
Web: www.nemours.org
SIC: 8011 Pediatrician

(G-20455)
TT SPALON
1319 Mckennans Church Rd (19808-2132)
PHONE......................302 668-1477
EMP: 5 EST: 2016
SALES (est): 32.03K Privately Held
SIC: 7231 Manicurist, pedicurist

(G-20456)
TTNA ENERGY SYSTEMS LLC
3422 Old Capitol Trl # 1468 (19808-6124)
P.O. Box 4287 (23058-4287)
PHONE......................302 384-9147
EMP: 5 EST: 2012
SALES (est): 216.76K Privately Held
SIC: 3826 Differential thermal analysis instruments

(G-20457)
TTS TCNJA TCI SHIPG N AMER INC (PA)
1013 Centre Rd Ste 403s (19805-1270)
PHONE......................770 383-4604
Timo Tessen, CEO
Joel Paritz, CFO
Henry Roske, Sec
EMP: 6 EST: 2020
SALES (est): 716.2K
SALES (corp-wide): 716.2K Privately Held
Web: www.tts-northamerica.com
SIC: 4731 4581 Freight transportation arrangement; Air freight handling at airports

(G-20458)
TUCSON HOTELS LP (PA)
Also Called: John Q Hammons Hotels
2711 Centerville Rd Ste 400 (19808-1660)
PHONE......................678 830-2438
Chris Pawelko, VP
Jonathan Eilian, *
Ron Brown, *
EMP: 65 EST: 1989
SQ FT: 10,226
SALES (est): 384.1MM Privately Held
Web: www.holidayinn.com
SIC: 7011 Hotels

(G-20459)
TUMBLE-KIDS LLC
228 Oakwood Rd (19803-3133)
PHONE......................302 530-7800
Janine Watens, Prin
EMP: 6 EST: 2014
SALES (est): 51.54K Privately Held
SIC: 7999 Gymnastic instruction, non-membership

(G-20460)
TURBO DISTRIBUTORS LLC
1013 Centre Rd Ste 403d (19805-1270)
PHONE......................845 678-6700
EMP: 14 EST: 2020
SALES (est): 727.84K Privately Held
SIC: 6221 Commodity contracts brokers, dealers

(G-20461)
TURFHOUND INC
5500 Skyline Dr Ste 6 (19808-1772)
PHONE......................215 783-8143
Richard Reynolds, Prin
Richard Reynolds, Pr
Catherine De Marco, VP
EMP: 3 EST: 2011
SQ FT: 22,000
SALES (est): 738.77K Privately Held
Web: www.turfhound.com
SIC: 3523 Turf and grounds equipment

(G-20462)
TURING MACHINES INC
251 Little Falls Dr (19808-1674)
PHONE......................415 500-0217
Stanislavs Nevedomskis, Prin
EMP: 2 EST: 2019
SALES (est): 100K Privately Held
SIC: 3571 Computers, digital, analog or hybrid

(G-20463)
TURNER AND SELBY GROUP INC
1320 Philadelphia Pike Ste 202 (19809-1818)
PHONE......................302 666-2339
William Small, CEO
EMP: 22
SALES (est): 515.83K Privately Held
SIC: 1389 Construction, repair, and dismantling services

(G-20464)
TURNING POINT COLLECTION LLC
2055 Limestone Rd Ste 302 (19808-5536)
P.O. Box 4451 (19807-0451)
PHONE......................302 275-0167
EMP: 2 EST: 2009
SALES (est): 160.86K Privately Held
Web: www.turningpointfurniture.com
SIC: 2531 7389 Public building and related furniture; Brokers' services

(G-20465)
TUSI BROTHERS INC
1 Copper Dr Ste 1 (19804-2446)
P.O. Box 6057 (19804-0657)
PHONE......................302 998-6383
Francis Tusi, Pr
Donna Tusi, Treas
EMP: 18 EST: 1974
SQ FT: 5,000
SALES (est): 867.97K Privately Held
Web: www.tusibrotherselectric.com
SIC: 1731 General electrical contractor

(G-20466)
TUTOR TIME LEARNING CTRS LLC
5305 Limestone Rd (19808-1256)
PHONE......................302 235-5701
Jennifer Netta, Dir
EMP: 172
Web: www.tutortime.com
SIC: 8351 Preschool center
HQ: Tutor Time Learning Centers, Llc
21333 Haggerty Rd Ste 300
Novi MI 48375
248 697-9000

(G-20467)
TW CONTRACTING
202 New Rd Unit 1 (19805-4140)
PHONE......................302 384-6777
EMP: 5 EST: 2018
SALES (est): 126.11K Privately Held
Web: www.avnails.com
SIC: 1799 Special trade contractors, nec

(G-20468)
TWIN SPANS BUSINESS PARK LLC
405 Marsh Ln Ste 1 (19804-2445)
PHONE......................302 328-5713
Thomas Harvey, Prin
EMP: 5 EST: 2005
SALES (est): 139.29K Privately Held
SIC: 6512 Commercial and industrial building operation

(G-20469)
TWINCO ROMAX LLC
1 Crowell Rd (19804-3556)
PHONE......................302 998-3019
EMP: 8 EST: 2013
SALES (est): 170.95K Privately Held
SIC: 2899 Chemical preparations, nec

(G-20470)
TWINNING LLC ✪
1427 Kynlyn Dr (19809-2422)
PHONE......................609 793-3510
Elisa Diamanti, Managing Member
EMP: 5 EST: 2022
SALES (est): 207.81K Privately Held
SIC: 8742 7389 Management consulting services; Business Activities at Non-Commercial Site

(G-20471)
TWO BROTHERS ROOFING LLC
605 W Summit Ave (19804-1815)
PHONE......................302 650-8077
Moises Serrano, Prin
EMP: 7 EST: 2018
SALES (est): 363.18K Privately Held
Web: www.twobrothersroofingde.com
SIC: 1761 Roofing contractor

(G-20472)
TWS CHEWSY LLC
1209 N Orange St (19801-1120)
PHONE......................514 730-8040
EMP: 3 EST: 2020
SALES (est): 91.38K Privately Held
SIC: 2023 Dietary supplements, dairy and non-dairy based

(G-20473)
TXE GLOBAL LLC (PA)
500 Delaware Ave (19801-1490)
PHONE......................302 409-0234
EMP: 8 EST: 2018
SQ FT: 2,100
SALES (est): 656.42K
SALES (corp-wide): 656.42K Privately Held
Web: www.txeglobal.com
SIC: 8748 Business consulting, nec

(G-20474)
TY JENNIFER MD
1600 Rockland Rd (19803-3607)
PHONE......................302 651-4459
M Jennifer, Ofcr
EMP: 19 EST: 2013
SALES (est): 888.44K Privately Held
Web: www.nemours.org
SIC: 8011 Pediatrician

(G-20475)
TYBOUT REDFEARN & PELL PA
501 Carr Rd Ste 300 (19809-2866)
P.O. Box 2092 (19899-2092)
PHONE......................302 658-6901
David Culley, Pt
Danielle Yearick, *
EMP: 40 EST: 1965
SALES (est): 7.13MM Privately Held
Web: www.trplaw.com
SIC: 8111 General practice attorney, lawyer

(G-20476)
TYCHRON CORPORATION
1201 N Orange St Ste 7456 (19801-1293)
PHONE......................844 892-4766
Michael Burlingame, Pr
EMP: 15 EST: 2019
SALES (est): 1.67MM Privately Held
Web: www.tychron.com
SIC: 4813 7371 8748 Telephone communication, except radio; Computer software development; Telecommunications consultant

(G-20477)
TYCO ENGINEERING TECH LLC
501 Silverside Rd Ste 28 (19809-1375)
P.O. Box 10234 (22310-0234)
PHONE......................202 790-9648
EMP: 5 EST: 2015
SALES (est): 52.72K Privately Held
SIC: 8711 Engineering services

(G-20478)
TYCO TECHNOLOGY RESOURCES
4550 New Lnden Hl Rd Ste (19808)
PHONE......................877 706-0510
Lisa Burgin Vaccarelli, Prin
EMP: 6 EST: 2010
SALES (est): 93.83K Privately Held
SIC: 7382 Security systems services

(G-20479)
TYCOS GENERAL CONTRACTING INC
412 Meco Dr (19804-1112)
PHONE......................302 268-6766
EMP: 10 EST: 2019
SALES (est): 804.41K Privately Held
Web: www.tycosgencon.com
SIC: 1799 Special trade contractors, nec

(G-20480)
TYCOS GENERAL CONTRACTORS INC
2112 Silverside Rd (19810-4148)
PHONE......................302 478-9267
Sergio Solis, Pr
EMP: 9 EST: 2016
SALES (est): 753.21K Privately Held
Web: www.tycosgencon.com
SIC: 1542 Commercial and office building contractors

(G-20481)
TYDEN GROUP HOLDINGS CORP (HQ)
1209 N Orange St (19801-1120)
PHONE......................740 420-6777
Steve Oneil, CEO
Bruce Heinemann, CFO
◆ EMP: 15 EST: 1988
SALES (est): 418.09MM
SALES (corp-wide): 418.09MM Privately Held
SIC: 3953 2891 Figures (marking devices), metal; Sealants
PA: Crimson Capital Silicon Valley
601 California St # 1450
San Francisco CA 94108
650 233-6900

Wilmington - New Castle County (G-20482)

(G-20482)
TYRANT SPORTSGEAR INC
2017 W Newport Pike (19804-3724)
P.O. Box 1375 (19707-5375)
PHONE..................................302 530-3410
Cory Frederick, *Prin*
EMP: 6 **EST:** 2016
SALES (est): 386.51K **Privately Held**
Web: www.tyrantwrestling.com
SIC: 5199 Advertising specialties

(G-20483)
U PRIME FITNESS AND WELLNESS
2601 Tonbridge Dr (19810-1216)
PHONE..................................302 529-1966
Andrew Holtz, *Prin*
EMP: 6 **EST:** 2017
SALES (est): 130.05K **Privately Held**
SIC: 7991 Physical fitness facilities

(G-20484)
U YOGA
703 Halstead Rd (19803-2227)
PHONE..................................302 893-4585
Marie Wagner, *Owner*
EMP: 6 **EST:** 2010
SALES (est): 96.37K **Privately Held**
Web: www.yogau.org
SIC: 7999 Yoga instruction

(G-20485)
U-HAUL INTERNATIONAL INC
Also Called: U-Haul
2920 Governor Printz Blvd (19802-3706)
PHONE..................................302 762-6445
Mohamed Moustafa, *Brnch Mgr*
EMP: 7
SALES (corp-wide): 5.86B **Publicly Held**
Web: www.uhaul.com
SIC: 7513 Truck rental and leasing, no drivers
HQ: U-Haul International, Inc.
2727 N Central Ave
Phoenix AZ 85004
602 263-6011

(G-20486)
U-MATTER LEARNING PLACE
821 W 32nd St (19802-2505)
PHONE..................................302 482-1746
Verlyn Rayfield, *Prin*
EMP: 6 **EST:** 2015
SALES (est): 76.94K **Privately Held**
SIC: 7999 Amusement and recreation, nec

(G-20487)
U2R INC (PA)
251 Little Falls Dr (19808-1674)
PHONE..................................609 792-6575
William Callahen, *CEO*
EMP: 10 **EST:** 2021
SALES (est): 6MM
SALES (corp-wide): 6MM **Privately Held**
SIC: 7311 Advertising consultant

(G-20488)
UACJ TRADING & PROCESSING AMER (PA)
1209 N Orange St (19801-1120)
PHONE..................................312 636-5941
Michinori Morikawa, *Pr*
Yohei Hasegawa, *VP*
EMP: 4 **EST:** 2014
SQ FT: 700
SALES (est): 2.31MM
SALES (corp-wide): 2.31MM **Privately Held**
SIC: 8611 3353 5015 3354 Business associations; Aluminum sheet, plate, and foil; Automotive supplies, used: wholesale and retail; Aluminum extruded products

(G-20489)
UAG INTERNATIONAL HOLDINGS INC (HQ)
1105 N Market St Ste 1300 (19801-1241)
PHONE..................................302 427-9859
EMP: 41 **EST:** 1999
SALES (est): 9.45MM **Publicly Held**
SIC: 6282 7389 Investment advice; Financial services
PA: Penske Automotive Group, Inc.
2555 S Telegraph Rd
Bloomfield Hills MI 48302

(G-20490)
UBER
318 W Summit Ave (19804-1726)
PHONE..................................302 287-4866
Charles Martin, *Prin*
EMP: 27 **EST:** 2016
SALES (est): 105.02K **Privately Held**
Web: www.uber.com
SIC: 4121 Taxicabs

(G-20491)
UBINET INC
831 N Tatnall St (19801-1717)
PHONE..................................302 722-6015
Karl Smith, *CEO*
EMP: 5 **EST:** 2017
SALES (est): 500K **Privately Held**
SIC: 8733 Research institute

(G-20492)
UBIUM GROUP
1000 N West St (19801-1050)
PHONE..................................801 487-5000
EMP: 948
SALES (corp-wide): 300MM **Privately Held**
SIC: 8741 Management services
PA: Ubium Group
1800 Carey Ave
Cheyenne WY 82001
801 487-5000

(G-20493)
UBS FINANCIAL SERVICES INC
500 Delaware Ave Ste 901 (19801-7409)
PHONE..................................302 657-5331
Robert Ritterreiser, *Mgr*
EMP: 13
Web: www.ubs.com
SIC: 7389 Financial services
HQ: Ubs Financial Services Inc.
1200 Harbor Blvd Fl 10
Weehawken NJ 07086
212 713-2000

(G-20494)
UBS FINANCIAL SERVICES INC
20 Montchanin Rd Ste 170 (19807-2184)
PHONE..................................302 407-4700
EMP: 5
Web: www.ubs.com
SIC: 6211 Security brokers and dealers
HQ: Ubs Financial Services Inc.
1200 Harbor Blvd Fl 10
Weehawken NJ 07086
212 713-2000

(G-20495)
ULTERIOR TECHNOLOGIES INC (PA)
1201 N Orange St Ste 7495 (19801-1298)
PHONE..................................929 399-8964
EMP: 7 **EST:** 2020
SALES (est): 73.91K
SALES (corp-wide): 73.91K **Privately Held**
SIC: 7379 Online services technology consultants

(G-20496)
ULTIMATE FIRE PROTECTION LLC
1625 N Heald St (19802-5146)
PHONE..................................302 994-8371
Fidel Maxwell, *Prin*
EMP: 8 **EST:** 2012
SALES (est): 281.27K **Privately Held**
Web: ultimate-fire-protection-llc.business.site
SIC: 7389 Fire protection service other than forestry or public

(G-20497)
ULTIMATE IMAGES INC
3100 Naamans Rd Ste 8 (19810-2100)
PHONE..................................302 479-0292
Beth Laplante, *Pr*
EMP: 5 **EST:** 1990
SALES (est): 246.57K **Privately Held**
Web: www.myultimateimages.com
SIC: 7231 Unisex hair salons

(G-20498)
ULTIMATE TOURNAMENT INC
1305 Chadwick Rd (19803-4115)
PHONE..................................410 746-1637
EMP: 5 **EST:** 2020
SALES (est): 131.85K **Privately Held**
SIC: 7371 Computer software development and applications

(G-20499)
ULTIUS CSTM WRTING EDTING SVCS
1201 N Orange St Ste 7038 (19801-1189)
PHONE..................................702 690-4552
EMP: 11 **EST:** 2019
SALES (est): 1.12MM **Privately Held**
Web: www.ultius.com
SIC: 7338 Editing service

(G-20500)
ULTRA MODERN LAUNDRY SVCS LLC
Also Called: Um Laundry
24a Trolley Sq (19806-3334)
PHONE..................................302 533-8596
Terrell Powell, *CEO*
EMP: 2 **EST:** 2020
SALES (est): 100K **Privately Held**
SIC: 2842 3582 4212 3633 Laundry cleaning preparations; Dryers, laundry: commercial, including coin-operated; Delivery service, vehicular; Laundry dryers, household or coin-operated

(G-20501)
ULTRA PACKET LLC
501 Silverside Rd (19809-1374)
PHONE..................................240 219-8472
EMP: 5 **EST:** 2020
SALES (est): 56.54K **Privately Held**
SIC: 7372 Business oriented computer software

(G-20502)
ULTRAFINE TECHNOLOGIES INC
405 Derby Way (19810-2265)
PHONE..................................302 384-6513
EMP: 3 **EST:** 1995
SQ FT: 1,500
SALES (est): 479.7K **Privately Held**
Web: www.ultrafinetechnologies.com
SIC: 5169 3625 8731 Chemicals and allied products, nec; Electric controls and control accessories, industrial; Electronic research

(G-20503)
UNADA LLC
300 Delaware Ave Ste 210a (19801-6601)
PHONE..................................470 809-9077
EMP: 30 **EST:** 2019
SALES (est): 1.53MM **Privately Held**
Web: www.icraft.us
SIC: 5078 Refrigeration equipment and supplies

(G-20504)
UNCLAIMED PROPERTY
820 N French St (19801-3509)
PHONE..................................302 577-8220
Rebecca Goldsmith, *Mgr*
EMP: 6 **EST:** 2017
SALES (est): 96.26K **Privately Held**
Web: www.unclaimed-funds.org
SIC: 6512 Nonresidential building operators

(G-20505)
UNFOLD STUDIO LLC
1401 N Dupont St (19806-4029)
PHONE..................................415 993-0943
Timoleon Tokousbalides, *Pr*
EMP: 5 **EST:** 2014
SALES (est): 61.68K **Privately Held**
SIC: 7336 Creative services to advertisers, except writers

(G-20506)
UNIBET INTERACTIVE INC
1209 N Orange St (19801-1120)
PHONE..................................855 655-6310
EMP: 19 **EST:** 2018
SALES (est): 394.94K **Privately Held**
SIC: 7011 Casino hotel

(G-20507)
UNICODEZ INC
831 N Tatnall St (19801-1717)
PHONE..................................703 963-2738
Pramod Shukla, *CEO*
Amy Blair, *VP*
Saurav Yadav, *Dir*
Anmol Shrivastava, *COO*
EMP: 10 **EST:** 2020
SALES (est): 356.33K **Privately Held**
Web: www.unicodez.com
SIC: 7389 Business Activities at Non-Commercial Site

(G-20508)
UNIDEL FOUNDATION INC
3801 Kennett Pike Ste C303 (19807-2325)
P.O. Box 1146 (19899-1146)
PHONE..................................302 658-9200
Richard L Sution Esq, *Ch Bd*
David D Wakefield, *V Ch Bd*
G Arno Loessner, *Sec*
EMP: 9 **EST:** 1964
SALES (est): 18.81MM **Privately Held**
SIC: 8699 Charitable organization

(G-20509)
UNIFIED COMPANIES INC
Also Called: Unified Biz Club
1201 N Orange St Ste 600 (19801-1171)
P.O. Box 8189 (60079-8189)
PHONE..................................866 936-0515
Ronald Clark, *CEO*
Sheila Lantigua Clark, *Sec*
Deshon Wynn, *OF CREATIVE DESIGN*
EMP: 8 **EST:** 2009
SQ FT: 500
SALES (est): 999.81K **Privately Held**

SIC: 7311 Advertising consultant

(G-20510)
UNIFIED FITNESS NPB
4924 Hogan Dr (19808-1716)
PHONE..................302 528-5021
Nina Parkerbrison, *Prin*
EMP: 6 EST: 2017
SALES (est): 58.9K **Privately Held**
Web: www.ufit-npb.com
SIC: 7991 Physical fitness facilities

(G-20511)
UNIGO INC
108 W 13th St (19801-1145)
PHONE..................205 974-1962
Lingli Wu, *CEO*
EMP: 4 EST: 2020
SALES (est): 219.18K **Privately Held**
SIC: 5072 3541 Garden tools, hand; Robots for drilling, cutting, grinding, polishing, etc.

(G-20512)
UNIK MARKETING INC
1007 N Orange St (19801-1239)
PHONE..................302 830-9935
Pahartging Xirifu, *CEO*
EMP: 5
SALES (est): 199.4K **Privately Held**
SIC: 7371 Computer software development

(G-20513)
UNION PARK LAWNS
412 S Sycamore St (19805-3742)
PHONE..................302 757-5496
EMP: 5 EST: 2015
SALES (est): 54.81K **Privately Held**
Web: www.unionparklawns.com
SIC: 0782 Lawn and garden services

(G-20514)
UNION PRESS PRINTING INC
1723 W 8th St (19805-3153)
PHONE..................302 652-0496
Chrissy Grimes, *Pr*
John Bove, *VP*
EMP: 6 EST: 1935
SQ FT: 2,000
SALES (est): 826.36K **Privately Held**
Web: www.unionpress.com
SIC: 2752 2796 Offset printing; Letterpress plates, preparation of

(G-20515)
UNION WHL ACOUSTICAL SUP CO
500 E Front St Ste 1 (19801-5017)
PHONE..................302 656-4462
James F Mclaughlin Junior, *Pr*
Chad Morris, *VP*
William Stackhouse, *Sec*
EMP: 7 EST: 1977
SQ FT: 13,000
SALES (est): 2.19MM **Privately Held**
Web: www.uwco.com
SIC: 5039 Ceiling systems and products
PA: J & P Holding Co Inc
500 E Front St Ste 1
Wilmington DE 19801

(G-20516)
UNION WHOLESALE CO (HQ)
500 E Front St Ste 1 (19801-5017)
PHONE..................302 656-4462
James L Mclaughlin, *Pr*
James F Mclaughlin, *VP*
Christopher Milyo, *VP*
EMP: 5 EST: 1956
SQ FT: 13,000
SALES (est): 7.95MM **Privately Held**
Web: www.uwco.com

SIC: 1742 Acoustical and ceiling work
PA: J & P Holding Co Inc
500 E Front St Ste 1
Wilmington DE 19801

(G-20517)
UNIQUE CREATIONS BY CHLOE LLC
501 Silverside Rd Ste 512 (19809-1374)
PHONE..................855 942-0477
EMP: 25 EST: 2019
SALES (est): 3MM **Privately Held**
SIC: 8742 Management consulting services

(G-20518)
UNIQUE FABRICATING NA INC
1313 N Market St (19801-6114)
PHONE..................248 853-2333
B Douglas Cain, *CEO*
Richard L Baum Junior, *Ch Bd*
Thomas Tekiele, *CFO*
▲ EMP: 734 EST: 1998
SALES (est): 35.16MM **Privately Held**
Web: www.uniquefab.com
SIC: 3053 3086 3296 2671 Gaskets, all materials; Plastics foam products; Mineral wool; Paper; coated and laminated packaging

(G-20519)
UNIQUE IMAGE LLC
Also Called: Unique Image T-Shirts Company
118 Bromley Dr (19808-1370)
PHONE..................302 658-2266
EMP: 26 EST: 1979
SALES (est): 2.15MM **Privately Held**
Web: www.uniqueimagetshirts.com
SIC: 2396 7389 2759 Screen printing on fabric articles; Embroidery advertising; Promotional printing

(G-20520)
UNIQUE PRO-CO LLC
1301 Birch Ln (19809-2464)
PHONE..................302 723-2365
Gene Grady, *Dir Opers*
EMP: 5 EST: 2015
SALES (est): 220.72K **Privately Held**
SIC: 4212 Local trucking, without storage

(G-20521)
UNISCRAP PBC
1000 N West St Ste 1200 (19801-1058)
PHONE..................302 407-8002
Panagiotis Kollas, *Pr*
EMP: 7 EST: 2016
SALES (est): 386.89K **Privately Held**
SIC: 4953 Refuse systems

(G-20522)
UNISIGHT BIT INC ✪
1000 Nw St Ste1281-291 (19801-1050)
PHONE..................888 294-6414
EMP: 20 EST: 2023
SALES (est): 616.33K **Privately Held**
SIC: 7371 Custom computer programming services

(G-20523)
UNITED ACQUISITION CORP (HQ)
1011 Centre Rd Ste 310 (19805-1266)
PHONE..................302 651-9856
John A Catsimatidis, *Ch Bd*
Myron Turfitt, *VP*
Ralph G Schwab, *VP*
Mark Kassner, *Asst VP*
▲ EMP: 20 EST: 1985
SALES (est): 1.69B
SALES (corp-wide): 2.16B **Privately Held**
Web: www.mywebaddress.com

SIC: 2911 5541 2951 Petroleum refining; Filling stations, gasoline; Asphalt paving mixtures and blocks
PA: Red Apple Group, Inc.
800 3rd Ave Fl 5
New York NY 10022
212 956-5803

(G-20524)
UNITED CEREBRAL PALSY OF DE (PA)
Also Called: UNITED CEREBRAL PALSY
700 A River Rd (19809-2765)
PHONE..................302 764-2400
William J Mc Cool Iii, *Ex Dir*
EMP: 25 EST: 1953
SQ FT: 3,000
SALES (est): 1.24MM
SALES (corp-wide): 1.24MM **Privately Held**
Web: www.ucpde.org
SIC: 8322 Social service center

(G-20525)
UNITED OUTDOOR ADVERTISING
2502 W 6th St (19805-2909)
PHONE..................302 652-3177
Thomas Finn, *Pr*
Kevin Finn, *VP*
EMP: 5 EST: 1976
SQ FT: 10,000
SALES (est): 490.49K **Privately Held**
SIC: 7312 6512 Billboard advertising; Commercial and industrial building operation

(G-20526)
UNITED SECURITY ADVISORS LLC
Also Called: American Wellness Supplies
1000 N West St Ste 1200 (19801-1058)
PHONE..................610 310-2482
EMP: 5 EST: 2017
SALES (est): 98.53K **Privately Held**
SIC: 7381 Guard services

(G-20527)
UNITED SPECIALTY FOAM LLC
709 Ashford Rd (19803-2221)
PHONE..................302 650-5948
Chiu Chan, *Managing Member*
EMP: 9 EST: 2011
SALES (est): 180K **Privately Held**
SIC: 3086 Plastics foam products

(G-20528)
UNITED STTES GYPS ASB PER INJU
P.O. Box 1080 (19899-1080)
PHONE..................888 708-8925
EMP: 5 EST: 2015
SALES (est): 73K **Privately Held**
Web: www.usgasbestostrust.com
SIC: 6733 Trusts, nec

(G-20529)
UNITED TECH PROJECT FOUNDATION
300 Delaware Ave (19801-1607)
PHONE..................302 404-4099
Daniel Dejesus, *Admn*
Daniel Dejesus, *Ex Dir*
EMP: 10 EST: 2017
SALES (est): 496.02K **Privately Held**
SIC: 7377 Computer hardware rental or leasing, except finance leasing

(G-20530)
UNITED WAY OF DELAWARE INC (PA)
Also Called: UNITED WAY
625 N Orange St Fl 3 (19801-2247)

PHONE..................302 573-3700
Michelle A Taylor, *Pr*
Jerry Hunter, *
Elaine Mercier, *
John Moore, *
Jim Coyne, *
EMP: 42 EST: 1946
SQ FT: 18,000
SALES (est): 23.87MM
SALES (corp-wide): 23.87MM **Privately Held**
Web: www.uwde.org
SIC: 8322 Social service center

(G-20531)
UNITY CONSTRUCTION INC
Also Called: Unity Development
3301 Lancaster Pike Ste 9 (19805-1436)
PHONE..................302 998-0531
Michael Simeone, *Pr*
Harry Simeone, *VP*
EMP: 17 EST: 1964
SALES (est): 367.13K **Privately Held**
Web: www.unitycorp.com
SIC: 6512 8741 Nonresidential building operators; Construction management

(G-20532)
UNIV OF DELAWARE
1600 Rocky Run Pkwy (19803-5404)
PHONE..................302 383-0473
Della Scott, *Analyst*
EMP: 6 EST: 1909
SALES (est): 51.47K **Privately Held**
SIC: 7911 Dance studios, schools, and halls

(G-20533)
UNIVERSAL BAKING COMPANY
303 Robinson Ln (19805-4673)
PHONE..................302 290-3204
EMP: 5 EST: 2011
SALES (est): 80.04K **Privately Held**
SIC: 5084 Industrial machinery and equipment

(G-20534)
UNIVERSITY WHIST CLB OF WLMNGT
805 N Broom St (19806-4624)
PHONE..................302 658-5125
Ted Dwyer, *Pr*
EMP: 23 EST: 1924
SALES (est): 3.41MM **Privately Held**
Web: www.universityandwhistclub.com
SIC: 8641 5812 Social club, membership; Eating places

(G-20535)
UPBOUND GROUP INC
Also Called: Rent-A-Center
1932 Maryland Ave (19805-4605)
PHONE..................302 654-7700
Anabell Enciso, *Mgr*
EMP: 5
Web: www.rentacenter.com
SIC: 7359 Appliance rental
PA: Upbound Group, Inc.
5501 Headquarters Dr
Plano TX 75024

(G-20536)
UPLOADCARE INC
2711 Centerville Rd Ste 400 (19808-1660)
PHONE..................855 953-2006
Igor Debatur, *CEO*
EMP: 42 EST: 2017
SALES (est): 3.86MM **Privately Held**
SIC: 5045 Computer software

Wilmington - New Castle County (G-20537)

(G-20537)
UPSCALE INDUSTRIES PROPERTY MA
1207 Delaware Ave (19806-4743)
PHONE..................302 386-8855
Eugene Hutchings, *Managing Member*
EMP: 5 EST: 2018
SALES (est): 200K **Privately Held**
SIC: 6531 Real estate brokers and agents

(G-20538)
UPTREND CONSULTING & CREATIVE
408 S Bancroft Pkwy (19805-3708)
P.O. Box 1740 (19707-5740)
PHONE..................484 840-1200
EMP: 5 EST: 2013
SALES (est): 102.51K **Privately Held**
Web: www.uptrendcreative.com
SIC: 8748 Business consulting, nec

(G-20539)
UPYO INC
300 Delaware Ave (19801-1607)
PHONE..................737 444-8899
Ahmed Alsenan, *Prin*
EMP: 6
SALES (est): 249.23K **Privately Held**
SIC: 7371 Custom computer programming services

(G-20540)
UR-EXPRESS INC
7 Lewis Cir (19804-1618)
PHONE..................302 839-2008
Robert Huang Managing, *Prin*
EMP: 6 EST: 2016
SALES (est): 500K **Privately Held**
SIC: 4783 7389 Packing goods for shipping; Packaging and labeling services

(G-20541)
URBAN CYBER SECURITY INC
1007 N Orange St Fl 83 (19801-1239)
PHONE..................803 805-9980
EMP: 8 EST: 2012
SALES (est): 407.18K **Privately Held**
Web: www.urban-vpn.com
SIC: 7379 Computer related services, nec
HQ: B.I Science (2009) Ltd
   6 Hanechoshet
   Tel Aviv-Jaffa

(G-20542)
URBAN RETAIL PROPERTIES LLC
Also Called: Urban Retail Properties Co
4737 Concord Pike (19803-1442)
PHONE..................302 479-8314
EMP: 8
SALES (corp-wide): 49.26MM **Privately Held**
Web: www.urbanretail.com
SIC: 6512 Shopping center, property operation only
HQ: Urban Retail Properties, Llc
   925 Suth Fdral Hwy Ste 70
   Boca Raton FL 33432

(G-20543)
URBAN YOUTH GOLF PROGRAM ASSN
800 N Dupont Rd (19807-2920)
PHONE..................302 384-8759
EMP: 7
SALES (est): 288.83K **Privately Held**
SIC: 7999 Golf services and professionals

(G-20544)
URBANPROMISE WILMINGTON INC
2401 Thatcher St (19802-4539)
P.O. Box 326 (19899-0326)
PHONE..................302 425-5502
Robert Prestowitz, *Dir*
EMP: 12 EST: 2002
SALES (est): 2.71MM **Privately Held**
Web: www.urbanpromise.org
SIC: 8322 Youth center

(G-20545)
URIE & BLANTON INC
510 A St (19801-5397)
PHONE..................302 658-8604
Donald Urie, *Pr*
Robert Urie, *VP*
John M Urie Junior, *Sec*
EMP: 9 EST: 1951
SQ FT: 20,000
SALES (est): 1.34MM **Privately Held**
SIC: 5084 5085 Welding machinery and equipment; Industrial supplies

(G-20546)
URPAYROLL INC
1207 Delaware Ave (19806-4743)
PHONE..................323 922-3829
Francisco Haro, *CEO*
EMP: 5
SALES (est): 209.42K **Privately Held**
SIC: 8741 Management services

(G-20547)
US AUTO FUNDING TRUST 2020-1
919 N Market St Ste 202 (19801-3023)
PHONE..................770 280-3918
EMP: 5 EST: 2020
SALES (est): 259.31K **Privately Held**
SIC: 6733 Trusts, nec

(G-20548)
US AUTO GLASS LLC
2055 Limestone Rd Ste 200c (19808-5536)
PHONE..................302 803-4924
EMP: 5 EST: 2021
SALES (est): 381.68K **Privately Held**
Web: www.us-autoglass.com
SIC: 3519 Parts and accessories, internal combustion engines

(G-20549)
US IMMIGRATION TECHNOLOGY LLC
1000 N West St Ste 1200 (19801-1058)
PHONE..................888 418-3053
EMP: 10 EST: 2014
SALES (est): 336.55K **Privately Held**
Web: www.usimmigration.us
SIC: 7299 Visa procurement service

(G-20550)
US INSTALLATION GROUP INC
355 Water St (19804-2410)
PHONE..................302 994-1644
Manuel Gonzalez, *Mgr*
EMP: 17
SALES (corp-wide): 24.63MM **Privately Held**
Web: www.us-installations.com
SIC: 1799 Antenna installation
PA: U.S. Installation Group Inc.
   5030 Chmpn Blvd Ste G11
   Boca Raton FL 33496
   561 962-0452

(G-20551)
US TAX RESOLUTIONS PA
3213 Emerald Pl (19810-2234)
PHONE..................302 478-7977
Nancy Wolf, *Admn*
EMP: 5 EST: 1996
SALES (est): 65.6K **Privately Held**
Web: www.universaldestiny.com
SIC: 7291 Tax return preparation services

(G-20552)
US TELEX CORPORATION
4001 Kennett Pike Ste 300 (19807-2039)
PHONE..................302 652-2707
Robert L Larson, *Pr*
EMP: 7 EST: 2001
SALES (est): 72.33K **Privately Held**
SIC: 7539 7371 Electrical services; Custom computer programming services

(G-20553)
USA FORTESCUE FUTURE INDS INC (PA)
1209 N Orange St (19801-1120)
PHONE..................703 608-5217
Andrew Forrest, *Ch*
EMP: 7 EST: 2021
SALES (est): 1.33MM
SALES (corp-wide): 1.33MM **Privately Held**
SIC: 1731 Electric power systems contractors

(G-20554)
USERWAY INC
1007 N Orange St (19801-1239)
PHONE..................415 510-9335
Allon Mason, *CEO*
EMP: 100 EST: 2019
SALES (est): 4.93MM **Privately Held**
SIC: 7371 Software programming applications

(G-20555)
USS PORTFOLIO DELAWARE INC
501 Silverside Rd Ste 53 (19809-1388)
PHONE..................302 798-7890
Anthony Shmidt, *Prin*
EMP: 6 EST: 2014
SALES (est): 387.94K
SALES (corp-wide): 21.07B **Publicly Held**
SIC: 6799 Investors, nec
PA: United States Steel Corp
   600 Grant St
   Pittsburgh PA 15219
   412 433-1121

(G-20556)
UT INVESTMENT MANAGEMENT CORP
1209 N Orange St (19801-1120)
PHONE..................215 399-5900
Dale Frey, *Prin*
EMP: 6 EST: 2012
SALES (est): 550.64K **Privately Held**
SIC: 6722 Management investment, open-end

(G-20557)
UTECH GLOBAL SERVICES (PA)
251 Little Falls Dr (19808-1674)
PHONE..................630 531-0427
Mike Maziarka, *CEO*
EMP: 20 EST: 2017
SALES (est): 2.29MM
SALES (corp-wide): 2.29MM **Privately Held**
SIC: 7379 Computer related consulting services

(G-20558)
UTILITY LOCATOR LLC
14 Hadco Rd (19804-1014)
PHONE..................215 596-1234
EMP: 6 EST: 2019
SALES (est): 437.04K **Privately Held**
Web: www.utilitylocator.com
SIC: 1623 Underground utilities contractor

(G-20559)
V DIMA INC
2400 W 4th St (19805-3306)
PHONE..................302 427-0787
EMP: 5
SALES (est): 173.53K **Privately Held**
SIC: 8093 Mental health clinic, outpatient

(G-20560)
V SQUILLACE MASON CONTRACTOR
111 Valley Rd (19804-1310)
PHONE..................302 655-0934
Victor Squillace, *Owner*
EMP: 5 EST: 2007
SALES (est): 96.58K **Privately Held**
SIC: 1771 Concrete work

(G-20561)
VAIRASOFT INC
913 N Market St Ste 200 (19801-3097)
PHONE..................336 422-6499
Sumanth Yanala, *CEO*
EMP: 5 EST: 2020
SALES (est): 200K **Privately Held**
SIC: 7379 Computer related consulting services

(G-20562)
VAKOMS LLC
913 N Market St Ste 200 (19801-3097)
PHONE..................206 474-4319
EMP: 5 EST: 2020
SALES (est): 46.16K **Privately Held**
Web: www.vakoms.com
SIC: 7371 Computer software development

(G-20563)
VALIRAM USA INC
1013 Centre Rd Ste 403s (19805-1270)
PHONE..................562 652-1698
Maximillian Gunara, *Admn*
EMP: 5 EST: 2014
SALES (est): 100K **Privately Held**
SIC: 5047 Medical equipment and supplies

(G-20564)
VALLEY RUN APARTMENTS
102 Robino Ct Ste 301 (19804-2371)
PHONE..................302 994-2505
EMP: 5 EST: 2010
SALES (est): 523.08K **Privately Held**
Web: www.liveatvalleyrun.com
SIC: 6513 Apartment building operators

(G-20565)
VALUE CHAIN EXCELLENCE LLC
103 Downs Dr (19807-2556)
PHONE..................302 545-8011
EMP: 5 EST: 2011
SALES (est): 101.35K **Privately Held**
SIC: 5072 Chains

(G-20566)
VALUE XCHANGE GROUP OF CO LLC ✪
Also Called: Prime
1007 N Orange St Fl 4 (19801-1242)
PHONE..................708 420-7642
Afeez Ogunsola, *Managing Member*
EMP: 75 EST: 2022
SALES (est): 1.87MM **Privately Held**
SIC: 2841 Soap and other detergents

(G-20567)
VAN BUREN FINANCIAL GROUP LLC
615 W 18th St (19802-4707)
P.O. Box 10150 (19850-0150)
PHONE..................302 655-9505

EMP: 16 EST: 2017
SALES (est): 1.96MM Privately Held
Web: www.vanburenfinancial.com
SIC: 6282 Investment advice

(G-20568)
VANDEMARK & LYNCH INC
4305 Miller Rd (19802-1901)
PHONE..............................302 764-7635
Stephan Lehm, Pr
Stephen L Johns, *
Christopher M O'keefe, VP
John S Bianco, *
EMP: 35 EST: 1937
SQ FT: 12,335
SALES (est): 4.28MM Privately Held
Web: www.vdleng.com
SIC: 8711 Consulting engineer

(G-20569)
VANGUARD MANUFACTURING INC
11 Lewis Cir (19804-1618)
P.O. Box 6376 (19804-0976)
PHONE..............................302 994-9302
David S Miller, Pr
▲ EMP: 9 EST: 1987
SQ FT: 5,000
SALES (est): 980.25K Privately Held
Web: www.washpro200.com
SIC: 2393 7389 Bags and containers, except sleeping bags: textile; Sewing contractor

(G-20570)
VANTAGE ENERGY LLC ✪
300 Delaware Ave Ste 210 (19801-6601)
PHONE..............................302 261-9351
Matthew Pavilionis, Managing Member
EMP: 15 EST: 2023
SALES (est): 1.54MM Privately Held
SIC: 6231 Stock exchanges

(G-20571)
VARI DEVELOPMENT CORP
Also Called: Vari Builders
1309 Veale Rd Ste 20 (19810-4609)
PHONE..............................302 479-5571
Anthony Vari, Pr
Joan Vari, Sec
EMP: 8 EST: 1980
SQ FT: 18,000
SALES (est): 1.77MM Privately Held
SIC: 1542 1521 Commercial and office building, new construction; New construction, single-family houses

(G-20572)
VD&L HOLDINGS INC
4305 Miller Rd (19802-1901)
PHONE..............................302 764-7635
Stephan Lehm, Pr
EMP: 14 EST: 1985
SALES (est): 195.7K Privately Held
Web: www.vdleng.com
SIC: 8711 Civil engineering

(G-20573)
VECTORVANCE LLC (PA)
1201 N Orange St Ste 600 (19801-1171)
PHONE..............................347 779-9932
Yien Lung, Genl Mgr
EMP: 9 EST: 2015
SALES (est): 1.48MM
SALES (corp-wide): 1.48MM Privately Held
SIC: 5065 Electronic parts and equipment, nec

(G-20574)
VEDA HEALTH GROUP LLC
2207 Concord Pike (19803-2908)
PHONE..............................302 536-8332
EMP: 6 EST: 2011
SALES (est): 142.83K Privately Held
SIC: 8099 Health and allied services, nec

(G-20575)
VEDAHAM INC
2711 Centerville Rd # 400 (19808-1660)
PHONE..............................302 250-4594
Bhulakshmi Sathyasai, Dir
EMP: 15 EST: 2009
SALES (est): 191.03K Privately Held
SIC: 7371 Custom computer programming services

(G-20576)
VEENDHQ INC
2055 Limestone Rd (19808-5536)
PHONE..............................470 300-9787
Olufemi Olanipekun, CEO
EMP: 5
SALES (est): 68.89K Privately Held
SIC: 7371 Computer software development

(G-20577)
VEGA CONSULTING INC (PA) ✪
251 Little Falls Dr (19808-1674)
PHONE..............................302 636-5401
Rajiv Sardana, CEO
EMP: 57 EST: 2022
SALES (est): 885.39MM
SALES (corp-wide): 885.39MM Privately Held
Web: www.vegaconsulting.com
SIC: 8748 Business consulting, nec

(G-20578)
VEHICLE MAINTENANCE DEPT
1450 New York Ave (19801-5826)
PHONE..............................302 571-5857
Jerry Walker, Prin
EMP: 5 EST: 2016
SALES (est): 27.95K Privately Held
SIC: 7538 General automotive repair shops

(G-20579)
VELS HAIR SALON
1824 Conrad St (19805-3409)
P.O. Box 30413 (19805-7413)
PHONE..............................302 427-3819
EMP: 5 EST: 2018
SALES (est): 86.89K Privately Held
Web: www.velshairsalon.com
SIC: 7231 Unisex hair salons

(G-20580)
VENSOFT SOLUTIONS INC
Also Called: Sunglobal Technologies
3516 Silverside Rd Ste 21 (19810-4932)
PHONE..............................302 392-9000
Ravi Mandalapu, Pr
EMP: 17 EST: 2003
SALES (est): 920.78K Privately Held
Web: www.vensoftsol.com
SIC: 7379 7371 Computer related consulting services; Custom computer programming services

(G-20581)
VENTION INC US (PA)
1201 N Orange St Ste 7160 (19801-1197)
PHONE..............................514 222-0380
EMP: 7 EST: 2021
SALES (est): 78.16K
SALES (corp-wide): 78.16K Privately Held
SIC: 3999 Manufacturing industries, nec

(G-20582)
VENTURIST MEDIA INC
Also Called: Andbeyond
501 Silverside Rd Ste 105 (19809-1376)
PHONE..............................646 455-3031
Dharika Merchant, Pr
EMP: 6 EST: 2015
SALES (est): 232.84K Privately Held
SIC: 4899 Data communication services

(G-20583)
VENZEE INC
4023 Kennett Pike 57126 (19807-2018)
PHONE..............................855 650-4204
EMP: 7 EST: 2014
SALES (est): 171.06K Privately Held
SIC: 7371 Computer software development

(G-20584)
VERASET LLC
2810 N Church St # 38188 (19802-4447)
PHONE..............................801 657-2009
EMP: 10 EST: 2019
SALES (est): 692.03K Privately Held
Web: www.veraset.com
SIC: 7371 Computer software development

(G-20585)
VERDANT PLANT HEALTH CARE
200 Ohio Ave (19805-2543)
P.O. Box 158 (19710-0158)
PHONE..............................302 593-0444
EMP: 9 EST: 2016
SALES (est): 456.04K Privately Held
Web: www.verdantplanthealth.com
SIC: 8099 Health and allied services, nec

(G-20586)
VERDANTAS LLC
5400 Limestone Rd (19808-1232)
PHONE..............................302 239-6634
Gerry Salontai, CEO
EMP: 11 EST: 2021
SALES (est): 514.5K Privately Held
SIC: 8744 Environmental remediation

(G-20587)
VERDICT LLC
3411 Silverside Rd # 114 (19810-4812)
PHONE..............................888 837-4618
Alex Greg, Managing Member
EMP: 3 EST: 2018
SALES (est): 71.13K Privately Held
SIC: 7372 Publisher's computer software

(G-20588)
VERITI SECURITY INCORPORATED
251 Little Falls Dr (19808-1674)
PHONE..............................212 203-0100
Adi Ikan, Pr
Oren Koren, Sec
Modi Rosen, Dir
EMP: 31 EST: 2021
SALES (est): 799.72K Privately Held
SIC: 7389 Inspection and testing services

(G-20589)
VERITO TECHNOLOGIES LLC
251 Little Falls Dr (19808-1674)
PHONE..............................855 583-7486
Jatin Narang, Pt
Jatin Narang, CEO
EMP: 15 EST: 2016
SALES (est): 796.06K Privately Held
Web: www.verito.com
SIC: 7379 Computer related maintenance services

(G-20590)
VERIZON DELAWARE LLC (HQ)
Also Called: Verizon
901 N Tatnall St Fl 2 (19801-1644)
PHONE..............................302 571-1571
Bonnie L Metz, *
William F Heitmann, *
EMP: 225 EST: 1897
SALES (est): 101.15MM
SALES (corp-wide): 133.97B Publicly Held
Web: www.verizon.com
SIC: 4812 7373 2741 4813 Cellular telephone services; Computer integrated systems design; Directories, telephone: publishing only, not printed on site; Local telephone communications
PA: Verizon Communications Inc.
1095 Ave Of The Americas
New York NY 10036
212 395-1000

(G-20591)
VERIZON DELAWARE LLC
Also Called: Verizon
3900 N Washington St Fl 1 (19802-2126)
P.O. Box 5 (19899-0005)
PHONE..............................302 761-6079
Debbie Melvin, Mgr
EMP: 94
SALES (corp-wide): 133.97B Publicly Held
Web: www.delaware.gov
SIC: 4813 Telephone communication, except radio
HQ: Verizon Delaware Llc
901 N Tatnall St Fl 2
Wilmington DE 19801
302 571-1571

(G-20592)
VERIZON MASTER TRUST
1100 N Market St (19890-1100)
PHONE..............................302 636-6182
EMP: 12
SALES (est): 5.56MM Privately Held
SIC: 4812 Cellular telephone services

(G-20593)
VERIZON WIRELESS
1625 Newport Gap Pike (19808-6207)
PHONE..............................610 301-2395
Matthew Gentile, Ofcr
EMP: 6 EST: 2000
SALES (est): 141.28K Privately Held
Web: www.verizon.com
SIC: 4812 Cellular telephone services

(G-20594)
VERSAPRO GROUP LLC
5605 W Timberview Ct (19808-3650)
PHONE..............................315 430-2775
EMP: 6 EST: 2017
SALES (est): 47.32K Privately Held
SIC: 8742 Management consulting services

(G-20595)
VERSCOM LLC (PA)
Also Called: Verscom Carrier
501 Silverside Rd Ste 105 (19809-1376)
PHONE..............................866 238-9189
▼ EMP: 22 EST: 2002
SQ FT: 1,200
SALES (est): 46.29MM
SALES (corp-wide): 46.29MM Privately Held
Web: www.verscom.com
SIC: 8748 Telecommunications consultant

(G-20596)
VERSUS GAMING INC
919 N Market St (19801-3023)
PHONE..............................855 643-9945
Jessie Sulecki, CEO
EMP: 9
SALES (est): 313.29K Privately Held

Wilmington - New Castle County (G-20597)

(G-20597)
VERTEX INDUSTRIES INC
Also Called: Austenitex
818 S Heald St Ste C (19801-5790)
PHONE..................302 472-0601
Alexander Conforti, *Pr*
Adrienne Conforti, *VP*
Alexander Conforti, *Prin*
◆ **EMP:** 6 **EST:** 2002
SQ FT: 10,000
SALES (est): 2.4MM **Privately Held**
Web: www.verociousmotorsports.com
SIC: 5051 5074 5085 Pipe and tubing, steel; Plumbing fittings and supplies; Industrial fittings

SIC: 7371 Software programming applications

(G-20598)
VERTICAL BLIND FACTORY INC (PA)
Also Called: Margaret Keith's Draperies
3 Meco Cir (19804-1108)
PHONE..................302 998-9616
Margaret Keith, *Pr*
Richard W Keith, *VP*
EMP: 2 **EST:** 1972
SQ FT: 10,000
SALES (est): 1.46MM **Privately Held**
Web: www.blindfactoryinc.com
SIC: 2591 2211 7699 Window blinds; Draperies and drapery fabrics, cotton; Window blind repair services

(G-20599)
VETERANS HEALTH ADMINISTRATION
Also Called: Wilmington Vet Center
2710 Centerville Rd (19808-1644)
PHONE..................302 994-1660
Jones Sp'Yencer, *Mgr*
EMP: 7
Web: wilmington.va.gov
SIC: 8011 9451 Medical centers; Administration of veterans' affairs, Federal government
HQ: Veterans Health Administration
810 Vermont Ave Nw
Washington DC 20420

(G-20600)
VETERANS HEALTH ADMINISTRATION
Also Called: Wilmington VAM&roc
1601 Kirkwood Hwy (19805-4917)
PHONE..................302 994-2511
Lori Barbanel, *Brnch Mgr*
EMP: 466
Web: benefits.va.gov
SIC: 8011 9451 Clinic, operated by physicians; Administration of veterans' affairs, Federal government
HQ: Veterans Health Administration
810 Vermont Ave Nw
Washington DC 20420

(G-20601)
VETOSINE INC
251 Little Falls Dr (19808-1674)
PHONE..................424 258-0120
Jarne Elleholm, *Ch*
EMP: 7 **EST:** 2021
SALES (est): 74.42K **Privately Held**
SIC: 2835 Veterinary diagnostic substances

(G-20602)
VFW MAGAZINE
1601 Kirkwood Hwy (19805-4917)
PHONE..................302 994-2511
EMP: 6 **EST:** 2018

SALES (est): 46.63K **Privately Held**
Web: www.vfw.org
SIC: 8641 Veterans' organization

(G-20603)
VI DIMA INC
2400 W 4th St (19805-3306)
PHONE..................302 427-0787
EMP: 5
SALES (est): 173.53K **Privately Held**
SIC: 8093 Mental health clinic, outpatient

(G-20604)
VIA MDICAL DAY SPA PASCA SALON
3212 Brookline Rd (19808-2613)
PHONE..................302 757-2830
Toni Toomey, *Prin*
EMP: 7 **EST:** 2008
SALES (est): 118.28K **Privately Held**
Web: www.viamedicaldayspa.com
SIC: 7991 Spas

(G-20605)
VIA NETWORKS INC
2711 Centerville Rd Ste 400 (19808-1660)
PHONE..................314 727-2087
Vijay Reddy, *Prin*
EMP: 15 **EST:** 1997
SALES (est): 305.4K **Privately Held**
Web: www.vianetworks.com
SIC: 3672 Circuit boards, television and radio printed

(G-20606)
VIANAIR INC
3511 Silverside Rd (19810-4902)
PHONE..................646 403-4705
Stavros Sidiropoulous, *Pr*
EMP: 7 **EST:** 2017
SALES (est): 287.75K **Privately Held**
SIC: 7371 Computer software development and applications

(G-20607)
VIATICUM INCORPORATED
132 W Champlain Ave (19804-1749)
PHONE..................302 467-8353
Vernon Perry, *CEO*
EMP: 10 **EST:** 2011
SALES (est): 408.59K **Privately Held**
Web: www.viaticuminc.com
SIC: 7389 6531 1521 Building inspection service; Real estate managers; Single-family home remodeling, additions, and repairs

(G-20608)
VICENTE & PARTNERS LLC
1209 N Orange St (19801-1120)
PHONE..................646 209-5527
Michelle Garcia, *Mgr*
EMP: 5 **EST:** 2019
SALES (est): 126.89K **Privately Held**
SIC: 7389 Financial services

(G-20609)
VICTIMS VOICES HEARD
100 W 10th St (19801-6603)
PHONE..................302 407-3747
Kim Book, *Ex Dir*
EMP: 7 **EST:** 2014
SALES (est): 146.94K **Privately Held**
Web: www.victimsvoicesheard.org
SIC: 8322 Social service center

(G-20610)
VICTOR J VENTURENA DDS
1117 N Franklin St (19806-4331)
PHONE..................302 656-0558
Victor J Venturena D.d.s., *Owner*

EMP: 7 **EST:** 1987
SALES (est): 180.54K **Privately Held**
SIC: 8021 Dentists' office

(G-20611)
VICTOR L GREGORY JR DMD
5301 Limestone Rd Ste 211 (19808-1265)
PHONE..................302 239-1827
Victor Gregory Junior, *Owner*
Victor Gregory, *Owner*
EMP: 7 **EST:** 1999
SALES (est): 443.95K **Privately Held**
Web: www.victorgregorydmd.com
SIC: 8021 Dentists' office

(G-20612)
VICTORIOUS JAESETTES INC
801 W 9th St Ste 2 (19801-1308)
PHONE..................302 898-1946
Javaughn Talley, *VP*
Sabrina Thomas, *Dir*
Rynell Collins, *VP*
EMP: 6 **EST:** 2021
SALES (est): 120.88K **Privately Held**
Web: victorious-jaesettes.ueniweb.com
SIC: 7911 Dance studio and school

(G-20613)
VICTORY LANE EXPRESS WASH LLC
1715 Foulk Rd (19803-2733)
PHONE..................302 543-6445
John Recchiuti, *Managing Member*
EMP: 5 **EST:** 2011
SALES (est): 141.81K **Privately Held**
SIC: 7542 Carwashes

(G-20614)
VICTORYCONSULTING LLC
3 Germay Dr Unit 42970 (19804-1127)
PHONE..................203 275-9398
Assata Pitt, *Managing Member*
EMP: 6
SALES (est): 71.79K **Privately Held**
SIC: 8742 Management consulting services

(G-20615)
VICTRA
1722 Naamans Rd (19810-2610)
PHONE..................302 408-0999
EMP: 7 **EST:** 2018
SALES (est): 93.86K **Privately Held**
Web: www.victra.com
SIC: 4812 Cellular telephone services

(G-20616)
VICTRA
2131 Kirkwood Hwy (19805-4901)
PHONE..................302 593-2648
EMP: 6 **EST:** 2018
SALES (est): 60.57K **Privately Held**
Web: www.victra.com
SIC: 4812 Cellular telephone services

(G-20617)
VIDELLS DAY SPA
14b Trolley Sq (19806-3343)
PHONE..................302 656-1784
Videll W Long, *Owner*
EMP: 7 **EST:** 2016
SALES (est): 78.67K **Privately Held**
Web: www.videllsdayspa.com
SIC: 7991 Spas

(G-20618)
VIDHQ INC ◯
1007 N Orange St Ste 1382 (19801-1239)
PHONE..................512 660-7862
Omer Gok, *Prin*
EMP: 2 **EST:** 2023
SALES (est): 87.4K **Privately Held**

SIC: 7372 Prepackaged software

(G-20619)
VILLA COTTON CORPORATION
1000 N West St Ste 1200 (19801-1058)
PHONE..................302 439-1508
Nikolai Kisliakov, *Pr*
Alexey Fedunov, *CFO*
EMP: 11 **EST:** 2020
SALES (est): 647.11K **Privately Held**
Web: www.villacotton.com
SIC: 2392 5961 Blankets, comforters and beddings; Catalog and mail-order houses

(G-20620)
VILLAGE AT FOX POINT
1436 Kynlyn Dr (19809-2423)
PHONE..................302 762-7480
Chris Crampton, *Mgr*
Rosemarie Upchurch, *Owner*
EMP: 8
SALES (est): 610K **Privately Held**
Web: www.villageatfoxpoint.com
SIC: 6513 Apartment building operators

(G-20621)
VILLAGE OF ST JOHN LP
2020 N Tatnall St (19802-4856)
PHONE..................302 652-1690
EMP: 6 **EST:** 2019
SALES (est): 149.78K **Privately Held**
Web: www.villageofstjohn.org
SIC: 7389 Business services, nec

(G-20622)
VILLAGE TREE
1037 W 7th St (19805-3217)
PHONE..................302 298-6349
Cecelia Rich, *Prin*
EMP: 5 **EST:** 2018
SALES (est): 58.19K **Privately Held**
Web: www.thevillagetree.org
SIC: 8699 Charitable organization

(G-20623)
VINAY KANDULA MD
1600 Rockland Rd (19803-3607)
PHONE..................302 651-4200
Manjula Kari, *Prin*
EMP: 16 **EST:** 2013
SALES (est): 311.67K **Privately Held**
Web: www.nemours.org
SIC: 8011 Pediatrician

(G-20624)
VINCENT J MARMODO
2300 Pennsylvania Ave (19806-1392)
PHONE..................302 777-1697
Vincent J Marmodo, *Prin*
EMP: 10 **EST:** 2010
SALES (est): 101.64K **Privately Held**
SIC: 8011 Cardiologist and cardio-vascular specialist

(G-20625)
VINCENZA & MARGHERITA BISTRO
1717 Marsh Rd (19810-4607)
PHONE..................302 479-7999
Margherita Carrieri-russo, *Owner*
EMP: 14 **EST:** 2014
SALES (est): 102.8K **Privately Held**
Web: www.vmbistro.com
SIC: 5812 2032 American restaurant; Italian foods, nec: packaged in cans, jars, etc.

(G-20626)
VINOCUR CHARLES MD
1600 Rockland Rd (19803-3607)
PHONE..................302 651-5888
Charles Vinocur, *Prin*

EMP: 14 EST: 2015
SALES (est): 266.27K **Privately Held**
Web: www.nemours.org
SIC: 8011 Pediatrician

(G-20627)
VINTAGE PROPERTIES LLC
Also Called: Arbor Pointe
4000 Dawnbrook Dr (19804-3925)
PHONE.................................302 994-4442
Judy Stewart, *Mgr*
EMP: 8
SALES (corp-wide): 893.12K **Privately Held**
Web: www.liveatarborpointe.com
SIC: 6513 Apartment building operators
PA: Vintage Properties, Llc
102 Robino Ct Ste 101
Wilmington DE 19804
302 994-2505

(G-20628)
VIP SYSTEMS INC
251 Little Falls Dr (19808-1674)
PHONE.................................786 615-8622
EMP: 6 EST: 2002
SALES (est): 27.88K **Privately Held**
SIC: 8741 Management services

(G-20629)
VIRA GAMES INC
2810 N Church St (19802-4447)
PHONE.................................302 468-7152
Anton Yesin, *CEO*
EMP: 5
SALES (est): 63.12K **Privately Held**
SIC: 7371 Computer software development and applications

(G-20630)
VIRGINIA LINENS LLC
2107 Nicholby Dr (19808-4230)
PHONE.................................757 342-4225
Daniel Anthony, *Prin*
EMP: 5 EST: 2016
SALES (est): 27.18K **Privately Held**
SIC: 7213 Linen supply

(G-20631)
VIRGINIA TRANSPORTATION CORP
700 Cornell Dr (19801-5762)
PHONE.................................302 384-6767
Virginia Dewees, *Brnch Mgr*
EMP: 159
Web: www.virginiatransportation.com
SIC: 4789 Pipeline terminal facilities, independently operated
PA: Virginia Transportation Corp.
141 Jmes P Murphy Ind Hwy
West Warwick RI 02893

(G-20632)
VIRIDI MARATHON LLC ✪
3711 Kennett Pike Ste 212 (19807-2161)
PHONE.................................302 647-8280
Evan Kirchen, *Ex VP*
EMP: 22 EST: 2023
SALES (est): 661.1K **Privately Held**
SIC: 8731 Energy research

(G-20633)
VIRTUAL BUSINESS ENTPS LLC
Also Called: Stewart Management Company
Farmers Bank Bldg 301 Ste 1410 N Market Street (19801)
PHONE.................................302 472-9100
Charles Anthony Shippam, *CEO*
Joan L Yori, *Client Services Vice President*
Gregory S Harrison, *CFO*
Gordon W Stewart, *VP*
EMP: 8 EST: 1998
SQ FT: 10,000
SALES (est): 710.08K **Privately Held**
SIC: 8748 Business consulting, nec

(G-20634)
VIRTUAL PRO GAMING INC
2810 N Church St (19802-4447)
PHONE.................................302 285-9891
Arron Dellosa, *CEO*
EMP: 2 EST: 2017
SALES (est): 85.22K **Privately Held**
SIC: 7372 7993 5092 Home entertainment computer software; Video game arcade; Video games

(G-20635)
VIRTUAL TALK HUB LLC
1201 N Market St Ste 111 (19801-1147)
PHONE.................................302 406-0038
EMP: 50
SALES (est): 1.19MM **Privately Held**
SIC: 8742 Management consulting services

(G-20636)
VISA EUROPE SERVICES LLC (HQ)
1209 N Orange St (19801)
PHONE.................................302 658-7581
EMP: 32 EST: 2004
SALES (est): 250.58K **Publicly Held**
SIC: 8748 Business consulting, nec
PA: Visa Inc.
900 Metro Center Blvd
Foster City CA 94404

(G-20637)
VISIO GROUP INTERNATIONAL CORP
1007 N Orange St (19801-1239)
PHONE.................................302 485-0378
Mark-odean Grant, *CEO*
EMP: 5 EST: 2019
SALES (est): 273.82K **Privately Held**
SIC: 8742 7389 Training and development consultant

(G-20638)
VISION CAMPUS INC
Also Called: Vision Learning Center
2205 Lancaster Ave (19805-3733)
PHONE.................................302 543-6809
Tawina Ricks, *CEO*
EMP: 10
SALES (est): 480K **Privately Held**
SIC: 8351 Child day care services

(G-20639)
VISION CENTER OF DELAWARE INC (PA)
Also Called: Eye Center of Delaware
213 Greenhill Ave Ste A (19805-1800)
PHONE.................................302 656-8867
George Popel Md, *Pr*
EMP: 15 EST: 1974
SALES (corp-wide): 2.36MM **Privately Held**
Web: www.eyecenterofdelaware.com
SIC: 8011 Opthalmologist

(G-20640)
VISION TO LEARN
100 W 10th St Ste 115 (19801-1632)
PHONE.................................302 220-4820
Diane Delaney, *Prin*
EMP: 13 EST: 2018
SALES (est): 47.44K **Privately Held**
Web: www.visiontolearn.org
SIC: 8042 Offices and clinics of optometrists

(G-20641)
VISIONS HAIR DESIGN
2807 Concord Pike (19803-5008)
PHONE.................................302 477-0820
Margie Hartnett, *Owner*
EMP: 8 EST: 1991
SALES (est): 223.92K **Privately Held**
Web: www.visions-hair.com
SIC: 7231 7241 Hairdressers; Barber shops

(G-20642)
VITAE INVESTMENT COMPANY
300 Delaware Ave Ste 566 (19801-1607)
PHONE.................................302 656-8985
L Van V Dauler Junior, *Pr*
EMP: 72 EST: 1996
SALES (est): 412.64K
SALES (corp-wide): 48.5MM **Privately Held**
SIC: 6211 Investment firm, general brokerage
PA: Neville Chemical Company
2800 Neville Rd
Pittsburgh PA 15225
412 331-4200

(G-20643)
VITAL BERRY
1700 Shallcross Ave (19806-2344)
PHONE.................................302 691-5063
Berry Vital, *Prin*
EMP: 5 EST: 2012
SALES (est): 90.92K **Privately Held**
SIC: 5199 General merchandise, non-durable

(G-20644)
VITAL RENEWABLE ENERGY COMPANY
2711 Centerville Rd # 300 (19808-1660)
PHONE.................................202 595-2944
Ricardo Roccia, *CEO*
Douglas Costa, *Contrlr*
EMP: 2 EST: 2008
SALES (est): 339.23K **Privately Held**
SIC: 6722 2869 Management investment, open-end; Fuels

(G-20645)
VIVIAN A HOUGHTON ESQUIRE
800 N West St Fl 2 (19801-1565)
PHONE.................................302 658-0518
Vivian A Houghton, *Owner*
EMP: 5 EST: 2000
SALES (est): 496.99K **Privately Held**
Web: www.dplaw.com
SIC: 8111 General practice attorney, lawyer

(G-20646)
VIZIOCHRON INC
251 Little Falls Dr (19808-1674)
PHONE.................................206 745-0356
EMP: 5 EST: 2019
SALES (est): 46.16K **Privately Held**
Web: www.viziochron.com
SIC: 7371 Computer software development and applications

(G-20647)
VLOCKER NORTH AMERICA LLC
2810 N Church St (19802-4447)
PHONE.................................469 567-0956
EMP: 5 EST: 2016
SALES (est): 80.17K **Privately Held**
SIC: 5065 Electronic parts

(G-20648)
VOITURE NATIONALE LA SOCIETY
Also Called: VOITURE NATIONALE LA SOCIETY
1017 Faun Rd (19803-3312)
PHONE.................................302 478-7591
Chip Rossen, *Dir*
EMP: 7
SALES (corp-wide): 27.54K **Privately Held**
Web: www.fortyandeight.org
SIC: 8641 Fraternal associations
PA: Voiture Nationale La Societe Des Quarante Hommes Et Huit Che
250 E 38th St
Indianapolis IN 46205
317 634-1804

(G-20649)
VOLUNTEERS FOR ADOLESCENT
Also Called: Vapp
611 W 18th St (19802-4707)
PHONE.................................302 658-3331
Yvonne Gordon, *Pr*
Lisa Oglesby, *Admn*
EMP: 8 EST: 2015
SALES (est): 261.26K **Privately Held**
SIC: 8399 Social services, nec

(G-20650)
VOLVANT INC (PA)
919 N Market St Ste 950 (19801-3036)
PHONE.................................805 456-6464
Walter Gonzalez, *CEO*
EMP: 7 EST: 2011
SALES (est): 833.19K
SALES (corp-wide): 833.19K **Privately Held**
SIC: 7371 Computer software development

(G-20651)
VORTEX LABS LLC
1209 N Orange St (19801-1120)
PHONE.................................302 231-1294
Pierre Cazettes, *Managing Member*
EMP: 5 EST: 2015
SALES (est): 236.84K **Privately Held**
SIC: 7371 Computer software development

(G-20652)
VORTEX REFRIGERATION COMPANY
1201 N Orange St Ste 7150 (19801-1197)
PHONE.................................855 562-5222
EMP: 5 EST: 2016
SALES (est): 190.43K **Privately Held**
Web: www.vortexrefrigeration.com
SIC: 5046 Restaurant equipment and supplies, nec

(G-20653)
VOS ENERGY LLC
1209 N Orange St (19801-1120)
PHONE.................................302 658-7581
Brian Tang, *CEO*
Hanish Dayal, *CEO*
EMP: 10 EST: 2020
SALES (est): 260.24K **Privately Held**
SIC: 6799 Investors, nec

(G-20654)
VOYAGER DRILLING SERVICES LLC
913 N Market St Ste 200 (19801-3097)
PHONE.................................302 439-6030
Azhar Jamal, *Managing Member*
EMP: 11 EST: 2018
SALES (est): 844.55K **Privately Held**
Web: www.voyagerdrillinggroup.com
SIC: 1382 Oil and gas exploration services

(G-20655)
VPSIE INC
108 W 13th St (19801-1145)
PHONE.................................844 468-7743
Hany Mekhael, *CEO*
EMP: 10 EST: 2014
SALES (est): 444.29K **Privately Held**
Web: www.vpsie.com

Wilmington - New Castle County (G-20656)   GEOGRAPHIC SECTION

SIC: 7379 8742 Online services technology consultants; Management information systems consultant

(G-20656)
VU BINH THAI
Also Called: La Nails
4717 Kirkwood Hwy (19808-5007)
PHONE..................................302 999-7980
Thomas Phunt, *Prin*
EMP: 8 EST: 2010
SALES (est): 153.45K **Privately Held**
SIC: 7231 Manicurist, pedicurist

(G-20657)
VULCAN INTERNATIONAL CORP
103 Foulk Rd (19803-3742)
PHONE..................................302 656-1950
Benjamin Gettler, *CEO*
EMP: 13
SALES (corp-wide): 9.95MM **Privately Held**
SIC: 6531 Real estate agents and managers
PA: Vulcan International Corporation
300 Delaware Ave Ste 1704
Wilmington DE 19801
302 428-3181

(G-20658)
VULCAN INTERNATIONAL CORP (PA)
300 Delaware Ave Ste 1704 (19801-1612)
PHONE..................................302 428-3181
Benjamin Gettler, *Ch Bd*
Vernon E Bachman, *VP*
◆ EMP: 12 EST: 1928
SQ FT: 88,000
SALES (est): 9.95MM
SALES (corp-wide): 9.95MM **Privately Held**
SIC: 3069 2499 3949 Heels, boot or shoe: rubber, composition, or fiber; Lasts, boot and shoe; Bowling pins

(G-20659)
VULCRAFT SALES CORP (HQ)
300 Delaware Ave Ste 210 (19801-6601)
PHONE..................................302 427-5832
F Kenneth Iverson, *Ch*
▼ EMP: 11 EST: 1973
SALES (est): 28.83MM
SALES (corp-wide): 41.51B **Publicly Held**
Web: www.vulcraft.com
SIC: 5051 Steel
PA: Nucor Corporation
1915 Rexford Rd Ste 400
Charlotte NC 28211
704 366-7000

(G-20660)
VULTRAN CREATIVE MARKETING
301 W 6th St (19801-2113)
PHONE..................................302 981-3379
Gerald Hearne, *Mgr*
EMP: 5 EST: 2018
SALES (est): 23.63K **Privately Held**
SIC: 7374 Data processing and preparation

(G-20661)
VYBN INC (PA)
300 Delaware Ave Ste 210a (19801-6601)
PHONE..................................415 715-7945
Michael True, *Prin*
EMP: 5 EST: 2018
SALES (est): 800K
SALES (corp-wide): 800K **Privately Held**
SIC: 7371 Computer software development and applications

(G-20662)
W L GORE (PA)
200 Owls Nest Rd (19807-1130)
PHONE..................................302 584-8822
EMP: 9 EST: 2017
SALES (est): 147.71K
SALES (corp-wide): 147.71K **Privately Held**
Web: www.gore.com
SIC: 2821 Plastics materials and resins

(G-20663)
W R GRACE & CO
1521 Concord Pike Ste 341 (19803-3642)
PHONE..................................410 531-4000
Walter Raquet, *Brnch Mgr*
EMP: 9
SALES (corp-wide): 6.27B **Privately Held**
Web: www.grace.com
SIC: 2819 Catalysts, chemical
HQ: W. R. Grace & Co.
7500 Grace Dr
Columbia MD 21044
410 531-4000

(G-20664)
W23 S12 HOLDINGS LLC
Also Called: Hilo House
2000 Pennsylvania Ave Unit 106 (19806)
PHONE..................................610 348-3825
EMP: 5 EST: 2019
SALES (est): 49.69K **Privately Held**
Web: www.hilohousefitness.com
SIC: 7991 7371 Physical fitness facilities; Computer software development and applications

(G-20665)
WABTEC FINANCE LLC (DH)
1011 Centre Rd Ste 310 (19805-1266)
PHONE..................................412 825-1000
EMP: 15 EST: 2011
SALES (est): 2.32MM **Publicly Held**
SIC: 7389 Financial services
HQ: Wabtec Corporation
30 Isabella St Ste 300
Pittsburgh PA 15212

(G-20666)
WACHU INC ◊
1007 N Orange St Fl 4 (19801-1242)
PHONE..................................323 657-3889
Samira Esquina, *COO*
EMP: 3 EST: 2022
SALES (est): 128.34K **Privately Held**
SIC: 7372 Prepackaged software

(G-20667)
WAGGIES BY MAGGIE AND FRIENDS
1310 Carruthers Ln (19803-4604)
PHONE..................................302 598-2867
EMP: 6 EST: 2019
SALES (est): 38.26K **Privately Held**
Web: www.waggies.org
SIC: 8699 Charitable organization

(G-20668)
WAGSTAFF DAY CARE CENTER INC
310 Kiamensi Rd Rm 301 (19804-2959)
PHONE..................................302 998-7818
Freddie Anderson, *Pr*
EMP: 10 EST: 1989
SALES (est): 198.15K **Privately Held**
SIC: 8351 Group day care center

(G-20669)
WAHL FAMILY DENTISTRY
2003 Concord Pike (19803-2904)
PHONE..................................302 655-1228
Michael Whal, *Owner*
EMP: 16 EST: 2003
SALES (est): 911.69K **Privately Held**
Web: www.wahlfamilydentistry.com
SIC: 8021 Dentists' office

(G-20670)
WAHL FINANCIAL INC
628 Black Gates Rd (19803-2240)
PHONE..................................302 229-1933
Joseph Wahl, *Pr*
EMP: 6 EST: 2019
SALES (est): 150K **Privately Held**
SIC: 6411 Insurance brokers, nec

(G-20671)
WALA LLC
2810 N Church St (19802-4447)
PHONE..................................949 410-0568
EMP: 6
SALES (est): 71.34K **Privately Held**
SIC: 4813 Online service providers

(G-20672)
WALDEN LLC
Also Called: Walden Townhomes
1 Henry Ct (19808-2017)
PHONE..................................302 998-8112
EMP: 5
SALES (est): 484.88K **Privately Held**
SIC: 6513 Apartment building operators

(G-20673)
WALNUT GREEN ASSET MGT LL
1301 Walnut Green Rd (19807-1649)
P.O. Box 4016 (19807-0016)
PHONE..................................302 689-3798
Anthony Hitschler, *Prin*
EMP: 5 EST: 2013
SALES (est): 180.84K **Privately Held**
SIC: 8741 Financial management for business

(G-20674)
WALTER J KOBASA JR MD
1941 Limestone Rd (19808-5408)
PHONE..................................302 993-1191
EMP: 7 EST: 2018
SALES (est): 229.83K **Privately Held**
SIC: 8011 Offices and clinics of medical doctors

(G-20675)
WANDA ROLAND
127 W 20th St (19802-4806)
P.O. Box 1386 (19899-1386)
PHONE..................................773 573-3265
Wanda Roland, *Mgr*
EMP: 6 EST: 2017
SALES (est): 55.28K **Privately Held**
SIC: 8049 Offices of health practitioner

(G-20676)
WANG CONSULTANTS INC
4023 Kennett Pike Ste 603 (19807-2018)
PHONE..................................626 483-0265
Jay Wang, *Pr*
EMP: 5 EST: 2013
SQ FT: 300
SALES (est): 226.87K **Privately Held**
SIC: 8742 Business planning and organizing services

(G-20677)
WARD & TAYLOR LLC (PA)
2710 Centerville Rd Ste 200 (19808-1664)
PHONE..................................302 225-3350
William E Ward, *Managing Member*
EMP: 24 EST: 2004
SQ FT: 17,000
SALES (est): 8.19MM **Privately Held**
Web: www.wardtaylor.com
SIC: 8111 Real estate law

(G-20678)
WARD CHIROPRACTIC
5810 Kirkwood Hwy (19808-4868)
P.O. Box 7162 (19803-0162)
PHONE..................................302 225-9000
Patrick W Ward, *Prin*
EMP: 9 EST: 2008
SALES (est): 58.97K **Privately Held**
SIC: 8041 Offices and clinics of chiropractors

(G-20679)
WARSAL & AMURAO MD PA
2006 Limestone Rd Ste 4 (19808-5553)
PHONE..................................302 654-6245
Doctor Joseph A Arminio, *Pr*
Doctor Nabil Warsol, *VP*
Doctor Augusto Amurao, *Sec*
Nabil F Warsal Md, *Owner*
EMP: 12 EST: 1970
SQ FT: 2,000
SALES (est): 846.34K **Privately Held**
SIC: 8011 Surgeon

(G-20680)
WARTRUDE SERVICES INC
1601 Milltown Rd (19808-4027)
PHONE..................................302 213-3944
Holly Hamilton, *Pr*
Randy Cain, *Dir*
EMP: 6 EST: 2014
SQ FT: 200
SALES (est): 102.97K **Privately Held**
Web: www.wartrudeservices.com
SIC: 8742 Real estate consultant

(G-20681)
WASTE MANAGEMENT DELAWARE INC
Also Called: Waste Management
300 Harvey Dr (19804-2430)
PHONE..................................302 994-0944
Kevin Shegog, *Div Mgr*
EMP: 8
SALES (corp-wide): 19.7B **Publicly Held**
SIC: 4953 Refuse systems
HQ: Waste Management Of Delaware Inc.
1001 Fannin St Ste 4000
Houston TX 77002
713 512-6200

(G-20682)
WATER INGENUITY HOLDINGS CORP
2711 Centerville Rd Ste 4 (19808-1660)
PHONE..................................847 725-3000
Michael Madsen, *Brnch Mgr*
EMP: 2
SIC: 3589 Water treatment equipment, industrial
HQ: Water Ingenuity Holdings Corp.
5500 Wayzata Blvd Ste 900
Golden Valley MN 55416
763 545-1730

(G-20683)
WATERCRAFT LLC
801 Owls Nest Rd (19807-1611)
PHONE..................................302 757-0786
Nick Ganc, *Owner*
EMP: 2 EST: 2007
SALES (est): 170.45K **Privately Held**
SIC: 3589 5999 7389 Water treatment equipment, industrial; Water purification equipment; Water softener service

(G-20684)
WATSON BOYS TRUCKING LLC
501 Silverside Rd (19809-1374)

▲ = Import ▼ = Export
◆ = Import/Export

PHONE.............................302 635-4109
EMP: 5 EST: 2019
SALES (est): 478.65K **Privately Held**
SIC: **4212** Local trucking, without storage

(G-20685)
WATTS ELECTRIC COMPANY
2027 Harwyn Rd (19810-3870)
PHONE.............................302 529-1183
Michael Watts, *Owner*
EMP: 5
SALES (est): 450.69K **Privately Held**
Web: www.gowatts.com
SIC: **1731** General electrical contractor

(G-20686)
WATTS HTG HOT WTR SLUTIONS LLC
1209 N Orange St (19801-1120)
PHONE.............................817 335-9531
EMP: 73
SALES (corp-wide): 1.98B **Publicly Held**
SIC: **3433** Boilers, low-pressure heating: steam or hot water
HQ: Watts Heating And Hot Water Solutions Llc
  425 W Everman Pkwy # 101
  Fort Worth TX 76134

(G-20687)
WAVE GLOBAL EMPLOYMENT INC
3 Germay Dr Ste 4 (19804-1127)
PHONE.............................617 987-0152
Drew Durbin, *CEO*
EMP: 30 EST: 2020
SALES (est): 2.02MM **Privately Held**
SIC: **7361** Employment agencies

(G-20688)
WAVE LLC
1201 N Orange St (19801-1155)
Rural Route 135 Mad Ave (10016)
PHONE.............................212 849-2217
EMP: 6 EST: 2018
SALES (est): 219.01K **Privately Held**
SIC: **7371** Computer software development

(G-20689)
WAVEINNOVA INC
1209 N Orange St (19801-1120)
PHONE.............................650 507-5756
Anubhav Gupta, *CEO*
EMP: 3 EST: 2021
SALES (est): 50K **Privately Held**
SIC: **3674** Integrated circuits, semiconductor networks, etc.

(G-20690)
WAVEONE INC
1209 N Orange St (19801-1120)
PHONE.............................650 796-8637
Lubomir Bourdev, *CEO*
EMP: 8 EST: 2016
SALES (est): 346.54K
SALES (corp-wide): 383.29B **Publicly Held**
Web: www.wave.one
SIC: **7371** Computer software development
PA: Apple Inc.
  1 Apple Park Way
  Cupertino CA 95014
  408 996-1010

(G-20691)
WAYBETTER INC
4023 Kennett Pike (19807-2018)
PHONE.............................212 343-8238
James Rosen, *CEO*
Sean Conrad, *VP*
Matthew Daniel, *VP*

Alison Weick, *VP*
Andrew Appelbaum, *Dir*
EMP: 19 EST: 2012
SALES (est): 615.94K **Privately Held**
Web: www.dietbet.com
SIC: **8093** Weight loss clinic, with medical staff

(G-20692)
WAYFARER SOLUTIONS INC
251 Little Falls Dr (19808-1674)
PHONE.............................808 228-9989
Jeffrey Hoffman, *CEO*
EMP: 11 EST: 2019
SALES (est): 520.84K **Privately Held**
Web: www.wayfarerpoints.com
SIC: **7371** Custom computer programming services

(G-20693)
WAYMAN FIRE PROTECTION INC
3540 Old Capitol Trl (19808-6126)
PHONE.............................302 994-5757
Duane Wayman, *Pr*
Alisha Bryson, *
Trippe Wayman, *
Magdalena Manofu, *
EMP: 160 EST: 1974
SQ FT: 12,000
SALES (est): 22.04MM **Privately Held**
Web: www.waymanfireprotection.com
SIC: **3669** Fire alarm apparatus, electric

(G-20694)
WAYNE INDUSTRIES INC (PA)
1105 N Market St Ste 1300 (19801-1241)
P.O. Box 8985 (19899-8985)
PHONE.............................302 478-6160
Robert A Milnes, *Pr*
Franklin A Milnes, *Ex VP*
Harry E Evans, *VP*
Martha Heil, *Treas*
EMP: 5 EST: 1984
SQ FT: 143,000
SALES (est): 15.36MM
SALES (corp-wide): 15.36MM **Privately Held**
SIC: **2241** 5131 Bindings, textile; Piece goods and other fabrics

(G-20695)
WAYNE K PANSA JR LCSW LLC
1201 W 6th St (19805-3213)
PHONE.............................302 455-7065
Wayne Pansa Junior, *Prin*
EMP: 6 EST: 2018
SALES (est): 70.37K **Privately Held**
SIC: **8322** Social worker

(G-20696)
WBI CAPITAL ADVISORS LLC (PA)
251 Little Falls Dr (19808-1674)
PHONE.............................856 361-6362
San Zhang, *Managing Member*
EMP: 24 EST: 2018
SALES (est): 2.21MM
SALES (corp-wide): 2.21MM **Privately Held**
SIC: **6282** 7372 Investment advisory service; Application computer software

(G-20697)
WDBID DBA DOWNTOWN VISIONS
409 N Orange St (19801-2218)
PHONE.............................302 425-5374
EMP: 21 EST: 2011
SALES (est): 242.75K **Privately Held**
Web: www.downtownwilmingtonde.com
SIC: **7011** Hotels

(G-20698)
WDBID MANAGEMENT COMPANY
Also Called: DOWNTOWN VISIONS
409 N Orange St (19801-2218)
PHONE.............................302 425-5374
EMP: 20 EST: 1994
SALES (est): 3.36MM **Privately Held**
Web: www.downtownwilmingtonde.com
SIC: **8641** Civic and social associations

(G-20699)
WE COBBLE LLC
4023 Kennett Pike Ste 50098 (19807-2018)
PHONE.............................302 504-4294
Philip Moore, *CEO*
EMP: 15 EST: 2017
SALES (est): 1.43MM **Privately Held**
Web: www.wecobble.com
SIC: **5045** 7371 Computer software; Computer software development

(G-20700)
WEARWELL
314 Walden Rd (19803-2424)
PHONE.............................302 547-3337
Erin Houston, *Prin*
EMP: 7 EST: 2017
SALES (est): 48.31K **Privately Held**
Web: www.wearwell.com
SIC: **3069** Fabricated rubber products, nec

(G-20701)
WEATHER OR NOT DOG WALKERS
1300 Tulane Rd (19803-5140)
PHONE.............................302 304-8399
Lisa Mcgrath, *Prin*
EMP: 7 EST: 2016
SALES (est): 115.22K **Privately Held**
Web: www.weatherornotde.com
SIC: **7299** Pet sitting, in-home

(G-20702)
WEATHERHILL DENTAL
5317 Limestone Rd Ste 2 (19808-1252)
PHONE.............................302 239-6677
Erika Williams, *Prin*
EMP: 11 EST: 2014
SALES (est): 1.1MM **Privately Held**
Web: www.weatherhilldental.com
SIC: **8021** Dentists' office

(G-20703)
WEB ADVANTAGE INC
216 Paddock Ln (19803-1919)
PHONE.............................302 479-7634
Hollis Thomases, *Pr*
David Cease, *VP*
EMP: 10 EST: 2008
SALES (est): 321.93K **Privately Held**
Web: www.advantage-de.com
SIC: **2741** Internet publishing and broadcasting

(G-20704)
WEBB LLC
312 W 35th St (19802-2639)
PHONE.............................302 744-0029
Terrence Webb, *Pr*
EMP: 6 EST: 2011
SALES (est): 159.83K **Privately Held**
SIC: **1711** Heating and air conditioning contractors

(G-20705)
WEBBROWSER MEDIA INC
Also Called: Quick Browser
3422 Old Capitol Trl Ste 716 (19808-6124)
PHONE.............................302 830-3664
Tobyn Sowden, *CEO*
EMP: 7 EST: 2015

SALES (est): 290.83K **Privately Held**
SIC: **7371** Computer software development and applications

(G-20706)
WEBTIME CORPORATION
501 Silverside Rd Ste 105 (19809-1376)
PHONE.............................302 476-2350
EMP: 5 EST: 2019
SALES (est): 132.27K **Privately Held**
Web: www.replacemagic.com
SIC: **7371** Computer software development

(G-20707)
WEBWORK TIME TRACKER INC ✪
1207 Delaware Ave (19806-4743)
PHONE.............................415 707-3544
EMP: 30 EST: 2022
SALES (est): 677.83K **Privately Held**
SIC: **7371** Computer software development and applications

(G-20708)
WECANRUSH INC (PA)
501 Silverside Rd 373 (19809-1374)
PHONE.............................317 603-6622
Ibrahim Gidado, *Prin*
EMP: 6 EST: 2020
SALES (est): 74.74K
SALES (corp-wide): 74.74K **Privately Held**
SIC: **4212** Delivery service, vehicular

(G-20709)
WEE CARE DAY CARE SALV ARMY
400 N Orange St (19801-2219)
P.O. Box 308 (19899-0308)
PHONE.............................302 472-0712
Ann Jeuell, *Dir*
EMP: 9 EST: 1971
SALES (est): 55.23K **Privately Held**
SIC: **8351** Child day care services

(G-20710)
WEE WONDERS DOULAS
932 Rockwell Rd (19810-3121)
PHONE.............................302 275-7799
EMP: 6 EST: 2014
SALES (est): 49.27K **Privately Held**
Web: www.weewondersdoulas.com
SIC: **8351** Child day care services

(G-20711)
WEEPOR COMPANY INC
103 Foulk Rd Ste 202 (19803-3742)
PHONE.............................302 575-9945
John S Moore, *Pr*
A P Waterman Junior, *VP*
Sandra Keller, *VP*
Marian Wagner, *Sec*
Samuel A Gilliland, *Sec*
EMP: 5 EST: 1936
SALES (est): 526.41K **Privately Held**
SIC: **6799** Investors, nec

(G-20712)
WEG CLEANING SERVICE INC
300 Delaware Ave (19801-1607)
PHONE.............................302 343-5746
Wyman Guy, *Pr*
EMP: 5
SALES (est): 203.68K **Privately Held**
SIC: **7349** Cleaning service, industrial or commercial

(G-20713)
WEIK NITSCHE & DOUGHERTY
305 N Union St Unit 2 (19805-3454)
P.O. Box 2324 (19899-2324)
PHONE.............................302 655-4040
Garry Nitsche, *Mng Pt*

Wilmington - New Castle County (G-20714)   GEOGRAPHIC SECTION

Joseph Weik, *Pt*
Michael Galbraith, *Pt*
Shawn Dougherty, *Pt*
EMP: 18 **EST:** 1958
SALES (est): 1.89MM **Privately Held**
Web: www.nitschefredricks.com
SIC: 8111 General practice attorney, lawyer

(G-20714)
WEINER DEVELOPMENT LLC
4 Denny Rd Ste 1 (19809-3445)
PHONE.................................302 764-9430
Leon Weiner, *Prin*
Kevin Kelly, *
EMP: 8 **EST:** 1999
SALES (est): 256.59K **Privately Held**
SIC: 1521 Single-family housing construction

(G-20715)
WEIR GREENBLATT PIERCE LLP
1204 N King St (19801-3218)
PHONE.................................302 652-8181
Walter Weir Junior, *Brnch Mgr*
EMP: 6
Web: www.wgpllp.com
SIC: 8111 General practice attorney, lawyer
PA: Weir Greenblatt Pierce Llp
1339 Chestnut St Ste 500
Philadelphia PA 19107

(G-20716)
WEISS & SAVILLE PA
1105 N Market St Ste 200 (19801-1276)
P.O. Box 370 (19899-0370)
PHONE.................................302 656-0400
EMP: 5 **EST:** 1996
SALES (est): 498.29K **Privately Held**
Web: www.weissandsaville.com
SIC: 8111 General practice law office

(G-20717)
WEIYE LI MD
1801 Rockland Rd Ste 100 (19803-3650)
PHONE.................................302 651-4400
Weiye Li, *Prin*
EMP: 10 **EST:** 2001
SALES (est): 129.02K **Privately Held**
SIC: 8011 Pediatrician

(G-20718)
WELCOME2CITY GROUP CORP ◆
919 N Market St (19801-3023)
PHONE.................................347 897-9941
Aleksander Abroskin, *CEO*
EMP: 10 **EST:** 2022
SALES (est): 348.32K **Privately Held**
SIC: 7371 Software programming applications

(G-20719)
WELLINGTON MANAGEMENT GROUP
300 Delaware Ave Ste 1380 (19801-1658)
PHONE.................................215 569-8900
Carol Attwood Kleiman, *Pr*
Craig C Cole, *Dir*
EMP: 6 **EST:** 2010
SALES (est): 185.7K **Privately Held**
Web: www.wellingtonmg.com
SIC: 8741 Business management

(G-20720)
WELLNESS NATURAL USA INC
Also Called: Simplyprotein
2810 N Church St Pmb 47081 (19802-4447)
PHONE.................................800 547-5790
Michael Lines, *CEO*
EMP: 8 **EST:** 2020
SALES (est): 312.11K **Privately Held**
SIC: 2096 2064 2052 Potato chips and similar snacks; Breakfast bars; Cookies and crackers

(G-20721)
WELLNESS STRATEGIES LLC
1101 Wilson Rd (19803-3424)
PHONE.................................302 475-5062
Tracy Porter, *Prin*
EMP: 6 **EST:** 2015
SALES (est): 74.33K **Privately Held**
SIC: 8099 Health and allied services, nec

(G-20722)
WELLS FARGO BANK NATIONAL ASSN
Also Called: Wells Fargo
2024 Naamans Rd (19810-2655)
PHONE.................................302 529-2550
Rhonda Bishop, *Mgr*
EMP: 5
SALES (corp-wide): 82.86B **Publicly Held**
Web: www.wellsfargo.com
SIC: 6021 National commercial banks
HQ: Wells Fargo Bank, National Association
420 Montgomery St San
San Francisco CA 94104
605 575-6900

(G-20723)
WELLS FARGO BANK NATIONAL ASSN
814 Philadelphia Pike (19809-2357)
PHONE.................................302 761-1300
Joe Piccirelli, *Mgr*
EMP: 8
SALES (corp-wide): 82.86B **Publicly Held**
Web: www.wellsfargo.com
SIC: 6021 National commercial banks
HQ: Wells Fargo Bank, National Association
420 Montgomery St San
San Francisco CA 94104
605 575-6900

(G-20724)
WELLS FARGO BANK NATIONAL ASSN
100 W 10th St Lbby 1 (19801-1645)
PHONE.................................302 622-3350
Ruthine Ruth, *Brnch Mgr*
EMP: 8
SALES (corp-wide): 82.86B **Publicly Held**
Web: www.wellsfargo.com
SIC: 6021 National commercial banks
HQ: Wells Fargo Bank, National Association
420 Montgomery St San
San Francisco CA 94104
605 575-6900

(G-20725)
WELLS FARGO BANK NATIONAL ASSN
Also Called: Wells Fargo
4015 Kennett Pike (19807-2018)
PHONE.................................302 421-7820
Shaakira Marton, *Mgr*
EMP: 8
SALES (corp-wide): 82.86B **Publicly Held**
Web: www.wellsfargo.com
SIC: 6021 National commercial banks
HQ: Wells Fargo Bank, National Association
420 Montgomery St San
San Francisco CA 94104
605 575-6900

(G-20726)
WELLS FARGO CLEARING SVCS LLC
Also Called: Wells Fargo Advisors
3801 Kennett Pike Ste B200 (19807-2321)
P.O. Box 3740 (19807-0740)
PHONE.................................302 428-8600
Gary Gittings Junior, *Mgr*
EMP: 6
SALES (corp-wide): 82.86B **Publicly Held**
Web: www.wellsfargoadvisors.com
SIC: 6211 Brokers, security
HQ: Wells Fargo Clearing Services, Llc
1 N Jefferson Ave Fl 7
Saint Louis MO 63103

(G-20727)
WELLS FARGO DELAWARE TR CO NA
505 Carr Rd (19809-2870)
PHONE.................................302 575-2002
Sandra Carreker, *Pr*
Ann Dukart, *VP*
EMP: 7 **EST:** 2002
SALES (est): 16.61MM
SALES (corp-wide): 82.86B **Publicly Held**
SIC: 6021 National commercial banks
HQ: Wells Fargo Bank, National Association
420 Montgomery St San
San Francisco CA 94104
605 575-6900

(G-20728)
WELLSPRING FARM INC
Also Called: Wellspring Tack Shop
800 Carr Rd (19809-2163)
PHONE.................................302 798-2407
Katherine C Van Dyke, *Pr*
EMP: 6 **EST:** 1984
SALES (est): 326.11K **Privately Held**
Web: wellspringfarm.us.com
SIC: 7999 Riding stable

(G-20729)
WEN INTERNATIONAL INC
101 Wayland Rd (19807-2529)
PHONE.................................845 354-1773
Sharon Chang, *Pr*
Frank Zimdhal, *VP*
▲ **EMP:** 6 **EST:** 1999
SQ FT: 8,000
SALES (est): 949.08K **Privately Held**
Web: www.weninternational.com
SIC: 5149 Flavorings and fragrances

(G-20730)
WENDY M D SCHOFER
602 Geddes St (19805-3719)
PHONE.................................302 824-4411
Wendy Schofer, *Prin*
EMP: 8 **EST:** 2017
SALES (est): 56.41K **Privately Held**
SIC: 8011 Offices and clinics of medical doctors

(G-20731)
WENEURO INC
1209 N Orange St (19801-1120)
PHONE.................................760 607-7277
Kenneth Kaufman, *CEO*
EMP: 8
SALES (est): 400.53K **Privately Held**
SIC: 5045 Computer software

(G-20732)
WEPLAY ESPORTS MEDIA INC
1013 Centre Rd Ste 403b (19805-1270)
PHONE.................................818 274-2959
EMP: 5 **EST:** 2020
SALES (est): 118.07K **Privately Held**
Web: www.weplay.tv
SIC: 7371 Computer software development and applications

(G-20733)
WERB & SULLIVAN
300 Delaware Ave Ste 1300 (19801-1658)
P.O. Box 25046 (19899-5046)
PHONE.................................302 652-1100
Brian A Sullivan, *Pt*
EMP: 10 **EST:** 1988
SALES (est): 788.95K **Privately Held**
Web: www.werbsullivan.com
SIC: 8111 General practice attorney, lawyer

(G-20734)
WERTZ & CO
116 Valley Rd (19804-1300)
PHONE.................................302 658-5186
Robin L Becker, *Pr*
EMP: 16 **EST:** 1926
SALES (est): 1.94MM **Privately Held**
Web: www.wertzandco.com
SIC: 1521 1761 General remodeling, single-family houses; Roofing contractor

(G-20735)
WES SANDERS & SON LLC
7 Circle Dr (19804-2925)
PHONE.................................302 383-4991
Harland Sanders, *Prin*
EMP: 5 **EST:** 2017
SALES (est): 246.61K **Privately Held**
SIC: 1522 Residential construction, nec

(G-20736)
WESLEY NOVAK PHD
1521 Concord Pike Ste 301 (19803-3644)
PHONE.................................302 477-0470
Wesley G Novak Ph.d., *Owner*
EMP: 8 **EST:** 2018
SALES (est): 59.55K **Privately Held**
SIC: 8011 Offices and clinics of medical doctors

(G-20737)
WEST CENTER PLACE
622 N Jefferson St (19801-2130)
PHONE.................................302 426-0201
Dorothy Robbins, *Mgr*
EMP: 5 **EST:** 1997
SALES (est): 82.73K **Privately Held**
SIC: 6513 Apartment building operators

(G-20738)
WEST END MACHINE SHOP INC
1405 Brown St (19805-4777)
PHONE.................................302 654-8436
William Betley, *Pr*
EMP: 4 **EST:** 1936
SQ FT: 3,700
SALES (est): 404.95K **Privately Held**
Web: www.westendmachineshop.com
SIC: 3599 Machine shop, jobbing and repair

(G-20739)
WEST END NEIGHBORHOOD HSE INC
Also Called: West End Nghbrhood Child Care
1725 W 8th St (19805-3153)
PHONE.................................302 654-2131
Victoria Mells, *Dir*
EMP: 8
SALES (corp-wide): 6.99MM **Privately Held**
Web: www.westendnh.org
SIC: 8322 Multi-service center
PA: The West End Neighborhood House Incorporated
710 N Lincoln St
Wilmington DE 19805
302 658-4171

GEOGRAPHIC SECTION
Wilmington - New Castle County (G-20767)

(G-20740)
WEST END NEIGHBORHOOD HSE INC (PA)
Also Called: WEST END
710 N Lincoln St (19805-3016)
PHONE.................................302 658-4171
Paul F Calistro Junior, *Ex Dir*
Joseph Johnson, *
EMP: 34 **EST:** 1883
SALES (est): 6.99MM
SALES (corp-wide): 6.99MM **Privately Held**
Web: www.westendnh.org
SIC: 8322 Social service center

(G-20741)
WEST HOME LEASEHOLD LLC
1209 N Orange St (19801-1120)
PHONE.................................917 443-7451
Arthur Modell, *Managing Member*
EMP: 10 **EST:** 2019
SALES (est): 2MM **Privately Held**
SIC: 6531 7389 Real estate managers; Business services, nec

(G-20742)
WESTON SOUND
2 Stone Barn Ln (19807-2524)
PHONE.................................215 327-8646
EMP: 6 **EST:** 2013
SALES (est): 125.13K **Privately Held**
Web: www.westonsound.com
SIC: 1731 Sound equipment specialization

(G-20743)
WESTOVER CAPITAL ADVISORS LLC
1013 Centre Rd Ste 405 (19805-1270)
PHONE.................................302 427-9600
H Murray Sawyer Junior, *Managing Member*
EMP: 8 **EST:** 1999
SALES (est): 3.5MM **Privately Held**
Web: www.westovercapital.com
SIC: 6282 Investment advisory service

(G-20744)
WESTOVER SYSTEMS LLC
1521 Concord Pike Ste 301 (19803-3644)
PHONE.................................302 652-3500
EMP: 5 **EST:** 2019
SALES (est): 111.66K **Privately Held**
SIC: 4789 Transportation services, nec

(G-20745)
WESTSIDE FAMILY HEALTHCARE INC
908 E 16th St Ste B (19802-5145)
PHONE.................................302 575-1414
Pori Cobb, *Brnch Mgr*
EMP: 36
Web: www.westsidehealth.org
SIC: 8011 8021 Clinic, operated by physicians; Offices and clinics of dentists
PA: Westside Family Healthcare, Inc.
300 Water St Ste 200
Wilmington DE 19801

(G-20746)
WESTSIDE FAMILY HEALTHCARE INC (PA)
300 Water St Ste 200 (19801-5043)
PHONE.................................302 656-8292
Christopher Fraser, *Pr*
John Hundley, *COO*
Maggie Norris Bent, *EXTERNAL AFFAIRS*
Sarah Stroh, *CFO*
EMP: 17 **EST:** 1983
SQ FT: 23,000
SALES (est): 29.96MM **Privately Held**
Web: www.westsidehealth.org

SIC: 8011 8021 Clinic, operated by physicians; Offices and clinics of dentists

(G-20747)
WESTSIDE FAMILY HEALTHCARE INC
1802 W 4th St (19805-3420)
PHONE.................................302 656-8292
Lolita A Lopez, *Brnch Mgr*
EMP: 35
Web: www.westsidehealth.org
SIC: 8011 8021 Clinic, operated by physicians; Offices and clinics of dentists
PA: Westside Family Healthcare, Inc.
300 Water St Ste 200
Wilmington DE 19801

(G-20748)
WEVIDIT INC
224 A Trolley Sqre Number 1226 (19806)
PHONE.................................516 513-1659
EMP: 10 **EST:** 2020
SALES (est): 68.01K **Privately Held**
Web: www.wevidit.com
SIC: 4899 Communication services, nec

(G-20749)
WEYL ENTERPRISES INC
Also Called: Custom Satellite and Sound
1206 Kirkwood Hwy (19805-2120)
PHONE.................................302 993-1248
David Weyl, *Pr*
EMP: 5 **EST:** 1994
SALES (est): 494.84K **Privately Held**
Web: www.csscustom.com
SIC: 3571 Electronic computers

(G-20750)
WEYMOUTH SWYZE CRROON INSUR IN
Also Called: Nationwide
5710 Kennett Pike (19807-1312)
P.O. Box 3939 (19807-0939)
PHONE.................................302 655-3705
R Bruce Swayze, *Pr*
EMP: 10 **EST:** 1943
SQ FT: 2,000
SALES (est): 2.61MM **Privately Held**
Web: www.wscins.com
SIC: 6411 Insurance agents, brokers, and service

(G-20751)
WGAMES INCORPORATED
1209 N Orange St (19801-1120)
PHONE.................................206 618-3699
Daniel Kajouie, *Pr*
Erik Fisher, *VP*
EMP: 8 **EST:** 2016
SALES (est): 282.8K **Privately Held**
Web: www.wgames.com
SIC: 7371 Computer software development

(G-20752)
WH &C MANAGEMENT SERVICES INC
11 Camp David Rd (19810-3261)
PHONE.................................302 225-3000
EMP: 6 **EST:** 2013
SALES (est): 224.9K **Privately Held**
SIC: 8741 Management services

(G-20753)
WH2P INC
3704 Kennett Pike Ste 400 (19807-2176)
P.O. Box 22 (19736-0022)
PHONE.................................302 530-6555
Brian Havertine, *Pr*
Greg Williamson, *VP*
Roger Poole, *Sec*

Joseph Harris, *Treas*
EMP: 6 **EST:** 1991
SQ FT: 1,800
SALES (est): 441.94K **Privately Held**
Web: www.wh2p.com
SIC: 7311 Advertising consultant

(G-20754)
WHARTON LEVIN EHRMANTRAUT
300 Delaware Ave (19801-1612)
PHONE.................................302 252-0090
Andrew Vernick, *Brnch Mgr*
EMP: 6 **EST:** 2011
SALES (est): 807.82K **Privately Held**
Web: www.whartonlevin.com
SIC: 8111 General practice attorney, lawyer

(G-20755)
WHC PROPERTIES LLC
1831 Delaware Ave Ste 1 (19806-2337)
PHONE.................................302 225-3000
EMP: 11 **EST:** 2017
SALES (est): 359.45K **Privately Held**
SIC: 6512 Nonresidential building operators

(G-20756)
WHEATFIELD HOLDINGS LLC (PA)
3411 Silverside Rd Ste 104 (19810-4812)
PHONE.................................312 956-0198
Anna Wilczek, *Managing Member*
EMP: 6 **EST:** 2018
SALES (est): 1.67MM
SALES (corp-wide): 1.67MM **Privately Held**
SIC: 5149 Bakery products

(G-20757)
WHEEL LADY GARCIA
200 Valley Rd (19804-9005)
PHONE.................................302 588-9750
EMP: 5 **EST:** 2020
SALES (est): 101.33K **Privately Held**
Web: the-wheel-lady.business.site
SIC: 7538 General automotive repair shops

(G-20758)
WHEELER FINANCIAL LLC
2961 Centerville Rd Ste 150 (19808-1666)
PHONE.................................302 543-5585
EMP: 6 **EST:** 2019
SALES (est): 138.55K **Privately Held**
Web: www.wheelerfinancial-llc.com
SIC: 6282 Investment advice

(G-20759)
WHEELER WOLFENDEN & DWARES CPA
4550 Linden Hill Rd (19808)
PHONE.................................302 254-8240
John Wheeler, *Pr*
EMP: 23 **EST:** 1953
SALES (est): 2.72MM **Privately Held**
Web: www.wwd-cpa.com
SIC: 8721 Certified public accountant

(G-20760)
WHIMSTAY INC
Also Called: Wemaste
2810 N Church St (19802-4447)
PHONE.................................650 867-0076
James J Rossiter, *Prin*
EMP: 7 **EST:** 2018
SALES (est): 352.43K **Privately Held**
Web: www.whimstay.com
SIC: 7372 Prepackaged software

(G-20761)
WHISMAN JOHN
Also Called: Motorsport Series
5201 W Woodmill Dr Ste 31 (19808-4068)

PHONE.................................302 530-1676
John Whisman, *Owner*
EMP: 2 **EST:** 2000
SALES (est): 73.05K **Privately Held**
SIC: 2396 2395 Screen printing on fabric articles; Emblems, embroidered

(G-20762)
WHITAKER CORPORATION
4550 Linden Hill Rd Ste 140 (19808)
PHONE.................................302 633-2740
Mark Young, *Pr*
Driscoll Nina, *OF INTELLECTUAL PROPERTY*
EMP: 34 **EST:** 1972
SQ FT: 6,000
SALES (est): 607.63K **Privately Held**
SIC: 8111 Legal services
HQ: Te Connectivity Corporation
1050 Westlakes Dr
Berwyn PA 19312
610 893-9800

(G-20763)
WHITE AND WILLIAMS LLP
Also Called: White & Williams
600 N King St Ste 800 (19801-3778)
P.O. Box 709 (19899-0709)
PHONE.................................302 654-0424
John Balaguer, *Mgr*
EMP: 23
SALES (corp-wide): 65.85MM **Privately Held**
Web: www.whiteandwilliams.com
SIC: 8111 General practice attorney, lawyer
PA: White And Williams, Llp
1650 Market St Ste 1800
Philadelphia PA 19103
215 864-7000

(G-20764)
WHITE HORSE WINERY
15 Guyencourt Rd (19807-1415)
PHONE.................................302 388-4850
Brock Vinton, *Prin*
EMP: 5 **EST:** 2016
SALES (est): 188.96K **Privately Held**
Web: www.whitehorsewinery.com
SIC: 2084 Wines

(G-20765)
WHITE HORSE WINERY LLC
300 Water St Ste 300 (19801-5046)
PHONE.................................302 472-7200
EMP: 6 **EST:** 2019
SALES (est): 625.38K **Privately Held**
Web: www.whitehorsewinery.com
SIC: 2084 Wines

(G-20766)
WHITE OAK LANDSCAPE MGT INC
17 Owls Nest Rd (19807-1125)
PHONE.................................302 652-7533
William Duncan, *Pr*
EMP: 9 **EST:** 1997
SALES (est): 504.54K **Privately Held**
Web: www.whiteoaklandscape.net
SIC: 0781 Landscape services

(G-20767)
WHITE ROBBINS COMPANY
Also Called: White Robbins Condo & Assn
3513 Concord Pike Ste 2100 (19803-5027)
PHONE.................................302 478-5555
Tucker Robbins, *Owner*
EMP: 5 **EST:** 1998
SALES (est): 508.48K **Privately Held**
Web: www.whiterobbins.com
SIC: 6531 Real estate managers

Wilmington - New Castle County (G-20768)

(G-20768)
WHITECAP PIPELINE COMPANY LLC
251 Little Falls Dr (19808-1674)
PHONE..................925 842-1000
EMP: 22 **EST:** 2000
SALES (est): 8.66MM
SALES (corp-wide): 246.25B **Publicly Held**
SIC: 4612 Crude petroleum pipelines
PA: Chevron Corporation
6001 Bollinger Canyon Rd
San Ramon CA 94583
925 326-2189

(G-20769)
WHITECROW RESEARCH INC
2711 Centerville Rd Ste 300 Pmb 604 (19808)
PHONE..................908 752-4200
Prems Srampical, *Dir*
Swyta Bahuguna, *Dir*
Mark Swain, *Dir*
Neel Majithia, *Dir*
EMP: 10 **EST:** 2016
SALES (est): 509.4K **Privately Held**
Web: www.whitecrowresearch.com
SIC: 7361 Employment agencies

(G-20770)
WHITEFORD TAYLOR AND PRESTON
1220 N Market St Ste 608 (19801-2598)
PHONE..................302 353-4144
Murray Sawyer, *Prin*
EMP: 9 **EST:** 2007
SALES (est): 126.06K **Privately Held**
Web: www.whitefordlaw.com
SIC: 8111 Administrative and government law

(G-20771)
WHITES BODY SHOP
Also Called: Whites Auto Repair & Body Shop
436 S Buttonwood St (19801-5306)
PHONE..................302 655-4369
Clarence White, *Owner*
EMP: 5 **EST:** 1960
SALES (est): 331.46K **Privately Held**
SIC: 7532 Body shop, automotive

(G-20772)
WHITMAN REQUARDT AND ASSOC LLP
Also Called: Whitman Requardt and Assoc
1013 Centre Rd Ste 302 (19805-1265)
PHONE..................302 571-9001
Jeff Riegner, *Brnch Mgr*
EMP: 37
SALES (corp-wide): 104.66MM **Privately Held**
Web: www.wrallp.com
SIC: 8711 Consulting engineer
PA: Whitman, Requardt And Associates, Llp
801 S Caroline St
Baltimore MD 21231
410 235-3450

(G-20773)
WHITTAKERS LAWN CARE
324 Mcdaniel Ave (19803-2572)
PHONE..................302 478-2169
James Whittaker, *Prin*
EMP: 5 **EST:** 2010
SALES (est): 153.93K **Privately Held**
SIC: 0782 Lawn care services

(G-20774)
WHITTENS FINE JEWELRY
Also Called: Wholesale Jewelry Outlet
4719 Kirkwood Hwy (19808-5007)
PHONE..................302 995-7464
EMP: 5 **EST:** 1998
SALES (est): 396.58K **Privately Held**
Web: www.whittensfinejewelry.com
SIC: 7631 5944 Jewelry repair services; Jewelry stores

(G-20775)
WHOLESALE JEWELRY OUTLET INC
3616 Kirkwood Hwy (19808-5124)
PHONE..................302 994-5114
Craig Whitten, *Owner*
EMP: 5 **EST:** 1984
SALES (est): 309.87K **Privately Held**
SIC: 5094 5944 Jewelry; Jewelry, precious stones and precious metals

(G-20776)
WHYFLY LLC
218 W 9th St (19801-1620)
PHONE..................302 222-7171
EMP: 12 **EST:** 2016
SALES (est): 3.4MM **Privately Held**
Web: www.whyfly.com
SIC: 8999 Communication services

(G-20777)
WIBX LOGISTICS LLC
604 W 6th St Apt 1 (19801-2014)
PHONE..................302 299-8860
EMP: 5 **EST:** 2020
SALES (est): 175.41K **Privately Held**
SIC: 3537 Trucks, tractors, loaders, carriers, and similar equipment

(G-20778)
WILBRAHAM LAWLER & BUBA PC
Also Called: WILBRAHAM LAWLER & BUBA PC
901 N Market St Ste 800 (19801-3090)
PHONE..................302 421-9922
Edward Wilbraham, *Pr*
EMP: 5
Web: www.wlbdeflaw.com
SIC: 8111 General practice attorney, lawyer
PA: Wilbraham, Lawler & Buba
1818 Market St Ste 3100
Philadelphia PA 19103

(G-20779)
WILCOX & FETZER LTD
1330 N King St (19801-3230)
PHONE..................302 655-0477
Kurt A Fetzer, *Pr*
Robert W Wilcox Senior, *VP*
EMP: 21 **EST:** 1976
SQ FT: 2,500
SALES (est): 366.48K **Privately Held**
Web: www.lexitaslegal.com
SIC: 7338 Court reporting service

(G-20780)
WILDERMAN PHYSICAL THERAPY LLC
2626 Belaire Dr (19808-3835)
PHONE..................717 873-6836
David Wilderman, *Prin*.
EMP: 5 **EST:** 2015
SALES (est): 65.76K **Privately Held**
Web: www.wildermanphysicaltherapy.com
SIC: 8049 Physical therapist

(G-20781)
WILKINSON ROOFING & SIDING INC
1000 First State Blvd (19804-3575)
P.O. Box 1236 (19317-0670)
PHONE..................302 998-0176
Kenneth Balagur, *Pr*
EMP: 21 **EST:** 1949
SQ FT: 18,000
SALES (est): 1.54MM **Privately Held**
Web: www.wilkinsonroofing.com
SIC: 1761 Roofing contractor

(G-20782)
WILKINSON TECHNOLOGY SVCS LLC
4 Squirrel Run (19807-2030)
PHONE..................302 384-7770
EMP: 5 **EST:** 2013
SALES (est): 233.59K **Privately Held**
SIC: 7374 Service bureau, computer

(G-20783)
WILKS LUKOFF & BRACEGIRDLE LLC
4250 Lancaster Pike # 200 (19805-1520)
PHONE..................302 225-0850
EMP: 9 **EST:** 2009
SALES (est): 1.22MM **Privately Held**
Web: www.wilks.law
SIC: 8111 Specialized law offices, attorneys

(G-20784)
WILLIAM BLAIR & COMPANY LLC
500 Delaware Ave (19801-1490)
PHONE..................302 573-5000
EMP: 8
Web: www.williamblair.com
SIC: 6211 Stock brokers and dealers
HQ: William Blair & Company Llc
150 N Riverside Plz # 3500
Chicago IL 60606
312 236-1600

(G-20785)
WILLIAM D SHELLADY INC
112 A St (19801-5219)
P.O. Box 1588 (19899-1588)
PHONE..................302 652-3106
Eugene A Matlusky, *Pr*
James Wahl, *
EMP: 75 **EST:** 1909
SQ FT: 5,000
SALES (est): 3.66MM **Privately Held**
SIC: 1711 Plumbing contractors

(G-20786)
WILLIAM DELCAMPO MECHANICAL SE
2429 Hartley Pl (19808-4258)
PHONE..................302 992-9748
Williams Del Campo, *Owner*
EMP: 6 **EST:** 2004
SALES (est): 499.58K **Privately Held**
Web: www.delcampomechanical.com
SIC: 1711 Mechanical contractor

(G-20787)
WILLIAM E WARD PA
2710 Centerville Rd Ste 200 (19808-1644)
P.O. Box 4360 (19807-0360)
PHONE..................302 225-3350
William E Ward, *Pr*
EMP: 10 **EST:** 1997
SALES (est): 233.7K **Privately Held**
Web: www.wardtaylor.com
SIC: 8111 General practice attorney, lawyer

(G-20788)
WILLIAM F & MARGARET HARTNETT
21 Penarth Dr (19803-2011)
PHONE..................302 479-5918
William Hartnett, *Prin*
EMP: 6 **EST:** 2013
SALES (est): 141.13K **Privately Held**
SIC: 1711 Plumbing contractors

(G-20789)
WILLIAM G DAY COMPANY
405 Tyrone Ave (19804-1932)
P.O. Box 7548 (19803-0548)
PHONE..................302 476-2808
William Day, *Pr*
Kenneth Cloud, *Sec*
EMP: 21 **EST:** 1997
SALES (est): 2.42MM **Privately Held**
Web: www.williamgdayco.com
SIC: 1711 Warm air heating and air conditioning contractor

(G-20790)
WILLIAM G ROBELEN INC
3110 Lancaster Ave (19805-1461)
PHONE..................302 656-8726
William Masciantonio Junior, *Pr*
Phillip Masciantonio, *VP*
EMP: 6 **EST:** 1900
SQ FT: 2,500
SALES (est): 366.95K **Privately Held**
SIC: 1711 Plumbing contractors

(G-20791)
WILLIAM GRANT & SONS USA CORP
1011 Ctr Rd Ste 310 (19805-1266)
PHONE..................302 573-3880
Vickie Sivemore, *Mgr*
◆ **EMP:** 400 **EST:** 1964
SALES (est): 9.07MM
SALES (corp-wide): 2.07B **Privately Held**
Web: www.williamgrant.com
SIC: 5182 2085 Bottling wines and liquors; Distilled and blended liquors
HQ: William Grant & Sons Limited
Customer Service Centre
Bellshill ML4 3

(G-20792)
WILLIAM H LUNGER ATTY
1020 N Bancroft Pkwy Ste 100 (19805-2666)
PHONE..................302 888-2504
William Lunger, *Prin*
EMP: 6 **EST:** 2010
SALES (est): 151.14K **Privately Held**
SIC: 8111 General practice attorney, lawyer

(G-20793)
WILLIAM H MCDANIEL INC
734 Hertford Rd (19803-1618)
P.O. Box 9236 (19809-0236)
PHONE..................302 764-2020
William H Mcdaniel Junior, *Pr*
EMP: 10 **EST:** 1947
SALES (est): 905.58K **Privately Held**
SIC: 1711 Mechanical contractor

(G-20794)
WILLIAM HCKS ANDRSON CMNTY CTR
501 N Madison St (19801-2060)
PHONE..................302 571-4266
Romain Alexander, *Dir*
EMP: 11 **EST:** 2000
SALES (est): 245.37K **Privately Held**
Web: www.seniorcenter.us
SIC: 8322 Community center

(G-20795)
WILLIAM N CANN INC
Also Called: Cann Printing
1 Meco Cir (19804-1108)
PHONE..................302 995-0820
William Cann Junior, *CEO*
Frank T Griffin, *Pr*
Miriam Lane, *Sec*
Celeste Sheehan, *Treas*
EMP: 20 **EST:** 1932

▲ = Import ▼ = Export
◆ = Import/Export

SQ FT: 18,000
SALES (est): 3.6MM **Privately Held**
Web: www.cannprinting.com
SIC: 2752 2791 2789 Offset printing; Typesetting; Bookbinding and related work

(G-20796)
WILLIAM R LYNCH M D
1521 Concord Pike Ste 301 (19803-3644)
PHONE.................................302 319-4736
William R Lynch, *Owner*
EMP: 7 **EST:** 2019
SALES (est): 180.5K **Privately Held**
SIC: 8011 Offices and clinics of medical doctors

(G-20797)
WILLIAMS APPLIANCEE
41 Germay Dr Ste A (19804-1100)
P.O. Box 5803 (19808-0803)
PHONE.................................302 656-8581
FAX: 302 994-7491
EMP: 15 **EST:** 1950
SALES (est): 870K **Privately Held**
SIC: 7699 7623 5064 5722 General household repair services; Air conditioning repair; Appliance parts, household; Appliance parts

(G-20798)
WILLIAMS HUMPHREYS AND CO LLC
1831 Delaware Ave (19806-2357)
PHONE.................................302 225-3000
EMP: 9 **EST:** 2020
SALES (est): 975.22K **Privately Held**
Web: www.whcompany.com
SIC: 1521 Single-family housing construction

(G-20799)
WILLIAMS INSURANCE AGENCY INC
4550 Linden Hill Rd Ste 303 (19808-2955)
P.O. Box 1174 (19971-0814)
PHONE.................................302 384-7804
EMP: 14
SALES (corp-wide): 5.67MM **Privately Held**
Web: www.williamsagency.com
SIC: 6411 Insurance agents, nec
PA: Williams Insurance Agency Inc
 20220 Coastal Hwy
 Rehoboth Beach DE 19971
 302 227-2501

(G-20800)
WILLIAMS INSURANCE AGENCY INC
4543 Stoney Batter Rd Ste B (19808-1286)
P.O. Box 1240 (19707-5240)
PHONE.................................302 227-2501
EMP: 6 **EST:** 2020
SALES (est): 255.8K **Privately Held**
Web: www.williamsagency.com
SIC: 6411 Insurance agents, nec

(G-20801)
WILLIAMS INSURANCE AGENCY INC
Also Called: G N G Insurance
5301 Limestone Rd Ste 100 (19808-1251)
PHONE.................................302 239-5500
EMP: 8
SALES (corp-wide): 5.67MM **Privately Held**
Web: www.williamsagency.com
SIC: 6411 Insurance agents, nec
PA: Williams Insurance Agency Inc
 20220 Coastal Hwy
 Rehoboth Beach DE 19971
 302 227-2501

(G-20802)
WILLIAMS LAW FIRM PA
1201 N Orange St Ste 600 (19801-1171)
P.O. Box 511 (19899-0511)
PHONE.................................302 575-0873
David N Williams, *Pt*
EMP: 5 **EST:** 1974
SALES (est): 812.98K **Privately Held**
Web: www.trustwilliams.com
SIC: 8111 General practice attorney, lawyer

(G-20803)
WILLIE HARDY MD
2219 Robin Rd (19803-3036)
PHONE.................................610 450-4559
Willie Hardy, *Prin*
EMP: 6 **EST:** 2012
SALES (est): 71.85K **Privately Held**
Web: www.rockymountainquarries.com
SIC: 8011 Anesthesiologist

(G-20804)
WILLOW TREE PROPERTIES LLC
100 Warwick Drive, Windsor Hills (19803-2621)
PHONE.................................302 674-2266
EMP: 5
SALES (est): 76.34K **Privately Held**
SIC: 6531 Real estate agents and managers

(G-20805)
WILLY CAB
2929 N Market St (19802-3148)
PHONE.................................302 465-1252
Myron Willy, *Prin*
EMP: 5 **EST:** 2013
SALES (est): 75.64K **Privately Held**
SIC: 4121 Taxicabs

(G-20806)
WILM OTOLARNGOLOGY
2300 Pennsylvania Ave Ste 2a (19806-1379)
PHONE.................................302 658-0404
William Medford, *Pt*
Jay Luft, *Pt*
EMP: 10 **EST:** 2010
SALES (est): 246.79K **Privately Held**
SIC: 8011 Eyes, ears, nose, and throat specialist: physician/surgeon

(G-20807)
WILMINGTON
1201 N Orange St Ste 7463 (19801-1293)
PHONE.................................302 357-4509
Vincent Cooper, *Bd of Dir*
Jonathon Farmer, *Bd of Dir*
Shawn Davis, *Bd of Dir*
Kelsey Bacon, *Bd of Dir*
Jeffery Greene, *Bd of Dir*
EMP: 7
SALES (est): 279.31K **Privately Held**
SIC: 3523 5084 1542 2833 Irrigation equipment, self-propelled; Brewery products manufacturing machinery, commercial; Greenhouse construction; Organic medicinal chemicals: bulk, uncompounded

(G-20808)
WILMINGTON ANIMAL HOSPITAL
828 Philadelphia Pike (19809-2332)
PHONE.................................302 762-2694
Doctor Shelly Epstein, *Pt*
EMP: 22 **EST:** 1945
SQ FT: 5,000
SALES (est): 2.1MM **Privately Held**
Web: www.wilmingtonanimalhospital.com
SIC: 0742 Animal hospital services, pets and other animal specialties

(G-20809)
WILMINGTON BLUE ROCKS LP
Also Called: Wilmington Blue Rocks
801 Shipyard Dr (19801-5154)
PHONE.................................302 888-2015
Matt Minker, *Genl Pt*
EMP: 12 **EST:** 1993
SALES (est): 2.51MM **Privately Held**
Web: www.bluerocks.com
SIC: 7941 Baseball club, professional and semi-professional

(G-20810)
WILMINGTON BREW WORKS LLC
3201 Miller Rd (19802-2542)
PHONE.................................302 757-4971
Craig Wensell, *Prin*
EMP: 13 **EST:** 2017
SALES (est): 2.93MM **Privately Held**
Web: www.wilmingtonbrewworks.com
SIC: 2082 Beer (alcoholic beverage)

(G-20811)
WILMINGTON CLUB INC
1103 N Market St (19801-1223)
P.O. Box 433 (19899-0433)
PHONE.................................302 658-4287
John E Riteel, *Pr*
Marcus Meyer, *Genl Mgr*
Charles Cummy, *VP*
Christopher Patterson, *Treas*
Michael Ledyard, *Sec*
EMP: 16 **EST:** 1876
SQ FT: 20,000
SALES (est): 612.55K **Privately Held**
Web: www.wilmingtonclub.com
SIC: 8641 Bars and restaurants, members only

(G-20812)
WILMINGTON COLLISION CENTER
3304 S Rockfield Dr (19810-3235)
PHONE.................................484 702-2115
Zach Dillard, *Prin*
EMP: 6 **EST:** 2018
SALES (est): 48.25K **Privately Held**
Web: www.henryautobody.com
SIC: 7532 Body shop, automotive

(G-20813)
WILMINGTON COUNTRY CLUB
4825 Kennett Pike (19807-1813)
PHONE.................................302 655-6171
Philip Lannelli, *Genl Mgr*
S Daniel Pierson, *
EMP: 150 **EST:** 1901
SALES (est): 18.54MM **Privately Held**
Web: www.wilmingtoncc.com
SIC: 7997 5941 5813 5812 Country club, membership; Sporting goods and bicycle shops; Drinking places; Eating places

(G-20814)
WILMINGTON DENTAL ASSOC PA
2309 Pennsylvania Ave (19806-1318)
PHONE.................................302 654-6915
John J Lenz, *Pt*
Anthony Vattilana, *Pt*
EMP: 16 **EST:** 1964
SQ FT: 4,000
SALES (est): 1.26MM **Privately Held**
Web: www.wilmingtondentalassociates.com
SIC: 8021 Dentists' office

(G-20815)
WILMINGTON FAMILY EYE CARE
801 E Newport Pike (19804-1920)
PHONE.................................302 999-1286
Daniel Baruffi, *Owner*
EMP: 12 **EST:** 2014
SALES (est): 941.08K **Privately Held**
Web: www.wilmingtonfamilyeyecare.com
SIC: 8042 Offices and clinics of optometrists

(G-20816)
WILMINGTON FIREFIGHTERS ASSN
Also Called: Wilmington Fire Fighters Assn
804 Maryland Ave (19805-4835)
PHONE.................................302 365-0168
EMP: 10 **EST:** 1987
SALES (est): 466.71K **Privately Held**
Web: www.wilmingtonfirefighters.org
SIC: 7389 Fund raising organizations

(G-20817)
WILMINGTON GLASS CO
727 S Market St (19801-5212)
PHONE.................................302 777-7000
EMP: 9 **EST:** 1994
SQ FT: 6,000
SALES (est): 887.92K **Privately Held**
Web: www.wilmingtonglass.com
SIC: 3211 Flat glass

(G-20818)
WILMINGTON HEADSTART INC (PA)
100 W 10th St Ste 1016 (19801-6607)
PHONE.................................302 762-8038
Deborah Thomas, *Dir*
EMP: 40 **EST:** 1984
SALES (est): 4.78MM
SALES (corp-wide): 4.78MM **Privately Held**
Web: www.wilmingtonheadstartinc.com
SIC: 8351 Head Start center, except in conjunction with school

(G-20819)
WILMINGTON HT XXXIII OWNER LLC
Also Called: Hotel Du Pont
42 W 11th St (19801-1393)
P.O. Box 991 (19899-0991)
PHONE.................................302 594-3100
TOLL FREE: 800
Greg Kavanagh, *Genl Mgr*
EMP: 34
SALES (corp-wide): 2.48MM **Privately Held**
Web: www.hoteldupont.com
SIC: 7011 Hotels
PA: Wilmington Hotel Xxxiii Owner Llc
 5425 Wisconsin Ave # 700
 Chevy Chase MD 20815
 302 594-3100

(G-20820)
WILMINGTON INFRARED TECH
108 Shinn Cir (19808-1114)
PHONE.................................302 234-6761
Mei-wei Tsao, *Owner*
EMP: 5 **EST:** 2002
SQ FT: 800
SALES (est): 453.93K **Privately Held**
Web: www.witinc.us
SIC: 3826 Infrared analytical instruments

(G-20821)
WILMINGTON LITTLE LEAGUE INC
2323 W 16th St (19806-1306)
PHONE.................................302 559-7690
Jennifer Mench, *Prin*
EMP: 5 **EST:** 2018
SALES (est): 63.22K **Privately Held**

Wilmington - New Castle County (G-20822)

GEOGRAPHIC SECTION

SIC: 7997 Baseball club, except professional and semi-professional

(G-20822)
WILMINGTON LRG-CAP STRTEGY FUN
1100 N Market St 10th Fl (19890-1100)
PHONE.................302 636-8500
EMP: 5
SALES (est): 195.92K **Privately Held**
SIC: 6722 Money market mutual funds

(G-20823)
WILMINGTON MEDICAL ASSOCIATES
Also Called: Sokoloff, Bruce H MD
2700 Silverside Rd Ste 3 (19810-3724)
PHONE.................302 478-0400
Bruce Slkollff, *Pt*
EMP: 31 EST: 1995
SALES (est): 4.94MM **Privately Held**
SIC: 8011 General and family practice, physician/surgeon

(G-20824)
WILMINGTON MONTESSORI SCHOOL
1400 Harvey Rd (19810-4210)
PHONE.................302 475-0555
Lisa Lalama, *Dir*
EMP: 75 EST: 1964
SALES (est): 4.66MM **Privately Held**
Web: www.wmsde.org
SIC: 8351 8211 Preschool center; Private elementary school

(G-20825)
WILMINGTON NEW CASTLE PEDIATRI
519 Brentwood Dr (19803-4309)
PHONE.................302 762-1072
EMP: 6
SALES (est): 13.97K **Privately Held**
SIC: 8011 Pediatrician

(G-20826)
WILMINGTON NGHBRHOOD CNSRVNCY
1007 N Orange St Fl 4 (19801-1242)
PHONE.................302 409-1023
Elizabeth Willauer, *Prin*
EMP: 5 EST: 2017
SALES (est): 1.88MM **Privately Held**
Web: www.wilmingtonlandbank.org
SIC: 6099 Functions related to deposit banking

(G-20827)
WILMINGTON ORTHODONTIC CENTER
2300 Pennsylvania Ave Ste 5c (19806-1305)
PHONE.................302 658-7354
Nancy Pancko, *Prin*
EMP: 10 EST: 2016
SALES (est): 493.17K **Privately Held**
Web: www.orthodontistwilmington.com
SIC: 8021 Orthodontist

(G-20828)
WILMINGTON OTLRYNGLOGY ASSOC P
Also Called: Medford, William L Jr MD
2300 Pennsylvania Ave Ste 2a (19806-1379)
PHONE.................302 658-0404
W L Medford Junior Md, *Pr*
Jay D Luft Md, *Prin*
EMP: 8 EST: 1975

SALES (est): 959.93K **Privately Held**
Web: www.entad.org
SIC: 8011 Ears, nose, and throat specialist: physician/surgeon

(G-20829)
WILMINGTON PAIN/REHAB CNTR PA
1021 Gilpin Ave Ste 101 (19806-3271)
PHONE.................302 575-1776
Ross Ufberg, *Pr*
EMP: 6 EST: 1985
SALES (est): 734.8K **Privately Held**
Web: www.wilmpain.com
SIC: 8093 Rehabilitation center, outpatient treatment

(G-20830)
WILMINGTON PARKING AUTHORITY (PA)
625 N Orange St Ste 2c (19801-2250)
PHONE.................302 655-4442
Stanley Soja, *Ex Dir*
Karla Britt, *Dir Opers*
Drew Horseman, *Dir Fin*
EMP: 8 EST: 1951
SQ FT: 5,000
SALES (est): 5.02MM
SALES (corp-wide): 5.02MM **Privately Held**
Web: www.wilmingtonparking.com
SIC: 7521 Parking garage

(G-20831)
WILMINGTON PLICE FIRE FDRAL CR
1701 Shallcross Ave Ste B (19806-2347)
PHONE.................302 654-0818
Evelyn Vega, *Prin*
EMP: 6 EST: 2015
SALES (est): 420.47K **Privately Held**
Web: www.wpffcu.org
SIC: 6061 Federal credit unions

(G-20832)
WILMINGTON REAL ESTATE CO INC
2213 Concord Pike (19803-2908)
PHONE.................302 652-1700
Matt Fish, *Ofcr*
EMP: 5 EST: 2018
SALES (est): 240.78K **Privately Held**
SIC: 6531 Real estate agent, residential

(G-20833)
WILMINGTON RENAISSANCE CORP
100 W 10th St Ste 206 (19801-1632)
PHONE.................302 425-5500
EMP: 5 EST: 1993
SALES (est): 486.05K **Privately Held**
Web: www.bigideaswilmington.com
SIC: 8399 Community development groups

(G-20834)
WILMINGTON ROWING CENTER
501 A St (19801-5327)
PHONE.................302 652-5339
EMP: 5 EST: 2019
SALES (est): 125.79K **Privately Held**
Web: www.wilmingtonrowing.org
SIC: 8641 Civic and social associations

(G-20835)
WILMINGTON SAV FUND SOC FSB
Also Called: Operations Center Branch
500 Delaware Ave (19801-1490)
PHONE.................888 973-7226
Kathy Mccade, *Asstg*
EMP: 2500 EST: 2012
SALES (est): 622.03MM
SALES (corp-wide): 963.95MM **Publicly Held**
Web: www.wsfsbank.com

SIC: 6022 State commercial banks
HQ: Wilmington Savings Fund Society
500 Delaware Ave
Wilmington DE 19801
302 792-6000

(G-20836)
WILMINGTON SAVINGS FUND SOC (HQ)
Also Called: Wilmington Savings Fund Bank
500 Delaware Ave (19801-1490)
PHONE.................302 792-6000
Rodger Levenson, *Pr*
Marvin N Schoenhals, *
Calvert Morgan Junior, *V Ch Bd*
Mark A Turner, *
Joseph Murphy, *
EMP: 150 EST: 1832
SQ FT: 20,000
SALES (est): 924.5MM
SALES (corp-wide): 963.95MM **Publicly Held**
Web: www.wsfsbank.com
SIC: 6022 State commercial banks
PA: Wsfs Financial Corporation
500 Delaware Ave
Wilmington DE 19801
302 792-6000

(G-20837)
WILMINGTON SAVINGS FUND SOC
Also Called: First State Plaza
1600 W Newport Pike (19804-3500)
PHONE.................302 999-1227
EMP: 8
SALES (corp-wide): 641.85MM **Publicly Held**
Web: www.wsfsbank.com
SIC: 6022 State commercial banks
HQ: Wilmington Savings Fund Society
500 Delaware Ave
Wilmington DE 19801
302 792-6000

(G-20838)
WILMINGTON SAVINGS FUND SOC
211 N Union St (19805-3429)
PHONE.................302 571-6508
Meg Thomas, *Brnch Mgr*
EMP: 6
SALES (corp-wide): 963.95MM **Publicly Held**
Web: www.wsfsbank.com
SIC: 6022 State commercial banks
HQ: Wilmington Savings Fund Society
500 Delaware Ave
Wilmington DE 19801
302 792-6000

(G-20839)
WILMINGTON SAVINGS FUND SOC
2005 Concord Pike (19803-2983)
PHONE.................302 571-6500
Steven Agabides, *Brnch Mgr*
EMP: 5
SALES (corp-wide): 963.95MM **Publicly Held**
Web: www.wsfsbank.com
SIC: 6022 State commercial banks
HQ: Wilmington Savings Fund Society
500 Delaware Ave
Wilmington DE 19801
302 792-6000

(G-20840)
WILMINGTON SAVINGS FUND SOC
500 Delaware Ave Ste 3 (19801-7400)
PHONE.................302 571-7090
EMP: 9
SALES (corp-wide): 641.85MM **Publicly Held**

Web: www.wsfsbank.com
SIC: 6022 State commercial banks
HQ: Wilmington Savings Fund Society
500 Delaware Ave
Wilmington DE 19801
302 792-6000

(G-20841)
WILMINGTON SAVINGS FUND SOC
Also Called: Pike Creek Branch
4730 Limestone Rd (19808-1928)
PHONE.................302 633-5700
EMP: 9
SALES (corp-wide): 641.85MM **Publicly Held**
Web: www.wsfsbank.com
SIC: 6035 Federal savings and loan associations
HQ: Wilmington Savings Fund Society
500 Delaware Ave
Wilmington DE 19801
302 792-6000

(G-20842)
WILMINGTON SAVINGS FUND SOC
Also Called: Trolley Square Branch 307
1711 Delaware Ave (19806-2329)
PHONE.................302 571-6516
EMP: 9
SALES (corp-wide): 641.85MM **Publicly Held**
Web: www.wsfsbank.com
SIC: 6035 Federal savings banks
HQ: Wilmington Savings Fund Society
500 Delaware Ave
Wilmington DE 19801
302 792-6000

(G-20843)
WILMINGTON SENIOR CENTER INC (PA)
1901 N Market St (19802-4897)
PHONE.................302 651-3400
Kathleen Purcell, *Ex Dir*
Cynthia Stewart, *Dir Fin*
EMP: 19 EST: 1956
SQ FT: 15,000
SALES (est): 2.79MM
SALES (corp-wide): 2.79MM **Privately Held**
Web: www.wilmingtonseniorcenter.org
SIC: 8322 Senior citizens' center or association

(G-20844)
WILMINGTON SMALL-CAP STRATEGY
1100 N Market St 10th Fl (19890-1100)
PHONE.................302 636-8500
EMP: 5 EST: 2019
SALES (est): 221.6K **Privately Held**
SIC: 6722 Money market mutual funds

(G-20845)
WILMINGTON STONEWORKS LLC
Also Called: Mason Contractor
1908 Elm St (19805-3855)
PHONE.................302 723-7126
EMP: 5 EST: 2011
SALES (est): 192.27K **Privately Held**
Web: www.wilmingtonstoneworks.com
SIC: 1799 Special trade contractors, nec

(G-20846)
WILMINGTON TRUST CLLCTIVE INV
1100 N Market St (19890-1100)
PHONE.................800 724-2440
EMP: 28 EST: 2018
SALES (est): 1.34MM **Privately Held**
Web: www.wilmingtontrust.com

GEOGRAPHIC SECTION
Wilmington - New Castle County (G-20874)

SIC: 6733 Trusts, nec

(G-20847)
WILMINGTON TRUST COMPANY (DH)
1100 N Market St Ste 1300 (19890-1100)
PHONE..................................302 651-1000
Donald Foley, CEO
Michael Spychall, *
William J Farrell, *
Mark A Graham, *
Marie James, *
EMP: 518 **EST:** 1901
SQ FT: 200,000
SALES (est): 322.68MM
SALES (corp-wide): 8.6B **Publicly Held**
Web: www.wilmingtontrust.com
SIC: 6733 Trusts, nec
HQ: Manufacturers And Traders Trust Company
1 M&T Plz Fl 3
Buffalo NY 14203
716 842-4200

(G-20848)
WILMINGTON TRUST FRNKLIN US AG
1100 N Market St 10th Fl (19890-1100)
PHONE..................................302 636-8500
EMP: 6
SALES (est): 106.48K **Privately Held**
Web: www.wilmingtontrust.com
SIC: 6722 Money market mutual funds

(G-20849)
WILMINGTON TRUST SP SERVICES (DH)
1105 N Market St Ste 1300 (19801-1241)
PHONE..................................302 427-7650
Charles Hanlon, VP Fin
EMP: 975 **EST:** 1982
SALES (est): 125.04MM
SALES (corp-wide): 8.6B **Publicly Held**
Web: www.wilmingtontrust.com
SIC: 2711 Newspapers
HQ: Wilmington Trust Company
1100 N Market St Ste 1300
Wilmington DE 19890
302 651-1000

(G-20850)
WILMINGTON TRUST TMPLTON FGN C ✪
1100 N Market St (19890-1100)
PHONE..................................800 724-2440
EMP: 5 **EST:** 2022
SALES (est): 76.37K **Privately Held**
Web: www.wilmingtontrust.com
SIC: 6722 Money market mutual funds

(G-20851)
WILMINGTON TUG INC (PA)
11 Gist Rd Ste 200 (19801-5879)
P.O. Box 389 (19720-0389)
PHONE..................................302 652-1666
Christopher Rowland, Pr
H Hickman Rowland Junior, *
Christopher Rowland, Treas
EMP: 30 **EST:** 1965
SQ FT: 1,600
SALES (est): 6.74MM
SALES (corp-wide): 6.74MM **Privately Held**
Web: www.wilmingtontug.com
SIC: 4492 Marine towing services

(G-20852)
WILMINGTON TURNERS CLUB
Also Called: Wilmington Turners
701 S Clayton St (19805-4214)
PHONE..................................302 658-9011
Thomas Frick, Owner
EMP: 10 **EST:** 1963
SALES (est): 166.18K **Privately Held**
Web: www.turnersde.org
SIC: 7997 Membership sports and recreation clubs

(G-20853)
WILMINGTON YOUTH ORGANIZATION
615 W 37th St (19802-2028)
PHONE..................................302 761-9030
Keith Leke, Pr
EMP: 5 **EST:** 1993
SALES (est): 91.67K **Privately Held**
Web: www.wilmingtonjaycees.org
SIC: 8641 Youth organizations

(G-20854)
WILMINGTON YOUTH ROWING ASSN
500 E Front St Frnt (19801-5017)
PHONE..................................302 777-4533
Faith Pizor, Dir
EMP: 6 **EST:** 1989
SALES (est): 231.77K **Privately Held**
Web: www.wyra.org
SIC: 8699 Athletic organizations

(G-20855)
WIN FROM WTHIN XC CAMP/TATNALL
10 Courtney Rd (19807-2548)
PHONE..................................302 494-5312
Patrick Castagno, Pr
EMP: 5 **EST:** 2014
SALES (est): 44.82K **Privately Held**
SIC: 7032 7389 Summer camp, except day and sports instructional; Business services, nec

(G-20856)
WINDCREST ANIMAL HOSPITAL
3705 Lancaster Pike (19805-1510)
PHONE..................................302 239-9464
Bruce Damme, Owner
EMP: 30 **EST:** 1955
SALES (est): 2.41MM **Privately Held**
Web: www.windcrestanimal.com
SIC: 0742 Animal hospital services, pets and other animal specialties

(G-20857)
WINDOW TREATMENTS & MORE LLC
405 W 34th St (19802-2634)
PHONE..................................302 275-7019
EMP: 2 **EST:** 2018
SALES (est): 90.43K **Privately Held**
SIC: 2591 Drapery hardware and window blinds and shades

(G-20858)
WINGFIELD & ASSOCIATES INC
251 Little Falls Dr (19808-1674)
PHONE..................................626 252-6586
EMP: 7 **EST:** 2019
SALES (est): 707.2K **Privately Held**
SIC: 4581 Airports, flying fields, and services

(G-20859)
WINK TECH LIMITED ✪
300 E Delaware Ave (19809-1515)
PHONE..................................302 268-9232
Yu Wang, CEO
EMP: 5 **EST:** 2023
SALES (est): 199.4K **Privately Held**
SIC: 7371 Computer software development

(G-20860)
WINNER GROUP INC (PA)
911 Tatnall St (19801-1605)
P.O. Box 954 (19899-0954)
PHONE..................................302 764-5900
John Hynansky, Pr
EMP: 12 **EST:** 1980
SQ FT: 10,000
SALES (est): 49.87MM
SALES (corp-wide): 49.87MM **Privately Held**
Web: www.quicklane.com
SIC: 5511 7514 Automobiles, new and used; Rent-a-car service

(G-20861)
WINNER GROUP MANAGEMENT INC (PA)
Also Called: Winner Automotive Group
520 S Walnut St (19801-5230)
PHONE..................................302 571-5200
John Hynansky, Pr
EMP: 16 **EST:** 1984
SQ FT: 10,000
SALES (est): 2.43MM
SALES (corp-wide): 2.43MM **Privately Held**
Web: www.winnerauto.com
SIC: 8742 Business management consultant

(G-20862)
WINNER INFINITI INC
Also Called: Winner Porsche
1300 N Union St (19806-2534)
PHONE..................................302 764-5900
John Hynansky, Pr
EMP: 26 **EST:** 1989
SALES (est): 4.55MM **Privately Held**
Web: www.winnerauto.com
SIC: 5511 5531 7538 Automobiles, new and used; Automotive parts; General automotive repair shops

(G-20863)
WINNER PREMIER COLLISION CTR
520 S Walnut St (19801-5230)
PHONE..................................302 571-5200
John Hynansky, CEO
EMP: 25 **EST:** 1999
SQ FT: 30,000
SALES (est): 925.6K **Privately Held**
Web: www.winnerauto.com
SIC: 7532 Collision shops, automotive

(G-20864)
WINNERS CIRCLE INC
Also Called: Audi Wilmington
1300 N Union St (19806-2534)
PHONE..................................302 661-2100
Michael Hynansky, Pr
EMP: 50 **EST:** 1979
SALES (est): 8.3MM **Privately Held**
Web: www.audiwilmingtonde.com
SIC: 5511 7549 Automobiles, new and used; Automotive maintenance services

(G-20865)
WINTERTHUR MUSEUM
1520 N Rodney St (19806-3008)
PHONE..................................302 740-9771
EMP: 10 **EST:** 2018
SALES (est): 38.53K **Privately Held**
Web: www.winterthur.org
SIC: 8412 Museum

(G-20866)
WIRE 2 WIRE LLC
2711 Centerville Rd # 400 (19808-1660)
PHONE..................................512 684-9100
EMP: 5 **EST:** 2013
SALES (est): 33.14K **Privately Held**
SIC: 4813 Internet connectivity services

(G-20867)
WIT SERVICES LLC
Also Called: Whatever It Takes Services
1174 Elderon Dr (19808-1924)
PHONE..................................302 995-2983
EMP: 6 **EST:** 2004
SALES (est): 686.81K **Privately Held**
SIC: 1522 Hotel/motel and multi-family home renovation and remodeling

(G-20868)
WITHYOUWITHME INC
1209 N Orange St (19801-1120)
PHONE..................................202 377-9743
Sam Baynes, Pr
EMP: 4 **EST:** 2018
SALES (est): 275.55K **Privately Held**
Web: www.withyouwithme.com
SIC: 3699 Security devices

(G-20869)
WL TIMBERS INC
4023 Kennett Pike Ste 54708 (19807-2018)
PHONE..................................843 376-1099
Yash Mehta, Dir
EMP: 4
SALES (corp-wide): 5MM **Privately Held**
SIC: 2499 Logs of sawdust and wood particles, pressed
PA: WI Timbers Inc.
247 Jedburg Rd
Summerville SC 29483
843 376-1099

(G-20870)
WM DELCAMPO MECHANICAL SVCS
2429 Hartley Pl (19808-4258)
PHONE..................................302 543-2725
EMP: 6 **EST:** 2016
SALES (est): 41.33K **Privately Held**
SIC: 7032 Sporting and recreational camps

(G-20871)
WM SYSTEMS INC
2711 Centerville Rd Ste 400 (19808-1660)
PHONE..................................302 450-4482
EMP: 5 **EST:** 2007
SQ FT: 1,000
SALES (est): 797.74K **Privately Held**
SIC: 5082 8734 Oil field equipment; Food testing service

(G-20872)
WMK FINANCING INC
300 Delaware Ave (19801-1607)
PHONE..................................302 576-2697
EMP: 114 **EST:** 2014
SALES (est): 189.85K
SALES (corp-wide): 4.7B **Publicly Held**
SIC: 7389 Financial services
PA: Weis Markets, Inc.
1000 S 2nd St
Sunbury PA 17801
570 286-4571

(G-20873)
WODAQOTA INC
919 N Market St (19801-3023)
PHONE..................................800 246-2677
EMP: 5 **EST:** 2021
SALES (est): 68.89K **Privately Held**
SIC: 7371 Computer software development

(G-20874)
WOHLSEN CONSTRUCTION COMPANY
501 Carr Rd Ste 100 (19809-2866)

Wilmington - New Castle County (G-20875) GEOGRAPHIC SECTION

PHONE.............................302 324-9900
David B Brodie, *Brnch Mgr*
EMP: 11
SALES (corp-wide): 133.13MM **Privately Held**
Web: www.wohlsenconstruction.com
SIC: 1542 1541 8741 School building construction; Industrial buildings, new construction, nec; Construction management
PA: Wohlsen Construction Company Inc
548 Steel Way
Lancaster PA 17601
717 299-2500

(G-20875)
WOLF WOOD WORKS LLC
4 Star Pine Cir (19808-1012)
PHONE.............................302 275-7227
Kevin Creswell, *Prin*
EMP: 5 **EST:** 2016
SALES (est): 64.26K **Privately Held**
SIC: 2431 Millwork

(G-20876)
WOLFGANG M D RADTKE
1600 Rockland Rd (19803-3607)
PHONE.............................302 651-6660
Wolfgang Radtke, *Prin*
EMP: 15 **EST:** 2018
SALES (est): 260.58K **Privately Held**
Web: www.nemours.org
SIC: 8011 Pediatrician

(G-20877)
WOLFS ELITE AUTOS
2130 W Newport Pike (19804-3721)
PHONE.............................302 999-9199
Ryan D Wolf, *Owner*
EMP: 5 **EST:** 2008
SALES (est): 426.32K **Privately Held**
SIC: 7538 5521 General automotive repair shops; Used car dealers

(G-20878)
WOLOSHIN AND LYNCH ASSOCIATES (PA)
3200 Concord Pike (19803-5015)
P.O. Box 7329 (19803-0329)
PHONE.............................302 477-3200
Melvyn Woloshin, *Owner*
James Natalie, *Dir*
David Gagne, *Dir*
EMP: 24 **EST:** 1965
SQ FT: 6,000
SALES (est): 2.19MM
SALES (corp-wide): 2.19MM **Privately Held**
Web: www.wlnglaw.com
SIC: 8111 Bankruptcy referee

(G-20879)
WOMBLE BOND DICKINSON (US) LLP
1313 N Market St Fl 12 (19801-1151)
PHONE.............................302 252-4320
Frank Monaco, *Pt*
EMP: 25
SALES (corp-wide): 218.48MM **Privately Held**
Web: www.womblebonddickinson.com
SIC: 8111 General practice law office
PA: Womble Bond Dickinson (Us) Llp
1 W 4th St
Winston Salem NC 27101
336 721-3600

(G-20880)
WOMEN TO WOMEN OB/GYN ASSOC PA
532 Greenhill Ave (19805-1851)
PHONE.............................302 778-2229
Nancy Fan, *Pr*
EMP: 8 **EST:** 2000
SALES (est): 716.02K **Privately Held**
SIC: 8011 Obstetrician

(G-20881)
WOMENS HEALTH CTR CHRISTN CARE
501 W 14th St (19801-1013)
PHONE.............................302 428-5810
Mary T Lednum, *Dir*
EMP: 22 **EST:** 2002
SALES (est): 424.38K **Privately Held**
Web: www.christianacare.org
SIC: 8062 General medical and surgical hospitals

(G-20882)
WOOD VENEER HUB LIMITED INC
1000 N West St Ste 1281 Pmb 104 (19801-1050)
PHONE.............................302 216-6177
Callum Freed, *Sls Mgr*
Cameron Lewis, *Prin*
Laurence Freed, *Dir*
Harry Conquest, *Dir*
EMP: 7 **EST:** 2020
SALES (est): 2.62MM **Privately Held**
Web: www.thewoodveneerhub.com
SIC: 5031 Paneling, wood

(G-20883)
WOODLAND APARTMENTS LP
Also Called: Woodland Apartments
1201 Centre Rd (19805-1202)
PHONE.............................302 994-9003
Timothy O Fanning, *Pt*
Michael Bonner, *VP*
EMP: 7 **EST:** 1967
SALES (est): 679.2K **Privately Held**
SIC: 6513 Apartment hotel operation

(G-20884)
WOODLAWN TRUSTEES INCORPORATED
1020 N Bancroft Pkwy Ste 200 (19805-2666)
PHONE.............................302 655-6215
Richard Przywara, *CEO*
Jennifer Dembeck, *CFO*
EMP: 15 **EST:** 1902
SQ FT: 2,500
SALES (est): 2.46MM **Privately Held**
Web: www.woodlawntrustees.com
SIC: 6531 6552 Real estate managers; Subdividers and developers, nec

(G-20885)
WOODMILL DENTAL LLC
5185 W Woodmill Dr Ste 2 (19808-4067)
PHONE.............................302 998-8588
John Eum, *Prin*
EMP: 8 **EST:** 2018
SALES (est): 248.62K **Privately Held**
Web: www.woodmilldental.com
SIC: 8021 Dentists' office

(G-20886)
WOODS EDGE APARTMENTS
Also Called: Apartment Communities
1204 Terra Hill Dr Apt 3b (19809-3538)
PHONE.............................302 762-8300
Joetta Keys, *Mgr*
EMP: 5 **EST:** 1962
SALES (est): 343.56K **Privately Held**
SIC: 6513 Apartment building operators

(G-20887)
WOODSON MINISTRIES INC
4613 Big Rock Dr (19802-1001)
PHONE.............................512 350-9950
Brandon Woodson, *Pr*
EMP: 5 **EST:** 2018
SALES (est): 66.88K **Privately Held**
SIC: 8742 Management consulting services

(G-20888)
WOODSTOVES JUNCTION
2222 Silverside Rd (19810-4502)
PHONE.............................302 397-8424
EMP: 5 **EST:** 2017
SALES (est): 94.6K **Privately Held**
Web: woodstove-junction.business.site
SIC: 7699 Repair services, nec

(G-20889)
WOODWORKS
550 Copper Dr (19804-2418)
PHONE.............................302 995-0800
R Heck, *Prin*
EMP: 4 **EST:** 2007
SALES (est): 78.6K **Privately Held**
Web: www.woodworksofwilmington.com
SIC: 2431 Millwork

(G-20890)
WORKAWAY VENTURES INC
1521 Concord Pike Ste 303 (19803-3644)
PHONE.............................843 608-9108
Kerranna Williamson, *Pr*
EMP: 2
SALES (est): 69.51K **Privately Held**
SIC: 2741 Internet publishing and broadcasting

(G-20891)
WORKING TENS INC
300 Delaware Ave Ste 210 (19801-1607)
PHONE.............................612 685-0921
Julia Lull, *CEO*
EMP: 3
SALES (est): 135.7K **Privately Held**
SIC: 3861 Motion picture film

(G-20892)
WORKPRO
6 Larch Ave Ste 397 (19804-2356)
PHONE.............................302 300-4392
EMP: 9 **EST:** 2013
SALES (est): 172.23K **Privately Held**
Web: www.ohsde.org
SIC: 8099 Health and allied services, nec

(G-20893)
WORKROOM ENTERPRISES LLC
300 Delaware Ave Ste 210a (19801-6601)
PHONE.............................417 621-5577
Murphy Mastin, *Managing Member*
EMP: 7 **EST:** 2019
SALES (est): 40K **Privately Held**
SIC: 2834 Dermatologicals

(G-20894)
WORKS BODY WRAP BY TANYA
411 Northwood Rd (19803-3537)
PHONE.............................302 669-7839
Tonya Patton, *Prin*
EMP: 5 **EST:** 2016
SALES (est): 48.67K **Privately Held**
Web: fatfighters.itworks.com
SIC: 7231 Beauty shops

(G-20895)
WORLD AMPTEE FTBALL FEDERATION
1033 Creekside Dr (19804-3924)
PHONE.............................302 383-2665
Richard Hofmann, *Prin*
EMP: 6 **EST:** 2015
SALES (est): 74.96K **Privately Held**
Web: www.usampsoccer.org
SIC: 8641 Civic and social associations

(G-20896)
WORLD WRLESS SOLUTIONS USA INC
300 Delaware Ave Ste 200 (19801-1607)
PHONE.............................877 746-4997
Eduardo Harari, *CEO*
EMP: 5
SALES (est): 104.37K **Privately Held**
Web: www.worldwirelesssolutions.com
SIC: 7379 Computer related consulting services

(G-20897)
WRAPAROUND MARYLAND
105 Rogers Rd Ste A (19801-5619)
P.O. Box 649 (19720-0649)
PHONE.............................302 504-8487
Kimberly Cooke, *Ex Dir*
EMP: 6 **EST:** 2013
SALES (est): 67.42K **Privately Held**
Web: www.wraparoundmd.com
SIC: 8641 Youth organizations

(G-20898)
WRAY LISA MD
1600 Rockland Rd (19803-3607)
PHONE.............................302 651-4000
EMP: 8 **EST:** 2018
SALES (est): 236.81K **Privately Held**
SIC: 8011 Pediatrician

(G-20899)
WRC
100 W 10th St Ste 206 (19801-1632)
PHONE.............................302 425-5500
Jennifer Lawson, *Prin*
EMP: 6 **EST:** 2016
SALES (est): 51.49K **Privately Held**
Web: wrc.udel.edu
SIC: 7997 Membership sports and recreation clubs

(G-20900)
WRENCH PLUMBING
3401 Old Capitol Trl (19808-6123)
PHONE.............................302 482-1043
EMP: 10 **EST:** 2017
SALES (est): 528.51K **Privately Held**
Web: www.wrenchplumbing.com
SIC: 1711 Plumbing contractors

(G-20901)
WS COMPANY
4708 Kirkwood Hwy (19808-5022)
PHONE.............................302 660-8735
EMP: 5 **EST:** 2016
SALES (est): 20.3K **Privately Held**
SIC: 7291 Tax return preparation services

(G-20902)
WSFS FINANCIAL CORPORATION
Also Called: Wsfs Bank
9a Trolley Sq (19806-3334)
PHONE.............................302 571-6516
EMP: 26
SALES (corp-wide): 963.95MM **Publicly Held**
Web: www.wsfsbank.com
SIC: 6022 State commercial banks
PA: Wsfs Financial Corporation
500 Delaware Ave
Wilmington DE 19801
302 792-6000

GEOGRAPHIC SECTION
Wilmington - New Castle County (G-20929)

(G-20903)
WSFS FINANCIAL CORPORATION (PA)
Also Called: Wsfs
500 Delaware Ave (19801-1490)
PHONE..............................302 792-6000
Rodger Levenson, *Ch Bd*
Lisa Brubaker, *CIO*
Arthur J Bacci, *Co-Vice President*
Steve Clark, *Chief Commercial Lending Officer*
EMP: 126 **EST:** 1988
SQ FT: 78,432
SALES (est): 963.95MM
SALES (corp-wide): 963.95MM **Publicly Held**
Web: www.wsfsbank.com
SIC: 6022 State commercial banks

(G-20904)
WSFS INVESTMENT GROUP INC
838 N Market St (19801-3154)
PHONE..............................302 573-3258
Robert Mack, *Ofcr*
EMP: 5 **EST:** 2003
SALES (est): 107.31K
SALES (corp-wide): 963.95MM **Publicly Held**
Web: www.wsfsinvestments.com
SIC: 6799 Investors, nec
PA: Wsfs Financial Corporation
   500 Delaware Ave
   Wilmington DE 19801
   302 792-6000

(G-20905)
WTA INC
Also Called: Altitude Trampoline Park
510 Justison St (19801-5142)
PHONE..............................302 397-8142
Coner Smith, *Brnch Mgr*
EMP: 32
SALES (corp-wide): 2.29MM **Privately Held**
Web: www.altitudetrampolinepark.com
SIC: 7999 Trampoline operation
PA: Wta Inc.
   30174 Foskey Ln
   Delmar MD 21875
   410 896-2219

(G-20906)
WWD INC
Also Called: Miller's Beverage Center
5998 Kirkwood Hwy (19808-4815)
PHONE..............................302 994-4553
William Dickhart, *Pr*
EMP: 6
SALES (corp-wide): 981.01K **Privately Held**
Web: www.wwd.com
SIC: 6512 Nonresidential building operators
PA: Wwd Inc
   31 Wakefield Dr
   Newark DE 19711
   302 994-4553

(G-20907)
WYNDHAM GROUP INC
2207 Concord Pike # 696 (19803-2908)
PHONE..............................704 905-9750
Adam James, *Ex Dir*
EMP: 9 **EST:** 2008
SALES (est): 699.09K **Privately Held**
Web: www.wyndhamgroup.net
SIC: 7379 8742 Computer related consulting services; Management consulting services

(G-20908)
WYRA
206 Hoiland Dr (19803-3230)
PHONE..............................302 777-4533
EMP: 6 **EST:** 2010
SALES (est): 65.15K **Privately Held**
Web: www.wyra.org
SIC: 8699 Charitable organization

(G-20909)
X DIMA INC
2400 W 4th St (19805-3306)
PHONE..............................302 427-0787
Merton Briggs, *Dir*
EMP: 6
SALES (est): 70.95K **Privately Held**
SIC: 8361 Residential care

(G-20910)
X SEAMLESS INC
2055 Limestone Rd (19808-5536)
PHONE..............................650 770-0771
EMP: 5
SALES (est): 68.89K **Privately Held**
SIC: 7371 Computer software development and applications

(G-20911)
X-SENSE USA LLC
1209 N Orange St (19801-1120)
PHONE..............................857 998-3929
EMP: 5
SALES (est): 197.14K **Privately Held**
Web: www.x-sense.com
SIC: 7382 Security systems services

(G-20912)
X5 NETWORKS CORPORATION
1013 Centre Rd Ste 403s (19805-1270)
PHONE..............................800 784-5228
EMP: 6 **EST:** 2017
SALES (est): 151.45K **Privately Held**
Web: www.x5.net
SIC: 7371 7374 Computer software development; Data processing and preparation

(G-20913)
XANDER GROUP II LLC
103 Foulk Rd Ste 202 (19803-3742)
PHONE..............................302 656-1950
EMP: 6 **EST:** 2007
SALES (est): 137.69K **Privately Held**
SIC: 8742 Management consulting services

(G-20914)
XAVIER INC
Also Called: School For Young Children
1315 N Union St (19806-2533)
PHONE..............................302 655-1962
Colleen Conaty, *Pr*
EMP: 9 **EST:** 1999
SALES (est): 259.88K **Privately Held**
Web: www.xavierschoolde.org
SIC: 8351 Preschool center

(G-20915)
XCERTIFIED RESTORE LLC
1708 Tulip St (19805-3933)
PHONE..............................302 330-8850
EMP: 7 **EST:** 2019
SALES (est): 427.3K **Privately Held**
SIC: 1799 Special trade contractors, nec

(G-20916)
XCS CORPORATION
Also Called: Sky Trax
500 Water St (19804-2423)
P.O. Box 184 (19720-0184)
PHONE..............................302 514-0600
Richard Ungerbuehler, *Pr*
Larry G Mahan, *VP*
David C Emanuel, *VP*
EMP: 7 **EST:** 2002
SQ FT: 3,300
SALES (est): 769.25K **Privately Held**
Web: www.sky-trax.com
SIC: 8711 7336 7373 7375 Engineering services; Graphic arts and related design; Computer systems analysis and design; Data base information retrieval

(G-20917)
XEENOM INC
1220 N Market St Ste 60 (19801-2535)
PHONE..............................302 427-6970
Reg Agents Legal Serv, *Asst Sec*
EMP: 6 **EST:** 2002
SALES (est): 44.05K **Privately Held**
SIC: 7389 Business Activities at Non-Commercial Site

(G-20918)
XERAFY INC
3511 Silverside Rd Ste 10 (19810-4902)
PHONE..............................817 938-4197
EMP: 6 **EST:** 2019
SALES (est): 164.48K **Privately Held**
SIC: 3629 7371 Electrical industrial apparatus, nec; Computer software development and applications

(G-20919)
XONEX RELOCATION LLC
2751 Centerville Rd Ste 303 (19808-1632)
P.O. Box 3496 (19804-0496)
PHONE..............................302 323-9000
Katherine Holman, *Pr*
Katherine Holman, *Pr*
Robert B Holman, *
Robert Webster, *
EMP: 65 **EST:** 1995
SALES (est): 9.46MM **Privately Held**
Web: www.xonex.com
SIC: 4212 Moving services

(G-20920)
XTEND INC
427 N Tatnall St 51198 (19801-2230)
PHONE..............................305 204-0595
Patrick Imperato, *CEO*
EMP: 7 **EST:** 2019
SALES (est): 100K **Privately Held**
Web: www.xtendcu.com
SIC: 4724 Travel agencies

(G-20921)
YACHT DELAWARE REGISTRY LTD (HQ)
3511 Silverside Rd Ste 105 (19810-4902)
PHONE..............................302 477-9800
Barbara Stargatt, *Pr*
Daniel Stargatt, *VP*
EMP: 19 **EST:** 1975
SQ FT: 2,600
SALES (est): 2.79MM
SALES (corp-wide): 44.28MM **Privately Held**
SIC: 7389 8742 Marine reporting; Corporation organizing consultant
PA: Corporation Trust Company
   1209 N Orange St
   Wilmington DE 19801
   302 658-7581

(G-20922)
YACHT REGISTRY LTD
3511 Silverside Rd # 105 (19810-4902)
PHONE..............................302 477-9800
EMP: 20 **EST:** 1975
SALES (est): 371.53K
SALES (corp-wide): 5.66B **Privately Held**
SIC: 8111 Corporate, partnership and business law
PA: Wolters Kluwer N.V.
   Zuidpoolsingel 2
   Alphen Aan Den Rijn ZH
   172641400

(G-20923)
YANCI BRAND LLC ✪
1201 N Market St (19801-1147)
PHONE..............................844 242-7263
Lutricia Dillard, *Managing Member*
EMP: 5 **EST:** 2023
SALES (est): 276.99K **Privately Held**
SIC: 8742 Management consulting services

(G-20924)
YARDEX LLC ✪
1201 N Market St Ste 111 (19801-1156)
PHONE..............................302 406-0933
Walid Elhusseiny, *CEO*
EMP: 250 **EST:** 2022
SALES (est): 18.25MM **Privately Held**
SIC: 3523 1799 Turf equipment, commercial; Artificial turf installation

(G-20925)
YEAR UP WLMNGTON MOCK INTRVEWS
1200 N French St Fl 5 (19801-3239)
PHONE..............................302 256-7344
EMP: 10 **EST:** 2018
SALES (est): 55.66K **Privately Held**
Web: www.yearup.org
SIC: 8699 Charitable organization

(G-20926)
YENAFFIT INC ✪
1207 Delaware Ave (19806-4743)
PHONE..............................302 650-4818
Tiffaney Rideaux, *Managing Member*
EMP: 8 **EST:** 2022
SALES (est): 430.26K **Privately Held**
SIC: 7389 8742 7371 Business Activities at Non-Commercial Site; Management consulting services; Software programming applications

(G-20927)
YES HARDSOFT SOLUTIONS INC (PA)
3626 Silverside Rd (19810-5190)
PHONE..............................609 632-0397
Deepak Budaguppe, *Ofcr*
EMP: 55 **EST:** 2014
SALES (est): 1.44MM
SALES (corp-wide): 1.44MM **Privately Held**
Web: www.yesgroups.net
SIC: 7371 7379 Computer software development; Computer related consulting services

(G-20928)
YHP HOLDINGS LLC
251 Little Falls Dr (19808-1674)
PHONE..............................302 636-5401
Eli Hopson, *Prin*
Dewight Flinch, *Prin*
EMP: 5 **EST:** 2017
SIC: 6719 Holding companies, nec

(G-20929)
YMCA CENTRAL BRANCH LLC
Also Called: YMCA
501 W 11th St Ste 100 (19801-6408)
PHONE..............................302 571-6950
Jonathan Gershen, *VP*
EMP: 10 **EST:** 2015

Wilmington - New Castle County (G-20930)   GEOGRAPHIC SECTION

SALES (est): 488K **Privately Held**
Web: www.ymcade.org
SIC: 8641 Youth organizations

(G-20930)
YOCHANAN EL BEY
Also Called: Donum Adeo
3616 Kirkwood Hwy (19808-5124)
PHONE..............................610 726-4493
Yochanan El Bey, *Pt*
EMP: 5 EST: 2018
SALES (est): 108.31K **Privately Held**
SIC: 8399 Social services, nec

(G-20931)
YOMBU EVENTS INC ✪
Also Called: Yombu
2810 N Church St Pm72783 (19802-4447)
PHONE..............................385 406-3651
Seth Van Oudtshoorn, *CMO*
Rose Novotry, *CEO*
EMP: 20 EST: 2023
SALES (est): 285.56K **Privately Held**
SIC: 7929 Entertainment service

(G-20932)
YOUNG & RUBICAM LLC
201 N Walnut St Ste 1005 (19801-2920)
PHONE..............................302 888-3450
Terry W Dukes, *Brnch Mgr*
EMP: 15
SALES (corp-wide): 17.37B **Privately Held**
Web: www.vmlyr.com
SIC: 7311 Advertising agencies
HQ: Young & Rubicam Llc
175 Greenwich St Fl 28
New York NY 10007
212 210-3017

(G-20933)
YOUNG CNWAY STRGATT TAYLOR LLP (PA)
Also Called: Young, Conaway & Associates
1000 N King St (19801-3335)
P.O. Box 391 (19899-0391)
PHONE..............................302 571-6600
Bruce M Stargatt, *Pt*
William F Taylor, *OF*
Sheldon A Weinstein, *Mng Pt*
▲ EMP: 225 EST: 1955
SQ FT: 20,000
SALES (est): 38.89MM
SALES (corp-wide): 38.89MM **Privately Held**
Web: www.youngconaway.com
SIC: 8111 General practice law office

(G-20934)
YOUNG LOGISTICS LLC
100 Fulton St (19805-3525)
P.O. Box 26072 (19899-6072)
PHONE..............................302 232-3034
EMP: 5 EST: 2016
SALES (est): 387.79K **Privately Held**
SIC: 4212 Local trucking, without storage

(G-20935)
YOUNG MENS CHRISTIAN ASSN
501 Silverside Rd Ste 43 (19809-1388)
PHONE..............................302 571-6925
J Mix, *Asstg*
EMP: 5 EST: 2018
SALES (est): 218.41K **Privately Held**
SIC: 6411 Insurance agents, brokers, and service

(G-20936)
YOUNG MENS CHRISTIAN ASSN DEL (PA)
Also Called: ASSOCIATION BUSINESS OFFICE
100 W 10th St Ste 1100 (19801-6607)
PHONE..............................302 571-6968
Jarrett Royster, *CEO*
Jim Kelley, *Pr*
Joseph E Johnson, *V Ch Bd*
Lynn Jones, *Ch*
William Farrell Ii, *V Ch Bd*
EMP: 21 EST: 1889
SQ FT: 123,000
SALES (est): 40.98MM
SALES (corp-wide): 40.98MM **Privately Held**
Web: www.ymcade.org
SIC: 7011 7997 YMCA/YMHA hotel; Membership sports and recreation clubs

(G-20937)
YOUNG MENS CHRISTIAN ASSN DEL
Also Called: YMCA
501 W 11th St Ste 100 (19801-6408)
PHONE..............................302 571-6900
Michael Graves, *Pr*
EMP: 149
SALES (corp-wide): 40.98MM **Privately Held**
Web: www.ymcade.org
SIC: 8361 8351 8322 7997 Residential care; Child day care services; Individual and family services; Membership sports and recreation clubs
PA: Young Men's Christian Association Of Delaware
100 W 10th St Ste 1100
Wilmington DE 19801
302 571-6968

(G-20938)
YOUNG MENS CHRISTIAN ASSN DEL
Also Called: Walnut Street Y M C A
1000 N Walnut St (19801-3339)
PHONE..............................302 571-6935
Jack Booker, *Ex Dir*
EMP: 99
SALES (corp-wide): 40.98MM **Privately Held**
Web: www.ymcade.org
SIC: 7997 7991 Membership sports and recreation clubs; Physical fitness facilities
PA: Young Men's Christian Association Of Delaware
100 W 10th St Ste 1100
Wilmington DE 19801
302 571-6968

(G-20939)
YOUNG MENS CHRISTIAN ASSOCIAT
Also Called: Resource Center YMCA
1000 N Walnut St (19801-3339)
PHONE..............................302 472-9622
EMP: 10
SALES (corp-wide): 40.98MM **Privately Held**
Web: www.ymcade.org
SIC: 7999 7991 Recreation services; Physical fitness facilities
PA: Young Men's Christian Association Of Delaware
100 W 10th St Ste 1100
Wilmington DE 19801
302 571-6968

(G-20940)
YOUR DENTISTRY TODAY INC
3801 Kennett Pike Ste E207 # 207 (19807-2340)
P.O. Box 4480 (19807-0480)
PHONE..............................302 575-0100
Michael Matthias, *Prin*
EMP: 5 EST: 2009
SALES (est): 362.38K **Privately Held**
Web: www.yourdentistry.com
SIC: 8021 Dentists' office

(G-20941)
YUPICA INC (USA)
3411 Silverside Rd Ste 104 (19810-4812)
PHONE..............................707 387-9874
Sean Stewart, *Pr*
EMP: 9 EST: 2019
SALES (est): 2.21MM
SALES (corp-wide): 18.34MM **Privately Held**
SIC: 5141 Food brokers
PA: Yupi.Ca Inc.
993 Princess St Suite 200
Kingston ON K7L 1
855 438-9874

(G-20942)
YWCA DELAWARE (PA)
100 W 10th St Ste 515 (19801-6610)
PHONE..............................302 655-0039
Genevieve Marino, *Ex Dir*
EMP: 72 EST: 1896
SALES (est): 3.87MM
SALES (corp-wide): 3.87MM **Privately Held**
Web: www.ywcade.org
SIC: 7991 8641 Physical fitness facilities; Civic and social associations

(G-20943)
YWY INCORPORATED
919 N Market St Ste 950 (19801-3036)
PHONE..............................916 794-1607
Peter Dunning, *Ch Bd*
EMP: 7 EST: 2019
SALES (est): 361.82K **Privately Held**
SIC: 8742 Management consulting services

(G-20944)
Z&M ENTERPRISES LLC
1521 Concord Pike Ste 301 (19803-3644)
PHONE..............................302 384-1205
EMP: 20 EST: 2021
SALES (est): 543.25K **Privately Held**
SIC: 7311 Advertising consultant

(G-20945)
ZACHARY CHIPMAN DMD PA
5505 Kirkwood Hwy (19808-5001)
PHONE..............................302 994-8696
Zachary Chipman, *Prin*
EMP: 5 EST: 2008
SALES (est): 496.56K **Privately Held**
Web: www.dentistwilmingtonde.com
SIC: 8021 Dentists' office

(G-20946)
ZAMOLXIS LLC
300 De Ave (19801-1607)
PHONE..............................571 286-0413
Felix Milea-ciobanu, *Managing Member*
EMP: 13
SALES (corp-wide): 20K **Privately Held**
SIC: 7371 Computer software development and applications
PA: Zamolxis Llc
261 Dorland St
San Francisco CA 94114
571 286-0413

(G-20947)
ZAREK DONOHUE LLC
Also Called: Progressive Health of Delaware
3411 Silverside Rd Ste 100 (19810-4812)
PHONE..............................302 543-5454
EMP: 21 EST: 2005
SALES (est): 1.69MM **Privately Held**
Web: www.progressivehealthproject.com

SIC: 8011 Internal medicine practitioners

(G-20948)
ZAVIER J DECAIRE
Also Called: New York Life
300 Delaware Ave Ste 814 (19801)
PHONE..............................302 658-0218
Zavier J Decaire, *Pt*
Donald Fulton, *Pt*
Terry Wolf, *Pt*
EMP: 11 EST: 2001
SALES (est): 269.6K **Privately Held**
Web: www.newyorklife.com
SIC: 6411 Insurance agents and brokers

(G-20949)
ZEBRAFISH DISEASE MODELS SOC
1209 N Orange St (19801-1120)
PHONE..............................518 399-7181
Jill De Jong, *Treas*
EMP: 5 EST: 2018
SALES (est): 100.96K **Privately Held**
Web: www.zdmsociety.org
SIC: 8621 Professional organizations

(G-20950)
ZEN ACUPUNCTURE CLINIC
30 Weilers Bnd (19810-4156)
PHONE..............................302 559-1325
Dong Song, *Prin*
EMP: 6 EST: 2017
SALES (est): 80.06K **Privately Held**
SIC: 8099 Health and allied services, nec

(G-20951)
ZEN THERAPY & BODYWORK INC
201 S Maryland Ave (19804-1343)
PHONE..............................302 252-1733
Yuezhen Zhang, *Asst Sec*
EMP: 7 EST: 2018
SALES (est): 87.9K **Privately Held**
SIC: 8093 Rehabilitation center, outpatient treatment

(G-20952)
ZENCITY TECHNOLOGIES US INC ✪
1313 N Market St Ste 5100 (19801-6111)
PHONE..............................347 632-1225
Eyal Feder, *CEO*
EMP: 6 EST: 2022
SALES (est): 255.91K **Privately Held**
Web: www.zencity.io
SIC: 7371 Computer software development

(G-20953)
ZENECA HOLDINGS INC (HQ)
Also Called: Astra Zeneca Pharmaceuticals
1800 Concord Pike (19897-0001)
P.O. Box 15437 (19850-5437)
PHONE..............................302 886-3000
Jonathan R Symonds, *Ch Bd*
David R Brennan, *Pr*
▲ EMP: 54 EST: 1993
SQ FT: 1,200,000
SALES (est): 69.78MM
SALES (corp-wide): 44.35B **Privately Held**
SIC: 2899 2834 Chemical preparations, nec; Druggists' preparations (pharmaceuticals)
PA: Astrazeneca Plc
1 Francis Crick Avenue
Cambridge CAMBS CB2 0
203 749-5000

(G-20954)
ZENECA INC (DH)
1800 Concord Pike (19897-0001)
PHONE..............................302 886-3000
Steven Mohr, *Ch*
David E White, *Treas*
Mark Uhle, *CFO*

▲ = Import ▼ = Export
◆ = Import/Export

EMP: 5 **EST:** 1971
SQ FT: 1,200,000
SALES (est): 48.08MM
SALES (corp-wide): 44.35B **Privately Held**
SIC: 2834 Pharmaceutical preparations
HQ: Zeneca Holdings Inc.
1800 Concord Pike
Wilmington DE 19897
302 886-3000

(G-20955)
ZENITH MIND INC
1201 N Market St Ste 111-A (19801-1147)
PHONE 302 543-2075
Samik Sharma, *Prin*
EMP: 10 **EST:** 2021
SALES (est): 363K **Privately Held**
Web: www.zenithmind.com
SIC: 8742 Management consulting services

(G-20956)
ZEPHYR ALUMINUM LLC
50 Germay Dr Ste 2 (19804-1187)
PHONE 302 571-0585
Tom Tankersley, *Mgr*
EMP: 5
SALES (corp-wide): 9.83MM **Privately Held**
Web: www.zephyraluminum.com
SIC: 1793 Glass and glazing work
PA: Zephyr Aluminum, Llc
1539 Fannie Dorsey Rd
Sykesville MD 21784
717 397-3618

(G-20957)
ZERODAYLAB LLC
3524 Silverside Rd Ste 35b (19810-4929)
PHONE 302 498-8322
EMP: 5 **EST:** 2019
SALES (est): 305.94K **Privately Held**
Web: www.zdlgroup.com
SIC: 7379 Computer related consulting services

(G-20958)
ZEROWAIT CORPORATION
707 Kirkwood Hwy (19805-5110)
PHONE 302 996-9408
EMP: 15 **EST:** 1989
SQ FT: 7,000
SALES (est): 3.03MM **Privately Held**
Web: www.zerowait.com
SIC: 7378 3572 Computer maintenance and repair; Computer storage devices

(G-20959)
ZETWERK MANUFACTURING USA INC
3411 Silverside Rd Ste 104 (19810-4812)
PHONE 520 720-3085
Srinath Ramakkrushnan, *Pr*
EMP: 5 **EST:** 2021
SALES (est): 2.41MM **Privately Held**
Web: www.zetwerk.com
SIC: 3569 Filters, general line: industrial
PA: Zetwerk Manufacturing Businesses Private Limited
No. 461, Oriental Towers, 1st & 2nd Floor,
Bengaluru KA 56010

(G-20960)
ZEUSS LLC (PA)
1209 N Orange St (19801-1120)
PHONE 305 904-8078
Jonas Siuksta, *CEO*
EMP: 9 **EST:** 2020
SALES (est): 424.35K
SALES (corp-wide): 424.35K **Privately Held**

SIC: 8099 Nutrition services

(G-20961)
ZIETA TECHNOLOGIES LLC (PA)
501 Silverside Rd Ste 39 (19809-1388)
PHONE 302 252-5249
EMP: 36 **EST:** 2002
SALES (est): 4.75MM **Privately Held**
Web: www.zietatech.com
SIC: 8748 Business consulting, nec

(G-20962)
ZILLA FINANCE INC
2055 Limestone Rd Ste 200c (19808-5536)
PHONE 213 645-2133
Tolu Abiodun, *CEO*
EMP: 22
SALES (est): 629.49K **Privately Held**
SIC: 7371 Computer software development and applications

(G-20963)
ZONGURU HOLDINGS INC
1013 Centre Rd Ste 403b (19805-1270)
PHONE 310 266-1427
Jonathan Tilley, *Prin*
EMP: 50
SALES (est): 1.14MM **Privately Held**
Web: www.zonguru.com
SIC: 7371 Computer software development and applications

(G-20964)
ZOOM INNOVATIONS INC
Also Called: Zoom Zoom
251 Little Falls Dr (19808-1674)
PHONE 416 677-7288
Walid Al Hilaly, *CEO*
EMP: 5 **EST:** 2021
SALES (est): 100K **Privately Held**
SIC: 4789 Transportation services, nec

(G-20965)
ZR TACTICAL OUTFITTERS LLC
12 Glenbarry Dr (19808-1366)
PHONE 302 353-9818
EMP: 5 **EST:** 2013
SALES (est): 96.09K **Privately Held**
SIC: 7999 Outfitters, recreation

(G-20966)
ZRCN INC (PA)
2711 Centerville Rd # 400 (19808-1660)
PHONE 212 602-1188
Kenneth Charles Grainger, *Pr*
EMP: 70 **EST:** 2018
SALES (est): 6.67K
SALES (corp-wide): 6.67K **Privately Held**
SIC: 3691 Storage batteries

(G-20967)
ZUBER & ASSOCIATES INC
Also Called: Omega Physical Therapy
16 Burnett Dr (19810-2205)
PHONE 302 478-1618
Peter Zuber, *Pr*
EMP: 5 **EST:** 1989
SQ FT: 1,300
SALES (est): 132.1K **Privately Held**
SIC: 8049 Physiotherapist

(G-20968)
ZUMBA
16 Gristmill Ct (19803-4951)
PHONE 215 870-9867
Beth Sanchez, *Prin*
EMP: 8 **EST:** 2016
SALES (est): 20.78K **Privately Held**
Web: www.zumba.com

SIC: 7999 Racquetball club, non-membership

(G-20969)
ZUTZ RISK MANAGEMENT
300 Delaware Ave Ste 1600 (19801-1612)
PHONE 302 658-8000
Harry Zutz, *Owner*
EMP: 5 **EST:** 1999
SALES (est): 123.12K **Privately Held**
SIC: 8742 Management consulting services

(G-20970)
ZWALLY BROWN LISA
1105 N Market St Fl 15 (19801-1201)
PHONE 302 504-7803
Lisa Brown, *Prin*
EMP: 5 **EST:** 2001
SALES (est): 78.14K **Privately Held**
SIC: 8111 General practice attorney, lawyer

(G-20971)
ZYNG NAILS
3828 Kennett Pike (19807-2320)
PHONE 302 407-3849
EMP: 5 **EST:** 2014
SALES (est): 61.31K **Privately Held**
Web: www.zyngnailspa.com
SIC: 7231 Manicurist, pedicurist

Winterthur
New Castle County

(G-20972)
HENRY FRNCIS DPONT WNTRTHUR MS
Also Called: Winterthur Museum & Cntry Est
5105 Kennett Pike (19735-1819)
PHONE 302 888-4852
David Roselle, *Dir*
▲ **EMP:** 160 **EST:** 1930
SALES (est): 25.88MM **Privately Held**
Web: www.winterthur.org
SIC: 8412 Museum

(G-20973)
WINTERTHUR MUSEUM GARDEN & LIB
5105 Kennett Pike (19735-0002)
PHONE 302 888-4600
Carol B Cadou, *CEO*
Leslie Bowman, *
▲ **EMP:** 40 **EST:** 1980
SALES (est): 8.39MM **Privately Held**
Web: www.winterthur.org
SIC: 8412 Museum

Woodside
Kent County

(G-20974)
BULLDOG CONSTRUCTION
177 Jaacs Ln (19980-8000)
PHONE 302 632-4834
Samuel A Frank, *Prin*
EMP: 5 **EST:** 2015
SALES (est): 128.45K **Privately Held**
Web: www.bulldogcontractingde.com
SIC: 1521 Single-family housing construction

(G-20975)
DELAWARE LISTER
9 Fleming St (19980-8007)
PHONE 302 382-7059
EMP: 5 **EST:** 2018
SALES (est): 69.86K **Privately Held**
Web: www.delawarelister.com

SIC: 5099 Durable goods, nec

(G-20976)
ERICS HANDYMAN & LDSCPG SVCS
351 Tuxedo Ln (19980-8020)
PHONE 302 242-7712
Eric Battin, *Prin*
EMP: 5 **EST:** 2008
SALES (est): 59.8K **Privately Held**
SIC: 0781 Landscape services

(G-20977)
K & R GRAPHICS & SIGNS INC
1685 Main St (19980)
P.O. Box 384 (19980-0384)
PHONE 302 697-7725
Karen Johnson, *Pr*
EMP: 2 **EST:** 1991
SALES (est): 227.66K **Privately Held**
Web: www.krgraphicsigns.com
SIC: 3993 Signs and advertising specialties

(G-20978)
KRITTER SITTER
P.O. Box 162 (19980-0162)
PHONE 302 270-0963
Karen Kaufman, *Prin*
EMP: 5 **EST:** 2011
SALES (est): 46.7K **Privately Held**
Web: www.dekrittersitter.com
SIC: 0752 Grooming services, pet and animal specialties

Wyoming
Kent County

(G-20979)
A NOD TO STELLA EMBROIDERY
120 Pine St (19934-1142)
PHONE 302 697-6308
Barbara Menden, *Prin*
EMP: 4 **EST:** 2014
SALES (est): 46.17K **Privately Held**
SIC: 2395 Embroidery and art needlework

(G-20980)
AQUANTUO LLC
148 Southern Blvd (19934-1152)
PHONE 302 753-0435
EMP: 6 **EST:** 2016
SALES (est): 340.03K **Privately Held**
Web: www.aquantuo.com
SIC: 4789 Transportation services, nec

(G-20981)
CAMDEN DRYWALL INC
203 Harrison Ave (19934-1175)
PHONE 302 697-9653
Richard C Greene Junior, *Pr*
Florence Greene, *Sec*
Richard C Greene Senior, *VP*
EMP: 6 **EST:** 1991
SALES (est): 479.24K **Privately Held**
SIC: 1742 Drywall

(G-20982)
CORN EXCHANGE LLC
105 Harrison Ave (19934-1104)
PHONE 302 747-8752
EMP: 5 **EST:** 2015
SALES (est): 82K **Privately Held**
SIC: 5963 7389 Food service, mobile, except coffee-cart; Business services, nec

(G-20983)
DELMARVA POLE BUILDING SUP INC
317 N Layton Ave (19934-1235)
PHONE 302 698-3636

Frederick Ruhe, *Prin*
EMP: 9 **EST:** 2000
SALES (est): 5.55MM **Privately Held**
Web: www.ilovepolebuildings.com
SIC: 1542 Nonresidential construction, nec

(G-20984)
DELMARVA TRUSS AND PANEL LLC
317 N Layton Ave (19934-1235)
PHONE.................................302 270-8888
Vernon Beachy, *Prin*
EMP: 7 **EST:** 2015
SALES (est): 117.36K **Privately Held**
SIC: 2439 Structural wood members, nec

(G-20985)
G DAVID OUTTEN LLC
114 E Third St (19934-1166)
PHONE.................................302 747-4932
EMP: 5 **EST:** 2017
SALES (est): 103.91K **Privately Held**
SIC: 1522 Residential construction, nec

(G-20986)
IMPARTS INC
Also Called: Avenue Imparts
100 N Railroad Ave (19934-1024)
PHONE.................................302 697-0990
Kevin Maier, *Pr*
EMP: 6 **EST:** 1985
SQ FT: 4,000
SALES (est): 913.63K **Privately Held**
Web: www.avenueimparts.com
SIC: 5013 Automotive supplies and parts

(G-20987)
KRAMER KONSTRUCTION
317 N Layton Ave (19934-1235)
PHONE.................................717 466-6500
Joe Kramer, *CEO*
EMP: 8 **EST:** 2009
SALES (est): 216.06K **Privately Held**
Web: www.ilovepolebuildings.com
SIC: 1542 1522 Nonresidential construction, nec; Residential construction, nec

(G-20988)
QUALITY CONTRACTING INC
317 N Layton Ave (19934-1235)
PHONE.................................302 270-8888
Vernon Beachy, *Owner*
EMP: 6 **EST:** 2017
SALES (est): 58.79K **Privately Held**
Web: www.qualitycontracting.us
SIC: 1799 Special trade contractors, nec

(G-20989)
QUALITY GARAGE
317 N Layton Ave (19934-1235)
PHONE.................................302 678-3667
Fredrik Ruhe, *Pr*
EMP: 8 **EST:** 2016
SALES (est): 289.53K **Privately Held**
Web: www.itrustquality.com
SIC: 1751 Garage door, installation or erection

(G-20990)
SIMPLY CHARMING
2 S Railroad Ave (19934-1026)
PHONE.................................302 697-7377
Barbara Gooden, *Prin*
EMP: 5 **EST:** 2010
SALES (est): 179.91K **Privately Held**
SIC: 5099 Antiques

Yorklyn
New Castle County

(G-20991)
DAVIS-YOUNG ASSOCIATES INC (PA)
2896 Creek Rd (19736-9714)
P.O. Box 451 (19710-0451)
PHONE.................................610 388-0932
Zachary Davis, *Pr*
EMP: 8 **EST:** 1984
SQ FT: 1,000
SALES (est): 997.38K **Privately Held**
SIC: 0782 1741 Landscape contractors; Masonry and other stonework

(G-20992)
GENTLEMAN DOOR COMPANY INC
506 Dawson Tract Rd (19736)
P.O. Box 77 (19736-0077)
PHONE.................................302 239-4045
Ann Strab, *Pr*
Thomas Strab, *VP*
Tom Strab, *VP*
EMP: 2 **EST:** 1994
SALES (est): 155K **Privately Held**
SIC: 3699 Door opening and closing devices, electrical

(G-20993)
INFORMATION CONSULTANTS INC
Also Called: Infocon
2851 Creek Rd (19736-9715)
P.O. Box 303 (19736-0303)
PHONE.................................302 239-2942
Fernan Dominguez, *Pr*
Lester Smalley, *VP*
EMP: 11 **EST:** 1971
SQ FT: 4,600
SALES (est): 499.86K **Privately Held**
SIC: 7374 Data processing and preparation

(G-20994)
WHITTINGTON & AULGUR (PA)
2979 Barley Mill Rd (19736-9702)
PHONE.................................302 235-5800
Thomas D Whittington Junior, *Pt*
Robert Aulgar, *Pt*
EMP: 8 **EST:** 1984
SALES (est): 2.32MM
SALES (corp-wide): 2.32MM **Privately Held**
SIC: 8111 General practice attorney, lawyer

(G-20995)
YORKLYN STORYTELLING FESTIVAL
1155 Yorklyn Rd (19736)
PHONE.................................302 238-6200
Michael Wright, *Ex Dir*
Carlos Alejandro, *Treas*
Terry Foreman, *Sec*
David Scott, *Dir*
Leslie Kedash, *Dir*
EMP: 6 **EST:** 2019
SALES (est): 89.12K **Privately Held**
Web: www.yorklynstoryfest.com
SIC: 7922 Theatrical producers and services

SIC INDEX

Standard Industrial Classification Alphabetical Index

SIC NO   PRODUCT

A

3291 Abrasive products
6321 Accident and health insurance
8721 Accounting, auditing, and bookkeeping
2891 Adhesives and sealants
7322 Adjustment and collection services
9611 Administration of general economic programs
9431 Administration of public health programs
9441 Administration of social and manpower programs
9451 Administration of veterans' affairs
7311 Advertising agencies
7319 Advertising, nec
2879 Agricultural chemicals, nec
3563 Air and gas compressors
4513 Air courier services
4522 Air transportation, nonscheduled
4512 Air transportation, scheduled
3721 Aircraft
3724 Aircraft engines and engine parts
3728 Aircraft parts and equipment, nec
4581 Airports, flying fields, and services
2812 Alkalies and chlorine
3354 Aluminum extruded products
3365 Aluminum foundries
3353 Aluminum sheet, plate, and foil
7999 Amusement and recreation, nec
7996 Amusement parks
3826 Analytical instruments
2077 Animal and marine fats and oils
0279 Animal specialties, nec
0752 Animal specialty services
6513 Apartment building operators
2389 Apparel and accessories, nec
3446 Architectural metalwork
8712 Architectural services
7694 Armature rewinding shops
2952 Asphalt felts and coatings
2951 Asphalt paving mixtures and blocks
5531 Auto and home supply stores
7533 Auto exhaust system repair shops
3581 Automatic vending machines
7521 Automobile parking
5012 Automobiles and other motor vehicles
2396 Automotive and apparel trimmings
5599 Automotive dealers, nec
7536 Automotive glass replacement shops
7539 Automotive repair shops, nec
7549 Automotive services, nec
7537 Automotive transmission repair shops

B

2673 Bags: plastic, laminated, and coated
2674 Bags: uncoated paper and multiwall
3562 Ball and roller bearings
6712 Bank holding companies
7241 Barber shops
7231 Beauty shops
0212 Beef cattle, except feedlots
5181 Beer and ale
2836 Biological products, except diagnostic
2782 Blankbooks and looseleaf binders
3312 Blast furnaces and steel mills
3564 Blowers and fans
5551 Boat dealers
3732 Boatbuilding and repairing
3452 Bolts, nuts, rivets, and washers
2732 Book printing
2731 Book publishing
5942 Book stores
2789 Bookbinding and related work
5192 Books, periodicals, and newspapers
8422 Botanical and zoological gardens
2086 Bottled and canned soft drinks
7933 Bowling centers
2051 Bread, cake, and related products
5032 Brick, stone, and related material

1622 Bridge, tunnel, and elevated highway
2211 Broadwoven fabric mills, cotton
2221 Broadwoven fabric mills, manmade
0251 Broiler, fryer, and roaster chickens
3991 Brooms and brushes
7349 Building maintenance services, nec
4142 Bus charter service, except local
4173 Bus terminal and service facilities
8244 Business and secretarial schools
8611 Business associations
8748 Business consulting, nec
7389 Business services, nec

C

4841 Cable and other pay television services
5946 Camera and photographic supply stores
2064 Candy and other confectionery products
5441 Candy, nut, and confectionery stores
2091 Canned and cured fish and seafoods
2033 Canned fruits and specialties
2032 Canned specialties
2394 Canvas and related products
3624 Carbon and graphite products
3955 Carbon paper and inked ribbons
1751 Carpentry work
7217 Carpet and upholstery cleaning
2273 Carpets and rugs
7542 Carwashes
0119 Cash grains, nec
5961 Catalog and mail-order houses
2823 Cellulosic manmade fibers
6553 Cemetery subdividers and developers
3253 Ceramic wall and floor tile
2022 Cheese; natural and processed
1479 Chemical and fertilizer mining
2899 Chemical preparations, nec
5169 Chemicals and allied products, nec
0252 Chicken eggs
8351 Child day care services
5641 Children's and infants' wear stores
2066 Chocolate and cocoa products
8641 Civic and social associations
1459 Clay and related minerals, nec
3255 Clay refractories
5052 Coal and other minerals and ores
1241 Coal mining services
7993 Coin-operated amusement devices
7215 Coin-operated laundries and cleaning
3316 Cold finishing of steel shapes
8221 Colleges and universities
4939 Combination utilities, nec
7336 Commercial art and graphic design
6029 Commercial banks, nec
5046 Commercial equipment, nec
3582 Commercial laundry equipment
3646 Commercial lighting fixtures
8732 Commercial nonphysical research
7335 Commercial photography
8731 Commercial physical research
2754 Commercial printing, gravure
2752 Commercial printing, lithographic
2759 Commercial printing, nec
6221 Commodity contracts brokers, dealers
4899 Communication services, nec
3669 Communications equipment, nec
5734 Computer and software stores
7376 Computer facilities management
7373 Computer integrated systems design
7378 Computer maintenance and repair
3577 Computer peripheral equipment, nec
7379 Computer related services, nec
7377 Computer rental and leasing
3572 Computer storage devices
3575 Computer terminals
5045 Computers, peripherals, and software
3271 Concrete block and brick

3272 Concrete products, nec
1771 Concrete work
5145 Confectionery
5082 Construction and mining machinery
3531 Construction machinery
5039 Construction materials, nec
1442 Construction sand and gravel
2679 Converted paper products, nec
3535 Conveyors and conveying equipment
2052 Cookies and crackers
1021 Copper ores
2298 Cordage and twine
0115 Corn
9223 Correctional institutions
2653 Corrugated and solid fiber boxes
3961 Costume jewelry
4215 Courier services, except by air
9211 Courts
2021 Creamery butter
7323 Credit reporting services
0722 Crop harvesting
0721 Crop planting and protection
0723 Crop preparation services for market
1311 Crude petroleum and natural gas
4612 Crude petroleum pipelines
1429 Crushed and broken stone, nec
3643 Current-carrying wiring devices
2391 Curtains and draperies
7371 Custom computer programming services
3281 Cut stone and stone products
3421 Cutlery
2865 Cyclic crudes and intermediates

D

0241 Dairy farms
5143 Dairy products, except dried or canned
7911 Dance studios, schools, and halls
7374 Data processing and preparation
8243 Data processing schools
0175 Deciduous tree fruits
4424 Deep sea domestic transportation of freight
4412 Deep sea foreign transportation of freight
4481 Deep sea passenger transportation, except ferry
2034 Dehydrated fruits, vegetables, soups
3843 Dental equipment and supplies
8072 Dental laboratories
5311 Department stores
7381 Detective and armored car services
2835 Diagnostic substances
2675 Die-cut paper and board
1411 Dimension stone
7331 Direct mail advertising services
5963 Direct selling establishments
7342 Disinfecting and pest control services
2085 Distilled and blended liquors
2047 Dog and cat food
2591 Drapery hardware and blinds and shades
1381 Drilling oil and gas wells
5813 Drinking places
5122 Drugs, proprietaries, and sundries
2023 Dry, condensed, evaporated products
7216 Drycleaning plants, except rugs
5099 Durable goods, nec
6514 Dwelling operators, except apartments

E

5812 Eating places
4931 Electric and other services combined
3634 Electric housewares and fans
3641 Electric lamps
4911 Electric services
5063 Electrical apparatus and equipment
5064 Electrical appliances, television and radio
3699 Electrical equipment and supplies, nec
3629 Electrical industrial apparatus
7629 Electrical repair shops

SIC INDEX

SIC NO	PRODUCT
1731	Electrical work
3845	Electromedical equipment
3313	Electrometallurgical products
3675	Electronic capacitors
3677	Electronic coils and transformers
3679	Electronic components, nec
3571	Electronic computers
5065	Electronic parts and equipment, nec
8211	Elementary and secondary schools
3534	Elevators and moving stairways
7361	Employment agencies
3694	Engine electrical equipment
8711	Engineering services
7929	Entertainers and entertainment groups
3822	Environmental controls
7359	Equipment rental and leasing, nec
1794	Excavation work
9111	Executive offices

F

SIC NO	PRODUCT
2381	Fabric dress and work gloves
3499	Fabricated metal products, nec
3498	Fabricated pipe and fittings
3443	Fabricated plate work (boiler shop)
3069	Fabricated rubber products, nec
3441	Fabricated structural metal
2399	Fabricated textile products, nec
8744	Facilities support services
5651	Family clothing stores
5083	Farm and garden machinery
3523	Farm machinery and equipment
0762	Farm management services
5191	Farm supplies
5159	Farm-product raw materials, nec
3965	Fasteners, buttons, needles, and pins
6111	Federal and federally sponsored credit
6061	Federal credit unions
6035	Federal savings institutions
1061	Ferroalloy ores, except vanadium
2875	Fertilizers, mixing only
0139	Field crops, except cash grain
9311	Finance, taxation, and monetary policy
2261	Finishing plants, cotton
2262	Finishing plants, manmade
2269	Finishing plants, nec
9224	Fire protection
6331	Fire, marine, and casualty insurance
5146	Fish and seafoods
3211	Flat glass
2087	Flavoring extracts and syrups, nec
5713	Floor covering stores
1752	Floor laying and floor work, nec
5992	Florists
2041	Flour and other grain mill products
5193	Flowers and florists supplies
3824	Fluid meters and counting devices
2026	Fluid milk
3594	Fluid power pumps and motors
3492	Fluid power valves and hose fittings
0182	Food crops grown under cover
2099	Food preparations, nec
3556	Food products machinery
5139	Footwear
3149	Footwear, except rubber, nec
6081	Foreign bank and branches and agencies
6082	Foreign trade and international banks
0851	Forestry services
4731	Freight transportation arrangement
5148	Fresh fruits and vegetables
2092	Fresh or frozen packaged fish
2037	Frozen fruits and vegetables
2038	Frozen specialties, nec
5431	Fruit and vegetable markets
0179	Fruits and tree nuts, nec
5983	Fuel oil dealers
6099	Functions related to depository banking
7261	Funeral service and crematories
5021	Furniture
2599	Furniture and fixtures, nec
5712	Furniture stores

G

SIC NO	PRODUCT
3944	Games, toys, and children's vehicles
7212	Garment pressing and cleaners' agents
4932	Gas and other services combined
4925	Gas production and/or distribution
4923	Gas transmission and distribution
3053	Gaskets; packing and sealing devices
5541	Gasoline service stations
7538	General automotive repair shops
0291	General farms, primarily animals
0191	General farms, primarily crop
9199	General government, nec
3569	General industrial machinery,
8062	General medical and surgical hospitals
4225	General warehousing and storage
5947	Gift, novelty, and souvenir shop
2361	Girl's and children's dresses, blouses
2369	Girl's and children's outerwear, nec
1793	Glass and glazing work
5153	Grain and field beans
3321	Gray and ductile iron foundries
2771	Greeting cards
5149	Groceries and related products, nec
5141	Groceries, general line
5411	Grocery stores
3761	Guided missiles and space vehicles

H

SIC NO	PRODUCT
3423	Hand and edge tools, nec
3996	Hard surface floor coverings, nec
5072	Hardware
5251	Hardware stores
3429	Hardware, nec
2426	Hardwood dimension and flooring mills
2435	Hardwood veneer and plywood
2353	Hats, caps, and millinery
8099	Health and allied services, nec
3433	Heating equipment, except electric
7353	Heavy construction equipment rental
1629	Heavy construction, nec
7363	Help supply services
1611	Highway and street construction
5945	Hobby, toy, and game shops
0213	Hogs
6719	Holding companies, nec
8082	Home health care services
5023	Homefurnishings
0272	Horses and other equines
2252	Hosiery, nec
6324	Hospital and medical service plans
7011	Hotels and motels
5722	Household appliance stores
3639	Household appliances, nec
3651	Household audio and video equipment
3631	Household cooking equipment
2392	Household furnishings, nec
2519	Household furniture, nec
3633	Household laundry equipment
3635	Household vacuum cleaners
0971	Hunting, trapping, game propagation

I

SIC NO	PRODUCT
2024	Ice cream and frozen deserts
8322	Individual and family services
5113	Industrial and personal service paper
1541	Industrial buildings and warehouses
3567	Industrial furnaces and ovens
2813	Industrial gases
2819	Industrial inorganic chemicals, nec
7218	Industrial launderers
5084	Industrial machinery and equipment
3599	Industrial machinery, nec
2869	Industrial organic chemicals, nec
1446	Industrial sand
5085	Industrial supplies
3537	Industrial trucks and tractors
3491	Industrial valves
7375	Information retrieval services
2816	Inorganic pigments
4785	Inspection and fixed facilities
1796	Installing building equipment
3825	Instruments to measure electricity
6411	Insurance agents, brokers, and service
6399	Insurance carriers, nec
4131	Intercity and rural bus transportation
8052	Intermediate care facilities
3519	Internal combustion engines, nec
6282	Investment advice
6726	Investment offices, nec
6799	Investors, nec
0134	Irish potatoes
3462	Iron and steel forgings
1011	Iron ores
4971	Irrigation systems

J

SIC NO	PRODUCT
3915	Jewelers' materials and lapidary work
5094	Jewelry and precious stones
5944	Jewelry stores
3911	Jewelry, precious metal
8331	Job training and related services
8222	Junior colleges

K

SIC NO	PRODUCT
8092	Kidney dialysis centers
2253	Knit outerwear mills
2254	Knit underwear mills

L

SIC NO	PRODUCT
8631	Labor organizations
3821	Laboratory apparatus and furniture
2258	Lace and warp knit fabric mills
3083	Laminated plastics plate and sheet
9512	Land, mineral, and wildlife conservation
0781	Landscape counseling and planning
7219	Laundry and garment services, nec
3524	Lawn and garden equipment
0782	Lawn and garden services
3151	Leather gloves and mittens
3199	Leather goods, nec
3111	Leather tanning and finishing
8111	Legal services
8231	Libraries
6311	Life insurance
3648	Lighting equipment, nec
7213	Linen supply
5984	Liquefied petroleum gas dealers
5921	Liquor stores
0751	Livestock services, except veterinary
6163	Loan brokers
4111	Local and suburban transit
4141	Local bus charter service
4119	Local passenger transportation, nec
4214	Local trucking with storage
4212	Local trucking, without storage
2411	Logging
2992	Lubricating oils and greases
3161	Luggage
5211	Lumber and other building materials
5031	Lumber, plywood, and millwork

M

SIC NO	PRODUCT
3545	Machine tool accessories
3541	Machine tools, metal cutting type
3542	Machine tools, metal forming type
3695	Magnetic and optical recording media
2083	Malt
2082	Malt beverages
8742	Management consulting services
6722	Management investment, open-ended
8741	Management services
2761	Manifold business forms
2097	Manufactured ice
3999	Manufacturing industries, nec
4493	Marinas
4491	Marine cargo handling
3953	Marking devices
1741	Masonry and other stonework
2515	Mattresses and bedsprings
3829	Measuring and controlling devices, nec
3586	Measuring and dispensing pumps
5421	Meat and fish markets
2011	Meat packing plants
5147	Meats and meat products
5047	Medical and hospital equipment

SIC INDEX

SIC NO	PRODUCT
7352	Medical equipment rental
8071	Medical laboratories
2833	Medicinals and botanicals
8699	Membership organizations, nec
7997	Membership sports and recreation clubs
7041	Membership-basis organization hotels
5136	Men's and boy's clothing
2329	Men's and boy's clothing, nec
2321	Men's and boy's furnishings
2323	Men's and boy's neckwear
2311	Men's and boy's suits and coats
2325	Men's and boy's trousers and slacks
2326	Men's and boy's work clothing
5611	Men's and boys' clothing stores
5962	Merchandising machine operators
3411	Metal cans
3479	Metal coating and allied services
3442	Metal doors, sash, and trim
3398	Metal heat treating
2514	Metal household furniture
1081	Metal mining services
1099	Metal ores, nec
3469	Metal stampings, nec
5051	Metals service centers and offices
3549	Metalworking machinery, nec
2431	Millwork
3296	Mineral wool
3295	Minerals, ground or treated
3532	Mining machinery
5699	Miscellaneous apparel and accessories
6159	Miscellaneous business credit
3496	Miscellaneous fabricated wire products
5499	Miscellaneous food stores
5399	Miscellaneous general merchandise
5719	Miscellaneous homefurnishings
0919	Miscellaneous marine products
3449	Miscellaneous metalwork
1499	Miscellaneous nonmetallic mining
7299	Miscellaneous personal services
2741	Miscellaneous publishing
5999	Miscellaneous retail stores, nec
5271	Mobile home dealers
6515	Mobile home site operators
2451	Mobile homes
6162	Mortgage bankers and correspondents
7822	Motion picture and tape distribution
7812	Motion picture and video production
7829	Motion picture distribution services
7832	Motion picture theaters, except drive-in
3714	Motor vehicle parts and accessories
5015	Motor vehicle parts, used
5013	Motor vehicle supplies and new parts
3711	Motor vehicles and car bodies
5571	Motorcycle dealers
3751	Motorcycles, bicycles, and parts
3621	Motors and generators
8412	Museums and art galleries
5736	Musical instrument stores
3931	Musical instruments

N

SIC NO	PRODUCT
2441	Nailed wood boxes and shook
2241	Narrow fabric mills
6021	National commercial banks
9711	National security
4924	Natural gas distribution
1321	Natural gas liquids
5511	New and used car dealers
7383	News syndicates
2711	Newspapers
2873	Nitrogenous fertilizers
3297	Nonclay refractories
8733	Noncommercial research organizations
6091	Nondeposit trust facilities
5199	Nondurable goods, nec
3463	Nonferrous forgings
3369	Nonferrous foundries, nec
3356	Nonferrous rolling and drawing, nec
3357	Nonferrous wiredrawing and insulating
3299	Nonmetallic mineral products,
1481	Nonmetallic mineral services
6512	Nonresidential building operators
1542	Nonresidential construction, nec
2297	Nonwoven fabrics
8059	Nursing and personal care, nec

O

SIC NO	PRODUCT
5044	Office equipment
2522	Office furniture, except wood
3579	Office machines, nec
8041	Offices and clinics of chiropractors
8021	Offices and clinics of dentists
8011	Offices and clinics of medical doctors
8042	Offices and clinics of optometrists
8031	Offices and clinics of osteopathic physicians
8043	Offices and clinics of podiatrists
8049	Offices of health practitioner
1382	Oil and gas exploration services
3533	Oil and gas field machinery
1389	Oil and gas field services, nec
1531	Operative builders
3851	Ophthalmic goods
5048	Ophthalmic goods
5995	Optical goods stores
3827	Optical instruments and lenses
3489	Ordnance and accessories, nec
2824	Organic fibers, noncellulosic
0181	Ornamental nursery products
0783	Ornamental shrub and tree services
7312	Outdoor advertising services

P

SIC NO	PRODUCT
5142	Packaged frozen goods
3565	Packaging machinery
4783	Packing and crating
5231	Paint, glass, and wallpaper stores
1721	Painting and paper hanging
2851	Paints and allied products
5198	Paints, varnishes, and supplies
2621	Paper mills
2671	Paper; coated and laminated packaging
2672	Paper; coated and laminated, nec
2542	Partitions and fixtures, except wood
7515	Passenger car leasing
7514	Passenger car rental
6794	Patent owners and lessors
6371	Pension, health, and welfare funds
2721	Periodicals
6141	Personal credit institutions
2999	Petroleum and coal products, nec
5171	Petroleum bulk stations and terminals
5172	Petroleum products, nec
2911	Petroleum refining
2834	Pharmaceutical preparations
2874	Phosphatic fertilizers
7334	Photocopying and duplicating services
7384	Photofinish laboratories
3861	Photographic equipment and supplies
5043	Photographic equipment and supplies
7221	Photographic studios, portrait
7991	Physical fitness facilities
2035	Pickles, sauces, and salad dressings
5131	Piece goods and notions
1742	Plastering, drywall, and insulation
3085	Plastics bottles
3086	Plastics foam products
5162	Plastics materials and basic shapes
2821	Plastics materials and resins
3088	Plastics plumbing fixtures
3089	Plastics products, nec
2796	Platemaking services
3471	Plating and polishing
2395	Pleating and stitching
5074	Plumbing and hydronic heating supplies
3432	Plumbing fixture fittings and trim
1711	Plumbing, heating, air-conditioning
9221	Police protection
2842	Polishes and sanitation goods
8651	Political organizations
3264	Porcelain electrical supplies
2096	Potato chips and similar snacks
3269	Pottery products, nec
5144	Poultry and poultry products
0254	Poultry hatcheries
2015	Poultry slaughtering and processing
7211	Power laundries, family and commercial
3568	Power transmission equipment, nec
3546	Power-driven handtools
3448	Prefabricated metal buildings
2452	Prefabricated wood buildings
7372	Prepackaged software
2048	Prepared feeds, nec
3652	Prerecorded records and tapes
3229	Pressed and blown glass, nec
3692	Primary batteries, dry and wet
3399	Primary metal products
3672	Printed circuit boards
2893	Printing ink
3555	Printing trades machinery
3823	Process control instruments
3231	Products of purchased glass
5049	Professional equipment, nec
8621	Professional organizations
8063	Psychiatric hospitals
2531	Public building and related furniture
7992	Public golf courses
8743	Public relations services
2611	Pulp mills
3561	Pumps and pumping equipment

R

SIC NO	PRODUCT
7948	Racing, including track operation
3663	Radio and t.v. communications equipment
7622	Radio and television repair
4832	Radio broadcasting stations
5731	Radio, television, and electronic stores
7313	Radio, television, publisher representatives
4812	Radiotelephone communication
3743	Railroad equipment
4011	Railroads, line-haul operating
3273	Ready-mixed concrete
6531	Real estate agents and managers
6798	Real estate investment trusts
6519	Real property lessors, nec
2493	Reconstituted wood products
5735	Record and prerecorded tape stores
5561	Recreational vehicle dealers
4222	Refrigerated warehousing and storage
3585	Refrigeration and heating equipment
5078	Refrigeration equipment and supplies
7623	Refrigeration service and repair
4953	Refuse systems
9621	Regulation, administration of transportation
9651	Regulation, miscellaneous commercial sectors
3625	Relays and industrial controls
8661	Religious organizations
4741	Rental of railroad cars
7699	Repair services, nec
8361	Residential care
1522	Residential construction, nec
3645	Residential lighting fixtures
5461	Retail bakeries
5261	Retail nurseries and garden stores
7641	Reupholstery and furniture repair
2095	Roasted coffee
5033	Roofing, siding, and insulation
1761	Roofing, siding, and sheetmetal work
7021	Rooming and boarding houses
3052	Rubber and plastics hose and beltings

S

SIC NO	PRODUCT
2068	Salted and roasted nuts and seeds
2656	Sanitary food containers
2676	Sanitary paper products
4959	Sanitary services, nec
2013	Sausages and other prepared meats
6036	Savings institutions, except federal
2421	Sawmills and planing mills, general
3596	Scales and balances, except laboratory
4151	School buses
8299	Schools and educational services
5093	Scrap and waste materials
3451	Screw machine products
3812	Search and navigation equipment
3341	Secondary nonferrous metals
7338	Secretarial and court reporting

SIC INDEX

SIC NO	PRODUCT
6231	Security and commodity exchanges
6289	Security and commodity service
6211	Security brokers and dealers
7382	Security systems services
3674	Semiconductors and related devices
3263	Semivitreous table and kitchenware
5087	Service establishment equipment
3589	Service industry machinery, nec
7819	Services allied to motion pictures
8999	Services, nec
4952	Sewerage systems
5949	Sewing, needlework, and piece goods
3444	Sheet metalwork
3731	Shipbuilding and repairing
7251	Shoe repair and shoeshine parlors
5661	Shoe stores
6153	Short-term business credit
3993	Signs and advertising specialties
3914	Silverware and plated ware
1521	Single-family housing construction
8051	Skilled nursing care facilities
3484	Small arms
3482	Small arms ammunition
2841	Soap and other detergents
8399	Social services, nec
0711	Soil preparation services
0116	Soybeans
9661	Space research and technology
3544	Special dies, tools, jigs, and fixtures
3559	Special industry machinery, nec
1799	Special trade contractors, nec
4226	Special warehousing and storage, nec
8069	Specialty hospitals, except psychiatric
8093	Specialty outpatient clinics, nec
3566	Speed changers, drives, and gears
3949	Sporting and athletic goods, nec
5091	Sporting and recreation goods
7032	Sporting and recreational camps
5941	Sporting goods and bicycle shops
7941	Sports clubs, managers, and promoters
6022	State commercial banks
6062	State credit unions
5112	Stationery and office supplies
5943	Stationery stores
3324	Steel investment foundries
3317	Steel pipe and tubes
3493	Steel springs, except wire
3315	Steel wire and related products
3691	Storage batteries
3259	Structural clay products, nec
1791	Structural steel erection
2439	Structural wood members, nec
6552	Subdividers and developers, nec
6351	Surety insurance
2843	Surface active agents
3841	Surgical and medical instruments
3842	Surgical appliances and supplies
8713	Surveying services
3613	Switchgear and switchboard apparatus
2822	Synthetic rubber

T

SIC NO	PRODUCT
3795	Tanks and tank components
7291	Tax return preparation services
4121	Taxicabs
4822	Telegraph and other communications
3661	Telephone and telegraph apparatus
4813	Telephone communication, except radio
4833	Television broadcasting stations
1743	Terrazzo, tile, marble, mosaic work
8734	Testing laboratories
2393	Textile bags
2299	Textile goods, nec
7922	Theatrical producers and services
2282	Throwing and winding mills
0811	Timber tracts
7534	Tire retreading and repair shops
3011	Tires and inner tubes
5014	Tires and tubes
6541	Title abstract offices
6361	Title insurance
5194	Tobacco and tobacco products
5993	Tobacco stores and stands
2844	Toilet preparations
7532	Top and body repair and paint shops
4725	Tour operators
4492	Towing and tugboat service
5092	Toys and hobby goods and supplies
7033	Trailer parks and campsites
3612	Transformers, except electric
5088	Transportation equipment and supplies
3799	Transportation equipment, nec
4789	Transportation services, nec
4724	Travel agencies
0173	Tree nuts
3713	Truck and bus bodies
7513	Truck rental and leasing, without drivers
3715	Truck trailers
4231	Trucking terminal facilities
4213	Trucking, except local
6733	Trusts, nec
6732	Trusts: educational, religious, etc.
3511	Turbines and turbine generator sets
2791	Typesetting

U

SIC NO	PRODUCT
3081	Unsupported plastics film and sheet
3082	Unsupported plastics profile shapes
2512	Upholstered household furniture
9532	Urban and community development
5521	Used car dealers
5932	Used merchandise stores
7519	Utility trailer rental

V

SIC NO	PRODUCT
3494	Valves and pipe fittings, nec
5331	Variety stores
0161	Vegetables and melons
3647	Vehicular lighting equipment
0741	Veterinary services for livestock
0742	Veterinary services, specialties
7841	Video tape rental
3262	Vitreous china table and kitchenware
3261	Vitreous plumbing fixtures
8249	Vocational schools, nec

W

SIC NO	PRODUCT
5075	Warm air heating and air conditioning
7631	Watch, clock, and jewelry repair
3873	Watches, clocks, watchcases, and parts
4489	Water passenger transportation
4941	Water supply
4449	Water transportation of freight
1781	Water well drilling
1623	Water, sewer, and utility lines
2385	Waterproof outerwear
7692	Welding repair
2046	Wet corn milling
0111	Wheat
5182	Wine and distilled beverages
2084	Wines, brandy, and brandy spirits
3495	Wire springs
5632	Women's accessory and specialty stores
5137	Women's and children's clothing
2341	Women's and children's underwear
2331	Women's and misses' blouses and shirts
2339	Women's and misses' outerwear, nec
5621	Women's clothing stores
3171	Women's handbags and purses
2335	Women's, junior's, and misses' dresses
2449	Wood containers, nec
2511	Wood household furniture
2434	Wood kitchen cabinets
2521	Wood office furniture
2448	Wood pallets and skids
2541	Wood partitions and fixtures
2491	Wood preserving
2499	Wood products, nec
2517	Wood television and radio cabinets
1795	Wrecking and demolition work

X

SIC NO	PRODUCT
3844	X-ray apparatus and tubes

SIC INDEX

Standard Industrial Classification Numerical Index

| SIC NO | PRODUCT |

01 agricultural production - crops

0111 Wheat
0115 Corn
0116 Soybeans
0119 Cash grains, nec
0134 Irish potatoes
0139 Field crops, except cash grain
0161 Vegetables and melons
0173 Tree nuts
0175 Deciduous tree fruits
0179 Fruits and tree nuts, nec
0181 Ornamental nursery products
0182 Food crops grown under cover
0191 General farms, primarily crop

02 agricultural production - livestock and animal specialties

0212 Beef cattle, except feedlots
0213 Hogs
0241 Dairy farms
0251 Broiler, fryer, and roaster chickens
0252 Chicken eggs
0254 Poultry hatcheries
0272 Horses and other equines
0279 Animal specialties, nec
0291 General farms, primarily animals

07 agricultural services

0711 Soil preparation services
0721 Crop planting and protection
0722 Crop harvesting
0723 Crop preparation services for market
0741 Veterinary services for livestock
0742 Veterinary services, specialties
0751 Livestock services, except veterinary
0752 Animal specialty services
0762 Farm management services
0781 Landscape counseling and planning
0782 Lawn and garden services
0783 Ornamental shrub and tree services

08 forestry

0811 Timber tracts
0851 Forestry services

09 fishing, hunting and trapping

0919 Miscellaneous marine products
0971 Hunting, trapping, game propagation

10 metal mining

1011 Iron ores
1021 Copper ores
1061 Ferroalloy ores, except vanadium
1081 Metal mining services
1099 Metal ores, nec

12 coal mining

1241 Coal mining services

13 oil and gas extraction

1311 Crude petroleum and natural gas
1321 Natural gas liquids
1381 Drilling oil and gas wells
1382 Oil and gas exploration services
1389 Oil and gas field services, nec

14 mining and quarrying of nonmetallic minerals, except fuels

1411 Dimension stone
1429 Crushed and broken stone, nec
1442 Construction sand and gravel
1446 Industrial sand
1459 Clay and related minerals, nec
1479 Chemical and fertilizer mining
1481 Nonmetallic mineral services

1499 Miscellaneous nonmetallic mining

15 construction - general contractors & operative builders

1521 Single-family housing construction
1522 Residential construction, nec
1531 Operative builders
1541 Industrial buildings and warehouses
1542 Nonresidential construction, nec

16 heamy construction, except building construction, contractor

1611 Highway and street construction
1622 Bridge, tunnel, and elevated highway
1623 Water, sewer, and utility lines
1629 Heavy construction, nec

17 construction - special trade contractors

1711 Plumbing, heating, air-conditioning
1721 Painting and paper hanging
1731 Electrical work
1741 Masonry and other stonework
1742 Plastering, drywall, and insulation
1743 Terrazzo, tile, marble, mosaic work
1751 Carpentry work
1752 Floor laying and floor work, nec
1761 Roofing, siding, and sheetmetal work
1771 Concrete work
1781 Water well drilling
1791 Structural steel erection
1793 Glass and glazing work
1794 Excavation work
1795 Wrecking and demolition work
1796 Installing building equipment
1799 Special trade contractors, nec

20 food and kindred products

2011 Meat packing plants
2013 Sausages and other prepared meats
2015 Poultry slaughtering and processing
2021 Creamery butter
2022 Cheese; natural and processed
2023 Dry, condensed, evaporated products
2024 Ice cream and frozen deserts
2026 Fluid milk
2032 Canned specialties
2033 Canned fruits and specialties
2034 Dehydrated fruits, vegetables, soups
2035 Pickles, sauces, and salad dressings
2037 Frozen fruits and vegetables
2038 Frozen specialties, nec
2041 Flour and other grain mill products
2046 Wet corn milling
2047 Dog and cat food
2048 Prepared feeds, nec
2051 Bread, cake, and related products
2052 Cookies and crackers
2064 Candy and other confectionery products
2066 Chocolate and cocoa products
2068 Salted and roasted nuts and seeds
2077 Animal and marine fats and oils
2082 Malt beverages
2083 Malt
2084 Wines, brandy, and brandy spirits
2085 Distilled and blended liquors
2086 Bottled and canned soft drinks
2087 Flavoring extracts and syrups, nec
2091 Canned and cured fish and seafoods
2092 Fresh or frozen packaged fish
2095 Roasted coffee
2096 Potato chips and similar snacks
2097 Manufactured ice
2099 Food preparations, nec

22 textile mill products

2211 Broadwoven fabric mills, cotton
2221 Broadwoven fabric mills, manmade
2241 Narrow fabric mills
2252 Hosiery, nec
2253 Knit outerwear mills
2254 Knit underwear mills
2258 Lace and warp knit fabric mills
2261 Finishing plants, cotton
2262 Finishing plants, manmade
2269 Finishing plants, nec
2273 Carpets and rugs
2282 Throwing and winding mills
2297 Nonwoven fabrics
2298 Cordage and twine
2299 Textile goods, nec

23 apparel, finished products from fabrics & similar materials

2311 Men's and boy's suits and coats
2321 Men's and boy's furnishings
2323 Men's and boy's neckwear
2325 Men's and boy's trousers and slacks
2326 Men's and boy's work clothing
2329 Men's and boy's clothing, nec
2331 Women's and misses' blouses and shirts
2335 Women's, junior's, and misses' dresses
2339 Women's and misses' outerwear, nec
2341 Women's and children's underwear
2353 Hats, caps, and millinery
2361 Girl's and children's dresses, blouses
2369 Girl's and children's outerwear, nec
2381 Fabric dress and work gloves
2385 Waterproof outerwear
2389 Apparel and accessories, nec
2391 Curtains and draperies
2392 Household furnishings, nec
2393 Textile bags
2394 Canvas and related products
2395 Pleating and stitching
2396 Automotive and apparel trimmings
2399 Fabricated textile products, nec

24 lumber and wood products, except furniture

2411 Logging
2421 Sawmills and planing mills, general
2426 Hardwood dimension and flooring mills
2431 Millwork
2434 Wood kitchen cabinets
2435 Hardwood veneer and plywood
2439 Structural wood members, nec
2441 Nailed wood boxes and shook
2448 Wood pallets and skids
2449 Wood containers, nec
2451 Mobile homes
2452 Prefabricated wood buildings
2491 Wood preserving
2493 Reconstituted wood products
2499 Wood products, nec

25 furniture and fixtures

2511 Wood household furniture
2512 Upholstered household furniture
2514 Metal household furniture
2515 Mattresses and bedsprings
2517 Wood television and radio cabinets
2519 Household furniture, nec
2521 Wood office furniture
2522 Office furniture, except wood
2531 Public building and related furniture
2541 Wood partitions and fixtures
2542 Partitions and fixtures, except wood
2591 Drapery hardware and blinds and shades
2599 Furniture and fixtures, nec

26 paper and allied products

SIC INDEX

SIC NO	PRODUCT
2611	Pulp mills
2621	Paper mills
2653	Corrugated and solid fiber boxes
2656	Sanitary food containers
2671	Paper; coated and laminated packaging
2672	Paper; coated and laminated, nec
2673	Bags: plastic, laminated, and coated
2674	Bags: uncoated paper and multiwall
2675	Die-cut paper and board
2676	Sanitary paper products
2679	Converted paper products, nec

27 printing, publishing and allied industries

SIC NO	PRODUCT
2711	Newspapers
2721	Periodicals
2731	Book publishing
2732	Book printing
2741	Miscellaneous publishing
2752	Commercial printing, lithographic
2754	Commercial printing, gravure
2759	Commercial printing, nec
2761	Manifold business forms
2771	Greeting cards
2782	Blankbooks and looseleaf binders
2789	Bookbinding and related work
2791	Typesetting
2796	Platemaking services

28 chemicals and allied products

SIC NO	PRODUCT
2812	Alkalies and chlorine
2813	Industrial gases
2816	Inorganic pigments
2819	Industrial inorganic chemicals, nec
2821	Plastics materials and resins
2822	Synthetic rubber
2823	Cellulosic manmade fibers
2824	Organic fibers, noncellulosic
2833	Medicinals and botanicals
2834	Pharmaceutical preparations
2835	Diagnostic substances
2836	Biological products, except diagnostic
2841	Soap and other detergents
2842	Polishes and sanitation goods
2843	Surface active agents
2844	Toilet preparations
2851	Paints and allied products
2865	Cyclic crudes and intermediates
2869	Industrial organic chemicals, nec
2873	Nitrogenous fertilizers
2874	Phosphatic fertilizers
2875	Fertilizers, mixing only
2879	Agricultural chemicals, nec
2891	Adhesives and sealants
2893	Printing ink
2899	Chemical preparations, nec

29 petroleum refining and related industries

SIC NO	PRODUCT
2911	Petroleum refining
2951	Asphalt paving mixtures and blocks
2952	Asphalt felts and coatings
2992	Lubricating oils and greases
2999	Petroleum and coal products, nec

30 rubber and miscellaneous plastic products

SIC NO	PRODUCT
3011	Tires and inner tubes
3052	Rubber and plastics hose and beltings
3053	Gaskets; packing and sealing devices
3069	Fabricated rubber products, nec
3081	Unsupported plastics film and sheet
3082	Unsupported plastics profile shapes
3083	Laminated plastics plate and sheet
3085	Plastics bottles
3086	Plastics foam products
3088	Plastics plumbing fixtures
3089	Plastics products, nec

31 leather and leather products

SIC NO	PRODUCT
3111	Leather tanning and finishing
3149	Footwear, except rubber, nec
3151	Leather gloves and mittens
3161	Luggage
3171	Women's handbags and purses
3199	Leather goods, nec

32 stone, clay, glass, and concrete products

SIC NO	PRODUCT
3211	Flat glass
3229	Pressed and blown glass, nec
3231	Products of purchased glass
3253	Ceramic wall and floor tile
3255	Clay refractories
3259	Structural clay products, nec
3261	Vitreous plumbing fixtures
3262	Vitreous china table and kitchenware
3263	Semivitreous table and kitchenware
3264	Porcelain electrical supplies
3269	Pottery products, nec
3271	Concrete block and brick
3272	Concrete products, nec
3273	Ready-mixed concrete
3281	Cut stone and stone products
3291	Abrasive products
3295	Minerals, ground or treated
3296	Mineral wool
3297	Nonclay refractories
3299	Nonmetallic mineral products,

33 primary metal industries

SIC NO	PRODUCT
3312	Blast furnaces and steel mills
3313	Electrometallurgical products
3315	Steel wire and related products
3316	Cold finishing of steel shapes
3317	Steel pipe and tubes
3321	Gray and ductile iron foundries
3324	Steel investment foundries
3341	Secondary nonferrous metals
3353	Aluminum sheet, plate, and foil
3354	Aluminum extruded products
3356	Nonferrous rolling and drawing, nec
3357	Nonferrous wiredrawing and insulating
3365	Aluminum foundries
3369	Nonferrous foundries, nec
3398	Metal heat treating
3399	Primary metal products

34 fabricated metal products

SIC NO	PRODUCT
3411	Metal cans
3421	Cutlery
3423	Hand and edge tools, nec
3429	Hardware, nec
3432	Plumbing fixture fittings and trim
3433	Heating equipment, except electric
3441	Fabricated structural metal
3442	Metal doors, sash, and trim
3443	Fabricated plate work (boiler shop)
3444	Sheet metalwork
3446	Architectural metalwork
3448	Prefabricated metal buildings
3449	Miscellaneous metalwork
3451	Screw machine products
3452	Bolts, nuts, rivets, and washers
3462	Iron and steel forgings
3463	Nonferrous forgings
3469	Metal stampings, nec
3471	Plating and polishing
3479	Metal coating and allied services
3482	Small arms ammunition
3484	Small arms
3489	Ordnance and accessories, nec
3491	Industrial valves
3492	Fluid power valves and hose fittings
3493	Steel springs, except wire
3494	Valves and pipe fittings, nec
3495	Wire springs
3496	Miscellaneous fabricated wire products
3498	Fabricated pipe and fittings
3499	Fabricated metal products, nec

35 industrial and commercial machinery and computer equipment

SIC NO	PRODUCT
3511	Turbines and turbine generator sets
3519	Internal combustion engines, nec
3523	Farm machinery and equipment
3524	Lawn and garden equipment
3531	Construction machinery
3532	Mining machinery
3533	Oil and gas field machinery
3534	Elevators and moving stairways
3535	Conveyors and conveying equipment
3537	Industrial trucks and tractors
3541	Machine tools, metal cutting type
3542	Machine tools, metal forming type
3544	Special dies, tools, jigs, and fixtures
3545	Machine tool accessories
3546	Power-driven handtools
3549	Metalworking machinery, nec
3555	Printing trades machinery
3556	Food products machinery
3559	Special industry machinery, nec
3561	Pumps and pumping equipment
3562	Ball and roller bearings
3563	Air and gas compressors
3564	Blowers and fans
3565	Packaging machinery
3566	Speed changers, drives, and gears
3567	Industrial furnaces and ovens
3568	Power transmission equipment, nec
3569	General industrial machinery,
3571	Electronic computers
3572	Computer storage devices
3575	Computer terminals
3577	Computer peripheral equipment, nec
3579	Office machines, nec
3581	Automatic vending machines
3582	Commercial laundry equipment
3585	Refrigeration and heating equipment
3586	Measuring and dispensing pumps
3589	Service industry machinery, nec
3594	Fluid power pumps and motors
3596	Scales and balances, except laboratory
3599	Industrial machinery, nec

36 electronic & other electrical equipment & components

SIC NO	PRODUCT
3612	Transformers, except electric
3613	Switchgear and switchboard apparatus
3621	Motors and generators
3624	Carbon and graphite products
3625	Relays and industrial controls
3629	Electrical industrial apparatus
3631	Household cooking equipment
3633	Household laundry equipment
3634	Electric housewares and fans
3635	Household vacuum cleaners
3639	Household appliances, nec
3641	Electric lamps
3643	Current-carrying wiring devices
3645	Residential lighting fixtures
3646	Commercial lighting fixtures
3647	Vehicular lighting equipment
3648	Lighting equipment, nec
3651	Household audio and video equipment
3652	Prerecorded records and tapes
3661	Telephone and telegraph apparatus
3663	Radio and t.v. communications equipment
3669	Communications equipment, nec
3672	Printed circuit boards
3674	Semiconductors and related devices
3675	Electronic capacitors
3677	Electronic coils and transformers
3679	Electronic components, nec
3691	Storage batteries
3692	Primary batteries, dry and wet
3694	Engine electrical equipment
3695	Magnetic and optical recording media
3699	Electrical equipment and supplies, nec

37 transportation equipment

SIC NO	PRODUCT
3711	Motor vehicles and car bodies
3713	Truck and bus bodies
3714	Motor vehicle parts and accessories
3715	Truck trailers
3721	Aircraft
3724	Aircraft engines and engine parts
3728	Aircraft parts and equipment, nec
3731	Shipbuilding and repairing
3732	Boatbuilding and repairing
3743	Railroad equipment

SIC INDEX

SIC NO	PRODUCT
3751	Motorcycles, bicycles, and parts
3761	Guided missiles and space vehicles
3795	Tanks and tank components
3799	Transportation equipment, nec

38 measuring, photographic, medical, & optical goods, & clocks

SIC NO	PRODUCT
3812	Search and navigation equipment
3821	Laboratory apparatus and furniture
3822	Environmental controls
3823	Process control instruments
3824	Fluid meters and counting devices
3825	Instruments to measure electricity
3826	Analytical instruments
3827	Optical instruments and lenses
3829	Measuring and controlling devices, nec
3841	Surgical and medical instruments
3842	Surgical appliances and supplies
3843	Dental equipment and supplies
3844	X-ray apparatus and tubes
3845	Electromedical equipment
3851	Ophthalmic goods
3861	Photographic equipment and supplies
3873	Watches, clocks, watchcases, and parts

39 miscellaneous manufacturing industries

SIC NO	PRODUCT
3911	Jewelry, precious metal
3914	Silverware and plated ware
3915	Jewelers' materials and lapidary work
3931	Musical instruments
3944	Games, toys, and children's vehicles
3949	Sporting and athletic goods, nec
3953	Marking devices
3955	Carbon paper and inked ribbons
3961	Costume jewelry
3965	Fasteners, buttons, needles, and pins
3991	Brooms and brushes
3993	Signs and advertising specialties
3996	Hard surface floor coverings, nec
3999	Manufacturing industries, nec

40 railroad transportation

SIC NO	PRODUCT
4011	Railroads, line-haul operating

41 local & suburban transit & interurban highway transportation

SIC NO	PRODUCT
4111	Local and suburban transit
4119	Local passenger transportation, nec
4121	Taxicabs
4131	Intercity and rural bus transportation
4141	Local bus charter service
4142	Bus charter service, except local
4151	School buses
4173	Bus terminal and service facilities

42 motor freight transportation

SIC NO	PRODUCT
4212	Local trucking, without storage
4213	Trucking, except local
4214	Local trucking with storage
4215	Courier services, except by air
4222	Refrigerated warehousing and storage
4225	General warehousing and storage
4226	Special warehousing and storage, nec
4231	Trucking terminal facilities

44 water transportation

SIC NO	PRODUCT
4412	Deep sea foreign transportation of freight
4424	Deep sea domestic transportation of freight
4449	Water transportation of freight
4481	Deep sea passenger transportation, except ferry
4489	Water passenger transportation
4491	Marine cargo handling
4492	Towing and tugboat service
4493	Marinas

45 transportation by air

SIC NO	PRODUCT
4512	Air transportation, scheduled
4513	Air courier services
4522	Air transportation, nonscheduled
4581	Airports, flying fields, and services

46 pipelines, except natural gas

SIC NO	PRODUCT
4612	Crude petroleum pipelines

47 transportation services

SIC NO	PRODUCT
4724	Travel agencies
4725	Tour operators
4731	Freight transportation arrangement
4741	Rental of railroad cars
4783	Packing and crating
4785	Inspection and fixed facilities
4789	Transportation services, nec

48 communications

SIC NO	PRODUCT
4812	Radiotelephone communication
4813	Telephone communication, except radio
4822	Telegraph and other communications
4832	Radio broadcasting stations
4833	Television broadcasting stations
4841	Cable and other pay television services
4899	Communication services, nec

49 electric, gas and sanitary services

SIC NO	PRODUCT
4911	Electric services
4923	Gas transmission and distribution
4924	Natural gas distribution
4925	Gas production and/or distribution
4931	Electric and other services combined
4932	Gas and other services combined
4939	Combination utilities, nec
4941	Water supply
4952	Sewerage systems
4953	Refuse systems
4959	Sanitary services, nec
4971	Irrigation systems

50 wholesale trade - durable goods

SIC NO	PRODUCT
5012	Automobiles and other motor vehicles
5013	Motor vehicle supplies and new parts
5014	Tires and tubes
5015	Motor vehicle parts, used
5021	Furniture
5023	Homefurnishings
5031	Lumber, plywood, and millwork
5032	Brick, stone, and related material
5033	Roofing, siding, and insulation
5039	Construction materials, nec
5043	Photographic equipment and supplies
5044	Office equipment
5045	Computers, peripherals, and software
5046	Commercial equipment, nec
5047	Medical and hospital equipment
5048	Ophthalmic goods
5049	Professional equipment, nec
5051	Metals service centers and offices
5052	Coal and other minerals and ores
5063	Electrical apparatus and equipment
5064	Electrical appliances, television and radio
5065	Electronic parts and equipment, nec
5072	Hardware
5074	Plumbing and hydronic heating supplies
5075	Warm air heating and air conditioning
5078	Refrigeration equipment and supplies
5082	Construction and mining machinery
5083	Farm and garden machinery
5084	Industrial machinery and equipment
5085	Industrial supplies
5087	Service establishment equipment
5088	Transportation equipment and supplies
5091	Sporting and recreation goods
5092	Toys and hobby goods and supplies
5093	Scrap and waste materials
5094	Jewelry and precious stones
5099	Durable goods, nec

51 wholesale trade - nondurable goods

SIC NO	PRODUCT
5112	Stationery and office supplies
5113	Industrial and personal service paper
5122	Drugs, proprietaries, and sundries
5131	Piece goods and notions
5136	Men's and boy's clothing
5137	Women's and children's clothing
5139	Footwear
5141	Groceries, general line
5142	Packaged frozen goods
5143	Dairy products, except dried or canned
5144	Poultry and poultry products
5145	Confectionery
5146	Fish and seafoods
5147	Meats and meat products
5148	Fresh fruits and vegetables
5149	Groceries and related products, nec
5153	Grain and field beans
5159	Farm-product raw materials, nec
5162	Plastics materials and basic shapes
5169	Chemicals and allied products, nec
5171	Petroleum bulk stations and terminals
5172	Petroleum products, nec
5181	Beer and ale
5182	Wine and distilled beverages
5191	Farm supplies
5192	Books, periodicals, and newspapers
5193	Flowers and florists supplies
5194	Tobacco and tobacco products
5198	Paints, varnishes, and supplies
5199	Nondurable goods, nec

52 building materials, hardware, garden supplies & mobile homes

SIC NO	PRODUCT
5211	Lumber and other building materials
5231	Paint, glass, and wallpaper stores
5251	Hardware stores
5261	Retail nurseries and garden stores
5271	Mobile home dealers

53 general merchandise stores

SIC NO	PRODUCT
5311	Department stores
5331	Variety stores
5399	Miscellaneous general merchandise

54 food stores

SIC NO	PRODUCT
5411	Grocery stores
5421	Meat and fish markets
5431	Fruit and vegetable markets
5441	Candy, nut, and confectionery stores
5461	Retail bakeries
5499	Miscellaneous food stores

55 automotive dealers and gasoline service stations

SIC NO	PRODUCT
5511	New and used car dealers
5521	Used car dealers
5531	Auto and home supply stores
5541	Gasoline service stations
5551	Boat dealers
5561	Recreational vehicle dealers
5571	Motorcycle dealers
5599	Automotive dealers, nec

56 apparel and accessory stores

SIC NO	PRODUCT
5611	Men's and boys' clothing stores
5621	Women's clothing stores
5632	Women's accessory and specialty stores
5641	Children's and infants' wear stores
5651	Family clothing stores
5661	Shoe stores
5699	Miscellaneous apparel and accessories

57 home furniture, furnishings and equipment stores

SIC NO	PRODUCT
5712	Furniture stores
5713	Floor covering stores
5719	Miscellaneous homefurnishings
5722	Household appliance stores
5731	Radio, television, and electronic stores
5734	Computer and software stores
5735	Record and prerecorded tape stores
5736	Musical instrument stores

58 eating and drinking places

SIC NO	PRODUCT
5812	Eating places
5813	Drinking places

59 miscellaneous retail

SIC NO	PRODUCT
5921	Liquor stores
5932	Used merchandise stores
5941	Sporting goods and bicycle shops
5942	Book stores

SIC INDEX

SIC NO	PRODUCT
5943	Stationery stores
5944	Jewelry stores
5945	Hobby, toy, and game shops
5946	Camera and photographic supply stores
5947	Gift, novelty, and souvenir shop
5949	Sewing, needlework, and piece goods
5961	Catalog and mail-order houses
5962	Merchandising machine operators
5963	Direct selling establishments
5983	Fuel oil dealers
5984	Liquefied petroleum gas dealers
5992	Florists
5993	Tobacco stores and stands
5995	Optical goods stores
5999	Miscellaneous retail stores, nec

60 depository institutions

SIC NO	PRODUCT
6021	National commercial banks
6022	State commercial banks
6029	Commercial banks, nec
6035	Federal savings institutions
6036	Savings institutions, except federal
6061	Federal credit unions
6062	State credit unions
6081	Foreign bank and branches and agencies
6082	Foreign trade and international banks
6091	Nondeposit trust facilities
6099	Functions related to depository banking

61 nondepository credit institutions

SIC NO	PRODUCT
6111	Federal and federally sponsored credit
6141	Personal credit institutions
6153	Short-term business credit
6159	Miscellaneous business credit
6162	Mortgage bankers and correspondents
6163	Loan brokers

62 security & commodity brokers, dealers, exchanges & services

SIC NO	PRODUCT
6211	Security brokers and dealers
6221	Commodity contracts brokers, dealers
6231	Security and commodity exchanges
6282	Investment advice
6289	Security and commodity service

63 insurance carriers

SIC NO	PRODUCT
6311	Life insurance
6321	Accident and health insurance
6324	Hospital and medical service plans
6331	Fire, marine, and casualty insurance
6351	Surety insurance
6361	Title insurance
6371	Pension, health, and welfare funds
6399	Insurance carriers, nec

64 insurance agents, brokers and service

SIC NO	PRODUCT
6411	Insurance agents, brokers, and service

65 real estate

SIC NO	PRODUCT
6512	Nonresidential building operators
6513	Apartment building operators
6514	Dwelling operators, except apartments
6515	Mobile home site operators
6519	Real property lessors, nec
6531	Real estate agents and managers
6541	Title abstract offices
6552	Subdividers and developers, nec
6553	Cemetery subdividers and developers

67 holding and other investment offices

SIC NO	PRODUCT
6712	Bank holding companies
6719	Holding companies, nec
6722	Management investment, open-ended
6726	Investment offices, nec
6732	Trusts: educational, religious, etc.
6733	Trusts, nec
6794	Patent owners and lessors
6798	Real estate investment trusts
6799	Investors, nec

70 hotels, rooming houses, camps, and other lodging places

SIC NO	PRODUCT
7011	Hotels and motels
7021	Rooming and boarding houses
7032	Sporting and recreational camps
7033	Trailer parks and campsites
7041	Membership-basis organization hotels

72 personal services

SIC NO	PRODUCT
7211	Power laundries, family and commercial
7212	Garment pressing and cleaners' agents
7213	Linen supply
7215	Coin-operated laundries and cleaning
7216	Drycleaning plants, except rugs
7217	Carpet and upholstery cleaning
7218	Industrial launderers
7219	Laundry and garment services, nec
7221	Photographic studios, portrait
7231	Beauty shops
7241	Barber shops
7251	Shoe repair and shoeshine parlors
7261	Funeral service and crematories
7291	Tax return preparation services
7299	Miscellaneous personal services

73 business services

SIC NO	PRODUCT
7311	Advertising agencies
7312	Outdoor advertising services
7313	Radio, television, publisher representatives
7319	Advertising, nec
7322	Adjustment and collection services
7323	Credit reporting services
7331	Direct mail advertising services
7334	Photocopying and duplicating services
7335	Commercial photography
7336	Commercial art and graphic design
7338	Secretarial and court reporting
7342	Disinfecting and pest control services
7349	Building maintenance services, nec
7352	Medical equipment rental
7353	Heavy construction equipment rental
7359	Equipment rental and leasing, nec
7361	Employment agencies
7363	Help supply services
7371	Custom computer programming services
7372	Prepackaged software
7373	Computer integrated systems design
7374	Data processing and preparation
7375	Information retrieval services
7376	Computer facilities management
7377	Computer rental and leasing
7378	Computer maintenance and repair
7379	Computer related services, nec
7381	Detective and armored car services
7382	Security systems services
7383	News syndicates
7384	Photofinish laboratories
7389	Business services, nec

75 automotive repair, services and parking

SIC NO	PRODUCT
7513	Truck rental and leasing, without drivers
7514	Passenger car rental
7515	Passenger car leasing
7519	Utility trailer rental
7521	Automobile parking
7532	Top and body repair and paint shops
7533	Auto exhaust system repair shops
7534	Tire retreading and repair shops
7536	Automotive glass replacement shops
7537	Automotive transmission repair shops
7538	General automotive repair shops
7539	Automotive repair shops, nec
7542	Carwashes
7549	Automotive services, nec

76 miscellaneous repair services

SIC NO	PRODUCT
7622	Radio and television repair
7623	Refrigeration service and repair
7629	Electrical repair shops
7631	Watch, clock, and jewelry repair
7641	Reupholstery and furniture repair
7692	Welding repair
7694	Armature rewinding shops
7699	Repair services, nec

78 motion pictures

SIC NO	PRODUCT
7812	Motion picture and video production
7819	Services allied to motion pictures
7822	Motion picture and tape distribution
7829	Motion picture distribution services
7832	Motion picture theaters, except drive-in
7841	Video tape rental

79 amusement and recreation services

SIC NO	PRODUCT
7911	Dance studios, schools, and halls
7922	Theatrical producers and services
7929	Entertainers and entertainment groups
7933	Bowling centers
7941	Sports clubs, managers, and promoters
7948	Racing, including track operation
7991	Physical fitness facilities
7992	Public golf courses
7993	Coin-operated amusement devices
7996	Amusement parks
7997	Membership sports and recreation clubs
7999	Amusement and recreation, nec

80 health services

SIC NO	PRODUCT
8011	Offices and clinics of medical doctors
8021	Offices and clinics of dentists
8031	Offices and clinics of osteopathic physicians
8041	Offices and clinics of chiropractors
8042	Offices and clinics of optometrists
8043	Offices and clinics of podiatrists
8049	Offices of health practitioner
8051	Skilled nursing care facilities
8052	Intermediate care facilities
8059	Nursing and personal care, nec
8062	General medical and surgical hospitals
8063	Psychiatric hospitals
8069	Specialty hospitals, except psychiatric
8071	Medical laboratories
8072	Dental laboratories
8082	Home health care services
8092	Kidney dialysis centers
8093	Specialty outpatient clinics, nec
8099	Health and allied services, nec

81 legal services

SIC NO	PRODUCT
8111	Legal services

82 educational services

SIC NO	PRODUCT
8211	Elementary and secondary schools
8221	Colleges and universities
8222	Junior colleges
8231	Libraries
8243	Data processing schools
8244	Business and secretarial schools
8249	Vocational schools, nec
8299	Schools and educational services

83 social services

SIC NO	PRODUCT
8322	Individual and family services
8331	Job training and related services
8351	Child day care services
8361	Residential care
8399	Social services, nec

84 museums, art galleries and botanical and zoological gardens

SIC NO	PRODUCT
8412	Museums and art galleries
8422	Botanical and zoological gardens

86 membership organizations

SIC NO	PRODUCT
8611	Business associations
8621	Professional organizations
8631	Labor organizations
8641	Civic and social associations
8651	Political organizations
8661	Religious organizations
8699	Membership organizations, nec

87 engineering, accounting, research, and management services

SIC NO	PRODUCT
8711	Engineering services
8712	Architectural services
8713	Surveying services

SIC INDEX

SIC NO	PRODUCT
8721	Accounting, auditing, and bookkeeping
8731	Commercial physical research
8732	Commercial nonphysical research
8733	Noncommercial research organizations
8734	Testing laboratories
8741	Management services
8742	Management consulting services
8743	Public relations services
8744	Facilities support services
8748	Business consulting, nec

89 services, not elsewhere classified
8999 Services, nec

91 executive, legislative & general government, except finance
9111 Executive offices
9199 General government, nec

92 justice, public order and safety
9211 Courts
9221 Police protection
9223 Correctional institutions
9224 Fire protection

93 public finance, taxation and monetary policy
9311 Finance, taxation, and monetary policy

94 administration of human resource programs
9431 Administration of public health programs
9441 Administration of social and manpower programs
9451 Administration of veterans' affairs

95 administration of environmental quality and housing programs
9512 Land, mineral, and wildlife conservation
9532 Urban and community development

96 administration of economic programs
9611 Administration of general economic programs
9621 Regulation, administration of transportation
9651 Regulation, miscellaneous commercial sectors
9661 Space research and technology

97 national security and international affairs
9711 National security

SIC SECTION

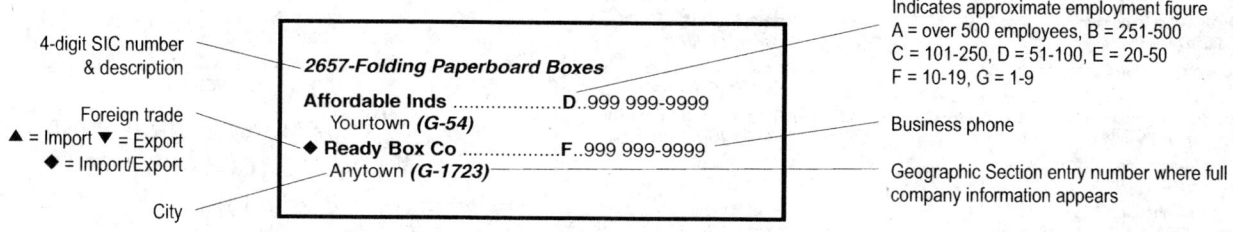

- 4-digit SIC number & description → **2657-Folding Paperboard Boxes**
- Foreign trade ▲ = Import ▼ = Export ◆ = Import/Export
- City
- **Affordable Inds** .... D..999 999-9999 Yourtown *(G-54)*
- ◆ **Ready Box Co** .... F..999 999-9999 Anytown *(G-1723)*
- Indicates approximate employment figure A = over 500 employees, B = 251-500, C = 101-250, D = 51-100, E = 20-50, F = 10-19, G = 1-9
- Business phone
- Geographic Section entry number where full company information appears

See footnotes for symbols and codes identification.
- The SIC codes in this section are from the latest Standard Industrial Classification manual published by the U.S. Government's Office of Management and Budget. For more information regarding SICs, see the Explanatory Notes.
- Companies may be listed under multiple classifications.

01 AGRICULTURAL PRODUCTION - CROPS

0111 Wheat

Elliott John.............................. G..... 302 846-2487
  Delmar *(G-1593)*
Pettyjohn Farms Inc................. G..... 302 684-4383
  Milton *(G-8684)*
Schiff Farms Inc...................... F..... 302 398-8014
  Harrington *(G-4828)*
Shadybrook Farms LLC........... F..... 302 734-9966
  Dover *(G-3538)*
T S Smith & Sons Inc............... F..... 302 337-8271
  Bridgeville *(G-774)*
Westwood Farms Incorporated.. F..... 302 238-7141
  Millsboro *(G-8504)*
Workmans Inc.......................... G..... 302 934-9228
  Georgetown *(G-4580)*

0115 Corn

Elliott John.............................. G..... 302 846-2487
  Delmar *(G-1593)*
Francis Bergold....................... G..... 302 284-8101
  Felton *(G-3976)*
J L Carpenter Farms LLC......... G..... 302 684-8601
  Milton *(G-8644)*
Murray Brothers....................... G..... 302 436-3639
  Selbyville *(G-13584)*
Rutkoske Bros Inc................... G..... 302 378-8181
  Middletown *(G-7528)*
Schiff Farms Inc...................... F..... 302 398-8014
  Harrington *(G-4828)*
Shadybrook Farms LLC........... F..... 302 734-9966
  Dover *(G-3538)*
Workmans Inc.......................... G..... 302 934-9228
  Georgetown *(G-4580)*

0116 Soybeans

Clifton Farms Inc..................... G..... 302 242-8806
  Milford *(G-7835)*
Elliott John.............................. G..... 302 846-2487
  Delmar *(G-1593)*
Murray Brothers....................... G..... 302 436-3639
  Selbyville *(G-13584)*
Schiff Farms Inc...................... F..... 302 398-8014
  Harrington *(G-4828)*
Shadybrook Farms LLC........... F..... 302 734-9966
  Dover *(G-3538)*
T S Smith & Sons Inc............... F..... 302 337-8271
  Bridgeville *(G-774)*

Workmans Inc.......................... G..... 302 934-9228
  Georgetown *(G-4580)*

0119 Cash grains, nec

Charles Dempsey Farms.......... G..... 302 734-4937
  Dover *(G-2057)*
Charles H West Farms Inc....... F..... 302 335-3936
  Milford *(G-7821)*
David R Daniels...................... G..... 410 275-8141
  Townsend *(G-13985)*
Donna Brittingham Ms.............. G..... 302 846-3661
  Delmar *(G-1590)*
Dulin Brothers......................... G..... 302 653-5365
  Clayton *(G-1360)*
Edward J Steen....................... G..... 302 732-6963
  Dagsboro *(G-1443)*
Francis Bergold....................... G..... 302 284-8101
  Felton *(G-3976)*
James L Carpenter & Son Inc.... G..... 302 684-8601
  Milton *(G-8647)*
Jumarally Chandra................... G..... 302 212-7027
  Millsboro *(G-8334)*
Kruger Farms Inc..................... G..... 302 856-2577
  Georgetown *(G-4395)*
Marshall Anthony Jr.................. G..... 302 398-3043
  Harrington *(G-4799)*
McBroom Jr Roger Dale........... G..... 302 228-0998
  Greenwood *(G-4651)*
T Harry Wheedleton.................. G..... 302 629-7414
  Seaford *(G-13424)*
Twin Creek Farms LLC............. G..... 302 249-2294
  Milford *(G-8122)*
Workmans Inc.......................... G..... 302 934-9228
  Georgetown *(G-4580)*

0134 Irish potatoes

Francis Bergold....................... G..... 302 284-8101
  Felton *(G-3976)*
Rutkoske Bros Inc................... G..... 302 378-8181
  Middletown *(G-7528)*
Shadybrook Farms LLC........... F..... 302 734-9966
  Dover *(G-3538)*

0139 Field crops, except cash grain

Donna Brittingham Ms.............. G..... 302 846-3661
  Delmar *(G-1590)*
Edward J Steen....................... G..... 302 732-6963
  Dagsboro *(G-1443)*
Gro-Connectcom Inc................ G..... 347 918-7437
  Lewes *(G-6066)*
Mark JB Inc............................. G..... 888 984-5845
  Newark *(G-11336)*

Self Care Holistic LLC.............. G..... 302 407-2456
  Wilmington *(G-19744)*

0161 Vegetables and melons

Baldwin Sayre Inc.................... G..... 302 337-0309
  Bridgeville *(G-671)*
C+m Farms LLC...................... G..... 302 841-1847
  Bridgeville *(G-679)*
Charles H West Farms Inc....... F..... 302 335-3936
  Milford *(G-7821)*
Dole Food Company Inc.......... C..... 302 652-6060
  Wilmington *(G-16122)*
Evans Farms LLC.................... G..... 302 337-8130
  Bridgeville *(G-699)*
▼ Fifer Orchards Inc................ C..... 302 697-2141
  Camden Wyoming *(G-944)*
J L Carpenter Farms LLC......... G..... 302 684-8601
  Milton *(G-8644)*
James L Carpenter & Son Inc.... G..... 302 684-8601
  Milton *(G-8647)*
Mernies Market........................ G..... 302 629-9877
  Seaford *(G-13280)*
Papen Farms Inc..................... F..... 302 697-3291
  Dover *(G-3267)*
Pine Breeze Farms Inc............. G..... 302 337-7717
  Bridgeville *(G-750)*

0173 Tree nuts

Walnut Grove Coop Inc............ G..... 302 545-3000
  Newark *(G-12346)*

0175 Deciduous tree fruits

▼ Fifer Orchards Inc................ C..... 302 697-2141
  Camden Wyoming *(G-944)*
Stag Run Farm Llc................... G..... 302 270-8435
  Georgetown *(G-4523)*
T S Smith & Sons Inc............... F..... 302 337-8271
  Bridgeville *(G-774)*

0179 Fruits and tree nuts, nec

Affordable Sod Inc................... G..... 302 545-0275
  Newark *(G-9794)*
Blessngs Grnhses Cmpost Fcilty.. F..... 302 684-8890
  Milford *(G-7795)*
Forest View Nursery................ G..... 302 653-7757
  Clayton *(G-1367)*
Gooden Floral Sp & Greenhouses.. G..... 302 422-4961
  Milford *(G-7909)*
Greenland Sod Farm LLC......... G..... 302 258-7543
  Bethel *(G-654)*

Employee Codes: A=Over 500 employees, B=251-500 C=101-250, D=51-100, E=20-50, F=10-19, G=1-9

01 AGRICULTURAL PRODUCTION - CROPS

Karizma Sparks LLC......................... G 302 607-5445
Newark (G-11143)

Lakeside Greenhouses Inc .... G 302 875-2457
Laurel (G-5544)

Old Country Garden Center Inc .... F 302 652-3317
Wilmington (G-18754)

Sandy Hill Greenhouses Inc .... F 302 856-2412
Georgetown (G-4498)

Sterling Nursery Inc .... G 302 653-7060
Smyrna (G-13901)

Yoders Greenhouse.......................... G 302 678-3530
Dover (G-3889)

0182 Food crops grown under cover

Ashanti Produce International .... F 800 295-9790
Wilmington (G-14578)

Gro-Connectcom Inc .... G 347 918-7437
Lewes (G-6066)

0191 General farms, primarily crop

A Farm Inc .... G 610 496-1504
Middletown (G-6822)

Ahmad Family Farm LLC .... G 302 349-5500
Greenwood (G-4590)

Alfred Moore................................... G 302 653-7600
Smyrna (G-13633)

Amanda F Bodine............................ G 302 270-5579
Hartly (G-4856)

Amick Farms LLC........................... C 302 846-9511
Delmar (G-1565)

Banks Farms LLC........................... G 302 542-4100
Dagsboro (G-1417)

Bellawood Kennels LLC .... G 302 738-0864
Newark (G-10015)

Bender Farms Llc............................ G 302 349-5574
Greenwood (G-4596)

Bennett Farms Inc........................... G 302 684-1627
Milford (G-7792)

Bonk Farms LLC............................. G 302 542-2431
Magnolia (G-6722)

C&S Farms Inc............................... G 302 249-0458
Laurel (G-5476)

Calloway Farms............................... G 302 875-0476
Bethel (G-653)

Carlisle Farms Inc........................... G 302 349-5692
Greenwood (G-4603)

Carlisle Farms Inc........................... G 302 349-5692
Farmington (G-3934)

Catherine L Kohland........................ G 302 335-1505
Frederica (G-4163)

Clover Farms Meats......................... G 610 428-8066
Ocean View (G-12490)

Cordrey Charities Inc....................... G 302 945-5855
Millsboro (G-8239)

E Lawrence Jester........................... G 302 378-8970
Townsend (G-13996)

Edward Krupka............................... G 302 492-0833
Hartly (G-4872)

Frozen Farmer LLC......................... G 302 337-8444
Bridgeville (G-702)

Gerald 1mccarthy............................ G 302 836-3171
Middletown (G-7156)

Green Acres Farm Inc...................... F 302 645-8652
Lewes (G-6057)

Grey Rock Farms LLC .... G 215 847-3478
Newark (G-10898)

Grimm Farms LLC.......................... G 302 841-8381
Greenwood (G-4632)

Honeys Farm Fresh......................... G 302 644-8400
Lewes (G-6102)

Hopkins Henlopen Homestead .... G 202 695-9302
Lewes (G-6104)

Hrupsa Farms Ltd Partnership .... G 302 270-1817
Harrington (G-4787)

Jeff Hopkins LLC............................. G 302 653-6413
Clayton (G-1375)

John R Gundry................................ G 302 629-9877
Seaford (G-13237)

Johns Farm Fresh Produce................ G 302 834-3747
Newark (G-11119)

K C Farms LLC............................... G 302 492-3439
Marydel (G-6802)

King of Mangoes.............................. G 302 547-2500
Newark (G-11178)

Lakeside Farms Inc.......................... G 302 841-8843
Laurel (G-5543)

Landslide Farm LLP......................... G 302 566-6418
Harrington (G-4796)

Larimore Inc................................... G 302 632-3618
Harrington (G-4797)

M Davis Farms LLC......................... G 302 856-7018
Georgetown (G-4410)

Mantis Farms................................. G 302 507-4851
Wilmington (G-18107)

Marie Willow & Co........................... G 302 632-0831
Lewes (G-6243)

Masc Farming LLC.......................... G 302 734-3602
Dover (G-3025)

Meadowbrook Farms Inc .... G 443 735-6244
Delmar (G-1619)

Michael Joseph Alexander................. G 302 670-0993
Felton (G-4002)

Mildford Neck Farms........................ G 302 422-6432
Milford (G-7998)

MJ Webb Farms Inc .... G 302 349-4453
Greenwood (G-4653)

Morris Farms LLC........................... G 302 875-1518
Laurel (G-5566)

Mountaire Farms LLC .... D 302 934-3011
Millsboro (G-8392)

◆ Mountaire Farms Delaware Inc .... A 302 934-1100
Millsboro (G-8393)

Mountaire Farms Inc........................ D 302 404-5057
Seaford (G-13291)

Mountaire Farms Inc........................ A 302 436-8241
Selbyville (G-13580)

O A Newton & Son Co...................... E 302 337-8211
Bridgeville (G-739)

Qomo Farms LLC........................... G 202 462-5449
Rehoboth Beach (G-12902)

Riverdale Park LLC.......................... G 302 945-2475
Millsboro (G-8446)

Royal Farms................................... G 410 725-9100
Laurel (G-5597)

Royal Farms................................... G 302 409-3992
Newark (G-11921)

Silk Grass Holdings Us LLC .... F 610 943-3047
Lewes (G-6471)

Snow Farms Inc.............................. G 302 653-7534
Smyrna (G-13898)

Suburban Farmhouse....................... G 302 250-6254
Milton (G-8717)

Tarachand Beharry.......................... G 302 875-0684
Laurel (G-5614)

Thomas Family Farms LLC................ G 302 492-3688
Marydel (G-6812)

Vincent Farms Inc............................ C 302 875-5707
Laurel (G-5619)

W C Farms LLC.............................. G 302 242-1770
Felton (G-4036)

Warner M Schlaupitz........................ G 302 492-3451
Camden Wyoming (G-985)

Wells Farms Inc.............................. G 302 422-4732
Milford (G-8148)

Wheatley Farms Inc......................... G 302 337-7286
Bridgeville (G-784)

William A ODay............................... G 302 629-7854
Seaford (G-13448)

Willin Farms LLC............................. G 302 629-2520
Seaford (G-13452)

02 AGRICULTURAL PRODUCTION - LIVESTOCK AND ANIMAL SPECIALTIES

0212 Beef cattle, except feedlots

Schiff Farms Inc.............................. F 302 398-8014
Harrington (G-4828)

0213 Hogs

Bi-State Feeders LLC .... G 302 398-3408
Harrington (G-4740)

Keystone Swine Services.................. G 302 329-9731
Milton (G-8651)

Murray Brothers.............................. G 302 436-3639
Selbyville (G-13584)

0241 Dairy farms

Charles Dempsey Farms................... G 302 734-4937
Dover (G-2057)

Dempsey Farms LLC....................... G 302 734-4937
Dover (G-2281)

Dulin Brothers................................ G 302 653-5365
Clayton (G-1360)

J E Bailey & Sons Inc....................... G 302 349-4376
Greenwood (G-4642)

James L Carpenter & Son Inc .... G 302 684-8601
Milton (G-8647)

Lewes Dairy Inc.............................. F 302 645-6281
Lewes (G-6194)

Natural Dairy Products Corp.............. G 302 455-1261
Newark (G-11492)

R Stanley Collier & Son Inc............... G 302 398-7855
Harrington (G-4817)

Robert C Thompson......................... G 302 492-1053
Hartly (G-4907)

0251 Broiler, fryer, and roaster chickens

Allen Harim Foods LLC .... E 302 629-9136
Millsboro (G-8167)

Country Store................................. G 302 653-5111
Kenton (G-5452)

Larry Hill Farms LLC........................ F 302 245-6657
Delmar (G-1614)

Murray Brothers.............................. G 302 436-3639
Selbyville (G-13584)

Perdue Farms Inc............................ E 302 855-5681
Laurel (G-5575)

State Line Farms LLC...................... G 302 628-4506
Seaford (G-13411)

T S Smith & Sons Inc....................... F 302 337-8271
Bridgeville (G-774)

Westwood Farms Incorporated .... F 302 238-7141
Millsboro (G-8504)

0252 Chicken eggs

Hatching Time LLC.......................... F 800 511-1369
Newark (G-10938)

Karizma Sparks LLC........................ G 302 607-5445
Newark (G-11143)

Puglisi Egg Farms Delaware LLC .... E 302 376-1200
Middletown (G-7479)

Red Bird Egg Farm Inc..................... E 302 834-2571
Bear (G-449)

SIC SECTION

07 AGRICULTURAL SERVICES

0254 Poultry hatcheries
Allen Harim Foods LLC .... B 302 732-9511
  Dagsboro *(G-1411)*
J E Bailey & Sons Inc .... G 302 349-4376
  Greenwood *(G-4642)*

0272 Horses and other equines
Country Comforts .... G 302 242-8527
  Camden Wyoming *(G-929)*
Crown Equine LLC .... G 302 629-2782
  Georgetown *(G-4273)*
Danielle Hill Training Center .... G 302 363-1484
  Dover *(G-2194)*
Pck Associates Inc .... G 302 378-7192
  Middletown *(G-7435)*
Thoroughbred Charities-America .... G 302 376-6289
  Middletown *(G-7639)*
Valour Arabians .... G 302 653-4066
  Smyrna *(G-13928)*

0279 Animal specialties, nec
Clean-A-Tank Inc .... G 302 250-4229
  Wilmington *(G-15472)*

0291 General farms, primarily animals
Last Chance Ranch .... G 518 369-9451
  Wilmington *(G-17814)*
Lc Ranch LLC .... G 302 654-3600
  Wilmington *(G-17840)*
Mary Del Ranch Inc .... G 302 492-8866
  Marydel *(G-6807)*
Rossakatum Ranch Inc .... G 302 875-5707
  Laurel *(G-5596)*

07 AGRICULTURAL SERVICES

0711 Soil preparation services
Agrolab Inc .... G 302 535-6591
  Harrington *(G-4724)*
Spec Processing Group Inc .... G 302 295-2197
  Bear *(G-504)*
Toubasam Inc .... G 302 299-2954
  Wilmington *(G-20375)*

0721 Crop planting and protection
Allen Chorman & Son Inc .... F 302 684-2770
  Milton *(G-8557)*
Danisco European Holding Inc .... F 302 999-4083
  Wilmington *(G-15787)*
Delcarm LLC .... F 610 345-9001
  Townsend *(G-13990)*
Dupont Electronics Holding LLC .... G 302 999-4083
  Wilmington *(G-16207)*
Dupont S&C Holding LLC .... G 302 999-4083
  Wilmington *(G-16215)*
Dupont US Holding LLC .... G 302 999-4083
  Wilmington *(G-16219)*
Performance Materials Intl LLC .... G 302 999-4083
  Wilmington *(G-18976)*
Performnce Spcalty Pdts NA LLC .... F 302 774-3034
  Wilmington *(G-18980)*
PM China Inc .... F 302 999-4083
  Wilmington *(G-19085)*
PM Taiwan Inc .... E 302 999-4083
  Wilmington *(G-19086)*
Sp Holding Et LLC .... G 302 999-4083
  Wilmington *(G-19947)*
Sp Holding Ib Inc .... G 302 999-4083
  Wilmington *(G-19948)*

0722 Crop harvesting
Clifton Farms Inc .... G 302 242-8806
  Milford *(G-7835)*
Nancy Cannone .... G 302 368-3572
  Newark *(G-11484)*

0723 Crop preparation services for market
Clifton Farms Inc .... G 302 242-8806
  Milford *(G-7835)*
Royalhalo LLC .... F 888 418-7692
  Wilmington *(G-19577)*

0741 Veterinary services for livestock
Gil Vansciver .... G 302 736-3000
  Dover *(G-2585)*
Peak Prfmce Globl Svcs LLC .... F 610 554-4773
  Lewes *(G-6357)*

0742 Veterinary services, specialties
A Caring Doctor Minnesota PA .... F 302 266-0122
  Newark *(G-9723)*
A Caring Doctor Minnesota PA .... G 302 478-3910
  Wilmington *(G-14160)*
A Little Veterinary Clinic PA .... F 302 398-3367
  Harrington *(G-4720)*
Alfred Idpont Hosp For Chldren .... B 302 629-5030
  Seaford *(G-13053)*
All Creatures Vet Services .... G 302 398-3367
  Lincoln *(G-6655)*
All Pets Medical Center .... G 302 653-2300
  Smyrna *(G-13635)*
Animal Haven Veterinary Center .... G 302 326-1400
  Bear *(G-37)*
Animal Veterinary Center LLC .... G 302 322-6488
  Bear *(G-38)*
Atlantic Veterinary Svcs Inc .... G 302 376-7506
  Middletown *(G-6883)*
Brandywine Hndred Vtrnary Hosp .... F 302 792-2777
  Wilmington *(G-15065)*
Brenford Animal Hospital P A .... E 302 678-9418
  Dover *(G-1976)*
Centerville Veterinary Hosp .... F 302 655-3315
  Wilmington *(G-15306)*
Circle Veterinary Clinic .... F 302 652-6587
  Wilmington *(G-15444)*
Coastal Veterinary LLC .... G 302 524-8550
  Selbyville *(G-13504)*
Country Roads Veterinary Svc .... G 302 514-9087
  Clayton *(G-1357)*
Craig Metzner .... G 302 629-9576
  Seaford *(G-13139)*
Crossroads Veterinary Clinic .... G 302 436-5984
  Selbyville *(G-13511)*
Dawn Mc Kenzie Dvm .... G 302 521-8206
  Bear *(G-136)*
Delaware S P C A .... E 302 998-2281
  Newark *(G-10475)*
Delaware Veterinary Med Assn .... G 302 242-7014
  Bear *(G-160)*
Delmarva Equine Clinic .... G 302 735-4735
  Dover *(G-2277)*
Dover Animal Hospital .... F 302 746-2688
  Dover *(G-2333)*
Duck Creek Animal Hospital .... G 302 663-6112
  Smyrna *(G-13716)*
Eastern Shore Veterinary Hosp .... F 302 875-5941
  Laurel *(G-5506)*
Elevate Dvm Inc .... G 302 761-9650
  Wilmington *(G-16356)*
Forrest Avenue Animal Hospital .... F 302 736-3000
  Dover *(G-2528)*
Four Paws Animal Hospital PA .... F 302 629-7297
  Bridgeville *(G-701)*

Georgetown Animal Hospital PA .... G 302 856-2623
  Georgetown *(G-4335)*
Golden Merger Corp .... F 302 737-8100
  Newark *(G-10862)*
Governors Ave Animal Hospital .... E 302 734-5588
  Dover *(G-2610)*
Haven Lake Animal Hospital .... F 302 422-8100
  Milford *(G-7923)*
Hockessin Animal Hospital .... G 302 239-9464
  Hockessin *(G-5240)*
Jeffrey Bowersox .... G 302 322-6933
  New Castle *(G-9257)*
Jr Robert M Thompson Dvm .... G 302 261-2683
  Bear *(G-313)*
Karli Flanagan Dvm .... G 302 893-7872
  Newark *(G-11144)*
Kim Gaines .... G 302 736-3000
  Dover *(G-2870)*
Kirkwood Anmal Brding Grooming ...... F 302 737-1098
  Newark *(G-11182)*
Lantana Veterinary Center Inc .... F 302 234-3275
  Hockessin *(G-5275)*
Limestone Veterinary Hospital .... F 302 239-5415
  Hockessin *(G-5281)*
Lums Pond Animal Hospital Inc .... E 302 836-5585
  Bear *(G-354)*
Middletown Veterinary Hospital .... G 302 378-2342
  Middletown *(G-7360)*
New London Veterinary Center .... G 302 738-5000
  Newark *(G-11524)*
Ocean View Animal Hospital .... G 302 539-2273
  Ocean View *(G-12555)*
Peninsula Anmal Hosp Orthpdics .... G 302 846-9011
  Delmar *(G-1628)*
Peninsula Veterinary Svcs LLC .... G 302 947-0719
  Millsboro *(G-8424)*
Pet Medical Center .... G 302 846-2869
  Delmar *(G-1630)*
Pike Creek Animal Hospital .... F 302 454-7780
  Newark *(G-11690)*
Precious Paws Animal Hospital .... F 302 539-2273
  Ocean View *(G-12560)*
Rbah Inc .... G 302 227-2009
  Rehoboth Beach *(G-12906)*
Rehoboth Animal Hospital .... G 302 227-2009
  Rehoboth Beach *(G-12913)*
Seaford Animal Hospital Inc .... F 302 629-7325
  Seaford *(G-13386)*
Sharon Alger-Little Dr .... G 302 398-3367
  Harrington *(G-4830)*
Summit Bridge Vet Hosp LLC .... G 302 834-7387
  Bear *(G-515)*
Sussex Veterinary Hospital .... G 302 732-9433
  Dagsboro *(G-1512)*
Tallyville Animal Hospital .... G 302 478-1194
  Wilmington *(G-20216)*
VCA Animal Hospitals Inc .... F 302 738-1738
  Newark *(G-12308)*
VCA Pike Creek Animal Hospital .... G 302 307-1077
  Newark *(G-12309)*
Veternary Specialty Ctr Del PA .... D 302 322-6933
  New Castle *(G-9670)*
Western Sussex Animal Hosp Inc .... G 302 337-7387
  Bridgeville *(G-782)*
White Clay Creek Vtrinary Hosp .... G 302 738-9611
  Wilmington *(G-12366)*
Willow Grace Vtrinary Hosp LLC .... G 302 378-9800
  Middletown *(G-7728)*
Wilmington Animal Hospital .... E 302 762-2694
  Wilmington *(G-20808)*
Windcrest Animal Hospital .... E 302 239-9464
  Wilmington *(G-20856)*

Employee Codes: A=Over 500 employees, B=251-500
C=101-250, D=51-100, E=20-50, F=10-19, G=1-9

2024 Harris Directory of
Delaware Businesses

07 AGRICULTURAL SERVICES

0751 Livestock services, except veterinary

Allen Harim Farms LLC .... E 302 629-9136
  Millsboro (G-8166)
Coastal Maintenance LLC .... E 302 536-1290
  Seaford (G-13127)

0752 Animal specialty services

Academy Dog Training & Agility .... G 302 588-4636
  Newark (G-9747)
Adandy Farm .... G 302 349-5116
  Greenwood (G-4589)
Alyce E Duffy .... G 302 383-5921
  Wilmington (G-14405)
American K9 Dggie Dycare Trnin ..... F 302 376-9663
  Middletown (G-6859)
Animal Inn Inc .... G 302 653-5560
  Dover (G-1796)
Apex Arabians Inc .... G 302 242-6272
  Houston (G-5436)
Augustin Stable .... G 302 571-8322
  Wilmington (G-14640)
Beach Cities Reptile Rescue .... G 949 412-6366
  Seaford (G-13080)
Brenford Animal Hospital P A .... E 302 678-9418
  Dover (G-1976)
Canine Creations .... G 302 593-2684
  Wilmington (G-15215)
Canine Cture Exprt Groming LLC .... G 302 500-1814
  Milford (G-7811)
Carlisle Group .... G 302 475-3010
  Wilmington (G-15253)
Delaware Blue Claws .... G 302 674-1123
  Leipsic (G-5630)
Delaware S P C A .... E 302 998-2281
  Newark (G-10475)
Delaware Zoological Soc Inc .... G 302 571-7747
  Wilmington (G-15985)
Dog House Ventures Inc .... F 302 738-2267
  Newark (G-10547)
Dog Stop .... G 302 376-9006
  Middletown (G-7067)
Dog Stop .... G 302 416-4646
  Wilmington (G-16117)
Dovington Training Center LLC .... G 302 284-2114
  Felton (G-3961)
Fur Baby .... G 302 725-5078
  Milford (G-7904)
Fur Baby Tracker LLC .... G 610 563-3294
  Wilmington (G-16772)
Grind Kennels LLC .... G 302 442-5599
  Wilmington (G-16980)
Groom Kings LLC .... G 302 744-9444
  Dover (G-2630)
Hall of Fame LLC .... G 443 373-4046
  Dagsboro (G-1458)
▲ Harrington Raceway Inc .... F 302 398-4920
  Harrington (G-4779)
Heavenly Hound Hotel .... G 302 436-2926
  Selbyville (G-13545)
Homeless Cat Helpers Inc .... F 302 344-3015
  Seaford (G-13214)
Jackie Heck .... G 302 856-1598
  Georgetown (G-4377)
Jenns Tail Waggers .... F 302 475-9621
  Wilmington (G-17528)
Jungle Jims Total Pet Care .... G 302 212-5055
  Dewey Beach (G-1672)
K-10 Dog Training .... G 302 236-2497
  Rehoboth Beach (G-12813)
K9 Service Companion Inc .... G 716 804-3830
  Dover (G-2827)

Kozy Kennels .... G 302 455-1152
  Newark (G-11201)
Kritter Sitter .... G 302 270-0963
  Woodside (G-20978)
Krm Stables .... G 302 653-3838
  Clayton (G-1382)
La Bella .... G 302 644-2572
  Milford (G-7969)
Love My Dog Inc .... G 240 441-7267
  Dover (G-2977)
Manmade Kennels LLC .... G 302 272-3625
  Felton (G-4000)
Mayer Racing Stables .... G 302 829-8673
  Ocean View (G-12544)
Michael Matthew Sponaugle .... G 302 566-1010
  Harrington (G-4802)
Miranda Enterprises LLC .... G 302 236-0897
  Ocean View (G-12548)
Never Nver Land Knnel Cttery I ...... G 302 645-6140
  Lewes (G-6310)
Oberle William A Jr St Rep .... G 302 738-6241
  Newark (G-11574)
Paws & People Too .... G 302 376-8234
  Middletown (G-7433)
Paws For Life Inc .... G 302 376-7297
  Middletown (G-7434)
Paws Love LLC .... G 267 770-0777
  Wilmington (G-18924)
Pet Bow Tique LLC .... G 302 856-7297
  Georgetown (G-4465)
Puppies and More Rescue Inc .... G 856 753-6538
  Wilmington (G-19257)
RAD Pets Inc .... G 302 335-5718
  Felton (G-4012)
Riverfront Pets .... G 302 428-9777
  Wilmington (G-19496)
Salty Paws RB LLC .... F 484 667-7122
  Rehoboth Beach (G-12944)
Sharp Farm .... F 302 378-9606
  Middletown (G-7559)
South Paw Acres .... G 302 945-1092
  Lewes (G-6493)
Tri-State Bird Rescue RES Inc .... E 302 737-9543
  Newark (G-12223)
Tri-State Pooper Scoopers Inc .... G 302 322-4522
  Newark (G-12226)
Uptown Pet Paws Grooming .... G 302 422-2229
  Milford (G-8132)
Wags To Riches .... G 302 436-4766
  Selbyville (G-13617)
Wash-N-Wag .... G 302 644-2466
  Lewes (G-6615)
Zoomin & Groomin .... G 302 985-3963
  Smyrna (G-13943)

0762 Farm management services

Claros Farm Inc .... G 415 347-1321
  Claymont (G-1089)
Clifton Farms Inc .... G 302 242-8806
  Milford (G-7835)
Los Verdor LLC .... G 971 344-0173
  Wilmington (G-17999)

0781 Landscape counseling and planning

A & V Ldscpg & Hardscaping LLC .. G 302 684-8609
  Milton (G-8553)
A 1 At Your Service .... G 302 369-7000
  Newark (G-9721)
A-1 Kevins Landscaping .... G 302 270-6914
  Smyrna (G-13626)
A&V Landscaping .... G 302 684-8609
  Milton (G-8554)

Addalli Landscaping .... G 302 836-2002
  Bear (G-14)
Albertini Landscaping .... G 302 998-7593
  Wilmington (G-14350)
All About Lawns Landscaping .... G 302 530-1868
  Wilmington (G-14360)
All Seasons Landscaping Inc .... G 302 423-8001
  Dover (G-1764)
Allure Outdoor Lighting LLC .... G 302 226-2532
  Lewes (G-5679)
Als Fare Green .... G 302 500-1871
  Millsboro (G-8169)
American Beauty Ldscpg LLC .... G 302 653-6460
  Smyrna (G-13638)
Anderson Landscaping .... F 302 423-3904
  Smyrna (G-13641)
Arborvine Landscaping LLC .... F 302 502-5605
  Wilmington (G-14525)
Atlantic Landscape Co .... G 302 661-1950
  Wilmington (G-14629)
Augusto & Sons Landscaping LLC . G 302 278-9196
  Bridgeville (G-669)
Autumn Hill Patio & Landscape .... G 302 293-1183
  Wilmington (G-14658)
Ayon Landscaping .... G 302 275-0205
  Wilmington (G-14687)
Bella Terra Landscapes LLC .... F 302 422-9000
  Lincoln (G-6658)
Bella Terra Nursery & Grdn Ctr .... G 302 422-9000
  Ellendale (G-3910)
Bernardon LLC .... F 302 622-9550
  Wilmington (G-14848)
Bethany Blooms .... G 302 829-8578
  Ocean View (G-12479)
Blue Rock Landscaping .... G 302 229-8861
  Wilmington (G-14973)
Blue Rock Landscaping .... G 302 408-0626
  Wilmington (G-14974)
Boni Landscaping LLC .... G 302 569-8852
  Georgetown (G-4237)
Borsello Inc .... E 302 472-2600
  Hockessin (G-5138)
Brandywine Nurseries Inc .... E 302 429-0865
  Wilmington (G-15075)
Brothers Landscaping LLC .... G 360 609-8131
  Laurel (G-5474)
Campbells Landscape Svc Inc .... G 302 266-0117
  Newark (G-10125)
Castaneda Landscaping & Patios ... G 302 377-1674
  Wilmington (G-15265)
Cheap-Scape Inc .... F 302 472-2600
  Hockessin (G-5157)
Cifuentes Landscaping LLC .... G 302 344-8108
  Millsboro (G-8228)
Coastal Edge Landscape LLC .... G 443 880-6270
  Selbyville (G-13502)
Coastal Landscaping LLC .... G 302 222-0098
  Camden Wyoming (G-925)
Coastal Landscaping LLC .... G 302 678-0983
  Dover (G-2106)
Coastal Life Patios .... G 301 944-4005
  Lewes (G-5844)
Complete Properties Services .... G 302 242-8666
  Camden Wyoming (G-926)
Contruction Jones and Ldscpg .... G 302 423-6456
  Camden Wyoming (G-928)
Corrin Tree & Landscape Co .... G 302 753-8733
  Townsend (G-13976)
Corrin Tree Landscape .... G 302 521-8333
  Wilmington (G-15645)
CP Lawn and Landscape .... G 302 396-7074
  Georgetown (G-4271)

2024 Harris Directory of Delaware Businesses

SIC SECTION — 07 AGRICULTURAL SERVICES

Company	Code	Phone
Creative Courtyards	G	302 253-8237
Georgetown *(G-4272)*		
Cutting Edge	F	302 834-8723
Delaware City *(G-1535)*		
Cutting Edge of Delaware Inc	F	302 834-8723
Wilmington *(G-15747)*		
Daniels Lawn and Tree LLC	F	302 218-0173
Wilmington *(G-15786)*		
Delaware Hardscape Supply LLC	G	302 996-6464
Wilmington *(G-15922)*		
Delaware Lawn & Tree Service	F	302 834-7406
Bear *(G-150)*		
Delaware Patio & Landscpg Inc	G	302 218-3738
Townsend *(G-13988)*		
Disabatino Landscaping Inc	D	302 764-0408
Wilmington *(G-16086)*		
Disabatino Ldscpg Tree Svc Inc	F	302 764-0408
Wilmington *(G-16087)*		
Distinctive Landscaping LLC	G	410 971-8466
Greenwood *(G-4619)*		
DOWntoearthlawn&landscapellc	G	302 381-5051
Dagsboro *(G-1442)*		
Dreamscape Landscaping	G	302 354-5247
Claymont *(G-1123)*		
Dutch Neck Lawn and Ldscp LLC	G	302 562-3651
Middletown *(G-7075)*		
E A Zando Custom Designs Inc	F	302 684-4601
Milton *(G-8613)*		
Edc LLC	G	302 645-0777
Lewes *(G-5948)*		
Edward Papiro	G	302 757-9813
Bear *(G-196)*		
Elite Landscape	G	302 543-7305
Wilmington *(G-16364)*		
Emerald Lawn and Ldscpg LLC	G	302 228-1468
Milford *(G-7880)*		
Erics Handyman & Ldscpg Svcs	G	302 242-7712
Woodside *(G-20976)*		
Evergreen Hardscaping Inc	G	302 633-4045
Wilmington *(G-16485)*		
Evergreen Landscaping De	G	302 724-0787
Smyrna *(G-13727)*		
Fantastic Landscaping Fen	G	302 494-9034
Newark *(G-10711)*		
Fast Action Landscaping Inc	G	302 332-7124
Newark *(G-10714)*		
First State Landscaping	G	302 420-8604
Bear *(G-228)*		
Garden Design Group Inc	G	302 234-3000
Hockessin *(G-5217)*		
Green Eyes Landscaping Inc	G	302 653-3800
Dover *(G-2623)*		
Greenleaf Landscapes LLC	G	302 762-5027
Wilmington *(G-16972)*		
Grizzlys Landscape Supl & Svc	G	302 644-0654
Lewes *(G-6064)*		
Habitat Design Group	G	302 335-4452
Frederica *(G-4169)*		
Hernandez Gustavo	G	302 354-1969
Newark *(G-10950)*		
Hockessin Landscaping	G	302 235-2141
Newark *(G-10956)*		
Hoerner Inc	F	302 762-4406
Wilmington *(G-17163)*		
Ibr Lndscping Lawn Care Svcs L	F	610 818-7127
Wilmington *(G-17256)*		
Irwin Landscaping Inc	G	302 239-9229
Hockessin *(G-5252)*		
Jack Kellys Ldscpg & Tree Svc	G	302 239-7185
Hockessin *(G-5257)*		
Jack R Kellys Landscape & Tre	G	302 218-6684
Newark *(G-11080)*		
Ji DCI Jv-II	G	302 652-4221
Wilmington *(G-17544)*		
Jimmy Smalls Landscaping LLC	F	302 730-0150
Camden Wyoming *(G-956)*		
Jobes Landscape Inc	G	302 945-0195
Lewes *(G-6143)*		
Joses Landscaping	G	302 584-2656
Wilmington *(G-17589)*		
Jrp Industrial Services LLC	G	302 439-4092
Claymont *(G-1202)*		
Juan Saucedo	G	302 233-4539
Dover *(G-2812)*		
Kairos Landscaping	G	302 399-4724
Clayton *(G-1378)*		
Kent Landscaping Co LLC	F	302 535-4296
Camden *(G-867)*		
Kinsler Landscaping LLC	G	302 745-0269
Millsboro *(G-8341)*		
Landscaping	G	302 438-3471
Wilmington *(G-17800)*		
Leons Garden World Ej Inc	F	410 392-8630
New Castle *(G-9308)*		
Leons Garden World Inc	E	302 999-9055
Wilmington *(G-17880)*		
Lord and Sons Landscaping	G	302 745-3001
Frankford *(G-4123)*		
Marenos Landscaping	G	302 531-7009
Dover *(G-3017)*		
Mark A Horne	G	302 381-6672
Rehoboth Beach *(G-12848)*		
MCB Landscaping LLC	G	215 421-1083
Wilmington *(G-18214)*		
Michael A Sinclair Inc	G	302 834-8144
Bear *(G-374)*		
Miguel Esparza	G	302 518-7873
Wilmington *(G-18349)*		
MRM Landscaping LLC	G	302 602-1203
Wilmington *(G-18473)*		
Natures Call LLC	G	302 777-7767
Wilmington *(G-18558)*		
Nichols Nursery Inc	E	302 834-2426
Newark *(G-11556)*		
Outside Services LLC	G	302 250-3317
Wilmington *(G-18840)*		
Paco Construction & Ldscpg LLC	G	302 359-2432
Dover *(G-3259)*		
Page Precision Cuts	G	302 272-2380
Smyrna *(G-13844)*		
Paradise Landscaping	G	302 654-4030
Wilmington *(G-18884)*		
Passwaters Landscaping	F	302 542-8077
Bridgeville *(G-745)*		
Penny Hill Lawn & Landscaping	G	302 762-4406
Wilmington *(G-18958)*		
Pqs Landscaping	G	302 690-6505
New Castle *(G-9487)*		
Precision Landscaping Inc	E	302 658-3855
Wilmington *(G-19156)*		
Precision Landscaping Svcs LLC	G	302 528-2935
Wilmington *(G-19157)*		
Precision Ldscpg & Lawn Care	G	302 492-1583
Hartly *(G-4904)*		
Prices Landscaping & Hardscap	G	302 280-3072
Bridgeville *(G-754)*		
R D Collins & Sons	F	302 834-3409
Bear *(G-444)*		
Ramones Landscaping	G	302 268-8023
Wilmington *(G-19327)*		
Ras Addis & Associates Inc	G	302 571-1683
Wilmington *(G-19335)*		
Rodney Rbnsn Ldscp Archts Inc	G	302 888-1544
Wilmington *(G-19549)*		
Ruppert Landscape LLC	D	302 537-2771
Dagsboro *(G-1502)*		
Ryan Gallo Tree Service Inc	F	302 239-1001
Hockessin *(G-5375)*		
Schools Landscaping	G	302 613-8224
Newark *(G-11960)*		
Shackleford Facilities Inc	F	877 735-3938
Frankford *(G-4141)*		
Shackleford Ldscp Grp LLC	G	302 883-9602
Bear *(G-486)*		
Shore Property Maintenance	F	302 947-4440
Harbeson *(G-4715)*		
Shortcutz Lawn Care Inc	G	302 538-6007
Dover *(G-3551)*		
Sposato Irrigation Company	E	302 645-4773
Milton *(G-8713)*		
Sposato Landscape Company Inc	E	302 645-4773
Milton *(G-8714)*		
Superior Yardworks Inc	G	610 274-2255
Hockessin *(G-5399)*		
Tlaloc Landscape LLC	G	302 562-9087
Bear *(G-534)*		
Waterfront Ldscpg Irrigation	G	302 645-8100
Lewes *(G-6617)*		
Whartons Landscaping LLC	F	302 426-4854
Rehoboth Beach *(G-13015)*		
White Oak Landscape MGT Inc	G	302 652-7533
Wilmington *(G-20766)*		

0782 Lawn and garden services

Company	Code	Phone
1-800-By-mulch	G	302 325-2257
New Castle *(G-8742)*		
Absolutely Green Inc	G	302 731-1616
Newark *(G-9746)*		
Apex Lawn & Home	G	302 670-4363
Dover *(G-1803)*		
Bartons Landscaping/Lawn Inc	E	302 629-2213
Seaford *(G-13076)*		
Borsello Inc	E	302 472-2600
Hockessin *(G-5138)*		
Bowden Landscaping	G	302 934-6567
Millsboro *(G-8202)*		
Brandywine Nurseries Inc	E	302 429-0865
Wilmington *(G-15075)*		
Bright Side Exteriors	G	302 674-4642
Dover *(G-1980)*		
Cavalier Lawn Care & Ldscpg	G	302 838-2005
Middletown *(G-6964)*		
Chambers Ldscpg & Lawncare Inc	G	302 328-1312
New Castle *(G-8925)*		
Charae Landscaping Inc	G	302 792-9411
Wilmington *(G-15334)*		
Coastal Plant Care LLC	G	703 994-6905
Ocean View *(G-12492)*		
Coastal Seafood LLC	G	302 242-6659
Lewes *(G-5846)*		
Common Sense Solutions LLC	F	302 875-4510
Laurel *(G-5484)*		
Country Lawn Care & Maint	F	302 593-3393
Harbeson *(G-4692)*		
Curbs Etc Inc	G	302 653-3511
Smyrna *(G-13690)*		
Custom Lawn Services Inc	G	302 540-4180
Wilmington *(G-15742)*		
Cutem Up Tree Care Del Inc	G	302 629-4655
Seaford *(G-13143)*		
Cutting Edge of Delaware Inc	F	302 834-8723
Wilmington *(G-15747)*		
Daniels Lawn and Tree LLC	F	302 218-0173
Wilmington *(G-15786)*		
David M Wagner	G	302 832-8336
Bear *(G-134)*		

07 AGRICULTURAL SERVICES

SIC SECTION

David Rockwell & Associates................ G 302 478-9900
  Wilmington *(G-15810)*

Davis-Young Associates Inc................. G 610 388-0932
  Yorklyn *(G-20991)*

De Turf Sports Complex....................... G 302 330-8873
  Frederica *(G-4164)*

Del Lawn Service.................................. G 302 525-4148
  Newark *(G-10412)*

Delaware Landscaping Inc................... G 302 698-3001
  Dover *(G-2248)*

Delaware Lawn Crew LLC.................... G 302 368-3344
  Wilmington *(G-15938)*

Delaware Lawnandlandscape............... G 302 276-1060
  New Castle *(G-9026)*

Delaware Secretary of State................. G 302 834-8046
  Bear *(G-155)*

Dick Ennis Inc....................................... G 302 945-2627
  Lewes *(G-5914)*

Dreamscape Design Cons LLC............. G 302 893-0984
  Newark *(G-10571)*

Eagle Building and Grounds................. G 302 508-5403
  Clayton *(G-1361)*

Edwards Lawn Care.............................. G 302 981-7751
  New Castle *(G-9082)*

Emerald Green...................................... G 302 836-6909
  Middletown *(G-7099)*

ER Lawn Care LLC............................... G 302 519-3173
  Bridgeville *(G-698)*

Ernie Deangelis.................................... F 302 226-9533
  Rehoboth Beach *(G-12746)*

Evan Hurst Property Management........ G 302 375-0398
  Claymont *(G-1137)*

Evs Lawn Service Inc........................... G 302 475-9222
  Wilmington *(G-16495)*

First Class Lawncare............................ F 302 753-0761
  Wilmington *(G-16616)*

Fish Lawn and Tree LLC....................... F 302 383-4202
  Townsend *(G-14002)*

Forever Green Landscaping Inc........... F 302 322-9535
  New Castle *(G-9140)*

Fresh Start Lawn Services................... G 302 279-6234
  Newark *(G-10783)*

George J Martino.................................. G 302 376-5162
  Townsend *(G-14007)*

Gildea Enterprises Inc......................... G 302 420-8900
  Wilmington *(G-16860)*

Grass Busters Landscaping Co........... E 302 292-1166
  Newark *(G-10881)*

Green Acres Lawn & Ldscpg Corp...... G 302 332-8239
  Newark *(G-10888)*

Green Blade Irrigation & Turf.............. G 302 736-8873
  Magnolia *(G-6748)*

Green Eyes Landscaping Inc.............. G 302 653-3800
  Dover *(G-2623)*

Green Side Up Lawn & Landscape..... G 302 999-7151
  Wilmington *(G-16967)*

Greenleaf Services Inc........................ G 302 836-9050
  Lewes *(G-6059)*

Greenleaf Turf Solutions Inc............... G 302 731-1075
  Newark *(G-10890)*

Grizzlys Landscape Sup & Svcs.......... G 302 644-0654
  Lewes *(G-6063)*

Hagy Landscaping Inc......................... G 707 935-6119
  Millsboro *(G-8311)*

Horsey Turf Farm LLC.......................... F 302 875-7299
  Laurel *(G-5532)*

Integrated Turf Management Sys........ F 302 266-8000
  Newark *(G-11031)*

Irwin Landscaping Inc......................... G 302 239-9229
  Hockessin *(G-5252)*

Isaacs Landscaping & Gardening........ G 302 947-1414
  Millsboro *(G-8322)*

Itea Inc.. G 302 328-3716
  Lewes *(G-6133)*

Izzys Lawn Service Inc........................ G 302 293-9221
  Wilmington *(G-17442)*

Jack Ennis Custom Lawn..................... G 302 422-8577
  Milford *(G-7949)*

Jamark Enterprises Inc....................... E 302 652-2000
  Wilmington *(G-17476)*

Jonny Nichols Ldscp Maint Inc........... G 302 697-2200
  Dover *(G-2802)*

Jordy Jael Lawn Care.......................... G 302 824-3748
  Georgetown *(G-4386)*

Kcs Total Lawn Care LLC.................... G 732 331-2454
  Millsboro *(G-8336)*

Keener-Sensenig Co............................ F 302 453-8584
  Newark *(G-11149)*

Kellys Lawn Care................................. G 302 584-1045
  Hockessin *(G-5267)*

Kenneth Dale Ralosky.......................... G 302 343-9464
  Dover *(G-2842)*

Kenneth J Hurley.................................. G 302 734-3251
  Dover *(G-2843)*

Kens Lawn Service Inc........................ G 302 478-2714
  Wilmington *(G-17690)*

Kevin M Miller...................................... G 302 514-7111
  Smyrna *(G-13791)*

Kst Land Design Inc............................ G 302 328-1879
  Wilmington *(G-17759)*

Lawnworks Inc..................................... F 302 368-5699
  Newark *(G-11233)*

Leounes Catered Affairs..................... G 302 547-3233
  Wilmington *(G-17882)*

Lets Get Green..................................... G 302 633-4733
  Wilmington *(G-17887)*

Lords Landscaping Inc....................... E 302 539-6119
  Millville *(G-8538)*

M Denight Lawn Care LLC................... G 302 528-4152
  Smyrna *(G-13812)*

Manicured Lawns................................. G 302 853-2222
  Seaford *(G-13272)*

Martom Landscaping Co Inc............... F 302 322-1920
  Saint Georges *(G-13037)*

Mary Annes Landscaping Inc............. G 302 335-5433
  Felton *(G-4001)*

McIlvain Lawn Mowing More LLC....... G 302 684-4213
  Milton *(G-8664)*

Michael J Truitt................................... G 302 436-4081
  Selbyville *(G-13571)*

Mid Atlantic.. G 302 393-4355
  Georgetown *(G-4427)*

Monkeys In Trees LLC......................... G 302 519-4551
  Bridgeville *(G-735)*

Moody Lawn Care & Renovations....... G 302 685-2338
  Wilmington *(G-18428)*

Nash Omniscaping LLC....................... G 302 654-4000
  Wilmington *(G-18535)*

Naturalawn of America Inc.................. F 302 652-2000
  Wilmington *(G-18556)*

New Creation Lawn Care Inc.............. G 302 698-0246
  Felton *(G-4005)*

Old Country Garden Center Inc.......... F 302 652-3317
  Wilmington *(G-18754)*

Outdoor Design Group LLC................ F 302 743-2363
  Newark *(G-11607)*

Outside Creations................................ G 302 757-5944
  New Castle *(G-9440)*

Paul Haller... G 302 737-0525
  Newark *(G-11643)*

Penwood Lawn Care............................ G 302 535-4464
  Felton *(G-4008)*

Perfection Lawncare Ltd..................... G 215 624-7410
  Middletown *(G-7441)*

Plant Retrievers Whl Nurs................... G 302 337-9833
  Georgetown *(G-4467)*

Pro Exteriors....................................... G 302 664-1700
  Milton *(G-8691)*

Professnl Arfication Svcs Inc.............. G 302 752-7003
  Georgetown *(G-4474)*

R D Collins & Sons.............................. F 302 834-3409
  Bear *(G-444)*

Rabbani-Tehrani Shahariar................. G 302 376-1081
  Middletown *(G-7497)*

Rentokil North America Inc................ E 302 733-0851
  Newark *(G-11855)*

Roger Summers Lawn Care Inc......... G 302 218-3319
  Hockessin *(G-5370)*

Royal Lawn Care & Property MAI....... G 302 436-9800
  Selbyville *(G-13601)*

Sacco Lawn Care................................. G 302 545-3803
  Bear *(G-478)*

Samuel Prettyman............................... G 302 858-8886
  Delmar *(G-1634)*

Seeney Electric LLC............................ G 302 494-3686
  New Castle *(G-9556)*

Serrano Inc.. G 302 607-1779
  Newark *(G-11982)*

Shortcutz Lawn and Landsca............. G 302 736-0906
  Dover *(G-3550)*

Shubert Enterprises Inc...................... F 302 846-3122
  Delmar *(G-1637)*

Simply Grand LLC............................... G 480 278-0367
  Wilmington *(G-19838)*

Simply Green....................................... F 302 256-0822
  Wilmington *(G-19839)*

Smith and Son Lawn Service.............. G 302 934-1778
  Dagsboro *(G-1505)*

Sposato Lawn Care.............................. G 302 645-4773
  Milton *(G-8715)*

Spring-Green Lawn Care.................... G 302 762-1499
  Wilmington *(G-19975)*

Stephen Hannig................................... G 302 792-1342
  Claymont *(G-1303)*

Stewart Bros Turf LLC......................... G 302 333-3707
  Wilmington *(G-20069)*

STI Landscape Solutions.................... G 302 645-6262
  Lewes *(G-6512)*

Superior Lawncare LLC...................... G 302 373-3289
  Townsend *(G-14075)*

Tender Lawn & Care............................ G 410 310-6550
  Seaford *(G-13428)*

Texas Lawn Care Svc.......................... G 302 547-5829
  Wilmington *(G-20282)*

Tramaine & Sons Lawn Care LLC....... G 302 897-0524
  Wilmington *(G-20390)*

Trugreen Limited Partnership............ E 302 724-6620
  Wilmington *(G-20445)*

Turf Pro Inc.. G 302 218-3530
  Newark *(G-12245)*

Union Park Lawns............................... G 302 757-5496
  Wilmington *(G-20513)*

US Lawns Dover.................................. G 302 703-2818
  Lewes *(G-6593)*

West Third Enterprises LLC............... G 302 732-3133
  Dagsboro *(G-1526)*

Whittakers Lawn Care......................... G 302 478-2169
  Wilmington *(G-20773)*

Wilcox Landscaping Inc..................... E 302 322-3002
  New Castle *(G-9682)*

William H Rdford Nurseries Inc.......... E 302 659-3130
  Smyrna *(G-13938)*

Wrights Lawn Care Inc....................... F 302 684-3058
  Milton *(G-8731)*

0783 Ornamental shrub and tree services

A+ Tree Service LLC............................... G 302 253-8612
  Georgetown (G-4193)
AAA Tree Work LLC................................ G 302 213-2917
  Millsboro (G-8158)
ABC Tree Svc... G 302 737-8473
  Wilmington (G-14197)
Afford-A-Tree Svc & Ldscpg LLC........ G 302 670-4154
  Hartly (G-4854)
All American Tree Experts.................... G 302 419-4876
  Bear (G-25)
American Tree Co LLC............................ G 302 836-1664
  Bear (G-33)
Ankor Tree Service LLC......................... G 302 514-7447
  Smyrna (G-13643)
Arbor Care... G 302 491-4392
  Lincoln (G-6657)
Arbor Care... F 302 258-8909
  Seaford (G-13068)
Beaver Tree Service Inc........................ G 302 226-3564
  Rehoboth Beach (G-12634)
Brandywine Tree and Shrub LLC......... G 302 475-7594
  Wilmington (G-15087)
Cheaps Tree Service.............................. G 302 750-4590
  New Castle (G-8927)
Complete Tree Care Inc........................ G 302 945-8289
  Millsboro (G-8237)
Cutem Up Tree Care Del Inc................ G 302 629-4655
  Seaford (G-13143)
Cypress Tree Care.................................. G 302 732-3227
  Frankford (G-4097)
Delmarva Arborists LLC....................... G 302 581-9494
  Dagsboro (G-1438)
Erosion Ctrl Specialists Inc................. G 302 367-6649
  Middletown (G-7108)
First State Rental Company LLC......... G 302 632-5699
  Houston (G-5441)
Fish and Son Services............................ G 302 383-4202
  Wilmington (G-16647)
Jason L Torlish Sr.................................... G 302 682-3874
  Seaford (G-13230)
Las Quality Tree Service LLC............. G 302 981-3243
  Newark (G-11223)
Loockermans Tree Stump Removal.... G 302 745-6446
  Dover (G-2975)
Mitsdarfer Bros Tree Service............... F 302 540-6029
  Wilmington (G-18388)
Randys Tree Service............................... G 302 856-7244
  Georgetown (G-4481)
Ryan Gallo Tree Service Inc................ F 302 239-1001
  Hockessin (G-5375)
Stein Tree Service Inc.......................... G 302 478-3511
  Wilmington (G-20047)
Strobert Tree Services.......................... G 302 633-3478
  Wilmington (G-20102)
▲ Strobert Tree Services Inc................ E 302 475-7089
  Wilmington (G-20103)
Sussex Tree Inc....................................... G 302 629-9899
  Bridgeville (G-772)
Tarburton Landscape.............................. G 302 932-1814
  Wilmington (G-20223)
Thomas E Cameron.................................. G 302 345-6708
  Claymont (G-1312)

08 FORESTRY

0811 Timber tracts

Dons Tree Farm.. G 302 349-0555
  Greenwood (G-4621)
Whitetail Country Log & Hlg................. G 302 846-3982
  Delmar (G-1656)

0851 Forestry services

Delaware Cy Vlntr Fire Co No 1........... E 302 834-9336
  Delaware City (G-1538)
Delmarva Arborists LLC....................... G 302 581-9494
  Dagsboro (G-1438)
Edward A Fufaro Inc.............................. G 302 934-6595
  Millsboro (G-8280)
U S Fire Forces Inc................................ F 302 270-8294
  Dover (G-3739)

09 FISHING, HUNTING AND TRAPPING

0919 Miscellaneous marine products

▲ Advance Marine LLC........................... G 302 656-2111
  Wilmington (G-14268)

0971 Hunting, trapping, game propagation

Deskzone LLC... G 212 608-7081
  Wilmington (G-16028)

10 METAL MINING

1011 Iron ores

▲ American Minerals Partnership........ F 302 652-3301
  New Castle (G-8800)
Oreomatic Mining Inc............................. E 725 255-8895
  Wilmington (G-18817)

1021 Copper ores

CC Enterprises LLC................................ F 302 265-3677
  Newark (G-10167)

1061 Ferroalloy ores, except vanadium

▲ American Minerals Partnership........ F 302 652-3301
  New Castle (G-8800)

1081 Metal mining services

Ivanhoe Electric Inc............................... D 720 933-1150
  Wilmington (G-17437)
Nanoshel LLC.. F 302 268-6163
  Wilmington (G-18531)

1099 Metal ores, nec

▲ American Minerals Partnership........ F 302 652-3301
  New Castle (G-8800)

12 COAL MINING

1241 Coal mining services

Oreomatic Mining Inc............................. E 725 255-8895
  Wilmington (G-18817)

13 OIL AND GAS EXTRACTION

1311 Crude petroleum and natural gas

Akbell Global Commodities LLC......... G 347 615-5014
  Dover (G-1759)
Firebird Energy II LLC............................ E 817 857-7800
  Wilmington (G-16611)
I-Pulse Inc... G 604 689-8765
  Wilmington (G-17250)
Kiwetinohk Marketing US Corp........... G 403 827-6958
  Dover (G-2879)
Nemours Energy....................................... G 302 655-4838
  Wilmington (G-18577)

1321 Natural gas liquids

Helix Services LLC................................. G 302 306-4880
  Middletown (G-7204)

1381 Drilling oil and gas wells

Ile LLC.. G 302 389-7911
  Wilmington (G-17279)
Pride International LLC........................ F 713 789-1400
  Wilmington (G-19190)
Regen III (usgc) Corporation............... G 604 806-5275
  Wilmington (G-19399)
◆ Scorpion Offshore Inc......................... B
  Wilmington (G-19711)

1382 Oil and gas exploration services

I-Pulse Inc... G 604 689-8765
  Wilmington (G-17250)
Lucid Colloids Amer.............................. G 302 475-2393
  Wilmington (G-18024)
Rangeland Nm LLC................................. G 800 316-6660
  Dover (G-3423)
Vault Oil & Gas LLC.............................. G 303 731-0080
  Dover (G-3776)
Voyager Drilling Services LLC........... F 302 439-6030
  Wilmington (G-20654)

1389 Oil and gas field services, nec

Accurate-Energy LLC............................. G 302 947-9560
  Lewes (G-5654)
Advanced Fuel Polsg Svc Inc.............. G 302 477-1040
  Claymont (G-1021)
Aim Metals & Alloys USA Inc.............. G 212 450-4519
  Wilmington (G-14333)
ARC Offshore Investments Inc........... G 561 670-9938
  Wilmington (G-14533)
Barry Management Group De LLC..... G 302 480-0519
  Wilmington (G-14769)
Carvers Construction LLC................... G 302 505-0260
  Camden (G-804)
Cobalt Pacific LLC................................. G 302 437-4761
  Townsend (G-13973)
D & J Welding LLC................................ F 347 706-5561
  Dover (G-2178)
Decennium Management Group.......... G 302 600-3644
  Dover (G-2205)
Delaware Storage & Pipeline Co........ G 302 736-1774
  Dover (G-2266)
DH Tech Wilmington De......................... G 215 680-9194
  Wilmington (G-16044)
Dick Ennis Inc.. G 302 945-2627
  Lewes (G-5914)
Do It Up Designs LLC........................... G 484 269-6142
  Millsboro (G-8273)
Dreams Unlimited LLC.......................... G 302 747-0527
  Dover (G-2382)
Ecg Industries Inc.................................. G 302 453-0535
  Newark (G-10603)
Empire Data Voice Networks LLC..... G 702 613-4900
  Millsboro (G-8281)
Estate Servicing LLC............................. G 302 731-1119
  Newark (G-10667)
I Do It Right 100 LLC............................. G 302 304-4467
  Wilmington (G-17246)
Jbm Petroleum Service LLC................. G 302 752-6105
  Lincoln (G-6677)
Keyrock LLC.. G 818 605-7772
  Wilmington (G-17705)
Lone Star Global Services Inc........... G 302 744-9800
  Dover (G-2974)
Mff Oilfield Solutions LLC.................. G 603 795-0617
  Wilmington (G-18297)
Mi-1 LLC... G 302 369-3447
  Newark (G-11398)
Monroe Enterprising Svcs LLC........... G 302 345-1527
  Wilmington (G-18418)
Next Level Home Improvements......... G 484 469-1767
  Claymont (G-1251)

13 OIL AND GAS EXTRACTION

O&G Knwldge Shring Pltform LLC......... G 303 872-0533
  Wilmington *(G-18724)*
Own Lane Construction LLC.................. G 302 579-8103
  Seaford *(G-13329)*
Padilla Konstruction LLC........................ G 302 276-6678
  Wilmington *(G-18861)*
Platinum Cnstr Renovations LLC............ G 302 288-0670
  Dover *(G-3329)*
Pride International LLC........................... F 713 789-1400
  Wilmington *(G-19190)*
Property Doctors LLC............................. G 302 249-7731
  Magnolia *(G-6777)*
Rawr Imports Group LLC........................ G 609 271-3455
  Claymont *(G-1274)*
Rock Solid Servicing LLC....................... G 302 233-2569
  Magnolia *(G-6780)*
Sn & Partners... G 312 826-3255
  Newark *(G-12044)*
T&G Construction LLC............................ G 302 922-1674
  Townsend *(G-14076)*
TEC-Con Inc... G 610 583-8770
  New Castle *(G-9621)*
Turner and Selby Group Inc................... E 302 666-2339
  Wilmington *(G-20463)*
Wallace Lamarr....................................... G 202 460-3477
  Dover *(G-3817)*
Willey and Co... G 302 629-3327
  Laurel *(G-5626)*

14 MINING AND QUARRYING OF NONMETALLIC MINERALS, EXCEPT FUELS

1411 Dimension stone
Dimensional Stone Products LLC........... F 302 322-3900
  New Castle *(G-9055)*

1429 Crushed and broken stone, nec
Contractors Materials LLC...................... F 302 656-6066
  Wilmington *(G-15624)*

1442 Construction sand and gravel
77 Legacy LLC....................................... G 404 576-7265
  Wilmington *(G-14147)*
Bear Materials LLC................................. G 302 658-5241
  New Castle *(G-8855)*
Cook Hauling LLC................................... G 302 378-6451
  Middletown *(G-7012)*
Goldsboro Sand and Gravel.................... G 410 310-0402
  Camden Wyoming *(G-949)*
Joseph M L Sand & Gravel Co................ E 302 856-7396
  Georgetown *(G-4387)*
Lewis Sand and Gravel LLC................... G 302 238-0169
  Millsboro *(G-8348)*
Material Transit Inc................................. E 302 395-0556
  New Castle *(G-9353)*
Parkway Gravel Inc................................. G 302 326-0554
  New Castle *(G-9451)*
Sussex Sand & Gravel Inc...................... G 302 628-6962
  Seaford *(G-13422)*

1446 Industrial sand
American Minerals Inc............................. G 302 652-3301
  New Castle *(G-8799)*
Stockley Materials LLC........................... F 302 856-7601
  Georgetown *(G-4526)*

1459 Clay and related minerals, nec
◆ Rhi Refractories Holding Company....... A 302 655-6497
  Wilmington *(G-19457)*

1479 Chemical and fertilizer mining
▲ Oceanport LLC.................................... F 302 792-2212
  Claymont *(G-1256)*

1481 Nonmetallic mineral services
Reliance Egleford Upstream LLC............ G 302 472-7437
  Wilmington *(G-19425)*

1499 Miscellaneous nonmetallic mining
Asbury Carbons Inc................................ F 302 652-0266
  Wilmington *(G-14576)*
Italtec Gold & Commodities Inc.............. F 302 446-3207
  Dover *(G-2755)*
◆ Rgp Holding Inc.................................. F 302 661-0117
  Wilmington *(G-19453)*

15 CONSTRUCTION - GENERAL CONTRACTORS & OPERATIVE BUILDERS

1521 Single-family housing construction
302 Properties LLC................................. G 302 525-4302
  Newark *(G-9708)*
36 Builders Inc....................................... E 302 349-9480
  Bridgeville *(G-657)*
A & Tc Builders Inc................................. G 443 736-0099
  Lewes *(G-5643)*
A J E Construction LLC........................... G 302 217-2268
  Seaford *(G-13044)*
A Js Fence Builders Inc.......................... G 302 731-0000
  Newark *(G-9725)*
A S Jacono LLC...................................... G 302 378-3000
  Middletown *(G-6824)*
A To Z First Builders LLC........................ G 302 393-9761
  Greenwood *(G-4587)*
Accord Restoration Inc........................... G 302 933-0991
  Millsboro *(G-8162)*
Ace Home Solutions Corp...................... G 302 743-8995
  New Castle *(G-8761)*
Acp Services LLC................................... G 302 299-4225
  Wilmington *(G-14239)*
Adel Construction.................................... G 302 286-7676
  Newark *(G-9764)*
Advance Construction Co Del................. F 302 697-9444
  Camden Wyoming *(G-906)*
Advance Construction Technique........... G 270 257-0377
  Wilmington *(G-14265)*
Advance Inc... F 302 324-8890
  Newark *(G-9771)*
Advance Wndw/Sprior Siding Inc............ G 302 324-8890
  Newark *(G-9772)*
Alka Construction LLC............................. G 443 944-9058
  Seaford *(G-13054)*
All In One Home Repairs LLC................ G 302 897-3845
  Newark *(G-9817)*
All Restored Inc...................................... G 302 697-7810
  Camden Wyoming *(G-909)*
Alltemp Air Inc... F 302 945-5734
  Lewes *(G-5678)*
American Builders Inc............................. G 856 287-0840
  Middletown *(G-6858)*
Americo Inc... F 302 981-9410
  Wilmington *(G-14446)*
Amish Tradesmen................................... G 302 349-5550
  Seaford *(G-13065)*
Amy Chilimidos C O Boa........................ G 302 388-1880
  Hockessin *(G-5124)*
Andrew B Price Custom Builde............... G 302 659-5368
  Smyrna *(G-13642)*

Andrews Construction LLC..................... G 302 604-8166
  Lincoln *(G-6656)*
Anythings Possible Cnstr........................ G 302 233-2357
  Harrington *(G-4733)*
AON Construction Services LLC............. G 302 858-6178
  Bethany Beach *(G-574)*
Apex Builders LLC.................................. G 302 242-1059
  Dover *(G-1802)*
Archadeck of Delaware........................... F 302 766-3698
  Hockessin *(G-5129)*
Archadeck of Delaware........................... G 302 766-3698
  Newark *(G-9899)*
Arivers Construction................................ G 302 299-2288
  Newark *(G-9903)*
Aruanno Enterprises Inc......................... G 302 530-1217
  Middletown *(G-6875)*
Astoria Builders LLC............................... G 302 892-9211
  Greenville *(G-4583)*
Astoria Builders LLC............................... G 302 993-7951
  Wilmington *(G-14605)*
Atlantic Coast Builders LLC.................... G 302 396-7824
  Frankford *(G-4062)*
Atlantic Homes LLC................................ G 302 947-0223
  Lewes *(G-5714)*
Avid Builders LLC.................................... G 302 233-0148
  Felton *(G-3944)*
B and B Contractors Inc......................... G 302 836-9207
  Newark *(G-9964)*
B Lawrence Homes LLC......................... G 302 559-1779
  Wilmington *(G-14702)*
B&S Home Imprv Envmtl Unvrsal........... G 302 310-4374
  Middletown *(G-6897)*
Bancroft Construction Company............. F 302 655-3434
  Dover *(G-1870)*
Bancroft Homes Inc................................ G 302 655-5461
  Wilmington *(G-14739)*
Banris Construction LLC......................... G 302 722-0958
  Wilmington *(G-14751)*
Bari Concrete Cnstr Corp....................... G 302 384-7093
  Wilmington *(G-14764)*
Basement Unlimited LLC........................ G 302 569-2211
  Lewes *(G-5736)*
Battaglia Mechanical Inc......................... E 302 325-6100
  New Castle *(G-8849)*
Bay 2 Bay Builders................................. G 302 632-7222
  Harrington *(G-4738)*
Bay Developers Inc................................ F 302 736-0924
  Dover *(G-1884)*
Bay To Beach Builders Inc..................... G 302 349-5099
  Farmington *(G-3933)*
Bb Builder Llc.. G 302 670-1972
  Dover *(G-1892)*
Beam Construction Inc........................... G 302 537-2787
  Fenwick Island *(G-4041)*
Bellaline Design LLC.............................. G 302 293-5676
  Bear *(G-68)*
Bellevue Contractors LLC....................... F 302 655-1522
  Wilmington *(G-14821)*
Benchmark Builders Inc......................... E 302 995-6945
  Wilmington *(G-14827)*
Benjamin B Smith Builders Inc............... G 302 537-1916
  Ocean View *(G-12477)*
Benoit Home Improvements LLC........... G 302 633-9284
  Wilmington *(G-14839)*
Benson Concrete Cnstr LLC................... G 410 382-5112
  Seaford *(G-13083)*
Beracah Homes Inc................................ E 302 349-4561
  Greenwood *(G-4597)*
Beracah Sales Office.............................. G 302 854-6700
  Milton *(G-8571)*
Bestfield Associates Inc......................... F 302 633-6361
  Wilmington *(G-14858)*

15 CONSTRUCTION - GENERAL CONTRACTORS & OPERATIVE BUILDERS

Black Dog Construction LLC .... G 302 530-4967
 Newark (G-10045)

Blenheim Management Company .... E 302 254-0100
 Newark (G-10051)

BNai BRith Claymont LP .... G 302 798-6846
 Claymont (G-1062)

Boardwalk Builders Inc .... F 302 227-5754
 Rehoboth Beach (G-12647)

Bowden Construction LLC .... G 302 907-0430
 Delmar (G-1568)

Bowles Construction LLC .... G 302 332-5641
 Wilmington (G-15018)

Boyds Custom Remodeling Inc .... G 302 698-1739
 Hartly (G-4859)

Brand Builder Solutions LLC .... G 302 234-4239
 Wilmington (G-15039)

Brandywine Contractors Inc .... G 302 325-2700
 New Castle (G-8886)

Brannan Construction LLC .... G 302 547-1659
 Newark (G-10081)

Bravos Construction LLC .... G 302 249-0039
 Bridgeville (G-674)

Breeze Construction LLC .... G 302 522-9201
 Townsend (G-13966)

Broadpoint Construction LLC .... G 302 228-8007
 Rehoboth Beach (G-12656)

Bromwell Construction Co LLC .... F 302 598-7072
 Wilmington (G-15125)

Bruce Mears Designer-Builder .... F 302 539-2355
 Ocean View (G-12483)

Bryant Guernsey Cnstr Co .... G 302 737-1841
 Newark (G-10097)

Bryton Hmes At Five Points LLC .... G 302 703-6633
 Frankford (G-4079)

Bulldog Construction .... G 302 632-4834
 Woodside (G-20974)

Bulwark Builders Inc .... G 302 299-3190
 Newark (G-10104)

Bunting Construction Corp .... F 302 436-5124
 Selbyville (G-13487)

Burton Construction Co LLC .... G 302 327-8650
 Hockessin (G-5145)

BV Teagarden & Son Cnstr LLC .... G 410 330-1733
 Delmar (G-1571)

Byers Electrical Construc .... G 302 420-8700
 Historic New Castle (G-4949)

Bz Construction Services Inc .... G 302 999-7505
 Wilmington (G-15167)

C & B Complete Clg Svc Inc .... E 302 436-9622
 Frankford (G-4081)

C & B Construct .... G 302 378-9862
 Milford (G-7809)

C & K Builders LLC .... G 302 324-9811
 Bear (G-87)

C M Construction Co LLC .... G 302 228-3570
 Frankford (G-4082)

C Vargas Construction LLC .... G 302 470-2004
 Seaford (G-13099)

C Wallace & Associates .... G 302 528-2182
 Hockessin (G-5146)

C&M Construction Company LLC .... E 302 663-0936
 Magnolia (G-6725)

C&M Custom Homes LLC .... G 302 736-5824
 Felton (G-3950)

C2 Construction LLC .... G 302 438-3901
 Wilmington (G-15180)

Cambria LLC .... G 703 898-9989
 Lewes (G-5786)

Capano Homes Inc .... E 302 384-7980
 Wilmington (G-15221)

Cape Financial Services Inc .... F 302 645-6274
 Lewes (G-5793)

Capstone Homes LLC .... E 302 644-0300
 Lewes (G-5800)

Carl Deputy & Son Builders LLC .... G 302 284-3041
 Felton (G-3951)

Carl M Freeman .... G 302 988-1669
 Selbyville (G-13491)

Carny Construction .... G 302 436-9738
 Selbyville (G-13493)

Carrie Construction Inc .... G 302 239-5386
 Hockessin (G-5149)

Carrow Construction LLC .... G 302 376-0520
 New Castle (G-8915)

Case Hndyman Svcs W Chster LLC ..... G 302 234-6558
 Hockessin (G-5151)

Castle Care Inc .... G 302 947-2277
 Lewes (G-5808)

Castle Services Inc .... G 302 481-6633
 Wilmington (G-15268)

Castle-Lambert Son Contg Inc .... G 410 329-8192
 Selbyville (G-13495)

Cavan Inc .... G 302 598-4176
 Wilmington (G-15281)

Cedar Rock Construction .... G 302 430-1276
 Harrington (G-4747)

Chandlee Projects LLC .... G 717 542-5919
 Frankford (G-4084)

Charles A Zonko Builders Inc .... F 302 436-0222
 Selbyville (G-13497)

Charles R Reed .... G 302 284-3353
 Felton (G-3953)

Choice Construction Co Inc .... G 302 226-1732
 Rehoboth Beach (G-12672)

Choice Rmdlg & Restoration Inc .... G 717 917-0601
 Hockessin (G-5162)

Chuck Coleman .... G 302 537-2071
 Frankford (G-4090)

Clark Construction Inc .... G 302 832-1288
 Bear (G-108)

Clendaniel Construction .... G 302 422-7415
 Milford (G-7834)

Cns Construction Corp .... G 302 224-0450
 Newark (G-10267)

Coastal Cttage Renovations LLC .... G 302 727-2443
 Lewes (G-5842)

Coastal Paint & Remodeling LLC .... F 302 278-5471
 Frankford (G-4091)

Coastal Sun Roms Prch Enclsres .... G 302 537-3679
 Frankford (G-4092)

Colonial Construction Company .... F 302 994-5705
 Wilmington (G-15535)

Colonial Home Improvements .... G 302 275-8247
 Bear (G-113)

Commonwealth Construction .... F 302 654-6611
 Wilmington (G-15551)

Commonwealth Contruction Co .... E 302 654-6611
 Wilmington (G-15552)

Communications Cnstr Group LLC ..... E 302 280-6926
 Laurel (G-5485)

Connell Construction Co .... G 302 738-9428
 Newark (G-10307)

Construction Resource MGT Inc .... G 302 778-2335
 Lewes (G-5857)

Continental Cnstr & Rmdlg .... G 302 332-6367
 Wilmington (G-15617)

Conway Construction Co .... G 302 598-5019
 Lewes (G-5858)

Country Builders Inc .... G 302 735-5530
 Dover (G-2144)

Country Life Homes Milford De .... G 302 265-2257
 Milford (G-7841)

Courtney Construction .... G 302 798-2393
 Wilmington (G-15659)

Courtney Construction Inc .... G 302 521-5865
 Wilmington (G-15660)

▲ Coverdeck Systems Inc .... F 302 427-7578
 Wilmington (G-15667)

Cpr Construction Inc .... G 302 322-5770
 Historic New Castle (G-4965)

Craftsman Builders of De .... G 302 542-0731
 Laurel (G-5488)

Craig Maurer .... G 302 293-2365
 Middletown (G-7018)

Critical Design and Cnstr Corp .... G 302 588-4406
 Wilmington (G-15707)

Crossroads Land Tech LLC .... F 302 841-0654
 Millsboro (G-8245)

Custom Improvers Inc .... G 302 731-9246
 Newark (G-10368)

D F Quillen & Sons Inc .... E 302 227-2531
 Rehoboth Beach (G-12709)

D S Builders .... G 302 242-3308
 Hartly (G-4865)

Daisy Construction Company .... G 302 658-4417
 New Castle (G-8994)

Dalco Construction Co .... G 302 475-2099
 Wilmington (G-15769)

Dan Miller and Sons Cnstr LLC .... G 302 492-8116
 Hartly (G-4867)

Daniels Custom Finishes LLC .... G 302 357-5806
 Wilmington (G-15785)

Daves Builders Inc .... G 302 539-4058
 Ocean View (G-12499)

Davis Samuel F Jr Gen Contr .... G 302 475-2607
 Wilmington (G-15816)

DC Chambers Construction LLC .... G 302 233-0148
 Felton (G-3957)

De Val Structurez .... G 302 575-9090
 Wilmington (G-15840)

Dead On Construction .... G 302 462-5023
 Selbyville (G-13516)

Deck Masters LLC .... G 302 563-4459
 Wilmington (G-15848)

Deco Crete Inc .... G 302 367-0151
 New Castle (G-9008)

Del Fab Construction LLC .... G 302 943-9131
 Clayton (G-1359)

Del Homes Inc .... F 302 730-1479
 Dover (G-2210)

Del Homes Inc .... F 302 697-8204
 Magnolia (G-6739)

Delaware Constructionology .... G 302 827-3072
 Middletown (G-7038)

Delaware Home Pros LLC .... G 302 894-7098
 Historic New Castle (G-4970)

Delaware Homes Inc .... F 302 378-9510
 Townsend (G-13987)

Delaware Landscape Cnstr LLC .... G 302 841-3010
 Rehoboth Beach (G-12718)

Delaware RE Answers LLC .... G 302 635-0375
 Wilmington (G-15958)

Delaware Remodeling Co .... G 302 545-0075
 Smyrna (G-13706)

Delmarva Builders Inc .... G 302 629-9123
 Bridgeville (G-692)

Delpa Builders LLC .... F 302 731-7304
 New Castle (G-9043)

Deshields Construction .... G 302 331-5214
 Magnolia (G-6740)

Deshong & Sons Contractors Inc .... G 302 453-8500
 Newark (G-10517)

Dewson Construction Co .... E 302 227-3095
 Rehoboth Beach (G-12724)

Dewson Construction Co .... G 302 427-2250
 Wilmington (G-16038)

Employee Codes: A=Over 500 employees, B=251-500
C=101-250, D=51-100, E=20-50, F=10-19, G=1-9

2024 Harris Directory of Delaware Businesses

15 CONSTRUCTION - GENERAL CONTRACTORS & OPERATIVE BUILDERS

Dewson Construction Company .... E 302 427-2250
Wilmington *(G-16039)*

Df Quillen Sons Inc DBA .... G 302 227-7368
Rehoboth Beach *(G-12725)*

Diamond State Homes & Rmdlg .... G 302 983-5574
Newark *(G-10527)*

Diane Austin .... G 302 856-3369
Georgetown *(G-4294)*

Dimple Construction Inc .... G 302 559-7535
Bear *(G-169)*

Dirickson Creek Construction L .... G 302 604-2482
Frankford *(G-4102)*

Disabatino Construction Co .... D 302 652-3838
Wilmington *(G-16084)*

Distinction LLC .... E 302 362-7574
Milton *(G-8607)*

Divergent LLC .... G 302 275-7019
Wilmington *(G-16092)*

Double Diamond Builders Inc .... F 302 945-2512
Millsboro *(G-8277)*

Double S Developers Inc .... G 302 838-8880
Bear *(G-178)*

Dream Home Remodeling LLC .... G 302 981-4919
Newark *(G-10570)*

Dream Werks LLC .... G 302 526-2415
Dover *(G-2381)*

Drw Construction .... G 302 945-9055
Lewes *(G-5937)*

DSM Commercial .... E 302 842-2450
Wilmington *(G-16183)*

Dsp Builders .... G 302 422-3515
Milford *(G-7872)*

Dugan Dt Roofing Inc .... G 302 636-9300
Wilmington *(G-16196)*

Dvele Partners LLC .... G 516 707-9357
Dover *(G-2396)*

E&S Home Improvement LLC .... G 302 559-2340
Newark *(G-10589)*

Eak Construction Inc .... G 302 893-8497
Bear *(G-186)*

East Coast Builders Inc .... F 302 629-3551
Seaford *(G-13165)*

Eastern Home Improvements Inc .... G 302 655-9920
Wilmington *(G-16258)*

Eastern Shore Porch Patio Inc .... E 302 436-9520
Selbyville *(G-13528)*

Edge Construction Corp .... G 302 778-5200
Wilmington *(G-16288)*

Ej Constructions .... G 302 272-2101
Laurel *(G-5508)*

Elite Developers Group LLC .... G 615 397-9732
Dover *(G-2434)*

Emerick Construction Group LLC .... G 302 547-0715
Newark *(G-10641)*

Empire Construction .... G 302 329-9256
Milton *(G-8618)*

Empire Construction Group LLC .... G 302 223-9208
Milton *(G-8619)*

Empire Investments Inc .... G 302 838-0631
New Castle *(G-9093)*

Ervin H Yoder .... G 302 492-1835
Camden Wyoming *(G-941)*

Estepp Construction Co Inc .... G 302 378-4958
Townsend *(G-13998)*

Exact Construction of De .... G 302 629-0464
Seaford *(G-13179)*

Eyetower LLC .... G 302 298-0944
Wilmington *(G-16513)*

EZ Construction Co .... G 302 723-5730
New Castle *(G-9112)*

EZ Deck LLC .... G 302 444-2268
Townsend *(G-14000)*

Falcon Construction LLC .... G 302 668-6874
Wilmington *(G-16531)*

Farrell Home Renovations LLC .... G 443 386-0885
Millsboro *(G-8287)*

Ferreira Builders LLC .... G 302 296-6014
Georgetown *(G-4318)*

Ferris Home Improvements .... G 302 377-8003
Wilmington *(G-16588)*

Ferris Home Imprvs Co LLC .... E 302 998-4500
Newark *(G-10725)*

Figgsy Builders .... G 302 875-2505
Laurel *(G-5512)*

Fix It Now .... G 302 293-7748
Hockessin *(G-5212)*

Flores Design and Construction .... G 302 635-7345
Wilmington *(G-16665)*

Francis Pollinger & Son Inc .... E 302 655-8097
Wilmington *(G-16723)*

Freedom At Home .... G 302 740-7054
Wilmington *(G-16740)*

G G + A LLC .... E 302 376-6122
Middletown *(G-7146)*

Gander Construction .... G 302 424-4007
Milford *(G-7907)*

Garrison Custom Homes .... G 302 644-4008
Lewes *(G-6027)*

Gator Construction Llc .... G 302 430-1160
Georgetown *(G-4331)*

Gemcraft Homes At Summercrest .... G 302 703-6763
Rehoboth Beach *(G-12767)*

George & Lynch Inc .... F 302 238-7289
Millsboro *(G-8298)*

Gerardi Construction Inc .... G 302 745-6252
Felton *(G-3978)*

Gfrs Construction One LLC .... G 484 357-5218
Ocean View *(G-12519)*

Gga Construction .... G 302 376-5193
Middletown *(G-7158)*

Gibellino Construction Co Inc .... G 302 455-0500
Newark *(G-10832)*

Give ME Shelter .... G 302 420-0402
Newark *(G-10841)*

Gleneagle Homes LLC .... G 914 262-1402
Millsboro *(G-8300)*

Graulich Builders .... G 302 313-4882
Lewes *(G-6053)*

Green Diamond Builders Inc .... G 302 284-1177
Felton *(G-3981)*

Gregg White Contracting .... G 302 542-9552
Bethany Beach *(G-605)*

Grimes Construction .... G 302 462-6533
Georgetown *(G-4347)*

Gsz Associates Inc .... G 302 824-2572
New Castle *(G-9182)*

Guardian Construction Co Inc .... G 302 656-1986
Wilmington *(G-17001)*

Gulfstream Development Corp .... G 302 539-6178
Millville *(G-8531)*

H & H Construction Company LLC .... G 936 825-6774
Dover *(G-2639)*

H B P Inc .... E 302 378-9693
Middletown *(G-7186)*

H H Builders Inc .... G 302 735-9900
Dover *(G-2640)*

H P Custom Trim LLC .... G 302 381-0802
Georgetown *(G-4350)*

Habitat For Hmnity New Cstle C .... F 302 652-0365
Wilmington *(G-17027)*

Handler Builders Inc .... F 302 999-9200
Wilmington *(G-17046)*

Handler Corporation .... E 302 999-9200
Wilmington *(G-17047)*

Handyman Housecalls Inc .... G 302 245-3816
Lewes *(G-6074)*

Hanso Home Inc .... G 760 437-2621
Wilmington *(G-17051)*

Harold Dutton Jr .... G 302 644-2992
Lewes *(G-6079)*

Hart Home Improvements LLC .... G 302 415-4764
Wilmington *(G-17067)*

Henlopen Homes Inc .... G 302 684-0860
Lewes *(G-6089)*

Herring Creek Builders Inc .... G 302 684-3015
Lewes *(G-6092)*

Hickory Hill Builders Inc .... G 302 934-6109
Dagsboro *(G-1463)*

Hoenen & Mitchell Inc .... G 302 645-6193
Lewes *(G-6094)*

Home Improvements .... G 302 537-1102
Dagsboro *(G-1465)*

Home Integrated .... G 302 656-1624
Wilmington *(G-17181)*

Home Services LLC .... G 302 510-4580
Wilmington *(G-17185)*

Homes For Laurel II Inc .... G 302 875-3525
Laurel *(G-5531)*

Homestar Remodeling LLC .... E 302 528-5898
Wilmington *(G-17190)*

Hope Reigns LLC .... F 302 406-0827
Wilmington *(G-17199)*

Hugh H Hickman & Sons Inc .... F 302 539-9741
Bethany Beach *(G-608)*

Humphries Construction Company .... G 302 349-9277
Greenwood *(G-4637)*

Hunter Construction .... G 410 392-5109
Newark *(G-10985)*

Inland Salem Square LLC .... F 302 472-9250
Wilmington *(G-17345)*

Innovative Home Imprvs LLC .... G 302 388-2950
Smyrna *(G-13771)*

Integrity Construction LLC .... G 302 241-6429
Marydel *(G-6801)*

Integrity MGT Solution Inc .... G 302 270-8976
Clayton *(G-1373)*

Interfaith Cmnty Hsing of Del .... F 302 652-3991
Wilmington *(G-17383)*

J & F Home Improvement LLC .... G 302 407-6845
Wilmington *(G-17443)*

J & L Services Inc .... F 410 943-3355
Seaford *(G-13226)*

J & S General Contractors .... G 302 658-4499
Wilmington *(G-17447)*

J A Ribinsky Builders .... F 302 542-7014
Millsboro *(G-8323)*

J B S Construction LLC .... G 302 349-5705
Greenwood *(G-4641)*

J I Beiler Homes LLC .... G 302 697-1553
Camden *(G-857)*

J&J Systems .... G 302 239-2969
Hockessin *(G-5256)*

J&M Remodeling .... G 443 736-0127
Frankford *(G-4117)*

Jack Hickman Real Estate .... F 302 539-8000
Bethany Beach *(G-611)*

Jackson Ed Home Improvements .... G 302 322-1566
New Castle *(G-9251)*

James A Peel & Sons Inc .... G 302 738-1468
Newark *(G-11088)*

James Rice Jr Construction Co .... G 302 731-9323
Newark *(G-11092)*

Jay Lynn Cnstr Solutions LLC .... G 302 349-5799
Millsboro *(G-8329)*

Jeffery Brannan .... G 302 547-1659
Bear *(G-302)*

15 CONSTRUCTION - GENERAL CONTRACTORS & OPERATIVE BUILDERS

Company	Code	Phone
Jeremy Sheiker, Wilmington (G-17531)	G	302 540-3741
JG Services, Dover (G-2787)	G	302 480-1900
Joel Crissman, Camden (G-860)	G	302 492-1757
John Campanelli & Sons Inc, Hockessin (G-5261)	G	302 239-8573
John T Elliott, Bridgeville (G-721)	G	302 337-7075
Joseph Devane Enterprises Inc, New Castle (G-9265)	F	302 703-0493
Joseph Truono, Wilmington (G-17585)	G	302 762-6822
Jrm Construction LLC, Seaford (G-13239)	G	302 362-7453
Jrs Homes LLC, New Castle (G-9269)	G	302 544-5911
Jsf Construction Co Inc, Wilmington (G-17605)	G	302 999-9573
Just Homes LLC, Wilmington (G-17617)	G	302 322-2233
K E Smart & Sons Inc, Laurel (G-5540)	G	302 875-7002
K Wolf Custom Homes Cnstr Inc, Middletown (G-7258)	G	302 598-2899
K&S Home Services LLC, Ocean View (G-12531)	G	302 604-3563
Kairos Home Pros LLC, Dover (G-2829)	G	302 233-7044
Kamax Construction LLC, Selbyville (G-13554)	G	302 296-8270
Karve Builders LLC, Camden (G-863)	G	403 471-2285
Kaye Construction, Seaford (G-13246)	G	302 628-6962
Kee Builders, Townsend (G-14022)	G	302 376-9858
Kelmon Construction, Wilmington (G-17682)	G	302 357-4391
Kenneth E Barrett, Magnolia (G-6757)	G	302 270-6056
Kevin A Johnson, Wilmington (G-17699)	G	302 762-7671
Kevin Hannah, Frederica (G-4176)	G	302 450-2867
Kirkley Construction LLC, Bear (G-331)	G	302 276-9795
Kleinhomers, Newark (G-11190)	G	302 234-2392
Kneesaverelectricalbox, Millsboro (G-8343)	G	732 239-7514
Knepps Construction, Delmar (G-1611)	G	302 846-3360
Knotts Construction Inc, Wilmington (G-17744)	G	302 475-7074
Kokoszka & Sons Inc, New Castle (G-9288)	G	302 328-4807
Kovach S Construction, Hartly (G-4892)	G	302 363-4130
Kurtz Construction LLC, Dover (G-2890)	G	302 943-4754
Lafond Construction, Georgetown (G-4400)	G	302 430-2834
Lane Builders LLC, Lewes (G-6178)	F	302 645-5555
Lane Builders Inc, Harbeson (G-4705)	G	302 644-1182
Laudato Home Improvements LLC, Millsboro (G-8346)	G	610 656-2944
Layton Builders, Milford (G-7974)	G	302 491-4571
Lc Construction Florida Inc, Wilmington (G-17838)	F	302 429-8700
Lc Homes, Townsend (G-14026)	G	302 376-7004
Leisure Home Builders LLC, Smyrna (G-13800)	G	302 528-4873
Lenape Builders Inc, Smyrna (G-13801)	F	302 376-3971
Leon N Weiner & Associates Inc, Wilmington (G-17877)	D	302 656-1354
Lessard Custom Homes, Lewes (G-6190)	G	302 645-7444
Liberto Development Ltd, Dover (G-2934)	G	302 698-1104
Lifestyle Communities LLC, Middletown (G-7301)	E	302 376-3066
Liii Construction Co, Wilmington (G-17911)	F	302 429-8700
LL Renovation LLC, New Castle (G-9320)	G	302 250-6449
Locker Construction Inc, Newark (G-11278)	G	302 239-2859
Lockhart Construction LLC, Claymont (G-1224)	G	302 753-5461
Lockwood Design Construction, Milton (G-8655)	G	302 684-4844
Lopesco Inc, Newark (G-11283)	G	908 482-5616
Lr Construction LLC, Bridgeville (G-726)	G	302 249-4507
Lynn Construction LLC, Seaford (G-13269)	G	302 236-6596
M L Morris Inc, Bridgeville (G-727)	G	302 956-0678
M L Parker Construction Inc, Claymont (G-1227)	F	302 798-8530
M W Fogarty Inc, Hockessin (G-5286)	G	302 658-5547
Macon Renovations LLC, Hockessin (G-5290)	G	302 244-9161
Make It New Construction LLC, Dover (G-3002)	G	302 423-7794
Man Around House, Milford (G-7982)	G	302 531-5124
Manor Creek Construction Inc, Selbyville (G-13565)	G	302 245-2887
Mark Gosser, Hockessin (G-5299)	G	302 388-8395
Mark Ventresca Associates Inc, Hockessin (G-5300)	G	302 239-3925
Marnie Custom Homes, Bethany Beach (G-618)	G	302 616-2664
Marra Landing LLC, Wilmington (G-18156)	G	302 530-5800
Marshall Kyle, Newark (G-11338)	F	302 454-7838
Martins Home Improvements, Wilmington (G-18172)	G	302 367-4789
Mazzola Systems Inc, Newark (G-11363)	G	302 738-6808
Mc Hunter LLC, Dover (G-3040)	G	302 672-0072
▲ McCove Construction Inc, Dover (G-3043)	G	302 363-0528
Mch Construction LLC, Magnolia (G-6764)	G	302 249-2765
McRogge LLC, Middletown (G-7336)	G	215 300-7975
Mebro Inc, Wilmington (G-18243)	E	302 992-0104
Messick and Johnson LLc, Seaford (G-13281)	G	302 628-3111
Michael A Mekulski Genera, Newark (G-11401)	G	302 834-8260
Michaels Home Repair Services, New Castle (G-9364)	G	302 333-2235
Mid Atlantic Builder Inc, Georgetown (G-4428)	F	302 344-7224
Miken Builders Inc, Millville (G-8542)	E	302 537-4444
Millennium Homes, Dover (G-3092)	G	302 678-2393
Minkers Construction Inc, Newark (G-11425)	F	302 239-9239
Miracle Builders LLC, Georgetown (G-4429)	G	302 236-1351
ML Whiteman and Sons Inc, Townsend (G-14038)	G	302 659-1001
Mmt Construction Services Inc, Wilmington (G-18393)	G	302 357-8506
Montchanin Builders, Wilmington (G-18420)	G	302 472-7213
Morales Gto Empire LLC, Wilmington (G-18440)	G	302 824-4315
Morgan Builders Inc, Wilmington (G-18444)	G	302 575-9943
Morning Star Construction LLC, Dagsboro (G-1483)	G	302 539-0791
Morse Home Improvement LLC, Dagsboro (G-1485)	E	302 663-0042
Mp Diversified Services LLC, Newark (G-11462)	G	302 828-1060
MR Custom Renovations LLC, Laurel (G-5568)	G	302 521-9663
Mullico General Construction, Wilmington (G-18482)	F	302 475-4400
Murphy Steel Inc, Newark (G-11473)	E	302 366-8676
Murphys Construction, Seaford (G-13297)	G	302 462-0319
Murray Bunting Constr, Selbyville (G-13585)	F	302 436-5144
MWM Construction, Townsend (G-14041)	G	302 218-5222
Nathan David Fretz, Clayton (G-1390)	G	302 218-3338
National Rstrtion Fclty Svcs I, Historic New Castle (G-5033)	E	856 401-0100
Ncd Remodeling LLC, Millsboro (G-8402)	G	302 604-3971
Neighborhood House Inc, Wilmington (G-18571)	F	302 658-5404
NM Construction Inc, Wilmington (G-18657)	G	302 478-6494
Noble Builders & Developers LL, Lewes (G-6318)	G	203 948-9396
Norman Johnson Builders, Ocean View (G-12552)	G	302 670-9201
Norman Yoder Construction, Hartly (G-4901)	G	302 492-3516
North Point Builders LLC, Newark (G-11565)	G	843 246-1516
Nvr Inc, Dagsboro (G-1492)	G	302 732-9900
Nvr Inc, Newark (G-11571)	F	302 731-5770
NY Construction, Smyrna (G-13839)	G	302 377-1846
Oak Construction, Lewes (G-6324)	G	302 703-2013
Ocean Services of De Inc, Selbyville (G-13588)	G	410 524-1518
Ocean Tower Construction LLC, Frankford (G-4129)	E	443 373-7096

Employee Codes: A=Over 500 employees, B=251-500, C=101-250, D=51-100, E=20-50, F=10-19, G=1-9

2024 Harris Directory of Delaware Businesses

15 CONSTRUCTION - GENERAL CONTRACTORS & OPERATIVE BUILDERS

Company		Phone
Ocean Tower Construction LLC Frankford (G-4130)	G	443 366-5556
ODonnell Services Newark (G-11578)	G	302 252-5134
Omar Kah Wilmington (G-18764)	G	718 552-6008
On Level Home Improvement Newark (G-11588)	G	302 368-7152
Onecall Services Inc Lewes (G-6335)	F	302 645-9008
Onsite Construction Inc Seaford (G-13325)	F	302 628-4244
Orjam Ltd Wilmington (G-18822)	F	302 482-5016
Ossandeep Associates LLC Newark (G-11604)	G	302 660-8545
Paddys Newark (G-11611)	F	302 388-3625
Paldor Inc Wilmington (G-18867)	G	302 999-9691
Pano Development Inc Wilmington (G-18877)	G	302 428-1062
Paoli Services Inc Wilmington (G-18878)	F	302 998-7031
Park Side Utility Construction New Castle (G-9449)	F	302 322-9760
Parker Builders LLC Harrington (G-4808)	G	302 398-6182
Patriot General Contractors New Castle (G-9458)	G	302 287-9000
Patriot Government Svcs Inc Wilmington (G-18910)	G	302 655-3434
Paul Dvis Emrgncy Svcs New CST Middletown (G-7432)	G	302 364-3139
Payne Enterprises LLC Georgetown (G-4457)	G	302 856-2899
Pdo Construction LLC Selbyville (G-13590)	G	302 542-0963
Pedro Rascon Cimarron Frankford (G-4132)	G	302 448-6806
Pelican Key LLC Brksdale A SRI Newark (G-11655)	G	302 563-9493
Philadlphia Arms Town Hmes Inc Ellendale (G-3928)	F	302 503-7216
Phoenix Construction LLC Milton (G-8685)	G	302 363-0453
Piccard Homes Rehoboth Beach (G-12891)	G	302 727-5145
Pientka Masonry Cnstr LLC Newark (G-11688)	G	302 420-6748
Pierson Culver LLC Dagsboro (G-1496)	G	302 732-1145
Pierson RE Construction Wilmington (G-19035)	F	302 407-3308
Pike Creek Construction Newark (G-11691)	G	302 453-0611
Pinnacle Home Improvement LLC Bridgeville (G-751)	G	302 569-5311
PJ Fitzpatrick Inc New Castle (G-9473)	D	302 325-2360
Polite Construction Jay New Castle (G-9483)	G	302 328-0390
Poolside Cnstr & Renovation Selbyville (G-13594)	G	302 436-9711
Powell Construction L L C Georgetown (G-4469)	G	302 745-1146
Precision Builders Inc Bear (G-434)	G	302 420-1391
Precision Hmes Rmdlg Group LLC Wilmington (G-19155)	G	302 293-0244
Precision Marine Construction Rehoboth Beach (G-12899)	G	302 227-2711
Preferred Contractors Inc Wilmington (G-19162)	G	302 798-5457
Premier Builders Inc Wilmington (G-19167)	G	302 999-8500
Premier Restoration Inc Lewes (G-6387)	F	302 645-1611
Preston & Remodeling Milton (G-8690)	G	302 604-0760
Princetonian Mhc LLC Wilmington (G-19194)	G	800 927-9800
Pro Carpet LLC Millsboro (G-8438)	G	443 757-7320
Proline Builders LLC Bridgeville (G-755)	G	302 956-0426
Purity Home Improvement Inc Wilmington (G-19265)	G	302 753-5454
Pw Construction LLC Wilmington (G-19270)	G	443 309-4082
Pyir Construction & Design Newark (G-11778)	G	302 824-9015
Quality Builders Inc Camden (G-887)	G	302 697-0664
Quality Construction Cleaning Bridgeville (G-758)	G	302 956-0752
Quality Construction De LLC New Castle (G-9505)	G	302 757-6185
Quality Finishers Inc Historic New Castle (G-5058)	G	302 325-1963
Quality Home Solutions LLC Millsboro (G-8439)	G	330 717-6793
R and JC Onstruction Inc Bear (G-443)	G	302 419-7393
R D Arnold Construction Inc Middletown (G-7495)	G	610 255-4739
R/T Decks Newark (G-11811)	G	302 983-4397
Ranco Construction Wilmington (G-19329)	G	302 322-3000
Rapid Renovation and Repr LLC Harrington (G-4818)	G	302 475-5400
Rays Plumbing & Heating Svcs Felton (G-4013)	F	302 697-3936
Read Construction Inc Smyrna (G-13863)	G	302 659-1144
Restoration Guys LLC Milford (G-8064)	G	302 542-4045
Reybold Homes Inc New Castle (G-9529)	C	302 834-3000
Riale System Services Bear (G-460)	G	302 328-3848
Richard Bratcher Dover (G-3467)	G	803 786-7322
Richard D Whaley Cnstr LLC Millsboro (G-8445)	G	302 934-9525
Richard Y Johnson & Son Inc Lincoln (G-6696)	E	302 422-3732
Risleus Properties LLC Dover (G-3473)	F	302 353-1255
Rkj Construction Inc Wilmington (G-19501)	G	302 690-0959
Rmm Builders LLC Newark (G-11893)	G	302 983-0734
Robert C Peoples Inc Bear (G-463)	D	302 834-5268
Robert E Davis Felton (G-4019)	G	302 535-9657
Robert Michael Corp Townsend (G-14061)	G	302 378-4164
Robert Miller Construction Inc Felton (G-4020)	G	302 335-4385
Rockland Builders Inc Wilmington (G-19539)	F	302 995-6800
Rons Mobile Home Sales Inc Harrington (G-4821)	G	302 398-9166
Royal Rsdntial Renovations LLC New Castle (G-9544)	G	302 377-0128
RSM Construction Dover (G-3492)	G	302 270-7099
Russell Smart Home Imprvs LLC Delmar (G-1633)	G	302 846-2404
Ryan Homes Milford (G-8076)	G	302 491-4442
Ryla Real Estate Options LLC New Castle (G-9550)	G	302 397-7402
S Finney Home Improvements Lewes (G-6436)	G	302 358-4562
S J Passwater General Cnstr Milford (G-8077)	G	302 422-1061
Sabcon Construction Company Wilmington (G-19617)	G	302 420-0467
Sams Construction LLC Wilmington (G-19649)	F	302 654-6542
Saxton Jack 3 Construction Wilmington (G-19687)	G	302 654-4553
SC&a Construction Inc Wilmington (G-19695)	E	302 478-6030
Schell Bros At Peninsula Lakes Millsboro (G-8455)	G	302 228-4488
Schell Brothers Georgetown (G-4501)	G	302 242-8334
Schell Brothers LLC Rehoboth Beach (G-12948)	E	302 226-1994
Shelde Construction Camden Wyoming (G-976)	G	561 723-5314
Shellys of Delaware Inc Wilmington (G-19794)	G	302 656-3337
Shelter Const Millsboro (G-8458)	G	302 829-8310
Shockley Brothers Construction Lincoln (G-6699)	G	302 424-3255
Shoreline Home Imprvs LLC Ocean View (G-12567)	G	302 616-1090
Signature Builders Felton (G-4029)	G	302 331-9095
Signature Cnstr Svcs LLC New Castle (G-9569)	F	302 691-1010
Signature Renovations Millsboro (G-8464)	G	302 858-2955
Silverside Contracting Inc Wilmington (G-19830)	G	302 798-1907
Sj Builders LLC Hartly (G-4908)	G	302 242-8222
Smith Home Improvements Wilmington (G-19889)	G	302 998-8294
Solid Construction LLC Lewes (G-6490)	G	571 451-4727
Spicer Bros Construction Inc Lewes (G-6501)	G	302 703-6754
Steimel Construction LLC Lewes (G-6510)	G	302 827-2471
Steven Rogers Milford (G-8104)	G	302 422-6285
Steven Soule Wilmington (G-20067)	G	302 690-3052
Stonehammer Construction Felton (G-4030)	G	302 233-3971
Stover Construction LLC Smyrna (G-13903)	G	302 653-6195
Summer Hill Custom Home Bldr Ocean View (G-12572)	G	302 462-5853
Sun Construction Inc Lewes (G-6521)	G	267 767-5047
Sussex Cnty Hbtat For Hmnity I Georgetown (G-4533)	G	302 855-1153

15 CONSTRUCTION - GENERAL CONTRACTORS & OPERATIVE BUILDERS

Sussex Home Imprv Contr LLC .... G 302 855-9679
  Georgetown (G-4539)
T J Lane Construction Inc .... G 302 734-1099
  Dover (G-3638)
Tag Water Restoration & Cnstr .... G 877 558-6646
  Wilmington (G-20207)
Th White General Contractor .... G 302 945-1829
  Millsboro (G-8483)
Thomas A Cofran & Sons Inc .... G 302 368-5157
  Newark (G-12190)
Thomas F Cavanaugh .... G 302 995-2859
  Wilmington (G-20307)
Three Little Builders .... G 302 317-1969
  Middletown (G-7640)
Tidemark LLC .... G 302 747-7737
  Dover (G-3684)
Tlbc LLC .... G 302 797-8700
  Lewes (G-6564)
Toback Builders .... G 302 644-1015
  Lewes (G-6566)
Todd Yerger Ta .... G 302 378-4196
  Middletown (G-7649)
Toll Njx 4 Corp .... F 302 652-3252
  Wilmington (G-20348)
Tolton Builders Inc .... G 302 239-5357
  Hockessin (G-5406)
Tom Rainey Builders LLC .... G 302 381-5339
  Lewes (G-6569)
Toner Jerome P Sr Patrici .... G 302 239-7271
  Newark (G-12209)
Top Tier Remodeling .... F 302 250-4845
  Wilmington (G-20356)
Transformers LLC .... G 302 757-3803
  Newark (G-12218)
Trevcon Construction Co .... G 908 413-7001
  Lewes (G-6579)
Tri State Construction Inc .... G 609 980-1000
  Smyrna (G-13918)
Triangle HM Imprvmnt Cntrctr L .... G 302 883-4943
  Dover (G-3724)
Tricon Construction MGT Inc .... E 302 838-6500
  New Castle (G-9639)
Trimark Enterprises Inc .... G 302 683-9065
  Wilmington (G-20422)
Tristate Remodeling Corp .... G 302 444-8314
  Newark (G-12236)
Troyer Construction Inc .... G 302 422-0745
  Milford (G-8120)
Tru Construction LLC .... G 302 740-9691
  Townsend (G-14086)
Tru General Contractor Inc .... G 302 354-0553
  Wilmington (G-20441)
Turnstone Builders LLC .... F 302 227-8876
  Rehoboth Beach (G-12998)
Turnstone Holdings LLC .... F 302 227-8876
  Rehoboth Beach (G-12999)
U and I Builders Inc .... G 302 697-1645
  Dover (G-3738)
V Colbert Inc .... G 302 420-5502
  Newark (G-12294)
Valliant Home Improvements .... G 302 363-7109
  Selbyville (G-13616)
Valor Construction LLC .... G 302 455-7994
  Newark (G-12302)
Vanguard Construction Inc .... G 302 697-9187
  Dover (G-3773)
Vari Development Corp .... G 302 479-5571
  Wilmington (G-20571)
Vetex Construction LLC .... G 302 670-0989
  Magnolia (G-6789)
Viaticum Incorporated .... F 302 467-8353
  Wilmington (G-20607)

Village Developers Inc .... G 302 732-3400
  Dagsboro (G-1524)
Vtech Engineering Group LLC .... G 267 253-2576
  Middletown (G-7697)
W D Pressley Inc .... G 302 653-4381
  Smyrna (G-13932)
Warfel Construction Co Inc .... E 302 422-8927
  Milford (G-8142)
Weiner Development LLC .... G 302 764-9430
  Wilmington (G-20714)
Wertz & Co .... F 302 658-5186
  Wilmington (G-20734)
Williams Humphreys and Co LLC .... G 302 225-3000
  Wilmington (G-20798)
Williamson Building Corp .... G 302 644-0605
  Lewes (G-6632)
Wilson Construction Co Inc .... G 302 856-3115
  Georgetown (G-4574)
Wn Builders Inc .... G 302 253-8640
  Georgetown (G-4577)
Wonderful Homes .... G 610 304-4744
  Rehoboth Beach (G-13021)
Woods General Contracting Inc .... G 302 856-4047
  Georgetown (G-4579)
Wtm Builders .... G 302 398-9522
  Harrington (G-4850)
Yellowfin Construction LLC .... F 302 293-0028
  Hockessin (G-5432)
Yencer Builders Inc .... G 302 284-9977
  Felton (G-4038)
Yoder and Sons Cnstr LLC .... F 302 349-0444
  Greenwood (G-4678)
Yorklyn Home LLC .... G 302 584-1219
  Hockessin (G-5433)

1522 Residential construction, nec

Albert Delpizzo LLC .... G 302 234-2994
  Newark (G-9806)
American Builder LLC .... G 302 841-2325
  Georgetown (G-4208)
American Craftsmen LLC .... G 302 545-3666
  Newark (G-9844)
Anthony Ferguson .... G 610 906-4998
  Selbyville (G-13464)
AR Campagnone LLC .... G 302 329-9323
  Milton (G-8562)
Aruanno Enterprises Inc .... G 302 530-1217
  Middletown (G-6875)
Ash Edward L I .... G 302 732-9181
  Frankford (G-4061)
Asset Assistance LLC .... G 302 364-3362
  Dover (G-1834)
B Doherty Inc .... G 302 239-3500
  Wilmington (G-14697)
Bekart Holding LLC .... F 302 600-7000
  Wilmington (G-14813)
Breeze Construction LLC .... G 302 522-9201
  Townsend (G-13966)
Brian K Mummert .... G 302 678-2260
  Dover (G-1977)
Bright Finish LLC .... G 888 974-4747
  Smyrna (G-13667)
Brobst Home Improvement LLC .... G 302 376-1656
  Townsend (G-13968)
Capano Management Company .... D 302 737-8056
  Newark (G-10132)
Cappo Dennis John .... G 302 245-2261
  Frankford (G-4083)
Carl M Freeman Associates Inc .... D 302 436-3000
  Ocean View (G-12486)
Chews Unlimited LLC .... G 302 280-6937
  Delmar (G-1578)

Cirillo Bros Inc .... E 302 326-1540
  New Castle (G-8943)
Cm Beach LLC .... G 202 521-1493
  Lewes (G-5834)
Cote Custom Works LLC .... G 302 359-2596
  Dover (G-2143)
Cretework LLC .... G 302 424-9970
  Ellendale (G-3912)
Custom Improvers Inc .... G 302 731-9246
  Newark (G-10368)
Dan Prinsloo .... G 302 373-8891
  Townsend (G-13984)
Daniel Shea .... G 302 349-5599
  Greenwood (G-4611)
David Dukes .... G 302 841-9481
  Millsboro (G-8254)
David Ira Jenkins .... G 302 335-3309
  Magnolia (G-6737)
David M Showalter .... G 302 462-5264
  Millsboro (G-8256)
Dec Home Services .... G 240 793-4818
  Selbyville (G-13517)
Deldeo Builders Inc .... F 302 791-0243
  Claymont (G-1116)
Dell Pump Company .... G 302 655-2436
  Wilmington (G-15995)
Diamond State Pole Bldings LLC .... G 302 387-1710
  Felton (G-3960)
Dieste Mark Design Build LLC .... F 301 921-9050
  Bethany Beach (G-597)
Disabatino Construction Co .... D 302 652-3838
  Wilmington (G-16084)
Divergent LLC .... G 302 275-7019
  Wilmington (G-16092)
Djlong Services .... G 302 541-4884
  Ocean View (G-12505)
Donald Goldsborough .... G 302 653-1081
  Smyrna (G-13712)
Donald Grebe .... G 302 945-7975
  Millsboro (G-8274)
Donald R Cordrey Jr .... G 302 875-4939
  Laurel (G-5501)
Douglas Randall Inc .... G 302 448-5826
  Lewes (G-5931)
Dream Structures LLC .... G 302 943-3974
  Hartly (G-4870)
E A Zando Custom Designs Inc .... F 302 684-4601
  Milton (G-8613)
East Coast Minority Supplier .... G 302 656-3337
  Wilmington (G-16252)
Ebanks Construction LLC .... G 302 420-7584
  New Castle (G-9080)
Ed Durynski .... G 302 994-6642
  Wilmington (G-16283)
Elegant Exteriors LLC .... G 302 218-8378
  Newark (G-10624)
Elite Developers Group LLC .... G 615 397-9732
  Dover (G-2434)
Everyone Can Achieve LLC .... E 404 317-1228
  Wilmington (G-16491)
Exantus and Son Homes .... G 302 745-3468
  Georgetown (G-4311)
Exterior Homeworks LLC .... G 302 249-0012
  Seaford (G-13180)
Falcon Crest Inv Intl Inc .... G 240 701-1746
  Wilmington (G-16532)
Fitch-It .... G 302 260-9657
  Rehoboth Beach (G-12758)
Flores Enterprises LLC .... G 484 880-5134
  Wilmington (G-16666)
Franklin Utilities LLC .... G 302 629-6658
  Georgetown (G-4325)

15 CONSTRUCTION - GENERAL CONTRACTORS & OPERATIVE BUILDERS

SIC SECTION

G David Outten LLC .... G 302 747-4932
 Wyoming (G-20985)
Garcia & Sons LLC .... G 302 562-8878
 Newark (G-10808)
Garret Thomas Pusey LLC .... G 302 875-9146
 Laurel (G-5517)
Garth Enterprises Ltd .... F 302 349-2298
 Frankford (G-4109)
General Service Contrs LLC .... G 302 220-1946
 New Castle (G-9161)
Geneva Hotel LLC .... G 440 901-2030
 Wilmington (G-16838)
Global Exterior .... G 302 449-1559
 Middletown (G-7164)
Good Neighbor LLC .... G 302 228-9910
 Selbyville (G-13538)
Grantlin Fabrication LLC .... G 302 270-3708
 Smyrna (G-13750)
H P Custom Trim LLC .... G 302 381-0802
 Georgetown (G-4350)
Hagerty Homes LLC .... G 302 234-4268
 Newark (G-10917)
Harold L Scott Sr .... G 302 343-9217
 Dover (G-2653)
Henlopen Homes LLC .... G 302 684-0860
 Milton (G-8636)
Homefix .... G 302 682-3837
 Lewes (G-6099)
Hospitality Essentials LLC .... G 732 874-0048
 Middletown (G-7218)
Improve Sussex LLC .... G 302 864-8559
 Lewes (G-6118)
Interstellar Cmnty Living LLC .... G 787 607-3939
 Wilmington (G-17399)
Interstllar Cmnty Lving MGT Co .... G 787 607-3939
 Wilmington (G-17400)
Jacobs Squared .... G 302 294-6607
 Newark (G-11081)
James Robert Kline .... G 302 633-3926
 Wilmington (G-17484)
James W McKee .... G 302 540-9191
 Middletown (G-7239)
Jeff Tetrick .... G 302 478-7185
 Wilmington (G-17515)
Jerry S Meiklejohn .... G 302 745-2632
 Dagsboro (G-1470)
Jl Solis LLC .... G 302 212-9521
 Millsboro (G-8332)
John Campanelli & Sons Inc .... G 302 239-8573
 Hockessin (G-5261)
John J Mast .... G 302 492-1356
 Hartly (G-4882)
John W Bateman .... G 302 644-1177
 Lewes (G-6148)
John W Petrofske .... G 410 422-1545
 Dover (G-2798)
Joseph D Allen .... G 302 685-4230
 Middletown (G-7253)
Joseph R Kasowski .... G 302 379-0523
 Wilmington (G-17584)
Jpl M&R .... G 302 883-9534
 Wilmington (G-17597)
Justin Maynard .... G 302 233-6086
 Hartly (G-4888)
K Squared Enterprises LLC .... G 302 402-3082
 Ocean View (G-12530)
Kenneth H Gladish .... G 302 270-2821
 Felton (G-3991)
Kevin Elzie .... G 302 697-6273
 Camden Wyoming (G-959)
Klh Enterprises .... F 302 245-0712
 Milton (G-8652)

Kms Servives .... G 302 502-5287
 Smyrna (G-13792)
Kramer Konstruction .... G 717 466-6500
 Wyoming (G-20987)
Larry Baker LLC .... G 302 703-2127
 Millsboro (G-8344)
Larrys Building .... G 302 670-8803
 Bridgeville (G-724)
Lions Group LLC .... G 302 535-6584
 Magnolia (G-6762)
Lloyd Richard LLC .... G 302 584-8798
 Newark (G-11275)
Lloyds Stoneworks .... G 302 492-0847
 Marydel (G-6804)
Lnw & A Construction Corp .... F 302 764-9430
 Wilmington (G-17964)
M & G Pro Services LLC .... G 302 420-1428
 Marydel (G-6805)
Mark Wanner .... G 302 478-6878
 Wilmington (G-18141)
Marshall Services Inc .... G 302 655-0076
 Wilmington (G-18160)
Martin Construction Svcs LLC .... F 302 200-0885
 Newark (G-11342)
Mast Homes LLC .... G 302 632-7735
 Camden (G-872)
Mazzola Systems Inc .... G 302 738-6808
 Newark (G-11363)
Michael A Madanat .... G 302 998-6613
 Wilmington (G-18303)
Michael Marino Inc .... G 302 764-5319
 Wilmington (G-18319)
Moore Services .... G 302 588-3984
 Wilmington (G-18437)
Mp Diversified Services LLC .... G 302 828-1060
 Newark (G-11462)
My 3 Sons .... G 302 559-7252
 Wilmington (G-18502)
Nail It Down General Contrs .... G 302 698-3073
 Dover (G-3145)
Newark Building Services LLC .... G 302 377-7687
 Newark (G-11530)
Nextmove Inc .... G 302 593-7830
 Townsend (G-14043)
Nvr Inc .... F 302 731-5770
 Newark (G-11571)
Orcurto Enterprises .... G 302 604-7039
 Bridgeville (G-743)
Parthian LLC .... G 240 441-8301
 Ocean View (G-12558)
Phillip T Bradley Inc .... G 302 947-2741
 Lewes (G-6365)
Platinum Heritage Entps LLC .... G 469 563-0411
 Dover (G-3330)
Portable Sheds Paul Yoder .... G 302 734-2681
 Dover (G-3352)
Powells General Services .... G 302 384-7817
 Wilmington (G-19135)
Preferred Construction Inc .... G 302 322-9568
 New Castle (G-9490)
Prestige Contractors Inc .... G 302 722-1032
 Wilmington (G-19181)
Price Edward A/Gnral Contractr .... G 302 571-9281
 Wilmington (G-19187)
Pro Clean Wilmington Inc .... G 302 836-8080
 Delaware City (G-1553)
Quarry Mill Craftsmen LLC .... G 302 388-6289
 Wilmington (G-19290)
R E Excavation LLC .... G 302 273-3669
 Newark (G-11806)
Ralph Del Signore Jr .... G 302 239-0803
 Hockessin (G-5353)

Raymond M Smith Jr .... G 302 670-3801
 Clayton (G-1400)
Raymond Shephard .... G 302 834-8405
 Bear (G-446)
Reinvex LLC .... G 484 259-7889
 Wilmington (G-19418)
Relocation Pettinar .... G 302 777-5240
 Wilmington (G-19427)
Resort Custom Homes .... G 302 645-8222
 Lewes (G-6418)
Richard W Krick Jr .... G 302 227-6974
 Rehoboth Beach (G-12935)
Risen Services .... G 302 858-8840
 Laurel (G-5592)
Robert Golebiowski .... G 302 234-6583
 Wilmington (G-19512)
Rockles Services LLC .... G 302 258-5357
 Milton (G-8702)
S and S LLC .... G 302 344-5990
 Milton (G-8705)
Sampson Interiors .... G 865 438-5097
 Rehoboth Beach (G-12946)
Sandhill Development Group LLC .... G 302 703-2140
 Milton (G-8706)
Scott Charles Foresman .... G 302 644-8418
 Lewes (G-6452)
Scuba World Inc .... G 302 698-1117
 Dover (G-3522)
Separe Inc .... G 302 736-5000
 Dover (G-3532)
Set FA Life LLC .... G 302 407-6773
 Wilmington (G-19767)
Soucialize Inc .... G 916 803-1057
 Lewes (G-6492)
Sunnyworld LLC .... G 240 506-8870
 Rehoboth Beach (G-12981)
Swarter Services LLC .... G 302 575-9943
 Wilmington (G-20170)
Thomas Brothers LLC .... G 302 366-1316
 Newark (G-12192)
Timothy P Collord .... G 302 448-9577
 Milton (G-8721)
Todd R Williams .... G 302 945-3662
 Lewes (G-6567)
Tom Can and Son General Contr .... G 302 737-5551
 Newark (G-12205)
Tony Ashburn Inc .... G 302 677-1940
 Dover (G-3697)
Top Notch Home Services .... G 302 275-2459
 Newark (G-12210)
Tristate Fbrcn and Machg .... G 302 533-5877
 Newark (G-12235)
Tropacool .... G 302 245-4078
 Georgetown (G-4562)
Turnkey Electric LLC .... G 302 858-3726
 Georgetown (G-4564)
Warren Reid .... E 302 877-0901
 Laurel (G-5620)
Weather or Not Inc .... F 302 436-7533
 Selbyville (G-13619)
Wes Sanders & Son LLC .... G 302 383-4991
 Wilmington (G-20735)
William Redding and Son .... G 302 562-4026
 Newark (G-12377)
Wirenut LLC .... G 302 858-7027
 Georgetown (G-4576)
Wit Services LLC .... G 302 995-2983
 Wilmington (G-20867)
Wm Companies LLC .... G 302 228-5122
 Greenwood (G-4675)
Wright Robert Steele .... G 302 423-2093
 Harrington (G-4849)

15 CONSTRUCTION - GENERAL CONTRACTORS & OPERATIVE BUILDERS

1531 Operative builders

A G M General Contractor Inc .... E 215 558-6880
Middletown *(G-6823)*

Bailey Builders LLC .... G 302 236-0035
Milton *(G-8567)*

Broadpoint Construction LLC .... G 302 567-2100
Rehoboth Beach *(G-12655)*

Cape Financial Services Inc .... F 302 645-6274
Lewes *(G-5793)*

Carl M Freeman Associates Inc .... D 302 539-6961
Bethany Beach *(G-589)*

Creative Builders Inc .... G 302 228-8153
Harbeson *(G-4693)*

Del Homes Inc .... F 302 697-8204
Magnolia *(G-6739)*

Eastern Property Assoc Inc .... G 302 998-0962
Wilmington *(G-16260)*

Gearhart Construction Inc .... G 302 674-5466
Dover *(G-2567)*

Global Touch Co .... E 302 321-5844
Dover *(G-2593)*

H P Custom Trim LLC .... G 302 381-0802
Georgetown *(G-4350)*

Hudson Management & Entps LLC ..... G 302 645-9464
Milton *(G-8641)*

J D Construction .... G 302 292-8789
Newark *(G-11071)*

No Joke I LLC .... G 302 395-0882
New Castle *(G-9421)*

NV Homes .... G 302 732-9900
Dagsboro *(G-1491)*

Nvr Inc .... F 302 731-5770
Newark *(G-11571)*

1541 Industrial buildings and warehouses

Advance Construction Co Del .... F 302 697-9444
Camden Wyoming *(G-906)*

▲ **Bancroft Construction Company** ..... C 302 655-3434
Wilmington *(G-14738)*

Bio-Diversified Ventures Inc .... F 720 680-9418
Wilmington *(G-14894)*

Breslin Contracting Inc .... E 302 322-0320
New Castle *(G-8891)*

Bristol Industrial Corporation .... F 302 322-1100
New Castle *(G-8893)*

Broadpoint Construction LLC .... G 302 567-2100
Rehoboth Beach *(G-12655)*

Building Concepts America Inc .... E 302 292-0200
Newark *(G-10101)*

Ci De Corp .... G 302 998-3944
Wilmington *(G-15430)*

Colonial Construction Company .... F 302 994-5705
Wilmington *(G-15535)*

Conventional Builders Inc .... F 302 422-2429
Houston *(G-5439)*

Crystal Holdings Inc .... D 302 421-5700
Wilmington *(G-15720)*

Dan H Beachy & Sons Inc .... G 302 492-1493
Hartly *(G-4866)*

Daystar Sills Inc .... D 302 633-1421
Wilmington *(G-15822)*

Deshong & Sons Contractors Inc .... G 302 453-8500
Newark *(G-10517)*

Disabatino Construction Co .... D 302 652-3838
Wilmington *(G-16084)*

Distinction LLC .... E 302 362-7574
Milton *(G-8607)*

Dover Afb .... G 302 677-3989
Dover *(G-2330)*

East Coast Minority Supplier .... G 302 656-3337
Wilmington *(G-16252)*

Eastern Metals Inc .... F 302 454-7886
Newark *(G-10598)*

Edis Company .... E 302 421-5700
Wilmington *(G-16294)*

Emment A Oat Contractor Inc .... G 302 999-1567
Wilmington *(G-16398)*

G TS Foods Inc .... G 302 376-3555
Middletown *(G-7147)*

Genspec Materials Inc .... G 302 777-1100
Wilmington *(G-16841)*

Gettier Staffing Services Inc .... G 302 478-0911
Wilmington *(G-16855)*

Gfp Cement Contractors LLC .... F 302 998-7687
Wilmington *(G-16856)*

Guardian Envmtl Svcs Co Inc .... D 302 918-3070
Newark *(G-10907)*

H&B Express Logistics .... G 815 201-0915
Dover *(G-2642)*

Hart Construction Co Inc .... G 302 737-7886
Newark *(G-10937)*

Healthy Snacks Holdings Inc .... G 917 540-6588
Middletown *(G-7201)*

Iclean LLC .... G 518 573-3446
Newark *(G-10993)*

▲ **Janette Redrow Ltd** .... G 302 659-3534
Townsend *(G-14020)*

John L Briggs & Co .... F 302 856-7033
Milton *(G-8649)*

Kent Construction Co .... E 302 653-6469
Smyrna *(G-13788)*

Louie Uncle Foods .... G 302 750-0117
Wilmington *(G-18005)*

Maccari Motors .... G 302 563-3361
Wilmington *(G-18065)*

Mario F Medori Inc .... G 302 239-4550
Wilmington *(G-18132)*

Miken Builders Inc .... E 302 537-4444
Millville *(G-8542)*

Mitten Construction Co .... F 302 697-2124
Dover *(G-3104)*

Nason Construction Inc .... E 302 529-2510
Wilmington *(G-18537)*

Penco Corporation .... G 302 629-7911
Seaford *(G-13332)*

Pettinaro Construction Co Inc .... G 302 999-0708
Wilmington *(G-19001)*

Reybold Construction Corp .... E 302 832-7100
Bear *(G-455)*

Salt Marsh Foods Inc .... G 302 260-9556
Rehoboth Beach *(G-12943)*

Shellys of Delaware Inc .... G 302 656-3337
Wilmington *(G-19794)*

Skanska USA Building Inc .... E 215 495-8790
Newark *(G-12019)*

Talley Brothers Inc .... E 302 224-5376
Newark *(G-12157)*

Udairy Creamery Prod Fcilty .... F 302 831-2486
Newark *(G-12260)*

Whayland Company Inc .... F 302 875-5445
Laurel *(G-5624)*

Whiting-Turner Contracting Co .... E 302 292-0676
Newark *(G-12369)*

Wohlsen Construction Company .... F 302 324-9900
Wilmington *(G-20874)*

1542 Nonresidential construction, nec

Absolute Equity .... G 302 983-2591
Delaware City *(G-1527)*

Advance Construction Co Del .... F 302 697-9444
Camden Wyoming *(G-906)*

Amakor Inc .... F 302 834-8664
Delaware City *(G-1530)*

Aviman Management LLC .... E 302 377-5788
Wilmington *(G-14669)*

B Doherty Inc .... G 302 239-3500
Wilmington *(G-14697)*

◆ **Balfour Beatty LLC** .... G 302 573-3873
Wilmington *(G-14721)*

Ballard Builders LLC .... F 302 363-1677
Clayton *(G-1352)*

Bancroft .... G 302 654-1408
Wilmington *(G-14733)*

▲ **Bancroft Construction Company** ..... C 302 655-3434
Wilmington *(G-14738)*

Bay Developers Inc .... F 302 736-0924
Dover *(G-1884)*

Benjamin B Smith Builders Inc .... G 302 537-1916
Ocean View *(G-12477)*

Bishop Cleaning and Maint LLC .... G 302 277-8815
Bear *(G-72)*

Blackstone Building Group LLC .... E 302 824-4632
Wilmington *(G-14948)*

Brandywine Contractors Inc .... E 302 325-2700
New Castle *(G-8885)*

Brandywine Contractors Inc .... G 302 325-2700
New Castle *(G-8886)*

Breeze Construction LLC .... G 302 522-9201
Townsend *(G-13966)*

Breslin Contracting Inc .... E 302 322-0320
New Castle *(G-8891)*

Broadpoint Construction LLC .... G 302 567-2100
Rehoboth Beach *(G-12655)*

Brs Consulting Inc .... G 302 786-2326
Harrington *(G-4741)*

Bunting Construction Corp .... F 302 436-5124
Selbyville *(G-13487)*

Cape Financial Services Inc .... F 302 645-6274
Lewes *(G-5793)*

Carl Deputy & Son Builders LLC .... G 302 284-3041
Felton *(G-3951)*

Chilimidos LLC .... G 302 388-1880
Hockessin *(G-5159)*

Christopher Companies .... G 302 539-2888
Millville *(G-8522)*

Cirillo Bros Inc .... E 302 326-1540
New Castle *(G-8943)*

Cobi Group Inc .... F 302 407-3085
Wilmington *(G-15511)*

Colonial Construction Company .... F 302 994-5705
Wilmington *(G-15535)*

Commonwealth Contruction Co .... E 302 654-6611
Wilmington *(G-15552)*

Consolidated LLC .... E 302 654-9001
Wilmington *(G-15609)*

Consolidated Contracting LLC .... G 302 727-9795
Dagsboro *(G-1431)*

Construction Unlimited Inc .... G 302 836-3140
Bear *(G-118)*

Conventional Builders Inc .... F 302 422-2429
Houston *(G-5439)*

Crystal Holdings Inc .... D 302 421-5700
Wilmington *(G-15720)*

Dal Construction .... G 302 538-5310
Camden *(G-813)*

Dan H Beachy & Sons Inc .... G 302 492-1493
Hartly *(G-4866)*

Daystar Sills Inc .... D 302 633-1421
Wilmington *(G-15822)*

Del Homes Inc .... F 302 697-8204
Magnolia *(G-6739)*

Deldeo Builders Inc .... F 302 791-0243
Claymont *(G-1116)*

Delmarva Builders Inc .... G 302 629-9123
Bridgeville *(G-692)*

15 CONSTRUCTION - GENERAL CONTRACTORS & OPERATIVE BUILDERS

Delmarva Pole Building Sup Inc............ G 302 698-3636
  Wyoming *(G-20983)*

Deshong & Sons Contractors Inc........... G 302 453-8500
  Newark *(G-10517)*

Dewson Construction Co....................... E 302 227-3095
  Rehoboth Beach *(G-12724)*

Diamond Hill Inc.................................... E 302 999-0302
  New Castle *(G-9050)*

Diamond State Pole Bldngs LLC............ G 302 387-1710
  Felton *(G-3960)*

Disabatino Construction Co................... D 302 652-3838
  Wilmington *(G-16084)*

Dry Wall Associates Ltd......................... D 302 737-3220
  Newark *(G-10574)*

Eastern Home Improvements Inc........... G 302 655-9920
  Wilmington *(G-16258)*

Ebanks Construction LLC...................... G 302 420-7584
  New Castle *(G-9080)*

Edge Construction Corp......................... G 302 778-5200
  Wilmington *(G-16288)*

Edis Company.. E 302 421-5700
  Wilmington *(G-16294)*

Empire Investments Inc.......................... G 302 838-0631
  New Castle *(G-9093)*

Essential Contracting LLC...................... G 330 984-1971
  Smyrna *(G-13726)*

Everyone Can Achieve LLC.................... E 404 317-1228
  Wilmington *(G-16491)*

From Ground Up Construction............... G 302 747-0996
  Newark *(G-10788)*

Garth Enterprises Ltd............................ F 302 349-2298
  Frankford *(G-4109)*

Gary P Simpson Contracting LLC........... G 302 398-7733
  Harrington *(G-4772)*

Gettier Staffing Services Inc................... G 302 478-0911
  Wilmington *(G-16855)*

Gga Construction.................................... E 302 376-6122
  Middletown *(G-7159)*

Greggo & Ferrara Inc............................. C 302 658-5241
  New Castle *(G-9180)*

Guardian Construction Co Inc................ D 302 834-1000
  New Castle *(G-9183)*

Hart Construction Co Inc........................ G 302 737-7886
  Newark *(G-10937)*

Humphries Construction Company......... G 302 349-9277
  Greenwood *(G-4637)*

Insite Constructors Inc........................... G 302 479-5555
  Wilmington *(G-17353)*

J & S General Contractors..................... G 302 658-4499
  Wilmington *(G-17447)*

J A Moore & Sons Inc............................ G 302 765-0110
  Wilmington *(G-17449)*

James Rice Jr Construction Co.............. G 302 731-9323
  Newark *(G-11092)*

JC General Construction Inc.................. G 302 383-3152
  Wilmington *(G-17508)*

Jni CCC Jv1 LLP.................................... F 302 654-6611
  Wilmington *(G-17559)*

John Campanelli & Sons Inc.................. G 302 239-8573
  Hockessin *(G-5261)*

John L Briggs & Co................................ F 302 856-7033
  Milton *(G-8649)*

Joseph A Santillo Inc.............................. G 302 661-7313
  Wilmington *(G-17578)*

JW Tull Contracting Svcs LLC................ F 302 494-8179
  Wilmington *(G-17625)*

KB Coldiron Inc..................................... D 302 436-4224
  Selbyville *(G-13556)*

Kent Construction Co............................. E 302 653-6469
  Smyrna *(G-13788)*

Kramer Konstruction.............................. G 717 466-6500
  Wyoming *(G-20987)*

Larry Hill Farms Inc............................... G 302 875-0886
  Delmar *(G-1613)*

Laurel Redevelopment Corp.................. G 302 875-0601
  Laurel *(G-5551)*

Leon N Weiner & Associates Inc............ D 302 656-1354
  Wilmington *(G-17877)*

Lighthouse Construction Inc.................. F 302 677-1965
  Magnolia *(G-6759)*

Linda McCormick................................... G 443 987-2099
  Wilmington *(G-17922)*

Locker Construction Inc........................ G 302 239-2859
  Newark *(G-11278)*

Lockwood Design Construction.............. G 302 684-4844
  Milton *(G-8655)*

Lofts 2nd and Loma.............................. G 302 300-1498
  Wilmington *(G-17975)*

Ltc Services LLC.................................... G 302 396-8598
  Seaford *(G-13267)*

M L Parker Construction Inc.................. G 302 798-8530
  Claymont *(G-1227)*

M W Fogarty Inc.................................... G 302 658-5547
  Hockessin *(G-5286)*

Martin Construction Svcs LLC............... F 302 200-0885
  Newark *(G-11342)*

Mason Building Group Inc..................... C 302 292-0600
  Newark *(G-11348)*

Mebro Inc.. G 302 992-0104
  Wilmington *(G-18243)*

Mike Molitor Contractor LLC................. G 302 528-6300
  Hockessin *(G-5309)*

Miken Builders Inc................................. G 302 537-4444
  Millville *(G-8542)*

Milestone Construction Co Inc............... F 302 442-4252
  Newark *(G-11419)*

Mitten Construction Co.......................... F 302 697-2124
  Dover *(G-3104)*

Moore Farms... F 302 629-4999
  Georgetown *(G-4434)*

Mp Diversified Services LLC.................. G 302 828-1060
  Newark *(G-11462)*

Mvl Structures Group LLC..................... G 302 652-7580
  Wilmington *(G-18498)*

Mvl-Al Othman Al Zamel JV LLC............ E 832 302-2757
  Wilmington *(G-18499)*

Mvl-Saqa JV LLC................................... E 832 302-2757
  Wilmington *(G-18500)*

Nason Construction Inc......................... E 302 529-2510
  Wilmington *(G-18537)*

National Rstrtion Fclty Svcs I................. E 856 401-0100
  Historic New Castle *(G-5033)*

North East Contractors Inc.................... G 302 286-6324
  Newark *(G-11564)*

Opus Design Build LLC......................... D 952 656-4444
  Wilmington *(G-18808)*

Paldor Inc.. G 302 999-9691
  Wilmington *(G-18867)*

Pettinaro Construction Co Inc................ D 302 999-0708
  Wilmington *(G-19001)*

Pettitt Construction LLC........................ G 302 690-0831
  Newark *(G-11677)*

Preferred Construction Inc.................... G 302 322-9568
  New Castle *(G-9490)*

Prestige Contractors Inc....................... G 302 722-1032
  Wilmington *(G-19181)*

Regal Contractors LLC.......................... G 302 736-5000
  Dover *(G-3445)*

Regional Builders Inc............................ F 302 628-8660
  Seaford *(G-13370)*

Renovate LLC.. G 302 378-1768
  Middletown *(G-7515)*

Reybold Construction Corp................... E 302 832-7100
  Bear *(G-455)*

Richard Y Johnson & Son Inc............... E 302 422-3732
  Lincoln *(G-6696)*

Robert C Peoples Inc............................ D 302 834-5268
  Bear *(G-463)*

SC&a Construction Inc.......................... E 302 478-6030
  Wilmington *(G-19695)*

Shellys of Delaware Inc......................... G 302 656-3337
  Wilmington *(G-19794)*

Shure-Line Construction Inc................. E 302 653-4610
  Kenton *(G-5454)*

Signature Furniture Svcs LLC................ E 302 691-1010
  New Castle *(G-9570)*

Silverside Contracting Inc..................... G 302 798-1907
  Wilmington *(G-19830)*

Skyline Roofing & Cnstr LLC................. G 610 929-4135
  Lewes *(G-6474)*

Smarter Home & Office LLC................. G 302 723-9313
  New Castle *(G-9574)*

SMI Services of Delaware LLC.............. G 302 514-9681
  Smyrna *(G-13889)*

Sumter Contracting Corp...................... G 703 323-7210
  Ocean View *(G-12573)*

Talley Brothers Inc................................ E 302 224-5376
  Newark *(G-12157)*

Taylor Kline Inc..................................... F 302 328-8306
  New Castle *(G-9618)*

Tycos General Contractors Inc.............. G 302 478-9267
  Wilmington *(G-20480)*

Universal Exteriors LLC........................ G 302 563-7900
  Dover *(G-3754)*

▲ Utopia Alley LLC................................ G 302 218-3108
  Hockessin *(G-5415)*

Vanguard Construction Inc................... G 302 697-9187
  Dover *(G-3773)*

Vari Development Corp......................... G 302 479-5571
  Wilmington *(G-20571)*

W D Pressley Inc................................... G 302 653-4381
  Smyrna *(G-13932)*

Warfel Construction Co Inc.................... E 302 422-8927
  Milford *(G-8142)*

Westwood Farms Incorporated............. F 302 238-7141
  Millsboro *(G-8504)*

Whayland Company Inc......................... F 302 875-5445
  Laurel *(G-5624)*

Whayland Company LLC....................... F 302 875-5445
  Laurel *(G-5625)*

White Eagle Integrations...................... G 302 464-0550
  Middletown *(G-7723)*

Whiting-Turner Contracting Co............. E 302 292-0676
  Newark *(G-12369)*

Whiting-Turner Contracting Co............. F 302 266-7450
  Newark *(G-12370)*

Wilmington.. G 302 357-4509
  Wilmington *(G-20807)*

Wohlsen Construction Company............ F 302 324-9900
  Wilmington *(G-20874)*

Woods General Contracting Inc............ G 302 856-4047
  Georgetown *(G-4579)*

Zacs Inc... G 302 242-4653
  Magnolia *(G-6793)*

16 HEAMY CONSTRUCTION, EXCEPT BUILDING CONSTRUCTION, CONTRACTOR

1611 Highway and street construction

A P Croll & Son Inc............................... D 302 856-6177
  Georgetown *(G-4189)*

A-Del Construction Company Inc.......... D 302 453-8286
  Newark *(G-9729)*

16 HEAVY CONSTRUCTION, EXCEPT BUILDING CONSTRUCTION, CONTRACTOR

Alex Evans Asphalt Paving LLC............ G 302 363-3796
  Bear *(G-24)*
All Tech Sealcoating LLC...................... G 302 907-0311
  Delmar *(G-1562)*
Allan Myers.. G 302 658-4417
  Newport *(G-12442)*
Allan Myers Md Inc............................... C 302 883-3501
  Dover *(G-1769)*
Alltech Pro Corporation....................... E 323 457-3225
  Middletown *(G-6854)*
Austin & Bednash Cnstr Inc.................. E 302 376-5590
  Newark *(G-9944)*
Baker & Sons Paving............................. G 302 945-6333
  Middletown *(G-6903)*
Bayside Sealcoating Supply................. G 302 697-6441
  Camden Wyoming *(G-916)*
Black Diamond Paving.......................... G 302 333-1987
  Newark *(G-10044)*
Black Magic Sealcoating....................... G 302 832-7906
  Bear *(G-73)*
Blacktop Sealcoating Inc...................... G 302 234-2243
  Newark *(G-10048)*
Bramble Construction Co Inc................ F 302 856-6723
  Georgetown *(G-4239)*
Brandywine Construction Co................ D 302 571-9773
  New Castle *(G-8884)*
Brick Doctor Inc.................................... F 302 678-3380
  Dover *(G-1978)*
Caleb G Stevens.................................... G 302 535-4202
  Harrington *(G-4744)*
Concrete Walls Inc............................... G 302 293-7061
  Bear *(G-117)*
Coppage Paving Inc............................. G 443 309-9796
  Bear *(G-121)*
Daisy Construction Company............... D 302 658-4417
  Wilmington *(G-15768)*
David G Horsey & Sons Inc................... D 302 875-3033
  Laurel *(G-5494)*
David M Sartin Sr.................................. G 302 838-1074
  Bear *(G-133)*
Delaware Department Trnsp................. E 302 326-8950
  Bear *(G-146)*
Delaware Department Trnsp................. E 302 653-4128
  Middletown *(G-7039)*
Diamond Materials............................... G 302 292-1100
  Newark *(G-10523)*
Disabatino Enterprises LLC.................. D 302 652-3838
  Wilmington *(G-16085)*
Don Rogers Inc..................................... F 302 658-6524
  Wilmington *(G-16132)*
Dover Kent County Mpo....................... G 302 387-6030
  Camden *(G-823)*
Dover Paving.. G 302 274-0743
  Dover *(G-2359)*
Dxi Construction Inc............................. C 302 858-5007
  Georgetown *(G-4301)*
E Earle Downing Inc.............................. E 302 656-9908
  Wilmington *(G-16238)*
Eastern States Cnstr Svc Inc................. D 302 995-2259
  Wilmington *(G-16264)*
Espinoza Orlando................................. G 302 442-5007
  Claymont *(G-1134)*
Evans Paving LLC.................................. G 302 322-6863
  Bear *(G-210)*
Everyone Can Achieve LLC................... E 404 317-1228
  Wilmington *(G-16491)*
Extreme Asphalt Maintenance.............. G 302 275-8996
  Newark *(G-10694)*
F & G Construction Co Inc..................... G 302 994-1406
  Wilmington *(G-16519)*
Ffi General Contractor In...................... G 302 420-1242
  Wilmington *(G-16592)*

First State Drvway Sealcoating............. G 302 478-2266
  Wilmington *(G-16628)*
First State Sealcoating......................... G 302 632-7522
  Felton *(G-3975)*
George & Lynch Inc.............................. D 302 736-3031
  Dover *(G-2573)*
George P Stewart.................................. G 302 737-4927
  Newark *(G-10824)*
Greggo & Ferrara Inc............................ C 302 658-5241
  New Castle *(G-9180)*
H Wells Paving & Sealcoating............... G 302 857-9243
  Bear *(G-260)*
H Wells Paving & Sealcoating............... G 302 838-2727
  Bear *(G-261)*
Harmony Construction Inc................... F 302 737-8700
  Newark *(G-10930)*
Highland Construction LLC................. F 302 286-6990
  Bear *(G-274)*
Hudson Scholastic................................ G 302 463-0840
  Dewey Beach *(G-1670)*
Isaacs Asphalt Paving.......................... G 302 251-2990
  Georgetown *(G-4374)*
J Stewart Paving Inc............................. G 610 359-9059
  Newark *(G-11077)*
James Docherty.................................... G 302 983-2653
  Newark *(G-11090)*
James L Webb Paving Co Inc................ G 302 697-2000
  Camden *(G-858)*
Jerrys Inc... E 302 422-7676
  Milford *(G-7952)*
Jjid Inc... E 302 836-0414
  Bear *(G-305)*
Jose A Fernandez................................. G 302 422-5903
  Ellendale *(G-3924)*
Joshuas Paving..................................... G 302 396-1221
  Dover *(G-2804)*
Lopez Gelasio....................................... G 302 377-2591
  Wilmington *(G-17993)*
Louis Dolente & Sons LLC..................... E 610 874-2100
  Claymont *(G-1226)*
Mark Jones Paving................................ G 302 355-0695
  Claymont *(G-1231)*
Material Supply Inc............................... E 302 658-6524
  Wilmington *(G-18191)*
Matts Management Family LLC............ G 302 732-3715
  Frankford *(G-4125)*
McJ Seal & Line Striping LLC................. G 302 416-1326
  Smyrna *(G-13821)*
McJ Seal & Line Striping LLC................. G 302 691-3255
  Middletown *(G-18231)*
McKenzie Paving Inc............................. F 302 376-8560
  Middletown *(G-7335)*
McNeil Paving....................................... G 302 945-7131
  Millsboro *(G-8371)*
Melvin L Joseph Cnstr Co...................... E 302 856-7396
  Georgetown *(G-4424)*
Mitten Construction Co........................ F 302 697-2124
  Dover *(G-3104)*
Mumford and Miller Con Inc................. C 302 378-7736
  Middletown *(G-7388)*
Naudain Enterprises LLC...................... F 302 239-6840
  Hockessin *(G-5319)*
New Castle County Flooring................. G 302 218-0507
  Newark *(G-11517)*
Palmer & Associates Inc....................... G 302 834-9329
  Bear *(G-412)*
Peninsula Pave & Seal LLC.................... F 302 226-7283
  Georgetown *(G-4459)*
Pitch Black Sealcoating LLC................. G 302 824-8125
  Wilmington *(G-19055)*
R S Widdoes & Son Inc......................... F 302 764-7455
  Wilmington *(G-19306)*

R&C Contractors LLC............................ F 302 284-9870
  Felton *(G-4011)*
RA Harrison Paving............................... G 302 363-7344
  Dover *(G-3417)*
Ralph Cahall & Son Paving................... F 302 653-4220
  Smyrna *(G-13862)*
Richard Harrison Jr Paving.................... G 302 875-4206
  Laurel *(G-5590)*
River Asphalt LLC................................. G 302 934-0881
  Dagsboro *(G-1500)*
Road Site Construction Inc.................. E 302 645-1922
  Lewes *(G-6424)*
Rock Bottom Paving Inc....................... G 800 728-3160
  Felton *(G-4021)*
Rp Ventures and Holdings Inc............. E 410 398-3000
  Wilmington *(G-19578)*
Sams Construction LLC........................ F 302 654-6542
  Wilmington *(G-19650)*
Sanco Construction Co Inc.................. G 302 633-4156
  Wilmington *(G-19655)*
Seal Pro Paving and Seal...................... G 302 379-8267
  Wilmington *(G-19721)*
Slurry Pavement Systems..................... G 609 500-3828
  Wilmington *(G-19867)*
Sme Masonry Contrs Ltd Lblty............. F 302 743-7338
  Wilmington *(G-19883)*
South Jersey Paving............................. G 856 498-8647
  Bear *(G-501)*
Straight Line Striping LLC.................... F 302 228-3335
  Milton *(G-8716)*
Stripe-A-Lot Inc.................................... E 302 654-9175
  Wilmington *(G-20101)*
Sweeten Companies Inc....................... G 302 737-6161
  Newark *(G-12140)*
Teal Construction Inc........................... D 302 276-6034
  Dover *(G-3661)*
Terra Firma of Delmarva Inc................. E 302 846-3350
  Delmar *(G-1640)*
Tersin Enterprises LLC.......................... G 614 260-3215
  Dover *(G-3671)*
Thelma Stanley..................................... G 302 604-8481
  Millsboro *(G-8485)*
Voshell Bros Welding Inc...................... E 302 674-1414
  Dover *(G-3810)*
Wb Paving LLC...................................... G 302 838-1886
  Bear *(G-560)*
Wilson Sealcoating.............................. G 302 653-0201
  Clayton *(G-1408)*
Zweemers Pav & Sealcoating LLC........ G 302 363-6116
  Magnolia *(G-6794)*

1622 Bridge, tunnel, and elevated highway

Aviman Management LLC................... E 302 377-5788
  Wilmington *(G-14669)*
Eastern Hwy Specialists Inc................ D 302 777-7673
  Wilmington *(G-16259)*
First State Crane Service Inc............... E 302 398-8885
  Felton *(G-3974)*
Greggo & Ferrara Inc............................ C 302 658-5241
  New Castle *(G-9180)*

1623 Water, sewer, and utility lines

Asplundh Tree Expert LLC.................... G 302 678-4702
  Dover *(G-1833)*
Blueocean Communications LLC......... G 617 586-6633
  Camden *(G-793)*
Bramble Construction Co Inc............... F 302 856-6723
  Georgetown *(G-4239)*
Brandywine Construction Co................ D 302 571-9773
  New Castle *(G-8884)*
Bunting & Murray Cnstr Corp.............. D 302 436-5144
  Selbyville *(G-13486)*

16 HEAVY CONSTRUCTION, EXCEPT BUILDING CONSTRUCTION, CONTRACTOR

Core & Main LP .... G 302 737-1500
   Newark *(G-10323)*

Crypto Trader LLC .... G 302 339-7500
   Rehoboth Beach *(G-12708)*

Current Solutions .... G 302 724-5243
   Dover *(G-2171)*

David Bridge .... G 302 429-3317
   Bear *(G-131)*

Dxi Construction Inc .... C 302 858-5007
   Georgetown *(G-4301)*

Dycom Industries Inc .... G 302 613-0958
   New Castle *(G-9071)*

Eastern States Cnstr Svc Inc .... D 302 995-2259
   Wilmington *(G-16264)*

Epb Associates Inc .... F 302 475-7301
   Wilmington *(G-16449)*

Fast Pipe Lining East Inc .... F 302 368-7414
   Newark *(G-10716)*

First State Underground Inc .... E 302 381-5601
   Dagsboro *(G-1447)*

Floleft LLC .... G 302 648-2088
   Dagsboro *(G-1448)*

Flood Rescue LLC .... G 302 547-4092
   Milford *(G-7899)*

George & Lynch Inc .... D 302 736-3031
   Dover *(G-2573)*

Gt Directional LLC .... G 714 417-2826
   Wilmington *(G-16997)*

Guardian Companies Inc .... E 302 834-1000
   Wilmington *(G-17000)*

H I E Contractors Inc .... F 302 224-3032
   Newark *(G-10913)*

Hopkins Construction Inc .... F 302 337-3366
   Bridgeville *(G-712)*

INA Acquisition Corp .... F 302 472-9258
   Wilmington *(G-17295)*

Joseph T Hardy & Son Inc .... E 302 328-9457
   New Castle *(G-9268)*

JT Enterprise LLC .... G 302 492-8119
   Hartly *(G-4887)*

Merit Construction Engineers .... F 302 992-9810
   Wilmington *(G-18284)*

Myralon Webb Ms .... G 302 684-3841
   Lewes *(G-6302)*

Nicoin Telecom LLC .... E 800 914-6177
   Lewes *(G-6313)*

R F Brown Inc .... G 302 737-1993
   Newark *(G-11808)*

Sprig .... G 302 753-6859
   Townsend *(G-14070)*

Standard Pipe Services LLC .... D 302 286-0701
   Newark *(G-12084)*

Teal Construction Inc .... D 302 276-6034
   Dover *(G-3661)*

Team Systems International LLC .... G 703 217-7648
   Lewes *(G-6545)*

Tri-State Grouting LLC .... G 302 286-0701
   Newark *(G-12225)*

Tri-State Underground Inc .... G 302 293-9352
   Bear *(G-540)*

Tri-State Underground Inc .... F 302 836-8030
   Townsend *(G-14084)*

Triton Construction Co Inc .... F 516 780-8100
   New Castle *(G-9641)*

Underground Locating Services .... G 302 856-9626
   Georgetown *(G-4565)*

Utilisite Inc .... F 302 945-5022
   Lewes *(G-6596)*

Utility Lines Cnstr Svcs LLC .... G 302 337-9980
   Bridgeville *(G-778)*

Utility Locator LLC .... G 215 596-1234
   Wilmington *(G-20558)*

Voshell Bros Welding Inc .... E 302 674-1414
   Dover *(G-3810)*

Yacht Anything Ltd .... G 302 226-3335
   Rehoboth Beach *(G-13026)*

Zober Contracting Services Inc .... G 302 270-3078
   Dover *(G-3903)*

1629 Heavy construction, nec

Advance Construction Technique .... G 270 257-0377
   Wilmington *(G-14265)*

Advanced Cnstr Techniques Inc .... D 302 273-2617
   Newark *(G-9773)*

Alpha Railroad & Piling .... G 318 377-8720
   Newark *(G-9835)*

Asplundh Tree Expert LLC .... G 302 678-4702
   Dover *(G-1833)*

Breakwater Construction Envmtl .... E 302 945-5800
   Millsboro *(G-8205)*

CBI Services LLC .... F 302 325-8400
   New Castle *(G-8922)*

Crimson Group LLC .... G 301 252-3779
   Newark *(G-10355)*

▲ Croda Uniqema Inc .... D 302 429-5599
   New Castle *(G-8988)*

Delaware City Refining Co LLC .... B 302 834-6000
   New Castle *(G-9016)*

Desalitech Inc .... E 508 981-7950
   Wilmington *(G-16022)*

Epb Associates Inc .... F 302 475-7301
   Wilmington *(G-16449)*

First State Crane Service Inc .... E 302 398-8885
   Felton *(G-3974)*

First State Rental Company LLC .... G 302 632-5699
   Houston *(G-5441)*

George & Lynch Inc .... D 302 736-3031
   Dover *(G-2573)*

Green Construction Services .... G 610 675-6337
   Wilmington *(G-16963)*

Interstate Construction Inc .... E 302 369-3590
   Newark *(G-11048)*

J & J Bulkheading .... G 302 436-2800
   Selbyville *(G-13550)*

▲ Janette Redrow Ltd .... G 302 659-3534
   Townsend *(G-14020)*

Jjid Inc .... E 302 836-0414
   Bear *(G-305)*

Kbr Inc .... G 302 452-9386
   Newark *(G-11146)*

Lavond Mackey .... G 484 466-8055
   Wilmington *(G-17827)*

Melvin L Joseph Cnstr Co .... E 302 856-7396
   Georgetown *(G-4424)*

Merritt Marine Cnstr Inc .... G 302 436-2881
   Selbyville *(G-13570)*

Msl Associates LLC .... E 207 391-4420
   Newark *(G-11466)*

Mumford and Miller Con Inc .... C 302 378-7736
   Middletown *(G-7388)*

Pauls Paving Inc .... F 302 539-9123
   Frankford *(G-4131)*

Pierson RE Construction .... F 302 407-3308
   Wilmington *(G-19035)*

Precision Marine Construction .... G 302 227-2711
   Rehoboth Beach *(G-12898)*

Ryan Gallo Tree Service Inc .... F 302 239-1001
   Hockessin *(G-5375)*

▼ Sun Marine Maintenance Inc .... E 302 539-6756
   Frankford *(G-4149)*

Sussex Marine Construction Inc .... G 302 436-9680
   Frankford *(G-4151)*

17 CONSTRUCTION - SPECIAL TRADE CONTRACTORS

1711 Plumbing, heating, air-conditioning

5 Star Hvacr LLC .... G 610 508-6464
   Claymont *(G-1013)*

A & A Air Services Inc .... E 302 436-4800
   Frankford *(G-4059)*

A & C Unlimited .... G 302 379-7112
   Bear *(G-6)*

A J Dauphin & Son Inc .... G 302 994-1454
   Wilmington *(G-14164)*

A Plumber .... G 302 249-7606
   Milford *(G-7757)*

A Ralph Woodrow Inc .... G 302 655-0297
   Newark *(G-9727)*

Abco Mech Htg & Coolg LLC .... G 302 353-4336
   New Castle *(G-8757)*

Above & Beyond Services .... F 443 614-2068
   Laurel *(G-5459)*

AC Home Solutions .... G 302 442-2516
   Wilmington *(G-14212)*

Accessheat Inc .... E 302 373-9524
   Wilmington *(G-14222)*

Accurate & Heating .... G 302 561-5749
   Bear *(G-13)*

Advanced Heating & Air Inc .... G 302 731-1000
   Newark *(G-9776)*

Advanced Home Services Inc .... G 302 339-7600
   Magnolia *(G-6714)*

Advanced Mechanical Inc .... F 302 734-5583
   Dover *(G-1725)*

Affordable Heating & AC .... G 302 328-9220
   Historic New Castle *(G-4924)*

Affordable Plumbing & Elc Inc .... G 443 235-9222
   Delmar *(G-1561)*

Air Doctorx Inc .... F 302 492-1333
   Hartly *(G-4855)*

Air One Htg Cooling Pros .... G 908 623-6154
   Millsboro *(G-8163)*

Air Temp Solutions LLC .... F 302 276-0532
   New Castle *(G-8775)*

Allied Elec Solutions Ltd .... G 302 893-0257
   Wilmington *(G-14380)*

Ambience Inc .... E 302 239-4822
   Wilmington *(G-14416)*

American Standard .... G 302 326-1349
   New Castle *(G-8801)*

Amstel Mechanical Contrs Inc .... G 302 836-6469
   New Castle *(G-8803)*

Anchor Plumbing Inc .... G 410 392-6520
   Newark *(G-9863)*

Angler Plumbing LLC .... G 302 293-5691
   Newark *(G-9870)*

Aqua Pro Inc .... G 302 659-6593
   Smyrna *(G-13647)*

Arctec Air Heating & Cooling .... G 302 629-7129
   Bridgeville *(G-666)*

Arctic Heating and AC .... G 302 537-6988
   Dagsboro *(G-1412)*

Ashley Wiper .... G 302 994-6838
   Wilmington *(G-14587)*

Associates Contracting Inc .... F 302 734-4311
   Dover *(G-1837)*

Assurance Plumbing Compnay .... G 302 324-0403
   New Castle *(G-8826)*

Atlantic Refrigeration Inc .... E 302 645-9321
   Lewes *(G-5717)*

Atlas Solar III LLC .... G 949 677-1308
   Wilmington *(G-14631)*

17 CONSTRUCTION - SPECIAL TRADE CONTRACTORS

B Walls Son Htg & A Conditions............. F 302 856-4045
  Georgetown *(G-4219)*
Back Bay Plumbing................................. G 302 945-1210
  Millsboro *(G-8179)*
Back Power Service LLC.......................... G 302 934-1901
  Millsboro *(G-8180)*
Barkley Heating & Air LLC...................... F 302 653-5971
  Smyrna *(G-13659)*
Battaglia Electric Inc................................ C 302 325-6100
  New Castle *(G-8847)*
Beaches Plumbing Plus............................ G 302 841-0171
  Milton *(G-8570)*
Beacon Air Inc.. G 302 323-1688
  New Castle *(G-8854)*
Bear Industries Inc.................................. D 302 368-1311
  Newark *(G-10005)*
Bella Hvac... G 302 561-4025
  Newark *(G-10014)*
Bennett Services Inc................................ G 302 656-4107
  Wilmington *(G-14838)*
Bethany Plumbing and Heating................ G 302 539-1022
  Ocean View *(G-12480)*
Blades H V A C Services.......................... G 302 539-4436
  Dagsboro *(G-1418)*
Blades Hvac Services............................... G 302 539-4436
  Frankford *(G-4073)*
Blue Skies Solar & Wind Power............... G 302 326-0856
  New Castle *(G-8871)*
Bob Davis Inc.. G 302 798-2561
  Wilmington *(G-14989)*
Bobs Plumbing Repair LLC..................... G 302 853-2259
  Georgetown *(G-4236)*
Booth Wyn Heating & AC....................... G 302 737-7170
  Hartly *(G-4857)*
Booths Services Plbg Htg & AC............... G 302 454-7385
  Newark *(G-10070)*
Boothwyn Heating & AC Inc.................. F 302 284-2772
  Hartly *(G-4858)*
Boulden Brothers..................................... E 302 368-3848
  Newark *(G-10072)*
Boulden Services LLC.............................. E 302 368-0100
  Newark *(G-10073)*
Braham Plumbing LLC............................ G 302 448-5708
  Laurel *(G-5473)*
Brandywine Contractors Inc.................... G 302 325-2700
  New Castle *(G-8886)*
Brandywine Heating & Air LLC.............. G 302 299-0180
  Wilmington *(G-15063)*
Breeding & Day Inc................................. E 302 478-4585
  Wilmington *(G-15100)*
Bronswerk Marine Corp.......................... G 619 813-4797
  Newark *(G-10092)*
Budget Rooter Inc.................................... F 302 322-3011
  New Castle *(G-8897)*
Burns & McBride Inc............................... D 302 656-5110
  New Castle *(G-8901)*
Burnsies Plumbing LLC........................... G 215 275-0723
  Bear *(G-85)*
Byrds Nest LLC.. G 302 475-4949
  Wilmington *(G-15165)*
Byron Outten Plumbing........................... G 302 236-4727
  Greenwood *(G-4601)*
C & D Contractors Inc............................. F 302 764-2020
  Wilmington *(G-15171)*
C & N Services LLC................................. G 302 883-1046
  Dover *(G-2005)*
C&S Mechanical Services Inc................... G 302 377-2343
  Wilmington *(G-15178)*
Cahill Plumbing & Heating Inc................ G 302 894-1802
  Newark *(G-10119)*
Calfo & Haight Inc................................... F 302 998-3852
  Wilmington *(G-15193)*

Calvert Mechanical Systems Inc............. E 302 998-0460
  Wilmington *(G-15202)*
Cape Climate Inc..................................... G 302 858-7160
  Georgetown *(G-4243)*
Carson City Ic LLC.................................. G 520 261-8094
  Dover *(G-2032)*
Castle Services Inc................................... G 302 481-6633
  Wilmington *(G-15268)*
Central Heating A Condtioning............... G 302 492-1169
  Hartly *(G-4863)*
Certified Mechanical Contrs.................... G 302 559-3727
  Wilmington *(G-15317)*
Cesn Partners Inc.................................... F 302 537-1814
  Ocean View *(G-12488)*
Charles A Klein & Sons Inc..................... G 410 549-6960
  Selbyville *(G-13496)*
Charles Moon Plumbing.......................... G 302 732-3555
  Dagsboro *(G-1425)*
Charles Moon Plumbing.......................... G 302 732-3555
  Dagsboro *(G-1426)*
Charles Moon Plumbing & Htg............... G 302 798-6666
  Claymont *(G-1083)*
Charles S Reskovitz Inc........................... G 302 999-9455
  Wilmington *(G-15339)*
Chesapeake Climate Control LLC............ E 302 732-6006
  Frankford *(G-4085)*
Chesapeake Home Services LLC............. G 302 732-6006
  Frankford *(G-4087)*
Chesapeake Plumbing & Htg Inc............. E 302 732-6006
  Frankford *(G-4089)*
Christensen Evert J Plumbing &.............. G 302 475-9249
  Wilmington *(G-15398)*
Christiana Mechanical Inc....................... F 302 378-7308
  Middletown *(G-6978)*
Clark Services Inc Delaware.................... G 302 834-0556
  Bear *(G-109)*
Clean Energy Usa LLC............................ G 302 227-1337
  Rehoboth Beach *(G-12675)*
Clendaniel Plbg Htg & Coolg.................. G 302 684-3152
  Milton *(G-8585)*
Climate Solutions Services...................... G 302 275-9919
  Wilmington *(G-15485)*
Cloudbrst Lawn Sprnklr Systems............ G 302 375-0446
  Middletown *(G-6998)*
CMI Electric Inc....................................... E 302 731-5556
  Newark *(G-10265)*
Cmp Fire LLC... G 410 620-2062
  Newark *(G-10266)*
Coastal Mechanical.................................. F 302 994-9100
  Wilmington *(G-15510)*
Collins Mechanical Inc............................. E 302 398-8877
  Harrington *(G-4752)*
Congo Capital Management LLC............ F 732 337-6643
  Wilmington *(G-15593)*
Congo Industries Inc................................ G 732 337-6643
  Wilmington *(G-15596)*
Coolersmart... G 302 323-2100
  Historic New Castle *(G-4964)*
Cooper Bros Inc....................................... F 302 323-0717
  New Castle *(G-8972)*
Costa and Rihl Inc.................................... C 856 534-7325
  Wilmington *(G-15649)*
Crystal Clear Mechanical LLC................. G 302 344-2531
  Selbyville *(G-13512)*
Cs Services LLC....................................... G 302 841-9420
  Lewes *(G-5873)*
Cs Webb Daughters & Son Inc................ G 302 239-2801
  Hockessin *(G-5174)*
Custom Mechanical Inc........................... E 302 537-1950
  Frankford *(G-4096)*
D B Mechanical LLC................................ G 302 722-0471
  Newark *(G-10375)*

D F Distribution Inc................................. E 302 798-5999
  Wilmington *(G-15760)*
Daniel D Rappa Inc.................................. G 302 994-1199
  Newport *(G-12447)*
Davis Services.. G 302 792-1754
  Claymont *(G-1110)*
DBA Heating Parts Hub........................... G 302 381-3705
  Greenwood *(G-4612)*
Del Campo Plumbing & Heating............. G 302 998-3648
  Wilmington *(G-15859)*
Delaware Heating & AC........................... F 302 738-4669
  Bear *(G-149)*
Delaware Heating & AC Svcs Inc............. E 302 738-4669
  Newark *(G-10451)*
Delaware Mech Contrs Assoc.................. G 302 235-2813
  Hockessin *(G-5180)*
Delcard Associates Inc............................. C 302 221-4822
  New Castle *(G-9041)*
Delmarva Plumbing LLC......................... G 571 274-4926
  Ocean View *(G-12502)*
Delmarva Refrigeration Inc..................... G 302 846-2727
  Delmar *(G-1588)*
Dewitt Heating & AC............................... G 267 228-7355
  Bear *(G-165)*
Dewitt Hvac... G 267 228-7355
  Bear *(G-166)*
Domenic Di Donato Plbg Htg Inc............ G 856 207-4919
  Wilmington *(G-16126)*
Done Right Today Inc.............................. G 302 528-4294
  Wilmington *(G-16139)*
Ducts Unlimited Inc................................. E 302 378-4125
  Smyrna *(G-13717)*
Durham Plumbing Service LLC............... G 302 653-5601
  Marydel *(G-6797)*
Dw Heating and Cooling Svcs.................. G 302 373-7786
  Townsend *(G-13995)*
Dynamic Air LLC..................................... G 302 612-1412
  Hartly *(G-4871)*
Eastern Air Service.................................. G 800 921-0392
  Georgetown *(G-4304)*
Eastern Shore Energy Inc........................ E 302 697-9230
  Camden *(G-824)*
Edward J Deseta Co Inc........................... F 302 420-0900
  Wilmington *(G-16302)*
Ehg Mechanical....................................... G 302 530-4438
  Wilmington *(G-16311)*
Elements Hvac Services LLC................... G 302 448-9641
  Selbyville *(G-13532)*
Elvin Schrock and Sons Inc..................... G 302 349-4384
  Greenwood *(G-4625)*
Enhanced Heating & AC.......................... G 302 836-1921
  Newark *(G-10649)*
Entek Manufacturing Inc......................... G 302 576-5860
  Wilmington *(G-16432)*
Esquire Plumbing & Heating Co.............. G 302 378-7001
  Middletown *(G-7109)*
Expert Refrigerationservice LL................ G 302 745-4181
  Bridgeville *(G-700)*
F & H Mechanical LLC............................ G 302 932-8034
  Hockessin *(G-5205)*
Falcone Truman Plbg & Htg Inc.............. E 302 376-7483
  Odessa *(G-12584)*
Family Heating & Cooling LLC............... G 302 229-4716
  New Castle *(G-9117)*
FE Mran Inc Fire Prtction E..................... E 302 453-9237
  Newark *(G-10719)*
Federal Mechanical Contractors.............. F 302 656-2998
  New Castle *(G-9123)*
Ferrell Cooling & Heating Inc................. G 302 436-2922
  Selbyville *(G-13535)*
First Class Heating & AC Inc................... D 302 934-8900
  Millsboro *(G-8289)*

Employee Codes: A=Over 500 employees, B=251-500
C=101-250, D=51-100, E=20-50, F=10-19, G=1-9

2024 Harris Directory of
Delaware Businesses

17 CONSTRUCTION - SPECIAL TRADE CONTRACTORS

Company	Code	Phone
First Class Heating AC — Newark (G-10728)	G	302 834-1036
First State Plumbing & Heating — New Castle (G-9131)	G	302 275-9746
Fletcher Plumbing Htg & AC Inc — Smyrna (G-13737)	F	302 653-6277
Flo Mechanical LLC — Hockessin (G-5213)	E	302 239-7299
Flo Mechanical LLC — Wilmington (G-16663)	F	302 543-5462
Flowrite — Historic New Castle (G-4989)	G	302 544-4042
Flowrite Inc — Bear (G-232)	G	302 547-5657
Frederick Enterprises Inc — Wilmington (G-16737)	E	302 994-5786
Freedom Drain Clg Pipe Svcs LL — Bear (G-238)	G	484 480-1368
General Refrigeration Company — Delmar (G-1598)	E	302 846-3073
George H Burns Inc — Wilmington (G-16845)	E	302 658-0752
Geter Done Mechanical — Laurel (G-5520)	G	302 727-3291
Godfrey Plumbing Services — Wilmington (G-16905)	G	302 985-1593
Gold Star Services LLC — New Castle (G-9171)	G	610 444-3333
Grace Mechanical — Rehoboth Beach (G-12776)	G	302 542-4102
Graydon Hurst & Son Inc — Wilmington (G-16952)	G	302 762-2444
Greensboro Heating & Air — Magnolia (G-6749)	G	302 598-5568
Greenway Comfort Solutions — Newark (G-10891)	G	302 200-4929
Gregg & Sons Mechanical LLC — Townsend (G-14011)	G	302 223-8145
H & R Heating & AC — New Castle (G-9188)	G	302 323-9919
Harry Caswell Inc — Millsboro (G-8313)	E	302 945-5322
Harry L Adams Inc — New Castle (G-9198)	G	302 328-5268
Harrys Heating & Cooling — Wilmington (G-17066)	G	302 438-5853
Harrys Nuts and Then Some — Millsboro (G-8314)	G	302 947-1344
Hellens Heating & Air I — Harbeson (G-4698)	G	302 945-1875
Henry Eashum & Son Inc — Camden (G-848)	F	302 697-6164
Henry Yee Plumbing Inc — Wilmington (G-17124)	G	914 980-2188
Hentkowski Inc — Wilmington (G-17126)	F	302 998-2257
Hillside Oil Company Inc — Newark (G-10953)	E	302 738-4144
Hns Plumbing Services LLC — Bear (G-276)	F	302 650-9010
Hollingsworth Heating & AC — Milford (G-7933)	G	302 422-7525
Honesty Service — Newark (G-10967)	G	302 690-2433
Horizon Services Inc — Newark (G-10971)	B	610 491-8800
Horizon Services Inc — Wilmington (G-17209)	C	302 762-1200
Hyett Refrigeration Inc — Harbeson (G-4701)	F	302 684-4600
ID Griffith Inc — Wilmington (G-17262)	D	302 656-8253
Innovative Heating & Coolg LLC — Newark (G-11023)	G	302 528-4172
Integrated Mechanical and Fire — Wilmington (G-17369)	G	302 420-0617
J E Pellegrino & Associates — Wilmington (G-17454)	G	302 655-2565
J F Sobieski Mech Contrs Inc — Wilmington (G-17456)	C	302 993-0103
J J White Inc — New Castle (G-9247)	A	215 722-1000
J Rihl Inc — Wilmington (G-17461)	F	856 778-5899
J Stachon Plumbing LLC — Wilmington (G-17464)	G	302 998-0938
Jam Air LLC — Dover (G-2767)	G	302 270-8236
Jeffs Total Heating N Air — Seaford (G-13234)	G	302 682-1816
Jenkins Mechanical — Georgetown (G-4382)	G	302 430-8211
Jmt Services Inc — Middletown (G-7250)	F	302 530-2807
John Hiott Refrigeration & AC — Camden Wyoming (G-957)	F	302 697-3050
Joseph T Richardson Inc — Harrington (G-4792)	E	302 398-8101
Jsf Construction Co Inc — Wilmington (G-17605)	G	302 999-9573
K and B Hvac Svcs LLC — Delmar (G-1609)	G	302 846-3111
K BS Plumbing Incorporated — Dover (G-2823)	G	302 678-2757
Kmp Mechanical LLC — Newark (G-11193)	G	410 392-6126
Kmp Mechanical LLC — Newark (G-11194)	G	410 392-6126
Kw Solar Solutions Inc — Bear (G-335)	G	302 838-8400
Kw Solar Solutions Inc — Bear (G-336)	G	302 838-8400
L & L Geothermal Hvac Svcs LLC — Seaford (G-13251)	G	302 536-7120
Leager Construction Inc — Smyrna (G-13797)	G	302 653-8021
Lig Energy Solutions LLC — Wilmington (G-17907)	C	646 918-8232
Lindale Plumbing LLC — Greenwood (G-4648)	G	302 242-2493
Listonburg Solar LLC — Wilmington (G-17933)	G	412 979-6872
Local Plumbing — Claymont (G-1223)	G	302 746-3101
M D Plumbing Drain Cleaning — Marydel (G-6806)	G	302 492-8880
M Davis & Sons Inc — Wilmington (G-18058)	G	302 998-3385
▲ M Davis & Sons Inc — Newark (G-11301)	C	302 998-3385
Maichle S Heating Air — New Castle (G-9337)	F	302 328-4822
Malins Jim E Plumbing & Htg — Hockessin (G-5293)	G	302 239-2755
Manley Hvac Inc — Wilmington (G-18105)	G	302 998-4654
Mary Annes Landscaping Inc — Felton (G-4001)	G	302 335-5433
Mason Mechanical LLC — Smyrna (G-13817)	G	302 653-4022
McCrea Equipment Company Inc — Bridgeville (G-729)	E	302 337-8249
McMahon Heating & AC — Lewes (G-6255)	F	302 945-4300
Mdm McHncal InstItItion USA LLC — Wilmington (G-18239)	G	617 938-9634
Mecham Mechanical — Milton (G-8665)	G	302 645-2793
Mechanical Solutions LLC — Camden (G-874)	G	302 900-1950
Megee Plumbing & Heating Co — Georgetown (G-4422)	D	302 856-6311
Mels Htg & A/C — Millsboro (G-8374)	G	302 947-1979
Mels Wells LLC — Lincoln (G-6684)	G	302 393-9017
Merit Mechanical Co Inc — Newark (G-11389)	D	302 366-8601
Merit Services Inc — Newark (G-11390)	E	302 366-8601
Messina Charles Plbg & Elc Co — Dover (G-3067)	D	302 674-5696
Mid Atlantic Mechanical Inc — Newark (G-11407)	E	302 999-9209
Midway Services Inc — Lincoln (G-6685)	G	302 422-8603
Miller Heating & Cooling LLC — Middletown (G-7371)	F	302 750-2409
Miller John H Plumbing & Htg — Camden (G-876)	F	302 697-1012
Mobile Air LLC — Newark (G-11435)	G	302 502-7743
Mobile Mechanical Services — Lincoln (G-6690)	G	302 503-7441
Modern Controls Inc — New Castle (G-9377)	C	302 325-6800
Monroe Mechanical Contracting — Clayton (G-1387)	G	302 223-6020
Morans Refrigeration Svc Inc — Rehoboth Beach (G-12861)	G	703 642-1200
Mr Rooter Plumbing of New — Newark (G-11464)	G	302 463-5720
My Cousin Vinnys Hvac — Newark (G-11476)	G	302 266-1888
Naegele Heating & Cooling — Greenwood (G-4654)	G	443 996-1881
National HVAC Service — New Castle (G-9397)	G	302 323-1776
National HVAC Service — Seaford (G-13313)	G	570 825-2894
Neuwing Renewable Energy LLC — Wilmington (G-18605)	G	267 319-1144
North East Pool Plumbing — New Castle (G-9426)	G	302 740-5071
North Star Heating & Air Inc — Dagsboro (G-1490)	E	302 732-3967
Ocean Air — Selbyville (G-13587)	G	302 524-8003
Ocean View Plumbing Inc — Dagsboro (G-1493)	E	302 732-9117
Old School Heating & Cooling — Claymont (G-1257)	G	302 383-7036
Oms Mechanical Inc — Bridgeville (G-742)	G	302 745-7424
One Hour Heating Air Cond — Wilmington (G-18781)	G	302 998-0460
Pencader Mechanical Contrs — Bear (G-421)	G	302 368-9144
Perfect Plumbing Partners Inc — Wilmington (G-18973)	G	610 521-6654
Petes Plumbing LLC — Dover (G-3305)	G	302 270-4990
Philadelphia Plumbing — New Castle (G-9471)	G	302 327-8545
Philadelphia Plumbing — Wilmington (G-19014)	G	302 468-5460

Phillip Fulton..G..... 302 995-6412 Wilmington *(G-19017)*	**Sabrs Home Comfort**..................................G..... 302 379-8133 Lewes *(G-6439)*	**Sussex Plumbing & Heating**........................G..... 302 344-2199 Laurel *(G-5611)*
Pierce Total Comfort LLC...........................F..... 302 378-7714 Middletown *(G-7448)*	**Schlosser Assoc Mech Cntrs Inc**................E..... 302 738-7333 Newark *(G-11958)*	**Synnove Energy Corporation LLC**..............G..... 805 215-8600 Dover *(G-3635)*
Pipe Pros Jetting & Plbg LLC.....................F..... 302 562-0522 Townsend *(G-14052)*	**Sears Heating and AC**..................................G..... 302 480-1382 Dover *(G-3525)*	**TA Austin Plumbing Inc**................................F..... 302 995-2282 Wilmington *(G-20203)*
Pluck Hvac..G..... 302 836-8596 Bear *(G-427)*	**Seiberlich Trane Energy Svcs**.....................D..... 302 395-0200 New Castle *(G-9557)*	**Telgian Corporation**.....................................E..... 480 753-5444 Wilmington *(G-20267)*
Plumbing Enterprises LLC..........................F..... 302 515-4620 Selbyville *(G-13591)*	**Service Air Tech Hvac**..................................G..... 302 335-8334 Magnolia *(G-6782)*	**Tesla Energy Operations Inc**......................G..... 650 638-1028 Newark *(G-12181)*
Plummer Co Inc...G..... 302 227-5000 Rehoboth Beach *(G-12892)*	**Service Unlimited Inc**....................................E..... 302 326-2665 New Castle *(G-9558)*	**Thomas A Cochran & Sons Inc**..................F..... 302 656-6054 Historic New Castle *(G-5085)*
Practical Systems..G..... 302 753-8885 Newark *(G-11720)*	**Sevo Indus Fire Protection LLC**..................G..... 913 677-1112 Middletown *(G-7557)*	**Thomas Francisconi**....................................G..... 302 995-2282 Wilmington *(G-20308)*
Preferred Fire Protection............................F..... 302 256-0607 Wilmington *(G-19163)*	**Shore Mechanical Services**.........................G..... 302 519-6540 Lewes *(G-6466)*	**Tj S Plumbing Heating L**..............................F..... 302 228-7129 Millsboro *(G-8486)*
Preferred Mechanical..................................F..... 302 668-1151 Wilmington *(G-19164)*	**Siegfried J Schulze Inc**................................F..... 302 737-0403 Newark *(G-12003)*	**Top Notch Htg & A C & Rfrgn**.....................G..... 302 645-7171 Lewes *(G-6571)*
Premier Comfort Services...........................G..... 302 740-0712 Townsend *(G-14054)*	**Skyline Roofing & Cnstr LLC**......................G..... 610 929-4135 Lewes *(G-6474)*	**Top Notch Plumbing LLC**.............................G..... 302 381-9096 Dagsboro *(G-1519)*
Pride Heating & Air Conditiong..................G..... 302 234-4751 Newark *(G-11738)*	**Smart Choice Hv/AC Svcs LLC**...................G..... 302 250-5762 Wilmington *(G-19876)*	**Total Climate Control Inc**............................G..... 302 836-6240 Newark *(G-12211)*
Pro Works Inc DH.......................................F..... 302 221-4200 New Castle *(G-9497)*	**Smile Heating & AC**.....................................G..... 302 542-7242 Frankford *(G-4145)*	**Traps Plumbing Heating A/C**.......................G..... 302 677-1775 Dover *(G-3716)*
Pucketts Heating Adn Air............................G..... 443 239-2129 Harrington *(G-4814)*	**Sneads Heating & AC**..................................G..... 302 524-8090 Selbyville *(G-13606)*	**Tri-State Technologies Inc**..........................F..... 302 658-5400 Wilmington *(G-20415)*
Quality Htg Ar-Cnditioning Inc...................E..... 302 654-5247 Wilmington *(G-19284)*	**Snyders Hvac Services LLC**.......................G..... 302 236-2517 Laurel *(G-5602)*	**Trinity Heating & Air**.....................................G..... 302 344-3628 Seaford *(G-13435)*
R & T Heating & Air....................................G..... 302 629-4011 Seaford *(G-13363)*	**Sobieski Services Inc**..................................E..... 302 993-0104 Newark *(G-12047)*	**Triple Tzz Hvac LLC**....................................G..... 302 846-3220 Delmar *(G-1647)*
R A Chance Plumbing Inc...........................G..... 302 324-8200 New Castle *(G-9511)*	**Solar Foundations Usa Inc**.........................G..... 855 738-7200 New Castle *(G-9576)*	**United Sun Systems US Inc**.........................G..... 650 460-8707 Lewes *(G-6590)*
R A Chance Plumbing Inc...........................G..... 302 292-1315 Newark *(G-11805)*	**Solar Frontiers Corp**....................................G..... 302 588-7600 Middletown *(G-7587)*	**Webb LLC**..G..... 302 744-0029 Wilmington *(G-20704)*
R S Bauer LLC...F..... 302 398-4668 Harrington *(G-4816)*	**Sole Contracting Inc**....................................E..... 302 420-4429 Rehoboth Beach *(G-12967)*	**Wegman Bros Inc**...F..... 302 738-4328 Newark *(G-12355)*
Radius Services LLC...................................D..... 302 993-0600 Wilmington *(G-19315)*	**Spring Rain Irrigation Inc**...........................G..... 302 838-9610 Bear *(G-505)*	**Wilkins Fuel Co**...G..... 302 422-5597 Milford *(G-8149)*
Ralph G Degli Obizzi & Sons.....................G..... 302 658-5127 Wilmington *(G-19323)*	**Ssm Industries Inc**......................................E..... 856 345-2525 Wilmington *(G-19989)*	**Willey and Co**..G..... 302 629-3327 Laurel *(G-5626)*
Ralph G Degli Obizzi & Sons Inc..............E..... 302 652-3593 Wilmington *(G-19324)*	**Stan Perkoskis Plumbing & Htg**................E..... 302 529-1220 Wilmington *(G-20010)*	**William D Shellady Inc**.................................D..... 302 652-3106 Wilmington *(G-20785)*
Rays and Sons Mechanical LLC................G..... 302 697-2100 Seaford *(G-13367)*	**Star Enrg**...G..... 302 743-6751 Wilmington *(G-20022)*	**William Delcampo Mechanical SE**.............G..... 302 992-9748 Wilmington *(G-20786)*
Rays Plumbing & Heating Svcs.................F..... 302 697-3936 Felton *(G-4013)*	**Star Enrg Cs LLC**..F..... 302 660-2187 Wilmington *(G-20023)*	**William F & Margaret Hartnett**...................G..... 302 479-5918 Wilmington *(G-20788)*
Real Hvac Services.....................................G..... 302 727-0272 Rehoboth Beach *(G-12910)*	**State Wide Plumbing Inc**.............................G..... 302 292-0924 Newark *(G-12092)*	**William G Day Company**..............................E..... 302 476-2808 Wilmington *(G-20789)*
Red Dog Plumbing and Htg Corp..............E..... 302 436-2922 Selbyville *(G-13596)*	**Statewide Mechanical Inc**...........................G..... 302 376-6117 Townsend *(G-14073)*	**William G Robelen Inc**.................................G..... 302 656-8726 Wilmington *(G-20790)*
Richard S Brown..G..... 302 438-6885 New Castle *(G-9533)*	**Stay True Plumbing**.....................................G..... 302 464-1198 Bear *(G-512)*	**William H McDaniel Inc**................................F..... 302 764-2020 Wilmington *(G-20793)*
Rigid Builders LLC......................................F..... 732 425-3443 Georgetown *(G-4488)*	**Steven Brown & Associates Inc**.................G..... 302 652-4722 Wilmington *(G-20064)*	**William H Metcaff & Sons Inc**......................G..... 301 868-6330 Seaford *(G-13450)*
Robert Gears..G..... 302 690-2590 Frankford *(G-4139)*	**Stratgic Slar Sltons Ltd Lblty**......................G..... 703 307-6761 Rehoboth Beach *(G-12977)*	**Williams Climate Control**.............................G..... 302 628-0440 Seaford *(G-13451)*
Ron Durr Mechanical...................................G..... 215 643-6990 Lewes *(G-6431)*	**Subcool Heating & Air Inc**...........................F..... 302 442-5658 New Castle *(G-9598)*	**Worth Co**...G..... 302 221-4822 New Castle *(G-9691)*
Ronnie Freeman...G..... 302 762-3252 Wilmington *(G-19563)*	**Summit Heating and AC LLC**......................G..... 302 378-1203 Townsend *(G-14074)*	**Wrench Plumbing**...F..... 302 482-1043 Wilmington *(G-20900)*
Roto-Rooter Services Company.................G..... 302 659-7637 Newark *(G-11917)*	**Summit Mechanical Inc**................................E..... 302 836-8814 Bear *(G-516)*	**Wswms Hvac**..G..... 302 454-1987 Newark *(G-12414)*
Rw Greer Inc..G..... 302 764-0376 Wilmington *(G-19597)*	**Summit Mechanical Inc**................................G..... 302 373-1132 Newark *(G-12121)*	**Yoders Central Air**..G..... 302 674-5144 Dover *(G-3888)*
Rw Heating & Air Inc...................................G..... 302 856-4330 Harbeson *(G-4714)*	**Sunlife LLC**..E..... 833 478-6669 Wilmington *(G-20131)*	**Zone Control Hvac Inc**................................G..... 302 752-6697 Bridgeville *(G-785)*
Rwm Plumbing...G..... 302 697-1705 Camden Wyoming *(G-972)*	**Sunnymac LLC**...G..... 844 786-6962 Wilmington *(G-20133)*	*1721 Painting and paper hanging*
Ryes Hvac LLC...G..... 302 981-7851 New Castle *(G-9549)*	**Super Heat**...G..... 302 276-0689 New Castle *(G-9605)*	**1st Choice Painting LLC**..............................G..... 302 278-2684 Bridgeville *(G-656)*
Sab Heating & Air..G..... 302 945-3117 Millsboro *(G-8451)*	**Sussex Heating and Air LLC**......................G..... 302 231-8446 Millsboro *(G-8476)*	**1touch Painting LLC**....................................G..... 302 703-6027 Lewes *(G-5636)*

Employee Codes: A=Over 500 employees, B=251-500
C=101-250, D=51-100, E=20-50, F=10-19, G=1-9

2024 Harris Directory of
Delaware Businesses

17 CONSTRUCTION - SPECIAL TRADE CONTRACTORS

Company	Code	Phone
360 Painting, Townsend (G-13948)	G	302 373-4867
A Pair of Painters, Magnolia (G-6712)	G	302 526-6761
A Rodriguez Painting LLC, Georgetown (G-4191)	G	302 559-7692
A1 Striping Inc, Newark (G-9730)	G	302 738-5016
All Right Painting, New Castle (G-8781)	G	302 983-7761
Alvarez Painting, Wilmington (G-14401)	G	302 287-1457
Armstrong Painting Inc, Millsboro (G-8175)	G	302 420-0415
Ayala Painting LLC, Wilmington (G-14685)	G	208 777-2654
B Boone Painting, Wilmington (G-14695)	G	302 740-2576
Bayside Painting, Lewes (G-5741)	G	302 344-6910
Bell Painting and Wall Cvg Inc, Newark (G-10013)	F	302 738-8854
Brian T Phillips, Wilmington (G-15105)	G	302 593-3815
Brighten Up Painting, Milford (G-7806)	G	302 424-4591
Brush of Color LLC, New Castle (G-8895)	G	302 932-0005
Bulls Home Services Co, Bear (G-84)	G	302 540-1381
Burke Painting Co Inc, Lewes (G-5781)	G	302 998-8500
C R Painting, Selbyville (G-13488)	G	302 519-3938
Cannon Sline LLC, New Castle (G-8912)	C	302 658-1420
Cassidy Painting Inc, New Castle (G-8918)	E	302 683-0710
Cassidy Painting Inc, New Castle (G-8919)	F	302 326-2412
CCS Painting LLC, Wilmington (G-15289)	G	302 438-4398
Certapro Painters of Rehoboth, Rehoboth Beach (G-12668)	G	302 212-5742
Chamberlain and Co Cstm Pntg, Bear (G-95)	G	610 633-2011
Christopher J Seivert, Newark (G-10237)	G	302 731-2719
Clean Hands LLC, Smyrna (G-13681)	F	215 681-1435
Coastal Custom Painting LLC, Rehoboth Beach (G-12682)	G	302 242-6134
Color Works Painting Inc, New Castle (G-8959)	F	302 324-8411
Colorwise and More, Lewes (G-5852)	G	302 703-6330
Connor Charles & Sons Painting, Georgetown (G-4266)	G	302 945-1746
Creekside Painting LLC, Selbyville (G-13509)	G	302 983-1914
D & S Painters LLC, Seaford (G-13144)	G	302 241-7221
Daypainters LLC, Wilmington (G-15821)	G	302 415-3365
Divine Painting and Cnstr, Newark (G-10539)	G	302 983-9405
Donovan Painting and Drywall, Rehoboth Beach (G-12731)	G	302 745-6306
Donovan Painting LLC, Rehoboth Beach (G-12732)	G	302 745-6306
Douglas Homewood, Greenwood (G-4622)	G	302 349-5964
DPs Custom Painting LLC, Frankford (G-4103)	G	302 732-3232
E&A Drywall and Painting Inc, Millsboro (G-8278)	G	302 393-1743
East Coast Painting LLC, Dover (G-2409)	G	302 678-9346
Eastern Shore Painters, Milford (G-7877)	G	443 373-3119
Edgar Silvestre Painting Svc, Bear (G-194)	G	302 670-7702
Esham Painting LLC, Frankford (G-4105)	G	302 381-7876
Everyone Can Achieve LLC, Wilmington (G-16491)	E	404 317-1228
F & F Pntg Faith & Fortune LLC, Dover (G-2477)	G	302 344-2512
F&M Custom Painting LLC, New Castle (G-9114)	G	302 391-4017
Facepainting, New Castle (G-9115)	G	302 344-3145
Final Finishes Inc, Wilmington (G-16606)	G	302 995-1850
Five Star Painting, Newark (G-10744)	G	302 743-6515
Floater Painting, New Castle (G-9135)	G	302 290-8520
Four C Painting, Dover (G-2529)	G	302 242-2497
Fresh Coat Painters of MOT, Townsend (G-14004)	G	302 313-6124
G Alvarez Painting, Seaford (G-13192)	G	443 783-2240
Gravatt Painting, Camden (G-840)	G	302 632-2835
Hampton Enterprises Inc, Townsend (G-14013)	G	302 378-7365
Harry Moore Painting Etc, Wilmington (G-17065)	G	302 803-1087
Henry M McElduff, New Castle (G-9209)	G	302 656-5561
Hernandez Painting, Georgetown (G-4355)	G	302 212-8425
Hinkle Husbands LLC, Wilmington (G-17152)	G	302 827-8202
Horning Bros Custom Painting, Wilmington (G-17212)	G	302 384-7675
J & R Painting and Wallpaper, Wilmington (G-17446)	G	302 438-9718
J G M Associates, Lewes (G-6134)	G	302 645-2159
J Michaels Painting Inc, Newark (G-11074)	G	302 738-8465
Jamestown Painting & Dctg Inc, Newark (G-11093)	E	302 454-7344
Jeff Warnock Carpentry Paintng, Wilmington (G-17516)	G	484 995-4812
JGm & Associates Custom Pntg, Lewes (G-6138)	F	302 645-2159
John Mobile Sndblst & Pain, Hartly (G-4883)	G	302 270-5627
Juan De Dios Painting, Frankford (G-4119)	G	302 841-0363
K and W Painting, Middletown (G-7256)	G	302 598-5663
Kent County Painting Inc, Wilmington (G-17692)	E	302 994-9628
Keystone Finishing Inc, Wilmington (G-17707)	F	925 825-2498
Kokoszka & Sons Inc, New Castle (G-9288)	G	302 328-4807
L&J Painting, Newark (G-11209)	G	267 423-6040
Lawrence E Haug III, Felton (G-3994)	G	302 222-7979
Lbm Painting LLC, Lincoln (G-6680)	G	302 569-1506
Lightning Painting LLC, Middletown (G-7303)	G	302 521-6033
Maccari Companies Inc, Wilmington (G-18064)	G	302 994-9628
Marinis Bros Inc, New Castle (G-9345)	F	302 322-9663
Martinez Painting LLC, Georgetown (G-4419)	G	302 448-1932
Master Painting and Remodeling, Millsboro (G-8368)	G	302 604-8978
Mayse Painting & Contg LLC, Middletown (G-7332)	G	443 553-6503
McElroy & Son Inc, Wilmington (G-18228)	G	302 995-2623
McNicholas Painting, Wilmington (G-18237)	G	302 995-0964
Middletown Painting LLC, Middletown (G-7357)	G	302 376-5419
Mike Morris Painting LLC, Frederica (G-4178)	G	302 423-3940
Navas Painting LLC, New Castle (G-9399)	G	302 685-1474
Paint By Bill LLC, Lewes (G-6347)	G	302 565-9013
Paintersrus, Georgetown (G-4454)	G	302 855-1317
Painting Parties, Newark (G-11614)	G	302 299-9355
Painting Solutions LLC, Dover (G-3261)	G	302 736-6483
Paintings By Sara, Greenwood (G-4659)	G	302 424-0376
Parients Painting LLC, Newark (G-11626)	G	302 738-6819
Perfection Custom Painting LLC, Seaford (G-13345)	G	303 536-7572
Philips Painting LLC, Seaford (G-13346)	G	302 344-0535
Pjhj LLC, Lewes (G-6374)	G	302 645-2159
Pro Quality East Coast Pntg, Lincoln (G-6694)	G	302 745-7753
Promax Painters, Bear (G-440)	G	302 312-8415
Quality Finishers Inc, Historic New Castle (G-5058)	G	302 325-1963
R & R Contractors LLC, Georgetown (G-4477)	G	302 344-6580
R L Wlkerson Assoc Ltd A/K/A R, Milford (G-8057)	G	302 503-3207
Red Eft Painting, Wilmington (G-19384)	G	302 636-9463
Regal Painting & Decorating, Wilmington (G-19398)	G	302 994-8943
Reis Enterprises LLC, Bear (G-451)	G	302 740-8382
Renovate Solutions, Frankford (G-4138)	G	717 951-4300
Rentz Painting LLC, Millsboro (G-8443)	G	302 363-6619
Reyes Painting LLC, Georgetown (G-4484)	G	302 470-1961
Reyes Painting LLC, Millsboro (G-8444)	G	302 519-4538
Robert G Burke Painting Co, Wilmington (G-19511)	F	302 998-2200
Robert J Peoples Inc, New Castle (G-9538)	F	302 984-2017

Robert J Peoples Inc .... F 302 322-0595
  Wilmington (G-19515)
Robert W Nagowski .... G 302 584-2326
  Middletown (G-7519)
Roluva Painting .... G 610 470-5207
  Hockessin (G-5372)
Ronald W Peacock Inc .... F 302 571-9313
  Wilmington (G-19562)
S&S Painting LLC .... G 302 766-2476
  Clayton (G-1403)
Sams Painting .... G 302 430-1241
  Dagsboro (G-1503)
Sebastians Painting .... G 302 725-8023
  Lincoln (G-6698)
Signature Painting Contractors .... G 267 571-6595
  Wilmington (G-19822)
Silbereisen S Painting LLC .... G 302 396-8135
  Lincoln (G-6701)
Sosa Painting LLC .... G 302 437-9282
  Middletown (G-7588)
Steve George Painting .... G 302 616-1456
  Ocean View (G-12570)
Sundew Painting Inc .... E 302 994-7004
  Wilmington (G-20130)
Sundew Painting Inc .... F 302 684-5858
  Harbeson (G-4717)
Superior Drywall Inc .... F 302 732-9800
  Dagsboro (G-1511)
Taylor & Sons Inc .... G 302 856-6962
  Georgetown (G-4545)
Three Bs Painting Contractors .... G 302 227-1497
  Rehoboth Beach (G-12994)
Tko Painting .... G 302 259-9450
  Georgetown (G-4556)
Top Qality Indus Finishers Inc .... G 302 778-5005
  Wilmington (G-20354)
V & A Painting LLC .... G 443 466-2344
  Bear (G-556)
Vango Painting .... G 302 689-8071
  Middletown (G-7682)
Wilkisons Marking Service Inc .... G 302 697-3669
  Dover (G-3850)

1731 Electrical work

A & B Electric .... G 302 349-4050
  Greenwood (G-4585)
A Plus Electric & Security .... G 302 455-1725
  Newark (G-9726)
Aaron and Sons Electric LLC .... G 302 764-5610
  Wilmington (G-14187)
Academy Sounds LLC .... G 302 276-5027
  Newport (G-12439)
Accessheat Inc .... E 302 373-9524
  Wilmington (G-14222)
Advanced Coatings Engrg LLC .... E 888 607-0000
  Newark (G-9774)
Advanced Networking .... G 302 368-7552
  Newark (G-9778)
Advanced Networking Inc .... F 302 442-6199
  Wilmington (G-14276)
Advanced Power Control Inc .... D 302 368-0443
  New Castle (G-8767)
Advanced Power Generation .... G 302 375-6145
  Claymont (G-1022)
Aezi Electrical Services LLC .... G 302 279-8344
  Wilmington (G-14301)
AK Electric Inc .... G 302 379-3728
  Lewes (G-5668)
Alarm Systems Co of Delaware .... G 302 239-7754
  Hockessin (G-5118)
Alliance Electric Inc .... F 302 366-0295
  Newark (G-9825)

Allied Elec Solutions Ltd .... G 302 893-0257
  Wilmington (G-14380)
American Electric LLC .... G 302 632-6724
  Lewes (G-5685)
AMP Electric LLC .... G 302 337-8050
  Bridgeville (G-665)
Anaconda Prtctive Concepts Inc .... F 302 834-1125
  Newark (G-9858)
Anchor Electric Inc .... G 302 221-6111
  New Castle (G-8807)
Apg Inc .... G 302 746-7167
  Claymont (G-1040)
Apple Electric Inc .... E 302 645-5105
  Rehoboth Beach (G-12609)
Artisan Electrical Inc .... G 302 645-5844
  Lewes (G-5702)
Arugie Enterprises Corp .... G 302 225-2000
  Wilmington (G-14573)
Associates Contracting Inc .... F 302 734-4311
  Dover (G-1837)
Assurance Media LLC .... E 302 892-3540
  Wilmington (G-14599)
Atr Electrical Services Inc .... F 302 373-7769
  Middletown (G-6886)
Atr Electrical Services Inc .... G 302 384-7044
  Wilmington (G-14635)
B & M Electric Inc .... G 302 745-3807
  Georgetown (G-4218)
B Safe Inc .... E 302 422-3916
  Dover (G-1865)
Baby Tel Communications Inc .... G 302 368-3969
  Newark (G-9970)
Battaglia Electric Inc .... C 302 325-6100
  New Castle (G-8847)
Bauguess Electrical Svcs Inc .... G 302 737-5614
  Newark (G-9993)
Bfpe International Inc .... G 302 346-4800
  Dover (G-1927)
Body Electric LLC .... G 302 559-5577
  Wilmington (G-14993)
Boulden Brothers .... E 302 368-3848
  Newark (G-10072)
Boulden Services LLC .... E 302 368-0100
  Newark (G-10073)
Boxwood Electric Inc .... G 302 368-3257
  New Castle (G-8880)
Brandywine Electronics Corp .... F 302 324-9992
  Bear (G-80)
Brewington Electric .... G 302 732-3570
  Dagsboro (G-1420)
Brown Electrical Services LLC .... G 302 245-4593
  Millsboro (G-8209)
BW Electric Inc .... E 302 566-6248
  Harrington (G-4743)
Byers Industrial Services LLC .... C 302 836-4790
  Bear (G-86)
Cahill Contracting .... F 302 378-9650
  Middletown (G-6950)
Cardenti Electric .... F 302 834-1278
  Bear (G-89)
Certified Lock & Access LLC .... G 302 383-7507
  Wilmington (G-15316)
Cg Global MGT Solutions LLC .... F 215 735-3745
  Wilmington (G-15321)
Chieffo Electric Inc .... G 302 292-6813
  Middletown (G-6974)
City Electric Contracting Co .... F 302 764-0775
  Wilmington (G-15451)
Clatchey Electrical Contr Inc .... G 443 845-3920
  Selbyville (G-13500)
Communications & Wiring Co .... G 302 539-0809
  Dagsboro (G-1429)

Compass Electric LLC .... G 302 731-0240
  Newark (G-10291)
Conectiv LLC .... C 202 872-2680
  Newark (G-10298)
Conectiv Communications Inc .... E 302 224-1177
  Newark (G-10299)
Conectiv Energy Supply Inc .... D 302 454-0300
  Newark (G-10300)
Construction MGT Svcs Inc .... A 302 478-4200
  Wilmington (G-15612)
Conti Electric of N J Inc .... G 302 996-3905
  Wilmington (G-15616)
CT Pete Crossan Inc .... F 302 737-0223
  Newark (G-10362)
Current Solutions Inc .... G 302 736-5210
  Camden Wyoming (G-931)
Cyberdefenders Inc .... G 510 999-3490
  Middletown (G-7023)
Daniel A Kinsler .... G 302 947-9790
  Millsboro (G-8253)
Daniel George Bebee Inc .... G 443 359-1542
  Laurel (G-5492)
Dawson Bedsworth Elec Contrs .... F 302 854-0210
  Georgetown (G-4275)
Delaware Electric Signal Co .... E 302 422-3916
  Dover (G-2235)
Delaware Energy Solutions .... G 302 242-6315
  Dover (G-2236)
Delcollo Security Tech Inc .... F 302 994-5400
  Wilmington (G-15991)
Delmarva Communications Inc .... F 302 324-1230
  New Castle (G-9042)
Diamond Electric Inc .... E 302 697-3296
  Dover (G-2290)
Digital Sounds .... G 302 644-9187
  Rehoboth Beach (G-12728)
Donaldson Electric Inc .... E 302 660-7534
  Wilmington (G-16138)
Drayton Electric LLC .... G 302 893-0884
  Wilmington (G-16173)
E Electric .... G 302 547-3151
  Claymont (G-1125)
East Coast Electric Inc .... F 302 998-1577
  Wilmington (G-16251)
Edward Hackendorn .... G 302 981-5000
  Middletown (G-7085)
Electric Fish LLC .... G 484 804-5149
  Rehoboth Beach (G-12740)
Electrical Associates Inc .... G 302 678-1068
  Hartly (G-4873)
Electrical Power Systems Inc .... G 302 325-3502
  New Castle (G-9088)
Electro Sound Systems .... G 302 367-9840
  Wilmington (G-16352)
Electronic Systems Specialist .... G 302 738-4165
  Newark (G-10623)
Emergncy Response Protocol LLC ...... G 302 994-2600
  Wilmington (G-16393)
Encentiv Energy LLC .... F 302 504-8506
  Wilmington (G-16404)
Envirotrols Group Inc .... G 302 846-9103
  Delmar (G-1594)
Eric C James .... G 302 841-0930
  Seaford (G-13178)
Erosion Control Services De .... F 302 218-8913
  Bear (G-206)
Favhometheater .... G 302 897-7168
  Bear (G-221)
Federal Energy Inf .... F 858 521-3300
  Wilmington (G-16569)
Fiber-One Inc .... G 302 834-0890
  Newark (G-10726)

Employee Codes: A=Over 500 employees, B=251-500
C=101-250, D=51-100, E=20-50, F=10-19, G=1-9

2024 Harris Directory of
Delaware Businesses

17 CONSTRUCTION - SPECIAL TRADE CONTRACTORS

Company		Phone
Filec Services LLC	F	302 328-7188
Middletown (G-7127)		
First State Electric Co	E	302 322-0140
New Castle (G-9128)		
Firstbase Inc	F	917 331-6863
Wilmington (G-16642)		
Frees Electric	G	302 752-8895
Rehoboth Beach (G-12761)		
Galloway Electric Co Inc	F	302 453-8385
Newark (G-10800)		
Gatesair Inc	E	513 459-3400
Wilmington (G-16814)		
Generation Electrical Svcs LLC	G	302 298-1868
Townsend (G-14006)		
George & Lynch Inc	D	302 736-3031
Dover (G-2573)		
Gerone C Hudson Elec Contr	F	302 539-3332
Frankford (G-4111)		
Globe Electric Company	G	302 328-8459
Hockessin (G-5223)		
Gnz LLC	C	302 499-2024
Lewes (G-6042)		
Gray Audograph Agency Inc	F	302 658-1700
New Castle (G-9176)		
H & A Electric Co	G	302 678-8252
Dover (G-2638)		
Hatzel and Buehler Inc	C	302 798-5422
Wilmington (G-17075)		
Hatzel and Buehler Inc	E	302 478-4200
Wilmington (G-17074)		
Hazzard Electrical Contrs Inc	G	302 645-8457
Lewes (G-6084)		
Hcs Electric	G	302 824-3743
Smyrna (G-13756)		
HK Electric LLC	G	302 927-0688
Frankford (G-4114)		
Hobe Sound LLC	G	302 529-7096
Wilmington (G-17160)		
Hockessin Electric Inc	G	302 239-9332
Hockessin (G-5242)		
Hts 20 LLP	G	800 690-2029
Milton (G-8640)		
I-Pulse Inc	G	604 689-8765
Wilmington (G-17250)		
Independent Elec Svcs LLC	D	302 383-2761
Claymont (G-1184)		
Infinity Electric LLC	G	302 635-4388
Hockessin (G-5251)		
Inflow Network LLC	G	424 303-0464
Newark (G-11019)		
Integrated Wirg Solutions LLC	E	302 999-8448
Saint Georges (G-13034)		
Integrity Tech Solutions Inc	G	302 369-9093
Newark (G-11038)		
Intellitek Inc	G	856 381-7650
Middletown (G-7228)		
Ips Development LLC	G	800 981-7183
Wilmington (G-17418)		
J E Parsley Electric LLC	G	302 396-9642
Milford (G-7947)		
J T Electric	G	302 275-6778
Newark (G-11078)		
J&A Electrical Services LLC	G	302 943-9894
Milton (G-8645)		
Jsf Construction Co Inc	G	302 999-9573
Wilmington (G-17605)		
Justitselectric	G	215 715-7314
Claymont (G-1203)		
Kam Electric Inc	G	302 998-5262
Wilmington (G-17641)		
Kent Electrical Services LLC	G	302 922-4631
Felton (G-3992)		
Kokoszka & Sons Inc	G	302 328-4807
New Castle (G-9288)		
Kriss Contracting Inc	E	302 492-3502
Hartly (G-4893)		
Kriss Contracting Inc	G	302 492-3502
Marydel (G-6803)		
Lattanzio Electrical Cntrctng	G	302 685-0711
Wilmington (G-17818)		
Leeman Electric	G	302 737-1753
Newark (G-11240)		
Leightner Electrical Contracto	G	302 723-1507
New Castle (G-9303)		
Light Action Inc	F	302 328-7800
Wilmington (G-17908)		
Lightscapes Inc	G	302 798-5451
Wilmington (G-17910)		
Loud & Clear H T Solutions LLC	G	302 985-1576
Smyrna (G-13810)		
◆ M Auger Enterprise Inc	F	302 992-9922
Wilmington (G-18057)		
▲ M Davis & Sons Inc	C	302 998-3385
Newark (G-11301)		
Martel Inc	G	302 674-5660
Dover (G-3023)		
Masten Electric Inc	G	302 653-4300
Smyrna (G-13818)		
Maximum Electrical Svcs LLC	G	302 521-2820
Newark (G-11361)		
Megee Plumbing & Heating Co	D	302 856-6311
Georgetown (G-4422)		
Mg Global Group LLC	G	302 217-3724
Newark (G-11397)		
Mid-Atlantic Elec Svcs Inc	E	302 945-2555
Millsboro (G-8379)		
Mid-County Electric Inc	F	302 934-8304
Millsboro (G-8380)		
Mills Electric LLC	G	302 257-8403
Dover (G-3094)		
Mister Sparky	G	302 751-6363
Magnolia (G-6768)		
Montgomery Electric	G	302 832-0945
Bear (G-378)		
Murphy Electric Inc	G	302 644-0404
Lewes (G-6296)		
Naked Feet Kitchen LLC	G	404 576-4426
Wilmington (G-18523)		
Nesmith & Company Inc	E	215 755-4570
Claymont (G-1249)		
Network Design Technologies	E	610 991-2929
Wilmington (G-18596)		
New Castle Counter	G	302 421-3940
Historic New Castle (G-5034)		
Nickle Elec Companies Inc	E	302 856-1006
Georgetown (G-4445)		
Nickle Elec Companies Inc	C	302 453-4000
Newark (G-11557)		
O Reilly Electric	F	302 381-6058
Seaford (G-13322)		
P S C Contracting Inc	F	302 838-2998
Delaware City (G-1550)		
P S C Electric Contractor Inc	F	302 838-2998
Delaware City (G-1551)		
Pace Elec & Generator Svcs	E	302 328-2600
Bear (G-411)		
Palmer & Sons Electric In	G	302 290-4899
Bear (G-413)		
Peter D Furness Elc Co Inc	C	302 764-6030
Wilmington (G-18992)		
Positive Energy Electric	G	267 902-1655
Historic New Castle (G-5051)		
Power Control Technologies Inc	G	203 560-2806
Wilmington (G-19136)		
Power Plus Elec Contg Inc	F	302 736-5070
Dover (G-3356)		
Powercomm LLC	E	302 235-8922
Wilmington (G-19138)		
Powwa Electric	G	302 236-2649
Seaford (G-13353)		
Preferred Electric Inc	D	302 322-1217
New Castle (G-9491)		
Preferred Security Inc	G	302 834-7800
Bear (G-435)		
Prince Telecom LLC	D	302 324-1800
New Castle (G-9494)		
Progressive Services Inc	E	302 658-7260
Wilmington (G-19220)		
Quandary Inc	F	302 757-6300
Wilmington (G-19286)		
Ram Electric	G	302 379-3351
Newark (G-11823)		
Ram Electric Inc	G	302 875-2356
Laurel (G-5584)		
Rays Plumbing & Heating Svcs	F	302 697-3936
Felton (G-4013)		
Renaissance Security LP	G	302 588-5975
Wilmington (G-19430)		
Rhino Cabling Group Inc	F	302 312-1333
Newark (G-11877)		
Ricks Electric LLC	G	410 924-6764
Felton (G-4016)		
Riley Electric	G	302 533-5918
Newark (G-11886)		
Riley Electric Inc	G	302 276-3581
Newark (G-11887)		
Roberts Electric Inc	G	302 233-3017
Magnolia (G-6779)		
▲ S J Desmond Inc	G	302 475-6520
Wilmington (G-19609)		
S J Desmond Inc	F	302 256-0801
Wilmington (G-19610)		
Sapere		888 727-3731
Dover (G-3509)		
Satterfield & Ryan Inc	F	302 422-4919
Milford (G-8085)		
Savannah Electric	G	302 645-5906
Lewes (G-6447)		
Security Instrument Corp Del	F	302 674-2891
Milton (G-8709)		
Security Instrument Corp Del	D	302 998-2261
Wilmington (G-19733)		
Service Unlimited Inc	E	302 326-2665
New Castle (G-9558)		
Shellysons Electrical Contract	G	302 275-8010
Newark (G-11995)		
Shore Electric Inc	G	302 645-4503
Lewes (G-6465)		
Shure Line Electrical Inc	G	302 856-3110
Georgetown (G-4512)		
Shure-Line Electrical Inc	D	302 389-1114
Smyrna (G-13885)		
Silver Electric LLC	G	302 227-1107
Rehoboth Beach (G-12959)		
Simplex Time Recorder LLC	G	302 325-6300
New Castle (G-9571)		
Skaggs Electric LLC	G	302 653-0576
Smyrna (G-13888)		
Smartis	G	302 653-8355
Dover (G-3578)		
Smith Electrical Services	G	302 423-5994
Marydel (G-6810)		
Smith-Spinella Electric LLC	G	302 228-4865
Laurel (G-5599)		
Sobieski Fire Protection LLC	C	302 993-0600
Wilmington (G-19906)		

Sound Body Products LLC .... G 302 660-2296
Wilmington (G-19932)

Sound Master Dj .... G 302 998-8235
Wilmington (G-19933)

Sound Solutions .... G 302 650-0950
Wilmington (G-19934)

Stapleford Electric LLC .... G 302 300-1377
Wilmington (G-20020)

Star Enrg Cs LLC .... F 302 660-2187
Wilmington (G-20023)

Star Sound Technologies LLC .... G 330 260-6767
Wilmington (G-20025)

Stuart Ja Inc .... G 302 378-8299
Newark (G-12109)

Sunstates Security LLC .... E 866 710-2019
New Castle (G-9604)

Superior Electric Service Co .... E 302 658-5949
Wilmington (G-20140)

Sure Line Electrical Inc .... G 302 856-3110
Georgetown (G-4531)

TA Rietdorf & Sons Inc .... G 302 429-0341
Wilmington (G-20204)

Tangent Cable Systems Inc .... E 302 994-4104
Wilmington (G-20218)

Taylor Electric Service Inc .... G 302 422-3966
Milford (G-8114)

Tc Electric Company Inc .... E 302 791-0378
Wilmington (G-20236)

Technicare Inc .... G 302 322-7766
Newark (G-12170)

Telgian Corporation .... E 480 753-5444
Wilmington (G-20267)

Towles Electric Inc .... G 302 674-4985
Dover (G-3706)

Tri-State SEC & Contrls LLC .... F 302 299-2175
Newark (G-12227)

Tri-State Technologies Inc .... F 302 658-5400
Wilmington (G-20415)

Triangle Electrical Svc Co .... G 302 856-7880
Georgetown (G-4560)

Tricomm Services Corporation .... G 302 454-2975
Newark (G-12228)

Tudor Electric Inc .... E 302 736-1444
Dover (G-3733)

Tusi Brothers Inc .... F 302 998-6383
Wilmington (G-20465)

USA Fortescue Future Inds Inc .... G 703 608-5217
Wilmington (G-20553)

Vassallo Michael Elec Contr .... F 302 455-9405
Newark (G-12307)

Wanex Electrical Service LLC .... F 302 326-1700
New Castle (G-9674)

Watts Electric Company .... G 302 529-1183
Wilmington (G-20685)

Wayne Bennett .... G 302 436-2379
Frankford (G-4158)

Weston Sound .... G 215 327-8646
Wilmington (G-20742)

White Eagle Electric .... G 302 533-7799
Newark (G-12367)

White Eagle Electrical Contg .... F 302 378-3366
Middletown (G-7722)

Wiz Electric .... G 302 293-0403
New Castle (G-9686)

Yacht Anything Ltd .... G 302 226-3335
Rehoboth Beach (G-13026)

1741 Masonry and other stonework

Aiken Masonry Scott Ta .... G 302 253-8179
Georgetown (G-4202)

Amer Masonry T A Marino .... G 302 834-1511
New Castle (G-8794)

American Masonry .... G 302 362-9962
Laurel (G-5463)

American Stone Crafters Inc .... G 302 834-8891
Bear (G-31)

Ashcraft Masonry Inc .... F 302 537-4298
Ocean View (G-12465)

Becks Masonry .... G 302 231-8872
Millsboro (G-8190)

Blair Carmean Masonry .... G 302 934-6103
Georgetown (G-4235)

Blair Carmean & Sons Masonry .... G 302 249-5783
Georgetown (G-8199)

Bliss Stone Masonry .... G 302 293-9194
Wilmington (G-14959)

Blue Hen Masonry Inc .... G 302 398-8737
Greenwood (G-4599)

Brick Doctor Inc .... F 302 678-3380
Dover (G-1978)

Cesars Vargas Stone Inc C .... G 302 296-7881
Seaford (G-13106)

Clean Sweep .... G 302 422-6085
Milford (G-7831)

Contractor Masonry .... G 302 945-1930
Millsboro (G-8238)

Corrado American LLC .... E 302 655-6501
New Castle (G-8975)

Countryside Masonry LLC .... G 302 945-5642
Millsboro (G-8241)

Czapp Masonry Inc .... G 302 238-7007
Millsboro (G-8250)

Davis-Young Associates Inc .... G 610 388-0932
Yorklyn (G-20991)

Dreamscape Design Cons LLC .... G 302 893-0984
Newark (G-10571)

Enterprise Masonry Corporation .... E 302 764-6858
Wilmington (G-16438)

Esposito Mansory LLC .... F 302 996-4961
Wilmington (G-16465)

Estepp Construction Co Inc .... G 302 378-4958
Townsend (G-13998)

Falasco Masonry Inc .... G 302 697-8971
Camden Wyoming (G-943)

Gullwing Contracting Inc .... F 302 943-0133
Harrington (G-4777)

Henlopen Masonry Inc .... G 302 947-9900
Milton (G-8637)

Hoppy LLC DBA Brick Works .... F 302 653-8961
Smyrna (G-13765)

J D Masonry Inc .... E 302 684-1009
Harbeson (G-4702)

Jackson Masonry .... G 302 397-4202
Wilmington (G-17472)

James Willey Masonry LLC .... G 302 258-6242
Dagsboro (G-1469)

Joseph Rizzo & Sons Cnstr Co .... E 302 656-8116
New Castle (G-9267)

Kevins Masonry Concrete Co .... G 302 382-7259
Felton (G-3993)

Kings Masonry LLC .... G 302 632-6783
Hartly (G-4891)

L A Masonary Inc .... F 302 239-6833
Newark (G-11206)

Lawrence Legates Masnry Co Inc ...... G 302 422-8043
Milford (G-7973)

Ldmasonry .... G 302 270-3386
Harrington (G-4798)

Lighthouse Masonry Inc .... G 302 945-1392
Lewes (G-6208)

Lower Sussex Masonry LLC .... G 302 249-3255
Laurel (G-5557)

M & L Contractors Inc .... F 302 436-9303
Selbyville (G-13563)

Mario F Medori Inc .... G 302 239-4550
Wilmington (G-18132)

Mario Medori Inc .... F 302 656-8432
Wilmington (G-18133)

Millers Masonry & Block LLC .... G 302 222-4091
Hartly (G-4897)

Moore Clinton Denver II .... G 302 856-3385
Georgetown (G-4433)

Morris Masonry .... G 410 726-6277
Delmar (G-1624)

Nu-Tech Masonry Inc .... G 302 934-5660
Millsboro (G-8409)

Paragon Masonry Corporation .... G 302 798-7314
Wilmington (G-18887)

Peninsula Masonry Inc .... G 302 684-3410
Harbeson (G-4711)

Petrovich Masonry .... G 302 697-2379
Dover (G-3309)

Premier Restoration Cnstr Inc .... G 302 832-1288
Middletown (G-7466)

R F Gentner & Son .... G 302 947-2733
Harbeson (G-4712)

◆ Rgp Holding Inc .... F 302 661-0117
Wilmington (G-19453)

Romano Masonry Inc .... F 302 368-4155
Newark (G-11913)

Shore Masonry Inc .... G 302 945-5933
Millsboro (G-8460)

Skyline Roofing & Cnstr LLC .... G 610 929-4135
Lewes (G-6474)

Sme Masonry Contrs Ltd Lblty .... F 302 743-7338
Wilmington (G-19883)

Snow & Assoc Gen Cnstr Co LLC ...... F 302 420-0564
Wilmington (G-19901)

South Delaware Masonry Inc .... G 302 378-1998
Townsend (G-14067)

Steven T Miller .... G 302 697-3541
Camden Wyoming (G-981)

Stonegate Granite .... G 302 500-8081
Georgetown (G-4527)

Stoneworks Lapidary .... G 814 528-1468
Lewes (G-6513)

Swedish Brickyard .... G 302 893-4143
Newark (G-12139)

Trenton Block Delaware Inc .... F 302 684-0112
Milton (G-8722)

Vivid Colors Carpet LLC .... G 302 335-3933
Frederica (G-4187)

Walter W Snyder .... G 302 378-1817
Middletown (G-7706)

Wilson Masonry Corp .... F 302 398-8240
Harrington (G-4847)

1742 Plastering, drywall, and insulation

A S A P Insulation Inc .... G 302 836-9040
Newark (G-9728)

ABC Drywall .... G 302 249-0389
Greenwood (G-4588)

Accurate Insulation LLC .... E 302 336-8401
Dover (G-1708)

Aln Construction Inc .... D 302 292-1580
Newark (G-9832)

American Stone Crafters Inc .... G 302 834-8891
Bear (G-31)

Aster Dry Wall LLC .... G 302 757-2750
Smyrna (G-13650)

Aster Drywall .... G 302 757-5876
New Castle (G-8827)

Atlantic Contracting Svcs LLC .... E 302 337-8360
Greenwood (G-4594)

B&F Drywall .... G 302 218-2467
Wilmington (G-14705)

17 CONSTRUCTION - SPECIAL TRADE CONTRACTORS

BDB Services .... G 302 536-1410
  Seaford (G-13079)
Blue Hen Insulation Inc .... G 302 424-4482
  Milford (G-7796)
Brothers Painting and Drywall .... G 302 737-9600
  Middletown (G-6945)
Camden Drywall Inc .... G 302 697-9653
  Wyoming (G-20981)
CC Drywall Contractors No .... G 302 307-6400
  Townsend (G-13970)
Circle Group Inc .... G 302 241-0018
  Dover (G-2076)
Cnc Drywall North .... G 302 307-6400
  Dover (G-2098)
Cook Plastering Inc .... G 302 737-0778
  Newark (G-10319)
Custom Drywall Inc .... G 302 369-3266
  Newark (G-10367)
Dale Insulation Co of Delaware .... G 302 324-9332
  New Castle (G-8995)
Delaware Spray Foam Inc .... G 302 234-4050
  Hockessin (G-5184)
Delmarva Spray Foam LLC .... F 302 752-1080
  Georgetown (G-4290)
Devere Insul HM Prfmce LLC .... G 302 854-0344
  Georgetown (G-4293)
Diaz Drywall LLC .... G 302 602-1110
  Newark (G-10528)
Dlc Drywall .... G 302 382-2213
  Greenwood (G-4620)
Drywall Inc .... E 302 838-6500
  New Castle (G-9065)
Eastern Industrial Svcs Inc .... D 302 455-1400
  Historic New Castle (G-4979)
Eastern Insulation Inc .... G 302 455-1400
  Newark (G-10595)
Ed Hileman Drywall Inc .... G 302 436-6277
  Selbyville (G-13530)
Erco Ceilings & Interiors Inc .... F 302 994-6200
  Wilmington (G-16455)
Fernandez Drywall Inc .... G 302 521-2760
  Newark (G-10723)
Freedom Drywall Supply LLC .... E 302 281-0085
  Newark (G-10777)
H & C Insulation LLC .... G 302 448-0777
  Greenwood (G-4634)
H & M Acoustical Services Inc .... G 302 218-7783
  Bear (G-258)
Hensco LLC .... G 302 423-1638
  Harrington (G-4784)
Heritage Interiors Inc .... F 302 369-3199
  Newark (G-10949)
Installed Building Pdts Inc .... F 302 480-1520
  Greenwood (G-4640)
J & G Acoustical Co .... E 302 285-3630
  Middletown (G-7233)
J Michaels Painting Inc .... G 302 738-8465
  Newark (G-11074)
Jdh Construction Inc .... G 302 993-0720
  Wilmington (G-17510)
Julio Drywall Inc .... G 302 218-8596
  New Castle (G-9270)
Kenco Drywall .... G 302 697-6489
  Felton (G-3990)
King Snipers Drywall LLC .... G 302 452-4515
  Magnolia (G-6758)
Lamart Drywall LLC .... G 302 723-8751
  New Castle (G-9294)
Lawson Home Services LLC .... G 302 684-3418
  Milton (G-8653)
M3 Contracting LLC .... E 302 781-3143
  Newark (G-11308)

Master Interiors Inc .... E 302 368-9361
  Milford (G-7988)
Master Interiors Inc .... E 302 368-9361
  Newark (G-11350)
N R O Drywall .... G 302 293-8811
  New Castle (G-9389)
Newark Insulation Co Inc .... G 302 731-8970
  Newark (G-11539)
O Morales Stucco Plaster Inc .... G 302 834-8891
  Bear (G-403)
Parsons PAInting&drywall LLC .... G 302 462-6169
  Millsboro (G-8414)
Pauls Plastering Inc .... F 302 654-5583
  New Castle (G-9462)
Peninsula Acoustical Co Inc .... G 302 653-3551
  Smyrna (G-13845)
Phillips Insulation Inc .... G 302 655-6523
  Wilmington (G-19020)
R&O Drywall LLC .... G 302 399-9480
  Dover (G-3416)
Rexmex Drywall LLC .... G 302 343-9140
  Hartly (G-4906)
Smogard & Associates LLC .... G 302 353-4717
  Wilmington (G-19896)
Smucker Company LLC .... E 302 322-9285
  Camden Wyoming (G-980)
Southland Insulators Del LLC .... D 302 854-0344
  Georgetown (G-4520)
Spacecon LLC .... F 302 322-9285
  New Castle (G-9583)
State Drywall Co Inc .... G 302 239-2843
  Hockessin (G-5390)
Superior Drywall Inc .... F 302 732-9800
  Dagsboro (G-1511)
Thomas Building Group Inc .... F 302 283-0600
  Newark (G-12193)
Three Bs Painting Contractors .... G 302 227-1497
  Rehoboth Beach (G-12994)
TNT Drywall LLC .... G 302 381-0114
  Lewes (G-6565)
Torresdrywall LLC .... G 302 228-6450
  Lincoln (G-6706)
Union Wholesale Co .... G 302 656-4462
  Wilmington (G-20516)

1743 Terrazzo, tile, marble, mosaic work

Aztek Tile .... G 302 875-0690
  Laurel (G-5465)
Bath Kitchen Tile DH .... G 302 992-9210
  Newark (G-9990)
Bella Tile and Stone LLC .... G 302 275-4550
  Bear (G-67)
◆ Casale Marble Imports Inc .... E 561 404-4213
  Wilmington (G-15262)
Ceramic Tile Supply Co .... G 302 737-4968
  Newark (G-10179)
Coastal Plains Wood & Tile LLC .... G 302 670-7853
  Rehoboth Beach (G-12685)
Coastal Tile AMP Stone In .... G 301 748-0754
  Selbyville (G-13503)
Coastal Tile and Hardwood .... G 302 339-7772
  Millsboro (G-8234)
Consolidated Construction Svcs .... F 302 629-6070
  Seaford (G-13135)
Creative Ceramics LLC .... G 302 275-9211
  Newark (G-10347)
Delaware Custom Tile .... G 302 841-9215
  Lewes (G-5896)
Dippold Marble Granite .... G 302 324-9101
  Middletown (G-7062)
Edward J Hennessy .... G 302 798-8019
  Claymont (G-1128)

Felixchem Corp Inc .... G 302 376-0199
  Middletown (G-7124)
Howarth Granite Holdings LLC .... G 302 543-6739
  Claymont (G-1182)
Inspiration Bennington Ceramic .... G 302 436-5544
  Selbyville (G-13549)
▲ Keystone Granite and Tile Inc .... F 302 323-0200
  New Castle (G-9280)
Kyles Tile LLC .... G 302 462-0959
  Ocean View (G-12535)
Mohawk Tile MBL Distrs of Del .... G 302 655-7164
  Wilmington (G-18401)
Old World Tile Works .... G 302 407-5552
  Wilmington (G-18757)
Pala Tile & Carpet Contrs Inc .... E 302 652-4500
  Wilmington (G-18865)
Peninsula Acoustical Co Inc .... G 302 653-3551
  Smyrna (G-13845)
Ruiz Flooring .... G 302 999-9350
  Wilmington (G-19588)
Sir Grout Delaware LLC .... G 302 401-1700
  Seaford (G-13403)
Smart-The Tile Rick Specialist .... G 302 331-5529
  Dover (G-3577)
Sosa Eloy .... G 302 275-3792
  Wilmington (G-19931)
Stone Age Tile and Flooring .... G 302 359-2166
  Frederica (G-4183)
Tile Guy .... G 302 382-7961
  Felton (G-4032)
Tile Market of Delaware Inc .... E 302 644-7100
  Lewes (G-6560)
◆ Tile Market of Delaware LLC .... E 302 777-4663
  Wilmington (G-20325)
Tile Shop LLC .... E 302 250-4889
  Wilmington (G-20326)
Upon A Once Tile Inc .... G 646 992-1376
  Lewes (G-6591)

1751 Carpentry work

AB Carpentry Services Inc .... G 302 276-2457
  New Castle (G-8755)
Affordable Custom Carpentry .... G 302 853-5582
  Laurel (G-5462)
American Wood Design .... G 302 792-2100
  Claymont (G-1034)
Andrew E Quesenberry Carpentry .... G 302 994-0700
  Wilmington (G-14475)
Artifex Carpentry .... G 484 557-7623
  Newark (G-9916)
Atlantic Mllwk Cabinetry Corp .... E 302 644-1405
  Lewes (G-5716)
Barracuda Carpentry LLC .... G 302 415-1588
  Millsboro (G-8181)
Beeline Services LLC .... G 302 376-7399
  Middletown (G-6910)
Bob Preston Carpentry .... G 302 234-8659
  Hockessin (G-5135)
Brad Allen Carpentry LLC .... G 302 228-4256
  Frankford (G-4075)
Brandywine Master Carpentry .... G 302 463-9773
  Wilmington (G-15072)
Cant Wait Overhead Door LLC .... G 302 546-3667
  Magnolia (G-6727)
Carroll M Carpenter .... G 302 654-7558
  Wilmington (G-15259)
Carvi Carpenter Inc .... G 302 722-3352
  Georgetown (G-4244)
Ceramic Tile Supply Co .... G 302 684-5691
  Harbeson (G-4687)
Clark & Sons Inc .... G 302 856-3372
  Georgetown (G-4257)

Company	Code	Phone
Clark & Sons Inc — Wilmington (G-15464)	E	302 998-7552
Clark & Sons Overhead Doors — Wilmington (G-15465)	F	302 998-7552
Coastal Cabinetry LLC — Seaford (G-13126)	F	302 542-4155
Construction Unlimited Inc — Bear (G-118)	G	302 836-3140
Craftsman Revisions — Bear (G-123)	G	302 834-9252
Creekside Carpentry LLC — Wilmington (G-15698)	G	302 218-4434
D J Byler — Clayton (G-1358)	G	302 653-4602
Delaware Express Gar Door Svc — Wilmington (G-15915)	G	302 562-5080
Delframing Inc — Ocean View (G-12501)	G	302 363-2658
Delmarva Coastal Cnstr LLC — Millsboro (G-8266)	G	302 259-5593
Dino Dicriscio — Wilmington (G-16074)	G	302 762-0610
Eavis and Sons Garage Doors — Newark (G-10600)	G	302 893-3783
Ecm Carpentry LLC — Wilmington (G-16281)	G	302 494-8995
Ed Turulski Custom Woodworking — Wilmington (G-16284)	G	302 658-2221
F W D Inc — New Castle (G-9113)	F	302 323-4999
Family Man Carpentry — Georgetown (G-4313)	G	302 542-8803
Ferris Home Imprvs Co LLC — Newark (G-10725)	E	302 998-4500
Francis Pollinger & Son Inc — Wilmington (G-16723)	E	302 655-8097
G2 Group Inc — Bear (G-244)	G	302 836-4202
Garcia Moises LLC — Camden Wyoming (G-948)	G	302 698-1930
Gjp & Sons LLC — Newark (G-10842)	G	302 690-8954
H P Custom Trim LLC — Georgetown (G-4350)	G	302 381-0802
Henlopen Overhead Door — Lewes (G-6091)	G	302 228-0561
Hrc Inc — Bridgeville (G-714)	G	302 604-3782
J & A Overhead Door Inc — Delmar (G-1603)	G	302 846-9915
J & L Services Inc — Seaford (G-13226)	F	410 943-3355
Jeanfreau Carpentry Services — Claymont (G-1198)	G	302 563-6449
John F Elder — Historic New Castle (G-5011)	G	302 544-6569
Js Carpenter Improvements — Middletown (G-7255)	G	302 540-0590
Kevin Garber — Bear (G-326)	G	302 834-0639
M&M Garage Doors Inc — Newark (G-11306)	G	302 304-1397
Mark Ventresca Associates Inc — Hockessin (G-5300)	G	302 239-3925
Martin & Calloway LLC — Wilmington (G-18166)	G	302 482-1180
Mason Building Group Inc — Newark (G-11348)	C	302 292-0600
Mastercrafters Inc — Dover (G-3029)	E	302 678-1470
Menchaca Building Corp — Wilmington (G-18271)	G	302 475-4581
Michael A OBrien & Sons — Wilmington (G-18306)	G	302 994-2894
Miner Ltd — Historic New Castle (G-5029)	C	302 516-7791
Mirandas Carpentry — Lewes (G-6279)	G	302 245-0298
Mitchell Associates Inc — Wilmington (G-18387)	F	302 594-9415
Mp Diversified Services LLC — Newark (G-11462)	G	302 828-1060
Newport Builders & Windowland — Wilmington (G-18632)	F	302 994-3537
Oceanic Ventures Inc — Lewes (G-6328)	G	302 645-5872
Overhead Door Co Delmar Inc — Milford (G-8039)	E	302 424-4400
Pinnacle Garage Door Co LLC — Frederica (G-4180)	G	302 505-4531
Quality Garage — Wyoming (G-20989)	G	302 678-3667
R & J Taylor Inc — Newark (G-11802)	G	302 368-7888
R W Harmon Carpentry Svcs LLC — Wilmington (G-19307)	G	302 477-1319
Rementer Brothers Inc — Milton (G-8695)	G	302 249-4250
Smiths Garage Doors Expert — Wilmington (G-19894)	G	302 803-5337
Superior Screen & Glass — Ocean View (G-12574)	G	302 541-5399
Thomas Building Group Inc — Newark (G-12193)	F	302 283-0600
United Garage Doors — Townsend (G-14087)	G	302 414-9220
V P Custom Finishers In — Middletown (G-7677)	G	302 415-0002
Yoder Overhead Door Company — Delmar (G-1660)	G	302 875-0663

1752 Floor laying and floor work, nec

Company	Code	Phone
Anderson Floor Coverings Inc — Rehoboth Beach (G-12604)	F	302 227-3244
Connolly Flooring Inc — Wilmington (G-15605)	E	302 996-9470
Creative Flooring Contrs Inc — Smyrna (G-13688)	E	302 653-7521
Delaware Wood Renewal Inc — Middletown (G-7049)	G	302 750-5167
Diaz and Costa Hardwood Flrng — Rehoboth Beach (G-12727)	G	302 212-5923
Dominic A Di Febo & Sons — Wilmington (G-16128)	G	302 425-5054
Edward Varnes Hardwood Floors — Newark (G-10612)	F	302 292-0919
Edwards Paul Crpt Installation — Dover (G-2427)	G	302 672-7847
▲ Facility Services Group Inc — Wilmington (G-16525)	G	302 317-3029
Fasttrak — Wilmington (G-16560)	F	302 761-5454
Floor Coatings Etc Inc — New Castle (G-9136)	E	302 322-4177
John S Kassees Inc — Lewes (G-6146)	G	302 838-1976
Margherita Vincent & Anthony — Newark (G-11330)	G	302 834-9023
Matt Carpet Guy LLC — Selbyville (G-13568)	G	443 497-3281
Modular Carpet Recycling Inc — New Castle (G-9379)	F	484 885-5890
New Castle County Flooring — Newark (G-11517)	G	302 218-0507
Nhance — Bear (G-397)	G	866 944-9663
Northstern Coating Systems Inc — Wilmington (G-18688)	G	302 328-6545
Ruiz Flooring — Wilmington (G-19588)	G	302 999-9350
Spacecon LLC — New Castle (G-9583)	F	302 322-9285
Unique Finishes Inc — Bear (G-549)	G	302 419-8557
Ziggys Inc — Newark (G-12434)	G	302 453-1285

1761 Roofing, siding, and sheetmetal work

Company	Code	Phone
Above All Gutter Svc — Middletown (G-6829)	G	302 561-0709
Affordable Roofing LLC — Dover (G-1735)	G	302 363-8429
All About Gutters LLC — Georgetown (G-4206)	G	302 853-2645
All Flats Roofing — Wilmington (G-14364)	G	302 383-6762
All Weather Roofing Co — Bear (G-27)	G	302 836-6400
Alpha Roofing & Siding Inc — Millsboro (G-8168)	G	302 249-2491
Amerimax Inc — New Castle (G-8802)	G	951 710-0899
Apex Exteriors Inc — Milford (G-7771)	G	302 858-1699
Avamer Roofing Inc — Milton (G-8566)	G	302 228-8673
Beckers Chimney and Roofg LLC — Wilmington (G-14811)	E	302 463-8294
Belusko Siding & Windows — Newark (G-10017)	G	302 366-8783
Best Roofing and Siding Co — Dover (G-1917)	G	302 678-5700
Beyond Gutters Inc — Wilmington (G-14870)	G	302 999-1422
Blue Hen Roofing LLC — Hockessin (G-5134)	G	302 545-2349
Bluefin LLC — Wilmington (G-14980)	G	302 731-5770
Brandywine Exteriors Corp — Wilmington (G-15056)	E	302 746-7134
Campbell Home Exteriors LLC — Magnolia (G-6726)	G	302 526-9663
Cannon Sline Industrial Inc — New Castle (G-8911)	F	302 658-1420
Coam Exterior Inc — Harbeson (G-4688)	G	302 329-9545
Coghan-Haes LLC — Wilmington (G-15518)	G	302 325-4210
CTA Roofing & Waterproofing — Newark (G-10363)	F	302 454-8551
Custom Metal Works Inc — Wilmington (G-15743)	G	302 765-2653
D Shinn Inc — Wilmington (G-15762)	E	302 792-2033
David Saunders General Contrs — Wilmington (G-15812)	G	302 998-0056
Del Coast Exterior LLC — Georgetown (G-4276)	G	302 752-6678
Del Coast Exteriors — Georgetown (G-4277)	G	302 236-5738
Del Coast Exteriors — Millsboro (G-8259)	G	302 542-8979
Delaware Siding Co Inc — Bear (G-156)	G	302 778-4771
Delaware Siding Company Inc — Bear (G-157)	G	302 836-6971

17 CONSTRUCTION - SPECIAL TRADE CONTRACTORS

Delaware Siding Company Inc .... G 302 732-1440
  Dagsboro *(G-1437)*
Delmarva Metal Roofing .... G 302 858-1699
  Milford *(G-7861)*
Delmarva Roofing & Coating Inc .... E 302 349-5174
  Greenwood *(G-4615)*
Dna Roofing and Siding .... G 302 455-2180
  Newark *(G-10542)*
Dream View Exteriors Group LLC .... G 302 358-9530
  Georgetown *(G-4299)*
Ducts Unlimited Inc .... E 302 378-4125
  Smyrna *(G-13717)*
Eastern Metals Inc .... F 302 454-7886
  Newark *(G-10598)*
Fadely LLC .... G 302 284-7389
  Felton *(G-3969)*
Farrell Roofing Inc .... E 302 378-7663
  Middletown *(G-7123)*
Ferris Home Imprvs Co LLC .... E 302 998-4500
  Newark *(G-10725)*
Francis Pollinger & Son Inc .... E 302 655-8097
  Wilmington *(G-16723)*
G Fedale General Contrs LLC .... E 302 225-7663
  Hockessin *(G-5216)*
G Fedale Roofing and Siding .... F 302 225-7663
  Wilmington *(G-16785)*
Gearhart Construction Inc .... G 302 674-5466
  Dover *(G-2567)*
Griffith Roofing and .... G 302 275-7123
  Harrington *(G-4775)*
Guys Gutter .... G 302 424-1931
  Milford *(G-7916)*
Guys Gutter .... F 302 325-4210
  Wilmington *(G-17010)*
H K Griffith Inc .... E 302 368-4635
  Newark *(G-10914)*
Hagertys Roofing .... G 302 650-3474
  Wilmington *(G-17031)*
Hard Hatters Roofg & Cnstr LLC .... G 302 766-3611
  Wilmington *(G-17055)*
Hard Hatters Roofg Constructi .... G 302 507-4459
  Wilmington *(G-17056)*
Hickman Overhead Door Company .... F 302 422-4249
  Milford *(G-7930)*
Home Services Unlimited .... G 302 293-8726
  Newark *(G-10964)*
Hurlock Roofing Company .... F 302 654-2783
  Wilmington *(G-17237)*
Interstate Steel Co Inc .... F 302 598-5159
  Newark *(G-11050)*
Invista Home LLC .... G 855 337-3200
  Newark *(G-11053)*
Jose Manuel Hernandez-Alvarez .... G 302 265-7873
  Millsboro *(G-8333)*
JR Walker Roofing Inc .... G 302 761-3744
  Wilmington *(G-17601)*
Jsf Construction Co Inc .... G 302 999-9573
  Wilmington *(G-17605)*
JW Tull Contracting Svcs LLC .... F 302 494-8179
  Wilmington *(G-17625)*
Kirkin Roofing LLC .... F 302 832-7663
  New Castle *(G-9284)*
Ko Gutters LLC .... G 302 943-8293
  Lewes *(G-6171)*
L & J Sheet Metal .... F 302 875-2822
  Laurel *(G-5542)*
Lane Group V LLC .... G 302 652-7663
  Wilmington *(G-17801)*
Lane Home Services Inc .... F 302 652-7663
  Wilmington *(G-17802)*
Let US Lift It Inc .... G 302 654-2221
  Wilmington *(G-17886)*

Lewis CK Construction .... G 443 910-1598
  Newark *(G-11249)*
Mastercraft Welding .... G 302 697-3932
  Dover *(G-3028)*
McConnell Bros Inc .... G 302 218-4240
  Wilmington *(G-18223)*
Miles Rs Son Roofing .... G 302 250-4992
  New Castle *(G-9370)*
Milford Gutter Guys LLC .... G 302 424-1931
  Lincoln *(G-6686)*
Mill Creek Metals Inc .... F 302 529-7020
  Claymont *(G-1236)*
Millers Roofing & Coating LLC .... G 302 943-8988
  Hartly *(G-4898)*
Morse Home Improvement LLC .... E 302 663-0042
  Dagsboro *(G-1485)*
Mumford Sheet Metal Works Inc .... F 302 436-8251
  Selbyville *(G-13583)*
N Barton Assoc .... G 302 575-9882
  Wilmington *(G-18514)*
P & C Roofing Inc .... E 302 322-6767
  New Castle *(G-9442)*
PJ Fitzpatrick Inc .... D 302 325-2360
  New Castle *(G-9473)*
Platinum Roofs .... G 302 226-4510
  Lewes *(G-6378)*
Quality Exteriors Inc .... E 302 398-9283
  Harrington *(G-4815)*
Quality Home Services Inc .... G 302 266-6113
  Newark *(G-11787)*
Quality Htg Ar-Cnditioning Inc .... E 302 654-5247
  Wilmington *(G-19284)*
Right As Rain Seamless Rain Gu .... G 302 272-2135
  Dover *(G-3471)*
Robert Grant Inc .... F 302 422-6090
  Milford *(G-8070)*
Rock Roofing .... G 302 757-2350
  Middletown *(G-7520)*
Roofers Inc .... E 302 995-7027
  Wilmington *(G-19564)*
Roofing Griffith .... G 302 762-1241
  Smyrna *(G-13870)*
Roofing Specialist .... G 302 344-2507
  Rehoboth Beach *(G-12939)*
Rshort Roofing LLC .... G 302 276-9531
  Townsend *(G-14062)*
Russell A Paulus & Son Inc .... G 302 998-4494
  Wilmington *(G-19593)*
S G Williams & Bros Co .... F 302 656-8167
  Wilmington *(G-19607)*
S M Commercial Roofing Inc .... G 302 478-3130
  Wilmington *(G-19611)*
Santanas Roofing LLC .... G 302 887-0067
  Newark *(G-11943)*
Sharp Raingutters .... F 302 398-4873
  Harrington *(G-4831)*
Sheet Metal Industry Advanceme .... G 302 994-7442
  Wilmington *(G-19788)*
Shingle Express Inc .... G 302 397-3773
  Wilmington *(G-19799)*
Skyline Roofing & Cnstr LLC .... G 610 929-4135
  Lewes *(G-6474)*
Star Enrg Cs LLC .... F 302 660-2187
  Wilmington *(G-20023)*
T R Roofing .... G 302 226-4510
  Rehoboth Beach *(G-12987)*
Tazelaar Roofing Service Inc .... G 302 697-2643
  Dover *(G-3656)*
Topmac LLC .... G 609 517-0585
  Wilmington *(G-20360)*
Two Brothers Roofing LLC .... G 302 650-8077
  Wilmington *(G-20471)*

Wertz & Co .... F 302 658-5186
  Wilmington *(G-20734)*
Wilkinson Roofing & Siding Inc .... E 302 998-0176
  Wilmington *(G-20781)*
Zanes Siding and Trim .... G 302 377-5394
  Bear *(G-572)*

1771 Concrete work

A G Concrete Works LLC .... G 302 841-2227
  Dagsboro *(G-1409)*
Absolution Inc .... G 302 528-2330
  Rehoboth Beach *(G-12595)*
All Types Concrete .... G 302 613-8400
  New Castle *(G-8784)*
American Stone Crafters Inc .... G 302 834-8891
  Bear *(G-31)*
Bari Concrete Contractors .... G 302 757-9512
  Wilmington *(G-14765)*
Beautiful Floors LLC .... G 302 690-5230
  Newark *(G-10007)*
Blue Heron Contracting LLC .... G 302 526-0648
  Greenwood *(G-4600)*
Boozer Excavation Co Inc .... F 302 542-0290
  Milton *(G-8573)*
Bradley & Sons Designer Con .... G 302 836-8031
  Bear *(G-79)*
Brick Doctor Inc .... F 302 678-3380
  Dover *(G-1978)*
Bridgestone Con & Masnry LLC .... G 302 462-5422
  Millsboro *(G-8207)*
Casey Battles Concrete .... G 302 312-3905
  Hartly *(G-4862)*
Chandlers Con Plcment Group LL ..... G 302 377-0017
  Dover *(G-2055)*
Chesco Coring & Cutng Del LLC .... G 302 276-7900
  New Castle *(G-8932)*
Chris Cocker .... F 302 744-9184
  Dover *(G-2071)*
Ci De Corp .... G 302 998-3944
  Wilmington *(G-15430)*
Cipolloni Brothers LLC .... F 302 449-0960
  Smyrna *(G-13678)*
Clarks Glasgow Pools Inc .... E 302 834-0200
  New Castle *(G-8953)*
Coastal Concrete Works LL .... G 302 684-2872
  Milton *(G-8586)*
Coastal Concrete Works LLC .... G 302 381-5261
  Harbeson *(G-4689)*
Compadre Concrete .... G 302 228-0763
  Bridgeville *(G-685)*
Complete Concrete Systems .... G 302 396-0013
  Milton *(G-8589)*
Concrete Bldg Systems Del Inc .... E 302 846-3645
  Delmar *(G-1583)*
Concrete Services Inc .... G 302 883-2883
  Dover *(G-2128)*
Contractors Flooring Del LLC .... G 302 698-4221
  Camden *(G-808)*
Curbs Etc Inc .... G 302 653-3511
  Smyrna *(G-13690)*
Custom Con Restoration LLC .... G 302 670-9525
  Dover *(G-2173)*
Custom Concrete Finishes .... G 302 463-0635
  Milton *(G-8595)*
Cutting of Precision Concrete .... G 302 543-5833
  Newport *(G-12446)*
D Gingerich Concrete & Masnry .... F 302 492-8662
  Hartly *(G-4864)*
Daisy Construction Company .... D 302 658-4417
  Wilmington *(G-15768)*
Delaware Concrete Coatings .... G 302 864-4014
  Lewes *(G-5892)*

17 CONSTRUCTION - SPECIAL TRADE CONTRACTORS

Delaware Concrete Specialists............... G 302 507-3038
  Newark (G-10427)
Delmarva Concrete Pumping Inc........... F 302 537-4118
  Frankford (G-4100)
Denn Con LLC....................................... F 443 941-4279
  Historic New Castle (G-4973)
Driveway Sealcoating............................ G 302 203-7451
  New Castle (G-9064)
Duncan S Concrete................................ G 302 395-1552
  Bear (G-183)
East Coast Poured Walls Inc................. F 302 430-0630
  Milford (G-7876)
F & N Vazquez Concrete LLC................. F 302 725-5305
  Lincoln (G-6667)
Farkas Concrete.................................... G 302 249-9172
  Lewes (G-5987)
Fasttrak Coatings Co............................. F 302 761-5454
  Wilmington (G-16561)
Francis Kelly Sons Inc........................... G 302 999-7400
  Wilmington (G-16720)
Frank Deramo & Son Inc....................... F 302 328-0102
  New Castle (G-9144)
GL Fluharty Jr Concrete LLC................. G 302 745-1290
  Lewes (G-6036)
Graydon Hurst & Son Inc....................... G 302 762-2444
  Wilmington (G-16952)
Healy Long & Jevin Inc.......................... F 302 654-8039
  Wilmington (G-17102)
Hh Concrete LLC................................... G 302 242-6342
  Milford (G-7929)
Highland Construction LLC.................... F 302 286-6990
  Bear (G-274)
J & T Concrete Inc................................ G 302 368-4949
  Newark (G-11068)
J E Rispoli Contractor Inc..................... G 302 999-1310
  Wilmington (G-17455)
James L Webb Paving Co Inc................. G 302 697-2000
  Camden (G-858)
Jaquez Concrete LLC............................ G 302 379-1148
  Middletown (G-7242)
JD Asphalt... F 302 514-7325
  Milford (G-7951)
JT Hoover Concrete Inc........................ E 302 832-2139
  Bear (G-315)
Lafazia Construction............................. G 302 234-1300
  Wilmington (G-17788)
Leager Construction Inc........................ G 302 653-8021
  Smyrna (G-13797)
Louis Dolente & Sons LLC..................... E 610 874-2100
  Claymont (G-1226)
Malone Cement Construction Inc........... F 302 239-9399
  Wilmington (G-18095)
Matt Carpet Guy LLC............................ G 443 497-3281
  Selbyville (G-13568)
Matthew Kirby..................................... G 302 427-0911
  Wilmington (G-18198)
Merit Construction Engineers................ F 302 992-9810
  Wilmington (G-18284)
Mike Mead Concrete LLC....................... G 816 588-6150
  Frederica (G-4177)
Mitchell E Morton................................. G 302 236-0878
  Lincoln (G-6689)
Mumford and Miller Con Inc.................. C 302 378-7736
  Middletown (G-7388)
New Castle Hot Mix Inc......................... G 302 655-2119
  Wilmington (G-18609)
North East Home Interiors LLC............. G 302 388-6262
  New Castle (G-9425)
O Morales Stucco Plaster Inc................ G 302 834-8891
  Bear (G-403)
Pargoe Flr Prep Lvlg Sltons LL.............. G 302 530-9450
  Wilmington (G-18890)

Pauls Paving Inc................................... F 302 539-9123
  Frankford (G-4131)
Peninsula Masonry Inc........................... G 302 684-3410
  Harbeson (G-4711)
Pioneer Products................................. G 302 678-0331
  Dover (G-3325)
Poured Foundations of De Inc............... F 302 234-2050
  Newark (G-11717)
Precision Con Cutng of Del MD.............. G 855 832-9876
  Wilmington (G-19153)
R S Widdoes & Son Inc......................... F 302 764-7455
  Wilmington (G-19306)
R&R Asphalt Paving.............................. G 302 312-8355
  Bear (G-445)
Ralph Cahall & Son Paving.................... G 302 653-4220
  Smyrna (G-13862)
Richard D Whaley Cnstr LLC.................. G 302 934-9525
  Millsboro (G-8445)
Rp Ventures and Holdings Inc............... E 410 398-3000
  Wilmington (G-19578)
Sanco Construction Co Inc.................... G 302 633-4156
  Wilmington (G-19655)
Santo Stucco....................................... G 302 453-0901
  Newark (G-11944)
Shea Concrete Ltd................................ G 302 422-7221
  Milford (G-8091)
Shore Masonry Inc................................ G 302 945-5933
  Millsboro (G-8460)
Smith Bill Concrete Masnry LLC............. G 302 250-4312
  Wilmington (G-19887)
Smith Concrete Inc............................... G 302 270-9251
  Milford (G-8094)
Sportsmans Hall LLC............................. G 410 429-6030
  Rehoboth Beach (G-12971)
Stone Technologies.............................. G 302 379-1759
  New Castle (G-9595)
Superior Sealing Services D................... F 610 717-6237
  Bear (G-520)
Talley Brothers Inc.............................. E 302 224-5376
  Newark (G-12157)
Terra Firma of Delmarva Inc.................. E 302 846-3350
  Delmar (G-1640)
Tomkat.. G 302 598-8823
  Wilmington (G-20349)
Tri County Materials............................. G 302 677-0156
  Dover (G-3722)
Triad Construction Company LLC........... G 302 652-3339
  New Castle (G-9637)
Trottys Concrete Pumping Inc............... G 302 732-3100
  Frankford (G-4154)
V Squillace Mason Contractor................ G 302 655-0934
  Wilmington (G-20560)
Victor Colbert Construction.................. G 302 368-7270
  Newark (G-12322)

1781 Water well drilling

A C Schultes of Delaware Inc................. F 302 337-0700
  Bridgeville (G-659)
American Water Well System................. F 302 629-3796
  Seaford (G-13064)
Bw Drilling Co...................................... G 302 658-0410
  Wilmington (G-15163)
Delmarva Builders Inc........................... G 302 629-9123
  Bridgeville (G-692)
Shore Well Drillers Inc......................... G 302 737-7707
  Newark (G-11999)
Water System Services Inc................... G 302 732-1490
  Dagsboro (G-1525)
White Drilling Corp............................... G 302 422-4057
  Lincoln (G-6708)

1791 Structural steel erection

▼ Amazon Steel Construction Inc............ G 302 751-1146
  Milford (G-7766)
Atlas Wldg & Fabrication Inc................. E 302 326-1900
  New Castle (G-8832)
Blue Heron Contracting LLC.................. G 302 526-0648
  Greenwood (G-4600)
Custom Iron Shop Inc........................... G 302 654-5201
  Wilmington (G-15741)
Deaven Development Corp.................... G 302 994-5793
  Wilmington (G-15847)
Donald F Deaven Inc............................. E 302 994-5793
  Wilmington (G-16135)
East Coast Erectors Inc....................... F 302 323-1800
  New Castle (G-9077)
Emlyn Construction Co......................... G 302 697-8247
  Dover (G-2441)
▲ Falcon Steel Co................................ E 302 571-0890
  Wilmington (G-16533)
LMS Ironworks..................................... G 302 300-7719
  Wilmington (G-17962)
▲ M Davis & Sons Inc........................... C 302 998-3385
  Newark (G-11301)
Metro Steel Incorporated..................... E 302 778-2288
  New Castle (G-9361)
R C Fabricators Inc............................. D 302 573-8989
  Wilmington (G-19303)
Steel Suppliers Inc.............................. C 302 654-5243
  Wilmington (G-20043)
Summit Steel Inc.................................. D 302 325-3220
  New Castle (G-9599)
Sykes Orna & Cstm Ir Works Inc............ G 302 757-2103
  Wilmington (G-20179)

1793 Glass and glazing work

Delaware Storefronts LLC..................... G 302 697-1850
  Dover (G-2267)
Eastern Home Improvements Inc........... G 302 655-9920
  Wilmington (G-16258)
New Castle Glass Inc............................ G 302 322-6164
  New Castle (G-9409)
Newark Glass & Mirror Inc..................... G 302 834-1158
  Bear (G-394)
Parags Glass Company......................... G 302 737-0101
  Newark (G-11625)
Premier Glass & Screen Inc................... F 302 732-3101
  Frankford (G-4134)
Service Glass Inc.................................. F 302 629-9139
  Seaford (G-13396)
Superior Screen & Glass....................... G 302 541-5399
  Ocean View (G-12574)
Zephyr Aluminum LLC........................... G 302 571-0585
  Wilmington (G-20956)

1794 Excavation work

Bobcat of New Castle LLC..................... E 732 780-6880
  Bear (G-77)
Bramble Construction Co Inc................. F 302 856-6723
  Georgetown (G-4239)
Brandywine Construction Co.................. D 302 571-9773
  New Castle (G-8884)
Bunting & Murray Cnstr Corp................. D 302 436-5144
  Selbyville (G-13486)
Bwb Inc... F 717 939-3679
  Millsboro (G-8211)
Castle Construction Del Inc................... E 302 326-3600
  New Castle (G-8920)
Central Backhoe Service....................... G 302 398-6420
  Milton (G-8581)
CHOPTANK EXCAVATION LLC................. G 302 420-0354
  New Castle (G-8936)
Christiana Excavating Company............. E 302 738-8660
  Newark (G-10228)

17 CONSTRUCTION - SPECIAL TRADE CONTRACTORS

Cirillo Bros Inc .... E 302 326-1540
  New Castle (G-8943)
Clean Delaware Inc .... G 302 684-4221
  Milton (G-8584)
Corrado American LLC .... E 302 655-6501
  New Castle (G-8975)
Corrado Construction Co LLC .... D 302 652-3339
  New Castle (G-8976)
Cygnet Construction Corp .... G 302 436-5212
  Selbyville (G-13513)
David G Horsey & Sons Inc .... D 302 875-3033
  Laurel (G-5494)
David P Roser Inc .... E 302 239-7605
  Hockessin (G-5175)
Dirt Works Inc .... F 302 947-2429
  Lewes (G-5921)
Dixon Contracting Inc .... G 302 653-4623
  Dover (G-2311)
Don Rogers Inc .... F 302 658-6524
  Wilmington (G-16132)
Edward J Kaye Construction .... F 302 629-7483
  Seaford (G-13170)
Guardian Companies Inc .... E 302 834-1000
  Wilmington (G-17000)
J & M Industries Inc .... G 302 575-0200
  Wilmington (G-17445)
Jerrys Inc .... E 302 422-7676
  Milford (G-7952)
Jth Excavating Inc .... G 302 832-7699
  Bear (G-316)
Kaye Construction .... G 302 628-6962
  Seaford (G-13246)
Leroy Betts Construction Inc .... G 302 284-9193
  Felton (G-3997)
Louis Dolente & Sons LLC .... E 610 874-2100
  Claymont (G-1226)
M G Hamex Corporation .... F 302 832-9072
  New Castle (G-9332)
Matthew W Spence Inc .... G 302 697-3284
  Camden (G-873)
Merit Construction Engineers .... F 302 992-9810
  Wilmington (G-18284)
Michael Robert Meibaum .... G 302 212-9969
  Lewes (G-6269)
Midway Services Inc .... G 302 422-8603
  Lincoln (G-6685)
Palmer & Associates Inc .... G 302 834-9329
  Bear (G-412)
Pearce & Moretto Inc .... E 302 326-0707
  Middletown (G-7436)
R & E Excavation LLC .... G 302 750-5226
  New Castle (G-9510)
Ralph Cahall & Son Paving .... G 302 653-4220
  Smyrna (G-13862)
Reybold Construction Group LLC .... F 302 832-7100
  Bear (G-456)
Ruark Inc .... G 302 846-2332
  Seaford (G-13381)
Swain Excavation Inc .... G 302 422-4349
  Lincoln (G-6705)
Talmo John .... G 302 547-9657
  Wilmington (G-20217)
Thomas Clark MASonry& Excav .... G 302 462-6039
  Frankford (G-4152)
Tru Grit LLC .... F 302 593-4700
  Smyrna (G-13919)
Walter W Snyder .... G 302 378-1817
  Middletown (G-7706)

1795 Wrecking and demolition work

AMA Resource LLC .... G 410 977-5101
  Wilmington (G-14407)
Design Contracting Inc .... G 302 429-6900
  Wilmington (G-16025)
Geotech LLC .... G 302 353-9769
  Wilmington (G-16849)
Green Earth Tech Group LLC .... F 302 257-5617
  Wilmington (G-16964)
Mid-Atlntic Dismantlement Corp .... E 302 678-9300
  Dover (G-3087)
Rpj Waste Services Inc .... G 302 653-9999
  Smyrna (G-13871)
Thomas Building Group Inc .... F 302 283-0600
  Newark (G-12193)

1796 Installing building equipment

▼ Amazon Steel Construction Inc .... G 302 751-1146
  Milford (G-7766)
Amrec Holdings Inc .... D 302 273-0000
  Dover (G-1788)
Brandywine Elevator Co Inc .... G 866 636-0102
  Wilmington (G-15055)
▲ Bruce Industrial Co Inc .... D 302 655-9616
  New Castle (G-8894)
Firebrick Wind LLC .... G 647 352-9533
  Wilmington (G-16613)
Greg Elect .... G 215 651-1477
  Hockessin (G-5229)
Harrold & Son Inc .... G 302 629-9504
  Seaford (G-13209)
Millwright Company LLC .... F 302 274-9590
  Wilmington (G-18367)
Northeast Missouri Wind LLC .... G 647 352-9533
  Wilmington (G-18682)
Oneals Millwright Services LLC .... G 302 542-5811
  Lincoln (G-6692)
Planned Poultry Renovation .... E 302 875-4196
  Laurel (G-5577)
Pradhan Energy Projects .... G 305 428-2123
  Hockessin (G-5351)
R & S Fabrication Inc .... G 302 629-0377
  Bridgeville (G-759)
Xwind Services Ltd .... G 916 367-2994
  Lewes (G-6644)
Xwind Services Ltd .... E 418 563-5453
  Lewes (G-6645)

1799 Special trade contractors, nec

2 Days Bath LLC .... F 302 798-0103
  Wilmington (G-14118)
2 Guys Pressure Washing .... G 302 250-3721
  Newark (G-9705)
302 Contracting LLC .... G 302 677-1912
  Dover (G-1685)
3w3d Inc .... F 858 263-5883
  Wilmington (G-14132)
911 Restoration of Delaware .... G 302 331-2033
  Middletown (G-6819)
A & B General Contracting .... G 302 604-9696
  Seaford (G-13043)
A E G Contracting LLC .... G 302 250-5438
  Wilmington (G-14162)
A L Merced General Contractors .... G 302 658-1618
  Wilmington (G-14166)
Accutrench Contracting LLC .... G 410 829-5157
  Seaford (G-13046)
Adkins Custom Contracting LLC .... G 302 841-3885
  Delmar (G-1560)
Advance Office Instltions Inc .... E 302 777-5599
  Historic New Castle (G-4922)
Affordable Contractor .... G 302 670-5699
  Historic New Castle (G-4923)
Affordable Delivery Svcs LLC .... E 302 276-0246
  New Castle (G-8771)
Ajko General Contractor .... G 302 373-4030
  Wilmington (G-14341)
Alan M Billingsley Jr .... G 302 998-7907
  Wilmington (G-14345)
Alberto Baez .... G 302 543-1212
  Elsmere (G-3930)
All American Fencing .... G 302 530-8155
  Middletown (G-6850)
All Restored Inc .... G 302 222-3537
  Camden Wyoming (G-910)
Allpro Services Group Inc .... G 302 750-1112
  Magnolia (G-6716)
Allura Bath & Kitchen Inc .... G 302 731-2851
  Newark (G-9828)
Aluminum Building Company .... G 302 423-8829
  Camden Wyoming (G-912)
▼ Amazon Steel Construction Inc .... G 302 751-1146
  Milford (G-7766)
American Restoration Carp .... G 302 993-7900
  Wilmington (G-14441)
American Seaboard Exteriors .... E 302 571-9896
  Wilmington (G-14442)
Amira Spray Foam .... G 302 464-0644
  Middletown (G-6860)
Andrew W Viohl .... G 302 388-7721
  Claymont (G-1038)
Apex Contractors LLC .... G 302 670-7799
  Bear (G-40)
Arcadia Fencing Inc .... G 302 398-7700
  Harrington (G-4735)
Aspire + Build LLC .... D 617 602-7400
  Wilmington (G-14590)
Astec Inc .... G 302 378-2717
  Middletown (G-6876)
At Contracting LLC .... G 302 678-4898
  Dover (G-1840)
Atd Contracting LLC .... G 302 535-1013
  Smyrna (G-13652)
Atechnologie LLC .... G 781 325-5230
  Wilmington (G-14617)
Atlantic Business Contracting .... G 302 337-7490
  Greenwood (G-4593)
Atlantic Contractor LL .... G 302 537-4361
  Ocean View (G-12466)
Atlantic Kitchen & Bath LLC .... G 302 947-9001
  Lewes (G-5715)
Atlantic Source Contg Inc .... G 302 645-5207
  Lewes (G-5718)
AW Viohl Contracting LLC .... G 302 375-6166
  Claymont (G-1047)
Aztech Contracting Inc .... F 302 526-2145
  Felton (G-3945)
B & T Contracting .... G 302 492-8415
  Camden Wyoming (G-914)
B G Halko & Sons Inc .... G 302 322-2020
  New Castle (G-8840)
B&H Contracting Group .... G 302 588-9774
  Newark (G-9967)
Basement Gurus LLC .... E 800 834-6584
  Wilmington (G-14773)
Basement Pros Inc .... G 302 266-0203
  Newark (G-9988)
Baypro Contracting .... G 703 593-7673
  Milford (G-7788)
Benny Bennett Contracting .... G 302 290-1613
  Bear (G-69)
Bethany Resort Furnishings .... G 302 539-4000
  Bethany Beach (G-585)
Bill Johnson Contracting .... G 302 245-4708
  Georgetown (G-4234)
Black Sea Contractor LLC .... G 856 558-1821
  Selbyville (G-13478)

17 CONSTRUCTION - SPECIAL TRADE CONTRACTORS

Black Star General Contractors............ G 302 275-4533
Newark *(G-10047)*

Blackstone Building Group................... F 302 660-5528
Rockland *(G-13028)*

Blackwells Welding Inc......................... G..... 301 498-5277
Milton *(G-8572)*

Blue Diamond Pools Inc........................ G 302 265-2165
Seaford *(G-13090)*

Bobot Robotics Inc................................ G 501 301-0612
Lewes *(G-5774)*

Boyds Trailor Hitches............................ G 302 697-9000
Camden Wyoming *(G-917)*

Brandywine Resurfacing........................ G..... 302 654-8744
Wilmington *(G-15083)*

Brandywine Waterproofing Del.............. G 302 482-4368
Wilmington *(G-15093)*

Breakwater Fence and Deck................. G 302 684-3333
Milford *(G-7804)*

Bright Finish LLC................................... G 888 974-4747
Smyrna *(G-13667)*

Builder Supply of Del Marva.................. G 302 829-8650
Ocean View *(G-12484)*

Builders LLC General............................. G 302 533-6528
Newark *(G-10100)*

Burkes Seal Coating.............................. G 302 697-7635
Dover *(G-1994)*

Buscemi Pressure Washing Llc............. G 302 223-6295
Smyrna *(G-13670)*

By The Sea Contracting LLC................. G 302 569-9701
Millsboro *(G-8212)*

Bylerwilliamr.. G 302 653-3727
Dover *(G-2003)*

C & C Contractors LLC.......................... G 302 934-1134
Millsboro *(G-8213)*

C & H Contracting LLC.......................... G 302 883-4339
Magnolia *(G-6723)*

C and C Drywall Contractors N............. F 302 242-3305
Dover *(G-2006)*

C&F Contractors Service LLC............... G 302 480-3002
Greenwood *(G-4602)*

CA Briggs Contracting........................... G 302 250-8858
Wilmington *(G-15182)*

Cannon Sline Industrial Inc................... F 302 658-1420
New Castle *(G-8911)*

Cannon Spas.. G 302 628-9404
Seaford *(G-13101)*

Capital Contracting LLC........................ G 302 690-0094
Newark *(G-10133)*

Cassidy Painting Inc............................. E 302 683-0710
New Castle *(G-8918)*

CD Installation.. G 302 588-7678
Newark *(G-10168)*

CDI Granite & MBL Fabrication............. G 302 235-7010
Wilmington *(G-15291)*

Cgc Geoservices LLC............................ F 302 489-2398
Newark *(G-10181)*

Chas Pools Inc....................................... F 302 376-5840
Middletown *(G-6971)*

Cherry Building Group........................... G 302 280-6876
Seaford *(G-13114)*

Choice Construction Co Inc.................. G 302 226-1732
Rehoboth Beach *(G-12672)*

Clark Benson Contracting..................... G 302 846-9119
Delmar *(G-1579)*

Clarks Glasgow Pools Inc..................... E 302 834-0200
New Castle *(G-8953)*

Clarks Swimming Pools Inc.................. G 302 629-8835
Seaford *(G-13123)*

Clean Pros... G 302 312-5666
Newark *(G-10255)*

Coastal Bath LLC.................................. G 302 742-9128
Delmar *(G-1581)*

Coastal Maintenance LLC..................... E 302 536-1290
Seaford *(G-13127)*

Coastal Pump & Tank Inc..................... G 302 398-3061
Harrington *(G-4751)*

Coastal Restorations Inc...................... G 443 859-4505
Dagsboro *(G-1428)*

Collett & Son Welding Inc.................... G 302 376-1830
Townsend *(G-13975)*

Colonial Marble of Delaware................ G 302 328-1735
New Castle *(G-8957)*

Contract PT LLC................................... G 302 628-0705
Seaford *(G-13136)*

Contractor Rashmi & Penny................. G 302 778-5771
Wilmington *(G-15623)*

Cornerstone Rbe Contg LLC................ G 443 480-6674
Middletown *(G-7014)*

County Environmental Inc.................... E 302 322-8946
New Castle *(G-8979)*

County Insulation Co............................ D 302 322-8946
New Castle *(G-8980)*

Crestview Services LLC....................... G 302 569-4909
Millsboro *(G-8244)*

Csrj Contracting................................... G 302 290-6208
Wilmington *(G-15725)*

CTA Roofing & Waterproofing............. F 302 454-8551
Newark *(G-10363)*

Curtiss Contracting LLC....................... G 302 604-1071
Milton *(G-8594)*

Custom Design Contracting LLC......... G 302 333-0547
Wilmington *(G-15740)*

Custom Framers Inc............................. F 302 684-5377
Harbeson *(G-4694)*

Custom Iron Shop Inc.......................... G 302 654-5201
Wilmington *(G-15741)*

Custom Porcelain Inc........................... G 302 659-6590
Townsend *(G-13981)*

D & C Bath LLC..................................... G 888 323-2284
Middletown *(G-7026)*

D H General Contracting..................... G 302 420-5269
Newark *(G-10377)*

Dal Contractors LLC............................. G 302 737-3220
Newark *(G-10382)*

DAndrea Contracting............................ G 302 893-4183
Middletown *(G-7028)*

Davis & Yoder Contracting Serv.......... G 302 369-8888
Newark *(G-10392)*

Delaware Crawl Space Co Inc............. G 302 930-0386
Lewes *(G-5894)*

Delaware Home & Envmtl Svcs........... G 302 313-2899
Lewes *(G-5898)*

Delaware Power Wash Plus LLC......... G 302 415-1066
Bear *(G-152)*

Delden Installations.............................. G 302 423-1279
Bear *(G-162)*

Delmarva Bath LLC............................... G 302 278-1717
Laurel *(G-5496)*

Delmarva Crawl Space Sltns............... G 302 265-0637
Harbeson *(G-4695)*

Delmarva Roofing & Coating Inc......... E 302 349-5174
Greenwood *(G-4615)*

Delmarva Spray Foam LLC.................. F 302 752-1080
Georgetown *(G-4290)*

Dezins Unlimited Inc............................ G 302 652-4545
Wilmington *(G-16043)*

Diamond State Wterproofing Sys........ G 302 325-0866
New Castle *(G-9053)*

Dickerson Fence Co Inc...................... G 302 846-2227
Delmar *(G-1589)*

Dippold Marble Granite........................ G 302 734-8505
Dover *(G-2299)*

Dogwatch of Delaware........................ G 302 268-3434
Wilmington *(G-16118)*

Double D Restoration LLC................... G 302 853-2176
Selbyville *(G-13522)*

Dover Pool & Patio Center Inc............ F 302 346-7665
Dover *(G-2361)*

Dreamscape Design Cons LLC........... G 302 893-0984
Newark *(G-10571)*

Dryzone LLC... G 302 684-5034
Ellendale *(G-3916)*

E Baumann Contracting...................... G 302 824-3765
Wilmington *(G-16235)*

E K Long General Contractors............ G 302 883-1463
Magnolia *(G-6742)*

E W Brown Inc...................................... G 302 652-6612
Wilmington *(G-16241)*

East Coast Elastomerics Inc............... F 302 524-8004
Selbyville *(G-13527)*

Eastern Industrial Svcs Inc................. D 302 455-1400
Historic New Castle *(G-4979)*

Eastern Shore Porch Patio Inc............ E 302 436-9520
Selbyville *(G-13528)*

Eastern States Cnstr Svc Inc.............. D 302 995-2259
Wilmington *(G-16264)*

Easy Living Service.............................. G 302 633-4849
Wilmington *(G-16268)*

Ecg Industries Inc................................ G 302 453-0535
Newark *(G-10603)*

Eclipes Erection Inc............................. G 302 633-1421
Wilmington *(G-16279)*

Eddie Simpson Stanley Contg............ G 302 276-0569
Bear *(G-193)*

Ellis Contracting LLC........................... G 302 559-5105
Wilmington *(G-16373)*

Epeius Contracting Service LLC......... G 302 533-8753
Newark *(G-10659)*

Expert Basement Waterproo............... G 302 655-8202
New Castle *(G-9110)*

Faranarium Inc...................................... F 716 235-5950
Middletown *(G-7122)*

Farrell Roofing Inc................................ E 302 378-7663
Middletown *(G-7123)*

Ferris Home Imprvs Co LLC................ E 302 998-4500
Newark *(G-10725)*

First General... G 302 381-2581
Georgetown *(G-4321)*

First State Petroleum Services........... G 302 398-9704
Harrington *(G-4770)*

First State Rental Company LLC........ G 302 632-5699
Houston *(G-5441)*

Freedom Kitchen and Bath.................. G 302 463-1659
Newark *(G-10778)*

FWd Contracting Entps LLC................ G 302 377-3459
Wilmington *(G-16782)*

G M Construction LLC.......................... G 302 462-5871
Lewes *(G-6025)*

G Parker Contracting........................... G 302 304-2940
Bear *(G-243)*

Gainor Awnings Inc.............................. G 302 998-8611
Wilmington *(G-16793)*

Garry F Kuhlman Gen Contractor........ G 302 482-3535
Hockessin *(G-5218)*

GAs Contracting Inc............................ G 302 875-2302
Laurel *(G-5518)*

Gateway Construction Inc................... G 302 653-4400
Clayton *(G-1368)*

Gemini Building Systems LLC............. F 302 654-5310
Wilmington *(G-16827)*

General Contractor.............................. G 302 241-8285
Wilmington *(G-16831)*

Generations Wldg & Contg LLC.......... G 302 430-4099
Laurel *(G-5519)*

Geosyntec Holdings LLC..................... G 561 995-0900
Wilmington *(G-16848)*

17 CONSTRUCTION - SPECIAL TRADE CONTRACTORS

Geotech LLC .... G 302 353-9769
  Wilmington (G-16849)
Giorgi Kitchens Inc .... F 302 762-1121
  Wilmington (G-16867)
Gotshadeonline Inc .... G 302 832-8468
  Bear (G-252)
Granite Central Distributors .... F 302 521-1584
  Newark (G-10880)
Grant Ireland Contracting LLC .... G 302 265-6112
  Felton (G-3980)
Gray Audograph Agency Inc .... F 302 658-1700
  New Castle (G-9176)
Gregg & Sons Mechanical LLC .... G 302 223-8145
  Townsend (G-14011)
Guardian Fence Company .... F 302 834-3044
  Middletown (G-7182)
Haines Contracting Inc .... G 443 877-7103
  New Castle (G-9191)
Hampton Enterprises Inc .... G 302 378-7365
  Townsend (G-14013)
Harmony Construction Inc .... F 302 737-8700
  Newark (G-10930)
Henderson Services Inc .... F 302 424-1999
  Milford (G-7926)
Heritage Painting .... G 302 270-2008
  Magnolia (G-6751)
Hernandez & Sons .... G 302 765-8476
  New Castle (G-9211)
Hertiage Builders & Improvemen .... G 302 275-8675
  Bear (G-270)
Hometown Fence LLC .... G 302 629-0415
  Georgetown (G-4364)
Hunts Family Contracting .... G 302 510-5585
  Wilmington (G-17236)
Hydrohero Franchising LLC .... G 302 321-7077
  Frankford (G-4115)
Hyland Restoration LLC .... G 516 713-6518
  Newark (G-10988)
Imperial Gunite .... G 631 244-0073
  Wilmington (G-17291)
Independence Contractors Inc .... G 302 530-3022
  Wilmington (G-17308)
Interiors By Kim Inc .... G 302 537-2480
  Ocean View (G-12525)
Iron Hill Fence .... G 302 453-9060
  Newark (G-11059)
J & G Acoustical Co .... E 302 285-3630
  Middletown (G-7233)
J & L Services Inc .... F 410 943-3455
  Seaford (G-13226)
J & M Fencing Inc .... G 302 284-9674
  Felton (G-3985)
J & M Fencing Inc .... G 302 284-9674
  Felton (G-3986)
J Dean Pusey Contractor Inc .... G 302 245-0432
  Ellendale (G-3922)
Jab Contracting LLC .... G 302 559-1905
  Wilmington (G-17469)
Jaffery & Jaffery Contractors .... G 302 766-3795
  Middletown (G-7236)
Jalal Bayar Contracting .... G 302 535-7294
  Smyrna (G-13780)
James Parker Contracting .... G 302 507-6200
  Bear (G-298)
Jbm Petroleum Service LLC .... G 302 752-6105
  Lincoln (G-6677)
Jbs Contracting .... G 302 543-7264
  Wilmington (G-17506)
JC Contractors LLC .... G 302 420-9338
  Middletown (G-7243)
Jeremey M Weddle .... G 410 829-7224
  Greenwood (G-4646)

Jh Contracting Inc .... F 302 893-4766
  Middletown (G-7248)
Jim Hutchison .... G 302 739-4758
  Dover (G-2789)
Jjc Independent Contractor LLC .... G 302 388-5499
  Wilmington (G-17552)
JM General Contractor .... G 302 464-9730
  New Castle (G-9260)
Joe Coover Contracting Inc .... G 302 540-5806
  New Castle (G-9261)
Joe Hallock Contracting LLC .... G 302 236-6423
  Rehoboth Beach (G-12806)
Joshua S Stevens .... G 302 492-3450
  Hartly (G-4886)
JW Tull Contracting Svcs LLC .... G 302 494-8179
  Wilmington (G-17625)
K C Contracting .... G 302 875-4661
  Laurel (G-5539)
Kent Contracting LLC .... G 302 233-3157
  Hartly (G-4889)
Kent Sign Company Inc .... F 302 697-2181
  Dover (G-2856)
Kgc Enterprises Inc .... G 302 668-1835
  Wilmington (G-17710)
Kitchen Gallery Inc .... G 302 655-7214
  Wilmington (G-17737)
Kreative Services .... G 302 545-5030
  Bear (G-334)
Kw Contracting Inc .... G 302 420-0159
  Townsend (G-14024)
Lacieah Inc .... G 302 365-5585
  Newark (G-11214)
Leak Stoppers LLC .... G 302 236-1652
  Lewes (G-6184)
Legacy Contractors LLC .... G 302 442-8817
  Newark (G-11241)
Linda McCormick .... G 443 987-2099
  Wilmington (G-17922)
Lopez General Contractors LLC .... G 302 377-2591
  New Castle (G-9325)
Louis L Rdding Cty/County Bldg .... G 302 576-2100
  Wilmington (G-18007)
Lupoli General Contracting .... G 302 449-1533
  Middletown (G-7316)
M J Bilecki Contracting .... G 302 357-7455
  Bear (G-356)
Maccari Companies Inc .... G 302 994-9628
  Wilmington (G-18064)
Macdonald Contracting LLC .... G 302 668-2022
  Wilmington (G-18066)
Marlings Inc .... F 302 325-1759
  Wilmington (G-18153)
Mastercrafters Inc .... E 302 678-1470
  Dover (G-3029)
Mayhorns Collisionandrestoratn .... G 302 779-2177
  Hartly (G-4895)
Mayscapes LLC .... G 302 389-5999
  Newark (G-11362)
Mebro Inc .... E 302 992-0104
  Wilmington (G-18243)
Messicks Mobile Homes Inc .... F 302 398-9166
  Harrington (G-4801)
Meta Mind Global Corp LLC .... G 267 471-3616
  Dover (G-3069)
Michael A Andreoli Contracting .... G 302 274-8709
  Newark (G-11400)
Mid-Atlntic Wtrproofing MD Inc .... F 301 206-9500
  Newark (G-11414)
Middletown Kitchen & Bath LLC .... F 302 464-1236
  Middletown (G-7354)
Midlantic Bldg Rstorations Inc .... G 302 475-8084
  Wilmington (G-18344)

Mike Molitor .... G 302 528-6300
  Wilmington (G-18351)
Millan Contractors .... G 302 983-9365
  Newark (G-11421)
Millcreekinvestments .... G 302 407-5034
  Wilmington (G-18361)
Millmar Contracting .... G 302 222-0823
  Milford (G-8012)
Millmar Contracting LLC .... G 302 697-6581
  Camden Wyoming (G-963)
Mobile Magic Pressure Washing .... G 302 697-1230
  Dover (G-3110)
Molinas Contracting LLC .... G 302 378-9316
  Middletown (G-7376)
N Mallari Gc Corp .... F 302 516-7738
  Newark (G-11479)
Nagin C Patel .... G 302 559-4357
  Wilmington (G-18520)
Nanticoke Fence LLC .... G 302 628-7808
  Seaford (G-13303)
Narissa Building Company LLC .... G 908 619-6419
  Wilmington (G-18534)
National Vinyl Products Inc .... F 817 913-5991
  Dover (G-3156)
Nepi Contracting Inc .... G 302 250-6820
  Wilmington (G-18584)
Newark Fence Co .... G 302 368-5329
  Newark (G-11537)
Newman Water PROofing&mold .... G 302 373-7579
  Newark (G-11550)
Newport Builders & Windowland .... F 302 994-3537
  Wilmington (G-18632)
Noble Contracting Group LLC .... G 302 219-4006
  Middletown (G-7407)
North East Home Interiors LLC .... G 302 388-6262
  New Castle (G-9425)
North Point Builders LLC .... G 843 246-1516
  Newark (G-11565)
Old House Restoration .... G 302 737-0806
  Newark (G-11583)
One Source Contracting .... G 302 893-3753
  Wilmington (G-18783)
Organized For Life .... G 302 792-1663
  Wilmington (G-18819)
Paramount Installations .... G 302 607-4243
  Dover (G-3270)
Paris Corporation .... F 302 427-5985
  Wilmington (G-18891)
Parker Construction Inc .... G 302 798-8530
  Claymont (G-1260)
Patio Systems Inc .... G 302 644-6540
  Lewes (G-6353)
Paul Dvis Rstoration Nthrn Del .... G 302 449-6941
  New Castle (G-9461)
Pen Pave Contractors Pave .... G 302 226-7283
  Rehoboth Beach (G-12885)
Pet Stop of Delmarva .... G 302 943-2310
  Harrington (G-4810)
Pierce Fence Company Inc .... F 302 674-1996
  Dover (G-3321)
Pieshalaamanda .... G 302 492-3227
  Camden Wyoming (G-965)
Pinnacle Restoration Corp .... G 302 650-0520
  Wilmington (G-19050)
Pioneer Fence Co Inc .... F 302 998-2892
  Wilmington (G-19052)
Pirate Pools LLC .... G 302 519-0624
  Lewes (G-6371)
Pole Buildings Unlimited .... G 302 399-3058
  Dover (G-3347)
Pool Man Inc .... G 302 737-8696
  Newark (G-11712)

Preferred Security Inc G 302 834-7800
Bear *(G-435)*

Premier Restoration G 302 645-1611
Milton *(G-8689)*

Pressure Washing G 302 393-0879
Greenwood *(G-4662)*

Prestige Building Co G 302 744-8282
Dover *(G-3369)*

Price Is Right Contracting LLC F 215 760-1416
Wilmington *(G-19188)*

Privacy Policy/United Custom C G 302 537-1717
Bethany Beach *(G-628)*

Pro Contractors G 302 894-2611
Newark *(G-11754)*

Proclean Inc E 302 656-8080
Delaware City *(G-1554)*

Professional Window Tinting G 302 456-3456
Newark *(G-11760)*

Pure Power Pressure Wshg LLC G 302 266-9933
Newark *(G-11772)*

Quality Contracting Inc G 302 270-8888
Wyoming *(G-20988)*

Quality Contracting & Developm G 302 438-0874
Middletown *(G-7486)*

Quality Contractor Svcs LLC G 302 502-6815
Newark *(G-11786)*

Quartz Mill Contracting G 302 750-6683
Newark *(G-11797)*

R & A Contracting G 302 669-7144
Wilmington *(G-19300)*

R & J Taylor Inc G 302 368-7888
Newark *(G-11802)*

R C Fabricators Inc D 302 573-8989
Wilmington *(G-19303)*

RAmaine&sons Contracting G 302 212-8330
Frankford *(G-4137)*

RE Bath of Northern De G 302 414-9751
Townsend *(G-14055)*

Reginald D Quail Sr G 302 335-3145
Felton *(G-4014)*

Remedy Restore Aesthetics LLC G 302 538-5261
Dover *(G-3451)*

Rhino Fence G 302 544-5225
New Castle *(G-9531)*

River Rock Contracting LLC G 302 538-7169
Camden Wyoming *(G-970)*

Rnh Installation G 302 731-8900
Newark *(G-11894)*

RNS Contracting G 302 384-4633
New Castle *(G-9537)*

Robinson Export & Import Corp G 410 219-7200
Millsboro *(G-8449)*

Rockhard Granite LLC G 302 737-9300
Newark *(G-11904)*

Rodney Square Services Inc E 302 652-5891
Wilmington *(G-19551)*

Romanos Original LLC G 215 796-3271
Wilmington *(G-19558)*

Rosario Ferrante General Contr G 302 234-1911
Newark *(G-11915)*

S and J Contracting LLC G 302 382-0769
Camden *(G-891)*

S&R Pressure Washing LLC G 410 430-9864
Selbyville *(G-13602)*

Sahaj Contractor LLC G 302 559-4357
Wilmington *(G-19632)*

Sandra M Cmpos Restoration LLC G 302 883-7663
Lewes *(G-6446)*

Sangree Construction Inc G 717 576-7144
Milton *(G-8707)*

Seaside Pressure Wash LLC G 302 470-4035
Greenwood *(G-4667)*

SEdoyle General Contractor G 302 531-5371
Felton *(G-4025)*

Shackleford Facilities Inc F 877 735-3938
Frankford *(G-4141)*

Shore Tint & More Inc G 302 947-4624
Harbeson *(G-4716)*

Silver Lake Restoration G 302 241-3931
Dover *(G-3561)*

SMS Contracting F 610 721-9943
Wilmington *(G-19898)*

Social Contract LLC E 302 357-5193
Wilmington *(G-19907)*

Somar General Contracting LLC G 302 561-3360
Claymont *(G-1295)*

Spacecon Specialty Contractors F 302 503-3824
Lincoln *(G-6704)*

Starrett Design Build G 302 598-6607
Hockessin *(G-5389)*

Stb Contracting LLC G 302 992-0570
Wilmington *(G-20042)*

Sum-R-Fun Pool Products Inc E 302 998-9288
Wilmington *(G-20122)*

Sunnyfield Contractors Inc F 302 674-8610
Dover *(G-3623)*

Superior Exterior Contracting G 302 287-8391
Hockessin *(G-5398)*

Superior Screen & Glass G 302 541-5399
Ocean View *(G-12574)*

Sussex Fence Co G 302 945-7008
Millsboro *(G-8474)*

Sussex Fencing G 302 945-7008
Millsboro *(G-8475)*

Sussex Machine Works Inc G 302 875-7958
Laurel *(G-5610)*

Swift Pools Inc E 302 738-9800
Newark *(G-12142)*

That Granite Place G 302 236-0820
Milford *(G-8118)*

That Granite Place LLC G 302 337-7490
Greenwood *(G-4671)*

Thomas Scott Gillespie G 302 750-0813
Bear *(G-531)*

Tier Two Contracting LLC G 443 928-0089
Georgetown *(G-4555)*

Tint World G 302 595-9100
Wilmington *(G-20333)*

Tm Crist Contracting Inc G 302 632-7557
Frederica *(G-4185)*

Toby W Miller G 302 270-1057
Dover *(G-3696)*

Tom McDonald Contracting G 302 219-7939
Newark *(G-12206)*

Total Basement Care G 302 367-4789
Wilmington *(G-20366)*

Total Bath Transformations G 302 985-7649
Townsend *(G-14083)*

Trivett Contracting G 302 275-6452
Wilmington *(G-20432)*

▲ **Troy Granite Inc** G 302 292-1750
Newark *(G-12240)*

TW Contracting G 302 384-6777
Wilmington *(G-20467)*

Tycos General Contracting Inc F 302 268-6766
Wilmington *(G-20479)*

US Installation Group Inc F 302 994-1644
Wilmington *(G-20550)*

Walkers Contracting LLC G 302 331-0425
Magnolia *(G-6790)*

White Drilling Corp G 302 422-4057
Lincoln *(G-6708)*

William Chambers and Son G 302 284-9655
Viola *(G-14098)*

William H Groton Construc G 302 697-4744
Seaford *(G-13449)*

Wilmington Stoneworks LLC G 302 723-7126
Wilmington *(G-20845)*

Xcertified Restore LLC G 302 330-8850
Wilmington *(G-20915)*

Xpress Contracting G 703 932-8565
Millsboro *(G-8509)*

Yardex LLC C 302 406-0933
Wilmington *(G-20924)*

20 FOOD AND KINDRED PRODUCTS

2011 Meat packing plants

Allen Harim Foods LLC E 302 684-1640
Harbeson *(G-4681)*

Cbbc Opco LLC G 863 967-0636
Wilmington *(G-15284)*

2013 Sausages and other prepared meats

AES Foods G 302 420-8377
Newark *(G-9790)*

Kirby & Holloway Provisions Co E 302 398-3705
Harrington *(G-4794)*

New B & M Meats Inc F 302 655-5331
Wilmington *(G-18607)*

Ralph and Paul Adams Inc B 800 338-4727
Bridgeville *(G-760)*

Rehoboth House of Jerky G 215 272-4217
Rehoboth Beach *(G-12928)*

2015 Poultry slaughtering and processing

Allen Biotech LLC A 302 629-9136
Millsboro *(G-8165)*

Eastern Shore Poultry Company B 302 855-1350
Georgetown *(G-4306)*

Harim Usa Ltd E 302 629-9136
Seaford *(G-13208)*

Jcr Enterprises Inc E 302 629-9163
Seaford *(G-13232)*

Karizma Sparks LLC G 302 607-5445
Newark *(G-11143)*

Mountaire Farms Inc C 302 934-1100
Millsboro *(G-8394)*

Mountaire Farms Inc C 302 934-1100
Millsboro *(G-8395)*

Mountaire Farms Inc B 302 988-6200
Selbyville *(G-13581)*

Mountaire of Delmarva Inc E 302 988-6207
Selbyville *(G-13582)*

New B & M Meats Inc F 302 655-5331
Wilmington *(G-18607)*

▼ **Omtron USA LLC** A 302 855-7131
Georgetown *(G-4452)*

Perdue Farms Inc C 302 337-2210
Bridgeville *(G-746)*

Perdue Farms Inc A 302 424-2600
Milford *(G-8046)*

Perdue Farms Incorporated G 302 855-5635
Georgetown *(G-4461)*

Perdue Farms Incorporated G 302 629-3216
Seaford *(G-13343)*

2021 Creamery butter

CD Cream G 302 832-5425
Delaware City *(G-1533)*

2022 Cheese; natural and processed

▲ **Roos Foods Inc** F 302 653-0600
Kenton *(G-5453)*

S
I
C

20 FOOD AND KINDRED PRODUCTS

2023 Dry, condensed, evaporated products

Brainiac Brands USA Inc............................. G 778 869-4099
  Wilmington (G-15037)
Buoy Hydration Inc.................................... G 314 230-5106
  Camden (G-795)
Candelay Industries LLC............................ G 302 696-2464
  Rockland (G-13029)
Codonrx LLC.. G 773 612-5828
  Dover (G-2109)
Golo LLC.. E 302 781-4260
  Newark (G-10864)
Harrock Properties LLC............................. G 302 202-1421
  Dover (G-2657)
Hembal Labs Inc.. G 800 414-4741
  Dover (G-2674)
In10sity Fitness United.............................. G 302 677-1010
  Dover (G-2723)
Kappa Bioscience Usa Inc........................ G 609 201-1459
  Dover (G-2830)
Lifespan Health Science LLC................... G 203 273-4037
  Wilmington (G-17904)
LLC Quick Shield....................................... G 514 730-8040
  Wilmington (G-17956)
Mellon Care Inc.. G 800 406-0281
  Middletown (G-7339)
Miracle Moo LLC.. G 321 948-4678
  Wilmington (G-18385)
Nuchido Inc.. G 314 260-7874
  Wilmington (G-18709)
Rophe Living Inc....................................... G 302 500-9238
  Middletown (G-7523)
▲ Roxlor LLC.. G 302 778-4166
  Wilmington (G-19574)
Skipwith Organics LLC.............................. G 908 573-2930
  Dover (G-3573)
Tc Nutrition Corp....................................... G 306 290-7457
  Wilmington (G-20237)
Tesla Nootropics Inc.................................. G 514 718-2270
  Dover (G-3672)
Tws Chewsy LLC....................................... G 514 730-8040
  Wilmington (G-20472)
Vulcan Wizard LLC.................................... G 914 326-6023
  Lewes (G-6612)
Wellabs Inc... G 816 774-4030
  Dover (G-3829)
Yumi Nutrition Inc..................................... G 917 909-2166
  Newark (G-12424)

2024 Ice cream and frozen deserts

Dana E Herbert... G 302 721-5798
  Bear (G-130)
La Banca... G 302 464-3005
  Middletown (G-7286)

2026 Fluid milk

Dfa Dairy Brands Fluid LLC...................... F 302 398-8321
  Harrington (G-4762)
Hy-Point Dairy Farms Inc......................... C 302 478-1414
  Wilmington (G-17240)
Lechia Inc... G 302 261-5733
  Dover (G-2922)
▲ Roos Foods Inc...................................... F 302 653-0600
  Kenton (G-5453)

2032 Canned specialties

Freakin Fresh Salsa Inc............................. G 302 750-9789
  Wilmington (G-16233)
Mariachi House.. G 302 635-7361
  Hockessin (G-5297)
Patafoods Inc... F 267 981-6411
  Newark (G-11632)

Vincenza & Margherita Bistro................... F 302 479-7999
  Wilmington (G-20625)

2033 Canned fruits and specialties

Denali Canning LLC.................................. G 272 226-6464
  Middletown (G-7054)
Fresh Industries Ltd................................. G 205 737-3747
  Lewes (G-6015)
Longbottom Drinks USA Inc.................... G 302 966-9177
  Wilmington (G-17983)
Loop Mission Corp.................................... E 514 994-7625
  Newark (G-11282)
▲ Mushroom Supply & Services Inc....... G 610 268-0800
  Newark (G-11475)
Produce Spot LLC..................................... F 267 864-1232
  Wilmington (G-19209)
Trisco Foods LLC...................................... D 719 352-3218
  Wilmington (G-20429)

2034 Dehydrated fruits, vegetables, soups

Ajwadates Inc.. G 323 999-1998
  Middletown (G-6846)
Pico Largo LLC.. G 915 710-2375
  Wilmington (G-19034)

2035 Pickles, sauces, and salad dressings

Calima Group LLC..................................... G 443 742-2134
  Wilmington (G-15196)
Kenny Brothers Produce LLC.................. G 302 337-3007
  Bridgeville (G-722)
Rhythm and Heat LLC............................... G 302 897-5259
  Wilmington (G-19462)

2037 Frozen fruits and vegetables

Baby Apron LLC... G 800 796-4406
  Claymont (G-1050)
Egm LLC.. G 302 932-1700
  New Castle (G-9083)
Juiceplus+... G 302 322-2616
  Historic New Castle (G-5013)
Kencko Foods Inc...................................... G 616 253-6256
  Newark (G-11153)
Nowadays Inc Pbc..................................... G 415 279-6802
  Dover (G-3207)
Tridge Trade Inc.. F 954 512-3734
  Dover (G-3726)
United Lemon Sales LLC.......................... F 513 368-6107
  New Castle (G-9654)

2038 Frozen specialties, nec

Baby Apron LLC... G 800 796-4406
  Claymont (G-1050)
◆ H&H Trading International LLC............ G 480 580-3911
  Wilmington (G-17022)
Nicola Pizza Inc... E 302 227-6211
  Lewes (G-6314)
Pictsweet Company................................... D 302 337-8206
  Bridgeville (G-749)

2041 Flour and other grain mill products

Kraft Heinz Company................................ A 302 734-6100
  Dover (G-2886)

2046 Wet corn milling

Milpa Nativa Inc.. G 512 668-9033
  Wilmington (G-18369)
◆ Staley Holdings Inc............................... A 302 793-0289
  Wilmington (G-20007)

2047 Dog and cat food

Petmex Company LLC.............................. G 800 829-4933
  Dover (G-3306)

2048 Prepared feeds, nec

B Diamond Feed Company....................... G 302 697-7576
  Camden Wyoming (G-915)
Best Veterinary Solutions Inc.................. F 302 934-1109
  Millsboro (G-8195)
Bi-State Feeders LLC................................ G 302 398-3408
  Harrington (G-4740)
Green Recovery Tech LLC....................... G 302 317-0062
  Historic New Castle (G-4998)
Jbs Souderton Inc..................................... G 302 629-0725
  Seaford (G-13231)
Natures Rule LLC...................................... G 518 961-5196
  Wilmington (G-18559)
Simmons Animal Nutrition Inc................. F 302 337-8223
  Bridgeville (G-766)
Simmons Animal Nutrition Inc................. D 302 337-5500
  Bridgeville (G-767)
Southern States Coop Inc........................ E 302 732-6651
  Dagsboro (G-1507)
Southern States Coop Inc........................ G 302 629-7991
  Seaford (G-13410)
Springhaus LLC... F 302 397-5261
  Wilmington (G-19977)
Unique Biotech Inc.................................... G 888 478-2799
  Lewes (G-6588)

2051 Bread, cake, and related products

Bevs Crafting Supplies LLC..................... G 302 252-7583
  Historic New Castle (G-4942)
Busymama Cupcakes................................ G 302 259-9988
  Seaford (G-13098)
Cake Sisters... G 302 838-1958
  Delaware City (G-1532)
Cupcake Kouture Bakery LLC................. G 302 602-6058
  Newport (G-12445)
Diane Lacash Inc....................................... G 302 608-2477
  Claymont (G-1118)
Dm KTure LLC.. G 201 892-3028
  Bear (G-172)
Feelz LLC.. G 347 860-5813
  Wilmington (G-16576)
Flawless Inbound LLC.............................. F 929 324-1132
  Dover (G-2514)
Goodbite USA Inc...................................... G 516 761-4386
  Bethany Beach (G-604)
International Food Co LLC....................... G 404 333-3434
  Newark (G-11044)
Kaan Cakes LLC... G 302 260-0647
  Millsboro (G-8335)
Kraft Heinz Company................................ A 302 734-6100
  Dover (G-2886)
Pembina Health Inc................................... F 701 314-7895
  Lewes (G-6359)
Pennsylvania Brand Co............................ G 302 674-5774
  Dover (G-3294)
Posh Cupcake.. G 302 234-4451
  Hockessin (G-5348)
Serpe & Sons Inc....................................... F 302 994-1868
  Wilmington (G-19759)
Signature Intl Foods LLC......................... G 833 463-0004
  Wilmington (G-19821)
Smackerals By Michelle LLC................... G 302 376-8272
  Middletown (G-7575)
Sweet Venom Effect LLC......................... E 302 674-5831
  Wilmington (G-20173)
Sweets By Samantha LLC........................ G 302 740-2218
  Newark (G-12141)
Yumitos LLC... G 704 819-6745
  Lewes (G-6646)

2052 Cookies and crackers

20 FOOD AND KINDRED PRODUCTS

Stauffer Family LLC.................................G..... 302 227-5820
 Rehoboth Beach *(G-12974)*

Supper Solutions LLC............................G..... 302 478-5935
 Wilmington *(G-20148)*

Wellness Natural USA Inc.....................G..... 800 547-5790
 Wilmington *(G-20720)*

2064 Candy and other confectionery products

Candyman Industries Inc......................G..... 970 319-8404
 Lewes *(G-5790)*

Hopes Caramels Inc.............................G..... 302 290-7506
 Wilmington *(G-17200)*

La Vie Chocolat LLC..............................G..... 302 750-4540
 Newark *(G-11210)*

Leiny Snacks...F..... 302 494-2499
 Wilmington *(G-17871)*

Wellness Natural USA Inc.....................G..... 800 547-5790
 Wilmington *(G-20720)*

2066 Chocolate and cocoa products

7th Heaven Inc......................................G..... 201 282-1925
 Wilmington *(G-14150)*

Chocolate Editions Inc..........................G..... 302 479-8400
 Claymont *(G-1085)*

Interntnal Agrclture Prod Grou..............G..... 302 450-2008
 Smyrna *(G-13776)*

Kraft Heinz Company............................A..... 302 734-6100
 Dover *(G-2886)*

◆ United Cocoa Processor Inc.............E..... 302 731-0825
 Newark *(G-12269)*

2068 Salted and roasted nuts and seeds

▲ Sunshine Nut Company LLC............G..... 781 352-7766
 Lewes *(G-6524)*

2077 Animal and marine fats and oils

Horizon Rendering Co Inc......................G..... 302 239-4950
 Wilmington *(G-17208)*

2082 Malt beverages

Chesapeakemaine Trey........................G..... 302 226-3600
 Rehoboth Beach *(G-12671)*

Delaware Beer Works Inc......................E..... 302 836-2739
 Bear *(G-142)*

Dewey Beer & Food Company LLC.......F..... 302 227-1182
 Dewey Beach *(G-1668)*

Dewey Beer Company LLC...................G..... 302 329-9759
 Milton *(G-8603)*

▲ Dogfish Head Craft Brewery LLC......C..... 302 684-1000
 Milton *(G-8610)*

Dogfish Head Inc..................................F..... 302 226-2739
 Rehoboth Beach *(G-12730)*

First State Brewing Co LLC...................E..... 302 285-9535
 Middletown *(G-7131)*

Jakl Beer Works LLC.............................G..... 610 442-0878
 Middletown *(G-7237)*

Volunteer Brewing Company LLC.........G..... 610 721-2836
 Middletown *(G-7694)*

Wilmington Brew Works LLC................F..... 302 757-4971
 Wilmington *(G-20810)*

2083 Malt

Proximity Malt LLC...............................F..... 414 755-8388
 Laurel *(G-5580)*

2084 Wines, brandy, and brandy spirits

Cargimex World LLC.............................G..... 514 701-4224
 Newark *(G-10144)*

◆ Chatam International Incorporated....C..... 302 478-6185
 Wilmington *(G-15347)*

Delaware Meat Company LLC...............G..... 302 438-0252
 Wilmington *(G-15941)*

Harvest Ridge Winery LLC....................G..... 302 250-6583
 Marydel *(G-6799)*

Nassau Vly Vineyards & Winery............G..... 302 645-9463
 Lewes *(G-6306)*

Piceno...G..... 302 545-6406
 Wilmington *(G-19033)*

Pizzadili Partners LLC...........................G..... 302 284-9463
 Felton *(G-4009)*

Rotten Apples Cider Co LLC..................G..... 609 602-7811
 Georgetown *(G-4493)*

Terrance R Hester................................G..... 856 905-8196
 Middletown *(G-7636)*

Texavino LLC..G..... 302 295-0829
 Wilmington *(G-20283)*

Universal Bev Importers LLC................G..... 302 276-0619
 Middletown *(G-7673)*

White Horse Winery..............................G..... 302 388-4850
 Wilmington *(G-20764)*

White Horse Winery LLC.......................G..... 302 472-7200
 Wilmington *(G-20765)*

Wine Worx LLC.....................................E..... 302 436-1500
 Frankford *(G-4161)*

2085 Distilled and blended liquors

Beach Time..G..... 302 644-2850
 Lewes *(G-5743)*

Bear Trap Spirits Inc.............................G..... 302 537-8008
 Millville *(G-8518)*

Breakthru Beverage Group LLC............D..... 302 356-3500
 New Castle *(G-8890)*

◆ Chatam International Incorporated....C..... 302 478-6185
 Wilmington *(G-15347)*

Dogfish Head Companies LLC..............C..... 302 684-1000
 Milton *(G-8609)*

Legacy Distilling LLC............................F..... 302 983-1269
 Smyrna *(G-13799)*

R J Baker Distillery...............................G..... 302 745-0967
 Laurel *(G-5583)*

Titan Spirits LLC...................................G..... 205 568-3338
 Wilmington *(G-20336)*

◆ William Grant & Sons USA Corp.......B..... 302 573-3880
 Wilmington *(G-20791)*

2086 Bottled and canned soft drinks

629 Market Retail LLC..........................G..... 302 691-2100
 Wilmington *(G-14144)*

Dope Venture Studio Inc.......................G..... 302 257-5936
 Dover *(G-2325)*

Food and Bev Innovations LLC.............G..... 302 722-8058
 Wilmington *(G-16681)*

Genki Forest (america) Inc....................F..... 626 456-2664
 Wilmington *(G-16839)*

Global Brands Usa Inc..........................G..... 314 401-2477
 Wilmington *(G-16885)*

Krave Like LLC......................................G..... 302 482-4550
 Wilmington *(G-17752)*

Maurten US Corporation.......................G..... 302 669-9085
 Wilmington *(G-18202)*

Minor Figures Inc..................................G..... 714 875-3449
 Camden *(G-877)*

Moon Shot Energy LLC.........................G..... 512 297-2626
 Lewes *(G-6289)*

Ooso Drinks Co LLC..............................G..... 919 808-7605
 Dover *(G-3235)*

Pepsi-Cola Btlg of Wilmington..............C..... 302 761-4848
 Wilmington *(G-18966)*

Taylor Made Waters Inc........................F..... 302 352-9979
 Wilmington *(G-20234)*

True Spirit Beverage Company.............G..... 520 356-4730
 Wilmington *(G-20444)*

Wize Monkey USA Inc...........................G..... 604 839-7640
 Dover *(G-3863)*

2087 Flavoring extracts and syrups, nec

Baboon Bubble Inc...............................G..... 302 307-2979
 New Castle *(G-8841)*

Bettys...G..... 302 233-2675
 Milford *(G-7793)*

Le Herbe LLC..G..... 949 317-1100
 Wilmington *(G-17842)*

Psychedelic Water Inc..........................G..... 855 337-7924
 Wilmington *(G-19246)*

Trisco Foods LLC..................................D..... 719 352-3218
 Wilmington *(G-20429)*

2091 Canned and cured fish and seafoods

Caveggo Inc..G..... 201 213-4630
 Wilmington *(G-15282)*

2092 Fresh or frozen packaged fish

Arkshell Corporation.............................F..... 917 985-8529
 Claymont *(G-1042)*

Boldy Foods LLC...................................G..... 415 616-2965
 Camden *(G-794)*

Lobster Made Easy Corp.......................G..... 902 818-9958
 Wilmington *(G-17969)*

Steven P Copp......................................G..... 302 645-9112
 Lewes *(G-6511)*

2095 Roasted coffee

Bdb LLC..G..... 469 288-7672
 Wilmington *(G-14797)*

Cofinet LLC...F..... 614 301-8082
 Lewes *(G-5849)*

2096 Potato chips and similar snacks

Fishers Popcorn Fenwick LLC...............E..... 302 539-8833
 Fenwick Island *(G-4050)*

Utz Quality Food Inc.............................G..... 302 266-6982
 Newark *(G-12292)*

Wellness Natural USA Inc.....................G..... 800 547-5790
 Wilmington *(G-20720)*

2097 Manufactured ice

Blue Marlin Ice LLC..............................G..... 302 697-7800
 Dover *(G-1952)*

2099 Food preparations, nec

Actual Veggies LLC...............................G..... 818 825-0531
 Lewes *(G-5659)*

Agventure Inc.......................................G..... 302 992-5940
 Wilmington *(G-14323)*

Cargill Meat Solutions Corp..................E..... 305 826-3699
 Wilmington *(G-15246)*

◆ Carlyle Cocoa Co LLC........................G..... 302 428-3800
 New Castle *(G-8914)*

Danisco USA Inc...................................D..... 866 583-2583
 Wilmington *(G-15788)*

Diyo Inc..G..... 647 354-8859
 Dover *(G-2312)*

Doselva PBC...E..... 510 299-7997
 Dover *(G-2328)*

Fly By Jing Inc......................................F..... 646 875-2465
 Lewes *(G-6005)*

Genco...G..... 302 588-5872
 Claymont *(G-1157)*

Godwits LLC...G..... 424 242-4462
 Wilmington *(G-16907)*

Grub-Busters Grub Bus LLC..................G..... 610 931-9406
 Wilmington *(G-16991)*

Hutzpah Kitchen LLC............................G..... 202 641-2916
 Wilmington *(G-17238)*

20 FOOD AND KINDRED PRODUCTS

Kraft Heinz Company............................ A 302 734-6100
  Dover (G-2886)
Martin Grey LLC.................................... G 302 990-0675
  Lewes (G-6246)
My Red Tea LLC..................................... G 415 259-4166
  Wilmington (G-18509)
Pure Anatolia LLC................................... G 571 660-0007
  Dover (G-3396)
Rosas Diner LLC.................................... G 302 336-8243
  Camden (G-890)
Saratoga Food Specialties LLC............... F 951 270-9600
  Dover (G-3511)
Shore Smoke Seasonings LLC................ G 302 943-4675
  Smyrna (G-13884)
▲ Supreme Trading LLC............................ G 302 415-3188
  Wilmington (G-20159)
Trisco Foods LLC................................... D 719 352-3218
  Wilmington (G-20429)
Vpho... G 302 369-3993
  Newark (G-12338)
Waffles & Wifi LLC.................................. G 267 909-0174
  Newark (G-12343)

22 TEXTILE MILL PRODUCTS

2211 Broadwoven fabric mills, cotton

Authentik Chick...................................... G 267 815-4132
  Wilmington (G-14649)
Boa Financial LLC.................................. G 888 444-5371
  Dover (G-1956)
C and C Alpaca Factory......................... G 609 752-7894
  Lewes (G-5785)
Classic Canvas LLC............................... G 443 359-0150
  Delmar (G-1580)
Coolpop Nation...................................... G 302 584-8833
  Wilmington (G-15631)
Dejour Reign CL & AP Co LLC............... G 302 981-2568
  New Castle (G-9010)
Eanerep Holdings LLC........................... G 888 837-2685
  Dover (G-2405)
H D Lee Company Inc............................ G 302 477-3930
  Wilmington (G-17018)
Japan Modern Art LLC........................... G 832 458-1536
  Dover (G-2771)
Keiths Boat Canvas............................... G 302 841-8081
  Georgetown (G-4392)
Pointe Snaps... G 260 602-0898
  Wilmington (G-19102)
Printify Inc... G 415 978-6351
  Wilmington (G-19197)
Selfx Innovations Inc............................. D 551 277-9665
  Wilmington (G-19745)
Spunkchild LLC...................................... F 917 504-4529
  Middletown (G-7595)
Threads N Denims................................. G 302 678-0642
  Dover (G-3681)
Uncorked Canvas Parties....................... G 302 724-7625
  Dover (G-3748)
Vertical Blind Factory Inc....................... G 302 998-9616
  Wilmington (G-20598)

2221 Broadwoven fabric mills, manmade

Baker Safety Equipment Inc.................. G 302 376-9302
  Bear (G-55)
Chester Ross.. G 267 461-1568
  New Castle (G-8933)
Lycra Company LLC.............................. B 302 731-6800
  Newark (G-11298)

2241 Narrow fabric mills

Ay Tech LLC.. G 302 861-6610
  Newark (G-9960)

Conlin Corporation................................ G 302 633-9174
  Wilmington (G-15597)
Wayne Industries Inc............................ G 302 478-6160
  Wilmington (G-20694)

2252 Hosiery, nec

Heated Wear LLC.................................. G 347 510-7965
  Wilmington (G-17109)

2253 Knit outerwear mills

Flapdoodles Inc.................................... D 302 731-9793
  Newark (G-10750)

2254 Knit underwear mills

Ginch Gonch Corp.................................. G 713 240-9900
  Newark (G-10837)
Lumia Home LLC................................... F 516 373-5269
  Lewes (G-6228)

2258 Lace and warp knit fabric mills

Moore Ltd.. G 302 427-5760
  Wilmington (G-18435)

2261 Finishing plants, cotton

Carter Printing and Design.................... G 302 655-2343
  Historic New Castle (G-4952)
D By D Printing LLC............................... G 302 659-3373
  Dover (G-2180)
James Thompson & Company Inc.......... E 302 349-4501
  Greenwood (G-4644)

2262 Finishing plants, manmade

Abbott Dynamics LLC............................ G 951 923-5996
  Talleyville (G-13944)

2269 Finishing plants, nec

James Thompson & Company Inc.......... E 302 349-4501
  Greenwood (G-4644)

2273 Carpets and rugs

Bentley Mills Inc................................... G 800 423-4709
  Wilmington (G-14840)
Indo Foreign Trade Craft LLC................ E 818 927-2872
  Newark (G-11014)
Josephine Keir Limited.......................... G 302 422-0270
  Milford (G-7960)
Kurtz Collection.................................... G 302 654-0442
  Wilmington (G-17767)
Maneto Inc.. E 302 656-4285
  Wilmington (G-18103)
Storyboards Inc.................................... G 214 272-0222
  Newark (G-12103)
Vivid Colors Carpet LLC........................ G 302 335-3933
  Frederica (G-4187)

2282 Throwing and winding mills

Hempville Inc.. G 336 862-0107
  Middletown (G-7205)

2297 Nonwoven fabrics

Dow Chemical Company........................ E 302 368-4169
  Newark (G-10558)

2298 Cordage and twine

Eidp Inc.. G 302 773-6287
  Wilmington (G-16327)

2299 Textile goods, nec

Be Blessed Design Group LLC.............. G 302 561-3793
  Bear (G-59)
◆ Fibre Processing Corporation............... D 302 654-3659
  Wilmington (G-16597)

Garage... G 302 453-1930
  Newark (G-10807)
Hodges International Inc....................... G 310 874-8516
  Dover (G-2685)
Oilminers Cbd LLC................................. G 484 885-9417
  Newark (G-11582)
Szovet & Co LLC.................................... G 908 656-5114
  Dover (G-3636)

23 APPAREL, FINISHED PRODUCTS FROM FABRICS & SIMILAR MATERIALS

2311 Men's and boy's suits and coats

Boa Financial LLC.................................. G 888 444-5371
  Dover (G-1956)
Cross Over Camo LLC........................... G 302 798-1898
  Claymont (G-1104)
Zuhatrend LLC....................................... G 302 883-2656
  Dover (G-3908)

2321 Men's and boy's furnishings

Lee Bell Inc... F 302 477-3930
  Wilmington (G-17853)

2323 Men's and boy's neckwear

Aptustech LLC....................................... G 347 254-5619
  Wilmington (G-14516)

2325 Men's and boy's trousers and slacks

Blue Mountain Apparel La LLC.............. G 646 787-5679
  Newark (G-10062)
Lee Bell Inc... F 302 477-3930
  Wilmington (G-17853)
True Religion Apparel Inc...................... G 302 894-9425
  Newark (G-12241)

2326 Men's and boy's work clothing

Nixon Uniform Service Inc.................... C 302 325-2875
  Historic New Castle (G-5040)
South Paxon LLC................................... G 302 918-5226
  Newark (G-12060)

2329 Men's and boy's clothing, nec

Avier Unltd LLC..................................... G 909 436-6964
  Middletown (G-6891)
Carpediem Health LLC.......................... G 347 467-4444
  Dover (G-2031)
Gemini Kustoms LLC............................. G 267 318-4121
  New Castle (G-9160)
Gmw Haberdashery LLC....................... G 718 864-7817
  Dover (G-2598)
Heated Wear LLC.................................. G 347 510-7965
  Wilmington (G-17109)
◆ Huzala Inc.. G 313 404-6941
  Newark (G-10987)
Kha-Neke Inc.. G 302 440-4728
  Newark (G-11168)
Lee Bell Inc... F 302 477-3930
  Wilmington (G-17853)
▲ Majdell Group USA Inc........................ G 302 722-8223
  Newark (G-11316)
Oluwaseyi David Popoola...................... G 302 331-3684
  Dover (G-3221)

2331 Women's and misses' blouses and shirts

Janice James & Joan LLC..................... G 845 682-1886
  Newark (G-11096)

2335 Women's, junior's, and misses' dresses
Arcangel Inc................................. G 347 771-0789
  Wilmington (G-14539)

2339 Women's and misses' outerwear, nec
Body Double Swimwear.................. G 302 537-1444
  Selbyville (G-13479)
Carpediem Health LLC................... G 347 467-4444
  Dover (G-2031)
City Theater Co Inc........................ G 302 831-2206
  Newark (G-10246)
Lee Bell Inc................................... F 302 477-3930
  Wilmington (G-17853)
Mommin With Swag LLC.................. G 302 373-6316
  Newark (G-11439)
Moxie Apparel Inc........................... F 844 894-1435
  Wilmington (G-18468)
True Religion Apparel Inc................ G 302 894-9425
  Newark (G-12241)

2341 Women's and children's underwear
Perteh... G 302 200-0912
  Wilmington (G-18991)
Victorias Secret Stores LLC............. G 302 644-1035
  Rehoboth Beach (G-13003)

2353 Hats, caps, and millinery
Vannies Hats.................................. G 302 765-7094
  New Castle (G-9666)

2361 Girl's and children's dresses, blouses
Carters Inc.................................... G 302 731-1432
  Newark (G-10156)
TT Luxury Group LLC...................... G 732 242-9795
  Newark (G-12243)

2369 Girl's and children's outerwear, nec

2381 Fabric dress and work gloves
Kaul Glove and Mfg Co.................... D 302 292-2660
  Historic New Castle (G-5014)
Masley Enterprises Inc.................... E 302 427-9885
  Wilmington (G-18183)

2385 Waterproof outerwear
Neilsen Clothing Inc....................... G 302 342-1370
  Dover (G-3167)

2389 Apparel and accessories, nec
Advacare LLC................................. G 302 448-5045
  Wilmington (G-14263)
DCB Apparel LLC............................ G 267 473-0895
  Newark (G-10394)
Ewe-Nited States of Fiber................ G 302 690-5084
  Newark (G-10680)
Faithful Servant Inc........................ G 302 597-6387
  Dover (G-2480)
G2 Performance Band ACC.............. G 800 554-8523
  Wilmington (G-16787)
John M Cooper Reverand.................. G 302 684-8639
  Lewes (G-6145)
Liberated World LLC....................... G 347 688-4943
  Dover (G-2933)
Mymoroccanbazar Inc...................... G 323 238-5747
  Newark (G-11478)
Nagorka.. G 302 537-2392
  Bethany Beach (G-622)
Roo Official LLC............................. G 267 614-2811
  Dover (G-3483)
Serrano Inc.................................... G 302 607-1779
  Newark (G-11982)

▲ Shaker Revolution LLC.................. G 302 219-4838
  Wilmington (G-19777)

2391 Curtains and draperies
Barlows Upholstery Inc.................... G 302 655-3955
  Wilmington (G-14766)
G L K Inc....................................... F 302 697-3838
  Dover (G-2551)

2392 Household furnishings, nec
▲ Bethany Resort Furn Whse............ G 302 251-4101
  Selbyville (G-13476)
Bethrant Industries LLC................... G 484 343-5435
  New Castle (G-8864)
G L K Inc....................................... F 302 697-3838
  Dover (G-2551)
Villa Cotton Corporation.................. F 302 439-1508
  Wilmington (G-20619)

2393 Textile bags
▲ Vanguard Manufacturing Inc.......... G 302 994-9302
  Wilmington (G-20569)

2394 Canvas and related products
Callaway Furniture Inc.................... G 302 398-8858
  Harrington (G-4745)
E W Brown Inc................................ G 302 652-6612
  Wilmington (G-16241)
Gainor Awnings Inc........................ G 302 998-8611
  Wilmington (G-16793)
Tee Pees From Rattlesnks................ G 302 654-0709
  Wilmington (G-20262)

2395 Pleating and stitching
A Nod To Stella Embroidery............. G 302 697-6308
  Wyoming (G-20979)
A Stitch In Time............................. G 302 395-1306
  New Castle (G-8751)
Actors Attic................................... G 302 734-8214
  Dover (G-1714)
Andrew Pipon................................. G 949 337-2249
  Milford (G-7768)
Creative Embroidery Inc.................. G 302 661-7313
  Wilmington (G-15691)
Five Stars Embroidery..................... G 443 466-9692
  Middletown (G-7136)
Flutterby Stitches & EMB................. G 302 531-7784
  Dover (G-2520)
In A Stitch.................................... G 302 678-2260
  Dover (G-2722)
Initially Yours Inc........................... G 302 999-0562
  Wilmington (G-17341)
Just One Embroiderer..................... G 302 832-9655
  Bear (G-317)
Kitschy Stitch................................ G 302 200-9889
  Lewes (G-6168)
Lids Corporation............................ G 302 736-8465
  Dover (G-2939)
Penny Cooper Sportswear & EMB...... G 302 325-3710
  New Castle (G-9465)
Pineapple Stitchery........................ G 302 500-8050
  Georgetown (G-4466)
Rwm Embroidery & More LLC........... G 302 653-8384
  Smyrna (G-13874)
Signature Stitches.......................... G 302 736-6500
  Dover (G-3556)
Stamford Screen Printing Inc........... G 302 654-2442
  Wilmington (G-20008)
Stitch-Stash LLC............................ G 302 227-1943
  Rehoboth Beach (G-12975)
T&T Custom Embroidery Inc............ G 302 420-9454
  Bear (G-522)

Whisman John................................ G 302 530-1676
  Wilmington (G-20761)

2396 Automotive and apparel trimmings
Atlantic Sun Screen Prtg Inc............ F 302 731-5100
  Newark (G-9936)
Be Blessed Design Group LLC.......... G 302 561-3793
  Bear (G-59)
Delaware Dept Hlth Social Svcs........ D 302 255-9800
  New Castle (G-9020)
Delaware Screen Printing Inc........... G 302 378-4231
  Middletown (G-7044)
Elwyn Pennsylvania and Del............. D 302 658-8860
  Wilmington (G-16382)
First State Manufacturing Inc........... D 302 424-4520
  Milford (G-7896)
Jairus Enterprises Inc..................... G 302 834-1625
  Bear (G-296)
Kayava Creations LLC..................... G 302 430-2231
  Seaford (G-13245)
Lasting Impression Inc A................. G 302 762-9200
  Wilmington (G-17815)
New Process Fibre Company............ D 302 349-4535
  Greenwood (G-4657)
Original Tube T Shirt Com............... G 845 291-7031
  Seaford (G-13327)
Red Sun Custom Apparel Inc........... F 302 988-8230
  Selbyville (G-13597)
Unique Image LLC......................... E 302 658-2266
  Wilmington (G-20519)
Whisman John................................ G 302 530-1676
  Wilmington (G-20761)

2399 Fabricated textile products, nec
Crochet Creations By Debbie............ G 302 287-2462
  Wilmington (G-15708)
◆ Custom Decor Inc......................... F 302 735-7600
  Dover (G-2174)
Fairway Manufacturing Company...... F 302 398-4630
  Harrington (G-4768)
Goodblue Inc.................................. G 801 755-5301
  Dover (G-2605)
Nina Woof LLC............................... G 210 492-6617
  Dover (G-3190)

24 LUMBER AND WOOD PRODUCTS, EXCEPT FURNITURE

2411 Logging
D&C Logging.................................. G 302 846-3982
  Delmar (G-1586)
High Vue Logging Inc...................... G 302 697-3606
  Camden (G-851)
Summers Logging LLC..................... G 302 234-8725
  Hockessin (G-5395)
Whitetail Country Log & Hlg............. G 302 846-3982
  Delmar (G-1656)

2421 Sawmills and planing mills, general
Byler Sawmill................................. G 302 730-4208
  Dover (G-2002)
Gordys Lumber Inc......................... F 302 875-3502
  Laurel (G-5524)
Grubb Lumber Company Inc............. E 302 652-2800
  Wilmington (G-16992)
Swartzentruber Sawmill Co.............. G 302 492-1665
  Hartly (G-4909)
Woodchuck Enterprises Inc.............. G 302 239-8336
  Hockessin (G-5430)

2426 Hardwood dimension and flooring mills

24 LUMBER AND WOOD PRODUCTS, EXCEPT FURNITURE

Agile Coliving Systems LLC............... F 310 980-0644
  Dover (G-1741)
Delmarva Hardwood Products Inc........ F 302 349-4101
  Laurel (G-5497)
Gordys Lumber Inc............................ F 302 875-3502
  Laurel (G-5524)
Grubb Lumber Company Inc............... E 302 652-2800
  Wilmington (G-16992)
Hardwood Direct LLC......................... G 302 378-3692
  Middletown (G-7196)
Old Wood & Co LLC........................... F 302 684-3600
  Harbeson (G-4710)
Stark Truss Company Inc.................... F 302 368-8566
  Newark (G-12090)

2431 Millwork

Aderyn Woodworks............................ G 219 229-5070
  New Castle (G-8763)
Aldas Refinishing Company................. G 302 528-5028
  Hockessin (G-5119)
Allmark Door Company LLC................ F 302 323-4999
  New Castle (G-8786)
Atlantic Aluminum Products Inc.......... D 302 349-9091
  Greenwood (G-4592)
Bancroft Carpentry Company.............. G 302 655-3434
  Wilmington (G-14737)
Brandywine Mill Work......................... G 302 652-3008
  Wilmington (G-15073)
Craigs Woodworks LLC....................... G 302 998-4201
  Selbyville (G-13508)
Daniel A Yoder................................... G 302 730-4076
  Dover (G-2191)
Delaware Millwork.............................. G 302 376-8324
  Middletown (G-7043)
Doug Green Woodworking................... G 302 652-6522
  Wilmington (G-16154)
▲ Dover Millwork Inc.......................... F 302 349-5070
  Harrington (G-4764)
Espositos Woodworking & Cnstr.......... G 302 245-5474
  Milton (G-8621)
Frankford Custom Woodworks Inc....... G 302 732-9570
  Frankford (G-4108)
Group Three Inc................................. G 302 658-4158
  Wilmington (G-16988)
Grubb Lumber Company Inc................ G 302 652-2800
  Wilmington (G-16992)
Johns Woodworking LLC..................... G 302 492-3527
  Hartly (G-4884)
Lanning Woodworks............................ G 302 353-4726
  Wilmington (G-17805)
Lulla Woodworking LLC....................... G 302 841-8800
  Ocean View (G-12541)
Mary Costas Woodworking.................. G 302 227-6255
  Rehoboth Beach (G-12851)
Mastermark Woodworking Inc............. G 302 945-9131
  Millsboro (G-8369)
Monge Woodworking LLC.................... G 302 455-0175
  Newark (G-11442)
New Look Home Inc........................... G 302 994-4397
  Wilmington (G-18622)
OBryan Woodworks............................. G 302 398-8202
  Harrington (G-4807)
ONeill Woodworking LLC..................... G 443 669-3458
  Lewes (G-6336)
Peirce James Townsend III.................. G 302 449-2279
  Middletown (G-7438)
Pinnacle Garage Door Co LLC............. G 302 505-4531
  Frederica (G-4180)
Richard Hrrmann Strbilders Inc........... G 302 654-4329
  Wilmington (G-19469)
Saienni Stairs LLC.............................. E 302 292-2699
  Newark (G-11934)

Tj Custom Woodworks Inc................... G 302 563-8535
  Newark (G-12200)
Wolf Wood Works LLC........................ G 302 275-7227
  Wilmington (G-20875)
Woodworks.. G 302 995-0800
  Wilmington (G-20889)
Wyoming Millwork Co......................... G 302 684-3150
  Milton (G-8732)
Wyoming Millwork Co......................... E 302 697-8650
  Camden (G-899)

2434 Wood kitchen cabinets

At Home Cabinetry & Design LLC....... G 302 853-5305
  Milford (G-7773)
Atlantic Cabinetry Corporation........... F 302 644-1407
  Lewes (G-5713)
Bancroft Carpentry Company.............. G 302 655-3434
  Wilmington (G-14737)
Cabinets To Go LLC........................... G 302 439-4989
  Claymont (G-1069)
Cedar Creek Cstm Cabinets LLC......... G 302 542-7794
  Milford (G-7814)
Coastal Cabinetry LLC....................... F 302 542-4155
  Seaford (G-13126)
Countertop Shop LLC......................... G 302 654-0700
  Wilmington (G-15656)
Culiquip LLC...................................... E 302 654-4974
  Wilmington (G-15732)
Custom Cabinet Shop Inc................... F 302 337-8241
  Greenwood (G-4609)
Diamond State Cabinetry.................... G 302 250-3531
  Millsboro (G-8271)
Driftwood Cabinetry LLC.................... G 302 645-4876
  Lewes (G-5936)
East Coast Cstm Cabinetry LLC......... G 302 245-3040
  Georgetown (G-4302)
Michael A OBrien & Sons................... G 302 994-2894
  Wilmington (G-18306)
Moores Cabinet Refinishing Inc.......... G 302 378-3055
  Middletown (G-7380)
Nardi Cabinetry LLC........................... G 302 945-7918
  Millsboro (G-8400)
Phippins Cabinetry............................. G 302 212-2189
  Rehoboth Beach (G-12890)
Stones and Cabinets City LLC............ G 302 729-4201
  New Castle (G-9596)
Sylvester Custom Cabinetry............... G 302 398-6050
  Harrington (G-4838)
Taylor Woodworks.............................. G 302 745-2049
  Dover (G-3655)
Toms Cabinet Shop Inc...................... G 302 258-6285
  Bridgeville (G-775)
Walnut Grove Cabinets LLC................ G 302 678-2694
  Dover (G-3818)
Zenith Products................................. G 302 322-2190
  Historic New Castle (G-5105)
◆ Zwd Products Corporation.............. B 302 326-8200
  Historic New Castle (G-5106)

2435 Hardwood veneer and plywood

Maneto Inc.. E 302 656-4285
  Wilmington (G-18103)

2439 Structural wood members, nec

Delmarva Truss and Panel LLC........... G 302 270-8888
  Wyoming (G-20984)
Sam Yoder and Son LLC.................... C 302 398-4711
  Greenwood (G-4666)
Stark Truss Company Inc.................... G 302 337-9470
  Bridgeville (G-769)
Stark Truss Company Inc.................... F 302 368-8566
  Newark (G-12090)

SIC SECTION

2441 Nailed wood boxes and shook

Elwyn Pennsylvania and Del............... D 302 658-8860
  Wilmington (G-16382)

2448 Wood pallets and skids

1st State Pallets LLC......................... G 302 743-3993
  Newark (G-9704)
Greenwood Pallet Co......................... G 302 337-8181
  Bridgeville (G-705)
Rcd Timber Products Inc................... G 302 384-6243
  New Castle (G-9513)
Rcd Timber Products Inc................... G 302 778-5700
  New Castle (G-9512)
Stephens Enterprises Inc.................. G 302 629-0322
  Seaford (G-13413)

2449 Wood containers, nec

H&H Customs Inc.............................. G 302 378-0810
  Middletown (G-7187)

2451 Mobile homes

Atlantic Realty Management.............. G 302 629-0770
  Seaford (G-13073)
Hippo Trailer.................................... G 302 854-6661
  Georgetown (G-4357)
Ictclean Inc...................................... F 315 216-5121
  Wilmington (G-17261)

2452 Prefabricated wood buildings

Beracah Homes Inc............................ E 302 349-4561
  Greenwood (G-4597)
Cool Branch Associates LLC.............. G 302 629-5363
  Laurel (G-5486)
Fox Pointe....................................... G 302 744-9442
  Dover (G-2530)
Great Outdoor Cottages LLC............. F 215 760-4971
  Georgetown (G-4346)
Henlopen Homes Inc......................... G 302 684-0860
  Lewes (G-6089)
Howard M Joseph Inc........................ G 302 335-1300
  Milford (G-7936)
Simpsons Log Homes Inc................... G 302 674-1900
  Dover (G-3566)

2491 Wood preserving

Glory Contracting............................. G 302 275-5430
  Townsend (G-14008)
Kustom Additions LLC....................... G 302 468-6865
  Wilmington (G-17769)
Wood Expressions Incorporated......... G 302 738-6189
  Newark (G-12401)

2493 Reconstituted wood products

Jcr Systems LLC................................ G 302 420-6072
  Historic New Castle (G-5010)
Southside Construction LLC............... G 302 500-9268
  Bear (G-502)

2499 Wood products, nec

Artisan Woodworks LLC..................... G 302 841-5182
  Harbeson (G-4683)
Bally Holding Company Delaware....... G 610 845-7511
  Wilmington (G-14725)
Carol Boyd Heron.............................. G 302 645-0551
  Lewes (G-5803)
Carspecken-Scott Inc........................ G 302 762-7955
  Wilmington (G-15260)
Cedar Neck Decor LLC...................... G 918 497-7179
  Dagsboro (G-1424)
Custom Framers Inc.......................... F 302 684-5377
  Harbeson (G-4694)

Delaware Animal Products LLC.............. G ..... 302 423-7754 Milford (G-7851)	Mattress Firm Milford................... G ..... 302 422-6585 Milford (G-7990)	**2611 Pulp mills**
Harvest Consumer Products LLC............. D ..... 302 732-6624 Dagsboro (G-1460)	Moving Club LLC.................... G ..... 929 377-9332 New Castle (G-9384)	Eco Plastic Products Del Inc................ F ..... 302 575-9227 Wilmington (G-16282)
Hillandale Farms Delaware Inc........... E ..... 302 492-3644 Hartly (G-4878)	Rattan Company Inc.................. G ..... 302 226-2404 Rehoboth Beach (G-12905)	Penco Corporation................... G ..... 302 629-7911 Seaford (G-13332)
J R Brooks Custom Framing LLC........... G ..... 302 538-3637 Felton (G-3988)	**2521 Wood office furniture**	Revolution Recovery Del LLC............. E ..... 302 356-3000 New Castle (G-9527)
Jdjs LLC........................ E ..... 844 967-3748 Georgetown (G-4380)	Corporate Interiors Inc................ F ..... 800 690-9101 New Castle (G-8973)	Sodra Cell USA Inc.................. G ..... 503 855-3032 Wilmington (G-19912)
Kenco Trophy Sales................. G ..... 302 846-3339 Delmar (G-1610)	▲ Corporate Interiors Inc............... D ..... 302 322-1008 New Castle (G-8974)	**2621 Paper mills**
Kustom Additions LLC............... G ..... 302 468-6865 Wilmington (G-17769)	Elevation Office Furn LLC.............. F ..... 267 261-0124 Wilmington (G-16359)	Action Unlimited Resources Inc........... E ..... 302 323-1455 Historic New Castle (G-4919)
Lempat Foods LLC.................. G ..... 914 449-1803 Dover (G-2928)	Heirloom Creations.................. G ..... 302 659-1817 Smyrna (G-13758)	Deadcow Computers................. G ..... 302 239-5974 Newark (G-10400)
Nanticoke Industries LLC.............. G ..... 302 245-8825 Seaford (G-13306)	**2522 Office furniture, except wood**	Henninger Printing Co Inc.............. G ..... 302 934-8119 Millsboro (G-8317)
Rodney Pratt Framing Gallery............ G ..... 302 593-6108 Historic New Castle (G-5060)	Coffeedge Inc.................... G ..... 585 294-2726 Middletown (G-7001)	Oxypaper Inc..................... B ..... 302 202-4897 Dover (G-3256)
Stockley Materials LLC............... F ..... 302 856-7601 Georgetown (G-4526)	Hirsh Industries Inc................. G ..... 302 678-3456 Dover (G-2682)	**2653 Corrugated and solid fiber boxes**
Urban Dweller.................... G ..... 973 402-7400 Milton (G-8724)	**2531 Public building and related furniture**	True-Pack Ltd.................... F ..... 302 326-2222 New Castle (G-9644)
◆ Vulcan International Corp............. F ..... 302 428-3181 Wilmington (G-20658)	Acorn Site Furnishings................ G ..... 302 249-4979 Bridgeville (G-661)	**2656 Sanitary food containers**
WI Timbers Inc................... G ..... 843 376-1099 Wilmington (G-20869)	Clarios LLC..................... C ..... 302 996-0309 New Castle (G-8952)	Rennies Rolled Ice Cream LLC............ G ..... 551 273-8925 New Castle (G-9521)
25 FURNITURE AND FIXTURES	Johnson Controls Inc................. F ..... 302 715-5208 Delmar (G-1608)	Solo Cup Operating Corporation.......... B ..... 800 248-5960 New Castle (G-9577)
2511 Wood household furniture	Tangtring Seating Tech USA LLC........... G ..... 269 365-4030 Wilmington (G-20219)	**2671 Paper; coated and laminated packaging**
Brandywine Valley Woodworking........... G ..... 302 743-5640 Wilmington (G-15091)	Turning Point Collection LLC............. G ..... 302 275-0167 Wilmington (G-20464)	Derprosa Spclty Films USA LLC........... G ..... 856 845-7524 Wilmington (G-16021)
Fairwood Corporation................ A ..... 302 884-6749 Wilmington (G-16530)	**2541 Wood partitions and fixtures**	Mercantile Press Inc................. F ..... 302 764-6884 Wilmington (G-18274)
Group Three Inc.................. G ..... 302 658-4158 Wilmington (G-16988)	3-D Fabrications Inc................. E ..... 302 292-3501 Newark (G-9707)	Oxypaper Inc..................... B ..... 302 202-4897 Dover (G-3256)
Kenton Chair Shop.................. F ..... 302 653-2411 Clayton (G-1381)	Cabinetry Unlimited LLC.............. E ..... 302 436-5030 Selbyville (G-13489)	Printpack Inc.................... C ..... 302 323-4000 New Castle (G-9495)
Mtb Artisans LLC.................. G ..... 303 475-9024 Wilmington (G-18480)	Counterparts LLC................. G ..... 302 349-0400 Greenwood (G-4605)	▲ Unique Fabricating Na Inc............. A ..... 248 853-2333 Wilmington (G-20518)
Quilted Heirlooms.................. G ..... 302 354-6061 Middletown (G-7492)	Michael A OBrien & Sons............... G ..... 302 994-2894 Wilmington (G-18306)	Zacros America Inc................. C ..... 302 391-2200 Newark (G-12429)
Slice of Wood LLC................. G ..... 315 335-0917 Delaware City (G-1558)	Solid Image Inc................... E ..... 302 877-0901 Laurel (G-5603)	**2672 Paper; coated and laminated, nec**
2512 Upholstered household furniture	**2542 Partitions and fixtures, except wood**	Mercantile Press Inc................. F ..... 302 764-6884 Wilmington (G-18274)
Barlows Upholstery Inc................ G ..... 302 655-3955 Wilmington (G-14766)	▲ J and J Display.................. G ..... 302 628-4190 Seaford (G-13227)	Oxypaper Inc..................... B ..... 302 202-4897 Dover (G-3256)
Fairwood Corporation................ A ..... 302 884-6749 Wilmington (G-16530)	Perry Enterprise LLC................ G ..... 302 505-4458 Dover (G-3301)	▲ The Crowell Corporation.............. D ..... 302 998-0558 Wilmington (G-20291)
2514 Metal household furniture	**2591 Drapery hardware and blinds and shades**	**2673 Bags: plastic, laminated, and coated**
Pony Run Kitchens LLC.............. G ..... 302 492-3006 Hartly (G-4903)	Local Vertical.................... G ..... 302 242-2552 Dover (G-2968)	Castle Bag Company................. G ..... 302 656-1001 Wilmington (G-15266)
◆ Zwd Products Corporation............. B ..... 302 326-8200 Historic New Castle (G-5106)	Vertical Blind Factory Inc.............. G ..... 302 998-9616 Wilmington (G-20598)	▲ Grayling Industries Inc.............. F ..... 770 751-9095 Frederica (G-4168)
2515 Mattresses and bedsprings	Window Treatments & More LLC.......... G ..... 302 275-7019 Wilmington (G-20857)	Ingenious Inventions AG LLC............ G ..... 818 578-8266 Wilmington (G-17334)
▲ Design Specific US Inc............... G ..... 650 318-6473 Wilmington (G-16026)	**2599 Furniture and fixtures, nec**	JEB Plastics Inc................... G ..... 302 479-9223 Wilmington (G-17513)
Plushbeds Inc.................... G ..... 888 758-7423 Wilmington (G-19082)	Cubic Products LLC................ G ..... 781 990-3886 Wilmington (G-15731)	Long Life Food Safety Pdts LLC........... G ..... 302 229-1207 Lewes (G-6218)
2517 Wood television and radio cabinets	Superior Luxe LLC................. G ..... 800 325-6262 Wilmington (G-20142)	Printpack Inc.................... C ..... 302 323-4000 New Castle (G-9495)
Jordan Cabinetry & WD Turning........... G ..... 302 792-1009 Claymont (G-1200)	**26 PAPER AND ALLIED PRODUCTS**	Richard Earl Fisher................. G ..... 302 598-1957 Wilmington (G-19468)
2519 Household furniture, nec		Toyo Fibre USA Inc................. G ..... 302 475-3699 Wilmington (G-20379)
Borne Legacy Logistics LLC............. G ..... 609 346-0380 New Castle (G-8876)		**2674 Bags: uncoated paper and multiwall**

Employee Codes: A=Over 500 employees, B=251-500
C=101-250, D=51-100, E=20-50, F=10-19, G=1-9

2024 Harris Directory of
Delaware Businesses

26 PAPER AND ALLIED PRODUCTS

Oxypaper Inc... B 302 202-4897
  Dover (G-3256)

2675 Die-cut paper and board

Cann-Erikson Bindery Inc.......................... F 302 995-6636
  Wilmington (G-15216)
Prescotech Inc.. D 502 585-5866
  Wilmington (G-19178)

2676 Sanitary paper products

Best Periodt LLC.. G 302 291-2275
  Dover (G-1916)
BETz&betz Enterprises LLC...................... G 302 602-0613
  Wilmington (G-14865)
Docs Medical LLC...................................... G 301 401-1489
  Bear (G-175)
Edgewell Personal Care LLC..................... E 302 678-6000
  Dover (G-2422)
Edgewell Personal Care Company............ A 302 678-6191
  Dover (G-2423)
Playtex Manufacturing Inc........................ D 302 678-6000
  Dover (G-3336)
Procter & Gamble Paper Pdts Co............. A 302 678-2600
  Dover (G-3376)
Sassy Kitty and Lash Spa LLC.................. G 443 983-1125
  Newark (G-11952)
Socal Auto Supply Inc............................... F 818 717-9982
  Lewes (G-6485)

2679 Converted paper products, nec

K&B Investors LLC..................................... G 302 357-9723
  Wilmington (G-17631)

27 PRINTING, PUBLISHING AND ALLIED INDUSTRIES

2711 Newspapers

Cape Gazette Ltd...................................... E 302 645-7700
  Lewes (G-5794)
Coastal Point.. F 302 539-1788
  Ocean View (G-12493)
Community Publications Inc..................... F 302 239-4644
  Middletown (G-7004)
County Women S Journal......................... G 302 236-1435
  Lewes (G-5865)
Dover Post Co Inc..................................... G 302 378-9531
  Dover (G-2363)
Dover Post Co Inc..................................... D 302 653-2083
  Dover (G-2362)
Dover Post Inc.. G 304 222-6025
  Milford (G-7871)
First State Press LLC................................. G 302 731-9058
  Newark (G-10737)
Gatehouse Media Inc................................ E 302 678-3616
  Dover (G-2564)
Hearst Media Services Conn LLC.............. E 203 330-6231
  Wilmington (G-17103)
High Tide News.. G 302 727-0390
  Selbyville (G-13546)
Hoy En Delaware LLC................................ G 302 854-0240
  Georgetown (G-4366)
Independent Newsmedia Inc USA............. E 302 674-3600
  Dover (G-2728)
Independent Newsmedia Inc USA............. G 302 422-1200
  Milford (G-7941)
▲ Independent Newsmedia Inc USA......... D 302 674-3600
  Dover (G-2729)
Info Titan LLC... G 510 495-4117
  Dover (G-2731)
Ini Holdings Inc... G 302 674-3600
  Dover (G-2734)

John T Tedesco... G 703 357-0797
  Georgetown (G-4385)
L E York Law LLC...................................... G 302 234-8338
  Wilmington (G-17776)
Middletown De.. G 302 449-2547
  Middletown (G-7349)
Middletown De.. G 302 655-9494
  Middletown (G-7350)
Morning Report Research Inc.................... G 302 730-3793
  Dover (G-3123)
Morning Star Publications Inc................... F 302 629-9788
  Seaford (G-13289)
News-Journal Company............................ C 302 324-2500
  New Castle (G-9417)
Renegade Entrmt & Media Co................... F 904 789-2897
  Middletown (G-7513)
Review... E 302 831-2771
  Newark (G-11874)
Spark... G 302 324-2203
  New Castle (G-9584)
Sussex Post.. G 302 629-5505
  Milford (G-8110)
Whitner House Publishing LLC................... G 267 338-9741
  Smyrna (G-13937)
Wilmington Trust Sp Services................... A 302 427-7650
  Wilmington (G-20849)

2721 Periodicals

AB Creative Publishing LLC....................... G 202 802-6909
  Wilmington (G-14190)
Action Enterprise Inc................................ G 302 537-7223
  Fenwick Island (G-4039)
Advance Magazine Publs Inc..................... G 302 830-4630
  Wilmington (G-14267)
Boldlatina Digital Group Pbc..................... G 415 754-0143
  Dover (G-1960)
Business History Conference.................... G 302 658-2400
  Wilmington (G-15157)
CIO Story LLC... G 408 915-5559
  Wilmington (G-15442)
Conde Nast International Inc.................... C 515 243-3273
  Wilmington (G-15587)
Crafts Report Publishing Co...................... G 302 656-2209
  Wilmington (G-15680)
Delaware Beach Life.................................. F 302 227-9499
  Rehoboth Beach (G-12715)
Delaware National Estuarine..................... G 302 739-3436
  Dover (G-2250)
Diversity In Beauty Inc............................. G 323 840-8801
  Wilmington (G-16097)
Envision It Publications LLC..................... G 800 329-9411
  Bear (G-204)
Henlopen Design LLC................................ G 302 265-4330
  Lewes (G-6088)
Hypebeast Inc.. E 714 791-0755
  Dover (G-2711)
Martinelli Holdings LLC............................. F 302 656-1809
  Wilmington (G-18170)
Shoutdel Magazine LLC............................. G 302 533-6070
  Newark (G-12001)
Simply Styling-Schl of Csmtlgy................. G 302 778-1885
  Wilmington (G-19840)
▲ Student Media Group............................ F 302 607-2580
  Newark (G-12110)
Suburban Publishing Inc........................... E 302 656-1809
  Wilmington (G-20116)
T S N Publishing Co Inc............................ G 302 655-6483
  Wilmington (G-20199)
TFT Media LLC.. G 302 645-7400
  Lewes (G-6553)
U Transit Inc.. G 302 227-1197
  Rehoboth Beach (G-13000)

World Economic Magazine Inc................... G 302 499-2016
  Lewes (G-6640)
Wutopia Group US Ltd.............................. F 302 488-0248
  Dover (G-3877)

2731 Book publishing

A Chance To Write It LLC......................... G 202 256-4524
  Lewes (G-5644)
Appointed Partners Pubg Inc.................... G 302 446-3675
  Dover (G-1807)
▲ Cedar Lane Inc..................................... F 302 328-7232
  Historic New Castle (G-4953)
Cosmic Strands LLC.................................. E 302 660-3268
  Wilmington (G-15648)
Dragon Cloud Inc..................................... G 702 508-2676
  Wilmington (G-16171)
Heartfelt Books Publishing....................... G 866 557-6522
  Wilmington (G-17107)
Hero Family Collection LLC...................... G 833 732-3432
  Wilmington (G-17132)
▲ Infobase Holdings Inc........................... E 212 967-8800
  Wilmington (G-17329)
Kardmaster Brochures Inc........................ G 610 434-5262
  Wilmington (G-17652)
Linguatext Ltd.. G 302 453-8695
  Newark (G-11262)
Liveware Inc... F 302 791-9446
  Claymont (G-1221)
Medical Society of Delaware..................... E 302 366-1400
  Newark (G-11377)
Mobetta Books LLC................................... G 904 762-7043
  New Castle (G-9376)
Narleyapps Inc... G 323 744-1398
  Dover (G-3150)
New Leaf Publishing Inc........................... G 408 502-8706
  Dover (G-3179)
Rah Books International........................... G 917 288-1064
  Dover (G-3419)
Readhowyouwant LLC............................... G 302 730-4560
  Dover (G-3431)
Seabrix LLC.. G 224 578-3191
  Dover (G-3524)
Wellthy Investors LLC............................... G 267 847-3486
  Dover (G-3831)

2732 Book printing

Pmb Associates LLC.................................. G 302 436-0111
  Selbyville (G-13592)

2741 Miscellaneous publishing

1300 Publishing Company LLC.................. G 302 268-2684
  Wilmington (G-14106)
360wise Live Inc...................................... G 844 360-9473
  Newark (G-9710)
Akimbo Inc... G 302 204-5299
  Claymont (G-1028)
▲ Associates International Inc.................. D 302 656-4500
  Wilmington (G-14592)
Blakgold Innovative Inc........................... G 302 220-0530
  Clayton (G-1355)
Bloom Daily Planners Inc......................... F 302 607-2580
  Newark (G-10055)
Bogo Publications LLC.............................. G 877 514-4052
  Christiana (G-993)
Bottle of Smoke Press............................... G 302 399-1856
  Dover (G-1966)
Bravin Publishing LLC............................... G 347 921-0443
  Dover (G-1975)
Byzantium Sky Press................................. G 302 258-6116
  Milton (G-8578)
Cameck Publishing................................... G 302 598-4799
  Wilmington (G-15204)

Castos Inc .... G 800 677-3394
Wilmington *(G-15270)*

Chatty Press .... G 617 712-3882
Lewes *(G-5810)*

Chesapeake Seaglass Jewelry .... G 410 778-4999
Selbyville *(G-13498)*

Chip Vickio .... G 302 448-0211
Millsboro *(G-8223)*

Cnwynn Publications .... G 484 753-1568
Dover *(G-2101)*

Coastal Images Inc .... G 302 539-6001
Fenwick Island *(G-4045)*

Conecmi LLC .... G 302 740-9261
Wilmington *(G-15589)*

Crossover Sports Entrmt LLC .... G 516 728-5360
Camden *(G-810)*

Cruz Publishing Group .... G 302 287-2938
Dover *(G-2164)*

Crystal Diamond Publishing .... G 302 737-2130
Newark *(G-10359)*

Dgc Publishing LLC .... G 302 634-0461
Newark *(G-10521)*

Divinity Press .... G 267 981-4002
Bear *(G-171)*

Donnas Garden Goodies .... G 302 399-3691
Townsend *(G-13993)*

Edit Inc .... G 302 478-7069
Wilmington *(G-16295)*

Eliyahna Creative LLC .... G 530 683-5463
Dover *(G-2435)*

Emw Publications .... G 302 438-9879
Hockessin *(G-5200)*

Fruitbearer Publishing LLC .... G 302 856-6649
Georgetown *(G-4327)*

Galerie Media Inc .... G 917 685-4168
Newark *(G-10799)*

Glimpse Global Inc .... G 305 216-7667
Dover *(G-2590)*

Gotti Boyz Entertainment .... G 302 409-2901
Bear *(G-253)*

Govbizconnect Inc .... G 860 341-1925
Dover *(G-2609)*

Grey Matter Inc .... G 302 764-5900
Wilmington *(G-16977)*

Hither Creek Press .... G 603 387-3444
Milford *(G-7932)*

Hotelrunner Inc .... E 650 665-6405
Newark *(G-10975)*

Ilj International LLC .... G 786 332-8535
Lewes *(G-6116)*

Independent School MGT Inc .... E 302 656-4944
Wilmington *(G-17310)*

Intouch Inc .... G 332 223-0720
Dover *(G-2749)*

Kardmaster Brochures Inc .... G 610 434-5262
Wilmington *(G-17652)*

Kat Postcard Solutions Inc .... G 614 288-1733
Hockessin *(G-5265)*

Kitty Jazzy Publishing .... G 302 897-8842
Newark *(G-11188)*

L & B Publishing .... G 302 743-4061
Newark *(G-11204)*

Litcharts LLC .... G 646 481-4807
Wilmington *(G-17934)*

Lsf Networks LLC .... G 213 537-2402
Wilmington *(G-18021)*

Lumhaa LLC .... G 916 517-9972
Wilmington *(G-18027)*

Melody Entertainment USA Inc .... G 305 505-7659
Wilmington *(G-18267)*

MJM Publishing LLC .... G 302 943-3590
Felton *(G-4003)*

Mobile Engagement LLC .... G 646 583-2775
Lewes *(G-6284)*

Moscova Enterprises Inc .... F 347 973-2522
Wilmington *(G-18460)*

New Castle Cnty Shoppers Guide .... G 302 325-6600
New Castle *(G-9406)*

Newspaper Archive Inc .... E 612 590-3401
Wilmington *(G-18633)*

Open Court TV LLC .... G 646 975-1509
Dover *(G-3236)*

Pagetech .... G 845 624-4911
Lewes *(G-6346)*

Pandia Press Inc .... F 352 789-8156
Wilmington *(G-18872)*

Percebe Music Inc .... G 850 341-9594
Dover *(G-3296)*

Phaction Inc .... G 240 459-5198
Wilmington *(G-19008)*

Pixorize Inc .... G 737 529-4404
Wilmington *(G-19058)*

PMC Publications LLC .... G 302 268-4480
Newark *(G-11705)*

Pole Press LLC .... G 260 209-4628
Newark *(G-11710)*

Postimpressions Incorporated .... G 302 656-2271
Wilmington *(G-19131)*

Powers Publishing Group .... G 302 519-8575
Millsboro *(G-8436)*

Prepared LLC .... G 650 825-5996
Wilmington *(G-19176)*

Press Media Group Inc .... G 323 205-5488
Middletown *(G-7468)*

Prestwick House Inc .... E 302 659-2070
Smyrna *(G-13854)*

Pretty Girl Press .... G 484 668-0770
Wilmington *(G-19184)*

Proofed Inc .... G 888 851-8179
Dover *(G-3381)*

Psych Ward Genius .... G 267 237-4528
Wilmington *(G-19245)*

Qoro LLC .... G 302 322-5900
New Castle *(G-9504)*

Raad360 LLC .... F 855 722-3360
Newark *(G-11812)*

Reed Elsevier Capital Inc .... E 302 427-9299
Wilmington *(G-19391)*

Reel Inc .... F 302 319-3522
Middletown *(G-7508)*

Responsible Publishing .... G 609 412-9621
Wilmington *(G-19442)*

Review .... E 302 831-2771
Newark *(G-11874)*

Rhino Smart Publications .... G 302 737-3422
Newark *(G-11879)*

Rlk Press Inc .... G 267 565-5138
Wilmington *(G-19502)*

Rockford Map Gallery LLC .... G 302 740-1851
Wilmington *(G-19536)*

Russell D Earnest & Assoc .... G 302 659-0730
Clayton *(G-1402)*

Rwk Ventures LLC .... G 305 494-4011
Wilmington *(G-19599)*

She Podcasts .... G 302 588-2317
Wilmington *(G-19785)*

Signatureone Media LLC .... G 347 849-3740
Dover *(G-3557)*

Socraticlaw Co Inc .... G 302 654-9191
Wilmington *(G-19910)*

Sonic Sights Incorporated .... G 312 498-9977
Dover *(G-3587)*

Soulscape Publishing LLC .... G 303 834-7060
Newark *(G-12058)*

Speedy Publishing LLC .... G 888 248-4521
Newark *(G-12066)*

Spotlight Publications LLC .... G 302 504-1329
Wilmington *(G-19971)*

Streameq Inc .... G 951 807-4938
Lewes *(G-6517)*

Street Knowledge Book Ctr LLC .... G 888 401-1114
Wilmington *(G-20096)*

Sussex Printing Corp .... E 302 629-9303
Seaford *(G-13420)*

Syncretic Press LLC .... G 443 723-8355
Wilmington *(G-20185)*

T S N Publishing Co Inc .... G 302 655-6483
Wilmington *(G-20199)*

Unprivileged Drinkers LLC .... G 215 800-5475
Felton *(G-4035)*

Verizon Delaware LLC .... C 302 571-1571
Wilmington *(G-20590)*

Vylo Inc .... G 310 902-9693
Newark *(G-12339)*

Wazoplus LLC .... G 302 496-0042
Newark *(G-12350)*

Web Advantage Inc .... F 302 479-7634
Wilmington *(G-20703)*

Wherebyus Enterprises Inc .... F 305 988-0808
Claymont *(G-1336)*

Wide Range Inc .... G 302 234-1193
Hockessin *(G-5425)*

Willow Winters Publishing LLC .... G 570 885-2513
Middletown *(G-7729)*

Wilson Publications LLC .... G 215 237-2344
Bear *(G-565)*

Wna Infotech LLC .... E 302 668-5977
Newark *(G-12392)*

Workaway Ventures Inc .... G 843 608-9108
Wilmington *(G-20890)*

Writers Relief .... G 866 405-3003
Rehoboth Beach *(G-13025)*

X Leader LLC .... G 800 345-2677
Lewes *(G-6642)*

Yellow Light Publishing LLC .... G 302 242-0990
Greenwood *(G-4677)*

2752 Commercial printing, lithographic

A+ Printing .... G 302 273-3147
Wilmington *(G-14175)*

Academy Business Mch & Prtg Co .... G 302 654-3200
Wilmington *(G-14214)*

Allied Printing Co Inc .... G 503 626-0669
New Castle *(G-8785)*

AlphaGraphics Franchising Inc .... G 302 559-8369
Wilmington *(G-14394)*

Ancar Enterprises LLC .... G 302 453-2600
Newark *(G-9861)*

Ancar Enterprises LLC .... G 302 477-1884
Wilmington *(G-14468)*

Armor Graphics Inc .... G 302 737-8790
Newark *(G-9905)*

▲ Associates International Inc .... D 302 656-4500
Wilmington *(G-14592)*

Aztec Copies LLC .... F 302 575-1993
Wilmington *(G-14688)*

Ben-Dom Printing Company .... F 302 737-9144
Newark *(G-10019)*

Bgdedge Inc .... G 302 477-1734
New Castle *(G-8866)*

Brandywine Graphics Inc .... G 302 655-7571
Wilmington *(G-15062)*

Chapis Drafting & Blue Print .... G 302 629-6373
Seaford *(G-13112)*

Coastal Printing Company .... G 302 537-1700
Ocean View *(G-12494)*

27 PRINTING, PUBLISHING AND ALLIED INDUSTRIES

Coko Prints .... G 302 507-1683
  Wilmington (G-15523)
Communications Printing Inc .... G 302 229-9369
  Newark (G-10287)
Conventioneer Pubg Co Inc .... G 301 487-3907
  Georgetown (G-4267)
D & B Printing and Mailing Inc .... G 302 838-7111
  Newark (G-10373)
D & D Screen Printing .... G 302 349-4231
  Greenwood (G-4610)
DC Printing Inc .... G 302 545-6666
  Wilmington (G-15826)
Delaware Dept Hlth Social Svcs .... G 302 255-9855
  New Castle (G-9017)
Delaware Dept Hlth Social Svcs .... D 302 255-9800
  New Castle (G-9020)
Delaware Screen Printing Inc .... G 302 378-4231
  Middletown (G-7044)
Delaware State Printing .... E 302 228-9431
  Dover (G-2264)
Delta Forms Inc .... F 302 652-3266
  Wilmington (G-16003)
Depro-Serical USA Inc .... G 302 368-8040
  Townsend (G-13991)
DMD Business Forms & Prtg Co .... G 302 998-8200
  Wilmington (G-16107)
Dover Litho Printing Co .... G 302 698-5292
  Dover (G-2351)
Dover Post Co Inc .... E 302 678-3616
  Dover (G-2364)
Dover Post Co Inc .... D 302 653-2083
  Dover (G-2362)
Edythe L Pridgen .... G 302 652-8887
  Bear (G-197)
Eidp Inc .... G 302 992-2012
  Wilmington (G-16315)
Factors Etc Inc .... G 302 834-1625
  Bear (G-218)
Fannon Color Printing LLC .... G 302 227-2164
  Rehoboth Beach (G-12750)
Fishtail Print Company .... G 302 408-4800
  Rehoboth Beach (G-12756)
Fishtail Print Company .... G 302 682-3053
  Rehoboth Beach (G-12757)
◆ Foxfire Printing and Packaging Inc ..... C 302 533-2240
  Newark (G-10769)
G & B Comp & Creative Design .... G 302 284-3856
  Felton (G-3977)
Garile Inc .... E 302 366-0848
  Newark (G-10809)
Grm Pro Imaging LLC .... G 302 999-8162
  Wilmington (G-16984)
Horizon Aeronautics Inc .... G 409 504-2645
  Wilmington (G-17204)
▲ Independent Newsmedia Inc USA .... D 302 674-3600
  Dover (G-2729)
Ini Holdings Inc .... G 302 674-3600
  Dover (G-2734)
Jerry O Thompson Prntng .... G 302 832-1509
  Bear (G-303)
Job Printing .... G 302 907-0416
  Delmar (G-1607)
Joseph W Small Associates Inc .... F
  Wilmington (G-17588)
Kardmaster Brochures Inc .... G 610 434-5262
  Wilmington (G-17652)
Litho-Print Inc .... G 302 239-1341
  Hockessin (G-5283)
Lord Printing LLC .... G 302 439-3253
  Wilmington (G-17994)
Love City Prints LLC .... G 302 245-5702
  Lewes (G-6224)

Luke Destefano Inc .... G 302 455-0710
  Newark (G-11294)
Markizon Printing .... G 610 715-7989
  Wilmington (G-18148)
Marthann Print Center LLC .... G 267 884-8130
  Dover (G-3024)
McClafferty Printing Company .... E 302 652-8112
  Wilmington (G-18220)
Mercantile Press Inc .... F 302 764-6884
  Wilmington (G-18274)
Mgl Screen Printing .... G 302 450-6250
  Clayton (G-1386)
Millennium Marketing Solutions .... E 301 725-8000
  Lewes (G-6274)
Morales Screen Printing .... G 302 465-8179
  Dover (G-3122)
New Image Inc .... G 302 738-6824
  Newark (G-11523)
News Print Shop .... G 302 337-8283
  Bridgeville (G-738)
Nexsigns LLC .... G 302 508-2615
  Clayton (G-1391)
OConnell Speedy Printing Inc .... G 302 656-1475
  Wilmington (G-18743)
One Hour Printing .... G 302 220-1684
  Newark (G-11592)
Patio Printing Co Inc .... G 302 328-6881
  New Castle (G-9457)
Penney Enterprises Inc .... G 302 629-4430
  Seaford (G-13340)
Print Coast 2 Coast .... G 302 381-4610
  Lewes (G-6391)
Print On This .... G 302 235-9475
  Newark (G-11747)
Print Shack Inc .... G 302 629-4430
  Seaford (G-13358)
Print-N-Press Inc .... G 302 994-6665
  Wilmington (G-19196)
Printcurement .... G 302 249-6100
  Historic New Castle (G-5054)
▲ Printed Solid Inc .... F 302 439-0098
  Newark (G-11748)
Printit Solutions LLC .... G 302 380-3838
  Dover (G-3373)
Prints and Princesses .... G 703 881-1057
  Newark (G-11749)
Pulsar Print LLC .... G 302 394-9202
  Historic New Castle (G-5057)
Quick Copies .... G 302 374-0798
  Claymont (G-1273)
Rescue Printig .... G 302 286-7266
  Newark (G-11861)
Rogers Graphics Inc .... G 302 422-6694
  Harbeson (G-4713)
Rogers Graphics Inc .... F 302 856-0028
  Georgetown (G-4490)
Shamrock Printing Company .... G 302 368-8888
  Newark (G-11990)
Skinify LLC .... E 302 212-5689
  Rehoboth Beach (G-12962)
Sprint Quality Printing Inc .... G 302 478-0720
  Wilmington (G-19980)
Stanley Golden .... G 302 652-5626
  Wilmington (G-20018)
Star Art Inc .... G 302 261-6732
  Bear (G-510)
Stratis Visuals LLC .... F 860 482-1208
  Newark (G-12107)
Studio B Milford LLC .... G 302 491-7910
  Milford (G-8106)
UNI Printing Solutionsllc .... G 631 438-6045
  New Castle (G-9651)

Union Press Printing Inc .... G 302 652-0496
  Wilmington (G-20514)
US Flexo Solutions LLC .... G 302 838-7805
  Newark (G-12289)
W B Mason Co Inc .... E 888 926-2766
  Newark (G-12340)
William N Cann Inc .... E 302 995-0820
  Wilmington (G-20795)
Windswept Enterprises .... G 302 678-0805
  Dover (G-3857)

2754 Commercial printing, gravure

Ancar Enterprises LLC .... G 302 477-1884
  Wilmington (G-14468)
Blue Heron Ent Inc .... G 302 834-1521
  Bear (G-76)
Promotion Zone LLC .... G 302 832-8565
  Newark (G-11763)

2759 Commercial printing, nec

70 Inc .... G 310 529-1526
  Dover (G-1690)
AIA .... G 302 407-2252
  New Castle (G-8774)
◆ Amer Inc .... G 302 654-2498
  Wilmington (G-14421)
Anthem Graphix .... G 302 270-5111
  Magnolia (G-6718)
Best Office Pros .... G 302 629-4561
  Seaford (G-13084)
Candlestick Publishing Inc .... G 817 939-1306
  Wilmington (G-15214)
Compass Graphics .... G 302 378-1977
  Middletown (G-7005)
Corlo Services Inc .... G 302 737-3207
  Newark (G-10324)
Cosmic Custom Screen Printing .... G 302 933-0920
  Millsboro (G-8240)
Creative Promotions .... G 302 697-7896
  Camden (G-809)
Delaware Screen Printing Inc .... G 302 378-4231
  Middletown (G-7044)
Diamond State Graphics Inc .... F 302 325-1100
  New Castle (G-9051)
Distinctive Stationery LLC .... G 410 247-5600
  Milton (G-8608)
Dragons Lair Printing LLC .... G 302 798-4465
  Claymont (G-1122)
Dream Graphics .... G 302 328-6264
  New Castle (G-9063)
Factors Etc Inc .... G 302 834-1625
  Bear (G-218)
Fbk Graphico Inc .... G 302 743-4784
  Wilmington (G-16564)
Fedex Office & Print Svcs Inc .... G 302 996-0264
  Wilmington (G-16573)
Go Tees LLC .... G 708 703-1788
  Middletown (G-7168)
Growth Inc .... E 302 366-0848
  Newark (G-10903)
JEB Plastics Inc .... G 302 479-9223
  Wilmington (G-17513)
Lasting Impression Inc A .... G 302 762-9200
  Wilmington (G-17815)
Logo Motive Inc .... G 302 645-2959
  Rehoboth Beach (G-12836)
Max One Printing .... G 302 897-9050
  Bear (G-368)
Meade Inc .... G 302 262-3394
  Seaford (G-13278)
▲ Middletown Ink LLC .... G 302 725-0705
  Middletown (G-7353)

28 CHEMICALS AND ALLIED PRODUCTS

Midnight Blue Inc .... F 302 436-9665
  Selbyville (G-13576)
New Image Inc .... G 302 738-6824
  Newark (G-11523)
Newphoenix Screen Printing .... G 302 747-8991
  Dover (G-3183)
Personalized Luggage Inc .... G 786 431-3118
  Wilmington (G-18989)
Promotion Zone LLC .... G 302 832-8565
  Newark (G-11763)
Proper-Tees LLC .... G 323 981-9809
  Camden (G-886)
Sportz Tees .... G 302 280-6076
  Laurel (G-5605)
Stamford Screen Printing Inc .... G 302 654-2442
  Wilmington (G-20008)
Stanley Golden .... G 302 652-5626
  Wilmington (G-20018)
Sussex Printing Corp .... E 302 629-9303
  Seaford (G-13420)
◆ Ten Talents Enterprises Inc .... G 302 409-0718
  Middletown (G-7634)
To A Tee Printing .... G 302 525-6336
  Newark (G-12202)
Unique Image LLC .... E 302 658-2266
  Wilmington (G-20519)
Zzhouse Inc .... F 302 354-3474
  New Castle (G-9701)

2761 Manifold business forms

Brandywine Graphics Inc .... G 302 655-7571
  Wilmington (G-15062)
Go Mozaic LLC .... G 302 438-4141
  Claymont (G-1166)

2771 Greeting cards

Chaukiss LLC .... G 551 655-5181
  Lewes (G-5811)
Sussex Printing Corp .... E 302 629-9303
  Seaford (G-13420)

2782 Blankbooks and looseleaf binders

Cann-Erikson Bindery Inc .... F 302 995-6636
  Wilmington (G-15216)
L E Stansell Inc .... G 302 475-1534
  Wilmington (G-17775)
SE Lavi Productions LLC .... G 727 457-2625
  Dover (G-3523)

2789 Bookbinding and related work

◆ Amer Inc .... G 302 654-2498
  Wilmington (G-14421)
Ben-Dom Printing Company .... F 302 737-9144
  Newark (G-10019)
Dover Post Co Inc .... E 302 678-3616
  Dover (G-2364)
▼ Dupont Txtles Intriors Del Inc .... E 302 774-1000
  Wilmington (G-16218)
Fox Specialties Inc .... F 302 322-5200
  Historic New Castle (G-4990)
Garile Inc .... E 302 366-0848
  Newark (G-10809)
L E Stansell Inc .... G 302 475-1534
  Wilmington (G-17775)
William N Cann Inc .... E 302 995-0820
  Wilmington (G-20795)

2791 Typesetting

◆ Amer Inc .... G 302 654-2498
  Wilmington (G-14421)
▲ Associates International Inc .... D 302 656-4500
  Wilmington (G-14592)

Ben-Dom Printing Company .... F 302 737-9144
  Newark (G-10019)
Dover Post Co Inc .... E 302 678-3616
  Dover (G-2364)
Garile Inc .... E 302 366-0848
  Newark (G-10809)
Stanley Golden .... G 302 652-5626
  Wilmington (G-20018)
Sussex Printing Corp .... E 302 629-9303
  Seaford (G-13420)
William N Cann Inc .... E 302 995-0820
  Wilmington (G-20795)

2796 Platemaking services

Union Press Printing Inc .... G 302 652-0496
  Wilmington (G-20514)

28 CHEMICALS AND ALLIED PRODUCTS

2812 Alkalies and chlorine

FMC Corporation .... D 302 366-5107
  Newark (G-10752)
Kuehne Chemical Company Inc .... E 302 834-4557
  New Castle (G-9291)
Safrax Inc .... E 302 404-0388
  Dover (G-3505)

2813 Industrial gases

AAL Drtc .... F 302 229-5891
  Newark (G-9733)
Air Lqide Advanced Separations .... F 302 225-1100
  Newport (G-12440)
Air Lqide Advanced Tech US LLC .... A 302 225-1100
  Newark (G-9799)
Air Lqide Advanced Tech US LLC .... F 302 225-1100
  Newport (G-12441)
Airgas Usa LLC .... F 302 834-7404
  Delaware City (G-1529)
Eidp Inc .... G 302 366-5763
  Newark (G-10616)
Grep Biogas I LLC .... G 212 390-8110
  Lewes (G-6060)
Helium3 Tech and Services LLC .... G 302 766-2856
  Newark (G-10945)
Keen Compressed Gas Co .... E 302 594-4545
  New Castle (G-9276)
Keen Compressed Gas Co .... F 302 594-4545
  New Castle (G-9277)
Keen Compressed Gas Co .... F 302 594-4545
  Wilmington (G-17674)
Messer LLC .... D 302 798-9342
  Claymont (G-1234)
Milwood Hydrogen LLC .... D 424 330-5739
  Lewes (G-6276)
Pure Air Holdings Corp .... G 302 655-7130
  Wilmington (G-19258)
Vernon Green Hydrogen LLC .... G 609 772-7979
  Dover (G-3786)

2816 Inorganic pigments

Ampacet Ohio LLC .... E 914 631-6600
  Wilmington (G-14461)
◆ Chemours Company Fc LLC .... E 302 773-1000
  Wilmington (G-15358)
Lanxess Corporation .... G 267 205-1969
  Wilmington (G-17806)

2819 Industrial inorganic chemicals, nec

7elements Inc .... F 302 294-1791
  Newark (G-9716)

Affinity Research Chemicals .... G 302 525-4060
  Wilmington (G-14305)
Brandywine Chemical Company .... G 302 656-5428
  New Castle (G-8883)
Celanese International Corp .... D 972 443-4000
  Wilmington (G-15298)
Chemours Company Fc LLC .... C 302 545-0072
  Wilmington (G-15357)
Ddh Advanced Mtls Systems Inc .... G 515 441-1313
  Newark (G-10397)
Degussa International Inc .... G 302 731-9250
  Newark (G-10409)
Delaware Chemical Corporation .... E 302 427-8752
  Wilmington (G-15883)
Divine Element Hbb .... G 302 538-5209
  Dover (G-2308)
Dow Chemical Company .... E 302 366-0500
  Newark (G-10557)
▼ Du Pont Chem Enrgy Oprtons Inc .... C 302 774-1000
  Wilmington (G-16188)
Dupont Athntcation Systems LLC .... F 800 345-9999
  Wilmington (G-16202)
Dupont John Gardner .... G 302 777-3730
  Wilmington (G-16211)
Dupont Prfmce Coatings Inc .... D 302 892-1064
  Wilmington (G-16213)
Dupont Specialty Pdts USA LLC .... E 800 972-7252
  Newark (G-10577)
Dupont Specialty Systems .... G 302 273-6955
  Newark (G-10578)
E I Du Pont De Nemours & Co .... F 302 733-8134
  Newark (G-10588)
Eidp Inc .... D 302 834-5901
  Delaware City (G-1539)
Eidp Inc .... G 302 239-9424
  Newark (G-10617)
Eidp Inc .... G 302 366-5583
  Newark (G-10618)
Eidp Inc .... E 302 266-7101
  Newark (G-10619)
Eidp Inc .... E 302 774-1000
  Wilmington (G-16314)
Eidp Inc .... E 302 999-3301
  Wilmington (G-16316)
Eidp Inc .... B 302 892-8832
  Wilmington (G-16317)
Eidp Inc .... G 302 999-2874
  Wilmington (G-16318)
Eidp Inc .... G 302 892-8832
  Wilmington (G-16319)
Eidp Inc .... F 302 695-7228
  Wilmington (G-16320)
Eidp Inc .... G 302 999-4356
  Wilmington (G-16321)
Eidp Inc .... E 302 792-4371
  Wilmington (G-16322)
Eidp Inc .... E 302 774-2102
  Wilmington (G-16323)
Eidp Inc .... G 302 774-1000
  Wilmington (G-16324)
Eidp Inc .... G 302 888-0200
  Wilmington (G-16325)
Eidp Inc .... F 302 668-8644
  Wilmington (G-16326)
Eidp Inc .... G 302 999-4329
  Wilmington (G-16328)
Eidp Inc .... G 302 999-2533
  Wilmington (G-16329)
Eidp Inc .... D 302 695-3742
  Wilmington (G-16330)
Eidp Inc .... G 302 999-5072
  Wilmington (G-16331)

28 CHEMICALS AND ALLIED PRODUCTS

Eidp Inc .... E 302 999-4321
   Wilmington *(G-16332)*
Eidp Inc .... G 302 774-1000
   Wilmington *(G-16333)*
Eidp Inc .... G 302 774-1000
   Wilmington *(G-16334)*
Eidp Inc .... G 302 695-5300
   Wilmington *(G-16335)*
Element .... G 302 645-0777
   Lewes *(G-5956)*
Essential Minerals LLC .... G 602 377-9878
   New Castle *(G-9100)*
Honeywell International Inc .... E 302 791-6700
   Claymont *(G-1181)*
Indo Amines Americas LLC .... F 301 466-9902
   Wilmington *(G-17312)*
John J Buckley Associates Inc ...... G 302 475-5443
   Wilmington *(G-17565)*
Kuehne Chemical Company Inc ..... E 302 834-4557
   New Castle *(G-9291)*
Lanxess Corporation .... G 267 205-1969
   Wilmington *(G-17806)*
Mastering Mrcury Dsign Elments ... G 302 344-4323
   Georgetown *(G-4420)*
Oreomatic Mining Inc .... E 725 255-8895
   Wilmington *(G-18817)*
Rohm Haas Electronic Mtls LLC .... E 302 366-0500
   Newark *(G-11909)*
Rohm Haas Electronic Mtls LLC .... E 302 366-0500
   Newark *(G-11910)*
Sinomine Resources (us) Inc .... G 204 340-6696
   Wilmington *(G-19842)*
Solvay Spclty Polymers USA LLC ... F 302 452-6609
   Newark *(G-12054)*
Timtec Inc .... F 302 292-8500
   Newark *(G-12196)*
W R Grace & Co .... G 410 531-4000
   Wilmington *(G-20663)*

2821 Plastics materials and resins

Aearo Technologies LLC .... B 302 283-5497
   Newark *(G-9787)*
ARC Resin Corp .... G 859 230-7063
   Wilmington *(G-14534)*
Biome Bioplastics Inc .... G 917 724-2850
   Newark *(G-10036)*
Celanese International Corp .... D 972 443-4000
   Wilmington *(G-15298)*
Celanese Polymer Products LLC .... D 302 774-1000
   Wilmington *(G-15299)*
Delaware Thrmplastic Specialty ...... G 302 424-4722
   Milford *(G-7859)*
Delmarva Plastics Co .... G 302 398-1000
   Harrington *(G-4760)*
Delrin Usa LLC .... F 302 295-5900
   Wilmington *(G-16001)*
Dow Chemical Company .... E 302 366-0500
   Newark *(G-10557)*
Dupont De Nemours Inc .... A 302 774-3034
   Wilmington *(G-16205)*
Dupont Indus Bsciences USA LLC . E 302 774-1000
   Wilmington *(G-16210)*
◆ Dupont Prfmce Elastomers LLC ... B
   Wilmington *(G-16214)*
Dupont Specialty Pdts USA LLC ..... E 302 992-2941
   Wilmington *(G-16216)*
Eidp Inc .... G 302 654-8198
   Wilmington *(G-16336)*
Eidp Inc .... G 302 999-2826
   Wilmington *(G-16339)*
Industrial Sls Factoring Corp .... G 302 573-2500
   Wilmington *(G-17317)*

▲ Intech Services Inc .... G 302 366-8530
   Newark *(G-11030)*
Invista Capital Management LLC .... D 302 731-6882
   Newark *(G-11052)*
Invista Capital Management LLC .... C 877 446-8478
   Wilmington *(G-17410)*
▲ Invista Capital Management LLC . G 302 683-3000
   Newark *(G-17409)*
Invistas Applied RES Centre .... G 302 731-6800
   Newark *(G-11054)*
Lanxess Corporation .... G 267 205-1969
   Wilmington *(G-17806)*
◆ Liveo Research Inc .... C 302 838-3200
   New Castle *(G-9318)*
Macro Polymers NA LLC .... G 302 660-6926
   Wilmington *(G-18072)*
Neko Colors USA Inc .... G 844 365-6356
   Newark *(G-11501)*
New Process Fibre Company .... D 302 349-4535
   Greenwood *(G-4657)*
Nova Polymers .... G 302 858-4677
   Georgetown *(G-4448)*
▲ Oci Melamine Americas Inc .... G 800 615-8284
   Wilmington *(G-18742)*
Performnce Solutions Holdg Inc ..... G 302 774-1000
   Wilmington *(G-18979)*
◆ Polymer Technologies Inc .... D 302 738-9001
   Newark *(G-11711)*
Presidium USA Inc .... G 203 803-2980
   Dover *(G-3366)*
Rohm and Haas Equity Corp .... G 302 366-0500
   Newark *(G-11907)*
Specialty Products Us LLC .... E 302 774-1000
   Wilmington *(G-19955)*
T P Composites Inc .... G 610 358-9001
   Historic New Castle *(G-5078)*
W L Gore .... G 302 584-8822
   Wilmington *(G-20662)*
W L Gore & Associates Inc .... C 302 368-3700
   Newark *(G-12341)*
▲ W L Gore & Associates Inc .... D 302 738-4880
   Newark *(G-12342)*

2822 Synthetic rubber

▲ Arlon LLC .... G 302 834-2100
   Bear *(G-44)*
Lanxess Corporation .... G 267 205-1969
   Wilmington *(G-17806)*
Rogers Corporation .... C 302 834-2100
   Bear *(G-467)*

2823 Cellulosic manmade fibers

FMC Corporation .... D 302 451-0100
   Newark *(G-10751)*

2824 Organic fibers, noncellulosic

Dupont Indus Bsciences USA LLC . E 302 774-1000
   Wilmington *(G-16210)*
◆ Durafiber Tech DFT Entps Inc ...... D 704 912-3770
   Wilmington *(G-16220)*
Gambers LLC .... G 402 218-7929
   Middletown *(G-7149)*
Specialty Products N&H Inc .... C 302 774-1000
   Wilmington *(G-19954)*

2833 Medicinals and botanicals

Dreamspell LLC .... G 786 633-1520
   Dover *(G-2383)*
Euphoric Hrbals Apothecary LLC ... G 302 491-4443
   Milford *(G-7884)*
◆ Glaxosmthkline Hldngs Amrcas I .. C 302 984-6932
   Wilmington *(G-16882)*

Go Shopping Inc .... G 305 370-4704
   Newark *(G-10856)*
Nutradrill LLC .... G 772 277-2201
   Wilmington *(G-18720)*
Personal Health PDT Dev LLC .... E 888 901-6150
   Wilmington *(G-18987)*
Pure Shaka LLC .... G 302 438-7105
   Wilmington *(G-19261)*
Wilmington .... G 302 357-4509
   Wilmington *(G-20807)*
Zeequest Inc .... G 760 212-7378
   Lewes *(G-6648)*

2834 Pharmaceutical preparations

A2a Intgrted Phrmceuticals LLC ..... G 270 202-2461
   Lewes *(G-5648)*
A66 Inc .... G 800 444-0446
   Wilmington *(G-14180)*
▲ Accelerated Intelligence Inc .... G 800 765-3628
   Wilmington *(G-14217)*
▲ Adesis Inc .... E 302 323-4880
   New Castle *(G-8764)*
▲ Amylin Pharmaceuticals LLC ...... A 858 552-2200
   Wilmington *(G-14466)*
Angita Pharmard LLC .... G 302 234-6794
   Hockessin *(G-5126)*
Anip Acquisition Company .... G 302 652-2021
   Wilmington *(G-14485)*
Anp Technologies Inc .... E 302 283-1730
   Newark *(G-9875)*
▲ Astrazeneca LP .... A 302 886-3000
   Wilmington *(G-14609)*
Astrazeneca Pharmaceuticals LP ... B 302 286-3500
   Newark *(G-9929)*
◆ Astrazeneca Pharmaceuticals LP . A 800 456-3669
   Wilmington *(G-14610)*
Auragin LLC .... G 800 383-5109
   Wilmington *(G-14643)*
Biosion Usa Inc .... F 302 257-5085
   Newark *(G-10037)*
Bristol-Myers Squibb Company ..... G 800 321-1335
   Wilmington *(G-15119)*
Champions + Legends Corp .... G 702 605-2522
   Wilmington *(G-15328)*
Colgate-Palmolive Company .... G 302 428-1554
   Wilmington *(G-15527)*
Cpex Pharmaceuticals Inc .... F 302 651-8300
   Wilmington *(G-15676)*
Delaware Dermatologic .... G 302 593-8625
   Wilmington *(G-15904)*
FMC Corporation .... D 302 451-0100
   Newark *(G-10751)*
Fulcrum Pharmacy MGT Inc .... G 302 658-8020
   Wilmington *(G-16768)*
Gap Innovations Pbc .... E 203 464-7048
   Dover *(G-2556)*
Genesis Laboratories Inc .... G 832 217-8585
   Wilmington *(G-16837)*
Glanbia Inc .... G 208 733-7555
   Wilmington *(G-16880)*
Glaxosmithkline Capital Inc .... E 302 656-5280
   Wilmington *(G-16881)*
◆ Glaxosmthkline Hldngs Amrcas I . C 302 984-6932
   Wilmington *(G-16882)*
Glycomira LLC .... G 704 651-9789
   Dover *(G-2597)*
Hopewell Pharma Ventures Inc ..... G 203 273-1350
   Wilmington *(G-17201)*
Incyte Holdings Corporation .... E 302 498-6700
   Wilmington *(G-17307)*
International N&H Usa Inc .... D 302 451-0176
   Newark *(G-11047)*

28 CHEMICALS AND ALLIED PRODUCTS

Iqure Pharma Inc .... F 908 294-1212
  Wilmington (G-17421)
Lavoisier Inc .... G 302 446-3244
  Dover (G-2910)
Leiluna LLC .... F 813 512-2213
  Wilmington (G-17870)
◆ LRC North America Inc .... E 302 427-2845
  Wilmington (G-18018)
Marlex Pharmaceuticals Inc .... E 302 328-3355
  New Castle (G-9348)
Mc2 Therapeutics Inc .... G 202 505-0891
  Dover (G-3041)
Medical Sup Support Svcs LLC ..... F 302 446-3658
  Dover (G-3052)
Medimmune LLC .... G 301 398-1200
  Wilmington (G-18255)
▲ Merck & Co Inc .... E 302 934-8051
  Millsboro (G-8377)
Mommas Mountain LLC .... G 410 236-6717
  Magnolia (G-6769)
Nanoskin LLC .... G 310 345-4768
  Middletown (G-7391)
Natural Stacks Inc .... G 855 678-2257
  Lewes (G-6307)
Neuracon Biotech Inc .... G 813 966-3129
  Wilmington (G-18601)
New Life Medicals LLC .... G 610 615-1483
  Dover (G-3180)
Nikang Therapeutics Inc .... E 302 415-5127
  Wilmington (G-18649)
Noramco Inc .... G 302 652-3840
  Wilmington (G-18670)
Noramco LLC .... E 302 761-2923
  Wilmington (G-18671)
Novaeo LLC .... E 832 643-2153
  Wilmington (G-18692)
Novartis Corporation .... G 302 992-5610
  Wilmington (G-18694)
Novo Nordisk Pharmaceuticals ..... G 302 345-0229
  Wilmington (G-18700)
Novo Nrdisk US Coml Hldngs Inc .. D 302 691-6181
  Wilmington (G-18701)
Penn Labs Inc .... E 215 751-4000
  Wilmington (G-18952)
Pharma E Market LLC .... F 302 737-3711
  Hockessin (G-5344)
Pharmunion LLC .... G 415 307-5128
  Wilmington (G-19009)
Platinum US Distribution Inc .... G 905 364-8713
  Wilmington (G-19073)
Plx Pharma Winddown Corp .... G 973 381-7408
  Dover (G-3339)
Prelude Therapeutics Inc .... D 302 467-1280
  Wilmington (G-19166)
Sangita Scientific LLC .... G 866 272-6432
  Wilmington (G-19664)
Sarkana Pharma Inc .... G 649 332-4417
  Wilmington (G-19673)
Scov3 LLC .... G 973 387-9771
  Wilmington (G-19714)
Scov3 LLC .... G 973 387-9771
  Wilmington (G-19715)
Shinlaza Inc .... G 800 206-0051
  Wilmington (G-19800)
Shire North American Group Inc .. D 484 595-8800
  Wilmington (G-19804)
Smithkline Beecham Intl Co .... E 302 479-5804
  Wilmington (G-19893)
▲ Snow Pharmaceuticals LLC .... G 302 436-8855
  Frankford (G-4146)
SPI Pharma Inc .... G 302 360-7200
  Lewes (G-6500)

Tesla Biohealing Inc .... E 302 265-2213
  Milford (G-8117)
Workroom Enterprises LLC .... G 417 621-5577
  Wilmington (G-20893)
▲ Zeneca Holdings Inc .... D 302 886-3000
  Wilmington (G-20953)
Zeneca Inc .... G 302 886-3000
  Wilmington (G-20954)
Zenw LLC .... G 302 722-7379
  Newark (G-12433)

2835 Diagnostic substances

Alcheme Bio Inc .... G 858 291-9708
  Dover (G-1760)
Anp Technologies Inc .... E 302 283-1730
  Newark (G-9875)
Aqua Science LLC .... G 302 757-5241
  Newark (G-9896)
Eidp Inc .... G 302 695-5300
  Wilmington (G-16335)
Enzymetrics Bioscience Inc .... G 302 763-3658
  Wilmington (G-16447)
Farma Quimica LLC .... G 703 537-9789
  Lewes (G-5988)
Siemens Hlthcare Dgnostics Inc ... G 302 631-8006
  Historic New Castle (G-5071)
Siemens Hlthcare Dgnostics Inc ... D 302 631-7357
  Newark (G-12005)
Standard Merger Sub LLC .... E 302 456-6785
  Newark (G-12083)
Vetosine Inc .... G 424 258-0120
  Wilmington (G-20601)

2836 Biological products, except diagnostic

Analytical Biological Svcs Inc .... E 302 654-4492
  New Castle (G-8806)
Artevet LLC .... G 443 255-0016
  Wilmington (G-14564)
Cleamol LLC .... G 513 885-3462
  Wilmington (G-15469)
◆ Glaxosmthkline Hldngs Amrcas I ..C 302 984-6932
  Wilmington (G-16882)
Mommas Mountain LLC .... G 410 236-6717
  Magnolia (G-6769)
One EDM LLC .... E 908 399-0536
  Wilmington (G-18780)
Orphagenix Inc .... G 267 334-5153
  Wilmington (G-18825)
Plume Serum LLC .... G 302 697-9044
  Magnolia (G-6775)
Reflection Biotechnologies Inc ..... G 212 765-2200
  Wilmington (G-19396)
Uvax Bio LLC .... E 818 859-3988
  Newark (G-12293)

2841 Soap and other detergents

111 Medco LLC .... G 888 711-7090
  Dover (G-1678)
Acosh Enterprise LLC .... G 631 767-4501
  Newark (G-9758)
Capriottis of Milford .... G 302 424-3309
  Camden Wyoming (G-922)
Ecolab Pest Elimination .... F 302 322-3600
  New Castle (G-9081)
Value Xchange Group of Co LLC .. D 708 420-7642
  Wilmington (G-20566)

2842 Polishes and sanitation goods

A Kleensweep .... G 302 764-7964
  Wilmington (G-14165)
Alcosm LLC .... G 302 703-7635
  Lewes (G-5671)

Beauty Max Inc .... G 302 735-1705
  Dover (G-1900)
Chem Tech Inc .... G 302 798-9675
  Wilmington (G-15353)
Cleaner Brands Worldwide LLC .... G 646 867-8328
  Dover (G-2091)
Coastal Chem-Dry .... G 302 234-0200
  Lewes (G-5838)
Diligent Detail .... G 302 482-2836
  Wilmington (G-16071)
Dow Chemical Company .... E 302 368-4169
  Newark (G-10558)
Eon Mist LLC .... G 310 500-2140
  Wilmington (G-16448)
Floor Guy Supply LLC .... G 302 325-3801
  New Castle (G-9137)
Gearhalo US Inc .... G 780 239-2120
  Dover (G-2566)
▼ Halosil International Inc .... G 302 543-8095
  Wilmington (G-17040)
Hampton Enterprises Inc .... G 302 378-7365
  Townsend (G-14013)
New Pendulum Corporation .... F 302 478-6160
  Wilmington (G-18624)
Playtex Manufacturing Inc .... D 302 678-6000
  Dover (G-3336)
Purple4s Inc .... G 443 504-9755
  Magnolia (G-6778)
Quip Laboratories Incorporated ... E 302 761-2600
  Wilmington (G-19297)
Sanosil International LLC .... G 302 454-8102
  Wilmington (G-19667)
Ultra Modern Laundry Svcs LLC ... G 302 533-8596
  Wilmington (G-20500)

2843 Surface active agents

James Thompson & Company Inc .. E 302 349-4501
  Greenwood (G-4644)
Richard Earl Fisher .... G 302 598-1957
  Wilmington (G-19468)

2844 Toilet preparations

5n1-Mc Cosmetics LLC .... G 866 561-6226
  Wilmington (G-14142)
Adrion & Co LLC .... G 302 313-1392
  Lewes (G-5660)
Aikym Essentials LLC .... G 215 910-9479
  Middletown (G-6842)
Arovo US Inc .... E 952 290-0799
  Dover (G-1818)
Boldify Inc .... G 240 396-0247
  Middletown (G-6929)
Brand Evangelists For Buty Inc .... G 973 970-0812
  Dover (G-1971)
Brandywine Botanicals LLC .... G 302 354-4650
  Wilmington (G-15046)
Claudiva Kae & Co LLC .... G 302 283-9803
  Newark (G-10250)
Code509com Inc .... G 941 263-3509
  Dover (G-2108)
Dab Deodorant LLC .... G 973 512-2703
  New Castle (G-8993)
Gladys Walker .... G 302 480-0713
  Wilmington (G-16879)
◆ Glaxosmthkline Hldngs Amrcas I ..C 302 984-6932
  Wilmington (G-16882)
Goodales Naturals .... G 302 743-6455
  Newark (G-10867)
Khaos Beauty LLC .... A 302 427-0119
  Wilmington (G-17712)
Khmisat LLC .... G 302 533-1303
  Newark (G-11170)

28 CHEMICALS AND ALLIED PRODUCTS

Matykos Beauty LLC................................G..... 302 213-6879
  Wilmington *(G-18200)*

Melanin Mixx Beauty Brand Inc...............G..... 302 266-1010
  Newark *(G-11385)*

My Lip Stuff..G..... 302 945-5922
  Lewes *(G-6300)*

N Daisy Jax Inc......................................E..... 302 387-3543
  Dover *(G-3142)*

Nabeel and Huzaif LLC..........................G..... 302 445-7483
  Lewes *(G-6303)*

Naked and Thriving Inc..........................G..... 855 943-0521
  Wilmington *(G-18522)*

Overtone Color LLC...............................G..... 520 448-3305
  Wilmington *(G-18842)*

Playtex Manufacturing Inc......................D..... 302 678-6000
  Dover *(G-3336)*

Remarle LLC..G..... 215 245-6448
  Middletown *(G-7511)*

Richard Earl Fisher.................................G..... 302 598-1957
  Wilmington *(G-19468)*

Succulents Soap Sand Scents...............G..... 302 757-0697
  Newark *(G-12117)*

◆ Sun Pharmaceuticals Corp..................E..... 302 678-6000
  Dover *(G-3622)*

Vegan Skin Clinic LLC............................G..... 302 932-1920
  Hockessin *(G-5416)*

Vvardis Inc...G..... 917 940-3009
  Middletown *(G-7698)*

Wellthy Investors LLC............................G..... 267 847-3486
  Dover *(G-3831)*

2851 Paints and allied products

▲ C P M Industries Inc...........................G..... 302 478-8200
  Wilmington *(G-15175)*

Coatings With A Purpose Inc.................G..... 302 462-1465
  Georgetown *(G-4260)*

Modified Thermoset Resins Inc..............G..... 302 235-3710
  Wilmington *(G-18399)*

PPG Architectural Finishes Inc...............G..... 302 736-6081
  Dover *(G-3357)*

PPG Architectural Finishes Inc...............G..... 302 454-9091
  Wilmington *(G-19140)*

PPG Architectural Finishes Inc...............G..... 302 762-0555
  Wilmington *(G-19141)*

T B Painting Restoration........................G..... 610 283-4100
  Newark *(G-12152)*

2865 Cyclic crudes and intermediates

BASF Corporation..................................C..... 302 992-5600
  Wilmington *(G-14774)*

◆ Chemfirst Inc.....................................D..... 302 774-1000
  Wilmington *(G-15354)*

Dupont Indus Bsciences USA LLC.........E..... 302 774-1000
  Wilmington *(G-16210)*

Eidp Inc...E..... 302 656-9626
  Wilmington *(G-16337)*

Eidp Inc...G..... 302 999-2826
  Wilmington *(G-16339)*

Orient Corporation of America................E..... 302 628-1300
  Seaford *(G-13326)*

2869 Industrial organic chemicals, nec

◆ Ashland Spcalty Ingredients GP..........C..... 302 594-5000
  Wilmington *(G-14584)*

Basell Capital Corporation.....................F..... 302 683-8000
  Wilmington *(G-14772)*

BASF Corporation..................................C..... 302 992-5600
  Wilmington *(G-14774)*

Breakthru Beverage Group LLC.............D..... 302 356-3500
  New Castle *(G-8890)*

Butamax Advanced Biofuels LLC...........G..... 302 695-6787
  Wilmington *(G-15160)*

Celanese International Corp...................D..... 972 443-4000
  Wilmington *(G-15298)*

Cfg Lab Inc..G..... 302 261-3403
  Wilmington *(G-15319)*

Ddp Spclty Elctrnic Mtls US 9................G..... 302 774-1000
  Wilmington *(G-15835)*

Dupont Tate Lyle Bio Pdts LLC...............G..... 865 408-1962
  Wilmington *(G-16217)*

Eidp Inc...E..... 302 656-9626
  Wilmington *(G-16337)*

Elcriton Inc..G..... 864 921-5146
  New Castle *(G-9086)*

Ensyn Renewables Inc..........................F..... 302 425-3740
  Wilmington *(G-16430)*

▲ Grayling Industries Inc......................F..... 770 751-9095
  Frederica *(G-4168)*

◆ Hercules LLC.....................................E..... 302 594-5000
  Wilmington *(G-17128)*

Honeywell International Inc....................G..... 302 791-6700
  Claymont *(G-1181)*

Iogen Bmthane Sup Chain III LL............G..... 613 218-2045
  Wilmington *(G-17412)*

Judy Tim Fuel Inc..................................G..... 302 349-5895
  Greenwood *(G-4647)*

Lynch Heights Fuel Corp........................G..... 302 422-9195
  Milford *(G-7980)*

Memorial Super Fuel..............................G..... 215 512-1012
  New Castle *(G-9357)*

Milana Colors LLC.................................G..... 872 274-4321
  Middletown *(G-7368)*

Nutrition & Biosciences Inc....................A..... 212 765-5500
  Wilmington *(G-18721)*

Plaza Fuel..G..... 302 275-6242
  Wilmington *(G-19076)*

Rohm Haas Electronic Mtls LLC.............E..... 302 366-0500
  Newark *(G-11909)*

▲ Royale Pigments & Chem Inc.............E..... 201 845-4666
  Bear *(G-474)*

Sas Nanotechnologies Inc.....................G..... 214 235-1008
  Newark *(G-11951)*

Simar Fuel Inc.......................................G..... 302 304-1969
  Smyrna *(G-13886)*

Specialty Products Us LLC....................E..... 302 774-1000
  Wilmington *(G-19955)*

SPI Holding Company............................E..... 800 789-9755
  Wilmington *(G-19961)*

Stereochemical Inc................................G..... 302 266-0700
  Newark *(G-12100)*

Syntec Corporation................................F..... 302 421-8393
  Wilmington *(G-20191)*

Vital Renewable Energy Company.........E..... 202 595-2944
  Wilmington *(G-20644)*

2873 Nitrogenous fertilizers

Aztech Industries Inc.............................G..... 302 653-1430
  Smyrna *(G-13657)*

◆ Growmark Fs LLC..............................D..... 302 422-3002
  Milford *(G-7913)*

2874 Phosphatic fertilizers

Growmark Fs LLC.................................G..... 302 422-3001
  Milford *(G-7912)*

◆ Growmark Fs LLC..............................D..... 302 422-3002
  Milford *(G-7913)*

2875 Fertilizers, mixing only

◆ Emerald Bioagriculture Corp...............F..... 517 882-7370
  Hockessin *(G-5199)*

◆ Growmark Fs LLC..............................D..... 302 422-3002
  Milford *(G-7913)*

Harvest Consumer Products LLC..........D..... 302 732-6624
  Dagsboro *(G-1460)*

Southern States Coop Inc......................E..... 302 732-6651
  Dagsboro *(G-1507)*

2879 Agricultural chemicals, nec

Ai Dupont..G..... 302 528-6520
  Wilmington *(G-14326)*

▲ Arkion Life Sciences LLC..................F..... 800 468-6324
  New Castle *(G-8822)*

Ashanti Produce International................F..... 800 295-9790
  Wilmington *(G-14578)*

Belchim Crop Prtection US Corp............F..... 302 407-3590
  Wilmington *(G-14814)*

Chemours Company Fc LLC..................C..... 678 427-1530
  Wilmington *(G-15359)*

◆ Chemours Company Fc LLC..............E..... 302 773-1000
  Wilmington *(G-15358)*

Corteva (china) LLC..............................E..... 833 267-8382
  Wilmington *(G-15646)*

Corteva Agriscience LLC.......................E..... 302 485-3000
  Wilmington *(G-15647)*

Dupont Electronics & Imaging................G..... 302 273-6958
  Newark *(G-10576)*

Dupont Indus Bsciences USA LLC.........E..... 302 774-1000
  Wilmington *(G-16210)*

E C I Motorsports Inc............................G..... 302 239-6376
  Newark *(G-10587)*

Eidp Inc...G..... 302 695-7141
  Bear *(G-198)*

Eidp Inc...C..... 302 992-2065
  Wilmington *(G-16338)*

Eidp Inc...G..... 302 999-2826
  Wilmington *(G-16339)*

Eidp Inc...E..... 844 773-2436
  Wilmington *(G-16340)*

Ft Dupont Redevelopment A..................G..... 302 838-7374
  Delaware City *(G-1545)*

HB Dupont Plaza...................................G..... 302 998-7271
  Wilmington *(G-17082)*

Meherrin AG & Chem Co.......................G..... 302 337-0330
  Bridgeville *(G-730)*

Specialty Products N&H Inc...................C..... 302 774-1000
  Wilmington *(G-19954)*

◆ Syngenta Corporation........................E..... 302 425-2000
  Wilmington *(G-20189)*

2891 Adhesives and sealants

Delchem Inc..E..... 302 426-1800
  Wilmington *(G-15990)*

◆ Hercules LLC.....................................E..... 302 594-5000
  Wilmington *(G-17128)*

▼ Max Seal Inc......................................F..... 619 946-2650
  Lewes *(G-6252)*

◆ Tyden Group Holdings Corp...............F..... 740 420-6777
  Wilmington *(G-20481)*

2893 Printing ink

C & A Ink..G..... 302 565-9866
  Newark *(G-10111)*

Colors & Effects USA LLC.....................G..... 302 996-2910
  Newport *(G-12444)*

Digital Ink Sciences LLC.......................G..... 951 757-0027
  Wilmington *(G-16065)*

◆ Fujifilm Imaging Colorants Inc............E..... 800 552-1609
  New Castle *(G-9150)*

2899 Chemical preparations, nec

Amino-Chem (us) LLC...........................G..... 281 305-8668
  Dover *(G-1787)*

Aquacast Liner LLC...............................F..... 302 535-3728
  Newark *(G-9897)*

Blue Sky Clean.......................................G..... 302 584-5800
  Wilmington *(G-14975)*

SIC SECTION

30 RUBBER AND MISCELLANEOUS PLASTIC PRODUCTS

Championx LLC .... G 856 423-6417
  Historic New Castle *(G-4955)*
Chemours Co Fc LLC .... F 302 353-5003
  Wilmington *(G-15355)*
▲ Chemours Company .... B 302 773-1000
  Wilmington *(G-15356)*
Chemours Company Fc LLC .... D 302 540-5423
  Wilmington *(G-15360)*
◆ Chemours Company Fc LLC .... E 302 773-1000
  Wilmington *(G-15358)*
Croda Inc .... G 302 429-5200
  New Castle *(G-8986)*
Croda Inc .... G 302 429-5249
  New Castle *(G-8987)*
Cytec Industries Inc .... E 302 530-7665
  Wilmington *(G-15756)*
Diversified Chemical Pdts Inc .... G 302 656-5293
  Wilmington *(G-16095)*
Dynasep LLC .... G 302 368-4540
  Newark *(G-10586)*
E I Du Pont De Nemours & Co .... E 843 335-5934
  Wilmington *(G-16239)*
Economic Laundry Solutions .... G 302 234-7627
  Hockessin *(G-5198)*
Euphoric Hrbals Apothecary LLC .... G 302 491-4443
  Milford *(G-7884)*
Franklin Jester PA .... G 302 368-3080
  Newark *(G-10772)*
Frontier Scientific Svcs Inc .... E 302 266-6891
  Newark *(G-10789)*
H2og Fogger Inc .... G 414 333-7024
  Wilmington *(G-17025)*
Honeywell International Inc .... E 302 791-6700
  Claymont *(G-1181)*
Hrd Products Inc .... G 302 757-3587
  Newark *(G-10983)*
Jcr Systems LLC .... G 302 420-6072
  Historic New Castle *(G-5010)*
Khaos Beauty LLC .... A 302 427-0119
  Wilmington *(G-17712)*
Lignolix Inc .... G 516 660-2558
  Newark *(G-11258)*
Management Chemical Co .... G 410 326-0964
  Dover *(G-3007)*
Orient Corporation of America .... E 302 628-1300
  Seaford *(G-13326)*
▲ Polydel Corporation .... F 302 655-8200
  Wilmington *(G-19113)*
Quikstamp LLC .... F 302 659-7555
  Newark *(G-11800)*
Rg3 Texas LLC .... G 778 891-5569
  Wilmington *(G-19452)*
Royal Delta Specialties LLC .... G 908 410-7478
  Rehoboth Beach *(G-12940)*
Saltverk Inc .... F 412 413-9193
  Wilmington *(G-19642)*
▲ Shore Chem LLC .... F 201 845-4666
  Bear *(G-490)*
Solenis Holdings 1 LLC .... F 866 337-1533
  Wilmington *(G-19920)*
Terra Systems of Delaware LLC .... G 302 798-9553
  Claymont *(G-1311)*
Thrupore Technologies Inc .... G 205 657-0714
  New Castle *(G-9627)*
Twinco Romax LLC .... G 302 998-3019
  Wilmington *(G-20469)*
▲ Zeneca Holdings Inc .... D 302 886-3000
  Wilmington *(G-20953)*

29 PETROLEUM REFINING AND RELATED INDUSTRIES

2911 Petroleum refining

Air Products and Chemicals Inc .... G 302 834-6033
  Delaware City *(G-1528)*
D150 Fueling LLC .... E 215 559-1132
  Newark *(G-10378)*
Eidp Inc .... G 302 772-0016
  New Castle *(G-9084)*
Eidp Inc .... F 302 452-9000
  Newark *(G-10620)*
Eidp Inc .... E 615 847-6920
  Wilmington *(G-16341)*
Greentec Laboratories LLC .... G 301 744-7336
  Historic New Castle *(G-4999)*
Honeywell International Inc .... E 302 791-6700
  Claymont *(G-1181)*
Innospec Inc .... F 302 454-8100
  Newark *(G-11022)*
O2diesel Fuels Inc .... F 302 266-6000
  Newark *(G-11572)*
▲ Prime Products Usa Inc .... G 302 528-3866
  Wilmington *(G-19192)*
Reliance Egleford Upstream LLC .... G 302 472-7437
  Wilmington *(G-19425)*
Rg3 Texas Holdings LLC .... G 778 891-7569
  Wilmington *(G-19451)*
Transstate Jet Service Inc .... F 302 346-3102
  Dover *(G-3715)*
▲ United Acquisition Corp .... E 302 651-9856
  Wilmington *(G-20523)*

2951 Asphalt paving mixtures and blocks

Asphalt Kingdom LLC .... G 866 399-5562
  Wilmington *(G-14589)*
Chemstar Corp .... G 302 465-3175
  Milford *(G-7824)*
Christiana Materials Inc .... F 302 633-5600
  Wilmington *(G-15411)*
Diamond Materials LLC .... D 302 658-6524
  Wilmington *(G-16051)*
Driveway Mint Pvng/Slcting LLC .... G 302 228-2644
  Bridgeville *(G-696)*
Gardner-Gibson Mfg Inc .... F 302 628-4290
  Seaford *(G-13196)*
Material Supply Inc .... E 302 658-6524
  Wilmington *(G-18191)*
▲ United Acquisition Corp .... E 302 651-9856
  Wilmington *(G-20523)*

2952 Asphalt felts and coatings

Goldis Holdings Inc .... D 302 764-3100
  Wilmington *(G-16914)*
Iko Production Inc .... E 302 764-3100
  Wilmington *(G-17273)*
▲ Iko Production Inc .... D 302 764-3100
  Wilmington *(G-17274)*
Ipm Inc .... F 302 328-4030
  New Castle *(G-9241)*
Kings Sealcoating .... G 302 674-1568
  Dover *(G-2877)*
Monroe Iko Inc .... F 302 764-3100
  Wilmington *(G-18419)*

2992 Lubricating oils and greases

Chem Tech Inc .... G 302 798-9675
  Wilmington *(G-15353)*
Restore Incorporated .... F 302 655-6257
  Wilmington *(G-19443)*
Robert Elgart Automotive .... G 800 220-7777
  Newark *(G-11898)*

2999 Petroleum and coal products, nec

Act & Associates LLC .... G 302 318-6842
  Newark *(G-9759)*

30 RUBBER AND MISCELLANEOUS PLASTIC PRODUCTS

3011 Tires and inner tubes

JS Tire Corporation .... G 302 558-2320
  Wilmington *(G-17604)*
Movarna LLC .... G 805 501-5821
  Middletown *(G-7385)*
Smart Tire Company Inc .... G 909 358-0987
  Middletown *(G-7577)*
Spm Tire Service LLC .... G 302 731-1004
  Newark *(G-12070)*

3052 Rubber and plastics hose and beltings

Industrial Valves & Fittings .... F 302 326-2494
  New Castle *(G-9233)*

3053 Gaskets; packing and sealing devices

Century Seals Inc .... E 302 629-0324
  Seaford *(G-13105)*
Greene Tweed of Delaware Inc .... E 302 888-2560
  Wilmington *(G-16971)*
▲ Miller Metal Fabrication Inc .... D 302 337-2291
  Bridgeville *(G-734)*
New Process Fibre Company .... D 302 349-4535
  Greenwood *(G-4657)*
▲ Unique Fabricating Na Inc .... A 248 853-2333
  Wilmington *(G-20518)*
▲ Watson-Marlow Flow Smart Inc .... E 302 536-6388
  Seaford *(G-13445)*

3069 Fabricated rubber products, nec

Brandywine Rubber Mills LLC .... G 267 499-3993
  Wilmington *(G-15084)*
Fabreeka Intl Holdings Inc .... G 302 452-2500
  Newark *(G-10700)*
▲ Forcebeyond Inc .... E 302 995-6588
  Wilmington *(G-16688)*
Forte Sports Incorporated .... G 302 731-0776
  Newark *(G-10766)*
I Love Myself LLC .... G 470 474-3347
  Wilmington *(G-17248)*
◆ LRC North America Inc .... E 302 427-2845
  Wilmington *(G-18018)*
Pascale Industries Inc .... F 302 421-9400
  New Castle *(G-9454)*
Rowe Industries Inc .... G 302 855-0585
  Milford *(G-8073)*
Twash LLC .... G 302 488-0248
  Dover *(G-3735)*
◆ Vulcan International Corp .... F 302 428-3181
  Wilmington *(G-20658)*
Wearwell .... G 302 547-3337
  Wilmington *(G-20700)*

3081 Unsupported plastics film and sheet

Aearo Technologies LLC .... B 302 283-5497
  Newark *(G-9787)*
▲ Ajedium Film Group LLC .... G 302 452-6609
  Newark *(G-9803)*
Axess Corporation .... G 302 292-8500
  Historic New Castle *(G-4937)*
◆ Delstar Technologies Inc .... C 302 378-8888
  Middletown *(G-7051)*
Dupont De Nemours Inc .... A 302 774-3034
  Wilmington *(G-16205)*
Dupont Specialty Pdts USA LLC .... E 302 992-2941
  Wilmington *(G-16216)*

30 RUBBER AND MISCELLANEOUS PLASTIC PRODUCTS

Eidp Inc .... G 302 992-2458
  Wilmington *(G-16344)*
Fuji Film .... E 302 477-8000
  New Castle *(G-9149)*
▲ Grayling Industries Inc .... F 770 751-9095
  Frederica *(G-4168)*
Ilc Dover LP .... B 302 629-6860
  Frederica *(G-4173)*
Mativ Holdings Inc .... F 302 378-8888
  Middletown *(G-7331)*
Printpack Inc .... C 302 323-4000
  New Castle *(G-9495)*
◆ Taghleef Industries Inc .... D 302 326-5500
  Newark *(G-12155)*
▲ Wilmington Fibre Specialty Co .... E 302 328-7525
  Historic New Castle *(G-5102)*

3082 Unsupported plastics profile shapes

Fbk Medical Tubing Inc .... F 302 855-0585
  Georgetown *(G-4315)*
Thermoplastic Processes Inc .... F 888 554-6400
  Georgetown *(G-4552)*
Tpi Partners Inc .... E 302 855-0139
  Georgetown *(G-4558)*

3083 Laminated plastics plate and sheet

Fbk Medical Tubing Inc .... F 302 855-0585
  Georgetown *(G-4315)*
▲ Franklin Fibre-Lamitex Corp .... E 302 652-3621
  Wilmington *(G-16728)*
Ipd Technologies LLC .... G 302 533-8850
  Newark *(G-11055)*

3085 Plastics bottles

▲ Shaker Revolution LLC .... G 302 219-4838
  Wilmington *(G-19777)*

3086 Plastics foam products

103 WHOlesale&distribution LLC .... G 302 344-2093
  Wilmington *(G-14102)*
Aearo Technologies LLC .... B 302 283-5497
  Newark *(G-9787)*
Baytown Packhouse Inc .... G 936 340-2122
  Newark *(G-9998)*
Cargo Aligeorgia LLC .... G 302 899-1025
  Smyrna *(G-13674)*
Dart Container Sales Company .... G 305 759-5044
  New Castle *(G-8998)*
Dupont De Nemours Inc .... A 302 774-3034
  Wilmington *(G-16205)*
Dupont Specialty Pdts USA LLC .... E 302 992-2941
  Wilmington *(G-16216)*
Fluorogistx LLC .... E 302 479-7614
  Wilmington *(G-16674)*
Prezoom LLC .... G 732 837-1170
  Historic New Castle *(G-5053)*
▲ Unique Fabricating Na Inc .... A 248 853-2333
  Wilmington *(G-20518)*
United Specialty Foam LLC .... G 302 650-5948
  Wilmington *(G-20527)*

3088 Plastics plumbing fixtures

Atlantic Source Contg Inc .... G 302 645-5207
  Lewes *(G-5718)*

3089 Plastics products, nec

3imachinecom Inc .... G 301 233-7562
  Wilmington *(G-14129)*
A&J Products Inc .... F 302 424-0750
  Houston *(G-5434)*
Artisan Interiors Group LLC .... F 302 537-4811
  Ocean View *(G-12464)*

Atlantic Aluminum Products Inc .... D 302 349-9091
  Greenwood *(G-4592)*
▲ Atlantis Industries Corp .... D 302 684-8542
  Georgetown *(G-4217)*
Axess Corporation .... G 302 292-8500
  Historic New Castle *(G-4937)*
Aztech Industries Inc .... G 302 653-1430
  Smyrna *(G-13657)*
Berry Global Inc .... E 302 378-9853
  Middletown *(G-6914)*
BF Rich Co Inc .... C 302 369-2512
  Newark *(G-10030)*
Cara Plastics Inc .... G 302 622-7070
  Wilmington *(G-15239)*
Charles Williams .... F 302 274-2996
  Wilmington *(G-15342)*
Covation Biomaterials LLC .... C 865 279-1414
  Newark *(G-10339)*
CP Cases Inc .... G 410 352-9450
  Frankford *(G-4095)*
▲ Craig Technologies Inc .... E 302 628-9900
  Seaford *(G-13140)*
Cramaro Tarpaulin Systems Inc .... G 302 292-2170
  Newark *(G-10344)*
▲ Custom America .... G 856 516-1103
  Wilmington *(G-15738)*
Dongjin Usa Inc .... F 302 691-8510
  Wilmington *(G-16140)*
Ensinger Penn Fibre Inc .... E 302 349-4505
  Greenwood *(G-4626)*
First State Container LLC .... E 603 888-1315
  Newark *(G-10730)*
▲ Forcebeyond Inc .... E 302 995-6588
  Wilmington *(G-16688)*
Itskins Americas Inc .... G 805 422-6700
  New Castle *(G-9245)*
JG Plastics .... G 302 545-4888
  Wilmington *(G-17541)*
Justin Tanks LLC .... G 302 856-3521
  Georgetown *(G-4389)*
Lonjew LLC .... G 803 994-9888
  Lewes *(G-6219)*
Molded Components Inc .... G 302 588-2240
  Wilmington *(G-18404)*
▲ Negri Bossi North America Inc .... G 302 328-8020
  New Castle *(G-9400)*
New Castle Engraving Co .... G 302 652-7551
  New Castle *(G-9408)*
New Process Fibre Company .... D 302 349-4535
  Greenwood *(G-4657)*
Oxford Plastic Systems LLC .... G 800 567-9182
  Wilmington *(G-18845)*
Pacifico Industrial Ltd .... F 213 435-1181
  Newark *(G-11610)*
Plasti Pallets Corp .... G 302 737-1977
  Christiana *(G-1007)*
Polytechnic Resources Inc .... G 302 629-4221
  Seaford *(G-13350)*
Pony Run Kitchens LLC .... G 302 492-3006
  Hartly *(G-4903)*
Quantum Polymers Corporation .... F 302 737-7012
  Newark *(G-11796)*
▲ Resource Intl Inc .... F 302 762-4501
  New Castle *(G-9524)*
Richard Earl Fisher .... G 302 598-1957
  Wilmington *(G-19468)*
Solo Cup Operating Corporation .... B 800 248-5960
  New Castle *(G-9577)*
▲ Wilmington Fibre Specialty Co .... E 302 328-7525
  Historic New Castle *(G-5102)*

31 LEATHER AND LEATHER PRODUCTS

3111 Leather tanning and finishing

Exco Inc .... D 905 477-3065
  Wilmington *(G-16502)*
Fairway Manufacturing Company .... F 302 398-4630
  Harrington *(G-4768)*
Patricea and Co LLC .... G 929 374-9761
  Dover *(G-3280)*

3149 Footwear, except rubber, nec

Shooshoos LLC .... G 302 256-5355
  Wilmington *(G-19807)*

3151 Leather gloves and mittens

Kaul Glove and Mfg Co .... D 302 292-2660
  Historic New Castle *(G-5014)*
Masley Enterprises Inc .... E 302 427-9885
  Wilmington *(G-18183)*

3161 Luggage

Bey Hollywood LLC .... G 209 789-5132
  Dover *(G-1925)*
Continental Case .... G 302 322-1765
  Newark *(G-10313)*
CP Cases Inc .... G 410 352-9450
  Frankford *(G-4095)*
Grease City Inc .... G 302 661-5675
  Wilmington *(G-16957)*
ID By Oliver LLC .... G 202 643-5536
  Middletown *(G-7220)*
Leallure LLC .... G 302 386-8886
  Wilmington *(G-17847)*
Makkari Globl Vsion A Sries LL .... G 571 308-6032
  Dover *(G-3003)*
Slaybelles LLC .... G 302 304-1027
  Wilmington *(G-19862)*
Snickers Ditch Trunk Company .... G 302 325-1762
  Historic New Castle *(G-5073)*
Ukhi LLC .... G 833 511-1977
  New Castle *(G-9649)*

3171 Women's handbags and purses

Frontgate LLC .... G 302 245-6654
  Bethany Beach *(G-602)*

3199 Leather goods, nec

Fairway Manufacturing Company .... F 302 398-4630
  Harrington *(G-4768)*
Jarel Industries LLC .... G 336 782-0697
  Camden *(G-859)*

32 STONE, CLAY, GLASS, AND CONCRETE PRODUCTS

3211 Flat glass

Wilmington Glass Co .... G 302 777-7000
  Wilmington *(G-20817)*

3229 Pressed and blown glass, nec

Bellaa Bomb LLC .... G 800 409-2521
  Wilmington *(G-14819)*
Psp Corp .... G 302 764-7730
  Wilmington *(G-19244)*
R and H Filter Co Inc .... G 302 856-2129
  Georgetown *(G-4479)*
Studio On 24 Inc .... G 302 644-4424
  Lewes *(G-6519)*

Te Connectivity Corporation................ F 800 522-6752
  Wilmington (G-20243)

3231 Products of purchased glass

Elevations In Ecom LLC....................... G 302 797-1709
  Wilmington (G-16360)
Hensco LLC... G 302 423-1638
  Harrington (G-4784)
◆ Miles Scientific Corporation................ E 302 737-6960
  Newark (G-11418)
Shamrock Glass Co Inc........................ F 302 629-5500
  Seaford (G-13399)
Venice International Pdts LLC.............. G 630 571-7171
  Newark (G-12312)

3253 Ceramic wall and floor tile

GE Energy Ceramic Composi................ D 302 631-1300
  Newark (G-10817)
Intelligent Building Mtls LLC................. G 302 261-9922
  Newark (G-11040)
Maneto Inc... E 302 656-4285
  Wilmington (G-18103)
Monopy International Inc...................... G 312 339-8751
  Wilmington (G-18417)

3255 Clay refractories

Frc Global Inc.. D 800 609-5711
  Wilmington (G-16732)
◆ Rgp Holding Inc.................................. F 302 661-0117
  Wilmington (G-19453)
◆ Rhi Refractories Holding Company..... A 302 655-6497
  Wilmington (G-19457)

3259 Structural clay products, nec

▲ Northern Roof Tiles US Inc................ G 888 678-6866
  Wilmington (G-18685)

3261 Vitreous plumbing fixtures

Aquatica Plumbing Group Inc............. G 866 606-2782
  New Castle (G-8817)
Sylvester Custom Cabinetry................ G 302 398-6050
  Harrington (G-4838)

3262 Vitreous china table and kitchenware

Saenger Porcelain................................ G 302 738-5349
  Newark (G-11932)

3263 Semivitreous table and kitchenware

▲ Mauviel Usa Inc................................. E 302 326-4800
  Historic New Castle (G-5025)
Monopy International Inc...................... G 312 339-8751
  Wilmington (G-18417)
Pony Run Kitchens LLC....................... G 302 492-3006
  Hartly (G-4903)

3264 Porcelain electrical supplies

◆ NGK North America Inc..................... G 302 654-1344
  Wilmington (G-18640)
▲ Niterra (USA) Holding Inc................... C 302 288-0131
  Wilmington (G-18650)

3269 Pottery products, nec

B & F Ceramics.................................... G 302 475-4721
  Wilmington (G-14691)
Intelligent Building Mtls LLC................. G 302 261-9922
  Newark (G-11040)
Joel Gonzalez...................................... G 302 562-6878
  Wilmington (G-17561)
Katlyn Co Ceramics............................. G 302 528-1322
  Bear (G-323)
Robert McMann................................... G 302 329-9413
  Milton (G-8701)

Valuewrite... G 302 593-0694
  Middletown (G-7681)

3271 Concrete block and brick

All Rock & Mulch LLC.......................... G 302 838-7625
  Bear (G-26)
Valley Landscaping and Con Inc......... G 302 922-5020
  Dover (G-3772)

3272 Concrete products, nec

American Precast................................. G 302 629-6688
  Seaford (G-13063)
▲ Ballistics Technology Intl Ltd............. G 877 291-1111
  Wilmington (G-14724)
Best Stoneworks Inc........................... G 302 765-3497
  Wilmington (G-14857)
Bio Riot Technologies Mfg Inc............. G 407 399-3413
  Lewes (G-5766)
Blue Heron Contracting LLC............... G 302 526-0648
  Greenwood (G-4600)
Cecil Vault & Memorial Co Inc............. G 302 994-3806
  Wilmington (G-15293)
Cooper-Wilbert Vault Co Inc................ G 302 376-1331
  Middletown (G-7013)
Delaware Monument and Vault............ G 302 540-2387
  Hockessin (G-5181)
F Sartin Tyson Inc................................ F 302 834-4571
  Saint Georges (G-13033)
National Concrete Products LLC......... E 302 349-5528
  Greenwood (G-4656)
Oldcastle Inc.. G 302 836-6492
  Bear (G-406)
◆ Rhi Refractories Holding Company..... A 302 655-6497
  Wilmington (G-19457)
Smw Sales LLC................................... E 302 875-7958
  Laurel (G-5600)

3273 Ready-mixed concrete

Atlantic Concrete Company Inc........... D 302 422-8017
  Milford (G-7777)
Chaney Enterprises............................. F 302 990-5039
  Seaford (G-13111)
Concrete Co Inc................................... G 302 652-1101
  Wilmington (G-15586)
Gfp Mobile Mix Supply LLC................. F 302 998-7687
  Wilmington (G-16857)
HMA Concrete LLC............................. F 302 777-1235
  Wilmington (G-17158)
Legacy Vulcan LLC............................. G 302 875-0748
  Georgetown (G-4405)
Legacy Vulcan LLC............................. G 302 875-5733
  Seaford (G-13258)
Material Transit Inc.............................. E 302 395-0556
  New Castle (G-9353)
Southgate Concrete Company............. F 302 376-5280
  Middletown (G-7591)
Thoro-Goods Concrete Co Inc............. E 302 934-8102
  Dagsboro (G-1516)

3281 Cut stone and stone products

H&K Group Inc..................................... G 302 934-7635
  Dagsboro (G-1457)
▲ Keystone Granite and Tile Inc........... F 302 323-0200
  New Castle (G-9280)
Sovereigntactical LLC.......................... G 858 336-9471
  Wilmington (G-19945)
Stone Express...................................... G 302 376-8876
  Middletown (G-7600)

3291 Abrasive products

3dsteel Inc.. G 713 677-2027
  Middletown (G-6817)

Dow Chemical Company...................... E 302 368-4169
  Newark (G-10558)
Spectrum Hone & Lace Llc.................. G 313 268-5455
  Newark (G-12065)

3295 Minerals, ground or treated

Iko Southeast Inc................................. E 302 764-3100
  Wilmington (G-17277)

3296 Mineral wool

Ipm Inc.. F 302 328-4030
  New Castle (G-9241)
▲ Unique Fabricating Na Inc................. A 248 853-2333
  Wilmington (G-20518)

3297 Nonclay refractories

3299 Nonmetallic mineral products,

Atlantic Industrial Optics...................... G 302 856-7905
  Selbyville (G-13467)
Best Stucco LLC.................................. G 302 650-3620
  New Castle (G-8862)
Santo Stucco....................................... G 302 453-0901
  Newark (G-11944)

33 PRIMARY METAL INDUSTRIES

3312 Blast furnaces and steel mills

AMP Manufacturing LLC...................... G 302 691-8883
  Wilmington (G-14460)
Apex Piping Systems Inc.................... D 302 995-6136
  Wilmington (G-14506)
◆ Chemfirst Inc..................................... D 302 774-1000
  Wilmington (G-15354)
◆ CMC Steel Holding Company............ G 302 691-6200
  Wilmington (G-15500)
Eagle Erectors Inc................................ F 302 832-9586
  Bear (G-185)
◆ Evraz Claymont Steel Holdings Inc.... B 302 792-5400
  Claymont (G-1140)
Evraz Claymont Steel Inc.................... B 302 792-5400
  Claymont (G-1141)
Lohmann Steel LLC............................ G 844 488-1790
  Wilmington (G-17977)
Seaside Service LLC........................... G 302 827-3775
  Lewes (G-6455)
Stainless Steel Invest Inc.................... D 800 499-7833
  Wilmington (G-20006)
Tire 24 X 7 Inc...................................... E 833 847-3247
  Newark (G-12199)
Tms Nrhlth Ctrs Tysons Crnr LL......... G 302 994-4010
  Bear (G-535)

3313 Electrometallurgical products

American Minerals Inc......................... G 302 652-3301
  New Castle (G-8799)

3315 Steel wire and related products

National Vinyl Products Inc.................. F 817 913-5991
  Dover (G-3156)
Priscilla Lancaster............................... G 302 792-8305
  Claymont (G-1267)

3316 Cold finishing of steel shapes

Joseph T Ryerson & Son Inc............... F 215 736-8970
  Newark (G-11129)
Stainless Alloys Inc............................. D 800 499-7833
  Wilmington (G-20005)
Stainless Steel Invest Inc.................... D 800 499-7833
  Wilmington (G-20006)

3317 Steel pipe and tubes

Employee Codes: A=Over 500 employees, B=251-500
C=101-250, D=51-100, E=20-50, F=10-19, G=1-9

33 PRIMARY METAL INDUSTRIES

Apex Piping Systems Inc .... D 302 995-6136
  Wilmington *(G-14506)*
▲ Emeca/Spe Usa LLC .... G 302 875-0760
  Laurel *(G-5509)*
Handy & Harman .... F 302 697-9521
  Camden *(G-843)*
▲ Handytube Corporation .... C 302 697-9521
  Camden *(G-844)*
Jaguar Tubulars Inc .... G 438 778-6535
  Newark *(G-11085)*
Psp Corp .... G 302 764-7730
  Wilmington *(G-19244)*

3321 Gray and ductile iron foundries

Ej Usa Inc .... E 302 378-1100
  Middletown *(G-7087)*

3324 Steel investment foundries

Consoldted Fabrication Constrs .... C 302 654-9001
  Wilmington *(G-15608)*
▲ Forcebeyond Inc .... E 302 995-6588
  Wilmington *(G-16688)*
S P S International Inv Co .... G 302 478-9055
  Wilmington *(G-19612)*
Tajan Hldings Investments Inc .... G 302 300-1183
  Middletown *(G-7619)*

3341 Secondary nonferrous metals

Diamond State Recycling Corp .... E 302 655-1501
  Wilmington *(G-16058)*
Negative Emissions Mtls Inc .... G 929 388-3352
  Claymont *(G-1248)*

3353 Aluminum sheet, plate, and foil

UACJ Trading & Processing Amer .... G 312 636-5941
  Wilmington *(G-20488)*

3354 Aluminum extruded products

UACJ Trading & Processing Amer .... G 312 636-5941
  Wilmington *(G-20488)*

3356 Nonferrous rolling and drawing, nec

Energy Tech Holdings LLC .... E 212 356-6130
  Wilmington *(G-16418)*

3357 Nonferrous wiredrawing and insulating

First State Controls Inc .... G 302 559-7822
  Wilmington *(G-16626)*
Nouvir Lighting Corporation .... F 302 628-9933
  Seaford *(G-13319)*
Nouvir Lightning Corporation .... G 302 628-9888
  Seaford *(G-13320)*
W L Gore & Associates Inc .... C 302 368-3700
  Newark *(G-12341)*
▲ W L Gore & Associates Inc .... D 302 738-4880
  Newark *(G-12342)*

3365 Aluminum foundries

Cushman Foundry LLC .... E 513 984-5570
  Dover *(G-2172)*

3369 Nonferrous foundries, nec

Diamond State Props .... G 302 528-7146
  Bear *(G-167)*

3398 Metal heat treating

Industrial Metal Treating Corp .... F 302 656-1677
  Wilmington *(G-17215)*

3399 Primary metal products

Ametek Inc .... D 302 456-4400
  Newark *(G-9851)*

34 FABRICATED METAL PRODUCTS

3411 Metal cans

▼ Crown Cork Seal Rcvbles De Cor .... G 215 698-5100
  Wilmington *(G-15716)*
▲ Jmt Inter LLC .... G 302 312-5177
  Bear *(G-306)*
Reynolds Metals Company LLC .... A 302 366-0555
  Newark *(G-11876)*

3421 Cutlery

Arovo US Inc .... E 952 290-0799
  Dover *(G-1818)*
Cobra Razors .... G 302 540-0464
  Wilmington *(G-15513)*
Dalstrong America Inc .... G 716 380-4998
  Wilmington *(G-15772)*
Delaware Diamond Knives Inc .... E 302 999-7476
  Wilmington *(G-15906)*
◆ LRC North America Inc .... E 302 427-2845
  Wilmington *(G-18018)*
Macknyfe Specialties .... G 302 239-4904
  Hockessin *(G-5289)*

3423 Hand and edge tools, nec

Black & Decker Inc .... G 860 827-3861
  Newark *(G-10043)*
▼ Easy Lawn Inc .... E 302 815-6500
  Greenwood *(G-4624)*
Pkg LLC .... G 269 651-8640
  Wilmington *(G-19062)*

3429 Hardware, nec

Buck Algonquin Co .... G 302 659-6900
  Smyrna *(G-13669)*
D C Mitchell LLC .... G 302 998-1181
  Wilmington *(G-15759)*
Gibbons Innovations Inc .... G 302 265-4220
  Lincoln *(G-6671)*
Pacbak Inc .... F 907 268-0802
  Lewes *(G-6345)*
Pennengineering Holdings LLC .... C 302 576-2746
  Wilmington *(G-18954)*
Wibdi Aviation Co Corp .... F 305 677-9685
  Dover *(G-3847)*

3432 Plumbing fixture fittings and trim

Ferguson Enterprises LLC .... G 302 747-2032
  Dover *(G-2492)*
Speakman Company .... F 302 765-0204
  Historic New Castle *(G-5074)*

3433 Heating equipment, except electric

Aztech Industries Inc .... G 302 653-1430
  Smyrna *(G-13657)*
Solar Foundations Usa Inc .... G 855 738-7200
  New Castle *(G-9576)*
Watts Htg Hot Wtr Slutions LLC .... D 817 335-9531
  Wilmington *(G-20686)*
World Class Products LLC .... G 302 737-1441
  Newark *(G-12408)*

3441 Fabricated structural metal

▼ Amazon Steel Construction Inc .... G 302 751-1146
  Milford *(G-7766)*
Anchor Enterprises .... G 302 629-7969
  Seaford *(G-13066)*
Asa V Peugh Inc .... E 302 629-7969
  Seaford *(G-13069)*

◆ CMC Steel Holding Company .... G 302 691-6200
  Wilmington *(G-15500)*
Crystal Steel Fabricators Inc .... F 302 846-0277
  Delmar *(G-1584)*
Crystal Steel Fabricators Inc .... D 302 846-0613
  Delmar *(G-1585)*
Deaven Development Corp .... G 302 994-5793
  Wilmington *(G-15847)*
Donald F Deaven Inc .... E 302 994-5793
  Wilmington *(G-16135)*
Eagle Erectors Inc .... F 302 832-9586
  Bear *(G-185)*
East Coast Erectors Inc .... F 302 323-1800
  New Castle *(G-9077)*
Engineering Incorporated .... G 302 995-6862
  Wilmington *(G-16424)*
First State Fabrication LLC .... G 302 875-2417
  Seaford *(G-13186)*
Hardcore Cmpstes Oprations Llc .... F 302 442-5900
  New Castle *(G-9196)*
Helmark Steel Inc C
  Wilmington *(G-17118)*
Industrial Products of Del .... G 302 328-6648
  New Castle *(G-9231)*
Interebar Fabricators LLC .... F 513 310-1782
  New Castle *(G-9238)*
Iron Works Inc .... F 302 684-1887
  Milton *(G-8643)*
Leland Oakley .... G 302 430-3403
  Felton *(G-3995)*
Mancor US Inc .... D 302 573-3858
  Wilmington *(G-18102)*
Messick & Gray Cnstr Inc .... E 302 337-8777
  Bridgeville *(G-731)*
Mid-Atlantic Steel LLC .... E 302 323-1800
  New Castle *(G-9368)*
▲ Miller Metal Fabrication Inc .... D 302 337-2291
  Bridgeville *(G-734)*
MJM Fabrications Inc .... G 302 764-0163
  Wilmington *(G-18390)*
Newarc Welding & Fabricating .... G 302 658-5214
  Wilmington *(G-18630)*
Phillips Fabrication .... G 302 875-4424
  Laurel *(G-5576)*
▼ Potts Wldg Boiler Repr Co Inc .... C 302 453-2550
  Newark *(G-11716)*
R C Fabricators Inc .... D 302 573-8989
  Wilmington *(G-19303)*
Rivas Ulises .... G 302 454-8595
  Newark *(G-11890)*
Spg International LLC .... G 404 823-3934
  Marydel *(G-6811)*
Steel Suppliers Inc .... C 302 654-5243
  Wilmington *(G-20043)*
Summit Steel Inc .... D 302 325-3220
  New Castle *(G-9599)*

3442 Metal doors, sash, and trim

Allmark Door Company LLC .... F 302 323-4999
  New Castle *(G-8786)*
◆ Alutech United Inc .... G 302 436-6005
  Selbyville *(G-13461)*
Axiom Dist & Fulfillment .... G 519 620-2000
  Wilmington *(G-14682)*
BF Rich Co Inc .... C 302 369-2512
  Newark *(G-10030)*
Cheslantic Overhead Door .... G 443 880-0378
  Delmar *(G-1577)*
Delmarvalous .... G 302 200-2001
  Dagsboro *(G-1439)*
Herbstar Industries LLC .... G 302 888-9207
  Newark *(G-10947)*

34 FABRICATED METAL PRODUCTS

Herbstar Industries LLC.................................. G 754 273-4204
  Newark (G-10948)
Shore Shutters and Shade........................... G 302 569-1738
  Millsboro (G-8462)

3443 Fabricated plate work (boiler shop)

Amer Industrial Tech Inc................................ E 302 765-3318
  Wilmington (G-14422)
Apex Piping Systems Inc.............................. D 302 995-6136
  Wilmington (G-14506)
Atom Alloys LLC... F 786 975-3771
  Wilmington (G-14633)
Baltimore Aircoil Company Inc..................... C 302 424-2583
  Milford (G-7781)
Contractor Materials LLC.............................. E 302 658-5241
  New Castle (G-8970)
Creative Assemblies Inc............................... F 302 956-6194
  Bridgeville (G-688)
Elanco Inc... G 302 731-8500
  Bear (G-199)

3444 Sheet metalwork

A & H Metals Inc... E 302 366-7540
  Newark (G-9720)
Accurate Metal Solutions LLC...................... A
  Wilmington (G-14228)
AG & G Sheet Metal Inc................................ G 302 653-4111
  Townsend (G-13954)
Allied Precision Inc....................................... G 302 376-6844
  Middletown (G-6852)
Alu-Rex USA Inc.. E 418 832-7632
  Wilmington (G-14399)
Atlantic Screen & Mfg Inc............................ G 302 684-3197
  Milton (G-8565)
Atlas Wldg & Fabrication Inc....................... E 302 326-1900
  New Castle (G-8832)
Costa and Rihl Inc.. C 856 534-7325
  Wilmington (G-15649)
CP Cases Inc... G 410 352-9450
  Frankford (G-4095)
Custom Mechanical Inc................................ E 302 537-1150
  Frankford (G-4096)
Custom Sheet Metal of Delaware................ G 302 998-6865
  Wilmington (G-15744)
D M Iannone Inc.. G 302 999-0893
  Wilmington (G-15761)
Ducts Unlimited Inc...................................... E 302 378-4125
  Smyrna (G-13717)
East Coast Machine Works.......................... G 302 349-5180
  Greenwood (G-4623)
Faust Sheet Metal Works Inc....................... G 302 645-9509
  Lewes (G-5991)
Keystone Flashing Company........................ G 215 329-8500
  Wilmington (G-17708)
L & J Sheet Metal.. F 302 875-2822
  Laurel (G-5542)
M Cubed Technologies Inc........................... D 302 454-8600
  Newark (G-11300)
Mastercraft Welding..................................... G 302 697-3932
  Dover (G-3028)
McCabes Mechanical Service Inc................ F 302 854-9001
  Georgetown (G-4421)
Metal-Tech Inc... E 302 322-7770
  New Castle (G-9360)
Metro Eqp & Sheetmetal Pdts..................... G 302 337-8249
  Bridgeville (G-732)
Murphy Steel Inc.. E 302 366-8676
  Newark (G-11473)
Phillips Fabrication...................................... G 302 875-4424
  Laurel (G-5576)
Pilepro Inc... F 866 666-7453
  Wilmington (G-19044)

Power Electronics Inc................................... E 302 653-4822
  Clayton (G-1398)
Quality Htg Ar-Cnditioning Inc.................... E 302 654-5247
  Wilmington (G-19284)
Ramco Solutions LLC.................................. G 302 715-5432
  Laurel (G-5585)
S G Williams & Bros Co............................... F 302 656-8167
  Wilmington (G-19607)
Seaside Service LLC.................................... G 302 827-3775
  Lewes (G-6455)
Sheet Metal Contracting Co........................ E 302 834-3727
  Bear (G-488)
V E Guerrazzi Inc.. F 302 369-5557
  Newark (G-12295)

3446 Architectural metalwork

Access4u Inc... F 800 355-7025
  Lewes (G-5652)
Asa V Peugh Inc... E 302 629-7969
  Seaford (G-13069)
Atlantic Aluminum Products Inc................. D 302 349-9091
  Greenwood (G-4592)
Deaven Development Corp.......................... G 302 994-5793
  Wilmington (G-15847)
Delaware Flooring Supply Inc..................... G 302 276-0031
  Historic New Castle (G-4969)
Donald F Deaven Inc.................................... E 302 994-5793
  Wilmington (G-16135)
Iron Source 2.. G 302 653-7562
  Smyrna (G-13777)
Murphy Steel Inc.. E 302 366-8676
  Newark (G-11473)

3448 Prefabricated metal buildings

▼ All-Span Inc... E 302 349-9460
  Bridgeville (G-662)
Coastal Sun Roms Prch Enclsres................ G 302 537-3679
  Frankford (G-4092)
Regional Builders Inc.................................. F 302 628-8660
  Seaford (G-13370)
Steel Buildings Inc...................................... G 302 644-0444
  Lewes (G-6508)
Street Core Utility Service.......................... F 302 239-4110
  Hockessin (G-5392)
Sweeten Companies Inc.............................. G 302 737-6161
  Newark (G-12140)

3449 Miscellaneous metalwork

Confab Inc... G 302 429-0140
  Wilmington (G-15592)
Cox Industries Inc....................................... G 302 332-8470
  Newark (G-10340)

3451 Screw machine products

Advanced Prttyping Sltionv LLC................. G 302 375-6048
  Wilmington (G-14278)

3452 Bolts, nuts, rivets, and washers

Advanced Prttyping Sltionv LLC................. G 302 375-6048
  Wilmington (G-14278)
Black & Decker Inc....................................... G 860 827-3861
  Newark (G-10043)
Mr Window Washer...................................... G 302 588-3624
  Claymont (G-1245)

3462 Iron and steel forgings

A T I Funding Corporation........................... F 302 656-8937
  Wilmington (G-14173)
Eager Gear... G 302 727-5831
  Lewes (G-5943)
Oakville Industries LLC................................ F 513 436-5007
  Wilmington (G-18729)

Square One Electric Service Co.................. F 302 678-0400
  Dover (G-3601)
Tdy Holdings LLC... E 302 254-4172
  Wilmington (G-20242)
Timken Gears & Services Inc...................... E 302 633-4600
  Historic New Castle (G-5086)

3463 Nonferrous forgings

Delaware Capital Formation Inc.................. G 302 793-4921
  Wilmington (G-15878)

3469 Metal stampings, nec

Arovo US Inc... E 952 290-0799
  Dover (G-1818)
Bear Forge and Machine Co Inc.................. G 302 322-5199
  Bear (G-63)
George Products Company Inc................... F 302 449-0199
  Middletown (G-7155)

3471 Plating and polishing

Aurista Technologies Inc............................ F 302 792-4900
  Claymont (G-1046)
Europlish Prcsion Fnshg USA In................ G 302 451-9241
  Newark (G-10673)
Felixcem Corporation Inc............................ G 302 324-9101
  New Castle (G-9124)
Industraplate Corp....................................... F 302 654-5210
  Wilmington (G-17314)
Industrial Metal Treating Corp.................... F 302 656-1677
  Wilmington (G-17315)
Rohm Haas Elctrnic Mtls Cmp In............... E
  Newark (G-11908)
Wendy Dixon LLC... G 302 387-7103
  Dover (G-3834)

3479 Metal coating and allied services

Ancatt... G 302 513-9392
  Wilmington (G-14469)
Chemring North Amer Group Inc................ G 302 658-5687
  Wilmington (G-15362)
Coastal Coatings Inc................................... G 302 645-1399
  Lewes (G-5840)
Crazy Coatings.. G 302 378-0888
  Middletown (G-7019)
E M C Process Company Inc....................... G 302 999-9204
  Wilmington (G-16240)
General Coatings LLC.................................. G 302 841-7958
  Millsboro (G-8297)
Metal-Tech Inc... E 302 322-7770
  New Castle (G-9360)
Orville Sammons Ardens............................. G 302 492-8620
  Dover (G-3246)
Perfect Finish Powder Coating................... G 302 566-6189
  Harrington (G-4809)
Prestige Powder Finishing Inc.................... F 302 737-7500
  Newark (G-11736)
Raymond Harner.. G 302 737-0755
  Newark (G-11830)
Top Qality Indus Finishers Inc.................... G 302 778-5005
  Wilmington (G-20354)

3482 Small arms ammunition

▼ Du Pont Chem Enrgy Oprtons Inc........... C 302 774-1000
  Wilmington (G-16188)

3484 Small arms

Stockmarket.. G 302 697-8878
  Magnolia (G-6785)

3489 Ordnance and accessories, nec

Cds Global LLC... E 302 307-6831
  Claymont (G-1078)

34 FABRICATED METAL PRODUCTS

JP McFarlane LLC...................................G.....302 709-1515
Bear (G-311)

3491 Industrial valves

▼ Potts Wldg Boiler Repr Co Inc...........C.....302 453-2550
Newark (G-11716)

3492 Fluid power valves and hose fittings

JC Industrial Solutions Inc..................G.....484 720-8381
Claymont (G-1197)

▲ Mto Hose Solutions Inc....................G.....302 266-6555
Newark (G-11469)

3493 Steel springs, except wire

Betts Inc..G.....302 475-3754
Wilmington (G-14864)

3494 Valves and pipe fittings, nec

Evraz Claymont Steel Inc....................B.....302 792-5400
Claymont (G-1141)

FPL Energy American Wind LLC........G.....302 655-0632
Wilmington (G-16717)

3495 Wire springs

▼ Delmaco Manufacturing Inc............F.....302 856-6345
Georgetown (G-4288)

3496 Miscellaneous fabricated wire products

◆ Bio Medic Corporation......................F.....302 628-4300
Seaford (G-13089)

Mid Atlantic Indus Belting..................G.....302 453-7453
Newark (G-11406)

3498 Fabricated pipe and fittings

Apex Piping Systems Inc...................D.....302 995-6136
Wilmington (G-14506)

Atlantic Screen & Mfg Inc..................G.....302 684-3197
Milton (G-8565)

Baltimore Aircoil Company Inc..........G.....302 424-2583
Milford (G-7781)

▼ Thermal Pipe Systems Inc..............G.....302 999-1588
Wilmington (G-20297)

3499 Fabricated metal products, nec

A B Fab & Machining LLC..................G.....302 293-4945
New Castle (G-8748)

▼ Delmaco Manufacturing Inc............F.....302 856-6345
Georgetown (G-4288)

Hickory Hill Metal Fabrication............G.....302 382-6727
Dover (G-2677)

▲ Independent Metal Strap Co Inc.....E.....516 621-0030
Dover (G-2727)

Mesys Inc...G.....917 566-7011
Dover (G-3068)

Scigate Holdings LLC.........................G.....970 481-4949
Newark (G-11962)

Visionary Energy Systems Inc..........G.....410 739-4342
Dover (G-3802)

35 INDUSTRIAL AND COMMERCIAL MACHINERY AND COMPUTER EQUIPMENT

3511 Turbines and turbine generator sets

Danfoss Power Solutions US Co........E.....515 956-5185
Wilmington (G-15780)

Everlift Wind Technology...................G.....240 683-9787
Lewes (G-5978)

Garrett Motion Inc..............................F.....973 867-7017
Wilmington (G-16807)

Kissangen Inc....................................G.....414 446-4182
Newark (G-11187)

3519 Internal combustion engines, nec

Cummins Power Generation Inc........E.....302 762-2027
Wilmington (G-15733)

US Auto Glass LLC.............................G.....302 803-4924
Wilmington (G-20548)

3523 Farm machinery and equipment

Cnh Cptal Oprting Lase Eqp Rcv........A.....262 636-6011
Wilmington (G-15504)

▼ Easy Lawn Inc.................................E.....302 815-6500
Greenwood (G-4624)

▲ Farmers Harvest Inc.......................G.....302 734-7708
Dover (G-2486)

Hog Slat Incorporated.......................E.....302 875-0889
Laurel (G-5529)

Lumi Cases LLC..................................G.....302 525-6971
Newark (G-11295)

Macknyfe Specialties.........................G.....302 239-4904
Hockessin (G-5289)

Redhead Farms LLC...........................G.....443 235-3990
Laurel (G-5587)

Turfhound Inc.....................................G.....215 783-8143
Wilmington (G-20461)

Wilmington...G.....302 357-4509
Wilmington (G-20807)

Yardex LLC...C.....302 406-0933
Wilmington (G-20924)

3524 Lawn and garden equipment

▼ Easy Lawn Inc.................................E.....302 815-6500
Greenwood (G-4624)

Hydroseeding Company LLC.............E.....302 815-6500
Greenwood (G-4638)

Varigle LLC...F.....858 336-9471
Dover (G-3775)

3531 Construction machinery

▲ Advance Marine LLC......................G.....302 656-2111
Wilmington (G-14268)

Arianna & Angelina Entps LLC..........E.....484 574-8119
Wilmington (G-14550)

Assured Affluence LLC......................G.....609 468-0250
Dover (G-1838)

Bob Reynolds Backhoe Services.......G.....302 239-4711
Hockessin (G-5136)

Bos Construction Company...............G.....302 875-9120
Laurel (G-5471)

Central Backhoe Service...................G.....302 398-6420
Milton (G-8581)

Cnh Cptal Oprting Lase Eqp Rcv........A.....262 636-6011
Wilmington (G-15504)

Duane Edward Ruark.........................G.....302 846-2332
Delmar (G-1591)

E-Berk Corporation............................G.....925 643-2375
Lewes (G-5941)

Js Sheds LLC......................................F.....484 918-0633
Wilmington (G-17603)

Marking Services Inc........................G.....302 478-0381
Wilmington (G-18147)

Smw Sales LLC..................................E.....302 875-7958
Laurel (G-5600)

Stockley Materials LLC......................F.....302 856-7601
Georgetown (G-4526)

Teksolv Usd Inc.................................G.....302 738-1050
Newark (G-12176)

Wolfe Backhoe Service.....................G.....302 737-2628
Newark (G-12393)

3532 Mining machinery

K-Tron Technologies Inc...................D.....302 421-7361
Wilmington (G-17632)

3533 Oil and gas field machinery

◆ Delaware Capital Holdings Inc.......G.....302 793-4921
Wilmington (G-15879)

Tdw Delaware Inc..............................F.....302 594-9880
New Castle (G-9620)

Us Engineering Corporation..............F.....302 645-7400
Lewes (G-6592)

3534 Elevators and moving stairways

Atlantic Elevators..............................G.....302 537-8304
Dagsboro (G-1414)

Brandywine Balustrades....................G.....302 893-1837
Newark (G-10077)

M K Customer Elevator Pads............G.....302 698-3110
Dover (G-2990)

MV Farinola Inc..................................G.....302 545-8492
Wilmington (G-18497)

3535 Conveyors and conveying equipment

Airsled Inc..G.....302 292-8911
Newark (G-9802)

CDI Inc Sofr System LLC....................G.....302 536-7325
Seaford (G-13103)

3537 Industrial trucks and tractors

3M Company.......................................C.....302 286-2480
Newark (G-9712)

Airsled Inc..G.....302 292-8911
Newark (G-9802)

All State Transport LLC.....................G.....443 735-6453
Newark (G-9818)

Arthur Coppedge................................G.....302 229-7581
Bear (G-49)

Cls Trucking & Logistics Inc..............G.....609 380-3399
Lewes (G-5832)

DD&k Logistics LLC............................G.....301 523-5984
Townsend (G-13986)

Dung Beetle Trucking LLC.................G.....312 843-1118
Lewes (G-5938)

Garretts Trucking LLC.......................G.....302 415-1794
Newark (G-10810)

Golsonel Global LLC..........................G.....267 461-8400
Camden Wyoming (G-950)

Green Team Moving & Design LLC....G.....252 406-7001
Wilmington (G-16968)

H&J Trucking Corp.............................G.....516 737-9134
Newark (G-10915)

Handy Logistics LLC..........................G.....570 905-4173
New Castle (G-9195)

K 1 Ng Logistics LLC..........................G.....516 459-3316
Wilmington (G-17626)

Neso Trucking LLC.............................G.....302 358-7878
New Castle (G-9403)

New Trinity Transport LLC................G.....215 457-5700
Felton (G-4007)

Plug Transportation LLC...................G.....302 644-5511
Middletown (G-7458)

S&N Logistics LLC..............................G.....302 303-3037
Middletown (G-7532)

Slr Transport LLC..............................G.....302 316-3306
Newark (G-12033)

T&B Logistics Inc...............................G.....301 304-3255
Dover (G-3639)

Tolbert Enterprise Inc.......................G.....866 986-5237
Newark (G-12204)

Wibx Logistics LLC.............................G.....302 299-8860
Wilmington (G-20777)

Wwc III Trucking LLC.........................G.....302 238-7778
Millsboro (G-8508)

SIC SECTION
35 INDUSTRIAL AND COMMERCIAL MACHINERY AND COMPUTER EQUIPMENT

Xpedient Freight LLC..................................G..... 267 826-6170
  Middletown (G-7740)

3541 Machine tools, metal cutting type

Diy Tool Supply LLC..................................G..... 302 253-8461
  Georgetown (G-4295)

Mazzpac LLC..G..... 973 641-9159
  Newark (G-11364)

Mot Cnc Works LLC.....................................G..... 302 379-2114
  Middletown (G-7382)

Paul A Lange..G..... 302 378-1706
  Middletown (G-7431)

Seaford Machine Works Inc......................F..... 302 629-6034
  Seaford (G-13389)

Unigo Inc...G..... 205 974-1962
  Wilmington (G-20511)

3542 Machine tools, metal forming type

Delaware Capital Formation Inc.................G..... 302 793-4921
  Wilmington (G-15878)

▲ Eastern Shore Metals LLC........................F..... 302 629-6629
  Seaford (G-13169)

▲ Miller Metal Fabrication Inc.....................D..... 302 337-2291
  Bridgeville (G-734)

3544 Special dies, tools, jigs, and fixtures

▲ Duhadaway Tool and Die Sp Inc............D..... 302 366-0113
  Newark (G-10575)

▲ Forcebeyond Inc.......................................E..... 302 995-6588
  Wilmington (G-16688)

Ox Pond Industries.....................................G..... 703 608-7769
  Dagsboro (G-1495)

3545 Machine tool accessories

Advanced Metal Concepts Inc..................F..... 302 421-9905
  Middletown (G-6836)

Aerosmith LLC..G..... 302 546-5465
  Dover (G-1730)

Agilent Technologies Inc...........................G..... 302 633-7337
  Historic New Castle (G-4925)

Alexis Wirt..G..... 302 654-4236
  Wilmington (G-14354)

Ddk..G..... 302 999-1132
  Wilmington (G-15834)

Mechanical Systems Intl Corp..................G..... 302 453-8315
  Newark (G-11371)

Petal Pushers LLC.....................................G..... 302 945-0350
  Lewes (G-6364)

3546 Power-driven handtools

◆ Rhi Refractories Holding Company.........A..... 302 655-6497
  Wilmington (G-19457)

3549 Metalworking machinery, nec

Gop Precision Machining..........................G..... 302 875-8875
  Laurel (G-5523)

Pennengineering Holdings LLC...............C..... 302 576-2746
  Wilmington (G-18954)

3555 Printing trades machinery

Aon3d Inc..G..... 650 410-3120
  Wilmington (G-14500)

Arihant Enterprise LLC..............................G..... 302 353-4400
  Bear (G-43)

Eidp Inc...E..... 302 733-9200
  Christiana (G-994)

Ferrante & Associates Inc........................G..... 781 891-4328
  Newark (G-10724)

Laser Marking Works LLC.........................G..... 786 307-6203
  Wilmington (G-17812)

My Qme Inc...G..... 302 218-8730
  Wilmington (G-18508)

Roller Service Corporation........................E..... 302 737-5000
  Newark (G-11912)

Spratley Publishing...................................G..... 267 779-7353
  Wilmington (G-19973)

3556 Food products machinery

Eidp Inc...G..... 302 695-5300
  Wilmington (G-16335)

Formidable Foods Inc................................G..... 415 877-9691
  Dover (G-2527)

Future 50 Inc..G..... 302 648-4665
  Dover (G-2547)

◆ Metal Msters Fdservice Eqp Inc.............C..... 302 653-3000
  Clayton (G-1385)

Motivated Juicery LLC..............................G..... 302 603-4619
  Dover (G-3127)

Tomasi Usa LLC...G..... 302 449-6492
  Middletown (G-7651)

3559 Special industry machinery, nec

◆ Cae(us) Inc..G..... 813 885-7481
  Wilmington (G-15189)

Canekast Inc..G..... 952 448-2801
  Dover (G-2020)

Cott Electronics LLC..................................D..... 302 520-2838
  Lewes (G-5862)

Dynasep Inc..G..... 302 268-6464
  Wilmington (G-16232)

Ermak Metals Inc.......................................G..... 952 448-2801
  Dover (G-2462)

Manatec Electronics LLC..........................G..... 248 653-1245
  Middletown (G-7325)

▲ Negri Bossi Usa Inc.................................E..... 302 328-8020
  New Castle (G-9401)

Roar Pedal LLC..G..... 412 301-6002
  Dover (G-3474)

3561 Pumps and pumping equipment

C H P T Manufacturing Inc.........................G..... 302 856-7660
  Georgetown (G-4242)

Constellation Pumps Corp.........................F..... 301 323-9000
  Wilmington (G-15610)

3562 Ball and roller bearings

Roller Service Corporation........................E..... 302 737-5000
  Newark (G-11912)

3563 Air and gas compressors

De Sales and Service................................G..... 302 456-1660
  Newark (G-10399)

▼ Easy Lawn Inc..E..... 302 815-6500
  Greenwood (G-4624)

Linne Industries LLC.................................G..... 302 454-1439
  Newark (G-11263)

3564 Blowers and fans

Air Natures Way Inc...................................G..... 302 738-3063
  Newark (G-9800)

Airlock389 Inc...G..... 213 393-1785
  Lewes (G-5667)

Aura Smart Air Inc.....................................G..... 847 909-5822
  Wilmington (G-14642)

Planet Iot Inc..F..... 314 585-9924
  Middletown (G-7455)

▲ Ptm Manufacturing LLC..........................G..... 302 455-9733
  Historic New Castle (G-5056)

3565 Packaging machinery

Ames Engineering Corp............................F..... 302 658-6945
  Wilmington (G-14455)

Telesonic PC Inc...G..... 302 658-6945
  Wilmington (G-20266)

Telesonic PC Inc...G..... 302 658-6945
  Middletown (G-7632)

3566 Speed changers, drives, and gears

◆ David Brown Gear Systems USA I..........G..... 540 416-2062
  Wilmington (G-15803)

Power Transmission Svcs Inc...................G..... 302 378-7925
  Middletown (G-7462)

TOLedo&giron USA LLC............................G..... 302 261-3771
  Lewes (G-6568)

3567 Industrial furnaces and ovens

◆ Chemfirst Inc...D..... 302 774-1000
  Wilmington (G-15354)

▲ Nabertherm Inc...G..... 302 322-3665
  New Castle (G-9390)

3568 Power transmission equipment, nec

Ggb Solutions Inc......................................G..... 202 999-5313
  Dover (G-2580)

◆ SSS Clutch Company Inc........................G..... 302 322-8080
  New Castle (G-9588)

3569 General industrial machinery,

Atlantic Screen & Mfg Inc.........................G..... 302 684-3197
  Milton (G-8565)

Graver Separations Inc.............................F..... 302 731-1700
  Newark (G-10882)

Kissangen Inc...G..... 414 446-4182
  Newark (G-11187)

Medal LP...D..... 302 225-1100
  Wilmington (G-18245)

Precision Airconvey Corp.........................F..... 302 999-8000
  Newark (G-11723)

Rhewum America Inc................................G..... 215 804-7977
  Wilmington (G-19456)

Siemens Industry Inc................................G..... 302 631-8410
  Newark (G-12006)

Zetwerk Manufacturing USA Inc..............G..... 520 720-3085
  Wilmington (G-20959)

3571 Electronic computers

Anatrope Inc...G..... 202 507-9441
  Dover (G-1791)

Axtra3d Inc...E..... 302 288-0670
  Dover (G-1861)

Broadberry Data Systems LLC................E..... 302 295-1086
  Wilmington (G-15121)

Broadberry Data Systems LLC................G..... 800 496-9918
  Wilmington (G-15122)

Crata Inc...F..... 214 606-1731
  Dover (G-2151)

Ecomo Inc...G..... 412 567-3867
  Dover (G-2417)

Itdw Group LLC..G..... 917 503-3574
  Dover (G-2757)

Longevity Health Corp..............................F..... 619 288-3922
  Wilmington (G-17984)

Neurastack Inc...G..... 512 760-3149
  Middletown (G-7397)

One Tech Sol LLC......................................G..... 302 551-6777
  Historic New Castle (G-5043)

Sheriff Electronic LLC...............................G..... 302 654-8090
  Lewes (G-6463)

Sumuri LLC...E..... 302 570-0015
  Magnolia (G-6786)

Turing Machines Inc.................................G..... 415 500-0217
  Wilmington (G-20462)

Weyl Enterprises Inc.................................G..... 302 993-1248
  Wilmington (G-20749)

Yeaher Inc..E..... 513 293-4347
  New Castle (G-9694)

35 INDUSTRIAL AND COMMERCIAL MACHINERY AND COMPUTER EQUIPMENT

3572 Computer storage devices

Milieux LLC .... G 302 770-5868
  Wilmington *(G-18356)*
Quantum Alchemy LLC .... G 484 299-8016
  New Castle *(G-9507)*
Quantum Corporation .... G 302 737-7012
  Newark *(G-11794)*
Zerowait Corporation .... F 302 996-9408
  Wilmington *(G-20958)*

3575 Computer terminals

Isaac Fair Corporation .... G 302 324-8015
  New Castle *(G-9243)*

3577 Computer peripheral equipment, nec

Aim God Society .... F 207 299-3881
  Middletown *(G-6843)*
Ametek Inc .... D 302 456-4400
  Newark *(G-9851)*
Creative Micro Designs Inc .... G 302 456-5800
  Newark *(G-10349)*
East Coast Games Inc .... F 302 838-0669
  Bear *(G-189)*
Nerdit Now LLC .... F 302 482-5979
  Wilmington *(G-18587)*
On Demand Services LLC .... G 302 388-1215
  Newark *(G-11587)*

3579 Office machines, nec

B Williams Holding Corp .... F 302 656-8596
  Wilmington *(G-14704)*
Black & Decker Inc .... G 860 827-3861
  Newark *(G-10043)*
Tritek Corporation .... F 302 239-1638
  Hockessin *(G-5411)*
Tritek Technologies Inc .... G 302 573-5096
  Wilmington *(G-20431)*
Tritek Technologies Inc .... G 302 239-1638
  Hockessin *(G-5412)*

3581 Automatic vending machines

Exquisite Taste Vending LLC .... G 856 278-3091
  Magnolia *(G-6745)*
Ompai & Co LLC .... G 302 632-4077
  Wilmington *(G-18772)*
Promo Builder LLC .... F 773 502-5796
  Bear *(G-441)*
Sunshine Vending Machines LLC .... G 800 670-6557
  Wilmington *(G-20137)*
Wolf Stone Enterprises LLC .... G 302 765-7456
  New Castle *(G-9688)*

3582 Commercial laundry equipment

Service General Corporation .... F 302 218-4279
  Georgetown *(G-4507)*
Ultra Modern Laundry Svcs LLC .... G 302 533-8596
  Wilmington *(G-20500)*

3585 Refrigeration and heating equipment

Baltimore Aircoil Company Inc .... C 302 424-2583
  Milford *(G-7781)*
Beach Mobile Home Supply .... G 302 945-5611
  Millsboro *(G-8189)*
Bluchill Inc .... G 302 658-2538
  New Castle *(G-8869)*
Climate Solutions Service .... G 302 824-2293
  Wilmington *(G-15484)*
Creative Assemblies Inc .... F 302 956-6194
  Bridgeville *(G-688)*
General Refrigeration Company .... E 302 846-3073
  Delmar *(G-1598)*
Munters Corporation .... F 302 798-2455
  Claymont *(G-1247)*
Omega Industries Inc .... G 302 734-3835
  Dover *(G-3224)*
Trane US Inc .... G 302 395-0200
  New Castle *(G-9632)*

3586 Measuring and dispensing pumps

Saker Energy Solutions Inc .... G 808 398-8326
  Historic New Castle *(G-5065)*

3589 Service industry machinery, nec

Aztech Industries Inc .... G 302 653-1430
  Smyrna *(G-13657)*
Better Business RE Inc .... G 609 746-9833
  Claymont *(G-1060)*
◆ Coffee Artisan LLC .... G 302 297-8800
  Millsboro *(G-8235)*
▲ Eagle Mhc Company .... G 302 653-3000
  Clayton *(G-1363)*
Evoqua Water Technologies LLC .... G 302 322-6247
  Historic New Castle *(G-4984)*
◆ Graver Technologies LLC .... C 302 731-1700
  Newark *(G-10883)*
◆ Metal Msters Fdservice Eqp Inc .... C 302 653-3000
  Clayton *(G-1385)*
One Tuch Prperty Solutions LLC .... G 302 765-8519
  Bear *(G-408)*
Sanosil International LLC .... G 302 454-8102
  Wilmington *(G-19667)*
◆ Severn Trent Inc .... F 302 427-5990
  Wilmington *(G-19771)*
Superior Services Group LLC .... G 888 683-8288
  Wilmington *(G-20143)*
Verisoft Inc .... G 602 908-7151
  Dover *(G-3785)*
Water Ingenuity Holdings Corp .... G 847 725-3000
  Wilmington *(G-20682)*
Watercraft LLC .... G 302 757-0786
  Wilmington *(G-20683)*

3594 Fluid power pumps and motors

Smw Sales LLC .... E 302 875-7958
  Laurel *(G-5600)*

3596 Scales and balances, except laboratory

Clover Logistics LLC .... G 713 474-4094
  Middletown *(G-6999)*

3599 Industrial machinery, nec

A & F Machine & Development .... F 302 368-4303
  Newark *(G-9719)*
Able Whelling and Machiene .... G 302 436-1929
  Selbyville *(G-13458)*
Advanced Prttyping Sltionv LLC .... G 302 375-6048
  Wilmington *(G-14278)*
Airespa Worldwide Whl LLC .... G 908 227-4441
  Dover *(G-1757)*
All Metals Fabricators Inc .... F 302 691-8805
  Wilmington *(G-14366)*
Allied Precision Inc .... G 302 376-6844
  Middletown *(G-6852)*
Apex Manufacturing Group Inc .... G 484 888-6252
  Newark *(G-9884)*
Automation Inc .... G 302 999-0971
  Wilmington *(G-14652)*
C & C Technologies Inc .... G 302 653-7623
  Smyrna *(G-13671)*
Chpt Mfg Inc .... G 302 645-4314
  Lewes *(G-5817)*
Chuck George Inc .... E 302 994-7444
  Wilmington *(G-15427)*
Croesus Inc .... F 302 472-9260
  Wilmington *(G-15709)*
Custom Sheet Metal of Delaware .... G 302 998-6865
  Wilmington *(G-15744)*
Delmarva Precision Grinding .... G 302 393-3008
  Milford *(G-7862)*
Dess Machine & Manufacturing .... G 302 736-7457
  Hartly *(G-4868)*
Diamond State Machining Inc .... F 302 398-8437
  Farmington *(G-3935)*
East Coast Machine Works .... G 302 349-5180
  Greenwood *(G-4623)*
Extreme Machining LLC .... F 302 368-7595
  Newark *(G-10696)*
Flyingparts International Inc .... G 610 400-1110
  Lewes *(G-6006)*
Hage Tool and Machine Inc .... G 302 836-4850
  Bear *(G-262)*
Haines Fabrication & Mch LLC .... F 302 436-1929
  Selbyville *(G-13541)*
Heritage Machine Shop LLC .... G 302 656-3313
  Wilmington *(G-17130)*
High-Tech Machine Company Inc .... F 302 636-0267
  Wilmington *(G-17142)*
Horns Machine Shop Inc .... G 302 653-6663
  Smyrna *(G-13766)*
HP Motors Inc .... G 302 368-4543
  Newark *(G-10981)*
Innovative Machine LLC .... G 302 455-1466
  Newark *(G-11024)*
J & A Grinding Inc .... F 302 368-8760
  Newark *(G-11065)*
James Machine Shop Inc .... G 302 798-5679
  Claymont *(G-1194)*
Manufacturing Support Inds Inc .... F 410 334-6140
  Seaford *(G-13274)*
Metal-Tech Inc .... E 302 322-7770
  New Castle *(G-9360)*
Michael A Beecher .... G 302 285-3357
  Townsend *(G-14035)*
Nanticoke Consulting Inc .... G 302 424-0750
  Greenwood *(G-4655)*
New Castle Precision Mch LLC .... G 302 650-7849
  New Castle *(G-9411)*
Next Hydrogen Usa Inc .... E 416 953-6657
  Dover *(G-3184)*
▲ O A Newton & Son Company .... E 302 337-3782
  Bridgeville *(G-740)*
Pauls Inc .... G 302 328-0191
  Bear *(G-420)*
▲ Polarstar Engineering & Mch .... G 302 368-4639
  Newark *(G-11709)*
Prototek Machining & Dev .... G 302 368-1226
  Newark *(G-11766)*
R & K Motors & Machine Shop .... G 302 737-4596
  Newark *(G-11803)*
Red Clay Inc .... G 302 239-2018
  Hockessin *(G-5360)*
Riemel of Delaware LLC .... G 302 998-5806
  Wilmington *(G-19482)*
Rumpstich Machine Works Inc .... G 302 422-4816
  Milford *(G-8075)*
Sachetta Machine & Development .... F 302 378-5468
  Middletown *(G-7534)*
Seaford Machine Works Inc .... F 302 629-6034
  Seaford *(G-13389)*
Sheet Metal Contracting Co .... E 302 834-3727
  Bear *(G-488)*
Standard Technologies & Machine Co ... F 302 994-0229
  Wilmington *(G-20015)*
State Line Machine Inc .... F 302 875-2248
  Laurel *(G-5607)*

36 ELECTRONIC & OTHER ELECTRICAL EQUIPMENT & COMPONENTS

Summit Industrial Corporation............... G 302 368-2718
  Newark *(G-12120)*

Tri-Tek Corporation............................... G 302 239-1638
  Wilmington *(G-20416)*

Troutman Machine Company Inc........... G 302 674-3540
  Dover *(G-3731)*

West End Machine Shop Inc.................. G 302 654-8436
  Wilmington *(G-20738)*

36 ELECTRONIC & OTHER ELECTRICAL EQUIPMENT & COMPONENTS

3612 Transformers, except electric

Continental Africa LLC........................... G 302 540-0069
  Newark *(G-10312)*

TMC Transformers USA Inc.................... G 716 548-0825
  Dover *(G-3692)*

3613 Switchgear and switchboard apparatus

Atlantic Control Systems Inc.................. G 302 284-9700
  Felton *(G-3943)*

Deride Igo... G 302 234-4121
  Newark *(G-10516)*

Panelmatic Inc....................................... G 302 324-9193
  New Castle *(G-9447)*

▼ Panelmatic East Inc........................... F 302 324-9193
  New Castle *(G-9448)*

Power Electronics Inc............................ E 302 653-4822
  Clayton *(G-1398)*

3621 Motors and generators

AC Engineering..................................... G 215 873-6482
  Bear *(G-11)*

Ametek Inc.. D 302 456-4400
  Newark *(G-9851)*

Amrec Holdings Inc................................ D 302 273-0000
  Dover *(G-1788)*

Cummins Power Generation Inc............. E 302 762-2027
  Wilmington *(G-15733)*

Emission Free Generators Inc............... G 440 503-7405
  Claymont *(G-1131)*

Kissangen Inc.. G 414 446-4182
  Newark *(G-11187)*

Opengrid Technologies Co..................... G 202 677-2794
  Wilmington *(G-18800)*

Reelve Inc... G 312 459-2669
  Dover *(G-3442)*

Star Enrg Cs LLC................................... F 302 660-2187
  Wilmington *(G-20023)*

▲ Totaltrax Inc...................................... D 302 514-0600
  New Castle *(G-9630)*

Ukraine Power Resources LLC............... G 508 280-6910
  Dover *(G-3744)*

3624 Carbon and graphite products

Ev Gg1 LLC... G 313 269-4175
  Newark *(G-10675)*

Nanoselect Inc....................................... E 302 355-1795
  Newark *(G-11486)*

3625 Relays and industrial controls

Automation Inc...................................... F 302 999-0971
  Wilmington *(G-14652)*

Envirotech LLC...................................... G 302 834-5011
  Bear *(G-203)*

Redarc Corporation................................ G 704 247-5150
  Dover *(G-3441)*

Tricklestar Inc....................................... F 888 700-1098
  Wilmington *(G-20420)*

Ultrafine Technologies Inc...................... G 302 384-6513
  Wilmington *(G-20502)*

Val-Tech Inc.. E 302 738-0500
  Newark *(G-12298)*

Williams Engrg Solutions LLC................. G 302 670-4841
  Magnolia *(G-6791)*

Xrosswater USA LLC.............................. G 917 310-1344
  Newark *(G-12417)*

3629 Electrical industrial apparatus

Dane Waters... G 302 377-9999
  Claymont *(G-1108)*

Hywatts Inc... G 650 460-4488
  Wilmington *(G-17245)*

McV Microwave East Inc........................ E 302 877-8079
  Laurel *(G-5562)*

Orange Power Electric Inc..................... G 205 886-5815
  Wilmington *(G-18813)*

Pixstory Global Holding Inc................... G 202 615-6777
  Lewes *(G-6373)*

Wirelisity Inc... G 213 816-1957
  Lewes *(G-6634)*

Xerafy Inc... G 817 938-4197
  Wilmington *(G-20918)*

3631 Household cooking equipment

Arovo US Inc... E 952 290-0799
  Dover *(G-1818)*

My Life Care LLC................................... D 302 760-9248
  Dover *(G-3138)*

3633 Household laundry equipment

Laundry Love Services LLC.................... G 302 367-7075
  Wilmington *(G-17822)*

Ultra Modern Laundry Svcs LLC............. G 302 533-8596
  Wilmington *(G-20500)*

3634 Electric housewares and fans

Econat Inc... G 302 504-4207
  Middletown *(G-7081)*

Urbie Inc... G 302 572-4243
  Dover *(G-3761)*

3635 Household vacuum cleaners

Healthy Homes De Inc........................... G 302 998-1001
  Wilmington *(G-17100)*

3639 Household appliances, nec

Meticulous Home Inc............................. F 302 878-7879
  Claymont *(G-1235)*

3641 Electric lamps

Papilla LLC.. G 302 558-7581
  Wilmington *(G-18880)*

3643 Current-carrying wiring devices

Crazy Eight... G 302 227-7429
  Rehoboth Beach *(G-12703)*

DMC Power Inc..................................... F 302 276-0303
  Historic New Castle *(G-4976)*

Leggs Hanes Bali Playtex Otlt................ G 302 227-8943
  Rehoboth Beach *(G-12829)*

◆ Niterra (USA) Holding Inc.................. C 302 288-0131
  Wilmington *(G-18650)*

Nouvir Lightning Corporation................. G 302 628-9888
  Seaford *(G-13320)*

Security Satellite.................................. G 302 376-0241
  Middletown *(G-7549)*

3645 Residential lighting fixtures

Fme Lighting LLC................................... G 877 234-8460
  Lewes *(G-6007)*

New Standard Product Dist Inc.............. F 844 312-6517
  Newark *(G-11525)*

3646 Commercial lighting fixtures

▲ Bwt Lighting Inc................................ G 302 709-0808
  Newark *(G-10110)*

Illumination Technology Inc................... G 410 430-5349
  Delmar *(G-1602)*

Pemco Lighting Products LLC................ F 302 892-9000
  Wilmington *(G-18947)*

▲ Whiteoptics LLC................................ G 302 476-2055
  New Castle *(G-9681)*

3647 Vehicular lighting equipment

Esafety Lights LLC................................ G 800 236-8621
  Wilmington *(G-16462)*

3648 Lighting equipment, nec

Detweilers Lighting............................... G 302 678-5804
  Hartly *(G-4869)*

Esafety Lights LLC................................ G 800 236-8621
  Wilmington *(G-16462)*

Evergreen Led...................................... G 302 218-7819
  Townsend *(G-13999)*

Globe Electric Company USA Inc........... G 514 694-0444
  Dover *(G-2596)*

▲ Jaykal Led Solutions Inc.................... G 302 295-0015
  Georgetown *(G-4379)*

Ledtolight... G 941 323-6664
  Wilmington *(G-17852)*

Main Light Industries Inc...................... C 302 998-8017
  Wilmington *(G-18089)*

Newport.. F 302 995-2840
  Wilmington *(G-18631)*

Smb Lighting... G 302 733-0664
  Newark *(G-12037)*

Sun-In-One Inc...................................... F 302 762-3100
  Wilmington *(G-20127)*

3651 Household audio and video equipment

Acoustic Audio Tek LLC......................... G 302 685-2113
  Wilmington *(G-14238)*

Balanced Audio Technology.................... G 302 996-9496
  Wilmington *(G-14719)*

Bat Electronics Inc............................... G 302 999-8855
  Wilmington *(G-14777)*

Beetronics Inc...................................... G 302 455-2070
  Claymont *(G-1055)*

Brandywine Electronics Corp................. F 302 324-9992
  Bear *(G-80)*

Helix Inc Ta Audioworks........................ G 302 285-0555
  Middletown *(G-7203)*

Major Mahh Levels LLC.......................... G 973 494-4767
  Wilmington *(G-18092)*

Mmm TV Mounting & Entrmt LLC............ G 267 310-5925
  Claymont *(G-1242)*

Padrino Records LLC............................. G 609 353-4683
  Hst Newcastle *(G-5451)*

Sound-N-Secure Inc.............................. G 302 424-3670
  Milford *(G-8095)*

Soundboks Inc....................................... G 213 436-5888
  Wilmington *(G-19935)*

3652 Prerecorded records and tapes

Routerabbit Inc..................................... G 508 596-8735
  Newark *(G-11919)*

Saregama India Limited......................... G 859 490-0156
  Newark *(G-11950)*

3661 Telephone and telegraph apparatus

2nu Photonics LLC................................ G 302 388-2261
  Newark *(G-9706)*

B Williams Holding Corp........................ F 302 656-8596
  Wilmington *(G-14704)*

36 ELECTRONIC & OTHER ELECTRICAL EQUIPMENT & COMPONENTS

Central Firm LLC .... G 610 470-9836
  Wilmington (G-15308)
Gfc Logistics LLC .... G 302 203-9511
  Newark (G-10829)
Onex Global Inc .... G 801 413-6375
  Wilmington (G-18789)
Photon Programming .... G 302 328-2925
  New Castle (G-9472)
Polycom Inc .... G 302 420-8618
  Wilmington (G-19112)
Shiv Baba LLC .... F 703 314-1203
  Dover (G-3546)
Siemens .... E 302 220-1544
  Wilmington (G-19815)
Siemens AG .... G 302 836-2933
  Bear (G-491)
Siemens Corporation .... E 302 220-1544
  Historic New Castle (G-5070)
Versitron Inc .... D 302 894-0699
  Newark (G-12318)

3663 Radio and t.v. communications equipment

3d Microwave LLC .... G 302 497-0223
  Laurel (G-5457)
C4-Nvis USA LLC .... G 213 465-5089
  Dover (G-2009)
Executive Brdband Cmmnctons LL .... G 302 463-4335
  Newark (G-10687)
Gatesair Inc .... E 513 459-3400
  Wilmington (G-16814)
▲ Integrated Data Corp .... G 302 295-5057
  Wilmington (G-17368)
Interdgital Communications Inc .... D 610 878-7800
  Wilmington (G-17379)
Interdigital Inc .... E 302 281-3600
  Wilmington (G-17380)
Interdigital Wireless Inc .... E 302 281-3600
  Wilmington (G-17381)
Newcosmos LLC .... G 302 838-1935
  Bear (G-396)
Omarichet LLC .... G 302 442-0812
  Newark (G-11584)
Oros Communications LLC .... G 954 228-7399
  Wilmington (G-18824)
Positron Access Solutions Inc .... F 888 577-5254
  Wilmington (G-19128)
Quinteccent Inc .... G 443 838-5447
  Selbyville (G-13595)
Ted Johnson Enterprises .... G 302 349-5925
  Greenwood (G-4670)
Vital-Gh Media Group LLC .... G 302 437-4258
  Middletown (G-7691)

3669 Communications equipment, nec

Eastern Shore Metal Detectors .... G 302 628-1985
  Seaford (G-13168)
Spare Cs Inc .... F 424 744-0155
  Lewes (G-6496)
Sumuri LLC .... E 302 570-0015
  Magnolia (G-6786)
Versitron Inc .... D 302 894-0699
  Newark (G-12318)
Wayman Fire Protection Inc .... C 302 994-5757
  Wilmington (G-20693)

3672 Printed circuit boards

Rogers Corporation .... C 302 834-2100
  Bear (G-467)
Seryalda LLC .... G 914 861-5974
  Wilmington (G-19764)

Suretronix Solutions LLC .... G 302 407-3146
  Wilmington (G-20161)
Via Networks Inc .... F 314 727-2087
  Wilmington (G-20605)

3674 Semiconductors and related devices

Accelerated Virtual Solutions .... G 302 494-3215
  Newark (G-9749)
Bloom Energy Corporation .... G 408 543-1227
  Newark (G-10056)
Dupont De Nemours Inc .... A 302 774-3034
  Wilmington (G-16205)
Dupont Displays Inc .... E 805 562-9293
  Wilmington (G-16206)
Dupont Specialty Pdts USA LLC .... E 302 992-2941
  Wilmington (G-16216)
Fractal Mobius LLC .... G 646 209-8559
  Dover (G-2531)
Ganvix Inc .... G 508 904-3045
  Wilmington (G-16801)
Gen Digital Inc .... G 650 527-8000
  Wilmington (G-16829)
Hirotec Inc .... G 248 836-5100
  Wilmington (G-17154)
▲ Jaykal Led Solutions Inc .... G 302 295-0015
  Georgetown (G-4379)
▲ Petro International Corp .... G 302 884-6755
  Wilmington (G-19000)
Thermoelectrics Unlimited Inc .... G 302 764-6618
  Wilmington (G-20299)
Waveinnova Inc .... G 650 507-5756
  Wilmington (G-20689)
Wiregateit LLC .... G 302 538-1304
  Middletown (G-7730)

3675 Electronic capacitors

Microhm Inc .... G 302 543-2178
  Wilmington (G-18329)

3677 Electronic coils and transformers

Ffi Ionix Inc .... F 302 629-5768
  Harrington (G-4769)

3679 Electronic components, nec

AC Group Inc .... G 201 840-5566
  Wilmington (G-14211)
Atlantic Industrial Optics .... G 302 856-7905
  Selbyville (G-13467)
Ef Technologies Inc .... G 302 451-1088
  Newark (G-10615)
Eidp Inc .... C 302 774-1000
  Wilmington (G-16342)
Hollingsead International LLC .... B 302 855-5888
  Georgetown (G-4360)
Intelexmicro Inc .... G 302 907-9545
  Laurel (G-5535)
Kinetic Oasis LLC .... G 508 202-0559
  Newark (G-11177)
Lexatys LLC .... F 302 715-5029
  Laurel (G-5555)
Pbtv Global Inc .... F 302 292-1400
  Wilmington (G-18931)
Suretronix Solutions LLC .... G 302 407-3146
  Wilmington (G-20161)
Val-Tech Inc .... E 302 738-0500
  Newark (G-12298)

3691 Storage batteries

Clarios LLC .... C 302 696-3221
  Middletown (G-6986)
Omareva Energy Inc .... G 514 660-0291
  Dover (G-3222)

Storm Energia Inc .... E 404 550-4862
  Wilmington (G-20088)
Talostech LLC .... G 302 332-9236
  Historic New Castle (G-5081)
Zrcn Inc .... D 212 602-1188
  Wilmington (G-20966)

3692 Primary batteries, dry and wet

Talostech LLC .... G 302 332-9236
  Historic New Castle (G-5081)

3694 Engine electrical equipment

Advanced Defense Technology .... C 888 298-5775
  Wilmington (G-14273)
Epic Charging Inc .... F 650 250-6811
  Dover (G-2456)
Ev Usa Inc .... G 973 674-1326
  Lewes (G-5976)
Evon Electric Enterprise Inc .... F 909 997-9599
  Lewes (G-5979)
Main Office Inc .... G 302 732-3460
  Dagsboro (G-1478)

3695 Magnetic and optical recording media

Currency Technics Metrics Inc .... E 302 482-4846
  Wilmington (G-15734)
Khaos Beauty LLC .... A 302 427-0119
  Wilmington (G-17712)
National Tape Duplicators .... G 302 999-1110
  Wilmington (G-18549)

3699 Electrical equipment and supplies, nec

Chimes Metro Inc .... A 302 452-3400
  Historic New Castle (G-4957)
Dp Fire & Safety Inc .... F 302 998-5430
  Wilmington (G-16159)
Eidp Inc .... E 302 733-9200
  Christiana (G-994)
Excape Entertainment US Ltd .... G 949 943-9219
  Wilmington (G-16498)
Gdt Properties Inc .... E 302 737-3778
  Newark (G-10816)
Gentleman Door Company Inc .... G 302 239-4045
  Yorklyn (G-20992)
◆ Graham Global Corporation .... F 302 839-3000
  Wilmington (G-16945)
Inc Chimes .... G 302 449-1926
  Townsend (G-14015)
Independent Elec Svcs LLC .... D 302 383-2761
  Claymont (G-1184)
Metatron Inc .... G 619 550-4668
  Dover (G-3072)
Mohawk Electrical Systems Inc .... E 302 422-2500
  Milford (G-8018)
▲ North American Brands Inc .... E 519 680-0385
  Wilmington (G-18676)
Precision Systems Inds LLC .... G 224 388-9837
  Wilmington (G-19158)
Primex Composites LLC .... G 302 981-1470
  Hockessin (G-5352)
Psp Corp .... G 302 764-7730
  Wilmington (G-19244)
RPS LLC .... G 302 653-2598
  Dover (G-3491)
Securitech Inc .... F 302 996-9230
  Wilmington (G-19732)
Thermal Transf Composites LLC .... G 302 635-7156
  Hockessin (G-5404)
Withyouwithme Inc .... G 202 377-9743
  Wilmington (G-20868)

37 TRANSPORTATION EQUIPMENT

3711 Motor vehicles and car bodies

Aetna Hose Hook and Ladder Co........... G..... 302 454-3300
  Newark (G-9792)
Commonwealth Motor Inc....................... G..... 302 505-5555
  Wilmington (G-15554)
Ford International Fin Corp..................... D..... 313 845-5712
  Wilmington (G-16689)
International Std Elc Corp...................... F..... 302 427-3769
  Wilmington (G-17391)
Miles Per Hour Inc............................... G..... 800 370-3050
  Wilmington (G-18353)
North ATL Intl Ocean Carier.................... E..... 786 275-5352
  New Castle (G-9423)
Penske Performance Inc........................ D..... 302 656-2082
  Wilmington (G-18959)
Star Campus II................................... G..... 302 514-7586
  Newark (G-12087)

3713 Truck and bus bodies

Kruger Trailers Inc............................... G..... 302 856-2577
  Georgetown (G-4396)
▼ T & J Murray Worldwide Svcs............. F..... 302 736-1790
  Dover (G-3637)

3714 Motor vehicle parts and accessories

Aaron Anderson.................................. G..... 804 986-1666
  New Castle (G-8754)
Airnav Group LLC................................ G..... 954 798-5509
  Middletown (G-6844)
▼ Autoport Inc.................................... E..... 302 658-5100
  New Castle (G-8834)
Fsvap Usa Inc.................................... F..... 248 639-8635
  Dover (G-2541)
Gif North America LLC......................... G..... 703 969-9243
  Rehoboth Beach (G-12771)
Globally Srced Vhcles Prts LLC.............. E..... 240 755-4935
  Dover (G-2595)
Horizon Intl Holdings LLC...................... C..... 302 636-5401
  Wilmington (G-17207)
Kautex Inc... B..... 302 456-1455
  Newark (G-11145)
Lion Electric Mfg USA Inc...................... F..... 833 512-5466
  Newark (G-11264)
Lkq Northeast Inc................................ G..... 800 223-0171
  Dover (G-2962)
Martinrea International US Inc................. G..... 615 212-0586
  Wilmington (G-18171)
Muldoons Diesel Prfmce LLC................. G..... 302 276-2882
  Historic New Castle (G-5030)
NAPA M3 Inc...................................... G..... 719 660-6263
  Middletown (G-7392)
◆ NGK North America Inc..................... G..... 302 654-1344
  Wilmington (G-18640)
Performnce Injction Equipmentc.............. G..... 302 858-5145
  Georgetown (G-4462)
Premium Diesel Parts LLC..................... G..... 205 723-1510
  Wilmington (G-19173)
Pressair International............................ F..... 302 636-5440
  Wilmington (G-19179)
Pro Fabricating Inc.............................. G..... 302 424-7700
  Milford (G-8053)
Sword Parts LLC................................. G..... 302 246-1346
  Rehoboth Beach (G-12986)
▲ Wilmington Fibre Specialty Co............ E..... 302 328-7525
  Historic New Castle (G-5102)

3715 Truck trailers

Integral Enterprise LLC......................... G..... 302 722-0827
  Wilmington (G-17366)
Kruger Trailers Inc............................... G..... 302 856-2577
  Georgetown (G-4396)
Utility/Stern Shore Trlr Sls I.................... G..... 302 337-7400
  Bridgeville (G-779)

3721 Aircraft

Boeing Company................................. G..... 302 735-2922
  Dover (G-1959)
Central Kansas Arospc Mfg LLC............. C..... 314 406-6550
  Wilmington (G-15309)
Dassault Falcon Jet - Wilmington Corp..... C..... 302 322-7000
  New Castle (G-9000)
Grindstone Aviation LLC........................ G..... 302 324-1993
  New Castle (G-9181)
Hel Ecrane Inc.................................... G..... 604 519-0200
  Dover (G-2671)
▲ Ilc Dover LP.................................... B..... 302 335-3911
  Frederica (G-4174)
Pats Aircraft LLC................................. D..... 855 236-1638
  Georgetown (G-4456)
Santos Aircraft LLC............................. G..... 302 608-6637
  New Castle (G-9552)

3724 Aircraft engines and engine parts

General Electric Company..................... C..... 302 631-1300
  Newark (G-10819)
Greenwich Aerogroup Inc...................... F..... 302 834-5400
  Middletown (G-7178)
Honeywell International Inc.................... G..... 302 322-4071
  New Castle (G-9220)
Rtx Corporation.................................. G..... 800 227-7437
  Historic New Castle (G-5064)
Santos Aircraft LLC............................. G..... 302 608-6637
  New Castle (G-9552)
▲ Tesla Industries Inc......................... F..... 302 324-8910
  Historic New Castle (G-5083)

3728 Aircraft parts and equipment, nec

Advantage Futuretech Company............. G..... 347 592-5667
  Lewes (G-5662)
Avacore LLC...................................... G..... 302 327-8830
  Wilmington (G-14661)
Barrel Fuel Technologies Inc.................. G..... 832 405-4806
  Dover (G-1874)
Dassault Falcon Jet - Wilmington Corp..... C..... 302 322-7000
  New Castle (G-9000)
Envoy Flight Systems Inc...................... G..... 302 738-1788
  Newark (G-10657)
▼ Exploration Systems & Tech............... G..... 302 335-3911
  Wilmington (G-16506)
Global Air Strategy Inc......................... G..... 302 229-5889
  Newark (G-10849)
Nakuuruq Solutions.............................. G..... 302 526-2223
  Dover (G-3148)
Nighthawk Aircraft LLC........................ G..... 703 994-0523
  Wilmington (G-18648)
Patrick Aircraft Group LLC..................... F..... 302 854-9300
  Georgetown (G-4455)
Pats Aircraft LLC................................. D..... 855 236-1638
  Georgetown (G-4456)

3731 Shipbuilding and repairing

Mv Cruise Partners LLC........................ G..... 561 329-3209
  Wilmington (G-18496)
Navalt Inc.. G..... 551 273-2773
  Dover (G-3161)
Sea Transport Corporation LLC.............. E..... 786 208-2433
  Wilmington (G-19719)

3732 Boatbuilding and repairing

Broadwater Oyster Company LLC........... G..... 610 220-7776
  Rehoboth Beach (G-12657)
Croker Oars Usa Inc............................ G..... 302 897-6705
  Townsend (G-13979)
Dunworth Machines LLC....................... G..... 434 977-4790
  Selbyville (G-13526)
Escape Yachts Inc............................... G..... 302 691-9070
  Wilmington (G-16463)
F & S Boat Works................................ F..... 302 838-5500
  Bear (G-217)
Nanticoke Industries LLC....................... G..... 302 245-8825
  Seaford (G-13306)
S & J Haftl Inc.................................... G..... 302 378-7571
  Middletown (G-7530)

3743 Railroad equipment

Delaware Car Company........................ E..... 302 655-6665
  Wilmington (G-15880)

3751 Motorcycles, bicycles, and parts

Apollo Imports Inc............................... E..... 514 895-9410
  Newark (G-9885)
Beno Inc.. G..... 814 796-7686
  Middletown (G-6913)
Delfast Inc... E..... 323 540-5155
  Dover (G-2275)
Infinity Choppers................................. G..... 302 249-7282
  Georgetown (G-4368)
Propel Bikes LLC................................. G..... 631 678-1946
  Wilmington (G-19231)
Ross Bicycles LLC............................... G..... 888 392-5628
  Lewes (G-6433)
Sfa America Inc.................................. G..... 206 265-3148
  Wilmington (G-19772)

3761 Guided missiles and space vehicles

4TH PHASE THECHNOLOGIES INC........ F..... 610 420-5765
  Wilmington (G-14138)
Merida Aerospace Inc........................... F..... 305 396-1471
  Lewes (G-6264)
Space Industries Inc............................ G..... 510 219-1005
  Dover (G-3592)

3795 Tanks and tank components

Intech Services................................... G..... 302 366-1442
  Newark (G-11029)

3799 Transportation equipment, nec

Ingenuity 213 LLC............................... G..... 647 303-5116
  Dover (G-2733)
J&L Logistic Group LLC........................ G..... 917 499-0019
  Wilmington (G-17468)
Michael C Rapa.................................. G..... 302 236-4423
  Laurel (G-5563)
No Pressure LLC................................. G..... 347 693-3116
  Millsboro (G-8405)
Pessagno Equipment Inc....................... G..... 302 738-7001
  Newark (G-11671)
Rd Transport & Logistics LLC................. F..... 302 893-8568
  Wilmington (G-19356)
Stallard Chassis Co............................. F..... 302 292-1800
  Newark (G-12082)

38 MEASURING, PHOTOGRAPHIC, MEDICAL, & OPTICAL GOODS, & CLOCKS

3812 Search and navigation equipment

Advanced Defense Technology............... C..... 888 298-5775
  Wilmington (G-14273)

38 MEASURING, PHOTOGRAPHIC, MEDICAL, & OPTICAL GOODS, & CLOCKS

First Line Defense LLC .... G 302 287-2764
  Smyrna *(G-13734)*
Lockheed Martin Corporation .... G 302 741-2004
  Dover *(G-2970)*
Pasadena Digital Inc .... G 310 774-6740
  Dover *(G-3277)*
Pilots Assn For Bay River Del .... E 302 645-2229
  Lewes *(G-6369)*
Precision Technic Defence Inc .... G 801 404-4626
  Wilmington *(G-19159)*
Russell Associates Inc .... G 443 992-5777
  Newark *(G-11928)*
Special Support Tech Inc .... G 804 620-6072
  Lewes *(G-6498)*
▲ Tesla Industries Inc .... F 302 324-8910
  Historic New Castle *(G-5083)*

3821 Laboratory apparatus and furniture

Azzota Corporation .... G 877 649-2746
  Claymont *(G-1048)*
◆ Bio Medic Corporation .... F 302 628-4300
  Seaford *(G-13089)*
Boa Financial LLC .... G 888 444-5371
  Dover *(G-1956)*
Delaware Technology Park Inc .... G 302 452-1100
  Newark *(G-10491)*
Heart To Heart Health Svcs LLC .... G 302 603-3976
  Dover *(G-2666)*
L F Systems Corp .... F 302 322-0460
  New Castle *(G-9292)*
Life Sciences Intl LLC .... G 603 436-9444
  Wilmington *(G-17901)*
Safeguard Dx Laboratory .... G 888 919-8275
  Wilmington *(G-19626)*

3822 Environmental controls

Accessheat Inc .... E 302 373-9524
  Wilmington *(G-14222)*
Energy Systems Tech Inc .... G 302 368-0443
  New Castle *(G-9096)*
▲ Totaltrax Inc .... D 302 514-0600
  New Castle *(G-9630)*
Val-Tech Inc .... E 302 738-0500
  Newark *(G-12298)*

3823 Process control instruments

Acorn Energy Inc .... G 410 654-3315
  Wilmington *(G-14237)*
▲ American Meter Holdings Corp .... A 302 477-0208
  Wilmington *(G-14437)*
Ametek Inc .... D 302 456-4400
  Newark *(G-9851)*
Applied Analytics Inc .... E 781 791-5005
  Newark *(G-9890)*
Delaware Capital Formation Inc .... G 302 793-4921
  Wilmington *(G-15878)*
Ecomo Inc .... G 412 567-3867
  Dover *(G-2417)*
Engineered Systems & Designs .... G 302 456-0446
  Wilmington *(G-16423)*
McCabes Mechanical Service Inc .... F 302 854-9001
  Georgetown *(G-4421)*
Retrotekusa Inc .... G 469 619-0899
  Wilmington *(G-19446)*
Romer Labs Technology Inc .... E 855 337-6637
  Newark *(G-11914)*
Senzors Inc .... G 866 736-9677
  Dover *(G-3531)*

3824 Fluid meters and counting devices

▲ American Meter Holdings Corp .... A 302 477-0208
  Wilmington *(G-14437)*

3825 Instruments to measure electricity

AC Group Inc .... G 201 840-5566
  Wilmington *(G-14211)*
Agilent Technologies Inc .... D 408 345-8886
  Wilmington *(G-14318)*
Agilent Technologies Inc .... A 877 424-4536
  Wilmington *(G-14319)*
Aim Research Co .... G 302 235-5940
  Hockessin *(G-5117)*
Cloud Collected LLC .... G 302 273-4010
  Newark *(G-10262)*
Engineered Systems & Designs .... G 302 456-0446
  Wilmington *(G-16423)*
Hunt Energy Netwrk Land Co LLC .... G 214 978-8000
  Dover *(G-2706)*
Pulsar360 Corp .... E 855 578-5727
  Newark *(G-11771)*
Suretronix Solutions LLC .... G 302 407-3146
  Wilmington *(G-20161)*

3826 Analytical instruments

Advanced Particle Sensors LLC .... G 302 695-4883
  Wilmington *(G-14277)*
Alphasense Inc .... G 302 294-0116
  Newark *(G-9836)*
Apollo Scitech LLC .... G 302 861-6557
  Newark *(G-9886)*
Axess Corporation .... G 302 292-8500
  Historic New Castle *(G-4937)*
▲ B & W Tek Inc .... D 855 692-9835
  Newark *(G-9963)*
Bia Separations Inc .... G 510 740-4045
  Wilmington *(G-14875)*
Bonna-Agela Technologies Inc .... D 302 438-8798
  Hockessin *(G-5137)*
▲ Bonna-Agela Technologies Inc .... E 302 438-8798
  Wilmington *(G-15000)*
▲ Creative Devices Inc .... G 302 378-5433
  Middletown *(G-7020)*
◆ Denovix Inc .... E 302 442-6911
  Wilmington *(G-16011)*
Joint Anlytcl Systms (amrcs) .... G 302 607-0088
  Newark *(G-11122)*
Kindwell Inc .... G 302 588-2895
  Wilmington *(G-17725)*
M&M Mass Spec Consulting LLC .... G 302 250-4488
  Newark *(G-11307)*
Markes International Inc .... G 302 656-5500
  Wilmington *(G-18143)*
◆ Miles Scientific Corporation .... E 302 737-6960
  Newark *(G-11418)*
Mstm LLC .... G 302 239-4447
  Newark *(G-11467)*
Nanodrop Technologies LLC .... G 302 479-7707
  Wilmington *(G-18530)*
Ribodynamics LLC .... G 518 339-6605
  Wilmington *(G-19464)*
Scientific Systems Corp .... G 302 655-5500
  Wilmington *(G-19706)*
Separation Methods Tech Inc .... F 302 368-0610
  Newark *(G-11979)*
Standard Merger Sub LLC .... E 302 456-6785
  Newark *(G-12083)*
Supercritical Fluid Tech .... G 302 738-3420
  Newark *(G-12128)*
▲ Supercritical Fluid Tech Inc .... G 302 738-3420
  Newark *(G-12129)*
▲ Ta Instruments - Waters LLC .... G 302 427-4000
  Historic New Castle *(G-5079)*
Ta Instruments-Waters LLC .... F 781 233-1717
  Historic New Castle *(G-5080)*

Thermo Fisher Scientific Inc .... G 302 479-7707
  Wilmington *(G-20298)*
Ttna Energy Systems LLC .... G 302 384-9147
  Wilmington *(G-20456)*
Wilmington Infrared Tech .... G 302 234-6761
  Wilmington *(G-20820)*

3827 Optical instruments and lenses

Atlantic Industrial Optics .... G 302 856-7905
  Selbyville *(G-13467)*
Docs Medical LLC .... G 301 401-1489
  Bear *(G-175)*

3829 Measuring and controlling devices, nec

Arrim LLC .... G 617 697-7914
  Wilmington *(G-14559)*
Avatar Instruments Inc .... G 302 703-6865
  Lewes *(G-5724)*
Boa Financial LLC .... G 888 444-5371
  Dover *(G-1956)*
Hanbang Group .... G 626 506-7585
  Newark *(G-10924)*
Horney Industrial Elec Inc .... G 302 337-3600
  Bridgeville *(G-713)*
Industrial Physics Inc .... E 302 613-5600
  New Castle *(G-9230)*
Rapta Inc .... G 408 627-2556
  Camden *(G-888)*
▲ Sepax Technologies Inc .... F 302 366-1101
  Newark *(G-11980)*
Solvetech Inc .... G 302 798-5400
  Wilmington *(G-19927)*
Terran Global Corporation .... G 702 626-5704
  Lewes *(G-6552)*
Testex Inc .... G 302 731-5693
  Newark *(G-12182)*
▲ Testing Machines Inc .... E 302 613-5600
  New Castle *(G-9625)*
Thomas B Davis .... G 302 692-0871
  Newark *(G-12191)*
Toxtrap Inc .... G 302 698-1400
  Dover *(G-3708)*
▲ United Testing Systems Inc .... E 714 638-2322
  New Castle *(G-9657)*

3841 Surgical and medical instruments

Caveman Design Inc .... G 302 234-9969
  Hockessin *(G-5153)*
Cydallia Inc .... G 860 682-0947
  Lewes *(G-5876)*
Datwyler Pharma Packg USA Inc .... F 302 603-8020
  Middletown *(G-7030)*
Denco Inc .... G 302 798-4200
  Wilmington *(G-16007)*
Direct Medical LLC .... G 781 640-7474
  Wilmington *(G-16078)*
Docs Medical LLC .... G 301 401-1489
  Bear *(G-175)*
Eidp Inc .... G 302 996-4000
  Wilmington *(G-16343)*
Endospace Corporation .... G 732 271-8700
  Newport *(G-12451)*
Enovis Corporation .... C 301 252-9160
  Wilmington *(G-16428)*
Fbk Medical Tubing Inc .... F 302 855-0585
  Georgetown *(G-4315)*
Med Tech Equipment Inc .... G 800 322-2609
  Wilmington *(G-18244)*
Medical Sup Support Svcs LLC .... F 302 446-3658
  Dover *(G-3052)*
Moor Instruments Inc .... G 302 798-7470
  Wilmington *(G-18433)*

39 MISCELLANEOUS MANUFACTURING INDUSTRIES

Perivision Usa Inc .... F 302 665-0866
  Dover *(G-3300)*
Promixco USA Corp .... G 814 810-3643
  Wilmington *(G-19229)*
Pulse Technologies Inc .... G 785 258-6423
  Claymont *(G-1270)*
Shummi US LLC .... G 847 987-1686
  Wilmington *(G-19812)*
▲ Smith & Nephew Holdings Inc .... E 302 884-6720
  Wilmington *(G-19886)*
Taro Medical Incorporated .... F 818 245-2202
  Lewes *(G-6542)*
W L Gore & Associates Inc .... C 302 368-3700
  Newark *(G-12341)*
▲ W L Gore & Associates Inc .... D 302 738-4880
  Newark *(G-12342)*

3842 Surgical appliances and supplies

Advanced Defense Technology .... C 888 298-5775
  Wilmington *(G-14273)*
Ascent Research LLC .... G 703 801-1490
  Dover *(G-1828)*
Choy Wilson Cdgn .... G 302 424-4141
  Milford *(G-7826)*
Christana Ctr For Wns Wellness .... F 302 454-9800
  Newark *(G-10212)*
Dads Workwear Inc .... G 302 663-0068
  Laurel *(G-5491)*
Elgood Solutions Inc .... G 610 420-7207
  Camden *(G-829)*
Enovis Corporation .... C 301 252-9160
  Wilmington *(G-16428)*
Harry J Lawall & Son Inc .... G 302 429-7630
  Wilmington *(G-17064)*
Howmedica Osteonics Corp .... G 302 655-3239
  Wilmington *(G-17220)*
Hygieia Shield Inc .... F 302 388-7350
  Dover *(G-2710)*
▲ Ilc Dover LP .... B 302 335-3911
  Frederica *(G-4174)*
Jarel Industries LLC .... G 336 782-0697
  Camden *(G-859)*
Johnson & Johnson .... E 302 652-3840
  Wilmington *(G-17570)*
M&M Pure Air Systems LLC .... G 403 801-2925
  Lewes *(G-6233)*
Marins Med LLC .... G 302 245-4596
  Georgetown *(G-4413)*
Mih International LLC .... G 301 908-4233
  Newark *(G-11417)*
Mt Foreign Holdings Inc .... D 301 252-9160
  Wilmington *(G-18479)*
Nestal Mdsphere Consulting LLC .... G 302 404-6506
  Wilmington *(G-18588)*
New Ilc Dover Inc .... B 302 335-3911
  Frederica *(G-4179)*
Ric Investments LLC .... G 302 656-8996
  Wilmington *(G-19465)*
Roll-A-Bout Corporation .... G 302 736-6151
  Frederica *(G-4181)*
Zimmer US Inc .... F 617 272-0062
  Camden Wyoming *(G-987)*

3843 Dental equipment and supplies

Cravitysci LLC .... G 571 208-6421
  New Castle *(G-8984)*
Delmarva 2000 Ltd .... G 302 645-2226
  Milton *(G-8601)*
Dentsply Sirona Inc .... D 302 422-4511
  Milford *(G-7864)*
Dentsply Sirona Inc .... F 302 422-1043
  Milford *(G-7865)*
Dentsply Sirona Inc .... G 302 430-7474
  Milford *(G-7866)*
Tc Dental Equipment Services .... G 302 740-9049
  Townsend *(G-14078)*

3844 X-ray apparatus and tubes

▲ Direct Radiography Corp .... C 302 631-2700
  Newark *(G-10536)*
Eidp Inc .... E 302 733-9200
  Christiana *(G-994)*
Eidp Inc .... G 302 996-4000
  Wilmington *(G-16343)*

3845 Electromedical equipment

▲ Direct Radiography Corp .... C 302 631-2700
  Newark *(G-10536)*
Drowsy Digital Inc .... G 833 438-6956
  Dover *(G-2387)*
Hearx Usa Inc .... D 415 212-5500
  Camden *(G-847)*
Hologic Inc .... D 302 631-2846
  Newark *(G-10960)*
Hologic Inc .... D 302 631-2700
  Newark *(G-10961)*
Mtrigger LLC .... G 302 502-7262
  Newark *(G-11470)*
Silverside Open Mri Imaging .... G 302 246-2000
  Wilmington *(G-19831)*
Slimstim Inc .... G 310 560-4950
  Wilmington *(G-19866)*

3851 Ophthalmic goods

Essilor America Holding Co Inc .... C 214 496-4000
  Wilmington *(G-16467)*
Furrer Inc .... G 302 273-3109
  Newark *(G-10792)*
Jim Knnas Optmtrsts Optcans In .... F 302 722-6197
  Wilmington *(G-11112)*
Jim Knnas Optmtrsts Optcans In .... G 302 722-6197
  Wilmington *(G-17549)*
Nordic Projekt Co .... G 302 208-7296
  Wilmington *(G-18673)*

3861 Photographic equipment and supplies

360 DC Rentals LLC .... G 202 432-3655
  Wilmington *(G-14125)*
B Williams Holding Corp .... F 302 656-8596
  Wilmington *(G-14704)*
Jollylook Inc .... F 754 267-1885
  Wilmington *(G-17571)*
Perryfilms Production Co LLC .... G 302 505-4458
  Lewes *(G-6363)*
Working Tens Inc .... G 612 685-0921
  Wilmington *(G-20891)*

3873 Watches, clocks, watchcases, and parts

Aurista Technologies Inc .... F 302 792-4900
  Claymont *(G-1046)*

39 MISCELLANEOUS MANUFACTURING INDUSTRIES

3911 Jewelry, precious metal

Alex and Ani LLC .... G 302 731-1420
  Newark *(G-9808)*
Alex and Ani LLC .... G 302 227-7360
  Rehoboth Beach *(G-12600)*
Joolala LLC .... E 302 444-0178
  Newark *(G-11124)*
Lightbox Jewelry Inc .... F 833 270-3737
  Dover *(G-2945)*
Manoj Ornaments Inc .... G 916 779-7916
  Dover *(G-3011)*
Nava .... G 515 495-4577
  Wilmington *(G-18560)*
Rck Soliatire LLC .... F 551 358-8400
  Rehoboth Beach *(G-12907)*
Stackd Studio LLC .... G 240 304-1085
  Newark *(G-12081)*

3914 Silverware and plated ware

◆ Bio Medic Corporation .... F 302 628-4300
  Seaford *(G-13089)*
◆ Leeber Limited USA .... F 302 733-0991
  Newark *(G-11239)*
Select Stainless Products LLC .... G 302 653-3062
  Clayton *(G-1405)*

3915 Jewelers' materials and lapidary work

Harlem Watch Company LLC .... G 646 354-7644
  Lewes *(G-6078)*

3931 Musical instruments

Ajam Inc .... G 267 323-5005
  Middletown *(G-6845)*
Bb Custom Instruments .... G 302 339-3826
  Georgetown *(G-4226)*
Cara Guitars Manufacturing .... G 302 521-0119
  Wilmington *(G-15238)*
Imperial Dynsty Arts Prgram In .... F 302 521-8551
  Wilmington *(G-17290)*
Jammy Instruments US Corp .... F 209 813-4052
  Claymont *(G-1195)*

3944 Games, toys, and children's vehicles

▼ Aero-Marine Laminates Inc .... F 302 628-3944
  Seaford *(G-13051)*
Affiliate Venture Group .... G 302 379-6961
  Wilmington *(G-14304)*
Co-Op Kitchen LLC .... G 407 342-2295
  Dover *(G-2102)*
Dti Direct Inc .... G 855 374-7836
  Wilmington *(G-16186)*
▲ Kid Agains Inc .... G 631 830-5228
  Dover *(G-2864)*
Sandebbarnanricway Corp .... G 302 475-2705
  Wilmington *(G-19657)*
Str8up Games Inc .... F 315 523-8216
  Dover *(G-3614)*
Tetris Company LLC .... G 302 656-1950
  Wilmington *(G-20280)*
Time4machine Inc .... E 302 999-7604
  Wilmington *(G-20328)*
Top Dog Best Games LLC .... G 949 859-8869
  Wilmington *(G-20352)*
▲ Zone Systems Inc .... E 302 730-8888
  Dover *(G-3906)*

3949 Sporting and athletic goods, nec

Abbey Lein Inc .... G 302 239-2712
  Newark *(G-9737)*
Agilite Systems Incorporated .... G 870 298-4152
  Wilmington *(G-14320)*
Allan B Stanley .... G 302 678-4774
  Dover *(G-1768)*
Asferik LLC .... G 302 981-6519
  Wilmington *(G-14577)*
▲ Beachballs Com LLC .... G 302 628-8888
  Seaford *(G-13081)*
Black & Decker Inc .... G 860 827-3861
  Newark *(G-10043)*
Bubba Game Calls .... G 302 332-2004
  Townsend *(G-13969)*

39 MISCELLANEOUS MANUFACTURING INDUSTRIES

Competition Game Calls .... G 302 345-7463
 Wilmington (G-15570)
Dahcor LLC .... G 302 257-2803
 Dover (G-2184)
Devastator Game Calls LLC .... G 302 875-5328
 Laurel (G-5500)
Disrupt Industries Deleware .... G 424 229-9300
 Dover (G-2303)
Doc Foals .... G 302 632-0424
 Dover (G-2316)
Fells Point Surf Co LLC .... G 302 212-2005
 Dewey Beach (G-1669)
Fells Points Surf .... G 302 537-7873
 Bethany Beach (G-601)
▲ Foldfast Goals LLC .... G 302 478-7881
 Wilmington (G-16680)
Golfclub LLC .... G 908 770-7892
 Wilmington (G-16917)
Hague Surfboards .... G 302 745-9336
 Lewes (G-6069)
J & V Shooters Supply LP .... G 302 422-5417
 Milford (G-7945)
Kinetic Skateboarding .... G 856 375-2236
 Wilmington (G-17726)
M B Cues .... G 443 309-3495
 Dagsboro (G-1476)
Masley Enterprises Inc .... E 302 427-9885
 Wilmington (G-18183)
Movetec Fitness Equipment LLC .... G 302 563-4487
 Newark (G-11460)
Msgg LLC .... G 917 565-8306
 Dover (G-3131)
Par 4 Golf Inc .... G 302 227-5663
 Rehoboth Beach (G-12883)
Planet X Skateboards .... G 484 886-9287
 Wilmington (G-19066)
Prouse Enterprises LLC .... G 302 846-9000
 Milford (G-8055)
Resurrektion Athletics Inc .... E 302 300-1900
 Middletown (G-7518)
Rope-It Golf LLC .... G 305 767-3481
 Wilmington (G-19566)
◆ Rukket LLC .... F 855 478-5538
 Wilmington (G-19589)
Sjm Sales Inc .... G 302 697-6748
 Camden Wyoming (G-979)
Terrain and Tactical LLC .... G 302 521-9290
 Wilmington (G-20275)
Turquoise Americallc .... G 302 608-7008
 Newark (G-12247)
◆ Vulcan International Corp .... F 302 428-3181
 Wilmington (G-20658)

3953 Marking devices

Franklin Rubber Stamp Co Inc .... G 302 654-8841
 Wilmington (G-16730)
Hot Shot Concepts .... G 302 947-1808
 Harbeson (G-4700)
◆ Tyden Group Holdings Corp .... F 740 420-6777
 Wilmington (G-20481)

3955 Carbon paper and inked ribbons

Identisource LLC .... G 888 716-7498
 Lewes (G-6114)
Kent-Sussex Industries Inc .... B 302 422-4014
 Milford (G-7964)

3961 Costume jewelry

▲ Goldmine Enterprises Inc .... G 302 834-4314
 Bear (G-251)
Mission Bracelets LLC .... G 302 528-5065
 Smyrna (G-13826)

Swarovski US Holding Limited .... G 302 737-4811
 Newark (G-12138)
T K O Designs Inc .... G 302 539-6992
 Bethany Beach (G-645)

3965 Fasteners, buttons, needles, and pins

Iron Lion Enterprises Inc .... G 302 628-8320
 Seaford (G-13225)
Tantalum Bolt & Fastener LLC .... F 888 393-4517
 Newark (G-12159)

3991 Brooms and brushes

◆ Dupont Flaments - Americas LLC .... E 302 774-1000
 Wilmington (G-16209)

3993 Signs and advertising specialties

9193 4323 Quebec Inc .... G 855 824-0795
 Newark (G-9717)
Ad-Art Signs Georgetown Inc .... G 302 856-7446
 Georgetown (G-4197)
Alli Inc .... G 302 733-0740
 Newark (G-9824)
Arena Signs .... G 302 644-8300
 Lewes (G-5698)
Aster Bouquet Flower Shop LLC .... G 302 258-9242
 Lewes (G-5708)
Banacom Signs Inc .... G 302 429-6243
 Wilmington (G-14727)
Barbara Graphics Inc .... G 302 636-9040
 Wilmington (G-14755)
Beachview Mgmt Inc .... G 302 227-3280
 Lewes (G-5744)
Clear Channel Outdoor LLC .... E 302 658-5520
 Wilmington (G-15476)
Cw Signs LLC .... G 302 533-5492
 Newark (G-10369)
D By D Printing LLC .... G 302 659-3373
 Dover (G-2180)
Da Vinci Painting .... G 302 229-0644
 Newark (G-10379)
Dandy Signs .... G 301 399-8746
 Ocean View (G-12498)
Delaware Dept Hlth Social Svcs .... G 302 255-9855
 New Castle (G-9017)
Delaware Dept Hlth Social Svcs .... D 302 255-9800
 New Castle (G-9020)
Delaware Sign Co .... G 302 469-5656
 Felton (G-3959)
Delmarva Sign Co .... G 302 934-6188
 Georgetown (G-4289)
DOT Pop Inc .... G 302 691-3160
 Wilmington (G-16153)
Electro-Art Sign Company .... G 302 322-1108
 New Castle (G-9089)
First State Signs Inc .... F 302 744-9990
 Dover (G-2510)
Friends and Sign .... G 302 368-4794
 Newark (G-10786)
Galaxy Sign & Lighting .... G 302 757-5349
 Wilmington (G-16794)
Gary M Munch Inc .... G 302 525-8301
 Newark (G-10812)
Gotshadeonline Inc .... G 302 832-8468
 Bear (G-252)
Gotshadeonline Inc .... G 302 384-2932
 Newark (G-10871)
Grier Signs .... G 302 737-4823
 Newark (G-10899)
Griffs Signs LLC .... G 302 784-5596
 Wilmington (G-16979)
Guedon Co .... G 302 375-6151
 Wilmington (G-17002)

Harting Graphics Ltd .... G 302 762-6397
 Wilmington (G-17068)
Hes Sign Services Inc .... E 302 257-5150
 Wilmington (G-17135)
Impact Graphix .... F 302 337-7076
 Seaford (G-13221)
Incolor Inc .... G 302 984-2695
 Wilmington (G-17301)
Insta Signs Plus Inc .... F 302 324-8800
 New Castle (G-9234)
JD Sign Company LLC .... G 302 786-2761
 Harrington (G-4790)
Jdjs LLC .... E 844 967-3748
 Georgetown (G-4380)
Jenner Enterprises Inc .... G 302 479-5686
 Wilmington (G-17524)
Jenner Enterprises Inc .... F 302 998-6755
 Wilmington (G-17523)
K & R Graphics & Signs Inc .... G 302 697-7725
 Woodside (G-20977)
Kalisign USA .... G 302 268-6946
 Wilmington (G-17638)
Kent Sign Company Inc .... F 302 697-2181
 Dover (G-2856)
Kgc Enterprises Inc .... G 302 668-1835
 Wilmington (G-17710)
Lane Sign Inc .... G 610 558-2630
 Wilmington (G-17803)
Led Sign City LLC .... G 866 343-4011
 Wilmington (G-17851)
Lewis Lettering Co .... G 610 209-0998
 Lewes (G-6204)
Marjano LLC .... G 302 454-7446
 Bear (G-363)
Mimesis Signs .... G 302 674-5566
 Dover (G-3095)
Mr Copy Inc .... G 302 227-4666
 Rehoboth Beach (G-12866)
Penney Enterprises Inc .... G 302 629-4430
 Seaford (G-13340)
Phillips Signs Inc .... F 302 629-3550
 Seaford (G-13347)
Prestige Powder Inc .... G 302 737-7086
 Newark (G-11735)
Quillen Signs LLC .... G 302 684-3661
 Seaford (G-13362)
Rentzs Sign Service .... G 302 378-9607
 Townsend (G-14057)
Rocket Signs .... G 302 645-1425
 Lewes (G-6428)
Rogers Sign Company Inc .... F 302 684-8338
 Milton (G-8703)
Sabion Sound Reinforcement Co .... G 302 427-0551
 Wilmington (G-19618)
Shekinah Glory Sign Company .... G 302 256-0426
 Wilmington (G-19790)
Sign Crafters .... G 302 832-8300
 Bear (G-492)
Sign Express .... G 302 999-0893
 Wilmington (G-19820)
Signs By Tomorrow .... G 302 744-9396
 Dover (G-3558)
Signscape Designs & Signs .... G 302 798-2926
 Wilmington (G-19824)
Southern Delaware Signs .... G 302 645-1425
 Lewes (G-6495)
Stop Traffic .... G 302 604-1176
 Millsboro (G-8468)
Towers Signs LLC .... G 302 629-7450
 Seaford (G-13433)
Trademark Signs .... G 484 832-5770
 Wilmington (G-20386)

39 MISCELLANEOUS MANUFACTURING INDUSTRIES

Traffic Sign Solutions Inc .... G 302 295-4836
  Wilmington (G-20387)
Trophy Shop .... G 302 656-4438
  Wilmington (G-20438)
Tylaur Inc .... G 302 894-9330
  Newark (G-12251)
Weber Sign Co .... F 302 732-1429
  Frankford (G-4160)
X Screen Graphix .... G 302 422-4550
  Milford (G-8154)

3996 Hard surface floor coverings, nec

Maneto Inc .... E 302 656-4285
  Wilmington (G-18103)

3999 Manufacturing industries, nec

Acosh Enterprise LLC .... G 631 767-4501
  Newark (G-9758)
Advanced Prttyping Sltionv LLC .... G 302 375-6048
  Wilmington (G-14278)
American Industries LLC .... G 302 585-0129
  Milton (G-8559)
Avkin Inc .... F 302 562-7468
  Wilmington (G-14673)
Azextensions LLC .... G 609 202-2098
  New Castle (G-8838)
Bambu Candles LLC .... G 917 903-2563
  Newark (G-9977)
Barbosa Manufacturing .... G 302 856-6343
  Georgetown (G-4221)
Baumann Industries Inc .... G 302 593-1049
  Wilmington (G-14781)
Beauty Barrettes LLC .... G 302 883-7532
  Newark (G-10008)
Bell Manufacturing Company Inc .... G 302 703-2684
  Lewes (G-5754)
Bleu Safe Inc .... G 619 416-6166
  Wilmington (G-14956)
Bold Industries LLC .... G 302 858-7237
  Frankford (G-4074)
Bombshell Beauty Inc .... G 302 559-3011
  Wilmington (G-14997)
▲ Brandywine PDT Group Intl Inc .... E 302 472-1463
  Wilmington (G-15080)
Candle Parlour .... G 302 408-0890
  Claymont (G-1072)
Cbd Pro LLC .... G 443 736-9002
  Laurel (G-5480)
Chemax Manufacturing Corp .... G 302 328-2440
  New Castle (G-8929)
Citystlecollections LLC .... G 302 219-0259
  Milton (G-8583)
Close Cuts Lawn Svc & Ldscpg .... G 302 422-2248
  Milford (G-7836)
Club 6 Barbershop .... G 302 276-1624
  Bear (G-111)
Conjured Jewells .... G 267 240-2263
  Newark (G-10305)
CT Innovations LLC .... G 209 559-3595
  Dover (G-2167)
Denices Ragged Wreath .... G 302 220-7377
  Newark (G-10513)
▲ Design Specific US Inc .... G 650 318-6473
  Wilmington (G-16026)
Discount Cigarette Depot .... G 302 398-4447
  Harrington (G-4763)
Dog Anya .... G 302 456-0108
  Newark (G-10546)
DXquisite Hair Factory LLC .... G 267 298-0821
  Smyrna (G-13718)
East Park Brands LLC .... G 201 668-7089
  Dover (G-2410)

Eastern Shore Lite Industries .... G 302 653-8687
  Clayton (G-1365)
Epix Industries Inc .... G 302 550-9007
  Lewes (G-5968)
Falco Industries Inc .... G 302 628-1170
  Seaford (G-13182)
Footcare Technologies Inc .... G 704 301-6966
  Milton (G-8625)
Gardner Industries Inc .... G 302 448-9195
  Seaford (G-13195)
Good Manufacturing Practices .... G 302 222-6808
  Dover (G-2604)
Gr Group Holdings Inc .... G 416 618-2676
  Dover (G-2614)
Grapefruit Usa Inc .... G 310 575-1175
  Wilmington (G-16950)
Hair By Ashleighmonai LLC .... G 215 201-6874
  Wilmington (G-17032)
High Confectionary Company .... G 213 807-6218
  Wilmington (G-17140)
▼ Hirsh Industries Inc .... G 302 678-4990
  Dover (G-2681)
Ice Cremee Creations .... G 516 450-2144
  Camden (G-854)
Infarm - Indoor Urban Frming U .... E 201 616-1441
  Dover (G-2730)
Invisible Hand Labs LLC .... G 434 989-9642
  Wilmington (G-17408)
ISA Professional Ltd .... G 647 869-1552
  Wilmington (G-17424)
Island Genius LLC .... G 888 529-5506
  Wilmington (G-17427)
J M Industries .... G 302 893-0363
  Hockessin (G-5254)
Jjs Industries LP .... G 302 690-2957
  Wilmington (G-17553)
K Lush Extensions LLC .... G 347 274-4353
  Middletown (G-7257)
K9 Natural Foods USA LLC .... E 855 596-2887
  Wilmington (G-17633)
Kangsters Inc .... G 716 563-8225
  Wilmington (G-17647)
Kershaw Industries .... G 302 464-1051
  Middletown (G-7268)
Klh Industries LLC .... G 800 348-0758
  Lewes (G-6169)
Lashedbyindie LLC .... G 267 734-4850
  Dover (G-2905)
Laytons Umbrellas .... G 302 249-1958
  Laurel (G-5553)
Limitless Flames LLC .... G 302 559-8712
  Wilmington (G-17918)
Loyalty Is Earned Inc .... G 347 606-6383
  Wilmington (G-18015)
Loyalty Soap and Candle Co LLC .... G 302 373-5854
  Townsend (G-14028)
Macknyfe Specialties .... G 302 239-4904
  Hockessin (G-5289)
Maf Industries .... G 302 249-1254
  Seaford (G-13271)
Manatec Electronics LLC .... G 248 653-1245
  Middletown (G-7325)
Manufactured Housing .... G 302 744-2383
  Dover (G-3012)
Martial Industries LLC .... G 302 983-5742
  Middletown (G-7330)
Maws Tails Mfg .... G 302 740-7664
  Milton (G-8663)
Mia Bellas Candles .... G 302 331-7038
  Hartly (G-4896)
Michael J Munroe .... G 804 240-7188
  Magnolia (G-6765)

MMR Industries Inc .... G 302 999-9561
  Wilmington (G-18392)
Mnr Industries LLC .... G 443 485-6213
  Dover (G-3108)
Monogram Specialties .... G 302 292-2424
  Newark (G-11445)
National Industries For The Bl .... G 302 477-0860
  Wilmington (G-18544)
Nature Impact Inc .... G 650 241-8301
  Wilmington (G-18557)
Northernsigs Mfg LLC .... G 302 383-9270
  Wilmington (G-18686)
Nova Industries LLC .... G 302 218-4837
  Bear (G-399)
Opulence Collection LLC .... G 267 808-1781
  Newark (G-11597)
Oski Industries .... G 646 369-5799
  New Castle (G-9438)
Pet Shop LLC .... G 646 345-8844
  Dover (G-3304)
PHM Springboard Bidco Inc .... G 919 678-7700
  Wilmington (G-19023)
Pierce Multi Solutions LLC .... G 302 609-7000
  Newark (G-11689)
Poshsistahs Hair LLC .... F 302 464-2469
  Middletown (G-7460)
Purebred LLC .... G 929 777-7770
  New Castle (G-9501)
R M Bell Industries Inc .... G 302 542-3747
  Lewes (G-6404)
Raymond Chung Industries Corp .... G 302 384-9796
  Wilmington (G-19345)
Rosas Greek Btq .... G 302 678-2147
  Dover (G-3485)
Rowe Industries Inc .... G 443 458-5569
  Georgetown (G-4495)
S&D Industries LLC .... G 703 801-3643
  Wilmington (G-19614)
Sandebbarnanricway Corp .... G 302 475-2705
  Wilmington (G-19657)
SBS Global LLC .... G 302 898-2911
  Newark (G-11955)
Scigate Holdings LLC .... G 970 481-4949
  Newark (G-11962)
Shalex Industries US Corp .... G 323 540-5586
  Middletown (G-7558)
Soft Life Beauty Suite LLC .... G 267 496-7655
  Wilmington (G-19913)
Spinlifecom LLC .... F 888 398-2267
  New Castle (G-9586)
Staging Dimensions Inc .... E 302 328-4100
  New Castle (G-9589)
Syf Industries .... G 302 384-6214
  Wilmington (G-20178)
Tdock Services & Holding Inc .... G 305 924-3653
  Dover (G-3659)
Think66 LLC .... G 949 326-8188
  Wilmington (G-20300)
Top Impact LLC .... G 646 830-4324
  Dover (G-3699)
Tributarymarinecom LLC .... G 443 553-9485
  New Castle (G-9638)
Under Whistle .... G 302 250-8400
  Newark (G-12264)
US Green Battery Inc .... G 347 723-5963
  New Castle (G-9665)
Uzin Utz Manufacturing N Amer .... F 336 456-4624
  Dover (G-3768)
Vention Inc US .... G 514 222-0380
  Wilmington (G-20581)
Vintage Candle Company .... G 302 643-9343
  Bridgeville (G-780)

39 MISCELLANEOUS MANUFACTURING INDUSTRIES

Westmor Industries .... G 302 956-0243
  Bridgeville (G-783)
Westmor Industries .... G 302 398-3253
  Harrington (G-4846)
Whet Industries Inc .... G 302 236-2182
  Newark (G-12365)
Wlg Equity Inc .... E 302 738-4880
  Newark (G-12391)

40 RAILROAD TRANSPORTATION

4011 Railroads, line-haul operating

CSX Transportation Inc .... G 302 998-8613
  Wilmington (G-15726)
Delaware Coast Line RR Co .... G 302 422-9200
  Milford (G-7855)
Delmarva Central Railroad .... G 302 449-1576
  Middletown (G-7050)
ITEL Rail Holdings Corporation .... D 302 656-5476
  Wilmington (G-17432)
Transflo Terminal Services Inc .... F 302 994-3853
  Wilmington (G-20397)

41 LOCAL & SUBURBAN TRANSIT & INTERURBAN HIGHWAY TRANSPORTATION

4111 Local and suburban transit

Arrow Express Inc .... G 302 836-3658
  Newark (G-9909)
Delaware Express Shuttle Inc .... C 302 454-7800
  Newark (G-10441)
Delaware Transportation Auth .... G 302 760-2000
  Dover (G-2271)
Delmarva Transportation Inc .... G 302 349-0840
  Greenwood (G-4616)
Direct Mobile Transit Inc .... F 302 218-5106
  Wilmington (G-16079)
Dover Leasing Co Inc .... F 302 674-2300
  Dover (G-2350)
Exp Growth LLC .... G 804 855-8910
  Wilmington (G-16505)
Gold Label Transportation LLC .... G 302 668-2383
  Newark (G-10860)
High Transit Us LLC .... G 302 286-5192
  Newark (G-10952)
Power Trans Inc .... G 302 918-7674
  Bear (G-431)
Preferred Trnsp Systems LLC .... G 302 323-0828
  Bear (G-436)
Shamrock Services LLC .... F 302 519-7609
  Lewes (G-6461)
Shuttle Runners .... G 302 245-0945
  Millsboro (G-8463)
U Transit Inc .... G 302 227-1197
  Rehoboth Beach (G-13000)
Vision Limousine .... G 302 584-0622
  Claymont (G-1329)
We Dem Boys Transportation LLC .... G 302 727-6164
  Milton (G-8728)

4119 Local passenger transportation, nec

Ace Your Party .... G 302 415-1670
  Claymont (G-1018)
Air Methods Corporation .... E 302 363-3168
  Georgetown (G-4203)
Ayea LLC .... G 302 319-3329
  Wilmington (G-14686)
Bayside Limousine .... F 302 644-6999
  Millsboro (G-8185)

Beebz Inc .... G 832 692-7558
  Middletown (G-6909)
Bill M Douthat Jr .... G 407 977-2273
  Lewes (G-5765)
Buker Limousine & Trnsp Svc .... F 302 234-7600
  Newark (G-10103)
Cft Ambulance Service Inc .... G 302 984-2255
  Bear (G-94)
Christiana Care Health Sys Inc .... C 302 623-3970
  New Castle (G-8938)
Christiana Fire Company .... G 302 834-2433
  Bear (G-100)
City Wide Transportation Inc .... G 302 792-1225
  Claymont (G-1088)
Citywide Transportation Inc .... G 302 792-0159
  Wilmington (G-15457)
Class Limousine Service .... G 302 653-1166
  Smyrna (G-13679)
Confidntial Exec Trnsp Intl In .... G 800 316-0802
  Middletown (G-7009)
Delaware Cy Vlntr Fire Co No 1 .... E 302 834-9336
  Delaware City (G-1538)
Delaware Express Shuttle Inc .... C 302 454-7800
  Newark (G-10441)
Delaware Premier Trnsp .... G 616 617-2598
  New Castle (G-9030)
Dnd Limousine Service .... G 302 998-5856
  Wilmington (G-16111)
Dynasty Car Collection LLC .... E 855 700-6530
  Middletown (G-7076)
Eagle Limousine Inc .... C 302 325-4200
  New Castle (G-9075)
Executive Transportation Inc .... G 302 337-3455
  Greenwood (G-4628)
Felton Community Fire Co Inc .... E 302 284-9552
  Felton (G-3971)
First State Trolley Co LLC .... G 302 500-0526
  Lewes (G-5999)
Flag Ride LLC .... G 202 390-4850
  Wilmington (G-16659)
Genes Limousine Service Inc .... G 410 479-8470
  Bridgeville (G-703)
Hart To Heart Ambulance .... G 302 697-9395
  Lewes (G-6080)
Jeffrey L Whitters Jr LLC .... G 800 563-6006
  Wilmington (G-17520)
Lifenet Inc .... G 973 698-6881
  Lewes (G-6207)
Limo Exchange .... F 302 322-1200
  Historic New Castle (G-5018)
Limousine Unlimited LLC .... F 302 284-1100
  Felton (G-3998)
Macklyn Home Care .... G 302 690-9397
  Wilmington (G-18071)
Maxicare Ambulance Services .... G 302 990-3777
  Newark (G-11360)
Mid Atlantic Care LLC .... G 302 266-8306
  Wilmington (G-18332)
Miles1 Inc .... G 267 506-0004
  Wilmington (G-18354)
New Castle Shuttle and Taxi SE .... G 302 326-1855
  New Castle (G-9413)
Preferred Trnsp Systems LLC .... G 302 323-0828
  Bear (G-436)
Roadrunner Express Inc .... G 302 426-9551
  Wilmington (G-19504)
Transcare .... G 302 322-2454
  New Castle (G-9634)

4121 Taxicabs

Aryvve Technologies LLC .... G 678 977-1252
  Dover (G-1827)

City Cab Inc .... F 302 628-2588
  Seaford (G-13121)
City Cab of Delware Inc .... G 302 227-8294
  Rehoboth Beach (G-12673)
City Cab of Delware Inc .... G 302 734-5968
  Dover (G-2079)
Gokart Transportation LLC .... G 302 202-9171
  Wilmington (G-16908)
Ladycar LLC .... G 984 389-9913
  Dover (G-2899)
Lyft Inc .... G 302 747-0124
  Wilmington (G-18044)
Tookuai Inc .... G 302 291-1505
  Lewes (G-6570)
U S Express Taxi Company LLC .... G 302 357-1908
  New Castle (G-9645)
Uber .... E 302 287-4866
  Wilmington (G-20490)
Willy Cab .... G 302 465-1252
  Wilmington (G-20805)
Zizo Taxi Cab LLC .... G 302 528-5663
  Newark (G-12436)

4131 Intercity and rural bus transportation

Chambers Bus Service Inc .... G 302 284-9655
  Viola (G-14093)
Hilton Bus Service .... G 302 697-7676
  Camden (G-852)
Matthew Smith Bus Service .... G 302 734-9311
  Dover (G-3035)
RE Calloway Trnsp Inc .... E 302 422-2471
  Houston (G-5449)

4141 Local bus charter service

Belkins Inc .... D 302 261-5393
  Dover (G-1906)
Deans Bus Service Inc .... G 302 335-5095
  Milford (G-7848)
Delaware Department Trnsp .... G 302 658-8960
  Wilmington (G-15902)
Edward L Ballard .... G 302 363-4302
  Townsend (G-13997)
Krapfs Coaches Inc .... E 302 993-7855
  Wilmington (G-17751)
R J K Transportation Inc .... G 302 422-3188
  Houston (G-5448)
Rohans Bus Service Inc .... G 302 332-8498
  Bear (G-468)
Staplefords Sales and Service .... G 302 834-4568
  Saint Georges (G-13039)

4142 Bus charter service, except local

Dawson Bus Service Inc .... D 302 697-9501
  Camden (G-814)
First Student Inc .... F 302 995-9607
  Newark (G-10739)
Jor-Lin Inc .... F 302 424-4445
  Milford (G-7958)
Krapfs Coaches Inc .... E 302 993-7855
  Wilmington (G-17751)
Matthew Smith Bus Service .... G 302 734-9311
  Dover (G-3035)

4151 School buses

Achieve Lgstic Systems Trnsp L .... F 302 654-4701
  Wilmington (G-14231)
Advanced Student Trnsp Inc .... C 302 998-6726
  Wilmington (G-14281)
B&P Transit .... G 302 653-8466
  Smyrna (G-13658)
Boulden Buses Inc .... F 302 998-5463
  Wilmington (G-15013)

42 MOTOR FREIGHT TRANSPORTATION

Cedar Creek Market Inc.................................. G 302 249-0725
  Milford (G-7815)
Colonial School District................................. E 302 323-2700
  New Castle (G-8958)
D&N Bus Service Inc..................................... F 302 422-3869
  Milford (G-7846)
Dawson Bus Service Inc................................ D 302 697-9501
  Camden (G-814)
Dianes Bus Service....................................... G 302 629-4336
  Seaford (G-13160)
First Student Inc.. F 302 995-9607
  Newark (G-10739)
Happy Hnds Feet Kidz Trnsp LLC................ G 302 897-2375
  Newark (G-10926)
Knotts Incorporated....................................... E 302 322-0554
  Historic New Castle (G-5015)
Lambden Bus Service LLC........................... G 302 629-4358
  Seaford (G-13256)
Larkins Bus Service LLC............................... G 302 653-5855
  Clayton (G-1383)
Lehanes Bus Service Inc.............................. F 302 328-7100
  Historic New Castle (G-5016)
Sutton Bus & Truck Co Inc............................ E 302 995-7444
  Wilmington (G-20166)

4173 Bus terminal and service facilities

Elite Facility Services LLC............................. D 302 566-7031
  Newark (G-10629)
Iag Service Corp.. G 302 577-1333
  Newark (G-10990)

42 MOTOR FREIGHT TRANSPORTATION

4212 Local trucking, without storage

A Collins Trucking Inc................................... G 302 438-8334
  Bear (G-9)
Advance Trucking Solutions LLC................. G 302 281-4191
  Dover (G-1722)
Affordable Delivery Svcs LLC...................... E 302 276-0246
  New Castle (G-8771)
Akita Trucking LLC.. G 302 463-8152
  Newark (G-9804)
All American Truck Brokers.......................... G 302 654-6101
  Wilmington (G-14362)
All Around Moverz... G 302 494-9925
  Wilmington (G-14363)
Allan Hughes Exp Inc................................... G 302 230-6666
  Wilmington (G-14371)
Armstrong Trnsf Stor Inc/Rmstr.................... B 302 323-9000
  New Castle (G-8823)
Asd Trucking Inc.. G 302 744-9832
  Dover (G-1829)
Asi Transport LLC... G 302 349-9460
  Bridgeville (G-668)
Atkison Trucking.. G 302 396-0322
  Seaford (G-13071)
Atlas World Express LLC............................. G 202 536-5238
  Middletown (G-6884)
Badillo Trucking LLC..................................... G 302 368-4207
  Middletown (G-6901)
Baggage Hub Inc... G 628 666-0150
  Dover (G-1867)
Banker Steel Co LLC..................................... G 708 478-0111
  Wilmington (G-14749)
Berry International Inc................................... G 302 674-1300
  Dover (G-1915)
Beth Trucking Inc... G 918 814-2970
  Newark (G-10028)
Big Jims Trucking.. G 214 504-1320
  Seaford (G-13088)

Bjc-5 LLC.. G 302 230-6733
  Middletown (G-6923)
Blair Materials Inc.. G 815 278-0999
  Wilmington (G-14950)
Bnjs LLC... G 302 465-6105
  Middletown (G-6928)
Bowmans Repair and Hauling...................... G 302 803-0098
  Newark (G-10075)
C & M Service Inc.. G 302 453-5228
  Newark (G-10112)
College Hunks Hauling Junk Mvg................. G 302 232-6200
  Wilmington (G-15532)
Connolly Options LLC................................... F 302 998-2016
  New Castle (G-8967)
Courtesy Trnsp Svcs Inc............................... F 302 322-9722
  New Castle (G-8982)
Cr Newlin Trucking Inc.................................. G 302 678-9124
  Dover (G-2150)
D & J Sweeping LLC..................................... G 302 875-3393
  Laurel (G-5490)
Dawn Arrow Inc.. G 302 328-9695
  New Castle (G-9002)
De Cheaper Trash LLC................................. G 302 325-0670
  New Castle (G-9005)
De Express Inc.. G 302 387-7178
  Smyrna (G-13693)
Dedicated and Driven Hlg LLC..................... G 404 909-6031
  Newark (G-10406)
Delmar Trucking.. G 240 353-3553
  Newark (G-10500)
Dependable Trucking Inc.............................. F 302 655-6271
  New Castle (G-9047)
Donkey Trucking LLC.................................... G 302 507-2380
  New Castle (G-9059)
Eastern Mail Transport Inc........................... F 302 838-0500
  Bear (G-191)
Estestwins Trucking LLC.............................. G 267 773-2991
  Camden Wyoming (G-942)
Evans Trucking Inc.. G 302 344-9375
  Milton (G-8622)
F S D Trucking... G 302 629-7498
  Seaford (G-13181)
Fedex Ground Package Sys Inc................... G 800 463-3339
  Seaford (G-13184)
First Class Hauling LLC................................ G 302 535-2338
  Smyrna (G-13733)
Foraker Oil Inc.. G 302 834-7595
  Delaware City (G-1541)
FSA Network Inc.. G 302 316-3200
  Dover (G-2539)
Geared Up Trucks and More........................ G 302 927-0147
  Frankford (G-4110)
Geotech LLC.. G 302 353-9769
  Wilmington (G-16849)
GM Trucking LLC... G 412 609-8818
  Newark (G-10855)
Grab DC LLC.. F 310 866-0560
  Dover (G-2615)
Grab-Ur-Bite Inc... G 415 568-1717
  Wilmington (G-16940)
Gregory A Maahs Sr..................................... G 302 359-9077
  Newark (G-10897)
H G Investments LLC................................... F 302 734-5017
  Magnolia (G-6750)
Hab Nab Trucking Inc................................... G 302 245-6900
  Bridgeville (G-707)
Halen Technologies Inc................................ F 302 290-3075
  Wilmington (G-17037)
Harmony Trucking Inc................................... G 302 633-5600
  Wilmington (G-17060)
Highland Construction LLC.......................... F 302 286-6975
  Bear (G-274)

Isha Brothers Inc.. G 302 299-3156
  Newark (G-11060)
J & S Moving & Dlvry Svc LLC..................... G 302 357-5675
  Newark (G-11067)
Jkb Corp... E 302 734-5017
  Dover (G-2792)
Jsm Transport & Haulage LLC..................... G 302 836-8057
  Bear (G-314)
K2 Trucking LLC... G 302 257-3135
  Dover (G-2826)
Keep It - Moving & Labor LLC...................... F 302 469-1161
  Camden (G-865)
Kld Trucking Corporation.............................. G 347 399-7619
  New Castle (G-9286)
Ktf Enterprise LLC... G 302 932-6039
  Wilmington (G-17760)
Le Luxe Nuit... E 855 535-8935
  Wilmington (G-17843)
Load 2 Go Inc... G 302 722-8844
  Lewes (G-6215)
Lotus Logistics LLC....................................... E 573 240-4154
  Wilmington (G-18002)
Lucky Star Farms LLC................................... G 302 841-5177
  Georgetown (G-4409)
M & W Trucking Inc....................................... G 302 655-6994
  New Castle (G-9331)
Mark Duphily Trucking Inc............................ G 302 292-2271
  Newark (G-11333)
Michael A Sinclair Inc.................................... G 302 834-8144
  Bear (G-374)
Morris CT Trucking Inc.................................. G 302 653-2396
  Smyrna (G-13827)
Morris E Justice Inc....................................... G 302 539-7731
  Dagsboro (G-1484)
Move Mint... G 267 289-4545
  New Castle (G-9383)
Murry Trucking Llc... F 302 653-4811
  Smyrna (G-13830)
Muvers Inc.. G 888 508-4849
  Wilmington (G-18495)
My Install Pro Ltd Lblty Co........................... E 803 486-3831
  Wilmington (G-18506)
Overnight Movers LLC.................................. F 302 345-1142
  New Castle (G-9441)
Patriot Trucking LLC..................................... G 302 469-3774
  New Castle (G-9459)
PB Trucking Inc... F 302 841-3209
  Greenwood (G-4660)
Perry Enterprise LLC.................................... G 302 505-4458
  Dover (G-3301)
Quantae L Jennings...................................... G 561 537-0821
  Millsboro (G-8440)
Qwintry LLC... F 858 633-6353
  Newark (G-11801)
R & W Transportation Corp.......................... G 703 670-5483
  Wilmington (G-19301)
Rifenburg Trucking Inc.................................. F 302 349-5969
  Greenwood (G-4664)
Riverside Farms LLC................................... G 302 222-0760
  Felton (G-4018)
Robert F Clendenin....................................... G 302 396-7922
  Seaford (G-13376)
Ron English Trucking Inc............................. F 302 328-2059
  New Castle (G-9540)
Samuel Coraluzzo Co Inc............................. E 302 322-1195
  New Castle (G-9551)
Santay Trucking Inc...................................... G 302 245-6012
  Ellendale (G-3929)
▲ Sardo & Sons Warehousing Inc.............. G 302 369-2100
  Christiana (G-1008)
Sentinel Transportation LLC........................ F 302 477-1640
  Wilmington (G-19753)

42 MOTOR FREIGHT TRANSPORTATION

Ser Trucking Inc .... G 302 328-0782
   Historic New Castle *(G-5068)*

SF Express Corporation .... G 302 407-6155
   New Castle *(G-9562)*

Sh Haughton Trucking Moving Co .... G 302 324-9505
   New Castle *(G-9564)*

Shirkey Trucking Corp .... G 302 349-2791
   Greenwood *(G-4668)*

Smart Choice Trucking Inc .... G 302 945-7100
   Lewes *(G-6481)*

Smooth Mves Elite Mvg Svcs LLC .... G 302 521-0973
   Wilmington *(G-19897)*

Specialized Carier Systems Inc .... G 302 424-4548
   Milford *(G-8099)*

Stallion Trucking Inc .... G 803 757-4366
   Dover *(G-3603)*

Stovoo Inc .... G 302 451-9589
   Newark *(G-12104)*

Sutton Bus & Truck Co Inc .... E 302 995-7444
   Wilmington *(G-20166)*

T J Irvin Trucking .... G 302 270-8475
   Milford *(G-8113)*

Triglias Transportation Co .... E 302 846-2141
   Delmar *(G-1645)*

Ultra Modern Laundry Svcs LLC .... G 302 533-8596
   Wilmington *(G-20500)*

Unique Pro-Co LLC .... G 302 723-2365
   Wilmington *(G-20520)*

Veer Trucking LLC .... G 484 802-1452
   Middletown *(G-7683)*

Wagner N J & Sons Trucking .... F 302 242-7731
   Felton *(G-4037)*

Walleys Trucking Inc .... G 302 893-8652
   Bear *(G-558)*

Wasteflo LLC .... G 410 202-0802
   Laurel *(G-5622)*

Watson Boys Trucking LLC .... G 302 635-4109
   Wilmington *(G-20684)*

Wecanrush Inc .... G 317 603-6622
   Wilmington *(G-20708)*

Whitetail Country Log & Hlg .... G 302 846-3982
   Delmar *(G-1656)*

Workhorse II LLC .... F 302 533-5342
   New Castle *(G-9689)*

Xavier Entertainment Inc .... G 215 356-8314
   Bear *(G-569)*

Xlr8 Logistics LLC .... G 682 622-1546
   Dover *(G-3881)*

Xonex Relocation LLC .... D 302 323-9000
   Wilmington *(G-20919)*

Young Logistics LLC .... G 302 232-3034
   Wilmington *(G-20934)*

4213 Trucking, except local

2yum Inc .... G 626 420-4851
   Dover *(G-1684)*

A Duie Pyle Inc .... D 302 326-9440
   Historic New Castle *(G-4917)*

A1 Express Trucking Inc .... F 302 544-9273
   Wilmington *(G-14176)*

Adam Hobbs & Son Inc .... F 302 697-2090
   Felton *(G-3938)*

Amber Waves One LLC .... G 302 653-4641
   Smyrna *(G-13637)*

Ameribulk Transport LLC .... F 302 792-1190
   Claymont *(G-1033)*

American Van Storage Corp .... F 302 369-0900
   Newark *(G-9850)*

Amh Enterprises LLC .... E 302 337-0300
   Bridgeville *(G-664)*

Andrew Simoff Horse Trnsp .... G 302 994-1533
   Wilmington *(G-14477)*

Asi Transport LLC .... G 302 349-9460
   Bridgeville *(G-668)*

Atlantic Bulk Carriers .... G 302 378-6300
   Middletown *(G-6880)*

Atlantic Bulk Carriers Inc .... F 302 378-4522
   Middletown *(G-6881)*

Attention To Dtils Strtgies LL .... G 877 870-2837
   Wilmington *(G-14638)*

Auto Express Transport Inc .... F 302 628-4601
   Seaford *(G-13074)*

Banks Farms LLC .... G 302 542-4100
   Dagsboro *(G-1417)*

▲ Bayshore Trnsp Sys Inc .... G 302 366-0220
   Newark *(G-9997)*

Big Day Trucking LLC .... G 302 900-1190
   Dover *(G-1934)*

Bl Own UP LLC .... G 609 509-8388
   Milford *(G-7794)*

Bloomfield Trucking Inc .... G 302 834-6922
   Middletown *(G-6925)*

Blue Hen Lines Inc .... E 302 422-6206
   Milford *(G-7797)*

Bowman Group LLC .... G 302 494-7476
   New Castle *(G-8879)*

Burris Logistics .... C 302 221-4100
   Historic New Castle *(G-4948)*

Burroughs Express LLC .... G 410 476-1764
   Dover *(G-1996)*

Chesapeake Carriers Inc .... E 302 628-3838
   Seaford *(G-13116)*

Christiana Motor Freight Inc .... F 302 655-6271
   New Castle *(G-8940)*

Cirrus Enterprises .... G 302 650-1648
   Wilmington *(G-15445)*

City Mist LLC .... G 302 342-1377
   New Castle *(G-8950)*

Co Fs Holding Company LLC .... F 302 894-1244
   Newark *(G-10268)*

Coast 2 Coast Logistics LLC .... G 857 212-9832
   Dover *(G-2104)*

Cobb Trucking Inc .... G 917 561-6263
   Smyrna *(G-13683)*

College Hunks Hauling Junk Mvg .... G 302 232-6200
   Wilmington *(G-15532)*

Contractual Carriers Inc .... E 302 453-1420
   Newark *(G-10316)*

Cowan Systems LLC .... C 302 656-1403
   Wilmington *(G-15670)*

Cs Associates LLC .... G 909 827-2335
   Wilmington *(G-15721)*

D 4 Brown LLC .... G 518 986-6809
   Dover *(G-2179)*

Delaware Moving & Storage Inc .... D 302 322-0311
   Bear *(G-151)*

Diamond State Corporation .... D 302 674-1300
   Dover *(G-2294)*

Donkey Trucking LLC .... G 302 507-2380
   New Castle *(G-9059)*

Eagle Express .... G 302 898-2247
   New Castle *(G-9074)*

Eastern Mail Transport Inc .... F 302 838-0500
   Bear *(G-191)*

Eric Hobbs Trucking Inc .... E 302 697-2090
   Viola *(G-14094)*

Family Freight LLC .... G 302 212-0708
   Dover *(G-2483)*

Foodliner Inc .... D 302 368-4204
   Newark *(G-10756)*

George Scott Paving .... G 302 588-0024
   New Castle *(G-9164)*

George W Oppel .... G 302 398-4433
   Houston *(G-5442)*

Getcarrier LLC .... G 302 763-3040
   Dover *(G-2575)*

Godspeed Transport LLC .... G 302 803-2929
   Wilmington *(G-16906)*

Hab Nab Trucking Inc .... G 302 245-6900
   Bridgeville *(G-707)*

Hackett Industries LLC .... G 302 516-0836
   Wilmington *(G-17029)*

Hobbs Enterprises Inc .... G 302 697-2090
   Viola *(G-14096)*

◆ Holman Moving Systems LLC .... E 302 323-9000
   New Castle *(G-9216)*

Igm Logistics LLC .... G 302 409-9404
   Newark *(G-10999)*

JG Allstar Trucking LLC .... F 609 372-8636
   Dover *(G-2786)*

Joshua Tilghman .... G 302 582-1491
   Middletown *(G-7254)*

Krh Trucking LLC .... G 302 535-8407
   Dover *(G-2887)*

Kzy Group Inc .... G 302 684-3078
   Lewes *(G-6174)*

Larrimore Logistics LLC .... G 302 265-2290
   Lincoln *(G-6679)*

Marine Lubricants Inc .... G 302 429-7570
   Wilmington *(G-18131)*

Material Transit LLC .... E 302 395-0556
   New Castle *(G-9353)*

Messicks Mobile Homes Inc .... F 302 398-9166
   Harrington *(G-4801)*

Mit Shah LLC .... G 469 307-6571
   Wilmington *(G-18386)*

Montgomery Kenneth John .... G 302 992-0484
   Wilmington *(G-18426)*

National Trucking LLC .... G 302 465-3692
   Bridgeville *(G-737)*

Next Trucking Inc .... E 213 568-0388
   Wilmington *(G-18635)*

Old Dominion Freight Line Inc .... G 302 337-8793
   Bridgeville *(G-741)*

Phoenix Trnsp & Logistics Inc .... F 302 348-8814
   Wilmington *(G-19027)*

Pierson Culver LLC .... G 302 732-1145
   Dagsboro *(G-1496)*

Pink Ape Logistics Inc .... G 210 570-1033
   Wilmington *(G-19047)*

Pyramid Transport Inc .... E 302 337-9340
   Bridgeville *(G-757)*

R W Morgan Farms Inc .... G 302 542-7740
   Lincoln *(G-6695)*

Reed Trucking Company .... D 302 684-8585
   Milton *(G-8694)*

Ruan Transport Corporation .... D 302 696-3270
   Middletown *(G-7526)*

Schwerman Trucking Co .... E 302 832-3103
   Bear *(G-482)*

Shade Merchant LLC .... G 571 634-0670
   Dover *(G-3537)*

Showbiz Trucking LLC .... G 302 526-6337
   Camden *(G-893)*

Superior Dedicated Svcs LLC .... F 443 497-4410
   Laurel *(G-5608)*

T A H First Inc .... G 302 653-6114
   Smyrna *(G-13910)*

Tax-E Logistics Inc .... G 877 829-3669
   Dover *(G-3654)*

Top Tier Trucking Inc .... G 917 545-5170
   Dover *(G-3700)*

Triglias Transportation Co .... E 302 846-2141
   Delmar *(G-1645)*

Trinity 3 Enterprises Inc .... G 267 973-2666
   Bear *(G-541)*

Ultimate Express Inc .... F 443 523-0800
  Selbyville (G-13615)
Xavier Entertainment Inc .... G 215 356-8314
  Bear (G-569)
Xpedient Freight LLC .... G 267 826-6170
  Middletown (G-7740)
Xpo Logistics Freight Inc .... E 302 629-5228
  Seaford (G-13456)

4214 Local trucking with storage

15 Division LLC .... G 667 334-0861
  Wilmington (G-14111)
Advance Office InstIItions Inc .... E 302 777-5599
  Historic New Castle (G-4922)
Aruna Network Inc .... G 832 303-3628
  Lewes (G-5704)
▲ Bayshore Trnsp Sys Inc .... D 302 366-0220
  Newark (G-9997)
Bonnie Relocation LLC .... G 302 538-0673
  Dover (G-1961)
Buntings Garage Inc .... F 302 732-9021
  Dagsboro (G-1421)
Christiana Motor Freight Inc .... F 302 655-6271
  New Castle (G-8940)
Contractual Carriers Inc .... E 302 453-1420
  Newark (G-10316)
Davis Trucking & Family LLC .... F 302 381-6358
  Frankford (G-4099)
Delaware Moving & Storage Inc .... D 302 322-0311
  Bear (G-151)
Diamond State Corporation .... D 302 674-1300
  Dover (G-2294)
Docuvault Delaware Valley LLC .... F 302 366-0220
  Newark (G-10545)
Dunkley Enterprises LLC .... G 302 275-0100
  Odessa (G-12583)
◆ Holman Moving Systems LLC .... E 302 323-9000
  New Castle (G-9216)
Kmk Portable Moving & Stor LLC .... G 302 734-0410
  Newark (G-11192)
New Creation Logistics Inc .... F 302 438-3154
  Newark (G-11520)
Penske Truck Leasing Corp .... G 302 449-9294
  Middletown (G-7439)
Wiggins Group LLC .... F 800 590-8070
  Dover (G-3848)
Xavier Entertainment Inc .... G 215 356-8314
  Bear (G-569)

4215 Courier services, except by air

Blue Marble Logistics LLC .... G 302 221-4674
  Historic New Castle (G-4943)
Blue Phoenix Logistics LLC .... G 347 424-7491
  Wilmington (G-14970)
Brooks Courier Service Inc .... C 302 762-4661
  Wilmington (G-15126)
Carr Courier Service Inc .... G 302 846-9826
  Delmar (G-1573)
Charles E Carlson .... G 302 284-3184
  Camden Wyoming (G-923)
Darlington Postal Company LLC .... G 410 917-4147
  Newark (G-10389)
Delaware Medical Courier .... G 302 670-1247
  Milton (G-8599)
Dt Transit LLC .... G 302 216-3547
  Hockessin (G-5194)
Freeman Courier Express .... G 610 803-3933
  Wilmington (G-16743)
Harrymrmax Lgstics Crier Svcs .... G 302 784-5578
  New Castle (G-9199)
Honestly Service LLC .... F 302 844-2214
  Wilmington (G-17193)

K Diamond Delivery Inc .... F 215 882-2585
  Wilmington (G-17629)
Kaebox LLC .... G 919 777-3939
  Middletown (G-7259)
Kenkay Inc .... G 302 838-7797
  Bear (G-325)
Levels Express Logistics LLC .... F 302 760-3750
  Dover (G-2931)
Lit Xpress LLC .... G 302 690-9520
  Newark (G-11269)
M&M Courier Service LLC .... G 302 430-2740
  Middletown (G-7319)
Parcels Inc .... G 302 736-1777
  Dover (G-3271)
Parcels Inc .... C 302 888-1718
  Wilmington (G-18889)
Persha LLC .... G 786 925-2952
  Dover (G-3303)

4222 Refrigerated warehousing and storage

Blue Marlin Ice LLC .... G 302 697-7800
  Dover (G-1952)
Burris Logistics .... C 302 221-4100
  Historic New Castle (G-4948)
Citrosuco North America Inc .... F 302 652-8763
  Wilmington (G-15450)
Realcold Manager LLC .... G 332 264-7077
  Wilmington (G-19372)
United States Cold Storage Inc .... E 302 422-7536
  Milford (G-8127)
United States Cold Storage Inc .... F 302 422-7536
  Milford (G-8128)

4225 General warehousing and storage

Advance Office InstIItions Inc .... E 302 777-5599
  Historic New Castle (G-4922)
Allstate Van & Storage Corp .... G 302 369-0230
  Wilmington (G-9827)
AmazonCom Services LLC .... D 206 266-1000
  Historic New Castle (G-4930)
American Van Storage Corp .... F 302 369-0900
  Newark (G-9850)
Barami De Inc .... G 201 993-9678
  Wilmington (G-14753)
Bayside Mini Storage .... G 302 524-2096
  Frankford (G-4070)
Brandywine Chemical Company .... G 302 656-5428
  New Castle (G-8883)
Burris Logistics .... C 302 398-5050
  Harrington (G-4742)
Burris Logistics .... C 302 221-4100
  Historic New Castle (G-4948)
Cannon Cold Storage LLC .... E 302 337-5500
  Bridgeville (G-680)
Ceco Inc .... E 302 732-3919
  Dagsboro (G-1423)
Cool Spring Storage Center Inc .... G 302 448-8164
  Rehoboth Beach (G-12699)
D & S Warehousing Inc .... G 302 731-7440
  Bear (G-129)
▲ D & S Warehousing Inc .... E 302 731-7440
  Newark (G-10374)
Delaware Beach Storage Center .... G 302 644-7774
  Lewes (G-5891)
Delaware Freeport Holdings LLC .... E 302 366-1150
  Newark (G-10447)
Delaware Moving & Storage Inc .... D 302 322-0311
  Bear (G-151)
Delaware Prep Center LLC .... E 302 932-1208
  Newark (G-10470)
Destorage .... G 302 424-6902
  Milford (G-7868)

Destorage Rehoboth LLC .... G 302 231-2127
  Rehoboth Beach (G-12722)
DOT Foods Inc .... D 302 300-4239
  Bear (G-177)
Eduardo McEdo Lite De Oliveira .... G 302 476-2285
  Lewes (G-5950)
First State Warehousing .... F 302 426-0802
  New Castle (G-9134)
Globbing LLC .... E 408 903-4209
  Claymont (G-1165)
Golo LLC .... E 302 781-4260
  Newark (G-10865)
Hardy Development .... G 302 436-4496
  Selbyville (G-13542)
Heavens Treasures Thrift and .... G 267 387-0030
  Wilmington (G-17112)
Hermann Warehouse Corporation .... F 732 297-5333
  Historic New Castle (G-5003)
Intercontinental Chem Svcs Inc .... E 302 654-6800
  Wilmington (G-17377)
◆ Iovate Health Sciences USA Inc .... G 888 334-4448
  Wilmington (G-17414)
Istorage .... G 302 798-6661
  Claymont (G-1189)
Istorage New Castle .... G 302 396-6224
  New Castle (G-9244)
Jkb Corp .... E 302 734-5017
  Dover (G-2792)
Kenco Group Inc .... G 302 629-4295
  Seaford (G-13248)
Lan Chester Sheds Gazebos .... G 302 653-7392
  Smyrna (G-13795)
Love Creek Marina MBL Hm Site .... F 302 448-6492
  Lewes (G-6225)
Maritime Logistics Corp LLC .... G 302 420-3007
  Wilmington (G-18134)
New Creation Logistics Inc .... F 302 438-3154
  Newark (G-11520)
Pencader Self Storage .... G 302 709-3180
  Newark (G-11661)
Penco Corporation .... G 302 629-3061
  Seaford (G-13333)
Penco Corporation .... D 302 629-7911
  Seaford (G-13334)
Pretty Damn Quick Inc .... G 201 613-2296
  Wilmington (G-19183)
Pure Storage Inc .... G 302 383-2492
  Wilmington (G-19262)
Salesinusa Inc .... G 973 771-4420
  Wilmington (G-19639)
Sardo & Sons Warehousing Inc .... G 302 737-3000
  Newark (G-11948)
Sardo & Sons Warehousing Inc .... G 302 369-0852
  Newark (G-11949)
▲ Sardo & Sons Warehousing Inc .... G 302 369-2100
  Christiana (G-1008)
Secure Self Storage .... G 302 832-0400
  New Castle (G-9555)
Simmons Animal Nutrition Inc .... D 302 337-5500
  Bridgeville (G-767)
Southern States Coop Inc .... G 302 629-7991
  Seaford (G-13410)
Standard Distributing Co Inc .... E 302 674-4591
  Dover (G-3604)
Storage Rentals of America .... G 302 838-7405
  New Castle (G-9597)
Storage Rentals of America .... G 302 313-1430
  Wilmington (G-20085)
Storage Squad LLC .... F 830 200-0269
  Lewes (G-6514)
Storageos Inc .... G 617 971-8470
  Wilmington (G-20086)

42 MOTOR FREIGHT TRANSPORTATION

Tops International Corp .... G 302 738-8889
 Wilmington (G-20361)
U-Haul Neighborhd Dealr Budget .... G 302 349-2167
 Greenwood (G-4673)
USA Fulfillment .... G 410 810-0880
 Dover (G-3766)
USA Fulfillment Inc .... F 410 810-0880
 Dover (G-3767)
▲ Westech Industries Inc .... G 302 453-0301
 Newark (G-12361)
Zenith Home Corp .... A 302 322-2190
 Historic New Castle (G-5104)

4226 Special warehousing and storage, nec

All Climate Storage Cente .... G 302 645-0006
 Lewes (G-5672)
Delaware Direct Inc .... G 302 658-8223
 Wilmington (G-15908)
Delaware Freeport LLC .... F 302 366-1150
 Newark (G-10446)
Doculogica Corp .... G 302 753-5944
 Wilmington (G-16113)
Fidelitrade Incorporated .... F 302 762-6200
 Wilmington (G-16598)
Globbing LLC .... E 408 903-4209
 Claymont (G-1165)
Houston Self Storage .... G 302 422-9660
 Houston (G-5444)
Lifestyle Document MGT Inc .... G 302 856-6387
 Georgetown (G-4407)
Meherrin AG & Chem Co .... G 302 337-0330
 Bridgeville (G-730)
Reybold Group of Companies Inc .... E 302 838-7405
 New Castle (G-9528)
Secure Self Storage .... G 302 832-0400
 New Castle (G-9555)

4231 Trucking terminal facilities

H & E Trucking Co LLC .... G 302 287-2113
 Middletown (G-7183)
Kan Trucking LLC .... G 413 358-7832
 Wilmington (G-17645)
Kimbles AVI Lgistical Svcs Inc .... G 334 663-4954
 Georgetown (G-4394)
Tnjd Diamond LLC .... G 614 902-9431
 Dover (G-3693)

44 WATER TRANSPORTATION

4412 Deep sea foreign transportation of freight

New Hope Vehicle Exports LLC .... G 302 275-6482
 Wilmington (G-18619)

4424 Deep sea domestic transportation of freight

Auto Express Transport Inc .... F 302 628-4601
 Seaford (G-13074)
Maritime Logistics Corp LLC .... G 302 420-3007
 Wilmington (G-18135)

4449 Water transportation of freight

American Eli Truck Network Inc .... E 210 842-2134
 Lewes (G-5686)
Delaware Bay Launch Service .... F 302 422-7604
 Milford (G-7853)
Family Legacy Llccom .... G 302 256-1406
 Wilmington (G-16541)

4481 Deep sea passenger transportation, except ferry

Cruise One .... G 302 698-6468
 Camden Wyoming (G-930)

4489 Water passenger transportation

Delaware Bay Launch Service .... F 302 422-7604
 Milford (G-7853)

4491 Marine cargo handling

▲ Advance Marine LLC .... G 302 656-2111
 Wilmington (G-14268)
Delaware River Stevedores Inc .... G 302 657-0472
 Wilmington (G-15962)
Diamond State Port Corporation ...... C 302 472-7678
 Wilmington (G-16055)
Iap Holding LLC .... G 302 394-9795
 Wilmington (G-17254)
Murphy Marine Services Inc .... B 302 571-4700
 Wilmington (G-18489)

4492 Towing and tugboat service

Buntings Garage Inc .... F 302 732-9021
 Dagsboro (G-1421)
Dick Ennis Inc .... G 302 945-2627
 Lewes (G-5914)
Wilmington Tug Inc .... E 302 652-1666
 Wilmington (G-20851)

4493 Marinas

Bayshore Inc .... G 302 539-7200
 Ocean View (G-12470)
Cedar Creek Marine Center .... G 302 629-3581
 Seaford (G-13104)
Chester Marina LLC .... G 302 829-8218
 Bethany Beach (G-590)
Delaware Bay Launch Service .... F 302 422-7604
 Milford (G-7853)
Freedom Boat Club Delaware .... G 302 219-3549
 Lewes (G-6014)
Indian Rver Cptins Assoc Wbmst ..... G 302 227-3071
 Rehoboth Beach (G-12794)
Jack Hickman Real Estate .... F 302 539-8000
 Bethany Beach (G-611)
Jamc LLC .... G 410 639-2224
 Millsboro (G-8327)
Love Creek Marina MBL Hm Site ..... F 302 448-6492
 Lewes (G-6225)
LP Smoked LLC .... G 302 379-3059
 Wilmington (G-18016)
Midlantic Marine Center Inc .... F 302 436-2628
 Selbyville (G-13575)
Misty Rivers Ltd .... G 315 415-2826
 Dover (G-3102)
North Bay Marina Incorporated .... E 302 436-4211
 Selbyville (G-13586)
South Shore Provisions LLC .... G 443 614-2442
 Selbyville (G-13607)
Summit North Marina .... F 302 836-1800
 Bear (G-517)
Summit North Marina LLC .... G 302 836-1800
 Bear (G-518)

45 TRANSPORTATION BY AIR

4512 Air transportation, scheduled

Penobscot Properties LLC .... G 302 322-4477
 New Castle (G-9466)
United Parcel Service Inc .... D 302 453-7462
 Newark (G-12270)

4513 Air courier services

Federal Express Corporation .... F 800 463-3339
 New Castle (G-9122)
Federal Express Corporation .... G 800 463-3339
 Wilmington (G-16570)
Fedex Corporation .... G 302 286-6570
 Newark (G-10721)
Penobscot Properties LLC .... G 302 322-4477
 New Castle (G-9466)

4522 Air transportation, nonscheduled

Aero Taxi Inc .... G 302 328-3430
 Wilmington (G-14296)
Horizon Helicopters Inc .... G 302 368-5135
 Newark (G-10970)
Interjet West Inc .... G 209 848-0290
 Wilmington (G-17384)
Penobscot Properties LLC .... G 302 322-4477
 New Castle (G-9466)
Transcontinental Airways Corp .... G 202 817-2020
 Wilmington (G-20396)

4581 Airports, flying fields, and services

Aero Enterprises Inc .... G 302 378-1396
 Townsend (G-13953)
Aircrafters Inc .... G 302 777-5000
 Wilmington (G-14337)
Bootcamp Helicopters LLC .... G 301 717-5455
 Middletown (G-6931)
Djh Enterprises Vii LLC .... G 410 749-0100
 Dagsboro (G-1441)
Dumont Aircraft Charter LLC .... F 610 266-1369
 New Castle (G-9066)
Dumont Aviation Group Inc .... G 302 777-1003
 New Castle (G-9067)
Dumont Aviation Group Inc .... F 302 777-1003
 New Castle (G-9068)
East Coast Aviation LLC .... G 302 650-9889
 Clayton (G-1364)
Georgetown Air Services .... G 302 855-2355
 Georgetown (G-4333)
Georgetown Air Services LLC .... F 302 855-2355
 Georgetown (G-4334)
Lowes Airport (fa77) .... G 813 366-7655
 Wilmington (G-18012)
Pats Aircraft LLC .... D 855 236-1638
 Georgetown (G-4456)
Rayco Auto & Marine Uphl Inc .... G 302 323-8844
 Hockessin (G-5356)
Savaren Corporate Arcft Svcs .... G 443 207-1372
 New Castle (G-9553)
Tts Tcnja TCI Shipg N Amer Inc ...... G 770 383-4604
 Wilmington (G-20457)
Wingfield & Associates Inc .... G 626 252-6586
 Wilmington (G-20858)

46 PIPELINES, EXCEPT NATURAL GAS

4612 Crude petroleum pipelines

Magellan Midstream Partners LP .... F 302 654-3717
 Wilmington (G-18078)
Whitecap Pipeline Company LLC .... E 925 842-1000
 Wilmington (G-20768)

47 TRANSPORTATION SERVICES

4724 Travel agencies

AAA Club Alliance Inc .... D 302 674-8020
 Dover (G-1700)
AAA Club Alliance Inc .... B 302 299-4700
 Wilmington (G-14181)

47 TRANSPORTATION SERVICES

AAA Washington .... E 860 371-9783
 Wilmington (G-14183)
Aba Travl & Ent Inc .... G 800 696-0838
 Lewes (G-5649)
Ans Corporation .... G 410 296-8330
 Rehoboth Beach (G-12607)
Avvinue Inc .... G 929 444-0554
 Middletown (G-6894)
Bethany Travel Inc .... G 302 933-0955
 Millsboro (G-8196)
Creative Travel Inc .... G 302 658-2900
 Newark (G-10350)
Cruise Holidays Brandywine Vly .... F 302 239-6400
 Hockessin (G-5173)
Cruise One .... G 302 698-6468
 Camden Wyoming (G-930)
Cruise Planners .... G 302 858-1996
 Lewes (G-5869)
Cruise Planners .... G 302 381-9249
 Lewes (G-5870)
Cruise Planners .... G 302 503-3694
 Milford (G-7844)
Cruise Planners .... G 302 731-9548
 Newark (G-10357)
Cruise Ship Centers .... G 302 999-0202
 Newark (G-10358)
Cruise Shoppe Inc .... G 302 737-7220
 Bear (G-128)
Dduberry LLC .... G 703 798-5280
 Newark (G-10398)
Expedia Cruiseshipcenters .... G 302 444-8447
 Bear (G-215)
Expedia Cruiseshipcenters .... G 484 483-3272
 Newark (G-10691)
Faremart Inc .... G 800 965-5819
 Wilmington (G-16553)
Flight Centre Travel Group USA .... G 302 479-7581
 Wilmington (G-16661)
Front Row Enterprises LLC .... G 646 862-6380
 Wilmington (G-16762)
Greenville Travel Agency Inc .... G 302 658-3585
 Milton (G-8632)
Inspire African Safaris LLC .... F 302 250-5763
 Wilmington (G-17356)
International Travel Network .... G 415 840-0207
 Wilmington (G-17392)
Iweekender Inc .... G 347 696-1010
 Wilmington (G-17440)
Jetset Travel Inc .... G 302 678-5050
 Rehoboth Beach (G-12805)
Misty Travel .... G 302 628-1815
 Seaford (G-13286)
My World Travel Inc .... F 610 358-3744
 Wilmington (G-18511)
Mymoroccanbazar Inc .... G 323 238-5747
 Newark (G-11478)
Our Services - Travelers Q .... G 302 660-3680
 Wilmington (G-18835)
Plane James and Janes LLC .... G 267 716-6723
 Middletown (G-7452)
Planiversity LLC .... G 315 498-0986
 Wilmington (G-19067)
Red Carpet Travel Agency Inc .... F 302 475-1220
 Wilmington (G-19383)
Reservation Centre LLC .... E 888 284-0908
 Dover (G-3459)
See The World Travel Agency .... G 302 559-4514
 Middletown (G-7550)
Skyworld Traveler Inc .... F 844 591-9060
 Wilmington (G-19860)
Tenon Tours LLC .... G 781 435-0425
 Lewes (G-6550)

Ticket To Travel .... G 302 442-0225
 Middletown (G-7644)
Timon Financials Inc .... G 620 464-4247
 Dover (G-3689)
Travel Offshore .... G 410 246-6648
 Selbyville (G-13613)
Travelbook Inc .... G 646 575-6731
 Lewes (G-6578)
Travelers Joy Inc .... G 888 878-5569
 Wilmington (G-20405)
Travly US LLC .... G 901 228-5882
 Dover (G-3719)
Welcome Aboard Travel Ltd .... G 302 678-9480
 Lewes (G-6621)
Wilson Travel and Getaway .... G 302 559-3412
 Claymont (G-1338)
Xtend Inc .... G 305 204-0595
 Wilmington (G-20920)
Zenner Inc .... F 302 781-9833
 Newark (G-12431)

4725 Tour operators

Cape Water Tours & Taxi .... G 302 245-4794
 Lewes (G-5798)
Case Tour Duty .... G 302 668-6998
 New Castle (G-8917)
Delaware Express Tours Inc .... F 302 454-7800
 Newark (G-10442)
Emerging Travel Inc .... G 302 295-3838
 Wilmington (G-16392)
Grand View Tour & Travel .... G 610 361-7979
 Ocean View (G-12520)
Jet Setting Tours LLC .... G 707 217-6967
 Wilmington (G-17537)
Posidon Adventure Inc .... F 302 543-5024
 Wilmington (G-19123)
U Transit Inc .... G 302 227-1197
 Rehoboth Beach (G-13000)

4731 Freight transportation arrangement

Achieve Lgstic Systems Trnsp L .... F 302 654-4701
 Wilmington (G-14231)
Adroit Logistics LLC .... G 385 381-0007
 Dover (G-1719)
Aku Transport Inc .... G 302 500-8127
 Georgetown (G-4204)
All Logistics LLC .... F 800 748-4891
 Lewes (G-5673)
Ameenahko LLC .... G 302 601-3720
 Wilmington (G-14420)
APL Lgstics Trnsp MGT Svcs Ltd .... E 302 230-2656
 Wilmington (G-14507)
Bettan Trucking LLC .... E 302 841-3834
 Lewes (G-5759)
Boj Global Services LLC .... F 302 325-4018
 New Castle (G-8873)
Brantimus Logistics LLC .... E 302 990-4110
 Dover (G-1972)
Briscoe Trucking Inc .... G 302 836-1327
 Newark (G-10090)
Burris Freight Management LLC .... G 800 805-8135
 Milford (G-7807)
C V International Inc .... G 302 427-0440
 Wilmington (G-15177)
Central American Trade Co LLC .... G 305 440-0420
 Wilmington (G-15307)
Ceva Logistics .... F 512 356-1700
 Historic New Castle (G-4954)
City Mist LLC .... G 302 342-1937
 New Castle (G-8950)
Cubic Sct Inc .... F 845 977-3240
 Middletown (G-7022)

D1 Express Inc .... G 302 883-9572
 Dover (G-2183)
D150 Fueling LLC .... E 215 559-1132
 Newark (G-10378)
Destiny Way Logistics LLC .... F 866 526-4900
 Wilmington (G-16029)
Duha Logistics LLC .... F 888 493-5999
 Wilmington (G-16197)
Dynamic Trnsp & Logistics LLC .... G 302 991-1005
 Wilmington (G-16231)
Eikon Int Inc .... G 312 550-2648
 Wilmington (G-16345)
Ens Logistics LLC .... G 302 784-5155
 Newark (G-10650)
Evanix Enterprises LLC .... G 302 384-1806
 Middletown (G-7111)
Explorer New Build LLC .... G 305 436-4000
 Wilmington (G-16507)
Expotrade Inc .... G 818 212-8905
 Lewes (G-5981)
EZ Way Transport LLC .... G 302 367-5272
 Wilmington (G-16516)
Faramove Inc .... F 815 674-3114
 Middletown (G-7121)
Fastcold LLC .... G 302 240-4402
 Wilmington (G-16559)
Ff Group LLC .... F 302 608-0609
 Dover (G-2493)
▲ Freds Stores Tennessee Inc .... A 800 746-7287
 Bear (G-237)
GATX Trmnals Ovrseas Hldg Corp .... F 302 636-5400
 Wilmington (G-16816)
Gemini Qulty Frt Solutions LLC .... G 302 219-3310
 Dover (G-2569)
Global Container & Chassis LLC .... G 302 608-0822
 Historic New Castle (G-4996)
Global Shopaholics LLC .... F 302 725-0586
 Historic New Castle (G-4997)
Herms Freight LLC .... G 321 417-4884
 Middletown (G-7207)
Hey Logistics LLC .... F 706 350-5539
 Middletown (G-7209)
Hollywell Logistics LLC .... F 267 901-4272
 Wilmington (G-17170)
Hs Capital LLC .... G 302 598-2961
 Wilmington (G-17223)
Immensity Logistics LLC .... G 501 500-6667
 Wilmington (G-17284)
International Logistiks LLC .... G 302 521-6338
 Wilmington (G-17389)
J A S Logistic Inc .... G 302 339-1825
 Middletown (G-7235)
Jade Logistics Inc .... G 302 724-2649
 Hartly (G-4880)
Jet Carrier .... G 908 759-6938
 Newark (G-11109)
Johns Premier Services LLC .... G 347 992-3783
 Dover (G-2799)
Julian H Nicol .... G 484 390-1980
 Wilmington (G-17609)
Kango Express Inc .... E 808 725-1688
 Newark (G-11141)
KDi Solutions LLC .... G 302 406-0224
 Wilmington (G-17671)
Koam Corp .... G 302 422-4848
 Milford (G-7967)
Ktm 2 LLC .... G 302 856-2516
 Selbyville (G-13559)
L&L Logistics Inc .... F 720 232-5637
 Wilmington (G-17778)
Leonards Express Inc .... E 302 426-0802
 New Castle (G-9307)

Employee Codes: A=Over 500 employees, B=251-500
C=101-250, D=51-100, E=20-50, F=10-19, G=1-9

47 TRANSPORTATION SERVICES

Link Road Logistics Inc .... G 267 283-9370
  Lewes *(G-6210)*
Long Rd Ahead Shipg Lgstic LLC .... E 480 702-6438
  Wilmington *(G-17982)*
MA Transportation LLC .... G 302 588-5435
  Millsboro *(G-8358)*
Mexicom Usa Inc .... G 956 516-7201
  Newark *(G-11396)*
Mobility Unbound LLC .... G 786 925-4411
  Dover *(G-3112)*
Monster King Conglomerate LLC .... G 302 222-9742
  New Castle *(G-9380)*
Mtc Delaware LLC .... F 302 654-3400
  New Castle *(G-9388)*
New Creation Logistics Inc .... F 302 438-3154
  Newark *(G-11520)*
New Hope Vehicle Exports LLC .... G 302 275-6482
  Wilmington *(G-18619)*
North American Trnspt Co Inc .... G 856 696-5483
  New Castle *(G-9422)*
Oceanview Capital Inds LLC .... F 813 397-3706
  Dover *(G-3215)*
Penn Del Carriers LLC .... G 484 424-3768
  New Castle *(G-9464)*
Platinum Logistics LLC .... G 412 708-6476
  Newark *(G-11700)*
◆ Port To Port Intl Corp .... E 302 654-2444
  New Castle *(G-9484)*
Port To Port Logistics LLC .... G 302 654-2444
  New Castle *(G-9485)*
Post Shipper LLC .... F 302 444-8144
  Bear *(G-429)*
Pteris Global (usa) Inc .... F 516 593-5633
  Dover *(G-3392)*
Real Matter LLC .... G 302 291-2562
  Lewes *(G-6411)*
Right Knda Guys Car Sltons LLC .... G 302 772-8717
  Newark *(G-11884)*
Rock City Consulting Corp .... G 302 551-6844
  Wilmington *(G-19527)*
Rsl Logistics LLC .... G 302 521-3299
  Wilmington *(G-19582)*
Sacher .... G 302 792-0281
  Wilmington *(G-19621)*
Sahra Intl Holdings Inc .... G 202 660-0090
  Lewes *(G-6443)*
Seven Shipping Inc .... G 302 516-7150
  Wilmington *(G-19768)*
SF Logistics Limited .... E 302 317-3954
  New Castle *(G-9563)*
Shipping Center LLC .... G 302 543-4968
  Wilmington *(G-19802)*
Shipserv Inc .... F 732 738-6500
  Dover *(G-3545)*
Spare Cs Inc .... F 424 744-0155
  Lewes *(G-6496)*
Spedag Americas Inc .... G 201 857-3471
  Wilmington *(G-19957)*
Stepship LLC .... G 773 503-2110
  Newark *(G-12099)*
Tasha P Brown .... G 732 948-7591
  Newark *(G-12162)*
Tc Trans Inc .... G 302 339-7952
  Georgetown *(G-4546)*
The North Truckers Inc .... F 302 309-0786
  Lewes *(G-6554)*
Tradeally Incorporated .... E 832 997-2582
  Lewes *(G-6577)*
Transcore LP .... G 302 838-7429
  Middletown *(G-7658)*
Triglia Express Inc .... G 302 846-2248
  Delmar *(G-1643)*

Trinity Logistics Inc .... F 302 595-2116
  New Castle *(G-9640)*
Trinity Logistics Inc .... C 302 253-3900
  Seaford *(G-13436)*
Tts Tcnja TCI Shipg N Amer Inc .... G 770 383-4604
  Wilmington *(G-20457)*
Ukraine Express Inc .... G 973 253-0050
  New Castle *(G-9650)*
Umbrella Transport Group Inc .... G 301 919-1623
  Newark *(G-12263)*
UPS Supply Chain Solutions Inc .... F 302 631-5259
  Newark *(G-12287)*
US Ravens Logistics Inc .... D 302 401-4033
  Dover *(G-3765)*
Vallejo Vzquez Sons Hrvstg LLC .... G 616 902-5851
  Delmar *(G-1653)*
Walker International Trnsp LLC .... F 302 325-4180
  Historic New Castle *(G-5100)*
Wentzel Transportation .... G 302 355-9465
  Smyrna *(G-13935)*
Xpedient Freight LLC .... G 267 826-6170
  Middletown *(G-7740)*
Yental Empire LLC .... G 404 423-0454
  Middletown *(G-7745)*
Zipline Xpress Corp .... G 302 531-6417
  Dover *(G-3902)*

4741 Rental of railroad cars

Dana Container Inc .... F 302 652-8550
  Wilmington *(G-15776)*
Dana Railcare Inc .... E 302 652-8550
  Wilmington *(G-15777)*
Road & Rail Services Inc .... D 302 731-2552
  Newark *(G-11895)*
We Got Cars 4 Cash Inc .... G 215 399-6978
  Claymont *(G-1334)*

4783 Packing and crating

Atlas Van Lines Agents .... G 302 369-0900
  Newark *(G-9940)*
Cirkla Inc .... E 415 851-4635
  Dover *(G-2077)*
Globbing LLC .... E 408 903-4209
  Claymont *(G-1165)*
Marlex Pharmaceuticals Inc .... E 302 328-3355
  New Castle *(G-9348)*
Pack Usa Inc .... G 443 655-8927
  Wilmington *(G-18860)*
Prescotech Inc .... D 502 585-5866
  Wilmington *(G-19178)*
Ur-Express Inc .... G 302 839-2008
  Wilmington *(G-20540)*

4785 Inspection and fixed facilities

Delaware River & Bay Authority .... C 302 571-6303
  New Castle *(G-9034)*
Drba Police Fund .... F 302 571-6326
  New Castle *(G-9062)*
Ooga Technologies Inc .... G 585 503-6047
  Dover *(G-3234)*

4789 Transportation services, nec

4rb Logistics LLC .... G 302 290-8187
  Newark *(G-9714)*
7 Jewel Logistics LLC .... G 409 350-9759
  Bear *(G-5)*
Acia Freight & Logistics LLC .... G 800 362-8837
  Wilmington *(G-14234)*
Adkess Transport Services LLC .... G 978 235-3924
  Bear *(G-16)*
Advanced Logistics LLC .... G 302 345-8921
  New Castle *(G-8765)*

AEG International LLC .... G 302 750-6411
  Laurel *(G-5461)*
All In One Transportation LLC .... D 302 482-3222
  Wilmington *(G-14365)*
Aloha Movers .... F 302 559-4310
  Wilmington *(G-14389)*
Altra Cargo Inc .... G 302 256-0748
  Wilmington *(G-14398)*
Amarch LLC .... G 484 478-1034
  New Castle *(G-8790)*
Apex Transportation Svcs LLC .... E 302 284-7463
  Felton *(G-3941)*
Aquantuo LLC .... G 302 753-0435
  Wyoming *(G-20980)*
Atlantic Bulk Ltd .... G 302 378-6300
  Middletown *(G-6882)*
Auxo Rail Holdings LLC .... D 304 325-7245
  Wilmington *(G-14659)*
B-Smart Logistics LLC .... F 609 388-6622
  Newark *(G-9969)*
Bay Shippers LLC .... G 302 652-5005
  New Castle *(G-8850)*
Bayshore Services LLC .... G 304 596-3788
  Georgetown *(G-4225)*
Beachy Transportation .... G 302 284-7202
  Harrington *(G-4739)*
Benlick Freight Forwarders LLC .... G 302 743-4990
  Newark *(G-10022)*
Best Warehouse and Trnsp LLC .... G 302 328-5371
  Historic New Castle *(G-4941)*
Big Box USA LLC .... G 302 595-3324
  Bear *(G-71)*
Blue Hen Route LLC .... E 347 863-5534
  Middletown *(G-6926)*
Book em Danni Logistics LLC .... G 302 983-2921
  Newark *(G-10068)*
Bull Head Transport LLC .... G 302 650-8544
  Middletown *(G-6946)*
Burris Logistics .... G 302 839-5129
  Dover *(G-1995)*
Burris Logistics .... G 302 737-5203
  Newark *(G-10106)*
◆ Burris Logistics .... D 302 839-4531
  Milford *(G-7808)*
C3 Wave Holdings LLC .... G 412 708-6476
  Newark *(G-10117)*
CAM-K Transport LLC .... G 267 693-1797
  New Castle *(G-8910)*
Cape May Lewes Ferry .... G 302 577-2011
  Wilmington *(G-15222)*
Changing My Direction LLC .... G 302 510-9873
  Claymont *(G-1082)*
CMS Logistics .... F 302 409-3138
  Wilmington *(G-15502)*
Coach Transport LLC .... G 302 983-7339
  Dover *(G-2103)*
Compassionate Care Trnspt LLC .... G 215 847-9836
  Wilmington *(G-15567)*
Dana Railcare Inc .... E 302 652-8550
  Wilmington *(G-15777)*
Delaware Car Company .... E 302 655-6665
  Wilmington *(G-15880)*
Dixon Brothers LLC .... D 302 377-8289
  Wilmington *(G-16100)*
Dry Bulk Transportation LLC .... G 561 409-7818
  Camden Wyoming *(G-936)*
Durham Transport LLC .... G 302 270-2178
  Camden Wyoming *(G-938)*
E-Lyte Transportation .... G 808 269-0283
  Dover *(G-2400)*
Ed Hunt Inc .... G 302 339-8443
  Dover *(G-2418)*

48 COMMUNICATIONS

Edison Trnspt & Logistics Inc .... G 302 332-6878
  Newark (G-10609)
Elite Auto Transport .... G 302 252-5847
  Middletown (G-7093)
Elite Trnspt & Logistics Inc .... G 302 348-8480
  Wilmington (G-16367)
Erik Lemus .... G 302 293-5178
  Wilmington (G-16458)
Flou Holding Inc .... G 832 267-3372
  Dover (G-2519)
Fox Logistics LLC .... G 302 444-4750
  Wilmington (G-16713)
Freehold Cartage Inc .... E 302 658-2005
  New Castle (G-9145)
Gisco Logistics LLC .... G 800 226-3696
  Newark (G-10840)
GO Underground LLC .... G 732 740-1127
  Lewes (G-6043)
Grace Logistics LLC .... G 302 287-4838
  Townsend (G-14010)
Gsi Express Logistics Inc .... G 201 345-3532
  Wilmington (G-16995)
Halen Technologies Inc .... F 302 290-3075
  Wilmington (G-17037)
Hands On Deck Moving Co LLC .... G 302 489-9251
  Dover (G-2649)
Harrymrmax Lgstics Crier Svcs .... G 302 784-5578
  New Castle (G-9199)
Hauleet Inc .... F 302 434-6384
  Dover (G-2663)
Helton and Moorehead Trnsp LLC .... G 443 842-3360
  Dover (G-2673)
J & J Bus Service .... F 302 744-9002
  Dover (G-2758)
J M Aja Transportation LLC .... G 302 562-6028
  Wilmington (G-17458)
Jager Transport LLC .... G 302 858-2962
  Greenwood (G-4643)
Jet Green Transporters LLC .... G 302 861-8918
  Dover (G-2785)
Jones Logistics LLC .... G 302 724-5663
  Dover (G-2801)
Justlabormovers Inc .... G 302 444-7599
  Newark (G-11139)
K&L Enterprise LLC .... G 302 514-1136
  Dover (G-2825)
King La Express .... G 215 607-9997
  New Castle (G-9283)
Lantransit Enterprises LLC .... G 302 722-4800
  Lewes (G-6179)
Larrimore Logistics LLC .... G 302 265-2290
  Lincoln (G-6679)
Latham Logistics .... G 215 760-4724
  Townsend (G-14025)
Legend Transportation LLC .... E 215 713-7472
  New Castle (G-9301)
M P Logistics Inc .... G 302 562-0420
  New Castle (G-9333)
Meridian Limo LLC .... G 800 462-1550
  Dover (G-3064)
Movendi Moving .... G 302 542-9346
  Rehoboth Beach (G-12865)
Moving Experience Delaware .... G 302 241-0899
  Dover (G-3129)
Moving On Time .... G 302 613-4066
  Newark (G-11461)
Moving Out .... G 302 470-5308
  Seaford (G-13292)
Naqeebi Transport Inc .... G 267 246-9321
  Wilmington (G-18533)
National Auto Movers LLC .... G 302 229-9256
  Smyrna (G-13833)

New Life Moving Inc .... G 704 969-0858
  Milford (G-8028)
Nexus Services America LLC .... G 800 946-4626
  Wilmington (G-18638)
North Atlantic Ocean Ship .... G 302 652-3782
  New Castle (G-9424)
Otr 2 Otr Dispatching LLC .... G 862 249-9407
  New Castle (G-9439)
Pascal Ngalim .... G 302 983-2322
  Bear (G-415)
PCI of Virginia LLC .... F 302 655-7300
  Wilmington (G-18934)
Person 2 Person Trnsp LLC .... G 302 900-1061
  Clayton (G-1396)
▼ Port Contractors Inc .... E 302 655-7300
  Wilmington (G-19119)
Qwick Time Logistics LLC .... G 985 413-2217
  Middletown (G-7493)
Reddix Transportation Inc .... F 302 249-9331
  Lewes (G-6414)
Rivera Transportation Inc .... G 302 258-9023
  Laurel (G-5593)
Riverside Farms LLC .... G 302 222-0760
  Felton (G-4018)
Road & Rail Services Inc .... D 302 731-2552
  Newark (G-11895)
Rocket Express LLC .... F 609 854-6705
  Dover (G-3476)
Rss LLC .... G 866 801-0692
  Wilmington (G-19584)
Sabo Logistics LLC .... G 302 440-4544
  Hockessin (G-5377)
Savannah Logistics LLC .... G 302 893-7251
  Middletown (G-7538)
Sb Logistics LLC .... G 302 494-9756
  Wilmington (G-19690)
Schiff Transport LLC .... F 302 398-8014
  Harrington (G-4829)
Second Technologies Inc .... G 310 774-7518
  Dover (G-3526)
Skyylimit LLC .... G 302 256-3212
  Townsend (G-14064)
Slavia Transportation .... G 302 218-4474
  Middletown (G-7571)
Sling It LLC .... G 302 648-5488
  Newark (G-12031)
Srsl and Transportation LLC .... G 302 295-3599
  Wilmington (G-19987)
St Logistics 360 Inc .... G 302 607-8666
  Wilmington (G-19998)
State of De .... G 302 653-0593
  Smyrna (G-13900)
Sussex Superior Tools Inc .... G 302 752-6817
  Millsboro (G-8477)
T & F Logistics LLC .... G 302 602-1285
  Newark (G-12150)
Tap Transportation LLC .... G 302 217-2729
  Seaford (G-13425)
TNT Grand Lux LLC .... G 443 228-3193
  Dover (G-3694)
Trans Logistics LLC .... F 267 244-6550
  Wilmington (G-20393)
Trial Transport Logistics .... G 302 383-5907
  Wilmington (G-20417)
Trinity Freight Logistics Inc .... G 302 543-3128
  Newark (G-12232)
Urys Transportation LLC .... G 302 841-9464
  Bridgeville (G-777)
USA Transport LLC .... G 302 273-0806
  Harrington (G-4843)
Vany Productions Logistics LLC .... G 443 397-2949
  Laurel (G-5618)

Virginia Transportation Corp .... C 302 384-6767
  Wilmington (G-20631)
W P D Transport Inc .... G 302 449-3260
  Middletown (G-7700)
Westover Systems LLC .... G 302 652-3500
  Wilmington (G-20744)
Working Every Shift Trnsprting .... E 267 262-3453
  Bear (G-566)
Xpress Transport Logistics LLC .... G 610 800-2288
  Newark (G-12416)
Zoom Innovations Inc .... G 416 677-7288
  Wilmington (G-20964)

48 COMMUNICATIONS

4812 Radiotelephone communication

786 Cellular and Accessory .... G 302 482-3024
  Wilmington (G-14148)
ABC Virginia Wireless .... G 302 744-8473
  Dover (G-1702)
Appa Inc .... G 302 440-1448
  Dover (G-1804)
AT&T Mobility LLC .... F 302 674-4888
  Dover (G-1843)
Atlantic Cellular .... G 302 945-3334
  Millsboro (G-8177)
Beox LLC .... F
  Wilmington (G-14841)
Boost Mobile .... G 302 482-1193
  Wilmington (G-15006)
Boost Mobile By Infinity Wirel .... G 856 691-7800
  Wilmington (G-15007)
Bvi Group LLC .... G 954 604-9363
  Dover (G-2000)
Cellco Partnership .... F 302 933-0514
  Millsboro (G-8218)
Cellco Partnership .... G 302 530-4620
  Wilmington (G-15301)
Cellco Partnership .... E 814 946-5596
  Wilmington (G-15302)
Cellular Sales Ep Ch .... G 302 455-1092
  Newark (G-10170)
Cellular Sales Knoxville Inc .... G 302 455-1092
  Newark (G-10171)
Cricket .... G 302 482-3658
  Wilmington (G-15703)
Cricket Wireless LLC .... D 302 276-0496
  New Castle (G-8985)
Crossroads Wireless Holdg LLC .... F 405 946-1200
  Wilmington (G-15715)
Du Wireless .... G 302 407-5532
  Wilmington (G-16192)
Fuzzy Fibersnet .... G 302 737-0644
  Newark (G-10794)
Gagl Sales LLC .... G 302 299-0084
  Wilmington (G-16791)
Global Wireless Accesories LLC .... G 302 753-7337
  Wilmington (G-16896)
Grahams Wireless Solutions Inc .... G 717 943-0717
  Millsboro (G-8304)
GSM Planet Incorp .... G 302 455-1111
  Christiana (G-998)
Hola America LLC .... G 302 261-3460
  Lewes (G-6095)
Int Pay LLC .... G 347 698-8159
  Wilmington (G-17365)
Metro By T-Mobile .... G 302 724-7494
  Dover (G-3074)
Metro By T-Mobile .... G 302 744-8473
  Dover (G-3075)
Metro By T-Mobile .... G 302 378-3559
  Middletown (G-7345)

48 COMMUNICATIONS

Company	Code	Phone
Metro By T-Mobile — Smyrna (G-13822)	G	302 508-5123
Metro By T-Mobile — Wilmington (G-18293)	G	302 384-7158
Mobilelink — Wilmington (G-18395)	G	302 502-3062
Murrys Cash & Carry — Dover (G-3133)	G	302 736-6508
National Communications In — Hockessin (G-5316)	G	302 235-0677
Neocomm De — Wilmington (G-18582)	G	302 762-6678
New Cingular Wireless Svcs Inc — Wilmington (G-18610)	F	302 999-0055
Nextel Communications Inc — Wilmington (G-18636)	G	302 633-4330
Nextel Communications Inc — Wilmington (G-18637)	G	302 652-1301
Opalwire — Wilmington (G-18794)	G	302 502-2407
Peach Wireless LLC — Wilmington (G-18940)	G	646 941-4391
Redi Call Corp — Georgetown (G-4482)	F	302 856-9000
Sprint Spectrum LP — New Castle (G-9587)	F	302 322-1712
Sprint Spectrum LP — Wilmington (G-19981)	F	302 993-3700
Sugardumplin — Dover (G-3619)	G	302 423-8810
T and T Wireless — Newark (G-12151)	G	302 894-1189
T-Mobile — Wilmington (G-20200)	G	302 652-7738
T-Mobile Usa Inc — Dover (G-3641)	G	302 736-1980
T-Mobile Usa Inc — Newark (G-12153)	G	302 366-8380
T-Mobile Usa Inc — Wilmington (G-20201)	G	302 479-9691
T-Mobile Usa Inc — Wilmington (G-20202)	G	302 998-0112
Tdp Wireless Inc — Dover (G-3660)	G	302 424-1900
TP Wireless Inc — Hockessin (G-5409)	G	302 235-0402
Verizon Authorized Ret Tcc — Smyrna (G-13929)	G	302 653-8183
Verizon Delaware LLC — Wilmington (G-20590)	C	302 571-1571
Verizon Master Trust — Wilmington (G-20592)	F	302 636-6182
Verizon Wireless — Wilmington (G-20593)	G	610 301-2395
Verizon Wireless Inc — Newark (G-12316)	G	302 737-5028
Victra — Wilmington (G-20615)	G	302 408-0999
Victra — Wilmington (G-20616)	G	302 593-2648
We R Wireless — Millsboro (G-8502)	G	443 880-0308
WER Wireless of Smyrna Inc — Smyrna (G-13936)	F	302 653-8183
Wicket Wireless LLC — Middletown (G-7725)	G	302 376-1788
Wireless Center — Newark (G-12390)	G	302 455-7220
Wireless Nation — Middletown (G-7731)	G	443 841-0116

4813 Telephone communication, except radio

Company	Code	Phone
3d Internet Group Inc — Middletown (G-6816)	G	302 376-7900
8mesh Inc — Lewes (G-5642)	G	888 627-4331
Adectra LLC — Middletown (G-6835)	F	203 424-2800
Adeox Technologies Inc — Newark (G-9765)	G	347 884-7131
Arma Tel LLC — Dover (G-1815)	E	302 480-9394
Azur Gcs Inc — Wilmington (G-14689)	G	302 884-6713
Bbi-Fiber LLC — Middletown (G-6906)	G	224 633-1288
Better Earth LLC — Dover (G-1922)	G	302 242-3644
C & B Internet Services LLC — Wilmington (G-15169)	G	302 384-9804
C4-Nvis USA LLC — Dover (G-2009)	G	213 465-5089
Callsynetwork LLC — Wilmington (G-15198)	G	785 241-7841
Capitol Broadband Dev Co LLC — Wilmington (G-15232)	E	
Carisma Telecom Inc — Wilmington (G-15251)	G	302 357-3650
Centrix Web Services LLC — Wilmington (G-15312)	G	302 319-5122
Clickssl — Newark (G-10259)	G	302 355-0692
Coachhub — Wilmington (G-15506)	G	929 930-1450
Coastal Images Inc — Fenwick Island (G-4045)	G	302 539-6001
Comcast Clfrn/Clrd/Llns/ndn/tx — Wilmington (G-15542)	D	248 233-4724
Conectiv Communications Inc — Newark (G-10299)	E	302 224-1177
Consult Dynamics Inc — Wilmington (G-15613)	E	302 654-1019
Dedicted Fibr Cmmnications LLC — Wilmington (G-15852)	G	302 416-3088
Delta Centric LLC — Wilmington (G-16002)	F	302 268-9359
Elli Creators Inc — Middletown (G-7097)	F	269 742-4057
Ewebvalet Co Inc — Wilmington (G-16497)	G	302 893-0903
Excede Brdband Stllite Intrnet — Felton (G-3968)	G	302 289-0147
Excede Brdband Stllite Intrnet — New Castle (G-9108)	G	302 613-0669
Fiberstate LLC — Historic New Castle (G-4987)	E	800 575-8921
Free Hosting LLC — Wilmington (G-16739)	G	302 421-5750
Global Marine Networks LLC — Lewes (G-6039)	G	215 327-2814
Global Tellink — Dover (G-2592)	G	302 672-7867
Globaltec Networks Inc — Wilmington (G-16897)	G	646 321-8627
Home Media One LLC — Georgetown (G-4361)	G	302 644-0307
Hughes Network Systems LLC — Frederica (G-4172)	G	302 335-4138
Ing Bank Fsb — Wilmington (G-17331)	D	302 255-3750
Instacall LLC — Wilmington (G-17358)	F	302 496-1166
Itglobalcom Corp — Claymont (G-1190)	G	302 498-8359
Jsi Group LLC — Hockessin (G-5263)	A	267 582-1850
Keep In Touch Systems Inc — Wilmington (G-17675)	G	510 868-8088
Keepgo USA Inc — Wilmington (G-17676)	G	832 998-8753
Key-Tel Communications Inc — Wilmington (G-17702)	G	302 475-3066
Latitude Sh LLC — Wilmington (G-17817)	E	712 481-2400
Lnh Inc — Newark (G-11277)	F	302 731-4948
Mancomtec LLC — Wilmington (G-18101)	G	234 243-4256
Maya Virtual Inc — Dover (G-3039)	G	213 587-7995
MCI Communications Corporation — Wilmington (G-18230)	F	302 791-4900
Mgj Enterprises Inc — Wilmington (G-18299)	E	866 525-8529
Minklist Digital Inc — Wilmington (G-18379)	G	917 364-8868
Mobile Direct LLC — Dover (G-3109)	F	908 342-8994
Neterra Communications LLC — Dover (G-3175)	F	302 497-3881
New Concept Technologies LLC — Wilmington (G-18614)	G	518 533-5367
Nextdns Inc — Middletown (G-7403)	E	831 854-7227
Nobelone Inc — Newark (G-11559)	G	617 283-8871
Obhost LLC — Lewes (G-6326)	G	302 440-1447
Oculus Networks Inc — Wilmington (G-18744)	F	732 841-1624
Painless Hosting LLC — Wilmington (G-18864)	F	703 688-2828
Progressive Telecom LLC — Wilmington (G-19222)	E	302 883-8883
Pulsar360 Corp — Newark (G-11771)	E	855 578-5727
Purple Wifi Inc — Wilmington (G-19266)	G	216 292-5760
Qsr Group LLC — Wilmington (G-19278)	G	302 268-6909
Quadix LLC — Middletown (G-7485)	G	877 669-8680
Quick Server Hosting LLC — New Castle (G-9508)	E	800 586-6126
Rehoboth Beach — Rehoboth Beach (G-12917)	G	302 245-0304
Reliance Communications Inc — Wilmington (G-19424)	F	888 673-5426
Rfpmart LLC — Wilmington (G-19450)	F	315 627-3333
Rippl Labs Inc — Wilmington (G-19485)	G	551 427-1997
Sigma Telecom LLC — Wilmington (G-19818)	F	347 741-8397
Simplica Corporation — Wilmington (G-19837)	F	302 594-9899
Skynethostingnet Inc — Wilmington (G-19858)	F	302 384-1784
Sprint Spectrum LP — Milford (G-8101)	F	302 393-2060
Switch Enterprises LLC — Dover (G-3632)	E	212 227-9191
Tata Communications Amer Inc — Wilmington (G-20226)	E	703 547-5900
Telco Envirotrols Inc — Delmar (G-1639)	F	302 846-9103

Toptel Inc .... G 310 999-4320
  Dover *(G-3702)*

Traitel Telecom Corp .... E 619 331-1913
  Wilmington *(G-20389)*

Trunk Tel LLC .... G 302 476-2370
  Wilmington *(G-20448)*

Tychron Corporation .... F 844 892-4766
  Wilmington *(G-20476)*

Ultahost Inc .... G 302 966-3941
  Middletown *(G-7671)*

Under/Comm Inc .... F 302 424-1554
  Milford *(G-8126)*

Verge Internet Inc .... G 202 827-5120
  Dover *(G-3783)*

Verizon Delaware LLC .... D 302 422-1430
  Milford *(G-8134)*

Verizon Delaware LLC .... C 302 738-3000
  Newark *(G-12315)*

Verizon Delaware LLC .... E 302 629-4502
  Seaford *(G-13440)*

Verizon Delaware LLC .... D 302 761-6079
  Wilmington *(G-20591)*

Verizon Delaware LLC .... C 302 571-1571
  Wilmington *(G-20590)*

Verizon Wireless Inc .... G 302 737-5028
  Newark *(G-12316)*

Voip Supplier LLC .... G 302 760-9237
  Dover *(G-3807)*

Vps International LLC .... G 800 493-9356
  Lewes *(G-6610)*

Wala LLC .... G 949 410-0568
  Wilmington *(G-20671)*

Wire 2 Wire LLC .... G 512 684-9100
  Wilmington *(G-20866)*

4822 Telegraph and other communications

Browse Contacts .... G 302 261-9495
  Wilmington *(G-15132)*

Soprano Design Limited .... F 206 446-4401
  Wilmington *(G-19929)*

4832 Radio broadcasting stations

302 Sports .... G 302 650-8479
  Wilmington *(G-14124)*

887 The Bridge .... F 302 422-6909
  Milford *(G-7755)*

Beasley FM Acquisition Corp .... F 302 765-1160
  Wilmington *(G-14806)*

Christian Reachfm Radio Netwrk .... G 302 731-0690
  Newark *(G-10214)*

First Media Radio LLC .... G 410 253-9406
  Rehoboth Beach *(G-12755)*

Gamefort LLC .... E 302 645-7400
  Lewes *(G-6026)*

Gamma Theta Lmbda Edcatn Fndti .... G 302 983-9429
  Bear *(G-245)*

God Said I Love You Ltd .... G 302 697-0647
  Camden *(G-839)*

Heart Ministry Radio .... G 215 847-6664
  Newark *(G-10942)*

Heritage Sports Rdo Netwrk LLC .... G 302 492-1132
  Hartly *(G-4877)*

I Heart Media .... G 302 730-3783
  Dover *(G-2714)*

La Zmx Radio .... G 302 702-2952
  Seaford *(G-13254)*

Larger Story Inc .... G 302 834-5712
  Middletown *(G-7289)*

Mals Sports .... G 302 598-8247
  Newark *(G-11320)*

News In Bullets LLC .... E 831 250-6955
  Middletown *(G-7400)*

Porter Broadcasting .... G 302 535-8809
  Dover *(G-3353)*

Priority Radio Inc .... G 302 540-5690
  Newark *(G-11750)*

Radio Rehoboth .... G 302 754-1444
  Rehoboth Beach *(G-12904)*

Resort Broadcasting Co LP .... F 302 945-2050
  Lewes *(G-6417)*

Royal Broadcasting Inc .... G 302 838-4543
  Bear *(G-472)*

Sussex Amateur Radio Assn .... G 302 629-4949
  Lewes *(G-6529)*

Trade News Inc .... G 212 884-8089
  Wilmington *(G-20385)*

Voice Radio LLC .... F 302 858-5118
  Georgetown *(G-4570)*

Wafl Wyus Broadcasting Inc .... G 302 422-7575
  Milford *(G-8136)*

4833 Television broadcasting stations

Eternal Word Television Inc .... G 302 734-8434
  Dover *(G-2465)*

Forecast Inc .... G 302 413-0675
  Dover *(G-2525)*

4841 Cable and other pay television services

A Dish Network .... G 302 495-5709
  Greenwood *(G-4586)*

A Dish Network .... G 302 565-4175
  Newark *(G-9724)*

A Dish Network .... G 302 223-5754
  Smyrna *(G-13624)*

Ayon Cable Technology LLC .... G 302 465-8999
  Newark *(G-9961)*

Bombonais Cable Tech LLC .... F 302 444-1199
  New Castle *(G-8874)*

Cable Connections LLC .... F 302 397-9014
  Laurel *(G-5477)*

Central Firm LLC .... G 610 470-9836
  Wilmington *(G-15308)*

Comcast Cablevision of Del .... E 302 661-4465
  New Castle *(G-8960)*

Comcast Cablevision of Del .... F 302 856-4591
  Georgetown *(G-4261)*

Comcast Cble Cmmunications LLC .... F 410 497-4600
  Dover *(G-2114)*

Comcast Cble Cmmunications LLC .... G 302 323-9200
  New Castle *(G-8961)*

Comcast Clfrn/Clrd/Llns/ndn/tx .... D 248 233-4724
  Wilmington *(G-15542)*

Comcast Corporation .... G 800 266-2278
  Dover *(G-2115)*

Comcast Corporation .... G 302 495-5612
  Greenwood *(G-4604)*

Comcast Corporation .... G 302 526-0109
  Seaford *(G-13129)*

Comcast Corporation .... G 302 262-8996
  Seaford *(G-13130)*

Comcast MO Investments LLC .... G 302 594-8705
  Wilmington *(G-15543)*

Comcast of Delmarva LLC .... E 215 286-3345
  Dover *(G-2116)*

Digital Technologies .... G 302 731-1928
  Newark *(G-10531)*

Directv .... G 302 203-9162
  Wilmington *(G-16081)*

Executive Brdband Cmmnctons LL .... G 302 463-4335
  Newark *(G-10687)*

Fscom Inc .... D 888 468-7419
  Historic New Castle *(G-4994)*

Mediacom LLC .... F 302 732-9352
  Dagsboro *(G-1481)*

NTL (triangle) LLC .... E 302 525-0027
  Wilmington *(G-18708)*

Rs Marks Inc .... G 302 478-4371
  Wilmington *(G-19579)*

Satellite Connection Inc .... G 302 328-2462
  Wilmington *(G-19676)*

4899 Communication services, nec

52nd & Forever Media LLC .... G 302 463-0014
  Claymont *(G-1014)*

Alive With Media .... G 302 746-7831
  Wilmington *(G-14358)*

Authority Media Group .... G 302 894-7700
  Newark *(G-9945)*

Axxess Marine LLC .... G 954 225-1744
  Lewes *(G-5731)*

Bethel Multimedia Dept .... G 302 563-0918
  Wilmington *(G-14861)*

Bilingual Access Media LLC .... G 302 738-4782
  Newark *(G-10033)*

Cleat Lrng & Communications .... G 845 527-3754
  Middletown *(G-6989)*

Cloudli Communications Inc .... F 877 808-8647
  Newark *(G-10263)*

Communications Cnstr Group LLC .... E 302 280-6926
  Laurel *(G-5485)*

Delaware Digital Media LLC .... G 302 278-8080
  Bethany Beach *(G-596)*

Delaware First Media Corp .... E 302 857-7096
  Dover *(G-2239)*

Delmarva Voice & Internet LLC .... G 302 496-0054
  Newark *(G-10507)*

Diamond Minds LLC .... G 302 359-5069
  Camden Wyoming *(G-932)*

Digitizing America LLC .... G 315 882-9516
  Historic New Castle *(G-4974)*

Doc REO Media LLC .... G 818 824-2885
  Lewes *(G-5925)*

ECR Communications LLC .... G 302 865-3118
  Magnolia *(G-6743)*

Fiberstate LLC .... E 800 575-8921
  Historic New Castle *(G-4987)*

Fireside It LLC .... G 302 284-4961
  Felton *(G-3973)*

Fizz Media Corporation .... G 630 730-7200
  Dover *(G-2513)*

Forester Communications .... G 302 545-6169
  Newark *(G-10762)*

Fronza Media LLC .... G 856 693-0975
  Wilmington *(G-16765)*

Gai Communications Inc .... G 609 254-1470
  Newark *(G-10798)*

Harvest Media LLC .... G 415 712-9702
  Wilmington *(G-17070)*

Hola Media Network LLC .... G 302 228-8942
  Lewes *(G-6096)*

Jerry A Fletcher .... G 302 875-9057
  Delmar *(G-1605)*

La Communication LLC .... G 302 653-1210
  Smyrna *(G-13794)*

Legist Media Ltd .... G 302 655-2730
  Wilmington *(G-17867)*

Leighton Communications .... G 610 513-6930
  Wilmington *(G-17869)*

LLC Forever Media of De .... D 412 221-1629
  Wilmington *(G-17955)*

Main Social Media .... F 302 268-6979
  Wilmington *(G-18090)*

Martech Communications .... G 703 989-6390
  Milton *(G-8661)*

Maya Virtual Inc .... G 213 587-7995
  Dover *(G-3039)*

48 COMMUNICATIONS

Medirents and Sales Inc .... G 302 286-7999
  Newark *(G-11378)*
Mesa Jame Corp .... G 302 528-9106
  Middletown *(G-7343)*
Milton Worldwide Media LLC .... G 302 353-4470
  Newark *(G-11423)*
Partyrite Events & Rentals .... G 302 743-5691
  New Castle *(G-9453)*
Positron Access Solutions Inc .... F 888 577-5254
  Wilmington *(G-19128)*
Quadix LLC .... G 877 669-8680
  Middletown *(G-7485)*
Renegade Entrmt & Media Co .... F 904 789-2897
  Middletown *(G-7513)*
Rising Star Communication .... G 302 462-5474
  Seaford *(G-13374)*
Rushstan Group LLC .... G 302 376-0259
  Middletown *(G-7527)*
S2 Groupe LLC .... G 917 512-1971
  Wilmington *(G-19615)*
Social Media Grabs .... G 281 603-2803
  Middletown *(G-7583)*
Stoudmire Media Group LLC .... G 302 689-3151
  Wilmington *(G-20090)*
Talents List Inc .... G 650 618-1040
  Lewes *(G-6539)*
Texnikos Inc .... G 302 656-8088
  Wilmington *(G-20284)*
Venturist Media Inc .... G 646 455-3031
  Wilmington *(G-20582)*
Voicely Social Inc .... F 302 446-4011
  Dover *(G-3806)*
Westchester Communications Svc .. G 302 827-2939
  Lewes *(G-6624)*
Wevidit Inc .... F 516 513-1659
  Wilmington *(G-20748)*

49 ELECTRIC, GAS AND SANITARY SERVICES

4911 Electric services

4 Elements Es LLC .... G 302 670-5575
  Dover *(G-1686)*
Aci Energy Inc .... D 302 588-3024
  Wilmington *(G-14233)*
AGE Electric Ltd .... G 302 632-2968
  Lincoln *(G-6654)*
Atlantic City Electric Co .... G 302 429-3200
  Wilmington *(G-14627)*
Atlantic City Electric Co .... G 302 588-6675
  Wilmington *(G-14628)*
Bid On Energy LLC .... F 302 360-8110
  Lewes *(G-5763)*
Blue Hen Utility Services Inc .... G 302 273-3167
  New Castle *(G-8870)*
Carroll Brothers Electric LLC .... G 302 947-4754
  Millsboro *(G-8216)*
Check-It Electric LLC .... G 302 650-1921
  Wilmington *(G-15350)*
Chesapeake Utilities Corp .... C 302 734-6799
  Dover *(G-2059)*
City of Dover .... E 302 736-7070
  Dover *(G-2081)*
City of Milford .... E 302 422-1110
  Milford *(G-7829)*
Clay White Electrical Inc .... G 302 994-7748
  Newark *(G-10252)*
Cleanbay Renewables LLC .... G 866 691-1519
  Wilmington *(G-15473)*
CMI Electric Inc .... E 302 731-5556
  Newark *(G-10265)*

Cogentrix Delaware Holdings .... B 847 908-2800
  Wilmington *(G-15517)*
Conectiv LLC .... A 302 429-3018
  Newark *(G-10297)*
Conectiv LLC .... F 800 375-7117
  Wilmington *(G-15590)*
Conectiv LLC .... C 202 872-2680
  Newark *(G-10298)*
Copia Power Opco LLC .... F 612 961-5783
  Dover *(G-2135)*
Country Coop Inc .... G 302 249-1985
  Greenwood *(G-4607)*
Cwp Energy Solution Inc .... G 514 360-0270
  Wilmington *(G-15748)*
Delaware Electric Cooperative Inc .. C 302 349-9090
  Greenwood *(G-4613)*
Delaware Municipal Elc Corp .... G 302 659-0200
  Smyrna *(G-13701)*
Delmarva Power & Light Company .. F 302 454-4040
  Newark *(G-10503)*
Delmarva Power & Light Company .. G 302 454-4450
  Newark *(G-10504)*
Delmarva Power & Light Company .. F 302 668-3809
  Wilmington *(G-15997)*
Delmarva Power & Light Company .. D 302 454-0300
  Newark *(G-10502)*
Elec Integrity .... G 302 388-3430
  Dover *(G-2431)*
Electrical Integrity LLC .... F 302 388-3430
  New Castle *(G-9087)*
Emera US Finance LP .... G 302 636-5400
  Wilmington *(G-16390)*
Energy Center Dover LLC .... F 302 678-4666
  Dover *(G-2449)*
Enersource Electrical Svc LLC .... G 302 842-8714
  Wilmington *(G-16419)*
Evolution Energy Partners LLC .... G 302 425-5008
  Wilmington *(G-16493)*
Flemings Electrical Service .... G 302 258-9386
  Laurel *(G-5513)*
FPL Energy American Wind LLC .... F 302 655-0632
  Wilmington *(G-16716)*
Garrison Calpine .... G 302 562-5661
  Dover *(G-2559)*
Hv Sunrise LLC .... F 612 961-5783
  Wilmington *(G-17239)*
J Fredericks & Son Elec C .... G 302 733-0307
  Newark *(G-11072)*
KB Electrical Services .... G 302 276-5733
  Wilmington *(G-17669)*
Kids Kingdom Elc LLC .... G 302 377-1698
  Wilmington *(G-17715)*
Marianas Energy Company LLC ..... E 671 477-3060
  Dover *(G-3018)*
Mocean Energy Corp .... G 410 449-4286
  Dover *(G-3114)*
Moltex Energy USA LLC .... G 775 346-7520
  Wilmington *(G-18405)*
Municipal Services Commission ..... G 302 323-2330
  Historic New Castle *(G-5031)*
Naes Corporation .... E 856 299-0020
  New Castle *(G-9391)*
NRG Energy Inc .... F 302 934-3537
  Millsboro *(G-8408)*
Nuclear Service Organization .... G 302 888-3000
  Wilmington *(G-18711)*
Omniptntial Enrgy Partners LLC ..... G 888 429-6664
  Wilmington *(G-18770)*
P H I Pepco .... E 302 454-4085
  Newark *(G-11609)*
Peg Gilson Membership Chair .... G 302 734-5190
  Dover *(G-3289)*

Pepco Holdings LLC .... F 202 872-2000
  Wilmington *(G-18965)*
Raymond M Cook .... G 302 236-0087
  Seaford *(G-13366)*
Renewable Energy Holdings LLC ... E 817 213-6041
  Dover *(G-3456)*
Resurrected Electric Llc .... G 302 841-8989
  Laurel *(G-5589)*
Ridgewood Electric Pwr Tr III .... G 302 888-7444
  Wilmington *(G-19480)*
Ross Electrical Services LLC .... G 443 614-7294
  Delmar *(G-1632)*
Scituate Solar I LLC .... G 212 419-4843
  Wilmington *(G-19709)*
Solar Electric Power Assoc .... G 302 893-1354
  Newark *(G-12052)*
St Delware Electrical .... G 302 857-5316
  Dover *(G-3602)*
Statewise Energy Ohio LLC .... F 855 862-1185
  Wilmington *(G-20036)*
Stephen Devary .... G 302 674-4560
  Dover *(G-3612)*
Stork Electric Associates LLC .... G 302 654-9427
  Wilmington *(G-20087)*
Summerfield Elec Solutions LLC ..... G 302 824-3045
  Clayton *(G-1407)*
Sun-In-One Inc .... F 302 762-3100
  Wilmington *(G-20127)*
Taporterelectric .... G 302 366-0108
  Newark *(G-12161)*
USS Wind Technologies LLC .... G 646 770-6265
  Lewes *(G-6595)*

4923 Gas transmission and distribution

Chesapeake Utilities Corp .... C 302 734-6799
  Dover *(G-2059)*
Delmarva Services .... G 302 934-8750
  Millsboro *(G-8267)*
Mexigas Group LLC .... F 302 645-7400
  Lewes *(G-6268)*
Sandpiper Energy Inc .... F 302 736-7656
  Dover *(G-3508)*

4924 Natural gas distribution

Avco Energy LLC .... G 302 597-0034
  Newark *(G-9952)*
Chesapeake Service Company .... G 302 734-6799
  Dover *(G-2058)*
Conectiv LLC .... C 202 872-2680
  Newark *(G-10298)*
Conectiv Energy Supply Inc .... D 302 454-0300
  Newark *(G-10300)*
Eastern Shore Natural Gas Co .... F 302 734-6716
  Dover *(G-2412)*
Eastern Shore Real Estate Inc .... G 302 734-6799
  Dover *(G-2413)*
Inoven Solutions LLC .... E 302 273-0177
  Wilmington *(G-17350)*
Pepco Holdings LLC .... F 202 872-2000
  Wilmington *(G-18965)*
Statewise Energy Ohio LLC .... F 855 862-1185
  Wilmington *(G-20036)*

4925 Gas production and/or distribution

Conectiv Energy Supply Inc .... D 302 454-0300
  Newark *(G-10300)*

4931 Electric and other services combined

AOP Holding Company LLC .... G 346 561-4123
  Dover *(G-1800)*
Balanceco2 Inc .... G 302 494-9476
  Wilmington *(G-14718)*

49 ELECTRIC, GAS AND SANITARY SERVICES

Delmarva Power Financing I.................... G 202 872-2000
  Wilmington (G-15998)
Indian River Power LLC............................ G 302 934-3527
  Dagsboro (G-1466)

4932 Gas and other services combined

Peninsula Energy Svcs Co Inc.................. G 302 734-6799
  Dover (G-3293)

4939 Combination utilities, nec

On The Mark Locators LLC...................... G 888 272-6065
  Newark (G-11589)

4941 Water supply

Artesian Resources Corporation............. G 302 453-6900
  Newark (G-9911)
Artesian Utility Dev Inc............................ F 800 332-5114
  Newark (G-9912)
Artesian Wastewater MD Inc.................. E 302 453-6900
  Newark (G-9913)
Artesian Water Company Inc.................. F 800 332-5114
  Milton (G-8564)
Artesian Water Maryland Inc.................. E 302 453-6900
  Newark (G-9914)
Camdenwyoming Sewer & Wtr Auth...... F 302 697-6372
  Camden (G-801)
City of Wilmington.................................... F 302 576-2584
  Wilmington (G-15454)
Core & Main LP... G 302 684-3054
  Milton (G-8591)
Core & Main LP... G 302 737-1500
  Newark (G-10323)
Long Neck Water Co................................ G 302 947-9600
  Millsboro (G-8351)
Middlesex Water Company..................... G 302 376-1501
  Dover (G-3088)
Middlesex Water Company..................... G 302 436-4625
  Selbyville (G-13574)
Municipal Services Commission.............. G 302 323-2330
  Historic New Castle (G-5031)
Naamans Creek Watershed..................... G 302 475-3037
  Wilmington (G-18517)
Siemens Industry Inc................................ F 302 322-6247
  Historic New Castle (G-5072)
Suez Water Delaware Inc......................... D 302 633-5900
  Wilmington (G-20119)
Sussex Shores Water Co Corp................. G 302 539-7611
  Bethany Beach (G-644)
Tidewater Envmtl Svcs Inc....................... G 302 674-8056
  Dover (G-3685)
Tidewater Utilities Inc.............................. D 302 674-8056
  Dover (G-3686)

4952 Sewerage systems

Camdenwyoming Sewer & Wtr Auth...... F 302 697-6372
  Camden (G-801)
Core & Main LP... G 302 684-3054
  Milton (G-8591)
Core & Main LP... G 302 737-1500
  Newark (G-10323)
Wolfe Neck Treatment Plant................... G 302 644-2761
  Rehoboth Beach (G-13020)

4953 Refuse systems

Abe Junk Removal & Home Svcs............ G 302 540-3722
  Smyrna (G-13628)
Advant-Dge Sltons Mddle ATL In............ G 302 533-6858
  Newark (G-9785)
Advik Republic Inc................................... G 844 987-4238
  Hockessin (G-5115)
Agile Waste LLC.. G 302 772-4882
  Wilmington (G-14316)
All Star Shredding LP............................... F 302 325-9998
  New Castle (G-8782)
Asi Comprehensive Waste MGT............... G 302 533-6858
  Newark (G-9923)
Bestrans Inc... D 302 824-0909
  New Castle (G-8863)
Blue Hen Bzzrds Dspose-All Inc.............. G 302 945-3500
  Millsboro (G-8200)
Cannon Iron and Metal Inc...................... G 302 492-8091
  Hartly (G-4860)
Cherry Island LLC..................................... F 302 658-5241
  New Castle (G-8930)
Ciancon Global LLC.................................. F 302 365-0956
  Wilmington (G-15431)
Clean Delaware Inc.................................. G 302 684-4221
  Milton (G-8584)
Commodities Plus Inc.............................. G 302 376-5219
  Newark (G-10285)
Complete Disposal Service LLC.............. G 302 448-1021
  Georgetown (G-4264)
D & J Recycling Inc.................................. G 302 422-0163
  Milford (G-7845)
Data Guard Recycling Inc....................... G 302 337-8870
  Bridgeville (G-689)
Delaware Material Recovery & R........... F 302 652-3150
  Wilmington (G-15940)
Delaware Recyclable Products............... E 302 655-1360
  New Castle (G-9032)
Delaware Recycling Center..................... G 215 921-7508
  New Castle (G-9033)
Delaware Solid Waste Authority............. G 302 764-2732
  Wilmington (G-15966)
Delaware Solid Waste Authority............. E 302 739-5361
  Dover (G-2260)
Diamond State Recycling Corp.............. E 302 655-1501
  Wilmington (G-16058)
Ecg Industries Inc.................................... G 302 453-0535
  Newark (G-10603)
Evergreen Waste Services LLC............... E 302 635-7055
  New Castle (G-9107)
First State Disposal................................. G 302 644-3885
  Lewes (G-5998)
First State Plastics Inc............................ E 302 325-3700
  New Castle (G-9130)
First State Towing LLC............................ G 302 322-1777
  New Castle (G-9133)
Gold Medal Envmtl De LLC..................... G 302 652-3150
  Wilmington (G-16909)
Goodeals Inc... G 302 999-1737
  Wilmington (G-16924)
Green Opportunities Corp...................... F 302 535-2235
  Camden Wyoming (G-951)
Holland Mulch Inc................................... F 302 765-3100
  Wilmington (G-17166)
Independent Disposal Services.............. G 302 378-5400
  Townsend (G-14016)
Independent Transfer Operators........... G 302 420-4289
  Hockessin (G-5249)
James Powell.. G 302 539-2351
  Frankford (G-4118)
Juliana Recycling Corporation............... G 347 753-6584
  Newark (G-11136)
Kaye Construction................................... G 302 628-6962
  Seaford (G-13246)
Kroegers Salvage Inc.............................. F 302 381-7082
  Bridgeville (G-723)
Magnus Environmental Corp................. G 302 655-4443
  New Castle (G-9336)
Mid Atlantic Compost & RE.................... G 302 644-2977
  Lewes (G-6271)
Mid Atlantic Waste System..................... G 610 497-2405
  New Castle (G-9366)
Mid-Shore Envmtl Svcs Inc..................... G 302 736-5504
  Bridgeville (G-733)
Millville Organic Center.......................... G 302 423-2601
  Ocean View (G-12547)
Modular Carpet Recycling Inc................ F 484 885-5890
  New Castle (G-9379)
Newark Recycling Center Inc................. G 302 737-7300
  Newark (G-11545)
Pacific Green Technologies Inc.............. F 302 601-4659
  Dover (G-3258)
Perdue-Agrirecycle LLC........................... C 302 628-2360
  Seaford (G-13344)
Recyclers of Delaware LLC...................... G 856 466-9067
  Bear (G-448)
Recycling Swift & Demolition................. G 302 328-8283
  New Castle (G-9515)
Republic Services Inc.............................. G 302 658-4097
  Wilmington (G-19434)
RJR Recycling Co..................................... G 610 647-1555
  New Castle (G-9536)
Route 24 Got Junk................................... G 302 258-7990
  Millsboro (G-8450)
Scottons Sanitation LLC.......................... G 302 382-5743
  Clayton (G-1404)
Service Disposal of Delaware................. G 302 326-9155
  Wilmington (G-19760)
Sustainable Envmtl MGT LLC.................. E 302 832-8000
  New Castle (G-9608)
Uniscrap Pbc.. G 302 407-8002
  Wilmington (G-20521)
Waste Industries...................................... G 302 367-5511
  New Castle (G-9675)
Waste Industries Delaware LLC............. G 302 934-1364
  Millsboro (G-8500)
Waste Management Delaware Inc......... G 302 854-5301
  Laurel (G-5621)
Waste Management Delaware Inc......... G 302 994-0944
  Wilmington (G-20681)
Waste Management Michigan Inc......... F 302 655-1360
  New Castle (G-9676)
Waste Masters Solutions LLC................. G 302 824-0909
  New Castle (G-9677)
Wasteflo LLC... G 410 202-0802
  Laurel (G-5622)

4959 Sanitary services, nec

A1 Striping Inc... G 302 738-5016
  Newark (G-9730)
▲ Aurora Corporation.............................. G 302 656-6717
  Wilmington (G-14645)
County Environmental Inc...................... E 302 322-8946
  New Castle (G-8979)
D & J Sweeping LLC................................ G 302 875-3393
  Laurel (G-5490)
Geosyntec Holdings LLC........................ G 561 995-0900
  Wilmington (G-16848)
Green Eyes Landscaping Inc.................. G 302 653-3800
  Dover (G-2623)
Guardian Envmtl Svcs Co Inc................. D 302 918-3070
  Newark (G-10907)
Hazardous Waste..................................... G 302 739-9403
  Dover (G-2664)
Preferred Enviromental.......................... G 610 364-1106
  Clayton (G-1399)
Reilly Sweeping Inc................................. C 302 738-8961
  Newark (G-11847)
Seaway Service Inc.................................. F 302 834-7101
  Delaware City (G-1557)
Shackleford Facilities Inc........................ F 877 735-3938
  Frankford (G-4141)
Terra Systems Inc.................................... E 302 798-9553
  Claymont (G-1310)

49 ELECTRIC, GAS AND SANITARY SERVICES

4971 Irrigation systems

Company		Phone
All About Lawns Irrigation	G	302 242-6861
Camden (G-788)		
AP Irrigation Inc	G	302 233-2357
Harrington (G-4734)		
Atlantic Water Products	E	302 326-1166
New Castle (G-8831)		
Borsello Irrigation Inc	G	302 652-6717
Wilmington (G-15008)		
Circle D Enterprises Inc	G	302 544-2654
Bear (G-104)		
County of Sussex	F	302 947-0864
Millsboro (G-8243)		
Delmarva Irrigation Inc	F	302 490-1588
Laurel (G-5498)		
Eagle Irrigation Inc	G	302 223-1176
Clayton (G-1362)		
Impact Irrgation Solutions Inc	G	484 723-3500
Wilmington (G-17286)		
Impact Irrigation	G	484 723-3500
Wilmington (G-17287)		
Integrity Irrigation Serv	G	302 542-7694
Frankford (G-4116)		
Jobes Landscape Inc	G	302 945-0195
Lewes (G-6143)		
Shore Irrigation Services	F	302 542-1206
Millsboro (G-8459)		
Vincent Farms Inc	C	302 875-5707
Laurel (G-5619)		

50 WHOLESALE TRADE - DURABLE GOODS

5012 Automobiles and other motor vehicles

Company		Phone
▼ Autoport Inc	E	302 658-5100
New Castle (G-8834)		
Cool Customs Inc	G	302 894-0406
Newark (G-10320)		
Dd Inc De LLC	G	302 669-9269
Claymont (G-1111)		
Delaware Public Auto Auction	F	302 656-0500
New Castle (G-9031)		
Delmarva Pump Center Inc	F	302 492-1245
Marydel (G-6796)		
Diamond Motor Sports Inc	D	302 697-3222
Dover (G-2292)		
Diamond State Truck Center LLC	G	302 275-9050
New Castle (G-9052)		
Greg Motors USA Inc	G	302 266-8200
Newark (G-10892)		
Harvey Mack Sales & Svc Inc	E	302 324-8340
New Castle (G-9202)		
Iaa Inc	G	302 322-1808
New Castle (G-9226)		
Lee Mc Neill Associates	G	302 593-6172
Wilmington (G-17854)		
Pafs Auto LLC	G	302 213-3881
Newark (G-11612)		
Porter Nissan Buick Newark	E	302 368-6300
Newark (G-11714)		
Staplefords Sales and Service	G	302 834-4568
Saint Georges (G-13039)		
Utility/Stern Shore Trlr Sls I	G	302 337-7400
Bridgeville (G-779)		
Walls Farm and Garden Ctr Inc	G	302 422-4565
Milford (G-8137)		
Winner Group Inc	F	302 292-8200
Newark (G-12389)		

5013 Motor vehicle supplies and new parts

Company		Phone
Action Automotive Inc	G	302 429-0643
Wilmington (G-14240)		
Adams Auto Parts LLC	F	302 655-9693
Wilmington (G-14250)		
All American Truck Brokers	G	302 654-6101
Wilmington (G-14362)		
Arundel Trailer Sales	G	302 398-6288
Harrington (G-4736)		
Berrodin Co	G	302 395-1100
Claymont (G-1059)		
Berrodin South Inc	E	302 575-0500
New Castle (G-8860)		
Bridgestone Ret Operations LLC	G	302 422-4508
Milford (G-7805)		
C & W Auto Parts Co Inc	G	302 697-2684
Magnolia (G-6724)		
Carl King Tire Co Inc	E	302 697-9506
Camden (G-803)		
Clarksville Auto Service Ctr	E	302 539-1700
Ocean View (G-12489)		
Coveys Car Care Inc	G	302 629-2746
Seaford (G-13138)		
Delaware Tire Center Inc	F	302 674-0234
Dover (G-2270)		
Dover Automotive Inc	G	302 653-9234
Smyrna (G-13714)		
Elite Lubricants LLC	G	302 629-3301
Seaford (G-13173)		
Fisher Auto Parts Inc	G	302 856-2507
Georgetown (G-4324)		
Fisher Auto Parts Inc	G	302 934-8088
Millsboro (G-8291)		
Fisher Auto Parts Inc	G	302 653-9241
Smyrna (G-13736)		
Fisher Auto Parts Inc	G	302 998-3111
Wilmington (G-16648)		
Fishers Auto Parts Inc	G	302 934-8088
Millsboro (G-8292)		
Fitzgerald Auto Salvage Inc	D	302 422-7584
Lincoln (G-6669)		
Future Ford Sales Inc	D	302 999-0261
Wilmington (G-16776)		
Garage	G	302 645-7288
Rehoboth Beach (G-12766)		
Genuine Parts Company	G	610 494-6355
Claymont (G-1160)		
Greg Smith Equipment Sales LLC	G	302 894-9333
Newark (G-10894)		
Harvey Mack Sales & Svc Inc	E	302 324-8340
New Castle (G-9202)		
Ieh Auto Parts LLC	E	302 994-7171
Wilmington (G-17267)		
IG Burton & Company Inc	D	302 629-2800
Seaford (G-13219)		
Imparts Inc	G	302 697-0990
Wyoming (G-20986)		
Irondt Corp	G	347 539-6471
Wilmington (G-17422)		
J N Grillo & Sons Co	G	302 658-7020
Wilmington (G-17460)		
Johns Auto Parts Inc	F	302 322-3273
Bear (G-308)		
Meineke Care Care Center	G	302 368-0700
Newark (G-11383)		
▲ Mto Hose Solutions Inc	G	302 266-6555
Newark (G-11469)		
◆ NGK North America Inc	G	302 654-1344
Wilmington (G-18640)		
Parts World USA LLC	G	302 451-9920
Newark (G-11631)		
Ploeners Automotive Pdts Co	G	302 655-4418
Wilmington (G-19080)		
Safelite Glass Corp	G	877 800-2727
Dover (G-3504)		
Safelite Glass Corp	E	302 656-4640
Wilmington (G-19628)		
Scott Muffler LLC	G	302 378-9247
Middletown (G-7545)		
Single Source Inc	G	302 697-6156
Camden Wyoming (G-977)		
Sp Auto Parts Inc	G	302 337-8897
Bridgeville (G-768)		
Sports Car Tire Inc	E	302 571-8473
Wilmington (G-19970)		
▼ T & J Murray Worldwide Svcs	F	302 736-1790
Dover (G-3637)		
▲ Tabor Auto Parts Inc	E	302 395-1100
New Castle (G-9615)		
Townsend Bros Inc	F	302 674-0100
Dover (G-3707)		
Transaxle LLC	G	302 322-8300
New Castle (G-9633)		
▲ Tri State Btry & Auto Elc Inc	F	302 292-2330
Newark (G-12220)		
Tri-State Btry Alternator LLC	E	320 292-2330
Newark (G-12224)		
Utility/Stern Shore Trlr Sls I	G	302 337-7400
Bridgeville (G-779)		

5014 Tires and tubes

Company		Phone
Admiral Tire	G	302 734-5911
Dover (G-1718)		
Bargain Tire & Service Inc	F	302 764-8900
Wilmington (G-14763)		
BLW Enterprise Inc	G	302 384-7459
Wilmington (G-14985)		
Bridgestone Ret Operations LLC	G	302 422-4508
Milford (G-7805)		
Carl King Tire Co Inc	F	302 644-4070
Lewes (G-5802)		
Carl King Tire Co Inc	E	302 697-9506
Camden (G-803)		
Delaware Tire Center Inc	F	302 674-0234
Dover (G-2270)		
Delaware Tire Center Inc	F	302 368-2531
Newark (G-10492)		
Els Tire Service Inc	F	302 834-1997
Newark (G-10633)		
EZ Manufacturing Company LLC	G	302 653-6567
Clayton (G-1366)		
Goodyear Tire & Rubber Company	G	302 998-0428
Wilmington (G-16929)		
Mavis Tire Express Svcs Corp	F	727 440-5435
Dover (G-3038)		
Tire Rack Inc	E	302 325-8260
Historic New Castle (G-5087)		
Tire Sales & Service Inc	F	302 658-8955
Wilmington (G-20335)		
Traction Wholesale Center Inc	G	302 743-8473
Wilmington (G-20381)		
Wellers Tire Service Inc	F	302 337-8228
Bridgeville (G-781)		

5015 Motor vehicle parts, used

Company		Phone
Arundel Trailer Sales	G	302 398-6288
Harrington (G-4736)		
Auto Parts of Greenwood	G	302 349-9601
Farmington (G-3932)		
Bridgeville Auto Center Inc	G	302 337-3100
Bridgeville (G-675)		
Delaware Auto Salvage Inc	G	302 322-2328
Wilmington (G-15869)		
Deltrans Inc	G	302 453-8213
Newark (G-10510)		

Donovan Salvage Works Inc............... F 302 856-9501
Georgetown (G-4296)

Fitzgerald Auto Salvage Inc.............. D 302 422-7584
Lincoln (G-6669)

Fred Drake Automotive Inc............... G 302 378-4877
Townsend (G-14003)

Goodchild Inc................................. G 302 368-1681
Newark (G-10868)

Hammond Enterprises Inc................ G 302 934-1700
Milford (G-7919)

Lkq Northeast Inc........................... G 800 223-0171
Dover (G-2962)

Mid Atlantic Tire ADI....................... G 302 221-2000
Historic New Castle (G-5027)

Parts Plus More LLC....................... E 302 480-1495
Dover (G-3276)

Pineal Consulting Group LLC........... G 302 446-3794
Dover (G-3324)

Pinnacle Garage Door Co LLC........... G 302 505-4531
Frederica (G-4180)

Ssmmd LLC.................................. G 302 249-1045
Laurel (G-5606)

Tire 24 X 7 Inc............................... G 833 847-3247
Newark (G-12199)

UACJ Trading & Processing Amer..... G 312 636-5941
Wilmington (G-20488)

Vehattire LLC................................. G 302 221-2000
New Castle (G-9667)

5021 Furniture

Automation Solutions Inc................ G 302 478-9060
Wilmington (G-14654)

Corporate Interiors Inc................... F 800 690-9101
New Castle (G-8973)

▲ Corporate Interiors Inc................ D 302 322-1008
New Castle (G-8974)

Demco.. G 302 399-6118
Middletown (G-7052)

Docs Medical LLC.......................... G 301 401-1489
Bear (G-175)

Furniture Whl Connection Inc.......... F 302 836-6000
Bear (G-241)

L F Systems Corp.......................... F 302 322-0460
New Castle (G-9292)

Laytons Umbrellas......................... G 302 249-1958
Laurel (G-5553)

Renewed Environments................. F 302 323-9100
New Castle (G-9520)

Richert Inc................................... F 302 684-0696
Milton (G-8698)

Saphic Innovations Inc................... G 820 888-0099
Wilmington (G-19670)

5023 Homefurnishings

A + Floor Store Inc........................ G 302 698-2166
Camden Wyoming (G-903)

Aaquaone Inc................................ G 949 331-5405
Wilmington (G-14185)

Advacare LLC................................ G 302 448-5045
Wilmington (G-14263)

Art Floor Inc................................. F 302 636-9201
Wilmington (G-14560)

◆ Avs Industries LLC.................... G 302 221-1705
New Castle (G-8836)

▲ Duralex Usa Inc........................ F 302 326-4804
Historic New Castle (G-4978)

F Schumacher & Co LLC................. E 302 454-3200
Newark (G-10699)

Gb Shades LLC............................. G 302 798-3028
Claymont (G-1155)

Indo Foreign Trade Craft LLC........... E 818 927-2872
Newark (G-11014)

L & L Carpet Discount Ctrs Inc......... G 302 292-3712
Newark (G-11205)

▲ Lekue USA Inc.......................... F 302 326-4805
Historic New Castle (G-5017)

Matt Carpet Guy LLC..................... G 443 497-3281
Selbyville (G-13568)

Middletown Kitchen and Bath.......... G 302 376-5766
Middletown (G-7355)

Nickles Arcade LLC........................ F 302 376-1794
Middletown (G-7406)

▲ Ready Set Textiles Inc............... G 302 518-6583
Rehoboth Beach (G-12909)

Reiver Hyman & Co Inc.................. G 302 764-2040
Wilmington (G-19419)

Rite Way Distributors..................... E 302 535-8507
Felton (G-4017)

▲ Rosle U S A Corp...................... E 302 326-4801
Historic New Castle (G-5062)

Selling Dreams LLC....................... G 302 746-7999
Wilmington (G-19747)

Suburban Floor Coverings.............. G 302 430-8494
Rehoboth Beach (G-12979)

Sunflixx LLC................................. G 302 206-0859
Newark (G-12123)

Urban Dweller............................... G 973 402-7400
Milton (G-8724)

Veritable USA Inc.......................... D 302 326-4800
Historic New Castle (G-5097)

Willey Farms Inc........................... D 302 378-8441
Townsend (G-14091)

Zawadius Inc................................ G 888 979-6929
Lewes (G-6647)

Zenith Home Corp......................... E 302 326-8200
Historic New Castle (G-5103)

5031 Lumber, plywood, and millwork

A Window To Wellness................... G 302 567-5468
Rehoboth Beach (G-12594)

Allura Bath & Kitchen Inc............... G 302 731-2851
Newark (G-9828)

American Cedar & Millwork Inc....... E 302 645-9580
Lewes (G-5683)

Atlantic Mllwk Cabinetry Corp......... E 302 644-1405
Lewes (G-5716)

Bair & Goff Sales LLC.................... E 302 292-2546
Newark (G-9975)

Bayside Millwork Inc..................... G 443 324-4376
Selbyville (G-13470)

Cabinetry Unlimited LLC................ E 302 436-5030
Selbyville (G-13489)

Ceramic Tile Supply Co.................. D 302 992-9200
Wilmington (G-15313)

Clearview Windows LLC................. G 302 491-6768
Milford (G-7833)

Dack Trading LLC.......................... G 917 576-4432
Rehoboth Beach (G-12710)

Delaware Building Supply Corp....... E 302 424-3505
Milford (G-7854)

Delaware Flooring Supply Inc......... G 302 276-0031
Historic New Castle (G-4969)

Global Lime & Lumber Co Inc......... G 609 579-1778
New Castle (G-9170)

Greenwood Pallet Co..................... G 302 337-8181
Bridgeville (G-705)

Grubb Lumber Company Inc.......... E 302 652-2800
Wilmington (G-16992)

Hathworth Inc............................... G 302 884-7616
Wilmington (G-17073)

Hickman Overhead Door Company.. F 302 422-4249
Milford (G-7930)

Kris Window Tint LLC.................... G 302 384-6185
Wilmington (G-17756)

La Floresta Perdida Inc.................. F 302 478-8900
Wilmington (G-17781)

Lowes Home Centers LLC............... C 302 697-0700
Camden (G-870)

Lowes Home Centers LLC............... C 302 735-7500
Dover (G-2979)

Lowes Home Centers LLC............... C 302 645-0900
Lewes (G-6226)

Lowes Home Centers LLC............... D 302 376-3006
Middletown (G-7315)

Lowes Home Centers LLC............... D 302 934-3740
Millsboro (G-8354)

Lowes Home Centers LLC............... D 302 252-3228
New Castle (G-9328)

Lowes Home Centers LLC............... C 302 781-1154
Newark (G-11291)

Lowes Home Centers LLC............... D 302 536-4000
Seaford (G-13265)

Lowes Home Centers LLC............... C 302 479-7799
Wilmington (G-18013)

M/S Hollow Metal Wholesale LLC..... G 302 349-9471
Greenwood (G-4650)

Manchester Trading Co.................. F 302 500-4010
Newark (G-11321)

Marjam Supply Co Inc................... F 302 283-1020
Newark (G-11332)

Moso North America Inc................ G 855 343-8444
Milford (G-8021)

Mumford Sheet Metal Works Inc..... F 302 436-8251
Selbyville (G-13583)

North American Hardwoods Ltd...... G 516 848-7729
Wilmington (G-18677)

Oasis Home Inc............................. F 949 331-5405
Wilmington (G-18732)

P D Supply Inc.............................. G 302 655-3358
Wilmington (G-18852)

Rcd Timber Products Inc................ G 302 778-5700
New Castle (G-9512)

Rehrig Penn Logistics Inc............... D 302 659-3337
Smyrna (G-13865)

Russell Plywood Inc...................... F 302 689-0137
Wilmington (G-19595)

Stanton Door Co Inc...................... F 302 731-4167
Newark (G-12086)

Window Man................................. G 302 381-4888
Delmar (G-1659)

Wood Veneer Hub Limited Inc........ G 302 216-6177
Wilmington (G-20882)

5032 Brick, stone, and related material

Asphalt Paving Eqp & Sups............ G 302 683-0105
Harbeson (G-4684)

Bari Concrete Cnstr Corp................ G 302 384-7093
Wilmington (G-14764)

Batholite Natural Stone Inc............. G 206 707-2298
Hockessin (G-5131)

Berkshire At Limestone.................. G 302 635-7495
Wilmington (G-14843)

Blue Sky Stones Inc....................... G 201 359-1368
Wilmington (G-14976)

◆ Casale Marble Imports Inc........... E 561 404-4213
Wilmington (G-15262)

Chesapeake Hearth Stone Co LLC... G 302 943-5276
Seaford (G-13117)

Christiana Materials Inc................. F 302 633-5600
Wilmington (G-15411)

Consolidated Construction Svcs...... F 302 629-6070
Seaford (G-13135)

Delaware Brick Company................ G 302 883-2807
Dover (G-2219)

Delaware Brick Company................ E 302 994-0948
Wilmington (G-15876)

50 WHOLESALE TRADE - DURABLE GOODS

Depro-Serical USA Inc .... G 302 368-8040
Townsend (G-13991)

East Bay Aggregates LLC .... G 302 337-0311
Bridgeville (G-697)

Edgemoor Materials Inc .... F 302 655-1510
Wilmington (G-16290)

◆ Fedmet Resources Corporation .... E 514 931-5711
Wilmington (G-16575)

Freedom Drywall Supply LLC .... E 302 281-0085
Newark (G-10777)

Gerardos Marble & Granite LLC .... G 302 344-6150
New Castle (G-9166)

▲ Jet Products LLC .... G 877 453-8868
Wilmington (G-17536)

▲ Landis Ltd .... G 302 656-9024
Wilmington (G-17797)

Limestone Acres Maintenance .... G 302 222-8457
Wilmington (G-17914)

Marcus Materials Co .... G 302 731-7519
Newark (G-11329)

Michael McCarthy Stones .... G 302 539-8056
Millville (G-8541)

Parker Block Co Inc .... E 302 934-9237
Millsboro (G-8413)

Porter Sand & Gravel Inc .... G 302 335-5132
Harrington (G-4813)

Steering Committee .... G 302 994-7533
Wilmington (G-20046)

Stucco Repairs .... G 302 442-0795
Middletown (G-7603)

5033 Roofing, siding, and insulation

Goldis Holdings Inc .... D 302 764-3100
Wilmington (G-16914)

Iko Sales Inc .... E 302 764-3100
Wilmington (G-17276)

J & L Building Materials Inc .... E 302 504-0350
Historic New Castle (G-5009)

Mill Creek Metals Inc .... F 302 529-7020
Claymont (G-1236)

Quality Rofg Sup Lancaster Inc .... G 302 322-8322
New Castle (G-9506)

S G Williams of Dover Inc .... F 302 678-1080
Dover (G-3499)

5039 Construction materials, nec

Aspen Meadows .... G 302 227-4266
Rehoboth Beach (G-12612)

Building Concepts America Inc .... E 302 292-0200
Newark (G-10101)

Door & Gate Co LLC .... F 888 505-6962
Claymont (G-1120)

Ducts Unlimited Inc .... G 302 378-4125
Smyrna (G-13717)

Edis Building Systems Inc .... G 302 421-5700
Wilmington (G-16293)

Erco Ceilings & Interiors Inc .... F 302 398-3200
Harrington (G-4767)

EZ Sips Corporation .... G 888 747-7488
Wilmington (G-16515)

J & M Fencing Inc .... G 302 284-9674
Felton (G-3986)

Master-Halco Inc .... G 302 475-6714
Wilmington (G-18188)

Pet Stop of Delaware .... G 302 922-7572
Greenwood (G-4661)

T & C Enterprise Incorporated .... G 302 934-8080
Millsboro (G-8479)

Union Whl Acoustical Sup Co .... G 302 656-4462
Wilmington (G-20515)

5043 Photographic equipment and supplies

▲ Autotype Holdings (usa) Inc .... D 302 378-3100
Middletown (G-6889)

Cameras Etc Inc .... F 302 764-9400
Wilmington (G-15206)

Elementice Inc .... G 302 444-5406
Newark (G-10625)

Scigate Holdings LLC .... G 970 481-4949
Newark (G-11962)

5044 Office equipment

Blue Marble Logistics LLC .... G 302 661-4390
Wilmington (G-14969)

Canon Solutions America Inc .... E 302 792-8700
Wilmington (G-15218)

Digital Office Solutions Inc .... F 302 286-6706
Newark (G-10530)

Esupply LLC .... G 415 315-9963
Wilmington (G-16472)

Hilyards Inc .... E 302 995-2201
Wilmington (G-17149)

K Conte .... G 302 283-9613
Wilmington (G-17628)

Michelet Finance Inc .... E 302 427-8751
Wilmington (G-18326)

No Nonsense Office Mchs LLC .... F 302 856-7381
Georgetown (G-4447)

5045 Computers, peripherals, and software

Agile Cockpit LLC .... G 646 220-3377
Dover (G-1740)

AK Multinational LLC .... E 845 542-8155
Wilmington (G-14343)

Aorel Tech Investments LLC .... G 610 674-1516
Wilmington (G-14501)

Aries Security LLC .... G 302 365-0026
Wilmington (G-14551)

Artificial Brain Tech Inc .... G 302 601-7201
Wilmington (G-14566)

Baytown Systems Inc .... G 302 689-3421
Wilmington (G-14791)

Bb Technologies Inc .... G 302 652-2300
Wilmington (G-14792)

Bigben1613 LLC .... E 305 926-3872
Wilmington (G-14885)

Bitcarter Inc .... F 518 512-9238
Wilmington (G-14898)

Bits & Bytes Inc .... G 302 674-2999
Dover (G-1942)

Blujin Corp .... G 973 219-2638
Wilmington (G-14984)

Blumatter Inc .... G 415 318-6857
Newark (G-10064)

Boomset Inc .... F 860 266-6738
Wilmington (G-15004)

Broadberry Data Systems LLC .... E 302 295-1086
Wilmington (G-15121)

Broadberry Data Systems LLC .... G 800 496-9918
Wilmington (G-15122)

Buygoods Inc .... G 302 573-2500
Wilmington (G-15162)

Chaingpt LLC .... G 302 382-7528
Dover (G-2054)

Cutler Industries Inc .... G 302 689-3779
Wilmington (G-15746)

Diversio Inc .... E 855 647-4155
Claymont (G-1119)

DOE Legal LLC .... E 302 798-7500
Wilmington (G-16115)

▲ Eluktronics Inc .... G 302 380-3242
Newark (G-10635)

Esupply LLC .... G 415 315-9963
Wilmington (G-16472)

Etailflow LLC .... E 302 894-8862
Newark (G-10669)

Express Vpn LLC .... G 310 601-8492
Newark (G-10692)

Firebolt Analytics Inc .... F 302 314-3135
Wilmington (G-16612)

Future Analytica Software Inc .... F 437 771-2947
Dover (G-2548)

Geo-Plus Corporation .... F 800 672-1733
Newark (G-10821)

Golden Recursion Inc .... F 415 779-4053
Claymont (G-1167)

Home Innovations .... G 302 448-9555
Lewes (G-6097)

Hoover Computer Services Inc .... G 302 529-7050
Wilmington (G-17195)

Hypertec Usa Inc .... G 480 626-9000
Dover (G-2712)

Info Systems LLC .... C 302 633-9800
Wilmington (G-17328)

Kovan Studio Inc .... F 855 964-3748
Middletown (G-7282)

Kvm Depot Inc .... G 302 472-9190
Wilmington (G-17770)

Licensing Assurance LLC .... E 305 851-3545
Lewes (G-6205)

Lisa Insurtech LLC .... G 612 470-1009
Lewes (G-6211)

Magus LLC .... G 213 332-9117
Dover (G-2997)

Meta Humans Ltd .... F 904 690-1589
Lewes (G-6267)

Modena Software Inc .... G 650 326-1136
Lewes (G-6286)

Neoteric Ascension LLC .... G 302 250-7243
Newark (G-11505)

Net Merge Ltd .... G 631 816-1145
Dover (G-3174)

Opti-Mag Inc .... G 302 738-2903
Newark (G-11596)

Ossum Inc .... G 516 851-4607
Wilmington (G-18829)

Partner Vantage Point LLC .... G 312 927-8990
Newark (G-11630)

PC Supplies Inc .... G 302 368-4800
Newark (G-11648)

Pebbles Inc .... F 408 600-8953
Wilmington (G-18944)

Point To Point Tech USA Inc .... G 302 359-5343
Newark (G-11707)

Popeyco LLC .... G 202 368-3842
Lewes (G-6382)

Quantum Leap Technology Inc .... G 614 254-1698
Wilmington (G-19287)

Quinn Data Corporation .... G 302 429-7450
Wilmington (G-19295)

Red Buffer LLC .... G 628 228-6024
Dover (G-3439)

Stm Consulting Inc .... F 408 341-6900
Claymont (G-1304)

Sumuri LLC .... E 302 570-0015
Magnolia (G-6786)

Taplistic LLC .... F 516 362-1890
Wilmington (G-20220)

Tech Now Mobile LLC .... G 484 480-0648
Wilmington (G-20251)

Threatmate Inc .... F 302 219-4714
Dover (G-3682)

Threesixtytrade LLC .... G 214 810-2922
Camden (G-896)

Timezest Inc .... F 702 582-6850
Wilmington (G-20330)

50 WHOLESALE TRADE - DURABLE GOODS

Tops International Corp............................ G 302 738-8889
  Wilmington *(G-20361)*

Trikorp Inc... G 970 690-6285
  Dover *(G-3727)*

Uploadcare Inc.. E 855 953-2006
  Wilmington *(G-20536)*

Vinyo Inc... G 856 493-2042
  Middletown *(G-7688)*

We Cobble LLC...................................... F 302 504-4294
  Wilmington *(G-20699)*

Weedim Inc... G 202 773-9244
  Middletown *(G-7714)*

Weneuro Inc.. G 760 607-7277
  Wilmington *(G-20731)*

5046 Commercial equipment, nec

Brewster Products Inc............................. G 302 764-4463
  Wilmington *(G-15103)*

Burke Equipment Company..................... E 302 248-7070
  Delmar *(G-1570)*

Cafection Corp.. G 800 561-6162
  Newark *(G-10118)*

Delmarva Automotive Eqp Inc................. G 302 349-9411
  Ellendale *(G-3913)*

Elmer Schultz Services Inc..................... G 302 655-8900
  Wilmington *(G-16376)*

▲ Greg Smith Equipment Inc.................. G 302 894-9333
  Newark *(G-10893)*

Hospitality Essentials LLC....................... G 732 874-0048
  Middletown *(G-7218)*

Hy-Point Equipment Co........................... F 302 478-0388
  Wilmington *(G-17241)*

Jesco Inc... C 302 376-6946
  Middletown *(G-7247)*

JLE Inc.. E 302 656-3590
  Wilmington *(G-17555)*

Kent Sign Company Inc........................... F 302 697-2181
  Dover *(G-2856)*

Peninsula Polymers Inc........................... G 302 422-2002
  Milford *(G-8044)*

Singer Equipment Co Inc........................ G 484 332-3386
  Smyrna *(G-13887)*

South Forks Inc...................................... G 302 731-0344
  Newark *(G-12059)*

Vending Solutions LLC............................ G 302 674-2222
  Dover *(G-3781)*

Vortex Refrigeration Company................ G 855 562-5222
  Wilmington *(G-20652)*

Webstaurant Store Inc............................. F 302 654-1247
  New Castle *(G-9679)*

Widgeon Enterprises Inc......................... G 302 846-9763
  Delmar *(G-1657)*

5047 Medical and hospital equipment

Agile Medical Systems LLC.................... F 310 980-0644
  Dover *(G-1744)*

◆ Anderson Group Inc............................ A 302 478-6160
  Wilmington *(G-14472)*

AR Pro Inc.. F 323 677-0503
  Wilmington *(G-14520)*

Aracent Healthcare LLC......................... G 302 478-8865
  Wilmington *(G-14522)*

Athena Biotechnologies Inc.................... G 302 224-3450
  Newark *(G-9931)*

Baker Safety Equipment Inc................... G 302 376-9302
  Bear *(G-55)*

Benco... G 302 650-0053
  Wilmington *(G-14829)*

Broad Creek Medical Service................. F 302 629-0202
  Seaford *(G-13093)*

Dentsply Sirona Inc................................ G 302 422-4511
  Milford *(G-7867)*

Dienay Distribution Corp........................ G 732 766-0814
  Middletown *(G-7060)*

Elgood Solutions Inc.............................. G 610 420-7207
  Camden *(G-829)*

Enovis Corporation................................ C 301 252-9160
  Wilmington *(G-16428)*

First Choice Home Med Equipt.............. G 302 424-2510
  Milford *(G-7892)*

First Choice Home Med Equipt.............. E 302 323-8700
  Historic New Castle *(G-4988)*

First State Dme LLC.............................. G 302 394-0301
  Dover *(G-2502)*

Global PHI Trading Company LLC......... G 404 759-8409
  Middletown *(G-7165)*

Good Stockx LLC................................... G 949 609-9533
  Newark *(G-10866)*

Granford Inc... D 413 474-6919
  Wilmington *(G-16947)*

Hannas Phrm Sup Co Inc....................... F 302 571-8761
  Wilmington *(G-17050)*

Hyper Gizmo LLC................................... G 888 487-1550
  Lewes *(G-6111)*

Hysiotherapy Associates Inc.................. G 610 444-1270
  Wilmington *(G-17244)*

Jaco LLC.. G 302 645-8068
  Milton *(G-8646)*

June Medical USA Inc............................ G 302 408-0084
  New Castle *(G-9271)*

Junior Bd of Christiana Care.................. G 302 733-1100
  Newark *(G-11137)*

Lamer Group LLC.................................. G 302 893-0500
  Wilmington *(G-17794)*

Linda McCormick................................... G 443 987-2099
  Wilmington *(G-17922)*

Marosa Surgical Industries.................... F 302 674-0907
  New Castle *(G-9349)*

Med Tech Equipment Inc........................ G 800 322-2609
  Wilmington *(G-18244)*

Medical Technologies Intl...................... F 760 837-4778
  Dover *(G-3053)*

Medrep Inc... G 302 571-0263
  Wilmington *(G-18257)*

Medtix LLC... G 302 736-0172
  Dover *(G-3054)*

Medtix LLC... F 302 265-4550
  Lewes *(G-6258)*

Medtix LLC... E 302 645-8070
  Milford *(G-7994)*

Motion Composites Corp........................ F 302 266-8200
  Newark *(G-11459)*

Neobex Corp.. G 833 460-2027
  Newark *(G-11504)*

Nestal Mdsphere Consulting LLC.......... G 302 404-6506
  Wilmington *(G-18588)*

Opera Products LLC.............................. E 413 331-3669
  Wilmington *(G-18802)*

Para Scientific Co.................................. G 215 736-0225
  Wilmington *(G-18882)*

Penglai Bioventures LLC....................... G 302 219-3259
  Dover *(G-3291)*

Peninsula Home Health Care................. F 302 629-5672
  Seaford *(G-13337)*

Personal Health PDT Dev LLC.............. E 888 901-6150
  Wilmington *(G-18987)*

Platinum World LLC............................... G 302 321-5040
  Dover *(G-3331)*

Purushas Picks Inc................................ G 302 918-7663
  Bear *(G-442)*

Quinn-Miller Group Inc........................... G 302 738-9742
  Wilmington *(G-19296)*

Rhondium Corporation........................... F 800 771-4364
  Wilmington *(G-19461)*

Sentryppe Inc... G 480 250-1721
  Dover *(G-3530)*

Siemens Hlthcare Dgnostics Inc............ D 302 631-7357
  Newark *(G-12005)*

Sivad Ppe LLC....................................... E 302 208-2233
  Bear *(G-494)*

▲ Smith & Nephew Holdings Inc........... E 302 884-6720
  Wilmington *(G-19886)*

Synergy Medical USA Inc...................... F 302 444-0163
  Newark *(G-12147)*

Tru American Enterprises LLC.............. G 801 404-1124
  Middletown *(G-7662)*

USA Angelalign Technology................... F 570 573-3515
  Newark *(G-12290)*

Valiram USA Inc..................................... G 562 652-1698
  Wilmington *(G-20563)*

Viro Inc... G 857 207-8174
  Middletown *(G-7689)*

Wexmon LLC.. G 302 746-2472
  Middletown *(G-7720)*

World Wide Trading Brokers................. G 302 368-7041
  Newark *(G-12410)*

Yanimed LLC.. F 929 556-6522
  Claymont *(G-1342)*

5048 Ophthalmic goods

Essilor America Holding Co Inc............. C 214 496-4000
  Wilmington *(G-16467)*

Jim Knnas Optmtrsts Optcans In........... F 302 722-6197
  Newark *(G-11112)*

Jim Knnas Optmtrsts Optcans In........... F 302 722-6197
  Wilmington *(G-17549)*

5049 Professional equipment, nec

1st Engineering Solutions LLC.............. G 302 966-9439
  Wilmington *(G-14115)*

◆ Bio Medic Corporation........................ F 302 628-4300
  Seaford *(G-13089)*

▲ Buchi Corporation............................... E 302 652-3000
  Historic New Castle *(G-4947)*

Elsicon Inc.. G 302 266-7030
  Newark *(G-10634)*

Gilante Scientific LLC............................ G 302 317-6060
  Newark *(G-10835)*

Igal Biochemical LLC............................. G 302 525-2090
  Newark *(G-10997)*

Joint Anlytcl Systms (amrcs)................. G 302 607-0088
  Newark *(G-11122)*

Main Light Industries Inc....................... C 302 998-8017
  Wilmington *(G-18089)*

◆ Miles Scientific Corporation................ E 302 737-6960
  Wilmington *(G-11418)*

Nestal Mdsphere Consulting LLC.......... G 302 404-6506
  Wilmington *(G-18588)*

▼ Pco-Tech Inc....................................... F 248 276-8820
  Wilmington *(G-18936)*

Reprographics Center Inc...................... G 302 328-5019
  New Castle *(G-9522)*

Scientific Holdings Corp........................ G 302 225-5065
  Wilmington *(G-19705)*

Survey Supply Inc.................................. G 302 422-3338
  Milford *(G-8109)*

Toxtrap Inc... G 302 698-1400
  Dover *(G-3708)*

Trimble Inc... G 302 368-2434
  Newark *(G-12230)*

5051 Metals service centers and offices

B & B Industries Inc............................... F 302 655-6156
  Wilmington *(G-14690)*

Boyds Trailor Hitches............................. G 302 697-9000
  Camden Wyoming *(G-917)*

50 WHOLESALE TRADE - DURABLE GOODS

Bushwick Metals LLC .... G 302 328-0590
   New Castle *(G-8902)*
◆ Calmet .... F 714 505-6765
   Wilmington *(G-15201)*
Coastal Aluminum Products .... G 302 242-4868
   Magnolia *(G-6732)*
Delta Sales Corp .... F 302 436-6063
   Selbyville *(G-13520)*
East Coast Stainless Inc .... G 302 366-0675
   Newark *(G-10591)*
East Coast Stainless & Alloys .... F 302 366-0675
   Newark *(G-10592)*
Eastern Metal Supply .... F 302 391-1370
   Newark *(G-10597)*
Handytube Corporation .... D 302 697-9521
   Camden *(G-845)*
Industrial Stl Structures Inc .... E 302 275-8892
   New Castle *(G-9232)*
Joseph T Ryerson & Son Inc .... F 215 736-8970
   Newark *(G-11129)*
Keystone Flashing Company .... G 215 329-8500
   Wilmington *(G-17708)*
Kloeckner Metals .... F 302 652-3326
   New Castle *(G-9287)*
Metal Partners Rebar LLC .... F 215 791-3491
   New Castle *(G-9359)*
▲ Miller Metal Fabrication Inc .... D 302 337-2291
   Bridgeville *(G-734)*
Petroserv Inc .... G 302 398-3260
   Harrington *(G-4811)*
Ryerson Geralyn .... G 302 547-3060
   Wilmington *(G-19602)*
S G Williams & Bros Co .... F 302 656-8167
   Wilmington *(G-19607)*
Steel Suppliers Inc .... C 302 654-5243
   Wilmington *(G-20043)*
Steel Suppliers Erectors Inc .... D 302 654-5243
   Wilmington *(G-20044)*
Superior Metals Alloys USA Inc .... G 860 208-6438
   Newark *(G-12130)*
Taffy Tubes LLC .... G 302 200-9255
   Lewes *(G-6538)*
◆ Vertex Industries Inc .... G 302 472-0501
   Wilmington *(G-20597)*
▼ Vulcraft Sales Corp .... F 302 427-5832
   Wilmington *(G-20659)*

5052 Coal and other minerals and ores

Bowie Refined Coal LLC .... G 302 636-5401
   Wilmington *(G-15017)*
Network Scrap Metal Corp .... G 702 354-0500
   Wilmington *(G-18598)*

5063 Electrical apparatus and equipment

Allpower Generator Sales & Svc .... G 302 793-1690
   Claymont *(G-1030)*
American Neon Products Company .... F 302 856-3400
   Milford *(G-7767)*
◆ Anderson Group Inc .... A 302 478-6160
   Wilmington *(G-14472)*
Anixter Inc .... G 302 325-2590
   New Castle *(G-8810)*
Anixter Power Solutions Inc .... F 302 298-3601
   Historic New Castle *(G-4932)*
Bainbridge Company .... G 302 509-3185
   Newark *(G-9974)*
Billows Electric Supply Co Inc .... G 302 996-9133
   Wilmington *(G-14892)*
C & S Battery Inc .... G 610 459-2227
   Wilmington *(G-15172)*
City Electric Supply Company .... G 302 777-5300
   Wilmington *(G-15452)*

Colonial Electric Supply Co .... F 302 998-9993
   Historic New Castle *(G-4960)*
Conectiv Energy Supply Inc .... D 302 454-0300
   Newark *(G-10300)*
Denney Electric Supply Del Inc .... G 302 934-8885
   Millsboro *(G-8270)*
Diversified Lighting Assoc Inc .... G 302 286-6370
   Wilmington *(G-16096)*
Dover Electric Supply Co Inc .... E 302 674-0115
   Dover *(G-2341)*
Electric Motor Wholesale Inc .... F 302 653-1844
   Camden Wyoming *(G-939)*
Electric Motor Wholesale Inc .... F 302 653-1844
   Camden Wyoming *(G-940)*
Ep Supply Corp .... G 909 969-5122
   Lewes *(G-5966)*
Fire Alarm Supplier LLC .... G 302 444-0801
   Milton *(G-8623)*
Globe Electric Company USA Inc .... G 514 694-0444
   Dover *(G-2596)*
Graybar Electric Company Inc .... D 302 322-2200
   New Castle *(G-9177)*
John R Seiberlich Inc .... D 302 356-2400
   New Castle *(G-9262)*
Kpss Government Solutions Inc .... F 302 992-7950
   Wilmington *(G-17749)*
Led Company Intl Llc .... F 302 668-8370
   Wilmington *(G-17850)*
Ledtolight .... G 941 323-6664
   Wilmington *(G-17852)*
LLC Sales Inc .... G 416 996-1856
   Wilmington *(G-17857)*
◆ NGK North America Inc .... G 302 654-1344
   Wilmington *(G-18640)*
Ploeners Automotive Pdts Co .... G 302 655-4418
   Wilmington *(G-19080)*
Powerback Service LLC .... G 302 934-1901
   Millsboro *(G-8435)*
Rumsey Electric Co .... G 302 368-9161
   Newark *(G-11927)*
Sentrylight Inc .... G 302 420-8844
   Newark *(G-11978)*
Sevenshopper Inc .... E 302 407-6905
   Wilmington *(G-19769)*
Siemens Corporation .... E 302 690-2046
   Newark *(G-12004)*
Siemens Industry Inc .... G 302 631-8410
   Newark *(G-12006)*
Simplex Time Recorder LLC .... G 302 325-6300
   New Castle *(G-9571)*
Switchgearus LLC .... E 302 232-3209
   Milford *(G-8112)*
▲ Tri State Btry & Auto Elc Inc .... F 302 292-2330
   Newark *(G-12220)*
Tsb Inc .... G 302 292-2330
   Newark *(G-12242)*
United Electric Supply Co Inc .... G 302 732-1291
   Dagsboro *(G-1522)*
United Electric Supply Co Inc .... G 302 674-8351
   Dover *(G-3751)*
United Electric Supply Co Inc .... C 800 322-3374
   New Castle *(G-9653)*
W W Grainger Inc .... G 302 322-1840
   Historic New Castle *(G-5098)*
Warren Electric Co Inc .... G 302 629-9134
   Seaford *(G-13444)*
▲ Way To Go Led Lighting Company .... F 844 312-4574
   Newark *(G-12349)*

5064 Electrical appliances, television and radio

ABC Sales & Service Inc .... F 302 652-3683
   Wilmington *(G-14196)*
Appliances Zone .... G 302 280-6073
   Delmar *(G-1566)*
Artisan Electrical Inc .... G 302 645-5844
   Lewes *(G-5702)*
Awaken Atusky LLC .... E 302 231-0818
   Lewes *(G-5727)*
Brandywine Electronics Corp .... F 302 324-9992
   Bear *(G-80)*
Cooltrade Inc .... E 844 356-2952
   Wilmington *(G-15632)*
Ensinger Penn Fibre Inc .... F 302 349-4505
   Greenwood *(G-4627)*
Gt World Machineries Usa Inc .... G 800 242-4935
   Christiana *(G-999)*
Lowes Home Centers LLC .... C 302 697-0700
   Camden *(G-870)*
Lowes Home Centers LLC .... C 302 735-7500
   Dover *(G-2979)*
Lowes Home Centers LLC .... C 302 645-0900
   Lewes *(G-6226)*
Lowes Home Centers LLC .... D 302 376-3006
   Middletown *(G-7315)*
Lowes Home Centers LLC .... D 302 934-3740
   Millsboro *(G-8354)*
Lowes Home Centers LLC .... D 302 252-3228
   New Castle *(G-9328)*
Lowes Home Centers LLC .... C 302 781-1154
   Newark *(G-11291)*
Lowes Home Centers LLC .... D 302 536-4000
   Seaford *(G-13265)*
Lowes Home Centers LLC .... C 302 479-7799
   Wilmington *(G-18013)*
Ryno Iron .... G 302 464-2973
   Townsend *(G-14063)*
Tanner Operations Inc .... F 302 464-2194
   Townsend *(G-14077)*
Williams Appliancee .... F 302 656-8581
   Wilmington *(G-20797)*

5065 Electronic parts and equipment, nec

A Plus Electric & Security .... G 302 455-1725
   Newark *(G-9726)*
A V C Inc .... G 302 227-2549
   Rehoboth Beach *(G-12593)*
▲ Alvatek Electronics LLC .... F 302 655-5870
   Wilmington *(G-14402)*
Atechnologie LLC .... G 781 325-5230
   Wilmington *(G-14617)*
Avirm Inc .... D 626 603-1000
   Wilmington *(G-14670)*
B F P Trading LLC .... F 347 927-0535
   Wilmington *(G-14699)*
Barrier Integrated Systems LLC .... G 302 502-2727
   Newark *(G-9985)*
Delmarva Communications Inc .... F 302 324-1230
   New Castle *(G-9042)*
Electronics Exchange Inc .... G 302 322-5401
   Historic New Castle *(G-4981)*
Exclusive Group LLC .... F 917 207-7299
   Wilmington *(G-16501)*
Granford Inc .... D 413 474-6919
   Wilmington *(G-16947)*
Iodparts Technologies Inc .... G 732 369-9939
   Bear *(G-288)*
Jag Industrials LLC .... G 267 334-7999
   Dover *(G-2765)*
John R Seiberlich Inc .... D 302 356-2400
   New Castle *(G-9262)*
▲ Lumenty Technologies Inc .... F 971 331-3113
   Wilmington *(G-18026)*

SIC SECTION 50 WHOLESALE TRADE - DURABLE GOODS

Metz Jade Associates................................ G 302 239-2414
  Newark *(G-11395)*

Nano Magnetics.. G 888 629-6266
  Wilmington *(G-18527)*

Nano Magnetics Usa Inc......................... G 888 629-6266
  Wilmington *(G-18528)*

Netatmo LLC... G 302 703-7680
  Wilmington *(G-18591)*

Quality Distributors Inc........................... G 917 335-6662
  Wilmington *(G-19283)*

Rosenberger Usa Corp........................... G 717 859-8900
  Wilmington *(G-19569)*

S & B Pro Security LLC........................... G 800 841-9907
  Dover *(G-3496)*

Securitech Inc.. F 302 996-9230
  Wilmington *(G-19732)*

▼ Servo2gocom Ltd.................................. G 877 378-0240
  Wilmington *(G-19763)*

Sgm Socher Inc... G 718 484-4253
  Historic New Castle *(G-5069)*

Tti Inc... G 302 725-5189
  Lincoln *(G-6707)*

Vectorvance LLC....................................... G 347 779-9932
  Wilmington *(G-20573)*

Velocity Eu Inc... F 331 226-1818
  Middletown *(G-7684)*

Vlocker North America LLC................... G 469 567-0956
  Wilmington *(G-20647)*

5072 Hardware

Acuity Spcialty Pdts Group Inc............... G 302 369-6949
  Wilmington *(G-14247)*

Allied Lock & Safe Company................. G 302 658-3172
  Wilmington *(G-14381)*

Bair & Goff Sales LLC.............................. E 302 292-2546
  Newark *(G-9975)*

Brass Sales Company Inc...................... F 302 284-4574
  Felton *(G-3947)*

Building Fasteners Inc............................ G 302 738-0671
  Newark *(G-10102)*

C M D Inc... G 302 894-1776
  Newark *(G-10113)*

Clark & Sons Overhead Doors............... G 302 998-7552
  Wilmington *(G-15465)*

Committee To Elect Brad Eaby............... G 302 670-4806
  Dover *(G-2117)*

Foss-Brown Inc... G 610 940-6040
  Wilmington *(G-16699)*

Integrity Corporation Inc......................... F 410 392-8665
  Newark *(G-11033)*

Lilly Fasteners & Customization Llc....... E 302 366-7640
  Newark *(G-11260)*

Mumford Sheet Metal Works Inc........... F 302 436-8251
  Selbyville *(G-13583)*

Petroserv Inc... G 302 398-3260
  Harrington *(G-4811)*

Robert S Brady... G 302 571-6690
  Wilmington *(G-19520)*

Rome Solutions LLC................................ G 302 261-3794
  Wilmington *(G-19559)*

Southco.. G 302 475-2140
  Wilmington *(G-19938)*

Standard Industrial Supply Co............... G 302 656-1631
  Wilmington *(G-20013)*

T & C Enterprise Incorporated............... G 302 934-8080
  Millsboro *(G-8479)*

Tantalum Bolt & Fastener LLC............... F 888 393-4517
  Newark *(G-12159)*

Unigo Inc... G 205 974-1962
  Wilmington *(G-20511)*

Value Chain Excellence LLC................... G 302 545-8011
  Wilmington *(G-20565)*

5074 Plumbing and hydronic heating supplies

Bemark Associates................................... G 302 373-6417
  Newark *(G-10018)*

Brass Sales Company Inc...................... F 302 284-4574
  Felton *(G-3947)*

Bristol Industrial Corporation................. F 302 322-1100
  New Castle *(G-8893)*

Condor Technologies Inc........................ G 302 698-4444
  Camden *(G-807)*

Core & Main LP.. G 302 684-3054
  Milton *(G-8591)*

Delmarva Refrigeration Inc..................... G 302 846-2727
  Delmar *(G-1588)*

Dover Plumbing Supply Co..................... F 302 674-0333
  Dover *(G-2360)*

Ferguson Enterprises LLC..................... G 302 747-2032
  Dover *(G-2492)*

Ferguson Enterprises LLC..................... G 302 500-8051
  Georgetown *(G-4317)*

Ferguson Enterprises LLC..................... G 302 732-0940
  Lewes *(G-5994)*

Ferguson Enterprises LLC..................... F 302 934-6040
  Millsboro *(G-8288)*

Ferguson Enterprises LLC..................... F 302 656-4421
  Wilmington *(G-16581)*

Ferguson Enterprises LLC..................... G 302 429-5850
  Wilmington *(G-16582)*

Ferguson Enterprises LLC..................... G 302 225-4082
  Wilmington *(G-16583)*

◆ Graver Technologies LLC.................... C 302 731-1700
  Newark *(G-10883)*

Greenberg Supply Co Inc....................... E 302 656-4496
  Wilmington *(G-16970)*

Hajoca Corporation................................... F 302 764-6000
  Wilmington *(G-17036)*

Hd Supply Waterworks Ltd..................... F 302 684-3054
  Milton *(G-8634)*

John Eisenbrey III.................................... G 302 422-5845
  Milford *(G-7955)*

Mumford Sheet Metal Works Inc........... F 302 436-8251
  Selbyville *(G-13583)*

North East Htg AC................................... G 410 299-1773
  Dover *(G-3196)*

Northeastern Supply Inc......................... G 302 698-1414
  Camden *(G-880)*

Northeastern Supply Inc......................... G 302 378-7880
  Middletown *(G-7411)*

Penco Corporation................................... G 302 698-3108
  Camden *(G-884)*

Penco Corporation................................... G 302 738-3212
  Newark *(G-11662)*

Penco Corporation................................... G 302 227-9188
  Rehoboth Beach *(G-12886)*

Penco Corporation................................... D 302 629-7911
  Seaford *(G-13334)*

Philadlphia Slar For Rnwble En............. G 412 297-4866
  Wilmington *(G-19015)*

Schagrin Gas Co....................................... E 302 378-2000
  Middletown *(G-7541)*

Sid Harvey Industries Inc....................... G 302 746-7760
  Claymont *(G-1290)*

Sun-In-One Inc... F 302 762-3100
  Wilmington *(G-20127)*

Sweeten Companies Inc......................... G 302 737-6161
  Newark *(G-12140)*

◆ Vertex Industries Inc............................. G 302 472-0601
  Wilmington *(G-20597)*

5075 Warm air heating and air conditioning

Berry Refrigeration Co............................ E 302 733-0933
  Newark *(G-10025)*

▲ Building Systems and Svcs Inc........ E 302 996-0900
  Wilmington *(G-15146)*

Greenberg Supply Co Inc....................... E 302 656-4496
  Wilmington *(G-16970)*

John R Seiberlich Inc.............................. D 302 356-2400
  New Castle *(G-9262)*

Kompressed Air Delaware Inc............... G 302 275-1985
  New Castle *(G-9289)*

R E Michel Company LLC...................... G 302 678-0250
  Dover *(G-3414)*

R E Michel Company LLC...................... G 302 645-0585
  Lewes *(G-6403)*

R E Michel Company LLC...................... G 302 368-9410
  Newark *(G-11807)*

United Refrigeration Inc......................... G 302 322-1836
  New Castle *(G-9655)*

W W Grainger Inc.................................... G 302 322-1840
  Historic New Castle *(G-5098)*

WJC of Delaware LLC............................. F 302 323-9600
  New Castle *(G-9687)*

5078 Refrigeration equipment and supplies

Berry Refrigeration Co............................ E 302 733-0933
  Newark *(G-10025)*

Delmarva Refrigeration Inc..................... G 302 846-2727
  Delmar *(G-1588)*

Greenberg Supply Co Inc....................... E 302 656-4496
  Wilmington *(G-16970)*

John R Seiberlich Inc.............................. D 302 356-2400
  New Castle *(G-9262)*

R E Michel Company LLC...................... G 302 678-0250
  Dover *(G-3414)*

R E Michel Company LLC...................... G 302 645-0585
  Lewes *(G-6403)*

Thermo King Corporation....................... G 302 907-0345
  Delmar *(G-1641)*

Thermo King LLC..................................... G 302 907-0345
  Delmar *(G-1642)*

Unada LLC... E 470 809-9077
  Wilmington *(G-20503)*

United Refrigeration Inc......................... G 302 322-1836
  New Castle *(G-9655)*

W W Grainger Inc.................................... G 302 322-1840
  Historic New Castle *(G-5098)*

5082 Construction and mining machinery

Alban Tractor LLC.................................... G 302 284-4100
  Felton *(G-3939)*

Alpine Contractors LLC.......................... F 302 343-9954
  Dover *(G-1775)*

Atlantic Tractor LLC................................ F 302 834-0114
  Newark *(G-9937)*

Bristol Industrial Corporation................. F 302 322-1100
  New Castle *(G-8893)*

Chesapeake Supply & Eqp Co.............. G 302 284-1000
  Felton *(G-3955)*

Delaware Brick Company....................... G 302 883-2807
  Dover *(G-2219)*

Ditch Witch of Virginia............................ G 302 629-3602
  Seaford *(G-13162)*

E-Industrial Suppliers LLC..................... G 302 251-6210
  Wilmington *(G-16243)*

Eagle Power and Equipment Corp........ F 302 652-3028
  New Castle *(G-9076)*

Evans Charles Contracting.................... G 701 340-9530
  Bear *(G-209)*

F and M Equipment Ltd.......................... F 302 449-2850
  Townsend *(G-14001)*

Foulk Lawn & Equipment Co Inc.......... G 302 475-3233
  Wilmington *(G-16701)*

50 WHOLESALE TRADE - DURABLE GOODS

◆ Graham Global Corporation .... F 302 839-3000
   Wilmington (G-16945)
Industrial Products of Del .... G 302 328-6648
   New Castle (G-9231)
▼ Iron Source LLC .... G 302 856-7545
   Georgetown (G-4373)
Jesco Inc .... C 302 376-6946
   Middletown (G-7247)
Kwik & Crafty Contracting .... G 302 227-2550
   Rehoboth Beach (G-12826)
Oakville Industries LLC .... F 513 436-5007
   Wilmington (G-18729)
S G Williams & Bros Co .... F 302 656-8167
   Wilmington (G-19607)
▲ Sun Piledriving Equipment LLC .. G 302 539-6756
   Frankford (G-4150)
Th White General Contract .... G 302 945-1829
   Millsboro (G-8482)
Thomas Building Group Inc .... F 302 283-0600
   Newark (G-12193)
Wm Systems Inc .... G 302 450-4482
   Wilmington (G-20871)
Yellow and Green Machinery LLC . G 302 526-4990
   Dover (G-3885)

5083 Farm and garden machinery

AG Industrial Inc .... G 888 289-1779
   Dover (G-1737)
All Rock & Mulch LLC .... G 302 838-7625
   Bear (G-26)
Atlantic Tractor LLC .... E 302 653-8536
   Clayton (G-1351)
Baxter Farms Inc .... G 302 856-1818
   Georgetown (G-4223)
Bluewater Wind LLC .... E 302 731-7020
   Lewes (G-5773)
Bunting & Bertrand Inc .... F 302 732-6836
   Frankford (G-4080)
Burke Equipment Company .... E 302 248-7070
   Delmar (G-1570)
Burke Equipment Company .... F 302 697-3200
   Felton (G-3949)
Delaware Hardscape Supply LLC . G 302 996-6464
   Wilmington (G-15923)
Hoober Inc .... E 717 768-8231
   Middletown (G-7214)
Hoober Inc .... F 302 629-3075
   Seaford (G-13216)
Messick & Gray Cnstr Inc .... E 302 337-8777
   Bridgeville (G-731)
Newark Kubota Inc .... F 302 365-6000
   Newark (G-11540)
Northeast Agri Systems Inc .... G 302 875-1886
   Laurel (G-5570)
▲ O A Newton & Son Company ..... E 302 337-3782
   Bridgeville (G-740)
Peninsula Poultry Eqp Co Inc .... E 302 875-0889
   Laurel (G-5573)
Peninsula Poultry Eqp Co Inc .... F 302 875-0886
   Laurel (G-5574)
Taylor and Messick Inc .... E 302 398-3729
   Harrington (G-4839)
▲ Thomas E Moore Inc .... F 302 674-1500
   Dover (G-3678)
Walls Irrigation Inc .... G 302 422-2262
   Milford (G-8138)
Whaleys Seed Store Inc .... G 302 875-7833
   Laurel (G-5623)
Willard Agri Service Greenw .... G 302 349-4100
   Farmington (G-3936)
Woodward Enterprises Inc .... F 302 378-2849
   Middletown (G-7736)

Yellow and Green Machinery LLC . G 302 526-4990
   Dover (G-3885)

5084 Industrial machinery and equipment

Accudyne Systems Inc .... E 302 369-5390
   Newark (G-9750)
Adash Inc .... G 302 654-3977
   Wilmington (G-14252)
▲ Advance Marine LLC .... G 302 656-2111
   Wilmington (G-14268)
▲ Advanced Machinery Sales Inc .. G 302 322-2226
   New Castle (G-8766)
Airgas Inc .... G 302 575-1822
   Wilmington (G-14338)
Airgas Usa LLC .... E 302 286-5400
   Newark (G-9801)
Airsled Inc .... G 302 292-8911
   Newark (G-9802)
Aquaflow Pump & Supply Company .... F 302 834-1311
   Bear (G-41)
▲ Arnold International Inc .... G 302 266-4441
   Newark (G-9907)
◆ Asw Machinery Inc .... F 866 792-5288
   Historic New Castle (G-4936)
Atlantic Elevators .... G 302 537-8304
   Dagsboro (G-1414)
Automation Air Inc .... G 973 875-6676
   Bridgeville (G-670)
Automation Partnership .... G 302 478-9060
   Wilmington (G-14653)
▲ Autotype Holdings (usa) Inc .... D 302 378-3100
   Middletown (G-6889)
Benz Hydraulics Inc .... F 302 328-6648
   New Castle (G-8858)
Billy Warren & Son LLC .... G 302 349-5767
   Greenwood (G-4598)
Brandywine Elevator Co Inc .... G 866 636-0102
   Wilmington (G-15055)
Brooks Machine Inc .... G 302 674-5900
   Dover (G-1984)
▲ Bruce Industrial Co Inc .... D 302 655-9616
   New Castle (G-8894)
◆ Careys Diesel Inc .... F 302 678-3797
   Leipsic (G-5629)
Catalyst Handling Resources .... F 302 798-2200
   Claymont (G-1076)
Cheshire Enterprise LLC .... G 302 365-6225
   Bear (G-98)
Cintas Corporation No 2 .... G 302 765-6460
   Wilmington (G-15441)
Cognitive Tech Solutions Inc .... G 302 207-1824
   Wilmington (G-15519)
CP Cases Inc .... G 410 352-9450
   Frankford (G-4095)
Delaware Capital Formation Inc ... G 302 793-4921
   Wilmington (G-15878)
◆ Delaware Capital Holdings Inc ... G 302 793-4921
   Wilmington (G-15879)
Delaware Elevator Inc .... G 800 787-0436
   Newark (G-10439)
Delaware Filter Corp .... G 302 326-3950
   New Castle (G-9023)
E E Rosser Inc .... G 302 762-9643
   Wilmington (G-16237)
Eastern Lift Truck Co Inc .... E 302 875-4031
   Laurel (G-5505)
Eastern Lift Truck Co Inc .... C 302 286-6660
   Newark (G-10596)
▲ Eastern Shore Metals LLC .... F 302 629-6629
   Seaford (G-13169)
▲ Easy Lift Equipment Co Inc .... E 302 737-7000
   Newark (G-10599)

Elevator Organization Inc .... G 847 431-2927
   Wilmington (G-16361)
Fiduks Industrial Services Inc ...... F 302 994-2534
   Wilmington (G-16602)
Fiduks Industrial Services Inc ...... F 302 994-2534
   Wilmington (G-16601)
Finger Lakes Metrology LLC .... G 607 742-7240
   Ellendale (G-3918)
First State Automation LLC .... G 302 743-4798
   New Castle (G-9127)
First State Distributors Inc .... G 302 655-8266
   Wilmington (G-16627)
Firstchoice Group America LLC ... G 425 242-8626
   Lewes (G-6000)
Four States LLC .... F 302 655-3400
   New Castle (G-9143)
G & E Welding Supply Co .... F 302 322-9353
   New Castle (G-9155)
◆ Graham Global Corporation .... F 302 839-3000
   Wilmington (G-16945)
Groff Tractor & Equipment LLC .... F 302 349-5760
   Greenwood (G-4633)
Hydroseeding Co LLC .... G 302 858-8171
   Bridgeville (G-715)
Jbcompany LLC .... G 406 623-8593
   Claymont (G-1196)
▼ JLJ Enterprises Inc .... F 302 398-0229
   Georgetown (G-4384)
John J Buckley Associates Inc .... G 302 475-5443
   Wilmington (G-17565)
▲ Jorc Industrial LLC .... G 302 395-0310
   New Castle (G-9264)
Kaeser Compressors Inc .... G 410 242-8793
   New Castle (G-9274)
Kahl Company Inc .... G 302 478-8450
   Wilmington (G-17634)
Karcher Municipal North Amer ..... E 401 230-3296
   Wilmington (G-17651)
Keen Compressed Gas Co .... F 302 594-4545
   Wilmington (G-17674)
Liberty Elevator Experts LLC .... E 302 650-4688
   Newark (G-11252)
Liberty Elevator Experts LLC .... G 844 542-3538
   Newark (G-11253)
Linde Gas & Equipment Inc .... G 302 654-8755
   Wilmington (G-17923)
Linde North America .... F 302 654-9348
   New Castle (G-9312)
Lweco Group LLC .... G 302 296-8035
   Millsboro (G-8355)
M Hs Lift of Delaware Inc .... F 302 629-4490
   Seaford (G-13270)
Material Handling Supply Inc .... F 302 571-0176
   Historic New Castle (G-5024)
McCabes Mechanical Service Inc .... F 302 854-9001
   Georgetown (G-4421)
Mecatech Indus Equipments LLC . G 617 586-4224
   Dover (G-3048)
Mechanics Paradise Inc .... F 302 652-8863
   New Castle (G-9355)
Messick & Gray Cnstr Inc .... E 302 337-8777
   Bridgeville (G-731)
Mfr Manufacturing Corp Inc .... G 815 552-3333
   Wilmington (G-18298)
▲ Mitusha International Corp .... G 302 674-2977
   Dover (G-3105)
National Metering Service Inc ...... G 302 516-7418
   Wilmington (G-18545)
Nerdit Now LLC .... F 302 482-5979
   Wilmington (G-18587)
Northeast Controls Inc .... F 201 419-6111
   Rehoboth Beach (G-12871)

50 WHOLESALE TRADE - DURABLE GOODS

▲ O A Newton & Son Company .... E 302 337-3782
   Bridgeville *(G-740)*

Pascale Industries Inc .... F 302 421-9400
   New Castle *(G-9454)*

▼ Pco-Tech Inc .... F 248 276-8820
   Wilmington *(G-18936)*

Power Trans Inc .... F 302 337-3016
   Bridgeville *(G-753)*

Processflo Inc .... G 302 633-4200
   Wilmington *(G-19208)*

Progressive Systems Inc .... G 302 732-3321
   Frankford *(G-4135)*

Senso Dynamics LLC .... G 302 257-5926
   Lewes *(G-6459)*

Square One Electric Service Co .... F 302 678-0400
   Dover *(G-3601)*

Standard Direct LLC .... G 855 550-0606
   Wilmington *(G-20012)*

Steven Brown & Associates Inc .... G 302 652-4722
   Wilmington *(G-20064)*

▲ Supercritical Fluid Tech Inc .... G 302 738-3420
   Newark *(G-12129)*

Sussex Protection Service LLC .... F 302 832-5700
   Newark *(G-12136)*

Technicare Inc .... G 302 322-7766
   Newark *(G-12170)*

▲ Testing Machines Inc .... E 302 613-5600
   New Castle *(G-9625)*

▲ Totaltrax Inc .... D 302 514-0600
   New Castle *(G-9630)*

Traction Wholesale Center Inc .... G 302 743-8473
   Wilmington *(G-20381)*

Tri-State Lift Truck Ltd .... G 302 427-2800
   Wilmington *(G-20414)*

United States Power Eqp LLC .... G 302 294-2562
   Newark *(G-12271)*

▲ United Testing Systems Inc .... E 714 638-2322
   New Castle *(G-9657)*

Universal Baking Company .... G 302 290-3204
   Wilmington *(G-20533)*

Urie & Blanton Inc .... G 302 658-8604
   Wilmington *(G-20545)*

W W Grainger Inc .... G 302 322-1840
   Historic New Castle *(G-5098)*

Wilmington .... G 302 357-4509
   Wilmington *(G-20807)*

World Wide Trading Brokers .... G 302 368-7041
   Newark *(G-12410)*

Wynright Corp .... G 302 239-9796
   Newark *(G-12415)*

Yellow and Green Machinery LLC .... G 302 526-4990
   Dover *(G-3885)*

5085 Industrial supplies

American Insert Flange Co Inc .... G 302 777-7464
   Wilmington *(G-14433)*

Arlon Med International LLC .... F 302 834-2100
   Bear *(G-45)*

Arlon Partners Inc .... G 302 595-1234
   Bear *(G-46)*

Bdi Inc .... C 570 299-7679
   Newark *(G-10000)*

Bristol Industrial Corporation .... F 302 322-1100
   New Castle *(G-8893)*

Building Fasteners Inc .... G 302 738-0671
   Newark *(G-10102)*

Bulk Mro Industrial Supply Inc .... G 646 713-1060
   Wilmington *(G-15147)*

C M D Inc .... G 302 894-1776
   Newark *(G-10113)*

Case Construction Inc .... G 302 737-3800
   Newark *(G-10158)*

Cobalt Pacific LLC .... G 302 437-4761
   Townsend *(G-13973)*

Delmarva Rubber & Gasket Co .... G 302 424-8300
   Bridgeville *(G-693)*

Dfc Industries Inc .... G 215 292-1572
   New Castle *(G-9048)*

E-Industrial Suppliers LLC .... G 302 251-6210
   Wilmington *(G-16243)*

Eastern Shore Equipment Co .... G 302 697-3300
   Camden *(G-825)*

Electric Motor Wholesale Inc .... F 302 653-1844
   Camden Wyoming *(G-939)*

Electric Motor Wholesale Inc .... F 302 653-1844
   Camden Wyoming *(G-940)*

First State Steel Drum Co .... G 302 655-2422
   New Castle *(G-9132)*

Forcebeyond LLC .... F 302 995-6588
   New Castle *(G-9139)*

G & E Welding Supply Co .... F 302 322-9353
   New Castle *(G-9155)*

Greenberg Supply Co Inc .... E 302 656-4496
   Wilmington *(G-16970)*

GTS Technical LLC .... F 302 778-1362
   Wilmington *(G-16998)*

Hartzell Industries Inc .... G 302 322-4900
   Historic New Castle *(G-5002)*

HK Paper .... G 302 475-3699
   Wilmington *(G-17156)*

Hose Pros .... G 302 663-0016
   Millsboro *(G-8318)*

Industrial Products of Del .... G 302 328-6648
   New Castle *(G-9231)*

Industrial Resource Netwrk Inc .... F 302 888-2905
   Wilmington *(G-17316)*

Industrial Valves & Fittings .... F 302 326-2494
   New Castle *(G-9233)*

Keen Compressed Gas Co .... E 302 594-4545
   New Castle *(G-9276)*

Keen Compressed Gas Co .... E 302 594-4545
   Wilmington *(G-17674)*

Ladder Mart USA LLC .... E 866 524-4536
   Dover *(G-2897)*

Makk-O Industries Inc .... G 302 376-0160
   Townsend *(G-14029)*

▲ Mitusha International Corp .... G 302 674-2977
   Dover *(G-3105)*

Motion Industries Inc .... E 302 462-3130
   Delmar *(G-1625)*

National Industrial LLC .... G 302 407-6233
   Wilmington *(G-18543)*

▲ OConnor Belting Intl Inc .... E 302 452-2500
   Newark *(G-11576)*

Petroserv Inc .... G 302 398-3260
   Harrington *(G-4811)*

Polymart Inc .... G 302 656-1470
   Hockessin *(G-5346)*

PQ Holding Inc .... E 302 478-6160
   Wilmington *(G-19142)*

Precision Flow LLC .... F 302 544-4417
   New Castle *(G-9489)*

Reybold Group .... G 302 834-1740
   Bear *(G-457)*

Rhino Lnngs Del Auto Style Inc .... F 302 368-4660
   Newark *(G-11878)*

Roberts Oxygen Company Inc .... G 302 337-9666
   Seaford *(G-13377)*

Royal Instruments Inc .... G 302 328-5900
   Historic New Castle *(G-5063)*

Skyline Supply Inc .... G 302 894-9190
   Newark *(G-12029)*

Standard Industrial Supply Co .... G 302 656-1631
   Wilmington *(G-20013)*

State Line Machine Inc .... F 302 478-0285
   Wilmington *(G-20035)*

Tantalum Bolt & Fastener LLC .... F 888 393-4517
   Newark *(G-12159)*

Texcel LLC .... G 302 738-4313
   Newark *(G-12185)*

Triangle Fastener Corporation .... F 302 322-0600
   Historic New Castle *(G-5091)*

Urie & Blanton Inc .... G 302 658-8604
   Wilmington *(G-20545)*

◆ Vertex Industries Inc .... G 302 472-0601
   Wilmington *(G-20597)*

W T Schrider & Sons Inc .... G 302 934-1900
   Millsboro *(G-8498)*

5087 Service establishment equipment

Agile Dcntmination Systems LLC ..... F 310 980-0644
   Dover *(G-1742)*

Allston Chemical Supply Inc .... G 302 322-3952
   Historic New Castle *(G-4927)*

Blue Sky Clean .... G 302 584-5800
   Wilmington *(G-14975)*

▲ Cad Import Inc .... E 302 628-4178
   Historic New Castle *(G-4950)*

Central America Distrs LLC .... F 302 628-4178
   Georgetown *(G-4248)*

Club 6 Barbershop .... G 302 276-1624
   Bear *(G-111)*

Cosmoprof .... G 302 674-5360
   Dover *(G-2142)*

Diamond Chemical & Supply Co ...... E 302 656-7786
   Wilmington *(G-16049)*

East Coast Cleaning Co LLC .... G 302 762-6820
   Wilmington *(G-16250)*

Grime Busters USA Inc .... G 302 834-7006
   Newark *(G-10900)*

Hoopes Fire Prevention Inc .... F 302 323-0220
   Newark *(G-10968)*

Lightscapes Inc .... G 302 798-5451
   Wilmington *(G-17910)*

Matt Carpet Guy LLC .... G 443 497-3281
   Selbyville *(G-13568)*

Mod Vellum Inc .... G 415 310-7354
   Milton *(G-8674)*

Philip Rosenau Co Inc .... G 302 322-3952
   Historic New Castle *(G-5048)*

Robo Wunderkind Inc .... F 857 353-8899
   Claymont *(G-1281)*

Sally Beauty Supply LLC .... G 302 674-2201
   Dover *(G-3507)*

Sally Beauty Supply LLC .... G 302 731-0285
   Newark *(G-11935)*

Sally Beauty Supply LLC .... G 302 737-8837
   Newark *(G-11936)*

Simply Styling-Schl of Csmtlgy .... G 302 778-1885
   Wilmington *(G-19840)*

Sky Touch LLC .... G 302 454-7040
   Newark *(G-12025)*

Source Supply Inc .... G 302 328-5110
   New Castle *(G-9580)*

South Forks Inc .... G 302 731-0344
   Newark *(G-12059)*

State Janitorial Supply Co .... G 302 734-4814
   Dover *(G-3607)*

Steven Brown & Associates Inc .... G 302 652-4722
   Wilmington *(G-20064)*

Total Beauty Supply Inc .... G 302 798-4647
   Wilmington *(G-20367)*

Vending Solutions LLC .... G 302 674-2222
   Dover *(G-3781)*

5088 Transportation equipment and supplies

50 WHOLESALE TRADE - DURABLE GOODS

Company		Phone
Aircrafters LLC	F	302 777-5000
Historic New Castle *(G-4926)*		
Arteaga Properties LLC	G	808 339-6906
Wilmington *(G-14562)*		
Auric Jets LLC	G	866 887-5414
Wilmington *(G-14644)*		
C & N Freight LLC	G	302 897-4061
New Castle *(G-8906)*		
Chambers Bros Logistics LLC	G	302 307-3668
Bear *(G-96)*		
Clicoh Inc	G	415 987-3261
Middletown *(G-6990)*		
Dassault Aircraft Svcs Corp	C	302 322-7000
New Castle *(G-8999)*		
Delta Engineering Corporation	E	302 325-9320
New Castle *(G-9045)*		
Dimo Corp	E	302 324-8100
New Castle *(G-9056)*		
▼ Eastern Group Inc	E	302 737-6603
Newark *(G-10594)*		
GA Telesis LLC	F	845 356-8390
Wilmington *(G-16788)*		
J & D Custom Golf Carts LLC	G	302 218-1505
Middletown *(G-7232)*		
▲ Janette Redrow Ltd	G	302 659-3534
Townsend *(G-14020)*		
Kinneys Enterprises LLC	G	302 300-2012
Newark *(G-11180)*		
Portable Pilot Solutions LLC	G	302 644-2775
Milton *(G-8687)*		
Quick To Go Shipping Center	G	302 327-0499
Historic New Castle *(G-5059)*		
Rawr Imports Group LLC	G	609 271-3455
Claymont *(G-1274)*		
Zat3 Transport LLC	G	302 470-6172
Laurel *(G-5627)*		

5091 Sporting and recreation goods

Company		Phone
Body Matrix	G	302 220-8406
New Castle *(G-8872)*		
Clearblue Pools & Spas LLC	F	888 630-7665
Millsboro *(G-8230)*		
▼ Eastern Group Inc	E	302 737-6603
Newark *(G-10594)*		
Gone Hunting Inc	G	302 659-5010
Townsend *(G-14009)*		
James Sutton	F	302 328-5438
New Castle *(G-9252)*		
Jerry L Burkert	G	302 736-1116
Dover *(G-2782)*		
Millers Gun Center Inc	G	302 328-4747
New Castle *(G-9371)*		
Odess Products Inc	G	253 394-0442
Wilmington *(G-18747)*		
Old Inlet Bait and Tackle Inc	F	302 227-7974
Rehoboth Beach *(G-12878)*		
Posidon Adventure Inc	F	302 543-5024
Wilmington *(G-19123)*		
Seagreen Bicycle	G	302 645-7008
Lewes *(G-6454)*		
Seagreen Bicycle LLP	G	302 226-2323
Rehoboth Beach *(G-12952)*		
Sgodde Inc	F	858 336-9471
Wilmington *(G-19774)*		
Stepr Inc	G	866 861-1281
Wilmington *(G-20062)*		
▲ Versatile Impex Inc	G	302 369-9480
Newark *(G-12317)*		

5092 Toys and hobby goods and supplies

Company		Phone
Balatroon Games Inc	G	647 986-9268
Dover *(G-1869)*		
Domestic Marketing Svcs LLC	G	646 361-9827
Wilmington *(G-16127)*		
Ealing Media & Tech (us) Ltd	G	909 576-4828
Bear *(G-187)*		
Eyliden Homelife Inc	F	858 336-9471
Wilmington *(G-16514)*		
Furobinc LLC	G	302 202-4551
Claymont *(G-1153)*		
Gamestop Inc	F	302 266-7362
Newark *(G-10805)*		
Genun Games Inc	G	425 344-4883
Wilmington *(G-16843)*		
Retrolio Games LLC	F	423 873-8768
Claymont *(G-1279)*		
Virtual Pro Gaming Inc	G	302 285-9891
Wilmington *(G-20634)*		

5093 Scrap and waste materials

Company		Phone
Billy Warren & Son LLC	G	302 349-5767
Greenwood *(G-4598)*		
Delaware Auto Salvage Inc	G	302 322-2328
Wilmington *(G-15869)*		
Diamond State Recycling Corp	E	302 655-1501
Wilmington *(G-16058)*		
Ecotrade Group North Amer LLC	G	302 724-6975
Newark *(G-10606)*		
Ewaste Express	G	302 691-8052
Wilmington *(G-16496)*		
Exim Routes Inc	G	302 551-6829
Claymont *(G-1143)*		
Joseph Smith & Sons Inc	G	302 492-8091
Hartly *(G-4885)*		
Lkq Northeast Inc	G	800 223-0171
Dover *(G-2962)*		
Network Scrap Metal Corp	G	702 354-0600
Wilmington *(G-18598)*		
Trash Porters LLC	G	302 709-1550
Wilmington *(G-20402)*		

5094 Jewelry and precious stones

Company		Phone
Aurista Technologies Inc	F	302 792-4900
Claymont *(G-1046)*		
Certified Assets MGT Intl LLC	G	302 765-3352
Wilmington *(G-15315)*		
First State Coin Co	G	302 734-7776
Dover *(G-2500)*		
Marches Jewelers Inc	G	856 858-4463
Lewes *(G-6241)*		
Rand Accessories USA Inc	G	302 266-8200
Newark *(G-11825)*		
▲ Stuart Kingston Inc	G	302 227-2524
Rehoboth Beach *(G-12978)*		
Vance Gems LLC	G	954 205-3982
Newark *(G-12304)*		
Wholesale Jewelry Outlet Inc	G	302 994-5114
Wilmington *(G-20775)*		

5099 Durable goods, nec

Company		Phone
A1 Sanitation Service Inc	G	302 653-9591
Smyrna *(G-13627)*		
AME Life LLC	G	305 517-7707
Dover *(G-1783)*		
♦ Anderson Group Inc	A	302 478-6160
Wilmington *(G-14472)*		
City Electric Supply Dover	G	302 672-3100
Dover *(G-2080)*		
Clubtac Supply Crates Ltd LLC	G	855 258-2822
Rehoboth Beach *(G-12680)*		
Cmv Audio LLC	E	929 229-9926
Wilmington *(G-15503)*		
De Alcoholic Beverage Whl Assn	G	302 356-3500
New Castle *(G-9004)*		
Delaware City Fire Co No 1	G	302 834-9336
Delaware City *(G-1536)*		
Delaware Lister	G	302 382-7059
Woodside *(G-20975)*		
Direct Importer LLC	G	302 838-2183
Newark *(G-10535)*		
Diverse Supply Solutions LLC	G	215 588-8300
Millsboro *(G-8272)*		
Econotransfer Company Inc	G	302 365-6664
Bear *(G-192)*		
Evergreen Wood Products LLC	G	302 697-2588
Hartly *(G-4874)*		
Fedex Office & Print Svcs Inc	G	302 996-0264
Wilmington *(G-16573)*		
Flw Wood Products Inc	G	410 259-4674
Dagsboro *(G-1450)*		
▼ Global Entp Worldwide LLC	F	713 260-9687
Wilmington *(G-16888)*		
▼ Honeywell Safety Pdts USA Inc	E	302 636-5401
Wilmington *(G-17194)*		
Igt Inc	B	302 674-3177
Dover *(G-2720)*		
Infinit Ventures LLC	G	800 966-9023
Middletown *(G-7225)*		
Instocking LLC	G	302 595-1595
Lewes *(G-6129)*		
JG Townsend Jr & Co Inc	E	302 856-2525
Georgetown *(G-4383)*		
K Supply Company Inc	F	302 629-3925
Seaford *(G-13242)*		
Kelitch Inc	G	847 910-6620
Dover *(G-2838)*		
Kratom Foundation	G	302 645-7400
Lewes *(G-6172)*		
Marcone	G	800 482-6022
Wilmington *(G-18123)*		
McDonald Safety Equipment Inc	E	302 999-0151
Wilmington *(G-18227)*		
MidatIntic Auto Rstration Sups	G	302 422-3812
Milford *(G-7997)*		
Minfon Group Inc	F	408 930-2190
Lewes *(G-6278)*		
Paradise Grill	F	302 945-4500
Millsboro *(G-8412)*		
Patpet LLC	G	855 888-9922
Dover *(G-3279)*		
Prestige Powder Inc	G	302 737-7086
Newark *(G-11735)*		
Simply Charming	G	302 697-7377
Wyoming *(G-20990)*		
Thomas B Davis	G	302 692-0871
Newark *(G-12191)*		
Town & Country Homes of Keller	G	302 252-5911
Middletown *(G-7655)*		

51 WHOLESALE TRADE - NONDURABLE GOODS

5112 Stationery and office supplies

Company		Phone
Brandywine Graphics Inc	G	302 655-7571
Wilmington *(G-15062)*		
Coordle Inc	G	419 618-0949
Dover *(G-2134)*		
Elite Worldwide Inc	G	833 200-5185
Claymont *(G-1130)*		
Endlesspens LLC	F	813 550-5501
Lewes *(G-5962)*		
Intelligent Change LLC	G	818 997-7712
Dover *(G-2744)*		
L E Stansell Inc	G	302 475-1534
Wilmington *(G-17775)*		

Nitro Impact Inc .... F 347 694-7000
  Wilmington (G-18652)
Safeguard Systems Inc .... G 609 822-6111
  Wilmington (G-19627)
Scigate Holdings LLC .... G 970 481-4949
  Newark (G-11962)
Total Services Inc .... G 302 575-1132
  Wilmington (G-20373)

5113 Industrial and personal service paper

A E Moore Incorporated .... F 302 934-7055
  Millsboro (G-8157)
Container Home Fund .... G 915 433-4817
  Newark (G-10311)
Diamond Chemical & Supply Co .... E 302 656-7786
  Wilmington (G-16049)
Forever Inc .... G 302 449-2100
  Middletown (G-7139)
Forever Inc .... F 302 594-0400
  Wilmington (G-16692)
Fulton Paper Company .... F 302 594-0400
  Wilmington (G-16770)
Orlando J Camp & Associates .... G 302 478-3720
  Wilmington (G-18823)
▼ Pet Poultry Products LLC .... E 302 337-8223
  Bridgeville (G-748)
Service First Container LLC .... G 302 527-5939
  Felton (G-4026)

5122 Drugs, proprietaries, and sundries

A2a Intgrted Phrmceuticals LLC .... G 270 202-2461
  Lewes (G-5648)
A66 Inc .... G 800 444-0446
  Wilmington (G-14180)
Agile Ip LLC .... F 310 980-0644
  Dover (G-1743)
Amaira Ntral Skncare Sltons In .... G 424 330-5231
  Wilmington (G-14408)
American Nutra Group LLC .... G 305 610-9448
  Wilmington (G-14439)
Animal Health Sales Inc .... F 302 436-8286
  Selbyville (G-13462)
Astrazeneca LLC .... D 800 236-9933
  Wilmington (G-14606)
◆ Astrazeneca Pharmaceuticals LP .... A 800 456-3669
  Wilmington (G-14610)
Cerobrand LLC .... G 740 971-2576
  Wilmington (G-15314)
CTB Intl LLC .... G 217 415-4843
  Dover (G-2168)
Delaware Pharmacist Society .... G 302 659-3088
  Smyrna (G-13704)
Dermal Health Science LLC .... G 302 213-8348
  Dover (G-2285)
Disrupt Pharma Tech Africa Inc .... G 312 945-8002
  Dover (G-2304)
Ds Supply LLC .... G 302 377-3974
  Wilmington (G-16281)
Foresee Pharmaceuticals Inc .... F 302 396-5243
  Newark (G-10760)
Fulcrum Pharmacy MGT Inc .... G 302 658-8020
  Wilmington (G-16768)
Goodscents Inc .... G 302 628-8042
  Bridgeville (G-704)
Hannas Phrm Sup Co Inc .... F 302 571-8761
  Wilmington (G-17050)
Harford Health Services Inc .... G 410 420-8108
  Selbyville (G-13543)
Harrock Properties LLC .... G 302 202-1321
  Dover (G-2657)
Hrc Medics LLC .... F 561 856-6180
  Newark (G-10982)

Jem Therapeutics Pbc .... G 561 462-1809
  Dover (G-2779)
Kerahealth France LLC .... G 302 351-3377
  Wilmington (G-17695)
L2 Trade LLC .... F 603 921-7930
  Dover (G-2893)
Lice Lifters Distribution LLC .... G 864 680-4030
  Dover (G-2938)
Maelys Cosmetics USA Inc .... F 312 888-5007
  Wilmington (G-18076)
Matrix Life Science Inc .... G 281 419-7942
  Wilmington (G-6249)
Melanin Mixx Beauty Brand Inc .... G 302 266-1010
  Newark (G-11385)
Mellon Care Inc .... G 800 406-0281
  Middletown (G-7339)
Mid States Sales & Marketing .... F 302 888-2475
  Wilmington (G-18336)
New Castle Rx LLC .... G 302 356-5600
  Historic New Castle (G-5037)
Normopharm Inc .... G 954 210-4812
  Wilmington (G-18674)
Olgam Life LLC .... F 917 635-1989
  Wilmington (G-18759)
▲ Pharmadel LLC .... G 302 322-1329
  Historic New Castle (G-5047)
Pharmerica Long-Term Care LLC .... E 302 454-8234
  Newark (G-11679)
Physicians Beauty Group LLC .... E 866 270-9290
  Dover (G-3318)
Pumas-Ai Inc .... E 551 207-6084
  Dover (G-3395)
Qps LLC .... C 302 369-3753
  Newark (G-11784)
Radius Rx Direct Inc .... G 302 658-9196
  Wilmington (G-19314)
Resh LLC .... F 302 543-5469
  New Castle (G-9523)
Sally Beauty Supply LLC .... G 302 629-5160
  Seaford (G-13383)
Sekoiya Inc .... G 323 761-9028
  Newark (G-11972)
▼ Sinuswars LLC .... F 212 901-0805
  Wilmington (G-19843)
So Hair and Beauty Supply .... G 302 407-3381
  Wilmington (G-19905)
▼ SPI Pharma Inc .... E 800 789-9755
  Wilmington (G-19962)
Sunshine Nutrition LLC .... G 971 456-1000
  Lewes (G-6525)
Xynomic Pharmaceuticals Inc .... F 650 430-7561
  Dover (G-3883)

5131 Piece goods and notions

F Schumacher & Co LLC .... E 302 454-3200
  Newark (G-10699)
Loomcraft Textile & Supply Co .... F 302 454-3232
  Newark (G-11281)
W L Gore & Associates Inc .... C 302 368-3700
  Newark (G-12341)
▲ W L Gore & Associates Inc .... D 302 738-4880
  Newark (G-12342)
Wayne Industries Inc .... G 302 478-6160
  Wilmington (G-20694)

5136 Men's and boy's clothing

Antoinette Xavier .... F 980 549-3272
  Harrington (G-4732)
Fenwick Island Nautical Sports .... G 443 397-0619
  Fenwick Island (G-4048)
H D Lee Company Inc .... G 302 477-3930
  Wilmington (G-17018)

Kaul Glove and Mfg Co .... D 302 292-2660
  Historic New Castle (G-5014)
▲ Majdell Group USA Inc .... G 302 722-8223
  Newark (G-11316)
Sui Trading Co .... G 302 239-2012
  Hockessin (G-5394)
Throat Threads Apparel USA Inc .... D 905 681-8437
  Dover (G-3683)

5137 Women's and children's clothing

Aquamarine Boutique LLC .... G 302 644-4550
  Lewes (G-5696)
Desires Lingerie .... G 302 744-9969
  Dover (G-2287)
Fenwick Island Nautical Sports .... G 443 397-0619
  Fenwick Island (G-4048)
Flapdoodles Inc .... D 302 731-9793
  Newark (G-10750)
H D Lee Company Inc .... G 302 477-3930
  Wilmington (G-17018)
◆ Huzala Inc .... G 313 404-6941
  Newark (G-10987)
Jiffyshirtscom (us) LP .... F 302 319-2063
  Wilmington (G-17546)
Lycra Company LLC .... G 540 949-2972
  Wilmington (G-18043)
Petite Plume LLC .... F 800 298-1381
  Wilmington (G-18998)
Throat Threads Apparel USA Inc .... D 905 681-8437
  Dover (G-3683)

5139 Footwear

Elite Feet LLC .... G 302 464-1028
  Middletown (G-7094)
Silver Bay International LLC .... G 302 213-3006
  Wilmington (G-19826)
Young Soles Inc .... G 516 643-0445
  Camden (G-900)

5141 Groceries, general line

Acm Corp .... G 302 736-3864
  Dover (G-1711)
Amazon Commodities LLC .... G 302 715-1427
  Newark (G-9840)
Brandywine Food Services LLC .... G 302 276-5165
  Wilmington (G-15058)
Camels Hump Inc .... F 302 227-5719
  Rehoboth Beach (G-12662)
El Bluebird LLC .... G 775 773-3255
  Wilmington (G-16347)
El Nopalito Distributors Inc .... F 302 393-2050
  Milford (G-7879)
Everest Foods Enterprises Inc .... F 215 896-8902
  Wilmington (G-16484)
Eztz Inc .... G 302 376-5641
  Historic New Castle (G-4986)
Heavenly Harvest LLC .... G 302 487-0974
  Dover (G-2669)
Hughes Delaware Maid Scrapple .... G 302 284-4370
  Felton (G-3983)
Oppenheimer Group Inc .... E 302 533-0779
  Newark (G-11595)
Petra Investments LLC .... G 312 887-1558
  Newark (G-11674)
Piffert Inc .... F 302 407-6185
  Historic New Castle (G-5049)
Premium Brands Inc .... G 925 566-8863
  Dover (G-3364)
Refix Commodities LLC .... G 888 465-8020
  Dover (G-3443)
Supermarket Associates Inc .... G 302 547-1977
  Wilmington (G-20146)

51 WHOLESALE TRADE - NONDURABLE GOODS

Thomas E Moore Inc .... F 302 674-1500
  Kenton (G-5456)
World Foods USA LLC .... G 302 288-0670
  Dover (G-3873)
Yupica Inc (usa) .... G 707 387-9874
  Wilmington (G-20941)

5142 Packaged frozen goods

Burris Logistics .... C 302 398-5050
  Harrington (G-4742)
DOT Foods Inc .... D 302 300-4239
  Bear (G-177)
H C Davis Inc .... G 302 337-7001
  Bridgeville (G-706)
JG Townsend Jr & Co Inc .... E 302 856-2525
  Georgetown (G-4383)
Nowadays Inc Pbc .... G 415 279-6802
  Dover (G-3207)
Produce Spot LLC .... F 267 864-1232
  Wilmington (G-19209)
Riverside Foods Inc .... G 888 546-8810
  Lewes (G-6423)
Sankhya Ventures LLC .... G 415 905-0887
  Wilmington (G-19666)

5143 Dairy products, except dried or canned

Burris Logistics .... C 302 398-5050
  Harrington (G-4742)
Dfa Dairy Brands Fluid LLC .... F 302 398-8321
  Harrington (G-4762)
Glacierpoint Enterprises Inc .... E 302 636-5401
  Wilmington (G-16878)
H C Davis Inc .... G 302 337-7001
  Bridgeville (G-706)
Hy-Point Dairy Farms Inc .... C 302 478-1414
  Wilmington (G-17240)
Queso Time De 3 LLC .... G 302 368-4541
  Newark (G-11799)
Yogo Factory .... G 302 266-4506
  Newark (G-12421)

5144 Poultry and poultry products

Egg .... G 302 227-3447
  Rehoboth Beach (G-12739)
Jabez Corp .... F 302 475-7600
  Wilmington (G-17470)
▼ Pet Poultry Products LLC .... E 302 337-8223
  Bridgeville (G-748)
Puglisi Egg Farms Delaware LLC .... E 302 376-1200
  Middletown (G-7479)

5145 Confectionery

A E Moore Incorporated .... F 302 934-7055
  Millsboro (G-8157)
Harry Kenyon Incorporated .... E 302 762-7776
  Historic New Castle (G-5001)
Herr Foods Incorporated .... E 302 628-9161
  Seaford (G-13210)
Imperial Popcorn Corp .... E 847 641-0991
  Newark (G-11005)
J & J Snack Foods Corp PA .... G 302 571-0884
  Wilmington (G-17444)
King of Sweets Inc .... F 302 730-8200
  Dover (G-2873)

5146 Fish and seafoods

Big Fish Wholesale LLC .... G 302 226-3474
  Rehoboth Beach (G-12643)
Febys Fishery Inc .... E 302 998-9501
  Wilmington (G-16566)
▲ Harbor House Seafood Inc .... D 302 629-0444
  Seaford (G-13207)

J A E Seafood .... G 302 765-2546
  Wilmington (G-17448)
Jesse Jmes Safood Barbeque LLC ...... G 302 883-3518
  Dover (G-2783)
Lewes Fishhouse & Produce Inc .... E 302 827-4074
  Lewes (G-6196)
Manoa Fresh Food LLC .... G 561 453-0521
  Dover (G-3010)
Meltrone Inc .... F 302 998-3457
  Wilmington (G-18268)
Oceanside Seafood Mkt Deli LLC .... F 302 313-5158
  Lewes (G-6330)
Paul Sorvino Foods Inc .... G 302 547-1977
  Wilmington (G-18922)
Seafood City Inc .... G 302 284-8486
  Felton (G-4024)
Southern Crab Company .... G 302 478-0181
  Wilmington (G-19939)
Venus On Halfshell .... G 302 227-9292
  Dewey Beach (G-1676)
Wooley Bully Inc .... G 302 542-3613
  Millsboro (G-8507)

5147 Meats and meat products

B & M Meats Inc .... F 302 655-5521
  Wilmington (G-14692)
Diamond State Meats LLC .... G 302 270-0009
  Rehoboth Beach (G-12726)
Estia Hospitality Group Inc .... G 302 798-5319
  Claymont (G-1136)
H C Davis Inc .... G 302 337-7001
  Bridgeville (G-706)
▲ Haass Family Butcher Shop .... G 302 734-5447
  Dover (G-2643)
Kit International Inc .... G 201 342-7753
  Wilmington (G-17736)
Lewes Fishhouse & Produce Inc .... E 302 827-4074
  Lewes (G-6196)
Ralph and Paul Adams Inc .... B 800 338-4727
  Bridgeville (G-760)
South Forks Inc .... G 302 731-0344
  Newark (G-12059)
Sure Good Foods USA LLC .... E 905 288-1136
  Newark (G-12131)

5148 Fresh fruits and vegetables

Chiquita Brands LLC .... F 302 571-9781
  Wilmington (G-15385)
David Oppenheimer and Co I LLC ...... E 302 533-0779
  Newark (G-10391)
Dole Fresh Fruit Company .... F 302 652-6484
  Wilmington (G-16123)
Dole Fresh Fruit Company .... F 302 652-2215
  Wilmington (G-16124)
Ernie Deangelis .... F 302 226-9533
  Rehoboth Beach (G-12746)
Estia Hospitality Group Inc .... G 302 798-5319
  Claymont (G-1136)
Pandol Bros Inc .... E 302 571-8923
  Wilmington (G-18873)
Robert T Minner Jr .... G 302 422-9206
  Greenwood (G-4665)
Tgfmx Inc .... G 302 613-0128
  Wilmington (G-20287)
Thomas E Moore Inc .... F 302 674-1500
  Kenton (G-5456)
▲ Thomas E Moore Inc .... F 302 674-1500
  Dover (G-3678)
Willey Farms Inc .... D 302 378-8441
  Townsend (G-14091)

5149 Groceries and related products, nec

Angry 8 LLC .... F 888 417-5477
  Newark (G-9871)
Beach Break & Bakrie .... G 302 537-3800
  Bethany Beach (G-576)
Beaverdam Pet Food .... G 302 349-5299
  Greenwood (G-4595)
Chara Tea LLC .... G 856 250-7180
  Dover (G-2056)
Chocolette Distribution LLC .... G 917 547-8905
  Lewes (G-5816)
Classic Cookies of Dowingtown .... G 302 494-9662
  Wilmington (G-15467)
Custom Creams LLC .... G 302 582-8862
  New Castle (G-8991)
Dfa Dairy Brands Fluid LLC .... F 302 398-8321
  Harrington (G-4762)
Elizabeth Beverage Company LLC ...... G 302 322-9895
  Historic New Castle (G-4982)
Four Ever Green Inc .... G 302 424-2393
  Milford (G-7902)
Freakin Fresh Salsa Inc .... G 302 750-9789
  Wilmington (G-16733)
Georges Trees Plus LLC .... G 302 539-0660
  Dagsboro (G-1452)
▲ Good Good Ntural Sweetness LLC ... G 302 364-0015
  Lewes (G-6048)
Green Roots LLC .... G 516 643-2621
  Lewes (G-6058)
Ism .... F 302 656-2376
  Wilmington (G-17428)
Kees Cookies & Cupcakes LLC .... G 302 223-6784
  Clayton (G-1380)
King of Sweets Distribution .... G 302 730-8200
  Dover (G-2874)
King of Sweets Online Inc .... F 302 730-8200
  Dover (G-2875)
Legacy Foods LLC .... E 302 656-5540
  Wilmington (G-17857)
Mateina US Inc .... G 514 443-4945
  Newark (G-11352)
Mekhala Living Inc .... G 650 443-8235
  Dover (G-3056)
Mr Natural Bottled Water Inc .... G 302 436-7700
  Ocean View (G-12549)
My Red Tea LLC .... G 415 259-4166
  Wilmington (G-18509)
Nectar Lifesciences Usa LLC .... G 518 229-8228
  Wilmington (G-18569)
P-Ks Wholesale Grocer Inc .... F 302 656-5540
  Wilmington (G-18855)
Panamerican Coffee Trdg Co LLC ...... G 786 538-9547
  Dover (G-3264)
Peppers Inc .... F 302 644-6900
  Lewes (G-6361)
Peppers Inc .... G 302 645-0812
  Lewes (G-6360)
Pepperscom Inc .... G 302 703-6355
  Lewes (G-6362)
Pepsi-Cola Btlg of Wilmington .... C 302 761-4848
  Wilmington (G-18966)
Pioneer Distributors Inc .... G 302 644-0791
  Milton (G-8686)
Point Coffee Shop and Bakery .... F 302 260-9734
  Rehoboth Beach (G-12894)
Raw Essential Juice Bar .... G 302 235-8019
  Wilmington (G-19341)
▲ Real Ch Inc .... G 347 433-8945
  Wilmington (G-19364)
Scotts Co .... G 302 777-4779
  Wilmington (G-19712)
Sn & Partners .... G 312 826-3255
  Newark (G-12044)

51 WHOLESALE TRADE - NONDURABLE GOODS

South Forks Inc .... G 302 731-0344
  Newark *(G-12059)*
Tail Bangers Inc .... F 302 947-4900
  Millsboro *(G-8480)*
Tailbangers Inc .... F 302 934-1125
  Millsboro *(G-8481)*
Three Sheep and A Mill LLC .... G 616 820-5668
  Middletown *(G-7641)*
Touch of Italy Bakery LLC .... G 302 827-2132
  Lewes *(G-6574)*
Valentina Liquors .... G 302 368-3264
  Newark *(G-12300)*
▲ Wen International Inc .... G 845 354-1773
  Wilmington *(G-20729)*
Wheatfield Holdings LLC .... G 312 956-0198
  Wilmington *(G-20756)*

5153 Grain and field beans

Against Grain LLC .... G 302 388-1667
  Wilmington *(G-14311)*
Allen Harim Foods LLC .... D 302 629-9460
  Seaford *(G-13056)*
Baldwin Sayre Inc .... G 302 337-0309
  Bridgeville *(G-671)*
Dack Trading LLC .... G 917 576-4432
  Rehoboth Beach *(G-12710)*
Delaware Intl Agrclture Entp L .... G 302 450-2008
  Smyrna *(G-13699)*
Johnson Jr Henry & Son Farm .... G 302 436-8501
  Selbyville *(G-13552)*
Laurel Grain Company .... G 302 875-4231
  Laurel *(G-5547)*
Lombard Trading International .... G 786 659-5010
  Newark *(G-11279)*
Mountaire Farms Delaware Inc .... G 302 398-3296
  Harrington *(G-4805)*
Mountaire Farms Delaware Inc .... G 302 378-2271
  Townsend *(G-14039)*
Suresrce Cmmdties LLC - Orgnic .... F 866 697-5960
  Wilmington *(G-20160)*

5159 Farm-product raw materials, nec

African Wood Inc .... G 302 884-6738
  Middletown *(G-6839)*
Baxter Farms Inc .... G 302 856-1818
  Georgetown *(G-4223)*
Complete Hemp LLC .... E 888 901-6150
  Wilmington *(G-15573)*
Grapefruit Usa Inc .... G 310 575-1175
  Wilmington *(G-16950)*
Kirkwood Smoke Shop .... G 302 525-6718
  Newark *(G-11185)*
Southern Delaware Horse .... G 302 856-1598
  Georgetown *(G-4519)*
Tops International Corp .... G 302 738-8889
  Wilmington *(G-20361)*

5162 Plastics materials and basic shapes

Delrin Usa LLC .... F 302 295-5900
  Wilmington *(G-16001)*
Fluorogistx Ct LLC .... F 800 373-7811
  Wilmington *(G-16675)*
Industrial Resource Netwrk Inc .... F 302 888-2905
  Wilmington *(G-17316)*
Osterman & Company Inc .... G 203 272-2233
  Wilmington *(G-18830)*
Polymart Inc .... G 302 656-1470
  Hockessin *(G-5346)*

5169 Chemicals and allied products, nec

A E Moore Incorporated .... F 302 934-7055
  Millsboro *(G-8157)*

Action Unlimited Resources Inc .... E 302 323-1455
  Historic New Castle *(G-4919)*
Airgas Usa LLC .... F 302 834-7404
  Delaware City *(G-1529)*
Alliance Chemicals Global LLC .... F 507 202-6872
  Wilmington *(G-14377)*
Amfine Chemical Corp .... G 302 559-2948
  Newark *(G-9852)*
Ancatt Company .... G 302 897-8366
  Newark *(G-9862)*
AR Pro Inc .... F 323 677-0503
  Newark *(G-14520)*
Arrow Chemical Inc .... G 302 731-7403
  Newark *(G-9908)*
Ashland Chemco Inc .... E 302 995-4180
  Wilmington *(G-14582)*
Ashland Inc .... C 302 995-3000
  Wilmington *(G-14583)*
Brainerd LLC .... F 918 622-1214
  Seaford *(G-13092)*
Cfg Lab Inc .... G 302 261-3403
  Wilmington *(G-15319)*
Ciba Specialty Chem N Amer .... G 302 992-5600
  Wilmington *(G-15432)*
Cibt America Inc .... G 302 318-1300
  Newark *(G-10241)*
Croda Inc .... G 302 429-5200
  New Castle *(G-8986)*
Diamond Chemical & Supply Co .... E 302 656-7786
  Wilmington *(G-16049)*
E E Rosser Inc .... G 302 762-9643
  Wilmington *(G-16237)*
Eidp Inc .... E 302 774-1000
  Wilmington *(G-16314)*
Elchemy Inc .... G 908 663-8750
  Lewes *(G-5954)*
▲ Grayling Industries Inc .... F 770 751-9095
  Frederica *(G-4168)*
Interntional Mkt Suppliers Inc .... F 302 392-1840
  Bear *(G-286)*
Isp International Corp .... G 302 594-5000
  Wilmington *(G-17429)*
Keen Compressed Gas Co .... E 302 594-4545
  New Castle *(G-9276)*
Keen Compressed Gas Co .... F 302 594-4545
  Wilmington *(G-17674)*
Magco Kissner Milling Co .... G 913 713-0612
  New Castle *(G-9334)*
Management Chemical Co .... G 410 326-0964
  Dover *(G-3007)*
▲ Mil International LLC .... G 302 234-7501
  Wilmington *(G-18352)*
Noramco of Delaware Inc .... C 302 761-2900
  Wilmington *(G-18672)*
▲ PDM Incorporated .... G 302 478-0768
  Wilmington *(G-18938)*
Progressive Systems Inc .... G 302 732-3321
  Frankford *(G-4135)*
Quaker Chemical Corporation .... E 302 791-9171
  Wilmington *(G-19281)*
▲ Rath Incorporated .... F 302 294-4446
  Newark *(G-11828)*
Recticel US Inc .... A 248 393-2100
  Wilmington *(G-19381)*
Roberts Oxygen Company Inc .... G 302 337-9666
  Seaford *(G-13377)*
Rockwood Specialties Inc .... E 302 765-6012
  Wilmington *(G-19547)*
Royale Group Inc .... G 201 845-4666
  Bear *(G-473)*
▲ Royale Pigments & Chem Inc .... E 201 845-4666
  Bear *(G-474)*

▲ Royale Pigments and Chem LLC .... G 201 845-4666
  Bear *(G-475)*
▲ Sepax Technologies Inc .... F 302 366-1101
  Newark *(G-11980)*
▲ Shore Chem LLC .... F 201 845-4666
  Bear *(G-490)*
Solenis Holdings 3 LLC .... A 866 337-1533
  Wilmington *(G-19921)*
Solenis LLC .... B 302 594-5000
  Wilmington *(G-19923)*
▼ Solenis LLC .... B 866 337-1533
  Wilmington *(G-19922)*
Syntec Corporation .... F 302 421-8393
  Wilmington *(G-20191)*
◆ Tenmat Inc .... G 302 633-6600
  Wilmington *(G-20273)*
▲ Thornley Company Inc .... G 302 224-8300
  Newark *(G-12194)*
Ultrafine Technologies Inc .... G 302 384-6513
  Wilmington *(G-20502)*

5171 Petroleum bulk stations and terminals

Du Pont Elastomers LP .... E 302 774-1000
  Wilmington *(G-16190)*
Eidp Inc .... G 302 772-0016
  New Castle *(G-9084)*
Merit Inc .... G 302 778-4732
  Wilmington *(G-18285)*
Peninsula Oil Co Inc .... E 302 422-6691
  Seaford *(G-13338)*
Service Oil Company .... G 302 734-7433
  Dover *(G-3535)*
Sunlite Energy Intll .... G 302 598-2984
  Historic New Castle *(G-5077)*

5172 Petroleum products, nec

Adams Oil Co Inc .... G 302 629-4531
  Seaford *(G-13048)*
C L Burchenal Oil Co Inc .... G 302 697-1517
  Camden *(G-798)*
Chemours Company Fc LLC .... D 302 773-1267
  Wilmington *(G-15361)*
Conectiv LLC .... C 202 872-2680
  Newark *(G-10298)*
Conectiv Energy Supply Inc .... E 302 454-0300
  Newark *(G-10301)*
J William Gordy Fuel Co .... G 302 846-3425
  Delmar *(G-1604)*
Pep-Up Inc .... G 302 645-2600
  Rehoboth Beach *(G-12888)*
Pep-Up Inc .... F 302 856-2555
  Georgetown *(G-4460)*
Performance Lubricants Inc .... G 302 239-5661
  Hockessin *(G-5338)*
Petroleum Equipment Inc .... F 302 422-4281
  Dover *(G-3308)*
▲ Petroleum Equipment Inc .... E 302 734-7433
  Dover *(G-3307)*
Sandy Brae Laboratories .... G 302 456-0446
  Wilmington *(G-19663)*
Service Energy LLC .... F 302 645-9050
  Lewes *(G-6460)*
Service Energy LLC .... D 302 734-7433
  Dover *(G-3534)*
Shellhorn & Hill Inc .... D 302 654-4200
  Wilmington *(G-19793)*
Sherman Heating Oils Inc .... G 302 684-4008
  Milton *(G-8711)*
◆ Ultrachem Inc .... F 302 325-9880
  Historic New Castle *(G-5094)*
Vp Racing Fuels Inc .... G 302 368-1500
  Newark *(G-12337)*

Employee Codes: A=Over 500 employees, B=251-500
C=101-250, D=51-100, E=20-50, F=10-19, G=1-9

51 WHOLESALE TRADE - NONDURABLE GOODS

5181 Beer and ale

Argilla Brewing Company............................ G 302 731-8200
  Newark *(G-9901)*
▲ Delaware Importers Inc............................ D 302 656-4487
  New Castle *(G-9025)*
NKS Distributors Inc................................... F 302 422-1220
  Milford *(G-8029)*
▲ NKS Distributors Inc............................... D 302 322-1811
  Smyrna *(G-13835)*
Prime Beverage Group LLC........................ G 302 327-0002
  New Castle *(G-9493)*
Southern Glzers Wine Sprits LL.................. E 302 656-4487
  New Castle *(G-9581)*
▲ Standard Distributing Co Inc.................... D 302 655-5511
  New Castle *(G-9590)*

5182 Wine and distilled beverages

Breakthru Beverage Group LLC.................. B 443 631-2597
  Middletown *(G-6936)*
Country Vintner LLC................................... E 877 946-3620
  Newark *(G-10335)*
▲ Delaware Importers Inc........................... D 302 656-4487
  New Castle *(G-9025)*
Empirical Inc... G 347 828-4528
  Dover *(G-2444)*
▲ HB Wine Merchants LLC......................... G 302 384-5991
  Hartly *(G-4876)*
Js Liquors... G 302 656-4066
  Wilmington *(G-17602)*
Lawrence Boone Selections LLC................ G 757 602-5173
  Bear *(G-339)*
▲ NKS Distributors Inc............................... D 302 322-1811
  Smyrna *(G-13835)*
Order Department...................................... G 302 654-3116
  New Castle *(G-9437)*
Outlet Liquors... G 302 227-7700
  Rehoboth Beach *(G-12881)*
Pk Fire LLC.. G 253 880-9025
  Dover *(G-3327)*
Robert M Panzer.. G 302 571-0717
  Wilmington *(G-19519)*
S & S Wines and Spirits............................. G 302 678-9987
  Dover *(G-3497)*
Sleigh Financial Inc.................................... G 302 684-2929
  Milton *(G-8712)*
Southern Glzers Wine Sprits LL.................. E 302 656-4487
  New Castle *(G-9581)*
▲ Southern Wine Spirits Del LLC................ E 800 292-7890
  New Castle *(G-9582)*
▲ Standard Distributing Co Inc................... D 302 655-5511
  New Castle *(G-9590)*
Universal Bev Importers LLC...................... G 302 322-7900
  New Castle *(G-9659)*
◆ William Grant & Sons USA Corp.............. B 302 573-3880
  Wilmington *(G-20791)*
Wine Worx LLC.. E 302 436-1500
  Frankford *(G-4161)*

5191 Farm supplies

B Diamond Feed Company......................... G 302 697-7576
  Camden Wyoming *(G-915)*
Bryan & Brittingham Inc............................. F 302 846-9500
  Delmar *(G-1569)*
◆ Chick Harness & Supply Inc.................... E 302 398-4630
  Harrington *(G-4748)*
◆ Emerald Bioagriculture Corp.................... F 517 882-7370
  Hockessin *(G-5199)*
Growmark Fs LLC...................................... G 302 422-3001
  Milford *(G-7912)*
◆ Growmark Fs LLC................................... D 302 422-3002
  Milford *(G-7913)*

Harvest Consumer Products LLC............... D 302 732-6624
  Dagsboro *(G-1460)*
Helena Agri-Enterprises LLC...................... G 302 337-3881
  Bridgeville *(G-710)*
Hudson Farm Supply Co Inc....................... G 302 398-3654
  Middletown *(G-7219)*
Joseph M L Sand & Gravel Co.................... E 302 856-7396
  Georgetown *(G-4387)*
Leons Garden World Ej Inc........................ F 410 392-8630
  New Castle *(G-9308)*
Leotech LLC... G 908 829-3813
  Wilmington *(G-17881)*
Nutrien AG Solutions Inc............................ F 302 422-3570
  Milford *(G-8034)*
◆ Q Vandenberg & Sons Inc....................... E 800 242-2852
  Wilmington *(G-19272)*
Soil Service Inc... G 302 629-7054
  Seaford *(G-13406)*
◆ Syngenta Corporation.............................. E 302 425-2000
  Wilmington *(G-20189)*
▲ Thomas E Moore Inc............................... F 302 674-1500
  Dover *(G-3678)*
Tractor Supply Company............................ F 302 629-3627
  Seaford *(G-13434)*
Tractor Supply Company............................ F 302 659-3333
  Smyrna *(G-13917)*
Whaleys Seed Store Inc............................. G 302 875-7833
  Laurel *(G-5623)*

5192 Books, periodicals, and newspapers

Acorn Books Inc... G 302 508-2219
  Smyrna *(G-13631)*
Around Again and Again Bks LLC.............. G 302 439-3847
  Wilmington *(G-14558)*
Books & Tobaccos Inc................................ G 302 994-3156
  Wilmington *(G-15003)*
Delaware Beach Book LLC......................... G 302 249-1030
  Milton *(G-8598)*
Distribution Marketing of Del...................... G 302 658-6397
  Wilmington *(G-16089)*
Hispano Magazine...................................... G 302 668-6118
  Newark *(G-10955)*
Linguatext Ltd... G 302 453-8695
  Newark *(G-11262)*
Suburban Marketing Associates................. E 302 656-8440
  Wilmington *(G-20114)*
Thomas B Davis... G 302 692-0871
  Newark *(G-12191)*

5193 Flowers and florists supplies

Gro-Connectcom Inc................................... G 347 918-7437
  Lewes *(G-6066)*
Harvest Consumer Products LLC............... D 302 732-6624
  Dagsboro *(G-1460)*
Hoek Flowers Usa Inc................................ G 786 999-5767
  Dover *(G-2686)*
Lakeside Greenhouses Inc......................... G 302 875-2457
  Laurel *(G-5544)*
Sieck Wholesale Florist Inc........................ G 302 356-2000
  New Castle *(G-9568)*
Sterling Nursery Inc................................... G 302 653-7060
  Smyrna *(G-13901)*
Village Green Inc.. E 302 764-2234
  New Castle *(G-9671)*

5194 Tobacco and tobacco products

BAt Capital Corporation.............................. E 302 691-6323
  Wilmington *(G-14776)*
Camden Cigars... G 302 698-1000
  Dover *(G-2015)*
Cigarette City Inc.. F 302 836-4889
  Newark *(G-10242)*

Guy & Lady Barrel LLC............................... G 302 399-3069
  Dover *(G-2635)*
Harry Kenyon Incorporated........................ E 302 762-7776
  Historic New Castle *(G-5001)*
Unreal Vapors... G 302 322-2600
  New Castle *(G-9661)*
Unreal Vapors... G 302 750-6213
  Smyrna *(G-13924)*
Unreal Vapors LLC..................................... G 302 449-2547
  Middletown *(G-7674)*

5198 Paints, varnishes, and supplies

Arthouse USA Incorporated....................... G 800 677-3394
  Wilmington *(G-14565)*
◆ Avt Paints LLC.. G 800 476-1634
  Wilmington *(G-14675)*
B F Shin of Salisbury Inc........................... G 302 652-3521
  Wilmington *(G-14700)*
B Frank Shinn Paint Co.............................. F 302 652-3521
  Wilmington *(G-14701)*
Bair & Goff Sales LLC................................ E 302 292-2546
  Newark *(G-9975)*
Boero Usa Inc.. G 800 935-6596
  Wilmington *(G-14996)*
F Schumacher & Co LLC............................ E 302 454-3200
  Newark *(G-10699)*
First State Distributors Inc........................ G 302 655-8266
  Wilmington *(G-16627)*
Mammeles Inc.. F 302 998-0541
  Wilmington *(G-18097)*
T B Painting Restoration........................... G 610 283-4100
  Newark *(G-12152)*

5199 Nondurable goods, nec

◆ AB Group Packaging Inc......................... F 302 607-3281
  Newark *(G-9736)*
Adventum LLC... G 518 620-1441
  Wilmington *(G-14288)*
Animal Health Sales Inc............................. F 302 436-8286
  Selbyville *(G-13462)*
Avenue 121.. G 302 354-1839
  Middletown *(G-6890)*
Badges Sports Bar..................................... G 302 256-0202
  Wilmington *(G-14714)*
Books & Tobaccos Inc................................ G 302 994-3156
  Wilmington *(G-15003)*
Bradley Distributing Inc............................ G 302 245-7508
  Seaford *(G-13091)*
Brandywine Rver Representative............... G 302 984-2861
  Wilmington *(G-15085)*
Candor Trading Corp.................................. G 302 268-6800
  Historic New Castle *(G-4951)*
Cannons Cake and Candy Sups................. G 302 738-3321
  Newark *(G-10129)*
Convention Coach...................................... G 302 335-5459
  Magnolia *(G-6735)*
Cramaro Tarpaulin Systems Inc................. G 302 292-2170
  Newark *(G-10344)*
Creative Promotions................................... G 302 697-7896
  Camden *(G-809)*
Daikin Comfort Tech Mfg LP....................... G 302 894-1010
  Newark *(G-10380)*
Day By Day Calendars............................... G 302 477-1763
  Wilmington *(G-15820)*
Diamond State Promotions........................ G 302 999-1900
  Wilmington *(G-16056)*
Digitalzone Inc.. E 646 771-6969
  Lewes *(G-5918)*
Direct Trends USA LLC.............................. G 347 354-2899
  Wilmington *(G-16080)*
Domian International Svc LLC................... G 804 837-3616
  Smyrna *(G-13711)*

East Coast Swag .... G 302 628-2674
  Seaford *(G-13167)*
Family of All Trades .... G 302 334-2710
  Ocean View *(G-12510)*
Forever Inc. .... F 302 594-0400
  Wilmington *(G-16692)*
▲ Francis Enterprises LLC .... F 302 276-1316
  Historic New Castle *(G-4991)*
Goddess Scent Candles LLC .... G 973 885-0606
  Bear *(G-250)*
Graham Packaging Pet Tech Inc .... E 302 453-9464
  Newark *(G-10878)*
Grupo Acosta Ecuador Limited .... C 302 231-2981
  Wilmington *(G-16993)*
Guinevere Associates Inc .... G 302 635-7798
  Wilmington *(G-17004)*
Hamilton Distributors Inc .... G 302 542-7860
  Seaford *(G-13205)*
Hayjay Auto Exports .... G 302 266-0266
  Newark *(G-10940)*
Joseph W Small Associates Inc .... F
  Wilmington *(G-17588)*
LC Distributors Inc .... G 484 326-9805
  Claymont *(G-1212)*
Lohmann Steel LLC .... G 844 488-1790
  Wilmington *(G-17977)*
Masley Enterprises Inc .... E 302 427-9885
  Wilmington *(G-18183)*
◆ Mid-Atlantic Packaging Company ...... E 800 284-1332
  Dover *(G-3086)*
Modise Imports & Exports LLC .... G 800 274-1240
  Dover *(G-3116)*
▲ Monseco Leather LLC .... G 302 235-1777
  Hockessin *(G-5311)*
New Image Inc .... G 302 738-6824
  Newark *(G-11523)*
Other Side LLC .... G 410 829-1053
  Greenwood *(G-4658)*
P&A River Gallery Promotion .... G 302 947-1805
  Lewes *(G-6344)*
Packaging Mania (not Inc) .... G 917 410-6835
  Milford *(G-8041)*
Papona LLC .... F 302 285-9559
  Middletown *(G-7424)*
Perch Acquisition Co 17 LLC .... G 617 206-3761
  Wilmington *(G-18968)*
Perch Foreign Acquisition Corp .... G 617 206-3761
  Wilmington *(G-18969)*
Prescotech Inc .... D 502 585-5866
  Wilmington *(G-19178)*
Promotion Zone LLC .... G 302 832-8565
  Newark *(G-11763)*
▲ Remline Corp .... E 302 737-7228
  Newark *(G-11850)*
Self Care Holistic LLC .... G 302 407-2456
  Wilmington *(G-19744)*
SM Snacks LLC .... G 973 229-2845
  Wilmington *(G-19868)*
Stamford Screen Printing Inc .... G 302 654-2442
  Wilmington *(G-20008)*
Systems Corporation .... G 323 984-7401
  Wilmington *(G-20194)*
Trovety Inc .... G 302 291-2252
  Lewes *(G-6580)*
Tyrant Sportsgear Inc .... G 302 530-3410
  Wilmington *(G-20482)*
Tz Distributors .... G 302 562-1029
  Historic New Castle *(G-5093)*
Union Building Trades Fcu .... G 973 263-0001
  New Castle *(G-9652)*
Vital Berry .... G 302 691-5063
  Wilmington *(G-20643)*

Zuminex Inc .... G 302 325-3200
  New Castle *(G-9700)*

52 BUILDING MATERIALS, HARDWARE, GARDEN SUPPLIES & MOBILE HOMES

5211 Lumber and other building materials

African Wood Inc .... G 302 884-6738
  Middletown *(G-6839)*
American Cedar & Millwork Inc .... E 302 645-9580
  Lewes *(G-5683)*
Cabinetry Unlimited LLC .... E 302 436-5030
  Selbyville *(G-13489)*
◆ Casale Marble Imports Inc .... E 561 404-4213
  Wilmington *(G-15262)*
Case Construction Inc .... G 302 737-3800
  Newark *(G-10158)*
Custom Cabinet Shop Inc .... F 302 337-8241
  Greenwood *(G-4609)*
D F Quillen & Sons Inc .... E 302 227-2531
  Rehoboth Beach *(G-12709)*
Delaware Brick Company .... E 302 994-0948
  Wilmington *(G-15876)*
Dick Ennis Inc .... G 302 945-2627
  Lewes *(G-5914)*
Dippold Marble Granite .... G 302 324-9101
  Middletown *(G-7062)*
East Coast Minority Supplier .... G 302 656-3337
  Wilmington *(G-16252)*
Erco Ceilings & Interiors Inc .... F 302 398-3200
  Harrington *(G-4767)*
Erco Ceilings & Interiors Inc .... F 302 994-6200
  Wilmington *(G-16455)*
Hickman Overhead Door Company ..... F 302 422-4249
  Milford *(G-7930)*
Home Depot USA Inc .... D 302 735-8864
  Dover *(G-2688)*
Home Depot USA Inc .... C 302 395-1260
  New Castle *(G-9218)*
Home Depot USA Inc .... D 302 838-6818
  Newark *(G-10962)*
Lowes Home Centers LLC .... C 302 697-0700
  Camden *(G-870)*
Lowes Home Centers LLC .... C 302 735-7500
  Dover *(G-2979)*
Lowes Home Centers LLC .... C 302 645-0900
  Lewes *(G-6226)*
Lowes Home Centers LLC .... D 302 376-3006
  Middletown *(G-7315)*
Lowes Home Centers LLC .... D 302 934-3740
  Millsboro *(G-8354)*
Lowes Home Centers LLC .... D 302 252-3228
  New Castle *(G-9328)*
Lowes Home Centers LLC .... C 302 781-1154
  Newark *(G-11291)*
Lowes Home Centers LLC .... D 302 536-4000
  Seaford *(G-13265)*
Lowes Home Centers LLC .... C 302 479-7799
  Wilmington *(G-18013)*
Marjam Supply Co Inc .... F 302 283-1020
  Newark *(G-11332)*
Mark Ventresca Associates Inc .... G 302 239-3925
  Hockessin *(G-5300)*
Mechanics Paradise Inc .... F 302 652-8863
  New Castle *(G-9355)*
Newport Builders & Windowland .... F 302 994-3537
  Wilmington *(G-18632)*
P D Supply Inc .... G 302 655-3358
  Wilmington *(G-18852)*

Precision Door Service .... G 302 343-6394
  Wilmington *(G-19154)*
Ruiz Flooring .... G 302 999-9350
  Wilmington *(G-19588)*
Stanton Door Co Inc .... F 302 731-4167
  Newark *(G-12086)*

5231 Paint, glass, and wallpaper stores

B Frank Shinn Paint Co .... F 302 652-3521
  Wilmington *(G-14701)*
East Coast Minority Supplier .... G 302 656-3337
  Wilmington *(G-16252)*
Interiors By Kim Inc .... G 302 537-2480
  Ocean View *(G-12525)*
Mammeles Inc .... F 302 998-0541
  Wilmington *(G-18097)*
Moorway Painting Management .... G 302 764-5002
  Wilmington *(G-18439)*
Newark Glass & Mirror Inc .... G 302 834-1158
  Bear *(G-394)*

5251 Hardware stores

Allied Lock & Safe Company .... G 302 658-3172
  Wilmington *(G-14381)*
Bawa Inc .... G 302 698-3200
  Dover *(G-1882)*
Baybiw Development LLC .... F 302 537-9700
  Ocean View *(G-12469)*
Bryan & Brittingham Inc .... F 302 846-9500
  Delmar *(G-1569)*
Case Construction Inc .... G 302 737-3800
  Newark *(G-10158)*
D F Quillen & Sons Inc .... E 302 227-2531
  Rehoboth Beach *(G-12709)*
Mechanics Paradise Inc .... F 302 652-8863
  New Castle *(G-9355)*
Suburban Lawn & Equipment Inc .... G 302 475-4300
  Wilmington *(G-20113)*

5261 Retail nurseries and garden stores

Atlantic Tractor LLC .... F 302 834-0114
  Newark *(G-9937)*
Bartons Landscaping/Lawn Inc .... E 302 629-2213
  Seaford *(G-13076)*
Burke Equipment Company .... F 302 697-3200
  Felton *(G-3949)*
Delaware Hardscape Supply LLC .... G 302 996-6464
  Wilmington *(G-15923)*
Delaware Lawn & Tree Service .... F 302 834-7406
  Bear *(G-150)*
Foulk Lawn & Equipment Co Inc .... G 302 475-3233
  Wilmington *(G-16701)*
Green Eyes Landscaping Inc .... G 302 653-3800
  Dover *(G-2623)*
Hockessin Tractor Inc .... G 302 239-4201
  Hockessin *(G-5247)*
Hudson Farm Supply Co Inc .... G 302 398-3654
  Middletown *(G-7219)*
Isaacs Landscaping & Gardening .... G 302 947-1414
  Millsboro *(G-8322)*
Itea Inc .... G 302 328-3716
  Lewes *(G-6133)*
Leons Garden World Ej Inc .... F 410 392-8630
  New Castle *(G-9308)*
Leons Garden World Inc .... E 302 999-9055
  Wilmington *(G-17880)*
Lords Landscaping Inc .... E 302 539-6119
  Millville *(G-8538)*
Old Country Garden Center Inc .... F 302 652-3317
  Wilmington *(G-18754)*
Pughs Service Inc .... F 302 678-2408
  Dover *(G-3394)*

52 BUILDING MATERIALS, HARDWARE, GARDEN SUPPLIES & MOBILE HOMES

Soil Service Inc .... G 302 629-7054
 Seaford (G-13406)
Suburban Lawn & Equipment Inc .... G 302 475-4300
 Wilmington (G-20113)
Talleys Garage Inc .... G 302 652-0463
 Wilmington (G-20214)
Walls Farm and Garden Ctr Inc .... G 302 422-4565
 Milford (G-8137)
Willey Farms Inc .... D 302 378-8441
 Townsend (G-14091)
Woodward Enterprises Inc .... F 302 378-2849
 Middletown (G-7736)

5271 Mobile home dealers

Bayshore Inc .... G 302 539-7200
 Ocean View (G-12470)
Love Creek Marina MBL Hm Site .... F 302 448-6492
 Lewes (G-6225)
Rons Mobile Home Sales Inc .... G 302 398-9166
 Harrington (G-4821)
T & C Enterprise Incorporated .... G 302 934-8080
 Millsboro (G-8479)
Theta Vest Inc .... G 302 227-3745
 Rehoboth Beach (G-12993)

53 GENERAL MERCHANDISE STORES

5311 Department stores

5331 Variety stores

▲ Freds Stores Tennessee Inc .... A 800 746-7287
 Bear (G-237)
◆ Historical Society of Delaware .... E 302 655-7161
 Wilmington (G-17155)
J Nichols Enterprises LLC .... G 302 579-0720
 Dover (G-2759)
▲ Stuart Kingston Inc .... G 302 227-2524
 Rehoboth Beach (G-12978)
Vinisia Inc .... F 252 297-6730
 Dover (G-3799)

5399 Miscellaneous general merchandise

AMC Museum Foundation .... G 302 677-5938
 Dover (G-1782)
Country Store .... G 302 653-5111
 Kenton (G-5452)
Domian International Svc LLC .... G 804 837-3616
 Smyrna (G-13711)

54 FOOD STORES

5411 Grocery stores

Hs Capital LLC .... G 302 598-2961
 Wilmington (G-17223)
J William Gordy Fuel Co .... G 302 846-3425
 Delmar (G-1604)
Newport Ventures Inc .... F 302 998-1693
 Middletown (G-7399)
Peninsula Oil Co Inc .... E 302 422-6491
 Seaford (G-13338)
Service Energy LLC .... D 302 734-7433
 Dover (G-3534)

5421 Meat and fish markets

Febys Fishery Inc .... E 302 998-9501
 Wilmington (G-16566)
▲ Haass Family Butcher Shop .... G 302 734-5447
 Dover (G-2643)
Jabez Corp .... F 302 475-7600
 Wilmington (G-17470)

Lewes Fishhouse & Produce Inc .... E 302 827-4074
 Lewes (G-6196)
Meltrone Inc .... F 302 998-3457
 Wilmington (G-18268)
Seafood City Inc .... G 302 284-8486
 Felton (G-4024)

5431 Fruit and vegetable markets

Willey Farms Inc .... D 302 378-8441
 Townsend (G-14091)

5441 Candy, nut, and confectionery stores

Fishers Popcorn Fenwick LLC .... E 302 539-8833
 Fenwick Island (G-4050)
King of Sweets Inc .... F 302 730-8200
 Dover (G-2873)

5461 Retail bakeries

Kaan Cakes LLC .... G 302 260-0647
 Millsboro (G-8335)
Swami Enterprises Inc .... G 302 999-8077
 Wilmington (G-20168)

5499 Miscellaneous food stores

Fresh Juice Partners LLC .... G 302 364-0909
 Lewes (G-6016)
Hockessin Chrpractic Centre PA .... G 302 239-8550
 Hockessin (G-5241)
Mark JB Inc .... G 888 984-5845
 Newark (G-11336)
Mommas Mountain LLC .... G 410 236-6717
 Magnolia (G-6769)
Petra Investments LLC .... G 312 887-1558
 Newark (G-11674)
Trexgen Nutrascience LLC .... G 302 520-2406
 Newark (G-12219)

55 AUTOMOTIVE DEALERS AND GASOLINE SERVICE STATIONS

5511 New and used car dealers

▼ Bayshore Ford Truck Sales Inc .... D 302 656-3160
 New Castle (G-8853)
Brandywine Chrysler Jeep Dodge .... D 302 998-0458
 Wilmington (G-15050)
Bullfeathers Auto Sound Inc .... G 302 846-0434
 Laurel (G-5475)
Clifton Leasing Co Inc .... E 302 674-2300
 Dover (G-2093)
Delaware Motor Sales Inc .... D 302 656-3100
 Wilmington (G-15945)
Delmarva Pump Center Inc .... F 302 492-1245
 Marydel (G-6796)
Diamond Motor Sports Inc .... D 302 697-3222
 Dover (G-2292)
Diamond State Truck Center LLC .... G 302 275-9050
 New Castle (G-9052)
Donright Services LLC .... G 302 685-7540
 Wilmington (G-16143)
Dover Volkswagen Inc .... E 302 734-4761
 Dover (G-2368)
Future Ford Sales Inc .... D 302 999-0261
 Wilmington (G-16776)
Harvey Mack Sales & Svc Inc .... E 302 324-8340
 New Castle (G-9202)
IG Burton & Company Inc .... D 302 424-3041
 Milford (G-7939)
IG Burton & Company Inc .... D 302 629-2800
 Seaford (G-13219)
IG Burton & Company Inc .... D 302 422-3041
 Milford (G-7938)

Indian River Golf Cars Dr Wldg .... G 302 947-2044
 Millsboro (G-8320)
Lee Mc Neill Associates .... G 302 593-6172
 Wilmington (G-17854)
Martin Dealership .... G 302 738-5200
 Newark (G-11343)
Martin Newark Dealership Inc .... D 302 454-9300
 Newark (G-11345)
NAPA M3 Inc .... G 719 660-6263
 Middletown (G-7392)
New Car Connection .... G 302 328-7000
 New Castle (G-9405)
Noel Auto Sales LLC .... G 302 286-7355
 Newark (G-11561)
Porter Nissan Buick Newark .... E 302 368-6300
 Newark (G-11714)
Richard Addington Co .... G 302 422-2668
 Milford (G-8068)
Smart Professions Inc .... E 603 289-6263
 Dover (G-3576)
Townsend Bros Inc .... F 302 674-0100
 Dover (G-3707)
Wellers Tire Service Inc .... F 302 337-8228
 Bridgeville (G-781)
Willis Ford Inc .... G 302 653-5900
 Smyrna (G-13939)
Winner Ford of Dover Ltd .... B 302 734-0444
 Dover (G-3860)
▼ Winner Ford of Newark Inc .... F 302 731-2415
 Newark (G-12388)
Winner Group Inc .... G 302 764-5900
 Wilmington (G-20860)
Winner Infiniti Inc .... E 302 764-5900
 Wilmington (G-20862)
Winners Circle Inc .... E 302 661-2100
 Wilmington (G-20864)

5521 Used car dealers

Armigers Auto Center Inc .... G 302 875-7642
 Laurel (G-5464)
Automotive Services Inc .... F 302 762-0100
 Wilmington (G-14656)
Brasures Body Shop Inc .... G 302 732-6157
 Frankford (G-4077)
Commonwealth Motor Inc .... G 302 505-5555
 Wilmington (G-15554)
Deals On Wheels Inc .... E 302 999-9955
 Wilmington (G-15845)
Delaware Public Auto Auction .... F 302 656-0500
 New Castle (G-9031)
European Coach Werkes Inc .... G 302 436-2277
 Frankford (G-4106)
Future Ford Sales Inc .... D 302 999-0261
 Wilmington (G-16776)
Lifetime Skills Services LLC .... G 302 378-2911
 Middletown (G-7302)
M L Morris Inc .... G 302 956-0678
 Bridgeville (G-727)
Sports Car Service Inc .... G 302 764-7439
 Wilmington (G-19969)
United Auto Sales Inc .... G 302 325-3000
 Newark (G-12266)
Wolfs Elite Autos .... G 302 999-9199
 Wilmington (G-20877)

5531 Auto and home supply stores

Action Automotive Inc .... G 302 429-0643
 Wilmington (G-14240)
Adams Auto Parts LLC .... F 302 655-9693
 Wilmington (G-14250)
Admiral Tire .... G 302 734-5911
 Dover (G-1718)

Ajacks Tire Service Inc............................. G..... 302 834-5200
  New Castle (G-8776)
Bargain Tire & Service Inc........................ F..... 302 764-8900
  Wilmington (G-14763)
Bill Cannons Garage Inc............................ F..... 302 436-4200
  Selbyville (G-13477)
Boyds Trailor Hitches................................. G..... 302 697-9000
  Camden Wyoming (G-917)
Bridgestone Ret Operations LLC............. G..... 302 734-4522
  Dover (G-1979)
Bridgestone Ret Operations LLC............. G..... 302 422-4508
  Milford (G-7805)
Bridgestone Ret Operations LLC............. G..... 302 656-2529
  New Castle (G-8892)
Bridgestone Ret Operations LLC............. G..... 302 995-2487
  Wilmington (G-15108)
C & W Auto Parts Co Inc.......................... G..... 302 697-2684
  Magnolia (G-6724)
Carl King Tire Co Inc................................ F..... 302 644-4070
  Lewes (G-5802)
Carl King Tire Co Inc................................ E..... 302 697-9506
  Camden (G-803)
Clarksville Auto Service Ctr..................... E..... 302 539-1700
  Ocean View (G-12489)
Delaware Tire Center Inc.......................... F..... 302 674-0234
  Dover (G-2270)
Delaware Tire Center Inc.......................... F..... 302 368-2531
  Newark (G-10492)
Deltrans Inc... G..... 302 453-8213
  Newark (G-10510)
Diamond State Tire Inc............................. G..... 302 836-1919
  Bear (G-168)
Diamond State Truck Center LLC............ G..... 302 275-9050
  New Castle (G-9052)
Dover Automotive Inc............................... G..... 302 653-9234
  Smyrna (G-13714)
Els Tire Service Inc................................... F..... 302 834-1997
  Newark (G-10633)
Fisher Auto Parts Inc................................ G..... 302 934-8088
  Millsboro (G-8291)
Fisher Auto Parts Inc................................ G..... 302 998-3111
  Wilmington (G-16648)
Fishers Auto Parts Inc.............................. G..... 302 934-8088
  Millsboro (G-8292)
Fitzgerald Auto Salvage Inc..................... D..... 302 422-7584
  Lincoln (G-6669)
Furrs Tire Service Inc............................... G..... 302 678-0800
  Dover (G-2546)
Genuine Parts Company........................... G..... 610 494-6355
  Claymont (G-1160)
Goodyear Tire & Rubber Company.......... G..... 302 737-2461
  Newark (G-10869)
Goodyear Tire & Rubber Company.......... G..... 302 998-0428
  Wilmington (G-16929)
IG Burton & Company Inc........................ D..... 302 424-3041
  Milford (G-7939)
Kirkwood Tires Inc.................................... G..... 302 737-2460
  Newark (G-11186)
Monro Inc... G..... 302 846-2732
  Delmar (G-1623)
New Creation Logistics Inc....................... F..... 302 438-3154
  Newark (G-11520)
Ocean Pines Auto Svc Ctr Inc................. F..... 410 641-7800
  Ocean View (G-12554)
Rhino Lnngs Del Auto Style Inc............... F..... 302 368-4660
  Newark (G-11878)
Service Tire Truck Center Inc.................. E..... 302 629-5533
  Seaford (G-13397)
Sports Car Tire Inc................................... E..... 302 571-8473
  Wilmington (G-19970)
▼ T & J Murray Worldwide Svcs............. F..... 302 736-1790
  Dover (G-3637)

Tire Sales & Service Inc........................... F..... 302 658-8955
  Wilmington (G-20335)
Transaxle LLC... G..... 302 322-8300
  New Castle (G-9633)
True Mobility Inc....................................... G..... 302 836-4110
  New Castle (G-9643)
Wellers Tire Service Inc............................ F..... 302 337-8228
  Bridgeville (G-781)
Willis Ford Inc... E..... 302 653-5900
  Smyrna (G-13939)
▼ Winner Ford of Newark Inc................. F..... 302 731-2415
  Newark (G-12388)
Winner Group Inc..................................... F..... 302 292-8200
  Newark (G-12389)
Winner Infiniti Inc..................................... E..... 302 764-5900
  Wilmington (G-20862)
Wreck Masters Demo Derby..................... F..... 302 368-5544
  Bear (G-568)

5541 Gasoline service stations

Air Products and Chemicals Inc............... G..... 302 834-6033
  Delaware City (G-1528)
Careys Inc.. F..... 302 875-5674
  Laurel (G-5478)
Conectiv Energy Supply Inc..................... E..... 302 454-0300
  Wilmington (G-10301)
Eidp Inc.. G..... 302 772-0016
  New Castle (G-9084)
J William Gordy Fuel Co.......................... G..... 302 846-3425
  Delmar (G-1604)
Logue Brothers Inc................................... F..... 302 762-1896
  Wilmington (G-17976)
Manor Exxon Inc....................................... G..... 302 834-6691
  Bear (G-360)
Meadowood Mobil Station........................ G..... 302 731-5602
  Newark (G-11369)
Millcreek Texaco Station.......................... G..... 302 571-8489
  Wilmington (G-18360)
Newport Ventures Inc............................... F..... 302 998-1693
  Middletown (G-7399)
Sals Auto Services Inc............................. G..... 302 654-1168
  Wilmington (G-19640)
Shellhorn & Hill Inc.................................. D..... 302 654-4200
  Wilmington (G-19793)
▲ United Acquisition Corp...................... E..... 302 651-9856
  Wilmington (G-20523)
Walls Service Center Inc.......................... G..... 302 422-8110
  Milford (G-8139)

5551 Boat dealers

Almars Outboard Service & Sls................ G..... 302 328-8541
  Historic New Castle (G-4928)
Bobs Marine Service Inc........................... F..... 302 539-3711
  Ocean View (G-12482)
▼ Eastern Group Inc............................... E..... 302 737-6603
  Newark (G-10594)
North Bay Marina Incorporated............... E..... 302 436-4211
  Selbyville (G-13586)
Rudy Marine Inc.. F..... 302 999-8735
  Dagsboro (G-1501)

5561 Recreational vehicle dealers

Delmarva Rv Center Inc........................... E..... 302 424-4505
  Milford (G-7863)

5571 Motorcycle dealers

Commonwealth Motor Inc......................... G..... 302 505-5555
  Wilmington (G-15554)
NAPA M3 Inc.. G..... 719 660-6263
  Middletown (G-7392)
Rommel Cycles LLC.................................. E..... 302 658-8800
  Smyrna (G-13869)

Walls Farm and Garden Ctr Inc............... G..... 302 422-4565
  Milford (G-8137)

5599 Automotive dealers, nec

Avacore LLC.. G..... 302 327-8830
  Wilmington (G-14661)
Dimo Corp.. E..... 302 324-8100
  New Castle (G-9056)
Utility/Stern Shore Trlr Sls I.................... G..... 302 337-7400
  Bridgeville (G-779)

56 APPAREL AND ACCESSORY STORES

5611 Men's and boys' clothing stores

Dads Workwear Inc................................... G..... 302 663-0068
  Laurel (G-5491)
Designer Braids and Trade....................... G..... 718 783-9078
  Middletown (G-7055)
Oluwaseyi David Popoola......................... G..... 302 331-3684
  Dover (G-3221)
Private Society LLC.................................. G..... 302 319-7126
  Newark (G-11753)

5621 Women's clothing stores

Boutique The Bridal Ltd........................... G..... 302 335-5948
  Milford (G-7800)
Bridal & Tuxedo Outlet Inc...................... G..... 302 731-8802
  Newark (G-10084)
Designer Braids and Trade....................... G..... 718 783-9078
  Middletown (G-7055)
Garage.. G..... 302 453-1930
  Newark (G-10807)
Golden Jewelry.. G..... 302 777-2121
  Wilmington (G-16913)
Ukap Trading LLC..................................... F..... 617 447-6490
  Dover (G-3743)

5632 Women's accessory and specialty stores

Bethany Sea-Crest Inc............................. G..... 302 539-7621
  Bethany Beach (G-586)
Danceworks.. G..... 302 286-1492
  Newark (G-10385)
Garage.. G..... 302 453-1930
  Newark (G-10807)
Stackd Studio LLC.................................... G..... 240 304-1085
  Newark (G-12081)
Victorias Secret Stores LLC..................... G..... 302 644-1035
  Rehoboth Beach (G-13003)

5641 Children's and infants' wear stores

Carters Inc... G..... 302 731-1432
  Newark (G-10156)

5651 Family clothing stores

Delave Denim Co LLC............................... G..... 302 308-5161
  Dover (G-2215)
Garage.. G..... 302 453-1930
  Newark (G-10807)
Johns El Family Industries Inc................ G..... 310 701-5678
  Lewes (G-6149)
Middle Room LLC...................................... G..... 302 220-9979
  New Castle (G-9369)
On Glo LLC.. G..... 205 567-3434
  Dover (G-3226)
Royalrose302 LLC..................................... G..... 800 259-7918
  New Castle (G-9547)
True Religion Apparel Inc........................ G..... 302 894-9425
  Newark (G-12241)

Employee Codes: A=Over 500 employees, B=251-500
C=101-250, D=51-100, E=20-50, F=10-19, G=1-9

56 APPAREL AND ACCESSORY STORES

5661 Shoe stores

◆ Chick Harness & Supply Inc............E 302 398-4748
   Harrington (G-4748)
Elite Feet LLC.....................................G 302 464-1028
   Middletown (G-7094)
Rare Royals Incorporated..................G 833 288-7171
   Middletown (G-7502)

5699 Miscellaneous apparel and accessories

Be Blessed Design Group LLC...........G 302 561-3793
   Bear (G-59)
Body Double Swimwear......................G 302 537-1444
   Selbyville (G-13479)
Candlelight Bridal Formal Tlrg...........G 302 934-8009
   Millsboro (G-8215)
◆ Chick Harness & Supply Inc............E 302 398-4630
   Harrington (G-4748)
Formal Affairs Inc..............................G 302 737-1519
   Newark (G-10765)
▲ Francis Enterprises LLC..................F 302 276-1316
   Historic New Castle (G-4991)
◆ Huzala Inc..G 313 404-6941
   Newark (G-10987)
Lids Corporation................................G 302 736-8465
   Dover (G-2939)
Rockeias Journey LLC.......................G 302 304-3055
   Newark (G-11903)
Slater Fireplaces Inc..........................G 302 999-1200
   Wilmington (G-19861)

57 HOME FURNITURE, FURNISHINGS AND EQUIPMENT STORES

5712 Furniture stores

Able Whelling and Machiene..............G 302 436-1929
   Selbyville (G-13458)
Callaway Furniture Inc.......................G 302 398-8858
   Harrington (G-4745)
Carolina Street Garden & Home........G 302 539-2405
   Fenwick Island (G-4043)
Couture Denim LLC..........................G 302 220-8339
   New Castle (G-8983)
Eastern Shore Porch Patio Inc...........E 302 436-9520
   Selbyville (G-13528)
Furniture Whl Connection Inc............F 302 836-6000
   Bear (G-241)
G2 Group Inc....................................G 302 836-4202
   Bear (G-244)
Group Three Inc................................G 302 658-4158
   Wilmington (G-16988)
▲ Johnny Janosik Inc........................C 302 875-5955
   Laurel (G-5537)
Kenton Chair Shop.............................F 302 653-2411
   Clayton (G-1381)
Mattress Firm Milford........................G 302 422-6585
   Milford (G-7990)
Plushbeds Inc....................................G 888 758-7423
   Wilmington (G-19082)
Rite Way Distributors........................E 302 535-8507
   Felton (G-4017)
W B Mason Co Inc............................G 888 926-2766
   Newark (G-12340)

5713 Floor covering stores

A + Floor Store Inc............................G 302 698-2166
   Camden Wyoming (G-903)
Anderson Floor Coverings Inc...........F 302 227-3244
   Rehoboth Beach (G-12604)
Art Floor Inc......................................F 302 636-9201
   Wilmington (G-14560)

Brasures Carpet Care Inc..................G 302 436-5652
   Selbyville (G-13483)
Brasures Pest Control Inc..................E 302 436-8140
   Selbyville (G-13484)
Callaway Furniture Inc......................G 302 398-8858
   Harrington (G-4745)
Connolly Flooring Inc........................E 302 996-9470
   Wilmington (G-15605)
Delaware Rug Co Inc.........................G 302 998-8881
   Wilmington (G-15963)
Edwards Paul Crpt Installation..........G 302 672-7847
   Dover (G-2427)
Interiors By Kim Inc..........................G 302 537-2480
   Ocean View (G-12525)
L & L Carpet Discount Ctrs Inc.........G 302 292-3712
   Newark (G-11205)
Pala Tile & Carpet Contrs Inc............E 302 652-4500
   Wilmington (G-18865)
Proclean Inc......................................E 302 656-8080
   Delaware City (G-1554)
Reiver Hyman & Co Inc.....................G 302 764-2040
   Wilmington (G-19419)
▲ Stuart Kingston Inc........................G 302 227-2524
   Rehoboth Beach (G-12978)

5719 Miscellaneous homefurnishings

Colonial Electric Supply Co...............F 302 998-9993
   Historic New Castle (G-4960)
Denney Electric Supply Del Inc.........G 302 934-8885
   Millsboro (G-8270)
Led Company Intl Llc........................F 302 668-8370
   Wilmington (G-17850)
Light Action Inc..................................F 302 328-7800
   Wilmington (G-17908)
Rementer Brothers Inc......................G 302 249-4250
   Milton (G-8695)
Slater Fireplaces Inc..........................G 302 999-1200
   Wilmington (G-19861)
Walls Farm and Garden Ctr Inc.........G 302 422-4565
   Milford (G-8137)

5722 Household appliance stores

ABC Sales & Service Inc...................F 302 652-3683
   Wilmington (G-14196)
C B Joe TV & Appliances Inc............G 302 322-7600
   New Castle (G-8907)
Del-Mar Appliance of Delaware........G 302 674-2414
   Dover (G-2211)
Hawkins & Sons Inc..........................G 302 426-9290
   Wilmington (G-17078)
Hayes Sewing Machine Co Inc..........G 302 764-9033
   Wilmington (G-17081)
Interiors By Kim Inc..........................G 302 537-2480
   Ocean View (G-12525)
Johns Washer Repair........................G 302 792-2333
   Claymont (G-1199)
Lowes Home Centers LLC................C 302 697-0700
   Camden (G-870)
Lowes Home Centers LLC................C 302 735-7500
   Dover (G-2979)
Lowes Home Centers LLC................C 302 645-0900
   Lewes (G-6226)
Lowes Home Centers LLC................D 302 376-3006
   Middletown (G-7315)
Lowes Home Centers LLC................D 302 934-3740
   Millsboro (G-8354)
Lowes Home Centers LLC................D 302 252-3228
   New Castle (G-9328)
Lowes Home Centers LLC................C 302 781-1154
   Newark (G-11291)
Lowes Home Centers LLC................D 302 536-4000
   Seaford (G-13265)

Lowes Home Centers LLC................C 302 479-7799
   Wilmington (G-18013)
Master Klean Company......................G 302 539-4290
   Ocean View (G-12543)
Schagrin Gas Co................................E 302 378-2000
   Middletown (G-7541)
Williams Appliancee..........................F 302 656-8581
   Wilmington (G-20797)

5731 Radio, television, and electronic stores

Avokadio Inc......................................G 302 291-4080
   Lewes (G-5726)
C B Joe TV & Appliances Inc............G 302 322-7600
   New Castle (G-8907)
Cameras Etc Inc................................F 302 764-9400
   Wilmington (G-15206)
Delmarva Communications Inc.........F 302 324-1230
   New Castle (G-9042)
G & S TV & Antenna..........................G 302 422-5733
   Milford (G-7905)
Redi Call Corp....................................F 302 856-9000
   Georgetown (G-4482)
Video Den...G 302 628-9835
   Seaford (G-13441)

5734 Computer and software stores

Altr Solutions LLC.............................F 888 757-2587
   Dover (G-1777)
Antenna House Inc............................G 302 566-7225
   Newark (G-9876)
Bits & Bytes Inc.................................G 302 674-2999
   Dover (G-1942)
Creative Micro Designs Inc...............G 302 456-5800
   Newark (G-10349)
Dignisys Inc......................................F 845 213-1121
   Dover (G-2298)
Ezdorms Inc......................................F 202 599-2953
   Wilmington (G-16517)
Famoid Technology LLC....................G 530 601-7284
   Newark (G-10710)
Gamestop Inc....................................F 302 266-7362
   Newark (G-10805)
Gro-Connectcom Inc.........................G 347 918-7437
   Lewes (G-6066)
Harrock Properties LLC....................G 302 202-1321
   Dover (G-2657)
Laser Images of Delaware Inc...........G 302 836-8610
   Bear (G-338)
Load Miles Inc...................................F 323 842-7038
   Dover (G-2965)
Mtc Usa LLC......................................F 980 999-8888
   Newark (G-11468)
Nerdit Now LLC.................................F 302 482-5979
   Wilmington (G-18587)
Opti-Mag Inc......................................G 302 738-2903
   Newark (G-11596)
PC Supplies Inc.................................G 302 368-4800
   Newark (G-11648)
Quinn Data Corporation....................G 302 429-7450
   Wilmington (G-19295)
Response Computer Group Inc.........F 302 335-3400
   Milford (G-8063)
Ryzenlink Technologies LLC.............G 786 536-0349
   Hockessin (G-5376)
SE Gaming Services Inc....................E 303 867-8090
   Newark (G-11966)
Software Services of De Inc..............E 302 654-3172
   Wilmington (G-19915)
Stylere LLC.......................................F 650 206-7721
   Dover (G-3618)
Tamp Inc..F 302 283-9195
   Newark (G-12158)

SIC SECTION

59 MISCELLANEOUS RETAIL

Tower Business Machines Inc	G	302 395-1445
Historic New Castle *(G-5088)*		
Wherebyus Enterprises Inc	F	305 988-0808
Claymont *(G-1336)*		

5735 Record and prerecorded tape stores

Video Den	G	302 628-9835
Seaford *(G-13441)*		
Video Scene of Delaware Inc	G	302 678-8526
Dover *(G-3793)*		

5736 Musical instrument stores

Earle Teate Music	G	302 736-1937
Dover *(G-2406)*		
Flute Pro Shop Inc	G	302 479-5000
Wilmington *(G-16676)*		

58 EATING AND DRINKING PLACES

5812 Eating places

1000 Degrees Pizzeria	F	609 382-3022
Wilmington *(G-14101)*		
Acosh Enterprise LLC	G	631 767-4501
Newark *(G-9758)*		
Baynum Enterprises Inc	E	302 875-4477
Laurel *(G-5467)*		
Baynum Enterprises Inc	E	302 934-8699
Millsboro *(G-8183)*		
Baynum Enterprises Inc	D	302 629-6104
Seaford *(G-13078)*		
Baywood Greens Golf Club	E	302 947-9225
Millsboro *(G-8186)*		
Bbdotq USA Inc	C	302 533-6589
Newark *(G-9999)*		
Blue Hen Hospitality LLC	F	302 530-5066
Wilmington *(G-14968)*		
Boardwalk Plaza Incorporated	E	302 227-0441
Rehoboth Beach *(G-12648)*		
Butler Hospitality LLC	D	888 288-5846
Wilmington *(G-15161)*		
Camels Hump Inc	F	302 227-5719
Rehoboth Beach *(G-12662)*		
Chuck Lager LLC	D	302 482-1773
Wilmington *(G-15428)*		
Coastal Properties I LLC	E	302 227-5800
Rehoboth Beach *(G-12686)*		
Country Villa Motel	G	814 938-8330
Milford *(G-7842)*		
D&C Concepts LLC	F	770 335-2503
Wilmington *(G-15763)*		
De Catering Inc	E	302 607-7200
Wilmington *(G-15837)*		
Delaware Beer Works Inc	E	302 836-2739
Bear *(G-142)*		
Delcastle Golf Club Management	F	302 998-9505
Wilmington *(G-15988)*		
Diamond State Pty Rentl & Sls	G	302 777-6677
Wilmington *(G-16057)*		
Dogfish Head Inc	F	302 226-2739
Rehoboth Beach *(G-12730)*		
Efficient Services Inc	G	302 629-2124
Seaford *(G-13171)*		
Estia Hospitality Group Inc	G	302 798-5319
Claymont *(G-1136)*		
Febys Fishery Inc	E	302 998-9501
Wilmington *(G-16566)*		
First State Bowling Center	G	302 762-3883
Wilmington *(G-16625)*		
First State Brewing Co LLC	E	302 285-9535
Middletown *(G-7131)*		

Fresh Juice Partners LLC	G	302 364-0909
Lewes *(G-6016)*		
Greenville Country Club Inc	E	302 652-3255
Wilmington *(G-16973)*		
Harrington Raceway Inc	D	302 398-5346
Harrington *(G-4780)*		
Hollywood Grill Restaurant	D	302 655-1348
Wilmington *(G-17171)*		
Jbs Kitchen LLC	G	302 487-3830
New Castle *(G-9256)*		
Kaan Cakes LLC	G	302 260-0647
Millsboro *(G-8335)*		
Kohr Brothers Inc	E	302 227-9354
Rehoboth Beach *(G-12825)*		
Leounes Catered Affairs	G	302 547-3233
Wilmington *(G-17882)*		
Lilian USA LLC	F	800 246-2677
Wilmington *(G-17912)*		
M & P Adventures Inc	G	302 645-6271
Lewes *(G-6232)*		
Newark Country Club	D	302 368-7008
Newark *(G-11532)*		
Nicola Pizza Inc	E	302 227-6211
Lewes *(G-6314)*		
Oceanside Seafood Mkt Deli LLC	F	302 313-5158
Lewes *(G-6330)*		
Pagoda Hotel Inc	F	808 922-1233
Historic New Castle *(G-5045)*		
Point Coffee Shop and Bakery	F	302 260-9734
Rehoboth Beach *(G-12894)*		
Premium Brands Inc	G	925 566-8863
Dover *(G-3364)*		
Routzhan Jessman	E	302 398-4206
Harrington *(G-4822)*		
Seafood City Inc	G	302 284-8486
Felton *(G-4024)*		
Swami Enterprises Inc	G	302 999-8077
Wilmington *(G-20168)*		
University Whist CLB of Wlmngt	E	302 658-5125
Wilmington *(G-20534)*		
Venus On Halfshell	G	302 227-9292
Dewey Beach *(G-1676)*		
Vincenza & Margherita Bistro	F	302 479-7999
Wilmington *(G-20625)*		
Wilmington Country Club	C	302 655-6171
Wilmington *(G-20813)*		

5813 Drinking places

Camels Hump Inc	F	302 227-5719
Rehoboth Beach *(G-12662)*		
Country Villa Motel	G	814 938-8330
Milford *(G-7842)*		
Delcastle Golf Club Management	F	302 998-9505
Wilmington *(G-15988)*		
Dewey Beer & Food Company LLC	F	302 227-1182
Dewey Beach *(G-1668)*		
First State Bowling Center	G	302 762-3883
Wilmington *(G-16625)*		
First State Brewing Co LLC	E	302 285-9535
Middletown *(G-7131)*		
Harrington Raceway Inc	D	302 398-5346
Harrington *(G-4780)*		
Hollywood Grill Restaurant	D	302 655-1348
Wilmington *(G-17171)*		
Millsboro Lanes Inc	F	302 934-0400
Millsboro *(G-8387)*		
Sinkeeas Lounge & Bar LLC	F	302 434-2530
Newark *(G-12013)*		
Wilmington Country Club	C	302 655-6171
Wilmington *(G-20813)*		

59 MISCELLANEOUS RETAIL

5921 Liquor stores

| Pizzadili Partners LLC | G | 302 284-9463 |
| Felton *(G-4009)* | | |

5932 Used merchandise stores

Black Gods and Goddess LLC	G	708 665-0949
Dover *(G-1943)*		
Fred Drake Automotive Inc	G	302 378-4877
Townsend *(G-14003)*		
Goodeals Inc	G	302 999-1737
Wilmington *(G-16924)*		
Goodwill Inds Del Del Cnty Inc	E	302 761-4640
Wilmington *(G-16927)*		
Houston Self Storage	G	302 422-9660
Houston *(G-5444)*		
Yental Empire LLC	G	404 423-0454
Middletown *(G-7745)*		

5941 Sporting goods and bicycle shops

Baywood Greens Golf Club	E	302 947-9225
Millsboro *(G-8186)*		
Bethany Cycle & Fitness Inc	G	302 537-9982
Bethany Beach *(G-584)*		
Carmalt Stuart LLC	G	302 366-8920
Newark *(G-10149)*		
◆ Chick Harness & Supply Inc	E	302 398-4630
Harrington *(G-4748)*		
Midway Fitness Center	G	302 645-0407
Rehoboth Beach *(G-12856)*		
Millers Gun Center Inc	G	302 328-9747
New Castle *(G-9371)*		
Noble Eagle Sales LLC	G	302 736-5166
Dover *(G-3191)*		
Old Inlet Bait and Tackle Inc	F	302 227-7974
Rehoboth Beach *(G-12878)*		
Pike Creek Bike Line Inc	G	610 747-1200
Wilmington *(G-19038)*		
Pleasant Hill Lanes Inc	F	302 998-8811
Wilmington *(G-19077)*		
Police & Fire Rod & Gun Club	G	302 655-0304
New Castle *(G-9481)*		
◆ Rukket LLC	F	855 478-5538
Wilmington *(G-19589)*		
Scuba World Inc	G	302 698-1117
Dover *(G-3522)*		
Shooters Choice Inc	G	302 736-5166
Dover *(G-3548)*		
South Shore Provisions LLC	G	443 614-2442
Selbyville *(G-13607)*		
Summit North Marina	F	302 836-1800
Bear *(G-517)*		
Wilmington Country Club	C	302 655-6171
Wilmington *(G-20813)*		

5942 Book stores

Biblion	G	302 644-2210
Lewes *(G-5762)*		
Prestwick House Inc	E	302 659-2070
Smyrna *(G-13854)*		
Wellthy Investors LLC	G	267 847-3486
Dover *(G-3831)*		

5943 Stationery stores

Creative Promotions	G	302 697-7896
Camden *(G-809)*		
Fulton Paper Company	F	302 594-0400
Wilmington *(G-16770)*		
Henninger Printing Co Inc	G	302 934-8119
Millsboro *(G-8317)*		

5944 Jewelry stores

Employee Codes: A=Over 500 employees, B=251-500
C=101-250, D=51-100, E=20-50, F=10-19, G=1-9

2024 Harris Directory of Delaware Businesses

59 MISCELLANEOUS RETAIL

Alex and Ani LLC .... G 302 731-1420
   Newark (G-9808)
Alex and Ani LLC .... G 302 227-7360
   Rehoboth Beach (G-12600)
Bridgewater Jewelers .... G 302 328-2101
   Historic New Castle (G-4945)
Continental Jewelers Inc .... G 302 475-2000
   Wilmington (G-15620)
Del Haven of Wilmington Inc .... G 302 999-9040
   Newark (G-10411)
First State Coin Co .... G 302 734-7776
   Dover (G-2500)
Golden Jewelry .... G 302 777-2121
   Wilmington (G-16913)
Marches Jewelers Inc .... G 856 858-4463
   Lewes (G-6241)
Michael Gallagher Jewelers .... G 302 836-2925
   Bear (G-375)
Nanticoke River Arts Council .... G 302 628-2787
   Seaford (G-13309)
Precision Jewelry Inc .... G 302 422-7138
   Milford (G-8051)
Stuart Kingston Galleries Inc .... G 302 652-7978
   Wilmington (G-20104)
T K O Designs Inc .... G 302 539-6992
   Bethany Beach (G-645)
Turquoise Shop Inc .... F 302 366-7448
   Newark (G-12248)
Whittens Fine Jewelry .... G 302 995-7464
   Wilmington (G-20774)
Wholesale Jewelry Outlet Inc .... G 302 994-5114
   Wilmington (G-20775)

5945 Hobby, toy, and game shops

▼ Aero-Marine Laminates Inc .... F 302 628-3944
   Seaford (G-13051)
Days of Knights .... G 302 366-0963
   Newark (G-10393)
Gamestop Inc .... F 302 266-7362
   Newark (G-10805)

5946 Camera and photographic supply stores

Cameras Etc Inc .... G 302 453-9400
   Newark (G-10124)
Cameras Etc Inc .... F 302 764-9400
   Wilmington (G-15206)

5947 Gift, novelty, and souvenir shop

Bethany Sea-Crest Inc .... G 302 539-7621
   Bethany Beach (G-586)
Casual Colors Inc .... G 302 298-0523
   Wilmington (G-15272)
Forever Inc .... G 302 594-0400
   Wilmington (G-16692)
Fulton Paper Company .... F 302 594-0400
   Wilmington (G-16770)
Good Samaritan Aid .... G 302 875-2425
   Laurel (G-5522)
Henninger Printing Co Inc .... G 302 934-8119
   Millsboro (G-8317)
Jdjs LLC .... E 844 967-3748
   Georgetown (G-4380)
Junior Bd of Christiana Care .... G 302 733-1100
   Newark (G-11137)
Old Country Garden Center Inc .... F 302 652-3317
   Wilmington (G-18754)
Sea Shell Shop Inc .... F 302 227-4323
   Rehoboth Beach (G-12950)
Self Care Holistic LLC .... G 302 407-2456
   Wilmington (G-19744)

Stuart Kingston Galleries Inc .... G 302 652-7978
   Wilmington (G-20104)
Studio B Milford LLC .... G 302 491-7910
   Milford (G-8106)

5949 Sewing, needlework, and piece goods

Hayes Sewing Machine Co Inc .... G 302 764-9033
   Wilmington (G-17081)
Loomcraft Textile & Supply Co .... F 302 454-3232
   Newark (G-11281)

5961 Catalog and mail-order houses

2yum Inc .... G 626 420-4851
   Dover (G-1684)
Arklight Arsenal LLC .... G 844 722-3766
   Dover (G-1814)
Atlas Beauty LLC .... G 904 382-3487
   Dover (G-1850)
Brysk Inc .... F 224 508-9542
   Wilmington (G-15138)
Canadian Sunpal Power LLC .... G 905 926-6681
   Lewes (G-5788)
Carzaty Inc .... F 650 396-0144
   Dover (G-2033)
▲ Cedar Lane Inc .... F 302 328-7232
   Historic New Castle (G-4953)
Chpter Holdings Inc .... F 650 223-1786
   Wilmington (G-15393)
Click2buy LLC .... G 347 698-7660
   Dover (G-2092)
Dakk Holdings LLC .... G 571 335-7844
   Dover (G-2186)
Dell Oem Inc .... G 302 294-0060
   Newark (G-10498)
DOT Matrix Inc .... G 917 657-4918
   Dover (G-2329)
F D Hammond Enterprises Inc .... F 302 424-8455
   Milford (G-7886)
Faithful Servant Inc .... G 302 597-6387
   Dover (G-2480)
Floor Guy Supply LLC .... G 302 325-3801
   New Castle (G-9137)
Jiffyshirtscom (us) LP .... F 302 319-2063
   Wilmington (G-17546)
Joolala LLC .... E 302 444-0178
   Newark (G-11124)
Kdg Solutions LLC .... G 302 494-4693
   Smyrna (G-13786)
Kintyre Solutions Inc .... G 888 636-0010
   Wilmington (G-17729)
Lamer Group LLC .... G 302 893-0500
   Wilmington (G-17794)
Lkb Management Group LLC .... G 919 561-2815
   Dover (G-2961)
Loadbalancerorginc .... G 888 867-9504
   Wilmington (G-17966)
Manners Brand LLC .... G 470 830-1114
   Dover (G-3009)
Mellon Care Inc .... G 800 406-0281
   Middletown (G-7339)
Mommas Mountain LLC .... G 410 236-6717
   Magnolia (G-6769)
Mymoroccanbazar Inc .... G 323 238-5747
   Newark (G-11478)
Netatmo LLC .... G 302 703-7680
   Wilmington (G-18591)
Nickles Arcade LLC .... F 302 376-1794
   Middletown (G-7406)
Opti-Mag Inc .... G 302 738-2903
   Newark (G-11596)
Rockeias Journey LLC .... G 302 304-3055
   Newark (G-11903)

Rs Marks Inc .... G 302 478-4371
   Wilmington (G-19579)
Safe Home Control .... F 302 401-4379
   Wilmington (G-19624)
Sqs Global Solutions LLC .... F 302 691-9682
   Wilmington (G-19984)
Tjs & Associates LLC .... E 302 563-5593
   Middletown (G-7647)
Villa Cotton Corporation .... F 302 439-1508
   Wilmington (G-20619)
Wna Infotech LLC .... E 302 668-5977
   Newark (G-12392)

5962 Merchandising machine operators

Cafection Corp .... G 800 561-6162
   Newark (G-10118)
Columbia Vending Service Inc .... F 302 856-7000
   Delmar (G-1582)
Efficient Services Inc .... G 302 629-2124
   Seaford (G-13171)
Optima Iq Investments Inc .... E 302 279-5750
   Middletown (G-7417)
Take-A-Break Inc .... E 302 658-8571
   Wilmington (G-20209)
Vending Solutions LLC .... G 302 674-2222
   Dover (G-3781)

5963 Direct selling establishments

Baby Apron LLC .... G 800 796-4406
   Claymont (G-1050)
Corn Exchange LLC .... G 302 747-8752
   Wyoming (G-20982)
Stuart Kingston Galleries Inc .... G 302 652-7978
   Wilmington (G-20104)
Sunshine Vending Machines LLC .... G 800 670-6557
   Wilmington (G-20137)
Take-A-Break Inc .... E 302 658-8571
   Wilmington (G-20209)

5983 Fuel oil dealers

Burns & McBride Inc .... D 302 656-5110
   New Castle (G-8901)
C L Burchenal Oil Co Inc .... G 302 697-1517
   Camden (G-798)
Clark Services Inc Delaware .... G 302 834-0556
   Bear (G-109)
Conectiv Energy Supply Inc .... E 302 454-0300
   Newark (G-10301)
Foraker Oil Inc .... G 302 834-7595
   Delaware City (G-1541)
Hillside Oil Company Inc .... E 302 738-4144
   Newark (G-10953)
Schlosser Assoc Mech Cntrs Inc .... E 302 738-7333
   Newark (G-11958)
Service Energy LLC .... F 302 645-9050
   Lewes (G-6460)
Service Energy LLC .... D 302 734-7433
   Dover (G-3534)
Shellhorn & Hill Inc .... D 302 654-4200
   Wilmington (G-19793)
Wilkins Fuel Co .... G 302 422-5597
   Milford (G-8149)

5984 Liquefied petroleum gas dealers

Keen Compressed Gas Co .... E 302 594-4545
   New Castle (G-9276)
Pep-Up Inc .... G 302 645-2600
   Rehoboth Beach (G-12888)
Pep-Up Inc .... F 302 856-2555
   Georgetown (G-4460)
▲ Petroleum Equipment Inc .... E 302 734-7433
   Dover (G-3307)

Schagrin Gas Co .... E 302 378-2000
  Middletown (G-7541)

5992 Florists

Kirks Flowers Inc .... G 302 737-3931
  Newark (G-11181)
Lakeside Greenhouses Inc .... G 302 875-2457
  Laurel (G-5544)
Self Care Holistic LLC .... G 302 407-2456
  Wilmington (G-19744)
Village Green Inc .... E 302 764-2234
  New Castle (G-9671)

5993 Tobacco stores and stands

Cigarette City Inc .... F 302 836-4889
  Newark (G-10242)
Guy & Lady Barrel LLC .... G 302 399-3069
  Dover (G-2635)
Pure Shaka LLC .... G 302 438-7105
  Wilmington (G-19261)

5995 Optical goods stores

Jim Knnas Optmtrsts Optcans In .... F 302 722-6197
  Newark (G-11112)
Jim Knnas Optmtrsts Optcans In .... G 302 722-6197
  Wilmington (G-17549)

5999 Miscellaneous retail stores, nec

A Plus Electric & Security .... G 302 455-1725
  Newark (G-9726)
A V C Inc .... G 302 227-2549
  Rehoboth Beach (G-12593)
A V Resources Inc .... G 302 994-1488
  Wilmington (G-14174)
Actors Attic .... G 302 734-8214
  Dover (G-1714)
American Homepatient Inc .... E 302 454-4941
  Newark (G-9845)
Analyttica Datalab Inc .... E 917 300-3325
  Wilmington (G-14467)
Avkin Inc .... F 302 562-7468
  Wilmington (G-14673)
B Merit Co .... F 888 263-7481
  Dover (G-1863)
Bryan & Brittingham Inc .... F 302 846-9500
  Delmar (G-1569)
Cannon Spas .... G 302 628-9404
  Seaford (G-13101)
Cannons Cake and Candy Sups .... G 302 738-3321
  Newark (G-10129)
Carol Boyd Heron .... G 302 645-0551
  Lewes (G-5803)
Cecil Vault & Memorial Co Inc .... G 302 994-3806
  Wilmington (G-15293)
Chesapeake Rehab Equipment Inc .... G 302 266-6234
  Newark (G-10198)
Clarks Swimming Pools Inc .... G 302 629-8835
  Seaford (G-13123)
Coastal Sun Roms Prch Enclsres .... G 302 537-3679
  Frankford (G-4092)
Collins Mechanical Inc .... E 302 398-8877
  Harrington (G-4752)
Crossroads Wireless Holdg LLC .... F 405 946-1200
  Wilmington (G-15715)
Denney Electric Supply Del Inc .... G 302 934-8885
  Millsboro (G-8270)
Dentsply Sirona Inc .... G 302 422-4511
  Milford (G-7867)
Designer Braids and Trade .... G 718 783-9078
  Middletown (G-7055)
Digibox LLC .... G 302 203-0088
  Dover (G-2296)

Dover Pool & Patio Center Inc .... F 302 346-7665
  Dover (G-2361)
Dp Fire & Safety Inc .... F 302 998-5430
  Wilmington (G-16159)
Elgood Solutions Inc .... G 610 420-7207
  Camden (G-829)
Enterprise Flasher Co Inc .... E 302 999-0856
  Wilmington (G-16433)
Excel Business Systems Inc .... E 302 453-1500
  Newark (G-10683)
Famglam LLC .... F 302 930-0026
  Ellendale (G-3917)
▲ Farmers Harvest Inc .... G 302 734-7708
  Dover (G-2486)
First State Coin Co .... G 302 734-7776
  Dover (G-2500)
Fscom Inc .... D 888 468-7419
  Historic New Castle (G-4994)
Fur Baby .... G 302 725-5078
  Milford (G-7904)
Girley Bells LLC .... G 347 922-6398
  Newark (G-10839)
◆ Graver Technologies LLC .... C 302 731-1700
  Newark (G-10883)
Gray Audograph Agency Inc .... F 302 658-1700
  New Castle (G-9176)
Haloali Teeth Whitening LLC .... G 302 300-4042
  Claymont (G-1174)
Happily Active LLC .... G 307 317-7277
  Wilmington (G-17053)
Hardwood Direct LLC .... G 302 378-3692
  Middletown (G-7196)
Hearsay Services of Delaware .... G 302 422-3312
  Milford (G-7925)
Henninger Printing Co Inc .... G 302 934-8119
  Millsboro (G-8317)
Hoosier Osteotronix Corp .... G 410 241-7627
  Rehoboth Beach (G-12791)
HP Motors Inc .... G 302 368-4543
  Newark (G-10981)
Hustleofficial247 LLC .... G 302 465-8965
  Dover (G-2708)
Hydroseeding Company LLC .... E 302 815-6500
  Greenwood (G-4638)
Interdgital Communications Inc .... D 610 878-7800
  Wilmington (G-17379)
Interdigital Inc .... E 302 281-3600
  Wilmington (G-17380)
Interdigital Wireless Inc .... E 302 281-3600
  Wilmington (G-17381)
Jdjs LLC .... E 844 967-3748
  Georgetown (G-4380)
Key-Tel Communications Inc .... G 302 475-3066
  Wilmington (G-17702)
Lawall Prsthtics - Orthtics In .... F 302 427-3668
  Wilmington (G-17834)
Local Mobile LLC .... F 619 759-0114
  Dover (G-2967)
Mark JB Inc .... G 888 984-5845
  Newark (G-11336)
Marosa Surgical Industries .... F 302 674-0907
  New Castle (G-9349)
Mellon Care Inc .... G 800 406-0281
  Middletown (G-7339)
Mid Atlntic Scientific Svc Inc .... G 302 328-4440
  New Castle (G-9367)
Mtrigger LLC .... G 302 502-7262
  Newark (G-11470)
Nanticoke River Arts Council .... G 302 628-2787
  Seaford (G-13309)
Nerdit Now LLC .... F 302 482-5979
  Wilmington (G-18587)

Newark Kubota Inc .... F 302 365-6000
  Newark (G-11540)
Power Trans Inc .... F 302 337-3016
  Bridgeville (G-753)
Prestige Powder Inc .... G 302 737-7086
  Newark (G-11735)
Purushas Picks Inc .... G 302 918-7663
  Bear (G-442)
Qoe Inc .... G 302 455-1234
  Newark (G-11783)
Quinn-Miller Group Inc .... F 302 738-9742
  Wilmington (G-19296)
Rawr Imports Group LLC .... G 609 271-3455
  Claymont (G-1274)
Redgate Tech Inc .... G 302 377-6563
  Wilmington (G-19388)
Roys Electrical Service Inc .... G 302 674-3199
  Cheswold (G-989)
Sally Beauty Supply LLC .... G 302 629-5160
  Seaford (G-13383)
Schillng-Dglas Schl Hair Dsign .... F 737 510-0101
  Newark (G-11957)
Short Funeral Home Inc .... G 302 846-9814
  Delmar (G-1636)
▲ Stuart Kingston Inc .... G 302 227-2524
  Rehoboth Beach (G-12978)
Swift Pools Inc .... E 302 738-9800
  Newark (G-12142)
Tee Pees From Rattlesnks .... G 302 654-0709
  Wilmington (G-20262)
Total Beauty Supply Inc .... G 302 798-4647
  Wilmington (G-20367)
Tower Business Machines Inc .... G 302 395-1445
  Historic New Castle (G-5088)
Trovety Inc .... G 302 291-2252
  Lewes (G-6580)
True Mobility Inc .... G 302 836-4110
  New Castle (G-9643)
True-Pack Ltd .... F 302 326-2222
  New Castle (G-9644)
Vending Solutions LLC .... G 302 674-2222
  Dover (G-3781)
Visual Communications Inc .... G 302 792-9500
  Claymont (G-1330)
Watercraft LLC .... G 302 757-0786
  Wilmington (G-20683)
Wellthy Investors LLC .... G 267 847-3486
  Dover (G-3831)
WER Wireless of Smyrna Inc .... F 302 653-8183
  Smyrna (G-13936)
Westward LLC .... G 570 609-3500
  Dover (G-3839)
◆ Xenopia LLC .... G 302 703-7050
  Lewes (G-6643)

60 DEPOSITORY INSTITUTIONS

6021 National commercial banks

Advisory Trust Co of Delaware .... F 302 636-8500
  Wilmington (G-14291)
Applied Bank .... E 302 326-4200
  Wilmington (G-14511)
Bancorp Inc .... D 302 385-5000
  Wilmington (G-14729)
Bank America National Assn .... F 888 550-6433
  Newark (G-9981)
Bank America National Assn .... F 302 765-2108
  Wilmington (G-14742)
Bank America National Assn .... G 302 478-1005
  Wilmington (G-14743)
Bank America National Assn .... G 302 656-5399
  Wilmington (G-14744)

Employee Codes: A=Over 500 employees, B=251-500
C=101-250, D=51-100, E=20-50, F=10-19, G=1-9

60 DEPOSITORY INSTITUTIONS

Bank America National Assn................... G 704 386-8539
  Wilmington (G-14745)
Bank America National Assn................... G 704 386-8539
  Wilmington (G-14746)
Bessemer Trust Company Del NA............. E 212 708-9182
  Wilmington (G-14851)
Bryn Mawr Capital MGT LLC................... G 302 429-8436
  Wilmington (G-15137)
Capital One National Assn........................ F 877 383-4802
  Wilmington (G-15230)
Capital One National Assn........................ B 302 658-3302
  Wilmington (G-15231)
Citibank National Association.................. G 302 477-5418
  New Castle (G-8944)
Citicorp Banking Corporation................... C 302 323-3140
  New Castle (G-8946)
Citicorp Delaware Services Inc................ F 302 323-3124
  New Castle (G-8948)
▲ Citigroup Asia PCF Holdg Corp............ G 302 323-3100
  New Castle (G-8949)
County Bank... G 302 537-0900
  Millville (G-8526)
Deutsche Bank Tr Co Americas............... E 302 636-3301
  Wilmington (G-16031)
Deutsche Bank Trust Co Del.................... C 302 636-3300
  Wilmington (G-16032)
First National Bnk of Wyoming................ E 302 697-2666
  Camden (G-835)
◆ Hsbc Bank USA..................................... A 302 778-0169
  Wilmington (G-17224)
JP Morgan Trust Company Del................ C 302 634-3800
  Newark (G-11132)
Jpmorgan Chase & Co............................. G 800 935-9935
  Bear (G-312)
Jpmorgan Chase & Co............................. F 312 732-2801
  Newark (G-11133)
Jpmorgan Chase Bank Nat Assn............. G 302 282-9000
  Wilmington (G-17598)
Meridian Bank.. E 302 477-9449
  Wilmington (G-18282)
PNC Bancorp Inc..................................... C 302 427-5896
  Wilmington (G-19088)
PNC Bank National Association.............. G 302 832-8750
  Bear (G-428)
PNC Bank National Association.............. G 302 337-3500
  Bridgeville (G-752)
PNC Bank National Association.............. F 302 735-2160
  Dover (G-3341)
PNC Bank National Association.............. G 302 735-3117
  Dover (G-3342)
PNC Bank National Association.............. G 302 855-0400
  Georgetown (G-4468)
PNC Bank National Association.............. G 302 645-4500
  Lewes (G-6379)
PNC Bank National Association.............. G 302 378-4441
  Middletown (G-7459)
PNC Bank National Association.............. G 302 422-1015
  Milford (G-8050)
PNC Bank National Association.............. G 302 934-3106
  Millsboro (G-8431)
PNC Bank National Association.............. G 302 326-4710
  New Castle (G-9477)
PNC Bank National Association.............. G 302 326-4701
  New Castle (G-9478)
PNC Bank National Association.............. G 302 733-7190
  Newark (G-11706)
PNC Bank National Association.............. G 302 629-5000
  Seaford (G-13349)
PNC Bank National Association.............. G 302 436-4500
  Selbyville (G-13593)
PNC Bank National Association.............. G 302 653-2475
  Smyrna (G-13850)

PNC Bank National Association.............. G 302 235-4010
  Wilmington (G-19089)
PNC Bank National Association.............. G 302 993-3000
  Wilmington (G-19090)
PNC Bank National Association.............. G 302 994-6337
  Wilmington (G-19091)
PNC Bank National Association.............. G 302 429-2266
  Wilmington (G-19092)
PNC Bank National Association.............. F 302 479-4529
  Wilmington (G-19093)
PNC Bank National Association.............. F 302 479-4520
  Wilmington (G-19094)
PNC Bank National Association.............. G 302 993-3013
  Wilmington (G-19095)
PNC Financial Svcs Group Inc................. F 302 429-1364
  Wilmington (G-19097)
Psci.. E 302 479-9700
  Wilmington (G-19242)
Reliance Trust Company LLC.................. G 302 246-5400
  Wilmington (G-19426)
Sen Tom Carper (d-D.............................. G 302 573-6291
  Wilmington (G-19749)
Stifel Trust Co Del Nat Assn.................... G 302 351-8900
  Wilmington (G-20074)
SunTrust Delaware Trust Co.................... E 302 892-9930
  Wilmington (G-20138)
Td Bank NA... G 302 644-0952
  Rehoboth Beach (G-12991)
Td Bank NA... G 302 655-5031
  Wilmington (G-20240)
Td Bank NA... G 508 793-4188
  Wilmington (G-20241)
Wells Fargo Bank National Assn............. G 302 832-6104
  Bear (G-562)
Wells Fargo Bank National Assn............. G 302 235-4304
  Hockessin (G-5422)
Wells Fargo Bank National Assn............. G 302 449-5485
  Middletown (G-7716)
Wells Fargo Bank National Assn............. F 302 326-4304
  New Castle (G-9680)
Wells Fargo Bank National Assn............. G 302 631-1500
  Newark (G-12358)
Wells Fargo Bank National Assn............. F 302 644-6351
  Rehoboth Beach (G-13012)
Wells Fargo Bank National Assn............. G 302 529-2550
  Wilmington (G-20722)
Wells Fargo Bank National Assn............. G 302 761-1300
  Wilmington (G-20723)
Wells Fargo Bank National Assn............. G 302 622-3350
  Wilmington (G-20724)
Wells Fargo Bank National Assn............. G 302 421-7820
  Wilmington (G-20725)
Wells Fargo Delaware Tr Co NA.............. G 302 575-2002
  Wilmington (G-20727)
Wells Fargo Home Mortgage Inc............. G 302 239-6300
  Hockessin (G-5423)
Wells Fargo Home Mortgage Inc............. G 302 227-5700
  Rehoboth Beach (G-13013)
Wells Krystal... G 302 738-4191
  Newark (G-12360)

6022 State commercial banks

Bank of Delmarva.................................... G 302 875-5901
  Laurel (G-5466)
Bank of Delmarva.................................... G 302 226-8900
  Rehoboth Beach (G-12622)
Bank of Delmarva.................................... G 302 629-2700
  Seaford (G-13075)
Bmo Delaware Trust Company............... G 302 652-1660
  Wilmington (G-14986)
Bny Investment MGT Svcs LLC.............. C 212 495-1784
  Wilmington (G-14988)

Cbc Holding Inc....................................... A 302 254-2000
  Wilmington (G-15285)
Citicorp Del-Lease Inc............................. D 302 323-3801
  New Castle (G-8947)
Citizens Bank National Assn................... F 302 834-2611
  Bear (G-106)
Citizens Bank National Assn................... E 302 734-0200
  Dover (G-2078)
Citizens Bank National Assn................... G 302 645-2024
  Lewes (G-5821)
Community Bank Delaware..................... E 302 348-8600
  Lewes (G-5854)
County Bank.. G 302 855-2000
  Georgetown (G-4269)
County Bank.. G 302 645-8880
  Lewes (G-5864)
County Bank.. G 302 424-2500
  Milford (G-7843)
County Bank.. G 302 947-7300
  Millsboro (G-8242)
County Bank.. G 302 684-2300
  Milton (G-8592)
County Bank.. F 302 226-9800
  Rehoboth Beach (G-12702)
Discover Bank... C 302 349-4512
  Greenwood (G-4618)
Farmers Bank of Willards........................ G 302 934-6300
  Millsboro (G-8286)
Fulton Bank National Assn...................... G 302 855-2406
  Georgetown (G-4328)
Fulton Bank National Assn...................... G 302 644-4900
  Lewes (G-6021)
Fulton Bank National Assn...................... G 302 378-4575
  Middletown (G-7144)
Fulton Bank National Assn...................... G 302 737-7766
  Newark (G-10790)
Fulton Bank National Assn...................... G 302 539-8031
  Ocean View (G-12515)
Fulton Bank National Assn...................... G 302 407-3291
  Wilmington (G-16769)
Govplus LLC... G 302 734-0231
  Dover (G-2612)
Govplus LLC... F 302 235-4321
  Hockessin (G-5226)
Govplus LLC... F 302 360-6101
  Lewes (G-6049)
Govplus LLC... G 302 376-3641
  Middletown (G-7172)
Govplus LLC... G 302 422-5010
  Milford (G-7910)
Govplus LLC... F 302 322-0525
  New Castle (G-9174)
Govplus LLC... G 302 292-6401
  Newark (G-10873)
Govplus LLC... F 302 456-7100
  Newark (G-10874)
Govplus LLC... F 302 283-5600
  Newark (G-10875)
Govplus LLC... F 302 628-6150
  Seaford (G-13200)
Govplus LLC... G 302 653-9245
  Smyrna (G-13749)
Govplus LLC... G 302 633-4503
  Wilmington (G-16933)
Govplus LLC... E 302 421-2248
  Wilmington (G-16934)
Govplus LLC... F 302 633-3080
  Wilmington (G-16935)
Govplus LLC... G 302 529-6100
  Wilmington (G-16936)
Govplus LLC... E 302 421-2229
  Wilmington (G-16937)

SIC SECTION
60 DEPOSITORY INSTITUTIONS

Govplus LLC .... G 302 477-1205
  Wilmington *(G-16938)*

K Bank .... G 302 645-9700
  Lewes *(G-6157)*

M & F Financial Corp .... F 302 427-5755
  Wilmington *(G-18055)*

Manufacturers & Traders Tr Co .... G 302 651-8828
  Bear *(G-362)*

Manufacturers & Traders Tr Co .... G 302 472-3262
  Claymont *(G-1230)*

Manufacturers & Traders Tr Co .... G 302 855-2297
  Delmar *(G-1616)*

Manufacturers & Traders Tr Co .... F 302 735-2020
  Dover *(G-3013)*

Manufacturers & Traders Tr Co .... G 302 735-2010
  Dover *(G-3014)*

Manufacturers & Traders Tr Co .... F 302 472-3177
  Hockessin *(G-5295)*

Manufacturers & Traders Tr Co .... G 302 855-2873
  Laurel *(G-5559)*

Manufacturers & Traders Tr Co .... G 302 855-2218
  Lewes *(G-6240)*

Manufacturers & Traders Tr Co .... G 302 449-2780
  Middletown *(G-7326)*

Manufacturers & Traders Tr Co .... G 302 285-3277
  Middletown *(G-7327)*

Manufacturers & Traders Tr Co .... G 302 855-2160
  Milford *(G-7983)*

Manufacturers & Traders Tr Co .... G 302 855-2891
  Millsboro *(G-8362)*

Manufacturers & Traders Tr Co .... G 302 855-2184
  Milton *(G-8660)*

Manufacturers & Traders Tr Co .... G 302 472-3249
  New Castle *(G-9343)*

Manufacturers & Traders Tr Co .... G 302 651-1618
  Newark *(G-11323)*

Manufacturers & Traders Tr Co .... G 302 472-3335
  Newark *(G-11324)*

Manufacturers & Traders Tr Co .... G 302 855-2227
  Rehoboth Beach *(G-12847)*

Manufacturers & Traders Tr Co .... G 302 856-4470
  Seaford *(G-13273)*

Manufacturers & Traders Tr Co .... G 302 651-8738
  Wilmington *(G-18108)*

Manufacturers & Traders Tr Co .... G 302 472-3161
  Wilmington *(G-18109)*

Manufacturers & Traders Tr Co .... F 302 636-6000
  Wilmington *(G-18110)*

Manufacturers & Traders Tr Co .... G 302 472-3309
  Wilmington *(G-18111)*

Manufacturers & Traders Tr Co .... G 302 472-3233
  Wilmington *(G-18112)*

Manufacturers & Traders Tr Co .... G 302 651-1757
  Wilmington *(G-18113)*

Manufacturers & Traders Tr Co .... F 302 651-1803
  Wilmington *(G-18114)*

Manufacturers & Traders Tr Co .... G 302 651-1544
  Wilmington *(G-18115)*

Manufacturers & Traders Tr Co .... F 302 656-1260
  Wilmington *(G-18116)*

PNC Bank Delaware .... A 302 655-7221
  Wilmington *(G-19096)*

PNC National Bank of Delaware .... D 302 479-4529
  Wilmington *(G-19099)*

Royal Bank America Leasing LLC .... F 302 798-1790
  Wilmington *(G-19575)*

Santander Bank NA .... F 302 654-5182
  Wilmington *(G-19668)*

Wilmington Sav Fund Soc Fsb .... A 888 973-7226
  Wilmington *(G-20835)*

Wilmington Savings Fund Soc .... G 302 792-6435
  Claymont *(G-1337)*

Wilmington Savings Fund Soc .... G 302 677-1891
  Dover *(G-3855)*

Wilmington Savings Fund Soc .... F 302 456-6404
  Newark *(G-12382)*

Wilmington Savings Fund Soc .... G 302 360-0440
  Seaford *(G-13453)*

Wilmington Savings Fund Soc .... G 302 999-1227
  Wilmington *(G-20837)*

Wilmington Savings Fund Soc .... G 302 571-6508
  Wilmington *(G-20838)*

Wilmington Savings Fund Soc .... G 302 571-6500
  Wilmington *(G-20839)*

Wilmington Savings Fund Soc .... G 302 571-7090
  Wilmington *(G-20840)*

Wilmington Savings Fund Soc .... C 302 792-6000
  Wilmington *(G-20836)*

Wsfs Financial Corporation .... E 302 571-6516
  Wilmington *(G-20902)*

Wsfs Financial Corporation .... C 302 792-6000
  Wilmington *(G-20903)*

6029 Commercial banks, nec

Artisans Bank Inc .... G 302 834-8800
  Bear *(G-50)*

Artisans Bank Inc .... G 302 430-7681
  Milford *(G-7772)*

Artisans Bank Inc .... G 302 738-3744
  Wilmington *(G-14572)*

Bancorp Bank National Assn .... E 302 385-5000
  Wilmington *(G-14730)*

Bank of Delmarva .... G 302 875-5901
  Laurel *(G-5466)*

Bank of Delmarva .... G 302 226-8900
  Rehoboth Beach *(G-12622)*

Bank of Delmarva .... G 302 629-2700
  Seaford *(G-13075)*

County Bank .... G 302 537-0900
  Millville *(G-8526)*

Hsbc Bank USA National Assn .... G 800 975-4722
  New Castle *(G-9223)*

Hsbc North America Inc .... F 302 652-4673
  Wilmington *(G-17225)*

K Bank .... G 302 645-9700
  Lewes *(G-6157)*

Td Bank NA .... G 302 644-0952
  Rehoboth Beach *(G-12991)*

Tiger LLC .... G 302 378-8700
  Middletown *(G-7645)*

6035 Federal savings institutions

Artisans Bank Inc .... G 302 674-3214
  Dover *(G-1825)*

Barclays Bank Delaware .... B 302 255-8000
  Wilmington *(G-14759)*

Beneficial Oklahoma Inc .... F 302 529-8701
  Wilmington *(G-14832)*

Home Savings America Newark .... G 302 286-7814
  Newark *(G-10963)*

Ing Bank Fsb .... D 302 658-2200
  Wilmington *(G-17332)*

▲ Ing USA Holding Corp .... A 302 658-2200
  Wilmington *(G-17333)*

Wilmington Savings Fund Soc .... G 302 633-5700
  Wilmington *(G-20841)*

Wilmington Savings Fund Soc .... G 302 571-6516
  Wilmington *(G-20842)*

6036 Savings institutions, except federal

Artisans Bank Inc .... G 302 834-8800
  Bear *(G-50)*

Artisans Bank Inc .... G 302 674-3214
  Dover *(G-1825)*

Artisans Bank Inc .... G 302 430-7681
  Milford *(G-7772)*

Artisans Bank Inc .... G 302 838-6700
  Newark *(G-9917)*

Artisans Bank Inc .... G 302 296-0155
  Rehoboth Beach *(G-12611)*

Artisans Bank Inc .... G 302 656-8188
  Wilmington *(G-14567)*

Artisans Bank Inc .... G 302 479-2553
  Wilmington *(G-14569)*

Artisans Bank Inc .... G 302 479-2550
  Wilmington *(G-14570)*

Artisans Bank Inc .... G 302 993-8220
  Wilmington *(G-14571)*

Artisans Bank Inc .... G 302 738-3744
  Wilmington *(G-14572)*

Artisans Bank Inc .... D 302 658-6881
  Wilmington *(G-14568)*

Midcoast Community Bank .... F 302 482-4250
  Wilmington *(G-18341)*

6061 Federal credit unions

American Spirit Federal Cr Un .... E 302 738-4515
  Newark *(G-9848)*

Chestnut Run Federal Cr Un .... F 302 999-2967
  Wilmington *(G-15369)*

Community Pwered Federal Cr Un ...... D 302 324-1441
  Historic New Castle *(G-4963)*

Community Pwered Federal Cr Un ...... G 302 368-2396
  Bear *(G-114)*

Community Twered Federal Cr Un ...... G 302 994-3617
  Wilmington *(G-15565)*

Community Twered Federal Cr Un ...... F 302 368-2396
  Newark *(G-10290)*

Del-One Federal Credit Union .... G 302 739-2390
  Dover *(G-2213)*

Del-One Federal Credit Union .... G 302 424-2969
  Milford *(G-7850)*

Del-One Federal Credit Union .... G 302 739-4496
  Smyrna *(G-13697)*

Del-One Federal Credit Union .... G 302 577-2667
  Wilmington *(G-15860)*

Del-One Federal Credit Union .... E 302 734-4496
  Dover *(G-2214)*

Delaware First Federal Cr Un .... F 302 998-0665
  Wilmington *(G-15919)*

Delaware Rver Bay Auth Emplyee ...... G 302 571-6320
  New Castle *(G-9035)*

Delaware State Plice Fdral Cr .... F 800 288-1080
  Georgetown *(G-4284)*

Delaware State Plice Fdral Cr .... G 302 324-8141
  New Castle *(G-9038)*

Delaware State Plice Fdral Cr .... F 302 856-3501
  Georgetown *(G-4285)*

Dexsta Federal Credit Union .... G 302 996-4893
  Wilmington *(G-16040)*

Dexsta Federal Credit Union .... F 302 695-3888
  Wilmington *(G-16042)*

Dexsta Federal Credit Union .... E 302 996-4893
  Wilmington *(G-16041)*

Dfs Corporate Services LLC .... E 302 349-4512
  Greenwood *(G-4617)*

Dover Federal Credit Union .... D 302 678-8000
  Dover *(G-2344)*

Eagle One Federal Credit Union .... G 302 798-7749
  Claymont *(G-1126)*

First State Federal Credit Un .... F 302 674-5281
  Dover *(G-2503)*

Louviers Federal Credit Union .... E 302 571-9513
  Wilmington *(G-18010)*

Louviers Federal Credit Union .... F 302 733-0426
  Newark *(G-11287)*

Employee Codes: A=Over 500 employees, B=251-500
C=101-250, D=51-100, E=20-50, F=10-19, G=1-9

60 DEPOSITORY INSTITUTIONS

New Cstle Cnty Del Emplyees Fd............ F 302 395-5350
  New Castle *(G-9414)*
New Cstle Cnty Schl Emplyees F........... E 302 613-5330
  Historic New Castle *(G-5038)*
Provident Federal Credit Union............. F 302 734-1133
  Dover *(G-3386)*
Sun East Federal Credit Union.............. G 610 485-2960
  Wilmington *(G-20126)*
▲ Tidemark Federal Credit Union........... F 302 629-0100
  Seaford *(G-13430)*
Wilmington Plice Fire Fdral Cr................ G 302 654-0818
  Wilmington *(G-20831)*

6062 State credit unions

Community Twered Federal Cr Un......... F 302 368-2396
  Newark *(G-10290)*
Dexsta Federal Credit Union.................. F 302 695-3888
  Wilmington *(G-16042)*
Dover Federal Credit Union.................... D 302 678-8000
  Dover *(G-2344)*

6081 Foreign bank and branches and agencies

Axis Capital Usa LLC............................... F 855 205-5577
  Dover *(G-1860)*

6082 Foreign trade and international banks

Gunnar Advik EI....................................... G 302 867-0424
  Hockessin *(G-5231)*
Lakpura LLC... F 302 786-0908
  Wilmington *(G-17789)*
Senso Dynamics LLC............................. G 302 257-5926
  Lewes *(G-6459)*

6091 Nondeposit trust facilities

Depository Trust Co Del LLC.................. E 302 762-2635
  Wilmington *(G-16018)*
First State Trust Company...................... E 302 573-5967
  Wilmington *(G-16637)*
Pfpc Trust Company................................ B 302 791-2000
  Wilmington *(G-19004)*

6099 Functions related to depository banking

Argo Financial Services Inc.................... G 302 322-7788
  New Castle *(G-8820)*
Beach Break... G 302 226-3450
  Dewey Beach *(G-1664)*
Cash Connect Inc.................................... E 302 283-4100
  Newark *(G-10159)*
Cash Plus 231.. G 302 526-2386
  Dover *(G-2035)*
Churchfunerals Direct Inc...................... G 800 308-3590
  Wilmington *(G-15429)*
Citigroup Inc... E 302 631-3530
  Newark *(G-10244)*
Coinbase Global Inc................................ D 302 777-0200
  Wilmington *(G-15522)*
Concord Corporate Services Inc............ B 302 791-8200
  Wilmington *(G-15579)*
Delaware Depository Svc Co LLC.......... G 302 762-2635
  Wilmington *(G-15903)*
Easy Money Emg..................................... G 302 421-3610
  Wilmington *(G-16269)*
Juni Holdings Inc..................................... F 415 949-4860
  Wilmington *(G-17614)*
Juniper Bank.. F 302 255-8000
  Wilmington *(G-17615)*
Loan Til Payday....................................... G 302 428-3925
  Wilmington *(G-17968)*
Nfinity Inc... F 852 642-9800
  Wilmington *(G-18639)*

Oink Oink LLC... G 302 924-5034
  Dover *(G-3217)*
Pfpc Worldwide Inc.................................. F 302 791-1700
  Wilmington *(G-19005)*
Service General Corp.............................. G 302 629-9701
  Seaford *(G-13395)*
United Check Cashing............................ G 302 792-2545
  Claymont *(G-1322)*
Wilmington Nghbrhood Cnsrvncy........... G 302 409-1023
  Wilmington *(G-20826)*

61 NONDEPOSITORY CREDIT INSTITUTIONS

6111 Federal and federally sponsored credit

Agfirst Farm Credit Bank........................ G 302 734-7534
  Dover *(G-1739)*
Agfirst Farm Credit Bank........................ G 302 856-9081
  Georgetown *(G-4201)*
Clean Cooking Africa Corp..................... G 706 691-9813
  Wilmington *(G-15471)*
Credit Insider LLC.................................. G 302 232-5644
  Dover *(G-2157)*
Mid Atlantic Farm Credit Aca.................. G 302 734-7534
  Dover *(G-3084)*
Navient Prvate Edcatn Ln Tr 20.............. G 302 636-3300
  Wilmington *(G-18561)*
Navient Solutions LLC............................ C 703 810-3000
  Wilmington *(G-18562)*
RKL Financial Corporation..................... E 302 283-8000
  Newark *(G-11891)*
SLM Corporation..................................... B 302 451-0200
  Newark *(G-12032)*
Triumph Worldwide Inc........................... E 302 465-6898
  Newark *(G-12238)*

6141 Personal credit institutions

Atlantic Finance....................................... G 302 730-1988
  Dover *(G-1847)*
Atlantic Finance....................................... G 302 629-6266
  Seaford *(G-13072)*
Bank of New Castle................................. E 800 347-3301
  New Castle *(G-8846)*
Beneficial Consumer Disc Co................. G 302 425-2500
  Wilmington *(G-14831)*
Cash Advance... G 302 730-1988
  Dover *(G-2034)*
Cash Advance Plus................................. G 302 846-3900
  Delmar *(G-1574)*
Citifinancial Credit Company.................. G 302 834-6677
  Bear *(G-105)*
Citifinancial Credit Company.................. G 302 422-9657
  Milford *(G-7828)*
Citifinancial Credit Company.................. G 302 628-9253
  Seaford *(G-13120)*
Citifinancial Credit Company.................. F 302 683-4917
  Wilmington *(G-15448)*
College Avenue Student Ln LLC............ D 302 684-6070
  Wilmington *(G-15531)*
Delaware Title Loans Inc........................ F 302 653-8315
  Smyrna *(G-13707)*
E Z Cash of Delaware Inc....................... G 302 846-2920
  Delmar *(G-1592)*
Eastern Specialty Finance Inc................ F 302 697-4290
  Camden *(G-826)*
Eastern Specialty Finance Inc................ F 302 736-1348
  Dover *(G-2414)*
Eastern Specialty Finance Inc................ F 302 658-5431
  Wilmington *(G-16263)*
EZ Loans Inc... F 302 934-5563
  Millsboro *(G-8285)*

First Advance Loan Center Inc............... G 302 482-7294
  Wilmington *(G-16614)*
Glance Capital Inc................................... G 800 825-9889
  Middletown *(G-7162)*
Horizon Farm Credit................................ G 302 856-9081
  Georgetown *(G-4365)*
Integrated Cash Logistics LLC............... E 302 652-9193
  Wilmington *(G-17367)*
John Lovett Inc... F 302 455-9460
  Newark *(G-11114)*
Jpmorgan Chase & Co............................ G 800 935-9935
  Bear *(G-312)*
Loan Simple Inc....................................... G 302 510-4808
  Wilmington *(G-17967)*
Loan Till Payday LLC.............................. G 302 536-2183
  Millsboro *(G-8350)*
Loanmax... G 302 747-2005
  Dover *(G-2966)*
Loanmax... G 302 326-0123
  New Castle *(G-9321)*
Minute Loan Center................................. G 302 791-9557
  Claymont *(G-1239)*
Minute Loan Center................................. G 302 607-2202
  Newark *(G-11426)*
Minute Loan Center................................. G 302 629-5366
  Seaford *(G-13285)*
Minute Loan Center................................. G 302 427-8041
  Wilmington *(G-18383)*
Minute Loan Center................................. G 302 994-6588
  Wilmington *(G-18384)*
Moneykey - TX Inc................................... E 866 255-1668
  Wilmington *(G-18414)*
Northeastern Title Loans........................ G 302 326-2210
  New Castle *(G-9427)*
Reevoy Corporation................................. F 631 769-6681
  Wilmington *(G-19394)*
Score Revive LLC.................................... G 302 455-2100
  Dover *(G-3519)*
Sears Roebuck Acceptance Corp......... G 302 434-3100
  Wilmington *(G-19725)*
SLM Corporation..................................... B 302 451-0200
  Newark *(G-12032)*
Weltio LLC.. F 305 307-9815
  Dover *(G-3832)*

6153 Short-term business credit

Access Funding 2010-A LLC.................. F 484 653-3300
  Wilmington *(G-14220)*
Access Funding 2013-1 LLC................... G 302 477-4071
  Wilmington *(G-14221)*
Acquisition Intl Holdings Inc................... G 302 603-7795
  Dover *(G-1712)*
Americas Got Funding............................ G 866 975-8363
  Bear *(G-34)*
Armstrong Cork Finance LLC................. E 302 652-1520
  Wilmington *(G-14556)*
BASF Uk Finance LLC............................ G 973 245-6000
  Wilmington *(G-14775)*
Bcp Finance Corp A Del Corp................ G 225 673-6121
  Wilmington *(G-14796)*
Best Egg Technologies LLC................... D 302 358-2730
  Wilmington *(G-14853)*
Business Funding Pro.............................. G 888 705-8278
  Wilmington *(G-15156)*
Cabicash Solutions Inc........................... E 315 961-2005
  Wilmington *(G-15183)*
Citifinancial Credit Company.................. G 302 834-6677
  Bear *(G-105)*
Dfs Corporate Services LLC.................. D 302 735-3902
  Dover *(G-2289)*
Innovations Funding LLC........................ G 302 743-6213
  Smyrna *(G-13770)*

62 SECURITY & COMMODITY BROKERS, DEALERS, EXCHANGES & SERVICES

Interntnal Fnding Slutions LLC............ G 212 765-4349
  Wilmington *(G-17395)*

John Lovett Inc............................. F 302 455-9460
  Newark *(G-11114)*

Moneykey-Mo Inc........................... F 866 255-1668
  Wilmington *(G-18415)*

New American Funding..................... G 302 200-4607
  Newark *(G-11513)*

Oink Oink LLC............................... G 302 924-5034
  Dover *(G-3217)*

Red Target LLC.............................. F 302 752-4449
  Harrington *(G-4819)*

Swift Financial LLC......................... D 302 374-7019
  Wilmington *(G-20175)*

6159 Miscellaneous business credit

Adr Investments LLC....................... G 800 710-6184
  Wilmington *(G-14262)*

Ally Auto Assets LLC........................ G 313 656-5500
  Wilmington *(G-14386)*

American Air Lease Finance LLC........... G 646 643-6303
  Wilmington *(G-14424)*

American Finance LLC...................... D 302 674-0365
  Harrington *(G-4727)*

Delaware Title Loans Inc.................... F 302 328-7482
  New Castle *(G-9039)*

Delaware Title Loans Inc.................... F 302 368-2131
  Newark *(G-10493)*

Delaware Title Loans Inc.................... F 302 629-8843
  Seaford *(G-13153)*

Ev Flux Inc................................... G 510 880-3737
  Newark *(G-10674)*

Frascella Enterprises Inc.................... G 267 467-4496
  Claymont *(G-1152)*

Greystone Business Credit.................. G 410 456-6559
  Millsboro *(G-8308)*

Mid Atlantic Farm Credit Aca............... G 302 734-7534
  Dover *(G-3084)*

Star States Leasing Corp.................... E 302 283-4500
  Newark *(G-12088)*

6162 Mortgage bankers and correspondents

About Angela Angelas Home Ln............ G 302 598-7799
  Newark *(G-9742)*

Academy Mortgage.......................... G 484 680-8092
  Wilmington *(G-14215)*

Accelerate Mortgage LLC.................. E 866 986-1245
  Newark *(G-9748)*

Acopia Home Loans......................... G 302 242-6272
  Rehoboth Beach *(G-12596)*

Acre Mortgage & Financial.................. G 302 737-5853
  Christiana *(G-990)*

Anniemac Home Mortgage LLC........... C 302 234-2956
  Wilmington *(G-14494)*

Atlantic Home Loans Inc.................... G 302 363-3950
  Dover *(G-1848)*

Caliber Home Loans......................... G 302 584-0580
  Middletown *(G-6952)*

Caliber Home Loans Inc..................... G 302 483-7587
  Newark *(G-10121)*

Castle Mortgage Services Inc............... F 302 366-0912
  Newark *(G-10161)*

Continental Mortgage Corp.................. G 302 996-5807
  Wilmington *(G-15621)*

Delaware Community Inv Corp.............. G 302 655-1420
  Wilmington *(G-15891)*

Embrace Home Loans Inc................... G 302 635-7998
  Wilmington *(G-16388)*

Equity Plus Inc............................... F 302 762-3122
  Wilmington *(G-16453)*

Evolve Bank & Trust......................... F 302 286-7838
  Newark *(G-10679)*

Fair Mortgage Co............................. G 202 904-4843
  Dover *(G-2479)*

Federal Home Loan ADM Inc................ G 855 345-2669
  Wilmington *(G-16571)*

Freedom Mortgage Corporation............. G 302 368-7100
  Newark *(G-10779)*

Gilpin Mortgage.............................. G 302 656-5400
  Wilmington *(G-16864)*

Gsf Mortgage Corporation................... D 302 373-5853
  Christiana *(G-997)*

Homestead Funding Corp.................... F 302 628-2828
  Seaford *(G-13215)*

Integrity First Mortgage LLC................ G 302 318-6858
  Newark *(G-11034)*

Jet Fast Loans............................... G 302 934-6794
  Millsboro *(G-8331)*

Jia Finance Inc............................... G 202 341-1031
  Wilmington *(G-17545)*

Jpmorgan Chase & Co....................... G 800 935-9935
  Bear *(G-312)*

Keystone Funding Inc........................ F 484 798-9084
  Dover *(G-2861)*

Keystone Funding Inc........................ F 610 644-6423
  Dover *(G-2862)*

M & F Financial Corp......................... F 302 427-5755
  Wilmington *(G-18055)*

Meridian Bank................................ G 302 635-7500
  Wilmington *(G-18281)*

Mortgage America Inc....................... G 302 239-0600
  Wilmington *(G-18456)*

Mortgage Network Solutions LLC........... F 302 252-0100
  Wilmington *(G-18458)*

Mortgage Network Solutions LLC........... E 302 252-0100
  Wilmington *(G-18457)*

Motto Mortgage Prosperity LLC............ G 302 313-5145
  Milton *(G-8675)*

Movement Mortgage LLC................... F 302 344-6758
  Lewes *(G-6294)*

N V R Mortgage.............................. G 302 732-1570
  Dagsboro *(G-1486)*

New Penn Financial LLC..................... G 240 475-4741
  Rehoboth Beach *(G-12870)*

Oakwood Funding Corporation.............. G 336 855-2400
  Wilmington *(G-18730)*

On Q Financial............................... G 866 667-3279
  Dover *(G-3227)*

Orchard Mortgage LLC..................... F 888 627-0677
  Wilmington *(G-18816)*

PNC Bank National Association............ G 302 429-2266
  Wilmington *(G-19092)*

Premier Capital Holding..................... G 302 730-1010
  Dover *(G-3359)*

Primary Residential Mrtg Inc................ E 302 292-1009
  Newark *(G-11742)*

Primelending A Plainscapital................ F 302 733-7599
  Newark *(G-11744)*

RKL Financial Corporation................... E 302 283-8000
  Newark *(G-11891)*

Shallcross Mortgage Co Inc.................. G 302 999-9800
  Wilmington *(G-19778)*

Supreme Lending............................ G 302 268-6244
  Wilmington *(G-20157)*

True Access Capital Corp................... F 302 652-6774
  Wilmington *(G-20442)*

Waterstone Mortgage Corp.................. G 302 227-8252
  Rehoboth Beach *(G-13008)*

6163 Loan brokers

ABC Lending Corp........................... G 302 369-5626
  Newark *(G-9739)*

Aca Mortgage Co Inc........................ G 302 225-1390
  Wilmington *(G-14213)*

American Spirit Federal Cr Un.............. E 302 738-4515
  Newark *(G-9848)*

Del-One Federal Credit Union............... E 302 734-4496
  Dover *(G-2214)*

Delaware Financial Capital.................. G 302 266-9500
  Newark *(G-10444)*

Delaware First Federal Cr Un................ F 302 998-0665
  Wilmington *(G-15919)*

Delaware Title Loans Inc.................... F 302 644-3640
  Lewes *(G-5901)*

Delaware Title Loans Inc.................... F 302 478-8505
  Wilmington *(G-15976)*

Equity Plus Inc............................... F 302 762-3122
  Wilmington *(G-16453)*

First Atlantic Mrtg Svcs LLC................ G 302 841-8435
  Lewes *(G-5996)*

Geris Auto Financial Svcs LLC.............. G 302 660-9719
  Newark *(G-10826)*

Interstate Mortgage Corp Inc................ G 302 733-7620
  Newark *(G-11049)*

John Lovett Inc............................. F 302 455-9460
  Newark *(G-11114)*

Lending Manager Holdings LLC............ G 888 501-0335
  Newark *(G-11245)*

Loan Till Payday LLC........................ F 302 792-5001
  Claymont *(G-1222)*

Louviers Mortgage Corporation............. G 302 234-4129
  Wilmington *(G-18011)*

Mercury Financial LLC...................... F 302 588-0107
  Wilmington *(G-18277)*

Pike Creek Mortgage Services.............. G 302 892-2811
  Newark *(G-11692)*

Provident Federal Credit Union.............. F 302 734-1133
  Dover *(G-3386)*

Resource Mortgage Corp.................... F 302 657-0181
  Wilmington *(G-19439)*

Ssbv LLC..................................... F 844 585-0656
  Wilmington *(G-19988)*

Synergy Direct Mortgage.................... G 302 283-0833
  Christiana *(G-1011)*

Van Buren Mortgage LLC................... G 302 945-1109
  Millsboro *(G-8492)*

Van Buren Mortgage LLC................... G 302 725-0723
  Ocean View *(G-12579)*

62 SECURITY & COMMODITY BROKERS, DEALERS, EXCHANGES & SERVICES

6211 Security brokers and dealers

Accessheat Inc.............................. E 302 373-9524
  Wilmington *(G-14222)*

Assurance Partners Intl..................... F 302 478-0173
  Wilmington *(G-14600)*

Brittingham Inc.............................. G 302 656-8173
  Wilmington *(G-15120)*

Cananwill Corp............................... G 302 576-3499
  Wilmington *(G-15212)*

▲ Cawsl Enterprises Inc..................... G 302 478-6160
  Wilmington *(G-15283)*

CG Jcf Corp.................................. G 302 658-7581
  Wilmington *(G-15322)*

Charles Schwab & Co Inc................... F 800 435-4000
  Wilmington *(G-15340)*

Citibank Overseas Inv Corp.................. F 302 323-3600
  New Castle *(G-8945)*

Citigroup Globl Mkts Fncl Pdts.............. F 212 559-1000
  Wilmington *(G-15449)*

CRH Investments Inc........................ G 302 427-0924
  Wilmington *(G-15702)*

62 SECURITY & COMMODITY BROKERS, DEALERS, EXCHANGES & SERVICES

Delaware Valley Brokerage Inc............ G 302 477-9700
  Wilmington (G-15978)
Deutsche Bank Tr Co Americas............ E 302 636-3301
  Wilmington (G-16031)
Fjs Capital Management Inc............... G 267 850-1123
  Wilmington (G-16658)
Freemarkets Investment Co Inc........... G 302 427-2089
  Wilmington (G-16744)
FTC Energy Ltd LLC............................ G 405 410-9040
  Wilmington (G-16766)
Futuretech Inv Group Inc..................... F 302 476-9529
  Newark (G-10793)
Gates and Company LLC..................... F 302 428-1338
  Wilmington (G-16813)
Gund Securities Corporation................ F 302 479-9210
  Wilmington (G-17006)
Inamco Air LLC.................................. G 630 830-4007
  Dover (G-2724)
Ing Bank Fsb..................................... D 302 658-2200
  Wilmington (G-17332)
Interactive Tech Holdings LLC............. A 302 478-9356
  Wilmington (G-17374)
John Lovett Inc................................. F 302 455-9460
  Newark (G-11114)
Jpmorgan Chase & Co........................ G 800 935-9935
  Bear (G-312)
Kensington Cross Ltd........................ F 888 999-9360
  Rehoboth Beach (G-12820)
Laurel Oak Capitl Partners LLC........... G 302 658-7581
  Wilmington (G-17824)
Markvell Delarie Gilmore Trust............. G 772 742-1499
  Wilmington (G-18151)
MBNA Consumer Services Inc............. A 302 453-9930
  Wilmington (G-18212)
Merrill Lynch Prce Fnner Smith............ G 302 736-7700
  Dover (G-3065)
Merrill Lynch Prce Fnner Smith............ F 302 571-5100
  Wilmington (G-18287)
Metl Technology Inc.......................... F 954 309-4589
  Wilmington (G-18291)
Metropolitan Wealth MGT LLC............. G 212 607-2488
  Wilmington (G-18294)
Morgan Garanty Intl Fincl Corp........... E 302 634-1000
  Newark (G-11453)
Morgan Stnley Smith Barney LLC......... C 302 636-5500
  Wilmington (G-18449)
Neptune Global Holdings LLC.............. G 302 256-5080
  Wilmington (G-18585)
Peters Alan E Peters & Assoc.............. G 302 656-1007
  Wilmington (G-18996)
Preferred Term Securities Xxvi............ G 302 651-7642
  Wilmington (G-19165)
Raymond James & Associates Inc........ G 302 656-1534
  Wilmington (G-19346)
Raymond James Financial................... F 302 384-8446
  Wilmington (G-19347)
Rbc... E 302 892-5901
  Wilmington (G-19350)
Rsl Investors Inc.............................. A 302 478-5142
  Wilmington (G-19581)
Safahi Corp..................................... G 925 503-4551
  Dover (G-3501)
Sap Investments Inc......................... F 302 427-7889
  Wilmington (G-19669)
SecondSTAX Inc............................... E 862 368-0413
  Wilmington (G-19729)
Skajaquoda Capital LLC..................... G 302 504-4448
  Wilmington (G-19852)
Sks Enterprise................................. D 302 310-2511
  Newark (G-12024)
TH King US LLC................................ F 617 903-7472
  Wilmington (G-20290)

UBS Financial Services Inc.................. G 302 407-4700
  Wilmington (G-20494)
Vitae Investment Company................. D 302 656-8985
  Wilmington (G-20642)
Wells Fargo Clearing Svcs LLC............ G 302 731-2131
  Newark (G-12359)
Wells Fargo Clearing Svcs LLC............ G 302 428-8600
  Wilmington (G-20726)
William Blair & Company LLC.............. G 302 573-5000
  Wilmington (G-20784)

6221 Commodity contracts brokers, dealers

Abitechno Inc.................................. G 302 213-6700
  Wilmington (G-14204)
Dvr International Inc......................... F 800 958-9000
  Laurel (G-5503)
Emaep LLC...................................... E 202 836-7886
  Wilmington (G-16385)
Gt Commodities LLC.......................... D 203 609-8300
  Wilmington (G-16996)
International Fresh Prod Assn............. E 302 738-7100
  Newark (G-11045)
Italtec Gold & Commodities Inc........... F 302 446-3207
  Dover (G-2755)
Mefta LLC.. F 804 433-3566
  Wilmington (G-18260)
Monterey SW LLC............................. F 302 504-4901
  Newark (G-11446)
Monterey Swf LLC............................ F 302 504-4901
  Newark (G-11447)
Trade Cafe USA Inc........................... F 647 694-2656
  Wilmington (G-20384)
Turbo Distributors LLC...................... F 845 678-6700
  Wilmington (G-20460)
Vtraderio LLC.................................. G 646 952-1189
  Dover (G-3814)

6231 Security and commodity exchanges

Delaware Bd Trade Holdings Inc.......... F 302 298-0600
  Wilmington (G-15871)
Justtai.. G 781 771-0329
  Wilmington (G-17623)
Smart Altcoins Inc............................ G 626 540-9415
  Lewes (G-6480)
Vantage Energy LLC.......................... F 302 261-9351
  Wilmington (G-20570)

6282 Investment advice

A Registered Agent Inc...................... G 302 288-0670
  Dover (G-1696)
Alvini & Assoc Fincl Planners............. G 302 397-8135
  Wilmington (G-14403)
Amazand Theta LLC.......................... G 302 285-9586
  Wilmington (G-14414)
American Air Lease Finance LLC......... G 646 643-6303
  Wilmington (G-14424)
Ameriprise Financial Inc.................... G 302 235-5765
  Hockessin (G-5122)
Ameriprise Financial Services............. G 302 476-8000
  Wilmington (G-14448)
Ameriprise Financial Svcs Inc............. F 302 543-5784
  Wilmington (G-14449)
Ameriprise Financial Svcs Inc............. F 302 475-5105
  Laurel (G-14450)
Ameriprise Financial Svcs Inc............. F 302 468-8200
  Wilmington (G-14451)
Ameriprise Financial Svcs LLC............ F 302 475-2357
  Wilmington (G-14452)
Ameriprise... G 302 656-7773
  Wilmington (G-14453)
Ashford Capital Management.............. F 302 655-1750
  Wilmington (G-14580)

Ashford Consulting Group Inc............. G 302 691-0228
  Wilmington (G-14581)
Axion Financial Group LLC................. G 267 261-4177
  Bethany Beach (G-575)
Barclays Financial Corporation........... A 302 652-6201
  Wilmington (G-14760)
Bell Rock Capital Llc........................ G 302 227-7607
  Rehoboth Beach (G-12639)
Brown Advisory Incorporated............. G 302 351-7600
  Wilmington (G-15128)
Campbell Fincl Solutions LLC.............. G 302 202-9029
  Wilmington (G-15211)
Chatham Financial Corporation........... G 570 510-0490
  Wilmington (G-15348)
Chicksx LLC..................................... E 518 727-1890
  Wilmington (G-15370)
Cibc Private Wealth Groups LLC......... G 302 478-4050
  Wilmington (G-15433)
Cloud Financial Corporation............... G 845 729-5513
  Wilmington (G-15489)
Coastal... E 302 319-4061
  Wilmington (G-15508)
Cobra Investments MGT Inc............... E 302 691-6333
  Wilmington (G-15512)
Courage Capital Management............. G 302 658-2459
  Wilmington (G-15657)
Covr Financial Tech Inc.................... F 800 377-6344
  Wilmington (G-15668)
Creative Financial Group................... G 302 738-0888
  Newark (G-10348)
Crude Gold Research LLC.................. F 646 681-7317
  Dover (G-2162)
Delaware Ave Wealth Planners........... G 302 254-2400
  Wilmington (G-15870)
Diversified LLC................................ E 302 765-3500
  Wilmington (G-16094)
Donovan Capital Group LLC............... G 202 642-4360
  Dover (G-2323)
Dravo Bay LLC................................. G 302 660-3350
  Wilmington (G-16172)
Egs Financial Care Inc..................... G 800 227-4000
  Wilmington (G-16310)
First Command Brkg Svcs Inc............. G 302 535-8132
  Dover (G-2498)
Futureadvisor Inc............................. F 302 797-2000
  Wilmington (G-16779)
Glenmede Trust Co Nat Assn............. G 302 661-2900
  Wilmington (G-16884)
Goat Financial LLC........................... G 800 843-4608
  Wilmington (G-16903)
Goodtymes Inc................................ G 302 598-6673
  Wilmington (G-16926)
Great Valley Advisor Group............... F 302 483-7200
  Wilmington (G-16960)
Greenville Capital Management........... G 302 429-9799
  Rockland (G-13031)
Guardian Advisors LLC...................... G 302 220-8729
  Seaford (G-13202)
Hf Administrators Ltd....................... G 302 884-6723
  Wilmington (G-17137)
Indepndnce Wealth Advisors Inc........ G 302 763-1180
  Hockessin (G-5250)
Infocus Financial Advisors Inc............ G 410 677-4848
  Georgetown (G-4369)
Investment Property Services L......... G 302 994-3907
  Wilmington (G-17406)
John Koziol Inc................................ G 302 234-5430
  Hockessin (G-5262)
JP Morgan Intl Fin Ltd..................... G 212 270-6000
  Newark (G-11131)
Kalmar Investments Inc.................... F 302 658-7575
  Wilmington (G-17639)

Kendall James Advisors LLC............... G 302 463-0720
  Hockessin (G-5268)
Lawter Planning Group Inc............... G 302 736-6065
  Dover (G-2917)
Lincoln Financial Advisors................. G 302 875-8300
  Laurel (G-5556)
Lindenberg Financial........................... F 302 235-8672
  Wilmington (G-17929)
Lovett Financial Advisors LLC............ G 302 250-4740
  Newark (G-11290)
Mallard Advisors LLC........................... F 302 239-1654
  Hockessin (G-5294)
Mallard Advisors LLC.......................... G 302 239-1654
  Newark (G-11318)
Mallard Financial Partners Inc............ C 302 737-4546
  Newark (G-11319)
Management PI Investme.................. G 888 654-5449
  Wilmington (G-18100)
Marvin & Palmer Associates............... E 302 573-3570
  Wilmington (G-18174)
Maxwell Financial Firm LLC................ E 302 332-3454
  Wilmington (G-18208)
Morgan Stanley & Co LLC................... G 302 573-4000
  Wilmington (G-18447)
Morgan Stnley Smith Barney LLC...... C 302 644-6600
  Rehoboth Beach (G-12862)
Ms Financing LLC................................ D 212 276-1206
  Wilmington (G-18474)
National Financial LLC......................... G 302 328-1370
  New Castle (G-9395)
Natixis Globl Asset MGT Hldngs......... G 617 449-2100
  Wilmington (G-18552)
New Visions Inv Group LLC................ G 302 299-6234
  Newark (G-11527)
Northern Cross Investments............... G 302 655-9074
  Wilmington (G-18684)
Onemain... G 812 492-2156
  Wilmington (G-18788)
Onemain Financial Group LLC........... G 302 628-9253
  Seaford (G-13324)
Parkwood Trust Company................... G 302 426-1220
  Wilmington (G-18897)
Peninsula Financial Group Inc............ G 302 856-0970
  Georgetown (G-4458)
Perella Weinberg Partners LLC.......... G 267 746-0569
  Wilmington (G-18970)
Pfpc Worldwide Inc............................... F 302 791-1700
  Wilmington (G-19005)
Pollintion Capitl Partners LLC............. G 872 201-1168
  Wilmington (G-19109)
Primerica.. G 302 455-9460
  Newark (G-11745)
Primerica.. G 302 439-0206
  Wilmington (G-19193)
Prudential Intl Invstmnts Corp............. G 302 778-1729
  Wilmington (G-19240)
Qbean International LLC...................... G 917 781-6274
  Claymont (G-1271)
Race Advisors LLC............................... G 302 245-1895
  Lewes (G-6405)
Ragaman Services Inc......................... F 339 221-6757
  Wilmington (G-19316)
Riversedge... G 267 342-6984
  Wilmington (G-19498)
Rk Advisors LLC.................................... G 302 561-5258
  Hockessin (G-5366)
Saggio Management Group Inc.......... G 302 659-6560
  Smyrna (G-13877)
Silver Bridge Capital Mgmt LLC.......... G 302 575-9215
  Wilmington (G-19827)
Standard & Poors Intl LLC................... G 212 512-2000
  Wilmington (G-20011)

Staples & Associates Insurance........... G 302 398-3276
  Harrington (G-4835)
Subaru Investment Inc......................... G 302 472-9266
  Wilmington (G-20109)
Tjm Financial Group LLC..................... G 302 674-7033
  Wilmington (G-20337)
Topkis Financial Advisors LLC............ G 302 654-4444
  Wilmington (G-20359)
Trade Investors LLC............................. G 888 579-0286
  Dover (G-3711)
Uag International Holdings Inc............. E 302 427-9859
  Wilmington (G-20489)
Union Fnosa Fincl Svcs USA LLC....... F 302 738-6680
  Newark (G-12265)
United Brokerage Packaging................ G 302 294-6782
  Newark (G-12268)
US Cherry LLC..................................... G 305 339-5318
  Dover (G-3763)
Van Buren Financial Group LLC.......... F 302 655-9505
  Wilmington (G-20567)
Wbi Capital Advisors LLC.................... E 856 361-6362
  Wilmington (G-20696)
Wealth Management Group................. G 302 734-5826
  Dover (G-3824)
Westover Capital Advisors LLC........... G 302 427-9600
  Wilmington (G-20743)
Wheeler Financial LLC.......................... G 302 543-5585
  Wilmington (G-20758)

6289 Security and commodity service

1 Konto Inc... F 215 783-8166
  Lewes (G-5634)
Fuinre Inc... E 402 480-6465
  Lewes (G-6020)

63 INSURANCE CARRIERS

6311 Life insurance

Alvini & Assoc Fincl Planners.............. G 302 397-8135
  Wilmington (G-14403)
Better Life Enerprise............................. G 302 312-9156
  Bear (G-70)
Chesapeake Brokerage LLC................ G 410 517-1592
  Rehoboth Beach (G-12670)
Cigna Global Holdings Inc................... F 302 797-3469
  Claymont (G-1086)
Cigna Holdings Inc............................... F 215 761-1000
  Claymont (G-1087)
Citicorp Del-Lease Inc.......................... D 302 323-3801
  New Castle (G-8947)
Cruise A Lifetime Usa Inc.................... G 302 697-2139
  Dover (G-2163)
Delaware American Lf Insur Co........... D 302 594-2871
  Wilmington (G-15864)
Donald C Savoy Inc.............................. F 888 992-6755
  Newark (G-10549)
Eea Life Settlements Inc...................... G 302 472-7429
  Wilmington (G-16306)
First Lincoln Holdings Inc..................... F 302 429-4900
  Wilmington (G-16619)
Hackney Business Solutions LLC......... G 843 496-7236
  Newark (G-10916)
Highmarks Inc....................................... G 302 421-3000
  Wilmington (G-17145)
New York Life Ins Co............................ G 302 537-7060
  Ocean View (G-12551)
Northwestern Mutl Fincl Netwrk........... G 414 299-2508
  Dover (G-3199)
Openeyes Insur Holdings Inc............... G 737 222-9132
  Wilmington (G-18799)
Rbc Insurance Holdings USA Inc......... A 302 651-8356
  Wilmington (G-19351)

6321 Accident and health insurance

American Life Insurance Co................. D 302 594-2000
  Wilmington (G-14435)
Architect Engineer Ins Co Risk............ G 302 658-2342
  Wilmington (G-14542)
Chesapeake Rehab Equipment Inc...... G 302 266-6234
  Newark (G-10198)
Cigna Holdings Inc............................... F 215 761-1000
  Claymont (G-1087)
Citicorp Del-Lease Inc.......................... D 302 323-3801
  New Castle (G-8947)
Delphi Financial Group Inc................... C 302 478-5142
  Wilmington (G-16000)
Highmarks Inc....................................... B 302 421-3000
  Wilmington (G-17144)
Rbc Insurance Holdings USA Inc......... A 302 651-8356
  Wilmington (G-19351)

6324 Hospital and medical service plans

Aetna Hose Hook & Ladder Co 9......... E 302 454-3305
  Newark (G-9791)
American Life Insurance Co................. D 302 594-2000
  Wilmington (G-14435)
Amerihalth Integrated Benefits............. E 302 777-6400
  Wilmington (G-14447)
Highmarks Inc....................................... G 302 421-3000
  Wilmington (G-17145)
Soul Purpose.. G 302 420-1254
  Townsend (G-14066)

6331 Fire, marine, and casualty insurance

AAA Club Alliance Inc.......................... D 302 674-8020
  Dover (G-1700)
AAA Club Alliance Inc.......................... B 302 299-4700
  Wilmington (G-14181)
Allstate Insur Ryan Nichols.................. G 302 864-2230
  Middletown (G-6853)
American Centennial Insur Co............. G 302 479-2100
  Wilmington (G-14426)
Chrissinger and Baumberger............... G 302 777-0100
  Wilmington (G-15395)
Cigna Holdings Inc............................... F 215 761-1000
  Claymont (G-1087)
Cowchok Tf Inc..................................... G 302 475-4510
  Wilmington (G-15671)
Highmarks Inc....................................... G 302 421-3000
  Wilmington (G-17145)
Homewatch Concierge......................... G 302 542-4087
  Rehoboth Beach (G-12790)
Nuclear Electric Insurance Ltd............. D 302 888-3000
  Wilmington (G-18710)
Progressive Casualty Insur Co............ G 302 734-7360
  Dover (G-3377)

6351 Surety insurance

A & R Bail Bonds LLC.......................... G 302 357-1221
  Wilmington (G-14157)
AAA Club Alliance Inc.......................... B 302 299-4700
  Wilmington (G-14181)
Anderson Catania Suretly Svc............. F 302 762-7599
  Wilmington (G-14471)
Bail Enforcement Agent....................... G 302 543-6305
  Wilmington (G-14715)
Chesapeake Brokerage LLC................ G 410 517-1592
  Rehoboth Beach (G-12670)
Highmarks Inc....................................... G 302 421-3000
  Wilmington (G-17145)
Martello RE Holdings Ltd LLC............. G 302 636-5401
  Wilmington (G-18164)
Pexmall Ltd Liability Company............ G 347 414-9879
  Newark (G-11678)

Employee Codes: A=Over 500 employees, B=251-500
C=101-250, D=51-100, E=20-50, F=10-19, G=1-9

63 INSURANCE CARRIERS

6361 Title insurance

Flowers Real Estate LLC................ G 302 383-8955
  Wilmington *(G-16668)*
Intercoastal Title Agency Inc........... G 302 478-7752
  Wilmington *(G-17375)*
Michelangelo Technologies Inc........ E 949 382-1899
  Lewes *(G-6270)*
Northwest Title Planet Inc.............. G 248 278-4080
  Lewes *(G-6319)*
Old Republic Nat Title Insur............ G 302 734-3570
  Dover *(G-3219)*
Old Republic Nat Title Insur............ F 302 661-1997
  Wilmington *(G-18755)*
Old Republic Title Company........... E 302 661-1997
  Wilmington *(G-18756)*
Pennmuni-Tiaa US RE Fund LLC..... G 302 636-5401
  Wilmington *(G-18956)*

6371 Pension, health, and welfare funds

Benefit Services Unlimited............. F 302 479-5696
  Wilmington *(G-14833)*
New Cstle Cnty Emplyees Pnsion..... G 302 395-5555
  New Castle *(G-9415)*
Sntc Holding Inc............................ F 302 777-5261
  Wilmington *(G-19902)*

6399 Insurance carriers, nec

Allstate Insur Ryan Nichols............ G 302 864-2230
  Middletown *(G-6853)*
Coveragex LLC............................. G 310 854-2677
  Wilmington *(G-15666)*
Gem Group LP.............................. F 302 762-2008
  Wilmington *(G-16826)*
Mid Atlantic Warranty..................... G 302 893-4220
  Wilmington *(G-18335)*

64 INSURANCE AGENTS, BROKERS AND SERVICE

6411 Insurance agents, brokers, and service

21st Century Insurance Group........ E 302 478-3109
  Wilmington *(G-14120)*
21st Century N Amer Insur Co........ A 877 310-5687
  Wilmington *(G-14121)*
A M Clay Onroe Inc....................... G 302 645-6565
  Lewes *(G-5646)*
AAA Club Alliance Inc.................... E 302 283-4300
  Newark *(G-9732)*
AAA Environmental Services......... G 302 284-4334
  Felton *(G-3937)*
AAA Mid-Atlantic........................... E 302 299-4230
  Wilmington *(G-14182)*
AAA Midatlantic Inc........................ F 800 999-4952
  Historic New Castle *(G-4918)*
Abby Pubusky............................... G 302 897-8932
  Wilmington *(G-14194)*
Abby Pubusky Insurance................ G 302 434-3333
  Wilmington *(G-14195)*
Affordable Insur Netwrk Del........... G 800 681-7261
  Bear *(G-20)*
AFLAC... G 302 376-9880
  Middletown *(G-6838)*
AFLAC District Offcie.................... G 302 375-6885
  Claymont *(G-1025)*
Aim Inc.. G 302 424-1424
  Milford *(G-7762)*
Allen Insurance Group.................. G 302 654-8823
  Wilmington *(G-14374)*
Allstate Insrnce Bob Sbraccia........ G 302 300-4500
  Wilmington *(G-14385)*
Allstate Insur Agnt Intgrity I............ G 302 368-6279
  Newark *(G-9826)*
Allstate Insurance........................ G 302 248-8500
  Lewes *(G-5677)*
Always Insurance Agency LLC....... G 302 566-6529
  Harrington *(G-4726)*
American Life Insurance Co........... D 302 594-2000
  Wilmington *(G-14435)*
Andrew Bobich............................ G 312 384-9323
  Wilmington *(G-14474)*
Angle Planning Concepts.............. G 302 735-7526
  Dover *(G-1795)*
Ansel Health Inc........................... F 844 987-1070
  Wilmington *(G-14495)*
Ascela... E 888 298-5151
  Newark *(G-9918)*
Assurance Partners Intl................. F 302 478-0173
  Wilmington *(G-14600)*
At-Bay Insurance Services LLC...... G 888 338-9522
  Wilmington *(G-14615)*
Auspice Risk LLC......................... G 484 467-1963
  Lewes *(G-5720)*
Auto Cheap Quotes Ins-Wlmgtn..... G 302 992-9736
  Wilmington *(G-14650)*
B+h Insurance LLC....................... E 302 995-2247
  Newark *(G-9968)*
Bankers Life................................. G 302 232-5006
  Dover *(G-1873)*
Bill Burris Insurance...................... G 302 239-6661
  Hockessin *(G-5133)*
Bishop Associates........................ G 302 838-1270
  Newark *(G-10039)*
Bob Mobley.................................. G 302 652-2005
  Wilmington *(G-14991)*
Bob Simmons Agency................... G 302 698-1970
  Dover *(G-1957)*
Bosco Insurance Agency............... G 302 678-0647
  Dover *(G-1964)*
Braun Agency Inc......................... G 302 998-1412
  Wilmington *(G-15096)*
Bs Insurance LLC......................... E 302 645-2356
  Lewes *(G-5779)*
Business Insurance Services........ G 302 655-5300
  New Castle *(G-8903)*
C Edgar Wood Inc........................ E 302 674-3500
  Dover *(G-2007)*
Cambridge Insurance Group Inc..... G 302 888-2440
  Wilmington *(G-15203)*
Carey Jr James E Inc.................... G 302 934-8383
  Dagsboro *(G-1422)*
Cbm Insurance Agency LLC......... E 302 322-2261
  New Castle *(G-8923)*
Ccgsr Inc..................................... G 800 927-9800
  Wilmington *(G-15288)*
Cedar Hamilton Insur Svcs LLC..... G 302 573-3000
  Wilmington *(G-15295)*
Chad Wiswall Agency.................... G 302 791-7600
  Wilmington *(G-15326)*
Chambers Insurance Agency Inc.... G 302 655-5300
  New Castle *(G-8924)*
Charlene Webb............................. G 302 424-8490
  Milford *(G-7820)*
Charles L Saulsbery Agt................ G 302 894-1430
  Newark *(G-10190)*
Charles M Wallace........................ G 302 998-1412
  Wilmington *(G-15338)*
Chesapeak Insurance Advisors..... G 610 793-6885
  Fenwick Island *(G-4044)*
Chesapeake Insurance Advisors.... F 302 544-6900
  New Castle *(G-8931)*
Chris Haist................................... G 302 234-1116
  Newark *(G-10210)*
Chubb US Holdings Inc................. C 215 640-1000
  Wilmington *(G-15426)*
Chuck Hall Agt.............................. G 302 934-8083
  Millsboro *(G-8226)*
Chuck Redstone - State Farm In..... G 302 832-0345
  Newark *(G-10238)*
Cigna Global Holdings Inc............. F 302 797-3469
  Claymont *(G-1086)*
Coastal Equities Inc..................... D 302 543-2784
  Wilmington *(G-15509)*
Commercial Insurance Assoc........ G 610 436-4608
  Newark *(G-10284)*
Concord Agency Inc..................... G 302 478-4000
  Wilmington *(G-15578)*
Davis Insurance Group Inc........... G 302 652-4700
  Montchanin *(G-8737)*
Debra McAfee............................... G 302 655-7999
  New Castle *(G-9007)*
Delaware All-State Theatre............ G 302 559-6667
  Wilmington *(G-15862)*
Delaware Deadly Weapons............ G 302 736-5159
  Dover *(G-2225)*
Delmarva Insurance Group........... G 302 248-8500
  Lewes *(G-5906)*
Denise Beam............................... G 302 539-1900
  Ocean View *(G-12504)*
Desanctis Insurance Agency LLC... G 302 629-8841
  Seaford *(G-13159)*
Dewberry Insurance Agency Inc.... G 302 995-9550
  Wilmington *(G-16037)*
Diann Jones Agcy - Nationwide..... G 302 530-1234
  Middletown *(G-7058)*
Donald C Savoy Inc..................... F 302 697-4100
  Dover *(G-2322)*
Donald C Savoy Inc..................... F 888 992-6755
  Newark *(G-10549)*
Douglas C Loew & Associates...... G 302 453-0550
  Newark *(G-10555)*
Eia Insurers Group LLC................ G 302 543-4572
  Wilmington *(G-16313)*
Elsmere Insurance Agency LLC..... F 317 574-2861
  Wilmington *(G-16379)*
Endurnce Reinsurance Corp Amer... E 973 898-9575
  Wilmington *(G-16414)*
Esis Inc....................................... C 215 640-1000
  Wilmington *(G-16464)*
Fair Insurance Agency Inc............. G 302 395-0740
  Bear *(G-219)*
Farmers Mutl Fire Insur Slem C...... E 856 935-1851
  Wilmington *(G-16554)*
Fidelity National Info Svcs............. F 302 658-2102
  Wilmington *(G-16599)*
Fowler & Williams Inc................... F 302 875-7518
  Laurel *(G-5514)*
Fox Point Programs Inc................ G 302 765-6018
  Wilmington *(G-16714)*
Fox Point Programs Inc................ F 800 499-7242
  Claymont *(G-1151)*
Fraim Monnarae.......................... G 302 761-1313
  Wilmington *(G-16718)*
Fred S Smalls Insurance............... F 302 633-1980
  Wilmington *(G-16736)*
Fusura LLC.................................. D 302 397-2200
  Wilmington *(G-16774)*
Garland Thompson Agency........... G 302 407-6260
  Wilmington *(G-16805)*
Garland Thompson Agency........... G 302 407-6262
  Wilmington *(G-16806)*
George H Bunting Jr..................... G 302 227-3891
  Rehoboth Beach *(G-12768)*
George J Weiner Associates......... F 302 658-0218
  Wilmington *(G-16846)*

SIC SECTION
64 INSURANCE AGENTS, BROKERS AND SERVICE

Harrington Realty Inc................................. E 302 736-0800
  Dover (G-2654)
Hartle Brian State Farm Agency............. G 302 322-1741
  New Castle (G-9200)
Heather Broujos Agt................................. G 302 368-8080
  Newark (G-10943)
Henaghan Insurance................................ G 302 235-3111
  Hockessin (G-5237)
Hetrick-Drake Associates Inc.................. G 302 998-7500
  Middletown (G-7208)
High Point Preferred Insur Co.................. D 800 245-2425
  Wilmington (G-17141)
Hoeschel Inv & Insur Group..................... F 302 738-3535
  Newark (G-10957)
Impact Insurance Agency......................... G 302 363-7785
  Clayton (G-1371)
Independent School MGT Inc.................. E 302 656-4944
  Wilmington (G-17310)
Ins Regulatory Insurance Svcs................. G 302 256-0455
  Wilmington (G-17351)
Insley Insur & Finanial Svcs..................... G 302 677-1888
  Dover (G-2738)
Insley Insur & Fincl Svcs Inc.................... F 302 286-0777
  Newark (G-11025)
Insley Jr Harry Agt.................................... G 302 656-1800
  Wilmington (G-17354)
Insurance & Financial Svcs Inc................ E 302 239-5895
  New Castle (G-9235)
Insurance Administrators Inc................... G 302 239-1688
  Wilmington (G-17361)
Insurance Associates Inc......................... F 302 368-0888
  Newark (G-11028)
Insurance Market Inc................................ G 302 934-9006
  Millsboro (G-8321)
Insurance Market Inc................................ F 302 875-7591
  Laurel (G-5534)
Insurance Office America Inc.................. G 302 764-1000
  Wilmington (G-17363)
Integra ADM Group Inc............................ F 800 959-3518
  Seaford (G-13223)
Iroquois New England Inc....................... F 716 373-5511
  Wilmington (G-17423)
James N Walsh Jr.................................... G 302 235-7777
  Wilmington (G-17483)
Jamie Laber.. G 302 373-7890
  Newark (G-11095)
Jeanine ODonnell..................................... G 302 644-3276
  Lewes (G-6137)
Jessica Yang Inc....................................... G 612 217-0220
  Wilmington (G-17534)
John Borden.. G 302 674-2992
  Dover (G-2796)
John Koziol Inc.. G 302 234-5430
  Hockessin (G-5262)
John Wingate Insurance........................... G 302 339-5185
  Seaford (G-13238)
Juno Insurance Services LLC.................. G 650 380-8449
  Wilmington (G-17616)
Katie Bennett.. G 302 697-2650
  Camden (G-864)
Kelly & Assoc Insur Group Inc................. G 302 661-6324
  Wilmington (G-17679)
Kim Jones Agcy State Frm Insur.............. G 302 934-9393
  Millsboro (G-8340)
L & D Insurance Services LLC................. G 302 235-2288
  Hockessin (G-5273)
L & W Insurance Inc................................. E 302 674-3500
  Dover (G-2892)
Lawrence Agencies Inc............................ G 302 995-6936
  Wilmington (G-17835)
Lexisnexis Risk Assets Inc....................... A 800 458-9410
  Wilmington (G-17889)

Lisa Broadbent Insurance Inc.................. G 302 731-0044
  Newark (G-11266)
Loss Pay Inc... G 833 567-7729
  Lewes (G-6223)
Lyons Companies LLC............................. D 302 658-5508
  Wilmington (G-18052)
Lyons Insurance Agency Inc.................... D 302 227-7100
  Wilmington (G-18054)
Mark Penuel... G 302 856-7724
  Georgetown (G-4415)
Martin Direct Insurance............................ G 302 452-2700
  Newark (G-11344)
Marvel Agency Inc.................................... G 302 422-7844
  Milford (G-7986)
Mary Bryan Inc... G 302 875-2087
  Laurel (G-5560)
Matt Basile State Farm Insur................... G 302 659-9000
  Smyrna (G-13819)
McCall Brooks Insurance Agency............ G 302 475-8200
  Newark (G-11366)
McComrick Insurance Services............... G 302 732-6655
  Dagsboro (G-1480)
Mercury Research LLC............................ F 860 532-3480
  Middletown (G-7341)
Metlife Inc.. E 302 594-2085
  Wilmington (G-18292)
MetLife Svcs & Solutions LLC.................. F 302 734-5803
  Dover (G-3073)
Michael Frankos....................................... G 302 531-0831
  Dover (G-3078)
Mizu Business Services Inc..................... G 302 321-5001
  Dover (G-3106)
Moore Insurance & Financial................... G 302 999-9101
  Wilmington (G-18434)
Mountain W Insur Fncl Svcs LLC............. F 970 824-8185
  Wilmington (G-18466)
Muncie Ins & Fncl Svcs Inc...................... G 302 398-9100
  Harrington (G-4806)
Muncie Ins & Fncl Svcs Inc...................... G 302 761-9611
  Wilmington (G-18486)
Muncie Insurance & Fincl Svcs................ G 302 645-7740
  Rehoboth Beach (G-12867)
Muncie Insurance Services...................... G 302 629-9414
  Seaford (G-13296)
Nationwide Insrnce Crey Insur................. F 302 934-8383
  Dagsboro (G-1487)
Nationwide Insrnce Wswall Agcy............. G 302 791-7600
  Wilmington (G-18550)
Nationwide Insur - Wlgus Insur................ G 302 629-5140
  Seaford (G-13314)
Nationwide Insurance............................... G 919 644-6535
  Dover (G-3157)
Nationwide Insurance............................... G 302 515-1851
  Georgetown (G-4443)
Nationwide Insurance............................... G 302 402-5188
  Milford (G-8025)
Nationwide Insurance............................... G 302 453-9698
  Newark (G-11491)
Nationwide Insurance Co......................... G 302 678-2223
  Dover (G-3158)
Nationwide Mutual Insurance Co............. F 302 234-5430
  Hockessin (G-5317)
Nationwide Mutual Insurance Co............. G 434 426-9410
  Wilmington (G-18551)
New Castle Insurance Ltd........................ F 302 328-6111
  Historic New Castle (G-5036)
Nickle Insurance....................................... G 302 654-0347
  Wilmington (G-18643)
Nickle Insurance Agency Inc................... G 302 834-9700
  Delaware City (G-1549)
Notch Insurance Inc................................. E 616 622-2554
  Dover (G-3201)

Nova Wave Credit LLC............................ G 929 263-4212
  Dover (G-3202)
Novo Insurance LLC................................ F 408 245-3800
  Wilmington (G-18699)
Occidental L Transamerica...................... F 302 477-9700
  Wilmington (G-18739)
October Phoenix Rlty Group LLC............ G 302 722-5125
  Newark (G-11577)
Options or Fast Cash Inc......................... G 310 867-9171
  Middletown (G-7418)
OSullivan Insurance Agency................... G 302 927-0927
  Dagsboro (G-1494)
Pennock Insurance Inc............................ G 302 235-8258
  Hockessin (G-5337)
Penteco LLC.. G 302 472-9105
  Wilmington (G-18962)
Peoples First Insurance Inc..................... G 302 449-4777
  Middletown (G-7440)
Perry and Associates Services................ G 302 581-3092
  Wilmington (G-18984)
Peter Renzi.. G 302 265-1309
  Milford (G-8049)
Phil Hill... G 302 678-0499
  Dover (G-3312)
Phly LLC... G 778 882-2391
  Wilmington (G-19022)
Planet Payment Solutions Inc.................. E 516 670-3200
  New Castle (G-9476)
Poland & Sullivan Insur Inc..................... F 302 738-3535
  Newark (G-11708)
Progressive Casualty Insur Co................ G 302 734-7360
  Dover (G-3377)
Prominent Insurance Svcs Inc................. G 302 351-3368
  Wilmington (G-19228)
Quikstamp LLC.. F 302 659-7555
  Newark (G-11800)
Rawlins Ferguson Jones & Lewis............ G 302 337-8231
  Seaford (G-13365)
Raymond Babiarz Agt.............................. G 302 993-8047
  Wilmington (G-19344)
Records - Gebhart Agency Inc................ G 302 653-9211
  Smyrna (G-13864)
Regina McLarnon..................................... G 800 903-8114
  Wilmington (G-19403)
Regulatory Insurance Services................ G 302 678-2004
  Dover (G-3447)
Rhue & Associates Inc............................ G 302 422-3058
  Milford (G-8067)
Richard A Parsons Agency Inc................ G 302 674-2810
  Dover (G-3466)
Richard P Horgan Insurance................... G 302 934-9494
  Wilmington (G-19473)
Robert F Mullen Insurance Agcy............. G 302 322-5331
  Bear (G-464)
Rockwood Programs Inc......................... E 302 765-6000
  Claymont (G-1282)
Ronnie Carter... G 302 284-9321
  Felton (G-4022)
S T Good Insurance Inc.......................... F 215 969-8385
  Newark (G-11929)
Sanderson Albidress Agency.................. G 302 368-3010
  Wilmington (G-19658)
Savoy Associates.................................... G 302 658-8770
  Wilmington (G-19685)
Schanne Mark State Farm Insur.............. G 302 422-7231
  Milford (G-8086)
Scor Globl Lf Amrcas Rnsurance............. C 704 344-2700
  Wilmington (G-19710)
Sean Ohagan LLC................................... G 302 798-7572
  Claymont (G-1287)
Sedgwick.. F 302 691-8871
  Wilmington (G-19734)

64 INSURANCE AGENTS, BROKERS AND SERVICE

Sentinel Insurance .... G 302 858-4962
  Georgetown *(G-4504)*

Sharon Farm Insurance .... G 215 333-5544
  Rehoboth Beach *(G-12955)*

Sierentz Advisors LLC .... G 423 665-9444
  Wilmington *(G-19816)*

Smith Health & Life LLC .... G 302 596-0641
  Wilmington *(G-19888)*

Standard Insurance Company .... D 302 322-9922
  New Castle *(G-9591)*

Staples & Associates Insurance .... G 302 398-3276
  Harrington *(G-4835)*

Starfish Spclty Insur Svcs LLC .... G 914 556-3200
  Newark *(G-12089)*

Starr Wright Insur Agcy Inc .... E 302 483-0190
  Wilmington *(G-20028)*

State Farm .... G 302 258-9989
  Dagsboro *(G-1509)*

State Farm .... G 302 678-5656
  Dover *(G-3606)*

State Farm .... G 302 344-3514
  Wilmington *(G-20031)*

State Farm Insurance .... E 302 834-5467
  Bear *(G-511)*

State Farm Insurance .... G 302 934-8083
  Millsboro *(G-8467)*

State Farm Insurance .... G 302 547-7478
  Wilmington *(G-20032)*

State Farm Insurance .... G 302 353-6636
  Wilmington *(G-20033)*

State Farm Insurance Co .... G 302 547-4117
  Wilmington *(G-20034)*

State Farmjeff Gardiner .... G 302 286-7130
  Newark *(G-12091)*

Steadfast Insurance Company .... G 847 605-6000
  Dover *(G-3610)*

Steele Insurance Group LLC .... G 302 898-6797
  Wilmington *(G-20045)*

Steinebach Robert and Assoc .... G 302 328-1212
  Christiana *(G-1010)*

Surplus & Excess Line Ltd .... G 302 653-5016
  Smyrna *(G-13905)*

Task Force Security Svcs LLC .... G 302 476-4064
  Bear *(G-525)*

Taylor Professional Insurance .... G 302 660-3685
  Wilmington *(G-20235)*

Terry White .... G 302 652-4969
  Newark *(G-12180)*

Terry White-State Farm Ins .... G 302 353-6636
  Wilmington *(G-20278)*

Thomas Weisenfels .... G 302 571-5244
  Wilmington *(G-20312)*

Tiffany Kistler Benefits .... D 302 425-5010
  Wilmington *(G-20320)*

Tom Wiseley Insurance Agency .... G 302 832-7700
  Newark *(G-12207)*

Tony Milam - State Farm Ins AG .... G 302 732-3220
  Dagsboro *(G-1518)*

Tri Valley Agency Inc .... G 302 482-3802
  Wilmington *(G-20411)*

Truitt Insurance Agency Inc .... G 302 645-9344
  Lewes *(G-6582)*

Virgil P Ellwanger .... G 302 934-8083
  Millsboro *(G-8495)*

Wahl Financial Inc .... G 302 229-1933
  Wilmington *(G-20670)*

Weymouth Swyze Crroon Insur In .... F 302 655-3705
  Wilmington *(G-20750)*

Wilgus Associates Inc .... G 302 644-2960
  Lewes *(G-6630)*

Wilgus Associates Inc .... E 302 539-7511
  Bethany Beach *(G-650)*

Wilgus Insur Agcy Inc - Mllsbo .... G 302 934-1502
  Millsboro *(G-8506)*

William Heydt .... G 302 678-1161
  Dover *(G-3851)*

Williams Insurance Agency Inc .... F 302 384-7804
  Wilmington *(G-20799)*

Williams Insurance Agency Inc .... G 302 227-2501
  Wilmington *(G-20800)*

Williams Insurance Agency Inc .... G 302 239-5500
  Wilmington *(G-20801)*

Williams Insurance Agency Inc .... E 302 227-2501
  Rehoboth Beach *(G-13019)*

Young Mens Christian Assn .... G 302 571-6925
  Wilmington *(G-20935)*

Zach Philippe Sate Farm Ins .... G 302 327-0120
  Bear *(G-571)*

Zavier J Decaire .... F 302 658-0218
  Wilmington *(G-20948)*

65 REAL ESTATE

6512 Nonresidential building operators

20 Mont LLC .... G 302 999-0708
  Wilmington *(G-14119)*

302 Properties LLC .... G 302 525-4302
  Newark *(G-9708)*

AAA Club Alliance Inc .... B 302 299-4700
  Wilmington *(G-14181)*

Advertising Is Simple .... G 302 407-0431
  Wilmington *(G-14290)*

Aftermath Services LLC .... E 302 357-3780
  Dover *(G-1736)*

Amy Kellenberger Inc .... F 302 381-7901
  Milton *(G-8560)*

Arcadia Properties LLC .... F 302 747-5050
  Dover *(G-1810)*

Atlantic Management Ltd .... F 302 645-9511
  Rehoboth Beach *(G-12615)*

Belco Inc .... G 302 655-1561
  Wilmington *(G-14815)*

Beshore Lawn Service LLC .... G 302 313-6924
  Townsend *(G-13963)*

Bestfield Properties LLC .... G 302 658-1000
  Wilmington *(G-14859)*

Better Days Properties LLC .... G 718 644-0163
  Middletown *(G-6917)*

Bulton Properties LLC .... G 302 945-0967
  Milton *(G-8577)*

Capitol Title Loans .... G 302 652-3591
  Wilmington *(G-15234)*

Carver Gardens Properties LLC .... G 302 420-2662
  Newark *(G-10157)*

CAs Prperty Preservation LLC .... G 302 416-2377
  Claymont *(G-1075)*

Cfg Properties .... G 302 993-1260
  Wilmington *(G-15320)*

Cigna Global Holdings Inc .... F 302 797-3469
  Claymont *(G-1086)*

Cigna Holdings Inc .... F 215 761-1000
  Claymont *(G-1087)*

Cigna Real Estate Inc .... G 302 476-3337
  Wilmington *(G-15436)*

Ckq Properties LLC .... G 302 378-2560
  Middletown *(G-6985)*

Concepcion Properties LLC .... G 302 691-9233
  New Castle *(G-8964)*

Concord Mall LLC .... E 302 478-9271
  Wilmington *(G-15582)*

Connections CSP .... G 302 384-8140
  Wilmington *(G-15600)*

Conserve Property Group .... G 302 275-8616
  Wilmington *(G-15607)*

Covenant Properties I .... G 302 234-5655
  Wilmington *(G-15663)*

Covenant Wealth Strategies .... F 302 234-5655
  Wilmington *(G-15664)*

Dack Realty Corp .... G 302 792-2737
  Claymont *(G-1107)*

Dannemann & Danneman LLC .... G 302 368-4685
  Wilmington *(G-15791)*

Delaware Corporate Center .... G 302 690-3789
  Wilmington *(G-15892)*

Delaware Occptnal Hlth Svcs LL .... E 302 368-5100
  Newark *(G-10464)*

Delmarva Ice LLC .... G 302 593-7095
  Seaford *(G-13154)*

Delport Holding Company .... G 302 655-7300
  New Castle *(G-9044)*

DMS Solution .... G 302 689-6558
  Bear *(G-174)*

Donovan Property Service Inc .... G 917 841-2396
  Hockessin *(G-5191)*

Dover Afb .... G 321 634-2016
  Dover *(G-2331)*

Dover Commons LLC .... F 302 678-4000
  Dover *(G-2336)*

Dover Mall LLC .... F 302 678-4000
  Dover *(G-2353)*

Dover Mall LLC .... E 302 678-4000
  Dover *(G-2354)*

Dover Rent-All Inc .... E 302 739-0860
  Dover *(G-2366)*

Doyjul Apartments .... F 302 998-0088
  Wilmington *(G-16157)*

Eagle Plaza Associates Inc .... G 302 999-0708
  Wilmington *(G-16246)*

Emory Hill RE Svcs Inc .... D 302 322-9500
  New Castle *(G-9091)*

Emz Properties .... G 302 730-8250
  Dover *(G-2447)*

Envision Property Solvers LLC .... G 888 478-0744
  Hockessin *(G-5202)*

Equity Lifestyle .... G 302 595-2833
  Bear *(G-205)*

Fairchild Rental Prpts LLC .... G 302 745-1144
  Greenwood *(G-4629)*

Faw Casson .... G 302 226-1082
  Rehoboth Beach *(G-12751)*

Ferris Properties Inc .... G 302 472-0875
  Wilmington *(G-16589)*

First Data .... G 302 793-5945
  Wilmington *(G-16617)*

First State Hobbies LLC .... G 302 595-2475
  Newark *(G-10732)*

Foresee Pharma .... G 302 368-1758
  Newark *(G-10759)*

Free Properties .... G 914 474-1980
  Lewes *(G-6012)*

Fusco Enterprises .... G 302 328-6251
  New Castle *(G-9152)*

Fusco Management Inc .... E 302 328-6251
  New Castle *(G-9153)*

Gaea Property Development LLC .... G 302 536-7646
  Seaford *(G-13194)*

Glasgow Shopping Center Corp .... G 302 836-1503
  Bear *(G-249)*

Gordy Management Inc .... G 302 322-3723
  New Castle *(G-9172)*

Habitat America LLC .... F 302 875-3525
  Laurel *(G-5526)*

Holland Properties .... G 201 965-9272
  Wilmington *(G-17167)*

Ideal Property Solutions .... G 302 266-0451
  Newark *(G-10995)*

SIC SECTION

65 REAL ESTATE

Keith Properties Inc .... G 302 258-9224
  Selbyville *(G-13557)*
Kenco Group Inc .... G 302 629-4295
  Seaford *(G-13248)*
Kirkwood Property .... G 302 981-0966
  Wilmington *(G-17733)*
Lewis Environmental Group Inc .... F 302 669-6010
  New Castle *(G-9309)*
Maple Crest LLC .... G 302 540-9937
  Newark *(G-11325)*
Market Street Center Inc .... G 302 856-9024
  Georgetown *(G-4417)*
Marketing Momma .... G 302 259-1644
  Smyrna *(G-13815)*
Marnie Properties .... G 302 462-5312
  Bethany Beach *(G-619)*
McLeen Properties .... G 302 482-1486
  Wilmington *(G-18235)*
Melchiorre and Melchiorre .... F 302 645-6311
  Lewes *(G-6260)*
Memorial Hall of Tllyvlle Fire .... F 302 478-1110
  Wilmington *(G-18269)*
Meris Property LLC .... G 301 928-6519
  Bethany Beach *(G-621)*
Meyer Properties LLC .... G 302 278-4100
  Wilmington *(G-18296)*
Morningstar Property Group LLC .... G 302 543-4093
  Wilmington *(G-18452)*
Mpi Properties LLC .... G 302 635-7143
  Newark *(G-11463)*
Papaleo Rosen & Chelf PA .... G 302 482-3283
  Wilmington *(G-18879)*
Parkway Gravel Inc .... D 302 658-5241
  New Castle *(G-9450)*
Pbe Companies LLC .... D 617 346-7459
  Wilmington *(G-18930)*
Presentable Properties .... G 302 853-5111
  Seaford *(G-13356)*
Pride Home Warranty .... G 302 894-1689
  Newark *(G-11739)*
Prime Time Properties LLC .... G 302 763-6050
  Bear *(G-438)*
Properties For Life LLC .... G 302 293-9465
  Middletown *(G-7475)*
Property Advisory Service .... G 401 453-4455
  Newark *(G-11765)*
Property Improvements LLC .... G 610 692-5343
  Bethany Beach *(G-629)*
Prudential Gallo Realty .... F 302 645-6661
  Lewes *(G-6396)*
PSC Properties LLC .... G 302 832-2076
  Delaware City *(G-1555)*
Rbw Properties II .... G 302 236-5155
  Seaford *(G-13368)*
Regional Properties LLC .... G 302 740-9740
  Newark *(G-11844)*
Reliable Prperty Solutions LLC .... G 302 753-1299
  Newark *(G-11849)*
Rentwell Leasemanagemaintain .... G 302 256-5356
  Wilmington *(G-19431)*
Renu ME Property Solutions .... G 267 440-6863
  Wilmington *(G-19432)*
Resortquest Service Center .... G 302 541-5977
  Bethany Beach *(G-635)*
Rodney Square Associates .... G 302 652-1536
  Wilmington *(G-19550)*
S & A Holding Associates Inc .... G 302 479-8314
  Wilmington *(G-19603)*
S & C Properties Ltd .... G 302 995-1537
  Wilmington *(G-19604)*
Sbh Group Properties LLC .... G 302 588-1656
  Wilmington *(G-19691)*

Schwartz Center For Arts .... G 302 678-3583
  Dover *(G-3517)*
Schwarz Properties LLC .... G 302 376-1696
  Middletown *(G-7543)*
SGS Properties LLC .... G 302 588-4010
  Wilmington *(G-19775)*
Shipwrecked .... F 410 271-9563
  Dagsboro *(G-1504)*
Silver Lining Solutions LLC .... G 302 691-7100
  Wilmington *(G-19828)*
Solari Commercial Prpts LLC .... G 302 757-2956
  Wilmington *(G-19919)*
Sovereign Property MGT LLC .... E 302 994-2505
  Wilmington *(G-19943)*
Stat Office Solutions .... G 302 884-6746
  Wilmington *(G-20030)*
Steady Inc .... G 302 266-4144
  Newark *(G-12093)*
Talleyville Towne Shoppes .... G 302 478-1969
  Wilmington *(G-20215)*
Tanger Outlet Ctr Midway .... G 302 645-2525
  Rehoboth Beach *(G-12988)*
Three Little Bird Prpts LLC .... G 302 475-2981
  Wilmington *(G-20317)*
Tudor Enterprises L L C .... G 302 736-8255
  Hartly *(G-4910)*
Twin Spans Business Park LLC .... G 302 328-5713
  Wilmington *(G-20468)*
Unclaimed Property .... G 302 577-8220
  Wilmington *(G-20504)*
United Outdoor Advertising .... G 302 652-3177
  Wilmington *(G-20525)*
Unity Construction Inc .... F 302 998-0531
  Wilmington *(G-20531)*
Urban Retail Properties LLC .... G 302 479-8314
  Wilmington *(G-20542)*
Wertz & Co .... G 302 727-5643
  Rehoboth Beach *(G-13014)*
Whc Properties LLC .... G 302 225-3000
  Wilmington *(G-20755)*
Wwd Inc .... G 302 994-4553
  Wilmington *(G-20906)*

6513 Apartment building operators

15 Renwick Street LLC .... G 302 652-2900
  Wilmington *(G-14112)*
Acts Rtrmnt-Life Cmmnities Inc .... C 302 629-4368
  Seaford *(G-13047)*
Alban Associates .... G 302 656-1827
  Wilmington *(G-14348)*
Apartment Communities Corp .... G 302 656-7781
  Wilmington *(G-14503)*
Apartment Communities Inc .... F 302 798-9100
  Claymont *(G-1039)*
Apartments Sdk .... G 302 478-1215
  Wilmington *(G-14504)*
Appleby Apartments Assoc LP .... G 302 219-5014
  New Castle *(G-8815)*
Appoquinimink Development Inc .... G 302 378-0878
  Middletown *(G-6871)*
Barrettes Run Apartments .... G 302 368-3400
  Newark *(G-9984)*
Belmont Villa Condominiums .... G 302 368-1633
  Newark *(G-10016)*
Berman Development Corp .... G 302 323-1197
  New Castle *(G-8859)*
Bethel Villa Associates LP .... E 302 426-9688
  Wilmington *(G-14862)*
Better Homes of Seaford Inc .... F 302 629-6522
  Seaford *(G-13086)*
Better Homes of Seaford Inc .... F 302 629-8048
  Seaford *(G-13085)*

BNai Brith Snior Ctzens Hsing .... G 302 798-6846
  Claymont *(G-1063)*
Boston Land Co Mgt Svcs Inc .... G 302 571-0100
  Wilmington *(G-15009)*
Brandywine Apartment Assoc LP .... G 302 475-8600
  Wilmington *(G-15042)*
Brandywine Hills Apartments .... G 302 764-3242
  Wilmington *(G-15064)*
Brandywine I & 2 Apts .... F 302 475-8600
  Wilmington *(G-15068)*
Brookside Plaza Apartments LLC .... G 302 737-2008
  Newark *(G-10094)*
Capano Management Company .... D 302 737-8056
  Newark *(G-10132)*
Carl M Freeman Associates Inc .... D 302 539-6961
  Bethany Beach *(G-589)*
Carleton Court Associates LP .... F 302 454-1800
  Wilmington *(G-15252)*
Carriage House Assoc .... G 302 225-2040
  Wilmington *(G-15258)*
Cascades LLC .... G 856 662-1730
  Milford *(G-7813)*
Cavalier Group .... E 302 368-7437
  Newark *(G-10165)*
Cavalier Group .... G 302 429-8700
  Wilmington *(G-15280)*
Chelten Apartments Assoc LP .... G 302 322-6323
  Wilmington *(G-15352)*
Christiana Meadows LLC .... F 302 322-6161
  Bear *(G-102)*
Christiana Wood LLC .... G 302 322-1172
  New Castle *(G-8941)*
Clyde Spinelli .... G 302 328-7679
  New Castle *(G-8954)*
Coastal Funding Corporation .... G 302 328-4113
  Historic New Castle *(G-4959)*
Colonial Inv Managment Co .... G 302 736-0674
  Dover *(G-2113)*
Colonial Rlty Assoc Ltd Partnr .... F 302 737-1254
  Newark *(G-10278)*
Colony North Apartments .... F 302 762-0405
  Wilmington *(G-15537)*
Community Housing Inc .... G 302 652-3991
  Wilmington *(G-15561)*
Compton Pk Prsrvtion Assoc LLC .... G 302 654-4369
  Wilmington *(G-15574)*
Coral Sands Apts .... G 302 539-9559
  Fenwick Island *(G-4046)*
Cornell Property MGT Corp .... G 302 674-1460
  Dover *(G-2139)*
Country Village Apartments .... G 302 674-0991
  Dover *(G-2145)*
County Seat Apartments LL .... G 302 856-7577
  Dover *(G-2146)*
Cranston Hall Apartments .... G 302 999-7001
  Wilmington *(G-15685)*
Crescent Business Center LLC .... G 302 683-0300
  Wilmington *(G-15699)*
Crescent Communities LLC .... G 302 798-8400
  Claymont *(G-1102)*
Dack Realty Corp .... G 302 792-2737
  Claymont *(G-1107)*
Delaware Equity Fund IV .... G 302 655-1420
  Wilmington *(G-15914)*
Doyjul Apartments .... F 302 998-0088
  Wilmington *(G-16157)*
Eagle Meadows LLC .... G 302 698-1073
  Dover *(G-2402)*
Eastern Property Group Inc .... G 302 764-7112
  Wilmington *(G-16261)*
Eastern Prosperity Group .... G 302 764-7112
  Wilmington *(G-16262)*

65 REAL ESTATE

Eden Rock .... E 302 475-9400
  Wilmington *(G-16287)*

Evergreen Apartment Group Inc .... E 302 998-0322
  New Castle *(G-9105)*

Evergreen Properties MGT Inc .... G 302 998-0322
  New Castle *(G-9106)*

Evergreen Realty .... F 302 999-8805
  Wilmington *(G-16486)*

Evergreen Realty Inc .... G 302 998-0354
  Wilmington *(G-16487)*

Fairville Management Co LLC .... G 302 798-1736
  Claymont *(G-1144)*

Fairway Village .... G 302 354-1021
  Ocean View *(G-12509)*

First Montgomery Properties .... E 302 834-8272
  Bear *(G-225)*

Forest Park Apartments .... G 302 737-6151
  Wilmington *(G-16691)*

Frankel Enterprises Inc .... G 302 652-6364
  Wilmington *(G-16726)*

Galman Group Ltd .... F 215 886-2000
  Newark *(G-10802)*

Galman Group Inc .... G 302 737-5550
  Newark *(G-10803)*

Georgetown Manor Apartments .... G 302 328-6231
  New Castle *(G-9165)*

Governors Place Townhomes .... G 302 653-6655
  Smyrna *(G-13748)*

Grande Apartments .... G 302 734-8344
  Dover *(G-2619)*

Greenville Towers LLC .... G 302 397-8016
  Wilmington *(G-16974)*

Harbor Club Apartments .... G 302 738-3561
  Newark *(G-10929)*

Harbour Towne Associates LP .... G 302 645-1003
  Lewes *(G-6077)*

Harmony Mill LP .... G 302 731-7948
  Newark *(G-10931)*

Hockessin .... G 302 234-4100
  Hockessin *(G-5239)*

Homeview Group LLC .... F 508 686-6669
  Middletown *(G-7213)*

Hospitality House LLC .... G 929 262-1790
  Newark *(G-10973)*

Hub Associates .... G 302 674-2200
  Dover *(G-2700)*

Iacono - Summer Chase .... F 302 994-2505
  Wilmington *(G-17252)*

Ingleside Homes Inc .... E 302 984-0950
  Wilmington *(G-17336)*

Ingleside Rtrment Aprtmnts LLC .... F 302 575-0250
  Wilmington *(G-17337)*

Iron Hill Apartments Assoc .... G 302 366-8228
  Newark *(G-11058)*

J & S General Contractors .... G 302 658-4499
  Wilmington *(G-17447)*

Justison Apts LLC .... G 302 691-2100
  Wilmington *(G-17621)*

Justison Investors LLC .... G 302 691-2100
  Wilmington *(G-17622)*

Kendal Corporation .... C 610 335-1200
  Newark *(G-11155)*

Kendal Management Services .... E 610 388-5594
  Newark *(G-11156)*

Kimberton Apartments Assoc LP .... G 302 368-0116
  Newark *(G-11175)*

Leon N Weiner & Associates Inc .... G 302 798-3446
  Claymont *(G-1215)*

Leon N Weiner & Associates Inc .... E 302 322-6233
  New Castle *(G-9306)*

Lexington Green Apartments .... G 302 322-8959
  Newark *(G-11251)*

Linkside Apts LLC .... G 302 697-0378
  Magnolia *(G-6760)*

Linkside LLC .... G 302 697-8312
  Magnolia *(G-6761)*

Lorelton .... E 302 573-3580
  Wilmington *(G-17995)*

Lsref4 Lighthouse Corp Acqstn .... G 302 737-8500
  Newark *(G-11293)*

Luther Towers III Dover Inc .... F 302 674-1408
  Dover *(G-2983)*

Luther Towers IV Dover Inc .... F 302 674-1408
  Dover *(G-2984)*

Luther Towers of Dover Inc .... F 302 674-1408
  Dover *(G-2985)*

Luther Village I Dover Inc .... F 302 674-1408
  Dover *(G-2986)*

Luther Village II Dover Inc .... F 302 674-1408
  Dover *(G-2987)*

Lutheran Senior Services Inc .... F 302 654-4490
  Wilmington *(G-18032)*

Lutheran Snior Svcs of Sssex C .... G 302 684-1668
  Milton *(G-8657)*

Luxiasuites LLC .... F 302 654-8527
  Wilmington *(G-18039)*

Management Associates Inc .... F 302 652-3991
  Wilmington *(G-18098)*

Mid-Atlantic Realty Co Inc .... G 302 737-3110
  Newark *(G-11411)*

Milford Housing Development .... E 302 678-0300
  Dover *(G-3090)*

Millsboro Hsing For Prgress In .... G 302 934-6491
  Millsboro *(G-8385)*

Millsboro Village I LLC .... G 302 678-9400
  Millsboro *(G-8389)*

Mispillion III .... G 302 422-4429
  Milford *(G-8016)*

ML Newark LLC .... A 302 737-2868
  Newark *(G-11432)*

New Colony North Enterprises .... G 302 762-0405
  Wilmington *(G-18612)*

New Wndsor Apartments Assoc LP .... G 302 656-1354
  Wilmington *(G-18628)*

Nohotel Enterprises LLC .... G 917 970-1974
  Dover *(G-3193)*

Old Landing II LP .... G 302 934-1871
  Millsboro *(G-8410)*

One Easton .... G 302 509-3900
  Newark *(G-11591)*

Owens Manor Ltd Partnership .... G 302 678-1065
  Dover *(G-3253)*

Palladian Management LLC .... F 302 737-1971
  Newark *(G-11616)*

Panco Management Corporation .... E 302 366-1875
  Newark *(G-11619)*

Panco Management Corporation .... G 302 995-6152
  Wilmington *(G-18870)*

Panco Management Corporation .... G 302 475-9337
  Wilmington *(G-18871)*

Park View .... G 302 429-7288
  Wilmington *(G-18894)*

Parq At Square Websit .... G 302 656-8543
  Wilmington *(G-18898)*

Pettinaro Enterprises LLC .... E 302 999-0708
  Wilmington *(G-19002)*

Phase Flats II L P .... G 717 291-1911
  Wilmington *(G-19010)*

Phase I Flats L P .... G 717 291-1911
  Wilmington *(G-19011)*

Prides Court Apartments .... G 302 737-2085
  Newark *(G-11741)*

Prudential Gallo Realty .... F 302 645-6661
  Lewes *(G-6396)*

R&M Real Estate Company LLC .... G 610 715-0906
  Middletown *(G-7496)*

Reserve At Darley Green .... G 302 525-8450
  Claymont *(G-1278)*

Retreat At Newark .... G 302 294-6520
  Newark *(G-11872)*

Reybold .... F 302 584-7975
  Bear *(G-454)*

Rockland Place .... F 302 777-3099
  Wilmington *(G-19540)*

Rockwood Apartments .... F 302 832-8823
  Newark *(G-11905)*

Roizman & Associates Inc .... G 302 426-9688
  Wilmington *(G-19556)*

School Bell Apartments LP .... G 302 328-9500
  Bear *(G-480)*

Schuster Management Corp .... G 302 653-1235
  Smyrna *(G-13881)*

Seaford Apartment Ventures LLC .... G 302 629-0909
  Seaford *(G-13387)*

Seaford Preservation Assoc LLC .... G 302 629-6416
  Seaford *(G-13393)*

Service General Corporation .... F 302 218-4279
  Georgetown *(G-4507)*

Sheldon Limited Partnership .... G 302 738-3048
  Newark *(G-11994)*

Shelter Development LLC .... G 302 737-4999
  Newark *(G-11996)*

St Andrews Apartments .... G 302 834-8600
  Bear *(G-508)*

Stoltz Realty Co .... F 302 798-8500
  Claymont *(G-1305)*

Stoltz Realty Co .... D 302 656-8543
  Wilmington *(G-20078)*

Stoneybrook Associates LP .... G 302 764-6450
  Wilmington *(G-20081)*

Stoneybrook Prsrvtion Assoc LL .... F 302 764-9430
  Claymont *(G-1306)*

Studio Green Apartments .... G 302 544-9070
  Newark *(G-12111)*

Summit Properties Inc .... G 302 737-3747
  Newark *(G-12122)*

Top of Hllbrndywine Apartments .... G 302 482-8544
  Wilmington *(G-20353)*

Town and Country Trust .... E 302 328-8700
  Bear *(G-538)*

Tsionas Management Co Inc .... F 302 369-8895
  Wilmington *(G-20453)*

Udr Inc .... G 302 674-8887
  Dover *(G-3742)*

University Garden Associates .... G 302 368-3823
  Newark *(G-12275)*

Valley Run Apartments .... G 302 994-2505
  Wilmington *(G-20564)*

Victoria Mews Group Invstors L .... G 610 543-0303
  Newark *(G-12323)*

Victoria Mews LP Delnware Vall .... G 302 489-2000
  Hockessin *(G-5419)*

Village At Blue Hen .... G 302 450-1265
  Dover *(G-3796)*

Village At Fox Point .... G 302 762-7480
  Wilmington *(G-20620)*

Vintage Properties LLC .... G 302 994-4442
  Wilmington *(G-20627)*

Walden LLC .... G 302 998-8112
  Wilmington *(G-20672)*

West Center Place .... G 302 426-0201
  Wilmington *(G-20737)*

Westover Management Company LP ...... G 302 738-5775
  Newark *(G-12362)*

Westover Management Company LP ...... F 302 731-1638
  Newark *(G-12363)*

65 REAL ESTATE

Whatcoat Village Assoc LLC .... F 856 596-0500
Dover *(G-3843)*

Woodacres Associates LP .... F 302 792-0243
Claymont *(G-1339)*

Woodland Apartments LP .... G 302 994-9003
Wilmington *(G-20883)*

Woods Edge Apartments .... G 302 762-8300
Wilmington *(G-20886)*

Zwaanendael LLC .... G 302 645-6466
Lewes *(G-6652)*

6514 Dwelling operators, except apartments

302 Properties LLC .... G 302 525-4302
Newark *(G-9708)*

Baynum Enterprises Inc .... E 302 875-4477
Laurel *(G-5467)*

Baynum Enterprises Inc .... E 302 934-8699
Millsboro *(G-8183)*

Baynum Enterprises Inc .... D 302 629-6104
Seaford *(G-13078)*

Broccworth Housing Firm LLC .... G 860 937-6308
Wilmington *(G-15123)*

Chandler Heights II LP .... G 302 629-8048
Seaford *(G-13110)*

Chelten Preservation Assoc LLC .... G 302 322-6323
New Castle *(G-8928)*

Interfaith Cmnty Hsing of Del .... F 302 652-3991
Wilmington *(G-17383)*

J & S General Contractors .... G 302 658-4499
Wilmington *(G-17447)*

Lux Paradise Properties LLC .... G 502 631-2008
Wilmington *(G-18036)*

Melchiorre and Melchiorre .... F 302 645-6311
Lewes *(G-6260)*

PII Group Inc .... G 917 455-7438
Dover *(G-3322)*

Prudential Gallo Realty .... F 302 645-6661
Lewes *(G-6396)*

Wild Meadows Homes .... G 302 730-4700
Dover *(G-3849)*

Zwaanendael LLC .... G 302 645-6466
Lewes *(G-6652)*

6515 Mobile home site operators

Bayshore Inc .... G 302 539-7200
Ocean View *(G-12470)*

Carlisle Group .... G 302 475-3010
Wilmington *(G-15253)*

Colonial East LP .... F 302 644-4758
Lewes *(G-5851)*

Edward M Tingle .... G 302 436-5539
Selbyville *(G-13531)*

Holly Hill Estates .... G 302 653-7503
Smyrna *(G-13762)*

Love Creek Marina MBL Hm Site .... F 302 448-6492
Lewes *(G-6225)*

Malone Bayside Marina .... G 302 947-0234
Millsboro *(G-8361)*

Millcreek Mobile Hm Pk Land Co .... G 302 998-3045
Wilmington *(G-18359)*

Mobile Home Remedies LLC .... G 717 879-9176
Lewes *(G-6285)*

Nanticoke Shores Assoc LLC .... G 302 945-1500
Millsboro *(G-8399)*

Pine Acres Inc .... F 302 945-2000
Lewes *(G-6370)*

Rehoboth Professional Ctr LLC .... G 302 226-8334
Rehoboth Beach *(G-12931)*

Reybold Group of Companies Inc .... G 302 834-2544
Bear *(G-459)*

Theta Vest Inc .... G 302 227-3745
Rehoboth Beach *(G-12993)*

Tunnell Companies LP .... F 302 945-9300
Millsboro *(G-8488)*

White House Beach Inc .... F 302 945-3032
Millsboro *(G-8505)*

6519 Real property lessors, nec

1320 Cbw LLC .... G 302 656-5599
Wilmington *(G-14109)*

Accuvention LLC .... G 302 369-5390
Newark *(G-9754)*

Amedee Enterprises LLC .... G 302 482-7442
New Castle *(G-8792)*

Bpg Justison P4 B1 LLC .... G 302 652-1876
Wilmington *(G-15022)*

Bpg Office .... F 302 654-8535
Wilmington *(G-15023)*

Burlington Mnor Prsrvtion Asso .... G 302 761-7306
Wilmington *(G-15153)*

Carl M Freeman Associates Inc .... D 302 539-6961
Bethany Beach *(G-589)*

Chestnut Hill Plaza .... G 302 731-0643
Newark *(G-10199)*

Cigna Real Estate Inc .... G 302 476-3337
Wilmington *(G-15436)*

Coldwell Bnkr Coml Amato Assoc .... G 302 224-7700
Wilmington *(G-15524)*

Davidson Lane LLC .... G 302 326-1540
New Castle *(G-9001)*

Davitron LLC .... G 302 239-1383
Hockessin *(G-5176)*

Disab LLC .... G 302 645-6987
Lewes *(G-5922)*

Double R Holdings Inc .... G 302 645-5555
Lewes *(G-5929)*

East Coast Sales & Lease LLC .... G 302 995-7505
Wilmington *(G-16254)*

Galman Group Ltd .... F 302 328-8149
New Castle *(G-9158)*

Hensco LLC .... G 302 423-1638
Harrington *(G-4784)*

Insight Homes .... G 302 858-4281
Georgetown *(G-4370)*

JG Townsend Jr & Co Inc .... E 302 856-2525
Georgetown *(G-4383)*

Kjoy LLC .... G 302 588-5420
Newark *(G-11189)*

Langdon Group LLC .... G 240 578-5400
Dover *(G-2903)*

Located In The Village Fenwick .... G 302 539-2242
Fenwick Island *(G-4052)*

Long & Foster Real Estate Inc .... G 302 227-3821
Rehoboth Beach *(G-12837)*

Mark H Davidson .... G 302 422-0646
Lincoln *(G-6682)*

Mori America LLC .... G 703 918-4663
Wilmington *(G-18450)*

Parkway Gravel Inc .... D 302 658-5241
New Castle *(G-9450)*

Pettinaro Construction Co Inc .... D 302 999-0708
Wilmington *(G-19001)*

Platinum (us) Acquisition LLC .... G 404 414-7768
Wilmington *(G-19072)*

Pods Inc New Castle .... G 856 217-4685
Historic New Castle *(G-5050)*

Resortquest Delaware RE LLC .... G 302 541-8999
Bethany Beach *(G-634)*

Riveredge III LLC .... G 302 656-3631
Wilmington *(G-19492)*

Shipyard Center LLC .... G 302 999-0708
Wilmington *(G-19803)*

Troi LLC .... G 302 528-0229
Wilmington *(G-20433)*

Tunnell Companies LP .... F 302 945-9300
Millsboro *(G-8488)*

Walter T Wilson .... G 302 542-6753
Georgetown *(G-4572)*

Wilgus Associates Inc .... G 302 644-2960
Lewes *(G-6630)*

6531 Real estate agents and managers

1st State Real Estate LLC .... F 302 319-4051
Wilmington *(G-14116)*

A C Emsley & Associates .... G 302 429-9191
Wilmington *(G-14159)*

A2z Property Management LLC .... G 302 239-6000
Hockessin *(G-5110)*

AB Brown Real Estate Inc .... G 302 731-1031
Wilmington *(G-14189)*

Advanced Real Estate Inc .... G 302 994-7424
Wilmington *(G-14280)*

AIG Global Real Estate Inc .... G 302 655-2141
Wilmington *(G-14331)*

Alex Property Management LLC .... A 302 384-9845
Dover *(G-1761)*

All About Housing LLC .... G 302 465-3246
Townsend *(G-13956)*

Alliance RE Professionals .... G 302 519-7735
Seaford *(G-13057)*

Alliance Real Estate Pros .... G 302 536-1838
Seaford *(G-13058)*

Allied Properties .... F 302 479-8314
Wilmington *(G-14382)*

Andy Mulrine .... G 302 547-7139
Newark *(G-9866)*

Andy Staton Real Estate Inc .... G 302 703-9090
Rehoboth Beach *(G-12605)*

Anne Powell LLC .... G 302 245-9245
Ocean View *(G-12463)*

Aparta Hospitality Tech .... G 617 383-3239
Dover *(G-1801)*

ARB Heavenly Homes LLC .... G 215 919-8272
Clayton *(G-1350)*

Arbor Management LLC .... C 302 764-6450
Wilmington *(G-14524)*

Asset Management Alliance .... F 302 656-5238
Wilmington *(G-14591)*

At Home Property MGT LLC .... G 623 216-8052
New Castle *(G-8828)*

Atlas Awaits LLC .... G 724 715-3774
Dover *(G-1849)*

Avanti Homes LLC .... G 302 374-0999
Wilmington *(G-14665)*

Avello Holdings LLC .... G 631 533-2634
Lewes *(G-5725)*

B F P Sothebys Intl Realty .... G 302 545-5266
Wilmington *(G-14698)*

Baiz Nancy Miller- .... G 302 576-6821
Wilmington *(G-14716)*

Battaglia Management Inc .... F 302 325-6100
New Castle *(G-8848)*

Bay Rose Homes .... G 302 945-9510
Lewes *(G-5739)*

Bear De .... G 302 836-6050
Bear *(G-62)*

Bee Wise LLC .... G 302 601-4171
Lewes *(G-5746)*

Bellevue Realty Co .... F 302 655-1818
Wilmington *(G-14823)*

Berkshire Hataway Home Svcs .... E 302 235-6431
Hockessin *(G-5132)*

Berkshire Hathaway Global .... E 302 477-5500
Wilmington *(G-14844)*

Berkshire Hathaway Home .... F 302 227-6554
Rehoboth Beach *(G-12641)*

65 REAL ESTATE

Berkshire Hathaway Home Servic......... F 302 373-7220
  Newark *(G-10023)*
Bethany Area Realty.......................... G 302 539-7500
  Bethany Beach *(G-578)*
Bethany Beach Vacation Rentals......... G 302 539-9400
  Bethany Beach *(G-582)*
Better Homes Laurel II Inc.................. G 302 875-4282
  Laurel *(G-5469)*
Blue Hen CC LLC............................... G 302 999-0708
  Wilmington *(G-14967)*
Boston Land Co Mgt Svcs Inc.............. G 302 571-0100
  Wilmington *(G-15009)*
Bpg Office Invstors III/IV LLC............... F 302 691-2100
  Wilmington *(G-15024)*
Bpg Real Estate Services LLC.............. G 302 478-1190
  Wilmington *(G-15026)*
Bpg Real Estate Services LLC.............. F 302 777-2000
  Wilmington *(G-15027)*
Bpg Rsdential Partners III LLC............. G 302 691-2100
  Wilmington *(G-15028)*
Bradford Enterprises Inc..................... G 302 378-0662
  Middletown *(G-6934)*
Brandywine Fine Properties................. F 302 691-3052
  Wilmington *(G-15057)*
Brandywine Realty Management.......... G 302 656-1058
  Wilmington *(G-15082)*
Brandywine Valley Properties.............. G 302 475-7660
  Wilmington *(G-15089)*
Broker Post....................................... G 302 628-8467
  Seaford *(G-13094)*
Brokers Realty Network...................... G 302 593-3998
  Wilmington *(G-15124)*
Burton Realty Inc............................... G 302 945-5100
  Millsboro *(G-8210)*
C and C Management Group LLC........ G 302 946-4179
  Wilmington *(G-15173)*
C21 Gold Key Realty........................... E 302 250-6801
  Newark *(G-10116)*
Cal Agents Realty Inc......................... G 408 219-1728
  Claymont *(G-1070)*
Cap Title of Delaware LLC................... G 302 537-3788
  Ocean View *(G-12485)*
Capano Management Company........... D 302 737-8056
  Newark *(G-10132)*
Capital Commercial Realty LLC........... G 302 734-4400
  Wilmington *(G-15228)*
Capitols of Jcs LLC............................. G 302 918-5599
  Dover *(G-2024)*
Caprini Suites LLC............................. F 302 200-8904
  Dover *(G-2025)*
Carl M Freeman Associates Inc............ D 302 539-6961
  Bethany Beach *(G-589)*
Carroll Group Inc............................... G 302 836-6180
  Bear *(G-91)*
Castles By Sea LLC........................... G 302 539-2508
  Ocean View *(G-12487)*
Cbre Inc... G 302 661-6700
  Wilmington *(G-15287)*
Century 21 Gold Key Realty................. G 405 315-1105
  Newark *(G-10177)*
Century 21 Mann & Sons..................... F 302 227-9477
  Rehoboth Beach *(G-12667)*
Century 21 Tom Livizos Inc.................. G 302 737-9000
  Newark *(G-10178)*
Chichester Business Park LLC............. G 302 685-2997
  Middletown *(G-6973)*
Christina Crescent............................. G 302 528-9182
  Wilmington *(G-15414)*
Chubb Realty Group........................... G 302 388-8699
  Wilmington *(G-15425)*
Cigna Real Estate Inc......................... G 302 476-3337
  Wilmington *(G-15436)*

Classic Financial LLC......................... E 302 476-0948
  Middletown *(G-6987)*
Coastal Funding Corporation............... G 302 328-4113
  Historic New Castle *(G-4959)*
Coldwell Banker................................. F 302 539-4086
  Bethany Beach *(G-591)*
Coldwell Banker................................. G 302 541-5790
  Millville *(G-8525)*
Coldwell Banker Resort Realtty............. G 302 864-0053
  Rehoboth Beach *(G-12687)*
Coldwell Banker Resort Realty.............. G 302 422-8200
  Milford *(G-7839)*
Coldwell Banker Resort Realty.............. G 302 645-2881
  Millsboro *(G-8236)*
Coldwell Banker Resort Realty.............. G 302 841-8470
  Rehoboth Beach *(G-12688)*
Coldwell Banker Resort Realty.............. G 302 245-2145
  Seaford *(G-13128)*
Coldwell Banker Village Green.............. G 302 227-3818
  Rehoboth Beach *(G-12689)*
Coldwell Bnkr Coml Amato Assoc......... G 302 224-7700
  Wilmington *(G-15524)*
Coldwell Bnkr Rhboth Rsort Rlt............. E 302 227-5000
  Rehoboth Beach *(G-12690)*
Cole Realty Inc.................................. G 302 764-4700
  Wilmington *(G-15525)*
Commonwealth Group LLC.................. E 302 472-7200
  Wilmington *(G-15553)*
Commonwealth Trust Co...................... F 302 658-7214
  Wilmington *(G-15556)*
Cor3 Capital LLC............................... G 941 402-8101
  Dover *(G-2136)*
Cozy Stays LLC................................. G 424 207-0157
  Newark *(G-10341)*
Cressona Associates LLC.................... G 302 792-2737
  Claymont *(G-1103)*
Crowley and Assoc Rlty Inc.................. F 302 227-6131
  Rehoboth Beach *(G-12705)*
Crystal Holdings Inc............................ D 302 421-5700
  Wilmington *(G-15720)*
D M F Associates Inc.......................... G 302 539-0606
  Bethany Beach *(G-592)*
Dack Realty Corp............................... G 302 792-2737
  Claymont *(G-1107)*
Daisy Hora....................................... G 302 727-6299
  Bethany Beach *(G-593)*
Dalou Property Management................ F 866 575-9387
  Wilmington *(G-15771)*
Deaton McCue & Co Inc...................... G 302 658-7789
  Hockessin *(G-5177)*
Deballi Distinctive Properties............... G 302 376-1113
  Bear *(G-139)*
Debbie Brittingham - Coldwell.............. G 302 745-1886
  Seaford *(G-13149)*
Debbie Reed..................................... F 302 227-3818
  Rehoboth Beach *(G-12713)*
Debora Reed Team............................. G 302 227-3818
  Rehoboth Beach *(G-12714)*
Dee & Doreens Team.......................... G 302 677-0030
  Dover *(G-2207)*
Delaware RE Advisors LLC................... G 302 998-4030
  Wilmington *(G-15957)*
Delaware Real Estate Search............... G 302 437-6516
  Bear *(G-153)*
Delaware Real Estate Search............... G 302 437-6516
  Newark *(G-10474)*
Delaware Realty Group Inc.................. G 302 227-4800
  Rehoboth Beach *(G-12719)*
Delaware Valley Dev Group LLC........... G 302 235-2500
  Wilmington *(G-15979)*
Delaware Valley RE Solutions.............. G 302 668-1694
  Wilmington *(G-15983)*

Delmarva Group................................. G 302 200-9053
  Lewes *(G-5905)*
Deltrust Group Inc.............................. G 302 362-9900
  Georgetown *(G-4292)*
Don Wllams Group - Kller Wllam............ G 302 545-6859
  Lewes *(G-5927)*
Donna D Planck.................................. G 302 733-7056
  Newark *(G-10550)*
Dover Community Partnership.............. G 302 678-1965
  Dover *(G-2337)*
Dream America LLC............................ G 305 509-9201
  Lewes *(G-5934)*
Dreamville LLC.................................. G 662 524-0917
  Lewes *(G-5935)*
Dsr Drew Sparks Realty LLC................ G 302 743-1210
  Middletown *(G-7074)*
Ducos Realty Inc................................ G 302 563-6902
  Townsend *(G-13994)*
E B D Management Inc........................ G 302 428-1313
  Wilmington *(G-16234)*
Eldertrust.. G 302 993-1022
  Wilmington *(G-16350)*
Empire Group International.................. G 302 791-1100
  Claymont *(G-1132)*
Empowering Realty LLC....................... G 302 744-8169
  Dover *(G-2446)*
En Properties LLC.............................. G 302 738-4201
  Hockessin *(G-5201)*
English Realty LLC............................. E 302 295-4845
  Wilmington *(G-16425)*
ERA Harrington Realty......................... G 302 363-1796
  Dover *(G-2459)*
ERA Harrington Realty......................... E 302 674-4663
  Dover *(G-2460)*
Estate Planning Council of Del.............. G 610 581-4748
  Wilmington *(G-16468)*
Excel Property Management LLC........... G 302 541-5312
  Millville *(G-8528)*
Exit King Realty................................. G 941 961-4925
  New Castle *(G-9109)*
Exp Realty.. E 302 382-5039
  Dover *(G-2472)*
Fairville Management Co LLC............... G 302 489-2000
  Hockessin *(G-5206)*
Faze II Inc.. G 302 328-7891
  Bear *(G-222)*
First Choice Real Estate Svcs............... G 302 525-4970
  Hockessin *(G-5209)*
First Montgomery Properties................ E 302 834-8272
  Bear *(G-225)*
Foster Long Real Estate...................... G 302 864-3216
  Ocean View *(G-12513)*
Franchise Co LLC USA......................... G 868 280-5272
  Lewes *(G-6010)*
Freedom Plaza Enterprises LLC............ G 302 653-9676
  Smyrna *(G-13738)*
Gallo Realty Inc................................. G 888 624-6794
  Bethany Beach *(G-603)*
Gallo Realty Inc................................. G 302 945-7368
  Rehoboth Beach *(G-12765)*
Galloway Leasing Inc.......................... G 302 453-8385
  Newark *(G-10801)*
Ganc Commercial Realty LLC............... G 302 292-1131
  Newark *(G-10806)*
GM Capital Investments Inc................. G 302 722-0558
  Newark *(G-10854)*
GM Realestate................................... G 302 376-9462
  Middletown *(G-7166)*
Gold Key Realty................................. F 302 369-5397
  Newark *(G-10859)*
Golden Coastal Realty........................ F 302 360-0226
  Lewes *(G-6045)*

SIC SECTION — 65 REAL ESTATE

Grayden Appraisals Inc .... G 302 598-8511
Newark *(G-10884)*

Green Oak Real Estate LP .... D 212 359-7800
Wilmington *(G-16965)*

Griffin Higgins Team LLC .... G 302 856-1458
Seaford *(G-13201)*

Guardian Property MGT LLC .... F 302 227-7878
Lewes *(G-6067)*

H D C Inc .... G 302 323-9300
Wilmington *(G-17017)*

H T G Consulting LLC .... G 302 322-4100
New Castle *(G-9189)*

Habash Commercial Realty LLC .... G 302 218-3025
Wilmington *(G-17026)*

Harrington Realty Inc .... F 302 422-2424
Dover *(G-2655)*

Harrington Realty Inc .... E 302 736-0800
Dover *(G-2654)*

Harris Property Management LLC .... F 302 588-8601
Wilmington *(G-17063)*

Harvey Development Co .... E 302 323-9300
New Castle *(G-9201)*

Herman/Turner Group .... G 302 322-4100
New Castle *(G-9210)*

Hollywood Grill Restaurant .... D 302 655-1348
Wilmington *(G-17171)*

Home Finders Real Estate Co .... G 302 655-8091
Wilmington *(G-17177)*

Home Team Realty .... F 302 629-7711
Seaford *(G-13213)*

Howard M Joseph Inc .... G 302 335-1300
Milford *(G-7936)*

Hybrid Property LLC .... F 302 289-6226
Wilmington *(G-17243)*

Incredible Care Inc .... G 302 428-6093
Wilmington *(G-17305)*

Insight Homes .... G 302 927-0235
Dagsboro *(G-1467)*

Insight Homes .... G 302 858-4281
Georgetown *(G-4370)*

J A Banks & Associates LLC .... F 914 260-2003
Smyrna *(G-13779)*

Jack Lingo Inc Realtor .... E 302 947-9030
Lewes *(G-6135)*

Jack Lingo Inc Realtor .... E 302 227-3883
Rehoboth Beach *(G-12798)*

Jack Lingo Realtor .... F 302 645-2207
Lewes *(G-6136)*

Jack Lingo Realtor .... G 302 344-9188
Rehoboth Beach *(G-12799)*

Jan Patrick RES .... G 302 234-6046
Hockessin *(G-5258)*

JG Townsend Jr & Co Inc .... E 302 856-2525
Georgetown *(G-4383)*

Joe Maggio Realty .... G 302 539-9300
Bethany Beach *(G-612)*

Joe Maggio Realty .... G 302 251-8792
Rehoboth Beach *(G-12807)*

Jones Enterprises Incorporated .... G 888 639-1194
Wilmington *(G-17574)*

Julie Gritton Team LLC .... G 302 645-1111
Lewes *(G-6155)*

Kat Geralis Home Team .... E 302 383-5412
Wilmington *(G-17657)*

Kats Meow Inc .... G 302 383-5412
Hockessin *(G-5266)*

Keller Williams At Beach Rlty .... G 302 363-0453
Milton *(G-8650)*

Keller Williams Realty .... G 302 360-0300
Lewes *(G-6164)*

Keller Williams Realty .... G 302 293-8654
Newark *(G-11150)*

Keller Williams Realty .... G 302 519-1683
Ocean View *(G-12532)*

Keller Williams Realty .... F 862 588-1342
Rehoboth Beach *(G-12817)*

Keller Williams Realty At Bch .... F 302 360-0300
Rehoboth Beach *(G-12818)*

Keller Williams Realty Ce .... G 302 653-3624
Dover *(G-2839)*

Keller Williams Realty Central .... G 302 465-7562
New Castle *(G-9278)*

Keller Williams Rlty Delmarva .... G 410 430-2721
Selbyville *(G-13558)*

Keller Wllams Rlty - Lsko To B .... G 302 581-9101
Millville *(G-8535)*

Kim Simpson Realty Group .... G 302 690-0245
Middletown *(G-7273)*

King Josiah Companies LLC .... G 855 312-3300
Dover *(G-2872)*

King-Edwards Residences LLC .... G 646 389-5830
Dover *(G-2876)*

Kubasko McKee Group RE .... G 877 302-7747
Wilmington *(G-17761)*

Kumar Properties LLC .... G 337 284-5975
Claymont *(G-1209)*

L3d LLC .... G 302 677-0031
Dover *(G-2894)*

Lake Properties Group LLC .... G 516 695-1441
Dover *(G-2900)*

Landex LLC .... G 903 293-9466
Newark *(G-11217)*

Landmark Associates of Del .... G 302 645-7070
Lewes *(G-6176)*

Lbg Homes LLC .... G 302 360-0300
Dagsboro *(G-1474)*

Lc Homes Inc .... G 302 429-8700
Wilmington *(G-17839)*

Lee Ann Wilkinson Group .... G 302 645-6664
Lewes *(G-6186)*

Lee Sells Houses Team .... G 302 516-7674
Wilmington *(G-17855)*

Legree & Fmly Investments LLC .... G 302 245-5218
Rehoboth Beach *(G-12830)*

Legum & Norman Mid-West LLC .... G 302 537-9499
Bethany Beach *(G-614)*

Legum & Norman Mid-West LLC .... G 302 227-8448
Lewes *(G-6188)*

Lenape Properties MGT Inc .... G 302 426-0200
Wilmington *(G-17873)*

Leslie Kopp Inc .... F 302 541-5207
Bethany Beach *(G-615)*

Lexan Group LLC .... G 704 900-0190
Newark *(G-11250)*

Liborio-Louviers LLC .... G 302 656-9400
Wilmington *(G-17898)*

Lighthouse Realty Group Inc .... G 302 864-0952
Ocean View *(G-12539)*

Lighthouse Realty Group I .... G 302 541-4440
Bethany Beach *(G-616)*

Linda Brannock .... G 302 346-3124
Dover *(G-2951)*

Linda Vista Real Estate .... F 302 313-1600
Rehoboth Beach *(G-12832)*

Lisa Johannsen .... G 302 270-5082
Middletown *(G-7306)*

Littljohn Blckston Hldings LLC .... G 302 468-6680
Wilmington *(G-17945)*

Livingston Enterprise .... G 302 588-5722
New Castle *(G-9319)*

Long & Foster .... G 302 569-0012
Dagsboro *(G-1475)*

Long & Foster Real Estate Inc .... G 302 542-0811
Milford *(G-7976)*

Long & Foster Real Estate Inc .... G 302 227-3821
Rehoboth Beach *(G-12837)*

Long and Foster .... G 925 699-4783
Lewes *(G-6217)*

Long and Foster .... G 302 858-7805
Selbyville *(G-13562)*

Long and Foster .... G 302 239-2636
Wilmington *(G-17981)*

Los Jardines Inc .... G 302 652-6390
Wilmington *(G-17998)*

Luther Martin Foundation Dover .... G 302 674-1408
Dover *(G-2982)*

Lutheran Senior Svcs of Dover .... E 302 674-1408
Dover *(G-2988)*

Madison Real Estate Inc .... G 718 947-6350
Wilmington *(G-18074)*

Maggio/Shields Teams .... G 302 226-3770
Rehoboth Beach *(G-12843)*

Malave Property Group LLC .... G 844 203-4610
Dover *(G-3004)*

Mann & Sons Inc .... F 302 841-0077
Rehoboth Beach *(G-12846)*

Manufctured Hsing Concepts LLC .... D 302 934-8848
Millsboro *(G-8363)*

Margaret Harris-Nemtuda .... G 302 477-5500
Wilmington *(G-18124)*

Mark Adcock .... G 302 660-0909
Wilmington *(G-18137)*

Marshall Manor LP .... G 302 422-8255
Milford *(G-7985)*

Marvel Agency Inc .... G 302 422-7844
Milford *(G-7986)*

Mary Kate Johnston .... G 302 388-5654
Newark *(G-11346)*

Maverick Realty LLC .... F 302 373-6591
Newark *(G-11357)*

Max RE Associates Inc .... E 302 453-3200
Newark *(G-11358)*

Max RE Associates Inc .... E 302 477-3900
Newark *(G-11359)*

Max RE Central .... F 302 234-3800
Hockessin *(G-5304)*

McConnell Johnson RE Co LLC .... E 302 421-2000
Wilmington *(G-18224)*

Meadow Edge Corp .... G 302 530-7339
Hockessin *(G-5306)*

Megan Aitken Team LLC .... G 302 376-9836
Middletown *(G-7338)*

Meyer & Meyer Inc .... F 302 994-9600
Wilmington *(G-18295)*

Michael A Kelczewski .... G 302 654-6500
Wilmington *(G-18302)*

Mid-Atlantic Realty Co Inc .... G 302 737-3110
Newark *(G-11411)*

Mid-Atlantic Realty Co Inc .... E 302 658-7642
Newark *(G-11412)*

Midway Realty Corp .... E 302 645-9511
Rehoboth Beach *(G-12857)*

Mike Difonzo .... G 302 764-0100
Wilmington *(G-18350)*

Milford Housing Development .... F 302 422-8255
Milford *(G-8001)*

Moore & Lind Inc .... G 302 934-8818
Millsboro *(G-8390)*

More Property Recovery .... G 302 834-4788
Newark *(G-11452)*

Mosap Global Inc .... E 302 559-3036
Newark *(G-11457)*

Mrt LLC .... G 856 685-1602
Bear *(G-381)*

Musi Commercial Properties Inc .... G 302 594-1000
Wilmington *(G-18493)*

65 REAL ESTATE

Company	Class	Phone
My Beach Agent Realty Group — Lewes (G-6298)	G	302 858-2370
Nanticoke Shores Assoc LLC — Millsboro (G-8399)	G	302 945-1500
Nest Properties LLC — Middletown (G-7395)	G	302 373-8015
Networks Programs — Newark (G-11510)	E	302 454-2233
New Castle Cnty Bd of Realtors — Wilmington (G-18608)	G	302 762-4800
Nexthome Prefer — Dover (G-3187)	G	302 526-2886
Nickle Insurance Agency Inc — Delaware City (G-1549)	G	302 834-9700
Nnn 824 North Market St LLC — Wilmington (G-18658)	G	302 652-8013
Noble Property LLC — Dover (G-3192)	E	718 502-4806
Nt Philadelphia LLC — Wilmington (G-18707)	D	302 384-8967
NVR Homes National — Rehoboth Beach (G-12872)	G	302 278-7099
Oberod Estates LLC — Wilmington (G-18735)	G	302 521-0250
Ocean Atlantic Agency Inc — Rehoboth Beach (G-12873)	D	302 227-6767
Ocean Atlantic Associates LLC — Rehoboth Beach (G-12874)	F	302 227-3573
Ocean Atlantic Sothebys Intl — Bethany Beach (G-624)	F	302 539-1033
October Phoenix Rlty Group LLC — Newark (G-11577)	G	302 722-5125
Olson Realty — Dover (G-3220)	G	302 448-6000
Ome Lake Vista III & IV LLC — Dover (G-3223)	G	619 787-5592
One Hundred West Tenth St — Wilmington (G-18782)	G	302 651-1469
P R C Management Co Inc — Wilmington (G-18853)	G	302 475-7643
P&H Realty LLC — Townsend (G-14047)	G	302 378-3484
Panco Management Corporation — Newark (G-11619)	E	302 366-1875
Panco Management Corporation — Wilmington (G-18870)	G	302 995-6152
Panco Management Corporation — Wilmington (G-18871)	G	302 475-9337
Parker Group — Bridgeville (G-744)	F	302 217-6692
Passavant Memorial Homes — Townsend (G-14049)	G	302 449-2202
Paterson Schwartz Real Estate — Bethany Beach (G-625)	F	302 537-1300
Patterson Price — Wilmington (G-18914)	G	302 378-9852
Patterson & Schwartz — Millsboro (G-8416)	F	302 945-5568
Patterson Price RE LLC — Newark (G-11640)	G	302 366-0200
Patterson Price RE LLC — Townsend (G-14050)	G	302 378-9550
Patterson-Schwartz — Bear (G-419)	G	215 805-8238
Patterson-Schwartz & Assoc Inc — Dover (G-3284)	D	302 672-9400
Patterson-Schwartz & Assoc Inc — Hockessin (G-5333)	F	302 234-3606
Patterson-Schwartz & Assoc Inc — Middletown (G-7430)	D	302 285-5100
Patterson-Schwartz & Assoc Inc — Newark (G-11641)	E	302 733-7000
Patterson-Schwartz & Assoc Inc — Wilmington (G-18915)	D	302 429-4500
Patterson-Schwartz & Assoc Inc — Hockessin (G-5334)	C	302 234-5250
Patterson-Schwartz Real Estate — Wilmington (G-18916)	G	302 690-7746
Penflex III LLC — Wilmington (G-18948)	G	302 998-0683
Perpetual Invstments Group LLC — Wilmington (G-18982)	F	718 795-3394
Pettinaro Construction Co Inc — Newark (G-11675)	E	302 832-8823
Pettinaro Construction Co Inc — Wilmington (G-19001)	D	302 999-0708
Platform Gallery LLC — Wilmington (G-19071)	G	844 244-2940
Porro Realty Group — Wilmington (G-19118)	G	302 384-6056
Powers Appraising LLC — Rehoboth Beach (G-12897)	G	410 337-8664
Prelude TX — Newark (G-11725)	G	302 273-3369
Princeton Coml Holdings LLC — Newark (G-11746)	G	302 449-4836
Prudential Gallo Realty — Lewes (G-6396)	F	302 645-6661
R R Commercial Realty — Georgetown (G-4480)	G	302 856-4000
Rbcmneusa LLC — Wilmington (G-19353)	G	607 316-5355
RE Max of Wilmington — Wilmington (G-19359)	E	302 657-8000
RE Max of Wilmington — Wilmington (G-19358)	E	302 234-2500
Re/Max — Bethany Beach (G-631)	G	302 381-2540
Re/Max Coast Country — Delmar (G-1631)	G	302 846-0200
RE/Max Horizons Inc — Dover (G-3428)	F	302 678-4300
Re/Max Premier Properties — Bear (G-447)	G	302 883-9202
Re/Max Realty Group-Rentals — Rehoboth Beach (G-12908)	F	302 227-4800
Real Estate Market — Laurel (G-5586)	G	302 715-5640
Real Estate Partners LLC — Wilmington (G-19367)	G	302 656-0251
Real Pro Holdings Inc — Wilmington (G-19370)	G	541 743-8500
Realty Mogul 14 LLC — Dover (G-3437)	G	877 977-2776
Red Brick Realty LLC — Wilmington (G-19382)	G	302 540-1128
Rehoboth Home Sales Inc — Rehoboth Beach (G-12927)	G	609 924-7701
Rehoboth Real Estate — Rehoboth Beach (G-12932)	G	302 226-6417
Rehoboth Realty Inc — Rehoboth Beach (G-12933)	E	302 227-5000
Remax 1st Choice LLC — Middletown (G-7512)	G	302 378-8700
Remax By Sea — Bethany Beach (G-632)	G	302 541-5000
Remax Sunvest Realty — Wilmington (G-19428)	F	302 995-1589
Remax Sunvest Realty Corp — Wilmington (G-19429)	E	302 995-1589
Resolute Industrial — Newark (G-11866)	F	267 401-0973
Resortquest Delaware RE LLC — Bethany Beach (G-634)	G	302 541-8999
Restu Stay LLC — New Castle (G-9526)	G	347 522-0919
Reybold Group of Companies Inc — Bear (G-458)	E	302 832-7100
Rhonda Frick — Bethany Beach (G-636)	G	302 236-1456
RHS Realty — Selbyville (G-13599)	G	302 436-6478
Riggin Group — Hockessin (G-5363)	G	302 235-2903
Rita Gasz Real Estate — Hockessin (G-5365)	G	302 234-6043
Rob Watson — Wilmington (G-19505)	G	302 234-8877
Robino Management Group Inc — Wilmington (G-19522)	E	302 633-6001
Robinson Realestate — Seaford (G-13378)	G	302 629-4574
Rock River Real Estate Inc — Wilmington (G-19531)	G	302 778-1000
Rocky Lac LLC — Bear (G-466)	F	302 440-5561
Rosedale Development LLC — Dover (G-3486)	E	281 968-9426
Rrr Realty Group LLC — Bear (G-476)	G	302 836-9836
Rush Realty LLC — Smyrna (G-13873)	G	302 219-6707
Salt Air Homes — Camden Wyoming (G-973)	G	302 698-4146
Saundra Wright — Wilmington (G-19680)	G	302 298-0324
Sea Play Homes LLC — Fenwick Island (G-4054)	G	302 564-7557
Seagreen Bicycle LLP — Rehoboth Beach (G-12952)	G	302 226-2323
Shirley I Blackburn Real Estat — Newark (G-11998)	G	302 292-6684
Shirley Price Sells — Bethany Beach (G-642)	G	302 236-7046
Showtime Real Estate — Wilmington (G-19811)	G	302 377-1292
Signature Property Management — Lewes (G-6468)	F	302 212-2381
Simple Stays LLC — Newark (G-12011)	G	949 290-5775
Simpsons Log Homes Inc — Dover (G-3566)	G	302 674-1900
Skipjack Inc — Dover (G-3572)	D	302 734-6755
Sks Enterprise — Newark (G-12024)	D	302 310-2511
Smalls Real Estate Company — Wilmington (G-19873)	F	302 633-1985
Smt Real Estate Holdings LLC — Newark (G-12043)	G	302 668-3512
Springside LLC — Newark (G-12077)	G	302 838-7223
Statera Homes — Rehoboth Beach (G-12973)	G	302 313-9949
Stenta Appraisal Portions — Wilmington (G-20051)	G	302 477-9562
Stephen J Crifasi Real Estate — Wilmington (G-20059)	G	302 658-9572
Stephens Management Corp — Seaford (G-13414)	G	302 629-4393
Steven Sachs Appraisal Access — Talleyville (G-13947)	G	302 477-9676
Stewart Valuation Services LLC — Wilmington (G-20072)	E	888 751-9234
Stoltz Real Estate Partners — Wilmington (G-20076)	G	302 654-3600

67 HOLDING AND OTHER INVESTMENT OFFICES

Stoltz Realty Co. .... F 302 798-8500
  Claymont (G-1305)
Stoltz Realty Co. .... D 302 656-8543
  Wilmington (G-20078)
Stoltz Realty Co. .... G 302 656-2852
  Wilmington (G-20077)
Summit Bridge Inv Prpts LLC .... G 410 499-1456
  Newark (G-12119)
Sunnyville Resort LLC .... G 706 255-9765
  New Castle (G-9603)
Sunrise RE Partners LLC .... G 302 644-0300
  Lewes (G-6523)
Sunrise Real Estate .... G 302 313-9949
  Rehoboth Beach (G-12982)
Supreme Servicez LLC .... G 302 932-5724
  Wilmington (G-20158)
Susan S Bryde .... G 302 239-2343
  Hockessin (G-5401)
Svn Delaware LLC .... G 302 536-1838
  Seaford (G-13423)
Thrive Real Lf Indpendence LLC .... G 302 261-2139
  Middletown (G-7643)
Tidemark LLC .... G 302 359-4646
  Camden Wyoming (G-982)
TMI Realty LLC .... F 302 613-5600
  New Castle (G-9628)
Tom Wright Real Estate .... G 302 234-6026
  Hockessin (G-5407)
Topaz & Associates LLC .... F 302 448-8914
  Wilmington (G-20357)
Trans Un Sttlment Slutions Inc .... D 800 916-8800
  Wilmington (G-20394)
Travelpad Rentals LLC .... G 203 751-1569
  Wilmington (G-20406)
Tunnell Companies LP .... F 302 945-9300
  Millsboro (G-8488)
United Group Real Estate LLC .... E 929 999-1277
  Historic New Castle (G-5095)
Upscale Industries Property Ma .... G 302 386-8855
  Wilmington (G-20537)
Veezys Holding Company LLC .... F 302 307-2418
  Dover (G-3779)
Viaticum Incorporated .... F 302 467-8353
  Wilmington (G-20607)
Vintage Realty .... G 302 731-1000
  Newark (G-12326)
Vulcan International Corp .... F 302 656-1950
  Wilmington (G-20657)
Wagamons Schell Brothers .... G 302 664-1680
  Rehoboth Beach (G-13004)
Walk By Faith LLC .... F 737 529-5869
  Lewes (G-6614)
Warner Tansey Inc .... G 302 539-3001
  Bethany Beach (G-648)
Watermark At North Bethany .... G 302 539-3223
  Bethany Beach (G-649)
Watsons Auction & Realty Svc .... G 302 422-2392
  Milford (G-8143)
Weed Real Estate LLC .... G 302 981-6388
  Newark (G-12354)
Welcome Home Getaways LLC .... G 724 426-5534
  Bear (G-561)
West Home Leasehold LLC .... F 917 443-7451
  Wilmington (G-20741)
White Robbins Company .... G 302 478-5555
  Wilmington (G-20767)
Wilgus Associates Inc .... G 302 644-2960
  Lewes (G-6630)
Wilgus Associates Inc .... E 302 539-7511
  Bethany Beach (G-650)
Willow Tree Properties LLC .... G 302 674-2266
  Wilmington (G-20804)

Wilmington Real Estate Co Inc .... G 302 652-1700
  Wilmington (G-20832)
Wilsons Auction Sales Inc .... G 302 422-3454
  Lincoln (G-6709)
Woodlawn Trustees Incorporated .... F 302 655-6215
  Wilmington (G-20884)
Yvonne Hall Inc .... G 302 677-1300
  Dover (G-3895)

6541 Title abstract offices

Brennan Title Company .... G 302 541-0400
  Frankford (G-4078)
Delaware Settlement Services .... G 302 731-2500
  Newark (G-10478)
First American Title Insur Co .... F 302 855-2120
  Georgetown (G-4320)
First American Title Insur Co .... G 302 421-9440
  Wilmington (G-16615)
Liberty Title Services .... G 302 559-4500
  Wilmington (G-17895)
Pna Title Services LLC .... G 302 294-6219
  Wilmington (G-19087)
Spn Title Services .... G 302 537-1540
  Dagsboro (G-1508)
Stewart Lender Services Inc .... G 302 433-8047
  Wilmington (G-20071)
Trans Un Sttlment Slutions Inc .... D 800 916-8800
  Wilmington (G-20394)
Webber Title LLC .... G 302 218-0911
  Dover (G-3826)

6552 Subdividers and developers, nec

Allcap Development Group LLC .... G 302 429-8700
  Wilmington (G-14372)
AT&e Developers Ltd .... F 302 467-1100
  Middletown (G-6877)
Barclay Farms .... G 302 697-6939
  Camden (G-792)
Commonwealth Group LLC .... E 302 472-7200
  Wilmington (G-15553)
Compton Twne Prsrvtion Assoc L ...... G 302 764-6450
  Wilmington (G-15575)
Del Homes Inc .... F 302 697-8204
  Magnolia (G-6739)
Del-Charter Associates LP .... G 302 325-1111
  Newark (G-10414)
Delaware Valley Dev LLC .... F 302 235-2500
  Wilmington (G-15980)
Donne Delle & Associates Inc .... E 302 325-1111
  Newark (G-10551)
Eastern States Develpment Inc .... G 302 998-0683
  Wilmington (G-16265)
Edward B De Seta & Associates .... G 302 428-1313
  Wilmington (G-16301)
Ferm Development LLC .... F 302 792-1102
  Wilmington (G-16584)
First Power LLC .... G 610 247-5750
  Wilmington (G-16621)
Gulfstream Development Corp .... G 302 539-6178
  Millville (G-8531)
Harvest Power Inc .... G 270 765-6268
  Milford (G-7921)
Interfaith Cmnty Hsing of Del .... F 302 652-3991
  Wilmington (G-17383)
Jack Hickman Real Estate .... F 302 539-8000
  Bethany Beach (G-611)
Kidmore End Developers LLC .... G 302 562-5110
  Claymont (G-1206)
Lang Development Group LLC .... G 302 731-1340
  Newark (G-11220)
Lang Development Group LLC .... G 302 731-1340
  Newark (G-11221)

Leon N Weiner & Associates Inc .... D 302 656-1354
  Wilmington (G-17877)
Medshifts Inc .... G 856 834-0074
  Wilmington (G-18258)
Newark Afrc .... G 302 292-1050
  Newark (G-11529)
Ocean Atlantic Management LLC ...... G 302 227-3573
  Rehoboth Beach (G-12875)
Pangro Development LLC .... G 302 351-3575
  Wilmington (G-18875)
Parkway Gravel Inc .... D 302 658-5241
  New Castle (G-9450)
Patterson Price RE LLC .... G 302 366-0200
  Newark (G-11640)
Patterson Price RE LLC .... G 302 378-9550
  Townsend (G-14050)
Post Rdge Prsrvation Assoc LLC .... G 302 761-7303
  Wilmington (G-19130)
Reybold Construction Corp .... E 302 832-7100
  Bear (G-455)
Riverfront Dev Corp Del .... F 302 425-4890
  Wilmington (G-19493)
Riverfront Development Corp .... E 302 425-4890
  Wilmington (G-19494)
Roizman & Associates Inc .... G 302 426-9688
  Wilmington (G-19556)
Salt Pond Associates .... E 302 539-2750
  Bethany Beach (G-638)
Stokelan Estate Winery LLC .... G 609 451-5535
  Hockessin (G-5391)
Tim Latham .... G 302 530-4002
  Wilmington (G-20327)
Titan Retail LLC .... F 205 291-1305
  Middletown (G-7646)
Villages of Nobles Pond Phase .... G 302 736-5000
  Dover (G-3797)
Woodlawn Trustees Incorporated .... F 302 655-6215
  Wilmington (G-20884)
Y and Y Garden Associates Inc .... G 302 684-0383
  Milton (G-8733)

6553 Cemetery subdividers and developers

Catholic Cemetaries Inc .... G 302 737-2524
  Wilmington (G-15276)
Catholic Cemetaries Inc .... F 302 254-4701
  Wilmington (G-15275)
Gracelawn Memorial Park Inc .... E 302 654-6158
  New Castle (G-9175)
Odd Fellows Cmtry of Milford .... G 302 422-4619
  Milford (G-8036)
Silverbrook Cemetery Co .... G 302 658-0953
  Wilmington (G-19829)

67 HOLDING AND OTHER INVESTMENT OFFICES

6712 Bank holding companies

Advantage Delaware .... G 302 365-5398
  Bear (G-18)
Cbc Holding Inc .... A 302 254-2000
  Wilmington (G-15285)
First State Bancorp Inc .... G 302 427-3637
  Wilmington (G-16624)
PNC Holding LLC .... G 302 427-5897
  Wilmington (G-19098)

6719 Holding companies, nec

302 Hemp Co .... G 302 854-4367
  Georgetown (G-4188)
Amerisource Heritage Corp .... G 800 829-3132
  Wilmington (G-14454)

67 HOLDING AND OTHER INVESTMENT OFFICES

Amrec Holdings Inc .... D 302 273-0000
  Dover (G-1788)
Anglin Associates LLC .... F 302 653-3500
  Clayton (G-1349)
Basigo Inc .... D 510 735-6240
  Claymont (G-1052)
Belchim Crop Prtection US Corp .... F 302 407-3590
  Wilmington (G-14814)
Braswell Enterprises LLC .... F 470 588-2087
  Dover (G-1973)
Capsula Inc .... G 562 466-0155
  Claymont (G-1073)
Dmac Enterprises LLC .... E 917 504-4529
  Middletown (G-7065)
Dormakaba US Holding Ltd .... B 252 200-5414
  Wilmington (G-16148)
Duns Investing Corporation .... G 302 651-2050
  Wilmington (G-16201)
Ema Corp .... E 302 479-9434
  Wilmington (G-16384)
Empower Healthcare Assets Inc .... G 604 789-2146
  Camden (G-831)
Eri Investments Inc .... F 302 656-8089
  Wilmington (G-16456)
Erm-Delaware Inc .... B 302 651-8300
  Wilmington (G-16461)
Exco Inc .... D 905 477-3065
  Wilmington (G-16502)
Faith Fmly Friends Holdg LLC .... F 202 256-4524
  Lewes (G-5985)
Famglam LLC .... F 302 930-0026
  Ellendale (G-3917)
Gallium US Holdings Inc .... G 713 213-0644
  Wilmington (G-16796)
Goliaths Haven Inc .... F 888 793-9311
  Wilmington (G-16918)
Griffen Corporate Services .... F 302 576-2890
  Wilmington (G-16978)
H-V Technical Services Inc .... G 302 427-5801
  Wilmington (G-17024)
Horton Holdings Inc .... E 855 501-5834
  Middletown (G-7217)
Hsi Service Corp .... F 302 369-3709
  Newark (G-10984)
Hunte Corporate Enterprise LLC .... G 212 710-1341
  Wilmington (G-17235)
Ieg Glbal Mdia Invstmnts Acqst .... G 720 290-9347
  Dover (G-2718)
Instant Global Services Corp .... G 302 514-1047
  Dover (G-2740)
Jacksun Inc .... E 800 861-7050
  Claymont (G-1193)
Ksre Capital LLC .... F 281 501-3777
  Dover (G-2888)
Labware Global Services Inc .... F 302 658-8444
  Wilmington (G-17786)
Labware Holdings Inc .... E 302 658-8444
  Wilmington (G-17787)
Landville Group LLC .... F 727 557-6149
  Lewes (G-6177)
Laohio Holdings LLC .... G 302 200-9685
  Lewes (G-6180)
Lela Capital LLC .... F 917 428-0304
  Ocean View (G-12537)
Maestro Media Holdings Inc .... F 855 313-3437
  Dover (G-2995)
Matador Companies LLC .... G 855 303-4229
  Lewes (G-6248)
Mater Ellis LLC .... G 302 508-0938
  Wilmington (G-18190)
Midway LLC .... G 302 378-9156
  Middletown (G-7367)

Morgan Stnley Intl Hldings Inc .... D 302 657-2000
  Wilmington (G-18448)
Nazhat Enterprises Holdings .... G 302 450-1418
  Dover (G-3164)
Nestl Holdings Inc .... G 203 629-7482
  Wilmington (G-18589)
Oni Acquisition Corp .... G 212 271-3800
  Wilmington (G-18790)
P&L Transportation Inc .... G 800 444-2580
  Wilmington (G-18854)
Phat Holdings Inc .... F 775 438-7428
  Wilmington (G-19012)
◆ Playtex Marketing Corp .... G 302 678-6000
  Dover (G-3337)
Qps Holdings LLC .... F 302 369-5601
  Newark (G-11785)
Savant International Holdings .... E 305 768-9395
  Newark (G-11953)
Sherpa Brokers LLC .... F 917 455-0094
  Middletown (G-7560)
Sia Netjer Corp .... F 302 319-5190
  Dover (G-3554)
Smithkline Bcham Phrmceuticals ...... F 302 984-6932
  Wilmington (G-19892)
Stewart Law Firm .... F 302 652-5200
  Wilmington (G-20070)
Stratos Holdings Inc .... F 800 927-9800
  Wilmington (G-20092)
Symack US Corp .... F 469 607-6092
  Smyrna (G-13909)
Tripleone Inc .... D 833 391-0111
  Dover (G-3728)
Ua Services Corp .... G 302 467-3700
  Middletown (G-7670)
Willow Tree Equity Holding LLC .... F 213 479-4077
  Lewes (G-6633)
X Trillion Inc 347 370-9117
  Middletown (G-7737)
Yhp Holdings LLC .... G 302 636-5401
  Wilmington (G-20928)
Zeon Enterprises Inc .... F 302 898-7167
  New Castle (G-9698)
Zuludynasty LLC .... G 815 909-4236
  Middletown (G-7752)

6722 Management investment, open-ended

1 Righter LLC .... G 302 479-9257
  Wilmington (G-14099)
ADP Capital Management Inc .... G 302 657-4060
  Wilmington (G-14259)
Bank of New York Mellon Corp .... G 302 421-2207
  Wilmington (G-14748)
Blackrock Advntage Esg Emrging ..... G 302 797-2000
  Wilmington (G-14904)
Blackrock Bond Fund Inc .... G 800 441-7762
  Wilmington (G-14905)
Blackrock Cal Mnicpl Income Tr .... G 800 882-0052
  Wilmington (G-14906)
Blackrock Corp High Yeld Fund .... C 800 441-7762
  Wilmington (G-14909)
Blackrock Cpitl Inv Advsors LL .... G 800 882-0052
  Wilmington (G-14910)
Blackrock Emrging Mkts LNG/Sho ..... G 302 797-2000
  Wilmington (G-14911)
Blackrock Fincl Institutions S .... G 800 441-7762
  Wilmington (G-14913)
Blackrock Funds V .... G 302 797-2000
  Wilmington (G-14915)
Blackrock Future US Themes Etf ...... G 302 797-2000
  Wilmington (G-14916)
Blackrock Globl Smllcap Fund I .... F 800 441-7762
  Wilmington (G-14917)

Blackrock Instnl Mgt Corp .... E 302 797-2000
  Wilmington (G-14921)
Blackrock LNG-Hrzon Eqity Fund ...... F 800 441-7762
  Wilmington (G-14922)
Blackrock Lrge Cap Grwth VI Fu .... D 302 797-2000
  Wilmington (G-14923)
Blackrock Macro Themes Fund .... D 302 797-2000
  Wilmington (G-14924)
Blackrock Midcap Index Fund .... D 302 797-2000
  Wilmington (G-14925)
Blackrock Mlt-Sector Income Tr .... F 800 882-0052
  Wilmington (G-14926)
Blackrock Mncpl Income Inv Qlt .... G 800 441-7762
  Wilmington (G-14928)
Blackrock Muniassets Fund Inc .... G 302 797-2000
  Wilmington (G-14932)
Blackrock Municipal Bond Trust .... F 888 825-2257
  Wilmington (G-14933)
Blackrock Municipal Income Tr .... G 888 882-0052
  Wilmington (G-14934)
Blackrock Municpl Income Tr II .... G 302 797-2000
  Wilmington (G-14935)
Blackrock Natural Resources Tr .... F 212 810-5300
  Wilmington (G-14937)
Blackrock NY Municpl Income Tr ...... G 800 882-0052
  Wilmington (G-14940)
Blackrock Science & Tech Tr .... G 302 797-2000
  Wilmington (G-14941)
Blackrock Small Cap Gro .... G 302 797-2000
  Wilmington (G-14942)
Blackrock Small Cap Grwth Fund ...... G 212 810-5300
  Wilmington (G-14943)
Blackrock SMD-Cap Grwth Eqity .... G 302 797-2000
  Wilmington (G-14944)
Blackrock Sstnble Blnced Prtfl .... G 800 537-4942
  Wilmington (G-14945)
Blackrock US Gvrnment Bond VI .... D 302 797-2000
  Wilmington (G-14946)
Blackrock Vlue Opprtnties VI F .... G 302 797-2000
  Wilmington (G-14947)
Brandywine Fund Inc .... F 302 656-3017
  Wilmington (G-15060)
Brandywine Global Investement .... G 610 380-2110
  Wilmington (G-15061)
CA All Wrld Ex US Eqity CEF Fu .... G 610 380-2110
  Wilmington (G-15181)
Castle HI Ttal Return Fund LLC .... G 626 844-4862
  Wilmington (G-15267)
Consulting Group Cpitl Mkts FN .... F 302 888-4104
  Wilmington (G-15614)
Dupont Capital Management Corp ..... G 302 477-6000
  Wilmington (G-16203)
Ferrara Asset Management Inc .... G 401 286-8464
  Wilmington (G-16585)
Fidelity Oxford Street Trust .... G 214 281-6351
  Wilmington (G-16600)
Franklin Tmplton Companies LLC ..... G 800 632-2301
  Wilmington (G-16731)
Frontier Emerging Markets Fund .... G 610 380-2110
  Wilmington (G-16763)
Global Currents Inv MGT LLC .... E 302 476-3800
  Wilmington (G-16886)
Gotham Index 500 Plus Fund .... G 877 974-6852
  Wilmington (G-16932)
Government Portfolio LLC .... F 301 718-9742
  Rehoboth Beach (G-12775)
H S B C Overseas Corp De .... D 302 657-8400
  Wilmington (G-17021)
Ishares US Scrtzed Bond Index .... G 800 441-7762
  Wilmington (G-17426)
Janus Hndrson Blnced Cllctive .... G 800 724-2440
  Wilmington (G-17497)

67 HOLDING AND OTHER INVESTMENT OFFICES

JP Morgan Multi-Manager Altern............ F 866 541-2724
 Wilmington *(G-17596)*
Marvin & Palmer US Equity LP................ G 302 573-3570
 Wilmington *(G-18175)*
Master Extnded Mkt Index Sries................ G 800 441-7762
 Wilmington *(G-18185)*
Master Focus Growth LLC............................ G 800 441-7762
 Wilmington *(G-18186)*
Mellon Private Wealth MGT......................... G 302 421-2306
 Wilmington *(G-18265)*
Mondrian Focused Global.............................. G 302 428-3839
 Wilmington *(G-18410)*
Mondrian International Small........................ G 302 428-3839
 Wilmington *(G-18411)*
Principal Lf Globl Funding II........................ G 302 636-6392
 Wilmington *(G-19195)*
Related RE Fund III LP................................... F 212 801-1013
 Wilmington *(G-19421)*
Resistance Energy Fund LP......................... F 514 871-2120
 Wilmington *(G-19438)*
Rockford RE Fund IV LP................................ G 302 220-4786
 Wilmington *(G-19538)*
Sierra Tmshare Cnduit Rcvbles..................... F 702 562-8316
 Wilmington *(G-19817)*
Smb Education Funding LLC....................... G 302 451-0537
 Newark *(G-12036)*
UT Investment Management Corp................ G 215 399-5900
 Wilmington *(G-20556)*
Vital Renewable Energy Company................ G 202 595-2944
 Wilmington *(G-20644)*
Wilmington Lrg-Cap Strtegy Fun.................. G 302 636-8500
 Wilmington *(G-20822)*
Wilmington Small-Cap Strategy.................... G 302 636-8500
 Wilmington *(G-20844)*
Wilmington Trust Frnklin US AG.................. G 302 636-8500
 Wilmington *(G-20848)*
Wilmington Trust Tmpltn Fgn C................... G 800 724-2440
 Wilmington *(G-20850)*

6726 Investment offices, nec

Atlas Management Inc.................................... E 302 576-2749
 Wilmington *(G-14630)*
Blackrock 2022 Globl Income Op.................. G 212 754-5560
 Wilmington *(G-14903)*
Blackrock Cal Mnicpl Income Tr................... G 800 882-0052
 Wilmington *(G-14906)*
Blackrock Capitl Allocation Tr....................... G 800 882-0052
 Wilmington *(G-14907)*
Blackrock Core Bond Trust............................ G 800 882-0052
 Wilmington *(G-14908)*
Blackrock Health Sciences Tr........................ G 800 882-0052
 Wilmington *(G-14918)*
Blackrock Income Trust Inc.......................... G 800 441-7762
 Wilmington *(G-14920)*
Blackrock Mncpl 2030 Trget Ter................... G 800 882-0052
 Wilmington *(G-14927)*
Blackrock Mnhldngs Cal Qlty Fu.................. G 800 882-0052
 Wilmington *(G-14929)*
Blackrock Mnhldngs NJ Qlty Fun................. G 800 882-0052
 Wilmington *(G-14930)*
Blackrock Mnyeld Cal Qlty Fund................... G 800 882-0052
 Wilmington *(G-14931)*
Blackrock Municipal Income Tr..................... G 888 882-0052
 Wilmington *(G-14934)*
Blackrock Muniyield Fund Inc...................... G 800 441-7762
 Wilmington *(G-14936)*
Blackrock NY Mncpl Income Qlty................. G 800 441-7762
 Wilmington *(G-14938)*
Blackrock NY Municpl Income Tr................. G 800 882-0052
 Wilmington *(G-14940)*
Delaware Kids Fund.. G 302 323-9300
 Newport *(G-12448)*

Ema Corp.. E 302 479-9434
 Wilmington *(G-16384)*
Freedom Central Holdings LLC..................... G 803 567-6400
 Wilmington *(G-16741)*
Jack Lingo Asset MGT LLC........................... F 302 226-6645
 Rehoboth Beach *(G-12797)*
Merrill Lynch Prce Fnner Smith.................... F 302 571-5100
 Wilmington *(G-18287)*
▲ National Holding Investment Co.............. D 302 573-3887
 Wilmington *(G-18540)*
Saint James Holdg & Inv Co Tr.................... F 877 690-9052
 Wilmington *(G-19634)*
Symack Capital MGT US Corp...................... F 469 607-6092
 Smyrna *(G-13906)*

6732 Trusts: educational, religious, etc.

Delaware Community Foundation................. G 302 571-8004
 Wilmington *(G-15890)*
Galtogether Group.. G 302 562-9170
 Wilmington *(G-16797)*
Hbcu Week Foundation Inc......................... G 302 544-0799
 Wilmington *(G-17085)*
Inka and Ezra Foundation Inc...................... G 301 535-1000
 Bear *(G-284)*
Larry Shelton.. F 678 948-6096
 New Castle *(G-9295)*
Lith AF Gamal Tru LLC................................. G 833 552-0181
 Rehoboth Beach *(G-12833)*
Milton & Hattie Kutz Foundaton................... G 302 427-2100
 Wilmington *(G-18370)*
Play For Good Inc... G 312 520-9788
 Wilmington *(G-19075)*
Simply Stylng-Schl of Csmtlgy..................... G 302 778-1885
 Wilmington *(G-19840)*
Smith-Jones Society....................................... G 302 203-9702
 Wilmington *(G-19891)*
Thomas Fenimore... G 302 464-2633
 Townsend *(G-14079)*
Udaan Inc.. G 267 408-3001
 Bear *(G-547)*

6733 Trusts, nec

AEsimmons LLC.. E 347 864-6294
 Dover *(G-1731)*
Ally Auto Rceivables Tr 2017-1.................... G 313 656-5500
 Wilmington *(G-14387)*
Ally Auto Rceivables Tr 2019-1.................... F 313 656-5500
 Wilmington *(G-14388)*
Ba Credit Card Trust...................................... E 704 386-5681
 Wilmington *(G-14707)*
Bancorp Coml Mrtg 2018-Cre4 Tr................ G 302 385-5000
 Wilmington *(G-14731)*
Bancorp Coml Mrtg 2019-Cre6 Tr................ G 302 385-5000
 Wilmington *(G-14732)*
Bfc Investors Trust... G 302 636-6466
 Wilmington *(G-14871)*
Blackrock Enhnced Globl Dvdend................. G 800 882-0052
 Wilmington *(G-14912)*
Blackrock Funds IV.. G 800 441-7762
 Wilmington *(G-14914)*
Blackrock Hlth Sciences Tr II....................... G 800 882-0052
 Wilmington *(G-14919)*
Blackrock NY Mncpl Income Tr I................. G 800 441-7762
 Wilmington *(G-14939)*
Brandywine Trust Co..................................... D 302 234-5750
 Hockessin *(G-5141)*
Capital Auto Receivables............................... F 313 656-6304
 Wilmington *(G-15227)*
College Ave Stdnt Ln 2021-B LL.................. G 302 497-0701
 Wilmington *(G-15530)*
Commonwealth Trust Co................................ F 302 658-7214
 Wilmington *(G-15556)*

Computershare Inc... A 781 575-2000
 Wilmington *(G-15576)*
Credit Accptnce Auto Ln Tr 201................... G 302 576-3706
 Wilmington *(G-15696)*
Delaware Claims Proc Fcilty......................... D 302 427-8913
 Wilmington *(G-15884)*
Dupont Capital MGT Gem Tr......................... G 302 477-6000
 Wilmington *(G-16204)*
Eleutherian Trust Co...................................... G 302 294-0821
 Wilmington *(G-16354)*
Embarcdero Arcft Scrtzation Tr.................... G 302 651-1000
 Wilmington *(G-16387)*
Goal Capital Funding Tr 2010-1................... G 302 636-6188
 Wilmington *(G-16902)*
Goldman Sachs Tr Co Nat Assn.................... E 302 793-3276
 Wilmington *(G-16915)*
Hillman/Dover Ltd Partnership..................... G 302 655-4133
 New Castle *(G-9214)*
Impact Shares Trust I.................................... G 469 442-8424
 Wilmington *(G-17288)*
Lefrak Trust Company................................... G 302 656-2390
 Wilmington *(G-17856)*
Legacy Trust Company NA............................ G 302 252-9991
 Wilmington *(G-17860)*
Marriott Vctons Wrldwide Owner................. G 302 636-6128
 Wilmington *(G-18157)*
Millennium Inv Group LLC............................ G 703 586-7968
 Wilmington *(G-18363)*
Neuberger & Berman Trust Co...................... G 302 658-8522
 Wilmington *(G-18599)*
Neuberger Berman Tr Co Del NA.................. G 302 830-4340
 Wilmington *(G-18600)*
One Hundred West Tenth St.......................... G 302 651-1469
 Wilmington *(G-18782)*
Osfs Wlmngtn-Phldlphia Prvnce................... G 302 656-8529
 Wilmington *(G-18828)*
Panthera Senior Living LLC.......................... G 786 540-0040
 Dover *(G-3266)*
Rbc Trust Company Delaware Ltd................ E 302 892-6900
 Wilmington *(G-19352)*
Rodney Trust Co... G 302 737-1205
 Newark *(G-11906)*
Smb Prvate Edcatn Ln Tr 2020-A................. G 302 451-0537
 Newark *(G-12038)*
Smb Prvate Edcatn Ln Tr 2022-A................. G 302 451-0537
 Newark *(G-12039)*
Thdxngrp LLC... G 443 993-6414
 New Castle *(G-9626)*
Tiedemann Trust Company........................... G 302 656-5644
 Wilmington *(G-20318)*
United Sttes Gyps Asb Per Inju................... G 888 708-8925
 Wilmington *(G-20528)*
US Auto Funding Trust 2020-1..................... G 770 280-3918
 Wilmington *(G-20547)*
Wilmington Trust Cllctive Inv....................... E 800 724-2440
 Wilmington *(G-20846)*
Wilmington Trust Company.......................... A 302 651-1000
 Wilmington *(G-20847)*

6794 Patent owners and lessors

1000 Degrees Pizzeria................................... F 609 382-3022
 Wilmington *(G-14101)*
6 8 Medical Solutions LLC............................ G 843 481-5550
 Lewes *(G-5641)*
Affilate Marks Investments Inc.................... G 302 478-7451
 Wilmington *(G-14302)*
Bbdotq USA Inc... C 302 533-6589
 Newark *(G-9999)*
Chuck Lager LLC.. D 302 482-1773
 Wilmington *(G-15428)*
Forbes Mrktplace Oprations Inc.................... E 973 393-0073
 Wilmington *(G-16687)*

67 HOLDING AND OTHER INVESTMENT OFFICES

Kohr Brothers Inc .... E 302 227-9354
  Rehoboth Beach (G-12825)
Lilian USA LLC .... F 800 246-2677
  Wilmington (G-17912)
Ripe Tech Corp .... G 786 633-2228
  Wilmington (G-19484)

6798 Real estate investment trusts

333 Rei LLC .... F 808 758-3095
  Middletown (G-6815)
All United Prpts Solutions LLC .... F 310 853-2223
  Camden (G-789)
Bekart Holding LLC .... F 302 600-7000
  Wilmington (G-14813)
Bpg Office Partners Viii LLC .... E 302 250-3065
  Wilmington (G-15025)
Divergent LLC .... G 302 275-7019
  Wilmington (G-16092)
Eldertrust .... G 302 993-1022
  Wilmington (G-16350)
EZ Investment Group LLC .... G 917 215-9887
  Dover (G-2475)
K&B Investors LLC .... G 302 357-9723
  Wilmington (G-17631)
Kennis Capital (usa) LLC .... G 302 605-6228
  Wilmington (G-17689)
Luxy Stay Imperial LLC .... G 844 483-5383
  Rehoboth Beach (G-12841)
Perpetual Invstments Group LLC .... F 718 795-3394
  Wilmington (G-18982)
Recadia Capital LLC .... G 866 671-1280
  Wilmington (G-19374)
Southwest American Corp .... G 302 652-7003
  Wilmington (G-19940)
St Lawrence Grant Ave Trust .... G 302 652-7978
  Wilmington (G-19997)

6799 Investors, nec

Abri Spac 2 Inc .... G 424 732-1021
  Newark (G-9744)
Accolade Global Inc .... G 209 645-0225
  Wilmington (G-14225)
Ackrell Spac Partners I Co .... G 650 560-4753
  Claymont (G-1019)
Acopia LLC .... D 302 286-5172
  Newark (G-9756)
Aetolia Captial LLC .... G 302 397-8238
  Wilmington (G-14300)
Affiliate Investment Inc .... C 302 478-7451
  Wilmington (G-14303)
Ajj Trades and Investment LLC .... G 302 403-7165
  Wilmington (G-14340)
Allen Estates LLC .... G 302 496-7250
  Dover (G-1770)
Amitra Vitta Incorporated .... E 267 905-3766
  Wilmington (G-14458)
Astrazneca Cllbrtion Vntres LL .... E 302 886-3000
  Wilmington (G-14611)
Aurum Capital Ventures Inc .... G 877 467-7780
  Dover (G-1854)
Bell Rock Capital LLC .... F 302 227-7607
  Rehoboth Beach (G-12638)
Best Holding LLC .... G 302 691-6023
  Wilmington (G-14854)
Bkl Ventures LLC .... G 302 317-2377
  Newark (G-10041)
Bri US LLC .... G 408 550-6354
  Lewes (G-5777)
Bsr Trade LLC .... G 646 250-4409
  Dover (G-1988)
Capital and Worth .... G 302 477-0660
  Wilmington (G-15225)

Capital Auto Rcvbles Asset Tr .... G 212 250-6864
  Wilmington (G-15226)
Capital Markets Iq LLC .... G 310 882-6380
  Wilmington (G-15229)
Cei Capital LLC .... G 302 573-3875
  Wilmington (G-15297)
Chelsea Creek Capital Co LLC .... G 312 977-4583
  Wilmington (G-15351)
Cigna Real Estate Inc .... G 302 476-3337
  Wilmington (G-15436)
Cinnaire Registered Investment .... F 302 655-1420
  Wilmington (G-15440)
Dd & E Investment Group Inc .... G 302 319-2780
  Wilmington (G-15831)
De/RE Investment Group .... G 302 450-6202
  Smyrna (G-13695)
Divine Legacy Group LLC .... G 973 986-7896
  Middletown (G-7064)
Dmm International Group Inc .... F 214 233-6898
  Wilmington (G-16109)
Dt Investment Partners LLC .... F 302 442-6203
  Wilmington (G-16185)
E-Cube .... G 302 290-7413
  Wilmington (G-16242)
Egw Capital Inc .... G 302 261-2008
  Lewes (G-5952)
Eloim Enterprises LLC .... F 510 209-3670
  Wilmington (G-16377)
Farazad Investments Inc .... G 302 573-2320
  Wilmington (G-16552)
Fas Mart / Shore Stop 286 LLC .... G 302 366-9694
  Newark (G-10713)
Gilliam & Garca RE Inv Co LLC .... G 302 377-5764
  Wilmington (G-16861)
Golden Gate Investments LLC .... G 302 894-8922
  Middletown (G-7169)
Good Life Group LLC .... G 720 759-9089
  Wilmington (G-16922)
Good Rputation Investments LLC .... G 888 382-1552
  Wilmington (G-16923)
GPM Investments LLC .... F 302 436-6330
  Selbyville (G-13539)
Green DOT Capital LLC .... G 302 395-0500
  Bear (G-256)
Guardian Investments .... G 302 541-2114
  Millsboro (G-8309)
Gulf Coast Investments Inc .... F 929 359-4439
  Dover (G-2633)
Hack Vc Management Company LLC .... G 650 575-4613
  Wilmington (G-17028)
Harrock Properties LLC .... G 302 202-1321
  Dover (G-2657)
Hs Capital LLC .... G 302 317-3614
  Wilmington (G-17222)
Iconix LLC .... G 215 850-9337
  New Castle (G-9228)
Ideatree Inc .... F 310 844-7447
  Wilmington (G-17264)
Imperial Realty Group LLC .... G 215 850-3142
  Newark (G-11006)
Independent Investors Inc .... G 302 366-1187
  Newark (G-11013)
Inheritnow Inc .... G 877 846-4374
  Wilmington (G-17339)
J A Banks & Associates LLC .... F 914 260-2003
  Smyrna (G-13779)
JC Marks Investments LLC .... G 302 602-4021
  Dover (G-2776)
Jsc Ventures LLC .... D 302 336-8151
  Dover (G-2810)
King-Edwards Residences LLC .... G 646 389-5830
  Dover (G-2876)

Landmark Homes .... G 302 388-8557
  Dover (G-2902)
Lc Associates LLC .... F 302 235-2500
  Hockessin (G-5279)
Legacy Global Developments LLC .... G 310 929-9862
  Dover (G-2926)
Linx Realty 2 LLC .... G 888 233-8901
  Dover (G-2953)
Llb Acquisition LLC .... F 212 750-8300
  Wilmington (G-17953)
Lubill Properties LLC .... G 302 946-4188
  Wilmington (G-18023)
Luxury Residence LLC .... F 302 216-2102
  Wilmington (G-18042)
M R Plumbing .... G 302 738-7978
  Newark (G-11304)
Medici Ventures Inc .... E 801 319-7029
  Wilmington (G-18251)
Miller Investments LLC .... G 949 836-2511
  Milford (G-8011)
Nestl Holdings Inc .... G 203 629-7482
  Wilmington (G-18589)
New Edge Enterprises LLC .... G 908 892-2856
  Milton (G-8676)
Nikko Capital Investments Ltd .... G 832 324-5335
  Lewes (G-6315)
Novin LLC .... G 315 670-7979
  Wilmington (G-18696)
Oasis Realty Inv Group LLC .... F 302 277-6885
  Newark (G-11573)
Ojo Investments LLC .... G 215 934-0855
  Dover (G-3218)
Oldfather Capital Inc .... G 302 296-6644
  Rehoboth Beach (G-12879)
One Ventures East LLC .... G 412 477-2754
  Lewes (G-6334)
Opportunity Investments .... G 302 887-3082
  Wilmington (G-18805)
Optima Iq Investments Inc .... E 302 279-5750
  Middletown (G-7417)
Patel Sandip .... G 302 363-9761
  Dover (G-3278)
PBL & 5js Holdings Inc .... G 404 832-5038
  Dover (G-3287)
PCA Acquisitions V LLC .... F 302 355-3500
  Wilmington (G-18932)
Perpetual Invstments Group LLC .... F 718 795-3394
  Wilmington (G-18982)
Pgim Foreign Investments Inc .... E 302 427-9530
  Wilmington (G-19007)
Philanthrovest LLC .... F 201 563-9179
  Dover (G-3313)
Pillar Wealth Advisors LLC .... G 302 409-3502
  Wilmington (G-19045)
Pipeline Funding Company LLC .... C 302 421-2287
  Wilmington (G-19054)
Prime Time Properties LLC .... G 302 763-6050
  Bear (G-438)
Progressive Investment Co Inc .... F 302 656-8597
  Wilmington (G-19219)
Pusan RE Newark LLC .... G 302 737-3087
  Newark (G-11776)
Quantum Temple Inc .... E 917 900-7452
  Middletown (G-7489)
Questar Capital Corporation .... G 302 856-9778
  Georgetown (G-4476)
Ral Group .... G 302 427-6970
  Wilmington (G-19321)
Rapid Hmmngbird Homebuyers LLC .... G 347 671-7761
  Dover (G-3424)
Recadia Corp Llc .... G 866 671-1280
  Wilmington (G-19375)

70 HOTELS, ROOMING HOUSES, CAMPS, AND OTHER LODGING PLACES

Regulation Holdco LLC .... F 800 521-1114
  Wilmington (G-19410)
Risq Trading Corp .... G 332 877-9934
  Wilmington (G-19487)
Rite Way Distributors .... E 302 535-8507
  Felton (G-4017)
Riverbend Inv MGT LLC Is A Rgs .... G 302 219-3080
  Rehoboth Beach (G-12936)
Rock Springs Capital LLC .... G 415 669-4545
  Wilmington (G-19532)
Rockford Capital Partners .... G 302 220-4786
  Wilmington (G-19535)
Ross Capital Partners LLC .... G 302 300-4220
  Hockessin (G-5373)
Round Table Men LLC .... G 302 287-8200
  New Castle (G-9542)
Sap Investments Inc .... F 302 427-7889
  Wilmington (G-19669)
Saving Our Slves Prprty Invsto .... G 267 879-0464
  Smyrna (G-13879)
Sb Global Advisers (us) Inc .... D 650 562-8100
  Wilmington (G-19689)
Scottish Ventures LLC .... G 302 382-6057
  New Castle (G-9554)
Scout Level LLC .... G 336 500-2067
  Middletown (G-7546)
Second Foundation US Trdg LLC .... F 253 777-4400
  Wilmington (G-19727)
Sqs Global Solutions LLC .... G 302 691-9682
  Wilmington (G-19984)
Svea Real Estate Group LLC .... G 855 262-9665
  Dover (G-3630)
Symack Capital US Corp .... F 469 607-6092
  Smyrna (G-13907)
Tcg High Yeld Inv Holdings LLC .... F 302 421-7361
  Wilmington (G-20238)
Third Sigma Investment Advisor .... G 302 656-1111
  Wilmington (G-20302)
Thirteen Svnty Six Cpitl MGT L .... G 561 247-1521
  Dover (G-3676)
Three Fields Capital LP .... G 302 636-5401
  Wilmington (G-20315)
Trolley Square Investors LLC .... G 302 658-1000
  Wilmington (G-20436)
Unity Growth Fund LLC .... G 703 585-7915
  Newark (G-12274)
USS Portfolio Delaware Inc .... G 302 798-7890
  Wilmington (G-20555)
Vos Energy LLC .... F 302 658-7581
  Wilmington (G-20653)
W Powell Investments .... G 443 523-2476
  Millsboro (G-8497)
Wealth Capital Investors LLC .... G 202 596-2280
  Lewes (G-6618)
Weepor Company Inc .... G 302 575-9945
  Wilmington (G-20711)
Ws One Investment Usa LLC .... F 302 317-2610
  New Castle (G-9692)
Wsfs Investment Group Inc .... G 302 573-3258
  Wilmington (G-20904)
Zehden Properties LLC .... G 310 773-8529
  Dover (G-3896)
Zeon Enterprises Inc .... F 302 898-7167
  New Castle (G-9698)

70 HOTELS, ROOMING HOUSES, CAMPS, AND OTHER LODGING PLACES

7011 Hotels and motels

1102 West Street Ltd Partnr .... D 302 429-7600
  Wilmington (G-14103)
1825 Inn .... F 717 838-8282
  Milton (G-8552)
190 Stadium LLC .... F 302 659-3635
  Smyrna (G-13623)
300 Gateway LLC .... F 302 655-4100
  New Castle (G-8745)
44 Aasha Hospitality Assoc LLC .... E 302 674-3784
  Dover (G-1688)
44 New England Management Co .... D 302 477-9500
  Wilmington (G-14135)
44 New England Management Co .... E 302 479-7900
  Wilmington (G-14136)
700 Nrth King St Wlmington LLC .... C 302 655-0400
  Wilmington (G-14146)
900 F Street Owner LLC .... D 212 355-1500
  Wilmington (G-14154)
Adams Oceanfront Resort .... F 302 227-3030
  Dewey Beach (G-1661)
Admiral Hotel .... G 302 227-2103
  Rehoboth Beach (G-12597)
Admiral On Baltimore .... E 302 227-1300
  Rehoboth Beach (G-12598)
Admiral West Inc .... E 609 729-0031
  Wilmington (G-14257)
Amaa Management Corporation .... E 302 677-0505
  Dover (G-1779)
Ambrux Hospitality LLC .... G 302 521-2492
  Wilmington (G-14418)
AmericInn By Wyndham .... F 302 398-3900
  Harrington (G-4729)
Anchorage Motel Inc .... G 302 645-8320
  Rehoboth Beach (G-12603)
Ark of Refuge Mission-Shelter .... F 302 381-2143
  Millsboro (G-8173)
Atlantic View Motel .... F 302 227-3878
  Dewey Beach (G-1662)
Bank House .... F 302 422-4824
  Milford (G-7782)
Bay Resort .... F 302 227-1598
  Dewey Beach (G-1663)
Bayside Resort Golf Club .... F 410 652-7705
  Millville (G-8516)
Beach House Resources .... F 703 980-3336
  Bethany Beach (G-577)
Beach House Services .... G 302 645-2554
  Milton (G-8569)
Beacon Hospitality .... E 302 249-0502
  Georgetown (G-4228)
Beacon Hospitality .... F 302 567-2213
  Rehoboth Beach (G-12630)
Beacon Motel .... G 302 645-4888
  Lewes (G-5745)
Bear Hospitality Inc .... G 302 326-2500
  Bear (G-64)
Bell Buoy Motel .... G 302 227-6000
  Dewey Beach (G-1665)
Best Western Goldleaf Ht LLC .... E 302 226-1100
  Rehoboth Beach (G-12642)
Bethany Bch Ocean Stes Rsdnce .... E 302 539-3201
  Bethany Beach (G-579)
Bethany Beach Bed & Breakfast .... G 301 651-2278
  Bethany Beach (G-580)
Bethany Sea-Crest Inc .... G 302 539-7621
  Bethany Beach (G-586)
Bfb Hospitality LLC .... F 302 829-1418
  Ocean View (G-12481)
Blenheim Hospitality LLC .... F 302 677-0900
  Dover (G-1948)
Blue Hen Hotel LLC .... E 302 266-0354
  Newark (G-10059)

Boardwalk Plaza Incorporated .... E 302 227-0441
  Rehoboth Beach (G-12648)
Breakers Associates .... E 302 227-6688
  Rehoboth Beach (G-12652)
Brick Hotel On The Circle .... F 302 745-0115
  Millsboro (G-8206)
Brighton Hotels LLC .... F 302 227-5780
  Rehoboth Beach (G-12654)
Buccini/Pollin Group Inc .... E 302 691-2100
  Wilmington (G-15139)
Butler Hospitality LLC .... D 888 288-5846
  Wilmington (G-15161)
Cambridge Trs Inc .... F 302 453-9200
  Newark (G-10123)
Candlewood Suites .... F 302 266-8184
  Newark (G-10128)
Canon Hospitality MGT LLC .... E 302 737-5050
  Newark (G-10134)
Ch Associates Viii LLC .... F 302 456-3800
  Newark (G-10182)
Ch Wilmington LLC .... E 302 438-4504
  Newark (G-10183)
Changing Place Inc .... F 302 357-6107
  Wilmington (G-15332)
Chapman Hospitality Inc .... D 302 738-3400
  Newark (G-10189)
Chillax Inn At Lewes Beach .... G 302 685-8845
  Lewes (G-5815)
Christiana Inn .... F 302 276-1659
  Bear (G-101)
Chudasama Enterprises LLC .... G 302 856-7532
  Georgetown (G-4255)
Chudasama Enterprises LLC .... G 302 934-7968
  Millsboro (G-8227)
Coastal Cottage .... G 302 539-7821
  Ocean View (G-12491)
Coastal Properties I LLC .... E 302 227-5800
  Rehoboth Beach (G-12686)
Colonial Oaks Hotel LLC .... C 302 645-7766
  Rehoboth Beach (G-12693)
Colonial Oaks Hotel LLC .... G 302 645-7766
  Rehoboth Beach (G-12694)
Comfort Inn & Suites .... E 302 737-3900
  Newark (G-10283)
Comfort Suites .... E 302 628-5400
  Seaford (G-13131)
Comfort Suites Motel .... G 302 266-6600
  Hockessin (G-5167)
Concord Towers Inc .... D 302 737-2700
  Newark (G-10296)
Cooper Simpler Associates Inc .... G 302 227-2999
  Rehoboth Beach (G-12700)
Country Inns Suites .... G 302 266-6400
  Newark (G-10334)
Country Villa Motel .... G 814 938-8330
  Milford (G-7842)
Courtyard Management Corp .... E 302 456-3800
  Newark (G-10336)
Courtyard Management Corp .... E 302 429-7600
  Wilmington (G-15661)
Courtyard Newark At Ud .... E 302 737-0900
  Newark (G-10337)
Covered Bridge Inn .... F 302 542-9605
  Lewes (G-5866)
Dan Licale .... F 302 888-2133
  Montchanin (G-8736)
Day 1 Motel .... F 302 397-8412
  Wilmington (G-15819)
Days Inn and Suites Seaford .... F 302 629-4300
  Seaford (G-13148)
Days Inn Dover Downtown .... E 302 674-8002
  Dover (G-2200)

70 HOTELS, ROOMING HOUSES, CAMPS, AND OTHER LODGING PLACES — SIC SECTION

Delaware Hotel Associates LP .... D 302 792-2700
  Claymont (G-1113)
Delaware Hotel-Motel Assn .... G 302 674-0630
  New Castle (G-9024)
Delaware Motel and Rv Park .... G 302 328-3114
  New Castle (G-9027)
Dewey Beach House .... F 302 227-4000
  Dewey Beach (G-1666)
Dhm Wilmington LLC .... E 302 656-8952
  Wilmington (G-16045)
Dillons Driftwood Entp LLC .... G 302 645-7500
  Lewes (G-5919)
Dinner Bell Inn .... F 302 227-2561
  Rehoboth Beach (G-12729)
Dipna Inc .... C 302 478-0300
  Wilmington (G-16076)
Divas Inn .... F 302 753-2170
  Wilmington (G-16091)
Dogfish Inn .... F 302 644-8292
  Lewes (G-5926)
Dolphin Beach LLC .... F 302 654-3543
  Wilmington (G-16125)
Dover Downs Inc .... A 302 674-4600
  Dover (G-2338)
Dover Downs Gaming MGT Corp .... F 302 730-3800
  Dover (G-2339)
Dover Garden Suites .... G 302 883-2417
  Dover (G-2345)
Dover Hospitality Group LLC .... E 302 677-0900
  Dover (G-2347)
Dpnl LLC .... F 302 366-8097
  Newark (G-10559)
Driftwood Hospitality MGT LLC .... E 302 655-0400
  Wilmington (G-16179)
Dunes Manor Hotel .... F 610 256-4307
  Selbyville (G-13525)
Dutch Village Motel Inc .... E 302 328-6246
  New Castle (G-9070)
Eastern Hospitality Management .... E 302 322-9480
  New Castle (G-9079)
Econo Lodge Inn Suites Resort .... E 302 227-0500
  Rehoboth Beach (G-12738)
Eventide Hospitality LLC .... F 202 725-6357
  Bethany Beach (G-600)
Everest Hotel Group LLC .... F 213 272-0088
  Camden (G-832)
Express Hotel Inc .... F 302 227-4030
  Rehoboth Beach (G-12748)
Fairways Inn .... F 302 653-7044
  Smyrna (G-13729)
First State Hospitality LLC .... F 302 538-5858
  Dover (G-2505)
George Metz .... G 302 227-4343
  Rehoboth Beach (G-12769)
Georgetown Hotel LLC .... E 302 515-2100
  Georgetown (G-4339)
Green Room Restaurant .... E 302 594-3100
  Wilmington (G-16966)
Grey Mountain Equities LLC .... G 623 387-0744
  Claymont (G-1171)
Greystone Bed & Breakfa .... F 302 645-0699
  Lewes (G-6061)
Gulab Management Inc .... G 302 398-4206
  Harrington (G-4776)
Gulab Management Inc .... E 302 934-6126
  Milford (G-7914)
Gulab Management Inc .... F 302 422-8089
  Milford (G-7915)
Gulab Management Inc .... E 302 734-4433
  Dover (G-2632)
Gurukrupa Inc .... G 302 328-6691
  New Castle (G-9184)

Hampton Inn .... E 302 422-4320
  Milford (G-7920)
Hampton Inn Middletown .... E 302 378-5656
  Middletown (G-7191)
Hampton Inn Seaford .... F 302 629-4500
  Seaford (G-13206)
Hampton Inn-Dover .... G 302 736-3500
  Dover (G-2648)
Harborside Development II LLC .... E 302 644-3377
  Rehoboth Beach (G-12780)
Hawthorn Suites Hotels Intl .... F 302 369-6212
  Newark (G-10939)
Henlopen Hotel Inc .... F 302 227-2551
  Rehoboth Beach (G-12786)
Hilltop Hostel .... F 202 291-9591
  Dagsboro (G-1464)
Hilton Garden Inn Dover .... F 302 465-3061
  Middletown (G-7210)
Holiday Inn .... F 302 655-0400
  Wilmington (G-17165)
Holiday Inn Express .... E 302 398-8800
  Harrington (G-4785)
Holiday Inn Express .... F 302 227-4030
  Rehoboth Beach (G-12787)
Holiday Inn Select .... F 302 792-2700
  Claymont (G-1180)
Hollywood Grill Restaurant .... D 302 737-3900
  Newark (G-10958)
Hollywood Grill Restaurant .... D 302 629-4500
  Seaford (G-13211)
Hollywood Grill Restaurant .... F 302 479-2000
  Wilmington (G-17172)
Hollywood Grill Restaurant .... D 302 655-1348
  Wilmington (G-17171)
Home2 Suites By Hilton .... F 302 291-1616
  Lewes (G-6098)
Homestead At Rehoboth Bb .... G 302 226-7625
  Rehoboth Beach (G-12788)
Homestead Newark - Christiana .... F 302 283-0800
  Newark (G-10965)
Homewood Stes By Hlton Wlmngto .... E 302 565-2100
  Wilmington (G-17191)
Hotel Rodney .... G 302 645-6466
  Lewes (G-6105)
House To House Incorporation .... F 302 450-8445
  Newark (G-10978)
Hyatt Hse Lewes / Rehoboth Bch .... F 302 783-1000
  Lewes (G-6109)
Hyatt Place .... E 302 864-9100
  Dewey Beach (G-1671)
Inn At Rehobeth Apartments .... G 302 226-1760
  Rehoboth Beach (G-12795)
Inn At Wilmington .... F 302 479-7900
  Wilmington (G-17346)
Inn LLC A-1 Dash .... F 302 368-7964
  Newark (G-11021)
Inns of Rehoboth Beach LLC .... E 302 645-8003
  Rehoboth Beach (G-12796)
Interstate Hotels LLC .... G 302 658-7581
  Wilmington (G-17398)
Interstate Hotels Resorts Inc .... F 302 792-2700
  Claymont (G-1188)
J & P Management Inc .... E 302 854-9400
  Georgetown (G-4375)
Jamc LLC .... G 410 639-2224
  Millsboro (G-8327)
Jay Ambe Inc .... F 302 654-5400
  New Castle (G-9254)
Jay Devi Inc .... E 302 777-4700
  New Castle (G-9255)
Jaysons LLC .... E 302 656-9436
  Wilmington (G-17502)

K W Lands North LLC .... D 302 678-0600
  Dover (G-2824)
Kenny Simpler .... G 302 226-2900
  Rehoboth Beach (G-12819)
Keval Corp .... F 302 453-9100
  Newark (G-11160)
Keval Corporation .... E 302 453-9100
  Newark (G-11161)
Khanna Entps Ltd A Ltd Partnr .... F 302 266-6400
  Newark (G-11169)
Knights Inn .... F 302 798-9914
  Claymont (G-1208)
Kw Garden .... F 302 735-7770
  Dover (G-2891)
Last Nickel Inn LLC .... F 302 945-4880
  Millsboro (G-8345)
Laughing Horse LLC .... F 917 513-5255
  Lewes (G-6182)
Lila Keshav Hospitality LLC .... F 302 696-2272
  Middletown (G-7304)
Luxiasuites LLC .... F 302 426-1200
  Wilmington (G-18041)
Luxiasuites LLC .... G 302 778-2900
  Wilmington (G-18040)
MainStay Suites .... E 302 678-8383
  Dover (G-2999)
Mandip LLC .... F 302 218-7449
  Newark (G-11322)
Mark One LLC .... E 302 735-4700
  Dover (G-3019)
Meris Gardens Bed & Breakfast .... F 302 752-4962
  Bethany Beach (G-620)
Milford Lodging LLC .... E 302 839-5000
  Milford (G-8003)
Milford Microtel LLC .... F 302 503-7615
  Milford (G-8005)
Mj Wilmington Hotel Assoc LP .... C 302 454-1500
  Newark (G-11430)
Mj Wilmington Hotel Assoc LP .... C 302 454-1500
  Newark (G-11431)
Monadnock Inn .... F 603 532-7800
  Felton (G-4004)
Moore Partnership .... F 302 227-5253
  Dewey Beach (G-1674)
Moores Enterprises Inc .... F 302 227-8200
  Rehoboth Beach (G-12860)
Motel 6 .... F 302 990-5291
  Seaford (G-13290)
My Salon Suites .... G 302 575-9035
  Wilmington (G-18510)
Nab Motel Inc .... F 302 983-0849
  Newark (G-11480)
Nab Motel Inc .... F 302 656-9431
  Wilmington (G-18518)
Nacstar .... E 302 453-1700
  Newark (G-11482)
Nazar Dover LLC .... E 302 747-5050
  Dover (G-3163)
New Beginnings Cnslng Cnst .... G 302 525-6268
  Newark (G-11514)
New Castle Lodging Corporation .... D 302 654-5544
  New Castle (G-9410)
New Orleans Hotel Equity LLC .... G 302 757-7300
  Wilmington (G-18623)
Newark Knights Ftbll and .... F 302 846-7776
  Bear (G-395)
Newark Land Group Inc .... F 302 453-1700
  Newark (G-11541)
Ocean CLB Rsort Rservation Ctr .... G 302 369-1420
  Newark (G-11575)
Ocean Glass Inn .... F 302 227-2844
  Rehoboth Beach (G-12876)

70 HOTELS, ROOMING HOUSES, CAMPS, AND OTHER LODGING PLACES

Packem Associates Partnership............ G 302 227-5780
  Rehoboth Beach *(G-12882)*
Pagoda Hotel Inc.................................... F 808 922-1233
  Historic New Castle *(G-5045)*
Park Hotels & Resorts Inc..................... F 703 883-1000
  Newark *(G-11628)*
Paul Amos... E 302 541-9200
  Bethany Beach *(G-626)*
Pde I LLC.. D 302 654-8300
  Wilmington *(G-18937)*
Pelican Bay Group Inc.......................... G 302 945-5900
  Millsboro *(G-8418)*
Perfect Grand Lodge Stdavid................ F 302 689-3579
  Wilmington *(G-18972)*
Polkamotion Rehoboth.......................... F 410 729-9697
  Rehoboth Beach *(G-12895)*
Premier Entertainment III LLC............... A 302 674-4600
  Dover *(G-3360)*
Quality Inn... F 302 292-1500
  Newark *(G-11789)*
Quality Inn... G 302 659-3635
  Smyrna *(G-13860)*
Quality Inn Newark............................... G 707 622-5339
  Newark *(G-11790)*
Quality Reside LLC............................... G 484 957-0564
  Middletown *(G-7488)*
Quintasian LLC..................................... E 302 674-3784
  Dover *(G-3412)*
Rama Corporation................................ E 302 266-6600
  Hockessin *(G-5354)*
Rdu Instahotels LLC............................. G 919 297-8399
  Middletown *(G-7506)*
Red Roof Inns Inc................................ E 302 292-2870
  Newark *(G-11840)*
Rehoboth Inn LLC................................ G 302 226-2410
  Rehoboth Beach *(G-12929)*
Relax Inn.. G 302 875-1554
  Laurel *(G-5588)*
Residence Inn....................................... E 302 777-7373
  Wilmington *(G-19437)*
Residence Inn By Mariott..................... F 302 539-3200
  Bethany Beach *(G-633)*
Residence Inn By Marriott LLC............. D 302 453-9200
  Newark *(G-11863)*
Residence Inn Dover............................ E 302 677-0777
  Dover *(G-3460)*
Residnce Inn Wlmngton Nwrk/CHR..... G 302 453-9200
  Newark *(G-11864)*
Resort Hotel LLC.................................. E 302 226-1515
  Rehoboth Beach *(G-12934)*
Resortquest.. F 302 616-1040
  Ocean View *(G-12563)*
Riverdale Park LLC.............................. G 302 945-2475
  Millsboro *(G-8446)*
Riverfront Hotel LLC............................. E 302 803-5888
  Wilmington *(G-19495)*
Rodeway Inn.. E 302 227-0401
  Rehoboth Beach *(G-12937)*
Routzhan Jessman............................... E 302 398-4206
  Harrington *(G-4822)*
Rp Hospitality LLC............................... F 302 398-4206
  Harrington *(G-4823)*
Sage Hospitality Resources LLC.......... C 302 292-1500
  Newark *(G-11933)*
SAI Ram Hospitality Inc....................... F 302 422-8089
  Milford *(G-8079)*
Sands Inc... D 302 227-2511
  Rehoboth Beach *(G-12947)*
Savannah Inn....................................... F 302 645-0330
  Lewes *(G-6448)*
Sea Colony LLC................................... F 302 537-8888
  Bethany Beach *(G-640)*

Sea Esta 4.. G 302 354-1245
  Rehoboth Beach *(G-12949)*
Sekhon Travels LLC............................. G 661 706-6459
  Dover *(G-3528)*
Seper 8 Motel....................................... E 302 734-5701
  Dover *(G-3533)*
Shiv Sagar Inc...................................... F 302 674-3800
  Dover *(G-3547)*
Shree Kishna Inc.................................. F 302 839-5000
  Milford *(G-8092)*
Shree Lalji LLC.................................... G 302 730-8009
  Dover *(G-3552)*
Shri SAI Dover LLC............................. E 302 747-5050
  Dover *(G-3553)*
Shri Swami Narayan LLC..................... D 302 738-3198
  Newark *(G-12002)*
Shriji Hospitality (not Llc)..................... D 302 654-5544
  New Castle *(G-9567)*
Simpler and Sons LLC......................... F 302 296-4400
  Rehoboth Beach *(G-12960)*
Skyways Motor Lodge Corp................. E 302 328-6666
  New Castle *(G-9572)*
Sleep Inn & Suites............................... F 302 645-6464
  Lewes *(G-6477)*
Sonesta Intl Hotels Corp...................... E 302 453-9200
  Newark *(G-12055)*
Soucialize Inc....................................... G 916 803-1057
  Lewes *(G-6492)*
Springhill Suites Newark Downt............ F 888 205-7322
  Newark *(G-12076)*
Ssn Christiana LLC.............................. E 302 266-6600
  Newark *(G-12079)*
State Street Inn.................................... G 302 734-2294
  Dover *(G-3609)*
Staybridge Suites................................. F 302 738-3400
  Wilmington *(G-20040)*
Studio302... F 302 462-0857
  Dover *(G-3617)*
Sun Hotel Inc....................................... G 302 322-0711
  New Castle *(G-9600)*
Sunny Hospitality LLC.......................... E 302 226-0700
  Rehoboth Beach *(G-12980)*
Sunny Hospitality LLC.......................... E 302 398-3900
  Harrington *(G-4837)*
Super Eight Dover................................ E 302 734-5701
  Dover *(G-3626)*
Superlodge... F 302 654-5544
  Wilmington *(G-20145)*
Surf Club.. G 302 227-7059
  Dewey Beach *(G-1675)*
Sussex Sands Inc................................ G 302 539-8200
  Fenwick Island *(G-4057)*
Theluxestay LLC.................................. F 802 234-1410
  Middletown *(G-7638)*
Towne Place Suites By Marriott............ D 302 369-6212
  Newark *(G-12214)*
Travel Inn New..................................... F 302 322-4500
  New Castle *(G-9636)*
Tucson Hotels LP................................. D 678 830-2438
  Wilmington *(G-20458)*
Umiya Inc... G 302 674-4011
  Dover *(G-3746)*
Unibet Interactive Inc........................... F 855 655-6310
  Wilmington *(G-20506)*
Veer Hotels Inc.................................... G 302 398-3900
  Harrington *(G-4844)*
Vivky of Delaware Inc.......................... F 302 798-9914
  Claymont *(G-1331)*
Wdbid DBA Downtown Visions............ E 302 425-5374
  Wilmington *(G-20697)*
Willis Hspitality Partners LLC............... F 302 544-5054
  New Castle *(G-9683)*

Wilmington Christiana Cou................... F 302 456-3800
  Newark *(G-12380)*
Wilmington Ht Xxxiii Owner LLC........... E 302 594-3100
  Wilmington *(G-20819)*
Winner Dover 1387 LLC....................... F 302 257-3500
  Dover *(G-3859)*
Wyndham Franchisor LLC.................... E 302 487-0234
  Dover *(G-3879)*
Young Mens Christian Assn Del........... E 302 571-6968
  Wilmington *(G-20936)*
Zwaanendael LLC................................ G 302 645-6466
  Lewes *(G-6652)*

7021 Rooming and boarding houses

Beacon Hospitality............................... E 302 249-0502
  Georgetown *(G-4228)*
DSU Student Housing LLC................... G 302 857-7966
  Dover *(G-2391)*
Ezdorms Inc... F 202 599-2953
  Wilmington *(G-16517)*
Kasa Enterprise LLC............................ G 302 634-0138
  Middletown *(G-7262)*
Ministry of Caring Inc.......................... G 302 652-0904
  Wilmington *(G-18374)*
Paragon Serenity LLC.......................... F 302 784-4979
  Newark *(G-11624)*
Pot-Nets Bywood Vacation Rentl......... F 302 945-9300
  Millsboro *(G-8434)*
Reva Stays LLC................................... G 347 599-8599
  Townsend *(G-14059)*

7032 Sporting and recreational camps

Basket Fundamentals LLC.................... G 302 360-8617
  Lewes *(G-5737)*
Bear-Glasgow YMCA............................ G 302 836-9622
  Newark *(G-10006)*
Camp Arrowhead Busine...................... F 302 448-6919
  Wilmington *(G-15208)*
Cedarbrook Camp In PA...................... G 302 463-0137
  Bear *(G-93)*
Division One Basketball LLC................ F 302 573-2528
  Wilmington *(G-16099)*
Ed Hunt Inc.. G 302 339-8443
  Dover *(G-2418)*
Ehs LLC.. G 302 332-4247
  Wilmington *(G-16312)*
Excel Education Day Care LLC............ G 302 832-1833
  Bear *(G-214)*
Hope House Daycare........................... G 302 407-3404
  Wilmington *(G-17197)*
Matts Fish Camp Lewes De LLC.......... F 302 539-4415
  Lewes *(G-6251)*
Mt Aire... G 302 629-8739
  Seaford *(G-13293)*
Piranha Sports LLC.............................. G 302 893-1997
  Bear *(G-426)*
Relyance Skim Camp........................... G 717 343-3588
  Ocean View *(G-12561)*
Win From Wthin Xc Camp/Tatnall........ G 302 494-5312
  Wilmington *(G-20855)*
Wm Delcampo Mechanical Svcs........... G 302 543-2725
  Wilmington *(G-20870)*
Young MNS Chrstn Assn Wlmngton..... C 302 296-9622
  Rehoboth Beach *(G-13027)*
YWCA Delaware.................................. F 302 224-4060
  Newark *(G-12425)*

7033 Trailer parks and campsites

Barsgr LLC... F 302 945-3410
  Millsboro *(G-8182)*
Bayshore Inc.. G 302 539-7200
  Ocean View *(G-12470)*

70 HOTELS, ROOMING HOUSES, CAMPS, AND OTHER LODGING PLACES

Cedarcreeklandingcgcom......................... G 302 491-6614
  Lincoln *(G-6659)*

Delaware Beaches Jellystone Pk................ F 302 491-4531
  Lincoln *(G-6662)*

Delaware Motel and Rv Park....................... G 302 328-3114
  New Castle *(G-9027)*

Gulls Way Campground.............................. G 302 732-6383
  Dagsboro *(G-1454)*

Gulls Way Campground.............................. G 302 732-6383
  Dagsboro *(G-1455)*

Gulls Way Inc... G 302 732-9629
  Dagsboro *(G-1456)*

Homestead Camping Inc............................ G 302 684-4278
  Georgetown *(G-4363)*

Masseys Landing Park Inc......................... F 302 947-2600
  Millsboro *(G-8367)*

Oak Forest Park LLC.................................. G 302 947-9328
  Smyrna *(G-13840)*

Pine Acres Inc... F 302 945-2000
  Lewes *(G-6370)*

Port Del-Mar-Va Inc.................................... G 302 227-7409
  Rehoboth Beach *(G-12896)*

S B Trailer Park.. G 302 697-0699
  Magnolia *(G-6781)*

Steamboat Landing.................................... G 302 645-6500
  Lewes *(G-6507)*

Tall Pines Associates Llc.......................... F 302 684-0300
  Lewes *(G-6541)*

Tuckahoe Acres Camping Resort............... G 302 539-1841
  Dagsboro *(G-1520)*

Yogi Bear Campground.............................. F 302 491-6514
  Lincoln *(G-6711)*

7041 Membership-basis organization hotels

Airbnb Inc.. F 415 800-5959
  Wilmington *(G-14336)*

Alpha Gmma RHO Almni Assn of T........... G 301 490-9972
  Selbyville *(G-13460)*

Delta Epsilon Tau....................................... G 302 541-0450
  Ocean View *(G-12503)*

Glasgow Court Enterprises LLC................. F 302 834-1633
  Newark *(G-10844)*

Innpros Inc.. F 302 326-2500
  Bear *(G-285)*

72 PERSONAL SERVICES

7211 Power laundries, family and commercial

AP Linens Inc.. E 302 430-0851
  Milford *(G-7770)*

Five Point Chinese Laundry........................ G 302 656-6051
  Wilmington *(G-16652)*

Harbour Textile Rental Svc Inc................... G 302 656-2300
  Historic New Castle *(G-5000)*

Harry Louies Laundry & Dry Clg................. G 302 734-8195
  Dover *(G-2658)*

Laurel Linen Service Inc............................. F 804 732-3315
  New Castle *(G-9296)*

Main Gate Laundry..................................... G 302 998-9949
  Wilmington *(G-18088)*

Selbyville Cleaners Inc............................... E 302 249-3444
  Selbyville *(G-13604)*

Thompson Cleaners................................... G 302 998-0935
  Wilmington *(G-20313)*

7212 Garment pressing and cleaners' agents

Blue Swan Cleaners Inc.............................. F 302 652-7607
  Wilmington *(G-14977)*

Capitol Cleaners & Ldrers Inc..................... D 302 674-1511
  Dover *(G-2022)*

Main Street Cleaners.................................. G 302 738-4385
  Newark *(G-11313)*

Marvi Cleaners Limited Inc......................... G 302 764-3077
  Wilmington *(G-18173)*

McKelvey Hires Dry Cleaning..................... F 302 998-9191
  Wilmington *(G-18232)*

Sissys Closet Inc.. G 302 698-1327
  Camden Wyoming *(G-978)*

7213 Linen supply

All Star Linen and Uniform Co.................... G 302 897-9003
  Wilmington *(G-14368)*

Alsco Inc... E 302 322-2136
  New Castle *(G-8788)*

Capitol Cleaners & Ldrers Inc..................... D 302 674-1511
  Dover *(G-2022)*

G K Services 238.. G 302 629-6729
  Seaford *(G-13193)*

Harbour Textile Rental Svc Inc................... G 302 656-2300
  Historic New Castle *(G-5000)*

Laurel Linen Service Inc............................. F 804 732-3315
  New Castle *(G-9296)*

Mayflower Laundry and Lin Sups................ G 302 652-1416
  New Castle *(G-9354)*

Medlanta Inc... G 610 991-2929
  Wilmington *(G-18256)*

Palace Laundry Inc.................................... A 302 322-2136
  New Castle *(G-9445)*

Selbyville Cleaners Inc............................... E 302 249-3444
  Selbyville *(G-13604)*

Socal Auto Supply Inc................................. F 818 717-9982
  Lewes *(G-6485)*

Virginia Linens LLC.................................... G 757 342-4225
  Wilmington *(G-20630)*

7215 Coin-operated laundries and cleaning

13 Laundromat... G 302 322-1910
  New Castle *(G-8743)*

Brookside Laundromat................................ G 302 369-3366
  Newark *(G-10093)*

Emerald City Wash World.......................... G 302 734-1230
  Dover *(G-2438)*

Gigis Laundry Room................................... G 302 764-7777
  Wilmington *(G-16859)*

Lazybones Inc.. G 302 530-7114
  Bear *(G-340)*

Ocean Suds Laundromat............................ G 302 856-3002
  Georgetown *(G-4450)*

Ocean Suds Laundry Mat........................... G 302 703-6601
  Rehoboth Beach *(G-12877)*

Royal Cleaners... G 302 478-0955
  Wilmington *(G-19576)*

Smart Laundromat...................................... G 302 854-0300
  Georgetown *(G-4513)*

Sparklean Laundromat............................... G 302 365-6665
  Bear *(G-503)*

Sparklean Laundromat............................... G 302 838-2226
  Newark *(G-12062)*

Splash Laundromat.................................... G 302 503-3325
  Milford *(G-8100)*

Splash Lndrmat LLC - Gorgetown.............. G 302 249-8231
  Georgetown *(G-4522)*

Surf N Suds Laundries............................... G 302 836-9120
  Bear *(G-521)*

Trolley Laundry.. G 302 654-3538
  Wilmington *(G-20434)*

7216 Drycleaning plants, except rugs

Blue Swan Cleaners Inc.............................. F 302 652-7607
  Wilmington *(G-14977)*

Brasures Carpet Care Inc........................... G 302 436-5652
  Selbyville *(G-13483)*

C & L Cleaners Inc..................................... G 302 736-5171
  Dover *(G-2004)*

City One Hour Cleaners............................. G 302 658-0001
  Wilmington *(G-15455)*

Curzon Corp... F 302 655-5551
  Wilmington *(G-15737)*

Dry Cleaning Home Service Inc.................. G 302 777-7444
  Wilmington *(G-16180)*

Dun Rite Cleaners...................................... G 302 654-3958
  Wilmington *(G-16199)*

Harry Louies Laundry & Dry Clg................. G 302 734-8195
  Dover *(G-2658)*

Joy Cleaners Inc... G 302 656-3537
  Wilmington *(G-17593)*

Linden Hill Cleaners Inc.............................. G 302 368-9795
  Wilmington *(G-17926)*

Main Gate Laundry..................................... G 302 998-9949
  Wilmington *(G-18088)*

Marvi Cleaners Limited Inc......................... G 302 764-3077
  Wilmington *(G-18173)*

McKelvey Hires Dry Cleaning..................... F 302 998-9191
  Wilmington *(G-18232)*

North Hills Cleaners Inc.............................. G 302 764-1234
  Wilmington *(G-18680)*

Ohs Liberty Cleaners Inc............................ G 302 454-1322
  Newark *(G-11581)*

Oneclick Cleaners...................................... G 302 697-8000
  Camden *(G-881)*

Park Avenue Dry Cleaners LLC................. G 302 725-9430
  Rehoboth Beach *(G-12884)*

Proclean Inc.. E 302 656-8080
  Delaware City *(G-1554)*

Schroedl Company..................................... D 410 358-5500
  Wilmington *(G-19698)*

7217 Carpet and upholstery cleaning

ABM Janitorial Services Inc....................... E 302 571-9900
  Wilmington *(G-14205)*

Apple Cleaning Systems LLC.................... F 302 368-7507
  New Castle *(G-8814)*

Brasures Carpet Care Inc........................... G 302 436-5652
  Selbyville *(G-13483)*

C & B Complete Clg Svc Inc...................... E 302 436-9622
  Frankford *(G-4081)*

Coastal Chem-Dry...................................... G 302 645-2800
  Lewes *(G-5837)*

Coit Clg Rstoration Wilmington.................. G 302 322-1099
  Claymont *(G-1097)*

Colonial Cleaning Services Inc................... G 302 660-2067
  Wilmington *(G-15534)*

Crystal Kleen Inc.. G 302 326-1140
  New Castle *(G-8990)*

Delaware Rug Co Inc................................. G 302 998-8881
  Wilmington *(G-15963)*

Dibiasos Clg Rstration Svc Inc................... G 302 376-7111
  Townsend *(G-13992)*

EBc Carpet Services Corp......................... E 302 995-7461
  Wilmington *(G-16273)*

Ebc National Inc... F 302 995-7461
  Wilmington *(G-16274)*

Edwards Paul Crpt Installation................... G 302 672-7847
  Dover *(G-2427)*

Greener Cleaner Sussex Corp................... G 302 497-7123
  Millsboro *(G-8307)*

Grime Busters USA Inc.............................. G 302 834-7006
  Newark *(G-10900)*

Hampton Enterprises Inc............................ G 302 378-7365
  Townsend *(G-14013)*

L & M Services Inc..................................... G 302 658-3735
  Wilmington *(G-17773)*

Lopesco Inc.. E 732 985-7776
  Newark *(G-11284)*

Marlings Inc.. F 302 325-1759
  Wilmington *(G-18153)*

72 PERSONAL SERVICES

Oceanside Elite Clg Bldg Svcs............... E 302 339-7777
  Lewes (G-6329)
Oxi Fresh Dover Carpet Clg................... F 302 526-5035
  Dover (G-3255)
Positive Results Cleaning Inc................ G 302 575-1146
  Wilmington (G-19126)
Proclean Inc.. E 302 656-8080
  Delaware City (G-1554)
Schrider Enterprises Inc......................... G 302 539-1036
  Ocean View (G-12566)
Stanley Steemer Intl Inc........................ E 302 293-2879
  New Castle (G-9592)
Steam Wizards LLC................................ G 302 548-5942
  Frankford (G-4148)
Tri State Cleaning................................. G 302 644-6554
  Milton (G-8723)
Vivid Colors Carpet LLC........................ G 302 335-3933
  Frederica (G-4187)
Worms Quality Carpet Care.................. F 302 629-3114
  Seaford (G-13455)
Worthys Property MGT LLC................. F 302 265-8301
  Lincoln (G-6710)

7218 Industrial launderers

Domain Hr Solutions............................. F 302 357-9401
  Middletown (G-7068)
Harbour Textile Rental Svc Inc.............. G 302 656-2300
  Historic New Castle (G-5000)
Jwr 1 LLC... G 302 379-9951
  Bear (G-320)
Nixon Uniform Service Inc................... C 302 325-2875
  Historic New Castle (G-5040)

7219 Laundry and garment services, nec

Authentic Tailoring Service................... G 302 740-1185
  Wilmington (G-14648)
Candlelight Bridal Formal Tlrg.............. G 302 934-8009
  Millsboro (G-8215)
Curzon Corp... F 302 655-5551
  Wilmington (G-15737)
Delaware Seamstress............................. G 302 286-8210
  Wilmington (G-15965)
Harry Louies Laundry & Dry Clg.......... G 302 734-8195
  Dover (G-2658)
Honey Alteration.................................... G 302 519-2031
  Lewes (G-6101)
Joy Cleaners Inc..................................... G 302 656-3537
  Wilmington (G-17593)
Marvi Cleaners Limited Inc................... G 302 764-3077
  Wilmington (G-18173)
North Hills Cleaners Inc........................ G 302 764-1234
  Wilmington (G-18680)

7221 Photographic studios, portrait

Delaware Color Lab................................ G 302 529-1339
  Wilmington (G-15889)
Dsd Photography Inc............................. G 678 622-5910
  Bear (G-182)
Gramonoli Enterprises Inc..................... G 302 227-1288
  Rehoboth Beach (G-12777)
Heather Baker.. G 302 382-7466
  Harrington (G-4783)
Jlquick Photography.............................. G 302 674-3794
  Dover (G-2793)
Kerry Harrison Photography................. G 302 494-4141
  Wilmington (G-17698)
Lifetouch Portrait Studios Inc................ F 302 734-9870
  Dover (G-2944)
Lifetouch Portrait Studios Inc................ G 302 453-8080
  Newark (G-11256)
Moonloop Photography LLC................. G 484 748-0812
  Wilmington (G-18431)

Nicholls Photography............................ G 302 543-3879
  New Castle (G-9420)
NKita Enterprises LLC........................... G 302 295-2363
  Bear (G-398)
Portrait Innovations Inc........................ G 302 477-1696
  Wilmington (G-19120)
Sugarhill International.......................... G 302 275-9257
  Wilmington (G-20121)
Tpp Acquisition Inc............................... F 302 674-4805
  Dover (G-3710)

7231 Beauty shops

2520 Hair Salon & Day Spa................... G 717 845-2241
  Rehoboth Beach (G-12590)
A Gentlemans Touch Inc....................... F 302 585-5805
  Wilmington (G-14163)
A Hair Hub LLC..................................... G 267 206-0569
  Bear (G-10)
A R Nails.. G 302 858-4592
  Georgetown (G-4190)
Abbey Hair Styling................................ G 302 697-1186
  Magnolia (G-6713)
Afterglo Beauty Spa.............................. G 302 537-7546
  Millville (G-8512)
Alchemy of Hair.................................... G 302 525-6676
  Newark (G-9807)
All About U Evada Concept................. G 302 539-1925
  Millville (G-8514)
An Event 2 Remember........................... G 215 783-9744
  Claymont (G-1037)
Angel Nails.. F 302 449-5067
  Middletown (G-6864)
April Mries Hair Design Studio............ G 302 981-3386
  Historic New Castle (G-4933)
Artistic Designs Salon........................... G 302 644-2009
  Lewes (G-5703)
Artistry Salon Studio............................. G 302 513-9225
  New Castle (G-8825)
Avenue Cuts Inc.................................... G 302 655-1718
  Wilmington (G-14666)
Babe Styling Studio Inc........................ G 302 543-7738
  Wilmington (G-14710)
Baby Bubba Dj & Event Planning........ G 302 373-4653
  New Castle (G-8843)
Bad Hair Day Inc................................... E 302 226-4247
  Rehoboth Beach (G-12621)
Barbara Baker....................................... G 302 238-7415
  Frankford (G-4067)
Beauty and Beach Hair Boutique......... G 302 260-9383
  Rehoboth Beach (G-12633)
Beauty By Jamie.................................... G 302 784-5311
  New Castle (G-8856)
Beauty Max Inc..................................... G 302 735-1705
  Dover (G-1900)
Bella Mia Aesthetics LLC...................... G 302 548-0660
  Middletown (G-6911)
Bethany Bch Hair Snippery Inc............ G 302 539-8344
  Millville (G-8520)
Billie Stevens Carlins............................. G 302 436-0856
  Frankford (G-4072)
Boundaries New..................................... G 302 658-3486
  New Castle (G-8877)
Braid Nation LLC................................. G 302 508-5913
  Smyrna (G-13666)
Brandon Tatum...................................... G 302 564-7428
  Selbyville (G-13480)
Brenda Anns Hair Salon........................ G 302 312-7658
  Bear (G-81)
Carme LLC.. F 302 832-8418
  Newark (G-10150)
Carols... G 302 448-0734
  Milford (G-7812)

Cartessa Aesthetics................................ G 302 332-1991
  Hockessin (G-5150)
Cartino Nail Spa.................................... G 302 212-2510
  Rehoboth Beach (G-12665)
Cathy Ann Mitchell............................... G 302 875-7018
  Laurel (G-5479)
CEst Moi Infinity Inc............................. G 267 455-2455
  Newark (G-10180)
Charlotte Wilson.................................... G 302 500-1440
  Seaford (G-13113)
Che Studio Inc....................................... G 856 246-8440
  New Castle (G-8926)
Cheveux Inc... G 302 731-9202
  Newark (G-10200)
Christophers Hair Design...................... G 302 378-1988
  Middletown (G-6980)
Cielo Salon & Spa Inc........................... F 302 575-0400
  Wilmington (G-15435)
CK Skin & Makeup LLC....................... G 302 317-2367
  Wilmington (G-15458)
Claymont Nails....................................... G 302 798-8220
  Claymont (G-1093)
CMC Corporation of Hockessin........... G 302 239-1960
  Hockessin (G-5164)
Coiffure Ltd... G 302 652-3463
  Wilmington (G-15521)
Cole Janeika.. G 302 838-1868
  Newark (G-10271)
Colecarol... G 302 313-6698
  Newark (G-10272)
Color ME Crazy Hair LLC.................... G 484 838-6027
  Middletown (G-7003)
Complete Family Care Inc.................... F 302 232-5002
  Wilmington (G-15572)
Crowning Glory Styling Salon............. G 302 999-8237
  Wilmington (G-15717)
Crumpton Starline................................. G 302 832-1342
  New Castle (G-8989)
Currie Hair Skin Nails........................... G 302 777-7755
  Wilmington (G-15735)
Daniel Halvorsen................................... G 302 645-1761
  Lewes (G-5879)
Danny Thach.. G 302 645-7779
  Lewes (G-5880)
Dawn Runs With Scissors..................... G 302 293-4517
  Wilmington (G-15817)
Deer Client Hair Salon.......................... G 302 983-3353
  Newark (G-10407)
Delaware Lrng Inst Csmtlogy In........... F 302 732-6704
  Dagsboro (G-1434)
Designer Braids and Trade.................... G 718 783-9078
  Middletown (G-7055)
Dianes Nail and Spa.............................. G 302 538-7185
  Camden (G-818)
Dionne Michelles Luxury Hair............. G 484 362-9242
  Bear (G-170)
Divine Profiles Inc................................ G 302 633-3400
  Wilmington (G-16098)
Donnas Family Cut & Curl Inc............ G 302 436-8999
  Selbyville (G-13521)
Dynasty Styling Studios LLC............... G 302 595-3042
  Bear (G-184)
Eco Centric Salon................................... G 302 378-1988
  Middletown (G-7080)
Efflorescence Skin Care........................ G 302 250-3232
  Wilmington (G-16309)
Eiva Nails & Spa LLC........................... G 302 537-1888
  Ocean View (G-12508)
Elayne James Salon & Spa LLC........... G 302 376-5290
  Middletown (G-7090)
Elegant Images LLP.............................. G 302 698-5250
  Camden (G-828)

Employee Codes: A=Over 500 employees, B=251-500
C=101-250, D=51-100, E=20-50, F=10-19, G=1-9

2024 Harris Directory of Delaware Businesses

72 PERSONAL SERVICES — SIC SECTION

Elite Nails .... G 302 745-5988
   Lewes *(G-5958)*

Encore Lashes Lash Lounge LLC .... G 844 408-0004
   New Castle *(G-9094)*

European Wax Center .... G 302 731-2700
   Newark *(G-10672)*

Fantasy Beauty Salon .... G 302 629-6762
   Seaford *(G-13183)*

Ferrari Hair Studio Ltd .... G 302 731-7505
   Wilmington *(G-16587)*

First State Wax LLC .... G 302 529-8888
   Wilmington *(G-16639)*

Fringe Hair Studio .... G 302 313-5213
   Lewes *(G-6017)*

Fusion .... G 302 479-9444
   Wilmington *(G-16773)*

Gc New Castle Inc .... G 302 544-6128
   New Castle *(G-9159)*

Gemini Hair Designs .... G 302 654-9371
   Wilmington *(G-16828)*

George Marcus Salon Inc .... G 302 475-7530
   Wilmington *(G-16847)*

Girls Auto Clinic LLC .... G 484 679-6394
   New Castle *(G-9167)*

Give Back Beauty LLC .... F 571 439-2321
   Dover *(G-2587)*

GL Robins Co Inc .... G 302 834-1272
   Bear *(G-248)*

GL Robins Co Inc .... G 302 475-5001
   Wilmington *(G-16874)*

GL Robins Co Inc .... G 302 654-4477
   Wilmington *(G-16875)*

Glitzy and Glamour Hair Salon .... G 302 325-9565
   New Castle *(G-9169)*

Glossgirl Inc .... G 302 888-4520
   Wilmington *(G-16898)*

Glossgirl Inc .... G 302 737-8080
   Newark *(G-10853)*

Goddess Beauty Supply LLC .... G 302 858-4649
   Georgetown *(G-4343)*

Goddess of Barn .... G 302 363-1062
   Smyrna *(G-13745)*

Great Clips .... G 302 737-2887
   Newark *(G-10885)*

Great Clips .... G 302 514-9819
   Smyrna *(G-13751)*

Great Clips .... G 302 995-2887
   Wilmington *(G-16958)*

Great Clips For Hair .... G 302 677-1838
   Cheswold *(G-988)*

Great Clips For Hair .... G 302 858-4871
   Georgetown *(G-4345)*

Great Clips For Hair .... G 302 235-2887
   Hockessin *(G-5227)*

Growing & Glowing LLC .... G 302 500-9220
   Newark *(G-10902)*

H & J Unisex Salon .... G 302 983-6833
   Newark *(G-10911)*

Hair Academy Llc .... G 302 738-6251
   Newark *(G-10918)*

Hair Day .... G 302 538-5198
   Dover *(G-2644)*

Hair Experience .... G 302 293-0359
   New Castle *(G-9192)*

Hair Gallerie .... G 302 373-4774
   Wilmington *(G-17033)*

Hair Sensations Inc .... G 302 731-0920
   New Castle *(G-9193)*

Hair Studio .... G 302 740-4804
   Newark *(G-10919)*

Hair Studio II .... G 302 945-5110
   Millsboro *(G-8312)*

Hair Yard .... G 302 264-0594
   Middletown *(G-7189)*

Hairworks Inc .... G 302 656-0566
   Wilmington *(G-17034)*

Hanthej Hulio .... G 302 478-3080
   Wilmington *(G-17052)*

Hawa African Hair Braiding .... G 302 654-9456
   Wilmington *(G-17077)*

Hc Salon Holdings Inc .... E 302 378-8565
   Middletown *(G-7199)*

Hc Salon Holdings Inc .... E 302 537-4624
   Millville *(G-8533)*

Hc Salon Holdings Inc .... G 302 999-7724
   Wilmington *(G-17086)*

Hc Salon Holdings Inc .... F 302 478-9978
   Wilmington *(G-17087)*

Hillary J White Soho Slon Spa .... G 302 838-2110
   Bear *(G-275)*

Hitrust LLC .... G 302 525-6223
   New Castle *(G-9215)*

HLS Event Solutions LLC .... G 484 293-4272
   Harbeson *(G-4699)*

Hockessin Day Spa .... G 302 234-7573
   Wilmington *(G-17162)*

Hockessin Salon .... G 302 740-3638
   Hockessin *(G-5245)*

Holiday Hair .... G 302 856-2575
   Georgetown *(G-4359)*

Hollywood Nails .... G 302 477-4849
   Wilmington *(G-17173)*

Hollywood Nails & Spa .... G 302 762-1800
   Wilmington *(G-17174)*

House of Harmony Hair Salon .... G 302 420-4565
   Bear *(G-279)*

Hughy Inc .... G 302 398-8826
   Harrington *(G-4788)*

Hype Hair LLC .... G 302 898-3145
   New Castle *(G-9224)*

Island of Misfits LLC .... G 302 732-6704
   Dagsboro *(G-1468)*

J Stanley Salon LLC .... G 302 778-1885
   Wilmington *(G-17465)*

James & Jesses Barbr & Buty Sp .... G 302 658-9617
   Wilmington *(G-17478)*

James C Wang .... G 302 737-6000
   Newark *(G-11089)*

Jamroxk LLC .... G 302 423-5377
   Dover *(G-2770)*

Jersey Clippers LLC .... G 302 956-0138
   Bridgeville *(G-718)*

Jk Tangles Hair Salon .... G 302 698-1006
   Dover *(G-2791)*

JMB Glamsquad LLC .... F 844 695-4526
   Wilmington *(G-17556)*

Justin Brian Salon LLC .... G 302 597-8945
   Wilmington *(G-17619)*

Justyce Barber & Beauty Salon .... G 302 998-7788
   Wilmington *(G-17624)*

Kathleens Creations .... G 302 492-8749
   Clayton *(G-1379)*

Kays Nail & Spa LLC .... G 302 376-7788
   Middletown *(G-7264)*

Kd Nails .... G 302 422-0998
   Milford *(G-7961)*

Kelf LLC .... G 302 229-2195
   Wilmington *(G-17678)*

Kellies Hair Place .... G 302 827-2715
   Lewes *(G-6166)*

Kjp LLC .... G 302 765-0134
   Wilmington *(G-17738)*

KS Nail and Spa .... G 302 703-6158
   Lewes *(G-6173)*

Kustom Kutz .... G 302 424-7556
   Milford *(G-7968)*

La Bella Nails Inc .... G 302 475-6216
   Wilmington *(G-17779)*

LA BELLE ARTISTRY LLC .... F 302 656-0555
   Wilmington *(G-17780)*

Lash Beauty Bar .... G 302 827-2160
   Lewes *(G-6181)*

Lasting Looks .... G 302 635-7327
   Hockessin *(G-5276)*

Lavish Nail Spa LLC .... G 302 829-3008
   Wilmington *(G-17826)*

Le Salone Hair Salon .... G 302 384-6788
   New Castle *(G-9298)*

Lee Nails .... G 302 674-5001
   Dover *(G-2925)*

Les Nails .... G 302 449-5290
   Middletown *(G-7295)*

Linden Nails & Spa .... G 302 510-4794
   Wilmington *(G-17928)*

Lindner LLC .... G 302 827-2160
   Lewes *(G-6209)*

Lorgus Enterprises Inc .... G 610 431-7453
   Dover *(G-2976)*

Lovely Nails & Spa LLC .... G 302 260-9231
   Rehoboth Beach *(G-12839)*

Lux Spa & Nails .... G 302 834-4899
   Bear *(G-355)*

Makeup & Love .... G 856 524-1966
   Lewes *(G-6238)*

Mane Attraction .... G 302 526-2013
   Dover *(G-3008)*

Mark IV Beauty Salon Inc .... G 302 737-4994
   Newark *(G-11335)*

Maureen Freebery .... G 302 234-7800
   Wilmington *(G-18201)*

Maxim Hair & Nails LLC .... G 410 920-8656
   Selbyville *(G-13569)*

Maxines Hair Happenings Inc .... G 302 875-4055
   Laurel *(G-5561)*

Michaelangelos Hair Designs .... G 302 734-8343
   Dover *(G-3082)*

My Roots LLC .... G 302 883-2693
   Dover *(G-3139)*

My Salon Suite .... G 302 233-6947
   Camden Wyoming *(G-964)*

N&D Nail Salon .... G 302 834-4899
   Bear *(G-387)*

Nail Art .... G 302 999-7807
   Wilmington *(G-18521)*

Nail Pros .... G 302 674-2988
   Dover *(G-3146)*

Nails At Taormina .... G 302 519-7528
   Millsboro *(G-8397)*

Nanas Butter LLC .... G 302 510-3937
   Wilmington *(G-18524)*

Natural Hair Consortium LLC .... G 240 508-1494
   Wilmington *(G-18553)*

Natural Nail Studio .... G 302 478-0077
   Wilmington *(G-18555)*

Natural Salon .... G 302 239-5000
   Hockessin *(G-5318)*

Ncc Cooperative Extension Off .... G 302 831-8965
   Newark *(G-11496)*

Neitao Express Nails .... G 302 276-1027
   New Castle *(G-9402)*

New Care Spa .... G 302 292-2067
   Newark *(G-11515)*

New Trend Hair Salon .... G 302 998-3331
   Wilmington *(G-18626)*

No 3 Eline Pwers Fgure Salons .... G 302 256-5015
   Wilmington *(G-18659)*

72 PERSONAL SERVICES

Noche Azul Spa ..... G 302 345-0070
　Wilmington (G-18662)
Not Your Mothers Makeup ..... G 302 538-1612
　Dover (G-3200)
Nu Attitude Styling Salon Ltd ..... G 302 734-8638
　Dover (G-3210)
Nu Image Landscaping Inc ..... G 302 366-8699
　Newark (G-11567)
Oerigo Consulting LLC ..... G 302 353-4719
　Smyrna (G-13841)
One Step Ahead Childcare ..... G 302 292-1162
　Newark (G-11593)
Otto Clips Company ..... G 267 918-9985
　Wilmington (G-18832)
Padens Hair Studio ..... G 267 718-8109
　New Castle (G-9444)
Pamper ME Pink LLC ..... F 302 200-2635
　Selbyville (G-13589)
Pamper Perfect Mobile Spa ..... G 866 947-9994
　Dover (G-3263)
Peachy Keen Sion + Buty Bar LL ..... G 302 519-5572
　Milford (G-8043)
Penache Beauty Salon ..... G 302 731-5912
　Newark (G-11657)
Perfect Nails ..... G 302 731-1964
　Newark (G-11665)
Perfect Ten Nail Salon Da ..... G 302 545-3001
　Wilmington (G-18974)
Perry Anthony Salon Spa Netwrk ..... G 302 239-6161
　Wilmington (G-18985)
Petite Hair Designs ..... G 302 945-2595
　Millsboro (G-8427)
Pin Up Girls Salon LLC ..... G 302 537-1325
　Ocean View (G-12559)
Pizazz Beauty Studio ..... G 302 761-9820
　Wilmington (G-19060)
Platinum LLC ..... G 302 492-1850
　Marydel (G-6809)
Platinum Salon LLC ..... G 302 653-6125
　Smyrna (G-13848)
Posh Salon ..... G 302 655-7000
　Wilmington (G-19122)
Premier Salons Intl Inc ..... G 302 477-3459
　Wilmington (G-19170)
Premiere Hair Design ..... G 302 368-7711
　Middletown (G-7467)
Pretty Nails ..... G 302 628-3937
　Seaford (G-13357)
Qbs Beauty Salon ..... G 302 691-3449
　Wilmington (G-19276)
Rape of The Locke Inc ..... G 302 368-5370
　Newark (G-11827)
Regis Corporation ..... F 302 834-9916
　Bear (G-450)
Regis Corporation ..... G 302 697-6220
　Camden (G-889)
Regis Corporation ..... G 302 376-6165
　Middletown (G-7509)
Regis Corporation ..... G 302 430-0881
　Milford (G-8061)
Regis Corporation ..... G 302 227-9730
　Rehoboth Beach (G-12912)
Regis Corporation ..... G 302 629-2916
　Seaford (G-13371)
Regis Corporation ..... G 302 628-0484
　Seaford (G-13372)
Rehoboth Nails & Spa ..... G 302 703-6481
　Rehoboth Beach (G-12930)
Rejuvntion Skin Wllness Asthti ..... G 302 537-8318
　Millville (G-8545)
Rene Delyn Designs Inc ..... F 302 736-6070
　Dover (G-3455)

Resh LLC ..... F 302 543-5469
　New Castle (G-9523)
Rhoyal Extensions ..... G 318 572-2549
　Newark (G-11880)
Rita Porter Darnetta ..... G 302 419-3877
　New Castle (G-9534)
Robins Hair & Tanning ..... G 302 529-9000
　Wilmington (G-19523)
Royal Vanity Hair Studio ..... G 302 322-4680
　New Castle (G-9546)
Salon 828 LLC ..... G 302 376-8282
　Middletown (G-7536)
Salon By Dominic ..... E 302 239-8282
　Hockessin (G-5378)
Salon Lala Mamoune ..... G 302 737-5264
　Newark (G-11937)
Salon On Central LLC ..... G 302 539-1882
　Ocean View (G-12565)
Salon Rispoli LLC ..... F 302 731-9202
　Newark (G-11938)
Sassy Spa ..... G 302 668-8008
　Wilmington (G-19675)
Savarna Inc ..... G 757 446-0101
　Historic New Castle (G-5066)
Savvy Artistry LLC ..... G 302 339-1712
　Historic New Castle (G-5067)
Savvy Hair Studios ..... G 302 724-5629
　Dover (G-3512)
SBS Global LLC ..... G 302 898-2911
　Newark (G-11955)
Schilling-Dglas Schl Hair Dsign ..... F 737 510-0101
　Newark (G-11957)
Shankias Best Braids ..... G 302 507-9891
　Wilmington (G-19779)
Shannlls Crtive Styles Brids L ..... G 302 508-9215
　Dover (G-3540)
Shear Collection Salon By Mel ..... G 302 543-6854
　Wilmington (G-19786)
Sinkor Beauty Salon ..... G 302 464-3292
　Middletown (G-7569)
Skin Solutions By Wendi ..... G 302 312-1569
　Newark (G-12022)
Sola Salon Studios ..... G 302 283-9216
　Wilmington (G-19918)
Sophisticuts Inc ..... G 302 834-7427
　Bear (G-500)
Sport Clips ..... G 302 294-1774
　Newark (G-12071)
Sport Clips ..... G 302 836-9900
　Newark (G-12072)
Sport Clips ..... G 302 456-9900
　Newark (G-12073)
Sport Clips Hrcuts Dver - Dpon ..... G 302 677-1622
　Dover (G-3599)
Sport Clips Hrcuts Rhboth Bch ..... F 302 291-2391
　Rehoboth Beach (G-12970)
Stephanie Saroukos ..... G 302 654-1614
　Wilmington (G-20055)
Steve Styles ..... G 302 540-4965
　Wilmington (G-20063)
Styles By US ..... G 302 629-3244
　Seaford (G-13415)
Styles Celebrity ..... G 302 286-7825
　Newark (G-12112)
Styles Divine Unlimited ..... G 302 409-4612
　Smyrna (G-13904)
Styling Her Esteem ..... G 302 494-1010
　Newark (G-12114)
Sundae Body LLC ..... F 480 430-5675
　Middletown (G-7609)
Sunlight Salon LLC ..... G 302 456-1799
　Newark (G-12125)

Supercuts ..... G 302 698-1988
　Camden (G-894)
Supercuts ..... G 302 422-8448
　Milford (G-8108)
Supercuts ..... G 302 934-6534
　Millsboro (G-8471)
Supercuts ..... G 302 644-4288
　Rehoboth Beach (G-12983)
Sylvia Saienna ..... G 302 683-9082
　Wilmington (G-20180)
Tess Afrcan Hair Brding Buty S ..... G 302 384-6439
　Wilmington (G-20279)
Todds ..... F 302 658-0387
　Wilmington (G-20343)
Top Notch Beauty ..... G 302 501-5442
　Bear (G-537)
Town and Country Salon ..... G 302 322-2929
　Historic New Castle (G-5089)
Town Hair Salon ..... G 302 803-4535
　Newark (G-12213)
Trendz Salon and Spa ..... G 302 632-3045
　Dover (G-3720)
Tresses Hair Studio ..... G 302 670-7356
　Dover (G-3721)
Trilogy Salon and Day Spa Inc ..... F 302 292-3511
　Newark (G-12229)
TT Spalon ..... G 302 668-1477
　Wilmington (G-20455)
Twisted Hair Designs ..... G 302 533-6104
　Newark (G-12249)
Ultimate Images Inc ..... G 302 479-0292
　Wilmington (G-20497)
Ultimate Tan Millsboro Inc ..... G 302 934-1400
　Dagsboro (G-1521)
Uppercut Inc ..... G 302 736-1661
　Dover (G-3760)
US Male Modern Barbershop ..... F 302 635-7370
　Hockessin (G-5414)
Vels Hair Salon ..... G 302 427-3819
　Wilmington (G-20579)
Visions Hair Design ..... G 302 477-0820
　Wilmington (G-20641)
Vivians Style ..... G 302 645-9444
　Lewes (G-6607)
Vu Binh Thai ..... G 302 999-7980
　Wilmington (G-20656)
White Mink Beauty Salon ..... G 302 737-2081
　Newark (G-12368)
Womens Wellness Ctr & Med Spa ..... G 302 643-2500
　Newark (G-12399)
Works Body Wrap By Tanya ..... G 302 669-7839
　Wilmington (G-20894)
Xanadu Concepts LLC ..... G 302 449-2677
　Middletown (G-7738)
Yankee Clippers Hair Designer ..... G 302 422-2748
　Milford (G-8155)
Young Divas LLC ..... G 302 354-6232
　New Castle (G-9695)
Zuri Hair Collection LLC ..... G 804 296-7534
　Dover (G-3909)
Zyng Nails ..... G 302 407-3849
　Wilmington (G-20971)

7241 Barber shops

A Gentlemans Touch Inc ..... F 302 585-5805
　Wilmington (G-14163)
All In Wrist ..... G 302 659-1010
　Smyrna (G-13634)
Amstel Barber Shop ..... G 302 696-2300
　Middletown (G-6861)
Amstel Barber Shop ..... G 302 378-5300
　Middletown (G-6862)

72 PERSONAL SERVICES

Amstel Barber Shop... G 302 543-4515
  Wilmington (G-14464)
Amstel Barbershop LLC..................................... G 302 635-7686
  Hockessin (G-5123)
Amstel Barbershop LLC..................................... G 302 299-5926
  Newark (G-9855)
Anna Vassallo Piera.. G 302 529-2607
  Wilmington (G-14490)
Artful Barber... G 302 672-0818
  Dover (G-1821)
Barber Shop At Rehoboth Beach....................... G 240 743-9064
  Harbeson (G-4685)
Bethany Bch Hair Snippery Inc........................... G 302 539-8344
  Millville (G-8520)
CMC Corporation of Hockessin......................... G 302 239-1960
  Hockessin (G-5164)
Cutting Edge of Delaware Inc............................ F 302 834-8723
  Wilmington (G-15747)
Cutting Edge Treatment Center......................... G 302 258-5710
  Harrington (G-4755)
Diamond State Express LLC............................. E 302 563-3514
  Hockessin (G-5187)
Fite LLC.. G 302 478-1002
  Wilmington (G-16650)
Georve V Sawyer.. G 302 736-1474
  Dover (G-2574)
Grooming Bar LLC.. G 302 803-8304
  Wilmington (G-16985)
Hair Studio II.. G 302 945-5110
  Millsboro (G-8312)
Haircut & Company Inc...................................... G 302 239-3236
  Newark (G-10920)
Headquarter Barber Shop.................................. G 302 378-7372
  Middletown (G-7200)
House of Kings Inc... G 302 319-8724
  New Castle (G-9221)
Jesse W Stone... G 302 677-0500
  Dover (G-2784)
Josue Barber Shop.. G 302 650-5362
  Wilmington (G-17591)
Larry Coverdale.. G 302 855-9305
  Georgetown (G-4401)
Napoleon Hernandez... G 302 368-2237
  Newark (G-11487)
New Castle Shop Rental Inc............................. G 302 328-8346
  New Castle (G-9412)
Professionals... G 302 764-5501
  Wilmington (G-19215)
Rape of The Locke Inc....................................... G 302 368-5370
  Newark (G-11827)
Toms Barber Shop... G 302 992-9635
  Wilmington (G-20350)
Uplift Barbershop.. G 302 883-3001
  Dover (G-3759)
US Male Modern Barbershop............................ F 302 635-7370
  Hockessin (G-5414)
Visions Hair Design... G 302 477-0820
  Wilmington (G-20641)

7251 Shoe repair and shoeshine parlors

Curzon Corp... F 302 655-5551
  Wilmington (G-15737)

7261 Funeral service and crematories

Bell Funeral Home... G 302 658-1555
  Wilmington (G-14817)
Bennie Smith Funeral Home Inc........................ G 302 934-9019
  Millsboro (G-8194)
Bennie Smith Funeral Home Inc........................ G 302 678-8747
  Dover (G-1913)
Ccci- Celebrants Christn Chpel......................... G 302 690-4890
  Middletown (G-6967)
Congo Funeral Home... G 302 652-8887
  Wilmington (G-15595)
Congo Funeral Home... F 302 652-6640
  Wilmington (G-15594)
Delaware Prof Fnrl Svcs Inc.............................. E 302 731-5459
  Newark (G-10471)
Direct Cremation Services Del.......................... F 302 656-6873
  Wilmington (G-16077)
Dohery Funeral Homes Inc................................ G 302 999-8277
  Wilmington (G-16120)
Evan W Smith Funeral Home............................. G 302 526-4662
  Dover (G-2466)
Evan W Smith Funeral Services........................ G 302 494-1847
  Bear (G-208)
Ews Funeral Home... G 302 494-1847
  Bear (G-213)
Family First Funeral Svcs LLC........................... G 800 377-6949
  Dover (G-2482)
Family First Funeral Svcs LLC........................... G 800 377-6949
  Newport (G-12452)
Gebhart Funeral Home Inc................................ G 302 798-7726
  Claymont (G-1156)
Gore Funeral Services....................................... G 610 364-9900
  New Castle (G-9173)
Grieco... G 302 792-1293
  Claymont (G-1172)
Hamilton Home Services LLC........................... G 302 430-6505
  Dagsboro (G-1459)
Hannigan Short Disharoonk............................... G 302 875-3637
  Laurel (G-5528)
House of Wright Mortuary................................... G 302 659-5517
  Smyrna (G-13768)
House of Wright Mortuary................................... G 302 762-8448
  Wilmington (G-17216)
Interntnal Soc For Hylrnan Scn......................... G 212 992-5971
  Wilmington (G-17396)
James B Crissman... G 302 475-1365
  Wilmington (G-17479)
James T Chandler & Son Inc............................. G 302 478-7100
  Wilmington (G-17487)
John F Yasik Funeral Services........................... G 302 428-9986
  Wilmington (G-17562)
McCrery Funeral Homes Inc.............................. G 302 478-2204
  Wilmington (G-18225)
Melson Funeral Services................................... G 302 945-9000
  Millsboro (G-8375)
Melson Funeral Services Ltd............................. G 302 732-9000
  Frankford (G-4126)
Melsons Cape Hnlopen Crematory.................... G 302 537-2441
  Frankford (G-4127)
Michael A Mealey & Sons Inc............................ F 302 654-3005
  Wilmington (G-18305)
Michael A Mealey & Sons Inc............................ F 302 652-5913
  Wilmington (G-18304)
Miller Fnrl HM & Cremation Svc........................ G 302 947-1144
  Laurel (G-5565)
Parsell Funeral Entps Inc................................... G 302 645-9520
  Lewes (G-6351)
Regulatory Datacorp Inc................................... G 302 299-2284
  Wilmington (G-19411)
Rkb Funerals Inc.. G 302 934-7842
  Millsboro (G-8447)
Robert T Jones & Foard Inc............................... G 302 731-4627
  Newark (G-11900)
Short Funeral Home Inc..................................... G 302 846-9814
  Delmar (G-1636)
Smith Harvey C Jr Funeral Dire........................ G 302 376-0200
  Odessa (G-12587)
Spicer Mullikin Funeral Homes.......................... G 302 368-9500
  Newark (G-12067)
Spicer Mullikin Funeral Homes.......................... G 302 368-9500
  New Castle (G-9585)
Starks Funeral Service LLC............................... G 202 361-0603
  Wilmington (G-20027)
Timothy J Meyers Inc... G 302 438-3709
  Wilmington (G-20332)
Torbert Fnrl Chpel Ambince Svc........................ G 302 734-3341
  Dover (G-3703)
Torbert Funeral Chapel Inc................................ F 302 734-3341
  Dover (G-3704)
Watson Funeral Home Inc.................................. F 302 934-7842
  Millsboro (G-8501)
Welcome Home Getaways LLC......................... G 724 426-5534
  Bear (G-561)
Zwaanendael LLC.. G 302 645-6466
  Lewes (G-6652)

7291 Tax return preparation services

Abacus Tax Service.. G 302 543-5619
  Wilmington (G-14192)
AC Tax Group LLC... G 844 378-1040
  Middletown (G-6831)
Accutax... G 302 735-9747
  Dover (G-1709)
Adkins & Assoc CPA.. G 302 737-2390
  Wilmington (G-14256)
Advantage Corp.. G 302 478-7977
  Wilmington (G-14284)
Advantage Delaware LLC.................................. G 302 479-7764
  Wilmington (G-14285)
Aguilera Tax Preparation.................................... G 302 746-7253
  Wilmington (G-14322)
Atm The Bottom Line Ltd.................................. G 302 322-0452
  Newark (G-9941)
Basic Block Corp.. F 302 645-2000
  Rehoboth Beach (G-12623)
Cjm Bookkeeping and Taxes LLC...................... G 302 999-8755
  Newark (G-10247)
Colonial Income Tax Service.............................. G 302 322-6881
  Historic New Castle (G-4961)
Cornerstone Group LLC..................................... G 302 377-7165
  Newark (G-10325)
Counting House.. G 302 249-5596
  Greenwood (G-4606)
Craig Weiner.. G 267 226-8511
  Wilmington (G-15682)
Dbw Tax Services... G 302 276-0428
  Bear (G-137)
Delaware Tax & Accounting Svcs..................... G 302 504-4063
  Newark (G-10488)
Delaware Tax Services...................................... G 302 453-1040
  Newark (G-10489)
Delaware Taxes LLC... G 302 368-7040
  Newark (G-10490)
Elite Tax Services LLC....................................... G 302 256-0401
  Wilmington (G-16366)
F & S Tax Solutions Inc..................................... G 302 477-4357
  Wilmington (G-16520)
Grc & Associates LLC....................................... G 770 484-9082
  Middletown (G-7173)
H & R Block.. G 302 856-3272
  Georgetown (G-4349)
H & R Block.. G 302 398-8730
  Harrington (G-4778)
H & R Block.. G 302 378-1538
  Middletown (G-7184)
H & R Block.. F 302 324-1040
  New Castle (G-9185)
H & R Block.. G 302 368-7500
  Newark (G-10912)
H & R Block.. G 302 436-0260
  Selbyville (G-13540)
H & R Block.. G 302 999-8100
  Wilmington (G-17012)

SIC SECTION — 72 PERSONAL SERVICES

H & R Block Inc .... G 302 836-2700
  Bear *(G-259)*
H & R Block Inc .... G 302 378-8931
  Middletown *(G-7185)*
H & R Block Inc .... G 302 934-6178
  Millsboro *(G-8310)*
H & R Block Inc .... G 302 328-7320
  New Castle *(G-9186)*
H & R Block Inc .... G 302 652-3286
  New Castle *(G-9187)*
H & R Block Inc .... G 302 999-7488
  Wilmington *(G-17013)*
H & R Block Inc .... F 302 478-9140
  Wilmington *(G-17014)*
H & R Block Inc .... G 302 478-6300
  Wilmington *(G-17015)*
H&R Block Eastern Enterpres .... G 302 656-7212
  Wilmington *(G-17023)*
Hopkins and Associates LLC .... G 302 660-8476
  Wilmington *(G-17203)*
Hopkins Tax & Accounting LLC .... G 302 846-2303
  Delmar *(G-1601)*
Horty & Horty PA .... F 302 730-4560
  Dover *(G-2695)*
Jackson Hewitt .... G 302 382-2140
  Dover *(G-2764)*
Jackson Hewitt Tax Service .... G 302 761-9626
  Wilmington *(G-17471)*
Jackson Hewitt Tax Service .... G 302 629-4548
  Seaford *(G-13228)*
Jackson Hewitt Tax Service Inc .... G 302 934-7430
  Millsboro *(G-8325)*
Jay Katz Lmm Taxation LLC .... G 302 894-9446
  Wilmington *(G-17501)*
Jpv Tax Services .... G 302 740-6383
  Wilmington *(G-17599)*
Judith A Smith .... G 302 322-9396
  Historic New Castle *(G-5012)*
Kelly Robert & Assoc LLC .... F 302 737-7785
  Newark *(G-11151)*
Liberty Tax .... G 302 678-3101
  Dover *(G-2937)*
Liberty Tax .... G 302 526-1611
  Middletown *(G-7297)*
Liberty Tax .... G 302 543-8840
  Wilmington *(G-17892)*
Liberty Tax .... G 302 304-8714
  Wilmington *(G-17893)*
Liberty Tax Service .... G 302 762-1010
  Claymont *(G-1217)*
Liberty Tax Service .... G 302 404-2140
  Seaford *(G-13260)*
Liberty Tax Service .... G 302 270-4135
  Smyrna *(G-13802)*
Liberty Tax Service .... G 302 691-9279
  Wilmington *(G-17894)*
Mark E Handley .... G 302 284-9550
  Camden Wyoming *(G-960)*
Michael Eller Income Tax Svc .... G 302 652-5916
  Wilmington *(G-18311)*
Miller & Associates PA .... G 302 234-0678
  Wilmington *(G-18364)*
Mobile Tax LLC .... G 302 297-8325
  Georgetown *(G-4430)*
Multi Michel Services .... G 302 628-3288
  Seaford *(G-13295)*
Multiwave Investment Inc .... E 302 658-9200
  Wilmington *(G-18484)*
National Income Tax Service .... G 302 777-1040
  Wilmington *(G-18542)*
Nikki Sykes Tax Preparation As .... G 302 399-6363
  Dover *(G-3189)*

No Tax Mall LLC .... G 215 554-5380
  Hockessin *(G-5323)*
Oates Consultants LLC .... G 302 477-0109
  Wilmington *(G-18734)*
Papaleo Rosen Chelf & Pinder .... G 302 644-8600
  Lewes *(G-6348)*
Personal Tax Services .... G 302 562-5051
  Newark *(G-11669)*
Prefered Tax Service Inc .... G 302 654-4388
  Wilmington *(G-19161)*
Preferred Tax Svc Inc .... G 302 945-3700
  Millsboro *(G-8437)*
R E WIlliams Prof Acctg Frm Tax .... G 302 598-7171
  Wilmington *(G-19304)*
Ronald Midaugh .... F 410 860-1040
  Dover *(G-3482)*
Sad Enterprises Inc .... G 302 422-6100
  Milford *(G-8078)*
Sam Your Taxes LLC .... G 302 482-9601
  Wilmington *(G-19647)*
Shore Tax Service Inc .... G 302 226-9792
  Rehoboth Beach *(G-12958)*
Slacum & Doyle Tax Service LLC .... G 302 734-1850
  Dover *(G-3575)*
Smart Tax Free Rtrment HM of I .... G 302 472-4897
  Wilmington *(G-19880)*
Summit Tax Solutions LLC .... G 302 464-1016
  Middletown *(G-7607)*
Tax Authority Inc .... G 302 633-0777
  Wilmington *(G-20230)*
Tax Giants LLC .... G 908 822-1090
  Middletown *(G-7622)*
Tax With Us LLC .... G 302 378-2627
  Middletown *(G-7623)*
Taxdone .... G 302 388-5796
  Wilmington *(G-20232)*
Taxes Its Your Money .... G 302 322-0452
  New Castle *(G-9617)*
Thomson Reuters (grc) Inc .... G 212 227-7357
  Wilmington *(G-20314)*
US Tax Resolutions PA .... G 302 478-7977
  Wilmington *(G-20551)*
Utax 4 Less Tax Svc .... G 302 743-6905
  Newark *(G-12291)*
Wahid Consultants LLC .... E 315 400-0955
  Historic New Castle *(G-5099)*
Watkins-Davis Kinard JV .... G 240 479-7273
  Rehoboth Beach *(G-13011)*
Wentworth Inc .... G 302 629-6284
  Seaford *(G-13446)*
Ws Company .... G 302 660-8735
  Wilmington *(G-20901)*

7299 Miscellaneous personal services

3h Agent Services Inc .... F 518 583-0639
  Wilmington *(G-14128)*
A Balanced Life Massage .... G 302 543-4004
  Wilmington *(G-14158)*
A Magcal Escape Thrptic Bdywrk ...... G 302 375-6533
  Wilmington *(G-14168)*
A1 Handyman Services .... G 302 398-4235
  Harrington *(G-4721)*
Ace Handyman Services .... G 302 899-7300
  Dover *(G-1710)*
Adpese LLC .... G 302 223-5411
  Wilmington *(G-14261)*
Advanced Massage of Delaware .... G 443 485-7024
  Ocean View *(G-12457)*
Aesthetics Center .... G 302 827-2125
  Lewes *(G-5664)*
Affair Events .... G 302 762-5765
  Wilmington *(G-14307)*

Alora LLC .... G 302 670-3066
  Milford *(G-7765)*
Alternative Therapy LLC .... G 302 368-0800
  Newark *(G-9838)*
Ambience of Excellence LLC .... G 302 751-0778
  New Castle *(G-8791)*
American Handyman Services .... G 302 616-2559
  Ocean View *(G-12460)*
Angelas Massage and Bodywork .... G 302 547-9390
  Newark *(G-9869)*
Anointed Creative Creations .... G 302 650-7033
  New Castle *(G-8812)*
Anytime Fitness Main Line .... G 302 239-4800
  Hockessin *(G-5128)*
Aqorn Inc .... G 916 123-4567
  Wilmington *(G-14517)*
Arcadia Therapeutic Massage .... G 302 438-3251
  Wilmington *(G-14537)*
At The G Spot LLC .... G 302 998-5010
  Wilmington *(G-14613)*
Back Road Studio .... G 302 381-6060
  Georgetown *(G-4220)*
Bayete Corp .... G 302 562-7415
  New Castle *(G-8852)*
Beach Tans and Hair Design .... G 302 645-8267
  Rehoboth Beach *(G-12629)*
Beginning .... G 302 491-6545
  Milford *(G-7791)*
Bijin .... G 302 777-4040
  Wilmington *(G-14890)*
Blab Studios LLC .... G 302 602-5211
  Newark *(G-10042)*
Blue Diamond RPS & Svcs LLC .... G 856 242-0480
  Wilmington *(G-14964)*
Blue Falls Grove Inc .... G 610 926-4017
  Newark *(G-10057)*
Blue Massage .... G 302 934-7378
  Millsboro *(G-8201)*
Body Images Tanning .... G 302 622-8267
  Wilmington *(G-14994)*
Body Interact Inc .... F 512 910-8350
  Dover *(G-1958)*
Boutique The Bridal Ltd .... G 302 335-5948
  Milford *(G-7800)*
Bridal & Tuxedo Outlet Inc .... G 302 731-8802
  Newark *(G-10084)*
Brookeside Studio .... G 302 629-2829
  Seaford *(G-13095)*
Candlelight Bridal Formal Tlrg .... G 302 934-8009
  Millsboro *(G-8215)*
Capiche Event Planning LLC .... G 302 743-1522
  Wilmington *(G-15224)*
Chicos Crows Nest Tttoo Studio .... G 302 475-6805
  Wilmington *(G-15371)*
Cnu Fit LLC .... G 302 744-9037
  Dover *(G-2100)*
Community Services Corporation ...... F 302 368-4400
  Newark *(G-10289)*
Concierge Beach Service .... G 302 541-0303
  Dagsboro *(G-1430)*
Concierge By Sea Inc .... G 302 228-2014
  Lewes *(G-5856)*
Concierge Home Services .... G 302 539-6178
  Ocean View *(G-12496)*
Deborah L Wayland .... G 443 669-3106
  Bethany Beach *(G-594)*
Deep Muscle Therapy Center Del ...... G 302 397-8073
  Wilmington *(G-15853)*
Delaware AG Museum Assn .... G 302 734-1618
  Dover *(G-2216)*
Delaware Mobile Signings LLC .... G 302 316-3926
  Millsboro *(G-8263)*

72 PERSONAL SERVICES

Delcastle Golf Club Management......... F 302 998-9505
  Wilmington (G-15988)
Dennis M Hughes......................... G 302 632-4503
  Harrington (G-4761)
Devstringx Technologies Inc............. G 650 209-7815
  Lewes (G-5913)
DI Holding and Design Inc............... F 302 219-4922
  Lewes (G-5924)
Docklands Riverfront.................... G 302 658-6626
  Wilmington (G-16112)
Domian International Svc LLC............ G 804 837-3616
  Smyrna (G-13711)
Dorothy A Carroll....................... G 302 455-0243
  Newark (G-10553)
East Coast Property MGT Inc............. G 302 654-2196
  Wilmington (G-16253)
Electric Tiger Tattoo................... G 302 226-1138
  Rehoboth Beach (G-12741)
Elevee Events........................... G 302 212-2112
  Rehoboth Beach (G-12742)
Empire Data Voice Networks LLC.......... G 702 613-4900
  Millsboro (G-8281)
Evan Hooper............................. G 302 682-5617
  Laurel (G-5511)
Evans Handyman Services................. G 302 422-2758
  Lincoln (G-6666)
Eventsbynye LLC......................... G 302 256-3971
  New Castle (G-9104)
Explosive Tattoo Northside.............. G 302 762-1650
  Wilmington (G-16508)
Faqx Inc................................ G 646 437-6797
  Claymont (G-1148)
Fonbnk Inc.............................. F 703 585-3288
  Dover (G-2523)
Formal Affairs Inc...................... G 302 737-1519
  Newark (G-10765)
Frank Costa Constr Handyman............. G 302 561-5792
  Rehoboth Beach (G-12760)
Fremont Hall............................ G 302 731-2431
  Newark (G-10781)
Fresh Start Transformations............. G 302 219-0221
  Newark (G-10784)
Gauge Girl Training LLC................. G 267 471-7104
  Wilmington (G-16818)
Gb Home Improvement..................... G 302 654-5411
  Wilmington (G-16821)
Gpc Construction Services LLC........... G 302 390-1257
  Newark (G-10876)
Graceful Body & Wellness LLC............ G 302 612-3356
  Dover (G-2617)
Graphites............................... G 302 329-9182
  Milton (G-8629)
Grayson Home Improvements LLC........... G 302 685-1848
  Wilmington (G-16955)
Griz Inc................................ G 302 655-1344
  Wilmington (G-16983)
Grofos International LLC................ G 302 635-4805
  Newark (G-10901)
Half Pint Ink........................... G 302 381-5561
  Milton (G-8633)
Hand and Stone.......................... G 302 373-6608
  Wilmington (G-17045)
Hand Stone Massage Facial Spa........... G 302 261-9716
  Bear (G-264)
Hand Stone Massage Facial Spa........... G 302 643-2991
  Middletown (G-7192)
Handy Handyman.......................... G 267 307-5206
  Middletown (G-7193)
Handy Husband LLC....................... G 302 697-7552
  Camden Wyoming (G-952)
Handyman Bill........................... G 302 588-5887
  Wilmington (G-17048)

Handyman Mark........................... G 302 454-1170
  Newark (G-10925)
Handyman Mtters Nrthrn-Dlaware.......... G 302 540-8263
  Wilmington (G-17049)
Healthy Foot Care Inc................... G 302 235-7799
  Hockessin (G-5235)
Heaven & Health Massage T............... G 302 999-9565
  Wilmington (G-17111)
Helen Williams Inc...................... G 302 328-9656
  New Castle (G-9206)
Hollywood Tans.......................... G 302 367-5959
  Smyrna (G-13763)
Hollywood Tans.......................... G 302 478-8267
  Wilmington (G-17175)
Hollywood Tans of Elkton................ G 302 345-2510
  Newark (G-10959)
Homeward Tattoo......................... G 302 226-8145
  Rehoboth Beach (G-12789)
Hoppscotch LLC.......................... G 858 395-1737
  Dover (G-2694)
In The Nest Quilting.................... G 302 644-7316
  Lewes (G-6119)
Inclusive Innovations Inc............... G 781 962-9959
  Newark (G-11009)
Ink Therapy Tattoo Studios LLC.......... G 302 674-1900
  Dover (G-2735)
InkInk.................................. G 323 854-9549
  Wilmington (G-17343)
Integrated Restorative Massage.......... G 302 391-4692
  Wilmington (G-17370)
Its All About You MSSge&bdywrk.......... G 302 563-3443
  Clayton (G-1374)
Iuventase Biosciences Inc............... G 858 302-8583
  Newark (G-11063)
J Stanley Salon LLC..................... G 302 778-1885
  Wilmington (G-17465)
Janet Sue Winner........................ G 302 798-3731
  Wilmington (G-17494)
JC Weight Loss Centres Inc.............. G 302 477-9202
  Wilmington (G-17509)
Jenny Craig Holdings Inc................ A 302 477-9202
  Wilmington (G-17529)
Jerrys Handyman LLC..................... G 302 357-1589
  New Castle (G-9259)
Karma Theory Tattoo & Gallery........... G 302 526-2096
  Dover (G-2832)
Kennharr LLC............................ G 800 692-7970
  Dover (G-2844)
Km Klacko & Associate................... G 302 652-1482
  Wilmington (G-17742)
Kneading To Heel........................ G 302 740-4647
  Newark (G-11195)
La Bella Med Spa........................ G 302 990-8770
  Seaford (G-13252)
Lambert Kishayra........................ G 215 287-6252
  Newark (G-11216)
Landings................................ G 302 233-8421
  Dover (G-2901)
Legacy Tattoo........................... G 302 502-2163
  Wilmington (G-17859)
Lorcys Massage & Bdy Works LLC.......... G 302 240-3958
  Smyrna (G-13809)
Luxiasuites LLC......................... F 302 778-3000
  Wilmington (G-18038)
M & P Adventures Inc.................... G 302 645-6271
  Lewes (G-6232)
M T Investment Group.................... G 302 793-4917
  Wilmington (G-18061)
Macrostat Inc........................... F 302 239-7442
  Hockessin (G-5291)
Mal Ventures Inc........................ G 302 454-1170
  Newark (G-11317)

Malarkey Tattoo LLC..................... G 302 304-5382
  Bear (G-359)
Marsha Neal Studio LLC.................. G 302 559-6781
  Hockessin (G-5301)
Massage Envy - Christiana............... G 302 266-2762
  Newark (G-11349)
Massage Envy Lewes...................... G 302 703-4100
  Rehoboth Beach (G-12852)
Matt Matiaset........................... G 302 376-3042
  Townsend (G-14032)
Maverick Tattoo Company LLC............. G 443 858-1511
  Seaford (G-13276)
Men In Black Wdding Officiants.......... G 302 945-6903
  Lewes (G-6262)
Michelle Hand........................... G 302 422-0622
  Milford (G-7995)
Moon Bounce Mania....................... G 302 588-1300
  Newark (G-11448)
Moving As One LLC....................... F 301 701-0434
  Claymont (G-1244)
My Hands Handyman LLC................... G 302 387-2749
  Georgetown (G-4440)
Nflate Your Party....................... G 302 562-9774
  Newark (G-11553)
Nixon Unf Rntl Svc of Lncaster.......... G 302 656-2774
  Historic New Castle (G-5039)
Now Thats A Party LLC................... G 302 465-0928
  Dover (G-3206)
Nur Temple Aaonms....................... G 302 328-6100
  New Castle (G-9430)
Oink Oink LLC........................... G 302 924-5034
  Dover (G-3217)
Open Heart Studio LLC................... G 302 381-0212
  Lewes (G-6337)
Osprey Flight Solutions Inc............. G 302 318-1401
  Newark (G-11603)
Pampered Parties LLC.................... G 302 216-2362
  Wilmington (G-18869)
Party Princess Productions.............. G 302 378-7127
  Middletown (G-7427)
Passion Driven LLC...................... G 302 293-5960
  New Castle (G-9456)
Patricia J Avery Artist................. G 941 223-5546
  Wilmington (G-18909)
Paxful Inc.............................. E 917 609-3850
  Wilmington (G-18925)
Pelican Seven Studios................... G 302 764-6684
  Wilmington (G-18946)
Professional Handyman Svcs Inc.......... G 302 478-1237
  Wilmington (G-19210)
Purelife Therapeutic Massage............ G 302 379-5547
  Wilmington (G-19264)
Quail Associates Inc.................... E 302 697-4660
  Camden Wyoming (G-966)
Quantum Transformation Inc.............. G 315 795-4427
  Middletown (G-7490)
Rader Services LLC...................... G 302 454-0373
  Newark (G-11816)
Ralph E Willis.......................... G 302 422-7167
  Milford (G-8058)
Ramiglot Inc............................ G 929 203-5115
  Middletown (G-7501)
Ranuba Inc.............................. G 870 360-3372
  Lewes (G-6408)
Reliable Handyman Services LLC.......... G 302 943-0166
  Dover (G-3448)
Resourceful Rae LLC..................... G 302 220-7704
  Newark (G-11867)
Rikarbon Inc............................ G 765 237-7649
  Newark (G-11885)
Robins Hair & Tanning................... G 302 529-9000
  Wilmington (G-19523)

Rock of Ages Tattoos .... G 302 475-8050
　Wilmington *(G-19530)*
Rockwood Conference Center .... G 302 761-4342
　Wilmington *(G-19545)*
S B Porter Services .... G 302 378-0209
　Frederica *(G-4182)*
Safe Home Control .... F 302 401-4379
　Wilmington *(G-19624)*
Samantha Hudran Massage .... G 302 382-5851
　Harrington *(G-4826)*
Sanctuary Spa and Saloon .... F 302 475-1469
　Wilmington *(G-19656)*
SD&I Bail Bonds LLC .... G 302 407-6591
　Wilmington *(G-19717)*
Selwor Enterprises Inc .... F 302 454-9454
　Newark *(G-11974)*
Sew Happy Quilts LLC .... G 302 382-5565
　Camden Wyoming *(G-974)*
Shore Concierge Inc .... G 302 500-1162
　Lincoln *(G-6700)*
Simplecar LLC .... E 857 380-7275
　Claymont *(G-1291)*
Sniffies LLC .... G 302 265-4101
　Dover *(G-3580)*
Soiree Factory .... G 302 275-6576
　Wilmington *(G-19916)*
Southern Belle Barn Venue LLC .... G 410 896-5408
　Seaford *(G-13407)*
Stanley J Lepowski Jr .... G 302 378-7284
　Townsend *(G-14072)*
Stephanie Galbraith .... G 302 290-2235
　Wilmington *(G-20053)*
Studio 923 .... G 302 276-1413
　Bear *(G-514)*
Studio43 .... G 302 539-8577
　Ocean View *(G-12571)*
Stylin Image .... G 302 407-8698
　Newark *(G-12113)*
Sun Dazed Tanning .... G 302 430-0150
　Milford *(G-8107)*
Sunkist Tanning Inc .... G 302 539-8269
　Fenwick Island *(G-4055)*
Symbiancehr LLC .... G 302 276-3302
　Middletown *(G-7614)*
TAC Financial Corp .... G 302 691-6014
　Wilmington *(G-20206)*
Taggart Professional Center .... G 410 491-7311
　Bethany Beach *(G-646)*
Tantini LLC .... E 302 444-4024
　Newark *(G-12160)*
Tattoo Blue Moon .... G 302 449-1551
　Middletown *(G-7621)*
Tattoo Galaxy Rehobeth Beach .... G 302 226-8118
　Rehoboth Beach *(G-12990)*
Terry A Gray .... G 302 478-2042
　Wilmington *(G-20277)*
Therapy At Beach .... G 302 313-5555
　Lewes *(G-6555)*
TNT Grand Lux LLC .... G 443 228-3193
　Dover *(G-3694)*
Tracy Halterman .... G 302 545-9930
　Wilmington *(G-20382)*
Tranquil Spirit Massage & Spa .... G 302 538-1135
　Dover *(G-3712)*
Tropic Fever Tanning Salon .... G 302 875-1500
　Laurel *(G-5616)*
Tru Beauti LLC .... E 302 353-9249
　Middletown *(G-7663)*
Twin Angels Service .... G 302 545-6749
　Bear *(G-543)*
U Tan Inc .... G 302 674-8040
　Dover *(G-3740)*

Universal Assembling Entp LLC .... F 302 543-3629
　Dover *(G-3753)*
University of Delaware .... F 302 831-2792
　Newark *(G-12282)*
Upperstack Inc .... G 410 925-8216
　Newark *(G-12286)*
US Immigration Technology LLC .... F 888 418-3053
　Wilmington *(G-20549)*
Vinnys Handyman Servies .... G 302 265-9196
　Milton *(G-8727)*
Vyzer Inc .... F 530 446-2568
　Middletown *(G-7699)*
Weather or Not Dog Walkers .... G 302 304-8399
　Wilmington *(G-20701)*
Web Data Solutions LLC .... E 888 407-5089
　Dover *(G-3825)*
White Eagle Integrations .... G 302 464-0550
　Middletown *(G-7723)*
Wicked Witch Studio .... G 302 838-2011
　Bear *(G-564)*
Worcester Golf Club Inc .... F 610 222-0200
　Milton *(G-8730)*
Zk Technologies LLC .... G 980 246-4090
　Lewes *(G-6651)*

73 BUSINESS SERVICES

7311 Advertising agencies

Accera Digital LLC .... F 877 855-2501
　Wilmington *(G-14219)*
Ad Bits Advertising and PR .... G 954 467-8420
　Hockessin *(G-5113)*
Adapex LLC .... E 718 618-9982
　Wilmington *(G-14251)*
Adtelligent Inc .... D 833 222-2102
　Dover *(G-1721)*
AHM TV Prod Inc .... F 929 332-0350
　Dover *(G-1751)*
Aloysius Butlr Clark Assoc Inc .... D 302 655-1552
　Wilmington *(G-14390)*
Asombro Extremo LLC .... G 305 495-1471
　Wilmington *(G-14588)*
Bayshore Communications Inc .... F 302 737-2164
　Lewes *(G-9995)*
Beanstock Media Inc .... E 415 912-1530
　Wilmington *(G-14804)*
Beholder Agency LLC .... F 302 455-2451
　Newark *(G-10011)*
Chilay Inc .... G 302 559-6014
　Newark *(G-10201)*
Cohesive Strategies Inc .... E 302 429-9120
　Wilmington *(G-15520)*
Comrade Technologies Inc .... G 888 575-1225
　Lewes *(G-5855)*
Convention Coach .... G 302 335-5459
　Magnolia *(G-6735)*
Cool Nerds Marketing Inc .... F 302 304-3440
　Wilmington *(G-15629)*
Delaware Design Company .... G 302 737-9700
　Newark *(G-10435)*
Digital Generation Inc .... E 302 368-0002
　Newark *(G-10529)*
Duration Media LLC .... G 917 283-5971
　Wilmington *(G-16221)*
E Business Pages LLC .... G 302 504-4403
　Wilmington *(G-16236)*
Epic Marketing Cons Corp .... E 302 285-9790
　Middletown *(G-7105)*
Famous Wsi Results .... G 302 407-0430
　New Castle *(G-9118)*
From Top Ltd .... G 310 626-0090
　Middletown *(G-7143)*

Grind or Starve LLC .... G 302 322-1679
　Wilmington *(G-16981)*
High Ground Creative LLC .... G 302 505-1367
　Dover *(G-2678)*
Highland Consulting Group Inc .... G 301 408-0600
　Bethany Beach *(G-607)*
Inbound Ignite LLC .... G 866 314-4499
　Dover *(G-2725)*
Industrial Training Cons Inc .... E 302 266-6100
　Newark *(G-11016)*
Inflection Associates Inc .... G 484 678-7915
　Wilmington *(G-17325)*
Jay Gundel and Associates Inc .... G 302 658-1674
　Wilmington *(G-17500)*
K F Dunn & Associates .... F 302 328-3347
　Wilmington *(G-17630)*
Koncordia Group LLC .... E 302 427-1350
　Wilmington *(G-17746)*
Lead Economy LLC .... E 914 355-1671
　Dover *(G-2918)*
Levines Enterprises LLC .... F 203 212-8441
　Dover *(G-2932)*
Lifetour Solutions LLC .... F 215 964-5000
　Wilmington *(G-17906)*
LLC Cutler Parrish .... G 609 744-9871
　Middletown *(G-7311)*
Marketing Plus LLC .... G 205 952-6602
　Dover *(G-3021)*
Marquis Dorsey LLC .... F 832 693-0260
　Middletown *(G-7329)*
Mc Creative Group .... F 302 348-8977
　Millsboro *(G-8370)*
Mediasurfer Inc .... F 814 300-8335
　Wilmington *(G-18247)*
Miller-Mauro Group Inc .... G 302 426-6565
　Wilmington *(G-18366)*
Moscova Enterprises Inc .... F 347 973-2522
　Wilmington *(G-18460)*
Netskyads Media LLC .... F 302 476-2277
　Lewes *(G-6309)*
Paragon Design Inc .... F 302 292-1523
　Newark *(G-11623)*
Pear Media LLC .... E 505 932-6555
　Lewes *(G-6358)*
Popsycle LLC .... G 202 831-0211
　Newark *(G-11713)*
Promo Marketing .... G 302 324-2650
　New Castle *(G-9499)*
Real Entrepreneur Inc .... E 989 300-0975
　Wilmington *(G-19366)*
▲ Remline Corp .... E 302 737-7228
　Newark *(G-11850)*
Sasquatch Creative LLC .... G 302 502-3105
　Wilmington *(G-19674)*
Sem Revival LLC .... F 302 600-1497
　Wilmington *(G-19748)*
Sevenshopper LLC .... G 302 516-7150
　Wilmington *(G-19770)*
Shiny Agency LLC .... G 302 384-6494
　Wilmington *(G-19801)*
Shor Associates Inc .... G 302 764-1701
　Wilmington *(G-19809)*
Simplymiddle LLC .... G 302 217-3460
　Wilmington *(G-19841)*
▲ Springboard Inc .... G 302 607-2580
　Newark *(G-12075)*
Status Intl LLC DBA Sttus Brnd .... G 202 290-6387
　Wilmington *(G-20037)*
Tapp Networks LLC .... G 302 222-3384
　Rehoboth Beach *(G-12989)*
Target Markets LLC .... E 302 268-1010
　Wilmington *(G-20224)*

73 BUSINESS SERVICES — SIC SECTION

Top Rated Media Inc................................. G..... 888 550-9273
  Wilmington (G-20355)
U2r Inc.. F..... 609 792-6575
  Wilmington (G-20487)
Unified Companies Inc........................... G..... 866 936-0515
  Wilmington (G-20509)
Upbound Group Inc............................... G..... 302 734-2094
  Dover (G-3756)
Vrtii Corporation..................................... G..... 703 401-8963
  Lewes (G-6611)
Wh2p Inc... G..... 302 530-6555
  Wilmington (G-20753)
Young & Rubicam LLC........................... F..... 302 888-3450
  Wilmington (G-20932)
Z&M Enterprises LLC............................. E..... 302 384-1205
  Wilmington (G-20944)

7312 Outdoor advertising services

Clear Channel Outdoor LLC.................. E..... 302 658-0520
  Wilmington (G-15476)
Delaware Outdoor Advertising............... G..... 302 234-1975
  Hockessin (G-5183)
United Outdoor Advertising................... G..... 302 652-3177
  Wilmington (G-20525)

7313 Radio, television, publisher representatives

Emagination Store USA Inc................... G..... 302 884-6746
  Wilmington (G-16386)
Mediastreet LLC..................................... G..... 800 308-6579
  Newark (G-11373)
Melody Entertainment USA Inc............. G..... 305 505-7659
  Wilmington (G-18267)
Social Work Helper Pbc........................ G..... 302 233-7422
  Dover (G-3586)
Staysaf 3 LLC.. G..... 305 699-1454
  Wilmington (G-20041)
Tjs & Associates LLC............................. E..... 302 563-5593
  Middletown (G-7647)
Yield Nexus LLC..................................... F..... 308 380-3788
  Dover (G-3887)

7319 Advertising, nec

Cyclops Net Inc...................................... G..... 844 979-0222
  Camden (G-812)
Gkua Inc... F..... 415 971-5341
  Wilmington (G-16873)
Gotshadeonline Inc................................ G..... 302 832-8468
  Bear (G-252)
Klip-It LLC.. G..... 888 202-0533
  Middletown (G-7280)
Noony Media LLC................................... F..... 856 834-0074
  Wilmington (G-18669)
Powers Interactive Digital LLC............... G..... 267 334-6306
  Lewes (G-6385)
Stackadapt US Inc.................................. C..... 647 385-7698
  Lewes (G-6505)
U Transit Inc... G..... 302 227-1197
  Rehoboth Beach (G-13000)

7322 Adjustment and collection services

Advanced Rcvable Solutions Inc............ G..... 302 225-6001
  Wilmington (G-14279)
Advantage Assets II Inc......................... F..... 877 858-3855
  Wilmington (G-14283)
Beach Associates Inc............................ F..... 866 744-9911
  Dover (G-1896)
Bonded Business Services.................... G..... 302 438-6007
  Wilmington (G-14999)
Byron & Davis Cccc............................... G..... 302 792-2334
  Wilmington (G-15166)
Commtrak Corporation........................... G..... 302 644-1600
  Lewes (G-5853)
Datalogy Bus Solutions Inc................... G..... 832 713-4790
  Middletown (G-7029)
Firstcollect Inc....................................... G..... 302 644-6804
  Lewes (G-6001)
G & D Collection Group Inc.................. F..... 302 482-2512
  Wilmington (G-16783)
Health Care Practice MGT..................... E..... 302 633-5840
  Wilmington (G-17096)
Jsd Management Inc............................. E..... 302 735-4628
  Dover (G-2811)
Kearns Brinen & Monaghan Inc........... E..... 302 736-6481
  Dover (G-2836)
Matthews Pierce & Lloyd Inc................ E..... 302 678-5500
  Dover (G-3036)
Phillips & Cohen Assoc Ltd................... C..... 302 355-3500
  Newark (G-11685)
Phillips & Cohen Associates.................. D..... 609 518-9000
  Wilmington (G-19018)
Public Assets Recovery Service............ G..... 267 767-0452
  Wilmington (G-19252)
Simm Associates Inc............................. C..... 302 283-2800
  Newark (G-12009)
SLM Corporation.................................... B..... 302 451-0200
  Newark (G-12032)
Smith Cohen & Rosenberg LLC............ F..... 302 260-8007
  Dover (G-3579)
Stevens & James Inc............................ E..... 302 398-6066
  Harrington (G-4836)
Stevenson Ventures LLC....................... G..... 302 752-4449
  Milford (G-8105)
Wyatt & Brown Inc................................ G..... 302 786-2793
  Harrington (G-4851)

7323 Credit reporting services

Lexisnexis Risk Assets Inc.................... A..... 800 458-9410
  Wilmington (G-17889)
S Wallace Holdings LLC........................ G..... 917 304-1164
  Wilmington (G-19613)
Standard & Poors Intl LLC..................... G..... 212 512-2000
  Wilmington (G-20011)

7331 Direct mail advertising services

B2b Lists LLC.. D..... 302 601-7207
  Claymont (G-1049)
D & B Printing and Mailing Inc.............. G..... 302 838-7111
  Newark (G-10373)
Hibbert Company.................................... C..... 609 394-7500
  Historic New Castle (G-5004)
◆ Joseph J Sheeran Inc......................... E..... 302 324-0200
  New Castle (G-9266)
Mailbiz.. G..... 302 644-9035
  Rehoboth Beach (G-12844)
Marketing Resources Inc....................... G..... 302 855-9209
  Georgetown (G-4418)
Money Mailer of Delaware..................... F..... 302 235-7262
  Newark (G-11440)
Money Mailer Tri Counties..................... G..... 240 832-1340
  Selbyville (G-13579)
Provide LLC... E..... 302 391-1200
  Newark (G-11767)
Sequoia Properties Inc.......................... G..... 847 599-9099
  Bear (G-483)
Trimark Inc... G..... 302 322-2143
  Historic New Castle (G-5092)
Valassis Direct Mail Inc........................ C..... 302 861-3567
  Newark (G-12299)

7334 Photocopying and duplicating services

◆ Amer Inc.. G..... 302 654-2498
  Wilmington (G-14421)
Braun Engineering & Surveying............ G..... 302 698-0701
  Camden Wyoming (G-919)
Fedex Office & Print Svcs Inc............... G..... 302 652-2151
  Wilmington (G-16572)
Fedex Office & Print Svcs Inc............... G..... 302 996-0264
  Wilmington (G-16573)
Garile Inc... E..... 302 366-0848
  Newark (G-10809)
Mr Copy Inc... G..... 302 227-4666
  Rehoboth Beach (G-12866)
Reliable Copy Service Inc..................... D..... 302 654-8080
  Wilmington (G-19422)
Reprographics Center Inc..................... G..... 302 328-5019
  New Castle (G-9522)

7335 Commercial photography

Colourworks Photographic Svcs............ G..... 302 428-0222
  Wilmington (G-15540)
Dean Digital Imaging Inc....................... G..... 302 655-6992
  Wilmington (G-15846)
Elementice Inc....................................... G..... 302 444-5406
  Newark (G-10625)
Floyd Dean Inc....................................... G..... 302 655-7193
  Wilmington (G-16672)
Herbert Studios...................................... G..... 302 229-7108
  Wilmington (G-17127)
Horizon Helicopters Inc......................... G..... 302 368-5135
  Newark (G-10970)
Judah Road Productions LLC............... G..... 508 640-5022
  Dover (G-2813)
Lenzinifordelaware................................. G..... 302 836-6287
  Bear (G-345)
Perryfilms Production Co LLC............... G..... 302 505-4458
  Lewes (G-6363)
Superlative Image LLC......................... G..... 714 369-5412
  Wilmington (G-20144)
Vonogrphy-The Perfect Shot LLC......... G..... 202 923-9532
  Newark (G-12336)

7336 Commercial art and graphic design

9193 4323 Quebec Inc........................... G..... 855 824-0795
  Newark (G-9717)
Act Media... G..... 888 666-0786
  Lewes (G-5655)
Bear Associates LLC............................. G..... 302 735-5558
  Dover (G-1898)
Bhaoo Inc... E..... 832 888-3694
  Dover (G-1931)
Brand Design Co Inc............................. G..... 302 234-2356
  Wilmington (G-15040)
Creative Solutions Intl........................... G..... 302 234-7400
  Hockessin (G-5170)
De Novo Corporation............................. E..... 302 234-7407
  Wilmington (G-15839)
Green Crescent LLC............................. G..... 800 735-9620
  Dover (G-2622)
Growth Inc... E..... 302 366-0848
  Newark (G-10903)
Harmattan Design LLC......................... G..... 609 385-1041
  Dover (G-2652)
Harting Graphics Ltd............................. G..... 302 762-6397
  Wilmington (G-17068)
Heavenly Films LLC.............................. G..... 302 232-8988
  Dover (G-2668)
Initially Yours Inc................................... G..... 302 999-0562
  Wilmington (G-17341)
JP Graphics... G..... 302 678-0335
  Dover (G-2806)
Kustom Additions LLC.......................... G..... 302 468-6865
  Wilmington (G-17769)
Mad Macs.. G..... 302 737-4800
  Newark (G-11310)

Mitchell Associates Inc .... E 302 594-9400
  New Castle (G-9373)
Pixxy Solutions LLC .... E 631 609-6686
  Claymont (G-1263)
Plugdin Inc .... G 347 726-1831
  Dover (G-3338)
Precision Color Graphics LLC .... G 302 661-2595
  Wilmington (G-19152)
Premiere Studio LLC .... F 347 336-0791
  Claymont (G-1266)
Promotion Zone LLC .... G 302 832-8565
  Newark (G-11763)
Promotions Plus Inc .... G 302 836-2820
  Newark (G-11764)
▼ Seaside Graphics Corp .... G 302 436-9460
  Selbyville (G-13603)
Sumthin3Ise .... G 302 272-5435
  Dover (G-3621)
Uncharted Waters LLC .... E 302 213-6354
  Dover (G-3747)
Unfold Studio LLC .... G 415 993-0943
  Wilmington (G-20505)
Xcs Corporation .... G 302 514-0600
  Wilmington (G-20916)
Zzhouse Inc .... G 302 453-1180
  Newark (G-12438)

7338 Secretarial and court reporting

Chancery Court Reporters .... G 302 255-0515
  Wilmington (G-15329)
Dale Hawkins .... G 302 658-6697
  Wilmington (G-15770)
Doculogica Corp .... G 302 753-5944
  Wilmington (G-16113)
Evc Inc .... F 302 571-0510
  Wilmington (G-16481)
Federal Court Reporters .... G 302 573-6195
  Wilmington (G-16568)
Lasers Edge Inc .... G 302 479-5997
  Wilmington (G-17813)
Resume Tech Corp .... F 800 403-5610
  Middletown (G-7517)
Resume Writer Direct .... G 866 706-0973
  Wilmington (G-19445)
Ultius Cstm Wrting Edting Svcs .... F 702 690-4552
  Wilmington (G-20499)
Wilcox & Fetzer Ltd .... E 302 655-0477
  Wilmington (G-20779)

7342 Disinfecting and pest control services

Accurate Pest Control Company ...... F 302 875-2725
  Laurel (G-5460)
Activ Pest & Lawn Inc .... F 302 645-1502
  Lewes (G-5657)
Advanced Pest Management .... G 410 398-4378
  Newark (G-9779)
Aion Oakwood Venture LLC .... G 212 849-9200
  Wilmington (G-14334)
Air Masters Hvac Inc .... G 267 292-2204
  Wilmington (G-14335)
Air Quality Remediation LLC .... F 302 464-1050
  Townsend (G-13955)
All Clear Pest Control .... G 443 359-5623
  Seaford (G-13055)
Bay Area Wildlife LLC .... G 410 829-6368
  Seaford (G-13077)
Brasures Pest Control Inc .... E 302 436-8140
  Selbyville (G-13484)
Brightside Pest Services Inc .... G 302 893-5858
  Hockessin (G-5143)
Davis A Scott .... G 302 535-0570
  Magnolia (G-6738)
Delaware Mosquito Control LLC ...... G 302 504-6757
  Newark (G-10462)
Delmar Termite & Pest Control .... G 302 658-5010
  Wilmington (G-15996)
Diamond Pest Control .... G 302 654-2300
  Wilmington (G-16052)
Diamond State Pest Control Co ...... G 302 250-3403
  Camden Wyoming (G-933)
Elkton Exterminating Co Inc .... G 302 368-9116
  Newark (G-10630)
First State Hood & Duct LLC .... G 888 866-7389
  Wilmington (G-16629)
Green Pest Management LLC .... F 302 777-2390
  New Castle (G-9179)
Guy Bug .... G 302 242-5254
  Dover (G-2636)
Home Prmnt Pest Ctrl Cmpnies I .... G 302 894-9201
  New Castle (G-9219)
Its R Joy Llc .... E 215 315-8300
  Bear (G-291)
Ladybug Pest Management Inc ...... G 302 846-2295
  Delmar (G-1612)
Liberty Pest Control LLC .... G 302 734-1507
  Dover (G-2936)
Maguire & Sons Inc .... G 302 798-1200
  Wilmington (G-18085)
Middletown Mosquito Ctrl LLC ...... G 302 378-3378
  Middletown (G-7356)
Mosquito Authority .... F 302 346-2970
  Dover (G-3126)
Mosquito Authority .... G 302 228-5821
  Rehoboth Beach (G-12864)
Mosquito Authority Wilmington ..... G 302 299-5299
  Middletown (G-7381)
Moyer Pest Control .... G 302 353-4404
  Wilmington (G-18469)
Pest Pro LLC .... G 877 737-8360
  Milford (G-8048)
Pestex Pest Control Inc .... G 302 745-8366
  Georgetown (G-4464)
Professional Pest MGT De .... G 302 738-1036
  Wilmington (G-19211)
Qualdent LLC .... G 856 642-4078
  Wilmington (G-19282)
Rentokil North America Inc .... D 302 337-8100
  Bridgeville (G-761)
Rentokil North America Inc .... F 410 882-1000
  Newark (G-11853)
Rentokil North America Inc .... E 302 325-2687
  Newark (G-11854)
Rentokil North America Inc .... E 302 733-0851
  Newark (G-11855)
Rollins Inc .... C 302 325-4410
  Historic New Castle (G-5061)
Royal Pest Management Inc .... G 302 376-8243
  Middletown (G-7525)
Royal Pest Solutions Inc .... E 302 322-6665
  New Castle (G-9543)
Royal Termite & Pest Ctrl Inc .... E 302 322-3600
  New Castle (G-9545)
Terminix Intl Co Ltd Partnr .... F 302 653-4866
  Historic New Castle (G-5082)
Think Clean & Grounds Up LLC ..... F 904 250-1614
  Historic New Castle (G-5084)
Total Pest Solutions .... G 302 275-7159
  Camden Wyoming (G-984)
Total Pest Solutions .... F 302 368-8081
  Newark (G-12212)
Tri State Termite & Pest Ctrl .... G 302 239-0512
  Newark (G-12221)
Trigger Action LLC .... G 302 858-8629
  Georgetown (G-4561)
True Pest Control Services .... G 302 834-0867
  Middletown (G-7665)
Wilkins Wildlife & Bedbug 911 .... G 302 236-3533
  Delmar (G-1658)

7349 Building maintenance services, nec

A+ Cleaning Solutions Inc .... G 423 693-7554
  Dover (G-1698)
A1 Striping Inc .... G 302 738-5016
  Newark (G-9730)
Able Whelling and Machiene .... G 302 436-1929
  Selbyville (G-13458)
ABM Janitorial Services Inc .... E 302 571-9900
  Wilmington (G-14205)
Above and Beyond Cleaning Svcs .. E 484 206-5101
  Newark (G-9743)
Abrahams Seed LLC .... G 302 588-1913
  Clayton (G-1347)
Advanced Bizz Innovations LLC ...... G 302 397-1162
  Townsend (G-13951)
Advanced Plumbing & Maint LLC ... G 302 584-4001
  Bear (G-17)
All Clean Services .... G 302 378-7376
  Townsend (G-13957)
All JS Cleaning Services Inc .... G 302 299-9916
  New Castle (G-8780)
All Pro Maids Inc .... E 302 645-9247
  Lewes (G-5674)
All Pro Property Maint LLC .... G 302 531-6811
  Milford (G-7764)
Alvins Professional Services .... F 302 544-6634
  New Castle (G-8789)
Apple Cleaning Systems LLC .... F 302 368-7507
  New Castle (G-8814)
Aqua Pro Inc .... G 302 659-6593
  Smyrna (G-13647)
Better Home Services .... G 302 250-9860
  Dover (G-1923)
Bravo Building Services Inc .... A 302 322-5959
  New Castle (G-8889)
Brenda Radick .... G 302 945-8982
  Harbeson (G-4686)
Briggs Services LLC .... G 302 569-5230
  Ellendale (G-3911)
C & B Complete Clg Svc Inc .... E 302 436-9622
  Frankford (G-4081)
Catch-A-Web Cleaning Inc .... G 302 836-1970
  Bear (G-92)
Chaffin Cleaning Service Inc .... G 302 369-2704
  Newark (G-10185)
Chesapeake Home Services LLC ... G 302 732-6006
  Frankford (G-4087)
Chimes Metro Inc .... E 302 838-1202
  Newark (G-10207)
Christopher Handy .... G 302 934-1018
  Millsboro (G-8225)
City Wide Maintenance Co Inc .... C 302 526-2833
  Dover (G-2085)
City Window Cleaning of Del .... E 302 633-0633
  Wilmington (G-15456)
Claw Blue Maintenance .... G 717 487-2808
  Georgetown (G-4258)
Clean Hands LLC .... F 215 681-1435
  Smyrna (G-13681)
Clean Sweep .... G 302 422-6085
  Milford (G-7831)
Cleaners Sunny .... G 302 827-2095
  Lewes (G-5825)
Cleanith LLC .... G 571 269-8213
  Magnolia (G-6731)
Clearview Windows LLC .... G 302 491-6768
  Milford (G-7833)

73 BUSINESS SERVICES

Business	Code	Phone
Coastal Chem-Dry, Lewes (G-5838)	G	302 234-0200
Coastal Cleaning Services Inc, Millsboro (G-8232)	G	302 858-8857
Coleman Cleaning Services Inc, Magnolia (G-6733)	G	302 335-1868
Colonial Cleaning Services Inc, Wilmington (G-15534)	G	302 660-2067
Community Services Corporation, Newark (G-10289)	F	302 368-4400
Continental Green Janitorial, New Castle (G-8969)	G	302 324-8063
County Building Services Inc, Middletown (G-7016)	G	302 377-4213
D A Jones Inc, Selbyville (G-13514)	G	302 836-9238
D C S Company, New Castle (G-8992)	G	302 328-5138
De Property Maintenance LLC, Middletown (G-7033)	G	302 241-5567
Delmar Corporate Clg Svcs Inc, Newark (G-10499)	E	302 861-8006
Delmarva Shore Maintenance, Millsboro (G-8268)	G	302 519-8657
Delmarva Soap & Powerwash Sls, Laurel (G-5499)	G	302 875-2012
Delores Welch, Georgetown (G-4291)	G	302 856-7989
Don-Lee Margin Corporation, Seaford (G-13163)	E	302 629-7567
Dover Nunan LLC, Dover (G-2356)	G	302 697-9776
Dss - Integrity LLC, Dover (G-2388)	F	302 677-0111
Dss Services Inc, Dover (G-2389)	F	302 677-0111
Dss Urban Joint Venture LLC, Dover (G-2390)	G	302 677-0111
Ducts R US LLC, Felton (G-3962)	G	302 284-0006
Dust Away Cleaning Svcs Inc, Wilmington (G-16222)	F	302 658-8803
Eckels Family LLC, Felton (G-3966)	E	302 465-5224
Efficient Services Inc, Seaford (G-13171)	G	302 629-2124
Elite Cleaning Company Inc, Wilmington (G-16363)	A	302 439-4430
Elite Commercial Cleaning Inc, Newark (G-10628)	D	302 366-8900
Elite Facility Services LLC, Newark (G-10629)	D	302 566-7031
Elite Property Maintenance, Delaware City (G-1540)	G	302 836-1865
Elite Property Maintenance, Middletown (G-7095)	G	302 836-8878
Empire Data Voice Networks LLC, Millsboro (G-8281)	G	702 613-4900
Focus Solutions Services Inc, Newark (G-10753)	F	302 318-1345
Fortress Home Maintenance Serv, Dagsboro (G-1451)	G	302 539-3446
Foshee Property Maintenance, Ocean View (G-12512)	G	302 344-6410
Fresh Cut Lndscping Mintenance, Millsboro (G-8295)	G	302 841-1848
Gale Force Cleaning & Restore, Ocean View (G-12517)	G	302 539-6244
Gemini Building Systems LLC, Wilmington (G-16827)	F	302 654-5310
Generation Cleaning Svc LLC, Claymont (G-1158)	G	302 492-2772
Go Go Prof Clg Svcs LLC, Middletown (G-7167)	F	302 729-2883
Golden Inc, Newark (G-10861)	E	800 878-1356
Gutter Connection LLC, Dover (G-2634)	F	302 736-0105
H&S Cleaning Service Inc, Townsend (G-14012)	G	302 449-2928
Heaven Maid Services Inc, Smyrna (G-13757)	G	302 223-6086
Hitz Mechanical, Frankford (G-4113)	G	727 742-6315
Home Works, Smyrna (G-13764)	G	302 514-9974
Hood Man LLC, Lincoln (G-6676)	G	302 422-4564
J & W Mc Cormick Ltd, Newark (G-11069)	F	302 798-0336
James Maintenance Services LLC, Millsboro (G-8328)	G	302 934-7625
JBA Enterprises LLC, Bear (G-301)	G	302 834-6685
John Eisenbrey III, Milford (G-7955)	G	302 422-5845
JV s Cleaning Services, Bear (G-318)	G	302 345-7679
Kc Janitorial Services, Smyrna (G-13785)	G	302 653-5435
Kevin Smith, Newark (G-11163)	E	800 878-1356
Kimberly Tucker, Middletown (G-7274)	G	302 358-0574
L & M Services Inc, Wilmington (G-17773)	G	302 658-3735
L Maintenance, Frankford (G-4122)	G	302 841-1698
Logiclean LLC, Claymont (G-1225)	G	302 298-0054
M N K Maintenance and REM, Dagsboro (G-1477)	G	302 841-5884
M T O Clean of Sussex County, Milton (G-8658)	G	302 854-0204
Mahmood B Omaid, Smyrna (G-13814)	G	302 399-7849
Maid For Shore, Lewes (G-6237)	G	302 344-1857
Maid My Day Cleaning Svc, Millsboro (G-8359)	G	302 947-9355
Maidpro, Middletown (G-7323)	G	302 327-4250
Maids For You Inc, New Castle (G-9338)	G	302 328-9050
Main Street Staffing Agcy LLC, Dover (G-2998)	G	302 608-7052
Maintenance Tech, New Castle (G-9340)	G	302 322-6410
Maintenance Troubleshooti, Wilmington (G-18091)	G	302 477-1045
Maintenance Unlimited LLC, Magnolia (G-6763)	G	302 387-1868
Marlings Inc, Wilmington (G-18153)	F	302 325-1759
Master Klean Company, Ocean View (G-12543)	G	302 539-4290
McClain Custodial Service, Lewes (G-6254)	G	302 645-6597
Mebro Inc, Wilmington (G-18243)	E	302 992-0104
Merry Maids, Christiana (G-1005)	G	302 223-9259
Merry Maids, Newark (G-11391)	G	302 266-6243
Merry Maids Inc, Dover (G-3066)	F	302 698-9038
Merry Maids of Ocean View, Ocean View (G-12545)	G	410 729-6661
Mid-Atlantic Services A-Team, Wilmington (G-18337)	D	302 984-9559
Mid-Atlantic Services A-Team, Seaford (G-13283)	E	302 628-3403
Ms Neat Cleaning Services LLC, Dover (G-3130)	G	302 535-7236
New Image Property Maintenance, Delmar (G-1626)	G	302 396-0451
Oceanside Elite Clg Bldg Svcs, Lewes (G-6329)	E	302 339-7777
Oe Performance Repr Maint Inc, Milton (G-8679)	G	302 664-1264
Optima Cleaning Systems Inc, Wilmington (G-18807)	E	302 652-3979
Otis Kamara, Dover (G-3247)	G	443 207-2643
Phoenix Home Theater Inc, Wilmington (G-19025)	F	302 295-1390
Pride Cleaning, Laurel (G-5579)	G	302 228-0755
Priority Services LLC, Newark (G-11751)	E	302 918-3070
Prolific Professionals LLC, Dover (G-3380)	G	302 497-4136
Property Maintenance, Lewes (G-6395)	G	302 645-5921
Purnells General Clg Svcs LLC, Felton (G-4010)	F	302 430-1170
R & R Power Washing, Georgetown (G-4478)	G	302 259-4012
Ras Addis & Associates Inc, Wilmington (G-19335)	G	302 571-1683
Rock Maintenance Services LLC, Wilmington (G-19528)	G	607 624-2341
Room2room Cleaning LLC, Wilmington (G-19565)	G	302 202-9140
Schoon Inc, Newark (G-11961)	G	302 894-7574
Schweizer Cleaning Service, Wilmington (G-19702)	G	302 995-2816
Service Master of Newark, Wilmington (G-19761)	G	302 654-8145
ServiceMaster of Newark, Newark (G-11985)	F	302 834-8006
SERVPRO Bear-New Castle Inc, Bear (G-484)	F	302 392-6000
SERVPRO of Norwalk/Wilton, Newark (G-11986)	G	203 866-2871
SERVPRO of Upper Darby, Bear (G-485)	G	302 392-6000
Shine Through Window Clg LLC, Bear (G-489)	G	302 261-6459
Ship Shape Marine Inc, Seaford (G-13401)	G	302 841-7355
Signature Clean Solutions LLC, Middletown (G-7565)	G	571 565-1270
Simply Clean, Newark (G-12012)	G	302 894-1569
Simply Clean Jantr Svcs Inc, Dover (G-3564)	G	302 744-9100
Sims Team Cleaning LLC, Middletown (G-7568)	E	610 990-1950
Slater Fireplaces Inc, Wilmington (G-19861)	G	302 999-1200
SMI Services of Delaware LLC, Selbyville (G-13605)	D	302 436-4410
St Andrews Maintenance, Bear (G-509)	G	302 832-2675

SIC SECTION
73 BUSINESS SERVICES

Stl & Associates LLC .... G 302 359-2801
  Smyrna (G-13902)
Stratus Building Solutions .... G 302 414-9749
  Newark (G-12108)
Sunshine Cleaning Services LLC .... G 302 430-8416
  Seaford (G-13416)
Supreme Servicez LLC .... G 302 932-5724
  Wilmington (G-20158)
Swamps Property Maint LLC .... G 302 841-1162
  Millsboro (G-8478)
Swift Services Inc .... G 302 328-1145
  New Castle (G-9610)
T & M Property Maintenance LLC .... G 302 462-1080
  Middletown (G-7617)
Teagle and Sons .... G 302 682-8639
  Seaford (G-13426)
Teff Inc .... F 302 856-9768
  Georgetown (G-4547)
Tlaloc Building Services Inc .... G 302 559-6459
  Bear (G-533)
TNT Window Cleaning .... G 302 326-2411
  Newark (G-12201)
Todds Janitorial Service Inc .... G 302 378-8212
  Middletown (G-7650)
Top of The Line Jantr Svcs .... G 302 645-2668
  Lewes (G-6572)
Tornado II Janitorial Svc LLC .... F 302 898-1370
  Wilmington (G-20364)
Tri-State Carpet Maint Inc .... G 302 654-8193
  Wilmington (G-20412)
Triniiity Group LLC .... G 302 402-1726
  Wilmington (G-20424)
Ventura Maintenance Company .... F 302 376-9060
  Middletown (G-7685)
Vicks Commercial Clg & Maint .... G 302 697-9591
  Dover (G-3791)
Weg Cleaning Service Inc .... G 302 343-5746
  Wilmington (G-20712)
Whaleys Seed Store Inc .... G 302 875-7833
  Laurel (G-5623)
Yoders Maintenance .... G 302 492-0203
  Hartly (G-4913)

7352 Medical equipment rental

American Homepatient Inc .... E 302 454-4941
  Newark (G-9845)
Apria Healthcare LLC .... F 302 737-7979
  New Castle (G-8816)
Broad Creek Medical Service .... F 302 629-0202
  Seaford (G-13093)
Hatfield Medical Instrs Inc .... G 301 468-0011
  Millsboro (G-8315)
Lincare .... G 302 736-1210
  Dover (G-2950)
Lincare Inc .... G 302 424-8302
  Felton (G-3999)
Quinn-Miller Group Inc .... F 302 738-9742
  Wilmington (G-19296)

7353 Heavy construction equipment rental

Active Crane Rentals Inc .... E 302 998-1000
  Wilmington (G-14243)
Chesapeake Supply & Eqp Co .... G 302 284-1000
  Felton (G-3955)
Delaware Valley Safety Council .... G 302 607-2758
  Newark (G-10495)
Don D Corp .... G 302 994-5793
  Wilmington (G-16131)
Dozr Ltd .... F 844 218-3697
  Wilmington (G-16158)
Eagle Power and Equipment Corp .... F 302 652-3028
  New Castle (G-9076)

First State Crane Service Inc .... E 302 398-8885
  Felton (G-3974)
Heavy Equipment Rental Inc .... F 302 654-5716
  New Castle (G-9205)
▼ Iron Source LLC .... G 302 856-7545
  Georgetown (G-4373)
Milford Rental Center Inc .... G 302 422-0315
  Dover (G-3091)
MSP Equip Rental .... F 302 322-5394
  New Castle (G-9387)
Rent Equipment .... G 302 537-9797
  Ocean View (G-12562)
Sunbelt Rentals Inc .... G 302 907-1921
  Delmar (G-1638)
Sunbelt Rentals Inc .... G 302 322-5394
  New Castle (G-9601)
Sunbelt Rentals Inc .... G 302 669-0595
  New Castle (G-9602)
Temp-Air Inc .... F 302 369-3880
  Newark (G-12177)

7359 Equipment rental and leasing, nec

A V Resources Inc .... G 302 994-1488
  Wilmington (G-14174)
A-1 Sanitation Service Inc .... E 302 322-1074
  New Castle (G-8752)
AAA Portable Restroom Co Inc .... G 909 981-0090
  Camden Wyoming (G-904)
Aarons Sales & Leasing .... G 302 628-8870
  Seaford (G-13045)
Academy Sounds LLC .... G 302 276-5027
  Newport (G-12439)
ACS Aero 2 Gamma Us LLC .... G 800 483-1140
  Dover (G-1713)
Action Rental Inc .... G 302 366-0749
  Newark (G-9760)
Action Unlimited Resources Inc .... E 302 323-1455
  Historic New Castle (G-4919)
Actors Attic .... G 302 734-8214
  Dover (G-1714)
◆ Aggreko Holdings Inc .... A 302 652-4076
  Wilmington (G-14313)
All For Fun Party Rentals .... G 302 322-3844
  New Castle (G-8779)
American Furniture Rentals Inc .... E 302 323-1682
  New Castle (G-8798)
American Traffic Pd LLC .... E 302 883-7263
  Historic New Castle (G-4931)
Arrow Leasing Corp .... F 302 834-4546
  Bear (G-47)
Atlantic Pumping Inc .... F 302 436-5047
  Selbyville (G-13468)
Awas Leasing One LLC .... F 425 440-6000
  Wilmington (G-14677)
B Williams Holding Corp .... F 302 656-8596
  Wilmington (G-14704)
Bawa Inc .... G 302 698-3200
  Dover (G-1882)
Bay Area Inflatables LLC .... G 302 379-2821
  Wilmington (G-14783)
Baybiw Development LLC .... F 302 537-9700
  Ocean View (G-12469)
Bethany Beach Goods & Rentals .... G 207 266-1682
  Bethany Beach (G-581)
Bk Rentals .... G 302 331-1984
  Felton (G-3946)
Brandywine Electronics Corp .... F 302 324-9992
  Bear (G-80)
Budget Rent A Car .... G 302 227-3041
  Rehoboth Beach (G-12660)
Burke Equipment Company .... F 302 697-3200
  Felton (G-3949)

Celera Services Inc .... G 302 378-7778
  Middletown (G-6968)
Chesapeake Supply & Eqp Co .... G 302 284-1000
  Felton (G-3955)
Cityline Rental .... G 302 834-3142
  Bear (G-107)
Coastal Rentals Hydraulics LLC .... G 302 251-3103
  Millville (G-8523)
Coastal Tented Events .... G 302 539-5211
  Millville (G-8524)
Darby Leasing LLC .... G 302 477-0500
  Wilmington (G-15793)
Diamond Chemical & Supply Co .... E 302 656-7786
  Wilmington (G-16049)
Diamond State Pty Rentl & Sls .... G 302 777-6677
  Wilmington (G-16057)
Dover Rent-All Inc .... E 302 739-0860
  Dover (G-2366)
Downtown Beach Rentals .... G 410 472-9480
  Rehoboth Beach (G-12735)
Eb Rental Ltd .... G 310 951-8931
  Newark (G-10601)
Enterprise Flasher Co Inc .... E 302 999-0856
  Wilmington (G-16433)
Enz Party Rental .... G 302 287-5995
  Wilmington (G-16445)
Excape Entertainment US Ltd .... G 949 943-9219
  Wilmington (G-16498)
First State Rental Company LLC .... G 302 632-5699
  Houston (G-5441)
Foster Long Vacation Rentals .... G 302 226-2919
  Rehoboth Beach (G-12759)
Gfc Leasing LLC .... G 302 449-5006
  Middletown (G-7157)
Gge Amusements .... G 302 227-0661
  Rehoboth Beach (G-12770)
Gian-Co .... F 302 798-7100
  Claymont (G-1161)
Gray Rental Properties LLC .... G 302 382-0439
  Milford (G-7911)
Groff Tractor & Equipment LLC .... F 302 349-5760
  Greenwood (G-4633)
Home Depot USA Inc .... D 302 735-8864
  Dover (G-2688)
Home Depot USA Inc .... C 302 395-1260
  New Castle (G-9218)
Home Depot USA Inc .... D 302 838-6818
  Newark (G-10962)
J R Rents Inc .... F 302 266-8090
  Newark (G-11076)
Kustom Additions LLC .... G 302 468-6865
  Wilmington (G-17769)
Lotus Lease Hospitality .... G 302 357-4699
  Wilmington (G-18001)
Margarita Man .... G 302 947-4000
  Lewes (G-6242)
Margarita Man of Delaware .... G 302 344-5837
  Millsboro (G-8365)
Material Handling Supply Inc .... F 302 571-0176
  Historic New Castle (G-5024)
MHS Lift of Delaware Inc .... F 302 629-4490
  Seaford (G-13282)
Middletown Tent Rentals Inc .... G 302 376-7010
  Middletown (G-7359)
Morton Electric Co .... G 302 645-9414
  Lewes (G-6292)
NS Air Leasing LLC .... G 302 396-6546
  Wilmington (G-18705)
Ownlease Inc .... G 855 447-4921
  Wilmington (G-18844)
Penske Truck Leasing Co LP .... G 302 325-9290
  New Castle (G-9467)

73 BUSINESS SERVICES

Professional Leasing Inc .... G 302 629-4350
  Seaford *(G-13359)*
Queen B Tbl Chair Rentals LLC .... G 215 960-6303
  Dover *(G-3409)*
Quillens Rent All Inc .... G 302 227-3151
  Rehoboth Beach *(G-12903)*
RAC Acceptance .... G 302 477-1513
  Wilmington *(G-19310)*
Rent Co Inc .... E 302 739-0860
  Dover *(G-3457)*
Rent Equipment .... G 302 537-9797
  Ocean View *(G-12562)*
Right Way Flagging and Sign Co .... F 302 698-5229
  Camden Wyoming *(G-969)*
Ryder Truck Rental Inc .... G 302 798-1472
  Wilmington *(G-19601)*
Seachange Vacation Rentals .... G 302 727-5566
  Rehoboth Beach *(G-12951)*
Sheets At Beach .... G 302 362-0876
  Lewes *(G-6462)*
Shell We Bounce .... G 302 727-5411
  Rehoboth Beach *(G-12956)*
Shore Rv Rentals .... G 443 235-2183
  Delmar *(G-1635)*
Storage Rentals of America .... G 302 786-0792
  Wilmington *(G-20084)*
Sunshine Vending Machines LLC .... G 800 670-6557
  Wilmington *(G-20137)*
Superior Equipment Rental Co .... F 302 658-6193
  Wilmington *(G-20141)*
Sussex Protection Service LLC .... F 302 832-5700
  Newark *(G-12136)*
◆ Ten Talents Enterprises Inc .... G 302 409-0718
  Middletown *(G-7634)*
Tucker Vacation Rentals Inc .... G 302 668-3512
  Newark *(G-12244)*
United Rentals North Amer Inc .... G 302 907-0292
  Delmar *(G-1649)*
United Rentals North Amer Inc .... F 302 846-0955
  Delmar *(G-1650)*
United Rentals North Amer Inc .... E 302 328-2900
  New Castle *(G-9656)*
Upbound Group Inc .... G 302 838-7333
  Bear *(G-553)*
Upbound Group Inc .... G 302 798-0663
  Claymont *(G-1324)*
Upbound Group Inc .... G 302 734-2094
  Dover *(G-3756)*
Upbound Group Inc .... G 302 678-4676
  Dover *(G-3757)*
Upbound Group Inc .... G 302 734-3505
  Dover *(G-3758)*
Upbound Group Inc .... G 302 856-9200
  Georgetown *(G-4566)*
Upbound Group Inc .... G 302 422-1230
  Milford *(G-8131)*
Upbound Group Inc .... G 302 934-6700
  Millsboro *(G-8490)*
Upbound Group Inc .... G 302 731-7900
  Newark *(G-12284)*
Upbound Group Inc .... G 302 629-8925
  Seaford *(G-13438)*
Upbound Group Inc .... G 302 653-3701
  Smyrna *(G-13925)*
Upbound Group Inc .... G 302 654-7700
  Wilmington *(G-20535)*
Vacuum Group Inc .... G 212 377-2073
  Newark *(G-12297)*
Video Den .... G 302 628-9835
  Seaford *(G-13441)*
Wyndham Vacation Rentals .... G 877 893-2487
  Bethany Beach *(G-652)*

7361 Employment agencies

1st-Recruit LLC .... F 732 666-4106
  Wilmington *(G-14117)*
924 Inc .... E 302 656-6100
  Hockessin *(G-5109)*
Access Labor Service Inc .... E 302 326-2575
  New Castle *(G-8760)*
Accu Personnel Inc .... F 302 384-8777
  Wilmington *(G-14227)*
Agent Staffing Services Llc .... G 302 244-2676
  Dover *(G-1738)*
Alium Consultancy LLC .... E 347 414-8851
  Dover *(G-1762)*
Allen Spolden LLC .... F 267 226-2160
  Middletown *(G-6851)*
Alpha Tech Consulting LLC .... F 302 898-2862
  Townsend *(G-13958)*
Altea Resources LLC .... F 713 242-1460
  Dover *(G-1776)*
Ark Recruiting Solutions Inc .... G 302 947-1877
  Millsboro *(G-8174)*
Array Corporation .... F 650 241-1382
  Claymont *(G-1043)*
Atwork Personnel Services .... G 302 660-1062
  Wilmington *(G-14639)*
Au-Naturel Services LLC .... G 775 484-5210
  Dover *(G-1853)*
Barbizon of Delaware Inc .... E 302 658-6666
  Wilmington *(G-14757)*
Barrett Business Services Inc .... G 302 674-2206
  Dover *(G-1875)*
Bestemps .... G 302 674-4357
  Dover *(G-1918)*
Bgm Compliance LLC .... F 302 450-1149
  Dover *(G-1929)*
Blueberry Staffing LLC .... G 302 445-6300
  Wilmington *(G-14979)*
Careerminds .... E 302 352-0511
  Wilmington *(G-15242)*
Careeronestop Dover One Stop .... G 302 739-5473
  Dover *(G-2030)*
Caring N Action Nursing .... G 302 368-2273
  Newark *(G-10146)*
Carter Aston .... G 302 561-6315
  New Castle *(G-8916)*
Carter Aston .... G 302 561-6315
  Newark *(G-10155)*
CBI Group LLC .... E 302 266-0860
  Newark *(G-10166)*
Centrix Hr .... G 302 777-7818
  Wilmington *(G-15311)*
Christana Care HM Hlth Cmnty S .... C 302 698-4300
  Camden *(G-806)*
Community Integrated Services .... E 215 238-7411
  Milford *(G-7840)*
Comprise It Solutions LLC .... E 302 337-4036
  Dover *(G-2126)*
Conducerent Incorporated .... G 302 543-8525
  Wilmington *(G-15588)*
Congruence Consulting Group .... G 320 290-6155
  Newark *(G-10304)*
Continntal Search Outplacement .... G 302 927-0200
  Dagsboro *(G-1432)*
D-Staffing Consulting Svcs LLC .... D 302 402-5678
  Dover *(G-2182)*
Delaware Registry Ltd .... G 302 477-9800
  Wilmington *(G-15959)*
Delaware Valley Group LLC .... G 302 777-7007
  Wilmington *(G-15982)*
Dkmrbh Inc .... F 302 250-4428
  Wilmington *(G-16103)*
Ekeo Group LLC .... G 973 489-1962
  New Castle *(G-9085)*
Excella Staffing Solutions LLC .... E 302 985-7373
  Dover *(G-2471)*
Exclusive Srch Connections LLC .... G 610 864-8000
  Newark *(G-10686)*
Exclusively Legal Inc .... F 302 239-5990
  Hockessin *(G-5204)*
Exec-Pro Recruiting .... G 302 379-7553
  Claymont *(G-1142)*
First State Stffing Sltion LLC .... E 302 285-9044
  Wilmington *(G-16636)*
Fladger & Associates Inc .... F 302 836-3100
  Bear *(G-230)*
Global Network Executive Inc .... F 302 251-8940
  Wilmington *(G-16892)*
Global Recruiters Network Inc .... G 302 455-9500
  Newark *(G-10851)*
Global Recruiters Wilmingto .... G 302 455-9500
  Newark *(G-10852)*
Greenlight Connections LLC .... G 843 209-1675
  Dover *(G-2627)*
High5 Global Corporation .... F 732 248-1900
  Lewes *(G-6093)*
Hornberger Management Company .... G 302 573-2541
  Wilmington *(G-17211)*
Infigage LLC .... G 302 207-2148
  Wilmington *(G-17320)*
Insignia Global Corporation .... G 302 310-4107
  Wilmington *(G-17352)*
Integrity Staffing Solutions .... A 302 661-8770
  Newark *(G-11036)*
Intello Group Inc .... F 832 827-3779
  Wilmington *(G-17373)*
International Esl Services LLC .... G 305 934-3769
  Wilmington *(G-17388)*
J S & Assoc .... G 302 765-2300
  Wilmington *(G-17462)*
Jbs Technologies Inc .... F 302 683-1098
  Wilmington *(G-17507)*
Kathleen Looney .... G 302 762-0106
  Wilmington *(G-17664)*
Ken Crest Services .... G 302 741-0256
  Dover *(G-2840)*
Lyneer Staffing Solutions .... F 302 892-9494
  Wilmington *(G-18048)*
Moore Staffing Agency LLC .... G 215 300-2770
  Bear *(G-379)*
Mwidm Inc .... E 302 298-0101
  Wilmington *(G-18501)*
Next Level Staffing Solutions .... F 302 281-4777
  Dover *(G-3185)*
Nurses Connection .... G 302 421-3687
  Wilmington *(G-18719)*
Nurses Next Staffing LLC .... F 302 446-3200
  Dover *(G-3211)*
Opportunity Center Inc .... D 302 762-0300
  New Castle *(G-9435)*
Opus Financial Svcs USA Inc .... G 646 435-5616
  Wilmington *(G-18809)*
Paramunt Hlthcare Rsources LLC .... F 302 722-5484
  Middletown *(G-7425)*
Personal Touch Memories .... G 302 598-3987
  Wilmington *(G-18988)*
Phrst .... G 302 739-2260
  Dover *(G-3316)*
Placers Inc of Delaware .... F 302 709-0973
  Newark *(G-11698)*
Populus LLC .... G 412 973-2340
  Dover *(G-3351)*
Premier Employee Solutions .... G 843 421-5579
  Newark *(G-11727)*

SIC SECTION

73 BUSINESS SERVICES

Premier Staffing Solutions Inc................. D 302 628-7700
  Seaford *(G-13355)*
Premier Staffing Solutions Inc................. E 302 344-5996
  Georgetown *(G-4471)*
Pridestaffing LLC.................................... E 302 525-2561
  Lewes *(G-6390)*
Professional Recruiting Cons................. G 302 479-9550
  Wilmington *(G-19212)*
Professional Selection Inc...................... F 905 392-7313
  Wilmington *(G-19213)*
Quality Staffing Services........................ F 302 990-5623
  Seaford *(G-13360)*
Randstad Professionals Us LLC............. F 302 658-6181
  Wilmington *(G-19330)*
Rapport It Services LLC.......................... E 302 304-8729
  Wilmington *(G-19334)*
Ready 4 Work LLC................................. F 302 229-9701
  Dover *(G-3433)*
Redleo Software Inc............................... F 302 691-9072
  Wilmington *(G-19390)*
Relig Staffing Inc.................................... E 312 219-6786
  Dover *(G-3449)*
Rmv Workforce Corp.............................. F 302 408-1061
  Milton *(G-8700)*
Robert Half International Inc.................. G 302 252-3162
  Wilmington *(G-19513)*
Sean E Reilly... G 302 690-9487
  Wilmington *(G-19723)*
Service General Corporation.................. F 302 218-4279
  Georgetown *(G-4507)*
Servicesource Inc.................................... G 302 322-0904
  New Castle *(G-9559)*
Servicexpress Corporation..................... A 302 424-3500
  Milford *(G-8089)*
Servicexpress Corporation..................... A 302 854-9118
  Seaford *(G-13398)*
Servicexpress Corporation..................... E 302 856-3500
  Georgetown *(G-4509)*
Sk Services LLC...................................... G 302 834-9133
  Bear *(G-495)*
Smiths Work At HM Slutions LLC........... G 302 367-6671
  New Castle *(G-9575)*
SOS Personnel Ltd Liability Co.............. G 267 357-9124
  New Castle *(G-9579)*
Staffmark Investment LLC...................... G 302 422-0606
  Milford *(G-8102)*
State of De... G 302 328-3573
  New Castle *(G-9593)*
Stm Consulting Inc.................................. F 408 341-6900
  Claymont *(G-1304)*
Synerfac Inc... F 302 324-9400
  New Castle *(G-9612)*
Talent Hire Consulting Inc...................... E 302 414-8235
  Wilmington *(G-20211)*
Trinity Cloud Company........................... E 973 494-8190
  Wilmington *(G-20425)*
Trinity Ems Educators Staffing.............. G 302 373-7276
  Newark *(G-12231)*
Trinity Hlthcare Staffing LLC.................. G 302 420-3782
  Middletown *(G-7661)*
Urban Avenue Inc.................................... G 302 420-1105
  New Castle *(G-9662)*
Varida-Tech Inc.. F 781 819-0259
  Claymont *(G-1326)*
Wave Global Employment Inc................ E 617 987-0152
  Wilmington *(G-20687)*
Whitecrow Research Inc......................... F 908 752-4200
  Wilmington *(G-20769)*

7363 Help supply services

Access Labor Service Inc....................... E 302 741-2575
  Dover *(G-1707)*
Adecco Usa Inc....................................... G 302 669-4005
  New Castle *(G-8762)*
Adecco Usa Inc....................................... G 302 457-4059
  Newark *(G-9763)*
Aero Ways Inc.. C 302 324-9970
  New Castle *(G-8768)*
Aerotek Inc.. G 302 561-6300
  New Castle *(G-8770)*
Aerotek Inc.. G 302 318-8760
  Newark *(G-9789)*
B&B Transports LLC............................... G 223 877-6812
  Middletown *(G-6896)*
Barrett Business Services Inc................ G 302 674-2206
  Dover *(G-1875)*
BP Staffing Inc.. F 302 999-7213
  Wilmington *(G-15021)*
Career Associates Inc............................ G 302 674-4357
  Dover *(G-2029)*
Cloud Financial Corporation.................. G 845 729-5513
  Wilmington *(G-15489)*
County of Sussex.................................... F 302 854-5050
  Georgetown *(G-4270)*
Eden Hill Express Care LLC................... G 302 674-1999
  Dover *(G-2420)*
Employers Bench Inc.............................. F 973 757-1912
  Christiana *(G-995)*
Fenway Aviation LLC............................... G 800 981-7183
  Wilmington *(G-16580)*
First State Stffing Sltion LLC................. E 302 285-9044
  Wilmington *(G-16636)*
Fritz Staffing Group LLC........................ F 844 581-5873
  Historic New Castle *(G-4993)*
Frontier SGS 360 LLC............................. G 609 919-1133
  Wilmington *(G-16764)*
GSM Systems Inc.................................... F 302 284-8304
  Viola *(G-14095)*
Ics - Worldwide Inc................................. D 800 266-5254
  Wilmington *(G-17258)*
Integrity Staffing Solutions.................... A 520 276-7775
  Newark *(G-11037)*
Interim Healthcare Del LLC.................... F 302 322-2743
  Smyrna *(G-13775)*
J&J Staffing Resources Inc.................... G 302 738-7800
  Newark *(G-11079)*
Jiga Inc.. F 408 878-3213
  Middletown *(G-7249)*
Kelly Services Inc................................... G 302 323-4748
  New Castle *(G-9279)*
Kelly Services Inc................................... G 302 366-1741
  Newark *(G-11152)*
Maxim Healthcare Services Inc............. B 302 478-3434
  Wilmington *(G-18205)*
Pilots4rent Inc... G 561 704-2885
  Bear *(G-425)*
Service General Corporation.................. G 302 856-3500
  Georgetown *(G-4508)*
Star Services LLC................................... G 302 373-5210
  Middletown *(G-7596)*
Stm Consulting Inc.................................. F 408 341-6900
  Claymont *(G-1304)*
Synerfac Inc... F 302 324-9400
  New Castle *(G-9612)*
Talent4health LLC................................... D 302 314-1677
  Wilmington *(G-20212)*
Tedron Inc... G 302 529-1838
  Wilmington *(G-20261)*
Timber Ridge Inc.................................... F 302 239-9239
  Hockessin *(G-5405)*
Triglia Trans Co....................................... G 302 846-3795
  Delmar *(G-1644)*
Virtually Fortified Staffing..................... G 302 547-9065
  Townsend *(G-14088)*

7371 Custom computer programming services

1000x LLC.. F 919 584-5420
  Middletown *(G-6814)*
114 Ai Inc... G 719 394-0606
  Lewes *(G-5635)*
2yum Inc.. G 626 420-4851
  Dover *(G-1684)*
4BOA LLC... E 323 747-7771
  Claymont *(G-1012)*
6clicks Inc... F 925 699-6304
  Middletown *(G-6818)*
9junio Inc.. G 239 946-6374
  Middletown *(G-6820)*
A Shared Space LLC............................... G 240 727-9917
  Wilmington *(G-14172)*
Abandon Inc.. G 858 863-7190
  Dover *(G-1701)*
Accuretix LLC.. G 646 434-6917
  Claymont *(G-1017)*
Advertised Media Inc.............................. G 415 967-8100
  Wilmington *(G-14289)*
Aeronex LLC.. G 206 809-0009
  Dover *(G-1729)*
Aetho LLC.. F 215 821-7290
  Dover *(G-1733)*
Agent Launch LLC................................... F 302 200-5574
  Newark *(G-9796)*
Agitek Softworks Inc.............................. G 240 356-3034
  Lewes *(G-5665)*
Aglide Inc.. G 302 213-0357
  Dover *(G-1746)*
Ai Athena LLC.. G 212 247-6400
  Wilmington *(G-14325)*
Al Whoo LLC.. G 302 494-6952
  Newark *(G-9798)*
Air Apps Inc... D 302 339-3843
  Dover *(G-1754)*
Air Temp Solutions LLC.......................... F 302 276-0532
  New Castle *(G-8775)*
Ais.. G 302 407-0430
  Wilmington *(G-14339)*
Albion Investments LLC......................... G 876 575-7371
  Lewes *(G-5670)*
Alchemy Software Solutions LLC........... E 201 627-0638
  Wilmington *(G-14351)*
Alias Technology LLC............................. G 302 856-9488
  Georgetown *(G-4205)*
Alivio Health Corp.................................. G 754 230-0234
  Newark *(G-9811)*
Alpha Technologies USA Inc.................. D 302 510-8205
  Wilmington *(G-14392)*
Alternate Cmmodities Index Inc............ G 302 238-1077
  Newark *(G-9837)*
Amalgama Digital Inc............................. G 302 387-0140
  Middletown *(G-6856)*
Amazed Apps LLC................................... G 916 934-9210
  Dover *(G-1781)*
Amazingdoc Inc....................................... G 847 909-0409
  Wilmington *(G-14415)*
Analytica LLC.. F 214 223-2055
  Dover *(G-1789)*
Annalise-Ai Inc.. G 440 281-5115
  Dover *(G-1797)*
Aola Inc... G 610 245-8231
  Wilmington *(G-14499)*
Apollo Software Inc................................ G 800 992-0847
  Newark *(G-9887)*
Apphive Inc... G 240 898-4661
  Newark *(G-9888)*

73 BUSINESS SERVICES

Apphud Inc... G 415 936-8741
   Newark *(G-9889)*

Appic Stars LLC..................................... G 903 224-6469
   Dover *(G-1805)*

Applied Control Engrg Inc...................... D 302 738-8800
   Newark *(G-9891)*

Apploye Inc... G 925 452-6102
   Newark *(G-9893)*

Apply Co... G 775 343-5307
   Claymont *(G-1041)*

Appointiv Inc... G 415 877-4339
   Middletown *(G-6869)*

Appricot Inc... G 484 291-8922
   Dover *(G-1808)*

Apptrium Inc.. D 800 888-0706
   Wilmington *(G-14514)*

Apriorit LLC... C 202 780-9339
   Wilmington *(G-14515)*

Aquia Inc.. F 530 215-7158
   Millsboro *(G-8171)*

Arbitexch LLC....................................... G 302 490-0111
   Wilmington *(G-14523)*

ARC Studio Labs Inc............................. G 323 990-8787
   Wilmington *(G-14535)*

Arcade Services Inc.............................. F 630 777-8092
   New Castle *(G-8818)*

Arcasoft LLC... G 402 575-1234
   Wilmington *(G-14540)*

Ardeun Biometrics Corp LLC................. F 949 662-1096
   Lewes *(G-5697)*

Ardexo Inc.. G 855 617-7500
   Dover *(G-1811)*

Aries Security LLC................................ G 302 365-0026
   Wilmington *(G-14551)*

Arnab Mobility Inc................................. F 774 316-6767
   Newark *(G-9906)*

Aros Design Studio LLC........................ G 505 560-0603
   Wilmington *(G-14557)*

Artid LLC... G 302 898-6307
   Dover *(G-1823)*

Arua Inc.. G 302 396-9868
   Dover *(G-1826)*

Ascent Technologies Inc....................... G 302 491-0545
   Newark *(G-9919)*

Ashweb Inc... G 844 493-6249
   Dover *(G-1832)*

Asphalt Kingdom LLC........................... G 866 399-5562
   Wilmington *(G-14589)*

Assanis & Associates Inc..................... G 734 277-0846
   Newark *(G-9927)*

Atlan Inc... G 650 288-6722
   Wilmington *(G-14626)*

Atlas Software LLC............................... F 312 576-2247
   Newark *(G-9939)*

Atomic Development Inc....................... G 424 354-9865
   Dover *(G-1851)*

Auditbot.. G 302 494-9476
   Newark *(G-9943)*

Aum LLC... F 302 385-6767
   Wilmington *(G-14641)*

Autoawards Inc..................................... F 302 696-6000
   Odessa *(G-12581)*

Automizy Inc... G 361 253-8238
   Wilmington *(G-14655)*

Autoweb Technologies Inc.................... G 443 485-4200
   Wilmington *(G-14657)*

Auxility Inc.. E 610 245-8039
   Lewes *(G-5722)*

Avanta Inc.. E 925 818-4760
   Dover *(G-1856)*

Avni Adtech Inc..................................... F 628 600-5009
   Middletown *(G-6892)*

Avokadio Inc... G 302 291-4080
   Lewes *(G-5726)*

Avomd Inc.. F 631 786-3867
   Dover *(G-1857)*

Axa Zara LLC....................................... G 513 206-4606
   Lewes *(G-5730)*

Axes Global Inc.................................... F 415 602-4049
   Wilmington *(G-14681)*

Axmos Technologies Inc....................... E 650 229-9094
   Wilmington *(G-14684)*

B+h Insurance LLC............................... E 302 995-2247
   Newark *(G-9968)*

Backdoor Global Inc.............................. G 386 465-2646
   Middletown *(G-6900)*

Bagel Technologies Inc........................ G 650 410-8018
   Middletown *(G-6902)*

Bands CA Inc....................................... G 206 396-7035
   Dover *(G-1872)*

Bartech Agency Inc.............................. F 302 317-2399
   Bear *(G-57)*

Base-2 Solutions LLC........................... D 202 215-2152
   Lewes *(G-5735)*

Base86 Inc... G 619 781-2670
   Newark *(G-9987)*

Basedash Inc.. G 302 244-0916
   Dover *(G-1878)*

Basetwo Artfcal Intllgnce USA............... G 519 400-8770
   Dover *(G-1880)*

Bastion Research Ltd........................... G 307 370-3767
   Lewes *(G-5738)*

Baxet Group Inc................................... G 917 938-7088
   Wilmington *(G-14782)*

Be Humane Co..................................... G 720 419-5362
   Dover *(G-1894)*

Beacon Interactive Inc.......................... F 414 306-5978
   Dover *(G-1897)*

Beamm Technologies Inc..................... G 302 402-5551
   Wilmington *(G-14802)*

Beejug Games LLC.............................. G 310 382-0746
   Lewes *(G-5753)*

Beforesunset Inc................................... F 812 341-0038
   Wilmington *(G-14812)*

Beneree Inc.. G 814 526-4238
   Middletown *(G-6912)*

Best High Technologies LLC................. D 917 742-6658
   Newark *(G-10026)*

Betworks Corporation............................ F 310 866-0365
   Lewes *(G-5760)*

Bhaoo Inc... E 832 888-3694
   Dover *(G-1931)*

Bhapi Inc.. G 859 475-1924
   Wilmington *(G-14873)*

Bid 4 Lease Corp.................................. G 302 244-9943
   Wilmington *(G-14876)*

Bidr TV LLC.. G 561 569-0931
   Wilmington *(G-14878)*

Big Data Elements LLC........................ G 917 620-2337
   Dover *(G-1933)*

Big Eld LLC.. G 302 549-0333
   Dover *(G-1935)*

Big Moose Exterior LLC........................ G 302 722-1969
   Middletown *(G-6918)*

Big Plan Inc.. G 910 556-9311
   Wilmington *(G-14881)*

Bigcloud Solutions Inc........................... G 917 972-6891
   Newark *(G-10032)*

Bipgo Inc.. F 708 586-9016
   Middletown *(G-6921)*

Birdie Ssot LLC.................................... G 857 361-6883
   Dover *(G-1941)*

Bits & Bytes Inc.................................... G 302 674-2999
   Dover *(G-1942)*

Bizdata Inc... G 650 283-1644
   Wilmington *(G-14899)*

Black Math Labs Inc............................. G 858 349-9446
   Dover *(G-1945)*

Blackwell Solution................................. G 302 660-2054
   Bear *(G-74)*

Blair Computing Systems Inc................ F 302 453-8947
   Newark *(G-10049)*

Blaze Systems Corporation................... G 302 733-7235
   Newark *(G-10050)*

Blb Services LLC.................................. G 678 989-7908
   Wilmington *(G-14953)*

Bleeks LLC... G 443 990-0496
   Wilmington *(G-14954)*

Blinqio Inc.. F 718 710-4529
   Wilmington *(G-14958)*

Blips Digital Inc..................................... F 661 520-1539
   Middletown *(G-6924)*

Blix Inc... E 347 753-8035
   Newark *(G-10052)*

Blue Hen Hospitality LLC...................... F 302 530-5066
   Wilmington *(G-14968)*

Booke AI Inc... G 650 540-1316
   Wilmington *(G-15001)*

Bookitngo Corp..................................... G 949 899-7684
   Dover *(G-1962)*

Bookme Ai Inc...................................... G 650 436-9210
   Wilmington *(G-15002)*

Boomerang Returns Ltd........................ G 347 205-1275
   Middletown *(G-6930)*

Boomset Inc... F 860 266-6738
   Wilmington *(G-15004)*

Boonoob Inc... G 302 288-0670
   Dover *(G-1963)*

Botix Inc... G 239 600-8116
   Middletown *(G-6933)*

Bounded Bits LLC................................ G 949 291-7358
   Newark *(G-10074)*

Breezle LLC... G 774 435-1566
   Wilmington *(G-15102)*

Brittons Wise Computers Inc................. G 302 659-0343
   Smyrna *(G-13668)*

Bryant Technologies Inc....................... G 302 289-2044
   Felton *(G-3948)*

Brysk Inc.. F 224 508-9542
   Wilmington *(G-15138)*

Bueno Technologies Inc....................... G 559 785-9800
   Newark *(G-10099)*

Bullseye Entertainment Tech Co........... E 302 924-5034
   Dover *(G-1992)*

Busability Corporation........................... G 845 821-4609
   Wilmington *(G-15155)*

Busibud Inc... D 626 228-1855
   Claymont *(G-1068)*

Buze Mobile Inc.................................... G 630 331-0553
   Dover *(G-1999)*

Buzzspark Labs LLC............................. G 302 828-0969
   Middletown *(G-6948)*

Bydarkmatter LLC................................. G 850 801-2732
   Dover *(G-2001)*

Byte Technology Systems Inc............... G 347 687-7240
   Lewes *(G-5784)*

Calcom Inc... E 442 227-3200
   Wilmington *(G-15191)*

Callvu Inc... G 646 506-4915
   Wilmington *(G-15199)*

Camelo LLC... G 302 574-6556
   Wilmington *(G-15205)*

Camio LLC... F 585 851-8550
   Dover *(G-2018)*

Canopy Interactive LLC........................ G 631 258-1552
   Newark *(G-10131)*

73 BUSINESS SERVICES

Capb Infotek LLC... G..... 347 277-7125
  Lewes (G-5791)

Capsa Solutions LLC.. G..... 800 437-6633
  Dover (G-2026)

Capton LLC.. G..... 510 766-2803
  Wilmington (G-15235)

Carda Health Inc... F..... 415 497-8417
  Dover (G-2028)

Carebnb Inc.. G..... 904 303-6825
  Middletown (G-6956)

Carewallet Inc... G..... 732 477-4149
  Wilmington (G-15245)

Carmedis Inc... G..... 725 712-2559
  Wilmington (G-15254)

Carpal Enterprise Inc....................................... F..... 917 985-8293
  Lewes (G-5804)

Carted Inc.. G..... 415 967-8691
  Middletown (G-6961)

Carzaty Inc.. F..... 650 396-0144
  Dover (G-2033)

Casting Arabia LLC... G..... 917 832-5287
  Middletown (G-6962)

Castor Research Inc.. F..... 415 484-5347
  Wilmington (G-15269)

Catalyst Foundry Inc.. F..... 917 471-0947
  Wilmington (G-15273)

Catovera Corp... G..... 804 814-0301
  Dover (G-2040)

Centrallo Corporation...................................... G..... 212 355-0880
  Wilmington (G-15310)

Centriq Technologies Inc............................... G..... 651 353-0691
  Claymont (G-1079)

Centrito LLC.. E..... 919 728-9401
  Claymont (G-1080)

Certified Code Inc.. G..... 347 508-6396
  Middletown (G-6970)

Cg Global MGT Solutions LLC....................... F..... 215 735-3745
  Wilmington (G-15321)

Channelape Inc.. E..... 570 351-9335
  Wilmington (G-15333)

Channelpro Mobile LLC.................................. F..... 757 620-4635
  Newark (G-10188)

Cheersrx Inc.. G..... 801 210-1658
  Felton (G-3954)

Cherry Island Rnwble Enrgy LLC................. G..... 302 379-0722
  Wilmington (G-15364)

Chores R Us Inc... F..... 844 442-4673
  Dover (G-2069)

Chotcut Inc.. G..... 706 437-7890
  Wilmington (G-15392)

Chpter Holdings Inc... F..... 650 223-1786
  Wilmington (G-15393)

Cignitix Global LLC.. G..... 408 638-9350
  Wilmington (G-15437)

Cim Concepts Incorporated.......................... F..... 302 613-5400
  New Castle (G-8942)

Cinenso Inc... G..... 424 245-5799
  Dover (G-2074)

Cinnamon Technologies Inc.......................... G..... 530 413-5533
  Dover (G-2075)

Cited Inc... G..... 302 384-9810
  Wilmington (G-15447)

Cks Global Ventures LLC............................... E..... 302 355-0511
  Newark (G-10248)

Clean Connect Inc... E..... 331 330-5662
  Wilmington (G-15470)

Cleared For Use Inc.. G..... 206 636-5222
  Lewes (G-5826)

Clew Medical Inc.. G..... 623 414-9009
  Wilmington (G-15480)

Client Monster LLC.. G..... 866 799-5433
  Newark (G-10260)

Clifton Enterprises LLC................................... G..... 630 220-7435
  Middletown (G-6992)

Climate Action Systems Inc......................... G..... 802 356-6541
  Wilmington (G-15483)

Cline Labs Inc... G..... 901 834-5102
  Middletown (G-6994)

Clinpharma Clinical RES LLC....................... E..... 646 961-3437
  Wilmington (G-15487)

Clootrack Software Labs Inc....................... G..... 302 204-1872
  Claymont (G-1095)

Cloud Software Development LLC............. G..... 703 957-9847
  Wilmington (G-15492)

Cloudarmee Ltd... F..... 714 673-8104
  Wilmington (G-15493)

Cloudbees Inc.. G..... 323 842-7783
  Lewes (G-5830)

Clutterbot Inc... G..... 425 679-1348
  Claymont (G-1096)

Clymene LLC.. G..... 888 679-3310
  Lewes (G-5833)

Cnct App Inc.. G..... 724 288-3212
  Lewes (G-5835)

Codeship Inc.. E..... 617 515-3664
  Lewes (G-5848)

Cognicor Technologies Inc........................... G..... 650 444-2076
  Dover (G-2111)

Coliving Inc... G..... 650 449-4448
  Newark (G-10273)

Comeet Technologies Inc............................. G..... 650 433-9027
  Wilmington (G-15544)

Commtrak Corporation.................................. G..... 302 644-1600
  Lewes (G-5853)

Compassred Inc.. G..... 302 383-2856
  Wilmington (G-15568)

Comprise It Solutions LLC............................. E..... 302 337-4036
  Dover (G-2126)

Computer Aid Inc.. G..... 302 831-5500
  Newark (G-10294)

Computools Llc.. F..... 617 861-0016
  Camden Wyoming (G-927)

Conci LLC.. D..... 847 665-9285
  Wilmington (G-15577)

Conquest Tech Solutions Inc....................... G..... 302 356-1423
  Wilmington (G-15606)

Conrep Inc.. E..... 302 528-8383
  Middletown (G-7010)

Construct App Inc... G..... 415 702-0634
  Wilmington (G-15611)

Contlo Inc.. G..... 860 775-7179
  Newark (G-10315)

Coolautomation Inc.. G..... 941 587-2287
  Wilmington (G-15630)

Copiri Inc... G..... 703 863-4304
  Wilmington (G-15635)

Cora Systems Us Inc..................................... F..... 833 269-5756
  Wilmington (G-15636)

Coral Technology LLC.................................... G..... 201 793-7127
  Lewes (G-5859)

Corblocks Inc... G..... 832 217-0864
  Wilmington (G-15637)

Core Results Inc.. G..... 805 552-6624
  Wilmington (G-15640)

Coremond LLC... G..... 267 797-7090
  Dover (G-2138)

Corticalio USA Inc... F..... 415 350-8588
  Newark (G-10331)

Corvant LLC.. F..... 302 299-1570
  Newark (G-10332)

Cosls LLC... F..... 877 900-7473
  Claymont (G-1101)

Cotalker Inc.. E..... 954 643-1497
  Wilmington (G-15650)

Counterfeit Combat Technology................ G..... 614 874-7414
  Wilmington (G-15654)

Coupert Science LLC..................................... E..... 206 445-0706
  Dover (G-2147)

Covant Solutions Inc...................................... F..... 302 607-2678
  Newark (G-10338)

Cr24 Inc... G..... 888 427-9357
  Wilmington (G-15678)

Cradleapps LLC... G..... 202 492-7953
  Wilmington (G-15679)

Cratis Solutions Inc.. G..... 515 423-7259
  Dover (G-2152)

Creative Xchange Inc..................................... G..... 888 502-5618
  Wilmington (G-15695)

Creator Studios Inc.. G..... 323 992-4350
  Lewes (G-5868)

Crediblockcom LLC... G..... 803 619-9458
  Dover (G-2156)

Crrraw Holdings LLC....................................... G..... 832 917-9442
  Wilmington (G-15718)

Cruisingapp LLC.. G..... 302 645-7400
  Lewes (G-5871)

Cryptlex LLC... G..... 786 269-0931
  Lewes (G-5872)

Crypto World Journal Inc............................. F..... 302 213-8136
  Dover (G-2165)

Cryptofi Inc... E..... 312 813-7188
  Dover (G-2166)

Cto Lab Inc... G..... 415 702-5014
  Claymont (G-1105)

Cubic Logics Inc.. G..... 480 382-8242
  Wilmington (G-15730)

Cyberdefenders Inc.. G..... 510 999-3490
  Middletown (G-7023)

D & G Inc... F..... 302 378-4877
  Townsend (G-13982)

D&C Concepts LLC... F..... 770 335-2503
  Wilmington (G-15763)

Daabo Inc.. F..... 816 559-4169
  Wilmington (G-15765)

Daily Byte LLC... G..... 516 236-9638
  Dover (G-2185)

Dama International LLC................................ F..... 813 778-5495
  Middletown (G-7027)

Danoffice It Inc.. G..... 703 579-0180
  Newark (G-10387)

Darwell Inc.. G..... 302 204-0939
  Dover (G-2196)

Data Unblocked Inc.. G..... 540 424-0801
  Lewes (G-5882)

Data-Bi LLC.. G..... 302 290-3138
  Wilmington (G-15798)

Datamola LLC.. G..... 347 474-1003
  Lewes (G-5883)

Datascope Solutions Corp........................... G..... 562 373-0209
  Wilmington (G-15799)

Datatech Enterprises Inc............................. F..... 540 370-0010
  Selbyville (G-13515)

Davait Inc.. G..... 302 930-0095
  Dover (G-2198)

Dayshape Corp.. G..... 929 512-5582
  Dover (G-2201)

Dbaza Inc.. G..... 302 467-3081
  Dover (G-2202)

DC Consulting Service LLC.......................... F..... 617 594-9780
  Wilmington (G-15824)

Dealer Automation Services LLC............... F..... 305 803-3201
  Wilmington (G-15844)

Deauthorized Inc... G..... 512 769-3026
  Newark (G-10402)

Decisivedge LLC.. D..... 302 299-1570
  Newark (G-10404)

73 BUSINESS SERVICES — SIC SECTION

Company	Code	Phone
Deckrobot Inc — Wilmington (G-15849)	F	617 765-7494
Deepen Inc — Middletown (G-7036)	G	813 813-9053
Defa Inc — Wilmington (G-15854)	E	302 219-5994
Delaware Pride Inc — Claymont (G-1114)	G	302 265-3020
DEMC Academia Institute — Dover (G-2280)	G	301 215-1056
Dendi Inc — Claymont (G-1117)	F	919 448-5511
Denim Inc — Dover (G-2282)	G	302 401-6502
Derived Data LLC — Wilmington (G-16019)	G	845 300-1805
Dialog Engineers Inc — Middletown (G-7056)	G	302 581-8080
Digibox LLC — Dover (G-2296)	G	302 203-0088
Digilence — Middletown (G-7061)	G	678 296-9198
Digital ARC LLC — Wilmington (G-16063)	F	855 275-2770
Digitalpaye Inc — Dover (G-2297)	F	302 232-5116
Digitlogy LLC DBA Exprttexting — Milton (G-8606)	G	302 703-9672
Dijitru Inc — New Castle (G-9054)	G	903 345-4878
Dining Software Group Inc — Camden (G-820)	G	720 236-9572
Discidium Technology Inc — Newark (G-10538)	G	347 220-5979
Disclo Inc — Dover (G-2301)	G	607 280-8949
Dish Quo LLC — Dover (G-2302)	G	845 709-1674
Dito Ventures Inc — Wilmington (G-16090)	G	305 424-9877
Diversion Company Inc — Dover (G-2307)	G	415 800-4136
Django Stars Ltd Liability Co — Wilmington (G-16101)	F	415 996-8054
Dlt Federal Bus Syst Corp — Wilmington (G-16106)	G	302 358-2229
DOE Technologies Inc — Wilmington (G-16116)	E	302 792-1285
Dopple Labs Inc — Wilmington (G-16144)	G	754 216-8175
Dori Inc — Dover (G-2326)	F	858 344-8699
Dorleeon LLC — Wilmington (G-16147)	G	302 415-3106
Dpsg - Dlgtion Pymnt Systems G — Wilmington (G-16160)	F	201 755-0912
Dr Hivey Corp — Dover (G-2373)	G	580 670-2046
Dream Conception LLC — Wilmington (G-16175)	G	302 319-9822
Dream Forge LLC — Dover (G-2380)	G	802 342-4647
Dream Weaver LLC — Wilmington (G-16177)	G	302 352-9473
Dreamtouch Games LLC — Dover (G-2385)	G	408 550-6042
Dukka Inc — Dover (G-2394)	G	401 659-6948
Dyatech LLC — Wilmington (G-16226)	F	845 666-0786
Dygital Technology LLC — Newark (G-10582)	G	302 283-9160
Dyte Inc — Lewes (G-5940)	G	669 577-4571
E2e LLC — Hockessin (G-5195)	G	703 906-5353
Eagan US Holdco LLC — Wilmington (G-16245)	A	414 339-8275
Easy Send Inc — Wilmington (G-16271)	F	610 389-0622
Ecom Technologies LLC — Dover (G-2416)	F	424 362-5155
Eden Care Group Holding LLC — Dover (G-2419)	G	929 461-7247
Edge Case LLC — Middletown (G-7083)	E	302 207-1291
Edgility Inc — Dover (G-2424)	G	650 382-2346
Efectibo LLC — Wilmington (G-16308)	G	305 498-8630
Egm LLC — New Castle (G-9083)	G	302 932-1700
Ehelp Health Corporation — Camden (G-827)	G	404 964-0906
Eice International LLC — Lewes (G-5953)	G	281 451-7328
Elevate Cdb Inc — Dover (G-2433)	E	844 903-4443
Elomia Health Inc — Dover (G-2437)	G	302 244-7193
Empire Data Voice Networks LLC — Millsboro (G-8281)	G	702 613-4900
Empirical Cre Holdings Corp — Wilmington (G-16400)	G	816 582-8041
Encompass Corporation US Inc — Wilmington (G-16406)	G	212 523-0340
Encross LLC — Wilmington (G-16407)	F	302 351-2593
Endevor LLC — Wilmington (G-16409)	G	302 543-5055
Engage Xr LLC — Wilmington (G-16421)	G	302 877-2028
Engati Technologies Inc — Wilmington (G-16422)	G	215 368-3551
Enou Labs LLC — Wilmington (G-16426)	F	321 343-4362
Enpass Technologies Inc — Wilmington (G-16429)	G	415 671-5123
Ente Technologies Inc — Dover (G-2450)	G	917 924-8450
Entertech Inc — Wilmington (G-16441)	G	415 840-0204
Envision Infosolutions Inc — Newark (G-10656)	E	302 565-4289
Enyumba Inc — Dover (G-2452)	G	818 272-9383
Enzigma LLC — Wilmington (G-16446)	G	415 830-3694
Eonscope Inc — Newark (G-10658)	G	312 319-4484
Epd Tech LLC — Lewes (G-5967)	G	415 508-7580
Episode Interactive LLC — Dover (G-2457)	G	858 220-0946
Epotec Inc — Wilmington (G-16451)	G	302 654-3090
Eptikar It Solutions Inc — Middletown (G-7106)	F	720 422-8441
Eshopperlists Com Inc — Hockessin (G-5203)	G	302 235-5743
Essen Technologies Inc — Middletown (G-7110)	G	617 959-9495
Estimators Corp — Wilmington (G-16470)	G	760 492-6405
Eswap Global Inc — Newark (G-10668)	G	323 244-2927
Ethereal Tech US Corp — Wilmington (G-16474)	E	567 694-8888
Etlgr LLC — Wilmington (G-16475)	G	302 204-0596
Ev Usa Inc — Lewes (G-5976)	G	973 674-1326
Evervault Inc — Wilmington (G-16490)	F	213 527-8608
Everytale Inc — Claymont (G-1139)	E	650 989-9807
Excelling LLC — Magnolia (G-6744)	G	302 276-3908
Expansion Platforms Inc — Newark (G-10690)	E	866 928-3098
Extenship LLC — Wilmington (G-16510)	G	302 400-5480
Extravaganza International Inc — New Castle (G-9111)	G	302 321-7117
Extreme Scale Solutions LLC — Newark (G-10697)	F	302 540-7149
Eztrackit Inc — Rehoboth Beach (G-12749)	G	800 371-5956
Fabby Inc — Wilmington (G-16522)	F	408 891-7991
Fabit Corp — Wilmington (G-16523)	G	832 217-0864
Factory Technologies Inc — Newark (G-10701)	G	302 266-1290
Factory Universe Co — Wilmington (G-16527)	F	302 216-2025
Famoid Technology LLC — Newark (G-10710)	G	530 601-7284
Fan Payment Solutions LLC — Wilmington (G-16549)	F	617 901-3970
Fanhouse Inc — Claymont (G-1147)	F	415 598-7628
Fantasy Nft LLC — Camden (G-834)	G	423 313-3436
Fantasythrone LLC — Wilmington (G-16550)	G	512 431-8658
Faramove Inc — Middletown (G-7121)	F	815 674-3114
Fast Af Inc — Newark (G-10715)	G	415 770-5235
Fast Fce Inc — Wilmington (G-16557)	G	833 327-8323
Featly Inc — Wilmington (G-16565)	G	505 305-6844
Fedi Inc — Wilmington (G-16574)	G	797 372-0606
Femispace Co — Wilmington (G-16578)	F	917 764-9943
File Right LLC — Middletown (G-7126)	G	302 757-7107
Filmustage Inc — Wilmington (G-16605)	F	260 225-3050
Finders Entertainment LLC — Dover (G-2496)	G	407 765-1826
Finnchat Inc — Middletown (G-7128)	G	517 258-6991
◆ Fiorano Software Inc — Lewes (G-5995)	D	650 326-1136
Fixcom Inc — Wilmington (G-16657)	G	916 534-8872
Flackon Inc — Newark (G-10749)	G	701 369-0789
Flagpole Corp — Lewes (G-6003)	G	302 261-5170
Flip App LLC — Dover (G-2516)	G	248 662-6875

73 BUSINESS SERVICES

Flipride Inc .... G 208 471-0007
  Dover *(G-2517)*
Flo Health Inc .... E 302 498-8369
  Wilmington *(G-16662)*
Flowpay Corporation .... G 720 425-3244
  Wilmington *(G-16670)*
FLUENTAAI INC .... G 323 739-5417
  Wilmington *(G-16673)*
Fnx Technologies Ltd .... G 844 969-0070
  Wilmington *(G-16678)*
Folderly Inc .... F 302 966-9083
  Dover *(G-2522)*
Fondeadora Inc .... G 925 413-3654
  Dover *(G-2524)*
Foreignerds Inc .... F 201 381-5152
  Newark *(G-10758)*
Fotomaster LLC .... G 646 233-3371
  Wilmington *(G-16700)*
Freckle Holdings LLC .... G 302 260-6385
  Dover *(G-2534)*
Friday Games Inc .... E 847 246-2189
  Newark *(G-10785)*
Frontierx Inc .... E 201 313-6998
  Dover *(G-2538)*
Ftl Technologies Corporation .... E 703 634-6910
  Lewes *(G-6019)*
Fuel Labs Inc .... G 302 364-0442
  Wilmington *(G-16767)*
Funfull Inc .... F 888 386-3855
  Delmar *(G-1597)*
Future Cmpus - Tech Innvtion L .... F 737 217-0321
  Lewes *(G-6024)*
Galaxyworks LLC .... F 404 894-8703
  Dover *(G-2555)*
Gamefort LLC .... E 302 645-7400
  Lewes *(G-6026)*
Gamers4gamers LLC .... G 302 722-6289
  Newark *(G-10804)*
Gamersunite Inc .... F 760 284-5588
  Middletown *(G-7150)*
Garri Inc .... G 319 538-4071
  Newark *(G-10811)*
Gastro Girl Inc .... G 202 579-1057
  Dover *(G-2563)*
Gatello Inc .... F 725 333-3830
  Newark *(G-10814)*
Gatesair Inc .... E 513 459-3400
  Wilmington *(G-16814)*
Gather Social Tech Corp .... G 604 356-0981
  Newark *(G-10815)*
Gbc Business Group LLC .... G 970 644-6319
  Wilmington *(G-16823)*
GBS Backup LLC .... G 302 907-9099
  Lewes *(G-6028)*
Gdk Services LLC .... E 929 242-8422
  Dover *(G-2565)*
Geeksoft Inc .... G 669 278-8022
  Dover *(G-2568)*
Generation Glory Ministries .... G 302 438-4335
  Wilmington *(G-16833)*
Genohm Inc .... G 646 616-7531
  Newark *(G-10820)*
Geospot Community LLC .... G 570 504-4115
  Newark *(G-10825)*
Gesso Labs Inc .... F 888 206-4024
  Wilmington *(G-16853)*
Getbit Technologies Inc .... G 425 647-3121
  Lewes *(G-6033)*
Getresponse Inc .... E 302 573-3895
  Wilmington *(G-16854)*
Giesela Inc .... G 855 556-4338
  Newark *(G-10833)*

Giftpass App Inc .... G 310 529-7566
  Dover *(G-2583)*
Gigkloud Inc .... F 301 375-5008
  Lewes *(G-6035)*
Girasol Payment Solutions LLC .... G 561 866-4343
  Wilmington *(G-16868)*
Gitduck Inc .... G 415 969-3825
  Claymont *(G-1162)*
Global Essentials Inc .... G 703 483-9544
  Wilmington *(G-16889)*
Global Telecom Group LLC .... G 302 295-2883
  Wilmington *(G-16895)*
Globaling Inc .... G 619 657-0070
  Dover *(G-2594)*
Gmdh Inc .... G 347 470-4634
  Lewes *(G-6040)*
Gmetri Inc .... F 704 260-6116
  Lewes *(G-6041)*
Golance Inc .... E 888 478-0358
  Dover *(G-2599)*
Golden Inc .... F 408 384-9136
  Lewes *(G-6046)*
Good Driver Mutuality Inc .... E 713 979-8257
  Dover *(G-2603)*
Goodsize Inc .... G 415 481-7330
  Wilmington *(G-16925)*
Gotit Inc .... F 408 382-1300
  Dover *(G-2608)*
Gourmetcarte Inc .... G 631 418-6170
  Middletown *(G-7171)*
Govsimplified LLC .... G 888 629-8008
  Claymont *(G-1169)*
Gr Dispatch Inc .... G 888 985-3440
  Lewes *(G-6050)*
Green Candy Solutions Inc .... E 302 599-7944
  Claymont *(G-1170)*
Greet 26 Inc .... G 310 601-2648
  Camden *(G-841)*
Greggii Inc .... F 647 606-3348
  Newark *(G-10896)*
Greynote LLC .... G 646 287-0705
  Dover *(G-2628)*
Grlla Gmng LLC .... G 302 291-2075
  Lewes *(G-6065)*
Groovvx Inc .... G 828 399-1549
  Wilmington *(G-16986)*
Growth Cave LLC .... E 323 688-5042
  Newark *(G-10904)*
Gw Solutions LLC .... G 240 578-5981
  Bethany Beach *(G-606)*
Haltia Inc .... E 302 244-7425
  Wilmington *(G-17042)*
Hank Technologies Inc .... G 812 223-5984
  Dover *(G-2650)*
Hasten Inc .... G 818 867-8151
  Dover *(G-2661)*
Hbm Apps Inc .... G 302 387-0052
  Middletown *(G-7198)*
Headtotoe Mhealth Inc .... G 438 867-1908
  Wilmington *(G-17091)*
Heal Room Inc .... G 770 597-3366
  Claymont *(G-1175)*
Healex Systems Ltd .... F 302 235-5750
  Wilmington *(G-17092)*
Healthylongevitycafe Inc .... G 408 599-6369
  Wilmington *(G-17101)*
Hedge Capital Markets Inc .... F 714 515-2645
  Dover *(G-2670)*
Helloguru Inc .... G 754 303-3278
  Claymont *(G-1178)*
Herdify LLC .... G 619 405-3952
  Middletown *(G-7206)*

Hidden Lake Games LLC .... G 302 305-1070
  Claymont *(G-1179)*
Hint America Inc .... F 646 845-1895
  Wilmington *(G-17153)*
Hirewise Inc .... G 888 899-4980
  Middletown *(G-7211)*
Hockey Labs Inc .... G 929 909-6607
  Dover *(G-2684)*
Home Innovations .... G 302 448-9555
  Lewes *(G-6097)*
Hoover Computer Services Inc .... G 302 529-7050
  Wilmington *(G-17195)*
Hopshop Inc .... G 323 745-1115
  Middletown *(G-7216)*
Howard Industries LLC .... G 217 836-4476
  Camden *(G-853)*
Hubgets Inc .... G 239 206-2995
  Wilmington *(G-17228)*
Hubioid Inc .... F 312 912-1515
  Wilmington *(G-17229)*
Hybridthory Digital Entrmt LLC .... G 864 973-5753
  Dover *(G-2709)*
Ibidd Holdings LLC .... G 800 960-9221
  Dover *(G-2716)*
Iconico LLC .... G 650 681-9211
  Claymont *(G-1183)*
Ideatree Inc .... F 310 844-7447
  Wilmington *(G-17264)*
iDreams Hub Inc .... G 740 990-2232
  Wilmington *(G-17266)*
Iexperto Inc .... G 347 808-3708
  Middletown *(G-7221)*
Il USA Corporation .... E 310 570-2928
  Wilmington *(G-17270)*
Ikarus Nest Inc .... F 415 727-2401
  Bear *(G-283)*
Ikkar Inc .... F 814 351-9394
  Newark *(G-11001)*
Imagic LLC .... G 628 600-5244
  Lewes *(G-6117)*
Impactful Technology LLC .... G 646 374-9004
  Wilmington *(G-17289)*
Implify Inc .... E 302 533-2345
  Newark *(G-11007)*
Inaccel LLC .... G 408 915-5548
  Wilmington *(G-17296)*
Incapp Inc .... G 318 880-7622
  Wilmington *(G-17299)*
Incite Solutions Inc .... G 302 655-8952
  Wilmington *(G-17300)*
Inclind Inc .... G 302 856-2802
  Lewes *(G-6120)*
Infinite Improbabilities Inc .... G 763 516-5825
  Wilmington *(G-17321)*
Inkit Inc .... F 612 712-1245
  Wilmington *(G-17342)*
Innoventic Inc .... G 302 476-2396
  Wilmington *(G-17349)*
Inova Business Solutions LLC .... G 251 316-0180
  Claymont *(G-1185)*
Insight Engineering Solutions .... G 302 378-4842
  Townsend *(G-14018)*
Insightzen LLC .... G 647 227-9325
  Lewes *(G-6128)*
Inspire African Safaris LLC .... F 302 250-5763
  Wilmington *(G-17356)*
Instasafe Inc .... G 408 400-3673
  Dover *(G-2741)*
Insurance Toolkits LLC .... G 302 272-5488
  Wilmington *(G-17364)*
Integrated Solutions Gate Inc .... G 302 404-6080
  Wilmington *(G-17371)*

Employee Codes: A=Over 500 employees, B=251-500
C=101-250, D=51-100, E=20-50, F=10-19, G=1-9

Interlace Global Inc .... G ..... 917 719-6811 　Wilmington *(G-17385)*	Knowt Inc .... F ..... 848 391-0575 　Lewes *(G-6170)*	Liveboard Inc .... G ..... 888 412-8882 　Middletown *(G-7310)*
Intermedia Analytics LLC .... F ..... 305 921-9647 　Dover *(G-2745)*	Kodo Digital Systems Inc .... G ..... 909 843-0946 　Dover *(G-2882)*	Livetrade Ltd .... G ..... 302 305-1797 　Lewes *(G-6214)*
Interpres Security Inc .... F ..... 570 971-9876 　Wilmington *(G-17397)*	Korsgy Technologies LLC .... G ..... 302 504-6201 　Wilmington *(G-17748)*	Lizard Soft Inc .... G ..... 619 618-0368 　Dover *(G-2960)*
Intouch Inc .... G ..... 332 223-0720 　Dover *(G-2749)*	Kortech Consulting Inc .... F ..... 302 559-4612 　Bear *(G-333)*	LLC Smart Bean .... G ..... 302 894-2323 　Dover *(G-2963)*
Inumsoft Inc .... G ..... 302 533-5403 　Bear *(G-287)*	Krayo Inc .... G ..... 415 851-6250 　Wilmington *(G-17753)*	Logicjunction Inc .... G ..... 216 292-5760 　Dover *(G-2971)*
Io Projects Inc .... G ..... 302 416-5776 　Wilmington *(G-17411)*	Kuest Inc .... G ..... 786 840-0842 　Middletown *(G-7284)*	Logique Inc .... G ..... 302 330-8866 　New Castle *(G-9323)*
Isolvrisk Inc .... G ..... 508 838-7708 　Smyrna *(G-13778)*	Kushim Inc .... G ..... 609 919-9889 　Wilmington *(G-17768)*	Lokalise Inc .... G ..... 302 498-9091 　Dover *(G-2973)*
Ispapp Inc .... F ..... 302 310-5009 　Dover *(G-2753)*	Labware .... G ..... 302 521-0250 　Newark *(G-11213)*	Lokblok Inc .... F ..... 408 640-8644 　Wilmington *(G-17979)*
Itango Inc .... G ..... 302 648-2646 　Wilmington *(G-17431)*	Labware Inc .... E ..... 302 658-8444 　Wilmington *(G-17785)*	Lookback App Co .... G ..... 508 735-1903 　Wilmington *(G-17990)*
Itexus LLC .... G ..... 917 618-9804 　Camden *(G-856)*	Labware Global Services Inc .... F ..... 302 658-8444 　Wilmington *(G-17786)*	Loom Network Inc .... F ..... 404 939-1294 　Wilmington *(G-17992)*
Itg Cloud Software LLC .... E ..... 786 708-6560 　Wilmington *(G-17433)*	Labware Holdings Inc .... E ..... 302 658-8444 　Wilmington *(G-17787)*	Lutinx Inc .... F ..... 718 502-6961 　Lewes *(G-6229)*
Iyper LLC .... E ..... 929 269-5699 　Wilmington *(G-17441)*	Laconic Innovations Co .... F ..... 302 501-6069 　Dover *(G-2896)*	Maad Africa Inc .... D ..... 847 927-0519 　Middletown *(G-7320)*
Jana Analysis Inc .... E ..... 724 584-0545 　Middletown *(G-7240)*	Lambdatest Inc .... D ..... 678 701-3618 　Wilmington *(G-17791)*	Macappstudio Inc .... G ..... 415 799-7415 　Newark *(G-11309)*
Jia Finance Inc .... G ..... 202 341-1031 　Wilmington *(G-17545)*	Lance Technologies LLC .... G ..... 404 934-4730 　Wilmington *(G-17796)*	Maestrik Inc .... E ..... 312 925-3116 　Newark *(G-11311)*
Jkings Mining Company LLC .... F ..... 628 600-9522 　Lewes *(G-6140)*	Landell Labs LLC .... G ..... 917 722-5166 　Middletown *(G-7288)*	Magic Bytes LLC .... F ..... 813 995-7343 　Lewes *(G-6236)*
Joincube Inc .... F ..... 214 532-9997 　Dover *(G-2800)*	Lattice Industries Inc .... G ..... 708 702-4664 　Wilmington *(G-17819)*	Magipop Inc .... G ..... 217 898-3115 　Wilmington *(G-18083)*
Joozoor Iptv LLC .... F ..... 302 635-4092 　Newark *(G-11125)*	Launcharm Inc .... G ..... 320 520-3818 　Middletown *(G-7290)*	Makave International Trdg LLC .... E ..... 302 288-0670 　Dover *(G-3001)*
◆ Joseph J Sheeran Inc .... E ..... 302 324-0200 　New Castle *(G-9266)*	Le Artist Lucratif N Amer LLC .... G ..... 438 223-3788 　Lewes *(G-6183)*	Malong LLC .... E ..... 516 336-9992 　Wilmington *(G-18096)*
Joyn Experiences Inc .... G ..... 214 437-8349 　Wilmington *(G-17595)*	Leadific Solutions LLC .... G ..... 866 265-0771 　Dover *(G-2920)*	Malwation Inc .... F ..... 302 208-9661 　Lewes *(G-6239)*
Julieth Ai Technologies Inc .... F ..... 512 680-1855 　Camden *(G-862)*	Leanscout Inc .... G ..... 628 236-9599 　Newark *(G-11237)*	Mara Labs Inc .... E ..... 650 564-4971 　Wilmington *(G-18117)*
Junction Expert Insights Corp .... G ..... 202 710-9258 　Dover *(G-2819)*	Learn Game LLC .... F ..... 484 841-9709 　Middletown *(G-7292)*	Marketforce Technologies Inc .... A ..... 339 674-0529 　Dover *(G-3020)*
Juni Holdings Inc .... F ..... 415 949-4860 　Wilmington *(G-17614)*	Legacy Labs Inc .... G ..... 302 550-9966 　Wilmington *(G-17858)*	Masstech Americas Inc .... D ..... 905 946-5700 　Dover *(G-3026)*
Kaebox LLC .... G ..... 919 777-3939 　Middletown *(G-7259)*	Legaledge Software .... G ..... 302 761-9304 　Wilmington *(G-17863)*	Master Kit Inc .... G ..... 650 743-5126 　Dover *(G-3027)*
Kagoal Technology LLC .... G ..... 617 818-0588 　Middletown *(G-7260)*	Legit Global Inc .... G ..... 661 444-9085 　Newark *(G-11243)*	Matchapro Inc .... G ..... 213 573-9882 　Hockessin *(G-5302)*
Kalanaai LLC .... G ..... 516 701-3977 　Wilmington *(G-17636)*	Legit Marketplace Intl LLC .... G ..... 929 273-0505 　Wilmington *(G-17868)*	Matium Inc .... G ..... 703 457-9997 　Dover *(G-3031)*
Kaleido Health Solutions Inc .... G ..... 843 303-9168 　Wilmington *(G-17637)*	Lemonface Technologies Corp .... G ..... 844 615-3666 　Lewes *(G-6189)*	Matrica Labs Inc .... F ..... 818 573-7394 　Wilmington *(G-18193)*
Kanu Inc .... G ..... 401 533-6112 　Wilmington *(G-17648)*	Letterhead Inc .... G ..... 305 988-0808 　Claymont *(G-1216)*	Meaningteam Inc .... F ..... 213 669-5804 　Dover *(G-3047)*
Kaplan Software Group .... G ..... 646 498-8275 　Lewes *(G-6160)*	Liblab Inc .... G ..... 302 415-3344 　Wilmington *(G-17897)*	Medici Ventures Inc .... E ..... 801 319-7029 　Wilmington *(G-18251)*
Katabat LLC .... E ..... 302 830-9262 　Wilmington *(G-17658)*	Liferithms Inc .... F ..... 770 885-6565 　Wilmington *(G-17903)*	Medshifts Inc .... G ..... 856 834-0074 　Wilmington *(G-18258)*
Katu Software Global LLC .... F ..... 302 803-5330 　Wilmington *(G-17667)*	Liftoff Agent Inc .... G ..... 925 462-5001 　Claymont *(G-1218)*	Medzoomer Inc .... G ..... 239 595-8899 　Middletown *(G-7337)*
Keble Inc .... G ..... 810 893-3352 　Wilmington *(G-17672)*	Lightrun Inc .... E ..... 646 453-6616 　Wilmington *(G-17909)*	Meetrecord Inc .... G ..... 281 407-7338 　Wilmington *(G-18259)*
Kenzz Inc .... E ..... 310 254-6927 　Middletown *(G-7267)*	Likehoop Inc .... G ..... 646 643-7738 　Dover *(G-2947)*	MEI App Inc .... G ..... 617 877-6603 　Newark *(G-11382)*
Keylent Inc .... D ..... 401 864-6498 　Wilmington *(G-17703)*	Lime Ccnut Data Intllgnce Lcdi .... G ..... 302 272-2858 　Dover *(G-2949)*	Melento Inc .... F ..... 571 989-1300 　Dover *(G-3057)*
Kgs Digital Inc .... G ..... 302 213-3979 　Dover *(G-2863)*	Linkers Inc .... F ..... 408 757-0021 　Dover *(G-2952)*	Mello Financial Inc .... G ..... 801 877-7787 　Wilmington *(G-18264)*
Kidberry Inc .... G ..... 857 559-3043 　Wilmington *(G-17713)*	Linkmeup Inc .... F ..... 302 440-3393 　Wilmington *(G-17930)*	Menehariya LLC .... F ..... 240 432-0082 　Dover *(G-3060)*
Knowcrunch Inc .... G ..... 210 300-7214 　Newark *(G-11198)*	Live Typing Inc .... G ..... 415 670-9601 　Wilmington *(G-17949)*	Mentor Consultants Inc .... G ..... 610 566-4004 　Wilmington *(G-18273)*

73 BUSINESS SERVICES

Mercurysend LLC .... G 917 267-8627
  Wilmington *(G-18278)*
Metamax Technology Inc .... F 302 587-0060
  Newark *(G-11393)*
Metanium Corp .... E 302 669-9084
  Dover *(G-3070)*
Metaquotes Software Corp .... E 657 859-6918
  Wilmington *(G-18289)*
Mh-Teq LLC .... G 302 897-2182
  Wilmington *(G-18301)*
Mican Technologies Inc .... C 302 703-0708
  Bear *(G-372)*
Microcom Tech LLC .... G 858 775-5559
  Rehoboth Beach *(G-12853)*
Microlog Corporation Maryland .... G 301 540-5501
  Rehoboth Beach *(G-12854)*
Micropets LLC .... E 925 341-2398
  Dover *(G-3083)*
Microtelecom Systems LLC .... D 718 707-0012
  Wilmington *(G-18331)*
Middleware Inc .... E 415 213-2625
  Wilmington *(G-18343)*
Mighty Acorn Digital Inc .... G 877 277-8805
  Wilmington *(G-18348)*
Mightyinvoice LLC .... G 302 415-3000
  Dover *(G-3089)*
Mindspaceweb LLC .... G 302 360-8744
  Claymont *(G-1238)*
Minimum Corporation .... F 857 928-0317
  Wilmington *(G-18372)*
Mintflint Inc .... G 236 991-3735
  Wilmington *(G-18381)*
Miops Inc .... G 302 451-9571
  Newark *(G-11427)*
Misaka Network Inc .... G 323 999-1409
  Dover *(G-3100)*
Mithril Cable Network Inc .... F 213 373-4381
  Claymont *(G-1240)*
Mjlinkcom Inc .... G 303 324-7668
  Lewes *(G-6281)*
Mnboost Corp .... G 302 645-7400
  Lewes *(G-6282)*
Mobeasy LLC .... G 628 251-1274
  Lewes *(G-6283)*
Mobility Route Inc .... G 302 273-0770
  Dover *(G-3111)*
Mobio Global Inc .... G 484 263-4845
  Dover *(G-3113)*
Mocha Technologies Inc .... F 408 556-9930
  Claymont *(G-1243)*
Moeco Iot Inc .... G 626 869-7140
  Wilmington *(G-18400)*
Mojio .... G 831 747-5141
  Wilmington *(G-18402)*
Monada Inc .... F 302 253-7382
  Wilmington *(G-18408)*
Monarch Nascent Inc .... F 310 601-4702
  Wilmington *(G-18409)*
Monetran LLC .... G 732 984-1983
  Hockessin *(G-5310)*
Money Factory LLC .... G 620 755-5215
  Dover *(G-3119)*
Monofor Inc .... G 415 800-4925
  Newark *(G-11444)*
Monster Gaming LLC .... F 251 281-8906
  Lewes *(G-6288)*
Moon Buyer Inc .... F 302 636-5401
  Wilmington *(G-18429)*
Moon Devices Inc .... G 650 206-8011
  Wilmington *(G-18430)*
Moonsworth LLC .... G 302 439-6039
  Wilmington *(G-18432)*

Morrow Limited .... D 213 631-3534
  Montchanin *(G-8739)*
Motameet LLC .... G 302 242-4483
  Lewes *(G-6293)*
Moving Sciences LLC .... G 617 871-9892
  Wilmington *(G-18467)*
Moxelle Inc .... G 646 226-9430
  Middletown *(G-7386)*
Mphasis Corporation .... F 212 686-6655
  Wilmington *(G-18471)*
Msd Business Solutions LLC .... G 609 375-8461
  Lewes *(G-6295)*
Msm Foods LLC .... G 302 524-4470
  Wilmington *(G-18476)*
Muni Tech LLC .... G 302 383-1487
  Wilmington *(G-18487)*
Must App Corp .... F 905 537-5522
  Wilmington *(G-18494)*
My Health Group Inc .... E 401 400-0015
  Dover *(G-3137)*
My Kase LLC .... E 647 686-7202
  Lewes *(G-6299)*
Mymedchoices Inc .... G 302 932-1920
  Hockessin *(G-5315)*
Nano Wallet Company LLC .... G 443 610-3402
  Wilmington *(G-18529)*
Narleyapps Inc .... G 323 744-1398
  Dover *(G-3150)*
National Home Rentals LP .... G 302 636-5401
  Wilmington *(G-18541)*
Native Grid LLC .... G 917 893-7544
  Dover *(G-3159)*
Navenu Inc .... G 416 543-9617
  Dover *(G-3162)*
Navigine Corporation .... G 339 234-0827
  Wilmington *(G-18563)*
Nayachi Inc .... G 302 400-0072
  Wilmington *(G-18566)*
Neodata LLC .... E 302 666-2848
  Dover *(G-3169)*
Neofithub Inc .... F 408 365-4156
  Wilmington *(G-18583)*
Neon USA LLC .... F 360 433-7512
  Dover *(G-3171)*
Net Journey LLC .... G 818 584-2519
  Dover *(G-3173)*
Netdata Inc .... E 650 407-3589
  Newark *(G-11507)*
Netfoundry Inc .... D 855 284-2007
  Wilmington *(G-18592)*
Neural Heaven Inc .... F 631 485-4205
  Middletown *(G-7396)*
Neuralight Inc .... F 203 615-1333
  Wilmington *(G-18602)*
Neuroscience Software Inc .... G 855 712-1818
  Dover *(G-3176)*
Neutec Corp .... G 302 697-6752
  Dover *(G-3177)*
New Concept Technologies LLC .... G 518 533-5367
  Wilmington *(G-18614)*
New Cstle Cnty Del Emplyees Fd .... F 302 395-5350
  New Castle *(G-9414)*
New Live Ventures Inc .... G 914 960-1877
  Lewes *(G-6311)*
Newtone Communications Inc .... G 650 727-0998
  Middletown *(G-7402)*
Nextera Robotic Systems Inc .... F 617 899-7323
  Middletown *(G-7404)*
Ngrow Inc .... F 603 764-7274
  Claymont *(G-1252)*
Niebex International Inc .... F 415 735-4718
  Wilmington *(G-18647)*

Ninety One Holding Inc .... E 212 203-7900
  Bethany Beach *(G-623)*
Ninjasalary Inc .... G 888 201-1107
  Claymont *(G-1253)*
Nitrility Inc .... F 848 702-6091
  Wilmington *(G-18651)*
Nixope Inc .... G 888 991-1606
  Wilmington *(G-18653)*
No Code Software Inc .... F 833 366-2633
  Lewes *(G-6317)*
Node Technologies Inc .... G 866 366-1862
  Middletown *(G-7408)*
Nole-Sec Inc .... F 561 693-9934
  Wilmington *(G-18663)*
Nomadic Capital LLC .... G 650 441-5796
  Wilmington *(G-18665)*
Nomod LLC .... G 917 480-7432
  Wilmington *(G-18666)*
Noramp Inc .... G 914 266-0153
  Newark *(G-11562)*
Nortal LLC .... G 425 233-0164
  Wilmington *(G-18675)*
Novo Financial Corp .... F 844 260-6800
  Dover *(G-3205)*
Nucural Inc .... G 408 625-7047
  Wilmington *(G-18712)*
Nueve Ceros LLC .... G 415 513-0332
  Wilmington *(G-18713)*
Nuix North America Inc .... G 302 584-7542
  Wilmington *(G-18714)*
Nurdsoft LLC .... G 332 203-2920
  Middletown *(G-7412)*
Nursecareai Inc .... F 717 439-0314
  Wilmington *(G-18718)*
Nuyka Inc .... E 707 400-5444
  Lewes *(G-6323)*
Nvcomputers Inc .... G 860 878-0525
  Wilmington *(G-18722)*
Oaks Lab Academy LLC .... G 509 481-5630
  Wilmington *(G-18728)*
Oasis Security Inc .... G 332 867-8141
  Wilmington *(G-18733)*
Objects Worldwide Inc .... G 703 623-7861
  Wilmington *(G-18737)*
Ociety LLC .... G 760 408-1992
  Lewes *(G-6331)*
Ollang Inc .... G 212 706-1883
  Wilmington *(G-18760)*
Omni Interactive Holding LLC .... G 779 612-8747
  Wilmington *(G-18767)*
Omninet International Inc .... E 208 246-5022
  Wilmington *(G-18769)*
Omnix Labs Inc .... G 917 640-4949
  Wilmington *(G-18771)*
One Codex Inc .... G 226 406-8524
  Wilmington *(G-18778)*
One Sententia Ltd .... G 646 284-0321
  Dover *(G-3228)*
One System Incorporated .... F 888 311-1110
  Wilmington *(G-18784)*
Onebill Inc .... G 619 292-8493
  Dover *(G-3229)*
Onebox Technologies Inc .... G 415 799-8830
  Wilmington *(G-18787)*
Onengine Corp .... G 949 872-0339
  Dover *(G-3230)*
Onnec USA Inc .... G 703 309-7338
  Middletown *(G-7416)*
Open Text Inc .... E 248 986-6927
  Wilmington *(G-18798)*
Openeducat Inc .... G 302 261-5133
  Claymont *(G-1258)*

73 BUSINESS SERVICES

Company	Code	Phone
Opinr Inc — Wilmington (G-18804)	D	646 207-3000
Orbixplay LLC — Dover (G-3239)	F	408 337-6490
Orderhive Inc — Newark (G-11599)	G	888 878-5538
Organic Intelligence LLC — Wilmington (G-18818)	G	949 423-3665
Orgnostic Inc — Newark (G-11600)	E	617 871-9987
Otc Trade LLC — Camden (G-883)	G	603 820-5820
Otherworld Co — Newark (G-11605)	G	424 335-5671
Out of Galaxy Inc — Wilmington (G-18837)	G	814 441-8058
Outburst Ai Limited — Wilmington (G-18838)	F	516 303-2097
Outland Art Inc — Dover (G-3249)	F	800 918-1587
Outmarch Inc — Dover (G-3250)	G	508 289-1233
Overscout Inc — Lewes (G-6342)	G	415 687-3005
Owlii Inc — Dover (G-3254)	G	626 695-6607
Oyster HR Americas Inc — Wilmington (G-18846)	C	912 219-2356
Oyster HR Inc — Wilmington (G-18847)	B	912 219-2356
Pantheon Technologies LLC — Dover (G-3265)	G	855 927-9387
Paper Street LLC — Newark (G-11622)	G	614 515-1259
Paradiso Solutions LLC — Wilmington (G-18885)	D	800 513-5902
Paralleldots Inc — Lewes (G-6349)	F	224 587-0022
Parchive Analytics Inc — Middletown (G-7426)	G	903 683-5878
Partytickets Inc — Wilmington (G-18901)	G	718 395-9590
Pathscale Inc — Wilmington (G-18904)	G	408 384-9948
Pattern Labs Tech Inc — Wilmington (G-18913)	G	516 340-3369
Payshiga Technologies Inc — Dover (G-3286)	E	214 447-0677
Peak Uptime Solutions LLC — Wilmington (G-18942)	G	856 243-5838
Pebble Stack LLC — Middletown (G-7437)	G	732 910-9701
People Tech Group Inc — New Castle (G-9469)	G	833 202-3555
Perficient Inc — Wilmington (G-18975)	G	302 690-2087
Perks Express Inc — Wilmington (G-18981)	G	855 924-7424
Perkwiz Inc — Hockessin (G-5341)	G	702 866-9122
Personas Inc — Wilmington (G-18990)	G	416 815-7000
Petcy Inc — Middletown (G-7443)	G	920 240-4312
Pfs Ltd — Dover (G-3310)	G	202 709-9755
Pick Winners Inc — Dover (G-3320)	F	516 206-0777
Pike Creek Computer Company — Wilmington (G-19039)	F	302 239-5113
Pintalk Inc — Newark (G-11694)	G	844 386-0178
Pixstar Inc — Wilmington (G-19059)	E	
Plane Software Inc — Middletown (G-7453)	E	857 693-9321
Play US Media LLC — Dover (G-3332)	G	302 924-5034
Playphone Inc — Dover (G-3334)	G	415 307-0246
Plugilo Inc — Newark (G-11701)	F	628 202-4444
Ply Fashion Inc — Wilmington (G-19084)	G	323 723-5337
Pmsa It Services LLC — Rehoboth Beach (G-12893)	G	301 806-5163
Poc Inc — Dover (G-3345)	F	415 853-4762
Polar Signals Inc — Claymont (G-1265)	G	765 679-9318
Polar Strategy Inc — Lewes (G-6381)	G	703 628-0001
Polaro Inc — Dover (G-3346)	F	415 240-0442
Poliquicks LLC — Wilmington (G-19105)	G	512 915-7919
Power Financial Wellness Inc — Wilmington (G-19137)	G	313 413-2345
Power On US Inc — Lewes (G-6384)	E	212 317-1010
Praktikaai Co — Wilmington (G-19144)	F	959 300-0719
Praval Technologies LLC — Wilmington (G-19147)	D	206 693-2443
Precisioncure LLC — Wilmington (G-19160)	G	302 622-9119
Premo Technologies Inc — Wilmington (G-19174)	G	951 514-6993
Prescience Corporation — Wilmington (G-19177)	E	208 599-3441
Prestige Labs Inc — Dover (G-3370)	G	917 698-3453
Prime Directive Inc — Newark (G-11743)	G	302 383-5607
Prime Security Corp — Middletown (G-7469)	G	803 281-0378
Prisma Holding Inc — Wilmington (G-19199)	E	903 480-4880
Problem Consulting Co — Newark (G-11757)	G	347 809-3402
Productive Co Inc — Claymont (G-1268)	G	415 304-6782
Professionals LLC — Wilmington (G-19217)	G	302 295-2330
Progressive Software Cmpt Inc — Wilmington (G-19221)	C	302 479-9700
Project Assistants Inc — Wilmington (G-19223)	E	302 477-9711
Protocol Labs Inc — Wilmington (G-19235)	C	302 703-7194
Proven Pass Inc — Middletown (G-7477)	F	888 404-2775
Prudent Technology & Svcs LLC — Dover (G-3387)	F	302 481-6399
Ps3g Inc — Wilmington (G-19241)	F	302 298-0270
Public Mint Inc — Dover (G-3393)	F	833 386-0182
Pullable Inc — Wilmington (G-19253)	F	302 574-6379
Pulse and Pixel Corp — Wilmington (G-19255)	F	845 366-1219
Pumas-Ai Inc — Dover (G-3395)	E	551 207-6084
Pumpkin Space Latte Co — Middletown (G-7480)	G	765 326-0517
Pumpkin Spice Latte Co — Middletown (G-7481)	G	765 326-0517
Purple Thinkers Inc — Newark (G-11775)	G	760 349-7603
Purple Wifi Inc — Dover (G-3398)	G	877 286-2631
Purplenow Inc — Dover (G-3399)	E	302 751-5226
Purse Money Technologies LLC — Dover (G-3400)	F	302 208-0184
Puzzle Investments LLC — Wilmington (G-19268)	F	774 516-6447
Pxe Group LLC — Dover (G-3401)	G	561 295-1451
Qcortex LLC — Dover (G-3403)	E	213 257-4004
Qodebotics LLC — Dover (G-3405)	G	617 312-7733
Qsr Group LLC — Wilmington (G-19278)	G	302 268-6909
Quadrotech Solutions Inc — Wilmington (G-19279)	C	302 660-0166
Quality Unit LLC — Wilmington (G-19285)	F	888 257-8754
Quantconnect Corporation — Lewes (G-6400)	F	917 327-0556
Quantum Leap Innovations Inc — Newark (G-11795)	F	302 894-8045
Quavo Inc — Wilmington (G-19291)	D	484 257-9846
Queskr Inc — Lewes (G-6401)	G	302 527-6007
Quest Global Digital Inc — Wilmington (G-19293)	B	650 267-1334
Quetext Software LLC — Wilmington (G-19294)	E	800 403-9067
Quiver Finance Inc — Wilmington (G-19298)	G	302 803-6006
Qwintry LLC — New Castle (G-9509)	G	844 794-6879
Raad360 LLC — Newark (G-11812)	F	855 722-3360
Raas Infotek LLC — Newark (G-11813)	E	302 894-3184
Rackdog LLC — Wilmington (G-19311)	G	224 803-4912
Radiant Technologies Inc — Newark (G-11818)	G	800 301-0980
Ragaman Services Inc — Wilmington (G-19316)	F	339 221-6757
Railbus Inc — Lewes (G-6406)	G	302 725-3185
Rainmaker Software Group LLC — Wilmington (G-19320)	G	800 616-6701
Ram Tech Systems Inc — Middletown (G-7500)	E	302 832-6600
Ravnur Inc — Wilmington (G-19340)	G	239 963-4404
Rayda Inc — Wilmington (G-19343)	G	302 261-5184
Rct Studio Inc — Wilmington (G-19354)	G	669 255-1562
Reach Apps Inc — Dover (G-3429)	G	707 812-0285
Reackt LLC — Newark (G-11833)	G	267 210-4743
Readmark Inc — Dover (G-3432)	G	650 450-9110
Real Messenger Inc — Wilmington (G-19368)	F	657 237-5918

SIC SECTION
73 BUSINESS SERVICES

Real Ones Inc .... G 408 857-0262
 Wilmington *(G-19369)*

Realassist Inc .... F 888 309-1114
 Dover *(G-3435)*

Rebatus Inc .... G 929 393-5529
 Lewes *(G-6412)*

Red Spark LP .... E 215 695-5002
 Claymont *(G-1275)*

Redcircle Technologies Inc .... F 844 404-2525
 Claymont *(G-1276)*

Redgate Tech Inc .... G 302 377-6563
 Wilmington *(G-19388)*

Refermate LLC .... G 951 892-8159
 Wilmington *(G-19395)*

Regal Technologies LLC .... G 321 695-4142
 Lewes *(G-6415)*

Rentdrop Inc .... G 302 250-2525
 Claymont *(G-1277)*

Rently Software LLC .... F 718 502-6575
 Newark *(G-11852)*

Reporting Solutions LLC .... G 857 284-3583
 Newark *(G-11859)*

Resistbot Inc .... G 408 599-2094
 Newark *(G-11865)*

Resulticks Solution Inc .... E 347 416-7673
 Wilmington *(G-19444)*

Retouch Salon LLC .... G 929 247-7095
 Lewes *(G-6420)*

Revoltion Freedom Platform LLC .... F 301 653-9207
 Lewes *(G-6421)*

Revolve Technologies LLC .... G 302 528-2647
 Townsend *(G-14060)*

Rfpmart LLC .... F 315 627-3333
 Wilmington *(G-19450)*

Rhyze Solutions LLC .... G 850 376-4201
 Wilmington *(G-19463)*

Riddle Inc .... G 724 901-1810
 Wilmington *(G-19478)*

Ridge It Solutions Inc .... G 302 455-8566
 Bear *(G-461)*

Riftwalker Game Studio Inc .... G 213 215-7165
 Dover *(G-3470)*

Ritchie Sawyer Corporation .... F 302 475-1971
 Wilmington *(G-19488)*

Riversedge Advisors LLC .... F 302 573-6864
 Wilmington *(G-19499)*

Rocaccion Inc .... G 617 902-8779
 Newark *(G-11902)*

Rocketchat Technologies Corp .... C 213 725-2428
 Wilmington *(G-19533)*

Rockey & Associates Inc .... G 800 338-7734
 Lewes *(G-6429)*

Rockoly Inc .... F 508 527-1939
 Dover *(G-3478)*

Romantic Ai Inc .... F 415 404-9188
 Claymont *(G-1283)*

Rooah LLC .... G 305 233-7557
 Dover *(G-3484)*

Rotobot Ai LLC .... G 978 305-5794
 Middletown *(G-7524)*

Roundrobin Corporation .... G 212 634-9193
 Dover *(G-3487)*

Roz Health LLC .... G 415 259-8992
 Newark *(G-11923)*

Rozdoum Inc .... G 315 707-7517
 Dover *(G-3489)*

Ruby Digital Agency Inc .... G 801 971-1681
 Wilmington *(G-19585)*

Rumz Inc .... G 571 733-0693
 Wilmington *(G-19591)*

Rwazi Inc .... F 800 597-5871
 Wilmington *(G-19598)*

Ryzenlink Technologies LLC .... G 786 536-0349
 Hockessin *(G-5376)*

Safeagain Inc .... G 929 276-2732
 Dover *(G-3503)*

Safeup US LLC .... G 480 526-5152
 Lewes *(G-6441)*

Sain Cosmos LLC .... F 936 244-7017
 Wilmington *(G-19633)*

Sales Documents Inc .... F 302 867-9957
 Wilmington *(G-19637)*

Sam8sara Inc .... F 347 605-0693
 Lewes *(G-6444)*

Satodesign LLC .... G 989 710-2029
 Wilmington *(G-19677)*

Satori Ci LLC .... G 302 526-0557
 Claymont *(G-1285)*

Savantis Group .... G 415 297-6926
 Wilmington *(G-19681)*

Savantis Solutions LLC .... B 732 906-3200
 Wilmington *(G-19682)*

Saverd LLC .... G 347 565-5586
 Wilmington *(G-19683)*

Scanpoint Inc .... G 603 429-0777
 Wilmington *(G-19696)*

Scanta Inc .... E 302 645-7400
 Lewes *(G-6450)*

Scorelogix LLC .... F 302 294-6532
 Newark *(G-11963)*

Screen Zone Enterprises LLC .... E 302 316-0705
 Dover *(G-3521)*

Scrubmoney Inc .... G 240 671-5379
 Wilmington *(G-19716)*

Seal Cybrscurity Solutions Inc .... G 302 636-5401
 Wilmington *(G-19720)*

Second Technologies Inc .... G 310 774-7518
 Dover *(G-3526)*

Securelayer7 LLC .... F 302 391-0803
 Middletown *(G-7548)*

Seecubic Inc .... E 267 400-1565
 Wilmington *(G-19736)*

Seemetrics Inc .... F 818 533-9806
 Wilmington *(G-19738)*

Sendchamp Inc .... G 510 423-3457
 Wilmington *(G-19750)*

Sendible Usa Inc .... G 646 569-9029
 Newark *(G-11975)*

Sendlink Inc .... G 650 505-5299
 Middletown *(G-7551)*

Senhasegura USA LLC .... G 469 620-7643
 Lewes *(G-6458)*

Sensedia LLC .... G 631 764-4544
 Wilmington *(G-19751)*

Sensiai Inc .... G 646 665-7668
 Middletown *(G-7552)*

Sensofusion Inc .... F 570 239-4912
 Milton *(G-8710)*

Servicevet Technologies LLC .... G 302 659-0343
 Smyrna *(G-13882)*

Sesimi LLC .... G 302 574-6280
 Wilmington *(G-19765)*

Sessions Technologies Inc .... G 302 202-0551
 Wilmington *(G-19766)*

Seven Tech LLC .... G 302 464-6488
 Middletown *(G-7556)*

◆ Severn Trent Inc .... F 302 427-5990
 Wilmington *(G-19771)*

Shammah LLC .... G 302 533-7359
 Newark *(G-11989)*

She Bash LLC .... G 302 204-6700
 Claymont *(G-1289)*

Shipthis Inc .... F 209 395-1293
 Newark *(G-11997)*

Shop Club USA Network Holding .... G 858 304-0044
 Wilmington *(G-19808)*

Shouldr LLC .... G 917 331-1384
 Lewes *(G-6467)*

Siditech LLC .... G 302 384-5088
 Wilmington *(G-19813)*

Signall Technologies Inc .... G 240 623-5800
 Dover *(G-3555)*

Signatureone Media LLC .... G 347 849-3740
 Dover *(G-3557)*

Signin Soft Inc .... F 315 966-6699
 Wilmington *(G-19823)*

Silly Monkey Studios LLC .... E 415 517-0830
 Wilmington *(G-19825)*

Simbiose Inc .... D 708 459-8068
 Newark *(G-12008)*

Simbull Sports Exchange Inc .... G 319 899-6223
 Lewes *(G-6472)*

Simplecode LLC .... G 302 703-7231
 Lewes *(G-6473)*

Simplelife Apps Inc .... G 954 591-8413
 Dover *(G-3562)*

Simpliigence Inc .... D 404 528-7646
 Dover *(G-3563)*

Simplylab Inc .... F 919 663-2800
 Dover *(G-3565)*

Sirqil LLC .... F 213 204-9333
 Dover *(G-3569)*

Sivil Technologies Inc .... G 214 893-9797
 Wilmington *(G-19845)*

Six Days Inc .... E 888 463-5898
 Wilmington *(G-19847)*

Sketches and Pixels LLC .... G 312 834-4402
 Newark *(G-12020)*

Skittle Inc .... F 855 575-4885
 Wilmington *(G-19855)*

Skoruz Holding Corporation .... G 510 766-2803
 Wilmington *(G-19856)*

Skygate Inc .... G 310 601-4201
 Newark *(G-12027)*

Sleepagotchi Inc .... F 617 852-7380
 Middletown *(G-7573)*

Sleepy Coach Inc .... G 310 372-5770
 Wilmington *(G-19863)*

SM Technomine Inc .... F 312 492-4386
 Wilmington *(G-19870)*

Smarketics Inc .... G 929 265-0177
 Middletown *(G-7576)*

Smart Invest Yam LLC .... G 302 721-5278
 Wilmington *(G-19878)*

Smart Professions Inc .... E 603 289-6263
 Dover *(G-3576)*

Smart Union Blockchain LLC .... F 919 872-5631
 Lewes *(G-6483)*

Smartprofyl LLC .... G 832 412-5803
 Middletown *(G-7578)*

Smjs Co .... G 415 326-4441
 Claymont *(G-1292)*

Snapify Corp .... F 646 814-6388
 Wilmington *(G-19899)*

Sniper Labs Inc .... F 925 321-0931
 Wilmington *(G-19900)*

Social Africa Inc .... E 763 670-3452
 Dover *(G-3583)*

Social Keyboard Inc .... F 650 519-8383
 Dover *(G-3585)*

Social Money Inc .... G 212 810-7540
 Lewes *(G-6486)*

Social Wonder Inc .... F 646 419-8009
 Wilmington *(G-19908)*

Socialpilot Technologies Inc .... G 415 450-6060
 Lewes *(G-6487)*

Employee Codes: A=Over 500 employees, B=251-500
C=101-250, D=51-100, E=20-50, F=10-19, G=1-9

2024 Harris Directory of
Delaware Businesses

73 BUSINESS SERVICES — SIC SECTION

Socradar Cyber Intelligence .... F 571 249-4598
  Middletown (G-7584)
Softlinn LLC .... G 718 926-2170
  Wilmington (G-19914)
Software Radio Systems USA Inc .... F 339 368-6321
  Newark (G-12051)
Software Services of De Inc .... E 302 654-3172
  Wilmington (G-19915)
Solo Global Inc .... G 302 307-1673
  Wilmington (G-19924)
Solon Labs Corp .... G 860 876-7766
  Newark (G-12053)
Sophistor Inc .... G 415 800-1028
  Claymont (G-1296)
Sortd Inc .... G 415 870-1075
  Newark (G-12056)
Soutron Global Inc .... F 760 519-3328
  Middletown (G-7592)
Space Soft Inc .... G 413 337-7223
  Claymont (G-1297)
Spare Cs Inc .... F 424 744-0155
  Lewes (G-6496)
Speed Auto Systems LLC .... E 888 446-7102
  Lewes (G-6499)
Speedrid Ltd .... D 213 550-5462
  Dover (G-3595)
Spire Innovations Inc .... D 646 583-1839
  Wilmington (G-19966)
Spiro Health Inc .... G 302 645-7400
  Lewes (G-6502)
▲ Springboard Inc .... G 302 607-2580
  Newark (G-12075)
Squadcast Studios Inc .... G 916 320-7761
  Wilmington (G-19985)
Stable App LLC .... G 310 767-7832
  Wilmington (G-20003)
Stackadapt US Inc .... C 647 385-7698
  Lewes (G-6505)
Stanga Games Inc .... G 415 549-6537
  Wilmington (G-20017)
Starkit Studio LLC .... G 302 467-2017
  Lewes (G-6506)
Stm Consulting Inc .... F 408 341-6900
  Claymont (G-1304)
Stones Soup Inc .... G 803 835-7123
  Newark (G-12102)
Stormx Inc .... F 425 998-8762
  Dover (G-3613)
Streameq Inc .... G 951 807-4938
  Lewes (G-6517)
Subcodevs Inc .... G 704 234-6780
  Wilmington (G-20110)
Subscript Inc .... G 302 470-8144
  Claymont (G-1307)
Sunlight Insur Holdings LLC .... D 952 808-6312
  Wilmington (G-20132)
Superops Inc .... G 510 330-2676
  Claymont (G-1308)
Superpower Entertainment LLC .... G 650 667-0266
  Wilmington (G-20147)
▼ Supply Chain Consultants Inc .... E 302 738-9215
  Wilmington (G-20149)
Surge Automated Inc .... G 800 457-9713
  Lewes (G-6526)
Surge Networks Inc .... G 206 432-5047
  Newark (G-12132)
Swipes Incorporated .... G 650 686-0223
  Lewes (G-6534)
Swordfish Security USA Inc .... F 302 327-8580
  Wilmington (G-20177)
Syft Analytics Inc .... F 862 308-0525
  Newark (G-12145)

Sygul Inc .... E 315 384-1848
  Newark (G-12146)
Symend US Inc .... E 855 579-6363
  Wilmington (G-20182)
SYNCOGAI CORP .... G 302 307-4500
  Dover (G-3634)
Syncologi LLC .... E 408 549-9559
  Lewes (G-6537)
Syncretic Software Inc .... F 302 762-2600
  Wilmington (G-20186)
Synnefa Inc .... G 302 565-4405
  Wilmington (G-20190)
Synup .... E 844 228-2852
  Wilmington (G-20193)
Systima Inc .... F 929 551-4849
  Wilmington (G-20195)
Tabletopia Corp .... F 305 548-8407
  Dover (G-3642)
Taiga Express LLC .... G 718 577-2028
  Wilmington (G-20208)
Talentmatch Inc .... G 508 825-6171
  Newark (G-12156)
Talents Digital Services Corp .... E 888 508-2503
  Dover (G-3647)
▲ Tangome Inc .... F 650 362-8086
  Dover (G-3649)
Tappit Technologies (us) Inc .... G 570 898-1399
  Wilmington (G-20221)
Task Analytics Inc .... G 631 388-3120
  Wilmington (G-20225)
Teachedison Inc .... G 973 902-8026
  Middletown (G-7624)
Tech Central LLC .... G 717 273-3301
  Wilmington (G-20246)
Tech Learn LLC .... G 305 600-0775
  Wilmington (G-20250)
Technlogy Expiration Group Inc .... G 202 222-0794
  New Castle (G-9622)
Tectanic LLC .... G 302 440-2788
  Lewes (G-6547)
Teerhub Inc .... G 281 223-3466
  Dover (G-3663)
Tej Studio LLC .... G 302 205-3224
  Wilmington (G-20263)
Tekgeminus Solutions Inc .... G 503 336-5259
  Middletown (G-7629)
Telivity Inc .... F 312 585-8485
  Wilmington (G-20269)
Telorca LLC .... G 315 693-8488
  Lewes (G-6549)
Tennr Inc .... G 650 288-8264
  Wilmington (G-20274)
Ternary Inc .... E 650 759-5277
  Claymont (G-1309)
Thinkhat Software Inc .... F 917 379-2638
  Wilmington (G-20301)
Thinksecurenet .... F 302 703-9717
  Lewes (G-6556)
Thirty Birds Inc .... G 351 910-5520
  Wilmington (G-20304)
Thrive Physical Therapy Inc .... F 302 834-8400
  Middletown (G-7642)
Ticket Sports and Entrmt Corp .... G 224 522-3517
  Newark (G-12195)
Tidy Technologies Inc .... G 888 788-2445
  Lewes (G-6559)
Tiers Inc .... G 302 298-3338
  Wilmington (G-20319)
Tilebox Inc .... G 206 741-0883
  Dover (G-3687)
Tis Group Inc .... F 929 322-8811
  Lewes (G-6562)

Tonic Health LLC .... F 510 386-2530
  Wilmington (G-20351)
Toptracker LLC .... B 415 230-0131
  Wilmington (G-20363)
Total Resistance LLC .... G 302 384-3077
  Wilmington (G-20372)
Total Wellness Innovations Inc .... G 404 543-9061
  Wilmington (G-20374)
Touchstone Systems Inc .... F 302 324-5322
  New Castle (G-9631)
Town of Middletown .... E 302 376-9950
  Middletown (G-7656)
Transactional Web Inc .... G 908 216-5054
  Wilmington (G-20395)
Translateai LLC .... E 213 675-6702
  Dover (G-3713)
Translucence Research Inc .... E 425 753-8886
  Middletown (G-7659)
Travelapp Inc .... G 617 580-7978
  Wilmington (G-20404)
Treinta Inc .... C 786 400-2430
  Middletown (G-7660)
Tretek LLC .... G 888 407-9737
  Wilmington (G-20409)
Triagons LLC .... G 619 761-0797
  Dover (G-3723)
Trialogics LLC .... F 302 313-9000
  Wilmington (G-20418)
Tribetech Solutions LLC .... G 302 597-7890
  Dover (G-3725)
Tribute Interactive Inc .... G 302 803-5432
  Wilmington (G-20419)
Trio Academy LLC .... G 646 330-9211
  Wilmington (G-20428)
Triprobotics Inc .... F 646 798-7137
  Claymont (G-1318)
Triumph Labs Inc .... G 561 886-7121
  Claymont (G-1319)
Truck Lagbe Inc .... E 860 810-8677
  Lewes (G-6581)
Twisty Systems LLC .... G 571 331-7093
  Lewes (G-6585)
Txthinking Inc .... G 646 820-1235
  Newark (G-12250)
Tychron Corporation .... F 844 892-4766
  Wilmington (G-20476)
U Good Enterprises LLC .... F 302 566-8038
  Newark (G-12253)
Ultimate Tournament Inc .... G 410 746-1637
  Wilmington (G-20498)
Ultra Fitness Inc .... G 310 890-9025
  Dover (G-3745)
Ultraworking Inc .... G 848 243-0008
  Newark (G-12262)
Unik Marketing Inc .... G 302 830-9935
  Wilmington (G-20512)
Unikie Inc .... F 408 839-1920
  Dover (G-3749)
Unisight Bit Inc .... E 888 294-6414
  Wilmington (G-20522)
Universal Algorithm Inc .... G 302 446-3562
  Dover (G-3752)
Universum Inc .... G 973 873-2636
  Dover (G-3755)
Uploop Technologies LP .... F 514 922-0399
  Newark (G-12285)
Upyo Inc .... G 737 444-8899
  Wilmington (G-20539)
US Telex Corporation .... G 302 652-2707
  Wilmington (G-20552)
Userway Inc .... D 415 510-9335
  Wilmington (G-20554)

73 BUSINESS SERVICES

Utopie Technologies Inc .... F 628 251-1312
  Lewes (G-6597)
Vakoms LLC .... G 206 474-4319
  Wilmington (G-20562)
Vanilla Innovations Inc .... G 305 815-7586
  Newark (G-12305)
Vedaham Inc .... F 302 250-4594
  Wilmington (G-20575)
Veendhq Inc .... G 470 300-9787
  Wilmington (G-20576)
Vel Micro Works Incorporated .... G 302 239-4661
  Hockessin (G-5417)
Vensoft Solutions Inc .... F 302 392-9000
  Wilmington (G-20580)
Venzee Inc .... G 855 650-4204
  Wilmington (G-20583)
Veraset LLC .... F 801 657-2009
  Wilmington (G-20584)
Verifiedly LLC .... G 240 708-9025
  Middletown (G-7686)
Verisign Inc .... E 571 325-7916
  New Castle (G-9669)
Versus Gaming Inc .... G 855 643-9945
  Wilmington (G-20596)
Vertrius Corp .... F 800 770-1913
  Lewes (G-6600)
Veryutils Inc .... G 858 939-9928
  Newark (G-12319)
Veteran It Pro LLC .... F 302 824-3111
  Hockessin (G-5418)
Vianair Inc .... G 646 403-4705
  Wilmington (G-20606)
Viaprogram Technology Inc .... G 917 292-5433
  Milton (G-8725)
Vidalytics .... F 303 500-5715
  Milton (G-8726)
Viinex Inc .... G 510 443-5114
  Lewes (G-6605)
Vira Games Inc .... G 302 468-7152
  Wilmington (G-20629)
Virtual Oplossing Pvt Ltd .... G 866 268-0333
  Newark (G-12329)
Viziochron Inc .... G 206 745-0356
  Wilmington (G-20646)
Voiceloft Inc .... F 678 882-5024
  Middletown (G-7692)
Voicemix Inc .... G 305 981-0518
  Middletown (G-7693)
Volvant Inc .... G 805 456-6464
  Wilmington (G-20650)
Vortex Labs LLC .... G 302 231-1294
  Wilmington (G-20651)
Vybn Inc .... G 415 715-7945
  Wilmington (G-20661)
W23 S12 Holdings LLC .... G 610 348-3825
  Wilmington (G-20664)
Wagefi Inc .... G 646 853-0165
  Middletown (G-7702)
Wajba Corp .... G 650 307-0070
  Middletown (G-7703)
Wave LLC .... G 212 849-2217
  Wilmington (G-20688)
Waveone Inc .... G 650 796-8637
  Wilmington (G-20690)
Wayfarer Solutions Inc .... F 808 228-9989
  Wilmington (G-20692)
We Are Friends Inc .... G 302 501-7521
  Middletown (G-7709)
We Are Future Tech Inc .... E 832 224-5528
  Middletown (G-7710)
We Cobble LLC .... F 302 504-4294
  Wilmington (G-20699)

Wearexalt LLC .... F 203 913-5286
  Middletown (G-7711)
Webbrowser Media Inc .... G 302 830-3664
  Wilmington (G-20705)
Webill Inc .... F 628 227-7780
  Middletown (G-7712)
Websays Inc .... G 424 385-9361
  Middletown (G-7713)
Webstudy Inc .... G 888 326-4058
  Harbeson (G-4718)
Webtime Corporation .... G 302 476-2350
  Wilmington (G-20706)
Webtrit Inc .... G 954 364-8888
  Lewes (G-6619)
Webwork Time Tracker Inc .... E 415 707-3544
  Wilmington (G-20707)
WEKEEP TRAVEL SERVICES LLC .... G 786 814-0722
  Lewes (G-6620)
Welcome2city Group Corp .... F 347 897-9941
  Wilmington (G-20718)
Wellford Corporation .... G 302 288-0670
  Dover (G-3830)
Weltron Technology Ltd Co .... G 508 353-6752
  Lewes (G-6623)
Weplay Esports Media Inc .... G 818 274-2959
  Wilmington (G-20732)
Wgames Incorporated .... G 206 618-3699
  Wilmington (G-20751)
Wifiesta Inc .... F 206 923-9206
  Lewes (G-6629)
Wink Tech Limited .... G 302 268-9232
  Wilmington (G-20859)
Witt Butch Inc .... G 706 883-0539
  Lewes (G-6635)
Wixfi Inc .... G 415 504-2607
  Lewes (G-6636)
Wna Infotech LLC .... E 302 668-5977
  Wilmington (G-12392)
Wodaqota Inc .... G 800 246-2677
  Wilmington (G-20873)
Wonderlust LLC .... G 662 312-8390
  Lewes (G-6639)
Workativ Sftwr Solutions LLC .... F 312 375-1062
  Newark (G-12404)
Workforce Cloud Tech Inc .... G 915 800-2362
  Newark (G-12405)
Workwall Inc .... F 415 800-2809
  Newark (G-12407)
Workweek Inc .... G 423 708-4565
  Dover (G-3872)
World Web Technology Pvt Ltd .... E 646 755-9276
  Dover (G-3875)
Wormhole Soft LLC .... G 302 424-4374
  Rehoboth Beach (G-13022)
Wutopia Group US Ltd .... F 302 488-0248
  Dover (G-3877)
X Seamless Inc .... G 650 770-0771
  Wilmington (G-20910)
X5 Networks Corporation .... G 800 784-5228
  Wilmington (G-20912)
Xerafy Inc .... G 817 938-4197
  Wilmington (G-20918)
Xi Global LLC .... F 332 456-6969
  Middletown (G-7739)
Yclas Inc .... G 929 377-1239
  Newark (G-12418)
Yenaffit Inc .... G 302 650-4818
  Wilmington (G-20926)
Yenasys LLC .... G 302 956-9277
  Middletown (G-7744)
Yes Hardsoft Solutions Inc .... D 609 632-0397
  Wilmington (G-20927)

Yevma Inc .... G 888 338-2221
  Dover (G-3886)
Young Music LLC .... G 302 307-1997
  Smyrna (G-13941)
Youshop Inc .... G 302 526-0521
  Dover (G-3894)
Z Data Inc .... G 800 676-5614
  Newark (G-12426)
Z Data Inc .... G 800 676-5614
  Newark (G-12427)
Zamolxis LLC .... F 571 286-0413
  Wilmington (G-20946)
Zarla Inc .... G 833 469-2752
  Claymont (G-1344)
Zelcore Technologies Inc .... G 408 829-6352
  Dover (G-3897)
Zenbanx Holding Ltd .... G 310 749-3101
  Claymont (G-1345)
Zencity Technologies US Inc .... G 347 632-1225
  Wilmington (G-20952)
Zenkoders LLC .... G 302 261-2627
  Claymont (G-1346)
Zenpli LLC .... F 302 314-5231
  Newark (G-12432)
Zeon Enterprises Inc .... F 302 898-7167
  New Castle (G-9698)
Zeroant Inc .... G 567 342-1530
  Middletown (G-7750)
Zilla Finance Inc .... E 213 645-2133
  Wilmington (G-20962)
Zonguru Holdings Inc .... E 310 266-1427
  Wilmington (G-20963)
Zowie Inc .... D 725 201-0590
  Dover (G-3907)

7372 Prepackaged software

4gurus LLC .... G 571 789-0012
  Lewes (G-5640)
8figures Inc .... G 484 291-8881
  Wilmington (G-14152)
A Successful Woman .... G 234 567-8910
  Rehoboth Beach (G-12592)
Accendustry LLC .... G 469 777-6186
  Lewes (G-5650)
Accessquint LLC .... F 302 351-4064
  Wilmington (G-14223)
Accurate Media LLC .... G 301 943-9428
  Lewes (G-5653)
Acmegrc Limited .... G 401 626-7684
  Wilmington (G-14235)
Acorn Energy Inc .... G 410 654-3315
  Wilmington (G-14237)
Acumen Health Technologies LLC .... F 800 941-0356
  Wilmington (G-14248)
AEG International LLC .... G 302 750-6411
  Laurel (G-5461)
Aegis-CC LLC .... G 814 661-5844
  Dover (G-1727)
AEj Ltd Liability Company .... G 847 274-1084
  Dover (G-1728)
Aerona Solutions Inc .... G 302 601-4332
  Lewes (G-5663)
Afinclic Financial Tech Inc .... G 646 946-1687
  Wilmington (G-14309)
Agave Tech Inc .... G 805 394-3112
  Claymont (G-1026)
Ailink Technology Corporation .... G 858 568-2137
  Dover (G-1753)
All Lives Matter LLC .... G 252 767-9291
  Dover (G-1763)
Altr Solutions LLC .... F 888 757-2587
  Dover (G-1777)

73 BUSINESS SERVICES

Company		Phone
Amadex LLC	G	302 722-6027
Newark (G-9839)		
Analyttica Datalab Inc	E	917 300-3325
Wilmington (G-14467)		
Anamo Inc	G	702 852-2992
Dover (G-1790)		
Annabella Technologies Inc	F	833 716-1909
Lewes (G-5693)		
Anutio Inc	F	647 607-8378
Wilmington (G-14496)		
Appcano LLC	G	951 285-3632
Wilmington (G-14509)		
Appgenius Labs LLC	F	412 953-5064
Middletown (G-6868)		
Apploye Inc	G	925 452-6102
Newark (G-9893)		
Appmotion Inc	G	347 513-6333
Wilmington (G-14513)		
Apps By Cs LLC	G	866 235-9752
Dover (G-1809)		
Ardexo Inc	G	855 617-7500
Dover (G-1811)		
Assetbook	F	301 387-3238
Bear (G-51)		
Aurelium Inc	E	415 636-6892
Lewes (G-5719)		
Baabao Inc	G	415 990-6767
Wilmington (G-14708)		
Babble Platforms Inc	G	416 825-0502
Wilmington (G-14709)		
Backupta Inc	G	828 337-8957
Newark (G-9972)		
Basemark Inc	G	832 483-7093
Dover (G-1879)		
Batescainelli LLC	G	202 618-2040
Rehoboth Beach (G-12624)		
Bayesian Health Inc	G	408 205-8035
Wilmington (G-14788)		
Beez Drivers Inc	G	917 392-9111
Dover (G-1903)		
Benga Inc	F	617 579-8636
Claymont (G-1058)		
Better Search Corporation	G	415 610-4825
Wilmington (G-14863)		
Big Sofa Technologies Inc	G	630 839-9332
Dover (G-1936)		
Bigthinx Inc	G	401 300-0494
Middletown (G-6919)		
Bijoti Inc	F	908 916-7764
Wilmington (G-14891)		
Black Feather Entrmt LLC	G	248 787-8060
Wilmington (G-14901)		
Blaze Systems Corporation	G	302 733-7235
Newark (G-10050)		
Blue Ridge Consultants LLC	G	248 345-2294
Dover (G-1953)		
Bluevault LLC	E	302 425-4367
Wilmington (G-14983)		
Bond App LLC	G	415 418-4017
Wilmington (G-14998)		
Boundless Enterprises Inc	G	628 201-9286
Wilmington (G-15015)		
Breakout Trading Group LLC	G	302 365-0947
Wilmington (G-15097)		
Bridgesoft Infosec LLC	F	270 799-4779
Wilmington (G-15107)		
Brightminds Social Inc	F	424 333-8879
Wilmington (G-15114)		
Bullioncom LLC	G	833 629-3927
Wilmington (G-15149)		
Butter Games LLC	G	650 867-2492
Newark (G-10109)		
C & A Management Inc	G	302 888-2786
Wilmington (G-15168)		
Cansurround Pbc	G	302 540-2270
Wilmington (G-15219)		
Caytu Inc	G	202 670-9288
Middletown (G-6965)		
Cegis Cyber Inc	G	800 809-2599
Wilmington (G-15296)		
Certinal Inc	G	609 799-5664
Wilmington (G-15318)		
Chart Exchange	G	850 376-6435
Claymont (G-1084)		
Charter Dynamics LLC	G	888 260-4579
Wilmington (G-15344)		
Chirofusion LLC	G	877 210-3230
Wilmington (G-15387)		
Claimmybadge LLC	G	347 236-8109
Dover (G-2086)		
Clairvyant Technosolutions Inc	F	302 999-7172
Wilmington (G-15460)		
Clerk Chat Inc	G	415 943-6084
Lewes (G-5827)		
Clover View Inc	G	561 779-2423
Newark (G-10264)		
Clovyr Co	G	302 636-5401
Wilmington (G-15497)		
Cmplify LLC	G	248 716-5136
Wilmington (G-15501)		
Code Vanguard LLC	G	302 463-8265
Selbyville (G-13505)		
Code-Masters LLC	G	408 508-9955
Newark (G-10269)		
Color Guru LLC	G	267 972-4447
Wilmington (G-15538)		
Confabulous Inc	G	917 727-5919
Dover (G-2130)		
Conferatu Inc	G	415 599-6407
Dover (G-2131)		
Conformit Corp	G	302 451-9167
Newark (G-10303)		
Connected Inc	G	858 833-8768
Dover (G-2132)		
Core Purchase LLC	G	616 328-5715
Wilmington (G-15639)		
Cosine Solutions LLC	E	267 398-8995
Lewes (G-5861)		
Counseling Insight LLC	G	805 341-9020
Newark (G-10333)		
Counterpoint Software Inc	G	302 426-6500
Wilmington (G-15655)		
Crawlr Innovations Inc	G	912 515-9087
Dover (G-2153)		
Cropsoft Solutions LLC	E	201 284-1535
Wilmington (G-15710)		
Crossrate Technologies LLC	G	323 643-5178
Dover (G-2160)		
Cryptomarket Inc	G	860 222-0318
Wilmington (G-15719)		
CT Corporation System	G	302 658-4968
Wilmington (G-15727)		
Cybele Software Inc	E	302 892-9625
Wilmington (G-15750)		
Cyber 20/20 Inc	F	203 802-8742
Newark (G-10370)		
Cyberlete Inc	G	440 983-8647
Middletown (G-7024)		
Cyph Inc	G	931 297-4462
Claymont (G-1106)		
Damon Baca	G	858 837-0800
Dover (G-2188)		
Datasea Inc	C	267 752-9029
Dover (G-2197)		
Datatech Enterprises Inc	F	540 370-0010
Selbyville (G-13515)		
Dbaza Inc	G	302 467-3081
Dover (G-2202)		
Demo Easel LLC	G	408 242-2770
Middletown (G-7053)		
Derby Software LLC	F	502 435-1371
Dover (G-2284)		
Digitalxc Inc	F	650 319-7249
Wilmington (G-16070)		
Directrestore LLC	E	650 276-0384
Dover (G-2300)		
Discidium Technology Inc	G	347 220-5979
Newark (G-10538)		
Divvz Inc	G	571 238-1722
Lewes (G-5923)		
Do Nothing Corp	G	216 780-1910
Newark (G-10543)		
Dodd Health Innovation LLC	G	410 598-7266
Ocean View (G-12506)		
Dokan Inc	G	386 259-8587
Dover (G-2319)		
Donr LLC	G	857 400-8679
Wilmington (G-16142)		
DOT and Line Inc	E	650 391-4837
Wilmington (G-16152)		
Dream Weaver LLC	G	302 352-9473
Wilmington (G-16177)		
Drop Fake Inc	G	707 563-1529
Dover (G-2386)		
Dux Technologies Inc	G	507 312-9687
Wilmington (G-16223)		
Dxc Technology Company	G	302 391-2762
Newark (G-10581)		
E2lingo Inc	G	800 345-2677
Lewes (G-5942)		
Eagan US Holdco LLC	A	414 339-8275
Wilmington (G-16245)		
Easy Analytic Software Inc	G	302 762-4271
Wilmington (G-16267)		
Echofin Inc	G	844 700-6060
Newark (G-10604)		
Eclipse Software Inc	G	212 727-1136
Wilmington (G-16280)		
Edaura Inc	G	707 330-9836
Wilmington (G-16285)		
Edify Inc	G	302 520-2403
Wilmington (G-16292)		
Edtech Consulting LLC	G	661 644-2990
Wilmington (G-16297)		
Educup Inc	G	305 504-1073
Middletown (G-7084)		
Eitv USA Inc	G	305 517-7715
Wilmington (G-16346)		
Elenore Inc	G	720 702-9390
Dover (G-2432)		
Emma Systems Inc	G	407 773-8536
Wilmington (G-16396)		
Enclave Digital Development Co	G	203 807-0400
Lewes (G-5961)		
Endless Os Foundation LLC	G	415 413-4159
Wilmington (G-16410)		
Entrilia Inc	F	954 372-1715
Wilmington (G-16442)		
Equine Technologies Inc	G	669 306-6009
Middletown (G-7107)		
Estarei LLC	F	508 494-7260
Dover (G-2464)		
Eurosoft Tech Inc	G	737 263-0307
Wilmington (G-16477)		
Everstage Inc	G	518 882-3489
Wilmington (G-16489)		

73 BUSINESS SERVICES

Famoid Technology LLC..................G..... 530 601-7284
Newark *(G-10710)*

Fetch Social Inc..................G..... 813 858-5774
Wilmington *(G-16591)*

◆ **Fiorano Software Inc**..................D..... 650 326-1136
Lewes *(G-5995)*

First Halthcare Compliance LLC..................F..... 302 416-4329
Wilmington *(G-16618)*

Flowpay Corporation..................G..... 720 425-3244
Wilmington *(G-16670)*

Foodstr Inc..................G..... 707 500-0599
Wilmington *(G-16683)*

Formclick LLC..................G..... 302 212-0311
Wilmington *(G-16695)*

Freshbooks Usa Inc..................G..... 416 525-5384
Wilmington *(G-16750)*

Ftl Technologies Corporation..................E..... 703 634-6910
Lewes *(G-6019)*

Fun Bakery LLC..................G..... 858 220-0946
Dover *(G-2544)*

Fuzebits Inc..................G..... 302 533-8623
Wilmington *(G-16780)*

Fyve By Corp..................G..... 770 862-9152
Dover *(G-2550)*

Game Genius Innovations LLC..................F..... 321 588-7798
Wilmington *(G-16798)*

Game Labs Inc..................E..... 385 444-5639
Wilmington *(G-16799)*

Garde-Robe Inc..................G..... 347 986-0455
Dover *(G-2557)*

Gastromind Inc..................G..... 302 252-8401
Wilmington *(G-16811)*

Germ Network Inc..................G..... 773 965-7004
Wilmington *(G-16851)*

Get Takeout LLC..................G..... 800 785-6218
Lewes *(G-6032)*

Gevme Inc..................G..... 302 335-7150
Dover *(G-2577)*

Giesela Inc..................G..... 855 556-4338
Newark *(G-10833)*

Gleam Mdrn Parenting Solutions..................G..... 302 416-6460
Wilmington *(G-16883)*

Global Computers Networks LLC..................G..... 484 686-8374
Middletown *(G-7163)*

Global Gaming Business..................G..... 302 994-3898
Wilmington *(G-16890)*

Golden Inc..................F..... 408 384-9136
Lewes *(G-6046)*

Golden Recursion Inc..................F..... 415 779-4053
Claymont *(G-1167)*

Golden Star Enterprises Ltd..................G..... 888 680-8033
Claymont *(G-1168)*

Golden TV Inc..................G..... 213 260-0070
Lewes *(G-6047)*

Govwell Technologies Inc..................G..... 920 360-4496
Dover *(G-2613)*

Grassrots Data Innovations Inc..................G..... 267 664-9905
Lewes *(G-6052)*

Gratz LLC..................G..... 719 581-9645
Dover *(G-2620)*

Great Thing Inc..................G..... 302 314-3909
Middletown *(G-7175)*

Grnmeta Inc..................G..... 425 362-3228
Dover *(G-2629)*

Guard Prostamp Inc..................G..... 626 290-3357
Newark *(G-10905)*

Halley LLC..................G..... 650 628-8501
Lewes *(G-6071)*

Halligan Inc..................G..... 314 488-9400
Lewes *(G-6072)*

Happyrobot Inc..................G..... 972 837-9213
Dover *(G-2651)*

Hawksbill Systems LLC..................G..... 302 494-1678
Wilmington *(G-17080)*

Helical Software Corp..................G..... 323 544-5348
Lewes *(G-6087)*

Hells Kitchen Software Ltd..................G..... 302 983-5644
Newark *(G-10946)*

HI Neo Inc..................G..... 917 514-9010
Camden *(G-849)*

Hivemq Inc..................G..... 888 803-3966
Middletown *(G-7212)*

Hoard Incorporated..................F..... 980 333-1703
Wilmington *(G-17159)*

Hopin US Inc..................E..... 250 896-8450
Wilmington *(G-17202)*

Hostigger Inc..................G..... 650 618-9818
Newark *(G-10974)*

Hourly Inc..................C..... 844 800-2211
Dover *(G-2696)*

Houseventure Inc..................G..... 786 481-7390
Wilmington *(G-17217)*

Hullo Inc..................G..... 415 939-6534
Dover *(G-2704)*

Humandata Inc..................G..... 302 698-1287
Dover *(G-2705)*

Idf Connect Inc..................G..... 888 765-1611
Wilmington *(G-17265)*

Iexperienceilearn LLC..................G..... 718 704-4870
Historic New Castle *(G-5007)*

IH Technologies (iht) LLC..................G..... 718 679-2613
Wilmington *(G-17268)*

Ihandy LLC..................F..... 708 239-1234
Wilmington *(G-17269)*

Impact Care Inc..................F..... 610 628-2004
Wilmington *(G-17285)*

Incountry Inc..................G..... 415 323-0322
Wilmington *(G-17304)*

▲ **Infobase Holdings Inc**..................E..... 212 967-8800
Wilmington *(G-17329)*

Innova Bus Applications Inc..................G..... 405 845-6871
Dover *(G-2736)*

Inputsoft Inc..................G..... 312 358-4509
Lewes *(G-6126)*

Inspectware..................G..... 302 999-9601
Wilmington *(G-17355)*

Instaworks Inc..................G..... 925 389-9799
Newark *(G-11027)*

Isaac Fair Corporation..................G..... 302 324-8015
New Castle *(G-9243)*

Island Boy Enterprise LLC..................G..... 904 347-4563
Bethany Beach *(G-610)*

Itango Inc..................G..... 302 648-2646
Wilmington *(G-17431)*

Jacks Life Management Inc..................G..... 347 757-0720
Dover *(G-2762)*

Jhana Inc..................G..... 530 863-7269
Dover *(G-2788)*

Judie Ai Inc..................F..... 407 401-4421
Wilmington *(G-17608)*

Juega LLC..................G..... 716 256-3186
Dover *(G-2815)*

Kanga Rew Software..................G..... 302 335-3546
Magnolia *(G-6756)*

Kanu Inc..................G..... 401 533-6112
Wilmington *(G-17648)*

Kidya Prschool Lrng Gmes For T..................F..... 302 483-7778
Wilmington *(G-17717)*

Kiefa Inc..................G..... 845 803-5924
Dover *(G-2869)*

Kissflow Inc..................C..... 650 396-7692
Wilmington *(G-17735)*

Klip-It LLC..................G..... 888 202-0533
Middletown *(G-7280)*

Knowt Inc..................F..... 848 391-0575
Lewes *(G-6170)*

Koheric LLC..................G..... 646 801-6741
Dover *(G-2883)*

Kortex Enterprises LLC..................F..... 678 551-8260
Dover *(G-2884)*

Kurb Systems Inc..................G..... 732 490-1741
Wilmington *(G-17765)*

Kurrensy Inc..................G..... 347 228-9306
Dover *(G-2889)*

Kutbu LLC..................G..... 848 225-8848
Middletown *(G-7285)*

Kyber Corp..................F..... 609 203-1413
Wilmington *(G-17772)*

Labware Inc..................E..... 302 658-8444
Wilmington *(G-17784)*

Labware Global Services Inc..................F..... 302 658-8444
Wilmington *(G-17786)*

Labware Holdings Inc..................E..... 302 658-8444
Wilmington *(G-17787)*

Lattice Social LLC..................G..... 916 580-9951
Wilmington *(G-17820)*

Laurel Bridge Software Inc..................G..... 302 453-0222
Newark *(G-11227)*

Legends of Venari Inc..................G..... 226 338-6622
Claymont *(G-1214)*

Liberty Universal Tech Inc..................G..... 404 719-4728
Wilmington *(G-17896)*

Lifesquared Inc..................G..... 415 475-9090
Dover *(G-2942)*

Lityx LLC..................G..... 888 548-9947
Wilmington *(G-17948)*

Liv180 Inc..................G..... 561 235-9669
Dover *(G-2958)*

Living Pixels Studio LLC..................G..... 650 464-6899
Camden *(G-868)*

Loadbalancerorginc..................G..... 888 867-9504
Wilmington *(G-17966)*

Localspin LLC..................G..... 917 232-7203
Wilmington *(G-17971)*

Lundgren Chaizhunussov Ltd LLC..................G..... 508 828-0058
Wilmington *(G-18028)*

Marble City Software Inc..................G..... 302 658-2583
Wilmington *(G-18118)*

Market Black LLC..................G..... 267 257-3017
New Castle *(G-9347)*

Matter Music Inc..................F..... 650 793-7749
Wilmington *(G-18194)*

Max Value Software LLC..................F..... 630 254-8804
Wilmington *(G-18204)*

Medblob Inc..................G..... 813 308-9273
Dover *(G-3050)*

Meme US Holdings LLC..................G..... 619 342-4340
Dover *(G-3058)*

Merix LLC..................G..... 425 659-1425
Lewes *(G-6265)*

Metanode Inc..................G..... 302 782-9758
Dover *(G-3071)*

Metawork Corporation..................G..... 347 756-1222
Wilmington *(G-18290)*

Mh Software Inc..................G..... 919 306-0163
Dover *(G-3077)*

Microtelecom Systems LLC..................D..... 718 707-0012
Wilmington *(G-18331)*

Miles1 Inc..................G..... 267 506-0004
Wilmington *(G-18354)*

Mimix Company..................G..... 305 916-8602
Dover *(G-3096)*

Mizzen Education Inc..................G..... 213 262-6196
Wilmington *(G-18389)*

Mokka LLC..................G..... 646 388-2449
Wilmington *(G-18403)*

73 BUSINESS SERVICES — SIC SECTION

Company	Code	Phone
Monster Incorporation Inc, Middletown (G-7378)	G	920 349-7947
More Than Shy Inc, Wilmington (G-18442)	G	603 918-1612
Motiverse Labs Inc, Camden (G-878)	G	206 391-7995
Motorfyx Inc, Wilmington (G-18465)	G	858 500-6677
Moving Sciences LLC, Wilmington (G-18467)	G	617 871-9892
Mresource LLC, Wilmington (G-18472)	G	312 608-4789
Mushu Inc, Wilmington (G-18492)	G	650 862-8863
Musick LLC, Middletown (G-7390)	G	201 962-0023
Mwidm Inc, Wilmington (G-18501)	E	302 298-0101
My Live Life World Corp, Wilmington (G-18507)	G	347 560-5425
Mybite Holdings LLC, Wilmington (G-18512)	G	647 225-1385
Myfurtribe Inc, Hockessin (G-5314)	G	210 904-3036
Myruck Inc, Dover (G-3140)	G	310 462-3342
Mysegmenter Technologies Inc, Dover (G-3141)	G	302 549-2288
Neon Fun LLC, Dover (G-3170)	G	858 220-0946
Nerd Boy LLC, Dover (G-3172)	G	302 857-0243
▼ Nevron Software LLC, Wilmington (G-18606)	F	855 370-5511
Norman Nielsen Group Inc, Dover (G-3195)	E	415 685-4230
Novlt LLC, Wilmington (G-18698)	G	925 332-6379
Omnisets LLC, Dover (G-3225)	G	425 229-1592
Onollo Inc, Dover (G-3232)	G	925 286-4797
Oppameet LLC, Lewes (G-6338)	G	732 540-0308
Paperbasket LLC, Dover (G-3268)	G	516 360-3500
Parcly LLC, Dover (G-3272)	G	347 305-6820
Paxo Assist LLC, Wilmington (G-18926)	G	786 351-0114
Paypergigs Inc, Newark (G-11646)	A	917 336-2162
Pbtv Global Inc, Wilmington (G-18931)	F	302 292-1400
Percebe Music Inc, Dover (G-3296)	G	850 341-9594
Perceri LLC, Dover (G-3297)	G	217 721-8731
Perisphere Inc, Dover (G-3299)	G	908 581-8058
Pfpc Worldwide Inc, Wilmington (G-19005)	F	302 791-1700
Piks Company, Wilmington (G-19043)	G	310 372-5770
Pixel Ninja Studios LLC, Wilmington (G-19057)	G	218 398-1374
Play Better Inc, Middletown (G-7457)	G	407 815-2719
Play US Media LLC, Dover (G-3332)	G	302 924-5034
Plotly (us) Inc, Wilmington (G-19081)	D	781 974-4062
Pluspoint Inc, Wilmington (G-19083)	G	305 901-2676
Pobbles Corporation, Dover (G-3344)	G	510 371-1627
Pony Up Inc, Dover (G-3350)	G	323 205-7669
Postly Technologies Inc, Middletown (G-7461)	F	315 215-0320
Pricetweakers LLC, Wilmington (G-19189)	G	424 325-0597
Process Academy LLC, Wilmington (G-19207)	G	302 415-3104
Qare Inc, Wilmington (G-19273)	G	408 475-7569
Qbench Inc, Newark (G-11782)	E	888 680-5834
Qrepublik Inc, Claymont (G-1272)	G	559 475-8262
Quadrosense LLC, Dover (G-3406)	G	302 608-0779
Quail Technologies, Dover (G-3407)	G	201 497-4902
Quantica Electronics LLC, Newark (G-11793)	G	302 648-4684
Quantus Innovations LLC, Wilmington (G-19289)	G	302 356-1661
Quavo Inc, Wilmington (G-19291)	D	484 257-9846
Queryloop Inc, Newark (G-11798)	G	412 253-6265
Raad360 LLC, Newark (G-11812)	F	855 722-3360
Ram Tech Systems Inc, Middletown (G-7500)	E	302 832-6600
Rated10 LLC, Middletown (G-7504)	G	310 699-9537
Re-Up App Inc, Wilmington (G-19360)	G	267 972-1183
Readyb Inc, Dover (G-3434)	G	323 813-8710
Realm Software Inc, Dover (G-3436)	G	734 799-0793
Recipero Inc, Wilmington (G-19377)	E	888 551-1159
Red Rhino Labs LLC, Newark (G-11839)	G	650 275-2464
Reform LLC, Dover (G-3444)	G	813 299-5726
Relytv LLC, Dover (G-3450)	G	213 373-5988
Remora Company, Lewes (G-6416)	G	845 532-5172
Renderapps LLC, Dover (G-3454)	G	919 274-0582
Rfx Analyst Inc, Dover (G-3463)	G	302 244-5650
Riko Inc, Wilmington (G-19483)	G	216 810-5083
Ringlet LLC, Dover (G-3472)	G	802 238-5858
Rocketchat Technologies Corp, Wilmington (G-19533)	C	213 725-2428
Ruabit LLC, Claymont (G-1284)	G	765 772-0806
Rumble League Studios Inc, Dover (G-3495)	G	800 564-5300
Saas Digital Technologies Inc, Newark (G-11930)	G	302 994-2000
Saasant Inc, Lewes (G-6438)	E	619 377-0977
Salesbox LLC, Wilmington (G-19638)	G	415 361-4080
Sanattest LLC, Wilmington (G-19653)	G	623 337-7849
Scholarjet PBC, Lewes (G-6451)	G	617 407-9851
Sdn Essentials LLC, Newark (G-11965)	F	415 902-5702
SE Gaming Services Inc, Newark (G-11966)	E	303 867-8090
Sensibo Inc, Wilmington (G-19752)	G	302 572-2572
Sertifier Inc, Newark (G-11983)	G	302 487-3193
SGS Telekom Inc, Newark (G-11988)	G	774 482-2236
Shire Civics Co, Middletown (G-7561)	G	423 520-6705
Signup Software Inc, Dover (G-3559)	G	302 531-1139
Siriusiq Mobile LLC, Newark (G-12015)	F	888 414-2047
Smappy Inc, Lewes (G-6479)	G	650 360-0713
Smart 360 Co, Wilmington (G-19875)	G	617 657-4360
Smartcard Mktg Systems Inc, Wilmington (G-19881)	G	844 843-7296
Smartcookiewifi Inc, Wilmington (G-19882)	G	424 205-4450
Smartprofyl LLC, Middletown (G-7578)	G	832 412-5803
Smartwnnr Inc, Lewes (G-6484)	E	415 534-9794
Smileback LLC, Wilmington (G-19885)	F	646 401-0024
Sneakylinks Com Inc, Middletown (G-7581)	F	470 312-3827
Software Bananas LLC, Newark (G-12050)	G	302 348-8488
Software Radio Systems USA Inc, Newark (G-12051)	F	339 368-6321
Solufy Corp, Wilmington (G-19925)	E	877 476-5839
Spinrack Corp, Dover (G-3598)	G	209 965-7746
Spotters Inc, Wilmington (G-19972)	G	646 662-6025
Sqella Technologies Corp, Wilmington (G-19983)	G	302 592-6747
Standard Magic Corporation, Wilmington (G-20014)	G	347 756-1222
Statwhiz Ventures LLC, Wilmington (G-20038)	G	310 819-5427
Stay Prime Inc, Wilmington (G-20039)	G	612 770-6753
Storeskipper Inc, Middletown (G-7601)	G	505 850-5878
Stream App LLC, Wilmington (G-20093)	G	610 420-5864
Studium Inc, Wilmington (G-20107)	G	614 402-0359
Submix Holdings Inc, Wilmington (G-20111)	G	858 336-6467
Sumuri LLC, Magnolia (G-6786)	E	302 570-0015
Supportcom Inc, Wilmington (G-20151)	D	650 556-9440
Sute Media Inc, Lewes (G-6532)	G	617 774-9499
Sweat Social LLC, Dover (G-3631)	G	504 510-1973
Swiirl Inc, Newark (G-12143)	G	650 430-5256

73 BUSINESS SERVICES

Swype Inc .... G 619 736-1410
  Lewes (G-6535)
Synthezai Corp .... G 415 980-9792
  Wilmington (G-20192)
Tale Innovations Inc .... G 301 887-7587
  Wilmington (G-20210)
Talk Aware LLC .... G 302 645-7400
  Lewes (G-6540)
Tech Beach Retreat Inc .... F 786 790-5922
  Newark (G-12167)
Tellerone Inc .... F 302 261-9062
  Middletown (G-7633)
Thoroughbred Software Intl .... G 302 339-8383
  Georgetown (G-4554)
Tiplab Inc .... G 917 586-9649
  Lewes (G-6561)
Toivotek Inc .... G 224 805-9554
  Wilmington (G-20346)
Toosacom Inc .... G 415 240-0442
  Middletown (G-7652)
Topiary Tech LLC .... G 302 636-5440
  Wilmington (G-20358)
Transmed Systems Inc .... G 650 584-3316
  Wilmington (G-20399)
Travelory Inc .... G 925 216-0718
  Dover (G-3718)
Trikorp Inc .... G 970 690-6285
  Dover (G-3727)
Truehost Cloud LLC .... G 972 674-3814
  Middletown (G-7666)
Trumove Inc .... G 917 379-7427
  Lewes (G-6583)
Trumpet LLC .... G 303 910-7444
  Wilmington (G-20447)
Ultra Packet LLC .... G 240 219-8472
  Wilmington (G-20501)
Ur World Inc .... G 313 241-0060
  Middletown (G-7676)
Veeglife LLC .... G 310 866-8249
  Dover (G-3778)
Veho Tech Inc .... E 720 466-3788
  Claymont (G-1327)
Velocity Eu Inc .... F 331 226-1818
  Middletown (G-7684)
Verdict LLC .... G 888 837-4618
  Wilmington (G-20587)
Version 40 Software LLC .... G 302 270-0245
  Magnolia (G-6788)
Vidalytics .... F 303 500-5715
  Milton (G-8726)
Vidhq Inc .... G 512 660-7862
  Wilmington (G-20618)
Viewbix Inc .... F 302 645-7400
  Lewes (G-6604)
Virtual Pro Gaming Inc .... G 302 285-9891
  Wilmington (G-20634)
Visueats Imagery Solutions LLC .... G 954 687-5112
  Middletown (G-7690)
Vizzie 360 .... G 323 239-0690
  Lewes (G-6608)
Vox Ai Inc .... G 302 288-0670
  Dover (G-3811)
Voxpopin Inc .... G 202 567-7483
  Claymont (G-1332)
Vshield Software Corp .... G 302 531-0855
  Dover (G-3812)
Wachu Inc .... G 323 657-3889
  Wilmington (G-20666)
Warring Nation Inc .... G 757 323-6312
  Dover (G-3821)
Wbi Capital Advisors LLC .... E 856 361-6362
  Wilmington (G-20696)

Webstudy Inc .... G 888 326-4058
  Harbeson (G-4718)
Whagons North America Inc .... E 781 241-5946
  Middletown (G-7721)
Whatarethose Inc .... G 443 467-3687
  Dover (G-3840)
Whimstay Inc .... G 650 867-0076
  Wilmington (G-20760)
Whoop Labs Inc .... G 425 442-2137
  Lewes (G-6627)
Whstle Corporation .... G 925 413-3316
  Dover (G-3846)
Whuups LLC .... G 808 393-6240
  Lewes (G-6628)
Wicked Pay LLC .... G 646 785-1143
  Middletown (G-7724)
Women Leading Innovation Inc .... G 540 798-4023
  Lewes (G-6637)
Yallery Inc .... G 571 351-3820
  Middletown (G-7743)
Zodiac Inc .... G 800 969-4170
  Middletown (G-7751)
Zolak Inc .... G 302 889-0556
  Dover (G-3904)

7373 Computer integrated systems design

22d LLC .... G 347 857-8807
  Wilmington (G-14122)
924 Inc .... E 302 656-6100
  Hockessin (G-5109)
Adapty Inc .... G 415 800-3343
  Claymont (G-1020)
Advanced Global Networks Inc .... G 302 308-6460
  Wilmington (G-14274)
Aething Inc .... G 917 640-2582
  Dover (G-1732)
Agts LLC .... G 800 496-3379
  Dover (G-1749)
Aigc Games Inc .... G 214 499-8654
  Lewes (G-5666)
Alpha Comm LLC .... F 302 784-0645
  Bear (G-29)
Applied Control Engrg Inc .... D 302 738-8800
  Newark (G-9891)
Ardexo Inc .... G 855 617-7500
  Dover (G-1811)
Avant Digital Inc .... G 660 726-2416
  Newark (G-9950)
Base-2 Solutions LLC .... D 202 215-2152
  Lewes (G-5735)
Batescainelli LLC .... G 202 618-2040
  Rehoboth Beach (G-12624)
Beverage Infosystems Ltd Lblty .... E 732 762-5299
  Wilmington (G-14866)
Blue Sky Web Solutions Inc .... G 302 261-2654
  Newark (G-10063)
◆ Bluent LLC .... E 832 476-8459
  Lewes (G-5771)
Boomn Inc .... G 844 808-2666
  Lewes (G-5775)
Bothub Ai Limited .... F 669 278-7485
  Newark (G-10071)
Bridgeway Digital LLC .... G 212 684-6931
  Lewes (G-5778)
Brittons Wise Computers Inc .... G 302 659-0343
  Smyrna (G-13668)
Bullseye Entertainment Tech Co .... E 302 924-5034
  Dover (G-1992)
Care Mentor Ai LLC .... E 302 830-3700
  Wilmington (G-15241)
Casper Hosting LLC .... G 480 442-7112
  Lewes (G-5807)

Central Firm LLC .... G 610 470-9836
  Wilmington (G-15308)
Cim Concepts Incorporated .... F 302 613-5400
  New Castle (G-8942)
Cited Inc .... G 302 384-9810
  Wilmington (G-15447)
City of Dover .... F 302 736-5071
  Dover (G-2084)
Cks Global Ventures LLC .... E 302 355-0511
  Newark (G-10248)
Cloudxperts LLC .... G 302 257-5686
  Dover (G-2097)
Conexiam Solutions Inc .... G 302 884-6746
  Wilmington (G-15591)
Conquest Tech Solutions Inc .... G 302 356-1423
  Wilmington (G-15606)
Consult Dynamics Inc .... E 302 654-1019
  Wilmington (G-15613)
Data-Bi LLC .... G 302 290-3138
  Wilmington (G-15798)
Datatech Enterprises Inc .... F 540 370-0010
  Selbyville (G-13515)
Delaware Business Systems Inc .... E 302 395-0900
  New Castle (G-9015)
Digitalai Software Inc .... F 678 268-3340
  Wilmington (G-16069)
Dodd Health Innovation LLC .... G 410 598-7266
  Ocean View (G-12506)
Dopamine World Inc .... G 650 933-8003
  Dover (G-2324)
Ebc Systems LLC .... G 302 472-1896
  Wilmington (G-16275)
Encross LLC .... F 302 351-2593
  Wilmington (G-16407)
GIERD INC .... E 206 289-0011
  Wilmington (G-16858)
Gigahub Inc .... G 916 304-4710
  Dover (G-2584)
Ifi Techsolutions Inc .... G 332 456-0765
  Middletown (G-7222)
Inclind Inc .... G 302 856-2802
  Lewes (G-6120)
Indelible Blue Inc .... F 302 231-5200
  Lewes (G-6122)
Infinite Solutions LLC .... F 302 438-5310
  Wilmington (G-17322)
Info Systems LLC .... C 302 633-9800
  Wilmington (G-17328)
Insight Engineering Solutions .... G 302 378-4842
  Townsend (G-14018)
Integration Logistics Inc .... E 302 832-7300
  Newark (G-11032)
Internet Business Pubg Corp .... F 302 875-7700
  Laurel (G-5536)
Itiyam LLC .... F 703 291-1600
  Wilmington (G-17434)
Kagoal Technology LLC .... G 617 818-0588
  Middletown (G-7260)
Luut Technologies Inc .... G 302 658-7581
  Wilmington (G-18035)
M C Tek LLC .... G 302 644-9695
  Rehoboth Beach (G-12842)
Medictek Inc .... G 302 351-4924
  Wilmington (G-18252)
Microtelecom Systems LLC .... D 718 707-0012
  Wilmington (G-18331)
Miners Supply Co LLC .... G 541 203-6826
  Dover (G-3098)
Obhost LLC .... G 302 440-1447
  Lewes (G-6326)
Omnimaven Inc .... G 302 378-8918
  Middletown (G-7414)

73 BUSINESS SERVICES

Pentius Inc .... E 855 825-3778
  Wilmington *(G-18963)*
PHD Technology Solutions LLC .... E 410 961-7895
  Newark *(G-11681)*
Play US Media LLC .... G 302 924-5034
  Dover *(G-3332)*
Pmsa It Services LLC .... G 301 806-5163
  Rehoboth Beach *(G-12893)*
Polar Strategy Inc .... G 703 628-0001
  Lewes *(G-6381)*
Progressive Software Cmpt Inc .... C 302 479-9700
  Wilmington *(G-19221)*
Public Systems Inc .... G 302 326-4500
  New Castle *(G-9500)*
Purplenow Inc .... E 302 751-5226
  Dover *(G-3399)*
Ram Tech Systems Inc .... E 302 832-6600
  Middletown *(G-7500)*
Rave Business Systems LLC .... F 302 407-2270
  Lewes *(G-6409)*
Riders App Inc .... G 347 484-4344
  Wilmington *(G-19479)*
Second Front Systems Inc .... D 301 744-7318
  Wilmington *(G-19728)*
Sensofusion Inc .... F 570 239-4912
  Milton *(G-8710)*
Sharlay Computer Systems .... G 302 588-3170
  Smyrna *(G-13883)*
She Bash LLC .... G 302 204-6700
  Claymont *(G-1289)*
Smartis .... G 302 653-8355
  Dover *(G-3578)*
SNMP3 Security LLC .... G 302 448-8501
  Newark *(G-12045)*
Staircase Inc .... E 215 693-5686
  Claymont *(G-1300)*
Supportyourapp Inc .... E 888 959-3556
  Wilmington *(G-20154)*
Talkpush LLC .... D 415 818-5083
  Dover *(G-3648)*
Tcp/Ip Solutions LLC .... F 302 219-0224
  Dover *(G-3657)*
Tpf Technologies LLC .... G 703 665-4588
  Wilmington *(G-20380)*
Transformify Inc .... G 302 205-0685
  Claymont *(G-1316)*
Urspayce Inc .... G 302 440-2880
  Claymont *(G-1325)*
Verizon Delaware LLC .... C 302 571-1571
  Wilmington *(G-20590)*
Very LLC .... D 630 945-5539
  Dover *(G-3787)*
Virtual Enterprises Inc .... F 302 324-5322
  New Castle *(G-9672)*
Watchdogdevelopmentcom LLC .... G 888 488-7531
  Dover *(G-3822)*
Webstudy Inc .... G 888 326-4058
  Harbeson *(G-4718)*
Xcs Corporation .... G 302 514-0600
  Wilmington *(G-20916)*
Xeroictech Inc .... F 302 252-1617
  Claymont *(G-1341)*
Xtalos LLC .... G 800 383-0662
  Middletown *(G-7741)*

7374 Data processing and preparation

Alpha Comm LLC .... F 302 784-0645
  Bear *(G-29)*
▼ Ample Business Solutions Inc .... F 302 752-4270
  Wilmington *(G-14462)*
Analyttica Datalab Inc .... E 917 300-3325
  Wilmington *(G-14467)*
Argo Ai Corporation .... G 516 602-9295
  Dover *(G-1812)*
Braincx Inc .... F 954 892-9101
  Wilmington *(G-15036)*
Brainstorm Force US LLC .... G 302 330-8557
  Wilmington *(G-15038)*
Brandywine Cad Design Inc .... G 302 478-8334
  Wilmington *(G-15047)*
Cadrender Inc .... G 302 657-0700
  Wilmington *(G-15188)*
Casper Hosting LLC .... G 480 442-7112
  Lewes *(G-5807)*
Cgs Infotech Inc .... E 302 351-2434
  Wilmington *(G-15324)*
Chief Web Design .... G 302 542-8409
  Georgetown *(G-4250)*
Clms LLC .... G 703 629-3231
  Rehoboth Beach *(G-12679)*
Cognitro LLC .... G 347 983-9785
  Lewes *(G-5850)*
Computer Aid Inc .... G 302 831-5500
  Newark *(G-10294)*
Computer Services of Delaware .... G 302 697-8644
  Dover *(G-2127)*
Court Record & Data MGT Svcs .... F 302 476-8976
  Wilmington *(G-15658)*
Creaform USA Inc .... G 407 732-4103
  Newark *(G-10345)*
Dastor LLC .... E 610 337-5560
  Wilmington *(G-15795)*
Data Cloud Partners LLC .... G 805 729-1088
  Wilmington *(G-15796)*
Data Drum Inc .... G 347 502-8485
  Newark *(G-10390)*
Data-Bi LLC .... G 302 290-3138
  Wilmington *(G-15798)*
Ddh (north America) Inc .... G 617 893-9004
  Lewes *(G-5884)*
Deeptrace Inc .... E 424 413-8787
  Lewes *(G-5886)*
Doculogica Corp .... G 302 753-5944
  Wilmington *(G-16113)*
Ecircular LLC .... F 713 514-4675
  Wilmington *(G-16278)*
Everlast Interactive LLC .... G 347 992-3783
  Bear *(G-212)*
Ezangacom Inc .... E 888 439-2642
  Middletown *(G-7116)*
Fis Investment Ventures LLC .... E 484 582-2000
  Wilmington *(G-16643)*
Fiserv Wrldwide Sltions II LLC .... F 800 872-7882
  Wilmington *(G-16644)*
Ftl Technologies Corporation .... E 703 634-6910
  Lewes *(G-6019)*
Global Comm Innovations LLC .... G 302 546-5010
  Claymont *(G-1163)*
GOBLIN Technologies LLC .... G 302 644-5599
  Newark *(G-10857)*
Hap LLC .... G 302 645-7400
  Lewes *(G-6075)*
Helical Software Corp .... G 323 544-5348
  Lewes *(G-6087)*
Iamag Inc .... G 317 487-9338
  Wilmington *(G-17253)*
Information Consultants Inc .... F 302 239-2942
  Yorklyn *(G-20993)*
Integrated Home LLC .... G 302 656-1624
  New Castle *(G-9236)*
Invensis Inc .... C 470 260-0084
  Wilmington *(G-17404)*
Ipr International LLC .... E 302 304-8774
  Wilmington *(G-17417)*
J P Morgan Services Inc .... C 302 634-1000
  Newark *(G-11075)*
John Snow Labs Inc .... E 302 786-5227
  Lewes *(G-6147)*
Kinsta Inc .... E 310 736-9306
  Dover *(G-2878)*
Label Your Data .... G 844 935-2538
  Wilmington *(G-17783)*
Lan-Tech Inc .... G 877 311-1030
  Claymont *(G-1211)*
Logically Ai Inc .... F 202 768-9876
  Camden *(G-869)*
Lokblok Inc .... F 408 640-8644
  Wilmington *(G-17979)*
Mobius New Media Inc .... G 302 475-9880
  Wilmington *(G-18397)*
Monet Intermediate LLC .... E 929 559-5423
  Wilmington *(G-18412)*
Morning Hornet LLC .... F 650 543-4800
  Wilmington *(G-18451)*
My Qme Inc .... G 302 218-8730
  Wilmington *(G-18508)*
National Dcument MGT Solutions .... G 302 535-9263
  Marydel *(G-6808)*
Nino Finance Inc .... G 415 236-7591
  Claymont *(G-1254)*
Pendulum It LLC .... G 302 480-9433
  Dover *(G-3290)*
Planet Payment Solutions Inc .... E 516 670-3200
  New Castle *(G-9476)*
Priv Social Inc .... G 501 301-4197
  Middletown *(G-7470)*
Professionsale Inc .... G 646 262-9101
  Bear *(G-439)*
Raad360 LLC .... F 855 722-3360
  Newark *(G-11812)*
Resulticks Solution Inc .... E 347 416-7673
  Wilmington *(G-19444)*
Rfx Analyst Inc .... G 302 244-5650
  Dover *(G-3463)*
Rocketchat Technologies Corp .... C 213 725-2428
  Wilmington *(G-19533)*
Rsf Managed Services LLC .... G 302 345-7162
  Wilmington *(G-19580)*
Search Optics LLC .... D 858 678-0707
  Wilmington *(G-19724)*
Sixteenpenny LLC .... G 302 463-7992
  Newark *(G-12018)*
Starbelt LLC .... G 256 724-9200
  Wilmington *(G-20026)*
Supportcom Inc .... D 650 556-9440
  Wilmington *(G-20151)*
Symmetry Data Solutions Inc .... E 805 708-4506
  Wilmington *(G-20183)*
Technigy Expiration Group Inc .... G 202 222-0794
  New Castle *(G-9622)*
Techno Goober .... F 302 645-7177
  Lewes *(G-6546)*
Tecpresso Inc .... G 302 240-0025
  Wilmington *(G-20260)*
Trolley Web .... G 302 468-7247
  Wilmington *(G-20437)*
Truveris Inc .... C 800 430-1430
  Wilmington *(G-20450)*
Usacarrecordcom LLC .... G 302 645-7400
  Lewes *(G-6594)*
Valiu Inc .... G 317 853-5081
  Lewes *(G-6598)*
Vic Victor Imagination Co LLC .... G 714 262-4426
  Lewes *(G-6603)*
Vultran Creative Marketing .... G 302 981-3379
  Wilmington *(G-20660)*

SIC SECTION
73 BUSINESS SERVICES

Webmost.. G 302 345-0807
  Newark *(G-12353)*
Webstudy Inc... G 888 326-4058
  Harbeson *(G-4718)*
Wilkinson Technology Svcs LLC............ G 302 384-7770
  Wilmington *(G-20782)*
X5 Networks Corporation......................... G 800 784-5228
  Wilmington *(G-20912)*
Your Superfoods Inc.................................. G 424 387-6165
  Newark *(G-12423)*

7375 Information retrieval services

Dawn US Holdings LLC............................ F 619 322-2799
  Wilmington *(G-15818)*
Derived Data LLC...................................... G 201 275-1111
  Wilmington *(G-16020)*
Ftl Technologies Corporation................... E 703 634-6910
  Lewes *(G-6019)*
Homeland SEC Verification LLC............. G 888 791-4614
  Wilmington *(G-17186)*
Ipr International LLC................................. E 302 304-8774
  Wilmington *(G-17417)*
Lexisnexis Risk Assets Inc...................... A 800 458-9410
  Wilmington *(G-17889)*
Merix LLC... G 425 659-1425
  Lewes *(G-6265)*
Post Media Inc... E 203 244-8424
  Wilmington *(G-19129)*
Quantumfly LLC... F 312 618-5739
  Dover *(G-3408)*
Rever Cre Inc... F 201 380-4566
  Dover *(G-3461)*
Rfx Analyst Inc... G 302 244-5650
  Dover *(G-3463)*
Sabi Ai Corp.. G 415 800-4641
  Dover *(G-3500)*
Veteran It Pro LLC.................................... F 302 824-3111
  Hockessin *(G-5418)*
Xcs Corporation... G 302 514-0600
  Wilmington *(G-20916)*

7376 Computer facilities management

Absolute Computer Support LLC............. G 717 917-8900
  Newark *(G-9745)*
Alpha Technologies USA Inc.................... D 302 510-8205
  Wilmington *(G-14392)*
Cks Global Ventures LLC......................... E 302 355-0511
  Newark *(G-10248)*
Gga Global Consulting LLC..................... F 302 238-1751
  Dover *(G-2579)*
Herbert R Martin Associates.................... G 302 239-1700
  Hockessin *(G-5238)*
Insight Engineering Solutions.................. G 302 378-4842
  Townsend *(G-14018)*
Ipr International LLC................................. E 302 304-8774
  Wilmington *(G-17417)*
Nuyka Inc.. E 707 400-5444
  Lewes *(G-6323)*
Supportyourapp Inc................................... E 888 959-3556
  Wilmington *(G-20154)*

7377 Computer rental and leasing

United Tech Project Foundation.............. F 302 404-4099
  Wilmington *(G-20529)*

7378 Computer maintenance and repair

AAA Computing.. G 302 430-9048
  Milford *(G-7758)*
Coastal It Consulting................................ G 302 226-9395
  Rehoboth Beach *(G-12683)*
Computer Jocks.. G 302 544-6448
  Bear *(G-116)*

Confluent Corporation............................... G 301 440-4100
  Georgetown *(G-4265)*
Curvature Inc.. G 302 525-9525
  Newark *(G-10366)*
Feddly Jeanniton.. G 302 325-1000
  New Castle *(G-9121)*
First Tech.. F 302 421-3650
  Wilmington *(G-16640)*
Handytech Solutions LLC.......................... G 302 449-4497
  Middletown *(G-7194)*
Information Technology Afforda............... G 302 525-6252
  Newark *(G-11020)*
Laser Images of Delaware Inc................. G 302 836-8610
  Bear *(G-338)*
Mauna Services LLC................................. G 302 446-4409
  Dover *(G-3037)*
ME Geek Squad Llc.................................. G 302 990-8092
  Wilmington *(G-18241)*
PC Supplies Inc... G 302 368-4800
  Newark *(G-11648)*
Response Computer Group Inc.............. F 302 335-3400
  Milford *(G-8063)*
Software Services of De Inc.................... E 302 654-3172
  Wilmington *(G-19915)*
TCS Inc... G 302 858-1389
  Milton *(G-8718)*
Teamlogic It.. G 302 446-4100
  Wilmington *(G-20245)*
Tech Impact.. F 302 256-5015
  Wilmington *(G-20248)*
Tech Now Mobile LLC............................... G 484 480-0648
  Wilmington *(G-20251)*
Technicare Inc... G 302 322-7766
  Newark *(G-12170)*
Teleplan Vdeocom Solutions Inc............. E 302 323-8503
  New Castle *(G-9624)*
Tower Business Machines Inc................. G 302 395-1445
  Historic New Castle *(G-5088)*
Zerowait Corporation................................. F 302 996-9408
  Wilmington *(G-20958)*

7379 Computer related services, nec

01 Hire Inc... E 408 599-2693
  Middletown *(G-6813)*
1st-Recruit LLC.. F 732 666-4106
  Wilmington *(G-14117)*
22 Solutions LLC....................................... F 901 672-0006
  Dover *(G-1681)*
2ndquadrant Inc.. E 650 378-1218
  Wilmington *(G-14123)*
3d Tech LLC... G 610 268-2350
  Hockessin *(G-5108)*
4sight Group LLC...................................... G 800 490-2131
  Wilmington *(G-14137)*
Acbusa Inc.. E 302 985-9395
  Wilmington *(G-14216)*
Access It Services Inc.............................. G 408 520-9069
  Middletown *(G-6832)*
Adectra LLC.. F 203 424-2800
  Middletown *(G-6835)*
Advanced Technology Sales.................... G 732 446-9681
  Townsend *(G-13952)*
Advent Cad LLC... G 302 569-1793
  Wilmington *(G-14287)*
Agilebits USA Inc....................................... G 416 371-3328
  Wilmington *(G-14317)*
Ahu Technologies Inc................................ F 302 397-7091
  Newark *(G-9797)*
Ait Advanced Infotech Inc........................ G 302 454-8620
  Bear *(G-22)*
Aleric International Inc............................. F 302 547-4846
  Middletown *(G-6848)*

Alpha Technologies Inc............................. F 917 412-9211
  Wilmington *(G-14391)*
Alpha Technologies USA Inc.................... D 302 510-8205
  Wilmington *(G-14392)*
Alphaforce Tech Solutions Inc................. G 917 231-3796
  Wilmington *(G-14393)*
Altairis Tech Partners LLC...................... G 302 354-0662
  Middletown *(G-6855)*
Alvissai Inc... G 470 202-3431
  Dover *(G-1778)*
American Solutions Inc............................ E 302 456-9600
  Newark *(G-9847)*
Antenna House Inc.................................... G 302 566-7225
  Newark *(G-9876)*
Applied Control Engrg Inc....................... D 302 738-8800
  Newark *(G-9891)*
Applied Technologies Inc.......................... G 302 670-4601
  Camden Wyoming *(G-913)*
Arrowtech LLC.. F 704 833-8777
  Middletown *(G-6873)*
ATA Technology Inc................................... G 862 233-0007
  Wilmington *(G-14616)*
Atiba Music Services................................ G 302 981-7157
  Claymont *(G-1045)*
Attentis Consulting Inc............................. F 570 575-7283
  Dover *(G-1852)*
Avixia LLC.. G 781 882-2200
  Newark *(G-9956)*
Axiom Resources LLC.............................. F 410 756-0440
  Dover *(G-1859)*
Axitech Inc.. G 248 318-9067
  Wilmington *(G-14683)*
Baba Sali LLC.. G 917 647-0561
  Dover *(G-1866)*
Bamboozle Web Services Inc................. G 833 380-4600
  Newark *(G-9976)*
Base-2 Solutions LLC............................... D 202 215-2152
  Lewes *(G-5735)*
Bell Info Solutions LLC............................ G 302 541-1200
  Wilmington *(G-14818)*
Biginsights LLC.. F 618 819-0902
  Dover *(G-1937)*
Binary Technology LLC............................. F 302 455-7400
  Dover *(G-1939)*
Blocksite LP... F 302 449-4227
  Wilmington *(G-14960)*
Blockware Solutions LLC......................... F 512 905-5209
  Dover *(G-1950)*
◆ Bluent LLC... E 832 476-8459
  Lewes *(G-5771)*
Body Interact Inc...................................... F 512 910-8350
  Dover *(G-1958)*
Bravatics LLC... G 703 966-0516
  Dover *(G-1974)*
Brightminds Social Inc............................. F 424 333-8879
  Wilmington *(G-15114)*
Brik Labs Inc.. F 302 499-4423
  Wilmington *(G-15115)*
Burgeon It Services LLC.......................... F 302 613-0999
  Wilmington *(G-15152)*
By Lore Tech Solutions Inc..................... G 302 202-9499
  Middletown *(G-6949)*
Call Rings LLC... E 302 250-4030
  Dover *(G-2014)*
Capgemini America Inc............................ G 302 656-7491
  Wilmington *(G-15223)*
Casper Hosting LLC.................................. G 480 442-7112
  Lewes *(G-5807)*
Centrien Consulting Svcs LLC................ E 844 741-0000
  Dover *(G-2052)*
Cgw Corp.. G 631 903-5700
  Seaford *(G-13107)*

Employee Codes: A=Over 500 employees, B=251-500
C=101-250, D=51-100, E=20-50, F=10-19, G=1-9

73 BUSINESS SERVICES — SIC SECTION

Cirrus Nexus Corp .... E 302 492-2700
  Wilmington (G-15446)
Cks Global Ventures LLC .... E 302 355-0511
  Newark (G-10248)
Clings Blings & Things .... G 302 734-9103
  Dover (G-2094)
Cloud Big Data Tech LLC .... D 573 201-5937
  Wilmington (G-15488)
Cloudokyo Technologies Inc .... G 845 551-8627
  Wilmington (G-15495)
Computer Sciences Corporation .... G 302 391-8347
  Newark (G-10295)
Conectiv Communications Inc .... E 302 224-1177
  Newark (G-10299)
Congruence Consulting Group .... G 320 290-6155
  Newark (G-10304)
Conquest Tech Solutions Inc .... G 302 356-1423
  Wilmington (G-15606)
Consol Usa Inc .... G 302 401-6537
  Dover (G-2133)
Convergetel LLC .... G 347 688-0922
  Newark (G-10317)
Csols Inc .... E 302 731-5290
  Newark (G-10361)
Culturetech Solutions LLC .... G 415 936-5799
  Dover (G-2169)
Data-Bi LLC .... G 302 290-3138
  Wilmington (G-15798)
Datatech Enterprises Inc .... F 540 370-0010
  Selbyville (G-13515)
Dbeaver Corporation .... E 347 809-3202
  Wilmington (G-15823)
Delasoft Inc .... C 302 533-7912
  New Castle (G-9011)
Delcomps LLC .... G 302 754-1543
  Lewes (G-5902)
Delica Inc .... G 917 566-7308
  Wilmington (G-15993)
Delmarva Furniture Svcs LLC .... F 302 644-4970
  Lewes (G-5904)
Delmarvavoip LLC .... G 855 645-8647
  Lewes (G-5909)
Delt LLC .... G 215 869-7409
  Newark (G-10508)
Dew Softech Inc .... F 302 834-2555
  Newark (G-10520)
Diamond Technologies Inc .... E 302 421-8252
  Wilmington (G-16060)
Digital Technica LLC .... F 416 829-8400
  Wilmington (G-16068)
Diligent Bus Solutions LLC .... G 302 897-5993
  Newark (G-10532)
Discidium Technology Inc .... G 347 220-5979
  Newark (G-10538)
Dwh System Inc .... F 551 208-5354
  Felton (G-3963)
Dx Tech Solutions Inc .... G 302 397-3500
  Newark (G-10580)
E2e LLC .... G 703 906-5353
  Hockessin (G-5195)
Easy Sales Solutions Inc .... G 929 273-0505
  Wilmington (G-16270)
Einstein Technologies LLC .... G 407 614-7404
  Newark (G-10621)
Electranet Enterprises .... G 302 309-8320
  Newark (G-10622)
Empire Blue .... G 302 324-1015
  New Castle (G-9092)
Encross LLC .... F 302 351-2593
  Wilmington (G-16407)
Enovante LLC .... F 917 960-8384
  Wilmington (G-16427)

Epatriotcrm LLC .... G 419 967-6812
  Dover (G-2454)
Epic Tides LLC .... G 646 535-6523
  Claymont (G-1133)
Eros Technologies Inc .... E 650 242-9262
  Lewes (G-5972)
Ets & Ycp LLC .... G 302 525-4111
  Newark (G-10671)
Even & Odd Minds LLC .... F 619 663-7284
  Wilmington (G-16482)
Evernex USA Inc .... B 888 630-9396
  Newark (G-10678)
Evocati Group Corporation .... F 206 551-9087
  Dover (G-2468)
Evonsys LLC .... G 302 544-2156
  Wilmington (G-16494)
Ewgcs Inc .... F 415 935-5884
  Dover (G-2470)
Ezra Consulting LLC .... F 912 695-5925
  Dover (G-2476)
Florient Contracting Firm LLC .... G 888 250-1915
  Wilmington (G-16667)
Forward Discovery Inc .... G 703 647-6364
  Camden Wyoming (G-947)
G B Tech Inc .... E 302 378-5600
  Middletown (G-7145)
Genesec Inc .... G 917 656-5742
  Claymont (G-1159)
Genovesius Solutia Llc .... G 302 252-7506
  Hockessin (G-5221)
Geo-Plus Corporation .... F 800 672-1733
  Newark (G-10821)
Gga Consulting Group LLC .... F 302 307-3443
  Dover (G-2578)
GIERD INC .... E 206 289-0011
  Wilmington (G-16858)
Global Bridging Corp .... G 202 318-7119
  Lewes (G-6038)
Gmg Solutions LLC .... E 302 781-3008
  Wilmington (G-16899)
Goodworld Inc .... G 845 325-2232
  Wilmington (G-16928)
Graceblood LLC .... F 302 703-2524
  Lewes (G-6051)
Headstream Inc .... F 302 356-0156
  Wilmington (G-17090)
Homeries LLC .... F 570 575-8008
  Wilmington (G-17188)
Hoover Computer Services Inc .... G 302 529-7050
  Wilmington (G-17195)
Icrush Technologies LLC .... G 302 613-2500
  Newark (G-10994)
Iji Inc .... E 732 485-9427
  Wilmington (G-17271)
Implify Inc .... E 302 533-2345
  Newark (G-11007)
Inetworkz LLC .... F 407 401-9384
  Lewes (G-6123)
Info Solutions LLC .... E 302 793-9200
  Wilmington (G-17326)
Info Solutions North Amer LLC .... F 302 793-9200
  Wilmington (G-17327)
Intellectual LLC .... F 202 769-1986
  Dover (G-2743)
Intellitec Solutions LLC .... E 302 652-3480
  Newark (G-11041)
Internet Working Technologies .... G 302 424-1855
  Milford (G-7942)
Intrinsic Partners LLC .... F 610 388-0853
  Wilmington (G-17401)
Inumsoft Inc .... G 302 533-5403
  Bear (G-287)

Investor Cash MGT Holdings Inc .... E 312 736-7700
  Wilmington (G-17407)
It Resources Inc .... E 203 521-6945
  Newark (G-11062)
It Tigers LLC .... G 732 898-2793
  Lewes (G-6132)
Itump Inc .... E 302 985-9406
  Wilmington (G-17436)
Jivosite Inc .... G 408 604-0183
  Wilmington (G-17551)
Kagoal Technology LLC .... G 617 818-0588
  Middletown (G-7260)
Karizma Sparks LLC .... G 302 607-5445
  Newark (G-11143)
Kogut Tech Consulting Inc .... G 302 455-0388
  Newark (G-11199)
Korsgy Technologies LLC .... G 302 504-6201
  Wilmington (G-17748)
Kortech Consulting Inc .... F 302 559-4612
  Bear (G-333)
Kwa Analytics US LLC .... E 914 629-6744
  Wilmington (G-17771)
Lambro Technologies LLC .... G 302 351-2559
  Wilmington (G-17792)
Latam Corporate Services LLC .... F 301 375-0714
  Dover (G-2906)
Layercake LLC .... G 571 449-7538
  Newark (G-11235)
Lel Wealth MGT & Tech Svc LLC .... G 804 243-0009
  Wilmington (G-17872)
Level Up Consulting Group Inc .... G 855 967-5550
  Middletown (G-7296)
Lifesquared Inc .... G 415 475-9090
  Dover (G-2942)
Liveware Inc .... F 302 791-9446
  Claymont (G-1221)
Load Balancer Crew LLC .... G 805 202-9953
  Dover (G-2964)
Luxcore LLC .... F 302 777-0538
  Wilmington (G-18037)
Matrix Network Solutions LLC .... G 302 331-7330
  Camden Wyoming (G-961)
Maven Security Consulting Inc .... G 302 365-6862
  Bear (G-367)
Menainfosec Inc .... E 217 650-7167
  Middletown (G-7340)
Menark Technologies Inc .... G 302 379-2185
  Bear (G-370)
Mercuri Inc .... G 425 395-5238
  Wilmington (G-18276)
Mgmis .... G 302 744-8645
  Dover (G-3076)
Mh-Teq LLC .... G 302 897-2182
  Wilmington (G-18301)
Mohan Consulting LLC .... G 314 583-9140
  Dover (G-3117)
Msrcosmos LLC .... F 925 218-6919
  Wilmington (G-18477)
My Digital Shield .... G 423 310-8977
  Wilmington (G-18504)
Netjectiives .... G 302 998-4436
  Newark (G-11508)
Network Design Technologies .... E 610 991-2929
  Wilmington (G-18596)
Next Pace Technologies Inc .... G 415 900-0876
  Dover (G-3186)
Oaks Lab Academy LLC .... G 509 481-5630
  Wilmington (G-18728)
Online Publishers LLC .... E 786 617-8896
  Wilmington (G-18792)
Opentact Inc .... F 484 424-9683
  Wilmington (G-18801)

SIC SECTION
73 BUSINESS SERVICES

Opusai Inc .... E 817 440-4609
  Dover (G-3238)
Partners Plus Inc .... G 302 529-3700
  New Castle (G-9452)
Pathscale Inc .... G 408 384-9948
  Wilmington (G-18904)
▲ Paymenex Inc .... F 302 504-6044
  Wilmington (G-18928)
Pding LLC .... G 252 201-8458
  Lewes (G-6356)
Pendulum It LLC .... G 302 480-9433
  Dover (G-3290)
Pixstar Inc .... E
  Wilmington (G-19059)
Play US Media LLC .... G 302 924-5034
  Dover (G-3332)
Poc Inc .... F 415 853-4762
  Dover (G-3345)
Prithvi Technologies LLC .... E 302 313-9273
  Wilmington (G-19200)
Proglo 2 LLC .... F 702 494-7877
  Middletown (G-7474)
Proteam LLC .... G 847 707-1074
  Wilmington (G-19233)
Qase Inc .... E 650 459-1800
  Wilmington (G-19274)
Quantum Leap Innovations Inc .... F 302 894-8045
  Newark (G-11795)
Raas Infotek LLC .... E 302 894-3184
  Newark (G-11813)
Raiden Tech Group Inc .... G 302 330-8514
  Newark (G-11820)
Ramping Technology LLC .... G 954 893-2909
  Dover (G-3422)
Rave Business Systems LLC .... F 302 407-2270
  Lewes (G-6409)
Republix Sourcestrike Corp .... F 647 206-1503
  Dover (G-3458)
Resulticks Solution Inc .... E 347 416-7673
  Wilmington (G-19444)
Roi International LLC .... G 704 340-1289
  Lewes (G-6430)
Rsf Managed Services LLC .... G 302 345-7162
  Wilmington (G-19580)
Ruby Moriarty LLC .... G 917 587-1511
  Dover (G-3493)
Sanjaban Corp .... G 612 805-5971
  Wilmington (G-19665)
Savantis Solutions LLC .... B 732 906-3200
  Wilmington (G-19682)
Savemunch Inc .... G 469 473-1601
  Lewes (G-6449)
SC Foster LLC .... E 302 383-0201
  Wilmington (G-19693)
Scinorx Technologies Inc .... G 302 268-5447
  Wilmington (G-19708)
SE Gaming Services Inc .... E 303 867-8090
  Newark (G-11966)
Securelayer7 LLC .... F 302 391-0803
  Middletown (G-7548)
Securenetmd LLC .... E 302 645-7770
  Lewes (G-6456)
Sendsafely LLC .... F 917 375-5891
  Newark (G-11976)
Sharp Tech Systems LLC .... G 302 956-9525
  Bridgeville (G-765)
Sigma Data Systems Inc .... F 302 453-8812
  Newark (G-12007)
Silicon Partners Inc .... F 646 571-2324
  Lewes (G-6470)
Silverbullet USA Inc .... F 203 216-2414
  Middletown (G-7567)

Simplica Corporation .... F 302 594-9899
  Wilmington (G-19837)
Skiplist Inc .... G 440 855-0319
  Newark (G-12023)
Skyward Solutions LLC .... G 469 563-0411
  Dover (G-3574)
Slice Global Inc .... G 415 801-6537
  Wilmington (G-19865)
SM Technomine Inc .... F 312 492-4386
  Wilmington (G-19870)
Smart Armor Protected LLC .... E 480 823-8122
  Newark (G-12034)
Sn & Partners .... G 312 826-3255
  Newark (G-12044)
Social Selling LLC .... G 888 384-3710
  Rehoboth Beach (G-12964)
Sokowatch Inc .... E 805 479-5544
  Claymont (G-1294)
Solid Idea Solutions LLC .... G 646 982-2890
  Lewes (G-6491)
Sortd Inc .... G 415 870-1075
  Newark (G-12056)
Southworks LLC .... G 302 295-5008
  Wilmington (G-19941)
Sparksphere Solutions LLC .... G 302 742-9048
  Dover (G-3594)
Sreeven Infotech Inc .... G 302 465-2402
  Wilmington (G-12078)
Sruplex LLC .... F 331 901-0011
  Lewes (G-6504)
Standards Site Inc .... G 917 449-4078
  Wilmington (G-20016)
Strang & Edson LLC .... G 917 664-0298
  Lewes (G-6515)
Support Services Group Inc .... G 404 939-1782
  Dover (G-3628)
Supportyourapp Inc .... E 888 959-3556
  Wilmington (G-20154)
Symbiosys Consulting LLC .... F 302 507-7649
  Wilmington (G-20181)
Synccore Inc .... G 833 612-0999
  Lewes (G-6536)
Syncretic Software Inc .... F 302 762-2600
  Wilmington (G-20186)
Systemonex Inc .... G 201 688-7663
  Middletown (G-7615)
Tamp Inc .... F 302 283-9195
  Newark (G-12158)
Tapp Networks LLC .... G 302 222-3384
  Rehoboth Beach (G-12989)
Target Integration Inc .... G 254 845-5684
  Middletown (G-7620)
Tatnall Technology LLC .... G 302 212-0959
  Wilmington (G-20227)
Tconcepts Resources Inc .... F 302 309-2490
  Lewes (G-6543)
Tech International Corp .... G 302 478-2301
  Wilmington (G-20249)
Techmap Integrated Inc .... G 770 800-3561
  Wilmington (G-20252)
Technical Media Solutions .... G 302 376-7588
  Middletown (G-7626)
Technlogy Explration Group Inc .... G 202 222-0794
  New Castle (G-9622)
Technology Extreme LLC .... F 213 325-5455
  Wilmington (G-20256)
Techsolutions Inc .... E 302 656-8324
  Wilmington (G-20257)
Tecs Plus .... F 302 437-6890
  Newark (G-12173)
Tek International Inc .... G 302 543-8035
  Middletown (G-7628)

Tekstrom Inc .... D 302 709-5900
  Wilmington (G-20264)
Tera Technology Group .... G 302 994-0500
  Elsmere (G-3931)
Teranetwork LLC .... G 302 257-7782
  Lewes (G-6551)
Tesis Time Inc .... G 302 613-0789
  Middletown (G-7637)
Thinklever LLC .... G 302 388-7461
  Newark (G-12189)
Toptal LLC .... D 414 550-3054
  Wilmington (G-20362)
Troposphere Technologies LLC .... G 613 833-0984
  Dover (G-3730)
Ublerb .... G 773 569-9686
  Dover (G-3741)
Ulterior Technologies Inc .... G 929 399-8964
  Wilmington (G-20495)
Ultraworking Inc .... G 848 243-0008
  Newark (G-12262)
University of Delaware .... F 302 831-6041
  Newark (G-12277)
Urban Cyber Security Inc .... G 803 805-9980
  Wilmington (G-20541)
UTECH Global Services .... E 630 531-0427
  Wilmington (G-20557)
Vairasoft Inc .... G 336 422-6499
  Wilmington (G-20561)
Vensoft Solutions Inc .... F 302 392-9000
  Wilmington (G-20580)
Verbspace Solutions Inc .... F 626 524-3003
  Dover (G-3782)
Veridian Solutions LLC .... F 832 867-7263
  Dover (G-3784)
Verito Technologies LLC .... F 855 583-7486
  Wilmington (G-20589)
Villa Token Inc .... G 831 227-9878
  Hockessin (G-5420)
Visavis Inc .... G 858 952-4175
  Dover (G-3800)
Visionary Cnslting Prtners LLC .... G 302 487-4200
  Dover (G-3801)
Vls It Consulting Inc .... F 302 368-5656
  Newark (G-12333)
Vonexpy Softech LLC .... G 512 484-8340
  Newark (G-12335)
Vpsie Inc .... F 844 468-7743
  Wilmington (G-20655)
Vsg Business Solutions LLC .... E 302 261-3209
  Bear (G-557)
Wahid Consultants LLC .... E 315 400-0955
  Historic New Castle (G-5099)
Wavetec North America Inc .... E 323 284-5084
  Claymont (G-1333)
Webbit .... G 302 725-6024
  Milford (G-8146)
Webeeta LLC .... E 720 316-1876
  Dover (G-3827)
World Wrless Solutions USA Inc .... G 877 746-4997
  Wilmington (G-20896)
Wyndham Group Inc .... G 704 905-9750
  Wilmington (G-20907)
Yes Hardsoft Solutions Inc .... G 609 632-0397
  Claymont (G-1343)
Yes Hardsoft Solutions Inc .... D 609 632-0397
  Wilmington (G-20927)
Yesamerica Corporation .... F 800 872-1548
  Middletown (G-7746)
Z Data Inc .... G 800 676-5614
  Newark (G-12427)
Zerodaylab LLC .... G 302 498-8322
  Wilmington (G-20957)

Employee Codes: A=Over 500 employees, B=251-500
C=101-250, D=51-100, E=20-50, F=10-19, G=1-9

2024 Harris Directory of
Delaware Businesses

73 BUSINESS SERVICES

Ziras Technologies Inc ..... F 302 286-7303
Newark (G-12435)

7381 Detective and armored car services

Alert Security & Technologies ..... G 302 294-9100
Wilmington (G-14353)

Alliedbarton Security Svcs LLC ..... G 302 498-0450
Wilmington (G-14383)

Axess Corp ..... G 910 270-2077
Newark (G-9958)

Bennett Det Prtective Agcy Inc ..... G 302 734-2480
Dover (G-1912)

Berkana Defense Security LLC ..... G 302 504-4455
Wilmington (G-14842)

Black Dragon Corporation ..... G 617 470-9230
Newark (G-10046)

Boulares Innovations LLC ..... G 504 575-2386
Wilmington (G-15012)

Conmac Security Systems Inc ..... G 302 529-9286
Wilmington (G-15598)

Delaware Acdemy Pub Safety SEC ..... G 302 377-1465
New Castle (G-9012)

Delaware Mobile Signings LLC ..... G 302 316-3926
Millsboro (G-8263)

Diamond State Ghost Invstgtors ..... G 302 463-4589
Wilmington (G-16054)

Dmp Security Agency LLC ..... F 302 384-3745
Wilmington (G-16110)

Dunbar Armored Inc ..... E 302 628-5401
Seaford (G-13164)

Dunbar Armored Inc ..... E 302 892-4950
Wilmington (G-16200)

Dupont Esl Security ..... G 302 695-1657
Wilmington (G-16208)

G4s Secure Solutions USA Inc ..... F 215 957-7503
Claymont (G-1154)

Garda CL Atlantic Inc ..... E 302 762-5444
Wilmington (G-16803)

Gettier Security ..... F 302 652-2700
Newark (G-10828)

Global Protection MGT LLC ..... B 302 425-4190
Wilmington (G-16894)

Govsimplified LLC ..... G 888 629-8008
Claymont (G-1169)

Great Gaines LLC ..... G 443 248-3952
Delmar (G-1599)

Groupe EHc LLC ..... F 302 309-9154
Dover (G-2631)

Gw Consulting Inc ..... B 302 294-2114
Wilmington (G-17011)

Home Security Wilmington ..... G 302 231-1142
Wilmington (G-17184)

J F Goetz Associates LLC ..... G 302 537-2485
Ocean View (G-12526)

JR Gettier & Associates Inc ..... E 302 478-0911
Wilmington (G-17600)

Lenar Detective Agency Inc ..... D 302 322-3700
New Castle (G-9305)

Matter Gray Security LLC ..... G 302 235-8627
Hockessin (G-5303)

Philadlphia Prtection Unit LLC ..... G 267 505-2671
Middletown (G-7445)

Professional Security Co ..... G 302 383-7142
Middletown (G-7473)

Resort Investigation & Patrol ..... G 302 539-5808
Millville (G-8546)

S & H Enterprises Inc ..... F 302 999-9911
Wilmington (G-19605)

Security Watch Corp ..... G 302 286-6728
Newark (G-11971)

Shadow Protective Services ..... G 410 903-3455
Millsboro (G-8457)

SOS Security Incorporated ..... G 302 425-4755
Wilmington (G-19930)

T & B Invstgtions SEC Agcy LLC ..... G 302 476-4087
Middletown (G-7616)

Tri-County Security ..... G 302 709-2244
Newark (G-12222)

United Security Advisors LLC ..... G 610 310-2482
Wilmington (G-20526)

Zicherheit LLC ..... G 302 510-3718
Selbyville (G-13622)

7382 Security systems services

A Plus Electric & Security ..... G 302 455-1725
Newark (G-9726)

ABM Security Services Inc ..... D 302 992-9733
Wilmington (G-14206)

Action Security ..... G 302 838-2852
Newark (G-9761)

Addlestone LLC ..... G 302 373-1598
Wilmington (G-14253)

ADT LLC ..... D 313 778-1493
Dover (G-1720)

ADT LLC ..... C 302 613-4745
Historic New Castle (G-4921)

ADT LLC ..... C 302 918-1016
Newark (G-9770)

Advanced Protection LLC ..... G 302 539-6041
Ocean View (G-12458)

Advantage Security Inc ..... F 302 652-3060
Wilmington (G-14286)

Advantech Inc ..... E 302 674-8405
Dover (G-1726)

Anaconda Prtctive Concepts Inc ..... F 302 834-1125
Newark (G-9858)

Aquia Nava II LLC ..... E 410 245-8990
Millsboro (G-8172)

B Safe Inc ..... E 302 422-3916
Dover (G-1865)

B Safe Inc ..... E 302 633-1833
Wilmington (G-14703)

Berley Security Systems Inc ..... F 302 791-9056
Wilmington (G-14845)

Besecure LLC ..... G 855 897-0650
Lewes (G-5756)

Cyproteck Inc ..... G 860 890-1889
Middletown (G-7025)

Dataspindle LLC ..... G 302 448-4988
Wilmington (G-15800)

Delaware Electric Signal Co ..... E 302 422-3916
Dover (G-2235)

Emergncy Response Protocol LLC ..... G 302 994-2600
Wilmington (G-16393)

Gatekeeper Systems USA Inc ..... G 434 477-6596
Wilmington (G-16812)

Instasafe Inc ..... G 408 400-3673
Dover (G-2741)

Integrated Tech Systems LLC ..... G 302 613-2111
New Castle (G-9237)

Integration Logistics Inc ..... E 302 832-7300
Newark (G-11032)

Ip Camera Warehouse LLC ..... G 302 358-2690
Wilmington (G-17415)

Johnson Cntrls SEC Sltions LLC ..... D 302 328-2800
New Castle (G-9263)

Laksh Cybersecurity & Def LLC ..... G 224 258-6564
Wilmington (G-17790)

Linx Security Inc ..... F 302 907-9848
Dover (G-2954)

Lokblok Inc ..... F 408 640-8644
Wilmington (G-17979)

M&S Group International LLC ..... G 302 592-6006
Dover (G-2993)

Novoquad Inc ..... F 800 916-6486
Wilmington (G-18702)

Prevent Alarm Company LLC ..... G 302 478-6647
Historic New Castle (G-5052)

Reolink Innovation Inc ..... G 833 424-0499
Wilmington (G-19433)

S & B Pro Security LLC ..... G 800 841-9907
Dover (G-3496)

Securitas Technology Corp ..... E 302 992-7950
Wilmington (G-19731)

Security 101 Philadlephia LLC ..... F 484 369-7101
Newark (G-11969)

Security Instrument Corp Del ..... D 302 998-2261
Wilmington (G-19733)

Security Quality ..... G 302 286-1200
Newark (G-11970)

Skylark Labs Inc ..... G 415 609-3633
Newark (G-12028)

Skypher Inc ..... F 510 570-5843
Wilmington (G-19859)

Sobieski Life Safety ..... E 800 321-1332
Newark (G-12046)

Sound-N-Secure Inc ..... G 302 424-3670
Milford (G-8095)

Tyco Technology Resources ..... G 877 706-0510
Wilmington (G-20478)

Wahid Consultants LLC ..... E 315 400-0955
Historic New Castle (G-5099)

X-Sense USA LLC ..... G 857 998-3929
Wilmington (G-20911)

7383 News syndicates

Dover Post Co Inc ..... E 302 678-3616
Dover (G-2364)

7384 Photofinish laboratories

▲ Avalanche Strategies LLC ..... C 302 436-7060
Selbyville (G-13469)

Cameras Etc Inc ..... G 302 453-9400
Newark (G-10124)

Colourworks Photographic Svcs ..... G 302 428-0222
Wilmington (G-15540)

Fujifilm Imaging Colorants Inc ..... D 302 472-1245
New Castle (G-9151)

7389 Business services, nec

1313 Innovation ..... G 302 407-0420
Wilmington (G-14107)

208 Social ..... G 610 762-3793
Lewes (G-5637)

2yum Inc ..... G 626 420-4851
Dover (G-1684)

3d Cad Design ..... G 302 373-7750
Newark (G-9711)

3d Exhibits Inc ..... G 302 319-1051
Historic New Castle (G-4914)

4dimensions LLC ..... D 302 339-0082
New Castle (G-8747)

4gurus LLC ..... G 571 789-0012
Lewes (G-5640)

4rb Logistics LLC ..... G 302 290-8187
Newark (G-9714)

550 Suites LLC ..... G 508 651-8197
Rehoboth Beach (G-12591)

6 Star Fundraising LLC ..... G 302 250-5085
Newark (G-9715)

730 Enterprises LLC ..... G 216 355-3008
Historic New Castle (G-4915)

8fig Growth LLC ..... E 442 888-4303
Wilmington (G-14151)

8figures Inc ..... G 484 291-8881
Wilmington (G-14152)

73 BUSINESS SERVICES

A B W Services LLC .... G 856 449-1329
  Townsend (G-13950)

A Hair Hub LLC .... G 267 206-0569
  Bear (G-10)

A Peaceful Pl Intgrted Care LLC ..... F 302 264-3692
  Dover (G-1695)

A-To-Z Management LLC .... G 302 500-5230
  Dover (G-1699)

A1 Nationwide LLC .... G 302 327-9302
  Wilmington (G-14177)

A2a Intgrted Phrmceuticals LLC ... G 270 202-2461
  Lewes (G-5648)

Aaron and Sons Electric LLC .... G 302 764-5610
  Wilmington (G-14187)

Abha Architects Inc .... E 302 658-6426
  Wilmington (G-14201)

Abled Directions LLC .... F 206 265-3928
  Middletown (G-6828)

Accelsiors LLC .... G 302 450-1883
  Dover (G-1705)

Accommodating Nurses LLC .... G 302 390-8065
  Wilmington (G-14226)

Acentium Inc .... F 617 938-3938
  Wilmington (G-14229)

Achievers Holdings Inc .... B 647 265-9032
  Wilmington (G-14232)

Acorn Site Furnishings .... G 302 249-4979
  Bridgeville (G-661)

Acosh Enterprise LLC .... G 631 767-4501
  Newark (G-9758)

ADd Marketing Group LLC .... G 347 668-0992
  Dover (G-1716)

Adriel Inc .... F 860 595-4602
  Newark (G-9768)

Advanced Logistics LLC .... G 302 345-8921
  New Castle (G-8765)

Advanced Modern Care LLC .... F 267 235-6922
  Newark (G-9777)

Advantage Futuretech Company .. G 347 592-5667
  Lewes (G-5662)

Aerospace Dsign Compliance LLC ... G 302 407-6825
  New Castle (G-8769)

Afford-A-Tree Svc & Ldscpg LLC ... G 302 670-4154
  Hartly (G-4854)

AFmensah LLC .... G 302 777-0538
  Wilmington (G-14310)

Agent Launch LLC .... F 302 200-5574
  Newark (G-9796)

AGS Royalty Management LLC ... G 888 292-6995
  Dover (G-1748)

Aids Delaware Inc .... E 302 652-6776
  Wilmington (G-14329)

Ajm Enterprises Inc .... G 302 212-2020
  Rehoboth Beach (G-12599)

Ajp Financial Services LLC .... G 302 798-7582
  Wilmington (G-14342)

Ajusta Tu Corona Inc .... F 203 434-0356
  Dover (G-1758)

Aldas Refinishing Company .... G 302 528-5028
  Hockessin (G-5119)

Alex Property Management LLC .. A 302 384-9845
  Dover (G-1761)

Alixpartners LLP .... F 302 824-7139
  Wilmington (G-14359)

All JS Cleaning Services Inc .... G 302 299-9916
  New Castle (G-8780)

All Lives Matter LLC .... G 252 767-9291
  Dover (G-1763)

All Star Shredding LP .... F 302 325-9998
  New Castle (G-8782)

Allegiant Fire Protection LLC .... G 302 276-1300
  Newark (G-9822)

Alliance Bus Dev Concepts LLC .. F 803 814-4004
  Clayton (G-1348)

Alpha Comm LLC .... F 302 784-0645
  Bear (G-29)

Amazed Apps LLC .... G 916 934-9210
  Dover (G-1781)

American Builder LLC .... G 302 841-2325
  Georgetown (G-4208)

American Chmber Cmmrce In Ukri ... E 352 505-9709
  Wilmington (G-14428)

American-Eurasian Exch Co LLC .. E 202 701-4009
  Wilmington (G-14445)

Ames Music Studio .... G 302 222-4648
  Harrington (G-4730)

Amtrak Material Control .... G 302 319-7270
  New Castle (G-8804)

Amwal Tech Inc .... F 650 391-5496
  Wilmington (G-14465)

Anax Designs .... G 877 908-8719
  Newark (G-9860)

Ankor Tree Service LLC .... G 302 514-7447
  Smyrna (G-13643)

Annadale Oladimeji .... G 267 357-9718
  Wilmington (G-14491)

Antoinette Xavier .... F 980 549-3272
  Harrington (G-4732)

Anybodies Inc .... G 646 699-8781
  Wilmington (G-14497)

Anymoney LLC .... F 818 431-5251
  Dover (G-1798)

AOP Holding Company LLC .... G 346 561-4123
  Dover (G-1800)

Aparta Hospitality Tech .... G 617 383-3239
  Dover (G-1801)

Appcano LLC .... G 951 285-3632
  Wilmington (G-14509)

Apphive Inc .... G 240 898-4661
  Wilmington (G-9888)

Appletree Answering Services Inc ... B 302 227-9015
  Wilmington (G-14510)

Applied Card Holdings Inc .... F 302 326-4200
  Wilmington (G-14512)

Applied Virtual Solutions LLC ..... G 302 312-8548
  Wilmington (G-9892)

Aptustech LLC .... G 347 254-5619
  Wilmington (G-14516)

Aquatic Management .... G 302 235-1818
  Wilmington (G-14519)

Aquia Nava II LLC .... E 410 245-8990
  Millsboro (G-8172)

ARC Falcon I Inc .... G 302 636-5401
  Wilmington (G-14526)

Argo US Feeder Fund LP .... G 345 769-4154
  Wilmington (G-14549)

Arion LLC .... G 215 531-1673
  Dover (G-1813)

Arklight Arsenal LLC .... G 844 722-3766
  Dover (G-1814)

Arrim LLC .... G 617 697-7914
  Wilmington (G-14559)

Artimus LLC .... F 302 546-5350
  Dover (G-1824)

Artsense Inc .... G 302 613-1870
  Middletown (G-6874)

Arvi Vr Inc .... G 844 615-8194
  Wilmington (G-14575)

Arya Life Coaching LLC .... G 610 590-1440
  Lewes (G-5705)

Ascension Industries LLC .... G 302 659-1778
  Smyrna (G-13648)

Assured Affluence LLC .... G 609 468-0250
  Dover (G-1838)

Aster Bouquet Flower Shop LLC .. G 302 258-9242
  Lewes (G-5708)

Astrazeneca Finance LLC .... G 800 677-3394
  Wilmington (G-14607)

At Systems Atlantic Inc .... G 302 762-5444
  Wilmington (G-14612)

At Wilmington .... G 302 235-2554
  Wilmington (G-14614)

Atlantic Sun Screen Prtg Inc .... F 302 731-5100
  Newark (G-9936)

Atlantic Water Products .... E 302 326-1166
  New Castle (G-8831)

Atlas Beauty LLC .... G 904 382-3487
  Dover (G-1850)

Atlas Sp Partners LP .... G 212 325-2777
  Wilmington (G-14632)

Atr Electrical Services Inc .... F 302 373-7769
  Middletown (G-6886)

Au-Naturel Services LLC .... G 775 484-5210
  Dover (G-1853)

Aura Smart Air Inc .... G 847 909-5822
  Wilmington (G-14642)

Automation Machine Design SE ... G 302 335-3911
  Magnolia (G-6720)

Aviman Management LLC .... E 302 377-5788
  Wilmington (G-14669)

Avirm Inc .... D 626 603-1000
  Wilmington (G-14670)

Axalta Coating Systems LLC ...... G 925 838-9876
  Wilmington (G-14678)

B Lawrence Homes LLC .... G 302 559-1779
  Wilmington (G-14702)

Baboon Bubble Inc .... G 302 307-2979
  New Castle (G-8841)

Baibi Wise LLC .... G 201 375-0170
  Newark (G-9973)

Bar & Associates Ltd .... G 302 999-9233
  Wilmington (G-14752)

Baronsky Patrick & Associates ... G 302 529-7585
  Wilmington (G-14767)

Batescainelli LLC .... G 202 618-2040
  Rehoboth Beach (G-12624)

Bayshore Communications Inc ... F 302 737-2164
  Newark (G-9995)

Bayville Postal Svc .... G 302 436-2715
  Selbyville (G-13473)

Be Blessed Design Group LLC ... G 302 561-3793
  Bear (G-59)

Be Humane Co .... G 720 419-5362
  Dover (G-1894)

Beautiful Floors LLC .... G 302 690-5230
  Newark (G-10007)

Beauty Barrettes LLC .... G 302 883-7532
  Newark (G-10008)

Beecanvas Inc .... G 415 800-4980
  Newark (G-10009)

Beeline Services LLC .... G 302 376-7399
  Middletown (G-6910)

Benefactory Ventures Inc .... G 646 693-6186
  Newark (G-10021)

Bernardon LLC .... F 302 622-9550
  Wilmington (G-14848)

Best Processing Solutions LLC .. G 212 739-7845
  Wilmington (G-14856)

Beth Stewart Vo LLC .... G 302 540-7782
  Wilmington (G-14860)

Bethany Beach Vlntr Fire Co ...... E 302 539-7700
  Bethany Beach (G-583)

BETz&betz Enterprises LLC ...... G 302 602-0613
  Wilmington (G-14865)

Big Day Trucking LLC .... G 302 900-1190
  Dover (G-1934)

73 BUSINESS SERVICES

Big Springs Inc .... G 443 570-3003
  Wilmington *(G-14882)*
Big Tomorrow LLC .... F 650 714-3912
  Wilmington *(G-14883)*
Bill Torbert .... F 302 734-9804
  Smyrna *(G-13661)*
Biotech Mentor LLC .... E 617 460-4983
  Dover *(G-1940)*
Bitta Monk Entertainment Inc .... G 916 969-4430
  Newark *(G-10040)*
Biya Global LLC .... G 302 645-7400
  Lewes *(G-5767)*
Bjc-5 LLC .... G 302 230-6733
  Middletown *(G-6923)*
Black Gods and Goddess LLC .... G 708 665-0949
  Dover *(G-1943)*
Blak Mpire LLC .... G 803 966-7648
  Lewes *(G-5769)*
Blaze Coin LLC .... G 509 768-2249
  Dover *(G-1946)*
BLJ&d Flagging Llc .... F 302 272-0574
  Dover *(G-1949)*
Blockware Solutions LLC .... F 512 905-5209
  Dover *(G-1950)*
Blue Collar Utilities LLC .... G 410 422-0886
  Bridgeville *(G-673)*
Blue Diamond RPS & Svcs LLC .... G 856 242-0480
  Wilmington *(G-14964)*
Blue Fin Services LLC .... G 302 633-3354
  Wilmington *(G-14966)*
Blue Heron Contracting LLC .... G 302 526-0648
  Greenwood *(G-4600)*
Bluepoint Systems LLC .... G 817 714-2320
  Lewes *(G-5772)*
Body Matrix .... G 302 220-8406
  New Castle *(G-8872)*
Bogo Publications LLC .... G 877 514-4052
  Christiana *(G-993)*
Bookitngo Corp .... G 949 899-7684
  Dover *(G-1962)*
Boomn Inc .... G 844 808-2666
  Lewes *(G-5775)*
Borne Legacy Logistics LLC .... G 609 346-0480
  New Castle *(G-8876)*
Bosphorus Textile LLC .... F 202 629-6563
  Dover *(G-1965)*
Boulden Brothers .... E 302 368-3848
  Newark *(G-10072)*
Bqt Inc .... G 347 443-8911
  Wilmington *(G-15031)*
Braincx Inc .... F 954 892-9101
  Wilmington *(G-15036)*
Brand Iq Group Inc .... G 302 924-8558
  Lewes *(G-5776)*
Brandywine Hundred Fire Co 1 .... D 302 764-4901
  Wilmington *(G-15067)*
Brandywine Marketing Services .... E 302 761-9755
  Wilmington *(G-15071)*
Brandywine Process Servers .... G 302 475-2600
  Wilmington *(G-15081)*
Brian Patterson PA .... G 203 466-9972
  Milton *(G-8574)*
Brik Labs Inc .... F 302 499-4423
  Wilmington *(G-15115)*
Brittney Ann Fischbeck LLC .... G 302 219-6491
  Dover *(G-1982)*
Broccworth Housing Firm LLC .... G 860 937-6308
  Wilmington *(G-15123)*
Brooks Courier Service Inc .... C 302 762-4661
  Wilmington *(G-15126)*
Brothers Gannon Inc .... G 302 422-2734
  Houston *(G-5437)*

Browns Unlimited 4u LLC .... G 800 940-5880
  Wilmington *(G-15131)*
Brute Performance Inc .... G 757 477-7136
  Camden Wyoming *(G-920)*
Buck Simpers Archt + Assoc Inc ...... F 302 658-9300
  Wilmington *(G-15141)*
Bullent Investment LLC .... G 877 214-7707
  Dover *(G-1991)*
Burkhan International Dev Corp .... E 202 790-8050
  Camden *(G-796)*
Burroughs Express LLC .... G 410 476-1764
  Dover *(G-1996)*
Business At International LLC .... E 605 610-4885
  Lewes *(G-5782)*
Business Move Solutions Inc .... E 302 324-0080
  New Castle *(G-8904)*
Buycrypt Inc .... G 309 733-4157
  Dover *(G-1998)*
By Lore Tech Solutions Inc .... G 302 202-9499
  Middletown *(G-6949)*
C & N Freight LLC .... G 302 897-4061
  New Castle *(G-8906)*
C4-Nvis USA LLC .... G 213 465-5089
  Dover *(G-2009)*
▲ Cad Import Inc .... E 302 628-4178
  Historic New Castle *(G-4950)*
Caliber Club Shooting Spt Inc .... G 703 283-3533
  Dover *(G-2012)*
Cameron Jones .... F 610 880-7700
  Claymont *(G-1071)*
Capade LLC .... G 302 786-5775
  Wilmington *(G-15220)*
Caprini Suites LLC .... F 302 200-8904
  Dover *(G-2025)*
Car Part Planet .... G 888 412-2772
  Rehoboth Beach *(G-12664)*
Care Constitution LLC .... G 201 240-3661
  Middletown *(G-6955)*
Carekraken LLC .... G 410 808-0333
  Middletown *(G-6957)*
Cargo Cube Licensing LLC .... G 844 200-2823
  Wilmington *(G-15247)*
Caribe Technologies Inc .... G 205 590-5767
  Middletown *(G-6959)*
Carolina Street Garden & Home ...... G 302 539-2405
  Fenwick Island *(G-4043)*
Carter Pool Management LLC .... G 302 236-6952
  Lewes *(G-5805)*
Carvers Construction LLC .... G 302 505-0260
  Camden *(G-804)*
Casual Colors Inc .... G 302 298-0523
  Wilmington *(G-15272)*
Catleza LLC .... G 415 812-2676
  Wilmington *(G-15279)*
Center For A Pstive Hmnity LLC ...... G 302 703-1036
  Felton *(G-3952)*
Center For Community Justice .... G 302 424-0890
  Milford *(G-7816)*
Ces Enterprises LLC .... G 302 313-5229
  Rehoboth Beach *(G-12669)*
Chara Tea LLC .... G 856 250-7180
  Dover *(G-2056)*
Chesapeake Design Center LLC ..... G 302 875-8570
  Laurel *(G-5481)*
Chicksx LLC .... E 518 727-1890
  Wilmington *(G-15370)*
Chime Inc .... D 978 844-1162
  Wilmington *(G-15382)*
Chores R Us Inc .... F 844 442-4673
  Dover *(G-2069)*
Christiana Auction Gallery .... G 570 441-7503
  Newark *(G-10216)*

Citigroup Inc .... E 302 631-3530
  Newark *(G-10244)*
City of Dover .... F 302 736-7035
  Dover *(G-2083)*
Clarip Inc .... G 888 252-5653
  Wilmington *(G-15463)*
Clayton Fire Company Prpts LLC ..... G 302 653-7317
  Clayton *(G-1356)*
Clearblue Pools & Spas LLC .... F 888 630-7665
  Millsboro *(G-8230)*
Clearvue Solutions .... G 301 213-3358
  Wilmington *(G-15477)*
Clerk Chat Inc .... G 415 943-6084
  Lewes *(G-5827)*
Click2buy LLC .... G 347 698-7660
  Dover *(G-2092)*
Clinton Craddock .... F 267 505-2671
  Middletown *(G-6995)*
Clipping Beast LLC .... G 850 312-8223
  Middletown *(G-6996)*
Clothes and Crystals LLC .... G 302 316-3405
  Dover *(G-2095)*
Cloudinfo Inc .... G 302 314-5748
  Wilmington *(G-15494)*
Cloudstaff USA LLC .... G 800 730-8615
  Dover *(G-2096)*
Cmd Interiors Inc .... G 917 826-8867
  Rehoboth Beach *(G-12681)*
Cmp Fire LLC .... G 410 620-2062
  Newark *(G-10266)*
Cnooc Finance 2015 USA LLC .... F 302 636-5400
  Wilmington *(G-15505)*
Coastline Realty LLC .... G 302 735-7526
  Dover *(G-2107)*
Cobb Trucking Inc .... G 917 561-6263
  Smyrna *(G-13683)*
Codonrx LLC .... G 773 612-5828
  Dover *(G-2109)*
Coinbase Global Inc .... D 302 777-0200
  Wilmington *(G-15522)*
Cointigo LLC .... F 817 681-7131
  Middletown *(G-7002)*
Collect Africa Inc .... G 657 204-4749
  Wilmington *(G-15529)*
Communication Concepts LLC .... G 302 658-9800
  Wilmington *(G-15557)*
Compete Hr Inc .... E 310 989-9857
  Wilmington *(G-15569)*
Comprehensive Bus Svcs LLC .... F 302 994-2000
  Newark *(G-10292)*
Conducerent Incorporated .... G 302 543-8525
  Wilmington *(G-15588)*
Conference Group LLC .... E 302 224-8255
  Newark *(G-10302)*
Continental Cr Protection LLC .... G 302 456-1930
  Newark *(G-10314)*
Continental Finance Co LLC .... F 302 456-1930
  Wilmington *(G-15618)*
Continental Funding LLC .... G 302 456-1930
  Wilmington *(G-15619)*
Contract Environments Inc .... G 302 658-0668
  Wilmington *(G-15622)*
Conzurge Inc .... F 267 507-6039
  Newark *(G-10318)*
Coolpop Nation .... G 302 584-8833
  Wilmington *(G-15631)*
Cordjia LLC .... F 302 743-1297
  Newark *(G-10322)*
Core Functions LLC .... G 443 956-9626
  Selbyville *(G-13506)*
Coremond LLC .... G 267 797-7090
  Dover *(G-2138)*

SIC SECTION

73 BUSINESS SERVICES

Corn Exchange LLC .... G 302 747-8752
Wyoming *(G-20982)*

Corpomax Inc .... E 302 266-8200
Newark *(G-10326)*

Couture Denim LLC .... G 302 220-8339
New Castle *(G-8983)*

Cowries & Calabash LLC .... G 917 727-8940
Dover *(G-2149)*

Cpf Ckd LLC .... E 855 386-2799
Wilmington *(G-15677)*

Crata Inc .... F 214 606-1731
Dover *(G-2151)*

Crazy Maple Interactive Inc .... F 408 603-7526
Dover *(G-2154)*

Creations By Mae Entps LLC .... G 302 985-5797
Wilmington *(G-15689)*

Creativbar LLC .... G 510 260-3011
Newark *(G-10346)*

Creative Marketing Concepts .... G 302 367-7100
Wilmington *(G-15694)*

Creativity Diversified LLC .... G 302 897-5961
Middletown *(G-7021)*

Credit Lifestyle LLC .... G 302 317-1812
Newark *(G-10351)*

Crossrate Technologies LLC .... G 323 643-5178
Dover *(G-2160)*

Cryptofi Inc .... E 312 813-7188
Dover *(G-2166)*

CSC Networks Inc .... G 302 636-5401
Wilmington *(G-15724)*

CT Innovations LLC .... G 209 559-3595
Dover *(G-2167)*

Culturetech Solutions LLC .... G 415 936-5799
Dover *(G-2169)*

Custom Creations By Design .... G 302 482-2267
Wilmington *(G-15739)*

Customs Benefits .... G 302 798-2884
Wilmington *(G-15745)*

Cws Ballantyne II 99 LLC .... G 302 636-5401
Wilmington *(G-15749)*

Cyber 20/20 Inc .... F 203 802-8742
Newark *(G-10370)*

Cyclops Net Inc .... G 844 979-0222
Camden *(G-812)*

Cycology 202 LLC .... F 610 202-0518
Lewes *(G-5875)*

Cydallia Inc .... G 860 682-0947
Lewes *(G-5876)*

D & F Bussing Inc .... G 302 934-9461
Millsboro *(G-8251)*

D & J Welding LLC .... F 347 706-5561
Dover *(G-2178)*

D A B Productions .... G 302 670-9407
Harrington *(G-4756)*

Dab Deodorant LLC .... G 973 512-2703
New Castle *(G-8993)*

Dabvasan Inc .... G 302 529-1100
Wilmington *(G-15766)*

Dahcor LLC .... G 302 257-2803
Dover *(G-2184)*

Dakk Holdings LLC .... G 571 335-7844
Dover *(G-2186)*

Damon Baca .... G 858 837-0800
Dover *(G-2188)*

Daniel Mitsdarfer T A Dan .... G 302 998-1295
Wilmington *(G-15783)*

Daniel T Metzgar LLC .... G 302 602-4451
Newark *(G-10386)*

Dannys Garage LLC .... G 702 752-9964
Historic New Castle *(G-4967)*

Dark Knight Services Inc .... F 302 468-6237
Wilmington *(G-15794)*

▲ Data MGT Internationale Inc .... E 302 656-1151
Historic New Castle *(G-4968)*

Davait Inc .... G 302 930-0095
Dover *(G-2198)*

David G Horsey & Sons Inc .... D 302 875-3033
Laurel *(G-5494)*

Davin Management Group LLC .... F 302 367-6563
Bear *(G-135)*

DC Consulting Service LLC .... F 617 594-9780
Wilmington *(G-15824)*

DCB Apparel LLC .... G 267 473-0895
Newark *(G-10394)*

Dcc Design Group LLC .... G 302 777-2100
Wilmington *(G-15827)*

Dcoder Inc .... G 716 638-0426
Wilmington *(G-15829)*

DD&k Logistics LLC .... G 301 523-5984
Townsend *(G-13986)*

Ddh (north America) Inc .... G 617 893-9004
Lewes *(G-5885)*

Deafinitions & Interpreting .... F 302 563-7714
Bear *(G-138)*

Deall LLC .... F 305 790-0109
Dover *(G-2204)*

Decoryoucrazy .... F 302 357-8175
Wilmington *(G-15851)*

Dedicated and Driven Hlg LLC .... G 404 909-6031
Newark *(G-10406)*

Delave Denim Co LLC .... G 302 308-5161
Dover *(G-2215)*

Delaware Bail Bonds .... G 302 734-9881
Dover *(G-2217)*

Delaware Barter Corp .... G 800 343-1322
Newark *(G-10420)*

Delaware Company House LLC .... F 302 526-4784
Dover *(G-2223)*

Delaware Fncl Edcatn Alnce Inc .... G 302 674-0288
Dover *(G-2240)*

Delaware Hlth Eqity Cltion Inc .... G 302 383-1701
Middletown *(G-7040)*

Delaware Innovation Space Inc .... G 302 695-2201
Wilmington *(G-15933)*

Delaware Merchant Services .... G 302 838-9100
Wilmington *(G-15944)*

Delaware Mobile Signings LLC .... G 302 316-3926
Millsboro *(G-8263)*

Delaware Mosquito Control LLC .... G 302 504-6757
Newark *(G-10462)*

Delaware Retired Schl Prsnl .... E 302 674-8252
Wilmington *(G-15960)*

Delaware Signing Services LLC .... G 302 464-5038
Middletown *(G-7045)*

Delaware Taxes LLC .... G 302 368-7040
Newark *(G-10490)*

Delaware Trust Company .... E 302 636-5404
Wilmington *(G-15977)*

Delaware Valley Field Svcs LLC .... G 302 384-8617
Wilmington *(G-15981)*

Delco Modular .... G 302 934-7704
Millsboro *(G-8265)*

Dell Oem Inc .... G 302 294-0060
Newark *(G-10498)*

Delmar Process Servers LLC .... F 302 306-2805
Dover *(G-2276)*

Delmarva Irrigation Inc .... F 302 490-1588
Laurel *(G-5498)*

Delmarva Water Solutions .... G 302 674-0509
Dover *(G-2279)*

Delverde Corporation .... G 302 656-1950
Wilmington *(G-16005)*

Dempsey Farms LLC .... G 302 734-4937
Dover *(G-2281)*

Denise Crothers .... G 302 629-7390
Seaford *(G-13157)*

Derby Software LLC .... F 502 435-1371
Dover *(G-2284)*

Design LLC .... G 888 520-7070
Wilmington *(G-16023)*

Designer Consigner Inc .... E 302 373-6318
Rehoboth Beach *(G-12721)*

Dewitt Heating & AC .... G 267 228-7355
Bear *(G-165)*

Dfs Corporate Services LLC .... D 302 735-3902
Dover *(G-2289)*

Dfs Corporate Services LLC .... C 302 323-7191
New Castle *(G-9049)*

Dgc Publishing LLC .... G 302 634-0461
Newark *(G-10521)*

Diamond Standard LLC .... G 917 676-6312
Wilmington *(G-16053)*

Diavaeh Luxury Car Rental LLC .... G 302 497-3443
Middletown *(G-7059)*

Dibiasos Clg Rstration Svc Inc .... G 302 376-7111
Townsend *(G-13992)*

Digiapp LLC .... G 855 217-2744
Lewes *(G-5917)*

Digital Broadcast Corporation .... F 215 285-0912
Wilmington *(G-16064)*

Digital Interxion Holding LLC .... F 737 281-0101
Wilmington *(G-16066)*

Dignisys Inc .... F 845 213-1121
Dover *(G-2298)*

Direct & Correct Inc .... G 302 697-7117
Camden Wyoming *(G-934)*

Disclo Inc .... G 607 280-8949
Dover *(G-2301)*

Divine Legacy Group LLC .... G 973 986-7896
Middletown *(G-7064)*

Divinity Assets LLC .... D 323 508-4130
Dover *(G-2310)*

▲ DLS Discovery LLC .... E 302 888-2060
Wilmington *(G-16105)*

Dm KTure LLC .... G 201 892-3028
Bear *(G-172)*

DMai Boyd LLC .... G 302 330-8293
Dover *(G-2313)*

Dmg Clearances Inc .... G 302 239-6337
Hockessin *(G-5188)*

Do It Up Designs LLC .... G 484 269-6142
Millsboro *(G-8273)*

Doculogica Corp .... G 302 753-5944
Wilmington *(G-16113)*

Document Advisor Inc .... E 786 206-0756
Dover *(G-2318)*

Documo Inc .... E 858 299-5295
Wilmington *(G-16114)*

DOE Technologies Inc .... E 302 792-1285
Wilmington *(G-16116)*

Domestic Gen USA Resources LLC ...... G 312 730-2437
Dover *(G-2320)*

Domian International Svc LLC .... G 804 837-3616
Smyrna *(G-13711)*

Donkey Trucking LLC .... G 302 507-2380
New Castle *(G-9059)*

Donright Services LLC .... G 302 685-7540
Wilmington *(G-16143)*

DOT Matrix Inc .... G 917 657-4918
Dover *(G-2329)*

Dow Advanced Materials .... G 302 607-3061
Bear *(G-179)*

Dr Hivey Corp .... G 580 670-2046
Dover *(G-2373)*

Drafting By Design Inc .... G 302 292-8304
Newark *(G-10569)*

73 BUSINESS SERVICES

Dreams Unlimited LLC .... G 302 747-0527
  Dover (G-2382)
Dreamscape Design Cons LLC .... G 302 893-0984
  Newark (G-10571)
Dreamspell LLC .... G 786 633-1520
  Dover (G-2383)
Du Pont Foreign Sales Corp .... E 302 774-1000
  Wilmington (G-16191)
Duration Media LLC .... G 917 283-5971
  Wilmington (G-16221)
Dustntime .... G 302 858-7876
  Rehoboth Beach (G-12736)
DWK LLC .... G 917 370-7106
  Newark (G-10579)
DXquisite Hair Factory LLC .... G 267 298-0821
  Smyrna (G-13718)
E-Carauctions LLC .... G 302 677-1552
  New Castle (G-9072)
E&A Drywall and Painting Inc .... G 302 393-1743
  Millsboro (G-8278)
Earthborne Equipment & Svc Co .... D 215 343-2000
  Felton (G-3965)
▲ Eastern Shore Metals LLC .... F 302 629-6629
  Seaford (G-13169)
Eastern Shore Onsite Svcs LLC .... G 302 736-0366
  Leipsic (G-5632)
Eazifunds Inc .... F 909 697-6422
  Middletown (G-7079)
EC Innovations USA Inc .... E 312 863-1966
  Wilmington (G-16277)
Echelon Interiors LLC .... G 302 519-9151
  Rehoboth Beach (G-12737)
Ecomo Inc .... G 412 567-3867
  Dover (G-2417)
Eden Care Group Holding LLC .... G 929 461-7247
  Dover (G-2419)
Edmonds Business Ventures LLC .... G 302 772-9112
  Newark (G-10610)
Edokk LLC .... G 305 434-7227
  Lewes (G-5949)
Edtech Consulting LLC .... G 661 644-2990
  Wilmington (G-16297)
Eduqc LLC .... F 800 346-4646
  Dover (G-2425)
Elenore Inc .... G 720 702-9390
  Dover (G-2432)
Elevate Cdb Inc .... E 844 903-4443
  Dover (G-2433)
Elevate RCM Consulting .... G 484 655-8733
  Wilmington (G-16357)
Elite Lubricants LLC .... G 302 629-3301
  Seaford (G-13173)
Elite USA Fashion LLC .... G 810 410-5403
  Claymont (G-1129)
Elsmere Fire Co 1 Inc .... G 302 999-0183
  Wilmington (G-16378)
Ema Corp .... E 302 479-9434
  Wilmington (G-16384)
Emendo Bio Inc .... G 516 595-1849
  Wilmington (G-16389)
Emerging Impact Group Corp .... G 404 625-1530
  Lewes (G-5960)
Emitt LLC .... F 302 757-2353
  Bear (G-201)
Empire Flippers LLC .... E 323 638-0438
  Wilmington (G-16399)
Enclave Digital Development Co .... G 203 807-0400
  Lewes (G-5961)
Encore Lashes Lash Lounge LLC .... G 844 408-0004
  New Castle (G-9094)
END Imports Inc .... G 302 393-2050
  Milford (G-7881)

Endospace Corporation .... G 732 271-8700
  Newport (G-12451)
Endure Walls .... G 302 479-7614
  Wilmington (G-16413)
Enf Ventures LLC .... G 443 475-0175
  Milton (G-8620)
Envision It Publications LLC .... G 800 329-9411
  Bear (G-204)
Epatriotcrm LLC .... G 419 967-6812
  Dover (G-2454)
Esource Systems LLC .... G 302 444-4228
  Newark (G-10666)
Estestwins Trucking LLC .... G 267 773-2991
  Camden Wyoming (G-942)
Estu Inc .... E 407 881-6177
  Wilmington (G-16471)
Etekserve Inc .... G 302 497-4301
  Newark (G-10670)
European Coach Werkes Inc .... G 302 436-2277
  Frankford (G-4106)
Evans Farms LLC .... G 302 337-8130
  Bridgeville (G-699)
Eventsbynye LLC .... G 302 256-3971
  New Castle (G-9104)
Everest Foods Enterprises Inc .... F 215 896-8902
  Wilmington (G-16484)
Evolution Cloud Services Inc .... G 516 507-4026
  Dover (G-2469)
Excella Staffing Solutions LLC .... E 302 985-7373
  Dover (G-2471)
Exclusive Group LLC .... F 917 207-7299
  Wilmington (G-16501)
Exeire Inc .... G 302 232-3555
  Newark (G-10688)
Exercomm Inc .... G 302 438-6130
  Middletown (G-7114)
Ezdorms Inc .... F 202 599-2953
  Wilmington (G-16517)
Ezra Consulting LLC .... F 912 695-5925
  Dover (G-2476)
Falcone Truman Plbg & Htg Inc .... E 302 376-7483
  Odessa (G-12584)
Family Creations .... G 302 239-4275
  Newark (G-10706)
Family Legacy Llccom .... E 302 256-1406
  Wilmington (G-16541)
Fanticipate Inc .... G 763 777-4232
  Wilmington (G-16551)
Fast Bailbonds LLC .... G 302 778-4400
  Wilmington (G-16556)
Federal Business Systems .... D 877 489-2111
  Wilmington (G-16567)
Federal Technical Associates .... G 302 697-7951
  Dover (G-2491)
Fenway Barr LLC .... G 302 222-1913
  Rehoboth Beach (G-12753)
Ferrara Asset Management Inc .... G 401 286-8464
  Wilmington (G-16585)
Ferreira Builders LLC .... G 302 296-6014
  Georgetown (G-4318)
Fetch Social Inc .... G 813 858-5774
  Wilmington (G-16591)
Ff Group LLC .... F 302 608-0609
  Dover (G-2493)
Fia Card Services Nat Assn .... A 302 457-0517
  Wilmington (G-16593)
Fia Card Services Nat Assn .... B 302 458-0365
  Wilmington (G-16595)
Fia Card Services Nat Assn .... B 302 432-1573
  Wilmington (G-16596)
▲ Fia Card Services Nat Assn .... E 800 362-6255
  Wilmington (G-16594)

First Halthcare Compliance LLC .... F 302 416-4329
  Wilmington (G-16618)
First Love Ministries Inc .... G 302 655-1776
  Middletown (G-7130)
First Shipment Inc .... G 206 747-1237
  Lewes (G-5997)
First State Inspection Agency .... G 302 449-5383
  Middletown (G-7132)
First State Inspection Agency .... G 302 422-3859
  Milford (G-7895)
Fiyah B Music LLC .... G 949 656-3246
  Newark (G-10748)
Flute Pro Shop Inc .... G 302 479-5000
  Wilmington (G-16676)
Focal Point Products .... G 800 662-5550
  Greenwood (G-4630)
Food Equipment Service Inc .... G 302 996-9363
  Wilmington (G-16682)
Foos Construction Inc .... G 302 753-3667
  Wilmington (G-16684)
Forged Bdc Inc .... G 561 802-8919
  Newark (G-10764)
Forum To Advnce Mnrties In Eng .... E 302 777-3254
  Wilmington (G-16697)
Founding Principals LLC .... G 917 693-7533
  Bear (G-233)
Fourth Floor .... G 302 472-8416
  Wilmington (G-16710)
Frances Ann Owens .... G 302 436-2333
  Frankford (G-4107)
Free Pdf Technologies Inc .... F 872 204-6733
  Lewes (G-6011)
Freedom Tech Consulting LLC .... G 215 485-7383
  Middletown (G-7140)
Freeman Courier Express .... G 610 803-3933
  Wilmington (G-16743)
Fresh Harvest Hydroponics .... G 302 934-7506
  Millsboro (G-8296)
Fresh Start Transformations .... G 302 219-0221
  Newark (G-10784)
Freshbooks Usa Inc .... G 416 525-5384
  Wilmington (G-16750)
Freshpac LLC .... F 559 648-2210
  Wilmington (G-16751)
Fsd Inc .... G 302 629-7498
  Seaford (G-13191)
FTC Energy Ltd LLC .... G 405 410-9040
  Wilmington (G-16766)
Fujifilm Imaging Colorants Inc .... D 302 472-1298
  Historic New Castle (G-4995)
Fundomundo .... G 617 606-1650
  Wilmington (G-16771)
Future Analytica Software Inc .... F 437 771-2947
  Dover (G-2548)
Galaxy Plus Fund - Lrr Mstr Fu .... G 312 504-0096
  Dover (G-2554)
Galtogether Group .... G 302 562-9170
  Wilmington (G-16797)
Gamers4gamers LLC .... G 302 722-6289
  Newark (G-10804)
Gary Chorman .... G 302 645-2972
  Milton (G-8627)
Generation Cleaning Svc LLC .... G 302 492-2772
  Claymont (G-1158)
Gensource Fincl Asrn Co LLC .... F 302 415-3030
  Wilmington (G-16840)
George Minkalis .... G 302 983-6475
  Newark (G-10823)
Get Takeout LLC .... G 800 785-6218
  Lewes (G-6032)
Getblend Inc .... G 800 720-3722
  Lewes (G-6034)

73 BUSINESS SERVICES

Giesela Inc... G 855 556-4338
  Newark (G-10833)
Gifted Hands 2 LLC.................................... G 302 643-2005
  Dover (G-2582)
Giles Enterprise... G 302 559-2577
  Newark (G-10836)
Girley Bells LLC.. G 347 922-6398
  Newark (G-10839)
Givesendgo LLC... G 302 404-6778
  Dover (G-2588)
Global Lime & Lumber Co Inc.................. G 609 579-1778
  New Castle (G-9170)
Global Shipping Center LLC..................... F 302 798-4321
  Claymont (G-1164)
Globally Srced Vhcles Prts LLC............... E 240 755-4935
  Dover (G-2595)
GM Capital Investments Inc...................... G 302 722-0558
  Newark (G-10854)
Go Marketplace LLC................................. G 630 624-9079
  Wilmington (G-16900)
Goddess Scent Candles LLC................... G 973 885-0606
  Bear (G-250)
Gold Standard Insptn Co LLC.................. G 302 381-0590
  Dagsboro (G-1453)
Goldberry LLC.. G 800 268-4956
  Wilmington (G-16910)
Golden Globe Intl Svcs Ltd....................... C 302 487-0022
  Wilmington (G-16912)
Golden Jewelry... G 302 777-2121
  Wilmington (G-16913)
Goldfinch Group Inc................................... G 646 300-0716
  Dover (G-2601)
Golsonel Global LLC.................................. G 267 461-8400
  Camden Wyoming (G-950)
Good 4 Legacy... G 302 690-4515
  Dover (G-2602)
Goodness Enterprises LLC....................... G 302 674-1400
  Dover (G-2606)
Goodworld Inc.. G 845 325-2232
  Wilmington (G-16928)
Grahams Wireless Solutions Inc.............. G 717 943-0717
  Millsboro (G-8304)
Grayson Home Improvements LLC......... G 302 685-1848
  Wilmington (G-16955)
Grease City Inc.. G 302 661-5675
  Wilmington (G-16957)
Great I AM Prod Studios Inc..................... G 302 463-2483
  New Castle (G-9178)
Great Spirit Ventures LLC......................... G 302 573-3820
  Wilmington (G-16959)
Green Crescent LLC................................. G 800 735-9620
  Dover (G-2622)
Green Lunar LLC....................................... G 650 507-9049
  Rehoboth Beach (G-12778)
Greynote LLC... G 646 287-0705
  Dover (G-2628)
Growing & Glowing LLC............................ G 302 500-9220
  Newark (G-10902)
GSM Systems Inc...................................... F 302 284-8304
  Viola (G-14095)
Gt Designs Inc... G 302 275-8100
  Middletown (G-7181)
Guy & Lady Barrel LLC.............................. G 302 399-3069
  Dover (G-2635)
H S Troyer.. G 302 678-2694
  Dover (G-2641)
H&B Express Logistics.............................. G 815 201-0915
  Dover (G-2642)
◆ H&H Trading International LLC............. G 480 580-3911
  Wilmington (G-17022)
Haloali Teeth Whitening LLC.................... G 302 300-4042
  Claymont (G-1174)

Hanbrun LLC.. G 929 302-6393
  Lewes (G-6073)
Handy Logistics LLC.................................. G 570 905-4173
  New Castle (G-9195)
Happily Active LLC.................................... G 307 317-7277
  Wilmington (G-17053)
Hardwick Tactical Corporation.................. F 787 466-6728
  Wilmington (G-17058)
Harriet Tubman Safe House Inc............... G 302 351-4434
  Wilmington (G-17061)
HART Group LLC...................................... G 302 782-9742
  Dover (G-2660)
Hashout Technologies Inc........................ G 703 622-1689
  Lewes (G-6082)
Hawksbill Systems LLC............................. G 302 494-1678
  Wilmington (G-17080)
Heartland Payment Systems LLC........... G 302 228-9365
  Selbyville (G-13544)
Heavenly Effects LLC................................ G 302 446-3521
  Dover (G-2667)
Helton and Moorehead Trnsp LLC........... G 443 842-3360
  Dover (G-2673)
Henderson Services Inc............................ F 302 424-1999
  Milford (G-7926)
Hibner Group Inc....................................... G 717 281-1918
  Dover (G-2676)
Highway Traffic Controllers....................... G 302 697-7117
  Camden Wyoming (G-953)
Holland Corp... G 302 245-5645
  Selbyville (G-13548)
Homni Health Solution Inc........................ G 408 469-4956
  Dover (G-2691)
Hoosier Osteotronix Corp......................... G 410 241-7627
  Rehoboth Beach (G-12791)
How Medical Marketing Inc...................... F 302 283-9565
  Dover (G-2697)
Hq Global Workplaces Inc........................ G 302 295-4800
  Wilmington (G-17221)
Hts 20 LLP.. G 800 690-2029
  Milton (G-8640)
Hunter Green Inc....................................... F 973 986-3114
  Dover (G-2707)
Hustleofficial247 LLC................................ G 302 465-8965
  Dover (G-2708)
I Love Myself LLC...................................... G 470 474-3347
  Wilmington (G-17248)
Icase LLC.. F 302 703-7854
  Lewes (G-6113)
Ice Cremee Creations............................... G 516 450-2144
  Camden (G-854)
ICS America Inc... F 215 979-1620
  Wilmington (G-17259)
Ict Enterprises Inc...................................... F 302 576-2840
  Wilmington (G-17260)
Ifcf LLC.. G 351 773-4853
  Dover (G-2719)
Imagineyu Designs LLC............................ G 302 387-1230
  Camden Wyoming (G-954)
Imperial Music Group LLC........................ G 302 289-6145
  Newark (G-11004)
Imperial Popcorn Corp.............................. E 847 641-0991
  Newark (G-11005)
Inbound Ignite LLC.................................... G 866 314-4499
  Dover (G-2725)
Inc Plan (usa)... G 302 428-1200
  Wilmington (G-17297)
Incapp Inc... G 318 880-7622
  Wilmington (G-17299)
Industrial Training Cons Inc...................... E 302 266-6100
  Newark (G-11016)
Inetworkz LLC.. F 407 401-9384
  Lewes (G-6123)

Infinite Solutions LLC................................ F 302 438-5310
  Wilmington (G-17322)
Inka and Ezra Foundation Inc.................. G 301 535-1000
  Bear (G-284)
Innova Bus Applications Inc..................... G 405 845-6871
  Dover (G-2736)
Innovative Concepts MGT LLC................ F 866 952-7066
  Wilmington (G-17347)
Insider Insight LLC.................................... G 480 548-0440
  Middletown (G-7226)
Inspiun Tech Solutions LLC...................... G 302 304-3949
  Wilmington (G-17357)
Insta Answer LLC...................................... G 973 303-1764
  Newark (G-11026)
INSTABASE INC....................................... F 628 261-7600
  Dover (G-2739)
Interactive Marketing Services................. E 302 456-9810
  Newark (G-11042)
Interiors Judith Davidson.......................... G 302 841-5500
  Georgetown (G-4372)
International Trade Fin LLC...................... F 302 440-1492
  Dover (G-2748)
Internet Activism Inc.................................. G 206 861-5106
  Wilmington (G-17393)
Intrinsic Realty LLC................................... G 302 425-1025
  Middletown (G-7230)
Introspction Cunseling Ctr LLC................ G 302 213-6158
  Dover (G-2750)
Ipwe Inc.. E 214 438-0820
  Dover (G-2751)
Is2 LLC.. F 302 379-1265
  Hockessin (G-5253)
Isaac F Davis... G 302 656-2050
  Bear (G-290)
Iswich LLC.. G 302 528-0229
  Wilmington (G-17430)
Itconnectus Inc... G 302 531-1139
  Dover (G-2756)
Itdw Group LLC... G 917 503-3574
  Dover (G-2757)
Itl (usa) Limited.. G 302 691-6158
  Wilmington (G-17435)
Its R Joy Llc... E 215 315-8300
  Bear (G-291)
Itskins Americas Inc.................................. G 805 422-6700
  New Castle (G-9245)
J L Carpenter Farms LLC......................... G 302 684-8601
  Milton (G-8644)
J Mamasian & Co LLC.............................. G 302 219-2880
  Milford (G-7948)
J Nichols Enterprises LLC........................ G 302 579-0720
  Dover (G-2759)
Jacks Life Management Inc..................... G 347 757-0720
  Dover (G-2762)
Jamaika.. G 302 521-4842
  Wilmington (G-17475)
James & Patricia Booth............................ G 302 378-9139
  Middletown (G-7238)
James Ray Family & Friends LLC........... G 302 670-0305
  Hartly (G-4881)
James Stewart Rostocki........................... G 302 250-5541
  Wilmington (G-17486)
Jamroxk LLC.. G 302 423-5377
  Dover (G-2770)
Janice James & Joan LLC....................... G 845 682-1886
  Newark (G-11096)
Jarel Industries LLC.................................. G 336 782-0697
  Camden (G-859)
Jason Lewis Pusey.................................... G 302 245-6545
  Bridgeville (G-717)
JBA Enterprises LLC................................. G 302 834-6685
  Bear (G-301)

73 BUSINESS SERVICES

Company	Location (ID)	Code	Phone
Jbj Enterprise LLC	Rehoboth Beach (G-12802)	G	302 227-6080
Jbm Petroleum Service LLC	Lincoln (G-6677)	G	302 752-6105
Jbs Kitchen LLC	New Castle (G-9256)	G	302 487-3830
JC Industrial Solutions Inc	Claymont (G-1197)	G	484 720-8381
Jefferson Group LLC	Wilmington (G-17517)	G	302 764-1550
Jeffrey Glenn Minor	Greenwood (G-4645)	G	302 422-3403
Jet Green Transporters LLC	Dover (G-2785)	G	302 861-8918
Ji DCI Jv-II	Wilmington (G-17544)	G	302 652-4221
Jill L Alfree	Clayton (G-1376)	G	302 653-9107
Jira LLC	Dover (G-2790)	G	302 202-4615
Jl Mechanical Inc	Bridgeville (G-719)	G	302 337-7855
Jmt Services Inc	Middletown (G-7250)	F	302 530-2807
Joff Capital LLC	Dover (G-2795)	G	216 682-6822
John Li-Ameriprise Finvl Srvcs	Lewes (G-6144)	G	302 200-9548
▲ Johnny Janosik Inc	Laurel (G-5537)	C	302 875-5955
Jonathan Lopez	Magnolia (G-6754)	G	302 752-5229
Jonathon Gordon	Wilmington (G-17573)	G	302 690-0614
Jones Property Company	Wilmington (G-17575)	G	302 213-2695
◆ Joseph J Sheeran Inc	New Castle (G-9266)	E	302 324-0200
Joshua Tilghman	Middletown (G-7254)	G	302 582-1491
Js Sheds LLC	Wilmington (G-17603)	F	484 918-0633
Jthan LLC	Wilmington (G-17606)	G	302 994-2534
Juega LLC	Dover (G-2815)	G	716 256-3186
Junction Expert Insights Corp	Dover (G-2819)	G	202 710-9258
Just Wallet Inc	Wilmington (G-17618)	G	770 925-5098
K&D Inc	Harbeson (G-4704)	G	302 945-7036
Kairon Corp	Lewes (G-6158)	F	347 688-3993
Kamara LLC	Wilmington (G-17643)	G	302 220-9570
Kamina LLC	Wilmington (G-17644)	G	347 200-0935
Kancapi LLC	Lewes (G-6159)	E	949 508-0350
Katherine Nwman Dsign Intl LLC	Wilmington (G-17662)	G	416 922-5806
Kdg Solutions LLC	Smyrna (G-13786)	G	302 494-4693
Kevin McDaniel	Georgetown (G-4393)	E	302 236-1451
Keys R US LLC	Lincoln (G-6678)	G	619 886-8774
Khmisat LLC	Newark (G-11170)	G	302 533-1303
▲ Kid Agains Inc	Dover (G-2864)	G	631 830-5228
Kids University LLC	Dover (G-2868)	G	302 514-8187
Kings Towing Company LLC	Newark (G-11179)	G	302 345-3134
Kintyre Solutions Inc	Wilmington (G-17729)	G	888 636-0010
Kirks Flowers Inc	Newark (G-11181)	G	302 737-3931
Kjan Innovations LLC	Middletown (G-7278)	G	954 388-1293
Klh Properties Ltd Lblty Co	Wilmington (G-17741)	G	352 208-8964
Klick Inc	Newark (G-11191)	F	302 292-8455
Knowt Inc	Lewes (G-6170)	F	848 391-0575
Knrp LLC	Dover (G-2881)	G	408 480-8501
Korsgy Technologies LLC	Wilmington (G-17748)	G	302 504-6201
Kriss Contracting Inc	Hartly (G-4893)	E	302 492-3502
Kristian Express LLC	Newark (G-11202)	G	302 528-7577
L & K Real Estate LLC	Bear (G-337)	F	484 410-4898
L&L Logistics Inc	Wilmington (G-17778)	F	720 232-5637
L2 Trade LLC	Dover (G-2893)	F	603 921-7930
Lake Properties Group LLC	Dover (G-2900)	G	516 695-1441
Laksh Cybersecurity & Def LLC	Wilmington (G-17790)	G	224 258-6564
Land Lock LLC	Middletown (G-7287)	G	302 747-6124
Langdon Group LLC	Dover (G-2903)	G	240 578-5400
Language Liaisons LLC	Wilmington (G-17804)	F	302 545-4257
Lashedbyindie LLC	Dover (G-2905)	G	267 734-4850
Latam Corporate Services LLC	Dover (G-2906)	F	301 375-0714
Latham Logistics	Townsend (G-14025)	G	215 760-4724
Lawing Musical Products LLC	Newark (G-11232)	G	302 533-7548
Legend Enterprises LLC	Bear (G-343)	G	267 278-9892
Lel Wealth MGT & Tech Svc LLC	Wilmington (G-17872)	G	804 243-0009
Liberty Consultancy Firm LLC	Dover (G-2935)	E	302 493-4344
Lifehuse Erly Chldhood Ctr LLC	Townsend (G-14027)	E	302 464-1105
Lifescore Inc	Middletown (G-7300)	G	808 780-4645
Lifesquared Inc	Dover (G-2942)	G	415 475-9090
Lifetime Financial Svcs LLC	Dover (G-2943)	G	302 678-1300
Lightrun Inc	Wilmington (G-17909)	E	646 453-6616
Likehoop Inc	Dover (G-2947)	G	646 643-7738
Lily B LLC	Bear (G-348)	F	302 290-5223
Lineage Auto Group L L C	New Castle (G-9313)	G	302 595-2119
Linkers Inc	Dover (G-2952)	F	408 757-0021
Linx Realty 2 LLC	Dover (G-2953)	G	888 233-8901
Lions Group LLC	Magnolia (G-6762)	G	302 535-6584
Lit Xpress LLC	Newark (G-11269)	G	302 690-9520
Litcharts LLC	Wilmington (G-17934)	G	646 481-4807
Liv180 Inc	Dover (G-2958)	G	561 235-9669
Live Typing Inc	Wilmington (G-17949)	G	415 670-9601
Lkb Management Group LLC	Dover (G-2961)	G	919 561-2815
LLC Gage Park	Newark (G-11274)	G	302 738-6680
Lne Power LLC	Wilmington (G-17963)	G	913 777-7552
Load Miles Inc	Dover (G-2965)	F	323 842-7038
Local Life Marketing Group LLC	Bear (G-352)	G	877 514-4052
Local Mobile LLC	Dover (G-2967)	F	619 759-0114
Longview Capital MGT LLC	Wilmington (G-17987)	F	302 353-4720
Looksiebin LLC	Wilmington (G-17991)	G	410 869-2192
Lotus Separations LLC	Newark (G-11286)	G	302 345-2510
Loudoun Modern LLC	Dewey Beach (G-1673)	G	703 447-6688
Love & Hope Rescue Mission Inc	Newark (G-11288)	G	302 332-3829
Lumber Industries Inc	Wilmington (G-18025)	G	302 655-9651
M & M Detail Wrap and Tint LLC	Wilmington (G-18056)	G	302 260-8988
MA Adas LLC	Wilmington (G-18062)	G	302 420-8158
Maciels Imports LLC	Wilmington (G-18069)	G	562 295-6773
Maggie Magpie Inc	Middletown (G-7321)	G	302 331-5061
Mail Express	Middletown (G-7324)	G	302 376-5151
Mail Stop	Millsboro (G-8360)	G	302 947-4704
Makatuu Inc	Dover (G-3000)	G	650 431-5582
Manners Brand LLC	Dover (G-3009)	G	470 830-1114
Mariano Lozano	Wilmington (G-18128)	G	302 478-6710
Mark Showell Interiors Ltd	Rehoboth Beach (G-12849)	F	302 227-2272
Markland Affiliates LLC	Wilmington (G-18149)	G	302 633-9134
Matrixport Inc	Dover (G-3032)	G	626 474-8738
Matter Music Inc	Wilmington (G-18194)	F	650 793-7749
Maxweb Inc	Wilmington (G-18207)	G	302 208-8361
Mazzpac Inc	Newark (G-11364)	G	973 641-9159
MBNA Marketing Systems Inc	Wilmington (G-18213)	A	302 456-8588
McConnell Bros Inc	Wilmington (G-18223)	G	302 218-4240
McRogge LLC	Middletown (G-7336)	G	215 300-7975

73 BUSINESS SERVICES

Mdaas Global Corp .... G 410 905-1213
  Dover *(G-3045)*

Mdnewsline Inc .... G 773 759-4363
  Dover *(G-3046)*

Medarch Inc .... F 405 638-3126
  Dover *(G-3049)*

Medical Sup Support Svcs LLC .... F 302 446-3658
  Dover *(G-3052)*

Medusind Solutions Inc .... B 800 250-7063
  Newark *(G-11379)*

Megan Gorelick Interiors Inc .... G 302 482-1325
  Montchanin *(G-8738)*

Mekhala Living Inc .... G 650 443-8235
  Dover *(G-3056)*

Melanated Minds Foundation LLC .... G 302 312-5303
  Wilmington *(G-18262)*

Melanin Mixx Beauty Brand Inc .... G 302 266-1010
  Newark *(G-11385)*

Mello Financial Inc .... G 801 877-7787
  Wilmington *(G-18264)*

Mercantile Processing Inc .... E 302 524-8000
  Millville *(G-8540)*

Merchant Global Assistance LLC .... G 914 522-4871
  Dover *(G-3062)*

Mercuri Inc .... G 425 395-5238
  Wilmington *(G-18276)*

Mergers Acqstons Strtegies LLC .... G 302 992-0400
  Wilmington *(G-18280)*

Merix LLC .... G 425 659-1425
  Lewes *(G-6265)*

Metal Shop LLC .... F 302 846-2988
  Delmar *(G-1620)*

Metaquotes Software Corp .... E 657 859-6918
  Wilmington *(G-18289)*

Metawork Corporation .... G 347 756-1222
  Wilmington *(G-18290)*

Mg Global Group LLC .... G 302 217-3724
  Newark *(G-11397)*

Mgts Global Inc .... G 302 385-6636
  Wilmington *(G-18300)*

Mhyhwh LLC .... G 302 518-0992
  Bear *(G-371)*

Microcom Tech LLC .... G 858 775-5559
  Rehoboth Beach *(G-12853)*

Middle Dept Insptn Agcy Inc .... F 302 875-4514
  Laurel *(G-5564)*

Middle Room LLC .... G 302 220-9979
  New Castle *(G-9369)*

Midnight Blue Inc .... F 302 436-9665
  Selbyville *(G-13576)*

Milfordlivecom .... G 302 542-9231
  Milford *(G-8010)*

Millenium Loan Fund LLC .... G 302 996-4811
  Wilmington *(G-18362)*

Milpa Nativa Inc .... G 512 668-9033
  Wilmington *(G-18369)*

Milton Mail Boxes .... G 302 664-2623
  Milton *(G-8672)*

Mission Movement Transport LLC .... G 302 480-9401
  Lincoln *(G-6688)*

Mitchell Associates Inc .... E 302 594-9400
  New Castle *(G-9373)*

Mitek Holdings Inc .... D 302 429-1816
  New Castle *(G-9374)*

ML Ruiz Enterprises Inc .... G 302 894-9000
  Newark *(G-11433)*

Mommin With Swag LLC .... G 302 373-6316
  Newark *(G-11439)*

Money Ex Pos Solutions US Inc .... E 866 946-6773
  Dover *(G-3118)*

Monica Bumbrey .... G 302 538-1942
  Dover *(G-3120)*

Montesino Technologies Inc .... G 302 888-2355
  Wilmington *(G-18423)*

Montrae Denorris Jones LLC .... G 770 851-3836
  Dover *(G-3121)*

Morgan Louise Fndtn LLC .... F 302 670-5792
  Clayton *(G-1388)*

Morning After Inc .... G 302 562-5190
  Hartly *(G-4899)*

Moscova Svrign Irrvcble Prvate .... G 347 973-2522
  Wilmington *(G-18461)*

Movetec Fitness Equipment LLC .... G 302 563-4487
  New Castle *(G-11460)*

Moving Club LLC .... G 929 377-9332
  New Castle *(G-9384)*

Moving Sciences LLC .... G 617 871-9892
  Wilmington *(G-18467)*

Ms Neat Cleaning Services LLC .... G 302 535-7236
  Dover *(G-3130)*

Msb Enterprise Partners LLC .... G 302 947-0736
  Millsboro *(G-8396)*

Msgg LLC .... G 917 565-8306
  Dover *(G-3131)*

Mt Cuba Center Inc .... C 302 239-4244
  Hockessin *(G-5313)*

Multiples Adams Service LLC .... F 302 792-0710
  Claymont *(G-1246)*

Mumford-Bjorkman Assoc Inc .... F 302 655-8234
  Wilmington *(G-18485)*

Muncie Insurance & Fincl Svcs .... G 302 645-7740
  Rehoboth Beach *(G-12867)*

Murry Trucking Llc .... F 302 653-4811
  Smyrna *(G-13830)*

Myfurtribe Inc .... G 210 904-3036
  Hockessin *(G-5314)*

Mystash Inc .... F 202 867-8874
  Wilmington *(G-18513)*

N J Jackson Realestate Inv LLC .... F 602 783-4064
  Wilmington *(G-18515)*

Nabu Casa Inc .... E 747 477-3105
  Dover *(G-3143)*

Nancy Dufresne .... G 302 378-7236
  Townsend *(G-14042)*

Nano Wallet Company LLC .... G 443 610-3402
  Wilmington *(G-18529)*

Nanticoke Consulting Inc .... G 302 424-0750
  Greenwood *(G-4655)*

National Opprtnities Unlimited .... G 913 905-2261
  New Castle *(G-9398)*

National Signing Source LLC .... G 773 885-3285
  Wilmington *(G-18546)*

Nautical Flfllment Lgstics LLC .... G 816 810-3118
  Dover *(G-3160)*

Nava .... G 515 495-4577
  Wilmington *(G-18560)*

Neil Services Inc .... G 302 573-2265
  Wilmington *(G-18574)*

Neodata LLC .... E 302 666-2848
  Dover *(G-3169)*

Neso Trucking LLC .... G 302 358-7878
  New Castle *(G-9403)*

Nettel Partners LLC .... F 215 290-7383
  Rehoboth Beach *(G-12869)*

New Vision Services Inc .... G 484 350-6495
  Newark *(G-11526)*

Newark Wings LLC .... E 302 455-9464
  Newark *(G-11549)*

Newton Management Holding Inc .... F 800 784-8714
  Middletown *(G-7401)*

Next Level Home Improvements .... G 484 469-1767
  Claymont *(G-1251)*

Next Level Staffing Solutions .... F 302 281-4777
  Dover *(G-3185)*

Nfinity Inc .... F 852 642-9800
  Wilmington *(G-18639)*

Nickels Arcade LLC .... G 800 979-3224
  Middletown *(G-7405)*

Nimbis Designs LLC .... F 302 494-7584
  Hockessin *(G-5321)*

Nina Woof LLC .... G 210 492-6617
  Dover *(G-3190)*

Niru LLC .... G 617 893-7317
  Lewes *(G-6316)*

No Joke I LLC .... G 302 395-0882
  New Castle *(G-9421)*

Noble Property LLC .... E 718 502-4806
  Dover *(G-3192)*

Noel Auto Sales LLC .... G 302 286-7355
  Newark *(G-11561)*

Notary Ltd .... G 302 635-1176
  Wilmington *(G-18690)*

Nouvir Lightning Corporation .... G 302 628-9888
  Seaford *(G-13320)*

Novo Financial Corp .... F 844 260-6800
  Dover *(G-3205)*

Nrai Services LLC .... F 302 674-4089
  Dover *(G-3208)*

Nutax Financial Services LLC .... G 302 834-9357
  Newark *(G-11570)*

Nvcomputers Inc .... G 860 878-0525
  Wilmington *(G-18722)*

Oak Lane Court Associates LP .... F 302 764-6450
  Wilmington *(G-18726)*

Oaks Lab Academy LLC .... G 509 481-5630
  Wilmington *(G-18728)*

Oasis Home Inc .... F 949 331-5405
  Wilmington *(G-18732)*

Oasis Security Inc .... G 332 867-8141
  Wilmington *(G-18733)*

Oasm Corp .... F 203 679-9124
  Dover *(G-3213)*

Objects Worldwide Inc .... G 703 623-7861
  Wilmington *(G-18737)*

Oerigo Consulting LLC .... G 302 353-4719
  Smyrna *(G-13841)*

Oink Oink LLC .... G 302 924-5034
  Dover *(G-3217)*

Olsen Enterprises Inc .... G 443 928-0089
  Georgetown *(G-4451)*

Olympus Consulting LLC .... G 302 353-7329
  Smyrna *(G-13842)*

Om Ganesh Two LLC .... G 410 720-9374
  Delmar *(G-1627)*

Omnisets LLC .... G 425 229-1592
  Dover *(G-3225)*

Omogs Group Corp .... G 302 645-7400
  Lewes *(G-6333)*

One Codex Inc .... G 226 406-8524
  Wilmington *(G-18778)*

Onollo Inc .... G 925 286-4797
  Dover *(G-3232)*

Oobla Inc .... G 416 230-9119
  Dover *(G-3233)*

Oracle Enterprises LLC .... G 407 900-2828
  Wilmington *(G-18810)*

Organic Intelligence LLC .... G 949 423-3665
  Wilmington *(G-18818)*

Otc Trade LLC .... G 603 820-5820
  Camden *(G-883)*

Out-Train Fitness & Prfmce LLC .... G 610 470-3196
  Milton *(G-8680)*

P A Cnmri .... D 302 678-8100
  Dover *(G-3257)*

Packaging Mania (not Inc) .... G 917 410-6835
  Milford *(G-8041)*

Employee Codes: A=Over 500 employees, B=251-500
C=101-250, D=51-100, E=20-50, F=10-19, G=1-9

73 BUSINESS SERVICES

Company	Code	Phone
Padi Technology Ltd — Middletown (G-7421)	G	832 646-6926
Padrino Records LLC — Hst Newcastle (G-5451)	G	609 353-4683
Pagos Solutions Inc — Middletown (G-7422)	F	310 245-3591
Palm Nft Studio Inc — Dover (G-3262)	G	216 870-9066
Pango Financial LLC — Wilmington (G-18874)	G	855 949-7264
Paragon Serenity LLC — Newark (G-11624)	G	302 784-4979
Paramunt Hlthcare Rsources LLC — Middletown (G-7425)	F	302 722-5484
Parcel Tech Inc — Wilmington (G-18888)	G	720 663-0558
Parcly LLC — Dover (G-3272)	G	347 305-6820
Parkobility LLC — Dover (G-3273)	E	877 298-5550
Pat & Ray Enterprises — Lewes (G-6352)	G	302 945-1367
Patrick Gaydos — Middletown (G-7429)	G	302 378-8753
Patriot Systems Inc — Wilmington (G-18912)	G	302 472-9727
Paul C Cunningham & Assoc LLC — Lewes (G-6355)	G	302 258-4163
Payourse Technologies Inc — Wilmington (G-18929)	F	206 922-8971
Pcd Solutions LLC — Wilmington (G-18933)	G	877 723-7552
Pen Enterprises LLC — Claymont (G-1261)	F	302 798-0268
Pennie Mgmt LLC — Wilmington (G-18955)	G	847 682-1644
Percebe Music Inc — Dover (G-3296)	G	850 341-9594
Perceri LLC — Dover (G-3297)	G	217 721-8731
Perisphere Inc — Dover (G-3299)	G	908 581-8058
Perkwiz Inc — Hockessin (G-5341)	G	702 866-9122
Persha LLC — Dover (G-3303)	G	786 925-2952
Pettinaro Residential LLC — Wilmington (G-19003)	F	302 999-0708
Phazebreak Coatings LLC — Wilmington (G-19013)	G	844 467-4293
Pheonixfire L L C — Newark (G-11682)	G	302 588-8220
Piis Global LLC — Lewes (G-6368)	E	628 600-5249
Pillar To Post — Magnolia (G-6774)	G	410 804-8626
Pillar To Post — Millsboro (G-8428)	G	908 319-4493
Pk & Associates Group Inc — Wilmington (G-19061)	G	302 394-9052
Plain & Fancy Inc — Wilmington (G-19063)	G	302 656-9901
Planet Payment Inc — New Castle (G-9475)	D	516 670-3200
Platformavr Inc — Dover (G-3328)	G	302 330-8980
Platinum Plus Enterprise LLC — Middletown (G-7456)	G	302 200-2257
Platinum World LLC — Dover (G-3331)	G	302 321-5040
Playpower Labs Inc — Dover (G-3335)	F	917 544-4171
Pmbtexas Enterprises LLC — Newark (G-11704)	G	254 993-1530
Polyjohn Acquisition LLC — Wilmington (G-19114)	G	800 292-1305
Pony Up Inc — Dover (G-3350)	G	323 205-7669
Pop-A-Docs All Ntral Hrbal Spp — Wilmington (G-19116)	G	302 622-5788
Poshlife Acquisitions LLC — Dover (G-3354)	G	516 376-7402
Positioneering LLC — Wilmington (G-19124)	G	302 415-3200
Postal Connections Inc — Hockessin (G-5349)	G	302 239-1129
Pradhan Energy Projects — Hockessin (G-5351)	G	305 428-2123
Pretty Girl Press — Wilmington (G-19184)	G	484 668-0770
Private Society LLC — Newark (G-11753)	G	302 319-7126
Process Academy LLC — Wilmington (G-19207)	G	302 415-3104
Prognstc Hlthcare Rsurces LLC — Smyrna (G-13857)	G	762 217-6323
Proksy Research LLC — Wilmington (G-19227)	F	737 238-0104
Promofill — Historic New Castle (G-5055)	G	302 276-2700
Prospect De — Dover (G-3382)	G	302 382-6579
Prospect Inspection Services — Dover (G-3383)	F	302 381-0110
Provaxus Inc — Dover (G-3385)	G	773 832-8015
Prudent Technology & Svcs LLC — Dover (G-3387)	F	302 481-6399
Prysm Financial Technology Inc — Middletown (G-7478)	F	323 333-7698
Pucketts Heating Adn Air — Harrington (G-4814)	G	443 239-2129
Pulsar360 Corp — Newark (G-11771)	E	855 578-5727
Pyle Hlg & Junk Removal LLC — Newark (G-11779)	G	302 750-7227
Python Software Foundation — Dover (G-3402)	F	970 305-9455
Qisstpay Inc — Dover (G-3404)	G	817 239-3900
Quadrosense LLC — Dover (G-3406)	G	302 608-0779
Quaestor Global Holdings Inc — Wilmington (G-19280)	F	610 745-3115
Qualdent LLC — Wilmington (G-19282)	G	856 642-4078
Quality Distributors Inc — Wilmington (G-19283)	G	917 335-6662
Quality Pool Care — Middletown (G-7487)	G	302 378-7486
Quantum Alchemy LLC — New Castle (G-9507)	G	484 299-8016
Quikstamp LLC — Newark (G-11800)	F	302 659-7555
Quotanda LLC — Dover (G-3413)	G	917 971-7585
R A Baba A Holdings Inc — Newark (G-11804)	G	302 533-8441
R&C Contractors LLC — Felton (G-4011)	F	302 284-9870
Rage Recording Studio LLC — Middletown (G-7499)	G	302 313-1699
Raiden Tech Group Inc — Newark (G-11820)	G	302 330-8514
Rainbow Xpress Lrng Acdemy LLC — Smyrna (G-13861)	G	302 659-0750
Ralph Paul Inc — Wilmington (G-19325)	G	302 764-9162
Rare Royals Incorporated — Middletown (G-7502)	G	833 288-7171
Rays and Sons Mechanical LLC — Seaford (G-13367)	G	302 697-2100
Reachable Solutions Inc — Dover (G-3430)	G	908 962-8076
Reagan-Watson Auctions LLC — Milford (G-8060)	G	302 422-2392
Realassist Inc — Dover (G-3435)	F	888 309-1114
Rebatus Inc — Lewes (G-6412)	G	929 393-5529
Reciprocity Health LLC — Wilmington (G-19378)	G	302 530-5244
Recreate Inc — Wilmington (G-19380)	G	404 625-3387
Red Stone USA Inc — Lewes (G-6413)	E	919 931-5078
Red Sun Custom Apparel Inc — Selbyville (G-13597)	F	302 988-8230
Redgait 2530 LLC — Wilmington (G-19387)	G	302 683-0978
Regal Painting & Decorating — Wilmington (G-19398)	G	302 994-8943
Registered Agents Ltd — Wilmington (G-19407)	F	302 421-5750
Registred Agnts Legal Svcs LLC — Wilmington (G-19409)	G	302 427-6970
Rehoboth Bch Sister Cites Assn — Rehoboth Beach (G-12916)	G	302 249-7878
Reliable Home Inspection — Wilmington (G-19423)	G	302 455-1200
Renderapps LLC — Dover (G-3454)	G	919 274-0582
Rennies Rolled Ice Cream LLC — New Castle (G-9521)	G	551 273-8925
Reservation Centre LLC — Dover (G-3459)	E	888 284-0908
Retrotekusa Inc — Wilmington (G-19446)	G	469 619-0899
Revolutionary Identity Elusion — Dover (G-3462)	G	618 780-1755
Revolve Training Staffing LLC — Wilmington (G-19448)	G	833 973-8658
Reyes Rebeca — New Castle (G-9530)	G	302 276-9132
Richard E Williams — Seaford (G-13373)	G	302 956-0374
Right Knda Guys Car Sltons LLC — Newark (G-11884)	G	302 772-8717
Right Way Flagging and Sign Co — Camden Wyoming (G-969)	F	302 698-5229
Risleus Properties LLC — Dover (G-3473)	F	302 353-1255
River Tower Ventures LLC — Wilmington (G-19491)	G	302 691-2100
Riverbend Inv MGT LLC Is A Rgs — Rehoboth Beach (G-12936)	G	302 219-3080
Rmdc Inc — Claymont (G-1280)	G	302 798-8800
Rock City Consulting Corp — Wilmington (G-19527)	G	302 551-6844
Rockeias Journey LLC — Newark (G-11903)	G	302 304-3055
Rockwood Conference Center — Wilmington (G-19545)	G	302 761-4342
Rohma Inc — Newark (G-11911)	G	909 234-5381

73 BUSINESS SERVICES

Roll Out Transit LLC .... G 800 233-1680
   Hockessin *(G-5371)*

Ron English Enterprises Inc .... G 302 981-9276
   Middletown *(G-7522)*

Round Table Men LLC .... G 302 287-8200
   New Castle *(G-9542)*

Royalrose302 LLC .... G 800 259-7918
   New Castle *(G-9547)*

Roz Health LLC .... G 415 259-8992
   Newark *(G-11923)*

Ryes Hvac LLC .... G 302 981-7851
   New Castle *(G-9549)*

S & S Mgnt Co LLC .... G 302 353-9249
   Middletown *(G-7531)*

S Brown Appraisals LLC .... G 302 672-0694
   Harrington *(G-4825)*

S3staffingusa Inc .... F 248 986-6062
   Middletown *(G-7533)*

Safra Inc .... G 302 305-0755
   Wilmington *(G-19629)*

Saisha Spices LLC .... G 786 288-3344
   Dover *(G-3506)*

Sakempire Distribution LLC .... F 800 838-0615
   Wilmington *(G-19635)*

Sanad Cash Inc .... G 302 314-8170
   Middletown *(G-7537)*

Savemunch Inc .... G 469 473-1501
   Lewes *(G-6449)*

Sbr Enterprises LLC .... G 302 836-6909
   Middletown *(G-7539)*

SC Ennis Incorporated .... F 302 629-8771
   Seaford *(G-13384)*

Schwartz Center For Arts .... G 302 678-3583
   Dover *(G-3517)*

Scientific USA Inc .... G 425 681-9462
   Wilmington *(G-19707)*

Scottish Ventures LLC .... G 302 382-6057
   New Castle *(G-9554)*

Sensofusion Inc .... F 570 239-4912
   Milton *(G-8710)*

Sergios Pool Service Inc .... G 302 655-1972
   Wilmington *(G-19758)*

Serrano Inc .... G 302 607-1779
   Newark *(G-11982)*

Servant Support Services LLC .... F 215 201-5990
   Newark *(G-11984)*

Shanills Crtive Styles Brids L .... G 302 508-9215
   Dover *(G-3540)*

Shawnee 1892 LLC .... G 302 738-6680
   Newark *(G-11991)*

Shelton Laday Hammond Jr .... G 302 832-6257
   New Castle *(G-9566)*

Shes Filming Productions LLC .... G 302 563-0336
   Dover *(G-3543)*

Shore Answer LLC .... G 302 253-8381
   Georgetown *(G-4511)*

Shore Smoke Seasonings LLC .... G 302 943-4675
   Smyrna *(G-13884)*

Showbiz Trucking LLC .... G 302 526-6337
   Camden *(G-893)*

Sibacpay Inc .... G 302 257-5784
   Middletown *(G-7563)*

Sigmasat USA Inc .... G 561 488-8048
   Wilmington *(G-19819)*

Signin Soft Inc .... F 315 966-6699
   Wilmington *(G-19823)*

Silpada Designs .... G 302 376-6964
   Middletown *(G-7566)*

Silver Bridge Capital Mgmt LLC .... G 302 575-9215
   Wilmington *(G-19827)*

Simple Space LLC .... G 801 520-3680
   Wilmington *(G-19835)*

Simpliigence Inc .... D 404 528-7646
   Dover *(G-3563)*

Sinkeeas Lounge & Bar LLC .... F 302 434-2530
   Newark *(G-12013)*

Sirqil LLC .... F 213 204-9333
   Dover *(G-3569)*

Sister Sister Covid Clean LLC .... G 267 467-8803
   Dover *(G-3570)*

Six Angels Development Inc .... G 302 218-1548
   Wilmington *(G-19846)*

Six Days Inc .... E 888 463-5898
   Wilmington *(G-19847)*

Six Sigma Telecom LLC .... G 302 636-5440
   Wilmington *(G-19849)*

Skjaldborg Artisans LLC .... G 302 698-7552
   Milford *(G-8093)*

Skylines One LLC .... G 646 400-0535
   Lewes *(G-6475)*

Slaybelles LLC .... G 302 304-1027
   Wilmington *(G-19862)*

SM Technomine Inc .... F 312 492-4386
   Wilmington *(G-19869)*

SM Technomine Inc .... F 312 492-4386
   Wilmington *(G-19870)*

Smart Altcoins Inc .... G 626 540-9415
   Lewes *(G-6480)*

Smart Hospitality & MGT LLC .... G 212 444-1989
   Wilmington *(G-19877)*

Sme Masonry Contrs Ltd Lblty .... F 302 743-7338
   Wilmington *(G-19883)*

Smiths Work At HM Slutions LLC .... G 302 367-6671
   New Castle *(G-9575)*

Snow & Assoc Gen Cnstr Co LLC .... F 302 420-0564
   Wilmington *(G-19901)*

Social Finance Inc .... G 707 473-3000
   Claymont *(G-1293)*

Social Keyboard Inc .... F 650 519-8383
   Dover *(G-3585)*

Social Wonder Inc .... F 646 419-8009
   Wilmington *(G-19908)*

Socialcash Inc .... F 310 293-6072
   Wilmington *(G-19909)*

Society For Acpuncture RES Inc .... G 302 222-1832
   Lewes *(G-6488)*

Solution Seeker Cons LLC .... G 347 230-8558
   Wilmington *(G-19926)*

South Wellington LLC .... G 954 736-7418
   Georgetown *(G-4517)*

Southern Del Trck Growers Assn .... G 302 875-3147
   Laurel *(G-5604)*

Sovereign Dealer Finance Inc .... G 302 691-6139
   Wilmington *(G-19942)*

Sp Holding Dps Inc .... G 302 999-2806
   Wilmington *(G-19946)*

Spec Simple Inc .... F 212 352-2002
   Historic New Castle *(G-5075)*

Specialized Carier Systems Inc .... G 302 424-4548
   Milford *(G-8099)*

Specialty Products Us LLC .... G 212 765-5500
   Wilmington *(G-19956)*

Speeder Solutions LLC .... F 302 448-8668
   Historic New Castle *(G-5076)*

Spences Bazaar & Auction LLC .... G 302 734-3441
   Dover *(G-3596)*

Spin4spin Inc .... G 720 547-2126
   Dover *(G-3597)*

Spirelio Inc .... G 302 467-3444
   Wilmington *(G-19967)*

Sportera Events Usa Inc .... G 514 978-2648
   Dover *(G-3600)*

Springleaf Fincl Holdings LLC .... B 302 543-6767
   Wilmington *(G-19978)*

Srhk Enterprises LLC .... G 302 834-2345
   Bear *(G-506)*

Staclar Inc .... G 628 213-1140
   Claymont *(G-1299)*

Staikos Associates Architects .... G 302 764-1678
   Wilmington *(G-20004)*

Stampede Btq & Vintage LLC .... G 215 668-5714
   Wilmington *(G-20009)*

Stan T Lepkowski .... G 302 393-9093
   Clayton *(G-1406)*

Standard Direct LLC .... G 855 550-0606
   Wilmington *(G-20012)*

Statwhiz Ventures LLC .... G 310 819-5427
   Wilmington *(G-20038)*

Stauffer Family LLC .... G 302 227-5820
   Rehoboth Beach *(G-12974)*

Stems Labs Inc .... F 708 834-3706
   Wilmington *(G-20049)*

Steph1official Inc .... F 302 744-0990
   Dover *(G-3611)*

Stl & Associates LLC .... G 302 359-2801
   Smyrna *(G-13902)*

Stora Central LLC .... E 929 273-0505
   Wilmington *(G-20083)*

Stovoo Inc .... G 302 451-9589
   Newark *(G-12104)*

Strands Prprty Prservation LLC .... G 302 381-9792
   Millsboro *(G-8469)*

Strategic Fund Raising Inc .... E 651 649-0404
   Wilmington *(G-20091)*

Stream App LLC .... G 610 420-5864
   Wilmington *(G-20093)*

Stride-360 Incorporated .... G 302 421-5752
   Wilmington *(G-20100)*

Strike Exchange Inc .... G 310 995-5653
   Lewes *(G-6518)*

Stuart Kingston Galleries Inc .... G 302 652-7978
   Wilmington *(G-20104)*

Studio B Milford LLC .... G 302 491-7910
   Milford *(G-8106)*

Stylere LLC .... F 650 206-7721
   Dover *(G-3618)*

Sumthin3lse .... G 302 272-5435
   Dover *(G-3621)*

Sun Exchange Inc .... G 917 747-9527
   Lewes *(G-6522)*

Sunflowers .... G 302 731-3150
   Newark *(G-12124)*

Superstar Holdings Inc .... G 302 289-8931
   Dover *(G-3627)*

Supportive Accountability Hub .... F 615 579-3533
   Wilmington *(G-20152)*

Sussex Financial Services Inc .... G 302 227-7814
   Rehoboth Beach *(G-12984)*

Suzette Noecker .... G 301 814-8003
   Millville *(G-8548)*

Swami Enterprises Inc .... G 302 999-8077
   Wilmington *(G-20168)*

Swave LLC .... F 302 766-3125
   Wilmington *(G-20171)*

Swift Financial LLC .... D 302 374-7019
   Wilmington *(G-20175)*

Swipetech Limited Inc .... G 929 293-8175
   Newark *(G-12144)*

Switchgearus LLC .... E 302 232-3209
   Milford *(G-8112)*

Swoop Payment Processing Inc .... E 479 586-2952
   Wilmington *(G-20176)*

Synerfac Inc .... F 302 324-9400
   New Castle *(G-9612)*

Systems Approach Ltd .... G 302 743-6331
   Newark *(G-12148)*

Employee Codes: A=Over 500 employees, B=251-500
C=101-250, D=51-100, E=20-50, F=10-19, G=1-9

73 BUSINESS SERVICES — SIC SECTION

Business	Code	Phone
T & B Invstgtions SEC Agcy LLC — Middletown (G-7616)	G	302 476-4087
T & H Bail Bonds Agency LLC — Wilmington (G-20197)	G	302 777-7982
T&B Logistics Inc — Dover (G-3639)	G	301 304-3255
TAI Group LLC — Dover (G-3643)	E	561 819-4231
Tailor Made Group LLC — Dover (G-3644)	G	347 824-0325
Take-A-Break Inc — Wilmington (G-20209)	E	302 658-8571
Talentlab Inc — Dover (G-3646)	G	310 999-4320
Tax Take LLC — Wilmington (G-20231)	G	302 760-9758
Teambrella Inc — Wilmington (G-20244)	G	347 630-0528
Tech Craft Solutions LLC — Wilmington (G-20247)	G	607 761-0376
Techadox Inc — Newark (G-12168)	F	302 691-9130
Techxponent Inc — Newark (G-12172)	F	410 701-0089
Teepee Fantasys LLC — Bear (G-527)	G	267 334-1270
Terrain and Tactical LLC — Wilmington (G-20275)	G	302 521-9290
The Real Established Inc — Wilmington (G-20292)	F	917 843-8580
The Tondo Group LLC — Newark (G-12187)	G	302 893-8449
Thirdwave Systems Inc — Dover (G-3675)	G	650 804-1385
This Is Cala Inc — Dover (G-3677)	F	512 900-4746
Thomas Phillips — Frankford (G-4153)	G	302 238-7130
Threatmate Inc — Dover (G-3682)	F	302 219-4714
Three Sheep and A Mill LLC — Middletown (G-7641)	G	616 820-5668
Tiny Token Trckg & Trnsp LLC — Smyrna (G-13913)	G	929 602-5512
Tirupati Inc — Delaware City (G-1559)	G	302 836-8335
Tjs & Associates LLC — Middletown (G-7647)	E	302 563-5593
Token Security Inc — Wilmington (G-20347)	G	972 546-9803
Top Tier Remodeling — Wilmington (G-20356)	F	302 250-4845
Toptel Inc — Dover (G-3702)	G	310 999-4320
Tospay Inc — Lewes (G-6573)	E	347 474-0402
TP It Group LLC — Dover (G-3709)	G	302 444-0441
Trexgen Nutrascience LLC — Newark (G-12219)	G	302 520-2406
Tristate Courier & Carriage — Wilmington (G-20430)	G	302 654-3345
Turning Point Collection LLC — Wilmington (G-20464)	G	302 275-0167
Turquoise Americallc — Newark (G-12247)	G	302 608-7008
Twin Creek Farms LLC — Milford (G-8122)	G	302 249-2294
Twinning LLC — Wilmington (G-20470)	G	609 793-3510
Two Cougars LLC — Hockessin (G-5413)	G	302 358-0197
Tyne Sunderland LLC — Bear (G-544)	G	302 526-1608
Tytrix Inc — Dover (G-3737)	E	877 489-8749
Uag International Holdings Inc — Wilmington (G-20489)	G	302 427-9859
UBS Financial Services Inc — Wilmington (G-20493)	G	302 657-5331
Ukap Trading LLC — Dover (G-3743)	F	617 447-6490
Ukhi LLC — New Castle (G-9649)	G	833 511-1977
Ultimate Fire Protection LLC — Wilmington (G-20496)	G	302 994-8371
Uncharted Waters LLC — Dover (G-3747)	E	302 213-6354
Unicodez Inc — Wilmington (G-20507)	F	703 963-2738
Unikie Inc — Dover (G-3749)	F	408 839-1920
Unique Image LLC — Wilmington (G-20519)	E	302 658-2266
University of De Printing — Newark (G-12276)	F	302 831-2153
UPS Authorized Retailer — Bear (G-554)	G	302 834-1600
UPS Store — Delmar (G-1651)	G	302 907-0455
UPS Store — Rehoboth Beach (G-13002)	G	302 360-0264
Upside Gaming Inc — Middletown (G-7675)	G	937 475-6908
Ur-Express Inc — Wilmington (G-20540)	G	302 839-2008
US Ravens Logistics Inc — Dover (G-3765)	D	302 401-4033
Utility Sales Associates Inc — Ocean View (G-12578)	G	410 479-0646
Uzin Utz North America Inc — Dover (G-3769)	D	302 450-1715
Val Capital Holdings LLC — Dover (G-3771)	E	800 997-4166
▲ Vanguard Manufacturing Inc — Wilmington (G-20569)	G	302 994-9302
Vany Productions Logistics LLC — Laurel (G-5618)	G	443 397-2949
Veezys Holding Company LLC — Dover (G-3779)	F	302 307-2418
Vegan Skin Clinic LLC — Hockessin (G-5416)	G	302 932-1920
Veriti Security Incorporated — Wilmington (G-20588)	E	212 203-0100
Veteran It Pro LLC — Hockessin (G-5418)	F	302 824-3111
Viaticum Incorporated — Wilmington (G-20607)	F	302 467-8353
Vicente & Partners LLC — Wilmington (G-20608)	G	646 209-5527
Victorous Kngdom Ctzens Ntwrk — Smyrna (G-13931)	G	302 409-0701
Victory Cleaning LLC — Dover (G-3792)	G	267 330-9422
Vie Incorporated — Dover (G-3795)	G	512 200-7638
Village Green Inc — New Castle (G-9671)	E	302 764-2234
Village of St John LP — Wilmington (G-20621)	G	302 652-1690
Vinisia Inc — Dover (G-3799)	F	252 297-6730
Vir Consultant LLC — Newark (G-12327)	E	747 666-2169
Vircap LLC — Newark (G-12328)	F	302 261-9892
Visio Group International Corp — Wilmington (G-20637)	G	302 485-0378
Vision Capital III LLC — Newark (G-12330)	F	312 576-2247
Vision Capital Vi LLC — Newark (G-12331)	F	312 576-2247
Vizzie 360 — Lewes (G-6608)	G	323 239-0690
Voitlex Corp — Dover (G-3808)	F	302 288-0670
Volvox Biologic Inc — Lewes (G-6609)	G	801 722-5942
Vtms LLC — Dover (G-3813)	G	302 264-9094
Vue Events Inc — Dover (G-3815)	G	301 812-3800
Vylo Inc — Newark (G-12339)	G	310 902-9693
Wabtec Finance LLC — Wilmington (G-20665)	F	412 825-1000
Wahid Consultants LLC — Historic New Castle (G-5099)	E	315 400-0955
Wallace Lamarr — Dover (G-3817)	G	202 460-3377
Walters Auctioneering — Viola (G-14097)	G	302 284-0914
Wartimeaction LLC — Middletown (G-7708)	F	203 685-8868
Watercraft LLC — Wilmington (G-20683)	G	302 757-0786
Watkins Consulting Inc — Rehoboth Beach (G-13009)	G	240 479-7273
We Got Cars 4 Cash Inc — Claymont (G-1334)	G	215 399-6978
Webb & Family LLC — Camden Wyoming (G-986)	G	302 697-7108
Welcome Home Getaways LLC — Bear (G-561)	G	724 426-5534
Weltio LLC — Dover (G-3832)	F	305 307-9815
West Home Leasehold LLC — Wilmington (G-20741)	F	917 443-7451
Western Union — Seaford (G-13447)	G	302 629-3001
Westward LLC — Dover (G-3839)	G	570 609-3500
Whstle Corporation — Dover (G-3846)	G	925 413-3316
Wibdi Aviation Co Corp — Dover (G-3847)	F	305 677-9685
William C Leager — Greenwood (G-4674)	G	302 398-7525
William D Emmert — Rehoboth Beach (G-13017)	G	302 227-1433
William H Burkhardt — Middletown (G-7726)	G	302 376-1193
Williamson Building Corp — Lewes (G-6632)	G	302 644-0605
Wilmington Firefighters Assn — Wilmington (G-20816)	F	302 365-0168
Wilsons Auction Sales Inc — Lincoln (G-6709)	G	302 422-3454
Win From Wthin Xc Camp/Tatnall — Wilmington (G-20855)	G	302 494-5312
Windy Inc — Dover (G-3858)	F	224 707-0442
Wis International — Dover (G-3861)	G	302 264-9343
Wmk Financing Inc — Wilmington (G-20872)	C	302 576-2697

Company	Code	Phone
Woohoo Inc	G	302 233-7272
Dover (G-3868)		
Woolleyenterprisesmx LLC	G	302 674-4089
Dover (G-3869)		
Workwall Inc	F	415 800-2809
Newark (G-12407)		
World Web Technology Pvt Ltd	E	646 755-9276
Dover (G-3875)		
Wsfs Financial Corporation	F	302 254-3569
New Castle (G-9693)		
Wuji Inc	G	815 274-6777
Dover (G-3876)		
Xeenom Inc	G	302 427-6970
Wilmington (G-20917)		
◆ Xenopia LLC	G	302 703-7050
Lewes (G-6643)		
Yacht Delaware Registry Ltd	F	302 477-9800
Wilmington (G-20921)		
Yenaffit Inc	G	302 650-4818
Wilmington (G-20926)		
Zat3 Transport LLC	G	302 470-6172
Laurel (G-5627)		
Zenind Inc	G	845 300-3310
Dover (G-3898)		
Zenpli LLC	F	302 314-5231
Newark (G-12432)		
Zicherheit LLC	G	302 510-3718
Selbyville (G-13622)		
Zogo Inc	G	978 810-8895
Newark (G-12437)		

75 AUTOMOTIVE REPAIR, SERVICES AND PARKING

7513 Truck rental and leasing, without drivers

Company	Code	Phone
Action Rental Inc	G	302 366-0749
Newark (G-9760)		
▼ Bayshore Ford Truck Sales Inc	D	302 656-3160
New Castle (G-8853)		
Clifton Leasing Co Inc	E	302 674-2300
Dover (G-2093)		
Dependable Trucking Inc	F	302 655-6271
New Castle (G-9047)		
Dover Leasing Co Inc	F	302 674-2300
Dover (G-2350)		
Lee Mc Neill Associates	G	302 593-6172
Wilmington (G-17854)		
Martin Newark Dealership Inc	D	302 454-9300
Newark (G-11345)		
Morton Electric Co	G	302 645-9414
Lewes (G-6292)		
Penske Performance Inc	D	302 656-2082
Wilmington (G-18959)		
Penske Truck Leasing Co LP	G	302 325-9290
New Castle (G-9467)		
Penske Truck Leasing Co LP	G	302 994-7899
Wilmington (G-18960)		
Penske Truck Leasing Corp	G	302 449-9294
Middletown (G-7439)		
Penske Truck Leasing Corp	G	302 260-7039
Rehoboth Beach (G-12887)		
Penske Truck Leasing Corp	G	302 629-5373
Seaford (G-13342)		
Penske Truck Leasing Corp	G	302 658-3255
Wilmington (G-18961)		
Penske Truck Rental	F	302 746-3020
Claymont (G-1262)		
Penske Truck Rental	G	302 648-3199
Millsboro (G-8425)		
▲ Rollins Leasing LLC	C	302 426-2700
Wilmington (G-19557)		
Ryder Truck	G	302 398-5106
Harrington (G-4824)		
Ryder Truck Rental Inc	G	302 798-1472
Wilmington (G-19601)		
Tat Trucking Inc	F	302 832-2667
Bear (G-526)		
U Haul Co Independent Dealers	G	302 424-3189
Milford (G-8123)		
U Haul Neighborhood Dealer	G	302 613-0207
Bear (G-545)		
U Haul Neighborhood Dealer	G	302 832-1433
Bear (G-546)		
U Haul Neighborhood Dealer	G	302 284-6051
Felton (G-4034)		
U Haul Neighborhood Dealer	G	302 393-2999
Milford (G-8124)		
U-Haul	G	302 565-4423
Newark (G-12255)		
U-Haul	G	302 514-0034
Smyrna (G-13923)		
U-Haul Co	G	302 628-8197
Seaford (G-13437)		
U-Haul International	G	302 934-1601
Millsboro (G-8489)		
U-Haul International	G	302 565-4056
Newark (G-12256)		
U-Haul International Inc	G	302 762-6445
Wilmington (G-20485)		
U-Haul International Inc	G	336 667-0147
New Castle (G-9646)		
U-Haul Neighorhd Dealr Budget	G	302 349-2167
Greenwood (G-4673)		
U-Haul Neighborhood Dealer	G	302 721-6064
Bridgeville (G-776)		
U-Haul Neighborhood Dealer	G	302 321-6032
Frankford (G-4156)		
U-Haul Neighborhood Dealer	G	302 343-7497
Hartly (G-4911)		
U-Haul Neighborhood Dealer	G	302 644-4316
Lewes (G-6586)		
U-Haul Neighborhood Dealer	G	302 703-0376
Lewes (G-6587)		
U-Haul Neighborhood Dealer	G	302 376-6858
Middletown (G-7668)		
U-Haul Neighborhood Dealer	G	302 449-7379
Middletown (G-7669)		
U-Haul Neighborhood Dealer	G	302 725-4525
Milford (G-8125)		
U-Haul Neighborhood Dealer	G	302 250-4422
New Castle (G-9647)		
U-Haul Neighborhood Dealer	G	302 544-9178
New Castle (G-9648)		
U-Haul Neighborhood Dealer	G	302 722-8016
Newark (G-12257)		
Watkins System Inc	E	302 658-8561
New Castle (G-9678)		
▼ Winner Ford of Newark Inc	F	302 731-2415
Newark (G-12388)		

7514 Passenger car rental

Company	Code	Phone
Ace Rent-A-Car Inc	F	302 368-5950
Newark (G-9755)		
Avis Car Rental	G	302 368-5950
Newark (G-9955)		
Avis Car Rental	G	302 227-1507
Rehoboth Beach (G-12620)		
Avis Car Rental	G	302 654-8044
Wilmington (G-14671)		
Avis Car Rental	G	302 762-3825
Wilmington (G-14672)		
Avis Rent A Car System Llc	G	302 322-2092
New Castle (G-8835)		
Budget Rent A Car	G	302 322-2026
New Castle (G-8896)		
Budget Rent A Car	G	302 227-3041
Rehoboth Beach (G-12660)		
Budget Rent A Car	G	302 762-4824
Wilmington (G-15143)		
Budget Rent A Car System Inc	G	302 652-0629
Wilmington (G-15144)		
Budget Truck LLC	G	302 731-5067
Newark (G-10098)		
Budget Truck Rental	G	302 325-9111
New Castle (G-8898)		
Budget Truck Rental	G	302 328-1282
New Castle (G-8899)		
Budget Truck Rental	G	302 436-5416
Selbyville (G-13485)		
Budget Truck Rental LLC	B	302 644-0132
Rehoboth Beach (G-12661)		
Dela Belle Inv Group Corp	G	901 279-2742
Middletown (G-7037)		
Diavaeh Luxury Car Rental LLC	G	302 497-3443
Middletown (G-7059)		
Ean Holdings LLC	G	302 674-5553
Dover (G-2403)		
Ean Holdings LLC	G	302 376-5606
Middletown (G-7077)		
Ean Holdings LLC	G	302 422-1167
Milford (G-7875)		
Enterprise Lsg Phladelphia LLC	G	302 732-3534
Dagsboro (G-1445)		
Enterprise Lsg Phladelphia LLC	G	302 266-7777
Newark (G-10652)		
Enterprise Lsg Phladelphia LLC	G	302 292-0524
Newark (G-10653)		
Enterprise Lsg Phladelphia LLC	G	302 425-4404
Wilmington (G-16435)		
Enterprise Lsg Phladelphia LLC	G	302 479-7829
Wilmington (G-16436)		
Enterprise Lsg Phladelphia LLC	G	302 761-4545
Wilmington (G-16437)		
Enterprise Rent A Car	G	302 856-6380
Georgetown (G-4309)		
Enterprise Rent A Car	G	302 454-2939
Newark (G-10654)		
Enterprise Rent A Car	G	302 636-0660
Wilmington (G-16439)		
Enterprise Rent-A-Car	G	302 376-5606
Middletown (G-7102)		
Enterprise Rent-A-Car	G	302 934-1216
Millsboro (G-8282)		
Enterprise Rent-A-Car	G	717 968-1966
Wilmington (G-16440)		
Enterprise Rentacar	G	302 645-5005
Rehoboth Beach (G-12744)		
Enterprise Rentacar	G	302 628-2931
Seaford (G-13176)		
Getrentacar Inc	G	786 460-8707
Dover (G-2576)		
Go4spin Corporation	G	310 400-2588
Wilmington (G-16901)		
Golden Chariot Transportaion	G	302 730-3882
Dover (G-2600)		
Hertz Corporation	E	302 428-0637
New Castle (G-9212)		
Hertz Corporation	E	302 428-0637
New Castle (G-9213)		
Hertz Corporation	G	302 654-8312
Wilmington (G-17134)		
Hertz Local Edition Corp	G	302 678-0700
Dover (G-2675)		

75 AUTOMOTIVE REPAIR, SERVICES AND PARKING

Kent Leasing Company Inc .... G 302 697-3000
  Dover *(G-2852)*
Provada Enterprise .... G 302 999-7553
  Wilmington *(G-19236)*
Spallco Enterprises Inc .... G 302 368-5950
  Newark *(G-12061)*
True Legacy Rentals LLC .... G 844 857-2271
  Middletown *(G-7664)*
Winner Group Inc .... F 302 764-5900
  Wilmington *(G-20860)*
Wreck Masters Demo Derby .... F 302 368-5544
  Bear *(G-568)*

7515 Passenger car leasing

Delaware Motor Sales Inc .... D 302 656-3100
  Wilmington *(G-15945)*
Future Ford Sales Inc .... D 302 999-0261
  Wilmington *(G-16776)*
Martin Newark Dealership Inc .... D 302 454-9300
  Newark *(G-11345)*
New Car Connection .... G 302 328-7000
  New Castle *(G-9405)*
Professional Leasing Inc .... G 302 629-4350
  Seaford *(G-13359)*
Star States Leasing Corp .... E 302 283-4500
  Newark *(G-12088)*
▼ Winner Ford of Newark Inc .... F 302 731-2415
  Newark *(G-12388)*
Winner Group Inc .... F 302 292-8200
  Newark *(G-12389)*

7519 Utility trailer rental

Complete Rsrvtion Slutions LLC .... F 800 672-8522
  Dover *(G-2123)*
Morton Electric Co .... G 302 645-9414
  Lewes *(G-6292)*
Penske Truck Leasing Co LP .... G 302 325-9290
  New Castle *(G-9467)*

7521 Automobile parking

Colonial Parking Inc .... E 302 651-3600
  Wilmington *(G-15536)*
Landmark Parking Inc .... G 302 651-3610
  Wilmington *(G-17799)*
Laz Parking .... F 302 654-7730
  Wilmington *(G-17837)*
Parkobility LLC .... E 877 298-5550
  Dover *(G-3273)*
Sp Plus Corporation .... G 302 652-1410
  Wilmington *(G-19949)*
SSC Parking LLC Sam Stanford .... G 302 561-0088
  Bear *(G-507)*
Toms Sealing & Striping Co .... G 302 531-7039
  Townsend *(G-14082)*
Wilmington Parking Authority .... G 302 655-4442
  Wilmington *(G-20830)*

7532 Top and body repair and paint shops

3e Ventures Inc .... G 302 773-8658
  New Castle *(G-8746)*
A R Myers Corporation .... F 302 652-3164
  Wilmington *(G-14170)*
ABRA Auto Body & Glass .... G 302 674-4525
  Dover *(G-1703)*
ABRA Auto Body & Glass LP .... G 302 279-1007
  Middletown *(G-6830)*
Anthonys Collision Cstm Works .... G 302 542-2489
  Harrington *(G-4731)*
Armigers Auto Center Inc .... G 302 875-7642
  Laurel *(G-5464)*
Auto Works Collision Ctr LLC .... F 302 732-3902
  Lewes *(G-5721)*
Automotive Services Inc .... F 302 762-0100
  Wilmington *(G-14656)*
▼ Autoport Inc .... E 302 658-5100
  New Castle *(G-8834)*
Balanced Body Inc .... G 302 373-3463
  Wilmington *(G-14720)*
Betts Texaco and B & G GL Inc .... F 302 834-2284
  Newark *(G-10029)*
Body Works .... G 302 275-2750
  Newark *(G-10067)*
Brandywine Body Shop Inc .... G 302 998-0424
  Wilmington *(G-15044)*
Brandywine Bodyworks .... G 302 798-0801
  Wilmington *(G-15045)*
Brasures Body Shop Inc .... G 302 732-6157
  Frankford *(G-4077)*
Caliber Bodyworks Texas Inc .... E 302 832-1660
  Bear *(G-88)*
Caliber Collision .... G 302 674-4525
  Dover *(G-2013)*
Caliber Collision .... G 302 279-1007
  Middletown *(G-6951)*
Caliber Collision .... G 302 731-1200
  Newark *(G-10120)*
Car Tech Auto Center .... G 302 368-4104
  Newark *(G-10138)*
Christiana Body Shop Inc .... G 302 655-1085
  Wilmington *(G-15399)*
Classic Auto Body Inc .... G 302 655-4044
  Wilmington *(G-15466)*
Clear Definition LLC .... G 302 503-7560
  Milford *(G-7832)*
Colliers Trim Shop Inc .... G 302 227-8398
  Rehoboth Beach *(G-12691)*
Commonwealth Motor Inc .... G 302 505-5555
  Wilmington *(G-15554)*
Complete Auto Body Inc .... F 302 629-3955
  Seaford *(G-13132)*
Dent Pro Inc .... G 302 628-0978
  Seaford *(G-13158)*
Dominos Body Shop .... G 302 697-3801
  Camden Wyoming *(G-935)*
Doug Richmonds Body Shop .... G 302 453-1173
  Newark *(G-10554)*
E & M Enterprises Inc .... G 302 736-6391
  Dover *(G-2398)*
East Coast Auto Body Inc .... G 302 265-6830
  Dover *(G-2408)*
Ellmore Auto Collision .... G 302 762-2301
  Wilmington *(G-16374)*
England Collision Center LLC .... G 240 440-1111
  New Castle *(G-9097)*
Eurshall Millers Autobody .... G 410 742-7329
  Delmar *(G-1595)*
Executive Auto Repairs Inc .... G 302 995-6220
  Wilmington *(G-16503)*
Gas & Go Inc .... G 302 734-8234
  Dover *(G-2562)*
Glasgow Auto Body .... G 302 292-1201
  Newark *(G-10843)*
Henry Bros Autobody & Pnt Sp .... G 302 994-4438
  Wilmington *(G-17123)*
Hertrich Collision Ctr of .... F 302 839-0550
  Milford *(G-7928)*
J Henry Edward & Sons Inc .... F 302 658-4324
  Wilmington *(G-17457)*
Jewell Enterprises Inc .... F 302 737-8460
  Newark *(G-11110)*
Jorge & Evonnes Auto Body LLC .... G 302 382-1460
  Camden *(G-861)*
JW Striping .... G 302 832-7762
  Bear *(G-319)*
King .... G 302 930-0139
  Claymont *(G-1207)*
Kpkm Inc .... G 302 678-0271
  Dover *(G-2885)*
Lewes Body Works Inc .... G 302 645-5595
  Lewes *(G-6191)*
LS Auto Experience LLC .... G 302 983-9668
  Wilmington *(G-18020)*
Maaco Collision Repair .... G 302 753-8721
  Bear *(G-358)*
Maaco Collision Repr Auto Pntg .... G 610 628-3867
  Wilmington *(G-18063)*
Martin Dealership .... G 302 738-5200
  Newark *(G-11343)*
Master Tech Inc .... F 302 832-1660
  Bear *(G-365)*
New Car Connection .... G 302 328-7000
  New Castle *(G-9405)*
No Evi-Dents Inc .... G 302 363-7788
  Wilmington *(G-18660)*
Omniway Corporation .... F 302 738-5076
  Newark *(G-11586)*
On Glo LLC .... G 205 567-3434
  Dover *(G-3226)*
One Off Rod & Custom Inc .... F 302 449-1489
  Middletown *(G-7415)*
Pine Valley Corvettes .... G 302 834-1268
  Middletown *(G-7449)*
Puzs Body Shop Inc .... G 302 368-8265
  Newark *(G-11777)*
Quillen Signs LLC .... G 302 684-3661
  Seaford *(G-13362)*
Rayco Auto & Marine Uphl Inc .... G 302 323-8844
  Hockessin *(G-5356)*
Red Barn Inc .... F 302 678-0271
  Dover *(G-3438)*
Rex Auto Body Inc .... G 302 731-4707
  Newark *(G-11875)*
Rickards Auto Body .... G 302 934-9600
  Dagsboro *(G-1499)*
Rockfield Collision LLC .... G 302 658-4324
  Wilmington *(G-19534)*
Rudlyn Inc .... F 302 764-5677
  Wilmington *(G-19586)*
Stokes Garage Inc .... G 302 994-0613
  Wilmington *(G-20075)*
Thomas Karmanski .... G 302 438-1458
  Wilmington *(G-20311)*
Whites Body Shop .... G 302 655-4369
  Wilmington *(G-20771)*
Willis Ford Inc .... E 302 653-5900
  Smyrna *(G-13939)*
Wilmington Collision Center .... G 484 702-2115
  Wilmington *(G-20812)*
Winner Premier Collision Ctr .... E 302 571-5200
  Wilmington *(G-20863)*

7533 Auto exhaust system repair shops

Bernard Limpert .... G 302 674-8280
  Dover *(G-1914)*
Best Custom Exhaust .... G 302 278-3555
  Georgetown *(G-4232)*
C-Met Inc .... G 302 652-1884
  New Castle *(G-8909)*
Car Shoppe LLC .... G 302 992-9669
  Wilmington *(G-15236)*
Daves Disc Mfflers of Dver De .... G 302 678-8803
  Dover *(G-2199)*
Lewes Meineke .... G 302 827-2054
  Lewes *(G-6197)*
Meineke Muffler .... G 302 644-8544
  Lewes *(G-6259)*

75 AUTOMOTIVE REPAIR, SERVICES AND PARKING

Rcs Mufflers Inc... G 302 328-7788
 New Castle *(G-9514)*

Walls Service Center Inc............................... G 302 422-8110
 Milford *(G-8139)*

7534 Tire retreading and repair shops

Ajacks Tire Service Inc................................. G 302 834-5200
 New Castle *(G-8776)*

Bridgestone Ret Operations LLC.................. G 302 734-4522
 Dover *(G-1979)*

Bridgestone Ret Operations LLC.................. G 302 656-2529
 New Castle *(G-8892)*

Bridgestone Ret Operations LLC.................. G 302 995-2487
 Wilmington *(G-15108)*

Clarksville Auto Service Ctr........................ E 302 539-1700
 Ocean View *(G-12489)*

Diamond State Tire Inc................................. F 302 836-1919
 Bear *(G-168)*

M & M Tire Services Inc................................ G 302 731-1004
 Newark *(G-11299)*

Service Tire Truck Center Inc..................... E 302 629-5533
 Seaford *(G-13397)*

Ssmmd LLC.. G 302 249-1045
 Laurel *(G-5606)*

7536 Automotive glass replacement shops

A R Myers Corporation............................... F 302 652-3164
 Wilmington *(G-14170)*

Aaron Auto Glass... G 302 297-8008
 Middletown *(G-6827)*

Caliber Collision... G 302 674-4525
 Dover *(G-2013)*

Caliber Collision... G 302 279-1007
 Middletown *(G-6951)*

Delaware Auto Glass.................................... G 302 709-2300
 Newark *(G-10417)*

Ght Autoglass.. G 302 494-4369
 Newark *(G-10830)*

Parags Glass Company.............................. G 302 737-0101
 Newark *(G-11625)*

Safelite Fulfillment Inc.............................. G 302 856-7175
 Georgetown *(G-4497)*

Safelite Glass Corp.................................... G 877 800-2727
 Dover *(G-3504)*

Safelite Glass Corp.................................... E 302 656-4640
 Wilmington *(G-19628)*

U A G Inc.. G 302 731-2747
 Newark *(G-12252)*

7537 Automotive transmission repair shops

A&M Transportation Inc............................. G 781 227-1257
 Dover *(G-1697)*

All Trans Transmission Inc....................... G 302 366-0104
 Newark *(G-9820)*

Benchmark Transmission Inc.................... G 302 792-2300
 Claymont *(G-1056)*

Benchmark Transmissions......................... G 302 221-5380
 Historic New Castle *(G-4940)*

Benchmark Transmissions Inc.................. G 302 999-9400
 Wilmington *(G-14828)*

Challenge Automotive Svcs Inc................ F 302 629-3058
 Seaford *(G-13108)*

Cottman Transmission.............................. G 302 322-4600
 New Castle *(G-8978)*

Dynamic Converters LLC........................... G 302 454-9203
 Newark *(G-10583)*

Jld Auto Repair and Transm..................... G 302 650-8613
 Wilmington *(G-17554)*

Js Automotive AAMCO................................ G 302 678-5660
 Dover *(G-2809)*

Powertrain Technology Inc....................... G 302 368-4900
 Newark *(G-11719)*

Scott Muffler LLC....................................... G 302 378-9247
 Middletown *(G-7545)*

Trans Plus Inc... G 302 323-3051
 Historic New Castle *(G-5090)*

Walls Service Center Inc........................... G 302 422-8110
 Milford *(G-8139)*

World Transmissions Inc........................... G 302 735-5535
 Dover *(G-3874)*

7538 General automotive repair shops

A2b Auto Group... G 302 786-2331
 Wilmington *(G-14179)*

Accurate Auto Service Inc......................... G 302 737-7998
 Newark *(G-9752)*

Admiral Tire.. G 302 734-5911
 Dover *(G-1718)*

Aiden Auto Repair Center........................... G 302 898-5777
 Bear *(G-21)*

Alderman Automotive Enterprise............. G 302 652-3733
 New Castle *(G-8777)*

All American Truck Brokers..................... G 302 654-6101
 Wilmington *(G-14362)*

All Tune & Lube.. G 302 744-9081
 Dover *(G-1767)*

All Tune & Lube.. G 302 367-6369
 Wilmington *(G-14369)*

Allisons Auto Cycle Kstomz LLC.............. G 302 836-4222
 Bear *(G-28)*

Allserve Allscpes Allstrctures................ G 302 684-1414
 Harbeson *(G-4682)*

Ameri Auto LLC.. G 302 607-9113
 Bear *(G-8795)*

Anthonys Automotive................................. G 302 420-9804
 New Castle *(G-8813)*

Area 51 Automotive................................... G 302 993-9114
 Wilmington *(G-14548)*

Army National Guard Delaware............... G 302 855-7456
 Dagsboro *(G-1413)*

ARS Fleet Service...................................... G 302 482-1305
 New Castle *(G-8824)*

Atlantic Auto Repair LLC......................... G 302 539-7352
 Millville *(G-8515)*

Atomic Garage.. G 302 898-1380
 Wilmington *(G-14634)*

Auto Evrything At Slepy Hllow................ G 302 376-3010
 Smyrna *(G-13656)*

Auto Plus Auto Parts................................ G 302 678-8400
 Dover *(G-1855)*

Autolab Inc... E 416 820-1636
 Wilmington *(G-14651)*

Automotive Diagnostic Sol...................... G 443 466-6108
 Newark *(G-9948)*

AV Auto Worx LLC...................................... F 302 384-7646
 Wilmington *(G-14660)*

B & F Towing Co... E 302 328-4146
 New Castle *(G-8839)*

B and B Automotive................................... G 302 559-2087
 Wilmington *(G-14693)*

Bavarian Cllision New Grdn Inc............... G 610 268-3966
 Bear *(G-58)*

▼ Bayshore Ford Truck Sales Inc............. D 302 656-3160
 New Castle *(G-8853)*

Bcb Diesel Mechanics Llc......................... G 302 422-3787
 Milford *(G-7789)*

Bear Alignment Center.............................. G 302 655-9219
 Wilmington *(G-14805)*

Bernard Limpert.. G 302 674-8280
 Dover *(G-1914)*

Bill Cannons Garage Inc........................... F 302 436-4200
 Selbyville *(G-13477)*

Blue Hen Spring Works Inc...................... F 302 422-6600
 Milford *(G-7798)*

Bradleys Auto Center Inc......................... G 302 762-2247
 Middletown *(G-6935)*

Buckleys Inc... G 302 999-8285
 Wilmington *(G-15142)*

Buds Auto... G 302 690-3838
 New Castle *(G-8900)*

Bullfeathers Auto Sound Inc.................... G 302 846-0434
 Laurel *(G-5475)*

C & C Autobrokers.................................... G 302 442-5464
 Wilmington *(G-15170)*

Camco Tire & Auto LLC.............................. G 302 664-1264
 Milton *(G-8579)*

Cammock Boys Auto.................................. G 302 409-0645
 Wilmington *(G-15207)*

Campbells... G 302 359-9918
 Harrington *(G-4746)*

Capital Trail Service Center.................... G 302 731-0999
 Newark *(G-10134)*

Car Doc.. G 301 302-3362
 Delmar *(G-1572)*

◆ Careys Diesel Inc................................... F 302 678-3797
 Leipsic *(G-5629)*

Careys Inc.. F 302 875-5674
 Laurel *(G-5478)*

Caribb Transport Inc................................ G 302 274-2112
 Wilmington *(G-15248)*

Carrillos Auto Care................................... G 302 339-7234
 Houston *(G-5438)*

Ccdiesel LLC.. G 302 353-0842
 Newport *(G-12443)*

Chriss Car Care Road................................ G 302 628-4695
 Bridgeville *(G-682)*

CJ S Autos.. G 302 500-0822
 Bridgeville *(G-683)*

Cjs Autos LLC.. G 302 337-8880
 Bridgeville *(G-684)*

CJs Beach Bays Inc................................... F 302 645-8478
 Lewes *(G-5823)*

Classic Auto Restoration Svcs................ G 302 398-9652
 Harrington *(G-4750)*

Coastal Towing Inc.................................... G 302 645-6300
 Lewes *(G-5847)*

Community Auto Repair............................. G 302 856-3333
 Georgetown *(G-4262)*

Coveys Car Care Inc................................. G 302 629-2746
 Seaford *(G-13138)*

Croosroads Auto Repair Inc.................... G 302 436-9100
 Selbyville *(G-13510)*

Cw Mobile Automotive Repa.................... G 302 663-0035
 Millsboro *(G-8248)*

D H Automotive Towing............................. G 302 368-5590
 Newark *(G-10376)*

D S Auto... G 302 542-3023
 Millsboro *(G-8252)*

Daly Concepts.. G 215 266-0866
 Wilmington *(G-15774)*

Daves Auto Restoration........................... G 302 258-7981
 Laurel *(G-5493)*

Daves Service Center................................ G 302 798-1776
 Claymont *(G-1109)*

Deals On Wheels Inc................................. E 302 999-9955
 Wilmington *(G-15845)*

Delmarva Pump Center Inc....................... F 302 492-1245
 Marydel *(G-6796)*

Delmarva Rv Center Inc........................... E 302 424-4505
 Milford *(G-7863)*

Dempseys Service Center Inc.................. G 302 239-4996
 Newark *(G-10511)*

Diamond State Diesel................................ G 864 784-6608
 Smyrna *(G-13710)*

Diamond State Truck Center LLC........... G 302 275-9050
 New Castle *(G-9052)*

Employee Codes: A=Over 500 employees, B=251-500
C=101-250, D=51-100, E=20-50, F=10-19, G=1-9

2024 Harris Directory of
Delaware Businesses

75 AUTOMOTIVE REPAIR, SERVICES AND PARKING

Business	Code	Phone
Dnr Auto, Dover (G-2314)	G	302 698-7829
Donald Briggs, Middletown (G-7069)	G	267 476-2712
Donaway Corporation, Millsboro (G-8275)	G	302 934-6226
Dover Volkswagen Inc, Dover (G-2368)	E	302 734-4761
E D S of Milford Inc, Milford (G-7873)	G	302 245-8813
Eds Auto Repair, Felton (G-3967)	G	302 382-0079
Eds Auto Repair, Wilmington (G-16296)	G	302 468-0955
Elite Auto LLC, Middletown (G-7092)	G	302 690-2948
Elite Auto Works LLC, Wilmington (G-16362)	G	302 252-1045
Empire Auto Protect LLC, Dover (G-2443)	G	888 345-0084
Enclosed Auto Solutions LLC, Middletown (G-7100)	G	302 437-9858
Ep Engine Performance, Smyrna (G-13723)	G	302 521-0435
Ericsons Garage, Smyrna (G-13724)	G	302 653-5032
European Performance Inc, Wilmington (G-16476)	G	302 633-1122
Evco Auto Inc DBA A To Z Auto, Bear (G-211)	G	302 595-3078
Everest Auto Repair LLC, Newark (G-10676)	G	302 737-8424
Everest Autoworks Auto Spa LLC, Newark (G-10677)	G	302 737-8424
Firestone Complete Auto C, Middletown (G-7129)	G	302 437-0497
First State Auto Glass, Wilmington (G-16622)	G	302 559-8902
First State Fleet Service Inc, New Castle (G-9129)	G	302 598-9500
Five Friends Auto, Wilmington (G-16651)	G	302 407-6236
Four Brothers Auto Service, Wilmington (G-16708)	F	302 482-2932
Four States LLC, New Castle (G-9143)	F	302 655-3400
Fox Run Automotive Inc, Bear (G-234)	F	302 834-1200
Freedom Rides Auto, Seaford (G-13190)	G	302 422-4559
Fromms Automotive, Laurel (G-5515)	G	717 202-9918
Furrs Tire Service Inc, Dover (G-2546)	G	302 678-0800
G Custom Work LLC, New Castle (G-9156)	G	302 353-2137
Gaby Auto, New Castle (G-9157)	G	856 469-1378
Garcias Auto Repair, Middletown (G-7151)	G	302 464-1118
Gears Garage LLC, Townsend (G-14005)	G	302 653-3684
Genesis Automobile Acquirers, Bear (G-247)	G	757 717-1673
Geo Transport Auto Export LLC, New Castle (G-9162)	G	302 322-9001
Girls Auto Clinic LLC, New Castle (G-9167)	G	484 679-6394
Glacier Autos, Wilmington (G-16877)	G	302 510-6771
Golden Car Care, Georgetown (G-4344)	G	302 856-2219
Goobers Garage, Wilmington (G-16920)	G	443 309-0328
Goodyear Tire & Rubber Company, Newark (G-10869)	G	302 737-2461
Gumboro Service Center Inc, Frankford (G-4112)	G	302 238-7040
H & C Auto Care, Bear (G-257)	G	302 494-8989
Harris Towing and Auto Service, Dover (G-2656)	G	302 736-9901
Harvey Road Automotive Inc, Wilmington (G-17071)	G	302 654-7500
Hazzard Auto Repairs Inc, Lewes (G-6083)	G	302 645-4543
HB&t Automotive LLC, Townsend (G-14014)	G	302 378-3333
Henrys Car Care Inc, Wilmington (G-17125)	G	302 994-5766
Hertrchs Fmly Auto Dealerships, Bear (G-271)	G	302 276-2554
High Horse Performance Inc, Smyrna (G-13760)	G	302 894-1115
Hoban Auto & Machineshop Inc, Selbyville (G-13547)	G	302 436-8013
Holly Oak Towing and Service, Wilmington (G-17169)	G	302 792-1500
IG Burton & Company Inc, Milford (G-7939)	D	302 424-3041
IG Burton & Company Inc, Milford (G-7938)	D	302 422-3041
Intune Automotive Inc, Newark (G-11051)	G	302 824-9893
Ivy Boy Auto Works, Wilmington (G-17438)	G	302 669-8842
J & K Auto Repair Inc, Bear (G-292)	G	302 834-8025
J V Auto Service Inc, Wilmington (G-17466)	F	302 999-0786
J&J Fleet Service, New Castle (G-9249)	F	484 632-1647
J&R Auto Repair, Ellendale (G-3923)	G	240 863-8653
Jamies Auto Repair South, Townsend (G-14019)	G	302 378-7933
Jays Auto Repair LLC, Newark (G-11101)	G	302 273-2811
Joes Auto and Equipment Repair, Harbeson (G-4703)	G	302 990-5845
Justin David Ennis, Smyrna (G-13784)	G	302 650-4934
Justin Oneill, Dover (G-2822)	G	631 346-7333
Kaminski Service Center, Claymont (G-1204)	G	302 375-6379
Kaspar Karrs, Wilmington (G-17656)	G	302 660-2256
Kent Sussex Auto Care Inc, Dover (G-2857)	G	302 422-3337
Kevins Road Svc, Saint Georges (G-13036)	G	302 218-2869
Kirkwood Tires Inc, Newark (G-11186)	G	302 737-2460
Kunkun Auto Group LLC, Wilmington (G-17763)	G	917 499-0019
Lee Lynn Inc, Dover (G-2923)	F	302 678-9978
Lekuche Autos & General Merch, Bear (G-344)	G	302 887-6748
Lineage Auto Group L L C, New Castle (G-9313)	G	302 595-2119
Lube Depot, Smyrna (G-13811)	G	302 659-3329
Luxz Auto Tech LLC, Newark (G-11296)	G	302 305-5899
M & M Automotive LLC, Historic New Castle (G-5022)	G	302 325-8140
M&M Small Engine Repair, Hartly (G-4894)	G	302 270-3941
M&S Auto Group Inc, Bear (G-357)	G	302 834-7905
Macs Auto Services, Smyrna (G-13813)	G	302 223-6771
Maliks Auto Repair, New Castle (G-9341)	G	302 325-2555
Manor Exxon Inc, Bear (G-360)	G	302 834-6691
Mark T Droney, Millville (G-8539)	G	302 537-2305
Martel & Son Foreign Car Ctr, Dover (G-3022)	G	302 674-5556
Martin Newark Dealership Inc, Newark (G-11345)	D	302 454-9300
Martinez Automotive, New Castle (G-9350)	G	302 250-5933
Matt S Auto Care, Lewes (G-6250)	G	302 226-2407
McCar Auto Group LLC, Wilmington (G-18217)	G	302 478-3049
Meineke Car Care Center 671, Claymont (G-1232)	F	302 746-2026
Middletown Car Care, Middletown (G-7346)	G	302 449-1550
Millcreek Texaco Station, Wilmington (G-18360)	G	302 571-8492
Monro Inc, Delmar (G-1623)	G	302 846-2732
Monro Inc, Middletown (G-7377)	E	302 378-3801
Moppert Auto Collision of, Newark (G-11449)	G	302 453-2900
New Car Connection, New Castle (G-9405)	G	302 328-7000
Nu - Vision Auto Glass LLC, Clayton (G-1393)	G	302 389-8700
Ocean Pines Auto Svc Ctr Inc, Ocean View (G-12554)	F	410 641-7800
OEM Auto Parts, Newark (G-11579)	G	302 983-6475
Oil Spot Express Lube Center, Seaford (G-13323)	G	302 628-9866
Omar Auto Repair LLC, Wilmington (G-18763)	G	302 502-3204
Onsite Semi Truck Repair, Milford (G-8038)	G	302 526-0517
Patriot Auto & Truck Care LLC, Dover (G-3282)	G	302 257-5715
Paul F Campanella Inc, Wilmington (G-18917)	F	302 777-7170
Paul F Campanella Inc, Wilmington (G-18918)	F	302 218-5374
Pen Del Auto & Marine Inc, Frankford (G-4133)	G	302 430-3046
Phillips Truck and Trailer, Middletown (G-7446)	G	302 502-5046
Pike Creek Automotive Inc, Wilmington (G-19037)	F	302 998-2234
Pleasant Hill Auto Svc LLC, Smyrna (G-13849)	G	302 376-6712
Poorman Auto, Seaford (G-13351)	G	302 628-0404
Powertrain Technology Inc, Newark (G-11719)	G	302 368-4900
Precision Auto LLC, Wilmington (G-19151)	G	302 384-6169

75 AUTOMOTIVE REPAIR, SERVICES AND PARKING

Prestige Auto .... G 302 898-5486
  Wilmington (G-19180)
Price Automotive Group .... E 302 383-8669
  Newark (G-11737)
Professionals Auto Salon .... G 302 420-5691
  Wilmington (G-19216)
Pughs Service Inc .... F 302 678-2408
  Dover (G-3394)
R & K Motors & Machine Shop .... G 302 737-4596
  Newark (G-11803)
Rbs Auto Repair Inc .... G 302 678-8803
  Dover (G-3426)
RE Auto Repair .... G 302 384-6508
  Wilmington (G-19357)
Redmill Auto Repair .... G 302 292-2155
  Newark (G-11842)
Reincarnatio Inc .... G 703 479-1337
  Wilmington (G-19417)
Rinehimer Body Shop Inc .... F 302 737-7350
  Newark (G-11888)
Robin Drive Auto LLC .... G 302 326-2437
  Bear (G-465)
Roccos Automotive Service .... G 302 998-2234
  Wilmington (G-19526)
Rock Ranch Auto LLC .... G 302 670-9992
  Houston (G-5450)
Rockaway Auto Repair .... G 302 644-1485
  Lewes (G-6427)
Route 9 Auto Center .... G 302 856-3941
  Georgetown (G-4494)
Royal Tech Auto Repair LLC .... G 302 737-6852
  Newark (G-11922)
RPM Automotive of Dover LLC .... G 302 734-9495
  Dover (G-3490)
Rs Werks .... G 302 740-1516
  Newark (G-11924)
Rudys European Motorcars .... G 302 645-6410
  Lewes (G-6434)
Rush Auto LLC .... G 302 323-9070
  New Castle (G-9548)
S Wilson Auto Repair .... G 302 856-3839
  Georgetown (G-4496)
S&M Small Engine Repair LLC .... G 302 893-7341
  Ocean View (G-12564)
Sals Garage Inc .... G 302 655-4981
  Wilmington (G-19641)
Sammys Auto LLC .... G 302 368-5203
  Newark (G-11939)
Scott Muffler LLC .... G 302 378-9247
  Middletown (G-7545)
Select Auto Inc .... G 215 423-6522
  Claymont (G-1288)
Sevys Auto Service Inc .... G 302 328-0839
  New Castle (G-9560)
Sharks Service Center LLC .... G 302 337-8233
  Bridgeville (G-764)
Shockleys Auto Service .... G 302 537-7663
  Frankford (G-4143)
Site-On Auto Inc .... G 302 505-5100
  Lincoln (G-6702)
Smalleys Automotive Group Inc .... G 302 450-0983
  Kenton (G-5455)
Smiths Jack Towing & Svc Ctr .... G 302 798-6667
  Wilmington (G-19895)
Smittys Auto Repair Inc .... G 302 398-8419
  Harrington (G-4833)
Sonnys Auto Services Inc .... G 302 287-7677
  Bear (G-499)
Sparkys Auto Repair LLC .... G 302 495-7525
  Greenwood (G-4669)
Sports Car Service Inc .... G 302 764-7439
  Wilmington (G-19969)

Star Gas & Diesel .... G 302 998-2002
  Wilmington (G-20024)
Steerr Inc .... G 412 303-5840
  Lewes (G-6509)
Stokes Garage Inc .... G 302 994-0613
  Wilmington (G-20075)
Sun Gas & Diesel .... G 302 376-8200
  Middletown (G-7608)
Sussex Diesel Inc .... G 302 877-0330
  Laurel (G-5609)
Td Automotive .... G 443 794-3453
  New Castle (G-9619)
Three Js Disc Tire & Auto Svc .... G 302 995-6141
  Wilmington (G-20316)
Trou Auto .... G 302 762-3200
  Wilmington (G-20439)
Truck Tech Inc .... G 302 832-8000
  New Castle (G-9642)
True Street Automotive LLC .... G 302 480-4119
  Smyrna (G-13921)
Turn of Wrench .... G 302 584-1824
  Smyrna (G-13922)
Unique Auto Accessories LLC .... G 302 841-0983
  Laurel (G-5617)
United Auto Sales Inc .... G 302 325-3000
  Newark (G-12266)
Universalfleet .... G 302 428-0661
  New Castle (G-9660)
Vehicle Maintenance Dept .... G 302 571-5857
  Wilmington (G-20578)
Wallis Repair Inc .... G 302 378-4301
  Middletown (G-7705)
Wheel Lady Garcia .... G 302 588-9750
  Wilmington (G-20757)
White Deer Auto .... G 302 846-0547
  Delmar (G-1655)
Wiedman Enterprises Inc .... G 302 226-2407
  Rehoboth Beach (G-13016)
William Chambers and Son .... G 302 284-9655
  Viola (G-14098)
William Craft .... G 302 945-5798
  Lewes (G-6631)
William T Wadkins Garage Inc .... G 302 422-0265
  Milford (G-8151)
Willis Ford Inc .... E 302 653-5900
  Smyrna (G-13939)
Winner Ford of Dover Ltd .... B 302 734-0444
  Dover (G-3860)
Winner Group Inc .... F 302 292-8200
  Newark (G-12389)
Winner Infiniti Inc .... E 302 764-5900
  Wilmington (G-20862)
Wolfs Elite Autos .... G 302 999-9199
  Wilmington (G-20877)
Zeglins Automotive Inc .... G 302 947-1414
  Millsboro (G-8511)

7539 Automotive repair shops, nec

A Minor Tune Up LLC .... G 302 658-1587
  Wilmington (G-14169)
Automotiveonly .... G 302 727-1064
  Rehoboth Beach (G-12618)
B & E Tire Alignment Inc .... G 302 732-6091
  Frankford (G-4066)
Bargain Tire .... G 302 764-8900
  Wilmington (G-14762)
Bargain Tire & Service Inc .... F 302 764-8900
  Wilmington (G-14763)
Benchmark Transmission Inc .... G 302 792-2300
  Claymont (G-1056)
Bernard Limpert .... G 302 674-8280
  Dover (G-1914)

Blue Hen Spring Works Inc .... F 302 422-6600
  Milford (G-7798)
Brandywine Chrysler Jeep Dodge .... D 302 998-0458
  Wilmington (G-15050)
Buntings Garage Inc .... F 302 732-9021
  Dagsboro (G-1421)
Capital Trail Service Center .... G 302 731-0999
  Newark (G-10134)
Coastal Towing Inc .... G 302 645-6300
  Lewes (G-5847)
D & H Automotive & Towing Inc .... G 302 655-7611
  Wilmington (G-15757)
Daves Service Center .... G 302 798-1776
  Claymont (G-1109)
Elite Meetings International .... G 302 516-7997
  Wilmington (G-16365)
Els Tire Service Inc .... F 302 834-1997
  Newark (G-10633)
Ewings Towing Service Inc .... G 302 366-8806
  Newark (G-10681)
Garage .... G 302 645-7288
  Rehoboth Beach (G-12766)
Goodchild Inc .... G 302 368-1681
  Newark (G-10868)
H&H Services Electrical Contrs .... G 302 373-4950
  New Castle (G-9190)
Highfield Electric LLC .... G 302 836-4300
  Bear (G-273)
Independent Elec Svcs LLC .... D 302 383-2761
  Claymont (G-1184)
J & K Auto Repair Inc .... G 302 834-8025
  Bear (G-292)
Kent Sign Company Inc .... F 302 697-2181
  Dover (G-2856)
Lees Best Car Wash .... G 302 328-0770
  New Castle (G-9299)
Martin Collision Center .... G 302 452-2711
  Newark (G-11341)
Meadowood Mobil Station .... G 302 731-5602
  Newark (G-11369)
Meineke Care Care Center .... G 302 368-0700
  Newark (G-11383)
Paul A Nicle Inc .... G 302 453-4000
  Newark (G-11642)
Reliable Trailer Inc .... F 856 962-7900
  Felton (G-4015)
Sb Electric LLC .... G 610 721-5361
  Wilmington (G-19688)
Schrider Enterprises Inc .... G 302 934-1900
  Millsboro (G-8456)
Sevys Auto Service Inc .... G 302 328-0839
  New Castle (G-9560)
Staplefords Sales and Service .... G 302 834-4568
  Saint Georges (G-13039)
Super Service Automotive Inc .... F 302 464-1149
  Middletown (G-7612)
US Telex Corporation .... G 302 652-2707
  Wilmington (G-20552)
V A Truck & Trailer Repair LLC .... G 302 653-7936
  Smyrna (G-13927)
Wrenchtime Auto LLC .... G 302 500-5558
  Newark (G-12412)

7542 Carwashes

Attention To Detail In Smyrna .... G 302 388-1267
  Smyrna (G-13655)
B and D Detailing .... G 302 543-6221
  Wilmington (G-14694)
Beyond Details .... G 302 223-6156
  Clayton (G-1354)
Big Toy Custom Car Care Inc .... G 302 668-6729
  Wilmington (G-14884)

Employee Codes: A=Over 500 employees, B=251-500
C=101-250, D=51-100, E=20-50, F=10-19, G=1-9

2024 Harris Directory of Delaware Businesses

75 AUTOMOTIVE REPAIR, SERVICES AND PARKING

Blue Hen Car Wash .... G 302 273-2100
   Newark *(G-10058)*

Car Wash of Prices Corner .... F 302 994-9274
   Wilmington *(G-15237)*

Carolines Spa & Goods LLC .... G 302 200-2635
   Selbyville *(G-13494)*

Coastal Car Wash LLC .... E 302 883-3554
   Dover *(G-2105)*

Damions Solar Shades .... G 302 661-1500
   Wilmington *(G-15775)*

Detail Stone Works .... G 302 357-7065
   Newark *(G-10518)*

Detailing Good Brothers .... G 302 482-3348
   Wilmington *(G-16030)*

Ferguson Ventures .... G 484 561-3510
   Middletown *(G-7125)*

Gas & Go Inc .... G 302 734-8234
   Dover *(G-2562)*

Greenhill Car Wash .... G 302 420-5961
   Middletown *(G-7176)*

Greenhill Express Car Wash .... G 302 464-1031
   Middletown *(G-7177)*

HI Line Auto Detailing .... G 302 420-5368
   Wilmington *(G-17138)*

Kjs Detailing LLC .... G 302 420-9121
   Wilmington *(G-17739)*

L L Detailing .... G 302 453-8000
   Newark *(G-11207)*

Logue Brothers Inc .... F 302 762-1896
   Wilmington *(G-17976)*

Maaco Collision Repr Auto Pntg .... G 610 628-3867
   Wilmington *(G-18063)*

Magic Car Wash .... G 302 750-2197
   Hockessin *(G-5292)*

Magic Car Wash II Inc .... G 302 660-8066
   Wilmington *(G-18079)*

Magic Car Wash Inc .... F 302 479-5911
   Wilmington *(G-18080)*

Magic Touch .... G 302 655-6430
   Historic New Castle *(G-5023)*

Mikes Expert Detailing .... G 302 853-5368
   Greenwood *(G-4652)*

Mobile Magic Detailing LLC .... G 302 444-8644
   Newark *(G-11436)*

Newport Ventures Inc .... F 302 998-1693
   Middletown *(G-7399)*

On-Site Detailing Inc .... G 302 540-9680
   Wilmington *(G-18776)*

One The Spot .... G 302 858-2957
   Laurel *(G-5572)*

Pwp Pike Creek LLC .... G 302 635-7837
   Wilmington *(G-19271)*

Ravis Car Detailing .... G 302 945-8253
   Lewes *(G-6410)*

Rehoboth Car Wash Inc .... G 302 227-6177
   Rehoboth Beach *(G-12923)*

Rehoboth Car Wash Inc .... G 302 245-6839
   Rehoboth Beach *(G-12924)*

Richard Addington Co .... G 302 422-2668
   Milford *(G-8068)*

Schaffers Mobile Detailing LLC .... G 302 284-7636
   Felton *(G-4023)*

Super Wash .... G 302 384-6111
   Wilmington *(G-20139)*

Triumph Bike Detailing .... G 302 463-3606
   Newark *(G-12237)*

Victory Lane Express Wash LLC .... G 302 543-6445
   Wilmington *(G-20613)*

Willies Auto Detail Service .... G 302 734-1010
   Dover *(G-3852)*

7549 Automotive services, nec

30215 Motorsports .... G 302 293-6193
   Newark *(G-9709)*

4 Points Twing Radside Svc LLC .... G 302 538-8935
   Camden Wyoming *(G-902)*

A M Towing Co .... G 302 357-5159
   New Castle *(G-8749)*

A-One Towing Inc .... G 302 853-2326
   Lewes *(G-5647)*

Alan Passwaters .... G 302 245-9114
   Seaford *(G-13052)*

All Star Towing LLC .... G 302 388-4221
   New Castle *(G-8783)*

▼ Autoport Inc .... E 302 658-5100
   New Castle *(G-8834)*

B & F Towing Co .... E 302 328-4146
   New Castle *(G-8839)*

Basher & Son Enterprises Inc .... G 302 239-6584
   Hockessin *(G-5130)*

Blueprint Motorsport .... G 302 333-2746
   Wilmington *(G-14981)*

Capital Trail Service Center .... G 302 731-0999
   Newark *(G-10134)*

Careys Inc .... F 302 875-5674
   Laurel *(G-5478)*

Chambers Motors Inc .... E 302 629-3553
   Seaford *(G-13109)*

City Towing Services .... G 302 561-7979
   New Castle *(G-8951)*

Coastal Towing Inc .... G 302 645-6300
   Lewes *(G-5847)*

Continental Warranty Corp .... E 302 375-0401
   Claymont *(G-1100)*

Coosco Auto Tech LLC .... G 302 391-6043
   Wilmington *(G-15634)*

Cr Lube Run LLC .... G 302 875-1641
   Laurel *(G-5487)*

D & G Inc .... F 302 378-4877
   Townsend *(G-13982)*

D & H Automotive & Towing Inc .... G 302 655-7611
   Wilmington *(G-15757)*

Delmarva Auto Repair LLC .... G 302 727-3237
   Greenwood *(G-4614)*

Donald Briggs .... G 267 476-2712
   Middletown *(G-7069)*

Dover Lubricants Inc .... G 302 674-8282
   Dover *(G-2352)*

Ellmore Auto Collision .... G 302 762-2301
   Wilmington *(G-16374)*

Ewings Towing Service Inc .... G 302 366-8806
   Newark *(G-10681)*

Fast4wrd Towing & Recovery .... G 302 331-5157
   Felton *(G-3970)*

Fred Drake Automotive Inc .... G 302 378-4877
   Townsend *(G-14003)*

Goodchild Inc .... G 302 368-1681
   Newark *(G-10868)*

Harold D Shockley .... G 302 275-8500
   Lincoln *(G-6675)*

Harris Towing and Auto Service .... G 302 736-9901
   Dover *(G-2656)*

Harris Towing Service .... G 302 736-5473
   Frederica *(G-4170)*

Hazzard Auto Repairs Inc .... G 302 645-4543
   Lewes *(G-6083)*

Hound Dog Recovery LLC .... G 302 836-3806
   Smyrna *(G-13767)*

Joeys Towing LLC .... G 610 342-7417
   Bridgeville *(G-720)*

Joseph Cartwright Jr .... G 302 658-9487
   Wilmington *(G-17580)*

Kanaci Technologies Inc .... F 302 658-7581
   Wilmington *(G-17646)*

Kings Towing Company LLC .... G 302 345-3134
   Newark *(G-11179)*

Loyalty Is Earned Inc .... G 347 606-6383
   Wilmington *(G-18015)*

M & M Detail Wrap and Tint LLC .... G 302 260-8988
   Wilmington *(G-18056)*

Martel & Son Foreign Car Ctr .... G 302 674-5556
   Dover *(G-3022)*

Matthews Towing & Recovery .... F 302 463-1108
   Smyrna *(G-13820)*

Middletown Towing .... G 302 357-6484
   Townsend *(G-14037)*

Midway Towing Inc .... G 302 323-4850
   Wilmington *(G-18345)*

Monro Inc .... G 302 846-2732
   Delmar *(G-1623)*

Nicastros Inc .... G 302 425-5555
   New Castle *(G-9419)*

Non Stop Towing LLC .... F 302 647-1399
   Wilmington *(G-18667)*

On Demand Oil Change LLC .... G 855 959-1599
   Wilmington *(G-18773)*

Positive Vibes Only Brand .... G 302 500-1369
   Wilmington *(G-19127)*

Predator Recovery & Towing LLC .... G 302 381-2135
   Laurel *(G-5578)*

Pughs Service Inc .... F 302 678-2408
   Dover *(G-3394)*

Right-Away Auto Assistance LLC .... G 302 438-9970
   Hockessin *(G-5364)*

Sals Auto Services Inc .... G 302 654-1168
   Wilmington *(G-19640)*

Sanchasegroup .... G 302 516-7373
   Wilmington *(G-19654)*

Schrider Enterprises Inc .... G 302 934-1900
   Millsboro *(G-8456)*

Shocker Towing & Recovery .... G 302 259-1123
   Frankford *(G-4142)*

Shore Tint & More Inc .... G 302 947-4624
   Harbeson *(G-4716)*

Smiths Jack Towing & Svc Ctr .... G 302 798-6667
   Wilmington *(G-19895)*

Swift Towing & Recovery .... G 302 650-4579
   New Castle *(G-9611)*

Tikana Motorsports .... G 302 290-0869
   Townsend *(G-14080)*

Tow Plus .... G 302 468-5987
   Wilmington *(G-20377)*

Truck Store LLC .... G 302 724-5918
   Dover *(G-3732)*

Tuff Tasks LLC .... G 302 983-5990
   Middletown *(G-7667)*

Uris LLC .... G 302 469-7000
   Millsboro *(G-8491)*

Wilson Fleet & Equipment .... G 302 422-7159
   Milford *(G-8152)*

Winners Circle Inc .... E 302 661-2100
   Wilmington *(G-20864)*

76 MISCELLANEOUS REPAIR SERVICES

7622 Radio and television repair

Als TV Service .... G 302 653-3711
   Smyrna *(G-13636)*

C B Joe TV & Appliances Inc .... G 302 322-7600
   New Castle *(G-8907)*

Corporate Arcft Technical Svcs .... G 302 383-9400
   Wilmington *(G-15643)*

ET Communications LLC .... F 302 322-2222
   Historic New Castle *(G-4983)*

76 MISCELLANEOUS REPAIR SERVICES

Far Rezolutions Inc .... G 302 547-6850
  Newark (G-10712)
G & S TV & Antenna .... G 302 422-5733
  Milford (G-7905)
Quality Crawlspace & More LLC .... G 443 944-5163
  Laurel (G-5581)

7623 Refrigeration service and repair

Berry Refrigeration Co .... E 302 733-0933
  Newark (G-10025)
Burns & McBride Inc .... D 302 656-5110
  New Castle (G-8901)
Commercial Equipment Service .... G 302 475-6682
  Wilmington (G-15547)
Delmarva Refrigeration Inc .... G 302 846-2727
  Delmar (G-1588)
Jam Air LLC .... G 302 270-8236
  Dover (G-2767)
Morans Refrigeration Svc Inc .... G 703 642-1200
  Rehoboth Beach (G-12861)
Roto-Rooter Services Company .... G 302 659-7637
  Newark (G-11917)
Smt Htg and Air Cond LLC .... G 302 285-9219
  Townsend (G-14065)
◆ Weitron Inc .... E 800 398-3816
  Newark (G-12356)
Williams Appliancee .... F 302 656-8581
  Wilmington (G-20797)

7629 Electrical repair shops

ABC Sales & Service Inc .... F 302 652-3683
  Wilmington (G-14196)
Bigcentric Appliance .... G 302 691-8510
  Wilmington (G-14886)
Bigcentric Inc .... G 410 456-1968
  Wilmington (G-14887)
Blue Skies Solar & Wind Power .... G 302 326-0856
  New Castle (G-8871)
Commercial Equipment Svc .... G 302 475-6682
  Wilmington (G-15548)
Del-Mar Appliance of Delaware .... G 302 674-2414
  Dover (G-2211)
Excel Business Systems Inc .... E 302 453-1500
  Newark (G-10683)
Food Equipment Service Inc .... G 302 996-9363
  Wilmington (G-16682)
Johns Washer Repair .... G 302 792-2333
  Claymont (G-1199)
Martel Inc .... G 302 674-5660
  Dover (G-3023)
Master Klean Company .... G 302 539-4290
  Ocean View (G-12543)
Modern Controls Inc .... C 302 325-6800
  New Castle (G-9377)
Morton Electric Co .... G 302 645-9414
  Lewes (G-6292)
Mr Appliance Sussex County .... E 302 752-3747
  Laurel (G-5567)
Qoe Inc .... G 302 455-1234
  Newark (G-11783)
Ram Tech Systems Inc .... E 302 832-6600
  Middletown (G-7500)
Roys Electrical Service Inc .... G 302 674-3199
  Cheswold (G-989)
Shootle Inc .... G 941 866-2135
  Lewes (G-6464)
Smith Brothers Communication .... G 302 293-5224
  Newark (G-12041)
Tower Business Machines Inc .... G 302 395-1445
  Historic New Castle (G-5088)
Visual Communications Inc .... G 302 792-9500
  Claymont (G-1330)

7631 Watch, clock, and jewelry repair

Bridgewater Jewelers .... G 302 328-2101
  Historic New Castle (G-4945)
Continental Jewelers Inc .... G 302 475-2000
  Wilmington (G-15620)
Del Haven of Wilmington Inc .... G 302 999-9040
  Newark (G-10411)
Golden Jewelry .... G 302 777-2121
  Wilmington (G-16913)
Michael Gallagher Jewelers .... G 302 836-2925
  Bear (G-375)
Precision Jewelry Inc .... G 302 422-7138
  Milford (G-8051)
Turquoise Shop Inc .... F 302 366-7448
  Newark (G-12248)
Whittens Fine Jewelry .... G 302 995-7464
  Wilmington (G-20774)

7641 Reupholstery and furniture repair

Advance Office Instiltions Inc .... E 302 777-5599
  Historic New Castle (G-4922)
Artcraft Upholstery LLC .... G 302 764-2067
  Wilmington (G-14561)
Barlows Upholstery Inc .... G 302 655-3955
  Wilmington (G-14766)
Colliers Trim Shop Inc .... G 302 227-8398
  Rehoboth Beach (G-12691)
Color Dye Systems and Co .... G 302 454-1754
  Newark (G-10279)
East Coast .... G 302 249-8867
  Lewes (G-5944)
Fibrenew Northern & Central De .... G 833 427-3639
  Smyrna (G-13731)
New Life Furniture Systems .... G 302 994-9054
  Wilmington (G-18620)

7692 Welding repair

3rd State Welding Supply LLC .... G 302 777-1088
  Wilmington (G-14131)
A and J Welding .... G 302 229-2000
  Middletown (G-6821)
Allied Precision Inc .... G 302 376-6844
  Middletown (G-6852)
Basher & Son Enterprises Inc .... G 302 239-6584
  Hockessin (G-5130)
Bear Forge and Machine Co Inc .... G 302 322-5199
  Bear (G-63)
Bg Welding LLC .... G 302 228-7260
  Bridgeville (G-672)
Blackwells Welding Inc .... G 301 498-5277
  Milton (G-8572)
Boyds Trailor Hitches .... G 302 697-9000
  Camden Wyoming (G-917)
Boyds Welding Inc .... G 302 697-9000
  Camden Wyoming (G-918)
Bruces Welding Inc .... G 302 629-3891
  Seaford (G-13097)
C&C Welding .... G 402 414-2485
  New Castle (G-8908)
Cat Welding LLC .... G 302 846-3509
  Delmar (G-1575)
Chuck George Inc .... E 302 994-7444
  Wilmington (G-15427)
Collett and Sons Welding .... E 302 223-6525
  Smyrna (G-13686)
D M Iannone Inc .... G 302 999-0893
  Wilmington (G-15761)
Davis Welding Service Llc .... G 302 465-3004
  Seaford (G-13147)
Dempseys Specialized Svcs LLC .... F 302 530-7856
  Newark (G-10512)
Diamond State Welding LLC .... G 302 644-8489
  Milton (G-8604)
Donaway Corporation .... G 302 934-6226
  Millsboro (G-8275)
East Coast Machine Works .... G 302 349-5180
  Greenwood (G-4623)
George Swire Sr .... G 302 690-6995
  Clayton (G-1369)
▲ George W Plummer & Son Inc .... G 302 645-9531
  Lewes (G-6030)
GJ Chalfant Welding LLC .... G 302 983-0822
  Port Penn (G-12588)
Graydie Welding LLC .... G 302 753-0695
  Wilmington (G-16951)
Hot Rod Welding .... G 302 725-5485
  Harrington (G-4786)
Indian River Golf Cars Dr Wldg .... G 302 947-2044
  Millsboro (G-8320)
K L Vincent Welding Svc Inc .... F 302 398-9357
  Harrington (G-4793)
L & J Sheet Metal .... F 302 875-2822
  Laurel (G-5542)
Leland Oakley Welding .... G 302 469-5746
  Felton (G-3996)
Lloyds Wldg & Fabrication LLC .... G 302 384-7662
  Wilmington (G-17958)
Marvel Portable Welding Inc .... G 302 732-9480
  Dagsboro (G-1479)
Mastercraft Welding .... G 302 697-3932
  Dover (G-3028)
Metal-Tech Inc .... E 302 322-7770
  New Castle (G-9360)
Miller JW Wldg Boiler Repr Co .... G 302 449-1575
  Middletown (G-7372)
Moore Quality Welding Fab .... G 302 250-7136
  Middletown (G-7379)
Nicks Welding Repair LLC .... G 302 545-1494
  Wilmington (G-18644)
Pauls Inc .... G 302 328-0191
  Bear (G-420)
Peninsula Technical Services I .... G 302 907-0554
  Delmar (G-1629)
Pts Professional Welding .... G 302 632-2079
  Houston (G-5447)
R & J Welding & Fabrication .... G 302 236-5618
  Laurel (G-5582)
R C Fabricators Inc .... D 302 573-8989
  Wilmington (G-19303)
Richard M White Welding .... G 302 684-4461
  Milton (G-8697)
Rm Industrial Welding .... G 302 407-6685
  Wilmington (G-19503)
Rrp Mechanical Welding LLC .... G 302 448-1051
  Bridgeville (G-763)
Sapps Welding Service .... G 302 491-6319
  Lincoln (G-6697)
Seaford Machine Works Inc .... F 302 629-6034
  Seaford (G-13389)
Truck Tech Inc .... G 302 832-8000
  New Castle (G-9642)
Welding By Jackson .... G 302 846-3090
  Delmar (G-1654)
William Stele Wldg Fabrication .... G 302 422-7444
  Milford (G-8150)

7694 Armature rewinding shops

Dills Electric .... G 302 674-3444
  Camden (G-819)
Electric Motor Repair Svc .... G 302 322-1179
  Historic New Castle (G-4980)
F and D Equipment & Repair LLC .... G 302 378-1999
  Middletown (G-7117)

Employee Codes: A=Over 500 employees, B=251-500
C=101-250, D=51-100, E=20-50, F=10-19, G=1-9

76 MISCELLANEOUS REPAIR SERVICES

HP Motors Inc..G..... 302 368-4543
  Newark *(G-10981)*

Roys Electrical Service Inc..........................G..... 302 674-3199
  Cheswold *(G-989)*

Warren Electric Co Inc.................................G..... 302 629-9134
  Seaford *(G-13444)*

7699 Repair services, nec

1st State Power Clean LLC........................G..... 302 735-7974
  Dover *(G-1680)*

3e Cleaning Services...................................G..... 215 359-8323
  Townsend *(G-13949)*

3phase Excel Elevator LLC..........................G..... 508 350-9900
  Wilmington *(G-14130)*

5-Star Cleaning Services............................G..... 302 476-9604
  Wilmington *(G-14141)*

A Smarter Clean LLC...................................F..... 302 841-8419
  Harbeson *(G-4679)*

A-1 Sanitation Service Inc..........................E..... 302 322-1074
  New Castle *(G-8752)*

A-Team Cleaning LLC..................................G..... 302 858-8709
  Bridgeville *(G-660)*

A&T Cleaning Services.................................G..... 302 752-5520
  Laurel *(G-5458)*

A1 Sanitation Service Inc...........................G..... 302 653-9591
  Smyrna *(G-13627)*

A2z Auto Rpair Auto Mble Rpair..................G..... 302 856-2219
  Georgetown *(G-4194)*

Acn Cleaning LLC...G..... 302 588-7485
  Wilmington *(G-14236)*

Adams Custom Leather...............................G..... 302 462-0187
  Harbeson *(G-4680)*

Adept Cleaning & Restoration....................G..... 302 385-6653
  Bear *(G-15)*

Alas Cleaners & Alterations........................G..... 302 366-1638
  Newark *(G-9805)*

All Bright Cleaning Svcs LLC........................F..... 302 219-7016
  New Castle *(G-8778)*

All Clean Power Washing.............................F..... 877 325-3215
  Selbyville *(G-13459)*

All County Cleaning......................................G..... 302 504-4719
  Felton *(G-3940)*

All County Cleaning......................................G..... 914 497-1477
  Magnolia *(G-6715)*

All JS Cleaning Services Inc........................G..... 302 299-9916
  New Castle *(G-8780)*

All Mighty Clean Company...........................G..... 302 798-1013
  Claymont *(G-1029)*

All Work Services..G..... 302 345-2695
  Newark *(G-9821)*

Allerfree Cleaning...G..... 302 593-6261
  Lewes *(G-5675)*

Allied Lock & Safe Company........................G..... 302 658-3172
  Wilmington *(G-14381)*

Almars Outboard Service & Sls...................G..... 302 328-8541
  Historic New Castle *(G-4928)*

Alvarenga Cleaner..G..... 302 427-2308
  Wilmington *(G-14400)*

Alvins Professional Services.......................F..... 302 544-6634
  New Castle *(G-8789)*

Always Duwell Clean....................................G..... 610 905-0779
  Wilmington *(G-14404)*

◆ Anderson Group Inc..................................A..... 302 478-6160
  Wilmington *(G-14472)*

Angel Pizzaro..G..... 302 653-4844
  Townsend *(G-13960)*

Angies Super Clean......................................G..... 302 519-0828
  Seaford *(G-13067)*

Anointed To Clean..G..... 302 284-7243
  Magnolia *(G-6717)*

Arrow Leasing Corp......................................F..... 302 834-4546
  Bear *(G-47)*

Arteaga Properties LLC................................G..... 808 339-6906
  Wilmington *(G-14562)*

ASAP Cleaning Services..............................G..... 302 519-6607
  Greenwood *(G-4591)*

Atlantic Pumping Inc....................................F..... 302 436-5047
  Selbyville *(G-13468)*

Avantish Cleaners..G..... 302 947-1632
  Lewes *(G-5723)*

Awesome Cleaning Services LLC...............G..... 302 585-3115
  Lewes *(G-5728)*

B-Dun Cleaning..G..... 302 542-7869
  Lewes *(G-5733)*

B&O Cleaning Service..................................G..... 302 604-0108
  Dagsboro *(G-1416)*

Bay Spray..G..... 302 245-2715
  Frankford *(G-4069)*

Beachside Cleaning LLC.............................G..... 717 875-3141
  Selbyville *(G-13474)*

Best Choice LLC...G..... 302 722-4249
  New Castle *(G-8861)*

Bethany Beach Cleaning LLC......................G..... 302 858-6524
  Ocean View *(G-12478)*

Bethany Cycle & Fitness Inc.......................G..... 302 537-9982
  Bethany Beach *(G-584)*

Biamby Cleaning Services..........................G..... 302 519-1604
  Georgetown *(G-4233)*

Bingnear Cleaning.......................................G..... 302 519-7318
  Millsboro *(G-8197)*

Blue Profit Cleaning LLC.............................G..... 302 377-3286
  Wilmington *(G-14971)*

Blue Shore Inc..G..... 301 890-9797
  Bethany Beach *(G-587)*

Blue Sky Clean..G..... 302 584-5800
  Wilmington *(G-14975)*

Bobs Marine Service Inc.............................F..... 302 539-3711
  Ocean View *(G-12482)*

Bollinger Cleaning Service LLC...................G..... 410 620-1953
  Historic New Castle *(G-4944)*

Bradfords Quality Care Inc..........................G..... 302 436-2467
  Frankford *(G-4076)*

Brisyn Pros Cleaning Service......................G..... 302 399-7366
  Dover *(G-1981)*

Broken Spoke Outfitters Inc........................E..... 604 558-0248
  Newark *(G-10091)*

Brooks Machine Inc.....................................G..... 302 674-5900
  Dover *(G-1984)*

▲ Bruce Industrial Co Inc...........................D..... 302 655-9616
  New Castle *(G-8894)*

Budget Rooter Inc..F..... 302 322-3011
  New Castle *(G-8897)*

Burns & McBride Inc....................................D..... 302 656-5110
  New Castle *(G-8901)*

C & B Complete Clg Svc Inc........................E..... 302 436-9622
  Frankford *(G-4081)*

C & S Battery Inc..G..... 610 459-2227
  Wilmington *(G-15172)*

C H P T Manufacturing Inc..........................G..... 302 856-7660
  Georgetown *(G-4242)*

C White & Sons LLC....................................G..... 302 629-4848
  Seaford *(G-13100)*

Candlelight Cleaning...................................G..... 302 270-1218
  Smyrna *(G-13673)*

Carspecken-Scott Inc..................................G..... 302 655-7173
  Wilmington *(G-15261)*

Cayley J Carson...G..... 302 328-2561
  New Castle *(G-8921)*

Cell Surgeon...G..... 302 423-4441
  Dover *(G-2045)*

Certified Lock & Access LLC.......................G..... 302 383-7507
  Wilmington *(G-15316)*

Cgm Repair..G..... 302 344-4222
  Millsboro *(G-8219)*

Charlie Square Cleaners LLC.....................G..... 302 778-3807
  Wilmington *(G-15343)*

Check Plus Cleaning LLC............................G..... 302 837-7308
  Wilmington *(G-15349)*

Cinderellas Cleaning LLC............................G..... 302 632-6036
  Dover *(G-2073)*

Clean A Lot LLC..F..... 302 218-2755
  Newark *(G-10253)*

Clean Bee...G..... 302 416-1723
  Newark *(G-10254)*

Clean Bees..G..... 302 470-1125
  Seaford *(G-13124)*

Clean Cars Inc..G..... 302 734-8234
  Dover *(G-2087)*

Clean Conscience LLC................................G..... 410 746-1315
  Lewes *(G-5824)*

Clean Cut Thread...G..... 302 491-4336
  Milford *(G-7830)*

Clean Delaware..G..... 302 462-1451
  Dover *(G-2088)*

Clean Delaware Inc......................................G..... 302 684-4221
  Milton *(G-8584)*

Clean Energy USA LLC................................G..... 302 227-1337
  Rehoboth Beach *(G-12676)*

Clean Genie..G..... 302 241-4708
  Dover *(G-2089)*

Clean Green Horizons.................................G..... 302 258-9808
  Rehoboth Beach *(G-12677)*

Clean ME Out Cleaning Svcs LLC..............G..... 302 480-4788
  Dover *(G-2090)*

Cleaning Authority.......................................G..... 302 508-5080
  Smyrna *(G-13682)*

Cleaning Bees..G..... 302 723-2421
  Townsend *(G-13972)*

Cleaning Bussiness.....................................G..... 302 260-9023
  Rehoboth Beach *(G-12678)*

Cleaning By Diana.......................................G..... 302 345-8904
  Wilmington *(G-15474)*

Cleaning Fairies...G..... 302 753-3617
  Wilmington *(G-15475)*

Cleaning Frenzy LLC....................................G..... 302 453-8800
  Newark *(G-10256)*

Clifton Leasing Co Inc.................................E..... 302 674-2300
  Dover *(G-2093)*

Clyde V Bush Sr..G..... 302 697-1723
  Camden Wyoming *(G-924)*

Coastal Services LLC..................................F..... 302 616-2906
  Ocean View *(G-12495)*

Columbia Vending Service Inc....................F..... 302 856-7000
  Delmar *(G-1582)*

Comfort Boyce Systems..............................F..... 302 419-4748
  Newark *(G-10281)*

Commercial Cleaning Services...................G..... 302 764-3424
  Wilmington *(G-15546)*

Coney Steam and Clean..............................G..... 302 670-0183
  Dover *(G-2129)*

Costline Cleaning Service...........................G..... 302 420-3000
  Harbeson *(G-4691)*

Crystal Blu Services LLC.............................G..... 302 404-5389
  Seaford *(G-13141)*

Crystal Clean..G..... 302 864-4032
  Millsboro *(G-8246)*

Crystal Kleen Inc..G..... 302 326-1140
  New Castle *(G-8990)*

Dag Residential Coml Svcs LLC.................G..... 302 513-6646
  Felton *(G-3956)*

Danis Home Cleaning Services..................G..... 302 525-8286
  New Castle *(G-8997)*

Daves Truck Repair LLC..............................G..... 302 362-2578
  Frankford *(G-4098)*

David Jenkins...G..... 302 304-5568
  Bear *(G-132)*

76 MISCELLANEOUS REPAIR SERVICES

David Robinson .... G 302 324-3253
   Wilmington *(G-15809)*

Davis Lock and Safe LLC .... G 302 628-5397
   Seaford *(G-13146)*

Del Mar Onsite Solutions .... G 302 629-2568
   Seaford *(G-13150)*

Del-State Cleaning Services .... G 302 563-0606
   Felton *(G-3958)*

◆ Delaware Capital Holdings Inc .... G 302 793-4921
   Wilmington *(G-15879)*

Delaware Rural Water Assn .... G 302 398-9633
   Harrington *(G-4757)*

Delawares Finest Services .... G 302 607-9288
   Newark *(G-10496)*

Delfis Clean LLC .... G 302 740-0989
   Wilmington *(G-15992)*

Delmarva Kleaning Klub LLC .... G 302 629-4706
   Seaford *(G-13155)*

Delmarva Performance and Repr .... G 302 858-3546
   Delmar *(G-1587)*

Delmarva Repair .... G 302 313-6900
   Lewes *(G-5907)*

Dependable Elec Svc & Repr .... G 302 877-0770
   Frankford *(G-4101)*

Dominion Cars LLC .... G 302 730-3882
   Dover *(G-2321)*

Doris House Cleaning .... G 302 235-8239
   Newark *(G-10552)*

Drain Kings LLC .... G 302 399-8980
   Smyrna *(G-13715)*

Duct Cleaning Corp .... G 302 310-4060
   Wilmington *(G-16194)*

Dukes Septic .... G 302 362-6010
   Milton *(G-8612)*

Dustntime .... G 302 858-7876
   Rehoboth Beach *(G-12736)*

Earls Place LLC .... G 302 538-8909
   Felton *(G-3964)*

Eastern Shore Cleaning LLC .... G 302 752-8856
   Georgetown *(G-4305)*

Eat Clean Juice Bar LLC .... F 856 397-9112
   Wilmington *(G-16272)*

Ecolistic Living Inc .... E 888 432-6547
   Lewes *(G-5947)*

Elite Chemical and Supply Inc .... G 302 366-8900
   Newark *(G-10627)*

Elite Cleaning Services LLC .... G 571 359-7751
   Lewes *(G-5957)*

Emmanuel Troumouhis .... G 302 762-3200
   Wilmington *(G-16397)*

Energy Services Group .... F 302 324-8400
   New Castle *(G-9095)*

Equinox Cleaning LLC .... G 240 419-9077
   Newark *(G-10660)*

F and S Commercial Cleaning .... G 302 250-1736
   Lewes *(G-5982)*

F M Repairs .... G 302 422-7229
   Milford *(G-7887)*

Fantastic Green Cleaning Svc .... G 302 981-8259
   New Castle *(G-9119)*

Fern Cleaning .... G 302 480-0241
   Newark *(G-10722)*

Fiduks Industrial Services Inc .... F 302 994-2534
   Wilmington *(G-16601)*

Filth-Fighters Clg Svcs LLC .... G 302 423-4684
   Dover *(G-2494)*

Final Touch Cleaning .... G 302 730-1495
   Dover *(G-2495)*

First Caliber Services LLC .... G 302 328-3049
   New Castle *(G-9126)*

First State Plumbing & Heating .... G 302 275-9746
   New Castle *(G-9131)*

First State Roof Extrior Clean .... G 302 751-0439
   Millsboro *(G-8290)*

Five-Star Cleaning Services .... G 302 746-7178
   Wilmington *(G-16656)*

Flute Pro Shop Inc .... G 302 479-5000
   Wilmington *(G-16676)*

Flying Locksmiths LLC .... G 302 607-7999
   Claymont *(G-1150)*

Fonzis LLC .... G 302 858-8024
   Greenwood *(G-4631)*

Foulk Lawn & Equipment Co Inc .... G 302 475-3233
   Wilmington *(G-16701)*

Framemakers Shop .... G 302 999-9968
   Wilmington *(G-16719)*

Freedom Cycle LLC .... G 302 286-6900
   Newark *(G-10775)*

General Merchandise & Svcs LLC ...... G 302 690-8662
   Hockessin *(G-5219)*

Genesis Cleaners .... G 302 827-2095
   Lewes *(G-6029)*

Glens Exterior Cleaning .... G 302 725-7222
   Lincoln *(G-6672)*

Goode Cleaning LLC .... G 302 398-4520
   Harrington *(G-4774)*

Gracefull Hands Cleaning LLC .... G 302 228-3841
   Ellendale *(G-3919)*

Greens Cleaning Expert LLC .... G 302 697-2848
   Felton *(G-3982)*

Grime 2 Shine LLC .... G 302 264-6709
   Smyrna *(G-13754)*

Groff Tractor & Equipment LLC .... F 302 349-5760
   Greenwood *(G-4633)*

Gtech Cleaning Services LLC .... E 302 494-2102
   Claymont *(G-1173)*

Gustavo E Espinosa .... G 302 731-5203
   Newark *(G-10908)*

Gutter Cleaning .... G 302 293-8461
   Wilmington *(G-17009)*

Hawkins & Sons Inc .... G 302 426-9290
   Wilmington *(G-17078)*

Hayes Sewing Machine Co Inc .... G 302 764-9033
   Wilmington *(G-17081)*

Heathers Home Works LLC .... G 302 927-0016
   Dagsboro *(G-1462)*

Heavy Equipment Rental Inc .... F 302 654-5716
   New Castle *(G-9205)*

Hershey Exteriors LLC .... G 302 278-2004
   Ocean View *(G-12522)*

Hickman Overhead Door Company .... F 302 422-4249
   Milford *(G-7930)*

Hockessin Tractor Inc .... G 302 239-4201
   Hockessin *(G-5247)*

Home Base Arms .... G 302 983-6816
   Bear *(G-278)*

Home Sweep Home .... G 302 536-7339
   Seaford *(G-13212)*

Hydroshield Delmarva .... G 302 542-5923
   Lewes *(G-6110)*

Igal Biochemical LLC .... G 302 525-2090
   Newark *(G-10997)*

Industrial Resource Netwrk Inc .... F 302 888-2905
   Wilmington *(G-17316)*

Integrity Cleaning Svcs LLC .... G 302 353-9315
   Clayton *(G-1372)*

J & J Services .... F 302 422-2684
   Milford *(G-7944)*

J & V Cleaning LLC .... G 302 245-5230
   Georgetown *(G-4376)*

J Hooked Twing Rcvery Auto Rep ...... G 302 335-3043
   Felton *(G-3987)*

J&J Cleaning .... G 302 507-5082
   Wilmington *(G-17467)*

Jacks Cleaning Services LLC .... G 302 494-8887
   New Castle *(G-9250)*

Janies Angel LLC .... G 302 669-1516
   Newark *(G-11098)*

Jbm Petroleum Service LLC .... G 302 752-6105
   Lincoln *(G-6677)*

Jewels Cleaning Service .... G 302 841-2948
   Milford *(G-7953)*

Jolly Joes Cleaning Service .... G 302 853-5681
   Laurel *(G-5538)*

Junes Touch .... G 631 603-9293
   Clayton *(G-1377)*

K and C Cleaning Services .... G 302 897-8661
   New Castle *(G-9272)*

Kc Service Cleaning .... G 410 845-1988
   Frankford *(G-4120)*

Ken Bertrand Realty Repairs .... G 302 436-2872
   Frankford *(G-4121)*

Keturahs Cleaning .... G 302 242-3967
   Dover *(G-2860)*

Kings Cust Clean & HM Ser LLC .... G 302 542-3920
   Seaford *(G-13250)*

Klean Team of Wilmington .... G 302 298-5558
   Wilmington *(G-17740)*

Kompressed Air Delaware Inc .... G 302 275-1985
   New Castle *(G-9289)*

Kream Puff Clean .... F 251 509-1639
   Smyrna *(G-13793)*

La Bendicion Cleaning Svcs LL .... G 302 276-6468
   New Castle *(G-9293)*

Lee Lynn Inc .... F 302 678-9978
   Dover *(G-2923)*

Lems Appliance Repair LLC .... G 302 539-2200
   Bridgeville *(G-725)*

Level & Clean LLC .... G 302 616-1585
   Ocean View *(G-12538)*

Lion Totalcare Inc .... G 610 444-1700
   Wilmington *(G-17931)*

Lnc Cleaning Company LLC .... G 302 437-6547
   Bear *(G-351)*

Longhorn Enterprises Inc .... G 302 737-7444
   Newark *(G-11280)*

Looks New Powerwashing LLC .... G 302 569-0172
   Millsboro *(G-8353)*

Lucys Cleaning Service .... G 302 893-9946
   New Castle *(G-9329)*

Lucys Housekeppers .... G 302 893-9946
   Bear *(G-353)*

Luttrell Guitars .... G 404 325-7977
   Lewes *(G-6230)*

M M Marine Service .... G 302 841-7689
   Millsboro *(G-8356)*

M&L Cleaning Service .... G 302 249-8634
   Millsboro *(G-8357)*

Magic Cleaning .... G 302 723-4328
   Wilmington *(G-18081)*

Maid Easy Cleaning Delaware .... G 302 858-1883
   Georgetown *(G-4412)*

Man Maid Cleaning Inc .... G 302 226-5050
   Rehoboth Beach *(G-12845)*

Map Hauiling .... G 267 235-6712
   New Castle *(G-9344)*

Markatos Services Inc .... F 302 792-0606
   Wilmington *(G-18142)*

Martin & Calloway .... G 302 268-6655
   Wilmington *(G-18165)*

Masters Touch Cleaning LLC .... G 302 650-8165
   New Castle *(G-9352)*

Mc Mullen Septic Service Inc .... G 302 629-6221
   Seaford *(G-13277)*

McLean Masonry Contractors LLC ..... G 215 349-0719
   Dover *(G-3044)*

76 MISCELLANEOUS REPAIR SERVICES

Med Tech Equipment Inc .... G 800 322-2609
  Wilmington *(G-18244)*
Messick & Gray Cnstr Inc .... E 302 337-8777
  Bridgeville *(G-731)*
Metal Shop LLC .... F 302 846-2988
  Delmar *(G-1620)*
Michael Matthew Sponaugle .... G 302 566-1010
  Harrington *(G-4802)*
Mid Atlntic Scientific Svc Inc .... G 302 328-4440
  New Castle *(G-9367)*
Midlantic Marine Center Inc .... F 302 436-2628
  Selbyville *(G-13575)*
Milford Machine LLC .... G 410 924-3211
  Houston *(G-5445)*
Mj Brunin LLC .... G 302 945-9467
  Harbeson *(G-4709)*
Modern Controls Inc .... C 302 325-6800
  New Castle *(G-9377)*
Moms Cleaning Service Inc .... G 302 547-5729
  Wilmington *(G-18407)*
Montgomery Carpet Cleaning .... G 302 258-6036
  Seaford *(G-13288)*
Mr Kleen II .... G 302 324-8797
  New Castle *(G-9385)*
Mrs Kleen Inc .... G 302 530-7330
  Townsend *(G-14040)*
Multi Koastal Services .... G 302 436-8822
  Frankford *(G-4128)*
Neat As A Pin LLC .... G 302 519-4504
  Seaford *(G-13315)*
Nls Machinery Inc .... G 302 416-3077
  Wilmington *(G-18656)*
Nobles Hvac Duct Cleaning .... G 302 538-5909
  Magnolia *(G-6771)*
Norwex .... G 817 691-7759
  Lewes *(G-6320)*
Oceanside Cleaning Inc .... G 302 526-4400
  Milton *(G-8678)*
One Way Source LLC .... G 302 894-8359
  Wilmington *(G-18786)*
Our Maids Inc .... G 302 389-5221
  Dover *(G-3248)*
Pat T Clean Inc .... G 302 239-5354
  Hockessin *(G-5332)*
Peak Equipment Repair .... G 302 526-4729
  Dover *(G-3288)*
Pecks Drain Cleaning .... G 302 345-4101
  Newark *(G-11652)*
Perfect Finish LLC .... G 302 480-3167
  Bear *(G-422)*
Perfectional Cleaning .... G 302 864-7112
  Bridgeville *(G-747)*
Pike Creek Bike Line Inc .... G 610 747-1200
  Wilmington *(G-19038)*
Pinnacle Garage Door Co LLC .... G 302 505-4531
  Frederica *(G-4180)*
Pop-A-Lock Wilmington .... G 866 866-6368
  Wilmington *(G-19117)*
Precision Door Service .... G 302 343-6394
  Wilmington *(G-19154)*
Premier Pro Cleaning Solutions .... G 302 743-5337
  Middletown *(G-7464)*
Prestige Frog Cleaning Svcs .... G 302 654-8459
  Wilmington *(G-19182)*
Priority Cleaning LLC .... G 302 519-4998
  Lincoln *(G-6693)*
Pristine Clean Co .... G 302 465-8274
  Magnolia *(G-6776)*
Product Service and Repair .... G 443 466-0566
  New Castle *(G-9498)*
Progressive Systems Inc .... G 302 732-3321
  Frankford *(G-4135)*

Providencias Cleaning .... G 302 507-7931
  Wilmington *(G-19237)*
Pughs Service Inc .... F 302 678-2408
  Dover *(G-3394)*
Pure Cleaning Services Inc .... G 302 494-2693
  Wilmington *(G-19260)*
Quick Clean - Quick Fix LLC .... G 302 245-9494
  Seaford *(G-13361)*
Ravana C Starks Cleaning Svcs .... G 215 647-2467
  Middletown *(G-7505)*
Razor Rick .... G 302 604-1339
  Milford *(G-8059)*
Reliable Trailer Inc .... F 856 962-7900
  Felton *(G-4015)*
Repair My Place LLC .... G 302 286-7721
  Newark *(G-11858)*
Richards Investment Group Corp .... G 302 399-0450
  Smyrna *(G-13866)*
Ricos Cleaning Services Inc .... G 302 357-8155
  Newark *(G-11883)*
Rmb Cleaning Services LLC .... G 302 753-0622
  Newark *(G-11892)*
Robert Westley .... G 302 645-2301
  Lewes *(G-6425)*
Roger C Perry .... G 302 604-7912
  Georgetown *(G-4489)*
Rommel Cycles LLC .... E 302 658-8800
  Smyrna *(G-13869)*
Rosy Cleaning Services .... G 302 723-7610
  Bear *(G-471)*
Roto-Rooter Plbg & Wtr Cleanup .... F 302 256-5022
  Wilmington *(G-19573)*
Roto-Rooter Services Company .... G 302 659-7637
  Newark *(G-11917)*
Rsg Cleaning Services .... G 302 650-3702
  Hockessin *(G-5374)*
Rt Taxidermy LLC .... G 302 629-7501
  Seaford *(G-13380)*
Rudy Marine Inc .... F 302 999-8735
  Dagsboro *(G-1501)*
Sara Cleaning Service .... G 856 498-3244
  Bear *(G-479)*
Sawyers Sanitation Service .... G 302 678-8240
  Leipsic *(G-5633)*
Seagreen Bicycle LLP .... G 302 226-2323
  Rehoboth Beach *(G-12952)*
Service Cleaning .... G 302 376-7258
  Middletown *(G-7555)*
Sharks Service Center LLC .... G 302 337-8233
  Bridgeville *(G-764)*
Signature Clean Solutions LLC .... G 571 565-1270
  Middletown *(G-7565)*
Spartan Cleaning .... G 302 345-7591
  Middletown *(G-7593)*
Square One Electric Service Co .... F 302 678-0400
  Dover *(G-3601)*
Squeaky Clean & Dry .... G 302 327-6240
  Hockessin *(G-5388)*
State Line Machine Inc .... F 302 478-0285
  Wilmington *(G-20035)*
Streak Free Clg By Ptticom LLC .... G 302 261-6933
  Bear *(G-513)*
Suburban Lawn & Equipment Inc .... G 302 475-4300
  Wilmington *(G-20113)*
Suck It Up Inc .... G 410 258-8023
  Dagsboro *(G-1510)*
Super C Inc .... G 302 533-6024
  Newark *(G-12127)*
Superior Maids .... F 302 284-2012
  Felton *(G-4031)*
Supreme Legacy Inc .... G 973 567-3115
  Wilmington *(G-20156)*

Sweep Dream Cleaning Services .... G 302 569-5519
  Bridgeville *(G-773)*
T & M Exhaust Hood Cleaning .... G 302 362-8816
  Georgetown *(G-4544)*
T&T Cleaning LLC .... F 609 575-0458
  Dover *(G-3640)*
Talleys Garage Inc .... G 302 652-0463
  Wilmington *(G-20214)*
Tc Clean .... G 302 737-3360
  Newark *(G-12164)*
That Cleaning Solutions LLC .... G 302 442-8148
  Bear *(G-528)*
The-Dirt-Squad .... G 302 723-5916
  Wilmington *(G-20293)*
Tighten Up Cleaning Services .... G 302 482-9970
  Wilmington *(G-20324)*
Tis Group Inc .... F 929 322-8811
  Lewes *(G-6562)*
Tjs Repair LLC .... G 302 422-8383
  Milford *(G-8119)*
Top Notch Cleaning .... G 302 893-7643
  Hockessin *(G-5408)*
Top Notch Cleaning Service .... G 302 854-6611
  Georgetown *(G-4557)*
Touch Class Cleaning Service .... G 302 482-5357
  Middletown *(G-7653)*
Tracy B Harris .... G 302 644-1477
  Lewes *(G-6576)*
Triple A Cleaning Services Inc .... G 302 236-0407
  Millsboro *(G-8487)*
True Mobility Inc .... G 302 836-4110
  New Castle *(G-9643)*
U S A Repair Shop .... G 302 545-5991
  Newark *(G-12254)*
Vertical Blind Factory Inc .... G 302 998-9616
  Wilmington *(G-20598)*
Vesta Wash LLC .... G 302 559-7533
  Newark *(G-12320)*
Victory Cleaning LLC .... G 267 330-9422
  Dover *(G-3792)*
Wahoo Repair LLC .... G 302 430-4588
  Georgetown *(G-4571)*
Walton Farm & Truck Repair .... G 302 245-3479
  Georgetown *(G-4573)*
We Are Family Cleaning Service .... G 302 524-8294
  Frankford *(G-4159)*
We Clean For A Reason .... G 302 930-0237
  Milford *(G-8145)*
Widgeon Enterprises Inc .... G 302 846-9763
  Delmar *(G-1657)*
Williams Appliancee .... F 302 656-8581
  Wilmington *(G-20797)*
Winmill Cleaning .... G 302 731-4139
  Newark *(G-12387)*
Wojo Home Cleaning LLC .... G 302 241-5866
  Dover *(G-3864)*
Wooden Wheels Svc & Repr LLC .... G 302 368-2453
  Newark *(G-12402)*
Woodstoves Junction .... G 302 397-8424
  Wilmington *(G-20888)*
Woodward Enterprises Inc .... F 302 378-2849
  Middletown *(G-7736)*
Xtreme Cleaning .... G 302 331-1084
  Harrington *(G-4852)*
Yhk Elm Cleaners Inc .... G 302 378-2017
  Middletown *(G-7747)*
Yoder Overhead Door Company .... G 302 875-0663
  Delmar *(G-1660)*

78 MOTION PICTURES

7812 Motion picture and video production

79 AMUSEMENT AND RECREATION SERVICES

Angry Reels Inc .... F 336 906-1797
  Middletown *(G-6865)*
Arden Media Resources .... G 256 656-8631
  Wilmington *(G-14547)*
Bardell Video Productions .... G 302 377-9936
  Wilmington *(G-14761)*
California Explosion LLC .... G 516 404-9892
  Wilmington *(G-15194)*
Delaware Digital Video Facc .... G 302 888-2737
  Wilmington *(G-15907)*
Delaware Sports .... G 302 731-1676
  Newark *(G-10483)*
Digital Memories Videography .... G 302 682-9180
  Seaford *(G-13161)*
Digital Peak Inc .... G 214 215-9054
  Wilmington *(G-16067)*
Dreya Inc .... G 302 265-0759
  Middletown *(G-7072)*
Edify Inc .... G 302 520-2403
  Wilmington *(G-16292)*
Electro Sound Systems Inc .... F 302 543-2292
  Newport *(G-12450)*
Floyd Allan Gregory .... G 302 658-0295
  Wilmington *(G-16671)*
Heavenly Films LLC .... G 302 232-8988
  Dover *(G-2668)*
Joozoor Iptv LLC .... F 302 635-4092
  Newark *(G-11125)*
Ken-Del Productions Inc .... G 302 999-1111
  Wilmington *(G-17683)*
King Creative LLC .... G 302 593-1595
  Wilmington *(G-17728)*
Marvelous Lghts Prductions LLC ..... G 215 678-2013
  New Castle *(G-9351)*
Melody Entertainment USA Inc .... G 305 505-7659
  Wilmington *(G-18267)*
Office Magic .... G 302 229-9520
  Wilmington *(G-18748)*
OK Video .... G 302 762-2333
  Wilmington *(G-18751)*
Orishun Company LLC .... E 302 538-2120
  Dover *(G-3240)*
▲ Petes Big Tvs Inc .... G 302 328-3551
  Historic New Castle *(G-5046)*
Pieholetv LLC .... G 415 287-3566
  Lewes *(G-6367)*
Pocket FM Corp .... E 408 896-7038
  Lewes *(G-6380)*
Point Eght Third Prdctions LLC .... G 302 317-9419
  Wilmington *(G-19100)*
Press Media Group Inc .... G 323 205-5488
  Middletown *(G-7468)*
Productions For Purpose Inc .... G 302 388-9883
  Middletown *(G-7472)*
Satodesign LLC .... G 989 710-2029
  Wilmington *(G-19677)*
Schiff Group LLC .... G 301 325-1359
  Bethany Beach *(G-639)*
Shes Filming Productions LLC .... G 302 563-0336
  Dover *(G-3543)*
Teleduction Associates Inc .... G 302 429-0303
  Wilmington *(G-20265)*
Vidfluencer LLC .... G 917 745-3713
  Dover *(G-3794)*

7819 Services allied to motion pictures

4 Youth Productions Inc .... G 347 338-8243
  Wilmington *(G-14133)*
Andy Is My Coach LLC .... G 302 943-4819
  Milford *(G-7769)*
Big Wlly Style Productions LLC .... G 973 897-8661
  New Castle *(G-8867)*
Deyas Honest Solutions LLC .... G 302 682-1830
  Magnolia *(G-6741)*
Jet Phynx Films LLC .... G 302 803-0109
  Wilmington *(G-17535)*
Make Productions .... G 302 593-1595
  Wilmington *(G-18093)*
Red Ladder Productions LLC .... G 781 970-6124
  Wilmington *(G-19385)*
Steph1official Inc .... F 302 744-0990
  Dover *(G-3611)*
Wruff Wryder Productions .... G 602 803-7620
  Lewes *(G-6641)*

7822 Motion picture and tape distribution

Amantya Technologies Inc .... G 302 439-6030
  Wilmington *(G-14413)*
Bew Productions .... G 302 547-8661
  Wilmington *(G-14869)*
Brewster Products .... G 302 463-3531
  Middletown *(G-6937)*
Bug Eyed Weasel Productions LL ... G 302 547-8661
  Wilmington *(G-15145)*
Bullseye Products LLC .... G 302 468-5086
  Wilmington *(G-15150)*
Diamond Standard Productions ...... G 302 508-2931
  Smyrna *(G-13709)*
Eastern Shore Vinyl Produ .... G 302 436-9520
  Selbyville *(G-13529)*
Fish & Monkey Productions LLC .... G 302 897-4318
  Wilmington *(G-16645)*
Gem Productions .... G 302 650-6725
  Newark *(G-10818)*
Gpc Productions .... G 302 530-4547
  Newark *(G-10877)*
Iko Sales Inc .... F 360 988-9103
  Wilmington *(G-17275)*
J Alexander Productions LLC .... G 302 559-6667
  Wilmington *(G-17451)*
J Chance Productions .... G 302 322-2251
  New Castle *(G-9246)*
Jam Productions .... G 302 369-3629
  Newark *(G-11086)*
Ls Anderson Reproductions Inc ...... G 302 999-9940
  Wilmington *(G-18019)*
Mark Perry Productions LLC .... G 443 521-4382
  Georgetown *(G-4416)*
New Cndlelight Productions Inc ...... F 302 475-2313
  Wilmington *(G-18611)*
Njl Productions .... G 302 898-9187
  Wilmington *(G-18654)*
Orishun Company LLC .... E 302 538-2120
  Dover *(G-3240)*
Outerhaven Productions .... G 302 792-9169
  Claymont *(G-1259)*
Party Princess Productions .... G 302 307-3804
  Middletown *(G-7428)*
Perfectly OK Productions .... G 302 233-3208
  Clayton *(G-1395)*
Peristalsis Productions Inc .... G 302 366-1106
  Newark *(G-11667)*
Red Spear LLC .... G 757 301-1052
  Dover *(G-3440)*
Short Order Production House .... G 302 656-1638
  Wilmington *(G-19810)*
T & T Produce LLC .... G 302 245-6235
  Selbyville *(G-13611)*
Trauma Film Production Pr LLC ..... G 623 582-2287
  Dover *(G-3717)*
Viacom Limited .... F 484 857-7116
  Dover *(G-3789)*

7829 Motion picture distribution services

No More Screts-Mind Bdy Spirit ...... G 215 485-7881
  Wilmington *(G-18661)*

7832 Motion picture theaters, except drive-in

Atlantic Theaters LLC .... E 302 645-9511
  Rehoboth Beach *(G-12616)*
Cinemark Usa Inc .... G 302 994-7280
  Wilmington *(G-15439)*
Everett Inc .... G 302 378-7038
  Middletown *(G-7112)*
Foot Light Production Inc .... F 302 645-7220
  Lewes *(G-6009)*
Main Street Movies 5 LLC .... G 302 738-4555
  Newark *(G-11315)*
Penn Cinema Riverfront LLC .... G 717 438-4800
  Wilmington *(G-18950)*
Regal Cinemas Inc .... E 302 479-0753
  Wilmington *(G-19397)*
Rich Hebert & Associates .... G 202 255-3474
  Selbyville *(G-13600)*
South Newport Co Inc .... F 302 732-9606
  Dagsboro *(G-1506)*
Theatre N At Nemours .... G 302 600-1923
  Wilmington *(G-20294)*
Westown Movies LLC .... G 330 244-1633
  Middletown *(G-7719)*

7841 Video tape rental

California Video 2 .... G 302 477-6944
  Wilmington *(G-15195)*
Dvd and Game Exchange De .... G 302 530-1199
  Wilmington *(G-16224)*
Extreme Audio & Video .... G 302 533-7404
  Newark *(G-10695)*
Foto Video Genesis .... G 302 422-6988
  Milford *(G-7901)*
Quality In-House Video Inc .... G 302 834-5654
  Newark *(G-11788)*
Sky4video .... G 302 377-3748
  Newark *(G-12026)*
Video Den .... G 302 628-9835
  Seaford *(G-13441)*
Video Scene of Delaware Inc .... G 302 678-8526
  Dover *(G-3793)*

79 AMUSEMENT AND RECREATION SERVICES

7911 Dance studios, schools, and halls

Blueballroom Dance Studio .... G 302 765-3511
  Wilmington *(G-14978)*
Brandywine Ctr For Dnce The PR ... G 302 416-6959
  Wilmington *(G-15054)*
Center For Grwing Tlent By Pma .... F 302 738-7100
  Newark *(G-10174)*
Dance Conservatory .... G 302 734-9717
  Dover *(G-2189)*
Dancedelaware .... G 302 998-1222
  Wilmington *(G-15778)*
Danceworks .... G 302 286-1492
  Newark *(G-10385)*
Danceworks Dance Studio LLC ...... G 302 244-8570
  New Castle *(G-8996)*
De-Infnty All Star Cheer Tmble .... G 302 383-0945
  Wilmington *(G-15842)*
Delaware Arts Conservatory .... G 302 595-4160
  Bear *(G-141)*
Delaware Dance Center .... E 302 229-9334
  Newark *(G-10431)*
Delaware Dance Center Inc .... G 302 454-1440
  Wilmington *(G-15900)*

79 AMUSEMENT AND RECREATION SERVICES — SIC SECTION

Delaware Dance Company Inc .... E 302 738-2023
   Newark *(G-10432)*

Devadasi .... G 302 229-7216
   Wilmington *(G-16033)*

Encore Dance Academy .... G 302 824-9669
   Newark *(G-10645)*

Fierce Dance Academy .... G 302 414-9191
   New Castle *(G-9125)*

First State Academy of D .... G 302 422-2633
   Milford *(G-7893)*

First State Ballet Theatre Inc .... G 302 658-7897
   Wilmington *(G-16623)*

Future Legacy of Dance .... G 610 400-7433
   New Castle *(G-9154)*

Iheart Dance Studio LLC .... G 267 249-8367
   Middletown *(G-7223)*

Il Extreme Entertainment .... G 302 389-8525
   New Castle *(G-9229)*

Lighthouse Dance and Yoga LLC .... G 302 564-7611
   Selbyville *(G-13561)*

New Castle Dance Academy .... F 302 836-2060
   Bear *(G-392)*

Premier Centre For Arts LLC .... G 302 684-3038
   Milton *(G-8688)*

Rehoboth Beach Dance & Company .... G 302 245-8132
   Rehoboth Beach *(G-12919)*

Stars On 9 Dance Center LLC .... G 302 855-9595
   Georgetown *(G-4524)*

Univ of Delaware .... G 302 383-0473
   Wilmington *(G-20532)*

Victorious Jaesettes Inc .... G 302 898-1946
   Wilmington *(G-20612)*

7922 Theatrical producers and services

Aihs Theater .... G 302 651-2626
   Wilmington *(G-14332)*

Annalissas Playhouse .... G 302 653-3529
   Smyrna *(G-13644)*

Arabian Lights Dance Co Inc .... G 410 543-4538
   Delmar *(G-1567)*

Bang Bang Media Corp .... G 213 374-0555
   Middletown *(G-6905)*

Blue Money Music Group Inc .... F 302 413-1304
   Middletown *(G-6927)*

Brass Unlimited .... G 302 322-2529
   New Castle *(G-8888)*

Colemans Healthcr Stffngffing .... F 302 423-9385
   Smyrna *(G-13684)*

Dct .... G 302 420-6350
   Newark *(G-10396)*

Delaware Theatre Company .... E 302 594-1100
   Wilmington *(G-15975)*

Earle Teate Music .... G 302 736-1937
   Dover *(G-2406)*

Evolution Enterprise LLC .... G 302 602-1875
   Middletown *(G-7113)*

Fears Promotions LLC .... G 302 437-6364
   Dover *(G-2490)*

Firebrand Entertainment Inc .... G 571 330-8983
   Newark *(G-10727)*

First State Ballet Theatre Inc .... G 302 658-7897
   Wilmington *(G-16623)*

For Them Inc .... F 646 623-4041
   Middletown *(G-7138)*

Freeman Arts Pavilion Inc .... G 302 436-6241
   Selbyville *(G-13536)*

Funfull Inc .... F 888 386-3855
   Delmar *(G-1597)*

Gbana Entertainment LLC .... G 302 307-1695
   Wilmington *(G-16822)*

Glewed Media LLC .... E 844 445-3933
   Newark *(G-10848)*

Grand Opera House Inc .... E 302 652-5577
   Wilmington *(G-16946)*

Heidis Academy of Prfrmg Arts .... F 302 293-7868
   Bear *(G-268)*

Henry Box Brown LLC .... F 917 749-3746
   Wilmington *(G-17122)*

Herstory Ensemble .... G 216 288-8759
   Wilmington *(G-17133)*

Ideal Venue LLC .... F 302 250-9208
   Wilmington *(G-17263)*

Joshua M Freeman Foundation .... F 302 436-3003
   Selbyville *(G-13553)*

Light Action Inc .... F 302 328-7800
   Wilmington *(G-17908)*

Magnolia Home Theatre .... G 302 677-7215
   Dover *(G-2996)*

Main Light Industries Inc .... C 302 998-8017
   Wilmington *(G-18089)*

Megara Inc .... F 914 487-4702
   Dover *(G-3055)*

Michael Schwartz .... F 302 791-9999
   Wilmington *(G-18324)*

Milton Theatre .... G 302 684-4232
   Milton *(G-8673)*

Mirworth Enterprise Inc .... G 302 846-0218
   Delmar *(G-1621)*

Molly Williams .... G 302 436-3015
   Selbyville *(G-13578)*

Operadelaware Inc .... G 302 658-8063
   Wilmington *(G-18803)*

Performing Systems Inc .... G 302 275-5409
   Wilmington *(G-18978)*

Power House Global Entps Inc .... D 215 660-0071
   Bear *(G-430)*

Premier Centre For Arts LLC .... G 302 684-3038
   Milton *(G-8688)*

Queen Theater .... G 608 359-5507
   Wilmington *(G-19292)*

Renegade Entrmt & Media Co .... F 904 789-2897
   Middletown *(G-7513)*

Rep .... G 910 622-0252
   Newark *(G-11857)*

Rhodeside Incorporated .... G 505 261-4568
   Wilmington *(G-19459)*

Tkxai LLC .... G 202 670-8818
   Lewes *(G-6563)*

Yorklyn Storytelling Festival .... G 302 238-6200
   Yorklyn *(G-20995)*

7929 Entertainers and entertainment groups

Affordable Wedding Entrmt .... G 302 258-3027
   Georgetown *(G-4200)*

Alawar Entertainment Inc .... G 646 413-5757
   Lewes *(G-5669)*

Anchors Aweigh Entrmt LLC .... G 302 236-1587
   Ocean View *(G-12462)*

Anlatan LLC .... G 618 318-5334
   Wilmington *(G-14487)*

Ashtray Management LLC .... G 424 258-9228
   Dover *(G-1831)*

Bank Fillers Entertainment LLC .... F 302 930-0262
   Wilmington *(G-14747)*

Before & After Entrmt LLC .... G 302 857-9659
   Smyrna *(G-13660)*

Bender .... G 302 366-8637
   Newark *(G-10020)*

Bihbrand Inc .... F 302 223-4330
   Lewes *(G-5764)*

Blackhouse Campaign LLC .... G 302 465-0980
   Wilmington *(G-14902)*

Caribbean Clture Awareness Inc .... G 888 595-1259
   Middletown *(G-6958)*

Chesapake Slver Crnet Brass Ba .... G 302 530-2915
   Millsboro *(G-8220)*

Coastal Concerts Inc .... G 302 645-1539
   Lewes *(G-5841)*

Comfort Zone Jazz LLC .... G 302 745-2019
   Milton *(G-8588)*

Craig and Company LLC .... G 609 221-9959
   Wilmington *(G-15681)*

Crazy Maple Interactive Inc .... F 408 603-7526
   Dover *(G-2154)*

Cre8tive Minds Ent LLC .... G 302 293-3461
   Wilmington *(G-15686)*

Cube Media LLC .... G 716 239-2789
   Wilmington *(G-15729)*

Division One Basketball LLC .... F 302 573-2528
   Wilmington *(G-16099)*

Dj First Class .... F 302 345-0602
   New Castle *(G-9058)*

Dover Symphony Orchestra Inc .... G 302 734-1701
   Dover *(G-2367)*

Dreamstage Inc .... G 901 286-5207
   Dover *(G-2384)*

Electric Lady Studios LLC Elec .... G 212 677-4700
   Wilmington *(G-16351)*

Entertainment Factory .... G 302 824-1428
   Newark *(G-10655)*

Event Enhancers .... G 267 217-3868
   Wilmington *(G-16483)*

Exodus Escape Rooms .... G 302 407-5362
   Wilmington *(G-16504)*

Exodus Escape Rooms LLC .... G 302 366-8250
   Newark *(G-10689)*

Exodus Escape Rooms LLC .... G 302 278-7679
   Rehoboth Beach *(G-12747)*

FBBc LLC .... G 302 442-3004
   Newark *(G-10718)*

First State Strings Inc .... G 302 331-7362
   Camden Wyoming *(G-945)*

Fiyah B Music LLC .... G 949 656-3246
   Newark *(G-10748)*

From Harps To Halos .... G 302 932-0956
   Wilmington *(G-16761)*

Funfull Inc .... F 888 386-3855
   Delmar *(G-1597)*

G2 Performance .... G 302 293-1847
   Newark *(G-10795)*

Gaming Entertainment Del LLC .... G 302 398-4920
   Harrington *(G-4771)*

Gbana Entertainment LLC .... G 302 307-1695
   Wilmington *(G-16822)*

Gge Amusements .... G 302 227-0661
   Rehoboth Beach *(G-12770)*

Hidden Jewel Tickets LLC .... G 571 425-6522
   Newark *(G-10951)*

Highlife Entrmt Group LLC .... G 478 250-1862
   Dover *(G-2679)*

Honeybee Arts LLC .... G 646 664-5511
   Dover *(G-2692)*

Ikenrock Entertainment LLC .... G 302 981-8532
   Wilmington *(G-17272)*

Jammin Productions .... G 302 670-7302
   Dover *(G-2769)*

K&B Investors LLC .... G 302 357-9723
   Wilmington *(G-17631)*

Klf Music Factory .... G 302 598-8770
   Middletown *(G-7279)*

Lets Gather LLC .... G 607 210-0581
   Dover *(G-2929)*

Lituation Entertainment .... G 302 543-6424
   Wilmington *(G-17947)*

Lune Rouge Entrmt USA Inc .... E 514 556-2101
   Wilmington *(G-18029)*

79 AMUSEMENT AND RECREATION SERVICES

Maddcitylive LLC .... G 302 591-3471
 Dover (G-2994)
Master G Entertainment .... G 302 547-9367
 Wilmington (G-18187)
Matthew and Richard Entp LLC .... G 267 767-0290
 Bear (G-366)
Mid Atlantic Grand Prix LLC .... G 302 656-5278
 New Castle (G-9365)
Mih Enterprises .... G 302 480-4443
 Smyrna (G-13825)
Milford Community Band Inc .... G 302 422-6304
 Milford (G-8000)
Mixx Entertainment LLC .... G 302 635-9966
 Newark (G-11429)
Mobile Muzic Inc .... G 302 998-5951
 Wilmington (G-18394)
Money Never Sleeps Entrmt LLC .... G 646 234-7285
 Wilmington (G-18413)
Niru LLC .... G 617 893-7317
 Lewes (G-6316)
Nkotb LLC .... G 302 286-5243
 Wilmington (G-18655)
Plyma Entertainment LLC .... F 302 248-4567
 Dover (G-3340)
Pop Pop Magic Clown .... G 302 764-5494
 Wilmington (G-19115)
Premier Entertainment III LLC .... A 302 674-4600
 Dover (G-3360)
Rainbow Chorale of Del Inc .... F 302 803-4440
 Wilmington (G-19319)
Raymond Entrmt Group LLC .... G 302 731-2000
 Newark (G-11829)
Renegade Entrmt & Media Co .... F 904 789-2897
 Middletown (G-7513)
Renegade Entrmt & Media Co LLC ... F 267 648-7916
 Middletown (G-7514)
Serena Joy LLC .... G 302 312-3318
 Wilmington (G-19755)
Smooth Sound Dance Band .... G 302 398-8467
 Harrington (G-4834)
Socallova LLC .... F 347 721-6416
 Middletown (G-7582)
Soucialize Inc .... G 916 803-1057
 Lewes (G-6492)
Souf Mode LLC .... G 332 220-6189
 Middletown (G-7589)
Spinwizards DJS .... G 302 252-1727
 Wilmington (G-19965)
Systems Orchestration LLC .... G 302 363-5168
 Camden (G-895)
Wastecost Corporation .... G 512 562-0888
 Lewes (G-6616)
Westland Entertainment LLC .... G 630 988-9684
 Dover (G-3837)
Yombu Events Inc .... E 385 406-3651
 Wilmington (G-20931)
Yomi Entertainment Inc .... G 838 588-8888
 Dover (G-3890)
Younity Lounge LLC .... G 302 359-5609
 Smyrna (G-13942)
Zone Laser Tag Inc .... F 302 730-8888
 Dover (G-3905)

7933 Bowling centers

AMF Bowling Centers Inc .... E 302 998-5316
 Wilmington (G-14456)
Bowlerama Inc .... E 302 654-0263
 New Castle (G-8878)
Brunswick Doverama .... G 302 734-7501
 Dover (G-1987)
Delaware Womens Bowling Assn ...... G 302 834-7002
 Bear (G-161)
First State Bowling Center .... G 302 762-3883
 Wilmington (G-16625)
Inspection Lanes .... G 302 853-1003
 Georgetown (G-4371)
Keglers Korner Pro Shop .... G 302 526-2249
 Dover (G-2837)
Leftys Alley & Eats .... F 302 864-6000
 Lewes (G-6187)
Leftys Alley & Eats .... G 302 344-5858
 Rehoboth Beach (G-12828)
Main Event Entrmt Wilmington .... G 302 722-9466
 Newark (G-11312)
Milford Bowling Lanes Inc .... F 302 422-9456
 Milford (G-7999)
Millsboro Lanes Inc .... F 302 934-0400
 Millsboro (G-8387)
Pleasant Hill Lanes Inc .... F 302 998-8811
 Wilmington (G-19077)
Spare Parts LLC .... G 302 333-2683
 Townsend (G-14068)

7941 Sports clubs, managers, and promoters

302 Elite Athletes .... G 302 834-7991
 Bear (G-1)
Awl LLC .... G 610 299-3322
 Lewes (G-5729)
Bernard Hopkins Boxing Inc .... G 302 239-7170
 Newark (G-10024)
Chase Fieldhouse .... G 610 996-0425
 Wilmington (G-15346)
Combat Zone Wresting LLC .... G 302 345-1077
 Newark (G-10280)
D1 Sports Basketball Training .... G 317 985-5125
 Wilmington (G-15764)
Delaware Professional Squash .... G 302 655-6171
 Wilmington (G-15954)
Family Depository Alliance .... F 888 332-6275
 Middletown (G-7120)
Fears Promotions LLC .... G 302 437-6364
 Dover (G-2490)
Five Star Franchising LLC .... G 646 838-3992
 Wilmington (G-16654)
Fwc2026 Us Inc .... E 469 505-2635
 Wilmington (G-16781)
Hockessin Soccer Club .... G 302 234-1444
 Hockessin (G-5246)
Ilovekickboxing-Wilmington De .... G 518 593-3463
 Newark (G-11002)
M Level Inc .... G 302 762-3910
 Hockessin (G-5285)
M O T Youth Ftball & Cheerldng ...... G 302 345-6182
 Middletown (G-7318)
Melodic Mvmnts Prfrmg Arts Prg ...... F 302 543-5257
 Wilmington (G-18266)
North East High Schl Football .... G 330 338-2993
 Clayton (G-1392)
Nside Wrestling .... G 302 697-9633
 Dover (G-3209)
Soccer Network LLC .... G 302 724-6951
 Dover (G-3582)
Southern Delaware Roller Derby .... G 410 253-9798
 Dover (G-3590)
Spring League LLC .... G 917 257-5801
 Wilmington (G-19974)
Volleyball .... G 302 593-4414
 Townsend (G-14089)
Wilmington Blue Rocks LP .... F 302 888-2015
 Wilmington (G-20809)

7948 Racing, including track operation

Action Track USA .... G 610 780-2290
 Lewes (G-5656)
Centaur Training LLC .... G 302 629-8783
 Bridgeville (G-681)
Delaware Racing Association .... B 302 355-1000
 Newark (G-10473)
▲ Delaware Racing Association .... A 302 994-2521
 Wilmington (G-15956)
Dover Motorsports Inc .... D 302 883-6500
 Dover (G-2355)
Edge Racing LLC .... G 302 519-6680
 Laurel (G-5507)
Gerard Joseph Capano .... G 302 658-3505
 Greenville (G-4584)
▲ Harrington Raceway Inc .... F 302 398-4920
 Harrington (G-4779)
Highbred Horse Racing .... G 302 519-6676
 Milford (G-7931)
Nashville Speedway Usa Inc .... E 615 547-7500
 Dover (G-3151)
Premier Entertainment III LLC .... A 302 674-4600
 Dover (G-3360)
Sharp Farm .... F 302 378-9606
 Middletown (G-7559)
U S 13 Dragway Inc .... D 302 875-1911
 Delmar (G-1648)
US 13 Speedway .... G 302 846-3911
 Delmar (G-1652)
Wj McDougall Racing Inc .... G 302 492-8248
 Hartly (G-4912)

7991 Physical fitness facilities

1 On 1 Personal Trainer LLC .... G 717 418-2719
 Selbyville (G-13457)
1110 On Parkway Nedi Spa .... G 302 576-1110
 Wilmington (G-14104)
24/7 Club Fitness .... G 302 226-4853
 Rehoboth Beach (G-12589)
409 Fitness .... G 302 354-7011
 Wilmington (G-14134)
6-4-3 Fitness Corp .... G 347 441-9690
 Dover (G-1689)
6am Run .... G 302 521-0023
 Wilmington (G-14145)
7chakras Spa Lounge .... G 302 584-7793
 Wilmington (G-14149)
9round .... G 302 365-5590
 Newark (G-9718)
9round .... G 302 543-2545
 Wilmington (G-14155)
9round .... G 302 525-6045
 Wilmington (G-14156)
9round Fitness .... G 302 504-4787
 Claymont (G-1015)
9zest Inc .... F 703 666-8122
 Dover (G-1692)
Achieving Physiques Inc .... G 302 593-7067
 Hockessin (G-5112)
ACorn Fitnes Well-Being LLC .... G 302 545-3032
 Newark (G-9757)
Afterglo Beauty Spa .... G 302 537-7546
 Millville (G-8512)
Alternative Therapy LLC .... G 302 368-0800
 Newark (G-9838)
American Karate Studios .... G 302 737-9500
 Newark (G-9846)
▼ American Martial Arts Inst .... F 302 834-4060
 Bear (G-30)
Anyone Fitness .... E 302 226-4653
 Rehoboth Beach (G-12608)
Anytime Fitness .... G 302 834-2348
 Bear (G-39)
Anytime Fitness .... G 302 229-1716
 Dover (G-1799)

Employee Codes: A=Over 500 employees, B=251-500
C=101-250, D=51-100, E=20-50, F=10-19, G=1-9

79 AMUSEMENT AND RECREATION SERVICES

Anytime Fitness .... F 302 212-6151
   Lewes *(G-5694)*

Anytime Fitness .... F 302 533-7773
   Newark *(G-9882)*

Anytime Fitness .... G 302 738-3040
   Newark *(G-9883)*

Anytime Fitness .... G 302 653-4496
   Smyrna *(G-13645)*

Anytime Fitness .... F 302 475-2404
   Wilmington *(G-14498)*

Anytime Fitness Lewes .... G 856 340-9252
   Milton *(G-8561)*

Anytime Fitness Main Line .... G 302 239-4800
   Hockessin *(G-5128)*

Art Fitness .... G 302 373-5148
   Bear *(G-48)*

Avenue Day Spa .... F 302 227-5649
   Rehoboth Beach *(G-12619)*

B Fit Enterprises .... G 302 292-1785
   Newark *(G-9966)*

Balanced Plates & Weights .... G 302 632-0953
   Marydel *(G-6795)*

Basement Circuit Training .... G 302 824-8078
   Claymont *(G-1051)*

Bayside Fitness .... G 302 231-8982
   Millsboro *(G-8184)*

Bear-Glasgow YMCA .... G 302 836-9622
   Newark *(G-10006)*

Bella Donna Spa .... G 703 313-7945
   Rehoboth Beach *(G-12640)*

Bella Medispa Inc .... G 302 736-6334
   Dover *(G-1907)*

Body Sclpting Prfessionals LLC .... G 986 999-8238
   Wilmington *(G-14995)*

Built Fitness LLC .... G 302 645-1932
   Milton *(G-8576)*

Catalyst Fitness LLC .... G 302 379-3883
   Hockessin *(G-5152)*

Charles H Hutson III .... G 302 378-9001
   Wilmington *(G-15335)*

Charmed Medi Spa .... G 302 273-2827
   Newark *(G-10192)*

Charmed Medispa Inc .... G 302 593-1994
   Newark *(G-10193)*

Christophers Hair Design .... G 302 378-1988
   Middletown *(G-6980)*

Cnu Fit LLC .... G 302 744-9037
   Dover *(G-2100)*

Coastal Funding Corporation .... G 302 328-4113
   Historic New Castle *(G-4959)*

County of New Castle .... F 302 571-4004
   New Castle *(G-8981)*

CP Fitness Wilmington LLC .... F 302 797-1400
   Wilmington *(G-15675)*

Cross Fit API .... G 302 235-8763
   Wilmington *(G-15712)*

Crossfit 1st State .... G 302 382-0603
   Townsend *(G-13980)*

Crossfit Bear .... G 302 540-4394
   Bear *(G-127)*

Crossfit Diamond State LLC .... G 201 803-1159
   Wilmington *(G-15713)*

Crossfit Dover LLC .... G 302 242-5400
   Magnolia *(G-6736)*

Crossfit Petram .... G 302 345-2560
   Newark *(G-10356)*

Crossfit Riverfront .... G 302 462-5176
   Rehoboth Beach *(G-12704)*

Crossfit Riverfront .... G 302 745-2348
   Wilmington *(G-15714)*

Curves International Inc .... G 302 698-1481
   Camden *(G-811)*

Cycology 202 LLC .... F 610 202-0518
   Lewes *(G-5875)*

Dalton Personal Training LLC .... G 302 266-7005
   Newark *(G-10384)*

David L Townsend Co Inc .... G 302 378-7967
   Smyrna *(G-13692)*

Dawn Somer Fitness .... G 229 325-9173
   Middletown *(G-7032)*

Del Hardbat LLC .... G 484 256-0465
   Newark *(G-10410)*

Delaware Rock Gym Inc .... G 302 838-5850
   Bear *(G-154)*

Delaware Swim & Fitness Center .... F 302 234-8500
   Wilmington *(G-15974)*

Dream Spa .... G 646 717-5397
   Wilmington *(G-16176)*

E-Volve Fitness Studio .... G 302 513-9641
   Wilmington *(G-16244)*

East Coast Health & Fitnes LLC .... G 410 213-7697
   Seaford *(G-13166)*

Eastern Athletic Clubs LLC .... C 302 239-6688
   Hockessin *(G-5197)*

Edge Fitness LLC .... G 302 613-0721
   Newark *(G-10608)*

End Result Gym .... G 302 280-6603
   Laurel *(G-5510)*

Energy Gym .... G 302 436-9001
   Selbyville *(G-13533)*

Equinox LLC .... G 856 364-5615
   Newark *(G-10661)*

Essential Luxuries Spa .... G 302 244-6875
   Dover *(G-2463)*

Evolve Health and Fitness LLC .... G 302 265-2560
   Milford *(G-7885)*

Family Unit Fitness .... G 267 403-6695
   Claymont *(G-1146)*

Fist Fit .... G 302 399-7095
   Dover *(G-2511)*

Fitbody Personal Training .... G 302 442-3685
   Wilmington *(G-16649)*

Fitness Performance Corp .... G 866 710-2227
   Newark *(G-10742)*

Flash Training Center .... G 302 943-4668
   Bear *(G-231)*

Flex World Fitness LLC .... G 302 856-7771
   Lewes *(G-6004)*

Forever Fit Foundation .... G 302 698-5201
   Dover *(G-2526)*

Fortaleza Fitness .... G 302 448-0922
   Seaford *(G-13189)*

Fresh Juice Partners LLC .... G 302 364-0909
   Lewes *(G-6016)*

Frontline Crossfit .... G 302 229-6467
   New Castle *(G-9148)*

Fun Fit Vibe LLC .... G 302 249-8000
   Lewes *(G-6022)*

Gilpin Avenue Fitness Inc .... G 302 654-6385
   Wilmington *(G-16862)*

Go Curves Ladies .... G 302 541-4681
   Millville *(G-8530)*

Golden Apple Spa .... G 302 375-6505
   Wilmington *(G-16911)*

Golds Gym .... G 302 226-4653
   Rehoboth Beach *(G-12772)*

Hand & Spa .... G 302 478-1700
   Wilmington *(G-17044)*

Harmony Spa .... G 302 563-7723
   Newark *(G-10932)*

Harper Fitness .... G 302 286-0474
   Newark *(G-10933)*

Haus of Lacquer LLC .... E 302 690-0309
   Wilmington *(G-17076)*

HB Fitness Concord Inc .... F 302 478-9692
   Wilmington *(G-17083)*

HB Fitness Delaware Inc .... F 302 384-7245
   Wilmington *(G-17084)*

Hday Spa .... G 302 482-1041
   Wilmington *(G-17088)*

Hockessin Day Spa .... G 302 234-7573
   Wilmington *(G-17162)*

Inspiration Empire .... G 302 535-9920
   Greenwood *(G-4639)*

Jacta Alea Est LLC .... F 302 731-7360
   Newark *(G-11083)*

Jazzercise .... G 302 690-3447
   Bear *(G-300)*

Jazzercise .... G 302 730-8177
   Dover *(G-2773)*

Jazzercise .... G 302 698-3020
   Dover *(G-2774)*

Jazzercise .... G 610 485-9044
   Wilmington *(G-17504)*

Jeffko Inc .... F 302 235-2180
   Hockessin *(G-5259)*

Jennifers Spa .... G 302 740-6363
   Newark *(G-11106)*

Jeremiah 29 11 Fitness LLC .... G 302 376-1287
   Middletown *(G-7246)*

Jube Medical Spa LLC .... G 302 478-4020
   Wilmington *(G-17607)*

Keystone Nfp Middletown LLC .... G 302 378-2777
   Middletown *(G-7269)*

Kingdom Spa Inc .... G 302 897-8255
   Middletown *(G-7277)*

Kirkwood Ftnes Racquetball CLB .... F 302 529-1865
   Wilmington *(G-17732)*

La Bella Vita Salon & Day Spa .... G 302 883-2597
   Dover *(G-2895)*

Last Tangle Salon and Spa .... G 302 653-6638
   Smyrna *(G-13796)*

Legion Sports Performance .... G 302 543-4922
   Wilmington *(G-17864)*

Legion Transformation Center .... G 302 464-1081
   Middletown *(G-7294)*

Legion Transformation Center .... G 302 533-6178
   Newark *(G-11242)*

Legion Transformation Ctr LLC .... G 302 543-4922
   Wilmington *(G-17865)*

Legion Trnsfrmtion Ctr Wlmngto .... G 302 543-4922
   Wilmington *(G-17866)*

Life Strong Fitness LLC .... G 302 312-9673
   Middletown *(G-7299)*

Lifestyle Fitness .... G 302 998-2942
   Wilmington *(G-17905)*

Lynn Victoria COSm&med Skin .... G 302 388-5459
   Hockessin *(G-5284)*

Mar Fitness Enterprises Inc .... G 302 730-1234
   Dover *(G-3016)*

Melanin Mixx Beauty Brand Inc .... Gt 302 266-1010
   Newark *(G-11385)*

Midway Fitness Center .... G 302 645-0407
   Rehoboth Beach *(G-12856)*

Millsboro Fitness LLC .... D 302 933-0722
   Millsboro *(G-8384)*

Mindbody Fitness .... G 302 893-6212
   Rehoboth Beach *(G-12858)*

Mindset Nutrition & Fitness .... G 302 219-0777
   New Castle *(G-9372)*

Mission Fitness Studio LLC .... G 302 535-1129
   Delmar *(G-1622)*

Modern Samurai Combat Fitness .... G 302 229-5399
   Newark *(G-11437)*

More Than Fitness Inc .... G 302 690-5655
   Wilmington *(G-18441)*

My Seaside Spa.................................. G 302 313-5174
  Lewes (G-6301)
Nail Spa By Tr................................... G 302 678-2122
  Dover (G-3147)
Neuro Fitness Therapy....................... G 302 753-2700
  Wilmington (G-18603)
New Relaxation Inc........................... G 302 934-9344
  Millsboro (G-8404)
Nursery Fitness LLC.......................... G 410 609-0106
  Newark (G-11569)
Orangetheory Fitness........................ G 302 426-2284
  Middletown (G-7419)
Orangetheory Fitness Pike................. G 302 426-2030
  Wilmington (G-18814)
Osx Fitness Training Center................ G 302 256-0667
  Wilmington (G-18831)
Out-Train Fitness & Prfmce LLC........... G 610 470-3196
  Milton (G-8680)
Paladin Sports Club Inc...................... F 302 764-5335
  Wilmington (G-18866)
Pamper Perfect Mobile Spa................ G 302 482-5938
  Newark (G-11617)
Phoenix Fitness LLC........................... G 302 786-2435
  Harrington (G-4812)
Pike Creek Court Club Inc.................. F 302 239-6688
  Wilmington (G-19041)
Planet Fitness................................... G 302 378-2777
  Middletown (G-7454)
Planet Fitness................................... F 302 501-7220
  New Castle (G-9474)
Planet Fitness................................... G 302 262-8676
  Seaford (G-13348)
Planet Fitness................................... G 302 543-5604
  Wilmington (G-19064)
Planet Fitness Inc.............................. G 302 483-7740
  Wilmington (G-19065)
Plexus Fitness.................................. F 302 654-9642
  Wilmington (G-19078)
Powerhouse Gym.............................. G 302 262-0262
  Seaford (G-13352)
Praize Fitness................................... G 302 312-7416
  Bear (G-433)
Press Fitness LLC.............................. G 973 441-9397
  New Castle (G-9492)
Pure Barre.. G 302 691-3618
  Wilmington (G-19259)
Rainbow Seven Spa........................... G 302 533-6916
  Newark (G-11822)
Rehoboth Fitness LLC........................ E 410 742-7990
  Rehoboth Beach (G-12925)
Renove Med Spa............................... G 302 584-3216
  Dagsboro (G-1497)
Retired-N-Fit.................................... F 302 478-4191
  Townsend (G-14058)
Retro Fitness.................................... F 302 276-0828
  Bear (G-453)
Ricks Fitness & Health Inc.................. G 302 684-0316
  Milton (G-8699)
Riv Athletics.................................... G 610 229-9092
  Wilmington (G-19489)
Rowing and Fitness........................... G 302 722-5445
  Newark (G-11920)
Sanctuary Spa and Saloon................. F 302 475-1469
  Wilmington (G-19656)
Sea Barre Fitness.............................. G 610 202-0518
  Lewes (G-6453)
Serenity Spa..................................... G 302 668-9534
  Wilmington (G-19757)
Shore Pride All-Stars Inc.................... G 302 245-1347
  Millsboro (G-8461)
Sites Fitness of Delaware LLC............ G 302 533-6040
  Newark (G-12017)

Smakkfitness LLC.............................. G 800 417-2558
  Wilmington (G-19871)
Small Wonder Fitness........................ G 302 838-0865
  Bear (G-497)
Smart Fit LLC................................... G 302 200-9803
  Lewes (G-6482)
Stada Fitness Concept LLC................. G 215 589-0914
  Townsend (G-14071)
Stone Powerhouse Training............... G 302 658-5077
  Wilmington (G-20079)
Stretch 1 LLC................................... G 253 255-7345
  Wilmington (G-20098)
Style 2 Fitness................................. G 215 254-0221
  Wilmington (G-20108)
Summit Fitness 180.......................... G 610 574-3587
  Wilmington (G-20124)
Team Demarco Fitness LLC................ G 347 743-3170
  Smyrna (G-13912)
This N That Fitness.......................... G 302 542-7115
  Dagsboro (G-1515)
Toppers Spa..................................... F 302 857-2020
  Dover (G-3701)
Train Hard Win Big Inc..................... G 302 993-6189
  Wilmington (G-20388)
Training Center................................ G 302 538-0847
  Newark (G-12215)
Tranquility By Tara Colazo................ G 302 668-4032
  Wilmington (G-20392)
Trilogy Salon & Spa........................... G 302 388-1210
  Wilmington (G-20421)
Tru Beauti LLC.................................. E 302 353-9249
  Middletown (G-7663)
True Rival Fitness............................. G 302 570-0530
  Wilmington (G-20443)
U Prime Fitness and Wellness............. G 302 529-1966
  Wilmington (G-20483)
Unified Fitness Npb.......................... G 302 528-5021
  Wilmington (G-20510)
Via Mdical Day Spa Pasca Salon......... G 302 757-2830
  Wilmington (G-20604)
Vidells Day Spa................................ G 302 656-1784
  Wilmington (G-20617)
Vogue On 24 Salon & Spa LLC............ G 302 947-5667
  Millsboro (G-8496)
W23 S12 Holdings LLC...................... G 610 348-3825
  Wilmington (G-20664)
Young Mens Christian Assn Del.......... D 302 571-6935
  Wilmington (G-20938)
Young Mens Christian Associat........... F 302 472-9622
  Wilmington (G-20939)
Young MNS Chrstn Assn Wlmngtn...... C 302 709-9622
  Newark (G-12422)
Young MNS Chrstn Assn Wlmngtn...... C 302 296-9622
  Rehoboth Beach (G-13027)
Younique... G 302 632-3060
  Camden (G-901)
YWCA Delaware................................ F 302 224-4060
  Newark (G-12425)
YWCA Delaware................................ D 302 655-0039
  Wilmington (G-20942)

7992 Public golf courses

American Classic Golf Club LLC......... G 302 703-6662
  Lewes (G-5684)
Back Creek Golf Club......................... E 302 378-6499
  Middletown (G-6898)
Bayside Golf LLC DBA Bear Trap........ F 302 537-5600
  Ocean View (G-12472)
Bayside Resort Golf Club................... F 302 436-3400
  Selbyville (G-13471)
Baywood Greens Golf Club................. E 302 947-9225
  Millsboro (G-8186)

Baywood Greens Golf Club................. G 302 947-9800
  Millsboro (G-8187)
Baywood Greens Golf Mntnc.............. G 757 460-5584
  Millsboro (G-8188)
Bear Trap Partners............................ F 302 537-5600
  Ocean View (G-12473)
City of Seaford................................. G 302 629-2890
  Seaford (G-13122)
Delaware Park Racing LLC.................. F 302 994-6700
  Wilmington (G-15952)
Delcaste Golf Course......................... F 302 225-9821
  Wilmington (G-15987)
Delcastle Golf Club Management........ F 302 998-9505
  Wilmington (G-15988)
Delcastle Golf Management LLC........ F 302 998-9505
  Wilmington (G-15989)
Dover Golf Center............................. G 302 674-8275
  Dover (G-2346)
▲ Fieldstone Golf Club LP.................. D 302 254-4569
  Wilmington (G-16603)
Frog Hollow Golf Course.................... F 302 376-6500
  Middletown (G-7142)
Garrisons Lake Golf Club Inc.............. F 302 659-1206
  Smyrna (G-13741)
Golf Course At Garrisons Lake........... G 302 659-1206
  Smyrna (G-13747)
Greens At Broadview LLC.................. E 302 684-3000
  Milton (G-8631)
Home Course Creators LLC................ G 302 419-6305
  Wilmington (G-17176)
Jonathans Landing............................. E 302 697-8204
  Magnolia (G-6755)
Meadowbrook Golf Group Inc............. E 302 571-9041
  Wilmington (G-18242)
Mulligans Pointe LLC......................... F 302 856-6283
  Georgetown (G-4438)
Odessa National Golf Crse LLC........... G 302 464-1007
  Townsend (G-14046)
Par 3 Inc... G 302 674-8275
  Dover (G-3269)
Peninsula.. G 410 342-8111
  Millsboro (G-8419)
Peninsula At Long Neck LLC............... G 302 947-4717
  Millsboro (G-8420)
Rock Manor Golf Course.................... G 302 295-1400
  Wilmington (G-19529)
Rookery Golf Courses South............... F 302 422-7010
  Milford (G-8072)
Tee It Up Golf Camp......................... G 302 684-1808
  Milton (G-8719)
Vinces Sports Center Inc.................... G 302 738-4859
  Newark (G-12325)
Worcester Golf Club Inc..................... F 610 222-0200
  Milton (G-8730)

7993 Coin-operated amusement devices

Bandai Namco Amus Amer Inc............ G 302 734-3623
  Dover (G-1871)
Beach Arcade Central........................ G 302 227-1043
  Rehoboth Beach (G-12626)
Delaware Racing Association.............. B 302 355-1000
  Newark (G-10473)
▲ Delaware Racing Association.......... A 302 994-2521
  Wilmington (G-15956)
Full-Tilt Security.............................. G 302 722-0275
  Bear (G-240)
Harrington Raceway Inc..................... D 302 398-5346
  Harrington (G-4780)
Midway Slots & Simulcast.................. G 302 398-4920
  Harrington (G-4804)
Orbit Research LLC........................... G 302 683-1063
  Wilmington (G-18815)

79 AMUSEMENT AND RECREATION SERVICES

Seaside Amusements Inc .... G 302 227-1921
   Rehoboth Beach *(G-12953)*

Touchmagix Inc .... G 310 230-5083
   Wilmington *(G-20376)*

Virtual Pro Gaming Inc .... G 302 285-9891
   Wilmington *(G-20634)*

7996 Amusement parks

Fun Adventures LLC .... G 302 223-5182
   Christiana *(G-996)*

Jungle Jims Adventure World .... D 302 227-8444
   Rehoboth Beach *(G-12812)*

7997 Membership sports and recreation clubs

Adkins Management Company .... F 302 684-3000
   Milford *(G-7760)*

AMC Museum Foundation .... G 302 677-5938
   Dover *(G-1782)*

American Sports Licensing Inc .... F 302 288-0122
   Wilmington *(G-14444)*

Bayside At Bthany Lkes Clbhuse .... G 302 539-4378
   Ocean View *(G-12471)*

Bayside Resort Golf Club .... F 302 436-3400
   Selbyville *(G-13471)*

Bayside Sports Club LLC .... F 302 436-3550
   Selbyville *(G-13472)*

Bear Trap Sales .... G 302 541-5454
   Ocean View *(G-12474)*

Beast of East Baseball LLC .... G 302 545-9094
   Historic New Castle *(G-4939)*

Bob Lafazia .... G 302 633-1456
   Wilmington *(G-14990)*

Brandywine Country Club .... G 302 478-4604
   Wilmington *(G-15053)*

Brandywine Lacrosse Club .... G 302 249-1840
   Wilmington *(G-15069)*

Brandywine Volleyball Club .... G 302 898-6452
   Wilmington *(G-15092)*

Bridgeville Lions Club Inc .... G 302 629-9543
   Bridgeville *(G-677)*

Cambridge CLB Assoc Ltd Partnr .... G 302 674-3500
   Hockessin *(G-5148)*

Camden-Wyoming Rotary Club .... G 302 697-2724
   Camden Wyoming *(G-921)*

Capitol Little League Inc .... F 302 999-1184
   Wilmington *(G-15233)*

Champions Club .... G 215 380-1273
   Magnolia *(G-6728)*

Chisel Creek Golf Club .... G 302 379-6011
   Wilmington *(G-15389)*

Clementes Clubhouse .... G 302 455-0936
   Newark *(G-10257)*

Cloud Kings RC Club .... G 717 284-0164
   Wilmington *(G-15490)*

Club Brennan .... G 302 838-9530
   Bear *(G-112)*

Club Mantis Boxing LLC .... G 302 943-2580
   Lincoln *(G-6661)*

Club Washington LLC .... G 215 594-1332
   Wilmington *(G-15499)*

Coastal Club Schell Brothers .... G 302 966-0063
   Lewes *(G-5839)*

Community Athc Solutions LLC .... G 302 468-5493
   Wilmington *(G-15559)*

Concord High School Baseball .... G 302 475-2537
   Wilmington *(G-15581)*

County Seat Cruisers Inc .... G 302 398-8999
   Harrington *(G-4754)*

Cripple Creek Golf & Cntry CLB .... E 302 539-1446
   Dagsboro *(G-1433)*

Dale Maple Country Club Inc .... E 302 674-2505
   Dover *(G-2187)*

Delaware Cobras Inc .... G 302 983-3500
   Bear *(G-143)*

Delaware Elite Track Club .... G 302 521-2243
   Bear *(G-147)*

Delaware Fury Inc .... G 302 838-3120
   Bear *(G-148)*

Delaware Lacrosse Foundation .... G 302 831-8661
   Wilmington *(G-15937)*

Delaware Mud Hens Baseball .... G 703 939-7828
   Frederica *(G-4165)*

Delaware Riders Basbal CLB Inc .... G 302 475-1915
   Wilmington *(G-15961)*

Delaware Sports League Inc .... F 302 654-8787
   Wilmington *(G-15967)*

Delaware Trail Spinners .... G 302 738-0177
   Newark *(G-10494)*

Delaware Union .... G 484 645-7064
   New Castle *(G-9040)*

Delmarva Whiskey Club .... G 215 815-1706
   Selbyville *(G-13519)*

Diamond State Curling Club .... G 856 577-3747
   Hockessin *(G-5186)*

Down Under Boxing Club .... G 302 745-4392
   Bridgeville *(G-695)*

Drummond Hill Swim Club .... G 302 366-9882
   Newark *(G-10573)*

Emblem At Christiana Clubhouse .... G 302 525-6692
   Newark *(G-10638)*

Factory Sports .... G 302 313-4186
   Lewes *(G-5984)*

Felton Little League Inc .... G 302 284-3713
   Felton *(G-3972)*

First State Pickleball CLB Inc .... G 302 387-1030
   Camden *(G-837)*

Five 1 Five Ice Sports Group L .... G 302 266-0777
   Newark *(G-10743)*

Forewinds Hospitality LLC .... F 302 368-6640
   Newark *(G-10763)*

Graylyn Crest III Swim Club .... G 302 547-5809
   Wilmington *(G-16953)*

Greater Newark Baseball L .... G 302 635-0562
   Newark *(G-10886)*

Greenville Country Club Inc .... E 302 652-3255
   Wilmington *(G-16973)*

Hagerty Drivers Club LLC .... F 302 504-6086
   Wilmington *(G-17030)*

Hellenic Univ CLB Wilmington .... G 302 479-8811
   Wilmington *(G-17117)*

Henlopen Acres Beach Club Inc .... G 302 227-9919
   Rehoboth Beach *(G-12784)*

Hunt Vicmead Club .... E 302 655-3336
   Wilmington *(G-17233)*

Hunt Vicmead Club .... E 302 655-9601
   Wilmington *(G-17234)*

Hunt Wandendale Club .... G 302 945-3369
   Millsboro *(G-8319)*

Indian River Soccer Club .... G 302 542-6397
   Ocean View *(G-12524)*

J P Blandin Baseball LLC .... G 302 535-8694
   Dover *(G-2760)*

Kids Clubhouse .... G 302 464-1134
   Middletown *(G-7271)*

Kings Creek Country Club Inc .... F 302 227-8951
   Rehoboth Beach *(G-12823)*

Kirkwood Ftnes Racquetball CLB .... F 302 529-1865
   Wilmington *(G-17732)*

Little League Baseball Inc .... G 302 276-0475
   New Castle *(G-9316)*

Little League Baseball Inc .... G 302 227-0888
   Rehoboth Beach *(G-12834)*

Lumber Jacks Axe Club LLC .... F 215 900-0318
   Historic New Castle *(G-5021)*

Major League Bocce LLC .... G 240 476-5801
   Milton *(G-8659)*

Mako Swim Club LLC .... G 631 682-2131
   Harbeson *(G-4707)*

Michael Lo Sapio .... G 201 919-2643
   Townsend *(G-14036)*

Middletown Sports Complex LLC .... F 302 299-8630
   Middletown *(G-7358)*

Milford Little League .... G 302 424-3100
   Milford *(G-8002)*

Millsboro Landing Inc .... F 302 934-6073
   Millsboro *(G-8386)*

Millsboro Little League .... F 302 934-1806
   Millsboro *(G-8388)*

Milton Garden Club .... G 302 684-8315
   Milton *(G-8670)*

Mrb Golf LLC .... G 302 368-7008
   Newark *(G-11465)*

National Cllgate Rgby Orgnztio .... E 603 748-1947
   Wilmington *(G-18539)*

New Castle 100 Archers Club .... G 302 722-7997
   Bear *(G-391)*

Newark Country Club .... D 302 368-7008
   Newark *(G-11532)*

Newark National Little League .... F 302 738-0881
   Newark *(G-11543)*

Northeast Rally Club .... G 302 934-1246
   Millsboro *(G-8406)*

Out-Train Fitness & Prfmce LLC .... G 610 470-3196
   Milton *(G-8680)*

Paladin Sports Club Inc .... F 302 764-5335
   Wilmington *(G-18866)*

Patriot Ice Arena LLC .... F 302 266-0777
   Newark *(G-11639)*

Pike Creek Court Club Inc .... F 302 239-6688
   Wilmington *(G-19041)*

Police & Fire Rod & Gun Club .... G 302 655-0304
   New Castle *(G-9481)*

Polish American Civic Assn .... G 302 652-9324
   Wilmington *(G-19106)*

Premier Volleyball Delaware .... G 302 593-4593
   Newark *(G-11731)*

Quail Associates Inc .... E 302 697-4660
   Camden Wyoming *(G-966)*

Rehoboth Bay Sailing Assn .... G 302 227-9008
   Rehoboth Beach *(G-12914)*

Rehoboth Beach Country Club .... D 302 227-3811
   Rehoboth Beach *(G-12918)*

Resort Poker League .... G 302 604-8706
   Selbyville *(G-13598)*

Right Coast Pro .... G 302 832-1517
   Bear *(G-462)*

Rockland Sports LLC .... D 302 654-4435
   Wilmington *(G-19541)*

Ronald L Barrows .... G 302 227-3616
   Rehoboth Beach *(G-12938)*

Salem County Amateur Radio CLB .... G 302 689-8127
   Wilmington *(G-19636)*

Salt Pond Associates .... E 302 539-2750
   Bethany Beach *(G-638)*

Saltwater Cowgirls .... G 302 745-3632
   Millsboro *(G-8452)*

Shellcrest Swim Club .... G 302 529-1464
   Wilmington *(G-19792)*

Shockwaves Aquatic Club LLC .... G 302 478-8800
   Wilmington *(G-19806)*

Silverside Club Inc .... G 302 478-4568
   Talleyville *(G-13946)*

Sisu Fit Club .... G 302 562-3920
   Newark *(G-12016)*

79 AMUSEMENT AND RECREATION SERVICES

Skim USA .... G 302 227-4011
  Rehoboth Beach *(G-12961)*
Slims Sports Complex LLC .... G 302 464-1058
  Middletown *(G-7574)*
Smyrna Clayton Little League I .... F 302 653-7550
  Smyrna *(G-13891)*
Softball World LLC .... G 302 856-7922
  Georgetown *(G-4516)*
Studio 11 .... G 302 622-9959
  Wilmington *(G-20105)*
Sussex Pines Country Club .... F 302 856-6283
  Georgetown *(G-4541)*
Team Horne LLC .... G 302 376-0579
  Middletown *(G-7625)*
Tennis String King .... G 215 280-2783
  Dagsboro *(G-1514)*
TSE Sports .... G 856 889-4913
  Rehoboth Beach *(G-12996)*
Vacation Club .... G 302 628-1144
  Seaford *(G-13439)*
Velo Amis .... G 302 757-2783
  Newark *(G-12310)*
Wilmington Aquatic Club Inc .... G 302 322-2487
  New Castle *(G-9684)*
Wilmington Country Club .... C 302 655-6171
  Wilmington *(G-20813)*
Wilmington Little League Inc .... G 302 559-7690
  Wilmington *(G-20821)*
Wilmington Trail Club .... G 302 521-3815
  Newark *(G-12383)*
Wilmington Turners Club .... F 302 658-9011
  Wilmington *(G-20852)*
Womens Civic Club Bethany Bch .... G 302 539-7515
  Bethany Beach *(G-651)*
Womens Tennis Club of New .... G 302 731-1456
  Newark *(G-12398)*
Woodland Ferry Beagle Club .... F 302 856-2186
  Georgetown *(G-4578)*
Wrc .... G 302 425-5500
  Wilmington *(G-20899)*
Young Mens Christian Assn Del .... C 302 571-6900
  Wilmington *(G-20937)*
Young Mens Christian Assn Del .... D 302 571-6935
  Wilmington *(G-20938)*
Young Mens Christian Assn Del .... E 302 571-6968
  Wilmington *(G-20936)*
Young MNS Chrstn Assn Wlmngton .... C 302 709-9622
  Newark *(G-12422)*
Young MNS Chrstn Assn Wlmngton .... C 302 296-9622
  Rehoboth Beach *(G-13027)*

7999 Amusement and recreation, nec

About - Per Rush Adventures .... G 302 270-7886
  Harrington *(G-4722)*
Agape Learning Academy .... G 302 491-4890
  Houston *(G-5435)*
American Art Tatttoo .... G 484 889-1663
  Newark *(G-9842)*
American Karate Studio .... F 302 529-7800
  Wilmington *(G-14434)*
American Karate Studios .... G 302 737-9500
  Newark *(G-9846)*
▼ American Martial Arts Inst .... F 302 834-4060
  Bear *(G-30)*
American Responder Svcs LLC .... G 302 567-2530
  Lewes *(G-5687)*
Awareness Center .... G 302 426-5050
  Newark *(G-9957)*
Axxiom Escape Rooms .... G 732 606-2844
  Newark *(G-9959)*
Barnes Camp .... G 302 539-7775
  Frankford *(G-4068)*

Battle Axe LLC .... G 302 437-4283
  Historic New Castle *(G-4938)*
Battleboost Inc .... G 302 499-2000
  Claymont *(G-1053)*
Blue Falls Grove Inc .... G 610 926-4017
  Newark *(G-10057)*
Bluecoast Rehoboth .... G 302 278-7395
  Rehoboth Beach *(G-12646)*
Bones Innovations In Art .... G 302 430-3592
  Laurel *(G-5470)*
Books & Tobaccos Inc .... G 302 994-3156
  Wilmington *(G-15003)*
Brandywine Art .... G 302 234-7874
  Hockessin *(G-5140)*
Brandywine Arts Festival .... G 302 363-5955
  Wilmington *(G-15043)*
Bunker Hill Equestrian Center .... G 302 312-9890
  Middletown *(G-6947)*
Camp Adventureland LLC .... G 302 449-2267
  Middletown *(G-6953)*
Cape Water Taxi .... G 302 644-7334
  Lewes *(G-5797)*
Carmalt Stuart LLC .... G 302 366-8920
  Newark *(G-10149)*
Cheer Force .... G 302 218-7384
  Newark *(G-10195)*
Chelsea King .... G 302 684-5227
  Milton *(G-8582)*
Childrens Beach House Inc .... E 302 645-9184
  Lewes *(G-5812)*
City of Newark .... E 302 366-7060
  Newark *(G-10245)*
Cobalt Art Studio .... G 201 819-9087
  Milton *(G-8587)*
Cowries & Calabash LLC .... G 917 727-8940
  Dover *(G-2149)*
Dagers Waterfowl Hunting .... G 302 659-1766
  Townsend *(G-13983)*
David Price .... G 410 708-7133
  Bridgeville *(G-690)*
Days of Knights .... G 302 366-0963
  Newark *(G-10393)*
De Wild Cheer and Tumble LLC .... G 302 438-7740
  Wilmington *(G-15841)*
Defy Technologies Inc .... G 732 213-7165
  Wilmington *(G-15856)*
Del Bay Charter Fishing LLC .... G 302 542-1930
  Milton *(G-8597)*
Delaware Div Parks Recreation .... F 302 571-7788
  Wilmington *(G-15909)*
Delaware Diy LLC .... G 302 318-8007
  Newark *(G-10437)*
Delaware Lrng Inst Csmtlogy In .... F 302 732-6704
  Dagsboro *(G-1434)*
Delaware River Adventures LLC .... G 302 422-2000
  Milford *(G-7857)*
Delaware School For Deaf .... D 302 454-2301
  Newark *(G-10477)*
Delaware Skating Center Ltd .... D 302 697-3218
  Dover *(G-2259)*
Delaware Skating Center Ltd .... E 302 366-0473
  Newark *(G-10479)*
Delaware State Fair Inc .... G 302 398-3269
  Harrington *(G-4758)*
Delaware State Pistol Club .... G 302 328-6836
  Newark *(G-10486)*
Delaware Surf Fishing LLC .... G 302 296-7812
  Millsboro *(G-8264)*
Delaware Womens Golf Assn .... G 302 598-0566
  Middletown *(G-7048)*
Delcaste Golf Course .... F 302 225-9821
  Wilmington *(G-15987)*

Dewey Beach Yoga LLC .... G 443 250-6770
  Dewey Beach *(G-1667)*
Dover Downs Inc .... A 302 674-4600
  Dover *(G-2338)*
Dream Chasers Gymnastics .... G 302 276-0457
  Historic New Castle *(G-4977)*
Dream Chasers Gymnastics .... G 302 559-5561
  Wilmington *(G-16174)*
Elevated Studios Hq .... G 302 407-3229
  Wilmington *(G-16358)*
Emitt LLC .... F 302 757-2353
  Bear *(G-201)*
Empowered Yoga .... F 302 654-9642
  Wilmington *(G-16401)*
Empowered Yoga .... G 302 409-0192
  Wilmington *(G-16402)*
Escape Rehoboth .... G 302 645-7653
  Lewes *(G-5973)*
Experience Sail LLC .... G 302 545-8149
  Bear *(G-216)*
Festival of Cheer .... G 302 227-4325
  Rehoboth Beach *(G-12754)*
First State Gymnstcs Athc Ass .... F 302 368-7107
  Newark *(G-10731)*
Fish Whisperer Charters .... G 302 363-2597
  Milford *(G-7898)*
Fitar Inc .... G 416 347-8099
  Middletown *(G-7135)*
Flex Fantasy Inc .... G 201 417-7692
  Dover *(G-2515)*
Fly High Cheer and Tumble LLC .... G 585 317-1442
  Camden Wyoming *(G-946)*
Flyogi LLC .... G 302 298-0926
  Wilmington *(G-16677)*
Frank Gillen .... G 302 894-1023
  Newark *(G-10770)*
Freestyles Ltd .... G 302 584-8601
  Wilmington *(G-16745)*
Frightland LLC .... G 302 838-0256
  Middletown *(G-7141)*
Fun Sport Inc .... G 302 644-2042
  Rehoboth Beach *(G-12762)*
G Rehoboth .... E 302 278-7677
  Rehoboth Beach *(G-12764)*
Gallery 37 .... G 413 297-2690
  Milford *(G-7906)*
Goat Joy LLC .... G 302 542-1062
  Harbeson *(G-4697)*
Gold Medal Gymnastics Inc .... G 302 659-5569
  Smyrna *(G-13746)*
Graceful Yoga .... G 302 994-3114
  Wilmington *(G-16943)*
Great Stemporium .... G 302 313-5139
  Lewes *(G-6055)*
Guided Footsteps .... G 302 494-6680
  Wilmington *(G-17003)*
Gym Starz LLC .... G 302 747-7218
  Dover *(G-2637)*
Gymstarz Gymnastics Academy .... G 302 697-1221
  Camden *(G-842)*
H & H Stables Inc .... G 302 629-5100
  Seaford *(G-13204)*
Harrington Raceway Inc .... D 302 398-5346
  Harrington *(G-4780)*
Higher Power Yoga .... G 302 354-5826
  Smyrna *(G-13761)*
Hook Em & Cook Em LLC .... G 302 226-8220
  Milford *(G-7934)*
Horse Power Show Hunters LLC .... G 302 265-2881
  Milford *(G-7935)*
House of Yoga LLC .... G 302 373-9534
  Newark *(G-10977)*

79 AMUSEMENT AND RECREATION SERVICES

IH Technologies (iht) LLC .... G 718 679-2613
   Wilmington *(G-17268)*
Iptl Global Inc .... F 408 306-8888
   Wilmington *(G-17419)*
Its my Art LLC .... G 302 750-1380
   Claymont *(G-1191)*
Jamaican MI Hungry .... G 302 287-3337
   Wilmington *(G-17474)*
▲ Johnny Fitness LLC .... G 302 654-9642
   Wilmington *(G-17568)*
Judy V .... G 302 226-2214
   Rehoboth Beach *(G-12810)*
Juicefresh Dimitra Yoga .... G 302 645-9100
   Rehoboth Beach *(G-12811)*
Kensington Tours Ltd .... E 888 903-2001
   Wilmington *(G-17691)*
Kent Cnty Rgnal Spt Cmplex Cor .... G 302 330-8873
   Frederica *(G-4175)*
Kent County Community School .... G 302 734-9011
   Dover *(G-2848)*
Kindred Kids Yoga .... G 302 741-2240
   Dover *(G-2871)*
Knights Golf Inc .... G 484 553-1119
   Townsend *(G-14023)*
Korean Martial Arts Institute .... G 302 992-7999
   Wilmington *(G-17747)*
Lady Lifters Gym .... G 302 222-2321
   Dover *(G-2898)*
Legacy Martial Arts .... G 302 345-8515
   New Castle *(G-9300)*
Lewes Yoga & Meditation Center .... G 302 245-6133
   Lewes *(G-6203)*
Lhr-Fine Arts Studios .... G 302 981-8553
   Wilmington *(G-17890)*
Linda Celestian Art Studio .... G 302 364-0278
   Wilmington *(G-17919)*
Lineage Bjj .... G 201 788-8167
   Greenwood *(G-4649)*
Little Gym .... G 302 856-2310
   Seaford *(G-13263)*
Little Gym of Ncc .... G 302 543-5524
   Wilmington *(G-17939)*
Mansion House Farm Paintball .... G 302 650-3141
   Bear *(G-361)*
Martha Marie Charters .... G 302 222-5637
   Lincoln *(G-6683)*
Marylou Sheaffer .... G 302 422-4118
   Milford *(G-7987)*
Meadowwood .... G 302 286-7004
   Newark *(G-11370)*
Megara Inc .... F 914 487-4702
   Dover *(G-3055)*
Michael Schwartz .... F 302 791-9999
   Wilmington *(G-18324)*
Michael Wescott .... G 302 423-7094
   Georgetown *(G-4426)*
Mid Atlantic Grand Prix LLC .... G 302 656-5278
   New Castle *(G-9365)*
Midcoast Gymnstics Dnce Studio .... G 302 436-6007
   Selbyville *(G-13573)*
Moneyball Dfs LLC .... G 302 240-0051
   Newark *(G-11441)*
Mystic Energy Guides Inc .... G 302 518-2068
   Bear *(G-385)*
Noble Eagle Sales LLC .... G 302 736-5166
   Dover *(G-3191)*
Nothing But Net Inc .... G 302 476-0453
   New Castle *(G-9428)*
ONeills Fly Fishing LLC .... G 302 898-6911
   Hockessin *(G-5329)*
Patriot Self Defense .... G 302 420-3503
   Wilmington *(G-18911)*

Petite Yogi .... G 570 840-5999
   Wilmington *(G-18999)*
Phluffy Rides LLC .... G 302 521-0092
   Wilmington *(G-19021)*
Pirates of Lewes Expeditions .... G 302 249-3538
   Lewes *(G-6372)*
Pjk Golf Operations LLC .... G 302 376-6500
   Middletown *(G-7451)*
Planke App LLC .... G 607 287-0794
   Wilmington *(G-19068)*
Plaza Mexico .... G 301 643-5701
   Millsboro *(G-8430)*
Poseidon Adventures Inc .... G 302 533-7815
   Newark *(G-11715)*
Posidon Adventure Inc .... F 302 543-5024
   Wilmington *(G-19123)*
Premier Entertainment III LLC .... A 302 674-4600
   Dover *(G-3360)*
Premier Mrtial Arts Nshvlle LL .... G 302 674-1985
   Dover *(G-3361)*
Premier Soccer .... G 302 533-7340
   Newark *(G-11730)*
Pure Self Coaching LLC .... G 302 345-0356
   Middletown *(G-7483)*
PUSH Yoga .... G 302 547-4807
   Wilmington *(G-19267)*
Rage World LLC .... G 302 397-4400
   Wilmington *(G-19317)*
Raw Tennis Inc .... G 302 507-8687
   Hockessin *(G-5355)*
Raw Tennis Inc .... G 302 421-2012
   Wilmington *(G-19342)*
Rehoboth Beach Yoga Centr .... G 302 226-7646
   Rehoboth Beach *(G-12922)*
Rehoboth Golf Park .... G 302 542-1295
   Rehoboth Beach *(G-12926)*
Restarant Actn Md-Tlantic Whse .... G 302 462-6678
   Dagsboro *(G-1498)*
Richardson Building Dnrec .... G 772 215-7625
   Dover *(G-3469)*
Rittenhouse Sq Fine Art Show .... G 610 299-1343
   New Castle *(G-9535)*
Riverwalk Mini Golf .... G 302 425-4890
   Wilmington *(G-19500)*
Rodney Street Tennis .... F 302 384-7498
   Wilmington *(G-19552)*
Ryans Mini Golf .... G 302 227-2667
   Rehoboth Beach *(G-12942)*
Sand Dollar Dewey LLC .... G 302 858-7030
   Lewes *(G-6445)*
Sarahs Art Scene .... G 302 792-2631
   Wilmington *(G-19671)*
Schutte Park .... G 302 349-4898
   Dover *(G-3515)*
Sea Shell Shop Inc .... F 302 227-4323
   Rehoboth Beach *(G-12950)*
Seagreen Bicycle .... G 302 645-7008
   Lewes *(G-6454)*
Shaddai I El .... G 302 632-7535
   Camden Wyoming *(G-975)*
Shakti Yoga LLC .... G 302 696-2288
   Dover *(G-3539)*
Shooters Choice Inc .... G 302 736-5166
   Dover *(G-3548)*
Shoshin Karate LLC .... G 302 369-9300
   Newark *(G-12000)*
Skateworld Inc .... G 302 875-2121
   Seaford *(G-13404)*
Skating Club of Wilmington Inc .... F 302 656-5005
   Wilmington *(G-19853)*
Sky Zone Trampoline Park .... G 302 449-1252
   Middletown *(G-7570)*

Soflete LLC .... G 773 983-4692
   Rehoboth Beach *(G-12966)*
Space Happens Game .... G 302 563-1949
   Wilmington *(G-19950)*
Sportsmans Hall LLC .... G 410 429-6030
   Rehoboth Beach *(G-12971)*
Spring Mix Sport Fshing Chrter .... G 443 463-8902
   Selbyville *(G-13609)*
Stick It Gymnastics .... G 302 678-8780
   Wilmington *(G-20073)*
Stumpys Hatchet House .... G 302 378-4737
   Middletown *(G-7605)*
Sundari Kula LLC .... F 302 373-7538
   Middletown *(G-7610)*
Surf and Soul Yoga .... G 302 539-5861
   Fenwick Island *(G-4056)*
Swellinfocom .... G 302 588-6241
   Lewes *(G-6533)*
Taekwondo Fitness Ctr of Del .... G 302 836-8264
   Bear *(G-524)*
Tiffgoyogaflow .... G 302 793-9455
   Wilmington *(G-20321)*
Tula Yoga Reiki Professionals .... G 302 359-9790
   Dover *(G-3734)*
Tumble-Kids LLC .... G 302 530-7800
   Wilmington *(G-20459)*
U Yoga .... G 302 893-4585
   Wilmington *(G-20484)*
U-Matter Learning Place .... G 302 482-1746
   Wilmington *(G-20486)*
Urban Youth Golf Program Assn .... G 302 384-8759
   Wilmington *(G-20543)*
V Power Fit Inc .... G 832 743-7116
   Middletown *(G-7678)*
Vickers Ballooning LLC .... G 302 462-1830
   Dagsboro *(G-1523)*
Vinces Sports Center Inc .... G 302 738-4859
   Newark *(G-12325)*
Wellspring Farm Inc .... G 302 798-2407
   Wilmington *(G-20728)*
Weltri Inc .... F 818 962-8834
   Dover *(G-3833)*
Works of Art .... G 302 562-3597
   New Castle *(G-9690)*
Write To Point .... G 302 235-7149
   Hockessin *(G-5431)*
Wta Inc .... E 302 397-8142
   Wilmington *(G-20905)*
Yoga For You .... G 302 832-0675
   Bear *(G-570)*
Yogo Factory .... G 302 266-4506
   Newark *(G-12421)*
Yoloha Yoga .... G 443 223-8651
   Milton *(G-8734)*
Young Mens Christian Associat .... F 302 472-9622
   Wilmington *(G-20939)*
Young MNS Chrstn Assn Wlmngton .... C 302 709-9622
   Newark *(G-12422)*
Zr Tactical Outfitters LLC .... G 302 353-9818
   Wilmington *(G-20965)*
Zumba .... G 215 870-9867
   Wilmington *(G-20968)*

80 HEALTH SERVICES

8011 Offices and clinics of medical doctors

8th & Market Spinal Center .... G 302 652-6000
   Wilmington *(G-14153)*
A Douglas Chervenak Do .... F 302 653-1050
   Smyrna *(G-13625)*
Abad & Salameda PA .... G 302 652-4705
   Wilmington *(G-14193)*

SIC SECTION
80 HEALTH SERVICES

Abby L Allen Fnp.................................. G 302 856-1773
Georgetown *(G-4195)*

Abby Medical Center............................ G 302 999-0003
Newark *(G-9738)*

Abel Center For Oculofacial................ G 302 998-3220
Wilmington *(G-14200)*

Abigail E Martin M D............................. F 302 651-4000
Wilmington *(G-14202)*

Abigail Family Medicine LLC............... G 302 738-3770
Newark *(G-9741)*

Abuwen Anesthesia Services LLC...... G 301 526-4584
New Castle *(G-8758)*

Accelcare Wund Prfssnals Del P........ G 800 261-0048
Dover *(G-1704)*

Ada L Gonzalez M D.............................. F 302 724-4567
Dover *(G-1715)*

Adriane Hohmann................................. G 302 253-2020
Georgetown *(G-4199)*

Adrienne B Neithardt MD..................... F 302 623-4242
Newark *(G-9769)*

Advance Physical Therapy LLC........... G 302 407-3592
Wilmington *(G-14269)*

Advanced Anesthesiology & Pain....... G 302 283-3300
Wilmington *(G-14270)*

Advanced Biomedical Inc..................... G 302 730-1880
Dover *(G-1723)*

Advanced Care Obgyn........................... G 302 633-9083
Wilmington *(G-14271)*

Advanced Care Obsttrics Gynclo........ F 302 275-2202
Wilmington *(G-14272)*

Advanced Endoscopy Center LLC....... G 302 678-0725
Dover *(G-1724)*

Advanced Plastic Surgery Cente......... F 302 623-4004
Newark *(G-9780)*

Advanced Plastic Surgery Ctr.............. F 302 355-0005
Newark *(G-9781)*

Advanced Surgical Specialists............ F 302 475-4900
Wilmington *(G-14282)*

Advoserv Inc.. D 302 365-8050
Wilmington *(G-14292)*

Aesthtic Plstic Surgery Del PA............. F 302 656-0214
Wilmington *(G-14298)*

Affinity Womens Health LLC............... G 302 468-4320
Bear *(G-19)*

Aiec.. F 302 993-0931
Wilmington *(G-14330)*

Alice R OBrien Ms Lpcmh..................... G 302 521-3859
Wilmington *(G-14357)*

Alicia Kendorski Ncc............................. G 302 448-5054
Millville *(G-8513)*

All About Pain and Spine...................... G 302 595-3670
Newark *(G-9813)*

All About Women................................... G 302 832-8331
Newark *(G-9814)*

All About Women................................... G 302 995-7073
Wilmington *(G-14361)*

All About Women LLC........................... E 302 224-8400
Newark *(G-9815)*

Allergy Associates PA........................... G 302 834-3401
Newark *(G-9823)*

Allergy Associates PA........................... G 302 570-0865
Wilmington *(G-14375)*

Allergy Associates PA Inc.................... F 302 798-8070
Wilmington *(G-14376)*

Allied Anesthesia Assoc LLC............... G 302 547-3620
Dover *(G-1771)*

Allison Scrivani LLC.............................. G 302 841-2320
Frankford *(G-4060)*

Alpha Care Medical LLC....................... G 302 398-0888
Harrington *(G-4725)*

Amanda C Szymczak............................. G 302 678-3020
Dover *(G-1780)*

Amanda L Porter................................... G 302 234-2026
Wilmington *(G-14410)*

Amanda Lynn Ferenc LPn..................... G 302 841-2498
Bridgeville *(G-663)*

Ambient Care Express.......................... G 302 629-3099
Delmar *(G-1563)*

Ambient Medical Care.......................... G 302 629-3099
Seaford *(G-13060)*

Ambulatorys Surgery Ctr..................... G 302 633-9416
Wilmington *(G-14419)*

American Cllge of Physicians.............. G 540 631-0426
Wilmington *(G-14430)*

American Surgery Center..................... F 302 266-9166
Bear *(G-32)*

Amick Mart J MD................................... F 302 633-1700
Wilmington *(G-14457)*

Andre M D Hoffman............................... G 302 892-2710
Newark *(G-9865)*

Andrea M D Arellano............................. G 302 678-0510
Dover *(G-1792)*

Andreas Rauer MD PA.......................... G 302 734-1760
Dover *(G-1793)*

Andrew J Glick MD................................ E 302 652-8990
Wilmington *(G-14476)*

Andrew W Donohue Do......................... G 302 235-3725
Wilmington *(G-14479)*

Andrew Weinstein MD Inc.................... G 302 428-1675
Wilmington *(G-14480)*

Anesthesiology & Pain MGT................ G 302 235-8074
Newark *(G-9867)*

Angela Saldarriaga................................ G 302 633-1182
Wilmington *(G-14482)*

Angelo Joseph Chiari Rph.................... G 302 239-5949
Hockessin *(G-5125)*

Ann White.. G 302 365-4664
Newark *(G-9872)*

Anthony Lee Cucuzzella MD................. G 302 623-4370
Newark *(G-9879)*

Antonio C Narvaez MD.......................... G 302 453-1002
Newark *(G-9881)*

Arlen D Stone M D................................. G 302 999-0933
Newark *(G-9904)*

Armand De MD Sanctic......................... F 302 475-2535
Wilmington *(G-14553)*

Armin Marefat Do.................................. F 302 645-9325
Lewes *(G-5700)*

Arun Jain Advicoach............................. G 302 442-0053
Wilmington *(G-14574)*

Ashesh I Modi.. F 302 452-3000
Newark *(G-9921)*

Ashish Anand Md................................... G 617 953-5914
Claymont *(G-1044)*

Ashish B Parikh..................................... F 302 338-9444
Newark *(G-9922)*

Associates In Medicine PA................... G 302 645-6644
Lewes *(G-5707)*

Assoctes Hmtlogy Oncology Group.... G 302 421-4860
Wilmington *(G-14594)*

Assoction Pathology Chairs Inc.......... G 302 660-4940
Wilmington *(G-14598)*

Asthma and Allergy Care Del............... G 302 995-2952
Wilmington *(G-14603)*

Athena T Jolly M D................................ G 302 454-3020
Newark *(G-9932)*

Atlantic Adult & Pediatric..................... F 302 644-1300
Lewes *(G-5711)*

Atlantic Family Physician LLC............ G 302 856-4092
Georgetown *(G-4215)*

Atlantic Physicians Billing................... G 914 490-3741
Milford *(G-7778)*

Attitude LLC None................................. G 302 422-3356
Milford *(G-7779)*

Avery Institute....................................... G 302 803-6784
Wilmington *(G-14668)*

Azhar H Khan MD.................................. F 302 454-8880
Newark *(G-9962)*

Balu Ganesh R MD................................ G 302 992-9191
Wilmington *(G-14726)*

Barbara Socha MD................................ G 302 541-4460
Ocean View *(G-12467)*

Barry Goldstein MD............................... G 302 734-4130
Dover *(G-1877)*

Bay Anesthesia Associates LLC......... F 302 598-9139
Dover *(G-1883)*

Bayada Home Health Care Inc............ D 302 424-8200
Milford *(G-7784)*

Bayhealth Hematology Oncology........ F 302 430-5072
Milford *(G-7787)*

Bayhealth Medical Group Ent.............. F 302 339-8040
Georgetown *(G-4224)*

Bayhealth Primary Care........................ F 302 855-1349
Milton *(G-8568)*

Bayside Health Assn Chartered.......... D 302 645-4700
Lewes *(G-5740)*

Beacon Pediatrics LLC........................ F 302 645-8212
Rehoboth Beach *(G-12632)*

Beck Jr Thomas D Do........................... G 302 541-4500
Ocean View *(G-12475)*

Beebe Medical Center Inc................... G 302 856-9729
Georgetown *(G-4231)*

Bellevue Heart Group LLC................... G 302 468-4500
Wilmington *(G-14822)*

Benjamin M D Cooper........................... G 302 652-3331
Wilmington *(G-14836)*

Berman Loren MD.................................. F 302 651-4000
Wilmington *(G-14846)*

Beth A Renzulli M D.............................. G 302 449-0420
Middletown *(G-6915)*

Beth R Schubert MD............................. F 302 224-9400
Newark *(G-10027)*

Bijan K Sorouri MD............................... G 302 652-1218
Wilmington *(G-14889)*

Birth Cnter Hlstic Wns Hlth CA............ F 302 658-2229
Newark *(G-10038)*

Blanca O Lim MD................................... F 302 653-1669
Smyrna *(G-13663)*

BMA Milford.. G 302 424-0552
Milford *(G-7799)*

Body Brain Sync Inc............................. G 302 498-9234
Bear *(G-78)*

Bonie L Burnquist M D P A.................. G 302 537-6110
Bethany Beach *(G-588)*

Bonnie L Burnquist MD PA................... G 302 537-2260
Millville *(G-8521)*

Boudreaux Ilene Lefkowitz MD............ F 302 479-5505
Wilmington *(G-15011)*

Bradford Family Physicians LLC......... G 302 730-3750
Dover *(G-1969)*

Bradley J Sandella Do.......................... G 302 477-3300
Wilmington *(G-15032)*

Brandi Wine Pediatric Inc.................... E 302 478-7805
Wilmington *(G-15041)*

Brandywine Care L L C......................... F 302 658-5822
Wilmington *(G-15048)*

Brandywine Cnseling Cmnty Svcs...... G 302 856-4700
Milford *(G-7803)*

Brandywine Cosmetic Surgery............ G 302 652-3331
Newark *(G-10079)*

Brandywine Hundred Family Mdcn..... F 302 478-5650
Wilmington *(G-15066)*

Brandywine Ob Gyn.............................. G 302 477-1375
Wilmington *(G-15076)*

Brandywine Pain Center....................... F 302 998-2585
Wilmington *(G-15078)*

Employee Codes: A=Over 500 employees, B=251-500
C=101-250, D=51-100, E=20-50, F=10-19, G=1-9

2024 Harris Directory of
Delaware Businesses

80 HEALTH SERVICES

Name	Code	Phone
Brandywine Urology Cons PA	G	302 652-8990
Newark (G-10080)		
Brandywine Urology Cons PA	F	302 652-8990
Wilmington (G-15088)		
Brian J Galinat M D	G	302 633-3555
Wilmington (G-15104)		
Bruce M Dopler MD	G	302 628-7730
Seaford (G-13096)		
Burke Dermatology	E	302 703-6585
Lewes (G-5780)		
Burke Dermatology	G	302 734-3376
Dover (G-1993)		
Burke Dermatology	G	302 230-3376
Newark (G-10105)		
Business Interface MD LLC	G	302 735-7739
Dover (G-1997)		
Butt Kambiz R MD	G	708 927-7169
Newark (G-10108)		
Call Care 24 Inc	F	832 217-0864
Wilmington (G-15197)		
Camden Primary Care	G	302 698-1100
Dover (G-2016)		
Camden Walk-In LLC	F	302 698-1100
Dover (G-2017)		
Camp Chiropractic Inc	G	302 378-2899
Middletown (G-6954)		
Cape Medical Associates PA	F	302 645-2805
Lewes (G-5795)		
Capital Orthopaedic	G	302 628-7702
Seaford (G-13102)		
Cardiac Rehab	F	302 832-5414
Newark (G-10139)		
Cardio-Kinetics Inc	E	302 738-6635
Newark (G-10140)		
Cardiology Consultants	E	302 645-1233
Lewes (G-5801)		
Cardiology Physicans PA Inc	E	302 366-8600
Newark (G-10141)		
Caridad Rosal MA MD	F	302 653-6174
Smyrna (G-13675)		
Caring Minds Medical Center	G	267 243-9102
Middletown (G-6960)		
Caring Minds Medical Ctr LLC	G	302 516-7936
Wilmington (G-15250)		
Carl R Yacoub	F	302 996-9010
Newark (G-10148)		
Carol A Tavani MD	G	302 454-9900
Newark (G-10152)		
Caruso Richard F MD PA	G	302 645-6698
Lewes (G-5806)		
Castro Jose MD	G	302 999-8169
Wilmington (G-15271)		
Cataract and Laser Center LLC	F	302 454-8802
Newark (G-10162)		
Center For Cosmetic Surgery	G	302 994-8492
Newark (G-10173)		
Center For Human Reproduction	F	302 738-4600
Newark (G-10175)		
Center For Neurology	F	302 422-0800
Milford (G-7817)		
Center For Surgical Studies	F	302 225-0177
Newark (G-10176)		
Center of Excellence In	F	302 503-0741
Milford (G-7818)		
Central Delaware Fmly Medicine	F	302 735-1616
Dover (G-2050)		
Cerebral Med Group A Prof Corp	D	415 403-2156
Claymont (G-1081)		
Charles L Hobbs DPM	G	302 655-7735
Wilmington (G-15337)		
Charles Wang MD PA	G	302 655-1500
Wilmington (G-15341)		
Cheryl Cantrell	G	610 793-9202
Wilmington (G-15365)		
Chesapeake Bay Orthopedics	G	302 404-5954
Seaford (G-13115)		
Chesapeake Neurology Service	G	302 563-7253
Wilmington (G-15367)		
Childers IV Henry E MD	G	302 258-8853
Georgetown (G-4252)		
Children Yuth Their Fmlies Del	G	302 633-2600
Wilmington (G-15377)		
Chistine E Woods	F	302 709-4497
Newark (G-10208)		
Chitiki Dhadha Gautamy MD	G	302 393-5006
Milford (G-7825)		
Choudhary Chitra MD	G	302 401-1500
Dover (G-2070)		
Chris Curry Dr	G	302 365-5457
Bear (G-99)		
Christana Ctr For Wns Wellness	G	302 454-9800
Newark (G-10212)		
Christana Inst Advnced Srgery	E	302 892-9900
Newark (G-10213)		
Christiana Care Health Sys Inc	C	302 733-2410
Newark (G-10224)		
Christiana Care Health Sys Inc	G	302 659-4401
Smyrna (G-13676)		
Christiana Care Health Sys Inc	G	302 477-6500
Wilmington (G-15400)		
Christiana Care Health System	F	302 674-1390
Townsend (G-13971)		
Christiana Care Hlth Svcs Inc	G	302 477-3960
Wilmington (G-15408)		
Christiana Cent	F	302 368-3257
Newark (G-10227)		
Christiana Counseling	G	302 995-1680
Wilmington (G-15409)		
Christiana Hernia Center	G	302 996-6400
Newark (G-10231)		
Christiana Neonatal Practice	F	302 733-2410
Newark (G-10232)		
Christiana Phys Therpy & Spine	G	302 731-2660
Wilmington (G-15412)		
Christina H Bovelsky M D	G	302 514-3371
Smyrna (G-13677)		
Christine Metzing	G	302 376-5148
Middletown (G-6979)		
Christine W Maynard M D	F	302 225-6110
Newark (G-10235)		
Christncare Ctr For Cmprhnsive	D	302 320-9108
Wilmington (G-15419)		
Christncare Prmry Care Fmly MD	F	302 477-3300
Wilmington (G-15421)		
Christopher A Bowens MD	G	302 834-3700
Newark (G-10236)		
Christopher H Wendel Md PA	F	302 540-2979
Hockessin (G-5163)		
Claravall Odilon	G	302 875-7753
Laurel (G-5483)		
Clement Ogunwande Do	G	302 762-4545
Wilmington (G-15478)		
Clinic By Sea	G	302 644-0999
Lewes (G-5829)		
Clinical Crdlgy Spcialists LLC	G	302 834-3700
Newark (G-10261)		
Cnmri	G	302 422-0800
Milford (G-7837)		
Cntrl De Gstroenterolgyassoc I	F	302 678-9002
Dover (G-2099)		
Coastal Care & Dermatology LLC	F	302 542-4999
Millsboro (G-8231)		
Coastal Direct Prmry Care LLC	G	786 897-2550
Lewes (G-5843)		
Coastal Kid Watch	F	302 537-0793
Rehoboth Beach (G-12684)		
Coastal Pain Care Physicans PA	G	302 644-8330
Lewes (G-5845)		
Coastline Medical Ctr Milford	F	302 265-2893
Milford (G-7838)		
Collabrting For Nvel Sltons LL	G	619 252-6060
Wilmington (G-15528)		
Colmorgen	F	302 744-6220
Dover (G-2112)		
Colon Rectal Surgery Assoc Del	E	302 737-5444
Newark (G-10276)		
Complete Family Care Inc	G	302 482-3347
Wilmington (G-15571)		
Complete Family Care Inc	F	302 232-5002
Wilmington (G-15572)		
Comprhensive Neurology Ctr LLC	G	302 996-9010
Newark (G-10293)		
Concord Med Spine & Pain Ctr	F	302 652-1107
Wilmington (G-15583)		
Connections Development Corp	F	302 984-3380
Wilmington (G-15601)		
Continental Insight	G	302 273-4458
Milton (G-8590)		
Cook Robinson Eyes Srgcal Asso	E	302 645-2300
Rehoboth Beach (G-12698)		
Corballis Emergency Medicine R	G	302 224-5678
Newark (G-10321)		
Craig D Sternberg MD	F	302 733-0980
Newark (G-10343)		
Craig Smucker MD Orthopaedics	G	610 869-5757
Hockessin (G-5169)		
Creative Med Consulting LLC	G	302 313-1411
Odessa (G-12582)		
Crestview Medical Center	G	302 762-4545
Wilmington (G-15701)		
Ctm Medical Associates LLC	F	302 945-9730
Millsboro (G-8247)		
Curt M Watkins M D	G	302 856-1773
Georgetown (G-4274)		
Curtis A Smith	G	302 875-6800
Laurel (G-5489)		
Curtis D Froehlich M D	F	302 651-4000
Wilmington (G-15736)		
Cynthia P Mangubat M D	G	302 883-3677
Dover (G-2176)		
Dale F Sutherland MD LLC	F	302 827-4376
Lewes (G-5878)		
Daniel Marelli	F	302 744-7980
Dover (G-2193)		
DAntuono Vincenzo S MD	G	302 628-8300
Seaford (G-13145)		
Danyo Plastic Surgery	F	302 753-6424
Wilmington (G-15792)		
David D Scheid M D	G	302 633-1700
Wilmington (G-15805)		
David M Pressel M D	F	302 651-4000
Wilmington (G-15807)		
David Rappaport	F	302 651-6040
Wilmington (G-15808)		
David S Jezyk M D	G	302 261-6343
Wilmington (G-15811)		
David T Springer MD	G	302 477-1830
Wilmington (G-15813)		
David V Martini MD	G	302 945-9730
Millsboro (G-8257)		
David W West M D	G	302 651-4317
Wilmington (G-15814)		
Dcmfm At Christiana Care	G	302 543-7543
Newark (G-10395)		
De Neurology Group	G	302 893-5301
Wilmington (G-15838)		

SIC SECTION

80 HEALTH SERVICES

Debay Surgical Service .... F 302 644-4954
  Lewes *(G-5885)*
Debbie D Takats Rn .... F 302 737-4552
  Newark *(G-10403)*
Deborah Kirk .... G 302 653-6022
  Smyrna *(G-13696)*
Dedicated To Women Obgyn .... F 302 285-5545
  Middletown *(G-7035)*
Del Marva Hand Specialists LLC .... E 302 644-0940
  Lewes *(G-5887)*
Delaware Advanced Vein Center .... F 302 737-0857
  Newark *(G-10416)*
Delaware Back Pain & Sports .... F 302 733-0980
  Newark *(G-10418)*
Delaware Behavioral Health .... G 302 397-8958
  Wilmington *(G-15872)*
Delaware Clncal Lab Physcans P .... E 302 737-7700
  Newark *(G-10426)*
Delaware Coastal Anesthesia LL .... G 302 275-5777
  Dover *(G-2222)*
Delaware Crdovascular Assoc PA .... F 302 734-7676
  Dover *(G-2224)*
Delaware Crdovascular Assoc PA .... F 302 235-4100
  Hockessin *(G-5178)*
Delaware Crdovascular Assoc PA .... E 302 644-7676
  Lewes *(G-5895)*
Delaware Crdovascular Assoc PA .... G 302 993-7676
  Newark *(G-10428)*
Delaware Ctr For Mtrnal Ftal M .... E 302 319-5680
  Newark *(G-10430)*
Delaware Dermatolgy PA .... G 302 736-1800
  Dover *(G-2231)*
Delaware Diagnostic Group LLC .... F 302 472-5555
  Wilmington *(G-15905)*
Delaware Ear Nose & Throat Hea .... G 302 738-6014
  Newark *(G-10438)*
Delaware Eye Institute PA .... E 302 645-2300
  Rehoboth Beach *(G-12716)*
Delaware Eye Surgeons .... G 302 956-0285
  Wilmington *(G-15916)*
Delaware Eye Surgery Center .... G 302 645-2300
  Rehoboth Beach *(G-12717)*
Delaware Hlth Eqity Cltion Inc .... G 302 383-1701
  Middletown *(G-7040)*
Delaware Imaging Network .... G 302 449-5400
  Middletown *(G-7041)*
Delaware Imaging Network .... G 302 836-4200
  Newark *(G-10454)*
Delaware Imaging Network Inc .... D 302 427-9855
  Newark *(G-10455)*
Delaware Intrvntnal Spine Asso .... G 302 674-8444
  Dover *(G-2247)*
Delaware Medical Associates PA .... F 302 475-2535
  Wilmington *(G-15942)*
Delaware Medical Care Inc .... E 302 225-6868
  Wilmington *(G-15943)*
Delaware Modern Pediatrics .... F 302 392-2077
  Newark *(G-10461)*
Delaware Nurosurgical Group PA .... F 302 366-7671
  Newark *(G-10463)*
Delaware Obgyn & Womens Health .... G 302 730-0633
  Dover *(G-2251)*
Delaware Obs LLC .... G 302 743-4798
  New Castle *(G-9029)*
Delaware Ophthalmology Co .... G 302 451-5022
  Newark *(G-10465)*
Delaware Ophthalmology Cons PA .... E 302 479-3937
  Wilmington *(G-15949)*
Delaware Orthopaedic Specialis .... D 302 633-3555
  Wilmington *(G-15951)*
Delaware Otolaryngology Consul .... F 302 644-2232
  Lewes *(G-5899)*

Delaware Otptent Ctr For Srger .... E 302 738-0300
  Newark *(G-10467)*
Delaware Pediatrics PA .... G 302 762-6222
  Townsend *(G-13989)*
Delaware Physiatry LLC .... G 302 387-1407
  Dover *(G-2253)*
Delaware Plastic & Recon .... F 302 994-8492
  Newark *(G-10469)*
Delaware Plastic Surgery .... G 302 632-7750
  Dover *(G-2254)*
Delaware Primary Care LLC .... G 302 730-0554
  Dover *(G-2255)*
Delaware Psychiatry LLC .... G 302 397-8516
  Wilmington *(G-15955)*
Delaware Scuba LLC .... G 302 236-6350
  Laurel *(G-5495)*
Delaware Sleep Dsrders Ctrs Lt .... G 302 669-6141
  Newark *(G-10480)*
▲ Delaware Surgery Center LLC .... E 302 730-0217
  Dover *(G-2268)*
Delaware Surgery Ctr .... F 302 730-0217
  Dover *(G-2269)*
Delaware Surgical Arts .... G 302 225-0177
  Newark *(G-10487)*
Delaware Surgical Group PA .... G 302 892-2100
  Wilmington *(G-15973)*
Delaware Valley Pathology .... G 302 239-3729
  Hockessin *(G-5185)*
Delaware Vascular & Vein Cente .... F 302 354-4671
  Wilmington *(G-15984)*
Deliri Hamid .... F 302 468-4500
  Wilmington *(G-15994)*
Delmarva Pain & Spine Ctr LLC .... G 302 355-0900
  Newark *(G-10501)*
Delmarva Skin PA .... G 302 564-0001
  Selbyville *(G-13518)*
Delmarva Surgery Assoc .... G 302 644-8880
  Lewes *(G-5908)*
Delmarva Surgery Center .... G 302 369-1700
  Newark *(G-10505)*
Digitizing America LLC .... G 315 882-9516
  Historic New Castle *(G-4974)*
Dimitrios M D Barmpouletos .... G 302 644-7676
  Lewes *(G-5920)*
Doc Optics Center .... G 302 477-2626
  Middletown *(G-7066)*
Doctors Pathology Services PA .... E 302 677-0000
  Dover *(G-2317)*
Don Baag MD .... F 302 235-2351
  Hockessin *(G-5190)*
Donald A Girard MD .... G 302 633-5755
  Wilmington *(G-16134)*
Douglas B Allen Do .... G 302 659-4545
  Smyrna *(G-13713)*
Dover Family Physicians PA .... E 302 734-2500
  Dover *(G-2343)*
Dover Ophthalmology Asc LLC .... F 302 724-4720
  Dover *(G-2357)*
Dover Pulmonary PA .... G 302 734-0400
  Dover *(G-2365)*
Dover Surgicenter LLC .... E 302 346-3171
  Middletown *(G-7071)*
Doyle Timothy F M Do .... G 302 836-5410
  Bear *(G-180)*
Dr Azarcon & Assoc .... G 302 478-2969
  Wilmington *(G-16162)*
Dr Beth Duncan .... G 302 644-2232
  Lewes *(G-5932)*
Dr Caroline M Wieczorek .... G 302 635-1430
  Newark *(G-10560)*
Dr Douglas A Palma MD .... F 302 655-9494
  Newark *(G-10562)*

Dr James Soor .... G 302 684-4682
  Milton *(G-8611)*
Dr Julie Hattier .... F 302 539-7063
  Millville *(G-8527)*
Dr Junfang Jiao .... F 302 453-1342
  Newark *(G-10563)*
Dr Lawernce Lewandowski .... G 302 387-1516
  Dover *(G-2376)*
Dr Mae Gaskins .... G 302 731-0439
  Newark *(G-10564)*
Dr Monika Gupta PA .... G 302 737-5074
  Newark *(G-10566)*
Dr Quan Nguyen .... G 302 453-1342
  Newark *(G-10567)*
Dr Rajshekar Narasimaiah MD .... G 302 537-1100
  Bethany Beach *(G-598)*
Dr Rene Badillo .... G 301 827-1800
  Newark *(G-10568)*
Dr Scott Schulze .... G 302 644-0940
  Lewes *(G-5933)*
Dr Sharon M Sifford-Wilson MD .... G 302 698-3725
  Dover *(G-2379)*
Dr Thomas C Scott Do .... G 302 328-0650
  New Castle *(G-9061)*
Drs Pahnke Penman & Whitney .... F 302 656-1950
  Newark *(G-10572)*
Du Pont Lynne M MD .... F 302 777-7966
  Wilmington *(G-16187)*
Duggal Manveen MD .... G 302 734-2782
  Dover *(G-2393)*
Dustin Davis .... G 302 856-2254
  Georgetown *(G-4300)*
E Mark Johnson .... F 302 422-6050
  Milford *(G-7874)*
E N T Associates .... E 302 674-3752
  Dover *(G-2399)*
Ear Nose Throat & Allergy .... F 302 998-0300
  Newark *(G-10590)*
Eastern Allrgy Asthma Spclsts .... G 732 789-7982
  Lewes *(G-5945)*
Eden Hill Expresscare LLC .... G 302 696-2129
  Smyrna *(G-13721)*
Edward Hu MD .... G 302 422-5155
  Milford *(G-7878)*
Edward L Alexander MD Facs .... F 302 674-4070
  Dover *(G-2426)*
Edward S Jaoude .... F 302 684-2020
  Milton *(G-8615)*
Edwin C Katzman MD .... G 302 368-2501
  Newark *(G-10613)*
EGNM LLC .... F 302 644-3466
  Lewes *(G-5951)*
Eileen Davis Do .... G 302 856-2254
  Georgetown *(G-4307)*
Elkton Mddltown Ashtma Allergy .... G 302 378-1887
  Middletown *(G-7096)*
Ellen A Spurrier M D .... F 302 651-6660
  Wilmington *(G-16372)*
Endoscopy Suite Partners LLC .... G 267 243-3850
  Wilmington *(G-16411)*
Eng Jerald MD .... F 302 478-4845
  Wilmington *(G-16420)*
Ent Allergy Center .... G 302 629-3400
  Seaford *(G-13175)*
Ent and Allergy Delaware LLC .... F 302 998-0300
  Wilmington *(G-16431)*
Ent and Allergy Delaware LLC .... G 302 478-8467
  Newark *(G-10651)*
Ephraim A Ayoola M D .... G 302 741-0204
  Dover *(G-2455)*
Eranga Cardiology .... G 302 422-2496
  Milford *(G-7882)*

Employee Codes: A=Over 500 employees, B=251-500
C=101-250, D=51-100, E=20-50, F=10-19, G=1-9

2024 Harris Directory of
Delaware Businesses

80 HEALTH SERVICES

Eranga Cardiology PA .... F 302 747-7486
  Dover (G-2461)
Erik A Underhill MD .... G 302 652-3772
  Wilmington (G-16457)
Ernest Soffronoff Dr .... G 302 827-2284
  Lewes (G-5971)
Eschbach Jr Leo H Do .... F 302 645-4700
  Lewes (G-5974)
Evagoras G Economides .... G 302 645-1233
  Lewes (G-5977)
Evan H Crain M D .... F 302 322-3400
  New Castle (G-9102)
Eye Care of Delaware .... F 302 454-8800
  Newark (G-10698)
Eye Consultants LLC .... G 302 998-2333
  Wilmington (G-16511)
Eye Physicians and Surgeons PA .... E 302 225-1018
  Wilmington (G-16512)
Eye Specialists of Delaware .... F 302 450-3028
  Dover (G-2474)
F H Everett & Associates Inc .... G 302 674-2380
  Dover (G-2478)
Family Ear Nose Throat Physcan .... E 302 998-0300
  Wilmington (G-16539)
Family Ent Physicians Inc .... E 302 998-0300
  Wilmington (G-16540)
Family Health Delaware Inc .... G 302 734-2444
  Dover (G-2484)
Family Medical Assoc Delaware .... G 302 655-0355
  Wilmington (G-16542)
Family Medical Centre PA .... F 302 678-0510
  Dover (G-2485)
Family Medicine At Greenville .... F 302 429-5870
  Wilmington (G-16543)
Family Practice Association PA .... E 302 656-5416
  Wilmington (G-16545)
Family Practice Center .... F 302 645-2833
  Lewes (G-5986)
Family Practice Hockessin PA .... G 302 239-4500
  Hockessin (G-5207)
Family Prctice Ctr of New Cstl .... G 302 999-0933
  Newark (G-10709)
Famlee Fertility Inc .... G 503 388-6915
  Camden (G-833)
Fataneh M Ziari MD .... G 302 836-8533
  Newark (G-10717)
Feathers Group LLC .... G 302 300-5967
  Newark (G-10720)
Felix C Vergara M D .... G 856 624-4312
  Wilmington (G-16577)
Feng Wang .... G 315 677-1685
  Wilmington (G-16579)
Figueroa T Ernesto MD .... F 302 651-5980
  Wilmington (G-16604)
First Care Physicians PA .... G 302 424-6995
  Milford (G-7891)
First State Endocrinology .... G 302 836-6969
  Bear (G-226)
First State Ent Association .... F 302 836-8961
  Bear (G-227)
First State Gastroenterology A .... F 302 677-1617
  Dover (G-2504)
First State Infctious Diseases .... F 302 535-4608
  Dover (G-2506)
First State Medical Assoc LLC .... G 302 999-8169
  Wilmington (G-16630)
First State Neurology LLC .... G 302 293-7524
  Middletown (G-7133)
First State Orthopaedics PA .... G 302 234-2600
  Hockessin (G-5210)
First State Orthopaedics PA .... F 302 322-3400
  Newark (G-10733)
First State Orthopaedics PA .... G 302 683-0700
  Newark (G-10735)
First State Orthopaedics PA .... G 302 653-5100
  Smyrna (G-13735)
First State Orthopaedics PA .... E 302 731-2888
  Newark (G-10734)
First State Pediatrics LLC .... F 302 292-1559
  Newark (G-10736)
First State Spine and Pain Ctr .... G 302 439-3063
  Wilmington (G-16634)
First State Surgery Center LLC .... F 302 683-0700
  Newark (G-10738)
First State Vein and Laser Ctr .... F 302 294-0700
  Wilmington (G-16638)
Fizul H Bacchus .... G 302 734-3331
  Dover (G-2512)
Forwood Chiropractic Center .... G 302 652-0411
  Wilmington (G-16698)
Francis Mase MD PA .... G 302 762-5656
  Wilmington (G-16721)
Francis Mase Pediatrics .... F 302 762-5656
  Wilmington (G-16722)
Francisco J Rodriguez .... G 302 424-7522
  Milford (G-7903)
Frank Falco MD .... F 302 392-6501
  Bear (G-236)
Frederick M Williams MD .... G 302 738-0103
  Newark (G-10774)
Frensenius Medical Ctr .... F 302 762-2903
  Wilmington (G-16748)
Fresenius Medical Care Souther .... E 302 678-2181
  Dover (G-2536)
Future Bright Pediatrics .... E 302 883-3266
  Dover (G-2549)
Future Bright Pediatrics .... G 609 744-2265
  Magnolia (G-6746)
Future Bright Pediatrics LLC .... G 302 538-6258
  Camden (G-838)
Gabbaud Health LLC .... F 267 512-1750
  Newark (G-10796)
Gabriel Jr Timoteo R MD .... G 302 998-0300
  Wilmington (G-16789)
Gadde & Chirra Inc .... F 302 384-6384
  Wilmington (G-16790)
Gaetano N Pastore MD .... G 302 994-3685
  Newark (G-10797)
Garg Manish MD .... G 302 355-2383
  Wilmington (G-16804)
Gary Quiroga .... G 302 697-3352
  Dover (G-2561)
Gastroenterology Associates PA .... E 302 738-5300
  Newark (G-10813)
Georgetown Family Medicine .... E 302 856-4092
  Georgetown (G-4338)
Georgetown Medical Assoc LLC .... F 302 856-3737
  Georgetown (G-4340)
GI Associates of Delaware .... G 302 678-5008
  Dover (G-2581)
GI Specialists of De .... F 302 832-1545
  Newark (G-10831)
Gifty A Nyinaku LPN .... G 571 224-2660
  Newark (G-10834)
Gilpin Medical Center .... G 302 623-4250
  Wilmington (G-16863)
Gina Health LLC .... G 573 529-9858
  Dover (G-2586)
Gina K Alderson MD .... G 302 628-7730
  Seaford (G-13198)
Glasgow Imaging LLC .... F 302 993-2330
  Newark (G-10845)
Glasgow Medical Associates PA .... G 302 836-3539
  Newark (G-10847)
Glasgow Medical Associates PA .... F 302 836-8350
  Newark (G-10846)
Glen D Rowe Dr .... G 302 730-4366
  Dover (G-2589)
Got A Doc - Walk In Med Ctr .... G 302 947-4111
  Millsboro (G-8303)
Governors Family Practice .... G 302 734-9150
  Dover (G-2611)
Gregg Zoarski .... F 302 733-1487
  Newark (G-10895)
Habib Bolourchi MD Facc .... G 302 645-7672
  Rehoboth Beach (G-12779)
Halpern Opthalmology Assoc .... G 302 678-2210
  Dover (G-2647)
Harmonious Mind LLC .... G 302 668-1059
  Wilmington (G-17059)
Harrison Family Practice Inc .... G 302 956-6986
  Bridgeville (G-708)
Harry A Lehman III Md PA .... F 302 629-5050
  Bridgeville (G-709)
Harsha Tankala MD .... G 302 674-1818
  Dover (G-2659)
Harvey Y Lee M D .... G 302 682-4155
  Milford (G-7922)
Hatjis Christos G MD .... G 302 744-6220
  Dover (G-2662)
Hcsg Regal Hghts Regal41 .... F 302 998-0181
  Hockessin (G-5233)
Health Care Assoc PA .... G 302 684-2033
  Milton (G-8635)
Healthstat Inc .... G 704 936-5546
  Milford (G-7924)
Healthy Outcomes LLC .... G 302 856-4022
  Georgetown (G-4354)
Hearsay Services of Delaware .... G 302 422-3312
  Milford (G-7925)
Heart and Vascular Clinic PA .... G 302 261-8200
  Middletown (G-7202)
Heart Vsclar Clinic Wilmington .... F 302 518-6200
  Wilmington (G-17106)
Heather L Dealy M D .... G 302 998-2333
  Wilmington (G-17110)
Helena Schroyer MD .... F 302 429-5870
  Wilmington (G-17116)
Henlopen Cardiology PA .... G 302 645-7671
  Rehoboth Beach (G-12785)
Henrietta Johnson Medical .... E 302 761-4610
  Wilmington (G-17121)
Herbert Mrs Sheryl A .... G 215 668-1849
  Bear (G-269)
Heritage Medical Associates PA .... E 302 998-3334
  Wilmington (G-17131)
Hifu Services Inc .... G 650 867-4972
  Wilmington (G-17139)
Hockessin Family Practice Med .... F 302 234-5770
  Hockessin (G-5243)
Horizons Family Practice PA .... F 302 918-6300
  Wilmington (G-17210)
Hosmane Cardiology .... G 302 588-1646
  Wilmington (G-17214)
Howard Paul MD LLP .... F 302 644-2232
  Milton (G-8639)
Howard Z Arian M D .... G 302 674-2390
  Dover (G-2699)
Hummell James MD .... G 302 875-8127
  Laurel (G-5533)
Huy M Le .... G 302 738-7054
  Newark (G-10986)
Ian Myers MD LLC .... F 302 832-7600
  Newark (G-10991)
III John F Glenn MD .... G 302 735-8850
  Dover (G-2721)

80 HEALTH SERVICES

Imaging Group Delaware PA................ F 302 421-4300
Wilmington *(G-17281)*

Imaging Group of Delaware Inc........... F 302 888-2303
Wilmington *(G-17282)*

Independent Insur Consulting............... G 302 983-0298
Newark *(G-11012)*

Indian River Golf Cars Dr Wldg............ G 302 947-2044
Millsboro *(G-8320)*

Infectious Disease Association............ G 302 368-2883
Newark *(G-11017)*

Infectious Diseases Cons PA............... F 302 994-9692
Newark *(G-11018)*

Infectous Dsease Solutions LLC........... G 302 841-0634
Seaford *(G-13222)*

Infusion Solutions of De...................... E 302 674-4627
Dover *(G-2732)*

Innovative Dermatology....................... G 610 789-7546
Wilmington *(G-17348)*

Internal Medicine Associates............... F 302 633-1700
Wilmington *(G-17386)*

Internal Medicine Bridgeville................ G 302 337-3300
Bridgeville *(G-716)*

Internal Medicine Delaware LLC........... F 302 261-2269
Middletown *(G-7229)*

Internal Medicine Dover PA................. G 302 678-4488
Dover *(G-2746)*

International Spine Pain...................... G 302 478-7001
Wilmington *(G-17390)*

Ioannis Kehagias-Athana MD............... G 302 378-5494
Middletown *(G-7231)*

IPC Healthcare Inc............................. G 302 368-2630
Wilmington *(G-17416)*

Irena C Viola MD PA........................... F 302 645-7257
Lewes *(G-6131)*

Irene C Szeto MD LLC....................... G 302 832-1560
Bear *(G-289)*

Irgau Isaias MD.................................. G 302 892-9900
Newark *(G-11057)*

Ismail Hummayun............................... F 302 633-9033
Newark *(G-11061)*

Ivan Cohen & Assoc LLC.................... G 302 428-0205
Newark *(G-11064)*

J & B Md Crabs.................................. G 302 387-2161
Harrington *(G-4789)*

J Bartley Stewart MD.......................... G 302 737-3281
Newark *(G-11070)*

Jadali Seyedmehdi MD....................... G 302 738-4300
Newark *(G-11084)*

Jamal G Misleh M D........................... G 302 658-7533
Newark *(G-11087)*

James B Salva MD............................. G 302 762-2283
Wilmington *(G-17480)*

James Boyland................................... G 302 838-0800
Bear *(G-297)*

James Fierro Do PA........................... G 302 529-2255
Wilmington *(G-17481)*

James Moran Do................................ F 302 731-2888
Newark *(G-11091)*

James S Reilly M D............................ F 302 651-4200
Wilmington *(G-17485)*

Jane A Ierardi M D.............................. F 302 651-4000
Wilmington *(G-17492)*

Jani Uday... G 302 684-0990
Milton *(G-8648)*

Janice Tildon-Burton MD..................... G 302 832-1124
Newark *(G-11097)*

Jarrell Benson Giles & Sweeney.......... F 302 678-4488
Dover *(G-2772)*

Jay D Lufty MD................................... F 302 658-0404
Wilmington *(G-17499)*

Jay J Dave Do.................................... G 302 422-0800
Milford *(G-7950)*

Jayant H Shukla Dr............................. G 302 834-0222
Bear *(G-299)*

Jeanes Radiology Associates PC........ G 302 738-1700
Newark *(G-11102)*

Jeffrey Goldstein Dr............................ G 302 478-5433
Wilmington *(G-17519)*

▼ Jennifer.. G 302 738-3020
Newark *(G-11104)*

Jennifer M D Hung.............................. G 302 644-0690
Rehoboth Beach *(G-12803)*

Jerry L Case Dr................................... G 302 368-5500
Newark *(G-11108)*

Jerry P Gluckman M D........................ G 302 426-8012
Wilmington *(G-17532)*

Jing Jin MD PHD................................ F 302 651-5040
Wilmington *(G-17550)*

Joan A Procaccio Inc.......................... G 302 542-6394
Lewes *(G-6142)*

Joaquin Cabrera MD........................... G 302 629-8977
Seaford *(G-13235)*

Joel Chodos Dr................................... G 302 455-1980
Newark *(G-11113)*

▲ Joel R Temple MD........................... G 302 678-1343
Dover *(G-2794)*

John Butler MD................................... G 302 674-8066
Dover *(G-2797)*

John Fenice MD................................. F 302 998-3334
Wilmington *(G-17563)*

John Johnson Dr................................ G 302 999-7104
Wilmington *(G-17566)*

John M D Murphy............................... G 302 368-2501
Newark *(G-11115)*

John R Stump MD.............................. G 302 422-3937
Felton *(G-3989)*

John T Malcynski MD.......................... G 302 424-7522
Milford *(G-7956)*

Jonathan L Patterson MD.................... G 302 242-6176
Milford *(G-7957)*

Jose A Pando MD............................... G 302 644-2302
Lewes *(G-6150)*

Jose H Austria MD.............................. G 302 645-8954
Lewes *(G-6151)*

Jose M Saez Do................................. G 302 424-3694
Milford *(G-7959)*

Jose Picazo M D P A.......................... G 302 738-6535
Newark *(G-11126)*

Joseph A Kuhn MD LLC...................... G 302 656-3801
Wilmington *(G-17577)*

Joseph G Goldberg Od....................... G 302 999-1286
Wilmington *(G-17581)*

Joseph H Piatt MD.............................. F 302 651-4000
Wilmington *(G-17582)*

Joseph J Thornton............................. G 302 355-0055
Newark *(G-11127)*

Joseph M Farrell Do........................... G 302 424-4141
Lewes *(G-6153)*

Joseph Napoli MD.............................. F 302 651-5981
Wilmington *(G-17583)*

Joseph Schwartz Psyd....................... G 302 213-3287
Rehoboth Beach *(G-12809)*

Joseph Straight Md............................ F 302 731-2888
Newark *(G-11128)*

Joshua Kalin MD................................ F 302 737-6900
Newark *(G-11130)*

Journeys... G 443 945-0615
Claymont *(G-1201)*

Jr Anesthesia LLC.............................. G 302 678-0725
Dover *(G-2807)*

Judith Rippert................................... F 302 734-1414
Dover *(G-2814)*

Just For Women Ob/Gyn PA................ F 302 224-9400
Newark *(G-11138)*

Justin Connor MD LLC........................ G 302 483-7115
Dover *(G-2821)*

Justin R Connor M D.......................... F 302 651-4200
Wilmington *(G-17620)*

K V Associates Inc............................. G 302 322-1353
New Castle *(G-9273)*

Kalin Eye Assoc................................. G 302 292-2020
Newark *(G-11140)*

Kapur Neeraj MD................................ G 302 789-0545
Wilmington *(G-17650)*

Karl W McIntosh M D.......................... G 302 594-9000
Wilmington *(G-17654)*

Kate W Bernstein............................... G 302 597-9911
Claymont *(G-1205)*

Katherine M King RN.......................... G 302 449-3625
Middletown *(G-7263)*

Kathleen M Cronan MD...................... F 302 651-5860
Wilmington *(G-17665)*

Kathryn L Ford Fmly Practice.............. G 302 674-8088
Dover *(G-2834)*

Katy E Crowe MD.............................. G 302 230-4965
Wilmington *(G-17668)*

Kaza Medical Group Inc..................... E 302 674-2616
Dover *(G-2835)*

Keith A Sargent Do............................ F 302 990-3300
Seaford *(G-13247)*

Kendall G Ritz M D............................ G 302 652-3586
Wilmington *(G-17684)*

Kennedy Heather Ann MD.................. F 302 655-7108
Wilmington *(G-17685)*

Kenny K Vu....................................... G 302 678-0510
Dover *(G-2845)*

Kenny Vu.. G 302 526-2361
Dover *(G-2846)*

Kent General Hospital Inc.................. A 302 430-5705
Milford *(G-7963)*

Kent Pediatrics.................................. G 302 747-7279
Dover *(G-2853)*

Kent Pediatrics LLC........................... F 302 264-9691
Dover *(G-2854)*

Kent Pulmonary Associates LLC........ G 302 674-7155
Dover *(G-2855)*

Kentmere Hlthcare Cnslting Cor......... F 302 478-7600
Wilmington *(G-17693)*

Kerry S Kirifides MD PA..................... E 302 918-6400
Newark *(G-11159)*

Kevin Keough Dr................................ G 302 384-8173
Wilmington *(G-17700)*

Kewmars E Dadmarz MD................... G 302 691-5179
Wilmington *(G-17701)*

Khaja Yezdani MD............................. F 302 322-1794
New Castle *(G-9281)*

Kiara M Moore................................... G 412 953-2791
Middletown *(G-7270)*

Kiddocs... G 302 892-3300
Wilmington *(G-17714)*

Kids Teens Pediatrics of Dover........... G 302 538-5624
Dover *(G-2867)*

Kieran Py MD.................................... G 302 541-4460
Ocean View *(G-12534)*

Kingstown LLC.................................. G 302 645-7050
Lewes *(G-6167)*

Kirk Family Practice.......................... G 302 423-2049
Wilmington *(G-17730)*

Kremer Eye Center............................ E 866 206-4322
Wilmington *(G-17754)*

Krishna White MD.............................. F 302 651-6040
Wilmington *(G-17757)*

Lakeside Physical Therapy LLC......... F 302 280-6920
Laurel *(G-5545)*

Lanza Silvano MD.............................. G 302 656-3305
Wilmington *(G-17807)*

Employee Codes: A=Over 500 employees, B=251-500
C=101-250, D=51-100, E=20-50, F=10-19, G=1-9

2024 Harris Directory of Delaware Businesses

80 HEALTH SERVICES — SIC SECTION

Larry R Glazerman M D .... G 302 655-7296
  Wilmington (G-17810)
Laser & Plastic Surgery Center ...... G 302 674-4865
  Dover (G-2904)
Laura B Moylan MD .... F 302 674-0223
  Dover (G-2907)
Laura J Manfield Do .... G 302 999-0137
  Wilmington (G-17823)
Laura M Gravelin M D .... G 302 734-1414
  Dover (G-2909)
Laurel Medical Group .... G 302 875-7753
  Laurel (G-5550)
Laurie B Jacobs .... G 302 764-7714
  Wilmington (G-17825)
Lawall Prosthetics - Orthotics .... G 302 677-0693
  Dover (G-2914)
Lawall Prsthtics - Orthtics In .... F 302 427-3668
  Wilmington (G-17834)
Lawrence M Lewandoski MD .... G 302 698-1100
  Dover (G-2916)
Le-Gen Medical LLC .... G 216 496-7113
  Wilmington (G-17844)
▲ Lee M Dennis MD .... G 302 735-1888
  Dover (G-2924)
Lennihan Richard Jr MD Office ..... G 302 994-7821
  Wilmington (G-17876)
Leonard H Seltzer M D .... F 302 229-8506
  Wilmington (G-17878)
Lewes Spine Center LLC .... G 302 231-4333
  Rehoboth Beach (G-12831)
Lewes Surgery Center .... G 302 644-3466
  Lewes (G-6201)
Lewes Surgical and Med Assoc .... F 302 945-9730
  Millsboro (G-8347)
Lifeline Bltmore MD Mllvlle De .... G 410 262-0875
  Millville (G-8536)
Limestone Open Mri LLC .... G 302 246-2001
  Bear (G-349)
Limestone Open Mri LLC .... G 302 246-2001
  Wilmington (G-17917)
Longneck Family Practice .... G 302 947-9767
  Millsboro (G-8352)
Look Great MD Centers .... G 302 658-1232
  Wilmington (G-17989)
Lorna Lee PC .... G 302 761-9191
  Wilmington (G-17997)
Loughran Medical Group PA .... G 302 479-8464
  Wilmington (G-18004)
Lowell Scott MD PA .... G 302 684-1119
  Milton (G-8656)
Lowell Scott MD PA .... G 302 684-1119
  Rehoboth Beach (G-12840)
Luis L David MD PA .... G 302 422-9768
  Milford (G-7979)
Lutwin-Kawalec Malgorzata MD .... F 302 651-4000
  Wilmington (G-18034)
Lynch Jim Heather E .... G 302 562-6336
  Wilmington (G-18046)
Lynda D Arai M D .... F 302 651-5350
  Wilmington (G-18047)
Lyndon B Cagampan .... F 302 730-8848
  Dover (G-2989)
Lynn M Fuchs M D .... F 302 651-4000
  Wilmington (G-18050)
Lynnanne Kasarda MD .... F 302 655-5822
  Wilmington (G-18051)
M Diana Metzger MD .... F 302 731-0942
  Newark (G-11302)
M Imran MD .... G 302 453-7399
  Newark (G-11303)
M Scott Bovelsky MD .... G 302 674-0223
  Dover (G-2991)

Mac Physician LLC .... G 302 235-8808
  Hockessin (G-5288)
Macfarlane A Radford MD PA .... F 302 633-6338
  Wilmington (G-18068)
Magan Forman .... G 443 394-9534
  Wilmington (G-18077)
Magnifaskin Medspa .... G 302 516-7287
  Wilmington (G-18084)
Manveen Duggal MD .... G 302 734-5438
  Dover (G-3015)
Marc Kattelman Do .... G 260 485-4580
  Milford (G-7984)
Marcelle L Paschall DSC .... G 302 376-1768
  Townsend (G-14030)
Maria Rubino Watkins .... F 405 532-4023
  Wilmington (G-18126)
Marian Thurrell .... G 302 239-1269
  Hockessin (G-5298)
Marie Bernier .... G 240 731-1555
  Ocean View (G-12542)
Marita F Fallorina MD .... G 302 322-0660
  New Castle (G-9346)
Mark E Case M D .... G 302 449-1710
  Middletown (G-7328)
Mark Evangelista MD .... G 302 629-4569
  Seaford (G-13275)
Mark Glassner MD .... F 302 369-9002
  Newark (G-11334)
Mark Menendez .... G 302 644-8500
  Georgetown (G-4414)
Mark Neurology LLC .... G 302 933-0111
  Millsboro (G-8366)
Marquez Misael MD .... G 302 995-6192
  Wilmington (G-18155)
Marshall T Williams MD PHD .... G 302 994-9692
  Newark (G-11339)
Mary Hazlett .... G 302 653-8823
  Smyrna (G-13816)
Maryland Center For Therapeuti ... G 302 727-8832
  Lewes (G-6247)
Maternity Gynecology Assoc PA .. F 302 368-9000
  Newark (G-11353)
Maternity Womens Health .... G 302 994-0979
  Wilmington (G-18192)
Mattern & Piccioni Md PA .... F 302 730-8060
  Dover (G-3033)
Mattern and Associates MD .... G 302 724-5062
  Dover (G-3034)
Matthew Eicherbaum .... F 302 655-9494
  Wilmington (G-18196)
Matthew W Lawrence Do .... F 302 652-6050
  Wilmington (G-18199)
Mawi Inc .... G 888 937-6868
  Wilmington (G-18203)
Mayflower Healthcare LLC .... G 908 414-8026
  Wilmington (G-18209)
Mds Interpreting LLC .... G 302 507-2393
  Wilmington (G-18240)
Mds Services Inc .... G 302 547-3861
  Newark (G-11368)
Medblob Inc .... G 813 308-9273
  Dover (G-3050)
Medexpress .... D 302 477-1406
  Wilmington (G-18246)
Medhat Iskander .... G 302 422-2020
  Milford (G-7992)
Medical Associates Bear Inc .... G 302 832-6768
  Bear (G-369)
Medical Oncology Hmtlogy Cons P ... E 302 366-1200
  Newark (G-11376)
Medical Tourism Agency LLC .... G 855 753-3833
  Wilmington (G-18250)

Meg A Frizzola Do .... F 302 651-4000
  Wilmington (G-18261)
Melissa M Damiano Do .... F 302 449-2570
  Townsend (G-14034)
Mercy Care For Wns Hlth Ob/Gyn ... G 302 883-3677
  Dover (G-3063)
Metroform Group Inc .... F 302 737-1165
  Newark (G-11394)
Michael Bober MD .... G 302 651-5916
  Wilmington (G-18309)
Michael Butterworth Dr .... F 302 732-9850
  Dagsboro (G-1482)
Michael D Johnson M D .... G 267 760-7195
  New Castle (G-9363)
Michael D Merrill .... G 302 994-2511
  Wilmington (G-18310)
Michael G Sugarman MD .... G 302 366-7671
  Newark (G-11402)
Michael G Sweeney M D .... G 302 678-4488
  Dover (G-3079)
Michael K Rosenthal .... F 302 652-3469
  Wilmington (G-18315)
Michael L Mattern MD PA .... G 302 734-3416
  Dover (G-3080)
Michael L Saruk MD .... G 302 478-8532
  Wilmington (G-18317)
Michael M Wydila M D .... G 302 798-8070
  Wilmington (G-18318)
Michael Matthias .... G 302 575-0100
  Wilmington (G-18320)
Michael P Rosenthal MD .... F 302 255-1300
  Wilmington (G-18322)
Michael Zaragoza Md Facs .... G 302 736-1320
  Dover (G-3081)
Michelle E Papa Do .... G 302 656-5424
  Wilmington (G-18328)
Mid Atlantic Cardiovascular .... G 302 294-1044
  Newark (G-11405)
Mid Atlantic Retina .... F 800 331-6634
  Newark (G-11408)
Mid Atlantic Spine .... F 302 369-1700
  Newark (G-11409)
Mid Atlantic Surgical LLC .... G 302 652-6050
  Wilmington (G-18333)
Mid Atlantic Surgical Practice .... G 302 652-6050
  Wilmington (G-18334)
Mid Delaware Imaging Inc .... D 302 734-9888
  Dover (G-3085)
Mid-Atlantic Fmly Practice LLC .... F 302 644-6860
  Lewes (G-6272)
Middletown Family Medicine Ctr .. F 302 449-3030
  Middletown (G-7352)
Middltown Familycare Assoc LLC ... E 302 378-4779
  Middletown (G-7363)
Milford Medical Associates PA ..... F 302 424-0600
  Milford (G-8004)
Milford Primary Care Assoc LLC .. F 302 536-2580
  Milford (G-8006)
Milford Pulmonary Assoc LLC ...... G 302 424-3100
  Milford (G-8007)
Miller Samuel MD .... G 302 629-8662
  Seaford (G-13284)
Miller Dr Elinor M D .... G 302 654-8291
  Wilmington (G-18365)
Mills James MD .... G 302 526-1470
  Dover (G-3093)
Millsboro Eye Care LLC .... E 302 684-2020
  Milton (G-8668)
Millsboro Family Practice PA .... G 302 934-5626
  Millsboro (G-8383)
Milton Family Practice .... F 302 684-2000
  Lewes (G-6275)

SIC SECTION

80 HEALTH SERVICES

Mind and Body Consortium LLC......... D 302 674-2380
Dover (G-3097)

Minimlly Invsive Srgcal Nrscnc................. C 302 738-0300
Newark (G-11424)

Mint & Needle LLC .... G 302 696-2484
Middletown (G-7373)

Mitchell C Stickler MD Inc .... F 302 644-6400
Lewes (G-6280)

Mohammad A Khan MD........................ G 302 449-5791
Middletown (G-7375)

Mohammed M Ali M D .... G 302 328-2895
Bear (G-376)

Morgan Kalman Clinic PA...................... E 302 529-5500
Wilmington (G-18443)

Morgan Kalman Clinic........................... F 610 869-5757
Wilmington (G-18445)

Morris Carol Jamie Do......................... G 302 393-5006
Milford (G-8020)

Mosiac of Delaware.............................. G 302 653-8889
Smyrna (G-13828)

Mr Counseling LLC............................... G 302 855-9598
Georgetown (G-4437)

Mujib R Obeidy................................... G 302 478-5900
Wilmington (G-18481)

Murray James..................................... G 302 629-3923
Seaford (G-13298)

Music Art & Culture Foundation............. G 347 746-9047
Lewes (G-6297)

Mymedchoices Inc............................... G 302 932-1920
Hockessin (G-5315)

Nancy A Mondero Do........................... G 302 644-9641
Lewes (G-6304)

Nancy Cotugna Dr............................... G 302 261-6255
Bear (G-388)

Nanticoke Bariatric Services................... F 302 536-5398
Seaford (G-13300)

Nanticoke Cardiology............................ F 302 629-9099
Seaford (G-13301)

Nanticoke Dbtes Endcrnlogy Ctr............. F 302 629-0452
Seaford (G-13302)

Nanticoke Gastroenterology................... G 302 629-2229
Seaford (G-13304)

Nanticoke Obgyn Associates P A........... F 302 629-2434
Seaford (G-13307)

Nanticoke River Physicians LLC............. F 302 629-9735
Seaford (G-13310)

Nanticoke Weight Loss & Gen................ F 302 536-5395
Seaford (G-13312)

Narinder Singh MD............................... G 302 737-2600
Newark (G-11488)

Nashed Maher MD............................... G 302 378-1887
Middletown (G-7393)

Neftali Ayeras Martinez MD .... G 302 827-2330
Lewes (G-6308)

Nemours Childrens Health Sys.............. F 610 642-4040
Wilmington (G-18576)

Nemours Dpont Pediatrics Dover........... G 302 672-5650
Dover (G-3168)

Nemours Foundation............................ G 302 422-4559
Milford (G-8027)

Nemours Foundation............................ F 302 836-7820
Newark (G-11502)

Nemours Foundation............................ E 302 651-6811
Wilmington (G-18578)

Nemours Foundation............................ F 302 576-5050
Wilmington (G-18579)

Nemours Foundation............................ F 302 651-4400
Wilmington (G-18580)

Nemours Fundation Pension Plan.......... A 302 836-7820
Newark (G-11503)

Nemours Fundation Pension Plan.......... A 302 629-5030
Seaford (G-13316)

Nemours Pediatrics.............................. F 302 934-6073
Millsboro (G-8403)

Nephrology Associates PA.................... E 302 225-0451
Newark (G-11506)

Neuro Ophthalmologic Asso.................. G 302 792-1616
Claymont (G-1250)

Neurology Associates PA...................... E 302 731-3017
Newark (G-11511)

Neurology Center South Del.................. F 443 944-9733
Seaford (G-13318)

Neurostar Inc...................................... G 302 778-0100
New Castle (G-9404)

Neurosurgery Consultants PA................ G 302 738-9145
Newark (G-11512)

New Castle Family Care PA.................. F 302 275-3428
Newark (G-11519)

Newark Emergency Center Inc............... E 302 738-4300
Newark (G-11536)

Newark Pediatrician Inc........................ F 302 738-4800
Newark (G-11544)

Newark Urgent Care............................. G 302 738-4300
Newark (G-11548)

Niaz M A MD...................................... G 302 368-2563
Newark (G-11554)

Nicole Smith....................................... G 302 383-8233
Wilmington (G-18646)

Noel Anupol.. F 302 424-6511
Milford (G-8030)

North Bay Medical Associates................ F 302 731-4620
Newark (G-11563)

North East Open Mri Inc....................... G 610 259-3200
Wilmington (G-18679)

Nouveau Inc....................................... F 302 235-4961
Hockessin (G-5326)

Nurses N Kids.................................... F 302 528-6902
Smyrna (G-13838)

Ob-Gyn Associates of Dover P A........... E 302 674-0223
Dover (G-3214)

Ocean Medical Imaging Del LLC............ F 302 684-5151
Milton (G-8677)

Ofc of Preachess Vellah MD.................. G 302 645-2245
Lewes (G-6332)

Omar A Khan M D............................... G 302 478-7160
Wilmington (G-18762)

Omega Imaging Associates LLC............ E 302 738-9300
Newark (G-11585)

Open Mri At Trolley Square LLC............ F 302 472-5555
Wilmington (G-18796)

Orthopaedic Specialists........................ G 302 730-0840
Dover (G-3244)

Orthopaedic Specialists PA................... F 302 655-9494
Wilmington (G-18827)

Orthopdic Assoc Suthern Del PA........... B 302 644-3311
Lewes (G-6340)

Orthopedic Properties LLC.................... F 302 998-2310
Newark (G-11601)

Orthopedic Specialists......................... E 302 351-4848
Newark (G-11602)

Orthopedic Spine Center P A................ G 302 734-9700
Dover (G-3245)

Otolaryngology Consultants.................. F 302 328-1331
Hockessin (G-5330)

Outpatent Ansthsia Spclists PA............. F 302 995-1860
Wilmington (G-18839)

Outpatient Procedure Ctrs LLC............. G 302 734-7246
Dover (G-3251)

Owens Jr Louis F MD PA..................... F 302 629-0448
Seaford (G-13328)

P A Alfieri Cardiology........................... E 302 836-2003
Newark (G-11608)

P A Alfieri Cardiology........................... F 302 731-0001
Wilmington (G-18848)

P A Anesthesia Services....................... G 302 709-4709
New Castle (G-9443)

P A Brandywine Pediatrics.................... F 302 479-9610
Wilmington (G-18850)

P A Cnmri.. D 302 678-8100
Dover (G-3257)

Pain MGT & Rehabilitation Ctr............... F 302 734-7246
Dover (G-3260)

Pain Solution Centers.......................... F 215 750-9600
Newark (G-11613)

Palermo Francis A MD Facc PA............. G 302 994-1100
Newark (G-11615)

Papastvros Assoc Med Imging LL.......... D 302 644-2590
Newark (G-11621)

Papastvros Assoc Med Imging LL.......... E 302 652-3016
Newark (G-11620)

Parikh Mona Ashish MD....................... G 302 300-4246
Newark (G-11627)

Pasquale Fucci MD.............................. G 302 652-4705
Wilmington (G-18902)

Patel Asit... G 302 502-3181
Newark (G-11633)

Patibanda Suguna M D........................ G 302 453-1550
Wilmington (G-18905)

Patient First Medical LLC..................... G 302 536-7740
Seaford (G-13330)

Patricia Chavarry Dr............................ G 302 747-7895
Dover (G-3281)

Patricia H Purcell MD........................... G 302 428-1142
Wilmington (G-18907)

Patricia Heinemann MD........................ G 302 778-2229
Wilmington (G-18908)

Patrick Swier Mdpa Kar........................ G 302 645-7737
Lewes (G-6354)

Paul H Aguillon MD.............................. G 302 629-6664
Seaford (G-13331)

Paul Imber Do.................................... G 302 478-5647
Wilmington (G-18919)

Paul J Gitlin MD.................................. F 302 678-3020
Dover (G-3285)

Paul Rosen MD................................... F 302 651-4000
Wilmington (G-18921)

Pearce Rupertus Kathleen M................. G 302 388-7515
Wilmington (G-18943)

Pediatric & Adolescent Center............... F 302 684-0561
Milton (G-8683)

Pediatric Associates PA....................... E 302 368-8612
Newark (G-11654)

Peninsula Allergy and Asthma............... F 302 734-4434
Dover (G-3292)

Peninsula Plastic Surgery PC................ G 302 663-0119
Millsboro (G-8423)

Peninsula Urology Assoc PA................. G 302 628-4222
Seaford (G-13339)

Persante Sleep Center......................... F 302 724-5128
Dover (G-3302)

Persante Sleep Center......................... F 302 508-2130
Smyrna (G-13846)

Persephone Jones MD.......................... F 302 651-4000
Wilmington (G-18986)

Peter Dunckley................................... G 302 234-1561
Hockessin (G-5343)

Peter F Townsend MD.......................... F 302 633-3555
Wilmington (G-18994)

Peter M D Rocca................................. F 302 683-9400
Newark (G-11672)

Peter R Coggins MD............................ G 302 655-1115
Wilmington (G-18995)

Peter Zorach...................................... G 302 377-5874
Middletown (G-7444)

Peterson Josha.................................. G 302 656-5416
Wilmington (G-18997)

Employee Codes: A=Over 500 employees, B=251-500
C=101-250, D=51-100, E=20-50, F=10-19, G=1-9

2024 Harris Directory of
Delaware Businesses

80 HEALTH SERVICES

Philips B Eric DMD PA................................ F 302 738-7303
  Newark *(G-11684)*
Physiatrist... G 302 993-0282
  Newark *(G-11687)*
Physicans Dspnsing Sltons Lwes.............. G 302 313-4883
  Lewes *(G-6366)*
Physician Dspnsng Solutions.................... E 302 734-7246
  Wilmington *(G-19030)*
Pike Creek Assoc In Wns Care................. F 302 995-7062
  Wilmington *(G-19036)*
Pike Creek Pediatric Assoc....................... F 302 239-7755
  Wilmington *(G-19042)*
Plastic Csmtc Priph Nrve Srger................ F 302 645-7737
  Lewes *(G-6377)*
Platinum World LLC................................... G 302 321-5040
  Dover *(G-3331)*
Premier Drmtlgy Csmtc Surgery................ E 302 633-7550
  Newark *(G-11726)*
Premier Pediatrics LLC............................. F 302 836-4440
  Newark *(G-11729)*
Premiere Oral and Facial Surg.................. F 302 273-8300
  Wilmington *(G-19171)*
Premiere Physicians PA........................... F 302 584-6799
  Newark *(G-11732)*
Pro RAD Onc... F 302 709-4508
  Newark *(G-11755)*
Professional Technicians Inc..................... E 215 364-4911
  Newark *(G-11759)*
Progressive Radiology............................... F 302 730-9300
  Dover *(G-3378)*
Psych Total Care LLC............................... F 302 478-7981
  Rehoboth Beach *(G-12901)*
Psychiatry Delaware................................. F 302 478-1450
  Wilmington *(G-19247)*
Pulmonary Associates PA......................... G 302 656-2213
  Wilmington *(G-19254)*
Puri Vineet MD.. G 302 744-9645
  Dover *(G-3397)*
Quinn Pediatric Dentistry........................... F 302 674-8000
  Dover *(G-3411)*
R Macpherson Dr...................................... G 302 834-8308
  Newark *(G-11809)*
Raafat Z Abdel-Misih MD........................... G 302 658-7533
  Wilmington *(G-19309)*
Radfertility... E 302 602-8822
  Newark *(G-11817)*
Radiation Oncology................................... G 302 733-1830
  Newark *(G-11819)*
Radiology Associates Inc.......................... E 302 832-5590
  Wilmington *(G-19313)*
Rafael Zaragoza Dr................................... G 302 697-2336
  Camden Wyoming *(G-968)*
Ramachandra U Hosmane MD................. G 302 645-2274
  Lewes *(G-6407)*
Ramani Natwarlal V MD........................... G 302 465-3002
  Dover *(G-3420)*
Ramesh Vemulapalli MD........................... G 302 674-9141
  Dover *(G-3421)*
Rangaswamy Leela MD........................... G 267 256-0721
  Wilmington *(G-19332)*
Rao D Bhaskar MD................................... G 302 733-5700
  Newark *(G-11826)*
Rebecca Jaffee MD................................... F 302 992-0200
  Wilmington *(G-19373)*
Reddy Dr Veena....................................... G 302 998-0304
  Newark *(G-11841)*
Reetz Family Practice LLC....................... G 215 806-0318
  Townsend *(G-14056)*
Regent Open Mri....................................... G 252 430-6246
  Seaford *(G-13369)*
Regional Hmatology Oncology PA............. G 302 731-7782
  Newark *(G-11843)*
Regional Hmatology Oncology PA............. G 302 731-7782
  Wilmington *(G-19404)*
Regional Medical Associates PA.............. G 302 734-7246
  Dover *(G-3446)*
Regional Orthopaedic Assoc.................... F 302 633-3555
  Wilmington *(G-19406)*
Rehabilitation Associates PA.................... E 302 832-8894
  Newark *(G-11846)*
Reproductive Associates Del PA............... F 302 602-8822
  Newark *(G-11860)*
Rescue Surgical Solutions LLC................ G 302 722-5877
  Newark *(G-11862)*
Rheumatology Center-Delaware............... G 302 994-2345
  Wilmington *(G-19455)*
Rhonda Replogle Horses.......................... F 301 730-3100
  Harrington *(G-4820)*
Riar Jehan MD.. G 302 855-1349
  Georgetown *(G-4485)*
Richard C Paul.. E 302 645-2666
  Lewes *(G-6422)*
Richard Dale Rodgers............................... G 814 323-0450
  Newark *(G-11882)*
Richard L Cruz MD................................... G 302 577-4270
  New Castle *(G-9532)*
Richard L Sherry MD................................ F 302 475-1880
  Wilmington *(G-19471)*
Richelle L Clark....................................... G 302 448-8094
  Georgetown *(G-4487)*
Ricks Fitness & Health Inc....................... G 302 684-0316
  Milton *(G-8699)*
Riverview Medical Center......................... F 302 396-1204
  Seaford *(G-13375)*
Robert A Heinle M D................................. F 302 651-6400
  Wilmington *(G-19506)*
Robert A Steele M D................................. G 302 234-2600
  Hockessin *(G-5368)*
Robert A Steele M D................................. G 302 478-5500
  Wilmington *(G-19507)*
Robert Davison.. G 301 518-0516
  Bridgeville *(G-762)*
Robert Donlick MD.................................... G 302 653-8916
  Smyrna *(G-13867)*
Robert Dressler MD.................................. F 302 733-6343
  Newark *(G-11897)*
Robert E Measley MD PC......................... G 302 543-4233
  Wilmington *(G-19509)*
Robert Kopecki Do.................................... G 302 230-4955
  Wilmington *(G-19517)*
Robert L Grzonka M D.............................. G 302 503-2460
  Milford *(G-8071)*
Robert S Callahan MD PA........................ F 302 731-0942
  Newark *(G-11899)*
Robin J Simpson Do................................. G 302 838-4750
  Newark *(G-11901)*
Rockland Surgery Center LP.................... E 302 999-0200
  Wilmington *(G-19542)*
Roderick M Relova Do.............................. G 302 346-3171
  Dover *(G-3479)*
Rodney Baltazar....................................... G 302 283-3300
  Middletown *(G-7521)*
Ron G Williams M D.................................. G 302 838-2238
  Bear *(G-469)*
Ronald A Beard.. G 302 883-7883
  Dover *(G-3480)*
Ronald A Luna M D................................... G 302 629-4569
  Seaford *(G-13379)*
Ronald F Feinberg MD............................. F 302 674-1390
  Dover *(G-3481)*
Ronald N Brown.. G 302 478-1108
  Wilmington *(G-19561)*
Rose Strab.. G 302 584-2074
  Wilmington *(G-19568)*
Rowe Robert L Dr Rev.............................. G 302 422-8814
  Milford *(G-8074)*
Ryan R Davies M D.................................. G 302 651-6660
  Wilmington *(G-19600)*
S Gregory Smith MD & Assoc PA............. G 302 993-1900
  Wilmington *(G-19608)*
Sabini Paul MD Facs................................ F 302 998-8007
  Newark *(G-11931)*
Samaha Michel R MD............................... G 302 422-3100
  Milford *(G-8081)*
Sameena Malhan..................................... G 302 422-3311
  Milford *(G-8082)*
Sandra Jackson.. G 302 510-3576
  Wilmington *(G-19659)*
Sandra Sue Retzky DO............................. G 302 540-3463
  Wilmington *(G-19661)*
Savvyderm Skin Clinic LLC..................... F 302 257-5089
  Millville *(G-8547)*
Schultz Corinna L MD.............................. G 302 651-4000
  Wilmington *(G-19699)*
Schwartz Eric MD..................................... G 302 730-0840
  Dover *(G-3516)*
Schwartz Eric Wm MD.............................. F 302 234-5770
  Hockessin *(G-5379)*
Scott A Hammer Md Faafp....................... G 302 725-2033
  Milford *(G-8087)*
Scott Pediatrics.. G 302 684-1119
  Milton *(G-8708)*
Seaford Endoscopy Center...................... G 302 629-7177
  Seaford *(G-13388)*
Seager Insight.. G 302 526-0597
  Claymont *(G-1286)*
Sedrak Wagdy MD................................... G 302 651-6386
  Wilmington *(G-19735)*
Seiff Jenna L MD..................................... G 302 633-6859
  Wilmington *(G-19739)*
Serene Minds... F 302 478-6199
  Wilmington *(G-19756)*
Serene Minds LLC................................... G 302 478-6199
  Newark *(G-11981)*
Seth L Ivins MD LLC................................ F 302 824-7280
  Newark *(G-11987)*
Seymour Sasha Rene C N A.................... G 302 543-1180
  New Castle *(G-9561)*
Shalini Sehgal MD.................................... F 302 424-3694
  Milford *(G-8090)*
Shariyfa A Fields...................................... F 302 552-3574
  Wilmington *(G-19781)*
Sharon MD.. G 302 239-2600
  Hockessin *(G-5381)*
Shashi Patel... G 302 737-5074
  Hockessin *(G-5382)*
Shavers Conswalla U MD........................ G 267 975-9571
  Bear *(G-487)*
Shaylin M Shorts...................................... G 302 494-2451
  Newark *(G-11992)*
Shore Accountants Md Inc....................... G 410 758-6900
  Middletown *(G-7562)*
Shore Community Medical....................... G 302 827-4365
  Rehoboth Beach *(G-12957)*
Silverside Open Mri Imaging.................... G 302 246-2000
  Wilmington *(G-19831)*
Singh Priya C MD.................................... G 302 674-4700
  Dover *(G-3568)*
Slay By Jere... G 302 723-0034
  Middletown *(G-7572)*
Sleep Emporium LLC............................... G 302 313-5061
  Rehoboth Beach *(G-12963)*
Smyrna Medical Associates PA................ F 302 653-6174
  Smyrna *(G-13896)*
Soares Dr Neha M................................... G 248 707-4931
  Dover *(G-3581)*

Sofp..G......302 354-3543
  Lewes *(G-6489)*
Southbrdge Med Advsory Council.......E......302 655-6187
  Wilmington *(G-19937)*
Southern Delaware Imaging LLP..........E......302 645-7919
  Lewes *(G-6494)*
Southern Delaware Med Group...........G......302 424-3900
  Dover *(G-3589)*
Southern Delaware Med Group PA.......F......302 424-3900
  Milford *(G-8098)*
Spana Gregory MD..............................G......302 736-1320
  Dover *(G-3593)*
Spine Care of Delaware........................G......302 894-1900
  Newark *(G-12069)*
Spine Group LLC.................................G......302 595-3030
  Wilmington *(G-19964)*
Sport Spine Chiropractic Ctrs..................G......302 600-1675
  Newark *(G-12074)*
St Johns Community Services...............G......302 292-1044
  Newark *(G-12080)*
State of De...G......302 376-5125
  Middletown *(G-7597)*
Stefanie N Marshall Do..........................G......302 454-9800
  Newark *(G-12095)*
Stephen J Duggan Do...........................F......302 449-3030
  Middletown *(G-7599)*
Stephen M Beneck M D.........................F......302 733-0980
  Newark *(G-12097)*
Stephen M D Carey...............................G......302 629-8662
  Seaford *(G-13412)*
Stephen S Grubbs M D..........................G......302 366-1200
  Newark *(G-12098)*
Steven M Dellose..................................F......302 655-9494
  Wilmington *(G-20066)*
Stone Harbor Square LLC.......................F......302 227-5227
  Rehoboth Beach *(G-12976)*
Stoney Btter Fmly Mdcine Assoc.............E......302 234-9109
  Wilmington *(G-20080)*
Studio 13 Skin By Christina....................G......302 258-4205
  Middletown *(G-7604)*
Summit Orthopaedic HM Care LLC.........E......302 703-0800
  Lewes *(G-6520)*
Sunwise Drmatology Surgery LLC...........F......302 378-7981
  Middletown *(G-7611)*
Surgical Assoc of Newark.......................G......302 737-4990
  Newark *(G-12133)*
Surgical Associates PA..........................E......302 346-4502
  Dover *(G-3629)*
Surgical Critical Assoc..........................G......302 623-4370
  Newark *(G-12134)*
Surgical Focus.....................................G......215 518-2138
  Middletown *(G-7613)*
Surgical Nanticoke Assoc PA..................G......302 629-8662
  Seaford *(G-13417)*
Susan Kelly MD....................................G......302 644-9080
  Lewes *(G-6527)*
▲ Sussex Eye Care & Medical Asso.......G......302 644-8007
  Lewes *(G-6530)*
Sussex Pain Relief Center LLC...............E......302 519-0100
  Georgetown *(G-4540)*
Sussex Regen Specialists.....................G......302 727-6669
  Georgetown *(G-4543)*
Svastijaya Daviratanasilp MD.................G......302 424-3694
  Milford *(G-8111)*
Tami S Creech....................................F......302 670-7798
  Smyrna *(G-13911)*
Tammi Lea Dr.....................................G......302 335-2563
  Frederica *(G-4184)*
Tamp Inc...F......302 283-9195
  Newark *(G-12158)*
Tankala Harsha MD............................G......302 346-0101
  Dover *(G-3650)*

Teresa H Keller MD.............................G......302 422-2022
  Milford *(G-8116)*
Textronics Inc...................................E......302 351-2109
  Wilmington *(G-20285)*
Theresa Little MD...............................G......302 735-1616
  Dover *(G-3674)*
Tidalhlth Pnnsula Regional Inc..............F......302 732-8400
  Dagsboro *(G-1517)*
Tidalhlth Pnnsula Regional Inc..............G......302 436-8004
  Selbyville *(G-13612)*
Tooze & Easter MD PA.........................F......302 735-8700
  Dover *(G-3698)*
Torregiani Seth DDo PA........................G......302 407-5412
  Wilmington *(G-20365)*
Toshiko N Reckner Rph........................G......302 697-6407
  Dover *(G-3705)*
Total Care Physicians.........................E......302 998-2977
  Wilmington *(G-20368)*
Total Care Physicians.........................E......302 798-0666
  Wilmington *(G-20369)*
Total Health & Rehabilitation................G......302 999-9202
  Wilmington *(G-20371)*
Treatment Access Ctr.........................G......302 856-5487
  Georgetown *(G-4559)*
Trinity Medical Center PA....................G......302 846-0618
  Delmar *(G-1646)*
Trolley Sq Opn Mri & Imgng Ctr.............F......302 472-5555
  Wilmington *(G-20435)*
Trudy L Hastings...............................G......302 653-3145
  Smyrna *(G-13920)*
Tsuda Takeshi MD.............................F......302 651-6660
  Newark *(G-20454)*
Turning Crnrs-Hand In Hand LLC..........G......302 689-3562
  Newark *(G-12246)*
Ty Jennifer MD..................................F......302 651-4459
  Wilmington *(G-20474)*
United Medical Clinic LLC...................G......302 451-5610
  Bear *(G-550)*
United Medical LLC............................D......302 266-9166
  Bear *(G-552)*
University of Delaware........................E......302 831-2226
  Newark *(G-12281)*
Urology Associates Dover PA...............E......302 674-1728
  Dover *(G-3762)*
VA Medical Ctr Wilmington De..............G......302 563-6024
  Middletown *(G-7680)*
Valerie Rivera...................................G......302 387-5334
  Frederica *(G-4186)*
Vascular Specialists Del PA..................F......302 733-5700
  Newark *(G-12306)*
Vein Center At Eden H........................G......302 735-8850
  Dover *(G-3780)*
Veterans Health Administration............G......302 994-1660
  Wilmington *(G-20599)*
Veterans Health Administration............B......302 994-2511
  Wilmington *(G-20600)*
Vinay Hosmane MD...........................G......302 836-2727
  Newark *(G-12324)*
Vinay Kandula MD.............................F......302 651-4200
  Wilmington *(G-20623)*
Vincent Abbrescia.............................G......302 734-1414
  Dover *(G-3798)*
Vincent B Killeen M D........................G......302 645-4700
  Lewes *(G-6606)*
Vincent J Marmodo............................F......302 777-1697
  Wilmington *(G-20624)*
Vinocur Charles MD..........................G......302 651-5888
  Wilmington *(G-20626)*
Vision Center of Delaware Inc..............F......302 656-8867
  Wilmington *(G-20639)*
Wagner & Prigg Family Medicine...........G......302 684-2000
  Lewes *(G-6613)*

Waked Hammoud Tarek M MD............F......302 536-5395
  Seaford *(G-13443)*
Walter J Kobasa Jr MD........................G......302 993-1191
  Wilmington *(G-20674)*
Walter Stark Dr.................................G......302 227-4990
  Rehoboth Beach *(G-13005)*
Warren G Butt M D............................G......302 738-5300
  Newark *(G-12347)*
Warsal & Amurao MD PA....................F......302 654-6245
  Wilmington *(G-20679)*
Wayne I Tucker.................................G......302 838-1100
  Bear *(G-559)*
Wayne R Bonlie M D..........................G......302 436-0901
  Selbyville *(G-13618)*
We Care Nephrology LLC....................G......302 242-0531
  Milford *(G-8144)*
Webster Dermatology PA....................F......302 234-9305
  Hockessin *(G-5421)*
Weiye LI MD....................................G......302 651-4400
  Wilmington *(G-20717)*
Well Primary Care LLC.....................G......302 449-0070
  Middletown *(G-7715)*
Wendy M D Schofer..........................G......302 824-4411
  Wilmington *(G-20730)*
Wesley Novak PHD...........................G......302 477-0470
  Wilmington *(G-20736)*
Western Kentucky Ambulatory.............G......302 542-2770
  Lewes *(G-6625)*
Westover Cardiology.........................G......302 482-2035
  Middletown *(G-7717)*
Westside Family Healthcare Inc...........E......302 836-2864
  Bear *(G-563)*
Westside Family Healthcare Inc...........E......302 678-4622
  Dover *(G-3838)*
Westside Family Healthcare Inc...........E......302 455-0900
  Newark *(G-12364)*
Westside Family Healthcare Inc...........E......302 575-1414
  Wilmington *(G-20745)*
Westside Family Healthcare Inc...........E......302 656-8292
  Wilmington *(G-20747)*
Westside Family Healthcare Inc...........E......302 656-8292
  Wilmington *(G-20746)*
William B Funk MD...........................F......302 731-0900
  Newark *(G-12373)*
William R Atkins MD.........................G......302 633-4525
  Newark *(G-12376)*
William R Lynch M D.........................G......302 319-4736
  Wilmington *(G-20796)*
William V Gallery Dr..........................G......302 945-5943
  Harbeson *(G-4719)*
Willie Hardy MD...............................G......610 450-4559
  Wilmington *(G-20803)*
Wilm Otolarngology...........................F......302 658-0404
  Wilmington *(G-20806)*
Wilmington Medical Associates............E......302 478-0400
  Wilmington *(G-20823)*
Wilmington New Castle Pediatri...........G......302 762-1072
  Wilmington *(G-20825)*
Wilmington Otlryngology Assoc P.........G......302 658-0404
  Wilmington *(G-20828)*
Wm H Jeppe Dr................................G......302 234-1785
  Hockessin *(G-5428)*
Wolf Creek Surgeons PA....................F......302 678-3627
  Dover *(G-3865)*
Wolfgang M D Radtke.......................G......302 651-6660
  Wilmington *(G-20876)*
Women First LLC.............................G......302 635-9800
  Hockessin *(G-5429)*
Women First LLC.............................F......302 368-3257
  Newark *(G-12394)*
Women To Women Ob/Gyn Assoc PA....G......302 778-2229
  Wilmington *(G-20880)*

80 HEALTH SERVICES

Name	Type	Phone
Womens Center At Milford Meml — Milford (G-8153)	G	302 430-5540
Womens Health Center — Lewes (G-6638)	G	517 437-5390
Womens Medical Center Inc — Seaford (G-13454)	G	302 629-5409
Womens Wellness Ctr & Med Spa — Newark (G-12399)	G	302 643-2500
Wong Peter MD — Dover (G-3866)	F	302 674-0223
Workpro Health — Newark (G-12406)	F	302 722-4471
Wray Lisa MD — Wilmington (G-20898)	G	302 651-4000
Zabel PLStc&recnstrctve Surgry — Newark (G-12428)	F	302 996-6400
Zarek Donohue LLC — Wilmington (G-20947)	E	302 543-5454
Zarraga & Zarraga Internl Medc — Milford (G-8156)	G	302 422-9140
Zeina Jeha Md MPH — Lewes (G-6649)	G	302 503-4200
Zhang Shunli MD — Dover (G-3900)	F	302 744-7050

8021 Offices and clinics of dentists

Name	Type	Phone
A D Alpine DMD — Wilmington (G-14161)	F	302 239-4600
Aaron B Poleck DDS — Newark (G-9735)	G	302 533-7649
Access Dental LLC — Dover (G-1706)	G	302 674-3303
Aesthtic Special Care Assoc PA — Wilmington (G-14299)	E	302 482-4444
Ahl Orthodontics — Dover (G-1750)	F	302 678-3000
Alan R Levine DDS — Wilmington (G-14346)	G	302 475-3743
Alfred B Lauder DDS — Camden Wyoming (G-907)	F	302 697-7188
Alfred Lauder DDS — Camden Wyoming (G-908)	G	302 678-9742
Ali S Husain Orthodontist — Newark (G-9810)	F	302 838-1400
All Smiles Family & Cosme — Dover (G-1765)	G	302 734-5303
Allan C Goldfeder DMD — Wilmington (G-14370)	G	302 994-1782
Aloe & Carr PA — Dover (G-1773)	G	302 736-6631
Alpine Rafetto Orthodontics — Wilmington (G-14396)	F	302 239-2304
Alvis D Burris — Camden (G-791)	F	302 697-3125
Anna Marie Mazoch DDS PA — Wilmington (G-14489)	G	302 998-9594
Arthur L Young Dentist Jr — Newark (G-9915)	F	302 737-9065
Arthur W Henry DDS Inc — Dover (G-1822)	G	302 734-8101
Avalon Dental — Wilmington (G-14663)	F	302 999-8822
Avalon Dental LLC Bldg G4 — Newark (G-9949)	F	302 292-8899
Avalon Dental of Newport — Wilmington (G-14664)	G	267 312-3184
B James Rogge DDS — Dover (G-1862)	G	302 736-1423
Baker James Ccjr DDS — Wilmington (G-14717)	G	302 658-9511
Barksdale Dental Associates — Newark (G-9983)	G	302 731-4907
Barry Kayne DDS — Newark (G-9986)	G	302 456-0400
Bear Glasgow Dental — Newark (G-10004)	E	302 836-3750
Bear-Glasgow Dental LLC — Bear (G-66)	F	302 836-9330
Beautiful Smiles Delaware LLC — Wilmington (G-14809)	F	302 656-0558
Blair A Jones DDS — Lewes (G-5768)	G	302 226-1115
Blog - Care First Dental Team — Dover (G-1951)	G	302 741-2044
Blue Diamond Dental PA — Wilmington (G-14963)	G	302 655-8387
Blue Hen Dental LLC — Smyrna (G-13664)	F	302 538-0448
Brafman Family Dentistry PC — Dagsboro (G-1419)	F	302 732-3852
Brian McAllister DDS — Middletown (G-6938)	G	302 376-0617
Brianna Rafetto DMD PA — Middletown (G-6939)	G	302 376-7882
Bruce E Matthews DDS PA — Hockessin (G-5144)	G	302 234-2440
Bruce E Matthews DDS PA — Wilmington (G-15133)	G	302 475-9220
Bruce G Fay DMD PA — Wilmington (G-15135)	G	302 778-3822
Burris Cosmtc & Fmly Dentistry — Camden (G-797)	F	302 697-3125
Caimar Corporation — Smyrna (G-13672)	G	302 653-5011
Cathy L Harris DDS — Newark (G-10164)	G	302 453-1400
Cha Moon DDS — Newark (G-10184)	G	302 297-3750
Charles J Veith DMD — Wilmington (G-15336)	G	302 658-7354
Childrens Dntl Hlth Wlmngton W — Wilmington (G-15381)	F	302 803-6560
Christiana Center-Oral Surgery — Middletown (G-6977)	G	302 376-3700
Christiana Family Dental Care — Newark (G-10229)	G	302 623-4190
Christiana Family Dental Care — Newark (G-10230)	G	302 623-4190
Christiana Pleasant Denta — Newark (G-10233)	G	302 738-3666
Christine E Fox DDS — Dagsboro (G-1427)	G	302 732-9850
Christopher Baran DDS — Wilmington (G-15423)	F	903 968-7467
Christopher Fortin DDS — Milford (G-7827)	G	302 422-9791
Clay White Dental Associates — Newark (G-10251)	F	302 731-4225
Clifford L Anzilotti DDS PC — Middletown (G-6991)	G	302 378-2778
Clifford L Anzilotti DDS PC — Wilmington (G-15481)	F	302 475-2050
Collins Associates — Newark (G-10274)	F	302 834-4000
Concord Dental — Wilmington (G-15580)	F	302 836-3750
Conley & Wright DDS — Rehoboth Beach (G-12697)	G	302 645-6671
Connie F Cicorelli DDS PA — Wilmington (G-15603)	F	302 798-5797
Cook & Cook Ltd Partnership — Wilmington (G-15628)	F	302 428-0109
▲ Cook G Legih DDS& Cook Jefry — Middletown (G-7011)	G	302 378-4416
Crescent Dental Associates — Bear (G-126)	F	302 836-6968
Cynthia A Mumma DDS — Wilmington (G-15753)	G	302 652-2451
D B Nibouar DDS — Wilmington (G-15758)	F	302 239-0502
D R Deakyne DDS — Smyrna (G-13691)	G	302 653-6661
Daniel J Fay Dmd PA — Dover (G-2192)	G	302 734-8101
Dann J Gladnick Dmd PA — Wilmington (G-15789)	G	302 654-7243
David A King DDS — Wilmington (G-15802)	G	302 998-0331
David L Isaacs DDS — Wilmington (G-15806)	F	302 654-2904
Dd Snacks LLC — Wilmington (G-15832)	G	302 652-3850
Delaware Braces LLC — Newark (G-10421)	F	302 365-5971
Delaware Dental Care Centers — Dover (G-2226)	G	410 474-5520
Delaware Dental Solutions LLC — Bear (G-145)	F	302 409-3050
Delaware Dental Studio LLC — Wilmington (G-15901)	G	302 475-0600
Delaware Kids Dental Center — Wilmington (G-15935)	G	302 764-7714
Delaware Orthodontics — Newark (G-10466)	F	302 838-1400
Delaware Periodontics — Wilmington (G-15953)	G	302 658-7871
Delaware Smile Center — Middletown (G-7047)	F	302 285-7645
Delaware Star Dental — Wilmington (G-15968)	F	302 994-3093
Delmarva Prosthodontics — Dover (G-2278)	G	302 674-8331
Dental Associates PA — Wilmington (G-16012)	G	302 571-0878
Dental Associates Delaware PA — Wilmington (G-16013)	E	302 477-4900
Dental Associates Hockessin — Wilmington (G-16014)	F	302 239-5917
Dental Associates of Newark — Newark (G-10514)	G	302 737-6761
Dental Group — Lewes (G-5911)	G	302 645-8993
Dental Sleep Solution — Wilmington (G-16016)	G	302 235-8249
Dentistry At Walker Square — Dover (G-2283)	F	302 735-8940
Dentistry For Children — Wilmington (G-16017)	F	302 475-7640
Devon Sadlowski DMD — Dover (G-2288)	F	302 735-8940
Diamond State Dentistry — Milford (G-7869)	F	302 424-7976
Dominic Gioffre DDS PA — Wilmington (G-16129)	E	302 239-0410
Dougherty Dental Solutions LLC — Wilmington (G-16155)	F	302 475-3270
Douglas Ditty DMD MD — Lewes (G-5930)	F	302 644-2977
Dover Oral and Maxillofacial S — Dover (G-2358)	F	302 674-1140
Dr Christopher Burns — Dover (G-2371)	G	302 674-8331
Dr Dawn Grandison DDS — Dover (G-2372)	F	302 678-3384
Dr James Kramer — Selbyville (G-13524)	F	302 436-5133

SIC SECTION
80 HEALTH SERVICES

Dr Jeffrey E Felzer DMD PC .... F 302 995-6979
  Wilmington *(G-16166)*
Dr John Fontana III .... F 302 734-1950
  Dover *(G-2374)*
Dr Kaz Fmly Cosmtc Dentistry .... G 302 235-7645
  Hockessin *(G-5192)*
Dr Robert M Collins .... G 302 239-3655
  Wilmington *(G-16168)*
Dr Robert Webster .... G 302 674-1080
  Dover *(G-2378)*
Dr Shefali Pandya .... F 302 421-9960
  Wilmington *(G-16169)*
Dr Steven Scurnick .... F 410 442-1173
  Ocean View *(G-12507)*
Dr Weidong Yang Dental Office .... G 302 409-3050
  Bear *(G-181)*
Dsd App LLC .... G 302 465-6606
  Wilmington *(G-16182)*
Eco Dental Delaware .... G 302 836-3711
  Newark *(G-10605)*
Edward S Yalisove DDS PA .... G 302 658-4124
  Wilmington *(G-16303)*
Edwin S Kuipers DDS .... G 302 455-0333
  Newark *(G-10614)*
Edwin S Kuipers DDS .... G 302 652-3775
  Wilmington *(G-16305)*
Elkton Bear Dental .... G 302 836-1670
  Bear *(G-200)*
Emil W Tetzner D M D .... G 302 744-9900
  Dover *(G-2440)*
Enhanced Dental Care .... G 302 645-7200
  Rehoboth Beach *(G-12743)*
Equidental .... G 302 423-0851
  Dover *(G-2458)*
Eric S Balliet .... F 302 856-7423
  Georgetown *(G-4310)*
Erik S Bradley DDS .... G 302 239-5917
  Wilmington *(G-16459)*
Erin N Macko DDS LLC .... F 302 368-7463
  Newark *(G-10665)*
Exceptional Dentistry Delaware .... G 302 797-1212
  Wilmington *(G-16500)*
Family Denistry .... G 302 368-0054
  Newark *(G-10707)*
Family Dental Associates Inc .... F 302 674-8810
  Dover *(G-2481)*
Family Dental Care .... G 302 999-7600
  Wilmington *(G-16536)*
Family Dental Center .... D 302 656-8266
  Wilmington *(G-16537)*
Family Dentistry Milford PA .... G 302 422-6924
  Milford *(G-7888)*
Family Dentistry Wilmington .... G 302 656-2434
  Wilmington *(G-16538)*
First State Oral Mxllfcial Srg .... G 302 674-4450
  Dover *(G-2508)*
First State Oral Mxllfcial Srg .... G 302 883-6051
  Seaford *(G-13187)*
Foulk Road Dental & Associates .... F 302 652-3775
  Wilmington *(G-16704)*
Franklin Pancko DDS .... G 302 674-1140
  Dover *(G-2532)*
Fred L Wright DDS .... G 302 239-1641
  Wilmington *(G-16734)*
Fred S Fink Orthodontist .... F 302 478-6930
  Wilmington *(G-16735)*
Freedom Dental Management Inc ..... F 302 836-3750
  Newark *(G-10776)*
G B Lyons DDS .... G 302 654-1765
  Wilmington *(G-16784)*
G W Keller DDS .... E 302 652-3586
  Wilmington *(G-16786)*

Gary L Waite DMD .... G 302 239-8586
  Wilmington *(G-16809)*
Gary R Collins DDS .... G 302 239-3531
  Wilmington *(G-16810)*
Gentle Touch Dentistry .... G 302 765-3373
  Wilmington *(G-16842)*
George E Frattali DDS .... G 302 651-4408
  Wilmington *(G-16844)*
Glenwood Dental Associates LLP ..... G 302 653-5011
  Smyrna *(G-13744)*
Gonce William E Dr DDS PA .... G 302 235-2400
  Hockessin *(G-5225)*
Gordon C Honig DMD PA .... G 302 696-4020
  Middletown *(G-7170)*
Gordon C Honig DMD PA .... G 302 737-6333
  Newark *(G-10870)*
Graylyn Dental .... G 302 475-5555
  Wilmington *(G-16954)*
Greeley & Nista Orthodontics .... E 302 475-4102
  Wilmington *(G-16962)*
H Dean McSpadden DDS .... G 302 239-5917
  Hockessin *(G-5232)*
H Dean McSpadden DDS .... G 302 571-0680
  Wilmington *(G-17019)*
Hammond M Knox DDS .... G 302 383-6696
  Newark *(G-10923)*
Harry He DDS LLC .... G 302 836-3711
  Newark *(G-10936)*
House Call Dentistry Inc .... G 866 686-4423
  Lewes *(G-6106)*
Howard W Zucker D D S P A .... F 302 475-8174
  Wilmington *(G-17219)*
Isaacs Isaacs Fmly Dentistry PA .... E 302 654-1328
  Wilmington *(G-17425)*
J A Pyne Jr DDS PA .... G 302 994-7730
  Wilmington *(G-17450)*
J Michael Fay DDS PA .... F 302 998-2244
  Wilmington *(G-17459)*
J R Forshey DMD PA .... F 302 322-0245
  New Castle *(G-9248)*
J R Williamson DDS .... G 302 734-8887
  Dover *(G-2761)*
J S McKelvey DDS .... F 302 239-0303
  Wilmington *(G-17463)*
James S Pillsbury DDS .... G 302 734-0330
  Dover *(G-2768)*
James Tigani III DDS .... G 302 571-8740
  Wilmington *(G-17488)*
Jane Choung .... F 302 378-8740
  Middletown *(G-7241)*
Jay J Harris PC .... G 302 453-1400
  Newark *(G-11100)*
Jeanette Y Son Dentist .... G 302 998-8283
  Wilmington *(G-17512)*
Jeena M Jolly DDS .... G 302 655-2626
  Wilmington *(G-17514)*
Jeffrey A Bright DMD .... F 302 832-1371
  Middletown *(G-7244)*
Jeffrey L Cook D M D .... G 302 453-8700
  Newark *(G-11103)*
Jennifer L Joseph DDS .... F 302 239-6677
  Wilmington *(G-17525)*
Jerome C Kayatta DDS .... G 302 737-6761
  Newark *(G-11107)*
Jessica S Dicerbo DDS .... G 302 644-4460
  Rehoboth Beach *(G-12804)*
Jill Garrido DDS .... G 302 475-3110
  Wilmington *(G-17547)*
Jillann I Hounsell DDS .... F 302 239-5917
  Hockessin *(G-5260)*
Jillann I Hounsell DDS .... G 302 691-3000
  Wilmington *(G-17548)*

Jiten Patel DDS .... G 302 690-8629
  Milford *(G-7954)*
John C Lynch DDS PA .... G 302 629-7115
  Seaford *(G-13236)*
John N Russo DDS .... G 302 652-3775
  Wilmington *(G-17567)*
John Nista DDS .... F 302 292-1552
  Newark *(G-11117)*
John V Reitz .... G 610 320-9993
  Selbyville *(G-13551)*
John Wasniewski DMD .... F 302 266-0200
  Newark *(G-11118)*
John Wasniewski III DMD .... G 302 832-1371
  Bear *(G-307)*
Johnson Orthodontics .... G 302 645-5554
  Rehoboth Beach *(G-12808)*
Joseph C Kelly DDS .... F 302 475-5555
  Wilmington *(G-17579)*
Jr Walter J Kaminski DDS .... G 302 738-3666
  Christiana *(G-1000)*
Judith E McCann DMD .... G 302 368-7463
  Newark *(G-11134)*
Julie Q Nies DDS .... F 302 242-9085
  Dover *(G-2818)*
Jung B Kim DDS .... G 302 652-3556
  Wilmington *(G-17613)*
Karl J Zeren DDS .... G 302 644-2773
  Rehoboth Beach *(G-12814)*
Kelly Ann Hatton .... G 484 571-5369
  Wilmington *(G-17680)*
Kelly Walker DDS .... G 302 832-2200
  Bear *(G-324)*
Kidd Robert W III DDS .... F 302 678-1440
  Dover *(G-2865)*
King and Minsk PA .... G 302 475-3270
  Wilmington *(G-17727)*
Kirkwood Dental Associates PA .... G 302 834-7700
  Newark *(G-11183)*
Kirkwood Dental Associates PA .... G 302 834-7700
  Newark *(G-11184)*
Kirkwood Dental Associates PA .... F 302 994-2582
  Wilmington *(G-17731)*
L F Conlin DDS .... G 302 764-0930
  Wilmington *(G-17777)*
Laima V Anthaney DMD .... G 302 645-4726
  Lewes *(G-6175)*
Laurel Dental .... G 302 875-4271
  Laurel *(G-5546)*
Lawrence A Louie DMD .... G 302 674-5437
  Dover *(G-2915)*
Lisa A Fagioletti DMD LLC .... G 302 514-9064
  Smyrna *(G-13805)*
Lois James DDS .... G 302 537-4500
  Ocean View *(G-12540)*
Louis K Rafetto DMD .... G 302 477-1800
  Wilmington *(G-18006)*
Louis P Martin DDS .... G 302 994-4900
  Wilmington *(G-18008)*
Lrk Dental .... F 302 629-7115
  Seaford *(G-13266)*
Main Street Dental .... G 302 368-2558
  Newark *(G-11314)*
Mark A Fortunato .... E 302 477-4900
  Wilmington *(G-18136)*
Mark B Brown DDS .... G 302 537-1200
  Bethany Beach *(G-617)*
Mark C Gladnick DDS .... G 302 994-2660
  Wilmington *(G-18138)*
Mark Wieczorek Dmd PC .... F 302 838-3384
  Bear *(G-364)*
Marsico & Weinstien DDS .... G 302 998-8474
  Wilmington *(G-18161)*

Employee Codes: A=Over 500 employees, B=251-500
C=101-250, D=51-100, E=20-50, F=10-19, G=1-9

2024 Harris Directory of Delaware Businesses

80 HEALTH SERVICES — SIC SECTION

Marta Biskup DDS .... G 302 478-0000
  Wilmington (G-18162)
Marta Blackhurst DMD .... F 302 478-1504
  Wilmington (G-18163)
Mary Sweeney-Lehr .... F 302 764-0589
  Wilmington (G-18182)
Mary Ziomek DDS .... G 301 984-9646
  Milton (G-8662)
Maxillofacial Southern De Oral .... E 302 644-2977
  Lewes (G-6253)
Mercer Dental Associates .... G 302 664-1385
  Milton (G-8667)
Michael A Poleck DDS PA .... G 302 994-7730
  Wilmington (G-18307)
Michael Butterworth Dr .... F 302 732-9850
  Dagsboro (G-1482)
Michael Matthias .... G 302 575-0100
  Wilmington (G-18320)
Michael S Wirosloff DMD .... G 302 998-8588
  Wilmington (G-18323)
Middletown Family Dentist .... F 302 376-1959
  Middletown (G-7351)
Mill Creek Select .... G 302 995-2090
  Wilmington (G-18357)
Monica Mehring DDS .... F 302 368-0054
  Newark (G-11443)
Ms Governors Square Shopping C .... F 302 838-3384
  Bear (G-382)
Mullen Thomas R DMD PA .... G 302 629-3588
  Seaford (G-13294)
Nathaniel Jon Bent DDS PA .... F 302 731-4907
  Newark (G-11489)
Neil G McAneny DDS .... G 302 368-0329
  Newark (G-11498)
Neil G McAneny DDS PC .... F 302 731-4907
  Newark (G-11499)
New Castle Dental Assoc PA .... F 302 328-1513
  New Castle (G-9407)
New Concept Dental .... G 302 778-3822
  Wilmington (G-18613)
Newark Dental Assoc Inc .... E 302 737-5170
  Newark (G-11535)
Norman M Lippman DDS .... G 302 674-1140
  Dover (G-3194)
Norman S Steward DDS PA .... G 302 422-9791
  Milford (G-8031)
OConnor Orthodontics .... G 302 678-1441
  Dover (G-3216)
Oral & Maxillofacial Surgery .... F 302 998-0331
  Wilmington (G-18811)
Oral Mxllfcial Srgery Assoc PA .... F 302 655-6183
  Wilmington (G-18812)
Ortho On Silver Lake .... G 302 653-5636
  Smyrna (G-13843)
Orthodontics On Silver Lake PA .... G 302 672-7776
  Dover (G-3242)
P2 Dental PA .... G 302 422-6924
  Milford (G-8040)
Pace Enterprises LLC .... G 302 529-2500
  Wilmington (G-18857)
Paige King DMD .... G 302 475-3270
  Wilmington (G-18862)
Park Place Dental .... F 302 455-0333
  Newark (G-11629)
Park Place Dental .... G 302 652-3775
  Wilmington (G-18892)
Peninsula Dental LLC .... G 302 297-3750
  Millsboro (G-8421)
Penna Orthodontics .... G 302 998-8783
  Wilmington (G-18953)
Peter F Subach .... G 302 995-1870
  Wilmington (G-18993)

Practice Without Pressure .... G 302 635-7837
  Wilmington (G-19143)
Premier Comprehensive Dental .... G 302 378-3131
  Middletown (G-7463)
Progresive Dental Arts .... E 302 455-9569
  Newark (G-11761)
Progressive Dental Arts .... G 302 234-2222
  Wilmington (G-19218)
Prudent Endodontics .... G 302 475-3803
  Wilmington (G-19239)
R M Quinn DDS .... F 302 674-8000
  Dover (G-3415)
Ralph Tomases DDS PA .... G 302 652-8656
  Wilmington (G-19326)
Raymond L Para DDS .... F 302 234-2728
  Hockessin (G-5357)
Raymond W Petrunich DDS .... G 302 836-3565
  Newark (G-11832)
Rehoboth Beach Dent .... G 302 226-7960
  Rehoboth Beach (G-12920)
Richard E Chodroff DMD .... G 302 995-6979
  Wilmington (G-19467)
Richard J Tananis DDS LLC .... G 302 875-4271
  Laurel (G-5591)
Robert A Penna DMD .... G 302 623-4060
  Newark (G-11896)
Robert P Hart DDS .... G 302 328-1513
  New Castle (G-9539)
Rodriguez Marieve O Dmd PA .... G 302 655-5862
  Wilmington (G-19553)
Russell J Tibbetts DDS PA .... G 302 479-5959
  Wilmington (G-19594)
Rutledge Dental Assoc Inc .... F 302 378-8705
  Middletown (G-7529)
S D Nemcic DDS .... G 302 734-1950
  Dover (G-3498)
Sarah K Smith DDS .... G 302 442-3233
  Newark (G-11946)
Sattar A Syed DMD PA .... G 302 994-3093
  Wilmington (G-19678)
Sedation Center PA .... G 302 678-3384
  Dover (G-3527)
Smile Brite Dental Care LLC .... G 302 838-8306
  Newark (G-12040)
Smile Place .... F 302 514-6200
  Smyrna (G-13890)
Smile Solutions By Emmi Dental .... G 302 999-8113
  Wilmington (G-19884)
Smiles Jolly PA .... G 302 378-3384
  Middletown (G-7579)
Smyrna Dental Center PA .... G 302 223-6194
  Smyrna (G-13894)
Southern Delaware Dental Spec .... G 302 855-9499
  Georgetown (G-4518)
Southern Dental LLC .... F 302 536-7589
  Seaford (G-13409)
Stanley H Goloskov DDS PA .... G 302 475-0600
  Wilmington (G-20019)
Stephen A Niemoeller DMD PA .... G 302 737-3320
  Newark (G-12096)
Steven Alban DDS PA .... G 302 422-9637
  Milford (G-8103)
Suk-Young Carr DDS .... G 302 736-6631
  Dover (G-3620)
Swiatowicz Dental Associates .... F 302 476-8185
  Wilmington (G-20174)
Thomas Dougherty DDS .... G 302 239-2500
  Wilmington (G-20306)
Thomas Family Dentist LLC .... F 302 697-1152
  Dover (G-3679)
Thomas Jenkins DMD .... F 302 426-0526
  Wilmington (G-20310)

Thomas W Mercer DMD .... G 302 678-2942
  Dover (G-3680)
Tigani Family Dentistry PA .... F 302 571-8740
  Wilmington (G-20322)
Todd Rowen DMD .... G 302 994-5887
  Wilmington (G-20341)
Victor J Venturena DDS .... G 302 656-0558
  Wilmington (G-20610)
Victor L Gregory Jr DMD .... G 302 239-1827
  Wilmington (G-20611)
W H Thomas DDS .... G 302 697-1152
  Dover (G-3816)
Wahl Family Dentistry .... F 302 655-1228
  Wilmington (G-20669)
Walter Scott .... G 302 265-2383
  Milford (G-8141)
Weatherhill Dental .... F 302 239-6677
  Wilmington (G-20702)
West Dover Dental Llc .... F 302 734-0330
  Dover (G-3836)
Westown Dental LLC .... G 302 376-3750
  Middletown (G-7718)
Westside Family Healthcare Inc .... E 302 836-2864
  Bear (G-563)
Westside Family Healthcare Inc .... E 302 455-0900
  Newark (G-12364)
Westside Family Healthcare Inc .... E 302 575-1414
  Wilmington (G-20745)
Westside Family Healthcare Inc .... E 302 656-8292
  Wilmington (G-20747)
Westside Family Healthcare Inc .... E 302 656-8292
  Wilmington (G-20746)
William Gonce .... F 302 235-2400
  Rehoboth Beach (G-13018)
William H Ralston DDS Office .... G 336 957-4948
  Newark (G-12375)
Wilmington Dental Assoc PA .... F 302 654-6915
  Wilmington (G-20814)
Wilmington Orthodontic Center .... F 302 658-7354
  Wilmington (G-20827)
Woodmill Dental LLC .... G 302 998-8588
  Wilmington (G-20885)
Wright Bruce B DDS Office RES .... F 302 227-8707
  Rehoboth Beach (G-13023)
Wright Steven B DMD PA .... F 302 645-6671
  Rehoboth Beach (G-13024)
Your Dentistry Today Inc .... G 302 575-0100
  Wilmington (G-20940)
Zachary Chipman DMD PA .... G 302 994-8696
  Wilmington (G-20945)

8031 Offices and clinics of osteopathic physicians

Abby Medical Center .... G 302 999-0003
  Newark (G-9738)
Anthony A Vasile Do .... G 302 764-2072
  Newark (G-9877)
Battaglia Joseph A & Diamond .... G 302 655-8868
  Wilmington (G-14779)
Christiana Care Health Sys Inc .... C 302 659-4401
  Smyrna (G-13676)
Delaware Back Pain and Sports .... F 302 832-3369
  Newark (G-10419)
Delaware Behavioral Health .... G 302 397-8958
  Wilmington (G-15872)
Dr Jillian G Stevens Do .... G 302 762-7332
  Wilmington (G-16167)
Dr Marisa E Conti Do .... E 302 678-4488
  Dover (G-2377)
Dr Timothy G Cook Do .... G 215 823-5800
  Wilmington (G-16170)

80 HEALTH SERVICES

Family Doctors... G 302 368-3600
  Newark *(G-10708)*
Family Medicine Smyrna Clayton........... G 302 653-1050
  Smyrna *(G-13730)*
Family Practice Hockessin PA.................. G 302 239-4500
  Hockessin *(G-5207)*
Forwood Chiropractic Center..................... G 302 652-0411
  Wilmington *(G-16698)*
International Spine Pain............................. G 302 478-7001
  Wilmington *(G-17390)*
Jing Jin MD PHD... F 302 651-5040
  Wilmington *(G-17550)*
Joseph Parise Do.. G 302 735-8855
  Dover *(G-2803)*
Mujib R Obeidy.. G 302 478-5900
  Wilmington *(G-18481)*
Nicholas O Biasotto Co.............................. F 302 998-1235
  Newark *(G-11555)*
Noel Anupol... F 302 424-6511
  Milford *(G-8030)*
Paul Imber Do... G 302 478-5647
  Wilmington *(G-18919)*
Ralph Burdick Do.. G 302 834-3600
  Delaware City *(G-1556)*
Robert S Callahan MD PA........................ F 302 731-0942
  Newark *(G-11899)*
Sabini Paul MD Facs.................................. F 302 998-8007
  Newark *(G-11931)*
Southern Delaware Med Group................ G 302 424-3900
  Dover *(G-3589)*
Stephen J Duggan Do................................ F 302 449-3030
  Middletown *(G-7599)*
Trinity Medical Center PA......................... G 302 846-0618
  Delmar *(G-1646)*
Vincent Lobo Dr PA.................................... G 302 398-8163
  Harrington *(G-4845)*

8041 Offices and clinics of chiropractors

4th Street Chiro Pain Mgmt...................... G 302 656-5009
  Wilmington *(G-14139)*
Absolute Health LLC.................................. G 302 535-8236
  Camden *(G-786)*
American Chiropractic Center.................. G 302 450-3153
  Dover *(G-1784)*
American Chiropractic Center.................. G 302 407-3046
  Wilmington *(G-14427)*
Anthony Giantinoto DC.............................. G 302 294-1832
  Newark *(G-9878)*
Apex Chiropractic Services...................... G 302 598-9404
  Middletown *(G-6867)*
Athena Chiropractic................................... G 302 543-4227
  Wilmington *(G-14618)*
Atlantic Chiropractic Assoc..................... E 302 422-3100
  Milford *(G-7775)*
Atlantic Chiropractic Associat................. F 302 422-3100
  Milford *(G-7776)*
Back In Action Chiropractic..................... G 302 322-3304
  New Castle *(G-8845)*
Be Truly Well LLC...................................... F 302 525-4343
  Newark *(G-10002)*
Bear Chiropractic Center DC................... G 302 836-8361
  Bear *(G-61)*
Better Life Chiropractic............................ G 302 535-9204
  Dover *(G-1924)*
Brandywine Total Health Care................. G 302 478-3028
  Wilmington *(G-15086)*
C-Schell Spine Speclst-C Schel............... G 302 736-1223
  Dover *(G-2008)*
Camp Chiropractic Inc.............................. G 302 378-2899
  Middletown *(G-6954)*
Cape Spine & Disc.................................... F 302 644-2473
  Lewes *(G-5796)*

Chiro Med Chiropractic LLC................... F 302 256-0363
  Wilmington *(G-15386)*
Chiropractic Colonial................................ G 302 328-1444
  New Castle *(G-8935)*
Chirostaff LLC.. G 302 332-3312
  Wilmington *(G-15388)*
Claymont Chiropractic Office................... G 302 798-1587
  Claymont *(G-1090)*
Complete Accident Relief......................... G 302 375-5019
  Middletown *(G-7008)*
Comprehensive Accident Injury............... G 302 563-7442
  Bear *(G-115)*
Comprehensive Chiropractic.................... G 302 346-4744
  Dover *(G-2125)*
Concord Med Spine & Pain Ctr............... F 302 652-1107
  Wilmington *(G-15583)*
Cowan Chiropractic Rehab PA................ G 302 559-5261
  Wilmington *(G-15669)*
DC Mac... F 302 660-3350
  Wilmington *(G-15825)*
Delaware Health Management................. D 302 454-1200
  Newark *(G-10450)*
Delaware Injury Associates PA................ F 302 332-1932
  Wilmington *(G-15931)*
Delaware Injury Care................................. G 302 678-8866
  Dover *(G-2246)*
Delaware Injury Care................................. G 914 960-1145
  Wilmington *(G-15932)*
Delmarva Chiropractic Wel...................... G 302 682-7975
  Harrington *(G-4759)*
Delware Injury Care LLC.......................... G 302 235-1111
  Wilmington *(G-16006)*
Diamond Chiropractic................................ F 302 300-4242
  Wilmington *(G-16050)*
Diamond Chiropractic Inc........................ F 302 892-9355
  Newark *(G-10522)*
Diamond State Chiropractic..................... G 302 737-6037
  Newark *(G-10524)*
Douglas R Briggs....................................... G 302 645-6681
  Rehoboth Beach *(G-12733)*
Dover Chiropractic & Rehabilit................ G 302 883-3251
  Dover *(G-2335)*
Dover Family Chiropractic........................ G 302 531-1900
  Camden *(G-822)*
Dover Family Chiropractic........................ G 302 698-1515
  Dover *(G-2342)*
Dr Casey Mae Fouse DC........................... G 302 472-4878
  Wilmington *(G-16163)*
Dr David Defries Chiropractor................. G 610 494-0412
  Claymont *(G-1121)*
Dr Douglas Briggs..................................... G 302 654-4001
  Wilmington *(G-16164)*
Family Chiropractic Office PA.................. G 302 993-9113
  Wilmington *(G-16534)*
Feeney Chiropractic Care Ctr PA............ G 302 328-0200
  Bear *(G-223)*
First Choice Health Care Inc................... G 302 836-6150
  Bear *(G-224)*
First State Physicians Inc....................... G 302 836-6150
  Bear *(G-229)*
Forwood Chiropractic Center................... G 302 652-0411
  Wilmington *(G-16698)*
Geo B Schreppler III.................................. G 302 678-5959
  Dover *(G-2571)*
Healthsource of Dover South................... G 302 744-8526
  Dover *(G-2665)*
Healthsource of Wilmington..................... G 302 319-4623
  Wilmington *(G-17099)*
Himani J Patel DC...................................... G 302 635-7421
  Wilmington *(G-17150)*
Hockessin Chrpractic Centre PA............. G 302 239-8550
  Hockessin *(G-5241)*

Ken Decker DC... G 302 389-8915
  Smyrna *(G-13787)*
Kenneth De Grout DC................................ G 302 475-5600
  Wilmington *(G-17687)*
Kevin J Murray DC..................................... G 302 453-4043
  Newark *(G-11162)*
Kirkwood Pain & Injury Chiropr.............. G 302 422-2329
  Milford *(G-7966)*
L Squared Healthcare LLC....................... G 302 289-5425
  Newark *(G-11208)*
Lewes Chiropractic Center....................... G 302 645-9171
  Lewes *(G-6192)*
Lodes Chiropractic Center PA................. G 302 477-1565
  Wilmington *(G-17972)*
M C Chiropractic Clinic Inc..................... G 302 715-5035
  Laurel *(G-5558)*
Mark Mathew Mauragas Dc...................... G 302 750-8084
  Wilmington *(G-18139)*
Market St Chrprctic Rhblttion................. G 302 652-6000
  Wilmington *(G-18145)*
Matthew J McIlrath DC............................. G 302 798-7033
  Wilmington *(G-18197)*
Mid-Town Massage LLC........................... F 302 256-0363
  Wilmington *(G-18340)*
Middletown Chiropractic & Reha............ G 302 376-5830
  Middletown *(G-7347)*
Mot Family Chiro-Wilmington.................. G 302 593-0031
  Wilmington *(G-18462)*
Mot Family Chiropractic -........................ G 302 378-9191
  Middletown *(G-7384)*
New Life Spinal Centers........................... G 302 883-2504
  Dover *(G-3181)*
North American Spine and Pain.............. G 302 482-3637
  Wilmington *(G-18678)*
Nowcare LLC.. G 302 777-5551
  Wilmington *(G-18703)*
Peninsula Chiropractic Center................. G 302 629-4344
  Seaford *(G-13335)*
Physicians Plus Spine & Rehab.............. G 302 261-6221
  Bear *(G-424)*
Premier Chiropractic................................. G 302 384-7145
  Wilmington *(G-19168)*
Pro Rehab and Chiropractic.................... G 302 268-6129
  Wilmington *(G-19204)*
Pro Rehab Chiropractic............................ G 302 200-9102
  Lewes *(G-6392)*
Pro Rehab Chiropractors......................... G 302 652-2225
  Wilmington *(G-19205)*
Pro Rhab Chrprctic Rhblitation............... G 302 332-3312
  Wilmington *(G-19206)*
Pure Wellness LLC.................................... G 302 449-0149
  Middletown *(G-7484)*
Pure Wellness LLC.................................... G 302 543-5679
  Wilmington *(G-19263)*
Pure Wellness LLC.................................... F 302 365-5470
  Newark *(G-11773)*
Renu Chrprctic Wllness Injury................ F 302 368-0124
  Newark *(G-11856)*
Richard M Gold DC.................................... G 302 998-1424
  Wilmington *(G-19472)*
Ross Get Healthy Chiropractic................ G 302 407-5571
  Wilmington *(G-19572)*
Schreppler Chropractic Offs PA.............. G 302 653-5525
  Smyrna *(G-13880)*
Sheehan Chiropractic Ltd........................ G 302 545-7441
  Wilmington *(G-19787)*
Sk Chiropractic LLC................................. E 302 482-3410
  Wilmington *(G-19850)*
Stephen Jankovic Chiropractor............... G 302 384-8540
  Wilmington *(G-20060)*
Sussex Pain Relief Center LLC............... E 302 519-0100
  Georgetown *(G-4540)*

80 HEALTH SERVICES

Synergy Integrated Medical Ctr............ F 302 777-0778
  Wilmington (G-20187)
T Shane Palmer DC............................. G 302 328-2656
  New Castle (G-9613)
Tarak N Patel DC................................. G 856 904-3061
  Wilmington (G-20222)
Todd E Watson DC............................... G 615 500-6825
  Bear (G-536)
Walsh Chiropractic Center.................... G 302 422-0622
  Milford (G-8140)
Ward Chiropractic................................ G 302 225-9000
  Wilmington (G-20678)
Wellness Health Inc............................. G 302 424-4100
  Milford (G-8147)

8042 Offices and clinics of optometrists

Amy M Farrall OD LLC......................... G 302 737-5777
  Newark (G-9856)
Betts and Biddle Eye Care PA.............. F 302 697-2151
  Seaford (G-13087)
Delaware Eye Care Center................... G 302 674-1121
  Dover (G-2237)
Deleware Eye Clinics........................... G 302 684-2020
  Milton (G-8600)
Don D Balckburn Od............................ G 302 737-5777
  Newark (G-10548)
Douglas J Lavenburg MD PA................ F 302 993-0722
  Newark (G-10556)
Epstein Kplan OpthImlogist LLP........... G 302 322-4444
  New Castle (G-9099)
Eye Worx LLC...................................... F 302 934-9679
  Millsboro (G-8284)
Halpern Eye Associates Inc................. G 302 838-0800
  Bear (G-263)
Halpern Eye Associates Inc................. G 302 734-5861
  Middletown (G-7190)
Halpern Eye Associates Inc................. G 302 422-2020
  Milford (G-7917)
Halpern Eye Associates Inc................. G 302 537-0234
  Millville (G-8532)
Halpern Eye Associates Inc................. G 302 653-3400
  Smyrna (G-13755)
Halpern Eye Associates Inc................. E 302 734-5861
  Dover (G-2645)
Halpern Eye Associates-Midway........... G 302 993-7861
  Wilmington (G-17041)
Halpern Eye Care................................. G 302 346-2020
  Dover (G-2646)
Halpern Eye Care................................. G 302 678-1700
  Milford (G-7918)
Howard B Stromwasser....................... G 302 368-4424
  Newark (G-10979)
Hubert Headen.................................... G 347 952-9250
  Dover (G-2701)
In Vision Eye Care............................... G 302 655-1952
  Wilmington (G-17293)
In Vision Eye Care Inc......................... G 302 235-7031
  Hockessin (G-5248)
John M Otto Od.................................... G 302 623-0170
  Newark (G-11116)
Joseph G Goldberg Od......................... G 302 999-1286
  Wilmington (G-17581)
Kelli Armstrong MD.............................. G 203 783-9632
  Lewes (G-6165)
Kneisley Eye Care PA......................... G 302 224-3000
  Newark (G-11196)
Laura Castillo...................................... G 302 734-5861
  Dover (G-2908)
Lmg Associates In Eye Care................ G 302 993-0931
  Wilmington (G-17961)
Locchio Eyecare LLC........................... G 302 644-1039
  Millville (G-8537)

My Eye Dr Optometrists LLC................ G 302 838-0800
  Bear (G-383)
My Eye Dr Optometrists LLC................ G 302 346-4992
  Dover (G-3135)
My Eye Dr Optometrists LLC................ G 302 734-5861
  Dover (G-3136)
My Eye Dr Optometrists LLC................ G 302 422-2020
  Milford (G-8023)
My Eye Dr Optometrists LLC................ G 302 629-9197
  Seaford (G-13299)
My Eye Dr Optometrists LLC................ G 302 653-3400
  Smyrna (G-13831)
My Eye Dr Optometrists LLC................ G 302 999-7171
  Wilmington (G-18505)
Nice Vision LLC................................... G 267 259-8705
  Wilmington (G-18641)
Penny Hill Eye Center.......................... G 302 764-4613
  Wilmington (G-18957)
Simon Eye Associates.......................... G 302 239-1933
  Wilmington (G-19832)
Simon Eye Associates PA.................... F 302 834-4305
  Bear (G-493)
Simon Eye Associates PA.................... G 302 655-8180
  Wilmington (G-19833)
Simon Eye Associates PA.................... F 302 239-1389
  Wilmington (G-19834)
Stella C Ohanenye Od LLC.................. G 302 388-7288
  Middletown (G-7598)
Susan J Betts Od................................. G 302 629-6691
  Seaford (G-13418)
Sussex Eye Center PA......................... G 302 856-2020
  Georgetown (G-4537)
Talitha Dltalia Od................................. G 302 998-1395
  Wilmington (G-20213)
Vision To Learn................................... F 302 220-4820
  Wilmington (G-20640)
Visionquest Eye Care Center................ E 302 678-3545
  Dover (G-3803)
Wilmington Family Eye Care................ F 302 999-1286
  Wilmington (G-20815)

8043 Offices and clinics of podiatrists

Advanced Foot & Ankle Center............. G 302 355-0056
  Newark (G-9775)
Ankle and Foot Surgical Assoc............. G 302 425-5720
  Wilmington (G-14486)
Anthony M Caristo DPM....................... G 302 834-3575
  Newark (G-9880)
Bradleylemondpm Lemon.................... G 302 934-7100
  Millsboro (G-8204)
Brandywine Foot Care......................... G 302 478-8099
  Wilmington (G-15059)
Central Del Fmly Foot Care.................. G 302 678-3338
  Dover (G-2048)
Cody A Bowers DPM............................ G 302 998-0178
  Wilmington (G-15516)
Delaware Foot & Ankle Assoc.............. G 302 834-3575
  Newark (G-10445)
Excellent Choice LLC........................... G 818 322-6376
  Wilmington (G-16499)
First State Podiatry LLC...................... G 302 678-4612
  Dover (G-2509)
First State Podiatry LLC...................... G 302 678-4612
  Wilmington (G-16632)
Foot & Ankle Ctr of Delaware............... G 302 945-1221
  Millsboro (G-8294)
Foot and Ankle Associates LLC........... F 302 652-5767
  Wilmington (G-16685)
▲ Foot Care Group Inc......................... E 302 998-0178
  Wilmington (G-16686)
Garcia Podiatry Group......................... G 302 994-5956
  Wilmington (G-16802)

Gina M Freeman DPM......................... G 302 765-2505
  Wilmington (G-16865)
James B Salva MD.............................. G 302 762-2283
  Wilmington (G-17480)
James F Palmer.................................. G 302 629-6162
  Seaford (G-13229)
Jason Bell Dr....................................... G 302 993-0722
  Newark (G-11099)
Jonathan P Contompasis DPM............. G 302 983-8366
  Wilmington (G-17572)
Joseph V Bakanas DPM....................... G 302 898-3873
  Wilmington (G-17586)
Linda Lawton DPM............................... G 302 659-0500
  Smyrna (G-13803)
Linda Lawton DPM............................... G 302 659-0500
  Smyrna (G-13804)
Lisa Ryan Hobbs DPM......................... G 302 629-3000
  Seaford (G-13262)
Rakesh N Patel DPM........................... G 302 629-4569
  Seaford (G-13364)
Raymond V Feehery Jr DPM................ G 302 999-8511
  Newark (G-11831)
Southern Delaware Foot...................... F 302 404-5915
  Seaford (G-13408)
Southern Delaware Foot & Ankle......... G 302 629-3000
  Millsboro (G-8465)
Sussex Podiatry Group........................ G 302 645-8555
  Lewes (G-6531)
Tri State Foot Ankle Cent.................... F 302 239-1625
  Hockessin (G-5410)

8049 Offices of health practitioner

Aaron Alfano...................................... G 302 995-9600
  Wilmington (G-14186)
Abraxas Massage and Bodywork......... G 910 992-0350
  Millsboro (G-8159)
Active Life Acupuncture...................... G 302 827-2691
  Lewes (G-5658)
Adirondack Bhvral Hlthcare LLC......... G 302 832-1282
  Christiana (G-991)
Advance Forward LLC......................... G 302 762-1615
  Wilmington (G-14266)
Advance Mblity Physcl Thrapy L.......... G 443 359-0132
  Seaford (G-13050)
Advance Physical Therapy LLC............ G 302 407-3592
  Wilmington (G-14269)
Advanced Healing Inc.......................... G 302 363-5839
  Milford (G-7761)
Affiliated Psychological Svc................. G 302 507-3039
  Newark (G-9793)
Albert T Wood III................................. F 302 463-5386
  Middletown (G-6847)
Alfred I Dupont Hospital....................... D 302 651-4000
  Wilmington (G-14355)
Allison R Randall................................. G 302 893-3817
  Wilmington (G-14384)
Amanda Coppinger.............................. G 301 938-2346
  Ocean View (G-12459)
Amber Dragon Acupuncture................. G 206 227-0641
  Lewes (G-5682)
Amy Donovan...................................... G 302 245-8957
  Lewes (G-5689)
Amy Linzey... G 302 541-4447
  Ocean View (G-12461)
Andrea Meyer..................................... G 302 745-8823
  Georgetown (G-4211)
Andrew Hayden.................................. G 302 562-9236
  Middletown (G-6863)
Ann M Campagna................................ G 302 395-8950
  New Castle (G-8811)
April L Sarver..................................... G 302 559-0787
  Newark (G-9894)

SIC SECTION
80 HEALTH SERVICES

Aquacare Physical.................................. G 302 200-9159
  Lewes *(G-5695)*

Ariel C Rubin... G 443 854-9901
  Rehoboth Beach *(G-12610)*

Ashely B Morrison.................................. G 302 526-1959
  Dover *(G-1830)*

Ashley Lynn Kontra................................. G 302 543-5454
  Wilmington *(G-14586)*

Ashley N Kaczorowski............................. G 302 430-9610
  Smyrna *(G-13649)*

Assoctes In Hlth Psychlogy LLC............. F 302 428-0205
  Wilmington *(G-14595)*

Aston Home Health................................. F 302 421-3686
  Wilmington *(G-14604)*

ATI Holdings LLC................................... G 302 836-5670
  Bear *(G-52)*

ATI Holdings LLC................................... F 302 392-3400
  Bear *(G-53)*

ATI Holdings LLC................................... F 302 677-0100
  Dover *(G-1845)*

ATI Holdings LLC................................... G 302 747-5280
  Dover *(G-1846)*

ATI Holdings LLC................................... G 302 253-8296
  Georgetown *(G-4214)*

ATI Holdings LLC................................... G 302 786-3008
  Harrington *(G-4737)*

ATI Holdings LLC................................... F 302 827-5123
  Lewes *(G-5710)*

ATI Holdings LLC................................... G 302 285-0700
  Middletown *(G-6878)*

ATI Holdings LLC................................... G 302 696-1924
  Middletown *(G-6879)*

ATI Holdings LLC................................... G 302 422-6670
  Milford *(G-7774)*

ATI Holdings LLC................................... F 302 297-0700
  Millsboro *(G-8176)*

ATI Holdings LLC................................... G 302 654-1700
  New Castle *(G-8830)*

ATI Holdings LLC................................... G 302 838-2165
  Newark *(G-9933)*

ATI Holdings LLC................................... F 302 226-2230
  Rehoboth Beach *(G-12613)*

ATI Holdings LLC................................... G 302 536-5562
  Seaford *(G-13070)*

ATI Holdings LLC................................... G 302 524-5951
  Selbyville *(G-13465)*

ATI Holdings LLC................................... G 302 659-3102
  Smyrna *(G-13653)*

ATI Holdings LLC................................... G 302 993-1450
  Wilmington *(G-14619)*

ATI Holdings LLC................................... G 302 994-1200
  Wilmington *(G-14620)*

ATI Holdings LLC................................... G 302 475-7500
  Wilmington *(G-14621)*

ATI Holdings LLC................................... G 302 351-0302
  Wilmington *(G-14622)*

ATI Holdings LLC................................... F 302 656-2521
  Wilmington *(G-14623)*

ATI Holdings LLC................................... F 302 658-7800
  Wilmington *(G-14624)*

ATI Physical Therapy.............................. G 302 281-3072
  Wilmington *(G-14625)*

Atlantic Physcl Thrapy Rhbltti................. C 302 934-0304
  Millsboro *(G-8178)*

Aurora Reiki LLC..................................... G 443 553-3233
  Wilmington *(G-14646)*

Awareness & Therapeutic Attach.......... G 302 655-6555
  Wilmington *(G-14676)*

Back 2 Healthy Nutrition LLC................. G 302 857-9818
  New Castle *(G-8844)*

Back Clinic Inc.. F 302 995-2100
  Wilmington *(G-14712)*

Bancroft Behavioral Health.................... G 302 273-2319
  Wilmington *(G-14734)*

Barbara Kwakye-Safo.............................. G 302 559-1955
  Bear *(G-56)*

Barclay & Associates PC....................... G 515 292-3023
  Wilmington *(G-14758)*

Bariatric Beautiful Barbii LLC................. F 302 279-6938
  Clayton *(G-1353)*

Bayada Home Health Care Inc.............. D 302 424-8200
  Milford *(G-7784)*

Be Well Massage and Skin Care............ G 302 883-3066
  Dover *(G-1895)*

Belcher-Timme Dr Zoe........................... G 215 266-5859
  Newark *(G-10012)*

Blue Hen Physical Therapy Inc.............. E 302 453-1588
  Newark *(G-10060)*

Blue Heron Acupuncture & Herbs......... G 302 344-7333
  Lewes *(G-5770)*

Bounce Back Physical Therapy............. G 484 582-0660
  Wilmington *(G-15014)*

Brie D Bolger.. G 302 668-8268
  Bear *(G-82)*

Bryan Longhenry Man............................. G 302 369-3369
  Newark *(G-10096)*

CAM Physcal Thrapy Wllness Svc........ G 301 853-0093
  Newark *(G-10122)*

Candice Ryder.. G 954 296-5709
  Lewes *(G-5789)*

Careportmd LLC.................................... G 302 283-9001
  Newark *(G-10143)*

Catherine Kotalis................................... G 302 526-1470
  Dover *(G-2037)*

Cathy Brown Lbw Nctmb........................ G 302 475-1477
  Wilmington *(G-15278)*

CB Therapy Services Inc....................... G 302 381-7079
  Georgetown *(G-4246)*

Center For Conscious Healing............... G 302 376-6144
  Middletown *(G-6969)*

Central Delaware Speech....................... F 302 538-5696
  Dover *(G-2051)*

Cherry Psychological Services............. G 302 528-2235
  Newark *(G-10197)*

Choi Eunhwa.. G 302 559-3771
  Wilmington *(G-15390)*

Christiana Care Hlth Svcs Inc................ F 302 477-3300
  Wilmington *(G-15407)*

Christiana Phys Therpy & Spine........... G 302 731-2660
  Wilmington *(G-15412)*

Christina M Hanna................................. G 302 236-7280
  Selbyville *(G-13499)*

Christina Newton................................... G 302 454-2400
  Bear *(G-103)*

Christine Dipaolo................................... G 302 651-4000
  Wilmington *(G-15417)*

Christine W Maynard MD........................ G 302 995-7073
  Wilmington *(G-15418)*

Christopher A Bowens MD..................... G 302 834-3700
  Newark *(G-10236)*

Christopher Burke.................................. G 410 603-7450
  Millsboro *(G-8224)*

Christopher McGlinn PHD...................... G 302 478-1450
  Wilmington *(G-15424)*

Cindy Elko Psyd LLC.............................. G 302 229-2110
  Newark *(G-10243)*

Cindy L Tucker PHD............................... G 302 743-5775
  Wilmington *(G-15438)*

Claire Kubizne Pt................................... G 302 521-3305
  Newark *(G-10249)*

Claudio M Morel..................................... G 917 584-5236
  Millsboro *(G-8229)*

Clifford O Smith..................................... G 302 995-9600
  Wilmington *(G-15482)*

Coastal Care Physcl Thrapy Inc............ F 480 236-3863
  Selbyville *(G-13501)*

Cody H Hafner.. G 302 234-1030
  Hockessin *(G-5165)*

Collabrtive Effort To Rnfrce T................ D 302 731-0301
  Smyrna *(G-13685)*

Collabrtive Effort To Rnfrce T................ D 302 731-0301
  New Castle *(G-8956)*

Complete Family Care Inc..................... F 302 232-5002
  Wilmington *(G-15572)*

Connectons Cmnty Spport Prgram....... D 302 454-7520
  Newark *(G-10306)*

Connectons Cmnty Spport Prgram....... D 302 984-2302
  Claymont *(G-1099)*

Core Physical Therapy........................... F 302 423-0236
  Dover *(G-2137)*

Corey Kennedy....................................... G 201 233-8054
  Lewes *(G-5860)*

Creekview Psychological...................... G 302 731-3130
  Newark *(G-10353)*

Cynthia R Drew NP................................. G 302 933-0111
  Millsboro *(G-8249)*

Cynthia S Devine.................................... G 302 678-8447
  Dover *(G-2177)*

D Steven Caldwell.................................. G 302 245-9713
  Lewes *(G-5877)*

Darlene R N Sheeran.............................. G 845 297-9704
  Lewes *(G-5881)*

Deborra M Trres Msn Pmhnp Ltd.......... G 609 500-4018
  Millsboro *(G-8258)*

Debra Rose... G 302 519-3029
  Milton *(G-8596)*

Delaware Arthritis................................... G 302 644-2633
  Lewes *(G-5888)*

Delaware Behavioral Health.................. G 302 397-8958
  Wilmington *(G-15872)*

Delaware Curative.................................. G 302 836-5670
  Bear *(G-144)*

Delaware Curative Workshop................ D 302 656-2521
  Wilmington *(G-15899)*

Delaware Injury Care LLC...................... G 302 628-8008
  Seaford *(G-13152)*

Delaware Orthopedic and Sports.......... E 302 653-8389
  Smyrna *(G-13703)*

Delaware Psychological Svcs LLC....... G 302 703-6332
  Lewes *(G-5900)*

Delaware Spine Rehabilitation.............. G 302 273-0064
  Bear *(G-158)*

Delaware Vein Center............................. G 302 258-8853
  Georgetown *(G-4287)*

Delawrschoolofmassage Bodywork..... G 302 407-5986
  Wilmington *(G-15986)*

Deleware Acupuncture........................... G 302 273-2807
  Newark *(G-10497)*

Denise A Cunha PHD.............................. G 302 652-7733
  Wilmington *(G-16008)*

Department Psychlgcal Brain SC.......... G 302 831-4591
  Newark *(G-10515)*

Derek Lawson.. G 302 588-3618
  Bear *(G-164)*

Diane Newman....................................... G 302 994-6838
  Wilmington *(G-16061)*

Dina R Anderson.................................... F 302 623-4144
  Newark *(G-10533)*

Dona E Ortelli Slp.................................. G 302 734-2606
  Leipsic *(G-5631)*

Donald Lambert III................................. G 302 421-1081
  Wilmington *(G-16136)*

Donna Marie Kemp................................ G 302 645-7088
  Lewes *(G-5928)*

Dorilyn English PHD.............................. G 302 655-6506
  Wilmington *(G-16145)*

Employee Codes: A=Over 500 employees, B=251-500
C=101-250, D=51-100, E=20-50, F=10-19, G=1-9

2024 Harris Directory of
Delaware Businesses

80 HEALTH SERVICES

Name	Location	Phone
Dorilyn English PHD	Wilmington (G-16146)	G 302 652-7733
Dr Alvin L Turner	Wilmington (G-16161)	G 302 777-3202
Dr Michele Turley	Newark (G-10565)	G 302 266-4043
Dynamic Physical Therapy	Wilmington (G-16229)	F 302 668-1768
Dynamic Therapy Services LLC	Newark (G-10585)	G 302 292-3454
Eastern Health Care Ctr	Wilmington (G-16257)	G 302 543-4998
Easy Breezy Beauty	Lewes (G-5946)	G 302 562-6751
Elizabeth L Thomas-Bauer	Wilmington (G-16369)	G 302 798-0666
Elizabeth Sutton Mace Psyd	Wilmington (G-16370)	G 302 293-4920
Ellingsen & Associates	Newark (G-10631)	G 302 650-6437
Energy Healing Pathways LLC	Wilmington (G-16417)	G 302 478-6383
Eric Barsky	Newark (G-10663)	G 856 495-6988
Eric Kafka Psychologist	Lewes (G-5969)	G 302 644-8891
Erin Bendler	Rehoboth Beach (G-12745)	G 201 704-6252
Evelyn M Falkowski	New Castle (G-9103)	G 302 328-3125
Excel Through Action	Lewes (G-5980)	G 302 569-9564
Family Care Associates	Newark (G-10705)	G 302 454-8880
First State Rehab Home LLC	Wilmington (G-16633)	G 302 304-9729
Flora F Petillo	Wilmington (G-16664)	G 302 658-8191
Focus Behavioral Health	Lewes (G-6008)	G 302 827-4206
Forensic Associates Del LLC	Wilmington (G-16690)	G 302 415-4944
Frank Austin	Bear (G-235)	G 302 832-9167
Frederick Dimeo	Dover (G-2535)	G 302 674-3970
Furtado Kim ND	Rehoboth Beach (G-12763)	G 302 945-2107
Gabrielle Freels	Dover (G-2552)	G 213 808-4907
Gary Gerace	Wilmington (G-16808)	G 302 320-2100
Genesis Psychological Services	Hockessin (G-5220)	G 302 513-7156
Gover Counseling Psychology	Rehoboth Beach (G-12773)	G 302 226-3661
Grafton Reeves MD	Wilmington (G-16944)	G 302 651-5965
H+trace Inc	Middletown (G-7188)	G 954 381-1400
Hamlin Mona Liza BSN Rn Ibclc	Newark (G-10922)	G 302 235-8277
Hands Healing Massage Day Spa	New Castle (G-9194)	G 302 689-3183
Hartnett Physical Therapy	Wilmington (G-17069)	G 302 428-9420
Healing Adults & Adolescents	Bear (G-266)	F 302 836-4000
Healing Arts LLC	New Castle (G-9203)	G 302 530-9152
Healing Garden At Fndg Avalon	Camden (G-846)	G 302 535-7883
Healing Intentions LLC	Hockessin (G-5234)	G 302 690-3270
Healing Touch Massage	Claymont (G-1176)	G 302 791-0235
Helen Delvecchio Lpn	Millville (G-8534)	G 914 472-3837
Helen Maloney	Houston (G-5443)	G 302 422-5359
Hillside Center	Wilmington (G-17147)	E 302 652-1181
Hines Shekelia	Wilmington (G-17151)	G 302 575-8255
Hockessin Chrpractic Centre PA	Hockessin (G-5241)	G 302 239-8550
Holly Ann Semanchik PA	Milton (G-8638)	G 908 672-1163
Howell Juanquetta	Ellendale (G-3921)	G 302 682-1602
Hummingbird Hill Psychological	Lewes (G-6108)	G 302 864-8818
Igleisias Aquiles	Newark (G-10998)	G 302 831-7100
Il Alfred Collins	Seaford (G-13220)	G 302 542-7010
Imperial Nutrition	Milford (G-7940)	G 302 752-8220
Ingrid S Jackoway	Wilmington (G-17338)	G 302 478-3702
Inspirit Studios	Magnolia (G-6752)	G 302 222-4804
Integrtive Psychlogy Group LLC	Newark (G-11039)	F 302 307-3702
Irene Fisher PHD	Newark (G-11056)	F 302 733-0980
Jaimie Stafford	Dover (G-2766)	G 302 336-8307
Jasmine L Heath Ms	Wilmington (G-17498)	G 215 391-3553
Jean L Binkley	Wilmington (G-17511)	G 302 598-5582
Jennifer F Divita	Dover (G-2781)	F 302 734-8000
Jennifer L Kopazna	Wilmington (G-17526)	G 215 868-1466
Jennifer M Dragone	Wilmington (G-17527)	G 302 353-7133
Jennifer R Rodgers	Ocean View (G-12529)	G 302 542-7095
Jessica A Whisler Mrs	Wilmington (G-17533)	G 302 438-3720
Jessica L Desrosiers	Bear (G-304)	G 443 617-5152
Jill Riley	Lewes (G-6139)	G 802 272-7310
Jin Pen Feet Massage	Delmar (G-1606)	G 302 228-2846
John Johnson Dr	Wilmington (G-17566)	G 302 999-7104
John T Pearson	Camden Wyoming (G-958)	G 302 653-2322
Julia C Gorman	Dover (G-2816)	F 302 734-8000
Julia Tegarden Jorda	Newark (G-11135)	G 302 731-1901
Julie A Carson PA	Seaford (G-13240)	G 302 629-3099
Julie H Rementer	Seaford (G-13241)	G 302 628-4416
Just Breathe Home Therapy	Lewes (G-6156)	G 919 270-3347
Justin Oakley	Dagsboro (G-1471)	G 302 752-8277
Kalin Eye Assoc	Newark (G-11140)	G 302 292-2020
Karen Berrie	Hockessin (G-5264)	G 201 906-9789
Karen Healing Hands	Dagsboro (G-1472)	G 302 841-8933
Katherine T Samworth	Wilmington (G-17663)	G 302 478-7485
Kathi Jenks	Rehoboth Beach (G-12815)	G 302 226-7791
Kathleen Kenney	Seaford (G-13244)	G 302 541-5700
Kathleen McGuiness	Rehoboth Beach (G-12816)	G 302 245-7355
Kathryn M Gehret	Lewes (G-6162)	G 610 420-7233
Katie Butera	Wilmington (G-17666)	G 815 979-5129
Kee Jr Rayvann	Wilmington (G-17673)	G 267 975-2199
Keith Perry	Ellendale (G-3925)	G 302 841-1514
Kenneth D Morris	Middletown (G-7265)	G 415 760-0791
Kevin M Bielanski	Ocean View (G-12533)	G 908 752-8210
Kimberly N Ginsberg Dr	Wilmington (G-17720)	G 215 760-0751
Krista J Anderson Mrs	New Castle (G-9290)	G 239 247-1170
Lakeside Physcl Thrapy Metodio	Milford (G-7970)	G 302 422-2518
Lakeside Physical Therapy LLC	Laurel (G-5545)	F 302 280-6920
Lardear Anne Otr/L	Wilmington (G-17808)	G 302 478-7022
Laura D Halley MS CCC-Slp	Newark (G-11226)	G 302 738-0692
Leslie Connor	Wilmington (G-17884)	G 302 479-5568
Limestone Nutrition	Wilmington (G-17916)	G 302 397-8705
Linda Duffy	Wilmington (G-17920)	G 302 651-4000
Linda L Silvis	Wilmington (G-17921)	G 302 559-5577
Lisa A Deleonardo	Hockessin (G-5282)	G 302 234-3443
Lisa Burroughs	Newark (G-11267)	G 302 454-8010
Lisa Harkins	Milford (G-7975)	G 302 388-2856
Lisa Prisco Pt	Dover (G-2955)	G 302 698-4256
Lisa R Shannon Lmt	Middletown (G-7307)	G 302 468-9416
Loretta A Higgins	Lewes (G-6220)	F 302 645-2666
Lori Ryan Skye	Lewes (G-6221)	G 302 588-2588
Louise M Flynn	Wilmington (G-18009)	F 302 651-4000
Lucila Carmichael Rn	Historic New Castle (G-5020)	G 302 324-8901
Marc Richman PHD	Newark (G-11328)	G 302 834-3039
Margaret Wright-Stasi	Millsboro (G-8364)	G 302 745-1509
Marianna J McSweeney Pt	Wilmington (G-18127)	G 302 234-1803
Marie E Dye	Camden (G-871)	G 302 698-4280

80 HEALTH SERVICES

Mark Sanford .... G 302 593-9773
  Newark *(G-11337)*
Mary E Mahoney .... G 302 757-9656
  Clayton *(G-1384)*
Mary Huff .... G 302 650-2460
  Wilmington *(G-18179)*
Maryruth L Nich .... G 302 623-1929
  Newark *(G-11347)*
Matrix Rehabilitation Delaware .... G 302 424-1714
  Milford *(G-7989)*
Matthew & Michele Denn .... G 302 235-0175
  Newark *(G-11354)*
Medical Massage Delaware LLC .... G 888 757-1951
  Newark *(G-11375)*
Megan Couch .... G 302 981-0687
  Newark *(G-11380)*
Melissa A Wolf .... G 716 465-7093
  Lewes *(G-6261)*
Menton Elizabeth A Crna PC .... G 443 694-6769
  Millsboro *(G-8376)*
Mercatante Beatrice An .... G 302 995-7073
  Wilmington *(G-18275)*
Michelle M Manasseri Psyd LLC .... G 302 478-1578
  Newark *(G-11403)*
Michelle Menzer .... G 302 366-7456
  Newark *(G-11404)*
Mid-Atlantic Behavioral Health .... G 302 224-1400
  Newark *(G-11410)*
Midwinter Co LLC .... G 302 463-9578
  Wilmington *(G-18346)*
Mind & Matter .... G 302 345-0575
  Claymont *(G-1237)*
Mind and Body Consortium LLC .... D 302 674-2380
  Dover *(G-3097)*
Mind Mechanix LLC .... G 302 313-1288
  Magnolia *(G-6767)*
Miranda OBrien .... G 302 436-6411
  Selbyville *(G-13577)*
Mitchell Jamison .... G 302 359-4163
  Seaford *(G-13287)*
Monica Khan .... G 302 652-1994
  Wilmington *(G-18416)*
Moore Shaun Pt .... G 302 477-3998
  Wilmington *(G-18438)*
More About You Inc .... G 302 660-8899
  Newark *(G-11451)*
My Touch Works Massage .... G 302 943-9783
  Milford *(G-8024)*
Nancy Hastings .... G 302 396-2899
  Georgetown *(G-4441)*
Nancy T Brohawn .... G 302 453-1866
  Newark *(G-11485)*
Nanticoke Rehab .... G 302 629-6224
  Seaford *(G-13308)*
Natural Healing Traditions .... G 302 994-6838
  Wilmington *(G-18554)*
Ndon Jordona .... G 609 254-2620
  Middletown *(G-7394)*
New Perspectives Inc .... G 302 489-0220
  Wilmington *(G-18625)*
Nicole A Fisher .... G 302 674-0600
  Dover *(G-3188)*
Nicole Lowe .... G 302 858-4337
  Georgetown *(G-4446)*
Nicole Sestito PHD .... G 610 465-7312
  Wilmington *(G-18645)*
Ninjanurse LLC .... G 302 750-6666
  Hockessin *(G-5322)*
Novacare .... F 302 500-6363
  Georgetown *(G-4449)*
Novacare Rehabilitation .... E 302 597-9256
  Bear *(G-400)*

Novacare Rehabilitation .... G 302 674-4192
  Dover *(G-3203)*
Novacare Rehabilitation .... G 302 947-0781
  Millsboro *(G-8407)*
Novacare Rehabilitation .... G 302 537-7762
  Ocean View *(G-12553)*
Novacare Rehabilitation .... F 302 653-8389
  Smyrna *(G-13836)*
Novacare Rehabilitation .... F 302 655-5877
  Wilmington *(G-18691)*
Novacare Rhabilitation Milford .... G 302 393-5889
  Milford *(G-8032)*
Nurse Maggie Nursing Assist In .... G 302 660-7100
  Wilmington *(G-18717)*
Old Towne Pt - Millsboro .... G 302 945-5300
  Millsboro *(G-8411)*
Omega Project Pt LLC .... G 845 323-8739
  Wilmington *(G-18765)*
Opt Therapy Svc .... G 302 478-3702
  Wilmington *(G-18806)*
Orthopaedic & Sports Phys .... G 302 683-0782
  Wilmington *(G-18826)*
Patel Soniya .... G 803 524-4547
  Wilmington *(G-18903)*
Patel Vaidehi .... G 302 295-0435
  Newark *(G-11634)*
Pathways2healing .... G 302 540-4632
  Bear *(G-417)*
Patricia Ayers .... G 302 841-9909
  Milton *(G-8681)*
Patterson Mrs Darnetta L .... G 215 828-2597
  Magnolia *(G-6772)*
Paul Ojewoye .... G 443 844-1345
  Townsend *(G-14051)*
Peak Cryotherapy .... G 302 502-3160
  Wilmington *(G-18941)*
Performance Enhancement Profes .... G 302 423-0236
  Dover *(G-3298)*
Performance Physcl Therapy Inc .... F 302 234-2288
  Hockessin *(G-5339)*
Performance Pt Solutions LLC .... G 302 202-3155
  Hockessin *(G-5340)*
Peter Dunckley .... G 302 234-1561
  Hockessin *(G-5343)*
Physical Therapist .... G 302 983-4151
  Middletown *(G-7447)*
Physical Therapy Services Inc .... E 302 678-3100
  Dover *(G-3317)*
Physical Thrapy Bokkeeping LLC .... G 302 505-5721
  Hartly *(G-4902)*
Physiotherapy Associates Inc .... F 302 674-1269
  Dover *(G-3319)*
Physiotherapy Associates Inc .... G 302 655-8989
  Wilmington *(G-19031)*
Physiotherapy Associates Inc .... G 610 444-1270
  Wilmington *(G-19032)*
Pierce Pt Inc .... G 302 659-0821
  Clayton *(G-1397)*
Pike Creek Psychlogical Ctr PA .... G 302 738-6859
  Newark *(G-11693)*
Pivot Physical Therapy .... F 302 730-4800
  Dover *(G-3326)*
Pivot Physical Therapy .... F 302 449-7792
  Middletown *(G-7450)*
Pivot Physical Therapy .... G 302 504-6195
  Wilmington *(G-19056)*
Prana Bodyworks .... G 302 229-3880
  Wilmington *(G-19145)*
Premier Physical Therapy .... G 302 724-6344
  Dover *(G-3362)*
Premier Physical Therapy & .... E 302 389-7855
  Smyrna *(G-13851)*

Premier Physical Therapy and .... F 302 727-0075
  Lewes *(G-6386)*
Primary Care Delaware L L C .... G 302 744-9645
  Dover *(G-3371)*
Private Massage Bodywork .... G 302 387-7199
  Dover *(G-3375)*
Pro Physical Therapy .... G 302 422-6670
  Milford *(G-8054)*
Pro Physical Therapy .... G 610 368-1006
  Wilmington *(G-19202)*
Pro Physical Therapy PA .... F 302 654-1700
  New Castle *(G-9496)*
Pro Physl Therapy Ftns Acct .... G 302 658-7800
  Wilmington *(G-19203)*
Professional Therapeutics .... G 302 438-5859
  Wilmington *(G-19214)*
Psychological C Hockessin .... G 610 388-8585
  Wilmington *(G-19248)*
Psychological Services .... G 302 489-0213
  Wilmington *(G-19249)*
Psychotherapeutic Services .... E 302 678-9962
  Dover *(G-3388)*
Pt Works De LLC .... G 410 446-2589
  Milford *(G-8056)*
Rachel Anne Beaston .... G 302 449-1875
  Middletown *(G-7498)*
Rachel L Farley .... G 302 734-8000
  Dover *(G-3418)*
Rebecca E Orr .... G 302 521-4920
  Newark *(G-11834)*
Rebecca Smlak-Kettlehake Psy D .... G 302 261-6901
  Newark *(G-11835)*
Rehabilitation Consultants Inc .... G 302 655-5877
  Wilmington *(G-19412)*
Rehabilitation Consultants Inc .... G 302 478-5240
  Wilmington *(G-19413)*
Rehabilitation Service .... F 302 449-3050
  Middletown *(G-7510)*
Reiki Experience .... G 704 526-7092
  Millsboro *(G-8441)*
Reiki With Rebecca .... G 302 528-0582
  Wilmington *(G-19415)*
Rhd De Program .... G 302 883-2926
  Dover *(G-3464)*
Risa Malone MA CCC-Slp .... G 352 536-9187
  Clayton *(G-1401)*
Robin R Pratola .... G 302 653-5100
  Smyrna *(G-13868)*
Robin Sesan .... F 302 475-1880
  Wilmington *(G-19521)*
Rockin Reiki and Massage LLC .... G 302 423-3214
  Dover *(G-3477)*
Rosanne Tray Inc .... G 302 656-5776
  Wilmington *(G-19567)*
Roselle D Albert Pt .... G 302 373-5753
  Bear *(G-470)*
Rosemarie Ciarrocchi .... G 302 731-9225
  Newark *(G-11916)*
Russ Otr Hardesty .... G 302 598-0824
  Wilmington *(G-19592)*
Samuel Blumberg PHD .... G 302 652-7733
  Wilmington *(G-19651)*
Sara Elizabeth Novy Dpt .... G 201 783-5082
  Millsboro *(G-8454)*
Sarah B Neely-Collins .... G 814 282-6013
  Dover *(G-3510)*
Sarah Craig Lmt .... G 302 480-4792
  Smyrna *(G-13878)*
Sarah Lockhead .... G 484 941-4712
  Newark *(G-11947)*
Sean Thomas Joynt Mspt Atc .... G 302 286-6282
  Newark *(G-11967)*

80 HEALTH SERVICES

Name	Code	Phone
Select Physical Therapy	F	302 760-9966
Dover (G-3529)		
Shiatsu Bodywork	G	302 529-7882
Wilmington (G-19798)		
Slater Nursing Service	G	302 419-6237
Bear (G-496)		
Southern Del Physcl Therapy	G	302 659-0173
Smyrna (G-13899)		
Specialty Rehabilitation Inc	F	302 709-0440
Hockessin (G-5386)		
Spectrum Mill Inc	F	941 815-9454
Claymont (G-1298)		
Speech Clinic	F	302 999-0702
Wilmington (G-19959)		
Speech Therapeutics Inc	G	302 234-9226
Hockessin (G-5387)		
Spine & Orthopedic Specialist	F	302 633-1280
Newark (G-12068)		
St John Beloved	G	302 562-9129
Wilmington (G-19996)		
Stretchplex LLC	G	302 696-5966
Hockessin (G-5393)		
Suber Tanisha Lashay Lpn	G	215 910-8361
Newark (G-12115)		
Susan J Howlett	G	302 670-1055
Bridgeville (G-771)		
Susan McClain	G	302 655-5877
Wilmington (G-20164)		
Susan Peet Rn	G	302 945-5228
Lewes (G-6528)		
Suzanne S Townsend	G	302 593-6253
Newark (G-12137)		
Tara K Adams Mrs	G	302 450-3936
Dover (G-3653)		
Telemind Inc	G	725 333-2411
Middletown (G-7631)		
Therapeutic Moore Services LLC	G	302 654-8142
Wilmington (G-20296)		
Thrive Physical Therapy Inc	F	302 834-8400
Middletown (G-7642)		
Tidewater Physcl Thrpy and REB	G	302 398-7982
Harrington (G-4841)		
Tidewater Physcl Thrpy and REB	G	302 945-5111
Lewes (G-6558)		
Tidewater Physcl Thrpy and REB	G	302 684-2829
Milton (G-8720)		
Tidewater Physcl Thrpy and REB	G	302 537-7260
Ocean View (G-12576)		
Tidewater Physcl Thrpy and REB	G	302 629-4024
Seaford (G-13431)		
Tina Trner Cmt Thrptic Massage	G	302 242-5114
Felton (G-4033)		
Total Health & Rehabilitation	F	302 477-0800
Wilmington (G-20370)		
Total Health & Rehabilitation	G	302 999-9202
Wilmington (G-20371)		
Uppal Umsa	G	302 897-7434
Smyrna (G-13926)		
Wanda Roland	G	773 573-3265
Wilmington (G-20675)		
Wellness Health Inc	G	302 424-4100
Milford (G-8147)		
Wilderman Physical Therapy LLC	G	717 873-6836
Wilmington (G-20780)		
Your Cbd Store	G	302 480-4474
Dover (G-3893)		
Zehnacker Russ Crna PA	G	302 834-7523
Newark (G-12430)		
Zuber & Associates Inc	G	302 478-1618
Wilmington (G-20967)		

8051 Skilled nursing care facilities

Name	Code	Phone
100 St Clire Drv Oprations LLC	A	610 444-6350
Hockessin (G-5107)		
1080 Slver Lk Blvd Oprtons LLC	F	610 444-6350
Dover (G-1677)		
1100 Nrman Eskrdge Hwy Oprtons	B	302 629-3575
Seaford (G-13041)		
1203 Walker Rd Operations LLC	A	302 735-8800
Dover (G-1679)		
500 Suth Dpont Blvd Oprtons LL	B	302 422-8700
Milford (G-7753)		
700 Marvel Road Operations LLC	B	302 422-3303
Milford (G-7754)		
Arden Courts of Wilmington	G	302 762-7800
Wilmington (G-14545)		
Arden Courts Wilmington De LLC	F	302 764-0181
Wilmington (G-14546)		
Beebe School of Nursing	E	302 645-3251
Lewes (G-5752)		
Birth Cnter Hlstic Wns Hlth CA	F	302 658-2229
Newark (G-10038)		
Brandywine Nrsing Rhblttion CT	E	302 683-0444
Wilmington (G-15074)		
Brandywine Snior Lving MGT LLC	E	302 226-8750
Rehoboth Beach (G-12651)		
Brilliance Living Corporation	G	386 690-1709
Wilmington (G-15116)		
Broadmeadow Investment LLC	E	302 449-3400
Middletown (G-6944)		
Brookdale Dover	F	302 674-4407
Dover (G-1983)		
Cadia Rhabilitation Pike Creek	E	302 455-0808
Wilmington (G-15185)		
Cadia Rverside Healthcare Svcs	F	302 455-0808
Wilmington (G-15187)		
Capitol Nrsing Rhblttion Ctr L	E	302 734-1199
Dover (G-2023)		
Center At Eden Hill	F	302 677-7100
Dover (G-2046)		
Chancellor Care Ctr of Delmar	E	302 846-3077
Delmar (G-1576)		
Churchman De Snf MGT LLC	D	302 998-6900
Newark (G-10239)		
Churchman Village Center LLC	E	302 998-6900
Newark (G-10240)		
Collabrtive Effort To Rnfrce T	D	302 731-0301
Smyrna (G-13685)		
Collabrtive Effort To Rnfrce T	G	302 731-0301
New Castle (G-8956)		
Complete Care At Silver Lk LLC	E	302 734-5990
Dover (G-2122)		
Conexio Care Inc	E	302 442-6622
Claymont (G-1098)		
Courtland Manor Inc	E	302 674-0566
Dover (G-2148)		
Delaware Dept Hlth Social Svcs	C	302 223-1000
Smyrna (G-13698)		
Emeritus Corporation	C	302 674-4407
Dover (G-2439)		
Exceptional Care For Children	D	302 894-1001
Newark (G-10685)		
Five Star Quality Care Inc	G	302 266-9255
Newark (G-10745)		
Five Star Quality Care Inc	G	302 366-0160
Newark (G-10746)		
Five Star Senior Living Inc	E	302 283-0540
Newark (G-10747)		
Five Star Senior Living Inc	D	302 655-6249
Wilmington (G-16655)		
Genesis Healthcare Corporation	G	302 422-3754
Milford (G-7908)		
Genesis Hlthcare Ctrs Hldngs I	D	302 652-4720
Wilmington (G-16836)		

Name	Code	Phone
Gracious Hart Nursing Svcs LLC	G	302 343-9083
Marydel (G-6798)		
Green Acres Health Systems	B	302 934-7300
Millsboro (G-8305)		
Green Valley Pavilion	F	302 653-5085
Smyrna (G-13752)		
Green Valley Terrace Snf LLC	C	302 934-7300
Millsboro (G-8306)		
Greenvlle Retirement Cmnty LLC	C	302 658-6200
Wilmington (G-16975)		
Harbor Hlthcare Rhbltation Ctr	B	302 645-4664
Lewes (G-6076)		
Harrison Snior Lving Gorgetown	G	302 856-4574
Georgetown (G-4353)		
Hillside Center	E	302 652-1181
Wilmington (G-17147)		
Home For Aged Wmn-Mnquadale HM	C	302 654-1810
Wilmington (G-17178)		
Home of Merciful Rest Society	C	302 652-3311
Wilmington (G-17183)		
Ingleside Homes Inc	E	302 984-0950
Wilmington (G-17336)		
Ivy Gables LLC	F	302 475-9400
Wilmington (G-17439)		
Just Like Home	F	302 653-0605
Smyrna (G-13783)		
Kendal Corp Pension Plan	F	610 388-7001
Newark (G-11154)		
Kendal Outreach LLC	F	610 335-1200
Newark (G-11157)		
Living Well With Dementia LLC	G	302 753-9725
Wilmington (G-17951)		
Milton & Hattie Kutz Home Inc	C	302 764-7000
Wilmington (G-18371)		
Morgan Louise Fndtn LLC	F	302 670-5792
Clayton (G-1388)		
Nemours Foundation	F	302 424-5420
Milford (G-8026)		
New Cstle Hlth Rhblttion Ctr L	C	302 328-2580
New Castle (G-9416)		
Newark Heritage Partners I LLC	E	302 283-0540
Newark (G-11538)		
Nursing Board	E	302 744-4500
Dover (G-3212)		
Oak Hrc New Castle LLC	C	302 328-2580
New Castle (G-9432)		
Onix Silverside LLC	F	484 731-2500
Wilmington (G-18791)		
Parkview Covalescent Center	F	302 655-6135
Wilmington (G-18895)		
Parkview De Snf Management LLC	D	302 655-6135
Wilmington (G-18896)		
Peninsula Untd Mthdst Hmes Inc	B	302 235-6810
Hockessin (G-5336)		
Peninsula Untd Mthdst Hmes Inc	B	302 654-5101
Wilmington (G-18949)		
Pinnacle Rhbilitation Hlth Ctr	D	302 653-5085
Smyrna (G-13847)		
Post Acute Medical LLC	D	717 731-9660
Dover (G-3355)		
Premier Healthcare Inc	E	302 731-5576
Newark (G-11728)		
Presbyterian Homes Inc	B	302 744-3600
Dover (G-3365)		
Public Health Nursing	F	302 856-5136
Georgetown (G-4475)		
Regal Hts Hlthcare Rhab Ctr LL	D	302 998-0181
Hockessin (G-5361)		
Regency Hlthcare Rehab Ctr LLC	C	302 654-8400
Wilmington (G-19400)		
Seaside Pointe	F	302 226-8750
Rehoboth Beach (G-12954)		

SIC SECTION
80 HEALTH SERVICES

Steven E Diamond M D.................................G..... 302 655-8868
  Wilmington *(G-20065)*

Summit At Hockessin.................................E..... 302 235-8388
  Hockessin *(G-5396)*

Summit Retirement Community............F..... 888 933-2300
  Hockessin *(G-5397)*

Sunrise Senior Living LLC.......................D..... 302 475-9163
  Wilmington *(G-20134)*

8052 Intermediate care facilities

All About Pink Inc......................................F..... 302 947-0309
  Millsboro *(G-8164)*

American Unvrsal-Hockessin LLC...........E..... 302 239-4106
  Hockessin *(G-5121)*

Chancellor Care Ctr of Delmar..................E..... 302 846-3077
  Delmar *(G-1576)*

Community Systems and Svcs Inc..........C..... 302 325-1500
  New Castle *(G-8962)*

Delaware Hospice.......................................E..... 302 934-9018
  Millsboro *(G-8262)*

Delaware Hospice Inc................................E..... 302 678-4444
  Dover *(G-2245)*

Delaware Hospice Inc................................E..... 302 856-7717
  Milford *(G-7856)*

Elderly Comfort Corporation.....................G..... 302 530-6680
  Wilmington *(G-16349)*

Home of Merciful Rest Society..................C..... 302 652-3311
  Wilmington *(G-17183)*

Ingleside Homes Inc.................................E..... 302 984-0950
  Wilmington *(G-17336)*

Little Sisters of The Poor..........................D..... 302 368-5886
  Newark *(G-11273)*

Lutheran Senior Services Inc..................D..... 302 654-4490
  Wilmington *(G-18033)*

Mary Campbell Center Inc........................C..... 302 762-6025
  Wilmington *(G-18177)*

Milton & Hattie Kutz Home Inc.................C..... 302 764-7000
  Wilmington *(G-18371)*

Mosaic...D..... 302 456-5995
  Newark *(G-11455)*

Mosaic...D..... 302 456-5995
  Newark *(G-11456)*

Oakleaf Inc..E..... 412 881-8194
  Lewes *(G-6325)*

Parkview De Snf Management LLC..........D..... 302 655-6135
  Wilmington *(G-18896)*

Pratt-Fields Home Please Inc...................G..... 215 868-9028
  New Castle *(G-9488)*

Smiley Shiney...G..... 215 601-6036
  Middletown *(G-7580)*

Vitas Healthcare Corporation...................C..... 302 451-4000
  Newark *(G-12332)*

8059 Nursing and personal care, nec

A and H Nursing Administra.....................F..... 302 544-4474
  Bear *(G-7)*

Bk Temp Home Care..................................F..... 302 575-1400
  Wilmington *(G-14900)*

Bove Psychological Svcs LLC..................G..... 302 299-5193
  Wilmington *(G-15016)*

Capitol Nrsing Rhbltiion Ctr L..................E..... 302 734-1199
  Dover *(G-2023)*

Care At Home of Delaware LLC..............G..... 302 502-7138
  Wilmington *(G-15240)*

Caring Hnds Phlbotomy Svcs LLC...........G..... 302 559-5539
  Wilmington *(G-15249)*

Courtland Manor Inc.................................E..... 302 674-0566
  Dover *(G-2148)*

Edlyncare LLC..D..... 267 474-0486
  Bear *(G-195)*

Green Valley Pavilion...............................F..... 302 653-5085
  Smyrna *(G-13752)*

Hillside Center..E..... 302 652-1181
  Wilmington *(G-17147)*

Infusion Care Delaware Home..................F..... 302 423-2511
  Wilmington *(G-17330)*

Little Sisters of The Poor..........................D..... 302 368-5886
  Newark *(G-11273)*

Lodge Lane Assisted Living.....................F..... 302 757-8100
  Wilmington *(G-17973)*

Macklyn Home Care...................................G..... 302 253-8208
  Georgetown *(G-4411)*

My Careshare LLC.....................................G..... 901 848-5988
  Dover *(G-3134)*

Nicole L Scott Np-C Adult Prmr................G..... 302 690-1692
  Hockessin *(G-5320)*

North Eastern Waffles LLC.......................F..... 302 697-2226
  Dover *(G-3197)*

Oncology Care Home................................F..... 610 274-2437
  Newark *(G-11590)*

Parkview De Snf Management LLC..........D..... 302 655-6135
  Wilmington *(G-18896)*

Peninsula Home Care LLC.......................E..... 302 629-4914
  Seaford *(G-13336)*

Presbyterian Homes Inc..........................B..... 302 744-3600
  Dover *(G-3365)*

Prognstic Hlthcare Rsurces LLC............G..... 762 217-6323
  Smyrna *(G-13857)*

PSC Technology Incorporated.................F..... 866 866-1466
  Lewes *(G-6397)*

Quality Care Homes LLC..........................F..... 302 858-3999
  Lewes *(G-6399)*

Quality Lawn Care Home RE...................G..... 302 331-5892
  Camden Wyoming *(G-967)*

Serenity Gardens Assisted Livi................F..... 302 442-5330
  Middletown *(G-7554)*

Ten Blade Enterprises LLC......................G..... 484 843-4811
  Wilmington *(G-20271)*

Thomas F Allen...F..... 302 604-3357
  Georgetown *(G-4553)*

Turning Pt Counseling Ctr LLC................G..... 214 883-5148
  Camden *(G-898)*

8062 General medical and surgical hospitals

Ai Dupont Hosp For Children....................A..... 302 651-4620
  Wilmington *(G-14327)*

Alfred Idpont Hosp For Chldren................A..... 302 651-4000
  Wilmington *(G-14356)*

Atlantic General Hospital Corp.................E..... 302 524-5007
  Selbyville *(G-13466)*

Bayhealth Med Ctr Inc-OCC Hlth...............E..... 302 678-1303
  Dover *(G-1889)*

Bayhealth Medical Center Inc..................C..... 302 674-4700
  Dover *(G-1890)*

Bayhealth Primary Care Dover W............G..... 302 734-7834
  Dover *(G-1891)*

Bayview Endoscopy Center......................E..... 302 644-0455
  Lewes *(G-5742)*

Beacon Medical Group PA.......................G..... 302 947-9767
  Rehoboth Beach *(G-12631)*

Beebe Healthcare..F..... 302 249-1448
  Georgetown *(G-4229)*

Beebe Healthcare..F..... 302 934-5052
  Millsboro *(G-8191)*

Beebe Hospital Hs......................................F..... 302 645-3565
  Lewes *(G-5747)*

Beebe Lab Express Georgetown...............F..... 302 856-9729
  Georgetown *(G-4230)*

Beebe Lab Express Millboro.....................F..... 302 934-5052
  Millsboro *(G-8192)*

Beebe Medical Center Inc.........................G..... 302 856-9729
  Georgetown *(G-4231)*

Beebe Medical Center Inc.........................E..... 302 645-3300
  Lewes *(G-5749)*

Beebe Medical Center Inc.........................C..... 302 645-3629
  Lewes *(G-5750)*

Beebe Medical Center Inc.........................E..... 302 393-2056
  Milford *(G-7790)*

Beebe Medical Center Inc.........................E..... 302 947-9767
  Millsboro *(G-8193)*

Beebe Medical Center Inc.........................E..... 302 541-4175
  Millville *(G-8519)*

Beebe Medical Center Inc.........................E..... 302 645-3100
  Rehoboth Beach *(G-12635)*

Beebe Medical Center Inc.........................E..... 302 645-3289
  Rehoboth Beach *(G-12636)*

Beebe Medical Center Inc.........................E..... 302 645-3010
  Rehoboth Beach *(G-12637)*

Beebe Medical Center Inc.........................A..... 302 645-3300
  Lewes *(G-5748)*

Beebe Physician Network Inc...................B..... 302 645-1805
  Lewes *(G-5751)*

Bhaskar Palekar MD PA.............................G..... 302 645-1805
  Lewes *(G-5761)*

Brian Costleigh LLC...................................F..... 302 645-3775
  Rehoboth Beach *(G-12653)*

Cancer Care Ctrs At Bay Hlth....................F..... 302 674-4401
  Dover *(G-2019)*

Cedar Tree Surgical Center......................E..... 302 945-9766
  Millsboro *(G-8217)*

Center For Spine Surgery LLC..................F..... 302 366-7671
  Wilmington *(G-15304)*

Christ Care Cardiac Surgery....................G..... 302 644-4282
  Lewes *(G-5818)*

Christana Care Vsclar Spcalist................F..... 302 733-5700
  Newark *(G-10211)*

Christiana Care Corp.................................G..... 302 738-4596
  Newark *(G-10217)*

Christiana Care Health Sys Inc.................C..... 302 449-3000
  Middletown *(G-6976)*

Christiana Care Health Sys Inc.................C..... 302 838-4750
  Newark *(G-10218)*

Christiana Care Health Sys Inc.................G..... 302 366-1929
  Newark *(G-10219)*

Christiana Care Health Sys Inc.................G..... 302 733-5700
  Newark *(G-10221)*

Christiana Care Health Sys Inc.................B..... 302 623-7500
  Wilmington *(G-15401)*

Christiana Care Health Sys Inc.................C..... 302 428-6219
  Wilmington *(G-15402)*

Christiana Care Health Sys Inc.................C..... 302 623-1929
  Wilmington *(G-15403)*

Christiana Care Health Sys Inc.................C..... 302 733-1000
  Wilmington *(G-15404)*

Christiana Care Health Sys Inc.................G..... 302 733-1000
  Newark *(G-10220)*

Christiana Care Health System.................F..... 302 992-5545
  Wilmington *(G-15405)*

Christiana Care Hlth Svcs Inc...................C..... 302 327-3959
  New Castle *(G-8939)*

Christiana Care Hlth Svcs Inc...................G..... 302 733-1805
  Wilmington *(G-15406)*

Christiana Care Hlth Svcs Inc...................A..... 302 733-1000
  Newark *(G-10225)*

Christiana Hospital.....................................G..... 203 645-2903
  Historic New Castle *(G-4958)*

Christncare Prmry Care At Lnde...............G..... 302 623-2850
  Wilmington *(G-15420)*

Commonspirit Health LLC........................F..... 302 336-8212
  Dover *(G-2118)*

Complete Family Care Inc.........................F..... 302 232-5002
  Wilmington *(G-15572)*

Cuhiana Care Health System....................F..... 302 733-1780
  Newark *(G-10364)*

Cynthia Crosser DC Fiama.......................G..... 302 239-5014
  Wilmington *(G-15754)*

Employee Codes: A=Over 500 employees, B=251-500
C=101-250, D=51-100, E=20-50, F=10-19, G=1-9

2024 Harris Directory of Delaware Businesses

80 HEALTH SERVICES

Daniel W Cuozzo Do............................. F 302 645-4801
  Rehoboth Beach *(G-12711)*
Delaware Bay Surgical Svc PA................ E 302 645-5650
  Lewes *(G-5890)*
Delaware Heart & Vascular PA................ G 302 734-1414
  Dover *(G-2244)*
Endoscopy Center of Deleware................ E 302 892-2710
  Newark *(G-10647)*
Envision Healthcare Corp...................... F 302 644-3852
  Lewes *(G-5965)*
Erik M D Stancofski............................... F 302 645-7050
  Lewes *(G-5970)*
Frenius Medical Care............................. F 302 421-9177
  Wilmington *(G-16747)*
Friends & Family Practice....................... G 302 537-3740
  Millville *(G-8529)*
Hale J Eric MD.................................... F 302 644-2064
  Lewes *(G-6070)*
Iqarus Americas Inc.............................. E 407 222-5726
  Wilmington *(G-17420)*
Jing Jin MD PHD................................... F 302 651-5040
  Wilmington *(G-17550)*
Jr Board of Kent Gen Hospital................. G 302 744-7128
  Dover *(G-2808)*
Kent General Hospital............................ A 302 744-7688
  Dover *(G-2850)*
Kent General Hospital............................ G 302 378-1199
  Middletown *(G-7266)*
Kent General Hospital............................ A 302 430-5731
  Milford *(G-7962)*
Kent General Hospital............................ G 302 653-2010
  Smyrna *(G-13790)*
Kent General Hospital............................ D 302 674-4700
  Dover *(G-2851)*
Lewes Orthopedic Ctr............................ G 302 645-4939
  Lewes *(G-6199)*
Limestone Medical Center Inc................ D 302 992-0500
  Wilmington *(G-17915)*
Lisa Bartels... F 302 856-9596
  Georgetown *(G-4408)*
Medical Center of Harrington.................. G 302 398-8704
  Harrington *(G-4800)*
Mediguide International LLC................... D 302 425-5900
  Wilmington *(G-18253)*
Milton Enterprises Inc........................... G 302 684-2000
  Milton *(G-8669)*
Mudiwa Munyikwa MD........................... F 302 645-7050
  Milford *(G-8022)*
Nancy A Union MD................................ G 302 645-6644
  Lewes *(G-6305)*
Nanticoke Immediate Care..................... G 302 715-5214
  Laurel *(G-5569)*
Natural Hypertension Inst Inc................. G 302 533-7704
  Newark *(G-11494)*
Nemours Foundation............................. A 302 651-4000
  Wilmington *(G-18581)*
North Wilmington Womens Center........... G 302 529-7900
  Wilmington *(G-18681)*
Peri Srihari MD.................................... F 302 645-3770
  Rehoboth Beach *(G-12889)*
Quick Surface Solutions LLC.................. F 302 236-6941
  Milton *(G-8692)*
Scimedico LLC..................................... G 302 375-7500
  Middletown *(G-7544)*
Select Medical Corporation.................... E 302 421-4545
  Wilmington *(G-19741)*
Select Specialty Hospital....................... A 302 421-4590
  Wilmington *(G-19742)*
Southern Delaware Surgery Ctr............... D 302 644-6992
  Rehoboth Beach *(G-12969)*
St Francis Health Services Corporation.... A 302 575-8301
  Wilmington *(G-19992)*
St Francis Hospital Inc......................... A 616 685-3538
  Wilmington *(G-19993)*
Tidalhealth Nanticoke Inc..................... A 302 629-6611
  Seaford *(G-13429)*
Tidalhlth Pnnsula Regional Inc............... F 302 732-8400
  Dagsboro *(G-1517)*
Tidalhlth Pnnsula Regional Inc............... G 302 436-8004
  Selbyville *(G-13612)*
Tunnell Cancer Ctr............................... G 302 645-3770
  Rehoboth Beach *(G-12997)*
UHS of Rockford LLC............................ D 302 892-4224
  Newark *(G-12261)*
Womens Health Ctr Christn Care............. E 302 428-5810
  Wilmington *(G-20881)*
World Hospital Inc................................ ..... 609 254-3391
  Bear *(G-567)*

8063 Psychiatric hospitals

Children Yuth Their Fmlies Del............... F 302 577-4270
  New Castle *(G-8934)*
Delaware Dept Hlth Social Svcs.............. D 302 255-2700
  New Castle *(G-9018)*
Delaware Dept Hlth Social Svcs.............. D 302 255-2700
  New Castle *(G-9019)*
Phc Inc.. E 313 831-3500
  New Castle *(G-9470)*
Social Health Innovations Inc................. G 917 476-9355
  Dover *(G-3584)*
UHS of Rockford LLC............................ D 302 892-4224
  Newark *(G-12261)*

8069 Specialty hospitals, except psychiatric

1212 Corporation................................. G 302 764-4048
  Wilmington *(G-14105)*
Addiction Medical Facility LLC................ F 302 629-2300
  Seaford *(G-13049)*
ARS New Castle LLC............................. F 302 323-9400
  Historic New Castle *(G-4934)*
ARS of Rio Grande LLC......................... F 302 323-9400
  Historic New Castle *(G-4935)*
Children Fmilies First Del Inc................. D 302 856-2388
  Georgetown *(G-4253)*
Crest Central...................................... F 302 736-0576
  Dover *(G-2158)*
Delaware Dept Hlth Social Svcs.............. C 302 223-1000
  Smyrna *(G-13698)*
Home of Divine Providence Inc............... G 302 654-1184
  Wilmington *(G-17182)*
Jamie H Keskeny................................. F 302 651-6060
  Wilmington *(G-17489)*
Lawall Prosthetics - Orthotics................ G 302 677-0693
  Dover *(G-2914)*
Logos Community Dev Corp................... G 302 349-2779
  Dover *(G-2972)*
Memorial Sloan Kttring Cncer C.............. E 302 384-7588
  Wilmington *(G-18270)*
Nemours Foundation............................. A 302 651-4000
  Wilmington *(G-18581)*
Presbyterian Homes Inc........................ B 302 744-3600
  Dover *(G-3365)*
Thresholds Inc.................................... E 302 827-4478
  Lewes *(G-6557)*

8071 Medical laboratories

Agro Lab.. F 302 265-2734
  Harrington *(G-4723)*
Armed Forces Med Examiner Sys............. E 302 346-8653
  Dover *(G-1816)*
Bg Laboratory..................................... G 302 535-3954
  Dover *(G-1928)*
Blog Expecting Miracles LLC.................. G 302 533-6682
  Newark *(G-10053)*
Breast Imaging Center.......................... F 302 623-9729
  Newark *(G-10082)*
CD Diagnostics Inc.............................. E 302 367-7770
  Claymont *(G-1077)*
Christiana Care Health Sys Inc............... B 302 733-1601
  Newark *(G-10222)*
Clinical Breast Imaging......................... G 302 658-4800
  Wilmington *(G-15486)*
Clinpharma Clinical RES LLC................. E 646 961-3437
  Wilmington *(G-15487)*
Current Care Analytics Inc.................... G 248 425-3973
  Lewes *(G-5874)*
Delaware Imaging Network..................... G 302 449-5400
  Middletown *(G-7041)*
Delaware Public Health Lab................... E 302 223-1520
  Smyrna *(G-13705)*
Dynamic Mobile Imaging....................... F 302 645-2142
  Lewes *(G-5939)*
F P T & W Medical Associates................ F 800 421-2368
  Wilmington *(G-16521)*
Green Clinics Laboratory LLC................. E 302 734-5050
  Dover *(G-2621)*
Inspektlabs Inc................................... F 302 601-7191
  Middletown *(G-7227)*
Laboratory Corporation America.............. G 302 731-0244
  Newark *(G-11211)*
Lightwave Logic Inc............................. G 302 737-6412
  Newark *(G-11257)*
Maria Lazar MD................................... G 302 838-2210
  Hockessin *(G-5296)*
Mears Health Campus............................ G 302 628-6300
  Seaford *(G-13279)*
Medlab-Havertown Inc........................... G 302 655-5227
  New Castle *(G-9356)*
Molecular Imaging Services Inc............... G 302 450-4505
  Bear *(G-377)*
Papastvros Assoc Med Imging LL............ D 302 644-2590
  Newark *(G-11621)*
Paul Renzi... F 302 478-3166
  Wilmington *(G-18920)*
Peter M Witherell M D........................... G 302 478-7001
  Newark *(G-11673)*
Professional Imaging............................ G 302 653-3522
  Smyrna *(G-13856)*
Provision Group LLC............................ G 844 220-7200
  Newark *(G-11768)*
Quest Diagnostics Incorporated.............. G 302 376-8675
  Middletown *(G-7491)*
RSM Diagnostics Lab LLC..................... G 302 592-4106
  Wilmington *(G-19583)*

8072 Dental laboratories

Mittelman Dental Lab........................... G 302 798-7440
  Claymont *(G-1241)*
National Dentex LLC............................ C 302 661-6000
  Historic New Castle *(G-5032)*
R Smiley LLC...................................... G 302 463-5111
  Newark *(G-11810)*
Welsh Family Dentistry......................... G 302 836-3711
  Hockessin *(G-5424)*
Wilmington & Newark Dental.................. G 302 571-0526
  Newark *(G-12378)*

8082 Home health care services

4 Green Solutions Inc........................... G 954 770-5157
  Lewes *(G-5639)*
Acts Rtrmnt-Life Cmmnities Inc.............. B 302 654-5101
  Wilmington *(G-14245)*
Addus Healthcare Inc........................... C 302 424-4842
  Milford *(G-7759)*
Addus Healthcare Inc........................... G 302 995-9010
  Wilmington *(G-14254)*

80 HEALTH SERVICES

Advanced Modern Care LLC.................. F 267 235-6922
  Newark *(G-9777)*
Affinity Homecare Services.................. G 302 264-9363
  Dover *(G-1734)*
Alisi Home Care LLC.......................... G 302 268-8686
  Middletown *(G-6849)*
Alliance Total Care............................... G 302 225-9000
  Wilmington *(G-14379)*
Almost Home Day Care......................... G 302 220-6731
  Newark *(G-9830)*
Almost Home Day Care LLC................. G 302 220-6731
  Newark *(G-9831)*
Always Best Care................................. F 302 409-3710
  Milton *(G-8558)*
Amada Senior Care Southern Del........... F 302 272-9500
  Lewes *(G-5680)*
Amalgam Rx Inc................................... F 302 983-0001
  Wilmington *(G-14409)*
Angels Visiting..................................... D 302 691-8700
  Wilmington *(G-14483)*
Annadale Oladimeji............................. G 267 357-9718
  Wilmington *(G-14491)*
At Home Care Agency........................... G 302 883-2059
  Dover *(G-1841)*
At Home Infucare LLC.......................... G 302 883-2059
  Dover *(G-1842)*
Atkins Home Health Aid Agency............ G 302 832-0315
  Bear *(G-54)*
Aveanna Healthcare As LLC.................. F 302 504-4101
  Christiana *(G-992)*
Bayada... F 302 213-5024
  Dover *(G-1885)*
Bayada Home Health Care Inc.............. D 302 736-6001
  Dover *(G-1886)*
Bayada Home Health Care Inc.............. D 302 213-5040
  Dover *(G-1887)*
Bayada Home Health Care Inc.............. D 302 424-8200
  Milford *(G-7784)*
Bayada Home Health Care Inc.............. D 302 351-1244
  Milford *(G-7785)*
Bayada Home Health Care Inc.............. G 302 322-2300
  New Castle *(G-8851)*
Bayada Home Health Care Inc.............. D 302 836-1000
  Newark *(G-9994)*
Bayada Home Health Care Inc.............. D 302 351-1244
  Wilmington *(G-14784)*
Bayada Home Health Care Inc.............. D 302 351-3633
  Wilmington *(G-14785)*
Bayada Home Health Care Inc.............. D 302 658-3000
  Wilmington *(G-14786)*
Bayada Home Health Care Inc.............. D 302 351-3636
  Wilmington *(G-14787)*
Bc Home Health Care Services.............. E 302 746-7844
  Claymont *(G-1054)*
Bills Home Care Service LLC................ G 302 526-2071
  Dover *(G-1938)*
Biotek Remedys Inc.............................. E 877 246-9104
  New Castle *(G-8868)*
Blue Ridge Home Care Inc.................... G 302 397-8211
  Dover *(G-1954)*
By The Shore...................................... G 302 462-0496
  Georgetown *(G-4241)*
Careportmd LLC................................... G 302 202-3020
  Wilmington *(G-15244)*
Caring For Life Inc.............................. F 302 892-2214
  New Castle *(G-8913)*
Caring Hearts Home Care LLC............. F 302 734-9000
  Hartly *(G-4861)*
Caring Matters Home Care................... F 302 993-1121
  Camden *(G-802)*
Caroline M Wiesner............................. G 877 220-9755
  Wilmington *(G-15257)*

Chesapeakecaregivers LLC.................... G 302 841-9686
  Seaford *(G-13118)*
Christana Care HM Hlth Cmnty S........... C 302 698-4300
  Camden *(G-806)*
Christana Care HM Hlth Cmnty S........... B 302 995-8448
  Wilmington *(G-15397)*
Christana Care HM Hlth Cmnty S........... B 302 327-5583
  New Castle *(G-8937)*
Christiana Care Infusion....................... F 302 623-0345
  Newark *(G-10226)*
Cindys Home Away From Hme Fam....... G 302 378-0487
  Middletown *(G-6982)*
Comfort Care At Home Inc.................... F 302 737-8078
  Newark *(G-10282)*
Connections CSP Inc............................. G 302 327-0122
  New Castle *(G-8966)*
Dedicated To Home Care LLC................ G 484 470-5013
  New Castle *(G-9009)*
Del Premier Care Inc............................ E 302 533-5988
  Newark *(G-10413)*
Delaware 4 Sniors Homecare LLC.......... F 302 386-8080
  Wilmington *(G-15861)*
Delaware Hospice Inc........................... D 302 478-5707
  Newark *(G-10452)*
Dependable Cmnty HM Care LLC.......... G 302 893-3779
  New Castle *(G-9046)*
Empathy Home Care LLC...................... G 302 722-1538
  Newark *(G-10642)*
Excellent Home Care........................... G 302 327-0147
  Historic New Castle *(G-4985)*
Expert Home Care LLC......................... G 856 870-6691
  Middletown *(G-7115)*
Fast Pay Rx LLC................................... G 833 511-9500
  Wilmington *(G-16558)*
Fogarty LLC.. G 610 731-4804
  Seaford *(G-13188)*
Generations Home Care Inc.................. E 302 322-3100
  Wilmington *(G-16834)*
Generations Home Care Inc.................. C 302 856-7774
  Wilmington *(G-16835)*
Grace Miracle Home Care..................... G 302 257-1079
  Wilmington *(G-16942)*
Grace Visitation Services..................... D 302 329-9475
  Milton *(G-8628)*
Griswold Home Care............................. G 302 703-0130
  Lewes *(G-6062)*
Griswold Home Care............................. F 302 750-4564
  Wilmington *(G-16982)*
Guardian Angel HM Hlth Care AG.......... G 302 476-1281
  Newark *(G-10906)*
Gunning Partners LLC.......................... D 302 482-4305
  Newport *(G-12453)*
Health Care Consultants Inc................. D 302 892-9210
  Wilmington *(G-17094)*
Health Care Consultants Inc................. D 302 883-9462
  Wilmington *(G-17095)*
Healthy At Home Care LLC.................... G 571 228-5935
  Rehoboth Beach *(G-12782)*
Heart 2 Heart Services LLC................... G 302 293-0124
  New Castle *(G-9204)*
Home Health Corp America Inc............. D 302 678-4764
  Dover *(G-2689)*
Home Health Heartfel........................... G 302 660-2686
  Wilmington *(G-17179)*
Home Health Services By TLC............... F 302 322-5510
  Wilmington *(G-17180)*
Home Instead Senior Care.................... G 302 697-6435
  Dover *(G-2690)*
Home Sweet.. G 302 353-9733
  Greenwood *(G-4636)*
Homewatch Caregivers........................ F 302 644-1888
  Lewes *(G-6100)*

Ijn Health Systems LLC......................... F 855 202-5993
  Bear *(G-282)*
In Loving Handz Home Care LLC.......... G 302 530-6344
  Newark *(G-11008)*
Ingleside Homes Inc............................. D 302 575-0250
  Wilmington *(G-17335)*
Interim Health Care.............................. G 302 322-2743
  New Castle *(G-9239)*
Interim Healthcare Del LLC.................. F 302 322-2743
  Smyrna *(G-13775)*
Kindheart Home Care Inc..................... G 484 479-6582
  Middletown *(G-7276)*
La Red Health Care.............................. F 757 709-5072
  Georgetown *(G-4398)*
Lieske E2e Home Hlth Care Inc............. G 302 898-1563
  Middletown *(G-7298)*
Life Force Eldercare Corp.................... G 302 737-4400
  Newark *(G-11254)*
Lifetime Skills Services LLC................. G 302 378-2911
  Middletown *(G-7302)*
Macklyn Home Care............................. G 302 253-8208
  Georgetown *(G-4411)*
Macklyn Home Care............................. G 302 690-9397
  Wilmington *(G-18071)*
Makua Inc... G 310 923-8549
  Wilmington *(G-18094)*
Middltown Snior Lving Prtners............. G 302 828-0988
  Middletown *(G-7365)*
Mirage Health Services LLC.................. E 302 349-7227
  Dover *(G-3099)*
National Mentor Holdings Inc............... A 302 934-0512
  Millsboro *(G-8401)*
Near and Dear Home Care.................... G 302 530-6498
  Newark *(G-11497)*
Neighbor Care Home Care & Fmly......... G 302 290-0341
  Bear *(G-390)*
Neighborly Home Care......................... F 610 420-1868
  Wilmington *(G-18572)*
Next Step Quality HM Care LLC............ F 888 367-5722
  Smyrna *(G-13834)*
Nurse Angels LLC................................ G 302 765-8093
  Hockessin *(G-5327)*
Nurses N Kids Inc................................ E 302 424-1770
  Milford *(G-8033)*
Packd LLC.. E 302 467-3443
  Georgetown *(G-4453)*
Pennsula Home Care LLC..................... F 302 629-4914
  Seaford *(G-13341)*
Perry & Assoc..................................... G 302 472-8701
  Wilmington *(G-18983)*
Phyllis M Green................................... G 302 354-6986
  Bear *(G-423)*
Pro 2 Respiratory Services................... G 302 514-9843
  Smyrna *(G-13855)*
R&R Homecare..................................... G 302 478-3448
  Wilmington *(G-19308)*
Robert Bird... E 302 654-4003
  Wilmington *(G-19508)*
Roz Health LLC.................................... G 415 259-8992
  Newark *(G-11923)*
Saint Home Health Care....................... F 302 514-9597
  Milford *(G-8080)*
Sea Care LLC...................................... G 410 688-4230
  Seaford *(G-13385)*
Seasons Hspice Plltive Care De............ E 847 692-1000
  Newark *(G-11968)*
Seniortech Inc.................................... G 302 533-5988
  Newark *(G-11977)*
Servant Support Services LLC.............. F 215 201-5990
  Newark *(G-11984)*
Shorecare of Delaware......................... F 302 724-5235
  Dover *(G-3549)*

Employee Codes: A=Over 500 employees, B=251-500
C=101-250, D=51-100, E=20-50, F=10-19, G=1-9

80 HEALTH SERVICES

Solace Lifesciences Inc .... G 830 792-3123
  Middletown (G-7585)
Solace Lifesciences Inc .... G 302 383-1450
  Middletown (G-7586)
Solution On-Call Services LLC .... F 302 353-4328
  New Castle (G-9578)
Soma Breath Inc .... E 415 633-5359
  Wilmington (G-19928)
Special Care Inc .... G 302 644-6990
  Lewes (G-6497)
Special Care Inc .... G 302 456-9904
  Wilmington (G-19953)
Specimen Collection Svcs LLC .... G 302 465-0494
  Newark (G-12064)
Spwa Services LLC .... G 856 761-4621
  Ocean View (G-12568)
T & L Consulting Services LLC .... G 302 573-1585
  Wilmington (G-20198)
Tailored Care LLC .... G 302 883-1761
  Magnolia (G-6787)
TLC Home Care .... G 302 983-5720
  Wilmington (G-20338)
Tobola Health Care Svcs Inc .... D 302 389-8448
  Dover (G-3695)
Trinity Home Health Care Corp .... E 302 838-2710
  Newark (G-12233)
Trinity Home Health Care LLC .... G 410 620-9366
  Newark (G-12234)
Vicdania Health Services LLC .... E 302 672-0139
  Dover (G-3790)
Visiting Angels of Dover .... F 302 346-7777
  Dover (G-3805)
Vna of Delaware .... F 302 454-5422
  Newark (G-12334)

8092 Kidney dialysis centers

American Renal .... G 302 672-7901
  Dover (G-1786)
Bio-Mdical Applications of Del .... G 302 998-7568
  Newark (G-10034)
DSI Laurel LLC .... D 302 715-3060
  Laurel (G-5502)
Fresenius Med Care Nthrn Del L .... E 302 239-4704
  Hockessin (G-5214)
Fresenius Medical Care N Amer .... F 302 328-9044
  Historic New Castle (G-4992)
Fresenius Medical Care N Amer .... G 302 633-6228
  Wilmington (G-16749)
Liberty Dalysis-Wilmington LLC .... F 302 429-0142
  Wilmington (G-17891)
Renal Care Group Inc .... D 302 678-8744
  Dover (G-3453)

8093 Specialty outpatient clinics, nec

A Center For Mntal Wllness Cmn .... E 302 674-1397
  Dover (G-1693)
Aba2day Behavior Services .... G 302 494-4303
  Wilmington (G-14191)
Advanced Behavioral Care Inc .... G 410 599-7400
  Lewes (G-5661)
Advanced Treatment Systems .... G 302 792-0700
  Claymont (G-1023)
Advancxing Pain Rhblttion Clin .... F 302 384-7439
  Newark (G-9784)
Adyn Inc .... G 206 451-7105
  Claymont (G-1024)
Ah Therapy Services LLC .... G 302 379-0528
  Wilmington (G-14324)
All The Difference Inc .... F 302 738-6353
  Newark (G-9819)
Angelic Therapy .... G 717 870-4618
  Lewes (G-5691)

Aod Smyrna 43 .... G 302 659-5060
  Smyrna (G-13646)
Applied Biofeedback Solutions .... G 302 674-3225
  Dover (G-1806)
ARC Seminars LLC .... G 856 776-6758
  Middletown (G-6872)
Art and Therapy Services .... G 302 329-9794
  Milton (G-8563)
At Eaze Massage Therapy .... G 302 559-3019
  Smyrna (G-13651)
Back To Blance Healing Therapy .... G 302 478-6470
  Wilmington (G-14713)
Bancroft Behavioral Health Inc .... G 302 502-3255
  Wilmington (G-14736)
Bellwether Behavioral Health .... G 856 769-2042
  Wilmington (G-14825)
Blooming Speech .... G 302 528-6663
  Wilmington (G-14962)
Body Ease Therapy .... G 610 314-0780
  Newark (G-10066)
Brain Works & Mind Matters LLC .... G 302 324-5255
  New Castle (G-8882)
Brandywine Cnsling Cmnty Svcs .... E 302 454-3020
  Newark (G-10078)
Brandywine Counseling .... E 302 856-4700
  Georgetown (G-4240)
Brandywine Occpational Therapy .... F 302 740-4798
  Wilmington (G-15077)
Capitol Nrsing Rhblttion Ctr L .... E 302 734-1199
  Dover (G-2023)
Cardio-Kinetics Inc .... E 302 738-6635
  Newark (G-10140)
Chopra Hlco LLC .... F 631 413-4249
  Dover (G-2068)
Christiana Care Health Sys Inc .... C 302 623-0390
  Newark (G-10223)
Christina Care Vna .... F 302 327-5212
  Wilmington (G-15413)
Cimi Enterprises LLC .... F 302 803-2210
  Middletown (G-6981)
Claymont Cmprhnsive Trtmnt Ctr .... G 302 792-0700
  Claymont (G-1091)
Common Cooperative Company .... G 504 333-0731
  Wilmington (G-15550)
Connections .... F 302 221-6605
  New Castle (G-8965)
Connectons Cmnty Spport Prgram .... D 302 536-1952
  Seaford (G-13134)
Corinthian House .... G 302 858-1493
  Georgetown (G-4268)
De Sleep Disorder Centers LLC .... G 302 697-2749
  Camden (G-815)
Defy Therapy Services LLC .... G 302 290-9562
  Wilmington (G-15857)
Delaware Curative Workshop .... D 302 656-2521
  Wilmington (G-15899)
Delaware Dept Hlth Social Svcs .... G 302 857-5000
  Dover (G-2229)
Delaware Dept Hlth Social Svcs .... F 302 368-6700
  Newark (G-10433)
Delaware Dept Hlth Social Svcs .... G 302 283-7500
  Newark (G-10434)
Delaware Sleep Disorder C .... F 302 407-3349
  Middletown (G-7046)
Delaware Spine Rehabilitation .... F 302 883-2292
  Dover (G-2261)
Delaware Spine Rehabilitation .... G 302 563-7442
  Historic New Castle (G-4972)
Delmarva Surgery Ctr .... G 443 245-3470
  Newark (G-10506)
Devereux Foundation .... E 302 731-2500
  Newark (G-10519)

Dima II Inc .... F 302 427-0787
  Wilmington (G-16072)
Divine Transitional Life LLC .... G 215 432-4974
  Newark (G-10540)
Doris V Obenshain .... G 302 448-1450
  Middletown (G-7070)
Dr GS Weightloss .... G 302 232-5153
  Wilmington (G-16165)
Dynamic Therapy Services LLC .... G 302 566-6624
  Harrington (G-4765)
Dynamic Therapy Services LLC .... G 302 280-6953
  Laurel (G-5504)
Easter Sals Del Mrylnds Estrn .... D 302 678-3353
  Dover (G-2411)
Elwyn Pennsylvania and Del .... D 302 658-8860
  Wilmington (G-16382)
Emory Massage Therapy .... G 302 290-0003
  Dover (G-2442)
Encompass Health Corporation .... F 302 464-3400
  Middletown (G-7101)
Essential Bgnnngs Bhvior Lrng .... F 302 278-0052
  Smyrna (G-13725)
Essentials Recovery Delaware .... F 302 256-0454
  Wilmington (G-16466)
Family Planning .... G 302 856-5225
  Georgetown (G-4314)
Fellowship Hlth Resources Inc .... G 302 422-6699
  Milford (G-7890)
Focus Behavioral Health .... G 302 762-2285
  Wilmington (G-16679)
Focus Health Care Delaware LLC .... D 302 395-1111
  New Castle (G-9138)
Focus Rehabilitation & Fitness .... G 302 231-8982
  Millsboro (G-8293)
Henlopen Music Therapy SE .... G 302 593-7784
  Lewes (G-6090)
Holistic Elevation LLC .... G 302 278-0026
  Bear (G-277)
Hudson House Services .... G 302 856-4363
  Georgetown (G-4367)
Hysiotherapy Associates Inc .... G 610 444-1270
  Wilmington (G-17244)
Informed Tuch Mssage Thrapy LL .... G 302 229-8239
  Townsend (G-14017)
Intouch Body Therapy LLC .... G 302 537-0510
  Bethany Beach (G-609)
Introspction Cunseling Ctr LLC .... G 302 213-6158
  Dover (G-2750)
Intuitive Care Therapy .... G 302 200-6123
  Wilmington (G-17402)
Jameil Akeem Cngo Cres Fndtion .... G 302 409-0791
  Wilmington (G-17477)
Jan Stern Eqine Asssted Thrapy .... G 302 234-9835
  Wilmington (G-17491)
Janelle G Evans LLC .... G 302 562-6504
  Wilmington (G-17493)
Jans Hands Massage Therapy .... G 302 753-3962
  Wilmington (G-17496)
Joselow Beth Lpcmh .... F 302 644-0130
  Lewes (G-6152)
Journeys LLC .... E 302 384-7843
  Wilmington (G-17592)
Julie Lewicki .... F 302 531-0763
  Dover (G-2817)
Kent Sussex Community Services .... E 302 384-6926
  Dover (G-2858)
Knus Inc .... D 855 935-5687
  Wilmington (G-17745)
Lake Therapy Creations .... G 410 920-7130
  Newark (G-11215)
Lewes Expressive Therapy .... G 302 727-3275
  Lewes (G-6195)

SIC SECTION
80 HEALTH SERVICES

Lotus Rcvery Ctr Prces Crnr LL............ E 302 999-8900
  Wilmington *(G-18003)*

Management Pain LLC......................... G 302 543-5180
  Wilmington *(G-18099)*

Marc Wsburg Lpcmh Mntal Hlth C.......... G 302 798-4400
  Wilmington *(G-18120)*

McCormick Assoc Middletown LLC........ G 302 449-0710
  Middletown *(G-7333)*

Medi-Weightloss Clinics....................... G 302 763-3455
  Hockessin *(G-5307)*

Mental Health Assn In Del................... G 302 654-6833
  Wilmington *(G-18272)*

Merakey USA..................................... F 302 836-1809
  Newark *(G-11388)*

Midatlantic Pain Institute..................... F 302 369-1700
  Newark *(G-11415)*

Moore Physcial Therapy...................... G 302 654-8142
  Wilmington *(G-18436)*

More About You Inc............................ G 302 229-4414
  Bear *(G-380)*

Multispecialty Healthcare.................... G 302 575-9794
  Wilmington *(G-18483)*

National Alnce On Mntal Illnes.............. E 302 427-0787
  Wilmington *(G-18538)*

National Stress Clinic LLC................... G 646 571-8627
  Wilmington *(G-18548)*

Necessary Luxury.............................. G 302 764-4032
  Wilmington *(G-18568)*

New Body By Tomorrow LLC................ E 706 816-9255
  Dover *(G-3178)*

New Life Fndation Recovery Inc............ G 302 317-2212
  Bear *(G-393)*

Norkrisservices................................. G 302 450-6108
  Middletown *(G-7410)*

Northeast Treatment Ctrs Inc............... D 302 691-0140
  Wilmington *(G-18683)*

Northwestern Human Services............. G 302 996-4858
  Wilmington *(G-18689)*

Novacare Rehabilitation Dover............. G 302 760-9966
  Dover *(G-3204)*

Novacare Rehabilitation Seafor............ G 302 990-2951
  Seaford *(G-13321)*

Nu Beginning Center LLC................... G 302 276-8483
  Smyrna *(G-13837)*

Occupational Therapy........................ G 302 994-4566
  Wilmington *(G-18740)*

Occuptnl Thrpy of Delaware................ F 302 491-4813
  Milford *(G-8035)*

On The Spot Massage........................ G 302 545-5200
  Bear *(G-407)*

Oneness Massage Therapy................. G 302 893-0348
  Newark *(G-11594)*

Pace Inc.. F 302 999-9812
  Wilmington *(G-18858)*

Pain & Sleep Therapy Center............... F 302 314-1409
  Wilmington *(G-18863)*

Phoenix Ctr For Hlth Wllness L............. G 302 543-5321
  Wilmington *(G-19024)*

Planned Parenthood of Delaware.......... G 302 731-7801
  Newark *(G-11699)*

Planned Parenthood of Delaware.......... E 302 655-7293
  Wilmington *(G-19069)*

Point Hope Brain Injury Spport............. F 302 731-7676
  New Castle *(G-9479)*

Premier Spine & Rehab...................... G 302 730-4878
  Dover *(G-3363)*

Premier Spine and Rehab................... G 302 404-5293
  Seaford *(G-13354)*

Presicson Pain Rhbltation Svcs............ F 302 827-2321
  Rehoboth Beach *(G-12900)*

Pro Rehab Chiropractic...................... G 302 200-9102
  Lewes *(G-6392)*

Psychotherapeutic Services................. E 302 672-7159
  Dover *(G-3389)*

Psychotherapeutic Services................. E 302 737-1597
  Newark *(G-11770)*

Psychotherapeutic Svc Assn Inc............ G 302 284-8370
  Dover *(G-3390)*

R H D Brandywine Hills........................ F 302 764-3660
  Wilmington *(G-19305)*

Recovery Innovations Inc.................... G 302 660-7560
  Wilmington *(G-19379)*

Recovery Inovations Inc..................... G 602 636-4608
  Newark *(G-11837)*

Rehabilitation Associates Pa................ G 302 293-6877
  Newark *(G-11845)*

Rehabitation Consultants.................... G 302 478-2131
  Wilmington *(G-19414)*

Relax Massage Therapy..................... G 302 738-7300
  Newark *(G-11848)*

Relaxing Tours LLC............................ G 610 905-3852
  Greenwood *(G-4663)*

Richard L Todd PHD........................... G 302 853-0559
  Milton *(G-8696)*

S T Progressive Strides...................... G 410 775-8103
  Bear *(G-477)*

Safe Space Delaware Inc.................... F 302 691-7946
  Wilmington *(G-19625)*

Sleep Disorders Ctr-Christiana............. F 302 623-0650
  Newark *(G-12030)*

Sodat - Delaware Inc.......................... F 302 656-2810
  Wilmington *(G-19911)*

Soundingboard Project........................ G 302 956-1112
  Wilmington *(G-19936)*

Sussex Pregnancy Care Center............ G 302 856-4344
  Georgetown *(G-4542)*

Swedish Massage Therapy................. G 302 841-3166
  Ocean View *(G-12575)*

Tele-Help Inc.................................... G 888 247-5767
  New Castle *(G-9623)*

Therapy Concierge LLC...................... G 302 319-3040
  Bear *(G-529)*

Therapy Services of Delaw.................. G 302 239-2285
  Hockessin *(G-5403)*

Tidewater Physcl Thrpy and REB........... G 302 945-5111
  Lewes *(G-6558)*

Tidewater Physcl Thrpy and REB........... G 302 629-4024
  Seaford *(G-13431)*

Total Health & Rehabilitation................ G 302 999-9202
  Wilmington *(G-20371)*

Trauma Rehabilitation PA.................... G 302 777-7723
  Wilmington *(G-20403)*

Unique Massage Therapy.................... G 302 359-5982
  Dover *(G-3750)*

US Dept of the Air Force..................... E 302 677-2525
  Dover *(G-3764)*

V Dima Inc....................................... G 302 427-0787
  Wilmington *(G-20559)*

Verde Loma LLC................................ G 302 858-4040
  Georgetown *(G-4568)*

Veritas Judgment Recovery................. G 302 376-7076
  Middletown *(G-7687)*

VI Dima Inc...................................... G 302 427-0787
  Wilmington *(G-20603)*

Waybetter Inc................................... F 212 343-8238
  Wilmington *(G-20691)*

Weighted With Love LLC..................... G 302 378-2041
  Townsend *(G-14090)*

Wilmington Pain/Rehab Cntr PA............ G 302 575-1776
  Wilmington *(G-20829)*

Worlds Best Massage Therapy............. G 302 366-8777
  Newark *(G-12411)*

Zen Therapy & Bodywork Inc............... G 302 252-1733
  Wilmington *(G-20951)*

8099 Health and allied services, nec

166th Medical Squadron..................... F 302 323-3385
  New Castle *(G-8744)*

1source Safety Health........................ G 302 470-2001
  Wilmington *(G-14114)*

360 Wellness LLC.............................. G 302 286-0118
  Wilmington *(G-14126)*

Abundant Natural Health Inc............... G 302 652-2900
  Wilmington *(G-14210)*

Acadia Healthcare Company Inc.......... F 302 328-3330
  New Castle *(G-8759)*

Access Quality Healthcare................... G 302 698-2150
  Camden Wyoming *(G-905)*

Access Quality Healthcare................... G 302 947-4437
  Millsboro *(G-8161)*

Accss Qlty Healthcare Accss................ G 302 339-4112
  Georgetown *(G-4196)*

Acuhealth & Wellness........................ G 302 438-4493
  Middletown *(G-6833)*

Affinity Womens Health LLC................ F 302 234-8982
  Hockessin *(G-5116)*

Air Medics Hvac LLC.......................... G 302 439-4254
  Claymont *(G-1027)*

Akshar Medical Service...................... G 302 369-3533
  Bear *(G-23)*

All Things Inspiring Wellness............... G 302 943-5503
  Dover *(G-1766)*

Alpha Medical Distribution.................. F 302 738-9742
  Newark *(G-9833)*

Ambrogi Integrative Hlth Servi............. G 610 368-1006
  Wilmington *(G-14417)*

Amerihealth Caritas Delaware............. F 844 211-0966
  Bear *(G-35)*

Amy Corbitt..................................... F 302 635-7233
  New Castle *(G-8805)*

An Intgrative Hlth Ctr Med Spa............ G 484 550-2085
  Newark *(G-9857)*

Andrew W Donohue Do...................... G 302 235-3725
  Wilmington *(G-14479)*

Apollo Health & Wellness LLC.............. G 302 994-2273
  Wilmington *(G-14508)*

Arab Therapy Inc.............................. E 310 956-4252
  Wilmington *(G-14521)*

Ashley Lntti Holistic Hlth LLC............... G 804 347-2641
  Wilmington *(G-14585)*

Aspira Health LLC............................. D 302 567-1500
  Lewes *(G-5706)*

Aspire Wellness LLC.......................... G 302 366-1727
  Newark *(G-9925)*

Atlantic Adult Pdtrics Mdcine............... G 302 644-1300
  Lewes *(G-5712)*

Atlantic General Hospital.................... G 302 539-2399
  Fenwick Island *(G-4040)*

Bancroft Behavioral Health................. G 302 690-0626
  Wilmington *(G-14735)*

Bancroft Inc..................................... F 856 769-1300
  Newark *(G-9978)*

Bancroft Neuro Health........................ G 302 266-7054
  Newark *(G-9979)*

Bancroft Neurohealth......................... D 302 691-8531
  Wilmington *(G-14740)*

Bay Health Frezza Charles.................. F 302 430-5565
  Milford *(G-7783)*

Bayhealth Bariatric Program............... F 302 430-5454
  Milford *(G-7786)*

Bayhealth Ent of Dover...................... F 302 674-3752
  Dover *(G-1888)*

Bca Mental Health Counseling............. G 302 513-9565
  Wilmington *(G-14794)*

Beachview Family Health................... G 302 537-8318
  Millville *(G-8517)*

Employee Codes: A=Over 500 employees, B=251-500
C=101-250, D=51-100, E=20-50, F=10-19, G=1-9

2024 Harris Directory of Delaware Businesses

80 HEALTH SERVICES

Company	Location	Grade	Phone
Bear Int Med Peds	Bear (G-65)	G	302 595-2146
Beginners Choice Day Care Ctr	Selbyville (G-13475)	G	302 436-4460
Behavioral Health Center Inc	Ocean View (G-12476)	G	808 944-6900
Brain Love Neurotherapy	Rehoboth Beach (G-12650)	G	302 278-7828
Brandx Heirloom Tomatoes	Townsend (G-13965)	G	302 287-1782
Calm Medical Massage Exprt Inc	Wilmington (G-15200)	G	443 566-0655
Canna Care Docs Delaware LLC	Wilmington (G-15217)	G	302 594-0630
Care Constitution LLC	Middletown (G-6955)	G	201 240-3661
Careportmd LLC	Newark (G-10142)	G	302 202-3020
Caring For Womens Health	Newark (G-10145)	F	302 489-2420
Caritas Home Health Services	Newark (G-10147)	G	302 525-6331
Celeri Health Inc	Wilmington (G-15300)	F	302 438-0766
Celesstia Health LLC	Dover (G-2044)	G	302 241-0601
Chas Medicine	Lewes (G-5809)	G	302 644-5870
Chayil Healthcarellc	Milford (G-7823)	G	302 399-0991
Chopin Building	Newark (G-10209)	G	302 283-7130
Christiana Care Health System	Wilmington (G-15405)	F	302 992-5545
Claymont Nutrition	Claymont (G-1094)	G	302 792-7818
Clough Health and Wellness LLC	Wilmington (G-15496)	G	443 414-3764
Colon Health Centers Americ	Newark (G-10275)	G	302 995-2656
Common Sense Health Research	Rehoboth Beach (G-12695)	G	302 260-9811
Compassonate Certification Ctr	Middletown (G-7007)	G	888 316-9085
Consensus Medical Systems	Newark (G-10308)	G	302 453-1969
Continental Health Care Svcs	Bear (G-119)	G	240 461-8569
Cornerstone Health Partners	Wilmington (G-15642)	G	302 561-4080
Creekside Counseling & Wellnes	Newark (G-10352)	G	302 562-7953
CT Partners LLC	Wilmington (G-15728)	G	302 766-4176
Ctm Medical Associates LLC	Milton (G-8593)	G	302 645-8587
De Medical Care	Smyrna (G-13694)	F	302 653-1281
Deact Medical Solutions Inc	Wilmington (G-15843)	G	302 354-6575
Decisionrx Inc	Dover (G-2206)	F	800 957-3606
Dedo Ventures & Health Inc	Bear (G-140)	G	302 838-1445
Delaware Adlescent Program Inc	Newark (G-10415)	E	302 268-7218
Delaware Care Collaboration	Wilmington (G-15881)	F	302 575-8371
Delaware Center For Cnselng	Newark (G-10422)	G	302 353-7052
Delaware Center For Counseling	Newark (G-10423)	G	302 292-1334
Delaware Colon Hydrotherapy	Wilmington (G-15888)	G	302 543-5717
Delaware Eye Clinics	Lewes (G-5897)	G	302 645-2338
Delaware Foster Care	Wilmington (G-15920)	G	302 656-2655
Delaware Health and Fitnes LLC	Hockessin (G-5179)	G	302 584-7531
Delaware Health Corp	Wilmington (G-15924)	E	302 655-0955
Delaware Health Net Inc	Wilmington (G-15925)	G	410 788-9715
Delaware Imaging Network	Newark (G-10453)	D	302 737-5990
Delaware Integrative Medical C	Georgetown (G-4282)	G	302 559-5959
Delaware Med Care Assoc LLC	Newark (G-10458)	G	302 633-9033
Delaware Occptnal Hlth Svcs LL	Newark (G-10464)	E	302 368-5100
Denmark School	Wilmington (G-16010)	G	302 416-6180
Dental Health Center Del-Tech	Wilmington (G-16015)	G	302 657-5176
Diamond State Srgcal Assoc LLC	Middletown (G-7057)	F	302 449-9660
Douglas Morrow	Wilmington (G-16156)	G	302 750-9161
Dover Behavorl Hlth 249	Dover (G-2334)	E	302 741-0140
Dr Debra Wolf Encore Health	Newark (G-10561)	G	302 737-1918
Dr Kellyann LLC	Dover (G-2375)	C	888 871-2155
Ds Express LLC	Middletown (G-7073)	G	302 494-4957
Dysis Medical	Wilmington (G-16233)	G	813 997-8979
▲ Eagle Mhc Company	Clayton (G-1363)	B	302 653-3000
Elaine Willey	Seaford (G-13172)	G	302 536-1286
Ella Health Inc	Wilmington (G-16371)	G	302 543-4396
Elsmere Nutrition	Wilmington (G-16380)	G	302 502-2061
Emotinal Wllness Cunseling LLC	Houston (G-5440)	G	302 865-8098
Empire Medical LLC	Camden (G-830)	G	443 553-0057
Ephphatha Med Care Svcs LLC	Seaford (G-13177)	G	925 222-9572
Er At Home Llc	Newark (G-10662)	G	540 845-9499
Eternal Health LLC	Wilmington (G-16473)	G	302 635-7421
Exam Master Corporation	Newark (G-10682)	E	800 572-3627
Extensive Health Services LLC	Newark (G-10693)	G	302 733-0303
Fast Care Medical Aid Unit LLC	Claymont (G-1149)	G	302 793-7506
First Halthcare Compliance LLC	Wilmington (G-16618)	F	302 416-4329
First State Health & Wellness	Milton (G-8624)	G	302 684-1995
First State Nutrition	Wilmington (G-16631)	G	302 384-7104
Focus Rehabilitation & Fitness	Millsboro (G-8293)	G	302 231-8982
Footprnts Prof Wrting Svcs LLC	Milton (G-8626)	G	917 324-6941
Foundation of Health	Wilmington (G-16705)	F	302 762-5973
Four C Health Solutions	Wilmington (G-16709)	E	804 601-2628
Germantown Medical Associates	Wilmington (G-16852)	G	484 431-5226
Global Wellness	Hockessin (G-5222)	G	302 234-6550
Green Clinics Laboratory LLC	Dover (G-2621)	E	302 734-5050
Hcsg Harbor Hc Harbo44	Lewes (G-6085)	G	302 645-4664
Health Care Solutions of	Claymont (G-1177)	G	484 234-2427
Health Support Services	Wilmington (G-17097)	G	302 287-4952
Healthcare Oprtons MGT Enterpr	Bear (G-267)	G	302 832-9572
Healthy Directions Wellness	Millsboro (G-8316)	G	302 420-3927
Heckessin Health Partners	Hockessin (G-5236)	G	302 234-2597
Holistic Health Care Delaware	Ocean View (G-12523)	G	302 545-1552
Home Medic LLC	Georgetown (G-4362)	F	302 841-3861
Hope Health Systems Inc	Middletown (G-7215)	G	302 376-9619
Hope Wellness Opportunity	Newark (G-10969)	G	302 521-6421
Hospitalists of Delaware	Newark (G-10972)	G	302 757-1231
Ilara Health Inc	Wilmington (G-17278)	G	646 322-7452
Impact Sports & Health Inc	Newark (G-11003)	G	734 678-5726
In Wellness We Win	Middletown (G-7224)	G	917 509-5414
Infinity Health & Wellness Del	Wilmington (G-17323)	G	302 543-5717
Integrated Health Assoc LLC	Dover (G-2742)	F	302 264-1021
Integrity Home Health Llc	Newark (G-11035)	G	302 981-4475
Integrity Nursing and Hea	Smyrna (G-13774)	G	302 275-8838
Jmk Behavior LLC	Wilmington (G-17557)	G	302 384-7354
Jo Stefanie Armour	Middletown (G-7251)	G	302 838-5311
Joshi Medical PA	Bear (G-310)	G	302 838-8858
Journey2wellness	Smyrna (G-13782)	G	302 399-6755
Karo Healthcare Inc	Wilmington (G-17655)	G	973 975-8306
Kennedy Health Pain Relief and	Wilmington (G-17686)	G	302 691-0110
Kent Family Medicine	Dover (G-2849)	G	302 747-7903
Kent General Hospital Inc	Milford (G-7963)	A	302 430-5705
La Red Health Center Inc	Seaford (G-13253)	D	408 533-3189
La Red Health Center Inc	Georgetown (G-4399)	E	302 855-1233
Laurel Highschool Wellness Ctr	Laurel (G-5548)	G	302 875-6164
Level Funded Hlth Partners LLC	Dover (G-2930)	G	847 310-8190
Lewes Walk-In Medical LLC	Newark (G-11248)	G	302 561-5429

80 HEALTH SERVICES

Lewes Wellness Center.................................... G 302 313-9990
  Lewes (G-6202)
Life At St Frncis Hlthcare Inc......................... G 302 660-3297
  Wilmington (G-17899)
Life Behavioral Hlth Consulta......................... G 302 312-6104
  Bear (G-347)
Life Net.. G 302 855-0550
  Georgetown (G-4406)
Lily Intrnl Medicine Asscs LLC....................... G 302 424-1000
  Dover (G-2948)
Little Miracles Child Care Ctr......................... G 302 367-4838
  Newark (G-11270)
Living Great Medical Assoc LLC.................... G 302 734-9200
  Dover (G-2959)
Living Well Natural Health............................. G 302 653-9748
  Smyrna (G-13808)
Lk Rejoice Child Care Center......................... G 302 543-4621
  Wilmington (G-17952)
Lucky Wellness Center Inc............................. G 302 990-5441
  Seaford (G-13268)
Lux Medical Solutions LLC............................. G 302 440-4557
  Lewes (G-6231)
Mac Concussion Center.................................. G 302 379-1027
  Hockessin (G-5287)
Mamaste Doula and Birth Svcs..................... G 302 670-3188
  Dover (G-3005)
Mara Puglisi Holistic Hlth LLC........................ G 302 368-4245
  Newark (G-11326)
Mara Puglisi Holistic Hlth LLC........................ G 240 338-0137
  Newark (G-11327)
Mary L Kreider.. G 302 375-6232
  Wilmington (G-18180)
McLaren Health Care Corp.............................. G 214 257-7012
  Historic New Castle (G-5026)
Medical Alternative Care................................ G 302 430-5705
  Milford (G-7993)
Medical Joyworks LLC.................................... F 310 919-4287
  Wilmington (G-18249)
Medical Reimbursement Sol........................... G 516 809-6812
  Millsboro (G-8372)
Medicine Woman.. G 302 684-8048
  Milton (G-8666)
Medimaps Group USA LLC............................. G 302 416-3063
  Wilmington (G-18254)
Meghan Zgler Hlth Wellness LLC................... G 302 379-9967
  Townsend (G-14033)
Meher Health Services................................... G 302 947-0333
  Millsboro (G-8373)
Melaleuca Wellness Company....................... G 336 314-5635
  Newark (G-11384)
Mid Atlantic Wellness Gro.............................. G 302 864-7766
  Rehoboth Beach (G-12855)
Mind Mechanix.. G 302 503-5142
  Milford (G-8013)
Murphy Mental Health.................................... G 302 463-7903
  Newark (G-11472)
My Medicare Advisor LLC............................... G 302 602-9426
  Bear (G-384)
Myositis Spport Undrstnding As.................... F 888 696-7273
  Lincoln (G-6691)
Nanticoke Health Services Inc....................... B 302 629-6611
  Seaford (G-13305)
Navipoint Health Inc....................................... G 888 902-3998
  Wilmington (G-18564)
New Hope Family Medicine LLC.................... G 302 388-9304
  Wilmington (G-18618)
New U Nutrition Inc.. G 302 543-4555
  Wilmington (G-18627)
New York Blood Center Inc............................ G 302 737-8405
  Dagsboro (G-1488)
New York Blood Center Inc............................ D 302 737-8405
  Newark (G-11528)

New York Blood Ctr Inc D/B/A B................... F 302 734-4100
  Dover (G-3182)
New York Blood Ctr Inc D/B/A B................... F 302 737-8400
  Georgetown (G-4444)
New York Blood Ctr Inc D/B/A B................... G 302 737-8400
  Wilmington (G-18629)
Next Century Medical Care LLC.................... G 302 375-6746
  Newark (G-11552)
Now Care Pain Relief Center.......................... G 302 276-1951
  Bear (G-401)
Nuraxi Holdings Inc.. F 571 213-2519
  Wilmington (G-18716)
Nutra4health LLC... G 704 223-8677
  Lewes (G-6322)
Ocean Rach Intrnal Medicine PA................... G 302 644-7472
  Lewes (G-6327)
One Stop Medical Inc..................................... G 302 450-4479
  Milford (G-8037)
Open Systems Healthcare.............................. E 302 298-3260
  Wilmington (G-18797)
Out-Train Fitness & Prfmce LLC.................... G 610 470-3196
  Milton (G-8680)
Paradigm Healthcare Assoc Inc.................... F 302 352-0517
  Wilmington (G-18883)
Pearl Clinic LLC.. G 302 648-2099
  Millsboro (G-8417)
Peninsula Health LLC..................................... G 302 945-0440
  Millsboro (G-8422)
Perdue Wellness Center................................. G 302 424-2663
  Milford (G-8047)
Persante... F 302 253-8740
  Georgetown (G-4463)
Pharmd Live Corporation............................... D 908 803-3311
  Dover (G-3311)
Phoenix Intelligence Inc................................. G 844 663-4799
  Dover (G-3315)
Phoenix Nightingale....................................... G 302 377-6876
  Wilmington (G-19026)
Pivot Occupational Health LLC..................... F 302 368-5100
  Newark (G-11697)
Pivotal Medical... G 302 299-5795
  Bethany Beach (G-627)
Pneuma Wellness & Spa LLC........................ G 302 990-8907
  Dover (G-3343)
Premier Health Service LLC.......................... F 302 597-6810
  Bear (G-437)
Produce For Btter Hlth Fndtion..................... G 302 235-2329
  Newark (G-11758)
Pure Wellness LLC... G 302 389-8915
  Smyrna (G-13859)
Quakertown Wellness Center........................ G 302 644-0130
  Lewes (G-6398)
Quick Care Walk In and Medical................... G 302 313-4660
  Lewes (G-6402)
Quoretech LLC.. G 206 627-0030
  Wilmington (G-19299)
RC&ps LLC.. F 516 984-8184
  Dover (G-3427)
Reciprocity Health LLC.................................. G 302 530-5244
  Wilmington (G-19378)
Regional Medical Group LLC......................... G 302 993-7890
  Wilmington (G-19405)
Rekindle Family Medicine.............................. G 302 565-4799
  Wilmington (G-19420)
Reliance Healthcare LLC................................ G 302 838-3100
  Bear (G-452)
Renal Care Ctr.. G 302 453-8834
  New Castle (G-9519)
Renew Integrative Health.............................. G 302 444-4366
  Newark (G-11851)
Rosa Health Center Inc.................................. G 302 858-4381
  Georgetown (G-4492)

Samto Medical Services................................. G 302 266-4933
  Newark (G-11940)
Sandler Occupational Health........................ G 302 607-7365
  Newark (G-11942)
Sands Health Spa LLC................................... G 302 543-8385
  Wilmington (G-19662)
SB&b Wellness LLC.. G 484 681-1411
  Dover (G-3513)
Seaford Medical Specialists........................... G 302 628-8300
  Seaford (G-13390)
Seascape Lab... G 760 807-7983
  Milford (G-8088)
Select Health Services LLC........................... G 504 737-4300
  Newark (G-11973)
Shayona Health Inc.. G 570 677-5509
  Newark (G-11993)
Shayona Health Inc.. G 302 660-8847
  Wilmington (G-19784)
Shirleys Little Friends Llc............................. G 302 981-9991
  Wilmington (G-19805)
Skin Care School & Ctr.................................. G 302 328-0611
  Wilmington (G-19854)
Sleep Disorders Center.................................. G 302 645-3186
  Lewes (G-6476)
Smyrna Medical Aid Unit............................... G 302 659-4444
  Smyrna (G-13895)
Southeastern Home Health Svcs................... G 214 466-1351
  Christiana (G-1009)
Spinal Health & Wellness.............................. G 302 993-9113
  Wilmington (G-19963)
Spirits Path To Wellness LLC........................ G 302 998-0074
  Wilmington (G-19968)
Splash Day... G 302 238-7457
  Millsboro (G-8466)
State of Delaware... E 302 322-2303
  New Castle (G-9594)
Suburban Intrnal Medcne Assocs................. F 302 654-4800
  Wilmington (G-20112)
Sun Behavioral Delaware LLC....................... E 732 747-1800
  Georgetown (G-4530)
Sunrise Medical Center................................. G 302 854-9006
  Millsboro (G-8470)
Sunshine Health... F 302 463-7600
  Wilmington (G-20136)
Swank Memory Care Center.......................... F 302 320-2620
  Wilmington (G-20169)
TAB Wellness Inc.. G 914 396-4316
  New Castle (G-9614)
Tabitha Medical Care LLC.............................. G 302 251-8870
  Laurel (G-5613)
Techworld Corporation Inc............................ G 302 757-3866
  Hockessin (G-5402)
Telemind Clinic.. G 253 332-4110
  Middletown (G-7630)
TGI Rebate Center.. G 866 433-3009
  Wilmington (G-20288)
Tidalhlth Pnnsula Regional Inc..................... C 302 537-1457
  Millville (G-8549)
Transforming Wellness LLC.......................... G 302 249-2526
  Millville (G-8550)
Tri-State Integrative Hlth LLC....................... G 302 743-2328
  Wilmington (G-20413)
Trolley Square Nutrition................................ G 302 757-6669
  Newark (G-12239)
Ud Student Wellness Hlth Prom................... G 302 831-3457
  Newark (G-12259)
United Medical Clinics of De......................... F 302 451-5607
  Bear (G-551)
Up and Away Travel Health........................... G 302 455-8416
  Newark (G-12283)
VA Medical Ctr Wilmington De...................... G 302 563-6024
  Middletown (G-7680)

80 HEALTH SERVICES

Veda Health Group LLC............................... G 302 536-8332
  Wilmington (G-20574)
Vemo Acu LLC.. G 508 654-7885
  Newark (G-12311)
Verdant Plant Health Care............................. G 302 593-0444
  Wilmington (G-20585)
Waked Tarek MD.. G 703 342-7744
  Seaford (G-13442)
Wellness and Rejuvenation............................ G 732 977-6958
  Millsboro (G-8503)
Wellness By Sea LLC..................................... G 302 278-0093
  Fenwick Island (G-4058)
Wellness From Within..................................... G 717 884-3908
  Lewes (G-6622)
Wellness Plus... G 302 368-7990
  Newark (G-12357)
Wellness Strategies LLC................................ G 302 475-5062
  Wilmington (G-20721)
Wellness Wahine... G 302 841-4988
  Milton (G-8729)
Wilmington VA Medical Cent........................ G 302 294-6743
  Newark (G-12385)
Womens Imaging Center Delaware............ G 302 738-9494
  Newark (G-12397)
Workpro... G 302 300-4392
  Wilmington (G-20892)
Zen Acupuncture Clinic................................. G 302 559-1325
  Wilmington (G-20950)
Zendo Medical LLC... G 302 322-3442
  New Castle (G-9697)
Zeuss LLC.. G 305 904-8078
  Wilmington (G-20960)
Ziphealth Inc.. G 561 207-7140
  Lewes (G-6650)

81 LEGAL SERVICES

8111 Legal services

4dimensions LLC.. D 302 339-0082
  New Castle (G-8747)
Abrams & Bayliss LLP................................... F 302 778-1000
  Wilmington (G-14208)
Agents of Delaware Inc................................. F 302 544-2467
  New Castle (G-8772)
Agile Legal.. E 302 376-6710
  Middletown (G-6841)
Alan L Frank Law Associates PA................ G 302 502-2702
  Wilmington (G-14344)
Albert J Roop.. G 302 655-4600
  Wilmington (G-14349)
Alexis Legal Support Svcs Inc..................... G 646 494-3289
  Newark (G-9809)
Allen & Associates... F 302 234-8600
  Wilmington (G-14373)
Allmond & Eastburn....................................... G 302 764-2193
  Bethany Beach (G-573)
Amber B Woodland.. G 302 628-4140
  Seaford (G-13059)
American Income Lf - Ryan Bsan................ G 484 442-8148
  Wilmington (G-14431)
American Incorporators Ltd.......................... E 302 421-5752
  Wilmington (G-14432)
Andrews & Springer LLC.............................. F 302 504-4957
  Wilmington (G-14481)
Archer & Greiner A Prof Corp...................... G 302 777-4350
  Wilmington (G-14541)
Ashby & Geddes.. F 302 654-1888
  Wilmington (G-14579)
Ashley M Oland.. G 302 854-5406
  Georgetown (G-4213)
Atlantic Law Group LLC............................... D 302 854-0380
  Georgetown (G-4216)

Axencis Inc.. E 302 888-9002
  Wilmington (G-14680)
Baird Mandalas Brockstedt LLC.................. F 302 644-0302
  Lewes (G-5734)
Baird Mandalas Brockstedt LLC.................. F 302 677-0061
  Dover (G-1868)
Balick & Balick Pllc.. G 302 658-4265
  Wilmington (G-14722)
Ballard Spahr LLP.. G 302 252-4465
  Wilmington (G-14723)
Bankruptcy Anywhere.................................... G 302 426-4777
  Wilmington (G-14750)
Barnett Tom D Law Firm............................... G 302 855-9252
  Georgetown (G-4222)
Barros Mc Nmara Mlkwicz Tylor................. F 302 734-8400
  Dover (G-1876)
Bench Walk Advisors LLC............................ G 302 426-2100
  Wilmington (G-14826)
Benesch Attorneys At Law........................... F 302 442-7005
  Wilmington (G-14834)
Benesch FrdInder Cplan Arnoff................... F 216 363-4500
  Wilmington (G-14835)
Benjamin W Keenan....................................... G 302 654-1888
  Wilmington (G-14837)
Beverly L Bove PA.. G 302 777-3500
  Wilmington (G-14867)
Biden For AG Inc.. G 302 295-8340
  Wilmington (G-14877)
Bielli & Klauder LLC...................................... G 302 803-4600
  Wilmington (G-14879)
Bifferato Gentilotti LLC.................................. G 302 429-1900
  Wilmington (G-14880)
Biggs & Battaglia... F 302 655-9677
  Wilmington (G-14888)
Blank Rome LLP... G 302 425-6400
  Wilmington (G-14952)
Bodell Bove LLC... G 302 655-6749
  Wilmington (G-14992)
Boudart & Mensinger LLP............................ G 302 428-0100
  Wilmington (G-15010)
Brady Law Firm PA.. G 302 482-4124
  Wilmington (G-15034)
Brown Shiels & OBrien.................................. G 302 734-4766
  Dover (G-1985)
Brown Shels Bauregard LLC........................ G 302 226-2270
  Dover (G-1986)
Brown Stone Nimeroff LLC........................... E 302 428-8142
  Wilmington (G-15129)
Burr & Forman LLP.. F 302 425-6400
  Wilmington (G-15154)
Business Incorporators.................................. G 302 475-6596
  Wilmington (G-15158)
Campbell & Levine LLC................................ G 302 426-1900
  Wilmington (G-15210)
Carmella P Keener Atty................................. G 302 656-4333
  Wilmington (G-15255)
Carmine Potter & Associates....................... G 302 832-6000
  Newark (G-10151)
Carmine Potter & Associates....................... G 302 658-8940
  Wilmington (G-15256)
Casarino Chrstman Shalk Rnsom............... E 302 594-4500
  Wilmington (G-15263)
Catherines CSAC Inc..................................... C 302 478-6160
  Wilmington (G-15274)
Central Firm LLC.. G 610 470-9836
  Wilmington (G-15308)
Ch Wilmington LLC.. F 302 655-1641
  Wilmington (G-15325)
Charles Slanina... G 302 234-1605
  Hockessin (G-5156)
Chimicles Schwrtz Krner Dnldsn................. F 302 656-2500
  Wilmington (G-15383)

Ciconte Wasserman & Scerba LLC............ F 302 658-7101
  Wilmington (G-15434)
Cindy L Szabo.. G 302 855-9505
  Georgetown (G-4256)
Clayton E Bunting.. G 302 856-0017
  Georgetown (G-4259)
Cogency Global Inc....................................... E 800 483-1140
  Dover (G-2110)
Cole Schotz PC... G 302 984-9541
  Wilmington (G-15526)
Color Street... G 302 574-0409
  Wilmington (G-15539)
Community Legal Aid Society..................... G 302 674-8503
  Dover (G-2119)
Community Legal Aid Society..................... F 302 856-0038
  Georgetown (G-4263)
Community Legal Aid Society..................... D 302 757-7001
  Wilmington (G-15563)
Connolly Bove Lodge & Hutz LLP............. G 302 658-9141
  Wilmington (G-15604)
Cooch and Taylor A Prof Assn.................... E 302 984-3800
  Wilmington (G-15627)
Cooper Levenson PA..................................... G 302 838-2600
  Bear (G-120)
Corp1 Inc... F 302 736-3466
  Dover (G-2140)
▲ Corporation Service Company................. B 302 636-5400
  Wilmington (G-15644)
Countrmsres Asssssment SEC Expr........... G 302 322-9600
  Middletown (G-7015)
Cozen OConnor.. F 302 295-2000
  Wilmington (G-15673)
Cramer Dimichele... G 302 235-8561
  Wilmington (G-15684)
Cross & Simon LLC....................................... F 302 777-4200
  Wilmington (G-15711)
Crossland & Associates LLC...................... F 302 409-0120
  Hockessin (G-5171)
Crossland and Associates............................ G 302 658-2100
  Hockessin (G-5172)
CSC Corporate Domains Inc....................... D 866 403-5272
  Wilmington (G-15722)
CSC Domains LLC... E 302 636-5400
  Wilmington (G-15723)
Curley & Benton LLC.................................... G 302 674-3333
  Dover (G-2170)
Curran James P Law Offices....................... G 302 894-1111
  Newark (G-10365)
Cynthia L Carroll.. G 302 733-0411
  Newark (G-10371)
Dalton & Associates PA................................ G 302 652-2050
  Wilmington (G-15773)
Daniel P McCollom... F 302 888-6865
  Wilmington (G-15784)
Danneman Firm LLC...................................... F 302 793-9660
  Wilmington (G-15790)
David A Dorey Esq... G 302 425-6400
  Wilmington (G-15801)
David D Finocchiaro Attorney...................... G 302 764-7113
  Wilmington (G-15804)
Delaware Alnce Agnst Sxual Vln................ G 302 468-7731
  Wilmington (G-15863)
Delaware Bus Incorporators Inc................. G 302 996-5819
  Wilmington (G-15877)
Delaware Corporate Registry....................... G 302 655-6500
  Wilmington (G-15893)
Delaware Counsel Group LLP.................... E 302 543-4870
  Rockland (G-13030)
Delaware Counsel Group LLP.................... G 302 576-9600
  Wilmington (G-15894)
Delaware Department Finance.................... D 302 739-5291
  Dover (G-2227)

SIC SECTION
81 LEGAL SERVICES

Delaware Elder Law Center............... G 302 300-4390
  Wilmington *(G-15913)*
Delaware Offices LLC...................... G 302 295-1214
  Wilmington *(G-15948)*
Delaware Offices LLC...................... G 302 295-1215
  Wilmington *(G-15947)*
Delaware Tchncal Cmnty College...... E 302 259-6160
  Georgetown *(G-4286)*
Deval Patel-Lennon Esq PA Inc......... G 302 998-2000
  Wilmington *(G-16034)*
Devlin Law Firm LLC....................... E 302 449-9010
  Wilmington *(G-16036)*
Dla Piper LLP (us)........................... E 302 654-3025
  Wilmington *(G-16104)*
▲ DLS Discovery LLC....................... E 302 888-2060
  Wilmington *(G-16105)*
Don A Beskrone.............................. G 302 654-1888
  Wilmington *(G-16130)*
Donald M Brown.............................. G 302 777-1840
  Wilmington *(G-16137)*
Doroshow Psqale Krwitz Sgel Bh..... G 302 832-3200
  Bear *(G-176)*
Doroshow Psqale Krwitz Sgel Bh..... F 302 674-7100
  Dover *(G-2327)*
Doroshow Psqale Krwitz Sgel Bh..... G 302 424-7744
  Milford *(G-7870)*
Doroshow Psqale Krwitz Sgel Bh..... F 302 934-9400
  Millsboro *(G-8276)*
Doroshow Psqale Krwitz Sgel Bh..... F 302 998-0100
  Wilmington *(G-16150)*
Doroshow Psqale Krwitz Sgel Bh..... E 302 998-2397
  Wilmington *(G-16149)*
Dorsey & Whitney LLP..................... G 302 383-1011
  Wilmington *(G-16151)*
Douglas M Helfer............................. G 302 988-8127
  Selbyville *(G-13523)*
Draper & Goldberg Pllc.................... G 302 448-4040
  Georgetown *(G-4298)*
Duly Noted LLC............................... G 302 353-4585
  Wilmington *(G-16198)*
Elzufon Astin Rrdon Trlov Mnde....... E 302 428-3181
  Wilmington *(G-16383)*
Elzufon Austin Reardon Tarlov......... G 302 644-0144
  Lewes *(G-5959)*
Eric M Doroshow............................. G 302 934-9400
  Millsboro *(G-8283)*
Eugene Cummings PC..................... G 312 984-0144
  Bear *(G-207)*
Evans... G 302 998-3356
  Wilmington *(G-16479)*
Express Legal Documents LLC......... G 212 710-1374
  Wilmington *(G-16509)*
Faegre Drnker Biddle Reath LLP....... F 302 467-4200
  Wilmington *(G-16528)*
Faruqi & Faruqi LLP......................... G 302 482-3182
  Wilmington *(G-16555)*
Ferrara Haley & Bevis...................... G 302 656-7247
  Wilmington *(G-16586)*
Ferry Joseph & Pearce PA............... F 302 856-3706
  Georgetown *(G-4319)*
Ferry Joseph & Pearce PA............... F 302 575-1555
  Wilmington *(G-16590)*
Fineman Krekstein & Harris PC........ G 312 655-0800
  Wilmington *(G-16610)*
Fish & Richardson PC...................... C 302 652-5070
  Wilmington *(G-16646)*
Fox Rothschild LLP.......................... D 302 654-7444
  Wilmington *(G-16715)*
Franklin & Prokopik......................... G 302 594-9780
  Wilmington *(G-16727)*
Franklin and Prokopik...................... G 302 594-9780
  Newark *(G-10771)*

Frederick L Cottrell......................... G 302 651-7686
  Wilmington *(G-16738)*
Freibott Law Firm............................ F 302 633-9000
  Wilmington *(G-16746)*
Friedlander and Gorris..................... G 302 573-3500
  Wilmington *(G-16752)*
Funk & Bolton PA............................ G 302 735-8400
  Dover *(G-2545)*
Fuqua & Yori P A............................ G 302 856-7777
  Georgetown *(G-4329)*
Gawthrop Greenwood PC................ G 302 351-1273
  Wilmington *(G-16820)*
Gerry Gray...................................... G 302 856-4101
  Smyrna *(G-13742)*
Gibson Glynis.................................. G 302 730-1300
  Felton *(G-3979)*
Gill Edward Law Offices of.............. F 302 854-5400
  Georgetown *(G-4342)*
Giordano Delcollo & Werb LLC........ G 302 234-6855
  Wilmington *(G-16866)*
Global Law Centers......................... G 302 654-4800
  Wilmington *(G-16891)*
Goldfinch Group Inc......................... G 646 300-0716
  Dover *(G-2601)*
Gonser and Gonser P A................... G 302 478-4445
  Wilmington *(G-16919)*
Gordon Fournaris Mammarella PA... E 302 652-2900
  Wilmington *(G-16930)*
Grady & Hampton LLC..................... G 302 678-1265
  Dover *(G-2618)*
Grant & Eisenhofer PA.................... D 302 622-7000
  Wilmington *(G-16948)*
Grant Tani Barash & Altman Man..... G 302 651-7700
  Wilmington *(G-16949)*
Greenberg Praurig LLC..................... G 302 661-7000
  Wilmington *(G-16969)*
GSB&b LLC..................................... G 302 425-5800
  Wilmington *(G-16994)*
Haller & Hudson.............................. G 302 856-4525
  Georgetown *(G-4352)*
Halloran Farkas + Kittila LLP........... F 302 257-2011
  Wilmington *(G-17039)*
Harris Berger LLC............................ G 302 665-1140
  Wilmington *(G-17062)*
Harvard Business Services Inc......... E 302 645-7400
  Lewes *(G-6081)*
Heckler & Frabizzio PA.................... F 302 573-4800
  Wilmington *(G-17113)*
Heiman Gouge & Kaufman LLP........ G 302 658-1800
  Wilmington *(G-17114)*
Heiman Aber Goldlust & Baker........ G 302 658-1800
  Wilmington *(G-17115)*
Herdeg Dupont Dalle Pazze LLP...... G 302 655-6500
  Wilmington *(G-17129)*
Heyman Enerio Gattuso & Hirzel..... F 302 472-7300
  Wilmington *(G-17136)*
Hochman C Michael Atty................. G 302 656-8162
  Wilmington *(G-17161)*
Honorable Myron T Steele............... G 302 739-4214
  Dover *(G-2693)*
Huang Law LLC............................... G 302 248-5138
  Wilmington *(G-17227)*
Hudson Jnes Jaywork Fisher LLC.... F 302 227-9441
  Rehoboth Beach *(G-12792)*
Hudson Jnes Jaywork Fisher LLC.... E 302 734-7401
  Dover *(G-2702)*
Hudson Jnes Jywork Fsher Attys.... G 302 839-1153
  Milford *(G-7937)*
Hudson Jones Jaywork Fisher......... G 302 645-7999
  Lewes *(G-6107)*
I Barry Guerke................................ G 302 450-1098
  Dover *(G-2713)*

J Clayton Athey.............................. G 302 888-6507
  Wilmington *(G-17453)*
Jacobs & Crumplar PA.................... E 302 656-5445
  Wilmington *(G-17473)*
James E Deakyne Jr PA.................. G 302 226-1200
  Rehoboth Beach *(G-12800)*
James L Holzman............................ F 302 888-6500
  Wilmington *(G-17482)*
Jeffrey Schlerf Atty........................ G 302 622-4212
  Wilmington *(G-17521)*
John H Williams Jr Atty.................. F 302 571-4780
  Wilmington *(G-17564)*
Joseph A Hurley PA........................ G 302 658-8980
  Wilmington *(G-17576)*
Joseph W Benson PA...................... G 302 656-8811
  Wilmington *(G-17587)*
K and L Gates................................. D 302 416-7000
  Wilmington *(G-17627)*
Karen Y Vcks Law Offces of LLC..... G 302 674-1100
  Dover *(G-2831)*
Kate G Shumaker............................ G 302 327-1100
  Bear *(G-322)*
Katharine L Mayer Atty................... G 302 984-6312
  Wilmington *(G-17660)*
Katherine Laffey............................. G 302 651-7999
  Wilmington *(G-17661)*
Kimmel Crter Rman Pltz Onill P...... F 302 565-6100
  Christiana *(G-1001)*
Knepper & Stratton......................... G 302 658-1717
  Dover *(G-2880)*
Kurt F Gwynne................................ G 302 778-7550
  Wilmington *(G-17766)*
La Esperanza Inc............................ F 302 854-9262
  Georgetown *(G-4397)*
Labaton Sucharow LLP.................... E 302 573-6938
  Wilmington *(G-17782)*
Landis Rath & Cobb LLP.................. E 302 467-4400
  Wilmington *(G-17798)*
Larosa & Associates....................... G 302 250-4283
  Wilmington *(G-17809)*
Latin Chat Services........................ G 302 249-4151
  Georgetown *(G-4402)*
Law Firm... F 302 472-4900
  Wilmington *(G-17828)*
Law of Michele D............................ G 302 234-8600
  Hockessin *(G-5278)*
Law Offces Murray Phillips Gay...... G 302 855-9300
  Georgetown *(G-4403)*
Law Office Daniel C Herr LLC.......... G 302 595-9084
  Wilmington *(G-17829)*
Law Office Jnnfer Kate M Arnso..... G 302 655-4600
  Wilmington *(G-17830)*
Law Office Laura A Yiengst LLC...... G 302 264-9780
  Dover *(G-2911)*
Law Office of Andrew Whitehead.... G 302 248-2000
  Georgetown *(G-4404)*
Law Office of Ej Fornias PA............ G 302 656-2829
  Wilmington *(G-17831)*
Law Office of Melissa Green............ G 302 998-2049
  New Castle *(G-9297)*
Law Office of Michael Bednash....... G 302 838-9077
  Newark *(G-11230)*
Law Office of Rbert l Msten Jr....... G 302 358-2044
  Newark *(G-11231)*
Law Office of Robert Valihura......... G 302 426-1313
  Wilmington *(G-17832)*
Law Office of Shauna T Hagan........ G 302 651-7999
  Wilmington *(G-17833)*
Law Offices Gary R Dodge PA......... G 302 674-5400
  Dover *(G-2912)*
Law Offices of Sean M Lynn PA...... G 302 734-2000
  Dover *(G-2913)*

Employee Codes: A=Over 500 employees, B=251-500
C=101-250, D=51-100, E=20-50, F=10-19, G=1-9

2024 Harris Directory of
Delaware Businesses

81 LEGAL SERVICES

Law Offices Patrick Scanlon PA .... G .... 302 424-1996 Milford *(G-7972)*	McCollom Dmlio Smith Ubler LLC .... F .... 302 468-5960 Wilmington *(G-18222)*	Panitch Schwarze Belisario .... G .... 302 394-6030 Wilmington *(G-18876)*
Lawson Firm LLC .... G .... 302 212-0655 Rehoboth Beach *(G-12827)*	McGivney Kluger & Cook PC .... G .... 302 656-1200 Wilmington *(G-18229)*	Parcels Inc .... C .... 302 888-1718 Wilmington *(G-18889)*
Lawyerland .... G .... 757 805-6817 Wilmington *(G-17836)*	McLaughlin Gordon L Law Office .... G .... 302 651-7979 Wilmington *(G-18233)*	Parkowski Guerke & Swayze PA .... F .... 302 678-3262 Dover *(G-3274)*
Legal Services Corp Delaware .... F .... 302 575-0408 Wilmington *(G-17861)*	McLaughlin Morton Holdg Co LLC .... F .... 302 426-1313 Wilmington *(G-18234)*	Parkway Law LLC .... G .... 302 449-0400 Townsend *(G-14048)*
Legal Services of Delaware .... F .... 302 575-0408 Wilmington *(G-17862)*	Michael B Tumas .... G .... 302 984-6029 Wilmington *(G-18308)*	Parsons & Robinson PA .... G .... 302 539-2220 Ocean View *(G-12557)*
Legalnature LLC .... G .... 888 881-1139 Dover *(G-2927)*	Michael L Berman .... G .... 302 300-3450 Wilmington *(G-18316)*	Patrick Scanlon PA .... G .... 302 424-1996 Milford *(G-8042)*
Leroy A Tice Esquire PA .... G .... 302 658-6901 Wilmington *(G-17883)*	Michael P Morton PA .... G .... 302 426-1313 Wilmington *(G-18321)*	Phillips Gldman McLghlin Hall .... E .... 302 655-4200 Wilmington *(G-19019)*
Letsbelegalcom .... G .... 302 894-4357 Newark *(G-11247)*	Milewski Stephan .... G .... 302 467-4502 Wilmington *(G-18355)*	Pinckney Wdnger Urban Jyce LLC .... G .... 302 504-1497 Wilmington *(G-19046)*
Liguori Morris & Reddin .... G .... 302 678-9900 Dover *(G-2946)*	Mintzer Sarowitz Zeris Leovar .... G .... 302 655-2181 Wilmington *(G-18382)*	Pinter Law LLC .... G .... 302 409-0089 Wilmington *(G-19051)*
Linarducci & Butler PA .... G .... 302 325-2400 New Castle *(G-9310)*	Minute Center .... G .... 302 645-9396 Rehoboth Beach *(G-12859)*	Poliquin Firm LLC .... G .... 302 702-5501 Dover *(G-3349)*
Lippstone Law Pllc .... G .... 302 252-1481 Newark *(G-11265)*	Modern Mixture LLC .... G .... 302 249-6183 Milford *(G-8017)*	Polsinelli Shalton Flanni .... G .... 302 654-2984 Wilmington *(G-19111)*
Lisa M Andersen .... G .... 302 644-3668 Lewes *(G-6212)*	Montgomery McCrcken Wlker Rhads .... F .... 302 504-7800 Wilmington *(G-18425)*	Poolside Cnstr & Renovation .... G .... 302 436-9711 Selbyville *(G-13594)*
LLC Castle Law .... G .... 302 428-8800 Wilmington *(G-17954)*	Monzack Mrsky McLghlin Brwder .... E .... 302 656-8162 Wilmington *(G-18427)*	Potter Anderson & Corroon .... G .... 302 984-6078 Wilmington *(G-19133)*
LLP Connolly Gallagher .... D .... 302 757-7300 Newark *(G-11276)*	Mooney & Andrew PA .... G .... 302 856-3070 Georgetown *(G-4431)*	Potter Anderson & Corroon LLP .... C .... 302 984-6000 Wilmington *(G-19134)*
LLP Connolly Gallagher .... F .... 302 757-7300 Wilmington *(G-17959)*	Moore & Rutt PA .... G .... 302 856-9568 Georgetown *(G-4432)*	Pratcher Krayer LLC .... G .... 302 803-5291 Wilmington *(G-19146)*
LLP Shaw Keller .... G .... 302 298-0700 Wilmington *(G-17960)*	Morgan Lewis International LLC .... G .... 302 574-3000 Wilmington *(G-18446)*	Prentice-Hall Corp System Inc .... D .... 302 636-5440 Wilmington *(G-19175)*
Logan & Associates LLC .... G .... 302 325-3555 New Castle *(G-9322)*	Morris James LLP .... G .... 302 678-8815 Dover *(G-3124)*	Prepaid Legal Service .... G .... 302 376-1952 Smyrna *(G-13852)*
Loizides & Associates PC .... G .... 302 654-0248 Wilmington *(G-17978)*	Morris James LLP .... F .... 302 368-4200 Newark *(G-11454)*	Procino Wells & Woodland LLC .... G .... 302 313-5934 Lewes *(G-6393)*
Longobardi & Boyle LLC .... G .... 302 575-1502 Wilmington *(G-17986)*	Morris James LLP .... G .... 302 260-7290 Rehoboth Beach *(G-12863)*	Rahaim & Saints Attys At Law .... F .... 302 892-9200 Wilmington *(G-19318)*
Losco and Marconi PA .... G .... 302 656-7776 Wilmington *(G-18000)*	Morris James LLP .... G .... 302 655-2599 Wilmington *(G-18453)*	Ramunno & Ramunno & Scerba PA .... F .... 302 656-9400 Wilmington *(G-19328)*
Lyons David J Law Office .... G .... 302 777-5698 Wilmington *(G-18053)*	Morris James LLP .... D .... 302 888-6800 Wilmington *(G-18454)*	Ramunno Ramunno .... G .... 302 737-6909 Newark *(G-11824)*
Macelree & Harvey Ltd .... E .... 302 654-4454 Wilmington *(G-18067)*	Morris James Per Injury Group .... G .... 302 856-0017 Georgetown *(G-4436)*	Raskaukas Joseph C Aty Law .... G .... 302 537-2000 Bethany Beach *(G-630)*
Manning Gross + Massenburg LLP .... F .... 302 657-2100 Wilmington *(G-18106)*	Morris Nichols Arsht Tnnell LLP .... C .... 302 658-9200 Wilmington *(G-18455)*	Ratner & Prestia PC .... F .... 302 778-2500 Wilmington *(G-19338)*
Marin Bayard .... G .... 302 658-4200 Wilmington *(G-18129)*	Morton Valihura & Zerbato LLC .... G .... 302 426-1313 Wilmington *(G-18459)*	Raymond E Tomassetti Esq .... G .... 302 539-3041 Fenwick Island *(G-4053)*
▲ Mark W Eckard .... G .... 302 778-7518 Wilmington *(G-18140)*	Murphy & Landon PC .... F .... 302 472-8100 Wilmington *(G-18488)*	Reed Smith LLP .... F .... 302 778-7500 Wilmington *(G-19392)*
Marks Onill Obrien Dhrty Klly .... G .... 302 658-6538 Wilmington *(G-18150)*	Murphy Law Firm .... G .... 302 855-1055 Georgetown *(G-4439)*	Reger Rizzo & Darnall LLP .... G .... 302 652-3611 Wilmington *(G-19401)*
Maron Mrvel Brdley Anderson PA .... D .... 302 425-5177 Wilmington *(G-18154)*	Murray Phillips PA .... G .... 302 697-2499 Camden *(G-879)*	Reilly Janiczek & McDevitt PC .... F .... 302 777-1700 Wilmington *(G-19416)*
Marshall Dnnhey Wrner Clman Gg .... E .... 302 504-3341 Wilmington *(G-18158)*	Newrez LLC .... G .... 240 475-4741 Lewes *(G-6312)*	Reynolds Services Ltd .... G .... 877 404-2179 Wilmington *(G-19449)*
Marshall Dnnhey Wrner Clman Gg .... E .... 302 552-4300 Wilmington *(G-18159)*	Nolte & Brodoway PA .... G .... 302 777-1700 Wilmington *(G-18664)*	Rhoades & Morrow LLC .... G .... 302 422-6705 Milford *(G-8066)*
Martin D Hvrly Attorney At Law .... G .... 302 529-0121 Wilmington *(G-18167)*	Norman Law Firm .... F .... 302 537-3788 Dagsboro *(G-1489)*	Rhoades & Morrow LLC .... F .... 302 427-9500 Wilmington *(G-19458)*
Martin Daniel D & Assoc LLC .... G .... 302 658-2884 Wilmington *(G-18168)*	Novak Druce Cnnlly Bv+qigg LLP .... C .... 302 252-9922 Wilmington *(G-18693)*	Rhodunda & Williams LLC .... G .... 302 576-2000 Wilmington *(G-19460)*
Mastracci Mastracci .... G .... 410 869-3400 Selbyville *(G-13567)*	O Kelly Ernst Belli Wallen LLC .... G .... 302 778-4001 Wilmington *(G-18723)*	Richard S Cobb Esquire .... G .... 302 467-4430 Wilmington *(G-19474)*
Matthew B Lunn .... G .... 302 571-6646 Wilmington *(G-18195)*	Obrien Firm .... G .... 302 654-1515 Wilmington *(G-18738)*	Richards Layton & Finger P A .... E .... 302 651-7700 Wilmington *(G-19475)*
Mattleman Weinroth & Miller PC .... G .... 302 731-8349 Newark *(G-11355)*	Offit Kurman PA .... D .... 302 351-0900 Wilmington *(G-18750)*	Richards Layton & Finger P A .... B .... 302 651-7700 Wilmington *(G-19476)*
McCabe Weisberg Conway PC .... F .... 302 409-3520 Wilmington *(G-18216)*	P A Bayard .... D .... 302 429-4212 Wilmington *(G-18849)*	Richards Layton & Finger P A .... C .... 302 651-7700 Wilmington *(G-19477)*
McCarter & English LLP .... E .... 302 984-6300 Wilmington *(G-18218)*	P C Flaster/Greenberg .... G .... 302 351-1910 Wilmington *(G-18851)*	Ridrodsky & Long PA .... G .... 302 691-8822 Wilmington *(G-19481)*

82 EDUCATIONAL SERVICES

Robert J Kriner Jr .... G 302 656-2500
  Wilmington (G-19514)
Robert K Beste Jr .... G 302 425-5089
  Wilmington (G-19516)
Robert L Thomas .... G 302 571-6602
  Wilmington (G-19518)
Robinson Grayson and Ward PA .... G 302 655-6262
  Wilmington (G-19524)
Roeberg Moore & Associates PA .... F 302 658-4757
  Wilmington (G-19554)
Roger D Anderson .... G 302 652-8400
  Wilmington (G-19555)
Ronald D Jr Attorney At Law .... G 302 856-9860
  Georgetown (G-4491)
Rosenthal Monhait Goddess PA .... F 302 656-4433
  Wilmington (G-19570)
Ross Aronstam & Moritz LLP .... F 302 576-1600
  Wilmington (G-19571)
Ruff & Ruff LLC .... G 267 243-3906
  Smyrna (G-13872)
Schab & Barnett PA .... G 302 856-9024
  Georgetown (G-4500)
Schmittinger & Rodriguez Attys .... G 302 378-1697
  Middletown (G-7542)
Schmittinger and Rodriguez PA .... D 302 674-0140
  Dover (G-3514)
Schnader Hrrson Sgal Lewis LLP .... F 302 888-4554
  Wilmington (G-19697)
Schuster Jachetti LLP .... G 302 984-1000
  Wilmington (G-19700)
Schuster Jachetti LLP .... G 302 856-2400
  Georgetown (G-4503)
Schwartz Schwartz Attys At Law .... G 302 998-1500
  Wilmington (G-19701)
Schwartz Schwrtz Attys At Law .... G 302 678-8700
  Dover (G-3518)
Seitz Vanogtrop & Green .... F 302 888-0600
  Wilmington (G-19740)
Sergovic & Ellis PA .... F 302 855-9500
  Georgetown (G-4505)
Sergovic Crmean Wdman McCrtney .... G 302 855-1260
  Georgetown (G-4506)
Shanley Assoc .... G 302 691-6838
  Wilmington (G-19780)
Sharon M Zieg .... G 302 571-6655
  Wilmington (G-19783)
Silverman McDonald & Friedman .... G 302 629-3350
  Seaford (G-13402)
Skadden Arps Slate Mgher Flom .... C 302 651-3000
  Wilmington (G-19851)
Smith Firm LLC .... G 302 875-5595
  Seaford (G-13405)
Smith Fnberg McCrtney Berl LLP .... F 302 856-7082
  Georgetown (G-4514)
Smith Katzenstein & Furlow LLP .... E 302 652-8400
  Wilmington (G-19890)
Snyder Associates PA .... G 302 657-8300
  Wilmington (G-19904)
Steen Waehler Schrider Fox LLC .... G 302 539-7900
  Ocean View (G-12569)
Stephen E Jenkins .... G 302 654-1888
  Wilmington (G-20058)
Stern & Eisenberg PC .... G 302 731-7200
  Newark (G-12101)
Stevens & Lee PC .... F 302 654-5180
  Wilmington (G-20068)
Stewart Law Firm .... F 302 652-5200
  Wilmington (G-20070)
Street & Ellis P A .... G 302 735-8408
  Dover (G-3616)
Stumpf Vickers and Sandy .... G 302 856-3561
  Georgetown (G-4528)

Sunu Consulting LLC .... G 202 534-5864
  Dover (G-3625)
Susan C Over PC .... G 302 660-2913
  Hockessin (G-5400)
Tarabicos Grosso .... F 302 757-7800
  New Castle (G-9616)
Taylor Copeland LLC .... G 302 598-4412
  Wilmington (G-20233)
Telos Legal Corp .... G 302 242-4815
  Dover (G-3666)
Theresa Hayes .... G 302 854-5406
  Georgetown (G-4551)
Thomas D Law Shel .... G 302 887-9116
  Wilmington (G-20305)
Thomas J McWilliams .... G 312 287-5148
  Wilmington (G-20309)
Thomson Reuters (grc) Inc .... G 212 227-7357
  Wilmington (G-20314)
Tighe and Cottrell PA .... G 302 658-6400
  Wilmington (G-20323)
Troutman Ppper Hmlton Snders L .... E 302 777-6500
  Wilmington (G-20440)
Tunnell & Raysor PA .... G 302 644-4442
  Lewes (G-6584)
Tunnell & Raysor PA .... E 302 856-7313
  Georgetown (G-4563)
Tybout Redfearn & Pell PA .... E 302 658-6901
  Wilmington (G-20475)
UAW-GM Legal Services Plan .... F 302 562-8212
  Newark (G-12258)
Vance A Funk III .... G 302 368-2561
  Newark (G-12303)
Vivian A Houghton Esquire .... G 302 658-0518
  Wilmington (G-20645)
Vps Services LLC .... G 302 376-6710
  Middletown (G-7696)
Ward & Taylor LLC .... G 302 539-3537
  Bethany Beach (G-647)
Ward & Taylor LLC .... G 302 346-7000
  Dover (G-3820)
Ward & Taylor LLC .... G 302 225-3350
  Middletown (G-7707)
Ward & Taylor LLC .... G 302 227-1403
  Rehoboth Beach (G-13007)
Ward & Taylor LLC .... E 302 225-3350
  Wilmington (G-20677)
Weber Gallagher Simpson .... G 302 346-6377
  Dover (G-3828)
Weik Nitsche & Dougherty .... F 302 655-4040
  Wilmington (G-20713)
Weir Greenblatt Pierce LLP .... G 302 652-8181
  Wilmington (G-20715)
Weiss & Saville PA .... G 302 656-0400
  Wilmington (G-20716)
Werb & Sullivan .... F 302 652-1100
  Wilmington (G-20733)
Wharton Levin Ehrmantraut .... G 302 252-0090
  Wilmington (G-20754)
Whitaker Corporation .... E 302 633-2740
  Wilmington (G-20762)
White and Williams LLP .... E 302 654-0424
  Wilmington (G-20763)
Whiteford Taylor and Preston .... G 302 353-4144
  Wilmington (G-20770)
Whittington & Aulgur .... G 302 235-5800
  Yorklyn (G-20994)
Wilbraham Lawler & Buba PC .... G 302 421-9922
  Wilmington (G-20778)
Wilks Lukoff & Bracegirdle LLC .... G 302 225-0850
  Wilmington (G-20783)
William E Ward PA .... F 302 225-3350
  Wilmington (G-20787)

William H Lunger Atty .... G 302 888-2504
  Wilmington (G-20792)
Williams Law Firm PA .... G 302 575-0873
  Wilmington (G-20802)
Willis Law LLC .... G 302 535-3200
  Dover (G-3854)
Wilson Halbrook & Bayard PA .... D 302 856-0015
  Georgetown (G-4575)
Wolfe Associates LLC .... G 302 668-6178
  Middletown (G-7732)
Woloshin and Lynch Associates .... E 302 477-3200
  Wilmington (G-20878)
Womble Bond Dickinson (us) LLP .... E 302 252-4320
  Wilmington (G-20879)
Yacht Registry Ltd .... E 302 477-9800
  Wilmington (G-20922)
Young & McNelis .... G 302 674-8822
  Dover (G-3891)
Young and Malmberg PA .... F 302 672-5600
  Dover (G-3892)
▲ Young Cnway Strgatt Taylor LLP .... C 302 571-6600
  Wilmington (G-20933)
Zwally Brown Lisa .... G 302 504-7803
  Wilmington (G-20970)

82 EDUCATIONAL SERVICES

8211 Elementary and secondary schools

Cacc Montessori School .... F 302 239-2917
  Hockessin (G-5147)
Caesar Rodney School District .... D 302 697-3207
  Dover (G-2011)
Capital School District .... G 302 678-8394
  Dover (G-2021)
Chesapake Cnfrnce Svnth-Day Ad .... G 302 998-3961
  Wilmington (G-15366)
Independence School Inc .... D 302 239-0330
  Newark (G-11011)
Instasafe Inc .... G 408 400-3673
  Dover (G-2741)
Kindercare Learning Ctrs LLC .... F 302 834-6931
  Newark (G-11176)
Lake Forest School District .... E 302 398-8945
  Harrington (G-4795)
Newark Ctr For Creative Lrng .... F 302 368-7772
  Newark (G-11533)
Pressley Ridge Foundation .... G 302 366-0490
  Dover (G-3367)
Readhowyouwant LLC .... G 302 730-4560
  Dover (G-3431)
Smyrna School District .... D 302 653-3135
  Smyrna (G-13897)
Wilmington Montessori School .... D 302 475-0555
  Wilmington (G-20824)

8221 Colleges and universities

University of Delaware .... F 302 831-6041
  Newark (G-12277)
University of Delaware .... G 302 831-4811
  Newark (G-12278)
University of Delaware .... G 302 831-2833
  Newark (G-12279)
University of Delaware .... G 302 831-2501
  Newark (G-12280)
University of Delaware .... E 302 831-2226
  Newark (G-12281)
University of Delaware .... F 302 831-2792
  Newark (G-12282)

8222 Junior colleges

Delaware Tchncal Cmnty College .... E 302 259-6160
  Georgetown (G-4286)

Employee Codes: A=Over 500 employees, B=251-500
C=101-250, D=51-100, E=20-50, F=10-19, G=1-9

2024 Harris Directory of Delaware Businesses

82 EDUCATIONAL SERVICES

8231 Libraries

A Gentlemans Touch Inc .... F 302 585-5805
  Wilmington (G-14163)
Artisans Bank Inc .... G 302 738-3744
  Wilmington (G-14572)
Document Advisor Inc .... E 786 206-0756
  Dover (G-2318)
◆ Historical Society of Delaware .... E 302 655-7161
  Wilmington (G-17155)

8243 Data processing schools

Bits & Bytes Inc .... G 302 674-2999
  Dover (G-1942)
Discidium Technology Inc .... G 347 220-5979
  Newark (G-10538)
Galaxyworks LLC .... F 404 894-8703
  Dover (G-2555)
Global Computers Networks LLC .... G 484 686-8374
  Middletown (G-7163)
Kortech Consulting Inc .... F 302 559-4612
  Bear (G-333)
Mh-Teq LLC .... G 302 897-2182
  Wilmington (G-18301)
Process Academy LLC .... G 302 415-3104
  Wilmington (G-19207)
Sdn Essentials LLC .... F 415 902-5702
  Newark (G-11965)
Smartprofyl LLC .... G 832 412-5803
  Middletown (G-7578)

8244 Business and secretarial schools

H & R Block Inc .... G 302 652-3286
  New Castle (G-9187)
Project of Providence LLC .... G 302 438-8970
  Wilmington (G-19224)

8249 Vocational schools, nec

Tipton Communications Group .... F 302 454-7901
  Newark (G-12198)
Treehouse Wellness Center LLC .... G 302 893-1001
  Wilmington (G-20407)

8299 Schools and educational services

Agape Learning Academy .... G 302 491-4890
  Houston (G-5435)
Amani Birth .... F 302 668-7506
  Wilmington (G-14411)
Analyttica Datalab Inc .... E 917 300-3325
  Wilmington (G-14467)
Avkin Inc .... F 302 562-7468
  Wilmington (G-14673)
Barbizon of Delaware Inc .... E 302 658-6666
  Wilmington (G-14757)
Crypto World Journal Inc .... F 302 213-8136
  Dover (G-2165)
Delaware Adlescent Program Inc .... E 302 268-7218
  Newark (G-10415)
Delaware Fncl Edcatn Alnce Inc .... G 302 674-0288
  Dover (G-2240)
Dental Sleep Solution .... G 302 235-8249
  Wilmington (G-16016)
Design Tribe Republic LLC .... F 302 918-5279
  Wilmington (G-16027)
Discover Permaculture LLC .... G 850 970-7375
  Middletown (G-7063)
Enhanced Corporate Prfmce LLC .... G 302 545-5441
  Newark (G-10648)
Favored Childcare Academy Inc .... G 302 698-1266
  Dover (G-2488)
Horizon Helicopters Inc .... G 302 368-5135
  Newark (G-10970)

Larry Shelton .... F 678 948-6096
  New Castle (G-9295)
Learn Game LLC .... F 484 841-9709
  Middletown (G-7292)
Maggie Magpie Inc .... G 302 331-5061
  Middletown (G-7321)
Music Art & Culture Foundation .... G 347 746-9047
  Lewes (G-6297)
Neighborhood House Inc .... F 302 658-5404
  Wilmington (G-18571)
Northeast Early Lrng Ctr LLC .... G 302 475-7080
  Claymont (G-1255)
Pamper ME Pink LLC .... F 302 200-2635
  Selbyville (G-13589)
Pressley Ridge Foundation .... G 302 854-9782
  Georgetown (G-4472)
Reading Assist Institute .... G 302 425-4080
  Wilmington (G-19362)
Republix Sourcestrike Corp .... F 647 206-1503
  Dover (G-3458)
Rose Hill Community Center .... F 302 656-8513
  New Castle (G-9541)
Serena Joy LLC .... G 302 312-3318
  Wilmington (G-19755)
She Podcasts .... G 302 588-2317
  Wilmington (G-19785)
Sn & Partners .... G 312 826-3255
  Newark (G-12044)
Tamp Inc .... F 302 283-9195
  Newark (G-12158)
Young Music LLC .... G 302 307-1997
  Smyrna (G-13941)

83 SOCIAL SERVICES

8322 Individual and family services

A B W Services LLC .... G 856 449-1329
  Townsend (G-13950)
A C M S Inc .... F 302 738-6036
  Newark (G-9722)
A Center For Mntal Wllness Inc .... E 302 674-1397
  Dover (G-1694)
A Seed Hope Counseling Ctr LLC ...... G 302 605-6702
  Wilmington (G-14171)
A22 Community Connections .... G 302 213-9426
  New Castle (G-8753)
Ability Network of Delaware .... G 302 622-9177
  Wilmington (G-14203)
Absalom Jones Senior Center .... G 302 998-0363
  Wilmington (G-14209)
Absolutely Flawless Women Inc .... G 410 845-6930
  Millsboro (G-8160)
Achieve Solutions .... G 302 598-1457
  Hockessin (G-5111)
Acl Services .... G 302 423-0276
  Smyrna (G-13630)
Active Hope .... G 302 545-2494
  Wilmington (G-14244)
Adam Kleinmeulman .... G 302 757-4517
  Wilmington (G-14249)
Adoption House Inc .... G 302 477-0944
  Wilmington (G-14258)
Age Advantage Senior Care Svcs .... F 302 722-8240
  Newark (G-9795)
Agile Shelter Systems LLC .... F 310 980-0644
  Dover (G-1745)
Aid In Dover Inc .... G 302 734-7610
  Dover (G-1752)
Aids Care Group .... G 610 220-8058
  Wilmington (G-14328)
Aids Delaware Inc .... E 302 652-6776
  Wilmington (G-14329)

Air Force US Dept of .... E 302 674-0942
  Dover (G-1756)
Allison Veith Lpcmh .... G 302 645-5338
  Lewes (G-5676)
Alpha Omega Community Svc Ctr ...... G 302 323-1311
  Historic New Castle (G-4929)
Alston Associates Counseling .... G 302 223-4797
  Wilmington (G-14397)
Alternative Solutions .... G 302 542-9081
  Georgetown (G-4207)
Alzheimers Assn Del Chapter .... G 302 633-4420
  Wilmington (G-14406)
American National Red Cross .... F 215 451-4372
  Wilmington (G-14438)
AMS of Delaware .... G 302 227-1320
  Rehoboth Beach (G-12602)
Angels Messiahs Foundation .... F 302 365-5516
  Bear (G-36)
Anna J Blommer .... G 302 576-4136
  Wilmington (G-14488)
Appoqnmink Counseling Svcs LLC ..... G 302 898-1616
  Middletown (G-6870)
Aqua Infra Rehab Co LLC .... G 610 328-7714
  Newark (G-9895)
ARC HUD II Inc .... G 302 996-9400
  Wilmington (G-14529)
ARC of Delaware .... E 302 996-9400
  Wilmington (G-14532)
ARC Wilmington .... F 302 656-6620
  Wilmington (G-14536)
Arlene Weisman .... G 302 569-2822
  Lewes (G-5699)
Aspiring Change LLC .... G 302 689-3138
  Newark (G-9926)
Autism Delaware Inc .... E 302 224-6020
  Newark (G-9946)
B2w2 Inc .... G 302 658-5177
  Wilmington (G-14706)
Back Up Ctr .... G 302 758-4500
  Newark (G-9971)
Balanced Mind Cnseling Ctr LLC .... F 302 377-6911
  Middletown (G-6904)
Barshay Stephanie Lplmh .... G 302 312-6466
  Wilmington (G-14770)
Beautful Gate Outreach Ctr Inc .... F 302 472-3002
  Wilmington (G-14808)
Bellevue Community Center .... F 302 762-1391
  Wilmington (G-14820)
Bernard Ruth Sgel Jwish Cmnty .... D 302 478-5660
  Wilmington (G-14847)
Bernies Foundation Inc .... G 302 750-7117
  Wilmington (G-14850)
Beth A Canalichio Lcsw Ltd .... E 302 734-7760
  Dover (G-1919)
Beth A Canalichio Lcsw Ltd .... G 302 734-7760
  Dover (G-1920)
Beverlys Helping Hands .... G 302 651-9304
  Wilmington (G-14868)
Big Brthers Big Sisters of Del .... E 302 998-3577
  Dover (G-1932)
Bppn LLC .... G 302 384-5119
  Wilmington (G-15030)
Brandy Wine Senior Center .... G 302 798-5562
  Claymont (G-1065)
Brandywine Center For Autism .... F 302 503-3120
  Milford (G-7802)
Brandywine Center For Autism .... D 302 762-2636
  Wilmington (G-15049)
Brandywine Cnsling Cmnty Svcs .... D 302 655-9880
  Wilmington (G-15051)
Brandywine Counseling .... E 302 762-7120
  Wilmington (G-15052)

83 SOCIAL SERVICES

Brandywine Hundred Fire Co 1 .... D 302 764-4901
  Wilmington *(G-15067)*

Brandywine Senior Care Inc .... F 302 436-2920
  Selbyville *(G-13482)*

Bridges4kids .... G 302 841-3700
  Milton *(G-8575)*

Bridgeville Senior Center .... G 302 337-8771
  Bridgeville *(G-678)*

Cadia Rehabilitation .... E 302 734-1199
  Dover *(G-2010)*

Cadia Rhabilitation Silverside .... F 302 478-8889
  Wilmington *(G-15186)*

Camden Counseling LLC .... G 302 698-9109
  Camden *(G-800)*

Campus Life .... G 302 294-6520
  Newark *(G-10126)*

Cancer Support Cmnty Del Inc .... G 302 995-2850
  Wilmington *(G-15213)*

Cape Henlopen Senior Center .... G 302 227-2055
  Rehoboth Beach *(G-12663)*

Carpe Dia Organization .... G 302 333-7546
  Newark *(G-10153)*

Catholic Charities Inc .... G 302 674-1600
  Dover *(G-2038)*

Catholic Charities Inc .... G 302 674-1600
  Dover *(G-2039)*

Catholic Charities Inc .... G 302 856-9578
  Georgetown *(G-4245)*

Catholic Charities Inc .... G 302 684-8694
  Milton *(G-8580)*

Catholic Charities Inc .... E 302 655-9624
  Wilmington *(G-15277)*

Cayuga Centers .... F 302 257-5848
  Middletown *(G-6966)*

Cbhi Inc .... F 484 751-7752
  Wilmington *(G-15286)*

Center For A Pstive Hmnity LLC .... G 302 703-1036
  Felton *(G-3952)*

Changing Place .... G 302 397-8731
  Wilmington *(G-15331)*

Chase Center On River .... G 302 655-2187
  Wilmington *(G-15345)*

Chec Inc .... G 302 275-4709
  Newark *(G-10194)*

Cheer Inc .... F 302 856-5641
  Georgetown *(G-4249)*

Cheon IL Guk Incorporated .... G 302 332-2672
  Middletown *(G-6972)*

Cheryl L Chambers .... G 302 393-3854
  Magnolia *(G-6729)*

Child Inc .... C 302 832-5451
  Newark *(G-10202)*

Child Inc .... E 302 762-8989
  Wilmington *(G-15372)*

Child Support .... G 302 855-7462
  Georgetown *(G-4251)*

Children Youth & Their Fam .... G 302 577-6011
  Wilmington *(G-15374)*

Children Fmilies First Del Inc .... G 302 674-8384
  Dover *(G-2061)*

Children Fmilies First Del Inc .... D 302 856-2388
  Georgetown *(G-4253)*

Children Fmilies First Del Inc .... D 302 629-6996
  Seaford *(G-13119)*

Children Fmilies First Del Inc .... D 302 658-5177
  Wilmington *(G-15375)*

Children Fmlies Frst Endowment .... G 302 658-5177
  Wilmington *(G-15376)*

Childrens Advocacy Center .... G 302 651-4567
  Wilmington *(G-15378)*

Childrens Advocacy Ctr of Del .... G 302 854-0323
  Georgetown *(G-4254)*

Childrens Advocacy Ctr of Del .... G 302 651-4615
  Wilmington *(G-15379)*

Childrens Advocacy Ctr of Del .... G 302 741-2123
  Dover *(G-2063)*

Childrens Beach House Inc .... E 302 655-4288
  Wilmington *(G-15380)*

Childrens Choice Inc .... G 302 731-9512
  Newark *(G-10205)*

Chimes Inc .... E 302 730-0747
  Dover *(G-2065)*

Chimes Inc .... G 302 934-1450
  Millsboro *(G-8222)*

Choices 1st LLC .... G 302 674-4204
  Dover *(G-2067)*

Choices For Community .... G 302 378-3821
  Middletown *(G-6975)*

Christana Care HM Hlth Cmnty S .... B 302 995-8448
  Wilmington *(G-15397)*

Christncare Rhbltion Svcs At .... G 302 623-1500
  Wilmington *(G-15422)*

Clarifi .... G 267 546-0430
  Wilmington *(G-15462)*

Claymont Community Center Inc .... E 302 792-2757
  Claymont *(G-1092)*

Claymore Senior Center Inc .... G 302 428-3170
  Wilmington *(G-15468)*

Cleanpro Detail Center .... G 302 464-1017
  Middletown *(G-6988)*

Clg True Solutions LLC .... G 302 709-1312
  Newark *(G-10258)*

Clinical Pstral Cnsling Prgram .... G 302 632-8842
  Seaford *(G-13125)*

Cls Counseling LLC .... G 302 644-2633
  Lewes *(G-5831)*

Coastal Counseling LLC .... G 302 542-4271
  Millsboro *(G-8233)*

Communities In Schools Del .... E 704 724-3737
  Wilmington *(G-15558)*

Community Cllaboration Del Inc .... G 302 824-6896
  Historic New Castle *(G-4962)*

Community Day .... G 302 757-3700
  Wilmington *(G-15560)*

Community Interactions Inc .... D 302 993-7846
  Wilmington *(G-15562)*

Community Pride .... G 302 236-6591
  Rehoboth Beach *(G-12696)*

Community Solutions Inc .... G 302 660-8691
  Wilmington *(G-15564)*

Communityliving Inc .... G 302 735-4534
  Dover *(G-2120)*

Connectionscsp Inc .... G 302 383-8482
  Seaford *(G-13133)*

Connectons Cmnty Spport Prgram .... E 302 834-8400
  Delaware City *(G-1534)*

Connectons Cmnty Spport Prgram .... D 302 454-7520
  Newark *(G-10306)*

Connectons Cmnty Spport Prgram .... D 302 536-1952
  Seaford *(G-13134)*

Connectons Cmnty Spport Prgram .... D 302 984-2302
  Claymont *(G-1099)*

Constance P Deptula Lcsw .... G 302 323-0345
  New Castle *(G-8968)*

Contactlifeline Inc .... G 302 761-9800
  Wilmington *(G-15615)*

Cornerstone Community Ctr LLC .... G 302 258-6459
  Bridgeville *(G-686)*

Counseling Services Inc .... G 302 894-1477
  Wilmington *(G-15653)*

Counseling Services Corp .... G 302 898-5184
  Bear *(G-122)*

Created Life Coaching .... G 302 584-7112
  Wilmington *(G-15687)*

Crossroads of Delaware .... G 302 744-9999
  Dover *(G-2161)*

Cynthia L Rae .... G 302 985-7069
  Newark *(G-10372)*

Cypress Support LLC .... G 410 937-2511
  Wilmington *(G-15755)*

Danielle Wiggins .... G 302 494-3397
  Dover *(G-2195)*

Dean A Aman Lpcmh LLC .... F 302 858-3324
  Newark *(G-10401)*

Delaware Adlescent Program Inc .... E 302 531-0257
  Camden *(G-816)*

Delaware Association For Blind .... E 302 998-5913
  Wilmington *(G-15868)*

Delaware Back Pain and Sports .... F 302 832-3369
  Newark *(G-10419)*

Delaware Brast Cncer Cltion In .... G 302 778-1102
  Wilmington *(G-15875)*

Delaware Breast Cancer Coalit .... G 302 672-6435
  Dover *(G-2218)*

Delaware Charms .... G 302 480-4951
  Dover *(G-2220)*

Delaware Cltion Agnst Dom Vlnc .... G 302 658-2958
  Wilmington *(G-15885)*

Delaware Ctr For Hmless Vtrans .... E 302 384-2350
  Wilmington *(G-15896)*

Delaware Ctr For Hmless Vtrans .... G 302 898-2647
  Wilmington *(G-15897)*

Delaware Dept Hlth Social Svcs .... G 302 337-8261
  Bridgeville *(G-691)*

Delaware Dept Hlth Social Svcs .... G 302 857-5000
  Dover *(G-2229)*

Delaware Dept Hlth Social Svcs .... F 302 255-9500
  Dover *(G-2230)*

Delaware Dept Hlth Social Svcs .... G 302 856-5586
  Georgetown *(G-4280)*

Delaware Dept Hlth Social Svcs .... F 302 391-3505
  New Castle *(G-9021)*

Delaware Drnking Drver Program .... F 302 856-1835
  Georgetown *(G-4281)*

Delaware Drnking Drver Program .... G 302 736-4326
  Dover *(G-2233)*

Delaware Ecumenical Council .... G 302 225-1040
  Wilmington *(G-15912)*

Delaware Families For Han .... G 302 383-9890
  Newark *(G-10443)*

Delaware Family Policy Council .... G 302 296-8698
  Seaford *(G-13151)*

Delaware Family Voices Inc .... G 302 669-3030
  Wilmington *(G-15918)*

Delaware Gdnce Svcs For Chldre .... E 302 678-3020
  Dover *(G-2241)*

Delaware Gdnce Svcs For Chldre .... E 302 455-9333
  Newark *(G-10448)*

Delaware Gdnce Svcs For Chldre .... F 302 355-0132
  Newark *(G-10449)*

Delaware Gdnce Svcs For Chldre .... F 302 652-3948
  Wilmington *(G-15921)*

Delaware Hiv Services Inc .... E 302 654-5471
  Wilmington *(G-15927)*

Delaware Juniors Volleyball .... G 302 463-4218
  Newark *(G-10456)*

Delaware Nat Gard Yuth Fndtion .... G 302 326-7582
  New Castle *(G-9028)*

Delaware Pride Inc .... G 302 265-3020
  Claymont *(G-1114)*

Delaware S P C A .... E 302 998-2281
  Newark *(G-10475)*

Delaware Senior Olympics Inc .... G 302 736-5698
  Dover *(G-2258)*

Delaware Wic Program .... G 302 857-5000
  Dover *(G-2274)*

Employee Codes: A=Over 500 employees, B=251-500
C=101-250, D=51-100, E=20-50, F=10-19, G=1-9

83 SOCIAL SERVICES

Name	Code	Phone
Delaware Wic Program	G	302 741-2900
Dover (G-2273)		
Delmarva Teen Challenge	G	302 337-9100
Bridgeville (G-694)		
Delmarva Teen Challenge Inc	G	302 629-8824
Seaford (G-13156)		
Diamond State Counseling	G	302 683-1055
Newark (G-10525)		
Dima Ix Inc	G	302 427-0787
Wilmington (G-16073)		
Dimarquez Intl Ministries Inc	G	302 256-4847
Historic New Castle (G-4975)		
Division Svcs For Aging Adlts	G	302 255-9390
New Castle (G-9057)		
Doctors For Emergency Svc PC	E	302 733-1000
Newark (G-10544)		
Donahue Julie Ann Lpc Lpcmh	G	610 764-8652
Wilmington (G-16133)		
Dover Afb Youth Center	F	302 677-6376
Dover (G-2332)		
Dover Educational & Cmnty Ctr	F	302 883-3092
Dover (G-2340)		
Dover Interfaith Mission Walte	G	302 264-9021
Dover (G-2348)		
Dover Intrfith Mssion For Hsin	F	302 736-3600
Dover (G-2349)		
Dunamis Dominion LLC	G	302 470-0468
Dover (G-2395)		
Dunams-Hmes Dvine Intrvntion I	G	302 393-5778
Camden Wyoming (G-937)		
Earl Carter	G	302 375-0354
Claymont (G-1127)		
Easter Sals Del MryInds Estrn	D	302 324-4444
New Castle (G-9078)		
Edgemoor Rvtalization Coop Inc	G	302 293-3944
Wilmington (G-16291)		
Elicin Edeline	G	973 687-9930
Newark (G-10626)		
Elizabeth A Hussey	G	302 577-5400
Wilmington (G-16368)		
Embrace Change LLC	G	302 286-5288
Newark (G-10639)		
Embrace The Change Counseling	G	302 358-6237
Newark (G-10640)		
Emily Crawford PHD	G	302 995-9600
Wilmington (G-16394)		
Empowering Group LLC	G	302 450-3065
Dover (G-2445)		
End of Life Doula	G	302 478-6958
Wilmington (G-16408)		
F H Everett & Associates Inc	G	302 674-2380
Dover (G-2478)		
Family Care Connections	F	856 579-7303
Middletown (G-7119)		
Family Cnsling Ctr St Puls Inc	F	302 576-4136
Wilmington (G-16535)		
Family Prmise Nthrn New Cstle	G	302 998-2222
Wilmington (G-16546)		
Family Services	F	302 422-1400
Milford (G-7889)		
Family Services Div	G	302 577-3824
Wilmington (G-16547)		
Family Wrkplace Connection Inc	E	302 479-1660
Wilmington (G-16548)		
Fedcap Rehabilitation Services	F	302 544-6634
New Castle (G-9120)		
First State Cmnty Action Agcy	E	302 674-1355
Dover (G-2499)		
First State Cmnty Action Agcy	E	302 856-7761
Georgetown (G-4322)		
Food Bank of Delaware Inc	E	302 292-1305
Newark (G-10754)		
Forgotten Few Foundation Inc	G	302 494-6212
Wilmington (G-16693)		
Frederica Senior Center Inc	G	302 335-4555
Frederica (G-4167)		
Freedom Outreach	G	302 655-2724
Wilmington (G-16742)		
Friendship House Incorporated	F	302 652-8033
Wilmington (G-16759)		
Friendship House Incorporated	F	302 652-8133
Wilmington (G-16760)		
Friendship House Nec	G	302 731-5338
Newark (G-10787)		
Gail S Levinson	G	302 764-0474
Wilmington (G-16792)		
Geraldine M Vota	G	302 762-2283
Lewes (G-6031)		
Geriatric & Palliative Svcs	G	302 438-5440
Wilmington (G-16850)		
Girl Scuts of Chspake Bay Cnci	E	302 456-7150
Newark (G-10838)		
Good Samaritan Aid	G	302 875-2425
Laurel (G-5522)		
Greater Lewes Community Vlg	G	302 703-2568
Lewes (G-6056)		
Growing Edges Counseling	G	484 883-6523
Wilmington (G-16989)		
Gull House Adult Activity	G	302 226-2160
Lewes (G-6068)		
Habitat For Hmnity New Cstle C	F	302 652-0365
Wilmington (G-17027)		
Hands of Hope	F	302 519-2706
Laurel (G-5527)		
Harmon Larhonda	G	302 747-0700
Middletown (G-7197)		
Harrington Senior Center Inc	G	302 398-4224
Harrington (G-4781)		
Harrison Hse Cmnty Prgrams Inc	G	302 427-8438
New Castle (G-9197)		
Hawkins Counsel Group	G	302 660-0858
Wilmington (G-17079)		
Heal Well LLC	G	302 542-7095
Dagsboro (G-1461)		
Healing Goddess Inrterprises	G	301 751-0695
Wilmington (G-17093)		
Helpinghands	G	302 290-1146
Wilmington (G-17119)		
Hillside Center	E	302 652-1181
Wilmington (G-17147)		
Holly Jordyn Ann	G	443 945-0615
Wilmington (G-17168)		
Home For Aged Wmn-Mnquadale HM	C	302 654-1810
Wilmington (G-17178)		
Hope Hanks Inc	G	302 562-9309
Wilmington (G-17196)		
Hopes Helping Hands LLC	G	443 365-5115
Seaford (G-13217)		
Horizon House Delaware	G	302 577-3220
Wilmington (G-17205)		
Horizon House of Delaware Inc	E	302 658-2392
Wilmington (G-17206)		
Housing Alliance Delaware Inc	F	302 654-0126
Wilmington (G-17218)		
Howard Weston Senior Center	G	302 328-6425
New Castle (G-9222)		
Humphrey Jones Sherry H PHD	G	302 239-1076
Wilmington (G-17232)		
Idrch3 Ministries	G	302 344-6957
Camden (G-855)		
Ignite Your Light	G	302 766-0982
Newark (G-11000)		
Immanuel Shelter Inc	G	888 634-9992
Rehoboth Beach (G-12793)		
Immanuel Shelter Inc	G	302 227-7743
Nassau (G-8741)		
▲ Independent Resources Inc	G	302 765-0191
Wilmington (G-17309)		
Ingleside Homes Inc	D	302 575-0250
Wilmington (G-17335)		
Integrity Companions	G	302 659-2936
Smyrna (G-13773)		
Isocde Community Ctr Location	G	302 697-7276
Felton (G-3984)		
Iveh Latino Family Servic	G	302 381-0762
Milford (G-7943)		
Jeffrie J Silverberg PHD	G	302 507-3039
Wilmington (G-17522)		
Jennifer C Dombroski Msw Lcsw	G	302 422-3811
Dover (G-2780)		
Jennifer M Ewald	G	302 377-6911
Middletown (G-7245)		
Jennifer Sellitto-Penoza Lcsw	G	302 328-4936
New Castle (G-9258)		
Jennifer Trolio Lcsw	G	302 836-1131
Newark (G-11105)		
Jewish Community Center Inc	E	302 478-5660
Wilmington (G-17538)		
Jewish Family Services of Del	F	302 478-9411
Wilmington (G-17539)		
Jgcounseling	G	302 354-0074
Wilmington (G-17542)		
Joann M Schneidman	G	302 761-9119
Wilmington (G-17560)		
Joanne Parker-Henry Inc	G	302 378-7251
Middletown (G-7252)		
Johns El Family Industries Inc	G	310 701-5678
Lewes (G-6149)		
Johns Sally H Lcsw	G	302 547-7710
Wilmington (G-17569)		
Josh N Schmidt	G	302 668-1304
Wilmington (G-17590)		
Jungle Gym LLC	G	302 734-1515
Dover (G-2820)		
Karen Kim Zogheib Lcsw	G	786 897-3022
Wilmington (G-17653)		
Katharine N Snyder	G	302 381-7283
Georgetown (G-4391)		
Kent Cnty Cmnty Action Agcy In	F	302 678-1949
Dover (G-2847)		
Kentmere Rhbltition Hlthcare CT	E	302 652-3311
Wilmington (G-17694)		
Kevin Scott Cameron	G	515 314-3400
Rehoboth Beach (G-12821)		
Keystone Human Services	F	302 502-2158
Wilmington (G-17709)		
Kindred Counseling	G	302 478-8888
Wilmington (G-17724)		
Kristina Brandis	G	516 457-2717
Middletown (G-7283)		
La Esperanza Inc	F	302 854-9262
Georgetown (G-4397)		
Lamont Josey Lcsw	G	302 559-6654
Wilmington (G-17795)		
Latin American Cmnty Ctr Corp	D	302 655-7338
Wilmington (G-17816)		
Laurel Community Hardware Inc	F	302 598-0454
Middletown (G-7291)		
Laurel Senior Center Inc	G	302 875-2536
Laurel (G-5552)		
Lavante N Dorsey & Assoc LLC	F	302 956-9188
Newark (G-11229)		
Lcsw Ceap LLC	G	302 824-0290
Wilmington (G-17841)		
Lend Helping Hand Child C	G	302 521-5298
Wilmington (G-17874)		

83 SOCIAL SERVICES

Leounes Kirsten .... G 302 229-5029
  Bear (G-346)
Lewes Counseling LLC .... G 302 430-2127
  Lewes (G-6193)
Lewes Senior Citizens Center .... G 302 645-9293
  Lewes (G-6200)
Life Innovations .... G 302 525-6521
  Newark (G-11255)
Lisa R Savage .... G 302 353-7052
  Newark (G-11268)
Living Water Counseling LLC .... G 443 553-7317
  Wilmington (G-17950)
Lnz Consulting LLC .... G 302 543-6296
  Wilmington (G-17965)
Lost and Found Dog Rescue Adop .... G 302 613-0394
  New Castle (G-9327)
Lutheran Community Services .... G 302 654-8886
  Wilmington (G-18031)
Luz D Reynoso .... G 302 358-6237
  Newark (G-11297)
M Michelle Milligan Lcsw .... G 302 540-9136
  Wilmington (G-18059)
M O T Senior Citizen Center .... F 302 378-3041
  Middletown (G-7317)
Madison Adoption Associates .... G 302 475-8977
  Claymont (G-1228)
Marc V Felizzi .... G 302 897-4942
  Wilmington (G-18119)
Margo Lewis-Jah Leona .... G 610 800-9524
  Wilmington (G-18125)
Mary Mother Hope House 1 .... F 302 652-8532
  Wilmington (G-18181)
McC Foundation Inc .... F 302 762-6025
  Wilmington (G-18215)
McCarthy Cate .... G 302 477-0708
  Wilmington (G-18219)
McCloskey Barbara Lcsw .... G 302 479-5916
  Wilmington (G-18221)
Meals On Whels of Lwes Rhoboth .... G 302 645-7449
  Lewes (G-6256)
Megan Mc Graw Lcsw .... G 302 283-0414
  Newark (G-11381)
Mending Cove LLC .... G 856 803-9958
  Newark (G-11386)
Mental Edge Counseling .... E 302 382-8698
  Dover (G-3061)
Mental Fuel Inc .... G 302 291-4858
  Newark (G-11387)
Mentor De .... G 302 858-4644
  Georgetown (G-4425)
Merakey USA .... E 302 325-3540
  New Castle (G-9358)
Meryls .... G 302 475-7555
  Wilmington (G-18288)
Metanoia Counseling LLC .... G 302 559-4421
  Middletown (G-7344)
Michael A Peyton Lcsw .... G 302 836-5311
  Bear (G-373)
Michael H McGrath .... G 302 242-3849
  Smyrna (G-13823)
Michael J Di Salvo .... G 302 636-0169
  Wilmington (G-18314)
Michael J Hurd .... G 302 539-5986
  Ocean View (G-12546)
Michelle C Johnson Lcsw .... G 302 893-9235
  Wilmington (G-18327)
Mid-County Inc .... G 302 995-6555
  Wilmington (G-18339)
Middletown Counseling .... G 302 376-0621
  Middletown (G-7348)
Middletown Counseling .... G 302 540-9003
  Smyrna (G-13824)

Middltown Odssa Twnsend Snior .... E 302 378-4758
  Middletown (G-7364)
Milford Senior Center Inc .... F 302 422-3385
  Milford (G-8008)
Millville Rehabilitation Svc .... F 302 645-3100
  Millville (G-8543)
Mind and Body Consortium LLC .... D 302 674-2380
  Dover (G-3097)
Mindy Body Consortium .... G 302 424-1322
  Milford (G-8014)
Ministry of Caring Inc .... G 302 652-0904
  Wilmington (G-18374)
Ministry of Caring Inc .... G 302 652-0970
  Wilmington (G-18376)
Ministry of Caring Inc .... G 302 652-0969
  Wilmington (G-18377)
Ministry of Caring Inc .... G 302 658-6123
  Wilmington (G-18378)
Mlk Educational Community Ctr .... G 302 242-1165
  Dover (G-3107)
Modern Maturity Center Inc .... E 302 734-1200
  Dover (G-3115)
Mosaic .... D 302 456-5995
  Newark (G-11455)
Mrs Rita Fisher .... G 215 500-6280
  Smyrna (G-13829)
Music Art & Culture Foundation .... G 347 746-9047
  Lewes (G-6297)
My Health Group Inc .... E 401 400-0015
  Dover (G-3137)
My Sisters Place Inc .... G 302 737-5303
  Newark (G-11477)
N U Friendship Outreach Inc .... G 302 836-0404
  Bear (G-386)
Nancy M Ball .... G 302 655-8101
  Wilmington (G-18525)
Nanticoke Senior Ctr .... F 302 629-4939
  Seaford (G-13311)
Narrow Gate1 .... G 302 387-1838
  Magnolia (G-6770)
Natascha L Hughes .... G 302 856-4700
  Georgetown (G-4442)
Nehemiah Gtwy Cmnty Dev Corp .... G 302 655-0803
  Wilmington (G-18570)
Neighborhood House Inc .... F 302 658-5404
  Wilmington (G-18571)
New Direction Counseling Svcs .... G 302 289-3768
  Felton (G-4006)
New Hope Rcreation Dev Ctr Inc .... F 302 424-0767
  Ellendale (G-3927)
Newark Senior Center Inc .... E 302 737-2336
  Newark (G-11546)
Northnode Group Counseling LLC .... F 302 257-3135
  Dover (G-3198)
NU Friendship Outreach .... G 302 354-1517
  New Castle (G-9429)
Oak Grove Senior Center Inc .... G 302 998-3319
  Wilmington (G-18725)
Oasis Senior Advisors Delaware .... G 302 668-0298
  Hockessin (G-5328)
Olga Yatzus Lpcmh .... G 302 407-3743
  Wilmington (G-18758)
One Village Alliance Inc .... G 302 275-1715
  Wilmington (G-18785)
Our Youth Inc .... G 302 655-8250
  Wilmington (G-18836)
Out of Ashes LLC .... G 302 507-4623
  Newark (G-11606)
Outreach Team LLC .... G 302 744-9500
  Dover (G-3252)
Parkview De Snf Management LLC .... D 302 655-6135
  Wilmington (G-18896)

Patricia Ayers .... G 609 335-8923
  Wilmington (G-18906)
Patricia R Wood .... G 302 737-3674
  Newark (G-11638)
Pauls House Inc .... G 302 384-2350
  Wilmington (G-18923)
Peace By Piece Inc .... F 302 266-2556
  Newark (G-11649)
Peoples Place II Inc .... G 302 422-8033
  Milford (G-8045)
Peoples Sttlment Assn Wlmngton .... E 302 658-4133
  Wilmington (G-18964)
Phc Inc .... E 313 831-3500
  New Castle (G-9470)
Phoenix Rehabilitation .... G 302 533-5313
  Newark (G-11686)
Pike Creek Counseling .... G 302 898-9229
  Wilmington (G-19040)
Pike Creek Psychological Ctr PA .... G 302 738-6859
  Newark (G-11693)
Pioneer House .... G 302 286-0892
  Newark (G-11695)
Point of Hope Inc .... E 302 731-7676
  New Castle (G-9480)
Police Offcer Mses Wlker Jr In .... G 215 268-4146
  Dover (G-3348)
Positive Directions II LLC .... F 302 654-9444
  Wilmington (G-19125)
Precious Mmnts Edcatn Cmnty CT .... F 302 697-9374
  Dover (G-3358)
Pressley Ridge Foundation .... G 302 677-1590
  Dover (G-3368)
Prestwick Community Corp .... G 302 227-7878
  Lewes (G-6389)
Prevent Child Abuse Delaware .... G 302 425-7490
  Wilmington (G-19186)
Pulsar360 Corp .... E 855 578-5727
  Newark (G-11771)
Puzzles Lf Rntry Prgram For Wm .... G 302 339-0327
  Wilmington (G-19269)
Rain of Light Inc .... G 302 312-7642
  Newark (G-11821)
Randy L Christofferson .... G 302 540-2006
  Wilmington (G-19331)
Rauma Survivors Foundation .... G 302 275-9705
  Wilmington (G-19339)
Rd Innovative Planning .... G 302 635-0767
  Wilmington (G-19355)
Reach Riverside Dev Corp .... G 302 232-6612
  Wilmington (G-19361)
Recovery Destination Services .... G 302 559-1010
  Hockessin (G-5358)
Reeds Refuge Center Inc .... G 302 428-1830
  Wilmington (G-19393)
Renew Your Heart and Mind LLC .... G 302 344-7519
  Millsboro (G-8442)
Resources For Human Dev Inc .... E 215 951-0300
  Newark (G-11870)
Restoring Lf Rstrtion Ctr Corp .... G 862 772-5148
  New Castle (G-9525)
Retired Senior Volunteer Prog .... G 302 856-5815
  Georgetown (G-4483)
RI Int .... E 302 318-6032
  Newark (G-11881)
Ronald McDonald House Delaware .... F 302 428-5299
  Wilmington (G-19560)
Rose Hill Community Center .... F 302 656-8513
  New Castle (G-9541)
Rouleau Suzanne Lcsw .... G 302 479-5157
  Newark (G-11918)
Ruby Road LLC .... G 856 887-1422
  Newark (G-11925)

Employee Codes: A=Over 500 employees, B=251-500
C=101-250, D=51-100, E=20-50, F=10-19, G=1-9

2024 Harris Directory of
Delaware Businesses

83 SOCIAL SERVICES

Ruffin Tellie .... G 302 650-3151
  Wilmington *(G-19587)*
Salvation Army .... F 302 934-3730
  Millsboro *(G-8453)*
Salvation Army .... F 302 996-9400
  Wilmington *(G-19644)*
Salvation Army .... E 302 656-1696
  Wilmington *(G-19645)*
Samaritan Outreach .... G 302 594-9476
  Wilmington *(G-19648)*
Sanare Today LLC .... E 610 344-9600
  Wilmington *(G-19652)*
Sandra L Korines .... G 201 245-2003
  Wilmington *(G-19660)*
Sarah Wolfe Lcsw .... G 302 744-8046
  Milford *(G-8084)*
Saving Our Yuth Mtters Incrprt .... G 917 889-0086
  Newark *(G-11954)*
Scchs .... F 302 856-7524
  Georgetown *(G-4499)*
Sellers Senior Center Inc .... G 302 762-2050
  Wilmington *(G-19746)*
Senior Nanticoke Center Inc .... F 302 629-4939
  Seaford *(G-13394)*
Shannon A Fisch .... G 302 536-5667
  Seaford *(G-13400)*
Shapeup Sales Coaching .... G 850 585-3527
  Felton *(G-4027)*
Shelatia J Dennis .... G 302 465-0630
  Dover *(G-3541)*
Shepherd Place Inc .... G 302 678-1909
  Dover *(G-3542)*
Sojourners Place Inc .... G 302 764-4592
  Wilmington *(G-19917)*
South Coastal .... G 302 542-5668
  Frankford *(G-4147)*
Southern Meadow .... G 302 677-0800
  Magnolia *(G-6784)*
Special Olympics Delaware Inc .... F 302 831-4653
  Newark *(G-12063)*
Springboard Collaborative Inc .... G 302 864-5220
  Wilmington *(G-19976)*
Springs Rhbltttion At Brndywine .... D 302 998-0101
  Wilmington *(G-19979)*
St Anthonys Community Center .... F 302 421-3721
  Wilmington *(G-19990)*
St Patricks Center Inc .... G 302 652-6219
  Wilmington *(G-20002)*
State Senior Care LLC .... G 302 674-2144
  Dover *(G-3608)*
Stephanie Orr Lcsw LLC .... G 302 478-4373
  Wilmington *(G-20054)*
Strength For Jurney Counseling .... G 302 367-4266
  Wilmington *(G-20097)*
Suburban Psychiatric Svcs LLC .... F 302 999-9834
  Wilmington *(G-20115)*
Sunday Breakfast Mission .... F 302 656-8542
  Wilmington *(G-20129)*
Supreme Court United States .... F 302 252-2950
  Wilmington *(G-20155)*
Survivors Abuse In Rcovery Inc .... G 302 651-0181
  Wilmington *(G-20162)*
Susan Donges .... G 302 645-3100
  Millsboro *(G-8473)*
Susan L Barton .... G 302 655-3953
  Wilmington *(G-20163)*
Sussex Cmnty Crsis Hsing Svcs .... F 302 856-2246
  Georgetown *(G-4532)*
Sussex Cnty Snior Svcs Adult D .... G 302 854-2882
  Georgetown *(G-4534)*
Sussex Family Counseling LLC .... G 302 864-7970
  Georgetown *(G-4538)*
Sussex Pregnancy Care Center .... G 302 856-4344
  Georgetown *(G-4542)*
Suzanne Isenberg .... G 302 470-1166
  Wilmington *(G-20167)*
Symphony of Mind Counseling .... G 302 747-7286
  Dover *(G-3633)*
Synergy Empowerment Coaching .... G 302 362-0054
  Laurel *(G-5612)*
Systems Inc Communit .... G 302 294-1872
  Newark *(G-12149)*
Tatsapod-Aame .... G 302 897-8963
  Wilmington *(G-20228)*
Techno Relief Limited .... G 416 453-9393
  Wilmington *(G-20255)*
Teri Lyn Busch Msw/Lcsw .... G 302 731-9110
  Newark *(G-12179)*
Tidewater Physcl Thrpy and REB .... G 302 684-2829
  Milton *(G-8720)*
Timothy S Early .... G 302 387-7374
  Dover *(G-3690)*
Togetherall .... F 315 434-0911
  Wilmington *(G-20345)*
Tomaros Change .... G 856 542-8861
  Claymont *(G-1314)*
Tomaros Change .... G 844 222-8500
  Claymont *(G-1315)*
Tranquil Roots Counseling .... G 301 275-0225
  Wilmington *(G-20391)*
Tranquility Counseling Inc .... G 302 636-0700
  Newark *(G-12217)*
Transitional Fisher .... G 302 322-4124
  New Castle *(G-9635)*
Transitional Youth .... F 302 423-7543
  Greenwood *(G-4672)*
Troy Farmer .... G 888 711-0094
  Bear *(G-542)*
Turning Point At Peoples Place .... G 302 424-2420
  Milford *(G-8121)*
United Cerebral Palsy of De .... E 302 764-2400
  Wilmington *(G-20524)*
United Way of Delaware Inc .... E 302 573-3700
  Wilmington *(G-20530)*
Unity Perspectives Inc .... G 302 265-2854
  Milford *(G-8130)*
University of Delaware .... G 302 831-2501
  Newark *(G-12280)*
Unlimited Restoration Inc .... G 302 439-4213
  Claymont *(G-1323)*
Upper Darby Community Out .... F 610 352-7008
  Rehoboth Beach *(G-13001)*
Urbanpromise Wilmington Inc .... G 302 425-5502
  Wilmington *(G-20544)*
Veterans Untd Outreach Del Inc .... G 302 678-1285
  Dover *(G-3788)*
Victims Voices Heard .... G 302 407-3747
  Wilmington *(G-20609)*
Wayne K Pansa Jr Lcsw LLC .... G 302 455-7065
  Wilmington *(G-20695)*
We Deserve It Shs For Kids Inc .... G 302 521-7255
  Dover *(G-3823)*
Wellspring Counseling Services .... G 302 373-8904
  Smyrna *(G-13934)*
West End Neighborhood Hse Inc .... G 302 654-2131
  Wilmington *(G-20739)*
West End Neighborhood Hse Inc .... E 302 658-4171
  Wilmington *(G-20740)*
Whatcoat Social Service Agency .... E 302 734-0319
  Dover *(G-3842)*
William Hcks Andrson Cmnty Ctr .... F 302 571-4266
  Wilmington *(G-20794)*
Willow Counseling Services .... G 814 779-9653
  Smyrna *(G-13940)*
Wilmington Senior Center Inc .... F 302 651-3400
  Wilmington *(G-20843)*
Young Mens Christian Assn Del .... C 302 571-6900
  Wilmington *(G-20937)*

8331 Job training and related services

Advanced Training Acadmey .... G 302 369-8800
  Newark *(G-9783)*
Cadia Rehabilitation Rnssnc .... F 302 947-4200
  Millsboro *(G-8214)*
Careeronestop Dover One Stop .... G 302 739-5473
  Dover *(G-2030)*
Chimes Inc .... E 302 382-4500
  Historic New Castle *(G-4956)*
Delaware Bus Leadership Netwrk .... G 302 314-5070
  New Castle *(G-9014)*
Delaware Dept Hlth Social Svcs .... G 302 255-9855
  New Castle *(G-9017)*
Delaware Dept Hlth Social Svcs .... D 302 255-9800
  New Castle *(G-9020)*
Delmarva Clergy United Inc .... F 302 422-2350
  Ellendale *(G-3914)*
Easter Sals Del Mrylnds Estrn .... D 302 678-3353
  Dover *(G-2411)*
Easter Sals Del Mrylnds Estrn .... D 302 856-7364
  Georgetown *(G-4303)*
Easter Sals Del Mrylnds Estrn .... D 302 324-4444
  New Castle *(G-9078)*
Elwyn Pennsylvania and Del .... D 302 658-8860
  Wilmington *(G-16382)*
Forward Support LLC .... G 315 292-8770
  Newark *(G-10767)*
Goodwill .... F 302 934-9146
  Millsboro *(G-8302)*
Goodwill Inds Del Del Cnty Inc .... E 302 761-4640
  Wilmington *(G-16927)*
Industrial Training Cons Inc .... E 302 266-6100
  Newark *(G-11016)*
Leadership Institute Inc .... F 302 368-7292
  Newark *(G-11236)*
Nlcdd .... G 302 831-4728
  Newark *(G-11558)*
Opportunity Center Inc .... D 302 762-0300
  New Castle *(G-9435)*
Service Quest .... G 302 235-0173
  Hockessin *(G-5380)*
Skillbird LLC .... E 302 216-1811
  Newark *(G-12021)*
Telamon Corp/Early Chldhd Pgrm .... G 302 934-1642
  Georgetown *(G-4548)*
Telamon Corporation .... G 302 934-0925
  Georgetown *(G-4549)*
Telamon Corporation .... G 302 398-9196
  Harrington *(G-4840)*
Telamon Corporation .... G 302 424-2335
  Milford *(G-8115)*
Telamon Corporation .... G 302 629-5557
  Seaford *(G-13427)*
Telamon Corporation Headstart .... F 302 875-7718
  Laurel *(G-5615)*
Telamon Delaware Head Start .... F 302 934-1642
  Georgetown *(G-4550)*

8351 Child day care services

A Better Chnce For Our Chldren .... F 302 725-5008
  Milford *(G-7756)*
A Childs Potential .... G 302 249-6929
  Lewes *(G-5645)*
A Childs World LLC .... F 302 322-9386
  Bear *(G-8)*
A Leap of Faith Inc .... F 302 543-6256
  Wilmington *(G-14167)*

83 SOCIAL SERVICES

A Place To Grow Fmly Chld Care............ G 302 897-8944
  Claymont *(G-1016)*
Academy of Early Learning................... G 302 659-0750
  Smyrna *(G-13629)*
Acclaim Academy LLC......................... F 215 848-7827
  Wilmington *(G-14224)*
All About ME Day Care......................... F 302 424-8322
  Milford *(G-7763)*
All In Harmony Child Care..................... G 302 494-3618
  Newark *(G-9816)*
All My Children Inc............................... G 302 995-9191
  Wilmington *(G-14367)*
Amemg Inc... F 302 220-7132
  New Castle *(G-8793)*
American Universal LLC....................... G 302 836-9790
  Newark *(G-9849)*
Angela Daycar Nana Lil........................ G 302 672-9167
  Dover *(G-1794)*
Angels Lindas...................................... G 302 328-3700
  New Castle *(G-8809)*
Anniejwels Erly Child Dev Ctr................ G 302 981-1904
  Wilmington *(G-14493)*
Anns Family Daycare........................... G 302 836-8910
  Newark *(G-9873)*
Army & Air Force Exchange Svc........... F 302 677-3716
  Dover *(G-1817)*
Atlantic Dawn Ltd................................ F 302 737-8854
  Newark *(G-9934)*
Attic Away From Home........................ F 302 378-2600
  Townsend *(G-13961)*
Ave Preschool..................................... E 302 422-8775
  Milford *(G-7780)*
Babes On Square................................ G 302 477-9190
  Wilmington *(G-14711)*
Baby Bear Educare.............................. G 302 981-9571
  New Castle *(G-8842)*
Barbara L McKinney............................. G 302 266-9594
  Newark *(G-9982)*
Beach Babies Child Care...................... G 302 645-5010
  Rehoboth Beach *(G-12627)*
Beach Bbies Child Care At Twns........... G 302 378-4778
  Townsend *(G-13962)*
Beach Bbies Child Care At Twns........... E 302 644-1585
  Rehoboth Beach *(G-12628)*
Beacon Hope Christian Ministry............ G 302 764-7162
  Wilmington *(G-14800)*
Bear Early Education Center................. G 302 836-5000
  Newark *(G-10003)*
Bear-Glasgow YMCA........................... G 302 836-9622
  Newark *(G-10006)*
Beetles Playhouse Day Care................. G 302 593-7321
  Newark *(G-10010)*
Beginning Blssngs Chldcare LLC........... G 302 893-1726
  New Castle *(G-8857)*
Beginnings & Beyond Nurery Sch.......... F 302 678-0445
  Dover *(G-1904)*
Beginnings and Beyond Inc................... E 302 734-2464
  Dover *(G-1905)*
Bernices Edctl Schl Age Ctr In.............. G 302 651-0286
  Wilmington *(G-14849)*
Bethel United Methodist Church............ F 302 645-9426
  Lewes *(G-5758)*
Bethesda Child Devmnt Ctr................... F 302 378-8435
  Middletown *(G-6916)*
Bizzy Bees Home Daycare LLC............. G 302 376-9245
  Middletown *(G-6922)*
Blessed Beginnings Lrng Ctr................. F 302 838-9112
  Bear *(G-75)*
Boost Learning LLC............................. F 302 691-5821
  Wilmington *(G-15005)*
Brees Home Day Care.......................... G 302 762-0876
  Wilmington *(G-15101)*

Bright Beginnings Inc............................ G 302 376-8001
  Middletown *(G-6940)*
Bright Bgnnngs Child Care Ctr............... G 302 934-1249
  Millsboro *(G-8208)*
Bright Futures Inc................................ E 610 905-0506
  Middletown *(G-6941)*
Bright Horizons Chld Ctrs LLC............... E 302 456-8913
  Newark *(G-10086)*
Bright Horizons Chld Ctrs LLC............... F 302 453-2050
  Newark *(G-10087)*
Bright Horizons Chld Ctrs LLC............... G 302 282-6378
  Wilmington *(G-15109)*
Bright Horizons Chld Ctrs LLC............... G 302 475-6780
  Wilmington *(G-15110)*
Bright Horizons Chld Ctrs LLC............... F 302 477-1023
  Wilmington *(G-15111)*
Bright Kidz Inc..................................... F 302 369-6929
  Newark *(G-10088)*
Bright New Beginnings......................... G 610 637-9809
  Wilmington *(G-15112)*
Bright New Schlars Academy LLC......... F 302 668-6053
  Newark *(G-10089)*
Bright Stars Daycare............................ G 302 449-9198
  Townsend *(G-13967)*
Bright Stars Home Daycare.................. F 302 378-8142
  Middletown *(G-6942)*
Brilliant Little Minds............................. F 302 376-9889
  Middletown *(G-6943)*
Brown Lisha... G 302 832-9529
  Newark *(G-10095)*
Building Blocks For Learni.................... G 302 677-0248
  Dover *(G-1990)*
Butterfield Inspection Service............... G 301 322-1644
  Lewes *(G-5783)*
Cacc Montessori School....................... F 302 239-2917
  Hockessin *(G-5147)*
Caesar Rodney School District............. D 302 697-3207
  Dover *(G-2011)*
Capital School District.......................... G 302 678-8394
  Dover *(G-2021)*
Carmen R Benitez................................ G 302 793-2061
  Claymont *(G-1074)*
Catholic Charities Inc........................... G 302 674-1600
  Dover *(G-2039)*
Cdb Ventures Inc................................ E 302 235-0414
  Hockessin *(G-5154)*
Center For Child Developement............ G 302 292-1334
  Newark *(G-10172)*
Central Del Schl of The Arts F.............. G 302 943-2274
  Viola *(G-14092)*
Chesapake Cnfrnce Svnth-Day Ad........ G 302 998-3961
  Wilmington *(G-15366)*
Chester Bthel Untd Mthdst Pre............. F 302 475-3549
  Wilmington *(G-15368)*
Child Care Ctr..................................... G 302 652-8992
  Wilmington *(G-15373)*
Child Care Service............................... F 302 981-1328
  Newark *(G-10203)*
Child Inc... F 302 335-8652
  Magnolia *(G-6730)*
Children First Lrng Ctr Inc.................... G 302 674-5227
  Dover *(G-2060)*
Children S Secret Garden..................... G 302 730-1717
  Dover *(G-2062)*
Childrens Beach House Inc................... E 302 645-9184
  Lewes *(G-5812)*
Childrens Place................................... G 302 875-7733
  Laurel *(G-5482)*
Childrens Place Child Dev Ce................ F 302 947-4808
  Millsboro *(G-8221)*
Childs Play At Home LLC..................... G 302 644-3445
  Lewes *(G-5813)*

Childs Play By Bay............................... G 302 703-6234
  Lewes *(G-5814)*
Christ Ch Episcpal Preschool................ F 302 472-0021
  Wilmington *(G-15396)*
Church of God In Christ........................ F 302 678-1949
  Dover *(G-2072)*
Circle Time Learning Center................. G 302 384-7193
  Wilmington *(G-15443)*
Claremont School LLC......................... G 302 478-4531
  Wilmington *(G-15461)*
Concord Preschool Childca................... G 302 750-7082
  Wilmington *(G-15584)*
Connections Development Corp............ E 302 436-3292
  Frankford *(G-4093)*
Corporate Kids Lrng Ctr Inc.................. F 302 678-0688
  Dover *(G-2141)*
Country Kids Child Care Lrng C............ G 302 349-5888
  Greenwood *(G-4608)*
Country Kids Home Day Care............... G 302 653-4134
  Townsend *(G-13977)*
Covenant Preschool............................. F 302 764-8503
  Wilmington *(G-15662)*
Cozy Critters Child Care Corp.............. E 302 541-8210
  Frankford *(G-4094)*
Creative Beginnings............................. G 302 633-4575
  Wilmington *(G-15690)*
Creative Education Inc......................... F 610 268-2770
  Bear *(G-124)*
Creative Land Care.............................. G 302 482-1944
  Wilmington *(G-15692)*
Creative Learning Child Care................ G 302 691-3167
  Wilmington *(G-15693)*
Creative Minds Daycare....................... G 302 378-0741
  Townsend *(G-13978)*
Creative Play Day School..................... F 610 268-2770
  Bear *(G-125)*
Dawn L Conly..................................... F 302 378-1890
  Middletown *(G-7031)*
Day School For Children...................... G 302 652-4651
  New Castle *(G-9003)*
Dcc Inc... F 302 750-1207
  Wilmington *(G-15828)*
De Colores Family Child Care............... F 302 883-3298
  Dover *(G-2203)*
Deanne Naples Family Daycare............. F 302 376-1408
  Middletown *(G-7034)*
Dees Learning Care............................. G 908 623-7685
  Newark *(G-10408)*
Delaware Adlescent Program Inc........... E 302 268-7218
  Newark *(G-10415)*
Denise Miller Day Care Ce................... G 302 482-9347
  Wilmington *(G-16009)*
Developing Minds Preschool................. G 302 995-9611
  Wilmington *(G-16035)*
Diane Spence Day Care....................... F 302 335-4460
  Frederica *(G-4166)*
Diocesan Council Inc........................... F 302 475-4688
  Wilmington *(G-16075)*
Dis Daycare.. F 302 888-0350
  Wilmington *(G-16082)*
Discovery Island Preschool................... F 302 732-7529
  Dagsboro *(G-1440)*
Ditrocchio Maria Antonetta................... G 302 450-6790
  Dover *(G-2305)*
Dover Educational & Cmnty Ctr............ F 302 883-3092
  Dover *(G-2340)*
Dovers Childrens Villag......................... F 302 672-6476
  Dover *(G-2369)*
Dreams Childcare LLC......................... G 302 652-1085
  Wilmington *(G-16178)*
Eagle Nest Daycare............................. F 302 684-2765
  Milton *(G-8614)*

83 SOCIAL SERVICES — SIC SECTION

Early Childhood Lab .... G 302 857-6731
  Dover *(G-2407)*
Early Learning Center .... F 302 239-3033
  Hockessin *(G-5196)*
Early Learning Center .... F 302 831-0584
  Wilmington *(G-16249)*
Ebenezer United Methdst Chruch .... F 302 731-9495
  Newark *(G-10602)*
Eden Land Care .... F 302 379-2405
  Wilmington *(G-16286)*
Edgemoor Community Center Inc .... D 302 762-1391
  Wilmington *(G-16289)*
Education Svcs Unlimited LLC .... F 302 650-4210
  Wilmington *(G-16298)*
Educational Enrichment Center .... E 302 478-8697
  Wilmington *(G-16300)*
Einsteins School Age Center .... G 302 855-5766
  Georgetown *(G-4308)*
Eisele Celine .... G 302 684-3201
  Milton *(G-8616)*
Elaine Leonard .... G 302 376-5553
  Middletown *(G-7089)*
Elsmere Presbyterian Church .... F 302 998-6365
  Wilmington *(G-16381)*
Emma Jefferies Day Care .... G 302 762-3235
  Wilmington *(G-16395)*
Emma Kane & Valerie Taylor Day .... F 302 629-4347
  Seaford *(G-13174)*
Enchanted Child Care Intl Inc .... G 302 834-0436
  Bear *(G-202)*
Enterprise Learning Solutions .... G 302 762-6595
  Wilmington *(G-16434)*
Estelles Child Dev Ctr Inc .... F 302 792-9065
  New Castle *(G-9101)*
Esther V Graham .... G 302 422-6667
  Milford *(G-7883)*
Excellent Educatn Daycare LLC .... F 302 565-2200
  Newark *(G-10684)*
Expanding Our Kids World .... F 302 659-0293
  Smyrna *(G-13728)*
Ezion Fair Community Academy .... F 302 652-9114
  Wilmington *(G-16518)*
Faith Victory Christn Academy .... F 302 333-0855
  Claymont *(G-1145)*
Family Wrkplace Connection Inc .... E 302 479-1660
  Wilmington *(G-16548)*
Favored Childcare Academy Inc .... G 302 698-1266
  Dover *(G-2488)*
First Steps Preschool-Milford .... G 302 424-4470
  Milford *(G-7897)*
Foot Steps Two Heaven Daycare .... G 302 738-5519
  Newark *(G-10757)*
Foulk Pr-School Day Care Ctr I .... G 302 478-3047
  Wilmington *(G-16702)*
Foulk Pre-Schl & Day Cre Cntr .... G 302 529-1580
  Wilmington *(G-16703)*
Fun 2 Learn Day Care .... G 302 875-3393
  Laurel *(G-5516)*
Funstep Inc .... E 302 731-9618
  Newark *(G-10791)*
Future Dev Lrng Acdemy Fdla LL .... G 302 652-7500
  Wilmington *(G-16775)*
Future Leaders .... G 862 262-7312
  Smyrna *(G-13740)*
Gb Jacobs LLC .... F 302 378-9100
  Middletown *(G-7152)*
Gem School Inc .... F 302 464-1711
  Middletown *(G-7153)*
Gift Love Early Learning Ctr .... G 302 659-1984
  Smyrna *(G-13743)*
Gigglebugs Early Learning Ctr .... F 302 934-5437
  Millsboro *(G-8299)*

Goddard School .... F 302 454-9454
  Newark *(G-10858)*
Goddard Systems Inc .... F 302 651-7995
  Wilmington *(G-16904)*
Good Beginnings Preschool .... G 302 875-5507
  Laurel *(G-5521)*
Gordons Daycare Home .... G 302 658-7854
  Wilmington *(G-16931)*
Graceland Daycare .... G 302 698-0414
  Magnolia *(G-6747)*
Great Minds .... G 302 834-4906
  Bear *(G-254)*
Great New Bgnnngs Mddltown Inc .... E 302 378-5555
  Middletown *(G-7174)*
Great New Bgnnngs St Andrews I .... E 302 838-1000
  Bear *(G-255)*
Growing Palace .... F 302 376-5553
  Middletown *(G-7179)*
Growing Palace III .... G 302 376-5553
  Middletown *(G-7180)*
Guardian Angel Child Care .... G 302 428-3620
  Wilmington *(G-16999)*
Guardian Angel Day Care .... G 302 934-0130
  Georgetown *(G-4348)*
Hand -N- Hand Early Lrng Ctr .... F 302 422-0702
  Ellendale *(G-3920)*
Happy Kids Academy Inc .... F 302 369-6929
  Newark *(G-10927)*
Happy Pl Child Care Mddltown L .... F 302 449-3311
  Middletown *(G-7195)*
Happy Place Day Care LLC .... F 302 737-7603
  Newark *(G-10928)*
Happyland Childcare .... G 302 424-3868
  Lincoln *(G-6674)*
Harrison Heart Daycare .... G 302 836-8581
  Newark *(G-10934)*
Harrison House Cmnty Program .... E 302 595-3370
  Newark *(G-10935)*
Hartly Family Learning Ctr LLC .... F 302 492-1152
  Hartly *(G-4875)*
Head Start Harrington .... G 302 398-9196
  Harrington *(G-4782)*
Heart Start Er Training Inc .... G 302 420-1917
  Wilmington *(G-17105)*
Heart To Hand Daycare LLC .... F 202 256-4524
  Lewes *(G-6086)*
Helene Day Care Pre-School .... G 302 834-9060
  Delaware City *(G-1547)*
Helping Hands Child Care .... G 302 438-1656
  New Castle *(G-9208)*
Hill Luth Day Care Center .... G 302 656-3224
  Wilmington *(G-17146)*
Hilltop Lthran Nghbrhood Ctr I .... E 302 656-3224
  Wilmington *(G-17148)*
Hockessin Montessori School .... E 302 234-1240
  Hockessin *(G-5244)*
Hope House Daycare .... G 302 407-3404
  Wilmington *(G-17197)*
Hope Presbyterian Church .... F 302 764-8615
  Wilmington *(G-17198)*
I Have A Dream Child Care .... G 302 507-2310
  Wilmington *(G-17247)*
Independence School Inc .... D 302 239-0330
  Newark *(G-11011)*
Independent Bb Fellowship Ch .... G 302 734-2301
  Dover *(G-2726)*
It Takes A Village Preschool .... G 302 241-3988
  Dover *(G-2754)*
J N Hooker Inc .... E 302 838-5650
  Bear *(G-293)*
Jacqueline Allens Daycare .... G 302 368-3633
  Newark *(G-11082)*

Janis Dicristofaro Day Care .... G 302 998-6630
  Wilmington *(G-17495)*
Jeans Love-N-Care Childcare .... G 302 934-5665
  Millsboro *(G-8330)*
Jjs Learning Experience LLC .... F 302 398-9000
  Harrington *(G-4791)*
Johnson Shawanda .... G 302 722-1715
  Bear *(G-309)*
Jumpin Jacks .... G 302 762-7604
  Wilmington *(G-17611)*
Junebugs Little Rubies LLC .... G 302 494-7552
  Wilmington *(G-17612)*
Karen Schreiber .... G 302 875-7733
  Laurel *(G-5541)*
Karen Schreiber .... G 302 628-3007
  Seaford *(G-13243)*
Kathys Day Care .... G 302 436-4308
  Selbyville *(G-13555)*
Kenton Child Care .... G 302 674-8142
  Dover *(G-2859)*
Kerry & G Inc .... G 302 999-0022
  Wilmington *(G-17697)*
Kiddie International Academy .... G 302 838-2183
  Newark *(G-11171)*
Kids Cottage LLC .... E 302 644-7690
  Rehoboth Beach *(G-12822)*
Kids Inc .... G 302 422-9099
  Milford *(G-7965)*
Kids Kastle Day Care .... F 302 740-8803
  Newark *(G-11173)*
Kids Korner Day Care .... G 302 998-4606
  Wilmington *(G-17716)*
Kids Nest Day Care .... G 302 731-7017
  Newark *(G-11174)*
Kids R US Learning Center Inc .... G 302 678-1234
  Dover *(G-2866)*
Kidz Akademy Corp .... G 302 732-6077
  Dagsboro *(G-1473)*
Kidz Choice LLC .... F 302 365-6787
  Bear *(G-327)*
Kidz Ink .... G 302 327-0686
  Bear *(G-328)*
Kidz Ink .... G 302 838-1000
  Bear *(G-329)*
Kidz Ink .... F 302 376-1700
  Middletown *(G-7272)*
Kidz Ink .... F 302 838-1500
  Bear *(G-330)*
Kidz Klub .... G 302 652-5439
  Wilmington *(G-17718)*
Kind Mind Kids .... G 302 545-0380
  Wilmington *(G-17721)*
Kindercare Learning Ctrs LLC .... F 302 234-8680
  Hockessin *(G-5269)*
Kindercare Learning Ctrs LLC .... F 302 322-3102
  New Castle *(G-9282)*
Kindercare Learning Ctrs LLC .... F 302 834-6931
  Newark *(G-11176)*
Kindercare Learning Ctrs LLC .... F 302 475-2212
  Wilmington *(G-17722)*
Kindercare Learning Ctrs LLC .... F 302 731-7138
  Wilmington *(G-17723)*
Kingdom Kids Day Care .... F 302 492-0207
  Hartly *(G-4890)*
Kings Kids .... F 302 239-4961
  Hockessin *(G-5270)*
Kodys Kids Inc .... G 302 858-0884
  Rehoboth Beach *(G-12824)*
La Petite Academy Inc .... F 877 271-6466
  Hockessin *(G-5274)*
Lake Forest School District .... E 302 398-8945
  Harrington *(G-4795)*

Name	Code	Phone
Lambs of Zion Daycare	F	302 252-6440
Wilmington (G-17793)		
Lauras Child Care	G	302 690-1283
Hockessin (G-5277)		
Learning Circle Child Care	G	302 834-1473
Bear (G-342)		
Learning Ctr At Madison St LLC	F	302 543-7588
Wilmington (G-17848)		
Learning Express Preschool	F	302 737-8990
Newark (G-11238)		
Learning Is Fundamental Child	G	302 653-1047
Smyrna (G-13798)		
Learning Tree Academy	F	302 449-1711
Middletown (G-7293)		
Learning Years Preschool	G	302 241-4781
Dover (G-2921)		
Learning4 Lrng Professionals	G	302 994-0451
Wilmington (G-17849)		
Lessons Lrned Day Care Prschoo	F	302 777-2200
Wilmington (G-17885)		
Lewes Montessori School	G	302 644-7482
Lewes (G-6198)		
Lifehuse Erly Chldhood Ctr LLC	E	302 464-1105
Townsend (G-14027)		
Lil Einsteins Learning Academy	F	302 466-3003
Newark (G-11259)		
Lil Kritters Childcare	G	302 362-9047
Seaford (G-13261)		
Lil Red Hen Nursery Schl Inc	E	302 846-2777
Delmar (G-1615)		
Linda Putnam Day Care	G	302 836-1033
Bear (G-350)		
Lindas Angels Chldcare Dev Ctr	F	302 328-3700
New Castle (G-9311)		
Lisa Trabaudo Day Care	G	302 653-3529
Smyrna (G-13806)		
Little Blessings Childcare	G	215 510-4514
Claymont (G-1219)		
Little Blessings Day Care	G	302 762-3600
Wilmington (G-17935)		
Little Blessings Daycare	F	302 655-8962
Wilmington (G-17936)		
Little Einsteins Preschool	G	302 933-0600
Millsboro (G-8349)		
Little Folks Too Day Care	G	302 652-3420
Wilmington (G-17937)		
Little Folks Too Day Care	E	302 652-1238
Wilmington (G-17938)		
Little Friends Lrng Academy	F	302 655-0725
New Castle (G-9314)		
Little Giggles	G	678 770-2089
New Castle (G-9315)		
Little Hearts Child Care LLC	E	302 442-5746
Wilmington (G-17940)		
Little Kids Swagg Lrng Ctr LLC	F	302 480-4404
Smyrna (G-13807)		
Little Learner Inc	G	302 798-5570
Claymont (G-1220)		
Little People Big World	G	302 310-0965
Newark (G-11271)		
Little People Child Dev	F	302 328-1481
Christiana (G-1003)		
Little People Child Dev Ctr 3	G	302 832-1891
New Castle (G-9317)		
Little People Day Care	G	302 528-4336
Middletown (G-7308)		
Little Peoples College	F	302 998-4929
Wilmington (G-17941)		
Little Scholars Ctr	G	302 368-7584
Newark (G-11272)		
Little Scholars Learning Ctr	G	302 656-8785
Wilmington (G-17942)		
Little School Inc	F	302 734-3040
Dover (G-2957)		
Little Star Inc	F	302 995-2920
Wilmington (G-17943)		
Little Steps Daycare	G	302 654-4867
Wilmington (G-17944)		
Little Trooper Day Care	G	302 378-7355
Middletown (G-7309)		
Little World LLC	G	302 644-1530
Lewes (G-6213)		
Lorraine S Daycare	G	302 328-1333
New Castle (G-9326)		
Love Learn & Play DC	G	302 236-9888
Milford (G-7977)		
Love N Care Daycare	G	302 369-8092
Newark (G-11289)		
Love N Fun Family Daycare	G	302 601-3629
Middletown (G-7314)		
Love N Learn Nursery Too	G	302 678-0445
Dover (G-2978)		
Lullaby Learning Center Inc	F	302 703-2871
Harbeson (G-4706)		
M O T H E R S Inc	F	302 275-4163
Wilmington (G-18060)		
Maddix Owens Lillian	G	302 897-1997
Wilmington (G-18073)		
Magic Yrs Child Care Lrng Cntr	F	302 322-3102
New Castle (G-9335)		
Mahavir LLC	E	302 651-7995
Wilmington (G-18086)		
Malgiero Helen A Day Care	G	302 834-9060
Delaware City (G-1548)		
Marlette R Lofland	G	302 628-1521
Bridgeville (G-728)		
Mary E Herring Daycare Center	G	302 652-5978
Wilmington (G-18178)		
Marys Little Lambs Daycare	G	302 436-5796
Selbyville (G-13566)		
Maxines Daycare	G	302 652-7242
Wilmington (G-18206)		
Melissas Childcare	G	302 547-6722
Wilmington (G-18263)		
Mercy Land Academy Inc	G	302 378-2013
Middletown (G-7342)		
MI-Dee Inc	F	302 453-7326
Newark (G-11399)		
Milford Early Learning Center	F	302 331-6612
Camden Wyoming (G-962)		
Mom Home Daycare	G	302 265-2668
Milford (G-8019)		
Montessori Learning Center LLC	G	302 478-2575
Wilmington (G-18424)		
Mother Goose Childrens Center	G	302 934-8454
Millsboro (G-8391)		
Mother Hubbard Child Care Ctr	F	302 368-7584
Newark (G-11458)		
Ms Hathers Lrng Ctr Childcare	G	302 994-2448
Wilmington (G-18475)		
Ms Kims Day Care	G	304 689-8023
New Castle (G-9386)		
Nagengast Janet Day Care	G	302 656-6898
Wilmington (G-18519)		
Nannys Heavenly Daycare	G	302 276-7149
New Castle (G-9392)		
Neenee Wees Daycare	G	302 730-3630
Dover (G-3166)		
Neighborhood House Inc	F	302 658-5404
Wilmington (G-18571)		
New Castle County Head Start	F	302 452-1500
Newark (G-11518)		
New Cstle Cnty Chld Hse Mntsso	F	302 529-9259
Wilmington (G-18615)		
New Day Montessori	F	302 235-2554
Wilmington (G-18617)		
New Direction Early Headstart	F	302 831-0584
Newark (G-11521)		
Newark Christian Childcare	G	302 369-3000
Newark (G-11531)		
Newark Ctr For Creative Lrng	F	302 368-7772
Newark (G-11533)		
Newark Day-Nursery Association	E	302 731-4925
Newark (G-11534)		
Newark Montessori Preschool	G	302 366-1481
Newark (G-11542)		
Newark United Methodist	E	302 368-8774
Newark (G-11547)		
Next Gnration Lrng Academy LLC	G	302 691-5223
Wilmington (G-18634)		
Northeast Early Lrng Ctr LLC	G	302 475-7080
Claymont (G-1255)		
Nurses N Kids Inc	E	302 323-1118
New Castle (G-9431)		
Oasis Childcare	G	302 312-5255
Wilmington (G-18731)		
Odelias Early Lrng Academy Ela	F	302 482-3249
Wilmington (G-18746)		
Odessa Early Education Center	G	302 376-5254
Townsend (G-14044)		
Ogletown Baptist Church	F	302 737-2511
Newark (G-11580)		
Ol Babies LLC	G	302 570-0205
Wilmington (G-18752)		
Our Childrens Learning Ctr	G	302 565-1272
Bear (G-410)		
Our Future Child Care Ctr LLC	G	302 762-8645
Wilmington (G-18833)		
Our Future Christian Chld Care	F	302 287-4442
Wilmington (G-18834)		
Over Rainbow Daycare	G	302 328-6574
Historic New Castle (G-5044)		
Panda Early Education Ctr Inc	F	302 832-1891
Christiana (G-1006)		
Panda Early Education Ctr Inc	F	302 328-1481
New Castle (G-9446)		
Panda Early Education Ctr Inc	G	302 832-1891
Bear (G-414)		
Passion Care Services	G	302 834-9585
New Castle (G-9455)		
Passion Care Services Inc	F	302 832-2622
Bear (G-416)		
Patricia Degirolano Day Care	G	302 947-2874
Millsboro (G-8415)		
Patricia Disario Day Care	G	302 737-8889
Newark (G-11637)		
Patricia McKay	G	302 563-5334
Bear (G-418)		
Peace and Blessings Child Care	G	302 543-4762
Wilmington (G-18939)		
Peoples Place II Inc	D	302 730-1321
Dover (G-3295)		
Peoples Place II Inc	D	302 934-0300
Millsboro (G-8426)		
Peoples Sttlment Assn Wlmngton	E	302 658-4133
Wilmington (G-18964)		
Personal Touch Child Care	E	302 368-2229
Newark (G-11670)		
Pirulos Child Care Center LLC	G	302 836-3520
Newark (G-11696)		
Playhouse Nursery School	G	302 747-7007
Dover (G-3333)		
Precious Knwldg Erly Lrng Ctr	F	302 293-2588
Newark (G-11721)		
Precious Little Hands Childcar	G	302 298-5027
Wilmington (G-19148)		

Employee Codes: A=Over 500 employees, B=251-500
C=101-250, D=51-100, E=20-50, F=10-19, G=1-9

83 SOCIAL SERVICES

Precious Lttle Hnds Chldcare C............... G 302 256-0194
  Wilmington *(G-19149)*
Precious Lttle Lambs Childcare............... G 302 723-1403
  Wilmington *(G-19150)*
Precious Moments Day Care............... G 302 856-2346
  Georgetown *(G-4470)*
Premier IL Volo LLC............... G 847 201-1760
  Wilmington *(G-19169)*
Primeros Pasos Inc............... G 302 856-7406
  Georgetown *(G-4473)*
Pyle Child Development Center............... F 302 732-1443
  Frankford *(G-4136)*
Rainbow Xpress Lrng Acdemy LLC............... G 302 659-0750
  Smyrna *(G-13861)*
Regina Coleman............... G 215 476-4682
  Wilmington *(G-19402)*
Renzi Rust Inc............... F 302 424-4470
  Milford *(G-8062)*
Rising Stars Child Care Inc............... F 302 998-7682
  Wilmington *(G-19486)*
Robin S Wright............... G 302 249-2105
  Lewes *(G-6426)*
Roca Family Daycare............... G 302 656-8356
  Wilmington *(G-19525)*
Rose Hill Community Center............... F 302 656-8513
  New Castle *(G-9541)*
Salvation Army............... E 302 656-1696
  Wilmington *(G-19645)*
Scalias Day Care Center Inc............... F 302 366-1430
  Newark *(G-11956)*
Seeds of Jesus Day Care LLC............... G 302 494-6568
  Wilmington *(G-19737)*
Selwor Enterprises Inc............... F 302 454-9454
  Newark *(G-11974)*
Shavone Loves Kids Day Care............... G 302 544-6170
  New Castle *(G-9565)*
Shelias Childcare Center............... G 302 472-9648
  Wilmington *(G-19791)*
Shells Child Care Center III............... F 302 398-9778
  Harrington *(G-4832)*
Shells Early Lrng Ctr Camden............... F 302 698-1556
  Camden *(G-892)*
Sherrys Childcare............... G 302 654-4982
  Wilmington *(G-19796)*
Shining Star Daycare............... G 302 393-7775
  Dover *(G-3544)*
Shining Time Day Care Center............... G 302 335-2770
  Felton *(G-4028)*
Slaughter Neck Educational and............... G 302 684-1834
  Lincoln *(G-6703)*
Small Wonder Day Care Inc............... F 302 654-2269
  Wilmington *(G-19872)*
Small Wonders............... G 302 645-8410
  Lewes *(G-6478)*
Smalls Stepping Stone............... F 302 652-3011
  Wilmington *(G-19874)*
Smart Start............... F 302 256-5104
  Wilmington *(G-19879)*
Smarty Pants Early Education............... G 302 985-3770
  Bear *(G-498)*
Smyrna School District............... D 302 653-3135
  Smyrna *(G-13897)*
St Helenas Early Learning............... G 302 561-4044
  Wilmington *(G-19994)*
St Helenas Early Learning Ctr............... G 610 497-0435
  Wilmington *(G-19995)*
St Marks United Methodist Ch............... G 302 994-0400
  Wilmington *(G-19999)*
St Michaels School and Nursery............... E 302 353-6717
  Wilmington *(G-20000)*
St Michaels School Inc............... E 302 656-3389
  Wilmington *(G-20001)*

Step Up Daycare............... G 302 762-3183
  Wilmington *(G-20052)*
Stepping Stones College............... G 302 983-1437
  Wilmington *(G-20061)*
Sunshine Home Childcare............... G 302 674-2009
  Dover *(G-3624)*
Sunshine Kids Academy............... G 302 444-4270
  Bear *(G-519)*
Susan R Austin............... G 302 322-4685
  New Castle *(G-9607)*
Susan T Fischer............... G 302 832-2570
  Newark *(G-12135)*
Sussex Montessori............... F 302 404-5367
  Seaford *(G-13419)*
Sussex Prschool Erly Care Ctrs............... G 302 732-7529
  Seaford *(G-13421)*
Sweet Dreams Daycare............... G 302 425-0844
  Wilmington *(G-20172)*
Telamon Corporation............... G 302 736-5933
  Dover *(G-3664)*
Tender Hearts............... F 302 674-2565
  Dover *(G-3668)*
Tender Hearts............... G 302 234-1017
  Wilmington *(G-20272)*
Tender Loving Kare............... E 302 464-1014
  Middletown *(G-7635)*
The Lrning Tree Chld Acdemy LL............... G 302 841-0194
  Dover *(G-3673)*
Thirst 2 Learn............... F 302 293-2304
  Bear *(G-530)*
Thirst 2 Learn LLC............... G 302 475-7080
  Wilmington *(G-20303)*
Timber Heart Learning Center............... G 302 674-2565
  Dover *(G-3688)*
Tinas Tiny Tots Daycare............... G 302 536-7077
  Seaford *(G-13432)*
Tiny Tots and Toddlers Llc............... G 302 838-8787
  Bear *(G-532)*
Tiny Tots Childcare and Learni............... G 302 651-9060
  Wilmington *(G-20334)*
Tlk............... G 302 376-8554
  Middletown *(G-7648)*
To The Moon and Back Childcare............... G 302 508-2749
  Smyrna *(G-13914)*
Todays Kid Inc (not Inc)............... G 302 834-5620
  Newark *(G-12203)*
Toddlers Tech Inc............... F 302 655-4487
  Wilmington *(G-20342)*
Toddys Tots............... G 302 661-1912
  Wilmington *(G-20344)*
Toys Story LLC............... G 267 334-9822
  Smyrna *(G-13916)*
Truitts Hlping Hnds Chldcr/Prs............... G 302 426-6436
  Wilmington *(G-20446)*
Tutor Time Learning Ctrs LLC............... C 302 235-5701
  Wilmington *(G-20466)*
Universal Design Company............... G 302 328-8391
  Historic New Castle *(G-5096)*
V Quinton Inc............... F 302 449-1711
  Middletown *(G-7679)*
Village Sq Acdemy Lrng Ctr LLC............... G 302 539-5000
  Ocean View *(G-12580)*
Vision Campus Inc............... F 302 543-6809
  Wilmington *(G-20638)*
Vivis Daycare and Preschool............... G 302 607-4478
  New Castle *(G-9673)*
Wagstaff Day Care Center Inc............... F 302 998-7818
  Wilmington *(G-20668)*
Wee Care Day Care Salv Army............... G 302 472-0712
  Wilmington *(G-20709)*
Wee Wonders Doulas............... G 302 275-7799
  Wilmington *(G-20710)*

Wesley Play Care Center............... F 302 678-8987
  Dover *(G-3835)*
Whatcoat Christian Preschool............... G 302 698-2108
  Dover *(G-3841)*
White Oak Head Start............... G 302 736-5933
  Dover *(G-3845)*
Williams Family............... G 302 378-9493
  Middletown *(G-7727)*
Wilmington Headstart Inc............... E 302 762-8038
  Wilmington *(G-20818)*
Wilmington Montessori School............... D 302 475-0555
  Wilmington *(G-20824)*
Wilson Care Wilson Co............... G 302 897-5059
  Newark *(G-12386)*
Wonder Years Kids Club............... F 302 398-0563
  Harrington *(G-4848)*
Wonder Years Preschool LLC............... F 302 376-5553
  Middletown *(G-7734)*
Wright Choice Child Care............... G 302 798-0758
  Claymont *(G-1340)*
Xavier Inc............... G 302 655-1962
  Wilmington *(G-20914)*
Young Mens Christian Assn Del............... C 302 571-6900
  Wilmington *(G-20937)*
Young MNS Chrstn Assn Wlmngton............... C 302 296-9622
  Rehoboth Beach *(G-13027)*
YWCA Delaware............... F 302 224-4060
  Newark *(G-12425)*

8361 Residential care

Abled Directions LLC............... F 206 265-3928
  Middletown *(G-6828)*
Alerislife Inc............... E 302 478-4296
  Wilmington *(G-14352)*
Assisted Living Concepts LLC............... F 302 735-8800
  Dover *(G-1835)*
Associated Svc Specialist Inc............... F 302 672-7159
  Dover *(G-1836)*
Brandywine Asssted Lving At FN............... A 302 436-0808
  Selbyville *(G-13481)*
Brenda Radick............... G 302 945-8982
  Harbeson *(G-4686)*
Catholic Mnstry To Elderly Inc............... F 302 368-2784
  Newark *(G-10163)*
Changing Faces Inc............... G 302 397-4164
  Lincoln *(G-6660)*
Children Fmilies First Del Inc............... D 302 629-6996
  Seaford *(G-13119)*
Chimes Inc............... E 302 678-3270
  Dover *(G-2066)*
Chimes Inc............... E 302 452-3400
  Newark *(G-10206)*
Choices For Community Living............... G 302 398-0446
  Harrington *(G-4749)*
Churchman Village Center LLC............... E 302 998-6900
  Newark *(G-10240)*
Conexio Care Inc............... E 302 442-6622
  Claymont *(G-1098)*
Connectons Cmnty Spport Prgram............... E 302 834-8400
  Delaware City *(G-1534)*
Connectons Cmnty Spport Prgram............... D 302 454-7520
  Newark *(G-10306)*
Connectons Cmnty Spport Prgram............... D 302 984-2302
  Claymont *(G-1099)*
Connectons Csp0110 W Lberty St............... G 302 566-6078
  Harrington *(G-4753)*
Cottage At Curry Manor............... G 202 258-7674
  Lewes *(G-5863)*
Criswell House............... G 302 498-5174
  Wilmington *(G-15704)*
Delaware Department Correction............... C 302 856-5280
  Georgetown *(G-4279)*

83 SOCIAL SERVICES

Dunams-Hmes Dvine Intrvntion I............ G 302 393-5778
 Camden Wyoming *(G-937)*

Elderwood Village Dover LLC................. F 516 496-1505
 Dover *(G-2430)*

Elizabeth W Murphey School Inc............ E 302 734-7478
 Dover *(G-2436)*

Fellowship Hlth Resources Inc................ F 302 856-7642
 Georgetown *(G-4316)*

Friends of The Good Samarit................... G 302 762-4937
 Wilmington *(G-16758)*

Gateway House Inc.................................. F 302 571-8885
 Wilmington *(G-16815)*

Gaudenzia Inc.. F 302 836-8260
 Delaware City *(G-1546)*

Gaudenzia Inc.. G 302 421-9945
 Wilmington *(G-16817)*

Gr Loudon LLC.. G 302 475-9400
 Wilmington *(G-16939)*

Green Valley Pavilion............................... F 302 653-5085
 Smyrna *(G-13752)*

Green Valley Snf LLC.............................. G 302 653-5085
 Smyrna *(G-13753)*

Harborchase Wilmington LLC................. G 302 273-8630
 Wilmington *(G-17054)*

Heritage At Milford.................................. F 302 422-8700
 Milford *(G-7927)*

Home For Aged Wmn-Mnquadale HM... C 302 654-1810
 Wilmington *(G-17178)*

Ingleside Homes Inc................................ D 302 575-0250
 Wilmington *(G-17335)*

Kencrest Services.................................... G 302 834-3365
 Saint Georges *(G-13035)*

Keystone Autism Services...................... E 302 731-3115
 Newark *(G-11164)*

Keystone Service Systems Inc............... C 302 286-7234
 Newark *(G-11166)*

Life Solutions Inc..................................... G 302 622-8292
 Wilmington *(G-17902)*

Limen House Inc..................................... G 302 652-7969
 Wilmington *(G-17913)*

Little Sisters of The Poor......................... D 302 368-5886
 Newark *(G-11273)*

Lodge Lane Assisted Living.................... F 302 764-7000
 Wilmington *(G-17974)*

Mary Campbell Center Inc...................... C 302 762-6025
 Wilmington *(G-18177)*

Moorings At Lewes.................................. D 302 644-6382
 Lewes *(G-6290)*

Mother Teresa House Inc........................ G 302 652-5523
 Wilmington *(G-18463)*

Naomi Rising Inc..................................... G 803 840-1874
 Dover *(G-3149)*

National Mentor Holdings Inc.................. A 302 934-0512
 Millsboro *(G-8401)*

New Vision Services Inc......................... G 484 350-6495
 Newark *(G-11526)*

Peninsula Untd Mthdst Hmes Inc............ B 302 654-5101
 Wilmington *(G-18949)*

Peninsula Untd Mthdst Hmes Inc............ G 302 235-6800
 Hockessin *(G-5335)*

People In Transition Inc.......................... G 302 784-5214
 New Castle *(G-9468)*

Pressley Ridge Foundation..................... G 302 366-0490
 Dover *(G-3367)*

Promise of Light Inc................................ F 201 471-5848
 Newark *(G-11762)*

Sacred Heart Village I Inc....................... F 302 428-0801
 Wilmington *(G-19622)*

Sacred Heart Village II Inc...................... G 302 428-3702
 Wilmington *(G-19623)*

Springpoint At Lewes Inc........................ E 732 430-3660
 Lewes *(G-6503)*

Sunrise Senior Living LLC...................... D 302 475-9163
 Wilmington *(G-20134)*

Visionquest Nonprofit Corp..................... F 302 735-1666
 Dover *(G-3804)*

Windsor Place... G 302 239-3200
 Hockessin *(G-5427)*

X Dima Inc... G 302 427-0787
 Wilmington *(G-20909)*

Young Mens Christian Assn Del.............. C 302 571-6900
 Wilmington *(G-20937)*

8399 Social services, nec

4youthproductions................................... G 302 690-5602
 Wilmington *(G-14140)*

AARP.. F 202 434-2277
 Wilmington *(G-14188)*

Abcfoc A Btter Chnce For Our C............. F 302 746-7265
 Wilmington *(G-14198)*

Activating Change Inc............................. F 646 457-8067
 Wilmington *(G-14242)*

Admeal Inc... G 954 758-8699
 Milton *(G-8555)*

Admin-Support... G 302 368-6441
 Newark *(G-9767)*

Against All Odds Llc................................ G 302 943-7321
 Camden *(G-787)*

Agh Parent LLC....................................... A 919 298-2267
 Wilmington *(G-14314)*

Allan For Delaware.................................. G 410 920-2493
 Milton *(G-8556)*

American Cncil For An Enrgy Ef.............. G 202 507-4000
 Newark *(G-9843)*

ARC Finance Ltd..................................... G 914 478-3851
 Wilmington *(G-14527)*

Banana Spot Co...................................... F 916 342-9519
 Wilmington *(G-14728)*

Campus Elction Enggment Prj In............ G 614 735-1460
 Lewes *(G-5787)*

Center For Integrative Change............... G 302 230-1962
 Wilmington *(G-15303)*

Central Del Hbtat For Hmnity I................ F 302 526-2366
 Dover *(G-2049)*

Champions For Childrens Mh.................. G 302 249-6788
 Newark *(G-10186)*

Children Fmilies First Del Inc.................. G 302 674-8384
 Dover *(G-2061)*

Click For Savings LLC............................ G 302 300-0202
 Bear *(G-110)*

Coalition To Save Lives........................... G 267 579-2875
 Wilmington *(G-15507)*

Colonial Chpter of The Prlyzed............... G 302 861-6671
 Newark *(G-10277)*

Compassnate Hlth Intatives Inc.............. F 302 765-8256
 Middletown *(G-7006)*

Connections CSP.................................... G 302 535-8330
 Magnolia *(G-6734)*

Council On Hlth RES For Dev US........... G 202 255-5300
 Wilmington *(G-15652)*

Coverdale Community Council................ G 302 337-7179
 Bridgeville *(G-687)*

Crime Victims Ctr Chester Cnty.............. G 610 692-7420
 Newark *(G-10354)*

Delaware Center For Digestive............... F 302 565-6596
 Newark *(G-10424)*

Delaware Center For Justice................... E 302 658-7174
 Wilmington *(G-15882)*

Delaware Hmanities Council Inc............. G 302 657-0650
 Wilmington *(G-15928)*

Delaware Soc For Rsprtory Care............ G 302 834-2905
 Newark *(G-10482)*

Each One Teach One Inc........................ G 302 345-8744
 New Castle *(G-9073)*

Easter Sals Del Mrylnds Estrn................ D 302 856-7364
 Georgetown *(G-4303)*

Eastside Bluprt Cmnty Dev Corp............ F 302 384-2350
 Wilmington *(G-16266)*

Edgemoor Rvtalization Coop Inc............. G 302 293-3944
 Wilmington *(G-16291)*

Endless Pssblties In The Cmnty.............. G 302 528-4503
 Newark *(G-10646)*

Family Otrach Mlt-Prpose Cmnty............ G 302 422-2158
 Lincoln *(G-6668)*

Fathers Day Gala Inc.............................. G 302 981-4117
 Wilmington *(G-16562)*

First State Cmnty Action Agcy................ E 302 856-7761
 Georgetown *(G-4322)*

First State Squash Inc............................. G 312 919-6767
 Wilmington *(G-16635)*

Food Bank of Delaware Inc..................... E 302 424-3301
 Milford *(G-7900)*

Full Support Technologies LLC............... G 302 832-2307
 Bear *(G-239)*

Fund For The Walking Wounded............ G 302 947-9056
 Lewes *(G-6023)*

Georgetown Playground & Pk Inc........... G 302 856-7111
 Georgetown *(G-4341)*

Ggc Inc.. G 267 893-8052
 Lincoln *(G-6670)*

Goodness For Life Center Inc................. G 302 922-5055
 Dover *(G-2607)*

Grace For Dover...................................... G 302 319-4433
 Dover *(G-2616)*

Greene Business Support S.................... G 302 480-3725
 Dover *(G-2626)*

Gregory For Wilmington.......................... G 302 562-3117
 Wilmington *(G-16976)*

Habitat For Humanity Intl Inc................... G 302 855-1156
 Georgetown *(G-4351)*

Help Is On Way....................................... G 302 328-4510
 New Castle *(G-9207)*

Hidden Acres Rest Home Inc.................. G 302 492-1962
 Marydel *(G-6800)*

Hispanic Personal Dev LLC.................... G 302 738-4782
 Newark *(G-10954)*

Homes For Life Foundation.................... G 302 571-1217
 Wilmington *(G-17189)*

Homeward Bound Inc.............................. F 302 737-2241
 Newark *(G-10966)*

Icg Enterprises Inc.................................. G 302 373-7136
 Dover *(G-2717)*

Inititive For Med Access Knwld............... G 917 455-6601
 Lewes *(G-6124)*

Jewish Federation of Delaware............... F 302 478-5660
 Wilmington *(G-17540)*

Kenya Gather Foundation....................... F 302 382-8227
 Millsboro *(G-8339)*

Kirwa Foundation..................................... F 347 932-4911
 Wilmington *(G-17734)*

Laseana Ford.. G 215 201-8070
 Newark *(G-11224)*

Left For Dead.. G 302 684-4320
 Ellendale *(G-3926)*

Life Choice.. G 302 526-2080
 Dover *(G-2940)*

Loris Hands Inc....................................... G 302 440-5454
 Newark *(G-11285)*

Love Harrisburg LLC............................... G 717 710-1556
 Middletown *(G-7313)*

Lyme Yarnbombs Inc.............................. G 302 547-1340
 Wilmington *(G-18045)*

Mad Delaware Chapter........................... G 910 284-6286
 Lewes *(G-6235)*

March of Dimes Inc................................. G 302 225-1020
 Wilmington *(G-18121)*

83 SOCIAL SERVICES

Meghan House Inc .... G 302 253-8261
  Georgetown (G-4423)
Ministry of Caring Inc .... C 302 652-8947
  Wilmington (G-18375)
Missions For Life Inc .... G 302 981-1915
  Newark (G-11428)
Mot Community Fund Inc .... G 302 378-5494
  Middletown (G-7383)
Mothers In Unity .... G 302 442-1904
  Wilmington (G-18464)
Music Art & Culture Foundation .... G 347 746-9047
  Lewes (G-6297)
National African American Coal .... G 301 395-9033
  Dover (G-3152)
New Life Intl Cmnty Dev Corp .... G 302 529-1997
  Wilmington (G-18621)
Nexgen Technical Support Group .... G 302 345-1330
  New Castle (G-9418)
Operation Water Inc .... G 787 599-0555
  Rehoboth Beach (G-12880)
Pacific Global Inc .... G 510 870-0248
  Wilmington (G-18859)
Parkinsons Edcatn Spport Group .... G 302 644-3465
  Lewes (G-6350)
Partnership For Delaw .... F 800 445-4935
  Wilmington (G-18899)
Pay It Frward Ntwrking Group C .... G 302 213-2695
  Wilmington (G-18927)
Peachi Inc .... G 347 907-0138
  Newark (G-11650)
Plastic Free Delaware Inc .... G 302 981-1950
  Wilmington (G-19070)
Positive Growth Alliance Inc .... G 302 381-1610
  Millsboro (G-8432)
Powell Life Skills Inc .... G 302 378-2706
  Townsend (G-14053)
Purple Moon Herbs Studies LLC .... G 302 270-5095
  Hartly (G-4905)
Quinn-Miller Group Inc .... F 302 738-9742
  Wilmington (G-19296)
Rescue For Misunderstood Inc .... G 302 650-8123
  Wilmington (G-19436)
Restore Sssex Cnty Hbtat For H .... G 302 703-6388
  Lewes (G-6419)
Richard Allen Coalition .... G 302 258-7182
  Georgetown (G-4486)
Royal Mission & Ministries .... G 302 249-8863
  Laurel (G-5598)
Saint Georges Cultr & Arts Rev .... G 302 836-8202
  Saint Georges (G-13038)
Salvation Army .... E 302 654-8808
  Wilmington (G-19643)
Schfh Restore .... G 302 855-1156
  Georgetown (G-4502)
Shady Oak Mobile Home Cmnty .... G 302 245-4324
  Georgetown (G-4510)
Sigpa .... G 302 678-8780
  Dover (G-3560)
Simplymiddle LLC .... G 302 217-3460
  Wilmington (G-19841)
Supportive Care Solutions LLC .... G 302 598-4797
  Wilmington (G-20153)
Td For W Games .... G 302 883-3627
  Dover (G-3658)
Tender Touch Support LLC .... G 302 272-1638
  Dover (G-3669)
Thedigitalsupport LLC .... G 347 305-4006
  Wilmington (G-20295)
Tim 2 My Bro Awrness Blnce Fnd .... G 302 278-2191
  Townsend (G-14081)
Tranquil Solutions For A .... G 302 383-5011
  Middletown (G-7657)

Transforming Lives Inc .... D 302 379-1043
  Wilmington (G-20398)
Trash For Cash .... G 302 540-1513
  Bear (G-539)
Tsf Incorporated .... G 518 879-6571
  Wilmington (G-20452)
Unique Mnds Changing Lives Inc .... G 302 943-1945
  Lewes (G-6589)
Uzuakoli Dev & Cultural Assn .... E 302 465-3266
  Dover (G-3770)
Victims Voices Heard Inc .... G 302 242-1108
  Millsboro (G-8494)
Volunteers For Adolescent .... G 302 658-3331
  Wilmington (G-20649)
Walkers For Jocelyn .... G 302 465-7461
  Newark (G-12344)
Wilmington Renaissance Corp .... G 302 425-5500
  Wilmington (G-20833)
Women of More .... G 260 760-8083
  Newark (G-12395)
Woodbrdge High Schl Prfrmg Art .... G 302 495-7025
  Greenwood (G-4676)
Yochanan El Bey .... G 610 726-4493
  Wilmington (G-20930)

84 MUSEUMS, ART GALLERIES AND BOTANICAL AND ZOOLOGICAL GARDENS

8412 Museums and art galleries

AMC Museum Foundation .... G 302 677-5938
  Dover (G-1782)
Anita Barbara Peghini Raber GA .... G 302 227-2888
  Rehoboth Beach (G-12606)
Barbara Moore Fine Art .... G 610 357-6100
  Wilmington (G-14756)
Brandywine Lighting Gallery .... G 302 543-6939
  Wilmington (G-15070)
Bridgeville Historical Society .... G 302 337-7600
  Bridgeville (G-676)
Creative Impressions Art .... G 858 722-2252
  Lewes (G-5867)
Crozier Fine Arts .... G 302 325-2071
  Historic New Castle (G-4966)
Delaware AG Museum Assn .... G 302 734-1618
  Dover (G-2216)
Delaware Art Museum Inc .... E 302 571-9590
  Wilmington (G-15866)
Delaware Ctr For Cntmprary Art .... F 302 656-6466
  Wilmington (G-15895)
Delaware Div Hstrcal Cltral AF .... F 302 736-7400
  Dover (G-2232)
Delaware History Museum .... G 302 656-0637
  Wilmington (G-15926)
Delaware Mseum Ntral Hstory In .... E 302 658-9111
  Wilmington (G-15946)
Delaware Museum Association .... G 302 644-5005
  Smyrna (G-13702)
Delaware Orchid Society .... G 302 654-8883
  Wilmington (G-15950)
Eleuthrian Mlls-Hgley Fndtion .... C 302 658-2400
  Wilmington (G-16355)
Ellen Rice Gallery .... G 302 539-3405
  Bethany Beach (G-599)
Environmental Outpost & Mntjoy .... G 302 659-5003
  Smyrna (G-13722)
Fine Art Fabrication .... G 302 632-4371
  Smyrna (G-13732)
Fort Delaware Society .... G 302 834-1630
  Delaware City (G-1543)

Friends of Bellaca Airfield .... G 302 322-3816
  New Castle (G-9146)
Ft Miles Historic Site .... G 302 644-5007
  Lewes (G-6018)
Gallery One .... G 302 537-5055
  Ocean View (G-12518)
Gilbert Perry Center For Arts .... G 302 378-2932
  Middletown (G-7161)
Governor Ross Mansion & Plntn .... G 302 628-9500
  Seaford (G-13199)
Hale Byrnes House .... G 302 998-3792
  Newark (G-10921)
Hendrickson House Museum .... G 302 652-5629
  Wilmington (G-17120)
▲ Henry Frncis Dpont Wntrthur Ms ...... C 302 888-4852
  Winterthur (G-20972)
Historical Society of Delaware .... E 302 322-8411
  Historic New Castle (G-5005)
◆ Historical Society of Delaware .... E 302 655-7161
  Wilmington (G-17155)
Hofa Gallery USA Inc .... G 213 270-1972
  Wilmington (G-17164)
Juliet Thorburn .... G 302 598-1841
  Wilmington (G-17610)
Kalmar Nyckel Foundation .... G 302 429-7447
  Wilmington (G-17640)
Manifesta .... G 610 883-0202
  Wilmington (G-18104)
Mark JB Inc .... G 888 984-5845
  Newark (G-11336)
Midge Smith Fine Art Gallery .... G 302 245-4528
  Lewes (G-6273)
Milton Historical Society .... F 302 684-1010
  Milton (G-8671)
Museum Studies Program .... G 302 831-1251
  Newark (G-11474)
Nanticoke Indian Museum .... G 302 945-7022
  Millsboro (G-8398)
New Castle Historical Society .... F 302 322-2794
  Historic New Castle (G-5035)
Ocean View Historical Society .... G 302 258-7470
  Ocean View (G-12556)
Oddporium LLC .... G 302 757-9544
  Wilmington (G-18745)
Odessa Historic Foundation .... F 302 378-4119
  Odessa (G-12586)
Overfalls Maritime Museum .... D 302 644-8050
  Lewes (G-6341)
Rehoboth Beach Historical Soc .... F 302 227-7310
  Rehoboth Beach (G-12921)
Rh Gallery and Studios .... G 302 218-5182
  Hockessin (G-5362)
Rockwood Museum .... G 302 761-4340
  Wilmington (G-19546)
Sewell C Biggs Trust .... F 302 674-2111
  Dover (G-3536)
Sunny Gallery LLC .... G 302 757-3960
  Newark (G-12126)
Urban Dweller .... G 973 402-7400
  Milton (G-8724)
Winterthur Museum .... F 302 740-9771
  Wilmington (G-20865)
▲ Winterthur Museum Garden & Lib .... E 302 888-4600
  Winterthur (G-20973)

8422 Botanical and zoological gardens

Brandywine Zoo .... E 302 571-7747
  Wilmington (G-15094)
Delaware Botanic Gardens Inc .... G 202 262-9501
  Bethany Beach (G-595)
Premium Aquatics LLC .... G 302 994-7742
  Wilmington (G-19172)

86 MEMBERSHIP ORGANIZATIONS

Slam Aquatics LLC............................... G 302 668-0186
  Hockessin (G-5384)

86 MEMBERSHIP ORGANIZATIONS

8611 Business associations

100 Commerce LLC............................... G 302 738-3038
  Newark (G-9702)
Aaert Inc... G 302 765-3510
  Wilmington (G-14184)
ABC Contractors LLC............................ F 302 492-1116
  Hartly (G-4853)
ABC Delaware...................................... G 302 858-2185
  New Castle (G-8756)
Adams Business Developmen............... G 302 698-1709
  Middletown (G-6834)
African Violet Society-Amer.................. G 302 653-6449
  Smyrna (G-13632)
American Chmber Cmmrce In Uzbk...... G 202 590-9294
  Wilmington (G-14429)
American Public Gardens Assn............ G 610 708-3010
  Wilmington (G-14440)
Asterlab Advisors LLC........................... G 302 295-4888
  Wilmington (G-14602)
Bethany Fenwick Area Cham............... G 302 537-3839
  Frankford (G-4071)
Bethany-Fnwick Area Chmber Cmm..... G 302 539-2100
  Fenwick Island (G-4042)
Better Business Bureau of De.............. G 302 221-5255
  New Castle (G-8865)
Brucke Inc.. G 302 319-9614
  Wilmington (G-15136)
Builders & Remodelers Assoc De........ G 302 678-1520
  Dover (G-1989)
C S C Corporation Texas Inc............... F 302 636-5440
  Wilmington (G-15176)
CDM Institue.. G 302 482-3234
  Wilmington (G-15292)
Center Meeting Associates LLC........... G 302 740-9700
  Wilmington (G-15305)
Central Del Chmber of Commerce....... G 302 734-7513
  Dover (G-2047)
Cherrington Service Corp..................... G 302 777-4064
  Wilmington (G-15363)
Concord Soccer Association................ F 302 479-5030
  Wilmington (G-15585)
Del DOT Canal Dist............................... G 410 742-9361
  Dover (G-2209)
Delaware Cmnty Rnvstment Actio....... G 302 298-3250
  Wilmington (G-15886)
Delaware Cnnbis Advcacy Ntwrk......... G 302 404-4208
  Dover (G-2221)
Delaware Credit Union Leag Inc.......... G 302 322-9341
  Newark (G-10429)
Delaware Department Trnsp................ D 302 577-3278
  Dover (G-2228)
Delaware Div Parks Recreation............ F 302 761-6963
  Wilmington (G-15910)
Delaware Homes Performance............. G 302 233-3917
  Wilmington (G-15929)
Delaware Restaurant Assn.................. G 302 738-2545
  Dover (G-2256)
Delaware State Chmber Cmmrce I...... F 302 655-7221
  Wilmington (G-15971)
Delaware State Farm Bureau Inc........ G 302 697-3183
  Camden (G-817)
Delaware Stndrdbred Owners Ass...... G 302 678-3058
  Dover (G-2265)
Eec Incubator..................................... G 302 737-4343
  Wilmington (G-16307)
Elms Management Association........... G 302 738-5225
  Newark (G-10632)

Establishing Black Men LLC................ G 215 432-7469
  Claymont (G-1135)
First State Mnfctred Hsing Ins............. F 302 674-5868
  Dover (G-2507)
Florida Pub Utl Co............................... G 561 838-1813
  Dover (G-2518)
Green Team.. G 302 344-4512
  Milton (G-8630)
Healthy To Core.................................. G 240 506-4202
  Ocean View (G-12521)
Home Builders Assn Del Inc................ F 302 678-1520
  Dover (G-2687)
Hostgpo Inc... F 424 422-0486
  Wilmington (G-17215)
Insurance Networks Aliance LLC......... G 302 268-1010
  Wilmington (G-17362)
Lonnie Wright..................................... G 302 655-1632
  New Castle (G-9324)
Mendota Merchants LLC..................... G 302 401-6453
  Dover (G-3059)
Middltown Area Chmber Commerce... F 302 376-0222
  Middletown (G-7362)
Millsboro... G 302 231-1152
  Millsboro (G-8381)
Millsboro... G 302 934-0300
  Millsboro (G-8382)
National Assn Elec Distr..................... G 302 322-3333
  New Castle (G-9393)
National Barberz Association.............. G 302 365-6169
  Bear (G-389)
Nemours Hlth & Prevention Svcs........ E 302 628-8304
  Seaford (G-13317)
New Cstle Cnty Chmber Commerce... E 302 737-4343
  Wilmington (G-18616)
Port Lewes Assoc Unit Owner............. G 302 645-6110
  Lewes (G-6383)
Pos & Merchant Services LLC............. G 302 356-3030
  Wilmington (G-19121)
Pp of De... G 252 393-3691
  Wilmington (G-19139)
Pride of Del Ldge No 349 Imprv......... G 215 453-9236
  Newark (G-11740)
Refining Co.. F 302 832-1099
  New Castle (G-9517)
Rehoboth Bch Dwey Bch Chmber C.... F 302 227-2233
  Rehoboth Beach (G-12915)
Ron Lank/Cash................................... G 302 684-4667
  Milton (G-8704)
Soft Dig LLC.. G 302 629-6658
  Georgetown (G-4515)
Stapler Athletic Association................ G 302 652-9769
  Wilmington (G-20021)
Superior Outdoor LLC......................... G 302 841-9827
  Bridgeville (G-770)
Sussex County Volunteer................... G 302 515-3020
  Georgetown (G-4536)
Technology Student Association......... F 302 857-3336
  Dover (G-3662)
UACJ Trading & Processing Amer...... G 312 636-5941
  Wilmington (G-20488)

8621 Professional organizations

Accesscare Inc................................... G 302 836-9314
  Bear (G-12)
Amani Birth.. F 302 668-7506
  Wilmington (G-14411)
American Birding Assn Inc.................. G 302 838-3660
  Delaware City (G-1531)
Architectural Solutions....................... G 302 230-1809
  New Castle (G-8819)
Assoction For The Rghts Ctzens......... F 302 996-9400
  Wilmington (G-14597)

Assoction Pathology Chairs Inc........... G 302 660-4940
  Wilmington (G-14598)
Barroja Ventures LLC.......................... G 302 256-0883
  Wilmington (G-14768)
Blend Network Inc.............................. G 267 521-8845
  Dover (G-1947)
Bni... G 302 668-9467
  Wilmington (G-14987)
Cape Ent PA....................................... F 717 269-3106
  Lewes (G-5792)
Central and Southern Delaware.......... G 302 545-8067
  Milford (G-7819)
Cooter Brwns Twsted Sthern Kit........ G 302 567-2132
  Rehoboth Beach (G-12701)
Cramer & Dimichele PA...................... G 302 293-1230
  Wilmington (G-15683)
Daphne LLC.. G 302 525-6010
  Newark (G-10388)
Dcor... G 302 227-9341
  Rehoboth Beach (G-12712)
Delaware Assn For The Edcatn Y....... G 302 764-1500
  Wilmington (G-15867)
Delaware Health Care Comm............. F 302 739-2730
  Dover (G-2242)
Delaware Health Info Netwrk.............. E 302 678-0220
  Dover (G-2243)
Delaware Home Valuations PA........... G 302 933-8607
  Millsboro (G-8261)
Delaware Rural Water Assn................ G 302 424-3792
  Milford (G-7858)
Delaware State Bar Association.......... G 302 658-5279
  Wilmington (G-15970)
Delaware State Dental Society........... G 302 368-7634
  Claymont (G-1115)
DMS Solution..................................... G 302 753-0040
  Bear (G-173)
Dynamic Dental Solutions LLC........... F 888 908-8225
  Wilmington (G-16227)
East Coast Trans LLC........................ G 302 740-5458
  Newark (G-10593)
Em Beauty Bar Inc............................ G 302 525-3933
  Newark (G-10636)
Healthshield LLC................................ G 302 352-0517
  Wilmington (G-17098)
Hearts International Inc..................... G 215 585-5597
  Wilmington (G-17108)
Income & Est Plg Partners PA........... G 302 722-6000
  Wilmington (G-17302)
James E Deakyne Jr PA..................... G 302 226-1200
  Rehoboth Beach (G-12801)
Jeffrey D Karron LLC.......................... G 302 494-3724
  Wilmington (G-17518)
Kathy J King PA................................. G 302 827-4740
  Lewes (G-6163)
Ken Fibble Professional Svcs............. G 302 947-2430
  Millsboro (G-8337)
Length Weave Bar............................. G 302 502-3171
  Wilmington (G-17875)
Loyal Order of Moose......................... G 302 436-2088
  Frankford (G-4124)
Medical Society of Delaware.............. E 302 366-1400
  Newark (G-11377)
Mid-Atlntic Reg Comm On Hgher....... E 267 284-5024
  Wilmington (G-18338)
N Biggs Professional Svcs LLC.......... G 302 632-7598
  Smyrna (G-13832)
National Society Inc.......................... G 302 656-9572
  Wilmington (G-18547)
Navy League of United States........... G 302 456-4410
  Wilmington (G-18565)
Nerdit Foundation.............................. G 302 482-5979
  Wilmington (G-18586)

86 MEMBERSHIP ORGANIZATIONS

Nonprofit Bus Solutions LLC .... F 302 353-4606
Wilmington (G-18668)

Python Software Foundation .... F 970 305-9455
Dover (G-3402)

Regional Enterprises LLC .... G 302 227-0202
Rehoboth Beach (G-12911)

Rethmerica Accounting and .... G 302 317-2417
Newark (G-11871)

Rockham 5g PA LP .... G 302 239-1250
Hockessin (G-5369)

Schoenbeck PA .... G 302 584-4519
Newark (G-11959)

Seamens Center Wilmington Inc .... G 302 575-1300
Wilmington (G-19722)

Sharon Boyd M Ed Lpcmh .... G 302 529-0220
Wilmington (G-19782)

Society For Whole-Body Autorad .... G 302 369-5240
Newark (G-12049)

State Edcatn Agcy Dirs Arts Ed .... G 302 739-4111
Dover (G-3605)

Yellowfins .... G 302 381-2569
Millsboro (G-8510)

Zebrafish Disease Models Soc .... G 518 399-7181
Wilmington (G-20949)

8631 Labor organizations

American Fdrtion State Cnty MN .... G 302 698-5034
Dover (G-1785)

American Fdrtion State Cnty MN .... G 302 323-2600
New Castle (G-8796)

American Fdrtion State Cnty MN .... F 302 323-2121
New Castle (G-8797)

Christina Education Assn .... G 302 454-7700
Newark (G-10234)

Communctons Wkrs Amer Lcal 131 .... G 302 737-0400
Newark (G-10286)

Delaware Nature Society .... E 302 239-1283
Hockessin (G-5182)

Delaware State Aflcio .... G 302 256-0310
Wilmington (G-15969)

Delaware State Education Assn .... G 302 366-8440
Newark (G-10484)

Delaware State Education Assn .... F 302 734-5834
Dover (G-2263)

Diamond State Tele Coml Un .... G 302 999-1100
Wilmington (G-16059)

International Brthd 2271 Local .... G 302 559-9167
Wilmington (G-17387)

Interntnal Brthd Elec Wkrs Lca .... G 302 328-0773
New Castle (G-9240)

Jatc Local Union 313 .... G 302 322-5089
New Castle (G-9253)

Local Hands-Crafted In America .... G 302 645-9100
Lewes (G-6216)

Millwrights Local Union 1548 .... F 410 355-0011
Wilmington (G-18368)

National Assn Ltr Carriers .... G 302 652-2933
Newport (G-12455)

Npmhe Local 308 .... G 302 322-2430
Historic New Castle (G-5041)

Plumbers Ppfitters Local Un 74 .... G 302 636-7400
Newark (G-11702)

Promote Your Loc Bus Pwred By .... G 302 764-5588
Wilmington (G-19230)

Sheet Metal Workers Local 19 .... F 302 999-0573
Wilmington (G-19789)

Transport Wkrs Un Amer Intl Un .... G 302 652-1503
Wilmington (G-20401)

Ufcw Local 27 .... G 302 436-6105
Selbyville (G-13614)

United Auto Workers Local 435 .... F 302 995-6001
Newark (G-12267)

United Sttes Harn Wrters Assoc .... G 215 681-0697
Harrington (G-4842)

United Tele Wkrs Local 13101 .... G 302 737-0400
Newark (G-12272)

United Trnsp Un Insur Assn .... F 302 655-6084
New Castle (G-9658)

Usw Local 4-898 .... G 302 836-6689
Bear (G-555)

8641 Civic and social associations

1313 Owner LLC .... G 302 225-7896
Wilmington (G-14108)

1401 Condominium Association .... F 302 656-8171
Wilmington (G-14110)

3b Braes Brown Bags .... G 302 544-0779
Bear (G-2)

4-H .... G 302 831-8161
Newark (G-9713)

436 Aerial Port Squadron .... G 302 677-3169
Dover (G-1687)

4troy Foundation .... F 302 448-9203
Bridgeville (G-658)

Alana Rose Foundation Inc .... G 302 519-5973
Dagsboro (G-1410)

Alpha PHI Delta .... G 302 377-5789
Dover (G-1774)

Alpha PHI Delta Fraternity .... F 302 531-7854
Camden (G-790)

American Legion .... G 302 398-3566
Harrington (G-4728)

American Legion .... G 302 378-4882
Townsend (G-13959)

American Legion .... F 302 628-5221
Seaford (G-13061)

American Legion Ambulance .... G 302 653-3557
Smyrna (G-13639)

American Legion Aux Dept Del .... G 302 629-3435
Seaford (G-13062)

American Legion Auxiliary .... G 302 329-9090
Georgetown (G-4210)

American Legion Auxiliary .... G 302 235-0878
Hockessin (G-5120)

American Lgion Ambince Stn 64 .... E 302 653-6465
Smyrna (G-13640)

American Lgion Post 15 Glen Ry .... G 410 726-4580
Delmar (G-1564)

American Soc Cytopathology Inc .... G 302 543-6583
Wilmington (G-14443)

Amvets Post 22 .... G 302 945-2599
Millsboro (G-8170)

Amy Gabel .... G 703 598-0763
Lewes (G-5690)

Ancient Order Hbernians Ladies .... G 302 633-0810
Wilmington (G-14470)

Ancient Order of Hibernians .... G 302 368-0264
Newark (G-9864)

Angel Homeowner .... G 302 504-6895
Newark (G-9868)

Angola By The Bay Prprty Owner .... F 302 945-2700
Lewes (G-5692)

Anhui Xncheng High Schl Almni .... G 302 234-4351
Hockessin (G-5127)

Arise Africa Foundation Inc .... G 877 829-5500
New Castle (G-8821)

Art For A Purpose .... G 302 245-4528
Lewes (G-5701)

Attack Addiction .... G 302 994-1550
Wilmington (G-14637)

Atterbury VFW Post 3420 .... G 302 737-6903
Newark (G-9942)

Battle Proven Foundation .... G 703 216-1986
Dover (G-1881)

Bay Forest Homeowners Assn .... G 302 537-6580
Ocean View (G-12468)

Baynard House Condominiums .... G 302 319-3740
Wilmington (G-14789)

Be Bold .... G 302 415-5242
Dover (G-1893)

Bear-Glasgow YMCA .... G 302 836-9622
Newark (G-10006)

Beau Bden Fndtion For The Prtc .... F 302 598-1885
Wilmington (G-14807)

Benevlent Prtctive Order Elks .... F 302 629-2458
Seaford (G-13082)

Benevlent Prtective Order Elks .... G 302 736-1903
Dover (G-1910)

Best Buddies International Inc .... G 302 691-3187
Wilmington (G-14852)

Bethany Forest Hoa .... G 302 645-7242
Lewes (G-5757)

Big Cats Foundation .... G 302 897-7140
Newark (G-10031)

Bing Rchel Zhang Fmly Fndation .... G 302 294-1859
Wilmington (G-14893)

Birch Pointe Condo Assc .... G 302 685-4310
Wilmington (G-14896)

Blackbird Community Assn Inc .... G 302 598-7447
Townsend (G-13964)

Boca Raton Exch Foundation Inc .... G 302 286-6067
Newark (G-10065)

Boyer .... G 302 368-8489
Newark (G-10076)

Boys & Girls Club of De .... F 302 677-6376
Dover (G-1967)

Boys & Girls Club of Milford .... G 302 422-4453
Milford (G-7801)

Boys & Girls Clubs Del Inc .... F 302 792-3780
Claymont (G-1064)

Boys & Girls Clubs Del Inc .... G 302 678-5182
Dover (G-1968)

Boys & Girls Clubs Del Inc .... F 302 856-4903
Georgetown (G-4238)

Boys & Girls Clubs Del Inc .... F 302 655-8569
New Castle (G-8881)

Boys & Girls Clubs Del Inc .... B 302 658-1870
Wilmington (G-15020)

Boys & Girls Clubs of America .... G 302 875-1200
Laurel (G-5472)

Boys & Girls Clubs of America .... F 302 659-5610
Smyrna (G-13665)

Boys and Girls .... G 302 947-4600
Millsboro (G-8203)

Boys Girls Clubs .... G 302 260-9864
Rehoboth Beach (G-12649)

Brandywine Club Inc .... G 302 798-9891
Claymont (G-1066)

Brandywine Education Assn .... G 302 793-5048
Claymont (G-1067)

Brandywine Park Condos .... G 302 655-2262
Wilmington (G-15079)

Brenden Bley Chanl VFW Post 58 .... G 302 239-0797
Hockessin (G-5142)

Brookview Townhomes Redev LLC .... G 302 472-7200
Wilmington (G-15127)

Bruce G & Mary A Robert FML Fd .... G 302 598-1609
Wilmington (G-15134)

Camden - Wyoming Lions Club .... G 302 697-6565
Camden (G-799)

Camp Possibilities Foundation .... G 302 563-9460
Wilmington (G-15209)

Cape Henlopen Elks Lodge .... G 302 645-7016
Nassau (G-8740)

Center For Inland Bays Inc .... G 302 226-8105
Rehoboth Beach (G-12666)

86 MEMBERSHIP ORGANIZATIONS

Clayton Lions Club..................................F..... 302 450-6098
  Smyrna (G-13680)
Coffee Run Condo Council Inc................G..... 302 239-4134
  Hockessin (G-5166)
Colette W Bleistine Paying It....................G..... 609 217-1925
  Townsend (G-13974)
Committed Hearts Foundation.................G..... 402 850-4644
  Wilmington (G-15549)
Community Business Dev Corp..............G..... 302 544-1709
  Newark (G-10288)
Corrozi Fountainview LLC........................G..... 302 266-7501
  Newark (G-10330)
Council of Devon......................................G..... 302 658-5366
  Wilmington (G-15651)
Crab Meat For Kids..................................G..... 302 378-1327
  Middletown (G-7017)
Ddx3x Foundation....................................G..... 917 796-3514
  Wilmington (G-15836)
Del Ray Foundatins LLC..........................G..... 302 272-6153
  Milford (G-7849)
Del-Mr-Va Cncil Inc Boy Scouts...............F..... 302 622-3300
  Dover (G-2212)
Delaware City Recreation Club................G..... 302 834-9900
  Delaware City (G-1537)
Delaware College Scholars Inc................F..... 302 437-6144
  Wilmington (G-15887)
Delaware Con Fndtons Slabs LLC..........G..... 302 945-1223
  Millsboro (G-8260)
Delaware Dnce Edcatn Orgnztion...........G..... 302 897-6345
  Wilmington (G-15911)
Delaware Ffa Foundation Inc..................G..... 302 857-6493
  Dover (G-2238)
Delaware Mobile Surfisherman...............G..... 302 945-1320
  Dagsboro (G-1435)
Delaware Nature Society.........................E..... 302 239-1283
  Hockessin (G-5182)
Delaware Paralyzed Vets.........................G..... 302 861-6671
  Newark (G-10468)
Delaware Parents Association.................F..... 302 678-9288
  Dover (G-2252)
Delaware Retired Schl Prsnl....................E..... 302 674-8252
  Wilmington (G-15960)
Delaware Saengerbund Lib Assn............G..... 302 366-9454
  Newark (G-10476)
Delaware Seashore Preservation.............G..... 302 227-0478
  Dagsboro (G-1436)
Delaware State Grange Inc.....................G..... 302 994-0295
  Wilmington (G-15972)
Delaware Terry Farrell Fund....................G..... 302 242-4341
  Lincoln (G-6663)
Delaware Veterans Home Inc.................E..... 302 424-6000
  Milford (G-7860)
Delaware Veterans Inc.............................F..... 302 674-9956
  Bear (G-159)
Delaware Veterans Post...........................G..... 302 317-1123
  Dover (G-2272)
Delisle K-9 Offcer Sfety Fndti..................G..... 302 893-7324
  Bear (G-163)
Delmarva Community Wellnet.................G..... 704 779-3280
  Lewes (G-5903)
Delmarva Space Scnces Fndation..........G..... 302 236-2761
  Millsboro (G-8269)
Delray Foundations Inc...........................E..... 302 503-3341
  Lincoln (G-6664)
Delta Gamma LLC...................................G..... 347 387-6956
  Wilmington (G-16004)
Delta Kappa Gamma Society..................G..... 302 945-7174
  Lewes (G-5910)
Diamond State Home Auxiliary................G..... 302 652-9331
  Newport (G-12449)
Dominique Ho..G..... 302 234-2971
  Hockessin (G-5189)

Donnie Jones Foundation Inc..................G..... 302 745-6946
  Ellendale (G-3915)
Donorware Foundation.............................G..... 302 230-7171
  Wilmington (G-16141)
Dvfa Foundation......................................G..... 302 734-9390
  Dover (G-2397)
Early Foundations Therapeutic...............G..... 302 384-6905
  Wilmington (G-16248)
East Sussex Moose Lodge......................G..... 302 436-2088
  Frankford (G-4104)
Eastern Brndywine Hndred Crdnt............G..... 302 764-2476
  Wilmington (G-16255)
Ebright Foundation LL.............................G..... 215 370-2821
  Wilmington (G-16276)
Edfeed Foundation..................................F..... 917 459-2762
  Middletown (G-7082)
Empowerment Group Inc.........................G..... 302 930-8080
  Lincoln (G-6665)
Endure To Cure Foundation....................G..... 866 400-2121
  Wilmington (G-16412)
Evan David Foundation...........................G..... 302 778-4546
  Wilmington (G-16478)
Fairway Villas Condo Assn.....................G..... 302 539-0414
  Dagsboro (G-1446)
Fan Payment Solutions LLC....................F..... 617 901-3970
  Wilmington (G-16549)
Farpath Foundation.................................G..... 302 645-8328
  Lewes (G-5989)
Farr Family Foundation Inc.....................G..... 540 349-4103
  Lewes (G-5990)
Fbinaa..G..... 302 344-7700
  Lewes (G-5992)
Fenwick Towers Condo Assn..................G..... 302 281-5025
  Fenwick Island (G-4049)
Firemens Hstrcal Fndtion Dlmar...............G..... 302 846-3014
  Delmar (G-1596)
First Tee of Delaware.............................G..... 302 593-2062
  Wilmington (G-16641)
Forest Oak Elementary Pta.....................G..... 302 540-2873
  Newark (G-10761)
Foundation Delaware Islamic...................G..... 302 325-4149
  New Castle (G-9141)
Frank & Yetta Chaiken Fou.....................G..... 302 737-7427
  Wilmington (G-16725)
Fraternal Order of Eagles BR..................G..... 302 616-2935
  Ocean View (G-12514)
Fraternal Order of Police.........................G..... 302 674-3673
  Dover (G-2533)
Free Spirited Foundation.........................G..... 614 946-7358
  Lewes (G-6013)
Freelee Foundation..................................G..... 302 607-8053
  Newark (G-10780)
Friends of Colonial..................................G..... 302 323-2746
  New Castle (G-9147)
Friends of New Cties Fundation..............G..... 718 896-8900
  Wilmington (G-16756)
Friends of The African Union..................G..... 302 834-7525
  Delaware City (G-1544)
Future Promises Foundation...................G..... 302 365-5735
  Bear (G-242)
Future Promises Foundation Inc.............G..... 302 689-3392
  Wilmington (G-16778)
Georgetown Boys and Girls Club............F..... 302 856-4903
  Georgetown (G-4336)
Girl Scuts of Chspake Bay Cnci..............E..... 302 456-7150
  Newark (G-10838)
Girls Incorporate of Delaware..................F..... 302 575-1041
  Wilmington (G-16870)
Girls Incorporate of Delaware..................G..... 302 575-1041
  Wilmington (G-16869)
Girls On Run..G..... 302 668-1720
  Wilmington (G-16871)

Give From The Heart-The Doroth............G..... 302 322-7808
  New Castle (G-9168)
Good Ole Boy Foundation Inc.................G..... 302 249-0237
  Millsboro (G-8301)
Greatful Lives Foundation........................G..... 404 965-9300
  Wilmington (G-16961)
Gregory A Williams Jr Educ....................G..... 302 875-1218
  Laurel (G-5525)
Gulu Project Inc.......................................G..... 302 547-8106
  Hockessin (G-5230)
Hall Burke VFW Post 5447 Inc...............F..... 302 798-2052
  Wilmington (G-17038)
Hamilton House Condominium................G..... 302 658-7787
  Wilmington (G-17043)
Harry K Foundation.................................F..... 301 226-0675
  Rehoboth Beach (G-12781)
Hclinton Foundation.................................G..... 302 393-1448
  Greenwood (G-4635)
Heal Autism Now Del Foundation............G..... 302 456-1335
  Newark (G-10941)
Heart In Game Foundation Inc................G..... 302 494-3133
  Wilmington (G-17104)
Helopen Condominium Council...............G..... 302 227-6409
  Rehoboth Beach (G-12783)
Heroes Self Defense Foundation.............G..... 609 335-2391
  Clayton (G-1370)
Hogs Heroes Foundation De Ch1...........G..... 443 754-0343
  Laurel (G-5530)
Ideaspace Open Mnds Foundation.........G..... 808 444-4578
  Bear (G-281)
Illumina Corporate Foundation................F..... 516 870-7722
  Wilmington (G-17280)
Indo-American Association Del...............G..... 302 234-0214
  Newark (G-11015)
Intercollegiate Studies Inst......................D..... 302 656-3292
  Wilmington (G-17376)
Internet Activism Inc...............................G..... 206 861-5106
  Wilmington (G-17393)
J N N Foundation....................................G..... 800 493-1069
  Bear (G-294)
J Riley Eaton...G..... 302 539-4537
  Ocean View (G-12527)
Jamestown Sports....................................G..... 302 328-2770
  Newark (G-11094)
JB For Office) Hogan..............................G..... 302 922-0000
  Dover (G-2775)
Joseph Patrick Fabber Meml...................G..... 302 858-4040
  Georgetown (G-4388)
Joy Choose Foundation...........................G..... 302 286-7560
  Dover (G-2805)
Kappa Alpha Fdn For Lead Serv.............G..... 302 475-4917
  Wilmington (G-17649)
Katy Aukamp Mem Foundation...............G..... 302 328-6446
  New Castle (G-9275)
Kids Club Foundation Delaware..............G..... 302 733-0168
  Newark (G-11172)
Kim and Evans Fmly Fndtion Inc............G..... 302 629-7166
  Seaford (G-13249)
Kind-Charity Inc......................................G..... 302 867-6042
  Middletown (G-7275)
Kiwanis International Inc.........................G..... 302 325-0778
  New Castle (G-9285)
Knights Clmbus Del State Cncil..............G..... 302 836-8235
  Bear (G-332)
Knights of Columbus...............................G..... 703 615-3372
  Bethany Beach (G-613)
Kool Boiz Foundation LLC......................G..... 614 404-2396
  Middletown (G-7281)
Kristol Ctr For Jewish Lf Inc...................G..... 302 453-0479
  Newark (G-11203)
Laurel Lions Club Foundation.................G..... 302 875-9178
  Laurel (G-5549)

Employee Codes: A=Over 500 employees, B=251-500
C=101-250, D=51-100, E=20-50, F=10-19, G=1-9

2024 Harris Directory of Delaware Businesses

86 MEMBERSHIP ORGANIZATIONS

League of Wmen Vters New Cstle............ G..... 302 571-8948
  Wilmington (G-17845)
Leah & Alain Lebec Foundation............. G..... 800 839-1754
  Wilmington (G-17846)
Lincoln Community Hall Inc.................. G..... 302 242-1747
  Lincoln (G-6681)
Linden Building.. G..... 302 573-3705
  Wilmington (G-17925)
Linden Hill Elementary Pta..................... G..... 302 454-3406
  Wilmington (G-17927)
Longboat Condominium LLC................... G..... 302 227-4785
  Rehoboth Beach (G-12838)
Longview Farms Civic Assn..................... G..... 302 475-6684
  Wilmington (G-17988)
Lorelton Foundation................................ G..... 302 573-2500
  Wilmington (G-17996)
Loyal Order Mose Clymont Lodge............ G..... 302 764-9765
  Wilmington (G-18014)
Loyal Order Mose Lwes Rehoboth............ G..... 302 684-4004
  Lewes (G-6227)
Loyal Order of Moose............................. G..... 302 378-2624
  Historic New Castle (G-5019)
Ltr Private Foundation............................ G..... 610 745-5000
  Wilmington (G-18022)
Lupus Foundtn of Amer Phila Tr.............. F..... 302 622-8700
  Wilmington (G-18030)
Magic Inc.. F..... 415 319-6331
  Wilmington (G-18082)
Mallerd Lakes.. F..... 443 783-2993
  Selbyville (G-13564)
Md22 Lions Low Vision Rehab................. G..... 410 737-2671
  Wilmington (G-18238)
Met Technologies LLC............................. G..... 302 468-5243
  Newark (G-11392)
Michael Ercka Hynnsky Fmly Fnd............ G..... 302 545-4600
  Wilmington (G-18312)
Michael G Schwrtz Mem Fndation............ G..... 302 453-9233
  Wilmington (G-18313)
Middletown YMCA.................................. F..... 302 510-1166
  Middletown (G-7361)
Middltown Vlg Cmnty Foundation............ G..... 857 544-3954
  Middletown (G-7366)
Midway Lions Club Inc........................... G..... 302 945-5525
  Harbeson (G-4708)
Milford Lions Club Svc Fdn..................... G..... 302 422-2861
  Lincoln (G-6687)
Milford Veterans of Foreign WA............... G..... 302 422-4412
  Milford (G-8009)
Military Order of The Purple................... G..... 302 563-0435
  Newark (G-11420)
Murray Mnor Hmwners Assction LL......... G..... 302 298-5997
  Wilmington (G-18490)
Mvrp Foundation Inc.............................. G..... 347 683-1974
  Rehoboth Beach (G-12868)
National Assn of Hispnc Nrses................. G..... 302 325-9292
  New Castle (G-9394)
National Society of Sons......................... G..... 443 614-5437
  Dover (G-3155)
Network Connect Inc.............................. F..... 302 300-1222
  Wilmington (G-18595)
New Foundations LLC............................. F..... 302 753-3135
  Newark (G-11522)
Noor Foundation International................ G..... 302 234-8860
  Hockessin (G-5324)
North Star Pta....................................... G..... 302 234-7200
  Hockessin (G-5325)
Nur Shrners Ancent Arab Order............... G..... 302 328-6100
  Newark (G-11568)
Objective Zero Foundation...................... F..... 202 573-9660
  Wilmington (G-18736)
OHM Lshree Foundation......................... G..... 302 652-2900
  Middletown (G-7413)

Olacole Foundation................................ G..... 215 279-4742
  Bear (G-405)
Oluv C Joynor Foundation....................... G..... 302 793-3277
  Wilmington (G-18761)
One Commerce Ctr Condo Council........... G..... 302 573-2513
  Wilmington (G-18779)
Order of The Eastern Star Del.................. G..... 302 369-0729
  Newark (G-11598)
Park Plaza Condo Association.................. G..... 302 658-3526
  Wilmington (G-18893)
PCA Pto.. G..... 302 250-8377
  Clayton (G-1394)
Pearce Q Foundation Inc........................ G..... 302 753-8612
  Newark (G-11651)
Perry Initiative...................................... G..... 302 319-1113
  Newark (G-11668)
Pershing Foundation.............................. G..... 636 352-7122
  Middletown (G-7442)
PHI Service Co...................................... G..... 302 451-5224
  Newark (G-11683)
Plantation Lakes Homeowners................. G..... 302 934-5200
  Millsboro (G-8429)
Pointe Condominiums............................ G..... 302 656-2018
  Wilmington (G-19101)
Police Athletic League Del Inc................. G..... 302 656-9501
  New Castle (G-9482)
Police Athletic League of De................... G..... 302 792-0930
  Wilmington (G-19104)
Polish Library Association....................... G..... 302 652-9555
  Wilmington (G-19107)
Polish Nat Aliance of The US................... G..... 302 658-3324
  Wilmington (G-19108)
Porsche Club America Del Reg................ G..... 302 588-3511
  Hockessin (G-5347)
Power Over Pain Crps Fndtion I............... G..... 302 983-6412
  New Castle (G-9486)
Preserve At Deacons Walk...................... G..... 302 613-4775
  Newark (G-11733)
PSI Zeta Chapter of Omega PSI............... G..... 302 367-8216
  Wilmington (G-19243)
Pta Delaware Congress........................... G..... 302 792-3916
  Claymont (G-1269)
Pta Delaware Congress........................... F..... 302 454-3424
  Wilmington (G-19250)
Pta Delaware Military Academy............... G..... 302 998-0745
  Wilmington (G-19251)
Puppy Playdate Co................................. G..... 765 326-0517
  Middletown (G-7482)
Raskob Fndtion For Cthlic Actv................ F..... 302 655-4440
  Wilmington (G-19336)
Red Clay Consolidated Schl Dst............... F..... 302 235-6600
  Hockessin (G-5359)
Rehoboth Bch Sister Cites Assn............... G..... 302 249-7878
  Rehoboth Beach (G-12916)
River Ridge Homeowners Assn................ G..... 302 761-9592
  Wilmington (G-19490)
Rockford Park Condominium Home.......... G..... 302 658-7842
  Wilmington (G-19537)
Roland E Tice... G..... 302 629-3674
  Laurel (G-5594)
Salvation Army...................................... E..... 302 654-8808
  Wilmington (G-19643)
Savimbo Inc.. E..... 650 387-6648
  Wilmington (G-19684)
Sbm Landowner Inc............................... G..... 302 652-8314
  Wilmington (G-19692)
Schooltoolstv.. G..... 415 948-0668
  Bear (G-481)
Seaford Police Dept............................... G..... 302 629-6644
  Seaford (G-13392)
Secure Schools Alliance Inc.................... G..... 302 333-1416
  Wilmington (G-19730)

Sigma Theta Tau Inc.............................. G..... 302 584-5908
  Middletown (G-7564)
Skyline Swim Club................................. G..... 302 737-4696
  Wilmington (G-19857)
Smartdrive Foundation........................... G..... 302 463-6543
  New Castle (G-9573)
Smyrna Clyton Ldge 2046 Order.............. G..... 302 653-2046
  Smyrna (G-13892)
Smyrna De.. G..... 302 653-1166
  Smyrna (G-13893)
Solutions Property Management.............. G..... 302 581-9060
  Rehoboth Beach (G-12968)
Soroptomist Foundation Inc.................... G..... 302 698-3686
  Dover (G-3588)
Soucialize Inc.. G..... 916 803-1057
  Lewes (G-6492)
South Bowers Ladies Auxiliary................. G..... 302 335-4135
  Milford (G-8096)
Speech & Language For Kids LLC............. G..... 847 852-0928
  Wilmington (G-19958)
Springmill Community Assoc................... G..... 302 376-5466
  Middletown (G-7594)
Star of The Sea Assoc of Ownrs............... G..... 302 227-6006
  Rehoboth Beach (G-12972)
Starliters Dance Studio Inc..................... G..... 302 798-6330
  Claymont (G-1301)
Studio Groups Inc.................................. F..... 302 998-7895
  Wilmington (G-20106)
Success Wont Wait Inc........................... G..... 302 388-9669
  Wilmington (G-20118)
Surrender House.................................... G..... 302 249-6830
  Millsboro (G-8472)
Temple Masonic..................................... E..... 302 734-4147
  Dover (G-3667)
The Oak Orchrd-Rvrdale Post 28............. F..... 302 945-1673
  Millsboro (G-8484)
Tiffany Pines Condo Assn Inc.................. G..... 302 227-0913
  Rehoboth Beach (G-12995)
Trivedi Foundation LLC.......................... G..... 302 678-4629
  Dover (G-3729)
Trustees of Ardentown........................... G..... 302 475-8193
  Wilmington (G-20449)
United Tele Wkrs Local 13101................. G..... 302 737-0400
  Newark (G-12272)
University Whist CLB of Wlmngt.............. E..... 302 658-5125
  Wilmington (G-20534)
Urban Change Incorporated.................... G..... 215 749-2049
  New Castle (G-9663)
V F W Post Home.................................. G..... 302 366-8438
  Newark (G-12296)
Valley Stream Townhomes...................... G..... 302 613-4859
  Newark (G-12301)
Veteran Services.................................... D..... 302 864-0009
  Frankford (G-4157)
Veterans Development Co LLC................. G..... 302 945-5281
  Lewes (G-6601)
Veterans of Foreign Wars....................... G..... 302 366-8438
  Newark (G-12321)
Veterans of Foreign Wars Newmn............ G..... 302 653-8801
  Smyrna (G-13930)
Veterans Story Project Inc...................... G..... 302 644-4600
  Lewes (G-6602)
VFW Magazine....................................... G..... 302 994-2511
  Wilmington (G-20602)
VFW Post 6483...................................... G..... 302 422-4412
  Milford (G-8135)
Voiture Nationale La Society................... G..... 302 478-7591
  Wilmington (G-20648)
Walter L Fox Post 2 Inc.......................... G..... 302 674-1741
  Dover (G-3819)
Warrior Community Connect Inc.............. G..... 202 309-5729
  Millsboro (G-8499)

Wdbid Management Company............ E 302 425-5374
  Wilmington *(G-20698)*

Whites Creek Manor Poa................... G 302 541-9422
  Millville *(G-8551)*

Wilmington Club Inc............................ F 302 658-4287
  Wilmington *(G-20811)*

Wilmington Rowing Center................. G 302 652-5339
  Wilmington *(G-20834)*

Wilmington Trap Association.............. G 302 834-9320
  Newark *(G-12384)*

Wilmington Youth Organization........... G 302 761-9030
  Wilmington *(G-20853)*

Wilson Dunes Condo Counci.............. G 302 542-1899
  Dover *(G-3856)*

World Amptee Ftball Federation......... G 302 383-2665
  Wilmington *(G-20895)*

Wraparound Maryland......................... G 302 504-8487
  Wilmington *(G-20897)*

YMCA Central Branch LLC................. F 302 571-6950
  Wilmington *(G-20929)*

YMCA of Delaware B/A Sch Pgrm...... E 302 836-9622
  Newark *(G-12420)*

You Are Not Alone Vtrans Fndti.......... F 302 287-8533
  Middletown *(G-7749)*

Young MNS Chrstn Assn Wlmngton.... C 302 709-9622
  Newark *(G-12422)*

YWCA Delaware.................................. F 302 224-4060
  Newark *(G-12425)*

YWCA Delaware.................................. D 302 655-0039
  Wilmington *(G-20942)*

8651 Political organizations

Carper For Delaware Hq..................... G 302 328-5774
  Newark *(G-10154)*

Civic Influencers Inc........................... G 302 644-5757
  Lewes *(G-5822)*

Kent County Republican Party............ G 302 653-2355
  Smyrna *(G-13789)*

8661 Religious organizations

Bethel United Methodist Church......... F 302 645-9426
  Lewes *(G-5758)*

Chester Bthel Untd Mthdst Pre........... F 302 475-3549
  Wilmington *(G-15368)*

Christ Ch Episcpal Preschool............. F 302 472-0021
  Wilmington *(G-15396)*

Church of God In Christ...................... F 302 678-1949
  Dover *(G-2072)*

Diocesan Council Inc......................... F 302 475-4688
  Wilmington *(G-16075)*

Ebenezer United Methdst Chruch...... F 302 731-9495
  Newark *(G-10602)*

Elsmere Presbyterian Church............. F 302 998-6365
  Wilmington *(G-16381)*

Fairwinds Baptist Church Inc.............. G 302 322-1029
  Bear *(G-220)*

Fellowship Hlth Resources Inc........... F 302 856-7642
  Georgetown *(G-4316)*

First Love Ministries Inc..................... F 302 655-1776
  Middletown *(G-7130)*

Generation Glory Ministries................ G 302 438-4335
  Wilmington *(G-16833)*

Hilltop Lthran Nghbrhood Ctr I............ E 302 656-3224
  Wilmington *(G-17148)*

Hope Presbyterian Church................. F 302 764-8615
  Wilmington *(G-17198)*

Independent Bb Fellowship Ch........... G 302 734-2301
  Dover *(G-2726)*

Jewish Federation of Delaware.......... F 302 478-5660
  Wilmington *(G-17540)*

Larry Shelton..................................... F 678 948-6096
  New Castle *(G-9295)*

Linde North America.......................... F 302 654-9348
  New Castle *(G-9312)*

Ministry of Caring Inc......................... G 302 428-3702
  Wilmington *(G-18373)*

Newark United Methodist................... E 302 368-8774
  Newark *(G-11547)*

Ogletown Baptist Church................... F 302 737-2511
  Newark *(G-11580)*

Salvation Army................................... F 302 934-3730
  Millsboro *(G-8453)*

Seaford Mission Inc........................... G 302 629-2559
  Seaford *(G-13391)*

St Marks United Methodist Ch........... F 302 994-0400
  Wilmington *(G-19999)*

Victorous Kngdom Ctzens Ntwrk........ G 302 409-0701
  Smyrna *(G-13931)*

8699 Membership organizations, nec

18 Pomegranets Inc.......................... G 800 839-1754
  Wilmington *(G-14113)*

613 Foundation.................................. G 800 839-1754
  Wilmington *(G-14143)*

AAA Club Alliance Inc........................ D 302 674-8020
  Dover *(G-1700)*

AAA Club Alliance Inc........................ D 302 368-8175
  Newark *(G-9731)*

Afgceaa Corporation.......................... G 617 314-0814
  Wilmington *(G-14308)*

Amani Family Foundation................... G 800 839-1754
  Wilmington *(G-14412)*

American Birding Association............ G 610 864-0370
  Wilmington *(G-14425)*

Angels In Action Inc........................... G 302 397-7061
  New Castle *(G-8808)*

Anne Anstasi Chrtble Fundation........ G 800 839-1754
  Wilmington *(G-14492)*

Apache Software Foundation............. G 302 295-4884
  Wilmington *(G-14502)*

ARC of Delaware............................... F 302 996-9400
  Wilmington *(G-14531)*

Association Eductional Publr............. F 302 295-8350
  Wilmington *(G-14593)*

Association of Centers Study O......... G 302 831-1724
  Newark *(G-9928)*

Astrazeneca Foundation.................... G 302 886-3000
  Wilmington *(G-14608)*

Athari Inc... F 312 358-4933
  Dover *(G-1844)*

Avalanche Canyon Foundation.......... G 800 839-1754
  Wilmington *(G-14662)*

Bauer Family Foundation Inc............. G 800 639-1754
  Wilmington *(G-14780)*

Because Love Allows Compassion.... G 302 674-2496
  Dover *(G-1901)*

Bee A Queen Inc............................... G 267 235-8415
  Middletown *(G-6908)*

Bethany Beach Vlntr Fire Co.............. E 302 539-7700
  Bethany Beach *(G-583)*

Blindsight Delaware LLC................... E 302 998-5913
  Wilmington *(G-14957)*

Bowman Family Foundation............... G 302 234-5750
  Hockessin *(G-5139)*

Brain Injury Association Del............... G 302 346-2083
  Dover *(G-1970)*

Brandywine Valley Spca.................... F 302 516-1000
  New Castle *(G-8887)*

Brandywine Valley Spca.................... G 302 475-9294
  Wilmington *(G-15090)*

Buck Road East Association.............. F 302 658-2400
  Wilmington *(G-15140)*

Cape Henlopen Senior Center........... G 302 227-2055
  Rehoboth Beach *(G-12663)*

Cappa Inc... G 302 598-4762
  Newark *(G-10137)*

Career Rady Educatn Foundation...... G 302 540-2733
  Bear *(G-90)*

Carl M Freedman Communities......... G 302 436-4102
  Selbyville *(G-13490)*

Carl M Freeman Foundation Inc........ G 302 436-6241
  Selbyville *(G-13492)*

Challenge Program............................ G 302 655-0945
  Wilmington *(G-15327)*

Charity Crossing Inc.......................... F 302 983-2271
  Bear *(G-97)*

Child Inc... E 302 762-8989
  Wilmington *(G-15372)*

Child Help Foundation....................... G 302 533-7078
  Newark *(G-10204)*

Chris and Tracey Haverkamp Fam..... G 800 839-1754
  Wilmington *(G-15394)*

Christian Science Reading Room....... G 302 456-1428
  Newark *(G-10215)*

Christina Cultural Arts Center............. E 302 652-0101
  Wilmington *(G-15415)*

City Fare... G 302 421-3734
  Wilmington *(G-15453)*

Collegiate Network Inc...................... G 302 652-4600
  Wilmington *(G-15533)*

Compassnate Soc of Chrst St St....... G 914 482-2562
  Dover *(G-2121)*

Createyourscholarshiporg.................. G 415 822-8266
  Wilmington *(G-15688)*

Curiosity Service Foundation............. G 302 628-4140
  Seaford *(G-13142)*

Cynthia Dnnis Mther Foundation....... G 410 598-3819
  Fenwick Island *(G-4047)*

Daniel G Wnda K Odell Fmly Fnd...... G 800 839-1754
  Wilmington *(G-15781)*

Daniel Karen Berman Foundation...... G 800 839-1754
  Wilmington *(G-15782)*

Dcrac... G 302 298-3289
  Wilmington *(G-15830)*

Delaware Apartment Association....... G 302 998-0322
  New Castle *(G-9013)*

Delaware Apartment Association....... G 617 680-3463
  Wilmington *(G-15865)*

Delaware Bioscience Assn................ G 302 635-0445
  Wilmington *(G-15873)*

Delaware Boots On Ground............... G 302 326-7789
  Wilmington *(G-15874)*

Delaware Chpter of The Amrcn A...... G 302 218-1075
  Newark *(G-10425)*

Delaware Cmnty Rnvstment Actio..... G 302 298-3250
  Wilmington *(G-15886)*

Delaware Ctr For Hrtclture Inc........... E 302 658-6262
  Wilmington *(G-15898)*

Delaware Juneteenth Assn................ G 302 530-1605
  Middletown *(G-7042)*

Delaware Lacrosse Foundation......... G 302 831-8661
  Wilmington *(G-15937)*

Delaware Liberia Association............. G 302 983-2536
  Newark *(G-10457)*

Delaware Magical Wishes Assn........ G 302 653-6974
  Smyrna *(G-13700)*

Delaware S P C A.............................. E 302 998-2281
  Newark *(G-10475)*

Delaware Schl Counselors Assn....... G 302 323-2821
  New Castle *(G-9037)*

Delaware School Nutrition Assn........ G 302 323-2743
  Wilmington *(G-15964)*

Delaware Seaside Railroad Club....... G 302 682-4652
  Ocean View *(G-12500)*

Delaware State Pipe Trdes Assn...... G 302 636-7400
  Newark *(G-10485)*

86 MEMBERSHIP ORGANIZATIONS

Delcaps Inc .... G 302 242-6953
  Smyrna (G-13708)
Delmarva Paddlers Retreat .... G 302 542-0818
  Rehoboth Beach (G-12720)
Dental Health Center Del-Tech .... G 302 657-5176
  Wilmington (G-16015)
Deseu .... G 302 883-3048
  Dover (G-2286)
Diabuddies .... G 302 893-0311
  Wilmington (G-16047)
Dovers Childrens Village Too .... G 302 674-8142
  Dover (G-2370)
East Sussex Moose Lodge .... G 302 436-2088
  Frankford (G-4104)
Education Voices Inc .... G 302 559-7889
  Wilmington (G-16299)
Edwards Mther Earth Foundation .... G 800 839-1754
  Wilmington (G-16304)
Elaine Cnroy More Chrtblfndtio .... G 302 296-6580
  Dagsboro (G-1444)
Fairwinds Baptist Church Inc .... G 302 322-1029
  Bear (G-220)
Faithful Friends Inc .... D 302 427-8514
  New Castle (G-9116)
First Person Arts .... G 267 402-2055
  Wilmington (G-16620)
First State Animal Center .... F 302 943-6032
  Camden (G-836)
First State Bmx .... G 302 422-4133
  Milford (G-7894)
First State Patriots Inc .... G 302 378-6092
  Middletown (G-7134)
Fledgling Fund .... G 800 839-1754
  Wilmington (G-16660)
Foundation Source Char Fdn Inc .... G 800 839-1754
  Wilmington (G-16706)
Foundation Source Philanthropi .... D 800 839-1754
  Wilmington (G-16707)
Fowler Family Charitable Foun .... G 800 839-1754
  Wilmington (G-16711)
Francis X Norton Center .... F 302 594-9455
  Wilmington (G-16724)
Frets4vetsorg .... G 302 382-1426
  Georgetown (G-4326)
Friends Hckssin Clred Schl 107 .... G 302 540-5959
  Hockessin (G-5215)
Friends Inc .... G 302 764-4488
  Wilmington (G-16753)
Friends of Belmont Hall Inc .... G 302 653-9212
  Smyrna (G-13739)
Friends of Dlwres Gmbrnus Sttu .... G 302 981-5972
  Wilmington (G-16754)
Friends of James Spadola .... G 302 383-3798
  Wilmington (G-16755)
Friends of Old Dover .... G 302 674-1787
  Dover (G-2537)
Friends of Stb .... G 302 765-2566
  Wilmington (G-16757)
Gene Tffin A Ray Fmly Fndation .... G 800 839-1754
  Wilmington (G-16830)
George K Horeis .... G 302 398-8684
  Harrington (G-4773)
Guardian General .... G 443 205-1210
  Seaford (G-13203)
H Private Foundation .... G 800 839-1754
  Wilmington (G-17020)
Harrison House Cmnty Program .... E 302 595-3370
  Newark (G-10935)
Harvest Ministries Inc .... G 302 846-3001
  Delmar (G-1600)
Help Initiative Inc .... G 302 236-7773
  Dover (G-2672)

Highland West Civic Assoc .... G 302 415-5435
  Wilmington (G-17143)
Historic Georgetown Assn .... G 302 934-8818
  Georgetown (G-4358)
Homer Foundation .... G 800 839-1754
  Wilmington (G-17187)
Huang Family Foundation .... G 800 839-1754
  Wilmington (G-17226)
Humane Animal Partners Inc .... E 302 571-0111
  Wilmington (G-17231)
I AM My Sisters Keeper .... G 302 304-1070
  New Castle (G-9225)
Iaabo .... F 302 737-4396
  Wilmington (G-17251)
Iaad .... G 302 234-0214
  Newark (G-10989)
Insightxperts LLC .... G 412 608-4346
  Dover (G-2737)
International Assn Emrgncy .... G 302 731-5705
  Newark (G-11043)
International Literacy Assn .... E 302 731-1600
  Newark (G-11046)
Iridescent Dance Alliance Assn .... G 302 244-8570
  New Castle (G-9242)
Its All Good In Delaware Inc .... G 302 698-1232
  Camden Wyoming (G-955)
Joy-Hope Foundation .... G 302 379-1209
  Wilmington (G-17594)
Keith D Stoltz Foundation .... G 302 654-3600
  Wilmington (G-17677)
Kenneth Ssan King Fndation Inc .... G 800 839-1754
  Wilmington (G-17688)
Kent Cnty Soc For The Prvntion .... F 302 698-3006
  Camden (G-866)
Khan Family Foundation Inc .... G 800 839-1754
  Wilmington (G-17711)
Killhffer Chritable Foundation .... G 302 994-4762
  Wilmington (G-17719)
Knauer Association LLC .... G 302 947-2531
  Millsboro (G-8342)
Labours of Love Inc .... G 443 593-2776
  Newark (G-11212)
Latinicida Inc .... G 302 277-6645
  Newark (G-11225)
Leonard M Elzbeth T Tnnnbaum F ..... G 302 793-4917
  Wilmington (G-17879)
Leonardo Charitable I LLC .... G 302 571-1818
  Newark (G-11246)
Lewes Senior Citizens Center .... G 302 645-9293
  Lewes (G-6200)
Llfe Fndtion Love Is For Evr .... G 302 660-1792
  Wilmington (G-17900)
Little League Baseball Inc .... G 302 276-0375
  New Castle (G-9316)
Lituation Creative Designs Inc .... F 302 494-4399
  Wilmington (G-17946)
Localsorg Inc .... G 650 441-6464
  Dover (G-2969)
Lodge Lane Assisted Living .... F 302 757-8100
  Wilmington (G-17973)
Marian Rosella Foundation Inc .... G 888 977-1937
  Newark (G-11331)
Mass For The Homeless Inc .... G 302 368-1030
  Wilmington (G-18184)
Mathletics Inc .... G 302 724-0619
  Dover (G-3030)
Meenakshi Hindu Charitable .... G 302 588-0686
  Hockessin (G-5308)
Mid Del Charity Foundation .... G 302 398-7223
  Harrington (G-4803)
Middle Run Chrtable Foundation .... G 302 658-7796
  Wilmington (G-18342)

Mile For Melanoma De .... G 302 540-8073
  Middletown (G-7369)
Millville By The Sea Mstr Cmnty .... G 302 539-2888
  Millville (G-8544)
Ministry of Caring Inc .... G 302 428-3702
  Wilmington (G-18373)
Minor League Baseball .... G 302 658-6336
  Wilmington (G-18380)
Mispillion Art League Inc .... G 302 430-7646
  Milford (G-8015)
More Foundation Group .... G 302 645-4669
  Lewes (G-6291)
Morning After Inc .... G 302 562-5190
  Hartly (G-4899)
Nacurh Inc .... F 302 722-6933
  Newark (G-11483)
Nanticoke River Arts Council .... G 302 628-2787
  Seaford (G-13309)
National Assn For Rgltory Admi .... G 302 234-4152
  Newark (G-11490)
National Association Realto .... G 302 674-8640
  Dover (G-3153)
National Guard Association Del .... F 302 326-7125
  New Castle (G-9396)
Natural Hypertension Inst Inc .... G 302 533-7704
  Newark (G-11494)
Nehemiah Gtwy Cmnty Dev Corp ...... G 302 655-0803
  Wilmington (G-18570)
Neighbors To Nicaragua Inc .... G 302 362-2642
  Wilmington (G-18573)
Noble Hearts Inc .... G 215 908-6525
  Newark (G-11560)
Norbertine Fathers .... G 302 449-1840
  Middletown (G-7409)
Nur Temple Aaonms .... G 302 328-6100
  New Castle (G-9430)
Odessa National Civic Assn .... G 302 530-1804
  Townsend (G-14045)
One At A Time Foundation .... G 800 839-1754
  Wilmington (G-18777)
Organization Innovations .... G 443 280-3009
  Lewes (G-6339)
Paws For Life Inc .... G 302 376-7297
  Middletown (G-7434)
Pay It 4-Ward Inc .... G 424 268-1127
  Newark (G-11645)
Peaceworks .... G 302 727-2464
  Milton (G-8682)
Peak Performance Athletics .... G 443 404-6049
  Magnolia (G-6773)
Peery Foundation .... G 650 644-4660
  Wilmington (G-18945)
Pencader Group LLC .... G 302 366-0721
  Newark (G-11659)
Pencader Heritage Area Assn .... G 518 578-3559
  Newark (G-11660)
Penn Acres Civic Association .... G 302 328-8500
  New Castle (G-9463)
Penn Delco Education Assn .... G 610 800-8218
  Wilmington (G-18951)
Philanthropy Delaware Inc .... G 302 588-1342
  Wilmington (G-19016)
Piedmont Baseball League Inc .... G 302 234-9437
  Hockessin (G-5345)
Pinkerton Foundation .... G 800 839-1754
  Wilmington (G-19049)
Police Athc Leag Wlmington Inc .... G 302 764-6170
  Wilmington (G-19103)
Police Athletic League .... G 302 834-8460
  Delaware City (G-1552)
Positive Otlook Gdnce Svcs Inc .... G 240 761-3460
  Camden (G-885)

87 ENGINEERING, ACCOUNTING, RESEARCH, AND MANAGEMENT SERVICES

Potomac Chesapeake Assn For C.......... G 302 225-6248
  Wilmington *(G-19132)*
Pressley Ridge Foundation................... G 302 854-9782
  Georgetown *(G-4472)*
R and L Unified Foundation................... G 302 244-1777
  Wilmington *(G-19302)*
Rebuilding Tgther Philadelphia............. G 302 234-4417
  Newark *(G-11836)*
Retrosheet Inc... G 302 731-1570
  Newark *(G-11873)*
Richard A & James F Corroon Fd.......... G 302 425-4841
  Wilmington *(G-19466)*
Richard Kren Lfrak Chrtble Fnd.............. G 302 656-2390
  Wilmington *(G-19470)*
Rising Sunset Publishing LLC............... G 877 231-5425
  Newark *(G-11889)*
Rivers Family Foundation Inc................. G 800 839-1754
  Wilmington *(G-19497)*
Rosies PH LLC.. G 630 222-5155
  Lewes *(G-6432)*
Roxana Automobile Service Cent.......... G 302 436-6202
  Frankford *(G-4140)*
Ruth Van Pelt Beebe Mem Sch Tr.......... G 302 226-9498
  Rehoboth Beach *(G-12941)*
Salvatore Seeley.................................... G 302 270-5503
  Rehoboth Beach *(G-12945)*
Science House Foundation................... G 800 839-1754
  Wilmington *(G-19703)*
Secure Americas Future Economy......... G 302 464-2687
  Middletown *(G-7547)*
Sherwood Park Civic Assn.................... G 302 994-6604
  Wilmington *(G-19797)*
Sister Cities Wilmington Inc................. G 302 383-0968
  Wilmington *(G-19844)*
Skim USA... G 302 227-4011
  Rehoboth Beach *(G-12961)*
Southeast Delco Education Assn.......... G 302 420-4888
  Middletown *(G-7590)*
Spca Sussex Chapter............................ F 302 856-6361
  Georgetown *(G-4521)*
Startup Africa Inc................................... G 302 894-8971
  Wilmington *(G-20029)*
Stop Vlnce Pryer Chain Fndtion............. G 302 513-9520
  Wilmington *(G-20082)*
Suburban Plaza Merchants Assn.......... G 302 737-8072
  Newark *(G-12116)*
Summer Lrng Collaborative Inc............. E 302 757-3940
  Wilmington *(G-20123)*
Summit Centre Tr.................................... G 302 690-7235
  Middletown *(G-7606)*
Sussex Central High Schoo................... G 304 261-2873
  Selbyville *(G-13610)*
Sussex Shores Beach Assn................... F 302 539-7511
  Bethany Beach *(G-643)*
Terrie M Wlliams Expansion Inc............ G 302 214-0685
  Wilmington *(G-20276)*
Tourette Syndrome................................. F 302 547-6306
  Middletown *(G-7654)*
Unidel Foundation Inc............................ G 302 658-9200
  Wilmington *(G-20508)*
USS Delaware....................................... G 908 910-4812
  Milford *(G-8133)*
Village Tree.. G 302 298-6349
  Wilmington *(G-20622)*
Waggies By Maggie and Friends........... G 302 598-2867
  Wilmington *(G-20667)*
Warachai Thai Boxing Assn.................. G 302 257-9794
  Rehoboth Beach *(G-13006)*
Water Is Life Kenya Inc.......................... G 302 894-7335
  Newark *(G-12348)*
What Is Your Voice Inc........................... F 443 653-2067
  Lewes *(G-6626)*

Wilmington Manor Lions Service............ F 302 322-3250
  New Castle *(G-9685)*
Wilmington Youth Rowing Assn.............. G 302 777-4533
  Wilmington *(G-20854)*
Womens Harmony Brigade Assn........... G 610 659-0096
  Middletown *(G-7733)*
Woos Foundation.................................... G 302 366-0259
  Newark *(G-12403)*
Wwwlawfrmllncorg Assn Jim Cyle......... G 803 212-4978
  Dover *(G-3878)*
Wyra.. G 302 777-4533
  Wilmington *(G-20908)*
Year Up Wlmngton Mock Intrvews......... F 302 256-7344
  Wilmington *(G-20925)*
Yes U Can Corporation........................... G 302 286-1399
  Newark *(G-12419)*

87 ENGINEERING, ACCOUNTING, RESEARCH, AND MANAGEMENT SERVICES

8711 Engineering services

160 Engineers... G 302 326-7441
  Newark *(G-9703)*
AC Group Inc... G 201 840-5566
  Wilmington *(G-14211)*
Acorn Energy Inc................................... G 410 654-3315
  Wilmington *(G-14237)*
Aecom Global LLC................................ E 213 593-8100
  Wilmington *(G-14293)*
Aecom Usa Inc....................................... D 302 781-5963
  Newark *(G-9788)*
Ag6 Engineering & Defense LLC........... G 609 480-4823
  Middletown *(G-6840)*
Amatuzio Appraisal Svcs Inc................. G 302 378-9654
  Middletown *(G-6857)*
American Hardscapes LLC.................... F 302 253-8237
  Georgetown *(G-4209)*
Ames Engineering Corp......................... F 302 658-6945
  Wilmington *(G-14455)*
Apex Engineering Inc............................. E 302 994-1900
  Wilmington *(G-14505)*
Aquasoli... G 704 696-8400
  Wilmington *(G-14518)*
Arcadis US Inc....................................... F 302 658-1718
  Wilmington *(G-14538)*
Area Wide Protective............................. G 302 455-1900
  Newark *(G-9900)*
Aries Security LLC................................ G 302 365-0026
  Wilmington *(G-14551)*
Automation Research Group LLC......... G 302 897-7776
  Newark *(G-9947)*
B E & K Inc... G 302 452-9000
  Newark *(G-9965)*
Batta Ramesh C Associates PA............ E 302 998-9463
  Wilmington *(G-14778)*
BBA USA Holdings Inc........................... G 450 464-2111
  Wilmington *(G-14793)*
Beacon Engineering LLC....................... G 302 864-8825
  Georgetown *(G-4227)*
Becker Morgan Group Inc...................... E 302 734-7950
  Dover *(G-1902)*
Blake and Vaughan Engrg Inc............... E 302 888-1780
  Wilmington *(G-14951)*
Brandywine Cad Design Inc.................. E 302 478-8334
  Wilmington *(G-15047)*
Brightfields Inc....................................... E 302 656-9600
  Wilmington *(G-15113)*
Bronswerk Marine Corp......................... G 619 813-4797
  Newark *(G-10092)*

Cda Engineering Inc.............................. G 302 998-9202
  Wilmington *(G-15290)*
Cecon Group LLC................................. G 302 994-8000
  Wilmington *(G-15294)*
Century Engineering Inc........................ E 302 734-9188
  Dover *(G-2053)*
Cgc Consulting LLC.............................. G 302 489-2280
  Wilmington *(G-15323)*
Cgc Geoservices LLC........................... F 302 489-2398
  Newark *(G-10181)*
Chip Design Systems LLC.................... E 302 307-6831
  Hockessin *(G-5161)*
Civil Consulting Engineers LLC............. G 302 824-6041
  Middletown *(G-6983)*
Civil Engineering Assoc LLC................. G 302 376-8833
  Middletown *(G-6984)*
Cobalt Pacific LLC................................. G 302 437-4761
  Townsend *(G-13973)*
Commerce Global Inc............................ G 302 478-0853
  Wilmington *(G-15545)*
Corporate Arcft Technical Svcs............. G 302 383-9400
  Wilmington *(G-15643)*
Corrosion Probe..................................... G 302 836-0165
  Newark *(G-10328)*
Corrosion Testing Laboratories.............. F 302 454-8200
  Newark *(G-10329)*
Cotten Engineering LLC........................ G 302 628-9164
  Seaford *(G-13137)*
Criterium Jagiasi Engineers................... G 302 498-5600
  Wilmington *(G-15705)*
Cybercore Holding Inc.......................... D 410 560-7177
  Wilmington *(G-15751)*
Deco Engineering Corp......................... G 302 576-6564
  Wilmington *(G-15850)*
Dedc LLC... D 302 738-7172
  Newark *(G-10405)*
Delaware Engrg & Design Corp............. E 302 738-7172
  Newark *(G-10440)*
Delta Engineering Corporation.............. E 302 325-9320
  New Castle *(G-9045)*
Delta Engineering Corporation.............. G 302 750-1065
  Newark *(G-10509)*
Diamond Mechanical Inc....................... E 302 697-7694
  Dover *(G-2291)*
Diversfied Entps Worldwide LLC........... G 888 230-3703
  Wilmington *(G-16093)*
Drafting By Design Inc.......................... G 302 292-8304
  Newark *(G-10569)*
Duffield Associates Inc......................... D 302 747-7156
  Dover *(G-2392)*
Duffield Associates LLC........................ G 302 239-6634
  Wilmington *(G-16195)*
Dupont Aviation Corp............................. E 302 996-8000
  New Castle *(G-9069)*
E2 Engineering LLC.............................. G 302 659-9090
  Smyrna *(G-13719)*
East West Engineering Inc.................... G 302 528-0652
  Bear *(G-190)*
Edc LLC... G 302 645-0777
  Lewes *(G-5948)*
Em Photonics Inc.................................. F 302 456-9003
  Newark *(G-10637)*
Enercon.. F 302 407-3179
  Wilmington *(G-16416)*
Evocati Group Corporation.................... F 206 551-9087
  Dover *(G-2468)*
Fairwinds Technologies Engrg.............. G 732 674-0094
  Newark *(G-10703)*
Fidelity Engineering............................... F 302 536-7655
  Seaford *(G-13185)*
Flowline Technologies Inc..................... G 302 256-5825
  Wilmington *(G-16669)*

87 ENGINEERING, ACCOUNTING, RESEARCH, AND MANAGEMENT SERVICES

Fluor Corp .... G 302 934-7742
Dagsboro (G-1449)

Gaichu Managed Services LLC .... G 302 232-8420
Dover (G-2553)

Garrett Mechanical & Advanced .... F 302 632-6261
Dover (G-2558)

Gcora Corp .... G 302 310-1000
Wilmington (G-16825)

Geo-Technology Associates Inc .... G 302 855-5775
Georgetown (G-4332)

George Miles & Buhr LLC .... G 302 628-1421
Seaford (G-13197)

Geosyntec Holdings LLC .... G 561 995-0900
Wilmington (G-16848)

Gif North America LLC .... G 703 969-9243
Rehoboth Beach (G-12771)

Greene Lawn & Landscape .... G 302 379-4425
Newark (G-10889)

Hardcore Cmpstes Oprations Llc .... F 302 442-5900
New Castle (G-9196)

Hillis-Carnes Engrg Assoc Inc .... F 302 744-9855
Dover (G-2680)

Hough Associates Inc .... E 302 322-7800
Newark (G-10976)

I3a LLC .... G 302 659-9090
Smyrna (G-13769)

Ibi Group (us) Inc .... C 949 833-5588
Wilmington (G-17255)

Jaed Corporation .... F 302 832-1652
Bear (G-295)

Ji DCI Jv-II .... G 302 652-4221
Wilmington (G-17544)

Johnson Mirmiran Thompson Inc .... F 302 266-9600
Newark (G-11120)

Karins Engineering Inc .... F 302 856-6699
Georgetown (G-4390)

Karins Engineering Inc .... E 302 369-2900
Newark (G-11142)

Kbr Engineering Company LLC .... D 302 452-9000
Newark (G-11147)

Kci Technologies Inc .... E 302 731-9176
Newark (G-11148)

Kercher Group Inc .... G 302 894-1098
Newark (G-11158)

Kubota Research Associates .... G 302 683-0199
Hockessin (G-5272)

Landmark Engineering Inc .... G 302 734-9597
Newark (G-11219)

Landmark Engineering Inc .... D 302 323-9377
Newark (G-11218)

Larsen Landis .... G 302 475-3175
Wilmington (G-17811)

Larson Engineering Inc .... G 302 731-7434
Newark (G-11222)

Long & Tann & D Onofrio Inc .... G 302 477-1970
Wilmington (G-17980)

Luriware Consulting Agricultur .... G 302 244-1947
Dover (G-2981)

Macintosh Engineering .... G 302 448-2000
Lewes (G-6234)

Macintosh Engineering Inc .... F 302 252-9200
Wilmington (G-18070)

Mahaffy & Associates Inc .... E 302 656-8381
Middletown (G-7322)

Marine & Energy Trading Corp .... E 857 207-7999
Wilmington (G-18130)

McBride and Ziegler Inc .... E 302 737-9138
Newark (G-11365)

McCORMICK TAYLOR INC .... G 302 738-0208
Newark (G-11367)

Merestone Consultants Inc .... F 302 226-5880
Lewes (G-6263)

Merestone Consultants Inc .... G 302 992-7900
Wilmington (G-18279)

Merit Cnstr Engineers Inc .... F 302 992-9810
Wilmington (G-18283)

Meta Mind Global Corp LLC .... G 267 471-3616
Dover (G-3069)

Mig Consulting LLC .... G 302 999-1888
Wilmington (G-18347)

Mission Support Services LLC .... F 813 494-0795
Dover (G-3101)

Momenee and Associates Inc .... G 610 527-3030
Newark (G-11438)

Morris & Ritchie Assoc Inc .... E 302 855-5734
Georgetown (G-4435)

Morris & Ritchie Assoc Inc .... F 302 326-2200
New Castle (G-9382)

Mountain Consulting Inc .... E 302 744-9875
Dover (G-3128)

Mvl Structures Group LLC .... G 302 652-7580
Wilmington (G-18498)

Network Mapping Inc .... G 310 560-4142
Wilmington (G-18597)

Northpoint Engrg Svcs LLC .... G 302 994-3907
Wilmington (G-18687)

On-Board Engineering Corp .... F 302 613-5030
New Castle (G-9433)

Oreomatic Mining Inc .... E 725 255-8895
Wilmington (G-18817)

Panelmatic Inc .... G 302 324-9193
New Castle (G-9447)

▼ Panelmatic East Inc .... F 302 324-9193
New Castle (G-9448)

Paragon Engineering Corp .... E 302 762-6010
Wilmington (G-18886)

Pelsa Company Inc .... G 302 834-3771
Newark (G-11656)

Pennoni .... D 302 234-4600
Newark (G-11663)

Pennoni Associates Inc .... G 302 655-4451
Newark (G-11664)

Phase Snsitive Innovations Inc .... F 302 286-5191
Newark (G-11680)

Poc Inc .... F 415 853-4762
Dover (G-3345)

Power Delivery Solutions LLC .... E 302 260-3114
Newark (G-11718)

Precise Alignment Mch TI Co .... G 302 832-2922
Newark (G-11722)

Pride International LLC .... F 713 789-1400
Wilmington (G-19190)

Qbeck Inspection Group .... F 302 452-9257
Newark (G-11781)

Quantum Satis Engeneering LLC .... F 302 485-5448
Wilmington (G-19288)

Quinteccent Inc .... G 443 838-5447
Selbyville (G-13595)

Rgs Technology Group LLC .... G 302 397-3169
Wilmington (G-19454)

Robert A Chagnon .... G 302 489-1932
Hockessin (G-5367)

Rummel Klepper & Kahl LLP .... E 302 468-4880
Wilmington (G-19590)

Saf Engineering LLC .... G 302 645-7400
Lewes (G-6440)

Sargent & Lundy LLC .... G 302 622-7200
Wilmington (G-19672)

Sauer Holdings Inc .... E 302 656-8989
Wilmington (G-19679)

Scott Engineering Inc .... G 302 736-3058
Dover (G-3520)

South Bowers Volunteer Fire Co .... G 302 335-4666
Milford (G-8097)

Spaceport Support Services .... G 302 524-4020
Selbyville (G-13608)

Sprocket LLC .... G 678 231-3165
Wilmington (G-19982)

Summer Consultants Inc .... F 484 493-4150
Newark (G-12118)

Suretronix Solutions LLC .... G 302 407-3146
Wilmington (G-20161)

Synerfac Inc .... F 302 324-9400
New Castle (G-9612)

Synetics Corporation .... G 302 427-0787
Wilmington (G-20188)

Taylor McCormick Inc .... F 302 897-2171
Newark (G-12163)

Tech International Corp .... G 302 478-2301
Wilmington (G-20249)

Techncal Stffing Resources LLC .... C 302 452-9933
Newark (G-12169)

Technology Transfers Inc .... G 302 234-4718
Newark (G-12171)

Telgian Corporation .... E 480 753-5444
Wilmington (G-20267)

Telgian Engrg & Consulting LLC .... F 480 282-5392
Wilmington (G-20268)

Ten Bears Environmental LLC .... G 302 731-8633
Newark (G-12178)

Tetra Tech Inc .... F 302 738-7551
Newark (G-12183)

Tetra Tech Inc .... G 302 738-7551
Newark (G-12184)

Tg Advisers Inc .... G 302 691-3330
Wilmington (G-20286)

Torrengineering LLC .... F 302 367-8365
Smyrna (G-13915)

Trinity Subsurface LLC .... E 855 387-4648
Wilmington (G-20427)

Truvision LLC .... G 267 349-4550
Wilmington (G-20451)

Tyco Engineering Tech LLC .... G 202 790-9648
Wilmington (G-20477)

U Good Enterprises LLC .... F 302 566-8038
Newark (G-12253)

Ultimate Material Spraying LLC .... G 302 723-2356
Claymont (G-1321)

Unitrack Industries Inc .... E 302 424-5050
Milford (G-8129)

Urban Engineers Inc .... G 302 689-0260
New Castle (G-9664)

URS Group Inc .... C 302 731-7824
Newark (G-12288)

Vandemark & Lynch Inc .... E 302 764-7635
Wilmington (G-20568)

VD&I Holdings Inc .... F 302 764-7635
Wilmington (G-20572)

Vector Engineering Svcs Corp .... G 609 947-2580
Millsboro (G-8493)

Veolia Envmtl Svcs N Amer LLC .... A 302 444-9172
Newark (G-12313)

Verdantas LLC .... G 302 239-6634
Lewes (G-6599)

Wallace Montgomery & Assoc LLP .... D 302 510-1080
Newark (G-12345)

Whitman Requardt and Assoc LLP .... E 302 571-9001
Wilmington (G-20772)

Woodin + Associates LLC .... F 302 378-7300
Middletown (G-7735)

Wsp USA Solutions Inc .... E 302 737-1872
Newark (G-12413)

Xcs Corporation .... G 302 514-0600
Wilmington (G-20916)

8712 Architectural services

Abha Architects Inc	E	302 658-6426
Wilmington (G-14201)

| Architecture Plus PA | G | 302 999-1614 |
Wilmington (G-14543)

◆ Balfour Beatty LLC ... G ... 302 573-3873
Wilmington (G-14721)

Becker Morgan Group Inc ... E ... 302 734-7950
Dover (G-1902)

Bernardon LLC ... F ... 302 622-9550
Wilmington (G-14848)

Brandywine Cad Design Inc ... E ... 302 478-8334
Wilmington (G-15047)

Breckstone Group Inc ... G ... 302 654-3646
Wilmington (G-15099)

Buck Simpers Archt + Assoc Inc ... F ... 302 658-9300
Wilmington (G-15141)

Cadrender Inc ... G ... 302 657-0700
Wilmington (G-15188)

Cooperson Associates LLC ... G ... 302 655-1105
Wilmington (G-15633)

Davis Bowen & Friedel Inc ... E ... 302 424-1441
Milford (G-7847)

Delaware Architects LLC ... G ... 302 491-6047
Milford (G-7852)

Design Collaborative Inc ... F ... 302 652-4221
Wilmington (G-16024)

Edc LLC ... G ... 302 645-0777
Lewes (G-5948)

G A Hastings & Associates ... G ... 302 537-5760
Ocean View (G-12516)

Gilbert Architects Inc ... F ... 302 449-2492
Middletown (G-7160)

Homsey Architects Inc ... F ... 302 656-4491
Wilmington (G-17192)

J Matthew Pearson LLC ... G ... 302 834-4595
Newark (G-11073)

Jaed Corporation ... F ... 302 832-1652
Bear (G-295)

Ji DCI Joint Venture 1 ... G ... 302 652-4221
Wilmington (G-17543)

Ji DCI Jv-II ... G ... 302 652-4221
Wilmington (G-17544)

Kci Technologies Inc ... E ... 302 731-9176
Newark (G-11148)

Krn Architecture LLC ... G ... 302 536-8576
Wilmington (G-17758)

Montchanin Design Group Inc ... E ... 302 652-3008
Wilmington (G-18421)

Ryan Architecture LLC ... G ... 302 629-6458
Seaford (G-13382)

Sea Studio Architects ... G ... 302 364-0821
Bethany Beach (G-641)

Simpsons Log Homes Inc ... G ... 302 674-1900
Dover (G-3566)

Staikos Associates Architects ... G ... 302 764-1678
Wilmington (G-20004)

Tevebaugh Associates Inc ... F ... 302 984-1400
Wilmington (G-20281)

Zeribon Holding Group LLC ... C ... 844 205-1999
Dover (G-3899)

8713 Surveying services

Adams Kemp Associates Inc ... G ... 302 856-6699
Newark (G-9762)

Amplified Gchmical Imaging LLC ... F ... 302 266-2428
Newark (G-9853)

Axis Geospatial ... G ... 302 276-0160
New Castle (G-8837)

Batta Ramesh C Associates PA ... E ... 302 998-9463
Wilmington (G-14778)

Braun Engineering & Surveying ... G ... 302 698-0701
Camden Wyoming (G-919)

Clifton L Bakhsh Jr Inc ... F ... 302 378-8009
Middletown (G-6993)

Coast Survey ... G ... 302 645-7184
Lewes (G-5836)

Compass Point Associates LLC ... G ... 302 684-2980
Harbeson (G-4690)

Davis Bowen & Friedel Inc ... E ... 302 424-1441
Milford (G-7847)

Design Consultants Group LLC ... E ... 302 684-8030
Milton (G-8602)

F Pete Lisinski Land Surveyor ... G ... 302 378-3200
Middletown (G-7118)

Florian P Lisinski Inc ... G ... 302 378-3200
Middletown (G-7137)

Fuller Aerial Solutions LLC ... G ... 302 734-1541
Dover (G-2543)

Land Tech Associates Inc ... F ... 301 277-8878
Selbyville (G-13560)

Landmark Engineering Inc ... G ... 302 734-9597
Newark (G-11219)

Landmark Engineering Inc ... D ... 302 323-9377
Newark (G-11218)

Landtech LLC ... G ... 302 539-2366
Ocean View (G-12536)

Lewis Miller Inc ... G ... 302 629-9895
Seaford (G-13259)

Merestone Consultants Inc ... F ... 302 226-5880
Lewes (G-6263)

Merestone Consultants Inc ... G ... 302 992-7900
Wilmington (G-18279)

Morris & Ritchie Assoc Inc ... E ... 302 855-5734
Georgetown (G-4435)

Morris & Ritchie Assoc Inc ... F ... 302 326-2200
New Castle (G-9382)

Robert Larimore ... G ... 302 730-8682
Camden Wyoming (G-971)

Rod-AES Surveryors Co ... G ... 302 993-1059
Wilmington (G-19548)

Scott Engineering Inc ... G ... 302 736-3058
Dover (G-3520)

Simpler Surveying & Associates ... G ... 302 539-7873
Frankford (G-4144)

True North Group LLC ... F ... 302 539-2488
Frankford (G-4155)

Woodin + Associates LLC ... F ... 302 378-7300
Middletown (G-7735)

8721 Accounting, auditing, and bookkeeping

855 Inc ... G ... 302 325-9100
Historic New Castle (G-4916)

Accusheets ... G ... 302 266-1047
Newark (G-9753)

Adam R Necelis CPA LLC ... G ... 302 322-1135
Historic New Castle (G-4920)

Add-Inscom LLC ... G ... 302 584-1771
Hockessin (G-5114)

Advantdge Hlthcare Sltions Inc ... F ... 302 224-5678
Newark (G-9786)

Aero Dynamic Services Inc ... G ... 302 737-4920
Middletown (G-6837)

Alma Company ... G ... 302 731-4427
Newark (G-9829)

Andrew T Patterson CPA ... G ... 302 652-4194
Wilmington (G-14478)

Arseneau Cpa LLC ... G ... 302 854-0133
Dover (G-1819)

Audit Team LLC ... G ... 302 322-0452
New Castle (G-8833)

Automotive Accounting Service ... E ... 302 378-9551
Middletown (G-6888)

Barbacane Thornton & Company ... E ... 302 478-8940
Wilmington (G-14754)

Bastianelli Group Inc ... G ... 302 658-1500
Newark (G-9989)

Bdo Usa LLP ... D ... 302 656-5500
Wilmington (G-14798)

Belfint Lyons & Shuman PA ... D ... 302 225-0600
Wilmington (G-14816)

Bench Accounting Inc ... G ... 888 760-1940
Dover (G-1909)

Benjamin Wolf Group LLC ... G ... 302 487-1827
Dover (G-1911)

Beyond Ledger LLC ... G ... 313 471-0462
Dover (G-1926)

Bookkeeping Solutions ... G ... 302 650-5058
Newark (G-10069)

Boyer & Boyer ... G ... 302 998-3700
Wilmington (G-15019)

Brae Corp ... G ... 302 691-6043
Wilmington (G-15035)

Breakwter Accnting Advsory Gro ... E ... 302 543-4564
Wilmington (G-15098)

Bumpers & Company Prof Assn ... F ... 302 798-3300
Wilmington (G-15151)

Chandler Nichol & Sloan PA ... G ... 302 478-9800
Wilmington (G-15330)

Christiana Incorporators Inc ... G ... 302 998-2008
Wilmington (G-15410)

City of Dover ... G ... 302 736-7018
Dover (G-2082)

Corcoran & Associates PA CPA ... G ... 302 478-9515
Wilmington (G-15638)

Cover & Rossiter PA ... E ... 302 656-6632
Wilmington (G-15665)

D Laverne Beiler ... G ... 302 378-4644
Dover (G-2181)

Delaware CPA-Pac Inc ... G ... 302 854-0133
Georgetown (G-4278)

Delaware Medical MGT Svcs LLC ... E ... 302 283-3300
Newark (G-10459)

Delaware Occptnal Hlth Svcs LL ... E ... 302 368-5100
Newark (G-10464)

Delaware Taxes LLC ... G ... 302 368-7040
Newark (G-10490)

Delong Zhou ... G ... 302 256-0124
Wilmington (G-15999)

Diehl & Co CPA ... G ... 302 644-4441
Lewes (G-5915)

Diehl Foraker Cpas LLC ... G ... 800 748-0354
Lewes (G-5916)

Digitizing America LLC ... G ... 315 882-9516
Historic New Castle (G-4974)

Dingle & Kane PA ... G ... 302 731-5200
Newark (G-10534)

Diversified LLC ... E ... 302 765-3500
Wilmington (G-16094)

Dixon Hughes Goodman LLP ... G ... 336 714-8100
Camden (G-821)

Doherty & Associates Inc ... F ... 302 239-3500
Wilmington (G-16119)

DSouza and Associates Inc ... E ... 302 239-2300
Hockessin (G-5193)

Elevatum Consulting LLC ... G ... 571 330-9016
Middletown (G-7091)

Elite Tax Services LLC ... G ... 302 256-0401
Wilmington (G-16366)

Ellie Tax Inc ... G ... 917 459-2762
Middletown (G-7098)

Encompass Accounting ... G ... 302 648-5488
Newark (G-10644)

Encompass Accounting Inc ... G ... 302 229-3572
Wilmington (G-16405)

Estep Ralph V Ea PA ... G ... 302 998-2008
Wilmington (G-16469)

87 ENGINEERING, ACCOUNTING, RESEARCH, AND MANAGEMENT SERVICES

Family Office Solutions L .... G 610 255-0623
  Wilmington (G-16544)
Faw Casson & Co LLP .... E 302 674-4305
  Dover (G-2489)
Faw Casson .... G 302 226-1919
  Rehoboth Beach (G-12752)
Fields & Company Inc .... G 302 234-2775
  Hockessin (G-5208)
First State Cpas LLC .... G 302 736-6657
  Dover (G-2501)
Gallagher & Associates PA .... G 302 239-5501
  Wilmington (G-16795)
Grabowski Sprano Vnclette Cpas .... G 302 999-7300
  Wilmington (G-16941)
Grc & Associates LLC .... G 770 484-9082
  Middletown (G-7173)
Gunnip & Company .... C 302 225-5000
  Wilmington (G-17007)
H & R Block Inc .... G 302 999-7488
  Wilmington (G-17013)
H&R Block Eastern Enterpres .... G 302 656-7212
  Wilmington (G-17023)
Health Care Practice MGT .... E 302 633-5840
  Wilmington (G-17096)
Horty & Horty PA .... F 302 730-4560
  Dover (G-2695)
Horty & Horty PA .... E 302 652-4194
  Wilmington (G-17213)
Hospital Blling Cllctn Svc Ltd .... B 302 552-8000
  Historic New Castle (G-5006)
Integrity Billing Specialist .... G 302 383-1704
  Smyrna (G-13772)
Jag Payments Inc .... G 800 261-0240
  Millsboro (G-8326)
Jane L Stayton CPA .... F 302 856-4141
  Georgetown (G-4378)
Jefferson Urian Dane Strner PA .... F 302 678-1425
  Dover (G-2778)
Jefferson Urian Dane Strner PA .... F 302 539-5543
  Ocean View (G-12528)
Jefferson Urian Dane Strner PA .... E 302 856-3900
  Georgetown (G-4381)
Jeffrey L Premo .... G 302 877-0468
  Seaford (G-13233)
Karen E Starr CPA .... G 302 834-1718
  Bear (G-321)
Karl Marinaccio CPA .... G 914 736-0772
  Middletown (G-7261)
Keystone Family Office Inc .... F 302 377-4500
  Newark (G-11165)
Kupferman & Associates LLC .... G 302 656-7566
  Wilmington (G-17764)
L Cor Inc .... F 302 428-3929
  Wilmington (G-17774)
Lank Johnson and Tull .... G 302 629-9543
  Seaford (G-13257)
Lank Johnson and Tull .... G 302 422-3308
  Milford (G-7971)
Lexisnexis Risk Assets Inc .... A 800 458-9410
  Wilmington (G-17889)
Luff & Associates CPA PA .... G 302 422-9699
  Milford (G-7978)
M D N Billing Consulting LLC .... G 914 376-6100
  Milford (G-7981)
M Wilson Accnting Bkkping Svc .... G 302 735-1537
  Dover (G-2992)
Maillie LLP .... F 302 324-0780
  New Castle (G-9339)
Marshall Wagner & Associates .... G 302 227-2537
  Rehoboth Beach (G-12850)
Martin Zukoff CPA .... G 302 478-4734
  Wilmington (G-18169)

Master Sidlow & Associates PA .... E 302 652-3480
  Newark (G-11351)
MDN Billing Consulting Svcs .... G 914 376-6100
  Milford (G-7991)
Medical Billing & MGT Svcs Inc .... E 610 564-5314
  Newark (G-11374)
Miller & Associates PA .... G 302 234-0678
  Wilmington (G-18364)
Mitten & Winters CPA .... F 302 736-6100
  Dover (G-3103)
Murgency Inc .... E 650 308-9964
  Dover (G-3132)
Naf Dover Afb .... G 302 677-6950
  Dover (G-3144)
Nannas Haines & Schiavo PA .... E 302 479-8800
  Wilmington (G-18526)
Office Service Solutions LLC .... G 302 420-3958
  Historic New Castle (G-5042)
Orth & Kowalick PA .... G 302 697-2159
  Dover (G-3241)
Papaleo Rosen Chelf & Pinder .... G 302 644-8600
  Lewes (G-6348)
Paths LLC .... F 302 294-1494
  Newark (G-11636)
Payroll Management Assistants .... G 302 456-6816
  Newark (G-11647)
Pcmb LLC .... G 302 482-1360
  Wilmington (G-18935)
Perioperative Services LLC .... D 302 733-0806
  Newark (G-11666)
Pfpc Worldwide Inc .... G 302 791-1700
  Wilmington (G-19005)
Pks & Company PA .... G 302 645-5757
  Lewes (G-6375)
Progar & Co .... G 302 645-6216
  Lewes (G-6394)
Raymond F Book III .... F 302 734-5826
  Dover (G-3425)
Richard L Engle Jr & Assoc PA .... G 302 674-5685
  Dover (G-3468)
Ritchie Sawyer Corporation .... F 302 475-1971
  Wilmington (G-19488)
Robert B Gregg .... G 302 994-9300
  Newport (G-12456)
Robert G Starkey CPA .... G 302 422-0108
  Milford (G-8069)
Robert Hoyt & Co .... G 302 934-6688
  Millsboro (G-8448)
Robert L Fox MST CPA .... G 302 697-7889
  Dover (G-3475)
Rockwell Associates .... G 302 655-7151
  Wilmington (G-19544)
Sandra S Gulledge CPA .... G 302 422-5005
  Milford (G-8083)
Santora CPA Group Pa .... E 302 737-6200
  Newark (G-11945)
Scassociates Inc .... F 302 454-1100
  Middletown (G-7540)
Shah & Associates PA .... G 302 999-0420
  Wilmington (G-19776)
Siegfried Group LLP .... C 302 984-1800
  Wilmington (G-19814)
Simon Mstr & Sidlow Assoc Inc .... G 302 652-3480
  Newark (G-12010)
Snyder & Company PA .... F 302 475-1600
  Wilmington (G-19903)
Stayton and Dickens LLP .... G 302 856-4141
  Georgetown (G-4525)
Stephano Slack LLC .... G 302 777-7400
  Wilmington (G-20056)
Szewczyk Company P A .... G 302 998-1117
  Wilmington (G-20196)

Tabeling & Co CPA .... G 302 999-8020
  Wilmington (G-20205)
Tax Take LLC .... G 302 760-9758
  Wilmington (G-20231)
Thomson Reuters (grc) Inc .... G 212 227-7357
  Wilmington (G-20314)
Timothy D Humphreys .... F 302 225-3000
  Wilmington (G-20331)
Tukel Inc .... F 302 520-2380
  Claymont (G-1320)
Wheeler Wolfenden & Dwares CPA .... E 302 254-8240
  Wilmington (G-20759)
Whitaker & Rago .... G 302 414-0056
  Historic New Castle (G-5101)
William B Tabeling .... G 302 234-9401
  Newark (G-12374)
Zimny & Associates PA .... G 302 325-6900
  New Castle (G-9699)

8731 Commercial physical research

Accugenix Inc .... E 302 292-8888
  Newark (G-9751)
Acp Technologies Inc .... G 302 981-5976
  Lincoln (G-6653)
Advanced Materials Technology .... G 302 477-2510
  Wilmington (G-14275)
Alantys Technology .... G 302 573-2312
  Wilmington (G-14347)
Alpha Omega Scientific LLC .... G 302 415-4499
  New Castle (G-8787)
Alphataraxia Quicksilver LLC .... G 571 367-7133
  Wilmington (G-14395)
Amino Medical Science Inc .... F 213 232-8619
  Lewes (G-5688)
▲ Amylin Pharmaceuticals LLC .... A 858 552-2200
  Wilmington (G-14466)
Anp Biopharma LLC .... E 302 283-1730
  Newark (G-9874)
Anp Technologies Inc .... E 302 283-1730
  Newark (G-9875)
Aries Security LLC .... G 302 365-0026
  Wilmington (G-14551)
▲ Arkion Life Sciences LLC .... F 800 468-6324
  New Castle (G-8822)
Becoming Bio Inc .... G 415 980-9796
  Middletown (G-6907)
Best Planet Science LLC .... G 754 200-1913
  Wilmington (G-14855)
Biomatik Usa LLC .... G 800 836-8089
  Wilmington (G-14895)
C M-Tec Inc .... G 302 369-6166
  Newark (G-10114)
Carbon Direct Inc .... F 212 742-3719
  Dover (G-2027)
Celavie Biosciences LLC .... G 516 593-5633
  Dover (G-2043)
Celsia Inc .... F 408 577-1407
  Georgetown (G-4247)
Charles River Labs Intl Inc .... F 302 292-8888
  Newark (G-10191)
Childrens Hosp Nntal Cnsrtium .... G 215 873-9492
  Dover (G-2064)
Chip Diagnostics Inc .... G 302 752-1064
  Wilmington (G-15384)
Cowie Technology Corp .... G 302 998-7037
  Wilmington (G-15672)
De Novo Foods Inc .... G 302 613-1351
  Claymont (G-1112)
Dehumidification Tech LP .... G 317 228-2000
  Wilmington (G-15858)
Delaware Innovation Space Inc .... G 302 695-2201
  Wilmington (G-15933)

87 ENGINEERING, ACCOUNTING, RESEARCH, AND MANAGEMENT SERVICES

Delaware Sstnble Enrgy Utility............ E..... 302 883-3038
  Dover (G-2262)
Delta Centric LLC.............................. F..... 302 268-9359
  Wilmington (G-16002)
Diversified Chemical Pdts Inc............. G..... 302 656-5293
  Wilmington (G-16095)
Dualitybio Inc.................................... E..... 201 486-7858
  Wilmington (G-16193)
Dupont Displays Inc........................... E..... 805 562-9293
  Wilmington (G-16206)
Ener-G Group Inc............................... F..... 917 281-0020
  Wilmington (G-16415)
Environmental Consulting Svcs........... F..... 302 378-9881
  Middletown (G-7103)
Environmental Protection Agcy............ E..... 302 739-9917
  Dover (G-2451)
Environmental Testing Inc................... G..... 302 378-5341
  Middletown (G-7104)
Fbk Medical Tubing Inc...................... F..... 302 855-0585
  Georgetown (G-4315)
First State Robotics Inc...................... G..... 302 584-7152
  Hockessin (G-5211)
Fraunhofer Usa Inc............................ D..... 302 369-1708
  Newark (G-10773)
Frontier Scientific Svcs Inc.................. E..... 302 266-6891
  Newark (G-10789)
Galaxyworks LLC............................... F..... 404 894-8703
  Dover (G-2555)
Gene Guard Inc................................. G..... 248 479-3623
  Middletown (G-7154)
Gom Technologies LLC...................... G..... 410 275-8029
  Hockessin (G-5224)
Heart To Heart Health Svcs LLC........... G..... 302 603-3976
  Dover (G-2666)
IEC... G..... 302 831-6231
  Newark (G-10996)
Incyte Corporation............................. A..... 302 498-6700
  Wilmington (G-17306)
Inventia Scientific Corp....................... G..... 888 201-0798
  Wilmington (G-17405)
Jenrin Discovery LLC......................... G..... 302 379-1679
  Wilmington (G-17530)
Leucine Inc....................................... G..... 650 534-2101
  Wilmington (G-17888)
Lightwave Logic Inc........................... G..... 302 737-6412
  Newark (G-11257)
Lila Labs Inc..................................... G..... 949 371-3978
  Middletown (G-7305)
Lithos Carbon Inc.............................. F..... 425 274-3276
  Dover (G-2956)
MMR Group Inc................................. E..... 302 328-0500
  New Castle (G-9375)
Modern Water Inc.............................. E..... 302 669-6900
  New Castle (G-9378)
Napigen Inc....................................... G..... 302 644-5464
  Wilmington (G-18532)
Neurorx Inc....................................... F..... 202 340-1352
  Wilmington (G-18604)
Neuroscience Software Inc.................. G..... 855 712-1818
  Dover (G-3176)
▲ Nichino America Inc......................... D..... 302 636-9001
  Wilmington (G-18642)
Nikang Therapeutics Inc..................... E..... 302 415-5127
  Wilmington (G-18649)
▲ Novasep LLC.................................. E..... 610 494-2052
  Wilmington (G-18695)
Nuyka Inc.. E..... 707 400-5444
  Lewes (G-6323)
Old Ayala Inc.................................... F..... 857 444-0553
  Wilmington (G-18753)
Omnimaven Inc.................................. G..... 302 378-8918
  Middletown (G-7414)

Organox Inc....................................... G..... 216 243-2202
  Wilmington (G-18820)
Panarum Corp.................................... F..... 302 994-2000
  Newark (G-11618)
Partnrship For Del Estuary Inc............. G..... 302 655-4990
  Wilmington (G-18900)
Pluribus Technologies Inc.................... G..... 302 373-2670
  Newark (G-11703)
Red Clay Inc..................................... G..... 302 239-2018
  Hockessin (G-5360)
Sdix LLC... D..... 302 456-6789
  Newark (G-11964)
Separation Methods Tech Inc.............. F..... 302 368-0610
  Newark (G-11979)
Stedim N Sartorius Amer Inc............... E..... 800 635-2906
  Newark (G-12094)
Stereochemical Inc............................. G..... 302 266-0700
  Newark (G-12100)
Streamline Technologies Inc................ G..... 302 383-3146
  Wilmington (G-20094)
Stride Services Inc............................. F..... 302 540-4713
  Wilmington (G-20099)
Sug Biosciences LLC.......................... G..... 305 735-7009
  Wilmington (G-20120)
Sun Coal & Coke LLC......................... A..... 630 824-1000
  Wilmington (G-20125)
Superbrewed Food Inc........................ F..... 302 220-4760
  New Castle (G-9606)
Synchrgnix Info Strategies LLC............ E..... 302 892-4800
  Wilmington (G-20184)
Terran Global Corporation................... G..... 702 626-5704
  Wilmington (G-6552)
Timtec LLC....................................... F..... 302 292-8500
  Newark (G-12197)
Ultrafine Technologies Inc................... G..... 302 384-6513
  Wilmington (G-20502)
Viridi Marathon LLC............................ E..... 302 647-8280
  Wilmington (G-20632)
Volvox Biologic Inc............................. G..... 801 722-5942
  Lewes (G-6609)
Wilmington Pharmatech Co LLC........... E..... 302 737-9916
  Newark (G-12381)

8732 Commercial nonphysical research

3e Marketing Solutions....................... G..... 302 383-4325
  Wilmington (G-14127)
431 Corporation................................. F..... 352 385-1427
  Bear (G-3)
Chemours Company............................ F..... 302 773-6417
  Newark (G-10196)
Circus Associates Intelligence............. E..... 757 663-7864
  Lewes (G-5820)
Convida Wireless LLC......................... G..... 302 281-3707
  Wilmington (G-15626)
Davis Index Inc.................................. E..... 732 659-0456
  Wilmington (G-15815)
Digital Wish Inc.................................. G..... 802 375-6721
  Milton (G-8605)
Diverse Generations LLC.................... G..... 571 248-1806
  Dover (G-2306)
Envision It Publications LLC................ G..... 800 329-9411
  Bear (G-204)
Fast Intrcnnect Tchologies Inc............. G..... 302 465-5344
  Dover (G-2487)
Gbc International Corp........................ G..... 404 860-2533
  Wilmington (G-16824)
Global Market Insights Inc................... G..... 302 470-2829
  Selbyville (G-13537)
Ibope Media LLC................................ G..... 305 529-0062
  Lewes (G-6112)
IMS Software Services Ltd.................. F..... 302 472-9100
  Wilmington (G-17292)

Inc Plan USA..................................... G..... 302 428-1200
  Wilmington (G-17298)
Instapanel Inc.................................... G..... 415 727-7279
  Claymont (G-1186)
Ka Analytics & Tech LLC..................... G..... 800 520-8178
  Dover (G-2828)
Kc & Associates Inc........................... G..... 302 633-3300
  Wilmington (G-17670)
Keynova Group LLC............................ F..... 410 785-6257
  Wilmington (G-17704)
Market Research Reports Inc.............. G..... 302 703-9904
  Lewes (G-6244)
Parks Associates................................ G..... 302 674-3267
  Dover (G-3275)
Pelsa Company Inc............................. G..... 302 834-3771
  Newark (G-11656)
Poc Inc... F..... 415 853-4762
  Dover (G-3345)
Pro Rfp Inc....................................... G..... 302 265-3786
  Middletown (G-7471)
Proksy Research LLC......................... F..... 737 238-0104
  Wilmington (G-19227)
Rationalstat LLC................................ F..... 302 803-5429
  Wilmington (G-19337)
Readhowyouwant LLC......................... G..... 302 730-4560
  Dover (G-3431)
▲ Remline Corp.................................. E..... 302 737-7228
  Newark (G-11850)
Reuse Everything Institute Inc............. G..... 607 351-1770
  Wilmington (G-19447)
Sahra Intl Holdings Inc....................... G..... 202 660-0090
  Lewes (G-6442)
Sanosil International LLC..................... G..... 302 454-8102
  Wilmington (G-19667)
SM Technomine Inc............................ F..... 312 492-4386
  Wilmington (G-19870)
Sparkia Inc.. G..... 302 636-5440
  Wilmington (G-19951)
Taq Incorporated................................ G..... 302 734-8300
  Dover (G-3652)
Transparency Market RES Inc.............. G..... 518 618-1030
  Wilmington (G-20400)
Unimrkt Response Inc......................... G..... 646 712-9302
  Middletown (G-7672)
W500g Inc... G..... 302 252-7279
  Middletown (G-7701)
Weekfish LLC.................................... G..... 800 979-5501
  Smyrna (G-13933)

8733 Noncommercial research organizations

A66 Inc... G..... 800 444-0446
  Wilmington (G-14180)
Analytical Biological Svcs Inc.............. E..... 302 654-4492
  New Castle (G-8806)
Avantix Labratories Inc....................... F..... 302 832-1008
  Newark (G-9951)
Carelon Research Inc......................... F..... 302 230-2000
  Wilmington (G-15243)
Ceasar Rodney Institute..................... F..... 302 542-1781
  Newark (G-10169)
Delaware Community Foundation......... G..... 302 571-8004
  Wilmington (G-15890)
Delaware Nature Society.................... E..... 302 239-1283
  Hockessin (G-5182)
Disaster Research Center................... G..... 302 831-6618
  Newark (G-10537)
Eldersafe Technologies Inc................. G..... 617 852-3018
  Lewes (G-5955)
Epic Research LLC............................. E..... 302 510-1338
  Wilmington (G-16450)
Fairness Institute............................... G..... 302 559-4074
  Newark (G-10702)

87 ENGINEERING, ACCOUNTING, RESEARCH, AND MANAGEMENT SERVICES — SIC SECTION

Galvin Industries LLC .... G 703 505-7860
  Georgetown (G-4330)
Global Institute .... G 732 776-7360
  Newark (G-10850)
Hard Science Incubator Corp .... G 302 752-1055
  Wilmington (G-17057)
Institute of Mssage Hling Arts .... G 610 357-2925
  Wilmington (G-17360)
Life-Science AI LLC .... G 438 833-8504
  Lewes (G-6206)
Medblob Inc .... G 813 308-9273
  Dover (G-3050)
Mid Atlantic Pain Institute .... G 302 369-1700
  Milford (G-7996)
Minder Foundation .... G 917 477-7661
  Lewes (G-6277)
NA Institute Christia .... G 302 478-4020
  Wilmington (G-18516)
Python Software Foundation .... F 970 305-9455
  Dover (G-3402)
Society For Acpuncture RES Inc .... G 302 222-1832
  Lewes (G-6488)
Tdm Pharmaceutical RES LLC .... G 302 832-1008
  Newark (G-12166)
Thomson Reuters (grc) Inc .... G 212 227-7357
  Wilmington (G-20314)
Tmpaa Institute Inc .... G 302 268-1010
  Wilmington (G-20340)
Towle Institute .... G 302 993-1408
  Wilmington (G-20378)
Ubinet Inc .... G 302 722-6015
  Wilmington (G-20491)
University of Delaware .... G 302 831-4811
  Newark (G-12278)
University of Delaware .... G 302 831-2833
  Newark (G-12279)
Vizzie 360 .... G 323 239-0690
  Lewes (G-6608)
Wonchin Institute .... G 302 602-5753
  Newark (G-12400)
Worldwide Clinical Trials Inc .... G 317 297-2208
  Georgetown (G-4581)
Youth Sports Institute Del Inc .... G 302 275-5947
  New Castle (G-9696)
Zinger Enterprizes Inc .... G 302 381-6761
  Laurel (G-5628)

8734 Testing laboratories

A S T B Analytical Services .... E 302 571-8882
  New Castle (G-8750)
Agrorefiner LLC .... G 212 651-4865
  New Castle (G-8773)
Alias Technology LLC .... G 302 856-9488
  Georgetown (G-4205)
Arcpoint Labs .... G 302 268-6560
  Wilmington (G-14544)
Ardex Laboratories Inc .... G 302 363-1005
  Bridgeville (G-667)
Atlantic Radon Systems Inc .... G 610 869-9066
  Dagsboro (G-1415)
Bio Reference Laboratories .... G 302 223-6896
  Smyrna (G-13662)
Biochek USA Corp .... G 302 521-5554
  Millsboro (G-8198)
Borderx Lab Inc .... G 510 203-3974
  New Castle (G-8875)
Christiana Care Health Sys Inc .... G 302 477-6500
  Wilmington (G-15400)
Compact Membrane Systems Inc .... E 302 999-7996
  New Castle (G-8963)
Corrosion Testing Laboratories .... F 302 454-8200
  Newark (G-10329)

Delaware Diagnostic Labs LLC .... E 302 407-5903
  Newark (G-10436)
Element Mtls Tech Wlmngton Inc .... F 302 636-0202
  Wilmington (G-16353)
Envirocorp Inc .... F 302 398-3869
  Harrington (G-4766)
Geo-Technology Associates Inc .... G 302 326-2100
  New Castle (G-9163)
Headland Labs LLC .... G 415 425-1997
  Wilmington (G-17089)
High Tide Lab .... G 302 538-7041
  Camden (G-850)
Integrity Testlabs LLC .... D 302 325-2365
  Historic New Castle (G-5008)
▲ Lab Products LLC .... F 302 628-4300
  Seaford (G-13255)
Lehigh Testing Laboratories .... G 302 328-0500
  New Castle (G-9302)
Micron Incorporated .... G 302 998-1184
  Wilmington (G-18330)
Midi Labs Inc .... F 302 737-4297
  Newark (G-11416)
MMR Group Inc .... G 302 328-0500
  New Castle (G-9375)
MSI .... G 302 449-5508
  Middletown (G-7387)
Nanticoke EZ Lab .... G 302 337-8571
  Bridgeville (G-736)
Quikstamp LLC .... F 302 659-7555
  Newark (G-11800)
Quinteccent Inc .... G 443 838-5447
  Selbyville (G-13595)
Radiogenic Shielding Systems .... G 302 288-0644
  Wilmington (G-19312)
Red Lion Medical Safety Inc .... G 302 731-8600
  Newark (G-11838)
Stellar Labs Inc .... F 650 868-6796
  Wilmington (G-20048)
Stereochemical Inc .... G 302 266-0700
  Newark (G-12100)
Tecniplast USA Inc .... G 484 716-2145
  Wilmington (G-20258)
▲ United Testing Systems Inc .... E 714 638-2322
  New Castle (G-9657)
Vora Labs Inc .... G 860 559-8985
  Middletown (G-7695)
Wm Systems Inc .... G 302 450-4482
  Wilmington (G-20871)

8741 Management services

1995 Property Management Inc .... G 302 745-1187
  Seaford (G-13042)
Aark Network Inc .... G 302 399-3945
  Newark (G-9734)
Adams Construction & Managemen ...... G 302 856-2022
  Georgetown (G-4198)
Advance Central Services Inc .... F 302 830-9732
  Wilmington (G-14264)
Agile 1 .... F 302 791-6900
  Wilmington (G-14315)
Agmaf Inc .... E 302 508-6991
  Wilmington (G-14321)
AGS Royalty Management LLC .... G 888 292-6995
  Dover (G-1748)
Allens Termite & Pest Mgmt .... G 302 698-1496
  Camden Wyoming (G-911)
AMC - Commercial Inc .... G 302 229-0051
  Claymont (G-1031)
Ameken Network Group Inc .... F 302 545-3472
  Claymont (G-1032)
Amity Lodges Ltd .... E 833 462-6489
  Wilmington (G-14459)

Amschel Capital LLC .... F 302 298-1199
  Claymont (G-1035)
Amschel Capital LLC .... F 302 298-1199
  Claymont (G-1036)
Anesthesiology & Pain MGT .... G 302 235-8074
  Newark (G-9867)
Antebellum Hospitality Inc .... G 302 436-4375
  Selbyville (G-13463)
Apartment Communities Corp .... G 302 656-7781
  Wilmington (G-14503)
Arbor Management Alarm .... G 302 856-2876
  Georgetown (G-4212)
Ardexo Inc .... G 855 617-7500
  Dover (G-1811)
Ashby Management Corporation .... G 302 894-1200
  Newark (G-9920)
Asset Key Management LLC .... G 302 505-4603
  Felton (G-3942)
Atlantic Management .... G 302 222-3919
  Rehoboth Beach (G-12614)
Atlantic Management Ltd .... F 302 645-9511
  Rehoboth Beach (G-12615)
Atlantic Realty Management LLC .... G 302 875-9571
  Smyrna (G-13654)
Axia Management .... F 302 674-2200
  Dover (G-1858)
◆ Balfour Beatty LLC .... G 302 573-3873
  Wilmington (G-14721)
Bancroft Vlant Joint Ventr LLC .... G 717 553-0165
  Wilmington (G-14741)
Baynard Property MGT LLC .... G 302 225-3350
  Wilmington (G-14790)
Bayshore Records MGT LLC .... G 302 731-4477
  Newark (G-9996)
Bcg Management LLC .... F 302 278-7677
  Rehoboth Beach (G-12625)
Be Beautiful Bossy .... G 888 558-9047
  Wilmington (G-14799)
Beachview Mgmt Inc .... G 302 227-3280
  Lewes (G-5744)
Beacon Wealth Management LLC .... G 302 383-2671
  Wilmington (G-14801)
BEC Capital LLC .... G 917 658-5867
  Wilmington (G-14810)
Bpgs Construction LLC .... D 302 691-2111
  Wilmington (G-15029)
Brandywine Contractors Inc .... G 302 325-2700
  New Castle (G-8886)
Brantngham Crroll Holdings Inc .... G 724 266-0400
  Wilmington (G-15095)
Bridge Enterprises LLC .... E 302 750-0828
  Wilmington (G-15106)
Brisbie LLC .... F 650 690-1433
  Wilmington (G-15118)
Brownstone LLC .... G 302 300-4370
  Historic New Castle (G-4946)
Buck Simpers Archt + Assoc Inc .... F 302 658-9300
  Wilmington (G-15141)
Business Integration Solution .... G 302 355-3512
  Newark (G-10107)
C & S Consultants Inc .... G 302 236-5211
  Milford (G-7810)
C and L Bradford and Assoc .... G 302 529-8566
  Wilmington (G-15174)
Cactus Annies Restaurant & Bar .... F 302 655-9004
  Wilmington (G-15184)
Cafe Management Associates .... G 302 655-4959
  Wilmington (G-15190)
Case Management Services .... G 302 354-3711
  Wilmington (G-15264)
Cashion Media Management .... G 302 674-8321
  Dover (G-2036)

87 ENGINEERING, ACCOUNTING, RESEARCH, AND MANAGEMENT SERVICES

Censys Inc.................................... G 248 629-0125
　Camden (G-805)
Ceo-Hqcom LLC............................ G 302 883-8555
　Hockessin (G-5155)
Chesapeake Fire Systems LLC....... F 302 732-6006
　Frankford (G-4086)
Chesapeake Management Co LLC.... E 302 732-6006
　Frankford (G-4088)
Christiana Care Health Sys Inc....... B 302 733-1601
　Newark (G-10222)
Christiana Care Health Sys Inc....... C 302 623-0390
　Newark (G-10223)
Christiana Care Health Sys Inc....... C 302 733-1000
　Wilmington (G-15404)
Cht Holdings LLC.......................... G 954 864-2008
　Lewes (G-5819)
Cloud Services Solutions Inc......... E 888 335-3132
　Wilmington (G-15491)
Cobra Investments MGT Inc.......... E 302 691-6333
　Wilmington (G-15512)
Cogir Management USA Inc........... G 916 400-3985
　Newark (G-10270)
Colonial East Management............ G 302 644-6500
　Rehoboth Beach (G-12692)
Columbus Inn Management I........ G 302 429-8700
　Wilmington (G-15541)
Commonwealth Partners MGT LLC.... F 302 223-5941
　Wilmington (G-15555)
Connor Management LLC.............. G 302 539-1678
　Ocean View (G-12497)
Construction MGT Svcs Inc............ A 302 478-4200
　Wilmington (G-15612)
Conway Management Group.......... G 302 323-9522
　New Castle (G-8971)
Corrado Management Svcs LLC..... E 302 225-0700
　New Castle (G-8977)
Craftsman Cbntry Woodworks Inc.... G 302 841-5274
　Selbyville (G-13507)
Credit Concierge LLC..................... E 877 860-9877
　Wilmington (G-15697)
Crescent Management Inc............. G 302 449-4560
　Wilmington (G-15700)
Crystal Holdings Inc...................... D 302 421-5700
　Wilmington (G-15720)
Dalou Property Management......... F 866 575-9387
　Wilmington (G-15771)
Danella Line Services Co Inc.......... D 302 893-1253
　Dover (G-2190)
Davin Management Group LLC...... F 302 367-6563
　Bear (G-135)
Ddesk LLC..................................... G 302 407-1558
　Wilmington (G-15833)
Delaware Innovation Space Inc..... G 302 695-2201
　Wilmington (G-15933)
Dis Management............................ G 302 543-4481
　Wilmington (G-16083)
Dks Sports Development LLC........ G 302 222-6184
　Newark (G-10541)
Dnrec Air Waste Management....... G 302 739-9406
　Dover (G-2315)
Dover Parks Management LLC...... G 302 326-1540
　New Castle (G-9060)
Eagle Hospitality Group LLC.......... G 302 678-8388
　Dover (G-2401)
Earthship LLC................................ G 239 850-8682
　Bear (G-188)
Eastern Christian Management..... G 302 633-1421
　Wilmington (G-16256)
Easydmarc Inc............................... G 888 563-5277
　Middletown (G-7078)
El Legacy LLC................................ G 601 790-0636
　Dover (G-2428)

El Management Group LLC........... G 844 263-3335
　Middletown (G-7088)
Elm Properties Inc........................ G 302 762-3757
　Wilmington (G-16375)
Empire Realty Management Inc.... G 302 731-0784
　Newark (G-10643)
Enabld Technologies Inc................ F 917 340-1606
　Wilmington (G-16403)
Eom Healthcare Group LLC........... E 917 750-5089
　Dover (G-2453)
Eprintit Usa Inc............................. F 613 299-7105
　Wilmington (G-16452)
Erickson Management................... G 302 235-0855
　Newark (G-10664)
Espino LLC.................................... F 855 506-3862
　Lewes (G-5975)
Everest Hotel Group LLC............... F 213 272-0088
　Camden (G-832)
Evidence Management Center...... G 302 691-8944
　Wilmington (G-16492)
F S Property Management............ G 302 644-4403
　Lewes (G-5983)
Facilities Mgmt Div....................... G 302 856-5817
　Georgetown (G-4312)
Faith Family Management Co....... G 302 832-5936
　Newark (G-10704)
Fci of Delmarva LLC..................... G 443 614-1794
　Ocean View (G-12511)
First State Cnstr MGT LLC............ G 302 257-5438
　Newark (G-10729)
First State Management LLC........ G 302 648-4600
　Georgetown (G-4323)
Fitness Management Group Inc.... G 302 218-5644
　Newark (G-10741)
Food Works Management LLC..... G 302 397-3000
　Newark (G-10755)
Four Seasons Property Manageme.... G 302 275-4816
　New Castle (G-9142)
Geodesic Management LLC.......... G 302 737-2151
　Newark (G-10822)
Glen Playa Inc............................... G 302 703-7512
　Lewes (G-6037)
Harvey Development Co............... E 302 323-9300
　New Castle (G-9201)
Hiatus Business Solutions Inc....... G 302 883-7324
　Smyrna (G-13759)
Highwater Management Kent LLC.... G 302 245-7570
　Frederica (G-4171)
Highwater MGT Sussex LLC......... G 302 245-7570
　Georgetown (G-4356)
Hlh Construction MGT Svcs Inc.... F 302 654-7508
　Wilmington (G-17157)
Howard Management Group I...... G 302 562-5051
　Newark (G-10980)
Hyas US Inc.................................. G 877 572-6446
　Wilmington (G-17242)
Hydrological Solutions................. G 302 841-4444
　Milton (G-8642)
INIIWI LLC.................................... G 866 312-4536
　Wilmington (G-17340)
Inside & Out Property MGT LLC..... G 302 632-4467
　Hartly (G-4879)
J Amoako Operation LLC.............. G 302 246-1346
　Wilmington (G-17452)
J Lotter Management.................... G 302 308-3939
　Claymont (G-1192)
J P Morgan Services Inc................ G 302 634-1000
　Newark (G-11075)
J&D Management.......................... G 302 239-2489
　Hockessin (G-5255)
Jazminerenae................................ F 302 784-4710
　Wilmington (G-17503)

Katalist LLC................................... G 302 502-0091
　Wilmington (G-17659)
Keystate Corporate MGT LLC........ F 302 425-5158
　Wilmington (G-17706)
Kubera Global Solutions LLC........ G 480 241-5124
　Wilmington (G-17762)
L C K Managment Inc................... G 609 820-2980
　Claymont (G-1210)
Lau & Assoc Ltd............................ E 302 792-5955
　Wilmington (G-17821)
Lawrence Kennedy........................ F 302 533-5880
　Newark (G-11234)
Lc Management............................ F 302 439-3523
　Claymont (G-1213)
Lemon Fin-Vest Inc....................... F 905 442-8480
　Newark (G-11244)
Lenape Builders Inc...................... F 302 376-3971
　Smyrna (G-13801)
Lifetour Solutions LLC.................. F 215 964-5000
　Wilmington (G-17906)
Lighthouse Construction Inc......... F 302 677-1965
　Magnolia (G-6759)
Locker Construction Inc................ G 302 239-2859
　Newark (G-11278)
Lutheran Community Services...... G 302 654-8886
　Wilmington (G-18031)
M C Tek LLC................................. G 302 644-9695
　Rehoboth Beach (G-12842)
Mahle Industrial Thermal Syste..... G 915 612-1611
　Wilmington (G-18087)
Marta Group................................. G 302 737-2008
　Newark (G-11340)
Mat Site Management LLC........... G 302 397-8561
　Wilmington (G-18189)
McKee Group Mckee Management.... G 302 449-0778
　Middletown (G-7334)
McNeil and Fmly MGT Group LLC.... F 302 830-3267
　Wilmington (G-18236)
Medical Billing Management......... G 302 239-2235
　Wilmington (G-18248)
Merman Management Inc............. G 302 644-6990
　Lewes (G-6266)
Merman Management Inc............. G 302 456-9904
　Wilmington (G-18286)
Michael Spradley........................... G 404 475-2647
　Wilmington (G-18325)
Mid Atlantic Grand Prix LLC......... G 302 656-5278
　New Castle (G-9365)
Mid-Lantic Enterprises Inc............ G 302 436-2772
　Selbyville (G-13572)
Mk Management Group LLC........ G 302 543-4414
　Wilmington (G-18391)
Montchanin Design Group Inc...... E 302 652-3008
　Wilmington (G-18421)
Moore Staffing Agency LLC.......... G 215 300-2770
　Bear (G-379)
Moorway Painting Management... G 302 764-5002
　Wilmington (G-18439)
Mosaic... D 302 456-5995
　Newark (G-11455)
Multifmily MGT Phladelphia LLC.... G 302 322-8953
　Newark (G-11471)
Natural House Inc......................... F 302 218-0338
　Newark (G-11493)
Nb Retail Management Inc........... G 302 230-3065
　Newark (G-11495)
Ne Care Management Service LLC.... G 302 501-6449
　Wilmington (G-18567)
Oakford Acquisitions LLC............. G 302 406-1535
　Wilmington (G-18727)
Omg Mgmt LLC............................. G 609 221-4572
　Wilmington (G-18766)

87 ENGINEERING, ACCOUNTING, RESEARCH, AND MANAGEMENT SERVICES

Omniway Corporation............................ F 302 738-5076
  Newark (G-11586)
Open Lanes-Solutions LLC.................. F 888 410-4207
  Wilmington (G-18795)
Orion Group LLC................................... G 302 357-9137
  Wilmington (G-18821)
Pallino Asset Management LLC............ G 302 378-0686
  Middletown (G-7423)
Palmetto MGT & Engrg LLC................. F 302 993-2766
  Wilmington (G-18868)
Pats Management................................. D 302 322-3442
  New Castle (G-9460)
Patterson 3 Inv Group LLC................... G 302 469-4783
  Dover (G-3283)
Patterson-Schwartz & Assoc Inc.......... F 302 234-3606
  Hockessin (G-5333)
Pcmb LLC... G 302 482-1360
  Wilmington (G-18935)
Pettinaro Management LLC................. G 302 832-8823
  Newark (G-11676)
Power Brokers Holdings LLC............... G 800 901-8483
  Hockessin (G-5350)
Ppmi Inc... F 302 584-1972
  Bear (G-432)
Premier Property & Pool MGT............. G 302 357-6321
  Middletown (G-7465)
Pro Pest Management of De Inc.......... G 302 994-2847
  Wilmington (G-19201)
Property Maintenance MGT................. G 302 883-1441
  Smyrna (G-13858)
Prorank Business Solutions LLC......... F 302 256-0642
  Wilmington (G-19232)
Prosperity Unlimited Ente.................... G 302 379-2494
  Middletown (G-7476)
Providence At Heritage Sh.................. G 302 337-1040
  Bridgeville (G-756)
Ptci Management................................. G 302 538-6996
  Dover (G-3391)
Purebread.. G 302 528-5591
  Newark (G-11774)
Pyramid Group MGT Svcs Co.............. G 302 355-1760
  New Castle (G-9503)
R & L Property Management LLC........ G 267 825-3570
  Middletown (G-7494)
Registred Agnts Legal Svcs LLC......... G 302 427-6970
  Wilmington (G-19409)
Rfpmart LLC... F 315 627-3333
  Wilmington (G-19450)
Roberts Property MGT LLC................. G 302 537-5371
  Bethany Beach (G-637)
Rosemont Wealth Management........... G 302 875-8300
  Laurel (G-5595)
S A Atramco... G 302 310-3350
  Wilmington (G-19606)
Saggio Management Group Inc........... G 302 659-6560
  Smyrna (G-13876)
Saggio Management Group Inc........... F 302 696-2036
  Middletown (G-7535)
Service General Corporation............... F 302 218-4279
  Georgetown (G-4507)
◆ Severn Trent Inc............................... F 302 427-5990
  Wilmington (G-19771)
Six Plus Inc... G 302 652-3296
  Wilmington (G-19848)
Smart Printing MGT LLC..................... G 855 549-4900
  Newark (G-12035)
SNK Enterprises Inc........................... G 443 783-5717
  Laurel (G-5601)
Sodel Concepts II LLC......................... C 302 228-3786
  Rehoboth Beach (G-12965)
Soules Management Inc..................... G 302 335-1980
  Magnolia (G-6783)

Southern Rivers Management LLC........ G 302 674-4089
  Dover (G-3591)
Sovereign Property MGT LLC................ G 302 994-2505
  Wilmington (G-19944)
Speech Ladder Inc................................. G 770 355-0719
  Townsend (G-14069)
St Anthonys Housing Mgt Corp............. G 302 421-3756
  Wilmington (G-19991)
Strands Prprty Prservation LLC............. G 302 381-9792
  Millsboro (G-8469)
Sunset Property Management................ G 410 202-1679
  Wilmington (G-20135)
Supply Chain Mgmt Inc........................... E 302 467-2014
  Wilmington (G-20150)
◆ Syngenta Corporation......................... E 302 425-2000
  Wilmington (G-20189)
Tdc Partners Ltd.................................... G 302 827-2137
  Lewes (G-6544)
Teksolv Usd Inc..................................... F 302 738-1050
  Newark (G-12175)
Tgx Holdings LLC................................... C 212 260-6300
  Wilmington (G-20289)
Thepowermba Inc................................... G 917 508-5535
  Newark (G-12188)
Timet Finance Management Co............. F 302 472-9277
  Wilmington (G-20329)
Tm Management LLC............................. G 302 654-4940
  Wilmington (G-20339)
Totaltranslogistics LLC........................... G 302 325-4245
  New Castle (G-9629)
Tpw Management LLC........................... G 302 227-7878
  Lewes (G-6575)
Twin Hearts Management LLC.............. G 302 777-5700
  Dover (G-3736)
Ubium Group... A 801 487-5000
  Wilmington (G-20492)
Unique Business Solutions.................... G 302 750-0930
  Bear (G-548)
Unity Construction Inc........................... F 302 998-0531
  Wilmington (G-20531)
Urpayroll Inc.. G 323 922-3829
  Wilmington (G-20546)
Vanguard Construction MGT................. G 302 462-2161
  Georgetown (G-4567)
Vest Management Inc........................... G 302 856-3100
  Georgetown (G-4569)
VIP Systems Inc................................... G 786 615-8622
  Wilmington (G-20628)
Volumetric Format Association.............. G 760 803-8720
  Dover (G-3809)
Walnut Green Asset MGT LL................. G 302 689-3798
  Wilmington (G-20673)
We Manage Your Site Inc...................... G 916 586-7724
  Newark (G-12351)
Wellington Management Group.............. G 215 569-8900
  Wilmington (G-20719)
Wh &C Management Services Inc.......... G 302 225-3000
  Wilmington (G-20752)
Whispering Meadows LLC..................... G 302 698-1073
  Dover (G-3844)
Winifred Ellen Erbe................................ G 302 541-0889
  Frankford (G-4162)
Wohlsen Construction Company............ F 302 324-9900
  Wilmington (G-20874)

8742 Management consulting services

1st-Recruit LLC..................................... F 732 666-4106
  Wilmington (G-14117)
247 Digimedia Inc................................. E 302 401-6869
  Dover (G-1682)
280 Group LLC..................................... E 408 834-7518
  Dover (G-1683)

360 Digital Marketing LLC........................ G 214 247-7153
  Lewes (G-5638)
924 Inc.. E 302 656-6100
  Hockessin (G-5109)
A-To-Z Management LLC......................... G 302 500-5230
  Dover (G-1699)
A1g0 LLC.. E 855 661-0101
  Wilmington (G-14178)
AA Media Inc.. G 302 729-2882
  Middletown (G-6825)
AA Smith & Associates LLC.................... F 973 477-3052
  Middletown (G-6826)
Abeks Financial Consulting LLC.............. G 302 351-5910
  Wilmington (G-14199)
Above and Beyond Coverage LLC.......... E 201 417-5189
  Wilmington (G-14207)
Accenture... D 302 830-5800
  Wilmington (G-14218)
Access Purchasing Network Inc.............. G
  Lewes (G-5651)
Accurate Media LLC................................ G 301 943-9428
  Lewes (G-5653)
Acer Synergy Tech America Corp............ G 267 901-4569
  Wilmington (G-14230)
ADd Marketing Group LLC...................... G 347 668-0992
  Dover (G-1716)
Adex Corporation..................................... G 703 618-9670
  Dover (G-1717)
Adjuvant Research Services Inc............. F 302 737-5513
  Newark (G-9766)
ADP Pacific Inc.. E 302 657-4060
  Wilmington (G-14260)
Advanced Systems Inc............................ G 302 368-1211
  Newark (G-9782)
Affinity Wealth Management.................... E 302 652-6767
  Wilmington (G-14306)
Agents and Corporations Inc.................. G 302 575-0877
  Wilmington (G-14312)
Air Conditioning Products LLC................ G 800 483-1140
  Dover (G-1755)
Aljstar Global Holdings Inc..................... F 302 565-5249
  Newark (G-9812)
Alliance Bus Dev Concepts LLC............. F 803 814-4004
  Clayton (G-1348)
Alpha Net Consulting LLC....................... G 302 737-2532
  Newark (G-9834)
Altea Resources LLC.............................. F 713 242-1460
  Dover (G-1776)
Alvini & Assoc Fincl Planners................. G 302 397-8135
  Wilmington (G-14403)
America Group... G 302 529-1320
  Wilmington (G-14423)
American Air Lease Finance LLC........... G 646 643-6303
  Wilmington (G-14424)
American Marketing Agency Inc............. F 484 424-9683
  Wilmington (G-14436)
Arbiter Inc... G 404 939-2826
  Newark (G-9898)
Arm Chair Scouts LLC............................ F 315 360-8692
  Wilmington (G-14552)
Armehtech Solutions LLC....................... D 302 309-9645
  Wilmington (G-14554)
Ascension Industries LLC....................... G 302 659-1778
  Smyrna (G-13648)
Aston Digital LLC.................................... E 323 286-4365
  Lewes (G-5709)
Ath Solutions LLC................................... G 888 861-6657
  Newark (G-9930)
Atlantic H&S Consulting......................... G 302 222-5526
  Magnolia (G-6719)
Atom Tech Inc... G 510 789-3045
  Middletown (G-6885)

SIC SECTION — 87 ENGINEERING, ACCOUNTING, RESEARCH, AND MANAGEMENT SERVICES

Atrifico LLC .... G 302 858-0161
  Rehoboth Beach *(G-12617)*
Attabotics (us) Corp .... E 403 454-0995
  Wilmington *(G-14636)*
Austin Alliance Electric Inc .... E 843 297-8078
  Wilmington *(G-14647)*
▲ Avalanche Strategies LLC .... C 302 436-7060
  Selbyville *(G-13469)*
Avenue Montaigne Inc .... F 310 926-6678
  Wilmington *(G-14667)*
Avontro Inc .... G 510 766-2803
  Wilmington *(G-14674)*
B Merit Co .... F 888 263-7481
  Dover *(G-1863)*
B&P Brown & Partners Corp .... G 302 703-0522
  Lewes *(G-5732)*
Base Carriers LLC .... G 215 559-1132
  Wilmington *(G-14771)*
Base-2 Solutions LLC .... D 202 215-2152
  Lewes *(G-5735)*
Bcg Holding Corp .... E 617 850-3700
  Wilmington *(G-14795)*
Bcg Inc .... G 302 875-6013
  Laurel *(G-5468)*
Beacon Technologies LLC .... F 302 438-9728
  Bear *(G-60)*
Beane Assoc Inc .... G 302 559-1452
  Wilmington *(G-14803)*
Bear Financial Group LLC .... G 302 735-9909
  Dover *(G-1899)*
Beholder Agency LLC .... F 302 455-2451
  Newark *(G-10011)*
Bene Market LLC .... G 717 357-4117
  Wilmington *(G-14830)*
Benepass Inc .... G 917 540-2391
  Claymont *(G-1057)*
Beyond Expected LLC .... E 302 384-1205
  Claymont *(G-1061)*
Bhakti Consulting LLC .... G 302 742-1964
  Dover *(G-1930)*
Bhaoo Inc .... E 832 888-3694
  Dover *(G-1931)*
Big Tomorrow LLC .... F 650 714-3912
  Wilmington *(G-14883)*
Bingebuilder Inc .... E 415 529-8306
  Rehoboth Beach *(G-12644)*
Biobx Ltd .... G 626 898-5814
  Middletown *(G-6920)*
Biomarker Associates Inc .... F 302 239-7962
  Newark *(G-10035)*
Black Lotus Ventures LLC .... F 650 260-4684
  Dover *(G-1944)*
Blackwell Hr Solutions .... G 202 246-0084
  Wilmington *(G-14949)*
Bless Ya Hart Cnslting Group L .... F 844 748-9017
  Wilmington *(G-14955)*
Blokhaus Inc .... E 302 932-7704
  Newark *(G-10054)*
Bloom Consulting .... G 302 584-1592
  Wilmington *(G-14961)*
Blue Dmnd Hldg Investments LLC ... G 302 588-8946
  Wilmington *(G-14965)*
Blue Horizon Properties LLC .... G 347 731-5570
  Magnolia *(G-6721)*
Blue Level Inc .... G 337 623-4442
  Newark *(G-10061)*
Blue River Resources LLC .... E 302 652-3150
  Wilmington *(G-14972)*
Bnl Consulting LLC .... G 302 857-1057
  Dover *(G-1955)*
Bot Workshop LLC .... G 888 228-8799
  Middletown *(G-6932)*

BP Staffing Inc .... F 302 999-7213
  Wilmington *(G-15021)*
Bradsworth Digital Solutions .... G 630 200-2251
  Wilmington *(G-15033)*
Brim Prtners Cnslting Group In .... G 657 234-7424
  Wilmington *(G-15117)*
Browns Unlimited 4u LLC .... G 800 940-5880
  Wilmington *(G-15131)*
Brs Consulting Inc .... G 302 786-2326
  Harrington *(G-4741)*
Byron & Davis Cccc .... G 302 792-2334
  Wilmington *(G-15166)*
C-Stacks Inc .... G 617 480-2555
  Dover *(G-15179)*
Can Services LLC .... G 212 920-9348
  Newark *(G-10127)*
Canadian Sunpal Power LLC .... G 905 926-6681
  Lewes *(G-5788)*
Casper Hosting LLC .... G 480 442-7112
  Lewes *(G-5807)*
Cast .... G 781 245-2212
  Newark *(G-10160)*
Ce Buys LLC .... G 650 245-6238
  Dover *(G-2041)*
Cg Global MGT Solutions LLC .... F 215 735-3745
  Wilmington *(G-15321)*
Charles Graef Inc .... G 302 239-7924
  Montchanin *(G-8735)*
Chopin Imports Ltd .... F 612 226-9875
  Wilmington *(G-15391)*
Christina River Exchange LLC .... G 302 691-2139
  Wilmington *(G-15416)*
Circus Associates Intelligence .... E 757 663-7864
  Lewes *(G-5820)*
Clever ME Inc .... G 832 866-8866
  Wilmington *(G-15479)*
Cliktrucom .... G 302 827-1103
  Lewes *(G-5828)*
Clms LLC .... G 703 629-3231
  Rehoboth Beach *(G-12679)*
Cloud Financial Corporation .... G 845 729-5513
  Wilmington *(G-15489)*
Cloud Services Solutions Inc .... E 888 335-3132
  Wilmington *(G-15491)*
Clr Marketing Services LLC .... F 302 688-9059
  Wilmington *(G-15498)*
CMC-Kuhnke Inc .... G 302 613-5600
  New Castle *(G-8955)*
Code Guide LLC .... G 530 424-8919
  Wilmington *(G-15514)*
▲ Company Corporation .... E 302 636-5440
  Wilmington *(G-15566)*
Compete Hr Inc .... E 310 989-9857
  Wilmington *(G-15569)*
Conducerent Incorporated .... G 302 543-8525
  Wilmington *(G-15588)*
Congruence Consulting Group .... G 320 290-6155
  Newark *(G-10304)*
Connecting Generations Inc .... F 302 656-2122
  Wilmington *(G-15599)*
Connectnow Vrtual Call Ctr LLC .... E 888 226-4130
  Wilmington *(G-15602)*
Conspiracy Theory LLC .... G 201 566-1069
  Newark *(G-10309)*
Convergence Group Inc .... F 302 234-7400
  Wilmington *(G-15625)*
Core Functions LLC .... G 443 956-9266
  Selbyville *(G-13506)*
Core Value Global LLC .... G 908 312-4070
  Wilmington *(G-15641)*
Corporate Loyalty LLC .... G 732 455-9266
  Newark *(G-10327)*

Countrmsres Assssment SEC Expr .. G 302 322-9600
  Middletown *(G-7015)*
CR&us LLC .... G 678 429-6293
  Newark *(G-10342)*
Creativity Diversified LLC .... G 302 897-5961
  Middletown *(G-7021)*
Creatopy Inc .... D 339 217-6684
  Dover *(G-2155)*
Crimson Strategy Group LLP .... G 302 503-5698
  Dover *(G-2159)*
Csi Solutions LLC .... F 202 506-7573
  Newark *(G-10360)*
Dailey Resources .... G 302 655-1811
  Wilmington *(G-15767)*
Daimlerchrysler N Amrca Financ ..... F 302 292-6840
  Newark *(G-10381)*
Dale Carnegie Training .... G 302 368-7292
  Newark *(G-10383)*
Dane & Cash Enterprise LLC .... F 302 281-4031
  Wilmington *(G-15779)*
Data Systems & Solutions LLC .... E 858 826-5995
  Wilmington *(G-15797)*
David G Major Associates Inc .... G 703 642-7450
  Millsboro *(G-8255)*
Dduberry LLC .... G 703 798-5280
  Newark *(G-10398)*
De Catering Inc .... E 302 607-7200
  Wilmington *(G-15837)*
Decennium Management Group ...... G 302 600-3644
  Dover *(G-2205)*
Decisivedge LLC .... D 302 299-1570
  Newark *(G-10404)*
Defendant Data Solutions LLC .... G 302 440-3042
  Wilmington *(G-15855)*
Dehui Solar Power Inc .... G 864 326-7936
  Dover *(G-2208)*
Delaware Enterprises Inc .... F 302 324-5660
  New Castle *(G-9022)*
Delaware Incorporation Svcs .... F 302 658-1733
  Wilmington *(G-15930)*
Delaware Intercorp Inc .... G 302 266-9367
  Wilmington *(G-15934)*
Delaware Labor Resources Inc .... G 302 377-5752
  Wilmington *(G-15936)*
Delaware Last Mile Lgstics DLM ...... G 302 407-1415
  Historic New Castle *(G-4971)*
Delaware Marketing Partners .... G 302 575-1610
  Wilmington *(G-15939)*
Delaware Mfg EXT Partnr Inc .... G 302 283-3131
  Newark *(G-10460)*
Delaware Property Mgmt Co LLC .... G 302 366-0208
  Newark *(G-10472)*
Delaware State Education Assn ...... F 302 734-5834
  Dover *(G-2263)*
Design Tribe Republic LLC .... F 302 918-5279
  Wilmington *(G-16027)*
Dewitt & Associates LLC .... G 302 226-0521
  Rehoboth Beach *(G-12723)*
Diablo Works LLC .... E 302 559-2118
  Wilmington *(G-16046)*
Diamond State Fincl Group Inc .... D 302 366-0366
  Newark *(G-10526)*
Diga Funding LLC .... G 404 631-7127
  Dover *(G-2295)*
Discover Permaculture LLC .... G 850 970-7376
  Middletown *(G-7063)*
Displayplan Inc .... G 502 767-1946
  Wilmington *(G-16088)*
Divinity Assets LLC .... G 323 508-4130
  Dover *(G-2309)*
Divinity Assets LLC .... D 323 508-4130
  Dover *(G-2310)*

Employee Codes: A=Over 500 employees, B=251-500
C=101-250, D=51-100, E=20-50, F=10-19, G=1-9

2024 Harris Directory of Delaware Businesses

87 ENGINEERING, ACCOUNTING, RESEARCH, AND MANAGEMENT SERVICES — SIC SECTION

DJT Operations LLC .... G 302 498-9070
  Wilmington (G-16102)
Dmg Marketing Inc .... F 302 575-1610
  Wilmington (G-16108)
Dojupa LLC .... G 302 300-2009
  Wilmington (G-16121)
Dorey Financial Services Inc .... G 302 856-0970
  Georgetown (G-4297)
Douglas C Loew & Associates .... G 302 453-0550
  Newark (G-10555)
Dreamville LLC .... G 662 524-0917
  Lewes (G-5935)
Dss Sstnable Solutions USA Inc .... E 800 532-7233
  Wilmington (G-16184)
Dynamic Devices LLC .... F 302 994-2401
  Wilmington (G-16228)
Eamo Health LLC .... G 302 565-7528
  Wilmington (G-16247)
East Coast Computer Cons .... G 302 945-5089
  Millsboro (G-8279)
Eastmoor Digital .... G 302 514-7002
  Smyrna (G-13720)
Easy Trade LLC .... G 334 577-4530
  Dover (G-2415)
Ecsquared Inc .... G 302 750-8554
  Newark (G-10607)
Edmonds Business Ventures LLC .... G 302 772-9112
  Newark (G-10610)
El Diablo .... G 302 691-3081
  Wilmington (G-16348)
Elate Partners LLC .... G 408 335-4582
  Dover (G-2429)
Emergent Frest Fin Acclrtor In .... F 347 796-4450
  Wilmington (G-16391)
Emory Hill & Company .... D 302 322-4400
  New Castle (G-9090)
Enhanced Corporate Prfmce LLC .... G 302 545-8541
  Newark (G-10648)
Epic Marketing Cons Corp .... E 302 285-9790
  Middletown (G-7105)
Erban Mndset Lfstyle Sltons In .... F 407 608-0134
  Wilmington (G-16454)
Evander Grey Group LLC .... G 302 595-1402
  Dover (G-2467)
Even & Odd Minds LLC .... F 949 246-4789
  Claymont (G-1138)
Even & Odd Minds LLC .... F 619 663-7284
  Wilmington (G-16482)
Evolution Cloud Services Inc .... G 516 507-4026
  Dover (G-2469)
Express Legal Documents LLC .... G 212 710-1374
  Wilmington (G-16509)
F D Hammond Enterprises Inc .... F 302 424-8455
  Milford (G-7886)
Fabrics and Textiles LLC .... G 507 369-2641
  Wilmington (G-16524)
Factori Inc .... G 682 392-3913
  Wilmington (G-16526)
Fair Square Financial LLC .... D 571 205-0305
  Wilmington (G-16529)
Fbh Business Consulting LLC .... G 267 266-8149
  Wilmington (G-16563)
Femmepal Corporation .... G 888 406-0804
  Lewes (G-5993)
Finance Business Solutions LLC .... G 646 707-1290
  Wilmington (G-16607)
Financial House Inc .... E 302 654-5451
  Wilmington (G-16608)
Financial Services .... E 302 478-4707
  Wilmington (G-16609)
Fiscal Associates .... F 302 894-0500
  Newark (G-10740)

Five Sixty Enterprise LLC .... E 302 268-6530
  Wilmington (G-16653)
Five Star Home Delivery LLC .... F 302 213-3535
  Lewes (G-6002)
Fort Hill Company Inc .... G 302 651-9223
  Wilmington (G-16696)
Founding Principals LLC .... G 917 693-7533
  Bear (G-233)
Fountain Resurgence LLC .... F 302 518-5659
  Newark (G-10768)
Fox Logistics LLC .... G 302 444-4750
  Wilmington (G-16712)
Franklin Kennet LLC .... G 302 655-6536
  Wilmington (G-16729)
Fresh Healthy Markets LLC .... G 484 748-4791
  Newark (G-10782)
Fulcrum Assets LLC .... G 615 278-0969
  Dover (G-2542)
G5 Cyber Security (usa) Inc .... E 302 570-0905
  Middletown (G-7148)
Garritz Advertising LLC .... G 347 607-7030
  Dover (G-2560)
Gateway International 360 LLC .... F 302 250-4990
  Bear (G-246)
Gavinsolmonese .... G 302 655-8997
  Wilmington (G-16819)
Genovesius Solutia Llc .... G 302 252-7506
  Hockessin (G-5221)
Geological Survey US Dept .... F 302 734-2506
  Dover (G-2572)
GIERD INC .... E 206 289-0011
  Wilmington (G-16858)
Gkua Inc .... F 415 971-5341
  Wilmington (G-16873)
Global Infrstrcture Sltons Inc .... G 808 381-3666
  Dover (G-2591)
Goldenpgsus It Cnslting Svcs L .... G 804 742-0710
  Newark (G-10863)
Government Mrktplace Ltd Lblty .... G 302 297-9694
  Newark (G-10872)
Grand Designs It Solutions LLC .... G 302 299-3500
  Newark (G-10879)
Gravity-Techinc LLC .... G 346 258-1597
  Lewes (G-6054)
Gredell & Associates PA .... G 302 996-9500
  Newark (G-10887)
Green Interest Enterprises LLC .... G 228 355-0708
  Dover (G-2624)
Green River Consulting LLC .... G 302 494-4497
  Hockessin (G-5228)
Grind or Starve LLC .... G 302 322-1679
  Wilmington (G-16981)
Grofos International LLC .... G 302 635-4805
  Newark (G-10901)
Growth River Usa LLC .... G 617 905-5156
  Wilmington (G-16990)
Gulf Development Partners LLC .... G 646 334-1245
  Wilmington (G-17005)
Gwp Group LLC .... E 888 217-4497
  Newark (G-10910)
H&R Block Eastern Enterpres .... G 302 656-7212
  Wilmington (G-17023)
Haccp Navigator LLC .... G 302 531-7922
  Lincoln (G-6673)
Harvey Hanna & Associates Inc .... G 302 323-9300
  Newport (G-12454)
Health Care Practice MGT .... E 302 633-5840
  Wilmington (G-17096)
Heavenly Effects LLC .... G 302 446-3521
  Dover (G-2667)
Hnh Holdings LLC .... G 415 548-3871
  Dover (G-2683)

Hook PR Group .... G 302 858-5055
  Lewes (G-6103)
How Medical Marketing Inc .... F 302 283-9565
  Dover (G-2697)
Howard Morris Group LLC .... G 877 296-4726
  Dover (G-2698)
Human Resources .... G 302 573-3126
  Wilmington (G-17230)
Hybrid Property LLC .... F 302 289-6226
  Wilmington (G-17243)
I Need It I Want It LLC .... G 888 299-1341
  Wilmington (G-17249)
Ibr Group Inc .... F 610 986-8545
  Newark (G-10992)
Iconic Skus LLC .... G 302 722-4547
  Wilmington (G-17257)
Ignis Group LLC .... E 302 645-7400
  Lewes (G-6115)
IMG Universe LLC .... G 212 774-6704
  Wilmington (G-17283)
In Wilmington Mktg Group Inc .... G 302 495-9456
  Wilmington (G-17294)
Incredo Us LLC .... G 530 586-8995
  Lewes (G-6121)
Independent School MGT Inc .... E 302 656-4944
  Wilmington (G-17310)
Indus Insights US Inc .... G 312 238-9815
  Wilmington (G-17313)
Infinity Intellectuals Inc .... E 302 565-4830
  Wilmington (G-17324)
Inkwhy Inc .... G 267 243-8498
  Wilmington (G-17344)
Innovtive Cpitl Cnslting Group .... G 202 670-0797
  Lewes (G-6125)
Instellars Globl Cnsulting Inc .... G 302 613-4379
  Wilmington (G-17359)
Intelhouse Marketing LLC .... F 213 438-9667
  Lewes (G-6130)
Intellectual LLC .... G 202 769-1986
  Dover (G-2743)
Intellgent Sltions Aliance LLC .... E 754 300-0051
  Claymont (G-1187)
Intercontinental Marketing .... G 302 429-7555
  Wilmington (G-17378)
Interfacing Bus Solutions Inc .... G 514 962-1344
  Wilmington (G-17382)
Intrinsic Partners LLC .... F 610 388-0853
  Wilmington (G-17401)
Intrinsic Realty LLC .... G 302 425-1025
  Middletown (G-7230)
Ipwe Inc .... E 214 438-0820
  Dover (G-2751)
Iris Diagnostics Incorporated .... F 877 292-4747
  Dover (G-2752)
It Tigers LLC .... G 732 898-2793
  Lewes (G-6132)
J & O Business Inc .... G 917 504-6062
  Newark (G-11066)
J & S - LOE Incorporated .... G 302 608-7858
  Middletown (G-7234)
Jack Donovan .... G 410 715-0504
  Millsboro (G-8324)
Jazminerenae .... F 302 784-4710
  Wilmington (G-17503)
JC&a Trust .... E 302 579-0886
  Dover (G-2777)
Jira LLC .... G 302 202-4615
  Dover (G-2790)
JMJ Assoc .... G 410 320-0890
  Lewes (G-6141)
Joff Capital LLC .... G 216 682-6822
  Dover (G-2795)

87 ENGINEERING, ACCOUNTING, RESEARCH, AND MANAGEMENT SERVICES

Johnston Associates .... G 302 521-2984
  Newark *(G-11121)*
Jolttek Inc .... G 302 204-7629
  Newark *(G-11123)*
Jones Property Company .... G 302 213-2695
  Wilmington *(G-17575)*
◆ Joseph J Sheeran Inc .... E 302 324-0200
  New Castle *(G-9266)*
Journalname LLC .... G 302 522-7680
  Lewes *(G-6154)*
K and L Gates .... D 302 416-7000
  Wilmington *(G-17627)*
Kam Marketing Holdings Inc .... G 302 658-7778
  Wilmington *(G-17642)*
Kasmo Cloud Inc .... G 302 319-9952
  Lewes *(G-6161)*
Katu Software Global LLC .... F 302 803-5330
  Wilmington *(G-17667)*
Kc & Associates Inc .... G 302 633-3300
  Wilmington *(G-17670)*
Kelmar Associates LLC .... D 781 213-6926
  Wilmington *(G-17681)*
◆ Kfs Strategic MGT Svcs LLC .... G 302 757-6631
  Newark *(G-11167)*
Kintyre Solutions Inc .... G 888 636-0010
  Wilmington *(G-17729)*
Kirk & Associates LLC .... F 302 444-4733
  Christiana *(G-1002)*
Korsgy Technologies LLC .... G 302 504-6201
  Wilmington *(G-17748)*
Kortech Consulting Inc .... F 302 559-4612
  Bear *(G-333)*
Lauri Brockson .... G 302 383-0147
  Newark *(G-11228)*
Lbg Homes LLC .... G 302 542-4221
  Laurel *(G-5554)*
Lead Stock .... G 424 306-2700
  Dover *(G-2919)*
Learning Core LLC .... E 628 600-9644
  Lewes *(G-6185)*
Level Up Consulting Group Inc .... G 855 967-5550
  Middletown *(G-7296)*
Liberty Consultancy Firm LLC .... E 302 493-4344
  Dover *(G-2935)*
Lifesource Consulting Svcs LLC .... F 302 257-6247
  Dover *(G-2941)*
Lifetour Solutions LLC .... F 215 964-5000
  Wilmington *(G-17906)*
Limitless Consulting Mktg LLC .... E 302 743-0520
  Newark *(G-11261)*
Linda McCormick .... G 443 987-2099
  Wilmington *(G-17922)*
Lindell Partners LLC .... G 773 269-0837
  Wilmington *(G-17924)*
Lissner & Associates LLC .... G 302 777-4620
  Wilmington *(G-17932)*
Living Resources Inc .... G 302 227-6867
  Rehoboth Beach *(G-12835)*
Local Ad Ninja Inc .... F 877 894-1502
  Wilmington *(G-17970)*
Local Life Marketing Group LLC .... G 877 514-4052
  Bear *(G-352)*
Longo and Associates LLP .... G 302 477-7500
  Wilmington *(G-17985)*
Lorica Strategy Partners LLC .... G 301 535-8263
  Lewes *(G-6222)*
Lpl Financial .... F 302 737-6559
  Newark *(G-11292)*
Lpl Financial .... G 617 423-3644
  Wilmington *(G-18017)*
Lukerative Solutions Inc .... G 302 294-6468
  Christiana *(G-1004)*

Luminous Energy Corporation .... G 866 475-7504
  Dover *(G-2980)*
Lynkmax LLC .... G 302 573-3568
  Wilmington *(G-18049)*
Lynne Fardell & Associates LLC .... G 302 276-1541
  New Castle *(G-9330)*
M Team Creative .... G 302 275-5658
  Newark *(G-11305)*
Mado Creative Agency Inc .... G 302 223-9532
  Wilmington *(G-18075)*
Mallard Advisors LLC .... F 302 239-1654
  Hockessin *(G-5294)*
Management 24 LLC .... G 646 820-5224
  Dover *(G-3006)*
Management Systems Improvement .... G 860 478-7496
  Claymont *(G-1229)*
Mancon Inc .... G 302 395-5376
  New Castle *(G-9342)*
Markel and Associates LLC .... G 302 898-5684
  Townsend *(G-14031)*
Market Edge LLC .... G 302 442-6800
  Wilmington *(G-18144)*
Marketing Creators Inc .... G 302 409-0344
  Wilmington *(G-18146)*
Markland Affiliates LLC .... G 302 633-9134
  Wilmington *(G-18149)*
Marlette Services Inc .... G 302 358-2730
  Wilmington *(G-18152)*
Marvin Palmer Globl Equity LP .... G 302 573-3570
  Wilmington *(G-18176)*
Maven Workforce LLC .... G 551 214-8937
  Newark *(G-11356)*
Mayple Ltd .... G 917 558-0698
  Wilmington *(G-18210)*
Mc Creative Group .... F 302 348-8977
  Millsboro *(G-8370)*
MCA - Mdsg Cons Assoc USA Inc .... G 800 465-4755
  Dover *(G-3042)*
McCauley Enterprises LLC .... G 217 454-7056
  Hockessin *(G-5305)*
McCullough & Associates Inc .... G 302 250-7679
  Wilmington *(G-18226)*
Medfluencers Inc .... F 518 813-2788
  Lewes *(G-6257)*
Media Fusion US LLC .... G 256 532-3874
  Newark *(G-11372)*
Mentor Consultants Inc .... G 610 566-4004
  Wilmington *(G-18273)*
Metropolitan Revenue Assoc LLC .... G 302 449-7490
  New Castle *(G-9362)*
Mid States Sales & Marketing .... F 302 888-2475
  Wilmington *(G-18336)*
Mid-Atlntic Sls Mktg Group LLC .... G 215 515-6077
  Newark *(G-11413)*
Milieux LLC .... G 302 770-5868
  Wilmington *(G-18356)*
Millennial Informatics LLC .... G 302 446-3800
  Camden *(G-875)*
Millennial Ventures Group LLC .... F 877 533-3337
  Newark *(G-11422)*
MMS Enterprises LLC .... G 888 786-9290
  Newark *(G-11434)*
Modernthink LLC .... F 302 764-4477
  Wilmington *(G-18398)*
Mohandis Enterprises LLC .... G 302 261-2821
  Lewes *(G-6287)*
Momentum Management Group Inc .... G 302 477-9730
  Wilmington *(G-18406)*
Montesino Associates .... G 302 888-2455
  Wilmington *(G-18422)*
Morning Report Research Inc .... G 302 730-3793
  Dover *(G-3123)*

Mosaic Media Holdings Inc .... F 888 379-3553
  Dover *(G-3125)*
Moscova Enterprises Inc .... F 347 973-2522
  Wilmington *(G-18460)*
Mountain Consulting Inc .... E 302 744-9875
  Dover *(G-3128)*
Mpe Global Incorporated .... G 856 376-0434
  Wilmington *(G-18470)*
Mscooperhomeloans .... F 302 494-7712
  Hockessin *(G-5312)*
Mtc Usa LLC .... F 980 999-8888
  Newark *(G-11468)*
Muse Marketing & Creative LLC .... G 856 823-1601
  Wilmington *(G-18491)*
MV Farinola Inc .... G 302 545-8492
  Wilmington *(G-18497)*
Mwidm Inc .... E 302 298-0101
  Wilmington *(G-18501)*
My Qme Inc .... G 302 218-8730
  Wilmington *(G-18508)*
Nationwide Inventory Svcs Inc .... G 888 741-3039
  Hartly *(G-4900)*
Ned Davis Associates Inc .... G 302 670-5307
  Dover *(G-3165)*
Neilson Associates Inc .... F 610 793-2271
  Wilmington *(G-18575)*
Neitsch Ltd Liability Company .... G 708 634-8724
  Newark *(G-11500)*
Network Design Technologies .... E 610 991-2929
  Wilmington *(G-18596)*
Newton Management Holding Inc .... F 800 784-8714
  Middletown *(G-7401)*
Newton One Advisors .... F 302 731-1326
  Newark *(G-11551)*
North Point Mktg & MGT LLC .... F 855 931-4075
  Newark *(G-11566)*
Nova RE & Bus Consulting LLC .... G 302 258-2193
  Lewes *(G-6321)*
NS 360 Inc .... G 855 678-2257
  Wilmington *(G-18704)*
Numberbox Inc .... G 302 830-8800
  Wilmington *(G-18715)*
Nx Level Marketing LLC .... G 215 880-4749
  Bear *(G-402)*
Ocean First Enterprises LLC .... E 302 232-8547
  Wilmington *(G-18741)*
Oceanstar Technologies Inc .... G 302 542-1900
  Bear *(G-404)*
Omni Outreach Inc .... F 888 291-8952
  Wilmington *(G-18768)*
Omninet International Inc .... F 208 246-5022
  Wilmington *(G-18769)*
Omniway Corporation .... F 302 738-5076
  Newark *(G-11586)*
Onfido Inc .... G 415 855-7113
  Camden *(G-882)*
Online Catalyst LLC .... G 916 990-3150
  Dover *(G-3231)*
Onyx Business Alliance LLC .... G 888 368-0402
  Wilmington *(G-18793)*
Open Lanes-Solutions LLC .... F 888 410-4207
  Wilmington *(G-18795)*
Openexo Inc .... F 617 965-5057
  Dover *(G-3237)*
Opinr Inc .... D 646 207-3000
  Wilmington *(G-18804)*
Opus Marketing Group .... G 302 275-2336
  Bear *(G-409)*
Oracle Enterprises LLC .... G 407 900-2828
  Wilmington *(G-18810)*
Original Shoppers The LLC .... G 866 838-3224
  Middletown *(G-7420)*

Employee Codes: A=Over 500 employees, B=251-500
C=101-250, D=51-100, E=20-50, F=10-19, G=1-9

87 ENGINEERING, ACCOUNTING, RESEARCH, AND MANAGEMENT SERVICES

Owl Jumpstart LLC ... F ... 302 467-2061
Wilmington (G-18843)

Oyster HR Americas Inc ... C ... 912 219-2356
Wilmington (G-18846)

Oyster HR Inc ... B ... 912 219-2356
Wilmington (G-18847)

P A Aba Intl Inc ... G ... 800 979-5106
Lewes (G-6343)

Pabian Ventures LLC ... G ... 302 762-1992
Wilmington (G-18856)

Paul C Cunningham & Assoc LLC ... G ... 302 258-4163
Lewes (G-6355)

Paxelax ... G ... 302 722-7290
Newark (G-11644)

Pcd Solutions LLC ... G ... 877 723-7552
Wilmington (G-18933)

Perennial Dev & Cnstr Corp ... E ... 855 625-0046
Wilmington (G-18971)

Performance Based Results ... G ... 302 478-4443
Talleyville (G-13945)

Perry and Associates Inc ... F ... 302 898-2327
Hockessin (G-5342)

Pgi Commercial LLC ... G ... 800 686-8134
Wilmington (G-19006)

Phoenix Global Shop LLC ... F ... 347 227-2519
Dover (G-3314)

Phreesia Inc ... D ... 651 983-0426
Wilmington (G-19028)

Phs Corporate Services Inc ... G ... 302 571-1128
Wilmington (G-19029)

Pierce Multi Solutions LLC ... G ... 302 609-7000
Newark (G-11689)

Pikchabox LLC ... F ... 302 207-1770
Dover (G-3323)

Pineal Consulting Group LLC ... G ... 302 446-3794
Dover (G-3324)

Pioneer Natural Resources Co ... F ... 972 444-9001
Wilmington (G-19053)

Pk & Associates Group Inc ... G ... 302 394-9052
Wilmington (G-19061)

Platformavr Inc ... G ... 302 330-8980
Dover (G-3328)

Pllal International LLC ... E ... 786 235-7800
Wilmington (G-19079)

Poloniex LLC ... G ... 302 518-6536
Wilmington (G-19110)

Positioneering LLC ... G ... 302 415-3200
Wilmington (G-19124)

Pot-Nets Bayside LLC ... E ... 302 945-9300
Millsboro (G-8433)

Predictive Analytics Group ... F ... 844 733-5724
Newark (G-11724)

Presidio Holdings LLC ... F ... 240 219-8351
Lewes (G-6388)

Prestigious Solution LLC ... G ... 800 392-2103
Smyrna (G-13853)

Prime Insights Group LLC ... F ... 407 289-1577
Dover (G-3372)

Prime One Global LLC ... D ... 831 215-5123
Wilmington (G-19191)

Prime Time Properties LLC ... G ... 302 763-6050
Bear (G-438)

Printify LLC ... G ... 415 968-6351
Wilmington (G-19198)

Privado Inc ... G ... 916 730-4522
Dover (G-3374)

Proautomated Inc ... D ... 302 294-6121
Newark (G-11756)

Project of Providence LLC ... G ... 302 438-8970
Wilmington (G-19224)

Project Otr LLC ... G ... 404 964-2244
Wilmington (G-19225)

Prolific Consultants LLC ... G ... 302 219-0958
Dover (G-3379)

Protech Labs Inc ... G ... 201 328-7856
Dover (G-3384)

Prudent Capital Advisor ... G ... 302 569-9444
Newark (G-11769)

Pyramid Group MGT Svcs Corp ... G ... 302 737-1770
Newark (G-11780)

Qspark LLC ... G ... 646 504-4975
Wilmington (G-19277)

Qualityfastforyou LLC ... G ... 618 540-1209
Newark (G-11791)

Quanteam North America Inc ... G ... 929 262-8538
Wilmington (G-11792)

Quinteccent Inc ... G ... 443 838-5447
Selbyville (G-13595)

Radaar LLC ... G ... 855 623-0723
Newark (G-11815)

Rastan Enterprises LLC ... G ... 443 691-0232
Middletown (G-7503)

Raymond James Financial Svc ... G ... 302 778-2170
Wilmington (G-19348)

Raymond James Fincl Svcs Inc ... G ... 302 656-1534
Wilmington (G-19349)

Ready Alliance Group Inc ... G ... 866 229-0927
Wilmington (G-19363)

Real Deals LLC ... E ... 484 470-8582
Wilmington (G-19365)

Real World Endo ... G ... 302 477-0960
Wilmington (G-19371)

Red Clay Inc ... G ... 302 239-2018
Hockessin (G-5360)

Red Lion LLC ... G ... 202 559-9365
Wilmington (G-19386)

Redflag Marketing Corp ... G ... 302 464-8116
Middletown (G-7507)

Redland Mills Co ... G ... 706 288-6003
Wilmington (G-19389)

Redleo Software Inc ... F ... 302 691-9072
Wilmington (G-19390)

Registration LLC ... G ... 877 955-7111
Wilmington (G-19408)

Reliable Aid Inc ... E ... 302 419-3558
New Castle (G-9518)

Repurpose Global Inc ... G ... 732 322-3839
Wilmington (G-19435)

Resemble Ai Inc ... G ... 401 255-6004
Middletown (G-7516)

Resources For Human Dev ... G ... 215 848-1947
Newark (G-11868)

Resources For Human Dev ... G ... 215 951-0300
Wilmington (G-19440)

Resources For Human Dev Inc ... F ... 302 731-5283
Newark (G-11869)

Resources For Human Dev Inc ... F ... 302 691-7574
Wilmington (G-19441)

Rich Rising Enterprise LLC ... G ... 302 592-6697
Dover (G-3465)

Roll Out Transit LLC ... G ... 800 233-1680
Hockessin (G-5371)

Roxanne Rxnne Cnslting Group L ... G ... 470 333-8553
Dover (G-3488)

S & S Mgnt Co LLC ... G ... 302 353-9249
Middletown (G-7531)

SA Associates LLC ... G ... 302 275-7359
Wilmington (G-19616)

Sabre Associates LLC ... G ... 302 998-0100
Wilmington (G-19619)

Sabre International Newco Inc ... F ... 682 605-6223
Wilmington (G-19620)

Safe Driver Corporation ... G ... 601 207-1164
Dover (G-3502)

Sam Walts & Associates ... G ... 302 777-2211
Wilmington (G-19646)

Sawai LLC ... E ... 800 625-3680
Wilmington (G-19686)

Scottish Ventures LLC ... G ... 302 382-6057
New Castle (G-9554)

Second Chance Solutions LLC ... G ... 302 204-0551
Wilmington (G-19726)

Selection Solutions Inc ... G ... 800 600-6605
Wilmington (G-19743)

Selisav Corporation ... F ... 702 888-2175
Lewes (G-6457)

Seotwix LLC ... E ... 877 849-8777
Middletown (G-7553)

Sfin 3 Inc ... G ... 302 472-9276
Wilmington (G-19773)

Sherpa Financial Services ... F ... 302 235-1284
Hockessin (G-5383)

Signature Square LLC ... G ... 866 216-5792
Lewes (G-6469)

Simpler Logistics LLC ... G ... 800 619-8321
Wilmington (G-19836)

Sinapi LLC ... E ... 650 265-7180
Dover (G-3567)

Siren Group USA Inc ... G ... 302 298-3307
Newark (G-12014)

Siriusiq Mobile LLC ... F ... 888 414-2047
Newark (G-12015)

Skillfi LLC ... G ... 469 701-9614
Dover (G-3571)

Smartprofyl LLC ... G ... 832 412-5803
Middletown (G-7578)

Sociable Consulting LLC ... G ... 302 546-2750
Hockessin (G-5385)

Solution Seeker Cons LLC ... G ... 347 230-8558
Wilmington (G-19926)

Speak Biz Consulting LLC ... F ... 302 272-9294
Wilmington (G-19952)

Status Intl LLC DBA Sttus Brnd ... G ... 202 290-6387
Wilmington (G-20037)

Steneral Consulting Inc ... E ... 302 721-6124
Wilmington (G-20050)

Stephen A Covey ... G ... 302 478-0215
Wilmington (G-20057)

Storyiq Inc ... F ... 718 801-8556
Wilmington (G-20089)

Strategic Integration LLC ... F ... 714 227-0142
Middletown (G-7602)

Strategic Solutions Intl Inc ... G ... 302 525-6313
Newark (G-12105)

Strategic Wealth Cons Inc ... G ... 601 715-4174
Dover (G-3615)

Strategybrix LLC ... F ... 312 804-6768
Lewes (G-6516)

StreamIners MGT Consulting LLC ... G ... 864 884-5064
Wilmington (G-20095)

Sumthin3lse ... G ... 302 272-5435
Dover (G-3621)

Sun-Ray Valley Investments LLC ... G ... 302 406-1078
Wilmington (G-20128)

Superstar Holdings Inc ... G ... 302 289-8931
Dover (G-3627)

▼ Supply Chain Consultants Inc ... E ... 302 738-9215
Wilmington (G-20149)

Swarthmore Financial Svcs LLC ... G ... 302 325-0700
New Castle (G-9609)

Sweat Social LLC ... G ... 504 510-1973
Dover (G-3631)

Symack Prof Svcs US Corp ... F ... 469 607-6092
Smyrna (G-13908)

Taglatam Inc ... G ... 302 314-9898
Middletown (G-7618)

87 ENGINEERING, ACCOUNTING, RESEARCH, AND MANAGEMENT SERVICES

TAI Group LLC...................................... E 561 819-4231
  Dover *(G-3643)*

Talent Ola Inc...................................... E 732 421-3216
  Dover *(G-3645)*

Tapp Networks LLC............................. G 302 222-3384
  Rehoboth Beach *(G-12989)*

Tawkify Inc.. G 415 549-1928
  Wilmington *(G-20229)*

Tcim Services Inc................................ A 302 633-3000
  Wilmington *(G-20239)*

Techneplus Americas LLC................... G 678 200-4052
  Wilmington *(G-20253)*

Tecnologika Usa Inc........................... G 302 597-7611
  Wilmington *(G-20259)*

Telecom Consulting Group Inc............ G 302 645-7400
  Lewes *(G-6548)*

Telus Intl Holdg USA Corp................... G 720 726-0677
  Wilmington *(G-20270)*

Thomas B Davis................................... G 302 692-0871
  Newark *(G-12191)*

Timtec LLC.. F 302 292-8500
  Newark *(G-12197)*

Tipton Communications Group............ F 302 454-7901
  Newark *(G-12198)*

Title One & Associates Inc................... G 410 758-1831
  Ocean View *(G-12577)*

Tk Blier Incorporated........................... E 207 760-7076
  Camden *(G-897)*

Tomi Inc... G 650 488-3054
  Newark *(G-12208)*

TP It Group LLC................................... G 302 444-0441
  Dover *(G-3709)*

Training Solution................................. G 302 379-3070
  Newark *(G-12216)*

Transporttee Inc................................... E 302 330-8912
  Dover *(G-3714)*

Twinning LLC....................................... G 609 793-3510
  Wilmington *(G-20470)*

Tytrix Inc.. E 877 489-8749
  Dover *(G-3737)*

Uncharted Waters LLC........................ E 302 213-6354
  Dover *(G-3747)*

Unique Creations By Chloe LLC........... E 855 942-0477
  Wilmington *(G-20517)*

United Worldwide Express LLC........... F 347 651-5111
  Newark *(G-12273)*

Vanguard Venture Group LLC............. G 954 324-8736
  Dover *(G-3774)*

Vcg LLC... G 302 336-8151
  Dover *(G-3777)*

Versapro Group LLC............................ G 315 430-2775
  Wilmington *(G-20594)*

Veteran It Pro LLC............................... F 302 824-3111
  Hockessin *(G-5418)*

Vic Victor Imagination Co LLC............. G 714 262-4426
  Lewes *(G-6603)*

Victoryconsulting LLC.......................... G 203 275-9398
  Wilmington *(G-20614)*

Vir Consultant LLC............................... E 747 666-2169
  Newark *(G-12327)*

Virasoft Corporation............................. G 281 851-9080
  Claymont *(G-1328)*

Virtual Talk Hub LLC............................ E 302 406-0038
  Wilmington *(G-20635)*

Visio Group International Corp............. G 302 485-0378
  Wilmington *(G-20637)*

Vpsie Inc... F 844 468-7743
  Wilmington *(G-20655)*

Vtms LLC... G 302 264-9094
  Dover *(G-3813)*

Wallace Investments Group LLC......... G 323 407-2889
  Middletown *(G-7704)*

Wang Consultants Inc......................... G 626 483-0265
  Wilmington *(G-20676)*

Wartrude Services Inc......................... G 302 213-3944
  Wilmington *(G-20680)*

Watkins Consulting Group JV.............. G 202 861-0200
  Rehoboth Beach *(G-13010)*

Wealth Access Services LLC............... G 302 327-4174
  Newark *(G-12352)*

Weelwork Inc....................................... G 800 546-8607
  Claymont *(G-1335)*

Why Unified Corp................................. E 302 803-5892
  Newark *(G-12371)*

Willis North America Inc...................... E 302 239-2416
  Hockessin *(G-5426)*

Winner Group Management Inc.......... F 302 571-5200
  Wilmington *(G-20861)*

Wizard Media Inc................................. G 610 653-9722
  Dover *(G-3862)*

Woodson Ministries Inc........................ G 512 350-9950
  Wilmington *(G-20887)*

Workfar Inc.. F 650 800-3990
  Dover *(G-3871)*

World Trade Sponsor Inc..................... G 404 780-3333
  Newark *(G-12409)*

Wyndham Group Inc............................ G 704 905-9750
  Wilmington *(G-20907)*

Xander Group II LLC........................... G 302 656-1950
  Wilmington *(G-20913)*

Xcutivescom Inc................................... E 888 245-9996
  Dover *(G-3880)*

Yacht Delaware Registry Ltd............... F 302 477-9800
  Wilmington *(G-20921)*

Yalla Marketing LLC............................ G 209 201-0313
  Middletown *(G-7742)*

Yanci Brand LLC................................. G 844 242-7263
  Wilmington *(G-20923)*

Yebo Alpha Inc.................................... G 302 335-8887
  Magnolia *(G-6792)*

Yenaffit Inc.. G 302 650-4818
  Wilmington *(G-20926)*

Ywy Incorporated................................ G 916 794-1607
  Wilmington *(G-20943)*

Zenith Mind Inc................................... F 302 543-2075
  Wilmington *(G-20955)*

Zeribon Holding Group LLC................ C 844 205-1999
  Dover *(G-3899)*

Ziggyfli LLC.. F 302 503-5582
  Dover *(G-3901)*

Zutz Risk Management........................ G 302 658-8000
  Wilmington *(G-20969)*

8743 Public relations services

ADd Marketing Group LLC................... G 347 668-0992
  Dover *(G-1716)*

Aloysius Butlr Clark Assoc Inc............. D 302 655-1552
  Wilmington *(G-14390)*

Bgp Publicity Inc.................................. F 302 234-9500
  Wilmington *(G-14872)*

Blue Horizon Promotions LLC.............. G 302 547-0913
  Saint Georges *(G-13032)*

Broydrick & Associates Inc.................. G 414 224-9393
  Rehoboth Beach *(G-12658)*

Go-Givers LLC.................................... G 302 703-9293
  Lewes *(G-6044)*

▲ Kent & O Connor Inc........................ G 703 351-6222
  Millsboro *(G-8338)*

Lindsay Mumford LLC......................... G 302 841-2309
  Fenwick Island *(G-4051)*

Makatuu Inc.. G 650 431-5582
  Dover *(G-3000)*

Mid Atlantic Athc Promotions.............. G 302 535-8472
  Magnolia *(G-6766)*

Muse Global Consulting Inc................. E 325 221-3634
  Middletown *(G-7389)*

One System Incorporated.................... F 888 311-1110
  Wilmington *(G-18784)*

▲ Remline Corp................................... E 302 737-7228
  Newark *(G-11850)*

Ruggerio Willson & Assoc LLC............ G 302 345-8468
  Dover *(G-3494)*

SC Marketing US Inc........................... G 714 352-4992
  Wilmington *(G-19694)*

Slice Communications LLC.................. F 215 600-0050
  Wilmington *(G-19864)*

Square Promote.................................. G 302 478-0736
  Wilmington *(G-19986)*

The Ascendant Group Inc.................... F 302 450-4494
  Newark *(G-12186)*

Tipton Communications Group............ F 302 454-7901
  Newark *(G-12198)*

Willis Groupllc..................................... G 302 632-9898
  Dover *(G-3853)*

8744 Facilities support services

Bi Solutions Group LLC....................... E 253 366-5173
  Wilmington *(G-14874)*

Blessngs Grnhses Cmpost Fcilty......... F 302 684-8890
  Milford *(G-7795)*

Brightfields Inc.................................... E 302 656-9600
  Wilmington *(G-15113)*

Delmar Corporate Clg Svcs Inc............ E 302 861-8006
  Newark *(G-10499)*

Dibiasos Clg Rstration Svc Inc............. G 302 376-7111
  Townsend *(G-13992)*

Ecg Industries Inc............................... G 302 453-0535
  Newark *(G-10603)*

Focus Solutions Services Inc............... F 302 318-1345
  Newark *(G-10753)*

Ges-Bay West Joint Venture LLC........ G 302 918-3070
  Newark *(G-10827)*

Moore Staffing Agency LLC................. G 215 300-2770
  Bear *(G-379)*

Seaford Mission Inc............................. G 302 629-2559
  Seaford *(G-13391)*

Shackleford Facilities Inc..................... F 877 735-3938
  Frankford *(G-4141)*

Team Systems International LLC......... G 703 217-7648
  Lewes *(G-6545)*

Verdantas LLC.................................... F 302 239-6634
  Wilmington *(G-20586)*

8748 Business consulting, nec

10-4 Safety LLC.................................. G 847 997-5515
  Wilmington *(G-14100)*

280 Group LLC.................................... E 408 834-7518
  Dover *(G-1683)*

5linx... G 302 981-2529
  Bear *(G-4)*

9222 Enterprises LLC......................... G 888 551-1393
  Dover *(G-1691)*

ABC Systems Inc................................ G 302 528-8875
  Newark *(G-9740)*

AC Group Inc...................................... G 201 840-5566
  Wilmington *(G-14211)*

Action Environmental Service.............. G 302 798-3100
  Wilmington *(G-14241)*

Acuitive Inc... G 214 738-1099
  Wilmington *(G-14246)*

Adept Consulting................................. G 267 398-7449
  Wilmington *(G-14255)*

Aecom Usa Inc................................... D 302 781-5963
  Newark *(G-9788)*

Aegis Networks LLC............................ G 917 378-7524
  Wilmington *(G-14294)*

Employee Codes: A=Over 500 employees, B=251-500
C=101-250, D=51-100, E=20-50, F=10-19, G=1-9

87 ENGINEERING, ACCOUNTING, RESEARCH, AND MANAGEMENT SERVICES

Aegis PM Group Inc .... G 302 456-0402
　Wilmington (G-14295)
Aesir Capital Management LP .... G 302 656-9161
　Wilmington (G-14297)
African Wood Inc .... G 302 884-6738
　Middletown (G-6839)
Allen Jarmon Enterprises Inc .... G 302 745-5122
　Rehoboth Beach (G-12601)
Alliance Bus Dev Concepts LLC .... F 803 814-4004
　Clayton (G-1348)
Alliance Data .... G 302 256-0853
　Wilmington (G-14378)
Allkare Inc .... G 302 212-0917
　Dover (G-1772)
Ambient Procurement Group LLC .... F 718 925-7750
　Newark (G-9841)
Amerihalth Integrated Benefits .... E 302 777-6400
　Wilmington (G-14447)
Amsoft Corp .... G 859 351-7688
　Wilmington (G-14463)
Amsol Inc .... G 302 369-6969
　Newark (G-9854)
Analytics Realm LLC .... G 302 743-0342
　Newark (G-9859)
Anderson Rnee Charles Anderson .... G 302 529-7845
　Wilmington (G-14473)
Anglin Cnsulting Solutions LLC .... F 302 406-0233
　Wilmington (G-14484)
Anthogo Enterprises .... G 302 378-0235
　Middletown (G-6866)
Aquila of Delaware Inc .... F 302 999-1106
　Bear (G-42)
ARC HUD I Inc .... G 302 996-9400
　Wilmington (G-14528)
ARC HUD VII Inc .... G 302 996-9400
　Wilmington (G-14530)
Aria Solutions Inc .... G 302 453-8389
　Newark (G-9902)
Armodias LLC .... G 302 384-9794
　Wilmington (G-14555)
Artemundi LLC .... F 302 988-5002
　Wilmington (G-14563)
Ascent Technologies Inc .... G 302 491-0545
　Newark (G-9919)
Ashanti Produce International .... F 800 295-9790
　Wilmington (G-14578)
Aspira of Delaware Inc .... G 302 292-1463
　Newark (G-9924)
Assoction Brds Thlgcal Educatn .... G 302 654-7770
　Wilmington (G-14596)
AST Sports Internacional LLC .... G 786 445-8081
　Wilmington (G-14601)
Atlantic Duncan Inc .... F 302 383-0740
　Newark (G-9935)
Atlantic Resource Management .... G 302 539-2029
　Frankford (G-4063)
Atlantic Resource Management .... F 302 539-2029
　Frankford (G-4064)
Atlantic Training LLC .... F 302 464-0341
　Newark (G-9938)
Attac Consulting Group LLC .... G 443 766-9079
　Frankford (G-4065)
Automation Alliance Group LLC .... G 302 202-5433
　Middletown (G-6887)
Avery Enterprises LLC .... G 302 750-5468
　Newark (G-9953)
Aviant Cnsltng & Riva Pymnt .... G 302 584-0549
　Newark (G-9954)
Avs Solutions LLC .... G 302 562-0642
　Middletown (G-6893)
Axchem Holding Company .... G 336 632-0500
　Wilmington (G-14679)

B C Consulting .... G 215 534-3805
　Wilmington (G-14696)
B Rich Enterprises .... G 302 530-6865
　Middletown (G-6895)
Bangus Business Services .... G 302 266-7285
　Newark (G-9980)
Bastianelli Group Inc .... G 302 658-1500
　Newark (G-9989)
Batescainelli LLC .... G 202 618-2040
　Rehoboth Beach (G-12624)
Batta Inc .... F 302 737-3376
　Newark (G-9991)
Batta Environmental Assoc Inc .... E 302 737-3376
　Newark (G-9992)
Be Right There Consulting LLC .... G 302 727-5047
　Newark (G-10001)
Belluno Manager LLC .... G 650 395-8185
　Wilmington (G-14824)
Berkelyn Inc .... G 360 609-4981
　Lewes (G-5755)
Betsson US Corp .... G 800 316-6660
　Dover (G-1921)
Biotech Mentor LLC .... E 617 460-4983
　Dover (G-1940)
Bishop Enterprises Corporation .... G 302 379-2884
　Wilmington (G-14897)
Blue Planet .... G 410 977-3426
　Rehoboth Beach (G-12645)
Bluestone Communications Inc .... G 302 478-4200
　Wilmington (G-14982)
Breylacom .... G 302 731-7456
　Newark (G-10083)
Bridgeforce Inc .... G 302 325-7100
　Newark (G-10085)
Brightfields Inc .... E 302 656-9600
　Wilmington (G-15113)
Brodie Consulting Mick Group .... G 302 468-6425
　Bear (G-83)
Browne Consulting .... G 302 482-1410
　Wilmington (G-15130)
Bruce Palmer LLC .... G 302 654-1135
　Rehoboth Beach (G-12659)
Bulk Solutions LLC .... G 310 906-0901
　Wilmington (G-15148)
Bullseye Entertainment Tech Co .... E 302 924-5034
　Dover (G-1992)
Business Intrface Wrkfrce Svcs .... E 302 660-7123
　Wilmington (G-15159)
By Mail Eric Graham Intl .... G 816 368-1641
　Wilmington (G-15164)
Byrd Group Delaware .... G 302 757-8300
　New Castle (G-8905)
C and L Bradford and Assoc .... G 302 529-8566
　Wilmington (G-15174)
C S Consultants .... G 302 623-4144
　Newark (G-10115)
C4-Nvis USA LLC .... G 213 465-5089
　Dover (G-2009)
Calculus Bus Solutions Inc .... E 302 676-2162
　Wilmington (G-15192)
Cannon Cold Storage LLC .... E 302 337-5500
　Bridgeville (G-680)
Capitol Environmental Svcs Inc .... G 302 652-8999
　Newark (G-10136)
▲ Capitol Environmental Svcs Inc .... G 302 380-3737
　Newark (G-10135)
Capstone Homes LLC .... F 302 644-0300
　Lewes (G-5799)
Casus Consulting LLC .... G 972 532-6357
　Middletown (G-6963)
Cecon Group LLC .... G 302 994-8000
　Wilmington (G-15294)

Cedcomm LLC .... G 646 653-0233
　Dover (G-2042)
Cg Global MGT Solutions LLC .... F 215 735-3745
　Wilmington (G-15321)
Chance De Group LLC .... G 800 667-3082
　Newark (G-10187)
Charles Taylor Consulting Inc .... G 703 200-8057
　Milford (G-7822)
Cheryl Wagner .... G 302 635-7632
　Hockessin (G-5158)
Chip Design Systems Inc .... F 302 494-6220
　Hockessin (G-5160)
CL Walton Enterprises LLC .... F 443 360-1120
　Wilmington (G-15459)
Clayton West LLC .... G 302 530-3492
　Rehoboth Beach (G-12674)
Cloud Cystems LLC .... F 815 797-9929
　Middletown (G-6997)
Coach AK Enterprises LLC .... F 617 433-7560
　Middletown (G-7000)
Codeiscode Mktg Consulting LLC .... G 415 202-5303
　Wilmington (G-15515)
Community Consulting Corps .... G 614 348-7823
　Hockessin (G-5168)
Compliance Environmental Inc .... G 302 674-4427
　Dover (G-2124)
Congruence Consulting Group .... G 320 290-6155
　Newark (G-10304)
Consulttive Rview Rhbilitation .... F 302 366-0356
　Newark (G-10310)
Core Construction LLC .... G 302 449-4186
　Smyrna (G-13687)
Countrmsres Asssment SEC Expr .... G 302 322-9600
　Middletown (G-7015)
Creative Micro Designs Inc .... G 302 456-5800
　Newark (G-10349)
Creativity Diversified LLC .... G 302 897-5961
　Middletown (G-7021)
Critical Bs Holdings LLC .... G 833 479-5375
　Wilmington (G-15706)
Cruitcast Inc .... G 856 693-3869
　Smyrna (G-13689)
Crx Consulting LLC .... G 302 864-7377
　Rehoboth Beach (G-12706)
Crx Consulting LLC .... G 302 864-7377
　Rehoboth Beach (G-12707)
Cychet LLC .... F 929 265-8351
　Dover (G-2175)
Cyclops Net Inc .... G 844 979-0222
　Camden (G-812)
Cynash Inc .... G 415 850-7842
　Wilmington (G-15752)
De Novo Corporation .... E 302 234-7407
　Wilmington (G-15839)
Dearng Safety Office .... G 302 326-7100
　New Castle (G-9006)
Decennium Management Group .... G 302 600-3644
　Dover (G-2205)
Delaware Bay & River .... G 302 645-7861
　Lewes (G-5889)
Delaware Consulting Servi .... G 302 945-7936
　Lewes (G-5893)
Delaware Economic Dev Auth .... G 302 739-4271
　Dover (G-2234)
Delaware Family Voices Inc .... F 302 588-4908
　Wilmington (G-15917)
Delaware Innovation Space Inc .... G 302 695-2201
　Wilmington (G-15933)
Delaware Mltcltral Cvic Orgnzt .... F 302 399-6118
　Dover (G-2249)
Delaware Safety Council Inc .... G 302 276-0660
　New Castle (G-9036)

87 ENGINEERING, ACCOUNTING, RESEARCH, AND MANAGEMENT SERVICES

Delaware Small Bus Dev Ctr .... G 302 831-1555
  Georgetown (G-4283)
Delaware Small Bus Dev Ctr .... F 302 831-1555
  Newark (G-10481)
Design Tribe Republic LLC .... F 302 918-5279
  Wilmington (G-16027)
Diamond State CLT Inc .... F 800 282-0477
  Dover (G-2293)
Diff Consulting LLC .... G 302 689-3979
  Wilmington (G-16062)
Digitlogy LLC DBA Exprttexting .... G 302 703-9672
  Milton (G-8606)
Dover East LLC .... F 302 330-3040
  Rehoboth Beach (G-12734)
Drone Consulting Pros Inc .... G 561 766-5176
  Claymont (G-1124)
Dvhd Inc .... G 302 584-3547
  Wilmington (G-16225)
Dynamic Support Services Inc .... G 202 820-3113
  Wilmington (G-16230)
Eancenter Telecom LLC .... G 302 450-4514
  Dover (G-2404)
Edgerite Inc .... G 302 404-6665
  Dover (G-2421)
Eighth Street Enterprises LLC .... G 302 376-8222
  Middletown (G-7086)
Elevate RCM Consulting .... G 484 655-8733
  Wilmington (G-16357)
Ementum Inc .... G 866 984-1999
  Milton (G-8617)
◆ Emerald Bioagriculture Corp .... F 517 882-7370
  Hockessin (G-5199)
Encross LLC .... F 302 351-2593
  Wilmington (G-16407)
Endocrinology Consultant .... G 302 734-2782
  Dover (G-2448)
Environmental Alliance Inc .... E 302 234-4400
  Wilmington (G-16443)
Environmental Consulting Svcs .... F 302 378-9881
  Middletown (G-7103)
Environmental Resources Inc .... G 302 436-9637
  Selbyville (G-13534)
Environmental Services Inc .... G 302 669-6812
  New Castle (G-9098)
Environmental Testing Inc .... G 302 378-5341
  Middletown (G-7104)
Envirotech Envmtl Consulting .... G 302 684-5201
  Lewes (G-5963)
Envirtech Enviromental Consltg .... G 302 645-6491
  Lewes (G-5964)
Envision Consulting LLC .... G 302 658-9027
  Wilmington (G-16444)
Erm Emerald US Inc .... A 302 651-8300
  Wilmington (G-16460)
Evans Act Inc .... G 302 792-0355
  Wilmington (G-16480)
Exponentia Global LLC .... E 302 330-7967
  Dover (G-2473)
Fbh Business Consulting LLC .... G 267 266-8149
  Wilmington (G-16563)
Fireside Partners Inc .... G 302 613-2165
  Dover (G-2497)
Flexera Inc .... F 302 945-6870
  Harbeson (G-4696)
Fluttering Butterfly LLC .... G 267 974-7812
  Dover (G-2521)
Foris Solutions LLC .... G 302 343-6396
  Wilmington (G-16694)
Freedom Tech Consulting LLC .... G 215 485-7383
  Middletown (G-7140)
Fshery Mid-Atlntic MGT Council .... F 302 674-2331
  Dover (G-2540)

Future Gold Technology Inc .... F 302 786-1388
  Wilmington (G-16777)
Galerie Media Inc .... G 917 685-4168
  Newark (G-10799)
Gamut Color Inc .... G 302 652-7171
  Wilmington (G-16800)
Generate Nb Fuel Cells LLC .... G 415 360-3063
  Wilmington (G-16832)
Genex Strategies .... G 302 356-1522
  Dover (G-2570)
Geo-Technology Associates Inc .... G 302 326-2100
  New Castle (G-9163)
Georgetown Construction Co .... G 302 856-7601
  Georgetown (G-4337)
Geosyntec Holdings LLC .... G 561 995-0900
  Wilmington (G-16848)
GIERD INC .... E 206 289-0011
  Wilmington (G-16858)
Gkg Consulting LLC .... D 888 918-0718
  Wilmington (G-16872)
GLA Company Ltd .... F 502 267-7522
  Wilmington (G-16876)
Global Bridging Corp .... G 202 318-7119
  Lewes (G-6038)
Global Dev Partners Inc .... G 480 330-7931
  Wilmington (G-16887)
Global Partner LLC .... G 646 630-9128
  Wilmington (G-16893)
Goldstone & Associates LLC .... G 302 857-0051
  Wilmington (G-16916)
Good Home Solutions LLC .... G 302 540-3190
  Wilmington (G-16921)
Government Affairs .... G 302 226-2704
  Rehoboth Beach (G-12774)
Greanex .... G 606 477-9768
  Wilmington (G-16956)
Green Standards LLC .... E 855 632-8036
  Dover (G-2625)
Ground/Water Trtmnt & Tech LLC .... F 302 654-0206
  Wilmington (G-16987)
Gusher .... G 302 803-5900
  Wilmington (G-17008)
Gwantel Intl Corp Engrg & Tech .... G 302 377-6235
  Newark (G-10909)
H Clemons Consulting Inc .... G 302 295-5097
  Wilmington (G-17016)
Harvard Environmental Inc .... F 302 326-2333
  Bear (G-265)
Hatch Consulting .... G 302 658-4380
  Wilmington (G-17072)
Hedgeforce LLC .... G 305 600-0085
  Newark (G-10944)
Hibner Group Inc .... G 717 281-1918
  Dover (G-2676)
Highdef Transportation LLC .... G 610 212-8596
  Bear (G-272)
Hobday Group Ltd .... G 302 337-9567
  Bridgeville (G-711)
Holistic Elevation LLC .... G 302 278-0026
  Bear (G-277)
Huling Cove Housing Corp .... G 302 739-4263
  Dover (G-2703)
Hydropac .... G 410 306-6945
  Seaford (G-13218)
I AM Consulting Group Inc .... F 302 521-4999
  Bear (G-280)
Iayam Financial LLC .... G 800 585-5315
  Dover (G-2715)
Incorporators USA LLC .... G 800 441-5940
  Wilmington (G-17303)
Incredible One Enterprises LLC .... G 888 801-5794
  Newark (G-11010)

Indigo Telecom USA LLC .... E 727 537-0142
  Wilmington (G-17311)
Industry ARC .... F 614 588-8538
  Wilmington (G-17318)
Infant Solutions .... E 302 250-4336
  Wilmington (G-17319)
Inrg of Delaware Inc .... G 302 369-1412
  Lewes (G-6127)
Insight Engineering Solutions .... G 302 378-4842
  Townsend (G-14018)
Integrity Brands LLC .... G 302 853-0709
  Seaford (G-13224)
Intelligent Signage Inc .... G 302 762-4100
  Wilmington (G-17372)
International Cloud Company .... G 858 472-9648
  Dover (G-2747)
International Spine Pain .... G 302 478-7001
  Wilmington (G-17390)
Intus Smartcities Inc .... F 403 542-8879
  Wilmington (G-17403)
Ione Group LLC .... G 302 584-8377
  Wilmington (G-17413)
Ipwe Inc .... E 214 438-0820
  Dover (G-2751)
J C Wells & Sons LP .... G 302 422-4732
  Milford (G-7946)
Jackson Contracting Inc .... F 302 678-2011
  Dover (G-2763)
Jbiza Enterprises LLC .... G 302 764-3389
  Wilmington (G-17505)
Jfm Enterprises LLC .... G 302 836-4107
  Newark (G-11111)
Jgreenbergconsulting LLC .... F 610 572-2729
  Magnolia (G-6753)
JLW Consulting LLC .... G 302 653-7283
  Smyrna (G-13781)
Jmt Services Inc .... G 302 407-5978
  Wilmington (G-17558)
Joseph T Hardy & Son Inc .... E 302 328-9457
  New Castle (G-9268)
JR Gettier & Associates Inc .... E 302 478-0911
  Wilmington (G-17600)
▲ Kaiser Time Inc .... G 646 473-1640
  Wilmington (G-17635)
Kaleo Inc .... G 302 376-0327
  Townsend (G-14021)
Kathairos Solutions Us Inc .... E 855 285-2010
  Dover (G-2833)
Kencrest Services .... G 302 735-1664
  Dover (G-2841)
Kerlink Inc .... G 805 407-9208
  Wilmington (G-17696)
◆ Kfs Strategic MGT Svcs LLC .... G 302 757-6631
  Newark (G-11167)
Klm Consulting LLC .... G 302 763-2174
  Hockessin (G-5271)
KMC Management LLC .... G 866 943-2205
  Wilmington (G-17743)
Knight Insur Consulting Group .... G 973 704-1112
  Newark (G-11197)
Korn Consult Group US Inc .... G 304 933-5355
  Newark (G-11200)
Kramer Group LLC .... G 717 368-2117
  Wilmington (G-17750)
Krenee LLC .... G 302 200-1025
  Wilmington (G-17755)
L & K Real Estate LLC .... F 484 410-4898
  Bear (G-337)
Landmark Engineering Inc .... D 302 323-9377
  Newark (G-11218)
Latam Corporate Services LLC .... F 301 375-0714
  Dover (G-2906)

Employee Codes: A=Over 500 employees, B=251-500
C=101-250, D=51-100, E=20-50, F=10-19, G=1-9

2024 Harris Directory of Delaware Businesses

87 ENGINEERING, ACCOUNTING, RESEARCH, AND MANAGEMENT SERVICES

Company	Code	Phone
LCB Consulting Inc — Bear (G-341)	G	302 836-1396
Leiters Tools LLC — New Castle (G-9304)	G	302 538-3284
Lens Tolic LLC — Hockessin (G-5280)	G	800 343-5697
Lig Energy Solutions LLC — Wilmington (G-17907)	C	646 918-8232
Lisa Mathena Group — Milton (G-8654)	F	302 645-4804
Lityx LLC — Wilmington (G-17948)	G	888 548-9947
Longwood Assets LLC — Middletown (G-7312)	G	617 906-8882
Marcon John Solutions Inc — Wilmington (G-18122)	G	302 295-4806
Marlen D Schlabach — Delmar (G-1617)	G	302 236-5394
Marquis Consulting LLC — Lewes (G-6245)	G	480 438-5582
Mayr Enterprises LLC — Delmar (G-1618)	G	302 846-2999
MB Store LLC — Wilmington (G-18211)	F	425 310-2574
Mc Creative Group — Millsboro (G-8370)	F	302 348-8977
Medevice Services LLC — Dover (G-3051)	G	877 202-1588
Mefta LLC — Wilmington (G-18260)	F	804 433-3566
Mentor Consultants Inc — Wilmington (G-18273)	G	610 566-4004
Meratalk LLC — Claymont (G-1233)	G	914 241-5226
Meta Mind Global Corp LLC — Dover (G-3069)	G	267 471-3616
Mid-Atlantic Envmtl Labs Inc — Historic New Castle (G-5028)	F	302 654-1340
Milieux LLC — Wilmington (G-18356)	G	302 770-5868
Mill Wilmington LLC — Wilmington (G-18358)	G	302 218-7527
Millenium Services LLC — Middletown (G-7370)	F	888 507-9473
Mjp Enterprises — Middletown (G-7374)	G	302 584-4736
Mobilen Communications Inc — Wilmington (G-18396)	G	844 580-7233
Moran Environmental Recovery — New Castle (G-9381)	G	302 322-6008
Mrt Enterprises Inc — Clayton (G-1389)	G	302 593-3070
Mss Energy Holdings LLC — Wilmington (G-18478)	G	212 231-2505
My Benefit Advisor LLC — Wilmington (G-18503)	G	302 588-7242
Nabstar Hospitality — Newark (G-11481)	G	302 453-1700
Nally Ventures Cnstr LLC — Ocean View (G-12550)	G	302 581-9243
Nanticoke Consulting Inc — Houston (G-5446)	G	302 245-3465
Nashco Enterprises Ltd — Wilmington (G-18536)	G	403 590-0846
National Cncil On AG Lf Lbor R — Dover (G-3154)	E	302 678-9400
Neitsch Ltd Liability Company — Newark (G-11500)	G	708 634-8724
Nestal Mdsphere Consulting LLC — Wilmington (G-18588)	G	302 404-6506
Netinstincts Inc — Wilmington (G-18593)	G	302 521-9478
Netragy LLC — Newark (G-11509)	G	973 846-7018
Netwerx LLC — Wilmington (G-18594)	G	732 245-8521
Network Design Technologies — Wilmington (G-18596)	E	610 991-2929
New Castle Cnty Shoppers Guide — New Castle (G-9406)	G	302 325-6600
New Covenant Elec Svcs Inc — Middletown (G-7398)	G	302 454-1165
Novitex Intermediate LLC — Wilmington (G-18697)	A	302 278-0867
Nr Hudson Consulting Inc — Laurel (G-5571)	G	302 875-5276
Nt Marine Apps LLC — Wilmington (G-18706)	G	561 329-3209
Nucar Consulting Inc — Odessa (G-12585)	E	302 696-6000
Oasm Corp — Dover (G-3213)	F	203 679-9124
Office Prtners Xiv Bllvue Pk L — Wilmington (G-18749)	G	302 691-2100
Olympus Consulting LLC — Smyrna (G-13842)	G	302 353-7329
On Point Partners LLC — Wilmington (G-18775)	G	302 655-5606
Only Gods Speed LLC — New Castle (G-9434)	F	302 367-8366
Orchard Park Group Inc — New Castle (G-9436)	G	302 356-1139
Oversight Board LLC — Wilmington (G-18841)	G	302 898-2599
Owcp Claims Consulting LLC — Hockessin (G-5331)	G	302 559-7501
Patent Information Users Group — Newark (G-11635)	F	302 660-3275
Patterson 3 Inv Group LLC — Dover (G-3283)	G	302 469-4783
Peddie John — Newark (G-11653)	G	302 838-8771
Pencader Consulting Group — Newark (G-11658)	G	302 454-8004
Perastic LLC — Wilmington (G-18967)	G	917 592-4219
Performance Materials Na Inc — Wilmington (G-18977)	A	302 892-7009
Pineal Consulting Group LLC — Dover (G-3324)	G	302 446-3794
Placidify Inc — Lewes (G-6376)	E	833 752-2434
Play By Play LLC — Wilmington (G-19074)	G	302 703-7670
Plenteous Consulting LLC — Claymont (G-1264)	G	724 325-1660
Prevail Trial Consultants LLC — Wilmington (G-19185)	F	302 442-7836
Princeton Coml Holdings LLC — Newark (G-11746)	G	302 449-4836
Prism Events Inc — Newark (G-11752)	G	424 252-1070
Pro Benefits Plus — Milford (G-8052)	G	302 683-5546
Pro Physical Therapy — Milford (G-8054)	G	302 422-6670
Project Widgets Inc — Wilmington (G-19226)	G	302 439-3414
Protect Intl Risk Sfety Svcs C — Wilmington (G-19234)	G	877 736-0805
Providge Consulting LLC — Wilmington (G-19238)	E	888 927-6583
Puma Energy US Inc — Wilmington (G-19256)	G	787 966-7929
Pyramid Educational Cons — New Castle (G-9502)	E	302 368-2515
Qsr Group LLC — Wilmington (G-19278)	G	302 268-6909
Qualdent LLC — Wilmington (G-19282)	G	856 642-4078
Quic-Pro Inc — Dover (G-3410)	G	302 883-8305
Rallypoint Solutions LLC — Wilmington (G-19322)	F	302 543-8087
Range Inc — Wilmington (G-19333)	G	201 350-7636
Reading Assist Institute — Wilmington (G-19362)	G	302 425-4080
Real World Endo — Milton (G-8693)	G	302 827-4816
Recadia Corp Llc — Wilmington (G-19375)	G	866 671-1280
Redrum City Productions — New Castle (G-9516)	G	313 389-6836
Renaissance Square LLC — Dover (G-3452)	G	302 943-5118
Rgs Technology Group LLC — Wilmington (G-19454)	G	302 397-3169
Rheumatology Consultants — Milford (G-8065)	G	302 491-6659
Robert Fry Economics LLC — Wilmington (G-19510)	G	302 743-8553
Rockledge Global Partners Ltd — Wilmington (G-19543)	G	800 659-1102
Rulesware LLC — Newark (G-11926)	G	302 293-4077
Rutman Enterprises — Wilmington (G-19596)	G	302 777-5298
Rxbenefits Inc — Lewes (G-6435)	G	724 525-9080
S S I Group LLC — Lewes (G-6437)	G	877 778-7099
SA Ryan LLC — Smyrna (G-13875)	G	302 757-6440
Safs International Group LLC — Wilmington (G-19630)	G	954 707-4627
Sagacious Works — Wilmington (G-19631)	F	609 251-9265
Sandler Occptnal Mdicine Assoc — Newark (G-11941)	G	302 369-0171
Santora CPA Group Pa — Newark (G-11945)	E	302 737-6200
Schatz Messick Enterprises LLC — Harrington (G-4827)	G	302 398-8646
Schiff Group LLC — Bethany Beach (G-639)	G	301 325-1359
Scientific Chemical Solutions — Wilmington (G-19704)	G	208 490-2125
Scotts-Sierra Investments LLC — Wilmington (G-19713)	G	302 622-9269
SD&I Enterprises LLC — Wilmington (G-19718)	G	302 407-6591
Sentinel-Sg LLC — Wilmington (G-19754)	G	580 458-9184
Service Rsource Group Intl LLC — Wilmington (G-19762)	G	832 646-8756
Six Angels Development Inc — Wilmington (G-19846)	G	302 218-1548
Smp Enterprises Inc — Newark (G-12042)	G	302 252-5331
Social Enterprises — Newark (G-12048)	G	302 526-4800
SOS Call Center Inc — Newark (G-12057)	G	302 319-5988
Spence Holding — Wilmington (G-19960)	F	973 392-1218

SIC SECTION
89 SERVICES, NOT ELSEWHERE CLASSIFIED

Spine Group LLC... G 302 595-3030
  Wilmington *(G-19964)*

Sqs Global Solutions LLC.............................. F 302 691-9682
  Wilmington *(G-19984)*

Stantec Consulting Svcs Inc......................... G 302 395-1919
  Newark *(G-12085)*

Strategy House Inc...................................... G 302 658-1500
  Newark *(G-12106)*

Suburban Waste Services Inc....................... G 302 661-0161
  Wilmington *(G-20117)*

Suffex Conservation.................................... G 302 856-2105
  Georgetown *(G-4529)*

Sussex Plmnary Endocrine Cnslt................. G 302 249-9970
  Rehoboth Beach *(G-12985)*

Sustainable-Generation LLC........................ F 917 678-6947
  Wilmington *(G-20165)*

Systems Tech & Science LLC....................... G 703 757-2010
  Dagsboro *(G-1513)*

Ta Management & Consulting....................... G 302 317-1538
  Bear *(G-523)*

Tade Info Tech Solutions............................. G 302 832-1449
  Newark *(G-12154)*

Tappedn Holdings LLC................................ G 404 877-2525
  Dover *(G-3651)*

Tdm Pharmaceutical RES Inc....................... G 302 832-1008
  Newark *(G-12165)*

Team Systems International LLC.................. G 703 217-7648
  Lewes *(G-6545)*

Tek Electronics LLC.................................... G 302 449-6947
  Middletown *(G-7627)*

Tek Tree LLC... F 302 368-2730
  Newark *(G-12174)*

Tekmen Group... G 302 381-0161
  Rehoboth Beach *(G-12992)*

Telgian Corporation..................................... E 480 753-5444
  Wilmington *(G-20267)*

Ten Bears Environmental LLC...................... G 302 731-8633
  Newark *(G-12178)*

Tepuyi LLC.. F 954 991-0749
  Dover *(G-3670)*

Terra Systems Inc....................................... E 302 798-9553
  Claymont *(G-1310)*

Thrive Agritech.. F 800 205-7216
  Claymont *(G-1313)*

Tinman Enterprises LLC............................... G 302 698-1630
  Camden Wyoming *(G-983)*

Tle Ventures Ltd.. G 800 794-3867
  Dover *(G-3691)*

Trade & Consulting Group Corp................... C 302 477-9800
  Wilmington *(G-20383)*

Treehouse Wellness Center LLC.................. G 302 893-1001
  Wilmington *(G-20407)*

Trellist Inc.. F 302 593-1432
  Wilmington *(G-20408)*

Tri State Waste Solutions............................ G 302 323-0200
  Wilmington *(G-20410)*

Trinet Consultants Inc.................................. F 302 633-9348
  Wilmington *(G-20423)*

Trinity Enterprises LLC................................ G 302 449-1301
  Claymont *(G-1317)*

Trinity Gold Consulting LLC......................... G 302 498-9063
  Wilmington *(G-20426)*

Trio Enterprises LLC................................... G 302 832-5575
  Townsend *(G-14085)*

Txe Global LLC... G 302 409-0234
  Wilmington *(G-20473)*

Tychron Corporation.................................... F 844 892-4766
  Wilmington *(G-20476)*

Uptrend Consulting & Creative.................... G 484 840-1200
  Wilmington *(G-20538)*

Vega Consulting Inc.................................... D 302 636-5401
  Wilmington *(G-20577)*

Velocity Maint Solutions LLC....................... E 844 538-8349
  New Castle *(G-9668)*

Veritas Consultant Group LLC..................... G 302 893-9794
  Newark *(G-12314)*

▼ Verscom LLC.. E 866 238-9189
  Wilmington *(G-20595)*

Victor A Maldonado..................................... G 302 420-9749
  Saint Georges *(G-13040)*

Virtual Business Entps LLC......................... G 302 472-9100
  Wilmington *(G-20633)*

Visa Europe Services LLC........................... E 302 658-7581
  Wilmington *(G-20636)*

Vtms LLC.. G 302 264-9094
  Dover *(G-3813)*

Wik Associates Inc..................................... G 302 322-2558
  Newark *(G-12372)*

Wilmington Area Plg Council........................ F 302 737-6205
  Newark *(G-12379)*

Womens Healthcare Consultants................. G 443 553-1398
  Newark *(G-12396)*

Woods Hole Group Inc................................ E 302 222-6720
  Dover *(G-3867)*

Workbetterai Inc.. F 805 825-5216
  Dover *(G-3870)*

Wrpatrick Enterprises LLC........................... G 302 988-1061
  Selbyville *(G-13620)*

Xerimis Inc... G 215 815-1706
  Selbyville *(G-13621)*

Xpert Tek Solutions Inc............................... G 302 724-4857
  Dover *(G-3882)*

Yeezie Holdings LLC................................... G 917 970-1974
  Dover *(G-3884)*

Yorston and Co LLC.................................... G 302 415-1925
  Middletown *(G-7748)*

Zcorp Property Consultants LLC................. G 302 864-8581
  Georgetown *(G-4582)*

Zeribon Holding Group LLC......................... C 844 205-1999
  Dover *(G-3899)*

Zieta Technologies LLC............................... E 302 252-5249
  Wilmington *(G-20961)*

89 SERVICES, NOT ELSEWHERE CLASSIFIED

8999 Services, nec

1evans Environmental Serv......................... G 410 635-8304
  Bridgeville *(G-655)*

A&R Environmental LLC.............................. G 302 864-7534
  Georgetown *(G-4192)*

Aetho LLC.. F 215 821-7290
  Dover *(G-1733)*

Agriculture United States Dept.................... G 302 741-2600
  Dover *(G-1747)*

Ajusta Tu Corona Inc................................... F 203 434-0356
  Dover *(G-1758)*

Amalipo Smartduka Ltd................................ F 857 452-1692
  Lewes *(G-5681)*

Art Ture.. G 302 893-0156
  Dover *(G-1820)*

Artcomun Technologies Inc......................... G 302 266-1521
  Newark *(G-9910)*

Astro-Lyfe LLC.. F 240 410-9665
  Dover *(G-1839)*

Ateleir Art Services Inc............................... G 302 669-6400
  New Castle *(G-8829)*

B P Services... G 302 399-4132
  Dover *(G-1864)*

Backdoor Entertainment LLC....................... G 215 514-0915
  Middletown *(G-6899)*

Belle Energie LLC....................................... G 302 690-3188
  Dover *(G-1908)*

Biblion... G 302 644-2210
  Lewes *(G-5762)*

Brightfields Inc... E 302 656-9600
  Wilmington *(G-15113)*

Congo Capital Management LLC.................. F 732 337-6643
  Wilmington *(G-15593)*

Congo Industries Inc................................... G 732 337-6643
  Wilmington *(G-15596)*

Coztel LLC.. G 832 224-5638
  Wilmington *(G-15674)*

Delaware Arts Conservatory........................ G 302 595-4160
  Bear *(G-141)*

Delaware Secretary of State........................ F 302 736-7400
  Dover *(G-2257)*

Delmarva Communications Inc.................... F 302 324-1230
  New Castle *(G-9042)*

Destiny Rescue Intl Inc............................... G 574 529-2238
  Lewes *(G-5912)*

Dialog News Paper Inc................................ G 302 573-3109
  Wilmington *(G-16048)*

Dj First Class.. F 302 345-0602
  New Castle *(G-9058)*

▼ Du Pont Delaware Inc.............................. D 302 774-1000
  Wilmington *(G-16189)*

Dupont Operations Inc................................ E 302 992-5940
  Wilmington *(G-16212)*

Dynamic Packet Corp.................................. F 302 448-2222
  Newark *(G-10584)*

Eds Road Service Inc.................................. G 302 437-4103
  Newark *(G-10611)*

Envision It Publications LLC....................... G 800 329-9411
  Bear *(G-204)*

Evergreen Resources Group LLC................ G 302 477-0189
  Wilmington *(G-16488)*

Forged Creations.. G 302 832-1631
  Delaware City *(G-1542)*

Hajirs Touch LLC.. G 302 543-2302
  Wilmington *(G-17035)*

Holmes Smith Consulting Svcs.................... G 302 407-6691
  New Castle *(G-9217)*

Ibg Enterprise Inc....................................... G 302 494-5017
  New Castle *(G-9227)*

Internet Vikings East LLC........................... G 347 879-1452
  Wilmington *(G-17394)*

Jamaika... G 302 521-4842
  Wilmington *(G-17475)*

Jamland Studio... G 302 475-0204
  Wilmington *(G-17490)*

Landmark Engineering Inc........................... D 302 323-9377
  Newark *(G-11218)*

Lon Kieffer... G 888 466-2379
  Seaford *(G-13264)*

Meta Mind Global Corp LLC........................ G 267 471-3616
  Dover *(G-3069)*

Mid Sussex Rescue Squad Inc.................... F 302 945-2680
  Millsboro *(G-8378)*

Moran Envmtl Recovery LLC....................... C 302 322-6008
  Newark *(G-11450)*

Murgency Inc.. E 650 308-9964
  Dover *(G-3132)*

Net 2 Apps LLC... G 214 810-2592
  Wilmington *(G-18590)*

New Castle Conservation Dst...................... F 302 832-3100
  Newark *(G-11516)*

New Perspectives Inc.................................. G 302 489-0220
  Wilmington *(G-18625)*

On My Mind Designs.................................... F 302 494-8622
  Wilmington *(G-18774)*

Open Lanes-Solutions LLC.......................... F 888 410-4207
  Wilmington *(G-18795)*

Orthopaedic Consultants PA....................... G 302 724-5062
  Dover *(G-3243)*

89 SERVICES, NOT ELSEWHERE CLASSIFIED

Paques Environmental Tech Inc............ G 412 932-3540
  Wilmington (G-18881)
Pink App LLC.. E 408 654-4636
  Wilmington (G-19048)
Prestege LLC.. G 302 312-8548
  Newark (G-11734)
Qbr Telecom Inc................................... F 302 510-1155
  Wilmington (G-19275)
Qualdent LLC....................................... G 856 642-4078
  Wilmington (G-19282)
RAC National Product Service L........... G 972 801-1100
  Newark (G-11814)
Recentia Usa Inc.................................. G 847 977-7571
  Wilmington (G-19376)
Ribodynamics LLC................................ G 518 339-6605
  Wilmington (G-19464)
Sam8sara Inc....................................... F 347 605-0693
  Lewes (G-6444)
Schiff Group LLC.................................. G 301 325-1359
  Bethany Beach (G-639)
Shepherd Stffing Cnsulting LLC............ G 302 652-0899
  Wilmington (G-19795)
Steagle Consulting Group LLC.............. G 302 439-4301
  Claymont (G-1302)
Stride Services Inc............................... F 302 540-4713
  Wilmington (G-20099)
Sussex Conservation District................ E 302 856-2105
  Georgetown (G-4535)
Switch Enterprises LLC........................ E 212 227-9191
  Dover (G-3632)
Technical Writers Inc............................ F 302 477-1972
  Wilmington (G-20254)
Telcast Networks LLC.......................... G 833 835-2278
  Dover (G-3665)
Volvox Biologic Inc............................... G 801 722-5942
  Lewes (G-6609)
Whyfly LLC... F 302 222-7171
  Wilmington (G-20776)

91 EXECUTIVE, LEGISLATIVE & GENERAL GOVERNMENT, EXCEPT FINANCE

9111 Executive offices

Delaware Dept Hlth Social Svcs............ G 302 856-5586
  Georgetown (G-4280)
Delaware Div Hstrcal Cltral AF.............. F 302 736-7400
  Dover (G-2232)
Larry Shelton....................................... F 678 948-6096
  New Castle (G-9295)

9199 General government, nec

City of Dover.. F 302 736-7035
  Dover (G-2083)
City of Dover.. F 302 736-5071
  Dover (G-2084)
Delaware Secretary of State................. G 302 834-8046
  Bear (G-155)
Delaware Secretary of State................. F 302 736-7400
  Dover (G-2257)

92 JUSTICE, PUBLIC ORDER AND SAFETY

9211 Courts

Supreme Court United States............... F 302 252-2950
  Wilmington (G-20155)

9221 Police protection

Town of Middletown.............................. E 302 376-9950
  Middletown (G-7656)

9223 Correctional institutions

Delaware Department Correction.......... C 302 856-5280
  Georgetown (G-4279)

9224 Fire protection

Christiana Fire Company...................... G 302 834-2433
  Bear (G-100)

93 PUBLIC FINANCE, TAXATION AND MONETARY POLICY

9311 Finance, taxation, and monetary policy

Delaware Department Finance.............. D 302 739-5291
  Dover (G-2227)

94 ADMINISTRATION OF HUMAN RESOURCE PROGRAMS

9431 Administration of public health programs

Children Yuth Their Fmlies Del............. F 302 577-4270
  New Castle (G-8934)
Children Yuth Their Fmlies Del............. G 302 633-2600
  Wilmington (G-15377)
Delaware Dept Hlth Social Svcs........... G 302 857-5000
  Dover (G-2229)
Delaware Dept Hlth Social Svcs........... G 302 255-9855
  New Castle (G-9017)
Delaware Dept Hlth Social Svcs........... D 302 255-2700
  New Castle (G-9019)
Delaware Dept Hlth Social Svcs........... F 302 391-3505
  New Castle (G-9021)
Delaware Dept Hlth Social Svcs........... F 302 368-6700
  Newark (G-10433)
Delaware Dept Hlth Social Svcs........... G 302 283-7500
  Newark (G-10434)
Delaware Dept Hlth Social Svcs........... C 302 223-1000
  Smyrna (G-13698)

9441 Administration of social and manpower programs

Children Youth & Their Fam.................. G 302 577-6011
  Wilmington (G-15374)
Delaware Dept Hlth Social Svcs........... G 302 337-8261
  Bridgeville (G-691)
Delaware Dept Hlth Social Svcs........... F 302 255-9500
  Dover (G-2230)
Delaware Dept Hlth Social Svcs........... F 302 391-3505
  New Castle (G-9021)

9451 Administration of veterans' affairs

Delaware Secretary of State................. G 302 834-8046
  Bear (G-155)
Veterans Health Administration............. G 302 994-1660
  Wilmington (G-20599)
Veterans Health Administration............. B 302 994-2511
  Wilmington (G-20600)

95 ADMINISTRATION OF ENVIRONMENTAL QUALITY AND HOUSING PROGRAMS

9512 Land, mineral, and wildlife conservation

City of Newark..................................... E 302 366-7060
  Newark (G-10245)
Delaware Div Parks Recreation............. F 302 571-7788
  Wilmington (G-15909)
Delaware Div Parks Recreation............. F 302 761-6963
  Wilmington (G-15910)

9532 Urban and community development

One Village Alliance Inc....................... G 302 275-1715
  Wilmington (G-18785)

96 ADMINISTRATION OF ECONOMIC PROGRAMS

9611 Administration of general economic programs

City of Dover.. E 302 736-7070
  Dover (G-2081)

9621 Regulation, administration of transportation

Delaware Department Trnsp.................. E 302 326-8950
  Bear (G-146)
Delaware Department Trnsp.................. D 302 577-3278
  Dover (G-2228)
Delaware Department Trnsp.................. E 302 653-4128
  Middletown (G-7039)
Delaware Department Trnsp.................. G 302 658-8960
  Wilmington (G-15902)

9651 Regulation, miscellaneous commercial sectors

Zeribon Holding Group LLC.................. C 844 205-1999
  Dover (G-3899)

9661 Space research and technology

97 NATIONAL SECURITY AND INTERNATIONAL AFFAIRS

9711 National security

Air Force US Dept of............................ E 302 674-0942
  Dover (G-1756)
Armed Forces Med Examiner Sys......... E 302 346-8653
  Dover (G-1816)
Army & Air Force Exchange Svc........... F 302 677-3716
  Dover (G-1817)
Army National Guard Delaware............. G 302 855-7456
  Dagsboro (G-1413)
US Dept of the Air Force...................... E 302 677-2525
  Dover (G-3764)

ALPHABETIC SECTION

> **R & R Sealants (HQ)**...999 999-9999
> 651 Tally Blvd, Yourtown (99999) *(G-458)*
> **Ready Box Co** 999 999-9999
> 704 Lawrence Rd, Anytown (99999) *(G-1723)*
> **Rendall Mfg Inc, Anytown** Also Called RMI *(G-1730)*

- Designates this location as a headquarters
- Business phone
- Geographic Section entry number where full company information appears
- Address, city & ZIP

See footnotes for symbols and codes identification.
- Companies listed alphabetically.
- Complete physical or mailing address.

(Marianas Energy Company is a wholly owned subsidiary of Power Solutions Duns 855023819), Dover Also Called: Marianas Energy Company LLC *(G-3018)*
01 Hire Inc...408 599-2693
651 N Broad St Middletown (19709) *(G-6813)*
1 Hour Martinizing, Wilmington Also Called: McKelvey Hires Dry Cleaning *(G-18232)*
1 Konto Inc...215 783-8166
16192 Coastal Hwy Lewes (19958) *(G-5634)*
1 On 1 Personal Trainer LLC......................................717 418-2719
38792 Wilson Ave Selbyville (19975) *(G-13457)*
1 Righter LLC...302 479-9257
2 Righter Pkwy Wilmington (19803) *(G-14099)*
1 Smart Home, Dagsboro Also Called: Communications & Wiring Co *(G-1429)*
1-800-By-mulch..302 325-2257
1715 River Rd New Castle (19720) *(G-8742)*
10-4 Safety LLC (PA)...847 997-5515
3411 Silverside Rd Ttnallb Wilmington (19810) *(G-14100)*
100 Commerce LLC...302 738-3038
100 Commerce Dr Newark (19713) *(G-9702)*
100 St Clire Drv Oprations LLC.................................610 444-6350
100 Saint Claire Dr Hockessin (19707) *(G-5107)*
1000 Degrees Pizzeria...609 382-3022
4500 New Linden Rd Wilmington (19808) *(G-14101)*
1000 Degrees Pizzeria, Wilmington Also Called: 1000 Degrees Pizzeria *(G-14101)*
1000x LLC..919 584-5420
651 N Broad St Middletown (19709) *(G-6814)*
103 WHOlesale&distribution LLC..............................302 344-2093
2154 Grafton Dr Wilmington (19808) *(G-14102)*
1080 Slver Lk Blvd Oprtons LLC...............................610 444-6350
1080 Silver Lake Blvd Dover (19904) *(G-1677)*
1100 Nrman Eskrdge Hwy Oprtons...........................302 629-3575
1100 Norman Eskridge Hwy Seaford (19973) *(G-13041)*
1102 West Street Ltd Partnr......................................302 429-7600
1102 N West St Wilmington (19801) *(G-14103)*
111 Medco LLC..888 711-7090
8 The Grn Ste 8178 Dover (19901) *(G-1678)*
1110 On Parkway Nedi Spa.......................................302 576-1110
1110 N Bancroft Pkwy Ste 2 Wilmington (19805) *(G-14104)*
114 Ai Inc..719 394-0606
16192 Coastal Hwy Lewes (19958) *(G-5635)*
1203 Walker Rd Operations LLC..............................302 735-8800
1203 Walker Rd Dover (19904) *(G-1679)*
1212 Corporation..302 764-4048
2700 N Washington St Wilmington (19802) *(G-14105)*
13 Laundromat..302 322-1910
329 S Dupont Hwy New Castle (19720) *(G-8743)*
1300 Publishing Company LLC................................302 268-2684
1306 W 6th St Wilmington (19805) *(G-14106)*
1313 Innovation...302 407-0420
1313 N Market St Ste 1150nw Wilmington (19801) *(G-14107)*
1313 Owner LLC...302 225-7896
1201 N Market St Ste 400 Wilmington (19801) *(G-14108)*
1320 Cbw LLC...302 656-5599
1320 Clifford Brown Walk Wilmington (19801) *(G-14109)*

1401 Condominium Association...............................302 656-8171
1401 Pennsylvania Ave Wilmington (19806) *(G-14110)*
15 Division LLC...667 334-0861
2810 N Church St Wilmington (19802) *(G-14111)*
15 Renwick Street LLC...302 652-2900
1925 Lovering Ave Wilmington (19806) *(G-14112)*
160 Engineers..302 326-7441
1001 Ogletown Rd Newark (19711) *(G-9703)*
166th Medical Squadron...302 323-3385
2600 Spruance Dr New Castle (19720) *(G-8744)*
18 Pomegranets Inc..800 839-1754
501 Silverside Rd Wilmington (19809) *(G-14113)*
1825 Inn...717 838-8282
26285 Broadkill Rd Milton (19968) *(G-8552)*
190 Stadium LLC..302 659-3635
190 Stadium St Smyrna (19977) *(G-13623)*
1995 Property Management Inc..............................302 745-1187
25309 Church Rd Seaford (19973) *(G-13042)*
1evans Environmental Serv......................................410 635-8304
14844 Deer Forest Rd Bridgeville (19933) *(G-655)*
1source Safety Health..302 470-2001
200 Powder Mill Rd 361 Wilmington (19803) *(G-14114)*
1st Choice Painting LLC...302 278-2684
10795 Rifle Range Rd Bridgeville (19933) *(G-656)*
1st Choice Service, Greenwood Also Called: McBroom Jr Roger Dale *(G-4651)*
1st Engineering Solutions LLC.................................302 966-9439
1000 N West St Ste 1200 Wilmington (19801) *(G-14115)*
1st State Insulation, Greenwood Also Called: Installed Building Pdts Inc *(G-4640)*
1st State Pallets LLC..302 743-3993
2911 Frazer Rd Newark (19702) *(G-9704)*
1st State Power Clean LLC......................................302 735-7974
1609 Forrest Ave Dover (19904) *(G-1680)*
1st State Real Estate LLC (PA)................................302 319-4051
175 Fairhill Dr Wilmington (19808) *(G-14116)*
1st-Recruit LLC..732 666-4106
3 Germay Dr Unit 4-2031 Wilmington (19804) *(G-14117)*
1touch Painting LLC..302 703-6027
17527 Nassau Commons Blvd Lewes (19958) *(G-5636)*
2 Days Bath LLC..302 798-0103
6603 Governor Printz Blvd Wilmington (19809) *(G-14118)*
2 Guys Pressure Washing..302 250-3721
113 Meadowood Dr Newark (19711) *(G-9705)*
20 Mont LLC...302 999-0708
234 N James St Wilmington (19804) *(G-14119)*
208 Social...610 762-3793
17270 N Village Main Blvd Lewes (19958) *(G-5637)*
21st Century Insurance, Wilmington Also Called: 21st Century N Amer Insur Co *(G-14121)*
21st Century Insurance, Wilmington Also Called: High Point Preferred Insur Co *(G-17141)*
21st Century Insurance Group.................................302 478-3109
3 Beaver Valley Rd Wilmington (19803) *(G-14120)*
21st Century N Amer Insur Co (DH)........................877 310-5687
3 Beaver Valley Rd Wilmington (19803) *(G-14121)*

(PA)=Parent Co (HQ)=Headquarters (DH)=Div Headquarters

22 Solutions LLC.. 901 672-0006
  8 The Grn Dover (19901) *(G-1681)*
22d LLC.. 347 857-8807
  24a Trolley Sq Ste 2234 Wilmington (19806) *(G-14122)*
24/7 Club Fitness... 302 226-4853
  18908 Rehoboth Mall Blvd Ste 5 Rehoboth Beach (19971) *(G-12589)*
247 Digimedia Inc... 302 401-6869
  8 The Grn Dover (19901) *(G-1682)*
2520 Hair Salon & Day Spa... 717 845-2241
  11 Sea Bright Way Rehoboth Beach (19971) *(G-12590)*
2678266170, Middletown Also Called: Xpedient Freight LLC *(G-7740)*
280 Group LLC.. 408 834-7518
  1151 Walker Rd Dover (19904) *(G-1683)*
2ndquadrant Inc.. 650 378-1218
  1000 Nw St Ste 1200 Wilmington (19801) *(G-14123)*
2nu Photonics LLC... 302 388-2261
  113 E Main St Unit 404 Newark (19711) *(G-9706)*
2yum Inc (PA).. 626 420-4851
  8 The Grn Ste A Dover (19901) *(G-1684)*
3-D Fabrications Inc... 302 292-3501
  100 Gabor Dr Newark (19711) *(G-9707)*
300 Gateway LLC.. 302 655-4100
  1200 West Ave New Castle (19720) *(G-8745)*
302 Contracting LLC.. 302 677-1912
  2428 W Denneys Rd Dover (19904) *(G-1685)*
302 Elite Athletes... 302 834-7991
  213 Hazel Dr Bear (19701) *(G-1)*
302 Hemp Co... 302 854-4367
  18751 Dupont Blvd Georgetown (19947) *(G-4188)*
302 Properties LLC.. 302 525-4302
  250 Corporate Blvd Ste L Newark (19702) *(G-9708)*
302 Sports... 302 650-8479
  116 Winston Ave Wilmington (19804) *(G-14124)*
30215 Motorsports.. 302 293-6193
  715 Stanton Christiana Rd Newark (19713) *(G-9709)*
333 Rei LLC... 808 758-3095
  651 N Broad St Ste 205 Middletown (19709) *(G-6815)*
36 Builders Inc.. 302 349-9480
  16255 Sussex Hwy Bridgeville (19933) *(G-657)*
360 DC Rentals LLC... 202 432-3655
  401 Justison St Wilmington (19801) *(G-14125)*
360 Digital Marketing LLC... 214 247-7153
  16192 Coastal Hwy Lewes (19958) *(G-5638)*
360 Painting.. 302 373-4867
  310 Androssan Pl Townsend (19734) *(G-13948)*
360 Wellness LLC... 302 286-0118
  5519 E Timberview Ct Wilmington (19808) *(G-14126)*
360wise Live Inc... 844 360-9473
  254 Chapman Rd Newark (19702) *(G-9710)*
3b Braes Brown Bags.. 302 544-0779
  950 Rue Madora Bear (19701) *(G-2)*
3d Cad Design.. 302 373-7750
  12 Bunker Hill Ct Newark (19702) *(G-9711)*
3d Exhibits Inc.. 302 319-1051
  200 Centerpoint Blvd Ste A Historic New Castle (19720) *(G-4914)*
3d Internet Group Inc.. 302 376-7900
  609 Colchester Ct Middletown (19709) *(G-6816)*
3d Microwave LLC.. 302 497-0223
  7795 Bethel Rd Laurel (19956) *(G-5457)*
3d Tech LLC.. 610 268-2350
  7454 Lancaster Pike # 308 Hockessin (19707) *(G-5108)*
3dsteel Inc... 713 677-2027
  651 N Broad St Ste 206 Middletown (19709) *(G-6817)*
3e Cleaning Services... 215 359-8323
  401 Bassett Ct Townsend (19734) *(G-13949)*
3e Marketing Solutions.. 302 383-4325
  9 Kathlyn Ct Wilmington (19808) *(G-14127)*
3e Ventures Inc... 302 773-8658
  410 Churchmans Rd New Castle (19720) *(G-8746)*
3h Agent Services Inc... 518 583-0639
  1201 N Orange St Ste 710 Wilmington (19801) *(G-14128)*

3imachinecom Inc.. 301 233-7562
  1209 N Orange St Wilmington (19801) *(G-14129)*
3M, Newark Also Called: 3M Company *(G-9712)*
3M Company... 302 286-2480
  650 Dawson Dr Newark (19713) *(G-9712)*
3phase Excel Elevator LLC.. 508 350-9900
  300 B And O Ln Wilmington (19804) *(G-14130)*
3rd State Welding Supply LLC.................................... 302 777-1088
  32 Germay Dr Ste C Wilmington (19804) *(G-14131)*
3w3d Inc.. 858 263-5883
  1201 N Orange St Wilmington (19801) *(G-14132)*
4 Elements Es LLC... 302 670-5575
  1061 S Little Creek Rd Trlr 230 Dover (19901) *(G-1686)*
4 Green Solutions Inc (PA).. 954 770-5157
  16192 Coastal Hwy Lewes (19958) *(G-5639)*
4 Points Twing Radside Svc LLC................................ 302 538-8935
  5425 Willow Grove Rd Camden Wyoming (19934) *(G-902)*
4 Youth Productions Inc... 347 338-8243
  1900 Superfine Ln Ste 9 Wilmington (19802) *(G-14133)*
4-H... 302 831-8161
  461 Wyoming Rd Newark (19716) *(G-9713)*
409 Fitness.. 302 354-7011
  1701 Concord Pike Wilmington (19803) *(G-14134)*
431 Corporation... 352 385-1427
  4185 Kirkwood St Georges Rd Bear (19701) *(G-3)*
436 Aerial Port Squadron... 302 677-3169
  150 Patriot Way Dover (19902) *(G-1687)*
436th Medical Group, Dover Also Called: US Dept of the Air Force *(G-3764)*
44 Aasha Hospitality Assoc LLC................................. 302 674-3784
  1706 N Dupont Hwy Dover (19901) *(G-1688)*
44 New England Management Co............................. 302 477-9500
  320 Rocky Run Pkwy Wilmington (19803) *(G-14135)*
44 New England Management Co............................. 302 479-7900
  300 Rocky Run Pkwy Wilmington (19803) *(G-14136)*
4BOA LLC... 323 747-7771
  2803 Philadelphia Pike Ste 4027 Claymont (19703) *(G-1012)*
4dimensions LLC... 302 339-0082
  402 Rolling Green Ave New Castle (19720) *(G-8747)*
4gurus LLC (PA)... 571 789-0012
  33621 Union Cir Lewes (19958) *(G-5640)*
4rb Logistics LLC... 302 290-8187
  8 Bergen Ct Newark (19702) *(G-9714)*
4sight Group LLC.. 800 490-2131
  4023 Kennett Pike Wilmington (19807) *(G-14137)*
4TH PHASE THECHNOLOGIES INC............................. 610 420-5765
  501 Silverside Rd Ste 98 Wilmington (19809) *(G-14138)*
4th Street Chiro Pain Mgmt.. 302 656-5009
  318 N Market St Wilmington (19801) *(G-14139)*
4troy Foundation.. 302 448-9203
  12453 Redden Rd Bridgeville (19933) *(G-658)*
4youthproductions... 302 690-5602
  308 Campbell Rd Wilmington (19807) *(G-14140)*
5 A Day Warehouse, Newark Also Called: Produce For Btter Hlth Fndtion *(G-11758)*
5 Point Gloria Laundry & Clr, Wilmington Also Called: Five Point Chinese Laundry *(G-16652)*
5 Roads, Newark Also Called: Grofos International LLC *(G-10901)*
5 Star Hvacr LLC.. 610 508-6464
  2803 Philadelphia Pike Ste 1254 Claymont (19703) *(G-1013)*
5-Star Cleaning Services... 302 476-9604
  218 S Maryland Ave Wilmington (19804) *(G-14141)*
500 Suth Dpont Blvd Oprtons LL............................... 302 422-8700
  500 S Dupont Blvd Milford (19963) *(G-7753)*
50onred, Claymont Also Called: Red Spark LP *(G-1275)*
52nd & Forever Media LLC.. 302 463-0014
  302 Chapel Ave Claymont (19703) *(G-1014)*
550 Suites LLC... 508 651-8197
  18633 Fir Drive Ext Rehoboth Beach (19971) *(G-12591)*
5linx.. 302 981-2529
  729 Ellen Dr Bear (19701) *(G-4)*
5n1-Mc Cosmetics LLC... 866 561-6226
  1007 N Orange St Wilmington (19801) *(G-14142)*
6 8 Medical Solutions LLC... 843 481-5550
  16192 Coastal Hwy Lewes (19958) *(G-5641)*

6 Star Fundraising LLC 302 250-5085
 16 Revelstone Ct Newark (19711) *(G-9715)*

6-4-3 Fitness Corp 347 441-9690
 9 E Loockerman St Ste 3a Dover (19901) *(G-1689)*

613 Foundation 800 839-1754
 501 Silverside Rd Wilmington (19809) *(G-14143)*

629 Market Retail LLC 302 691-2100
 1000 N West St Ste 1000 # 1000 Wilmington (19801) *(G-14144)*

6am Run 302 521-0023
 108 Talleyrand Dr Wilmington (19810) *(G-14145)*

6clicks Inc (PA) 925 699-6304
 651 N Broad St Ste 206 Middletown (19709) *(G-6818)*

7 Jewel Logistics LLC 409 350-9759
 2 N Sherman Dr Bear (19701) *(G-5)*

7 Shipping, Wilmington Also Called: Seven Shipping Inc *(G-19768)*

70 Inc 310 529-1526
 8 The Grn Ste B Dover (19901) *(G-1690)*

700 Marvel Road Operations LLC 302 422-3303
 700 Marvel Rd Milford (19963) *(G-7754)*

700 Nrth King St Wlmington LLC 302 655-0400
 700 N King St Wilmington (19801) *(G-14146)*

730 Enterprises LLC 216 355-3008
 730 Ferry Cut Off St Historic New Castle (19720) *(G-4915)*

77 Legacy LLC 404 576-7265
 1209 N Orange St Wilmington (19801) *(G-14147)*

786 Cellular and Accessory 302 482-3024
 702 Wilmington Ave Wilmington (19805) *(G-14148)*

7chakras Spa Lounge 302 584-7793
 508 E 6th St Wilmington (19801) *(G-14149)*

7elements Inc 302 294-1791
 308 Suburban Dr Newark (19711) *(G-9716)*

7th Heaven Inc (PA) 201 282-1925
 910 Foulk Rd Ste 201 Wilmington (19803) *(G-14150)*

855 Inc 302 325-9100
 464 Moores Ln Historic New Castle (19720) *(G-4916)*

887 The Bridge 302 422-6909
 1977 Bay Rd Milford (19963) *(G-7755)*

8fig Growth LLC (PA) 442 888-4303
 1007 N Orange St Wilmington (19801) *(G-14151)*

8figures Inc 484 291-8881
 251 Little Falls Dr Wilmington (19808) *(G-14152)*

8mesh Inc 888 627-4331
 16192 Coastal Hwy Lewes (19958) *(G-5642)*

8th & Market Spinal Center 302 652-6000
 207 N Market St Wilmington (19801) *(G-14153)*

900 F Street Owner LLC 212 355-1500
 251 Little Falls Dr Wilmington (19808) *(G-14154)*

911 Restoration, Middletown Also Called: 911 Restoration of Delaware *(G-6819)*

911 Restoration of Delaware 302 331-2033
 105 E Lockwood St Middletown (19709) *(G-6819)*

9193 4323 Quebec Inc 855 824-0795
 2915 Ogletown Rd Unit 2385 Newark (19713) *(G-9717)*

9222 Enterprises LLC 888 551-1393
 8 The Grn Dover (19901) *(G-1691)*

924 Inc 302 656-6100
 724 Yorklyn Rd Ste 305 Hockessin (19707) *(G-5109)*

9junio Inc 239 946-6374
 651 N Broad St Middletown (19709) *(G-6820)*

9round 302 365-5590
 2826 Pulaski Hwy Newark (19702) *(G-9718)*

9round 302 543-2545
 1812 Marsh Rd Ste 405 Wilmington (19810) *(G-14155)*

9round 302 525-6045
 4565 Linden Hill Rd Wilmington (19808) *(G-14156)*

9round Fitness 302 504-4787
 3533 Philadelphia Pike Claymont (19703) *(G-1015)*

9zest Inc 703 666-8122
 8 The Grn Ste 5910 Dover (19901) *(G-1692)*

A & A Air Services Inc (PA) 302 436-4800
 35130 Bennett Rd Frankford (19945) *(G-4059)*

A & A Enterprises, Wilmington Also Called: Arianna & Angelina Entps LLC *(G-14550)*

A & B Electric 302 349-4050
 25 Adamsville Rd Greenwood (19950) *(G-4585)*

A & B General Contracting 302 604-9696
 25680 Covert St Seaford (19973) *(G-13043)*

A & C Unlimited 302 379-7112
 107 Bell Ct Bear (19701) *(G-6)*

A & D Enterprises, Ocean View Also Called: Clover Farms Meats *(G-12490)*

A & F Machine & Development 302 368-4303
 129 Sandy Dr Newark (19713) *(G-9719)*

A & H Metals Inc 302 366-7540
 249 E Chestnut Hill Rd Newark (19713) *(G-9720)*

A & J Custom Woodworking, Middletown Also Called: Peirce James Townsend III *(G-7438)*

A & R Bail Bonds LLC 302 357-1221
 1710 Philadelphia Pike Wilmington (19809) *(G-14157)*

A & Tc Builders Inc 443 736-0099
 32808 Pear Tree Ct Lewes (19958) *(G-5643)*

A & V Ldscpg & Hardscaping LLC 302 684-8609
 704 Chestnut St Milton (19968) *(G-8553)*

A + Floor Store Inc 302 698-2166
 166 Roundabout Trl Camden Wyoming (19934) *(G-903)*

A 1 At Your Service 302 369-7000
 74 Albe Dr Newark (19702) *(G-9721)*

A and H Nursing Administra 302 544-4474
 94 Dasher Ave Bear (19701) *(G-7)*

A and J Welding 302 229-2000
 4401 Summit Bridge Rd Ste 1 Middletown (19709) *(G-6821)*

A B C Ticket Co, Wilmington Also Called: Michael Schwartz *(G-18324)*

A B Fab & Machining LLC 302 293-4945
 170 Earland Dr New Castle (19720) *(G-8748)*

A B W Services LLC 856 449-1329
 281 Camerton Ln Townsend (19734) *(G-13950)*

A Balanced Life Massage 302 543-4004
 1 Murphy Rd # 2 Wilmington (19803) *(G-14158)*

A Better Chnce For Our Chldren 302 725-5008
 805 S Dupont Blvd Milford (19963) *(G-7756)*

A C Emsley & Associates 302 429-9191
 12 S Union St Wilmington (19805) *(G-14159)*

A C M S Inc 302 738-6036
 14 Thomas Ln N Newark (19711) *(G-9722)*

A C Schultes of Delaware Inc (HQ) 302 337-0700
 16289 Sussex Hwy Bridgeville (19933) *(G-659)*

A Caring Doctor Minnesota PA 302 266-0122
 1291 Churchmans Rd Newark (19713) *(G-9723)*

A Caring Doctor Minnesota PA 302 478-3910
 3010 Brandywine Pkwy Wilmington (19803) *(G-14160)*

A Center For Mntal Wllness Cmn 302 674-1397
 121 W Loockerman St Dover (19904) *(G-1693)*

A Center For Mntal Wllness Inc 302 674-1397
 121 W Loockerman St Dover (19904) *(G-1694)*

A Chance To Write It LLC 202 256-4524
 16192 Coastal Hwy Lewes (19958) *(G-5644)*

A Childs Potential 302 249-6929
 12 Gosling Dr Lewes (19958) *(G-5645)*

A Childs World LLC 302 322-9386
 300 Bear Christiana Rd Bear (19701) *(G-8)*

A Collins Trucking Inc 302 438-8334
 314 Turnberry Ct Bear (19701) *(G-9)*

A D Alpine DMD 302 239-4600
 4901 Limestone Rd Wilmington (19808) *(G-14161)*

A Dish Network 302 495-5709
 2 Schulze Rd Greenwood (19950) *(G-4586)*

A Dish Network 302 565-4175
 668 Paper Mill Rd Newark (19711) *(G-9724)*

A Dish Network 302 223-5754
 103 S Dupont Blvd Smyrna (19977) *(G-13624)*

A Douglas Chervenak Do 302 653-1050
 319 N Carter Rd Smyrna (19977) *(G-13625)*

A Duie Pyle Inc 302 326-9440
 204 Quigley Blvd Historic New Castle (19720) *(G-4917)*

A E G Contracting LLC 302 250-5438
 400 Valley Rd Wilmington (19804) *(G-14162)*

ALPHABETIC SECTION

A E Moore Incorporated 302 934-7055
25872 W State St Millsboro (19966) *(G-8157)*

A F R, New Castle Also Called: American Furniture Rentals Inc *(G-8798)*

A Farm Inc 610 496-1504
1482 Levels Rd Middletown (19709) *(G-6822)*

A G Concrete Works LLC 302 841-2227
31883 New St Dagsboro (19939) *(G-1409)*

A G M General Contractor Inc 215 558-6880
600 N Broad St Ste 5 Middletown (19709) *(G-6823)*

A Gentlemans Touch Inc 302 585-5805
1321 Lancaster Ave Ste A Wilmington (19805) *(G-14163)*

A Hair Hub LLC 267 206-0569
119 Banff St Bear (19701) *(G-10)*

A I Dupont Hosp For Children, Wilmington Also Called: Alfred Idpont Hosp For Chldren *(G-14356)*

A I O, Selbyville Also Called: Atlantic Industrial Optics *(G-13467)*

A I T, Wilmington Also Called: Amer Industrial Tech Inc *(G-14422)*

A J Dauphin & Son Inc 302 994-1454
3313 Elizabeth Ave Wilmington (19808) *(G-14164)*

A J E Construction LLC 302 217-2268
24705 Rosalyn Dr Seaford (19973) *(G-13044)*

A Js Fence Builders Inc 302 731-0000
11 Lawrence Ave Newark (19711) *(G-9725)*

A Kleensweep 302 764-7964
910 Marion Ave Wilmington (19809) *(G-14165)*

A L Merced General Contractors 302 658-1618
322 6th Ave Wilmington (19805) *(G-14166)*

A Leap Faith Child Dev Ctr, Wilmington Also Called: A Leap of Faith Inc *(G-14167)*

A Leap of Faith Inc 302 543-6256
1715 W 4th St Wilmington (19805) *(G-14167)*

A Little Veterinary Clinic PA 302 398-3367
6902 Milford Harrington Hwy Harrington (19952) *(G-4720)*

A M Clay Onroe Inc 302 645-6565
1143 Savannah Rd Lewes (19958) *(G-5646)*

A M T General Contracting, Dover Also Called: Troutman Machine Company Inc *(G-3731)*

A M Towing Co 302 357-5159
91 Villas Dr Apt 10 New Castle (19720) *(G-8749)*

A Magcal Escape Thrptic Bdywrk 302 375-6533
2502 Silverside Rd Ste 9 Wilmington (19810) *(G-14168)*

A Minor Tune Up LLC 302 658-1587
1704 N Scott St Wilmington (19806) *(G-14169)*

A Nod To Stella Embroidery 302 697-6308
120 Pine St Wyoming (19934) *(G-20979)*

A P Croll & Son Inc 302 856-6177
22997 Lewes Georgetown Hwy Georgetown (19947) *(G-4189)*

A P Linen Service, Milford Also Called: AP Linens Inc *(G-7770)*

A Pair of Painters 302 526-6761
191 Ponderosa Dr Magnolia (19962) *(G-6712)*

A Peacful Pl Intgrted Care LLC 302 264-3692
1001 S Bradford St Ste 7 Dover (19904) *(G-1695)*

A Place To Grow Fmly Chld Care 302 897-8944
3067 W Court Ave Claymont (19703) *(G-1016)*

A Plumber 302 249-7606
5923 Old Shawnee Rd Milford (19963) *(G-7757)*

A Plus Electric & Security 302 455-1725
94 Stardust Dr Newark (19702) *(G-9726)*

A Plus Floor Store, Camden Wyoming Also Called: A + Floor Store Inc *(G-903)*

A R Myers Auto Body, Wilmington Also Called: A R Myers Corporation *(G-14170)*

A R Myers Corporation 302 652-3164
1300 E 18th St Wilmington (19801) *(G-14170)*

A R Nails 302 858-4592
401 College Park Ln Georgetown (19947) *(G-4190)*

A Ralph Woodrow Inc 302 655-0297
116 Chadd Rd Newark (19711) *(G-9727)*

A Registered Agent Inc 302 288-0670
8 The Grn Ste 1 Dover (19901) *(G-1696)*

A Rodriguez Painting LLC 302 559-7692
417 Walter St Georgetown (19947) *(G-4191)*

A S A P Insulation Inc 302 836-9040
3019 Mcdaniel Ln Newark (19702) *(G-9728)*

A S C, Wilmington Also Called: American Soc Cytopathology Inc *(G-14443)*

A S I, Milton Also Called: Atlantic Screen & Mfg Inc *(G-8565)*

A S Jacono LLC 302 378-3000
865 Vance Neck Rd Middletown (19709) *(G-6824)*

A S T B Analytical Services 302 571-8882
4027 New Castle Ave New Castle (19720) *(G-8750)*

A Seed Hope Counseling Ctr LLC 302 605-6702
1601 Milltown Rd Ste 1 Wilmington (19808) *(G-14171)*

A Shared Space LLC 240 727-9917
3640 Concord Pike Unit 1136 Wilmington (19803) *(G-14172)*

A Smarter Clean LLC 302 841-8419
21 Pinewater Dr Harbeson (19951) *(G-4679)*

A Stitch In Time 302 395-1306
101 Harrison Ave New Castle (19720) *(G-8751)*

A Successful Woman 234 567-8910
21 Robins Ln Rehoboth Beach (19971) *(G-12592)*

A T I Funding Corporation (HQ) 302 656-8937
801 N West St 2nd Fl Wilmington (19801) *(G-14173)*

A To Z First Builders LLC 302 393-9761
87 Gardenia Blvd Greenwood (19950) *(G-4587)*

A Toll Building Systems, Newark Also Called: Case Construction Inc *(G-10158)*

A V C Inc 302 227-2549
20807 Coastal Hwy Ste 4 Rehoboth Beach (19971) *(G-12593)*

A V Resources Inc 302 994-1488
240 N James St Ste B2 Wilmington (19804) *(G-14174)*

A W Viohl General Contracting, Claymont Also Called: Andrew W Viohl *(G-1038)*

A Window To Wellness 302 567-5468
19606 Coastal Hwy Rehoboth Beach (19971) *(G-12594)*

A-1 Kevins Landscaping 302 270-6914
620 W South St Smyrna (19977) *(G-13626)*

A-1 Sanitation Service Inc 302 322-1074
1009 River Rd New Castle (19720) *(G-8752)*

A-Del Construction Company Inc 302 453-8286
10 Adel Dr Newark (19702) *(G-9729)*

A-One Towing Inc 302 853-2326
22467 John J Williams Hwy Lewes (19958) *(G-5647)*

A-Team Cleaning LLC 302 858-8709
7019 Seashore Hwy Bridgeville (19933) *(G-660)*

A-To-Z Management LLC 302 500-5230
8 The Grn Ste 14696 Dover (19901) *(G-1699)*

A&J Products Inc 302 424-0750
2860 Williamsville Rd Houston (19954) *(G-5434)*

A&M Transportation Inc 781 227-1257
120 N St Ate St Dover (19901) *(G-1697)*

A&R Environmental LLC 302 864-7534
25200 Governor Stockley Rd Georgetown (19947) *(G-4192)*

A&T Cleaning Services 302 752-5520
117 Washington St Laurel (19956) *(G-5458)*

A&V Landscaping 302 684-8609
704 Chestnut St Milton (19968) *(G-8554)*

A+ Cleaning Solutions Inc 423 693-7554
3500 S Dupont Hwy Dover (19901) *(G-1698)*

A+ Printing 302 273-3147
501 Birmingham Ave Wilmington (19804) *(G-14175)*

A+ Tree Service LLC 302 253-8612
21460 Park Ave Georgetown (19947) *(G-4193)*

A1 Express Trucking Inc 302 544-9273
3200 Kirkwood Hwy Ste 1068 Wilmington (19808) *(G-14176)*

A1 Handyman Services 302 398-4235
2199 Brownsville Rd Harrington (19952) *(G-4721)*

A1 Nationwide LLC 302 327-9302
1201 N Orange St Ste 7037 Wilmington (19801) *(G-14177)*

A1 Sanitation Service Inc 302 653-9591
27 E Chestnut St Smyrna (19977) *(G-13627)*

A1 Striping Inc 302 738-5016
902 Irish Bank Rd Newark (19702) *(G-9730)*

A1g0 LLC 855 661-0101
2055 Limestone Rd Ste 200c Wilmington (19808) *(G-14178)*

A22 Community Connections 302 213-9426
125 Rodney Dr New Castle (19720) *(G-8753)*

A2a Intgrted Phrmceuticals LLC 270 202-2461
16192 Coastal Hwy Lewes (19958) *(G-5648)*

(G-0000) Company's Geographic Section entry number

ALPHABETIC SECTION

A2b Auto Group 302 786-2331
   1211 E 15th St Wilmington (19802) *(G-14179)*

A2z Auto Rpair Auto Mble Rpair 302 856-2219
   19395 Substation Rd Georgetown (19947) *(G-4194)*

A2z Property Management LLC 302 239-6000
   2 White Briar Cir Hockessin (19707) *(G-5110)*

A66 Inc 800 444-0446
   2711 Centerville Rd Ste 400 Wilmington (19808) *(G-14180)*

AA Media Inc 302 729-2882
   307 S Cass St Middletown (19709) *(G-6825)*

AA Smith & Associates LLC 973 477-3052
   364 E Main St Ste 403 Middletown (19709) *(G-6826)*

AAA, Wilmington Also Called: AAA Washington *(G-14183)*

AAA Club Alliance Inc 302 674-8020
   124 Greentree Dr Dover (19904) *(G-1700)*

AAA Club Alliance Inc 302 368-8175
   200 Commerce Dr Newark (19713) *(G-9731)*

AAA Club Alliance Inc 302 283-4300
   200 Continental Dr Ste 402 Newark (19713) *(G-9732)*

AAA Club Alliance Inc (PA) 302 299-4700
   1 River Pl Wilmington (19801) *(G-14181)*

AAA Computing 302 430-9048
   306 S Washington St Milford (19963) *(G-7758)*

AAA Dover, Dover Also Called: AAA Club Alliance Inc *(G-1700)*

AAA Environmental Services 302 284-4334
   257 Deerwood Farm Ln Felton (19943) *(G-3937)*

AAA Keystone, Wilmington Also Called: AAA Club Alliance Inc *(G-14181)*

AAA Mid-Atlantic 302 299-4230
   1 River Pl Wilmington (19801) *(G-14182)*

AAA Midatlantic Inc 800 999-4952
   19 Lukens Dr Ste 100 Historic New Castle (19720) *(G-4918)*

AAA Portable Restroom Co Inc 909 981-0090
   108 Gardengate Rd Camden Wyoming (19934) *(G-904)*

AAA Tree & Shrub of Delaware, Claymont Also Called: Thomas E Cameron *(G-1312)*

AAA Tree Work LLC 302 213-2917
   28334 Wynikako Ave Millsboro (19966) *(G-8158)*

AAA Washington 860 371-9783
   1 River Pl Wilmington (19801) *(G-14183)*

Aaert Inc 302 765-3510
   2900 Fairhope Rd Wilmington (19810) *(G-14184)*

AAL Drtc 302 229-5891
   200 Gbc Dr Newark (19702) *(G-9733)*

AAMCO Transmissions, Dover Also Called: Js Automotive AAMCO *(G-2809)*

AAMCO Transmissions, Seaford Also Called: Challenge Automotive Svcs Inc *(G-13108)*

Aameenah Ali Muhammad, Wilmington Also Called: Ameenahko LLC *(G-14420)*

Aaquaone Inc 949 331-5405
   1226 N King St Ste 128 Wilmington (19801) *(G-14185)*

Aark Network Inc 302 399-3945
   1142 Elkton Rd Newark (19711) *(G-9734)*

Aaron Alfano 302 995-9600
   3608 Lancaster Pike Wilmington (19805) *(G-14186)*

Aaron and Sons Electric LLC 302 764-5610
   200 W 38th St Wilmington (19802) *(G-14187)*

Aaron Anderson 804 986-1666
   973 Red Lion Rd New Castle (19720) *(G-8754)*

Aaron Auto Glass 302 297-8008
   651 N Broad St Middletown (19709) *(G-6827)*

Aaron B Poleck DDS 302 533-7649
   50 Omega Dr Newark (19713) *(G-9735)*

Aaron's F244, Seaford Also Called: Aarons Sales & Leasing *(G-13045)*

Aaron's Rental Purchase, Newark Also Called: J R Rents Inc *(G-11076)*

Aarons Sales & Leasing 302 628-8700
   850 Norman Eskridge Hwy Seaford (19973) *(G-13045)*

AARP 202 434-2277
   222 Delaware Ave Ste 1610 Wilmington (19801) *(G-14188)*

AARP Delaware, Wilmington Also Called: AARP *(G-14188)*

AB Brown Real Estate Inc 302 731-1031
   4808 Plum Run Ct Wilmington (19808) *(G-14189)*

AB Carpentry Services Inc 302 276-2457
   217 Sykes Rd New Castle (19720) *(G-8755)*

AB Creative Publishing LLC 202 802-6909
   1104 Philadelphia Pike Wilmington (19809) *(G-14190)*

AB Group Packaging Inc 302 607-3281
   1800 Ogletown Rd Newark (19711) *(G-9736)*

AB&c, Wilmington Also Called: Aloysius Butlr Clark Assoc Inc *(G-14390)*

Aba PA, Lewes Also Called: P A Aba Intl Inc *(G-6343)*

Aba Travl & Ent Inc 800 696-0838
   16192 Coastal Hwy Lewes (19958) *(G-5649)*

Aba2day Behavior Services 302 494-4303
   1526 Villa Rd Wilmington (19809) *(G-14191)*

Abacus Tax Service 302 543-5619
   2604 Kirkwood Hwy Wilmington (19805) *(G-14192)*

Abad & Salameda PA 302 652-4705
   1508 Penns Ave Ste 1c Wilmington (19806) *(G-14193)*

Abandon Inc 858 863-7190
   8 The Grn Dover (19901) *(G-1701)*

Abbey Hair Styling 302 697-1186
   1309 Ponderosa Dr Magnolia (19962) *(G-6713)*

Abbey Lein Inc 302 239-2712
   28 Meteor Ct Newark (19711) *(G-9737)*

Abbey Walk Apts, Newark Also Called: Mid-Atlantic Realty Co Inc *(G-11411)*

Abbott Dynamics LLC 951 923-5996
   330 Delaware Ave 210-A Talleyville (19803) *(G-13944)*

Abby Family Practice, Newark Also Called: Family Prctice Ctr of New Cstl *(G-10709)*

Abby L Allen Fnp 302 856-1773
   20797 Professional Park Blvd Ste 214 Georgetown (19947) *(G-4195)*

Abby Medical Center 302 999-0003
   1 Centurian Dr Ste 301 Newark (19713) *(G-9738)*

Abby Pubusky 302 897-8932
   1805 Foulk Rd Ste A Wilmington (19810) *(G-14194)*

Abby Pubusky Insurance 302 434-3333
   1601 Concord Pike Ste 88 Wilmington (19803) *(G-14195)*

Abbycare, Newark Also Called: Abigail Family Medicine LLC *(G-9741)*

ABC Contractors LLC 302 492-1116
   4491 Arthursville Rd Hartly (19953) *(G-4853)*

ABC Delaware 302 858-2185
   31 Blevins Dr Ste B New Castle (19720) *(G-8756)*

ABC Drywall 302 249-0389
   14432 Owens Rd Greenwood (19950) *(G-4588)*

ABC Lending Corp 302 369-5626
   1007 S College Ave Newark (19713) *(G-9739)*

ABC Sales & Service Inc 302 652-3683
   2520 W 6th St Wilmington (19805) *(G-14196)*

ABC Systems Inc 302 528-8875
   92 White Clay Cres Newark (19711) *(G-9740)*

ABC Tree Svc 302 737-8733
   2204 Rodman Rd Wilmington (19805) *(G-14197)*

ABC Virginia Wireless 302 744-8473
   1616 S Governors Ave Dover (19904) *(G-1702)*

Abcfoc A Btter Chnce For Our C 302 746-7265
   1307 Philadelphia Pike Wilmington (19809) *(G-14198)*

Abco Mech Htg & Coolg LLC 302 353-4336
   14 Rambleton Dr New Castle (19720) *(G-8757)*

Abe Junk Removal & Home Svcs 302 540-3722
   16 Annie Gillis Ln Smyrna (19977) *(G-13628)*

Abeks Financial Consulting LLC 302 351-5910
   3501 Silverside Rd # 206 Wilmington (19810) *(G-14199)*

Abel Center For Oculofacial 302 998-3220
   1941 Limestone Rd Ste 201 Wilmington (19808) *(G-14200)*

ABG Designs, Middletown Also Called: Ten Talents Enterprises Inc *(G-7634)*

Abha Architects Inc 302 658-6426
   1621 N Lincoln St Wilmington (19806) *(G-14201)*

Abigail E Martin M D 302 651-4000
   1600 Rockland Rd Wilmington (19803) *(G-14202)*

Abigail Family Medicine LLC 302 738-3770
   412 Suburban Dr Newark (19711) *(G-9741)*

Ability Network of Delaware 302 622-9177
   100 W 10th St Ste 103 Wilmington (19801) *(G-14203)*

Abitechno Inc 302 213-6700
   3 Germay Dr Wilmington (19804) *(G-14204)*

Able Welding & Machine, Selbyville Also Called: Able Whelling and Machiene *(G-13458)*

ALPHABETIC SECTION

Able Whelling and Machiene...302 436-1929
  45 Railroad Ave Selbyville (19975) *(G-13458)*

Abled Directions LLC..206 265-3928
  1017 Ashland St Middletown (19709) *(G-6828)*

ABM Janitorial Services Inc..302 571-9900
  2110 Duncan Rd Wilmington (19808) *(G-14205)*

ABM Security Services Inc..302 992-9733
  2110 Duncan Rd Wilmington (19808) *(G-14206)*

About - Per Rush Adventures..302 270-7886
  1211 Sandbox Rd Harrington (19952) *(G-4722)*

About Angela Angelas Home Ln...302 598-7799
  22 Polly Drummond Hill Rd Newark (19711) *(G-9742)*

Above & Beyond Services..443 614-2068
  14461 Johnson Rd Laurel (19956) *(G-5459)*

Above All Gutter Svc...302 561-0709
  301 Senator Dr Middletown (19709) *(G-6829)*

Above and Beyond Cleaning Svcs...484 206-5101
  904 Vinings Way Newark (19702) *(G-9743)*

Above and Beyond Coverage LLC..201 417-5189
  3616 Kirkwood Hwy Wilmington (19808) *(G-14207)*

ABRA Auto Body & Glass..302 674-4525
  5825 W Denneys Rd Dover (19904) *(G-1703)*

ABRA Auto Body & Glass LP...302 279-1007
  5077 Summit Bridge Rd Middletown (19709) *(G-6830)*

ABRA Autobody & Glass, Dover Also Called: ABRA Auto Body & Glass *(G-1703)*

ABRA Autobody & Glass, Middletown Also Called: ABRA Auto Body & Glass LP *(G-6830)*

Abrahams Seed LLC..302 588-1913
  246 Coldwater Dr Clayton (19938) *(G-1347)*

Abrams & Bayliss LLP...302 778-1000
  20 Montchanin Rd Ste 200 Wilmington (19807) *(G-14208)*

Abraxas Massage and Bodywork...910 992-0350
  33010 Circle Dr Millsboro (19966) *(G-8159)*

Abri Spac 2 Inc..424 732-1021
  40 E Main St 1009 Newark (19711) *(G-9744)*

ABS, New Castle Also Called: Analytical Biological Svcs Inc *(G-8806)*

Absalom Jones Senior Center..302 998-0363
  310 Kiamensi Rd Ste B Wilmington (19804) *(G-14209)*

Absolute Computer Support LLC..717 917-8900
  249 E Main St Bldg 1 Newark (19711) *(G-9745)*

Absolute Equity..302 983-2591
  501 Clinton St Delaware City (19706) *(G-1527)*

Absolute Health LLC..302 535-8236
  301 E Camden Wyoming Ave Camden (19934) *(G-786)*

Absolute Locksmith, Magnolia Also Called: Jonathan Lopez *(G-6754)*

Absolutely Flawless Women Inc..410 845-6930
  19845 Lowes Crossing Rd Millsboro (19966) *(G-8160)*

Absolutely Green Inc...302 731-1616
  995 S Chapel St Ste 3 Newark (19713) *(G-9746)*

Absolution Inc...302 528-2330
  19119 Stonewood Ln Unit 48 Rehoboth Beach (19971) *(G-12595)*

Abundant Natural Health Inc..302 652-2900
  1925 Lovering Ave Wilmington (19806) *(G-14210)*

Abuwen Anesthesia Services LLC...301 526-4584
  516 Bluebill Dr New Castle (19720) *(G-8758)*

AC Engineering...215 873-6482
  135 Emerald Ridge Dr Bear (19701) *(G-11)*

AC Group Inc...201 840-5566
  3422 Old Capitol Trl 163 Wilmington (19808) *(G-14211)*

AC Home Solutions..302 442-2516
  1205 Lorrain Ave Wilmington (19808) *(G-14212)*

AC Tax Group LLC...844 378-1040
  801 Mapleton Ave Middletown (19709) *(G-6831)*

Aca Mortgage Co Inc..302 225-1390
  3202 Kirkwood Hwy Ste 205 Wilmington (19808) *(G-14213)*

Academy Bind Body Arts, Newark Also Called: American Karate Studios *(G-9846)*

Academy Business Mch & Prtg Co...302 654-3200
  12 S Maryland Ave Wilmington (19804) *(G-14214)*

Academy Dog Training & Agility...302 588-4636
  89b Albe Dr Newark (19702) *(G-9747)*

Academy Mortgage...484 680-8092
  4758 Limestone Rd Wilmington (19808) *(G-14215)*

Academy of Early Learning..302 659-0750
  310 N Main St Bldg A Smyrna (19977) *(G-13629)*

Academy Printing, Wilmington Also Called: Academy Business Mch & Prtg Co *(G-14214)*

Academy Sounds LLC...302 276-5027
  520 Copper Dr Newport (19804) *(G-12439)*

Acadia Healthcare Company Inc..302 328-3330
  575 S Dupont Hwy New Castle (19720) *(G-8759)*

Acbusa Inc...302 985-9395
  24a Trolley Sq Wilmington (19806) *(G-14216)*

Accelcare Wund Prfssnals Del P...800 261-0048
  73 Greentree Dr Dover (19904) *(G-1704)*

Accelcomm, Wilmington Also Called: AC Group Inc *(G-14211)*

Accelerate Mortgage LLC..866 986-1245
  750 Prides Xing Ste 303 Newark (19713) *(G-9748)*

Accelerated Intelligence Inc..800 765-3628
  717 N Union St Ste 150 Wilmington (19805) *(G-14217)*

Accelerated Virtual Solutions...302 494-3215
  57 E Periwinkle Ln Newark (19711) *(G-9749)*

Accelsiors LLC..302 450-1883
  3500 S Dupont Hwy Ste G101 Dover (19901) *(G-1705)*

Accendustry LLC...469 777-6186
  16192 Coastal Hwy Lewes (19958) *(G-5650)*

Accent Coatings, Newark Also Called: Raymond Harner *(G-11830)*

Accent Drapery Div Richert Inc, Milton Also Called: Richert Inc *(G-8698)*

Accent On Travel, Rehoboth Beach Also Called: Ans Corporation *(G-12607)*

Accenture..302 830-5800
  501 Carr Rd Ste 200 Wilmington (19809) *(G-14218)*

Accera Digital LLC...877 855-2501
  1201 N Market St Wilmington (19801) *(G-14219)*

Access Dental LLC..302 674-3303
  446 S New St A Dover (19904) *(G-1706)*

Access Funding 2010-A LLC..484 653-3300
  5500 Brandywine Pkwy Wilmington (19803) *(G-14220)*

Access Funding 2013-1 LLC..302 477-4071
  5500 Brandywine Pkwy Wilmington (19803) *(G-14221)*

Access It Services Inc...408 520-9069
  651 N Broad St Ste 206 Middletown (19709) *(G-6832)*

Access Labor Service Inc...302 741-2575
  1102 S State St Dover (19901) *(G-1707)*

Access Labor Service Inc (PA)..302 326-2575
  2203 N Dupont Hwy New Castle (19720) *(G-8760)*

Access Purchasing Network Inc (PA) 16192 Coastal Hwy Lewes (19958) *(G-5651)*

Access Quality Healthcare..302 698-2150
  608 Raven Cir Camden Wyoming (19934) *(G-905)*

Access Quality Healthcare..302 947-4437
  32026 Long Neck Rd Millsboro (19966) *(G-8161)*

Access4u Inc...800 355-7025
  510 Railroad Ave Lewes (19958) *(G-5652)*

Accesscare Inc...302 836-9314
  502 Beechwood Ct Bear (19701) *(G-12)*

Accessheat Inc...302 373-9524
  913 N Market St Ste 200 Wilmington (19801) *(G-14222)*

Accessquint LLC..302 351-4064
  300 Delaware Ave Ste 200 Wilmington (19801) *(G-14223)*

Acclaim Academy LLC..215 848-7827
  1521 Concord Pike Ste 301 Wilmington (19803) *(G-14224)*

Accolade Global, Wilmington Also Called: Accolade Global Inc *(G-14225)*

Accolade Global Inc..209 645-0225
  4023 Kennett Pike Ste 1000 Wilmington (19807) *(G-14225)*

Accommodating Nurses LLC...302 390-8065
  1521 Concord Pike Ste 301 Wilmington (19803) *(G-14226)*

Accord Restoration Inc...302 933-0991
  28368 John J Williams Hwy Millsboro (19966) *(G-8162)*

Accountemps, Wilmington Also Called: Robert Half International Inc *(G-19513)*

Accounting, Middletown Also Called: AC Tax Group LLC *(G-6831)*

Accss Qlty Healthcare Accss..302 339-4112
  20930 Dupont Blvd Georgetown (19947) *(G-4196)*

Accu Personnel Inc...302 384-8777
  1707 Concord Pike Wilmington (19803) *(G-14227)*

Accudyne Systems Inc (PA)..302 369-5390
  210 Executive Dr Ste 5 Newark (19702) *(G-9750)*

ALPHABETIC SECTION

Accugenix, Newark *Also Called: Charles River Labs Intl Inc (G-10191)*
   Accugenix Inc 302 292-8888
     223 Lake Dr Newark (19702) *(G-9751)*
   Accurate & Heating 302 561-5749
     17 Riva Ridge Ln Bear (19701) *(G-13)*
   Accurate Auto Service Inc 302 737-7998
     233 E Main St Newark (19711) *(G-9752)*
   Accurate Insulation LLC 302 336-8401
     143 Hatchery Rd Dover (19901) *(G-1708)*
   Accurate Media LLC 301 943-9428
     14689 Pleasant Pond Way Lewes (19958) *(G-5653)*
   Accurate Metal Solutions LLC
     1209 N Orange St Wilmington (19801) *(G-14228)*
   Accurate Pest Control Company 302 875-2725
     30139 Sussex Hwy Laurel (19956) *(G-5460)*
   Accurate Termite & Pest Ctrl, Laurel *Also Called: Accurate Pest Control Company (G-5460)*
   Accurate-Energy LLC 302 947-9560
     35180 South Dr Lewes (19958) *(G-5654)*
   Accuretix LLC 646 434-6917
     2803b Philadelphia Pike # 4177 Claymont (19703) *(G-1017)*
   Accusheets 302 266-1047
     218 W General Grey Ct Newark (19702) *(G-9753)*
   Accutax 302 735-9747
     408 Martin St Dover (19901) *(G-1709)*
   Accutrench Contracting LLC 410 829-5157
     407 Highland Dr Seaford (19973) *(G-13046)*
   Accuvention LLC 302 369-5390
     210 Executive Dr Newark (19702) *(G-9754)*
   Ace Global Solution, Wilmington *Also Called: Chubb US Holdings Inc (G-15426)*
   Ace Handyman Services 302 899-7300
     371 W North St Dover (19904) *(G-1710)*
   Ace Home Solutions Corp 302 743-8995
     5 Camino Ct New Castle (19720) *(G-8761)*
   Ace of Seed, Newark *Also Called: Napoleon Hernandez (G-11487)*
   Ace Rent-A-Car Inc 302 368-5950
     915 S Chapel St Newark (19713) *(G-9755)*
   Ace Your Party 302 415-1670
     904 Peachtree Rd Apt L Claymont (19703) *(G-1018)*
   Acentium Inc 617 938-3938
     251 Little Falls Dr Wilmington (19808) *(G-14229)*
   Acer Synergy Tech America Corp 267 901-4569
     251 Little Falls Dr Wilmington (19808) *(G-14230)*
   Achieve Lgstic Systems Trnsp L 302 654-4701
     510 A St Wilmington (19801) *(G-14231)*
   Achieve Solutions 302 598-1457
     1 Foxview Cir Hockessin (19707) *(G-5111)*
   Achievers Holdings Inc 647 265-9032
     1209 N Orange St Wilmington (19801) *(G-14232)*
   Achieving Physiques Inc 302 593-7067
     207 Hobson Dr Hockessin (19707) *(G-5112)*
   Aci Energy Inc 302 588-3024
     1105 N Market St Ste 650 Wilmington (19801) *(G-14233)*
   Acia Freight & Logistics LLC 800 362-8837
     2711 Centerville Rd Ste 400 Wilmington (19808) *(G-14234)*
   Ackrell Spac Partners I Co 650 560-4753
     2093 Philadelphia Pike # 1968 Claymont (19703) *(G-1019)*
   Acl Services 302 423-0276
     250 Ashton Ct Smyrna (19977) *(G-13630)*
   Acm Corp 302 736-3864
     218 Canal St Dover (19904) *(G-1711)*
   Acmegrc Limited 401 626-7684
     251 Little Falls Dr Wilmington (19808) *(G-14235)*
   Acn Cleaning LLC 302 588-7485
     1916 W 7th St Wilmington (19805) *(G-14236)*
   Acolyst, Selbyville *Also Called: Datatech Enterprises Inc (G-13515)*
   Acopia LLC 302 286-5172
     220 Continental Dr Ste 203 Newark (19713) *(G-9756)*
   Acopia Home Loans 302 242-6272
     405 Rehoboth Ave Rehoboth Beach (19971) *(G-12596)*
   Acorn, Wilmington *Also Called: Acorn Energy Inc (G-14237)*
   Acorn Books, Smyrna *Also Called: Acorn Books Inc (G-13631)*

   Acorn Books Inc 302 508-2219
     727 Lexington Ave Smyrna (19977) *(G-13631)*
   Acorn Energy Inc (PA) 410 654-3315
     1000 N West St Ste 1200 Wilmington (19801) *(G-14237)*
   ACorn Fitnes Well-Being LLC 302 545-3032
     903 Pickett Ln Newark (19711) *(G-9757)*
   Acorn Site Furnishings 302 249-4979
     5218 Federalsburg Rd Bridgeville (19933) *(G-661)*
   Acosh Enterprise LLC 631 767-4501
     1107 Lauren Pl Newark (19702) *(G-9758)*
   Acoustic Audio Tek LLC 302 685-2113
     1000 N West St Ste 1200 Wilmington (19801) *(G-14238)*
   Acp Services LLC 302 299-4225
     1 River Pl Wilmington (19801) *(G-14239)*
   Acp Technologies Inc 302 981-5976
     218 W Holly Dr Lincoln (19960) *(G-6653)*
   Acquisition Intl Holdings Inc 302 603-7795
     8 The Grn Ste 8382 Dover (19901) *(G-1712)*
   Acre Mortgage & Financial 302 737-5853
     56 W Main St Ste 107 Christiana (19702) *(G-990)*
   ACS Aero 2 Gamma Us LLC 800 483-1140
     850 New Burton Rd Ste 201 Dover (19904) *(G-1713)*
   Act & Associates LLC 302 318-6842
     3 Francis Cir Newark (19711) *(G-9759)*
   Act Media 888 666-0786
     16192 Coastal Hwy Lewes (19958) *(G-5655)*
   Act One, Wilmington *Also Called: Agile 1 (G-14315)*
   Act Program, Dover *Also Called: Delaware Gdnce Svcs For Chldre (G-2241)*
   Action Automotive Inc 302 429-0643
     2200 Rodman Rd Wilmington (19805) *(G-14240)*
   Action Enterprise Inc 302 537-7223
     27 W Bayard St Fenwick Island (19944) *(G-4039)*
   Action Environmental Service 302 798-3100
     501 Silverside Rd Ste 114 Wilmington (19809) *(G-14241)*
   Action Rental Inc 302 366-0749
     8 Mill Park Ct Newark (19713) *(G-9760)*
   Action Security 302 838-2852
     100 Peoples Dr Newark (19702) *(G-9761)*
   Action Track USA 610 780-2290
     33217 W Edgemoor St Lewes (19958) *(G-5656)*
   Action Unlimited Resources Inc 302 323-1455
     230 Quigley Blvd Historic New Castle (19720) *(G-4919)*
   Activ Pest & Lawn Inc 302 645-1502
     16861 New Rd Lewes (19958) *(G-5657)*
   Activating Change Inc 646 457-8067
     919 N Market St Ste 950 Wilmington (19801) *(G-14242)*
   Active Crane Rentals Inc 302 998-1000
     103 Water St Wilmington (19804) *(G-14243)*
   Active Hope 302 545-2494
     19 W 39th St Wilmington (19802) *(G-14244)*
   Active Life Acupuncture 302 827-2691
     33044 E Light Dr Lewes (19958) *(G-5658)*
   Actors Attic 302 734-8214
     525 Otis Dr Dover (19901) *(G-1714)*
   Acts Rtrmnt-Life Cmmnties Inc 302 629-4368
     1001 Middleford Rd Seaford (19973) *(G-13047)*
   Acts Rtrmnt-Life Cmmnties Inc 302 654-5101
     4830 Kennett Pike Wilmington (19807) *(G-14245)*
   Actual Veggies LLC 818 825-0531
     17500 Slipper Shell Way Unit 12 Lewes (19958) *(G-5659)*
   Acuhealth & Wellness 302 438-4493
     134 Tywyn Dr Middletown (19709) *(G-6833)*
   Acuitive Inc 214 738-1099
     4001 Kennett Pike Ste 134 Wilmington (19807) *(G-14246)*
   Acuity Spcialty Pdts Group Inc 302 369-6949
     2711 Keswick Ct Wilmington (19808) *(G-14247)*
   Acumen Health Technologies LLC 800 941-0356
     2207 Concord Pike 224 Wilmington (19803) *(G-14248)*
   Ad Bits Advertising and PR 954 467-8420
     754 Morris Rd Hockessin (19707) *(G-5113)*
   Ad-Art Signs Georgetown Inc 302 856-7446
     24383 Mariner Cir Georgetown (19947) *(G-4197)*

Ada L Gonzalez M D 302 724-4567
  156 S State St Dover (19901) *(G-1715)*
Adam Hobbs & Son Inc 302 697-2090
  344 Fitzbrian Dr Felton (19943) *(G-3938)*
Adam Kleinmeulman 302 757-4517
  3522 Silverside Rd Wilmington (19810) *(G-14249)*
Adam R Necelis CPA LLC 302 322-1135
  700 Delaware St Historic New Castle (19720) *(G-4920)*
Adams Auto Parts, Wilmington *Also Called: Adams Auto Parts LLC (G-14250)*
Adams Auto Parts LLC (HQ) 302 655-9693
  1601 Northeast Blvd Wilmington (19802) *(G-14250)*
Adams Business Developmen 302 698-1709
  17 Palmer Dr Middletown (19709) *(G-6834)*
Adams Construction & Managemen 302 856-2022
  23 Marcella St Georgetown (19947) *(G-4198)*
Adams Custom Leather 302 462-0187
  22089 Harbeson Rd Harbeson (19951) *(G-4680)*
Adams Kemp Associates Inc 302 856-6699
  17 Polly Drummond Shpg Ctr Ste 201 Newark (19711) *(G-9762)*
Adams Oceanfront Resort 302 227-3030
  4 Read Ave Dewey Beach (19971) *(G-1661)*
Adams Oceanfront Villas, Dewey Beach *Also Called: Adams Oceanfront Resort (G-1661)*
Adams Oil Co Inc 302 629-4531
  Pine St Extd Seaford (19973) *(G-13048)*
Adandy Farm 302 349-5116
  13450 Adandy Farm Ln Greenwood (19950) *(G-4589)*
Adapex LLC 718 618-9982
  3422 Old Capitol Trl Wilmington (19808) *(G-14251)*
Adapty Inc 415 800-3343
  2093 Philadelphia Pike Ste 9181 Claymont (19703) *(G-1020)*
Adash Inc 302 654-3977
  1740 W 4th St Wilmington (19805) *(G-14252)*
ADd Marketing Group LLC 347 668-0992
  611 S Dupont Hwy Ste 102 Dover (19901) *(G-1716)*
Add-Inscom LLC 302 584-1771
  144 Dewberry Dr Hockessin (19707) *(G-5114)*
Addalli Landscaping 302 836-2002
  2546 Red Lion Rd Bear (19701) *(G-14)*
Addiction Medical Facility LLC 302 629-2300
  1309 Bridgeville Hwy Seaford (19973) *(G-13049)*
Addlestone LLC 302 373-1598
  1511 New London Rd Wilmington (19807) *(G-14253)*
Addus Healthcare Inc 302 424-4842
  1675 S State Street Milford (19963) *(G-7759)*
Addus Healthcare Inc 302 995-9010
  3521 Silverside Rd Wilmington (19810) *(G-14254)*
Addy Sea, The, Bethany Beach *Also Called: Eventide Hospitality LLC (G-600)*
Adecco Staffing, Newark *Also Called: Adecco Usa Inc (G-9763)*
Adecco Usa Inc 302 669-4005
  40 Reads Way New Castle (19720) *(G-8762)*
Adecco Usa Inc 302 457-4059
  1000 Samoset Dr Newark (19713) *(G-9763)*
Adectra LLC 203 424-2800
  651 N Broad St Middletown (19709) *(G-6835)*
Adel Construction 302 286-7676
  300 Creek View Rd Newark (19711) *(G-9764)*
Adeox Technologies Inc 347 884-7131
  226 W Park Pl Ste 14 Newark (19711) *(G-9765)*
Adept Cleaning & Restoration 302 385-6653
  503 E Pompeii Dr Bear (19701) *(G-15)*
Adept Consulting 267 398-7449
  407 Eastlawn Ave Wilmington (19802) *(G-14255)*
Aderyn Woodworks 219 229-5070
  11 Villas Dr Apt 9 New Castle (19720) *(G-8763)*
Adesis Inc 302 323-4880
  27 Mccullough Dr New Castle (19720) *(G-8764)*
Adeva, Middletown *Also Called: Hirewise Inc (G-7211)*
Adex Corporation 703 618-9670
  8 The Grn Dover (19901) *(G-1717)*
Adirondack Bhvral Hlthcare LLC 302 832-1282
  1400 Peoples Plz Ste 204 Christiana (19702) *(G-991)*

Adjuvant Research Services Inc 302 737-5513
  1 Innovation Way Ste 400 Newark (19711) *(G-9766)*
Adkess Transport Services LLC 978 235-3924
  14 Winchester Ct Bear (19701) *(G-16)*
Adkins & Assoc CPA 302 737-2390
  2615 E Riding Dr Wilmington (19808) *(G-14256)*
Adkins & Associates CPA, Wilmington *Also Called: Adkins & Assoc CPA (G-14256)*
Adkins Custom Contracting LLC 302 841-3885
  18575 Line Church Rd Delmar (19940) *(G-1560)*
Adkins Management Company 302 684-3000
  421 Kings Hwy Milford (19963) *(G-7760)*
Admeal Inc 954 758-8699
  124 Broadkill Rd Milton (19968) *(G-8555)*
Admin-Support 302 368-6441
  12 Top View Ct Newark (19702) *(G-9767)*
Administrative Office, Dover *Also Called: Delaware Wic Program (G-2273)*
Admiral Hotel 302 227-2103
  2 Baltimore Ave Rehoboth Beach (19971) *(G-12597)*
Admiral Motel, Wilmington *Also Called: Admiral West Inc (G-14257)*
Admiral On Baltimore 302 227-1300
  2 Baltimore Ave Rehoboth Beach (19971) *(G-12598)*
Admiral Tire 302 734-5911
  280 Cowgill St Dover (19901) *(G-1718)*
Admiral West Inc 609 729-0031
  726 Greenwood Rd Wilmington (19807) *(G-14257)*
Adoption House Inc 302 477-0944
  3411 Silverside Rd # 101 Wilmington (19810) *(G-14258)*
ADP Capital Management Inc 302 657-4060
  800 Delaware Ave Ste 601 Wilmington (19801) *(G-14259)*
ADP Pacific Inc 302 657-4060
  800 Delaware Ave Ste 601 Wilmington (19801) *(G-14260)*
Adpese LLC 302 223-5411
  3616 Kirkwood Hwy Ste A-1011 Wilmington (19808) *(G-14261)*
Adr Investments LLC 800 710-6184
  2711 Centerville Rd # 400 Wilmington (19808) *(G-14262)*
Adriane Hohmann 302 253-2020
  501 College Park Ln Georgetown (19947) *(G-4199)*
Adriel Inc 860 595-4602
  2035 Sunset Lake Rd Ste B2 Newark (19702) *(G-9768)*
Adrienne B Neithardt MD 302 623-4242
  4735 Ogletown Stanton Rd Ste 3217 Newark (19713) *(G-9769)*
Adrion & Co LLC 302 313-1392
  16192 Coastal Hwy Lewes (19958) *(G-5660)*
Adroit Logistics LLC 385 381-0007
  8 The Grn Dover (19901) *(G-1719)*
ADS, New Castle *Also Called: Affordable Delivery Svcs LLC (G-8771)*
ADT LLC 313 778-1493
  263 N Dupont Hwy Dover (19901) *(G-1720)*
ADT LLC 302 613-4745
  140 Quigley Blvd Historic New Castle (19720) *(G-4921)*
ADT LLC 302 918-1016
  130 Executive Dr Ste 2 Newark (19702) *(G-9770)*
Adtelligent Inc 833 222-2102
  8 The Green Ste R Dover (19901) *(G-1721)*
Advacare LLC 302 448-5045
  3601 Old Capitol Trl Unit A5a6 Wilmington (19808) *(G-14263)*
Advance Central Services Inc (PA) 302 830-9732
  1313 N Mkt St Fl 10 Wilmington (19801) *(G-14264)*
Advance Construction Co Del 302 697-9444
  280 Banning Rd Camden Wyoming (19934) *(G-906)*
Advance Construction Technique 270 257-0377
  1000 N West St Ste 1200 Wilmington (19801) *(G-14265)*
Advance Forward LLC 302 762-1615
  222 Hawthorne Ln Wilmington (19803) *(G-14266)*
Advance Inc 302 324-8890
  645 Dawson Dr Ste A Newark (19713) *(G-9771)*
Advance Magazine Group, Wilmington *Also Called: Advance Magazine Publs Inc (G-14267)*
Advance Magazine Publs Inc 302 830-4630
  1201 N Market St Ste 600 Wilmington (19801) *(G-14267)*
Advance Marine LLC 302 656-2111
  900 Smiths Bridge Rd Wilmington (19807) *(G-14268)*

ALPHABETIC SECTION

Advance Mblity Physcl Thrapy L.. 443 359-0132
  24488 Sussex Hwy Ste 2 Seaford (19973) *(G-13050)*
Advance Office Instlltions Inc... 302 777-5599
  37 Lukens Dr Ste B Historic New Castle (19720) *(G-4922)*
Advance Paving Services, Wilmington *Also Called: Stripe-A-Lot Inc (G-20101)*
Advance Physical Therapy LLC... 302 407-3592
  1021 Gilpin Ave Wilmington (19806) *(G-14269)*
Advance Trucking Solutions LLC... 302 281-4191
  1151 Walker Rd Dover (19904) *(G-1722)*
Advance Windows, Newark *Also Called: Advance Inc (G-9771)*
Advance Wndw/Sprior Siding Inc.. 302 324-8890
  11 Mcmillan Way Ste A Newark (19713) *(G-9772)*
Advanced Anesthesiology & Pain.. 302 283-3300
  5307 Limestone Rd Ste 103 Wilmington (19808) *(G-14270)*
Advanced Behavioral Care Inc... 410 599-7400
  19 Cedarwood Dr Lewes (19958) *(G-5661)*
Advanced Biomedical Inc... 302 730-1880
  9 E Loockerman St Ste 3a Dover (19901) *(G-1723)*
Advanced Bizz Innovations LLC.. 302 397-1162
  405 South St Townsend (19734) *(G-13951)*
Advanced Care Obgyn.. 302 633-9083
  1941 Limestone Rd Ste 217 Wilmington (19808) *(G-14271)*
Advanced Care Obsttrics Gynclo... 302 275-2202
  1941 Limestone Rd Ste 217 Wilmington (19808) *(G-14272)*
Advanced Cnstr Techniques Inc.. 302 273-2617
  2860 Ogletown Rd Newark (19713) *(G-9773)*
Advanced Cnstrctons Techniques, Newark *Also Called: Advanced Cnstr Techniques Inc (G-9773)*
Advanced Coatings Engrg LLC.. 888 607-0000
  2915 Ogletown Rd Newark (19713) *(G-9774)*
Advanced Defense Technology... 888 298-5775
  3422 Old Capitol Trl Ste 200 Wilmington (19808) *(G-14273)*
Advanced Endoscopy Center LLC... 302 678-0725
  742 S Governors Ave Ste 2 Dover (19904) *(G-1724)*
Advanced Foot & Ankle Center... 302 355-0056
  774 Christiana Rd Ste 105 Newark (19713) *(G-9775)*
Advanced Foot & Ankle Center, Wilmington *Also Called: Ankle and Foot Surgical Assoc (G-14486)*
Advanced Fuel Polsg Svc Inc.. 302 477-1040
  950 Ridge Rd Ste A6 Claymont (19703) *(G-1021)*
Advanced Global Networks Inc.. 302 308-6460
  108 W 13th St Wilmington (19801) *(G-14274)*
Advanced Healing Inc... 302 363-5839
  919 Se 2nd St Milford (19963) *(G-7761)*
Advanced Heating & Air Inc... 302 731-1000
  667 Dawson Dr Ste C Newark (19713) *(G-9776)*
Advanced Home Services Inc... 302 339-7600
  126 Hunters Ridge Way Magnolia (19962) *(G-6714)*
Advanced Logistics LLC.. 302 345-8921
  13 Erbitea Ln New Castle (19720) *(G-8765)*
Advanced Machinery, New Castle *Also Called: Advanced Machinery Sales Inc (G-8766)*
Advanced Machinery Sales Inc... 302 322-2226
  2 Mccullough Dr Ste 2 New Castle (19720) *(G-8766)*
Advanced Massage of Delaware.. 443 485-7024
  29 Atlantic Ave Ste P Ocean View (19970) *(G-12457)*
Advanced Materials Technology... 302 477-2510
  3521 Silverside Rd Ste 1k Wilmington (19810) *(G-14275)*
Advanced Mechanical Inc... 302 734-5583
  509 Hatchery Rd Ste B Dover (19901) *(G-1725)*
Advanced Metal Concepts Inc.. 302 421-9905
  1823 Choptank Rd Middletown (19709) *(G-6836)*
Advanced Modern Care LLC... 267 235-6922
  16 N Bellwoode Dr Newark (19702) *(G-9777)*
Advanced Networking.. 302 368-7552
  36 Brookhill Dr Newark (19702) *(G-9778)*
Advanced Networking Inc... 302 442-6199
  1316 Philadelphia Pike Wilmington (19809) *(G-14276)*
Advanced Particle Sensors LLC... 302 695-4883
  2409 Raven Rd Wilmington (19810) *(G-14277)*
Advanced Performance Materials, Newark *Also Called: Chemours Company (G-10196)*
Advanced Pest Management.. 410 398-4378
  955 Dawson Dr Ste 2 Newark (19713) *(G-9779)*
Advanced Plastic Surgery Cente... 302 623-4004
  4735 Ogletown Stanton Rd Newark (19713) *(G-9780)*
Advanced Plastic Surgery Ctr... 302 355-0005
  774 Christiana Rd Ste 101 Newark (19713) *(G-9781)*
Advanced Plumbing & Maint LLC... 302 584-4001
  20 Valerie Dr Bear (19701) *(G-17)*
Advanced Power Control Inc (HQ)... 302 368-0443
  15 Reads Way Ste 101 New Castle (19720) *(G-8767)*
Advanced Power Generation.. 302 375-6145
  950 Ridge Rd Ste A6 Claymont (19703) *(G-1022)*
Advanced Protection LLC... 302 539-6041
  9 Briarcliffe Ct Ocean View (19970) *(G-12458)*
Advanced Prototyping Solutions, Wilmington *Also Called: Advanced Prttyping Sltionv LLC (G-14278)*
Advanced Prttyping Sltionv LLC... 302 375-6048
  6517 Governor Printz Blvd Wilmington (19809) *(G-14278)*
Advanced Rcvable Solutions Inc... 302 225-6001
  1300 First State Blvd Ste A Wilmington (19804) *(G-14279)*
Advanced Real Estate Inc... 302 994-7424
  903 Newgate Ln Wilmington (19808) *(G-14280)*
Advanced Student Trnsp Inc.. 302 998-6726
  1400 First State Blvd Wilmington (19804) *(G-14281)*
Advanced Surgical Specialists.. 302 475-4900
  1401 Foulk Rd Ste 207 Wilmington (19803) *(G-14282)*
Advanced Systems Inc.. 302 368-1211
  202 Cheltenham Rd Newark (19711) *(G-9782)*
Advanced Technology Sales... 732 446-9681
  556 Stonehaven Dr Townsend (19734) *(G-13952)*
Advanced Training Acadmey.. 302 369-8800
  9 Prospect Ave Newark (19711) *(G-9783)*
Advanced Treatment Systems.. 302 792-0700
  2999 Philadelphia Pike Claymont (19703) *(G-1023)*
Advancxing Pain Rhblttion Clin... 302 384-7439
  620 Stanton Christiana Rd Ste 202 Newark (19713) *(G-9784)*
Advant-Dge Sltons Mddle ATL In... 302 533-6858
  17 Shea Way Newark (19713) *(G-9785)*
Advantage Assets II Inc.. 877 858-3855
  1000 N West St Ste 1200 Wilmington (19801) *(G-14283)*
Advantage Corp.. 302 478-7977
  3213 Emerald Pl Wilmington (19810) *(G-14284)*
Advantage Delaware... 302 365-5398
  134 Antlers Ln Bear (19701) *(G-18)*
Advantage Delaware LLC.. 302 479-7764
  3524 Silverside Rd Wilmington (19810) *(G-14285)*
Advantage Futuretech Company.. 347 592-5667
  16192 Coastal Hwy Lewes (19958) *(G-5662)*
Advantage Security Inc.. 302 652-3060
  802 First State Blvd Wilmington (19804) *(G-14286)*
Advantdge Hlthcare Sltions Inc... 302 224-5678
  307 Ruthar Dr Newark (19711) *(G-9786)*
Advantech Inc.. 302 674-8405
  151 Garrison Oak Dr Dover (19901) *(G-1726)*
ADVANTEDGE HEALTHCARE SOLUTIONS INC., Newark *Also Called: Advantdge Hlthcare Sltions Inc (G-9786)*
Advent Cad LLC... 302 569-1793
  5017 The Pines Blvd Wilmington (19808) *(G-14287)*
Adventres In Lrng Erly Chldhoo, New Castle *Also Called: Amemg Inc (G-8793)*
Adventum LLC... 518 620-1441
  2701 Centerville Rd Wilmington (19808) *(G-14288)*
Advertised Media Inc... 415 967-8100
  3411 Silverside Rd Ste 104 Wilmington (19810) *(G-14289)*
Advertising Is Simple... 302 407-0431
  14 Ashley Pl Wilmington (19804) *(G-14290)*
Advertsing Archtctural Photogr, Wilmington *Also Called: Herbert Studios (G-17127)*
Advik Republic Inc... 844 987-4238
  7209 Lancaster Pike Ste 4-1112 Hockessin (19707) *(G-5115)*
Advisory Trust Co of Delaware.. 302 636-8500
  2710 Centerville Rd Ste 101 Wilmington (19808) *(G-14291)*
Advoserv Inc.. 302 365-8050
  750 Shipyard Dr Ste 213 Wilmington (19801) *(G-14292)*
Adyn Inc.. 206 451-7105
  2093 Philadelphia Pike Claymont (19703) *(G-1024)*

Ae Simmons, Dover *Also Called: AEsimmons LLC (G-1731)*

Aearo Technologies LLC.. 302 283-5497
650 Dawson Dr Newark (19713) *(G-9787)*

Aecom Global LLC (HQ).. 213 593-8100
Corporation Trust Company 1209 Orange St Wilmington (19801) *(G-14293)*

Aecom Usa Inc.. 302 781-5963
248 Chapman Rd Newark (19702) *(G-9788)*

Aeec, Wilmington *Also Called: American-Eurasian Exch Co LLC (G-14445)*

AEG International LLC.. 302 750-6411
30931 Sussex Hwy Laurel (19956) *(G-5461)*

Aegis Networks LLC.. 917 378-7524
251 Little Falls Dr Wilmington (19808) *(G-14294)*

Aegis PM Group Inc.. 302 456-0402
4023 Kennett Pike Wilmington (19807) *(G-14295)*

Aegis-CC LLC.. 814 661-5844
8 The Grn Ste A Dover (19901) *(G-1727)*

AEj Ltd Liability Company.. 847 274-1084
611 S Dupont Hwy Ste 102 Dover (19901) *(G-1728)*

Aero Dynamic Services Inc.. 302 737-4920
18 Manassas Dr Middletown (19709) *(G-6837)*

Aero Enterprises Inc.. 302 378-1396
1270 Caldwell Corner Rd Townsend (19734) *(G-13953)*

Aero Marine Laminates, Seaford *Also Called: Aero-Marine Laminates Inc (G-13051)*

Aero Taxi Inc.. 302 328-3430
1315 Chadwick Rd Wilmington (19803) *(G-14296)*

Aero Ways Inc.. 302 324-9970
131 N Dupont Hwy New Castle (19720) *(G-8768)*

Aero-Marine Laminates Inc.. 302 628-3944
22762 Sussex Hwy Seaford (19973) *(G-13051)*

Aerona Solutions Inc.. 302 601-4332
16192 Coastal Hwy Lewes (19958) *(G-5663)*

Aeronex LLC.. 206 809-0009
1111b S Governors Ave Ste 6573 Dover (19904) *(G-1729)*

Aerosmith LLC.. 302 546-5465
8 The Grn A Dover (19901) *(G-1730)*

Aerospace Dsign Compliance LLC.. 302 407-6825
10 Corporate Cir Ste 225 New Castle (19720) *(G-8769)*

Aerotek Inc.. 302 561-6300
100 W Commons Blvd Ste 425 New Castle (19720) *(G-8770)*

Aerotek Inc.. 302 318-8760
240 Continental Dr Ste 201 Newark (19713) *(G-9789)*

AEROTEK, INC., New Castle *Also Called: Aerotek Inc (G-8770)*

AEROTEK, INC., Newark *Also Called: Aerotek Inc (G-9789)*

AES Foods.. 302 420-8377
83 Albe Dr Ste F Newark (19702) *(G-9790)*

AES Surveyors, Wilmington *Also Called: Rod-AES Surveryors Co (G-19548)*

AEsimmons LLC (PA).. 347 864-6294
1221 College Park Dr # 116 Dover (19904) *(G-1731)*

Aesir Capital Management LP.. 302 656-9161
1105 N Market St Wilmington (19801) *(G-14297)*

Aesthetic Surgical Associates, Wilmington *Also Called: Peter R Coggins MD (G-18995)*

Aesthetics Center.. 302 827-2125
34172 Citizen Dr Lewes (19958) *(G-5664)*

Aesthetis Special Care Assoc, Wilmington *Also Called: Thomas Jenkins DMD (G-20310)*

Aesthtic Plstic Surgery Del PA.. 302 656-0214
1600 Pennsylvania Ave Ste A Wilmington (19806) *(G-14298)*

Aesthtic Special Care Assoc PA.. 302 482-4444
2323 Pennsylvania Ave Ste Ll Wilmington (19806) *(G-14299)*

Aet Films, Newark *Also Called: Taghleef Industries Inc (G-12155)*

Aething Inc.. 917 640-2582
1111b S Governors Ave # 6113 Dover (19904) *(G-1732)*

Aetho, Dover *Also Called: Aetho LLC (G-1733)*

Aetho LLC.. 215 821-7290
8 The Grn Ste A Dover (19901) *(G-1733)*

Aetna Banquet Hall, Newark *Also Called: Aetna Hose Hook & Ladder Co 9 (G-9791)*

Aetna Hose Hook & Ladder Co 9.. 302 454-3305
400 Ogletown Rd Newark (19711) *(G-9791)*

Aetna Hose Hook and Ladder Co.. 302 454-3300
31 Academy St Newark (19711) *(G-9792)*

Aetolia Captial LLC.. 302 397-8238
3828 Kennett Pike Wilmington (19807) *(G-14300)*

Aezi Electrical Services LLC.. 302 279-8344
302 Robinson Ln Wilmington (19805) *(G-14301)*

Affilate Marks Investments Inc.. 302 478-7451
3411 Silverside Rd Ste 205bc Wilmington (19810) *(G-14302)*

Affiliate Investment Inc.. 302 478-7451
3411 Silverside Rd Ste 205a Wilmington (19810) *(G-14303)*

Affiliate Venture Group.. 302 379-6961
2419 Kirkwood Hwy Wilmington (19805) *(G-14304)*

Affiliated Psychological Svc.. 302 507-3039
303 Shisler Ct Newark (19702) *(G-9793)*

Affinity Homecare Services.. 302 264-9363
1040 S State St Dover (19901) *(G-1734)*

Affinity Research Chemicals (PA).. 302 525-4060
406 Meco Dr Wilmington (19804) *(G-14305)*

Affinity Wealth Management.. 302 652-6767
2961 Centerville Rd Ste 310 Wilmington (19808) *(G-14306)*

Affinity Womens Health LLC.. 302 234-8982
614 Loveville Rd Ste F1a Hockessin (19707) *(G-5116)*

Affinity Womens Health LLC.. 302 468-4320
121 Becks Woods Dr Ste 100 Bear (19701) *(G-19)*

Afflair Events.. 302 762-5765
1 Paschall Ct Wilmington (19803) *(G-14307)*

Afford-A-Tree Svc & Ldscpg LLC.. 302 670-4154
118 Downes Dr Hartly (19953) *(G-4854)*

Affordable Contractor.. 302 670-5699
400 Delaware St Historic New Castle (19720) *(G-4923)*

Affordable Custom Carpentry.. 302 853-5582
525 King St Laurel (19956) *(G-5462)*

Affordable Delivery Svcs LLC.. 302 276-0246
217 Lisa Dr Ste D New Castle (19720) *(G-8771)*

Affordable Heating & AC.. 302 328-9220
1700 Wilmington Rd Historic New Castle (19720) *(G-4924)*

Affordable Insur Netwrk Del.. 800 681-7261
1218 Pulaski Hwy Ste 490 Bear (19701) *(G-20)*

Affordable Plumbing & Elc Inc.. 443 235-9222
36842 Red Berry Rd Delmar (19940) *(G-1561)*

Affordable Roofing LLC.. 302 363-8429
70 Humpsman Dr Dover (19904) *(G-1735)*

Affordable Sod Inc.. 302 545-0275
1 S Wynwyd Dr Newark (19711) *(G-9794)*

Affordable Wedding Entrmt.. 302 258-3027
715 Ingramtown Rd Georgetown (19947) *(G-4200)*

Afgceaa Corporation.. 617 314-0814
1521 Concord Pike Ste 303 Wilmington (19803) *(G-14308)*

Afinclic Financial Tech Inc.. 646 946-1687
1209 N Orange St Wilmington (19801) *(G-14309)*

AFLAC.. 302 376-9880
334 Senator Dr Middletown (19709) *(G-6838)*

AFLAC District Offcie.. 302 375-6885
1102 Society Dr Claymont (19703) *(G-1025)*

AFmensah LLC.. 302 777-0538
1521 Concord Pike Ste 301 Wilmington (19803) *(G-14310)*

African Violet Society-Amer.. 302 653-6449
36 S Main St Smyrna (19977) *(G-13632)*

African Wood Inc.. 302 884-6738
274 Liborio Dr Middletown (19709) *(G-6839)*

Afscme-Council 81, New Castle *Also Called: American Fdrtion State Cnty MN (G-8797)*

Afterglo Beauty Spa.. 302 537-7546
22 Cedar Dr Millville (19967) *(G-8512)*

Aftermath Services LLC.. 302 357-3780
160 Greentree Dr Ste 101 Dover (19904) *(G-1736)*

Afternoon Little, Dover *Also Called: Little School Inc (G-2957)*

AG & G Sheet Metal Inc.. 302 653-4111
470 Oak Hill School Rd Townsend (19734) *(G-13954)*

AG Concrete Works, Dagsboro *Also Called: A G Concrete Works LLC (G-1409)*

AG Industrial Inc.. 888 289-1779
36 Victory Chapel Rd Dover (19904) *(G-1737)*

AG Wholesale Marketplace, Lewes *Also Called: Gro-Connectcom Inc (G-6066)*

Ag6 Engineering & Defense LLC.. 609 480-4823
651 N Broad St Ste 2054626 Middletown (19709) *(G-6840)*

Against All Odds Llc.. 302 943-7321
27 Spring Ridge Way Camden (19934) *(G-787)*

ALPHABETIC SECTION

Against Grain LLC.. 302 388-1667
403 Grandview Ave Wilmington (19809) *(G-14311)*

Agape Learning Academy.. 302 491-4890
283 School St Houston (19954) *(G-5435)*

Agave Tech Inc... 805 394-7154
2093 Philadelphia Pike Claymont (19703) *(G-1026)*

Age Advantage Senior Care Svcs........................... 302 722-8240
2634 Kirkwood Highway Newark (19711) *(G-9795)*

AGE Electric Ltd... 302 632-2968
8768 Clendaniel Pond Rd Lincoln (19960) *(G-6654)*

Agent Launch LLC.. 302 200-5574
256 Chapman Rd Ste 1054 Newark (19702) *(G-9796)*

Agent Staffing Services Llc.................................... 302 244-2676
200 Nob Hill Rd Dover (19901) *(G-1738)*

Agents and Corporations Inc (PA)......................... 302 575-0877
1201 N Orange St Ste 600 Wilmington (19801) *(G-14312)*

Agents of Delaware Inc... 302 544-2467
257 Old Churchmans Rd New Castle (19720) *(G-8772)*

Agfirst Farm Credit Bank...................................... 302 734-7534
1410 S State St Dover (19901) *(G-1739)*

Agfirst Farm Credit Bank...................................... 302 856-9081
20816 Dupont Blvd Georgetown (19947) *(G-4201)*

Aggreko Holdings Inc.. 302 652-4076
1105 N Market St Wilmington (19801) *(G-14313)*

Agh Parent LLC... 919 298-2267
1209 N Orange St Wilmington (19801) *(G-14314)*

Agile 1.. 302 791-6900
1013 Centre Rd Ste 200 Wilmington (19805) *(G-14315)*

Agile Cockpit LLC... 646 220-3377
160 Greentree Dr Dover (19904) *(G-1740)*

Agile Coliving Systems LLC.................................. 310 980-0644
8 The Grn Ste R Dover (19901) *(G-1741)*

Agile Dcntmination Systems LLC......................... 310 980-0644
8 The Grn Ste R Dover (19901) *(G-1742)*

Agile Ip LLC.. 310 980-0644
8 The Grn Ste R Dover (19901) *(G-1743)*

Agile Legal... 302 376-6710
651 N Broad St Ste 308 Middletown (19709) *(G-6841)*

Agile Medical Systems LLC.................................. 310 980-0644
8 The Grn Ste R Dover (19901) *(G-1744)*

Agile Shelter Systems LLC................................... 310 980-0644
8 The Grn Ste R Dover (19901) *(G-1745)*

Agile Waste LLC... 302 772-4882
1209 N Orange St Wilmington (19801) *(G-14316)*

Agilebits USA Inc.. 416 371-3328
1000 N West St Ste 1200 Wilmington (19801) *(G-14317)*

Agilent Technologies Inc...................................... 408 345-8886
300 Century Blvd Wilmington (19808) *(G-14318)*

Agilent Technologies Inc...................................... 877 424-4536
2850 Centerville Rd Wilmington (19808) *(G-14319)*

Agilent Technologies Inc...................................... 302 633-7337
500 Ships Landing Way Historic New Castle (19720) *(G-4925)*

Agilite Systems Incorporated.............................. 870 298-4152
2711 Centerville Rd Wilmington (19808) *(G-14320)*

Agitek Softworks Inc.. 240 356-3034
16192 Coastal Hwy Lewes (19958) *(G-5665)*

Aglide Inc (PA)... 302 213-0357
1111b S Governors Ave Ste 6311 Dover (19904) *(G-1746)*

Agmaf Inc... 302 508-6991
300 Delaware Ave Ste 210 Wilmington (19801) *(G-14321)*

Agriculture /Chemicals, Wilmington Also Called: Ashanti Produce International *(G-14578)*

Agriculture United States Dept............................ 302 741-2600
800 S Bay Rd Ste 2 Dover (19901) *(G-1747)*

AGRICULTURE, UNITED STATES DEPARTMENT OF, Dover Also Called: Agriculture United States Dept *(G-1747)*

Agro Lab... 302 265-2734
101 Clukey Dr Harrington (19952) *(G-4723)*

Agrolab Inc... 302 535-6591
101 Cluckey Dr Harrington (19952) *(G-4724)*

Agrorefiner LLC.. 212 651-2865
51 Steel Dr Unit B New Castle (19720) *(G-8773)*

AGS Royalty Management LLC............................. 888 292-6995
8 The Grn Dover (19901) *(G-1748)*

Agts LLC... 800 496-3379
8 The Grn Ste 10746 Dover (19901) *(G-1749)*

Aguilera Tax Preparation..................................... 302 746-7253
1800 Philadelphia Pike Wilmington (19809) *(G-14322)*

Agventure Inc... 302 992-5940
974 Centre Rd Wilmington (19805) *(G-14323)*

Ah Therapy Services LLC..................................... 302 379-0528
725 Halstead Rd Wilmington (19803) *(G-14324)*

Ahl Orthodontics.. 302 678-3000
1004 S State St Dover (19901) *(G-1750)*

AHM TV Prod Inc... 929 332-0350
548 Roberta Ave Dover (19901) *(G-1751)*

Ahmad Family Farm LLC...................................... 302 349-5500
14699 B&R Rd Greenwood (19950) *(G-4590)*

Ahmir Media, Lewes Also Called: Doc REO Media LLC *(G-5925)*

AHP, Wilmington Also Called: Assoctes In Hlth Psychology LLC *(G-14595)*

Ahu Tech, Newark Also Called: Ahu Technologies Inc *(G-9797)*

Ahu Technologies Inc.. 302 397-7091
15 Prestbury Sq Ste 11 Newark (19713) *(G-9797)*

Ai Athena LLC... 212 247-6400
2711 Centerville Rd # 400 Wilmington (19808) *(G-14325)*

Ai Dupont.. 302 528-6520
2200 Concord Pike Wilmington (19803) *(G-14326)*

Ai Dupont Hosp For Children................................ 302 651-4620
1600 Rockland Rd Wilmington (19803) *(G-14327)*

AI Whoo LLC... 302 494-6952
88 Munro Rd Newark (19711) *(G-9798)*

AIA.. 302 407-2252
4058 New Castle Ave New Castle (19720) *(G-8774)*

Aid In Dover Inc.. 302 734-7610
801 W Division St Dover (19904) *(G-1752)*

Aiden Auto Repair Center..................................... 302 898-5777
804 Pulaski Hwy Bear (19701) *(G-21)*

Aids Care Group... 610 220-8058
209 Murphy Rd Wilmington (19803) *(G-14328)*

Aids Delaware Inc (PA).. 302 652-6776
100 W 10th St Ste 315 Wilmington (19801) *(G-14329)*

Aiec.. 302 993-0931
21 Oxford Way Wilmington (19807) *(G-14330)*

AIG Global Real Estate Inc.................................. 302 655-2141
600 N King St Wilmington (19801) *(G-14331)*

Aigc Games Inc.. 214 499-8654
16192 Coastal Hwy Lewes (19958) *(G-5666)*

Aihs Theater... 302 651-2626
50 Hillside Rd Wilmington (19807) *(G-14332)*

Aiken Masonry Scott Ta....................................... 302 253-8179
22451 Wood Branch Rd Georgetown (19947) *(G-4202)*

Aikym Essentials LLC.. 215 910-9479
1051 Sherbourne Rd Middletown (19709) *(G-6842)*

Ailink Technology Corporation............................ 858 568-2137
8 The Grn Ste A Dover (19901) *(G-1753)*

Aim God Society... 207 299-3881
651 N Broad St Ste 206 Middletown (19709) *(G-6843)*

Aim Inc... 302 424-1424
506 Heath Row Milford (19963) *(G-7762)*

Aim Metals & Alloys USA Inc (PA)....................... 212 450-4519
1209 N Orange St Wilmington (19801) *(G-14333)*

Aim Research Co.. 302 235-5940
5936 Limestone Rd Ste 302 Hockessin (19707) *(G-5117)*

Aims.gg, Middletown Also Called: Aim God Society *(G-6843)*

Aion Oakwood Venture LLC................................. 212 849-9200
2711 Centerville Rd Wilmington (19808) *(G-14334)*

Air Apps, Dover Also Called: Air Apps Inc *(G-1754)*

Air Apps Inc.. 302 339-3843
8 The Grn Dover (19901) *(G-1754)*

Air Conditioning Products LLC............................. 800 483-1140
850 New Burton Rd Ste 201 Dover (19904) *(G-1755)*

Air Doctorx Inc... 302 492-1333
4639 Halltown Rd Ste B Hartly (19953) *(G-4855)*

Air Force US Dept of 302 674-0942
262 Chad St Dover (19902) *(G-1756)*

Air Liquide, Wilmington Also Called: Medal LP *(G-18245)*

Air Liquide Advanced Tech, Newport Also Called: Air Lqide Advanced Tech US LLC *(G-12441)*

Air Lqide Advanced Separations 302 225-1100
305 Water St Newport (19804) *(G-12440)*

Air Lqide Advanced Tech US LLC 302 225-1100
200 Gbc Dr Newark (19702) *(G-9799)*

Air Lqide Advanced Tech US LLC 302 225-1100
305 Water St Newport (19804) *(G-12441)*

Air Masters Hvac Inc 267 292-2204
218 W Pembrey Dr Wilmington (19803) *(G-14335)*

Air Medics Hvac LLC 302 439-4254
950 Ridge Rd Ste C15 Claymont (19703) *(G-1027)*

Air Methods Corporation 302 363-3168
21479 Rudder Ln Georgetown (19947) *(G-4203)*

Air Methods Corporation, Georgetown Also Called: Air Methods Corporation *(G-4203)*

Air Natures Way Inc 302 738-3063
5 Myers Rd Newark (19713) *(G-9800)*

Air One Htg Cooling Pros 908 623-6154
34712 Ringbolt Ave Millsboro (19966) *(G-8163)*

Air Products, Delaware City Also Called: Air Products and Chemicals Inc *(G-1528)*

Air Products and Chemicals Inc 302 834-6033
4550 Wrangle Hill Rd Delaware City (19706) *(G-1528)*

Air Quality Remediation LLC 302 464-1050
1274 Caldwell Corner Rd Townsend (19734) *(G-13955)*

Air Temp Solutions LLC 302 276-0532
101 J And M Dr New Castle (19720) *(G-8775)*

Airbnb Inc 415 800-5959
2711 Centerville Rd Wilmington (19808) *(G-14336)*

Aircrafters LLC 302 777-5000
259 Quigley Blvd Ste 12-18 Historic New Castle (19720) *(G-4926)*

Aircrafters Inc 302 777-5000
320 Cornell Dr Wilmington (19801) *(G-14337)*

Airespa Worldwide Whl LLC 908 227-4441
8 The Grn Dover (19901) *(G-1757)*

Airgas, Wilmington Also Called: Airgas Inc *(G-14338)*

Airgas Inc 302 575-1822
1521 Concord Pike Ste 101 Wilmington (19803) *(G-14338)*

Airgas Usa LLC 302 834-7404
4442 Wrangle Rd Delaware City (19706) *(G-1529)*

Airgas Usa LLC 302 286-5400
200 Gbc Dr Newark (19702) *(G-9801)*

Airlock389 Inc 213 393-1785
16192 Postal Hwy Lewes (19958) *(G-5667)*

Airnav Group LLC 954 798-5509
651 N Broad St Ste 206 Middletown (19709) *(G-6844)*

Airsled Inc 302 292-8911
66 Albe Dr Newark (19702) *(G-9802)*

Airwick/Delaware, Wilmington Also Called: Diamond Chemical & Supply Co *(G-16049)*

Ais 302 407-0430
2625 Grubb Rd Wilmington (19810) *(G-14339)*

Ait Advanced Infotech Inc 302 454-8620
467 Carson Dr Bear (19701) *(G-22)*

Ajacks Tire Service Inc 302 834-5200
819 S Dupont Hwy New Castle (19720) *(G-8776)*

Ajam Inc 267 323-5005
10 Willow Grove Mill Dr Middletown (19709) *(G-6845)*

Ajedium Film Group LLC 302 452-6609
100 Interchange Blvd Newark (19711) *(G-9803)*

Ajj Trades and Investment LLC 302 403-7165
1207 Delaware Ave Ste 3314 Wilmington (19806) *(G-14340)*

Ajko General Contractor 302 373-4030
906 Shipley Rd Wilmington (19803) *(G-14341)*

Ajm Enterprises Inc 302 212-2020
19545 Camelot Dr Ste A Rehoboth Beach (19971) *(G-12599)*

Ajp Financial Services LLC 302 798-7582
506 Woodside Ave Wilmington (19809) *(G-14342)*

Ajusta Tu Corona Inc (PA) 203 434-0356
8 The Grn Ste A Dover (19901) *(G-1758)*

Ajwadates Inc 323 999-1998
651 N Broad St Middletown (19709) *(G-6846)*

AK Electric Inc 302 379-3728
31575 Gooseberry Way Lewes (19958) *(G-5668)*

AK Multinational LLC 845 542-8155
300 Delaware Ave Ste 210 Wilmington (19801) *(G-14343)*

Akbell Global Commodities LLC 347 615-5014
221 College Pk Dr Ste 116 Dover (19904) *(G-1759)*

Akimbo Inc 302 204-5299
2093 Philadelphia Pike # 3022 Claymont (19703) *(G-1028)*

Akita Trucking LLC 302 463-8152
6 Redwood Ct Newark (19702) *(G-9804)*

Akshar Medical Service 302 369-3533
417 Oregano Ct Bear (19701) *(G-23)*

Aku Transport Inc (PA) 302 500-8127
24559 Dupont Blvd Georgetown (19947) *(G-4204)*

Al's Additional Restoration, Elsmere Also Called: Alberto Baez *(G-3930)*

Alamo, Wilmington Also Called: Enterprise Lsg Phladelphia LLC *(G-16435)*

Alan B Evantash, Wilmington Also Called: Christiana Care Hlth Svcs Inc *(G-15406)*

Alan L Frank Law Associates PA 302 502-2702
521 N West St Wilmington (19801) *(G-14344)*

Alan M Billingsley Jr 302 998-7907
2502 Tigani Dr Wilmington (19808) *(G-14345)*

Alan Passwaters 302 245-9114
9551 N Shore Dr Seaford (19973) *(G-13052)*

Alan R Levine DDS 302 475-3743
2018 Naamans Rd Ste A2 Wilmington (19810) *(G-14346)*

Alana Rose Foundation Inc 302 519-5973
35017 Hoot Owl Ln Dagsboro (19939) *(G-1410)*

Alantys Technology 302 573-2312
1201 N Orange St Ste 700 Wilmington (19801) *(G-14347)*

Alarm Cmmncations Sytems Group, Rehoboth Beach Also Called: Yacht Anything Ltd *(G-13026)*

Alarm Systems Co of Delaware 302 239-7754
735 Montgomery Woods Dr Hockessin (19707) *(G-5118)*

Alas Cleaners & Alterations 302 366-1638
430 Old Baltimore Pike Newark (19702) *(G-9805)*

Alawar Entertainment Inc (PA) 646 413-5757
16192 Coastal Hwy Lewes (19958) *(G-5669)*

Alban Associates 302 656-1827
1600 Bonwood Rd Wilmington (19805) *(G-14348)*

Alban Tractor LLC 302 284-4100
13074 S Dupont Hwy Felton (19943) *(G-3939)*

Albert Delpizzo LLC 302 234-2994
224 Mercury Rd Newark (19711) *(G-9806)*

Albert J Roop 302 655-4600
8 E 13th St Wilmington (19801) *(G-14349)*

Albert T Wood III 302 463-5386
350 Noxontown Rd Middletown (19709) *(G-6847)*

Albertini Landscaping 302 998-7593
1 Glover Cir Wilmington (19804) *(G-14350)*

Alberto Baez 302 543-1212
119 Beech Ave Elsmere (19805) *(G-3930)*

Albion Investments LLC (PA) 876 575-7371
16192 Coastal Hwy Lewes (19958) *(G-5670)*

Albireo Energy, New Castle Also Called: Advanced Power Control Inc *(G-8767)*

Alcheme Bio Inc 858 291-9708
8 The Grn Ste 13081 Dover (19901) *(G-1760)*

Alchemy of Hair 302 525-6676
4633 Ogletown Stanton Rd Newark (19713) *(G-9807)*

Alchemy Software Solutions LLC 201 627-0638
1000 N West St Ste 1200 Wilmington (19801) *(G-14351)*

Alcoa, Newark Also Called: Reynolds Metals Company LLC *(G-11876)*

Alcosm LLC 302 703-7635
16192 Coastal Hwy Lewes (19958) *(G-5671)*

Aldas Refinishing, Hockessin Also Called: Aldas Refinishing Company *(G-5119)*

Aldas Refinishing Company 302 528-5028
606 Chanin Ct Hockessin (19707) *(G-5119)*

Alderman Automotive Enterprise 302 652-3733
2317 N Dupont Hwy New Castle (19720) *(G-8777)*

Alderman Automotive Machine Sp, New Castle Also Called: Alderman Automotive Enterprise *(G-8777)*

ALPHABETIC SECTION — All Seasons Landscaping Inc

Aleric International Inc 302 547-4846
  116 Saint Andrews Ct Middletown (19709) *(G-6848)*

Alerislife Inc 302 478-4296
  1212 Foulk Rd Ste 1 Wilmington (19803) *(G-14352)*

Alert Security & Technologies 302 294-9100
  704 N King St Wilmington (19801) *(G-14353)*

Alex and Ani, Newark *Also Called: Alex and Ani LLC (G-9808)*

Alex and Ani, Rehoboth Beach *Also Called: Alex and Ani LLC (G-12600)*

Alex and Ani LLC 302 731-1420
  132 Christiana Mall Newark (19702) *(G-9808)*

Alex and Ani LLC 302 227-7360
  36494 Seaside Outlet Dr Unit 1420 Rehoboth Beach (19971) *(G-12600)*

Alex Evans Asphalt Paving LLC 302 363-3796
  827 Sparrow Ln Bear (19701) *(G-24)*

Alex Property Management LLC 302 384-9845
  8 The Grn Ste 8678 Dover (19901) *(G-1761)*

Alexis Legal Support Svcs Inc 646 494-3289
  35 Fairway Rd Apt 3a Newark (19711) *(G-9809)*

Alexis Wirt 302 654-4236
  610 Harrington Ave Wilmington (19805) *(G-14354)*

Alfred B Lauder DDS 302 697-7188
  508 Eagle Nest Dr Camden Wyoming (19934) *(G-907)*

Alfred I Dupont Hospital 302 651-4000
  1600 Rockland Rd Wilmington (19803) *(G-14355)*

Alfred Idpont Hosp For Chldren 302 629-5030
  49 Fallon Ave Seaford (19973) *(G-13053)*

Alfred Idpont Hosp For Chldren (HQ) 302 651-4000
  1600 Rockland Rd Wilmington (19803) *(G-14356)*

Alfred Lauder DDS 302 678-9742
  508 Eagle Nest Dr Camden Wyoming (19934) *(G-908)*

Alfred Moore 302 653-7600
  1057 Wheatleys Pond Rd Smyrna (19977) *(G-13633)*

Algiclor Liquid Chlorine, Smyrna *Also Called: Aztech Industries Inc (G-13657)*

Ali S Husain Orthodontist (PA) 302 838-1400
  1400 Peoples Plz Ste 312 Newark (19702) *(G-9810)*

Alias Technology LLC 302 856-9488
  25100 Trinity Dr Georgetown (19947) *(G-4205)*

Alice R OBrien Ms Lpcmh 302 521-3859
  130 Downs Dr Wilmington (19807) *(G-14357)*

Alicia Kendorski Ncc 302 448-5054
  32630 Cedar Dr Unit A Millville (19967) *(G-8513)*

Alisi Home Care LLC 302 268-8686
  108 Patriot Dr Ste A Middletown (19709) *(G-6849)*

Alium Consultancy LLC 347 414-8851
  8 The Grn Ste A Dover (19901) *(G-1762)*

Alive With Media 302 746-7831
  18 Hemlock Pl Wilmington (19810) *(G-14358)*

Alivio Health Corp 754 230-0234
  256 Chapman Rd Newark (19702) *(G-9811)*

Alixpartners LLP 302 824-7139
  3711 Kennett Pike Ste 130 Wilmington (19807) *(G-14359)*

Aljstar Global Holdings Inc 302 565-5249
  200 Continental Dr Ste 401-1103 Newark (19713) *(G-9812)*

Alka Construction LLC 443 944-9058
  10730 Serenity Cir Seaford (19973) *(G-13054)*

All About Gutters LLC 302 853-2645
  24531 Bethesda Rd Georgetown (19947) *(G-4206)*

All About Housing LLC 302 465-3246
  126 Tweedsmere Dr Townsend (19734) *(G-13956)*

All About Kidz, Bear *Also Called: J N Hooker Inc (G-293)*

All About Lawns Irrigation 302 242-6861
  34 Deer Jump Cir Camden (19934) *(G-788)*

All About Lawns Landscaping 302 530-1868
  414 W Summit Ave Wilmington (19804) *(G-14360)*

All About ME Day Care 302 424-8322
  104 Mccoy St Milford (19963) *(G-7763)*

All About Pain and Spine 302 595-3670
  2600 Glasgow Ave Ste 102 Newark (19702) *(G-9813)*

All About Pink Inc 302 947-0309
  28903 Harmons Hill Rd Millsboro (19966) *(G-8164)*

All About U Evada Concept (PA) 302 539-1925
  35825 Atlantic Ave Millville (19967) *(G-8514)*

All About Women 302 832-8331
  2600 Glasgow Ave Ste 120 Newark (19702) *(G-9814)*

All About Women 302 995-7073
  4600 Linden Hill Rd Ste 202 Wilmington (19808) *(G-14361)*

All About Women LLC 302 224-8400
  4735 Ogletown Stanton Rd Ste 2300 Newark (19713) *(G-9815)*

All American Fencing 302 530-8155
  6 Jersey Ct Middletown (19709) *(G-6850)*

All American Tree Experts 302 419-4876
  107 Mahon Ln Bear (19701) *(G-25)*

All American Truck Brokers 302 654-6101
  2205 E Huntington Dr Wilmington (19808) *(G-14362)*

All Around Moverz 302 494-9925
  314 W 35th St Wilmington (19802) *(G-14363)*

All Bright Cleaning Svcs LLC 302 219-7016
  117 Malcolm Forest Rd New Castle (19720) *(G-8778)*

All Clean Power Washing 877 325-3215
  36668 Hudson Rd Selbyville (19975) *(G-13459)*

All Clean Services 302 378-7376
  859 Union Church Rd Townsend (19734) *(G-13957)*

All Clear Pest Control 443 359-5623
  46 Read St Seaford (19973) *(G-13055)*

All Climate Storage Cente 302 645-0006
  17485 Shady Rd Lewes (19958) *(G-5672)*

All County Cleaning 302 504-4719
  104 Lake Dr Felton (19943) *(G-3940)*

All County Cleaning 914 497-1177
  122 Church Creek Dr Magnolia (19962) *(G-6715)*

All Creatures Vet Services 302 398-3367
  10395 Clendaniel Pond Rd Lincoln (19960) *(G-6655)*

All Flats Roofing 302 383-6762
  410 Junction St Wilmington (19805) *(G-14364)*

All For Fun Party Rentals 302 322-3844
  200 Lisa Dr New Castle (19720) *(G-8779)*

All In Harmony Child Care 302 494-3618
  802 S Harmony Rd Newark (19713) *(G-9816)*

All In One Home Repairs LLC 302 897-3845
  596 Old Baltimore Pike Newark (19702) *(G-9817)*

All In One Transportation LLC 302 482-3222
  32 Brookside Dr Wilmington (19894) *(G-14365)*

All In Wrist 302 659-1010
  231 S Dupont Blvd Smyrna (19977) *(G-13634)*

All JS Cleaning Services Inc 302 299-9916
  21 Jennings Ct New Castle (19720) *(G-8780)*

All Lives Matter LLC 252 767-9291
  8 The Grn Ste A Dover (19901) *(G-1763)*

All Logistics LLC 800 748-4891
  30862 Saddleridge Way Lewes (19958) *(G-5673)*

All Metals Fabricators Inc 302 691-8805
  6 Hadco Rd Wilmington (19804) *(G-14366)*

All Mighty Clean Company 302 798-1013
  55 Denham Ave Claymont (19703) *(G-1029)*

All My Children Elsmere, Wilmington *Also Called: All My Children Inc (G-14367)*

All My Children Inc 302 995-9191
  8 Walnut Ave Wilmington (19805) *(G-14367)*

All Pets Medical Center 302 653-2300
  10 Artisan Dr Smyrna (19977) *(G-13635)*

All Pro Maids Inc 302 645-9247
  1546 Savannah Rd Lewes (19958) *(G-5674)*

All Pro Property Maint LLC 302 531-6811
  410 East St Milford (19963) *(G-7764)*

All Pro Security, Delmar *Also Called: Great Gaines LLC (G-1599)*

All Restored Inc 302 697-7810
  137 Sarah Cir Camden Wyoming (19934) *(G-909)*

All Restored Inc 302 222-3537
  1638 Thicket Rd Camden Wyoming (19934) *(G-910)*

All Right Painting 302 983-7761
  185 Edge Ave New Castle (19720) *(G-8781)*

All Rock & Mulch LLC 302 838-7625
  1570 Red Lion Rd Bear (19701) *(G-26)*

All Seasons Landscaping Inc 302 423-8001
  154 S Fairfield Dr Dover (19901) *(G-1764)*

ALPHABETIC SECTION

All Smiles Family & Cosme.. 302 734-5303
95 Wolf Creek Blvd Ste 3 Dover (19901) *(G-1765)*

All Star Linen and Uniform Co.. 302 897-9003
3217 Heathwood Rd Wilmington (19810) *(G-14368)*

All Star Shredding LP.. 302 325-9998
6 Dock View Dr Ste 1000 New Castle (19720) *(G-8782)*

All Star Towing LLC.. 302 388-4221
4030 New Castle Ave New Castle (19720) *(G-8783)*

All State Transport LLC... 443 735-6453
200 Continental Dr Newark (19713) *(G-9818)*

All Tech Sealcoating LLC... 302 907-0311
36834 Red Berry Rd Delmar (19940) *(G-1562)*

All The Difference Inc... 302 738-6353
119 Saint Regis Dr Newark (19711) *(G-9819)*

All Things Inspiring Wellness.. 302 943-5503
531 Pear St Dover (19904) *(G-1766)*

All Trans Transmission Inc... 302 366-0104
18 Albe Dr Newark (19702) *(G-9820)*

All Tune & Lube... 302 744-9081
4200 N Dupont Hwy Ste 5 Dover (19901) *(G-1767)*

All Tune & Lube... 302 367-6369
3 W Salisbury Dr Wilmington (19809) *(G-14369)*

All Tune & Lube, Dover *Also Called: All Tune & Lube (G-1767)*

All Tune & Lube, Wilmington *Also Called: All Tune & Lube (G-14369)*

All Types Concrete... 302 613-8400
63 Meadow Rd New Castle (19720) *(G-8784)*

All United Prpts Solutions LLC.. 310 853-2223
4034 Willow Grove Rd Camden (19934) *(G-789)*

All Weather Roofing Co... 302 836-6400
200 Suffolk Blvd Bear (19701) *(G-27)*

All Work Services... 302 345-2695
2433 Glasgow Ave Newark (19702) *(G-9821)*

All-Span Inc (PA).. 302 349-9460
9347 Allspan Dr Bridgeville (19933) *(G-662)*

Allan B Stanley... 302 678-4774
2571 Kenton Rd Dover (19904) *(G-1768)*

Allan C Goldfeder DMD... 302 994-1782
2415 Milltown Rd Wilmington (19808) *(G-14370)*

Allan For Delaware... 410 920-2493
13288 Sunland Dr Milton (19968) *(G-8556)*

Allan Hughes Exp Inc (PA)... 302 230-6666
701 Bennett St Wilmington (19801) *(G-14371)*

Allan Myers.. 302 658-4417
102 Larch Cir Ste 203 Newport (19804) *(G-12442)*

Allan Myers Md Inc... 302 883-3501
440 Twin Oak Dr Dover (19904) *(G-1769)*

Allandale Village Apartments, Newark *Also Called: Westover Management Company LP (G-12362)*

Allcap Development Group LLC.. 302 429-8700
105 Foulk Rd Fl 2 Wilmington (19803) *(G-14372)*

Allegiant Fire Protection LLC.. 302 276-1300
118 Sandy Dr Ste 6 Newark (19713) *(G-9822)*

Allen & Associates.. 302 234-8600
4250 Lancaster Pike # 230 Wilmington (19805) *(G-14373)*

Allen Biotech LLC... 302 629-9136
29984 Pinnacle Way Millsboro (19966) *(G-8165)*

Allen Chorman & Son Inc.. 302 684-2770
30475 E Mill Run Milton (19968) *(G-8557)*

Allen Estates LLC.. 302 496-7250
8 The Grn Ste F Dover (19901) *(G-1770)*

Allen Harim, Millsboro *Also Called: Allen Biotech LLC (G-8165)*

Allen Harim, Millsboro *Also Called: Allen Harim Foods LLC (G-8167)*

Allen Harim Farms LLC... 302 629-9136
29984 Pinnacle Way Millsboro (19966) *(G-8166)*

Allen Harim Foods LLC... 302 732-9511
26867 Nine Foot Rd Dagsboro (19939) *(G-1411)*

Allen Harim Foods LLC... 302 684-1640
18752 Harbeson Rd Harbeson (19951) *(G-4681)*

Allen Harim Foods LLC (HQ).. 302 629-9136
29984 Pinnacle Way Millsboro (19966) *(G-8167)*

Allen Harim Foods LLC... 302 629-9460
20799 Allen Rd Seaford (19973) *(G-13056)*

Allen Insurance Group (PA)... 302 654-8823
410 Delaware Ave Wilmington (19801) *(G-14374)*

Allen Jarmon Enterprises Inc.. 302 745-5122
317 Rehoboth Ave Rehoboth Beach (19971) *(G-12601)*

Allen Spolden LLC.. 267 226-2160
651 N Broad St Ste 205 Middletown (19709) *(G-6851)*

Allens Termite & Pest Mgmt... 302 698-1496
5991 Mud Mill Rd Camden Wyoming (19934) *(G-911)*

Allerfree Cleaning... 302 593-6261
428 W 4th St Lewes (19958) *(G-5675)*

Allergy Associates PA.. 302 834-3401
2600 Glasgow Ave Ste 201 Newark (19702) *(G-9823)*

Allergy Associates PA.. 302 570-0865
1403 Silverside Rd Ste 4b Wilmington (19810) *(G-14375)*

Allergy Associates PA Inc.. 302 798-8070
1400 Philadelphia Pike Ste A6 Wilmington (19809) *(G-14376)*

Alli Inc.. 302 733-0740
250 Pencader Plz Newark (19713) *(G-9824)*

Alliance Bus Dev Concepts LLC.. 803 814-4004
1480 Alley Corner Rd Clayton (19938) *(G-1348)*

Alliance Chemicals Global LLC (PA).................................. 507 202-6872
3524 Silverside Rd Ste 35b Wilmington (19810) *(G-14377)*

Alliance Data... 302 256-0853
2 Righter Pkwy Ste 310 Wilmington (19803) *(G-14378)*

Alliance Electric Inc... 302 366-0295
1003 S Chapel St Ste D Newark (19702) *(G-9825)*

Alliance RE Professionals.. 302 519-7735
26673 Sussex Hwy Seaford (19973) *(G-13057)*

Alliance Real Estate Pros... 302 536-1838
26673 Sussex Hwy Seaford (19973) *(G-13058)*

Alliance Total Care... 302 225-9000
1851 Marsh Rd Wilmington (19810) *(G-14379)*

Allied Anesthesia Assoc LLC.. 302 547-3620
75 Old Mill Rd Dover (19901) *(G-1771)*

Allied Barton Security Svcs, Wilmington *Also Called: Alliedbarton Security Svcs LLC (G-14383)*

Allied Behavioral Health, Christiana *Also Called: Adirondack Bhvral Hlthcare LLC (G-991)*

Allied Elec Solutions Ltd... 302 893-0257
4661 Malden Dr Wilmington (19803) *(G-14380)*

Allied Lock & Safe Company... 302 658-3172
709 N Shipley St Wilmington (19801) *(G-14381)*

Allied Precision Inc.. 302 376-6844
106 Sleepy Hollow Dr Ste C Middletown (19709) *(G-6852)*

Allied Printing Co Inc... 503 626-0669
2 Penns Way Ste 301 New Castle (19720) *(G-8785)*

Allied Properties... 302 479-8314
4737 Concord Pike Wilmington (19803) *(G-14382)*

Allied Retail Properties, Wilmington *Also Called: Allied Properties (G-14382)*

Alliedbarton Security Svcs LLC.. 302 498-0450
824 N Market St Ste 102 Wilmington (19801) *(G-14383)*

Allison R Randall... 302 893-3817
1307 Philadelphia Pike Wilmington (19809) *(G-14384)*

Allison Scrivani LLC... 302 841-2320
108 Ocean Farm Dr Frankford (19945) *(G-4060)*

Allison Veith Lpcmh... 302 645-5338
31168 Learning Ln Lewes (19958) *(G-5676)*

Allison's Auto, Bear *Also Called: Allisons Auto Cycle Kstomz LLC (G-28)*

Allisons Auto Cycle Kstomz LLC.. 302 836-4222
700 Julian Ln Bear (19701) *(G-28)*

Allkare Inc.. 302 212-0917
8 The Grn Ste 12777 Dover (19901) *(G-1772)*

Allmark Door Company LLC... 302 323-4999
502 Churchmans Rd New Castle (19720) *(G-8786)*

Allmond & Eastburn... 302 764-2193
34952 Belle Rd Bethany Beach (19930) *(G-573)*

Allmond, Charles M III, Bethany Beach *Also Called: Allmond & Eastburn (G-573)*

Allpower Generator Sales & Svc... 302 793-1690
100 Naamans Rd Ste 1h Claymont (19703) *(G-1030)*

Allpro Services Group Inc.. 302 750-1112
529 Tullamore Rd Magnolia (19962) *(G-6716)*

Allserve Allscpes Allstrctures.. 302 684-1414
26539 Lewes Georgetown Hwy Harbeson (19951) *(G-4682)*

ALPHABETIC SECTION

Allstate, Lewes *Also Called: Allstate Insurance (G-5677)*
Allstate, Middletown *Also Called: Allstate Insur Ryan Nichols (G-6853)*
Allstate, Milford *Also Called: Charlene Webb (G-7820)*
Allstate, Milford *Also Called: Marvel Agency Inc (G-7986)*
Allstate, New Castle *Also Called: Joseph Devane Enterprises Inc (G-9265)*
Allstate, Newark *Also Called: Tom Wiseley Insurance Agency (G-12207)*
Allstate Insrnce Bob Sbraccia 302 300-4500
   5307 Limestone Rd Ste 101 Wilmington (19808) *(G-14385)*
Allstate Insur Agnt Intgrity I 302 368-6279
   230 E Cleveland Ave Newark (19711) *(G-9826)*
Allstate Insur Ryan Nichols 302 864-2230
   704 Ash Blvd Middletown (19709) *(G-6853)*
Allstate Insurance 302 248-8500
   19413 Jingle Shell Way Lewes (19958) *(G-5677)*
Allstate Van & Storage Corp 302 369-0230
   910 Interchange Blvd Newark (19711) *(G-9827)*
Allstates Technical Services, Newark *Also Called: Techncal Stffing Resources LLC (G-12169)*
Allston Chemical, Historic New Castle *Also Called: Philip Rosenau Co Inc (G-5048)*
Allston Chemical Supply Inc 302 322-3952
   264 Quigley Blvd Historic New Castle (19720) *(G-4927)*
Alltech Pro Corporation 323 457-3225
   651 N Broad St Ste 205 Middletown (19709) *(G-6854)*
Alltemp Air Inc 302 945-5734
   21171 John J Williams Hwy Lewes (19958) *(G-5678)*
Allura Bath & Kitchen Inc 302 731-2851
   704 Interchange Blvd Newark (19711) *(G-9828)*
Allure Outdoor Lighting LLC 302 226-2532
   20187 Beaver Dam Rd Lewes (19958) *(G-5679)*
Allure Salon, Smyrna *Also Called: Platinum Salon LLC (G-13848)*
Ally Auto Assets LLC 313 656-5500
   1209 N Orange St Wilmington (19801) *(G-14386)*
Ally Auto Rceivables Tr 2017-1 .... 313 656-5500
   1209 N Orange St Wilmington (19801) *(G-14387)*
Ally Auto Rceivables Tr 2019-1 .... 313 656-5500
   1209 N Orange St Wilmington (19801) *(G-14388)*
Alma Company 302 731-4427
   625 Barksdale Rd Newark (19711) *(G-9829)*
Almars Outboard Service & Sls 302 328-8541
   701 Washington St Historic New Castle (19720) *(G-4928)*
Almost Home Child Care Center, Milford *Also Called: Renzi Rust Inc (G-8062)*
Almost Home Day Care 302 220-6731
   1129 Capitol Trl Newark (19711) *(G-9830)*
Almost Home Day Care LLC 302 220-6731
   201 Cain Rue Newark (19711) *(G-9831)*
Aln Construction Inc 302 292-1580
   104 Sandy Dr Newark (19713) *(G-9832)*
Aloe & Carr PA 302 736-6631
   850 S State St Ste 2 Dover (19901) *(G-1773)*
Aloft Aeroarchitects, Georgetown *Also Called: Pats Aircraft LLC (G-4456)*
Aloha Movers 302 559-4310
   4306 Miller Rd Wilmington (19802) *(G-14389)*
Alora LLC 302 670-3066
   5995 Williamsville Rd Milford (19963) *(G-7765)*
Aloysius Butlr Clark Assoc Inc 302 655-1552
   600 N King St Wilmington (19801) *(G-14390)*
Alpha Care Medical LLC (PA) 302 398-0888
   1000 Midway Dr Ste 3 Harrington (19952) *(G-4725)*
Alpha Chemicals, Hockessin *Also Called: Economic Laundry Solutions (G-5198)*
Alpha Comm LLC 302 784-0645
   717 Javelin Way Bear (19701) *(G-29)*
Alpha Gmma RHO Almni Assn of T 301 490-9972
   37805 Crab Bay Ln Selbyville (19975) *(G-13460)*
Alpha Medical Distribution 302 738-9742
   201 Ruthar Dr Ste 5 Newark (19711) *(G-9833)*
Alpha Net Consulting LLC 302 737-2532
   100 Commerce Dr Newark (19713) *(G-9834)*
Alpha Omega Community Svc Ctr 302 323-1311
   806 Tremont St Historic New Castle (19720) *(G-4929)*
Alpha Omega Scientific LLC 302 415-4499
   129 Freedom Trl New Castle (19720) *(G-8787)*
Alpha PHI Delta 302 377-5789
   236 N Governors Ave Dover (19904) *(G-1774)*
Alpha PHI Delta Fraternity 302 531-7854
   257 E Camden Wyoming Ave Ste A Camden (19934) *(G-790)*
Alpha Railroad & Piling 318 377-8720
   231 Executive Dr Ste 15 Newark (19702) *(G-9835)*
Alpha Roofing & Siding Inc 302 249-2491
   29758 Colonial Estates Ave Millsboro (19966) *(G-8168)*
Alpha Tech Consulting LLC 302 898-2862
   1405 Gibraltar Ct Townsend (19734) *(G-13958)*
Alpha Technologies, Wilmington *Also Called: Alpha Technologies USA Inc (G-14392)*
Alpha Technologies Inc 917 412-9211
   704 N King St Fl 4 Wilmington (19801) *(G-14391)*
Alpha Technologies USA Inc 302 510-8205
   704 N King St Fl 4 Wilmington (19801) *(G-14392)*
Alphaforce Tech Solutions Inc 917 231-3796
   108 W 13th St Wilmington (19801) *(G-14393)*
AlphaGraphics, Newark *Also Called: Ancar Enterprises LLC (G-9861)*
AlphaGraphics, Wilmington *Also Called: AlphaGraphics Franchising Inc (G-14394)*
AlphaGraphics, Wilmington *Also Called: Ancar Enterprises LLC (G-14468)*
AlphaGraphics Franchising Inc 302 559-8369
   248 Weldin Ridge Rd Wilmington (19803) *(G-14394)*
Alphasense Inc 302 294-0116
   28 Hillstream Rd Newark (19711) *(G-9836)*
Alphataraxia Quicksilver LLC 571 367-7133
   1209 N Orange St Wilmington (19801) *(G-14395)*
Alpine Contractors LLC 302 343-9954
   200 Weston Dr Dover (19904) *(G-1775)*
Alpine Rafetto Orthodontics 302 239-2304
   4901 Limestone Rd Ste 4 Wilmington (19808) *(G-14396)*
Als Fare Green 302 500-1871
   98 Rudder Rd Millsboro (19966) *(G-8169)*
Als TV Service 302 653-3711
   1200 Wheatleys Pond Rd Smyrna (19977) *(G-13636)*
Alsco Inc 302 322-2136
   30 Mccullough Dr New Castle (19720) *(G-8788)*
Alston Associates Counseling 302 223-4797
   1232 N King St Ste 305 Wilmington (19801) *(G-14397)*
Altairis Tech Partners LLC 302 354-0662
   257 Milford Dr Middletown (19709) *(G-6855)*
Altea Resources LLC 713 242-1460
   3500 S Dupont Hwy Dover (19901) *(G-1776)*
Alternate Cmmodities Index Inc 302 238-1077
   9 Innovation Way Newark (19711) *(G-9837)*
Alternative Solutions 302 542-9081
   532 S Bedford St Georgetown (19947) *(G-4207)*
Alternative Therapy LLC 302 368-0800
   4629 Ogletown Stanton Rd Newark (19713) *(G-9838)*
Altitude Trampoline Park, Wilmington *Also Called: Wta Inc (G-20905)*
Altr Solutions LLC 888 757-2587
   8 The Grn Ste A Dover (19901) *(G-1777)*
Altra Cargo Inc 302 256-0748
   4004 N Market St Wilmington (19802) *(G-14398)*
Alu-Rex USA Inc 418 832-7632
   108 W 13th St Wilmington (19801) *(G-14399)*
Aluminum Building Company 302 423-8829
   10957 Willow Grove Rd Camden Wyoming (19934) *(G-912)*
Alutech Awnings, Selbyville *Also Called: Alutech United Inc (G-13461)*
Alutech United Inc (PA) 302 436-6005
   117 Dixon St Selbyville (19975) *(G-13461)*
Alvarenga Cleaner 302 427-2308
   123 Lorewood Ave Wilmington (19804) *(G-14400)*
Alvarez Painting 302 287-1457
   29 2nd Ave Wilmington (19808) *(G-14401)*
Alvatek Electronics LLC 302 655-5870
   1200 Pennsylvania Ave Ste 101 Wilmington (19806) *(G-14402)*
Alvini & Assoc Fincl Planners 302 397-8135
   29 Bancroft Mills Rd Wilmington (19806) *(G-14403)*
Alvins Professional Services 302 544-6634
   241 Old Churchmans Rd New Castle (19720) *(G-8789)*
Alvis D Burris 302 697-3125
   199 South St Camden (19934) *(G-791)*

ALPHABETIC SECTION

Alvissai Inc 470 202-3431
   8 The Grn Dover (19901) *(G-1778)*

Always Best Care 302 409-3710
   624 Mulberry St Milton (19968) *(G-8558)*

Always Duwell Clean 610 905-0779
   2809 Landon Dr Wilmington (19810) *(G-14404)*

Always Insurance Agency LLC 302 566-6529
   16190 S Dupont Hwy Harrington (19952) *(G-4726)*

Alyce E Duffy 302 383-5921
   1880 Superfine Ln Apt 40 Wilmington (19802) *(G-14405)*

Alycia, Wilmington Also Called: Holly Oak Towing and Service *(G-17169)*

Alzheimers Assn Del Chapter 302 633-4420
   2306 Kirkwood Hwy Wilmington (19805) *(G-14406)*

AMA Resource LLC 410 977-5101
   6 Lombardy Dr Wilmington (19803) *(G-14407)*

Amaa Management Corporation 302 677-0505
   764 Dover Leipsic Rd Dover (19901) *(G-1779)*

Amada Senior Care, Lewes Also Called: Amada Senior Care Southern Del *(G-5680)*

Amada Senior Care Southern Del 302 272-9500
   1 Ashford Dr Lewes (19958) *(G-5680)*

Amadex LLC 302 722-6027
   254 Chapman Rd Ste 208 # 10451 Newark (19702) *(G-9839)*

Amaira Ntral Skncare Sltons In 424 330-5231
   2711 Centerville Rd Ste 400 Wilmington (19808) *(G-14408)*

Amakor Inc 302 834-8664
   72 Clinton St Delaware City (19706) *(G-1530)*

Amalgam Rx Inc (PA) 302 983-0001
   206 Alapocas Dr Wilmington (19803) *(G-14409)*

Amalgama Digital Inc 302 387-0140
   651 N Broad St Ste 206 Middletown (19709) *(G-6856)*

Amalipo Smartduka Ltd 857 452-1692
   16192 Coastal Hwy Lewes (19958) *(G-5681)*

Amanda C Szymczak 302 678-3020
   103 Mont Blanc Blvd Dover (19904) *(G-1780)*

Amanda Coppinger 301 938-2346
   37139 Lord Baltimore Ln Ocean View (19970) *(G-12459)*

Amanda F Bodine 302 270-5579
   1652 Hourglass Rd Hartly (19953) *(G-4856)*

Amanda L Porter 302 234-2026
   5307 Limestone Rd Ste 101 Wilmington (19808) *(G-14410)*

Amanda Lynn Ferenc LPn 302 841-2498
   6755 Cannon Rd Bridgeville (19933) *(G-663)*

AMANECER COUNSELING & RESOURCE, Wilmington Also Called: Family Cnsling Ctr St Puls Inc *(G-16535)*

Amani Birth 302 668-7506
   1401 Pennsylvania Ave Wilmington (19806) *(G-14411)*

Amani Family Foundation 800 839-1754
   501 Silverside Rd Wilmington (19809) *(G-14412)*

Amantya Technologies Inc 302 439-6030
   1201 N Market St Ste 111 Wilmington (19801) *(G-14413)*

Amarch LLC 484 478-1034
   1023 Matthew Way New Castle (19720) *(G-8790)*

Amatuzio Appraisal Svcs Inc 302 378-9654
   409 Waltham Dr Middletown (19709) *(G-6857)*

Amazand Theta LLC 302 285-9586
   3316 Cross Country Dr Wilmington (19810) *(G-14414)*

Amazed Apps LLC 916 934-9210
   8 The Grn Dover (19901) *(G-1781)*

Amazingdoc Inc 847 909-0409
   251 Little Falls Dr Wilmington (19808) *(G-14415)*

Amazon Commodities LLC (PA) 302 715-1427
   112 Capitol Trl Ste A455 Newark (19711) *(G-9840)*

Amazon Steel Construction Inc 302 751-1146
   2537 Bay Rd Milford (19963) *(G-7766)*

Amazon.Com, Historic New Castle Also Called: AmazonCom Services LLC *(G-4930)*

AmazonCom Services LLC 206 266-1000
   1 Centerpoint Blvd Historic New Castle (19720) *(G-4930)*

Amber B Woodland 302 628-4140
   225 High St Seaford (19973) *(G-13059)*

Amber Dragon Acupuncture 206 227-0641
   1143 Savannah Rd Ste 4 Lewes (19958) *(G-5682)*

Amber Waves One LLC 302 653-4641
   335 Ryan Rd Smyrna (19977) *(G-13637)*

Ambience Inc 302 239-4822
   3701 Oak Ridge Rd Wilmington (19808) *(G-14416)*

Ambience of Excellence LLC 302 751-0778
   9 Liborio Ln New Castle (19720) *(G-8791)*

Ambient Care Express 302 629-3099
   31010 Thornton Blvd Unit 2 Delmar (19940) *(G-1563)*

Ambient Medical Care 302 629-3099
   24459 Sussex Hwy Ste 2 Seaford (19973) *(G-13060)*

Ambient Procurement Group LLC 718 925-7750
   300 Creek View Rd Ste 209 Newark (19711) *(G-9841)*

Ambrogi Integrative Hlth Servi 610 368-1006
   2000 Pennsylvania Ave Wilmington (19806) *(G-14417)*

Ambrux Hospitality LLC 302 521-2492
   4409 Kennett Pike Wilmington (19807) *(G-14418)*

Ambulatorys Surgery Ctr 302 633-9416
   1941 Limestone Rd Ste 113 Wilmington (19808) *(G-14419)*

AMC - Commercial Inc 302 229-0051
   316 Governor Printz Blvd Claymont (19703) *(G-1031)*

AMC Museum Foundation 302 677-5938
   1301 Heritage Rd Dover (19902) *(G-1782)*

AME Life LLC 305 517-7707
   8 The Grn Ste 7302 Dover (19901) *(G-1783)*

AME-Life, Dover Also Called: AME Life LLC *(G-1783)*

Amedee Enterprises LLC 302 482-7442
   1 E Saxony Dr New Castle (19720) *(G-8792)*

Ameenahko LLC 302 601-3720
   201 Woodlawn Ave Apt B Wilmington (19805) *(G-14420)*

Ameken Network Group Inc 302 545-3472
   405 Maple Ln Claymont (19703) *(G-1032)*

Amemg Inc 302 220-7132
   32 Phoebe Farms Ln New Castle (19720) *(G-8793)*

Amer Inc 302 654-2498
   1010 N Union St Ste D Wilmington (19805) *(G-14421)*

Amer Industrial Tech Inc 302 765-3318
   100 Amer Rd Ste 200 Wilmington (19809) *(G-14422)*

Amer Masonry T A Marino 302 834-1511
   811 Reybold Dr New Castle (19720) *(G-8794)*

Ameri Auto LLC 302 607-9113
   150 Malcolm Forest Rd New Castle (19720) *(G-8795)*

Ameribulk Transport LLC (PA) 302 792-1190
   6300 Philadelphia Pike Claymont (19703) *(G-1033)*

America Group 302 529-1320
   2036 Foulk Rd Ste 104 Wilmington (19810) *(G-14423)*

American Air Lease Finance LLC 646 643-6303
   605 N Market St Fl 2 Wilmington (19801) *(G-14424)*

American Art Tatttoo 484 889-1663
   114 W Rutherford Dr Newark (19713) *(G-9842)*

American Beauty Landscaping, Smyrna Also Called: American Beauty Ldscpg LLC *(G-13638)*

American Beauty Ldscpg LLC 302 653-6460
   1578 Sunnyside Rd Smyrna (19977) *(G-13638)*

American Birding Assn Inc (PA) 302 838-3660
   93 Clinton St Ste Aba Delaware City (19706) *(G-1531)*

American Birding Association 610 864-0370
   20 Murphy Rd Wilmington (19803) *(G-14425)*

American Builder LLC 302 841-2325
   31 Fairway West Dr Georgetown (19947) *(G-4208)*

American Builders Inc 856 287-0840
   1212 Pimpernell Path Middletown (19709) *(G-6858)*

American Cedar & Millwork, Lewes Also Called: American Cedar & Millwork Inc *(G-5683)*

American Cedar & Millwork Inc (PA) 302 645-9580
   17993 American Way Lewes (19958) *(G-5683)*

American Centennial Insur Co 302 479-2100
   1415 Foulk Rd Ste 202 Wilmington (19803) *(G-14426)*

American Chiropractic Center 302 450-3153
   230 Beiser Blvd Ste 101 Dover (19904) *(G-1784)*

American Chiropractic Center 302 407-3046
   1324 N King St Wilmington (19801) *(G-14427)*

American Chmber Cmmrce In Ukri (PA) 352 505-9709
   1209 N Orange St Wilmington (19801) *(G-14428)*

ALPHABETIC SECTION — Americas Got Funding

American Chmber Cmmrce In Uzbk.. 202 590-9294
  1209 N Orange St Wilmington (19801) *(G-14429)*

American Classic Golf Club LLC.. 302 703-6662
  18485 Bethpage Dr Ste 1 Lewes (19958) *(G-5684)*

American Cllge of Physicians... 540 631-0426
  2 Richards Dr Wilmington (19810) *(G-14430)*

American Cncil For An Enrgy Ef... 202 507-4000
  1 Roy Ct Newark (19711) *(G-9843)*

American Consumer Marketing, Dover Also Called: Acm Corp *(G-1711)*

American Craftsmen LLC... 302 545-3666
  608 S Gerald Dr Newark (19713) *(G-9844)*

American Electric LLC.. 302 632-6724
  31019 Edgewood Dr Lewes (19958) *(G-5685)*

American Eli Truck Network Inc... 210 842-2134
  16192 Coastal Hwy Lewes (19958) *(G-5686)*

American Fdrtion State Cnty MN... 302 698-5034
  177 Candlewick Dr Dover (19901) *(G-1785)*

American Fdrtion State Cnty MN... 302 323-2600
  100 Churchmans Rd New Castle (19720) *(G-8796)*

American Fdrtion State Cnty MN... 302 323-2121
  91 Christiana Rd New Castle (19720) *(G-8797)*

American Finance LLC.. 302 674-0365
  17507 S Dupont Hwy Harrington (19952) *(G-4727)*

American Furniture Rentals Inc... 302 323-1682
  490 W Basin Rd New Castle (19720) *(G-8798)*

American Handyman Services... 302 616-2559
  30958 Maplewood Rd Ocean View (19970) *(G-12460)*

American Hardscapes LLC.. 302 253-8237
  20099 Gravel Hill Rd Georgetown (19947) *(G-4209)*

American Homepatient, Newark Also Called: American Homepatient Inc *(G-9845)*

American Homepatient Inc.. 302 454-4941
  701 Interchange Blvd Newark (19711) *(G-9845)*

American Ice, Milford Also Called: United States Cold Storage Inc *(G-8127)*

American Income Lf - Ryan Bsan... 484 442-8148
  300 Delaware Ave Ste 210 Wilmington (19801) *(G-14431)*

American Incorporators, Wilmington Also Called: Incorporators USA LLC *(G-17303)*

American Incorporators Ltd.. 302 421-5752
  1013 Centre Rd Ste 403a Wilmington (19805) *(G-14432)*

American Industries LLC.. 302 585-0129
  124 Broadkill Rd Ste 436 Milton (19968) *(G-8559)*

American Insert Flange Co Inc... 302 777-7464
  1603 Jessup St Ste 6 Wilmington (19802) *(G-14433)*

American K9 Dggie Dycare Trnin... 302 376-9663
  128 Patriot Dr Unit 12 Middletown (19709) *(G-6859)*

American Karate Studio.. 302 529-7800
  1812 Marsh Rd Ste 421 Wilmington (19810) *(G-14434)*

American Karate Studios.. 302 737-9500
  1150 Capitol Trl Newark (19711) *(G-9846)*

American Legion.. 302 398-3566
  17448 S Dupont Hwy Harrington (19952) *(G-4728)*

American Legion (PA)... 302 628-5221
  601 Bridgeville Hwy Ste 213 Seaford (19973) *(G-13061)*

American Legion.. 302 378-4882
  3 Owensby Dr Townsend (19734) *(G-13959)*

American Legion, Delmar Also Called: American Lgion Post 15 Glen Ry *(G-1564)*

American Legion, Seaford Also Called: American Legion Aux Dept Del *(G-13062)*

American Legion Ambulance... 302 653-3557
  210 E North St Smyrna (19977) *(G-13639)*

American Legion Aux Dept Del.. 302 629-3435
  386 Graham Branch Rd Seaford (19973) *(G-13062)*

American Legion Auxiliary.. 302 329-9090
  25109 Prettyman Rd Georgetown (19947) *(G-4210)*

American Legion Auxiliary.. 302 235-0878
  62 Wesley Dr Hockessin (19707) *(G-5120)*

American Legion Ckrt Post 7, Harrington Also Called: American Legion *(G-4728)*

American Lgion Amblnce Stn 64.. 302 653-6465
  900 Smyrna Clayton Blvd Smyrna (19977) *(G-13640)*

American Lgion Post 15 Glen Ry... 410 726-4780
  104 N 2nd St Delmar (19940) *(G-1564)*

American Life Insurance Co (HQ).. 302 594-2000
  1 Alico Plz 600 King St Wilmington (19801) *(G-14435)*

American Marketing Agency Inc... 484 424-9683
  3524 Silverside Rd 35b Wilmington (19810) *(G-14436)*

American Martial Arts Inst.. 302 834-4060
  402 Eden Cir Bear (19701) *(G-30)*

American Masonry.. 302 362-9962
  9602 Chris Ave Laurel (19956) *(G-5463)*

American Meter Holdings Corp.. 302 477-0208
  1105 N Market St Ste 1300 Wilmington (19801) *(G-14437)*

American Minerals Inc.. 302 652-3301
  301 Pigeon Point Rd New Castle (19720) *(G-8799)*

American Minerals Partnership.. 302 652-3301
  301 Pigeon Point Rd New Castle (19720) *(G-8800)*

American National Red Cross... 215 451-4372
  5329 Concord Pike Wilmington (19803) *(G-14438)*

American Neon Products Company.. 302 856-3400
  720 Mccolley St Milford (19963) *(G-7767)*

American Nutra Group LLC... 305 610-9448
  1000 N West St Ste 1200 Wilmington (19801) *(G-14439)*

American Precast.. 302 629-6688
  8506 Potts Ln Seaford (19973) *(G-13063)*

American Public Gardens Assn... 610 708-3010
  1207 Delaware Ave Wilmington (19806) *(G-14440)*

American Quality Construction, Townsend Also Called: EZ Deck LLC *(G-14000)*

American Records Management, Newark Also Called: American Van Storage Corp *(G-9850)*

American Renal... 302 672-7901
  107 Mont Blanc Blvd Dover (19904) *(G-1786)*

AMERICAN RENAL, Hockessin Also Called: American Unvrsal-Hockessin LLC *(G-5121)*

AMERICAN RENAL, Newark Also Called: American Universal LLC *(G-9849)*

American Responder Svcs LLC.. 302 567-2530
  16797 Coastal Hwy Lewes (19958) *(G-5687)*

American Restoration Carp.. 302 993-7900
  412 Greenwood Dr Wilmington (19808) *(G-14441)*

American Restoration Services, Wilmington Also Called: American Restoration Carp *(G-14441)*

American Seaboard Exteriors.. 302 571-9896
  14 Ashley Pl Wilmington (19804) *(G-14442)*

American Soc Cytopathology Inc.. 302 543-6583
  100 W 10th St Ste 605 Wilmington (19801) *(G-14443)*

American Solutions Inc.. 302 456-9600
  100 Commerce Dr Ste 103 Newark (19713) *(G-9847)*

American Speedy Printing, Wilmington Also Called: OConnell Speedy Printing Inc *(G-18743)*

American Spirit Federal Cr Un... 302 738-4515
  1110 Elkton Rd Newark (19711) *(G-9848)*

American Sports, Newark Also Called: Versatile Impex Inc *(G-12317)*

American Sports Licensing Inc (PA)... 302 288-0122
  1011 Ctr Rd Ste 310 Wilmington (19805) *(G-14444)*

American Standard... 302 326-1349
  66 Southgate Blvd New Castle (19720) *(G-8801)*

American Stone Crafters Inc... 302 834-8891
  7 Hawkins Ct Bear (19701) *(G-31)*

American Surgery Center... 302 266-9166
  161 Becks Woods Dr Bear (19701) *(G-32)*

American Traffic Pd LLC.. 302 883-7263
  122 Delaware St Historic New Castle (19720) *(G-4931)*

American Tree Co LLC... 302 836-1664
  915 Sugar Pine Dr Bear (19701) *(G-33)*

American Universal LLC.. 302 836-9790
  1415 Pulaski Hwy Ste 2 Newark (19702) *(G-9849)*

American Unvrsal-Hockessin LLC... 302 239-4106
  5936 Limestone Rd Ste 101 Hockessin (19707) *(G-5121)*

American Van Storage Corp.. 302 369-0900
  900 Interchange Blvd Newark (19711) *(G-9850)*

American Water Well System.. 302 629-3796
  1129 A Brickyard Rd Seaford (19973) *(G-13064)*

American Wellness Supplies, Wilmington Also Called: United Security Advisors LLC *(G-20526)*

American Wood Design.. 302 792-2100
  100 Naamans Rd Ste 4b Claymont (19703) *(G-1034)*

American-Eurasian Exch Co LLC... 202 701-4009
  4023 Kennett Pike 267 Wilmington (19807) *(G-14445)*

Americas Got Funding.. 866 975-8363
  1148 Pulaski Hwy Ste 404 Bear (19701) *(G-34)*

AmericInn — ALPHABETIC SECTION

AmericInn, Harrington *Also Called: AmericInn By Wyndham (G-4729)*
AmericInn, Harrington *Also Called: Sunny Hospitality LLC (G-4837)*
AmericInn, Milford *Also Called: Milford Lodging LLC (G-8003)*
AmericInn, Rehoboth Beach *Also Called: Sunny Hospitality LLC (G-12980)*

AmericInn By Wyndham 302 398-3900
1259 Corn Crib Rd Harrington (19952) *(G-4729)*

AmericInn Lodge & Suites, Bear *Also Called: Innpros Inc (G-285)*

Americo Inc 302 981-9410
117 Bunche Blvd Wilmington (19801) *(G-14446)*

Amerihalth Integrated Benefits (DH) 302 777-6400
919 N Market, Ste 1200 Wilmington (19801) *(G-14447)*

Amerihealth Caritas Delaware 844 211-0966
1142 Pulaski Hwy Bear (19701) *(G-35)*

Amerimax Inc 951 710-0899
3025 Bowlarama Dr New Castle (19720) *(G-8802)*

Ameriprise Financial Inc 302 235-5765
103 Brook Run Hockessin (19707) *(G-5122)*

Ameriprise Financial Services 302 476-8000
2 Righter Pkwy Wilmington (19803) *(G-14448)*

Ameriprise Financial Services, Hockessin *Also Called: Ameriprise Financial Inc (G-5122)*
Ameriprise Financial Services, Wilmington *Also Called: Ameriprise Financial Svcs Inc (G-14450)*
Ameriprise Financial Services, Wilmington *Also Called: Ameriprise Financial Svcs LLC (G-14452)*
AMERIPRISE FINANCIAL SERVICES, INC., Wilmington *Also Called: Ameriprise Financial Svcs Inc (G-14449)*
AMERIPRISE FINANCIAL SERVICES, INC., Wilmington *Also Called: Ameriprise Financial Svcs Inc (G-14451)*

Ameriprise Financial Svcs Inc 302 543-5784
5195 W Woodmill Dr 27 Wilmington (19808) *(G-14449)*

Ameriprise Financial Svcs Inc 302 475-5105
1805 Foulk Rd Ste A Wilmington (19810) *(G-14450)*

Ameriprise Financial Svcs Inc 302 468-8200
1011 Centre Rd Ste 100 Wilmington (19805) *(G-14451)*

Ameriprise Financial Svcs LLC 302 475-2357
2106 Silverside Rd Ste 201 Wilmington (19810) *(G-14452)*

Ameriprise 302 656-7773
1 Righter Pkwy Ste 250 Wilmington (19803) *(G-14453)*

Amerisource Heritage Corp 800 829-3132
1403 Foulk Rd Ste 106 Wilmington (19803) *(G-14454)*

Ames Engineering Corp 302 658-6945
805 E 13th St Wilmington (19802) *(G-14455)*

Ames Music Studio 302 222-4648
16 Fleming St Harrington (19952) *(G-4730)*

Ametek Inc 302 456-4400
455 Corporate Blvd Newark (19702) *(G-9851)*

AMF, Wilmington *Also Called: All Metals Fabricators Inc (G-14366)*
AMF, Wilmington *Also Called: AMF Bowling Centers Inc (G-14456)*

AMF Bowling Centers Inc 302 998-5316
3215 Kirkwood Hwy Wilmington (19808) *(G-14456)*

Amfine Chemical Corp 302 559-2948
602 Benham Ct Newark (19711) *(G-9852)*

Amh Enterprises LLC 302 337-0300
8805 Newton Rd Bridgeville (19933) *(G-664)*

Amick Farms LLC 302 846-9511
10392 Allens Mill Rd Delmar (19940) *(G-1565)*

Amick Mart J MD 302 633-1700
3105 Limestone Rd Ste 301 Wilmington (19808) *(G-14457)*

Amino Medical Science Inc 213 232-8619
16192 Coastal Hwy Ste 102 Lewes (19958) *(G-5688)*

Amino-Chem (us) LLC 281 305-8668
160 Greentree Dr Ste 101 Dover (19904) *(G-1787)*

Amira Spray Foam 302 464-0644
548 Red Fox Cir S Middletown (19709) *(G-6860)*

Amish Tradesmen 302 349-5550
26673 Sussex Hwy Seaford (19973) *(G-13065)*

Amitra Vitta Incorporated 267 905-3766
831 N Tatnall St Ste M148 Wilmington (19801) *(G-14458)*

Amity Lodges Ltd 833 462-6489
251 Little Falls Dr Wilmington (19808) *(G-14459)*

AMP Electric LLC 302 337-8050
302 Earlee Ave Bridgeville (19933) *(G-665)*

AMP Manufacturing LLC 302 691-8883
6 Hadco Rd Wilmington (19804) *(G-14460)*

Ampacet Ohio LLC 914 631-6600
300 Delaware Ave Ste 210 Wilmington (19801) *(G-14461)*

Amphitrades, Wilmington *Also Called: Emaep LLC (G-16385)*

Ample Business Solutions Inc 302 752-4270
501 Silverside Rd Wilmington (19809) *(G-14462)*

Amplified Gchmical Imaging LLC 302 266-2428
210 Executive Dr Ste 1 Newark (19702) *(G-9853)*

Amrec, Dover *Also Called: Amrec Holdings Inc (G-1788)*

Amrec Holdings Inc 302 273-0000
8 The Grn Ste 4257 Dover (19901) *(G-1788)*

Amrelieve, Middletown *Also Called: Wexmon LLC (G-7720)*
AMS, Rehoboth Beach *Also Called: AMS of Delaware (G-12602)*

AMS of Delaware 302 227-1320
20576 Coastal Hwy Rehoboth Beach (19971) *(G-12602)*

Amschel Capital LLC 302 298-1199
2093 Philadelphia Pike Ste 2711 Claymont (19703) *(G-1035)*

Amschel Capital LLC 302 298-1199
2093 Philadelphia Pike Claymont (19703) *(G-1036)*

Amsoft Corp 859 351-7688
4023 Kennett Pike Wilmington (19807) *(G-14463)*

Amsol Inc 302 369-6969
100 Commerce Dr Ste 103 Newark (19713) *(G-9854)*

Amstel Barber Shop 302 696-2300
2484 N Dupont Pkwy Middletown (19709) *(G-6861)*

Amstel Barber Shop 302 378-5300
712 Ash Blvd Middletown (19709) *(G-6862)*

Amstel Barber Shop 302 543-4515
1319 Mckennans Church Rd Wilmington (19808) *(G-14464)*

Amstel Barbershop LLC 302 635-7686
7313 Lancaster Pike Ste 4 Hockessin (19707) *(G-5123)*

Amstel Barbershop LLC 302 299-5926
1830 Capitol Trl Newark (19711) *(G-9855)*

Amstel Mechanical Contrs Inc 302 836-6469
1183 S Dupont Hwy New Castle (19720) *(G-8803)*

Amtrak Material Control 302 319-7270
5 Boulden Cir New Castle (19720) *(G-8804)*

Amvets Post 22 .... 302 945-2599
32369 Long Neck Rd Unit 18 Millsboro (19966) *(G-8170)*

Amwal Tech Inc 650 391-5496
2055 Limestone Rd Wilmington (19808) *(G-14465)*

Amy Chilimidos C O Boa 302 388-1880
108 Haddington Way Hockessin (19707) *(G-5124)*

Amy Corbitt 302 635-7233
632 Dane Ct New Castle (19720) *(G-8805)*

Amy Donovan 302 245-8957
32855 Ocean Reach Dr Lewes (19958) *(G-5689)*

Amy Gabel 703 598-0763
18370 Alpine Loop Lewes (19958) *(G-5690)*

Amy Kellenberger Inc 302 381-7901
22542 Hartschorn Dr Milton (19968) *(G-8560)*

Amy Linzey 302 541-4447
38241 Yacht Basin Rd # 9 Ocean View (19970) *(G-12461)*

Amy M Farrall OD LLC 302 737-5777
317 E Main St Newark (19711) *(G-9856)*

Amylin Pharmaceuticals LLC 858 552-2200
1800 Concord Pike Wilmington (19897) *(G-14466)*

An Event 2 Remember 215 783-9744
9 Colin Ct Claymont (19703) *(G-1037)*

An Intgrative Hlth Ctr Med Spa 484 550-2085
19 Haines St Newark (19711) *(G-9857)*

Anaconda Prtctive Concepts Inc 302 834-1125
210 Executive Dr Ste 6 Newark (19702) *(G-9858)*

Analtech, Newark *Also Called: Miles Scientific Corporation (G-11418)*

Analytica LLC 214 223-2055
800 N State St Ste 402 Dover (19901) *(G-1789)*

Analytical Biological Svcs Inc 302 654-4492
2 Reads Way New Castle (19720) *(G-8806)*

Analytics Realm LLC 302 743-0342
43 Anthony Dr Newark (19702) *(G-9859)*

ALPHABETIC SECTION

Analyttica Datalab Inc (PA) 917 300-3325
   1007 N Orange St Fl 4 Wilmington (19801) *(G-14467)*

Anamo Inc 702 852-2992
   28 Old Rudnick Ln Dover (19901) *(G-1790)*

Anatrope Inc 202 507-9441
   3500 S Dupont Hwy Dover (19901) *(G-1791)*

Anax Designs 877 908-8719
   200 Continental Dr Newark (19713) *(G-9860)*

Ancar Enterprises LLC 302 453-2600
   703 Interchange Blvd Newark (19711) *(G-9861)*

Ancar Enterprises LLC (PA) 302 477-1884
   3411 Silverside Rd # 103 Wilmington (19810) *(G-14468)*

Ancatt 302 513-9392
   9 Germay Dr Wilmington (19804) *(G-14469)*

Ancatt Company 302 897-8366
   20 Findail Dr Newark (19711) *(G-9862)*

Anchor Electric Inc 302 221-6111
   185 Old Churchmans Rd New Castle (19720) *(G-8807)*

Anchor Enterprises 302 629-7969
   22 W High St Seaford (19973) *(G-13066)*

Anchor Enterprises, Seaford *Also Called: Asa V Peugh Inc (G-13069)*

Anchor Plumbing Inc 410 392-6520
   207 Brennen Dr Newark (19713) *(G-9863)*

Anchorage Motel Inc 302 645-8320
   18809 Coastal Hwy Rehoboth Beach (19971) *(G-12603)*

Anchors Aweigh Entrmt LLC 302 236-1587
   37959 William Chandler Blvd Ocean View (19970) *(G-12462)*

Ancient Order Hbernians Ladies 302 633-0810
   401 Jackson Ave Wilmington (19804) *(G-14470)*

Ancient Order of Hibernians 302 368-0264
   11 Palmer Pl Newark (19713) *(G-9864)*

Andbeyond, Wilmington *Also Called: Venturist Media Inc (G-20582)*

Andels Home Care, Wilmington *Also Called: Annadale Oladimeji (G-14491)*

Anderson Catania Suretly Svc 302 762-7599
   707 Philadelphia Pike Wilmington (19809) *(G-14471)*

Anderson Floor Coverings Inc 302 227-3244
   4286 Highway One Rehoboth Beach (19971) *(G-12604)*

Anderson Group Inc 302 478-6160
   3411 Silverside Rd Ste 103 Wilmington (19810) *(G-14472)*

Anderson Landscaping 302 423-3904
   95 Jump Dr Smyrna (19977) *(G-13641)*

Anderson Rnee Charles Anderson 302 529-7845
   101 Maplewood Ln Wilmington (19810) *(G-14473)*

Andre M D Hoffman 302 892-2710
   1090 Old Churchmans Rd Newark (19713) *(G-9865)*

Andrea M D Arellano 302 678-0510
   811 S Governors Ave Dover (19904) *(G-1792)*

Andrea Meyer 302 745-8823
   24584 Hollytree Cir Georgetown (19947) *(G-4211)*

Andreas Rauer MD PA 302 734-1760
   16 Old Rudnick Ln Dover (19901) *(G-1793)*

Andrew B Price Custom Builde 302 659-5368
   312 W Mount Vernon St Smyrna (19977) *(G-13642)*

Andrew Bobich 312 384-9323
   1316 N Union St Wilmington (19806) *(G-14474)*

Andrew E Quesenberry Carpentry 302 994-0700
   1012 Stanton Rd Wilmington (19808) *(G-14475)*

Andrew Hayden 302 562-9236
   306 Seamans Ct Middletown (19709) *(G-6863)*

Andrew J Glick MD 302 652-8990
   2000 Foulk Rd Ste F Wilmington (19810) *(G-14476)*

Andrew Pipon 949 337-2249
   8231 Woods Edge Cir Milford (19963) *(G-7768)*

Andrew Simoff Horse Trnsp 302 994-1433
   3719 Old Capitol Trl Wilmington (19808) *(G-14477)*

Andrew T Patterson CPA 302 652-4194
   503 Carr Rd Ste 120 Wilmington (19809) *(G-14478)*

Andrew W Donohue Do 302 235-3725
   1906 Maryland Ave Wilmington (19805) *(G-14479)*

Andrew W Viohl 302 388-7721
   2405 Mckinley Ave Claymont (19703) *(G-1038)*

Andrew Weinstein MD Inc 302 428-1675
   111 Walnut Ridge Rd Wilmington (19807) *(G-14480)*

Andrews & Springer LLC 302 504-4957
   4001 Kennett Pike Ste 250 Wilmington (19807) *(G-14481)*

Andrews Construction LLC 302 604-8166
   126 Major St Lincoln (19960) *(G-6656)*

Andrews, Joseph F MD, Dover *Also Called: Delaware Dermatolgy PA (G-2231)*

Andy Is My Coach LLC 302 943-4819
   21 General Torbert Dr Milford (19963) *(G-7769)*

Andy Mulrine 302 547-7139
   228 Suburban Dr Newark (19711) *(G-9866)*

Andy Staton Real Estate Inc 302 703-9090
   309 Rehoboth Ave Rehoboth Beach (19971) *(G-12605)*

Anesthesiology & Pain MGT 302 235-8074
   1080 S Chapel St Ste 100 Newark (19702) *(G-9867)*

Angel Homeowner 302 504-6895
   25 Sunny Bnd Newark (19702) *(G-9868)*

Angel Nails 302 449-5067
   480 Middletown Warwick Rd Middletown (19709) *(G-6864)*

Angel Pizzaro 302 653-4844
   1760 Harvey Straughn Rd Townsend (19734) *(G-13960)*

Angela Daycar Nana Lil 302 672-9167
   117 Hitching Post Dr Dover (19904) *(G-1794)*

Angela Saldarriaga 302 633-1182
   5578 Kirkwood Hwy Wilmington (19808) *(G-14482)*

Angelas Massage and Bodywork 302 547-9390
   11 O Rourke Ct Newark (19702) *(G-9869)*

Angelic Therapy 717 870-4618
   17436 Slipper Shell Way Unit 11 Lewes (19958) *(G-5691)*

Angelo Joseph Chiari Rph 302 239-5949
   516 Defoe Rd Hockessin (19707) *(G-5125)*

Angels In Action Inc 302 397-7061
   23 Elks Trl New Castle (19720) *(G-8808)*

Angels Interaction, New Castle *Also Called: Angels In Action Inc (G-8808)*

Angels Lindas 302 328-3700
   6 Parkway Ct New Castle (19720) *(G-8809)*

Angels Messiahs Foundation 302 365-5516
   360 Foxhunt Dr Bear (19701) *(G-36)*

Angels Visiting 302 691-8700
   3101 Limestone Rd Ste E Wilmington (19808) *(G-14483)*

Angies Super Clean 302 519-0828
   223b N Willey St Seaford (19973) *(G-13067)*

Angita Pharmard LLC 302 234-6794
   24 Tall Oaks Dr Hockessin (19707) *(G-5126)*

Angle Planning Concepts 302 735-7526
   31 Saulsbury Rd # B Dover (19904) *(G-1795)*

Angler Plumbing LLC 302 293-5691
   37 Dempsey Dr Newark (19713) *(G-9870)*

Anglin Aircraft Recovery Svc, Clayton *Also Called: Anglin Associates LLC (G-1349)*

Anglin Associates LLC 302 653-3500
   4901 Holletts Corner Rd Clayton (19938) *(G-1349)*

Anglin Cnsulting Solutions LLC 302 406-0233
   1201 N Market St Wilmington (19801) *(G-14484)*

Angola By The Bay Prprty Owner 302 945-2700
   33457 Woodland Cir Lewes (19958) *(G-5692)*

Angry 8 LLC (PA) 888 417-5477
   200 Continental Dr Ste 401-796 Newark (19713) *(G-9871)*

Angry Reels Inc 336 906-1797
   651 N Broad St Ste 205 Middletown (19709) *(G-6865)*

Anhui Xncheng High Schl Almni 302 234-4351
   115 Hockessin Dr Hockessin (19707) *(G-5127)*

Animal Haven Veterinary Center 302 326-1400
   757 Pulaski Hwy Ste 6 Bear (19701) *(G-37)*

Animal Health Sales Inc 302 436-8286
   44 Rte 113 Selbyville (19975) *(G-13462)*

Animal Inn Inc 302 653-5560
   2308 Seeneytown Rd Dover (19904) *(G-1796)*

Animal Veterinary Center LLC 302 322-6488
   160 Bear Christiana Rd Bear (19701) *(G-38)*

Anip Acquisition Company 302 652-2021
   2003 Kentmere Pkwy Wilmington (19806) *(G-14485)*

Anita Barbara Peghini Raber GA 302 227-2888
  49 Baltimore Ave Rehoboth Beach (19971) *(G-12606)*
Anixter, Historic New Castle *Also Called: Anixter Power Solutions Inc (G-4932)*
Anixter Inc 302 325-2590
  51 Steel Dr New Castle (19720) *(G-8810)*
Anixter Power Solutions Inc 302 298-3601
  599 Ships Landing Way Historic New Castle (19720) *(G-4932)*
Ankle and Foot Surgical Assoc 302 425-5720
  701 N Clayton St Fl 4 Wilmington (19805) *(G-14486)*
Ankor Tree Service LLC 302 514-7447
  316 N School Ln Smyrna (19977) *(G-13643)*
Anlatan LLC 618 318-5334
  2055 Limestone Rd Ste 200c Wilmington (19808) *(G-14487)*
Ann M Campagna 302 395-8950
  2 Boulden Cir Ste 1 New Castle (19720) *(G-8811)*
Ann White 302 365-4664
  14 Newbrook Rd Newark (19711) *(G-9872)*
Anna J Blommer 302 576-4136
  1010 W 4th St Wilmington (19805) *(G-14488)*
Anna Marie Mazoch DDS PA 302 998-9594
  2601 Annand Dr Ste 18 Wilmington (19808) *(G-14489)*
Anna Vassallo Piera 302 529-2607
  1812 Marsh Rd Ste 423 Wilmington (19810) *(G-14490)*
Annabella Technologies Inc 833 716-1909
  16192 Coastal Hwy Lewes (19958) *(G-5693)*
Annadale Oladimeji (PA) 267 357-9718
  501 Silverside Rd Ste 28 Wilmington (19809) *(G-14491)*
Annalise-Ai Inc 440 281-5115
  8 The Grn Ste R Dover (19901) *(G-1797)*
Annalissas Playhouse 302 653-3529
  316 Lisa Ct Smyrna (19977) *(G-13644)*
Anne Anstasi Chrtble Fundation 800 839-1754
  501 Silverside Rd Wilmington (19809) *(G-14492)*
Anne Powell LLC 302 245-9245
  10 Daisey Ave Ocean View (19970) *(G-12463)*
Anniejwels Erly Child Dev Ctr 302 981-1904
  118 Bunche Blvd Wilmington (19801) *(G-14493)*
Anniemac Home Mortgage LLC 302 234-2956
  4839 Limestone Rd Wilmington (19808) *(G-14494)*
Anns Family Daycare 302 836-8910
  30 Reubens Cir Newark (19702) *(G-9873)*
Anointed Creative Creations 302 650-7033
  15 Meadow Rd New Castle (19720) *(G-8812)*
Anointed To Clean 302 284-7243
  135 Winding Wood Dr Magnolia (19962) *(G-6717)*
Anp Biopharma LLC 302 283-1730
  824 Interchange Blvd Newark (19711) *(G-9874)*
Anp Technologies Inc 302 283-1730
  824 Interchange Blvd Newark (19711) *(G-9875)*
Ans Corporation (PA) 410 296-8330
  37156 Rehoboth Avenue Ext Unit 3 Rehoboth Beach (19971) *(G-12607)*
Ansel Health Inc 844 987-1070
  1209 N Orange St Wilmington (19801) *(G-14495)*
Antebellum Hospitality Inc 302 436-4375
  118 W Church St Selbyville (19975) *(G-13463)*
Antenna House Inc 302 566-7225
  500 Creek View Rd Ste 107 Newark (19711) *(G-9876)*
Anthem Graphix 302 270-5111
  10 Cinnamon Way Magnolia (19962) *(G-6718)*
Anthogo Enterprises 302 378-0235
  535 Maiden Ct Middletown (19709) *(G-6866)*
Anthony A Vasile Do 302 764-2072
  620 Stanton Christiana Rd Newark (19713) *(G-9877)*
Anthony D'S Auto Repair, Historic New Castle *Also Called: 855 Inc (G-4916)*
Anthony Ferguson 610 906-4998
  37200 W White Tail Dr Selbyville (19975) *(G-13464)*
Anthony Giantinoto DC 302 294-1832
  260 Chapman Rd Ste 104e Newark (19702) *(G-9878)*
Anthony Lee Cucuzzella MD 302 623-4370
  4735 Ogletown Stanton Rd Ste 3302 Newark (19713) *(G-9879)*
Anthony M Caristo DPM 302 834-3575
  2600 Glasgow Ave Ste 106 Newark (19702) *(G-9880)*

Anthonys Automotive 302 420-9804
  252 Bassett Ave New Castle (19720) *(G-8813)*
Anthonys Collision Cstm Works 302 542-2489
  10 Clark St Harrington (19952) *(G-4731)*
Antoinette Xavier 980 549-3272
  17573 S Dupont Hwy Harrington (19952) *(G-4732)*
Antonio C Narvaez MD 302 453-1002
  2602 Eastburn Ctr Newark (19711) *(G-9881)*
Anutio Inc 647 607-8378
  704 N King St Ste 500 Wilmington (19801) *(G-14496)*
Anybodies Inc 646 699-8781
  2810 N Church St Wilmington (19802) *(G-14497)*
Anymoney LLC 818 431-5251
  8 The Grn Dover (19901) *(G-1798)*
Anyone Fitness 302 226-4653
  18908 Rehoboth Mall Blvd Ste 5 Rehoboth Beach (19971) *(G-12608)*
Anythings Possible Cnstr 302 233-2357
  1211 Sandbox Rd Harrington (19952) *(G-4733)*
Anytime Fitness 302 834-2348
  235 Governors Pl Bear (19701) *(G-39)*
Anytime Fitness 302 229-1716
  880 S Governors Ave Dover (19904) *(G-1799)*
Anytime Fitness 302 212-6151
  17400 N Village Main Blvd Lewes (19958) *(G-5694)*
Anytime Fitness 302 533-7773
  247 S Main St Newark (19711) *(G-9882)*
Anytime Fitness 302 738-3040
  201 Louviers Dr Newark (19711) *(G-9883)*
Anytime Fitness 302 653-4496
  599 Jimmy Dr Ste 18 Smyrna (19977) *(G-13645)*
Anytime Fitness 302 475-2404
  1851 Marsh Rd Wilmington (19810) *(G-14498)*
Anytime Fitness, Hockessin *Also Called: Anytime Fitness Main Line (G-5128)*
Anytime Fitness, Milton *Also Called: Anytime Fitness Lewes (G-8561)*
Anytime Fitness Lewes 856 340-9252
  23574 Holly Oak Dr Milton (19968) *(G-8561)*
Anytime Fitness Main Line 302 239-4800
  702 Lantana Dr Hockessin (19707) *(G-5128)*
Aod Smyma 43 .... 302 659-5060
  222 N Dupont Blvd Smyrna (19977) *(G-13646)*
Aola, Wilmington *Also Called: Aola Inc (G-14499)*
Aola Inc (PA) 610 245-8231
  919 N Market St Ste 950 Wilmington (19801) *(G-14499)*
AON Construction Services LLC 302 858-6178
  961b Hawksbill St Bethany Beach (19930) *(G-574)*
Aon3d Inc 650 410-3120
  1209 N Orange St Wilmington (19801) *(G-14500)*
AOP Holding Company LLC (PA) 346 561-4123
  8 The Grn Ste R Dover (19901) *(G-1800)*
Aorel Tech Investments LLC 610 674-1516
  3 Germay Dr Ste 4 Wilmington (19804) *(G-14501)*
AP Irrigation Inc 302 233-2357
  1211 Sandbox Rd Harrington (19952) *(G-4734)*
AP Linens Inc 302 430-0851
  713 S Washington St Milford (19963) *(G-7770)*
Apache Software Foundation 302 295-4884
  1000 Nw St Ste 1200 Wilmington (19801) *(G-14502)*
Aparta Hospitality Tech 617 383-3239
  8 The Grn Ste A Dover (19901) *(G-1801)*
Apartment Communities, Wilmington *Also Called: Woods Edge Apartments (G-20886)*
Apartment Communities Corp 302 656-7781
  402 Foulk Rd Apt 1a9 Wilmington (19803) *(G-14503)*
Apartment Communities Inc 302 798-9100
  31 Harbor Dr Apt 2 Claymont (19703) *(G-1039)*
Apartments Sdk 302 478-1215
  3120 Naamans Rd Wilmington (19810) *(G-14504)*
Apex Arabians Inc 302 242-6272
  671 Williamsville Rd Houston (19954) *(G-5436)*
Apex Builders LLC 302 242-1059
  152 Old Forge Dr Dover (19904) *(G-1802)*
Apex Chiropractic Services 302 598-9404
  404 N Hampton Ct Middletown (19709) *(G-6867)*

ALPHABETIC SECTION

Apex Contractors LLC 302 670-7799
   1148 Pulaski Hwy Bear (19701) *(G-40)*

Apex Engineering Inc 302 994-1900
   27 W Market St Wilmington (19804) *(G-14505)*

Apex Exteriors Inc 302 858-1699
   497 Bowman Rd Milford (19963) *(G-7771)*

Apex Lawn & Home 302 670-4363
   42 E Inner Cir Dover (19904) *(G-1803)*

Apex Manufacturing Group Inc 484 888-6252
   825 Dawson Dr Ste 1 Newark (19713) *(G-9884)*

Apex Piping Systems Inc (PA) 302 995-6136
   302 Falco Dr Wilmington (19804) *(G-14506)*

Apex Stable, Houston *Also Called: Apex Arabians Inc (G-5436)*

Apex Transportation Svcs LLC 302 284-7463
   12600 S Dupont Hwy Felton (19943) *(G-3941)*

Apg Inc 302 746-7167
   100 Naamans Rd Claymont (19703) *(G-1040)*

Apga, Wilmington *Also Called: American Public Gardens Assn (G-14440)*

API, Smyrna *Also Called: Aqua Pro Inc (G-13647)*

APL Lgstics Trnsp MGT Svcs Ltd 302 230-2656
   200 Powder Mill Rd Bldg 402 Wilmington (19803) *(G-14507)*

Apollo Health & Wellness LLC 302 994-2273
   5503 Kirkwood Hwy Wilmington (19808) *(G-14508)*

Apollo Imports Inc 514 895-9410
   2915 Ogletown Rd # 3696 Newark (19713) *(G-9885)*

Apollo Scitech LLC 302 861-6557
   18 Shea Way Ste 108 Newark (19713) *(G-9886)*

Apollo Software Inc 800 992-0847
   2035 Sunset Lake Rd B2 Newark (19702) *(G-9887)*

Aponte, Lourdes MD, Lewes *Also Called: Nancy A Union MD (G-6305)*

Appa Inc 302 440-1448
   8 The Grn Ste 7868 Dover (19901) *(G-1804)*

Appcano LLC 951 285-3632
   2810 N Church St # 42197 Wilmington (19802) *(G-14509)*

Appgenius Labs LLC 412 953-5064
   651 N Broad St Ste 201 Middletown (19709) *(G-6868)*

Apphive Inc 240 898-4661
   2035 Sunset Lake Rd Newark (19702) *(G-9888)*

Apphud Inc 415 936-8741
   200 Continental Dr Ste 401 Newark (19713) *(G-9889)*

Appic Stars LLC 903 224-6469
   8 The Grn Ste 4524 Dover (19901) *(G-1805)*

Apple Cleaning Systems LLC 302 368-7507
   34 Blevins Dr Ste 1 New Castle (19720) *(G-8814)*

Apple Electric Inc 302 645-5105
   18854 John J Williams Hwy Rehoboth Beach (19971) *(G-12609)*

Appleby Apartments Assoc LP 302 219-5014
   401 Bedford Ln New Castle (19720) *(G-8815)*

Appletree Answering Services Inc 302 227-9015
   1521 Concord Pike Ste 202 Wilmington (19803) *(G-14510)*

Appliances Zone 302 280-6073
   34936 Sussex Hwy Delmar (19940) *(G-1566)*

Applied Analytics Inc 781 791-5005
   113 Barksdale Professional Ctr Newark (19711) *(G-9890)*

Applied Bank (PA) 302 326-4200
   2200 Concord Pike Ste 102 Wilmington (19803) *(G-14511)*

Applied Biofeedback Solutions 302 674-3225
   1485 S Governors Ave Dover (19904) *(G-1806)*

Applied Card Holdings Inc 302 326-4200
   601 Delaware Ave Ste 100 Wilmington (19801) *(G-14512)*

Applied Control Engrg Inc (PA) 302 738-8800
   700 Creek View Rd Newark (19711) *(G-9891)*

Applied Technologies Inc 302 670-4601
   169 Roundabout Trl Camden Wyoming (19934) *(G-913)*

Applied Virtual Solutions LLC 302 312-8548
   16 N Bellwoode Dr Newark (19702) *(G-9892)*

Apploye Inc 925 452-6102
   2035 Sunset Lake Rd B2 Newark (19702) *(G-9893)*

Apply Co 775 343-5307
   2093 Philadelphia Pike Ste 3581 Claymont (19703) *(G-1041)*

Appmotion Inc 347 513-6333
   1000 N West St Ste 1200 Wilmington (19801) *(G-14513)*

Appointed Partners Pubg Inc 302 446-3675
   8 The Grn Ste 11910 Dover (19901) *(G-1807)*

Appointiv Inc 415 877-4339
   651 N Broad St Middletown (19709) *(G-6869)*

Appoqnmink Counseling Svcs LLC 302 898-1616
   11 Crawford St Middletown (19709) *(G-6870)*

Appoquinimink Development Inc 302 378-0878
   103 E Park Pl Middletown (19709) *(G-6871)*

Appricot Inc 484 291-8922
   8 The Grn Dover (19901) *(G-1808)*

Apps By Cs LLC 866 235-9752
   1041 N Dupont Hwy Dover (19901) *(G-1809)*

Apptrium Inc 800 888-0706
   1000 N West St Ste 1200 Wilmington (19801) *(G-14514)*

Apria Healthcare LLC 302 737-7979
   1 Mccullough Dr New Castle (19720) *(G-8816)*

April L Sarver 302 559-0787
   303 N Dillwyn Rd Newark (19711) *(G-9894)*

April Mries Hair Design Studio 302 981-3386
   202 E 6th St Ste D Historic New Castle (19720) *(G-4933)*

April's Healing Hand's, Newark *Also Called: April L Sarver (G-9894)*

Apriorit LLC 202 780-9339
   3524 Silverside Rd Ste 35b Wilmington (19810) *(G-14515)*

APS Cleaning Services, New Castle *Also Called: Alvins Professional Services (G-8789)*

Aptustech LLC 347 254-5619
   1209 Ornge St Corp Tr Ctr Wilmington (19801) *(G-14516)*

Aqorn Inc 916 123-4567
   427 N Tatnall St Wilmington (19801) *(G-14517)*

Aqua Infra Rehab Co LLC 610 328-7714
   567 Walther Rd Newark (19702) *(G-9895)*

Aqua Pro Inc 302 659-6593
   104 Big Woods Rd Smyrna (19977) *(G-13647)*

Aqua Science LLC 302 757-5241
   250 Corporate Blvd Ste K Newark (19702) *(G-9896)*

Aquacare Physical 302 200-9159
   34434 King Street Row Lewes (19958) *(G-5695)*

Aquacast Liner LLC 302 535-3728
   100 Lake Dr Ste 200 Newark (19702) *(G-9897)*

Aquaflow Pump & Supply Company (PA) 302 834-1311
   1561 Pulaski Hwy Bear (19701) *(G-41)*

Aquamarine Boutique LLC 302 644-4550
   114 2nd St Lewes (19958) *(G-5696)*

Aquamarine On Market, Lewes *Also Called: Aquamarine Boutique LLC (G-5696)*

Aquantuo LLC 302 753-0435
   148 Southern Blvd Wyoming (19934) *(G-20980)*

Aquasoli 704 696-8400
   3422 Old Capitol Trl Wilmington (19808) *(G-14518)*

Aquatic Management 302 235-1818
   4905 Mermaid Blvd Wilmington (19808) *(G-14519)*

Aquatica Plumbing Group Inc 866 606-2782
   414 Greenwood Dr New Castle (19720) *(G-8817)*

Aquia Inc 530 215-7158
   24408 Shady Ln Millsboro (19966) *(G-8171)*

Aquia Nava II LLC 410 245-8990
   24408 Shady Ln Millsboro (19966) *(G-8172)*

Aquila of Delaware Inc (PA) 302 999-1106
   4185 Kirkwood St Georges Rd Bear (19701) *(G-42)*

AR Campagnone LLC 302 329-9323
   14928 Hudson Rd Milton (19968) *(G-8562)*

AR Pro Inc 323 677-0503
   2055 Limestone Rd Ste 200c Wilmington (19808) *(G-14520)*

Arab Therapy Inc 310 956-4252
   108 W 13th St Wilmington (19801) *(G-14521)*

Arabian Lights Dance Co Inc 410 543-4538
   38052 Old Stage Rd Delmar (19940) *(G-1567)*

Aracent Healthcare LLC 302 478-8865
   3411 Silverside Rd Ste 202 Wilmington (19810) *(G-14522)*

ARB Heavenly Homes LLC 215 919-8272
   41 Andover Branch Rd Clayton (19938) *(G-1350)*

Arbiter Inc 404 939-2826
   2035 Sunset Lake Rd B2 Newark (19702) *(G-9898)*

Arbitexch LLC 302 490-0111
500 N King St Wilmington (19801) *(G-14523)*

Arbor Care 302 491-4392
21429 Bella Terra Dr Lincoln (19960) *(G-6657)*

Arbor Care 302 258-8909
31 Rivers End Dr Seaford (19973) *(G-13068)*

Arbor Management LLC (PA) 302 764-6450
4 Denny Rd Ste 1 Wilmington (19809) *(G-14524)*

Arbor Management Alarm 302 856-2876
200 Ingramtown Rd Georgetown (19947) *(G-4212)*

Arbor Pointe, Wilmington Also Called: Vintage Properties LLC *(G-20627)*

Arbor Pointe Rental Co, Wilmington Also Called: Sovereign Property MGT LLC *(G-19943)*

Arborvine Landscaping LLC 302 502-5605
114 Chatham Pl Wilmington (19810) *(G-14525)*

ARC Falcon I Inc (PA) 302 636-5401
251 Little Falls Dr Wilmington (19808) *(G-14526)*

ARC Finance Ltd 914 478-3851
251 Little Falls Dr Wilmington (19808) *(G-14527)*

ARC HUD I Inc 302 996-9400
2 S Augustine St Wilmington (19804) *(G-14528)*

ARC HUD II Inc 302 996-9400
2 S Augustine St Wilmington (19804) *(G-14529)*

ARC HUD VII Inc 302 996-9400
2 S Augustine St Wilmington (19804) *(G-14530)*

ARC of Delaware 302 996-9400
2 S Augustine St Ste B Wilmington (19804) *(G-14531)*

ARC of Delaware 302 996-9400
2 S Augustine St Ste B Wilmington (19804) *(G-14532)*

ARC OF DELAWARE, Wilmington Also Called: Assocition For The Rghts Ctzens *(G-14597)*

ARC Offshore Investments Inc 561 670-9938
3511 Silverside Rd # 105 Wilmington (19810) *(G-14533)*

ARC Resin Corp 859 230-7063
2112 Lindell Blvd Wilmington (19808) *(G-14534)*

ARC Seminars LLC 856 776-6758
406 S Cass St Middletown (19709) *(G-6872)*

ARC Studio Labs Inc 323 990-8787
2810 N Church St Pmb 65228 Wilmington (19802) *(G-14535)*

ARC Wilmington 302 656-6620
100 W 10th St Wilmington (19801) *(G-14536)*

Arcade Services Inc 630 777-8092
257 Old Churchmans Rd New Castle (19720) *(G-8818)*

Arcadia Fencing Inc 302 398-7700
166 Hopkins Cemetery Rd Harrington (19952) *(G-4735)*

Arcadia Properties LLC 302 747-5050
561 N Dupont Hwy Dover (19901) *(G-1810)*

Arcadia Therapeutic Massage 302 438-3251
918 Wilson Rd Wilmington (19803) *(G-14537)*

Arcadis US Inc 302 658-1718
1007 N Orange St Fl 1 Wilmington (19801) *(G-14538)*

Arcangel Inc 347 771-0789
1013 Centre Rd Ste 403 Wilmington (19805) *(G-14539)*

Arcasoft LLC 402 575-1234
1201 N Orange St Ste 7306 Wilmington (19801) *(G-14540)*

Archadeck, Hockessin Also Called: Archadeck of Delaware *(G-5129)*

Archadeck, Newark Also Called: Archadeck of Delaware *(G-9899)*

Archadeck of Delaware 302 766-3698
7465 Lancaster Pike Hockessin (19707) *(G-5129)*

Archadeck of Delaware 302 766-3698
31 Savoy Rd Newark (19702) *(G-9899)*

Archer & Greiner A Prof Corp 302 777-4350
300 Delaware Ave Ste 1100 Wilmington (19801) *(G-14541)*

Archer Group, The, Wilmington Also Called: Cohesive Strategies Inc *(G-15520)*

Archer Sweets, Dover Also Called: Monica Bumbrey *(G-3120)*

Architect Engineer Ins Co Risk 302 658-2342
4001 Kennett Pike Ste 318 Wilmington (19807) *(G-14542)*

Architects Engineers Loss Ctrl, Wilmington Also Called: Architect Engineer Ins Co Risk *(G-14542)*

Architectural Solutions 302 230-1809
23 Grady Ln New Castle (19720) *(G-8819)*

Architecture Plus PA 302 999-1614
234 N James St Wilmington (19804) *(G-14543)*

Arcpoint Labs 302 268-6560
222 Philadelphia Pike Ste 5 Wilmington (19809) *(G-14544)*

Arctec Air Heating & Cooling 302 629-7129
21965 Palomino Way Bridgeville (19933) *(G-666)*

Arctic Heating and AC 302 537-6988
28896 Hudson Rd Dagsboro (19939) *(G-1412)*

Arden Courts of Wilmington 302 762-7800
700 1/2 Foulk Rd Wilmington (19803) *(G-14545)*

Arden Courts of Wilmington, Wilmington Also Called: Arden Courts Wilmington De LLC *(G-14546)*

Arden Courts Wilmington De LLC 302 764-0181
700 One Half Foulk Rd Wilmington (19803) *(G-14546)*

Arden Media Resources 256 656-8631
1302 N West St Wilmington (19801) *(G-14547)*

Ardeun Biometrics Corp LLC 949 662-1096
16192 Coastal Hwy Lewes (19958) *(G-5697)*

Ardex Laboratories Inc 302 363-1005
5027 Dublin Hill Rd Bridgeville (19933) *(G-667)*

Ardexo Inc 855 617-7500
8 The Grn Ste 4810 Dover (19901) *(G-1811)*

Ardexo Housing Solutions, Dover Also Called: Ardexo Inc *(G-1811)*

Area 51 Automotive 302 993-9114
8 Hadco Rd Wilmington (19804) *(G-14548)*

Area Wide Protective 302 455-1900
12 Mill Park Ct Newark (19713) *(G-9900)*

Arena Signs 302 644-8300
34696 Jiffy Way Lewes (19958) *(G-5698)*

Arg Communications, Wilmington Also Called: Arugie Enterprises Corp *(G-14573)*

Argilla Brewing Company 302 731-8200
2667 Kirkwood Hwy Newark (19711) *(G-9901)*

Argo Ai Corporation 516 602-9295
8 The Grn Ste D Dover (19901) *(G-1812)*

Argo Financial Services Inc 302 322-7788
104 Penn Mart Shopping Ctr New Castle (19720) *(G-8820)*

Argo US Feeder Fund LP 345 769-4154
251 Little Falls Dr Wilmington (19808) *(G-14549)*

Aria Solutions Inc 302 453-8389
194 Mccormick Blvd Newark (19702) *(G-9902)*

Arianna & Angelina Entps LLC 484 574-8119
2801 Centerville Rd Wilmington (19808) *(G-14550)*

Ariel C Rubin 443 854-9901
5 Caroline Ln Rehoboth Beach (19971) *(G-12610)*

Aries Security LLC 302 365-0026
1226 N King St Wilmington (19801) *(G-14551)*

Arihant Enterprise LLC 302 353-4400
140 Foxhunt Dr Bear (19701) *(G-43)*

Arion LLC 215 531-1673
9 E Loockerman St Ste 311 Dover (19901) *(G-1813)*

Arise Africa Foundation Inc 877 829-5500
10 Elks Trl New Castle (19720) *(G-8821)*

Aritisans Wilmington Bank, Wilmington Also Called: Artisans Bank Inc *(G-14571)*

Arivers Construction 302 299-2288
43 Abbey Rd Newark (19702) *(G-9903)*

Ark of Refuge Mission-Shelter 302 381-2143
29687 Millsboro Hwy Millsboro (19966) *(G-8173)*

Ark Recruiting Solutions Inc 302 947-1877
27185 Barefoot Blvd Millsboro (19966) *(G-8174)*

Arkieva, Wilmington Also Called: Supply Chain Consultants Inc *(G-20149)*

Arkion, New Castle Also Called: Arkion Life Sciences LLC *(G-8822)*

Arkion Life Sciences LLC (PA) 800 468-6324
551 Mews Dr Ste J New Castle (19720) *(G-8822)*

Arklight Arsenal LLC 844 722-3766
8 The Grn Ste 8692 Dover (19901) *(G-1814)*

Arkshell Corporation 917 985-8529
2093a Philadelphia Pike Ste 279 Claymont (19703) *(G-1042)*

Arlen D Stone M D 302 999-0933
1 Centurian Dr Ste 105 Newark (19713) *(G-9904)*

Arlene Weisman 302 569-2822
119 W 3rd St Lewes (19958) *(G-5699)*

Arlon LLC (HQ) 302 834-2100
1100 Governor Lea Rd Bear (19701) *(G-44)*

Arlon Med International LLC 302 834-2100
1100 Governor Lea Rd Bear (19701) *(G-45)*

Arlon Mtl Tech Microwave Mtls, Bear *Also Called: Arlon LLC (G-44)*

Arlon Partners Inc 302 595-1234
1100 Governor Lea Rd Bear (19701) *(G-46)*

Arm Chair Scouts LLC 315 360-8692
427 N Tatnall St 24852 Wilmington (19801) *(G-14552)*

Arma Tel LLC 302 480-9394
8 The Grn Ste A Dover (19901) *(G-1815)*

Armand De MD Sanctic 302 475-2535
2101 Foulk Rd Wilmington (19810) *(G-14553)*

Armed Forces Med Examiner Sys 302 346-8653
115 Purple Heart Ave Dover (19902) *(G-1816)*

Armehtech Solutions LLC 302 309-9645
919 N Market St Ste 950 Wilmington (19801) *(G-14554)*

Armigers Auto Center Inc (PA) 302 875-7642
28866 Sussex Hwy Laurel (19956) *(G-5464)*

Armin Marefat Do 302 645-9325
33663 Bayview Medical Dr Lewes (19958) *(G-5700)*

Armodias LLC 302 384-9794
4023 Kennett Pike # 273 Wilmington (19807) *(G-14555)*

Armor Graphics Inc 302 737-8790
1102 Ogletown Rd Newark (19711) *(G-9905)*

Armstrong Cork Finance LLC 302 652-1520
818 N Washington St Wilmington (19801) *(G-14556)*

Armstrong Painting Inc 302 420-0415
25216 Harmony Woods Dr Millsboro (19966) *(G-8175)*

Armstrong Trnsf Stor Inc/Rmstr 302 323-9000
20 E Commons Blvd New Castle (19720) *(G-8823)*

Army & Air Force Exchange Svc 302 677-3716
260 Chad St Dover (19902) *(G-1817)*

Army National Guard Delaware 302 855-7456
Rd 2 Dagsboro (19939) *(G-1413)*

Arnab Mobility Inc 774 316-6767
2035 Sunset Lake Rd B2 Newark (19702) *(G-9906)*

Arnold International Inc 302 266-4441
573 Bellevue Rd Ste B Newark (19713) *(G-9907)*

Aroma, Lewes *Also Called: Flyingparts International Inc (G-6006)*

Aros Design Studio LLC 505 560-0603
2604 Whittier Pl Wilmington (19808) *(G-14557)*

Around Again and Again Bks LLC 302 439-3847
1400 Philadelphia Pike Wilmington (19809) *(G-14558)*

Arovo US Inc 952 290-0799
8 The Grn Ste 14569 Dover (19901) *(G-1818)*

Array Corporation 650 241-1382
2093 Philadelphia Pike # 5334 Claymont (19703) *(G-1043)*

Arrim LLC (PA) 617 697-7914
919 N Market St Ste 950 Wilmington (19801) *(G-14559)*

Arrow Chemical Inc 302 731-7403
4142 Ogletown Stanton Rd Newark (19713) *(G-9908)*

Arrow Express Inc 302 836-3658
26 Chambord Dr Newark (19702) *(G-9909)*

Arrow Leasing Corp 302 834-4546
1772 Pulaski Hwy Bear (19701) *(G-47)*

Arrow Safety Device Company, Selbyville *Also Called: Ktm 2 LLC (G-13559)*

Arrow Sanitary Service, Bear *Also Called: Arrow Leasing Corp (G-47)*

Arrowtech LLC 704 833-8777
651 N Broad St Middletown (19709) *(G-6873)*

ARS Fleet Service 302 482-1305
501 Lambson Ln New Castle (19720) *(G-8824)*

ARS New Castle LLC 302 323-9400
263 Quigley Blvd Ste 1b Historic New Castle (19720) *(G-4934)*

ARS of Rio Grande LLC 302 323-9400
263 Quigley Blvd Historic New Castle (19720) *(G-4935)*

Arseneau Cpa LLC (PA) 302 854-0133
65 N Dupont Hwy Dover (19901) *(G-1819)*

Art and Therapy Services 302 329-9794
120 S White Cedar Dr Milton (19968) *(G-8563)*

Art Fitness 302 373-5148
109 Faraday Ct Bear (19701) *(G-48)*

Art Floor Inc 302 636-9201
9 Jefferson Ave Wilmington (19805) *(G-14560)*

Art For A Purpose 302 245-4528
102 Savannah Rd Lewes (19958) *(G-5701)*

ART GROUP, Wilmington *Also Called: Studio Groups Inc (G-20106)*

Art Ture 302 893-0156
47 Rodney Rd Dover (19901) *(G-1820)*

Artcomun, Newark *Also Called: Artcomun Technologies Inc (G-9910)*

Artcomun Technologies Inc 302 266-1521
112 Capitol Trl Ste A153 Newark (19711) *(G-9910)*

Artcraft Upholstery LLC 302 764-2067
116 Center Ct Wilmington (19810) *(G-14561)*

Arteaga Properties LLC 808 339-6906
2711 Centerville Rd # 200 Wilmington (19808) *(G-14562)*

Artemundi LLC 302 988-5002
3411 Silverside Rd Ste 104 Wilmington (19810) *(G-14563)*

Artesian Resources, Newark *Also Called: Artesian Resources Corporation (G-9911)*

Artesian Resources Corporation (PA) 302 453-6900
664 Churchmans Rd Newark (19702) *(G-9911)*

Artesian Utility Dev Inc 800 332-5114
664 Churchmans Rd Newark (19702) *(G-9912)*

Artesian Wastewater MD Inc 302 453-6900
664 Churchmans Rd Newark (19702) *(G-9913)*

Artesian Water Company Inc 800 332-5114
14701 Coastal Hwy Milton (19968) *(G-8564)*

Artesian Water Maryland Inc 302 453-6900
664 Churchmans Rd Newark (19702) *(G-9914)*

Artevet, Wilmington *Also Called: Artevet LLC (G-14564)*

Artevet LLC 443 255-0016
1000 N West St Ste 1200 Wilmington (19801) *(G-14564)*

Artful Barber 302 672-0818
301 W Loockerman St Dover (19904) *(G-1821)*

Arthouse USA Incorporated 800 677-3394
1209 N Orange St Wilmington (19801) *(G-14565)*

Arthur Coppedge 302 229-7581
7 Paynter St Bear (19701) *(G-49)*

Arthur L Young Dentist Jr 302 737-9065
6 Millbourne Dr Newark (19711) *(G-9915)*

Arthur W Henry DDS Inc 302 734-8101
748 S New St Dover (19904) *(G-1822)*

Artid LLC (PA) 302 898-6307
8 The Grn Ste E Dover (19901) *(G-1823)*

Artifex Carpentry 484 557-7623
40 Fairway Rd Apt 3c Newark (19711) *(G-9916)*

Artificial Brain Tech Inc (PA) 302 601-7201
1209 N Orange St Wilmington (19801) *(G-14566)*

Artimus LLC 302 546-5350
8 The Grn Ste A Dover (19901) *(G-1824)*

Artisan Electrical Inc 302 645-5844
119 S Washington Ave Lewes (19958) *(G-5702)*

Artisan Interiors Group LLC 302 537-4811
30089 Cedar Neck Rd Ocean View (19970) *(G-12464)*

Artisan Woodworks LLC 302 841-5182
28205 Johnson Ln Harbeson (19951) *(G-4683)*

ARTISANS BANK, Wilmington *Also Called: Artisans Bank Inc (G-14568)*

Artisans Bank Clefco Branch, Newark *Also Called: Artisans Bank Inc (G-9917)*

Artisans Bank Inc 302 834-8800
1124 Pulaski Hwy Bear (19701) *(G-50)*

Artisans Bank Inc 302 674-3214
1555 S Governors Ave Dover (19904) *(G-1825)*

Artisans Bank Inc 302 430-7681
100 Aerenson Dr Milford (19963) *(G-7772)*

Artisans Bank Inc 302 838-6700
2424 Pulaski Hwy Newark (19702) *(G-9917)*

Artisans Bank Inc 302 296-0155
17211 Hood Rd Rehoboth Beach (19971) *(G-12611)*

Artisans Bank Inc 302 656-8188
223 W 9th St Wilmington (19801) *(G-14567)*

Artisans Bank Inc (PA) 302 658-6881
2961 Centerville Rd Ste 101 Wilmington (19808) *(G-14568)*

Artisans Bank Inc 302 479-2553
3631 Silverside Rd Wilmington (19810) *(G-14569)*

Artisans Bank Inc 302 479-2550
1706 Marsh Rd Wilmington (19810) *(G-14570)*

Artisans Bank Inc 302 993-8220
4901 Kirkwood Hwy Wilmington (19808) *(G-14571)*

Artisans Bank Inc 302 738-3744
4551 Linden Hill Rd Wilmington (19808) *(G-14572)*

Artistic Designs Salon 302 644-2009
20361 John J Williams Hwy Lewes (19958) *(G-5703)*

Artistry Salon Studio 302 513-9225
210 Sterling Ave New Castle (19720) *(G-8825)*

Artsense Inc 302 613-1870
651 N Broad St Ste 206 Middletown (19709) *(G-6874)*

Arty's Trucking, Bear Also Called: Arthur Coppedge *(G-49)*

Arua Inc 302 396-9868
8 The Grn Ste 300 Dover (19901) *(G-1826)*

Aruanno Enterprises Inc 302 530-1217
524 E Creek Ln Middletown (19709) *(G-6875)*

Arugie Enterprises Corp 302 225-2000
612 S Colonial Ave Ste A Wilmington (19805) *(G-14573)*

Arun Jain Advicoach 302 442-0053
2 Camp David Rd Wilmington (19810) *(G-14574)*

Aruna Network Inc 832 303-3628
16192 Coastal Hwy Lewes (19958) *(G-5704)*

Arundel Trailer Sales 302 398-6288
344 Jefferson Woods Dr Harrington (19952) *(G-4736)*

Arvi Vr Inc 844 615-8194
108 W 13th St Wilmington (19801) *(G-14575)*

Arya Life Coaching LLC 610 590-1440
16192 Coastal Hwy Lewes (19958) *(G-5705)*

Aryvve Technologies LLC 678 977-1252
1675 S State St Ste B Dover (19901) *(G-1827)*

Asa V Peugh Inc 302 629-7969
22 W High St Seaford (19973) *(G-13069)*

ASAP Cleaning Services 302 519-6607
14198 Cart Branch Rd Greenwood (19950) *(G-4591)*

ASAP Mass Spectrometry, Newark Also Called: M&M Mass Spec Consulting LLC *(G-11307)*

ASAP Tickets, Wilmington Also Called: International Travel Network *(G-17392)*

Asari, Julie Y MD, Wilmington Also Called: Christiana Care Health Sys Inc *(G-15401)*

Asbury Carbons Inc 302 652-0266
103 Foulk Rd Ste 202 Wilmington (19803) *(G-14576)*

Ascela 888 298-5151
200 Continental Dr Ste 305 Newark (19713) *(G-9918)*

Ascension Industries LLC 302 659-1778
104 Needham Dr Smyrna (19977) *(G-13648)*

Ascent Research LLC 703 801-1490
8 The Grn Ste 10331 Dover (19901) *(G-1828)*

Ascent Technologies Inc 302 491-0545
42 Prestbury Sq Ste 12 Newark (19713) *(G-9919)*

Asd Trucking Inc 302 744-9832
2505 White Oak Rd Dover (19901) *(G-1829)*

Asdi, Newark Also Called: Frontier Scientific Svcs Inc *(G-10789)*

Aserik LLC 302 981-6519
717 W Oakmeade Dr Wilmington (19810) *(G-14577)*

Ash Edward L I 302 732-9181
7 Thatcher St Frankford (19945) *(G-4061)*

Ashanti Produce International 800 295-9790
1000 N West St Ste 1200 Wilmington (19801) *(G-14578)*

Ashby & Geddes 302 654-1888
500 Delaware Ave Ste 8 Wilmington (19801) *(G-14579)*

Ashby Management Corporation 302 894-1200
108 W Main St Newark (19711) *(G-9920)*

Ashcraft Masonry Inc 302 537-4298
30171 Jump Ln Ocean View (19970) *(G-12465)*

Ashely B Morrison 302 526-1959
1001 S Bradford St Ste 9 Dover (19904) *(G-1830)*

Ashesh I Modi 302 452-3000
4745 Ogletown Stanton Rd # 134 Newark (19713) *(G-9921)*

Ashford Capital Management 302 655-1750
1 Walkers Mill Rd Wilmington (19807) *(G-14580)*

Ashford Consulting Group Inc 302 691-0228
2 Righter Pkwy Ste 105 Wilmington (19803) *(G-14581)*

Ashish Anand Md 617 953-5914
7403 Society Dr Claymont (19703) *(G-1044)*

Ashish B Parikh 302 338-9444
620 Stanton Christiana Rd Ste 203 Newark (19713) *(G-9922)*

Ashland, Wilmington Also Called: Ashland Inc *(G-14583)*

Ashland Chemco Inc 302 995-4180
500 Hercules Rd Wilmington (19808) *(G-14582)*

Ashland Credit Union, Wilmington Also Called: Ashland Chemco Inc *(G-14582)*

Ashland Inc (PA) 302 995-3000
8145 Blazer Dr Wilmington (19808) *(G-14583)*

Ashland Spcalty Ingredients GP (DH) 302 594-5000
8145 Blazer Dr Wilmington (19808) *(G-14584)*

Ashland Water Technologies, Wilmington Also Called: Solenis LLC *(G-19923)*

Ashley Lntti Holistic Hlth LLC 804 347-2641
2207 Brookline Rd Wilmington (19803) *(G-14585)*

Ashley Lynn Kontra 302 543-5454
3521 Silverside Rd Ste 2j Wilmington (19810) *(G-14586)*

Ashley M Oland 302 854-5406
16 N Bedford St Georgetown (19947) *(G-4213)*

Ashley N Kaczorowski 302 430-9610
255 W Pembrooke Dr Smyrna (19977) *(G-13649)*

Ashley Wiper 302 994-6838
204 Milltown Rd Wilmington (19808) *(G-14587)*

Ashtray Management LLC 424 258-9228
8 The Grn Ste A Dover (19901) *(G-1831)*

Ashweb Inc 844 493-6249
611 S Dupont Hwy Ste 102 Dover (19901) *(G-1832)*

Asi Comprehensive Waste MGT 302 533-6858
1 Shea Way Newark (19713) *(G-9923)*

Asi Transport LLC 302 349-9460
9347 Allspan Dr Bridgeville (19933) *(G-668)*

Asombro Extremo LLC 305 495-1471
3411 Silverside Rd Ste A Wilmington (19810) *(G-14588)*

Aspen Meadows 302 227-4266
36179 Palace Ln Rehoboth Beach (19971) *(G-12612)*

Asphalt Kingdom, Wilmington Also Called: Asphalt Kingdom LLC *(G-14589)*

Asphalt Kingdom LLC 866 399-5562
1209 N Orange St Wilmington (19801) *(G-14589)*

Asphalt Paving Eqp & Sups 302 683-0105
26822 Lewes Georgetown Hwy Harbeson (19951) *(G-4684)*

Aspira Health LLC 302 567-1500
18068 Coastal Hwy Lewes (19958) *(G-5706)*

Aspira of Delaware Inc 302 292-1463
326 Ruthar Dr Newark (19711) *(G-9924)*

Aspire + Build LLC 617 602-7400
427 N Tatnall St # 57021 Wilmington (19801) *(G-14590)*

Aspire Wellness LLC 302 366-1727
1220 Capitol Trl Newark (19711) *(G-9925)*

Aspiring Change LLC 302 689-3138
308 Scotland Dr Newark (19702) *(G-9926)*

Asplundh Tree Expert LLC 302 678-4702
100 Carlsons Way Ste 14 Dover (19901) *(G-1833)*

Assanis & Associates Inc 734 277-0846
47 Kent Way Newark (19711) *(G-9927)*

Asset Assistance LLC 302 364-3362
72 Representative Ln Dover (19904) *(G-1834)*

Asset Key Management LLC 302 505-4603
125 Dickens Ln Felton (19943) *(G-3942)*

Asset Management Alliance 302 656-5238
222 Delaware Ave Ste 109 Wilmington (19801) *(G-14591)*

Assetbook 301 387-3238
125 Rickey Blvd Unit 453 Bear (19701) *(G-51)*

Assetone, Newark Also Called: Cks Global Ventures LLC *(G-10248)*

Assisted Living Concepts LLC 302 735-8800
1203 Walker Rd Dover (19904) *(G-1835)*

Associated Svc Specialist Inc 302 672-7159
630 W Division St Ste E Dover (19904) *(G-1836)*

Associates Contracting Inc 302 734-4311
1661 S Dupont Hwy Dover (19901) *(G-1837)*

Associates In Medicine PA 302 645-6644
1302 Savannah Rd Lewes (19958) *(G-5707)*

Associates International Inc 302 656-4500
100 Rogers Rd Wilmington (19801) *(G-14592)*

ALPHABETIC SECTION — ATI Holdings LLC

ASSOCIATION BUSINESS OFFICE, Wilmington Also Called: Young Mens Christian Assn Del *(G-20936)*

Association Eductional Publr.. 302 295-8350
300 Martin Luther King Blvd Wilmington (19801) *(G-14593)*

Association of Centers Study O.. 302 831-1724
16 Allison Ln Newark (19711) *(G-9928)*

Assoctes Hmtlogy Onclogy Group... 302 421-4860
701 N Clayton St Ste 502 Wilmington (19805) *(G-14594)*

Assoctes In Hlth Psychlogy LLC (PA)... 302 428-0205
1521 Concord Pike Ste 103 Wilmington (19803) *(G-14595)*

Assoction Brds Thlgcal Educatn.. 302 654-7770
100 W 10th St Ste 703 Wilmington (19801) *(G-14596)*

Assoction For The Rghts Ctzens (PA).. 302 996-9400
1016 Centre Rd Ste 1 Wilmington (19805) *(G-14597)*

Assoction Pathology Chairs Inc.. 302 660-4940
100 W 10th St Ste 603 Wilmington (19801) *(G-14598)*

Assurance Media LLC... 302 892-3540
590 Century Blvd Ste B Wilmington (19808) *(G-14599)*

Assurance Partners Intl... 302 478-0173
1201 N Market St Ste 1600 Wilmington (19801) *(G-14600)*

Assurance Plumbing Compnay... 302 324-0403
87 Skyline Dr New Castle (19720) *(G-8826)*

Assured Affluence LLC.. 609 468-0250
8 The Grn Ste 8374 Dover (19901) *(G-1838)*

AST Sports Internacional LLC.. 786 445-8081
2711 Centerville Rd Wilmington (19808) *(G-14601)*

Astec Inc.. 302 378-2717
1554 Lorewood Grove Rd Middletown (19709) *(G-6876)*

Aster Bouquet Flower Shop, Lewes Also Called: Aster Bouquet Flower Shop LLC *(G-5708)*

Aster Bouquet Flower Shop LLC... 302 258-9242
624 Pilottown Rd Lewes (19958) *(G-5708)*

Aster Dry Wall LLC... 302 757-2750
1156 Paddock Rd Smyrna (19977) *(G-13650)*

Aster Drywall... 302 757-5876
103 Wedgefield Dr New Castle (19720) *(G-8827)*

Asterlab Advisors LLC... 302 295-4888
1000 N West St Ste 1200 Wilmington (19801) *(G-14602)*

Asthma Allergy Care Delaware, Wilmington Also Called: Andrew Weinstein MD Inc *(G-14480)*

Asthma and Allergy Care Del (PA).. 302 995-2952
1941 Limestone Rd Ste 209 Wilmington (19808) *(G-14603)*

Aston Digital LLC... 323 286-4365
16192 Coastal Hwy Lewes (19958) *(G-5709)*

Aston Home Health.. 302 421-3686
1021 Gilpin Ave Ste 100 Wilmington (19806) *(G-14604)*

Astoria Builders LLC... 302 892-9211
1107 Hillside Rd Greenville (19807) *(G-4583)*

Astoria Builders LLC... 302 993-7951
96 Wayland Rd Wilmington (19807) *(G-14605)*

Astra Zeneca Pharmaceuticals, Wilmington Also Called: Zeneca Holdings Inc *(G-20953)*

Astrazeneca, Wilmington Also Called: Astrazeneca LP *(G-14609)*

Astrazeneca, Wilmington Also Called: Astrazneca Cllbrtion Vntres LL *(G-14611)*

Astrazeneca LLC (HQ).. 800 236-9933
1800 Concord Pike Wilmington (19803) *(G-14606)*

Astrazeneca Finance LLC.. 800 677-3394
1209 N Orange St Wilmington (19801) *(G-14607)*

Astrazeneca Foundation.. 302 886-3000
1800 Concord Pike Wilmington (19850) *(G-14608)*

Astrazeneca LP (DH).. 302 886-3000
1800 Concord Pike Wilmington (19803) *(G-14609)*

Astrazeneca Pharmaceuticals LP.. 302 286-3500
587 Old Baltimore Pike Newark (19702) *(G-9929)*

Astrazeneca Pharmaceuticals LP (HQ).. 800 456-3669
1800 Concord Pike Wilmington (19850) *(G-14610)*

Astrazneca Cllbrtion Vntres LL... 302 886-3000
1800 Concord Pike Wilmington (19897) *(G-14611)*

Astro-Lyfe LLC... 240 410-9665
1041 N Dupont Hwy Dover (19901) *(G-1839)*

Asw Machinery Inc (DH)... 866 792-5288
2 Lukens Dr Ste 300 Historic New Castle (19720) *(G-4936)*

At Contracting LLC... 302 678-4898
391 Rose Valley School Rd Dover (19904) *(G-1840)*

At Eaze Massage Therapy... 302 559-3019
311 Arctic Ln Smyrna (19977) *(G-13651)*

At Home Cabinetry & Design LLC... 302 853-5305
219 S Walnut St Milford (19963) *(G-7773)*

At Home Care Agency.. 302 883-2059
57 Saulsbury Rd Dover (19904) *(G-1841)*

At Home Infucare LLC.. 302 883-2059
373 W North St Ste A Dover (19904) *(G-1842)*

At Home Property MGT LLC.. 623 216-8052
39 Winburne Dr New Castle (19720) *(G-8828)*

At Systems Atlantic Inc... 302 762-5444
4200 Governor Printz Blvd Wilmington (19802) *(G-14612)*

At The Bch Repr & Maintainance, Harbeson Also Called: Custom Framers Inc *(G-4694)*

At The G Spot LLC... 302 998-5010
2302 W Newport Pike Wilmington (19804) *(G-14613)*

At Wilmington.. 302 235-2554
1 Middletoh Dr Wilmington (19808) *(G-14614)*

At-Bay Insurance Services LLC.. 888 338-9522
1013 Centre Rd Ste 403s Wilmington (19805) *(G-14615)*

AT&e Developers Ltd.. 302 467-1100
600 N Broad St Middletown (19709) *(G-6877)*

AT&T Mobility LLC.. 302 674-4888
275 N Dupont Hwy Dover (19901) *(G-1843)*

AT&T Wireless, Wilmington Also Called: New Cingular Wireless Svcs Inc *(G-18610)*

ATA Technology Inc (PA).. 862 233-0007
1500 Shallcross Ave 2a-6 Wilmington (19806) *(G-14616)*

Atd Contracting LLC... 302 535-1013
93 N Fairfield Dr Smyrna (19977) *(G-13652)*

Atechnologie LLC... 781 325-5230
1521 Concord Pike Ste 301 Wilmington (19803) *(G-14617)*

Ateleir Art Services Inc... 302 669-6400
71 Southgate Blvd New Castle (19720) *(G-8829)*

Ath Solutions LLC (PA)... 888 861-6657
254 Chapman Rd Ste 209 Newark (19702) *(G-9930)*

Athari Inc.. 312 358-4933
278 Jordan Dr Dover (19904) *(G-1844)*

Athena Biotechnologies Inc... 302 224-3450
1090 Elkton Rd Newark (19711) *(G-9931)*

Athena Chiropractic.. 302 543-4227
222 Philadelphia Pike Wilmington (19809) *(G-14618)*

Athena T Jolly M D... 302 454-3020
24 Brookhill Dr Newark (19702) *(G-9932)*

ATI, New Castle Also Called: Pro Physical Therapy PA *(G-9496)*

ATI Funding, Wilmington Also Called: A T I Funding Corporation *(G-14173)*

ATI Holdings LLC... 302 836-5670
1015 E Songsmith Dr Bear (19701) *(G-52)*

ATI Holdings LLC... 302 392-3400
100 Becks Woods Dr Bear (19701) *(G-53)*

ATI Holdings LLC... 302 677-0100
1288 S Governors Ave Dover (19904) *(G-1845)*

ATI Holdings LLC... 302 747-5280
200 Banning St Ste 230 Dover (19904) *(G-1846)*

ATI Holdings LLC... 302 253-8296
401 College Park Ln Unit 3 Georgetown (19947) *(G-4214)*

ATI Holdings LLC... 302 786-3008
16819 S Dupont Hwy Ste 500 Harrington (19952) *(G-4737)*

ATI Holdings LLC... 302 827-5123
17252 N Village Main Blvd Unit 2 Lewes (19958) *(G-5710)*

ATI Holdings LLC... 302 285-0700
114 Sandhill Dr Ste 103 Middletown (19709) *(G-6878)*

ATI Holdings LLC... 302 696-1924
224 Dove Run Centre Dr Middletown (19709) *(G-6879)*

ATI Holdings LLC... 302 422-6670
941 N Dupont Blvd Ste C Milford (19963) *(G-7774)*

ATI Holdings LLC... 302 297-0700
28535 Dupont Blvd Unit 1 Millsboro (19966) *(G-8176)*

ATI Holdings LLC... 302 654-1700
2032 New Castle Ave New Castle (19720) *(G-8830)*

ATI Holdings LLC... 302 838-2165
2600 Glasgow Ave Ste 105 Newark (19702) *(G-9933)*

ATI Holdings LLC... 302 226-2230
19266 Coastal Hwy Unit 9 Rehoboth Beach (19971) *(G-12613)*

(PA)=Parent Co (HQ)=Headquarters (DH)=Div Headquarters

ATI Holdings LLC 302 536-5562
    22832 Sussex Hwy Seaford (19973) (G-13070)
ATI Holdings LLC 302 524-5951
    38394 Dupont Blvd Unit 1 Selbyville (19975) (G-13465)
ATI Holdings LLC 302 659-3102
    1000 Smyrna Clayton Blvd Ste 4 Smyrna (19977) (G-13653)
ATI Holdings LLC 302 993-1450
    1208 Kirkwood Hwy Wilmington (19805) (G-14619)
ATI Holdings LLC 302 994-1200
    100 Valley Center Rd Wilmington (19808) (G-14620)
ATI Holdings LLC 302 475-7500
    1812 Marsh Rd Ste 505 Wilmington (19810) (G-14621)
ATI Holdings LLC 302 351-0302
    914 Justison St Wilmington (19801) (G-14622)
ATI Holdings LLC 302 656-2521
    1600 N Washington St Wilmington (19802) (G-14623)
ATI Holdings LLC 302 658-7800
    213 Greenhill Ave Ste C Wilmington (19805) (G-14624)
ATI Physical Therapy 302 281-3072
    3620 Concord Pike Wilmington (19803) (G-14625)
ATI Physical Therapy, Bear Also Called: ATI Holdings LLC (G-52)
ATI Physical Therapy, Bear Also Called: ATI Holdings LLC (G-53)
ATI Physical Therapy, Dover Also Called: ATI Holdings LLC (G-1845)
ATI Physical Therapy, Georgetown Also Called: ATI Holdings LLC (G-4214)
ATI Physical Therapy, Harrington Also Called: ATI Holdings LLC (G-4737)
ATI Physical Therapy, Lewes Also Called: ATI Holdings LLC (G-5710)
ATI Physical Therapy, Middletown Also Called: ATI Holdings LLC (G-6878)
ATI Physical Therapy, Milford Also Called: ATI Holdings LLC (G-7774)
ATI Physical Therapy, Millsboro Also Called: ATI Holdings LLC (G-8176)
ATI Physical Therapy, New Castle Also Called: ATI Holdings LLC (G-8830)
ATI Physical Therapy, Newark Also Called: ATI Holdings LLC (G-9933)
ATI Physical Therapy, Rehoboth Beach Also Called: ATI Holdings LLC (G-12613)
ATI Physical Therapy, Seaford Also Called: ATI Holdings LLC (G-13070)
ATI Physical Therapy, Smyrna Also Called: ATI Holdings LLC (G-13653)
ATI Physical Therapy, Wilmington Also Called: ATI Holdings LLC (G-14619)
ATI Physical Therapy, Wilmington Also Called: ATI Holdings LLC (G-14620)
ATI Physical Therapy, Wilmington Also Called: ATI Holdings LLC (G-14622)
ATI Physical Therapy, Wilmington Also Called: ATI Holdings LLC (G-14623)
ATI Physical Therapy, Wilmington Also Called: ATI Holdings LLC (G-14624)
Atiba Music Services 302 981-7157
    41 2nd Ave Claymont (19703) (G-1045)
Atkins Home Health Aid Agency 302 832-0315
    18 Calvarese Dr Bear (19701) (G-54)
Atkison Trucking 302 396-0322
    40 Rivers End Dr Seaford (19973) (G-13071)
Atlan, Wilmington Also Called: Atlan Inc (G-14626)
Atlan Inc 650 288-6722
    1000 N West St Ste 1281 Pmb M171 Wilmington (19801) (G-14626)
Atlantic Adult & Pediatric 302 644-1300
    34453 King Street Row Ste 1 Lewes (19958) (G-5711)
Atlantic Adult Pdtrics Mdcine 302 644-1300
    34435 King Street Row # 1 Lewes (19958) (G-5712)
Atlantic Aluminum Products Inc 302 349-9091
    12136 Sussex Hwy Greenwood (19950) (G-4592)
Atlantic Auto Repair LLC 302 539-7352
    35252 Atlantic Ave Millville (19967) (G-8515)
Atlantic Barter, Newark Also Called: Delaware Barter Corp (G-10420)
Atlantic Bulk Carriers 302 378-6300
    364 E Main St Middletown (19709) (G-6880)
Atlantic Bulk Carriers Inc 302 378-4522
    1600 Belts Rd Middletown (19709) (G-6881)
Atlantic Bulk Ltd 302 378-6300
    421 Boyds Corner Rd Middletown (19709) (G-6882)
Atlantic Business Contracting 302 337-7490
    9599 Nanticoke Business Park Dr Greenwood (19950) (G-4593)
Atlantic Cabinetry Corporation 302 644-1407
    17527 Nassau Commons Blvd Lewes (19958) (G-5713)
Atlantic Cellular 302 945-3334
    31507 Trading Post Plz Unit 9 Millsboro (19966) (G-8177)

Atlantic Chiropractic Assoc 302 422-3100
    509 Lakeview Ave Milford (19963) (G-7775)
Atlantic Chiropractic Associat (PA) 302 422-3100
    375 Mullet Run Milford (19963) (G-7776)
Atlantic City Electric Co 302 429-3200
    800 N King St Ste 400 Wilmington (19895) (G-14627)
Atlantic City Electric Co 302 588-6675
    630 Martin Luther King Blvd Wilmington (19801) (G-14628)
Atlantic Coast Builders LLC 302 396-7824
    21538 Shell Station Rd Frankford (19945) (G-4062)
Atlantic Concrete Company Inc (PA) 302 422-8017
    New Wharf Rd Milford (19963) (G-7777)
Atlantic Contracting Svcs LLC 302 337-8360
    9599 Nanticoke Business Park Dr Greenwood (19950) (G-4594)
Atlantic Contractor LL 302 537-4361
    207 E Orlando Ave Ocean View (19970) (G-12466)
Atlantic Control Systems Inc 302 284-9700
    7873 S Dupont Hwy Ste 2 Felton (19943) (G-3943)
Atlantic Dawn Ltd 302 737-8854
    366 Old Baltimore Pike Newark (19702) (G-9934)
Atlantic Duncan Inc 302 383-0740
    5 Magil Ct Newark (19702) (G-9935)
Atlantic Elevators 302 537-8304
    27515 Hodges Ln Dagsboro (19939) (G-1414)
Atlantic Family Physician LLC 302 856-4092
    2 Lee Ave Unit 103 Georgetown (19947) (G-4215)
Atlantic Finance 302 730-1988
    71 Greentree Dr Dover (19904) (G-1847)
Atlantic Finance 302 629-6266
    22937 Sussex Hwy Seaford (19973) (G-13072)
Atlantic General Hospital 302 539-2399
    1209 Coastal Hwy Fenwick Island (19944) (G-4040)
Atlantic General Hospital, Selbyville Also Called: Atlantic General Hospital Corp (G-13466)
Atlantic General Hospital Corp 302 524-5007
    38394 Dupont Blvd Ste H Selbyville (19975) (G-13466)
Atlantic H&S Consulting 302 222-5526
    247 Cider Run Magnolia (19962) (G-6719)
Atlantic Heat Treat, Wilmington Also Called: Industrial Metal Treating Corp (G-17315)
Atlantic Home Loans Inc 302 363-3950
    1198 S Governors Ave Dover (19904) (G-1848)
Atlantic Homes LLC 302 947-0223
    20684 John J Williams Hwy Ste 1 Lewes (19958) (G-5714)
Atlantic Industrial Optics 302 856-7905
    38249 Bay Vista Dr Apt 1246 Selbyville (19975) (G-13467)
Atlantic Kitchen & Bath LLC 302 947-9001
    18355 Coastal Hwy Lewes (19958) (G-5715)
Atlantic Landscape Co 302 661-1950
    800 A St Wilmington (19801) (G-14629)
Atlantic Law Group LLC 302 854-0380
    512 E Market St Georgetown (19947) (G-4216)
Atlantic Management 302 222-3919
    34821 Derrickson Dr Rehoboth Beach (19971) (G-12614)
Atlantic Management Ltd 302 645-9511
    29 Midway Shopping Ctr Rehoboth Beach (19971) (G-12615)
Atlantic Mllwk Cabinetry Corp 302 644-1405
    17527 Nassau Commons Blvd Lewes (19958) (G-5716)
Atlantic Physcl Thrapy Rhbltti 302 934-0304
    358 E Dupont Hwy Millsboro (19966) (G-8178)
Atlantic Physicians Billing 914 490-3741
    9 Lake Crest Dr Milford (19963) (G-7778)
Atlantic Pumping Inc 302 436-5047
    10 Discovery Ln Selbyville (19975) (G-13468)
Atlantic Radon Systems Inc 610 869-9066
    30829 W Lagoon Rd Dagsboro (19939) (G-1415)
Atlantic Realty Management 302 629-0770
    100 Hitch Pond Cir Seaford (19973) (G-13073)
Atlantic Realty Management LLC 302 875-9571
    14 Village Sq Smyrna (19977) (G-13654)
Atlantic Refrigeration & AC, Lewes Also Called: Atlantic Refrigeration Inc (G-5717)
Atlantic Refrigeration Inc 302 645-9321
    17553 Nassau Commons Blvd Lewes (19958) (G-5717)

ALPHABETIC SECTION

Atlantic Resource Management 302 539-2029
  32717 Lavender Ln Frankford (19945) *(G-4063)*

Atlantic Resource Management 302 539-2029
  32582 Omar Rd Frankford (19945) *(G-4064)*

Atlantic Sands Hotel, Rehoboth Beach *Also Called: Sands Inc (G-12947)*

Atlantic Screen & Mfg Inc 302 684-3197
  142 Broadkill Rd Milton (19968) *(G-8565)*

Atlantic Shres Rhbltion Hlth, Millsboro *Also Called: Green Valley Terrace Snf LLC (G-8306)*

Atlantic Source Contg Inc 302 645-5207
  35 Bridle Ridge Cir Lewes (19958) *(G-5718)*

Atlantic Sun Screen Prtg Inc 302 731-5100
  700 Peoples Plz Newark (19702) *(G-9936)*

Atlantic Surgical, Milford *Also Called: John T Malcynski MD (G-7956)*

Atlantic Theaters LLC 302 645-9511
  18585 Coastal Hwy Unit 1 Rehoboth Beach (19971) *(G-12616)*

Atlantic Tractor LLC 302 653-8536
  315 Main St Clayton (19938) *(G-1351)*

Atlantic Tractor LLC 302 834-0114
  2688 Pulaski Hwy Newark (19702) *(G-9937)*

Atlantic Training LLC 302 464-0341
  200 Ruthar Dr Ste 4 Newark (19711) *(G-9938)*

Atlantic Veterinary Center, Middletown *Also Called: Atlantic Veterinary Svcs Inc (G-6883)*

Atlantic Veterinary Svcs Inc 302 376-7506
  411 Weston Dr Middletown (19709) *(G-6883)*

Atlantic View Motel 302 227-3878
  2 Clayton St Dewey Beach (19971) *(G-1662)*

Atlantic Water Products 302 326-1166
  74 Southgate Blvd New Castle (19720) *(G-8831)*

Atlantis Industries Corp 302 684-8542
  21490 Baltimore Ave Georgetown (19947) *(G-4217)*

Atlas Awaits LLC 724 715-3774
  8 The Grn Dover (19901) *(G-1849)*

Atlas Beauty LLC 904 382-3487
  8 The Grn Ste B Dover (19901) *(G-1850)*

Atlas Management Inc (DH) 302 576-2749
  103 Foulk Rd Wilmington (19803) *(G-14630)*

Atlas Privacy, Dover *Also Called: Roundrobin Corporation (G-3487)*

Atlas Scuritized Pdts Partners, Wilmington *Also Called: Atlas Sp Partners LP (G-14632)*

Atlas Software LLC 312 576-2247
  200 Continental Dr # 401 Newark (19713) *(G-9939)*

Atlas Solar III LLC 949 677-1308
  1209 N Orange St Wilmington (19801) *(G-14631)*

Atlas Sp Partners LP 212 325-2777
  251 Little Falls Dr Wilmington (19808) *(G-14632)*

Atlas Van Lines Agents 302 369-0900
  900 Interchange Blvd Newark (19711) *(G-9940)*

Atlas Welding, New Castle *Also Called: Atlas Wldg & Fabrication Inc (G-8832)*

Atlas Wldg & Fabrication Inc 302 326-1900
  728 Grantham Ln New Castle (19720) *(G-8832)*

Atlas World Express LLC 202 536-5238
  119 Plymouth Pl Middletown (19709) *(G-6884)*

Atm The Bottom Line Ltd 302 322-0452
  118 Astro Shopping Ctr Newark (19711) *(G-9941)*

Atom Alloys LLC 786 975-3771
  3411 Silverside Rd Ste 104 Wilmington (19810) *(G-14633)*

Atom Solutions United States, Wilmington *Also Called: Atom Alloys LLC (G-14633)*

Atom Tech Inc 510 789-3045
  221 N Broad St Ste 3 Middletown (19709) *(G-6885)*

Atomic Development Inc 424 354-9865
  850 New Burton Rd Dover (19904) *(G-1851)*

Atomic Garage 302 898-1380
  462 B And O Ln Wilmington (19804) *(G-14634)*

Atr Electrical Services Inc 302 373-7769
  14 Manassas Dr Middletown (19709) *(G-6886)*

Atr Electrical Services Inc 302 384-7044
  529 W Champlain Ave Wilmington (19804) *(G-14635)*

Atrifico LLC 302 858-0161
  179 Rehoboth Ave Unit 16 Rehoboth Beach (19971) *(G-12617)*

Attabotics (us) Corp 403 454-0995
  3 Germay Dr Ste 4 Wilmington (19804) *(G-14636)*

Attac Consulting Group LLC 443 766-9079
  33968 Monterray Ave Frankford (19945) *(G-4065)*

Attack Addiction 302 994-1550
  2615 Crossgate Dr Wilmington (19808) *(G-14637)*

Attention To Detail In Smyrna 302 388-1267
  5702 Dupont Pkwy Smyrna (19977) *(G-13655)*

Attention To Dtils Strtgies LL 877 870-2837
  2207 Concord Pike Ste 399 Wilmington (19803) *(G-14638)*

Attentis Consulting Inc 570 575-7283
  8 The Grn Ste 7066 Dover (19901) *(G-1852)*

Atterbury VFW Post 3420 .... 302 737-6903
  646 Churchmans Rd Newark (19702) *(G-9942)*

Attic Away From Home 302 378-2600
  893 Noxontown Rd Townsend (19734) *(G-13961)*

Attitude LLC None 302 422-3356
  617 N Dupont Blvd Milford (19963) *(G-7779)*

Attorney Rymond H Lemischs Off, Wilmington *Also Called: Benesch Frdlnder Cplan Arnoff (G-14835)*

Atwork Personnel Services 302 660-1062
  1021 Kent Rd Wilmington (19807) *(G-14639)*

Au-Naturel Services, Dover *Also Called: Au-Naturel Services LLC (G-1853)*

Au-Naturel Services Inc 775 484-5210
  8 The Grn Ste R Dover (19901) *(G-1853)*

Audi Wilmington, Wilmington *Also Called: Winners Circle Inc (G-20864)*

Audio Visual Communications, Rehoboth Beach *Also Called: A V C Inc (G-12593)*

Audit Team LLC 302 322-0452
  1 Bassett Ave New Castle (19720) *(G-8833)*

Auditbot 302 494-9476
  11 Latour Ln Newark (19702) *(G-9943)*

Augustin Stable 302 571-8322
  3801 Kennett Pike Wilmington (19807) *(G-14640)*

Augusto & Sons Landscaping LLC 302 278-9196
  17490 Cedar Corners Rd Bridgeville (19933) *(G-669)*

Aum LLC 302 385-6767
  20c Trolley Sq Wilmington (19806) *(G-14641)*

Aura Air, Wilmington *Also Called: Aura Smart Air Inc (G-14642)*

Aura Smart Air Inc 847 909-5822
  1007 N Orange St Fl 10 Wilmington (19801) *(G-14642)*

Auragin LLC 800 383-5109
  427 N Tatnall St Wilmington (19801) *(G-14643)*

Aurelium Inc 415 636-6892
  16192 Coastal Hwy Lewes (19958) *(G-5719)*

Auric Jets LLC 866 887-5414
  251 Little Falls Dr Wilmington (19808) *(G-14644)*

Aurista, Claymont *Also Called: Aurista Technologies Inc (G-1046)*

Aurista Technologies Inc 302 792-4900
  100 Naamans Rd Ste 3c Claymont (19703) *(G-1046)*

Aurora Corporation (PA) 302 656-6717
  3422 Old Capitol Trl Wilmington (19808) *(G-14645)*

Aurora Reiki LLC 443 553-3233
  506 N Union St Wilmington (19805) *(G-14646)*

Aurum Capital Ventures Inc 877 467-7780
  3500 S Dupont Hwy Dover (19901) *(G-1854)*

Auspice Risk LLC 484 467-1963
  11286 Hall Rd Lewes (19958) *(G-5720)*

Austenitex, Wilmington *Also Called: Vertex Industries Inc (G-20597)*

Austin, Newark *Also Called: Austin & Bednash Cnstr Inc (G-9944)*

Austin & Bednash Cnstr Inc 302 376-5590
  32 Brookhill Dr Newark (19702) *(G-9944)*

Austin Alliance Electric Inc 843 297-8078
  300 Delaware Ave Ste 210a Wilmington (19801) *(G-14647)*

Authentic Tailoring Service 302 740-1185
  3207 Miller Rd Wilmington (19802) *(G-14648)*

Authentik Chick 267 815-4132
  1412 Kynlyn Dr Wilmington (19809) *(G-14649)*

Authority Media Group 302 894-7700
  2035 Sunset Lake Rd Newark (19702) *(G-9945)*

Autism Delaware Inc 302 224-6020
  924 Old Harmony Rd Ste 201 Newark (19713) *(G-9946)*

Auto Cheap Quotes Ins-Wlmgtn 302 992-9736
  813 E Newport Pike Wilmington (19804) *(G-14650)*

Auto Evrything At Slepy Hllow 302 376-3010
  1231 S Dupont Blvd Ste 100 Smyrna (19977) *(G-13656)*

Auto Express Transport Inc 302 628-4601
  24290 Shufelt Rd Seaford (19973) *(G-13074)*
Auto Parts of Greenwood 302 349-9601
  8316 Greenwood Rd Farmington (19950) *(G-3932)*
Auto Plus Auto Parts 302 678-8400
  120 S Governors Ave Dover (19904) *(G-1855)*
Auto Works Collision Ctr LLC 302 732-3902
  1145 Savannah Rd Lewes (19958) *(G-5721)*
Auto-Lab, Wilmington *Also Called: Autolab Inc (G-14651)*
Autoawards Inc 302 696-6000
  313 N Dupont Hwy Odessa (19730) *(G-12581)*
Autolab Inc 416 820-1636
  1201 N Orange St Ste 600 Wilmington (19801) *(G-14651)*
Automation Air Inc 973 875-6676
  16782 Oak Rd Bridgeville (19933) *(G-670)*
Automation Alliance Group LLC 302 202-5433
  651 N Broad St Ste 206 Middletown (19709) *(G-6887)*
Automation Inc 302 999-0971
  408 Harvey Dr Wilmington (19804) *(G-14652)*
Automation Machine Design SE 302 335-3911
  164 Dogwood Dr Magnolia (19962) *(G-6720)*
Automation Partnership 302 478-9060
  502 First State Blvd Wilmington (19804) *(G-14653)*
Automation Research Group LLC 302 897-7776
  929 Crossan Rd Newark (19711) *(G-9947)*
Automation Solutions Inc 302 478-9060
  20 Montchanin Rd Ste 200 Wilmington (19807) *(G-14654)*
Automizy Inc 361 253-8238
  3422 Old Capitol Trl Ste 700 Wilmington (19808) *(G-14655)*
Automotive Accounting Service 302 378-9551
  680 N Broad St Middletown (19709) *(G-6888)*
Automotive Diagnostic Sol 443 466-6108
  1106 Ogletown Rd Newark (19711) *(G-9948)*
Automotive Services Inc 302 762-0100
  2510 Northeast Blvd Wilmington (19802) *(G-14656)*
Automotive/Construction, Bridgeville *Also Called: M L Morris Inc (G-727)*
Automotiveonly 302 727-1064
  57 Bryan Dr Rehoboth Beach (19971) *(G-12618)*
Autoport Inc 302 658-5100
  203 Pigeon Point Rd New Castle (19720) *(G-8834)*
Autoteam Delaware, Wilmington *Also Called: Delaware Motor Sales Inc (G-15945)*
Autotype Holdings (usa) Inc 302 378-3100
  701 Industrial Dr Middletown (19709) *(G-6889)*
Autoweb Technologies Inc 443 485-4200
  2801 Centerville Rd Wilmington (19808) *(G-14657)*
Autumn Hill Patio & Landscape 302 293-1183
  242 Barberry Dr Wilmington (19808) *(G-14658)*
Auxility, Lewes *Also Called: Auxility Inc (G-5722)*
Auxility Inc 610 245-8039
  16192 Coastal Hwy Lewes (19958) *(G-5722)*
Auxo Rail Holdings LLC 304 325-7245
  251 Little Falls Dr Wilmington (19808) *(G-14659)*
AV Auto Worx LLC 302 384-7646
  124 Middleboro Rd Wilmington (19804) *(G-14660)*
Avacore, Wilmington *Also Called: Avacore LLC (G-14661)*
Avacore LLC 302 327-8830
  3524 Silverside Rd Ste 35b Wilmington (19810) *(G-14661)*
Avalanche Canyon Foundation 800 839-1754
  501 Silverside Rd Wilmington (19809) *(G-14662)*
Avalanche Strategies LLC 302 436-7060
  144 Dixon St Selbyville (19975) *(G-13469)*
Avalon Dental 302 999-8822
  34 Kiamensi Rd Wilmington (19804) *(G-14663)*
Avalon Dental LLC Bldg G4 .... 302 292-8899
  420 Christiana Medical Ctr Newark (19702) *(G-9949)*
Avalon Dental of Newport 267 312-3184
  6 Larch Ave Ste 402 Wilmington (19804) *(G-14664)*
Avamer Roofing Inc 302 228-8673
  26483 Cave Neck Rd Milton (19968) *(G-8566)*
Avant Digital Inc 660 726-2416
  254 Chapman Rd Newark (19702) *(G-9950)*

Avanta Inc 925 818-4760
  8 The Grn Ste R Dover (19901) *(G-1856)*
Avanti Homes LLC 302 374-0999
  4023 Kennett Pike Wilmington (19807) *(G-14665)*
Avantish Cleaners 302 947-1632
  20231 Wil King Rd Lewes (19958) *(G-5723)*
Avantix Laboratories Inc 302 832-1008
  100 Biddle Ave Ste 202 Newark (19702) *(G-9951)*
Avatar Instruments Inc 302 703-6865
  16587 Coastal Hwy Lewes (19958) *(G-5724)*
Avco Energy LLC 302 597-0034
  200 Continental Dr Newark (19713) *(G-9952)*
Ave Preschool 302 422-8775
  20 N Church Ave Milford (19963) *(G-7780)*
Aveanna Healthcare As LLC 302 504-4101
  56 W Main St Ste 211 Christiana (19702) *(G-992)*
Avello Holdings LLC 631 533-2634
  16192 Coastal Hwy Ste 1 Lewes (19958) *(G-5725)*
Avenue 121 .... 302 354-1839
  809 Marsh Hawk Ct Middletown (19709) *(G-6890)*
Avenue Apothecary and Spa, Rehoboth Beach *Also Called: Avenue Day Spa (G-12619)*
Avenue Cuts Inc 302 655-1718
  1700 N Scott St Lowr Wilmington (19806) *(G-14666)*
Avenue Day Spa 302 227-5649
  110 Rehoboth Ave Ste A Rehoboth Beach (19971) *(G-12619)*
Avenue Imparts, Wyoming *Also Called: Imparts Inc (G-20986)*
Avenue Inn, Rehoboth Beach *Also Called: Kenny Simpler (G-12819)*
Avenue Medical, New Castle *Also Called: Marosa Surgical Industries (G-9349)*
Avenue Montaigne Inc 310 926-6678
  919 N Market St Ste 950 Wilmington (19801) *(G-14667)*
Avery Enterprises LLC 302 750-5468
  4 Georgian Cir Newark (19711) *(G-9953)*
Avery Institute 302 803-6784
  3 Germay Dr Ste 4 Wilmington (19804) *(G-14668)*
Aviant Cnsltng & Riva Pymnt 302 584-0549
  21 Somerset Ln Newark (19711) *(G-9954)*
Avid Builders LLC 302 233-0148
  1054 Paradise Alley Rd Felton (19943) *(G-3944)*
Avier Unltd LLC 909 436-6964
  651 N Broad St Ste 206 Middletown (19709) *(G-6891)*
Aviman Management LLC 302 377-5788
  3411 Silverside Rd Ste 101 Wilmington (19810) *(G-14669)*
Avirm Inc 626 603-1000
  1201 N Orange St Ste 600one Wilmington (19801) *(G-14670)*
Avis Car Rental 302 368-5950
  915 S Chapel St Newark (19713) *(G-9955)*
Avis Car Rental 302 227-1507
  19563 Coastal Hwy Unit A Rehoboth Beach (19971) *(G-12620)*
Avis Car Rental 302 654-8044
  100 French St Wilmington (19801) *(G-14671)*
Avis Car Rental 302 762-3825
  702 Philadelphia Pike Wilmington (19809) *(G-14672)*
Avis Rent A Car System Llc 302 322-2092
  151 N Dupont Hwy New Castle (19720) *(G-8835)*
Avis Rent A Car Systems, New Castle *Also Called: Avis Rent A Car System Llc (G-8835)*
Avixia LLC 781 882-2200
  254 Chapman Rd Ste 208 Pmb 12750 Newark (19702) *(G-9956)*
Avkin Inc 302 562-7468
  103 S James St Wilmington (19804) *(G-14673)*
Avni Adtech Inc 628 600-5009
  651 N Broad St Middletown (19709) *(G-6892)*
Avokadio Inc 302 291-4080
  19162 Coastal Hwy Lewes (19958) *(G-5726)*
Avokadio,, Lewes *Also Called: Avokadio Inc (G-5726)*
Avomd Inc 631 786-3867
  32 W Loockerman St Ste 107 Dover (19904) *(G-1857)*
Avontro Inc 510 766-2803
  251 Little Falls Dr Wilmington (19808) *(G-14674)*
Avs Industries LLC 302 221-1705
  21 Bellecor Dr Ste C New Castle (19720) *(G-8836)*
Avs Solutions LLC 302 562-0642
  730 Wood Duck Ct Middletown (19709) *(G-6893)*

ALPHABETIC SECTION

Avt Paints LLC 800 476-1634
   501 Silverside Rd Ste 105 Wilmington (19809) *(G-14675)*

Avvinue Inc (PA) 929 444-0554
   651 N Broad St Ste 20 Middletown (19709) *(G-6894)*

AW Viohl Contracting LLC 302 375-6166
   950 Ridge Rd Claymont (19703) *(G-1047)*

Awaken Atusky LLC 302 231-0818
   16192 Coastal Hwy Lewes (19958) *(G-5727)*

Awareness & Therapeutic Attach 302 655-6555
   309 Walden Rd Wilmington (19803) *(G-14676)*

Awareness Center 302 426-5050
   280 E Main St Ste 109 Newark (19711) *(G-9957)*

Awas Leasing One LLC 425 440-6000
   200 Bellevue Pkwy Ste 210 Wilmington (19809) *(G-14677)*

Awesome Cleaning Services LLC 302 585-3115
   31587 Siham Rd Lewes (19958) *(G-5728)*

Awl LLC 610 299-3322
   16192 Coastal Hwy Lewes (19958) *(G-5729)*

Awsm Industries, Bear *Also Called: Royale Pigments & Chem Inc (G-474)*

Axa Zara LLC 513 206-4606
   16192 Coastal Hwy Lewes (19958) *(G-5730)*

Axalta Coating Systems LLC 925 838-9876
   1007 Market St Wilmington (19898) *(G-14678)*

Axchem Holding Company (PA) 336 632-0500
   1209 N Orange St Wilmington (19801) *(G-14679)*

Axe Bail Bonds, Harrington *Also Called: D A B Productions (G-4756)*

Axencis Inc 302 888-9002
   1201 N Orange St Ste 7160 Wilmington (19801) *(G-14680)*

Axes, Wilmington *Also Called: Axes Global Inc (G-14681)*

Axes Global Inc 415 602-4049
   2055 Limestone Rd Ste 200c Wilmington (19808) *(G-14681)*

Axess Corp 910 270-2077
   100 Interchange Blvd Newark (19711) *(G-9958)*

Axess Corporation (PA) 302 292-8500
   91 Lukens Dr Ste E Historic New Castle (19720) *(G-4937)*

Axia Management 302 674-2200
   222 S Dupont Hwy Frnt Dover (19901) *(G-1858)*

Axiom Dist & Fulfillment 519 620-2000
   1007 N Orange St Fl 4 Wilmington (19801) *(G-14682)*

Axiom Resources LLC 410 756-0440
   160 Greentree Dr Ste 101 Dover (19904) *(G-1859)*

Axion Financial Group LLC 267 261-4177
   33258 Kent Ave Bethany Beach (19930) *(G-575)*

Axis Capital Usa LLC 855 205-5577
   1675 S State St Ste B Dover (19901) *(G-1860)*

Axis Geospatial 302 276-0160
   40 Mccullough Dr New Castle (19720) *(G-8837)*

Axitech Inc 248 318-9067
   3411 Silverside Rd Wilmington (19810) *(G-14683)*

Axmos Technologies Inc 650 229-9094
   2810 N Church St Wilmington (19802) *(G-14684)*

Axtra3d Inc 302 288-0670
   8 The Grn Ste A Dover (19901) *(G-1861)*

Axxess Marine LLC 954 225-1744
   16192 Coastal Hwy Lewes (19958) *(G-5731)*

Axxiom Escape Rooms 732 606-2844
   284 E Main St Newark (19711) *(G-9959)*

Ay Tech LLC 302 861-6610
   117 Ruthar Dr Newark (19711) *(G-9960)*

Ayala Painting LLC 208 777-2654
   3706 Old Capitol Trl Wilmington (19808) *(G-14685)*

Ayea LLC 302 319-3329
   2305 Pyle St Wilmington (19805) *(G-14686)*

Ayon Cable Technology LLC 302 465-8999
   72 Hobart Dr Apt C2 Newark (19713) *(G-9961)*

Ayon Landscaping 302 275-0205
   313 Orinda Dr Wilmington (19804) *(G-14687)*

Azap Finance, Dover *Also Called: Bullent Investment LLC (G-1991)*

Azextensions LLC 609 202-2098
   96 Freedom Trl New Castle (19720) *(G-8838)*

Azhar H Khan MD 302 454-8880
   111 Continental Dr Ste 406 Newark (19713) *(G-9962)*

Azie.ai, Dover *Also Called: Liv180 Inc (G-2958)*

Aztec Copies LLC 302 575-1993
   3636 Silverside Rd Wilmington (19810) *(G-14688)*

Aztec Printing and Design, Wilmington *Also Called: Aztec Copies LLC (G-14688)*

Aztech Contracting Inc 302 526-2145
   68 Elijah Ln Felton (19943) *(G-3945)*

Aztech Industries Inc (PA) 302 653-1430
   1501 S Dupont Blvd Smyrna (19977) *(G-13657)*

Aztek Tile 302 875-0690
   Road 451 Laurel (19956) *(G-5465)*

Azur Gcs Inc 302 884-6713
   1201 N Orange St Ste 7293 Wilmington (19801) *(G-14689)*

Azzota Corporation 877 649-2746
   100 Naamans Rd Ste 5i Claymont (19703) *(G-1048)*

B & B Contracting, Wilmington *Also Called: Alan M Billingsley Jr (G-14345)*

B & B Industries Inc 302 655-6156
   1507 A St Wilmington (19801) *(G-14690)*

B & E Tire Alignment Inc 302 732-6091
   Rr 113 Frankford (19945) *(G-4066)*

B & F Ceramics 302 475-4721
   2644 Boxwood Dr Wilmington (19810) *(G-14691)*

B & F Towing Co 302 328-4146
   449 Old Airport Rd New Castle (19720) *(G-8839)*

B & M Electric Inc 302 745-3807
   19460 Savannah Rd Georgetown (19947) *(G-4218)*

B & M Meats Inc 302 655-5521
   21 Commerce St Wilmington (19801) *(G-14692)*

B & T Contracting 302 492-8415
   4158 Westville Rd Camden Wyoming (19934) *(G-914)*

B & W Tek Inc 855 692-9835
   18 Shea Way Ste 103 Newark (19713) *(G-9963)*

B A C, Milford *Also Called: Baltimore Aircoil Company Inc (G-7781)*

B and B Automotive 302 559-2087
   305 Commercial Dr Wilmington (19805) *(G-14693)*

B and B Contractors Inc 302 836-9207
   503 Stewarton Ct Newark (19702) *(G-9964)*

B and D Detailing 302 543-6221
   2800 Governor Printz Blvd Wilmington (19802) *(G-14694)*

B Boone Painting 302 740-2576
   2029 Wildwood Dr Wilmington (19805) *(G-14695)*

B C Builders, Clayton *Also Called: Nathan David Fretz (G-1390)*

B C Consulting 215 534-3805
   1521 Concord Pike Ste 202 Wilmington (19803) *(G-14696)*

B Diamond Feed Company 302 697-7576
   2140 Jebb Rd Camden Wyoming (19934) *(G-915)*

B Doherty Inc 302 239-3500
   5301 Limestone Rd Ste 100 Wilmington (19808) *(G-14697)*

B E & K Inc 302 452-9000
   242 Chapman Rd Newark (19702) *(G-9965)*

B E & K, INC., Newark *Also Called: B E & K Inc (G-9965)*

B F P Sothebys Intl Realty 302 545-5266
   5701 Kennett Pike Wilmington (19807) *(G-14698)*

B F P Trading LLC 347 927-0535
   214 E Lea Blvd Wilmington (19802) *(G-14699)*

B F Shin of Salisbury Inc 302 652-3521
   1715 Lovering Ave Wilmington (19806) *(G-14700)*

B Fit Enterprises (PA) 302 292-1785
   35 Salem Church Rd Ste 23 Newark (19713) *(G-9966)*

B Frank Shinn Paint Co (PA) 302 652-3521
   1715 Lovering Ave Wilmington (19806) *(G-14701)*

B G Halko & Sons Inc 302 322-2020
   204 Old Churchmans Rd New Castle (19720) *(G-8840)*

B James Rogge DDS 302 736-1423
   838 Walker Rd Ste 21-1 Dover (19904) *(G-1862)*

B Lawrence Homes LLC 302 559-1779
   1907 Dorcas Ln Wilmington (19806) *(G-14702)*

B Merit Co 888 263-7481
   8 The Grn Ste A Dover (19901) *(G-1863)*

B P Services 302 399-4132
   547 N Bradford St Dover (19904) *(G-1864)*

B Rich Enterprises 302 530-6865
   808 Sweet Hollow Ct Middletown (19709) *(G-6895)*

B Safe Inc ... 302 422-3916
1490 E Lebanon Rd Dover (19901) *(G-1865)*

B Safe Inc (PA) ... 302 633-1833
109 Baltimore Ave Wilmington (19805) *(G-14703)*

B Walls Son Htg & A Conditions ... 302 856-4045
22424 Peterkins Rd Georgetown (19947) *(G-4219)*

B Williams Holding Corp (HQ) ... 302 656-8596
1011 Centre Rd Ste 319 Wilmington (19805) *(G-14704)*

B-Dun Cleaning ... 302 542-7869
33980 Yoshino Dr Lewes (19958) *(G-5733)*

B-Smart Logistics LLC ... 609 388-6622
524 Jacobsen Dr Newark (19702) *(G-9969)*

B'Nai B'Rith House, Claymont *Also Called: BNai Brith Snior Ctzens Hsing (G-1063)*

B&B Transports LLC ... 223 877-6812
651 N Broad St Ste 201 Middletown (19709) *(G-6896)*

B&F Drywall ... 302 218-2467
2896 Shipley Rd Wilmington (19810) *(G-14705)*

B&H Contracting Group ... 302 588-9774
505 W Hummock Ln Newark (19702) *(G-9967)*

B&O Cleaning Service ... 302 604-0108
30328 Bunting Rd Dagsboro (19939) *(G-1416)*

B&P Brown & Partners Corp ... 302 703-0522
16192 Coastal Hwy Lewes (19958) *(G-5732)*

B&P Transit ... 302 653-8466
979 Mount Friendship Rd Smyrna (19977) *(G-13658)*

B&S Home Imprv Envmtl Unvrsal ... 302 310-4374
600 N Broad St Ste 5 Middletown (19709) *(G-6897)*

B+h Insurance LLC ... 302 995-2247
111 Continental Dr Newark (19713) *(G-9968)*

B2b Lists LLC ... 302 601-7207
2093 Philadelphia Pike # 5376 Claymont (19703) *(G-1049)*

B2w2 Inc ... 302 658-5177
809 N Washington St Wilmington (19801) *(G-14706)*

Ba Credit Card Trust ... 704 386-5681
1100 N King St Wilmington (19884) *(G-14707)*

Baabao Inc ... 415 990-6767
300 Delaware Ave Ste 210a Wilmington (19801) *(G-14708)*

Baba Sali LLC ... 917 647-0561
9 E Looockerman St Ste 311 Dover (19901) *(G-1866)*

Babble Platforms Inc ... 416 825-0602
1007 N Orange St Wilmington (19801) *(G-14709)*

Babe Styling Studio Inc ... 302 543-7738
213 N Market St Wilmington (19801) *(G-14710)*

Babes On Square ... 302 477-9190
1413 Foulk Rd Ste 100 Wilmington (19803) *(G-14711)*

Baboon Bubble Inc ... 302 307-2979
406 John Vineyards Ln New Castle (19720) *(G-8841)*

Baby Apron LLC ... 800 796-4406
2093 Philadelphia Pike Ste 8950 Claymont (19703) *(G-1050)*

Baby Bear Educare ... 302 981-9571
202 Remi Dr New Castle (19720) *(G-8842)*

Baby Bubba Dj & Event Planning ... 302 373-4653
18 Crippen Dr New Castle (19720) *(G-8843)*

Baby Tel Communications Inc ... 302 368-3969
727 Art Ln Newark (19713) *(G-9970)*

Back 2 Healthy Nutrition LLC ... 302 857-9818
20 Blyth Ct New Castle (19720) *(G-8844)*

Back Bay Plumbing ... 302 945-1210
34140 Meadow Ln Millsboro (19966) *(G-8179)*

Back Clinic Inc ... 302 995-2100
5550 Kirkwood Hwy Wilmington (19808) *(G-14712)*

Back Creek Golf Club ... 302 378-6499
101 Back Creek Dr Middletown (19709) *(G-6898)*

Back Creek Golf Course, Middletown *Also Called: Back Creek Golf Club (G-6898)*

Back In Action Chiropractic ... 302 322-3304
819 Churchmans Road Ext New Castle (19720) *(G-8845)*

Back Power Service LLC ... 302 934-1901
25252 Summer Rd Millsboro (19966) *(G-8180)*

Back Road Studio ... 302 381-6060
23004 Seagull Ln Georgetown (19947) *(G-4220)*

Back To Blance Healing Therapy ... 302 478-6470
2844 Kennedy Rd Wilmington (19810) *(G-14713)*

Back Up Ctr ... 302 758-4500
400 White Clay Center Dr Newark (19711) *(G-9971)*

Backdoor Entertainment LLC ... 215 514-0915
137 Betsy Rawls Dr Middletown (19709) *(G-6899)*

Backdoor Global Inc ... 386 465-2646
651 N Broad St Ste 201 Middletown (19709) *(G-6900)*

Backupta Inc ... 828 337-8957
2915 Ogletown Rd Newark (19713) *(G-9972)*

Bacon, Alfred, Newark *Also Called: Infectious Disease Association (G-11017)*

Bad Hair Day Inc ... 302 226-4247
20 Lake Ave Rehoboth Beach (19971) *(G-12621)*

Badger Electric, Wilmington *Also Called: M Auger Enterprise Inc (G-18057)*

Badges Sports Bar ... 302 256-0202
300 N Union St Wilmington (19805) *(G-14714)*

Badillo Trucking LLC ... 302 368-4207
103 Night Heron Ln Middletown (19709) *(G-6901)*

Bafundo & Associates, Wilmington *Also Called: Let US Lift It Inc (G-17886)*

Bagel Technologies Inc ... 650 410-8018
651 N Broad St Ste 206 Middletown (19709) *(G-6902)*

Baggage Hub Inc ... 628 666-0150
3500 S Dupont Hwy Dover (19901) *(G-1867)*

Bahtiarian, Gregory Do, Lewes *Also Called: Bayside Health Assn Chartered (G-5740)*

Baibi Wise LLC ... 201 375-0170
4 Peddlers Row Pmb 285 Newark (19702) *(G-9973)*

Bail Enforcement Agent ... 302 543-6305
1601 Milltown Rd Wilmington (19808) *(G-14715)*

Bailey Builders LLC ... 302 236-0035
29615 Woodgate Dr Milton (19968) *(G-8567)*

Bainbridge Company ... 302 509-3185
1 Eaton Pl Newark (19711) *(G-9974)*

Bair & Goff Sales, Newark *Also Called: Bair & Goff Sales LLC (G-9975)*

Bair & Goff Sales LLC ... 302 292-2546
199 Kenneth Ct Newark (19711) *(G-9975)*

Baird Mandalas Brockstedt LLC (PA) ... 302 677-0061
6 S State St Dover (19901) *(G-1868)*

Baird Mandalas Brockstedt LLC ... 302 644-0302
1413 Savannah Rd Unit 1 Lewes (19958) *(G-5734)*

Baiz Nancy Miller- ... 302 576-6821
3711 Kennett Pike Ste 130 Wilmington (19807) *(G-14716)*

Baker James Ccjr DDS ... 302 658-9511
1304 N Broom St Uppr Wilmington (19806) *(G-14717)*

Baker & Sons Paving ... 302 945-6333
116 Bakerfield Dr Middletown (19709) *(G-6903)*

Baker Safety Equipment Inc ... 302 376-9302
107 Delilah Dr Bear (19701) *(G-55)*

Bakhsh Surveyors, Middletown *Also Called: Clifton L Bakhsh Jr Inc (G-6993)*

Balanceco2 Inc ... 302 494-9476
103 Ascension Dr Wilmington (19808) *(G-14718)*

Balanced Audio Technology ... 302 996-9496
26 Beethoven Dr Wilmington (19807) *(G-14719)*

Balanced Audio Technology, Wilmington *Also Called: Bat Electronics Inc (G-14777)*

Balanced Body Inc ... 302 373-3463
903 Shipley Rd Wilmington (19803) *(G-14720)*

Balanced Mind Cnseling Ctr LLC ... 302 377-6911
115 N Broad St Ste 4a Middletown (19709) *(G-6904)*

Balanced Plates & Weights ... 302 632-0953
1883 Westville Rd Marydel (19964) *(G-6795)*

Balatroon Games Inc ... 647 986-9268
8 The Grn Ste A Dover (19901) *(G-1869)*

Baldwin Sayre Inc ... 302 337-0309
17882 Potato Ln Bridgeville (19933) *(G-671)*

Balfour Beatty LLC (HQ) ... 302 573-3873
1011 Centre Rd Ste 322 Wilmington (19805) *(G-14721)*

Balick & Balick Pllc ... 302 658-4265
711 N King St Wilmington (19801) *(G-14722)*

Ballard Builders LLC ... 302 363-1677
101 S Bassett St Clayton (19938) *(G-1352)*

Ballard Business Services, Townsend *Also Called: Edward L Ballard (G-13997)*

Ballard Spahr LLP ... 302 252-4465
919 N Market St Ste 1201 Wilmington (19801) *(G-14723)*

Ballet Theatre of Dover, Dover *Also Called: Dance Conservatory (G-2189)*

Ballistics Technology Intl Ltd (PA).. 877 291-1111
2207 Concord Pike # 657 Wilmington (19803) *(G-14724)*

Bally Holding Company Delaware (HQ).................................. 610 845-7511
3411 Silverside Rd Ste 100 Wilmington (19810) *(G-14725)*

Baltazar Women's Care, Middletown Also Called: Rodney Baltazar *(G-7521)*

Baltimore Aircoil Company Inc.. 302 424-2583
1162 Holly Hill Rd Milford (19963) *(G-7781)*

Balu Ganesh R MD.. 302 992-9191
390 Mitch Rd Wilmington (19804) *(G-14726)*

Bamboozle Web Services Inc.. 833 380-4600
2035 Sunset Lake Rd Newark (19702) *(G-9976)*

Bambu Candles LLC... 917 903-2563
210 Cullen Way Newark (19711) *(G-9977)*

Banacom Signs Inc.. 302 429-6243
3201 Miller Rd Ste A Wilmington (19802) *(G-14727)*

Banana Boat Products, Dover Also Called: Sun Pharmaceuticals Corp *(G-3622)*

Banana Spot Co (PA)... 916 342-9519
1201 N Orange St Ste 600 Wilmington (19801) *(G-14728)*

Bancorp Inc (PA).. 302 385-5000
409 Silverside Rd Ste 105 Wilmington (19809) *(G-14729)*

Bancorp Bank National Assn (HQ)....................................... 302 385-5000
409 Silverside Rd Ste 105 Wilmington (19809) *(G-14730)*

Bancorp Bank, The, Wilmington Also Called: Bancorp Bank National Assn *(G-14730)*

Bancorp Coml Mrtg 2018-Cre4 Tr.. 302 385-5000
409 Silverside Rd Wilmington (19809) *(G-14731)*

Bancorp Coml Mrtg 2019-Cre6 Tr.. 302 385-5000
409 Silverside Rd Wilmington (19809) *(G-14732)*

Bancroft... 302 654-1408
904 N Broom St Wilmington (19806) *(G-14733)*

Bancroft Behavioral Health... 302 273-2319
1601 Milltown Rd Ste 12 Wilmington (19808) *(G-14734)*

Bancroft Behavioral Health... 302 690-0626
1601 Milltown Rd Wilmington (19808) *(G-14735)*

Bancroft Behavioral Health Inc... 302 502-3255
1601 Milltown Rd Ste 12 Wilmington (19808) *(G-14736)*

Bancroft Carpentry Company (HQ)..................................... 302 655-3434
44 Bancroft Mills Rd Wilmington (19806) *(G-14737)*

Bancroft Construction Company.. 302 655-3434
479 Chevron St Dover (19902) *(G-1870)*

Bancroft Construction Company (PA)................................ 302 655-3434
1300 N Grant Ave Ste 101 Wilmington (19806) *(G-14738)*

Bancroft Family Care, Wilmington Also Called: Helena Schroyer MD *(G-17116)*

Bancroft Homes Inc... 302 655-5461
1300 N Grant Ave Ste 204 Wilmington (19806) *(G-14739)*

Bancroft Inc... 856 769-1300
9 Thunder Gulch Newark (19702) *(G-9978)*

Bancroft Neuro Health... 302 266-7054
107 Lauren Pl Newark (19702) *(G-9979)*

Bancroft Neurohealth... 302 691-8531
321 E 11th St Wilmington (19801) *(G-14740)*

BANCROFT NEUROHEALTH, A NEW JERSEY NONPROFIT CORPORATION, Wilmington
Also Called: Bancroft Neurohealth *(G-14740)*

Bancroft Pkwy Open Mri & Imgng, Wilmington Also Called: Trolley Sq Opn Mri & Imgng Ctr *(G-20435)*

Bancroft Vlant Joint Ventr LLC... 717 553-0165
1300 N Grant Ave Ste 101 Wilmington (19806) *(G-14741)*

Bandai Namco Amus Amer Inc.. 302 734-3623
1365 N Dupont Hwy Ste 4004 Dover (19901) *(G-1871)*

Bands, Dover Also Called: Bands CA Inc *(G-1872)*

Bands CA Inc... 206 396-7035
8 The Grn Ste 6772 Dover (19901) *(G-1872)*

Banfield Pet Hospital 1103, Wilmington Also Called: A Caring Doctor Minnesota PA *(G-14160)*

Bang Bang Media Corp (HQ).. 213 374-0555
651 N Broad St Ste 308 Middletown (19709) *(G-6905)*

Bangus Business Services... 302 266-7285
18 Marvin Dr Apt B4 Newark (19713) *(G-9980)*

Bank Amer Child Dev Ctr - Nwar, Newark Also Called: Bright Horizons Chld Ctrs LLC *(G-10086)*

Bank America National Assn.. 888 550-6433
1000 Samoset Dr Newark (19713) *(G-9981)*

Bank America National Assn.. 302 765-2108
1100 N King St Wilmington (19884) *(G-14742)*

Bank America National Assn.. 302 478-1005
5215 Concord Pike Wilmington (19803) *(G-14743)*

Bank America National Assn.. 302 656-5399
3816 Kennett Pike Wilmington (19807) *(G-14744)*

Bank America National Assn.. 704 386-8539
5215 Concord Pike Wilmington (19803) *(G-14745)*

Bank America National Assn.. 704 386-8539
1020 N French St Wilmington (19884) *(G-14746)*

Bank Fillers Entertainment LLC... 302 930-0262
831 N Tatnall St Ste M Wilmington (19801) *(G-14747)*

Bank House.. 302 422-4824
5879 Old Shawnee Rd Milford (19963) *(G-7782)*

Bank of America, Wilmington Also Called: Bank America National Assn *(G-14742)*

Bank of America, Wilmington Also Called: Bank America National Assn *(G-14743)*

Bank of America, Wilmington Also Called: Bank America National Assn *(G-14744)*

Bank of America, N.a, Wilmington Also Called: Bank America National Assn *(G-14745)*

Bank of Delmar, Seaford Also Called: Bank of Delmarva *(G-13075)*

Bank of Delmarva... 302 875-5901
200 E Market St Laurel (19956) *(G-5466)*

Bank of Delmarva... 302 226-8900
18578 Coastal Hwy Rehoboth Beach (19971) *(G-12622)*

Bank of Delmarva... 302 629-2700
910 Norman Eskridge Hwy Seaford (19973) *(G-13075)*

Bank of New Castle.. 800 347-3301
12 Reads Way New Castle (19720) *(G-8846)*

Bank of New York Mellon Corp... 302 421-2207
4005 Kennett Pike Wilmington (19807) *(G-14748)*

Banker Steel Co LLC.. 708 478-0111
1209 N Orange St Wilmington (19801) *(G-14749)*

Bankers Life.. 302 232-5006
99 Wolf Creek Blvd Ste 1b Dover (19901) *(G-1873)*

Bankers Life, Dover Also Called: Bankers Life *(G-1873)*

Banknorth Massachusetts, Wilmington Also Called: Td Bank NA *(G-20241)*

Bankruptcy Anywhere.. 302 426-4777
922 New Rd Wilmington (19805) *(G-14750)*

Banks Farms LLC... 302 542-4100
30190 Whites Neck Rd Dagsboro (19939) *(G-1417)*

Banris Construction LLC... 302 722-0958
347 Mitchell Dr Wilmington (19808) *(G-14751)*

Bar & Associates Intr Design, Wilmington Also Called: Bar & Associates Ltd *(G-14752)*

Bar & Associates Ltd... 302 999-9233
3410 Old Capitol Trl Ste 2 Wilmington (19808) *(G-14752)*

Barami De Inc.. 201 993-9678
735 S Market St Ste A Wilmington (19801) *(G-14753)*

Barbacane Thornton & Company... 302 478-8940
3411 Silverside Rd Ste 202 Wilmington (19810) *(G-14754)*

Barbara Baker... 302 238-7415
37058 Triple B Farm Ln Frankford (19945) *(G-4067)*

Barbara Graphics Inc... 302 636-9040
506 First State Blvd Wilmington (19804) *(G-14755)*

Barbara Kwakye-Safo.. 302 559-1955
113 Faraday Ct Bear (19701) *(G-56)*

Barbara L McKinney.. 302 266-9594
5 Knickerbocker Dr Newark (19713) *(G-9982)*

Barbara Moore Fine Art.. 610 357-6100
1514 Ridge Rd Wilmington (19809) *(G-14756)*

Barbara Socha MD... 302 541-4460
96 Atlantic Ave Ste 103 Ocean View (19970) *(G-12467)*

Barber Shop At Rehoboth Beach... 240 743-9064
20187 Doddtown Rd Harbeson (19951) *(G-4685)*

Barbizon of Delaware Inc... 302 658-6666
17 Trolley Sq Ste B Wilmington (19806) *(G-14757)*

Barbizon School of Modeling, Wilmington Also Called: Barbizon of Delaware Inc *(G-14757)*

Barbosa Manufacturing.. 302 856-6343
24965 Kruger Rd Georgetown (19947) *(G-4221)*

Barclay & Associates PC.. 515 292-3023
2401 Kentmere Pkwy Wilmington (19806) *(G-14758)*

Barclay Farms.. 302 697-6939
1 Paynters Way Camden (19934) *(G-792)*

BARCLAYCARD US, Wilmington Also Called: Barclays Bank Delaware *(G-14759)*

Barclays Bank Delaware   ALPHABETIC SECTION

Barclays Bank Delaware (DH) 302 255-8000
   100 S West St Wilmington (19801) *(G-14759)*

Barclays Financial Corporation 302 652-6201
   100 S West St Wilmington (19801) *(G-14760)*

Bardell Video Productions 302 377-9936
   212 Potomac Rd Wilmington (19803) *(G-14761)*

Bargain Tire 302 764-8900
   3018 Governor Printz Blvd Wilmington (19802) *(G-14762)*

Bargain Tire & Service Inc 302 764-8900
   3415 N Market St Ste 17 Wilmington (19802) *(G-14763)*

Bari Concrete Cnstr Corp 302 384-7093
   202 New Rd Wilmington (19805) *(G-14764)*

Bari Concrete Contractors 302 757-9512
   1805 W 8th St Wilmington (19805) *(G-14765)*

Bariatric Beautiful Barbii LLC 302 279-6938
   148 Parma Dr Clayton (19938) *(G-1353)*

Barker Therapy Rehabilitation, Milford *Also Called: Matrix Rehabilitation Delaware (G-7989)*

Barker-Mtrix Thrapy Rhbltation, Dover *Also Called: Physiotherapy Associates Inc (G-3319)*

Barkley Heating & Air LLC 302 653-5971
   931 Boxwood Dr Smyrna (19977) *(G-13659)*

Barksdale Dental Associates 302 731-4907
   625 Barksdale Rd Ste 115-117 Newark (19711) *(G-9983)*

Barlow Upholstery, Wilmington *Also Called: Barlows Upholstery Inc (G-14766)*

Barlows Upholstery Inc 302 655-3955
   1002 W 28th St Wilmington (19802) *(G-14766)*

Barnes Camp 302 539-7775
   37171 Camp Barnes Rd Frankford (19945) *(G-4068)*

Barnett Tom D Law Firm 302 855-9252
   512 E Market St Georgetown (19947) *(G-4222)*

Barnett, Norman C, Georgetown *Also Called: Market Street Center Inc (G-4417)*

Barnhart, Ryan DDS, Lewes *Also Called: Dental Group (G-5911)*

Baronsky Patrick & Associates 302 529-7585
   2643 Bellows Dr Wilmington (19810) *(G-14767)*

Barracuda Carpentry LLC 302 415-1588
   9 Nelsa Ln Millsboro (19966) *(G-8181)*

Barrel Fuel Technologies Inc 832 405-4806
   3500 S Dupont Hwy Dover (19901) *(G-1874)*

Barrett Business Services Inc 302 674-2206
   116 E Water St Dover (19901) *(G-1875)*

Barrettes Run Apartments 302 368-3400
   100 N Barrett Ln Newark (19702) *(G-9984)*

Barrier Integrated Systems LLC 302 502-2727
   527 Stanton Christiana Rd Newark (19713) *(G-9985)*

Barroja, Wilmington *Also Called: Barroja Ventures LLC (G-14768)*

Barroja Ventures LLC 302 256-0883
   1709 Delaware Ave Wilmington (19806) *(G-14768)*

Barros Mc Nmara Mlkwicz Tylor 302 734-8400
   2 W Loockerman St Dover (19904) *(G-1876)*

Barry Goldstein MD 302 734-4130
   1325 S State St Ste 204 Dover (19901) *(G-1877)*

Barry Kayne DDS 302 456-0400
   58 Omega Dr Ste F58 Newark (19713) *(G-9986)*

Barry Management Group De LLC 302 480-0519
   1715 Montgomery Rd Wilmington (19805) *(G-14769)*

Barsgr LLC 302 945-3410
   32087 Holly Lake Rd Millsboro (19966) *(G-8182)*

Barshay Stephanie Lplmh 302 312-6466
   1200 N Van Buren St Wilmington (19806) *(G-14770)*

Bartech Agency Inc 302 317-2399
   1148 Pulaski Hwy Ste 107 Bear (19701) *(G-57)*

Bartol Research Institute, Newark *Also Called: University of Delaware (G-12278)*

Bartons Landscaping/Lawn Inc 302 629-2213
   20689 Sussex Hwy Seaford (19973) *(G-13076)*

Bartsch John C, Dover *Also Called: Sunnyfield Contractors Inc (G-3623)*

Base Carriers, Wilmington *Also Called: Base Carriers LLC (G-14771)*

Base Carriers LLC 215 559-1132
   501 Garasches Ln Wilmington (19801) *(G-14771)*

Base-2 Solutions, Lewes *Also Called: Base-2 Solutions LLC (G-5735)*

Base-2 Solutions LLC 202 215-2152
   12211 Collins Rd Lewes (19958) *(G-5735)*

Base86 Inc 619 781-2670
   2035 Sunset Lake Rd Ste B2 Newark (19702) *(G-9987)*

Basedash Inc 302 244-0916
   8 The Grn Ste 5775 Dover (19901) *(G-1878)*

Basell Capital Corporation 302 683-8000
   2 Righter Pkwy Ste 300 Wilmington (19803) *(G-14772)*

Basemark Inc (PA) 832 483-7093
   3500 S Dupont Hwy Dover (19901) *(G-1879)*

Basement Circuit Training 302 824-8078
   100 Naamans Rd Ste 5g Claymont (19703) *(G-1051)*

Basement Gurus LLC 800 834-6584
   244 W Champlain Ave Wilmington (19804) *(G-14773)*

Basement Pros Inc 302 266-0203
   569 Walther Rd Newark (19702) *(G-9988)*

Basement Unlimited LLC 302 569-2211
   17667 Gate Dr Unit 3 Lewes (19958) *(G-5736)*

Basetwo, Dover *Also Called: Basetwo Artfcal Intllgnce USA (G-1880)*

Basetwo Artfcal Intllgnce USA 519 400-8770
   838 Walker Rd Ste 21-2 Dover (19904) *(G-1880)*

BASF Corporation 302 992-5600
   205 S James St Wilmington (19804) *(G-14774)*

BASF Uk Finance LLC (PA) 973 245-6000
   1209 N Orange St Wilmington (19801) *(G-14775)*

Basher & Son Enterprises Inc 302 239-6584
   1072 Yorklyn Rd Hockessin (19707) *(G-5130)*

Basher & Son Welding, Hockessin *Also Called: Basher & Son Enterprises Inc (G-5130)*

Basic Block Corp 302 645-2000
   4590 Highway One Ste 118 Rehoboth Beach (19971) *(G-12623)*

Basigo Inc 510 735-6240
   2803 Philadelphia Pike Ste B Claymont (19703) *(G-1052)*

Basket Fundamentals LLC 302 360-8617
   16192 Coastal Hwy Lewes (19958) *(G-5737)*

Bastianelli Group Inc 302 658-1500
   231 Executive Dr Ste 15 Newark (19702) *(G-9989)*

Bastion Research Ltd 307 370-3767
   16192 Coastal Hwy Lewes (19958) *(G-5738)*

BAt Capital Corporation 302 691-6323
   103 Foulk Rd Ste 120 Wilmington (19803) *(G-14776)*

Bat Electronics Inc 302 999-8855
   1300 First State Blvd Ste A Wilmington (19804) *(G-14777)*

Batescainelli LLC 202 618-2040
   319 Byview Ave Rhboth Bch Rehoboth Beach Rehoboth Beach (19971) *(G-12624)*

Bath Kitchen Tile DH 302 992-9210
   23 Ridgewood Turn Newark (19711) *(G-9990)*

Bath, Kitchen & Tile Center, Wilmington *Also Called: Ceramic Tile Supply Co (G-15313)*

Batholite Natural Stone Inc 206 707-2298
   302 Wellspring Ct Hockessin (19707) *(G-5131)*

Batta Inc 302 737-3376
   6 Garfield Way Newark (19713) *(G-9991)*

Batta Environmental Assoc Inc (PA) 302 737-3376
   6 Garfield Way Newark (19713) *(G-9992)*

Batta Laboratory, Newark *Also Called: Batta Environmental Assoc Inc (G-9992)*

Batta Ramesh C Associates PA (PA) 302 998-9463
   4600 Linden Hill Rd Ste 102 Wilmington (19808) *(G-14778)*

Battaglia Electric Inc 302 325-6100
   11 Industrial Blvd New Castle (19720) *(G-8847)*

Battaglia Joseph A & Diamond 302 655-8868
   900 Foulk Rd Ste 200 Wilmington (19803) *(G-14779)*

Battaglia Management Inc 302 325-6100
   11 Industrial Blvd Ste B New Castle (19720) *(G-8848)*

Battaglia Mechanical Inc 302 325-6100
   11 Industrial Blvd New Castle (19720) *(G-8849)*

Battle Axe LLC 302 437-4283
   616 Delaware St Historic New Castle (19720) *(G-4938)*

Battle Proven Foundation 703 216-1986
   368 Artis Dr Dover (19904) *(G-1881)*

Battleboost Inc 302 499-2000
   2093 Philadelphia Pike Ste 4343 Claymont (19703) *(G-1053)*

Bauer Family Foundation Inc 800 639-1754
   501 Silverside Rd Wilmington (19809) *(G-14780)*

Bauguess Electrical Svcs Inc 302 737-5614
   1400 Interchange Blvd Newark (19711) *(G-9993)*

ALPHABETIC SECTION

Baumann Industries Inc 302 593-1049
   2412 W Heather Rd Ste 200 Wilmington (19803) *(G-14781)*

Bavarian Cllision New Grdn Inc 610 268-3966
   119 Pigeon Run Dr Bear (19701) *(G-58)*

Bawa Inc 302 698-3200
   45 Old Mill Rd Dover (19901) *(G-1882)*

Baxet Group Inc 917 938-7088
   919 N Market St Ste 950 Wilmington (19801) *(G-14782)*

Baxter Farms Inc 302 856-1818
   23073 Zoar Rd Georgetown (19947) *(G-4223)*

Bay 2 Bay Builders 302 632-7222
   396 Hayfield Rd Harrington (19952) *(G-4738)*

Bay Anesthesia Associates LLC 302 598-9139
   640 S State St Dover (19901) *(G-1883)*

Bay Area Inflatables LLC (PA) 302 379-2821
   28 Whitekirk Dr Wilmington (19808) *(G-14783)*

Bay Area Market Place, Wilmington Also Called: Hs Capital LLC *(G-17223)*

Bay Area Wildlife LLC 410 829-6368
   10533 Old Furnace Rd Seaford (19973) *(G-13077)*

Bay Developers Inc 302 736-0924
   200 Weston Dr Dover (19904) *(G-1884)*

Bay Forest Homeowners Assn 302 537-6580
   36115 Bay Forest Dr Ocean View (19970) *(G-12468)*

Bay Health Frezza Charles 302 430-5565
   21 W Clarke Ave Milford (19963) *(G-7783)*

Bay Resort 302 227-1598
   1607 Bayard Ave Dewey Beach (19971) *(G-1663)*

Bay Resort Motel, Dewey Beach Also Called: Moore Partnership *(G-1674)*

Bay Rose Homes 302 945-9510
   31767 Marsh Island Ave Lewes (19958) *(G-5739)*

Bay Shippers LLC 302 652-5005
   1535 Matassino Rd New Castle (19720) *(G-8850)*

Bay Spray 302 245-2715
   34199 Dianas Ln Frankford (19945) *(G-4069)*

Bay To Beach Builders Inc 302 349-5099
   11582 Sussex Hwy Farmington (19950) *(G-3933)*

Bayada 302 213-5024
   655 S Bay Rd Ste 1g Dover (19901) *(G-1885)*

Bayada Home Health Care Inc 302 736-6001
   655 S Bay Rd Ste 1g Dover (19901) *(G-1886)*

Bayada Home Health Care Inc 302 213-5040
   655 S Bay Rd Ste 1g Dover (19901) *(G-1887)*

Bayada Home Health Care Inc 302 424-8200
   1016 N Walnut St Milford (19963) *(G-7784)*

Bayada Home Health Care Inc 302 351-1244
   100 Silicato Pkwy Suite 104 Milford (19963) *(G-7785)*

Bayada Home Health Care Inc 302 322-2300
   15 Reads Way Ste 205 New Castle (19720) *(G-8851)*

Bayada Home Health Care Inc 302 836-1000
   200 Biddle Ave Ste 101 Newark (19702) *(G-9994)*

Bayada Home Health Care Inc 302 351-1244
   4250 Lancaster Pike Ste 310 Wilmington (19805) *(G-14784)*

Bayada Home Health Care Inc 302 351-3633
   4250 Lancaster Pike Ste 308 Wilmington (19805) *(G-14785)*

Bayada Home Health Care Inc 302 658-3000
   4250 Lancaster Pike Ste 300 Wilmington (19805) *(G-14786)*

Bayada Home Health Care Inc 302 351-3636
   4250 Lancaster Pike Ste 312 Wilmington (19805) *(G-14787)*

Bayada Nurses, Newark Also Called: Bayada Home Health Care Inc *(G-9994)*

Bayard House, Wilmington Also Called: Home of Divine Providence Inc *(G-17182)*

Bayard, Eugene H, Georgetown Also Called: Wilson Halbrook & Bayard PA *(G-4575)*

Baybiw Development LLC 302 537-9700
   123 Atlantic Ave Ocean View (19967) *(G-12469)*

Bayesian Health Inc 408 205-8035
   251 Little Falls Dr Wilmington (19808) *(G-14788)*

Bayete Corp 302 562-7415
   10 Shadwell Ct New Castle (19720) *(G-8852)*

Bayhealth Bariatric Program 302 430-5454
   100 Wellness Way Milford (19963) *(G-7786)*

Bayhealth Ent of Dover 302 674-3752
   826 S Governors Ave Dover (19904) *(G-1888)*

Bayhealth Hematology Oncology 302 430-5072
   21 W Clarke Ave Milford (19963) *(G-7787)*

Bayhealth Med Ctr Inc-OCC Hlth 302 678-1303
   1275 S State St Dover (19901) *(G-1889)*

Bayhealth Medical Center, Middletown Also Called: Kent General Hospital *(G-7266)*

Bayhealth Medical Center Inc (PA) 302 674-4700
   640 S State St Dover (19901) *(G-1890)*

Bayhealth Medical Group Ent 302 339-8040
   20930 Dupont Boulevard Unit 202 Georgetown (19947) *(G-4224)*

Bayhealth Primary Care 302 855-1349
   18383 Hudson Rd Milton (19968) *(G-8568)*

Bayhealth Primary Care Dover W 302 734-7834
   720 S Queen St Dover (19904) *(G-1891)*

Baymont Inn & Suites, Newark Also Called: Newark Land Group Inc *(G-11541)*

Baynard House Condominiums 302 319-3740
   2400 Baynard Blvd Wilmington (19802) *(G-14789)*

Baynard Property MGT LLC 302 225-3350
   2710 Centerville Rd Ste 200 Wilmington (19808) *(G-14790)*

Baynum Enterprises Inc 302 875-4477
   403 N Central Ave Unit A Laurel (19956) *(G-5467)*

Baynum Enterprises Inc 302 934-8699
   28632 Dupont Blvd Unit 20 Millsboro (19966) *(G-8183)*

Baynum Enterprises Inc (PA) 302 629-6104
   300 W Stein Hwy Seaford (19973) *(G-13078)*

Baypro Contracting 703 593-7673
   211 S Walnut St Milford (19963) *(G-7788)*

Bayshore Communications Inc 302 737-2164
   2839 Ogletown Rd Newark (19713) *(G-9995)*

Bayshore Ford Truck Sales Inc (PA) 302 656-3160
   4003 N Dupont Hwy New Castle (19720) *(G-8853)*

Bayshore Inc 302 539-7200
   Rr 1 Box 252 Ocean View (19970) *(G-12470)*

Bayshore Records MGT LLC 302 731-4477
   901 Dawson Dr Newark (19713) *(G-9996)*

Bayshore Services LLC 304 596-3788
   19102 Carey Ln Georgetown (19947) *(G-4225)*

Bayshore Trnsp Sys Inc (PA) 302 366-0220
   901 Dawson Dr Newark (19713) *(G-9997)*

Bayside At Bthany Lkes Clbhuse 302 539-4378
   38335 Old Mill Way Ocean View (19970) *(G-12471)*

Bayside Fitness 302 231-8982
   24784 Shoreline Dr Millsboro (19966) *(G-8184)*

Bayside Golf LLC DBA Bear Trap 302 537-5600
   7 Clubhouse Dr Ocean View (19970) *(G-12472)*

Bayside Health Assn Chartered (PA) 302 645-4700
   1535 Savannah Rd Lewes (19958) *(G-5740)*

Bayside Limousine 302 644-6999
   34026 Annas Way Unit 1 Millsboro (19966) *(G-8185)*

Bayside Millwork Inc 443 324-4376
   11062 Destination Dr Selbyville (19975) *(G-13470)*

Bayside Mini Storage 302 524-2096
   36097 Zion Church Rd Frankford (19945) *(G-4070)*

Bayside Painting 302 344-6910
   111 American Legion Rd Lewes (19958) *(G-5741)*

Bayside Resort Golf Club 410 652-7705
   31854 Mill Run Drive Millville (19970) *(G-8516)*

Bayside Resort Golf Club 302 436-3400
   31806 Lakeview Dr Selbyville (19975) *(G-13471)*

Bayside Sealcoating Supply 302 697-6441
   6453 Mud Mill Rd Camden Wyoming (19934) *(G-916)*

Bayside Sports Club LLC 302 436-3550
   31381 Sorsyphia Selbyville (19975) *(G-13472)*

Baytown Packhouse Inc 936 340-2122
   112 Capitol Trl Newark (19711) *(G-9998)*

Baytown Systems Inc 302 689-3421
   2711 Centerville Rd # 400 Wilmington (19808) *(G-14791)*

Bayview Endoscopy Center 302 644-0455
   33663 Bayview Medical Dr # 3 Lewes (19958) *(G-5742)*

Bayville Postal Svc 302 436-2715
   37232 Lighthouse Rd Selbyville (19975) *(G-13473)*

Baywood Greens Golf Club 302 947-9225
   24 Ofc Rt Millsboro (19966) *(G-8186)*

Baywood Greens Golf Club (PA) 302 947-9800
32267 Clubhouse Way Millsboro (19966) *(G-8187)*

Baywood Greens Golf Mntnc 757 460-5584
25258 Banks Rd Millsboro (19966) *(G-8188)*

Bb Builder Llc 302 670-1972
1452 W Denneys Rd Dover (19904) *(G-1892)*

Bb Custom Instruments 302 339-3826
300a Nancy St Georgetown (19947) *(G-4226)*

Bb Technologies Inc 302 652-2300
801 N West St 2nd Fl Wilmington (19801) *(G-14792)*

Bb.q Chicken South Main St Plz, Newark *Also Called: Bbdotq USA Inc (G-9999)*

BBA USA Holdings Inc (PA) 450 464-2111
2801 Centerville Rd Wilmington (19808) *(G-14793)*

Bbdg, Bear *Also Called: Be Blessed Design Group LLC (G-59)*

Bbdotq USA Inc 302 533-6589
165 S Main St Unit 117 Newark (19711) *(G-9999)*

Bbi-Fiber LLC (PA) 224 633-1288
364 E Main St Ste 410 Middletown (19709) *(G-6906)*

Bbsi, Dover *Also Called: Barrett Business Services Inc (G-1875)*

Bc Home Health Care Services 302 746-7844
3301 Green St Claymont (19703) *(G-1054)*

Bca Mental Health Counseling 302 513-9565
900 Philadelphia Pike Wilmington (19809) *(G-14794)*

Bcb Diesel Mechanics Llc 302 422-3787
404 Milford Harrington Hwy Milford (19963) *(G-7789)*

Bcg Holding Corp (HQ) 617 850-3700
1209 N Orange St Wilmington (19801) *(G-14795)*

Bcg Inc 302 875-6013
30739 Sussex Hwy Laurel (19956) *(G-5468)*

Bcg Management LLC 302 278-7677
234 Rehoboth Ave Rehoboth Beach (19971) *(G-12625)*

BCI, New Castle *Also Called: Brandywine Contractors Inc (G-8885)*

Bcp Finance Corp A Del Corp 225 673-6121
2711 Centerville Rd # 400 Wilmington (19808) *(G-14796)*

Bdb LLC 469 288-7672
1201 N Orange St Ste 600 Wilmington (19801) *(G-14797)*

BDB Services 302 536-1410
25560 Business Park Seaford (19973) *(G-13079)*

Bdc-Healthit, Ocean View *Also Called: Dodd Health Innovation LLC (G-12506)*

Bdi Inc 570 299-7679
706 Enter Chance Blvd Newark (19711) *(G-10000)*

Bdo Usa LLP 302 656-5500
4250 Lancaster Pike Ste 120 Wilmington (19805) *(G-14798)*

BDO USA, LLP, Wilmington *Also Called: Bdo Usa LLP (G-14798)*

Be Beautiful Bossy 888 558-9047
1207 D St Ste 2035 Wilmington (19801) *(G-14799)*

Be Blessed Design Group LLC 302 561-3793
808 Lowell Dr Bear (19701) *(G-59)*

Be Bold 302 415-5242
421 Ridgely Blvd Dover (19904) *(G-1893)*

Be Human E, Dover *Also Called: Be Humane Co (G-1894)*

Be Humane Co 720 419-5362
8 The Grn Dover (19901) *(G-1894)*

Be Right There Consulting LLC 302 727-5047
4 Peddlers Row Newark (19702) *(G-10001)*

Be Truly Well LLC 302 525-4343
218 E Main St Ste 112 Newark (19711) *(G-10002)*

Be Well Massage and Skin Care 302 883-3066
554 Garton Ln Dover (19904) *(G-1895)*

Be-Tech Group Company, Dover *Also Called: Bullseye Entertainment Tech Co (G-1992)*

BE&k, Newark *Also Called: Kbr Engineering Company LLC (G-11147)*

Beach Arcade Central 302 227-1043
101 S Boardwalk Rehoboth Beach (19971) *(G-12626)*

Beach Associates Inc 866 744-9911
9 E Loockerman St Ste 2a Dover (19901) *(G-1896)*

Beach Babies Child Care 302 645-5010
35245 Hudson Way Rehoboth Beach (19971) *(G-12627)*

BEACH BABIES CHILD CARE, Rehoboth Beach *Also Called: Beach Babies Child Care (G-12627)*

Beach Bbies Child Care At Twns (PA) 302 644-1585
104 Canal View Ct Rehoboth Beach (19971) *(G-12628)*

Beach Bbies Child Care At Twns 302 378-4778
6020 Summit Bridge Rd Townsend (19734) *(G-13962)*

Beach Break 302 226-3450
2104 Highway One Dewey Beach (19971) *(G-1664)*

Beach Break & Bakrie 302 537-3800
123 Garfield Pkwy Bethany Beach (19930) *(G-576)*

Beach Cities Reptile Rescue 949 412-6366
10333 Airport Rd Seaford (19973) *(G-13080)*

Beach House Dewey Hotel, Dewey Beach *Also Called: Dewey Beach House (G-1666)*

Beach House Resources 703 980-3336
29l Atlantic Ave # 199 Bethany Beach (19930) *(G-577)*

Beach House Services 302 645-2554
26 Cripple Creek Run Milton (19968) *(G-8569)*

Beach Mobile Home Supply 302 945-5611
32695 Long Neck Rd Unit 1 Millsboro (19966) *(G-8189)*

Beach Tans & Hair Designs, Rehoboth Beach *Also Called: Beach Tans and Hair Design (G-12629)*

Beach Tans and Hair Design 302 645-8267
23 Midway Shopping Ctr Rehoboth Beach (19971) *(G-12629)*

Beach Time 302 644-2850
32191 Nassau Rd Lewes (19958) *(G-5743)*

Beach View Motel, Rehoboth Beach *Also Called: Cooper Simpler Associates Inc (G-12700)*

Beach-Net.com, Fenwick Island *Also Called: Coastal Images Inc (G-4045)*

Beachballs Com LLC 302 628-8888
112 S Bradford St Seaford (19973) *(G-13081)*

Beaches Plumbing Plus 302 841-0171
14955 Orth Ln Milton (19968) *(G-8570)*

Beachside Cleaning LLC 717 875-3141
37080 Canvasback Rd Selbyville (19975) *(G-13474)*

Beachview Family Health 302 537-8318
550 Atlantic Ave Millville (19967) *(G-8517)*

Beachview Mgmt Inc 302 227-3280
33045 E Light Dr Lewes (19958) *(G-5744)*

Beachy Transportation 302 284-7202
177 Plummer Ln Harrington (19952) *(G-4739)*

Beacon Air Inc 302 323-1688
23 Parkway Cir Ste 9 New Castle (19720) *(G-8854)*

Beacon Engineering LLC 302 864-8825
23318 Cedar Ln Georgetown (19947) *(G-4227)*

Beacon Hope Christian Ministry 302 764-7162
4001 N Market St Wilmington (19802) *(G-14800)*

Beacon Hospitality 302 249-0502
22297 Dupont Blvd Georgetown (19947) *(G-4228)*

Beacon Hospitality 302 567-2213
36619 Tanger Blvd Rehoboth Beach (19971) *(G-12630)*

Beacon Interactive Inc 414 306-5978
8 The Grn Ste A Dover (19901) *(G-1897)*

Beacon Medical Group PA 302 947-9767
18947 John J Williams Hwy Unit 303 Rehoboth Beach (19971) *(G-12631)*

Beacon Motel 302 645-4888
514 E Savannah Rd Lewes (19958) *(G-5745)*

Beacon of Hope Daycare Center, Wilmington *Also Called: Beacon Hope Christian Ministry (G-14800)*

Beacon Pediatrics LLC 302 645-8212
18947 John J Williams Hwy Unit 212 Rehoboth Beach (19971) *(G-12632)*

Beacon Technologies LLC 302 438-9728
336 Brandywine Dr Bear (19701) *(G-60)*

Beacon Wealth Management LLC 302 383-2671
1018 Crestover Rd Wilmington (19803) *(G-14801)*

Beam Construction Inc 302 537-2787
1 E Atlantic St Fenwick Island (19944) *(G-4041)*

Beamm Technologies Inc 302 402-5551
3 Germay Dr Unit 41563 Wilmington (19804) *(G-14802)*

Beane Assoc Inc 302 559-1452
614 Haverhill Rd Wilmington (19803) *(G-14803)*

Beanstock Media Inc (PA) 415 912-1530
300 Delaware Ave Ste 1100 Wilmington (19801) *(G-14804)*

Bear Alignment Center 302 655-9219
1317 N Scott St Wilmington (19806) *(G-14805)*

Bear Associates LLC 302 735-5558
209 Massey Dr Dover (19904) *(G-1898)*

ALPHABETIC SECTION

Bear Chiropractic Center DC.. 302 836-8361
   811 Governors Pl Bear (19701) *(G-61)*

Bear De.. 302 836-6050
   258 E Scotland Dr Bear (19701) *(G-62)*

Bear Early Education Center.. 302 836-5000
   2884 Glasgow Ave Newark (19702) *(G-10003)*

Bear Financial Group LLC.. 302 735-9909
   846 Walker Rd Ste 31-2 Dover (19904) *(G-1899)*

Bear Forge and Machine Co Inc... 302 322-5199
   147 School Bell Rd Bear (19701) *(G-63)*

Bear Glasgow Dental.. 302 836-3750
   1290 Peoples Plz Newark (19702) *(G-10004)*

Bear Hospitality Inc.. 302 326-2500
   875 Pulaski Hwy Bear (19701) *(G-64)*

Bear Industries Inc.. 302 368-1311
   15 Albe Dr Newark (19702) *(G-10005)*

Bear Int Med Peds... 302 595-2146
   26 Dunleary Dr Bear (19701) *(G-65)*

Bear Materials LLC (PA).. 302 658-5241
   4048 New Castle Ave New Castle (19720) *(G-8855)*

Bear Mri & Imaging Center, Bear *Also Called: Limestone Open Mri LLC (G-349)*

Bear Trap Dunes, Ocean View *Also Called: Bear Trap Partners (G-12473)*

Bear Trap Partners.. 302 537-5600
   County Rte 84 Ocean View (19970) *(G-12473)*

Bear Trap Sales.. 302 541-5454
   21 Village Green Dr Ste 101 Ocean View (19970) *(G-12474)*

Bear Trap Spirits Inc... 302 537-8008
   38014 Town Center Dr Millville (19967) *(G-8518)*

Bear-Glasgow Dental LLC... 302 836-9330
   1106 Pulaski Hwy Bear (19701) *(G-66)*

Bear-Glasgow YMCA... 302 836-9622
   351 George Williams Way Newark (19702) *(G-10006)*

Beasley FM Acquisition Corp... 302 765-1160
   812 Philadelphia Pike Wilmington (19809) *(G-14806)*

Beast of East Baseball LLC.. 302 545-9094
   916 Gray St Historic New Castle (19720) *(G-4939)*

Beau Bden Fndtion For The Prtc... 302 598-1885
   4601 Concord Pike Wilmington (19803) *(G-14807)*

Beautful Gate Outreach Ctr Inc... 302 472-3002
   604 N Walnut St Wilmington (19801) *(G-14808)*

Beautiful Floors LLC.. 302 690-5230
   4 Lynford St Newark (19713) *(G-10007)*

Beautiful Smiles Delaware LLC.. 302 656-0558
   4901 Limestone Rd Ste 1 Wilmington (19808) *(G-14809)*

Beauty and Beach Hair Boutique.. 302 260-9383
   37169 Rehoboth Avenue Ext Rehoboth Beach (19971) *(G-12633)*

Beauty Barrettes LLC.. 302 883-7532
   24 Sandalwood Dr Newark (19713) *(G-10008)*

Beauty By Jamie.. 302 784-5311
   8 Nieole Ave New Castle (19720) *(G-8856)*

Beauty Max Inc... 302 735-1705
   1634 S Governors Ave Dover (19904) *(G-1900)*

Beaver Tree Service Inc.. 302 226-3564
   108 2nd St Rehoboth Beach (19971) *(G-12634)*

Beaverdam Pet Food.. 302 349-5299
   12933 Sussex Hwy Greenwood (19950) *(G-4595)*

BEC Capital LLC.. 917 658-5867
   3422 Old Capitol Trl Ste 438 Wilmington (19808) *(G-14810)*

Because Love Allows Compassion.. 302 674-2496
   270 Beechwood Ave Dover (19901) *(G-1901)*

Because We Care, Dover *Also Called: Independent Bb Fellowship Ch (G-2726)*

Beck Jr Thomas D Do.. 302 541-4500
   88 Atlantic Ave Ocean View (19970) *(G-12475)*

Becker Morgan Group Inc... 302 734-7950
   309 S Governors Ave Dover (19904) *(G-1902)*

Beckers Chimney and Roofg LLC.. 302 463-8294
   209 Main St Wilmington (19804) *(G-14811)*

Becks Masonry.. 302 231-8872
   26395 W Pintail Rd Millsboro (19966) *(G-8190)*

Becoming Bio Inc.. 415 980-9796
   651 N Broad St Ste 201 Middletown (19709) *(G-6907)*

Bee A Queen Inc.. 267 235-8415
   73 Cantwell Dr Middletown (19709) *(G-6908)*

Bee Wise LLC... 302 601-4171
   20028 John J Williams Hwy Lewes (19958) *(G-5746)*

Beebe Healthcare... 302 249-1448
   26179 Manor Way Georgetown (19947) *(G-4229)*

Beebe Healthcare... 302 934-5052
   28538 Dupont Blvd Unit 2 Millsboro (19966) *(G-8191)*

Beebe Healthcare, Lewes *Also Called: Beebe Medical Center Inc (G-5750)*

Beebe Hospital Hs.. 302 645-3565
   424 E Savannah Rd Lewes (19958) *(G-5747)*

Beebe Imaging, Georgetown *Also Called: Beebe Medical Center Inc (G-4231)*

Beebe Lab Express Georgetown.. 302 856-9729
   21635 Biden Ave Unit 101 Georgetown (19947) *(G-4230)*

Beebe Lab Express Millboro.. 302 934-5052
   28538 Dupont Blvd Unit 2 Millsboro (19966) *(G-8192)*

Beebe Medical Center Inc... 302 856-9729
   21635 Biden Ave Georgetown (19947) *(G-4231)*

Beebe Medical Center Inc (PA)... 302 645-3300
   424 Savannah Rd Lewes (19958) *(G-5748)*

Beebe Medical Center Inc... 302 645-3300
   440 Market St Lewes (19958) *(G-5749)*

Beebe Medical Center Inc... 302 645-3629
   431 Savannah Rd Bldg C Lewes (19958) *(G-5750)*

Beebe Medical Center Inc... 302 393-2056
   810 Seabury Ave Milford (19963) *(G-7790)*

Beebe Medical Center Inc... 302 947-9767
   Long Neck Rd Millsboro (19966) *(G-8193)*

Beebe Medical Center Inc... 302 541-4175
   32550 Docs Pl Millville (19967) *(G-8519)*

Beebe Medical Center Inc... 302 645-3100
   18947 John J Williams Hwy Unit 201 # 20 Rehoboth Beach (19971) *(G-12635)*

Beebe Medical Center Inc... 302 645-3289
   38149 Terrace Rd Rehoboth Beach (19971) *(G-12636)*

Beebe Medical Center Inc... 302 645-3010
   18941 John J Williams Hwy Rehoboth Beach (19971) *(G-12637)*

BEEBE MEDICAL CENTER HOME HEAL, Lewes *Also Called: Beebe Physician Network Inc (G-5751)*

Beebe Medical Ctr HM Hlth Svc, Lewes *Also Called: Beebe Medical Center Inc (G-5748)*

Beebe Physician Network Inc.. 302 645-1805
   1515 Savannah Rd Ste 103 Lewes (19958) *(G-5751)*

Beebe School of Nursing... 302 645-3251
   424 Savannah Rd Lewes (19958) *(G-5752)*

Beebz Inc... 832 692-7558
   221 N Broad St Ste 3a Middletown (19709) *(G-6909)*

Beecanvas Inc.. 415 800-4980
   2035 Sunset Lake Rd Ste B2 Newark (19702) *(G-10009)*

Beejug Games LLC... 310 382-0746
   16192 Coastal Hwy Lewes (19958) *(G-5753)*

Beeline Services LLC.. 302 376-7399
   865 Vance Neck Rd Middletown (19709) *(G-6910)*

Beetles Playhouse Day Care.. 302 593-7321
   1 Coronet Ct Newark (19713) *(G-10010)*

Beetronics Inc.. 302 455-2070
   2093 Philadelphia Pike # 4945 Claymont (19703) *(G-1055)*

Beez Drivers Inc.. 917 392-9111
   838 Walker Rd Ste 21-2 Dover (19904) *(G-1903)*

Before & After Entrmt LLC.. 302 857-9659
   486 Joseph Wick Dr Smyrna (19977) *(G-13660)*

Beforesunset Inc.. 812 341-0038
   24a Trolley Sq Wilmington (19806) *(G-14812)*

Beginners Choice Day Care Ctr... 302 436-4460
   38081 Community Ln Selbyville (19975) *(G-13475)*

Beginning... 302 491-6545
   303 Moyer Cir W Milford (19963) *(G-7791)*

Beginning Blessings Daycare, New Castle *Also Called: Beginning Blssngs Chldcare LLC (G-8857)*

Beginning Blssngs Chldcare LLC... 302 893-1726
   23 Karen Ct New Castle (19720) *(G-8857)*

Beginnings & Beyond Nurery Sch.. 302 678-0445
   710 Buckson Dr Dover (19901) *(G-1904)*

Beginnings and Beyond Inc..302 734-2464
  402 Cowgill St Dover (19901) *(G-1905)*

Behavioral Health Center Inc..808 944-6900
  33316 Heavenly Way Ocean View (19970) *(G-12476)*

Behind Closed Doors, Ocean View Also Called: Artisan Interiors Group LLC *(G-12464)*

Beholder Agency LLC..302 455-2451
  200 Continental Dr Ste 401 Newark (19713) *(G-10011)*

Bekart Holding LLC..302 600-7000
  1201 N Orange St Ste 7524 Wilmington (19801) *(G-14813)*

Belcher-Timme Dr Zoe..215 266-5859
  52 Omega Dr Newark (19713) *(G-10012)*

Belchim Crop Prtection US Corp (HQ)..302 407-3590
  2751 Centerville Rd Ste 100 Wilmington (19808) *(G-14814)*

Belco Inc..302 655-1561
  909 Delaware Ave Wilmington (19806) *(G-14815)*

Belfint Lyons & Shuman PA..302 225-0600
  1011 Ctr Rd Ste 310 Wilmington (19805) *(G-14816)*

Belkins Inc..302 261-5393
  8 The Grn Ste 4331 Dover (19901) *(G-1906)*

Bell Buoy Motel..302 227-6000
  21 Vandyke St Dewey Beach (19971) *(G-1665)*

Bell Funeral Home..302 658-1555
  909 Clifford Brown Walk Wilmington (19801) *(G-14817)*

Bell Info Solutions LLC..302 541-1200
  3522 Silverside Rd Ste 30 Wilmington (19810) *(G-14818)*

Bell Manufacturing Company Inc..302 703-2684
  31971 Carneros Ave Lewes (19958) *(G-5754)*

Bell Painting, Newark Also Called: Bell Painting and Wall Cvg Inc *(G-10013)*

Bell Painting and Wall Cvg Inc..302 738-8854
  667 Dawson Dr Ste F Newark (19713) *(G-10013)*

Bell Rock Capital LLC (DH)..302 227-7607
  35568 Airport Rd Rehoboth Beach (19971) *(G-12638)*

Bell Rock Capital Llc..302 227-7607
  35568 Airport Rd Rehoboth Beach (19971) *(G-12639)*

Bella Donna Spa..703 313-7945
  5 S Branch Way Rehoboth Beach (19971) *(G-12640)*

Bella Hvac..302 561-4025
  3 Linette Ct Newark (19702) *(G-10014)*

Bella Medispa Inc..302 736-6334
  435 S Dupont Hwy Dover (19901) *(G-1907)*

Bella Mia Aesthetics LLC..302 548-0660
  111 W Main St Middletown (19709) *(G-6911)*

Bella Terra Landscapes LLC..302 422-9000
  21429 Bella Terra Dr Lincoln (19960) *(G-6658)*

Bella Terra Nursery & Grdn Ctr..302 422-9000
  13482 Spicer Rd Ellendale (19941) *(G-3910)*

Bella Tile and Stone LLC..302 275-4550
  802 Archer Pl Bear (19701) *(G-67)*

Bellaa Bomb LLC..800 409-2521
  3911 Concord Pike Unit 8030 Wilmington (19803) *(G-14819)*

Bellaline Design LLC..302 293-5676
  106 Loretta Ln Bear (19701) *(G-68)*

Bellawood Kennels LLC..302 738-0864
  2131 Pleasant Valley Rd Newark (19702) *(G-10015)*

Bellbuoy Inn, Dewey Beach Also Called: Bell Buoy Motel *(G-1665)*

Belle Energie LLC..302 690-3188
  37 Richard Lee Ct Dover (19904) *(G-1908)*

Bellevue Community Center..302 762-1391
  500 Duncan Rd Ofc A Wilmington (19809) *(G-14820)*

Bellevue Contractors LLC..302 655-1522
  909 Delaware Ave Wilmington (19806) *(G-14821)*

Bellevue Heart Group LLC..302 468-4500
  1508 Pennsylvania Ave Ste 2a Wilmington (19806) *(G-14822)*

Bellevue Realty Co..302 655-1818
  909 Delaware Ave Wilmington (19806) *(G-14823)*

Bellevue State Park, Wilmington Also Called: Delaware Div Parks Recreation *(G-15910)*

Bellmoor, The, Rehoboth Beach Also Called: Coastal Properties I LLC *(G-12686)*

Bells of Hope, Historic New Castle Also Called: Dimarquez Intl Ministries Inc *(G-4975)*

Belluno Manager LLC..650 395-8185
  251 Little Falls Dr Wilmington (19808) *(G-14824)*

Bellwether Behavioral Health..856 769-2042
  750 Shipyard Dr Ste 213 Wilmington (19801) *(G-14825)*

Belmont Villa Condominiums..302 368-1633
  60 Welsh Tract Rd Ste 2b Newark (19713) *(G-10016)*

Belsham Technologies, Wilmington Also Called: Symbiosys Consulting LLC *(G-20181)*

Belusko Siding & Windows..302 366-8783
  30 Donegal Ct Newark (19711) *(G-10017)*

Bemark Associates..302 373-6417
  104 W Mill Station Dr Newark (19711) *(G-10018)*

Ben-Dom Printing Company..302 737-9144
  35 Salem Church Rd Ste 43e Newark (19713) *(G-10019)*

Bench Accounting Inc..888 760-1940
  874 Walker Rd Dover (19904) *(G-1909)*

Bench Walk Advisors LLC (PA)..302 426-2100
  123 S Justison St 7th Fl Wilmington (19801) *(G-14826)*

Benchmark Builders Inc (PA)..302 995-6945
  818 First State Blvd Wilmington (19804) *(G-14827)*

Benchmark Transmission Inc..302 792-2300
  2610 Philadelphia Pike Ste 1a Claymont (19703) *(G-1056)*

Benchmark Transmissions..302 221-5380
  1 Merit Dr Historic New Castle (19720) *(G-4940)*

Benchmark Transmissions, Newark Also Called: Powertrain Technology Inc *(G-11719)*

Benchmark Transmissions Inc..302 999-9400
  1301 Centerville Rd Wilmington (19808) *(G-14828)*

Benco..302 650-0053
  1914 Julian Rd Wilmington (19803) *(G-14829)*

Bender..302 366-8637
  501 E Hanna Dr Newark (19702) *(G-10020)*

Bender Farms Llc..302 349-5574
  13060 Bender Farm Rd Greenwood (19950) *(G-4596)*

Bendom Printing, Newark Also Called: Ben-Dom Printing Company *(G-10019)*

Bene Market LLC..717 357-4117
  1201 N Market St Wilmington (19801) *(G-14830)*

Benefactory Ventures Inc..646 693-6186
  2035 Sunset Lake Rd B2 Newark (19702) *(G-10021)*

Beneficial, Wilmington Also Called: Beneficial Consumer Disc Co *(G-14831)*

Beneficial, Wilmington Also Called: Beneficial Oklahoma Inc *(G-14832)*

Beneficial Consumer Disc Co (DH)..302 425-2500
  301 N Walnut St Wilmington (19801) *(G-14831)*

Beneficial Oklahoma Inc (DH)..302 529-8701
  301 N Walnut St Wilmington (19801) *(G-14832)*

Benefit Services Unlimited..302 479-5696
  2500 Grubb Rd Ste 140 Wilmington (19810) *(G-14833)*

Benepass Inc..917 540-2391
  2093 Philadelphia Pike Claymont (19703) *(G-1057)*

Beneree Inc..814 526-4238
  651 N Broad St Ste 201 Middletown (19709) *(G-6912)*

Benesch Attorneys At Law..302 442-7005
  222 Delaware Ave Wilmington (19801) *(G-14834)*

Benesch Frdlnder Cplan Arnoff..216 363-4500
  1313 N Market St Fl 12 Wilmington (19801) *(G-14835)*

Benevlent Prtctive Order Elks..302 629-2458
  8846 Elks Rd Seaford (19973) *(G-13082)*

Benevlent Prtctive Order Elks..302 736-1903
  200 Saulsbury Rd Dover (19904) *(G-1910)*

Benga Inc..617 579-8636
  2093 Philadelphia Pike Ste 3620 Claymont (19703) *(G-1058)*

Benjamin B Smith Builders Inc..302 537-1916
  54 Central Ave Ocean View (19970) *(G-12477)*

Benjamin F Rich Company, Newark Also Called: BF Rich Co Inc *(G-10030)*

Benjamin M D Cooper..302 652-3331
  410 Foulk Rd Ste 203 Wilmington (19803) *(G-14836)*

Benjamin W Keenan..302 654-1888
  500 Delaware Ave Ste 800 Wilmington (19801) *(G-14837)*

Benjamin Wolf Group LLC..302 487-1827
  8 The Grn Ste 11166 Dover (19901) *(G-1911)*

Benlick Freight Forwarders LLC..302 743-4990
  322 Jaymar Blvd Newark (19702) *(G-10022)*

Bennett Det Prtective Agcy Inc (PA)..302 734-2480
  335 Martin St Dover (19901) *(G-1912)*

Bennett Electric, Frankford Also Called: Wayne Bennett *(G-4158)*

Bennett Farms Inc..302 684-1627
  24139 Sugar Hill Rd Milford (19963) *(G-7792)*

ALPHABETIC SECTION

Bennett Realty, Bethany Beach *Also Called: D M F Associates Inc (G-592)*
Bennett Security Service, Dover *Also Called: Bennett Det Prtective Agcy Inc (G-1912)*
Bennett Services Inc.. 302 656-4107
   412 Rogers Rd Wilmington (19801) *(G-14838)*
Bennie Smith Funeral Home Inc (PA).................................... 302 678-8747
   717 W Division St Dover (19904) *(G-1913)*
Bennie Smith Funeral Home Inc.. 302 934-9019
   216 S Washington St Millsboro (19966) *(G-8194)*
Benny Bennett Contracting.. 302 290-1613
   637 S Huckleberry Ave Bear (19701) *(G-69)*
Beno Inc.. 814 796-7686
   651 N Broad St Middletown (19709) *(G-6913)*
Benoit Home Improvements LLC.. 302 633-9284
   103 Westgate Dr Wilmington (19808) *(G-14839)*
Benson Concrete Cnstr LLC... 410 382-5112
   26500 Asbury Rd Seaford (19973) *(G-13083)*
Bentley Mills Inc.. 800 423-4709
   2711 Centerville Rd Ste 400 Wilmington (19808) *(G-14840)*
Benz Hydraulic Service, New Castle *Also Called: Benz Hydraulics Inc (G-8858)*
Benz Hydraulics Inc (PA)... 302 328-6648
   153 S Dupont Hwy New Castle (19720) *(G-8858)*
Beox LLC
   501 Silverside Rd Ste 105 Wilmington (19809) *(G-14841)*
Beracah Homes Inc.. 302 349-4561
   9590 Nanticoke Business Park Dr Greenwood (19950) *(G-4597)*
Beracah Sales Office.. 302 854-6700
   18427 Josephs Rd Milton (19968) *(G-8571)*
Berkana Defense Security LLC... 302 504-4455
   2711 Centerville Rd Wilmington (19808) *(G-14842)*
Berkelyn Inc.. 360 609-4981
   16192 Coastal Hwy Lewes (19958) *(G-5755)*
Berkshire At Limestone... 302 635-7495
   1526 Braken Ave Wilmington (19808) *(G-14843)*
Berkshire Hataway Home Svcs.. 302 235-6431
   88 Lantana Dr Hockessin (19707) *(G-5132)*
Berkshire Hathaway Global.. 302 477-5500
   2200 Concord Pike Fl 1 Wilmington (19803) *(G-14844)*
Berkshire Hathaway Home.. 302 227-6554
   37230 Rehoboth Avenue Ext Rehoboth Beach (19971) *(G-12641)*
Berkshire Hathaway Home Servic.. 302 373-7220
   850 Library Ave Newark (19711) *(G-10023)*
Berley Security Systems Inc... 302 791-9056
   6701 Governor Printz Blvd Wilmington (19809) *(G-14845)*
Berman Loren MD.. 302 651-4000
   1600 Rockland Rd Wilmington (19803) *(G-14846)*
Berman Development Corp.. 302 323-1197
   30 Highland Blvd New Castle (19720) *(G-8859)*
Bernard Hopkins Boxing Inc... 302 239-7170
   38 Lakewood Cir Newark (19711) *(G-10024)*
Bernard Limpert.. 302 674-8280
   1465 S Governors Ave Dover (19904) *(G-1914)*
Bernard Personnel, Wilmington *Also Called: BP Staffing Inc (G-15021)*
Bernard Ruth Sgel Jwish Cmnty.. 302 478-5660
   101 Garden Of Eden Rd Ste 102 Wilmington (19803) *(G-14847)*
Bernardon LLC.. 302 622-9550
   123 S Justison St Ste 101 Wilmington (19801) *(G-14848)*
Bernices Edctl Schl Age Ctr In.. 302 651-0286
   2516 W 4th St Wilmington (19805) *(G-14849)*
Bernies Foundation Inc... 302 750-7111
   1523 W 6th St Wilmington (19805) *(G-14850)*
Berrodin Auto Parts, New Castle *Also Called: Tabor Auto Parts Inc (G-9615)*
Berrodin Co... 302 395-1100
   100 Naamans Rd Ste 4d Claymont (19703) *(G-1059)*
Berrodin Parts Warehouse, Claymont *Also Called: Berrodin Co (G-1059)*
Berrodin South Inc... 302 575-0500
   20 Mccullough Dr New Castle (19720) *(G-8860)*
Berry Global Inc.. 302 378-9853
   801 Industrial Dr Middletown (19709) *(G-6914)*
Berry International Inc.. 302 674-1300
   606 Pear St Unit 1 Dover (19904) *(G-1915)*
Berry Refrigeration Co... 302 733-0933
   2 Garfield Way Newark (19713) *(G-10025)*

Berry Van Lines, Dover *Also Called: Diamond State Corporation (G-2294)*
Besecure LLC.. 855 897-0650
   16192 Coastal Hwy Lewes (19958) *(G-5756)*
Beshore Lawn Service LLC... 302 313-6924
   251 Union Church Rd Townsend (19734) *(G-13963)*
Bessemer Trust Company Del NA (PA).................................. 212 708-9182
   20 Montchanin Rd Ste 1500 Wilmington (19807) *(G-14851)*
Best Periodt LLC.. 302 291-2275
   8 The Grn Ste 12587 Dover (19901) *(G-1916)*
Best Buddies International Inc... 302 691-3187
   1401 Pennsylvania Ave Ste 104 Wilmington (19806) *(G-14852)*
Best Choice LLC.. 302 722-4249
   209 Skelton Dr New Castle (19720) *(G-8861)*
Best Custom Exhaust... 302 278-3555
   20983 Dupont Blvd Georgetown (19947) *(G-4232)*
Best Egg, Wilmington *Also Called: Best Egg Technologies LLC (G-14853)*
Best Egg Technologies LLC.. 302 358-2730
   3419 Silverside Rd Wilmington (19810) *(G-14853)*
Best High Technologies LLC.. 917 742-6658
   200 Continental Dr Ste 401 Newark (19713) *(G-10026)*
Best Holding LLC... 302 691-6023
   103 Foulk Rd Wilmington (19803) *(G-14854)*
Best Office Pros.. 302 629-4561
   26082 Butler Branch Rd Seaford (19973) *(G-13084)*
Best Planet Science LLC... 754 200-1913
   1209 N Orange St Wilmington (19801) *(G-14855)*
Best Processing Solutions LLC... 212 739-7845
   1013 Centre Rd Ste 40 Wilmington (19805) *(G-14856)*
Best Roofing and Siding Co.. 302 678-5700
   5091 N Dupont Hwy Dover (19901) *(G-1917)*
Best Shot, Lewes *Also Called: American Responder Svcs LLC (G-5687)*
Best Stoneworks Inc... 302 765-3497
   3015 Bellevue Ave Wilmington (19802) *(G-14857)*
Best Stucco LLC... 302 650-3620
   304 Jefferson Ave New Castle (19720) *(G-8862)*
Best Value Inn, Millsboro *Also Called: Chudasama Enterprises LLC (G-8227)*
Best Veterinary Solutions Inc... 302 934-1109
   1381 Northern Ave Millsboro (19966) *(G-8195)*
Best Warehouse and Trnsp LLC.. 302 328-5371
   350 Anchor Mill Rd Historic New Castle (19720) *(G-4941)*
Best Western, Dover *Also Called: Mark One LLC (G-3019)*
Best Western, Rehoboth Beach *Also Called: Best Western Goldleaf Ht LLC (G-12642)*
Best Western Goldleaf Ht LLC... 302 226-1100
   1400 Hwy 1 Rehoboth Beach (19971) *(G-12642)*
Best Western Plus, Bear *Also Called: Bear Hospitality Inc (G-64)*
Best Western Smyrna Inn, Smyrna *Also Called: 190 Stadium LLC (G-13623)*
Bestemps... 302 674-4357
   385 W North St Dover (19904) *(G-1918)*
Bestemps Career Asso Resume Sv, Dover *Also Called: Career Associates Inc (G-2029)*
Bestemps of Dover, Dover *Also Called: Bestemps (G-1918)*
Bestfield Associates Inc... 302 633-6361
   200 Mary Ella Dr Wilmington (19805) *(G-14858)*
Bestfield Homes, Wilmington *Also Called: Bestfield Associates Inc (G-14858)*
Bestfield Properties LLC.. 302 658-1000
   1424 N Clayton St Wilmington (19806) *(G-14859)*
Bestrans Inc... 302 824-0909
   19 Davidson Ln Frnt Frnt New Castle (19720) *(G-8863)*
Bet.works, Lewes *Also Called: Betworks Corporation (G-5760)*
Beth A Canalichio Lcsw Ltd.. 302 734-7760
   884 Walker Rd Ste C Dover (19904) *(G-1919)*
Beth A Canalichio Lcsw Ltd (PA)... 302 734-7760
   863 Buttner Pl Dover (19904) *(G-1920)*
Beth A Renzulli M D.. 302 449-0420
   102 Sleepy Hollow Dr Ste 200 Middletown (19709) *(G-6915)*
Beth R Schubert MD.. 302 224-9400
   875 Aaa Blvd Newark (19713) *(G-10027)*
Beth Stewart Vo LLC.. 302 540-7782
   127 Alders Dr Wilmington (19803) *(G-14860)*
Beth Trucking Inc... 918 814-2970
   129 Crikmoe Blvd Newark (19702) *(G-10028)*

Bethany Area Realty 302 539-7500
   778 Garfield Pkwy Bethany Beach (19930) *(G-578)*

Bethany Bch Hair Snippery Inc 302 539-8344
   32566 Docs Pl Unit 6 Millville (19967) *(G-8520)*

Bethany Bch Ocean Stes Rsdnce 302 539-3201
   99 Hollywood St Bethany Beach (19930) *(G-579)*

Bethany Beach Bed & Breakfast 301 651-2278
   33391 Ocean Pines Ln Bethany Beach (19930) *(G-580)*

Bethany Beach Cleaning LLC 302 858-6524
   29 Atlantic Ave Ste L Ocean View (19970) *(G-12478)*

Bethany Beach Goods & Rentals 207 266-1682
   163 Scannell Blvd Bethany Beach (19930) *(G-581)*

Bethany Beach Vacation Rentals 302 539-9400
   39682 Sunrise Ct Bethany Beach (19930) *(G-582)*

Bethany Beach Vlntr Fire Co (PA) 302 539-7700
   215 Hollywood St Bethany Beach (19930) *(G-583)*

Bethany Blooms 302 829-8578
   27 Indian Hill Ln Ocean View (19970) *(G-12479)*

Bethany Cycle & Fitness Inc (PA) 302 537-9982
   792b Garfield Pkwy Bethany Beach (19930) *(G-584)*

Bethany Cycle and Fitness, Bethany Beach *Also Called: Bethany Cycle & Fitness Inc (G-584)*

Bethany Fenwick Area Cham 302 537-3839
   5 Main St Frankford (19945) *(G-4071)*

Bethany Forest Hoa 302 645-7242
   34634 Bay Crossing Blvd Lewes (19958) *(G-5757)*

Bethany Plumbing and Heating 302 539-1022
   37949 Muddy Neck Rd Ocean View (19970) *(G-12480)*

Bethany Resort Furn Whse 302 251-4101
   145 Dixon St Selbyville (19975) *(G-13476)*

Bethany Resort Furnishings 302 539-4000
   939 N Pennsylvania Ave Bethany Beach (19930) *(G-585)*

Bethany Resort Furnishings, Selbyville *Also Called: Bethany Resort Furn Whse (G-13476)*

Bethany Sea-Crest Inc 302 539-7621
   99 Atlantic Garfield Pkwy Bethany Beach (19930) *(G-586)*

Bethany Travel Inc 302 933-0955
   28436 Dupont Blvd Millsboro (19966) *(G-8196)*

Bethany-Fnwick Area Chmber Cmm 302 539-2100
   36913 Coastal Hwy Fenwick Island (19944) *(G-4042)*

Bethel Multimedia Dept 302 563-0918
   306 S Connell St Wilmington (19805) *(G-14861)*

Bethel United Methodist Church 302 645-9426
   129 W 4th St Lewes (19958) *(G-5758)*

Bethel Villa, Wilmington *Also Called: Bethel Villa Associates LP (G-14862)*

Bethel Villa Apartments, Wilmington *Also Called: Roizman & Associates Inc (G-19556)*

Bethel Villa Associates LP 302 426-9688
   506 E 5th St Fl 2 Wilmington (19801) *(G-14862)*

Bethesda Child Devmnt Ctr 302 378-8435
   116 E Main St Middletown (19709) *(G-6916)*

Bethrant Industries LLC 484 343-5435
   7 Midfield Rd New Castle (19720) *(G-8864)*

Betsson US Corp 800 316-6660
   1675 S State St Ste B Dover (19901) *(G-1921)*

Bettan Trucking LLC 302 841-3834
   19347 Beaver Dam Rd Lewes (19958) *(G-5759)*

Better Business Bureau of De 302 221-5255
   60 Reads Way New Castle (19720) *(G-8865)*

Better Business RE Inc 609 746-9833
   2803 Philadelphia Pike # 4036 Claymont (19703) *(G-1060)*

Better Days Properties LLC 718 644-0163
   204 Sheats Ln Middletown (19709) *(G-6917)*

Better Earth LLC 302 242-3644
   160 Greentree Dr Ste 101 Dover (19904) *(G-1922)*

Better Home Services 302 250-9860
   1183 Rose Dale Ln Dover (19904) *(G-1923)*

Better Homes Laurel II Inc 302 875-4282
   2900 Daniel St Laurel (19956) *(G-5469)*

Better Homes of Seaford Inc (PA) 302 629-8048
   101 Independence Dr Seaford (19973) *(G-13085)*

Better Homes of Seaford Inc 302 629-6522
   2 Chandler St Seaford (19973) *(G-13086)*

Better Life Chiropractic 302 535-9204
   1111 S Governors Ave Dover (19904) *(G-1924)*

Better Life Enerprise 302 312-9156
   187 Willamette Dr Bear (19701) *(G-70)*

Better Search Corporation 415 610-4825
   251 Little Falls Dr Wilmington (19808) *(G-14863)*

Betts and Biddle Eye Care PA 302 697-2151
   8500 Herring Run Rd Seaford (19973) *(G-13087)*

Betts Garage, Newark *Also Called: Betts Texaco and B & G GL Inc (G-10029)*

Betts Inc 302 475-3754
   3002 Fairhope Rd Wilmington (19810) *(G-14864)*

Betts Texaco and B & G GL Inc 302 834-2284
   2806 Pulaski Hwy Newark (19702) *(G-10029)*

Bettys 302 233-2675
   140 N Landing Dr Milford (19963) *(G-7793)*

Betworks Corporation (PA) 310 866-0365
   16192 Coastal Hwy Lewes (19958) *(G-5760)*

BETz&betz Enterprises LLC 302 602-0613
   528 W 3rd St Wilmington (19801) *(G-14865)*

Beverage Infosystems Ltd Lblty 732 762-5299
   501 Silverside Rd Ste 77 Wilmington (19809) *(G-14866)*

Beverage Trade Network, Wilmington *Also Called: Beverage Infosystems Ltd Lblty (G-14866)*

Beverly Bove Attorney At Law, Wilmington *Also Called: Beverly L Bove PA (G-14867)*

Beverly L Bove PA 302 777-3500
   1020 W 18th St Ste 2 Wilmington (19802) *(G-14867)*

Beverlys Helping Hands 302 651-9304
   400 W 9th St Ste 100 Wilmington (19801) *(G-14868)*

Bevs Crafting Supplies LLC 302 252-7583
   147 Quigley Blvd Historic New Castle (19720) *(G-4942)*

Bew Productions 302 547-8661
   1004 Berkeley Rd Wilmington (19807) *(G-14869)*

Bewitched, Dover *Also Called: Actors Attic (G-1714)*

Bey Hollywood LLC 209 789-5132
   8 The Grn Ste R Dover (19901) *(G-1925)*

Beyond Details 302 223-6156
   117 Cool Breeze Dr Clayton (19938) *(G-1354)*

Beyond Expected LLC 302 384-1205
   391 Harbor Dr Apt 5 Claymont (19703) *(G-1061)*

Beyond Fifty, Townsend *Also Called: Retired-N-Fit (G-14058)*

Beyond Gutters Inc 302 999-1422
   2002 Wildwood Dr Wilmington (19805) *(G-14870)*

Beyond Ledger LLC 313 471-0462
   8 The Grn Ste A Dover (19901) *(G-1926)*

BF Rich Co Inc 302 369-2512
   322 Ruthar Dr Newark (19711) *(G-10030)*

Bfb Hospitality LLC 302 829-1418
   30415 Cedar Neck Rd Ocean View (19970) *(G-12481)*

Bfc Investors Trust 302 636-6466
   1100 N Market St Wilmington (19890) *(G-14871)*

Bfe, Wilmington *Also Called: Bank Fillers Entertainment LLC (G-14747)*

Bfpe International Inc 302 346-4800
   155 Commerce Way Dover (19904) *(G-1927)*

Bg Laboratory 302 535-3954
   383 Mockingbird Ave Dover (19904) *(G-1928)*

Bg Welding LLC 302 228-7260
   14047 Redden Rd Bridgeville (19933) *(G-672)*

Bgdedge Inc 302 477-1734
   62 Southgate Blvd New Castle (19720) *(G-8866)*

Bgm Compliance LLC 302 450-1149
   8 The Grn Ste 7485 Dover (19901) *(G-1929)*

Bgp Publicity Inc 302 234-9500
   3106 Centerville Rd Wilmington (19807) *(G-14872)*

Bhakti Consulting LLC 302 742-1964
   614 N Dupont Hwy Ste 200 Dover (19901) *(G-1930)*

Bhaoo Inc 832 888-3694
   8 The Grn Dover (19901) *(G-1931)*

Bhapi Inc 859 475-1924
   2810 N Church St Wilmington (19802) *(G-14873)*

Bhaskar Palekar MD PA 302 645-1805
   1526 Savannah Rd Ste 1 Lewes (19958) *(G-5761)*

Bhhs Fox & Roach Brandywine, Wilmington *Also Called: Berkshire Hathaway Global (G-14844)*

Bi Solutions Group LLC 253 366-5173
   1000 N West St Wilmington (19801) *(G-14874)*

ALPHABETIC SECTION

Bi-State Feeders LLC 302 398-3408
16054 S Dupont Hwy Harrington (19952) *(G-4740)*

Bia Separations Inc 510 740-4045
1000 N West St Ste 1200 Wilmington (19801) *(G-14875)*

Biad, Dover *Also Called: Brain Injury Association Del (G-1970)*

Biamby Cleaning Services 302 519-1604
15453 Weigelia Dr Georgetown (19947) *(G-4233)*

Biblion 302 644-2210
205 2nd St Ste 6 Lewes (19958) *(G-5762)*

Bid 4 Lease Corp 302 244-9943
3616 Kirkwood Hwy Ste A # 1285 Wilmington (19808) *(G-14876)*

Bid On Energy LLC 302 360-8110
16192 Coastal Hwy Lewes (19958) *(G-5763)*

Bidc, Camden *Also Called: Burkhan International Dev Corp (G-796)*

Biden For AG Inc 302 295-8340
4 E 8th St Wilmington (19801) *(G-14877)*

BIDERMAN GOLF CLUB, Wilmington *Also Called: Hunt Vicmead Club (G-17234)*

Bidermann Golf Course, Wilmington *Also Called: Hunt Vicmead Club (G-17233)*

Bidr TV LLC 561 569-0931
3411 Silverside Rd 104b Wilmington (19810) *(G-14878)*

Bielli & Klauder LLC 302 803-4600
1204 N King St Wilmington (19801) *(G-14879)*

Bifferato Gentilotti LLC (PA) 302 429-1900
4250 Lancaster Pike Ste 130 Wilmington (19805) *(G-14880)*

Big Box USA LLC 302 595-3324
459 Carson Dr Bear (19701) *(G-71)*

Big Brthers Big Sisters of Del 302 998-3577
1001 S Bradford St Ste 1 Dover (19904) *(G-1932)*

Big Cats Foundation 302 897-7140
617 5th St Newark (19711) *(G-10031)*

Big Centric, Wilmington *Also Called: Dongjin Usa Inc (G-16140)*

Big Data Elements LLC (PA) 917 620-2337
8 The Grn Ste A Dover (19901) *(G-1933)*

Big Day Trucking LLC 302 900-1190
8 The Grn Ste 14688 Dover (19901) *(G-1934)*

Big Eld LLC 302 549-0333
8 The Grn Dover (19901) *(G-1935)*

Big Fish Wholesale LLC (PA) 302 226-3474
37369 Martin St Rehoboth Beach (19971) *(G-12643)*

Big Fish Wholesales Sea Fd Co, Rehoboth Beach *Also Called: Big Fish Wholesale LLC (G-12643)*

Big Jims Trucking 214 504-1320
73 Hitch Pond Cir Seaford (19973) *(G-13088)*

Big Moose Exterior LLC 302 722-1969
1057 Boyds Corner Rd Middletown (19709) *(G-6918)*

Big Plan Inc (PA) 910 556-9311
108 W 13th St Wilmington (19801) *(G-14881)*

Big Sofa Technologies Inc 630 839-9332
874 Walker Rd Ste C Dover (19904) *(G-1936)*

Big Springs Inc 443 570-3003
1209 N Orange St Wilmington (19801) *(G-14882)*

Big Tomorrow LLC 650 714-3912
800 Delaware Ave Wilmington (19801) *(G-14883)*

Big Toy Custom Car Care Inc 302 668-6729
1806 Tulip St Wilmington (19805) *(G-14884)*

Big Wlly Style Productions LLC 973 897-8661
5 Nicole Ct New Castle (19720) *(G-8867)*

Bigben1613 LLC 305 926-3872
1400 Vandever Ave Wilmington (19802) *(G-14885)*

Bigcentric Appliance 302 691-8510
151 Edgemoor Rd Wilmington (19809) *(G-14886)*

Bigcentric Inc 410 456-1968
151 Edgemoor Rd Wilmington (19809) *(G-14887)*

Bigcloud Solutions Inc 917 972-6891
260 Chapman Rd Ste 206 Newark (19702) *(G-10032)*

Biggs & Battaglia 302 655-9677
921 N Orange St Wilmington (19801) *(G-14888)*

Biginsights LLC 618 819-0902
8 The Grn Ste A Dover (19901) *(G-1937)*

Bigthinx Inc (PA) 401 300-0494
651 N Broad St Middletown (19709) *(G-6919)*

Bihbrand Inc 302 223-4330
16192 Coastal Hwy Lewes (19958) *(G-5764)*

Bijan K Sorouri MD 302 652-1218
4014 Kennett Pike Wilmington (19807) *(G-14889)*

Bijin 302 777-4040
31 Sharons Way Wilmington (19808) *(G-14890)*

Bijoti Inc 908 916-7764
1808 N Washington St Wilmington (19802) *(G-14891)*

Bilingual Access Media LLC 302 738-4782
2 Rolling Dr Newark (19713) *(G-10033)*

Bill Burris Insurance 302 239-6661
7217 Lancaster Pike Ste B Hockessin (19707) *(G-5133)*

Bill Cannon's Garage, Selbyville *Also Called: Bill Cannons Garage Inc (G-13477)*

Bill Cannons Garage Inc 302 436-4200
Rd 2 Box 125 A Rt 113 North Selbyville (19975) *(G-13477)*

Bill Johnson Contracting 302 245-4708
29028 Black Pepper Ln Georgetown (19947) *(G-4234)*

Bill Luke Team, Wilmington *Also Called: Real Estate Partners LLC (G-19367)*

Bill M Douthat Jr 407 977-2273
17468 Slipper Shell Way Unit 16 Lewes (19958) *(G-5765)*

Bill Torbert 302 734-9804
347 Lake Como Cir Smyrna (19977) *(G-13661)*

Billie Stevens Carlins 302 436-0856
32427 Mccary Rd Frankford (19945) *(G-4072)*

Billows Electric Supply Co Inc 302 996-9133
480 First State Blvd Wilmington (19804) *(G-14892)*

Bills Home Care Service LLC 302 526-2071
160 Beech Dr Dover (19904) *(G-1938)*

Billy Warren & Son LLC 302 349-5767
7040 Hickman Rd Greenwood (19950) *(G-4598)*

Bilski, William F Do, Newark *Also Called: Family Doctors (G-10708)*

Binary Technology LLC 302 455-7400
8 The Grn Ste R Dover (19901) *(G-1939)*

Bing Rchel Zhang Fmly Fndation 302 294-1859
314 Oracle Rd Wilmington (19808) *(G-14893)*

Bingebuilder Inc 415 529-8306
18585 Coastal Hwy Unit 102006 Rehoboth Beach (19971) *(G-12644)*

Bingnear Cleaning 302 519-7318
26034 Redwing Ln Millsboro (19966) *(G-8197)*

Bio Medic Corporation (PA) 302 628-4300
742 Sussex Ave Seaford (19973) *(G-13089)*

Bio Reference Laboratories 302 223-6896
100 S Main St Smyrna (19977) *(G-13662)*

Bio Riot Technologies Mfg Inc 407 399-3413
16192 Coastal Hwy Lewes (19958) *(G-5766)*

Bio-Diversified Ventures Inc 720 680-9418
910 Foulk Rd Ste 201 Wilmington (19803) *(G-14894)*

Bio-Mdical Applications of Del 302 998-7568
4923 Ogletown Stanton Rd Ste 210 Newark (19713) *(G-10034)*

Biobx Ltd 626 898-5814
651 N Broad St Ste 205-1772 Middletown (19709) *(G-6920)*

Biochek USA Corp 302 521-5554
109 Woodland Way Millsboro (19966) *(G-8198)*

Biomarker Associates Inc 302 239-7962
25 Meteor Ct Newark (19711) *(G-10035)*

Biomatik Usa LLC 800 836-8089
105 Silverside Rd 501 Wilmington (19809) *(G-14895)*

Biome Bioplastics Inc 917 724-2850
200 Continental Dr Ste 401 Newark (19713) *(G-10036)*

Biosion Usa Inc 302 257-5085
1 Innovation Way Ste 300 Newark (19711) *(G-10037)*

Biotech Mentor LLC 617 460-4983
8 The Grn Dover (19901) *(G-1940)*

Biotek Remedys Inc (PA) 877 246-9104
2 Penns Way Ste 404 New Castle (19720) *(G-8868)*

Bipgo Inc 708 586-9016
651 N Broad St Ste 206 Middletown (19709) *(G-6921)*

Birch Pointe Condo Assc 302 685-4310
3411 Haley Ct Wilmington (19808) *(G-14896)*

Birdie, Dover *Also Called: Birdie Ssot LLC (G-1941)*

Birdie Ssot LLC 857 361-6883
3500 S Dupont Hwy Dover (19901) *(G-1941)*

Birth Center — ALPHABETIC SECTION

Birth Center, Newark *Also Called: Birth Cnter Hlstic Wns Hlth CA* *(G-10038)*
Birth Cnter Hlstic Wns Hlth CA..................302 658-2229
620 Churchmans Rd Ste 101 Newark (19702) *(G-10038)*

Bishop Associates..................302 838-1270
1235 Peoples Plz Newark (19702) *(G-10039)*

Bishop Cleaning and Maint LLC..................302 277-8815
1023 King James Ct Bear (19701) *(G-72)*

Bishop Enterprises Corporation..................302 379-2884
2207 Concord Pike Ste 412 Wilmington (19803) *(G-14897)*

Bitcarter Inc..................518 512-9238
925 N Orange St Wilmington (19801) *(G-14898)*

Bits & Bytes Inc..................302 674-2999
2953 Dyke Branch Rd Dover (19901) *(G-1942)*

Bitta Monk Entertainment Inc..................916 969-4430
25 Winchester Rd Apt G Newark (19713) *(G-10040)*

Biya Global LLC..................302 645-7400
16192 Coastal Hwy Lewes (19958) *(G-5767)*

Bizdata Inc..................650 283-1644
3422 Old Capitol Trl Ste 45 Wilmington (19808) *(G-14899)*

Bizzy Bees Home Daycare LLC..................302 376-9245
815 S Cass St Middletown (19709) *(G-6922)*

Bjc-5 LLC..................302 230-6733
7 Jackie Cir Middletown (19709) *(G-6923)*

Bk Rentals..................302 331-1984
7667 Canterbury Rd Felton (19943) *(G-3946)*

Bk Temp Home Care..................302 575-1400
2101 N Tatnall St Wilmington (19802) *(G-14900)*

Bkl Ventures LLC..................302 317-2377
22 Cedar Farms Dr Newark (19702) *(G-10041)*

Bl Own UP LLC..................609 509-8388
18 Little Pond Dr Milford (19963) *(G-7794)*

Blab Studios LLC..................302 602-5211
2 Hempstead Dr Newark (19702) *(G-10042)*

Black & Decker Inc (DH)..................860 827-3861
1207 Drummond Plz Newark (19711) *(G-10043)*

Black Diamond Paving..................302 333-1987
252 N Patrice Dr Newark (19702) *(G-10044)*

Black Dog Construction LLC..................302 530-4967
1104 Oakland Ct Newark (19711) *(G-10045)*

Black Dragon Corporation..................617 470-9230
40 E Main St 1010 Newark (19711) *(G-10046)*

Black Feather Entrmt LLC..................248 787-8060
3911 Concord Pike # 803 Wilmington (19803) *(G-14901)*

Black Gods and Goddess LLC (PA)..................708 665-0949
8 The Grn Ste A Dover (19901) *(G-1943)*

Black Lotus Ventures LLC..................650 260-4684
8 The Grn Ste R Dover (19901) *(G-1944)*

Black Magic Sealcoating..................302 832-7906
214 Edgewood Dr Bear (19701) *(G-73)*

Black Math Labs Inc..................858 349-9446
8 The Grn Ste A Dover (19901) *(G-1945)*

Black Sea Contractor LLC..................856 558-1821
3 Waterford Ln Selbyville (19975) *(G-13478)*

Black Star General Contractors..................302 275-4533
56 Gill Dr Newark (19713) *(G-10047)*

Blackbird Community Assn Inc..................302 598-7447
120 Blackbird Forest Rd Townsend (19734) *(G-13964)*

Blackhouse Campaign LLC..................302 465-0980
804 W 24th St Wilmington (19802) *(G-14902)*

Blackrock 2022 Globl Income Op..................212 754-5560
100 Bellevue Pkwy Wilmington (19809) *(G-14903)*

Blackrock Advntage Esg Emrging..................302 797-2000
100 Bellevue Pkwy Wilmington (19809) *(G-14904)*

Blackrock Bond Fund Inc..................800 441-7762
100 Bellevue Pkwy Wilmington (19809) *(G-14905)*

Blackrock Cal Mnicpl Income Tr..................800 882-0052
100 Bellevue Pkwy Wilmington (19809) *(G-14906)*

Blackrock Capitl Allocation Tr..................800 882-0052
100 Bellevue Pkwy Wilmington (19809) *(G-14907)*

Blackrock Core Bond Trust..................800 882-0052
100 Bellevue Pkwy Wilmington (19809) *(G-14908)*

Blackrock Corp High Yeld Fund..................800 441-7762
100 Bellevue Pkwy Wilmington (19809) *(G-14909)*

Blackrock Cpitl Inv Advsors LL..................800 882-0052
100 Bellevue Pkwy Wilmington (19809) *(G-14910)*

Blackrock Emrging Mkts LNG/Sho..................302 797-2000
100 Bellevue Pkwy Wilmington (19809) *(G-14911)*

Blackrock Enhnced Globl Dvdend..................800 882-0052
100 Bellevue Pkwy Wilmington (19809) *(G-14912)*

Blackrock Fincl Institutions S..................800 441-7762
100 Bellevue Pkwy Wilmington (19809) *(G-14913)*

Blackrock Funds IV..................800 441-7762
100 Bellevue Pkwy Wilmington (19809) *(G-14914)*

Blackrock Funds V..................302 797-2000
100 Bellevue Pkwy Wilmington (19809) *(G-14915)*

Blackrock Future US Themes Etf..................302 797-2000
100 Bellevue Pkwy Wilmington (19809) *(G-14916)*

Blackrock Globl Smllcap Fund I..................800 441-7762
100 Bellevue Pkwy Wilmington (19809) *(G-14917)*

Blackrock Health Sciences Tr..................800 882-0052
100 Bellevue Pkwy Wilmington (19809) *(G-14918)*

Blackrock Hlth Sciences Tr II..................800 882-0052
100 Bellevue Pkwy Wilmington (19809) *(G-14919)*

Blackrock Income Trust Inc..................800 441-7762
100 Bellevue Pkwy Wilmington (19809) *(G-14920)*

Blackrock Instnl Mgt Corp..................302 797-2000
100 Bellevue Pkwy Wilmington (19809) *(G-14921)*

Blackrock LNG-Hrzon Eqity Fund..................800 441-7762
100 Bellevue Pkwy Wilmington (19809) *(G-14922)*

Blackrock Lrge Cap Grwth VI Fu..................302 797-2000
100 Bellevue Pkwy Wilmington (19809) *(G-14923)*

Blackrock Macro Themes Fund..................302 797-2000
100 Bellevue Pkwy Wilmington (19809) *(G-14924)*

Blackrock Midcap Index Fund..................302 797-2000
100 Bellevue Pkwy Wilmington (19809) *(G-14925)*

Blackrock Mlt-Sector Income Tr..................800 882-0052
100 Bellevue Pkwy Wilmington (19809) *(G-14926)*

Blackrock Mncpl 2030 Trget Ter..................800 882-0052
100 Bellevue Pkwy Wilmington (19809) *(G-14927)*

Blackrock Mncpl Income Inv Qlt..................800 441-7762
100 Bellevue Pkwy Wilmington (19809) *(G-14928)*

Blackrock Mnhldngs Cal Qlty Fu..................800 882-0052
100 Bellevue Pkwy Wilmington (19809) *(G-14929)*

Blackrock Mnhldngs NJ Qlty Fun..................800 882-0052
100 Bellevue Pkwy Wilmington (19809) *(G-14930)*

Blackrock Mnyeld Cal Qlty Fund..................800 882-0052
100 Bellevue Pkwy Wilmington (19809) *(G-14931)*

Blackrock Muniassets Fund Inc..................302 797-2000
100 Bellevue Pkwy Wilmington (19809) *(G-14932)*

Blackrock Municipal Bond Trust..................888 825-2257
100 Bellevue Pkwy Wilmington (19809) *(G-14933)*

Blackrock Municipal Income Tr..................888 882-0052
100 Bellevue Pkwy Wilmington (19809) *(G-14934)*

Blackrock Municpl Income Tr II..................302 797-2000
100 Bellevue Pkwy Wilmington (19809) *(G-14935)*

Blackrock Muniyield Fund Inc..................800 441-7762
100 Bellevue Pkwy Wilmington (19809) *(G-14936)*

Blackrock Natural Resources Tr..................212 810-5300
100 Bellevue Pkwy Wilmington (19809) *(G-14937)*

Blackrock NY Mncpl Income Qlty..................800 441-7762
100 Bellevue Pkwy Wilmington (19809) *(G-14938)*

Blackrock NY Mncpl Income Tr I..................800 441-7762
100 Bellevue Pkwy Wilmington (19809) *(G-14939)*

Blackrock NY Municpl Income Tr..................800 882-0052
100 Bellevue Pkwy Wilmington (19809) *(G-14940)*

Blackrock Science & Tech Tr..................302 797-2000
100 Bellevue Pkwy Wilmington (19809) *(G-14941)*

Blackrock Small Cap Gro..................302 797-2000
100 Bellevue Pkwy Wilmington (19809) *(G-14942)*

Blackrock Small Cap Grwth Fund..................212 810-5300
100 Bellevue Pkwy Wilmington (19809) *(G-14943)*

Blackrock SMD-Cap Grwth Eqity..................302 797-2000
100 Bellevue Pkwy Wilmington (19809) *(G-14944)*

ALPHABETIC SECTION

Blackrock Sstnble Blnced Prtfl... 800 537-4942
  100 Bellevue Pkwy Wilmington (19809) *(G-14945)*
Blackrock US Gvrnment Bond VI... 302 797-2000
  100 Bellevue Pkwy Wilmington (19809) *(G-14946)*
Blackrock Vlue Opprtnties VI F... 302 797-2000
  100 Bellevue Pkwy Wilmington (19809) *(G-14947)*
Blackstone Building Group.. 302 660-5528
  100 S Rockland Falls Rd Rockland (19732) *(G-13028)*
Blackstone Building Group LLC.. 302 824-4632
  1705 Lovering Ave Wilmington (19806) *(G-14948)*
Blacktop Sealcoating Inc.. 302 234-2243
  511 Paisley Pl Newark (19711) *(G-10048)*
Blackwell Hr Solutions.. 202 246-0084
  1601 Concord Pike Ste 78 Wilmington (19803) *(G-14949)*
Blackwell Solution... 302 660-2054
  128 Emerald Ridge Dr Bear (19701) *(G-74)*
Blackwells Welding Inc.. 301 498-5277
  15491 Lavinia St Milton (19968) *(G-8572)*
Blades H V A C Services... 302 539-4436
  32798 Swamp Rd Dagsboro (19939) *(G-1418)*
Blades Hvac Services.. 302 539-4436
  Rte 1 Pa Frankford (19945) *(G-4073)*
Blair Carmean Masonry... 302 934-6103
  24373 Gravel Hill Rd Georgetown (19947) *(G-4235)*
Blair A Jones DDS.. 302 226-1115
  34359 Carpenters Way Lewes (19958) *(G-5768)*
Blair Carmean & Sons Masonry.. 302 249-5783
  26624 Gravel Hill Rd Millsboro (19966) *(G-8199)*
Blair Computing Systems Inc... 302 453-8947
  500 Creek View Rd Ste 200 Newark (19711) *(G-10049)*
Blair Materials Inc... 815 278-0999
  6 Denny Rd Ste 200 Wilmington (19809) *(G-14950)*
Blak Mpire LLC... 803 966-7648
  16192 Coastal Hwy Lewes (19958) *(G-5769)*
Blake and Vaughan Engrg Inc... 302 888-1780
  800 Woodlawn Ave Wilmington (19805) *(G-14951)*
Blakgold Innovative Inc.. 302 220-0530
  96 Penrose Branch Rd Clayton (19938) *(G-1355)*
Blanca O Lim MD... 302 653-1669
  38 Deak Dr Smyrna (19977) *(G-13663)*
Blank Rome LLP.. 302 425-6400
  1201 N Market St Ste 800 Wilmington (19801) *(G-14952)*
Blaze Coin LLC.. 509 768-2249
  8 The Grn Ste B Dover (19901) *(G-1946)*
Blaze Systems Corporation.. 302 733-7235
  300 Creek View Rd Ste 204 Newark (19711) *(G-10050)*
Blb Services LLC... 678 989-7908
  251 Little Falls Dr Wilmington (19808) *(G-14953)*
Bleeks LLC... 443 990-0496
  3575 Silverside Rd # 101 Wilmington (19810) *(G-14954)*
Blend Network Inc.. 267 521-8845
  8 The Grn Dover (19901) *(G-1947)*
Blenheim Homes, Newark *Also Called: Blenheim Management Company (G-10051)*
Blenheim Hospitality LLC... 302 677-0900
  655 N Dupont Hwy Dover (19901) *(G-1948)*
Blenheim Management Company.. 302 254-0100
  220 Continental Dr Ste 410 Newark (19713) *(G-10051)*
Bless Ya Hart Cnslting Group L... 844 748-9017
  300 Delaware Ave Ste 210 Wilmington (19801) *(G-14955)*
Blessed Beginnings Lrng Ctr... 302 838-9112
  117 Portside Ct Bear (19701) *(G-75)*
Blessngs Grnhses Cmpost Fcilty... 302 684-8890
  9372 Draper Rd Milford (19963) *(G-7795)*
Bleu Safe Inc.. 619 416-6166
  300 Delaware Ave Ste 210a Wilmington (19801) *(G-14956)*
Blindsight Delaware LLC... 302 998-5913
  2915 Newport Gap Pike Wilmington (19808) *(G-14957)*
Blinqio Inc... 718 710-4529
  1007 N Orange St Wilmington (19801) *(G-14958)*
Blips Digital Inc.. 661 520-1539
  651 N Broad St Middletown (19709) *(G-6924)*
Bliss Stone Masonry.. 302 293-9194
  106 S Marshall St Wilmington (19804) *(G-14959)*
Blix Inc.. 347 753-8035
  40 E Main St Ste 556 Newark (19711) *(G-10052)*
BLJ&d Flagging Llc.. 302 272-0574
  820 Carvel Dr Apt J12 Dover (19901) *(G-1949)*
Blocksite LP... 302 449-4227
  1007 N Orange St Wilmington (19801) *(G-14960)*
Blockware Solutions LLC... 512 905-5209
  8 The Grn Dover (19901) *(G-1950)*
Blog - Care First Dental Team.. 302 741-2044
  1250 S Governors Ave Dover (19904) *(G-1951)*
Blog Expecting Miracles LLC... 302 533-6682
  500 Christiana Medical Ctr Newark (19702) *(G-10053)*
Blokhaus Inc.. 302 932-7704
  200 Continental Dr Ste 401 Newark (19713) *(G-10054)*
Blood Bank of Delmarva, Newark *Also Called: New York Blood Center Inc (G-11528)*
Bloom 415, Millville *Also Called: Suzette Noecker (G-8548)*
Bloom Consulting.. 302 584-1592
  2812 Landon Dr Wilmington (19810) *(G-14961)*
Bloom Daily Planners Inc... 302 607-2580
  500 Creek View Rd Ste 302 Newark (19711) *(G-10055)*
Bloom Energy Corporation... 408 543-1227
  200 Christina Pkwy Newark (19713) *(G-10056)*
Bloomfield Trucking Inc.. 302 834-6922
  Middletown (19709) *(G-6925)*
Blooming Speech.. 302 528-6663
  12 Peirce Rd Wilmington (19803) *(G-14962)*
Bloomvp Spav2 Co., Middletown *Also Called: Soutron Global Inc (G-7592)*
Blossic, Tamara DC, Hockessin *Also Called: Hockessin Chrpractic Centre PA (G-5241)*
Bluchill Inc... 302 658-2638
  19 Davidson Ln Bldg 7 New Castle (19720) *(G-8869)*
Blue Collar Utilities LLC... 410 422-0886
  7003 Seashore Hwy Bridgeville (19933) *(G-673)*
Blue Cross, Wilmington *Also Called: Highmarks Inc (G-17145)*
Blue Diamond Dental PA.. 302 655-8387
  2300 Pennsylvania Ave Ste 2c Wilmington (19806) *(G-14963)*
Blue Diamond Pools Inc... 302 265-2165
  5669 Galestown Reliance Rd Seaford (19973) *(G-13090)*
Blue Diamond RPS & Svcs LLC (PA)................................... 856 242-0480
  1500-1506 N Hills Wilmington (19802) *(G-14964)*
Blue Dmnd Hldg Investments LLC.. 302 588-8946
  501 N Spruce St Wilmington (19801) *(G-14965)*
Blue Falls Grove Inc.. 610 926-4017
  913 Kenilworth Ave Newark (19711) *(G-10057)*
Blue Fin Services LLC... 302 633-3354
  103 Water St Wilmington (19804) *(G-14966)*
Blue Hen Bzzrds Dspose-All Inc... 302 945-3500
  34026 Annas Way Unit 3 Millsboro (19966) *(G-8200)*
Blue Hen Car Wash... 302 273-2100
  1008 Capitol Trl Newark (19711) *(G-10058)*
Blue Hen CC LLC... 302 999-0708
  234 N James St Wilmington (19804) *(G-14967)*
Blue Hen Courier, Camden Wyoming *Also Called: Charles E Carlson (G-923)*
Blue Hen Dental LLC... 302 538-0448
  231 S Dupont Blvd Smyrna (19977) *(G-13664)*
Blue Hen Hospitality LLC (PA)... 302 530-5066
  4579 Kirkwood Hwy Wilmington (19808) *(G-14968)*
Blue Hen Hotel LLC.. 302 266-0354
  400 David Hollowell Dr Newark (19716) *(G-10059)*
Blue Hen Insulation Inc.. 302 424-4482
  2844 Deer Valley Rd Milford (19963) *(G-7796)*
Blue Hen Lines Inc... 302 422-6206
  404 Milford Harrington Hwy Milford (19963) *(G-7797)*
Blue Hen Masonry Inc.. 302 398-8737
  3296 Andrewville Rd Greenwood (19950) *(G-4599)*
Blue Hen Physical Therapy Inc.. 302 453-1588
  407 New London Rd Newark (19711) *(G-10060)*
Blue Hen Roofing LLC.. 302 545-2349
  503 Hemingway Dr Hockessin (19707) *(G-5134)*
Blue Hen Route LLC.. 347 863-5534
  1102 White Ibis Ct Middletown (19709) *(G-6926)*

Blue Hen Spring Works Inc 302 422-6600
  112 N Rehoboth Blvd Milford (19963) *(G-7798)*
Blue Hen Surgery Center The, Dover Also Called: Dover Ophthalmology Asc LLC *(G-2357)*
Blue Hen Utility Services Inc 302 273-3167
  473 Old Airport Rd Bldg 4 New Castle (19720) *(G-8870)*
Blue Heron Acupuncture & Herbs 302 344-7333
  1307 Savannah Rd Lewes (19958) *(G-5770)*
Blue Heron Contracting LLC 302 526-0648
  45 Amanda Ave Greenwood (19950) *(G-4600)*
Blue Heron Discount Cards, Bear Also Called: Blue Heron Ent Inc *(G-76)*
Blue Heron Ent Inc 302 834-1521
  600 Garron Point Pass Bear (19701) *(G-76)*
Blue Horizon Promotions LLC 302 547-0913
  1 Delaware St Saint Georges (19733) *(G-13032)*
Blue Horizon Properties LLC 347 731-5570
  49 Heartleaf Ln Magnolia (19962) *(G-6721)*
Blue Level Inc 337 623-4442
  2915 Ogletown Rd Ste 3546 Newark (19713) *(G-10061)*
Blue Marble Logistics LLC 302 221-4674
  263 Quigley Blvd Ste 3 Historic New Castle (19720) *(G-4943)*
Blue Marble Logistics LLC (PA) 302 661-4390
  800 N King St Ste 102 Wilmington (19801) *(G-14969)*
Blue Marlin Ice LLC 302 697-7800
  273 Walnut Shade Rd Dover (19904) *(G-1952)*
Blue Massage 302 934-7378
  28408 Dupont Blvd Millsboro (19966) *(G-8201)*
Blue Money Music Group Inc 302 413-1304
  651 N Broad St Ste 205 Middletown (19709) *(G-6927)*
Blue Mountain Apparel La LLC 646 787-5679
  40 E Main St Ste 899 Newark (19711) *(G-10062)*
Blue Phoenix Logistics LLC 347 424-7491
  407 E Ayre St Ste 1071 Wilmington (19804) *(G-14970)*
Blue Planet 410 977-3426
  159 Columbia Ave Rehoboth Beach (19971) *(G-12645)*
Blue Profit Cleaning LLC 302 377-3286
  10 Tamarack Ave Wilmington (19805) *(G-14971)*
Blue Ridge Consultants LLC (PA) 248 345-2294
  8 The Grn Ste B Dover (19901) *(G-1953)*
Blue Ridge Home Care Inc 302 397-8211
  9 E Loockerman St Ste 210 Dover (19901) *(G-1954)*
Blue River Resources LLC 302 652-3150
  1000 S Heald St Wilmington (19801) *(G-14972)*
Blue Rock Landscaping 302 229-8861
  103 Farm Ave Wilmington (19810) *(G-14973)*
Blue Rock Landscaping 302 408-0626
  502 Beaver Valley Rd Wilmington (19803) *(G-14974)*
Blue Shore Inc 301 890-9797
  601 Holly Ct Bethany Beach (19930) *(G-587)*
Blue Skies Solar & Wind Power 302 326-0856
  261 Airport Rd New Castle (19720) *(G-8871)*
Blue Sky Clean 302 584-5800
  293 Carlow Dr Wilmington (19808) *(G-14975)*
Blue Sky Management, Frankford Also Called: Winifred Ellen Erbe *(G-4162)*
Blue Sky Stones Inc (PA) 201 359-1368
  1013 Centre Rd Ste 403b Wilmington (19805) *(G-14976)*
Blue Sky Web Solutions Inc 302 261-2654
  200 Continental Dr # 401 Newark (19713) *(G-10063)*
Blue Swan Cleaners Inc (PA) 302 652-7607
  2001 Delaware Ave Wilmington (19806) *(G-14977)*
Blueballroom Dance Studio 302 765-3511
  206 Weldin Ln Wilmington (19809) *(G-14978)*
Blueberry Staffing LLC 302 445-6300
  3 Germay Dr Ste 4 Wilmington (19804) *(G-14979)*
Bluecoast Rehoboth 302 278-7395
  30115 Veterans Way Rehoboth Beach (19971) *(G-12646)*
Bluefin LLC 302 731-5770
  191 Edgemoor Rd Wilmington (19809) *(G-14980)*
Bluent LLC 832 476-8459
  16192 Coastal Hwy Lewes (19958) *(G-5771)*
Blueocean Communications LLC 617 586-6633
  2140 S Dupont Hwy Camden (19934) *(G-793)*
Bluepoint Systems LLC 817 714-2320
  16192 Coastal Hwy Lewes (19958) *(G-5772)*
Blueprint Motorsport 302 333-2746
  112 A St Wilmington (19801) *(G-14981)*
Bluestone Communications Inc (DH) 302 478-4200
  3600 Silverside Rd Wilmington (19810) *(G-14982)*
Bluevault LLC 302 425-4367
  1300 N Broom St Wilmington (19806) *(G-14983)*
Bluewater Wind LLC 302 731-7020
  700 Pilottown Rd Lewes (19958) *(G-5773)*
Bluffs, The, Newark Also Called: Sheldon Limited Partnership *(G-11994)*
Blujin Corp 973 219-2638
  251 Little Falls Dr Wilmington (19808) *(G-14984)*
Blumatter Inc 415 318-6857
  2035 Sunset Lake Rd Newark (19702) *(G-10064)*
BLW Enterprise Inc 302 384-7459
  1701 Newport Gap Pike Wilmington (19808) *(G-14985)*
BMA Milford 302 424-0552
  656 N Dupont Blvd Ste D Milford (19963) *(G-7799)*
Bmo Delaware Trust Company 302 652-1660
  20 Montchanin Rd Ste 240 Wilmington (19807) *(G-14986)*
BNai BRith Claymont LP 302 798-6846
  8000 Society Dr Claymont (19703) *(G-1062)*
BNai Brith Snior Ctzens Hsing 302 798-6846
  8000 Society Dr Claymont (19703) *(G-1063)*
Bni 302 668-9467
  6 Oaknoll Rd Wilmington (19808) *(G-14987)*
Bnj's Trucking, Middletown Also Called: Bnjs LLC *(G-6928)*
Bnjs LLC 302 465-6105
  910 Benalli Dr Middletown (19709) *(G-6928)*
Bnl Consulting LLC 302 857-1057
  100 Campus Dr Dover (19904) *(G-1955)*
Bny Investment MGT Svcs LLC 212 495-1784
  103 Bellevue Pkwy Wilmington (19809) *(G-14988)*
Boa Financial LLC 888 444-5371
  8 The Grn Ste 1 Dover (19901) *(G-1956)*
Board & Brush, Newark Also Called: Delaware Diy LLC *(G-10437)*
Boardwalk Builders Inc 302 227-5754
  37395 Martin St Rehoboth Beach (19971) *(G-12647)*
Boardwalk Plaza Incorporated (PA) 302 227-0441
  2 Olive Ave Rehoboth Beach (19971) *(G-12648)*
Bob Davis Inc 302 798-2561
  7 Georgetown Ave Wilmington (19809) *(G-14989)*
Bob Lafazia 302 633-1456
  2635 Grendon Dr Wilmington (19808) *(G-14990)*
Bob Mobley 302 652-2005
  4007 Kennett Pike Ste D Wilmington (19807) *(G-14991)*
Bob Preston Carpentry 302 234-8659
  433 Bishop Dr Hockessin (19707) *(G-5135)*
Bob Reynolds Backhoe Services 302 239-4711
  1124 Old Wilmington Rd Hockessin (19707) *(G-5136)*
Bob Simmons Agency 302 698-1970
  1460 E Lebanon Rd Dover (19901) *(G-1957)*
Bob's Custom Clubs, Wilmington Also Called: Bob Lafazia *(G-14990)*
Bob's Touch of The Brush, Middletown Also Called: Robert W Nagowski *(G-7519)*
Bobcat of New Castle LLC (PA) 732 780-6880
  1872 Pulaski Hwy Bear (19701) *(G-77)*
Bobot Robotics Inc 501 301-0612
  16192 Coastal Hwy Lewes (19958) *(G-5774)*
Bobs Marine Service Inc 302 539-3711
  Routes 17 & 26 Ocean View (19970) *(G-12482)*
Bobs Plumbing Repair LLC 302 853-2259
  16956 Seashore Hwy Georgetown (19947) *(G-4236)*
Boca Raton Exch Foundation Inc 302 286-6067
  333 Stamford Dr Newark (19711) *(G-10065)*
Bodell Bove LLC 302 655-6749
  1225 N King St Ste 1000 Wilmington (19801) *(G-14992)*
Bodied By Tru, Middletown Also Called: Tru Beauti LLC *(G-7663)*
Body Brain Sync Inc 302 498-9234
  17 Perth St Bear (19701) *(G-78)*
Body Double Swimwear 302 537-1444
  1007 Coastal Hwy Selbyville (19944) *(G-13479)*

Body Ease Therapy..610 314-0780
  105 Louviers Dr Newark (19711) *(G-10066)*
Body Electric LLC...302 559-5577
  5700 Kirkwood Hwy Ste 205 Wilmington (19808) *(G-14993)*
Body Images Tanning..302 622-8267
  2900 Concord Pike Ste E Wilmington (19803) *(G-14994)*
Body Interact Inc..512 910-8350
  614 N Dupont Hwy Ste 210 Dover (19901) *(G-1958)*
Body Matrix...302 220-8406
  13 Oakmont Dr New Castle (19720) *(G-8872)*
Body Sclpting Prfessionals LLC..986 999-8238
  919 N Market St Ste 950 Wilmington (19801) *(G-14995)*
Body Works...302 275-2750
  78 Albe Dr Ste 1 Newark (19702) *(G-10067)*
Boeing, Dover *Also Called: Boeing Company (G-1959)*
Boeing Company...302 735-2922
  639 Evreux St Dover (19902) *(G-1959)*
Boero Usa Inc...800 935-6596
  1209 N Orange St Wilmington (19801) *(G-14996)*
Bogo Publications LLC..877 514-4052
  6 Donegal Ct Christiana (19702) *(G-993)*
Boj Global Services LLC..302 325-4018
  152 N Katrin Cir New Castle (19720) *(G-8873)*
Bold Industries LLC...302 858-7237
  37424 Dale Earnhardt Blvd Frankford (19945) *(G-4074)*
Boldify Inc...240 396-0247
  651 N Broad St Ste 206 Middletown (19709) *(G-6929)*
Boldlatina Digital Group Pbc..415 754-0143
  8 The Grn Dover (19901) *(G-1960)*
Boldy Foods LLC...415 616-2965
  2140 S Dupont Hwy Camden (19934) *(G-794)*
Bollinger Cleaning Service LLC..410 620-1953
  1403 Wilmington Rd Historic New Castle (19720) *(G-4944)*
Bombonais Cable Tech LLC...302 444-1199
  218 Mccallmont Rd New Castle (19720) *(G-8874)*
Bombshell Beauty Inc...302 559-3011
  331 Rockmeade Dr Wilmington (19810) *(G-14997)*
Bond App LLC...415 418-4017
  1207 Delaware Ave Wilmington (19806) *(G-14998)*
Bond, Donald T DDS, Newark *Also Called: Clay White Dental Associates (G-10251)*
Bonded Business Services...302 438-6007
  6 Colony Boulevard Apt 208 Wilmington (19802) *(G-14999)*
Bones Innovations In Art...302 430-3592
  9645 Chris Ave Laurel (19956) *(G-5470)*
Boni Landscaping LLC..302 569-8852
  307 Calhoun St Georgetown (19947) *(G-4237)*
Bonie L Burnquist M D P A..302 537-6110
  433 Canal Way W Bethany Beach (19930) *(G-588)*
Bonk Farms LLC...302 542-2431
  472 Barkers Landing Rd Magnolia (19962) *(G-6722)*
Bonna-Agela Technologies Inc..302 438-8798
  217 Cherry Blossom Pl Hockessin (19707) *(G-5137)*
Bonna-Agela Technologies Inc (PA)................................302 438-8798
  2038a Telegraph Rd Wilmington (19808) *(G-15000)*
Bonnie L Burnquist MD PA..302 537-2260
  118 Atlantic Ave Millville (19970) *(G-8521)*
Bonnie Relocation LLC..302 538-0673
  40 Ridgely St Dover (19904) *(G-1961)*
Book em Danni Logistics LLC..302 983-2921
  42 Teal Cir Newark (19702) *(G-10068)*
Booke AI Inc..650 540-1316
  919 N Market St Wilmington (19801) *(G-15001)*
Bookitngo Corp..949 899-7684
  8 The Grn Dover (19901) *(G-1962)*
Bookkeeping Solutions..302 650-5058
  414 Stafford Ave Newark (19711) *(G-10069)*
Bookme Ai Inc...650 436-9210
  2810 N Church St Wilmington (19802) *(G-15002)*
Books & Tobaccos Inc..302 994-3156
  4555 Kirkwood Hwy Wilmington (19808) *(G-15003)*
Boomerang Returns Ltd...347 205-1275
  651 N Broad St Middletown (19709) *(G-6930)*
Boomn, Lewes *Also Called: Boomn Inc (G-5775)*
Boomn Inc (PA)...844 808-2666
  16192 Coastal Hwy Lewes (19958) *(G-5775)*
Boomset, Wilmington *Also Called: Boomset Inc (G-15004)*
Boomset Inc..860 266-6738
  2810 N Church St Wilmington (19802) *(G-15004)*
Boone Selections, Bear *Also Called: Lawrence Boone Selections LLC (G-339)*
Boonoob Inc..302 288-0670
  8 The Grn Ste 12218 Dover (19901) *(G-1963)*
Boost Learning LLC...302 691-5821
  721 Ambleside Dr Wilmington (19808) *(G-15005)*
Boost Mobile...302 482-1193
  1200 Northeast Blvd Wilmington (19802) *(G-15006)*
Boost Mobile By Infinity Wirel...856 691-7800
  206 W Market St Wilmington (19804) *(G-15007)*
Bootcamp Helicopters LLC..301 717-5455
  364 E Main St Ste 985 Middletown (19709) *(G-6931)*
Booth Wyn Heating & AC...302 737-7170
  1052 Everetts Corner Rd Hartly (19953) *(G-4857)*
Booths Services Plbg Htg & AC.......................................302 454-7385
  1088 1/2 S Chapel St Newark (19702) *(G-10070)*
Boothwyn Heating & AC Inc..302 284-2772
  1052 Everetts Corner Rd Hartly (19953) *(G-4858)*
Boozer Excavation Co Inc...302 542-0290
  18208 Beech Tree Path Milton (19968) *(G-8573)*
BOPyer& Boyer CPA, Wilmington *Also Called: Boyer & Boyer (G-15019)*
Borderx Lab Inc...510 203-3974
  1140 River Rd New Castle (19720) *(G-8875)*
Born Again Beautiful Entps, New Castle *Also Called: Rita Porter Darnetta (G-9534)*
Borne Legacy Logistics LLC..609 346-0380
  7 E Lexton Rd New Castle (19720) *(G-8876)*
Borsello Inc...302 472-2600
  720 Yorklyn Rd Ste 5 Hockessin (19707) *(G-5138)*
Borsello Irrigation Inc..302 652-6717
  2001 Monroe Pl Wilmington (19802) *(G-15008)*
Borsello Landscaping, Hockessin *Also Called: Cheap-Scape Inc (G-5157)*
Bos Construction Company...302 875-9120
  7045 Sharptown Rd Laurel (19956) *(G-5471)*
Bosco Insurance Agency...302 678-0647
  625 S Dupont Hwy Ste 101 Dover (19901) *(G-1964)*
Bosphorus Textile LLC..202 629-6563
  8 The Grn Dover (19901) *(G-1965)*
Boston Land Co Mgt Svcs Inc...302 571-0100
  200 N Washington St Ofc 1 Wilmington (19801) *(G-15009)*
Bot Workshop LLC..888 228-8799
  600 N Broad St Ste 5 # 3349 Middletown (19709) *(G-6932)*
Bothub Ai Limited..669 278-7485
  113 Darksdale Prof Ctr Newark (19711) *(G-10071)*
Botix Inc (PA)..239 600-8116
  651 N Broad St Ste 205 Middletown (19709) *(G-6933)*
Bottle of Smoke Press...302 399-1856
  902 Wilson Dr Dover (19904) *(G-1966)*
Boudart & Mensinger LLP..302 428-0100
  2710 Centerville Rd Ste 101 Wilmington (19808) *(G-15010)*
Boudreaux Ilene Lefkowitz MD..302 479-5505
  3521 Silverside Rd Ste 1f Wilmington (19810) *(G-15011)*
Boulares Innovations LLC...504 575-2386
  300 Delaware Ave Wilmington (19801) *(G-15012)*
Boulden Brothers...302 368-3848
  107 Sandy Dr Unit 700 Newark (19713) *(G-10072)*
Boulden Brothers, Newark *Also Called: Boulden Services LLC (G-10073)*
Boulden Buses Inc..302 998-5463
  32 Honeysuckle Ln Wilmington (19804) *(G-15013)*
Boulden Services LLC...302 368-0100
  107 Sandy Dr Unit 700 Newark (19713) *(G-10073)*
Bounce Back Physical Therapy.......................................484 582-0660
  106 Dale Rd Wilmington (19810) *(G-15014)*
Boundaries New..302 658-3486
  103 E Hazeldell Ave Ste A New Castle (19720) *(G-8877)*
Bounded Bits LLC (PA)...949 291-7358
  2035 Sunset Lake Rd B2 Newark (19702) *(G-10074)*

ALPHABETIC SECTION

Boundless Enterprises Inc 628 201-9286
1207 Delaware Ave Wilmington (19806) *(G-15015)*

Boutique The Bridal Ltd 302 335-5948
2454 Bay Rd Milford (19963) *(G-7800)*

Bove Psychological Svcs LLC 302 299-5193
108 Peirce Rd Wilmington (19803) *(G-15016)*

Bowden Construction LLC 302 907-0430
14147 Line Rd Delmar (19940) *(G-1568)*

Bowden Landscaping 302 934-6567
25831 Gravel Hill Rd Millsboro (19966) *(G-8202)*

Bowie Refined Coal LLC 302 636-5401
2711 Centerville Rd # 400 Wilmington (19808) *(G-15017)*

Bowlerama Inc 302 654-0263
3031 New Castle Ave New Castle (19720) *(G-8878)*

Bowles Construction LLC 302 332-5641
1 Queens Ct Wilmington (19808) *(G-15018)*

Bowman Family Foundation 302 234-5750
7234 Lancaster Pike Ste 300a Hockessin (19707) *(G-5139)*

Bowman Group LLC 302 494-7476
1207 Canvasback Dr New Castle (19720) *(G-8879)*

Bowmans Repair and Hauling 302 803-0098
107 Burningbush Dr Newark (19711) *(G-10075)*

Boxwood Electric Inc 302 368-3257
10 King Ave New Castle (19720) *(G-8880)*

BOY SCOUTS OF AMERICA, Dover Also Called: Del-Mr-Va Cncil Inc Boy Scuts *(G-2212)*

Boyds Crane, Camden Wyoming Also Called: Boyds Trailor Hitches *(G-917)*

Boyds Custom Remodeling Inc 302 698-1739
2429 Tower Rd Hartly (19953) *(G-4859)*

Boyds Trailer Hitches 302 697-9000
3178 S State St Camden Wyoming (19934) *(G-917)*

Boyds Welding Inc 302 697-9000
3178 S State St Camden Wyoming (19934) *(G-918)*

Boyer 302 368-8489
110 Anglin Dr Newark (19713) *(G-10076)*

Boyer & Boyer (PA) 302 998-3700
2392 Limestone Rd Wilmington (19808) *(G-15019)*

Boys & Girls Club of De 302 677-6376
864 Center Rd Dover (19901) *(G-1967)*

Boys & Girls Club of Dover, Dover Also Called: Boys & Girls Clubs Del Inc *(G-1968)*

Boys & Girls Club of Milford 302 422-4453
105 Ne Front St Milford (19963) *(G-7801)*

Boys & Girls Clubs Del Inc 302 792-3780
500 Darley Rd Unit 2 Claymont (19703) *(G-1064)*

Boys & Girls Clubs Del Inc 302 678-5182
375 Simon Cir Dover (19904) *(G-1968)*

Boys & Girls Clubs Del Inc 302 856-4903
115 N Race St Georgetown (19947) *(G-4238)*

Boys & Girls Clubs Del Inc 302 655-8569
19 Lambson Ln New Castle (19720) *(G-8881)*

Boys & Girls Clubs Del Inc (PA) 302 658-1870
669 S Union St Wilmington (19805) *(G-15020)*

Boys & Girls Clubs of America 302 875-1200
454 Central Ave Laurel (19956) *(G-5472)*

Boys & Girls Clubs of America 302 659-5610
240 E Commerce St Smyrna (19977) *(G-13665)*

Boys and Girls 302 947-4600
32615 Oak Orchard Rd # 3 Millsboro (19966) *(G-8203)*

Boys Girls Clubs 302 260-9864
19285 Holland Glade Rd Rehoboth Beach (19971) *(G-12649)*

BP, Dover Also Called: B P Services *(G-1864)*

BP Staffing Inc 302 999-7213
5187 W Woodmill Dr Ste 1 Wilmington (19808) *(G-15021)*

Bpg, Wilmington Also Called: Bpg Office Invstors III/IV LLC *(G-15024)*

Bpg, Wilmington Also Called: Bpg Real Estate Services LLC *(G-15027)*

Bpg, Wilmington Also Called: Buccini/Pollin Group Inc *(G-15139)*

Bpg International, Wilmington Also Called: Brandywine PDT Group Intl Inc *(G-15080)*

Bpg Justison P4 B1 LLC 302 652-1876
340 S Madison St Wilmington (19801) *(G-15022)*

Bpg Office 302 654-8535
233 N King St Wilmington (19801) *(G-15023)*

Bpg Office Invstors III/IV LLC 302 691-2100
1000 N West St Ste 900 Wilmington (19801) *(G-15024)*

Bpg Office Partners Viii LLC 302 250-3065
1000 N West St Ste 900 Wilmington (19801) *(G-15025)*

Bpg Real Estate Services LLC 302 478-1190
3505 Silverside Rd Ste 105 Wilmington (19810) *(G-15026)*

Bpg Real Estate Services LLC (PA) 302 777-2000
1000 N West St Ste 1000 Wilmington (19801) *(G-15027)*

Bpg Rsdential Partners III LLC 302 691-2100
22 A St Ste 300 Wilmington (19801) *(G-15028)*

Bpgs Construction LLC 302 691-2111
1000 N West St Wilmington (19801) *(G-15029)*

Bppn LLC 302 384-5119
707 N Union St Wilmington (19805) *(G-15030)*

Bqt Inc 347 443-8911
3613 Kirkwood Hwy Ste F Wilmington (19808) *(G-15031)*

Brackenville Center, Hockessin Also Called: 100 St Clire Drv Oprations LLC *(G-5107)*

Brad Allen Carpentry LLC 302 228-4256
33133 Jess N Ray Way Frankford (19945) *(G-4075)*

Bradford Enterprises Inc 302 378-0662
503 Aspen Ct Middletown (19709) *(G-6934)*

Bradford Family Physicians LLC 302 730-3750
1055 S Bradford St Dover (19904) *(G-1969)*

Bradfords Quality Care Inc 302 436-2467
32303 Gum Rd Frankford (19945) *(G-4076)*

Bradley & Sons Designer Con 302 836-8031
1 Tammie Dr Bear (19701) *(G-79)*

Bradley Distributing Inc 302 245-7508
2929 Woodland Ferry Rd Seaford (19973) *(G-13091)*

Bradley J Sandella Do 302 477-3300
1401 Foulk Rd Ste 100 Wilmington (19803) *(G-15032)*

Bradley, Michael J Do, Dover Also Called: Dover Family Physicians PA *(G-2343)*

Bradleylemondpm Lemon 302 934-7100
28253 Dupont Blvd Millsboro (19966) *(G-8204)*

Bradleys Auto Center Inc 302 762-2247
1167 Bohemia Mill Rd Middletown (19709) *(G-6935)*

Bradsworth Digital Solutions 630 200-2251
251 Little Falls Dr Wilmington (19808) *(G-15033)*

Brady Law Firm PA 302 482-4124
240 N James St Wilmington (19804) *(G-15034)*

Brae Corp 302 691-6043
103 Foulk Rd Wilmington (19803) *(G-15035)*

Brafman Family Dentistry PC 302 732-3852
31381 Dogwood Acres Dr Unit 2 Dagsboro (19939) *(G-1419)*

Braham Plumbing LLC 302 448-5708
10682 Dorothy Rd Laurel (19956) *(G-5473)*

Braid Babe, Wilmington Also Called: Gladys Walker *(G-16879)*

Braid Nation LLC 302 508-5913
5609 Dupont Pkwy Ste 15 Smyrna (19977) *(G-13666)*

Brain Injury Association Del 302 346-2083
840 Walker Rd Ste A Dover (19904) *(G-1970)*

Brain Love Neurotherapy 302 278-7828
19633 Blue Bird Ln Unit 5 Rehoboth Beach (19971) *(G-12650)*

Brain Works & Mind Matters LLC 302 324-5255
42 Reads Way Ste 135-136 New Castle (19720) *(G-8882)*

Braincx Inc (PA) 954 892-9101
300 Dlware Ave Ste 210 Wilmington (19801) *(G-15036)*

Brainerd LLC 918 622-1214
100 Industrial Park Blvd Seaford (19973) *(G-13092)*

Brainiac Brands USA Inc 778 869-4099
919 N Market St Ste 950 Wilmington (19801) *(G-15037)*

Brainify.ai, Dover Also Called: Neuroscience Software Inc *(G-3176)*

Brainstorm Force US LLC 302 330-8557
300 Delaware Ave Ste 210a Wilmington (19801) *(G-15038)*

Bramble Construction Co Inc 302 856-6723
812 E Market St Georgetown (19947) *(G-4239)*

Brand Builder Solutions LLC 302 234-4239
232 Steeplechase Cir Wilmington (19808) *(G-15039)*

Brand Design Co Inc 302 234-2356
2927 Faulkland Rd Wilmington (19808) *(G-15040)*

Brand Evangelists For Buty Inc 973 970-0812
8 The Grn Ste R Dover (19901) *(G-1971)*

Brand Iq Group Inc 302 924-8558
16192 Coastal Hwy Lewes (19958) *(G-5776)*

ALPHABETIC SECTION

Brandi Wine Pediatric Inc..302 478-7805
  3521 Silverside Rd Ste 1f Wilmington (19810) *(G-15041)*

Brandon Tatum..302 564-7428
  36666 Bluewater Run W Unit 7 Selbyville (19975) *(G-13480)*

Brandx Heirloom Tomatoes..302 287-1782
  103 Ashley Ann Ct Townsend (19734) *(G-13965)*

Brandy Bine Medical Associates, Wilmington *Also Called: Abad & Salameda PA (G-14193)*

Brandy Wine Senior Center..302 798-5562
  3301 Green St Claymont (19703) *(G-1065)*

Brandywine, Wilmington *Also Called: Brandywine Fund Inc (G-15060)*

Brandywine Apartment Assoc LP..302 475-8600
  2702 Jacqueline Dr Apt H19 Wilmington (19810) *(G-15042)*

Brandywine Art..302 234-7874
  809 Grande Ln Hockessin (19707) *(G-5140)*

Brandywine Arts Festival..302 363-5955
  1302 W 9th St Wilmington (19806) *(G-15043)*

Brandywine Asssted Lving At FN..302 436-0808
  21111 Arrington Dr Unit 101 Selbyville (19975) *(G-13481)*

Brandywine Auto Parts, Wilmington *Also Called: Action Automotive Inc (G-14240)*

Brandywine Balustrades..302 893-1837
  1225 Old Coochs Bridge Rd Newark (19713) *(G-10077)*

Brandywine Body Shop Inc..302 998-0424
  1325 Newport Gap Pike Wilmington (19804) *(G-15044)*

Brandywine Bodyworks..302 798-0801
  1400 Philadelphia Pike Wilmington (19809) *(G-15045)*

Brandywine Botanicals LLC..302 354-4650
  318 Tindall Rd Wilmington (19805) *(G-15046)*

Brandywine Cad Design Inc..302 478-8334
  3204 Concord Pike Wilmington (19803) *(G-15047)*

Brandywine Care L L C..302 658-5822
  1300 Delaware Ave Ste 1 Wilmington (19806) *(G-15048)*

Brandywine Center For Autism..302 503-3120
  1010 Mattlind Way Milford (19963) *(G-7802)*

Brandywine Center For Autism..302 762-2636
  510 Philadelphia Pike Fl 2 Wilmington (19809) *(G-15049)*

Brandywine Chemical Company..302 656-5428
  600 Terminal Ave New Castle (19720) *(G-8883)*

Brandywine Chrysler Jeep, Wilmington *Also Called: Brandywine Chrysler Jeep Dodge (G-15050)*

Brandywine Chrysler Jeep Dodge (PA)..............................302 998-0458
  3807 Kirkwood Hwy Wilmington (19808) *(G-15050)*

Brandywine Club Inc..302 798-9891
  135 Princeton Ave Claymont (19703) *(G-1066)*

Brandywine Cnseling Cmnty Svcs......................................302 856-4700
  769 E Masten Cir Milford (19963) *(G-7803)*

Brandywine Cnsling Cmnty Svcs..302 454-3020
  24 Brookhill Dr Newark (19702) *(G-10078)*

Brandywine Cnsling Cmnty Svcs (PA)................................302 655-9880
  2713 Lancaster Ave Wilmington (19805) *(G-15051)*

BRANDYWINE COM RSRC CNCL, Claymont *Also Called: Claymont Community Center Inc (G-1092)*

Brandywine Construction Co..302 571-9773
  101 Pigeon Point Rd New Castle (19720) *(G-8884)*

Brandywine Contractors Inc..302 325-2700
  34 Industrial Blvd New Castle (19720) *(G-8885)*

Brandywine Contractors Inc..302 325-2700
  34 Industrial Blvd New Castle (19720) *(G-8886)*

Brandywine Cosmetic Surgery..302 652-3331
  Medical Arts Pavilion Ste 137 Newark (19713) *(G-10079)*

Brandywine Counseling..302 856-4700
  528 E Market St Georgetown (19947) *(G-4240)*

Brandywine Counseling..302 762-7120
  500 Duncan Rd Ofc 1 Wilmington (19809) *(G-15052)*

Brandywine Counseling, Newark *Also Called: Brandywine Cnsling Cmnty Svcs (G-10078)*

Brandywine Country Club..302 478-4604
  302 River Rd Apt D2 Wilmington (19809) *(G-15053)*

Brandywine Ctr For Dnce The PR......................................302 416-6959
  1812 Marsh Rd Ste 419 Wilmington (19810) *(G-15054)*

Brandywine Education Assn..302 793-5048
  1000 Pennsylvania Ave Claymont (19703) *(G-1067)*

Brandywine Elec Ltd Belcom, Bear *Also Called: Brandywine Electronics Corp (G-80)*

Brandywine Electronics Corp..302 324-9992
  611 Carson Dr Bear (19701) *(G-80)*

Brandywine Elevator Co Inc (PA)..866 636-0102
  300 B And O Ln Wilmington (19804) *(G-15055)*

Brandywine Exteriors Corp..302 746-7134
  221 Valley Rd Wilmington (19804) *(G-15056)*

Brandywine Eye Center, Wilmington *Also Called: Richard L Sherry MD (G-19471)*

Brandywine Fine Properties..302 691-3052
  5701 Kennett Pike Wilmington (19807) *(G-15057)*

Brandywine Food Services LLC..302 276-5165
  800 N King St Ste 303 Wilmington (19801) *(G-15058)*

Brandywine Foot Care..302 478-8099
  2106 Silverside Rd Ste 102 Wilmington (19810) *(G-15059)*

Brandywine Fund Inc..302 656-3017
  3711 Kennett Pike Ste 100 Wilmington (19807) *(G-15060)*

Brandywine Global Investement..610 380-2110
  4005 Kennett Pike Ste 250 Wilmington (19807) *(G-15061)*

Brandywine Graphics Inc..302 655-7571
  500 S Colonial Ave Wilmington (19805) *(G-15062)*

Brandywine Heating & Air LLC..302 299-0180
  216 S Maryland Ave Wilmington (19804) *(G-15063)*

Brandywine Hills Apartments..302 764-3242
  4310 Miller Rd Apt 106 Wilmington (19802) *(G-15064)*

Brandywine Hndred Vtrnary Hosp......................................302 792-2777
  806 Silverside Rd Wilmington (19809) *(G-15065)*

Brandywine Hundred Family Mdcn....................................302 478-5650
  1401 Foulk Rd Ste 202 Wilmington (19803) *(G-15066)*

Brandywine Hundred Fire Co 1..302 764-4901
  1006 Brandywine Blvd Wilmington (19809) *(G-15067)*

BRANDYWINE HUNDRED FIRE CO NO, Wilmington *Also Called: Brandywine Hundred Fire Co 1 (G-15067)*

Brandywine I & 2 Apts..302 475-8600
  2702 Jacqueline Dr H19 Wilmington (19810) *(G-15068)*

Brandywine Lacrosse Club..302 249-1840
  2403 W Heather Rd Wilmington (19803) *(G-15069)*

Brandywine Lighting Gallery..302 543-6939
  4723 Concord Pike Ste F Wilmington (19803) *(G-15070)*

Brandywine Management, Wilmington *Also Called: Brandywine Realty Management (G-15082)*

Brandywine Marketing Services..302 761-9755
  17 Stone Crop Rd Wilmington (19810) *(G-15071)*

Brandywine Master Carpentry..302 463-9773
  2824 W Oakland Dr Wilmington (19808) *(G-15072)*

Brandywine Mill Work..302 652-3008
  1907 N Market St Wilmington (19802) *(G-15073)*

Brandywine Nrsing Rhblttion CT..302 683-0444
  505 Greenbank Rd Wilmington (19808) *(G-15074)*

Brandywine Nurseries Inc..302 429-0865
  4 James Ct Wilmington (19801) *(G-15075)*

Brandywine Ob Gyn..302 477-1375
  3520 Silverside Rd Ste 2l1 Wilmington (19810) *(G-15076)*

Brandywine Occpational Therapy......................................302 740-4798
  800 Carr Rd Wilmington (19809) *(G-15077)*

Brandywine Pain Center..302 998-2585
  4512 Kirkwood Hwy Ste 200 Wilmington (19808) *(G-15078)*

Brandywine Park Condominiums, Wilmington *Also Called: Brandywine Park Condos (G-15079)*

Brandywine Park Condos..302 655-2262
  1704 N Park Dr Apt 115 Wilmington (19806) *(G-15079)*

Brandywine PDT Group Intl Inc..302 472-1463
  3 Mill Rd Ste 202 Wilmington (19806) *(G-15080)*

Brandywine Process Servers..302 475-2600
  2500 Delaware Ave Wilmington (19806) *(G-15081)*

Brandywine Realty Management..302 656-1058
  3200 Lancaster Ave Wilmington (19805) *(G-15082)*

Brandywine Resurfacing..302 654-8744
  2213 Brookline Rd Wilmington (19803) *(G-15083)*

Brandywine Rubber Mills LLC..267 499-3993
  1704 N Park Dr Apt 508 Wilmington (19806) *(G-15084)*

Brandywine Rver Representative..302 984-2861
  122 Brook Valley Rd Wilmington (19807) *(G-15085)*

Brandywine Senior Care Inc
ALPHABETIC SECTION

Brandywine Senior Care Inc 302 436-2920
  36413 Redwood Way Selbyville (19975) *(G-13482)*

Brandywine Senior Living, Rehoboth Beach *Also Called: Brandywine Snior Lving MGT LLC* *(G-12651)*

Brandywine Snior Lving MGT LLC 302 226-8750
  36101 Seaside Blvd Rehoboth Beach (19971) *(G-12651)*

Brandywine Sr Care, Selbyville *Also Called: Brandywine Asssted Lving At FN (G-13481)*

Brandywine Technology, Hockessin *Also Called: 924 Inc (G-5109)*

Brandywine Total Health Care 302 478-3028
  3214 Naamans Rd Wilmington (19810) *(G-15086)*

Brandywine Town Center 16, Wilmington *Also Called: Regal Cinemas Inc (G-19397)*

Brandywine Tree and Shrub LLC 302 475-7594
  214 Alders Dr Wilmington (19803) *(G-15087)*

Brandywine Trust Co 302 234-5750
  7234 Lancaster Pike Ste 300a Hockessin (19707) *(G-5141)*

Brandywine Urology Cons PA 302 652-8990
  4701 Ogletown Stanton Rd Ste 4500 Newark (19713) *(G-10080)*

Brandywine Urology Cons PA (PA) 302 652-8990
  2000 Foulk Rd Ste F Wilmington (19810) *(G-15088)*

Brandywine Valley Properties 302 475-7660
  1806 Breen Ln Wilmington (19810) *(G-15089)*

Brandywine Valley Spca 302 516-1000
  290 Churchmans Rd New Castle (19720) *(G-8887)*

Brandywine Valley Spca 302 475-9294
  1110 Graylyn Rd Wilmington (19803) *(G-15090)*

Brandywine Valley Woodworking 302 743-5640
  1212 Bruce Rd Wilmington (19803) *(G-15091)*

Brandywine Vending, Claymont *Also Called: Gian-Co (G-1161)*

Brandywine Vly Fire Safety Div, Wilmington *Also Called: McDonald Safety Equipment Inc (G-18227)*

Brandywine Volleyball Club 302 898-6452
  3023 Maple Shade Ln Wilmington (19810) *(G-15092)*

Brandywine Waterproofing Del 302 482-4368
  2407 Saint Francis St Wilmington (19808) *(G-15093)*

Brandywine Wods Aprtmnts Sites, Bear *Also Called: Town and Country Trust (G-538)*

Brandywine Zoo 302 571-7747
  1001 N Park Dr Wilmington (19802) *(G-15094)*

Brandywine Zoo, Wilmington *Also Called: Delaware Div Parks Recreation (G-15909)*

Brannan Construction LLC 302 547-1659
  35 Wenark Dr Apt 6 Newark (19713) *(G-10081)*

Brantimus Logistics LLC 302 990-4110
  8 The Grn Ste 8643 Dover (19901) *(G-1972)*

Brantngham Crroll Holdings Inc (PA) 724 266-0400
  1209 N Orange St Wilmington (19801) *(G-15095)*

Brass Sales Company Inc (PA) 302 284-4574
  8092 S Dupont Hwy Felton (19943) *(G-3947)*

Brass Unlimited 302 322-2529
  441 Park Ave New Castle (19720) *(G-8888)*

Brasures Body Shop Inc 302 732-6157
  Rte 113 Frankford (19945) *(G-4077)*

Brasures Carpet Care Inc (PA) 302 436-5652
  35131 Lighthouse Rd Selbyville (19975) *(G-13483)*

Brasures Pest Control Inc 302 436-8140
  38187 Dickerson Rd Selbyville (19975) *(G-13484)*

Braswell Enterprises LLC 470 588-2087
  8 The Grn Ste A Dover (19901) *(G-1973)*

Braun Agency Inc 302 998-1412
  1906 Newport Gap Pike Wilmington (19808) *(G-15096)*

Braun Engineering & Surveying 302 698-0701
  863 Allabands Mill Rd Camden Wyoming (19934) *(G-919)*

Bravatics LLC 703 966-0516
  8 The Grn Ste B Dover (19901) *(G-1974)*

Bravin Publishing LLC 347 921-0443
  1041 N Dupont Hwy Dover (19901) *(G-1975)*

Bravo Building Services Inc 302 322-5959
  34 Blevins Dr Ste 7 New Castle (19720) *(G-8889)*

Bravos Construction LLC 302 249-0039
  20871 Sanfilippo Rd Bridgeville (19933) *(G-674)*

Breakers Associates 302 227-6688
  105 2nd St Rehoboth Beach (19971) *(G-12652)*

Breakers Hotel, The, Rehoboth Beach *Also Called: Breakers Associates (G-12652)*

Breakout Trading Group LLC 302 365-0947
  2810 N Church St Pmb 544583 Wilmington (19802) *(G-15097)*

Breakthru Beverage Delaware, Middletown *Also Called: Breakthru Beverage Group LLC (G-6936)*

Breakthru Beverage Delaware, New Castle *Also Called: Breakthru Beverage Group LLC (G-8890)*

Breakthru Beverage Group LLC 443 631-2597
  922 Levels Rd Middletown (19709) *(G-6936)*

Breakthru Beverage Group LLC 302 356-3500
  411 Churchmans Rd New Castle (19720) *(G-8890)*

Breakwater Construction Envmtl 302 945-5800
  4 Chief Joseph Trl Millsboro (19966) *(G-8205)*

Breakwater Fence and Deck 302 684-3333
  9565 Bay Shore Dr Milford (19963) *(G-7804)*

Breakwter Accnting Advsory Gro 302 543-4564
  1601 Concord Pike Ste 100 Wilmington (19803) *(G-15098)*

Breast Imaging Center 302 623-9729
  4735 Ogletown Stanton Rd # 2112 Newark (19713) *(G-10082)*

Breckstone Architecture, Wilmington *Also Called: Breckstone Group Inc (G-15099)*

Breckstone Group Inc 302 654-3646
  2417 Lancaster Ave Wilmington (19805) *(G-15099)*

Breeding & Day Inc (PA) 302 478-4585
  3316 Silverside Rd Wilmington (19810) *(G-15100)*

Brees Home Day Care 302 762-0876
  915 E 26th St Wilmington (19802) *(G-15101)*

Breeze Construction LLC 302 522-9201
  39 Basalt St Townsend (19734) *(G-13966)*

Breezle LLC 774 435-1566
  1201 N Orange St Ste 6001 Wilmington (19801) *(G-15102)*

Brenda Anns Hair Salon 302 312-7658
  1745 Bear Corbitt Rd Bear (19701) *(G-81)*

Brenda Radick 302 945-8982
  11 Multiflora Dr Harbeson (19951) *(G-4686)*

Brenden Bley Chanl VFW Post 58 .... 302 239-0797
  7620 Lancaster Pike Hockessin (19707) *(G-5142)*

Brenford Animal Hospital P A (PA) 302 678-9418
  4118 N Dupont Hwy Dover (19901) *(G-1976)*

Brennan Title Company 302 541-0400
  31634 Hickory Manor Rd Frankford (19945) *(G-4078)*

Breslin Contracting Inc 302 322-0320
  18 King Ct New Castle (19720) *(G-8891)*

Brewington Electric 302 732-3570
  Rural Rt 26 Dagsboro (19939) *(G-1420)*

Brewster Products 302 463-3531
  205 Ruth Dr Middletown (19709) *(G-6937)*

Brewster Products Inc 302 764-4463
  3607 Downing Dr Ste E Wilmington (19802) *(G-15103)*

Breylacom 302 731-7456
  18 Argyle Rd Newark (19713) *(G-10083)*

Bri US LLC 408 550-6354
  16192 Coastal Hwy Lewes (19958) *(G-5777)*

Brian Costleigh LLC 302 645-3775
  1 Beach Ave Rehoboth Beach (19971) *(G-12653)*

Brian J Galinat M D 302 633-3555
  1941 Limestone Rd Ste 101 Wilmington (19808) *(G-15104)*

Brian K Mummert 302 678-2260
  526 Rose Dale Ln Dover (19904) *(G-1977)*

Brian McAllister DDS 302 376-0617
  200 Cleaver Farms Rd Ste 101 Middletown (19709) *(G-6938)*

Brian Patterson PA 203 466-9972
  122 Main Sail Dr Milton (19968) *(G-8574)*

Brian T Phillips 302 593-3815
  3 Main Ave Wilmington (19804) *(G-15105)*

Brianna Rafetto DMD PA 302 376-7882
  600 N Broad St Ste 7 Middletown (19709) *(G-6939)*

Brick Doctor Inc (PA) 302 678-3380
  130 Kruser Blvd Dover (19901) *(G-1978)*

Brick Hotel On The Circle 302 745-0115
  32344 River Rd Millsboro (19966) *(G-8206)*

Bridal & Tuxedo Outlet Inc (PA) 302 731-8802
  124 Astro Shopping Ctr Newark (19711) *(G-10084)*

ALPHABETIC SECTION

Bridal & Tuxedo Shoppe, Newark Also Called: Bridal & Tuxedo Outlet Inc *(G-10084)*

Bridge Enterprises LLC 302 750-0828
113 Marsh Rd Wilmington (19809) *(G-15106)*

Bridgeforce Inc 302 325-7100
155 Stanton Christiana Rd Newark (19702) *(G-10085)*

Bridges4kids 302 841-3700
110 W Shore Dr Milton (19968) *(G-8575)*

Bridgesoft Infosec LLC (HQ) 270 799-4779
1000 N West St Ste 1200 Wilmington (19801) *(G-15107)*

Bridgestone Con & Masnry LLC 302 462-5422
24242 Kent Dr Millsboro (19966) *(G-8207)*

Bridgestone Ret Operations LLC 302 734-4522
625 S Bay Rd Dover (19901) *(G-1979)*

Bridgestone Ret Operations LLC 302 422-4508
103 Causey Ave Bldg 103 Milford (19963) *(G-7805)*

Bridgestone Ret Operations LLC 302 656-2529
2098 New Castle Ave New Castle (19720) *(G-8892)*

Bridgestone Ret Operations LLC 302 995-2487
3301 Old Capitol Trl Wilmington (19808) *(G-15108)*

Bridgeville Auto Center Inc 302 337-3100
Rte 13 S Bridgeville (19933) *(G-675)*

Bridgeville Historical Society 302 337-7600
102 Willin Ave Bridgeville (19933) *(G-676)*

Bridgeville Lions Club Inc 302 629-9543
Bridgeville (19933) *(G-677)*

Bridgeville Machining, Bridgeville Also Called: Messick & Gray Cnstr Inc *(G-731)*

Bridgeville Senior Center 302 337-8771
414 Market St Bridgeville (19933) *(G-678)*

Bridgeville State Services, Bridgeville Also Called: Delaware Dept Hlth Social Svcs *(G-691)*

Bridgewater Jewelers 302 328-2101
318 Delaware St Historic New Castle (19720) *(G-4945)*

Bridgeway Digital LLC 212 684-6931
16192 Coastal Hwy Lewes (19958) *(G-5778)*

Brie D Bolger 302 668-8268
4 Emerald Ridge Dr Bear (19701) *(G-82)*

Briggs Company, Milton Also Called: John L Briggs & Co *(G-8649)*

Briggs Services LLC 302 569-5230
14546 S Old State Rd Ellendale (19941) *(G-3911)*

Bright Beginnings Inc 302 376-8001
341 W Windmill Way Middletown (19709) *(G-6940)*

Bright Bgnnngs Child Care Ctr 302 934-1249
29753 John J Williams Hwy Millsboro (19966) *(G-8208)*

Bright Dental, Middletown Also Called: Brianna Rafetto DMD PA *(G-6939)*

Bright Finish LLC 888 974-4747
56 Arrowood Dr Smyrna (19977) *(G-13667)*

Bright Future Pediatrics, Camden Also Called: Future Bright Pediatrics LLC *(G-838)*

BRIGHT FUTURE PEDIATRICS, Dover Also Called: Future Bright Pediatrics *(G-2549)*

Bright Futures Inc 610 905-0506
125 Sleepy Hollow Dr Middletown (19709) *(G-6941)*

Bright Horizons Child Care Ctr, Wilmington Also Called: Bright Horizons Chld Ctrs LLC *(G-15111)*

Bright Horizons Chld Ctrs LLC 302 456-8913
950 Samoset Dr Newark (19713) *(G-10086)*

Bright Horizons Chld Ctrs LLC 302 453-2050
1089 Prides Xing Newark (19713) *(G-10087)*

Bright Horizons Chld Ctrs LLC 302 282-6378
201 N Walnut St Wilmington (19801) *(G-15109)*

Bright Horizons Chld Ctrs LLC 302 475-6780
3511 Silverside Rd Wilmington (19810) *(G-15110)*

Bright Horizons Chld Ctrs LLC 302 477-1023
3515 Silverside Rd Ste 102 Wilmington (19810) *(G-15111)*

Bright Kidz Inc 302 369-6929
273 Old Baltimore Pike Newark (19702) *(G-10088)*

Bright New Beginnings 610 637-9809
8 W Holly Oak Rd Wilmington (19809) *(G-15112)*

Bright New Schlars Academy LLC 302 668-6053
355 Corporate Blvd Newark (19702) *(G-10089)*

Bright Side Exteriors 302 674-4642
615 Otis Dr Dover (19901) *(G-1980)*

Bright Stars Daycare 302 449-9198
24 Dornoch Way Townsend (19734) *(G-13967)*

Bright Stars Home Daycare 302 378-8142
302 Northhampton Way Middletown (19709) *(G-6942)*

Brighten Up Painting 302 424-4591
2 W Thrush Dr Milford (19963) *(G-7806)*

Brightfields Inc (PA) 302 656-9600
801 Industrial St Wilmington (19801) *(G-15113)*

Brightminds Social Inc 424 333-8879
3422 Old Capitol Trl # 558 Wilmington (19808) *(G-15114)*

Brighton Hotels LLC 302 227-5780
34 Wilmington Ave Rehoboth Beach (19971) *(G-12654)*

Brighton Suites Hotel, Rehoboth Beach Also Called: Brighton Hotels LLC *(G-12654)*

Brighton Suites Hotel, The, Rehoboth Beach Also Called: Packem Associates Partnership *(G-12882)*

Brightside Pest Services Inc 302 893-5858
27 Wesley Dr Hockessin (19707) *(G-5143)*

Brik Labs Inc 302 499-4423
1007 N Orange St Fl 4 Wilmington (19801) *(G-15115)*

Brilliance Living Corporation 386 690-1709
2711 Centerville Rd # 400 Wilmington (19808) *(G-15116)*

Brilliant Little Minds 302 376-9889
102 Sandhill Dr Middletown (19709) *(G-6943)*

Brillnce Asssted Lving Edgwter, Wilmington Also Called: Brilliance Living Corporation *(G-15116)*

Brim Prtners Cnslting Group In (PA) 657 234-7424
3911 Concord Pike # 8030 Wilmington (19803) *(G-15117)*

Brisbie LLC 650 690-1433
103 Foulk Rd Ste 202 Wilmington (19803) *(G-15118)*

Briscoe Trucking Inc 302 836-1327
28 Chambord Dr Newark (19702) *(G-10090)*

Bristol Industrial Corporation 302 322-1100
1010 River Rd New Castle (19720) *(G-8893)*

Bristol-Myers Squibb, Wilmington Also Called: Bristol-Myers Squibb Company *(G-15119)*

Bristol-Myers Squibb Company 800 321-1335
1209 N Orange St Wilmington (19801) *(G-15119)*

Brisyn Pros Cleaning Service 302 399-7366
55 Saint Bernadino Cir Dover (19904) *(G-1981)*

Brite Lite Supply, Historic New Castle Also Called: Colonial Electric Supply Co *(G-4960)*

Brittingham Inc 302 656-8173
5809 Kennett Pike Wilmington (19807) *(G-15120)*

Brittney Ann Fischbeck LLC 302 219-6491
8 The Grn Ste 14852 Dover (19901) *(G-1982)*

Brittons Wise Computers Inc 302 659-0343
777 Paddock Rd Smyrna (19977) *(G-13668)*

Broad Creek Medical Service 302 629-0202
1601 Middleford Rd Seaford (19973) *(G-13093)*

Broadberry Data Systems LLC 302 295-1086
1308 Delaware Ave Wilmington (19806) *(G-15121)*

Broadberry Data Systems LLC (PA) 800 496-9918
501 Silverside Rd Ste 119 Wilmington (19809) *(G-15122)*

Broadcreek Medical Service, Seaford Also Called: Broad Creek Medical Service *(G-13093)*

Broadmeadow Healthcare, Middletown Also Called: Broadmeadow Investment LLC *(G-6944)*

Broadmeadow Investment LLC 302 449-3400
500 S Broad St Middletown (19709) *(G-6944)*

Broadpoint Construction LLC 302 567-2100
37251 Rehoboth Avenue Ext Rehoboth Beach (19971) *(G-12655)*

Broadpoint Construction LLC 302 228-8007
70 Rehoboth Ave Rehoboth Beach (19971) *(G-12656)*

Broadpoint Custom Homes, Rehoboth Beach Also Called: Broadpoint Construction LLC *(G-12655)*

Broadwater Oyster Company LLC 610 220-7776
4 S Lake Ter Rehoboth Beach (19971) *(G-12657)*

Brobst Home Improvement LLC 302 376-1656
5909 Summit Bridge Rd Townsend (19734) *(G-13968)*

Broccworth Housing Firm LLC 860 937-6308
1207 Delaware Ave Wilmington (19806) *(G-15123)*

Brodie Consulting Mick Group 302 468-6425
4 Chilmark Ct Bear (19701) *(G-83)*

Broken Spoke Outfitters Inc 604 558-0248
40 E Main St Ste 959 Newark (19711) *(G-10091)*

Broker Post 302 628-8467
1310 Bridgeville Hwy Seaford (19973) *(G-13094)*

Brokers Realty Network — ALPHABETIC SECTION

Brokers Realty Network 302 593-3998
3203 Concord Pike Ste 3 Wilmington (19803) *(G-15124)*

Bromwell Construction Co LLC 302 598-7072
1800 Newport Gap Pike Wilmington (19808) *(G-15125)*

Bronswerk Marine Corp 619 813-4797
2915 Ogletown Rd Ste 869 Newark (19713) *(G-10092)*

Brookdale Dover 302 674-4407
150 Saulsbury Rd Dover (19904) *(G-1983)*

Brookeside Studio 302 629-2829
7 Woodland Dr Seaford (19973) *(G-13095)*

Brooks Courier Service Inc 302 762-4661
831 E 28th St Wilmington (19802) *(G-15126)*

Brooks Machine Inc (PA) 302 674-5900
716 S West St Dover (19904) *(G-1984)*

Brooks Metal Saws Repair, Dover Also Called: Brooks Machine Inc *(G-1984)*

Brookside Laundromat 302 369-3366
69 Marrows Rd Newark (19713) *(G-10093)*

Brookside Plaza Apartments LLC 302 737-2008
885 Marrows Rd Apt D6 Newark (19713) *(G-10094)*

Brookview Townhomes Redev LLC 302 472-7200
300 Water St Wilmington (19801) *(G-15127)*

Brothers Gannon Inc 302 422-2734
31 Oakglade Dr Houston (19954) *(G-5437)*

Brothers Landscaping LLC 360 609-8131
31871 Old Hickory Rd Laurel (19956) *(G-5474)*

Brothers Painting and Drywall 302 737-9600
709 Waterbird Ln Middletown (19709) *(G-6945)*

Brown Shiels & OBrien 302 734-4766
108 E Water St Dover (19901) *(G-1985)*

Brown Advisory Incorporated 302 351-7600
5701 Kennett Pike # 100 Wilmington (19807) *(G-15128)*

Brown Electrical Services LLC 302 245-4593
28881 Harmons Hill Rd Millsboro (19966) *(G-8209)*

Brown Lisha 302 832-9529
33 Wellington Dr Newark (19702) *(G-10095)*

Brown Shels Bauregard LLC 302 226-2270
148 S Bradford St Dover (19904) *(G-1986)*

Brown Stone Nimeroff LLC 302 428-8142
901 N Market St Wilmington (19801) *(G-15129)*

Browne Consulting 302 482-1410
3704 Wild Cherry Ln Wilmington (19808) *(G-15130)*

Browns Unlimited 4u LLC 800 940-5880
1303 Delaware Ave Apt 405 Wilmington (19806) *(G-15131)*

Brownstone LLC 302 300-4370
200 Centerpoint Blvd Ste A Historic New Castle (19720) *(G-4946)*

Browse Contacts 302 261-9495
3524 Silverside Rd 35b Wilmington (19810) *(G-15132)*

Broydrick & Associates Inc (PA) 414 224-9393
102 Saint Lawrence St Rehoboth Beach (19971) *(G-12658)*

Brs Consulting Inc 302 786-2326
293 Jackson Ditch Rd Harrington (19952) *(G-4741)*

Bruce E Matthews DDS PA 302 234-2440
451 Hockessin Cors Hockessin (19707) *(G-5144)*

Bruce E Matthews DDS PA (PA) 302 475-9220
1403 Silverside Rd Ste A Wilmington (19810) *(G-15133)*

Bruce G & Mary A Robert FML Fd 302 598-1609
501 W 9th St Wilmington (19801) *(G-15134)*

Bruce G Fay DMD PA 302 778-3822
900 Foulk Rd Ste 203 Wilmington (19803) *(G-15135)*

Bruce Industrial Co Inc 302 655-9616
4049 New Castle Ave New Castle (19720) *(G-8894)*

Bruce M Dopler MD 302 628-7730
24488 Sussex Hwy Ste 6 Seaford (19973) *(G-13096)*

Bruce Mears Designer-Builder 302 539-2355
31370 Railway Rd # 2 Ocean View (19970) *(G-12483)*

Bruce Palmer LLC 302 654-1135
20245 Bay Vista Rd Rehoboth Beach (19971) *(G-12659)*

Bruces Welding Inc 302 629-3891
21263 Nattell Ln Seaford (19973) *(G-13097)*

Brucke Inc 302 319-9614
1201 N Orange St Wilmington (19801) *(G-15136)*

Brunswick Doverama 302 734-7501
1600 S Governors Ave Dover (19904) *(G-1987)*

Brush of Color LLC 302 932-0005
28 Yorktown Rd New Castle (19720) *(G-8895)*

Brute Performance Inc 757 477-7136
303 Chanticleer Cir Camden Wyoming (19934) *(G-920)*

Bryan & Brittingham Inc 302 846-9500
38148 Bi State Blvd Delmar (19940) *(G-1569)*

Bryan Longhenry Man 302 369-3369
245 S Dillwyn Rd Newark (19711) *(G-10096)*

Bryant Guernsey Cnstr Co 302 737-1841
54 Montrose Dr Newark (19713) *(G-10097)*

Bryant Technologies Inc 302 289-2044
2368 Paradise Alley Rd Felton (19943) *(G-3948)*

Bryn Mawr Capital MGT LLC (HQ) 302 429-8436
5803 Kennett Pike Ste C Wilmington (19807) *(G-15137)*

Brysk Inc 224 508-9542
108 W 13th St Wilmington (19801) *(G-15138)*

Bryton Hmes At Five Points LLC 302 703-6633
30632 Redmon Rd Frankford (19945) *(G-4079)*

Bs Insurance LLC 302 645-2356
17527 Nassau Commons Blvd Lewes (19958) *(G-5779)*

Bsr Trade LLC 646 250-4409
8 The Grn Ste 6258 Dover (19901) *(G-1988)*

Bubba Game Calls 302 332-2004
158 Blackbird Station Rd Townsend (19734) *(G-13969)*

Buccini/Pollin Group Inc (PA) 302 691-2100
1000 N West St Ste 1000 Wilmington (19801) *(G-15139)*

Buchi Corporation (HQ) 302 652-3000
19 Lukens Dr Ste 400 Historic New Castle (19720) *(G-4947)*

Buck Algonquin Co 302 659-6900
370 N Main St Smyrna (19977) *(G-13669)*

Buck Road East Association 302 658-2400
1 River Pl Wilmington (19801) *(G-15140)*

Buck Simpers Archt + Assoc Inc 302 658-9300
954 Justison St Wilmington (19801) *(G-15141)*

Buck's Barber Shop, Dover Also Called: Georve V Sawyer *(G-2574)*

Buckingham Pl Twnhuse Aprtmnts, Newark Also Called: Galman Group Inc *(G-10803)*

Buckley's Autocare, Wilmington Also Called: Buckleys Inc *(G-15142)*

Buckleys Inc 302 999-8285
1604 E Newport Pike Wilmington (19804) *(G-15142)*

Budget Blinds, Milton Also Called: Rementer Brothers Inc *(G-8695)*

Budget Rent A Car 302 322-2026
151 N Dupont Hwy New Castle (19720) *(G-8896)*

Budget Rent A Car 302 227-3041
19563 Coastal Hwy Rehoboth Beach (19971) *(G-12660)*

Budget Rent A Car 302 762-4824
702 Philadelphia Pike Wilmington (19809) *(G-15143)*

Budget Rent A Car System Inc 302 652-0629
100 S Front St Wilmington (19801) *(G-15144)*

Budget Rent-A-Car, New Castle Also Called: Budget Rent A Car *(G-8896)*

Budget Rent-A-Car, New Castle Also Called: Budget Truck Rental *(G-8898)*

Budget Rent-A-Car, New Castle Also Called: Budget Truck Rental *(G-8899)*

Budget Rent-A-Car, Rehoboth Beach Also Called: Budget Rent A Car *(G-12660)*

Budget Rent-A-Car, Selbyville Also Called: Budget Truck Rental *(G-13485)*

Budget Rent-A-Car, Wilmington Also Called: Budget Rent A Car *(G-15143)*

Budget Rent-A-Car, Wilmington Also Called: Budget Rent A Car System Inc *(G-15144)*

Budget Rooter Inc 302 322-3011
1015 River Rd New Castle (19720) *(G-8897)*

Budget Truck LLC 302 731-5067
915 S Chapel St Newark (19713) *(G-10098)*

Budget Truck Rental 302 325-9111
211 S Dupont Hwy New Castle (19720) *(G-8898)*

Budget Truck Rental 302 328-1282
103 N Dupont Hwy New Castle (19720) *(G-8899)*

Budget Truck Rental 302 436-5416
34821 W Line Rd Unit 9 Selbyville (19975) *(G-13485)*

Budget Truck Rental LLC 302 644-0132
18744 John J Williams Hwy Rehoboth Beach (19971) *(G-12661)*

Buds Auto 302 690-3838
632 Dane Ct New Castle (19720) *(G-8900)*

ALPHABETIC SECTION

Bueno Technologies Inc 559 785-9800
  2035 Sunset Lake Rd Ste B2 Newark (19702) *(G-10099)*
Buffalo Consulting Group, New Castle *Also Called: Delaware Enterprises Inc (G-9022)*
Bug Eyed Weasel Productions LL 302 547-8661
  1004 Berkeley Rd Wilmington (19807) *(G-15145)*
Builder Supply of Del Marva 302 829-8650
  61 Atlantic Ave Ocean View (19970) *(G-12484)*
Builders & Remodelers Assoc De 302 678-1520
  109 E Division St Dover (19901) *(G-1989)*
Builders LLC General 302 533-6528
  99 Albe Dr Ste A Newark (19702) *(G-10100)*
Building Blocks For Learni 302 677-0248
  88 Beech Dr Dover (19904) *(G-1990)*
Building Concepts America Inc 302 292-0200
  101 Peoples Dr Newark (19702) *(G-10101)*
Building Fasteners Inc 302 738-0671
  955 Dawson Dr Ste 1 Newark (19713) *(G-10102)*
Building Systems and Svcs Inc 302 996-0900
  1504 Kirkwood Hwy Wilmington (19805) *(G-15146)*
Built Fitness LLC 302 645-1932
  29634 Woodgate Dr Milton (19968) *(G-8576)*
Buker Limousine & Trnsp Svc 302 234-7600
  517 Paisley Pl Newark (19711) *(G-10103)*
Bulk Mro Industrial Supply Inc (PA) 646 713-1060
  1013 Centre Rd Ste 403b Wilmington (19805) *(G-15147)*
Bulk Solutions LLC 310 906-0901
  704 N King St Wilmington (19801) *(G-15148)*
Bull Head Transport LLC 302 650-8544
  8 Chase Ln Middletown (19709) *(G-6946)*
Bulldog Construction 302 632-4834
  177 Jaacs Ln Woodside (19980) *(G-20974)*
Bullent Investment LLC 877 214-7707
  8 The Grn Ste A Dover (19901) *(G-1991)*
Bullfeathers Auto Sound Inc 302 846-0434
  28368 Beaver Dam Branch Rd Laurel (19956) *(G-5475)*
Bullioncom LLC 833 629-3927
  800 N King St Ste 304 Wilmington (19801) *(G-15149)*
Bulls Home Services Co 302 540-1381
  317 Manubay Ct Bear (19701) *(G-84)*
Bullseye Entertainment Tech Co 302 924-5034
  8 The Grn Ste 8136 Dover (19901) *(G-1992)*
Bullseye Products LLC 302 468-5086
  717 N Union St Wilmington (19805) *(G-15150)*
Bulton Properties LLC 302 945-0967
  29161 Stockley Rd Milton (19968) *(G-8577)*
Bulwark Builders Inc 302 299-3190
  15 Bender Dr Newark (19711) *(G-10104)*
Bumpers & Company Prof Assn 302 798-3300
  1104 Philadelphia Pike Wilmington (19809) *(G-15151)*
Bunker Hill Equestrian Center 302 312-9890
  1239 Bunker Hill Rd Middletown (19709) *(G-6947)*
Bunting & Bertrand Inc 302 732-6836
  15 Hickory St Frankford (19945) *(G-4080)*
Bunting & Murray Cnstr Corp 302 436-5144
  32996 Lighthouse Rd Selbyville (19975) *(G-13486)*
Bunting Construction Corp 302 436-5124
  32996 Lighthouse Rd Selbyville (19975) *(G-13487)*
Buntings Garage Inc 302 732-9021
  28506 Carebear Ln Dagsboro (19939) *(G-1421)*
Buoy Hydration Inc 314 230-5106
  2140 S Dupont Hwy Camden (19934) *(G-795)*
Burgeon It Services LLC 302 613-0999
  1601 Concord Pike Ste 36e Wilmington (19803) *(G-15152)*
Burke Dermatology (PA) 302 734-3376
  95 Wolf Creek Blvd Ste 1 Dover (19901) *(G-1993)*
Burke Dermatology 302 703-6585
  353 Savannah Rd Lewes (19958) *(G-5780)*
Burke Dermatology (PA) 302 230-3376
  774 Christiana Rd Ste 107 Newark (19713) *(G-10105)*
Burke Equipment Company 302 248-7070
  11196 E Snake Rd Delmar (19940) *(G-1570)*

Burke Equipment Company (PA) 302 697-3200
  54 Andrews Lake Rd Felton (19943) *(G-3949)*
Burke Painting Co Inc 302 998-8500
  119 E Quail Trl Lewes (19958) *(G-5781)*
Burkes Seal Coating 302 697-7635
  22 Howell St Dover (19901) *(G-1994)*
Burkhan International Dev Corp 202 790-8050
  2140 S Dupont Hwy Camden (19934) *(G-796)*
Burlington Mnor Prsrvtion Asso 302 761-7306
  4 Denny Rd Wilmington (19809) *(G-15153)*
Burns & McBride, New Castle *Also Called: Burns & McBride Inc (G-8901)*
Burns & McBride Inc (HQ) 302 656-5110
  18 Boulden Cir Ste 30 New Castle (19720) *(G-8901)*
Burnsies Plumbing LLC 215 275-0723
  20 Pear Dr Bear (19701) *(G-85)*
Burr & Forman LLP 302 425-6400
  1201 N Market St Ste 140 Wilmington (19801) *(G-15154)*
Burris Cosmtc & Fmly Dentistry 302 697-3125
  199 South St Camden (19934) *(G-797)*
Burris Freight Management LLC 800 805-8135
  501 Se 5th St Milford (19963) *(G-7807)*
Burris Logistics 302 839-5129
  309 Concord Rd Dover (19904) *(G-1995)*
Burris Logistics 302 398-5050
  111 Reese Ave Harrington (19952) *(G-4742)*
Burris Logistics 302 221-4100
  1000 Centerpoint Blvd Historic New Castle (19720) *(G-4948)*
Burris Logistics (PA) 302 839-4531
  501 Se 5th St Milford (19963) *(G-7808)*
Burris Logistics 302 737-5203
  650 Pencader Dr Newark (19702) *(G-10106)*
Burris Refrigerated Logistics, Historic New Castle *Also Called: Burris Logistics (G-4948)*
Burris Retail Logistics, Milford *Also Called: Burris Logistics (G-7808)*
Burroughs Express LLC 410 476-1764
  59 Stoney Dr Dover (19904) *(G-1996)*
Burton Construction Co LLC 302 327-8650
  530 Schoolhouse Rd Ste E Hockessin (19707) *(G-5145)*
Burton Realty Inc 302 945-5100
  24808 John J Williams Hwy Millsboro (19966) *(G-8210)*
Busability Corporation 845 821-4609
  1013 Centre Rd Ste 403s Wilmington (19805) *(G-15155)*
Buscemi Pressure Washing Llc 302 223-6295
  1960 Wheatleys Pond Rd Smyrna (19977) *(G-13670)*
Bushwick Metals LLC 302 328-0590
  100 Steel Dr New Castle (19720) *(G-8902)*
Busibud Inc 626 228-1855
  2093a Philadelphia Pike Ste 422 Claymont (19703) *(G-1068)*
Business At International LLC 605 610-4885
  16192 Coastal Hwy Lewes (19958) *(G-5782)*
Business Funding Pro 888 705-8278
  913 N Market St Ste 100 Wilmington (19801) *(G-15156)*
Business History Conference 302 658-2400
  298 Buck Rd Wilmington (19807) *(G-15157)*
Business Incorporators 302 475-6596
  1019 Cypress Rd Wilmington (19810) *(G-15158)*
Business Insurance Services 302 655-5300
  100 W Commons Blvd New Castle (19720) *(G-8903)*
Business Integration Solution 302 355-3512
  220 Continental Dr Ste 213 Newark (19713) *(G-10107)*
Business Interface MD LLC 302 735-7739
  1203 College Park Dr Ste 101 Dover (19904) *(G-1997)*
Business Intrface Wrkfrce Svcs 302 660-7123
  800 N King St Ste 101 Wilmington (19801) *(G-15159)*
Business Move Solutions Inc 302 324-0080
  11 Boulden Cir New Castle (19720) *(G-8904)*
Busy Bees Home Learning Center, Dover *Also Called: Ditrocchio Maria Antonetta (G-2305)*
Busymama Cupcakes 302 259-9988
  328 E Poplar St Seaford (19973) *(G-13098)*
Butamax Advanced Biofuels LLC (PA) 302 695-6787
  Route 141 & Henry Clay Wilmington (19880) *(G-15160)*
Butler Hospitality LLC 888 288-5846
  1204 N King St Wilmington (19801) *(G-15161)*

Butt Kambiz R MD..708 927-7169
  111 Continental Dr # 406 Newark (19713) *(G-10108)*
Butter Games LLC..650 867-2492
  254 Chapman Rd Ste 208 Newark (19702) *(G-10109)*
Butterfield Inspection Service................................301 322-1644
  113 Dewey Ave Lewes (19958) *(G-5783)*
Buy and Sell Rags, Newark Also Called: Commodities Plus Inc *(G-10285)*
Buycrypt Inc..309 733-4157
  8 The Grn Ste A Dover (19901) *(G-1998)*
Buygoods Inc..302 573-2500
  1201 N Orange St Ste 7223 Wilmington (19801) *(G-15162)*
Buze Mobile Inc..630 331-0553
  8 The Grn Ste 16808 Dover (19901) *(G-1999)*
Buzzspark Labs LLC..302 828-0969
  651 N Broad St Ste 201 Middletown (19709) *(G-6948)*
BV Teagarden & Son Cnstr LLC.............................410 330-1733
  36421 Saint George Rd Delmar (19940) *(G-1571)*
Bvi Group LLC..954 604-9363
  8 The Grn Ste 6006 Dover (19901) *(G-2000)*
Bw Drilling Co...302 658-0410
  100 W 10th St Wilmington (19801) *(G-15163)*
BW Electric Inc...302 566-6248
  15342 S Dupont Hwy Harrington (19952) *(G-4743)*
Bwb Inc...717 939-3679
  24115 Cari Dr Millsboro (19966) *(G-8211)*
Bwci Animal Hospital MGT Sys, Smyrna Also Called: Brittons Wise Computers Inc *(G-13668)*
Bwe Electric, Harrington Also Called: BW Electric Inc *(G-4743)*
Bwt Lighting Inc..302 709-0808
  825 Dawson Dr Ste 1 Newark (19713) *(G-10110)*
By Feel Farms, Felton Also Called: Francis Bergold *(G-3976)*
By Lore Tech Solutions Inc....................................302 202-9499
  743 Ashington Dr Middletown (19709) *(G-6949)*
By Mail Eric Graham Intl..816 368-1641
  427 N Tatnall St Wilmington (19801) *(G-15164)*
By The Sea Contracting LLC..................................302 569-9701
  32641 W Carteret Ct Millsboro (19966) *(G-8212)*
By The Shore..302 462-0496
  27303 Road Dawg Ln Georgetown (19947) *(G-4241)*
Bydarkmatter LLC..850 801-2732
  1111b S Governors Ave Ste 6502 Dover (19904) *(G-2001)*
Byers Electrical Construc......................................302 420-8700
  508 South St Historic New Castle (19720) *(G-4949)*
Byers Industrial Services LLC...............................302 836-4790
  1501 Porter Rd Bear (19701) *(G-86)*
Byler Sawmill..302 730-4208
  2846 Yoder Dr Dover (19904) *(G-2002)*
Bylerwilliamr..302 653-3727
  502 W Denneys Rd Dover (19904) *(G-2003)*
Byrd Group Delaware...302 757-8300
  10 Corporate Cir Ste 215 New Castle (19720) *(G-8905)*
Byrds Nest LLC..302 475-4949
  2627 Point Breeze Dr Wilmington (19810) *(G-15165)*
Byron & Davis Cccc...302 792-2334
  601 Philadelphia Pike Wilmington (19809) *(G-15166)*
Byron Outten Plumbing...302 236-4727
  10004 Woodyard Rd Greenwood (19950) *(G-4601)*
Byte Technology Systems Inc...............................347 687-7240
  16192 Coastal Hwy Lewes (19958) *(G-5784)*
Byzantium Sky Press..302 258-6116
  27567 Bristol Ct Milton (19968) *(G-8578)*
Bz Construction Services Inc...............................302 999-7505
  120 E Ayre St Wilmington (19804) *(G-15167)*
C & A Ink..302 565-9866
  42 Stallion Dr Newark (19713) *(G-10111)*
C & A Management Inc..302 888-2786
  919 Market Street Flr 2 Wilmington (19801) *(G-15168)*
C & B Complete Clg Svc Inc..................................302 436-9622
  36007 Zion Church Rd Frankford (19945) *(G-4081)*
C & B Construct...302 378-9862
  150 Vickers Rd Milford (19963) *(G-7809)*
C & B Internet Services LLC..................................302 384-9804
  704 N King St Ste 500 Wilmington (19801) *(G-15169)*

C & C Autobrokers..302 442-5464
  601 A St Wilmington (19801) *(G-15170)*
C & C Contractors LLC..302 934-1134
  11 Beacon Cir Millsboro (19966) *(G-8213)*
C & C Technologies Inc...302 653-7623
  441 Pier Head Blvd Smyrna (19977) *(G-13671)*
C & D Contractors Inc...302 764-2020
  734 Hertford Rd Wilmington (19803) *(G-15171)*
C & H Contracting LLC..302 883-4339
  3404 Irish Hill Rd Magnolia (19962) *(G-6723)*
C & K Builders LLC..302 324-9811
  334 Bear Christiana Rd Bear (19701) *(G-87)*
C & L Cleaners Inc...302 736-5171
  266 Galaxy St Bldg Afb Dover (19902) *(G-2004)*
C & M Roofing & Siding, Magnolia Also Called: C&M Construction Company LLC *(G-6725)*
C & M Service Inc..302 453-5228
  550 S College Ave Newark (19713) *(G-10112)*
C & N Freight LLC..302 897-4061
  354 Hackberry Dr New Castle (19720) *(G-8906)*
C & N Services LLC...302 883-1046
  126 Thornhill Ct Dover (19904) *(G-2005)*
C & S Battery Inc..610 459-2227
  12 Penarth Dr Wilmington (19803) *(G-15172)*
C & S Consultants Inc...302 236-5211
  6 E Clarke Ave Milford (19963) *(G-7810)*
C & W Auto Parts Co Inc.......................................302 697-2684
  851 Sorghum Mill Rd Magnolia (19962) *(G-6724)*
C and C Alpaca Factory...609 752-7894
  17219 Sweetbriar Rd Lewes (19958) *(G-5785)*
C and C Drywall Contractors N.............................302 242-3305
  730 Horsepond Rd Dover (19901) *(G-2006)*
C and C Management Group LLC.........................302 946-4179
  1201 N Market St Ste 111 Wilmington (19801) *(G-15173)*
C and L Bradford and Assoc.................................302 529-8566
  1604 Trevalley Rd Wilmington (19810) *(G-15174)*
C B Joe TV & Appliances Inc.................................302 322-7600
  348 Churchmans Rd New Castle (19720) *(G-8907)*
C Edgar Wood Inc (PA)..302 674-3500
  1154 S Governors Ave Dover (19904) *(G-2007)*
C H P T Manufacturing Inc....................................302 856-7660
  21388 Cedar Creek Ave Georgetown (19947) *(G-4242)*
C L Burchenal Oil Co Inc.......................................302 697-1517
  109 S Main St Camden (19934) *(G-798)*
C M C, Wilmington Also Called: CMC Steel Holding Company *(G-15500)*
C M Construction Co LLC.....................................302 228-3570
  89 Reed St Frankford (19945) *(G-4082)*
C M D Inc..302 894-1776
  62 Albe Dr Ste C Newark (19702) *(G-10113)*
C M-Tec Inc...302 369-6166
  1 Innovation Way Ste 100 Newark (19711) *(G-10114)*
C P M Industries Inc..302 478-8200
  3511 Silverside Rd Ste 210 Wilmington (19810) *(G-15175)*
C R Painting...302 519-3938
  28044 Puncheon Rd Selbyville (19975) *(G-13488)*
C S C, Wilmington Also Called: C S C Corporation Texas Inc *(G-15176)*
C S C, Wilmington Also Called: Corporation Service Company *(G-15644)*
C S C Corporation Texas Inc................................302 636-5440
  2711 Centerville Rd Ste 400 Wilmington (19808) *(G-15176)*
C S Consultants...302 623-4144
  4735 Ogletown Stanton Rd Newark (19713) *(G-10115)*
C V International Inc..302 427-0440
  603 Christiana Ave Wilmington (19801) *(G-15177)*
C Vargas Construction LLC..................................302 470-2004
  89 Monticello Ct Seaford (19973) *(G-13099)*
C Wallace & Associates..302 528-2182
  805 Grande Ln Hockessin (19707) *(G-5146)*
C White & Sons LLC..302 629-4848
  5635 Neals School Rd Seaford (19973) *(G-13100)*
C-Met Inc..302 652-1884
  1604 N Dupont Hwy New Castle (19720) *(G-8909)*
C-Schell Spine Speclst-C Schel............................302 736-1223
  1169 Walker Rd Dover (19904) *(G-2008)*

ALPHABETIC SECTION — Camco Tire & Auto LLC

C-Stacks Inc... 617 480-2555
   1313 N Market St Ste 5100 Wilmington (19801) *(G-15179)*

C.E.R.T.S., New Castle *Also Called: Collabrtive Effort To Rnfrce T* *(G-8956)*

C&B Complete Cleaning & Cnstr, Frankford *Also Called: C & B Complete Clg Svc Inc* *(G-4081)*

C&C Welding... 402 414-2485
   50 N Purdue Ave New Castle (19720) *(G-8908)*

C&F Contractors Service LLC.. 302 480-3002
   21033 S Dupont Hwy Greenwood (19950) *(G-4602)*

C&M Construction Company LLC................................. 302 663-0936
   49 Doris Ct Magnolia (19962) *(G-6725)*

C&M Custom Homes LLC... 302 736-5824
   7344 S Dupont Hwy Ste 1 Felton (19943) *(G-3950)*

C&S Farms Inc... 302 249-0458
   8947 Woodland Ferry Rd Laurel (19956) *(G-5476)*

C&S Mechanical Services Inc...................................... 302 377-2343
   202 S Van Buren St Wilmington (19805) *(G-15178)*

C+m Farms LLC... 302 841-1847
   11433 Michael Ave Bridgeville (19933) *(G-679)*

C2 Construction LLC... 302 438-3901
   2913 N Van Buren St Wilmington (19802) *(G-15180)*

C21 Gold Key Realty.. 302 250-6801
   260 E Main St Frnt Newark (19711) *(G-10116)*

C3 Solutions, Newark *Also Called: C3 Wave Holdings LLC* *(G-10117)*

C3 Wave Holdings LLC.. 412 708-6476
   35 Salem Church Rd Ste 80 Newark (19713) *(G-10117)*

C4-Nvis USA LLC.. 213 465-5089
   8 The Grn Ste 6794 Dover (19901) *(G-2009)*

CA All Wrld Ex US Eqity CEF Fu.................................. 610 380-2110
   4005 Kennett Pike Ste 250 Wilmington (19807) *(G-15181)*

CA Briggs Contracting... 302 250-8858
   307 3rd Ave Wilmington (19804) *(G-15182)*

Cabicash Solutions Inc... 315 961-2005
   1000 N West St Ste 1200 Wilmington (19801) *(G-15183)*

Cabinetry Unlimited LLC... 302 436-5030
   7 Hosier St Selbyville (19975) *(G-13489)*

Cabinets To Go LLC.. 302 439-4989
   203 Naamans Rd Ste 1 Claymont (19703) *(G-1069)*

Cable Connections LLC... 302 397-9014
   28838 E Trap Pond Rd Laurel (19956) *(G-5477)*

Cacc Montessori School... 302 239-2917
   1313 Little Baltimore Rd Hockessin (19707) *(G-5147)*

Cactus Annies Restaurant & Bar................................ 302 655-9004
   211 W 9th St Wilmington (19801) *(G-15184)*

Cad Import Inc.. 302 628-4178
   650 Centerpoint Blvd Historic New Castle (19720) *(G-4950)*

Cadia Rehabilitation... 302 734-1199
   1225 Walker Rd Dover (19904) *(G-2010)*

Cadia Rehabilitation Rnssnc...................................... 302 947-4200
   26002 John J Williams Hwy Millsboro (19966) *(G-8214)*

Cadia Rhabilitation Pike Creek.................................. 302 455-0808
   3540 Three Little Bakers Blvd Wilmington (19808) *(G-15185)*

Cadia Rhabilitation Silverside................................... 302 478-8889
   3322 Silverside Rd Wilmington (19810) *(G-15186)*

Cadia Rverside Healthcare Svcs................................ 302 455-0808
   3540 Three Little Bakers Blvd Wilmington (19808) *(G-15187)*

Cadrender Inc... 302 657-0700
   716 N Tatnall St Wilmington (19801) *(G-15188)*

Cae(us) Inc (HQ)... 813 885-7481
   1011 Ct Rd Ste 322 Wilmington (19805) *(G-15189)*

Caesar Rodney Chapter Sar, Dover *Also Called: National Society of Sons* *(G-3155)*

Caesar Rodney School District................................... 302 697-3207
   950 Center Dover (19901) *(G-2011)*

Cafe Management Associates..................................... 302 655-4959
   1428 N Clayton St Wilmington (19806) *(G-15190)*

Cafection Corp.. 800 561-6162
   2915 Ogletown Rd Newark (19713) *(G-10118)*

Cahill Contracting.. 302 378-9650
   104 Sleepy Hollow Dr Ste 201 Middletown (19709) *(G-6950)*

Cahill Electrical Contractors, Middletown *Also Called: Cahill Contracting* *(G-6950)*

Cahill Plumbing & Heating Inc................................... 302 894-1802
   325 Markus Ct Newark (19713) *(G-10119)*

Caimar Corporation... 302 653-5011
   17 W Glenwood Ave Smyrna (19977) *(G-13672)*

Cake Sisters.. 302 838-1958
   88 Clinton St Delaware City (19706) *(G-1532)*

Cal Agents Realty Inc.. 408 219-1728
   2093 Philadelphia Pike Ste 2828n Claymont (19703) *(G-1070)*

Calcom Inc.. 442 227-3200
   251 Little Falls Dr Wilmington (19808) *(G-15191)*

Calculus Bus Solutions Inc.. 302 676-2162
   1521 Concord Pike Ste 301 Wilmington (19803) *(G-15192)*

Caleb G Stevens.. 302 535-4202
   118 Mechanic St Harrington (19952) *(G-4744)*

Calfo & Haight Inc.. 302 998-3852
   21 Glover Cir Wilmington (19804) *(G-15193)*

Caliber Bodyworks Texas Inc..................................... 302 832-1660
   731 Rue Madora Bear (19701) *(G-88)*

Caliber Club Shooting Spt Inc................................... 703 283-3533
   8 The Grn Dover (19901) *(G-2012)*

Caliber Collision.. 302 674-4525
   5825 W Denneys Rd Dover (19904) *(G-2013)*

Caliber Collision.. 302 279-1007
   5077 Summit Bridge Rd Middletown (19709) *(G-6951)*

Caliber Collision.. 302 731-1200
   8 Mill Park Ct Newark (19713) *(G-10120)*

Caliber Collision Centers, Bear *Also Called: Caliber Bodyworks Texas Inc* *(G-88)*

Caliber Home Loans... 302 584-0580
   107 Brooks Ct Middletown (19709) *(G-6952)*

Caliber Home Loans Inc.. 302 483-7587
   200 Continental Dr Ste 201 Newark (19713) *(G-10121)*

Calibrant Energy, Wilmington *Also Called: Mss Energy Holdings LLC* *(G-18478)*

California Explosion LLC (PA)................................... 516 404-9892
   300 Delaware Ave Ste 210a Wilmington (19801) *(G-15194)*

California Video, Wilmington *Also Called: California Video 2* *(G-15195)*

California Video 2.. 302 477-6944
   1716 Marsh Rd Wilmington (19810) *(G-15195)*

Calima Group LLC... 443 742-2134
   704 N King St Ste 500 Wilmington (19801) *(G-15196)*

Call Care 24 Inc... 832 217-0864
   1201 N Orange St Ste 6001 Wilmington (19801) *(G-15197)*

Call Rings LLC... 302 250-4030
   8 The Grn Ste 13074 Dover (19901) *(G-2014)*

Callaway Furniture Inc... 302 398-8858
   15152 S Dupont Hwy Harrington (19952) *(G-4745)*

Calloway Farms.. 302 875-0476
   6445 Baileys Landing Dr Bethel (19931) *(G-653)*

Callsynetwork LLC... 785 241-7841
   2055 Limestone Rd 200c Wilmington (19808) *(G-15198)*

Callvu Inc... 646 506-4915
   1000 N West St Ste 1501 Wilmington (19801) *(G-15199)*

Calm Medical Massage Exprt Inc.............................. 443 566-0655
   1994 Carol Dr Wilmington (19808) *(G-15200)*

Calmet... 714 505-6765
   717 N Union St Ste 100 Wilmington (19805) *(G-15201)*

Calvert Comfort Cooling & Htg, Wilmington *Also Called: Calvert Mechanical Systems Inc* *(G-15202)*

Calvert Mechanical Systems Inc............................... 302 998-0460
   410 Meco Dr Wilmington (19804) *(G-15202)*

CAM Physcal Thrapy Wllness Svc (PA)..................... 301 853-0093
   100 Biddle Ave Ste 101a Newark (19702) *(G-10122)*

CAM-K Transport LLC.. 267 693-1797
   550 S Dupont Hwy Apt 15 New Castle (19720) *(G-8910)*

Cambria LLC... 703 898-9989
   16826 Forest Dr Lewes (19958) *(G-5786)*

Cambridge CLB Assoc Ltd Partnr.............................. 302 674-3500
   726 Yorklyn Rd Ste 200 Hockessin (19707) *(G-5148)*

Cambridge Insurance Group Inc................................ 302 888-2440
   1740 Lancaster Ave Wilmington (19805) *(G-15203)*

Cambridge Trs Inc.. 302 453-9200
   240 Chapman Rd Newark (19702) *(G-10123)*

Camco Tire & Auto LLC.. 302 664-1264
   200 Business Park Ln Milton (19968) *(G-8579)*

(PA)=Parent Co (HQ)=Headquarters (DH)=Div Headquarters

Camden - Wyoming Lions Club 302 697-6565
220 Weeks Dr Camden (19934) *(G-799)*

Camden Cigars 302 698-1000
4004 S Dupont Hwy Dover (19901) *(G-2015)*

Camden Counseling LLC 302 698-9109
258 E Camden Wyoming Ave Camden (19934) *(G-800)*

Camden Drywall Inc 302 697-9653
203 Harrison Ave Wyoming (19934) *(G-20981)*

Camden Metals, Camden Also Called: Handytube Corporation *(G-845)*

Camden Primary Care 302 698-1100
4601 S Dupont Hwy Ste 2 Dover (19901) *(G-2016)*

Camden Walk-In LLC 302 698-1100
4601 S Dupont Hwy Dover (19901) *(G-2017)*

Camden-Wyoming Rotary Club 302 697-2724
6 Bob White Pl Camden Wyoming (19934) *(G-921)*

Camdenwyoming Sewer & Wtr Auth 302 697-6372
16 Sw St Camden (19934) *(G-801)*

Cameck Publishing 302 598-4799
3306 Coachman Rd Wilmington (19803) *(G-15204)*

Camelo LLC 302 574-6556
2055 Limestone Rd Ste 200c Wilmington (19808) *(G-15205)*

Camels Hump Inc 302 227-5719
63 Fields End Rehoboth Beach (19971) *(G-12662)*

Cameras Etc Inc 302 453-9400
165 E Main St Newark (19711) *(G-10124)*

Cameras Etc Inc (PA) 302 764-9400
2303 Baynard Blvd Wilmington (19802) *(G-15206)*

Cameras Etc T V & Video, Wilmington Also Called: Cameras Etc Inc *(G-15206)*

Cameras Etc TV & Video, Newark Also Called: Cameras Etc Inc *(G-10124)*

Cameron Jones 610 880-7700
371 Harbor Dr Apt 9 Claymont (19703) *(G-1071)*

Camio LLC 585 851-8550
8 The Grn Dover (19901) *(G-2018)*

Cammarato & Aloe PA, Dover Also Called: Aloe & Carr PA *(G-1773)*

Cammock Boys Auto 302 409-0645
2103 Carter St Wilmington (19802) *(G-15207)*

Camp Adventureland LLC 302 449-2267
112 Patriot Dr Ste C Middletown (19709) *(G-6953)*

Camp Arrowhead Busine 302 448-6919
913 Wilson Rd Wilmington (19803) *(G-15208)*

Camp Bow Wow, Newark Also Called: Dog House Ventures Inc *(G-10547)*

Camp Chiropractic Inc 302 378-2899
272 Carter Dr Ste 120 Middletown (19709) *(G-6954)*

Camp Possibilities Foundation 302 563-9460
Wilmington (19807) *(G-15209)*

Campbell & Levine LLC 302 426-1900
222 Delaware Ave Ste 1600 Wilmington (19801) *(G-15210)*

Campbell Fincl Solutions LLC 302 202-9029
1201 N Market St Ste 111 Wilmington (19801) *(G-15211)*

Campbell Home Exteriors LLC 302 526-9663
276 Jury Dr Magnolia (19962) *(G-6726)*

Campbell's Custom Cabinet Shop, Greenwood Also Called: Custom Cabinet Shop Inc *(G-4609)*

Campbells 302 359-9918
332 Weiner Ave Harrington (19952) *(G-4746)*

Campbells Landscape Svc Inc 302 266-0117
22 Deer Run Newark (19711) *(G-10125)*

Campus Elction Enggment Prj In 614 735-1460
16192 Coastal Hwy Lewes (19958) *(G-5787)*

Campus Life 302 294-6520
501 Hamlet Way Newark (19711) *(G-10126)*

Can Services LLC 212 920-9348
254 Chapman Rd Newark (19702) *(G-10127)*

Canadian Sunpal Power LLC 905 926-6681
16192 Coastal Hwy Lewes (19958) *(G-5788)*

Cananwill Corp 302 576-3499
300 Delaware Ave Wilmington (19801) *(G-15212)*

Cananwill Premium Funding Co, Wilmington Also Called: Cananwill Corp *(G-15212)*

Canby Park Apartments, Wilmington Also Called: Alban Associates *(G-14348)*

Cancer Care Ctrs At Bay Hlth 302 674-4401
793 S Queen St Dover (19904) *(G-2019)*

Cancer Support Cmnty Del Inc 302 995-2850
4810 Lancaster Pike Wilmington (19807) *(G-15213)*

Candelay Industries LLC 302 696-2464
702 Rockland Rd Rockland (19732) *(G-13029)*

Candice Ryder 954 296-5709
17432 Slipper Shell Way # 1 Lewes (19958) *(G-5789)*

Candle Parlour 302 408-0890
12 Commonwealth Ave Claymont (19703) *(G-1072)*

Candlelight Bridal Formal Tlrg 302 934-8009
314 Main St Millsboro (19966) *(G-8215)*

Candlelight Cleaning 302 270-1218
379 Lake Dr Smyrna (19977) *(G-13673)*

Candlestick Publishing Inc 817 939-1306
4023 Kennett Pike Wilmington (19807) *(G-15214)*

Candlewood Suites 302 266-8184
1101 S College Ave Newark (19713) *(G-10128)*

Candor Trading Corp 302 268-6800
122 Delaware St Historic New Castle (19720) *(G-4951)*

Candyland Farm, Middletown Also Called: Pck Associates Inc *(G-7435)*

Candyman Industries Inc 970 319-8404
16192 Coastal Hwy Lewes (19958) *(G-5790)*

Canekast Inc (PA) 952 448-2801
1111 S Governors Ave Dover (19904) *(G-2020)*

Canine Creations 302 593-2684
5903 Orchard Ave Wilmington (19808) *(G-15215)*

Canine Cture Exprt Groming LLC 302 500-1814
217 N Rehoboth Blvd Milford (19963) *(G-7811)*

Cann Printing, Wilmington Also Called: William N Cann Inc *(G-20795)*

Cann-Erikson, Wilmington Also Called: Cann-Erikson Bindery Inc *(G-15216)*

Cann-Erikson Bindery Inc 302 995-6636
1 Meco Cir Wilmington (19804) *(G-15216)*

Canna Care Docs Delaware LLC 302 594-0630
9 Germay Dr Wilmington (19804) *(G-15217)*

Cannon Cold Storage, Bridgeville Also Called: Cannon Cold Storage LLC *(G-680)*

Cannon Cold Storage LLC 302 337-5500
8141 Seashore Hwy Bridgeville (19933) *(G-680)*

Cannon Iron and Metal Inc 302 492-8091
3221 Hartly Rd Hartly (19953) *(G-4860)*

Cannon Sline Industrial Inc (DH) 302 658-1420
103 Carroll Dr New Castle (19720) *(G-8911)*

Cannon Sline LLC 302 658-1420
103 Carroll Dr New Castle (19720) *(G-8912)*

Cannon Spas 302 628-9404
10747 Hastings Farm Rd Seaford (19973) *(G-13101)*

Cannon Spas & Pools, Seaford Also Called: Cannon Spas *(G-13101)*

Cannon's, Newark Also Called: Cannons Cake and Candy Sups *(G-10129)*

Cannons Cake and Candy Sups 302 738-3321
2638 Kirkwood Hwy Newark (19711) *(G-10129)*

Canon Hospitality MGT LLC 302 737-5050
268 E Main St Newark (19711) *(G-10130)*

Canon Solutions America Inc 302 792-8700
300 Bellevue Pkwy Ste 135 Wilmington (19809) *(G-15218)*

Canopy Interactive LLC (PA) 631 258-1552
2035 Sunset Lake Rd Newark (19702) *(G-10131)*

Cansurround Pbc 302 540-2270
1815 W 13th St Ste 5 Wilmington (19806) *(G-15219)*

Cant Wait Overhead Door LLC 302 546-3667
1554 Walnut Shade Rd Magnolia (19962) *(G-6727)*

Cap Title of Delaware LLC 302 537-3788
29 Atlantic Ave Ste E Ocean View (19970) *(G-12485)*

Capade LLC 302 786-5775
1222 Crestover Rd Wilmington (19803) *(G-15220)*

Capano Homes Inc 302 384-7980
4420 Limestone Rd Ste 202a Wilmington (19808) *(G-15221)*

Capano Management, Wilmington Also Called: Capano Homes Inc *(G-15221)*

Capano Management Company 302 737-8056
33 Marrows Rd Newark (19713) *(G-10132)*

Capb Infotek LLC 347 277-7125
16192 Coastal Hwy Lewes (19958) *(G-5791)*

Cape Climate Inc 302 858-7160
26411 Fells St Georgetown (19947) *(G-4243)*

Cape Ent PA..717 269-3106
  17005 Old Orchard Rd Lewes (19958) *(G-5792)*

Cape Financial Services Inc...................................302 645-6274
  16117 Willow Creek Rd Lewes (19958) *(G-5793)*

Cape Gazette Ltd..302 645-7700
  17585 Nassau Commons Blvd Ste 6 Lewes (19958) *(G-5794)*

Cape Henlopen Elks Lodge....................................302 645-7016
  Nassau (19969) *(G-8740)*

Cape Henlopen Senior Center................................302 227-2055
  11 Christian St Rehoboth Beach (19971) *(G-12663)*

Cape Hnlpen Nntcoke Drmatology, Lewes *Also Called: Mitchell C Stickler MD Inc (G-6280)*

Cape May Lewes Ferry..302 577-2011
  820 N French St Wilmington (19801) *(G-15222)*

Cape Medical Associates PA...................................302 645-2805
  701 Savannah Rd Ste B Lewes (19958) *(G-5795)*

Cape Orthopedic, Lewes *Also Called: Cape Medical Associates PA (G-5795)*

Cape Spine & Disc...302 644-2473
  1540 Savannah Rd Ste B Lewes (19958) *(G-5796)*

Cape Water Taxi..302 644-7334
  107 Anglers Rd Lewes (19958) *(G-5797)*

Cape Water Tours & Taxi..302 245-4794
  22549 Rocky Rd Lewes (19958) *(G-5798)*

Capgemini America Inc..302 656-7491
  405 N King St Wilmington (19801) *(G-15223)*

Capiche Event Planning LLC..................................302 743-1522
  520 Milton Dr Wilmington (19802) *(G-15224)*

Capital and Worth...302 477-0660
  1202 Foulk Rd Wilmington (19803) *(G-15225)*

Capital Auto Rcvbles Asset Tr.................................212 250-6864
  1209 N Orange St Wilmington (19801) *(G-15226)*

Capital Auto Receivables..313 656-6304
  301 Bellevue Pkwy Fl 3 Wilmington (19809) *(G-15227)*

Capital Commercial Realty LLC..............................302 734-4400
  5307 Limestone Rd Ste 102 Wilmington (19808) *(G-15228)*

Capital Contracting LLC..302 690-0094
  6 Noble Ln Newark (19713) *(G-10133)*

Capital Crematorium, Dover *Also Called: Torbert Funeral Chapel Inc (G-3704)*

Capital Hlthcare Svcs Nrsing R, Dover *Also Called: Capitol Nrsing Rhblttion Ctr L (G-2023)*

Capital Markets Iq LLC..310 882-6380
  427 N Tatnall St Ste 52811 Wilmington (19801) *(G-15229)*

Capital One National Assn......................................877 383-4802
  802 Delaware Ave Fl 1 Wilmington (19801) *(G-15230)*

Capital One National Assn......................................302 658-3302
  1 S Orange St Wilmington (19801) *(G-15231)*

Capital Orthopaedic..302 628-7702
  1320 Middleford Rd Seaford (19973) *(G-13102)*

Capital School District..302 678-8394
  126 Mourning Dove Ln Dover (19901) *(G-2021)*

Capital Trail Service Center....................................302 731-0999
  1530 Capitol Trl Newark (19711) *(G-10134)*

Capitaql Environmental, Newark *Also Called: Capitol Environmental Svcs Inc (G-10136)*

Capitol Broadband Dev Co LLC
  1000 N West St Fl 10 Wilmington (19801) *(G-15232)*

Capitol Cleaners & Ldrers Inc (PA).........................302 674-1511
  195 Commerce Way Dover (19904) *(G-2022)*

Capitol Environmental Svcs Inc (PA)......................302 380-3737
  200 Biddle Ave Ste 205 Newark (19702) *(G-10135)*

Capitol Environmental Svcs Inc..............................302 652-8999
  200 Biddle Ave Ste 205 Newark (19702) *(G-10136)*

Capitol Little League Inc..302 999-1184
  2148 Elder Dr Wilmington (19808) *(G-15233)*

Capitol Nrsing Rhblttion Ctr L.................................302 734-1199
  1225 Walker Rd Dover (19904) *(G-2023)*

Capitol Title Loans..302 652-3591
  101 N Union St Wilmington (19805) *(G-15234)*

Capitol Uniform & Linen Svc, Dover *Also Called: Capitol Cleaners & Ldrers Inc (G-2022)*

Capitols of Jcs LLC..302 918-5599
  73 Greentree Dr Ste 401 Dover (19904) *(G-2024)*

Cappa Inc...302 598-4762
  321 Possum Park Rd Newark (19711) *(G-10137)*

Cappo Dennis John..302 245-2261
  32776 Omar Rd Frankford (19945) *(G-4083)*

Caprini Suites LLC..302 200-8904
  8 The Grn Ste 12426 Dover (19901) *(G-2025)*

Capriottis of Milford..302 424-3309
  457 Banning Rd Camden Wyoming (19934) *(G-922)*

Capsa Solutions LLC...800 437-6633
  160 Greentree Dr Dover (19904) *(G-2026)*

Capstone Homes LLC..302 644-0300
  33712 Wescoats Rd Unit 5 Lewes (19958) *(G-5799)*

Capstone Homes LLC...302 644-0300
  28855 Lewes Georgetown Hwy Lewes (19958) *(G-5800)*

Capsula Inc..562 466-0155
  2093 Philadelphia Pike Claymont (19703) *(G-1073)*

Captain's Catch, Wilmington *Also Called: Meltrone Inc (G-18268)*

Capton LLC..510 766-2803
  1007 N Orange St Fl 4 Wilmington (19801) *(G-15235)*

Car Doc..301 302-3362
  9534 Shadow Point Ln Delmar (19940) *(G-1572)*

Car Part Planet..888 412-2772
  18585 Coastal Hwy Rehoboth Beach (19971) *(G-12664)*

Car Shoppe LLC..302 992-9669
  2205 Mitch Rd Wilmington (19804) *(G-15236)*

Car Tech Auto Center...302 368-4104
  102 Albe Dr Ste A Newark (19702) *(G-10138)*

Car Wash of Prices Corner.....................................302 994-9274
  3213 Kirkwood Hwy Wilmington (19808) *(G-15237)*

Cara Guitars Manufacturing...................................302 521-0119
  112 Water St Wilmington (19804) *(G-15238)*

Cara Plastics Inc..302 622-7070
  1201 N Market St Ste 2100 Wilmington (19801) *(G-15239)*

Carbon Direct Inc (PA)...212 742-3719
  850 New Burton Rd Ste 201 Dover (19904) *(G-2027)*

Carda Health Inc..415 497-8417
  8 The Grn Dover (19901) *(G-2028)*

Cardenti Electric..302 834-1278
  109 E Scotland Dr Bear (19701) *(G-89)*

Cardiac Diagnostic Center, Wilmington *Also Called: Christiana Care Health Sys Inc (G-15400)*

Cardiac Rehab...302 832-5414
  2600 Glasgow Ave Ste 220 Newark (19702) *(G-10139)*

Cardio-Kinetics Inc..302 738-6635
  52 N Chapel St Ste 101 Newark (19711) *(G-10140)*

Cardiology Consultants..302 645-1233
  16704 Kings Hwy Lewes (19958) *(G-5801)*

Cardiology Physicans PA Inc..................................302 366-8600
  1 Centurian Dr Ste 200 Newark (19713) *(G-10141)*

Care At Home of Delaware LLC............................302 502-7138
  20 Montchanin Rd Ste 50 Wilmington (19807) *(G-15240)*

Care Constitution LLC..201 240-3661
  651 N Broad St Middletown (19709) *(G-6955)*

Care Mentor Ai LLC..302 830-3700
  910 Foulk Rd Ste 201 Wilmington (19803) *(G-15241)*

Carebnb Inc..904 303-6825
  651 N Broad St Ste 206 Middletown (19709) *(G-6956)*

Career Associates Inc...302 674-4357
  385 W North St Ste A Dover (19904) *(G-2029)*

Career Rady Educatn Foundation..........................302 540-2733
  2595 Mccoy Rd Bear (19701) *(G-90)*

Careerminds..302 352-0511
  1601 Concord Pike Ste 82 Wilmington (19803) *(G-15242)*

Careeronestop Dover One Stop.............................302 739-5473
  655 S Bay Rd Dover (19901) *(G-2030)*

Carekraken LLC...410 808-0333
  221 N Broad St Ste 3a Middletown (19709) *(G-6957)*

Carelon Research Inc (HQ)...................................302 230-2000
  123 S Justison St Ste 200 Wilmington (19801) *(G-15243)*

Careportmd LLC...302 202-3020
  100 College Sq Newark (19711) *(G-10142)*

Careportmd LLC (PA)..302 283-9001
  1 Innovation Way Ste 400 Newark (19711) *(G-10143)*

Careportmd LLC...302 202-3020
  4365 Kirkwood Hwy Wilmington (19808) *(G-15244)*

Carewallet, Wilmington *Also Called: Carewallet Inc (G-15245)*

ALPHABETIC SECTION

Carewallet Inc (PA)..732 477-4149
1013 Ctr Rd Ste 403s Wilmington (19805) *(G-15245)*

Carey Jr James E Inc (PA)...............................302 934-8383
30618 Dupont Blvd Unit 1 Dagsboro (19939) *(G-1422)*

Careys Diesel Inc...302 678-3797
168 Denny St Leipsic (19901) *(G-5629)*

Careys Inc..302 875-5674
30986 Sussex Hwy Laurel (19956) *(G-5478)*

Careys Towing, Laurel Also Called: Careys Inc *(G-5478)*

Cargill Meat Solutions Corp.............................305 826-3699
1209 N Orange St Wilmington (19801) *(G-15246)*

Cargimex World LLC......................................514 701-4224
3390 Ogletown Rd Newark (19713) *(G-10144)*

Cargo Aligeorgia LLC.....................................302 899-1025
74 E Glenwood Ave Ste 5198 Smyrna (19977) *(G-13674)*

Cargo Cube Licensing LLC.............................844 200-2823
2711 Centerville Rd # 400 Wilmington (19808) *(G-15247)*

Caribb Moto Cars, Wilmington Also Called: Caribb Transport Inc *(G-15248)*

Caribb Transport Inc......................................302 274-2112
2800 Governor Printz Blvd Ste 3 Wilmington (19802) *(G-15248)*

Caribbean Clture Awareness Inc (PA)..............888 595-1259
610 Wesley Ct Middletown (19709) *(G-6958)*

Caribe Technologies Inc.................................205 590-5767
651 N Broad St Middletown (19709) *(G-6959)*

Caridad Rosal MA MD....................................302 653-6174
38 Deak Dr Smyrna (19977) *(G-13675)*

Caring For Life Inc..302 892-2214
92 Reads Way Ste 207 New Castle (19720) *(G-8913)*

Caring For Womens Health..............................302 489-2420
620 Stanton Christiana Rd Newark (19713) *(G-10145)*

Caring Hearts Home Care LLC........................302 734-9000
971 Burris Rd Hartly (19953) *(G-4861)*

Caring Hnds Phlbotomy Svcs LLC....................302 559-5539
301 6th Ave Wilmington (19805) *(G-15249)*

Caring Matters Home Care.............................302 993-1121
283 Orchard Grove Dr Camden (19934) *(G-802)*

Caring Minds Medical Center..........................267 243-9102
2 Hogan Cir Middletown (19709) *(G-6960)*

Caring Minds Medical Ctr LLC........................302 516-7936
5223 W Woodmill Dr Ste 41 Wilmington (19808) *(G-15250)*

Caring N Action Nursing.................................302 368-2273
15 Prestbury Sq Newark (19713) *(G-10146)*

Carisma Tel, Wilmington Also Called: Carisma Telecom Inc *(G-15251)*

Carisma Telecom Inc.....................................302 357-3650
501 Silverside Rd Ste 105 Wilmington (19809) *(G-15251)*

Caritas Home Health Services........................302 525-6331
30 Prestbury Sq Ste 325 Newark (19713) *(G-10147)*

Carl Deputy & Son Builders LLC.....................302 284-3041
981 Tomahawk Ln Felton (19943) *(G-3951)*

Carl King Tire Co Inc (PA)..............................302 697-9506
109 S Main St Camden (19934) *(G-803)*

Carl King Tire Co Inc....................................302 644-4070
96 Tulip Dr Lewes (19958) *(G-5802)*

Carl M Freedman Communities.......................302 436-4102
31822 Lakeview Dr Selbyville (19975) *(G-13490)*

Carl M Freeman..302 988-1669
36558 Wild Rose Cir Selbyville (19975) *(G-13491)*

Carl M Freeman Associates Inc.......................302 539-6961
Rte 1 & Pennsylvania Ave Bethany Beach (19930) *(G-589)*

Carl M Freeman Associates Inc.......................302 436-3000
21 Village Green Dr Ste 101 Ocean View (19970) *(G-12486)*

Carl M Freeman Foundation Inc......................302 436-6241
31255 Americana Pkwy Selbyville (19975) *(G-13492)*

Carl R Yacoub...302 996-9010
537 Stanton Christiana Rd Ste 106 Newark (19713) *(G-10148)*

Carleton Court Apartments, Wilmington Also Called: Carleton Court Associates LP *(G-15252)*

Carleton Court Associates LP.........................302 454-1800
4 Denny Rd Wilmington (19809) *(G-15252)*

Carlisle Farms Inc...302 349-5692
12733 Shawnee Rd Greenwood (19950) *(G-4603)*

Carlisle Farms Inc...302 349-5692
12733 Shawnee Rd Farmington (19950) *(G-3934)*

Carlisle Group...302 475-3010
2801 Ebright Rd Wilmington (19810) *(G-15253)*

Carlyle Cocoa Co LLC (PA)............................302 428-3800
23 Harbor View Dr New Castle (19720) *(G-8914)*

Carmalt Stuart LLC.......................................302 366-8920
801 Christiana Rd Newark (19713) *(G-10149)*

Carme LLC...302 832-8418
1420 Pulaski Hwy Newark (19702) *(G-10150)*

Carmedis Inc..725 712-2559
1207 Delaware Ave Wilmington (19806) *(G-15254)*

Carmella P Keener Atty.................................302 656-4333
919 N Market St Wilmington (19801) *(G-15255)*

Carmen R Benitez...302 793-2061
3047 Greenshire Ave Claymont (19703) *(G-1074)*

Carmine Potter & Associates..........................302 832-6000
1400 Peoples Plz Ste 104 Newark (19702) *(G-10151)*

Carmine Potter & Associates (PA)..................302 658-8940
1719 Delaware Ave Wilmington (19806) *(G-15256)*

Carny Construction......................................302 436-9738
36884 Chandler Dr Selbyville (19975) *(G-13493)*

Carol A Tavani MD.......................................302 454-9900
4745 Ogletown Stanton Rd Ste 124 Newark (19713) *(G-10152)*

Carol Boyd Heron..302 645-0551
520 E Savannah Rd Lewes (19958) *(G-5803)*

Carolina Street Garden & Home.....................302 539-2405
40118 East South Carolina St Fenwick Island (19944) *(G-4043)*

Caroline M Wiesner......................................877 220-9755
3322 Englewood Rd Wilmington (19810) *(G-15257)*

Carolines Spa & Goods LLC..........................302 200-2635
46 N Main St Selbyville (19975) *(G-13494)*

Carols..302 448-0734
7082 Pleasanton Dr Milford (19963) *(G-7812)*

Carpal Enterprise Inc....................................917 985-8293
16192 Coastal Hwy Lewes (19958) *(G-5804)*

Carpe Dia Organization................................302 333-7546
241 Goldfinch Turn Newark (19711) *(G-10153)*

Carpediem Health LLC..................................347 467-4444
8 The Grn Ste 240 Dover (19901) *(G-2031)*

Carpentry Unlimited, Bear Also Called: Kevin Garber *(G-326)*

Carper For Delaware Hq................................302 328-5774
218 E Main St Newark (19711) *(G-10154)*

Carpevita Home Care, Newport Also Called: Gunning Partners LLC *(G-12453)*

Carr Courier Service Inc...............................302 846-9826
12294 Coachmen Ln Delmar (19940) *(G-1573)*

Carriage House Assoc..................................302 225-2040
1100 N Grant Ave Wilmington (19805) *(G-15258)*

Carrie Construction Inc................................302 239-5386
403 Hockessin Hills Rd Hockessin (19707) *(G-5149)*

Carrillos Auto Care......................................302 339-7234
7 Sleepy Hollow Dr Houston (19954) *(G-5438)*

Carrington Way Apartments, Newark Also Called: Kimberton Apartments Assoc LP *(G-11175)*

Carroll Brothers Electric LLC........................302 947-4754
24853 Rivers Edge Rd Millsboro (19966) *(G-8216)*

Carroll Group Inc...302 836-6180
1271 Quintilio Dr Bear (19701) *(G-91)*

Carroll M Carpenter.....................................302 654-7558
600 Center Mill Rd Wilmington (19807) *(G-15259)*

Carrow Construction LLC.............................302 376-0520
1685 River Rd New Castle (19720) *(G-8915)*

Carson City Ic LLC......................................520 261-8094
3500 S Dupont Hwy Dover (19901) *(G-2032)*

Carspecken-Scott Inc...................................302 762-7955
3007 Rosemont Ave Wilmington (19802) *(G-15260)*

Carspecken-Scott Inc (PA)...........................302 655-7173
1707 N Lincoln St Wilmington (19806) *(G-15261)*

Carted Inc...415 967-8691
651 N Broad St Ste 206 Middletown (19709) *(G-6961)*

Carter Aston..302 561-6315
100 W Commons Blvd New Castle (19720) *(G-8916)*

Carter Aston..302 561-6315
240 Continental Dr Newark (19713) *(G-10155)*

ALPHABETIC SECTION

Carter Pool Management LLC 302 236-6952
   35740 Cutter Ct Lewes (19958) *(G-5805)*

Carter Printing and Design 302 655-2343
   427 Martin Dr Historic New Castle (19720) *(G-4952)*

Carters Inc 302 731-1432
   3132 Fashion Center Blvd Newark (19702) *(G-10156)*

Cartessa Aesthetics 302 332-1991
   210 Peoples Way Hockessin (19707) *(G-5150)*

Cartino Nail Spa 302 212-2510
   19330 Lighthouse Plaza Blvd Unit 1a Rehoboth Beach (19971) *(G-12665)*

Caruso Richard F MD PA 302 645-6698
   130 Savannah Rd Ste B Lewes (19958) *(G-5806)*

Carvel Gardens Annex, Laurel *Also Called: Better Homes Laurel II Inc (G-5469)*

Carver Gardens Properties LLC 302 420-2662
   482 W Chestnut Hill Rd Newark (19713) *(G-10157)*

Carvers Construction LLC 302 505-0260
   209 Eagle View Ln Camden (19934) *(G-804)*

Carvi Carpenter Inc 302 722-3352
   16562 Seashore Hwy Georgetown (19947) *(G-4244)*

Carzaty Inc 650 396-0144
   874 Walker Rd Ste C Dover (19904) *(G-2033)*

CAs Prperty Preservation LLC 302 416-2377
   7509 Governor Printz Blvd Claymont (19703) *(G-1075)*

Casa San Francisco, Milton *Also Called: Catholic Charities Inc (G-8580)*

Casale Marble Imports Inc 561 404-4213
   3518 Silverside Rd Ste 22 Wilmington (19810) *(G-15262)*

Casarino Chrstman Shalk Rnsom 302 594-4500
   1007 N Orange St Wilmington (19801) *(G-15263)*

Cascades LLC 856 662-1730
   151 Cascades Ln Milford (19963) *(G-7813)*

Case, Middletown *Also Called: Countrmsres Assssment SEC Expr (G-7015)*

Case Construction Inc 302 737-3800
   17 Mcmillan Way Newark (19713) *(G-10158)*

Case Hndyman Svcs W Chster LLC 302 234-6558
   510 Thorndale Dr Hockessin (19707) *(G-5151)*

Case Management Services 302 354-3711
   234 Philadelphia Pike Ste 6 Wilmington (19809) *(G-15264)*

Case Tour Duty 302 668-6998
   77 Mccullough Dr Ste 6 New Castle (19720) *(G-8917)*

Casey Battles Concrete 302 312-3905
   1423 Everetts Corner Rd Hartly (19953) *(G-4862)*

Cash Advance 302 730-1988
   71 Greentree Dr Dover (19904) *(G-2034)*

Cash Advance Plus 302 846-3900
   38650 Sussex Hwy Unit 8 Delmar (19940) *(G-1574)*

Cash Connect Inc 302 283-4100
   700 Prides Xing Newark (19713) *(G-10159)*

Cash Plus 231 .... 302 526-2386
   429 S New St Dover (19904) *(G-2035)*

Cashion Media Management 302 674-8321
   300 Stonewater Way Dover (19904) *(G-2036)*

Cashtoday Financial Centers, Claymont *Also Called: Frascella Enterprises Inc (G-1152)*

Casper Hosting LLC 480 442-7112
   16192 Coastal Hwy Lewes (19958) *(G-5807)*

Cassidy Painting Inc 302 683-0710
   17 Bellecor Dr New Castle (19720) *(G-8918)*

Cassidy Painting Inc 302 326-2412
   3128 New Castle Ave New Castle (19720) *(G-8919)*

Cast 781 245-1212
   500 N Wakefield Dr Newark (19702) *(G-10160)*

Castaneda Landscaping & Patios 302 377-1674
   1000 Stanton Rd Wilmington (19808) *(G-15265)*

Casting Arabia LLC (PA) 917 832-5287
   221 N Broad St Ste 3a Middletown (19709) *(G-6962)*

Castle Bag Company 302 656-1001
   115 Valley Rd Wilmington (19804) *(G-15266)*

Castle Care Inc 302 947-2277
   22530 Waterview Rd Lewes (19958) *(G-5808)*

Castle Construction Del Inc 302 326-3600
   185 Old Churchmans Rd New Castle (19720) *(G-8920)*

Castle Consultants, Wilmington *Also Called: Ciancon Global LLC (G-15431)*

Castle HI Ttal Return Fund LLC 626 844-4862
   2711 Centerville Rd # 400 Wilmington (19808) *(G-15267)*

Castle Mortage Services Inc 302 366-0912
   4 Vantage Ct Newark (19711) *(G-10161)*

Castle Services Inc 302 481-6633
   3 Germay Dr Ste 4 # 1095 Wilmington (19804) *(G-15268)*

Castle-Lambert Son Contg Inc 410 329-8192
   39034 Bayview W Selbyville (19975) *(G-13495)*

Castles By Sea LLC 302 539-2508
   154 Naomi Dr Ocean View (19970) *(G-12487)*

Castor Edc, Wilmington *Also Called: Castor Research Inc (G-15269)*

Castor Research Inc 415 484-5347
   1209 N Orange St Wilmington (19801) *(G-15269)*

Castos Inc 800 677-3394
   1209 N Orange St Wilmington (19801) *(G-15270)*

Castro Jose MD 302 999-8169
   2055 Limestone Rd Ste 111 Wilmington (19808) *(G-15271)*

Casual Colors Inc 302 298-0523
   1013 Centre Rd Ste 403s Wilmington (19805) *(G-15272)*

Casus Consulting LLC (PA) 972 532-6357
   651 N Broad St Ste 201 Middletown (19709) *(G-6963)*

Cat Welding LLC 302 846-3509
   37544 Horsey Church Rd Delmar (19940) *(G-1575)*

Catalyst Fitness LLC 302 379-3883
   40 Pierson Dr Hockessin (19707) *(G-5152)*

Catalyst Foundry LLC (PA) 917 471-0947
   1209 N Orange St Wilmington (19801) *(G-15273)*

Catalyst Handling Resources 302 798-2200
   950 Ridge Rd Ste E3 Claymont (19703) *(G-1076)*

Cataract and Laser Center LLC 302 454-8802
   4102 Ogletown Stanton Rd Ste 1 Newark (19713) *(G-10162)*

Catch-A-Web Cleaning Inc 302 836-1970
   2099 Red Lion Rd Bear (19701) *(G-92)*

Caterpillar Authorized Dealer, Felton *Also Called: Alban Tractor LLC (G-3939)*

Cathedral Cemetary, Wilmington *Also Called: Catholic Cemeteries Inc (G-15275)*

Catherine Deane, Wilmington *Also Called: Arcangel Inc (G-14539)*

Catherine Kotalis 302 526-1470
   540 S Governors Ave Dover (19904) *(G-2037)*

Catherine L Kohland 302 335-1505
   1696 Skeeter Neck Rd Frederica (19946) *(G-4163)*

Catherines CSAC Inc 302 478-6160
   1105 N Market St Ste 1300 Wilmington (19801) *(G-15274)*

Catholic Cemeteries Inc (PA) 302 254-4701
   2400 Lancaster Ave Wilmington (19805) *(G-15275)*

Catholic Cemeteries Inc 302 737-2524
   6001 Kirkwood Hwy Wilmington (19808) *(G-15276)*

Catholic Charities, Georgetown *Also Called: Catholic Charities Inc (G-4245)*

Catholic Charities, Wilmington *Also Called: Catholic Charities Inc (G-15277)*

Catholic Charities Inc 302 674-1600
   2099 S Dupont Hwy Dover (19901) *(G-2038)*

Catholic Charities Inc 302 674-1600
   1155 Walker Rd Dover (19904) *(G-2039)*

Catholic Charities Inc 302 856-9578
   406 S Bedford St Georgetown (19947) *(G-4245)*

Catholic Charities Inc 302 684-8694
   127 Broad St Milton (19968) *(G-8580)*

Catholic Charities Inc (PA) 302 655-9624
   2601 W 4th St Wilmington (19805) *(G-15277)*

CATHOLIC HEALTH EAST, Wilmington *Also Called: St Francis Hospital Inc (G-19993)*

Catholic Mnstry To Elderly Inc 302 368-2784
   135 Jeandell Dr Newark (19713) *(G-10163)*

Cathy Ann Mitchell 302 875-7018
   31894 Mitchell Ln Laurel (19956) *(G-5479)*

Cathy Brown Lbw Nctmb 302 475-1477
   Veale Rd Ardencroft Wilmington (19801) *(G-15278)*

Cathy L Harris DDS 302 453-1400
   220 Christiana Medical Ctr Newark (19702) *(G-10164)*

Catleza LLC 415 812-2676
   1521 Concord Pike Ste 301 Wilmington (19803) *(G-15279)*

Catovera Corp 804 814-0301
   8 The Grn Ste 300 Dover (19901) *(G-2040)*

Cavalier Apartments | **ALPHABETIC SECTION**

Cavalier Apartments, Wilmington *Also Called: Cavalier Group (G-15280)*
Cavalier Apts, Newark *Also Called: Cavalier Group (G-10165)*
Cavalier Group..302 368-7437
  25 Golf View Dr Ofc A4 Newark (19702) *(G-10165)*
Cavalier Group (PA)..302 429-8700
  105 Foulk Rd Wilmington (19803) *(G-15280)*
Cavalier Lawn Care & Ldscpg...302 838-2005
  724 New Brighton Ct Middletown (19709) *(G-6964)*
Cavan Inc..302 598-4176
  713 Ashford Rd Wilmington (19803) *(G-15281)*
Caveggo Inc (PA)..201 213-4630
  108 W 13th St Wilmington (19801) *(G-15282)*
Caveman Design Inc..302 234-9969
  359 Lower Snuff Mill Rd Hockessin (19707) *(G-5153)*
Cawsl Enterprises Inc (HQ)...302 478-6160
  3411 Silverside Rd Wilmington (19810) *(G-15283)*
Cayley J Carson..302 328-2561
  1 Lasalle Ave New Castle (19720) *(G-8921)*
Caytu Inc..202 670-9288
  651 N Broad St Ste 206 Middletown (19709) *(G-6965)*
Cayuga Centers..302 257-5848
  292 Carter Dr Ste A Middletown (19709) *(G-6966)*
CB Therapy Services Inc..302 381-7079
  22869 Zoar Rd Georgetown (19947) *(G-4246)*
Cbbc Opco LLC (PA)...863 967-0636
  200 Bellevue Pkwy Ste 210 Wilmington (19809) *(G-15284)*
Cbc Holding Inc..302 254-2000
  1201 N Market St 9th Fl Wilmington (19801) *(G-15285)*
Cbd Pro LLC...443 736-9002
  6625 Millcreek Rd Laurel (19956) *(G-5480)*
Cbhi Inc..484 751-7752
  3423 N Rockfield Dr Wilmington (19810) *(G-15286)*
CBI Group LLC (PA)...302 266-0860
  850 Library Ave Ste 106 Newark (19711) *(G-10166)*
CBI Services LLC...302 325-8400
  24 Reads Way New Castle (19720) *(G-8922)*
Cbm Insurance Agency LLC (PA)....................................302 322-2261
  100 W Commons Blvd Ste 302 New Castle (19720) *(G-8923)*
Cbre Inc..302 661-6700
  3711 Kennett Pike Wilmington (19807) *(G-15287)*
CBS, Delmar *Also Called: Concrete Bldg Systems Del Inc (G-1583)*
CC Drywall Contractors No..302 307-6400
  553 Money Rd Townsend (19734) *(G-13970)*
CC Enterprises LLC...302 265-3677
  105 Anita Dr Newark (19713) *(G-10167)*
Ccci- Celebrants Christn Chpel......................................302 690-4890
  410 N Ramunno Dr # 2304 Middletown (19709) *(G-6967)*
Ccdiesel LLC..302 353-0842
  401 S Dupont Rd Newport (19804) *(G-12443)*
Ccgsr Inc..800 927-9800
  2711 Centerville Rd # 400 Wilmington (19808) *(G-15288)*
Cchs Logistics Center, New Castle *Also Called: Christiana Care Health Sys Inc (G-8938)*
CCS Painting LLC..302 438-4398
  7 Sharons Way Wilmington (19808) *(G-15289)*
CD Cream...302 832-5425
  32 Clinton St Delaware City (19706) *(G-1533)*
CD Diagnostics Inc (HQ)...302 367-7770
  650 Naamans Rd Ste 100 Claymont (19703) *(G-1077)*
CD Installation..302 588-7678
  90 Old Red Mill Rd Newark (19711) *(G-10168)*
Cda Engineering Inc..302 998-9202
  6 Larch Ave Ste 401 Wilmington (19804) *(G-15290)*
Cdb Ventures Inc..302 235-0414
  157 Lantana Dr Hockessin (19707) *(G-5154)*
CDI, Seaford *Also Called: CDI Inc Sofr System LLC (G-13103)*
CDI Granite & MBL Fabrication.......................................302 235-7010
  811 Kiamensi Rd Wilmington (19804) *(G-15291)*
CDI Inc Sofr System LLC..302 536-7325
  1330 Middleford Rd Seaford (19973) *(G-13103)*
CDM Institue...302 482-3234
  3707 N Market St Wilmington (19802) *(G-15292)*

Cds Global LLC..302 307-6831
  2093 Philadelphia Pike # 5 Claymont (19703) *(G-1078)*
Ce Buys LLC..650 245-6238
  9 E Loockerman St Ste 205 Dover (19901) *(G-2041)*
Ceasar Rodney Institute..302 542-1781
  420 Corporate Blvd Newark (19702) *(G-10169)*
Cecil Vault & Memorial Co Inc...302 994-3806
  5701 Kirkwood Hwy Wilmington (19808) *(G-15293)*
Ceco Inc..302 732-3919
  27515 Hodges Ln Unit N1 Dagsboro (19939) *(G-1423)*
Cecon Group LLC..302 994-8000
  242 N James St Ste 202 Wilmington (19804) *(G-15294)*
Cedar Chase Apartments, Dover *Also Called: Udr Inc (G-3742)*
Cedar Creek Cstm Cabinets LLC....................................302 542-7794
  7816 Cedar Creek Ct Milford (19963) *(G-7814)*
Cedar Creek Marine Center...302 629-3581
  20676 Sussex Hwy Seaford (19973) *(G-13104)*
Cedar Creek Market Inc...302 249-0725
  20728 Sapp Rd Milford (19963) *(G-7815)*
Cedar Hamilton Insur Svcs LLC.....................................302 573-3000
  1201 N Market St Ste 1100 Wilmington (19801) *(G-15295)*
Cedar Lane Inc...302 328-7232
  310 Delaware St Historic New Castle (19720) *(G-4953)*
Cedar Neck Decor LLC..918 497-7179
  30980 Country Gdns Q1 Dagsboro (19939) *(G-1424)*
Cedar Rock Construction...302 430-1276
  5513 Whiteleysburg Rd Harrington (19952) *(G-4747)*
Cedar Tree Apartments, Wilmington *Also Called: Panco Management Corporation (G-18871)*
Cedar Tree Medical Center, Millsboro *Also Called: Lewes Surgical and Med Assoc (G-8347)*
Cedar Tree Surgical Center..302 945-9766
  32711 Long Neck Rd Millsboro (19966) *(G-8217)*
Cedarbrook Camp In PA..302 463-0137
  822 Percheron Dr Bear (19701) *(G-93)*
Cedarcreeklandingcgcom...302 491-6614
  8295 Brick Granary Rd Lincoln (19960) *(G-6659)*
Cedcomm LLC..646 653-0233
  8 The Grn Dover (19901) *(G-2042)*
Cegis Cyber Inc..800 809-2599
  251 Little Falls Dr Wilmington (19808) *(G-15296)*
Cei Capital LLC...302 573-3875
  1105 N Market St Ste 1300 Wilmington (19801) *(G-15297)*
Celanese International Corp...972 443-4000
  Silverside Rd Rodney 34 Wilmington (19810) *(G-15298)*
Celanese Polymer Products LLC (HQ)..........................302 774-1000
  200 Powder Mill Rd Bldg 304 Wilmington (19803) *(G-15299)*
Celavie Biosciences LLC..516 593-5633
  615 S Dupont Hwy Dover (19901) *(G-2043)*
Celebree Learning Centers, Bear *Also Called: Enchanted Child Care Intl Inc (G-202)*
Celera Services Inc...302 378-7778
  364 E Main St Middletown (19709) *(G-6968)*
Celeri Health Inc..302 438-0766
  1815 W 13th St Ste 5 Wilmington (19806) *(G-15300)*
Celesstia Health LLC...302 241-0601
  8 The Grn Unit 6121 Dover (19901) *(G-2044)*
Cell Surgeon...302 423-4441
  4004 S Dupont Hwy Dover (19901) *(G-2045)*
Cellco Partnership...302 933-0514
  26676 Centerview Dr Millsboro (19966) *(G-8218)*
Cellco Partnership...302 530-4620
  4407 Concord Pike Wilmington (19803) *(G-15301)*
Cellco Partnership...814 946-5596
  844 N King St Wilmington (19801) *(G-15302)*
Cellular Sales Ep Ch..302 455-1092
  379 E Chestnut Hill Rd Newark (19713) *(G-10170)*
Cellular Sales Knoxville Inc..302 455-1092
  379 E Chestnut Hill Rd Newark (19713) *(G-10171)*
Celsia Inc (PA)..408 577-1407
  26117 Kits Burrow Ct Georgetown (19947) *(G-4247)*
Censys Inc..248 629-0125
  3500 S Dupont Hwy Camden (19934) *(G-805)*
Centaur Training LLC..302 629-8783
  22000 Heritage Farm Rd Bridgeville (19933) *(G-681)*

ALPHABETIC SECTION

Center At Eden Hill..302 677-7100
   300 Banning St Dover (19904) *(G-2046)*

Center For A Pstive Hmnity LLC..302 703-1036
   86 Ludlow Ln Felton (19943) *(G-3952)*

Center For Advnced Srgcal Arts, Wilmington *Also Called: Rockland Surgery Center LP* *(G-19542)*

Center For Child Developement..302 292-1334
   256 Chapman Rd Ste 201 Newark (19702) *(G-10172)*

Center For Community Justice...302 424-0890
   1129 Airport Rd Milford (19963) *(G-7816)*

Center For Conscious Healing..302 376-6144
   101 W Park Pl Middletown (19709) *(G-6969)*

Center For Cosmetic Surgery...302 994-8492
   1 Centurian Dr Ste 301 Newark (19713) *(G-10173)*

Center For Grwing Tlent By Pma...302 738-7100
   1500 Casho Mill Rd Newark (19711) *(G-10174)*

Center For Human Reproduction (PA)....................................302 738-4600
   4745 Ogletown Stanton Rd Ste 111 Newark (19713) *(G-10175)*

Center For Inland Bays Inc...302 226-8105
   39375 Inlet Rd Rehoboth Beach (19971) *(G-12666)*

Center For Integrative Change...302 230-1962
   607 W 22nd St Wilmington (19802) *(G-15303)*

Center For Neurology...302 422-0800
   111 Neurology Way Milford (19963) *(G-7817)*

Center For Rehabilitation, Wilmington *Also Called: Christiana Care Health Sys Inc* *(G-15404)*

Center For Spine Surgery LLC...302 366-7671
   1219 Jefferson St Wilmington (19801) *(G-15304)*

Center For Surgical Studies...302 225-0177
   537 Stanton Christiana Rd Ste 109 Newark (19713) *(G-10176)*

CENTER FOR THE INLAND BAYS, Rehoboth Beach *Also Called: Center For Inland Bays Inc* *(G-12666)*

Center Meeting Associates LLC..302 740-9700
   300 Water St Ste 300 Wilmington (19801) *(G-15305)*

Center of Excellence In..302 503-0741
   305 Jefferson Ave Milford (19963) *(G-7818)*

Centerville Veterinary Hosp...302 655-3315
   5804 Kennett Pike Wilmington (19807) *(G-15306)*

Central Amer Hlth Buty Distrs, Georgetown *Also Called: Central America Distrs LLC* *(G-4248)*

Central America Distrs LLC...302 628-4178
   11 E Market St Ste 2 Georgetown (19947) *(G-4248)*

Central American Trade Co LLC...305 440-0420
   1209 N Orange St Wilmington (19801) *(G-15307)*

Central and Southern Delaware...302 545-8067
   221 S Rehoboth Blvd Milford (19963) *(G-7819)*

Central Backhoe Service...302 398-6420
   28247 Round Pole Bridge Rd Milton (19968) *(G-8581)*

Central Del Chmber of Commerce..302 734-7513
   435 N Dupont Hwy Dover (19901) *(G-2047)*

Central Del Fmly Foot Care...302 678-3338
   1326 S Governors Ave Ste B Dover (19904) *(G-2048)*

Central Del Hbtat For Hmnity I...302 526-2366
   2311 S Dupont Hwy Dover (19901) *(G-2049)*

Central Del Schl of The Arts F...302 943-2274
   8 Ruritan Ln Viola (19979) *(G-14092)*

Central Delaware Fmly Medicine...302 735-1616
   95 Wolf Creek Blvd Ste 2 Dover (19901) *(G-2050)*

Central Delaware Nursing, Dover *Also Called: Bayada Home Health Care Inc* *(G-1887)*

Central Delaware Speech..302 538-5696
   541 S Red Haven Ln Dover (19901) *(G-2051)*

Central Firm LLC...610 470-9836
   1201 N Orange St Ste 7016 Wilmington (19801) *(G-15308)*

Central Heating A Condtioning..302 492-1169
   2114 Fords Corner Rd Hartly (19953) *(G-4863)*

Central Kansas Arospc Mfg LLC...314 406-6550
   251 Little Falls Dr Wilmington (19808) *(G-15309)*

Centrallo Corporation (HQ)...212 355-0880
   1201 N Orange St Ste 600 Wilmington (19801) *(G-15310)*

Centrien Consulting Svcs LLC..844 741-0000
   8 The Grn Ste 10333 Dover (19901) *(G-2052)*

Centriq Technologies Inc...651 353-0691
   2093 Philadelphia Pike Ste 4321 Claymont (19703) *(G-1079)*

Centrito LLC...919 728-9401
   2093 Philadelphia Pike # 1434 Claymont (19703) *(G-1080)*

Centrix Hr..302 777-7818
   213 W 4th St Wilmington (19801) *(G-15311)*

Centrix Web Services LLC..302 319-5122
   831 N Tatnall St Ste M217 Wilmington (19801) *(G-15312)*

Century 21, Newark *Also Called: Century 21 Gold Key Realty* *(G-10177)*

Century 21, Newark *Also Called: Century 21 Tom Livizos Inc* *(G-10178)*

Century 21, Newark *Also Called: Gold Key Realty* *(G-10859)*

Century 21 Gold Key Realty...405 315-1105
   2 Magil Ct Newark (19702) *(G-10177)*

Century 21 Mann & Sons...302 227-9477
   19606 Coastal Hwy Unit 205 Rehoboth Beach (19971) *(G-12667)*

Century 21 Tom Livizos Inc...302 737-9000
   701 Capitol Trl Newark (19711) *(G-10178)*

Century Engineering Inc..302 734-9188
   550 S Bay Rd Dover (19901) *(G-2053)*

Century Seals Inc (PA)..302 629-0324
   503 Harrington St Seaford (19973) *(G-13105)*

Ceo-Hqcom LLC...302 883-8555
   7209 Lancaster Pike # 41023 Hockessin (19707) *(G-5155)*

Ceramic Tile Supply Co...302 684-5691
   26836 Lewes Georgetown Hwy Ste B1c Harbeson (19951) *(G-4687)*

Ceramic Tile Supply Co...302 737-4968
   375 Bellevue Rd Newark (19713) *(G-10179)*

Ceramic Tile Supply Co (PA)..302 992-9200
   103 Greenbank Rd Wilmington (19808) *(G-15313)*

Cerebral Med Group A Prof Corp..415 403-2156
   2093 Philadelphia Pike # 9898 Claymont (19703) *(G-1081)*

Cerobrand LLC..740 971-2576
   2810 N Church St Wilmington (19802) *(G-15314)*

Certapro Painters of Rehoboth..302 212-5742
   21810 D St Rehoboth Beach (19971) *(G-12668)*

Certified Assets MGT Intl LLC...302 765-3352
   100 Todds Ln Wilmington (19802) *(G-15315)*

Certified Code Inc..347 508-6396
   651 N Broad St Middletown (19709) *(G-6970)*

Certified Lock & Access LLC..302 383-7507
   3 Germay Dr Ste 7 Wilmington (19804) *(G-15316)*

Certified Mechanical Contrs..302 559-3727
   117 David Rd Wilmington (19804) *(G-15317)*

Certinal Inc...609 799-5664
   919 N Market St Ste 950 Wilmington (19801) *(G-15318)*

Ces Enterprises LLC..302 313-5229
   18585 Coastal Hwy Rehoboth Beach (19971) *(G-12669)*

Cesars Vargas Stone Inc C..302 296-7881
   220 High St Apt A Seaford (19973) *(G-13106)*

Cesn Partners Inc..302 537-1814
   34541 Atlantic Ave Ocean View (19970) *(G-12488)*

CEst Moi Infinity Inc...267 455-2455
   13 Brookfield Dr Newark (19702) *(G-10180)*

Ceva Logistics...512 356-1700
   800 Ships Landing Way Historic New Castle (19720) *(G-4954)*

Cfg Lab Inc..302 261-3403
   1521 Concord Pike Ste 301 Wilmington (19803) *(G-15319)*

Cfg Properties..302 993-1260
   113 Thissell Ln Wilmington (19807) *(G-15320)*

CFS Construction, Lewes *Also Called: Cape Financial Services Inc* *(G-5793)*

Cft Ambulance Service Inc..302 984-2255
   33 Pear Dr Bear (19701) *(G-94)*

Cg Global MGT Solutions LLC..215 735-3745
   501 Silverside Rd Ste 10 Wilmington (19809) *(G-15321)*

CG Jcf Corp...302 658-7581
   1209 N Orange St Wilmington (19801) *(G-15322)*

Cgc Consulting LLC..302 489-2280
   5400 Limestone Rd Ste 200 Wilmington (19808) *(G-15323)*

Cgc Geoservices LLC..302 489-2398
   1000 Dawson Dr Ste C Newark (19713) *(G-10181)*

Cgm Repair..302 344-4222
   22638 Bethel Rd Millsboro (19966) *(G-8219)*

Cgs Infotech Inc...302 351-2434
   501 Silverside Rd Ste 105 Wilmington (19809) *(G-15324)*

Cgw Corp.. 631 903-5700 9585 Cedar Ln Seaford (19973) *(G-13107)*	**Channelape Inc**.. 570 351-9335 2810 N Church St Pmb 82108 Wilmington (19802) *(G-15333)*
Ch Associates Viii LLC.. 302 456-3800 48 Geoffrey Dr Newark (19713) *(G-10182)*	**Channelpro Mobile LLC**.. 757 620-4635 19 Kris Ct Newark (19702) *(G-10188)*
Ch Wilmington LLC... 302 438-4504 268 E Main St Newark (19711) *(G-10183)*	**Chapis Drafting & Blue Print**.. 302 629-6373 8057 Hearns Pond Rd Seaford (19973) *(G-13112)*
Ch Wilmington LLC... 302 655-1641 1300 N Market St Wilmington (19801) *(G-15325)*	**Chapman Hospitality Inc**... 302 738-3400 260 Chapman Rd Newark (19702) *(G-10189)*
Cha Moon DDS.. 302 297-3750 1290 Peoples Plz Newark (19702) *(G-10184)*	**Chara Tea LLC (PA)**... 856 250-7180 8 The Grn Dover (19901) *(G-2056)*
Chad Wiswall Agency... 302 791-7600 520 Philadelphia Pike Wilmington (19809) *(G-15326)*	**Charae Landscaping Inc**... 302 792-9411 3201 Miller Rd Wilmington (19802) *(G-15334)*
Chaffin Cleaning Service Inc... 302 369-2704 3 Whitfield Rd Newark (19711) *(G-10185)*	**Charity Crossing Inc**.. 302 983-2271 2 Pear Dr Bear (19701) *(G-97)*
Chaingpt LLC... 302 382-7528 8 The Grn Ste A Dover (19901) *(G-2054)*	**Charlan Neighborhood Home, Newark** *Also Called: Mosaic (G-11456)*
Challenge Automotive Svcs Inc.. 302 629-3058 22598 Sussex Hwy Seaford (19973) *(G-13108)*	**Charlene Webb**... 302 424-8490 915 N Dupont Blvd Ste 102 Milford (19963) *(G-7820)*
Challenge Program.. 302 655-0945 1124 E 7th St Wilmington (19801) *(G-15327)*	**Charles A Klein & Sons Inc**... 410 549-6960 3 Mason Dr Selbyville (19975) *(G-13496)*
CHAMBER OF COMMERCE OF CENTRAL, Dover *Also Called: Central Del Chmber of Commerce (G-2047)*	**Charles A Zonko Builders Inc**... 302 436-0222 37116 Lighthouse Rd Selbyville (19975) *(G-13497)*
Chamberlain and Co Cstm Pntg.. 610 633-2011 142 Willow Oak Blvd Bear (19701) *(G-95)*	**Charles A. Klein & Sons, Selbyville** *Also Called: Charles A Klein & Sons Inc (G-13496)*
Chambers Bros Logistics LLC... 302 307-3668 4 Kerry Ct Bear (19701) *(G-96)*	**Charles Dempsey Farms**... 302 734-4937 1708 Fast Landing Rd Dover (19901) *(G-2057)*
Chambers Bus Service Inc... 302 284-9655 8964 S Dupont Hwy Viola (19979) *(G-14093)*	**Charles E Carlson**... 302 284-3184 3670 Willow Grove Rd Camden Wyoming (19934) *(G-923)*
Chambers Insurance Agency Inc.. 302 655-5300 100 W Commons Blvd New Castle (19720) *(G-8924)*	**Charles E Hill MD, Wilmington** *Also Called: Brandywine Care L L C (G-15048)*
Chambers Ldscpg & Lawncare Inc... 302 328-1312 41 Don Ave New Castle (19720) *(G-8925)*	**Charles Graef Inc**.. 302 239-7924 1302 Old Lancaster Pike Montchanin (19710) *(G-8735)*
Chambers Motors Inc... 302 629-3553 20610 Sussex Hwy Seaford (19973) *(G-13109)*	**Charles H Hutson III**... 302 378-9001 221 Westmoreland Ave Wilmington (19804) *(G-15335)*
Chamish, Steven E, New Castle *Also Called: New Castle Dental Assoc PA (G-9407)*	**Charles H West Farms, Milford** *Also Called: Charles H West Farms Inc (G-7821)*
Champion Builders, New Castle *Also Called: No Joke I LLC (G-9421)*	**Charles H West Farms Inc**.. 302 335-3936 2953 Tub Mill Pond Rd Milford (19963) *(G-7821)*
Champion Window Cleaners, Selbyville *Also Called: D A Jones Inc (G-13514)*	**Charles J Veith DMD**.. 302 658-7354 2300 Pennsylvania Ave Ste 5c Wilmington (19806) *(G-15336)*
Champions + Legends Corp... 702 605-2522 251 Little Falls Dr Wilmington (19808) *(G-15328)*	**Charles L Hobbs DPM**... 302 655-7735 1706 N Park Dr Apt 9 Wilmington (19806) *(G-15337)*
Champions Club... 215 380-1273 488 Augusta National Dr Magnolia (19962) *(G-6728)*	**Charles L Saulsbery Agt**... 302 894-1430 226 W Park Pl Ste 12 Newark (19711) *(G-10190)*
Champions For Childrens Mh.. 302 249-6788 119 Timberline Dr Newark (19711) *(G-10186)*	**Charles M Wallace**.. 302 998-1412 1906 Newport Gap Pike Wilmington (19808) *(G-15338)*
Championx LLC.. 856 423-6417 204 Quigley Blvd Historic New Castle (19720) *(G-4955)*	**Charles Moon Plumbing**... 302 732-3555 33214 Main St Dagsboro (19939) *(G-1425)*
Chance De Group LLC.. 800 667-3082 262 Chapman Rd Ste 205223 Newark (19702) *(G-10187)*	**Charles Moon Plumbing**... 302 732-3555 32980 Dupont Blvd Dagsboro (19939) *(G-1426)*
Chancellor Care Center Delmar, Delmar *Also Called: Chancellor Care Ctr of Delmar (G-1576)*	**Charles Moon Plumbing & Htg (PA)**.. 302 798-6666 2505 Philadelphia Pike Ste C Claymont (19703) *(G-1083)*
Chancellor Care Ctr of Delmar... 302 846-3077 101 Delaware Ave Delmar (19940) *(G-1576)*	**Charles Moon Plumbing & Htg, Ocean View** *Also Called: Cesn Partners Inc (G-12488)*
Chancery Court Reporters... 302 255-0515 500 N King St Ste 11400 Wilmington (19801) *(G-15329)*	**Charles R Reed**.. 302 284-3353 93 Paradise Cove Way Felton (19943) *(G-3953)*
Chandlee Projects LLC... 717 542-5919 35145 Chandlee Ln Frankford (19945) *(G-4084)*	**Charles River Labs Intl Inc**.. 302 292-8888 614 Interchange Blvd Newark (19711) *(G-10191)*
Chandler Nichol & Sloan PA.. 302 478-9800 3510 Silverside Rd Ste 4 Wilmington (19810) *(G-15330)*	**Charles S Reskovitz Inc**... 302 999-9455 1018 Liberty Rd Wilmington (19804) *(G-15339)*
Chandler Funeral Homes, Wilmington *Also Called: James T Chandler & Son Inc (G-17487)*	**Charles Schwab, Wilmington** *Also Called: Charles Schwab & Co Inc (G-15340)*
Chandler Heights II LP... 302 629-8048 802 Clementine Ct Seaford (19973) *(G-13110)*	**Charles Schwab & Co Inc**... 800 435-4000 4021 Kennett Pike Ste A Wilmington (19807) *(G-15340)*
Chandlers Con Plcment Group LL.. 302 377-0017 4604 N Dupont Hwy Dover (19901) *(G-2055)*	**Charles Slanina**.. 302 234-1605 724 Yorklyn Rd Ste 210 Hockessin (19707) *(G-5156)*
Chaney Enterprises.. 302 990-5039 22223 Eskridge Rd Seaford (19973) *(G-13111)*	**Charles Taylor Consulting Inc**.. 703 200-8057 8485 Glade Dr Milford (19963) *(G-7822)*
Changing Faces Inc... 302 397-4164 19500 Pine Rd Lincoln (19960) *(G-6660)*	**Charles Wang MD PA**... 302 655-1500 1700 Wawaset St Ste 200 Wilmington (19806) *(G-15341)*
Changing My Direction LLC... 302 510-9873 2803 Philadelphia Pike Ste B Claymont (19703) *(G-1082)*	**Charles Williams**.. 302 274-2996 1202 E 16th St Wilmington (19802) *(G-15342)*
Changing Place.. 302 397-8731 848 N Madison St Wilmington (19801) *(G-15331)*	**Charlie Square Cleaners LLC**.. 302 778-3807 2001 Delaware Ave Wilmington (19806) *(G-15343)*
Changing Place Inc.. 302 357-6107 809 Morrow St Wilmington (19801) *(G-15332)*	**Charlotte Wilson**... 302 500-1440 629 Rosemary Dr Seaford (19973) *(G-13113)*
	Charmed Medi Spa... 302 273-2827 48 Omega Dr Newark (19713) *(G-10192)*

ALPHABETIC SECTION — Chesapeake Utilities

Charmed Medispa Inc..302 593-1994
H48 Omega Dr Newark (19713) *(G-10193)*

Chart Exchange..850 376-6435
3001 Philadelphia Pike Claymont (19703) *(G-1084)*

Charter Dynamics LLC..888 260-4579
427 N Tatnall St Ste 70775 Wilmington (19802) *(G-15344)*

Chas Medicine..302 644-5870
34435 King Street Row Lewes (19958) *(G-5809)*

Chas Pools Inc..302 376-5840
600 N Broad St Ste 11 Middletown (19709) *(G-6971)*

Chase Center On River..302 655-2187
815 Justison St Ste B Wilmington (19801) *(G-15345)*

Chase Fieldhouse...610 996-0425
401 Garasches Ln Wilmington (19801) *(G-15346)*

Chatam International Incorporated.........................302 478-6185
1105 N Market St Ste 1300 Wilmington (19801) *(G-15347)*

Chatham Financial Corporation................................570 510-0490
1105 N Market St Wilmington (19801) *(G-15348)*

Chatty Press..617 712-3882
31210 Ringtail Dr Lewes (19958) *(G-5810)*

Chaukiss LLC (PA)...551 655-5181
16192 Coastal Hwy Lewes (19958) *(G-5811)*

Chayil Healthcarellc...302 399-0991
26 Patrick Henry Ln Milford (19963) *(G-7823)*

Che Studio Inc..856 246-8440
103 E Hazeldell Ave New Castle (19720) *(G-8926)*

Cheap-Scape Inc...302 472-2600
720 Yorklyn Rd Ste 5 Hockessin (19707) *(G-5157)*

Cheaps Tree Service...302 750-4590
110 Paisley Ln New Castle (19720) *(G-8927)*

Chec Inc...302 275-4709
1100 Helen Dr Apt 107 Newark (19702) *(G-10194)*

Check 'n Go 2801, Wilmington Also Called: Eastern Specialty Finance Inc *(G-16263)*

Check 'n Go 2846, Dover Also Called: Eastern Specialty Finance Inc *(G-2414)*

Check 'n Go 2907, Camden Also Called: Eastern Specialty Finance Inc *(G-826)*

Check Plus Cleaning LLC..302 837-7308
503 W 30th St Wilmington (19802) *(G-15349)*

Check-It Electric LLC..302 650-1921
40 Harlech Dr Wilmington (19807) *(G-15350)*

Cheer Inc (PA)..302 856-7541
546 S Bedford St Georgetown (19947) *(G-4249)*

Cheer Force..302 218-7384
20 Swansea Ln Newark (19702) *(G-10195)*

Cheersrx Inc..801 210-1658
13 W Main St Felton (19943) *(G-3954)*

Chelsea Creek Capital Co LLC..................................312 977-4583
251 Little Falls Dr Wilmington (19808) *(G-15351)*

Chelsea King...302 684-5227
108 Bangor Ln Milton (19968) *(G-8582)*

Chelten Apartments, New Castle Also Called: Chelten Preservation Assoc LLC *(G-8928)*

Chelten Apartments, New Castle Also Called: Leon N Weiner & Associates Inc *(G-9306)*

Chelten Apartments, Wilmington Also Called: Chelten Apartments Assoc LP *(G-15352)*

Chelten Apartments Assoc LP...................................302 322-6323
4 Denny Rd Wilmington (19809) *(G-15352)*

Chelten Preservation Assoc LLC...............................302 322-6323
431 Old Forge Rd New Castle (19720) *(G-8928)*

Chem Tech Inc..302 798-9675
6725 Governor Printz Blvd Wilmington (19809) *(G-15353)*

Chemax Manufacturing Corp....................................302 328-2440
1025 River Rd New Castle (19720) *(G-8929)*

Chemfirst Inc (HQ)..302 774-1000
1007 Market St Wilmington (19898) *(G-15354)*

Chemours, Wilmington Also Called: Chemours Company *(G-15356)*

Chemours, Wilmington Also Called: Chemours Company Fc LLC *(G-15358)*

Chemours Co Fc LLC...302 353-5003
200 Powder Mill Rd Wilmington (19803) *(G-15355)*

Chemours Company..302 773-6417
201 Discovery Blvd Newark (19713) *(G-10196)*

Chemours Company (PA)...302 773-1000
1007 Market St Wilmington (19898) *(G-15356)*

Chemours Company Fc LLC....................................302 545-0072
1007 Market St Wilmington (19898) *(G-15357)*

Chemours Company Fc LLC (HQ)..........................302 773-1000
1007 Market St Wilmington (19898) *(G-15358)*

Chemours Company Fc LLC....................................678 427-1530
4301 Lancaster Pike Wilmington (19805) *(G-15359)*

Chemours Company Fc LLC....................................302 540-5423
Chestnut Run Wilmington (19880) *(G-15360)*

Chemours Company Fc LLC....................................302 773-1267
1007 Market St Wilmington (19898) *(G-15361)*

Chemring North Amer Group Inc (DH)..................302 658-5687
1105 N Market St Wilmington (19801) *(G-15362)*

Chemstar Corp..302 465-3175
686 N Dupont Blvd Milford (19963) *(G-7824)*

Cheon IL Guk Incorporated......................................302 332-2672
500 Ethel Ct Middletown (19709) *(G-6972)*

Cherrington Service Corp...302 777-4064
106 Haywood Rd Wilmington (19807) *(G-15363)*

Cherry Building Group..302 280-6876
26739 Sussex Hwy Seaford (19973) *(G-13114)*

Cherry Island Landfill, Wilmington Also Called: Delaware Solid Waste Authority *(G-15966)*

Cherry Island LLC...302 658-5241
4048 New Castle Ave New Castle (19720) *(G-8930)*

Cherry Island Rnwble Enrgy LLC............................302 379-0722
1706 E 12th St Wilmington (19809) *(G-15364)*

Cherry Psychological Services.................................302 528-2235
218 Cullen Way Newark (19711) *(G-10197)*

Cheryl Cantrell...610 793-9202
1701 Augustine Cut Off Ste 100 Wilmington (19803) *(G-15365)*

Cheryl L Chambers..302 393-3854
689 Golf Links Ln Magnolia (19962) *(G-6729)*

Cheryl Wagner..302 635-7632
7217 Lancaster Pike Hockessin (19707) *(G-5158)*

Chesapake Cnfrnce Svnth-Day Ad..........................302 998-3961
3003 Mill Creek Rd Wilmington (19808) *(G-15366)*

Chesapeake Slver Crnet Brass Ba............................302 530-2915
23674 Samuel Adams Cir Millsboro (19966) *(G-8220)*

Chesapeak Insurance Advisors.................................610 793-6885
902 S Schulz Rd Fenwick Island (19944) *(G-4044)*

Chesapeake Bay Orthopedics...................................302 404-5954
1340 Middleford Rd Seaford (19973) *(G-13115)*

Chesapeake Brass Band, Millsboro Also Called: Chesapake Slver Crnet Brass Ba *(G-8220)*

Chesapeake Brokerage LLC......................................410 517-1592
18766 John J Williams Hwy Ste 4395 Rehoboth Beach (19971) *(G-12670)*

Chesapeake Carriers Inc...302 628-3838
518 Bridgeville Hwy Seaford (19973) *(G-13116)*

Chesapeake Climate Control LLC............................302 732-6006
34913 Delaware Ave Frankford (19945) *(G-4085)*

Chesapeake Design Center LLC...............................302 875-8570
32852 Sussex Hwy Laurel (19956) *(G-5481)*

Chesapeake Fire Systems LLC..................................302 732-6006
34913 Delaware Ave Frankford (19945) *(G-4086)*

Chesapeake Hearth Stone Co LLC...........................302 943-5276
26950 Danny Dr Seaford (19973) *(G-13117)*

Chesapeake Home Services LLC..............................302 732-6006
34913 Delaware Ave Frankford (19945) *(G-4087)*

Chesapeake Insurance Advisors...............................302 544-6900
10 Corporate Cir Ste 215 New Castle (19720) *(G-8931)*

Chesapeake Management Co LLC...........................302 732-6006
34913 Delaware Ave Frankford (19945) *(G-4088)*

Chesapeake Neurology Service.................................302 563-7253
12 Stable Ln Wilmington (19803) *(G-15367)*

Chesapeake Plumbing & Htg Inc.............................302 732-6006
34913 Delaware Ave Frankford (19945) *(G-4089)*

Chesapeake Rehab Equipment Inc..........................302 266-6234
810 Interchange Blvd Newark (19711) *(G-10198)*

Chesapeake Seaglass Jewelry...................................410 778-4999
11505 W Sand Cove Rd Selbyville (19975) *(G-13498)*

Chesapeake Service Company (HQ)........................302 734-6799
500 Energy Ln Ste 400 Dover (19901) *(G-2058)*

Chesapeake Supply & Eqp Co..................................302 284-1000
12915 S Dupont Hwy Felton (19943) *(G-3955)*

Chesapeake Utilities, Dover Also Called: Chesapeake Utilities Corp *(G-2059)*

Chesapeake Utilities Corp (PA)........................302 734-6799
 500 Energy Ln Dover (19901) *(G-2059)*
Chesapeakecaregivers LLC........................302 841-9686
 10105 Concord Rd Seaford (19973) *(G-13118)*
Chesapeakemaine Trey........................302 226-3600
 316 Rehoboth Ave Rehoboth Beach (19971) *(G-12671)*
Chesco Coring & Cutng Del LLC........................302 276-7900
 473 Old Airport Rd New Castle (19720) *(G-8932)*
Cheshire Enterprise LLC........................302 365-6225
 100 E Scotland Dr Bear (19701) *(G-98)*
Cheslantic Overhead Door........................443 880-0378
 23 Shannon St Delmar (19940) *(G-1577)*
Chester Bethel Preschool, Wilmington Also Called: Chester Bthel Untd Mthdst Pre *(G-15368)*
Chester Bthel Untd Mthdst Pre........................302 475-3549
 2619 Foulk Rd Wilmington (19810) *(G-15368)*
Chester Cnty Orthpd Spt Physcl, Wilmington Also Called: Hysiotherapy Associates Inc *(G-17244)*
Chester Marina LLC........................302 829-8218
 33309 Kent Ave Bethany Beach (19930) *(G-590)*
Chester Ross........................267 461-1568
 113 Stanley Ln New Castle (19720) *(G-8933)*
Chestnut Hill Plaza........................302 731-0643
 110 Christiana Med Ctr Newark (19702) *(G-10199)*
Chestnut Run Federal Cr Un (PA)........................302 999-2967
 974 Centre Rd Wilmington (19805) *(G-15369)*
Cheveux Inc........................302 731-9202
 1115 Churchmans Rd Newark (19713) *(G-10200)*
Chews Unlimited LLC........................302 280-6137
 38113 Brittingham Rd Delmar (19940) *(G-1578)*
CHI, Middletown Also Called: Compassnate Hlth Intatives Inc *(G-7006)*
Chichester Business Park LLC........................302 685-2997
 108 Patriot Dr Ste A Middletown (19709) *(G-6973)*
Chick Harness & Supply Inc (PA)........................302 398-4630
 18011 S Dupont Hwy Harrington (19952) *(G-4748)*
Chicksx LLC........................518 727-1890
 2055 Limestone Rd Ste 200 Pmb C Wilmington (19808) *(G-15370)*
Chicos Crows Nest Tttoo Studio........................302 475-6805
 2204 Grubb Rd Wilmington (19810) *(G-15371)*
Chief Web Design........................302 542-8409
 24787 Hollis Rd Georgetown (19947) *(G-4250)*
Chieffo Electric Inc........................302 292-6813
 108 W Cedarwood Dr Middletown (19709) *(G-6974)*
Chilay Inc........................302 559-6014
 40 E Main St 111 Newark (19711) *(G-10201)*
Child Inc........................302 832-5451
 148 Flamingo Dr Sparrow Run Newark (19702) *(G-10202)*
Child Inc (PA)........................302 762-8989
 507 Philadelphia Pike Wilmington (19809) *(G-15372)*
CHILD CARE, Harbeson Also Called: Lullaby Learning Center Inc *(G-4706)*
Child Care Ctr........................302 652-8992
 221 N Jackson St Wilmington (19805) *(G-15373)*
Child Care Service........................302 981-1328
 262 Chapman Rd Ste 202 Newark (19702) *(G-10203)*
Child Help Foundation........................302 533-7078
 6 Wyncliff Ln Newark (19711) *(G-10204)*
Child Inc........................302 335-8652
 776 Tullamore Ct Magnolia (19962) *(G-6730)*
Child Support........................302 855-7462
 22 The Cir Georgetown (19947) *(G-4251)*
Childers IV Henry E MD........................302 258-8853
 20930 Dupont Blvd Unit 202 Georgetown (19947) *(G-4252)*
Children Youth & Their Fam........................302 577-6011
 321 E 11th St Fl 1 Wilmington (19801) *(G-15374)*
Children & Families First, Dover Also Called: Children Fmilies First Del Inc *(G-2061)*
Children First Lrng Ctr Inc........................302 674-5227
 760 Townsend Blvd Dover (19901) *(G-2060)*
Children Fmilies First Del Inc........................302 674-8384
 91 Wolf Creek Blvd Dover (19901) *(G-2061)*
Children Fmilies First Del Inc........................302 856-2388
 410 S Bedford St Georgetown (19947) *(G-4253)*
Children Fmilies First Del Inc........................302 629-6996
 400 N Market Street Ext Seaford (19973) *(G-13119)*

Children Fmilies First Del Inc (PA)........................302 658-5177
 809 N Washington St Wilmington (19801) *(G-15375)*
Children Fmlies Frst Endowment........................302 658-5177
 809 N Washington St Wilmington (19801) *(G-15376)*
Children S Secret Garden........................302 730-1717
 717 Hatchery Rd Dover (19901) *(G-2062)*
Children Yuth Their Fmlies Del........................302 577-4270
 10 Central Ave New Castle (19720) *(G-8934)*
Children Yuth Their Fmlies Del........................302 633-2600
 1825 Faulkland Rd Wilmington (19805) *(G-15377)*
CHILDREN'S HOUSE MONTESSORI SC, Wilmington Also Called: New Cstle Cnty Chld Hse Mntsso *(G-18615)*
Children's Place, Laurel Also Called: Childrens Place *(G-5482)*
Children's Place, The, Magnolia Also Called: Child Inc *(G-6730)*
Children's Theater of Delmarva, Delmar Also Called: Mirworth Enterprise Inc *(G-1621)*
Childrens Advocacy Center........................302 651-4567
 Wilmington (19899) *(G-15378)*
Childrens Advocacy Ctr of Del (PA)........................302 741-2123
 611 S Dupont Hwy Ste 201 Dover (19901) *(G-2063)*
Childrens Advocacy Ctr of Del........................302 854-0323
 410 S Bedford St Georgetown (19947) *(G-4254)*
Childrens Advocacy Ctr of Del........................302 651-4615
 1600 Rockland Rd Rm 3f-27 Wilmington (19803) *(G-15379)*
Childrens Beach House Inc........................302 645-9184
 1800 Bay Ave Lewes (19958) *(G-5812)*
Childrens Beach House Inc (PA)........................302 655-4288
 100 W 10th St Ste 411 Wilmington (19801) *(G-15380)*
Childrens Choice Inc........................302 731-9512
 25 S Old Baltimore Pike Ste 101 Newark (19702) *(G-10205)*
Childrens Dntl Hlth Wlmngton W........................302 803-6560
 3301 Lancaster Pike Wilmington (19805) *(G-15381)*
Childrens Hosp Nntal Cnsrtium........................215 873-9492
 8 The Grn Ste 10426 Dover (19901) *(G-2064)*
Childrens Place........................302 875-7733
 12034 County Seat Hwy Laurel (19956) *(G-5482)*
Childrens Place Child Dev Ce........................302 947-4808
 32362 Long Neck Rd Millsboro (19966) *(G-8221)*
Childs Play At Home LLC........................302 644-3445
 11 Hartford Way Lewes (19958) *(G-5813)*
Childs Play By Bay........................302 703-6234
 1510 Savannah Rd Lewes (19958) *(G-5814)*
Chilimidos LLC........................302 388-1880
 7209 Lancaster Pike Ste 4 # 314 Hockessin (19707) *(G-5159)*
Chillax Inn At Lewes Beach........................302 685-8845
 4 Camden Ave Lewes (19958) *(G-5815)*
Chime Inc........................978 844-1162
 1013 Centre Rd Ste 403 Wilmington (19805) *(G-15382)*
Chimes Inc........................302 730-0747
 165 Commerce Way Dover (19904) *(G-2065)*
Chimes Inc........................302 678-3270
 3499 Cypress St Dover (19901) *(G-2066)*
Chimes Inc........................302 382-4500
 130 Quigley Blvd Historic New Castle (19720) *(G-4956)*
Chimes Inc........................302 452-3400
 514 Interchange Blvd Newark (19711) *(G-10206)*
Chimes Inc........................302 934-1450
 28393 Dupont Blvd Millsboro (19966) *(G-8222)*
Chimes Metro, Dover Also Called: Chimes Inc *(G-2065)*
Chimes Metro Inc........................302 452-3400
 323 E 14th St Historic New Castle (19720) *(G-4957)*
Chimes Metro Inc (HQ)........................302 838-1202
 514 Interchange Blvd Newark (19711) *(G-10207)*
Chimicles Schwrtz Krner Dnldsn........................302 656-2500
 2711 Centerville Rd Ste 201 Wilmington (19808) *(G-15383)*
Chip Design Systems Inc........................302 494-6220
 12 Longacre Ct Hockessin (19707) *(G-5160)*
Chip Design Systems LLC........................302 307-6831
 12 Longacre Ct Hockessin (19707) *(G-5161)*
Chip Diagnostics Inc (PA)........................302 752-1064
 1105 N Market St Ste 1800 Wilmington (19801) *(G-15384)*
Chip Vickio........................302 448-0211
 30845 Phillips Branch Rd Millsboro (19966) *(G-8223)*

ALPHABETIC SECTION — Christiana Care Health System

Chiquita, Wilmington *Also Called: Chiquita Brands LLC* *(G-15385)*
- **Chiquita Brands LLC**..302 571-9781
  101 River Rd Wilmington (19801) *(G-15385)*
- **Chiro Med Chiropractic LLC**...................................302 256-0363
  213 W 4th St Wilmington (19801) *(G-15386)*
- **Chirofusion LLC**..877 210-3230
  3411 Silverside Rd Ste 106 Wilmington (19810) *(G-15387)*
- **Chiropractic Colonial**..302 328-1444
  105 Penn Mart Shopping Ctr New Castle (19720) *(G-8935)*
- **Chirostaff LLC**...302 332-3312
  903 Shipley Rd Wilmington (19803) *(G-15388)*
- **Chisel Creek Golf Club**..302 379-6011
  2602 Belaire Dr Wilmington (19808) *(G-15389)*
- **Chistine E Woods**..302 709-4497
  111 Continental Dr # 412 Newark (19713) *(G-10208)*
- **Chitiki Dhadha Gautamy MD**..................................302 393-5006
  517 S Dupont Blvd Milford (19963) *(G-7825)*
- **Chocolate Editions Inc**..302 479-8400
  2614 Philadelphia Pike Claymont (19703) *(G-1085)*
- **Chocolette Distribution LLC**...................................917 547-8905
  16192 Coastal Hwy Lewes (19958) *(G-5816)*

Choctaw- Kaul Distribution Co, Historic New Castle *Also Called: Kaul Glove and Mfg Co* *(G-5014)*
- **Choi Eunhwa**..302 559-3771
  30 Weilers Bnd Wilmington (19810) *(G-15390)*
- **Choice Construction Co Inc**..................................302 226-1732
  Rr 2 Box 137b Rehoboth Beach (19971) *(G-12672)*
- **Choice Rmdlg & Restoration Inc**..........................717 917-0601
  110 Ramunno Cir Hockessin (19707) *(G-5162)*

Choicepoint, Wilmington *Also Called: Lexisnexis Risk Assets Inc* *(G-17889)*
- **Choices 1st LLC**..302 674-4204
  1326 S Governors Ave Dover (19904) *(G-2067)*
- **Choices For Community**...302 378-3821
  30 W Main St Middletown (19709) *(G-6975)*
- **Choices For Community Living (PA)**...................302 398-0446
  100 Kings Ct Harrington (19952) *(G-4749)*
- **Chopin Building**..302 283-7130
  258 Chapman Rd Newark (19702) *(G-10209)*
- **Chopin Imports Ltd**..612 226-9875
  3422 Old Capitol Trl Wilmington (19808) *(G-15391)*
- **Chopra Hlco LLC**..631 413-4249
  838 Walker Rd Ste 21-2 Dover (19904) *(G-2068)*
- **CHOPTANK EXCAVATION LLC**.............................302 420-0354
  1715 River Rd New Castle (19720) *(G-8936)*

Chorerelief, Dover *Also Called: Chores R Us Inc* *(G-2069)*
- **Chores R Us Inc**..844 442-4673
  8 The Grn Ste A Dover (19901) *(G-2069)*
- **Chotcut Inc**..706 437-7890
  2055 Limestone Rd Ste 200c Wilmington (19808) *(G-15392)*
- **Choudhary Chitra MD**..302 401-1500
  1058 S Governors Ave Dover (19904) *(G-2070)*
- **Choy Wilson Cdgn**...302 424-4141
  329 Mullet Run Milford (19963) *(G-7826)*

Chpt Manufacturing, Georgetown *Also Called: C H P T Manufacturing Inc* *(G-4242)*
- **Chpt Mfg Inc**...302 645-4314
  100 Dock Dr Lewes (19958) *(G-5817)*
- **Chpter Holdings Inc**..650 223-1786
  2810 N Church St Wilmington (19802) *(G-15393)*

Chrias, Newark *Also Called: Christana Inst Advnced Srgery* *(G-10213)*
- **Chris and Tracey Haverkamp Fam**......................800 839-1754
  501 Silverside Rd Ste 123 Wilmington (19809) *(G-15394)*
- **Chris Cocker**...302 744-9184
  300 Artis Dr Dover (19904) *(G-2071)*
- **Chris Curry Dr**..302 365-5457
  3 Dogwood Ct Bear (19701) *(G-99)*
- **Chris Haist**...302 234-1116
  33 Possum Park Mall Newark (19711) *(G-10210)*
- **Chriss Car Care Road**..302 628-4695
  473 Seaford Bridgeville (19933) *(G-682)*
- **Chrissinger and Baumberger**................................302 777-0100
  3 Mill Rd Ste 301 Wilmington (19806) *(G-15395)*

Chrissy Bees Honey, Georgetown *Also Called: Stag Run Farm Llc* *(G-4523)*
- **Christ Care Cardiac Surgery**................................302 644-4282
  400 Savannah Rd Ste C Lewes (19958) *(G-5818)*
- **Christ Ch Episcpal Preschool**...............................302 472-0021
  505 E Buck Rd Wilmington (19807) *(G-15396)*

Christana Care Crdiolgy Conslt, Newark *Also Called: Christiana Care Health Sys Inc* *(G-10219)*
- **Christana Care HM Hlth Cmnty S**.........................302 698-4300
  2116 S Dupont Hwy Ste 2 Camden (19934) *(G-806)*
- **Christana Care HM Hlth Cmnty S (HQ)**...............302 327-5583
  1 Reads Way Ste 100 New Castle (19720) *(G-8937)*
- **Christana Care HM Hlth Cmnty S**.........................302 995-8448
  3000 Newport Gap Pike Wilmington (19808) *(G-15397)*
- **Christana Care Vsclar Spcalist**.............................302 733-5700
  4765 Ogletown Stanton Rd Ste 1e20 Newark (19713) *(G-10211)*

Christana Care Vsting Nrse Ass, New Castle *Also Called: Christana Care HM Hlth Cmnty S* *(G-8937)*
- **Christana Ctr For Wns Wellness**..........................302 454-9800
  4745 Ogletown Stanton Rd Ste 105 Newark (19713) *(G-10212)*
- **Christana Inst Advnced Srgery**.............................302 892-9900
  537 Stanton Christiana Rd Ste 102 Newark (19713) *(G-10213)*

Christany Care Healthcare, Newark *Also Called: Christiana Care Health Sys Inc* *(G-10224)*
- **Christensen Evert J Plumbing &**..........................302 475-9249
  Dartmouth Woods St Wilmington (19810) *(G-15398)*
- **Christian Reachfm Radio Netwrk**........................302 731-0690
  179 Stanton Christiana Rd Newark (19702) *(G-10214)*

Christian Recovery Spa, Seaford *Also Called: Charlotte Wilson* *(G-13113)*
- **Christian Science Reading Room**........................302 456-1428
  92 E Main St Ste 7 Newark (19711) *(G-10215)*
- **Christiana Auction Gallery**.....................................570 441-7503
  314 E Main St Newark (19711) *(G-10216)*
- **Christiana Body Shop Inc**......................................302 655-1085
  96 Germay Dr Wilmington (19804) *(G-15399)*
- **Christiana Care Corp**..302 738-4596
  21 Nightingale Cir Newark (19711) *(G-10217)*

Christiana Care Dover, Camden *Also Called: Christana Care HM Hlth Cmnty S* *(G-806)*
- **Christiana Care Health Sys Inc**............................302 449-3000
  124 Sleepy Hollow Dr Ste 203 Middletown (19709) *(G-6976)*
- **Christiana Care Health Sys Inc**............................302 623-3970
  11 Boulden Cir New Castle (19720) *(G-8938)*
- **Christiana Care Health Sys Inc**............................302 838-4750
  300 Biddle Ave Ste 200 Newark (19702) *(G-10218)*
- **Christiana Care Health Sys Inc**............................302 366-1929
  252 Chapman Rd Ste 150 Newark (19702) *(G-10219)*
- **Christiana Care Health Sys Inc (HQ)**..................302 733-1000
  200 Hygeia Dr Newark (19713) *(G-10220)*
- **Christiana Care Health Sys Inc**............................302 733-5700
  4755 Ogletown Stanton Rd Newark (19718) *(G-10221)*
- **Christiana Care Health Sys Inc**............................302 733-1601
  4755 Stanton Ogletown Rd Ste Lo308 Newark (19718) *(G-10222)*
- **Christiana Care Health Sys Inc**............................302 623-0390
  200 Hygeia Dr Newark (19713) *(G-10223)*
- **Christiana Care Health Sys Inc**............................302 733-2410
  4745 Ogletown Stanton Rd Map 1 Ste 217 Newark (19718) *(G-10224)*
- **Christiana Care Health Sys Inc**............................302 659-4401
  100 S Main St Ste 105 Smyrna (19977) *(G-13676)*
- **Christiana Care Health Sys Inc**............................302 477-6500
  3521 Silverside Rd Ste 1a Wilmington (19810) *(G-15400)*
- **Christiana Care Health Sys Inc**............................302 623-7500
  4512 Kirkwood Hwy Ste 300 Wilmington (19808) *(G-15401)*
- **Christiana Care Health Sys Inc**............................302 428-6219
  4000 Nexus Dr Wilmington (19803) *(G-15402)*
- **Christiana Care Health Sys Inc**............................302 623-1929
  3506 Kennett Pike Wilmington (19807) *(G-15403)*
- **Christiana Care Health Sys Inc**............................302 733-1000
  501 W 14th St Wilmington (19801) *(G-15404)*
- **Christiana Care Health System**............................302 674-1390
  606 Union Church Rd Townsend (19734) *(G-13971)*
- **Christiana Care Health System**............................302 992-5545
  100 N Dupont Rd Wilmington (19807) *(G-15405)*

Christiana Care Health System, Newark *Also Called: Christiana Care Health Sys Inc* *(G-10221)*

Christiana Care Hlth Svcs Inc — ALPHABETIC SECTION

Christiana Care Hlth Svcs Inc 302 327-3959
1 Reads Way Ste 200 New Castle (19720) *(G-8939)*

Christiana Care Hlth Svcs Inc (PA) 302 733-1000
4755 Ogletown Stanton Rd Newark (19718) *(G-10225)*

Christiana Care Hlth Svcs Inc 302 733-1805
2302 W 16th St Wilmington (19806) *(G-15406)*

Christiana Care Hlth Svcs Inc 302 477-3300
1401 Foulk Rd Ste 100 Wilmington (19803) *(G-15407)*

Christiana Care Hlth Svcs Inc 302 477-3960
2501 Ebright Rd Wilmington (19810) *(G-15408)*

Christiana Care Infusion 302 623-0345
600 White Clay Center Dr Newark (19711) *(G-10226)*

Christiana Cent 302 368-3257
1082 Old Churchmans Rd Ste 100 Newark (19713) *(G-10227)*

Christiana Center-Oral Surgery 302 376-3700
114 Saint Annes Church Rd Middletown (19709) *(G-6977)*

Christiana Counseling 302 995-1680
5235 W Woodmill Dr Ste 47& Wilmington (19808) *(G-15409)*

Christiana Counseling, Wilmington *Also Called: Christiana Counseling (G-15409)*

Christiana Excavating Company 302 738-8660
2016 Sunset Lake Rd Newark (19702) *(G-10228)*

Christiana Family Dental Care 302 623-4190
50 Omega Dr Newark (19713) *(G-10229)*

Christiana Family Dental Care 302 623-4190
4735 Ogletown Stanton Rd Ste 1101 Newark (19713) *(G-10230)*

Christiana Fire Company 302 834-2433
1714 Porter Rd Bear (19701) *(G-100)*

Christiana Hernia Center 302 996-6400
550 Stanton Christiana Rd Ste 202 Newark (19713) *(G-10231)*

Christiana High Sch Wellness, Newark *Also Called: Vna of Delaware (G-12334)*

Christiana Hosp Satellite Off, Newark *Also Called: John M Otto Od (G-11116)*

Christiana Hospital 203 645-2903
9 W 9th St Historic New Castle (19720) *(G-4958)*

Christiana Hospital, Newark *Also Called: Christiana Care Health Sys Inc (G-10220)*

Christiana Hospital, Newark *Also Called: Christiana Care Hlth Svcs Inc (G-10225)*

Christiana Incorporators Inc 302 998-2008
508 Main St Wilmington (19804) *(G-15410)*

Christiana Inn 302 276-1659
875 Pulaski Hwy Bear (19701) *(G-101)*

Christiana Materials Inc 302 633-5600
305 W Newport Pike Wilmington (19804) *(G-15411)*

Christiana Meadows LLC 302 322-6161
265 Bear Christiana Rd Bear (19701) *(G-102)*

Christiana Meadows Apartments, Bear *Also Called: Christiana Meadows LLC (G-102)*

Christiana Mechanical Inc 302 378-7308
109 Sleepy Hollow Dr Ste A Middletown (19709) *(G-6978)*

Christiana Motor Freight Inc (PA) 302 655-6271
520 Terminal Ave Ste C New Castle (19720) *(G-8940)*

Christiana Neonatal Practice 302 733-2410
4745 Ogletown Stanton Rd Ste 217 Newark (19713) *(G-10232)*

Christiana Phys Therpy & Spine 302 731-2660
5307 Limestone Rd Ste 101 Wilmington (19808) *(G-15412)*

Christiana Physcl Therapy Plus, Wilmington *Also Called: Christiana Care Hlth Svcs Inc (G-15407)*

Christiana Pleasant Denta 302 738-3666
72 Omega Dr Newark (19713) *(G-10233)*

Christiana Psychiatric Svcs, Newark *Also Called: Carol A Tavani MD (G-10152)*

Christiana Skating Center, Newark *Also Called: Delaware Skating Center Ltd (G-10479)*

Christiana Wood LLC 302 322-1172
21- 8 Villas Dr New Castle (19720) *(G-8941)*

Christianity Care Pathology, Newark *Also Called: Christiana Care Health Sys Inc (G-10222)*

Christina Care Vna 302 327-5212
4000 Nexus Dr Wilmington (19803) *(G-15413)*

Christina Crescent 302 528-9182
125 S West St Wilmington (19801) *(G-15414)*

Christina Cultural Arts Center 302 652-0101
705 N Market St Wilmington (19801) *(G-15415)*

Christina Education Assn 302 454-7700
4135 Ogletown Stanton Rd Newark (19713) *(G-10234)*

Christina H Bovelsky M D 302 514-3371
320 E North St Smyrna (19977) *(G-13677)*

Christina Landing, Wilmington *Also Called: Luxiasuites LLC (G-18041)*

Christina M Hanna 302 236-7280
37680 Pine Rd Selbyville (19975) *(G-13499)*

Christina Mill Apartments, Newark *Also Called: ML Newark LLC (G-11432)*

Christina Newton 302 454-2400
925 Bear Corbitt Rd Bear (19701) *(G-103)*

Christina River Exchange LLC 302 691-2139
1000 N West St Ste 800 Wilmington (19801) *(G-15416)*

Christine Dipaolo 302 651-4000
1600 Rockland Rd Wilmington (19803) *(G-15417)*

Christine E Fox DDS 302 732-9850
31059 Dupont Blvd Dagsboro (19939) *(G-1427)*

Christine Metzing 302 376-5148
413 Meadow Ln Middletown (19709) *(G-6979)*

Christine W Maynard M D 302 225-6110
4735 Ogletown Stanton Rd Ste 2300 Newark (19713) *(G-10235)*

Christine W Maynard MD 302 995-7073
4600 New Lndn Hll Rd 20 Wilmington (19808) *(G-15418)*

Christncare Ctr For Cmprhnsive 302 320-9108
205 W 14th St Wilmington (19801) *(G-15419)*

Christncare Prmry Care At Lnde 302 623-2850
100 S Riding Blvd Wilmington (19808) *(G-15420)*

Christncare Prmry Care Fmly MD 302 477-3300
1401 Foulk Rd Wilmington (19803) *(G-15421)*

Christncare Rhblttion Svcs At 302 623-1500
5311 Limestone Rd Wilmington (19808) *(G-15422)*

Christopher A Bowens MD 302 834-3700
2600 Glasgow Ave Ste 108 Newark (19702) *(G-10236)*

Christopher Baran DDS 903 968-7467
1601 Milltown Rd Ste 19 Wilmington (19808) *(G-15423)*

Christopher Burke 410 603-7450
20766 Brunswick Ln Millsboro (19966) *(G-8224)*

Christopher Companies 302 539-2888
39008 Seascape Ct Millville (19967) *(G-8522)*

Christopher Fortin DDS 302 422-9791
214 S Walnut St Milford (19963) *(G-7827)*

Christopher H Wendel Md PA 302 540-2979
Hockessin (19707) *(G-5163)*

Christopher Handy 302 934-1018
24872 Doe Bridge Ln Millsboro (19966) *(G-8225)*

Christopher J Seivert 302 731-2719
3 Andrew Jackson Cir Newark (19702) *(G-10237)*

Christopher McGlinn PHD 302 478-1450
1415 Foulk Rd Ste 104 Wilmington (19803) *(G-15424)*

Christopher's Salon & Spa, Middletown *Also Called: Christophers Hair Design (G-6980)*

Christophers Hair Design 302 378-1988
423 N Broad St Ste 5 Middletown (19709) *(G-6980)*

Chruch Creek, Dover *Also Called: Liberto Development Ltd (G-2934)*

Cht Holdings LLC 954 864-2008
16192 Coastal Hwy Lewes (19958) *(G-5819)*

Chubb Realty Group 302 388-8699
505 Falkirk Rd Wilmington (19803) *(G-15425)*

Chubb US Holdings Inc 215 640-1000
1 Beaver Valley Rd # 4e Wilmington (19803) *(G-15426)*

Chuck Coleman 302 537-2071
34130 Burton Farm Rd Frankford (19945) *(G-4090)*

Chuck George Inc 302 994-7444
400 Water St Wilmington (19804) *(G-15427)*

Chuck Hall Agt 302 934-8083
29787 John J Williams Hwy Millsboro (19966) *(G-8226)*

Chuck Lager, Wilmington *Also Called: Chuck Lager LLC (G-15428)*

Chuck Lager LLC 302 482-1773
4500 Linden Hill Rd Wilmington (19808) *(G-15428)*

Chuck Redstone - State Farm In 302 832-0345
920 Peoples Plz Newark (19702) *(G-10238)*

Chudasama Enterprises LLC 302 856-7532
313 N Dupont Hwy Georgetown (19947) *(G-4255)*

Chudasama Enterprises LLC (PA) 302 934-7968
521 W Dupont Hwy Millsboro (19966) *(G-8227)*

Church of God In Christ 302 678-1949
120a S Governors Ave Dover (19904) *(G-2072)*

ALPHABETIC SECTION — Citizens Bank National Assn

Churchfunerals Direct Inc.. 800 308-3590
　1000 N West St Ste 1200 Wilmington (19801) *(G-15429)*

Churchman De Snf MGT LLC.. 302 998-6900
　4949 Ogletown Stanton Rd Newark (19713) *(G-10239)*

CHURCHMAN VILLAGE, Newark Also Called: Churchman De Snf MGT LLC *(G-10239)*

Churchman Village Center LLC... 302 998-6900
　4949 Ogletown Stanton Rd Newark (19713) *(G-10240)*

Churman Village Center, Newark Also Called: Churchman Village Center LLC *(G-10240)*

Ci Centre, Millsboro Also Called: David G Major Associates Inc *(G-8255)*

Ci De Corp (PA)... 302 998-3944
　39 Brookside Dr Wilmington (19804) *(G-15430)*

Ciancon Global LLC.. 302 365-0956
　501 Silverside Rd Ste 105 Wilmington (19809) *(G-15431)*

Ciba Specialty Chem N Amer.. 302 992-5600
　205 S James St Wilmington (19804) *(G-15432)*

Cibc ATL Tr Private Wealth MGT, Wilmington Also Called: Cibc Private Wealth Groups LLC *(G-15433)*

Cibc Private Wealth Groups LLC...................................... 302 478-4050
　1 Righter Pkwy Ste 180 Wilmington (19803) *(G-15433)*

Cibt America Inc... 302 318-1300
　200 Continental Dr # 401 Newark (19713) *(G-10241)*

Ciconte Wasserman & Scerba LLC.................................. 302 658-7101
　1300 N King St Wilmington (19801) *(G-15434)*

Cielo Salon & Spa Inc.. 302 575-0400
　600 Delaware Ave Wilmington (19801) *(G-15435)*

Cifuentes Landscaping LLC.. 302 344-8108
　29314 Ed Morris Ln Millsboro (19966) *(G-8228)*

Cigarette City Inc (PA)... 302 836-4889
　460 Peoples Plz Newark (19702) *(G-10242)*

Cigna, Claymont Also Called: Cigna Global Holdings Inc *(G-1086)*

Cigna, Claymont Also Called: Cigna Holdings Inc *(G-1087)*

Cigna, Wilmington Also Called: Cigna Real Estate Inc *(G-15436)*

Cigna Global Holdings Inc (DH)....................................... 302 797-3469
　590 Naamans Rd Claymont (19703) *(G-1086)*

Cigna Holdings Inc (DH)... 215 761-1000
　590 Naamans Rd Claymont (19703) *(G-1087)*

Cigna Real Estate Inc (DH)... 302 476-3337
　1 Beaver Valley Rd Wilmington (19803) *(G-15436)*

Cignitix Global LLC.. 408 638-9350
　2055 Limestone Rd Ste 200c Wilmington (19808) *(G-15437)*

Cim Concepts Incorporated.. 302 613-5400
　100 W Commons Blvd Ste 101 New Castle (19720) *(G-8942)*

Cimi Enterprises LLC.. 302 803-2210
　108 Patriot Dr Middletown (19709) *(G-6981)*

Cinderellas Cleaning LLC... 302 632-6036
　512 N Dupont Hwy Dover (19901) *(G-2073)*

Cindy Elko Psyd LLC... 302 229-2110
　260 Chapman Rd Ste 205c Newark (19702) *(G-10243)*

Cindy L Szabo.. 302 855-9505
　9 N Front St Georgetown (19947) *(G-4256)*

Cindy L Tucker PHD.. 302 743-5775
　2500 Grubb Rd Ste 240 Wilmington (19810) *(G-15438)*

Cindys Home Away From Hme Fam................................ 302 378-0487
　22 Canary Ct Middletown (19709) *(G-6982)*

Cinemark Movies 10, Wilmington Also Called: Cinemark Usa Inc *(G-15439)*

Cinemark Usa Inc.. 302 994-7280
　1796 W Newport Pike Wilmington (19804) *(G-15439)*

Cinenso Inc... 424 245-5799
　8 The Grn Ste R Dover (19901) *(G-2074)*

Cingular Wireless, Dover Also Called: AT&T Mobility LLC *(G-1843)*

Cinnaire Registered Investment....................................... 302 655-1420
　100 W 10th St Ste 302 Wilmington (19801) *(G-15440)*

Cinnamon Technologies Inc.. 530 413-5533
　8 The Grn Ste B Dover (19901) *(G-2075)*

Cintas Corporation No 2.. 302 765-6460
　2925 Governor Printz Blvd Wilmington (19802) *(G-15441)*

Cintas J98, Wilmington Also Called: Cintas Corporation No 2 *(G-15441)*

CIO Story LLC... 408 915-5559
　19c Trolley Sq Wilmington (19806) *(G-15442)*

Cipolloni Brothers LLC.. 302 449-0960
　879 Black Diamond Rd Smyrna (19977) *(G-13678)*

Circle D Enterprises Inc... 302 544-2654
　201 Silver Birch Ln Bear (19701) *(G-104)*

Circle Group Inc... 302 241-0018
　735 Holly Dr Dover (19904) *(G-2076)*

Circle Time Learning Center... 302 384-7193
　1002 S Grant Ave Wilmington (19805) *(G-15443)*

Circle Veterinary Clinic... 302 652-6587
　1212 E Newport Pike Wilmington (19804) *(G-15444)*

Circus Associates Intelligence... 757 663-7864
　16192 Coastal Hwy Lewes (19958) *(G-5820)*

Circus Associates, The, Lewes Also Called: Circus Associates Intelligence *(G-5820)*

Cirillo Bros Inc... 302 326-1540
　761 Grantham Ln New Castle (19720) *(G-8943)*

Cirkla Inc (PA)... 415 851-4635
　8 The Grn Ste R Dover (19901) *(G-2077)*

Cirrus Enterprises.. 302 650-1648
　19c Trolley Sq Wilmington (19806) *(G-15445)*

Cirrus Nexus Corp.. 302 492-2700
　300 Delaware Ave Wilmington (19801) *(G-15446)*

Ciseaux Hair Design Studio, Dover Also Called: Jk Tangles Hair Salon *(G-2791)*

Cited Inc.. 302 384-9810
　2711 Centerville Rd Wilmington (19808) *(G-15447)*

Citibank, New Castle Also Called: Citibank National Association *(G-8944)*

Citibank, New Castle Also Called: Citibank Overseas Inv Corp *(G-8945)*

Citibank, New Castle Also Called: Citigroup Asia PCF Holdg Corp *(G-8949)*

Citibank National Association.. 302 477-5418
　1 Penns Way New Castle (19721) *(G-8944)*

Citibank Overseas Inv Corp (DH)..................................... 302 323-3600
　1 Penns Way New Castle (19720) *(G-8945)*

Citicorp, New Castle Also Called: Citicorp Del-Lease Inc *(G-8947)*

Citicorp Banking Corporation (HQ).................................. 302 323-3140
　One Penn's Way New Castle (19721) *(G-8946)*

Citicorp Del-Lease Inc (HQ).. 302 323-3801
　1 Penn's Wy New Castle (19721) *(G-8947)*

Citicorp Delaware Services Inc.. 302 323-3124
　1 Penns Way New Castle (19721) *(G-8948)*

Citifinancial, Bear Also Called: Citifinancial Credit Company *(G-105)*

Citifinancial, Milford Also Called: Citifinancial Credit Company *(G-7828)*

Citifinancial, Seaford Also Called: Citifinancial Credit Company *(G-13120)*

Citifinancial, Wilmington Also Called: Citifinancial Credit Company *(G-15448)*

Citifinancial Credit Company... 302 834-6677
　619 Governors Pl Bear (19701) *(G-105)*

Citifinancial Credit Company... 302 422-9657
　660 N Dupont Blvd Milford (19963) *(G-7828)*

Citifinancial Credit Company... 302 628-9253
　22974 Sussex Hwy Seaford (19973) *(G-13120)*

Citifinancial Credit Company... 302 683-4917
　4500 Linden Hill Rd 3rd Fl Wilmington (19808) *(G-15448)*

Citigroup, New Castle Also Called: Citicorp Banking Corporation *(G-8946)*

Citigroup, Newark Also Called: Citigroup Inc *(G-10244)*

Citigroup Inc... 302 631-3530
　500 White Clay Center Dr Newark (19711) *(G-10244)*

Citigroup Asia PCF Holdg Corp (DH)............................... 302 323-3100
　1 Penns Way Street 1st Fl New Castle (19721) *(G-8949)*

Citigroup Globl Mkts Fncl Pdts.. 212 559-1000
　1209 N Orange St Wilmington (19801) *(G-15449)*

Citizens Bank, Bear Also Called: Citizens Bank National Assn *(G-106)*

Citizens Bank, Dover Also Called: Citizens Bank National Assn *(G-2078)*

Citizens Bank, Dover Also Called: Govplus LLC *(G-2612)*

Citizens Bank, Lewes Also Called: Citizens Bank National Assn *(G-5821)*

Citizens Bank, Milford Also Called: Govplus LLC *(G-7910)*

Citizens Bank, Smyrna Also Called: Govplus LLC *(G-13749)*

Citizens Bank, Wilmington Also Called: Govplus LLC *(G-16933)*

Citizens Bank, Wilmington Also Called: Govplus LLC *(G-16935)*

Citizens Bank, Wilmington Also Called: Govplus LLC *(G-16936)*

Citizens Bank, Wilmington Also Called: Govplus LLC *(G-16938)*

Citizens Bank National Assn.. 302 834-2611
　146 Foxhunt Dr Bear (19701) *(G-106)*

Citizens Bank National Assn.. 302 734-0200
　779 N Dupont Hwy Dover (19901) *(G-2078)*

Citizens Bank National Assn... 302 645-2024
  34161 Citizen Dr Lewes (19958) *(G-5821)*
Citrosuco North America Inc.. 302 652-8763
  1000 Ferry Rd Wilmington (19801) *(G-15450)*
City Cab, Rehoboth Beach *Also Called: City Cab of Delware Inc (G-12673)*
City Cab Inc... 302 628-2588
  704 Norman Eskridge Hwy Seaford (19973) *(G-13121)*
City Cab of Delware Inc (PA).. 302 734-5968
  1203 State College Rd Dover (19904) *(G-2079)*
City Cab of Delware Inc... 302 227-8294
  164 Henlopen Ave Rehoboth Beach (19971) *(G-12673)*
City Electric Contracting Co... 302 764-0775
  204 Channel Rd Wilmington (19809) *(G-15451)*
City Electric Supply Company... 302 777-5300
  6 Medori Blvd Wilmington (19801) *(G-15452)*
City Electric Supply Dover... 302 672-3100
  401 Cassidy Dr Ste A Dover (19901) *(G-2080)*
City Fare... 302 421-3734
  1703 W 10th St Wilmington (19805) *(G-15453)*
City Mist LLC.. 302 342-1377
  1005 Willings Way New Castle (19720) *(G-8950)*
City Mist Logistics, New Castle *Also Called: City Mist LLC (G-8950)*
City of Dover.. 302 736-7070
  860 Buttner Pl Dover (19904) *(G-2081)*
City of Dover.. 302 736-7018
  5 E Reed St Dover (19901) *(G-2082)*
City of Dover.. 302 736-7035
  5 E Reed St Ste 100 Dover (19901) *(G-2083)*
City of Dover.. 302 736-5071
  15 Loockerman Plz Dover (19901) *(G-2084)*
City of Milford.. 302 422-1110
  180 Vickers Rd Milford (19963) *(G-7829)*
City of Newark.. 302 366-7060
  220 S Main St Newark (19711) *(G-10245)*
City of Seaford... 302 629-2890
  1019 W Locust St Seaford (19973) *(G-13122)*
City of Wilmington.. 302 576-2584
  800 N French St Wilmington (19801) *(G-15454)*
City One Hour Cleaners... 302 658-0001
  615 N King St Wilmington (19801) *(G-15455)*
City Theater Co Inc... 302 831-2206
  110 Tanglewood Ln Newark (19711) *(G-10246)*
City Towing Services... 302 561-7979
  415 Old Airport Rd New Castle (19720) *(G-8951)*
City Wide Facility Solutions, Dover *Also Called: City Wide Maintenance Co Inc (G-2085)*
City Wide Maintenance Co Inc... 302 526-2833
  755 Walker Rd Ste A Dover (19904) *(G-2085)*
City Wide Transportation Inc.. 302 792-1225
  6705 Governor Printz Blvd Claymont (19703) *(G-1088)*
City Window Cleaning of Del... 302 633-0633
  130b Middleboro Rd Wilmington (19804) *(G-15456)*
Cityline Rental.. 302 834-3142
  146 Countryside Ln Bear (19701) *(G-107)*
Citystlecollections LLC... 302 219-0259
  124 Broadkill Rd Milton (19968) *(G-8583)*
Citywide Transportation Inc... 302 792-0159
  6705 Governor Printz Blvd Wilmington (19809) *(G-15457)*
Civic Influencers Inc... 302 644-5757
  16192 Coastal Hwy Lewes (19958) *(G-5822)*
Civil Consulting Engineers LLC.. 302 824-6041
  8 Berton Ct Middletown (19709) *(G-6983)*
Civil Engineering Assoc LLC.. 302 376-8833
  55 W Main St Middletown (19709) *(G-6984)*
CJ S Autos... 302 500-0822
  20354 Sussex Hwy Bridgeville (19933) *(G-683)*
Cjm Bookkeeping and Taxes LLC...................................... 302 999-8755
  10 Broadfield Dr Newark (19713) *(G-10247)*
Cjs Autos LLC... 302 337-8880
  20354 Sussex Hwy Bridgeville (19933) *(G-684)*
CJs Beach Bays Inc... 302 645-8478
  33711 Wescoats Rd Lewes (19958) *(G-5823)*
CK Skin & Makeup LLC.. 302 317-2367
  1035 N Lincoln St Wilmington (19805) *(G-15458)*
Ckq Properties LLC.. 302 378-2560
  5197 Summit Bridge Rd Middletown (19709) *(G-6985)*
Cks Global Ventures LLC... 302 355-0511
  792 Jacobsen Cir Newark (19702) *(G-10248)*
CL Walton Enterprises LLC.. 443 360-1120
  300 Delaware Ave Ste 210a Wilmington (19801) *(G-15459)*
Claimmybadge LLC... 347 236-8109
  8 The Grn Ste B Dover (19901) *(G-2086)*
Claire Kubizne Pt... 302 521-3305
  16 Tremont Ct Newark (19711) *(G-10249)*
Clairvyant Technosolutions Inc....................................... 302 999-7172
  5700 Kirkwood Hwy Ste 107 Wilmington (19808) *(G-15460)*
Claravall Odilon... 302 875-7753
  1124 S Central Ave Laurel (19956) *(G-5483)*
Claremont School LLC... 302 478-4531
  1501 Marsh Rd Wilmington (19803) *(G-15461)*
Clarifi... 267 546-0430
  710 N Lincoln St Wilmington (19805) *(G-15462)*
Clarios LLC.. 302 696-3221
  50 Patriot Dr Middletown (19709) *(G-6986)*
Clarios LLC.. 302 996-0309
  18 Boulden Cir Ste 24 New Castle (19720) *(G-8952)*
Clarip Inc.. 888 252-5653
  20 Montchanin Rd Ste 20 Wilmington (19807) *(G-15463)*
Clark & Sons Inc.. 302 856-3372
  500 W Market St Georgetown (19947) *(G-4257)*
Clark & Sons Inc (PA)... 302 998-7552
  314 E Ayre St Wilmington (19804) *(G-15464)*
Clark & Sons Overhead Doors.. 302 998-7552
  314 E Ayre St Wilmington (19804) *(G-15465)*
Clark Benson Contracting... 302 846-9119
  37034 Saint George Rd Delmar (19940) *(G-1579)*
Clark Construction Inc... 302 832-1288
  4542 Kirkwood St Georges Rd Bear (19701) *(G-108)*
Clark Services Inc Delaware... 302 834-0556
  900 Julian Ln Bear (19701) *(G-109)*
Clarks Glasgow Pools Inc (PA)... 302 834-0200
  109 J And M Dr New Castle (19720) *(G-8953)*
Clarks Pool and Spa, New Castle *Also Called: Clarks Glasgow Pools Inc (G-8953)*
Clarks Swimming Pools Inc... 302 629-8835
  22855 Sussex Hwy Seaford (19973) *(G-13123)*
Clarksville Auto Service Ctr (PA)..................................... 302 539-1700
  34461 Atlantic Ave Ocean View (19970) *(G-12489)*
Clarksville Parts Plus, Ocean View *Also Called: Clarksville Auto Service Ctr (G-12489)*
Claros Farm Inc... 415 347-1321
  2093a Philadelphia Pike Ste 410 Claymont (19703) *(G-1089)*
Class Limousine Service... 302 653-1166
  1271 S Dupont Blvd Smyrna (19977) *(G-13679)*
Classic Auto Body Inc.. 302 655-4044
  103 Brookside Dr Wilmington (19804) *(G-15466)*
Classic Auto Body Wilmington, Wilmington *Also Called: Classic Auto Body Inc (G-15466)*
Classic Auto Restoration Svcs.. 302 398-9652
  2782 Jackson Ditch Rd Harrington (19952) *(G-4750)*
Classic Canvas LLC.. 443 359-0150
  3505 May Twilley Rd Delmar (19940) *(G-1580)*
Classic Cookies of Dowingtown....................................... 302 494-9662
  2628 Longwood Dr Wilmington (19810) *(G-15467)*
Classic Financial LLC.. 302 476-0948
  764 Ashington Dr Ste 100 Middletown (19709) *(G-6987)*
Clatchey Electrical Contr Inc... 443 845-3720
  36892 Wood Duck Way Selbyville (19975) *(G-13500)*
Claudio M Morel... 917 584-5236
  31309 Olney Way Millsboro (19966) *(G-8229)*
Claudiva Kae & Co LLC.. 302 283-9803
  406 Suburban Dr Newark (19711) *(G-10250)*
Claw Blue Maintenance... 717 487-2808
  27902 Avalon Dr Georgetown (19947) *(G-4258)*
Clay White Dental Associates... 302 731-4225
  12 Polly Drummond Hill Rd Newark (19711) *(G-10251)*

ALPHABETIC SECTION

Clay White Electrical Inc... 302 994-7748
 17 New Haven Dr Newark (19713) *(G-10252)*
Claymont Boys and Girls Club, Claymont Also Called: Boys & Girls Clubs Del Inc *(G-1064)*
Claymont Chiropractic Office.. 302 798-1587
 2100 Philadelphia Pike Claymont (19703) *(G-1090)*
Claymont Cmprhnsive Trtmnt Ctr.................................. 302 792-0700
 2999 Philadelphia Pike Claymont (19703) *(G-1091)*
Claymont Community Center Inc................................... 302 792-2757
 3301 Green St Claymont (19703) *(G-1092)*
Claymont Foods, Claymont Also Called: Estia Hospitality Group Inc *(G-1136)*
Claymont Nails... 302 798-8220
 2081 Philadelphia Pike Claymont (19703) *(G-1093)*
Claymont Nutrition.. 302 792-7818
 8 Commonwealth Ave Claymont (19703) *(G-1094)*
Claymore Senior Center Inc.. 302 428-3170
 504 S Clayton St Wilmington (19805) *(G-15468)*
Clayton E Bunting... 302 856-0017
 107 W Market St Georgetown (19947) *(G-4259)*
Clayton Fire Company Prpts LLC................................. 302 653-7317
 300 East St Clayton (19938) *(G-1356)*
Clayton Lions Club.. 302 450-6098
 545 S Carter Rd Smyrna (19977) *(G-13680)*
Clayton Theatre, Dagsboro Also Called: South Newport Co Inc *(G-1506)*
Clayton West LLC.. 302 530-3492
 42 Rehoboth Ave Ste 23 Rehoboth Beach (19971) *(G-12674)*
Cleamol LLC... 513 885-3462
 330 Water St Ste 105 Wilmington (19804) *(G-15469)*
Clean A Lot LLC... 302 218-2755
 5 Jaymar Blvd Newark (19702) *(G-10253)*
Clean Bee... 302 416-1723
 6 Philip Ct Newark (19711) *(G-10254)*
Clean Bees... 302 470-1125
 308 Oak Rd Seaford (19973) *(G-13124)*
Clean Cars Inc... 302 734-8234
 805 Forest St Dover (19904) *(G-2087)*
Clean Connect Inc... 331 330-5662
 501 Silverside Rd Ste 201 Wilmington (19809) *(G-15470)*
Clean Conscience LLC... 410 746-1315
 20883 Iris Rd Lewes (19958) *(G-5824)*
Clean Cooking Africa Corp... 706 691-9813
 1201 N Orange St Wilmington (19801) *(G-15471)*
Clean Cut Interlocking Pavers, Lewes Also Called: Road Site Construction Inc *(G-6424)*
Clean Cut Thread... 302 491-4336
 125 Causey Ave Milford (19963) *(G-7830)*
Clean Delaware.. 302 462-1451
 3799 N Dupont Hwy Dover (19901) *(G-2088)*
Clean Delaware Inc.. 302 684-4221
 Rte 404 Milton (19968) *(G-8584)*
Clean Energy Usa LLC (PA)... 302 227-1337
 20184 Phillips St Rehoboth Beach (19971) *(G-12675)*
Clean Energy USA LLC.. 302 227-1337
 37342 Martin St Rehoboth Beach (19971) *(G-12676)*
Clean Genie.. 302 241-4708
 201 Charring Cross Dr Dover (19904) *(G-2089)*
Clean Green Horizons... 302 258-9808
 18585 Coastal Hwy Rehoboth Beach (19971) *(G-12677)*
Clean Hands, Smyrna Also Called: Clean Hands LLC *(G-13681)*
Clean Hands LLC... 215 681-1435
 60 Markham Ct Smyrna (19977) *(G-13681)*
Clean ME Out Cleaning Svcs LLC................................ 302 480-4788
 1008 Hayes Cir Dover (19904) *(G-2090)*
Clean Pros.. 302 312-5666
 27 Concord Dr Newark (19702) *(G-10255)*
Clean Sweep... 302 422-6085
 5862 Old Shawnee Rd Milford (19963) *(G-7831)*
Clean-A-Tank Inc... 302 250-4229
 207 S Ogle Ave Wilmington (19805) *(G-15472)*
Cleanbay Renewables LLC (PA).................................. 866 691-1519
 1209 N Orange St Wilmington (19801) *(G-15473)*
Cleaner Brands Worldwide LLC.................................... 646 867-8328
 8 The Grn Ste R Dover (19901) *(G-2091)*
Cleaners Sunny.. 302 827-2095
 17601 Coastal Hwy Lewes (19958) *(G-5825)*
Cleaning Authority... 302 508-5080
 222 E Glenwood Ave Smyrna (19977) *(G-13682)*
Cleaning Bees.. 302 723-2421
 1342 Caldwell Corner Rd Townsend (19734) *(G-13972)*
Cleaning Bussiness... 302 260-9023
 36181 Field Ln Rehoboth Beach (19971) *(G-12678)*
Cleaning By Diana... 302 345-8904
 3115 Acacia St Wilmington (19804) *(G-15474)*
Cleaning Fairies... 302 753-3617
 615 Curtis Ave Wilmington (19804) *(G-15475)*
Cleaning Frenzy LLC... 302 453-8800
 2860 Ogletown Rd Bldg 6-1 Newark (19713) *(G-10256)*
Cleanith LLC... 571 269-8213
 348 Cinnamon Way Magnolia (19962) *(G-6731)*
Cleanpro Detail Center.. 302 464-1017
 5221 Summit Bridge Rd Middletown (19709) *(G-6988)*
Clear Channel Outdoor LLC... 302 658-5520
 24 Germay Dr Wilmington (19804) *(G-15476)*
Clear Definition LLC.. 302 503-7560
 110 N Rehoboth Blvd Milford (19963) *(G-7832)*
Clearblue Pools & Spas LLC.. 888 630-7665
 26046 Matthews St Millsboro (19966) *(G-8230)*
Cleared For Use Inc (PA)... 206 636-5222
 16192 Coastal Hwy Lewes (19958) *(G-5826)*
Clearview Windows LLC.. 302 491-6768
 600 Ne Front Street Ext Ste H Milford (19963) *(G-7833)*
Clearvue Solutions.. 301 213-3358
 300 Delaware Ave Ste 210 Wilmington (19801) *(G-15477)*
Cleat Lrng & Communications...................................... 845 527-3754
 218 Wilgus Ct Middletown (19709) *(G-6989)*
Clement Ogunwande Do... 302 762-4545
 1800 N Broom St Ste 109 Wilmington (19802) *(G-15478)*
Clementes Clubhouse.. 302 455-0936
 321 Shisler Ct Newark (19702) *(G-10257)*
Clendaniel Construction.. 302 422-7415
 7632 N Union Church Rd Milford (19963) *(G-7834)*
Clendaniel Plbg Htg & Coolg....................................... 302 684-3152
 14677 Oyster Rocks Rd Milton (19968) *(G-8585)*
Clendaniel Plbg Htg & Coolg, Milton Also Called: Clendaniel Plbg Htg & Coolg *(G-8585)*
Clerk Chat, Lewes Also Called: Clerk Chat Inc *(G-5827)*
Clerk Chat Inc... 415 943-6084
 16192 Coastal Hwy Lewes (19958) *(G-5827)*
Clever ME Inc... 832 866-8866
 1209 N Orange St Wilmington (19801) *(G-15479)*
Cleverx, Newark Also Called: Blumatter Inc *(G-10064)*
Clew Medical Inc.. 623 414-9009
 1313 N Market St Ste 5100 Wilmington (19801) *(G-15480)*
Clg True Solutions LLC.. 302 709-1312
 130 Cannonball Ln Newark (19702) *(G-10258)*
Click For Savings LLC... 302 300-0202
 5104 Christiana Mdws Bear (19701) *(G-110)*
Click2buy LLC (PA)... 347 698-7660
 8 The Grn Ste B Dover (19901) *(G-2092)*
Clickssl... 302 355-0692
 40 E Main St Newark (19711) *(G-10259)*
Clicoh Inc.. 415 987-3261
 651 N Broad St Ste 206 Middletown (19709) *(G-6990)*
Client Monster LLC.. 866 799-5433
 1300 Helen Dr Apt 112 Newark (19702) *(G-10260)*
Clifford L Anzilotti DDS PC... 302 378-2778
 112 Saint Annes Church Rd Middletown (19709) *(G-6991)*
Clifford L Anzilotti DDS PC (PA).................................. 302 475-2050
 2101 Foulk Rd Wilmington (19810) *(G-15481)*
Clifford O Smith... 302 995-9600
 3 Woodbrook Cir Wilmington (19810) *(G-15482)*
Clifton Enterprises LLC... 630 220-7435
 651 N Broad St Ste 205 Middletown (19709) *(G-6992)*
Clifton Farms Inc... 302 242-8806
 306 Warner Rd Milford (19963) *(G-7835)*

Clifton L Bakhsh Jr Inc 302 378-8009
  4450 Summit Bridge Rd Middletown (19709) *(G-6993)*

Clifton Leasing Co Inc (PA) 302 674-2300
  613 Clara St Dover (19904) *(G-2093)*

Cliktrucom 302 827-1103
  20487 Old Meadow Ln Lewes (19958) *(G-5828)*

Climate Action Systems Inc 802 356-6541
  251 Little Falls Dr Wilmington (19808) *(G-15483)*

Climate Solutions Service 302 824-2293
  3605 Old Capitol Trl Wilmington (19808) *(G-15484)*

Climate Solutions Services 302 275-9919
  2426 Calf Run Dr Wilmington (19808) *(G-15485)*

Cline Labs Inc 901 834-5102
  651 N Broad St Middletown (19709) *(G-6994)*

Clings Blings & Things 302 734-9103
  913 Schoolhouse Ln Dover (19904) *(G-2094)*

Clinic By Sea 302 644-0999
  16295 Willow Creek Rd Lewes (19958) *(G-5829)*

Clinical Breast Imaging 302 658-4800
  2401 Pennsylvania Ave Ste 115 Wilmington (19806) *(G-15486)*

Clinical Crdlgy Spcialists LLC 302 834-3700
  1400 Peoples Plz Ste 111 Newark (19702) *(G-10261)*

Clinical Pstral Cnsling Prgram 302 632-8842
  54 South State St Seaford (19973) *(G-13125)*

Clinpharma Clinical RES LLC 646 961-3437
  1000 N West St Ste 1200 Wilmington (19801) *(G-15487)*

Clinton Craddock 267 505-2671
  511 Cilantro Ct Middletown (19709) *(G-6995)*

Clipping Beast LLC 850 312-8223
  364 E Main St Ste 1011 Middletown (19709) *(G-6996)*

Clms LLC 703 629-3231
  21136 Laguna Dr Rehoboth Beach (19971) *(G-12679)*

Clootrack Software Labs Inc 302 204-1872
  2093 Philadelphia Pike Claymont (19703) *(G-1095)*

Close Cuts Lawn Svc & Ldscpg 302 422-2248
  24 Ne 10th St Milford (19963) *(G-7836)*

Clothes and Crystals LLC 302 316-3405
  245 Charring Cross Dr Dover (19904) *(G-2095)*

Cloud, Newark *Also Called: Cloud Collected LLC (G-10262)*

Cloud Big Data Tech LLC 573 201-5937
  3524 Silverside Rd Ste 35b Wilmington (19810) *(G-15488)*

Cloud Collected LLC 302 273-4010
  560 Peoples Plz # 312 Newark (19702) *(G-10262)*

Cloud Cystems LLC 815 797-9929
  651 N Broad St Ste 201 Middletown (19709) *(G-6997)*

Cloud Financial Corporation 845 729-5513
  919 N Market St Ste 950 Wilmington (19801) *(G-15489)*

Cloud Kings RC Club 717 284-0164
  119 Kirkwood Sq Wilmington (19808) *(G-15490)*

Cloud Services Solutions Inc (PA) 888 335-3132
  1521 Concord Pike Ste 301 Wilmington (19803) *(G-15491)*

Cloud Software Development LLC 703 957-9847
  3411 Silverside Rd # 104 Wilmington (19810) *(G-15492)*

Cloudarmee Ltd 714 673-8104
  251 Little Falls Dr Wilmington (19808) *(G-15493)*

Cloudbees, Lewes *Also Called: Cloudbees Inc (G-5830)*

Cloudbees Inc (PA) 323 842-7783
  16192 Coastal Hwy Lewes (19958) *(G-5830)*

Cloudbrst Lawn Sprnklr Systems 302 375-0446
  212 Wilmore Dr Middletown (19709) *(G-6998)*

Cloudbrst Lawn Sprnklr Systems, Wilmington *Also Called: D F Distribution Inc (G-15760)*

Cloudburst Sprinkler Systems, Wilmington *Also Called: Lightscapes Inc (G-17910)*

Cloudinfo Inc 302 314-5748
  1000 N West St Ste 1263 Wilmington (19801) *(G-15494)*

Cloudli Communications Inc 877 808-8647
  2915 Ogletown Rd Newark (19713) *(G-10263)*

Cloudokyo Technologies Inc 845 551-8627
  251 Little Falls Dr Wilmington (19808) *(G-15495)*

Cloudstaff USA LLC 800 730-8615
  1221 College Park Dr Ste 116 Dover (19904) *(G-2096)*

Cloudxperts LLC 302 257-5686
  8 The Grn Ste 5210 Dover (19901) *(G-2097)*

Clough Health and Wellness LLC 443 414-3764
  115 Norris Rd Wilmington (19803) *(G-15496)*

Clover Farms Meats 610 428-8066
  15 William Ave Ocean View (19970) *(G-12490)*

Clover Logistics LLC 713 474-4094
  651 N Broad St Middletown (19709) *(G-6999)*

Clover View Inc 561 779-2423
  254 Chapman Rd Ste 208 Newark (19702) *(G-10264)*

Clovyr Co 302 636-5401
  251 Little Falls Dr Wilmington (19808) *(G-15497)*

Clr Marketing Services LLC 302 688-9059
  1201 N Market St Wilmington (19801) *(G-15498)*

Cls Counseling LLC 302 644-2633
  20268 Plantations Rd Lewes (19958) *(G-5831)*

Cls Trucking & Logistics Inc 609 380-3399
  16192 Coastal Hwy Lewes (19958) *(G-5832)*

Club 6 Barbershop 302 276-1624
  112 Mario Dr Bear (19701) *(G-111)*

Club Brennan 302 838-9530
  1 Primrose Dr Bear (19701) *(G-112)*

Club Mantis Boxing LLC 302 943-2580
  16424 Fitzgeralds Rd Lincoln (19960) *(G-6661)*

Club Pilates, Wilmington *Also Called: CP Fitness Wilmington LLC (G-15675)*

Club Washington LLC 215 594-1332
  143 Carpenters Row Wilmington (19807) *(G-15499)*

Clubtac Supply Crates Ltd LLC 855 258-2822
  18766 John J Williams Hwy # 4 Rehoboth Beach (19971) *(G-12680)*

Clutterbot Inc 425 679-1348
  2093 Philadelphia Pike Ste 1348 Claymont (19703) *(G-1096)*

Clyde Spinelli 302 328-7679
  500 S Dupont Hwy Apt 225 New Castle (19720) *(G-8954)*

Clyde V Bush Sr 302 697-1723
  95 Goshawk Ln Camden Wyoming (19934) *(G-924)*

Clyde V Bush Sr Arms, Camden Wyoming *Also Called: Clyde V Bush Sr (G-924)*

Clymene LLC 888 679-3310
  16192 Coastal Hwy Lewes (19958) *(G-5833)*

Cm Beach LLC 202 521-1493
  19830 Beaver Dam Rd Lewes (19958) *(G-5834)*

CMC Corporation of Hockessin 302 239-1960
  721 Yorklyn Rd Hockessin (19707) *(G-5164)*

CMC Steel Holding Company (HQ) 302 691-6200
  802 N West St Ste 302 Wilmington (19801) *(G-15500)*

CMC-Kuhnke Inc 302 613-5600
  40 Mccullough Dr New Castle (19720) *(G-8955)*

Cmd Interiors Inc 917 826-8867
  402 Rehoboth Ave Rehoboth Beach (19971) *(G-12681)*

CMI, Middletown *Also Called: Christiana Mechanical Inc (G-6978)*

CMI Electric Inc (PA) 302 731-5556
  83 Albe Dr Ste A Newark (19702) *(G-10265)*

CMI Solar Electric, Newark *Also Called: CMI Electric Inc (G-10265)*

Cmp Fire LLC 410 620-2062
  1820 Otts Chapel Rd Newark (19702) *(G-10266)*

Cmplify LLC 248 716-5136
  1201 N Orange St Ste 600 Wilmington (19801) *(G-15501)*

CMS, Wilmington *Also Called: Bluevault LLC (G-14983)*

CMS Logistics 302 409-3138
  1521 Concord Pike Wilmington (19803) *(G-15502)*

Cmv Audio LLC (PA) 929 229-9926
  1000 N West St Ste 1501 Wilmington (19801) *(G-15503)*

Cnc Drywall North 302 307-6400
  730 Horsepond Rd Dover (19901) *(G-2098)*

Cnct App Inc (PA) 724 288-3212
  16192 Coastal Hwy Lewes (19958) *(G-5835)*

Cnh Cptal Oprting Lase Eqp Rcv 262 636-6011
  1209 N Orange St Wilmington (19801) *(G-15504)*

Cnmri 302 422-0800
  111 Neurology Way Milford (19963) *(G-7837)*

Cnmri, Dover *Also Called: P A Cnmri (G-3257)*

Cnooc Finance 2015 USA LLC 302 636-5400
  2711 Centerville Rd Wilmington (19808) *(G-15505)*

Cns Construction Corp 302 224-0450
  116 Sandy Dr Ste B Newark (19713) *(G-10267)*

Cntrl De Gstroenterolgyassoc I.. 302 678-9002
  644 S Queen St Ste 106 Dover (19904) *(G-2099)*
Cnu Fit LLC... 302 744-9037
  1404 Forrest Ave Ste 9 Dover (19904) *(G-2100)*
CNW Enterprise, Wilmington Also Called: Brandywine Graphics Inc *(G-15062)*
Cnwynn Publications.. 484 753-1568
  1102 Dwight Ct Dover (19904) *(G-2101)*
Co Fs Holding Company LLC... 302 894-1244
  502 S College Ave Newark (19713) *(G-10268)*
Co-Op Kitchen LLC.. 407 342-2295
  8 The Grn Ste A Dover (19901) *(G-2102)*
Coach AK Enterprises Inc... 617 433-7560
  651 N Broad St Ste 205 Middletown (19709) *(G-7000)*
Coach Transport LLC.. 302 983-7339
  29 S Turnberry Dr Dover (19904) *(G-2103)*
Coachhub Inc... 929 930-1450
  1209 N Orange St Wilmington (19801) *(G-15506)*
Coalition To Save Lives... 267 579-2875
  1510 Bondridge Rd Wilmington (19805) *(G-15507)*
Coam Exterior Inc... 302 329-9545
  26826 Lewes Georgetown Hwy Harbeson (19951) *(G-4688)*
Coast 2 Coast Logistics LLC... 857 212-9832
  611 S Dupont Hwy Ste 102 Dover (19901) *(G-2104)*
Coast Survey.. 302 645-7184
  32261 Nassau Rd Lewes (19958) *(G-5836)*
Coastal... 302 319-4061
  1201 N Orange St Ste 700 Wilmington (19801) *(G-15508)*
Coastal Aluminum Products.. 302 242-4868
  814 Evergreen Rd Magnolia (19962) *(G-6732)*
Coastal Bath LLC.. 302 742-9128
  106 N Pennsylvania Ave Delmar (19940) *(G-1581)*
Coastal Cabinetry LLC... 302 542-4155
  400 Megan Ave Seaford (19973) *(G-13126)*
Coastal Car Wash LLC... 302 883-3554
  1117 S Dupont Hwy Dover (19901) *(G-2105)*
Coastal Care & Dermatology LLC... 302 542-4999
  230 Mitchell St Ste B Millsboro (19966) *(G-8231)*
Coastal Care Physcl Thrapy Inc.. 480 236-3863
  37197 E Stoney Run Selbyville (19975) *(G-13501)*
Coastal Chem-Dry.. 302 645-2800
  34043 Clematis St Lewes (19958) *(G-5837)*
Coastal Chem-Dry.. 302 234-0200
  112 Breakwater Reach Lewes (19958) *(G-5838)*
Coastal Cleaning Services Inc.. 302 858-8857
  24832 John J Williams Hwy Millsboro (19966) *(G-8232)*
Coastal Club Schell Brothers.. 302 966-0063
  31605 Exeter Way Lewes (19958) *(G-5839)*
Coastal Coatings Inc.. 302 645-1399
  17993 American Way Lewes (19958) *(G-5840)*
Coastal Concerts Inc... 302 645-1539
  Bethel United Methodist Church Hall Fourth & Market Streets Lewes (19958) *(G-5841)*
Coastal Concrete Works LL.. 302 684-2872
  14298 Isaacs Rd Milton (19968) *(G-8586)*
Coastal Concrete Works LLC... 302 381-5261
  27220 Buckskin Trl Harbeson (19951) *(G-4689)*
Coastal Cottage.. 302 539-7821
  101 Atlantic Ave Ocean View (19970) *(G-12491)*
Coastal Counseling LLC... 302 542-4271
  330 Blossom Way Millsboro (19966) *(G-8233)*
Coastal Cttage Renovations LLC.. 302 727-2443
  344 Pilottown Rd Lewes (19958) *(G-5842)*
Coastal Custom Painting LLC (PA)... 302 242-6134
  18977 Munchy Branch Rd Ste 3g Rehoboth Beach (19971) *(G-12682)*
Coastal Direct Prmry Care LLC... 786 897-2550
  1409 Savannah Rd Lewes (19958) *(G-5843)*
Coastal Edge Landscape LLC.. 443 880-6270
  37252 Hudson Rd Selbyville (19975) *(G-13502)*
Coastal Equities Inc.. 302 543-2784
  1201 N Orange St Wilmington (19801) *(G-15509)*
Coastal Funding Corporation (PA).. 302 328-4113
  216 Delaware St Historic New Castle (19720) *(G-4959)*

Coastal Hearth and Home, Greenwood Also Called: Atlantic Contracting Svcs LLC *(G-4594)*
Coastal Images Inc... 302 539-6001
  711 Coastal Hwy Fenwick Island (19944) *(G-4045)*
Coastal It Consulting.. 302 226-9395
  4 Tall Oaks Ct Rehoboth Beach (19971) *(G-12683)*
Coastal Kid Watch.. 302 537-0793
  34 Club House Dr Rehoboth Beach (19971) *(G-12684)*
Coastal Landscaping LLC... 302 222-0098
  1 Clubhouse Dr Camden Wyoming (19934) *(G-925)*
Coastal Landscaping LLC... 302 678-0983
  30 The Grn Dover (19901) *(G-2106)*
Coastal Life Patios.. 301 944-4005
  9 Greystone Dr Lewes (19958) *(G-5844)*
Coastal Maintenance LLC... 302 536-1290
  25731 Winners Circle Dr Seaford (19973) *(G-13127)*
Coastal Mechanical.. 302 994-9100
  1 Carsdale Ct Wilmington (19808) *(G-15510)*
Coastal Pain Care Physcians PA.. 302 644-8330
  1606 Savannah Rd Ste 8 Lewes (19958) *(G-5845)*
Coastal Paint & Remodeling LLC.. 302 278-5471
  153 Clayton Ave Frankford (19945) *(G-4091)*
Coastal Plains Wood & Tile LLC.. 302 670-7853
  2 Tall Oaks Ct Rehoboth Beach (19971) *(G-12685)*
Coastal Plant Care LLC... 703 994-6905
  32621 Bella Via Ct Ocean View (19970) *(G-12492)*
Coastal Point... 302 539-1788
  111 Atlantic Ave Ste 2 Ocean View (19970) *(G-12493)*
Coastal Printing, Ocean View Also Called: Coastal Printing Company *(G-12494)*
Coastal Printing Company.. 302 537-1700
  Rte 26, Shops Of Millville Ocean View (19970) *(G-12494)*
Coastal Properties I LLC... 302 227-5800
  6 Christian St Rehoboth Beach (19971) *(G-12686)*
Coastal Pump & Tank Inc.. 302 398-3061
  17401 S Dupont Hwy Harrington (19952) *(G-4751)*
Coastal Rentals Hydraulics LLC.. 302 251-3103
  35283 Atlantic Ave Millville (19967) *(G-8523)*
Coastal Restorations Inc... 443 859-4505
  104 Riverview Dr Dagsboro (19939) *(G-1428)*
Coastal Seafood LLC.. 302 242-6659
  34527 Maple Dr Lewes (19958) *(G-5846)*
Coastal Services LLC.. 302 616-2906
  30430 Cedar Neck Rd Ocean View (19970) *(G-12495)*
Coastal Sun Roms Prch Enclsres... 302 537-3679
  36017 Pine Bark Ln Frankford (19945) *(G-4092)*
Coastal Tented Events... 302 539-5211
  35283 Atlantic Ave Millville (19967) *(G-8524)*
Coastal Tile AMP Stone In.. 301 748-0754
  7 N Williams St Selbyville (19975) *(G-13503)*
Coastal Tile and Hardwood.. 302 339-7772
  28509 Ok Waw Ave Millsboro (19966) *(G-8234)*
Coastal Towing Inc... 302 645-6300
  33012 Cedar Grove Rd Lewes (19958) *(G-5847)*
Coastal Veterinary LLC... 302 524-8550
  33053 Lighthouse Rd Selbyville (19975) *(G-13504)*
Coastline Medical Ctr Milford.. 302 265-2893
  907 N Dupont Blvd Milford (19963) *(G-7838)*
Coastline Realty LLC... 302 735-7526
  830 Walker Rd Ste 11-1 Dover (19904) *(G-2107)*
Coating Effects Div, Wilmington Also Called: BASF Corporation *(G-14774)*
Coatings With A Purpose Inc.. 302 462-1465
  21166 Greenway Pl Georgetown (19947) *(G-4260)*
Cobalt Art Studio... 201 819-9087
  16394 Samuel Paynter Blvd Milton (19968) *(G-8587)*
Cobalt Pacific LLC.. 302 437-4761
  642 Courtly Rd Townsend (19734) *(G-13973)*
Cobb Trucking Inc.. 917 561-6263
  363 E Commerce St Apt 408 Smyrna (19977) *(G-13683)*
Cobi Group Inc... 302 407-3085
  3424 Old Capitol Trl Wilmington (19808) *(G-15511)*
Cobra Investments MGT Inc... 302 691-6333
  103 Foulk Rd Wilmington (19803) *(G-15512)*

Cobra Razors ... 302 540-0464
4007 Montchanin Rd Wilmington (19807) *(G-15513)*

Cochran Oil, New Castle Also Called: Federal Mechanical Contractors *(G-9123)*

Code Guide LLC ... 530 424-8919
1521 Concord Pike Ste 301 Wilmington (19803) *(G-15514)*

Code Vanguard LLC ... 302 463-8265
37105 Hudson Rd Selbyville (19975) *(G-13505)*

Code-Masters LLC ... 408 508-9955
254 Chapman Rd Ste 208 Newark (19702) *(G-10269)*

Code509com Inc ... 941 263-3509
8 The Grn Ste A Dover (19901) *(G-2108)*

Codeiscode Mktg Consulting LLC ... 415 202-5303
427 N Tatnall St Wilmington (19801) *(G-15515)*

Codeship Inc ... 617 515-3664
16192 Coastal Hwy Lewes (19958) *(G-5848)*

Codonrx LLC ... 773 612-5828
8 The Grn Dover (19901) *(G-2109)*

Cody A Bowers DPM ... 302 998-0178
1601 Milltown Rd Ste 24 Wilmington (19808) *(G-15516)*

Cody H Hafner ... 302 234-1030
100 Fitness Way Hockessin (19707) *(G-5165)*

Coffee Artisan LLC ... 302 297-8800
718 Phillips Hill Dr Millsboro (19966) *(G-8235)*

Coffee Run Condo Council Inc ... 302 239-4134
614 Loveville Rd Hockessin (19707) *(G-5166)*

Coffeedge Inc ... 585 294-2726
651 N Broad St Ste 206 Middletown (19709) *(G-7001)*

Cofinet LLC ... 614 301-8082
16192 Coastal Hwy Lewes (19958) *(G-5849)*

Cogency Global Inc ... 800 483-1140
850 New Burton Rd Ste 201 Dover (19904) *(G-2110)*

Cogentrix Delaware Holdings (DH) ... 847 908-2800
1105 N Market St Ste 1108 Wilmington (19801) *(G-15517)*

Coghan-Haes LLC ... 302 325-4210
101 S Mary St Wilmington (19804) *(G-15518)*

Cogir Management USA Inc ... 916 400-3985
2915 Ogletown Rd Newark (19713) *(G-10270)*

Cogir On NAPA Road, Newark Also Called: Cogir Management USA Inc *(G-10270)*

Cognicor Technologies Inc ... 650 444-2076
8 The Grn Dover (19901) *(G-2111)*

Cognitive Tech Solutions Inc ... 302 207-1824
1000 N West St Ste 1200 Wilmington (19801) *(G-15519)*

Cognitro LLC ... 347 983-9785
16192 Coastal Hwy Lewes (19958) *(G-5850)*

Cohesive Strategies Inc ... 302 429-9120
600 N King St Ste 2 Wilmington (19801) *(G-15520)*

Coiffure Ltd ... 302 652-3463
4031 Kennett Pike Wilmington (19807) *(G-15521)*

COINBASE, Wilmington Also Called: Coinbase Global Inc *(G-15522)*

Coinbase Global Inc (PA) ... 302 777-0200
1209 N Orange St Wilmington (19801) *(G-15522)*

Cointigo LLC ... 817 681-7131
651 N Broad St Ste 205 # 647 Middletown (19709) *(G-7002)*

Cointracker, Claymont Also Called: Nino Finance Inc *(G-1254)*

Coit Clg Rstoration Wilmington ... 302 322-1099
950 Ridge Rd Ste C2 Claymont (19703) *(G-1097)*

Coker Concrete, Dover Also Called: Chris Cocker *(G-2071)*

Cokesbury Village, Hockessin Also Called: Peninsula Untd Mthdst Hmes Inc *(G-5336)*

Coko Prints ... 302 507-1683
3 Doe Run Ct Apt 1b Wilmington (19808) *(G-15523)*

Coldwell Banker ... 302 539-4086
39682 Sunrise Ct Bethany Beach (19930) *(G-591)*

Coldwell Banker ... 302 541-5790
35786 Atlantic Ave Unit 2 Millville (19967) *(G-8525)*

Coldwell Banker, Millville Also Called: Coldwell Banker *(G-8525)*

Coldwell Banker, Rehoboth Beach Also Called: Coldwell Banker Resort Realtty *(G-12687)*

Coldwell Banker, Rehoboth Beach Also Called: Coldwell Banker Village Green *(G-12689)*

Coldwell Banker, Rehoboth Beach Also Called: Coldwell Bnkr Rhboth Rsort Rlt *(G-12690)*

Coldwell Banker, Wilmington Also Called: Coldwell Bnkr Coml Amato Assoc *(G-15524)*

Coldwell Banker Resort Realtty ... 302 864-0053
36462 E Estate Dr Rehoboth Beach (19971) *(G-12687)*

Coldwell Banker Resort Realty ... 302 422-8200
711 N Dupont Blvd Milford (19963) *(G-7839)*

Coldwell Banker Resort Realty ... 302 645-2881
100 White Pine Dr Millsboro (19966) *(G-8236)*

Coldwell Banker Resort Realty ... 302 841-8470
41 Bay Reach Rehoboth Beach (19971) *(G-12688)*

Coldwell Banker Resort Realty ... 302 245-2145
22350 Sussex Hwy Seaford (19973) *(G-13128)*

Coldwell Banker Resort Realty, Rehoboth Beach Also Called: Rehoboth Realty Inc *(G-12933)*

Coldwell Banker Village Green ... 302 227-3818
317 Rehoboth Ave Rehoboth Beach (19971) *(G-12689)*

Coldwell Bnkr Coml Amato Assoc ... 302 224-7700
413 Larch Cir Wilmington (19804) *(G-15524)*

Coldwell Bnkr Rhboth Rsort Rlt ... 302 227-5000
20184 Coastal Hwy Rehoboth Beach (19971) *(G-12690)*

Cole Janeika ... 302 838-1868
6 Lyon Ct Newark (19702) *(G-10271)*

Cole Realty Inc ... 302 764-4700
705 Philadelphia Pike Wilmington (19809) *(G-15525)*

Cole Schotz PC ... 302 984-9541
500 Delaware Ave Ste 1410 Wilmington (19801) *(G-15526)*

Colecarol ... 302 313-6698
1217 Churchmans Rd Newark (19713) *(G-10272)*

Coleman Cleaning Services, Magnolia Also Called: Coleman Cleaning Services Inc *(G-6733)*

Coleman Cleaning Services Inc ... 302 335-1868
831 Lexington Mill Rd Magnolia (19962) *(G-6733)*

Colemans Healthcr Stffngffing ... 302 423-9385
42 Liborio Ln Smyrna (19977) *(G-13684)*

Colette W Bleistine Paying It ... 609 217-1925
537 Stonehaven Dr Townsend (19734) *(G-13974)*

Colgate-Palmolive, Wilmington Also Called: Colgate-Palmolive Company *(G-15527)*

Colgate-Palmolive Company ... 302 428-1554
1105 N Market St Ste 1300 Wilmington (19801) *(G-15527)*

Coliving Inc ... 650 449-4448
2035 Sunset Lake Rd Ste B2 Newark (19702) *(G-10273)*

Collabrting For Nvel Sltons LL ... 619 252-6060
2711 Centerville Rd Ste 300 Wilmington (19808) *(G-15528)*

Collabrtive Effort To Rnfrce T (PA) ... 302 731-0301
52 Reads Way New Castle (19720) *(G-8956)*

Collabrtive Effort To Rnfrce T ... 302 731-0301
699 S Carter Rd Unit 1 Smyrna (19977) *(G-13685)*

Collect Africa Inc ... 657 204-4749
256 Chapman Rd Ste 105-4 Wilmington (19808) *(G-15529)*

College Ave Stdnt Ln 2021-B LL ... 302 497-0701
1105 N Market St 20th Fl Wilmington (19801) *(G-15530)*

College Ave Student Loans, Wilmington Also Called: College Avenue Student Ln LLC *(G-15531)*

College Avenue Student Ln LLC ... 302 684-6070
233 N King St Ste 400 Wilmington (19801) *(G-15531)*

College Hunks Hauling Junk Mvg ... 302 232-6200
12 Hadco Rd Wilmington (19804) *(G-15532)*

Collegiate Network Inc ... 302 652-4600
3901 Centerville Rd Wilmington (19807) *(G-15533)*

Collett & Son Welding Inc ... 302 376-1830
550 Green Giant Rd Townsend (19734) *(G-13975)*

Collett and Sons Welding ... 302 223-6525
370 N Main St Smyrna (19977) *(G-13686)*

Colliers Trim Shop Inc ... 302 227-8398
2206 Hwy One Rehoboth Beach (19971) *(G-12691)*

Collins Associates ... 302 834-4000
38 Peoples Plz Newark (19702) *(G-10274)*

Collins Mechanical Inc ... 302 398-8877
15294 S Dupont Hwy Harrington (19952) *(G-4752)*

Colmorgen ... 302 744-6220
640 S State St Dover (19901) *(G-2112)*

Colon Health Centers Americ ... 302 995-2656
537 Stanton Christiana Rd Newark (19713) *(G-10275)*

Colon Rectal Surgery Assoc Del ... 302 737-5444
4745 Ogletown Stanton Rd Ste 216 Newark (19713) *(G-10276)*

Colonial Chpter of The Prlyzed ... 302 861-6671
700 Barksdale Rd Ste 7 Newark (19711) *(G-10277)*

ALPHABETIC SECTION

Colonial Cleaning, Wilmington Also Called: Colonial Construction Company *(G-15535)*
Colonial Cleaning Services Inc 302 660-2067
126b Middleboro Rd Wilmington (19804) *(G-15534)*
Colonial Construction Company 302 994-5705
126 Middleboro Rd Wilmington (19804) *(G-15535)*
Colonial East LP 302 644-4758
16 Manor House Ln Lewes (19958) *(G-5851)*
Colonial East Management 302 644-6500
18389 Olde Coach Dr Rehoboth Beach (19971) *(G-12692)*
Colonial Electric Supply Co 302 998-9993
88 Quigley Blvd Historic New Castle (19720) *(G-4960)*
Colonial Garden Apartments, Newark Also Called: Colonial Rlty Assoc Ltd Partnr *(G-10278)*
Colonial Home Improvements 302 275-8247
807 Seymour Rd Bear (19701) *(G-113)*
Colonial Income Tax Service 302 322-6881
700 Delaware St Historic New Castle (19720) *(G-4961)*
Colonial Inv Managment Co 302 736-0674
9 E Loockerman St Ste C Dover (19901) *(G-2113)*
Colonial Marble of Delaware 302 328-1735
240 S Dupont Hwy Ste 100 New Castle (19720) *(G-8957)*
Colonial Oaks Hotel LLC 302 645-7766
18964 John J Williams Hwy Rehoboth Beach (19971) *(G-12693)*
Colonial Oaks Hotel LLC (PA) 302 645-7766
19113 Coastal Hwy Rehoboth Beach (19971) *(G-12694)*
Colonial Parking Inc (HQ) 302 651-3600
715 N Orange St Wilmington (19801) *(G-15536)*
Colonial Rlty Assoc Ltd Partnr 302 737-1254
334 E Main St Bldg B Newark (19711) *(G-10278)*
Colonial School District 302 323-2700
1617 Matassino Rd New Castle (19720) *(G-8958)*
Colonial Security Services, New Castle Also Called: Lenar Detective Agency Inc *(G-9305)*
Colony North Apartments 302 762-0405
319 E Lea Blvd Wilmington (19802) *(G-15537)*
Color Dye Systems and Co 302 454-1754
663 Dawson Dr Ste B Newark (19713) *(G-10279)*
Color Guru, Wilmington Also Called: Color Guru LLC *(G-15538)*
Color Guru LLC 267 972-4447
1605 Sunset Ln Wilmington (19810) *(G-15538)*
Color ME Crazy Hair LLC (PA) 484 838-6027
27 W Main St Middletown (19709) *(G-7003)*
Color Street 302 574-0409
911 Lovering Ave Wilmington (19806) *(G-15539)*
Color Works Painting Inc 302 324-8411
251 Edwards Ave New Castle (19720) *(G-8959)*
Colorful World Daycare, Bridgeville Also Called: Marlette R Lofland *(G-728)*
Colors & Effects USA LLC 302 996-2910
205 S James St Newport (19804) *(G-12444)*
Colorwise and More 302 703-6330
34732 Bookhammer Landing Rd Lewes (19958) *(G-5852)*
Colourworks Photographic Svcs 302 428-0222
1902 Superfine Ln Wilmington (19802) *(G-15540)*
Columbia Vending Service Inc 302 856-7000
10000 Old Racetrack Rd Delmar (19940) *(G-1582)*
Columbus Inn Management I 302 429-8700
105 Foulk Rd Wilmington (19803) *(G-15541)*
Combat Zone Wresting LLC 302 345-1077
208 Spruceglen Dr Newark (19711) *(G-10280)*
Comcast, Dover Also Called: Comcast Cble Cmmunications LLC *(G-2114)*
Comcast, Dover Also Called: Comcast of Delmarva LLC *(G-2116)*
Comcast, Georgetown Also Called: Comcast Cablevision of Del *(G-4261)*
Comcast, New Castle Also Called: Comcast Cablevision of Del *(G-8960)*
Comcast, New Castle Also Called: Comcast Cble Cmmunications LLC *(G-8961)*
Comcast, Wilmington Also Called: Comcast Clfrn/Clrd/Llns/ndn/tx *(G-15542)*
Comcast Cable, Seaford Also Called: Comcast Corporation *(G-13129)*
Comcast Cablevision of Del (HQ) 302 856-4591
426a N Dupont Hwy Georgetown (19947) *(G-4261)*
Comcast Cablevision of Del 302 661-4465
5 Bellecor Dr New Castle (19720) *(G-8960)*
Comcast Cble Cmmunications LLC 410 497-4600
5729 W Denneys Rd Dover (19904) *(G-2114)*
Comcast Cble Cmmunications LLC 302 323-9200
22 Reads Way New Castle (19720) *(G-8961)*
Comcast Clfrn/Clrd/Llns/ndn/tx 248 233-4724
1201 N Market St Ste 1000 Wilmington (19801) *(G-15542)*
Comcast Corporation 800 266-2278
1580 N Dupont Hwy Dover (19901) *(G-2115)*
Comcast Corporation 302 495-5612
2 Schulze Rd Greenwood (19950) *(G-4604)*
Comcast Corporation 302 526-0109
22992 Sussex Hwy Seaford (19973) *(G-13129)*
Comcast Corporation 302 262-8996
500 High St Seaford (19973) *(G-13130)*
Comcast MO Investments LLC 302 594-8705
1201 N Market St Ste 1000 Wilmington (19801) *(G-15543)*
Comcast of Delmarva LLC 215 286-3345
5729 W Denneys Rd Dover (19904) *(G-2116)*
Comeet Technologies Inc 650 433-9027
1313 N Market St Ste 5100 Wilmington (19801) *(G-15544)*
Comfort Boyce Systems 302 419-4748
134b Sandy Dr Newark (19713) *(G-10281)*
Comfort Care At Home Inc 302 737-8078
254 Chapman Rd Newark (19702) *(G-10282)*
Comfort Inn, Dover Also Called: Amaa Management Corporation *(G-1779)*
Comfort Inn, Georgetown Also Called: J & P Management Inc *(G-4375)*
Comfort Inn, Newark Also Called: Comfort Inn & Suites *(G-10283)*
Comfort Inn, Newark Also Called: Keval Corp *(G-11160)*
Comfort Inn, Rehoboth Beach Also Called: Resort Hotel LLC *(G-12934)*
Comfort Inn & Suites 302 737-3900
3 Concord Ln Newark (19713) *(G-10283)*
Comfort Keepers, New Castle Also Called: Caring For Life Inc *(G-8913)*
Comfort Service Company, Seaford Also Called: National HVAC Service *(G-13313)*
Comfort Suites 302 628-5400
23420 Sussex Hwy Seaford (19973) *(G-13131)*
Comfort Suites, Hockessin Also Called: Comfort Suites Motel *(G-5167)*
Comfort Suites, Seaford Also Called: Comfort Suites *(G-13131)*
Comfort Suites Motel 302 266-6600
181 Thompson Dr Hockessin (19707) *(G-5167)*
Comfort Zone Jazz LLC 302 745-2019
30515 Osprey Rd Milton (19968) *(G-8588)*
Commerce Global Inc 302 478-0853
2419 Dorval Rd Wilmington (19810) *(G-15545)*
Commercial Cleaning Services 302 764-3424
814 Philadelphia Pike Ste A Wilmington (19809) *(G-15546)*
Commercial Equipment Service 302 475-6682
2645 Longwood Dr Wilmington (19810) *(G-15547)*
Commercial Equipment Svc 302 475-6682
6603 Governor Printz Blvd Wilmington (19809) *(G-15548)*
Commercial Food Equipment Repr, Wilmington Also Called: Elmer Schultz Services Inc *(G-16376)*
Commercial Insurance Assoc 610 436-4608
256 Chapman Rd Ste 203 Newark (19702) *(G-10284)*
Commercial Residential Contrs, Dover Also Called: Scuba World Inc *(G-3522)*
Committed Hearts Foundation 402 850-4644
106 Country Club Dr Wilmington (19803) *(G-15549)*
Committee To Elect Brad Eaby 302 670-4806
233 Pebble Valley Dr Dover (19904) *(G-2117)*
Commodities Plus Inc 302 376-5219
132 Sandy Dr Newark (19713) *(G-10285)*
Common, Wilmington Also Called: Common Cooperative Company *(G-15550)*
Common Cooperative Company 504 333-0731
919 N Market St Ste 950 Wilmington (19801) *(G-15550)*
Common Sense Health Research 302 260-9811
46 Baltimore Ave Rehoboth Beach (19971) *(G-12695)*
Common Sense Solutions LLC 302 875-4510
14127 Rottwaller Rd Laurel (19956) *(G-5484)*
Commonspirit Health LLC 302 336-8212
838 Walker Rd Ste 21-2 Dover (19904) *(G-2118)*
Commonwealth Construction 302 654-6611
2317 Pennsylvania Ave Wilmington (19806) *(G-15551)*
Commonwealth Contruction Co 302 654-6611
2317 Pennsylvania Ave Wilmington (19806) *(G-15552)*

Commonwealth Group LLC (PA) 302 472-7200
  300 Water St Ste 300 Wilmington (19801) *(G-15553)*

Commonwealth Motor Inc 302 505-5555
  1126 Lodge St Wilmington (19802) *(G-15554)*

Commonwealth Partners MGT LLC 302 223-5941
  717 N Union St # 45 Wilmington (19805) *(G-15555)*

Commonwealth Trust Co 302 658-7214
  29 Bancroft Mills Rd Wilmington (19806) *(G-15556)*

Commtrak Corporation 302 644-1600
  17493 Nassau Commons Blvd Lewes (19958) *(G-5853)*

Communctons Wkrs Amer Lcal 131 .... 302 737-0400
  350 Gooding Dr Newark (19702) *(G-10286)*

Communication Concepts LLC 302 658-9800
  300 Delaware Ave Ste 210a Wilmington (19801) *(G-15557)*

Communications & Wiring Co 302 539-0809
  34423 Sylvan Vue Dr Dagsboro (19939) *(G-1429)*

Communications Cnstr Group LLC 302 280-6926
  1158 S Central Ave Laurel (19956) *(G-5485)*

Communications Printing Inc 302 229-9369
  2850 Ogletown Rd Newark (19713) *(G-10287)*

Communities In Schools Del 704 724-3737
  522 S Walnut St Wilmington (19801) *(G-15558)*

Community Athc Solutions LLC 302 468-5493
  913 N Market St Ste 200 Wilmington (19801) *(G-15559)*

Community Auto Repair 302 856-3333
  514 W Market St Georgetown (19947) *(G-4262)*

Community Bank Delaware (PA) 302 348-8600
  16982 Kings Hwy Lewes (19958) *(G-5854)*

Community Business Dev Corp 302 544-1709
  25 Hempstead Dr Newark (19702) *(G-10288)*

Community Cllaboration Del Inc 302 824-6896
  621 Delaware St Historic New Castle (19720) *(G-4962)*

Community Consulting Corps 614 348-7823
  3 Larchmont Ct Hockessin (19707) *(G-5168)*

Community Day 302 757-3700
  1501 Barley Mill Rd Wilmington (19807) *(G-15560)*

Community Housing Inc (PA) 302 652-3991
  613 N Washington St Wilmington (19801) *(G-15561)*

Community Integrated Services 215 238-7411
  24 Nw Front St Ste 300 Milford (19963) *(G-7840)*

Community Interactions Inc 302 993-7846
  625 W Newport Pike Wilmington (19804) *(G-15562)*

COMMUNITY INTERACTIONS, INC, Wilmington *Also Called: Community Interactions Inc (G-15562)*

Community Legal Aid Society 302 674-8503
  840 Walker Rd Dover (19904) *(G-2119)*

Community Legal Aid Society 302 856-0038
  20151 Office Cir Georgetown (19947) *(G-4263)*

Community Legal Aid Society (PA) 302 757-7001
  100 W 10th St Ste 801 Wilmington (19801) *(G-15563)*

Community Pride 302 236-6591
  72 Glade Cir E Rehoboth Beach (19971) *(G-12696)*

Community Publications Inc 302 239-4644
  24 W Main St Middletown (19709) *(G-7004)*

Community Pwered Federal Cr Un (PA) 302 368-2396
  1758 Pulaski Hwy Bear (19701) *(G-114)*

Community Pwered Federal Cr Un 302 324-1441
  4 Quigley Blvd Historic New Castle (19720) *(G-4963)*

Community Services Corporation 302 368-4400
  116 Haines St Newark (19711) *(G-10289)*

Community Solutions Inc 302 660-8691
  1421 Marsh Rd Wilmington (19802) *(G-15564)*

Community Systems and Svcs Inc 302 325-1500
  2 Penns Way Ste 301 New Castle (19720) *(G-8962)*

Community Twered Federal Cr Un (PA) 302 368-2396
  401 Eagle Run Rd Newark (19702) *(G-10290)*

Community Twered Federal Cr Un 302 994-3617
  3670 Kirkwood Hwy Wilmington (19808) *(G-15565)*

Communityliving Inc 302 735-4534
  145 Kings Hwy Dover (19901) *(G-2120)*

Compact Membrane Systems Inc 302 999-7996
  15 Reads Way New Castle (19720) *(G-8963)*

Compadre Concrete 302 228-0763
  100b John St Bridgeville (19933) *(G-685)*

Company Corporation (HQ) 302 636-5440
  251 Little Falls Dr Wilmington (19808) *(G-15566)*

Compass Electric LLC 302 731-0240
  935 Rahway Dr Newark (19711) *(G-10291)*

Compass Graphics 302 378-1977
  137 Back Creek Dr Middletown (19709) *(G-7005)*

Compass Point Associates LLC 302 684-2980
  26373 Lewes Georgetown Hwy Harbeson (19951) *(G-4690)*

Compassionate Care Trnspt LLC 215 847-9836
  510 Howard St Wilmington (19804) *(G-15567)*

Compassnate Hlth Intatives Inc 302 765-8256
  717 Dairy Dr Middletown (19709) *(G-7006)*

Compassnate Soc of Chrst St St 914 482-2562
  126 Cresthaven Ln Dover (19901) *(G-2121)*

Compassonate Certification Ctr 888 316-9085
  364 E Main St Ste 2001 Middletown (19709) *(G-7007)*

Compassred Inc 302 383-2856
  112 S French St # 4 Wilmington (19801) *(G-15568)*

Compete Hr Inc 310 989-9857
  1007 N Orange St Wilmington (19801) *(G-15569)*

Competition Game Calls 302 345-7463
  208 Brookland Ave Wilmington (19805) *(G-15570)*

Complete Accident Relief 302 375-5019
  222 Carter Dr Ste 103 Middletown (19709) *(G-7008)*

Complete Auto Body Inc 302 629-3955
  26907 Sussex Hwy Seaford (19973) *(G-13132)*

Complete Care At Silver Lk LLC 302 734-5990
  1080 Silver Lake Blvd Dover (19904) *(G-2122)*

Complete Concrete Systems 302 396-0013
  27403 Walking Run Milton (19968) *(G-8589)*

Complete Disposal Service LLC 302 448-1021
  18265 Deer Forest Rd Georgetown (19947) *(G-4264)*

Complete Family Care Inc 302 482-3347
  534 Greenhill Ave Wilmington (19805) *(G-15571)*

Complete Family Care Inc 302 232-5002
  2500 W 4th St Ste 6 Wilmington (19805) *(G-15572)*

Complete Hemp LLC 888 901-6150
  4023 Kennett Pike Ste 622 Wilmington (19807) *(G-15573)*

Complete Lawn Care, Millsboro *Also Called: Complete Tree Care Inc (G-8237)*

Complete Properties Services 302 242-8666
  116 Sarah Cir Ste D Camden Wyoming (19934) *(G-926)*

Complete Rsrvtion Slutions LLC 800 672-8522
  8 The Grn Ste 5863 Dover (19901) *(G-2123)*

Complete Tree Care Inc 302 945-8289
  30598 Cordrey Rd Millsboro (19966) *(G-8237)*

Compliance Environmental Inc 302 674-4427
  150 S Bradford St Dover (19904) *(G-2124)*

Comprehensive Accident Injury 302 563-7442
  131 Becks Woods Dr Bear (19701) *(G-115)*

Comprehensive Bus Svcs LLC (PA) 302 994-2000
  112 Capitol Trl Newark (19711) *(G-10292)*

Comprehensive Chiropractic 302 346-4744
  850 New Burton Rd Dover (19904) *(G-2125)*

Comprhensive Neurology Ctr LLC 302 996-9010
  1114 Drummond Plz Newark (19711) *(G-10293)*

Comprhnsive Spine Spt Medicine, Bear *Also Called: Frank Falco MD (G-236)*

Comprise It Solutions LLC 302 337-4036
  8th The Green Ste 14916 Dover (19901) *(G-2126)*

Compton Apartments, Wilmington *Also Called: Compton Pk Prsrvtion Assoc LLC (G-15574)*

Compton Pk Prsrvtion Assoc LLC 302 654-4369
  650 N Walnut St Wilmington (19801) *(G-15574)*

Compton Townehouse Apartments, Wilmington *Also Called: Compton Twne Prsrvtion Assoc L (G-15575)*

Compton Twne Prsrvtion Assoc L 302 764-6450
  831a Towne Ct Wilmington (19801) *(G-15575)*

Computer Aid Inc 302 831-5500
  500 Creek View Rd Ste 201 Newark (19711) *(G-10294)*

Computer Jocks 302 544-6448
  726 Pulaski Hwy Bear (19701) *(G-116)*

ALPHABETIC SECTION

Computer Sciences Corporation.. 302 391-8347
500 Creek View Rd Newark (19711) *(G-10295)*

Computer Services of Delaware.. 302 697-8644
1991 S State St Ste B Dover (19901) *(G-2127)*

Computershare Inc.. 781 575-2000
919 N Market St Ste 1600 Wilmington (19801) *(G-15576)*

Computing & Network Service, Newark Also Called: University of Delaware *(G-12277)*

Computools Llc.. 617 861-0016
341 Raven Cir Camden Wyoming (19934) *(G-927)*

Comrade Technologies Inc.. 888 575-1225
16192 Coastal Hwy Lewes (19958) *(G-5855)*

Concepcion Properties LLC.. 302 691-9233
141 Sweetbay Ln New Castle (19720) *(G-8964)*

Conci LLC.. 847 665-9285
1013 Centre Rd Wilmington (19805) *(G-15577)*

Concierge Beach Service.. 302 541-0303
30728 Irons Ln Dagsboro (19939) *(G-1430)*

Concierge By Sea Inc.. 302 228-2014
36269 Tarpon Dr Lewes (19958) *(G-5856)*

Concierge Home Services.. 302 539-6178
27 Atlantic Ave Fl 2 Ocean View (19970) *(G-12496)*

Concord Agency Inc.. 302 478-4000
3520 Silverside Rd Ste 28 Wilmington (19810) *(G-15578)*

Concord Corporate Services Inc (DH).. 302 791-8200
1100 Carr Rd Wilmington (19809) *(G-15579)*

Concord Dental.. 302 836-3750
2304 Concord Pike Wilmington (19803) *(G-15580)*

Concord High School Baseball.. 302 475-2537
2629 Epping Rd Wilmington (19810) *(G-15581)*

Concord Mall LLC.. 302 478-9271
4737 Concord Pike 3rd Fl Wilmington (19803) *(G-15582)*

Concord Med Spine & Pain Ctr.. 302 652-1107
6 Sharpley Rd Wilmington (19803) *(G-15583)*

Concord Preschool Childca.. 302 750-7082
1243 Lakewood Dr Wilmington (19803) *(G-15584)*

Concord Soccer Association.. 302 479-5030
2 Onyx Ct Wilmington (19810) *(G-15585)*

Concord Towers Inc.. 302 737-2700
1201 Christiana Rd Newark (19713) *(G-10296)*

Concrete Bldg Systems Del Inc.. 302 846-3645
9283 Old Racetrack Rd Delmar (19940) *(G-1583)*

Concrete Co Inc.. 302 652-1101
101 Brookside Dr Wilmington (19804) *(G-15586)*

Concrete Services Inc.. 302 883-2883
794 Rose Valley School Rd Dover (19904) *(G-2128)*

Concrete Walls Inc.. 302 293-7061
3415 Wrangle Hill Rd Ste 2 Bear (19701) *(G-117)*

Cond Nast's, Wilmington Also Called: Conde Nast International Inc *(G-15587)*

Conde Nast International Inc.. 515 243-3273
1313 N Market St Fl 11 Wilmington (19801) *(G-15587)*

Condor Technologies Inc.. 302 698-4444
110 N Main St Ste H Camden (19934) *(G-807)*

Conducerent Incorporated.. 302 543-8525
1011 Centre Rd Ste 104 Wilmington (19805) *(G-15588)*

Conecmi LLC.. 302 740-9261
3616 Kirkwood Hwy A117 Wilmington (19808) *(G-15589)*

Conectiv LLC.. 302 429-3018
375 N Wakefield Dr Newark (19702) *(G-10297)*

Conectiv LLC (HQ).. 202 872-2680
500 N Wakefield Dr Newark (19702) *(G-10298)*

Conectiv LLC.. 800 375-7117
630 Martin Luther King Blvd Wilmington (19801) *(G-15590)*

Conectiv Communications Inc.. 302 224-1177
500 N Wakefield Dr Newark (19702) *(G-10299)*

Conectiv Energy Supply Inc (DH).. 302 454-0300
500 N Wakefield Dr Newark (19702) *(G-10300)*

Conectiv Energy Supply Inc.. 302 454-0300
500 N Wakefield Dr Newark (19702) *(G-10301)*

Conexiam Solutions Inc.. 302 884-6746
1201 N Orange St Ste 700 Wilmington (19801) *(G-15591)*

Conexio Care Inc.. 302 442-6622
590 Naamans Rd Claymont (19703) *(G-1098)*

Coney Steam and Clean.. 302 670-0183
621 William St Dover (19904) *(G-2129)*

Confab Inc.. 302 429-0140
1216 D St Wilmington (19801) *(G-15592)*

Confabulous Inc.. 917 727-5919
3500 S Dupont Hwy Dover (19901) *(G-2130)*

Conferatu Inc.. 415 599-6407
850 New Burton Rd Ste 201 Dover (19904) *(G-2131)*

Conference Group LLC.. 302 224-8255
254 Chapman Rd Ste 200 Newark (19702) *(G-10302)*

Confidntial Exec Trnsp Intl In.. 800 316-0802
651 N Broad St Ste 205-1082 Middletown (19709) *(G-7009)*

Confluent Corporation.. 301 440-4100
19640 Buck Run Georgetown (19947) *(G-4265)*

Conformit Corp.. 302 451-9167
2915 Ogletown Rd Ste 2636 Newark (19713) *(G-10303)*

Congo Capital Management, Wilmington Also Called: Congo Capital Management LLC *(G-15593)*

Congo Capital Management LLC (HQ).. 732 337-6643
3911 Concord Pike Wilmington (19803) *(G-15593)*

Congo Funeral Home (PA).. 302 652-6640
2317 N Market St Wilmington (19802) *(G-15594)*

Congo Funeral Home.. 302 652-8887
201 N Gray Ave Wilmington (19805) *(G-15595)*

Congo Industries Inc (PA).. 732 337-6643
3911 Concord Pike Wilmington (19803) *(G-15596)*

Congruence Consulting, Newark Also Called: Congruence Consulting Group *(G-10304)*

Congruence Consulting Group.. 320 290-6155
87 Madison Dr Ste A Newark (19711) *(G-10304)*

Conjured Jewells.. 267 240-2263
17 Oakview Dr Newark (19702) *(G-10305)*

Conley & Wright DDS.. 302 645-6671
18913 John J Williams Hwy Rehoboth Beach (19971) *(G-12697)*

Conlin Corporation.. 302 633-9174
737 Ambleside Dr Wilmington (19808) *(G-15597)*

Conmac Security Systems Inc.. 302 529-9286
205 Beau Tree Dr Wilmington (19810) *(G-15598)*

Connected, Dover Also Called: Connected Inc *(G-2132)*

Connected Capital LLC, Claymont Also Called: We Got Cars 4 Cash Inc *(G-1334)*

Connected Inc.. 858 833-8768
8 The Grn Ste B Dover (19901) *(G-2132)*

Connecticut Metallurgical, New Castle Also Called: MMR Group Inc *(G-9375)*

Connecting Generations Inc.. 302 656-2122
100 W 10th St Ste 102 Wilmington (19801) *(G-15599)*

Connections.. 302 221-6605
204 Gordy Pl New Castle (19720) *(G-8965)*

Connections, Claymont Also Called: Connectons Cmnty Spport Prgram *(G-1099)*

Connections CSP.. 302 535-8330
27 Medal Way Magnolia (19962) *(G-6734)*

Connections CSP.. 302 384-8140
507 W 9th St Wilmington (19801) *(G-15600)*

Connections CSP Inc.. 302 327-0122
550 S Dupont Hwy New Castle (19720) *(G-8966)*

Connections Development Corp.. 302 436-3292
35906 Zion Church Rd Frankford (19945) *(G-4093)*

Connections Development Corp (PA).. 302 984-3380
3821 Lancaster Pike Wilmington (19805) *(G-15601)*

Connectionscsp Inc.. 302 383-8482
310 Virginia Ave Seaford (19973) *(G-13133)*

Connectnow Vrtual Call Ctr LLC.. 888 226-4130
3 Germay Dr Ste 42743 Wilmington (19804) *(G-15602)*

Connectons Cmnty Spport Prgram (PA).. 302 984-2302
590 Naamans Rd Claymont (19703) *(G-1099)*

Connectons Cmnty Spport Prgram.. 302 834-8400
New Castle Ave Delaware City (19706) *(G-1534)*

Connectons Cmnty Spport Prgram.. 302 454-7520
1423 Capitol Trl Polly Drummond Plz Bldg 3 Newark (19711) *(G-10306)*

Connectons Cmnty Spport Prgram.. 302 536-1952
105 N Front St Seaford (19973) *(G-13134)*

Connectons Csp0110 W Lberty St.. 302 566-6078
110 W Liberty St Harrington (19952) *(G-4753)*

Connell Construction Co 302 738-9428
  808 N Country Club Dr Newark (19711) *(G-10307)*

Connexion Technologies, Wilmington *Also Called: Capitol Broadband Dev Co LLC (G-15232)*

Connie F Cicorelli DDS PA 302 798-5797
  1401 Silverside Rd Ste 2a Wilmington (19810) *(G-15603)*

Connolly Bove Lodge & Hutz LLP 302 658-9141
  1007 N Orange St Ste 800 Wilmington (19801) *(G-15604)*

Connolly Flooring Inc 302 996-9470
  315 Water St Wilmington (19804) *(G-15605)*

Connolly Options LLC 302 998-2016
  83 Christiana Rd New Castle (19720) *(G-8967)*

Connor Charles & Sons Painting 302 945-1746
  14219 Road 526 Georgetown (19947) *(G-4266)*

Connor Management LLC 302 539-1678
  31685 Edith St Ocean View (19970) *(G-12497)*

Conquest Tech Solutions Inc 302 356-1423
  300 Delaware Ave Ste 210 Wilmington (19801) *(G-15606)*

Conrep Inc 302 528-8383
  292 Carter Dr Ste C Middletown (19709) *(G-7010)*

Consensus Medical Systems 302 453-1969
  131 Continental Dr Newark (19713) *(G-10308)*

Conserve Property Group 302 275-8616
  4302 Marlowe Rd Wilmington (19802) *(G-15607)*

Consol Usa Inc 302 401-6537
  8 The Grn Ste 8212 Dover (19901) *(G-2133)*

Consoldted Fabrication Constrs 302 654-9001
  1216 D St Wilmington (19801) *(G-15608)*

Consolidated LLC 302 654-9001
  1216 D St Wilmington (19801) *(G-15609)*

Consolidated Construction Svcs 302 629-6070
  7450 Rivershore Dr Seaford (19973) *(G-13135)*

Consolidated Contracting LLC 302 727-9795
  30237 Whites Neck Rd Dagsboro (19939) *(G-1431)*

Conspiracy Theory LLC 201 566-1069
  200 Continental Dr Ste 401 Newark (19713) *(G-10309)*

Constance P Deptula Lcsw 302 323-0345
  85 Commonwealth Blvd New Castle (19720) *(G-8968)*

Constellation Pumps Corp 301 323-9000
  2711 Centerville Rd Ste 400 Wilmington (19808) *(G-15610)*

Construct App Inc 415 702-0634
  2711 Centerville Rd # 400 Wilmington (19808) *(G-15611)*

Construction, Newark *Also Called: Valor Construction LLC (G-12302)*

Construction MGT Svcs Inc (PA) 302 478-4200
  3600 Silverside Rd Wilmington (19810) *(G-15612)*

Construction Resource MGT Inc 302 778-2335
  101 Quaker Rd Lewes (19958) *(G-5857)*

Construction Unlimited Inc 302 836-3140
  705 Elizabeth Ln Bear (19701) *(G-118)*

Consult Dynamics Inc (PA) 302 654-1019
  1016 Delaware Ave Wilmington (19806) *(G-15613)*

Consulting Experts Online, Hockessin *Also Called: Ceo-Hqcom LLC (G-5155)*

Consulting Group Cpitl Mkts FN 302 888-4104
  222 Delaware Ave Wilmington (19801) *(G-15614)*

Consulttive Rview Rhbilitation 302 366-0356
  630 Churchmans Rd Ste 105 Newark (19702) *(G-10310)*

Consumer Injury Alert, Newark *Also Called: Chilay Inc (G-10201)*

Contactlifeline Inc (PA) 302 761-9800
  314 Brandywine Blvd Wilmington (19809) *(G-15615)*

Container Home Fund 915 433-4817
  200 Continental Dr # 401 Newark (19713) *(G-10311)*

Conti Electric of N J Inc 302 996-3905
  2633 Skylark Rd Wilmington (19808) *(G-15616)*

Continental Africa LLC 302 540-0069
  35 Autumnwood Dr Newark (19711) *(G-10312)*

Continental Case 302 322-1765
  64 Shields Ln Newark (19702) *(G-10313)*

Continental Cnstr & Rmdlg 302 332-6367
  2508 Dorval Rd Wilmington (19810) *(G-15617)*

Continental Cr Protection LLC 302 456-1930
  121 Continental Dr # 108 Newark (19713) *(G-10314)*

Continental Finance Co LLC (PA) 302 456-1930
  4550 Linden Hill Rd Ste 400 Wilmington (19808) *(G-15618)*

Continental Funding LLC 302 456-1930
  4550 Linden Hill Rd Ste 400 Wilmington (19808) *(G-15619)*

Continental Green Janitorial 302 324-8063
  296 Churchmans Rd New Castle (19720) *(G-8969)*

Continental Health Care Svcs 240 461-8569
  113 Newton Dr Bear (19701) *(G-119)*

Continental Insight 302 273-4458
  124 Broadkill Rd Milton (19968) *(G-8590)*

Continental Jewelers Inc 302 475-2000
  2209 Silverside Rd Wilmington (19810) *(G-15620)*

Continental Mortgage Corp 302 996-5807
  3422 Old Capitol Trl Wilmington (19808) *(G-15621)*

Continental Warranty Corp 302 375-0401
  99 Wiltshire Rd Claymont (19703) *(G-1100)*

Continntal Search Outplacement 302 927-0200
  30022 Judson Ln Dagsboro (19939) *(G-1432)*

Contlo Inc 860 775-7179
  200 Continental Dr Ste 401 Newark (19713) *(G-10315)*

Contract Environments Inc 302 658-0668
  2055 Limestone Rd Ste 302 Wilmington (19808) *(G-15622)*

Contract PT LLC 302 628-0705
  10430 Gravelly Creek Ln Seaford (19973) *(G-13136)*

Contractor Masonary 302 945-1930
  30983 Phillips Branch Rd Millsboro (19966) *(G-8238)*

Contractor Materials LLC 302 658-5241
  4048 New Castle Ave New Castle (19720) *(G-8970)*

Contractor Rashmi & Penny 302 778-5771
  1980 Superfine Ln Apt 804 Wilmington (19802) *(G-15623)*

Contractors Flooring Del LLC 302 698-4221
  91 Brenda Ln Ste C Camden (19934) *(G-808)*

Contractors Materials, New Castle *Also Called: Contractor Materials LLC (G-8970)*

Contractors Materials LLC 302 656-6066
  925 S Heald St Wilmington (19801) *(G-15624)*

Contractual Carriers Inc 302 453-1420
  104 Alan Dr Newark (19711) *(G-10316)*

Contruction Jones and Ldscpg 302 423-6456
  5169 Mud Mill Rd Camden Wyoming (19934) *(G-928)*

Convention Coach 302 335-5459
  554 Lexington Mill Rd Magnolia (19962) *(G-6735)*

Conventional Builders Inc 302 422-2429
  846 School St Houston (19954) *(G-5439)*

Conventioneer Pubg Co Inc 301 487-3907
  24948 Green Fern Dr Georgetown (19947) *(G-4267)*

Convergence Group Inc 302 234-7400
  1011 Centre Rd Ste 104 Wilmington (19805) *(G-15625)*

Convergetel LLC 347 688-0922
  112 Capitol Trl Ste A Newark (19711) *(G-10317)*

Convida Wireless LLC 302 281-3707
  200 Bellevue Pkwy Ste 300 Wilmington (19809) *(G-15626)*

Conway Construction Co 302 598-5019
  29893 Vincent Ave Lewes (19958) *(G-5858)*

Conway Management Group 302 323-9522
  2801 Stonebridge Blvd New Castle (19720) *(G-8971)*

Conzurge Inc 267 507-6039
  2035 Sunset Lake Rd B2 Newark (19702) *(G-10318)*

Cooch and Taylor A Prof Assn (PA) 302 984-3800
  1007 N Orange St Ste 1120 Wilmington (19801) *(G-15627)*

Cooch and Taylor Attys At Law, Wilmington *Also Called: Cooch and Taylor A Prof Assn (G-15627)*

Cook & Cook Ltd Partnership 302 428-0109
  304 Centennial Cir Wilmington (19807) *(G-15628)*

Cook G Legih DDS& Cook Jefry 302 378-4416
  12 Pennington St Ste 300 Middletown (19709) *(G-7011)*

Cook Hauling LLC 302 378-6451
  350 Misty Vale Dr Middletown (19709) *(G-7012)*

Cook Plastering Inc 302 737-0778
  1026 Summit View Dr Newark (19713) *(G-10319)*

Cook Robinson Eyes Srgcal Asso 302 645-2300
  18791 John J Williams Hwy Rehoboth Beach (19971) *(G-12698)*

Cool Branch Associates LLC 302 629-5363
  31052 Shady Acres Ln Laurel (19956) *(G-5486)*

ALPHABETIC SECTION — Corteva Agriscience LLC

Cool Customs Inc 302 894-0406
  80 Aleph Dr Newark (19702) *(G-10320)*

Cool Nerds Marketing Inc 302 304-3440
  300 N Market St Ste 208 Wilmington (19801) *(G-15629)*

Cool Spring Storage Center Inc 302 448-8164
  18585 Coastal Hwy Unit 17 Rehoboth Beach (19971) *(G-12699)*

Coolautomation Inc 941 587-2287
  919 N Market St Ste 950 Wilmington (19801) *(G-15630)*

Coolersmart 302 323-2100
  88 Quigley Blvd Historic New Castle (19720) *(G-4964)*

Coolpop Nation 302 584-8833
  2418 Rambler Rd Wilmington (19810) *(G-15631)*

Cooltrade Inc 844 356-2952
  1013 Centre Rd Ste 403b Wilmington (19805) *(G-15632)*

Coon, Chris E Dvm, Dover *Also Called: Dover Animal Hospital (G-2333)*

Cooper Bros Inc 302 323-0717
  62 Southgate Blvd Frnt Frnt New Castle (19720) *(G-8972)*

Cooper Levenson PA 302 838-2600
  30 Foxhunt Dr U 30 Bear (19701) *(G-120)*

Cooper Simpler Associates Inc 302 227-2999
  6 Wilmington Ave Rehoboth Beach (19971) *(G-12700)*

Cooper-Wilbert Vault Co Inc 302 376-1331
  4971 Summit Bridge Rd Middletown (19709) *(G-7013)*

Cooper, Stephen MD, Dover *Also Called: E N T Associates (G-2399)*

Cooper's Place, Newark *Also Called: Galman Group Ltd (G-10802)*

Cooperson Associates LLC 302 655-1105
  1504 N French St Wilmington (19801) *(G-15633)*

Coordle Inc 419 618-0949
  8 The Grn Ste B Dover (19901) *(G-2134)*

Coosco Auto Tech LLC 302 391-6043
  1201 N Market St Ste 111 Wilmington (19801) *(G-15634)*

Cooter Brwns Twsted Sthern Kit 302 567-2132
  70 Rehoboth Ave Rehoboth Beach (19971) *(G-12701)*

Copia Power Opco LLC (PA) 612 961-5783
  850 New Burton Rd Dover (19904) *(G-2135)*

Copiri Inc 703 863-4304
  4023 Kennett Pike Wilmington (19807) *(G-15635)*

Copp Seafood, Lewes *Also Called: Steven P Copp (G-6511)*

Coppage Paving Inc 443 309-9796
  1378 Porter Rd Bear (19701) *(G-121)*

Copy Print, Georgetown *Also Called: Rogers Graphics Inc (G-4490)*

Copy Systems, Newark *Also Called: Digital Office Solutions Inc (G-10530)*

Cor3 Capital LLC 941 402-8101
  1675 S State St Ste B Dover (19901) *(G-2136)*

Cora Systems Us Inc 833 269-5756
  2801 Centerville Rd Fl 1 Wilmington (19808) *(G-15636)*

Coral Sands Apts 302 539-9559
  Bunting Ave Fenwick Island (19944) *(G-4046)*

Coral Sprng Rhab Halthcare Ctr, Wilmington *Also Called: Springs Rhblttion At Brndywine (G-19979)*

Coral Technology LLC (PA) 201 793-7127
  16192 Coastal Hwy Lewes (19958) *(G-5859)*

Corballis Emergency Medicine R 302 224-5678
  307 Ruthar Dr Newark (19711) *(G-10321)*

Corbett & Associates, Wilmington *Also Called: Evc Inc (G-16481)*

Corblocks Inc 832 217-0864
  1201 N Orange St Ste 600 Wilmington (19801) *(G-15637)*

Corcoran & Associates PA CPA 302 478-9515
  3801 Kennett Pike Ste C100 # 100 Wilmington (19807) *(G-15638)*

Corcoran & Company PA CPA, Wilmington *Also Called: Corcoran & Associates PA CPA (G-15638)*

Cordjia LLC (PA) 302 743-1297
  131 Continental Dr Ste 409 Newark (19713) *(G-10322)*

Cordrey Charities Inc 302 945-5855
  70 Creek Dr Millsboro (19966) *(G-8239)*

Core & Main LP 302 684-3054
  25414 Primehook Rd Ste 100 Milton (19968) *(G-8591)*

Core & Main LP 302 737-1500
  22 Garfield Way Newark (19713) *(G-10323)*

Core Construction LLC 302 449-4186
  115 E Glenwood Ave Smyrna (19977) *(G-13687)*

Core Functions LLC 443 956-9626
  21142 Arrington Dr Selbyville (19975) *(G-13506)*

Core Physical Therapy 302 423-0236
  71 Mcbry Dr Dover (19901) *(G-2137)*

Core Purchase LLC 616 328-5715
  910 Foulk Rd Ste 201 Wilmington (19803) *(G-15639)*

Core Results Inc (PA) 805 552-6624
  1209 N Orange St Wilmington (19801) *(G-15640)*

Core Value Global LLC 908 312-4070
  1209 N Orange St Wilmington (19801) *(G-15641)*

Coremond LLC 267 797-7090
  8 The Grn Dover (19901) *(G-2138)*

Corexcel, Wilmington *Also Called: Momentum Management Group Inc (G-18406)*

Corey Kennedy 201 233-8054
  31607 Exeter Way Lewes (19958) *(G-5860)*

Corinthian House 302 858-1493
  219 S Race St Georgetown (19947) *(G-4268)*

Corlo Services Inc 302 737-3207
  100 Peoples Dr Newark (19702) *(G-10324)*

Corn Exchange LLC 302 747-8752
  105 Harrison Ave Wyoming (19934) *(G-20982)*

Cornell Property MGT Corp 302 674-1460
  14 Rockford Xing Dover (19901) *(G-2139)*

Corner Stone Group, Wilmington *Also Called: Bigben1613 LLC (G-14885)*

Cornerstone Community Ctr LLC 302 258-6459
  55 Church St Bridgeville (19933) *(G-686)*

Cornerstone Group LLC 302 377-7165
  273 E Main St Ste E Newark (19711) *(G-10325)*

Cornerstone Health Partners 302 561-4080
  2303 Woods Rd Wilmington (19808) *(G-15642)*

Cornerstone Rbe Contg LLC 443 480-6674
  911 Lansdowne Rd Middletown (19709) *(G-7014)*

Corp1 Inc 302 736-3466
  614 N Dupont Hwy Ste 210 Dover (19901) *(G-2140)*

Corpomax Inc 302 266-8200
  2915 Ogletown Rd Newark (19713) *(G-10326)*

Corporate Arcft Technical Svcs 302 383-9400
  415 Riblett Ln Wilmington (19808) *(G-15643)*

Corporate Interiors Inc 800 690-9101
  240 Lisa Dr New Castle (19720) *(G-8973)*

Corporate Interiors Inc (PA) 302 322-1008
  223 Lisa Dr New Castle (19720) *(G-8974)*

Corporate Interiors Delaware, New Castle *Also Called: Corporate Interiors Inc (G-8974)*

Corporate Kids Lrng Ctr Inc 302 678-0688
  605 S Bay Rd Dover (19901) *(G-2141)*

Corporate Loyalty LLC 732 455-9266
  200 Continental Dr Ste 401 Newark (19713) *(G-10327)*

Corporation Service Company (PA) 302 636-5400
  251 Little Falls Dr Wilmington (19808) *(G-15644)*

Corrado American LLC 302 655-6501
  200 Marsh Ln New Castle (19720) *(G-8975)*

Corrado Construction Co LLC 302 652-3339
  210 Marsh Ln New Castle (19720) *(G-8976)*

Corrado Fleet Services, New Castle *Also Called: Heavy Equipment Rental Inc (G-9205)*

Corrado Management Svcs LLC 302 225-0700
  204 Marsh Ln New Castle (19720) *(G-8977)*

Corrin Expert Tree Care, Townsend *Also Called: Corrin Tree & Landscape Co (G-13976)*

Corrin Tree & Landscape Co 302 753-8733
  299 Saw Mill Rd Townsend (19734) *(G-13976)*

Corrin Tree Landscape 302 521-8333
  1307 N Rodney St Wilmington (19806) *(G-15645)*

Corrosion Probe 302 836-0165
  6 Verdun Ct Newark (19702) *(G-10328)*

Corrosion Testing Laboratories 302 454-8200
  60 Blue Hen Dr Newark (19713) *(G-10329)*

Corrozi Fountainview LLC 302 266-7501
  1000 Fountainview Cir Newark (19713) *(G-10330)*

Corteva (china) LLC (HQ) 833 267-8382
  974 Centre Rd Bldg 735 Wilmington (19805) *(G-15646)*

Corteva Agriscience LLC 302 485-3000
  974 Centre Rd Chestnut Run Plz 735 Wilmington (19805) *(G-15647)*

Cortical.io | ALPHABETIC SECTION

Cortical.io, Newark *Also Called: Corticalio USA Inc (G-10331)*
Corticalio USA Inc..415 350-8588
40 E Main St Ste 737 Newark (19711) *(G-10331)*
Corvant LLC..302 299-1570
131 Continental Dr Ste 409 Newark (19713) *(G-10332)*
Cosine Solutions LLC..267 398-8995
16192 Coastal Hwy Lewes (19958) *(G-5861)*
CosIs LLC...877 900-7373
2093 Philadelphia Pike Ste 3093 Claymont (19703) *(G-1101)*
Cosmic Custom Screen Printing..302 933-0920
28116 John J Williams Hwy Millsboro (19966) *(G-8240)*
COSMIC CUSTOM SCREEN PRINTING, Millsboro *Also Called: Cosmic Custom Screen Printing (G-8240)*
Cosmic Strands LLC..302 660-3268
1201 N Market St Ste 111 Wilmington (19801) *(G-15648)*
Cosmoprof..302 674-5360
261 N Dupont Hwy Dover (19901) *(G-2142)*
Cosmoprof, Newark *Also Called: Sally Beauty Supply LLC (G-11935)*
Costa and Rihl Inc...856 534-7325
3518 Silverside Rd Ste 22 Wilmington (19810) *(G-15649)*
Costa and Rihl Mech Contrs, Wilmington *Also Called: J Rihl Inc (G-17461)*
Costleigh, Brian J MD, Dover *Also Called: Cancer Care Ctrs At Bay Hlth (G-2019)*
Costline Cleaning Service...302 420-3000
22791 Dozer Ln Unit 5 Harbeson (19951) *(G-4691)*
Cotalker Inc..954 643-1497
251 Little Falls Dr Wilmington (19808) *(G-15650)*
Cote Custom Works LLC...302 359-2596
2457 Pearsons Corner Rd Dover (19904) *(G-2143)*
Cott Electronics LLC..302 520-2838
16192 Coastal Hwy Lewes (19958) *(G-5862)*
Cottage At Curry Manor..202 258-7674
6 Seashell Pl Lewes (19958) *(G-5863)*
Cotten Engineering LLC..302 628-9164
10087 Concord Rd Seaford (19973) *(G-13137)*
Cottman Transmission..302 322-4600
1600 N Dupont Hwy New Castle (19720) *(G-8978)*
Council of Devon...302 658-5366
2401 Pennsylvania Ave Apt 606 Wilmington (19806) *(G-15651)*
Council On Hlth RES For Dev US..202 255-5300
1 Wood Rd Wilmington (19806) *(G-15652)*
Counseling Insight LLC..805 341-9020
254 Chapman Rd Ste 208 Newark (19702) *(G-10333)*
Counseling Services Inc..302 894-1477
116 David Rd Wilmington (19804) *(G-15653)*
Counseling Services Corp...302 898-5184
29 E Savannah Dr Bear (19701) *(G-122)*
Counterfeit Combat Technology..614 874-7414
251 Little Falls Dr Wilmington (19808) *(G-15654)*
Counterparts LLC..302 349-0400
12952 Sussex Hwy Greenwood (19950) *(G-4605)*
Counterpoint Software Inc...302 426-6500
1901 N Lincoln St Wilmington (19806) *(G-15655)*
Countertop Shop LLC...302 654-0700
45 Germay Dr Ste B Wilmington (19804) *(G-15656)*
Counting House...302 249-5596
94 Mcewen Dr Greenwood (19950) *(G-4606)*
Countrmsres Asssment SEC Expr..302 322-9600
36 E Sarazen Dr Middletown (19709) *(G-7015)*
Country Builders Inc...302 735-5530
818 Nault Rd Dover (19904) *(G-2144)*
Country Comforts..302 242-8527
6309 Mud Mill Rd Camden Wyoming (19934) *(G-929)*
Country Coop Inc..302 249-1985
16048 Long Branch Rd Greenwood (19950) *(G-4607)*
Country House, Wilmington *Also Called: Acts Rtrmnt-Life Cmmnities Inc (G-14245)*
Country House, The, Wilmington *Also Called: Peninsula Untd Mthdst Hmes Inc (G-18949)*
Country Inns Suites..302 266-6400
1024 Old Churchmans Rd Newark (19713) *(G-10334)*
Country Kids Child Care, Greenwood *Also Called: Country Kids Child Care Lrng C (G-4608)*
Country Kids Child Care Lrng C...302 349-5888
14352 Staytonville Rd Greenwood (19950) *(G-4608)*

Country Kids Home Day Care...302 653-4134
1069 Vndyke Grenspring Rd Townsend (19734) *(G-13977)*
Country Lawn Care & Maint..302 593-3393
30435 Hollymount Rd Harbeson (19951) *(G-4692)*
Country Life Homes Milford De..302 265-2257
610 Marshall St Milford (19963) *(G-7841)*
Country Roads Veterinary Svc..302 514-9087
2681 Shaws Corner Rd Clayton (19938) *(G-1357)*
Country Store...302 653-5111
11 S Main St Kenton (19955) *(G-5452)*
Country Suites By Carlson, Newark *Also Called: Country Inns Suites (G-10334)*
Country Suites By Carlson, Newark *Also Called: Khanna Entps Ltd A Ltd Partnr (G-11169)*
Country Villa Motel..814 938-8330
1036 N Walnut St Milford (19963) *(G-7842)*
Country Village Apartments...302 674-0991
480 Country Dr Dover (19901) *(G-2145)*
Country Vintner LLC..877 946-3620
310 Ruthar Dr Newark (19711) *(G-10335)*
Countryside Masonry LLC..302 945-5642
28248 Cannon St Millsboro (19966) *(G-8241)*
County Bank...302 855-2000
13 N Bedford St Georgetown (19947) *(G-4269)*
County Bank...302 645-8880
1609 Savannah Rd Lewes (19958) *(G-5864)*
County Bank...302 424-2500
100 E Masten Cir Milford (19963) *(G-7843)*
County Bank...302 947-7300
25933 School Ln Millsboro (19966) *(G-8242)*
County Bank...302 537-0900
10 Old Mill Dr Millville (19967) *(G-8526)*
County Bank...302 684-2300
140 Broadkill Rd Milton (19968) *(G-8592)*
County Bank (PA)..302 226-9800
19927 Shuttle Rd Rehoboth Beach (19971) *(G-12702)*
County Building Services Inc..302 377-4213
8 Knightsbridge Rd Middletown (19709) *(G-7016)*
County Environmental Inc...302 322-8946
461 Churchmans Rd New Castle (19720) *(G-8979)*
County Group Companies, New Castle *Also Called: County Environmental Inc (G-8979)*
County Insulation Co..302 322-8946
461 Churchmans Rd New Castle (19720) *(G-8980)*
County of New Castle...302 571-4004
26 Karlyn Dr New Castle (19720) *(G-8981)*
County of Sussex..302 854-5050
9 S Dupont Hwy Georgetown (19947) *(G-4270)*
County of Sussex..302 947-0864
29445 Inland Bay Rd Millsboro (19966) *(G-8243)*
County Seat Apartments LL...302 856-7577
200 Weston Dr Dover (19904) *(G-2146)*
County Seat Cruisers Inc...302 398-8999
158 Central Park Dr Harrington (19952) *(G-4754)*
County Women S Journal...302 236-1435
17252 N Village Main Blvd Unit 9 Lewes (19958) *(G-5865)*
Coupert Science LLC..206 445-0706
8 The Grn Dover (19901) *(G-2147)*
Courage Capital Management...302 658-2459
1105 N Market St Ste 1300 Wilmington (19801) *(G-15657)*
Court Record & Data MGT Svcs..302 476-8976
1300 First State Blvd Ste H Wilmington (19804) *(G-15658)*
Courtesy Trnsp Svcs Inc..302 322-9722
4 Parkway Cir New Castle (19720) *(G-8982)*
Courtland Manor Inc...302 674-0566
889 S Little Creek Rd Dover (19901) *(G-2148)*
Courtney Construction...302 798-2393
7 Park Ln Wilmington (19809) *(G-15659)*
Courtney Construction Inc..302 521-5865
23 Selborne Dr Wilmington (19807) *(G-15660)*
Courtyard By Marriott, Newark *Also Called: Ch Wilmington LLC (G-10183)*
Courtyard By Marriott, Newark *Also Called: Courtyard Management Corp (G-10336)*
Courtyard By Marriott, Wilmington *Also Called: 1102 West Street Ltd Partnr (G-14103)*
Courtyard By Marriott, Wilmington *Also Called: 44 New England Management Co (G-14135)*

ALPHABETIC SECTION — Creative Builders Inc

Courtyard Management Corp 302 456-3800
48 Geoffrey Dr Newark (19713) *(G-10336)*

Courtyard Management Corp 302 429-7600
1102 N West St Wilmington (19801) *(G-15661)*

Courtyard Newark At Ud 302 737-0900
400 David Hollowell Dr Newark (19716) *(G-10337)*

Couture Denim LLC 302 220-8339
3 Silsbee Rd New Castle (19720) *(G-8983)*

Covant Solutions Inc 302 607-2678
220 Continental Dr Ste 314 Newark (19713) *(G-10338)*

Covation Biomaterials LLC 865 279-1414
800 Prides Xing Ste 201 Newark (19713) *(G-10339)*

Covenant Preschool 302 764-8503
503 Duncan Rd Wilmington (19809) *(G-15662)*

Covenant Properties I 302 234-5655
15 Middleton Dr Wilmington (19808) *(G-15663)*

Covenant Wealth Strategies 302 234-5655
11 Middleton Dr Wilmington (19808) *(G-15664)*

Cover & Rossiter PA 302 656-6632
2711 Centerville Rd Ste 100 Wilmington (19808) *(G-15665)*

Coveragex LLC 310 854-2677
919 N Market St Ste 950 Wilmington (19801) *(G-15666)*

Coverdale Community Council 302 337-7179
11575 Fisher Cir Bridgeville (19933) *(G-687)*

Coverdeck Systems Inc 302 427-7578
408 Meco Dr # A Wilmington (19804) *(G-15667)*

Covered Bridge Inn 302 542-9605
30249 Fisher Rd Lewes (19958) *(G-5866)*

Coveys Car Care Inc 302 629-2746
1300 Middleford Rd Seaford (19973) *(G-13138)*

Covr Financial Tech Inc 800 377-6344
1209 N Orange St Wilmington (19801) *(G-15668)*

Cowan Chiropractic Rehab PA 302 559-5261
2500 W 4th St Ste 3 Wilmington (19805) *(G-15669)*

Cowan Systems LLC 302 656-1403
603 Christiana Ave Wilmington (19801) *(G-15670)*

Cowchok Tf Inc 302 475-4510
2615 Kimbrough Dr Wilmington (19810) *(G-15671)*

Cowie Technology Corp 302 998-7037
510 First State Blvd Wilmington (19804) *(G-15672)*

Cowries & Calabash LLC 917 727-8940
8 The Grn Ste A Dover (19901) *(G-2149)*

Cox Industries Inc 302 332-8470
111 Lake Dr Ste C Newark (19702) *(G-10340)*

Cozen OConnor 302 295-2000
1201 N Market St Ste 1001 Wilmington (19801) *(G-15673)*

Coztel LLC 832 224-5638
300 Delaware Ave Ste 210233 Wilmington (19801) *(G-15674)*

Cozy Critters Child Care Corp 302 541-8210
35371 Beaver Dam Rd Frankford (19945) *(G-4094)*

Cozy Stays LLC 424 207-0157
254 Chapman Rd Newark (19702) *(G-10341)*

CP Cases Inc 410 352-9450
34607 Dupont Blvd Frankford (19945) *(G-4095)*

CP Fitness Wilmington LLC 302 797-1400
5610 Concord Pike Wilmington (19803) *(G-15675)*

CP Lawn and Landscape 302 396-7074
16963 Hardscrabble Rd Georgetown (19947) *(G-4271)*

Cpex Pharmaceuticals Inc 302 651-8300
1105 N Market St Ste 1300 Wilmington (19801) *(G-15676)*

Cpf Ckd LLC 855 386-2799
1209 N Orange St Wilmington (19801) *(G-15677)*

Cpr Construction Inc 302 322-5770
106 E 14th St Historic New Castle (19720) *(G-4965)*

Cr Lube Run LLC 302 875-1641
30053 Fire Tower Rd Laurel (19956) *(G-5487)*

Cr Newlin Trucking Inc 302 678-9124
2199 Fast Landing Rd Dover (19901) *(G-2150)*

CR&us LLC 678 429-6293
254 Chapman Rd Ste 208 Newark (19702) *(G-10342)*

Cr24 Inc 888 427-9357
1605 E Ayre St Ste 24 Wilmington (19804) *(G-15678)*

Crab Meat For Kids 302 378-1327
482 Brick Mill Rd Middletown (19709) *(G-7017)*

Crabby Dick's Creamery, Delaware City *Also Called: CD Cream (G-1533)*

Cradleapps LLC 202 492-7953
251 Little Falls Dr Wilmington (19808) *(G-15679)*

Craft Bookbinding Co, Wilmington *Also Called: L E Stansell Inc (G-17775)*

Crafts Report Publishing Co 302 656-2209
100 Rogers Rd Wilmington (19801) *(G-15680)*

Craftsman Builders of De 302 542-0731
16101 Willow Way Laurel (19956) *(G-5488)*

Craftsman Cbntry Woodworks Inc 302 841-5274
37357 Tree Top Ln Selbyville (19975) *(G-13507)*

Craftsman Revisions 302 834-9252
70 Bristle Cone Dr Bear (19701) *(G-123)*

Craig and Company LLC 609 221-9959
28 Sharons Way Wilmington (19808) *(G-15681)*

Craig D Sternberg MD 302 733-0980
87 Omega Dr Newark (19713) *(G-10343)*

Craig Maurer 302 293-2365
791 Idlewyld Dr Middletown (19709) *(G-7018)*

Craig Metzner 302 629-9576
22661 Atlanta Rd Seaford (19973) *(G-13139)*

Craig Smucker MD Orthopaedics 610 869-5757
5936 Limestone Rd Ste 202 Hockessin (19707) *(G-5169)*

Craig Technologies Inc (PA) 302 628-9900
103 Davis Dr Seaford (19973) *(G-13140)*

Craig Weiner 267 226-8511
209 N Pembrey Dr Wilmington (19803) *(G-15682)*

Craigs Woodworks LLC 302 998-4201
38208 Rock Elm Dr Selbyville (19975) *(G-13508)*

Cramaro Tarpaulin Systems Inc 302 292-2170
131 Sandy Dr Newark (19713) *(G-10344)*

Cramer & Dimichele PA 302 293-1230
1801 W Newport Pike Wilmington (19804) *(G-15683)*

Cramer Dimichele 302 235-8561
5305 Limestone Rd Ste 200 Wilmington (19808) *(G-15684)*

Cranston Hall Apartments 302 999-7001
3314 Old Capitol Trl Ofc 2 Wilmington (19808) *(G-15685)*

Crata Inc 214 606-1731
8 The Grn Ste A Dover (19901) *(G-2151)*

Cratis Solutions Inc 515 423-7259
8 The Grn Ste 5910 Dover (19901) *(G-2152)*

Cravitysci LLC 571 208-6421
19 Bellecor Dr New Castle (19720) *(G-8984)*

Crawlr Innovations Inc 912 515-9087
8 The Grn Ste B Dover (19901) *(G-2153)*

Crazy Coatings 302 378-0888
4783 Summit Bridge Rd Middletown (19709) *(G-7019)*

Crazy Eight 302 227-7429
36508 Seaside Outlet Dr Rehoboth Beach (19971) *(G-12703)*

Crazy Maple Interactive Inc 408 603-7526
8 The Grn Dover (19901) *(G-2154)*

Crds, Wilmington *Also Called: Court Record & Data MGT Svcs (G-15658)*

Cre8tive Minds Ent LLC 302 293-3461
5803 Highland Ct Wilmington (19802) *(G-15686)*

Creaform USA Inc 407 732-4103
220 E Delaware Ave Newark (19711) *(G-10345)*

Created Life Coaching 302 584-7112
442 S Bancroft Pkwy Wilmington (19805) *(G-15687)*

Createyourscholarshiporg 415 822-8266
2810 N Church St Ste 41193 Wilmington (19802) *(G-15688)*

Creations By Mae Entps LLC 302 985-5797
427 S Rodney St Wilmington (19805) *(G-15689)*

Creativbar LLC 510 260-3011
254 Chapman Rd Newark (19702) *(G-10346)*

Creative Assemblies Inc 302 956-6194
17053 Tatman Farm Rd Bridgeville (19933) *(G-688)*

Creative Beginnings 302 633-4575
3 Paoletti Dr Wilmington (19808) *(G-15690)*

Creative Builders Inc 302 228-8153
20593 Rust Rd Harbeson (19951) *(G-4693)*

ALPHABETIC SECTION

Creative Ceramics LLC 302 275-9211
112 Mccormick Blvd Newark (19702) *(G-10347)*

Creative Children, Wilmington *Also Called: Regina Coleman (G-19402)*

Creative Courtyards 302 253-8237
20099 Gravel Hill Rd Georgetown (19947) *(G-4272)*

Creative Devices Inc 302 378-5433
361 Misty Vale Dr Middletown (19709) *(G-7020)*

Creative Education, Bear *Also Called: Creative Education Inc (G-124)*

Creative Education Inc 610 268-2770
128 Pisces Dr Bear (19701) *(G-124)*

Creative Embroidery Inc 302 661-7313
47 Germay Dr Ste C Wilmington (19804) *(G-15691)*

Creative Financial Group 302 738-0888
111 Continental Dr Ste 305 Newark (19713) *(G-10348)*

Creative Flooring Contrs Inc 302 653-7521
100c E Glenwood Ave Smyrna (19977) *(G-13688)*

Creative Impressions Art 858 722-2252
17303 N Village Main Blvd Lewes (19958) *(G-5867)*

Creative Land Care 302 482-1944
520 Robinson Ln Wilmington (19805) *(G-15692)*

Creative Learning Child Care 302 691-3167
1220 Apple St Wilmington (19801) *(G-15693)*

Creative Marketing Concepts 302 367-7100
2419 W Newport Pike Wilmington (19804) *(G-15694)*

Creative Med Consulting LLC 302 313-1411
111 6th St S Dupont Hwy Odessa (19730) *(G-12582)*

Creative Micro Designs Inc 302 456-5800
645 Dawson Dr Ste B Newark (19713) *(G-10349)*

Creative Minds Daycare 302 378-0741
2 Mica St Townsend (19734) *(G-13978)*

Creative Play Day School 610 268-2770
128 Pisces Dr Bear (19701) *(G-125)*

Creative Promotions 302 697-7896
38 South St Camden (19934) *(G-809)*

Creative Solutions Intl (HQ) 302 234-7400
724 Yorklyn Rd Ste 240 Hockessin (19707) *(G-5170)*

Creative Solutions Intl, Wilmington *Also Called: De Novo Corporation (G-15839)*

Creative Travel Inc 302 658-2900
908 Old Harmony Rd Newark (19713) *(G-10350)*

Creative Xchange Inc 888 502-5618
919 N Market St Ste 950 Wilmington (19801) *(G-15695)*

Creativity Diversified LLC 302 897-5961
141 Gillespie Ave Middletown (19709) *(G-7021)*

Creatopy, Dover *Also Called: Creatopy Inc (G-2155)*

Creatopy Inc 339 217-6684
8 The Grn Ste R Dover (19901) *(G-2155)*

Creator Studios Inc 323 992-4350
16192 Coastal Hwy Lewes (19958) *(G-5868)*

Crediblockcom LLC 803 619-9458
8 The Grn Ste 8364 Dover (19901) *(G-2156)*

Credit Accptnce Auto Ln Tr 201 .... 302 576-3706
300 Delaware Ave Fl 9 Wilmington (19801) *(G-15696)*

Credit Concierge LLC 877 860-9877
427 N Ttnall St Unit 6571 Wilmington (19801) *(G-15697)*

Credit Insider LLC 302 232-5644
8 The Grn Ste 10494 Dover (19901) *(G-2157)*

Credit Lifestyle LLC 302 317-1812
200 Continental Dr Ste 401 Newark (19713) *(G-10351)*

Creekside Carpentry LLC 302 218-4434
400 N Augustine St Wilmington (19804) *(G-15698)*

Creekside Counseling & Wellnes 302 562-7953
318 N Dillwyn Rd Newark (19711) *(G-10352)*

Creekside Painting LLC 302 983-1914
34411 Waters Run Selbyville (19975) *(G-13509)*

Creekview Psychological 302 731-3130
300 Creek View Rd Ste 101b Newark (19711) *(G-10353)*

Crescent Business Center LLC 302 683-0300
4708 Kirkwood Hwy Wilmington (19808) *(G-15699)*

Crescent Communities LLC 302 798-8400
321 Harbor Dr Claymont (19703) *(G-1102)*

Crescent Dental Associates 302 836-6968
100 Becks Woods Dr Bear (19701) *(G-126)*

Crescent Management Inc 302 449-4560
4708 Kirkwood Hwy Ste C Wilmington (19808) *(G-15700)*

Cressona Associates LLC 302 792-2737
1308 Society Dr Claymont (19703) *(G-1103)*

Crest Central 302 736-0576
300 W Water St Dover (19904) *(G-2158)*

Crestview Medical Center 302 762-4545
1800 N Broom St Ste 109 Wilmington (19802) *(G-15701)*

Crestview Services LLC 302 569-4909
26212 Tucks Rd Millsboro (19966) *(G-8244)*

Crestwood Garden Apts, Georgetown *Also Called: Service General Corporation (G-4507)*

Cretework LLC 302 424-9970
16505 Beach Hwy Ellendale (19941) *(G-3912)*

CRH Investments Inc 302 427-0924
1105 N Market St Wilmington (19801) *(G-15702)*

Cricket 302 482-3658
1012 Wilmington Ave Ste A Wilmington (19805) *(G-15703)*

Cricket Wireless, Wilmington *Also Called: Opalwire (G-18794)*

Cricket Wireless LLC 302 276-0496
1405 N Dupont Hwy New Castle (19720) *(G-8985)*

Crime Victims Ctr Chester Cnty 610 692-7420
720 6th St Newark (19711) *(G-10354)*

Crimson Group LLC 301 252-3779
17 Dubb Dr Newark (19702) *(G-10355)*

Crimson Strategy Group LLP 302 503-5698
8 The Grn Ste 10235 Dover (19901) *(G-2159)*

Cripple Creek Golf & Cntry CLB 302 539-1446
29494 Cripple Creek Dr Dagsboro (19939) *(G-1433)*

Criswell House 302 498-5174
724 N Madison St Wilmington (19801) *(G-15704)*

Criterium Jagiasi Engineers 302 498-5600
1500 Shallcross Ave Wilmington (19806) *(G-15705)*

Critical Bs Holdings LLC 833 479-5375
1201 N Market St Ste 111 Wilmington (19801) *(G-15706)*

Critical Design and Cnstr Corp 302 588-4406
1525 Barley Mill Rd Wilmington (19807) *(G-15707)*

Crochet Creations By Debbie 302 287-2462
1219 Mckennans Church Rd Wilmington (19808) *(G-15708)*

Croda Inc 302 429-5200
315 Cherry Ln New Castle (19720) *(G-8986)*

Croda Inc 302 429-5249
321 Cherry Ln New Castle (19720) *(G-8987)*

Croda Atlas Point, New Castle *Also Called: Croda Uniqema Inc (G-8988)*

Croda Uniqema Inc 302 429-5599
315 Cherry Ln New Castle (19720) *(G-8988)*

Croesus Inc 302 472-9260
1007 N Orange St Wilmington (19801) *(G-15709)*

Croker Oars Usa Inc 302 897-6705
212 Karins Blvd Townsend (19734) *(G-13979)*

Croosroads Auto Repair Inc 302 436-9100
32469 Lighthouse Rd Selbyville (19975) *(G-13510)*

Cropsoft Solutions LLC 201 284-1535
3524 Silverside Rd Ste 35b Wilmington (19810) *(G-15710)*

Cross & Simon LLC 302 777-4200
913 N Market St Ste 1100 Wilmington (19801) *(G-15711)*

Cross Border It, Dover *Also Called: Damon Baca (G-2188)*

Cross Fit API 302 235-8763
4905 Mermaid Blvd Wilmington (19808) *(G-15712)*

Cross Over Camo LLC 302 798-1898
7205 Governor Printz Blvd Claymont (19703) *(G-1104)*

Crossfit 1st State 302 382-0603
36 Dornoch Way Townsend (19734) *(G-13980)*

Crossfit Bear 302 540-4394
2611 Del Laws Rd Bear (19701) *(G-127)*

Crossfit Diamond State LLC 201 803-1159
1801 Lincoln Ave Wilmington (19809) *(G-15713)*

Crossfit Dover LLC 302 242-5400
177 Windrow Way Magnolia (19962) *(G-6736)*

Crossfit Petram 302 345-2560
20 Shea Way Newark (19713) *(G-10356)*

Crossfit Riverfront 302 462-5176
21331 Catalina Cir Rehoboth Beach (19971) *(G-12704)*

Crossfit Riverfront..302 745-2348
512 Justison St Wilmington (19801) *(G-15714)*

Crossland & Associates LLC..........................302 409-0120
724 Yorklyn Rd Ste 100 Hockessin (19707) *(G-5171)*

Crossland and Associates.............................302 658-2100
724 Yorklyn Rd Ste 100 Hockessin (19707) *(G-5172)*

Crossover Grid, Camden Also Called: Crossover Sports Entrmt LLC *(G-810)*

Crossover Sports Entrmt LLC.........................516 728-5360
2140 S Dupont Hwy Camden (19934) *(G-810)*

Crossrate Technologies LLC............................323 643-5178
8 The Grn Dover (19901) *(G-2160)*

Crossroad Restaurant, Wilmington Also Called: Blue Hen Hospitality LLC *(G-14968)*

Crossroads Land Tech LLC.............................302 841-0654
34364 Fox Hound Ln Millsboro (19966) *(G-8245)*

Crossroads of Delaware..................................302 744-9999
2 Forest St Dover (19904) *(G-2161)*

Crossroads Veterinary Clinic..........................302 436-5984
36774 Dupont Blvd Selbyville (19975) *(G-13511)*

Crossroads Wireless, Wilmington Also Called: Crossroads Wireless Holdg LLC *(G-15715)*

Crossroads Wireless Holdg LLC......................405 946-1200
919 N Market St Ste 600 Wilmington (19801) *(G-15715)*

Crowley and Assoc Rlty Inc.............................302 227-6131
20250 Coastal Hwy Rehoboth Beach (19971) *(G-12705)*

Crown Cork Seal Rcvbles De Cor (HQ)............215 698-5100
5301 Limestone Rd Ste 221 Wilmington (19808) *(G-15716)*

Crown Cork Seal Receivables De, Wilmington Also Called: Crown Cork Seal Rcvbles De Cor *(G-15716)*

Crown Equine LLC..302 629-2782
14274 Cokesbury Rd Georgetown (19947) *(G-4273)*

Crowne Plaza Wilmington North, Claymont Also Called: Delaware Hotel Associates LP *(G-1113)*

Crowning Glory Styling Salon..........................302 999-8237
3808 Old Capitol Trl Wilmington (19808) *(G-15717)*

Crozier Fine Arts...302 325-2071
1400 Johnson Way Historic New Castle (19720) *(G-4966)*

Crrraw Holdings LLC......................................832 917-9442
2810 N Church St Unit 765891 Wilmington (19802) *(G-15718)*

Crude Gold Research LLC.............................646 681-7317
8 The Grn Ste A Dover (19901) *(G-2162)*

Cruise A Lifetime Usa Inc..............................302 697-2139
505 Brookfield Dr Dover (19901) *(G-2163)*

Cruise Holidays, Hockessin Also Called: Cruise Holidays Brandywine Vly *(G-5173)*

Cruise Holidays Brandywine Vly......................302 239-6400
7460 Lancaster Pike Ste 6 Hockessin (19707) *(G-5173)*

Cruise One...302 698-6468
159 Orchard Grove Ct Camden Wyoming (19934) *(G-930)*

Cruise Planners...302 858-1996
22424 S Acorn Way Lewes (19958) *(G-5869)*

Cruise Planners...302 381-9249
24343 Zinfandel Ln Unit 107 Lewes (19958) *(G-5870)*

Cruise Planners...302 503-3694
115 N Walnut St Milford (19963) *(G-7844)*

Cruise Planners...302 731-9548
4 High Pond Dr Newark (19711) *(G-10357)*

Cruise Ship Centers.......................................302 999-0202
760 Peoples Plz Newark (19702) *(G-10358)*

Cruise Shoppe Inc..302 737-7220
26 Valerie Dr Bear (19701) *(G-128)*

Cruisingapp LLC (PA)....................................302 645-7400
16192 Coastal Hwy Lewes (19958) *(G-5871)*

Cruitcast Inc...856 693-3869
285 W Pembrooke Dr Smyrna (19977) *(G-13689)*

Crumpton Starline..302 832-1342
5 Greenfield Dr New Castle (19720) *(G-8989)*

Cruz Publishing Group....................................302 287-2938
64 Representative Ln Dover (19904) *(G-2164)*

Crx Consulting LLC.......................................302 864-7377
20245 Bay Vista Rd Unit 305 Rehoboth Beach (19971) *(G-12706)*

Crx Consulting LLC.......................................302 864-7377
201 Lakeview Shrs Rehoboth Beach (19971) *(G-12707)*

Cryptlex LLC..786 269-0931
16192 Coastal Hwy Lewes (19958) *(G-5872)*

Crypto Trader LLC...302 339-7500
19266 Coastal Hwy Rehoboth Beach (19971) *(G-12708)*

Crypto World Journal Inc...............................302 213-8136
8 The Grn # A Dover (19901) *(G-2165)*

Cryptofi Inc..312 813-7188
8 The Grn Dover (19901) *(G-2166)*

Cryptomarket Inc (PA)...................................860 222-0318
1209 N Orange St Wilmington (19801) *(G-15719)*

Cryptomkt, Wilmington Also Called: Cryptomarket Inc *(G-15719)*

Crystal Blu Services LLC..............................302 404-5389
902 Heritage Dr Seaford (19973) *(G-13141)*

Crystal Clean..302 864-4032
22235 Westwoods Rd Millsboro (19966) *(G-8246)*

Crystal Clear Mechanical LLC......................302 344-2531
31950 Phillips Rd Selbyville (19975) *(G-13512)*

Crystal Diamond Publishing..........................302 737-2130
1 Mabry Ct Newark (19702) *(G-10359)*

Crystal Holdings Inc (PA).............................302 421-5700
110 S Poplar St Ste 400 Wilmington (19801) *(G-15720)*

Crystal Kleen Inc...302 326-1140
32 Appleby Rd New Castle (19720) *(G-8990)*

Crystal Metalworks Inc Fairfax, Delmar Also Called: Crystal Steel Fabricators Inc *(G-1585)*

Crystal Steel Fabricators Inc........................302 846-0277
N 2nd Delmar (19940) *(G-1584)*

Crystal Steel Fabricators Inc (PA)................302 846-0613
9317 Old Racetrack Rd Delmar (19940) *(G-1585)*

Cs Associates LLC (PA)...............................909 827-2335
3911 Concord Pike Unit 8030 Wilmington (19803) *(G-15721)*

Cs Services LLC...302 841-9420
30757 Conleys Chapel Rd Lewes (19958) *(G-5873)*

Cs Webb Daughters & Son Inc......................302 239-2801
1028 Yorklyn Rd Hockessin (19707) *(G-5174)*

CSC, Wilmington Also Called: Company Corporation *(G-15566)*

CSC, Wilmington Also Called: CSC Corporate Domains Inc *(G-15722)*

CSC, Wilmington Also Called: CSC Domains LLC *(G-15723)*

CSC Corporate Domains Inc (HQ)................866 403-5272
251 Little Falls Dr Wilmington (19808) *(G-15722)*

CSC Domains LLC (HQ)..............................302 636-5400
2711 Centerville Rd Ste 400 Wilmington (19808) *(G-15723)*

CSC Networks Inc..302 636-5401
251 Little Falls Dr Wilmington (19808) *(G-15724)*

Csi Solutions LLC (PA)................................202 506-7573
200 Continental Dr Ste 401 Newark (19713) *(G-10360)*

Csols Inc...302 731-5290
750 Prides Xing Ste 305 Newark (19713) *(G-10361)*

Csrj Contracting...302 290-6208
2007 Baird Ave Wilmington (19808) *(G-15725)*

CSX, Wilmington Also Called: CSX Transportation Inc *(G-15726)*

CSX Transportation Inc................................302 998-8613
1155 Centerville Rd Wilmington (19804) *(G-15726)*

CT Corporation System (PA).......................302 658-4968
1209 N Orange St Wilmington (19801) *(G-15727)*

CT Innovations LLC.....................................209 559-3595
8 The Grn Ste A Dover (19901) *(G-2167)*

CT Partners LLC..302 766-4176
4001 Kennett Pike Ste 242 Wilmington (19807) *(G-15728)*

CT Pete Crossan Inc....................................302 737-0223
420 Terrapin Ln Newark (19711) *(G-10362)*

CTA Roofing & Waterproofing......................302 454-8551
91 Blue Hen Dr Newark (19713) *(G-10363)*

CTB Intl LLC..217 415-4843
The Grn Ste 8325 Dover (19901) *(G-2168)*

Ctm Medical Associates LLC......................302 945-9730
32711 Long Neck Rd Millsboro (19966) *(G-8247)*

Ctm Medical Associates LLC (PA).............302 645-8587
109 Heronwood Dr Milton (19968) *(G-8593)*

Cto Lab Inc..415 702-5014
2093 Philadelphia Pike Ste 5021 Claymont (19703) *(G-1105)*

Cube Media LLC...716 239-2789
501 Silverside Rd 345 Wilmington (19809) *(G-15729)*

Cubic Logics Inc..480 382-8242
Twenty Four A Trolley Square #4058 Wilmington (19806) *(G-15730)*

Cubic Products LLC 781 990-3886
  2711 Centerville Rd Wilmington (19808) *(G-15731)*

Cubic Sct Inc 845 977-3240
  600 N Broad St Middletown (19709) *(G-7022)*

Cuhiana Care Health System 302 733-1780
  4755 Ogletown Stanton Rd Newark (19718) *(G-10364)*

Culcha Foundation, Lewes Also Called: Music Art & Culture Foundation *(G-6297)*

Culiquip LLC 302 654-4974
  20 Germay Dr Wilmington (19804) *(G-15732)*

Culturetech Solutions LLC (PA) 415 936-5799
  8 The Grn Ste A Dover (19901) *(G-2169)*

Cummins, Wilmington Also Called: Cummins Power Generation Inc *(G-15733)*

Cummins Power Generation Inc 302 762-2027
  1706 E 12th St Wilmington (19809) *(G-15733)*

Cupcake Kouture Bakery LLC 302 602-6058
  212 W Market St Newport (19804) *(G-12445)*

Curbs Etc Inc 302 653-3511
  3528 S Dupont Blvd Smyrna (19977) *(G-13690)*

Curiosity Service Foundation 302 628-4140
  2001 Bridgeville Hwy Seaford (19973) *(G-13142)*

Curley & Benton LLC 302 674-3333
  250 Beiser Blvd Ste 202 Dover (19904) *(G-2170)*

Curley and Funk, Dover Also Called: Curley & Benton LLC *(G-2170)*

Curran James P Law Offices 302 894-1111
  256 Chapman Rd Ste 107 Newark (19702) *(G-10365)*

Currency Technics Metrics Inc 302 482-4846
  4200 Governor Printz Blvd Wilmington (19802) *(G-15734)*

Current Care Analytics Inc 248 425-3973
  16192 Coastal Hwy Lewes (19958) *(G-5874)*

Current Solutions 302 724-5243
  1160 Rose Valley School Rd Dover (19904) *(G-2171)*

Current Solutions Inc 302 736-5210
  1100 Apple Grove School Rd Camden Wyoming (19934) *(G-931)*

Currie Hair Skin Nailss 302 777-7755
  317 Justison St Wilmington (19801) *(G-15735)*

CURRIE HAIR SKIN NAILSS, Wilmington Also Called: Currie Hair Skin Nailss *(G-15735)*

Curt M Watkins M D 302 856-1773
  20797 Professional Park Boulevard Georgetown (19947) *(G-4274)*

Curtis A Smith 302 875-6800
  314 S Central Ave Laurel (19956) *(G-5489)*

Curtis D Froehlich M D 302 651-4000
  1600 Rockland Rd Wilmington (19803) *(G-15736)*

Curtiss Contracting LLC 302 604-1071
  807 Atlantic Ave Milton (19968) *(G-8594)*

Curvature Inc 302 525-9525
  645 Paper Mill Rd Newark (19711) *(G-10366)*

Curves, Camden Also Called: Curves International Inc *(G-811)*

Curves International Inc 302 698-1481
  103 South St # 2 Camden (19934) *(G-811)*

Curzon Corp 302 655-5551
  900 N Union St Wilmington (19805) *(G-15737)*

Cushing Construction, Wilmington Also Called: S & C Properties Ltd *(G-19604)*

Cushman Foundry LLC 513 984-5570
  1111 S Governors Ave Dover (19904) *(G-2172)*

Custom America 856 516-1103
  173 Edgemoor Rd Wilmington (19809) *(G-15738)*

Custom Cabinet Shop Inc 302 337-8241
  Rte 13 Greenwood (19950) *(G-4609)*

Custom Ceramics, Wilmington Also Called: Joel Gonzalez *(G-17561)*

Custom Con Restoration LLC 302 670-9525
  131 Cantwell Dr Dover (19904) *(G-2173)*

Custom Concrete Finishes 302 463-0635
  103 W Apollo Ln Milton (19968) *(G-8595)*

Custom Creams LLC 302 582-8862
  128 Sunset Blvd Pmb 1211 New Castle (19720) *(G-8991)*

Custom Creations By Design 302 482-2267
  1 Murphy Rd Wilmington (19803) *(G-15739)*

Custom Decor Inc 302 735-7600
  1585 Mckee Rd # 1 Dover (19904) *(G-2174)*

Custom Design Contracting LLC 302 333-0547
  16 E Salisbury Dr Wilmington (19809) *(G-15740)*

Custom Drywall Inc 302 369-3266
  573 Bellevue Rd Ste C Newark (19713) *(G-10367)*

Custom Framers Inc 302 684-5377
  26526 Lewes Georgetown Hwy Harbeson (19951) *(G-4694)*

Custom Improvers Inc 302 731-9246
  89 Albe Dr Newark (19702) *(G-10368)*

Custom Iron Shop Inc 302 654-5201
  735 S Market St Ste A Wilmington (19801) *(G-15741)*

Custom Lawn Services Inc 302 540-4180
  4023 Kennett Pike Ste 258 Wilmington (19807) *(G-15742)*

Custom Mechanical Inc (PA) 302 537-1150
  34799 Daisey Rd Frankford (19945) *(G-4096)*

Custom Metal Works Inc 302 765-2653
  530 Ruxton Dr Wilmington (19809) *(G-15743)*

Custom Porcelain Inc 302 659-6590
  1245 Caldwell Corner Rd Townsend (19734) *(G-13981)*

Custom Satellite and Sound, Wilmington Also Called: Weyl Enterprises Inc *(G-20749)*

Custom Sheet Metal of Delaware 302 998-6865
  464 E Ayre St Wilmington (19804) *(G-15744)*

Customer Services Department, Dover Also Called: City of Dover *(G-2083)*

Customs Benefits 302 798-2884
  501 Silverside Rd Ste 120 Wilmington (19809) *(G-15745)*

Cutem Up Tree Care Del Inc 302 629-4655
  10404 Old Furnace Rd Seaford (19973) *(G-13143)*

Cutler Industries Inc 302 689-3779
  2711 Centerville Rd # 400 Wilmington (19808) *(G-15746)*

Cutting Edge 302 834-8723
  511 5th St Delaware City (19706) *(G-1535)*

Cutting Edge of Delaware Inc 302 834-8723
  511 E 5th St Wilmington (19801) *(G-15747)*

Cutting Edge Treatment Center 302 258-5710
  1000 Midway Dr Ste 3 Harrington (19952) *(G-4755)*

Cutting of Precision Concrete 302 543-5833
  213 Maryland Ave Newport (19804) *(G-12446)*

Cw Mobile Automotive Repa 302 663-0035
  26693 Jersey Rd Millsboro (19966) *(G-8248)*

Cw Signs LLC 302 533-5492
  812 Pencader Dr Unit E Newark (19702) *(G-10369)*

Cwp Energy Solution, Wilmington Also Called: Cwp Energy Solution Inc *(G-15748)*

Cwp Energy Solution Inc 514 360-0270
  1209 N Orange St Wilmington (19801) *(G-15748)*

Cws Ballantyne II 99 LLC 302 636-5401
  251 Little Falls Dr Wilmington (19808) *(G-15749)*

Cybele Software Inc 302 892-9625
  3422 Old Capitol Trl Ste 1125 Wilmington (19808) *(G-15750)*

Cyber 20/20 Inc 203 802-8742
  1 Innovation Way Unit 2 Newark (19711) *(G-10370)*

Cybercore Holding Inc 410 560-7177
  1209 N Orange St Wilmington (19801) *(G-15751)*

Cyberdefenders Inc 510 999-3490
  651 N Broad St Middletown (19709) *(G-7023)*

Cyberlete Inc 440 983-8647
  651 N Broad St Middletown (19709) *(G-7024)*

Cychet LLC 929 265-8351
  8 The Grn Dover (19901) *(G-2175)*

Cyclops Net Inc 844 979-0222
  2140 S Dupont Hwy Camden (19934) *(G-812)*

Cycology 202 LLC (PA) 610 202-0518
  23924 Sunny Cove Ct Lewes (19958) *(G-5875)*

Cydallia Inc (PA) 860 682-0947
  16192 Coastal Hwy Lewes (19958) *(G-5876)*

Cygnet Construction Corp 302 436-5212
  50 Saw Mill Ln Selbyville (19975) *(G-13513)*

Cynash Inc 415 850-7842
  1 Righter Pkwy Ste 260 Wilmington (19803) *(G-15752)*

Cynthia A Mumma DDS 302 652-2451
  1 Zachary Ct Wilmington (19803) *(G-15753)*

Cynthia Crosser DC Fiama 302 239-5014
  3101 Limestone Rd Ste B Wilmington (19808) *(G-15754)*

Cynthia Dnnis Mther Foundation 410 598-3819
  38892 Bunting Ave Fenwick Island (19944) *(G-4047)*

ALPHABETIC SECTION

Cynthia L Carroll 302 733-0411
  262 Chapman Rd Ste 108 Newark (19702) *(G-10371)*

Cynthia L Rae 302 985-7069
  254 E Main St Newark (19711) *(G-10372)*

Cynthia P Mangubat M D 302 883-3677
  819 S Governors Ave Dover (19904) *(G-2176)*

Cynthia R Drew NP 302 933-0111
  28467 Dupont Blvd Unit 6 Millsboro (19966) *(G-8249)*

Cynthia S Devine 302 678-8447
  240 Beiser Blvd Ste 101 Dover (19904) *(G-2177)*

Cynwood Apartments, Wilmington Also Called: Panco Management Corporation *(G-18870)*

Cynwyd Club Apartments, Wilmington Also Called: Delaware Equity Fund IV *(G-15914)*

Cyph, Claymont Also Called: Cyph Inc *(G-1106)*

Cyph Inc 931 297-4462
  2093a Philadelphia Pike Ste 152 Claymont (19703) *(G-1106)*

Cypress Support LLC 410 937-2511
  1202 Faun Rd Wilmington (19803) *(G-15755)*

Cypress Tree Care 302 732-3227
  33529 Fox Run Frankford (19945) *(G-4097)*

Cyproteck Inc 860 890-1889
  651 N Broad St Ste 201 Middletown (19709) *(G-7025)*

Cytec Industries Inc 302 530-7665
  3 Weldin Park Dr Wilmington (19803) *(G-15756)*

Czapp Masonry Inc 302 238-7007
  36171 Victory Ln Millsboro (19966) *(G-8250)*

D & B Printing and Mailing Inc 302 838-7111
  3 Brookmont Dr Newark (19702) *(G-10373)*

D & C Bath LLC 888 323-2284
  600 N Broad St Ste 4 Middletown (19709) *(G-7026)*

D & D Screen Printing 302 349-4231
  12794 Shawnee Rd Greenwood (19950) *(G-4610)*

D & F Bussing Inc 302 934-9461
  231 Laurel Rd Millsboro (19966) *(G-8251)*

D & G Inc 302 378-4877
  4195 Dupont Pkwy Townsend (19734) *(G-13982)*

D & H Automotive & Towing Inc 302 655-7611
  4016th Ave Ste B Wilmington (19805) *(G-15757)*

D & J Recycling Inc 302 422-0163
  5688 Betty St Milford (19963) *(G-7845)*

D & J Sweeping LLC 302 875-3393
  7119 Airport Rd Laurel (19956) *(G-5490)*

D & J Welding LLC 347 706-5561
  8 The Grn Dover (19901) *(G-2178)*

D & S Painters LLC 302 241-7221
  23415 Sussex Hwy Seaford (19973) *(G-13144)*

D & S Warehousing Inc 302 731-7440
  300 D And S Ln Bear (19701) *(G-129)*

D & S Warehousing Inc 302 731-7440
  104 Alan Dr Newark (19711) *(G-10374)*

D 4 Brown LLC 518 986-6809
  8 The Grn Ste 4000 Dover (19901) *(G-2179)*

D A B Productions 302 670-9407
  604 Fernwood Dr Harrington (19952) *(G-4756)*

D A Jones Inc 302 836-9238
  37479 Leisure Dr Selbyville (19975) *(G-13514)*

D B Mechanical LLC 302 722-0471
  13 Oaknoll Cir Newark (19711) *(G-10375)*

D B Nibouar DDS 302 239-0502
  5317 Limestone Rd Wilmington (19808) *(G-15758)*

D B S, New Castle Also Called: Delaware Business Systems Inc *(G-9015)*

D By D Printing LLC 302 659-3373
  5083 N Dupont Hwy Dover (19901) *(G-2180)*

D C A Net, Wilmington Also Called: Consult Dynamics Inc *(G-15613)*

D C I, Wilmington Also Called: Design Collaborative Inc *(G-16024)*

D C Mitchell LLC 302 998-1181
  8 Hadco Rd Ste B Wilmington (19804) *(G-15759)*

D C S Company 302 328-5138
  233 Gordy Pl New Castle (19720) *(G-8992)*

D E C, Greenwood Also Called: Delaware Electric Cooperative Inc *(G-4613)*

D F Distribution Inc 302 798-5999
  6603 Governor Printz Blvd Ste A Wilmington (19809) *(G-15760)*

D F Quillen & Sons Inc (PA) 302 227-2531
  803 Rehoboth Ave Ste F Rehoboth Beach (19971) *(G-12709)*

D Gingerich Concrete & Masnry 302 492-8662
  952 Myers Dr Hartly (19953) *(G-4864)*

D H Automotive Towing 302 368-5590
  80 Aleph Dr Newark (19702) *(G-10376)*

D H General Contracting 302 420-5269
  112 Kenmar Dr Newark (19713) *(G-10377)*

D J Byler 302 653-4602
  5290 Judith Rd Clayton (19938) *(G-1358)*

D L Printing, Claymont Also Called: Dragons Lair Printing LLC *(G-1122)*

D Lav Denim Co, Dover Also Called: Delave Denim Co LLC *(G-2215)*

D Laverne Beiler 302 378-4644
  220 Beiser Blvd Dover (19904) *(G-2181)*

D M F Associates Inc 302 539-0606
  Rte 1 Evergreen St Bethany Beach (19930) *(G-592)*

D M I, Historic New Castle Also Called: Data MGT Internationale Inc *(G-4968)*

D M Iannone Inc 302 999-0893
  103 S Augustine St Wilmington (19804) *(G-15761)*

D R Deakyne DDS 302 653-6661
  231 N New St Smyrna (19977) *(G-13691)*

D S Auto 302 542-3023
  23108 Country Living Rd Millsboro (19966) *(G-8252)*

D S Builders 302 242-3308
  1325 Tuxward Rd Hartly (19953) *(G-4865)*

D Shinn Inc 302 792-2033
  1409 Haines Ave Wilmington (19809) *(G-15762)*

D Steven Caldwell 302 245-9713
  34444 King Street Row Lewes (19958) *(G-5877)*

D-Staffing Consulting Svcs LLC 302 402-5678
  8 The Grn Ste 6060 Dover (19901) *(G-2182)*

D&B Mechanical, Newark Also Called: D B Mechanical LLC *(G-10375)*

D&C Concepts LLC 770 335-2503
  919 N Market St Ste 950 Wilmington (19801) *(G-15763)*

D&C Logging 302 846-3982
  16075 Russell Rd Delmar (19940) *(G-1586)*

D&N Bus Service Inc 302 422-3869
  140 Vickers Rd Milford (19963) *(G-7846)*

D1 Express Inc 302 883-9572
  15 Maggies Way Ste 1 Dover (19901) *(G-2183)*

D1 Sports Basketball Training 317 985-5125
  919 N Market St Ste 425 Wilmington (19801) *(G-15764)*

D150 Fueling LLC 215 559-1132
  150 East Chestnut Hill Rd Newark (19713) *(G-10378)*

D2cmed, Dover Also Called: L2 Trade LLC *(G-2893)*

Da Vinci Painting 302 229-0644
  5 Wenark Dr Apt 11 Newark (19713) *(G-10379)*

Daabo Inc 816 559-4169
  2055 Limestone Rd Wilmington (19808) *(G-15765)*

Dab Deodorant LLC 973 512-2703
  6 Tulip Ln Apt 36 New Castle (19720) *(G-8993)*

Dabvasan Inc 302 529-1100
  1812 Marsh Rd Ste 6 Wilmington (19810) *(G-15766)*

Dack Realty Corp (PA) 302 792-2737
  1308 Society Dr Claymont (19703) *(G-1107)*

Dack Trading LLC 917 576-4432
  18585 Coastal Hwy Unit 10 Rehoboth Beach (19971) *(G-12710)*

Dad's Workwear, Laurel Also Called: Dads Workwear Inc *(G-5491)*

Dads Workwear Inc (PA) 302 663-0068
  11480 Commercial Ln Laurel (19956) *(G-5491)*

Dag Residential Coml Svcs LLC 302 513-6646
  1129 Barney Jenkins Rd Felton (19943) *(G-3956)*

Dagers Waterfowl Hunting 302 659-1766
  166 Gardner Rd Townsend (19734) *(G-13983)*

Dagsboro Family Practice, Dagsboro Also Called: Tidalhlth Pnnsula Regional Inc *(G-1517)*

Dagsboro Serv-Dagsboro BR, Dagsboro Also Called: Southern States Coop Inc *(G-1507)*

Dahcor LLC 302 257-2803
  8 The Grn Ste A Dover (19901) *(G-2184)*

Daikin Comfort Tech Mfg LP 302 894-1010
  230 Executive Dr Ste 5 Newark (19702) *(G-10380)*

Dailey Resources 302 655-1811
  2302 Riddle Ave Wilmington (19806) *(G-15767)*

Daily Byte LLC 516 236-9638
   8 The Grn Ste A Dover (19901) *(G-2185)*

Daily Cart, Dover *Also Called: World Foods USA LLC (G-3873)*

Daily News-Sun, Dover *Also Called: Independent Newsmedia Inc USA (G-2729)*

Daimlerchrysler N Amrca Financ 302 292-6840
   131 Continental Dr Newark (19713) *(G-10381)*

Daisy Construction Company 302 658-4417
   3128 New Castle Ave New Castle (19720) *(G-8994)*

Daisy Construction Company 302 658-4417
   102 Larch Cir Ste 301 Wilmington (19804) *(G-15768)*

Daisy Hora 302 727-6299
   39682 Sunrise Ct Bethany Beach (19930) *(G-593)*

Dakk Holdings LLC 571 335-7844
   8 The Grn Dover (19901) *(G-2186)*

Dal Construction 302 538-5310
   8331 Willow Grove Rd Camden (19934) *(G-813)*

Dal Contractors LLC 302 737-3220
   50 Albe Dr Newark (19702) *(G-10382)*

Dalco Construction Co 302 475-2099
   1112 Marsh Rd Wilmington (19803) *(G-15769)*

Dale Carnegie Training 302 368-7292
   220 Continental Dr Ste 205 Newark (19713) *(G-10383)*

Dale F Sutherland MD LLC 302 827-4376
   35573 Peregrine Rd Lewes (19958) *(G-5878)*

Dale Hawkins 302 658-6697
   715 N King St Ste 200 Wilmington (19801) *(G-15770)*

Dale Insulation Co of Delaware 302 324-9332
   13 King Ct Ste 5 New Castle (19720) *(G-8995)*

Dale Maple Country Club Inc 302 674-2505
   180 Mapledale Cir Dover (19904) *(G-2187)*

Dales Lawn Care,, Dover *Also Called: Kenneth Dale Ralosky (G-2842)*

Dalou Property Management 866 575-9387
   3 Germay Dr Wilmington (19804) *(G-15771)*

Dalstrong America Inc 716 380-4998
   3411 Silverside Rd Ste 104 Wilmington (19810) *(G-15772)*

Dalton & Associates PA 302 652-2050
   1106 W 10th St Wilmington (19806) *(G-15773)*

Dalton Personal Training LLC 302 266-7005
   218 Megan Ct Newark (19702) *(G-10384)*

Daly Concepts 215 266-0866
   1607 W 13th St Apt 2 Wilmington (19806) *(G-15774)*

Dama International LLC 813 778-5495
   364 E Main St Ste 157 Middletown (19709) *(G-7027)*

Damions Solar Shades 302 661-1500
   2800 Kirkwood Hwy Wilmington (19805) *(G-15775)*

Damon Baca 858 837-0800
   8 The Grn Ste 8 Dover (19901) *(G-2188)*

Dan H Beachy & Sons Inc 302 492-1493
   1298 Lockwood Chapel Rd Hartly (19953) *(G-4866)*

Dan Licale 302 888-2133
   Corner Kirk Rd And 100 Montchanin (19710) *(G-8736)*

Dan Miller and Sons Cnstr LLC 302 492-8116
   5790 Halltown Rd Hartly (19953) *(G-4867)*

Dan Prinsloo 302 373-8891
   217 Olivine Cir Townsend (19734) *(G-13984)*

Dana Container Inc 302 652-8550
   1280 Railcar Ave Wilmington (19802) *(G-15776)*

Dana E Herbert 302 721-5798
   22 Peterson Pl Bear (19701) *(G-130)*

Dana Railcare, Wilmington *Also Called: Dana Container Inc (G-15776)*

Dana Railcare Inc 302 652-8550
   1280 Railcar Ave Wilmington (19802) *(G-15777)*

Dance Conservatory 302 734-9717
   522 Otis Dr Dover (19901) *(G-2189)*

Dancedelaware 302 998-1222
   2005 Concord Pike Ste 204 Wilmington (19803) *(G-15778)*

Danceworks 302 286-1492
   413 New London Rd Newark (19711) *(G-10385)*

Danceworks Dance Studio LLC 302 244-8570
   187 Penn Mart Shopping Ctr New Castle (19720) *(G-8996)*

Danceworks Studio, New Castle *Also Called: Danceworks Dance Studio LLC (G-8996)*

DAndrea Contracting 302 893-4183
   230 Milford Dr Middletown (19709) *(G-7028)*

Dandy Signs 301 399-8746
   37384 Club House Rd Ocean View (19970) *(G-12498)*

Dane & Cash Enterprise LLC 302 281-4031
   300 Delaware Ave Fl 10 Wilmington (19801) *(G-15779)*

Dane Waters 302 377-9999
   1 Hillside Rd Claymont (19703) *(G-1108)*

Danella Line Services Co Inc 302 893-1253
   874 Walker Rd Dover (19904) *(G-2190)*

Danfoss Power Solutions US Co 515 956-5185
   251 Little Falls Dr Wilmington (19808) *(G-15780)*

Daniel A Kinsler 302 947-9790
   28426 Wynikako Ave Millsboro (19966) *(G-8253)*

Daniel A Yoder 302 730-4076
   2956 Yoder Dr Dover (19904) *(G-2191)*

Daniel D Rappa Inc 302 994-1199
   302 Cedar St Newport (19804) *(G-12447)*

Daniel G Wnda K Odell Fmly Fnd 800 839-1754
   501 Silverside Rd Wilmington (19809) *(G-15781)*

Daniel George Bebee Inc 443 359-1542
   32353 Cobbs Creek Rd Laurel (19956) *(G-5492)*

Daniel Halvorsen 302 645-1761
   33095 Nassau Loop Lewes (19958) *(G-5879)*

Daniel J Fay Dmd PA 302 734-8101
   748 S New St Ste C Dover (19904) *(G-2192)*

Daniel Karen Berman Foundation 800 839-1754
   501 Silverside Rd Ste 123 Wilmington (19809) *(G-15782)*

Daniel Marelli 302 744-7980
   540 S Governors Ave Dover (19904) *(G-2193)*

Daniel Mitsdarfer T A Dan 302 998-1295
   1413 Oak Hill Dr Wilmington (19805) *(G-15783)*

Daniel P McCollom 302 888-6865
   222 Delaware Ave Wilmington (19801) *(G-15784)*

Daniel Shea 302 349-5599
   1859 Elliott Ln Greenwood (19950) *(G-4611)*

Daniel T Metzgar LLC 302 602-4451
   84 Kenmar Dr Newark (19713) *(G-10386)*

Daniel W Cuozzo Do 302 645-4801
   18947 John J Williams Hwy Unit 201 Rehoboth Beach (19971) *(G-12711)*

Danielle Hill Training Center 302 363-1484
   2075 Sharon Hill Rd Dover (19904) *(G-2194)*

Danielle Wiggins 302 494-3397
   121 W Loockerman St Dover (19904) *(G-2195)*

Daniels Custom Finishes LLC 302 357-5806
   9 W 26th St Wilmington (19802) *(G-15785)*

Daniels Lawn and Tree LLC 302 218-0173
   3210 Wilson Ave Wilmington (19808) *(G-15786)*

Danis Home Cleaning Services 302 525-8286
   6 Cresson Ave New Castle (19720) *(G-8997)*

Danisco European Holding Inc 302 999-4083
   974 Centre Rd Wilmington (19805) *(G-15787)*

Danisco USA, Wilmington *Also Called: Danisco USA Inc (G-15788)*

Danisco USA Inc 866 583-2583
   974 Centre Rd Crp735 Wilmington (19805) *(G-15788)*

Dann J Gladnick Dmd PA 302 654-7243
   1104 N Broom St Wilmington (19806) *(G-15789)*

Danneman Firm LLC 302 793-9660
   3411 Silverside Rd Ste 108wb Wilmington (19810) *(G-15790)*

Dannemann & Dannemann LLC 302 368-4685
   3411 Silverside Rd Ste 108wb Wilmington (19810) *(G-15791)*

Danny Thach 302 645-7779
   17601 Coastal Hwy Lewes (19958) *(G-5880)*

Dannys Garage LLC 702 752-9964
   606 Cherry St Historic New Castle (19720) *(G-4967)*

Danoffice It Inc 703 579-0180
   200 Continental Dr Ste 401 Newark (19713) *(G-10387)*

DAntuono Vincenzo S MD 302 628-8300
   1350 Middleford Rd # 502 Seaford (19973) *(G-13145)*

Danyo Plastic Surgery 302 753-6424
   4001 Kennett Pike Ste 234 Wilmington (19807) *(G-15792)*

ALPHABETIC SECTION — Davis Services

Dap, Milford *Also Called: Delaware Animal Products LLC (G-7851)*

Daphne LLC 302 525-6010
3 Chesmar Plz Newark (19713) *(G-10388)*

DAPI, Newark *Also Called: Delaware Adlescent Program Inc (G-10415)*

Dapple, Wilmington *Also Called: II USA Corporation (G-17270)*

Darby Leasing LLC 302 477-0500
3411 Silverside Rd Ste 104 Wilmington (19810) *(G-15793)*

Dark Knight Services Inc 302 468-6237
3 Germay Dr Ste 4-2158 Wilmington (19804) *(G-15794)*

Darlene R N Sheeran 845 297-9704
31247 Temple Rd Lewes (19958) *(G-5881)*

Darley Road Pta, Claymont *Also Called: Pta Delaware Congress (G-1269)*

Darlington Postal Company LLC 410 917-4147
1217 Old Coochs Bridge Rd Newark (19713) *(G-10389)*

Dart Container Sales Company 305 759-5044
2451 Bear Corbitt Rd New Castle (19720) *(G-8998)*

Dart First State, Dover *Also Called: Delaware Department Trnsp (G-2228)*

Darwell Inc 302 204-0939
874 Walker Rd Dover (19904) *(G-2196)*

Dassault Aircraft Svcs Corp 302 322-7000
191 N Dupont Hwy New Castle (19720) *(G-8999)*

Dassault Falcon Jet - Wilmington Corp 302 322-7000
191 N Dupont Hwy New Castle (19720) *(G-9000)*

Dastor LLC (PA) 610 337-5560
1201 N Market St Ste 201 Wilmington (19801) *(G-15795)*

Data Cloud Partners LLC 805 729-1088
1209 N Orange St Wilmington (19801) *(G-15796)*

Data Drum Inc 347 502-8485
2035 Sunset Lake Rd Newark (19702) *(G-10390)*

Data Guard Recycling Inc 302 337-8870
9174 Redden Rd Bridgeville (19933) *(G-689)*

Data MGT Internationale Inc (PA) 302 656-1151
55 Lukens Dr Ste A Historic New Castle (19720) *(G-4968)*

Data Systems & Solutions LLC 858 826-5995
1013 Centre Rd Wilmington (19805) *(G-15797)*

Data Unblocked Inc 540 424-0801
16192 Coastal Hwy Lewes (19958) *(G-5882)*

Data-Bi LLC 302 290-3138
601 Entwisle Ct Wilmington (19808) *(G-15798)*

Datalogy Bus Solutions Inc 832 713-4790
651 N Broad St Ste 206 Middletown (19709) *(G-7029)*

Datamola LLC 347 474-1003
16192 Coastal Hwy Lewes (19958) *(G-5883)*

Datascope Solutions Corp 562 373-0209
251 Little Falls Dr Wilmington (19808) *(G-15799)*

Datasea Inc 267 752-9029
8 The Grn Ste R Dover (19901) *(G-2197)*

Dataspindle LLC 302 448-4988
2207 Concord Pike Ste 425 Wilmington (19803) *(G-15800)*

Datatech Enterprises Inc (PA) 540 370-0010
36322 Sunflower Blvd Selbyville (19975) *(G-13515)*

Datwyler Pharma Packg USA Inc 302 603-8020
571 Merrimac Ave Middletown (19709) *(G-7030)*

Davait Inc 302 930-0095
8 The Grn Ste B Dover (19901) *(G-2198)*

Daves Auto Restoration 302 258-7981
28327 Woods Ln Laurel (19956) *(G-5493)*

Daves Builders Inc 302 539-4058
38308 Lu Lee Ct Ocean View (19970) *(G-12499)*

Daves Disc Mfflers of Dver De 302 678-8803
1312 S Dupont Hwy Dover (19901) *(G-2199)*

Daves Lawn Care & Landscaping, Bear *Also Called: David M Wagner (G-134)*

Daves Service Center 302 798-1776
950 Ridge Rd Ste A6 Claymont (19703) *(G-1109)*

Daves Truck Repair LLC 302 362-2578
24434 Cypress Rd Frankford (19945) *(G-4098)*

David A Dorey Esq 302 425-6400
1201 N Market St Ste 800 Wilmington (19801) *(G-15801)*

David A King DDS 302 998-0331
2601 Annand Dr Ste 10 Wilmington (19808) *(G-15802)*

David Bridge 302 429-3317
245 Benjamin Blvd Bear (19701) *(G-131)*

David Brown Gear Systems USA I (PA) 540 416-2062
300 Delaware Ave Ste 1370 Wilmington (19801) *(G-15803)*

David D Finocchiaro Attorney 302 764-7113
916 Cranbrook Dr Wilmington (19803) *(G-15804)*

David D Scheid M D 302 633-1700
3105 Limestone Rd Ste 301 Wilmington (19808) *(G-15805)*

David Dukes 302 841-9481
29622 Dirt Ln Millsboro (19966) *(G-8254)*

David G Horsey & Sons Inc 302 875-3033
28107 Beaver Dam Branch Rd Laurel (19956) *(G-5494)*

David G Major Associates Inc 703 642-7450
30165 Ethan Allen Ct Millsboro (19966) *(G-8255)*

David Ira Jenkins 302 335-3309
117 Barkers Landing Rd Magnolia (19962) *(G-6737)*

David Jenkins 302 304-5568
522 Liam Pl Bear (19701) *(G-132)*

David L Isaacs DDS 302 654-2904
707 Foulk Rd Ste 103 Wilmington (19803) *(G-15806)*

David L Townsend Co Inc 302 378-7967
1041 Clayton Greenspring Rd Smyrna (19977) *(G-13692)*

David M Pressel M D 302 651-4000
1600 Rockland Rd Wilmington (19803) *(G-15807)*

David M Sartin Sr 302 838-1074
1984 Porter Rd Bear (19701) *(G-133)*

David M Showalter 302 462-5264
4 Scott Dr Millsboro (19966) *(G-8256)*

David M Wagner 302 832-8336
812 Archer Pl Bear (19701) *(G-134)*

David Oppenheimer and Co I LLC 302 533-0779
200 Continental Dr Ste 301 Newark (19713) *(G-10391)*

David P Roser Inc (PA) 302 239-7605
19 Roser Ln Hockessin (19707) *(G-5175)*

David Price 410 708-7133
14655 Russell Rd Bridgeville (19933) *(G-690)*

David R Daniels 410 275-8141
375 Vandyke Maryland Line Rd Townsend (19734) *(G-13985)*

David Rappaport 302 651-6040
1600 Rockland Rd Wilmington (19803) *(G-15808)*

David Robinson 302 324-3253
2300 Naamans Rd Wilmington (19810) *(G-15809)*

David Rockwell & Associates 302 478-9900
208 W Pembrey Dr Wilmington (19803) *(G-15810)*

David S Jezyk M D 302 261-6343
4515 Griffin Dr Wilmington (19808) *(G-15811)*

David Saunders General Contrs 302 998-0056
1204 E Willow Run Dr Wilmington (19805) *(G-15812)*

David T Springer MD 302 477-1830
1228 Gilbert Ave Wilmington (19808) *(G-15813)*

David V Martini MD 302 945-9730
32711 Long Neck Rd Millsboro (19966) *(G-8257)*

David W West M D 302 651-4317
1701 Rockland Rd Wilmington (19803) *(G-15814)*

Davidson Lane LLC 302 326-1540
761 Grantham Ln New Castle (19720) *(G-9001)*

Davin Management Group LLC 302 367-6563
808 Jeffrey Pine Dr Bear (19701) *(G-135)*

Davis Bowen & Friedel Inc 302 424-1441
1 Park Ave Milford (19963) *(G-7847)*

Davis & Yoder Contracting Serv 302 369-8888
9 Cartier Ct Newark (19711) *(G-10392)*

Davis A Scott 302 535-0570
57 Snowdrift Cir Magnolia (19962) *(G-6738)*

Davis Index Inc 732 659-0456
919 N Market St Ste 950 Wilmington (19801) *(G-15815)*

Davis Insurance Group Inc 302 652-4700
Rte 100 And Rockland Rd Montchanin (19710) *(G-8737)*

Davis Lock and Safe LLC 302 628-5397
9758 Warrens Way Seaford (19973) *(G-13146)*

Davis Samuel F Jr Gen Contr 302 475-2607
2100 Brandywood Dr Wilmington (19810) *(G-15816)*

Davis Services 302 792-1754
3 N Avon Dr Claymont (19703) *(G-1110)*

Davis Trucking, Frankford *Also Called: Davis Trucking & Family LLC (G-4099)*
Davis Trucking & Family LLC 302 381-6358
22181 Charles West Rd Frankford (19945) *(G-4099)*
Davis Welding Service Llc 302 465-3004
26075 River Rd Seaford (19973) *(G-13147)*
Davis-Young Associates Inc (PA) 610 388-0932
2896 Creek Rd Yorklyn (19736) *(G-20991)*
Davitron LLC 302 239-1383
20 Longacre Ct Hockessin (19707) *(G-5176)*
Dawn Arrow Inc 302 328-9695
602 Brant Ave New Castle (19720) *(G-9002)*
Dawn L Conly 302 378-1890
266 Bucktail Dr Middletown (19709) *(G-7031)*
Dawn Mc Kenzie Dvm 302 521-8206
3052 Wrangle Hill Rd Bear (19701) *(G-136)*
Dawn Runs With Scissors 302 293-4517
1600 Delaware Ave Wilmington (19806) *(G-15817)*
Dawn Somer Fitness 229 325-9173
706 Worcester Ave Middletown (19709) *(G-7032)*
Dawn US Holdings LLC 619 322-2799
251 Little Falls Dr Wilmington (19808) *(G-15818)*
Dawson Bedsworth Elec Contrs 302 854-0210
19291 County Seat Hwy Georgetown (19947) *(G-4275)*
Dawson Bus Service Inc (PA) 302 697-9501
405 E Camden Wyoming Ave Camden (19934) *(G-814)*
Day 1 Motel 302 397-8412
5029 Governor Printz Blvd Wilmington (19809) *(G-15819)*
Day By Day Calendars 302 477-1763
4737 Concord Pike Wilmington (19803) *(G-15820)*
Day School For Children 302 652-4651
3071 New Castle Ave New Castle (19720) *(G-9003)*
Day Town Pack House, Newark *Also Called: Baytown Packhouse Inc (G-9998)*
Daypainters LLC 302 415-3365
214 S Ford Ave Wilmington (19805) *(G-15821)*
Days Inn, Dover *Also Called: Days Inn Dover Downtown (G-2200)*
Days Inn, New Castle *Also Called: Jay Ambe Inc (G-9254)*
Days Inn, Seaford *Also Called: Days Inn and Suites Seaford (G-13148)*
Days Inn and Suites Seaford 302 629-4300
23450 Sussex Hwy Seaford (19973) *(G-13148)*
Days Inn Dover Downtown 302 674-8002
272 N Dupont Hwy Dover (19901) *(G-2200)*
Days Inn Wilmington, Wilmington *Also Called: Dipna Inc (G-16076)*
Days of Knights 302 366-0963
173 E Main St Lowr Newark (19711) *(G-10393)*
Dayshape Corp (PA) 929 512-5582
874 Walker Rd Ste C Dover (19904) *(G-2201)*
Daystar Sills Inc 302 633-1421
330 Water St Ste 1 Wilmington (19804) *(G-15822)*
DBA Heating Parts Hub 302 381-3705
6953 Hickman Rd Greenwood (19950) *(G-4612)*
Dbaza Inc 302 467-3081
614 N Dupont Hwy Ste 210 Dover (19901) *(G-2202)*
Dbd Maangment, Wilmington *Also Called: Edward B De Seta & Associates (G-16301)*
Dbeaver Corporation 347 809-3202
1000 N West St Ste 1200 Wilmington (19801) *(G-15823)*
Dbot, Wilmington *Also Called: Delaware Bd Trade Holdings Inc (G-15871)*
Dbw Tax Services 302 276-0428
222 Guilford St Bear (19701) *(G-137)*
DC Chambers Construction LLC 302 233-0148
1054 Paradise Alley Rd Felton (19943) *(G-3957)*
DC Consulting Service LLC 617 594-9780
3422 Old Capitol Trl Ste 700 Wilmington (19808) *(G-15824)*
DC Mac 302 660-3350
1 Ave Of The Arts Wilmington (19801) *(G-15825)*
DC Printing Inc 302 545-6666
2305 Pennsylvania Ave Wilmington (19806) *(G-15826)*
DCB Apparel LLC 267 473-0895
5 Rudloff Ct Newark (19702) *(G-10394)*
Dcc Design Group LLC 302 777-2100
2 Mill Rd Ste 103 Wilmington (19806) *(G-15827)*
Dcc Inc 302 750-1207
2639 Grendon Dr Wilmington (19808) *(G-15828)*

DCCA, Wilmington *Also Called: Delaware Ctr For Cntmprary Art (G-15895)*
DCH, Wilmington *Also Called: Delaware Ctr For Hrtclture Inc (G-15898)*
Dchv, Wilmington *Also Called: Delaware Ctr For Hmless Vtrans (G-15896)*
Dcmfm At Christiana Care 302 543-7543
1 Centurian Dr Ste 312 Newark (19713) *(G-10395)*
Dcoder Inc 716 638-0426
251 Little Falls Dr Wilmington (19808) *(G-15829)*
Dcor 302 227-9341
37545 Atlantic Ave Rehoboth Beach (19971) *(G-12712)*
Dcrac 302 298-3289
600 S Harrison St Wilmington (19805) *(G-15830)*
Dct 302 420-6350
230 E Seneca Dr Newark (19702) *(G-10396)*
Dd & E Investment Group Inc 302 319-2780
1000 N. Street Wilmington (19801) *(G-15831)*
Dd Inc De LLC 302 669-9269
907 Providence Ave Claymont (19703) *(G-1111)*
Dd Snacks LLC 302 652-3850
230 Alban Dr Wilmington (19805) *(G-15832)*
DD&k Logistics LLC 301 523-5984
318 Sunnyside Ln Townsend (19734) *(G-13986)*
Ddesk LLC 302 407-1558
501 Silverside Rd Ste 105 Wilmington (19809) *(G-15833)*
Ddh (north America) Inc 617 893-9004
1100 Louisiana St Ste 2750 Lewes (19958) *(G-5884)*
Ddh Advanced Mtls Systems Inc 515 441-1313
625 Dawson Dr Ste B Newark (19713) *(G-10397)*
Ddk 302 999-1132
3825 Lancaster Pike Wilmington (19805) *(G-15834)*
Ddp Spclty Elctrnc Mtls US 9 (DH) 302 774-1000
974 Centre Rd Wilmington (19805) *(G-15835)*
Dduberry LLC 703 798-5280
200 Continental Dr Ste 401 Newark (19713) *(G-10398)*
Ddx3x Foundation 917 796-3514
322 A St Ste 300 Wilmington (19801) *(G-15836)*
De Alcoholic Beverage Whl Assn 302 356-3500
411 Churchmans Rd New Castle (19720) *(G-9004)*
De Atlantic Elevator, Dagsboro *Also Called: Atlantic Elevators (G-1414)*
De Catering Inc 302 607-7200
913 Brandywine Blvd Wilmington (19809) *(G-15837)*
De Cheaper Trash LLC 302 325-0670
22 Mark Dr New Castle (19720) *(G-9005)*
De Colores Family Child Care 302 883-3298
917 Monroe Ter Dover (19904) *(G-2203)*
De Express Inc 302 387-7178
334 W Pembrooke Dr Smyrna (19977) *(G-13693)*
De Homecare, Wilmington *Also Called: Maxim Healthcare Services Inc (G-18205)*
De Medical Care 302 653-1281
51 Deak Dr Smyrna (19977) *(G-13694)*
De Neurology Group 302 893-5301
708 Greenbank Rd Wilmington (19808) *(G-15838)*
De Novo Corporation (PA) 302 234-7407
1011 Centre Rd Ste 104 Wilmington (19805) *(G-15839)*
De Novo Foods Inc (PA) 302 613-1351
2093 Philadelphia Pike # 9 Claymont (19703) *(G-1112)*
De Property Maintenance LLC 302 241-5567
110 W Green St Middletown (19709) *(G-7033)*
De Sales and Service 302 456-1660
1210 Janice Dr Newark (19713) *(G-10399)*
De Sleep Disorder Centers LLC 302 697-2749
2116 S Dupont Hwy Ste 3 Camden (19934) *(G-815)*
De Turf Sports Complex 302 330-8873
4000 Bay Rd Frederica (19946) *(G-4164)*
De Turf Sports Complex, Frederica *Also Called: Kent Cnty Rgnal Spt Cmplex Cor (G-4175)*
De Val Structurez 302 575-9090
3329 Coachman Rd Unit B Wilmington (19803) *(G-15840)*
De Wild Cheer and Tumble LLC 302 438-7740
416 E Ayre St Wilmington (19804) *(G-15841)*
De-Infnty All Star Cheer Tmble 302 383-0945
6 N Clifton Ave Wilmington (19805) *(G-15842)*
De/RE Investment Group 302 450-6202
452 Greens Branch Ln Smyrna (19977) *(G-13695)*

ALPHABETIC SECTION — Del Mar Onsite Solutions

Deact Medical Solutions Inc 302 354-6575
 827 Jasmine Dr Wilmington (19808) *(G-15843)*

Dead On Construction 302 462-5023
 Selbyville (19975) *(G-13516)*

Deadcow Computers 302 239-5974
 14 Deer Track Ln Newark (19711) *(G-10400)*

Deafinitions & Interpreting 302 563-7714
 1148 Pulaski Hwy Ste 236 Bear (19701) *(G-138)*

Dealer Automation Services LLC 305 803-3201
 1007 N Market St Wilmington (19801) *(G-15844)*

Deall LLC 305 790-0109
 8 The Grn Dover (19901) *(G-2204)*

Deals On Wheels Inc (PA) 302 999-9955
 1220 Centerville Rd Wilmington (19808) *(G-15845)*

Deals On Wheels Used Cars, Wilmington *Also Called: Deals On Wheels Inc (G-15845)*

Dean A Aman Lpcmh LLC 302 858-3324
 260 Chapman Rd Ste 205c Newark (19702) *(G-10401)*

Dean Digital Imaging Inc 302 655-6992
 2 S Poplar St Ste B Wilmington (19801) *(G-15846)*

Deanne Naples Family Daycare 302 376-1408
 225 Manchester Way Middletown (19709) *(G-7034)*

Deans Bus Service Inc 302 335-5095
 1891 Fork Landing Rd Milford (19963) *(G-7848)*

Dearng Safety Office 302 326-7100
 1 Vavala Way New Castle (19720) *(G-9006)*

Deaton McCue & Co Inc 302 658-7789
 724 Yorklyn Rd Hockessin (19707) *(G-5177)*

Deauthorized Inc (PA) 512 769-3026
 2035 Sunset Lake Rd B2 Newark (19702) *(G-10402)*

Deaven Development Corp 302 994-5793
 1615 E Ayre St Wilmington (19804) *(G-15847)*

Deballi Distinctive Properties 302 376-1113
 1126 Pulaski Hwy Bear (19701) *(G-139)*

Debay Surgical Service 302 644-4954
 33664 Bayview Medical Dr Lewes (19958) *(G-5885)*

Debbie Brittingham - Coldwell 302 745-1886
 22350 Sussex Hwy Seaford (19973) *(G-13149)*

Debbie D Takats Rn 302 737-4552
 110 Elma Dr Newark (19711) *(G-10403)*

Debbie Reed 302 227-3818
 319 Rehoboth Ave Rehoboth Beach (19971) *(G-12713)*

Debora Reed Team 302 227-3818
 319 Rehoboth Ave Rehoboth Beach (19971) *(G-12714)*

Deborah Kirk 302 653-6022
 100 S Main St Ste 205 Smyrna (19977) *(G-13696)*

Deborah L Wayland 443 669-3106
 603 Sussex Ct Bethany Beach (19930) *(G-594)*

Deborra M Trres Msn Pmhnp Ltd 609 500-4018
 32853 Circle Dr Millsboro (19966) *(G-8258)*

Debra McAfee 302 655-7999
 2323 N Dupont Hwy New Castle (19720) *(G-9007)*

Debra Rose 302 519-3029
 506 Union St Milton (19968) *(G-8596)*

Dec Home Services 240 793-4818
 37116 Hudson Rd Selbyville (19975) *(G-13517)*

Decalgirl.com, Rehoboth Beach *Also Called: Skinify LLC (G-12962)*

Decennium Management Group 302 600-3644
 8 The Grn Ste 4738 Dover (19901) *(G-2205)*

Decg, Wilmington *Also Called: Delaware Counsel Group LLP (G-15894)*

Decisionrx Inc 800 957-3606
 8 The Grn Ste A Dover (19901) *(G-2206)*

Decisivedge LLC (PA) 302 299-1570
 131 Continental Dr Ste 409 Newark (19713) *(G-10404)*

Deck Masters LLC 302 563-4459
 123 S Clifton Ave Wilmington (19805) *(G-15848)*

Deckrobot Inc 617 765-7494
 300 Delaware Ave Ste 210 Wilmington (19801) *(G-15849)*

Deco Crete Inc 302 367-0151
 550 S Dupont Hwy New Castle (19720) *(G-9008)*

Deco Engineering Corp 302 576-6564
 1201 N Orange St Wilmington (19801) *(G-15850)*

Decoded USA, Wilmington *Also Called: Advanced Defense Technology (G-14273)*

Decoryoucrazy 302 357-8175
 220 W 35th St Wilmington (19802) *(G-15851)*

Dedc LLC 302 738-7172
 315 S Chapel St Newark (19711) *(G-10405)*

Dedicated and Driven Hlg LLC 404 909-6031
 14 Tarcote Ct Newark (19702) *(G-10406)*

Dedicated To Home Care LLC 484 470-5013
 2 Yorktown Rd New Castle (19720) *(G-9009)*

Dedicated To Women Obgyn 302 285-5545
 209 E Main St Middletown (19709) *(G-7035)*

Dedicted Fibr Cmmnications LLC 302 416-3088
 913 N Market St Ste 200 Wilmington (19801) *(G-15852)*

Dedo Ventures & Health Inc 302 838-1445
 26 Forsythia Ln Bear (19701) *(G-140)*

Dee & Doreens Team 302 677-0030
 1671 S State St Dover (19901) *(G-2207)*

Dee's Cleaning Service, Georgetown *Also Called: Delores Welch (G-4291)*

Deep Muscle Therapy Center Del 302 397-8073
 5700 Kirkwood Hwy Ste 206 Wilmington (19808) *(G-15853)*

Deepen Inc 813 813-9053
 651 N Broad St Ste 201 Middletown (19709) *(G-7036)*

Deeps On Massage, Wilmington *Also Called: Deep Muscle Therapy Center Del (G-15853)*

Deeptrace Inc 424 413-8787
 16192 Coastal Hwy Lewes (19958) *(G-5886)*

Deer Client Hair Salon 302 983-3353
 116 Astro Shopping Ctr Newark (19711) *(G-10407)*

Deerborne Woods Sales Center, Wilmington *Also Called: Handler Builders Inc (G-17046)*

Dees Learning Care 908 623-7685
 128 Auckland Dr Newark (19702) *(G-10408)*

Defa Inc 302 219-5994
 108 W 13th St Wilmington (19801) *(G-15854)*

Defendant Data Solutions LLC 302 440-3042
 1007 N Orange St Fl 4 Wilmington (19801) *(G-15855)*

Defy Technologies Inc 732 213-7165
 251 Little Falls Dr Wilmington (19808) *(G-15856)*

Defy Therapy Services LLC 302 290-9562
 2213 Beaumont Rd Wilmington (19803) *(G-15857)*

Degussa International Inc 302 731-9250
 220 Continental Dr Ste 204 Newark (19713) *(G-10409)*

Dehui Solar Power Inc 864 326-7936
 9 E Loockerman St Ste 311 Dover (19901) *(G-2208)*

Dehumidification Tech LP 317 228-2000
 1 Limousine Dr Wilmington (19803) *(G-15858)*

Dejour Reign CL & AP Co LLC 302 981-2568
 107 Hillview Ave New Castle (19720) *(G-9010)*

Del Bay Charter Fishing LLC 302 542-1930
 23602 Harvest Run Reach Milton (19968) *(G-8597)*

Del Campo Plumbing & Heating 302 998-3648
 2429 Hartley Pl Wilmington (19808) *(G-15859)*

Del Coast Exterior LLC 302 752-6678
 16732 Seashore Hwy Georgetown (19947) *(G-4276)*

Del Coast Exteriors 302 236-5738
 21825 Zoar Rd Georgetown (19947) *(G-4277)*

Del Coast Exteriors 302 542-8979
 35430 Sussex Ln Millsboro (19966) *(G-8259)*

Del DOT Canal Dist 410 742-9361
 800 S Bay Rd Ste 1 Dover (19901) *(G-2209)*

Del Fab Construction LLC 302 943-9131
 2373 Harvey Straughn Rd Clayton (19938) *(G-1359)*

Del Hardbat LLC 484 256-0465
 70 Aleph Dr Ste B Newark (19702) *(G-10410)*

Del Haven of Wilmington Inc 302 999-9040
 152 Kane Dr Newark (19702) *(G-10411)*

Del Homes Inc 302 730-1479
 1567 Mckee Rd Dover (19904) *(G-2210)*

Del Homes Inc (PA) 302 697-8204
 1309 Ponderosa Dr Magnolia (19962) *(G-6739)*

Del Lawn Service 302 525-4148
 5 Matthews Rd Newark (19713) *(G-10412)*

Del Mar Onsite Solutions 302 629-2568
 5635 Neals School Rd Seaford (19973) *(G-13150)*

Del Marva Hand Specialists LLC... 302 644-0940
701 Savannah Rd Ste B Lewes (19958) *(G-5887)*

Del Premier Care Inc... 302 533-5988
630 Churchmans Rd Ste 107 Newark (19702) *(G-10413)*

Del Ray Foundatins LLC.. 302 272-6153
48 Goosebriar Ln Milford (19963) *(G-7849)*

Del-Charter Associates LP... 302 325-1111
200 Continental Dr # 200 Newark (19713) *(G-10414)*

Del-Mar Appliance, Dover Also Called: Del-Mar Appliance of Delaware *(G-2211)*

Del-Mar Appliance of Delaware (PA).. 302 674-2414
230 S Governors Ave Dover (19904) *(G-2211)*

Del-Mr-Va Cncil Inc Boy Scuts (PA)... 302 622-3300
1910 Baden Powell Way Dover (19904) *(G-2212)*

Del-One Federal Credit Union.. 302 739-2390
150 E Water St Ste 1 Dover (19901) *(G-2213)*

Del-One Federal Credit Union (PA)... 302 734-4496
270 Beiser Blvd Dover (19904) *(G-2214)*

Del-One Federal Credit Union.. 302 424-2969
100 Credit Union Way Milford (19963) *(G-7850)*

Del-One Federal Credit Union.. 302 739-4496
201 Pharmacy Dr Smyrna (19977) *(G-13697)*

Del-One Federal Credit Union.. 302 577-2667
824 N Market St Ste 104 Wilmington (19801) *(G-15860)*

Del-State Cleaning Services... 302 563-0606
41 Rockwood Blvd Felton (19943) *(G-3958)*

Dela Belle Inv Group Corp... 901 279-2742
651 N Broad St Ste 205 Middletown (19709) *(G-7037)*

Delasoft Inc.. 302 533-7912
92 Reads Way Ste 204 New Castle (19720) *(G-9011)*

Delave Denim Co LLC (PA).. 302 308-5161
8 The Grn Ste 4000 Dover (19901) *(G-2215)*

Delaw Back Pain and, Newark Also Called: Delaware Back Pain and Sports *(G-10419)*

Delaware 4 Sniors Homecare LLC.. 302 386-8080
1000 N West St Ste 1200 Wilmington (19801) *(G-15861)*

Delaware Acdemy Pub Safety SEC.. 302 377-1465
179 Stanton Christiana Road New Castle (19720) *(G-9012)*

Delaware Adlescent Program Inc.. 302 531-0257
185 South St Camden (19934) *(G-816)*

Delaware Adlescent Program Inc (PA)... 302 268-7218
1901 S College Ave Newark (19702) *(G-10415)*

Delaware Advanced Vein Center... 302 737-0857
40 Omega Dr Bldg G Newark (19713) *(G-10416)*

Delaware AG Museum Assn... 302 734-1618
866 N Dupont Hwy Dover (19901) *(G-2216)*

Delaware All-State Theatre.. 302 559-6667
2208 Van Buren Pl Wilmington (19802) *(G-15862)*

Delaware Alnce Agnst Sxual Vln.. 302 468-7731
405 Foulk Rd Wilmington (19803) *(G-15863)*

Delaware American Lf Insur Co... 302 594-2871
600 N King St Wilmington (19801) *(G-15864)*

Delaware Animal Products LLC.. 302 423-7754
662 Log Cabin Rd Milford (19963) *(G-7851)*

Delaware Apartment Association.. 302 998-0322
1627 New Jersey Ave New Castle (19720) *(G-9013)*

Delaware Apartment Association.. 617 680-3463
240 N James St Ste 208 Wilmington (19804) *(G-15865)*

Delaware Architects LLC... 302 491-6047
16558 Retreat Cir Milford (19963) *(G-7852)*

Delaware Art Museum Inc... 302 571-9590
2301 Kentmere Pkwy Wilmington (19806) *(G-15866)*

Delaware Arthritis.. 302 644-2633
20268 Plantations Rd Lewes (19958) *(G-5888)*

Delaware Arts Conservatory.. 302 595-4160
723 Rue Madora Ste 4 Bear (19701) *(G-141)*

Delaware Assistive Care, Wilmington Also Called: Bayada Home Health Care Inc *(G-14784)*

Delaware Assn For The Edcatn Y.. 302 764-1500
2004 Foulk Rd Ste 6 Wilmington (19810) *(G-15867)*

Delaware Association For Blind (PA)... 302 998-5913
2915 Newport Gap Pike Wilmington (19808) *(G-15868)*

Delaware Auto Glass... 302 709-2300
810 Pencader Dr Unit A Newark (19702) *(G-10417)*

Delaware Auto Salvage Inc... 302 322-2328
155 Hay Rd Wilmington (19809) *(G-15869)*

Delaware Ave Wealth Planners.. 302 254-2400
1831 Delaware Ave Wilmington (19806) *(G-15870)*

Delaware Back Pain & Sports... 302 733-0980
87 Omega Dr Newark (19713) *(G-10418)*

Delaware Back Pain and Sports... 302 832-3369
2600 Glasgow Ave Ste 210 Newark (19702) *(G-10419)*

Delaware Bail Bonds... 302 734-9881
414 Denison St Dover (19901) *(G-2217)*

Delaware Barter Corp.. 800 343-1322
4 Mill Park Ct # F Newark (19713) *(G-10420)*

Delaware Bay & River.. 302 645-7861
700 Pilottown Rd Lewes (19958) *(G-5889)*

Delaware Bay Launch Service... 302 422-7604
100 Passwaters Dr Milford (19963) *(G-7853)*

Delaware Bay Surgical Svc PA.. 302 645-5650
33664 Bayview Medical Dr Ste 2 Lewes (19958) *(G-5890)*

Delaware Bd Trade Holdings Inc.. 302 298-0600
1313 N Market St Fl 8 Wilmington (19801) *(G-15871)*

Delaware Beach Book LLC... 302 249-1030
19401 Hunter Dr Milton (19968) *(G-8598)*

Delaware Beach Life... 302 227-9499
37587 Bay Harbor Dr Rehoboth Beach (19971) *(G-12715)*

Delaware Beach Storage Center... 302 644-7774
333 Market St Lewes (19958) *(G-5891)*

Delaware Beaches Jellystone Pk.. 302 491-4531
22444 Holly Branch Way Lincoln (19960) *(G-6662)*

Delaware Beer Works Inc... 302 836-2739
219 Governors Pl Bear (19701) *(G-142)*

Delaware Behavioral Health.. 302 397-8958
240 N James St Wilmington (19804) *(G-15872)*

Delaware Bioscience Assn.. 302 635-0445
2110 Concord Pike Wilmington (19803) *(G-15873)*

Delaware Blue Claws... 302 674-1123
354 Main St Leipsic (19901) *(G-5630)*

Delaware Boots On Ground.. 302 326-7789
Wilmington (19808) *(G-15874)*

Delaware Botanic Gardens Inc.. 202 262-9501
201 Ashwood St Bethany Beach (19930) *(G-595)*

Delaware Braces LLC... 302 365-5971
2444 Pulaski Hwy Ste 200 Newark (19702) *(G-10421)*

Delaware Brast Cncer Cltion In (PA)... 302 778-1102
100 W 10th St Ste 209 Wilmington (19801) *(G-15875)*

Delaware Brast Cncer Coalition, Dover Also Called: Delaware Breast Cancer Coalit *(G-2218)*

Delaware Breast Cancer Coalit... 302 672-6435
165 Commerce Way Ste 2 Dover (19904) *(G-2218)*

Delaware Brick Co, Wilmington Also Called: Delaware Brick Company *(G-15876)*

Delaware Brick Company.. 302 883-2807
492 Webbs Ln Dover (19904) *(G-2219)*

Delaware Brick Company (PA)... 302 994-0948
1114 Centerville Rd Wilmington (19804) *(G-15876)*

Delaware Building Supply Corp... 302 424-3505
141 Mullet Run Milford (19963) *(G-7854)*

Delaware Bus Incorporators Inc.. 302 996-5819
3422 Old Capitol Trl Ste 700 Wilmington (19808) *(G-15877)*

Delaware Bus Leadership Netwrk.. 302 314-5070
13 Reads Way Ste 101 New Castle (19720) *(G-9014)*

Delaware Business Systems Inc... 302 395-0900
191 Airport Rd New Castle (19720) *(G-9015)*

Delaware Capital Formation Inc (HQ)... 302 793-4921
501 Silverside Rd Ste 5 Wilmington (19809) *(G-15878)*

Delaware Capital Holdings Inc (DH).. 302 793-4921
501 Silverside Rd Ste 5 Wilmington (19809) *(G-15879)*

Delaware Car Company.. 302 655-6665
Second & Lombard St Wilmington (19801) *(G-15880)*

Delaware Care Collaboration... 302 575-8371
701 N Clayton St Wilmington (19805) *(G-15881)*

Delaware Center For Cnselng... 302 353-7052
262 Chapman Rd Ste 100 Newark (19702) *(G-10422)*

Delaware Center For Counseling.. 302 292-1334
262 Chapman Rd Ste 100 Newark (19702) *(G-10423)*

ALPHABETIC SECTION

Delaware Dept Hlth Social Svcs

Delaware Center For Digestive... 302 565-6596
   537 Stanton Christiana Rd Ste 203 Newark (19713) *(G-10424)*

Delaware Center For Justice... 302 658-7174
   100 W 10th St Ste 905 Wilmington (19801) *(G-15882)*

Delaware Center For Maternal, Newark *Also Called: Delaware Ctr For Mtrnal Ftal M (G-10430)*

Delaware Chapter, Wilmington *Also Called: March of Dimes Inc (G-18121)*

Delaware Charms.. 302 480-4951
   206 Richard Bassett Rd Dover (19904) *(G-2220)*

Delaware Chemical Corporation... 302 427-8752
   1105 N Market St Ste 1300 Wilmington (19801) *(G-15883)*

Delaware Chpter of The Amrcn A.. 302 218-1075
   4765 Ogletown Stanton Rd Ste L10 Newark (19713) *(G-10425)*

Delaware City Fire Co No 1... 302 834-9336
   815 5th St Delaware City (19706) *(G-1536)*

Delaware City Recreation Club... 302 834-9900
   5th And Wahington Delaware City (19706) *(G-1537)*

Delaware City Refining Co LLC... 302 834-6000
   4550 Wrangle Hill Rd New Castle (19720) *(G-9016)*

Delaware Claims Proc Fcilty.. 302 427-8913
   1007 N Orange St Fl 1 Wilmington (19801) *(G-15884)*

Delaware Clncal Lab Physcans P (PA)................................... 302 737-7700
   4701 Ogletown Stanton Rd Ste 4200 Newark (19713) *(G-10426)*

Delaware Cltion Agnst Dom Vlnc.. 302 658-2958
   100 W 10th St Ste 903 Wilmington (19801) *(G-15885)*

Delaware Cmnty Rnvstment Actio... 302 298-3250
   600 S Harrison St Wilmington (19805) *(G-15886)*

Delaware Cnnbis Advcacy Ntwrk.. 302 404-4208
   438 S State St Dover (19901) *(G-2221)*

Delaware Coast Line RR Co (PA)... 302 422-9200
   8266 N Union Church Rd Milford (19963) *(G-7855)*

Delaware Coastal Anesthesia LL.. 302 275-5777
   100 Scull Ter Dover (19901) *(G-2222)*

Delaware Cobras Inc.. 302 983-3500
   122 Honora Dr Bear (19701) *(G-143)*

Delaware College Scholars Inc... 302 437-6144
   4 E 8th St Wilmington (19801) *(G-15887)*

Delaware Colon Hydrotherapy.. 302 543-5717
   6 Larch Ave Wilmington (19804) *(G-15888)*

Delaware Color Lab.. 302 529-1339
   2107 Naamans Rd Wilmington (19810) *(G-15889)*

Delaware Community Foundation (PA).................................. 302 571-8004
   100 W 10th St Ste 115 Wilmington (19801) *(G-15890)*

Delaware Community Inv Corp... 302 655-1420
   100 W 10th St Ste 303 Wilmington (19801) *(G-15891)*

Delaware Company House LLC... 302 526-4784
   8 The Grn Ste R Dover (19901) *(G-2223)*

Delaware Con Fndtons Slabs LLC... 302 945-1223
   31241 Barnacle Blvd Millsboro (19966) *(G-8260)*

Delaware Concrete Coatings... 302 864-4014
   17569 Nassau Commons Blvd Lewes (19958) *(G-5892)*

Delaware Concrete Specialists... 302 507-3038
   26 Kenmar Dr Newark (19713) *(G-10427)*

Delaware Constructionology.. 302 827-3072
   314 White Pine Dr Middletown (19709) *(G-7038)*

Delaware Consulting Servi.. 302 945-7936
   19082 Robinsonville Rd Lewes (19958) *(G-5893)*

Delaware Corporate Center... 302 690-3789
   2 Righter Pkwy Wilmington (19803) *(G-15892)*

Delaware Corporate Registry.. 302 655-6500
   15 Center Meeting Rd Wilmington (19807) *(G-15893)*

Delaware Counsel Group LLP... 302 543-4870
   100 S Rockland Falls Rd Rockland (19732) *(G-13030)*

Delaware Counsel Group LLP (PA)....................................... 302 576-9600
   2 Mill Rd Ste 108 Wilmington (19806) *(G-15894)*

Delaware CPA Services, Georgetown *Also Called: Delaware CPA-Pac Inc (G-4278)*

Delaware CPA-Pac Inc.. 302 854-0133
   216 W Market St Unit A Georgetown (19947) *(G-4278)*

Delaware Crawl Space Co Inc.. 302 930-0386
   37101 Suzanne Ln Lewes (19958) *(G-5894)*

Delaware Crdovascular Assoc PA... 302 734-7676
   1113 S State St Ste 100 Dover (19901) *(G-2224)*

Delaware Crdovascular Assoc PA... 302 235-4100
   5936 Limestone Rd Hockessin (19707) *(G-5178)*

Delaware Crdovascular Assoc PA... 302 644-7676
   34453 King Street Row Lewes (19958) *(G-5895)*

Delaware Crdovascular Assoc PA... 302 993-7676
   537 Stanton Christiana Rd Ste 105 Newark (19713) *(G-10428)*

Delaware Credit Union Leag Inc... 302 322-9341
   262 Chapman Rd Ste 101 Newark (19702) *(G-10429)*

Delaware Ctr For Cntmprary Art... 302 656-6466
   200 S Madison St Wilmington (19801) *(G-15895)*

Delaware Ctr For Hmless Vtrans.. 302 384-2350
   10 Birch Knoll Rd Wilmington (19810) *(G-15896)*

Delaware Ctr For Hmless Vtrans.. 302 898-2647
   1405 Veale Rd Wilmington (19810) *(G-15897)*

Delaware Ctr For Hrtclture Inc.. 302 658-6262
   1810 N Dupont St Wilmington (19806) *(G-15898)*

Delaware Ctr For Mtrnal Ftal M... 302 319-5680
   1 Centurian Dr Ste 312 Newark (19713) *(G-10430)*

Delaware Curative.. 302 836-5670
   609 Governors Pl Bear (19701) *(G-144)*

Delaware Curative, Wilmington *Also Called: Delaware Curative Workshop (G-15899)*

Delaware Curative Workshop (PA)... 302 656-2521
   1600 N Washington St Wilmington (19802) *(G-15899)*

Delaware Custom Tile.. 302 841-9215
   125b Beach Plum Pl Lewes (19958) *(G-5896)*

Delaware Cy Vlntr Fire Co No 1... 302 834-9336
   815 5th St Delaware City (19706) *(G-1538)*

Delaware Dance Center... 302 229-9334
   11 Foxtail Ct Newark (19711) *(G-10431)*

Delaware Dance Center Inc.. 302 454-1440
   4751 Shopp Of Lindenhill Rd Wilmington (19808) *(G-15900)*

Delaware Dance Company Inc... 302 738-2023
   168 S Main St Ste 101 Newark (19711) *(G-10432)*

Delaware Day Treatment, Dover *Also Called: Catholic Charities Inc (G-2039)*

Delaware Deadly Weapons... 302 736-5159
   861 Silver Lake Blvd Ste 203 Dover (19904) *(G-2225)*

Delaware Dental Care Centers... 410 474-5520
   73 Greentree Dr 407 Dover (19904) *(G-2226)*

Delaware Dental Solutions LLC.. 302 409-3050
   131 Becks Woods Dr Bear (19701) *(G-145)*

Delaware Dental Studio LLC... 302 475-0600
   2500 Grubb Rd Wilmington (19810) *(G-15901)*

Delaware Department Correction... 302 856-5280
   23203 Dupont Blvd Georgetown (19947) *(G-4279)*

Delaware Department Finance... 302 739-5291
   1575 Mckee Rd Ste 102 Dover (19904) *(G-2227)*

Delaware Department Trnsp... 302 326-8950
   250 Bear Christiana Rd Bear (19701) *(G-146)*

Delaware Department Trnsp... 302 577-3278
   655 S Bay Rd Ste 4g Dover (19901) *(G-2228)*

Delaware Department Trnsp... 302 653-4128
   5369 Summit Bridge Rd Middletown (19709) *(G-7039)*

Delaware Department Trnsp... 302 658-8960
   119 Lower Beech St Ste 100 Wilmington (19805) *(G-15902)*

Delaware Depository Svc Co LLC.. 302 762-2635
   3601 N Market St Wilmington (19802) *(G-15903)*

Delaware Dept Hlth Social Svcs... 302 337-8261
   400 Mill St Bridgeville (19933) *(G-691)*

Delaware Dept Hlth Social Svcs... 302 857-5000
   805 River Rd Dover (19901) *(G-2229)*

Delaware Dept Hlth Social Svcs... 302 255-9500
   410 Federal St Ste 7 Dover (19901) *(G-2230)*

Delaware Dept Hlth Social Svcs... 302 856-5586
   20105 Office Cir Georgetown (19947) *(G-4280)*

Delaware Dept Hlth Social Svcs... 302 255-9855
   1901 N Dupont Hwy New Castle (19720) *(G-9017)*

Delaware Dept Hlth Social Svcs... 302 255-2700
   1901 N Dupont Hwy New Castle (19720) *(G-9018)*

Delaware Dept Hlth Social Svcs... 302 255-2700
   1901 N Dupont Hwy Fl 1 New Castle (19720) *(G-9019)*

Delaware Dept Hlth Social Svcs... 302 255-9800
   1901 N Dupont Hwy New Castle (19720) *(G-9020)*

Delaware Dept Hlth Social Svcs 302 391-3505
 1901 N Dupont Hwy Annex Entrance New Castle (19720) *(G-9021)*

Delaware Dept Hlth Social Svcs 302 368-6700
 501 Ogletown Rd Newark (19711) *(G-10433)*

Delaware Dept Hlth Social Svcs 302 283-7500
 501 Ogletown Rd 3rd Fl Newark (19711) *(G-10434)*

Delaware Dept Hlth Social Svcs 302 223-1000
 100 Sunnyside Rd Smyrna (19977) *(G-13698)*

Delaware Dermatolgy PA 302 736-1800
 737 S Queen St Ste 1 Dover (19904) *(G-2231)*

Delaware Dermatologic 302 593-8625
 14 Alders Ln Wilmington (19807) *(G-15904)*

Delaware Design Company 302 737-9700
 29 S Old Baltimore Pike Newark (19702) *(G-10435)*

Delaware Diagnostic Group LLC 302 472-5555
 2060 Limestone Rd Wilmington (19808) *(G-15905)*

Delaware Diagnostic Labs LLC 302 407-5903
 1 Centurian Dr Ste 103 Newark (19713) *(G-10436)*

Delaware Diamond Knives Inc 302 999-7476
 3825 Lancaster Pike Ste 200 Wilmington (19805) *(G-15906)*

Delaware Digital Media LLC 302 278-8080
 32895 Coastal Hwy Unit 201b Bethany Beach (19930) *(G-596)*

Delaware Digital Video Facc 302 888-2737
 1709 Concord Pike Wilmington (19803) *(G-15907)*

Delaware Direct Inc 302 658-8223
 220 Valley Rd Wilmington (19804) *(G-15908)*

Delaware Div Hstrcal Cltral AF (DH) 302 736-7400
 21 The Grn Dover (19901) *(G-2232)*

Delaware Div Parks Recreation 302 571-7788
 1001 N Park Dr Wilmington (19802) *(G-15909)*

Delaware Div Parks Recreation 302 761-6963
 800 Carr Rd Wilmington (19809) *(G-15910)*

Delaware Diy LLC 302 318-8007
 110 Peoples Plz Newark (19702) *(G-10437)*

Delaware Dnce Edcatn Orgnztion 302 897-6345
 208 Oakwood Rd Wilmington (19803) *(G-15911)*

Delaware Document Retrieval, Dover *Also Called: Parcels Inc (G-3271)*

Delaware Document Retrieval, Wilmington *Also Called: Parcels Inc (G-18889)*

Delaware Drnking Drver Program (PA) 302 736-4326
 1661 S Dupont Hwy Dover (19901) *(G-2233)*

Delaware Drnking Drver Program 302 856-1835
 6 N Railroad Ave Georgetown (19947) *(G-4281)*

Delaware Ear Nose & Throat Hea 302 738-6014
 4701 Ogletown Stanton Rd Ste 1200 Newark (19713) *(G-10438)*

Delaware Early Childhood Ctr, Harrington *Also Called: Lake Forest School District (G-4795)*

Delaware Economic Dev Auth 302 739-4271
 99 Kings Hwy Dover (19901) *(G-2234)*

Delaware Ecumenical Council 302 225-1040
 2629 W 19th St Wilmington (19806) *(G-15912)*

Delaware Elder Law Center 302 300-4390
 3711 Kennett Pike Wilmington (19807) *(G-15913)*

Delaware Electric Cooperative Inc 302 349-9090
 14198 Sussex Hwy Greenwood (19950) *(G-4613)*

Delaware Electric Signal, Dover *Also Called: B Safe Inc (G-1865)*

Delaware Electric Signal Co 302 422-3916
 1490 E Lebanon Rd Dover (19901) *(G-2235)*

Delaware Elevator Inc 800 787-0436
 2907 Ogletown Rd Newark (19713) *(G-10439)*

Delaware Elite Track Club 302 521-2243
 46 Owls Nest Cir Bear (19701) *(G-147)*

Delaware Elwyn, Wilmington *Also Called: Elwyn Pennsylvania and Del (G-16382)*

Delaware Energy Solutions 302 242-6315
 999 Long Point Rd Dover (19901) *(G-2236)*

Delaware Engrg & Design Corp 302 738-7172
 315 S Chapel St Newark (19711) *(G-10440)*

Delaware Enterprises Inc 302 324-5660
 42 Reads Way Ste B New Castle (19720) *(G-9022)*

Delaware Equity Fund IV 302 655-1420
 100 W 10th St Ste 303 Wilmington (19801) *(G-15914)*

Delaware Ex Shuttle & Tours, Newark *Also Called: Delaware Express Shuttle Inc (G-10441)*

Delaware Express Gar Door Svc 302 562-5080
 56 Lakeview Ct Wilmington (19810) *(G-15915)*

Delaware Express Shuttle Inc 302 454-7800
 2825 Ogletown Rd Newark (19713) *(G-10441)*

Delaware Express Tours Inc 302 454-7800
 2825 Ogletown Rd Newark (19713) *(G-10442)*

Delaware Eye Care Center (PA) 302 674-1121
 833 S Governors Ave Dover (19904) *(G-2237)*

Delaware Eye Clinic, Milton *Also Called: Millsboro Eye Care LLC (G-8668)*

Delaware Eye Clinics 302 645-2338
 31059 Sycamore Dr Lewes (19958) *(G-5897)*

Delaware Eye Institute PA 302 645-2300
 18791 John J Williams Hwy Ste 1 Rehoboth Beach (19971) *(G-12716)*

Delaware Eye Optical, Rehoboth Beach *Also Called: Delaware Eye Institute PA (G-12716)*

Delaware Eye Surgeons 302 956-0285
 2710 Centerville Rd Ste 102 Wilmington (19808) *(G-15916)*

Delaware Eye Surgery Center 302 645-2300
 18791 John J Williams Hwy Rehoboth Beach (19971) *(G-12717)*

Delaware Families For Han 302 383-9890
 4 Vista Dr Newark (19711) *(G-10443)*

Delaware Family Care Assoc, Wilmington *Also Called: Delaware Medical Care Inc (G-15943)*

Delaware Family Policy Council 302 296-8698
 1201 Bridgeville Hwy Seaford (19973) *(G-13151)*

Delaware Family Voices Inc 302 588-4908
 3301 Englewood Rd Wilmington (19810) *(G-15917)*

Delaware Family Voices Inc 302 669-3030
 222 Philadelphia Pike Ste 11 Wilmington (19809) *(G-15918)*

DELAWARE FARM BUREAU, Camden *Also Called: Delaware State Farm Bureau Inc (G-817)*

Delaware Federal Credit Union, Wilmington *Also Called: Del-One Federal Credit Union (G-15860)*

Delaware Ffa Foundation Inc 302 857-6493
 35 Commerce Way Ste 1 Dover (19904) *(G-2238)*

Delaware Film & Tape Vault Co, Wilmington *Also Called: Ken-Del Productions Inc (G-17683)*

Delaware Filter Corp 302 326-3950
 4 Bellecor Dr New Castle (19720) *(G-9023)*

Delaware Financial Capital (PA) 302 266-9500
 22 Polly Drummond Hill Rd Newark (19711) *(G-10444)*

Delaware First Federal Cr Un (PA) 302 998-0665
 1815 Newport Gap Pike Ste A Wilmington (19808) *(G-15919)*

Delaware First Media Corp 302 857-7096
 1200 N Dupont Hwy Dover (19901) *(G-2239)*

Delaware Flooring Supply Inc 302 276-0031
 520 South St Historic New Castle (19720) *(G-4969)*

Delaware Fncl Edcatn Alnce Inc 302 674-0288
 8 W Loockerman St Ste 200 Dover (19904) *(G-2240)*

Delaware Foot & Ankle Assoc 302 834-3575
 2600 Glasgow Ave Ste 101 Newark (19702) *(G-10445)*

Delaware Foster Care 302 656-2655
 2003 N Jefferson St Fl 1 Wilmington (19802) *(G-15920)*

Delaware Freeport LLC 302 366-1150
 111 Alan Dr Newark (19711) *(G-10446)*

Delaware Freeport Holdings LLC 302 366-1150
 111 Alan Dr Newark (19711) *(G-10447)*

Delaware Fury Inc 302 838-3120
 114 Greenbrier Dr Bear (19701) *(G-148)*

Delaware Gdnce Svcs For Chldre 302 678-3020
 103 Mont Blanc Blvd Dover (19904) *(G-2241)*

Delaware Gdnce Svcs For Chldre 302 455-9333
 1 Polly Drummond Shpg Ctr Newark (19711) *(G-10448)*

Delaware Gdnce Svcs For Chldre 302 355-0132
 261 Chapman Rd Ste 102 Newark (19702) *(G-10449)*

Delaware Gdnce Svcs For Chldre (PA) 302 652-3948
 1213 Delaware Ave Wilmington (19806) *(G-15921)*

Delaware Geological Survey, Newark *Also Called: University of Delaware (G-12279)*

Delaware Hardscape Supply LLC 302 996-6464
 401 B And O Ln Wilmington (19804) *(G-15922)*

Delaware Hardscape Supply LLC 302 996-6464
 4701 B And O Ln Wilmington (19804) *(G-15923)*

Delaware Health and Fitnes LLC 302 584-7531
 204 Lantana Dr Hockessin (19707) *(G-5179)*

Delaware Health Care Comm 302 739-2730
 410 Federal St Ste 7 Dover (19901) *(G-2242)*

Delaware Health Corp 302 655-0955
 2801 W 6th St Wilmington (19805) *(G-15924)*

ALPHABETIC SECTION — Delaware Millwork

Delaware Health Info Netwrk 302 678-0220
  107 Wolf Creek Blvd Ste 2 Dover (19901) *(G-2243)*

Delaware Health Management 302 454-1200
  1536 Capitol Trl Newark (19711) *(G-10450)*

Delaware Health Net Inc 410 788-9715
  601 New Castle Ave Wilmington (19801) *(G-15925)*

Delaware Heart & Vascular PA 302 734-1414
  200 Banning St Ste 340 Dover (19904) *(G-2244)*

Delaware Heating & AC 302 738-4669
  713 Millcreek Ln Bear (19701) *(G-149)*

Delaware Heating & AC Svcs Inc 302 738-4669
  11 Mcmillan Way Newark (19713) *(G-10451)*

Delaware History Museum 302 656-0637
  504 N Market St Wilmington (19801) *(G-15926)*

Delaware Hiv Services Inc 302 654-5471
  100 W 10th St Ste 415 Wilmington (19801) *(G-15927)*

Delaware Hlth Eqity Cltion Inc 302 383-1701
  239 Wickerberry Dr Middletown (19709) *(G-7040)*

Delaware Hmanities Council Inc 302 657-0650
  100 W 10th St Ste 509 Wilmington (19801) *(G-15928)*

Delaware Home & Envmtl Svcs 302 313-2899
  16141 Willow Creek Rd Lewes (19958) *(G-5898)*

Delaware Home Pros LLC 302 894-7098
  710 Wilmington Rd Ste 1 Historic New Castle (19720) *(G-4970)*

Delaware Home Valuations PA 302 933-8607
  305 Laurel Rd Millsboro (19966) *(G-8261)*

Delaware Homes Inc (PA) 302 378-9510
  401 Main St Townsend (19734) *(G-13987)*

Delaware Homes Performance 302 233-3917
  1603 Jessup St Ste 4 Wilmington (19802) *(G-15929)*

Delaware Hosp For Chrnclly Ill, Smyrna *Also Called: Delaware Dept Hlth Social Svcs* *(G-13698)*

Delaware Hospice 302 934-9018
  315 Old Landing Rd Unit 1 Millsboro (19966) *(G-8262)*

Delaware Hospice, Newark *Also Called: Delaware Hospice Inc* *(G-10452)*

Delaware Hospice Inc 302 678-4444
  911 S Dupont Hwy Dover (19901) *(G-2245)*

Delaware Hospice Inc 302 856-7717
  100 Patriots Way Milford (19963) *(G-7856)*

Delaware Hospice Inc (PA) 302 478-5707
  16 Polly Drummond Shpg Ctr Ste 2 Newark (19711) *(G-10452)*

Delaware Hotel Associates LP 302 792-2700
  630 Naamans Rd Claymont (19703) *(G-1113)*

Delaware Hotel-Motel Assn (PA) 302 674-0630
  1612 N Dupont Hwy New Castle (19720) *(G-9024)*

DELAWARE HUMANITIES, Wilmington *Also Called: Delaware Hmanities Council Inc* *(G-15928)*

Delaware Imaging Network 302 449-5400
  114 Sandhill Dr Ste 201 Middletown (19709) *(G-7041)*

Delaware Imaging Network 302 737-5990
  40 Polly Drummond Hill Rd Bldg 4 Newark (19711) *(G-10453)*

Delaware Imaging Network 302 836-4200
  2600 Glasgow Ave Ste 122 Newark (19702) *(G-10454)*

Delaware Imaging Network, Newark *Also Called: Delaware Imaging Network* *(G-10454)*

Delaware Imaging Network Inc 302 427-9855
  40 Polly Drummond Hill Rd # 4 Newark (19711) *(G-10455)*

Delaware Importers Inc 302 656-4487
  615 Lambson Ln New Castle (19720) *(G-9025)*

Delaware Incorporation Svcs 302 658-1733
  704 N King St Ste 500 Wilmington (19801) *(G-15930)*

Delaware Industrial Supply, Newark *Also Called: C M D Inc* *(G-10113)*

Delaware Industries For Blind, New Castle *Also Called: Delaware Dept Hlth Social Svcs* *(G-9017)*

Delaware Injury Associates PA 302 332-1932
  707 Foulk Rd Ste 102 Wilmington (19803) *(G-15931)*

Delaware Injury Care 302 678-8866
  240 Beiser Blvd Ste 101 Dover (19904) *(G-2246)*

Delaware Injury Care 914 960-1145
  4023 Kennett Pike Wilmington (19807) *(G-15932)*

Delaware Injury Care LLC 302 628-8008
  608 N Porter St Seaford (19973) *(G-13152)*

Delaware Innovation Space Inc 302 695-2201
  200 Powder Mill Rd E500 Wilmington (19803) *(G-15933)*

Delaware Inst For Rep, Newark *Also Called: Center For Human Reproduction* *(G-10175)*

Delaware Integrative Medical C 302 559-5959
  20930 Dupont Blvd Unit 203 Georgetown (19947) *(G-4282)*

Delaware Intercorp Inc 302 266-9367
  3511 Silverside Rd Ste 105 Wilmington (19810) *(G-15934)*

Delaware Intl Agrclture Entp L 302 450-2008
  22 Zion Dr Smyrna (19977) *(G-13699)*

Delaware Intl Speedway, Delmar *Also Called: U S 13 Dragway Inc* *(G-1648)*

Delaware Intrvntnal Spine Asso 302 674-8444
  1673 S State St Ste B Dover (19901) *(G-2247)*

Delaware Juneteenth Assn 302 530-1605
  139 Asbury Loop Middletown (19709) *(G-7042)*

Delaware Juniors Volleyball 302 463-4218
  4142 Ogletown Stanton Rd # 229 Newark (19713) *(G-10456)*

Delaware Kids Dental Center 302 764-7714
  708 Foulk Rd Wilmington (19803) *(G-15935)*

Delaware Kids Fund 302 323-9300
  405 Marsh Ln Ste 1 Newport (19804) *(G-12448)*

Delaware Labor Resources Inc 302 377-5752
  6 Coffee Run Ln Wilmington (19808) *(G-15936)*

Delaware Lacrosse Foundation 302 831-8661
  Wilmington (19810) *(G-15937)*

Delaware Landscape Cnstr LLC 302 841-3010
  30 Coventry Rd Rehoboth Beach (19971) *(G-12718)*

Delaware Landscaping Inc 302 698-3001
  106 Semans Dr Dover (19904) *(G-2248)*

Delaware Last Mile Lgstics DLM 302 407-1415
  1500 Johnson Way Historic New Castle (19720) *(G-4971)*

Delaware Lawn & Tree Service 302 834-7406
  1756 Bear Corbitt Rd Bear (19701) *(G-150)*

Delaware Lawn Crew LLC 302 368-3344
  1001 Garasches Ln Wilmington (19801) *(G-15938)*

Delaware Lawnandlandscape 302 276-1060
  467 Old Airport Rd New Castle (19720) *(G-9026)*

Delaware Liberia Association 302 983-2536
  27 Sandalwood Dr Apt 8 Newark (19713) *(G-10457)*

Delaware Limo, Wilmington *Also Called: Ayea LLC* *(G-14686)*

Delaware Lister 302 382-7059
  9 Fleming St Woodside (19980) *(G-20975)*

Delaware Lrng Inst Csmtlogy In 302 732-6704
  32448 Royal Blvd Unit A Dagsboro (19939) *(G-1434)*

Delaware Magical Wishes Assn 302 653-6974
  715 W South St Smyrna (19977) *(G-13700)*

Delaware Marketing Group, Wilmington *Also Called: Delaware Marketing Partners* *(G-15939)*

Delaware Marketing Partners 302 575-1610
  3801 Kennett Pike D301 Wilmington (19807) *(G-15939)*

Delaware Material Recovery & R 302 652-3150
  1000 S Heald St Wilmington (19801) *(G-15940)*

Delaware Meat Company LLC 302 438-0252
  28 Brookside Dr Wilmington (19804) *(G-15941)*

Delaware Mech Contrs Assoc 302 235-2813
  Hockessin (19707) *(G-5180)*

Delaware Med Care Assoc LLC 302 633-9033
  550 Stanton Christiana Rd Ste 103 Newark (19713) *(G-10458)*

Delaware Medical Associates PA 302 475-2535
  2101 Foulk Rd Ste 2 Wilmington (19810) *(G-15942)*

Delaware Medical Care Inc 302 225-6868
  2700 Silverside Rd Ste 2 Wilmington (19810) *(G-15943)*

Delaware Medical Courier 302 670-1247
  17048 W Holly Dr Milton (19968) *(G-8599)*

Delaware Medical MGT Svcs LLC 302 283-3300
  71 Omega Dr Newark (19713) *(G-10459)*

Delaware Mentor, Millsboro *Also Called: National Mentor Holdings Inc* *(G-8401)*

Delaware Merchant Services 302 838-9100
  510 Century Blvd Wilmington (19808) *(G-15944)*

Delaware Metals, Wilmington *Also Called: Chuck George Inc* *(G-15427)*

Delaware Mfg EXT Partnr Inc 302 283-3131
  400 Stanton Christiana Rd Ste 154 Newark (19713) *(G-10460)*

Delaware Millwork 302 376-8324
  110 W Green St Middletown (19709) *(G-7043)*

Delaware Mltcltral Cvic Orgnzt   **ALPHABETIC SECTION**

- **Delaware Mltcltral Cvic Orgnzt** 302 399-6118
  365 United Way Dover (19901) *(G-2249)*
- **DELAWARE MOBILE SIGNINGS, Millsboro** Also Called: Delaware Mobile Signings LLC *(G-8263)*
- **Delaware Mobile Signings LLC** 302 316-3926
  26976 Bethesda Rd Millsboro (19966) *(G-8263)*
- **Delaware Mobile Surfishermen** 302 945-1320
  Dagsboro (19939) *(G-1435)*
- **Delaware Modern Pediatrics** 302 392-2077
  300 Biddle Ave Ste 206 Newark (19702) *(G-10461)*
- **Delaware Monument and Vault** 302 540-2387
  203 Wyndtree Ct S Hockessin (19707) *(G-5181)*
- **Delaware Mosquito Control LLC** 302 504-6757
  4 Cobblestone Xing Newark (19702) *(G-10462)*
- **Delaware Motel and Rv Park** 302 328-3114
  235 S Dupont Hwy New Castle (19720) *(G-9027)*
- **Delaware Motor Sales Inc (PA)** 302 656-3100
  1606 Pennsylvania Ave Wilmington (19806) *(G-15945)*
- **Delaware Moving & Storage Inc** 302 322-0311
  214 Bear Christiana Rd Bear (19701) *(G-151)*
- **Delaware Mseum Ntral Hstory In** 302 658-9111
  4840 Kennett Pike Wilmington (19807) *(G-15946)*
- **Delaware Mud Hens Baseball** 703 939-7828
  584 Otter Way Frederica (19946) *(G-4165)*
- **Delaware Municipal Elc Corp** 302 659-0200
  22 Artisan Dr Smyrna (19977) *(G-13701)*
- **Delaware Museum Association** 302 644-5005
  165 Brick Store Lnding Rd Smyrna (19977) *(G-13702)*
- **Delaware Nat Gard Yuth Fndtion** 302 326-7582
  1 Vavala Way New Castle (19720) *(G-9028)*
- **Delaware National Estuarine** 302 739-3436
  818 Kitts Hummock Rd Dover (19901) *(G-2250)*
- **Delaware Nature Society (PA)** 302 239-1283
  3511 Barley Mill Rd Hockessin (19707) *(G-5182)*
- **Delaware Neurorehab, Dover** Also Called: Delaware Physiatry LLC *(G-2253)*
- **Delaware Nurosurgical Group PA** 302 366-7671
  774 Christiana Rd Ste 202 Newark (19713) *(G-10463)*
- **Delaware Nursing Adult, Wilmington** Also Called: Bayada Home Health Care Inc *(G-14787)*
- **Delaware Obgyn & Womens Health** 302 730-0633
  1057 S Bradford St Dover (19904) *(G-2251)*
- **Delaware Obs LLC** 302 743-4798
  305 Pennewill Dr New Castle (19720) *(G-9029)*
- **Delaware Occptnal Hlth Svcs LL** 302 368-5100
  15 Omega Dr Bldg K15 Newark (19713) *(G-10464)*
- **Delaware Odyssey of The Mind, Smyrna** Also Called: Delcaps Inc *(G-13708)*
- **Delaware Offices LLC (PA)** 302 295-1215
  4828 Kennett Pike Wilmington (19807) *(G-15947)*
- **Delaware Offices LLC** 302 295-1214
  219 W 9th St Ste 200 Wilmington (19801) *(G-15948)*
- **Delaware Open M R I, Newark** Also Called: Jeanes Radiology Associates PC *(G-11102)*
- **Delaware Ophthalmology Co** 302 451-5022
  401 Eagle Run Rd Newark (19702) *(G-10465)*
- **Delaware Ophthalmology Cons, Wilmington** Also Called: Delaware Ophthalmology Cons PA *(G-15949)*
- **Delaware Ophthalmology Cons PA (PA)** 302 479-3937
  3501 Silverside Rd Wilmington (19810) *(G-15949)*
- **Delaware Orchid Society** 302 654-8883
  9 Carriage Rd Wilmington (19807) *(G-15950)*
- **Delaware Orthodontics** 302 838-1400
  2444 Pulaski Hwy Newark (19702) *(G-10466)*
- **Delaware Orthopaedic Specialis** 302 633-3555
  1941 Limestone Rd Ste 101 Wilmington (19808) *(G-15951)*
- **Delaware Orthopedic and Sports** 302 653-8389
  208 N Dupont Blvd Smyrna (19977) *(G-13703)*
- **Delaware Otolaryngology Consul** 302 644-2232
  17316 Coastal Hwy Lewes (19958) *(G-5899)*
- **Delaware Otptent Ctr For Srger** 302 738-0300
  774 Christiana Rd Ste 2 Newark (19713) *(G-10467)*
- **Delaware Outdoor Advertising** 302 234-1975
  207 Golding Ct Hockessin (19707) *(G-5183)*
- **Delaware Paralyzed Vets** 302 861-6671
  700 Barksdale Rd Newark (19711) *(G-10468)*

- **Delaware Parents Association** 302 678-9288
  101 W Loockerman St Ste 3a Dover (19904) *(G-2252)*
- **Delaware Park, Wilmington** Also Called: Delaware Racing Association *(G-15956)*
- **Delaware Park Racing LLC** 302 994-6700
  777 Delaware Park Blvd Wilmington (19804) *(G-15952)*
- **Delaware Patio & Landscpg Inc** 302 218-3738
  176 Olivine Cir Townsend (19734) *(G-13988)*
- **Delaware Pediatrics PA (PA)** 302 762-6222
  3920 Dupont Pkwy Ste A Townsend (19734) *(G-13989)*
- **Delaware Periodontics** 302 658-7871
  1110 N Bancroft Pkwy Ste 1 Wilmington (19805) *(G-15953)*
- **Delaware Pharmacist Society** 302 659-3088
  27 N Main St Smyrna (19977) *(G-13704)*
- **Delaware Physiatry LLC** 302 387-1407
  1221 College Park Dr Ste 203 Dover (19904) *(G-2253)*
- **Delaware Plastic & Recon** 302 994-8492
  1 Centurian Dr Ste 301 Newark (19713) *(G-10469)*
- **Delaware Plastic & Recon, Newark** Also Called: Delaware Plastic & Recon *(G-10469)*
- **Delaware Plastic Surgery** 302 632-7750
  1695 S State St Dover (19901) *(G-2254)*
- **Delaware Power Wash Plus LLC** 302 415-1066
  36 Orchid Dr Bear (19701) *(G-152)*
- **Delaware Premier Trnsp** 616 617-2598
  30 Lanford Rd New Castle (19720) *(G-9030)*
- **Delaware Prep Center LLC** 302 932-1208
  250 Executive Dr Newark (19702) *(G-10470)*
- **Delaware Pride Inc** 302 265-3020
  10 Hickman Rd Claymont (19703) *(G-1114)*
- **Delaware Primary Care LLC** 302 730-0554
  810 New Burton Rd Ste 3 Dover (19904) *(G-2255)*
- **Delaware Prof Fnrl Svcs Inc** 302 731-5459
  635 Churchmans Rd Newark (19702) *(G-10471)*
- **Delaware Professional Squash** 302 655-6171
  4825 Kennett Pike Wilmington (19807) *(G-15954)*
- **Delaware Property Mgmt Co LLC** 302 366-0208
  1101 Millstone Dr Newark (19711) *(G-10472)*
- **Delaware Protection Agency, Middletown** Also Called: Clinton Craddock *(G-6995)*
- **Delaware Psychiatric Center, New Castle** Also Called: Delaware Dept Hlth Social Svcs *(G-9018)*
- **Delaware Psychiatry LLC** 302 397-8516
  5700 Kirkwood Hwy Wilmington (19808) *(G-15955)*
- **Delaware Psychological Svcs LLC** 302 703-6332
  16287 Willow Creek Rd Lewes (19958) *(G-5900)*
- **Delaware Public Auto Auction** 302 656-0500
  2323 N Dupont Hwy New Castle (19720) *(G-9031)*
- **Delaware Public Health Lab** 302 223-1520
  30 Sunnyside Rd Smyrna (19977) *(G-13705)*
- **Delaware Public Media, Dover** Also Called: Delaware First Media Corp *(G-2239)*
- **Delaware Racing Association** 302 355-1000
  2701 Kirkwood Hwy Newark (19711) *(G-10473)*
- **Delaware Racing Association (PA)** 302 994-2521
  777 Delaware Park Blvd Wilmington (19804) *(G-15956)*
- **Delaware RE Advisors LLC** 302 998-4030
  1013 Centre Rd Ste 201 Wilmington (19805) *(G-15957)*
- **Delaware RE Answers LLC** 302 635-0375
  2516 W 3rd St Wilmington (19805) *(G-15958)*
- **Delaware Real Estate Search** 302 437-6516
  1126 Pulaski Hwy Bear (19701) *(G-153)*
- **Delaware Real Estate Search** 302 437-6516
  5 Crabapple Ct Newark (19702) *(G-10474)*
- **Delaware Realty Group Inc** 302 227-4800
  317 Rehoboth Ave Rehoboth Beach (19971) *(G-12719)*
- **Delaware Recyclable Products** 302 655-1360
  246 Marsh Ln New Castle (19720) *(G-9032)*
- **Delaware Recycling Center** 215 921-7508
  1101 Lambson Ln New Castle (19720) *(G-9033)*
- **Delaware Registry Ltd** 302 477-9800
  3511 Silverside Rd Ste 105 Wilmington (19810) *(G-15959)*
- **Delaware Remodeling Co** 302 545-0075
  334 W Commerce St Smyrna (19977) *(G-13706)*
- **Delaware Restaurant Assn** 302 738-2545
  420 S State St Dover (19901) *(G-2256)*

ALPHABETIC SECTION — Delaware Storefronts LLC

Delaware Retired Schl Prsnl.. 302 674-8252
100 Galewood Ct Wilmington (19803) *(G-15960)*

Delaware Riders Basbal CLB Inc... 302 475-1915
2214 Nassau Dr Wilmington (19810) *(G-15961)*

Delaware River & Bay Authority (PA).................................. 302 571-6303
2162 New Castle Ave New Castle (19720) *(G-9034)*

Delaware River Adventures LLC... 302 422-2000
21 Nw Front St Milford (19963) *(G-7857)*

Delaware River Stevedores Inc... 302 657-0472
1 Hausel Rd Ste 115 Wilmington (19801) *(G-15962)*

Delaware Rock Gym Inc... 302 838-5850
520 Carson Dr Bear (19701) *(G-154)*

Delaware Rug Co Inc.. 302 998-8881
5 Forrest Ave Wilmington (19805) *(G-15963)*

Delaware Rural Water Assn... 302 398-9633
27 Commerce St Ste 27c Harrington (19952) *(G-4757)*

Delaware Rural Water Assn... 302 424-3792
210 Vickers Rd Milford (19963) *(G-7858)*

Delaware Rver Bay Auth Emplyee.. 302 571-6320
New Castle (19720) *(G-9035)*

Delaware S P C A (PA)... 302 998-2281
455 Stanton Christiana Rd Newark (19713) *(G-10475)*

Delaware Saengerbund Lib Assn... 302 366-9454
49 Salem Church Rd Newark (19713) *(G-10476)*

Delaware Safety Council Inc.. 302 276-0660
2 Penns Way Ste 201 New Castle (19720) *(G-9036)*

Delaware Schl Counselors Assn.. 302 323-2821
713 E Basin Rd New Castle (19720) *(G-9037)*

Delaware School For Deaf... 302 454-2301
630 E Chestnut Hill Rd Newark (19713) *(G-10477)*

Delaware School Nutrition Assn.. 302 323-2743
4 Mount Lebanon Rd Wilmington (19803) *(G-15964)*

Delaware Screen Printing, Middletown *Also Called: Delaware Screen Printing Inc (G-7044)*

Delaware Screen Printing Inc.. 302 378-4231
350 Strawberry Ln Middletown (19709) *(G-7044)*

Delaware Scuba LLC... 302 236-6350
31785 Katum Dr Laurel (19956) *(G-5495)*

Delaware Seamstress... 302 286-8210
2413 W 2nd St Wilmington (19805) *(G-15965)*

Delaware Seashore Preservation... 302 227-0478
200 Summer Ct Dagsboro (19939) *(G-1436)*

Delaware Seaside Railroad Club.. 302 682-4652
Ocean View (19970) *(G-12500)*

Delaware Secretary of State.. 302 834-8046
2465 Chesapeake City Rd Bear (19701) *(G-155)*

Delaware Secretary of State.. 302 736-7400
21 The Grn # A Dover (19901) *(G-2257)*

Delaware Senior Olympics Inc... 302 736-5698
1121 Forrest Ave Dover (19904) *(G-2258)*

Delaware Settlement Services... 302 731-2500
930 Old Harmony Rd Ste F1 Newark (19713) *(G-10478)*

Delaware Siding Co Inc.. 302 778-4771
3310 Wrangle Hill Rd Ste 113 Bear (19701) *(G-156)*

Delaware Siding Company Inc.. 302 836-6971
723 Rue Madora Ste 8 Bear (19701) *(G-157)*

Delaware Siding Company Inc.. 302 732-1440
27515 Hodges Ln Dagsboro (19939) *(G-1437)*

Delaware Sign Co... 302 469-5656
411 E Railroad Ave Felton (19943) *(G-3959)*

Delaware Signing Services LLC... 302 464-5038
163 Tywyn Dr Middletown (19709) *(G-7045)*

Delaware Skating Center Ltd... 302 697-3218
2201 S Dupont Hwy Dover (19901) *(G-2259)*

Delaware Skating Center Ltd (PA).. 302 366-0473
801 Christiana Rd Newark (19713) *(G-10479)*

Delaware Sleep Disorder C.. 302 407-3349
108 Patriot Dr Ste A Middletown (19709) *(G-7046)*

Delaware Sleep Dsrders Ctrs Lt (PA).................................... 302 669-6141
620 Stanton Christiana Rd Ste 101 Newark (19713) *(G-10480)*

Delaware Small Bus Dev Ctr.. 302 831-1555
103 W Pine St Georgetown (19947) *(G-4283)*

Delaware Small Bus Dev Ctr.. 302 831-1555
1 Innovation Way Ste 301 Newark (19711) *(G-10481)*

Delaware Smile Center.. 302 285-7645
201 Carter Dr Ste A Middletown (19709) *(G-7047)*

Delaware Soc For Rsprtory Care... 302 834-2905
111 Marabou Dr Newark (19702) *(G-10482)*

Delaware Soc Rdlgy Profession, Wilmington *Also Called: National Society Inc (G-18547)*

Delaware Solid Waste Authority (PA)................................... 302 739-5361
1128 S Bradford St Dover (19904) *(G-2260)*

Delaware Solid Waste Authority... 302 764-2732
1706 E 12th St Wilmington (19809) *(G-15966)*

Delaware Specialty Dist, Wilmington *Also Called: Fluorogistx LLC (G-16674)*

Delaware Spine Institute, Dover *Also Called: Delaware Intrvntnal Spine Asso (G-2247)*

Delaware Spine Rehabilitation... 302 273-0064
131 Becks Woods Dr Bear (19701) *(G-158)*

Delaware Spine Rehabilitation... 302 883-2292
642 S Queen St Dover (19904) *(G-2261)*

Delaware Spine Rehabilitation... 302 563-7442
216 E 2nd St Historic New Castle (19720) *(G-4972)*

Delaware Sports... 302 731-1676
338 Tamara Cir Newark (19711) *(G-10483)*

Delaware Sports League Inc... 302 654-8787
4 E 8th St Ste 300a Wilmington (19801) *(G-15967)*

Delaware Spray Foam Inc... 302 234-4050
585 Hemingway Dr Hockessin (19707) *(G-5184)*

Delaware Sstnble Enrgy Utility... 302 883-3038
500 W Loockerman St Ste 400 Dover (19904) *(G-2262)*

Delaware Star Dental... 302 994-3093
5507 Kirkwood Hwy Wilmington (19808) *(G-15968)*

Delaware State Aflcio.. 302 256-0310
3304 Old Capitol Trl Wilmington (19808) *(G-15969)*

Delaware State Bar Association.. 302 658-5279
405 N King St Ste 100 Wilmington (19801) *(G-15970)*

DELAWARE STATE CHAMBER OF COMM, Wilmington *Also Called: Delaware State Chmber Cmmrce I (G-15971)*

Delaware State Chmber Cmmrce I.. 302 655-7221
1201 N Orange St Ste 200 Wilmington (19801) *(G-15971)*

Delaware State Dental Society.. 302 368-7634
2803 Philadelphia Pike Claymont (19703) *(G-1115)*

Delaware State Education Assn (PA).................................... 302 734-5834
136 E Water St Dover (19901) *(G-2263)*

Delaware State Education Assn.. 302 366-8440
4135 Ogletown Stanton Rd Ste 101 Newark (19713) *(G-10484)*

Delaware State Fair Inc (PA).. 302 398-3269
18500 S Dupont Hwy Harrington (19952) *(G-4758)*

Delaware State Farm Bureau Inc.. 302 697-3183
3457 S Dupont Hwy Camden (19934) *(G-817)*

Delaware State Grange Inc... 302 994-0295
4201 Limestone Rd Wilmington (19808) *(G-15972)*

Delaware State Hospital, New Castle *Also Called: Delaware Dept Hlth Social Svcs (G-9019)*

Delaware State Hstric Prsrvtio, Dover *Also Called: Delaware Secretary of State (G-2257)*

Delaware State Lottery, Dover *Also Called: Delaware Department Finance (G-2227)*

Delaware State News, Dover *Also Called: Independent Newsmedia Inc USA (G-2728)*

Delaware State Pipe Trdes Assn... 302 636-7400
201 Executive Dr Newark (19702) *(G-10485)*

Delaware State Pistol Club.. 302 328-6836
36 Mercer Dr Newark (19713) *(G-10486)*

Delaware State Plice Fdral Cr... 800 288-1080
700 N Bedford St Georgetown (19947) *(G-4284)*

Delaware State Plice Fdral Cr (PA)...................................... 302 856-3501
700 N Bedford St Georgetown (19947) *(G-4285)*

Delaware State Plice Fdral Cr... 302 324-8141
235 Christiana Rd New Castle (19720) *(G-9038)*

Delaware State Printing... 302 228-9431
110 Galaxy Dr Dover (19901) *(G-2264)*

Delaware Stndrdbred Owners Ass.. 302 678-3058
830 Walker Rd Ste 11-2 Dover (19904) *(G-2265)*

Delaware Storage & Pipeline Co.. 302 736-1774
987 Port Mahon Rd Dover (19901) *(G-2266)*

Delaware Storefronts LLC (PA)... 302 697-1850
720 S Governors Ave Dover (19904) *(G-2267)*

Delaware Surf Fishing LLC — ALPHABETIC SECTION

Delaware Surf Fishing LLC 302 296-7812
  25728 Whispering Wind Ln Millsboro (19966) (G-8264)
Delaware Surgery Center LLC 302 730-0217
  200 Banning St Ste 110 Dover (19904) (G-2268)
Delaware Surgery Ctr 302 730-0217
  1326 S Governors Ave Ste C Dover (19904) (G-2269)
Delaware Surgical Arts 302 225-0177
  537 Stanton Christiana Rd Ste 109 Newark (19713) (G-10487)
Delaware Surgical Group PA (PA) 302 892-2100
  1941 Limestone Rd Ste 213 Wilmington (19808) (G-15973)
Delaware Surgical Service, Lewes Also Called: Debay Surgical Service (G-5885)
Delaware Swim & Fitness Center 302 234-8500
  4905 Mermaid Blvd Wilmington (19808) (G-15974)
Delaware Tax & Accounting Svcs 302 504-4063
  284 E Main St Newark (19711) (G-10488)
Delaware Tax Services 302 453-1040
  16 Tyre Ave Newark (19711) (G-10489)
Delaware Taxes LLC 302 368-7040
  14a Marrows Rd Newark (19713) (G-10490)
Delaware Tchncal Cmnty College 302 259-6160
  21179 College Dr Georgetown (19947) (G-4286)
Delaware Technology Park Inc 302 452-1100
  1 Innovation Way Ste 300 Newark (19711) (G-10491)
Delaware Terry Farrell Fund 302 242-4341
  18588 Sherman Ave Lincoln (19960) (G-6663)
Delaware Theatre Company 302 594-1100
  200 Water St Wilmington (19801) (G-15975)
Delaware Thrmplastic Specialty 302 424-4722
  720 Mccolley St Ste D Milford (19963) (G-7859)
Delaware Tire Center Inc 302 674-0234
  207 S Governors Ave Dover (19904) (G-2270)
Delaware Tire Center Inc (PA) 302 368-2531
  616 S College Ave Newark (19713) (G-10492)
Delaware Title Loans Inc 302 644-3640
  17672 Coastal Hwy Lewes (19958) (G-5901)
Delaware Title Loans Inc 302 328-7482
  505 N Dupont Hwy New Castle (19720) (G-9039)
Delaware Title Loans Inc 302 368-2131
  2431 Pulaski Hwy Ste 1 Newark (19702) (G-10493)
Delaware Title Loans Inc 302 629-8843
  22994 Sussex Hwy Seaford (19973) (G-13153)
Delaware Title Loans Inc 302 653-8315
  202 N Dupont Blvd Smyrna (19977) (G-13707)
Delaware Title Loans Inc 302 478-8505
  3300 Concord Pike Ste 2 Wilmington (19803) (G-15976)
Delaware Tool Cleaning, Wilmington Also Called: Conlin Corporation (G-15597)
Delaware Trail Spinners 302 738-0177
  1013 Tulip Tree Ln Newark (19713) (G-10494)
Delaware Transit, Wilmington Also Called: Delaware Department Trnsp (G-15902)
Delaware Transportation Auth 302 760-2000
  800 S Bay Rd Dover (19901) (G-2271)
Delaware Trenching, Newark Also Called: R F Brown Inc (G-11808)
Delaware Trust Company 302 636-5404
  251 Little Falls Dr Wilmington (19808) (G-15977)
Delaware Union 484 645-7064
  214 Harlequin Dr New Castle (19720) (G-9040)
Delaware Valley Brokerage Inc 302 477-9700
  1415 Foulk Rd Ste 103 Wilmington (19803) (G-15978)
Delaware Valley Dev Group LLC 302 235-2500
  5718 Kennett Pike Wilmington (19807) (G-15979)
Delaware Valley Dev LLC 302 235-2500
  5718 Kennett Pike Wilmington (19807) (G-15980)
Delaware Valley Field Svcs LLC 302 384-8617
  321 Robinson Ln Wilmington (19805) (G-15981)
Delaware Valley Group LLC 302 777-7007
  1720 Gilpin Ave Wilmington (19806) (G-15982)
Delaware Valley Housing Dev, Wilmington Also Called: Dvhd Inc (G-16225)
Delaware Valley Pathology 302 239-3729
  22 Withers Way Hockessin (19707) (G-5185)
Delaware Valley RE Solutions 302 668-1694
  502 Beaver Valley Rd Wilmington (19803) (G-15983)

Delaware Valley Safety Council 302 607-2758
  130 Executive Dr Newark (19702) (G-10495)
Delaware Vascular & Vein Cente 302 354-4671
  701 N Clayton St Wilmington (19805) (G-15984)
Delaware Vein Center 302 258-8853
  20930 Dupont Blvd Unit 202 Georgetown (19947) (G-4287)
Delaware Veterans Home Inc 302 424-6000
  100 Delaware Veterans Blvd Milford (19963) (G-7860)
Delaware Veterans Inc 302 674-9956
  2465 Chesapeake City Rd Bear (19701) (G-159)
Delaware Veterans Post 302 317-1123
  720 Pear St Dover (19904) (G-2272)
Delaware Veterinary Med Assn 302 242-7014
  3052 Wrangle Hill Rd Bear (19701) (G-160)
Delaware Wic Program (PA) 302 741-2900
  635 S Bay Rd # 1c Dover (19901) (G-2273)
Delaware Wic Program 302 857-5000
  805 River Rd Dover (19901) (G-2274)
Delaware Womens Bowling Assn 302 834-7002
  9 Winchester Ct Bear (19701) (G-161)
Delaware Womens Golf Assn 302 598-0566
  800 Shallcross Lake Rd Middletown (19709) (G-7048)
Delaware Wood Renewal Inc 302 750-5167
  2 Rebecca Ct Middletown (19709) (G-7049)
Delaware Zoological Soc Inc 302 571-7747
  1001 N Park Dr Wilmington (19802) (G-15985)
Delawares Finest Services 302 607-9288
  2914a Ogletown Rd Newark (19713) (G-10496)
Delawrschoolofmassage Bodywork 302 407-5986
  1601 Milltown Rd Ste 15 Wilmington (19808) (G-15986)
Delcaps Inc 302 242-6953
  4134 Wheatleys Pond Rd Smyrna (19977) (G-13708)
Delcard Associates Inc 302 221-4822
  31 Blevins Dr Ste C New Castle (19720) (G-9041)
Delcarm LLC (PA) 610 345-9001
  1482 Levels Rd Townsend (19734) (G-13990)
Delcaste Golf Course 302 225-9821
  3601 Miller Rd Wilmington (19802) (G-15987)
Delcastle Golf Club, Wilmington Also Called: Delcastle Golf Club Management (G-15988)
Delcastle Golf Club Management 302 998-9505
  3800 Valley Brook Dr Wilmington (19808) (G-15988)
Delcastle Golf Management LLC 302 998-9505
  801 Mckennans Church Rd Wilmington (19808) (G-15989)
Delchem Inc 302 426-1800
  1318 E 12th St Ste 1 Wilmington (19802) (G-15990)
Delco Modular 302 934-7704
  23581 Godwin School Rd Millsboro (19966) (G-8265)
Delcollo Security Tech Inc 302 994-5400
  226 Brookside Dr Wilmington (19804) (G-15991)
Delcomps, Lewes Also Called: Delcomps LLC (G-5902)
Delcomps LLC 302 754-1543
  31059 Sycamore Dr Lewes (19958) (G-5902)
Delden Installations 302 423-1279
  3125 Chipmunk Ct Bear (19701) (G-162)
Deldeo Builders Inc 302 791-0243
  100 Naamans Rd Ste 3f Claymont (19703) (G-1116)
Delduca, Vincent Jr MD, Newark Also Called: Medical Onclogy Hmtlogy Cons P (G-11376)
Deleware Acupuncture 302 273-2807
  7 Greenfield Ct Newark (19713) (G-10497)
Deleware Eye Clinics 302 684-2020
  28322 Lewes Georgetown Hwy Unit 1 Milton (19968) (G-8600)
Deleware Heart Group, Newark Also Called: Christopher A Bowens MD (G-10236)
Delfast Inc 323 540-5155
  160 Greentree Dr Ste 101 Dover (19904) (G-2275)
Delfis Clean LLC 302 740-0989
  3879 Evelyn Dr Wilmington (19808) (G-15992)
Delframing Inc 302 363-2658
  30897 Fresh Pond Dr Ocean View (19970) (G-12501)
Delica Inc 917 566-7308
  251 Little Falls Dr Wilmington (19808) (G-15993)
Delight Housing Complex, Lincoln Also Called: Ggc Inc (G-6670)

ALPHABETIC SECTION — Delmarva Water Solutions

Deliri Hamid 302 468-4500
1016 Delaware Ave Wilmington (19806) *(G-15994)*

Delisle K-9 Offcer Sfety Fndti 302 893-7324
413 Brandywine Dr Bear (19701) *(G-163)*

Dell Oem Inc 302 294-0060
705 Dawson Dr Newark (19713) *(G-10498)*

Dell Pump Company 302 655-2436
1507 A St Wilmington (19801) *(G-15995)*

Delmaco Manufacturing Inc 302 856-6345
21424 Cedar Creek Ave Georgetown (19947) *(G-4288)*

Delmar Corporate Clg Svcs Inc 302 861-8006
260 Chapman Rd Ste 104b Newark (19702) *(G-10499)*

Delmar Process Servers LLC 302 306-2805
8 The Grn Ste 17282 Dover (19901) *(G-2276)*

Delmar Termite & Pest Control 302 658-5010
700 Cornell Dr Wilmington (19801) *(G-15996)*

Delmar Trucking 240 353-3553
18 Top View Ct Newark (19702) *(G-10500)*

Delmarva 2000 Ltd 302 645-2226
21 Shay Ln Milton (19968) *(G-8601)*

Delmarva Adult Teen Challenge, Seaford *Also Called: Delmarva Teen Challenge Inc*
(G-13156)

Delmarva Arborists LLC 302 581-9494
32712 Swamp Rd Dagsboro (19939) *(G-1438)*

Delmarva Auto Repair LLC 302 727-3237
12313 Sussex Hwy Greenwood (19950) *(G-4614)*

Delmarva Automotive Eqp Inc 302 349-9411
14247 Oakley Rd Ellendale (19941) *(G-3913)*

Delmarva Bath LLC 302 278-1717
32097 Lous Discount Ln Laurel (19956) *(G-5496)*

Delmarva Builders Inc 302 629-9123
20846 Camp Rd Bridgeville (19933) *(G-692)*

Delmarva Central Railroad 302 449-1576
1275 Lorewood Grove Rd Middletown (19709) *(G-7050)*

Delmarva Chiropractic Wel 302 682-7975
1000 Midway Dr Harrington (19952) *(G-4759)*

Delmarva Clergy United Inc 302 422-2350
13724 S Old State Rd Ellendale (19941) *(G-3914)*

Delmarva Clrgy Untd In Scial A, Ellendale *Also Called: Delmarva Clergy United Inc (G-3914)*

Delmarva Coastal Cnstr LLC 302 259-5593
28464 Nanticoke Ave Millsboro (19966) *(G-8266)*

Delmarva Communications Inc 302 324-1230
113 J And M Dr New Castle (19720) *(G-9042)*

Delmarva Community Wellnet 704 779-3280
1307 Savannah Rd Lewes (19958) *(G-5903)*

Delmarva Concrete Pumping Inc 302 537-4118
34090 Central Ave Frankford (19945) *(G-4100)*

Delmarva Crawl Space Sltns 302 265-0637
28323 Johnson Ln Harbeson (19951) *(G-4695)*

Delmarva Digital Media Group, Laurel *Also Called: Internet Business Pubg Corp (G-5536)*

Delmarva Equine Clinic 302 735-4735
1008 S Governors Ave Dover (19904) *(G-2277)*

Delmarva Furniture Svcs LLC 302 644-4970
16192 Coastal Hwy Lewes (19958) *(G-5904)*

Delmarva Group 302 200-9053
1632 Savannah Rd Ste 2 Lewes (19958) *(G-5905)*

Delmarva Hardwood Products Inc 302 349-4101
28950 Seaford Rd Laurel (19956) *(G-5497)*

Delmarva Ice LLC 302 593-7095
24483 Sussex Hwy Seaford (19973) *(G-13154)*

Delmarva Insulation, Georgetown *Also Called: Southland Insulators Del LLC (G-4520)*

Delmarva Insurance Group 302 248-8500
19413 Jingle Shell Way Lewes (19958) *(G-5906)*

Delmarva Irrigation Inc 302 490-1588
11027 Delaware Ave Laurel (19956) *(G-5498)*

Delmarva Kenworth Trucks, Dover *Also Called: Clifton Leasing Co Inc (G-2093)*

Delmarva Kleaning Klub LLC 302 629-4706
24262 Chapel Branch Rd Seaford (19973) *(G-13155)*

Delmarva Metal Roofing 302 858-1699
497 Bowman Rd Milford (19963) *(G-7861)*

Delmarva Paddlers Retreat 302 542-0818
11 Eagle Dr Rehoboth Beach (19971) *(G-12720)*

Delmarva Pain & Spine Ctr LLC 302 355-0900
1 Centurian Dr Ste 110 Newark (19713) *(G-10501)*

Delmarva Pain and Spine Center, Newark *Also Called: Delmarva Pain & Spine Ctr LLC*
(G-10501)

Delmarva Performance and Repr 302 858-3546
502 N Bi State Blvd Delmar (19940) *(G-1587)*

Delmarva Plastics Co 302 398-1000
800 Pine Pitch Rd Harrington (19952) *(G-4760)*

Delmarva Plumbing LLC 571 274-4926
17 Longview Dr Ocean View (19970) *(G-12502)*

Delmarva Pole Building Sup Inc 302 698-3636
317 N Layton Ave Wyoming (19934) *(G-20983)*

Delmarva Power, Newark *Also Called: P H I Pepco (G-11609)*

Delmarva Power & Light Company (HQ) 302 454-0300
500 N Wakefield Dr Fl 2 Newark (19702) *(G-10502)*

Delmarva Power & Light Company 302 454-4040
401 Eagle Run Rd Newark (19702) *(G-10503)*

Delmarva Power & Light Company 302 454-4450
Rt 273 & I-95 Newark (19714) *(G-10504)*

Delmarva Power & Light Company 302 668-3809
800 Delmarva Lane Wilmington (19801) *(G-15997)*

Delmarva Power Financing I 202 872-2000
800 N King St Ste 400 Wilmington (19801) *(G-15998)*

Delmarva Precision Grinding 302 393-3008
906 Se 2nd St Milford (19963) *(G-7862)*

Delmarva Prosthodontics 302 674-8331
871 S Governors Ave Ste 1 Dover (19904) *(G-2278)*

Delmarva Pump Center Inc (PA) 302 492-1245
335 Strauss Ave Marydel (19964) *(G-6796)*

Delmarva Refrigeration Inc 302 846-2727
504 N Pennsylvania Ave Delmar (19940) *(G-1588)*

Delmarva Repair 302 313-6900
16557 Coastal Hwy Lewes (19958) *(G-5907)*

Delmarva Roofing & Coating Inc 302 349-5174
12982 Mennonite School Rd Greenwood (19950) *(G-4615)*

Delmarva Rubber & Gasket Co 302 424-8300
16356 Sussex Hwy Bridgeville (19933) *(G-693)*

Delmarva Rv Center Inc 302 424-4505
702 Milford Harrington Hwy Milford (19963) *(G-7863)*

Delmarva Services 302 934-8750
28528 Warwick Rd Millsboro (19966) *(G-8267)*

Delmarva Shore Maintenance 302 519-8657
35487 Skipjack Ln Millsboro (19966) *(G-8268)*

Delmarva Sign Co 302 934-6188
24835 Lawson Rd Georgetown (19947) *(G-4289)*

Delmarva Skin PA 302 564-0001
38394 Dupont Blvd Unit Fg Selbyville (19975) *(G-13518)*

Delmarva Soap & Powerwash Sls 302 875-2012
10759 N Laurel Plaza Rd Laurel (19956) *(G-5499)*

Delmarva Space Scnces Fndation 302 236-2761
10046 Iron Pointe Drive Ext Millsboro (19966) *(G-8269)*

Delmarva Sports Action Mag, Fenwick Island *Also Called: Action Enterprise Inc (G-4039)*

Delmarva Spray Foam LLC 302 752-1080
22976 Sussex Ave Georgetown (19947) *(G-4290)*

Delmarva Surgery Assoc 302 644-8880
36031 Tarpon Dr Lewes (19958) *(G-5908)*

Delmarva Surgery Center 302 369-1700
139 E Chestnut Hill Rd Newark (19713) *(G-10505)*

Delmarva Surgery Ctr 443 245-3470
100 Biddle Ave Ste 101 Newark (19702) *(G-10506)*

Delmarva Teen Challenge 302 337-9100
10968 Leadership Way Bridgeville (19933) *(G-694)*

Delmarva Teen Challenge Inc (PA) 302 629-8824
611 3rd St Seaford (19973) *(G-13156)*

Delmarva Transportation Inc 302 349-0840
101 Maryland Ave Greenwood (19950) *(G-4616)*

Delmarva Truss and Panel LLC 302 270-8888
317 N Layton Ave Wyoming (19934) *(G-20984)*

Delmarva Voice & Internet LLC 302 496-0054
432 S Barrington Ct Ste B Newark (19702) *(G-10507)*

Delmarva Water Solutions 302 674-0509
1039 Fowler Ct Dover (19901) *(G-2279)*

ALPHABETIC SECTION

Delmarva Whiskey Club..215 815-1706
36414 Azalea Ave Selbyville (19975) *(G-13519)*

Delmarvalous...302 200-2001
30748 Long Leaf Rd Dagsboro (19939) *(G-1439)*

Delmarvavoip LLC..855 645-8647
16557 Coastal Hwy Lewes (19958) *(G-5909)*

Delnet, Middletown *Also Called: Delstar Technologies Inc (G-7051)*

Delone, Hockessin *Also Called: Ralph Del Signore Jr (G-5353)*

Delong Zhou..302 256-0124
2115 Concord Pike Wilmington (19803) *(G-15999)*

Delores Welch...302 856-7989
22812 Cedar Ln Georgetown (19947) *(G-4291)*

Delpa Builders LLC...302 731-7304
10 King Ave New Castle (19720) *(G-9043)*

Delphi, Wilmington *Also Called: Delphi Financial Group Inc (G-16000)*

Delphi Financial Group Inc (HQ)..............................302 478-5142
1105 N Market St Ste 1230 Wilmington (19801) *(G-16000)*

Delport Holding Company..302 655-7300
529 Terminal Ave New Castle (19720) *(G-9044)*

Delray Foundations Inc...302 503-3341
7411 Marshall St Lincoln (19960) *(G-6664)*

Delrin Usa LLC..302 295-5900
Building 308 Experimental Station 200 Power Mill Rd Wilmington (19803) *(G-16001)*

Delstar Technologies Inc (DH)..................................302 378-8888
601 Industrial Dr Middletown (19709) *(G-7051)*

Delt LLC..215 869-7409
201 Ruthar Dr Ste 4 Newark (19711) *(G-10508)*

Delta Centric LLC...302 268-9359
251 Little Falls Dr Wilmington (19808) *(G-16002)*

Delta Engineering Corporation.................................302 325-9320
13 Drba Way New Castle (19720) *(G-9045)*

Delta Engineering Corporation.................................302 750-1065
20 Shea Way Newark (19713) *(G-10509)*

Delta Epsilon Tau..302 541-0450
31257 Bird Haven St Ocean View (19970) *(G-12503)*

Delta Forms Inc...302 652-3266
5 Germay Dr Wilmington (19804) *(G-16003)*

Delta Gamma LLC...347 387-6956
300 Delaware Ave Ste 210a Wilmington (19801) *(G-16004)*

Delta Kappa Gamma Society......................................302 945-7174
33676 Woodland Cir Lewes (19958) *(G-5910)*

Delta Sales Corp..302 436-6063
5 W Church St Unit 202 Selbyville (19975) *(G-13520)*

Deltrans Inc..302 453-8213
759 Old Baltimore Pike Newark (19702) *(G-10510)*

Deltrust Group Inc...302 362-9900
115 W Laurel St Georgetown (19947) *(G-4292)*

Delverde Corporation..302 656-1950
103 Foulk Rd Ste 202 Wilmington (19803) *(G-16005)*

Delware Injury Care LLC...302 235-1111
4901 Limestone Rd Wilmington (19808) *(G-16006)*

DEMC Academia Institute..301 215-1056
8 The Grn Ste 300 Dover (19901) *(G-2280)*

Demco..302 399-6118
102 E Kilts Ln Middletown (19709) *(G-7052)*

Demec, Smyrna *Also Called: Delaware Municipal Elc Corp (G-13701)*

DEMEP, Newark *Also Called: Delaware Mfg EXT Partnr Inc (G-10460)*

Demo Easel LLC..408 242-2770
221 N Broad St Ste 3a Middletown (19709) *(G-7053)*

Dempsey Farms, Dover *Also Called: Charles Dempsey Farms (G-2057)*

Dempsey Farms LLC..302 734-4937
1708 Fast Landing Rd Dover (19901) *(G-2281)*

Dempseys Service Center Inc....................................302 239-4996
604 Corner Ketch Rd Newark (19711) *(G-10511)*

Dempseys Specialized Svcs LLC...............................302 530-7856
304b Markus Ct Newark (19713) *(G-10512)*

Denali Canning LLC..272 226-6464
221 N Broad St 3a Middletown (19709) *(G-7054)*

Denco Inc..302 798-4200
501 Silverside Rd Ste 132 Wilmington (19809) *(G-16007)*

Dendi Inc..919 448-5511
2093 Philadelphia Pike # 1420 Claymont (19703) *(G-1117)*

Denices Ragged Wreath..302 220-7377
691 Churchmans Rd Newark (19702) *(G-10513)*

Denim Inc...302 401-6502
8 The Green Ste #4172 Dover (19901) *(G-2282)*

Denise A Cunha PHD...302 652-7733
1020 W 18th St Wilmington (19802) *(G-16008)*

Denise Beam...302 539-1900
112 Atlantic Ave Ocean View (19970) *(G-12504)*

Denise Crothers...302 629-7390
26378 Bethel Concord Rd Seaford (19973) *(G-13157)*

Denise Miller Day Care Ce...302 482-9347
2904 N West St Wilmington (19802) *(G-16009)*

Denmark School..302 416-6180
215 W 23rd St Wilmington (19802) *(G-16010)*

Denn Con LLC...443 941-4279
702 Delaware St Historic New Castle (19720) *(G-4973)*

Denney Electric Supply, Millsboro *Also Called: Denney Electric Supply Del Inc (G-8270)*

Denney Electric Supply Del Inc................................302 934-8885
28635 Dupont Blvd Millsboro (19966) *(G-8270)*

Dennis H Snyder Assoc, Wilmington *Also Called: Snyder & Company PA (G-19903)*

Dennis M Hughes...302 632-4503
597 Gallo Rd Harrington (19952) *(G-4761)*

Denovix, Wilmington *Also Called: Denovix Inc (G-16011)*

Denovix Inc..302 442-6911
3411 Silverside Rd Ste 101hb Wilmington (19810) *(G-16011)*

Dent Pro Inc..302 628-0978
14470 Baker Mill Rd Seaford (19973) *(G-13158)*

Dental Associates PA...302 571-0878
2300 Pennsylvania Ave Ste 6cd Wilmington (19806) *(G-16012)*

Dental Associates Delaware PA (PA)......................302 477-4900
1415 Foulk Rd Ste 200 Wilmington (19803) *(G-16013)*

Dental Associates Hockessin......................................302 239-5917
1415 Foulk Rd Ste 201 Wilmington (19803) *(G-16014)*

Dental Associates of Newark.....................................302 737-6761
301 S Chapel St Newark (19711) *(G-10514)*

Dental Group...302 645-8993
34359 Carpenters Way Lewes (19958) *(G-5911)*

Dental Health Assoc Pike Creek, Wilmington *Also Called: J S McKelvey DDS (G-17463)*

Dental Health Center Del-Tech.................................302 657-5176
333 N Shipley St Wilmington (19801) *(G-16015)*

Dental Sleep Solution..302 235-8249
4901 Limestone Rd Wilmington (19808) *(G-16016)*

Dentistry At Walker Square......................................302 735-8940
882 Walker Rd Ste A Dover (19904) *(G-2283)*

Dentistry For Children...302 475-7640
2036 Foulk Rd Ste 200 Wilmington (19810) *(G-16017)*

Dentsply Sirona Inc..302 422-4511
38 W Clarke Ave Milford (19963) *(G-7864)*

Dentsply Sirona Inc..302 422-1043
779 E Masten Cir Milford (19963) *(G-7865)*

Dentsply Sirona Inc..302 430-7474
412 Mccolley St Milford (19963) *(G-7866)*

Dentsply Sirona Inc..302 422-4511
38 W Clarke Ave Milford (19963) *(G-7867)*

Department Psychlgcal Brain SC.............................302 831-4591
105 The Grn Rm 108 Newark (19716) *(G-10515)*

Dependable Cmnty HM Care LLC............................302 893-3779
8 Peachleaf Trl New Castle (19720) *(G-9046)*

Dependable Elec Svc & Repr.....................................302 877-0770
37680 Hudson Rd Frankford (19945) *(G-4101)*

Dependable Trucking Inc..302 655-6271
520 Terminal Ave New Castle (19720) *(G-9047)*

Depository Trust Co Del LLC....................................302 762-2635
3601 N Market St Wilmington (19802) *(G-16018)*

Depro Serical, Townsend *Also Called: Depro-Serical USA Inc (G-13991)*

Depro-Serical USA Inc..302 368-8040
4676 Dupont Pkwy Townsend (19734) *(G-13991)*

Derby Software LLC (PA)...502 435-1371
8 The Grn Ste A Dover (19901) *(G-2284)*

Derco USA, Newark *Also Called: OConnor Belting Intl Inc (G-11576)*

Derek Lawson..302 588-3618
235 Rice Dr Bear (19701) *(G-164)*

ALPHABETIC SECTION

Deride Igo 302 234-4121
28 Findail Dr Newark (19711) *(G-10516)*

Derived Data LLC 845 300-1805
2801 Centerville Rd Wilmington (19808) *(G-16019)*

Derived Data LLC 201 275-1111
2801 Centerville Rd Pmb 610 Wilmington (19808) *(G-16020)*

Derlin USA, Wilmington *Also Called: Delrin Usa LLC (G-16001)*

Dermal Health Science LLC 302 213-8348
19 Holly Cove Ln Dover (19901) *(G-2285)*

Derprosa Spcalty Films USA LLC 856 845-7524
2751 Centerville Rd Ste 400 Wilmington (19808) *(G-16021)*

Desai, Parul MD, Wilmington *Also Called: Rebecca Jaffee MD (G-19373)*

Desalitech Inc 508 981-7950
974 Centre Rd Wilmington (19805) *(G-16022)*

Desanctis Insurance Agency LLC 302 629-8841
26982 Crest Dr Seaford (19973) *(G-13159)*

Deseu 302 883-3048
500 W Loockerman St Ste 400 Dover (19904) *(G-2286)*

Deshields Construction 302 331-5214
281 Sunny Meadow Dr Magnolia (19962) *(G-6740)*

Deshong & Sons Contractors Inc 302 453-8500
2606 Ogletown Rd Newark (19713) *(G-10517)*

Design LLC 888 520-7070
2711 Centerville Rd # 120 Wilmington (19808) *(G-16023)*

Design Collaborative Inc 302 652-4221
1211 Delaware Ave Ste Dc1 Wilmington (19806) *(G-16024)*

Design Consultants Group LLC 302 684-8030
10872d Davidson Dr Milton (19968) *(G-8602)*

Design Contracting Inc 302 429-6900
1000 N Heald St Wilmington (19802) *(G-16025)*

Design Specific US Inc 650 318-6473
501 Silverside Rd Ste 105 Wilmington (19809) *(G-16026)*

Design Technology, Seaford *Also Called: Nouvir Lightning Corporation (G-13320)*

Design Tribe Republic LLC 302 918-5279
300 Delaware Ave Ste 210a Wilmington (19801) *(G-16027)*

Designer Braids and Trade 718 783-9078
148 Vincent Cir Middletown (19709) *(G-7055)*

Designer Consigner Inc 302 373-6318
5 N 1st St Rehoboth Beach (19971) *(G-12721)*

Desires Lingerie 302 744-9969
4200 N Dupont Hwy Dover (19901) *(G-2287)*

Deskzone LLC 212 608-7081
4023 Kennett Pike Wilmington (19807) *(G-16028)*

Dess Machine & Manufacturing 302 736-7457
1426 Pearsons Corner Rd Hartly (19953) *(G-4868)*

Desserts By Dana, Bear *Also Called: Dana E Herbert (G-130)*

Destiny Rescue Intl Inc 574 529-2238
16192 Coastal Hwy Lewes (19958) *(G-5912)*

Destiny Way Logistics LLC 866 526-4900
1007 N Orange St Wilmington (19801) *(G-16029)*

Destorage 302 424-6902
1001 E Masten Cir Milford (19963) *(G-7868)*

Destorage Rehoboth LLC 302 231-2127
19659 Blue Bird Ln Rehoboth Beach (19971) *(G-12722)*

Detail Stone Works 302 357-7065
113 Pike Creek Rd Newark (19711) *(G-10518)*

Detailing Good Brothers 302 482-3348
1600 N Locust St Wilmington (19802) *(G-16030)*

Details Cleaning Service, Lewes *Also Called: Robert Westley (G-6425)*

Detweilers Lighting 302 678-5804
285 Pearsons Corner Rd R Hartly (19953) *(G-4869)*

Deutsche Bank Tr Co Americas 302 636-3301
1011 Centre Rd Ste 200 Wilmington (19805) *(G-16031)*

Deutsche Bank Trust Co Del 302 636-3300
1011 Centre Rd Ste 200 Wilmington (19805) *(G-16032)*

Devadasi 302 229-7216
4904 Old Hill Rd Wilmington (19807) *(G-16033)*

Deval Patel-Lennon Esq PA Inc 302 998-2000
5153 W Woodmill Dr # 18 Wilmington (19808) *(G-16034)*

Devastator Game Calls LLC 302 875-5328
12009 Lahoba Ln Laurel (19956) *(G-5500)*

Developers Concrete Con, Lincoln *Also Called: Mitchell E Morton (G-6689)*

Developing Minds Preschool 302 995-9611
2106 Saint James Church Rd Wilmington (19808) *(G-16035)*

Devere Insul HM Prfmce LLC 302 854-0344
22976 Sussex Ave Georgetown (19947) *(G-4293)*

Devereux Foundation 302 731-2500
930 Old Harmony Rd Ste B Newark (19713) *(G-10519)*

Devereux Foundation, Newark *Also Called: Devereux Foundation (G-10519)*

Devlin Law Firm LLC 302 449-9010
1526 Gilpin Ave Wilmington (19806) *(G-16036)*

Devon Sadlowski DMD 302 735-8940
882 Walker Rd Ste A Dover (19904) *(G-2288)*

Devstringx Technologies Inc 650 209-7815
16192 Coastal Hwy Lewes (19958) *(G-5913)*

Dew Softech Inc 302 834-2555
200 Biddle Ave Ste 212 Newark (19702) *(G-10520)*

Dewberry Insurance Agency Inc 302 995-9550
5700 Kirkwood Hwy Ste 103 Wilmington (19808) *(G-16037)*

Dewey Beach House 302 227-4000
1710 Coastal Hwy Dewey Beach (19971) *(G-1666)*

Dewey Beach Yoga LLC 443 250-6770
119 Jersey St Dewey Beach (19971) *(G-1667)*

Dewey Beer & Food Company LLC 302 227-1182
2100 Coastal Hwy Dewey Beach (19971) *(G-1668)*

Dewey Beer Company, Dewey Beach *Also Called: Dewey Beer & Food Company LLC (G-1668)*

Dewey Beer Company LLC 302 329-9759
21241 Iron Throne Dr Milton (19968) *(G-8603)*

Dewitt & Associates LLC 302 226-0521
55 Fields End Rehoboth Beach (19971) *(G-12723)*

Dewitt Heating & AC 267 228-7355
1 Joanne Ct Bear (19701) *(G-165)*

Dewitt Hvac 267 228-7355
1 Joanne Ct Bear (19701) *(G-166)*

Dewson Construction Co 302 227-3095
20616 Coastal Hwy Rehoboth Beach (19971) *(G-12724)*

Dewson Construction Co (PA) 302 427-2250
9 Jefferson Ave Wilmington (19805) *(G-16038)*

Dewson Construction Company (PA) 302 427-2250
7 S Lincoln St Wilmington (19805) *(G-16039)*

Dexsta Federal Credit Union 302 996-4893
300 Foulk Rd Ste 100 Wilmington (19803) *(G-16040)*

Dexsta Federal Credit Union (PA) 302 996-4893
1310 Centerville Rd Wilmington (19808) *(G-16041)*

Dexsta Federal Credit Union 302 695-3888
E 444-108 Wilmington (19880) *(G-16042)*

Deyas Honest Solutions LLC 302 682-1830
199 Wildflower Cir N Magnolia (19962) *(G-6741)*

Dezins Unlimited Inc 302 652-4545
323 Clubhouse Ln Wilmington (19810) *(G-16043)*

Df Quillen Sons Inc DBA 302 227-7368
19897 Hebron Rd Unit F Rehoboth Beach (19971) *(G-12725)*

Dfa Dairy Brands Fluid LLC 302 398-8321
17267 S Dupont Hwy Harrington (19952) *(G-4762)*

Dfc Industries, New Castle *Also Called: Dfc Industries Inc (G-9048)*

Dfc Industries Inc 215 292-1572
4 Bellecor Dr Unit B New Castle (19720) *(G-9048)*

Dfs Corporate Services LLC 302 735-3902
34 Starlifter Ave Dover (19901) *(G-2289)*

Dfs Corporate Services LLC 302 349-4512
502 E Market St Greenwood (19950) *(G-4617)*

Dfs Corporate Services LLC 302 323-7191
12 Reads Way New Castle (19720) *(G-9049)*

Dgc Publishing LLC 302 634-0461
31 Bass Ct Newark (19713) *(G-10521)*

Dgs, Newark *Also Called: Delaware Gdnce Svcs For Chldre (G-10448)*

DH Tech Wilmington De 215 680-9194
1 Limousine Dr Wilmington (19803) *(G-16044)*

Dhm Wilmington LLC 302 656-8952
700 N King St Wilmington (19801) *(G-16045)*

Di Sabatino, M P DDS, Smyrna *Also Called: Caimar Corporation (G-13672)*

(PA)=Parent Co (HQ)=Headquarters (DH)=Div Headquarters

Diablo Works LLC   ALPHABETIC SECTION

Diablo Works LLC 302 559-2118
  1521 Concord Pike Ste 301 Wilmington (19803) *(G-16046)*

Diabuddies 302 893-0311
  4023 Greenmount Dr Wilmington (19810) *(G-16047)*

Diagnostic Imaging Associates, Newark Also Called: Omega Imaging Associates LLC *(G-11585)*

Dialog Engineers Inc 302 581-8080
  600 N Broad St Ste 5 Middletown (19709) *(G-7056)*

Dialog News Paper Inc 302 573-3109
  1925 Delaware Ave Fl 3 Wilmington (19806) *(G-16048)*

Diamond Chemical & Supply Co 302 656-7786
  524 S Walnut St Ste B Wilmington (19801) *(G-16049)*

Diamond Chiropractic 302 300-4242
  2100 Baynard Blvd Ste B Wilmington (19802) *(G-16050)*

Diamond Chiropractic Inc 302 892-9355
  1101 Twin Ceiling Ln Ste 201 Newark (19713) *(G-10522)*

Diamond Electric Inc 302 697-3296
  3566 Peachtree Run Rd Ste 1 Dover (19901) *(G-2290)*

Diamond Glo Cleaning Solutions, Bear Also Called: David Jenkins *(G-132)*

Diamond Graphite, Wilmington Also Called: Frc Global Inc *(G-16732)*

Diamond Hill Inc 302 999-0302
  34 Industrial Blvd # 104 New Castle (19720) *(G-9050)*

Diamond Materials 302 292-1100
  394 S Chapel St Newark (19713) *(G-10523)*

Diamond Materials LLC 302 658-6524
  242 N James St Ste 102 Wilmington (19804) *(G-16051)*

Diamond Mechanical Inc 302 697-7694
  3588 Peachtree Run Rd Dover (19901) *(G-2291)*

Diamond Minds LLC 302 359-5069
  4470 Mud Mill Rd Camden Wyoming (19934) *(G-932)*

Diamond Motor Sports Inc 302 697-3222
  4595 S Dupont Hwy Dover (19901) *(G-2292)*

Diamond Pest Control 302 654-2300
  6 Weldin Park Dr Wilmington (19803) *(G-16052)*

Diamond Standard LLC 917 676-6312
  3 Germay Dr Wilmington (19804) *(G-16053)*

Diamond Standard Productions 302 508-2931
  359 E Frazier St Smyrna (19977) *(G-13709)*

Diamond State Cabinetry 302 250-3531
  32627 Millsboro Hwy Millsboro (19966) *(G-8271)*

Diamond State Chiropractic 302 737-6037
  215 Upper Pike Creek Rd Newark (19711) *(G-10524)*

Diamond State Chiropractic, Newark Also Called: Diamond Chiropractic Inc *(G-10522)*

Diamond State CLT Inc 800 282-0477
  9 E Loockerman St Ste 205 Dover (19901) *(G-2293)*

DIAMOND STATE COMMUNITY LAND T, Dover Also Called: Diamond State CLT Inc *(G-2293)*

Diamond State Corporation (PA) 302 674-1300
  602 Pear St Dover (19904) *(G-2294)*

Diamond State Counseling 302 683-1055
  2644 Kirkwood Highway Ste 250 Newark (19711) *(G-10525)*

Diamond State Curling Club 856 577-3747
  8 E Aldine Dr Hockessin (19707) *(G-5186)*

Diamond State Dentistry 302 424-7976
  215 W Liberty Way Milford (19963) *(G-7869)*

Diamond State Diesel 864 784-6608
  5585 Dupont Pkwy Smyrna (19977) *(G-13710)*

Diamond State Express LLC 302 563-3514
  105 E Bridle Path Hockessin (19707) *(G-5187)*

Diamond State Financial Group, Newark Also Called: Diamond State Fincl Group Inc *(G-10526)*

Diamond State Fincl Group Inc 302 366-0366
  900 Prides Xing Newark (19713) *(G-10526)*

Diamond State Ghost Invstgtors 302 463-4589
  37 Longspur Dr Wilmington (19808) *(G-16054)*

Diamond State Graphics Inc 302 325-1100
  200 Century Park New Castle (19720) *(G-9051)*

Diamond State Home Auxiliary 302 652-9331
  8 S Dupont Rd Newport (19804) *(G-12449)*

Diamond State Homes & Rmdlg 302 983-5574
  176 Starr Rd Newark (19711) *(G-10527)*

Diamond State Machining Inc (PA) 302 398-8437
  207 Main St Farmington (19950) *(G-3935)*

Diamond State Meats LLC 302 270-0009
  37369 Martin St Rehoboth Beach (19971) *(G-12726)*

Diamond State Pest Control Co 302 250-3403
  244 Morgans Choice Rd Camden Wyoming (19934) *(G-933)*

Diamond State Pole Bldings LLC (PA) 302 387-1710
  7288 S Dupont Hwy Felton (19943) *(G-3960)*

Diamond State Port Corporation 302 472-7678
  1 Hausel Rd Lbby Wilmington (19801) *(G-16055)*

Diamond State Promotions 302 999-1900
  3211 Dunlap Dr Wilmington (19808) *(G-16056)*

Diamond State Props 302 528-7146
  463 Granger Dr Bear (19701) *(G-167)*

Diamond State Pty Rentl & Sls 302 777-6677
  53 Germay Dr Wilmington (19804) *(G-16057)*

Diamond State Recycling Corp 302 655-1501
  1600 Bowers St Wilmington (19802) *(G-16058)*

Diamond State Srgcal Assoc LLC 302 449-9660
  102 Sleepy Hollow Dr Ste 101 Middletown (19709) *(G-7057)*

Diamond State Tele Coml Un 302 999-1100
  1819 Newport Rd Ste A Wilmington (19808) *(G-16059)*

Diamond State Tire Inc 302 836-1919
  3482 Wrangle Hill Rd Bear (19701) *(G-168)*

Diamond State Truck Center LLC 302 275-9050
  29 E Commons Blvd Ste 300 New Castle (19720) *(G-9052)*

Diamond State Welding LLC 302 644-8489
  13307 Jefferson Rd Milton (19968) *(G-8604)*

Diamond State Whsng & Dist, New Castle Also Called: First State Warehousing *(G-9134)*

Diamond State Wterproofing Sys 302 325-0866
  13 King Ct Ste 5 New Castle (19720) *(G-9053)*

Diamond Technologies Inc 302 421-8252
  4001 Miller Rd Ste 3 Wilmington (19802) *(G-16060)*

Diane Austin 302 856-3369
  15079 Wilson Hill Rd Georgetown (19947) *(G-4294)*

Diane Lacash Inc 302 608-2477
  8 Denham Ave Claymont (19703) *(G-1118)*

Diane Newman 302 994-6838
  204 Milltown Rd Wilmington (19808) *(G-16061)*

Diane Spence Day Care 302 335-4460
  19 Ruyter Dr Frederica (19946) *(G-4166)*

Dianes Bus Service 302 629-4336
  Rt 2 Box 79 Seaford (19973) *(G-13160)*

Dianes Nail and Spa 302 538-7185
  3469 S Dupont Hwy Camden (19934) *(G-818)*

Diann Jones Agcy - Nationwide 302 530-1234
  226 Horseshoe Dr Middletown (19709) *(G-7058)*

Diavaeh Luxury Car Rental LLC 302 497-3443
  1317 Darling Dr Middletown (19709) *(G-7059)*

Diaz and Costa Hardwood Flrng 302 212-5923
  19871 Coastal Hwy Rehoboth Beach (19971) *(G-12727)*

Diaz Drywall LLC 302 602-1110
  73 Auckland Dr Newark (19702) *(G-10528)*

Dibiasos Clg Rstration Svc Inc 302 376-7111
  690 Blackbird Station Rd Townsend (19734) *(G-13992)*

Dick Ennis Inc 302 945-2627
  22357 John J Williams Hwy Lewes (19958) *(G-5914)*

Dickerson Fence Co Inc 302 846-2227
  36947 Saint George Rd Delmar (19940) *(G-1589)*

Diehl & Co CPA 302 644-4441
  18306 Coastal Hwy Lewes (19958) *(G-5915)*

Diehl Foraker Cpas LLC 800 748-0354
  18306 Coastal Hwy Lewes (19958) *(G-5916)*

Dienay Distribution Corp 732 766-0814
  101 Trupenny Turn Ste 1b Middletown (19709) *(G-7060)*

Dieste Mark Design Build LLC 301 921-9050
  32895 Coastal Hwy Unit 201 Bethany Beach (19930) *(G-597)*

Diff Consulting LLC 302 689-3979
  919 N Market St Ste 725 Wilmington (19801) *(G-16062)*

Diga Funding LLC 404 631-7127
  8 The Grn Ste B Dover (19901) *(G-2295)*

Digen Auto Group, Middletown Also Called: Lifetime Skills Services LLC *(G-7302)*

Digiapp LLC 855 217-2744
  16192 Coastal Hwy Lewes (19958) *(G-5917)*

ALPHABETIC SECTION — Discover Financial Services

Digibox LLC 302 203-0088
8 The Grn Ste A Dover (19901) *(G-2296)*

Digilence LLC 678 296-9198
651 N Broad St Ste 201 Middletown (19709) *(G-7061)*

Digital ARC LLC 855 275-2770
1723a Marsh Rd Ste 117 Wilmington (19810) *(G-16063)*

Digital Broadcast Corporation 215 285-0912
2207 Concord Pike # 619 Wilmington (19803) *(G-16064)*

Digital Generation Inc 302 368-0002
450 Corporate Blvd Newark (19702) *(G-10529)*

Digital Ink Sciences LLC 951 757-0027
3 Germay Dr Ste 4 Wilmington (19804) *(G-16065)*

Digital Interxion Holding LLC (DH) 737 281-0101
1209 N Orange St Wilmington (19801) *(G-16066)*

Digital Legal, Wilmington *Also Called: DLS Discovery LLC* *(G-16105)*

Digital Marketing & Sales, Wilmington *Also Called: GIERD INC* *(G-16858)*

Digital Memories Videography 302 682-9180
217 N Bradford St Seaford (19973) *(G-13161)*

Digital Office Solutions Inc 302 286-6706
101 Sandy Dr Newark (19713) *(G-10530)*

Digital Peak Inc 214 215-9054
3422 Old Capitol Trl Ste 368 Wilmington (19808) *(G-16067)*

Digital Sounds 302 644-9187
24 Tiffany Dr Rehoboth Beach (19971) *(G-12728)*

Digital Technica LLC 416 829-8400
1201 N Orange St Ste 7167 Wilmington (19801) *(G-16068)*

Digital Technologies 302 731-1928
62 Albe Dr Ste B Newark (19702) *(G-10531)*

Digital Wish, Milton *Also Called: Digital Wish Inc* *(G-8605)*

Digital Wish Inc (PA) 802 375-6721
15187 Hudson Rd Milton (19968) *(G-8605)*

Digitalai Software Inc 678 268-3340
4023 Kennett Pike Unit 50128 Wilmington (19807) *(G-16069)*

Digitalpaye Inc 302 232-5116
8 The Grn Dover (19901) *(G-2297)*

Digitalxc Inc 650 319-7249
1013 Centre Rd Ste 403s Wilmington (19805) *(G-16070)*

Digitalzone Inc 646 771-6969
16192 Coastal Hwy Lewes (19958) *(G-5918)*

Digitizing America LLC 315 882-9516
147 Quigley Blvd Ste 12006 Historic New Castle (19720) *(G-4974)*

Digitlogy LLC DBA Exprttexting 302 703-9672
124 Broadkill Rd Milton (19968) *(G-8606)*

Dignan Group, Bethany Beach *Also Called: Highland Consulting Group Inc* *(G-607)*

Dignisys Inc 845 213-1121
8 The Grn Ste R Dover (19901) *(G-2298)*

Dijitru Inc 903 345-4878
257 Old Churchmans Rd New Castle (19720) *(G-9054)*

Diligent Bus Solutions LLC 302 897-5993
1 Marra Pl Newark (19702) *(G-10532)*

Diligent Detail 302 482-2836
2203 Mitch Rd Wilmington (19804) *(G-16071)*

Dillons Driftwood Entp LLC 302 645-7500
18282 Coastal Hwy Lewes (19958) *(G-5919)*

Dills Electric 302 674-3444
11924 Willow Grove Rd Camden (19934) *(G-819)*

Dima II Inc 302 427-0787
2400 W 4th St Wilmington (19805) *(G-16072)*

Dima Ix Inc 302 427-0787
2400 W 4th St Wilmington (19805) *(G-16073)*

Dimarquez Intl Ministries Inc 302 256-4847
417 Moores Ln Historic New Castle (19720) *(G-4975)*

Dimensional Stone Products LLC 302 322-3900
76 Southgate Blvd New Castle (19720) *(G-9055)*

Dimitrios M D Barmpouletos 302 644-7676
34453 King Street Row Lewes (19958) *(G-5920)*

Dimo Corp 302 324-8100
46 Industrial Blvd New Castle (19720) *(G-9056)*

Dimple Construction Inc 302 559-7535
3310 Wrangle Hill Rd Ste 112 Bear (19701) *(G-169)*

Dina R Anderson 302 623-4144
4735 Ogletown Stanton Rd Ste 2310 Newark (19713) *(G-10533)*

Dingle & Kane PA 302 731-5200
356 E Main St Ste A Newark (19711) *(G-10534)*

Dining Software Group Inc 720 236-9572
2140 S Dupont Hwy Camden (19934) *(G-820)*

Dinner Bell Inn 302 227-2561
2 Christian St Rehoboth Beach (19971) *(G-12729)*

Dino Dicriscio 302 762-0610
610 Foulk Rd Wilmington (19803) *(G-16074)*

Diocesan Council Inc 302 475-4688
2320 Grubb Rd Wilmington (19810) *(G-16075)*

Dionne Michelles Luxury Hair 484 362-9242
6 Ritchie Dr Bear (19701) *(G-170)*

Dipna Inc 302 478-0300
5209 Concord Pike Wilmington (19803) *(G-16076)*

Dippold Marble Granite 302 734-8505
101 Hatchery Rd Dover (19901) *(G-2299)*

Dippold Marble Granite (PA) 302 324-9101
110 W Main St Middletown (19709) *(G-7062)*

Direct & Correct Inc 302 697-7117
6236 Mud Mill Rd Camden Wyoming (19934) *(G-934)*

Direct Cremation Services Del 302 656-6873
1900 Delaware Ave Wilmington (19806) *(G-16077)*

Direct Importer LLC 302 838-2183
843 Salem Church Rd Newark (19702) *(G-10535)*

Direct Medical LLC 781 640-7474
1000n N West St Ste 1501 Wilmington (19801) *(G-16078)*

Direct Mobile Transit, Wilmington *Also Called: Direct Mobile Transit Inc* *(G-16079)*

Direct Mobile Transit Inc 302 218-5106
2110 Duncan Rd # 3 Wilmington (19808) *(G-16079)*

Direct Radiography Corp 302 631-2700
600 Technology Dr Newark (19702) *(G-10536)*

Direct Trends USA LLC 347 354-2899
2055 Limestone Rd Wilmington (19808) *(G-16080)*

Directrestore LLC 650 276-0384
3500 S Dupont Hwy Dover (19901) *(G-2300)*

Directv 302 203-9162
4901 Limestone Rd Wilmington (19808) *(G-16081)*

Dirickson Creek Construction L 302 604-2482
37377 Dirickson Creek Rd Frankford (19945) *(G-4102)*

Dirt Works Inc 302 947-2429
22547 Waterview Rd Lewes (19958) *(G-5921)*

Dis Daycare 302 888-0350
1725 W 7th St Wilmington (19805) *(G-16082)*

Dis Management 302 543-4481
713 Greenbank Rd Wilmington (19808) *(G-16083)*

Disab LLC 302 645-6987
805 Savannah Rd Lewes (19958) *(G-5922)*

Disabatino Construction Co 302 652-3838
1 S Cleveland Ave Wilmington (19805) *(G-16084)*

Disabatino Enterprises LLC 302 652-3838
1 S Cleveland Ave Wilmington (19805) *(G-16085)*

Disabatino Landscaping Inc 302 764-0408
471 B And O Ln Wilmington (19804) *(G-16086)*

Disabatino Ldscpg Tree Svc Inc 302 764-0408
471 B And O Ln Wilmington (19804) *(G-16087)*

Disabilities Law Program, Dover *Also Called: Community Legal Aid Society* *(G-2119)*

Disabilities Law Program, Georgetown *Also Called: Community Legal Aid Society* *(G-4263)*

Disanto, Joseph MD, Wilmington *Also Called: Brandi Wine Pediatric Inc* *(G-15041)*

Disaster Research Center 302 831-6618
111 Academy St Rm 166 Newark (19716) *(G-10537)*

Discidium Technologies, Newark *Also Called: Discidium Technology Inc* *(G-10538)*

Discidium Technology Inc 347 220-5979
100 Cullen Way Newark (19711) *(G-10538)*

Disclo Inc (PA) 607 280-8949
8 The Grn Ste 8372 Dover (19901) *(G-2301)*

Discount Central, Wilmington *Also Called: Lotus Logistics LLC* *(G-18002)*

Discount Cigarette Depot 302 398-4447
1 Liberty Plz Harrington (19952) *(G-4763)*

Discover Bank (HQ) 302 349-4512
502 E Market St Greenwood (19950) *(G-4618)*

Discover Financial Services, New Castle *Also Called: Dfs Corporate Services LLC* *(G-9049)*

Discover Permaculture LLC — 850 970-7376
  651 N Broad St Ste 206 Middletown (19709) (G-7063)
Discovery Cove Learning Center, Laurel Also Called: Karen Schreiber (G-5541)
Discovery Island Preschool — 302 732-7529
  32532 Smith Dr Dagsboro (19939) (G-1440)
Discovery Island Preschool, Seaford Also Called: Sussex Prschool Erly Care Ctrs (G-13421)
Dish Quo LLC (PA) — 845 709-1674
  874 Walker Rd Dover (19904) (G-2302)
Displayplan Inc — 502 767-1946
  1013 Centre Rd Ste 403a Wilmington (19805) (G-16088)
Disrupt Industries Deleware — 424 229-9300
  8 The Grn Dover (19901) (G-2303)
Disrupt Pharma Tech, Dover Also Called: Disrupt Pharma Tech Africa Inc (G-2304)
Disrupt Pharma Tech Africa Inc — 312 945-8002
  8 The Grn Ste A Dover (19901) (G-2304)
Distinction LLC — 302 362-7574
  22467 Ridgecrest Dr Milton (19968) (G-8607)
Distinctive Landscaping LLC — 410 971-8466
  12101 Tuckers Rd Greenwood (19950) (G-4619)
Distinctive Stationery LLC — 410 247-5600
  18801 Riverwalk Dr Milton (19968) (G-8608)
Distribution Headquarters, Wilmington Also Called: Casale Marble Imports Inc (G-15262)
Distribution Marketing of Del — 302 658-6397
  818 S Heald St Ste A Wilmington (19801) (G-16089)
Ditch Witch of Virginia — 302 629-3602
  182 Kent Dr Seaford (19973) (G-13162)
Dito Ventures Inc — 305 424-9877
  3 Germay Dr Unit 41736 Wilmington (19804) (G-16090)
Ditrocchio Maria Antonetta — 302 450-6790
  814 S Governors Ave Dover (19904) (G-2305)
Divas Inn — 302 753-2170
  223 E 35th St Wilmington (19802) (G-16091)
Divergent LLC — 302 275-7019
  405 W 34th St Wilmington (19802) (G-16092)
Divergent Real Estate & Inv, Wilmington Also Called: Divergent LLC (G-16092)
Diverse Generations LLC — 571 248-1806
  8 The Grn Dover (19901) (G-2306)
Diverse Supply Solutions LLC — 215 588-8300
  35486 Bayview Ln Millsboro (19966) (G-8272)
Diversfied Entps Worldwide LLC — 888 230-3703
  1000 N West St Ste 1200 Wilmington (19801) (G-16093)
Diversified LLC — 302 765-3500
  2200 Concord Pike Ste 104 Wilmington (19803) (G-16094)
Diversified Chemical Pdts Inc — 302 656-5293
  60 Germay Dr Wilmington (19804) (G-16095)
Diversified Lighting Assoc Inc — 302 286-6370
  5466 Fairmont Dr Wilmington (19808) (G-16096)
DIVERSIFIED LIGHTING ASSOCIATES, INC., Wilmington Also Called: Diversified Lighting Assoc Inc (G-16096)
Diversio Inc (PA) — 855 647-4155
  2093a Philadelphia Pike Ste 384 Claymont (19703) (G-1119)
Diversion Company Inc — 415 800-4136
  850 New Burton Rd Dover (19904) (G-2307)
Diversity In Beauty Inc — 323 840-8801
  919 N Market St Ste 950 Wilmington (19801) (G-16097)
Divine Element Hbb — 302 538-5209
  405 W Lebanon Rd Dover (19901) (G-2308)
Divine Legacy Group LLC — 973 986-7896
  1025 Sherbourne Rd Middletown (19709) (G-7064)
Divine Painting and Cnstr — 302 983-9405
  41 Martindale Dr Newark (19713) (G-10539)
Divine Profiles Inc — 302 633-3400
  2606 Kirkwood Hwy Wilmington (19805) (G-16098)
Divine Transitional Life LLC — 215 432-4974
  23 Eastwind Ct Newark (19713) (G-10540)
Divinity Assets, Dover Also Called: Divinity Assets LLC (G-2309)
Divinity Assets LLC — 323 508-4130
  8 The Grn Ste A Dover (19901) (G-2309)
Divinity Assets LLC — 323 508-4130
  8 The Grn Ste A Dover (19901) (G-2310)
Divinity Press — 267 981-4002
  1203 Hurlock Ct Bear (19701) (G-171)

Division Child Spport Enfrcmen, Georgetown Also Called: Delaware Dept Hlth Social Svcs (G-4280)
Division For Visually Impaired, New Castle Also Called: Delaware Dept Hlth Social Svcs (G-9020)
Division One Basketball LLC — 302 573-2528
  1201 N Orange St Ste 7193 Wilmington (19801) (G-16099)
Division Svcs For Aging Adlts — 302 255-9390
  1901 N Dupont Hwy Fl 1 New Castle (19720) (G-9057)
Divvz Inc — 571 238-1722
  16192 Coastal Hwy Lewes (19958) (G-5923)
Dixon Brothers LLC — 302 377-8289
  601 A St Wilmington (19801) (G-16100)
Dixon Contracting Inc — 302 653-4623
  1614 Seeneytown Rd Dover (19904) (G-2311)
Dixon Hughes Goodman LLP — 336 714-8100
  1 S Main St Camden (19934) (G-821)
Diy Tool Supply LLC — 302 253-8461
  23135 Lewes Georgetown Hwy Unit 15 Georgetown (19947) (G-4295)
Diyo Inc (PA) — 647 354-8859
  8 The Grn Ste R Dover (19901) (G-2312)
Dj First Class — 302 345-0602
  20 Robins Nest Ln New Castle (19720) (G-9058)
Django Stars Ltd Liability Co — 415 996-8054
  2711 Centerville Rd Ste 400 Wilmington (19808) (G-16101)
Djh Enterprises Vii LLC — 410 749-0100
  32442 Royal Blvd Unit 2 Dagsboro (19939) (G-1441)
Djlong Services — 302 541-4884
  23 Longview Dr Ocean View (19970) (G-12505)
DJT Operations LLC — 302 498-9070
  3 Germay Dr Ste 2475 Wilmington (19804) (G-16102)
Dkmrbh Inc — 302 250-4428
  704 N King St Ste 500 Wilmington (19801) (G-16103)
Dks Sports Development LLC — 302 222-6184
  24 Stage Rd Newark (19711) (G-10541)
Dl Holding and Design Inc — 302 219-4922
  16192 Coastal Hwy Lewes (19958) (G-5924)
Dla Piper LLP (us) — 302 654-3025
  919 N Market St Wilmington (19801) (G-16104)
Dlc Drywall — 302 382-2213
  1044 Abbotts Pond Rd Greenwood (19950) (G-4620)
DLS Discovery LLC — 302 888-2060
  1007 N Orange St Ste 510 Wilmington (19801) (G-16105)
Dlt Federal Bus Syst Corp — 302 358-2229
  1000 N West St Ste 1200 Wilmington (19801) (G-16106)
Dm KTure LLC — 201 892-3028
  15 Wisteria Way Bear (19701) (G-172)
Dmac Enterprises LLC — 917 504-4529
  221 N Broad St Middletown (19709) (G-7065)
DMai Boyd LLC — 302 330-8293
  8 The Grn # 4000 Dover (19901) (G-2313)
DMC Power Inc — 302 276-0303
  98 Quigley Blvd Historic New Castle (19720) (G-4976)
DMD Business Forms & Prtg Co — 302 998-8200
  204 S Maryland Ave Wilmington (19804) (G-16107)
Dmg Clearances Inc — 302 239-6337
  7209 Lancaster Pike Ste 4-330 Hockessin (19707) (G-5188)
Dmg Marketing Inc — 302 575-1610
  5722 Kennett Pike Wilmington (19807) (G-16108)
Dmi, Wilmington Also Called: Sign Express (G-19820)
Dml Creation, Newark Also Called: 9193 4323 Quebec Inc (G-9717)
Dmm International Group Inc — 214 233-6898
  1007 N Orange St Wilmington (19801) (G-16109)
Dmms, Newark Also Called: Delaware Medical MGT Svcs LLC (G-10459)
Dmp Security Agency LLC — 302 384-3745
  706 N West St Wilmington (19801) (G-16110)
DMS Solution — 302 753-0040
  26 Foxhunt Dr Bear (19701) (G-173)
DMS Solution — 302 689-6558
  2104 Christiana Mdws Bear (19701) (G-174)
Dna Roofing and Siding — 302 455-2180
  31 Savoy Rd Newark (19702) (G-10542)

ALPHABETIC SECTION

Dnd Limousine Service..302 998-5856
   104c S John St Wilmington (19804) *(G-16111)*
DNG YOUTH FOUNDATION, New Castle *Also Called: Delaware Nat Gard Yuth Fndtion* *(G-9028)*
Dnr Auto..302 698-7829
   2428 W Denneys Rd Dover (19904) *(G-2314)*
Dnrec Air Waste Management...302 739-9406
   30 S American Ave Dover (19901) *(G-2315)*
Do It Up Designs LLC..484 269-6142
   27569 Mayfield Rd Millsboro (19966) *(G-8273)*
Do Nothing Corp..216 780-1910
   254 Chapman Rd Ste 208 Newark (19702) *(G-10543)*
Doc Foals..302 632-0424
   1407 Woodmill Dr Dover (19904) *(G-2316)*
Doc Optics Center..302 477-2626
   272 Carter Dr Middletown (19709) *(G-7066)*
Doc REO Media LLC..818 824-2885
   16192 Coastal Hwy Lewes (19958) *(G-5925)*
Docklands Riverfront..302 658-6626
   110 S West St Wilmington (19801) *(G-16112)*
Docs Medical LLC..301 401-1489
   25 Dynasty Dr Bear (19701) *(G-175)*
Doctor Laubers Karate Plus, Bear *Also Called: Taekwondo Fitness Ctr of Del* *(G-524)*
Doctors For Emergency Svc PC..302 733-1000
   4755 Ogletown Stanton Rd Newark (19718) *(G-10544)*
Doctors Pathology Services PA..302 677-0000
   1253 College Park Dr Dover (19904) *(G-2317)*
Doculogica Corp..302 753-5944
   104 David Rd Wilmington (19804) *(G-16113)*
Document Advisor Inc...786 206-0756
   8 The Grn Dover (19901) *(G-2318)*
Documo Inc..858 299-5295
   919 N Market St Ste 950 Wilmington (19801) *(G-16114)*
Docuvault Delaware Valley LLC..302 366-0220
   300 Pencader Dr Newark (19702) *(G-10545)*
Dodd Health Innovation LLC...410 598-7266
   31027 Scissorbill Rd Ocean View (19970) *(G-12506)*
DOE Legal, Wilmington *Also Called: DOE Technologies Inc* *(G-16116)*
DOE Legal LLC..302 798-7500
   1200 Philadelphia Pike Ste 1 Wilmington (19809) *(G-16115)*
DOE Technologies Inc..302 792-1285
   1200 Philadelphia Pike Ste 1 Wilmington (19809) *(G-16116)*
Dog Anya..302 456-0108
   918 Kenilworth Ave Newark (19711) *(G-10546)*
Dog House Ventures Inc..302 738-2267
   21 Grosbeak Ln Newark (19711) *(G-10547)*
Dog Stop...302 376-9006
   108 Sleepy Hollow Dr Ste 100 Middletown (19709) *(G-7067)*
Dog Stop...302 416-4646
   101 Greenbank Rd Wilmington (19808) *(G-16117)*
Dogfish Head Brewings & Eats, Rehoboth Beach *Also Called: Dogfish Head Inc* *(G-12730)*
Dogfish Head Companies LLC...302 684-1000
   6 Cannery Vlg Milton (19968) *(G-8609)*
Dogfish Head Craft Brewery LLC...302 684-1000
   6 Cannery Vlg Milton (19968) *(G-8610)*
Dogfish Head Inc...302 226-2739
   320 Rehoboth Ave Rehoboth Beach (19971) *(G-12730)*
Dogfish Inn..302 644-8292
   105 Savannah Rd Lewes (19958) *(G-5926)*
Dogwatch of Delaware..302 268-3434
   1417 Spruce Ave Wilmington (19805) *(G-16118)*
Doherty & Associates Inc...302 239-3500
   4550 Linden Hill Rd Ste 130 Wilmington (19808) *(G-16119)*
Dohery Funeral Homes Inc...302 999-8277
   3200 Limestone Rd Wilmington (19808) *(G-16120)*
Dojupa LLC..302 300-2009
   5586 Kirkwood Hwy Wilmington (19808) *(G-16121)*
Dokan Inc...386 259-8587
   8 The Grn Dover (19901) *(G-2319)*
Dole, Wilmington *Also Called: Dole Fresh Fruit Company* *(G-16123)*
Dole, Wilmington *Also Called: Dole Fresh Fruit Company* *(G-16124)*
Dole Food, Wilmington *Also Called: Dole Food Company Inc* *(G-16122)*
Dole Food Company Inc...302 652-6060
   Port Of Wilmington Lbr Rd Wilmington (19899) *(G-16122)*
Dole Fresh Fruit Company..302 652-6484
   70 Gist Rd Wilmington (19801) *(G-16123)*
Dole Fresh Fruit Company..302 652-2215
   1 Hausel Rd Wilmington (19801) *(G-16124)*
Dolphin Beach LLC..302 654-3543
   2400 W 11th St Wilmington (19805) *(G-16125)*
Dolphin Design & Communic, Newark *Also Called: Delaware Design Company* *(G-10435)*
Domain Hr Solutions...302 357-9401
   364 E Main St Ste 1012 Middletown (19709) *(G-7068)*
Domenic Di Donato Plbg Htg Inc...856 207-4919
   128 Shrewsbury Dr Wilmington (19810) *(G-16126)*
Domestic Gen USA Resources LLC (PA).............................312 730-2437
   8 The Grn Ste R Dover (19901) *(G-2320)*
Domestic Marketing Svcs LLC...646 361-9827
   2711 Centerville Rd # 400 Wilmington (19808) *(G-16127)*
Domian International Svc LLC..804 837-3616
   22 Zion Dr Smyrna (19977) *(G-13711)*
Dominic A Di Febo & Sons...302 425-5054
   812 Rose St Wilmington (19805) *(G-16128)*
Dominic Gioffre DDS PA..302 239-0410
   4901 Limestone Rd Wilmington (19808) *(G-16129)*
Dominion Cars LLC...302 730-3882
   624 W Division St Dover (19904) *(G-2321)*
Dominique Ho..302 234-2971
   252 Pond Dr Hockessin (19707) *(G-5189)*
Dominos Body Shop..302 697-3801
   467 Moose Lodge Rd Camden Wyoming (19934) *(G-935)*
Don A Beskrone...302 654-1888
   500 Delaware Ave Ste 800 Wilmington (19801) *(G-16130)*
Don Baag MD...302 235-2351
   722 Yorklyn Rd Hockessin (19707) *(G-5190)*
Don D Balckburn Od...302 737-5777
   317 E Main St Newark (19711) *(G-10548)*
Don D Corp..302 994-5793
   1615 E Ayre St Wilmington (19804) *(G-16131)*
Don Noel Professional Services, Middletown *Also Called: Donald Briggs* *(G-7069)*
Don Rogers Inc (PA)...302 658-6524
   242 N James St Ste 102 Wilmington (19804) *(G-16132)*
Don Wllams Group - Kller Wllam..302 545-6859
   18344 Coastal Hwy Lewes (19958) *(G-5927)*
Don-Lee Margin Corporation...302 629-7567
   25271 Figgs Rd Seaford (19973) *(G-13163)*
Dona E Ortelli Slp..302 734-2606
   228 Front St Leipsic (19901) *(G-5631)*
Donahue Julie Ann Lpc Lpcmh..610 764-8652
   7 Pinecrest Dr Wilmington (19810) *(G-16133)*
Donald A Girard MD..302 633-5755
   2601 Annand Dr Ste 19 Wilmington (19808) *(G-16134)*
Donald Briggs...267 476-2712
   400 W Harvest Ln Middletown (19709) *(G-7069)*
Donald C Savoy Inc..302 697-4100
   5158 S Dupont Hwy Dover (19901) *(G-2322)*
Donald C Savoy Inc..888 992-6755
   200 Continental Dr Ste 209 Newark (19713) *(G-10549)*
Donald F Deaven Inc..302 994-5793
   1615 E Ayre St Wilmington (19804) *(G-16135)*
Donald Goldsborough...302 653-1081
   1784 Woodland Beach Rd Smyrna (19977) *(G-13712)*
Donald Grebe..302 945-7975
   31790 Schooner Dr Millsboro (19966) *(G-8274)*
Donald Jaffey Enterprises, Claymont *Also Called: Dack Realty Corp* *(G-1107)*
Donald Lambert III..302 421-1081
   1900 Newport Gap Pike Wilmington (19808) *(G-16136)*
Donald M Brown..302 777-1840
   2402 W 2nd St Wilmington (19805) *(G-16137)*
Donald R Cordrey Jr...302 875-4939
   33258 Shockley Rd Laurel (19956) *(G-5501)*
Donaldson Electric Inc...302 660-7534
   124 Middleboro Rd Ste A Wilmington (19804) *(G-16138)*

Donaway Corporation (PA) 302 934-6226
Route 24 Millsboro (19966) *(G-8275)*

Donaway Service Station, Millsboro *Also Called: Donaway Corporation (G-8275)*

Done Right Today Inc 302 528-4294
313 Goodley Rd Wilmington (19803) *(G-16139)*

Dongjin Usa Inc 302 691-8510
175 Edgemoor Rd Wilmington (19809) *(G-16140)*

Donkey Trucking LLC 302 507-2380
117 W Harvest Dr New Castle (19720) *(G-9059)*

Donna Brittingham Ms 302 846-3661
38076 Brittingham Rd Delmar (19940) *(G-1590)*

Donna D Planck 302 733-7056
680 S College Ave Newark (19713) *(G-10550)*

Donna Marie Kemp 302 645-7088
17232 N Village Main Blvd Lewes (19958) *(G-5928)*

Donnas Family Cut & Curl Inc 302 436-8999
106 Bayville Shopping Ctr Selbyville (19975) *(G-13521)*

Donnas Garden Goodies 302 399-3691
1412 Dexter Corner Rd Townsend (19734) *(G-13993)*

Donne Delle & Associates Inc (PA) 302 325-1111
200 Continental Dr Newark (19713) *(G-10551)*

Donnie Jones Foundation Inc 302 745-6946
200 Main St Ellendale (19941) *(G-3915)*

Donorware Foundation 302 230-7171
110 W 9th St Pmb 602 Wilmington (19801) *(G-16141)*

Donovan Capital Group LLC 202 642-4360
8 The Grn Ste A Dover (19901) *(G-2323)*

Donovan Painting and Drywall 302 745-6306
36983 Rehoboth Avenue Ext Unit C Rehoboth Beach (19971) *(G-12731)*

Donovan Painting LLC 302 745-6306
85 Bryan Dr Rehoboth Beach (19971) *(G-12732)*

Donovan Property Service Inc 917 841-2396
15 Foxview Cir Hockessin (19707) *(G-5191)*

Donovan Salvage Works Inc 302 856-9501
20262 Donovans Rd Georgetown (19947) *(G-4296)*

Donovan, Jack, Seminars, Millsboro *Also Called: Jack Donovan (G-8324)*

Donr LLC 857 400-8679
251 Little Falls Dr Wilmington (19808) *(G-16142)*

Donright Services LLC 302 685-7540
11 Deville Cir Wilmington (19808) *(G-16143)*

Dons Tree Farm 302 349-0555
6396 Hickman Rd Greenwood (19950) *(G-4621)*

Donum Adeo, Wilmington *Also Called: Yochanan El Bey (G-20930)*

Door & Gate Co LLC 888 505-6962
130 Hickman Rd Ste 26 Claymont (19703) *(G-1120)*

Dopamine, Dover *Also Called: Dopamine World Inc (G-2324)*

Dopamine World Inc (PA) 650 933-8003
3500 S Dupont Hwy Dover (19901) *(G-2324)*

Dope Venture Studio Inc 302 257-5936
8 The Grn Dover (19901) *(G-2325)*

Dopple Labs Inc 754 216-8175
251 Little Falls Dr Wilmington (19808) *(G-16144)*

Dorey Financial Services Inc 302 856-0970
13 Bridgeville Rd Georgetown (19947) *(G-4297)*

Dori Inc 858 344-8699
160 Greentree Dr Ste 101 Dover (19904) *(G-2326)*

Dorilyn English PHD 302 655-6506
18c Trolley Sq Wilmington (19806) *(G-16145)*

Dorilyn English PHD 302 652-7733
1020 W 18th St Wilmington (19802) *(G-16146)*

Doris House Cleaning 302 235-8239
9 Hillstream Rd Newark (19711) *(G-10552)*

Doris Obenshain Counseling, Middletown *Also Called: Doris V Obenshain (G-7070)*

Doris V Obenshain 302 448-1450
100 W Green St Middletown (19709) *(G-7070)*

Dorleeon LLC 302 415-3106
1007 N Orange St Fl 4 Wilmington (19801) *(G-16147)*

Dormakaba US Holding Ltd 252 200-5414
1201 N Market St Ste 1347 Wilmington (19801) *(G-16148)*

Doroshow Pasquale Law Offices, Millsboro *Also Called: Doroshow Psqale Krwitz Sgel Bh (G-8276)*

Doroshow Pasquale Law Offices, Wilmington *Also Called: Doroshow Psqale Krwitz Sgel Bh (G-16149)*

Doroshow Psqale Krwitz Sgel Bh 302 832-3200
1701 Pulaski Hwy Bear (19701) *(G-176)*

Doroshow Psqale Krwitz Sgel Bh 302 674-7100
500 W Loockerman St Ste 120 Dover (19904) *(G-2327)*

Doroshow Psqale Krwitz Sgel Bh 302 424-7744
903 Lakeview Ave Milford (19963) *(G-7870)*

Doroshow Psqale Krwitz Sgel Bh 302 934-9400
28535 Dupont Blvd Unit 2 Millsboro (19966) *(G-8276)*

Doroshow Psqale Krwitz Sgel Bh (PA) 302 998-2397
1202 Kirkwood Hwy Wilmington (19805) *(G-16149)*

Doroshow Psqale Krwitz Sgel Bh 302 998-0100
1208 Kirkwood Hwy Wilmington (19805) *(G-16150)*

Dorothy A Carroll 302 455-0243
17 Millwright Dr Newark (19711) *(G-10553)*

Dorsey & Whitney LLP 302 383-1011
1105 N Market St Ste 1600 Wilmington (19801) *(G-16151)*

Doselva PBC 510 299-7997
838 Walker Rd Dover (19904) *(G-2328)*

DOT and Line Inc 650 391-4837
221 W 9th St Wilmington (19801) *(G-16152)*

DOT Foods Inc 302 300-4239
301 American Blvd Bear (19701) *(G-177)*

DOT Matrix Inc (PA) 917 657-4918
3500 S Dupont Hwy Dover (19901) *(G-2329)*

DOT Pop Inc 302 691-3160
1010 N Union St Ste D Wilmington (19805) *(G-16153)*

Double D Restoration LLC 302 853-2176
33 W Church St Selbyville (19975) *(G-13522)*

Double Diamone Builders Inc 302 945-2512
25187 Banks Rd Millsboro (19966) *(G-8277)*

Double R Holdings Inc 302 645-5555
1009 Kings Hwy Lewes (19958) *(G-5929)*

Double S Co, Bear *Also Called: Double S Developers Inc (G-178)*

Double S Developers Inc 302 838-8880
1919 Red Lion Rd Bear (19701) *(G-178)*

Double Tree By Hilton, Wilmington *Also Called: Driftwood Hospitality MGT LLC (G-16179)*

Doubletree Downtown Wilmington, Wilmington *Also Called: 700 Nrth King St Wlmington LLC (G-14146)*

Doubletree Hotel Wilmington, Wilmington *Also Called: Dhm Wilmington LLC (G-16045)*

Doug Green Woodworking 302 652-6522
330 N Maryland Ave Wilmington (19804) *(G-16154)*

Doug Richmonds Body Shop 302 453-1173
5 Garfield Way Newark (19713) *(G-10554)*

Dougherty Dental Solutions LLC 302 475-3270
1805 Foulk Rd Ste D Wilmington (19810) *(G-16155)*

Douglas B Allen Do 302 659-4545
100 S Main St Ste 101 Smyrna (19977) *(G-13713)*

Douglas C Loew & Associates 302 453-0550
248 E Chestnut Hill Rd Ste 4 Newark (19713) *(G-10555)*

Douglas Ditty DMD MD 302 644-2977
37718 Wescoats Rd Lewes (19958) *(G-5930)*

Douglas Homewood 302 349-5964
12005 Woodbridge Rd Greenwood (19950) *(G-4622)*

Douglas J Lavenburg MD PA (PA) 302 993-0722
1 Centurian Dr Ste 114 Newark (19713) *(G-10556)*

Douglas M Helfer 302 988-8127
20 S Main St Selbyville (19975) *(G-13523)*

Douglas Morrow 302 750-9161
211 Beau Tree Dr Ste 100 Wilmington (19810) *(G-16156)*

Douglas R Briggs 302 645-6681
26 Midway Shopping Ctr Rehoboth Beach (19971) *(G-12733)*

Douglas Randall Inc 302 448-5826
20684 John J Williams Hwy Ste 1 Lewes (19958) *(G-5931)*

Dover, Dover *Also Called: Dover Motorsports Inc (G-2355)*

Dover Afb 302 677-3989
442 13th St Dover (19902) *(G-2330)*

Dover Afb 321 634-2016
1069 High St Dover (19901) *(G-2331)*

Dover Afb Child Care Center, Dover *Also Called: Army & Air Force Exchange Svc (G-1817)*

ALPHABETIC SECTION — Dpc Emergency Equipment

Dover Afb Youth Center.. 302 677-6376
864 Center Rd Dover (19901) *(G-2332)*

Dover Air Force Base, Dover *Also Called: Air Force US Dept of (G-1756)*

Dover Animal Hospital.. 302 746-2688
1151 S Governors Ave Dover (19904) *(G-2333)*

Dover Animal Hospital, Smyrna *Also Called: All Pets Medical Center (G-13635)*

Dover Auto Repair, Dover *Also Called: E & M Enterprises Inc (G-2398)*

Dover Automotive Inc.. 302 653-9234
5 E Glenwood Ave Smyrna (19977) *(G-13714)*

Dover Behaviorl Hlth 249.. 302 741-0140
725 Horsepond Rd Dover (19901) *(G-2334)*

Dover Budget Inn, Dover *Also Called: Gulab Management Inc (G-2632)*

Dover Chiropractic & Rehabilit.. 302 883-3251
222 S Dupont Hwy Ste 203 Dover (19901) *(G-2335)*

Dover Commons, Dover *Also Called: Dover Commons LLC (G-2336)*

Dover Commons LLC.. 302 678-4000
1365 N Dupont Hwy Sp 5601 Dover (19901) *(G-2336)*

Dover Community Partnership.. 302 678-1965
76 Stevenson Dr Dover (19901) *(G-2337)*

Dover Downs Inc.. 302 674-4600
1131 N Dupont Hwy Dover (19901) *(G-2338)*

Dover Downs Gaming & Entrmt, Dover *Also Called: Premier Entertainment III LLC (G-3360)*

Dover Downs Gaming MGT Corp.. 302 730-3800
1131 N Dupont Hwy Dover (19901) *(G-2339)*

Dover Downs Hotel & Casino, Dover *Also Called: Dover Downs Inc (G-2338)*

Dover East LLC.. 302 330-3040
19545 Camelot Dr Ste A Rehoboth Beach (19971) *(G-12734)*

Dover Educational & Cmnty Ctr.. 302 883-3092
744 River Rd Dover (19901) *(G-2340)*

Dover Electric Supply Co Inc (PA).. 302 674-0115
1631 S Dupont Hwy Dover (19901) *(G-2341)*

Dover Family Chiropractic.. 302 531-1900
120 Old Camden Rd Ste C Camden (19934) *(G-822)*

Dover Family Chiropractic.. 302 698-1515
119 Stuart Dr Dover (19901) *(G-2342)*

Dover Family Physicians PA.. 302 734-2500
1342 S Governors Ave Dover (19904) *(G-2343)*

Dover Federal Credit Union (PA).. 302 678-8000
1075 Silver Lake Blvd Dover (19904) *(G-2344)*

Dover Garden Court Apartments, Dover *Also Called: Colonial Inv Managment Co (G-2113)*

Dover Garden Suites.. 302 883-2417
520 Martin Luther King Jr Blvd Dover (19901) *(G-2345)*

Dover Golf Center.. 302 674-8275
924 Artis Dr Dover (19904) *(G-2346)*

Dover Hospitality Group LLC.. 302 677-0900
655 N Dupont Hwy Dover (19901) *(G-2347)*

Dover Inn, Dover *Also Called: Umiya Inc (G-3746)*

Dover Interfaith Mission Walte.. 302 264-9021
1155 Walker Rd Dover (19904) *(G-2348)*

Dover Intrfith Mssion For Hsin.. 302 736-3600
630 W Division St Dover (19904) *(G-2349)*

Dover Kent County Mpo.. 302 387-6030
1783 Friends Way Camden (19934) *(G-823)*

Dover Leasing Co Inc.. 302 674-2300
613 Clara St Dover (19904) *(G-2350)*

Dover Litho Printing Co.. 302 698-5292
21 Chadwick Dr Dover (19901) *(G-2351)*

Dover Lubricants Inc.. 302 674-8282
236 S Dupont Hwy Dover (19901) *(G-2352)*

Dover Mall, Dover *Also Called: Dover Mall LLC (G-2354)*

Dover Mall LLC.. 302 678-4000
1365 N Dupont Hwy Ste 5061 Dover (19901) *(G-2353)*

Dover Mall LLC.. 302 678-4000
1365 N Dupont Hwy Dover (19901) *(G-2354)*

Dover Millwork Inc.. 302 349-5070
10862 Shawnee Rd Harrington (19952) *(G-4764)*

Dover Mntessori Cntry Day Schl, Dover *Also Called: Capital School District (G-2021)*

Dover Motorsports Inc (DH).. 302 883-6500
1131 N Dupont Hwy Dover (19901) *(G-2355)*

Dover Nunan LLC.. 302 697-9776
607 Otis Dr Dover (19901) *(G-2356)*

Dover Ophthalmology Asc LLC.. 302 724-4720
655 S Bay Rd Ste 5b Dover (19901) *(G-2357)*

Dover Oral and Maxillofacial S.. 302 674-1140
1004 S State St Ste 1 Dover (19901) *(G-2358)*

Dover Parks Management LLC.. 302 326-1540
761 Grantham Ln New Castle (19720) *(G-9060)*

Dover Paving.. 302 274-0743
1475 S Governors Ave Dover (19904) *(G-2359)*

Dover Place, Dover *Also Called: Assisted Living Concepts LLC (G-1835)*

Dover Plumbing Supply Co.. 302 674-0333
3626 N Dupont Hwy Dover (19901) *(G-2360)*

Dover Pool & Patio Center Inc (PA).. 302 346-7665
1255 S State St Ste 1 Dover (19901) *(G-2361)*

Dover Post Co Inc (PA).. 302 653-2083
609 E Division St Dover (19901) *(G-2362)*

Dover Post Co Inc.. 302 378-9531
1196 S Little Creek Rd # 101 Dover (19901) *(G-2363)*

Dover Post Co Inc.. 302 678-3616
1196 S Little Creek Rd Dover (19901) *(G-2364)*

Dover Post Inc.. 304 222-6025
12 S Walnut St Milford (19963) *(G-7871)*

Dover Post News Paper, Dover *Also Called: Gatehouse Media Inc (G-2564)*

Dover Post Web Printing, Dover *Also Called: Dover Post Co Inc (G-2364)*

Dover Pulmonary PA.. 302 734-0400
31 Gooden Ave Dover (19904) *(G-2365)*

Dover Rent-All Inc.. 302 739-0860
35 Commerce Way Ste 180 Dover (19904) *(G-2366)*

Dover Rental, Dover *Also Called: Dover Rent-All Inc (G-2366)*

Dover Security, Dover *Also Called: Dover Mall LLC (G-2353)*

Dover Skating Center, Dover *Also Called: Delaware Skating Center Ltd (G-2259)*

Dover Surgicenter LLC.. 302 346-3171
108 Patriot Dr Ste A Middletown (19709) *(G-7071)*

Dover Symphony Orchestra Inc.. 302 734-1701
Dover (19901) *(G-2367)*

Dover Volkswagen Inc.. 302 734-4761
1387 N Dupont Hwy Dover (19901) *(G-2368)*

Dover Windows and Doors, Harrington *Also Called: Dover Millwork Inc (G-4764)*

Dovers Childrens Villag.. 302 672-6476
726 Woodcrest Dr Dover (19904) *(G-2369)*

Dovers Childrens Village Too.. 302 674-8142
1298 Mckee Rd Dover (19904) *(G-2370)*

Dovington Training Center LLC.. 302 284-2114
595 Black Swamp Rd Felton (19943) *(G-3961)*

Dow Advanced Materials.. 302 607-3061
200 D And S Ln Bear (19701) *(G-179)*

Dow Chemical, Newark *Also Called: Dow Chemical Company (G-10557)*

Dow Chemical, Newark *Also Called: Dow Chemical Company (G-10558)*

Dow Chemical Company.. 302 366-0500
231 Lake Dr Newark (19702) *(G-10557)*

Dow Chemical Company.. 302 368-4169
451 Bellevue Rd Bldg 9 Newark (19713) *(G-10558)*

Dow Electronic Materials, Newark *Also Called: Rohm Haas Electronic Mtls LLC (G-11909)*

Down To Earth Wines, Wilmington *Also Called: Robert M Panzer (G-19519)*

Down Under Boxing Club.. 302 745-4392
19124 Wesley Church Rd Bridgeville (19933) *(G-695)*

DOWntoearthlawn&landscapellc.. 302 381-5051
406 Walnut Ct Dagsboro (19939) *(G-1442)*

Downtown Beach Rentals.. 410 472-9480
20 Baltimore Ave Rehoboth Beach (19971) *(G-12735)*

DOWNTOWN VISIONS, Wilmington *Also Called: Wdbid Management Company (G-20698)*

Doyjul Apartments.. 302 998-0088
3403 Lancaster Pike Wilmington (19805) *(G-16157)*

Doyjul Center, Wilmington *Also Called: Doyjul Apartments (G-16157)*

Doyle Timothy F M Do.. 302 836-5410
1721 Pulaski Hwy Bear (19701) *(G-180)*

Dozr Ltd (PA).. 844 218-3697
3411 Silverside Rd Ste 104 Wilmington (19810) *(G-16158)*

Dp Fire & Safety Inc.. 302 998-5430
411 Orinda Dr Wilmington (19804) *(G-16159)*

Dpc Emergency Equipment, Marydel *Also Called: Delmarva Pump Center Inc (G-6796)*

Dpnl LLC 302 366-8097
270 Chapman Rd Newark (19702) *(G-10559)*

DPs Custom Painting LLC 302 732-3232
33099 Thunder Rd Frankford (19945) *(G-4103)*

Dpsg - Dlgtion Pymnt Systems G 201 755-0912
2711 Centerville Rd Ste 400 Wilmington (19808) *(G-16160)*

Dr Alvin L Turner 302 777-3202
222 Philadelphia Pike Wilmington (19809) *(G-16161)*

Dr Azarcon & Assoc 302 478-2969
3411 Silverside Rd Ste 107r Wilmington (19810) *(G-16162)*

Dr Beth Duncan 302 644-2232
17316 Coastal Hwy Lewes (19958) *(G-5932)*

Dr Caroline M Wieczorek 302 635-1430
50 Somerset Ln Newark (19711) *(G-10560)*

Dr Casey Mae Fouse DC 302 472-4878
3910 Concord Pike Wilmington (19803) *(G-16163)*

Dr Christopher Burns 302 674-8331
871 S Governors Ave Ste 1 Dover (19904) *(G-2371)*

Dr David Defries Chiropractor 610 494-0412
2 Drexel Rd Claymont (19703) *(G-1121)*

Dr Dawn Grandison DDS 302 678-3384
429 S Governors Ave Dover (19904) *(G-2372)*

Dr Debra Wolf Encore Health 302 737-1918
19 Green Meadow Ct Newark (19711) *(G-10561)*

Dr Douglas A Palma MD 302 655-9494
1096 Old Churchmans Rd Newark (19713) *(G-10562)*

Dr Douglas Briggs 302 654-4001
910 N Union St Wilmington (19805) *(G-16164)*

Dr GS Weightloss 302 232-5153
3801 Kennett Pike Ste E-126 Wilmington (19807) *(G-16165)*

Dr Hivey Corp 580 670-2046
8 The Grn Ste 300 Dover (19901) *(G-2373)*

Dr James Kramer 302 436-5133
13 S Main St # 348 Selbyville (19975) *(G-13524)*

Dr James Soor 302 684-4682
6 Meadowridge Ln Milton (19968) *(G-8611)*

Dr Jeffrey E Felzer DMD PC 302 995-6979
3105 Limestone Rd Ste 203 Wilmington (19808) *(G-16166)*

Dr Jillian G Stevens Do 302 762-7332
812 Bezel Rd Wilmington (19803) *(G-16167)*

Dr John Fontana III 302 734-1950
910 Walker Rd Ste A Dover (19904) *(G-2374)*

Dr John Reitz, Selbyville *Also Called: John V Reitz (G-13551)*

Dr Julie Hattier 302 539-7063
35202 Atlantic Ave Millville (19967) *(G-8527)*

Dr Junfang Jiao 302 453-1342
179 W Chestnut Hill Rd Ste 1 Newark (19713) *(G-10563)*

Dr Kaz Fmly Cosmtc Dentistry 302 235-7645
5936 Limestone Rd Ste 201 Hockessin (19707) *(G-5192)*

Dr Kellyann LLC 888 871-2155
8 The Grn Ste A Dover (19901) *(G-2375)*

Dr Lawernce Lewandowski 302 387-1516
4601 S Dupont Hwy Dover (19901) *(G-2376)*

Dr Mackler, Seaford *Also Called: Nanticoke Gastroenterology (G-13304)*

Dr Mae Gaskins 302 731-0439
22 Kayser Ct Newark (19711) *(G-10564)*

Dr Marisa E Conti Do 302 678-4488
725 S Queen St Dover (19904) *(G-2377)*

Dr Michele Turley 302 266-4043
300 Creek View Rd Newark (19711) *(G-10565)*

Dr Monika Gupta PA 302 737-5074
314 E Main St Ste 404 Newark (19711) *(G-10566)*

Dr Quan Nguyen 302 453-1342
1200 Peoples Plz Newark (19702) *(G-10567)*

Dr Rajshekar Narasimaiah MD 302 537-1100
33188 Coastal Hwy Unit 4 Bethany Beach (19930) *(G-598)*

Dr Rene Badillo 301 827-1800
1450 Pulaski Hwy Newark (19702) *(G-10568)*

Dr Robert M Collins 302 239-3655
5500 Skyline Dr Ste 3 Wilmington (19808) *(G-16168)*

Dr Robert Webster 302 674-1080
1522 S State St Dover (19901) *(G-2378)*

Dr Scott Schulze 302 644-0940
701 Savannah Rd Ste B Lewes (19958) *(G-5933)*

Dr Sharon M Sifford-Wilson MD 302 698-3725
38 Chadwick Dr Dover (19901) *(G-2379)*

Dr Shefali Pandya 302 421-9960
707 Foulk Rd Wilmington (19803) *(G-16169)*

Dr Steven Scurnick 410 442-1173
30958 Scissorbill Rd Ocean View (19970) *(G-12507)*

Dr Thomas C Scott Do 302 328-0650
11 Hodgkins Pl New Castle (19720) *(G-9061)*

Dr Timothy G Cook Do 215 823-5800
131 Parrish Ln Wilmington (19810) *(G-6170)*

Dr Weidong Yang Dental Office 302 409-3050
131 Becks Woods Dr Bear (19701) *(G-181)*

Dr. Armand Neal Dsanctis Jr MD, Wilmington *Also Called: Delaware Medical Associates PA (G-15942)*

Drafting By Design Inc 302 292-8304
170 E Main St Ste 1 Newark (19711) *(G-10569)*

Dragon Cloud Inc 702 508-2676
1 Cmmrce Ctr 1201 Ste 6 Wilmington (19899) *(G-16171)*

Dragons Lair Printing LLC 302 798-4465
130 Hickman Rd Ste 24 Claymont (19703) *(G-1122)*

Drain Kings LLC 302 399-8980
3867 Wheatleys Pond Rd Smyrna (19977) *(G-13715)*

Draper & Goldberg Pllc 302 448-4040
512 E Market St Georgetown (19947) *(G-4298)*

Dravo Bay LLC 302 660-3350
1 Ave Of The Arts Ste A Wilmington (19801) *(G-16172)*

Drayton Electric, Wilmington *Also Called: Drayton Electric LLC (G-16173)*

Drayton Electric LLC 302 893-0884
8 N Clifton Ave Wilmington (19805) *(G-16173)*

Drba Police Fund 302 571-6326
Route 9 And I-295 New Castle (19720) *(G-9062)*

Dream America LLC 305 509-9201
16192 Coastal Hwy Lewes (19958) *(G-5934)*

Dream Chasers Gymnastics 302 276-0457
245 Quigley Blvd Historic New Castle (19720) *(G-4977)*

Dream Chasers Gymnastics 302 559-5561
21 S Lloyd St Wilmington (19804) *(G-16174)*

Dream Conception LLC 302 319-9822
108 W 13th St Wilmington (19801) *(G-16175)*

Dream Forge LLC 802 342-4647
8 The Grn Ste 4000 Dover (19901) *(G-2380)*

Dream Graphics 302 328-6264
9 King Ave New Castle (19720) *(G-9063)*

Dream Home Remodeling LLC 302 981-4919
147 Woodshade Dr Newark (19702) *(G-10570)*

Dream Spa 646 717-5397
1408 N King St Wilmington (19801) *(G-16176)*

Dream Structures LLC 302 943-3974
1998 Tower Rd Hartly (19953) *(G-4870)*

Dream Vacations, Millsboro *Also Called: Bethany Travel Inc (G-8196)*

Dream View Exteriors Group LLC 302 358-9530
201 Primary Ave Georgetown (19947) *(G-4299)*

Dream Weaver LLC 302 352-9473
1521 Concord Pike Ste 301 Wilmington (19803) *(G-16177)*

Dream Werks LLC 302 526-2415
100 Carlsons Way Dover (19901) *(G-2381)*

Dreamreal Events, Newark *Also Called: Lambert Kishayra (G-11216)*

Dreams Childcare LLC 302 652-1085
725 N Union St Wilmington (19805) *(G-16178)*

Dreams Unlimited LLC 302 747-0527
2 Riverside Rd Dover (19904) *(G-2382)*

Dreamscape Design Cons LLC 302 893-0984
205 Roseman Ct Newark (19711) *(G-10571)*

Dreamscape Landscaping 302 354-5247
60 Colby Ave Claymont (19703) *(G-1123)*

Dreamspell LLC 786 633-1520
8 The Grn Ste B Dover (19901) *(G-2383)*

Dreamstage, Dover *Also Called: Dreamstage Inc (G-2384)*

Dreamstage Inc 901 286-5207
8 The Grn Dover (19901) *(G-2384)*

ALPHABETIC SECTION

Dreamtouch Games LLC 408 550-6042
614 N Dupont Hwy Ste 210 Dover (19901) *(G-2385)*

Dreamville LLC 662 524-0917
16192 Coastal Hwy Lewes (19958) *(G-5935)*

Dreya Inc 302 265-0759
651 N Broad St Ste 205 # 5784 Middletown (19709) *(G-7072)*

Driftwood Cabinetry LLC 302 645-4876
1009 Kings Hwy Lewes (19958) *(G-5936)*

Driftwood Club Apartments, Wilmington *Also Called: Evergreen Realty Inc (G-16487)*

Driftwood Hospitality MGT LLC 302 655-0400
700 N King St Wilmington (19801) *(G-16179)*

Driveway Mint Pvng/Slcting LLC 302 228-2644
7031 Cannon Rd Bridgeville (19933) *(G-696)*

Driveway Sealcoating 302 203-7451
12 Appleby Trlr Ct New Castle (19720) *(G-9064)*

Drone Consulting Pros Inc 561 766-5176
2093 Philadelphia Pike Claymont (19703) *(G-1124)*

Drop A Tot Pre-School Day Care, Dover *Also Called: Church of God In Christ (G-2072)*

Drop Fake Inc 707 563-1529
3500 S Dupont Hwy Dover (19901) *(G-2386)*

Drowsy Digital Inc 833 438-6956
850 New Burton Rd Ste 201 Dover (19904) *(G-2387)*

Drs Pahnke Penman & Whitney 302 656-1950
4701 Ogletown Stanton Rd Ste 1340 Newark (19713) *(G-10572)*

Drummond Hill Swim Club 302 366-9882
Alton Dr Newark (19711) *(G-10573)*

Drw Construction 302 945-9055
30777 Steeple Chase Run Lewes (19958) *(G-5937)*

Dry Bulk Transportation LLC 561 409-7818
303 Chanticleer Cir Camden Wyoming (19934) *(G-936)*

Dry Cleaning Home Service Inc 302 777-7444
2402 Shellpot Dr Wilmington (19803) *(G-16180)*

Dry Wall Associates Ltd 302 737-3220
58 Albe Dr Newark (19702) *(G-10574)*

Drywall Inc 302 838-6500
13 King Ct Ste 3 New Castle (19720) *(G-9065)*

Dryzone LLC 302 684-5034
16507 Beach Hwy Ellendale (19941) *(G-3916)*

Ds Express LLC 302 494-4957
108 Peachtree Ln Middletown (19709) *(G-7073)*

Ds Supply LLC 302 377-3974
3605 Old Capitol Trl Unit C4 Wilmington (19808) *(G-16181)*

Dsd App LLC (PA) 302 465-6606
1209 N Orange St Wilmington (19801) *(G-16182)*

Dsd Photography Inc 678 622-5910
43 Wicklow Rd Bear (19701) *(G-182)*

DSI Laurel LLC 302 715-3060
30214 Sussex Hwy Laurel (19956) *(G-5502)*

DSM Commercial 302 842-2450
3304 Old Capitol Trl Wilmington (19808) *(G-16183)*

DSouza and Associates Inc 302 239-2300
530 Schoolhouse Rd Ste A Hockessin (19707) *(G-5193)*

Dsp Builders 302 422-3515
7587 Shawnee Rd Milford (19963) *(G-7872)*

Dsr Drew Sparks Realty LLC 302 743-1210
408 Commodore Dr Middletown (19709) *(G-7074)*

Dss - Integrity LLC 302 677-0111
1679 S Dupont Hwy Ste 5 Dover (19901) *(G-2388)*

Dss Services Inc 302 677-0111
373 W North St Ste B Dover (19904) *(G-2389)*

Dss Sstnable Solutions USA Inc 800 532-7233
4023 Kennett Pike Pmb 282 Wilmington (19807) *(G-16184)*

Dss Urban Joint Venture LLC 302 677-0111
373 W North St Ste B Dover (19904) *(G-2390)*

Dssf, Millsboro *Also Called: Delmarva Space Scnces Fndation (G-8269)*

DSU Student Housing LLC 302 857-7966
430 College Rd Dover (19904) *(G-2391)*

Dt Investment Partners LLC 302 442-6203
1013 Centre Rd Wilmington (19805) *(G-16185)*

Dt Transit LLC 302 216-3547
7209 Lancaster Pike Hockessin (19707) *(G-5194)*

Dti Direct Inc 855 374-7836
251 Little Falls Dr Wilmington (19808) *(G-16186)*

Du Pont Lynne M MD 302 777-7966
910 Foulk Rd Wilmington (19803) *(G-16187)*

Du Pont Chem Enrgy Oprtons Inc (DH) 302 774-1000
974 Centre Rd Wilmington (19805) *(G-16188)*

Du Pont Delaware Inc (DH) 302 774-1000
974 Centre Rd Chestnut Run Plaza Bldg 730 Wilmington (19805) *(G-16189)*

Du Pont Elastomers LP 302 774-1000
974 Centre Rd Wilmington (19805) *(G-16190)*

Du Pont Foreign Sales Corp 302 774-1000
974 Centre Rd Wilmington (19805) *(G-16191)*

Du Wireless 302 407-5532
9 Courtyard Ln Wilmington (19802) *(G-16192)*

Dualitybio Inc 201 486-7858
3524 Silverside Rd 35b Wilmington (19810) *(G-16193)*

Duane Edward Ruark 302 846-2332
6988 Beagle Dr Delmar (19940) *(G-1591)*

Duck Creek Animal Hospital 302 663-6112
10 Artisan Dr Smyrna (19977) *(G-13716)*

Ducos Realty Inc 302 563-6902
217 Karins Blvd Townsend (19734) *(G-13994)*

Duct Cleaning Corp 302 310-4060
3 Germay Dr Ste 4 Wilmington (19804) *(G-16194)*

Ducts R US LLC 302 284-4006
7686 Burnite Mill Rd Felton (19943) *(G-3962)*

Ducts Unlimited Inc 302 378-4125
421 Smyrna Clayton Blvd Smyrna (19977) *(G-13717)*

Duffield, Wilmington *Also Called: Duffield Associates LLC (G-16195)*

Duffield Associates Inc 302 747-7156
1060 S Governors Ave Dover (19904) *(G-2392)*

Duffield Associates LLC (HQ) 302 239-6634
5400 Limestone Rd Wilmington (19808) *(G-16195)*

DUFFIELD ASSOCIATES, INC., Dover *Also Called: Duffield Associates Inc (G-2392)*

Dugan Dt Roofing Inc 302 636-9300
20 S Woodward Ave Wilmington (19805) *(G-16196)*

Dugan, Dt Roofing Co, Wilmington *Also Called: Dugan Dt Roofing Inc (G-16196)*

Duggal Manveen MD 302 734-2782
111 Wolf Creek Blvd Ste 3 Dover (19901) *(G-2393)*

Duha Logistics Inc 888 493-5999
3 Germay Dr Ste 4 # 2159 Wilmington (19804) *(G-16197)*

Duhadaway Tool and Die Sp Inc 302 366-0113
801 Dawson Dr Newark (19713) *(G-10575)*

Dukes Septic 302 362-6010
16653 Sand Hill Rd Milton (19968) *(G-8612)*

Dukka Inc 401 659-6948
8 The Grn Dover (19901) *(G-2394)*

Dulin Brothers 302 653-5365
938 Blackiston Church Rd Clayton (19938) *(G-1360)*

Duly Noted LLC 302 353-4585
427 N Tatnall St Wilmington (19801) *(G-16198)*

Dumont Aircraft Charter LLC 610 266-1369
1 Boulden Cir New Castle (19720) *(G-9066)*

Dumont Aviation, New Castle *Also Called: Dumont Aviation Group Inc (G-9067)*

Dumont Aviation Group Inc 302 777-1003
1 Boulden Cir New Castle (19720) *(G-9067)*

Dumont Aviation Group Inc 302 777-1003
15 Penns Way New Castle (19720) *(G-9068)*

Dumont Jets, New Castle *Also Called: Dumont Aircraft Charter LLC (G-9066)*

Dun Rite Cleaners 302 654-3958
132 Concord Ave Wilmington (19802) *(G-16199)*

Dunamis Dominion LLC 302 470-0468
100 Carlsons Way Dover (19901) *(G-2395)*

Dunams-Hmes Dvine Intrvntion I 302 393-5778
1328 Rising Sun Rd Ste 1 Camden Wyoming (19934) *(G-937)*

Dunbar Armored Inc 302 628-5401
186 Kent Dr Seaford (19973) *(G-13164)*

Dunbar Armored Inc 302 892-4950
320 Water St Ste A Wilmington (19804) *(G-16200)*

Duncan S Concrete 302 395-1552
324 N Red Lion Ter Bear (19701) *(G-183)*

Dunes Manor Hotel 610 256-4307
  38312 Ocean Vista Dr Selbyville (19975) *(G-13525)*
Dung Beetle Trucking LLC 312 843-1118
  16192 Coastal Hwy Lewes (19958) *(G-5938)*
Dunkin' Donuts, Wilmington Also Called: Swami Enterprises Inc *(G-20168)*
Dunkle, Mark F, Dover Also Called: Parkowski Guerke & Swayze PA *(G-3274)*
Dunkley Enterprises LLC 302 275-0100
  139 Wallace Rd Odessa (19730) *(G-12583)*
Duns Investing Corporation 302 651-2050
  801 N West St Fl 2 Wilmington (19801) *(G-16201)*
Dunworth Machines LLC 434 977-4790
  34676 Horseshoe Dr Selbyville (19975) *(G-13526)*
Dupont, Bear Also Called: Eidp Inc *(G-198)*
Dupont, Christiana Also Called: Eidp Inc *(G-994)*
Dupont, New Castle Also Called: Eidp Inc *(G-9084)*
Dupont, Newark Also Called: Dupont Specialty Pdts USA LLC *(G-10577)*
Dupont, Newark Also Called: Eidp Inc *(G-10617)*
Dupont, Newark Also Called: Eidp Inc *(G-10619)*
Dupont, Newark Also Called: Eidp Inc *(G-10620)*
Dupont, Wilmington Also Called: Celanese Polymer Products LLC *(G-15299)*
Dupont, Wilmington Also Called: Du Pont Chem Enrgy Oprtons Inc *(G-16188)*
Dupont, Wilmington Also Called: Du Pont Delaware Inc *(G-16189)*
Dupont, Wilmington Also Called: Dupont Prfmce Coatings Inc *(G-16213)*
Dupont, Wilmington Also Called: Eidp Inc *(G-16314)*
Dupont, Wilmington Also Called: Eidp Inc *(G-16316)*
Dupont, Wilmington Also Called: Eidp Inc *(G-16317)*
Dupont, Wilmington Also Called: Eidp Inc *(G-16321)*
Dupont, Wilmington Also Called: Eidp Inc *(G-16322)*
Dupont, Wilmington Also Called: Eidp Inc *(G-16324)*
Dupont, Wilmington Also Called: Eidp Inc *(G-16326)*
Dupont, Wilmington Also Called: Eidp Inc *(G-16327)*
Dupont, Wilmington Also Called: Eidp Inc *(G-16328)*
Dupont, Wilmington Also Called: Eidp Inc *(G-16329)*
Dupont, Wilmington Also Called: Eidp Inc *(G-16332)*
Dupont, Wilmington Also Called: Eidp Inc *(G-16333)*
Dupont, Wilmington Also Called: Eidp Inc *(G-16334)*
Dupont, Wilmington Also Called: Eidp Inc *(G-16336)*
Dupont, Wilmington Also Called: Eidp Inc *(G-16337)*
Dupont, Wilmington Also Called: Eidp Inc *(G-16338)*
Dupont, Wilmington Also Called: Eidp Inc *(G-16339)*
Dupont, Wilmington Also Called: Eidp Inc *(G-16340)*
Dupont, Wilmington Also Called: Eidp Inc *(G-16341)*
Dupont, Wilmington Also Called: Eidp Inc *(G-16342)*
Dupont, Wilmington Also Called: Eidp Inc *(G-16343)*
Dupont Athntcation Systems LLC 800 345-9999
  4417 Lancaster Pike Wilmington (19805) *(G-16202)*
Dupont Aviation Corp 302 996-8000
  199 N Dupont Hwy New Castle (19720) *(G-9069)*
Dupont Building Innovations, Wilmington Also Called: Eidp Inc *(G-16319)*
Dupont Capital Management Corp 302 477-6000
  974 Centre Rd Wilmington (19805) *(G-16203)*
Dupont Capital MGT Gem Tr 302 477-6000
  974 Centre Rd Wilmington (19805) *(G-16204)*
Dupont Children's Rehab, Wilmington Also Called: Alfred I Dupont Hospital *(G-14655)*
Dupont Corp Remediation Group, Wilmington Also Called: Eidp Inc *(G-16318)*
Dupont Country Club, Wilmington Also Called: Rockland Sports LLC *(G-19541)*
Dupont De Nemours Inc (PA) 302 774-3034
  974 Centre Rd Bldg 730 Wilmington (19805) *(G-16205)*
Dupont Displays Inc (DH) 805 562-9293
  974 Centre Rd Wilmington (19805) *(G-16206)*
Dupont Electronics & Imaging 302 273-6958
  231 Lake Dr Newark (19702) *(G-10576)*
Dupont Electronics Holding LLC 302 999-4083
  974 Centre Rd Wilmington (19805) *(G-16207)*
Dupont Esl Security 302 695-1657
  200 Powder Mill Rd Wilmington (19803) *(G-16208)*
Dupont Experimental Station, Wilmington Also Called: Eidp Inc *(G-16330)*

Dupont Flaments - Americas LLC 302 774-1000
  974 Centre Rd Chestnut Run Plaza Bldg 730 Wilmington (19805) *(G-16209)*
Dupont Indus Bsciences USA LLC (HQ) 302 774-1000
  974 Centre Rd Wilmington (19805) *(G-16210)*
Dupont Industrial Biosciences, Wilmington Also Called: Eidp Inc *(G-16320)*
Dupont John Gardner 302 777-3730
  2002 Woodlawn Ave Wilmington (19806) *(G-16211)*
Dupont Operations Inc 302 992-5940
  974 Centre Rd Wilmington (19805) *(G-16212)*
Dupont Prfmce Coatings Inc 302 892-1064
  4417 Lancaster Pike Wilmington (19805) *(G-16213)*
Dupont Prfmce Elastomers LLC (DH) 4417 Lancaster Pike Bldg 728 Wilmington (19805) *(G-16214)*
Dupont Red Lion, Delaware City Also Called: Eidp Inc *(G-1539)*
Dupont S&C Holding LLC 302 999-4083
  974 Centre Rd Wilmington (19805) *(G-16215)*
Dupont Specialty Pdts USA LLC 800 972-7252
  350 Bellevue Rd Newark (19713) *(G-10577)*
Dupont Specialty Pdts USA LLC (HQ) 302 992-2941
  974 Centre Rd Wilmington (19805) *(G-16216)*
Dupont Specialty Systems 302 273-6955
  231 Lake Dr Newark (19702) *(G-10578)*
Dupont Stine Haskell RES Ctr, Newark Also Called: Eidp Inc *(G-10618)*
Dupont Tate Lyle Bio Pdts LLC 865 408-1962
  1007 Market St Fl 2 Wilmington (19898) *(G-16217)*
Dupont Txtles Intriors Del Inc 302 774-1000
  974 Centre Rd Wilmington (19805) *(G-16218)*
Dupont US Holding LLC 302 999-4083
  974 Centre Rd Wilmington (19805) *(G-16219)*
Durafiber Tech DFT Entps Inc (HQ) 704 912-3770
  300 Delaware Ave Ste 1100 Wilmington (19801) *(G-16220)*
Durafiber Technologies, Wilmington Also Called: Durafiber Tech DFT Entps Inc *(G-16220)*
Duralex USA, Historic New Castle Also Called: Duralex Usa Inc *(G-4978)*
Duralex Usa Inc 302 326-4804
  802 Centerpoint Blvd Historic New Castle (19720) *(G-4978)*
Duration Media LLC 917 283-5971
  1209 N Orange St Wilmington (19801) *(G-16221)*
Durham Plumbing Service LLC 302 653-5601
  555 Parkers Chapel Rd Marydel (19964) *(G-6797)*
Durham Transport LLC 302 270-2178
  135 Goshawk Ln Camden Wyoming (19934) *(G-938)*
Dust Away Cleaning Svcs Inc 302 658-8803
  700 Cornell Dr Ste E1 Wilmington (19801) *(G-16222)*
Dustin Davis 302 856-2254
  25 Bridgeville Rd Georgetown (19947) *(G-4300)*
Dustntime 302 858-7876
  36181 Field Ln Rehoboth Beach (19971) *(G-12736)*
Dutch Neck Lawn and Ldscp Inc 302 562-3651
  1210 Dutch Neck Rd Middletown (19709) *(G-7075)*
Dutch Village Motel Inc 302 328-6246
  111 S Dupont Hwy New Castle (19720) *(G-9070)*
Dux Technologies Inc 507 312-9687
  251 Little Falls Dr Wilmington (19808) *(G-16223)*
Dvd and Game Exchange De 302 530-1199
  2707 Pecksniff Rd Wilmington (19808) *(G-16224)*
Dvele Partners LLC 516 707-9357
  3500 S Dupont Hwy Ste L-101 Dover (19901) *(G-2396)*
Dvfa Foundation 302 734-9390
  122a S Bradford St Dover (19904) *(G-2397)*
Dvhd Inc 302 584-3547
  1716 Shallcross Ave Ste 02 Wilmington (19806) *(G-16225)*
Dvr International Inc (PA) 800 958-9000
  12062 Laurel Rd Laurel (19956) *(G-5503)*
Dw Heating and Cooling Svcs 302 373-7786
  306 Androssan Pl Townsend (19734) *(G-13995)*
Dwh System Inc 551 208-5354
  225 Steamboat Ave Felton (19943) *(G-3963)*
DWK LLC 917 370-7106
  53 Cheswold Blvd Newark (19713) *(G-10579)*
Dx Tech Solutions Inc 302 397-3500
  107 Carriage Wood Ct Newark (19702) *(G-10580)*

ALPHABETIC SECTION — Eagle One Federal Credit Union

Dxc Technology Company 302 391-2762
   645 Paper Mill Rd Newark (19711) *(G-10581)*

Dxi Construction Inc 302 858-5007
   22237 Lewes Georgetown Hwy Georgetown (19947) *(G-4301)*

Dxl, Wilmington *Also Called: Dojupa LLC (G-16121)*

DXquisite Hair Factory LLC 267 298-0821
   79 Buckeye Ln Smyrna (19977) *(G-13718)*

Dyatech LLC 845 666-0786
   1000 N West St Ste 1200 Wilmington (19801) *(G-16226)*

Dycom Industries Inc 302 613-0958
   34 Blevins Dr Ste 5 New Castle (19720) *(G-9071)*

Dygital Technology LLC 302 283-9160
   130 Peoples Plz Newark (19702) *(G-10582)*

Dynamic Air LLC 302 612-1412
   3354 Arthursville Rd Hartly (19953) *(G-4871)*

Dynamic Converters LLC 302 454-9203
   122 Sandy Dr Ste F Newark (19713) *(G-10583)*

Dynamic Dental Solutions LLC 888 908-8225
   1007 N Orange St Wilmington (19801) *(G-16227)*

Dynamic Devices LLC 302 994-2401
   8 Lewis Cir Wilmington (19804) *(G-16228)*

Dynamic Mobile Imaging 302 645-2142
   17527 Nassau Commons Blvd Lewes (19958) *(G-5939)*

Dynamic Packet Corp 302 448-2222
   40 E Main St Ste 4000 Newark (19711) *(G-10584)*

Dynamic Physical Therapy 302 668-1768
   2701 Kirkwood Hwy Wilmington (19805) *(G-16229)*

Dynamic Physical Therapy, Newark *Also Called: Dynamic Therapy Services LLC (G-10585)*

Dynamic Recycling Enterprise, Wilmington *Also Called: Delaware Valley Group LLC (G-15982)*

Dynamic Support Services Inc 202 820-3113
   1209 N Orange St Wilmington (19801) *(G-16230)*

Dynamic Therapy Services LLC 302 566-6624
   2000 Midway Dr Harrington (19952) *(G-4765)*

Dynamic Therapy Services LLC 302 280-6953
   400 S Central Ave Laurel (19956) *(G-5504)*

Dynamic Therapy Services LLC 302 292-3454
   2717 Pulaski Hwy Newark (19702) *(G-10585)*

Dynamic Trnsp & Logistics LLC 302 991-1005
   1201 N Market St Wilmington (19801) *(G-16231)*

Dynasep LLC 302 368-4540
   134 Sandy Dr Newark (19713) *(G-10586)*

Dynasep Inc 302 268-6464
   4023 Kennett Pike Ste 278 Wilmington (19807) *(G-16232)*

Dynasty Car Collection LLC 855 700-6530
   651 N Broad St Ste 205 Middletown (19709) *(G-7076)*

Dynasty Styling Studios LLC 302 595-3042
   1661 Pulaski Hwy Bear (19701) *(G-184)*

Dysis Medical 813 997-8979
   920 N King St Lbby 2 Wilmington (19801) *(G-16233)*

Dyte Inc 669 577-4571
   16192 Coastal Hwy Lewes (19958) *(G-5940)*

E & M Enterprises Inc 302 736-6391
   5102 N Dupont Hwy Dover (19901) *(G-2398)*

E A Zando Custom Designs Inc 302 684-4601
   210 Chandler St Milton (19968) *(G-8613)*

E B D Management Inc 302 428-1313
   4001 Kennett Pike Ste 10 Wilmington (19807) *(G-16234)*

E Baumann Contracting 302 824-3765
   317 Marsh Rd Wilmington (19809) *(G-16235)*

E Business Pages LLC 302 504-4403
   1201 N Orange St Ste 600 Wilmington (19801) *(G-16236)*

E C I Motorsports Inc 302 239-6376
   9 Polaris Dr Newark (19711) *(G-10587)*

E D S of Milford Inc 302 245-8813
   2542 Deer Valley Rd Milford (19963) *(G-7873)*

E E Rosser Inc 302 762-9643
   5109 Governor Printz Blvd Wilmington (19809) *(G-16237)*

E Earle Downing Inc 302 656-9908
   1221 Bowers St Ste 5 Wilmington (19802) *(G-16238)*

E Electric 302 547-3151
   311 Delaware Ave Claymont (19703) *(G-1125)*

E I Du Pont De Nemours & Co 302 733-8134
   350 Bellevue Rd Newark (19713) *(G-10588)*

E I Du Pont De Nemours & Co 843 335-5934
   1 Righter Pkwy Wilmington (19803) *(G-16239)*

E K Long General Contractors 302 883-1463
   154 Loquitur Ln Magnolia (19962) *(G-6742)*

E Lawrence Jester 302 378-8970
   747 Green Giant Rd Townsend (19734) *(G-13996)*

E M C Process Company Inc 302 999-9204
   1663 E Ayre St Wilmington (19804) *(G-16240)*

E Mark Johnson 302 422-6050
   802 N Dupont Blvd Milford (19963) *(G-7874)*

E N T Associates 302 674-3752
   826 S Governors Ave Dover (19904) *(G-2399)*

E S Tile, Wilmington *Also Called: Sosa Eloy (G-19931)*

E W Brown Inc 302 652-6612
   1202 E 16th St Wilmington (19802) *(G-16241)*

E Z Cash of Delaware Inc (PA) 302 846-2920
   300 N Bi State Blvd Ste 1 Delmar (19940) *(G-1592)*

E-Berk Corporation 925 643-2375
   16192 Coastal Hwy Lewes (19958) *(G-5941)*

E-Carauctions LLC (PA) 302 677-1552
   1602 N Dupont Hwy New Castle (19720) *(G-9072)*

E-Cube 302 290-7413
   143 Carpenters Row Wilmington (19807) *(G-16242)*

E-Industrial Suppliers LLC 302 251-6210
   2207 Concord Pike Ste 648 Wilmington (19803) *(G-16243)*

E-Lyte Transportation 808 269-0283
   8 The Grn Dover (19901) *(G-2400)*

E-Volve Fitness Studio 302 513-9641
   3680 Kirkwood Hwy Wilmington (19808) *(G-16244)*

E&A Drywall and Painting Inc 302 393-1743
   27324 John J Williams Hwy Millsboro (19966) *(G-8278)*

E&S Home Improvement LLC 302 559-2340
   5 Clemson Ct Newark (19711) *(G-10589)*

E&Z Party Rental, Wilmington *Also Called: Enz Party Rental (G-16445)*

E2 Engineering LLC 302 659-9090
   106 W Commerce St Smyrna (19977) *(G-13719)*

E2e LLC 703 906-5353
   177 Thompson Dr Ste 888 Hockessin (19707) *(G-5195)*

E2lingo Inc 800 345-2677
   16192 Coastal Hwy Lewes (19958) *(G-5942)*

Each One Teach One Inc 302 345-8744
   550 S Dupont Hwy Apt 55w New Castle (19720) *(G-9073)*

Eagan US Holdco LLC 414 339-8275
   401 Old Kennett Rd Wilmington (19807) *(G-16245)*

Eager Gear 302 727-5831
   19413 Jingle Shell Way # 6 Lewes (19958) *(G-5943)*

Eagle 97.7 FM, Milford *Also Called: Wafl Wyus Broadcasting Inc (G-8136)*

Eagle Building and Grounds 302 508-5403
   2817 Shaws Corner Rd Clayton (19938) *(G-1361)*

Eagle Erectors Inc 302 832-9586
   3500 Wrangle Hill Rd Bear (19701) *(G-185)*

Eagle Express 302 898-2247
   101 J And M Dr Ste 101 New Castle (19720) *(G-9074)*

Eagle Foodservice, Clayton *Also Called: Metal Msters Fdservice Eqp Inc (G-1385)*

Eagle Group, Clayton *Also Called: Eagle Mhc Company (G-1363)*

Eagle Hospitality Group LLC 302 678-8388
   201 Stover Blvd Dover (19901) *(G-2401)*

Eagle Irrigation Inc 302 223-1176
   837 Daisey Rd Clayton (19938) *(G-1362)*

Eagle Limousine Inc (PA) 302 325-4200
   77 Mccullough Dr Ste 5 New Castle (19720) *(G-9075)*

Eagle Meadows LLC 302 698-1073
   4666 Carolina Ave Dover (19901) *(G-2402)*

Eagle Mhc Company 302 653-3000
   100 Industrial Blvd Clayton (19938) *(G-1363)*

Eagle Nest Daycare 302 684-2765
   Zion Church Rd Milton (19968) *(G-8614)*

Eagle One Federal Credit Union 302 798-7749
   3301 Philadelphia Pike Claymont (19703) *(G-1126)*

ALPHABETIC SECTION

Eagle Plaza Associates Inc 302 999-0708
  234 N James St Wilmington (19804) *(G-16246)*

Eagle Power and Equipment Corp 302 652-3028
  2211 N Dupont Hwy New Castle (19720) *(G-9076)*

Eagle Transportation, New Castle *Also Called: Eagle Limousine Inc (G-9075)*

Eagle's Nest, Wilmington *Also Called: Bright Horizons Chld Ctrs LLC (G-15109)*

Eak Construction Inc 302 893-8497
  2806 Christiana Mdws Bear (19701) *(G-186)*

Ealing Media & Tech (us) Ltd 909 576-4828
  139 Rickey Blvd Bear (19701) *(G-187)*

Eamo Health LLC 302 565-7528
  1201 N Market St Ste 1404 Wilmington (19801) *(G-16247)*

Ean Holdings LLC 302 674-5553
  580 S Bay Rd Dover (19901) *(G-2403)*

Ean Holdings LLC 302 376-5606
  5207 Summit Bridge Rd Middletown (19709) *(G-7077)*

Ean Holdings LLC 302 422-1167
  411 N Rehoboth Blvd Milford (19963) *(G-7875)*

Eancenter Telecom LLC 302 450-4514
  8 The Grn Ste R Dover (19901) *(G-2404)*

Eanerep Holdings LLC 888 837-2685
  445 Bank Ln Ste 148 Dover (19904) *(G-2405)*

Ear Nose Throat & Allergy 302 998-0300
  2600 Glasgow Ave Ste 221 Newark (19702) *(G-10590)*

Earl Carter 302 375-0354
  98 Harvey Rd Claymont (19703) *(G-1127)*

Earle Teate Music (PA) 302 736-1937
  3098 N Dupont Hwy Dover (19901) *(G-2406)*

Earls Place LLC 302 538-8909
  12605 S Dupont Hwy Felton (19943) *(G-3964)*

EARLY CHILDHOOD ASSISTANCE PRO, Wilmington *Also Called: Hilltop Lthran Nghbrhood Ctr I (G-17148)*

EARLY CHILDHOOD EDUCATION ARTS, Wilmington *Also Called: Christina Cultural Arts Center (G-15415)*

Early Childhood Lab 302 857-6731
  1200 N Dupont Hwy Dover (19901) *(G-2407)*

Early Education, Bear *Also Called: Great New Bgnnngs St Andrews I (G-255)*

Early Education, Middletown *Also Called: Great New Bgnnngs Mddltown Inc (G-7174)*

Early Essntals Prschool Innvti, Middletown *Also Called: Elaine Leonard (G-7089)*

Early Foundation Preschool, Wilmington *Also Called: Early Foundations Therapeutic (G-16248)*

Early Foundations Therapeutic 302 384-6905
  2814 W 2nd St Wilmington (19805) *(G-16248)*

Early Learning Center 302 239-3033
  7250 Lancaster Pike Hockessin (19707) *(G-5196)*

Early Learning Center 302 831-0584
  1218 B St Wilmington (19801) *(G-16249)*

Earthborne Equipment & Svc Co 215 343-2000
  12915 S Dupont Hwy Felton (19943) *(G-3965)*

Earthship LLC 239 850-8682
  465 Carson Dr Bear (19701) *(G-188)*

East Bay Aggregates LLC 302 337-0311
  8805 Newton Rd Bridgeville (19933) *(G-697)*

East Coast 302 249-8867
  909 Pilottown Rd Lewes (19958) *(G-5944)*

East Coast Auto Body Inc 302 265-6830
  216 South St Dover (19904) *(G-2408)*

East Coast Aviation LLC 302 650-9889
  1505 Clayton Delaney Rd Clayton (19938) *(G-1364)*

East Coast Builders Inc 302 629-3551
  Rte 1 Box 350 Seaford (19973) *(G-13165)*

East Coast Cleaning Co LLC 302 762-6820
  528 Ruxton Dr Wilmington (19809) *(G-16250)*

East Coast Computer Cons 302 945-5089
  295 Pond Rd Millsboro (19966) *(G-8279)*

East Coast Cstm Cabinetry LLC 302 245-3040
  23636 Saulsbury Ln Georgetown (19947) *(G-4302)*

East Coast Elastomerics Inc 302 524-8004
  35115 Johnson Store Rd Selbyville (19975) *(G-13527)*

East Coast Electric Inc 302 998-1577
  824 Kiamensi Rd Wilmington (19804) *(G-16251)*

East Coast Erectors Inc 302 323-1800
  1144 River Rd New Castle (19720) *(G-9077)*

East Coast Games Inc 302 838-0669
  24 Eaton Pl Bear (19701) *(G-189)*

East Coast Health & Fitnes LLC 410 213-7697
  620 W Stein Hwy Seaford (19973) *(G-13166)*

East Coast Machine Works 302 349-5180
  12773 Tuckers Rd Greenwood (19950) *(G-4623)*

East Coast Minority Supplier 302 656-3337
  610 W 8th St Wilmington (19801) *(G-16252)*

East Coast Painting LLC 302 678-9346
  64 River Chase Dr Dover (19901) *(G-2409)*

East Coast Poured Walls Inc 302 430-0630
  331 S Rehoboth Blvd Milford (19963) *(G-7876)*

East Coast Property MGT Inc 302 654-2196
  200 N Poplar St Wilmington (19801) *(G-16253)*

East Coast Sales & Lease LLC 302 995-7505
  3623 Kirkwood Hwy Wilmington (19808) *(G-16254)*

East Coast Stainless Inc 302 366-0675
  22 Albe Dr Newark (19702) *(G-10591)*

East Coast Stainless & Alloys 302 366-0675
  22 Albe Dr Newark (19702) *(G-10592)*

East Coast Swag 302 628-2674
  94 Rivers End Dr Seaford (19973) *(G-13167)*

East Coast Trans LLC 302 740-5458
  2 Hidlins Way Newark (19713) *(G-10593)*

East Park Brands LLC 201 668-7089
  8 The Grn Dover (19901) *(G-2410)*

East Sussex Moose Lodge 302 436-2088
  35993 Zion Church Rd Frankford (19945) *(G-4104)*

East West Engineering Inc 302 528-0652
  130 Wynnefield Rd Bear (19701) *(G-190)*

Easter Sals Del Mrylnds Estrn 302 678-3353
  100 Enterprise Pl Ste 1 Dover (19904) *(G-2411)*

Easter Sals Del Mrylnds Estrn 302 856-7364
  22317 Dupont Blvd Georgetown (19947) *(G-4303)*

Easter Sals Del Mrylnds Estrn (PA) 302 324-4444
  61 Corporate Cir New Castle (19720) *(G-9078)*

Easter Seals, Dover *Also Called: Easter Sals Del Mrylnds Estrn (G-2411)*

Eastern Air Service 800 921-0392
  26844 Governor Stockley Rd Georgetown (19947) *(G-4304)*

Eastern Allrgy Asthma Spclsts 732 789-7982
  750 Kings Hwy Ste 102 Lewes (19958) *(G-5945)*

Eastern Athletic Clubs LLC 302 239-6688
  100 Fitness Way Hockessin (19707) *(G-5197)*

Eastern Brndywine Hndred Crdnt 302 764-2476
  1212 Haines Ave Wilmington (19809) *(G-16255)*

Eastern Christian Management 302 633-1421
  330 Water St Wilmington (19804) *(G-16256)*

Eastern Group Inc 302 737-6603
  931 S Chapel St Newark (19713) *(G-10594)*

Eastern Health Care Ctr 302 543-4998
  813 N Market St Wilmington (19801) *(G-16257)*

Eastern Home Improvements Inc (PA) 302 655-9920
  3112 Lancaster Ave Wilmington (19805) *(G-16258)*

Eastern Hospitality Management 302 322-9480
  215 S Dupont Hwy New Castle (19720) *(G-9079)*

Eastern Hwy Specialists Inc 302 777-7673
  3604 Downing Dr Wilmington (19802) *(G-16259)*

Eastern Industrial Svcs Inc 302 455-1400
  196 Quigley Blvd Ste A Historic New Castle (19720) *(G-4979)*

Eastern Insulation Inc 302 455-1400
  401 Bellevue Rd Newark (19713) *(G-10595)*

Eastern Lift Truck Co Inc 302 875-4031
  11512 Commercial Ln Laurel (19956) *(G-5505)*

Eastern Lift Truck Co Inc 302 286-6660
  137 Sandy Dr Newark (19713) *(G-10596)*

Eastern Mail Transport Inc 302 838-0500
  900 Julian Ln Bear (19701) *(G-191)*

Eastern Metal Supply 302 391-1370
  231 Executive Dr Ste 11 Newark (19702) *(G-10597)*

ALPHABETIC SECTION — Econotransfer Company Inc

Eastern Metals Inc 302 454-7886
679 Dawson Dr Newark (19713) *(G-10598)*

Eastern Percision, Newark *Also Called: Trimble Inc* *(G-12230)*

Eastern Property Assoc Inc 302 998-0962
715 Dorcaster Dr Wilmington (19808) *(G-16260)*

Eastern Property Group Inc 302 764-7112
3408 Miller Rd Apt C7 Wilmington (19802) *(G-16261)*

Eastern Prosperity Group 302 764-7112
3408 Miller Rd Wilmington (19802) *(G-16262)*

Eastern Shore Cleaning LLC 302 752-8856
24337 Givens Cir Georgetown (19947) *(G-4305)*

Eastern Shore Energy Inc 302 697-9230
11550 Willow Grove Rd Camden (19934) *(G-824)*

Eastern Shore Equipment Co 302 697-3300
12244 Willow Grove Rd Camden (19934) *(G-825)*

Eastern Shore Gastroenterology, Lewes *Also Called: Bayview Endoscopy Center* *(G-5742)*

Eastern Shore Lite Industries 302 653-8687
5908 Judith Rd Clayton (19938) *(G-1365)*

Eastern Shore Metal Detectors 302 628-1985
20380 Wesley Church Rd Seaford (19973) *(G-13168)*

Eastern Shore Metals LLC 302 629-6629
102 Park Ave Seaford (19973) *(G-13169)*

Eastern Shore Natural Gas Co 302 734-6716
909 Silver Lake Blvd Dover (19904) *(G-2412)*

Eastern Shore Onsite Svcs LLC 302 736-0366
265 Front St Leipsic (19901) *(G-5632)*

Eastern Shore Painters 443 373-3119
405 Wisseman Ave Milford (19963) *(G-7877)*

Eastern Shore Porch Patio Inc 302 436-9520
17 Mason Dr Selbyville (19975) *(G-13528)*

Eastern Shore Poultry Company 302 855-1350
21724 Broad Creek Ave Georgetown (19947) *(G-4306)*

Eastern Shore Poultry Services, Laurel *Also Called: Hog Slat Incorporated* *(G-5529)*

Eastern Shore Real Estate Inc 302 734-6799
909 Silver Lake Blvd Dover (19904) *(G-2413)*

Eastern Shore Veterinary Hosp 302 875-5941
32384 Sussex Hwy Laurel (19956) *(G-5506)*

Eastern Shore Vinyl Produ 302 436-9520
17 Mason Dr Selbyville (19975) *(G-13529)*

Eastern Shore Wedding & Events, Bethany Beach *Also Called: Deborah L Wayland* *(G-594)*

Eastern Specialty Finance Inc 302 697-4290
374 Walmart Dr Ste 3 Camden (19934) *(G-826)*

Eastern Specialty Finance Inc 302 736-1348
283 N Dupont Hwy Ste B Dover (19901) *(G-2414)*

Eastern Specialty Finance Inc 302 658-5431
800 W 4th St Ste 401 Wilmington (19801) *(G-16263)*

Eastern States Cnstr Svc Inc 302 995-2259
702 First State Blvd Wilmington (19804) *(G-16264)*

Eastern States Develpment Inc 302 998-0683
702 First State Blvd Wilmington (19804) *(G-16265)*

Eastmoor Digital 302 514-7002
221 N Walnut St Smyrna (19977) *(G-13720)*

Eastside Bluprt Cmnty Dev Corp 302 384-2350
121 N Poplar St Wilmington (19801) *(G-16266)*

Easy Analytic Software Inc 302 762-4271
21 Paladin Dr Wilmington (19802) *(G-16267)*

Easy Analytic Software Inc, Wilmington *Also Called: Easy Analytic Software Inc* *(G-16267)*

Easy Breezy Beauty 302 562-6751
12 Pinewood Dr Lewes (19958) *(G-5946)*

Easy Lawn Inc 302 815-6500
9599 Nanticoke Business Park Dr Ste 1 Greenwood (19950) *(G-4624)*

Easy Lift Equipment, Newark *Also Called: Easy Lift Equipment Co Inc* *(G-10599)*

Easy Lift Equipment Co Inc 302 737-7000
2 Mill Park Ct Newark (19713) *(G-10599)*

Easy Living Service 302 633-4849
2301 W Newport Pike Wilmington (19804) *(G-16268)*

Easy Money Emg 302 421-3610
2501 Concord Pike Wilmington (19803) *(G-16269)*

Easy Sales Solutions Inc 929 273-0505
2055 Limestone Rd Wilmington (19808) *(G-16270)*

Easy Send Inc 610 389-0622
103 Center Ct Ste 403 Wilmington (19810) *(G-16271)*

Easy Trade LLC 334 577-4530
838 Walker Rd Ste 21-2 Dover (19904) *(G-2415)*

Easydmarc Inc 888 563-5277
651 N Broad St Ste 206 Middletown (19709) *(G-7078)*

Eat Clean Juice Bar LLC 856 397-9112
225 N Market St Wilmington (19801) *(G-16272)*

Eavis and Sons Garage Doors 302 893-3783
9 Ansonia Ct Newark (19711) *(G-10600)*

Eazifunds Inc 909 697-6422
651 N Broad St Ste 206 Middletown (19709) *(G-7079)*

Eb Rental Ltd 310 951-8931
2915 Ogletown Rd Newark (19713) *(G-10601)*

Ebanks Construction LLC 302 420-7584
507 Florence Fields Ln New Castle (19720) *(G-9080)*

EBc Carpet Services Corp 302 995-7461
1300 First State Blvd Ste I Wilmington (19804) *(G-16273)*

Ebc National Inc 302 995-7461
1300 First State Blvd Wilmington (19804) *(G-16274)*

Ebc Systems LLC 302 472-1896
1 Ave Of The Arts Wilmington (19801) *(G-16275)*

Ebenezer Preschool, Newark *Also Called: Ebenezer United Methdst Chruch* *(G-10602)*

Ebenezer United Methdst Chruch 302 731-9495
525 Polly Drummond Hill Rd Newark (19711) *(G-10602)*

Ebright Foundation LL 215 370-2821
607 W 18th St Wilmington (19802) *(G-16276)*

EC Innovations USA Inc 312 863-1966
501 Silverside Rd Ste 105 Wilmington (19809) *(G-16277)*

Ece Weatherguard, Selbyville *Also Called: East Coast Elastomerics Inc* *(G-13527)*

Ecg Industries Inc (PA) 302 453-0535
254 Chapman Rd Ste 203 Newark (19702) *(G-10603)*

Echelon Interiors LLC 302 519-9151
55 Cascade Ln Ste A Rehoboth Beach (19971) *(G-12737)*

Echofin Inc 844 700-6060
2035 Sunset Lake Rd Ste B2 Newark (19702) *(G-10604)*

Ecircular LLC 713 514-4675
2810 N Church St Ste 624369 Wilmington (19802) *(G-16278)*

Eckels Family LLC 302 465-5224
141 Hunters Run Blvd Felton (19943) *(G-3966)*

Eclipes Erection Inc 302 633-1421
330 Water St Wilmington (19804) *(G-16279)*

Eclipse Software Inc 212 727-1136
908 Greenhill Ave Wilmington (19805) *(G-16280)*

Ecm Carpentry LLC 302 494-8995
12 1st Ave Wilmington (19808) *(G-16281)*

Eco Centric Salon 302 378-1988
317 W Main St Middletown (19709) *(G-7080)*

Eco Dental Delaware 302 836-3711
1400 Peoples Plz Ste 207 Newark (19702) *(G-10605)*

Eco Plastic Products Del Inc 302 575-9227
18 Germay Dr Wilmington (19804) *(G-16282)*

Eco Safety Lights, Wilmington *Also Called: Esafety Lights LLC* *(G-16462)*

Ecolab Pest Elimination 302 322-3600
53 Mccullough Dr New Castle (19720) *(G-9081)*

Ecolistic Cleaning, Lewes *Also Called: Ecolistic Living Inc* *(G-5947)*

Ecolistic Living Inc 888 432-6547
17046 Oak Ct Lewes (19958) *(G-5947)*

Ecom Technologies LLC 424 362-5155
8 The Grn Ste A Dover (19901) *(G-2416)*

Ecommerence, Dover *Also Called: Dakk Holdings LLC* *(G-2186)*

Ecomo Inc 412 567-3867
160 Greentree Dr Ste 101 Dover (19904) *(G-2417)*

Econat Inc 302 504-4207
651 N Broad St Ste 206 Middletown (19709) *(G-7081)*

Econo Lodge, New Castle *Also Called: Sun Hotel Inc* *(G-9600)*

Econo Lodge, Rehoboth Beach *Also Called: Econo Lodge Inn Suites Resort* *(G-12738)*

Econo Lodge Inn Suites Resort 302 227-0500
19540 Coastal Hwy Rehoboth Beach (19971) *(G-12738)*

Econo Lodge Newark, Newark *Also Called: Keval Corporation* *(G-11161)*

Economic Laundry Solutions 302 234-7627
14 Cinnamon Dr Hockessin (19707) *(G-5198)*

Econotransfer Company Inc 302 365-6664
451 Carson Dr Bear (19701) *(G-192)*

Ecotrade Group North Amer LLC	302 724-6975
2915 Ogletown Rd Newark (19713) *(G-10606)*	
ECR Communications LLC	302 865-3118
190 Galway Ct Magnolia (19962) *(G-6743)*	
Ecsquared Inc	302 750-8554
717 Swarthmore Dr Newark (19711) *(G-10607)*	
Ed Durynski	302 994-6642
130 Landis Way N Wilmington (19803) *(G-16283)*	
Ed Hileman Drywall Inc	302 436-6277
36722 Roxana Rd Selbyville (19975) *(G-13530)*	
Ed Hunt Inc (PA)	302 339-8443
8 The Grn Ste 9487 Dover (19901) *(G-2418)*	
Ed Oliver Golf Club, Wilmington Also Called: Meadowbrook Golf Group Inc *(G-18242)*	
Ed Turulski Custom Woodworking	302 658-2221
1020 Liberty Rd Wilmington (19804) *(G-16284)*	
Edaura Inc	707 330-9836
1209 N Orange St Wilmington (19801) *(G-16285)*	
Edc LLC	302 645-0777
115 W Market St Fl 2 Lewes (19958) *(G-5948)*	
Eddie Simpson Stanley Contg	302 276-0569
104 Northwind Rd Bear (19701) *(G-193)*	
Edelsohn, Lanny MD, Newark Also Called: Neurology Associates PA *(G-11511)*	
Eden Care Group Holding LLC	929 461-7247
8 The Grn Dover (19901) *(G-2419)*	
Eden Hill Express Care LLC	302 674-1999
200 Banning St Ste 170 Dover (19904) *(G-2420)*	
Eden Hill Expresscare LLC	302 696-2129
300 Jimmy Dr Smyrna (19977) *(G-13721)*	
Eden Hill Medical Center, Dover Also Called: Surgical Associates PA *(G-3629)*	
Eden Land Care	302 379-2405
202 New Rd Unit 7 Wilmington (19805) *(G-16286)*	
Eden Rock	302 475-9400
2210 Swiss Ln Wilmington (19810) *(G-16287)*	
Edfeed Foundation	917 459-2762
909 Benalli Dr Middletown (19709) *(G-7082)*	
Edgar Silvestre Painting Svc	302 670-7702
230 Landau Way Bear (19701) *(G-194)*	
Edge Case LLC	302 207-1291
651 N Broad St Middletown (19709) *(G-7083)*	
Edge Construction Corp	302 778-5200
300 Martin Luther King Blvd Ste 300 Wilmington (19801) *(G-16288)*	
Edge Fitness LLC	302 613-0721
2800 Fashion Center Blvd Newark (19702) *(G-10608)*	
Edge Racing LLC	302 519-6680
34772 Hill Hvn Laurel (19956) *(G-5507)*	
Edge Water Tire, Dover Also Called: Admiral Tire *(G-1718)*	
Edgemoor Community Center Inc	302 762-1391
500 Duncan Rd Ofc A Wilmington (19809) *(G-16289)*	
Edgemoor Materials Inc	302 655-1510
1230 Railcar Ave Wilmington (19802) *(G-16290)*	
Edgemoor Rvtalization Coop Inc	302 293-3944
41 S Cannon Dr Wilmington (19809) *(G-16291)*	
Edgerite Inc	302 404-6665
8 The Grn Ste 8573 Dover (19901) *(G-2421)*	
Edgewell Personal Care LLC	302 678-6000
50 N Dupont Hwy Dover (19901) *(G-2422)*	
Edgewell Personal Care Company	302 678-6191
185 Saulsbury Rd Dover (19904) *(G-2423)*	
Edgility Inc	650 382-2346
108 Lakeland Ave Dover (19901) *(G-2424)*	
Edify Inc	302 520-2403
1007 N Orange St Fl 4 Wilmington (19801) *(G-16292)*	
Edis Building Systems Inc	302 421-5700
110 S Poplar St Wilmington (19801) *(G-16293)*	
Edis Company	302 421-5700
110 S Poplar St Ste 400 Wilmington (19801) *(G-16294)*	
Edison Trnspt & Logistics Inc	302 332-6878
200 Continental Dr Ste 401 Newark (19713) *(G-10609)*	
Edit Inc	302 478-7069
1026 Sedwick Dr Wilmington (19803) *(G-16295)*	
Edlyncare LLC	267 474-0486
821 Seymour Rd Bear (19701) *(G-195)*	

Edmonds Business Ventures LLC	302 772-9112
98 S Skyward Dr Newark (19713) *(G-10610)*	
Edokk LLC	305 434-7227
16192 Coastal Hwy Lewes (19958) *(G-5949)*	
EDS, Milford Also Called: E D S of Milford Inc *(G-7873)*	
Eds Auto Repair	302 382-0079
1772 Berrytown Rd Felton (19943) *(G-3967)*	
Eds Auto Repair	302 468-0955
4601 Governor Printz Blvd Wilmington (19809) *(G-16296)*	
Eds Road Service Inc	302 437-4103
1000 Dawson Dr Ste B Newark (19713) *(G-10611)*	
Edtech Consulting LLC	661 644-2990
1201 N Orange St Wilmington (19801) *(G-16297)*	
Edu-Care Preschool & Daycare, Newark Also Called: MI-Dee Inc *(G-11399)*	
Eduardo McEdo Lite De Oliveira	302 476-2285
16192 Coastal Hwy Lewes (19958) *(G-5950)*	
Education Svcs Unlimited LLC	302 650-4210
610 Westmont Dr Wilmington (19808) *(G-16298)*	
Education Voices Inc	302 559-7889
1510 W 5th St Wilmington (19805) *(G-16299)*	
Educational Enrichment Center	302 478-8697
730 Halstead Rd Wilmington (19803) *(G-16300)*	
Educup Inc	305 504-1073
651 N Broad St Ste 206 Middletown (19709) *(G-7084)*	
Edufar, Newark Also Called: Sygul Inc *(G-12146)*	
Eduqc LLC	800 346-4646
3500 S Dupont Hwy Dover (19901) *(G-2425)*	
Edward A Fufaro Inc	302 934-6595
29728 Springwood Dr Millsboro (19966) *(G-8280)*	
Edward B De Seta & Associates	302 428-1313
4001 Kennett Pike Ste 10 Wilmington (19807) *(G-16301)*	
Edward B De Seta & Associates, Wilmington Also Called: E B D Management Inc *(G-16234)*	
Edward Hackendorn	302 981-5000
417 N Broad St Middletown (19709) *(G-7085)*	
Edward Hennessy Tile, Claymont Also Called: Edward J Hennessy *(G-1128)*	
Edward Hu MD	302 422-5155
110 Ne Front St Milford (19963) *(G-7878)*	
Edward J Deseta Co Inc	302 420-0900
322 A St Ste 200 Wilmington (19801) *(G-16302)*	
Edward J Hennessy	302 798-8019
17 Franklin Ave Claymont (19703) *(G-1128)*	
Edward J Kaye Construction	302 629-7483
22822 Coverdale Rd Seaford (19973) *(G-13170)*	
Edward J Steen	302 732-6963
700 Cherry Dr Dagsboro (19939) *(G-1443)*	
Edward Krupka	302 492-0833
1079 Lockwood Chapel Rd Hartly (19953) *(G-4872)*	
Edward L Alexander MD Facs	302 674-4070
724 S New St Dover (19904) *(G-2426)*	
Edward L Ballard	302 363-4302
157 Wiggins Mill Rd Townsend (19734) *(G-13997)*	
Edward M Tingle	302 436-5539
209 Hosier Street Ext Selbyville (19975) *(G-13531)*	
Edward Papiro	302 757-9813
4 Heagy Ct Bear (19701) *(G-196)*	
Edward S Jaoude	302 684-2020
28322 Lewes Georgetown Hwy Milton (19968) *(G-8615)*	
Edward S Yalisove DDS PA	302 658-4124
1111 N Franklin St Wilmington (19806) *(G-16303)*	
Edward Varnes Hardwood Floors	302 292-0919
634 Old Baltimore Pike Newark (19702) *(G-10612)*	
Edwards Lawn Care	302 981-7751
258 Bassett Ave New Castle (19720) *(G-9082)*	
Edwards Mther Earth Foundation	800 839-1754
501 Silverside Rd Ste 123 Wilmington (19809) *(G-16304)*	
Edwards Paul Crpt Installation	302 672-7847
547 Otis Dr Dover (19901) *(G-2427)*	
Edwin C Katzman MD	302 368-2501
210 Christiana Med Ctr Newark (19702) *(G-10613)*	
Edwin S Kuipers DDS	302 455-0333
210 W Park Pl Newark (19711) *(G-10614)*	

ALPHABETIC SECTION

Edwin S Kuipers DDS ... 302 652-3775
300 Foulk Rd Ste 101 Wilmington (19803) *(G-16305)*

Edythe L Pridgen ... 302 652-8887
450 S Hyde Pl Bear (19701) *(G-197)*

Eea Life Settlements Inc ... 302 472-7429
1007 N Orange St Ste 1461 Wilmington (19801) *(G-16306)*

Eec, Wilmington *Also Called: Educational Enrichment Center (G-16300)*

Eec Incubator ... 302 737-4343
920 Justison St Wilmington (19801) *(G-16307)*

Ef Technologies Inc ... 302 451-1088
119b Sandy Dr Newark (19713) *(G-10615)*

Efectibo, Wilmington *Also Called: Efectibo LLC (G-16308)*

Efectibo LLC ... 305 498-8630
251 Little Falls Dr Wilmington (19808) *(G-16308)*

Efficient Services Inc ... 302 629-2124
24660 German Rd Seaford (19973) *(G-13171)*

Efflorescence Skin Care ... 302 250-3232
1207 Oak St Wilmington (19805) *(G-16309)*

Egg ... 302 227-3447
510 Rehoboth Ave Rehoboth Beach (19971) *(G-12739)*

Egli, Michelle D Dvm, Dover *Also Called: Delmarva Equine Clinic (G-2277)*

Egm LLC ... 302 932-1700
42 Valley Forge Rd New Castle (19720) *(G-9083)*

EGNM LLC ... 302 644-3466
17015 Old Orchard Rd Unit 4 Lewes (19958) *(G-5951)*

Egs Financial Care Inc ... 800 227-4000
Wilmington (19850) *(G-16310)*

Egw Capital Inc ... 302 261-2008
16192 Coastal Hwy Lewes (19958) *(G-5952)*

Ehc Group, Dover *Also Called: Groupe EHc LLC (G-2631)*

Ehelp Health Corporation (PA) ... 404 964-0906
2140 S Dupont Hwy Camden (19934) *(G-827)*

Ehg Mechanical ... 302 530-4438
115 Fallon Ave Wilmington (19804) *(G-16311)*

Ehrlich, J C Pest Control, Bridgeville *Also Called: Rentokil North America Inc (G-761)*

Ehrlich Pest Control, Newark *Also Called: Rentokil North America Inc (G-11853)*

Ehs LLC ... 302 332-4247
901 Merribrook Rd Wilmington (19810) *(G-16312)*

Eia Insurers Group LLC ... 302 543-4572
1601 Concord Pike Wilmington (19803) *(G-16313)*

Eice International LLC ... 281 451-7328
31794 Marsh Island Ave Lewes (19958) *(G-5953)*

Eice Texas, Lewes *Also Called: Eice International LLC (G-5953)*

Eidp Inc ... 302 695-7141
407 Cheer Ct Bear (19701) *(G-198)*

Eidp Inc ... 302 733-9200
600 Eagle Run Rd Christiana (19702) *(G-994)*

Eidp Inc ... 302 834-5901
755 Govonor Lea Rd Delaware City (19706) *(G-1539)*

Eidp Inc ... 302 772-0016
1001 Lambson Ln New Castle (19720) *(G-9084)*

Eidp Inc ... 302 366-5763
1090 Elkton Rd Newark (19711) *(G-10616)*

Eidp Inc ... 302 239-9424
6 Meteor Ln Newark (19711) *(G-10617)*

Eidp Inc ... 302 366-5583
1090 Elkton Rd Newark (19711) *(G-10618)*

Eidp Inc ... 302 266-7101
1090 Elkton Rd Newark (19711) *(G-10619)*

Eidp Inc ... 302 452-9000
242 Chapman Rd Newark (19702) *(G-10620)*

Eidp Inc ... 302 774-1000
16237 Brandywine Bldg Wilmington (19898) *(G-16314)*

Eidp Inc ... 302 992-2012
30 Barley Mill Dr Wilmington (19807) *(G-16315)*

Eidp Inc ... 302 999-3301
702 Canter Rd Wilmington (19810) *(G-16316)*

Eidp Inc ... 302 892-8732
4417 Lancaster Pike Wilmington (19805) *(G-16317)*

Eidp Inc ... 302 999-2874
974 Centre Rd Wilmington (19805) *(G-16318)*

Eidp Inc ... 302 892-8832
4417 Lancaster Pike Wilmington (19805) *(G-16319)*

Eidp Inc ... 302 695-7228
200 Powder Mill Rd Wilmington (19803) *(G-16320)*

Eidp Inc ... 302 999-4356
Chestnut Run Plz 708 Rm 141 Wilmington (19805) *(G-16321)*

Eidp Inc ... 302 792-4371
300 Delaware Ave Wilmington (19801) *(G-16322)*

Eidp Inc ... 302 774-2102
15305 Brandywine Bldg B Wilmington (19898) *(G-16323)*

Eidp Inc ... 302 774-1000
Barley Mill Plz Wilmington (19898) *(G-16324)*

Eidp Inc ... 302 888-0200
901 Market Wilmington (19801) *(G-16325)*

Eidp Inc ... 302 668-8644
22 Barley Mill Wilmington (19807) *(G-16326)*

Eidp Inc ... 302 773-6287
6235 Brandywine Building Wilmington (19898) *(G-16327)*

Eidp Inc ... 302 999-4329
Faulkland Rd & Centre Rd Wilmington (19808) *(G-16328)*

Eidp Inc ... 302 999-2533
1 Little Leaf Ct Wilmington (19810) *(G-16329)*

Eidp Inc ... 302 695-3742
200 Powder Mill Rd Wilmington (19803) *(G-16330)*

Eidp Inc ... 302 999-5072
4417 Lancaster Pike Wilmington (19805) *(G-16331)*

Eidp Inc ... 302 999-4321
Laurel Run Building Wilmington (19880) *(G-16332)*

Eidp Inc ... 302 774-1000
N-9541 Nemours Bldg Wilmington (19898) *(G-16333)*

Eidp Inc ... 302 774-1000
5537 Nemours Bldg Wilmington (19898) *(G-16334)*

Eidp Inc ... 302 695-5300
Experimental Station Bldg 400 Box 80400 Wilmington (19880) *(G-16335)*

Eidp Inc ... 302 654-8198
1011 Centre Rd Ste 200 Wilmington (19805) *(G-16336)*

Eidp Inc ... 302 656-9626
Bldg B14232 Wilmington (19898) *(G-16337)*

Eidp Inc ... 302 992-2065
Centre Rd Wilmington (19805) *(G-16338)*

Eidp Inc ... 302 999-2826
974 Centre Rd Bldg 730 Wilmington (19805) *(G-16339)*

Eidp Inc ... 844 773-2436
1007 Market St Wilmington (19898) *(G-16340)*

Eidp Inc ... 615 847-6920
Rte 41 & 48 Wilmington (19880) *(G-16341)*

Eidp Inc ... 302 774-1000
Barley Mill Plaza, Bldg 21 Wilmington (19880) *(G-16342)*

Eidp Inc ... 302 996-4000
Barley Mill Plz Bldg 24 Wilmington (19898) *(G-16343)*

Eidp Inc ... 302 992-2458
4417 Lancaster Pike Wilmington (19805) *(G-16344)*

Eighth Street Enterprises LLC ... 302 376-8222
12 W Main St Middletown (19709) *(G-7086)*

Eikon Int Inc ... 312 550-2648
300 Delaware Ave Ste 200 Wilmington (19801) *(G-16345)*

Eileen Davis Do ... 302 856-2254
201 W Market St Georgetown (19947) *(G-4307)*

Ein Taxid Registration, Claymont *Also Called: Govsimplified LLC (G-1169)*

Einstein Lighting, Newark *Also Called: Einstein Technologies LLC (G-10621)*

Einstein Technologies LLC ... 407 614-7404
2035 Sunset Lake Rd B2 Newark (19702) *(G-10621)*

Einsteins School Age Center ... 302 855-5766
21133 Sterling Ave Georgetown (19947) *(G-4308)*

Eisele Celine ... 302 684-3201
225 Bayport Business Park Milton (19968) *(G-8616)*

Eisi, Historic New Castle *Also Called: Eastern Industrial Svcs Inc (G-4979)*

Eitv USA Inc ... 305 517-7715
501 Silverside Rd Ste 105 Wilmington (19809) *(G-16346)*

Eiva Nails & Spa LLC ... 302 537-1888
29 Atlantic Ave Ste I Ocean View (19970) *(G-12508)*

Ej Constructions — ALPHABETIC SECTION

Ej Constructions 302 272-2101
  14726 Shiloh Church Rd Laurel (19956) *(G-5508)*

Ej Usa Inc 302 378-1100
  401 Industrial Dr Middletown (19709) *(G-7087)*

EKA Jewelers, Milford Also Called: Precision Jewelry Inc *(G-8051)*

Ekeo Group LLC 973 489-1962
  128 Sunset Blvd New Castle (19720) *(G-9085)*

El Bluebird LLC 775 773-3255
  1000 N West St Ste 1200 Wilmington (19801) *(G-16347)*

El Diablo 302 691-3081
  837 N Market St Wilmington (19801) *(G-16348)*

El Legacy LLC 601 790-0636
  8 The Grn Ste B Dover (19901) *(G-2428)*

El Management Group LLC 844 263-3335
  651 N Broad St Middletown (19709) *(G-7088)*

El Nopalito Distributors Inc 302 393-2050
  656 N Dupont Blvd Unit G Milford (19963) *(G-7879)*

Elaine Cnroy More Chrtblfndtio 302 296-6580
  29582 Vines Creek Rd Dagsboro (19939) *(G-1444)*

Elaine Leonard 302 376-5553
  111 Patriot Dr Ste A&B Middletown (19709) *(G-7089)*

Elaine Willey 302 536-1286
  24979 Len St Seaford (19973) *(G-13172)*

Elanco Inc 302 731-8500
  723 Rue Madora Ste 6 Bear (19701) *(G-199)*

Elate Partners LLC 408 335-4582
  8 The Grn Dover (19901) *(G-2429)*

Elayne James Salon & Spa LLC 302 376-5290
  221 Porky Oliver Dr Middletown (19709) *(G-7090)*

Elchemy Inc 908 663-8750
  16192 Coastal Hwy Lewes (19958) *(G-5954)*

Elcriton Inc 864 921-5146
  15 Reads Way New Castle (19720) *(G-9086)*

Eld, Wilmington Also Called: Express Legal Documents LLC *(G-16509)*

Elderly Comfort Corporation 302 530-6680
  800 N West St Ste 301 Wilmington (19801) *(G-16349)*

Eldersafe Technologies Inc (PA) 617 852-3018
  16192 Coastal Hwy Lewes (19958) *(G-5955)*

Eldertrust 302 993-1022
  2711 Centerville Rd Ste 108 Wilmington (19808) *(G-16350)*

Elderwood Village Dover LLC 516 496-1505
  21 N State St Dover (19901) *(G-2430)*

Elec Integrity 302 388-3430
  6253 N Dupont Hwy Dover (19901) *(G-2431)*

Electranet Enterprises 302 309-8320
  4 Belfort Loop Newark (19702) *(G-10622)*

Electric, Kenton Also Called: Shure-Line Construction Inc *(G-5454)*

Electric Department, Dover Also Called: City of Dover *(G-2081)*

Electric Department, Milford Also Called: City of Milford *(G-7829)*

Electric Fish LLC 484 804-5149
  42 Rehoboth Ave Ste 5 Rehoboth Beach (19971) *(G-12740)*

Electric Lady Studios LLC Elec 212 677-4700
  20 Montchanin Rd Ste 250 Wilmington (19807) *(G-16351)*

Electric Motor Repair Svc 302 322-1179
  263 Quigley Blvd Ste 12 Historic New Castle (19720) *(G-4980)*

Electric Motor Wholesale Inc 302 653-1844
  2575 Morgans Choice Rd Camden Wyoming (19934) *(G-939)*

Electric Motor Wholesale Inc 302 653-1844
  2575 Morgans Choice Rd Camden Wyoming (19934) *(G-940)*

Electric Tiger Tattoo 302 226-1138
  19972 Church St Rehoboth Beach (19971) *(G-12741)*

Electrical Associates Inc 302 678-1068
  959 Hazlettville Rd Hartly (19953) *(G-4873)*

Electrical Integrity Inc 302 388-3430
  117 J And M Dr New Castle (19720) *(G-9087)*

Electrical Power Systems Inc (PA) 302 325-3502
  240a Churchmans Rd New Castle (19720) *(G-9088)*

Electro Sound Systems 302 367-9840
  2310 Henlopen Ave Wilmington (19804) *(G-16352)*

Electro Sound Systems Inc 302 543-2292
  330 Water St Ste 108 Newport (19804) *(G-12450)*

Electro-Art Sign Company 302 322-1108
  107 J And M Dr New Castle (19720) *(G-9089)*

Electronic Security, Dover Also Called: S & B Pro Security LLC *(G-3496)*

Electronic Systems Specialist 302 738-4165
  Bldg 16 Polly Drummond Shp Ctr C Newark (19711) *(G-10623)*

Electronics Exchange Inc 302 322-5401
  282 Quigley Blvd Historic New Castle (19720) *(G-4981)*

Elegance, Newark Also Called: Leeber Limited USA *(G-11239)*

Elegant Exteriors LLC 302 218-8378
  47 Wedgewood Rd Newark (19711) *(G-10624)*

Elegant Images LLP 302 698-5250
  10 S West St Camden (19934) *(G-828)*

Elegantly Set In Stone, Claymont Also Called: Howarth Granite Holdings LLC *(G-1182)*

Element 302 645-0777
  115 W Market St Lewes (19958) *(G-5956)*

Element Design Group, Lewes Also Called: Edc LLC *(G-5948)*

Element Mtls Tech Wlmngton Inc 302 636-0202
  1300 First State Blvd Ste C Wilmington (19804) *(G-16353)*

Elementice Inc 302 444-5406
  2035 Sunset Lake Rd B2 Newark (19702) *(G-10625)*

Elements Hvac Services LLC 302 448-9641
  38015 Sunny Winters Dr Selbyville (19975) *(G-13532)*

Elenore Inc 720 702-9390
  8 The Grn Ste 16591 Dover (19901) *(G-2432)*

Eleutherian Trust Co 302 294-0821
  1105 N Market St Ste 900 Wilmington (19801) *(G-16354)*

Eleuthrian Mlls-Hgley Fndtion 302 658-2400
  200 Hawley St Wilmington (19807) *(G-16355)*

Elevate Cdb Inc 844 903-4443
  8 The Grn Ste B Dover (19901) *(G-2433)*

Elevate Dvm Inc 302 761-9650
  3 Penny Lane Ct Wilmington (19803) *(G-16356)*

Elevate RCM Consulting 484 655-8733
  300 Delaware Ave Wilmington (19801) *(G-16357)*

Elevated Studios Hq 302 407-3229
  34a Trolley Sq Wilmington (19806) *(G-16358)*

Elevation Office Furn LLC 267 261-0124
  2509 Duncan Rd Wilmington (19808) *(G-16359)*

Elevations In Ecom LLC 302 797-1709
  501 Silverside Rd Ste 516 Wilmington (19809) *(G-16360)*

Elevator Organization Inc 847 431-2927
  2055 Limestone Rd Ste 200c Wilmington (19808) *(G-16361)*

Elevatum Consulting LLC 571 330-9016
  221 N Broad St Ste 3a Middletown (19709) *(G-7091)*

Elevee Events 302 212-2112
  260 Sea Eagle Dr Unit 2 Rehoboth Beach (19971) *(G-12742)*

Elgood Solutions Inc 610 420-7207
  2140 S Dupont Hwy Camden (19934) *(G-829)*

Elicin Edeline 973 687-9930
  260 Chapman Rd Ste 100b Newark (19702) *(G-10626)*

Elite, Wilmington Also Called: Eagan US Holdco LLC *(G-16245)*

Elite Auto LLC 302 690-2948
  364 E Main St Ste 204 Middletown (19709) *(G-7092)*

Elite Auto Transport 302 252-5847
  1327 Darling Dr Middletown (19709) *(G-7093)*

Elite Auto Works LLC 302 252-1045
  2501 W 3rd St Wilmington (19805) *(G-16362)*

Elite Building Services, Wilmington Also Called: Elite Cleaning Company Inc *(G-16363)*

Elite Chemical and Supply Inc 302 366-8900
  630 Churchmans Rd Ste 106 Newark (19702) *(G-10627)*

Elite Cleaning Company, Newark Also Called: Elite Commercial Cleaning Inc *(G-10628)*

Elite Cleaning Company Inc 302 439-4430
  2200 Concord Pike Wilmington (19803) *(G-16363)*

Elite Cleaning Services LLC 571 359-7751
  13 Amberwood Way Lewes (19958) *(G-5957)*

Elite Commercial Cleaning Inc 302 366-8900
  630 Churchmans Rd Ste 106 Newark (19702) *(G-10628)*

Elite Developers Group LLC 615 397-9732
  8 The Grn Ste 8651 Dover (19901) *(G-2434)*

Elite Facility Services LLC 302 566-7031
  200 Continental Dr Ste 401 Newark (19713) *(G-10629)*

ALPHABETIC SECTION

Elite Feet LLC.. 302 464-1028
  5238 Summit Bridge Rd Middletown (19709) *(G-7094)*

Elite Landscape... 302 543-7305
  108 Boxwood Rd Wilmington (19804) *(G-16364)*

Elite Lubricants LLC... 302 629-3301
  8734 Concord Rd Seaford (19973) *(G-13173)*

Elite Meetings International... 302 516-7997
  100 Greenhill Ave Ste C Wilmington (19805) *(G-16365)*

Elite Nails... 302 745-5988
  34005 Wescoats Rd Unit 4 Lewes (19958) *(G-5958)*

Elite Property Maintenance... 302 836-1865
  201 5th St Delaware City (19706) *(G-1540)*

Elite Property Maintenance... 302 836-8878
  137 Pine Valley Dr Middletown (19709) *(G-7095)*

Elite Tax Services LLC... 302 256-0401
  30b Trolley Sq Wilmington (19806) *(G-16366)*

Elite Trnspt & Logistics Inc.. 302 348-8480
  300 Delaware Ave Ste 210 Wilmington (19801) *(G-16367)*

Elite USA Fashion LLC.. 810 410-5403
  650 Naamans Rd Ste 204 Claymont (19703) *(G-1129)*

Elite Worldwide Inc.. 833 200-5185
  2093 Philadelphia Pike Claymont (19703) *(G-1130)*

Eliyahna Creative LLC... 530 683-5463
  8 The Grn Dover (19901) *(G-2435)*

Elizabeth A Hussey.. 302 577-5400
  401 E 12th St Wilmington (19801) *(G-16368)*

Elizabeth Beverage Company LLC.................................. 302 322-9895
  650 Ships Landing Way Historic New Castle (19720) *(G-4982)*

Elizabeth Bottling Company, Historic New Castle *Also Called: Elizabeth Beverage Company LLC (G-4982)*

Elizabeth L Thomas-Bauer.. 302 798-0666
  1320 Philadelphia Pike Ste 101 Wilmington (19809) *(G-16369)*

Elizabeth Sutton Mace Psyd.. 302 293-4920
  501 Silverside Rd Ste 145 Wilmington (19809) *(G-16370)*

Elizabeth W Murphey School Inc..................................... 302 734-7478
  42 Kings Hwy Dover (19901) *(G-2436)*

ELKS LODGE, Seaford *Also Called: Benevlent Prtctive Order Elks (G-13082)*

ELKS LODGE 1903, Dover *Also Called: Benevlent Prtective Order Elks (G-1910)*

Elkton Bear Dental... 302 836-1670
  34 Waterton Dr Bear (19701) *(G-200)*

Elkton Exterminating Co Inc.. 302 368-9116
  1040 S Chapel St Newark (19702) *(G-10630)*

Elkton Mddltown Ashtma Allergy..................................... 302 378-1887
  12 Pennington St Ste 100 Middletown (19709) *(G-7096)*

Ella Health Inc.. 302 543-4396
  4600 Linden Hill Rd Wilmington (19808) *(G-16371)*

Ellen A Spurrier M D.. 302 651-6660
  1600 Rockland Rd Wilmington (19803) *(G-16372)*

Ellen Rice Gallery... 302 539-3405
  98 Garfield Pkwy Unit 109 Bethany Beach (19930) *(G-599)*

Elli Creators Inc.. 269 742-4057
  651 N Broad St Ste 201 Middletown (19709) *(G-7097)*

Ellie Tax Inc.. 917 459-2762
  909 Benalli Dr Middletown (19709) *(G-7098)*

Ellingsen & Associates... 302 650-6437
  113 Barksdale Professional Ctr Newark (19711) *(G-10631)*

Elliott John... 302 846-2487
  36411 August Rd Delmar (19940) *(G-1593)*

Ellis Contracting LLC... 302 559-5105
  238 Barberry Dr Wilmington (19808) *(G-16373)*

Ellmore Auto Collision... 302 762-2301
  4921 Governor Printz Blvd Wilmington (19809) *(G-16374)*

Elm Properties Inc... 302 762-3757
  301 Old Dupont Rd Ste G Wilmington (19804) *(G-16375)*

Elmer Schultz Services Inc... 302 655-8900
  36 Belmont Ave Wilmington (19804) *(G-16376)*

Elms Management Association....................................... 302 738-5225
  2201 London Way Newark (19713) *(G-10632)*

Eloim Enterprises LLC... 510 209-3670
  2711 Centerville Rd # 400 Wilmington (19808) *(G-16377)*

Elomia Health Inc... 302 244-7193
  8 The Grn Dover (19901) *(G-2437)*

Elrod, Michael E DC, Lewes *Also Called: Lewes Chiropractic Center (G-6192)*

Els Tire Service Inc.. 302 834-1997
  2724 Pulaski Hwy Newark (19702) *(G-10633)*

Elsicon Inc.. 302 266-7030
  5 Innovation Way Ste 100 Newark (19711) *(G-10634)*

Elsmere Fire Co 1 Inc.. 302 999-0183
  1107 Kirkwood Hwy Wilmington (19805) *(G-16378)*

Elsmere Insurance Agency LLC...................................... 317 574-2861
  1000 N West St Ste 1220 Wilmington (19801) *(G-16379)*

Elsmere Nutrition... 302 502-2061
  15 Sanders Rd Wilmington (19805) *(G-16380)*

Elsmere Presbyterian Church.. 302 998-6365
  606 New Rd Wilmington (19805) *(G-16381)*

Eluktronics Inc.. 302 380-3242
  9 Albe Dr Ste E Newark (19702) *(G-10635)*

Elvin Schrock and Sons Inc... 302 349-4384
  10725 Beach Hwy Greenwood (19950) *(G-4625)*

Elwyn Pennsylvania and Del... 302 658-8860
  321 E 11th St Fl 1 Wilmington (19801) *(G-16382)*

Elzufon Astin Rrdon Trlov Mnde (PA).............................. 302 428-3181
  300 Delaware Ave Ste 1700 Wilmington (19801) *(G-16383)*

Elzufon Austin Reardon Tarlov....................................... 302 644-0144
  1413 Savannah Rd Unit 1 Lewes (19958) *(G-5959)*

Em Beauty Bar Inc... 302 525-3933
  24 Prestbury Sq Newark (19713) *(G-10636)*

Em Photonics Inc... 302 456-9003
  51 E Main St Ste 203 Newark (19711) *(G-10637)*

Ema Corp (HQ)... 302 479-9434
  1105 N Market St Wilmington (19801) *(G-16384)*

Emaep LLC... 202 836-7886
  1201 N Orange St Wilmington (19801) *(G-16385)*

Emagination Store USA Inc... 302 884-6746
  1201 N Orange St Ste 7291 Wilmington (19801) *(G-16386)*

Embarcdero Arcft Scrtzation Tr....................................... 302 651-1000
  1100 N Market St Wilmington (19801) *(G-16387)*

Emblem At Christiana Clubhouse.................................... 302 525-6692
  1150 Helen Dr Newark (19702) *(G-10638)*

Embrace Change LLC... 302 286-5288
  179 W Chestnut Hill Rd Ste 6 Newark (19713) *(G-10639)*

Embrace Home Loans Inc... 302 635-7998
  5341 Limestone Rd Ste 101 Wilmington (19808) *(G-16388)*

Embrace The Change Counseling................................... 302 358-6237
  179 W Chestnut Hill Rd Ste 6 Newark (19713) *(G-10640)*

Embroidery Enterprises, Milford *Also Called: Andrew Pipon (G-7768)*

Emeca/Spe Usa LLC.. 302 875-0760
  200 W 10th St Laurel (19956) *(G-5509)*

Emendo Bio Inc.. 516 595-1849
  1811 Silverside Rd Wilmington (19810) *(G-16389)*

Ementum Inc (PA).. 866 984-1999
  2841 S Bay Shore Dr Milton (19968) *(G-8617)*

Emera US Finance LP... 302 636-5400
  2711 Centerville Rd Ste 400 Wilmington (19808) *(G-16390)*

Emerald Bioagriculture Corp (PA)................................... 517 882-7370
  726 Yorklyn Rd Ste 420 Hockessin (19707) *(G-5199)*

Emerald City Wash World.. 302 734-1230
  730 W Division St Dover (19904) *(G-2438)*

Emerald Green... 302 836-6909
  992 Port Penn Rd Middletown (19709) *(G-7099)*

Emerald Lawn and Ldscpg LLC....................................... 302 228-1468
  701 Lindsay Ln Milford (19963) *(G-7880)*

Emergency Medical Mgmnt, Wilmington *Also Called: Douglas Morrow (G-16156)*

Emergency Room, Wilmington *Also Called: Kathleen M Cronan MD (G-17665)*

Emergent Frest Fin Acclrtor In.. 347 796-4450
  251 Little Falls Dr Wilmington (19808) *(G-16391)*

Emerging Impact Group Corp... 404 625-1530
  16192 Coastal Hwy Apt 1 Lewes (19958) *(G-5960)*

Emerging Travel Group, Wilmington *Also Called: Emerging Travel Inc (G-16392)*

Emerging Travel Inc (PA)... 302 295-3838
  1000 N West St Ste 1200 Wilmington (19801) *(G-16392)*

Emergncy Response Protocol LLC.................................. 302 994-2600
  101 W Ayre St Wilmington (19804) *(G-16393)*

Emerick Construction Group LLC 302 547-0715
3205 Frazer Rd Newark (19702) *(G-10641)*

Emeritus Corporation 302 674-4407
150 Saulsbury Rd Dover (19904) *(G-2439)*

Emil W Tetzner D M D 302 744-9900
804 S State St Ste 1 Dover (19901) *(G-2440)*

Emily Crawford PHD 302 995-9600
3608 Lancaster Pike Wilmington (19805) *(G-16394)*

Emission Free Generators Inc 440 503-7405
2093 Philadelphia Pike Ste 2099 Claymont (19703) *(G-1131)*

Emitt LLC 302 757-2353
121 Hadrian Close Bear (19701) *(G-201)*

Emlyn Construction Co 302 697-8247
1341 Walnut Shade Rd Dover (19901) *(G-2441)*

Emma Jefferies Day Care 302 762-3235
603 W 39th St Wilmington (19802) *(G-16395)*

Emma Kane & Valerie Taylor Day 302 629-4347
23856 Dove Rd Seaford (19973) *(G-13174)*

Emma Systems Inc 407 773-8536
1013 Centre Rd Ste 403b Wilmington (19805) *(G-16396)*

Emmanuel Diningroom, Wilmington Also Called: Ministry of Caring Inc *(G-18378)*

Emmanuel Troumouhis 302 762-3200
735 Philadelphia Pike Wilmington (19809) *(G-16397)*

Emment A Oat Contractor Inc 302 999-1567
501 W Newport Pike Wilmington (19804) *(G-16398)*

Emory Hill & Company (PA) 302 322-4400
10 Corporate Cir Ste 100 New Castle (19720) *(G-9090)*

Emory Hill RE Svcs Inc (PA) 302 322-9500
10 Corporate Cir Ste 100 New Castle (19720) *(G-9091)*

Emory Massage Therapy 302 290-0003
155 Willis Rd Apt G Dover (19901) *(G-2442)*

Emotinal Wllness Cunseling LLC 302 865-8098
818 Williamsville Rd Houston (19954) *(G-5440)*

Empathy Home Care LLC 302 722-1538
57 Anglin Dr Newark (19713) *(G-10642)*

Empire, New Castle Also Called: Empire Investments Inc *(G-9093)*

Empire Auto Protect LLC 888 345-0084
8 The Grn Ste 11230 Dover (19901) *(G-2443)*

Empire Blue 302 324-1015
315 Schafer Blvd New Castle (19720) *(G-9092)*

Empire Construction 302 329-9256
221 Milton Ellendale Hwy Milton (19968) *(G-8618)*

Empire Construction Group LLC 302 223-9208
16791 Hudson Rd Milton (19968) *(G-8619)*

Empire Data Voice Networks LLC 702 613-4900
30851 Fowlers Path Millsboro (19966) *(G-8281)*

Empire Flippers LLC 323 638-0438
427 N Tatnall St # 34425 Wilmington (19801) *(G-16399)*

Empire Group International 302 791-1100
3506 Philadelphia Pike Claymont (19703) *(G-1132)*

Empire Investments Inc 302 838-0631
201 Jestan Blvd New Castle (19720) *(G-9093)*

Empire Medical LLC 443 553-0057
379 Walmart Dr Camden (19934) *(G-830)*

Empire Realty Management Inc 302 731-0784
54 Cheswold Blvd Newark (19713) *(G-10643)*

Empirical Cre Holdings Corp (PA) 816 582-8041
108 W 13th St Wilmington (19801) *(G-16400)*

Empirical Inc 347 828-4528
3500 S Dupont Hwy Ste Ek-101 Dover (19901) *(G-2444)*

Employers Bench Inc 973 757-1912
40 W Main St Ste 855 Christiana (19702) *(G-995)*

Empower Healthcare Assets Inc 604 789-2146
2140 S Dupont Hwy Camden (19934) *(G-831)*

Empowered Yoga 302 654-9642
2000 Pennsylvania Ave Apt 208 Wilmington (19806) *(G-16401)*

Empowered Yoga 302 409-0192
20 Montchanin Rd Ste 60 Wilmington (19807) *(G-16402)*

Empowering Group LLC 302 450-3065
371 W North St Dover (19904) *(G-2445)*

Empowering Realty LLC 302 744-8169
838 Walker Rd Ste 22-1 Dover (19904) *(G-2446)*

Empowerment Group Inc 302 930-8080
22761 Slaughter Neck Rd Lincoln (19960) *(G-6665)*

Emw Publications 302 438-9879
351 Mockingbird Hill Rd Hockessin (19707) *(G-5200)*

Emz Properties 302 730-8250
1447 S Governors Ave Dover (19904) *(G-2447)*

En Properties LLC 302 738-4201
11 Foxview Cir Hockessin (19707) *(G-5201)*

Enabld Technologies Inc (PA) 917 340-1606
3524 Silverside Rd Ste 35b Wilmington (19810) *(G-16403)*

Encentiv Energy LLC 302 504-8506
801 W Newport Pike Ste 202 Wilmington (19804) *(G-16404)*

Enchanted Child Care Intl Inc 302 834-0436
1205 Quintilio Dr Bear (19701) *(G-202)*

Enclave Digital Development Co (PA) 203 807-0400
16192 Coastal Hwy Lewes (19958) *(G-5961)*

Enclosed Auto Solutions LLC 302 437-9858
229 Liborio Dr Middletown (19709) *(G-7100)*

Encompass Accounting 302 648-5488
523 Capitol Trl Newark (19711) *(G-10644)*

Encompass Accounting Inc 302 229-3572
2607 Belaire Dr Wilmington (19808) *(G-16405)*

Encompass Corporation US Inc 212 523-0340
1209 N Orange St Wilmington (19801) *(G-16406)*

Encompass Elements, Historic New Castle Also Called: Fox Specialties Inc *(G-4990)*

Encompass Health Corporation 302 464-3400
250 E Hampden Rd Middletown (19709) *(G-7101)*

Encore Dance Academy 302 824-9669
1150 Capitol Trl Newark (19711) *(G-10645)*

Encore Lashes Lash Lounge LLC 844 408-0004
15 Dalton Ct New Castle (19720) *(G-9094)*

Encross LLC 302 351-2593
1521 Concord Pike Ste 301 Wilmington (19803) *(G-16407)*

END Imports Inc 302 393-2050
656 N Dupont Blvd Unit G Milford (19963) *(G-7881)*

End of Life Doula 302 478-6958
2511 Lori Ln N Wilmington (19810) *(G-16408)*

End Result Gym 302 280-6603
28167 Seaford Rd Laurel (19956) *(G-5510)*

Endevor, Wilmington Also Called: Endevor LLC *(G-16409)*

Endevor LLC 302 543-5055
3844 Kennett Pike Ste 210 Wilmington (19807) *(G-16409)*

Endless Os Foundation LLC 415 413-4159
24a Trolley Sq # 2319 Wilmington (19806) *(G-16410)*

Endless Pssblties In The Cmnty 302 528-4503
54 Winslow Rd Newark (19711) *(G-10646)*

Endlesspens LLC 813 550-5501
16192 Coastal Hwy Lewes (19958) *(G-5962)*

Endocrinology Consultant 302 734-2782
111 Wolf Creek Blvd Dover (19901) *(G-2448)*

Endoscopy Center of Delaware, Newark Also Called: Endoscopy Center of Deleware *(G-10647)*

Endoscopy Center of Deleware 302 892-2710
1090 Old Churchmans Rd Newark (19713) *(G-10647)*

Endoscopy Suite Partners LLC 267 243-3850
2207 Concord Pike Ste 167 Wilmington (19803) *(G-16411)*

Endospace Corporation 732 271-8700
240 N James St Ste 100 Newport (19804) *(G-12451)*

Endure To Cure Foundation 866 400-2121
1201 N Orange St Ste 7089 Wilmington (19801) *(G-16412)*

Endure Walls 302 479-7614
3704 Kennett Pike Wilmington (19807) *(G-16413)*

Endurnce Reinsurance Corp Amer 973 898-9575
1209 N Orange St Wilmington (19801) *(G-16414)*

Ener-G Group Inc 917 281-0020
3422 Old Capitol Trl Wilmington (19808) *(G-16415)*

Enercon 302 407-3179
3411 Silverside Rd Ste 100 Wilmington (19810) *(G-16416)*

Energy Assistance Program, Dover Also Called: Catholic Charities Inc *(G-2038)*

Energy Center Dover LLC 302 678-4666
1280 W North St Dover (19904) *(G-2449)*

ALPHABETIC SECTION — Envision Consulting LLC

Energy Gym 302 436-9001
36666 Bluewater Run W Unit 1 Selbyville (19975) *(G-13533)*

Energy Healing Pathways LLC 302 478-6383
5 Stones Throw Rd Wilmington (19803) *(G-16417)*

Energy Services Group 302 324-8400
2 King Ct Ste A New Castle (19720) *(G-9095)*

Energy Systems Tech Inc 302 368-0443
15 Reads Way Ste 101a New Castle (19720) *(G-9096)*

Energy Tech Holdings LLC (PA) 212 356-6130
1209 N Orange St Wilmington (19801) *(G-16418)*

Enersource Electrical Svc LLC 302 842-8714
831 N Tatnall St Wilmington (19801) *(G-16419)*

Enf Ventures LLC 443 475-0175
21884 Spring Forest Way Milton (19968) *(G-8620)*

Eng Jerald MD 302 478-4845
3521 Silverside Rd Ste 1f Wilmington (19810) *(G-16420)*

Engage Xr LLC 302 877-2028
251 Little Falls Dr Wilmington (19808) *(G-16421)*

Engati Technologies Inc 215 368-3551
919 N Market St Ste 950 Wilmington (19801) *(G-16422)*

Engineered Systems & Designs 302 456-0446
3 S Tatnall St Wilmington (19801) *(G-16423)*

Engineering Incorporated 302 995-6862
6 Lewis Cir Wilmington (19804) *(G-16424)*

England Collision Center LLC 240 440-1111
19 King Ct New Castle (19720) *(G-9097)*

English Realty LLC 302 295-4845
1000 N West St Ste 1200 Wilmington (19801) *(G-16425)*

English Village, Newark *Also Called: Panco Management Corporation (G-11619)*

Enhanced Corporate Prfmce LLC 302 545-8541
1 Morning Glen Ln Newark (19711) *(G-10648)*

Enhanced Dental Care 302 645-7200
18947 John J Williams Hwy Unit 301 Rehoboth Beach (19971) *(G-12743)*

Enhanced Heating & AC 302 836-1921
68 Albe Dr Newark (19702) *(G-10649)*

Enliv, Wilmington *Also Called: Thinkhat Software Inc (G-20301)*

Enou Labs LLC 321 343-4362
2055 Limestone Rd Ste 200c Wilmington (19808) *(G-16426)*

Enovante LLC 917 960-8384
2055 Limestone Rd Ste 200c Wilmington (19808) *(G-16427)*

Enovis Corporation (PA) 301 252-9160
2711 Centerville Rd Ste 400 Wilmington (19808) *(G-16428)*

Enpass Technologies Inc (PA) 415 671-5123
1201 N Market St Ste 111 Wilmington (19801) *(G-16429)*

Ens Logistics LLC 302 784-5155
39 O Rourke Ct Newark (19702) *(G-10650)*

Ensinger Penn Fibre Inc 302 349-4505
220 S Church & Snider St Greenwood (19950) *(G-4626)*

Ensinger Penn Fibre Inc 302 349-4505
221 S Church St Greenwood (19950) *(G-4627)*

Ensyn Renewables Inc 302 425-3740
1521 Concord Pike Ste 205 Wilmington (19803) *(G-16430)*

Ent Allergy Center 302 629-3400
8468 Herring Run Rd Seaford (19973) *(G-13175)*

Ent and Allergy Delaware LLC (PA) 302 478-8467
700 Prides Xing Ste 200 Newark (19713) *(G-10651)*

Ent and Allergy Delaware LLC 302 998-0300
1941 Limestone Rd Wilmington (19808) *(G-16431)*

Ente Technologies Inc 917 924-8450
1111b S Governors Ave Ste 6032 Dover (19904) *(G-2450)*

Entek Manufacturing Inc 302 576-5860
300 Delaware Ave Ste 800 Wilmington (19801) *(G-16432)*

Enteraxion, Wilmington *Also Called: Charter Dynamics LLC (G-15344)*

Enterprise Flasher Co Inc 302 999-0856
4 Hadco Rd Wilmington (19804) *(G-16433)*

Enterprise Learning Solutions 302 762-6595
236 Weldin Ridge Rd Wilmington (19803) *(G-16434)*

Enterprise Lsg Phladelphia LLC 302 732-3534
27424 Auto Works Ave Dagsboro (19939) *(G-1445)*

Enterprise Lsg Phladelphia LLC 302 266-7777
409 E Cleveland Ave Newark (19711) *(G-10652)*

Enterprise Lsg Phladelphia LLC 302 292-0524
430 Newark Shopping Ctr Newark (19711) *(G-10653)*

Enterprise Lsg Phladelphia LLC 302 425-4404
100 S French St Unit 115a Wilmington (19801) *(G-16435)*

Enterprise Lsg Phladelphia LLC 302 479-7829
4727 Concord Pike Wilmington (19803) *(G-16436)*

Enterprise Lsg Phladelphia LLC 302 761-4545
100 Philadelphia Pike Wilmington (19809) *(G-16437)*

Enterprise Masonry Corporation 302 764-6858
3010 Bellevue Ave Wilmington (19802) *(G-16438)*

Enterprise Rent A Car 302 856-6380
22694 Dupont Blvd Georgetown (19947) *(G-4309)*

Enterprise Rent A Car 302 454-2939
2405 Pulaski Hwy Newark (19702) *(G-10654)*

Enterprise Rent A Car 302 636-0660
1602 E Newport Pike Wilmington (19804) *(G-16439)*

Enterprise Rent-A-Car 302 376-5606
753 N Broad St Middletown (19709) *(G-7102)*

Enterprise Rent-A-Car 302 934-1216
28656 Dupont Blvd Millsboro (19966) *(G-8282)*

Enterprise Rent-A-Car 717 968-1966
4616 Kirkwood Hwy Wilmington (19808) *(G-16440)*

Enterprise Rent-A-Car, Dagsboro *Also Called: Enterprise Lsg Phladelphia LLC (G-1445)*

Enterprise Rent-A-Car, Dover *Also Called: Ean Holdings LLC (G-2403)*

Enterprise Rent-A-Car, Middletown *Also Called: Ean Holdings LLC (G-7077)*

Enterprise Rent-A-Car, Middletown *Also Called: Enterprise Rent-A-Car (G-7102)*

Enterprise Rent-A-Car, Milford *Also Called: Ean Holdings LLC (G-7875)*

Enterprise Rent-A-Car, Millsboro *Also Called: Enterprise Rent-A-Car (G-8282)*

Enterprise Rent-A-Car, Newark *Also Called: Enterprise Lsg Phladelphia LLC (G-10652)*

Enterprise Rent-A-Car, Newark *Also Called: Enterprise Lsg Phladelphia LLC (G-10653)*

Enterprise Rent-A-Car, Wilmington *Also Called: Enterprise Lsg Phladelphia LLC (G-16436)*

Enterprise Rent-A-Car, Wilmington *Also Called: Enterprise Lsg Phladelphia LLC (G-16437)*

Enterprise Rent-A-Car, Wilmington *Also Called: Enterprise Rent-A-Car (G-16440)*

Enterprise Rentacar 302 645-5005
18767 Coastal Hwy Rehoboth Beach (19971) *(G-12744)*

Enterprise Rentacar 302 628-2931
26876 Sussex Hwy Seaford (19973) *(G-13176)*

Entertainment, Georgetown *Also Called: Affordable Wedding Entrmt (G-4200)*

Entertainment Factory 302 824-1428
810 Broadfield Dr Newark (19713) *(G-10655)*

Entertainment Production Svcs, Wilmington *Also Called: Bew Productions (G-14869)*

Entertech Inc 415 840-0204
1521 Concord Pike Ste 301 Wilmington (19803) *(G-16441)*

Entrilia Inc (PA) 954 372-1715
919 N Market St Ste 950 Wilmington (19801) *(G-16442)*

Envirocorp Inc 302 398-3869
51 Clark St Harrington (19952) *(G-4766)*

Environmental Alliance Inc (HQ) 302 234-4400
5341 Limestone Rd Wilmington (19808) *(G-16443)*

Environmental Consulting Svcs (PA) 302 378-9881
100 S Cass St Middletown (19709) *(G-7103)*

Environmental Outpost & Mntjoy 302 659-5003
585 Big Oak Rd Smyrna (19977) *(G-13722)*

Environmental Protection Agcy 302 739-9917
89 Kings Hwy Dover (19901) *(G-2451)*

Environmental Resources Inc 302 436-9637
38173 Dupont Blvd Selbyville (19975) *(G-13534)*

Environmental Services Inc 302 669-6812
461 Churchmans Rd New Castle (19720) *(G-9098)*

Environmental Testing Inc 302 378-5341
100 S Cass St Middletown (19709) *(G-7104)*

Envirotech Envmtl Consulting 302 684-5201
17605 Nassau Commons Blvd Lewes (19958) *(G-5963)*

Envirotech LLC 302 834-5011
13 Bryan Cir Bear (19701) *(G-203)*

Envirotrols Group Inc 302 846-9103
105 E State St Delmar (19940) *(G-1594)*

Envirtech Enviromental Consltg 302 645-6491
34634 Bay Crossing Blvd Lewes (19958) *(G-5964)*

Envision Consulting LLC 302 658-9027
2008 Woodlawn Ave Wilmington (19806) *(G-16444)*

Envision Healthcare Corp.. 302 644-3852
    1451 Kings Hwy Ste 4a Lewes (19958) (G-5965)
Envision Infosolutions Inc... 302 565-4289
    260 Chapman Rd Ste 204d Newark (19702) (G-10656)
Envision It Publications LLC... 800 329-9411
    1148 Pulaski Hwy Bear (19701) (G-204)
Envision Property Solvers LLC... 888 478-0744
    7209 Lancaster Pike Hockessin (19707) (G-5202)
Envoy Flight Systems Inc... 302 738-1788
    201 Ruthar Dr Ste 3 Newark (19711) (G-10657)
Enyumba Inc... 818 272-9383
    8 The Grn Dover (19901) (G-2452)
Enz Party Rental... 302 287-5995
    2700 Lancaster Ave Wilmington (19805) (G-16445)
Enzigma LLC... 415 830-3694
    1201 N Orange St Ste 7403 Wilmington (19801) (G-16446)
Enzymetrics Bioscience Inc... 302 763-3658
    1 Righter Pkwy Ste 260 Wilmington (19803) (G-16447)
Eom Healthcare Group LLC.. 917 750-5089
    555 E Loockerman St Ste 120 Dover (19901) (G-2453)
Eon Mist LLC.. 310 500-2140
    427 N Tatnall St 85923 Wilmington (19801) (G-16448)
Eonscope Inc.. 312 319-4484
    2035 Sunset Lake Rd B2 Newark (19702) (G-10658)
Ep Engine Performance.. 302 521-0435
    32 W Pembrooke Dr Smyrna (19977) (G-13723)
Ep Supply Corp.. 909 969-5122
    16192 Coastal Hwy Lewes (19958) (G-5966)
EPA, Dover Also Called: Environmental Protection Agcy (G-2451)
Epatriotcrm LLC... 419 967-6812
    8 The Grn Ste A Dover (19901) (G-2454)
Epb Associates Inc... 302 475-7301
    107 W Sutton Pl Wilmington (19810) (G-16449)
Epd Tech LLC... 415 508-7580
    16192 Coastal Hwy Lewes (19958) (G-5967)
Epeius Contracting Service LLC... 302 533-8753
    30 Windy Ct Newark (19713) (G-10659)
Ephphatha Med Care Svcs LLC... 925 222-9572
    1350 Middleford Rd Ste 501 Seaford (19973) (G-13177)
Ephraim A Ayoola M D.. 302 741-0204
    4164 N Dupont Hwy Dover (19901) (G-2455)
Epic Charging Inc.. 650 250-6811
    8 The Grn Dover (19901) (G-2456)
Epic Manufacturing, Greenwood Also Called: Hydroseeding Company LLC (G-4638)
Epic Marketing Cons Corp... 302 285-9790
    10 Jackie Cir Middletown (19709) (G-7105)
Epic Research LLC... 302 510-1338
    1105 N Market St Ste 1600 Wilmington (19801) (G-16450)
Epic Tides LLC.. 646 535-6523
    2093a Philadelphia Pike Ste 246 Claymont (19703) (G-1133)
Episode Interactive LLC... 858 220-0946
    3500 S Dupont Hwy Dover (19901) (G-2457)
Epix Industries Inc... 302 550-9007
    16192 Coastal Hwy Lewes (19958) (G-5968)
Epotec Inc.. 302 654-3090
    62 Rockford Rd Wilmington (19806) (G-16451)
Eprintit Usa Inc.. 613 299-7105
    1000 N West St Wilmington (19801) (G-16452)
Epstein Kplan Opthlmlogist LLP... 302 322-4444
    169 Christiana Rd New Castle (19720) (G-9099)
Eptikar It Solutions Inc... 720 422-8441
    651 N Broad St Middletown (19709) (G-7106)
Equidental... 302 423-0851
    21 Wilder Rd Dover (19904) (G-2458)
Equine Technologies Inc.. 669 306-6009
    651 N Broad St Ste 205 Middletown (19709) (G-7107)
Equine Wholesalers, Harrington Also Called: Chick Harness & Supply Inc (G-4748)
Equinox Cleaning LLC.. 240 419-9077
    520 Capitol Trl Newark (19711) (G-10660)
Equinox LLC.. 856 364-5615
    131 King William St Newark (19711) (G-10661)

Equity Lifestyle.. 302 595-2833
    205 Joan Dr Bear (19701) (G-205)
Equity Plus Inc.. 302 762-3122
    500 Philadelphia Pike C Wilmington (19809) (G-16453)
Equity Plus Mortgage Company, Wilmington Also Called: Equity Plus Inc (G-16453)
Er, Wilmington Also Called: Erban Mndset Lfstyle Sltons In (G-16454)
Er At Home Llc... 540 845-9499
    11 Christina Woods Ct Ste B Newark (19702) (G-10662)
ER Lawn Care LLC... 302 519-3173
    14008 Deer Forest Rd Bridgeville (19933) (G-698)
ERA, Dover Also Called: Harrington Realty Inc (G-2654)
ERA, Dover Also Called: Harrington Realty Inc (G-2655)
ERA, Wilmington Also Called: Cole Realty Inc (G-15525)
ERA Harrington Realty.. 302 363-1796
    516 Jefferic Blvd Ste C Dover (19901) (G-2459)
ERA Harrington Realty (PA).. 302 674-4663
    1404 Forrest Ave Ste A Dover (19904) (G-2460)
Eranga Cardiology... 302 422-2496
    113 Neurology Way Milford (19963) (G-7882)
Eranga Cardiology PA.. 302 747-7486
    200 Banning St Ste 310 Dover (19904) (G-2461)
Erban Mndset Lfstyle Sltons In... 407 608-0134
    1412 Fresno Rd Wilmington (19803) (G-16454)
ERC, Wilmington Also Called: Edgemoor Rvtalization Coop Inc (G-16291)
Erco, Wilmington Also Called: Erco Ceilings & Interiors Inc (G-16455)
Erco Ceilings & Blinds, Harrington Also Called: Erco Ceilings & Interiors Inc (G-4767)
Erco Ceilings & Interiors Inc.. 302 398-3200
    512 Shaw Ave Harrington (19952) (G-4767)
Erco Ceilings & Interiors Inc (HQ)... 302 994-6200
    2 S Dupont Rd Wilmington (19805) (G-16455)
Eri Investments Inc.. 302 656-8089
    801 N West St Fl 2 Wilmington (19801) (G-16456)
Eric Barsky... 856 495-6988
    19 Autumnwood Dr Newark (19711) (G-10663)
Eric C James... 302 841-0930
    26735 Asbury Meadows Ln Seaford (19973) (G-13178)
Eric Hobbs Trucking Inc.. 302 697-2090
    3292 Turkey Point Rd Viola (19979) (G-14094)
Eric Kafka Psychologist... 302 644-8891
    216 W 3rd St Lewes (19958) (G-5969)
Eric M Doroshow.. 302 934-9400
    213 E Dupont Hwy Millsboro (19966) (G-8283)
Eric S Balliet.. 302 856-7423
    212 W Market St Georgetown (19947) (G-4310)
Erickson Management.. 302 235-0855
    447 Coldspring Run Newark (19711) (G-10664)
Erics Handyman & Ldscpg Svcs.. 302 242-7712
    351 Tuxedo Ln Woodside (19980) (G-20976)
Ericsons Garage... 302 653-5032
    742 Tush Rd Smyrna (19977) (G-13724)
Erik A Underhill MD.. 302 652-3772
    1806 N Van Buren St Ste 200 Wilmington (19802) (G-16457)
Erik Lemus... 302 293-5178
    7 Claire Pl Wilmington (19808) (G-16458)
Erik M D Stancofski.. 302 645-7050
    431 Savannah Rd Lewes (19958) (G-5970)
Erik S Bradley DDS.. 302 239-5917
    1415 Foulk Rd Ste 200 Wilmington (19803) (G-16459)
Erin Bendler.. 201 704-6252
    8 London Cir N Rehoboth Beach (19971) (G-12745)
Erin N Macko DDS LLC... 302 368-7463
    625 Barksdale Rd Ste 101 Newark (19711) (G-10665)
Erm Emerald US Inc... 302 651-8300
    1150 N Market St Ste 1300 Wilmington (19801) (G-16460)
Erm-Delaware Inc (HQ).. 302 651-8300
    1105 N Market St Ste 1300 Wilmington (19801) (G-16461)
Ermak Foundry & Machining, Dover Also Called: Ermak Metals Inc (G-2462)
Ermak Metals Inc (HQ)... 952 448-2801
    1111 S Governors Ave Dover (19904) (G-2462)
Ernest Soffronoff Dr... 302 827-2284
    36315 Tarpon Dr Lewes (19958) (G-5971)

ALPHABETIC SECTION

Ernie Deangelis (PA) 302 226-9343
19791 Coastal Hwy Rehoboth Beach (19971) *(G-12746)*

Eros Technologies Inc 650 242-9262
16192 Coastal Hwy Lewes (19958) *(G-5972)*

Erosion Control Services De 302 218-8913
1432 Elk Way Bear (19701) *(G-206)*

Erosion Ctrl Specialists Inc 302 367-6649
364 E Main St Pmb 332 Middletown (19709) *(G-7108)*

Ervin H Yoder 302 492-1835
5338 Mud Mill Rd Camden Wyoming (19934) *(G-941)*

Esafety Lights LLC 800 236-8621
251 Little Falls Dr Wilmington (19808) *(G-16462)*

Escape Rehoboth 302 645-7653
510 Kings Hwy Lewes (19958) *(G-5973)*

Escape Yachts Inc 302 691-9070
3511 Silverside Rd # 105 Wilmington (19810) *(G-16463)*

Eschbach Jr Leo H Do 302 645-4700
1535 Savannah Rd Lewes (19958) *(G-5974)*

Esd, Wilmington Also Called: Engineered Systems & Designs *(G-16423)*

Eseco, Camden Also Called: Eastern Shore Equipment Co *(G-825)*

Esham Painting LLC 302 381-7876
32419 Frankford School Rd Frankford (19945) *(G-4105)*

Eshopperlists Com Inc 302 235-5743
114 Hockessin Dr Hockessin (19707) *(G-5203)*

Esis Inc 215 640-1000
Wilmington (19850) *(G-16464)*

Esource Systems LLC 302 444-4228
750 Barksdale Rd Ste 4 Newark (19711) *(G-10666)*

Espino LLC 855 506-3862
16192 Coastal Hwy Lewes (19958) *(G-5975)*

Espinoza Orlando 302 442-5007
7 Virginia Ave Claymont (19703) *(G-1134)*

Esposito Mansory LLC 302 996-4961
471 B And O Ln Wilmington (19804) *(G-16465)*

Espositos Woodworking & Cnstr 302 245-5474
99 Falls Rd Milton (19968) *(G-8621)*

Esquire Plumbing & Heating Co 302 378-7001
7 Wood St Middletown (19709) *(G-7109)*

Essen Technologies Inc 617 959-9595
651 N Broad St Middletown (19709) *(G-7110)*

Essential Bgnnngs Bhvior Lrng 302 278-0052
28 E Mount Vernon St Smyrna (19977) *(G-13725)*

Essential Contracting LLC 330 984-1971
142 Belmont Ave Smyrna (19977) *(G-13726)*

Essential Luxuries Spa 302 244-6875
255 Webbs Ln Apt B21 Dover (19904) *(G-2463)*

Essential Minerals LLC 602 377-9878
901 Lambson Ln New Castle (19720) *(G-9100)*

Essentials Recovery Delaware 302 256-0454
3700 Lancaster Pike Wilmington (19805) *(G-16466)*

Essilor America Holding Co Inc (HQ) 214 496-4000
1209 N Orange St Wilmington (19801) *(G-16467)*

Est, Wilmington Also Called: Exploration Systems & Tech *(G-16506)*

Establishing Black Men LLC 215 432-7469
Claymont (19703) *(G-1135)*

Estarei LLC 508 494-7260
838 Walker Rd Ste 1-2 Dover (19904) *(G-2464)*

Estate Planning Council of Del 610 581-4748
2751 Centerville Rd Ste 310 Wilmington (19808) *(G-16468)*

Estate Planning Delaware Vly, Wilmington Also Called: Occidental L Transamerica *(G-18739)*

Estate Servicing LLC 302 731-1119
901 Barksdale Rd Newark (19711) *(G-10667)*

Estelles Child Dev Ctr Inc 302 792-9065
132 Colesbery Dr New Castle (19720) *(G-9101)*

Estep Ralph V Ea PA 302 998-2008
508 Main St Fl 1 Wilmington (19804) *(G-16469)*

Estepp Construction Co Inc 302 378-4958
1047 Dexter Corner Rd Townsend (19734) *(G-13998)*

Estestwins Trucking LLC 267 773-2991
5269 Mud Mill Rd Camden Wyoming (19934) *(G-942)*

Esther V Graham 302 422-6667
901 N Dupont Blvd Milford (19963) *(G-7883)*

Estia Hospitality Group Inc (PA) 302 798-5319
3526 Philadelphia Pike Claymont (19703) *(G-1136)*

Estimators, Wilmington Also Called: Estimators Corp *(G-16470)*

Estimators Corp 760 492-6405
1007 N Orange St Fl 777 Wilmington (19801) *(G-16470)*

Estu Inc 407 881-6177
1209 N Orange St Wilmington (19801) *(G-16471)*

Estu Life, Wilmington Also Called: Estu Inc *(G-16471)*

Esupply LLC 415 315-9963
1000 N West St Ste 1200 Wilmington (19801) *(G-16472)*

Eswap Global Inc 323 244-2927
2035 Sunset Lake Rd Newark (19702) *(G-10668)*

ET Communications LLC 302 322-2222
270 Quigley Blvd Historic New Castle (19720) *(G-4983)*

Etailflow LLC 302 894-8862
1800 Ogletown Rd Ste B Newark (19711) *(G-10669)*

Etekserve Inc 302 497-4301
100 Biddle Ave Ste 201 Newark (19702) *(G-10670)*

Eternal Health LLC 302 635-7421
5231 W Woodmill Dr Wilmington (19808) *(G-16473)*

Eternal Word Television Inc 302 734-8434
173 Continental Dr Dover (19904) *(G-2465)*

Ethereal Tech US Corp 567 694-8888
1013 Centre Rd Ste 403s Wilmington (19805) *(G-16474)*

Etlgr LLC 302 204-0596
913 N Market St Ste 200 Wilmington (19801) *(G-16475)*

Ets & Ycp LLC 302 525-4111
113 Barksdale Professional Ctr Newark (19711) *(G-10671)*

Eugene Cummings PC 312 984-0144
27 Craig Rd Bear (19701) *(G-207)*

Euphoric Herbals, Milford Also Called: Euphoric Hrbals Apothecary LLC *(G-7884)*

Euphoric Hrbals Apothecary LLC 302 491-4443
621 N Dupont Blvd Milford (19963) *(G-7884)*

European Coach Werkes Inc 302 436-2277
Rte 20 Frankford (19945) *(G-4106)*

European Performance Inc 302 633-1122
806 Wilmington Ave Wilmington (19805) *(G-16476)*

European Wax Center 302 731-2700
3162 Fashion Center Blvd Newark (19702) *(G-10672)*

European Wax Center, Wilmington Also Called: First State Wax LLC *(G-16639)*

Europlish Prcsion Fnshg USA In 302 451-9241
112 Capitol Trl Newark (19711) *(G-10673)*

Eurosoft Tech Inc 737 263-0307
910 Foulk Rd Wilmington (19803) *(G-16477)*

Eurshall Millers Autobody 410 742-7329
36371 Sussex Hwy Delmar (19940) *(G-1595)*

Ev Flux Inc 510 880-3737
2035 Sunset Lake Rd B2 Newark (19702) *(G-10674)*

Ev Gg1 LLC 313 269-4175
254 Chapman Rd Newark (19702) *(G-10675)*

Ev Usa Inc 973 674-1326
16192 Coastal Hwy Lewes (19958) *(G-5976)*

Evagoras G Economides 302 645-1233
16704 Kings Hwy Lewes (19958) *(G-5977)*

Evan David Foundation 302 778-4546
7 Barley Mill Dr Wilmington (19807) *(G-16478)*

Evan H Crain M D 302 322-3400
239 Christiana Rd New Castle (19720) *(G-9102)*

Evan Hooper 302 682-5617
400 Park Ln Laurel (19956) *(G-5511)*

Evan Hurst Lawn & Landscaping, Claymont Also Called: Evan Hurst Property Management *(G-1137)*

Evan Hurst Property Management 302 375-0398
100 Naamans Rd Claymont (19703) *(G-1137)*

Evan W Smith Funeral Home 302 526-4662
518 S Bay Rd Dover (19901) *(G-2466)*

Evan W Smith Funeral Services 302 494-1847
219 Niobrara Ln Bear (19701) *(G-208)*

Evander Grey Group LLC 302 595-1402
8 The Grn Ste 15251 Dover (19901) *(G-2467)*

Evanix Enterprises LLC 302 384-1806
49 W Sarazen Dr Middletown (19709) *(G-7111)*

Evans

Evans 302 998-3356
  203 Lauren Dr Wilmington (19804) *(G-16479)*

Evans Act Inc 302 792-0355
  501 Silverside Rd Wilmington (19809) *(G-16480)*

Evans Charles Contracting 701 340-9530
  509 Southwind Rd Bear (19701) *(G-209)*

Evans Farms LLC 302 337-8130
  9843 Seashore Hwy Bridgeville (19933) *(G-699)*

Evans Handyman Services 302 422-2758
  228 W Holly Dr Lincoln (19960) *(G-6666)*

Evans Paving LLC 302 322-6863
  828 Sparrow Ln Bear (19701) *(G-210)*

Evans Trucking Inc 302 344-9375
  604 Mulberry St Milton (19968) *(G-8622)*

Evc Inc 302 571-0510
  230 N Market St Wilmington (19801) *(G-16481)*

Evco Auto Inc DBA A To Z Auto 302 595-3078
  469 County Rd Bear (19701) *(G-211)*

Evelyn M Falkowski 302 328-3125
  335 Pennewill Dr New Castle (19720) *(G-9103)*

Even & Odd Minds LLC 949 246-4789
  3430 Philadelphia Pike Unit 55 Claymont (19703) *(G-1138)*

Even & Odd Minds LLC (PA) 619 663-7284
  1521 Concord Pike Ste 301 Wilmington (19803) *(G-16482)*

Even Flow Irrigation, Bear *Also Called: Circle D Enterprises Inc (G-104)*

Event Enhancers 267 217-3868
  2115 Exton Dr Wilmington (19810) *(G-16483)*

Event Guru Software, Lewes *Also Called: 4gurus LLC (G-5640)*

Eventide Hospitality LLC 202 725-6357
  99 Ocean View Pkwy Bethany Beach (19930) *(G-600)*

Eventsbynye LLC 302 256-3971
  6 Carvel Ave New Castle (19720) *(G-9104)*

Everest Auto Repair LLC 302 737-8424
  690 Capitol Trl Newark (19711) *(G-10676)*

Everest Autoworks Auto Spa LLC 302 737-8424
  690 Kirkwood Hwy Newark (19711) *(G-10677)*

Everest Foods Enterprises Inc 215 896-8902
  4603 Laura Dr Wilmington (19804) *(G-16484)*

Everest Hotel Group LLC (PA) 213 272-0088
  2140 S Dupont Hwy Camden (19934) *(G-832)*

Everett Inc 302 378-7038
  47 W Main St Middletown (19709) *(G-7112)*

Evergreen Apartment Group Inc 302 998-0322
  1627 New Jersey Ave New Castle (19720) *(G-9105)*

Evergreen Ctr Alzhmer Day Trtm, Wilmington *Also Called: Christana Care HM Hlth Cmnty S (G-15397)*

Evergreen Hardscaping Inc 302 633-4045
  21 W Ayre St Wilmington (19804) *(G-16485)*

Evergreen Landscaping De 302 724-0787
  11 Ferndale Dr Smyrna (19977) *(G-13727)*

Evergreen Led 302 218-7819
  29 Dornoch Way Townsend (19734) *(G-13999)*

Evergreen Properties MGT Inc 302 998-0322
  1627 New Jersey Ave New Castle (19720) *(G-9106)*

Evergreen Reallty, Wilmington *Also Called: Brandywine Hills Apartments (G-15064)*

Evergreen Realty 302 999-8805
  100 Ethan Ct Apt H Wilmington (19804) *(G-16486)*

Evergreen Realty Inc 302 998-0354
  125 Greenbank Rd Apt A4 Wilmington (19808) *(G-16487)*

Evergreen Resources Group LLC 302 477-0189
  2 Righter Pkwy Ste 120 Wilmington (19803) *(G-16488)*

Evergreen Waste Services LLC 302 635-7055
  619 Lambson Ln New Castle (19720) *(G-9107)*

Evergreen Wood Products LLC 302 697-2588
  4763 Halltown Rd Hartly (19953) *(G-4874)*

Everlast Interactive LLC 347 992-3783
  515 Equinox Dr Bear (19701) *(G-212)*

Everlift, Lewes *Also Called: Everlift Wind Technology (G-5978)*

Everlift Wind Technology 240 683-9787
  31798 Carneros Ave Lewes (19958) *(G-5978)*

Evernex USA Inc 888 630-9396
  2915 Ogletown Rd Ste 1844 Newark (19713) *(G-10678)*

Everstage Inc 518 882-3489
  3524 Silverside Rd Ste 35b Wilmington (19810) *(G-16489)*

Evervault Inc 213 527-8608
  1209 N Orange St Wilmington (19801) *(G-16490)*

Everyone Can Achieve LLC 404 317-1228
  405 S Claymont St Wilmington (19801) *(G-16491)*

Everytale Inc 650 989-9807
  2093 Philadelphia Pike # 221 Claymont (19703) *(G-1139)*

Evidence Management Center 302 691-8944
  3 Lewis Cir Wilmington (19804) *(G-16492)*

Evocati Group Corporation 206 551-9087
  9 E Loockerman St Ste 3a Dover (19901) *(G-2468)*

Evolution Cloud Services Inc 516 507-4026
  8 The Grn Ste 8371 Dover (19901) *(G-2469)*

Evolution Energy Partners LLC 302 425-5008
  2312 Ridgeway Rd Wilmington (19805) *(G-16493)*

Evolution Enterprise LLC 302 602-1875
  610 Wesley Ct Middletown (19709) *(G-7113)*

Evolve Bank & Trust 302 286-7838
  220 Continental Dr Ste 215 Newark (19713) *(G-10679)*

Evolve Health and Fitness LLC 302 265-2560
  1004 Mattlind Way Milford (19963) *(G-7885)*

Evon Electric Enterprise Inc 909 997-9599
  16192 Coastal Hwy Lewes (19958) *(G-5979)*

Evonsys LLC (PA) 302 544-2156
  4550 Linden Hill Rd Ste 104 Wilmington (19808) *(G-16494)*

Evoqua Water Technologies LLC 302 322-6247
  259 Quigley Blvd Historic New Castle (19720) *(G-4984)*

Evoque, Wilmington *Also Called: Dawn US Holdings LLC (G-15818)*

Evraz, Claymont *Also Called: Evraz Claymont Steel Holdings Inc (G-1140)*

Evraz Claymont Steel Holdings Inc 302 792-5400
  4001 Philadelphia Pike Claymont (19703) *(G-1140)*

Evraz Claymont Steel Inc 302 792-5400
  4001 Philadelphia Pike Claymont (19703) *(G-1141)*

Evs Lawn Service Inc 302 475-9222
  2609 Ebright Rd Wilmington (19810) *(G-16495)*

Ewaste Express 302 691-8052
  6 Rosetree Ct Wilmington (19810) *(G-16496)*

Ewe-Nited States of Fiber 302 690-5084
  512 Benham Ct Newark (19711) *(G-10680)*

Ewebvalet Co Inc 302 893-0903
  22 Center Meeting Rd Wilmington (19807) *(G-16497)*

Ewgcs Inc 415 935-5884
  8 The Grn Ste 4755 Dover (19901) *(G-2470)*

Ewings Towing Service Inc 302 366-8806
  30 Aleph Dr Newark (19702) *(G-10681)*

Ews Funeral Home 302 494-1847
  219 Niobrara Ln Bear (19701) *(G-213)*

Exact Construction of De 302 629-0464
  Rr 2 Box 308a Seaford (19973) *(G-13179)*

Exam Master Corporation 800 572-3627
  100 Lake Dr Ste 6 Newark (19702) *(G-10682)*

Exantus and Son Homes 302 745-3468
  58 Garden Cir Georgetown (19947) *(G-4311)*

Excape Entertainment US Ltd 949 943-9219
  704 N King St Ste 500 Wilmington (19801) *(G-16498)*

Excede Brdband Stllite Intrnet 302 289-0147
  11460 S Dupont Hwy Felton (19943) *(G-3968)*

Excede Brdband Stllite Intrnet 302 613-0669
  905 E Basin Rd New Castle (19720) *(G-9108)*

Excel Business Systems Inc (PA) 302 453-1500
  201 Ruthar Dr Ste 10 Newark (19711) *(G-10683)*

Excel Education Day Care LLC 302 832-1833
  234 Rickey Blvd Bear (19701) *(G-214)*

Excel Property Management LLC 302 541-5312
  35370 Atlantic Ave Millville (19967) *(G-8528)*

Excel Through Action 302 569-9564
  17021 Old Orchard Rd # 1 Lewes (19958) *(G-5980)*

Excella Staffing Solutions LLC 302 985-7373
  8 The Grn Ste A Dover (19901) *(G-2471)*

Excellent Choice LLC 818 322-6376
  1013 Centre Rd Ste 403s Wilmington (19805) *(G-16499)*

ALPHABETIC SECTION

Excellent Educatn Daycare LLC 302 565-2200
   1411 Old Baltimore Pike Newark (19702) *(G-10684)*

Excellent Home Care 302 327-0147
   122 Delaware St Historic New Castle (19720) *(G-4985)*

Excelling LLC 302 276-3908
   5121 S State St Magnolia (19962) *(G-6744)*

Exceptional Care For Children 302 894-1001
   11 Independence Way Newark (19713) *(G-10685)*

EXCEPTIONAL CARE FOR CHILDREN, Newark Also Called: Exceptional Care For Children *(G-10685)*

Exceptional Dentistry Delaware 302 797-1212
   900 Foulk Rd Ste 203 Wilmington (19803) *(G-16500)*

Exclusive Group LLC 917 207-7299
   108 W 13 St Wilmington (19801) *(G-16501)*

Exclusive Srch Connections LLC 610 864-8000
   103 Glen Avon Ct Newark (19702) *(G-10686)*

Exclusively Legal Inc 302 239-5990
   7301 Lancaster Pike Ste 2 Hockessin (19707) *(G-5204)*

Exco Inc (HQ) 905 477-3065
   1007 N Orange St Wilmington (19801) *(G-16502)*

Exec-Pro Recruiting 302 379-7553
   5 Dustin Dr Claymont (19703) *(G-1142)*

Executive Auto Repairs Inc 302 995-6220
   480 B And O Ln Wilmington (19804) *(G-16503)*

Executive Brdband Cmmnctons LL 302 463-4335
   6 Jaymar Blvd Newark (19702) *(G-10687)*

Executive Brdband Cmmnications, Newark Also Called: Executive Brdband Cmmnctons LL *(G-10687)*

Executive Transportation Inc 302 337-3455
   12643 Rock Rd Greenwood (19950) *(G-4628)*

Exeire Inc 302 232-3555
   15 Peddlers Row Newark (19702) *(G-10688)*

EXELON, Newark Also Called: Delmarva Power & Light Company *(G-10502)*

Exercomm Inc 302 438-6130
   335 Jessica Dr Middletown (19709) *(G-7114)*

Exim Routes Inc 302 551-6829
   2803 Philadelphia Pike B Claymont (19703) *(G-1143)*

Exit King Realty 941 961-4925
   18 Lovelace Ave New Castle (19720) *(G-9109)*

Exit Realty, New Castle Also Called: Exit King Realty *(G-9109)*

Exodus Escape Rooms 302 407-5362
   1708 Marsh Rd Wilmington (19810) *(G-16504)*

Exodus Escape Rooms LLC 302 366-8250
   280 E Main St Newark (19711) *(G-10689)*

Exodus Escape Rooms LLC 302 278-7679
   19266 Coastal Hwy Rehoboth Beach (19971) *(G-12747)*

Exp Growth LLC 804 855-8910
   3 Germay Dr Wilmington (19804) *(G-16505)*

Exp Realty 302 382-5039
   150 Seacroft Dr Dover (19904) *(G-2472)*

Expanding Our Kids World 302 659-0293
   3460 S Dupont Blvd Smyrna (19977) *(G-13728)*

Expansion Platforms Inc 866 928-3098
   200 Creek View Rd Newark (19711) *(G-10690)*

Expedia Cruiseshipcenters 302 444-8447
   126 Foxhunt Dr Bear (19701) *(G-215)*

Expedia Cruiseshipcenters 484 483-3272
   5 W Hawthorne Ct Newark (19702) *(G-10691)*

Experience Sail LLC 302 545-8149
   168 Willamette Dr Bear (19701) *(G-216)*

Expert Basement Waterproo 302 655-8202
   745 Cox Neck Rd New Castle (19720) *(G-9110)*

Expert Home Care LLC 856 870-6691
   504 Silverhill Xing Middletown (19709) *(G-7115)*

Expert Refrigerationservice LL 302 745-4181
   2932 Mcdowell Rd Bridgeville (19933) *(G-700)*

Exploration Systems & Tech 302 335-3911
   1209 N Orange St Wilmington (19801) *(G-16506)*

Explorer New Build LLC 305 436-4000
   2711 Centerville Rd Ste 400 Wilmington (19808) *(G-16507)*

Explosive Tattoo Northside 302 762-1650
   722 Philadelphia Pike Wilmington (19809) *(G-16508)*

Exponentia Global LLC 302 330-7967
   8 The Grn Ste 8309 Dover (19901) *(G-2473)*

Expotrade Inc 818 212-8905
   16192 Coastal Hwy Lewes (19958) *(G-5981)*

Express Hotel Inc 302 227-4030
   19953 Shuttle Rd Rehoboth Beach (19971) *(G-12748)*

Express Legal Documents LLC (HQ) 212 710-1374
   1201 N Orange St Wilmington (19801) *(G-16509)*

Express Vpn LLC 310 601-8492
   113 Barksdale Pro Ctr Newark (19711) *(G-10692)*

Exquisite Taste Vending LLC 856 278-3091
   745 Chestnut Ridge Dr Magnolia (19962) *(G-6745)*

Extenship LLC 302 400-5480
   520 Robinson Ln Unit 4 Wilmington (19805) *(G-16510)*

Extensive Health Services LLC 302 733-0303
   280 E Main St Ste 112 Newark (19711) *(G-10693)*

Exterior Homeworks LLC 302 249-0012
   18 E 6th St Seaford (19973) *(G-13180)*

Extravaganza International Inc 302 321-7117
   257 Old Churchmans Rd New Castle (19720) *(G-9111)*

Extreme Asphalt Maintenance 302 275-8996
   352 Matthew Flocco Dr Newark (19713) *(G-10694)*

Extreme Audio & Video 302 533-7404
   19a Albe Dr Newark (19702) *(G-10695)*

Extreme Bolt & Fastener, Newark Also Called: Tantalum Bolt & Fastener LLC *(G-12159)*

Extreme Machining LLC 302 368-7595
   111 Lake Dr Ste A Newark (19702) *(G-10696)*

Extreme Scale Solutions LLC 302 540-7149
   260 Chapman Rd Newark (19702) *(G-10697)*

Exxon, Middletown Also Called: Newport Ventures Inc *(G-7399)*

Exxon, Newark Also Called: Meadowood Mobil Station *(G-11369)*

Exxon Food Mart, Delmar Also Called: J William Gordy Fuel Co *(G-1604)*

Eye Care of Delaware 302 454-8800
   4102 Ogletown Rd Ste 1 Newark (19713) *(G-10698)*

Eye Center of Delaware, Wilmington Also Called: Vision Center of Delaware Inc *(G-20639)*

Eye Consultants LLC 302 998-2333
   1941 Limestone Rd Ste 200 Wilmington (19808) *(G-16511)*

Eye Physicians and Surgeons PA 302 225-1018
   1207 N Scott St Ste 1 Wilmington (19806) *(G-16512)*

Eye Specialists of Delaware 302 450-3028
   200 Banning St Ste 130 Dover (19904) *(G-2474)*

Eye Worx LLC 302 934-9679
   28544 Dupont Blvd Unit 1 Millsboro (19966) *(G-8284)*

Eyetower LLC 302 298-0944
   2711 Centerville Rd Ste 300 Wilmington (19808) *(G-16513)*

Eyliden Homelife Inc 858 336-9471
   1226 N King St 208 Wilmington (19801) *(G-16514)*

EZ Construction Co 302 723-5730
   4 Bellecor Dr New Castle (19720) *(G-9112)*

EZ Deck LLC 302 444-2268
   107 Ashley Ann Ct Townsend (19734) *(G-14000)*

EZ Investment Group LLC 917 215-9887
   8 The Grn Ste A Dover (19901) *(G-2475)*

EZ Loans Inc (PA) 302 934-5563
   28273 Dupont Blvd Millsboro (19966) *(G-8285)*

EZ Manufacturing Company LLC 302 653-6567
   500 N Bassett St Clayton (19938) *(G-1366)*

EZ Sips Corporation 888 747-7488
   501 Silverside Rd Ste 105 Wilmington (19809) *(G-16515)*

EZ Way Transport LLC 302 367-5272
   9 Durboraw Rd Wilmington (19810) *(G-16516)*

Ezangacom Inc 888 439-2642
   222 Carter Dr Ste 201 Middletown (19709) *(G-7116)*

Ezdorms Inc 202 599-2953
   300 Dlware Ave Ste 210-52 Wilmington (19801) *(G-16517)*

Ezion Fair Community Academy 302 652-9114
   1400 B St Wilmington (19801) *(G-16518)*

Ezra Consulting LLC 912 695-5925
   8 The Grn Ste A Dover (19901) *(G-2476)*

Eztrackit Inc 800 371-5956
   19266 Coastal Hwy Unit 4 # 6 Rehoboth Beach (19971) *(G-12749)*

Eztread

ALPHABETIC SECTION

Eztread, Historic New Castle *Also Called: Delaware Flooring Supply Inc (G-4969)*

Eztz Inc.. 302 376-5641
263 Quigley Blvd Ste 9 Historic New Castle (19720) *(G-4986)*

F & F Pntg Faith & Fortune LLC.. 302 344-2512
219 N Queen St Dover (19904) *(G-2477)*

F & G Construction Co Inc.. 302 994-1406
25 Maple Ave, B & O Ln Wilmington (19804) *(G-16519)*

F & H Mechanical LLC.. 302 932-8034
10 Arthur Dr Hockessin (19707) *(G-5205)*

F & N Vazquez Concrete LLC.. 302 725-5305
18679 Sherman Ave Lincoln (19960) *(G-6667)*

F & S Boat Works.. 302 838-5500
353 Summit Pointe Cir Bear (19701) *(G-217)*

F & S Property Management Co, Seaford *Also Called: Integra ADM Group Inc (G-13223)*

F & S Tax Solutions Inc.. 302 477-4357
2504 Tigani Dr Wilmington (19808) *(G-16520)*

F and D Equipment & Repair LLC.. 302 378-1999
213 W Lake St Unit F Middletown (19709) *(G-7117)*

F and M Equipment Ltd.. 302 449-2850
3272 Dupont Pkwy Townsend (19734) *(G-14001)*

F and S Commercial Cleaning.. 302 250-1736
32789 Ocean Reach Dr Lewes (19958) *(G-5982)*

F D Hammond Enterprises Inc.. 302 424-8455
1111 N Dupont Blvd Milford (19963) *(G-7886)*

F E Moran, Newark *Also Called: FE Mran Inc Fire Prtction E (G-10719)*

F H Everett & Associates Inc.. 302 674-2380
1151 Walker Rd Ste 100 Dover (19904) *(G-2478)*

F M C Biopolymore, Newark *Also Called: FMC Corporation (G-10751)*

F M Repairs.. 302 422-7229
19840 Beaver Dam Rd Milford (19963) *(G-7887)*

F P T & W Medical Associates.. 800 421-2368
1508 Penns Ave Ste 2b Wilmington (19806) *(G-16521)*

F Pete Lisinski Land Surveyor.. 302 378-3200
1848 Choptank Rd Middletown (19709) *(G-7118)*

F S C Wallcoverings, Newark *Also Called: F Schumacher & Co LLC (G-10699)*

F S D Trucking.. 302 629-7498
14596 Concord Rd Seaford (19973) *(G-13181)*

F S Property Management.. 302 644-4403
2500 Savannah West Sq Lewes (19958) *(G-5983)*

F Sartin Tyson Inc.. 302 834-4571
4376 Kirkwood St Georges Rd Saint Georges (19733) *(G-13033)*

F Schumacher & Co LLC.. 302 454-3200
131 Continental Dr Ste 300 Newark (19713) *(G-10699)*

F W D Inc.. 302 323-4999
502 Churchmans Rd New Castle (19720) *(G-9113)*

F&M Custom Painting LLC.. 302 391-4017
1208 Stonebridge Blvd New Castle (19720) *(G-9114)*

Fabby Inc.. 408 891-7991
1013 Centre Rd Ste 403b Wilmington (19805) *(G-16522)*

Fabit Corp.. 832 217-0864
1201 N Orange St Ste 775 Wilmington (19801) *(G-16523)*

Fabreeka Intl Holdings Inc.. 302 452-2500
315 Ruthar Dr Newark (19711) *(G-10700)*

Fabri-Zone Cleaning Systems, Ocean View *Also Called: Schrider Enterprises Inc (G-12566)*

Fabrics and Textiles LLC.. 507 369-2641
2711 Centerville Rd # 400 Wilmington (19808) *(G-16524)*

Facepainting.. 302 344-3145
260 Christiana Rd Apt F10 New Castle (19720) *(G-9115)*

Facibus, Dover *Also Called: Harrock Properties LLC (G-2657)*

Facilities Mgmt Div.. 302 856-5817
5 E Pine St Georgetown (19947) *(G-4312)*

Facility Services Group Inc.. 302 317-3029
300 Cornell Dr Ste A1 Wilmington (19801) *(G-16525)*

Factori Inc.. 682 392-3913
1207 Delaware Ave Wilmington (19806) *(G-16526)*

Factors Etc Inc.. 302 834-1625
1218 Pulaski Hwy Ste 484 Bear (19701) *(G-218)*

Factory Sports.. 302 313-4186
17543 Nassau Commons Blvd Lewes (19958) *(G-5984)*

Factory Technologies Inc.. 302 266-1290
2035 Sunset Lake Rd Ste B2 Newark (19702) *(G-10701)*

Factory Universe Co.. 302 216-2025
1201 N Market St Wilmington (19801) *(G-16527)*

Fadely LLC.. 302 284-7389
109 Logan Dr Felton (19943) *(G-3969)*

Faegre Drnker Biddle Reath LLP.. 302 467-4200
222 Delaware Ave Ste 1400 Wilmington (19801) *(G-16528)*

Fair Insurance Agency Inc.. 302 395-0740
881 Pulaski Hwy Bear (19701) *(G-219)*

Fair Mortgage Co.. 202 904-4843
8 The Grn Dover (19901) *(G-2479)*

Fair Square Financial LLC.. 571 205-0305
1000 N West St Ste 1100 Wilmington (19801) *(G-16529)*

Fairchild Rental Prpts LLC.. 302 745-1144
12916 Oak Rd Greenwood (19950) *(G-4629)*

Fairfax Eye Works, Wilmington *Also Called: In Vision Eye Care (G-17293)*

Fairfax Vision Center, Hockessin *Also Called: In Vision Eye Care Inc (G-5248)*

Fairfield Inn Stes Wlmngton New, New Castle *Also Called: Jay Devi Inc (G-9255)*

Fairfield Inn, Dover *Also Called: Dover Hospitality Group LLC (G-2347)*

Fairfield Inn, Newark *Also Called: Sage Hospitality Resources LLC (G-11933)*

Fairfield Inn Suites Rehoboth, Rehoboth Beach *Also Called: Colonial Oaks Hotel LLC (G-12694)*

Fairness Institute.. 302 559-4074
1000 Fountainview Cir Apt 216 Newark (19713) *(G-10702)*

Fairview Inn, Wilmington *Also Called: Nab Motel Inc (G-18518)*

Fairville Management Co LLC.. 302 798-1736
3207 E Brandywine Ave Claymont (19703) *(G-1144)*

Fairville Management Co LLC (PA).. 302 489-2000
726 Yorklyn Rd Ste 200 Hockessin (19707) *(G-5206)*

Fairway Manufacturing Company (HQ).. 302 398-4630
51 Clark St Harrington (19952) *(G-4768)*

Fairway Village.. 302 354-1021
101 Augusta Dr Ocean View (19970) *(G-12509)*

Fairway Villas Condo Assn.. 302 539-0414
1 Cripple Creek Dr Dagsboro (19939) *(G-1446)*

Fairways Inn.. 302 653-7044
296 W Clarendon Dr Smyrna (19977) *(G-13729)*

Fairwinds Baptist Church Inc.. 302 322-1029
801 Seymour Rd Bear (19701) *(G-220)*

Fairwinds Christian School, Bear *Also Called: Fairwinds Baptist Church Inc (G-220)*

Fairwinds Technologies Engrg.. 732 674-0094
111 Sandy Dr Newark (19713) *(G-10703)*

Fairwood Corporation.. 302 884-6749
1201 N Orange St Ste 7901 Wilmington (19801) *(G-16530)*

Faith Day Care and Preschool, Wilmington *Also Called: Hope Presbyterian Church (G-17198)*

Faith Family Management Co.. 302 832-5936
63 Marrows Rd Newark (19713) *(G-10704)*

Faith Fmly Friends Holdg LLC.. 202 256-4524
16192 Coastal Hwy Lewes (19958) *(G-5985)*

Faith Victory Christn Academy.. 302 333-0855
301 Commonwealth Ave Claymont (19703) *(G-1145)*

Faithful Friends Animal Soc, New Castle *Also Called: Faithful Friends Inc (G-9116)*

Faithful Friends Inc.. 302 427-8514
165 Airport Rd New Castle (19720) *(G-9116)*

Faithful Servant Inc.. 302 597-6387
8 The Grn Ste 16161 Dover (19901) *(G-2480)*

Falasco Masonry Inc.. 302 697-8971
3152 S State St Camden Wyoming (19934) *(G-943)*

Falco Industries Inc.. 302 628-1170
200 Bedford Falls Dr Unit 1 Seaford (19973) *(G-13182)*

Falcon Construction LLC.. 302 668-6874
104 Boxwood Rd Wilmington (19804) *(G-16531)*

Falcon Crest Inv Intl Inc.. 240 701-1746
1201 N Orange St Ste 600 Wilmington (19801) *(G-16532)*

Falcon Steel, Wilmington *Also Called: Falcon Steel Co (G-16533)*

Falcon Steel Co.. 302 571-0890
811 S Market St Wilmington (19801) *(G-16533)*

Falcone Truman Plbg & Htg Inc.. 302 376-7483
3891 South Dupont Parkway Odessa (19730) *(G-12584)*

Fame, Wilmington *Also Called: Forum To Advnce Mnrties In Eng (G-16697)*

Famglam LLC.. 302 930-0026
20100 Reynolds Pond Rd Ellendale (19941) *(G-3917)*

ALPHABETIC SECTION

Family Benefit Home Care, Wilmington Also Called: Caroline M Wiesner *(G-15257)*
Family Care Associates.. 302 454-8880
  510 Christiana Medical Ctr Newark (19702) *(G-10705)*
Family Care Associates, New Castle Also Called: K V Associates Inc *(G-9273)*
Family Care Connections.. 856 579-7303
  225 Armata Dr Middletown (19709) *(G-7119)*
Family Chiropractic Office PA.. 302 993-9113
  3105 Limestone Rd Ste 303 Wilmington (19808) *(G-16534)*
Family Cnsling Ctr St Puls Inc...................................... 302 576-4136
  301 N Van Buren St Wilmington (19805) *(G-16535)*
Family Creations.. 302 239-4275
  915 Doe Run Rd Newark (19711) *(G-10706)*
Family Denistry... 302 368-0054
  179 W Chestnut Hill Rd # 4 Newark (19713) *(G-10707)*
Family Dental Associates Inc....................................... 302 674-8810
  385 Saulsbury Rd Dover (19904) *(G-2481)*
Family Dental Care.. 302 999-7600
  1601 Milltown Rd Ste 19 Wilmington (19808) *(G-16536)*
Family Dental Center... 302 656-8266
  1 Winston Ave Wilmington (19804) *(G-16537)*
Family Dentistry Milford PA... 302 422-6924
  100 Sussex Ave Milford (19963) *(G-7888)*
Family Dentistry Wilmington.. 302 656-2434
  1708 Lovering Ave Ste 101 Wilmington (19806) *(G-16538)*
Family Depository Alliance... 888 332-6275
  651 N Broad St Ste 201 Middletown (19709) *(G-7120)*
Family Doctors... 302 368-3600
  4 Polly Drummond Hill Rd Newark (19711) *(G-10708)*
Family Ear Nose Throat Physcan................................. 302 998-0300
  1941 Limestone Rd Ste 210 Wilmington (19808) *(G-16539)*
Family Ear Nose Throat Physcn, Wilmington Also Called: Gabriel Jr Timoteo R MD *(G-16789)*
Family Ent Physicians Inc (PA)................................... 302 998-0300
  1941 Limestone Rd Ste 210 Wilmington (19808) *(G-16540)*
Family First Funeral Svcs LLC..................................... 800 377-6949
  614 S Dupont Hwy Dover (19901) *(G-2482)*
Family First Funeral Svcs LLC (PA)............................. 800 377-6949
  212 E Justis St Newport (19804) *(G-12452)*
Family Freight LLC... 302 212-0708
  8 The Grn Ste 1 Dover (19901) *(G-2483)*
Family Health Delaware Inc... 302 734-2444
  640 S Queen St Dover (19904) *(G-2484)*
Family Heating & Cooling LLC..................................... 302 229-4716
  11 Hardy Rd New Castle (19720) *(G-9117)*
Family Legacy Llccom... 302 256-1406
  1616 Bonwood Rd Apt P2 Wilmington (19805) *(G-16541)*
Family Man Carpentry.. 302 542-8803
  22236 Breasure Rd Georgetown (19947) *(G-4313)*
Family Mediation Services, Wilmington Also Called: Katherine Laffey *(G-17661)*
Family Medical Assoc Delaware................................... 302 655-0355
  2300 Pennsylvania Ave Ste 1a Wilmington (19806) *(G-16542)*
Family Medical Centre PA... 302 678-0510
  111 Wolf Creek Blvd Ste 2 Dover (19901) *(G-2485)*
Family Medicine At Greenville..................................... 302 429-5870
  213 Greenhill Ave Ste B Wilmington (19805) *(G-16543)*
Family Medicine Smyrna Clayton................................. 302 653-1050
  679 S Carter Rd Unit 4 Smyrna (19977) *(G-13730)*
Family of All Trades.. 302 334-2710
  31145 Whites Neck Dr Ocean View (19970) *(G-12510)*
Family Office Solutions L.. 610 255-0623
  3801 Kennett Pike Ste C30 Wilmington (19807) *(G-16544)*
Family Otrach Mlt-Prpose Cmnty................................. 302 422-2158
  19227 Young Ln Lincoln (19960) *(G-6668)*
Family Planning.. 302 856-5225
  544 S Bedford St Georgetown (19947) *(G-4314)*
Family Practice Association PA................................... 302 656-5416
  1100 S Broom St Ste 1 Wilmington (19805) *(G-16545)*
Family Practice Center.. 302 645-2833
  7 Dunes Ter Lewes (19958) *(G-5986)*
Family Practice Hockessin PA..................................... 302 239-4500
  5936 Limestone Rd Ste 202 Hockessin (19707) *(G-5207)*

Family Prctice Ctr of New Cstl..................................... 302 999-0933
  1 Centurian Dr Ste 105 Newark (19713) *(G-10709)*
Family Prmise Nthrn New Cstle................................... 302 998-2222
  2104 Saint James Church Rd Wilmington (19808) *(G-16546)*
Family Services... 302 422-1400
  247 Ne Front St Milford (19963) *(G-7889)*
Family Services Div... 302 577-3824
  119 Lower Beech St Ste 100 Wilmington (19805) *(G-16547)*
FAMILY TO FAMILY, Wilmington Also Called: Delaware Family Voices Inc *(G-15917)*
Family Unit Fitness.. 267 403-6695
  2309 Wilson Ave Claymont (19703) *(G-1146)*
Family Wrkplace Connection Inc (PA)....................... 302 479-1660
  2005 Baynard Blvd Wilmington (19802) *(G-16548)*
Famlee, Camden Also Called: Famlee Fertility Inc *(G-833)*
Famlee Fertility Inc.. 503 388-6915
  2140 S Dupont Hwy Camden (19934) *(G-833)*
Famoid Technology LLC.. 530 601-7284
  112 Capitol Trl Newark (19711) *(G-10710)*
Famous Wsi Results.. 302 407-0430
  12 Penns Way New Castle (19720) *(G-9118)*
Fan Payment Solutions LLC (PA)................................ 617 901-3970
  108 W 13th St Wilmington (19801) *(G-16549)*
Fandom Pay, Wilmington Also Called: Fan Payment Solutions LLC *(G-16549)*
Fanhouse Inc... 415 598-7628
  2093a Philadelphia Pike Claymont (19703) *(G-1147)*
Fannon Color Printing LLC... 302 227-2164
  20 Harbor Rd Rehoboth Beach (19971) *(G-12750)*
Fantastic Green Cleaning Svc..................................... 302 981-8259
  32 Valley Forge Rd New Castle (19720) *(G-9119)*
Fantastic Landscaping Fen.. 302 494-9034
  51 Greenridge Rd Newark (19711) *(G-10711)*
Fantasy Beauty Salon... 302 629-6762
  224 High St Seaford (19973) *(G-13183)*
Fantasy Nft LLC.. 423 313-3436
  2140 S Dupont Hwy Camden (19934) *(G-834)*
Fantasythrone LLC (PA).. 512 431-8658
  300 Delaware Ave Ste 210a Wilmington (19801) *(G-16550)*
Fanticipate Inc.. 763 777-4232
  251 Little Falls Dr Wilmington (19808) *(G-16551)*
Faqx Inc.. 646 437-6797
  2093 Philadelphia Pike Claymont (19703) *(G-1148)*
Far Rezolutions Inc.. 302 547-6850
  218 Margaux Cir Newark (19702) *(G-10712)*
Faramove Inc.. 815 674-3114
  651 N Broad St Middletown (19709) *(G-7121)*
Faranarium Inc... 716 235-5950
  600 N Broad St Ste 5 Middletown (19709) *(G-7122)*
Farazad Investments Inc.. 302 573-2320
  1201 N Orange St Wilmington (19801) *(G-16552)*
Faremart Inc (PA)... 800 965-5819
  3524 Silverside Rd Ste 35b Wilmington (19810) *(G-16553)*
Farkas Concrete.. 302 249-9172
  31632 Sarah Rd Lewes (19958) *(G-5987)*
Farma Quimica LLC.. 703 537-9789
  16192 Coastal Hwy Lewes (19958) *(G-5988)*
Farmers Bank, Millsboro Also Called: Farmers Bank of Willards *(G-8286)*
Farmers Bank of Willards... 302 934-6300
  28656 Dupont Blvd Millsboro (19966) *(G-8286)*
Farmers Harvest Inc.. 302 734-7708
  2826 Seven Hickories Rd Dover (19904) *(G-2486)*
Farmers Insurance, Wilmington Also Called: Farmers Mutl Fire Insur Slem C *(G-16554)*
Farmers Mutl Fire Insur Slem C (PA)......................... 856 935-1851
  1 Ave Of The Arts Wilmington (19801) *(G-16554)*
Farpath Foundation... 302 645-8328
  800 Bay Ave Lewes (19958) *(G-5989)*
Farr Family Foundation Inc.. 540 349-4103
  16192 Coastal Hwy Lewes (19958) *(G-5990)*
Farrell Home Renovations LLC.................................... 443 386-0885
  26310 Portside Ln Millsboro (19966) *(G-8287)*
Farrell Roofing Inc.. 302 378-7663
  201 W Lake St Middletown (19709) *(G-7123)*

(PA)=Parent Co (HQ)=Headquarters (DH)=Div Headquarters

2024 Harris Directory of Delaware Businesses

Faruqi & Faruqi LLP 302 482-3182
   3828 Kennett Pike Ste 201 Wilmington (19807) *(G-16555)*
Fas Mart / Shore Stop 286 LLC 302 366-9694
   1400 Capitol Trl Newark (19711) *(G-10713)*
Fast Action Landscaping Inc 302 332-7124
   3 Broadfield Dr Newark (19713) *(G-10714)*
Fast Af Inc 415 770-5235
   2035 Sunset Lake Rd B2 Newark (19702) *(G-10715)*
Fast Bailbonds, Wilmington *Also Called: Fast Bailbonds LLC (G-16556)*
Fast Bailbonds LLC 302 778-4400
   1224 N King St Wilmington (19801) *(G-16556)*
Fast Care Medical Aid Unit LLC 302 793-7506
   2722 Philadelphia Pike Claymont (19703) *(G-1149)*
Fast Fce Inc 833 327-8323
   2207 Concord Pike Ste 446 Wilmington (19803) *(G-16557)*
Fast Intrcnnect Tchologies Inc 302 465-5344
   73 Greentree Dr Ste 30 Dover (19904) *(G-2487)*
Fast Pay Rx LLC 833 511-9500
   108 W 13th St Wilmington (19801) *(G-16558)*
Fast Pipe Lining East Inc 302 368-7414
   563 Walther Rd Newark (19702) *(G-10716)*
Fast4wrd Towing & Recovery 302 331-5157
   98 Sanford St Felton (19943) *(G-3970)*
Fastcold LLC 302 240-4402
   221 W 9th St Wilmington (19801) *(G-16559)*
Fastsigns, Wilmington *Also Called: Jenner Enterprises Inc (G-17523)*
Fastsigns, Wilmington *Also Called: Jenner Enterprises Inc (G-17524)*
Fasttrak 302 761-5454
   1500 Eastlawn Ave Wilmington (19802) *(G-16560)*
Fasttrak Coatings Co 302 761-5454
   1500 Eastlawn Ave Wilmington (19802) *(G-16561)*
Fataneh M Ziari MD 302 836-8533
   2600 Glasgow Ave Ste 212 Newark (19702) *(G-10717)*
Fathers Day Gala Inc 302 981-4117
   436 S Buttonwood St Wilmington (19801) *(G-16562)*
Faust Sheet Metal Works Inc 302 645-9509
   1636 Savannah Rd Ste A Lewes (19958) *(G-5991)*
Favhometheater 302 897-7168
   11 Monferrato Ct Bear (19701) *(G-221)*
Favored Childcare Academy Inc 302 698-1266
   2319 S Dupont Hwy Dover (19901) *(G-2488)*
Faw Casson & Co LLP 302 674-4305
   160 Greentree Dr Ste 203 Dover (19904) *(G-2489)*
Faw Casson 302 226-1082
   20245 Bay Vista Rd Rehoboth Beach (19971) *(G-12751)*
Faw Casson 302 226-1919
   20376 Coastal Hwy Ste 204 Rehoboth Beach (19971) *(G-12752)*
Faw Casson & Co, Dover *Also Called: Faw Casson & Co LLP (G-2489)*
Faze II Inc 302 328-7891
   881 Pulaski Hwy Bear (19701) *(G-222)*
FBBc LLC 302 442-3004
   8 Spinet Rd Newark (19713) *(G-10718)*
Fbh Business Consulting LLC 267 266-8149
   24a Trolley Sq Ste 1162 Wilmington (19806) *(G-16563)*
Fbinaa 302 344-7700
   7 Anser Ln Lewes (19958) *(G-5992)*
Fbk Graphico Inc 302 743-4784
   2207 Concord Pike Wilmington (19803) *(G-16564)*
Fbk Medical Tubing Inc 302 855-0585
   21649 Cedar Creek Ave Georgetown (19947) *(G-4315)*
Fci of Delmarva LLC 443 614-1794
   111 Atlantic Ave 8 Ocean View (19970) *(G-12511)*
Fcw, Wilmington *Also Called: Carspecken-Scott Inc (G-15260)*
FE Mran Inc Fire Prtction E 302 453-9237
   301 Ruthar Dr Ste B Newark (19711) *(G-10719)*
Fears Promotions LLC 302 437-6364
   32 W Loockerman St Ste 109 Dover (19904) *(G-2490)*
Feathers Group LLC 302 300-5967
   13 Sheldrake Rd Newark (19713) *(G-10720)*
Featly Inc 505 305-6844
   2055 Limestone Rd Wilmington (19808) *(G-16565)*

Febys Fishery Inc 302 998-9501
   3701 Lancaster Pike Wilmington (19805) *(G-16566)*
Fedcap Rehabilitation Services 302 544-6634
   241 Old Churchmans Rd New Castle (19720) *(G-9120)*
Feddly Jeanniton 302 325-1000
   4 Bellecor Dr New Castle (19720) *(G-9121)*
Federal Business Systems, Wilmington *Also Called: Federal Business Systems Corporation Government Division (G-16567)*
Federal Business Systems Corporation Government Division 877 489-2111
   1000 N West St Ste 1200 Wilmington (19801) *(G-16567)*
Federal Court Reporters 302 573-6195
   844 N King St Unit 24 Wilmington (19801) *(G-16568)*
Federal Energy Inf 858 521-3300
   251 Little Falls Dr Wilmington (19808) *(G-16569)*
Federal Express Corporation 800 463-3339
   2 W Commons Blvd New Castle (19720) *(G-9122)*
Federal Express Corporation 800 463-3339
   1209 N Orange St Wilmington (19801) *(G-16570)*
Federal Home Loan ADM Inc 855 345-2669
   1201 N Orange St Ste 600 Wilmington (19801) *(G-16571)*
Federal Mechanical Contractors 302 656-2998
   229 Hillview Ave New Castle (19720) *(G-9123)*
Federal Technical Associates 302 697-7951
   50 Westview Ave Dover (19901) *(G-2491)*
Federated Auto Parts, Millsboro *Also Called: Fisher Auto Parts Inc (G-8291)*
Fedex, New Castle *Also Called: Federal Express Corporation (G-9122)*
Fedex, Seaford *Also Called: Fedex Ground Package Sys Inc (G-13184)*
Fedex, Wilmington *Also Called: Federal Express Corporation (G-16570)*
Fedex, Wilmington *Also Called: Fedex Office & Print Svcs Inc (G-16572)*
Fedex, Wilmington *Also Called: Fedex Office & Print Svcs Inc (G-16573)*
Fedex Corporation 302 286-6570
   701 Pencader Dr Ste C Newark (19702) *(G-10721)*
Fedex Ground Package Sys Inc 800 463-3339
   161 Venture Dr Seaford (19973) *(G-13184)*
Fedex Office & Print Svcs Inc 302 652-2151
   1201 N Market St Ste 1200 Wilmington (19801) *(G-16572)*
Fedex Office & Print Svcs Inc 302 996-0264
   4721a Kirkwood Hwy Wilmington (19808) *(G-16573)*
Fedi Inc (PA) 797 372-0606
   251 Little Falls Dr Wilmington (19808) *(G-16574)*
Fedmet Resources Corporation (PA) 514 931-5711
   1000 N West St Ste 1200 # 889 Wilmington (19801) *(G-16575)*
Feelz LLC 347 860-5813
   704 N King St Ste 500 Wilmington (19801) *(G-16576)*
Feeney Chiropractic Care Ctr PA 302 328-0200
   835 Pulaski Hwy Bear (19701) *(G-223)*
Feeney Chrprctic Care Cntre PA, Bear *Also Called: Feeney Chiropractic Care Ctr PA (G-223)*
Feick, Judith MD, Wilmington *Also Called: Pike Creek Pediatric Assoc (G-19042)*
Felder USA, Historic New Castle *Also Called: Asw Machinery Inc (G-4936)*
Felix C Vergara M D 856 624-4312
   2601 Annand Dr Ste 14 Wilmington (19808) *(G-16577)*
Felixcem Corporation Inc 302 324-9101
   314 Bay West Blvd New Castle (19720) *(G-9124)*
Felixchem Corp Inc 302 376-0199
   110 W Main St Middletown (19709) *(G-7124)*
Fellowship Hlth Resources Inc 302 856-7642
   16 Shortly Rd Georgetown (19947) *(G-4316)*
Fellowship Hlth Resources Inc 302 422-6699
   7549 Wilkins Rd Milford (19963) *(G-7890)*
Fells Point Surf Co LLC 302 212-2005
   23 Bellevue St Dewey Beach (19971) *(G-1669)*
Fells Points Surf 302 537-7873
   114 Garfield Pkwy Bethany Beach (19930) *(G-601)*
Felton Community Fire Co Inc 302 284-9552
   9 E Main St Felton (19943) *(G-3971)*
Felton Little League Inc 302 284-3713
   Felton (19943) *(G-3972)*
Felton Residential Trtmnt Ctr, Dover *Also Called: Psychotherapeutic Svc Assn Inc (G-3390)*
Femispace Co 917 764-9943
   2055 Limestone Rd Ste 200c Wilmington (19808) *(G-16578)*

ALPHABETIC SECTION

Femmepal Corporation.. 888 406-0804
  16192 Coastal Hwy Lewes (19958) *(G-5993)*

Feng Wang.. 315 677-1685
  808 First State Blvd Wilmington (19804) *(G-16579)*

Fenway Aviation LLC... 800 981-7183
  108 W 13th St Wilmington (19801) *(G-16580)*

Fenway Barr LLC... 302 222-1913
  107 Cotton Tail Ct S Rehoboth Beach (19971) *(G-12753)*

Fenwick Island Nautical Sports................................. 443 397-0619
  300 Coastal Hwy Fenwick Island (19944) *(G-4048)*

Fenwick Towers Condo Assn..................................... 302 281-5025
  40126 Fenwick Towers Rd Fenwick Island (19944) *(G-4049)*

Ferguson Enterprises LLC... 302 747-2032
  10 Maggies Way Dover (19901) *(G-2492)*

Ferguson Enterprises LLC... 302 500-8051
  25131 Dupont Blvd Georgetown (19947) *(G-4317)*

Ferguson Enterprises LLC... 302 732-0940
  32325 Lewes Georgetown Hwy Lewes (19958) *(G-5994)*

Ferguson Enterprises LLC... 302 934-6040
  28520 Dupont Blvd Millsboro (19966) *(G-8288)*

Ferguson Enterprises LLC... 302 656-4421
  2000 Maryland Ave Wilmington (19805) *(G-16581)*

Ferguson Enterprises LLC... 302 429-5850
  1000 First State Blvd Wilmington (19804) *(G-16582)*

Ferguson Enterprises LLC... 302 225-4082
  919 S Heald St Wilmington (19801) *(G-16583)*

Ferguson Enterprises 1861, Wilmington *Also Called: Ferguson Enterprises LLC (G-16582)*

Ferguson Enterprises 784, Lewes *Also Called: Ferguson Enterprises LLC (G-5994)*

Ferguson Ventures... 484 561-3510
  600 N Broad St Middletown (19709) *(G-7125)*

Ferm Development LLC.. 302 792-1102
  501 Silverside Rd Wilmington (19809) *(G-16584)*

Fern Cleaning... 302 480-0241
  605 Coventry Ln Newark (19713) *(G-10722)*

Fernandez Drywall Inc.. 302 521-2760
  379 Moir St Newark (19702) *(G-10723)*

Ferrante & Associates Inc... 781 891-4328
  501 Paisley Pl Newark (19711) *(G-10724)*

Ferrara Asset Management Inc................................. 401 286-8464
  2711 Centerville Rd Ste 400 Wilmington (19808) *(G-16585)*

Ferrara Haley & Bevis... 302 656-7247
  1716 Wawaset St Wilmington (19806) *(G-16586)*

Ferrari Hair Studio Ltd.. 302 731-7505
  4559 Linden Hill Rd Wilmington (19808) *(G-16587)*

Ferreira Builders LLC.. 302 296-6014
  22797 Rum Bridge Rd Georgetown (19947) *(G-4318)*

Ferrell Cooling & Heating Inc.................................... 302 436-2922
  32971 Lighthouse Rd Selbyville (19975) *(G-13535)*

Ferris Home Improvements.. 302 377-8003
  325 Oracle Rd Wilmington (19808) *(G-16588)*

Ferris Home Imprvs Co LLC...................................... 302 998-4500
  1908 Kirkwood Hwy Ste 3 Newark (19711) *(G-10725)*

Ferris Properties Inc... 302 472-0875
  818 S Broom St Apt 1a Wilmington (19805) *(G-16589)*

Ferry Joseph & Pearce PA... 302 856-3706
  6 W Market St Georgetown (19947) *(G-4319)*

Ferry Joseph & Pearce PA (PA)................................. 302 575-1555
  1521 Concord Pike Ste 202 Wilmington (19803) *(G-16590)*

Festival of Cheer... 302 227-4325
  19406 Coastal Hwy Rehoboth Beach (19971) *(G-12754)*

Fetch Social Inc... 813 858-5774
  251 Little Falls Dr Wilmington (19808) *(G-16591)*

Ff Group LLC.. 302 608-0609
  8 The Grn Dover (19901) *(G-2493)*

Ffi General Contractor In... 302 420-1242
  13 Perth Dr Wilmington (19803) *(G-16592)*

Ffi Ionix Inc... 302 629-5768
  299 Cluckey Dr Ste A Harrington (19952) *(G-4769)*

Fia Card Services Nat Assn....................................... 302 457-0517
  11 King St Wilmington (19884) *(G-16593)*

Fia Card Services Nat Assn (HQ)............................. 800 362-6255
  1100 N King St Wilmington (19884) *(G-16594)*

Fia Card Services Nat Assn....................................... 302 458-0365
  655 Paper Mill Rd Wilmington (19884) *(G-16595)*

Fia Card Services Nat Assn....................................... 302 432-1573
  1200 N French St Wilmington (19884) *(G-16596)*

Fiber-One Inc.. 302 834-0890
  2812 Old County Rd Newark (19702) *(G-10726)*

Fiberstate LLC.. 800 575-8921
  122 Delaware St Ste B8 Historic New Castle (19720) *(G-4987)*

Fiberstore, Historic New Castle *Also Called: Fscom Inc (G-4994)*

Fibre Processing Corporation.................................... 302 654-3659
  701 Garasches Ln Wilmington (19801) *(G-16597)*

Fibrenew, Smyrna *Also Called: Fibrenew Northern & Central De (G-13731)*

Fibrenew Northern & Central De............................... 833 427-3639
  88 Durham Ln Smyrna (19977) *(G-13731)*

Fidelitrade Incorporated (PA)................................... 302 762-6200
  3601 N Market St Wilmington (19802) *(G-16598)*

Fidelity Engineering.. 302 536-7655
  25600 Business Park Seaford (19973) *(G-13185)*

Fidelity National, Wilmington *Also Called: Fidelity National Info Svcs (G-16599)*

Fidelity National Info Svcs (PA)................................ 302 658-2102
  600 N King St Fl 10 Wilmington (19801) *(G-16599)*

Fidelity Oxford Street Trust....................................... 214 281-6351
  1201 N Market St Wilmington (19801) *(G-16600)*

Fiduks Industrial Services Inc (PA).......................... 302 994-2534
  7 Meco Cir Wilmington (19804) *(G-16601)*

Fiduks Industrial Services Inc................................... 302 994-2534
  7 Meco Cir Wilmington (19804) *(G-16602)*

Fields & Company Inc.. 302 234-2775
  7460 Lancaster Pike Ste 3 Hockessin (19707) *(G-5208)*

Fieldstone Golf Club LP... 302 254-4569
  1000 Dean Rd Wilmington (19807) *(G-16603)*

Fierce Dance Academy... 302 414-9191
  608 E Basin Rd New Castle (19720) *(G-9125)*

Fifer Orchards Inc... 302 697-2141
  1919 Allabands Mill Rd Camden Wyoming (19934) *(G-944)*

Figgsy Builders.. 302 875-2505
  5656 Broad Dr Laurel (19956) *(G-5512)*

Figueroa T Ernesto MD.. 302 651-5980
  1600 Rockland Rd Wilmington (19803) *(G-16604)*

File Right LLC... 302 757-7107
  364 E Main St Middletown (19709) *(G-7126)*

Filec Services LLC.. 302 328-7188
  680 Port Penn Rd Middletown (19709) *(G-7127)*

Filmustage Inc.. 260 225-3050
  2810 N Church St Pmb 68039 Wilmington (19802) *(G-16605)*

Filth-Fighters Clg Svcs LLC....................................... 302 423-4684
  4514a New Jersey Dr Dover (19901) *(G-2494)*

Final Finishes Inc.. 302 995-1850
  708 Woodtop Rd Wilmington (19804) *(G-16606)*

Final Touch Cleaning.. 302 730-1495
  2682 Seven Hickories Rd Dover (19904) *(G-2495)*

Finance Business Solutions LLC............................... 646 707-1290
  3616 Kirkwood Hwy Wilmington (19808) *(G-16607)*

Finance Department, Dover *Also Called: City of Dover (G-2082)*

Financial House Inc... 302 654-5451
  5818 Kennett Pike Wilmington (19807) *(G-16608)*

Financial Services... 302 478-4707
  1000 N West St Ste 1200 Wilmington (19801) *(G-16609)*

Finders Entertainment LLC.. 407 765-1826
  8 The Grn Ste A Dover (19901) *(G-2496)*

Fine Art Fabrication.. 302 632-4371
  581 Smyrna Landing Rd Smyrna (19977) *(G-13732)*

Fine Remodeling, Wilmington *Also Called: Delaware RE Answers LLC (G-15958)*

Fineman Krekstein & Harris PC................................. 312 655-0800
  1300 N King St Wilmington (19801) *(G-16610)*

Finger Lakes Metrology LLC...................................... 607 742-7240
  13478 Mustang Dr Ellendale (19941) *(G-3918)*

Finnchat Inc.. 517 258-6991
  651 N Broad St Ste 206 Middletown (19709) *(G-7128)*

Fiorano Software Inc.. 650 326-1136
  16192 Coastal Hwy Lewes (19958) *(G-5995)*

Fire Alarm Supplier LLC 302 444-0801
  124 Broadkill Rd Ste 600 Milton (19968) *(G-8623)*

Firebird Energy II LLC 817 857-7800
  251 Little Falls Dr Wilmington (19808) *(G-16611)*

Firebolt Analytics Inc (PA) 302 314-3135
  1007 N Orange St Wilmington (19801) *(G-16612)*

Firebrand Entertainment Inc 571 330-8983
  503 4th St Newark (19711) *(G-10727)*

Firebrick Wind LLC 647 352-9533
  251 Little Falls Dr Wilmington (19808) *(G-16613)*

Firemens Hstrcal Fndtion Dlmar 302 846-3014
  601 Delaware Ave Delmar (19940) *(G-1596)*

Fireside It LLC 302 284-4961
  130 Sumac Dr Felton (19943) *(G-3973)*

Fireside Partners Inc 302 613-2165
  60 Starlifter Ave Dover (19901) *(G-2497)*

Firestone, Dover *Also Called: Bridgestone Ret Operations LLC (G-1979)*

Firestone, Milford *Also Called: Bridgestone Ret Operations LLC (G-7805)*

Firestone, New Castle *Also Called: Bridgestone Ret Operations LLC (G-8892)*

Firestone, Wilmington *Also Called: Bridgestone Ret Operations LLC (G-15108)*

Firestone Complete Auto C 302 437-0497
  202 Casa Dr Middletown (19709) *(G-7129)*

First Advance Loan Center Inc 302 482-7294
  2100 Naamans Rd Wilmington (19810) *(G-16614)*

First American Title Insur Co 302 855-2120
  231 S Race St Georgetown (19947) *(G-4320)*

First American Title Insur Co 302 421-9440
  704 N King St Wilmington (19801) *(G-16615)*

First Atlantic Mortgage Svcs, Lewes *Also Called: First Atlantic Mrtg Svcs LLC (G-5996)*

First Atlantic Mrtg Svcs LLC 302 841-8435
  16678 Kings Hwy Ste 2 Lewes (19958) *(G-5996)*

First Caliber Services LLC 302 328-3049
  144 Dutton Ct New Castle (19720) *(G-9126)*

First Care Physicians PA 302 424-6995
  124 Ivy Ln Milford (19963) *(G-7891)*

First Choice Health Care Inc 302 836-6150
  12 Foxhunt Dr Bear (19701) *(G-224)*

First Choice Home Med Equipt (PA) 302 323-8700
  259 Quigley Blvd Ste 1 Historic New Castle (19720) *(G-4988)*

First Choice Home Med Equipt 302 424-2510
  1013 Mattlind Way Milford (19963) *(G-7892)*

First Choice Real Estate Svcs 302 525-4970
  724 Yorklyn Rd Hockessin (19707) *(G-5209)*

First Class Hauling LLC 302 535-2338
  304 Garnet Ln Smyrna (19977) *(G-13733)*

First Class Heating & AC Inc 302 934-8900
  28418 Dupont Blvd Millsboro (19966) *(G-8289)*

First Class Heating AC 302 834-1036
  6 Shea Way Newark (19713) *(G-10728)*

First Class Lawncare 302 753-0761
  4009 Greenmount Dr Wilmington (19810) *(G-16616)*

First Command Brkg Svcs Inc 302 535-8132
  4608 S Dupont Hwy Ste 1 Dover (19901) *(G-2498)*

First Data 302 793-5945
  101 Bellevue Pkwy Wilmington (19809) *(G-16617)*

First Data, Wilmington *Also Called: First Data (G-16617)*

First General 302 381-2581
  826 E Market St Georgetown (19947) *(G-4321)*

First Halthcare Compliance LLC 302 416-4329
  3903 Centerville Rd Wilmington (19807) *(G-16618)*

First Lincoln Holdings Inc 302 429-4900
  1219 N West St Wilmington (19801) *(G-16619)*

First Line Defense LLC 302 287-2764
  885 Mount Friendship Rd Smyrna (19977) *(G-13734)*

First Love Ministries Inc 302 655-1776
  853 Bullen Dr Middletown (19709) *(G-7130)*

First Media Radio LLC 410 253-9406
  9 Stockley St Rehoboth Beach (19971) *(G-12755)*

First Montgomery Properties 302 834-8272
  900 Woodchuck Pl Bear (19701) *(G-225)*

First National Bank, Camden *Also Called: First National Bnk of Wyoming (G-835)*

First National Bnk of Wyoming 302 697-2666
  4566 S Dupont Hwy Camden (19934) *(G-835)*

First Person Arts 267 402-2055
  1010 W 8th St Wilmington (19806) *(G-16620)*

First Power LLC 610 247-5750
  22 Peirce Rd Wilmington (19803) *(G-16621)*

First Shipment Inc 206 747-1237
  16192 Coastal Hwy Lewes (19958) *(G-5997)*

First State, Historic New Castle *Also Called: Fresenius Medical Care N Amer (G-4992)*

First State Academy of D 302 422-2633
  107 S Maple Ave Rm Main Milford (19963) *(G-7893)*

First State Animal Center 302 943-6032
  32 Shelter Cir Camden (19934) *(G-836)*

First State Auto Glass 302 559-8902
  605 Curtis Ave Wilmington (19804) *(G-16622)*

First State Automation LLC 302 743-4798
  34 Blevins Dr Ste 3 New Castle (19720) *(G-9127)*

First State Ballet Theatre Inc 302 658-7897
  818 N Market St Wilmington (19801) *(G-16623)*

First State Bancorp Inc (HQ) 302 427-3637
  1105 N Market St Ste 1300 Wilmington (19801) *(G-16624)*

First State Bmx 302 422-4133
  1045 N Walnut St Milford (19963) *(G-7894)*

First State Bowling Center 302 762-3883
  4601 Bedford Blvd Wilmington (19803) *(G-16625)*

First State Brewing Co LLC 302 285-9535
  109 Patriot Dr Middletown (19709) *(G-7131)*

First State Cmnty Action Agcy 302 674-1355
  655 S Bay Rd Ste 4j Dover (19901) *(G-2499)*

First State Cmnty Action Agcy (PA) 302 856-7761
  308 N Railroad Ave Georgetown (19947) *(G-4322)*

First State Cnstr MGT LLC 302 257-5438
  1802 Chelmsford Cir Newark (19713) *(G-10729)*

First State Coin Co 302 734-7776
  53 Greentree Dr Dover (19904) *(G-2500)*

First State Container LLC 603 888-1315
  100 Lake Dr Ste 106 Newark (19702) *(G-10730)*

First State Controls Inc 302 559-7822
  2207 Concord Pike 220 Wilmington (19803) *(G-16626)*

First State Cpas LLC 302 736-6657
  18 S State St Dover (19901) *(G-2501)*

First State Crane Service Inc 302 398-8885
  13326 S Dupont Hwy Felton (19943) *(G-3974)*

First State Disposal 302 644-3885
  15 Bridle Ridge Cir Lewes (19958) *(G-5998)*

First State Distributors Inc 302 655-8266
  222a 7th Ave Wilmington (19805) *(G-16627)*

First State Dme LLC 302 394-0301
  4115 N Dupont Hwy Dover (19901) *(G-2502)*

First State Drain Kings, Smyrna *Also Called: Drain Kings LLC (G-13715)*

First State Drvway Sealcoating 302 478-2266
  211 Waverly Rd Wilmington (19803) *(G-16628)*

First State Electric Co 302 322-0140
  25 King Ct New Castle (19720) *(G-9128)*

First State Endocrinology 302 836-6969
  1404 Olmsted Dr Bear (19701) *(G-226)*

First State Ent Association 302 836-8961
  1011 Powell Ct Bear (19701) *(G-227)*

First State Fabrication, Seaford *Also Called: First State Fabrication LLC (G-13186)*

First State Fabrication LLC 302 875-2417
  26546 Seaford Rd Seaford (19973) *(G-13186)*

First State Federal Credit Un 302 674-5281
  58 Carver Rd Dover (19904) *(G-2503)*

First State Fleet Service Inc 302 598-9500
  100 Carroll Dr New Castle (19720) *(G-9129)*

First State Gastroenterology A 302 677-1617
  644 S Queen St Ste 106 Dover (19904) *(G-2504)*

First State Gymnstics Athc Ass 302 368-7107
  131 John F Campbell Rd Newark (19711) *(G-10731)*

First State Health & Wellness 302 684-1995
  113 Union St Unit A Milton (19968) *(G-8624)*

ALPHABETIC SECTION

First State Hobbies LLC.. 302 595-2475
  600 Peoples Plz Newark (19702) *(G-10732)*

First State Hood & Duct LLC.. 888 866-7389
  23 S Clayton St Wilmington (19805) *(G-16629)*

First State Hospitality LLC.. 302 538-5858
  88 Wildswood Rd Dover (19901) *(G-2505)*

First State Infctious Diseases..................................... 302 535-4608
  200 Banning St Ste 230 Dover (19904) *(G-2506)*

First State Inspection Agency...................................... 302 449-5383
  811 N Broad St Ste 201 Middletown (19709) *(G-7132)*

First State Inspection Agency (PA)............................. 302 422-3859
  1001 Mattlind Way Milford (19963) *(G-7895)*

First State Landscaping.. 302 420-8604
  214 Springwood Dr Bear (19701) *(G-228)*

First State Lanes, Wilmington Also Called: First State Bowling Center *(G-16625)*

First State Management LLC....................................... 302 648-4600
  20856 Dupont Blvd Georgetown (19947) *(G-4323)*

First State Manufacturing Inc..................................... 302 424-4520
  301 Se 4th St Milford (19963) *(G-7896)*

First State Medical Assoc LLC.................................... 302 999-8169
  2055 Limestone Rd Ste 111 Wilmington (19808) *(G-16630)*

First State Mnfctred Hsing Ins................................... 302 674-5868
  1675 S State St Ste E Dover (19901) *(G-2507)*

First State Neurology LLC... 302 293-7524
  114 Sandhill Dr Ste 201a Middletown (19709) *(G-7133)*

First State Nutrition.. 302 384-7104
  910 N Union St Wilmington (19805) *(G-16631)*

First State Oral Mxllfcial Srg....................................... 302 674-4450
  1004 S State St Ste 1 Dover (19901) *(G-2508)*

First State Oral Mxllfcial Srg....................................... 302 883-6051
  9096 Riverside Dr Seaford (19973) *(G-13187)*

First State Orthopaedics, Newark Also Called: First State Surgery Center LLC *(G-10738)*

First State Orthopaedics PA.. 302 234-2600
  304 Lantana Dr Hockessin (19707) *(G-5210)*

First State Orthopaedics PA.. 302 322-3400
  4051 Ogletown Rd Ste 103 Newark (19713) *(G-10733)*

First State Orthopaedics PA (PA)............................... 302 731-2888
  4745 Ogletown Stanton Rd Ste 225 Newark (19713) *(G-10734)*

First State Orthopaedics PA.. 302 683-0700
  1000 Twin C Ln Ste 200 Newark (19713) *(G-10735)*

First State Orthopaedics PA.. 302 653-5100
  100 S Main St Ste 200 Smyrna (19977) *(G-13735)*

First State Patriots Inc... 302 378-6092
  103 Avian Way Middletown (19709) *(G-7134)*

First State Pediatrics LLC (PA).................................. 302 292-1559
  210 Christiana Medical Ctr Newark (19702) *(G-10736)*

First State Petroleum Services................................... 302 398-9704
  714 Gallo Rd Harrington (19952) *(G-4770)*

First State Physicians Inc (PA)................................... 302 836-6150
  12 Foxhunt Dr Bear (19701) *(G-229)*

First State Pickleball CLB Inc..................................... 302 387-1030
  32 Cox Ln Camden (19934) *(G-837)*

First State Plastics Inc... 302 325-3700
  955 River Rd New Castle (19720) *(G-9130)*

First State Plaza, Wilmington Also Called: Wilmington Savings Fund Soc *(G-20837)*

First State Plumbing & Heating................................. 302 275-9746
  47 Dunsinane Dr New Castle (19720) *(G-9131)*

First State Podiatry LLC.. 302 678-4612
  1177 S Governors Ave Dover (19904) *(G-2509)*

First State Podiatry LLC.. 302 678-4612
  390 Mitch Rd Wilmington (19804) *(G-16632)*

First State Press LLC... 302 731-9058
  14 Eileen Dr Newark (19711) *(G-10737)*

First State Printing, Newark Also Called: Luke Destefano Inc *(G-11294)*

First State Rehab Home LLC...................................... 302 304-9729
  111 Oxford Pl Wilmington (19803) *(G-16633)*

First State Rental Company LLC............................... 302 632-5699
  4414 Williamsville Rd Houston (19954) *(G-5441)*

First State Robotics Inc... 302 584-7152
  106 Meriden Dr Hockessin (19707) *(G-5211)*

First State Roof Extrior Clean.................................... 302 751-0439
  29257 Revel Rd Millsboro (19966) *(G-8290)*

First State Sealcoating.. 302 632-7522
  4860 Sandtown Rd Felton (19943) *(G-3975)*

First State Signs Inc... 302 744-9990
  2015 S Dupont Hwy Dover (19901) *(G-2510)*

First State Spine and Pain Ctr................................... 302 439-3063
  5311 Limestone Rd Ste 204 Wilmington (19808) *(G-16634)*

First State Squash Inc... 312 919-6767
  501 W 11th St Wilmington (19801) *(G-16635)*

First State Steel Drum Co... 302 655-2422
  4030 New Castle Ave New Castle (19720) *(G-9132)*

First State Stffing Sltion LLC..................................... 302 285-9044
  112 S French St Wilmington (19801) *(G-16636)*

First State Strings Inc.. 302 331-7362
  140 Metz Dr Camden Wyoming (19934) *(G-945)*

First State Surgery Center, Newark Also Called: First State Orthopaedics PA *(G-10735)*

First State Surgery Center LLC.................................. 302 683-0700
  1000 Twin C Ln Ste 200 Newark (19713) *(G-10738)*

First State Towing LLC.. 302 322-1777
  431 Old Airport Rd New Castle (19720) *(G-9133)*

First State Trolley Co LLC... 302 500-0526
  32099 Conleys Chapel Rd Lewes (19958) *(G-5999)*

First State Trust Company.. 302 573-5967
  1 Righter Pkwy Ste 120 Wilmington (19803) *(G-16637)*

First State Underground Inc...................................... 302 381-5601
  32353 Smith Dr Dagsboro (19939) *(G-1447)*

First State Vein and Laser Ctr.................................... 302 294-0700
  1300 N Franklin St Wilmington (19806) *(G-16638)*

First State Warehousing... 302 426-0802
  300 Pigeon Blvd New Castle (19720) *(G-9134)*

First State Wax LLC.. 302 529-8888
  5603 Concord Pike Wilmington (19803) *(G-16639)*

First Steps Preschool-Milford.................................... 302 424-4470
  104 Mccoy St Milford (19963) *(G-7897)*

First Steps Primeros Pasos, Georgetown Also Called: Primeros Pasos Inc *(G-4473)*

First Student, Newark Also Called: First Student Inc *(G-10739)*

First Student Inc... 302 995-9607
  750 Stanton Christiana Rd Newark (19713) *(G-10739)*

First Tech.. 302 421-3650
  700 Cornell Dr Ste E5 Wilmington (19801) *(G-16640)*

First Tee of Delaware... 302 593-2062
  800 N Dupont Rd Wilmington (19807) *(G-16641)*

Firstbase Inc (PA)... 917 331-6863
  251 Little Falls Drive Wilmington (19808) *(G-16642)*

Firstchoice Group America LLC................................. 425 242-8626
  16192 Coastal Hwy Lewes (19958) *(G-6000)*

Firstcollect Inc.. 302 644-6804
  12000 Old Vine Blvd Lewes (19958) *(G-6001)*

Fis Investment Ventures LLC (HQ)............................ 484 582-2000
  1105 N Market St Ste 1412 Wilmington (19801) *(G-16643)*

Fiscal Associates.. 302 894-0500
  16 Fairfield Dr Newark (19711) *(G-10740)*

Fiserv Wrldwide Sltions II LLC (HQ)........................ 800 872-7882
  251 Little Falls Dr Wilmington (19808) *(G-16644)*

Fish & Monkey Productions LLC............................... 302 897-4318
  1612 W 16th St Wilmington (19806) *(G-16645)*

Fish & Richardson PC.. 302 652-5070
  222 Delaware Ave Fl 17 Wilmington (19801) *(G-16646)*

Fish and Son Services.. 302 383-4202
  307 Brighton Ave Wilmington (19805) *(G-16647)*

Fish Lawn and Tree LLC.. 302 383-4202
  912 Dexter Corner Rd Townsend (19734) *(G-14002)*

Fish Whisperer Charters... 302 363-2597
  14 Rogers Dr Milford (19963) *(G-7898)*

Fish Window Cleaning Services, Milford Also Called: Clearview Windows LLC *(G-7833)*

Fisher Auto Parts Inc... 302 856-2507
  117 E Market St Georgetown (19947) *(G-4324)*

Fisher Auto Parts Inc... 302 934-8088
  422 Union St Millsboro (19966) *(G-8291)*

Fisher Auto Parts Inc... 302 653-9241
  5736 Dupont Pkwy Smyrna (19977) *(G-13736)*

Fisher Auto Parts Inc... 302 998-3111
  1600 E Newport Pike Ste C Wilmington (19804) *(G-16648)*

Fishers Auto Parts Inc ... 302 934-8088
422 Union St Millsboro (19966) *(G-8292)*

Fishers Popcorn Fenwick LLC ... 302 539-8833
37081 Coastal Hwy Fenwick Island (19944) *(G-4050)*

Fishtail Print Company ... 302 408-4800
18585 Coastal Hwy Rehoboth Beach (19971) *(G-12756)*

Fishtail Print Company ... 302 682-3053
36837 Winner Cir Rehoboth Beach (19971) *(G-12757)*

Fist Fit ... 302 399-7095
17 Manor Dr Dover (19901) *(G-2511)*

Fitar Inc ... 416 347-8099
651 N Broad St Ste 201 Middletown (19709) *(G-7135)*

Fitbody Personal Training ... 302 442-3685
727 N Market St Wilmington (19801) *(G-16649)*

Fitch-It ... 302 260-9657
21183 K St Rehoboth Beach (19971) *(G-12758)*

Fite LLC ... 302 478-1002
3464 Naamans Rd Wilmington (19810) *(G-16650)*

Fitness Management Group Inc ... 302 218-5644
247 S Main St Newark (19711) *(G-10741)*

Fitness Performance Corp ... 866 710-2227
2915 Ogletown Rd Ste 2839 Newark (19713) *(G-10742)*

Fitzgerald Auto Salvage Inc ... 302 422-7584
17115 Fitzgeralds Rd Lincoln (19960) *(G-6669)*

Five 1 Five Ice Sports Group L ... 302 266-0777
101 John F Campbell Rd Newark (19711) *(G-10743)*

Five Friends Auto ... 302 407-6236
199 Philadelphia Pike Wilmington (19809) *(G-16651)*

Five Point Chinese Laundry ... 302 656-6051
118 N Maryland Ave Wilmington (19804) *(G-16652)*

Five Points, Lewes Also Called: County Bank *(G-5864)*

Five Sixty Enterprise LLC ... 302 268-6530
501 Silverside Rd Ste 505 Wilmington (19809) *(G-16653)*

Five Star Franchising LLC (HQ) ... 646 838-3992
1209 N Orange St Wilmington (19801) *(G-16654)*

Five Star Home Delivery LLC ... 302 213-3535
16192 Coastal Hwy Lewes (19958) *(G-6002)*

Five Star Painting ... 302 743-6515
5 Beacon Ln Newark (19711) *(G-10744)*

Five Star Painting of Newark, Bear Also Called: Bulls Home Services Co *(G-84)*

Five Star Quality Care Inc ... 302 266-9255
501 S Harmony Rd Newark (19713) *(G-10745)*

Five Star Quality Care Inc ... 302 366-0160
255 Possum Park Rd Newark (19711) *(G-10746)*

Five Star Senior Living Inc ... 302 283-0540
4175 Ogletown Rd Newark (19713) *(G-10747)*

Five Star Senior Living Inc ... 302 655-6249
407 Foulk Rd Wilmington (19803) *(G-16655)*

Five Stars Embroidery ... 443 466-9692
224 Milford Dr Middletown (19709) *(G-7136)*

Five-Star Basketball, Wilmington Also Called: Five Star Franchising LLC *(G-16654)*

Five-Star Cleaning Services ... 302 746-7178
3207 Crystal Ct Wilmington (19810) *(G-16656)*

Fix It Now ... 302 293-7748
13 Rivendell Ct Hockessin (19707) *(G-5212)*

Fix.com, Wilmington Also Called: Fixcom Inc *(G-16657)*

Fixcom Inc ... 916 534-8872
251 Little Falls Dr Wilmington (19808) *(G-16657)*

Fiyah B, Newark Also Called: Fiyah B Music LLC *(G-10748)*

Fiyah B Music LLC (PA) ... 949 656-3246
140 Songsmith Dr Newark (19702) *(G-10748)*

Fizul H Bacchus ... 302 734-3331
863 Buttner Pl Dover (19904) *(G-2512)*

Fizz Media Corporation ... 630 730-7200
160 Greentree Dr Ste 101 Dover (19904) *(G-2513)*

Fjs Capital Management Inc ... 267 850-1123
300 Delaware Ave Ste 210 Wilmington (19801) *(G-16658)*

Fka Chronically Capable, Dover Also Called: Disclo Inc *(G-2301)*

Flackon Inc ... 701 369-0789
2035 Sunset Lake Rd Ste B2 Newark (19702) *(G-10749)*

Fladger & Associates Inc ... 302 836-3100
204 Stewards Ct Bear (19701) *(G-230)*

Flag Ride LLC (PA) ... 202 390-4850
942 Bennett St Fl 2nf Wilmington (19801) *(G-16659)*

Flagpole Corp ... 302 261-5170
16192 Coastal Hwy Lewes (19958) *(G-6003)*

Flapdoodles Inc (PA) ... 302 731-9793
725 Dawson Dr Newark (19713) *(G-10750)*

Flash Training Center ... 302 943-4668
1390 Red Lion Rd Bear (19701) *(G-231)*

Flashback Farms, Camden Wyoming Also Called: Country Comforts *(G-929)*

Flawless Inbound LLC ... 929 324-1132
8 The Grn Ste A Dover (19901) *(G-2514)*

Fledgling Fund ... 800 839-1754
501 Silverside Rd Ste 123 Wilmington (19809) *(G-16660)*

Flemings Electrical Service ... 302 258-9386
15199 Trap Pond Rd Laurel (19956) *(G-5513)*

Fletcher Plumbing Htg & AC Inc (PA) ... 302 653-6277
18 Myrtle St Smyrna (19977) *(G-13737)*

Flex Fantasy Inc ... 201 417-7692
874 Walker Rd Ste C Dover (19904) *(G-2515)*

Flex World Fitness LLC ... 302 856-7771
6 Nicole Way Lewes (19958) *(G-6004)*

Flexera Inc ... 302 945-6870
22791 Dozer Ln Unit 8 Harbeson (19951) *(G-4696)*

Flexible Packaging Group, New Castle Also Called: Printpack Inc *(G-9495)*

Flight Centre Travel Group USA ... 302 479-7581
4737 Concord Pike Ste 835 Wilmington (19803) *(G-16661)*

Flip App LLC (PA) ... 248 662-6875
8 The Grn Ste R Dover (19901) *(G-2516)*

Flipride Inc ... 208 471-0007
1221 College Park Dr # 116 Dover (19904) *(G-2517)*

Flo Health Inc (PA) ... 302 498-8369
1013 Centre Rd Ste 403b Wilmington (19805) *(G-16662)*

Flo Mechanical LLC ... 302 239-7299
507 Baxter Ct Hockessin (19707) *(G-5213)*

Flo Mechanical LLC ... 302 543-5462
1017 W 25th St Wilmington (19802) *(G-16663)*

Floater Painting ... 302 290-8520
36 Roxeter Rd New Castle (19720) *(G-9135)*

Floleft LLC ... 302 648-2088
29585 Carnoustie Ct Unit 802 Dagsboro (19939) *(G-1448)*

Flood Rescue LLC ... 302 547-4092
7851 Sugar Maple Dr Milford (19963) *(G-7899)*

Floor Coatings Etc Inc ... 302 322-4177
110 J And M Dr New Castle (19720) *(G-9136)*

Floor Guy Supply LLC ... 302 325-3801
12 Mccullough Dr Ste 10 New Castle (19720) *(G-9137)*

Flora F Petillo ... 302 658-8191
1600 N Washington St Wilmington (19802) *(G-16664)*

Flores Design and Construction ... 302 635-7345
2417 Lancaster Ave Wilmington (19805) *(G-16665)*

Flores Enterprises LLC ... 484 880-5134
3902 Newport Gap Pike Wilmington (19808) *(G-16666)*

Florian P Lisinski Inc ... 302 378-3200
1848 Choptank Rd Middletown (19709) *(G-7137)*

Florida Digital Media LLC, Bethany Beach Also Called: Delaware Digital Media LLC *(G-596)*

Florida Pub Utl Co ... 561 838-1813
909 Silver Lake Blvd Dover (19904) *(G-2518)*

Florient Contracting Firm LLC ... 888 250-1915
1201 N Market St Wilmington (19801) *(G-16667)*

Flou Holding Inc ... 832 267-3372
8 The Grn Dover (19901) *(G-2519)*

Flowers Real Estate LLC ... 302 383-8955
406 Robinson Dr Wilmington (19801) *(G-16668)*

Flowline Technologies Inc ... 302 256-5825
1201 N Orange St Ste 600 Wilmington (19801) *(G-16669)*

Flowpay Corporation ... 720 425-3244
221 W 9th St Ste 300 Wilmington (19801) *(G-16670)*

Flowrite ... 302 544-4042
1620 Wilmington Rd Historic New Castle (19720) *(G-4989)*

Flowrite Inc ... 302 547-5657
102 Country Woods Dr Bear (19701) *(G-232)*

ALPHABETIC SECTION — Forgotten Few Foundation Inc

Flowrite Plumbing, Bear Also Called: Flowrite Inc (G-232)
Floyd Allan Gregory..302 658-0295
 707 W 21st St Lower Level Wilmington (19802) (G-16671)
Floyd Dean Inc...302 655-7193
 2 S Poplar St Ste B Wilmington (19801) (G-16672)
FLUENTAAI INC..323 739-5417
 1209 N Orange St Wilmington (19801) (G-16673)
Fluor Corp...302 934-7742
 29416 Power Plant Rd Dagsboro (19939) (G-1449)
Fluorogistx LLC..302 479-7614
 3704 Kennett Pike Ste 100 Wilmington (19807) (G-16674)
Fluorogistx Ct LLC (PA)...800 373-7811
 3704 Kennett Pike Ste 100 Wilmington (19807) (G-16675)
Fluoroproducts, Wilmington Also Called: Chemours Company Fc LLC (G-15360)
Flute Pro Shop Inc..302 479-5000
 4023 Kennett Pike Ste 30 Wilmington (19807) (G-16676)
Flutterby Stitches & EMB..302 531-7784
 203 Doveview Dr Unit 403 Dover (19904) (G-2520)
Fluttering Butterfly LLC...267 974-7812
 8 The Grn Ste 4000 Dover (19901) (G-2521)
Flw Wood Products Inc..410 259-4674
 33290 Bayberry Ct Dagsboro (19939) (G-1450)
FLW WOOD PRODUCTS INC., Dagsboro Also Called: Flw Wood Products Inc (G-1450)
Fly Advanced, New Castle Also Called: Aero Ways Inc (G-8768)
Fly By Jing Inc...646 875-2465
 16192 Coastal Hwy Lewes (19958) (G-6005)
Fly High Cheer and Tumble LLC...............................585 317-1442
 149 Estates Dr Camden Wyoming (19934) (G-946)
Flying Locksmiths LLC..302 607-7999
 1002 Society Dr Claymont (19703) (G-1150)
Flyingparts International Inc....................................610 400-1110
 16192 Coastal Hwy Lewes (19958) (G-6006)
Flyogi LLC..302 298-0926
 605 N Market St Fl 2 Wilmington (19801) (G-16677)
FMC Corporation..302 451-0100
 1301 Ogletown Rd Newark (19711) (G-10751)
FMC Corporation..302 366-5107
 1090 Elkton Rd Newark (19711) (G-10752)
Fme Lighting LLC...877 234-8460
 34005 Wescoats Rd Unit A2 Lewes (19958) (G-6007)
Fnx Technologies Ltd (PA)..844 969-0070
 251 Little Falls Dr Wilmington (19808) (G-16678)
Foard R T & Jones Funeral Home, Newark Also Called: Robert T Jones & Foard Inc (G-11900)
Focal Point Products..800 662-5550
 9706 Nanticoke Business Park Dr Greenwood (19950) (G-4630)
Focus Behavioral Health...302 827-4206
 33712 Wescoats Rd Unit 4 Lewes (19958) (G-6008)
Focus Behavioral Health...302 762-2285
 410 Foulk Rd Ste 105 Wilmington (19803) (G-16679)
Focus Health Care Delaware LLC.............................302 395-1111
 575 S Dupont Hwy New Castle (19720) (G-9138)
Focus Rehabilitation & Fitness.................................302 231-8982
 34814 Long Neck Rd Millsboro (19966) (G-8293)
Focus Solutions Services Inc....................................302 318-1345
 262 Chapman Rd Ste 200 Newark (19702) (G-10753)
Fogarty LLC...610 731-4804
 5 Coty Ln Seaford (19973) (G-13188)
Folderly Inc..302 966-9083
 8 The Grn Ste 10781 Dover (19901) (G-2522)
Foldfast Goals LLC..302 478-7881
 1211 Stony Run Dr Wilmington (19803) (G-16680)
Fonbnk Inc...703 585-3288
 8 The Grn Dover (19901) (G-2523)
Fondeadora Inc (PA)..925 413-3654
 8 The Grn Ste 10849 Dover (19901) (G-2524)
Fonzis LLC..302 858-8024
 13149 Mennonite School Rd Greenwood (19950) (G-4631)
Food and Bev Innovations LLC.................................302 722-8058
 300 Delaware Ave Wilmington (19801) (G-16681)
Food Bank of Delaware Inc.......................................302 424-3301
 1040 Mattlind Way Milford (19963) (G-7900)

Food Bank of Delaware Inc (PA)...............................302 292-1305
 222 Lake Dr Newark (19702) (G-10754)
Food Equipment Service Inc.....................................302 996-9363
 3316a Old Capitol Trl Wilmington (19808) (G-16682)
Food Works Management LLC..................................302 397-3000
 560 Peoples Plz Ste 310 Newark (19702) (G-10755)
Foodliner Inc..302 368-4204
 206 Hansen Ct Newark (19713) (G-10756)
Foodstr Inc...707 500-0599
 251 Little Falls Dr Wilmington (19808) (G-16683)
Foos Construction Inc...302 753-3667
 230 Philadelphia Pike Wilmington (19809) (G-16684)
Foot & Ankle Ctr of Delaware...................................302 945-1221
 26744 John J Williams Hwy Millsboro (19966) (G-8294)
Foot and Ankle Associates LLC...............................302 652-5767
 3801 Kennett Pike Ste A102 Wilmington (19807) (G-16685)
Foot Care Group Inc (PA)..302 998-0178
 1601 Milltown Rd Ste 24 Wilmington (19808) (G-16686)
Foot Light Production Inc..302 645-7220
 516 Kings Hwy Lewes (19958) (G-6009)
Foot Steps Two Heaven Daycare..............................302 738-5519
 606 Lisbeth Rd Newark (19713) (G-10757)
Footcare Technologies Inc..704 301-6966
 124 Broadkill Rd Ste 472 Milton (19968) (G-8625)
Footprnts Prof Wrting Svcs LLC...............................917 324-6941
 22607 Deep Woods Rd Milton (19968) (G-8626)
For Them Inc...646 623-4041
 651 N Broad St Ste 206 Middletown (19709) (G-7138)
Foraker Oil Inc...302 834-7595
 5th & Clinton St Delaware City (19706) (G-1541)
Forbes Mrktplace Oprations Inc...............................973 393-0073
 251 Little Falls Dr Wilmington (19808) (G-16687)
Forcebeyond Inc...302 995-6588
 1521 Concord Pike Ste 301 Wilmington (19803) (G-16688)
Forcebeyond LLC (PA)..302 995-6588
 261 Quigley Blvd Ste 18 New Castle (19726) (G-9139)
Ford International Fin Corp.......................................313 845-5712
 1209 N Orange St Wilmington (19801) (G-16689)
Forecast Inc...302 413-0675
 8 The Grn Ste A Dover (19901) (G-2525)
Foreignerds Inc...201 381-5152
 2035 Sunset Lake Rd Ste B2 Newark (19702) (G-10758)
Forensic Associates Del LLC....................................302 415-4944
 2055 Limestone Rd Wilmington (19808) (G-16690)
Foresee Pharma..302 368-1758
 550 S College Ave Newark (19716) (G-10759)
Foresee Pharmaceuticals Inc....................................302 396-5243
 3 Innovation Way Ste 240 Newark (19711) (G-10760)
Forest Oak Elementary Pta..302 540-2873
 55 S Meadowood Dr Newark (19711) (G-10761)
Forest Park Apartments..302 737-6151
 5501 Limeric Cir Ofc 33 Wilmington (19808) (G-16691)
Forest View Nursery...302 653-7757
 1313 Blackbird Forest Rd Clayton (19938) (G-1367)
Forester Communications...302 545-6169
 887 Salem Church Rd Newark (19702) (G-10762)
Forever Inc...302 449-2100
 328 E Main St Middletown (19709) (G-7139)
Forever Inc (PA)..302 594-0400
 1006 W 27th St Wilmington (19802) (G-16692)
Forever Fit Foundation..302 698-5201
 1510 E Lebanon Rd Dover (19901) (G-2526)
Forever Green Landscaping Inc................................302 322-9535
 340 Churchmans Rd New Castle (19720) (G-9140)
Forewinds Hospitality LLC (HQ)...............................302 368-6640
 507 Thompson Station Rd Newark (19711) (G-10763)
Forged Bdc Inc..561 802-8919
 254 Chapman Rd Ste 209 Newark (19702) (G-10764)
Forged Creations..302 832-1631
 124 Clinton St Delaware City (19706) (G-1542)
Forgotten Few Foundation Inc..................................302 494-6212
 1927 W 4th St Wilmington (19805) (G-16693)

(PA)=Parent Co (HQ)=Headquarters (DH)=Div Headquarters

Foris Solutions LLC   ALPHABETIC SECTION

Foris Solutions LLC 302 343-6396
   330 Water St Ste 109 Wilmington (19804) *(G-16694)*

Formal Affairs Inc 302 737-1519
   257 E Main St # 100 Newark (19711) *(G-10765)*

Formclick LLC 302 212-0311
   1007 N Orange St Fl 4 Wilmington (19801) *(G-16695)*

Formidable Foods Inc (PA) 415 877-9691
   3500 S Dupont Hwy Dover (19901) *(G-2527)*

Formula One Tinting Graphics, Bear Also Called: Gotshadeonline Inc *(G-252)*

Forrest Avenue Animal Hospital 302 736-3000
   3156 Forrest Ave Dover (19904) *(G-2528)*

Forrest Fence, Felton Also Called: J & M Fencing Inc *(G-3985)*

Forrest Fencing, Felton Also Called: J & M Fencing Inc *(G-3986)*

Fort Delaware Society 302 834-1630
   33 Staff Ln Delaware City (19706) *(G-1543)*

Fort Hill Company Inc 302 651-9223
   1104 Philadelphia Pike Wilmington (19809) *(G-16696)*

Fortaleza Fitness 302 448-0922
   27431 Patricks Ln Seaford (19973) *(G-13189)*

Forte Sports Incorporated 302 731-0776
   314 E Main St Ste 1 Newark (19711) *(G-10766)*

Forthright Consulting, Wilmington Also Called: Trellist Inc *(G-20408)*

Fortress Home Maintenance Serv 302 539-3446
   31275 Gray Rd Dagsboro (19939) *(G-1451)*

Forum To Advnce Mnrties In Eng 302 777-3254
   2005 Baynard Blvd Wilmington (19802) *(G-16697)*

Forward Discovery Inc 703 647-6364
   27 Milbourn Manor Dr Camden Wyoming (19934) *(G-947)*

Forward Support LLC 315 292-8770
   903 S College Ave Newark (19713) *(G-10767)*

Forwood Chiropractic Center 302 652-0411
   6 Sharpley Rd Wilmington (19803) *(G-16698)*

Foschi Fine Photography, Wilmington Also Called: Delaware Color Lab *(G-15889)*

Foshee Property Maintenance 302 344-6410
   33403 Oak Street Ext Ocean View (19970) *(G-12512)*

Foss-Brown Inc (PA) 610 940-6040
   3411 Silverside Rd Ste 100wb Wilmington (19810) *(G-16699)*

Foster Long Real Estate 302 864-3216
   31045 Scissorbill Rd Ocean View (19970) *(G-12513)*

Foster Long Vacation Rentals 302 226-2919
   527 N Boardwalk Rehoboth Beach (19971) *(G-12759)*

Foto Video Genesis 302 422-6988
   635 Adams Dr Milford (19963) *(G-7901)*

Fotomaster LLC 646 233-3371
   1013 Centre Rd Ste 403b Wilmington (19805) *(G-16700)*

Foulk Lawn & Equipment Co Inc 302 475-3233
   2018 Foulk Rd Wilmington (19810) *(G-16701)*

Foulk Manor North, Wilmington Also Called: Alerislife Inc *(G-14352)*

Foulk Manor South, Wilmington Also Called: Five Star Senior Living Inc *(G-16655)*

Foulk Pr-School Day Care Ctr I (PA) 302 478-3047
   2 Tenby Dr Wilmington (19803) *(G-16702)*

Foulk Pre-Schl & Day Cre Cntr 302 529-1580
   2711 Carpenter Station Rd Wilmington (19810) *(G-16703)*

Foulk Road Dental & Associates 302 652-3775
   300 Foulk Rd Ste 101 Wilmington (19803) *(G-16704)*

Foundation Delaware Islamic 302 325-4149
   249 Appleby Rd New Castle (19720) *(G-9141)*

Foundation of Health 302 762-5973
   112 South Rd Wilmington (19809) *(G-16705)*

Foundation Source Char Fdn Inc 800 839-1754
   501 Silverside Rd Ste 123 Wilmington (19809) *(G-16706)*

Foundation Source Philanthropi 800 839-1754
   501 Silverside Rd Ste 123 Wilmington (19809) *(G-16707)*

Founding Principals LLC 917 693-7533
   936 King James Ct Bear (19701) *(G-233)*

Fountain Resurgence LLC 302 518-5659
   4 Peddlers Row Unit 31 Newark (19702) *(G-10768)*

Four Brothers Auto Service 302 482-2932
   101 N Union St Wilmington (19805) *(G-16708)*

Four C Health Solutions 804 601-2628
   3903 Centerville Rd Wilmington (19807) *(G-16709)*

Four C Painting 302 242-2497
   190 Mannering Dr Dover (19901) *(G-2529)*

Four Ever Green Inc 302 424-2393
   1 N Walnut St Milford (19963) *(G-7902)*

Four Paws Animal Hospital PA 302 629-7297
   21804 Eskridge Rd Bridgeville (19933) *(G-701)*

Four Pnts By Shrton Nwark Chrs, Newark Also Called: Ssn Christiana LLC *(G-12079)*

Four Seasons Property Manageme 302 275-4816
   162 Christiana Rd New Castle (19720) *(G-9142)*

Four Seasons Sunrooms, Wilmington Also Called: Eastern Home Improvements Inc *(G-16258)*

Four States LLC 302 655-3400
   520 Terminal Ave Ste G New Castle (19720) *(G-9143)*

Fourth Floor 302 472-8416
   1205 N Orange St Wilmington (19801) *(G-16710)*

Fowler & Williams Inc 302 875-7518
   314 S Central Ave Laurel (19956) *(G-5514)*

Fowler Family Charitable Foun 800 839-1754
   501 Silverside Rd Ste 123 Wilmington (19809) *(G-16711)*

Fox Logistics LLC 302 444-4750
   601 Cornell Dr Ste G10 Wilmington (19801) *(G-16712)*

Fox Logistics LLC 302 444-4750
   700 Cornell Dr Ste E16 Wilmington (19801) *(G-16713)*

Fox Point Programs Inc 302 765-6018
   706 Philadelphia Pike Ste 2 Wilmington (19809) *(G-16714)*

Fox Point Programs Inc 800 499-7242
   3001 Philadelphia Pike Claymont (19703) *(G-1151)*

Fox Pointe 302 744-9442
   352 Fox Pointe Dr Dover (19904) *(G-2530)*

Fox Rothschild LLP 302 654-7444
   919 N Market St Wilmington (19801) *(G-16715)*

Fox Run Apartments, Bear Also Called: First Montgomery Properties *(G-225)*

Fox Run Automotive Inc 302 834-1200
   610 Connor Blvd Bear (19701) *(G-234)*

Fox Specialties Inc 302 322-5200
   1500 Johnson Way Historic New Castle (19720) *(G-4990)*

Foxfire Printing and Packaging Inc 302 533-2240
   750 Dawson Dr Newark (19713) *(G-10769)*

FPL Energy American Wind LLC 302 655-0632
   3801 Kennett Pike Ste C200 Wilmington (19807) *(G-16716)*

FPL Energy American Wind LLC 302 655-0632
   201 W 29th St Wilmington (19802) *(G-16717)*

Fractal Mobius LLC 646 209-8559
   8 The Grn Ste A Dover (19901) *(G-2531)*

Fraim Monnarae 302 761-1313
   814 Philadelphia Pike Wilmington (19809) *(G-16718)*

Framemakers Shop 302 999-9968
   4416 Kirkwood Hwy Wilmington (19808) *(G-16719)*

Frances Ann Owens 302 436-2333
   34720 Pyle Center Rd Frankford (19945) *(G-4107)*

Franchise Co LLC USA 868 280-5272
   16192 Coastal Hwy Lewes (19958) *(G-6010)*

Francis Bergold 302 284-8101
   918 Midstate Rd Felton (19943) *(G-3976)*

Francis Enterprises LLC 302 276-1316
   261 Quigley Blvd Ste 10 Historic New Castle (19720) *(G-4991)*

Francis Kelly Sons Inc 302 999-7400
   8 Meco Cir Wilmington (19804) *(G-16720)*

Francis Mase MD PA 302 762-5656
   209 Sulky Cir Wilmington (19810) *(G-16721)*

Francis Mase Pediatrics 302 762-5656
   700 W Lea Blvd Ste 209 Wilmington (19802) *(G-16722)*

Francis Pollinger & Son Inc 302 655-8097
   57 Germay Dr Wilmington (19804) *(G-16723)*

Francis X Norton Center 302 594-9455
   917 N Madison St Wilmington (19801) *(G-16724)*

Francisco J Rodriguez 302 424-7522
   806 Seabury Ave Milford (19963) *(G-7903)*

Frank & Yetta Chaiken Fou 302 737-7427
   4002 Lakeview Dr Wilmington (19807) *(G-16725)*

Frank Austin 302 832-9167
   250 Mariners Way Bear (19701) *(G-235)*

ALPHABETIC SECTION — Fresh Coat Painters of MOT

Frank Costa Constr Handyman.. 302 561-5792
  5 N 1st St Rehoboth Beach (19971) *(G-12760)*

Frank Deramo & Son Inc... 302 328-0102
  10 King Ct New Castle (19720) *(G-9144)*

Frank Falco MD.. 302 392-6501
  100 Becks Woods Dr Ste 102 Bear (19701) *(G-236)*

Frank Gillen... 302 894-1023
  9 Stearrett Dr Newark (19702) *(G-10770)*

Frank Smths Twing Atobody Repr, Wilmington *Also Called: Ellmore Auto Collision (G-16374)*

Frankel Enterprises Inc... 302 652-6364
  1300 N Harrison St Ofc A100 Wilmington (19806) *(G-16726)*

Frankford Custom Woodworks Inc.. 302 732-9570
  34139 Dupont Blvd Frankford (19945) *(G-4108)*

Franklin & Prokopik... 302 594-9780
  300 Delaware Ave Ste 1340 Wilmington (19801) *(G-16727)*

Franklin and Prokopik.. 302 594-9780
  500 Creek View Rd Ste 502 Newark (19711) *(G-10771)*

Franklin Fibre-Lamitex Corp.. 302 652-3621
  903 E 13th St Wilmington (19802) *(G-16728)*

Franklin Jester PA... 302 368-3080
  603 Lisbeth Rd Newark (19713) *(G-10772)*

Franklin Kennet LLC... 302 655-6536
  1113 N Franklin St Wilmington (19806) *(G-16729)*

Franklin Pancko DDS.. 302 674-1140
  712 S Governors Ave Dover (19904) *(G-2532)*

Franklin Rubber Stamp Co Inc.. 302 654-8841
  301 W 8th St Frnt Wilmington (19801) *(G-16730)*

Franklin Tmplton Companies LLC... 800 632-2301
  919 N Market St Ste 600 Wilmington (19801) *(G-16731)*

Franklin Utilities LLC... 302 629-6658
  14619 Cokesbury Rd Georgetown (19947) *(G-4325)*

Frascella Enterprises Inc.. 267 467-4496
  650 Naamans Rd Ste 300 Claymont (19703) *(G-1152)*

Fraternal Order of Eagles BR.. 302 616-2935
  35083 Atlantic Ave Ocean View (19970) *(G-12514)*

FRATERNAL ORDER OF EAGLES, BRYAN AERIE 2233 OF BRYAN, OHIO, Ocean View *Also Called: Fraternal Order of Eagles BR (G-12514)*

Fraternal Order of Police.. 302 674-3673
  Kitts Hummock Rd Dover (19901) *(G-2533)*

Fraunhofer Center For Molecula, Newark *Also Called: Fraunhofer Usa Inc (G-10773)*

Fraunhofer Usa Inc... 302 369-1708
  9 Innovation Way Newark (19711) *(G-10773)*

Frc Global Inc... 800 609-5711
  1000 N West St Ste 3008 Wilmington (19801) *(G-16732)*

Freakin Fresh Salsa Inc.. 302 750-9789
  2 Biltmore Ct Wilmington (19808) *(G-16733)*

Freckle Holdings LLC... 302 260-6385
  8 The Grn Ste 12441 Dover (19901) *(G-2534)*

Fred Drake Automotive Inc... 302 378-4877
  4195 Dupont Pkwy Townsend (19734) *(G-14003)*

Fred Drake Salvage, Townsend *Also Called: Fred Drake Automotive Inc (G-14003)*

Fred L Wright DDS... 302 239-1641
  5309 Limestone Rd Wilmington (19808) *(G-16734)*

Fred S Fink Orthodontist.. 302 478-6930
  23 The Commons Wilmington (19810) *(G-16735)*

Fred S Smalls Insurance (PA).. 302 633-1980
  5227 W Woodmill Dr Ste 43 Wilmington (19808) *(G-16736)*

Fred's, Bear *Also Called: Freds Stores Tennessee Inc (G-237)*

Frederica Senior Center Inc... 302 335-4555
  216 S Market St Frederica (19946) *(G-4167)*

Frederick Dimeo... 302 674-3970
  540 S Governors Ave # 201 Dover (19904) *(G-2535)*

Frederick Enterprises Inc.. 302 994-5786
  810 Stanton Rd Wilmington (19804) *(G-16737)*

Frederick L Cottrell.. 302 651-7686
  920 N King St Lbby 1 Wilmington (19801) *(G-16738)*

Frederick M Williams MD... 302 738-0103
  4110 Ogletown Stanton Rd Newark (19713) *(G-10774)*

Freds Stores Tennessee Inc (PA).. 800 746-7287
  27 Crimson King Dr Bear (19701) *(G-237)*

Free Hosting LLC... 302 421-5750
  Suite 606-1220 N.Market S Wilmington (19801) *(G-16739)*

Free Pdf Technologies Inc... 872 204-6733
  16192 Coastal Hwy Lewes (19958) *(G-6011)*

Free Properties.. 914 474-1980
  31443 Falmouth Way Lewes (19958) *(G-6012)*

Free Spirited Foundation.. 614 946-7358
  23951 Creek Ln Lewes (19958) *(G-6013)*

Freedom At Home... 302 740-7054
  609 Ohio Ave Wilmington (19805) *(G-16740)*

Freedom Boat Club Delaware.. 302 219-3549
  909 Pilottown Rd Lewes (19958) *(G-6014)*

Freedom Central Holdings LLC.. 803 567-6400
  1209 N Orange St Wilmington (19801) *(G-16741)*

Freedom Cycle LLC.. 302 286-6900
  1110 Ogletown Rd Newark (19711) *(G-10775)*

Freedom Dental Management Inc.. 302 836-3750
  1290 Peoples Plz Newark (19702) *(G-10776)*

Freedom Drain Clg Pipe Svcs LL... 484 480-1368
  6 S Muirfield Ln Bear (19701) *(G-238)*

Freedom Drywall Supply LLC (HQ)... 302 281-0085
  721 Dawson Dr Newark (19713) *(G-10777)*

Freedom Kitchen and Bath... 302 463-1659
  159 E Green Valley Cir Newark (19711) *(G-10778)*

Freedom Materials, Newark *Also Called: Freedom Drywall Supply LLC (G-10777)*

Freedom Mortgage Corporation.. 302 368-7100
  220 Continental Dr Ste 315 Newark (19713) *(G-10779)*

Freedom Outreach.. 302 655-2724
  2506 N Market St Wilmington (19802) *(G-16742)*

Freedom Plaza Enterprises LLC... 302 653-9676
  20 York Dr Smyrna (19977) *(G-13738)*

Freedom Rides Auto... 302 422-4559
  26831 Sussex Hwy Seaford (19973) *(G-13190)*

Freedom Tech Consulting LLC... 215 485-7383
  221 N Broad St Ste 3a Middletown (19709) *(G-7140)*

Freehold Cartage Inc.. 302 658-2005
  350 Pigeon Point Rd New Castle (19720) *(G-9145)*

Freelee Foundation... 302 607-8053
  1400 Helen Dr Apt 104 Newark (19702) *(G-10780)*

Freeman Arts Pavilion Inc.. 302 436-6241
  31255 Americana Pkwy Selbyville (19975) *(G-13536)*

Freeman Courier Express.. 610 803-3933
  123 Governor House Cir Wilmington (19809) *(G-16743)*

Freemarkets Investment Co Inc... 302 427-2089
  1105 N Market St Ste 1300 Wilmington (19801) *(G-16744)*

Frees Electric... 302 752-8895
  19266 Coastal Hwy Unit 10 Rehoboth Beach (19971) *(G-12761)*

Freestyles Ltd... 302 584-8601
  4905 Mermaid Blvd Wilmington (19808) *(G-16745)*

Freibott Law Firm... 302 633-9000
  1711 E Newport Pike Wilmington (19804) *(G-16746)*

Fremont Hall.. 302 731-2431
  82 Possum Park Rd Newark (19711) *(G-10781)*

Frenius Medical Care... 302 421-9177
  7 S Clayton St Wilmington (19805) *(G-16747)*

Frensenius Medical Ctr.. 302 762-2903
  4000 N Washington St Wilmington (19802) *(G-16748)*

Fresenius Kidney Care Lantana, Hockessin *Also Called: Fresenius Med Care Nthrn Del L (G-5214)*

Fresenius Kidney Care N Dover, Dover *Also Called: Fresenius Medical Care Souther (G-2536)*

Fresenius Med Care Brndywine H, Newark *Also Called: Bio-Mdical Applications of Del (G-10034)*

Fresenius Med Care Nthrn Del L.. 302 239-4704
  214 Lantana Dr Hockessin (19707) *(G-5214)*

Fresenius Medical Care N Amer.. 302 328-9044
  608 Ferry Cut Off St Historic New Castle (19720) *(G-4992)*

Fresenius Medical Care N Amer.. 302 633-6228
  605 W Newport Pike Wilmington (19804) *(G-16749)*

FRESENIUS MEDICAL CARE NORTH AMERICA, Wilmington *Also Called: Fresenius Medical Care N Amer (G-16749)*

Fresenius Medical Care Souther.. 302 678-2181
  80 Salt Creek Dr Dover (19901) *(G-2536)*

Fresh Coat Painters of MOT... 302 313-6124
  413 Prestwick Pl Townsend (19734) *(G-14004)*

(PA)=Parent Co (HQ)=Headquarters (DH)=Div Headquarters

Fresh Cut Lndscping Mintenance 302 841-1848
314 Country Pl Millsboro (19966) *(G-8295)*

Fresh Harvest Hydroponics 302 934-7506
25345 Gravel Hill Rd Millsboro (19966) *(G-8296)*

Fresh Healthy Markets LLC 484 748-4791
304 S Chapel St Unit 5 Newark (19711) *(G-10782)*

Fresh Industries Ltd 205 737-3747
18388 Coastal Hwy Unit 10 Lewes (19958) *(G-6015)*

Fresh Juice Partners LLC 302 364-0909
18388 Coastal Hwy Unit 10 Lewes (19958) *(G-6016)*

Fresh Start Lawn Services 302 279-6234
213 N Oxford Dr Newark (19702) *(G-10783)*

Fresh Start Transformations 302 219-0221
4604 Tracy Dr Newark (19702) *(G-10784)*

Freshbooks Usa Inc 416 525-5384
2801 Centerville Rd Wilmington (19808) *(G-16750)*

Freshpac LLC 559 648-2210
1 Hausel Rd Wilmington (19801) *(G-16751)*

Frets4vetsorg 302 382-1426
300a Nancy St Georgetown (19947) *(G-4326)*

Friday Games Inc 847 246-2189
200 Continental Dr Ste 401 Newark (19713) *(G-10785)*

Friedlander and Gorris 302 573-3500
1201 N Market St Ste 2200 Wilmington (19801) *(G-16752)*

Friends & Family Practice 302 537-3740
609 Atlantic Ave Ste A Millville (19967) *(G-8529)*

Friends and Sign 302 368-4794
61 Matthews Rd Newark (19713) *(G-10786)*

Friends Hckssin Clred Schl 107 .... 302 540-5959
4266 Mill Creek Rd Hockessin (19707) *(G-5215)*

Friends Inc 302 764-4488
3209 Miller Rd Wilmington (19802) *(G-16753)*

Friends of Bellaca Airfield 302 322-3816
Rt 273 Ctr Pt Blvd New Castle (19720) *(G-9146)*

Friends of Belmont Hall Inc 302 653-9212
21 E Commerce St Smyrna (19977) *(G-13739)*

Friends of Colonial 302 323-2746
318 E Basin Rd New Castle (19720) *(G-9147)*

Friends of Dlwres Gmbrnus Sttu 302 981-5972
2313 W 16th St Wilmington (19806) *(G-16754)*

Friends of James Spadola 302 383-3798
1504 N Broom St Ste 18 Wilmington (19806) *(G-16755)*

Friends of New Cties Fundation 718 896-8900
1209 N Orange St Wilmington (19801) *(G-16756)*

Friends of Old Dover 302 674-1787
323 S State St Dover (19901) *(G-2537)*

Friends of Stb 302 765-2566
38 E Mccaulley Ct Wilmington (19801) *(G-16757)*

Friends of The African Union 302 834-7525
407 Clinton St Delaware City (19706) *(G-1544)*

Friends of The Good Samarit 302 762-4937
13 Lombardy Dr Wilmington (19803) *(G-16758)*

Friendship House Incorporated 302 652-8033
720 N Orange St Wilmington (19801) *(G-16759)*

Friendship House Incorporated (PA) 302 652-8133
1503 W 13th St Wilmington (19806) *(G-16760)*

Friendship House Nec 302 731-5338
69 E Main St Newark (19711) *(G-10787)*

Frightland LLC 302 838-0256
309 Port Penn Rd Middletown (19709) *(G-7141)*

Fringe Hair Studio 302 313-5213
1509 Savannah Rd Lewes (19958) *(G-6017)*

Fritz Staffing Group LLC (PA) 844 581-5873
508 South St Bldg D Historic New Castle (19720) *(G-4993)*

Frog Hollow Golf Course 302 376-6500
1 Wittington Way Middletown (19709) *(G-7142)*

From Ground Up Construction 302 747-0996
26 Evergreen Dr Newark (19702) *(G-10788)*

From Harps To Halos 302 932-0956
6 N Clifton Ave Wilmington (19805) *(G-16761)*

From Top Ltd (PA) 310 626-0090
651 N Broad St Ste 201 Middletown (19709) *(G-7143)*

Fromms Automotive 717 202-9918
14519 Arvey Rd Laurel (19956) *(G-5515)*

Front Row Enterprises LLC 646 862-6380
901 N Market St Ste 705 Wilmington (19801) *(G-16762)*

Frontgate LLC 302 245-6654
33258 Kent Ave Bethany Beach (19930) *(G-602)*

Frontier Emerging Markets Fund 610 380-2110
4005 Kennett Pike Ste 250 Wilmington (19807) *(G-16763)*

Frontier Scientific Svcs Inc 302 266-6891
601 Interchange Blvd Newark (19711) *(G-10789)*

Frontier SGS 360 LLC 609 919-1133
1521 Concord Pike Ste 302 Wilmington (19803) *(G-16764)*

Frontierx Inc 201 313-6998
3500 S Dupont Hwy Dover (19901) *(G-2538)*

Frontline Crossfit 302 229-6467
4060 N Dupont Hwy # 1 New Castle (19720) *(G-9148)*

Fronza Media LLC 856 693-0975
1833 W 8th St Wilmington (19805) *(G-16765)*

Frozen Farmer LLC 302 337-8444
9843 Seashore Hwy Bridgeville (19933) *(G-702)*

Frst State Ceramics & Marble, Milton *Also Called: Robert McMann (G-8701)*

Fruitbearer Publishing LLC 302 856-6649
107 Elizabeth St Georgetown (19947) *(G-4327)*

FSA Network Inc 302 316-3200
60 Starlifter Avenue Dover (19901) *(G-2539)*

Fscom Inc 888 468-7419
380 Centerpoint Blvd Historic New Castle (19720) *(G-4994)*

Fsd Inc 302 629-7498
14596 Concord Rd Seaford (19973) *(G-13191)*

Fshery Mid-Atlntic MGT Council 302 674-2331
800 N State St Ste 201 Dover (19901) *(G-2540)*

Fsvap Usa Inc 248 639-8635
108 Lakeland Ave Dover (19901) *(G-2541)*

Ft Dupont Redevelopment A 302 838-7374
260 Old Elm Ave Delaware City (19706) *(G-1545)*

Ft Miles Historic Site 302 644-5007
15099 Cape Henlopen Dr Lewes (19958) *(G-6018)*

FTC Energy Ltd LLC 405 410-9040
1201 N Orange St Ste 600 Wilmington (19801) *(G-16766)*

Ftl Technologies Corporation 703 634-6910
16192 Coastal Hwy Lewes (19958) *(G-6019)*

Fuel Labs Inc 302 364-0442
501 Silverside Rd Ste 105 Wilmington (19809) *(G-16767)*

Fuelshaker, Wilmington *Also Called: Shaker Revolution LLC (G-19777)*

Fuinre Inc 402 480-6465
16192 Coastal Hwy Lewes (19958) *(G-6020)*

Fuji Film 302 477-8000
233 Cherry Ln New Castle (19720) *(G-9149)*

Fujifilm, New Castle *Also Called: Fujifilm Imaging Colorants Inc (G-9151)*

Fujifilm Imaging Colorants Inc 302 472-1298
109 Lukens Dr Historic New Castle (19720) *(G-4995)*

Fujifilm Imaging Colorants Inc (DH) 800 552-1609
233 Cherry Ln New Castle (19720) *(G-9150)*

Fujifilm Imaging Colorants Inc 302 472-1245
233 Cherry Ln New Castle (19720) *(G-9151)*

Fulcrum Assets LLC 615 278-0969
8 The Grn Ste A Dover (19901) *(G-2542)*

Fulcrum Pharmacy, Wilmington *Also Called: Fulcrum Pharmacy MGT Inc (G-16768)*

Fulcrum Pharmacy MGT Inc 302 658-8020
501 N Shipley St Wilmington (19801) *(G-16768)*

Full Support Technologies LLC 302 832-2307
930 Mather Dr Bear (19701) *(G-239)*

Full-Tilt Security 302 722-0275
238 Cornwell Dr Bear (19701) *(G-240)*

Fuller Aerial Solutions LLC 302 734-1541
7 Nixon Ln Dover (19901) *(G-2543)*

Fulton Bank National Assn 302 855-2406
21035 Dupont Blvd Georgetown (19947) *(G-4328)*

Fulton Bank National Assn 302 644-4900
34346 Carpenters Way Lewes (19958) *(G-6021)*

Fulton Bank National Assn 302 378-4575
468 W Main St Middletown (19709) *(G-7144)*

ALPHABETIC SECTION

Fulton Bank National Assn... 302 737-7766
   287 E Main St Unit 105 Newark (19711) *(G-10790)*

Fulton Bank National Assn... 302 539-8031
   60 Atlantic Ave Ocean View (19970) *(G-12515)*

Fulton Bank National Assn... 302 407-3291
   800 Foulk Rd Wilmington (19803) *(G-16769)*

Fulton Financial Advisors, Georgetown *Also Called: Fulton Bank National Assn (G-4328)*

Fulton Financial Advisors, Lewes *Also Called: Fulton Bank National Assn (G-6021)*

Fulton Financial Advisors, Middletown *Also Called: Fulton Bank National Assn (G-7144)*

Fulton Financial Advisors, Newark *Also Called: Fulton Bank National Assn (G-10790)*

Fulton Financial Advisors, Ocean View *Also Called: Fulton Bank National Assn (G-12515)*

Fulton Financial Advisors, Wilmington *Also Called: Fulton Bank National Assn (G-16769)*

Fulton Mechanical, Wilmington *Also Called: Phillip Fulton (G-19017)*

Fulton Paper, Middletown *Also Called: Forever Inc (G-7139)*

Fulton Paper & Party Supply, Wilmington *Also Called: Forever Inc (G-16692)*

Fulton Paper Co, Wilmington *Also Called: Fulton Paper Company (G-16770)*

Fulton Paper Company... 302 594-0400
   1006 W 27th St Wilmington (19802) *(G-16770)*

Fun 2 Learn Day Care... 302 875-3393
   7119 Airport Rd Laurel (19956) *(G-5516)*

Fun Adventures LLC... 302 223-5182
   531 W Main St Christiana (19702) *(G-996)*

Fun Bakery LLC.. 858 220-0946
   3500 S Dupont Hwy Dover (19901) *(G-2544)*

Fun Fit Vibe LLC... 302 249-8000
   1604 Savannah Rd Unit A Lewes (19958) *(G-6022)*

Fun Sport Inc... 302 644-2042
   Rr 1 Rehoboth Beach (19971) *(G-12762)*

Fund For The Walking Wounded... 302 947-9056
   21338 N Acorn Way Lewes (19958) *(G-6023)*

Fundomundo... 617 606-1650
   1401 Pennsylvania Ave Wilmington (19806) *(G-16771)*

Funfull Inc... 888 386-3855
   31236 Meadowview Sq Delmar (19940) *(G-1597)*

Funk & Bolton PA.. 302 735-8400
   426 S State St Dover (19901) *(G-2545)*

Funland, Rehoboth Beach *Also Called: Seaside Amusements Inc (G-12953)*

Funstep Inc... 302 731-9618
   1805 Capitol Trl Newark (19711) *(G-10791)*

Fuqua & Yori P A.. 302 856-7777
   26 The Cir Georgetown (19947) *(G-4329)*

Fuqua, James A Jr, Georgetown *Also Called: Fuqua & Yori P A (G-4329)*

Fur Baby.. 302 725-5078
   301 Ne Front St Milford (19963) *(G-7904)*

Fur Baby Tracker LLC.. 610 563-3294
   302 Taft Ave Wilmington (19805) *(G-16772)*

Furniture Solution, Bear *Also Called: Furniture Whl Connection Inc (G-241)*

Furniture Whl Connection Inc.. 302 836-6000
   1890 Pulaski Hwy Bear (19701) *(G-241)*

Furobinc LLC.. 302 202-4551
   2803 Philadelphia Pike Claymont (19703) *(G-1153)*

Furrer Inc.. 302 273-3109
   38 Executive Dr Newark (19702) *(G-10792)*

Furrs Tire Service Inc.. 302 678-0800
   1251 S Bay Rd Dover (19901) *(G-2546)*

Furtado Kim ND.. 302 945-2107
   35252 Hudson Way Rehoboth Beach (19971) *(G-12763)*

Fusco Enterprises (PA).. 302 328-6251
   200 Airport Rd New Castle (19720) *(G-9152)*

Fusco Enterprises, New Castle *Also Called: Fusco Management Inc (G-9153)*

Fusco Management Inc.. 302 328-6251
   200 Airport Rd New Castle (19720) *(G-9153)*

Fusion.. 302 479-9444
   3444 Naamans Rd 1st Fl Wilmington (19810) *(G-16773)*

Fusura LLC.. 302 397-2200
   800 Delaware Ave Ste 500 Wilmington (19801) *(G-16774)*

Future 50 Inc... 302 648-4665
   8 The Grn Ste A Dover (19901) *(G-2547)*

Future Analytica Software Inc... 437 771-2947
   8 The Grn Dover (19901) *(G-2548)*

Future Bright Pediatrics.. 302 883-3266
   938 S Bradford St Dover (19904) *(G-2549)*

Future Bright Pediatrics.. 609 744-2265
   121 Windrow Way Magnolia (19962) *(G-6746)*

Future Bright Pediatrics LLC (PA)... 302 538-6258
   120 Old Camden Rd Ste B Camden (19934) *(G-838)*

Future Cmpus - Tech Innvtion L.. 737 217-0321
   16192 Coastal Hwy Lewes (19958) *(G-6024)*

Future Dev Lrng Acdemy Fdla LL... 302 652-7500
   500 Maryland Ave Wilmington (19805) *(G-16775)*

Future Ford Sales Inc (PA)... 302 999-0261
   4001 Kirkwood Hwy Wilmington (19808) *(G-16776)*

Future Gold Technology Inc... 302 786-1388
   865 Powder Mill Rd Wilmington (19803) *(G-16777)*

Future Leaders... 862 262-7312
   906 Boxwood Dr Smyrna (19977) *(G-13740)*

Future Legacy of Dance... 610 400-7433
   401 Llangollen Blvd New Castle (19720) *(G-9154)*

Future Option Trading Company, Newark *Also Called: Futuretech Inv Group Inc (G-10793)*

Future Promises Foundation... 302 365-5735
   1745 Bear Corbitt Rd Bear (19701) *(G-242)*

Future Promises Foundation Inc... 302 689-3392
   807 N Union St Wilmington (19805) *(G-16778)*

Futureadvisor Inc.. 302 797-2000
   400 Bellevue Pkwy Wilmington (19809) *(G-16779)*

Futuretech Inv Group Inc... 302 476-9529
   12 Timber Creek Ln Newark (19711) *(G-10793)*

Fuzebits Inc... 302 533-8623
   1201 N Orange St Ste 7452 Wilmington (19801) *(G-16780)*

Fuzzy Fibersnet.. 302 737-0644
   25 Glencoe Dr Newark (19702) *(G-10794)*

Fwc2026 Us Inc... 469 505-2635
   251 Little Falls Dr Wilmington (19808) *(G-16781)*

FWd Contracting Entps LLC.. 302 377-3459
   1705 Talley Rd Wilmington (19803) *(G-16782)*

Fyve By Corp... 770 862-9152
   611 S Dupont Hwy Ste 102 Dover (19901) *(G-2550)*

G & A Repairs & Improvements, Newark *Also Called: Gustavo E Espinosa (G-10908)*

G & B Comp & Creative Design... 302 284-3856
   331 Drapers Mill Rd Felton (19943) *(G-3977)*

G & D Collection Group Inc... 302 482-2512
   234 Philadelphia Pike Ste 9 Wilmington (19809) *(G-16783)*

G & D Lawn Service, Townsend *Also Called: George J Martino (G-14007)*

G & E Welding Supply, New Castle *Also Called: G & E Welding Supply Co (G-9155)*

G & E Welding Supply Co.. 302 322-9353
   281 Airport Rd New Castle (19720) *(G-9155)*

G & S TV & Antenna... 302 422-5733
   20450 Sapp Rd Milford (19963) *(G-7905)*

G A Hastings & Associates.. 302 537-5760
   102 Central Ave Ste 1 Ocean View (19970) *(G-12516)*

G Alvarez Painting... 443 783-2240
   12329 Concord Rd Seaford (19973) *(G-13192)*

G B Lyons DDS.. 302 654-1765
   100 W Rockwind Rd Wilmington (19801) *(G-16784)*

G B Tech Inc... 302 378-5600
   651 N Broad St Ste 301 Middletown (19709) *(G-7145)*

G Custom Work LLC.. 302 353-2137
   186 N Dupont Hwy Ste 27 New Castle (19720) *(G-9156)*

G David Outten LLC... 302 747-4932
   114 E Third St Wyoming (19934) *(G-20985)*

G E N, Wilmington *Also Called: Global Network Executive Inc (G-16892)*

G Fedale General Contrs LLC.. 302 225-7663
   160 Thompson Dr Hockessin (19707) *(G-5216)*

G Fedale Roofing & Siding, Hockessin *Also Called: G Fedale General Contrs LLC (G-5216)*

G Fedale Roofing and Siding.. 302 225-7663
   101 S Mary St Wilmington (19804) *(G-16785)*

G G + A LLC.. 302 376-6122
   1050 Industrial Dr Ste 110 Middletown (19709) *(G-7146)*

G I Associates of Delaware, Dover *Also Called: GI Associates of Delaware (G-2581)*

G K Services 238... 302 629-6729
   415 Harrington St Seaford (19973) *(G-13193)*

(PA)=Parent Co (HQ)=Headquarters (DH)=Div Headquarters   2024 Harris Directory of Delaware Businesses

G L K Inc (PA) 302 697-3838
   55 Beloit Ave Dover (19901) *(G-2551)*

G M Construction LLC 302 462-5871
   21618 W Conley Cir Lewes (19958) *(G-6025)*

G N G Insurance, Wilmington *Also Called: Williams Insurance Agency Inc (G-20801)*

G Parker Contracting 302 304-2940
   225 Shorewind Rd Bear (19701) *(G-243)*

G Rehoboth 302 278-7677
   234 Rehoboth Ave Rehoboth Beach (19971) *(G-12764)*

G Spot Tattoos, The, Wilmington *Also Called: At The G Spot LLC (G-14613)*

G TS Foods Inc 302 376-3555
   428 E Main St Middletown (19709) *(G-7147)*

G W Keller DDS 302 652-3586
   1110 N Bancroft Pkwy Ste 2 Wilmington (19805) *(G-16786)*

G2 Group Inc 302 836-4202
   88 Loblolly Ln Bear (19701) *(G-244)*

G2 Lab Group, Bear *Also Called: G2 Group Inc (G-244)*

G2 Performance 302 293-1847
   23 Beagle Club Way Newark (19711) *(G-10795)*

G2 Performance Band ACC 800 554-8523
   2207 Concord Pike Ste 220 Wilmington (19803) *(G-16787)*

G4s Secure Solutions USA Inc 215 957-7603
   650 Naamans Rd Ste 200 Claymont (19703) *(G-1154)*

G5 Cyber Security (usa) Inc 302 570-0905
   651 N Broad St Ste 206 Middletown (19709) *(G-7148)*

GA Telesis LLC 845 356-8390
   251 Little Falls Dr Wilmington (19808) *(G-16788)*

Gabbaud Health LLC 267 512-1750
   406 Anchorage Ct Newark (19702) *(G-10796)*

Gabriel Jr Timoteo R MD 302 998-0300
   1941 Limestone Rd Ste 210 Wilmington (19808) *(G-16789)*

Gabrielle Freels 213 808-4907
   200 Banning St Ste 200 Dover (19904) *(G-2552)*

Gaby Auto 856 469-1378
   425 Stahl Ave New Castle (19720) *(G-9157)*

Gadde & Chirra Inc 302 384-6384
   4524 Kirkwood Hwy Wilmington (19808) *(G-16790)*

Gaea Property Development LLC 302 536-7646
   27964 Sussex Hwy Seaford (19973) *(G-13194)*

Gaetano N Pastore MD 302 994-3685
   1 Centurian Dr Ste 200 Newark (19713) *(G-10797)*

Gagl Sales LLC 302 299-0084
   847 Cranbrook Dr Wilmington (19803) *(G-16791)*

Gai Communications Inc 609 254-1470
   560 Peoples Plz 136 Newark (19702) *(G-10798)*

Gaichu Managed Services LLC 302 232-8420
   8 The Grn Ste 11236 Dover (19901) *(G-2553)*

Gail S Levinson 302 764-0474
   1303 Delaware Ave Ste 103 Wilmington (19806) *(G-16792)*

Gainor Awnings Inc 302 998-8611
   1 Elm Ave Wilmington (19805) *(G-16793)*

Galaxy Plus Fund - Lrr Mstr Fu 312 504-0096
   850 New Burton Rd Ste 201 Dover (19904) *(G-2554)*

Galaxy Sign & Lighting 302 757-5349
   2117 Armour Dr Wilmington (19808) *(G-16794)*

Galaxyworks LLC 404 894-8703
   8 The Grn Ste 5008 Dover (19901) *(G-2555)*

Gale Force Cleaning & Restore 302 539-6244
   14 Atlantic Ave Ocean View (19970) *(G-12517)*

Galerie Media Inc 917 685-4168
   154 W Rutherford Dr Newark (19713) *(G-10799)*

Gallagher & Associates PA 302 239-5501
   5500 Skyline Dr Ste 6 Wilmington (19808) *(G-16795)*

Gallery 107, Seaford *Also Called: Nanticoke River Arts Council (G-13309)*

Gallery 37 .... 413 297-2690
   8 S Walnut St Milford (19963) *(G-7906)*

Gallery One 302 537-5055
   125 Atlantic Ave Ocean View (19967) *(G-12518)*

Gallium US Holdings Inc 713 213-0644
   1209 N Orange St Wilmington (19801) *(G-16796)*

Gallo Realty Inc 888 624-6794
   33292 Coastal Hwy Unit 1 Bethany Beach (19930) *(G-603)*

Gallo Realty Inc (PA) 302 945-7368
   37230 Rehoboth Avenue Ext Rehoboth Beach (19971) *(G-12765)*

Gallo Tree Service, Hockessin *Also Called: Ryan Gallo Tree Service Inc (G-5375)*

Galloway Electric Co Inc 302 453-8385
   19 Albe Dr Newark (19702) *(G-10800)*

Galloway Leasing Inc 302 453-8385
   19 Albe Dr Newark (19702) *(G-10801)*

Galman Group Ltd 302 328-8149
   30 Highland Blvd New Castle (19720) *(G-9158)*

Galman Group Ltd 215 886-2000
   146 Chestnut Crossing Dr Newark (19713) *(G-10802)*

Galman Group Inc 302 737-5550
   25b Windsor Cir Newark (19702) *(G-10803)*

Galtogether Group 302 562-9170
   187 Odyssey Dr Wilmington (19808) *(G-16797)*

Galvin Industries LLC 703 505-7860
   202 W Laurel St Georgetown (19947) *(G-4330)*

Gambers LLC 402 218-7929
   221 N Broad St Middletown (19709) *(G-7149)*

Game Genius Innovations LLC 321 588-7798
   1007 N Orange St Fl 4 Wilmington (19801) *(G-16798)*

Game Labs Inc 385 444-5639
   1000 N West St Ste 1200 Wilmington (19801) *(G-16799)*

Gamefort LLC 302 645-7400
   16192 Coastal Hwy Lewes (19958) *(G-6026)*

Gamers4gamers LLC 302 722-6289
   40 E Main St Ste 649 Newark (19711) *(G-10804)*

Gamersunite Inc 760 284-5588
   601 N Broad St Ste 201 Middletown (19709) *(G-7150)*

Gamestop Inc 302 266-7362
   326 Suburban Dr Newark (19711) *(G-10805)*

Gaming Entertainment Del LLC 302 398-4920
   15 W Rider Rd Harrington (19952) *(G-4771)*

Gaming Morning Report, Dover *Also Called: Morning Report Research Inc (G-3123)*

Gamma Theta Lmbda Edcatn Fndti 302 983-9429
   2 N Sherman Dr Bear (19701) *(G-245)*

Gamut Color Inc 302 652-7171
   1600 N Scott St Wilmington (19806) *(G-16800)*

Ganc Commercial Realty LLC 302 292-1131
   105 Briggs Ln Newark (19711) *(G-10806)*

Gander Construction 302 424-4007
   510 Caulk Rd Milford (19963) *(G-7907)*

Ganvix Inc 508 904-3045
   1 Righter Pkwy Wilmington (19803) *(G-16801)*

Gap Innovations Pbc 203 464-7048
   8 The Grn Ste B Dover (19901) *(G-2556)*

Garage 302 453-1930
   132 Christiana Mall Newark (19702) *(G-10807)*

Garage 302 645-7288
   4544 Highway One Rehoboth Beach (19971) *(G-12766)*

Garcia & Sons LLC 302 562-8878
   106 Fox Dr Newark (19713) *(G-10808)*

Garcia Moises LLC 302 698-1930
   507 Rising Sun Rd Camden Wyoming (19934) *(G-948)*

Garcia Podiatry Group 302 994-5956
   1941 Limestone Rd Ste 208 Wilmington (19808) *(G-16802)*

Garcia, Luis M Jr DPM, Wilmington *Also Called: Garcia Podiatry Group (G-16802)*

Garcias Auto Repair 302 464-1118
   213 W Lake St Middletown (19709) *(G-7151)*

Garda CL Atlantic Inc (HQ) 302 762-5444
   4200 Governor Printz Blvd Wilmington (19802) *(G-16803)*

Garde-Robe Inc 347 986-0455
   874 Walker Rd Ste C Dover (19904) *(G-2557)*

Garden Bears Landscaping, Rehoboth Beach *Also Called: Mark A Horne (G-12848)*

Garden Design Group Inc 302 234-3000
   787 Valley Rd Hockessin (19707) *(G-5217)*

Gardner Industries Inc 302 448-9195
   25938 Nanticoke Ave Seaford (19973) *(G-13195)*

Gardner-Gibson Mfg Inc 302 628-4290
   25938 Nanticoke Ave Seaford (19973) *(G-13196)*

Garg Manish MD 302 355-2383
   2006 Limestone Rd Ste 7 Wilmington (19808) *(G-16804)*

ALPHABETIC SECTION

Garile Inc 302 366-0848
  311 Ruthar Dr Newark (19711) *(G-10809)*

Garland Thompson Agency 302 407-6260
  4 E 8th St Ste 200 Wilmington (19801) *(G-16805)*

Garland Thompson Agency 302 407-6262
  1211 N King St Wilmington (19801) *(G-16806)*

Garret Thomas Pusey LLC 302 875-9146
  412 E 4th St Laurel (19956) *(G-5517)*

Garrett Mechanical & Advanced 302 632-6261
  134 S Shore Dr Dover (19901) *(G-2558)*

Garrett Motion Inc (DH) 973 867-7017
  251 Little Falls Dr Wilmington (19808) *(G-16807)*

Garretts Trucking LLC 302 415-1794
  632 Candlestick Ln Newark (19702) *(G-10810)*

Garri Inc 319 538-4071
  256 Chapman Rd Newark (19702) *(G-10811)*

Garrison Calpine 302 562-5661
  450 Garrison Oak Dr Dover (19901) *(G-2559)*

Garrison Custom Homes 302 644-4008
  19413 Jingle Shell Way Unit 5 Lewes (19958) *(G-6027)*

Garrisons Lake Golf Club Inc 302 659-1206
  101 W Fairways Cir Smyrna (19977) *(G-13741)*

Garritz Advertising LLC 347 607-7030
  8 The Grn Ste 6322 Dover (19901) *(G-2560)*

Garry F Kuhlman Gen Contractor 302 482-3535
  1580 Snuff Mill Rd Hockessin (19707) *(G-5218)*

Garth Enterprises Ltd 302 349-2298
  37428 Dirickson Creek Rd Frankford (19945) *(G-4109)*

Gary Chorman 302 645-2972
  29545 Canvasback Xing Milton (19968) *(G-8627)*

Gary Gerace 302 320-2100
  205 W 14th St Wilmington (19801) *(G-16808)*

Gary L Waite DMD 302 239-8586
  5500 Skyline Dr Ste 2 Wilmington (19808) *(G-16809)*

Gary M Munch Inc 302 525-8301
  995 S Chapel St Ste 1 Newark (19713) *(G-10812)*

Gary P Simpson Contracting LLC 302 398-7733
  1994 Fox Hunters Rd Harrington (19952) *(G-4772)*

Gary Quiroga 302 697-3352
  34 S Fairfield Dr Dover (19901) *(G-2561)*

Gary R Collins DDS 302 239-3531
  5500 Skyline Dr Ste 1 Wilmington (19808) *(G-16810)*

Gas & Go Inc 302 734-8234
  805 Forest St Dover (19904) *(G-2562)*

GAs Contracting Inc 302 875-2302
  16091 Willow Way Laurel (19956) *(G-5518)*

Gastro Girl Inc 202 579-1057
  8 The Grn Unit 8109 Dover (19901) *(G-2563)*

Gastroenterology Associates PA (PA) 302 738-5300
  4745 Ogletown Stanton Rd Ste 134 Newark (19713) *(G-10813)*

Gastromind Inc 302 252-8401
  1401 Pennsylvania Ave Ste 105 Wilmington (19806) *(G-16811)*

Gatehouse Media Inc 302 678-3616
  1196 S Little Creek Rd Dover (19901) *(G-2564)*

Gatekeeper Systems USA Inc 434 477-6596
  221 Valley Rd Wilmington (19804) *(G-16812)*

Gatello Inc 725 333-3830
  256 Chapman Rd Newark (19702) *(G-10814)*

Gates and Company, Wilmington *Also Called: Gates and Company LLC (G-16813)*

Gates and Company LLC 302 428-1338
  4914 Threadneedle Rd Wilmington (19807) *(G-16813)*

Gatesair Inc 513 459-3400
  2711 Centerville Rd Wilmington (19808) *(G-16814)*

Gateway Construction Inc 302 653-4400
  498 Sudlersville Rd Clayton (19938) *(G-1368)*

Gateway House Inc 302 571-8885
  121 N Poplar St Apt A11 Wilmington (19801) *(G-16815)*

Gateway International 360 LLC 302 250-4990
  159 Meridian Blvd Bear (19701) *(G-246)*

Gather Social Tech Corp 604 356-0981
  300 Creek View Rd Newark (19711) *(G-10815)*

Gator Construction Llc 302 430-1160
  26136 Gvernor Stockley Rd Georgetown (19947) *(G-4331)*

GATX Trmnals Ovrseas Hldg Corp 302 636-5400
  251 Little Falls Dr Wilmington (19808) *(G-16816)*

Gaudenzia Fresh Start, Wilmington *Also Called: Gaudenzia Inc (G-16817)*

Gaudenzia Inc 302 836-8260
  171 New Castle Ave Delaware City (19706) *(G-1546)*

Gaudenzia Inc 302 421-9945
  604 W 10th St Wilmington (19801) *(G-16817)*

Gauge Girl Training LLC 267 471-7104
  41 Ross Rd Wilmington (19810) *(G-16818)*

Gavinsolmonese 302 655-8997
  919 N Market St Wilmington (19801) *(G-16819)*

Gawthrop Greenwood PC 302 351-1273
  3711 Kennett Pike Ste 100 Wilmington (19807) *(G-16820)*

Gb Home Improvement 302 654-5411
  100 Greenhill Ave Ste F # G Wilmington (19805) *(G-16821)*

Gb Jacobs LLC 302 378-9100
  2486 N Dupont Pkwy Middletown (19709) *(G-7152)*

Gb Shades LLC (PA) 302 798-3028
  100 Naamans Rd Ste 5f Claymont (19703) *(G-1155)*

Gbana Entertainment LLC 302 307-1695
  28b Trolley Sq Wilmington (19806) *(G-16822)*

Gbc Business Group LLC 970 644-6319
  2055 Limestone Rd Ste 200c Wilmington (19808) *(G-16823)*

Gbc International Corp (PA) 404 860-2533
  2711 Centerville Rd Ste 400 Wilmington (19808) *(G-16824)*

GBS Backup LLC 302 907-9099
  16192 Coastal Hwy Lewes (19958) *(G-6028)*

Gc New Castle Inc 302 544-6128
  1508 Beaver Brook Plz New Castle (19720) *(G-9159)*

Gcl A, Wilmington *Also Called: Garda CL Atlantic Inc (G-16803)*

Gcora Corp 302 310-1000
  3616 Kirkwood Hwy Ste A Wilmington (19808) *(G-16825)*

Gdf Financial, Claymont *Also Called: United Check Cashing (G-1322)*

Gdk Services LLC 929 242-8422
  8 The Grn Ste 11464 Dover (19901) *(G-2565)*

Gdt Properties Inc 302 737-3778
  302 Gabor Dr Newark (19711) *(G-10816)*

GE, Newark *Also Called: General Electric Company (G-10819)*

GE Energy Ceramic Composite Products LLC 302 631-1300
  400 Bellevue Rd Newark (19713) *(G-10817)*

Geared Up Trucks and More 302 927-0147
  34407 Dupont Blvd Frankford (19945) *(G-4110)*

Gearhalo US Inc 780 239-2120
  8 The Grn Dover (19901) *(G-2566)*

Gearhart Construction Inc 302 674-5466
  5075 N Dupont Hwy Dover (19901) *(G-2567)*

Gears Garage LLC 302 653-3684
  282 Deer Run Rd Townsend (19734) *(G-14005)*

Gears Mechanical Company, Frankford *Also Called: Robert Gears (G-4139)*

Gebhart Funeral Home Inc 302 798-7726
  3401 Philadelphia Pike Claymont (19703) *(G-1156)*

Geeksoft, Dover *Also Called: Geeksoft Inc (G-2568)*

Geeksoft Inc 669 278-8022
  8 The Grn Ste 11988 Dover (19901) *(G-2568)*

Geekytek, Rehoboth Beach *Also Called: M C Tek LLC (G-12842)*

Gellert Scali Busenkell Brown, Wilmington *Also Called: GSB&b LLC (G-16994)*

Gem Group LP 302 762-2008
  501 Carr Rd Wilmington (19809) *(G-16826)*

Gem Productions 302 650-6725
  6 Amaranth Dr Newark (19711) *(G-10818)*

Gem School Inc 302 464-1711
  100 Patriot Dr Middletown (19709) *(G-7153)*

Gemcraft Homes At Summercrest 302 703-6763
  34795 Mute Swan Ln Rehoboth Beach (19971) *(G-12767)*

Gemini Building Systems LLC 302 654-5310
  1607 E Newport Pike Wilmington (19804) *(G-16827)*

Gemini Hair Designs 302 654-9371
  2207 Baynard Blvd Wilmington (19802) *(G-16828)*

Gemini Kustoms LLC 267 318-4121
  105 Fowler Ct New Castle (19720) *(G-9160)*

Gemini Qulty Frt Solutions LLC 302 219-3310
8 The Grn Ste 16368 Dover (19901) *(G-2569)*

Gen Digital Inc 650 527-8000
1209 N Orange St Wilmington (19801) *(G-16829)*

Genco 302 588-5872
2803 B Philly Pike Ste 112 Claymont (19703) *(G-1157)*

Gene Guard Inc (PA) 248 479-3623
651 N Broad St Ste 206 Middletown (19709) *(G-7154)*

Gene Tffin A Ray Fmly Fndation 800 839-1754
501 Silverside Rd Ste 123 Wilmington (19809) *(G-16830)*

General Automotive Repair, Dover *Also Called: Patriot Auto & Truck Care LLC (G-3282)*

General Chapter Eastern Star, Newark *Also Called: Order of The Eastern Star Del (G-11598)*

General Coatings LLC 302 841-7958
26492 Shasta Way Millsboro (19966) *(G-8297)*

General Contractor 302 241-8285
4306 Miller Rd Apt 109 Wilmington (19802) *(G-16831)*

General Electric Company 302 631-1300
400 Bellevue Rd Newark (19713) *(G-10819)*

General Freight, Wilmington *Also Called: Hackett Industries LLC (G-17029)*

General Merchandise & Svcs LLC 302 690-8662
11 Mccormick Dr Hockessin (19707) *(G-5219)*

General Refrigeration Company (PA) 302 846-3073
34971 Sussex Hwy Delmar (19940) *(G-1598)*

General Service Contrs LLC 302 220-1946
729 Grantham Ln New Castle (19720) *(G-9161)*

Generate Nb Fuel Cells LLC 415 360-3063
251 Little Falls Dr Wilmington (19808) *(G-16832)*

Generation Cleaning Svc LLC 302 492-2772
605 New York Ave Claymont (19703) *(G-1158)*

Generation Electrical Svcs LLC 302 298-1868
128 Edgar Rd Townsend (19734) *(G-14006)*

Generation Glory Ministries 302 438-4335
302 W Matson Run Pkwy Wilmington (19802) *(G-16833)*

Generations Home Care Inc 302 322-3100
5211 W Woodmill Dr Wilmington (19808) *(G-16834)*

Generations Home Care Inc 302 856-7774
5211 W Woodmill Dr # 36 Wilmington (19808) *(G-16835)*

Generations Wldg & Contg LLC 302 430-4099
14716 Laurel Rd Laurel (19956) *(G-5519)*

Genes Limousine Service Inc 410 479-8470
501 Market St Bridgeville (19933) *(G-703)*

Genesec Inc 917 656-5742
62 Lake Forest Blvd Claymont (19703) *(G-1159)*

Genesis, Wilmington *Also Called: Genesis Hlthcare Ctrs Hldngs I (G-16836)*

Genesis Automobile Acquirers 757 717-1673
138 Banff St Bear (19701) *(G-247)*

Genesis Cleaners 302 827-2095
17601 Coastal Hwy Lewes (19958) *(G-6029)*

Genesis Deer Farm, Hartly *Also Called: Edward Krupka (G-4872)*

GENESIS HEALTH CARE, Wilmington *Also Called: Hillside Center (G-17147)*

Genesis Healthcare Corporation 302 422-3754
700 Marvel Rd Milford (19963) *(G-7908)*

GENESIS HEALTHCARE CORPORATION, Milford *Also Called: Genesis Healthcare Corporation (G-7908)*

Genesis Hlthcare Ctrs Hldngs I 302 652-4720
103 Foulk Rd Ste 202 Wilmington (19803) *(G-16836)*

Genesis Laboratories Inc (PA) 832 217-8585
11 Middleton Dr Wilmington (19808) *(G-16837)*

Genesis Psychological Services 302 513-7156
7503 Lancaster Pike Hockessin (19707) *(G-5220)*

Geneva Hotel LLC 440 901-2030
251 Little Falls Dr Wilmington (19808) *(G-16838)*

Genex Strategies 302 356-1522
73 Greentree Dr Dover (19904) *(G-2570)*

Genki Forest (america) Inc 626 456-2664
108 W 13th St Wilmington (19801) *(G-16839)*

Genohm Inc 646 616-7531
2915 Ogletown Rd Newark (19713) *(G-10820)*

Genovesius Solutia Llc 302 252-7506
521 Cabot Dr Hockessin (19707) *(G-5221)*

Gensource, Wilmington *Also Called: Gensource Fincl Asrn Co LLC (G-16840)*

Gensource Fincl Asrn Co LLC 302 415-3030
3422 Old Capitol Trl Wilmington (19808) *(G-16840)*

Genspec Materials Inc 302 777-1100
1201 N Orange St Ste 700 Wilmington (19801) *(G-16841)*

Gentle Care Family Dentistry, Wilmington *Also Called: Rodriguez Marieve O Dmd PA (G-19553)*

Gentle Touch Dentistry 302 765-3373
303 E Lea Blvd Wilmington (19802) *(G-16842)*

Gentleman Door Company Inc 302 239-4045
506 Dawson Tract Rd Yorklyn (19736) *(G-20992)*

Genuine Parts Company 610 494-6355
319 Ridge Rd Claymont (19703) *(G-1160)*

Genun Games Inc 425 344-4883
1013 Centre Rd Ste 403b Wilmington (19805) *(G-16843)*

Geo B Schreppler III 302 678-5959
1425 New Burton Rd Dover (19904) *(G-2571)*

Geo Transport Auto Export LLC 302 322-9001
235 S Dupont Hwy New Castle (19720) *(G-9162)*

Geo-Plus Corporation 800 672-1733
2915 Ogletown Rd Newark (19713) *(G-10821)*

Geo-Technology Associates Inc 302 855-5775
21491 Baltimore Ave # 1 Georgetown (19947) *(G-4332)*

Geo-Technology Associates Inc 302 326-2100
18 Boulden Cir Ste 36 New Castle (19720) *(G-9163)*

Geodesic Management LLC 302 737-2151
15 Split Rail Ln Newark (19702) *(G-10822)*

Geological Survey US Dept 302 734-2506
300 S New St Dover (19904) *(G-2572)*

GEOLOGICAL SURVEY, UNITED STATES DEPARTMENT OF, Dover *Also Called: Geological Survey US Dept (G-2572)*

George Miles & Buhr LLC 302 628-1421
400 High St Seaford (19973) *(G-13197)*

George & Lynch Inc (PA) 302 736-3031
150 Lafferty Ln Dover (19901) *(G-2573)*

George & Lynch Inc 302 238-7289
20631 Betts Rd Millsboro (19966) *(G-8298)*

George E Frattali DDS 302 651-4408
1801 Rockland Rd Ste 100 Wilmington (19803) *(G-16844)*

George H Bunting Jr 302 227-3891
19716 Sea Air Ave # 1 Rehoboth Beach (19971) *(G-12768)*

George H Burns Inc 302 658-0752
200 N Ford Ave Wilmington (19805) *(G-16845)*

George J Martino 302 376-5162
440 Dogtown Rd Townsend (19734) *(G-14007)*

George J Weiner Associates 302 658-0218
2711 Centerville Rd Wilmington (19808) *(G-16846)*

George K Horeis 302 398-8684
3822 Fox Hunters Rd Harrington (19952) *(G-4773)*

George Marcus Salon Inc 302 475-7530
3629 Silverside Rd Ste 1 Wilmington (19810) *(G-16847)*

George Metz 302 227-4343
713 Rehoboth Ave Rehoboth Beach (19971) *(G-12769)*

George Minkalis 302 983-6475
104 Lynch Farm Dr Newark (19713) *(G-10823)*

George P Stewart 302 737-4927
488 Walther Rd Newark (19702) *(G-10824)*

George Products Company Inc 302 449-0199
110 Sleepy Hollow Dr Middletown (19709) *(G-7155)*

George Read II House, Historic New Castle *Also Called: Historical Society of Delaware (G-5005)*

George Scott Paving 302 588-0024
502 Isadore Dr New Castle (19720) *(G-9164)*

George Swire Sr 302 690-6995
790 Daisey Rd Clayton (19938) *(G-1369)*

George W Oppel 302 398-4433
3202 Gun And Rod Club Rd Houston (19954) *(G-5442)*

George W Plummer & Son Inc 302 645-9531
18370 Coastal Hwy Lewes (19958) *(G-6030)*

Georges Trees Plus LLC 302 539-0660
209 Woodland Ct Dagsboro (19939) *(G-1452)*

Georgetown, Georgetown *Also Called: Boys & Girls Clubs Del Inc (G-4238)*

ALPHABETIC SECTION

Georgetown Air Services.. 302 855-2355
  21553 Rudder Ln Unit 1 Georgetown (19947) *(G-4333)*
Georgetown Air Services LLC... 302 855-2355
  21553 Rudder Ln Unit 1 Georgetown (19947) *(G-4334)*
Georgetown Animal Hospital PA.. 302 856-2623
  20784 Dupont Blvd Georgetown (19947) *(G-4335)*
Georgetown Boys and Girls Club.. 302 856-4903
  115 N Race St Georgetown (19947) *(G-4336)*
Georgetown Construction Co... 302 856-7601
  25136 Dupont Blvd Georgetown (19947) *(G-4337)*
Georgetown Family Medicine... 302 856-4092
  201 W Market St Georgetown (19947) *(G-4338)*
Georgetown Hotel LLC.. 302 515-2100
  301 College Park Ln Georgetown (19947) *(G-4339)*
Georgetown Manor Apartments... 302 328-6231
  260 Christiana Rd Ofc B4 New Castle (19720) *(G-9165)*
Georgetown Medical Assoc LLC... 302 856-3737
  20930 Dupont Blvd Unit 101 Georgetown (19947) *(G-4340)*
Georgetown Playground & Pk Inc....................................... 302 856-7111
  212 Wilson St Georgetown (19947) *(G-4341)*
Georve V Sawyer.. 302 736-1474
  2296 Forrest Ave Dover (19904) *(G-2574)*
Geospot Community LLC... 570 504-4115
  211 Amstel Way Newark (19711) *(G-10825)*
Geosyntec Holdings LLC.. 561 995-0900
  251 Little Falls Dr Wilmington (19808) *(G-16848)*
Geotech LLC... 302 353-9769
  1600 Newport Gap Pike Wilmington (19808) *(G-16849)*
Gerald 1mccarthy... 302 836-3171
  1061 Dutch Neck Rd Middletown (19709) *(G-7156)*
Geraldine M Vota... 302 762-2283
  33712 Wescoats Rd Unit 4 Lewes (19958) *(G-6031)*
Gerard Joseph Capano.. 302 658-3505
  1105 Hillside Rd Greenville (19807) *(G-4584)*
Gerardi Construction Inc... 302 745-6252
  404 Jarrells Rd Felton (19943) *(G-3978)*
Gerardos Marble & Granite LLC... 302 344-6150
  314 Bay West Blvd New Castle (19720) *(G-9166)*
Geriatric & Palliative Svcs... 302 438-5440
  104 Jade Dr Wilmington (19810) *(G-16850)*
Geris Auto Financial Svcs LLC.. 302 660-9719
  23 Geneva Ct Apt B4 Newark (19702) *(G-10826)*
Germ Network Inc.. 773 965-7004
  2810 N Church St Pmb 57729 Wilmington (19802) *(G-16851)*
Germantown Medical Associates....................................... 484 431-5226
  420 Derby Way Wilmington (19810) *(G-16852)*
Gerone C Hudson Elec Contr... 302 539-3332
  35944 Bayard Rd Frankford (19945) *(G-4111)*
Gerry Gray.. 302 856-4101
  63 White Rabbit Dr Smyrna (19977) *(G-13742)*
Ges-Bay West Joint Venture LLC.. 302 918-3070
  70 Albe Dr Newark (19702) *(G-10827)*
Gesso Labs Inc... 888 206-4024
  2810 N Church St Wilmington (19802) *(G-16853)*
Get Takeout LLC... 800 785-6218
  16192 Coastal Hwy Lewes (19958) *(G-6032)*
Getbit Technologies Inc.. 425 647-3121
  16192 Coastal Hwy Lewes (19958) *(G-6033)*
Getbit.money, Lewes *Also Called: Getbit Technologies Inc (G-6033)*
Getblend Inc.. 800 720-3722
  16192 Coastal Hwy Lewes (19958) *(G-6034)*
Getcarrier LLC.. 302 763-3040
  8 The Grn Ste 7362 Dover (19901) *(G-2575)*
Geter Done Mechanical... 302 727-3291
  231 Lewis Dr Laurel (19956) *(G-5520)*
Getrentacar Inc (PA)... 786 460-8707
  9 E Loockerman St Dover (19901) *(G-2576)*
Getresponse Inc... 302 573-3895
  1011 Centre Rd Ste 322 Wilmington (19805) *(G-16854)*
Gettakeout.com, Lewes *Also Called: Get Takeout LLC (G-6032)*
Gettier Security.. 302 652-2700
  1901 Ogletown Rd Newark (19711) *(G-10828)*
Gettier Security, Wilmington *Also Called: JR Gettier & Associates Inc (G-17600)*
Gettier Staffing Services Inc.. 302 478-0911
  2 Centerville Rd Wilmington (19808) *(G-16855)*
Gevme Inc... 302 335-7150
  8 The Grn Ste A Dover (19901) *(G-2577)*
Gfc Leasing LLC.. 302 449-5006
  4783 Summit Bridge Rd Middletown (19709) *(G-7157)*
Gfc Logistics LLC.. 302 203-9511
  200 Continental Dr Ste 401 Newark (19713) *(G-10829)*
Gfl Environmental, Millsboro *Also Called: Waste Industries Delaware LLC (G-8500)*
Gfp Cement Contractors LLC... 302 998-7687
  14 Hadco Rd Wilmington (19804) *(G-16856)*
Gfp Mobile Mix Supply LLC.. 302 998-7687
  14 Hadco Rd Wilmington (19804) *(G-16857)*
Gfrs Construction One LLC.. 484 357-5218
  37138 Pinewood Rd Ocean View (19970) *(G-12519)*
Gga, Georgetown *Also Called: Geo-Technology Associates Inc (G-4332)*
Gga Construction.. 302 376-5193
  1285 Cedar Lane Rd Middletown (19709) *(G-7158)*
Gga Construction.. 302 376-6122
  1130 Industrial Dr Middletown (19709) *(G-7159)*
Gga Consulting Group LLC... 302 307-3443
  8 The Grn Ste 16721 Dover (19901) *(G-2578)*
Gga Global Consulting LLC.. 302 238-1751
  8 The Grn # 16722 Dover (19901) *(G-2579)*
Ggb Solutions Inc... 202 999-5313
  8 The Grn Ste G Dover (19901) *(G-2580)*
Ggc Inc... 267 893-8052
  19544 Pine Rd Lincoln (19960) *(G-6670)*
Gge Amusements... 302 227-0661
  34974 Oyster House Rd Rehoboth Beach (19971) *(G-12770)*
Ght Autoglass... 302 494-4369
  15 Merriman Rd Newark (19713) *(G-10830)*
GI Associates of Delaware... 302 678-5008
  742 S Governors Ave Ste 3 Dover (19904) *(G-2581)*
GI Ondemand, Dover *Also Called: Gastro Girl Inc (G-2563)*
GI Specialists of De.. 302 832-1545
  2600 Glasgow Ave Ste 106 Newark (19702) *(G-10831)*
Gian-Co... 302 798-7100
  2 Stockdale Ave Claymont (19703) *(G-1161)*
Gibbons Innovations Inc... 302 265-4220
  10633 W Yellowood Dr Lincoln (19960) *(G-6671)*
Gibellino Construction Co Inc... 302 455-0500
  1213 Old Coochs Bridge Rd Newark (19713) *(G-10832)*
Gibson Glynis... 302 730-1300
  186 Macananny Ln Felton (19943) *(G-3979)*
GIERD INC... 206 289-0011
  2810 N Church St Ste 24479 Wilmington (19802) *(G-16858)*
Giesela Inc.. 855 556-4338
  2035 Sunset Lake Rd Ste B2 Newark (19702) *(G-10833)*
Gif North America LLC.. 703 969-9243
  18227 Shockley Dr Rehoboth Beach (19971) *(G-12771)*
Gift Love Early Learning Ctr.. 302 659-1984
  115 E North St Smyrna (19977) *(G-13743)*
Gifted Hands 2 LLC... 302 643-2005
  500 Isabelle Isle Apt 106 Dover (19904) *(G-2582)*
Giftpass App Inc... 310 529-7566
  1675 S State St Ste B Dover (19901) *(G-2583)*
Gifty A Nyinaku LPN... 571 224-2660
  315 Valley Stream Dr Newark (19702) *(G-10834)*
Gigahub Inc... 916 304-4710
  8 The Grn Ste A Dover (19901) *(G-2584)*
Gigglebugs Early Learning Ctr... 302 934-5437
  213 W State St Millsboro (19966) *(G-8299)*
Gigis Laundry Room... 302 764-7777
  3612 Miller Rd Wilmington (19802) *(G-16859)*
Gigkloud Inc.. 301 375-5008
  16192 Coastal Hwy Lewes (19958) *(G-6035)*
Gil Vansciver... 302 736-3000
  3156 Forrest Ave Dover (19904) *(G-2585)*
Gilante Scientific LLC... 302 317-6060
  18 Shea Way Ste 106 Newark (19713) *(G-10835)*

Gilbert Architects Inc 302 449-2492
  100 S Broad St Middletown (19709) *(G-7160)*

Gilbert Perry Center For Arts 302 378-2932
  51 W Main St Middletown (19709) *(G-7161)*

Gildea Enterprises Inc 302 420-8900
  2100 Willow Way Wilmington (19810) *(G-16860)*

Giles Enterprise 302 559-2577
  4142 Ogletown Stanton Rd Newark (19713) *(G-10836)*

Giles, Christopher MD, Dover *Also Called: Jarrell Benson Giles & Sweeney (G-2772)*

Gill Edward Law Offices of 302 854-5400
  16 N Bedford St Georgetown (19947) *(G-4342)*

Gillespiehall, Wilmington *Also Called: Bgp Publicity Inc (G-14872)*

Gilliam & Garca RE Inv Co LLC 302 377-5764
  700 W 32nd St Wilmington (19802) *(G-16861)*

Gilpin Avenue Fitness Inc 302 654-6385
  1406 Gilpin Ave Wilmington (19806) *(G-16862)*

GILPIN HALL, Wilmington *Also Called: Home For Aged Wmn-Mnquadale HM (G-17178)*

Gilpin Medical Center 302 623-4250
  1021 Gilpin Ave Ste 100 Wilmington (19806) *(G-16863)*

Gilpin Mortgage 302 656-5400
  1400 N Dupont St Wilmington (19806) *(G-16864)*

Gina Health LLC 573 529-9858
  8 The Grn Ste R Dover (19901) *(G-2586)*

Gina K Alderson MD 302 628-7730
  24488 Sussex Hwy Ste 6 Seaford (19973) *(G-13198)*

Gina M Freeman DPM 302 765-2505
  1800 N Broom St Ste 109b Wilmington (19802) *(G-16865)*

Ginch Gonch Corp 713 240-9900
  2915 Ogletown Rd Newark (19713) *(G-10837)*

Giordano Delcollo & Werb LLC 302 234-6855
  5315 Limestone Rd Wilmington (19808) *(G-16866)*

Giordano, Delcollo Werb Gdw, Wilmington *Also Called: Giordano Delcollo & Werb LLC (G-16866)*

Giordano, Lawrence S, Wilmington *Also Called: Peter F Subach (G-18993)*

Giorgi Kitchens Inc 302 762-1121
  4 Meco Cir Wilmington (19804) *(G-16867)*

Girasol Payment Solutions LLC 561 866-4343
  1209 N Orange St Wilmington (19801) *(G-16868)*

Girl Scuts of Chspake Bay Cnci (PA) 302 456-7150
  225 Old Baltimore Pike Newark (19702) *(G-10838)*

Girley Bells LLC 347 922-6398
  28 Iris Ln Newark (19702) *(G-10839)*

Girleybells.com, Newark *Also Called: Girley Bells LLC (G-10839)*

Girls Auto Clinic LLC 484 679-6394
  35 Antioch Ct New Castle (19720) *(G-9167)*

Girls Incorporate of Delaware (PA) 302 575-1041
  1019 Brown St Wilmington (19805) *(G-16869)*

Girls Incorporate of Delaware 302 575-1041
  1501 N Market St Ste 100 Wilmington (19801) *(G-16870)*

Girls Incorporated of Delaware, Wilmington *Also Called: Girls Incorporate of Delaware (G-16870)*

Girls On Run 302 668-1720
  615 W 18th St Wilmington (19802) *(G-16871)*

Gisco Logistics LLC 800 226-3696
  462 Welsh Hill Rd Newark (19702) *(G-10840)*

Gitduck Inc 415 969-3825
  2093 Philadelphia Pike Claymont (19703) *(G-1162)*

Give Back Beauty LLC 571 439-2321
  8 The Grn Ste 4220 Dover (19901) *(G-2587)*

Give From The Heart-The Doroth 302 322-7808
  6 Fairhaven Ct New Castle (19720) *(G-9168)*

Give ME Shelter 302 420-0402
  209 Megan Ct Newark (19702) *(G-10841)*

Givesendgo, Dover *Also Called: Givesendgo LLC (G-2588)*

Givesendgo LLC 302 404-6778
  8 The Grn Ste A Dover (19901) *(G-2588)*

GJ Chalfant Welding LLC 302 983-0822
  119 S Congress St Port Penn (19731) *(G-12588)*

Gjp & Sons LLC 302 690-8954
  64 Sanford Dr Newark (19713) *(G-10842)*

Gkg Consulting LLC (PA) 888 918-0718
  517 Marsh Rd Wilmington (19809) *(G-16872)*

Gkua Inc 415 971-5341
  1000 N West St Ste 1200 Wilmington (19801) *(G-16873)*

GL Fluharty Jr Concrete LLC 302 745-1290
  3 Felicia Ln Lewes (19958) *(G-6036)*

GL Robins Co Inc 302 834-1272
  1233 Quintilio Dr Bear (19701) *(G-248)*

GL Robins Co Inc 302 475-5001
  2504 Foulk Rd Wilmington (19810) *(G-16874)*

GL Robins Co Inc 302 654-4477
  1406 N Dupont St Wilmington (19806) *(G-16875)*

GLA Company Ltd 502 267-7522
  5615 Kirkwood Hwy Wilmington (19808) *(G-16876)*

Glacier Autos 302 510-6771
  111 N Union St Wilmington (19805) *(G-16877)*

Glacierpoint Enterprises Inc (PA) 302 636-5401
  251 Little Falls Dr Wilmington (19808) *(G-16878)*

Gladys Walker 302 480-0713
  937 N Lombard St Apt 2 Wilmington (19801) *(G-16879)*

Glanbia Inc 208 733-7555
  3411 Silverside Rd Ste 104 Wilmington (19810) *(G-16880)*

Glance Capital Inc 800 825-9889
  651 N Broad St Middletown (19709) *(G-7162)*

Glasgow Auto Body 302 292-1201
  2905 Pulaski Hwy Newark (19702) *(G-10843)*

Glasgow Court Enterprises LLC 302 834-1633
  268 Cornell Dr Newark (19702) *(G-10844)*

Glasgow Imaging LLC 302 993-2330
  40 Polly Drummond Hill Rd Newark (19711) *(G-10845)*

Glasgow Medical Associates PA (PA) 302 836-8350
  2600 Glasgow Ave Ste 126 Newark (19702) *(G-10846)*

Glasgow Medical Associates PA 302 836-3539
  2600 Glasgow Ave Ste 106 Newark (19702) *(G-10847)*

Glasgow Medical Center, Newark *Also Called: Glasgow Medical Associates PA (G-10846)*

Glasgow Shopping Center Corp 302 836-1503
  2750 Wrangle Hill Rd Bear (19701) *(G-249)*

Glaxo Smithkline Beecham, Wilmington *Also Called: Smithkline Bcham Phrmceuticals (G-19892)*

Glaxosmithkline Capital Inc 302 656-5280
  1105 N Market St Ste 622 Wilmington (19801) *(G-16881)*

Glaxosmithkline Company, Wilmington *Also Called: Penn Labs Inc (G-18952)*

Glaxosmithkline Svcs Unlimited, Wilmington *Also Called: Glaxosmthkline Hldngs Amrcas I (G-16882)*

Glaxosmthkline Hldngs Amrcas I (DH) 302 984-6932
  1105 N Market St Ste 622 Wilmington (19801) *(G-16882)*

Gleam Mdrn Parenting Solutions 302 416-6460
  108 W 13th St Ste 100 Wilmington (19801) *(G-16883)*

Glen D Rowe Dr 302 730-4366
  1093 S Governors Ave Dover (19904) *(G-2589)*

Glen Eagle Villiage, Newark *Also Called: Westover Management Company LP (G-12363)*

Glen Playa Inc 302 703-7512
  16192 Coastal Hwy Lewes (19958) *(G-6037)*

Gleneagle Homes LLC 914 262-1402
  32653 Seaview Loop Millsboro (19966) *(G-8300)*

Glenmede Trust Co Nat Assn 302 661-2900
  1201 N Market St Ste 1501 Wilmington (19801) *(G-16884)*

Glens Exterior Cleaning 302 725-7222
  10316 Greentop Rd Lincoln (19960) *(G-6672)*

Glenwood Dental Associates LLP 302 653-5011
  17 W Glenwood Ave Smyrna (19977) *(G-13744)*

Glewed Media LLC 844 445-3933
  200 Continental Dr Ste 401 Newark (19713) *(G-10848)*

Glidden Professional Paint Ctr, Dover *Also Called: PPG Architectural Finishes Inc (G-3357)*

Glidden Professional Paint Ctr, Wilmington *Also Called: PPG Architectural Finishes Inc (G-19140)*

Glidden Professional Paint Ctr, Wilmington *Also Called: PPG Architectural Finishes Inc (G-19141)*

Glimpse Global Inc 305 216-7667
  8 The Grn Ste A Dover (19901) *(G-2590)*

Glitzy and Glamour Hair Salon 302 325-9565
  265 N Dupont Hwy New Castle (19720) *(G-9169)*

Global Air Strategy Inc 302 229-5889
  40 E Main St Ste 275 Newark (19711) *(G-10849)*

ALPHABETIC SECTION

Global Brands Usa Inc 314 401-2477
  251 Little Falls Dr Wilmington (19808) *(G-16885)*
Global Bridging Corp 202 318-7119
  16192 Coastal Hwy Lewes (19958) *(G-6038)*
Global Comm Innovations LLC 302 546-5010
  2093 Philadelphia Pike Claymont (19703) *(G-1163)*
Global Computers Networks LLC 484 686-8374
  718 Pinewood Dr Ste 2 Middletown (19709) *(G-7163)*
Global Container & Chassis LLC 302 608-0822
  607 Deemer Pl Historic New Castle (19720) *(G-4996)*
Global Currents Inv MGT LLC 302 476-3800
  2 Righter Pkwy Wilmington (19803) *(G-16886)*
Global Dev Partners Inc 480 330-7931
  2711 Centerville Rd # 400 Wilmington (19808) *(G-16887)*
Global Entp Worldwide LLC (PA) 713 260-9687
  1201 N Orange St Ste 700 # 7140 Wilmington (19801) *(G-16888)*
Global Essentials Inc 703 483-9544
  30b Trolley Sq Wilmington (19806) *(G-16889)*
Global Exterior 302 449-1559
  325 Clayton Manor Dr Middletown (19709) *(G-7164)*
Global Gaming Business 302 994-3898
  2413 Horace Dr Wilmington (19808) *(G-16890)*
Global Infrstrcture Sltons Inc 808 381-3666
  1675 S State St Ste B Dover (19901) *(G-2591)*
Global Institute 732 776-7360
  10 Eileen Dr Newark (19711) *(G-10850)*
Global Institute, The, Wilmington Also Called: Intercontinental Marketing *(G-17378)*
Global Law Centers 302 654-4800
  1403 N Rodney St Wilmington (19806) *(G-16891)*
Global Lime & Lumber Co Inc 609 579-1778
  732 Grantham Ln New Castle (19720) *(G-9170)*
Global Logistics and Trnsp, New Castle Also Called: Courtesy Trnsp Svcs Inc *(G-8982)*
Global Marine Networks LLC 215 327-2814
  205 E Savannah Rd Lewes (19958) *(G-6039)*
Global Market Insights Inc 302 470-2829
  4 N Main St Selbyville (19975) *(G-13537)*
Global Network Executive Inc 302 251-8940
  702 N West St Ste 101 Wilmington (19801) *(G-16892)*
Global Partner LLC (PA) 646 630-9128
  501 Silverside Rd Ste 105 Wilmington (19809) *(G-16893)*
Global PHI Trading Company LLC 404 759-8409
  651 N Broad St Ste 206 Middletown (19709) *(G-7165)*
Global Protection MGT LLC 302 425-4190
  1105 N Market St Ste 400 Wilmington (19801) *(G-16894)*
Global Recruiters Network Inc 302 455-9500
  3202 Drummond Plz Newark (19711) *(G-10851)*
Global Recruiters Wilmingto 302 455-9500
  1114 Drummond Plz Newark (19711) *(G-10852)*
Global Shipping Center LLC 302 798-4321
  2803 Philadelphia Pike Ste B Claymont (19703) *(G-1164)*
Global Shopaholics LLC 302 725-0586
  243 Quigley Blvd Ste E Historic New Castle (19720) *(G-4997)*
Global Space Organization, Lewes Also Called: Terran Global Corporation *(G-6552)*
Global Telecom Group LLC 302 295-2883
  1201 N Orange St Ste 6001 Wilmington (19801) *(G-16895)*
Global Tellink 302 672-7867
  300 W Water St Dover (19904) *(G-2592)*
Global Touch Co 302 321-5844
  8 The Grn Dover (19901) *(G-2593)*
Global Wellness 302 234-6550
  17 Raphael Rd Hockessin (19707) *(G-5222)*
Global Wireless Accesories LLC 302 753-7337
  21 W Market St Wilmington (19804) *(G-16896)*
Globaling Inc (PA) 619 657-0070
  3500 S Dunpont Hwy Dover (19901) *(G-2594)*
Globaling.io, Dover Also Called: Globaling Inc *(G-2594)*
Globally Srced Vhcles Prts LLC 240 755-4935
  8 The Grn Ste 8544 Dover (19901) *(G-2595)*
Globaltec Networks Inc 646 321-8627
  1013 Centre Rd Wilmington (19805) *(G-16897)*
Globbing LLC 408 903-4209
  950 Ridge Rd Claymont (19703) *(G-1165)*
Globe Electric Company 302 328-8809
  28 Longbow Ter Hockessin (19707) *(G-5223)*
Globe Electric Company USA Inc 514 694-0444
  874 Walker Rd Ste C Dover (19904) *(G-2596)*
Glory Contracting 302 275-5430
  231 Ratledge Rd Townsend (19734) *(G-14008)*
Gloss City, Newark Also Called: Glossgirl Inc *(G-10853)*
Glossgirl Inc (PA) 302 737-8080
  77 E Main St Newark (19711) *(G-10853)*
Glossgirl Inc 302 888-4520
  1320 N Union St Wilmington (19806) *(G-16898)*
Glycomira LLC 704 651-9789
  160 Greentree Dr Ste 101 Dover (19904) *(G-2597)*
GM Capital Investments Inc 302 722-0558
  41 Cannon Run Newark (19702) *(G-10854)*
GM Realestate 302 376-9462
  503 S Broad St Middletown (19709) *(G-7166)*
GM Trucking LLC 412 609-8818
  133 Torington Way Newark (19702) *(G-10855)*
Gmb - Seaford, Seaford Also Called: George Miles & Buhr LLC *(G-13197)*
Gmdh Inc 347 470-4634
  16192 Coastal Hwy Lewes (19958) *(G-6040)*
Gmetri Inc 704 260-6116
  16192 Coastal Hwy Lewes (19958) *(G-6041)*
Gmg Solutions LLC 302 781-3008
  4550 Linden Hill Rd Ste 301 Wilmington (19808) *(G-16899)*
Gmw Haberdashery LLC 718 864-7817
  8 The Grn Ste A Dover (19901) *(G-2598)*
Gnz LLC (HQ) 302 499-2024
  16192 Coastal Hwy Lewes (19958) *(G-6042)*
Go Curves Ladies 302 541-4681
  33077 Deer Trl Millville (19967) *(G-8530)*
Go Go Prof Clg Svcs LLC 302 729-2883
  1117 Westown Way Middletown (19709) *(G-7167)*
Go Marketplace LLC (PA) 630 624-9079
  1007 N Market St Ste G20 Wilmington (19801) *(G-16900)*
Go Mortgage, Christiana Also Called: Gsf Mortgage Corporation *(G-997)*
Go Mozaic LLC 302 438-4141
  3042 Greenshire Ave Claymont (19703) *(G-1166)*
Go Shopping Inc 305 370-4704
  200 Interchange Blvd Newark (19711) *(G-10856)*
Go Tees LLC 708 703-1788
  101 Arcadia Pkwy Middletown (19709) *(G-7168)*
GO Underground LLC 732 740-1127
  16192 Coastal Hwy Lewes (19958) *(G-6043)*
Go-Givers LLC 302 703-9293
  16192 Coastal Hwy Lewes (19958) *(G-6044)*
Go4spin Corporation 310 400-2588
  251 Little Falls Dr Wilmington (19808) *(G-16901)*
Goal Capital Funding Tr 2010-1 .... 302 636-6188
  1100 N Market St Wilmington (19890) *(G-16902)*
Goat Financial LLC 800 843-4608
  1521 Concord Pike Ste 102 Wilmington (19803) *(G-16903)*
Goat Joy LLC 302 542-1062
  22114 Ritter Ln Harbeson (19951) *(G-4697)*
GOBLIN Technologies LLC 302 644-5599
  100 Discovery Blvd Ste 802 Newark (19713) *(G-10857)*
God Said I Love You Ltd 302 697-0647
  401 Eagle Nest Dr Camden (19934) *(G-839)*
Goddard Early Learning Center, Newark Also Called: Selwor Enterprises Inc *(G-11974)*
Goddard School 302 454-9454
  50 Polly Drummond Hill Rd Newark (19711) *(G-10858)*
Goddard School, The, Wilmington Also Called: Mahavir LLC *(G-18086)*
Goddard Systems Inc 302 651-7995
  111 S West St Wilmington (19801) *(G-16904)*
Goddess Beauty Supply LLC 302 858-4649
  401 College Park Ln Unit 5 Georgetown (19947) *(G-4343)*
Goddess of Barn 302 363-1062
  295 Black Diamond Rd Smyrna (19977) *(G-13745)*
Goddess Scent Candles LLC 973 885-0606
  3 Berwick Ln Bear (19701) *(G-250)*

Godfrey Plumbing Services	302 985-1593
2606 Longwood Dr Wilmington (19810) *(G-16905)*	
Godspeed Transport LLC	302 803-2929
307 Pennsylvania Ave Wilmington (19804) *(G-16906)*	
Godwits LLC	424 242-4462
1207 Delaware Ave 1006 Wilmington (19806) *(G-16907)*	
Gokart Transportation LLC	302 202-9171
1201 N Market St Ste 111 Wilmington (19801) *(G-16908)*	
Golance Inc	888 478-0358
8 The Grn Ste 4753 Dover (19901) *(G-2599)*	
Gold Care Center, Newark Also Called: Abby Medical Center *(G-9738)*	
Gold Key Realty	302 369-5397
122 W Main St Newark (19711) *(G-10859)*	
Gold Label Transportation LLC	302 668-2383
36 Cardenti Ct Newark (19702) *(G-10860)*	
Gold Medal Envmtl De LLC	302 652-3150
1000 S Heald St Wilmington (19801) *(G-16909)*	
Gold Medal Gymnastics Inc	302 659-5569
56 Artisan Dr Ste 1 Smyrna (19977) *(G-13746)*	
Gold Standard Insptn Co LLC	302 381-0590
30838 Vines Creek Rd Dagsboro (19939) *(G-1453)*	
Gold Star Services LLC	610 444-3333
21a Industrial Blvd New Castle (19720) *(G-9171)*	
Goldberry LLC	800 268-4956
919 N Market St Wilmington (19801) *(G-16910)*	
Golden, Claymont Also Called: Golden Recursion Inc *(G-1167)*	
Golden Apple Spa	302 375-6505
2601 Carpenter Station Rd Wilmington (19810) *(G-16911)*	
Golden Car Care	302 856-2219
19395 Substation Rd Georgetown (19947) *(G-4344)*	
Golden Chariot Transportaion	302 730-3882
622 W Division St Dover (19904) *(G-2600)*	
Golden Coastal Realty	302 360-0226
33815 Clay Rd Ste 5 Lewes (19958) *(G-6045)*	
Golden Gate Investments LLC	302 894-8922
651 N Broad St Ste 205 Middletown (19709) *(G-7169)*	
Golden Globe Intl Svcs Ltd	302 487-0022
913 N Market St Ste 200 Wilmington (19801) *(G-16912)*	
Golden Inc	408 384-9136
16192 Coastal Hwy Lewes (19958) *(G-6046)*	
Golden Inc	800 878-1356
200 Continental Dr Ste 401 Newark (19713) *(G-10861)*	
Golden Incorporated, Newark Also Called: Kevin Smith *(G-11163)*	
Golden Jewelry	302 777-2121
1902 Maryland Ave Wilmington (19805) *(G-16913)*	
Golden Merger Corp	302 737-8100
245 E Cleveland Ave Newark (19711) *(G-10862)*	
Golden Recursion Inc	415 779-4053
2093a Philadelphia Pike Ste 206 Claymont (19703) *(G-1167)*	
Golden Star Enterprises Ltd	888 680-8033
2803 Philadelphia Pike Ste B Claymont (19703) *(G-1168)*	
Golden TV Inc	213 260-0070
16192 Coastal Hwy Lewes (19958) *(G-6047)*	
Goldenpgsus It Cnslting Svcs L	804 742-0710
112 Capitol Trl Ste A Newark (19711) *(G-10863)*	
Goldfinch Group Inc	646 300-0716
9 E Loockerman St Ste 3a Dover (19901) *(G-2601)*	
Goldis Holdings Inc (HQ)	302 764-3100
6 Denny Rd Ste 200 Wilmington (19809) *(G-16914)*	
Goldman Sachs, Wilmington Also Called: Goldman Sachs Tr Co Nat Assn *(G-16915)*	
Goldman Sachs Tr Co Nat Assn	302 793-3276
200 Bellevue Pkwy Ste 250 Wilmington (19809) *(G-16915)*	
Goldmine Enterprises Inc	302 834-4314
930 Woods Rd Bear (19701) *(G-251)*	
Golds Gym	302 226-4653
3712 Highway One Rehoboth Beach (19971) *(G-12772)*	
Goldsboro Sand and Gravel	410 310-0402
2904 Willow Grove Rd Camden Wyoming (19934) *(G-949)*	
Goldstone & Associates LLC	302 857-0051
1521 Concord Pike Ste 303 Wilmington (19803) *(G-16916)*	
Golf Bayside, Selbyville Also Called: Bayside Resort Golf Club *(G-13471)*	
Golf Course At Garrisons Lake	302 659-1206
101 W Fairways Cir Smyrna (19977) *(G-13747)*	
Golfclub, Wilmington Also Called: Golfclub LLC *(G-16917)*	
Golfclub LLC	908 770-7892
1209 Orange St Wilmington Wilmington (19801) *(G-16917)*	
Goliaths Haven Inc	888 793-9311
4023 Kennett Pike Ste 50142 Wilmington (19807) *(G-16918)*	
Golo LLC (PA)	302 781-4260
4051 Ogletown Rd Fl 3 Newark (19713) *(G-10864)*	
Golo LLC	302 781-4260
203 Gabor Dr Newark (19711) *(G-10865)*	
Golo For Life, Newark Also Called: Golo LLC *(G-10865)*	
Golsonel Global LLC	267 461-8400
33 Quigley Ct Camden Wyoming (19934) *(G-950)*	
Gom Technologies LLC	410 275-8029
724 Yorklyn Rd Ste 250 Hockessin (19707) *(G-5224)*	
Gonce William E Dr DDS PA	302 235-2400
1127 Valley Rd Ste 4 Hockessin (19707) *(G-5225)*	
Gone Hunting Inc	302 659-5010
112 Deer Run Rd Townsend (19734) *(G-14009)*	
Gonser and Gonser P A	302 478-4445
3411 Silverside Rd Ste 203hg Wilmington (19810) *(G-16919)*	
Goobers Garage	443 309-0328
3 Mill Rd Ste 102 Wilmington (19806) *(G-16920)*	
Good 4 Legacy	302 690-4515
8 The Grn Dover (19901) *(G-2602)*	
Good Beginnings Preschool	302 875-5507
10024 Woodland Ferry Rd Laurel (19956) *(G-5521)*	
Good Driver Mutuality Inc	713 979-8257
8 The Grn Ste R Dover (19901) *(G-2603)*	
Good Good Ntural Sweetness LLC	302 364-0015
16192 Coastal Hwy Lewes (19958) *(G-6048)*	
Good Home Solutions LLC	302 540-3190
20 North Ave Wilmington (19804) *(G-16921)*	
Good Life Group LLC	720 759-9089
1201 N Orange St Wilmington (19801) *(G-16922)*	
Good Manufacturing Practices	302 222-6808
80 Coventry Ct Dover (19901) *(G-2604)*	
Good Neighbor LLC	302 228-9910
37524 Leisure Dr Selbyville (19975) *(G-13538)*	
Good Ole Boy Foundation Inc	302 249-0237
20529 Laurel Rd Millsboro (19966) *(G-8301)*	
Good Rputation Investments LLC	888 382-1552
3 Germay Dr Ste 4 Wilmington (19804) *(G-16923)*	
Good Samaritan Aid	302 875-2425
115 W Market St Laurel (19956) *(G-5522)*	
GOOD SAMARITAN THRIFT SHOP, TH, Laurel Also Called: Good Samaritan Aid *(G-5522)*	
Good Stockx LLC	949 609-9533
12 Timber Creek Ln Newark (19711) *(G-10866)*	
Goodales Naturals	302 743-6455
84 Warren Dr Newark (19702) *(G-10867)*	
Goodbite USA Inc	516 761-4386
56140 Pine Cone Ln Bethany Beach (19930) *(G-604)*	
Goodblue Inc	801 755-5301
8 The Grn Dover (19901) *(G-2605)*	
Goodchild Inc	302 368-1681
6 Brookhill Dr Newark (19702) *(G-10868)*	
Goode Cleaning LLC (PA)	302 398-4520
229 Beaver Pond Rd Harrington (19952) *(G-4774)*	
Goodeals Inc	302 999-1737
537 Main St Wilmington (19804) *(G-16924)*	
Gooden Floral Sp & Greenhouses	302 422-4961
909 N Walnut St Milford (19963) *(G-7909)*	
Goodness Enterprises LLC	302 674-1400
4200 N Dupont Hwy Dover (19901) *(G-2606)*	
Goodness For Life Center Inc	302 922-5055
8 The Grn Ste 5312 Dover (19901) *(G-2607)*	
Goodnew Natural Foods, Milford Also Called: Four Ever Green Inc *(G-7902)*	
Goodscents Inc	302 628-8042
5270 Baker Rd Bridgeville (19933) *(G-704)*	
Goodsize Inc	415 481-7330
251 Little Falls Dr Wilmington (19808) *(G-16925)*	

ALPHABETIC SECTION

Grace Visitation Services

Goodtymes Inc 302 598-6673
  132 School Rd Wilmington (19803) *(G-16926)*
Goodwill 302 934-9146
  28595 Dupont Blvd Unit 1 Millsboro (19966) *(G-8302)*
GOODWILL CENTER, Wilmington Also Called: Goodwill Inds Del Del Cnty Inc *(G-16927)*
Goodwill Inds Del Del Cnty Inc (PA) 302 761-4640
  300 E Lea Blvd Wilmington (19802) *(G-16927)*
Goodwin Brothers Shading & Spc, Claymont Also Called: Gb Shades LLC *(G-1155)*
Goodworld Inc 845 325-2232
  2711 Centerville Rd Ste 400 Wilmington (19808) *(G-16928)*
Goodyear, Newark Also Called: Goodyear Tire & Rubber Company *(G-10869)*
Goodyear Tire & Rubber Company 302 737-2461
  1929 Kirkwood Hwy Newark (19711) *(G-10869)*
Goodyear Tire & Rubber Company 302 998-0428
  3217 Kirkwood Hwy Wilmington (19808) *(G-16929)*
Gop Precision Machining 302 875-8875
  5583 Watson Rd Laurel (19956) *(G-5523)*
Gordon C Honig DMD PA 302 696-4020
  104 Sleepy Hollow Dr Middletown (19709) *(G-7170)*
Gordon C Honig DMD PA (PA) 302 737-6333
  2707 Kirkwood Hwy Newark (19711) *(G-10870)*
Gordon Fournaris Mammarella PA 302 652-2900
  1925 Lovering Ave Wilmington (19806) *(G-16930)*
Gordons Daycare Home 302 658-7854
  2240 N Pine St Wilmington (19802) *(G-16931)*
Gordy Enterprises, New Castle Also Called: Gordy Management Inc *(G-9172)*
Gordy Management Inc 302 322-3723
  265 N Dupont Hwy Fl 2 New Castle (19720) *(G-9172)*
Gordys Lumber Inc 302 875-3502
  28950 Seaford Rd Laurel (19956) *(G-5524)*
Gore Funeral Services 610 364-9900
  812 Arthur Springs Ln New Castle (19720) *(G-9173)*
GORE FUNERAL SERVICES, New Castle Also Called: Gore Funeral Services *(G-9173)*
Got A Doc - Walk In Med Ctr 302 947-4111
  25935 Plaza Dr Unit 1 Millsboro (19966) *(G-8303)*
Gotadoc, Claymont Also Called: Fast Care Medical Aid Unit LLC *(G-1149)*
Gotham Index 500 Plus Fund 877 974-6852
  301 Bellevue Pkwy Wilmington (19809) *(G-16932)*
Gotit Inc 408 382-1300
  3500 S Dupont Hwy Dover (19901) *(G-2608)*
Gotshadeonline Inc 302 832-8468
  1700 Firedancer Ln Bear (19701) *(G-252)*
Gotshadeonline Inc 302 384-2932
  2860 Ogletown Rd Newark (19713) *(G-10871)*
Gotti Boyz Entertainment 302 409-2901
  1314 Elk Way Bear (19701) *(G-253)*
Gourmetcarte Inc 631 418-6170
  600 N Broad St Middletown (19709) *(G-7171)*
Govbizconnect Inc 860 341-1925
  850 New Burton Rd Dover (19904) *(G-2609)*
Gover Counseling Psychology 302 226-3661
  The Lndg Rehoboth Beach (19971) *(G-12773)*
Government Affairs 302 226-2704
  12 Beaver Dam Reach Rehoboth Beach (19971) *(G-12774)*
Government Mrktplace Ltd Lblty 302 297-9694
  200 Continental Dr Ste 401 Newark (19713) *(G-10872)*
Government Portfolio LLC 301 718-9742
  35546 Hatteras Ct Rehoboth Beach (19971) *(G-12775)*
Governor Ross Mansion & Plntn 302 628-9500
  203 High St Seaford (19973) *(G-13199)*
Governors Ave Animal Hospital 302 734-5588
  1008 S Governors Ave Dover (19904) *(G-2610)*
Governors Family Practice 302 734-9150
  1177 S Governors Ave Dover (19904) *(G-2611)*
Governors Place Townhomes 302 653-6655
  17 Providence Dr Smyrna (19977) *(G-13748)*
Govplus LLC 302 734-0231
  1399 Forrest Ave Dover (19904) *(G-2612)*
Govplus LLC 302 235-4321
  128 Lantana Dr Hockessin (19707) *(G-5226)*
Govplus LLC 302 360-6101
  34161 Citizen Dr Lewes (19958) *(G-6049)*
Govplus LLC 302 376-3641
  460 E Main St Middletown (19709) *(G-7172)*
Govplus LLC 302 422-5010
  610 N Dupont Blvd Milford (19963) *(G-7910)*
Govplus LLC 302 322-0525
  130 N Dupont Hwy New Castle (19720) *(G-9174)*
Govplus LLC 302 292-6401
  100 Suburban Dr Newark (19711) *(G-10873)*
Govplus LLC 302 456-7100
  40 Chestnut Hill Plz Newark (19713) *(G-10874)*
Govplus LLC 302 283-5600
  1 University Plz Newark (19702) *(G-10875)*
Govplus LLC 302 628-6150
  22870 Sussex Hwy Seaford (19973) *(G-13200)*
Govplus LLC 302 653-9245
  7 W Glenwood Ave Smyrna (19977) *(G-13749)*
Govplus LLC 302 633-4503
  4435 Kirkwood Hwy Wilmington (19808) *(G-16933)*
Govplus LLC 302 421-2248
  1422 N Dupont St Wilmington (19806) *(G-16934)*
Govplus LLC 302 633-3080
  4720 Limestone Rd Wilmington (19808) *(G-16935)*
Govplus LLC 302 529-6100
  2084 Naamans Rd Wilmington (19810) *(G-16936)*
Govplus LLC 302 421-2229
  919 N Market St Ste 200 Wilmington (19801) *(G-16937)*
Govplus LLC 302 477-1205
  1620 Marsh Rd Wilmington (19803) *(G-16938)*
GOVPLUS LLC, Hockessin Also Called: Govplus LLC *(G-5226)*
GOVPLUS LLC, Lewes Also Called: Govplus LLC *(G-6049)*
GOVPLUS LLC, Middletown Also Called: Govplus LLC *(G-7172)*
GOVPLUS LLC, New Castle Also Called: Govplus LLC *(G-9174)*
GOVPLUS LLC, Newark Also Called: Govplus LLC *(G-10873)*
GOVPLUS LLC, Newark Also Called: Govplus LLC *(G-10874)*
GOVPLUS LLC, Newark Also Called: Govplus LLC *(G-10875)*
GOVPLUS LLC, Seaford Also Called: Govplus LLC *(G-13200)*
GOVPLUS LLC, Wilmington Also Called: Govplus LLC *(G-16934)*
GOVPLUS LLC, Wilmington Also Called: Govplus LLC *(G-16937)*
Govsimplified LLC 888 629-8008
  2093 Philadelphia Pike # 3338 Claymont (19703) *(G-1169)*
Govwell Technologies Inc (PA) 920 360-4496
  614 N Dupont Hwy Ste 210 Dover (19901) *(G-2613)*
Gpc Construction Services LLC 302 390-1257
  9 Todd Ln Newark (19713) *(G-10876)*
Gpc Productions 302 530-4547
  38 Abelia Ln Newark (19711) *(G-10877)*
GPM Investments LLC 302 436-6330
  36345 Lighthouse Rd Ste 301 Selbyville (19975) *(G-13539)*
Gr Dispatch Inc 888 985-3440
  16192 Coastal Hwy Lewes (19958) *(G-6050)*
Gr Group Holdings Inc (PA) 416 618-2676
  108 Lakeland Ave Dover (19901) *(G-2614)*
Gr Loudon LLC 302 475-9400
  2210 Swiss Ln Wilmington (19810) *(G-16939)*
Grab DC LLC 310 866-0560
  8 The Grn Ste A Dover (19901) *(G-2615)*
Grab-Ur-Bite Inc 415 568-1717
  251 Little Falls Dr Wilmington (19808) *(G-16940)*
Grabowski Sprano Vnclette Cpas 302 999-7300
  1814 Newport Gap Pike Wilmington (19808) *(G-16941)*
Grace For Dover 302 319-4433
  350 Mckee Rd Dover (19904) *(G-2616)*
Grace Logistics LLC 302 287-4838
  328 Camerton Ln Townsend (19734) *(G-14010)*
Grace Mechanical 302 542-4102
  18746 Munchy Branch Rd Rehoboth Beach (19971) *(G-12776)*
Grace Miracle Home Care 302 257-1079
  3604 Miller Rd Wilmington (19802) *(G-16942)*
Grace Visitation Services 302 329-9475
  28350 Lewes Georgetown Hwy Milton (19968) *(G-8628)*

Graceblood LLC — ALPHABETIC SECTION

Graceblood LLC 302 703-2524
417 E Cape Shores Dr Lewes (19958) *(G-6051)*

Graceful Body & Wellness LLC 302 612-3356
2714 Kitts Hummock Rd Dover (19901) *(G-2617)*

Graceful Hands Cleaning Svc, Ellendale *Also Called: Gracefull Hands Cleaning LLC (G-3919)*

Graceful Yoga 302 994-3114
3315 Elizabeth Ave Wilmington (19808) *(G-16943)*

Gracefull Hands Cleaning LLC 302 228-3841
702 Main St Ellendale (19941) *(G-3919)*

Graceland Daycare 302 698-0414
342 Ponderosa Dr Magnolia (19962) *(G-6747)*

Gracelawn Memorial Park Inc (PA) 302 654-6158
2220 N Dupont Hwy New Castle (19720) *(G-9175)*

Gracious Hart Nursing Svcs LLC 302 343-9083
1884 Westville Rd Marydel (19964) *(G-6798)*

Grady & Hampton LLC 302 678-1265
6 N Bradford St Dover (19904) *(G-2618)*

Grafton Reeves MD 302 651-5965
Dupont Hosp For Children Wilmington (19801) *(G-16944)*

Graham Global Corporation 302 839-3000
3616 Kirkwood Hwy Ste A Wilmington (19808) *(G-16945)*

Graham Packaging Pet Tech Inc 302 453-9464
1601 Ogletown Rd Newark (19711) *(G-10878)*

Grahams Wireless Solutions Inc 717 943-0717
24817 Rivers Edge Rd Millsboro (19966) *(G-8304)*

Grainger 595, Historic New Castle *Also Called: W W Grainger Inc (G-5098)*

Gramonoli Enterprises Inc 302 227-1288
21 Rehoboth Ave Rehoboth Beach (19971) *(G-12777)*

Grand Designs It Solutions LLC 302 299-3500
113 Woodland Rd Newark (19702) *(G-10879)*

GRAND OPERA HOUSE, Wilmington *Also Called: Grand Opera House Inc (G-16946)*

Grand Opera House Inc 302 652-5577
818 N Market St Fl 2 Wilmington (19801) *(G-16946)*

Grand Rental Station, Rehoboth Beach *Also Called: Quillens Rent All Inc (G-12903)*

Grand View Tour & Travel 610 361-7979
20996 Cormorant Way Ocean View (19970) *(G-12520)*

Grande Apartments 302 734-8344
201 Doveview Dr Unit 101 Dover (19904) *(G-2619)*

Granford Inc 413 474-6919
1000 N West St Ste 1200 Wilmington (19801) *(G-16947)*

Granite Central Distributors 302 521-1584
131 Mute Swan Pl Newark (19711) *(G-10880)*

Grant & Eisenhofer PA (PA) 302 622-7000
123 S Justison St Ste 700 Wilmington (19801) *(G-16948)*

Grant & Sons Roofing & Siding, Milford *Also Called: Robert Grant Inc (G-8070)*

Grant Ireland Contracting LLC 302 265-6112
622 Mount Olive Cemetery Rd Felton (19943) *(G-3980)*

Grant Tani Barash & Altman Man 302 651-7700
1100 N Mkt St Rodney Sq Wilmington (19890) *(G-16949)*

Grantlin Fabrication LLC 302 270-3708
872 Blackbird Greenspring Rd Smyrna (19977) *(G-13750)*

Grapefruit Usa Inc (PA) 310 575-1175
1000 N West St Wilmington (19801) *(G-16950)*

Graphites 302 329-9182
12200 Cadet Dr Milton (19968) *(G-8629)*

Grass Busters Landscaping Co 302 292-1166
935 Rahway Dr Newark (19711) *(G-10881)*

Grassrots Data Innovations Inc 267 664-9905
16192 Coastal Hwy Lewes (19958) *(G-6052)*

Gratz LLC 719 581-9645
611 S Dupont Hwy Ste 102 Dover (19901) *(G-2620)*

Graulich Builders 302 313-4882
34697 Jiffy Way Lewes (19958) *(G-6053)*

Gravatt Painting 302 632-2835
217 Willow Ave Camden (19934) *(G-840)*

Gravely Hockessin, Hockessin *Also Called: Hockessin Tractor Inc (G-5247)*

Graver Separations Inc 302 731-1700
200 Lake Dr Newark (19702) *(G-10882)*

Graver Technologies LLC (DH) 302 731-1700
200 Lake Dr Frnt Newark (19702) *(G-10883)*

Gravity-Techinc LLC 346 258-1597
16192 Coastal Hwy Lewes (19958) *(G-6054)*

Gray Audograph Agency Inc 302 658-1700
2340 N Dupont Hwy New Castle (19720) *(G-9176)*

Gray Rental Properties LLC 302 382-0439
4771 Mills Rd Milford (19963) *(G-7911)*

Graybar Electric Company Inc 302 322-2200
43 Boulden Blvd New Castle (19720) *(G-9177)*

Grayden Appraisals Inc 302 598-8511
580 Timber Wood Blvd Newark (19702) *(G-10884)*

Graydie Welding LLC 302 753-0695
42 W Reamer Ave Wilmington (19804) *(G-16951)*

Graydon Hurst & Son Inc 302 762-2444
2901 Baynard Blvd Ste 4 Wilmington (19802) *(G-16952)*

Grayling Industries Inc (HQ) 770 751-9095
1 Moonwalker Rd Frederica (19946) *(G-4168)*

Graylyn Crest III Swim Club 302 547-5809
2015 Kynwyd Rd Wilmington (19810) *(G-16953)*

Graylyn Dental 302 475-5555
2205 Silverside Rd Ste 2 Wilmington (19810) *(G-16954)*

Grays Fine Printing, Wilmington *Also Called: Stanley Golden (G-20018)*

Grayson Home Improvements LLC 302 685-1848
911 E 27th St Wilmington (19802) *(G-16955)*

Grc & Associates LLC 770 484-9082
1419 Westown Way Middletown (19709) *(G-7173)*

Greanex 606 477-9768
1209 N Orange St Wilmington (19801) *(G-16956)*

Grease City Inc 302 661-5675
900 N Madison St Apt 2 Wilmington (19801) *(G-16957)*

Great American Switchgear, Milford *Also Called: Switchgearus LLC (G-8112)*

Great Clips 302 737-2887
212 Suburban Dr Newark (19711) *(G-10885)*

Great Clips 302 514-9819
232 E Glenwood Ave Smyrna (19977) *(G-13751)*

Great Clips 302 995-2887
4705 Kirkwood Hwy Wilmington (19808) *(G-16958)*

Great Clips, Bridgeville *Also Called: Jersey Clippers LLC (G-718)*

Great Clips, Cheswold *Also Called: Great Clips For Hair (G-988)*

Great Clips, Georgetown *Also Called: Great Clips For Hair (G-4345)*

Great Clips, Hockessin *Also Called: Great Clips For Hair (G-5227)*

Great Clips, Smyrna *Also Called: Great Clips (G-13751)*

Great Clips For Hair 302 677-1838
137 Jerome Dr Cheswold (19936) *(G-988)*

Great Clips For Hair 302 858-4871
401 College Park Ln Georgetown (19947) *(G-4345)*

Great Clips For Hair 302 235-2887
6292 Limestone Rd Hockessin (19707) *(G-5227)*

Great Clips Hair Cut Salon, New Castle *Also Called: Gc New Castle Inc (G-9159)*

Great Gaines LLC (PA) 443 248-3952
4574 White Deer Rd Delmar (19940) *(G-1599)*

Great I AM, New Castle *Also Called: Great I AM Prod Studios Inc (G-9178)*

Great I AM Prod Studios Inc 302 463-2483
25 Rose Ln New Castle (19720) *(G-9178)*

Great Minds 302 834-4906
54 Lochview Dr Bear (19701) *(G-254)*

Great New Bgnnngs Mddltown Inc 302 378-5555
210 Cleaver Farms Rd Ste 3 Middletown (19709) *(G-7174)*

Great New Bgnnngs St Andrews I 302 838-1000
14 Saint Andrews Dr Bear (19701) *(G-255)*

Great Outdoor Cottages LLC 215 760-4971
21498 Baltimore Ave Georgetown (19947) *(G-4346)*

Great Spirit Ventures LLC 302 573-3820
1011 Centre Rd Ste 310 Wilmington (19805) *(G-16959)*

Great Stemporium 302 313-5139
18388 Coastal Hwy Unit 10 Lewes (19958) *(G-6055)*

Great Thing Inc 302 314-3909
651 N Broad St Ste 201 Middletown (19709) *(G-7175)*

Great Valley Advisor Group 302 483-7200
1200 Pennsylvania Ave Ste 202 Wilmington (19806) *(G-16960)*

Greater Lewes Community Vlg 302 703-2568
16686 Kings Hwy # B Lewes (19958) *(G-6056)*

Greater Newark Baseball L 302 635-0562
Newark (19714) *(G-10886)*

ALPHABETIC SECTION

Greatful Lives Foundation.. 404 965-9300
   1007 N Orange St Ste 1450 Wilmington (19801) *(G-16961)*
Gredell & Associates PA.. 302 996-9500
   725 Art Ln Newark (19713) *(G-10887)*
Greeley & Nista Orthodontics.. 302 475-4102
   1405 Silverside Rd Ste A Wilmington (19810) *(G-16962)*
Green Acres Farm Inc.. 302 645-8652
   18186 Dairy Farm Rd Lewes (19958) *(G-6057)*
Green Acres Health Systems.. 302 934-7300
   231 S Washington St Millsboro (19966) *(G-8305)*
Green Acres Lawn & Ldscpg Corp.................................... 302 332-8239
   39 Brookhill Dr Newark (19702) *(G-10888)*
Green Blade Irrigation & Turf... 302 736-8873
   2203 Ponderosa Dr Magnolia (19962) *(G-6748)*
Green Candy Solutions Inc... 302 599-7944
   2093a Philadelphia Pike Ste 486 Claymont (19703) *(G-1170)*
Green Clinics Laboratory LLC... 302 734-5050
   1633 Sorghum Mill Rd Dover (19901) *(G-2621)*
Green Construction Services.. 610 675-6337
   3120 Naamans Rd Apt P2 Wilmington (19810) *(G-16963)*
Green Crescent LLC.. 800 735-9620
   8 The Grn Ste 4710 Dover (19901) *(G-2622)*
Green Crescent Translations, Dover Also Called: Green Crescent LLC *(G-2622)*
Green Diamond Builders Inc (PA)..................................... 302 284-1177
   24 Memorial Ave Felton (19943) *(G-3981)*
Green DOT Capital LLC... 302 395-0500
   203 Cornwell Dr Bear (19701) *(G-256)*
Green Earth Tech Group LLC... 302 257-5617
   1000 N West St Wilmington (19801) *(G-16964)*
Green Eyes Landscaping Inc.. 302 653-3800
   158 Attix Dr Dover (19904) *(G-2623)*
Green Interest Enterprises LLC... 228 355-0708
   81 Rye Oak Ct Dover (19904) *(G-2624)*
Green Lunar LLC.. 650 507-9049
   19266 Coastal Hwy Rehoboth Beach (19971) *(G-12778)*
Green Meadows At Latrobe, Dover Also Called: Emeritus Corporation *(G-2439)*
Green Oak Real Estate LP... 212 359-7800
   1209 N Orange St Wilmington (19801) *(G-16965)*
Green Opportunities Corp... 302 535-2235
   3051 Willow Grove Rd Camden Wyoming (19934) *(G-951)*
Green Pest Management LLC.. 302 777-2390
   18 Boulden Cir Ste 22 New Castle (19720) *(G-9179)*
Green Recovery Tech LLC.. 302 317-0062
   42 Lukens Dr Ste 100 Historic New Castle (19720) *(G-4998)*
Green River Consulting LLC... 302 494-4497
   Hockessin (19707) *(G-5228)*
Green Room Restaurant... 302 594-3100
   100 W 11th St Wilmington (19801) *(G-16966)*
Green Roots LLC.. 516 643-2621
   16192 Coastal Hwy Lewes (19958) *(G-6058)*
Green Side Up Lawn & Landscape................................... 302 999-7151
   406 1/2 Hillside Ave Wilmington (19805) *(G-16967)*
Green Standards LLC... 855 632-8036
   1675 S State St Ste B Dover (19901) *(G-2625)*
Green Team.. 302 344-4512
   405 Behringer Ave Milton (19968) *(G-8630)*
Green Team Moving & Design LLC................................... 252 406-7001
   1201 N Market St Ste 111 Wilmington (19801) *(G-16968)*
Green Valley Pavilion.. 302 653-5085
   3034 S Dupont Blvd Smyrna (19977) *(G-13752)*
Green Valley Snf LLC.. 302 653-5085
   3034 S Dupont Blvd Smyrna (19977) *(G-13753)*
Green Valley Terrace Snf LLC... 302 934-7300
   231 S Washington St Millsboro (19966) *(G-8306)*
Green Valley Terrance, Millsboro Also Called: Green Acres Health Systems *(G-8305)*
Greenberg Praurig LLC... 302 661-7000
   1007 N Orange St Ste 1200 Wilmington (19801) *(G-16969)*
Greenberg Supply Co Inc.. 302 656-4496
   809 E 5th St Wilmington (19801) *(G-16970)*
Greene Business Support S.. 302 480-3725
   3 Heritage Dr Dover (19904) *(G-2626)*
Greene Lawn & Landscape... 302 379-4425
   6 S Fawn Dr Newark (19711) *(G-10889)*
Greene Tweed of Delaware Inc... 302 888-2560
   1105 N Market St Ste 1300 Wilmington (19801) *(G-16971)*
Greener Cleaner Sussex Corp.. 302 497-7123
   31007 Conaway Rd Millsboro (19966) *(G-8307)*
Greenhill Car Wash... 302 420-5961
   890 Middletown Warwick Rd Middletown (19709) *(G-7176)*
Greenhill Express Car Wash... 302 464-1031
   299 E Main St Middletown (19709) *(G-7177)*
Greenland Sod Farm LLC... 302 258-7543
   8268 Snake Rd Bethel (19931) *(G-654)*
Greenleaf Landscapes LLC.. 302 762-5027
   301 Weldin Rd Wilmington (19803) *(G-16972)*
Greenleaf Services Inc... 302 836-9050
   20393 John J Williams Hwy Lewes (19958) *(G-6059)*
Greenleaf Turf Solutions Inc... 302 731-1075
   9 Albe Dr Ste C Newark (19702) *(G-10890)*
Greenlight Connections LLC... 843 209-1675
   8 The Grn Ste B Dover (19901) *(G-2627)*
Greens At Broadview LLC... 302 684-3000
   27052 Broadkill Rd Milton (19968) *(G-8631)*
Greens Cleaning Expert LLC.. 302 697-2848
   1129 Barney Jenkins Rd Felton (19943) *(G-3982)*
Greensboro Heating & Air... 302 598-5568
   126 Mystic Ln Magnolia (19962) *(G-6749)*
Greentec Laboratories LLC... 301 744-7336
   122 Delaware St Ste F7 Historic New Castle (19720) *(G-4999)*
Greenville Capital Management.. 302 429-9799
   100 S Rockland Falls Rd Rockland (19732) *(G-13031)*
Greenville Community Newspaper, Middletown Also Called: Community Publications Inc *(G-7004)*
Greenville Country Club Inc.. 302 652-3255
   201 Owls Nest Rd Wilmington (19807) *(G-16973)*
Greenville Towers LLC.. 302 397-8016
   220 Presidential Dr Wilmington (19807) *(G-16974)*
Greenville Travel Agency Inc... 302 658-3585
   16923 Beulah Blvd Milton (19968) *(G-8632)*
Greenvlle Retirement Cmnty LLC...................................... 302 658-6200
   4031 Kennett Pike Wilmington (19807) *(G-16975)*
Greenway Comfort Solutions.. 302 200-4929
   8 Westover Woods Dr Newark (19702) *(G-10891)*
Greenwich Aerogroup Inc.. 302 834-5400
   4200 Summit Bridge Rd Middletown (19709) *(G-7178)*
Greenwood Pallet Co.. 302 337-8181
   16849 Road Runner Dr Bridgeville (19933) *(G-705)*
Greet 26 Inc... 310 601-2648
   2140 S Dupont Hwy Camden (19934) *(G-841)*
Greg Elect.. 215 651-1477
   547 Ashland Ridge Rd Hockessin (19707) *(G-5229)*
Greg Motors USA Inc.. 302 266-8200
   2915 Ogletown Rd Newark (19713) *(G-10892)*
Greg Smith Equipment Inc.. 302 894-9333
   250 Executive Dr Ste 123 Newark (19702) *(G-10893)*
Greg Smith Equipment Sales LLC..................................... 302 894-9333
   250 Executive Dr Ste 1 Newark (19702) *(G-10894)*
Gregg & Sons Mechanical LLC... 302 223-8145
   256 Gum Bush Rd Townsend (19734) *(G-14011)*
Gregg Bus Service, Wilmington Also Called: Krapfs Coaches Inc *(G-17751)*
Gregg White Contracting.. 302 542-9552
   300 Hollywood St Bethany Beach (19930) *(G-605)*
Gregg Zoarski.. 302 733-1487
   4755 Ogletown Stanton Rd Newark (19718) *(G-10895)*
Greggii Inc... 647 606-3348
   200 Continental Dr Newark (19713) *(G-10896)*
Greggo & Ferrara Inc (PA).. 302 658-5241
   4048 New Castle Ave New Castle (19720) *(G-9180)*
Gregory A Maahs Sr.. 302 359-9077
   69 S Skyward Dr Newark (19713) *(G-10897)*
Gregory A Williams Jr Educ... 302 875-1218
   104 E 6th St Laurel (19956) *(G-5525)*

Gregory For Wilmington

Gregory For Wilmington..302 562-3117
401 W 22nd St Wilmington (19802) *(G-16976)*

Grep Biogas I LLC..212 390-8110
16192 Coastal Hwy Lewes (19958) *(G-6060)*

Grey Matter Inc..302 764-5900
2701 Centerville Rd Wilmington (19808) *(G-16977)*

Grey Mountain Equities LLC..623 387-0744
2803 Philadelphia Pike B-260 Claymont (19703) *(G-1171)*

Grey Rock Farms LLC..215 847-3478
189 N Star Rd Newark (19711) *(G-10898)*

Greynote LLC (PA)..646 287-0705
8 The Grn Ste B Dover (19901) *(G-2628)*

Greystone Bed & Breakfa..302 645-0699
303 Market St Lewes (19958) *(G-6061)*

Greystone Business Credit..410 456-6559
27191 Barefoot Blvd Millsboro (19966) *(G-8308)*

Grgh, Dover *Also Called: Gr Group Holdings Inc (G-2614)*

Grieco..302 792-1293
3401 Philadelphia Pike Claymont (19703) *(G-1172)*

Grier Signs..302 737-4823
4 Bridgeview Ct Newark (19711) *(G-10899)*

Griffen Corporate Services..302 576-2890
300 Delaware Ave Fl 9 Wilmington (19801) *(G-16978)*

Griffin Higgins Team LLC..302 856-1458
24994 Sussex Hwy Seaford (19973) *(G-13201)*

Griffith Roofing and..302 275-7123
205 Hanley St Harrington (19952) *(G-4775)*

Griffs Signs LLC..302 784-5596
101 Westmoreland Ave Wilmington (19804) *(G-16979)*

Grime 2 Shine LLC..302 264-6709
105 Oak Dr Smyrna (19977) *(G-13754)*

Grime Busters USA Inc..302 834-7006
3 Misty Ct Newark (19702) *(G-10900)*

Grimes Construction..302 462-6533
22242 Lewes Georgetown Hwy Georgetown (19947) *(G-4347)*

Grimm Farms LLC..302 841-8381
12620 Hunters Cove Rd Greenwood (19950) *(G-4632)*

Grind Kennels LLC (PA)..302 442-5599
24a Trolley Sq Unit 1259 Wilmington (19806) *(G-16980)*

Grind or Starve LLC..302 322-1679
608 W Lea Blvd Apt C4 Wilmington (19802) *(G-16981)*

Grindstone Aviation LLC..302 324-1993
13 1/2 Penns Way New Castle (19720) *(G-9181)*

Griswold Home Care..302 703-0130
18335 Coastal Hwy Ste A Lewes (19958) *(G-6062)*

Griswold Home Care..302 750-4564
115 Christina Landing Dr Apt 708 Wilmington (19801) *(G-16982)*

Griswold Special Care, Wilmington *Also Called: Special Care Inc (G-19953)*

Griz Inc..302 655-1344
2305 Pennsylvania Ave Wilmington (19806) *(G-16983)*

Grizzlys Landscape Sup & Svcs....................................302 644-0654
20144 John J Williams Hwy Lewes (19958) *(G-6063)*

Grizzlys Landscape Supl & Svc......................................302 644-0654
18412 The Narrow Rd Lewes (19958) *(G-6064)*

Grlla Gmng LLC..302 291-2075
16192 Coastal Hwy Lewes (19958) *(G-6065)*

Grm Pro Imaging LLC..302 999-8162
401 Marsh Ln Ste 3 Wilmington (19804) *(G-16984)*

Grn Wilmington, Newark *Also Called: Global Recruiters Network Inc (G-10851)*

Grnmeta Inc..425 362-3228
874 Walker Rd Dover (19904) *(G-2629)*

Gro-Connectcom Inc..347 918-7437
16192 Coastal Hwy Lewes (19958) *(G-6066)*

Groff Tractor & Equipment LLC......................................302 349-5760
12420 Sussex Hwy Greenwood (19950) *(G-4633)*

Grofos International LLC (PA)..302 635-4805
1 Innovation Way Ste 426 Newark (19711) *(G-10901)*

Groom Kings LLC..302 744-9444
331 W Loockerman St Dover (19904) *(G-2630)*

Grooming Bar LLC..302 803-8304
701 S Union St Ste 4 Wilmington (19805) *(G-16985)*

Groovvx Inc..828 399-1549
4 Guyenne Rd Wilmington (19807) *(G-16986)*

Ground/Water Trtmnt & Tech LLC..................................302 654-0206
1204 E 12th St Ste 4c Wilmington (19802) *(G-16987)*

Group Investments Associates, Wilmington *Also Called: Dental Associates Delaware PA (G-16013)*

Group Three Inc (PA)..302 658-4158
1100 Duncan St Ste A Wilmington (19805) *(G-16988)*

Groupe EHc LLC..302 309-9154
3500 S Dupont Hwy Dover (19901) *(G-2631)*

Grow & Learn Childcare Center, Middletown *Also Called: Gb Jacobs LLC (G-7152)*

Growing & Glowing LLC..302 500-9220
1 Smalleys Cv Newark (19702) *(G-10902)*

Growing Edges Counseling..484 883-6523
5149 W Woodmill Dr Ste 20 Wilmington (19808) *(G-16989)*

Growing Palace..302 376-5553
111 Patriot Dr Ste A Middletown (19709) *(G-7179)*

Growing Palace 3, The, Middletown *Also Called: Growing Palace III (G-7180)*

Growing Palace III..302 376-5553
111 Patriot Dr Ste A Middletown (19709) *(G-7180)*

Growmark Fs LLC..302 422-3001
339 Milford Harrington Hwy Milford (19963) *(G-7912)*

Growmark Fs LLC (HQ)..302 422-3002
308 Ne Front St Milford (19963) *(G-7913)*

Growth Inc..302 366-0848
311 Ruthar Dr Newark (19711) *(G-10903)*

Growth Cave LLC..323 688-5042
254 Chapman Rd Ste 208634 Newark (19702) *(G-10904)*

Growth River Usa LLC..617 905-5156
1201 N Orange St Ste 600 Wilmington (19801) *(G-16990)*

Grub-Busters Grub Bus LLC..610 931-9406
1201 N Market St Wilmington (19801) *(G-16991)*

Grubb Lumber Company Inc..302 652-2800
200 A St Wilmington (19801) *(G-16992)*

Grupo Acosta Ecuador Limited......................................302 231-2981
501 Silverside Rd 105-3 Wilmington (19809) *(G-16993)*

GSB&b LLC..302 425-5800
1201 N Orange St Ste 300 Wilmington (19801) *(G-16994)*

Gsf Mortgage Corporation..302 373-5853
56 W Main St Ste 204 Christiana (19702) *(G-997)*

Gsi Express Logistics Inc..201 345-3532
430 E Ayre St Wilmington (19804) *(G-16995)*

GSM Planet Incorp..302 455-1111
19 Peddlers Row Christiana (19702) *(G-998)*

GSM Systems Inc (PA)..302 284-8304
215 E Evens Rd Viola (19979) *(G-14095)*

Gsz Associates Inc..302 824-2572
7 Dunsinane Dr New Castle (19720) *(G-9182)*

Gt Commodities LLC..203 609-8300
3511 Silverside Rd Ste 10 Wilmington (19810) *(G-16996)*

Gt Designs Inc..302 275-8100
109 Wellington Way Middletown (19709) *(G-7181)*

Gt Directional LLC..714 417-2826
3524 Silverside Rd Ste 35b Wilmington (19810) *(G-16997)*

Gt World Machineries Usa Inc..800 242-4935
40 W Main St Christiana (19702) *(G-999)*

Gtech Cleaning Services LLC..302 494-2102
950 Ridge Rd Ste B5 Claymont (19703) *(G-1173)*

Gti Millwork, Wilmington *Also Called: Group Three Inc (G-16988)*

GTS Technical LLC..302 778-1362
122 Middleboro Rd Wilmington (19804) *(G-16998)*

Guap International Enterprise, Townsend *Also Called: Nancy Dufresne (G-14042)*

Guard Prostamp Inc..626 290-3357
4 Peddlers Row Unit 299 Newark (19702) *(G-10905)*

Guardian Advisors LLC..302 220-8729
60 Rivers End Dr Seaford (19973) *(G-13202)*

Guardian Angel Child Care..302 428-3620
1000 Wilson St Wilmington (19801) *(G-16999)*

Guardian Angel Day Care..302 934-0130
25193 Zoar Rd Georgetown (19947) *(G-4348)*

Guardian Angel HM Hlth Care AG..................................302 476-1281
30 Prestbury Sq Ste 301 Newark (19713) *(G-10906)*

ALPHABETIC SECTION — H & R Block

Guardian Companies Inc (PA) 302 834-1000
  101 Rogers Rd Ste 101 Wilmington (19801) *(G-17000)*

Guardian Construction Co Inc (HQ) 302 834-1000
  1617 Matassino Rd New Castle (19720) *(G-9183)*

Guardian Construction Co Inc 302 656-1986
  100 Rogers Rd Wilmington (19801) *(G-17001)*

Guardian Envmtl Svcs Co Inc 302 918-3070
  70 Albe Dr Newark (19702) *(G-10907)*

Guardian Fence Company 302 834-3044
  4783 Summit Bridge Rd Middletown (19709) *(G-7182)*

Guardian General 443 205-1210
  112 S Tull Dr Seaford (19973) *(G-13203)*

Guardian Investments 302 541-2114
  28371 Dupont Blvd Unit 3 Millsboro (19966) *(G-8309)*

Guardian Property MGT LLC 302 227-7878
  17298 Coastal Hwy Unit 1 Lewes (19958) *(G-6067)*

Guco, Wilmington *Also Called: Guedon Co (G-17002)*

Guedon Co 302 375-6151
  1106 Cypress Rd Wilmington (19810) *(G-17002)*

Guide Svcs, Townsend *Also Called: Dagers Waterfowl Hunting (G-13983)*

Guided Footsteps 302 494-6680
  2820 W 3rd St Wilmington (19805) *(G-17003)*

Guiding Hearts Family Daycare, New Castle *Also Called: Susan R Austin (G-9607)*

Guinevere Associates Inc 302 635-7798
  2 Nob Hill Rd Wilmington (19808) *(G-17004)*

Gulab Management Inc (PA) 302 734-4433
  1426 N Dupont Hwy Dover (19901) *(G-2632)*

Gulab Management Inc 302 398-4206
  17101 Dupont Hwy Harrington (19952) *(G-4776)*

Gulab Management Inc 302 934-6126
  729 Bay Rd Milford (19963) *(G-7914)*

Gulab Management Inc 302 422-8089
  1036 N Walnut St Milford (19963) *(G-7915)*

Gulf Coast Investments Inc 929 359-4439
  8 The Grn Dover (19901) *(G-2633)*

Gulf Development Partners LLC (PA) 646 334-1245
  910 Foulk Rd Ste 201 Wilmington (19803) *(G-17005)*

Gulfstream Development Corp 302 539-6178
  35477 Atlantic Ave Millville (19967) *(G-8531)*

Gull House Adult Activity 302 226-2160
  34382 Carpenters Way Ste 1 Lewes (19958) *(G-6068)*

Gull's Way Campground, Dagsboro *Also Called: Gulls Way Inc (G-1456)*

Gulls Way Campground 302 732-6383
  30738 Gulls Way Dr Dagsboro (19939) *(G-1454)*

Gulls Way Campground 302 732-6383
  Rte 26 Dagsboro (19939) *(G-1455)*

Gulls Way Inc 302 732-9629
  Dagsboro (19939) *(G-1456)*

Gullwing Contracting Inc 302 943-0133
  728 Toby Collins Ln Harrington (19952) *(G-4777)*

Gulu Project Inc 302 547-8106
  123 Dantes Dr Hockessin (19707) *(G-5230)*

Gumboro Service Center Inc 302 238-7040
  22181 Charles West Rd Frankford (19945) *(G-4112)*

Gund Securities Corporation 302 479-9210
  1105 N Market St Ste 1300 Wilmington (19801) *(G-17006)*

Gunnar Advik El 302 867-0424
  7209 Lancaster Pike Ste 4-1112 Hockessin (19707) *(G-5231)*

Gunning Partners LLC 302 482-4305
  240 N James St Ste 103 Newport (19804) *(G-12453)*

Gunnip & Company 302 225-5000
  2751 Centerville Rd Ste 300 Wilmington (19808) *(G-17007)*

Gunnip Employment Services, Wilmington *Also Called: Gunnip & Company (G-17007)*

Gurukrupa Inc 302 328-6691
  133 S Dupont Hwy New Castle (19720) *(G-9184)*

Gusher 302 803-5900
  405 N King St Wilmington (19801) *(G-17008)*

Gustavo E Espinosa 302 731-5203
  111 Radcliffe Dr Newark (19711) *(G-10908)*

Gutter Cleaning 302 293-8461
  2328 Thomas Ln Wilmington (19810) *(G-17009)*

Gutter Connection LLC 302 736-0105
  2559 Mckee Rd Dover (19904) *(G-2634)*

Guy & Lady Barrel Cigars, Dover *Also Called: Guy & Lady Barrel LLC (G-2635)*

Guy & Lady Barrel LLC 302 399-3069
  198 Hatteras Dr Dover (19904) *(G-2635)*

Guy Bug 302 242-5254
  1017 Westview Ter Dover (19904) *(G-2636)*

Guys Gutter 302 424-1931
  466 Bay Rd Milford (19963) *(G-7916)*

Guys Gutter 302 325-4210
  2406 W Newport Pike Wilmington (19804) *(G-17010)*

Gw Consulting Inc 302 294-2114
  4200 Governor Printz Blvd Wilmington (19802) *(G-17011)*

Gw Solutions LLC 240 578-5981
  237 Oyster Shell Cv Bethany Beach (19930) *(G-606)*

Gwantel Intl Corp Engrg & Tech 302 377-6235
  21 Hidden Valley Dr Fl B Newark (19711) *(G-10909)*

Gwantel-Usa, Newark *Also Called: Gwantel Intl Corp Engrg & Tech (G-10909)*

Gwp Group LLC 888 217-4497
  200 Continental Dr Ste 401 Newark (19713) *(G-10910)*

Gym Starz LLC 302 747-7218
  155 Commerce Way Ste D Dover (19904) *(G-2637)*

Gymstarz Gymnastics Academy 302 697-1221
  23 Cochran Ln Camden (19934) *(G-842)*

H & A Electric Co 302 678-8252
  59 Roosevelt Ave Dover (19901) *(G-2638)*

H & C Auto Care 302 494-8989
  1280 Porter Rd Bear (19701) *(G-257)*

H & C Insulation LLC 302 448-0777
  14329 Saint Johnstown Rd Greenwood (19950) *(G-4634)*

H & E Trucking Co LLC 302 287-2113
  581 Old State Rd Middletown (19709) *(G-7183)*

H & H Construction Company LLC 936 825-6774
  1365 N Dupont Hwy Dover (19901) *(G-2639)*

H & H Stables Inc 302 629-5100
  26705 River Rd Seaford (19973) *(G-13204)*

H & J Unisex Salon 302 983-6833
  15 Salem Village Sq Newark (19713) *(G-10911)*

H & M Acoustical Services Inc 302 218-7783
  777 White Rock Rd Bear (19701) *(G-258)*

H & R Block 302 856-3272
  21305 Berlin Rd Unit 1 Georgetown (19947) *(G-4349)*

H & R Block 302 398-8730
  16819 S Dupont Hwy Ste 200 Harrington (19952) *(G-4778)*

H & R Block 302 378-1538
  705 Middletown Warwick Rd Middletown (19709) *(G-7184)*

H & R Block 302 324-1040
  287 Christiana Rd Ste 24 New Castle (19720) *(G-9185)*

H & R Block 302 368-7500
  561 College Sq Newark (19711) *(G-10912)*

H & R Block 302 436-0260
  38445 Dupont Blvd Unit 3 Selbyville (19975) *(G-13540)*

H & R Block 302 999-8100
  2407 Kirkwood Hwy Wilmington (19805) *(G-17012)*

H & R Block, Bear *Also Called: H & R Block Inc (G-259)*

H & R Block, Georgetown *Also Called: H & R Block (G-4349)*

H & R Block, Harrington *Also Called: H & R Block (G-4778)*

H & R Block, Middletown *Also Called: H & R Block (G-7184)*

H & R Block, Middletown *Also Called: H & R Block Inc (G-7185)*

H & R Block, Millsboro *Also Called: H & R Block Inc (G-8310)*

H & R Block, New Castle *Also Called: H & R Block (G-9185)*

H & R Block, New Castle *Also Called: H & R Block Inc (G-9186)*

H & R Block, New Castle *Also Called: H & R Block Inc (G-9187)*

H & R Block, Newark *Also Called: H & R Block (G-10912)*

H & R Block, Rehoboth Beach *Also Called: Basic Block Corp (G-12623)*

H & R Block, Seaford *Also Called: Wentworth Inc (G-13446)*

H & R Block, Selbyville *Also Called: H & R Block (G-13540)*

H & R Block, Wilmington *Also Called: H & R Block (G-17012)*

H & R Block, Wilmington *Also Called: H & R Block Inc (G-17013)*

H & R Block, Wilmington *Also Called: H & R Block Inc (G-17014)*
H & R Block, Wilmington *Also Called: H & R Block Inc (G-17015)*
H & R Block Inc 302 836-2700
  54 Foxhunt Dr Bear (19701) *(G-259)*
H & R Block Inc 302 378-8931
  Middletown Shopping Ctr Middletown (19709) *(G-7185)*
H & R Block Inc 302 934-6178
  28417 Dupont Blvd Unit 4 Millsboro (19966) *(G-8310)*
H & R Block Inc 302 328-7320
  196 Penn Mart Shopping Ctr Unit 11 New Castle (19720) *(G-9186)*
H & R Block Inc 302 652-3286
  232 New Castle Ave New Castle (19720) *(G-9187)*
H & R Block Inc 302 999-7488
  4711 Kirkwood Hwy Wilmington (19808) *(G-17013)*
H & R Block Inc 302 478-9140
  1720 Marsh Rd Wilmington (19810) *(G-17014)*
H & R Block Inc 302 478-6300
  3629b Silverside Rd Wilmington (19810) *(G-17015)*
H & R Block-Milford, Milford *Also Called: Sad Enterprises Inc (G-8078)*
H & R Heating & AC 302 323-9919
  7 King Ct New Castle (19720) *(G-9188)*
H B P Inc (PA) 302 378-9693
  110 W Green St Middletown (19709) *(G-7186)*
H C Davis Inc 302 337-7001
  Pine Alley Bridgeville (19933) *(G-706)*
H Clemons Consulting Inc 302 295-5097
  1000 N West St Ste 1200 Wilmington (19801) *(G-17016)*
H D C Inc 302 323-9300
  405 Marsh Ln Ste 1 Wilmington (19804) *(G-17017)*
H D Lee Company Inc (HQ) 302 477-3930
  3411 Silverside Rd Ste 201 Wilmington (19810) *(G-17018)*
H Dean McSpadden DDS 302 239-5917
  500 Lantana Dr Hockessin (19707) *(G-5232)*
H Dean McSpadden DDS 302 571-0680
  11 Old Barley Mill Rd Wilmington (19807) *(G-17019)*
H G Investments LLC 302 734-5017
  27 E Walnut St Magnolia (19962) *(G-6750)*
H H Builders Inc 302 735-9900
  3947 Forrest Ave Dover (19904) *(G-2640)*
H I E Contractors Inc 302 224-3032
  324 Markus Ct Newark (19713) *(G-10913)*
H K Griffith Inc 302 368-4635
  115 Happy Ln Newark (19711) *(G-10914)*
H P Custom Trim LLC 302 381-0802
  22091 Lwes Georgetown Hwy Georgetown (19947) *(G-4350)*
H P Electric Motors, Newark *Also Called: HP Motors Inc (G-10981)*
H Private Foundation 800 839-1754
  501 Silverside Rd Ste 123 Wilmington (19809) *(G-17020)*
H S B C Overseas Corp De 302 657-8400
  300 Delaware Ave Ste 1400 Wilmington (19801) *(G-17021)*
H S Troyer 302 678-2694
  351 Rose Valley School Rd Dover (19904) *(G-2641)*
H T G Consulting LLC 302 322-4100
  2 Penns Way Ste 300 New Castle (19720) *(G-9189)*
H Wells Paving & Sealcoating 302 857-9243
  712 Cardinal Ave Bear (19701) *(G-260)*
H Wells Paving & Sealcoating 302 838-2727
  149 Hadrian Close Bear (19701) *(G-261)*
H-V Technical Services Inc 302 427-5801
  300 Delaware Ave Ste 525 Wilmington (19801) *(G-17024)*
H&B Express Logistics 815 201-0915
  8 The Grn Dover (19901) *(G-2642)*
H&H Customs Inc 302 378-0810
  708 Lorewood Grove Rd Middletown (19709) *(G-7187)*
H&H Services Electrical Contrs 302 373-4950
  507 Sterling Ave New Castle (19720) *(G-9190)*
H&H Trading International LLC 480 580-3911
  1201 N Orange St Ste 600 Wilmington (19801) *(G-17022)*
H&J Trucking Corp 516 737-9134
  254 Chapman Rd Ste 208 Newark (19702) *(G-10915)*
H&K Group Inc 302 934-7635
  30548 Thorogoods Rd Dagsboro (19939) *(G-1457)*

H&R Block Eastern Enterpres 302 656-7212
  106 S Union St Wilmington (19805) *(G-17023)*
H&S Cleaning Service Inc 302 449-2928
  684 Southerness Dr Townsend (19734) *(G-14012)*
H+trace Inc 954 381-1400
  651 N Broad St Middletown (19709) *(G-7188)*
H2og Fogger Inc 414 333-7024
  3200 Kirkwood Hwy Wilmington (19808) *(G-17025)*
Haart Program, Bear *Also Called: Healing Adults & Adolescents (G-266)*
Haass Family Butcher Shop 302 734-5447
  3997 Hazlettville Rd Dover (19904) *(G-2643)*
Hab Nab Trucking Inc 302 245-6900
  8805 Newton Rd Bridgeville (19933) *(G-707)*
Habash Commercial Realty LLC 302 218-3025
  205 Philadelphia Pike Wilmington (19809) *(G-17026)*
Habib Bolourchi MD Facc 302 645-7672
  4503 Hwy 1 Rehoboth Beach (19971) *(G-12779)*
Habitat America LLC 302 875-3525
  100 Laurel Commons Ln Laurel (19956) *(G-5526)*
Habitat Design Group 302 335-4452
  192 Bowers Beach Rd Frederica (19946) *(G-4169)*
Habitat For Hmnity New Cstle C (PA) 302 652-0365
  1920 Hutton St Wilmington (19802) *(G-17027)*
HABITAT FOR HUMANITY, Dover *Also Called: Central Del Hbtat For Hmnity I (G-2049)*
Habitat For Humanity, Georgetown *Also Called: Habitat For Humanity Intl Inc (G-4351)*
Habitat For Humanity Intl Inc 302 855-1156
  107 Depot St Georgetown (19947) *(G-4351)*
Haccp Navigator LLC 302 531-7922
  10256 Webb Farm Rd Lincoln (19960) *(G-6673)*
Hack Vc Management Company LLC 650 575-4613
  1209 N Orange St Wilmington (19801) *(G-17028)*
Hackett Industries LLC 302 516-0836
  701 S Franklin St Wilmington (19805) *(G-17029)*
Hackney Business Solutions LLC 843 496-7236
  930 Alexandria Dr Newark (19711) *(G-10916)*
Hage Tool and Machine Inc 302 836-4850
  3415 Wrangle Hill Rd Ste 7 Bear (19701) *(G-262)*
Hagerty Drivers Club LLC 302 504-6086
  2711 Centerville Rd Ste 400 Wilmington (19808) *(G-17030)*
Hagerty Homes LLC 302 234-4268
  42 E Periwinkle Ln Newark (19711) *(G-10917)*
Hagertys Roofing 302 650-3474
  102 Cambridge Dr Wilmington (19803) *(G-17031)*
HAGLEY MUSEUM AND LIBRARY, Wilmington *Also Called: Eleuthrian Mlls-Hgley Fndtion (G-16355)*
Hague Surfboards 302 745-9336
  102 Gosling Creek Rd Lewes (19958) *(G-6069)*
Hagy Landscaping Inc 707 935-6119
  16 Lenape Ln Millsboro (19966) *(G-8311)*
Haines Contracting Inc 443 877-7103
  1055 Lower Twin Lane Rd New Castle (19720) *(G-9191)*
Haines Fabrication & Mch LLC 302 436-1929
  45 Railroad Ave Selbyville (19975) *(G-13541)*
Hair Academy Llc 302 738-6251
  160 Pencader Plz Newark (19713) *(G-10918)*
Hair Acdemy Schl Brbering Buty, Newark *Also Called: Hair Academy Llc (G-10918)*
Hair By Ashleighmonai LLC 215 201-6874
  804 E 28th St Wilmington (19802) *(G-17032)*
Hair Cuttery, Middletown *Also Called: Hc Salon Holdings Inc (G-7199)*
Hair Cuttery, Millville *Also Called: Hc Salon Holdings Inc (G-8533)*
Hair Cuttery, Wilmington *Also Called: Hc Salon Holdings Inc (G-17086)*
Hair Cuttery, Wilmington *Also Called: Hc Salon Holdings Inc (G-17087)*
Hair Day 302 538-5198
  2459 S State St Dover (19901) *(G-2644)*
Hair Experience 302 293-0359
  11 Calwell Dr New Castle (19720) *(G-9192)*
Hair Gallerie 302 373-4774
  2747 Shipley Rd Wilmington (19810) *(G-17033)*
Hair Sensations Inc 302 731-0920
  55 Herbert Dr New Castle (19720) *(G-9193)*
Hair Snippery, Millville *Also Called: Bethany Bch Hair Snippery Inc (G-8520)*

ALPHABETIC SECTION

Hair Studio.. 302 740-4804
   133 E Elgin Ct Newark (19702) *(G-10919)*

Hair Studio II... 302 945-5110
   Long Neck Rd Millsboro (19966) *(G-8312)*

Hair Yard... 302 264-0594
   11 Wood St Ste D Middletown (19709) *(G-7189)*

Haircut & Co, Newark *Also Called: Haircut & Company Inc (G-10920)*

Haircut & Company Inc.. 302 239-3236
   47 Tenby Chase Dr Newark (19711) *(G-10920)*

Hairworks Inc.. 302 656-0566
   1601 Concord Pike Ste 21 Wilmington (19803) *(G-17034)*

Hajirs Touch LLC.. 302 543-2302
   704 W 9th St Wilmington (19801) *(G-17035)*

Hajoca Corporation.. 302 764-6000
   303 E 30th St Wilmington (19802) *(G-17036)*

Haldas Brothers, Wilmington *Also Called: Jabez Corp (G-17470)*

Hale J Eric MD.. 302 644-2064
   1305 Savannah Rd Lewes (19958) *(G-6070)*

Hale Byrnes House.. 302 998-3792
   606 Stanton Christiana Rd Newark (19713) *(G-10921)*

Halen, Wilmington *Also Called: Halen Technologies Inc (G-17037)*

Halen Technologies Inc.. 302 290-3075
   1007 N Market St Wilmington (19801) *(G-17037)*

Haley, David, Wilmington *Also Called: Foot Care Group Inc (G-16686)*

Half Pint Ink.. 302 381-5561
   114 Falls Rd Milton (19968) *(G-8633)*

Hall Burke VFW Post 5447 Inc.. 302 798-2052
   1605 Philadelphia Pike Wilmington (19809) *(G-17038)*

Hall of Fame LLC.. 443 373-4046
   30003 Pawley Island Ct Dagsboro (19939) *(G-1458)*

Haller & Hudson... 302 856-4525
   101 S Bedford St Georgetown (19947) *(G-4352)*

Halley LLC... 650 628-8501
   16192 Coastal Hwy Lewes (19958) *(G-6071)*

Halligan Inc.. 314 488-9400
   16192 Coastal Hwy Lewes (19958) *(G-6072)*

Halloran Farkas + Kittila LLP... 302 257-2011
   5801 Kennett Pike Ste C Wilmington (19807) *(G-17039)*

Haloali Teeth Whitening LLC.. 302 300-4042
   409 Fillmore Ct Claymont (19703) *(G-1174)*

Halosil International Inc.. 302 543-8095
   1500 Eastlawn Ave Wilmington (19802) *(G-17040)*

Halpern Eye Associates Inc... 302 838-0700
   1237 Quintilio Dr Bear (19701) *(G-263)*

Halpern Eye Associates Inc (PA).. 302 734-5861
   885 S Governors Ave Dover (19904) *(G-2645)*

Halpern Eye Associates Inc... 302 734-5861
   223 E Main St Middletown (19709) *(G-7190)*

Halpern Eye Associates Inc... 302 422-2020
   771 E Masten Cir Ste 109 Milford (19963) *(G-7917)*

Halpern Eye Associates Inc... 302 537-0234
   142 Atlantic Ave Ste A Millville (19967) *(G-8532)*

Halpern Eye Associates Inc... 302 653-3400
   201 Stadium St Smyrna (19977) *(G-13755)*

Halpern Eye Associates-Midway... 302 993-7861
   4605 Kirkwood Hwy Wilmington (19808) *(G-17041)*

Halpern Eye Care.. 302 346-2020
   1404 Forrest Ave Ste 1 Dover (19904) *(G-2646)*

Halpern Eye Care.. 302 678-1700
   1197 Airport Rd Milford (19963) *(G-7918)*

Halpern Eye Care, Dover *Also Called: Halpern Eye Associates Inc (G-2645)*

Halpern Medical, Dover *Also Called: Halpern Opthalmology Assoc (G-2647)*

Halpern Opthalmology Assoc.. 302 678-2210
   200 Banning St Dover (19904) *(G-2647)*

Haltia Inc... 302 244-7425
   2810 N Church St Pmb 29349 Wilmington (19802) *(G-17042)*

Hamilton Distributors Inc.. 302 542-7860
   6920 Robin Dr Seaford (19973) *(G-13205)*

Hamilton Home Services LLC.. 302 430-6505
   32889 Vines Creek Rd Dagsboro (19939) *(G-1459)*

Hamilton House Condominium... 302 658-7787
   1403 Shallcross Ave Apt 304 Wilmington (19806) *(G-17043)*

Hamlin Mona Liza BSN Rn Ibclc.. 302 235-8277
   306 Cox Rd Newark (19711) *(G-10922)*

Hammer, Greg S, Dover *Also Called: Brenford Animal Hospital P A (G-1976)*

Hammond Enterprises Inc.. 302 934-1700
   1111 N Dupont Blvd Milford (19963) *(G-7919)*

Hammond M Knox DDS... 302 383-6696
   13 Thomas Ln N Newark (19711) *(G-10923)*

Hampton By Hilton, Middletown *Also Called: Hampton Inn Middletown (G-7191)*

Hampton By Hilton, Seaford *Also Called: Hampton Inn Seaford (G-13206)*

Hampton Enterprises Inc.. 302 378-7365
   413 Prestwick Pl Townsend (19734) *(G-14013)*

Hampton Enterprises Delaware, Townsend *Also Called: Hampton Enterprises Inc (G-14013)*

Hampton Inn... 302 422-4320
   800 Karken Pit Rd Milford (19963) *(G-7920)*

Hampton Inn, Newark *Also Called: Hollywood Grill Restaurant (G-10958)*

Hampton Inn, Seaford *Also Called: Hollywood Grill Restaurant (G-13211)*

Hampton Inn Dover, Dover *Also Called: Hampton Inn-Dover (G-2648)*

Hampton Inn Middletown.. 302 378-5656
   117 Sandhill Dr Middletown (19709) *(G-7191)*

Hampton Inn Seaford... 302 629-4500
   799 N Dual Hwy Seaford (19973) *(G-13206)*

Hampton Inn-Dover... 302 736-3500
   1568 N Dupont Hwy Dover (19901) *(G-2648)*

Hampton Walk Apartments, New Castle *Also Called: Evergreen Apartment Group Inc (G-9105)*

Hanbang Group.. 626 506-7585
   201 Ruthar Dr Newark (19711) *(G-10924)*

Hanbrun LLC.. 929 302-6393
   16192 Coastal Hwy Lewes (19958) *(G-6073)*

Hand -N- Hand Early Lrng Ctr.. 302 422-0702
   13724 S Old State Rd Unit 3 Ellendale (19941) *(G-3920)*

Hand & Spa.. 302 478-1700
   3654 Concord Pike Wilmington (19803) *(G-17044)*

Hand and Stone.. 302 373-6608
   301 Alders Dr Wilmington (19803) *(G-17045)*

Hand Stone Massage Facial Spa... 302 261-9716
   213 Governors Pl Bear (19701) *(G-264)*

Hand Stone Massage Facial Spa... 302 643-2991
   401 S Ridge Ave Middletown (19709) *(G-7192)*

Handler Builders Inc... 302 999-9200
   5169 W Woodmill Dr Wilmington (19808) *(G-17046)*

Handler Corporation... 302 999-9200
   5169 W Woodmill Dr Ste 10 Wilmington (19808) *(G-17047)*

Hands Healing Massage Day Spa... 302 689-3183
   42 Reads Way New Castle (19720) *(G-9194)*

Hands of Hope.. 302 519-2706
   32104 S Spring Ct Laurel (19956) *(G-5527)*

Hands On Deck Moving Co LLC.. 302 489-9251
   312 Loganberry Ter Dover (19901) *(G-2649)*

Handy & Harman.. 302 697-9521
   12244 Willow Grove Rd Camden (19934) *(G-843)*

Handy & Harman, Camden *Also Called: Handytube Corporation (G-844)*

Handy Handyman... 267 307-5206
   630 Vivaldi Dr Middletown (19709) *(G-7193)*

Handy Husband LLC.. 302 697-7552
   8771 Willow Grove Rd Camden Wyoming (19934) *(G-952)*

Handy Logistics LLC.. 570 905-4173
   319 Elizabeth Sweetbriar Ln New Castle (19720) *(G-9195)*

Handy Man Maintenance, Millsboro *Also Called: Christopher Handy (G-8225)*

Handyman Bill.. 302 588-5887
   407 Cleveland Ave Wilmington (19804) *(G-17048)*

Handyman Housecalls Inc.. 302 245-3816
   34417 Skyler Dr Lewes (19958) *(G-6074)*

Handyman Mark... 302 454-1170
   213 Mulberry Rd Newark (19711) *(G-10925)*

Handyman Matters, Wilmington *Also Called: Handyman Mtters Nrthrn-Dlaware (G-17049)*

Handyman Mtters Nrthrn-Dlaware.. 302 540-8263
   4722 Mermaid Blvd Wilmington (19808) *(G-17049)*

Handymen USA, Townsend *Also Called: Stanley J Lepowski Jr (G-14072)*

Handytech Solutions LLC... 302 449-4497
   308 John Randal Dr Middletown (19709) *(G-7194)*

Handytube Corporation (DH) 302 697-9521
12244 Willow Grove Rd Camden (19934) *(G-844)*

Handytube Corporation 302 697-9521
124 Vepco Blvd Camden (19934) *(G-845)*

Hank Technologies Inc 812 223-5984
8 The Grn Dover (19901) *(G-2650)*

Hanker, James W., Dover Also Called: Management Chemical Co *(G-3007)*

Hannahs Christian HM Day Care, Bear Also Called: Phyllis M Green *(G-423)*

Hannas Phrm Sup Co Inc 302 571-8761
2505 W 6th St Wilmington (19805) *(G-17050)*

Hannigan Short Disharoonk 302 875-3637
700 West St Laurel (19956) *(G-5528)*

Hanso Home Inc 760 437-2621
1007 N Orange St Fl 4401 Wilmington (19801) *(G-17051)*

Hanthej Hulio 302 478-3080
4011 Concord Pike Ste A Wilmington (19803) *(G-17052)*

Hap LLC 302 645-7400
16192 Coastal Hwy Lewes (19958) *(G-6075)*

Happily Active LLC 307 317-7277
2055 Limestone Rd Wilmington (19808) *(G-17053)*

Happy Hnds Feet Kidz Trnsp LLC 302 897-2375
262 Chapman Rd Ste 221 Newark (19702) *(G-10926)*

Happy Hoofer, Harrington Also Called: Michael Matthew Sponaugle *(G-4802)*

Happy Kids Academy Inc 302 369-6929
273 Old Baltimore Pike Newark (19702) *(G-10927)*

Happy Pl Child Care Mddltown L 302 449-3311
4922 Summit Bridge Rd Middletown (19709) *(G-7195)*

Happy Place Day Care LLC 302 737-7603
4638 Ogletown Stanton Rd Newark (19713) *(G-10928)*

Happyland Childcare 302 424-3868
18073 Johnson Rd Lincoln (19960) *(G-6674)*

Happypath, Newark Also Called: Do Nothing Corp *(G-10543)*

Happyrobot Inc 972 837-9213
1111b S Governors Ave Ste 6189 Dover (19904) *(G-2651)*

Harbor Club Apartments 302 738-3561
26 Cheswold Blvd Apt 2a Newark (19713) *(G-10929)*

Harbor Hlthcare Rhbltation Ctr 302 645-4664
301 Ocean View Blvd Lewes (19958) *(G-6076)*

Harbor House Apts, Claymont Also Called: Apartment Communities Inc *(G-1039)*

Harbor House Seafood, Seaford Also Called: Harbor House Seafood Inc *(G-13207)*

Harbor House Seafood Inc (PA) 302 629-0444
504 Bridgeville Hwy Seaford (19973) *(G-13207)*

Harborchase Wilmington LLC 302 273-8630
2004 Shipley Rd Wilmington (19803) *(G-17054)*

Harborside Development II LLC 302 644-3377
18826 Coastal Hwy Rehoboth Beach (19971) *(G-12780)*

Harbour Textile Rental Svc Inc 302 656-2300
259 Quigley Blvd Ste 8 Historic New Castle (19720) *(G-5000)*

Harbour Towne Associates LP 302 645-1003
34232 Woods Edge Dr Unit 313 Lewes (19958) *(G-6077)*

Hard Hatters Roofg & Cnstr LLC 302 766-3611
1512 Lower Greenbriar Rd Wilmington (19810) *(G-17055)*

Hard Hatters Roofg Constructi 302 507-4459
2300 Inglewood Rd Apt B Wilmington (19803) *(G-17056)*

Hard Science Incubator Corp 302 752-1055
3411 Silverside Rd Wilmington (19810) *(G-17057)*

Hardcore Cmpstes Oprations Llc 302 442-5900
618 Lambson Ln New Castle (19720) *(G-9196)*

Hardcore Composites, New Castle Also Called: Hardcore Cmpstes Oprations Llc *(G-9196)*

Hardwick Tactical Corporation 787 466-6728
251 Little Falls Dr Wilmington (19808) *(G-17058)*

Hardwood Direct LLC 302 378-3692
4390 Summit Bridge Rd Ste 5 Middletown (19709) *(G-7196)*

Hardy Development 302 436-4496
32984 Lighthouse Rd Selbyville (19975) *(G-13542)*

Hardy Environmental Services, New Castle Also Called: Joseph T Hardy & Son Inc *(G-9268)*

Hardy's Development, Selbyville Also Called: Hardy Development *(G-13542)*

Harford Health Services Inc 410 420-8108
37454 Woods Run Cir Selbyville (19975) *(G-13543)*

Harim Usa Ltd (PA) 302 629-9136
126 N Shipley St Seaford (19973) *(G-13208)*

Harlem Watch Company LLC 646 354-7644
16192 Coastal Hwy Lewes (19958) *(G-6078)*

Harley-Davidson, Smyrna Also Called: Rommel Cycles LLC *(G-13869)*

Harmattan Design LLC 609 385-1041
3500 S Dupont Hwy Dover (19901) *(G-2652)*

Harmon Larhonda 302 747-0700
734 Rothwell Dr Middletown (19709) *(G-7197)*

Harmonious Mind LLC 302 668-1059
5189 W Woodmill Dr Ste 30a Wilmington (19808) *(G-17059)*

Harmony Construction Inc 302 737-8700
350 Salem Church Rd Newark (19702) *(G-10930)*

Harmony Mill LP 302 731-7948
26 Cheswold Blvd Newark (19713) *(G-10931)*

Harmony Spa 302 563-7723
550 Stanton Christiana Rd Ste 301 Newark (19713) *(G-10932)*

Harmony Trucking Inc 302 633-5600
305 W Newport Pike Wilmington (19804) *(G-17060)*

Harmony Yoga, Milford Also Called: Marylou Sheaffer *(G-7987)*

Harold D Shockley 302 275-8500
14686 Staytonville Rd Lincoln (19960) *(G-6675)*

Harold Dutton Builder, Lewes Also Called: Harold Dutton Jr *(G-6079)*

Harold Dutton Jr. 302 644-2992
14 Schaffer Ln Lewes (19958) *(G-6079)*

Harold L Scott Sr. 302 343-9217
2148 Lockwood Chapel Rd Dover (19904) *(G-2653)*

Harper Fitness 302 286-0474
266 Romney Blvd Newark (19702) *(G-10933)*

Harriet Tubman Safe House Inc 302 351-4434
914 E 7th St Wilmington (19801) *(G-17061)*

Harrington Medical & Optical, Harrington Also Called: Medical Center of Harrington *(G-4800)*

Harrington Raceway and Casino, Harrington Also Called: Harrington Raceway Inc *(G-4780)*

Harrington Raceway Inc 302 398-4920
15 W Rider Rd Harrington (19952) *(G-4779)*

Harrington Raceway Inc 302 398-5346
Rte 13-2nd Gate Harrington (19952) *(G-4780)*

Harrington Realty Inc (PA) 302 736-0800
516 Jefferic Blvd Ste C Dover (19901) *(G-2654)*

Harrington Realty Inc 302 422-2424
494 N Dupont Hwy Dover (19901) *(G-2655)*

Harrington Senior Center Inc 302 398-4224
102 Fleming St Harrington (19952) *(G-4781)*

Harris Berger LLC (PA) 302 665-1140
1105 N Market St Ste 1100 Wilmington (19801) *(G-17062)*

Harris Property Management LLC 302 588-8601
415 E 10th St Ofc 1c Wilmington (19801) *(G-17063)*

Harris Towing and Auto Service 302 736-9901
5360 N Dupont Hwy Dover (19901) *(G-2656)*

Harris Towing Service 302 736-5473
174 Albacore Dr Frederica (19946) *(G-4170)*

Harrison Family Practice Inc 302 956-6986
18119 Sussex Hwy Unit 1 Bridgeville (19933) *(G-708)*

Harrison Heart Daycare 302 836-8581
58 Wellington Dr Newark (19702) *(G-10934)*

Harrison House Cmnty Program 302 595-3370
1415 Pulaski Hwy Newark (19702) *(G-10935)*

Harrison Hse Cmnty Prgrams Inc 302 427-8438
6 Halcyon Dr New Castle (19720) *(G-9197)*

Harrison Snior Lving Gorgetown 302 856-4574
110 W North St Georgetown (19947) *(G-4353)*

Harrock Properties LLC 302 202-1321
8 The Grn Ste 8334 Dover (19901) *(G-2657)*

Harrold & Son Inc 302 629-9504
27129 Woodland Rd Seaford (19973) *(G-13209)*

Harry A Lehman III Md PA 302 629-5050
38 Snowy Egret Ct Bridgeville (19933) *(G-709)*

Harry Caswell Inc 302 945-5322
32645 Long Neck Rd Millsboro (19966) *(G-8313)*

Harry He DDS LLC 302 836-3711
1400 Peoples Plz Ste 207 Newark (19702) *(G-10936)*

Harry J Lawall & Son Inc 302 429-7630
1822 Augustine Cut Off Wilmington (19803) *(G-17064)*

ALPHABETIC SECTION

Harry K Foundation.. 301 226-0675
  313 S Boardwalk Rehoboth Beach (19971) *(G-12781)*
Harry Kenyon Incorporated... 302 762-7776
  259 Quigley Blvd Ste 1 Historic New Castle (19720) *(G-5001)*
Harry L Adams Inc... 302 328-5268
  23 Parkway Cir Ste 14 New Castle (19720) *(G-9198)*
Harry Louies Laundry & Dry Clg... 302 734-8195
  129 S Governors Ave Dover (19904) *(G-2658)*
Harry Moore Painting Etc.. 302 803-1087
  4514 Hendry Ave Wilmington (19808) *(G-17065)*
Harrymrmax Lgstics Crier Svcs.. 302 784-5578
  26 Bellecor Dr Ste B New Castle (19720) *(G-9199)*
Harrys Heating & Cooling.. 302 438-5853
  1 Lynbrook Rd Wilmington (19804) *(G-17066)*
Harrys Nuts and Then Some.. 302 947-1344
  32645 Long Neck Rd Millsboro (19966) *(G-8314)*
Harsha Tankala MD.. 302 674-1818
  1055 S Bradford St Dover (19904) *(G-2659)*
Hart Construction Co Inc... 302 737-7886
  109 Dallas Ave Newark (19711) *(G-10937)*
HART Group LLC... 302 782-9742
  8 The Grn Ste A Dover (19901) *(G-2660)*
Hart Home Improvements LLC.. 302 415-4764
  2418 Calf Run Dr Wilmington (19808) *(G-17067)*
Hart Management Group, Newark *Also Called: Hart Construction Co Inc (G-10937)*
Hart To Heart Ambulance.. 302 697-9395
  32413 Lewes Georgetown Hwy Lewes (19958) *(G-6080)*
Harting Graphics Ltd... 302 762-6397
  305 Brandywine Blvd Wilmington (19809) *(G-17068)*
Hartle Brian State Farm Agency... 302 322-1741
  239 Christiana Rd Ste C New Castle (19720) *(G-9200)*
Hartly Family Learning Ctr LLC.. 302 492-1152
  21 North St Hartly (19953) *(G-4875)*
Hartnett Physical Therapy.. 302 428-9420
  800 Woodlawn Ave Wilmington (19805) *(G-17069)*
Hartzell Industries Inc... 302 322-4900
  115 Quigley Blvd Historic New Castle (19720) *(G-5002)*
Harvard Business Services Inc (PA)... 302 645-7400
  16192 Coastal Hwy Lewes (19958) *(G-6081)*
Harvard Environmental Inc.. 302 326-2333
  760 Pulaski Hwy Bear (19701) *(G-265)*
Harvest Consumer Products LLC... 302 732-6624
  350 Clayton St Dagsboro (19939) *(G-1460)*
Harvest Media LLC... 415 712-9702
  19c Trolley Sq Wilmington (19806) *(G-17070)*
Harvest Ministries Inc... 302 846-3001
  305 N Bi State Blvd Delmar (19940) *(G-1600)*
Harvest Power Inc.. 270 765-6268
  1977 Bay Rd Milford (19963) *(G-7921)*
Harvest Ridge Winery LLC.. 302 250-6583
  447 Westville Rd Marydel (19964) *(G-6799)*
Harvey Development Co.. 302 323-9300
  29 E Commons Blvd Ste 100 New Castle (19720) *(G-9201)*
Harvey Development Company, Wilmington *Also Called: H D C Inc (G-17017)*
Harvey Hanna & Associates Inc... 302 323-9300
  405 Marsh Ln Ste 1 Newport (19804) *(G-12454)*
Harvey Mack Sales & Svc Inc (PA)... 302 324-8340
  29 E Commons Blvd Ste 300 New Castle (19720) *(G-9202)*
Harvey Road Automotive Inc.. 302 654-7500
  1004 W 25th St Wilmington (19802) *(G-17071)*
Harvey Truck Center, New Castle *Also Called: Harvey Mack Sales & Svc Inc (G-9202)*
Harvey Y Lee M D... 302 682-4155
  21 W Clarke Ave Milford (19963) *(G-7922)*
Hashout Technologies Inc... 703 622-1689
  16192 Coastal Hwy Lewes (19958) *(G-6082)*
Haskell Laboratory, Newark *Also Called: Eidp Inc (G-10616)*
Hasten Inc (PA).. 818 867-8151
  8 The Grn Ste R Dover (19901) *(G-2661)*
Hat World, Dover *Also Called: Lids Corporation (G-2939)*
Hatch Consulting.. 302 658-4380
  2100 Kentmere Pkwy Wilmington (19806) *(G-17072)*

Hatching Time LLC... 800 511-1369
  305 Ruthar Dr Ste C Newark (19711) *(G-10938)*
Hatfield Medical Instrs Inc (PA).. 301 468-0011
  29186 Baylis Ave Millsboro (19966) *(G-8315)*
Hathworth Inc... 302 884-7616
  913 N Market St Ste 200 Wilmington (19801) *(G-17073)*
Hatjis Christos G MD.. 302 744-6220
  1060 S Governors Ave Dover (19904) *(G-2662)*
Hatzel and Buehler Inc (HQ).. 302 478-4200
  3600 Silverside Rd Wilmington (19810) *(G-17074)*
Hatzel and Buehler Inc... 302 798-5422
  1 Righter Pkwy Ste 110 Wilmington (19803) *(G-17075)*
Hauleet Inc... 302 434-6384
  8 The Grn # 10713 Dover (19901) *(G-2663)*
Haus of Lacquer LLC (PA)... 302 690-0309
  300 N Market St Wilmington (19801) *(G-17076)*
Havc & Heating, Wilmington *Also Called: Bennett Services Inc (G-14838)*
Haven Lake Animal Hospital.. 302 422-8100
  300 Milford Harrington Hwy Milford (19963) *(G-7923)*
Hawa African Hair Braiding.. 302 654-9456
  6 E 7th St Wilmington (19801) *(G-17077)*
Hawkins & Sons Inc... 302 426-9290
  314 New Rd Wilmington (19805) *(G-17078)*
Hawkins Counsel Group... 302 660-0858
  521 N West St Wilmington (19801) *(G-17079)*
Hawkins Reporting Service, Wilmington *Also Called: Dale Hawkins (G-15770)*
Hawksbill Systems LLC... 302 494-1678
  3411 Silverside Rd Bynardb Wilmington (19810) *(G-17080)*
Hawthorn Suites Hotels Intl... 302 369-6212
  410 Eagle Run Rd Newark (19702) *(G-10939)*
Hayes Sewing Machine Co Inc.. 302 764-9033
  4425 Concord Pike Wilmington (19803) *(G-17081)*
Hayjay Auto Exports... 302 266-0266
  900 Old Harmony Rd Newark (19713) *(G-10940)*
Hazardous Waste... 302 739-9403
  89 Kings Hwy Dover (19901) *(G-2664)*
Hazzard Auto Repairs Inc... 302 645-4543
  1141 Savannah Rd Lewes (19958) *(G-6083)*
Hazzard Electric, Lewes *Also Called: Hazzard Electrical Contrs Inc (G-6084)*
Hazzard Electrical Contrs Inc.. 302 645-8457
  111 American Legion Rd Lewes (19958) *(G-6084)*
HB Dupont Plaza.. 302 998-7271
  422 Delaware Ave Wilmington (19801) *(G-17082)*
HB Fitness Concord Inc.. 302 478-9692
  4737 Concord Pike Wilmington (19803) *(G-17083)*
HB Fitness Delaware Inc.. 302 384-7245
  5810 Kirkwood Hwy Ste B Wilmington (19808) *(G-17084)*
HB Wine Merchants LLC.. 302 384-5991
  884 Arthursville Rd Hartly (19953) *(G-4876)*
HB&t Automotive LLC... 302 378-3333
  3171 Dupont Pkwy Townsend (19734) *(G-14014)*
Hbcs, Historic New Castle *Also Called: Hospital Blling Cllctn Svc Ltd (G-5006)*
Hbcu Week Foundation Inc... 302 544-0799
  1022 Coleman St Wilmington (19805) *(G-17085)*
Hbg Finest Carpet Cleaning, Dover *Also Called: Coney Steam and Clean (G-2129)*
Hbm Apps Inc.. 302 387-0052
  51 N Broad St Middletown (19709) *(G-7198)*
Hbnyc, Dover *Also Called: Hypebeast Inc (G-2711)*
Hbs, Lewes *Also Called: Harvard Business Services Inc (G-6081)*
Hbwm, Hartly *Also Called: HB Wine Merchants LLC (G-4876)*
Hc Salon Holdings Inc.. 302 378-8565
  659 Middletown Warwick Rd Middletown (19709) *(G-7199)*
Hc Salon Holdings Inc.. 302 537-4624
  38069 Town Center Dr Millville (19967) *(G-8533)*
Hc Salon Holdings Inc.. 302 999-7724
  3218 Kirkwood Hwy Wilmington (19808) *(G-17086)*
Hc Salon Holdings Inc.. 302 478-9978
  5607 Concord Pike Wilmington (19803) *(G-17087)*
Hce, Wilmington *Also Called: Hunte Corporate Enterprise LLC (G-17235)*
Hclinton Foundation.. 302 393-1448
  12363 Sussex Hwy Greenwood (19950) *(G-4635)*

Hcnrg Solutions, Wilmington *Also Called: H Clemons Consulting Inc* **(G-17016)**

Hcs Electric..302 824-3743
  206 N Canvasback Ct Smyrna (19977) **(G-13756)**

Hcsg Harbor Hc Harbo44...302 645-4664
  301 Ocean View Blvd Lewes (19958) **(G-6085)**

Hcsg Regal Hghts Regal41...302 998-0181
  6525 Lancaster Pike Hockessin (19707) **(G-5233)**

Hd Supply Waterworks Ltd..302 684-3054
  25414 Primehook Rd # 100 Milton (19968) **(G-8634)**

HD SUPPLY WATERWORKS LTD, Milton *Also Called: Hd Supply Waterworks Ltd* **(G-8634)**

Hday Spa..302 482-1041
  1900 Newport Gap Pike Wilmington (19808) **(G-17088)**

Head Start Harrington...302 398-9196
  112 East St Harrington (19952) **(G-4782)**

Headland Labs LLC...415 425-1997
  427 N Tatnall St Wilmington (19801) **(G-17089)**

Headquarter Barber Shop..302 378-7372
  217 E Main St Middletown (19709) **(G-7200)**

Headstream Inc..302 356-0156
  5301 Limestone Rd Ste 204 Wilmington (19808) **(G-17090)**

Headtotoe Mhealth Inc..438 867-1908
  1007 N Orange St Wilmington (19801) **(G-17091)**

Heal Autism Now Del Foundation....................................302 456-1335
  133 Pawnee Ct Newark (19702) **(G-10941)**

Heal Room Inc..770 597-3366
  2093 Philadelphia Pike # 1313 Claymont (19703) **(G-1175)**

Heal Well LLC..302 542-7095
  29967 Sawmill Dr Dagsboro (19939) **(G-1461)**

Healex Systems Ltd...302 235-5750
  11 Middleton Dr Wilmington (19808) **(G-17092)**

Healing Adults & Adolescents...302 836-4000
  3560 Wrangle Hill Rd Bear (19701) **(G-266)**

Healing Arts LLC..302 530-9152
  25 Jay Dr New Castle (19720) **(G-9203)**

Healing Garden At Fndg Avalon......................................302 535-7883
  102 S Main St Camden (19934) **(G-846)**

Healing Goddess Interprises...301 751-0695
  1201 Philadelphia Pike Ste 2 Wilmington (19809) **(G-17093)**

Healing Intentions LLC..302 690-3270
  120 Farm Meadows Ln Hockessin (19707) **(G-5234)**

Healing Touch Massage..302 791-0235
  613 Delancey Pl Claymont (19703) **(G-1176)**

Health & Beauty, Dover *Also Called: Lice Lifters Distribution LLC* **(G-2938)**

Health Care Assoc PA...302 684-2033
  616 Mulberry St Milton (19968) **(G-8635)**

Health Care Consultants Inc...302 892-9210
  240 N James St Ste 111 Wilmington (19804) **(G-17094)**

Health Care Consultants Inc...302 883-9462
  240 N James St Ste 209 Wilmington (19804) **(G-17095)**

Health Care Practice MGT...302 633-5840
  1602 Newport Gap Pike Wilmington (19808) **(G-17096)**

Health Care Solutions of...484 234-2427
  131 Woodgreen Rd Claymont (19703) **(G-1177)**

Health Insurance Associates, Dover *Also Called: Donald C Savoy Inc* **(G-2322)**

Health Support Services...302 287-4952
  732 E 11th St Wilmington (19801) **(G-17097)**

Healthcare Oprtons MGT Enterpr....................................302 832-9572
  221 Mariners Way Bear (19701) **(G-267)**

Healthshield LLC..302 352-0517
  1601 Milltown Rd Ste 3 Wilmington (19808) **(G-17098)**

Healthsource of Dover South..302 744-8526
  737 S Governors Ave Dover (19904) **(G-2665)**

Healthsource of Wilmington..302 319-4623
  1305 Kirkwood Hwy Wilmington (19805) **(G-17099)**

HealthSouth, Middletown *Also Called: Encompass Health Corporation* **(G-7101)**

Healthstat Inc...704 936-5546
  1162 Holly Hill Rd Milford (19963) **(G-7924)**

Healthworks, Dover *Also Called: Bayhealth Med Ctr Inc-OCC Hlth* **(G-1889)**

Healthy At Home Care LLC...571 228-5935
  7 Kendal Ln Rehoboth Beach (19971) **(G-12782)**

Healthy Directions Wellness...302 420-3927
  6 Arrowhead Trl Millsboro (19966) **(G-8316)**

Healthy Foot Care Inc...302 235-7799
  124 Lantana Dr Hockessin (19707) **(G-5235)**

Healthy Homes De Inc..302 998-1001
  3925 Kirkwood Hwy Wilmington (19808) **(G-17100)**

Healthy Kneads, Wilmington *Also Called: Stephanie Galbraith* **(G-20053)**

Healthy Outcomes LLC..302 856-4022
  2 Lee Ave Unit 103 Georgetown (19947) **(G-4354)**

Healthy Snacks Holdings Inc..917 540-6588
  651 N Broad St Ste 206 Middletown (19709) **(G-7201)**

Healthy To Core...240 506-4202
  57 Golden Eagle Dr Ocean View (19970) **(G-12521)**

Healthylongevitycafe Inc...408 599-6369
  2055 Limestone Rd Ste 200c Wilmington (19808) **(G-17101)**

Healy Long & Jevin Inc...302 654-8039
  2000 Rodman Rd Wilmington (19805) **(G-17102)**

Hearsay Services of Delaware..302 422-3312
  104 Ne Front St Milford (19963) **(G-7925)**

Hearst Media Services Conn LLC...................................203 330-6231
  1209 N Orange St Wilmington (19801) **(G-17103)**

Heart 2 Heart Services LLC..302 293-0124
  442 Pigeon View Ln New Castle (19720) **(G-9204)**

Heart and Vascular Clinic, Newark *Also Called: Ashish B Parikh* **(G-9922)**

Heart and Vascular Clinic PA..302 261-8200
  118 Sandhill Dr Ste 104 Middletown (19709) **(G-7202)**

Heart In Game Foundation Inc..302 494-3133
  3535 Silverside Rd Wilmington (19810) **(G-17104)**

Heart Ministry Radio..215 847-6664
  20 Ricci Ln Newark (19702) **(G-10942)**

Heart Start Er Training Inc...302 420-1917
  2724 Jacqueline Dr M33 Wilmington (19810) **(G-17105)**

Heart To Hand Daycare LLC..202 256-4524
  16192 Coastal Hwy Lewes (19958) **(G-6086)**

Heart To Heart Health Svcs LLC....................................302 603-3976
  896 S State St Dover (19901) **(G-2666)**

Heart Vsclar Clinic Wilmington.......................................302 518-6200
  410 Foulk Rd Ste 101 Wilmington (19803) **(G-17106)**

Heartfelt Books Publishing..866 557-6522
  1000 N West St Ste 1200 Wilmington (19801) **(G-17107)**

Heartland Payment Systems LLC...................................302 228-9365
  37126 E White Tail Dr Selbyville (19975) **(G-13544)**

Hearts International Inc...215 585-5597
  222 Delaware Ave Fl 9 Wilmington (19801) **(G-17108)**

Hearx Usa Inc..415 212-5500
  2140 S Dupont Hwy Camden (19934) **(G-847)**

Hearxgroup, Camden *Also Called: Hearx Usa Inc* **(G-847)**

Heated Wear LLC..347 510-7965
  427 N Tatnall St Ste 16278 Wilmington (19801) **(G-17109)**

Heather Baker..302 382-7466
  4320 Vernon Rd Harrington (19952) **(G-4783)**

Heather Broujos Agt..302 368-8080
  33 Possum Park Mall Newark (19711) **(G-10943)**

Heather L Dealy M D...302 998-2333
  1941 Limestone Rd Ste 200 Wilmington (19808) **(G-17110)**

Heather Ramadoss, Dover *Also Called: Edgility Inc* **(G-2424)**

Heathers Home Works LLC..302 927-0016
  29475 Vines Creek Rd Dagsboro (19939) **(G-1462)**

Heaven & Health Massage T..302 999-9565
  8 S Dupont Rd Wilmington (19805) **(G-17111)**

Heaven Maid Services Inc..302 223-6086
  272 Golden Plover Dr Smyrna (19977) **(G-13757)**

Heavenly Effects LLC..302 446-3521
  8 The Grn Ste 13403 Dover (19901) **(G-2667)**

Heavenly Films LLC..302 232-8988
  8 The Grn Ste 8571 Dover (19901) **(G-2668)**

Heavenly Harvest LLC...302 487-0974
  8 The Grn Ste R Dover (19901) **(G-2669)**

Heavenly Hound Hotel..302 436-2926
  33049 Lighthouse Rd Selbyville (19975) **(G-13545)**

Heavens Treasures Thrift and...267 387-0030
  1423 N Grant Ave Wilmington (19806) **(G-17112)**

Heavy Equipment Rental Inc..302 654-5716
  218 Marsh Ln New Castle (19720) **(G-9205)**

ALPHABETIC SECTION — Heritage Interiors Inc

Heckessin Health Partners 302 234-2597
  5850 Limestone Rd Hockessin (19707) *(G-5236)*

Heckler & Frabizzio PA 302 573-4800
  800 Delaware Ave Ste 200 Wilmington (19801) *(G-17113)*

Hedge Capital Markets Inc 714 515-2645
  8 The Grn Ste A Dover (19901) *(G-2670)*

Hedgeforce LLC 305 600-0085
  9 Majestic Dr Newark (19713) *(G-10944)*

Heidis Academy of Prfrmg Arts 302 293-7868
  1218 Pulaski Hwy Bear (19701) *(G-268)*

Heiman Gouge & Kaufman LLP 302 658-1800
  800 N King St Ste 303 Wilmington (19801) *(G-17114)*

Heiman Aber Goldlust & Baker 302 658-1800
  800 N King St Ste 303 Wilmington (19801) *(G-17115)*

Heiman, Henry A, Wilmington Also Called: Heiman Aber Goldlust & Baker *(G-17115)*

Heirloom Creations 302 659-1817
  5899 Underwoods Corner Rd Smyrna (19977) *(G-13758)*

Hel Ecrane Inc 604 519-0200
  8 The Grn Ste A Dover (19901) *(G-2671)*

Helen Delvecchio Lpn 914 472-3837
  30237 Seashore Park Dr Millville (19967) *(G-8534)*

Helen Maloney 302 422-5359
  184 Broad St Houston (19954) *(G-5443)*

Helen Williams Inc 302 328-9656
  179 S Dupont Hwy New Castle (19720) *(G-9206)*

Helen's Psychic Readings, New Castle Also Called: Helen Williams Inc *(G-9206)*

Helena Agri-Enterprises LLC 302 337-3881
  16635 Adams Rd Bridgeville (19933) *(G-710)*

Helena Schroyer MD 302 429-5870
  1010 N Bancroft Pkwy Ste L2 Wilmington (19805) *(G-17116)*

Helene Day Care Pre-School 302 834-9060
  311 Monroe St Delaware City (19706) *(G-1547)*

Helical Software Corp 323 544-5348
  16192 Coastal Hwy Lewes (19958) *(G-6087)*

Helium3 Tech and Services LLC 302 766-2856
  197 Harriet Ct Newark (19711) *(G-10945)*

Helix Inc Ta Audioworks 302 285-0555
  478 Middletown Warwick Rd Middletown (19709) *(G-7203)*

Helix Services LLC 302 306-4880
  651 N Broad St Ste 205-1930 Middletown (19709) *(G-7204)*

Hellenic Univ CLB Wilmington 302 479-8811
  1407 Foulk Rd Ste 100 Wilmington (19803) *(G-17117)*

Hellens Heating & Air I 302 945-1875
  20949 Harbeson Rd Harbeson (19951) *(G-4698)*

Helloguru Inc 754 303-3278
  2093 Philadelphia Pike # 4072 Claymont (19703) *(G-1178)*

Hells Kitchen Software Ltd 302 983-5644
  12 Furman Ct Newark (19713) *(G-10946)*

Helmark Steel Inc
  813 S Market St Wilmington (19801) *(G-17118)*

Helopen Condominium Council 302 227-6409
  527 N Boardwalk Rehoboth Beach (19971) *(G-12783)*

Help Initiative Inc 302 236-7773
  101 W Loockerman St Ste 1b Dover (19904) *(G-2672)*

Help Is On Way 302 328-4510
  211 Llangollen Blvd New Castle (19720) *(G-9207)*

Helpern Eye Associates, Milford Also Called: Halpern Eye Associates Inc *(G-7917)*

Helping Hands Child Care 302 438-1656
  4 Capo Ln New Castle (19720) *(G-9208)*

Helpinghands 302 290-1146
  8 Colony Blvd Apt 325 Wilmington (19802) *(G-17119)*

Helton and Moorehead Trnsp LLC 443 842-3360
  12 Royal Grant Way Dover (19901) *(G-2673)*

Hembal Labs Inc 800 414-4741
  1221 College Park Dr Dover (19904) *(G-2674)*

Hempville Inc 336 862-0107
  651 N Broad St Ste 206 Middletown (19709) *(G-7205)*

Henaghan Insurance 302 235-3111
  1302 Old Lancaster Pike Hockessin (19707) *(G-5237)*

Henderson Services Inc 302 424-1999
  219 N Rehoboth Blvd Milford (19963) *(G-7926)*

Hendrickson House Museum 302 652-5629
  606 N Church St Wilmington (19801) *(G-17120)*

Henlopen Acres Beach Club Inc 302 227-9919
  28 Dune Way Rehoboth Beach (19971) *(G-12784)*

Henlopen Cardiology, Rehoboth Beach Also Called: Habib Bolourchi MD Facc *(G-12779)*

Henlopen Cardiology PA (PA) 302 645-7671
  18959 Coastal Hwy Ste A Rehoboth Beach (19971) *(G-12785)*

Henlopen Condominiums, Rehoboth Beach Also Called: Helopen Condominium Council *(G-12783)*

Henlopen Design LLC 302 265-4330
  16192 Coastal Hwy Lewes (19958) *(G-6088)*

Henlopen Homes Inc 302 684-0860
  17644 Coastal Hwy Lewes (19958) *(G-6089)*

Henlopen Homes LLC 302 684-0860
  18427 Josephs Rd Milton (19968) *(G-8636)*

Henlopen Hotel Inc 302 227-2551
  511 N Boardwalk Rehoboth Beach (19971) *(G-12786)*

Henlopen Masonry Inc 302 947-9900
  20072 Cool Spring Rd Milton (19968) *(G-8637)*

Henlopen Music Therapy SE 302 593-7784
  31618 Holly Ct Lewes (19958) *(G-6090)*

Henlopen Overhead Door 302 228-0561
  31547 N Conley Cir Lewes (19958) *(G-6091)*

Henninger Printing Co Inc 302 934-8119
  208 Main St Millsboro (19966) *(G-8317)*

Henrietta Johnson Medical 302 761-4610
  601 New Castle Ave Wilmington (19801) *(G-17121)*

HENRIETTA JOHNSON MEDICAL CENT, Wilmington Also Called: Southbrdge Med Advsory Council *(G-19937)*

Henry Auto Body Shop, Wilmington Also Called: J Henry Edward & Sons Inc *(G-17457)*

Henry Box Brown LLC 917 749-3746
  412 N Monroe St Wilmington (19801) *(G-17122)*

Henry Bros, Wilmington Also Called: Henry Bros Autobody & Pnt Sp *(G-17123)*

Henry Bros Autobody & Pnt Sp 302 994-4438
  2013 W Newport Pike Wilmington (19804) *(G-17123)*

Henry Eashum & Son Inc 302 697-6164
  20 S Dupont Hwy Camden (19934) *(G-848)*

Henry Frncis Dpont Wntrthur Ms 302 888-4852
  5105 Kennett Pike Winterthur (19735) *(G-20972)*

Henry M McElduff 302 656-5561
  117 Rodney Dr New Castle (19720) *(G-9209)*

Henry Yee Plumbing Inc 914 980-2188
  300 Delaware Ave Wilmington (19801) *(G-17124)*

Henrys Car Care Inc 302 994-5766
  2207 Saint James Dr Wilmington (19808) *(G-17125)*

Hensco Glass Company, Harrington Also Called: Hensco LLC *(G-4784)*

Hensco LLC 302 423-1638
  155 Argos Choice Harrington (19952) *(G-4784)*

Hentkowski Inc 302 998-2257
  3420 Old Capitol Trl Wilmington (19808) *(G-17126)*

Herbert Mrs Sheryl A 215 668-1849
  135 Emerald Ridge Dr Bear (19701) *(G-269)*

Herbert R Martin Associates 302 239-1700
  489 Valley Brook Dr Hockessin (19707) *(G-5238)*

Herbert Studios 302 229-7108
  219 N Market St Wilmington (19801) *(G-17127)*

Herbstar Industries LLC 302 888-9207
  94 Albe Dr Ste 3 Newark (19702) *(G-10947)*

Herbstar Industries LLC 754 273-4204
  94 Albe Dr Ste 3 Newark (19702) *(G-10948)*

Hercules LLC (DH) 302 594-5000
  1313 N Market St Hercules Plz Wilmington (19894) *(G-17128)*

Herdeg Dupont Dalle Pazze LLP 302 655-6500
  15 Center Meeting Rd Wilmington (19807) *(G-17129)*

Herdify LLC 619 405-3952
  651 N Broad St Ste 205 Middletown (19709) *(G-7206)*

Heritage At Dover, Dover Also Called: 1203 Walker Rd Operations LLC *(G-1679)*

Heritage At Milford 302 422-8700
  500 S Dupont Blvd Milford (19963) *(G-7927)*

Heritage Concrete, Wilmington Also Called: HMA Concrete LLC *(G-17158)*

Heritage Interiors Inc 302 369-3199
  113 Sandy Dr Newark (19713) *(G-10949)*

Heritage Machine Shop LLC 302 656-3313
2 James Ct Wilmington (19801) *(G-17130)*

Heritage Medical Associates PA 302 998-3334
2601 Annand Dr Ste 4 Wilmington (19808) *(G-17131)*

Heritage Painting 302 270-2008
595 Augusta National Dr Magnolia (19962) *(G-6751)*

Heritage Sports Rdo Netwrk LLC 302 492-1132
1841 Bryants Corner Rd Hartly (19953) *(G-4877)*

Herman/Turner Group 302 322-4100
2 Penns Way Ste 300 New Castle (19720) *(G-9210)*

Hermann Warehouse Corporation 732 297-5333
400 Anchor Mill Rd Historic New Castle (19720) *(G-5003)*

Herms Freight LLC 321 417-4884
651 N Broad St Ste 205 Middletown (19709) *(G-7207)*

Hernandez & Sons 302 765-8476
308 Elwood Pl New Castle (19720) *(G-9211)*

Hernandez Contractor, Millsboro *Also Called: Jose Manuel Hernandez-Alvarez (G-8333)*

Hernandez Gustavo 302 354-1969
1 Neurys Ln Newark (19702) *(G-10950)*

Hernandez Landscaping, Newark *Also Called: Hernandez Gustavo (G-10950)*

Hernandez Painting 302 212-8425
14947 Wilson Hill Rd Georgetown (19947) *(G-4355)*

Hero Family Collection LLC 833 732-3432
1201 N Market St Ste 111-G25 Wilmington (19801) *(G-17132)*

Heroes Self Defense Foundation 609 335-2391
579 Coldwater Dr Clayton (19938) *(G-1370)*

Herr Foods Incorporated 302 628-9161
22706 Sussex Hwy Seaford (19973) *(G-13210)*

Herring Creek Builders Inc 302 684-3015
23130 Prince George Dr Lewes (19958) *(G-6092)*

Hershey Exteriors LLC 302 278-2004
33229 Parker House Rd Ocean View (19970) *(G-12522)*

Herstory Ensemble 216 288-8759
111 W 13th St # A Wilmington (19801) *(G-17133)*

Hertiage Builders & Improvemen 302 275-8675
9 Linn Ct Bear (19701) *(G-270)*

Hertrchs Fmly Auto Dealerships 302 276-2554
100 Buckley Blvd Bear (19701) *(G-271)*

Hertrich Collision Ctr of 302 839-0550
1449 Bay Rd Milford (19963) *(G-7928)*

Hertrich's Collision Center, Seaford *Also Called: Complete Auto Body Inc (G-13132)*

Hertz, Dover *Also Called: Hertz Local Edition Corp (G-2675)*

Hertz, New Castle *Also Called: Hertz Corporation (G-9212)*

Hertz, New Castle *Also Called: Hertz Corporation (G-9213)*

Hertz, Wilmington *Also Called: Hertz Corporation (G-17134)*

Hertz Corporation 302 428-0637
131 N Dupont Hwy New Castle (19720) *(G-9212)*

Hertz Corporation 302 428-0637
120 Old Churchmans Rd New Castle (19720) *(G-9213)*

Hertz Corporation 302 654-8312
100 S French St Ste D Wilmington (19801) *(G-17134)*

Hertz Local Edition Corp 302 678-0700
1679 S Dupont Hwy Ste 17 Dover (19901) *(G-2675)*

Hes Sign Services Inc 302 257-5150
200 Hadco Rd Wilmington (19804) *(G-17135)*

Hester Winery, Middletown *Also Called: Terrance R Hester (G-7636)*

Hetrick-Drake Associates Inc 302 998-7500
1220 N Olmsted Pkwy Middletown (19709) *(G-7208)*

Hetrick, C H Associates, Middletown *Also Called: Hetrick-Drake Associates Inc (G-7208)*

Hey Logistics LLC 706 350-5539
651 N Broad St Middletown (19709) *(G-7209)*

Heyman Enerio Gattuso & Hirzel 302 472-7300
300 Delaware Ave Wilmington (19801) *(G-17136)*

Hf Administrators Ltd 302 884-6723
1201 N Orange St Ste 7004 Wilmington (19801) *(G-17137)*

Hh Concrete LLC 302 242-6342
4927 Mills Rd Milford (19963) *(G-7929)*

HI Grade Dairy, Harrington *Also Called: Dfa Dairy Brands Fluid LLC (G-4762)*

HI Line Auto Detailing 302 420-5368
1618 Newport Gap Pike Wilmington (19808) *(G-17138)*

HI Neo Inc 917 514-9010
2140 S Dupont Hwy Camden (19934) *(G-849)*

Hiatus Business Solutions Inc 302 883-7324
56 Ogden Ct Smyrna (19977) *(G-13759)*

Hibbert Company 609 394-7500
890 Ships Landing Way Historic New Castle (19720) *(G-5004)*

Hibbert Group, The, Historic New Castle *Also Called: Hibbert Company (G-5004)*

Hibner Group Inc 717 281-1918
8 The Grn Dover (19901) *(G-2676)*

Hickman Overhead Door Company 302 422-4249
1625 Bay Rd Milford (19963) *(G-7930)*

Hickory Hill Builders Inc 302 934-6109
25714 Timmons Ln Dagsboro (19939) *(G-1463)*

Hickory Hill Metal Fabrication 302 382-6727
2134 Seven Hickories Rd Dover (19904) *(G-2677)*

Hidden Acres Rest Home Inc 302 492-1962
265 Mowely Ln Marydel (19964) *(G-6800)*

Hidden Jewel Tickets LLC 571 425-6522
40 E Main St # 830 Newark (19711) *(G-10951)*

Hidden Lake Games LLC 302 305-1070
2093 Philadelphia Pike # 8830 Claymont (19703) *(G-1179)*

Hie, Bridgeville *Also Called: Horney Industrial Elec Inc (G-713)*

Hifu Services Inc 650 867-4972
3411 Silverside Rd Ste 104 Wilmington (19810) *(G-17139)*

High Confectionary Company 213 807-6218
251 Little Falls Dr Wilmington (19808) *(G-17140)*

High Ground Creative LLC 302 505-1367
401 Cassidy Dr Ste F Dover (19901) *(G-2678)*

High Horse Performance Inc 302 894-1115
93 Artisan Dr Ste 6 Smyrna (19977) *(G-13760)*

High Point Preferred Insur Co 800 245-2425
3 Beaver Valley Rd Wilmington (19803) *(G-17141)*

High Tide Lab 302 538-7041
23 Cochran Ln Camden (19934) *(G-850)*

High Tide News 302 727-0390
11243 Signature Blvd Selbyville (19975) *(G-13546)*

High Transit Us LLC 302 286-5192
1263 Old Coochs Bridge Rd Newark (19713) *(G-10952)*

High Vue Logging Inc 302 697-3606
12090 Willow Grove Rd Camden (19934) *(G-851)*

High-Tech Machine Company Inc 302 636-0267
10 Lewis Cir Wilmington (19804) *(G-17142)*

High5 Global Corporation (PA) 732 248-1900
16192 Coastal Hwy Lewes (19958) *(G-6093)*

Highbred Horse Racing 302 519-6676
624 Cicada Ln Milford (19963) *(G-7931)*

Highdef Transportation LLC 610 212-8596
8 Dover Ct Bear (19701) *(G-272)*

Higher Power Yoga 302 354-5826
751 Dorchester Ct Smyrna (19977) *(G-13761)*

Highfield Electric LLC 302 836-4300
304 Genoa Dr Bear (19701) *(G-273)*

Highland Construction LLC 302 286-6990
3415 Wrangle Hill Rd Ste 10 Bear (19701) *(G-274)*

Highland Consulting Group Inc 301 408-0600
505 Fairway Dr Bethany Beach (19930) *(G-607)*

Highland West Civic Assoc 302 415-5435
213 Whitekirk Dr Wilmington (19808) *(G-17143)*

Highlife Entrmt Group LLC 478 250-1862
141 Stone Ridge Dr Dover (19901) *(G-2679)*

Highmark Blue Cross Blue Sheld, Wilmington *Also Called: Highmarks Inc (G-17144)*

Highmarks Inc (PA) 302 421-3000
800 Delaware Ave Ste 900 Wilmington (19801) *(G-17144)*

Highmarks Inc 302 421-3000
800 Delaware Ave Wilmington (19809) *(G-17145)*

Highwater Management Kent LLC 302 245-7570
4000 Bay Rd Frederica (19946) *(G-4171)*

Highwater MGT Sussex LLC 302 245-7570
22518 Lewes Georgetown Hwy Georgetown (19947) *(G-4356)*

Highway Operations, Middletown *Also Called: Delaware Department Trnsp (G-7039)*

Highway Traffic Controllers 302 697-7117
6236 Mud Mill Rd Camden Wyoming (19934) *(G-953)*

ALPHABETIC SECTION

Hildr Group, Dover *Also Called: Boa Financial LLC* *(G-1956)*

Hill Luth Day Care Center..302 656-3224
1018 W 6th St Wilmington (19805) *(G-17146)*

Hillandale Farms Delaware Inc...302 492-3644
149 Sydell Dr Hartly (19953) *(G-4878)*

Hillary J White Soho Slon Spa..302 838-2110
1582 Red Lion Rd Bear (19701) *(G-275)*

Hillis-Carnes Engrg Assoc Inc...302 744-9855
1277 Mcd Dr Dover (19901) *(G-2680)*

Hillman/Dover Ltd Partnership..302 655-4133
100 W Cmmons Blvd Ste 303 New Castle (19720) *(G-9214)*

Hillside Center...302 652-1181
810 S Broom St Wilmington (19805) *(G-17147)*

Hillside Oil Company Inc...302 738-4144
40 Brookhill Dr Newark (19702) *(G-10953)*

Hilltop Hostel...202 291-9591
34508 Quail Ln Dagsboro (19939) *(G-1464)*

Hilltop Lthran Nghbrhood Ctr I..302 656-3224
1018 W 6th St Wilmington (19805) *(G-17148)*

Hilo House, Wilmington *Also Called: W23 S12 Holdings LLC* *(G-20664)*

Hilton, Dover *Also Called: 44 Aasha Hospitality Assoc LLC* *(G-1688)*

Hilton, Dover *Also Called: Quintasian LLC* *(G-3412)*

Hilton, Newark *Also Called: Mj Wilmington Hotel Assoc LP* *(G-11431)*

Hilton Bus Service...302 697-7676
168 Vepco Blvd Camden (19934) *(G-852)*

Hilton Christiana, Newark *Also Called: Mj Wilmington Hotel Assoc LP* *(G-11430)*

Hilton Garden Inn Dover..302 465-3061
416 Tartan Dr Middletown (19709) *(G-7210)*

Hilton Garden Inns, Middletown *Also Called: Hilton Garden Inn Dover* *(G-7210)*

Hilyard's Business Solutions, Wilmington *Also Called: Hilyards Inc* *(G-17149)*

Hilyards Inc (PA)...302 995-2201
1616 Newport Gap Pike Wilmington (19808) *(G-17149)*

Himani J Patel DC..302 635-7421
4837 Limestone Rd Wilmington (19808) *(G-17150)*

Hines Shekelia...302 575-8255
1072 Justison St Wilmington (19801) *(G-17151)*

Hinkle Husbands LLC...302 827-8202
418 Geddes St Wilmington (19805) *(G-17152)*

Hint America Inc..646 845-1895
112 S French St Ste 105 Wilmington (19801) *(G-17153)*

Hippo Trailer..302 854-6661
14 Evergreen Dr Georgetown (19947) *(G-4357)*

Hirewise Inc...888 899-4980
651 N Broad St Middletown (19709) *(G-7211)*

Hirotec Inc...248 836-5100
1209 N Orange St Wilmington (19801) *(G-17154)*

Hirsh Industries Inc..302 678-4990
631 Ridgely St Dover (19904) *(G-2681)*

Hirsh Industries Inc..302 678-3456
1525 Mckee Rd Dover (19904) *(G-2682)*

Hispanic Personal Dev LLC..302 738-4782
2 Rolling Dr Newark (19713) *(G-10954)*

Hispano Magazine..302 668-6118
2 Rolling Dr Newark (19713) *(G-10955)*

Historic Georgetown Assn..302 934-8818
105 Spicer St Georgetown (19947) *(G-4358)*

Historical Society of Delaware..302 322-8411
42 The Strand Historic New Castle (19720) *(G-5005)*

Historical Society of Delaware (PA)....................................302 655-7161
505 N Market St Wilmington (19801) *(G-17155)*

Historical Society of Dover, Dover *Also Called: Friends of Old Dover* *(G-2537)*

Hither Creek Press..603 387-3444
197 Meadow Brook Ln Milford (19963) *(G-7932)*

Hitrust Hair, New Castle *Also Called: Hitrust LLC* *(G-9215)*

Hitrust LLC..302 525-6223
1140 River Rd New Castle (19720) *(G-9215)*

Hitz Mechanical..727 742-6315
37300 Dirickson Creek Rd Frankford (19945) *(G-4113)*

Hivemq Inc...888 803-3966
600 N Broad St Ste 5 Middletown (19709) *(G-7212)*

HK Electric LLC..302 927-0688
36207 Watch Hill Rd Frankford (19945) *(G-4114)*

HK Paper...302 475-3699
2706 Alexander Dr Wilmington (19810) *(G-17156)*

Hlh Construction MGT Svcs Inc..302 654-7508
2000 Rodman Rd Wilmington (19805) *(G-17157)*

HLS Event Solutions LLC...484 293-4272
21577 Capitan Loop Harbeson (19951) *(G-4699)*

HMA Concrete LLC..302 777-1235
270 Presidential Dr # 200 Wilmington (19807) *(G-17158)*

Hmi, Millsboro *Also Called: Hatfield Medical Instrs Inc* *(G-8315)*

Hnh Holdings LLC..415 548-3871
8 The Grn A Dover (19901) *(G-2683)*

Hns Plumbing Services LLC...302 650-9010
418 Pencader Ln Bear (19701) *(G-276)*

Hoard Incorporated..980 333-1703
251 Little Falls Dr Wilmington (19808) *(G-17159)*

Hoban Auto & Machineshop Inc...302 436-8013
19 N Main St Selbyville (19975) *(G-13547)*

Hoban Service Center, Selbyville *Also Called: Hoban Auto & Machineshop Inc* *(G-13547)*

Hobbs Enterprises Inc..302 697-2090
4398 Turkey Point Rd Viola (19979) *(G-14096)*

Hobday Group Ltd..302 337-9567
7222 Seashore Hwy Bridgeville (19933) *(G-711)*

Hobe Sound LLC..302 529-7096
2 Sunset Ct Wilmington (19810) *(G-17160)*

Hochman C Michael Atty..302 656-8162
1201 N Orange St Ste 400 Wilmington (19801) *(G-17161)*

Hockessin..302 234-4100
7503 Lancaster Pike Hockessin (19707) *(G-5239)*

Hockessin Animal Hospital...302 239-9464
643 Yorklyn Rd Hockessin (19707) *(G-5240)*

Hockessin Athletic Club, Hockessin *Also Called: Eastern Athletic Clubs LLC* *(G-5197)*

Hockessin Chrpractic Centre PA...302 239-8550
724 Yorklyn Rd Ste 150 Hockessin (19707) *(G-5241)*

Hockessin Day Spa..302 234-7573
1900 Newport Gap Pike Wilmington (19808) *(G-17162)*

Hockessin Electric Inc..302 239-9332
6 Fritze Ct Hockessin (19707) *(G-5242)*

Hockessin Family Practice Med..302 234-5770
726 Yorklyn Rd Ste 100 Hockessin (19707) *(G-5243)*

Hockessin Kinder Care 1633, Hockessin *Also Called: Kindercare Learning Ctrs LLC* *(G-5269)*

Hockessin Landscaping..302 235-2141
24 Donaldson Dr Newark (19713) *(G-10956)*

Hockessin Montessori School...302 234-1240
1000 Old Lancaster Pike Hockessin (19707) *(G-5244)*

Hockessin Salon...302 740-3638
117 Pumpkin Patch Ln Hockessin (19707) *(G-5245)*

Hockessin Soccer Club..302 234-1444
740 Evanson Rd Hockessin (19707) *(G-5246)*

Hockessin Tractor Inc...302 239-4201
654 Yorklyn Rd Hockessin (19707) *(G-5247)*

Hockey Labs Inc...929 909-6607
8 The Grn Ste 12995 Dover (19901) *(G-2684)*

Hodges International Inc..310 874-8516
8 The Grn Dover (19901) *(G-2685)*

Hoek Flowers Usa Inc..786 999-5767
160 Greentree Dr Dover (19904) *(G-2686)*

Hoenen & Mitchell Inc..302 645-6193
18548 Arabian Acres Rd Lewes (19958) *(G-6094)*

Hoerner Inc..302 762-4406
602 Elizabeth Ave Wilmington (19809) *(G-17163)*

Hoeschel Inv & Insur Group..302 738-3535
106 Haines St Ste A Newark (19711) *(G-10957)*

Hofa Gallery USA Inc...213 270-1972
2810 N Church St Wilmington (19802) *(G-17164)*

Hofa Gllery - Hse Fine Art - L, Wilmington *Also Called: Hofa Gallery USA Inc* *(G-17164)*

Hog Slat Incorporated..302 875-0889
30709 Sussex Hwy Laurel (19956) *(G-5529)*

Hogs Heroes Foundation De Ch1.......................................443 754-0343
31799 Katum Dr Laurel (19956) *(G-5530)*

Hola America LLC   ALPHABETIC SECTION

Hola America LLC 302 261-3460
   16192 Coastal Hwy Lewes (19958) *(G-6095)*

Hola Media Network LLC 302 228-8942
   17818 Cape Dr Lewes (19958) *(G-6096)*

Holiday Hair 302 856-2575
   6 College Park Ln Ste 1 Georgetown (19947) *(G-4359)*

Holiday Hair, Seaford *Also Called: Regis Corporation (G-13371)*

Holiday Hair 141, Rehoboth Beach *Also Called: Regis Corporation (G-12912)*

Holiday Hair 238, Bear *Also Called: Regis Corporation (G-450)*

Holiday Inn 302 655-0400
   700 N King St Wilmington (19801) *(G-17165)*

Holiday Inn, Bethany Beach *Also Called: Paul Amos (G-626)*

Holiday Inn, Claymont *Also Called: Holiday Inn Select (G-1180)*

Holiday Inn, Claymont *Also Called: Interstate Hotels Resorts Inc (G-1188)*

Holiday Inn, Dover *Also Called: K W Lands North LLC (G-2824)*

Holiday Inn, Dover *Also Called: Nazar Dover LLC (G-3163)*

Holiday Inn, Dover *Also Called: Shri SAI Dover LLC (G-3553)*

Holiday Inn, Harrington *Also Called: Holiday Inn Express (G-4785)*

Holiday Inn, Newark *Also Called: Concord Towers Inc (G-10296)*

Holiday Inn, Rehoboth Beach *Also Called: Holiday Inn Express (G-12787)*

Holiday Inn Express 302 398-8800
   17271 S Dupont Hwy Harrington (19952) *(G-4785)*

Holiday Inn Express 302 227-4030
   19953 Shuttle Rd Rehoboth Beach (19971) *(G-12787)*

Holiday Inn Express & Suites, Middletown *Also Called: Lila Keshav Hospitality LLC (G-7304)*

Holiday Inn Select 302 792-2700
   630 Naamans Rd Claymont (19703) *(G-1180)*

Holistic Elevation LLC 302 278-0026
   2220 Porter Rd Bear (19701) *(G-277)*

Holistic Health Care Delaware 302 545-1552
   796 Hickman Dr Ocean View (19970) *(G-12523)*

Holland Corp 302 245-5645
   33357 Deer Run Rd Selbyville (19975) *(G-13548)*

Holland Mulch Inc 302 765-3100
   135 Hay Rd Wilmington (19809) *(G-17166)*

Holland Properties 201 965-9272
   1515 Spring Ln Wilmington (19809) *(G-17167)*

Hollingsead International LLC 302 855-5888
   21583 Baltimore Ave Georgetown (19947) *(G-4360)*

Hollingsworth Heating & AC 302 422-7525
   719 S Dupont Blvd Milford (19963) *(G-7933)*

Holly Jordyn Ann 443 945-0615
   5201 W Woodmill Dr Wilmington (19808) *(G-17168)*

Holly Ann Semanchik PA 908 672-1163
   30241 Whitehall Dr Milton (19968) *(G-8638)*

Holly Hill Estates 302 653-7503
   271 Berry Dr Smyrna (19977) *(G-13762)*

Holly Lake Campsite, Millsboro *Also Called: Barsgr LLC (G-8182)*

Holly Oak Towing and Service 302 792-1500
   6521 Governor Printz Blvd Wilmington (19809) *(G-17169)*

Hollywell Logistics LLC 267 901-4272
   802 Nw St Ste 105 Wilmington (19801) *(G-17170)*

Hollywood Grill Restaurant 302 737-3900
   3 Concord Ln Newark (19713) *(G-10958)*

Hollywood Grill Restaurant 302 629-4500
   799 N Dual Hwy Seaford (19973) *(G-13211)*

Hollywood Grill Restaurant (PA) 302 655-1348
   3513 Concord Pike Ste 3300 Wilmington (19803) *(G-17171)*

Hollywood Grill Restaurant 302 479-2000
   350 Rocky Run Pkwy Wilmington (19803) *(G-17172)*

Hollywood Nails 302 477-4849
   3100 Naamans Rd Ste 7 Wilmington (19810) *(G-17173)*

Hollywood Nails & Spa 302 762-1800
   4101 N Market St Wilmington (19802) *(G-17174)*

Hollywood Tans 302 367-5959
   502 Greens Branch Ln Smyrna (19977) *(G-13763)*

Hollywood Tans 302 478-8267
   3100 Naamans Rd Ste 34 Wilmington (19810) *(G-17175)*

Hollywood Tans of Elkton 302 345-2510
   32 Belfort Loop Newark (19702) *(G-10959)*

Holman Moving Systems, New Castle *Also Called: Holman Moving Systems LLC (G-9216)*

Holman Moving Systems LLC (PA) 302 323-9000
   20 E Commons Blvd New Castle (19720) *(G-9216)*

Holmes Smith Consulting Svcs 302 407-6691
   19 Lambson Ln New Castle (19720) *(G-9217)*

Hologic Inc 302 631-2846
   18 Bay Blvd Newark (19702) *(G-10960)*

Hologic Inc 302 631-2700
   600 Technology Dr Newark (19702) *(G-10961)*

Holy See Global District, New Castle *Also Called: Larry Shelton (G-9295)*

Home Base Arms 302 983-6816
   2126 Old Kirkwood Rd Bear (19701) *(G-278)*

Home Builders Assn Del Inc 302 678-1520
   109 E Division St Dover (19901) *(G-2687)*

Home Course Creators LLC 302 419-6305
   206 Steeplechase Cir Wilmington (19808) *(G-17176)*

Home Depot USA Inc 302 735-8864
   801 N Dupont Hwy Dover (19901) *(G-2688)*

Home Depot USA Inc 302 395-1260
   138 Sunset Blvd New Castle (19720) *(G-9218)*

Home Depot USA Inc 302 838-6818
   2000 Peoples Plz Newark (19702) *(G-10962)*

Home Depot, The, Dover *Also Called: Home Depot USA Inc (G-2688)*

Home Depot, The, New Castle *Also Called: Home Depot USA Inc (G-9218)*

Home Depot, The, Newark *Also Called: Home Depot USA Inc (G-10962)*

Home Finders Real Estate, Wilmington *Also Called: Home Finders Real Estate Co (G-17177)*

Home Finders Real Estate Co 302 655-8091
   31 Trolley Sq Ste C Wilmington (19806) *(G-17177)*

Home For Aged Wmn-Mnquadale HM 302 654-1810
   1101 Gilpin Ave Wilmington (19806) *(G-17178)*

Home Health Corp America Inc 302 678-4764
   1221 College Park Dr Ste 203 Dover (19904) *(G-2689)*

Home Health Heartfel 302 660-2686
   5179 W Woodmill Dr Wilmington (19808) *(G-17179)*

Home Health Services By TLC 302 322-5510
   287 Christiana Ave Ste 24 Wilmington (19801) *(G-17180)*

Home Healthcare Agency, Bear *Also Called: Edlyncare LLC (G-195)*

Home Helpers, Claymont *Also Called: Bc Home Health Care Services (G-1054)*

Home Improvements 302 537-1102
   34816 Stream Ct Dagsboro (19939) *(G-1465)*

Home Innovations 302 448-9555
   17693 Coastal Hwy Lewes (19958) *(G-6097)*

Home Instead Senior Care 302 697-6435
   755 Walker Rd Ste A Dover (19904) *(G-2690)*

Home Instead Senior Care, Wilmington *Also Called: Robert Bird (G-19508)*

Home Integrated 302 656-1624
   325 Robinson Ln Wilmington (19805) *(G-17181)*

Home Media One LLC 302 644-0307
   22344 Lewes Georgetown Hwy Georgetown (19947) *(G-4361)*

Home Medic LLC 302 841-3861
   24617 Springfield Rd Georgetown (19947) *(G-4362)*

Home of Divine Providence Inc 302 654-1184
   300 Bayard Ave Wilmington (19805) *(G-17182)*

Home of Merciful Rest Society 302 652-3311
   1900 Lovering Ave Wilmington (19806) *(G-17183)*

Home Prmnt Pest Ctrl Cmpnies I 302 894-9201
   769 S Dupont Hwy New Castle (19720) *(G-9219)*

Home Savings America Newark 302 286-7814
   220 Continental Dr Newark (19713) *(G-10963)*

Home Security Wilmington 302 231-1142
   709 N Madison St Wilmington (19801) *(G-17184)*

Home Services LLC 302 510-4580
   3410 Old Capitol Trl Wilmington (19808) *(G-17185)*

Home Services Unlimited 302 293-8726
   22 Sailboat Cir Newark (19702) *(G-10964)*

Home Sweep Home 302 536-7339
   21 Crossgate Dr Seaford (19973) *(G-13212)*

Home Sweet 302 353-9733
   202 Governors Ave Greenwood (19950) *(G-4636)*

Home Team Realty 302 629-7711
   959 Norman Eskridge Hwy Seaford (19973) *(G-13213)*

ALPHABETIC SECTION

Home Theater, Dover *Also Called: Smartis (G-3578)*
Home Works 302 514-9974
   473 Pier Head Blvd Smyrna (19977) *(G-13764)*
Home2 Suites By Hilton 302 291-1616
   17388 Ocean One Plz Lewes (19958) *(G-6098)*
Homefix 302 682-3837
   17667 Gate Dr Unit 3 Lewes (19958) *(G-6099)*
Homeland SEC Verification LLC 888 791-4614
   4001 Kennett Pike Wilmington (19807) *(G-17186)*
Homeless Cat Helpers Inc 302 344-3015
   550 N Pine St Seaford (19973) *(G-13214)*
Homepay, Wilmington *Also Called: Safe Home Control (G-19624)*
Homer Foundation 800 839-1754
   501 Silverside Rd Wilmington (19809) *(G-17187)*
Homeries LLC 570 575-8008
   919 N Market St Ste 950 Wilmington (19801) *(G-17188)*
Homes For Laurel II Inc 302 875-3525
   100 Laurel Commons Ln Laurel (19956) *(G-5531)*
Homes For Life Foundation 302 571-1217
   1106 Berkeley Rd Wilmington (19807) *(G-17189)*
Homestar Remodeling LLC 302 528-5898
   405 Silverside Rd Ste 250 Wilmington (19809) *(G-17190)*
Homestead At Rehoboth Bb 302 226-7625
   35060 Warrington Rd Rehoboth Beach (19971) *(G-12788)*
Homestead Camping Inc 302 684-4278
   25165 Prettyman Rd Georgetown (19947) *(G-4363)*
Homestead Funding Corp 302 628-2828
   116 S Market St Seaford (19973) *(G-13215)*
Homestead Newark - Christiana 302 283-0800
   333 Continental Dr Newark (19713) *(G-10965)*
Hometown Fence LLC 302 629-0415
   23656 Fox Croft Ln Georgetown (19947) *(G-4364)*
Homeview Group LLC 508 686-6669
   651 N Broad St Ste 205 Middletown (19709) *(G-7213)*
Homeward Bound Inc 302 737-2241
   34 Continental Ave Newark (19711) *(G-10966)*
Homeward Tattoo 302 226-8145
   37169 Rehoboth Avenue Ext Unit 10 Rehoboth Beach (19971) *(G-12789)*
Homewatch Caregivers 302 644-1888
   17527 Nassau Commons Blvd Lewes (19958) *(G-6100)*
Homewatch Concierge 302 542-4087
   75 Kings Creek Cir Rehoboth Beach (19971) *(G-12790)*
Homewell Care Services, Georgetown *Also Called: Packd LLC (G-4453)*
Homewood Stes By Hilton Wlmngto 302 565-2100
   820 Justison St Wilmington (19801) *(G-17191)*
Homewood Suites, Wilmington *Also Called: Hollywood Grill Restaurant (G-17171)*
Homewood Suites, Wilmington *Also Called: Hollywood Grill Restaurant (G-17172)*
Homewood Suites, Wilmington *Also Called: Homewood Stes By Hlton Wlmngto (G-17191)*
Homework, Felton *Also Called: Kenneth H Gladish (G-3991)*
Homni Health Solution Inc 408 469-4956
   1221 College Park Dr # 116 Dover (19904) *(G-2691)*
Homsey Architects Inc 302 656-4491
   2003 N Scott St Wilmington (19806) *(G-17192)*
Honestly Service LLC 302 844-2214
   1201 N Market St Ste 111 Wilmington (19801) *(G-17193)*
Honesty Service 302 690-2433
   2213 Ogletown Rd Ste E Newark (19711) *(G-10967)*
Honey Alteration 302 519-2031
   17370 Coastal Hwy Lewes (19958) *(G-6101)*
Honeybee Arts LLC 646 664-5511
   6 Barrington Way Dover (19904) *(G-2692)*
Honeys Farm Fresh 302 644-8400
   329 Savannah Rd Lewes (19958) *(G-6102)*
Honeywell, Claymont *Also Called: Honeywell International Inc (G-1181)*
Honeywell, New Castle *Also Called: Honeywell International Inc (G-9220)*
Honeywell Authorized Dealer, Bear *Also Called: Delaware Heating & AC (G-149)*
Honeywell Authorized Dealer, Bridgeville *Also Called: JI Mechanical Inc (G-719)*
Honeywell Authorized Dealer, Dagsboro *Also Called: Blades H V A C Services (G-1418)*
Honeywell Authorized Dealer, Dagsboro *Also Called: North Star Heating & Air Inc (G-1490)*
Honeywell Authorized Dealer, Delmar *Also Called: K and B Hvac Svcs LLC (G-1609)*
Honeywell Authorized Dealer, Dover *Also Called: Associates Contracting Inc (G-1837)*
Honeywell Authorized Dealer, Dover *Also Called: Traps Plumbing Heating A/C (G-3716)*
Honeywell Authorized Dealer, Frankford *Also Called: A & A Air Services Inc (G-4059)*
Honeywell Authorized Dealer, Frankford *Also Called: Chesapeake Climate Control LLC (G-4085)*
Honeywell Authorized Dealer, Frankford *Also Called: Custom Mechanical Inc (G-4096)*
Honeywell Authorized Dealer, Georgetown *Also Called: Megee Plumbing & Heating Co (G-4422)*
Honeywell Authorized Dealer, Harbeson *Also Called: Hyett Refrigeration Inc (G-4701)*
Honeywell Authorized Dealer, Hartly *Also Called: Air Doctorx Inc (G-4855)*
Honeywell Authorized Dealer, Laurel *Also Called: Above & Beyond Services (G-5459)*
Honeywell Authorized Dealer, Middletown *Also Called: Pierce Total Comfort LLC (G-7448)*
Honeywell Authorized Dealer, New Castle *Also Called: Amstel Mechanical Contrs Inc (G-8803)*
Honeywell Authorized Dealer, New Castle *Also Called: National HVAC Service (G-9397)*
Honeywell Authorized Dealer, Newark *Also Called: Berry Refrigeration Co (G-10025)*
Honeywell Authorized Dealer, Newark *Also Called: Total Climate Control Inc (G-12211)*
Honeywell Authorized Dealer, Wilmington *Also Called: B Safe Inc (G-14703)*
Honeywell Authorized Dealer, Wilmington *Also Called: George H Burns Inc (G-16845)*
Honeywell Authorized Dealer, Wilmington *Also Called: Hentkowski Inc (G-17126)*
Honeywell International Inc 302 791-6700
   6100 Philadelphia Pike Claymont (19703) *(G-1181)*
Honeywell International Inc 302 322-4071
   3 Boulden Cir New Castle (19720) *(G-9220)*
Honeywell Safety Pdts USA Inc (HQ) 302 636-5401
   2711 Centerville Rd Ste 400 Wilmington (19808) *(G-17194)*
Honig, Gordon C DMD, Newark *Also Called: Gordon C Honig DMD PA (G-10870)*
Honorable Myron T Steele 302 739-4214
   800 N State St Ste 401 Dover (19901) *(G-2693)*
Hoober Inc 717 768-8231
   1130 Middletown Warwick Rd Middletown (19709) *(G-7214)*
Hoober Inc 302 629-3075
   6367 Stein Hwy Ste A Seaford (19973) *(G-13216)*
Hoober Equipment, Middletown *Also Called: Hoober Inc (G-7214)*
Hood Man LLC 302 422-4564
   10421 Jasmine Dr Lincoln (19960) *(G-6676)*
Hook Em & Cook Em LLC 302 226-8220
   24603 Bay Ave Milford (19963) *(G-7934)*
Hook PR Group 302 858-5055
   135 2nd St Fl 2 Lewes (19958) *(G-6103)*
Hooper's Landing, Seaford *Also Called: City of Seaford (G-13122)*
Hoopes Fire Prevention Inc 302 323-0220
   124 Sandy Dr Newark (19713) *(G-10968)*
Hoosier Osteotronix Corp 410 241-7627
   35669 Kiawah Path Rehoboth Beach (19971) *(G-12791)*
Hoover Computer Services Inc 302 529-7050
   4611 Bedford Blvd Wilmington (19803) *(G-17195)*
Hope Hanks Inc 302 562-9309
   1706 Pennrock Rd Wilmington (19809) *(G-17196)*
Hope Health Systems Inc 302 376-9619
   417 E Main St Middletown (19709) *(G-7215)*
Hope House Daycare 302 407-3404
   2814 W 2nd St Wilmington (19805) *(G-17197)*
Hope Presbyterian Church 302 764-8615
   720 Marsh Rd Wilmington (19803) *(G-17198)*
Hope Reigns LLC 302 406-0827
   1201 N Market St Ste 111 Wilmington (19801) *(G-17199)*
Hope Wellness Opportunity 302 521-6421
   2 Dempsey Dr Newark (19713) *(G-10969)*
Hopes Caramels Inc 302 290-7506
   36 Carpenter Plz Wilmington (19810) *(G-17200)*
Hopes Helping Hands LLC 443 365-5115
   1330 Middleford Rd Ste 303 Seaford (19973) *(G-13217)*
Hopewell Pharma Ventures Inc 203 273-1350
   1201 N Orange St Ste 717 Wilmington (19801) *(G-17201)*
Hopin US Inc 250 896-8450
   2810 N Church St Wilmington (19802) *(G-17202)*
Hopkins and Associates LLC 302 660-8476
   5143 W Woodmill Dr Wilmington (19808) *(G-17203)*

Hopkins Construction Inc...	302 337-3366
18904 Maranatha Way Unit 1 Bridgeville (19933) *(G-712)*	
Hopkins Henlopen Homestead..	202 695-9302
18186 Dairy Farm Rd Lewes (19958) *(G-6104)*	
Hopkins Tax & Accounting LLC......................................	302 846-2303
36885 Columbia Rd Delmar (19940) *(G-1601)*	
Hoppscotch LLC...	858 395-1737
8 The Grn Ste A Dover (19901) *(G-2694)*	
Hoppy LLC DBA Brick Works...	302 653-8961
230 S Dupont Blvd Smyrna (19977) *(G-13765)*	
Hopshop Inc...	323 745-1115
651 N Broad St Ste 201 Middletown (19709) *(G-7216)*	
Horizon Aeronautics Inc...	409 504-2645
300 Delaware Ave Ste 300 Wilmington (19801) *(G-17204)*	
Horizon and Co, Wilmington *Also Called: Kensington Tours Ltd (G-17691)*	
Horizon Farm Credit..	302 856-9081
20816 Dupont Blvd Georgetown (19947) *(G-4365)*	
Horizon Helicopters Inc..	302 368-5135
2035 Sunset Lake Rd Ste A Newark (19702) *(G-10970)*	
Horizon House Delaware...	302 577-3220
911 N Franklin St Wilmington (19806) *(G-17205)*	
Horizon House of Delaware Inc......................................	302 658-2392
1902 Maryland Ave Wilmington (19805) *(G-17206)*	
Horizon Intl Holdings LLC...	302 636-5401
251 Little Falls Dr Wilmington (19808) *(G-17207)*	
Horizon Rendering Co Inc..	302 239-4950
5802 Stone Pine Rd Wilmington (19808) *(G-17208)*	
Horizon Services Inc..	610 491-8800
307 Ruthar Dr Newark (19711) *(G-10971)*	
Horizon Services Inc (PA)..	302 762-1200
320 Century Blvd Wilmington (19808) *(G-17209)*	
Horizons Family Practice PA...	302 918-6300
3105 Limestone Rd Ste 301 Wilmington (19808) *(G-17210)*	
Hornberger Management Company (PA)........................	302 573-2541
1 Commerce Center Fl 7 Wilmington (19801) *(G-17211)*	
Horney Industrial Elec Inc (PA).......................................	302 337-3600
114 N Main St Bridgeville (19933) *(G-713)*	
Horning Bros Custom Painting..	302 384-7675
2408 Lanside Dr Wilmington (19810) *(G-17212)*	
Horns Machine Shop Inc...	302 653-6663
3652 Big Woods Rd Smyrna (19977) *(G-13766)*	
Horse Power Show Hunters LLC.....................................	302 265-2881
307 Hall Pl Milford (19963) *(G-7935)*	
Horsey Family, The, Laurel *Also Called: David G Horsey & Sons Inc (G-5494)*	
Horsey Turf Farm LLC..	302 875-7299
28107 Beaver Dam Branch Rd Laurel (19956) *(G-5532)*	
Horton Holdings Inc...	855 501-5834
651 N Broad St Ste 205 Middletown (19709) *(G-7217)*	
Horty, Wilmington *Also Called: Horty & Horty PA (G-17213)*	
Horty & Horty PA..	302 730-4560
3702 N Dupont Hwy Dover (19901) *(G-2695)*	
Horty & Horty PA (PA)..	302 652-4194
503 Carr Rd Ste 120 Wilmington (19809) *(G-17213)*	
Hose Pros..	302 663-0016
270 W State St Millsboro (19966) *(G-8318)*	
Hosford-Skapof, Martha A MD, Newark *Also Called: Regional Hmatology Oncology PA (G-11843)*	
Hosmane Cardiology..	302 588-1646
5515 Kirkwood Hwy Wilmington (19808) *(G-17214)*	
Hospital Blling Cllctn Svc Ltd (PA).................................	302 552-8000
118 Lukens Dr Historic New Castle (19720) *(G-5006)*	
Hospitalists of Delaware...	302 757-1231
5 Deville Ct Newark (19711) *(G-10972)*	
Hospitality Essentials LLC...	732 874-0048
811 N Broad St Ste 203 Middletown (19709) *(G-7218)*	
Hospitality House LLC..	929 262-1790
254 Chapman Rd Ste 208 Newark (19702) *(G-10973)*	
Hostgpo Inc...	424 422-0486
108 W 13th St Wilmington (19801) *(G-17215)*	
Hostigger Inc...	650 618-9818
2035 Sunset Lake Rd Ste B Newark (19702) *(G-10974)*	
Hosting.com, Newark *Also Called: Lnh Inc (G-11277)*	
Hot Rod Welding...	302 725-5485
258 Sika Dr Harrington (19952) *(G-4786)*	
Hot Shot Concepts..	302 947-1808
4 Sassafras Ln Harbeson (19951) *(G-4700)*	
Hotel Du Pont, Wilmington *Also Called: Wilmington Ht Xxxiii Owner LLC (G-20819)*	
Hotel Dupont Company, Wilmington *Also Called: Green Room Restaurant (G-16966)*	
Hotel Rodney...	302 645-6466
142 2nd St Unit 1 Lewes (19958) *(G-6105)*	
Hotelrunner Inc...	650 665-6405
2035 Sunset Lake Rd Ste B2 Newark (19702) *(G-10975)*	
Hough Associates Inc...	302 322-7800
2605 Eastburn Ctr Newark (19711) *(G-10976)*	
Hound Dog Recovery LLC...	302 836-3806
2151 S Dupont Blvd Smyrna (19977) *(G-13767)*	
Hourly Inc...	844 800-2211
3500 S Dupont Hwy Dover (19901) *(G-2696)*	
House Call Dentistry Inc...	866 686-4423
3 Bay Oak Dr Lewes (19958) *(G-6106)*	
House Industries, Wilmington *Also Called: Brand Design Co Inc (G-15040)*	
House of Harmony Hair Salon...	302 420-4565
35 Killane St Bear (19701) *(G-279)*	
House of Joseph, Wilmington *Also Called: Ministry of Caring Inc (G-18374)*	
House of Kings Inc..	302 319-8724
1511 N Dupont Hwy New Castle (19720) *(G-9221)*	
House of Wright Mortuary...	302 659-5517
48 E Commerce St Smyrna (19977) *(G-13768)*	
House of Wright Mortuary (PA).......................................	302 762-8448
208 E 35th St Wilmington (19802) *(G-17216)*	
House of Yoga LLC..	302 373-9534
7 Haileys Trl Newark (19711) *(G-10977)*	
House To House Incorporation..	302 450-8445
157 Chestnut Crossing Dr Newark (19713) *(G-10978)*	
Houseventure Inc..	786 481-7390
251 Little Falls Dr Wilmington (19808) *(G-17217)*	
Housing Alliance Delaware Inc..	302 654-0126
100 W 10th St Ste 611 Wilmington (19801) *(G-17218)*	
Houston Self Storage...	302 422-9660
Mill St Houston (19954) *(G-5444)*	
How Medical Marketing Inc...	302 283-9565
8 The Grn Ste B Dover (19901) *(G-2697)*	
Howard B Stromwasser...	302 368-4424
210 Suburban Dr Newark (19711) *(G-10979)*	
Howard Industries LLC (PA)...	217 836-4476
2140 S Dupont Hwy Camden (19934) *(G-853)*	
Howard Johnson, Newark *Also Called: Shri Swami Narayan LLC (G-12002)*	
Howard M Joseph Inc (PA)...	302 335-1300
3235 Bay Rd Milford (19963) *(G-7936)*	
Howard Management Group I...	302 562-5051
22 N Valley Stream Cir Newark (19702) *(G-10980)*	
Howard Morris Group LLC..	877 296-4726
910 Walker Rd Ste B Dover (19904) *(G-2698)*	
Howard Paul MD LLP..	302 644-2232
506 Union St Milton (19968) *(G-8639)*	
Howard W Zucker D D S P A...	302 475-8174
205 Hoyer Ct Wilmington (19803) *(G-17219)*	
Howard Weston Senior Center..	302 328-6425
1 Bassett Ave Ste 1 New Castle (19720) *(G-9222)*	
Howard Z Arian M D..	302 674-2390
95 Wolf Creek Blvd Ste 1 Dover (19901) *(G-2699)*	
Howarth Granite Holdings LLC..	302 543-6739
2703 Philadelphia Pike Ste D Claymont (19703) *(G-1182)*	
Howell Juanquetta..	302 682-1602
201 King Aly Ellendale (19941) *(G-3921)*	
Howmedica Osteonics Corp...	302 655-3239
2118 Kirkwood Hwy Ste A Wilmington (19805) *(G-17220)*	
Hoy En Delaware LLC...	302 854-0240
105 Depot St Georgetown (19947) *(G-4366)*	
Hoyt, Robert M & Co LLC CPA, Millsboro *Also Called: Robert Hoyt & Co (G-8448)*	
HP Motors Inc..	302 368-4543
38 Albe Dr Ste 14 Newark (19702) *(G-10981)*	

ALPHABETIC SECTION

Hq Global Workplaces Inc ... 302 295-4800
1000 N West St Ste 1200 Wilmington (19801) *(G-17221)*

Hrc Inc ... 302 604-3782
203 S Main St Bridgeville (19933) *(G-714)*

Hrc Medics LLC ... 561 856-6180
2608 Eastburn Ctr Newark (19711) *(G-10982)*

Hrd Products Inc ... 302 757-3587
68d Omega Dr Newark (19713) *(G-10983)*

Hrupsa Farms Ltd Partnership ... 302 270-1817
3418 Hopkins Cemetery Rd Harrington (19952) *(G-4787)*

Hs Capital LLC ... 302 317-3614
300 Delaware Ave Ste 1370 Wilmington (19801) *(G-17222)*

Hs Capital LLC ... 302 598-2961
300 Delaware Ave Ste 1370 Wilmington (19801) *(G-17223)*

Hsbc Bank, Wilmington *Also Called: Hsbc Bank USA (G-17224)*

Hsbc Bank USA (DH) ... 302 778-0169
300 Delaware Ave Ste 1400 Wilmington (19801) *(G-17224)*

Hsbc Bank USA National Assn ... 800 975-4722
90 Christiana Rd New Castle (19720) *(G-9223)*

Hsbc North America Inc ... 302 652-4673
1105 N Market St Fl 1 Wilmington (19801) *(G-17225)*

Hsi Service Corp ... 302 369-3709
220 Continental Dr Ste 115 Newark (19713) *(G-10984)*

Htm Management, Wilmington *Also Called: High-Tech Machine Company Inc (G-17142)*

Hts, Milton *Also Called: Hts 20 LLP (G-8640)*

Hts 20 LLP ... 800 690-2029
16394 Samuel Paynter Blvd Unit 103 Milton (19968) *(G-8640)*

Huang Family Foundation ... 800 839-1754
501 Silverside Rd Ste 123 Wilmington (19809) *(G-17226)*

Huang Law LLC ... 302 248-5138
3513 Concord Pike Ste 3100 Wilmington (19803) *(G-17227)*

Hub Associates ... 302 674-2200
222 S Dupont Hwy Dover (19901) *(G-2700)*

Hubert Headen ... 347 952-9250
295 Tea Party Trl Dover (19901) *(G-2701)*

Hubgets Inc ... 239 206-2995
4250 Lancaster Pike Ste 120 Wilmington (19805) *(G-17228)*

Hubioid Inc ... 312 912-1515
1000 N West St Ste 1200 Wilmington (19801) *(G-17229)*

Hudson Farm Supply Co Inc ... 302 398-3654
318 W Windmill Way Middletown (19709) *(G-7219)*

Hudson House Services ... 302 856-4363
11 W Pine St Georgetown (19947) *(G-4367)*

Hudson Jnes Jaywork Fisher LLC (PA) ... 302 734-7401
225 S State St Dover (19901) *(G-2702)*

Hudson Jnes Jaywork Fisher LLC ... 302 227-9441
309 Rehoboth Ave Rehoboth Beach (19971) *(G-12792)*

Hudson Jnes Jywork Fsher Attys ... 302 839-1153
995 N Dupont Blvd Milford (19963) *(G-7937)*

Hudson Jones, Rehoboth Beach *Also Called: Hudson Jnes Jaywork Fisher LLC (G-12792)*

Hudson Jones Jaywork Fisher ... 302 645-7999
34382 Carpenters Way # 3 Lewes (19958) *(G-6107)*

Hudson Management & Entps LLC ... 302 645-9464
30045 Eagles Crest Rd Milton (19968) *(G-8641)*

Hudson Scholastic ... 302 463-0840
109a Clayton St Dewey Beach (19971) *(G-1670)*

Hudson State Service Center, Newark *Also Called: Delaware Dept Hlth Social Svcs (G-10433)*

Hugh H Hickman & Sons Inc ... 302 539-9741
300 Ocean View Pkwy Bethany Beach (19930) *(G-608)*

Hughes Delaware Maid Scrapple ... 302 284-4370
8873 Burnite Mill Rd Felton (19943) *(G-3983)*

Hughes Network Systems LLC ... 302 335-4138
1 E David St Frederica (19946) *(G-4172)*

Hughy Inc ... 302 398-8826
111 E Center St Harrington (19952) *(G-4788)*

Huling Cove Housing Corp ... 302 739-4263
18 The Grn Dover (19901) *(G-2703)*

Hullo Inc ... 415 939-6534
3500 S Dupont Hwy Dover (19901) *(G-2704)*

Human Resources ... 302 573-3126
1626 N Union St Wilmington (19806) *(G-17230)*

Humandata, Dover *Also Called: Humandata Inc (G-2705)*

Humandata Inc ... 302 698-1287
8 The Grn Ste 11370 Dover (19901) *(G-2705)*

HUMANE ANIMAL PARTNERS, Wilmington *Also Called: Humane Animal Partners Inc (G-17231)*

Humane Animal Partners Inc ... 302 571-0111
701 A St Wilmington (19801) *(G-17231)*

Hummell James MD ... 302 875-8127
30867 Al Jan Dr Laurel (19956) *(G-5533)*

Hummingbird Hill Psychological ... 302 864-8818
1143 Savannah Rd Ste 4 Lewes (19958) *(G-6108)*

Hummingbird Lawn Care, Middletown *Also Called: Rabbani-Tehrani Shahariar (G-7497)*

Humphrey Jones Sherry H PHD ... 302 239-1076
3214 Charing Cross Wilmington (19808) *(G-17232)*

Humphries Construction Company ... 302 349-9277
11533 Holly Tree Ln Greenwood (19950) *(G-4637)*

Hungry Student Athletes, Odessa *Also Called: Dunkley Enterprises LLC (G-12583)*

Hunt Energy Netwrk Land Co LLC ... 214 978-8000
1675 S State St Ste B Dover (19901) *(G-2706)*

Hunt Vicmead Club ... 302 655-3336
601 Adams Dam Rd Wilmington (19807) *(G-17233)*

Hunt Vicmead Club (PA) ... 302 655-9601
903 Owls Nest Rd Wilmington (19807) *(G-17234)*

Hunt Wandendale Club ... 302 945-3369
34068 Village Way Millsboro (19966) *(G-8319)*

Hunte Corporate Enterprise LLC (PA) ... 212 710-1341
1201 N Orange St Ste 7377 Wilmington (19801) *(G-17235)*

Hunter Construction (PA) ... 410 392-5109
560 Peoples Plz 282 Newark (19702) *(G-10985)*

Hunter Green Inc ... 973 986-3114
260 Fieldcrest Dr Dover (19904) *(G-2707)*

Hunters Crossing, Newark *Also Called: Palladian Management LLC (G-11616)*

Hunters Run Associates, Bear *Also Called: Reybold Group of Companies Inc (G-459)*

Hunts Family Contracting ... 302 510-5585
522 Centerville Rd Wilmington (19808) *(G-17236)*

Hurlock Roofing Company ... 302 654-2783
26 Brookside Dr Wilmington (19804) *(G-17237)*

Husain, Ali S DMD Msd, Newark *Also Called: Ali S Husain Orthodontist (G-9810)*

Hustleofficial247 LLC ... 302 465-8965
544 N Bradford St Dover (19904) *(G-2708)*

Hutzpah Kitchen LLC ... 202 641-2916
2055 Limestone Rd 200c Wilmington (19808) *(G-17238)*

Huy M Le ... 302 738-7054
32 Omega Dr Newark (19713) *(G-10986)*

Huzala Inc (PA) ... 313 404-6941
4c Aleph Dr Newark (19702) *(G-10987)*

Hv Sunrise LLC (PA) ... 612 961-5783
919 N Market St Ste 950 Wilmington (19801) *(G-17239)*

Hy-Point Dairy Farms Inc ... 302 478-1414
425 Beaver Valley Rd Wilmington (19803) *(G-17240)*

Hy-Point Equipment Co ... 302 478-0388
425 Beaver Valley Rd Wilmington (19803) *(G-17241)*

Hyas US Inc ... 877 572-6446
251 Little Falls Dr Wilmington (19808) *(G-17242)*

Hyatt Hse Lewes / Rehoboth Bch ... 302 783-1000
17254 Five Points Sq Lewes (19958) *(G-6109)*

Hyatt Pl Wilmington Riverfront, Wilmington *Also Called: Riverfront Hotel LLC (G-19495)*

Hyatt Place ... 302 864-9100
1301 Coastal Hwy Dewey Beach (19971) *(G-1671)*

Hybrid Property LLC ... 302 289-6226
300 Delaware Ave Ste 210-252 Wilmington (19801) *(G-17243)*

Hybrid Property Group, Wilmington *Also Called: Hybrid Property LLC (G-17243)*

Hybridthory Digital Entrmt LLC ... 864 973-5753
8 The Grn Dover (19901) *(G-2709)*

Hydrohero Franchising LLC ... 302 321-7077
34407 Dupont Blvd Unit 8 Frankford (19945) *(G-4115)*

Hydrological Solutions ... 302 841-4444
27394 Round Pole Bridge Rd Milton (19968) *(G-8642)*

Hydropac ... 410 306-6345
742 Sussex Ave Seaford (19973) *(G-13218)*

Hydroseeding Co LLC ... 302 858-8171
22021 Eskridge Rd Bridgeville (19933) *(G-715)*

Hydroseeding Company LLC — 302 815-6500
9599 Nanticoke Business Park Dr Ste 3 Greenwood (19950) *(G-4638)*

Hydroshield Delmarva — 302 542-5923
30723 Molly B Rd Lewes (19958) *(G-6110)*

Hyett Refrigeration Inc — 302 684-4600
26451 Lewes Georgetown Hwy Harbeson (19951) *(G-4701)*

Hygieia Shield Inc — 302 388-7350
47 S West St Dover (19904) *(G-2710)*

Hyland Restoration LLC — 516 713-6518
2 Burleigh Ct Apt A5 Newark (19702) *(G-10988)*

Hype Hair LLC — 302 898-3145
550 S Dupont Hwy Apt 8i New Castle (19720) *(G-9224)*

Hypebeast Inc — 714 791-0755
3500 S Dupont Hwy Dover (19901) *(G-2711)*

Hyper Gizmo LLC — 888 487-1550
16192 Coastal Hwy Lewes (19958) *(G-6111)*

Hypertec Usa Inc — 480 626-9000
73 Greentree Dr Dover (19904) *(G-2712)*

Hysiotherapy Associates Inc — 610 444-1270
3411 Silverside Rd # 105 Wilmington (19810) *(G-17244)*

Hywatts Inc — 650 460-4488
919 N Market St Ste 950 Wilmington (19801) *(G-17245)*

I AM Consulting Group Inc — 302 521-4999
12 Dunleary Dr Bear (19701) *(G-280)*

I AM My Sisters Keeper — 302 304-1070
207 Highland Blvd Apt D New Castle (19720) *(G-9225)*

I Barry Guerke — 302 450-1098
116 E Water St Dover (19901) *(G-2713)*

I C S, Wilmington *Also Called: Intercontinental Chem Svcs Inc (G-17377)*

I Do It Right 100 LLC — 302 304-4467
1502 E Ayre St Wilmington (19804) *(G-17246)*

I G Burton Chrysler, Milford *Also Called: IG Burton & Company Inc (G-7939)*

I G Burton Imports, Milford *Also Called: IG Burton & Company Inc (G-7938)*

I Have A Dream Child Care — 302 507-2310
713 Vandever Ave Wilmington (19802) *(G-17247)*

I Heart Media — 302 730-3783
1575 Mckee Rd Ste 206 Dover (19904) *(G-2714)*

I K O Productions, Wilmington *Also Called: Goldis Holdings Inc (G-16914)*

I Love Myself LLC — 470 474-3347
2201 Carlton Ln Wilmington (19810) *(G-17248)*

I Need It I Want It LLC — 888 299-1341
1201 N Market St Ste 111 Wilmington (19801) *(G-17249)*

I T M S, Newark *Also Called: Integrated Turf Management Sys (G-11031)*

I V F, New Castle *Also Called: Industrial Valves & Fittings (G-9233)*

I-Pulse Inc (PA) — 604 689-8765
2711 Centerville Rd Ste 400 Wilmington (19808) *(G-17250)*

I3a LLC — 302 659-9090
5819 Underwoods Corner Rd Smyrna (19977) *(G-13769)*

I9 Directcom, Wilmington *Also Called: Homeland SEC Verification LLC (G-17186)*

Iaa Inc — 302 322-1808
417 Old Airport Rd New Castle (19720) *(G-9226)*

IAA, INC., New Castle *Also Called: Iaa Inc (G-9226)*

Iaabo — 302 737-4396
118 Belmont Dr Wilmington (19808) *(G-17251)*

Iaad — 302 234-0214
113 Jupiter Rd Newark (19711) *(G-10989)*

Iacono - Summer Chase — 302 994-2505
102 Robino Ct Ste 101 Wilmington (19804) *(G-17252)*

Iag Service Corp — 302 577-1333
200 Continental Dr Ste 401 Newark (19713) *(G-10990)*

Iamag Inc — 317 487-9338
2810 N Church St Pmb 99673 Wilmington (19802) *(G-17253)*

Ian Myers MD LLC — 302 832-7600
2600 Glasgow Ave Ste 218 Newark (19702) *(G-10991)*

Iap Holding LLC — 302 394-9795
3 Germay Dr Ste 42324 Wilmington (19804) *(G-17254)*

Iayam Financial LLC — 800 585-5315
8 The Grn Dover (19901) *(G-2715)*

Ibg Enterprise Inc — 302 494-5017
9 Nieole Ave New Castle (19720) *(G-9227)*

Ibi Group (us) Inc (DH) — 949 833-5588
501 Silverside Rd Unit 307 Wilmington (19809) *(G-17255)*

Ibidd Holdings LLC — 800 960-9221
8 The Grn Ste A12044 Dover (19901) *(G-2716)*

Ibope Media LLC — 305 529-0062
16192 Coastal Hwy Lewes (19958) *(G-6112)*

Ibr Group Inc — 610 986-8545
1098 Elkton Rd Newark (19711) *(G-10992)*

Ibr Lndscping Lawn Care Svcs L — 610 818-7127
1413 N Franklin St Wilmington (19806) *(G-17256)*

Icase LLC — 302 703-7854
16192 Coastal Hwy Lewes (19958) *(G-6113)*

Ice Cremee Creations — 516 450-2144
42 Doe Hill Ct Camden (19934) *(G-854)*

Icg Enterprises Inc — 302 373-7136
234 Red Tail Dr Dover (19904) *(G-2717)*

ICHDE, Wilmington *Also Called: Interfaith Cmnty Hsing of Del (G-17383)*

Iclean LLC (PA) — 518 573-3446
2035 Sunset Lake Rd Newark (19702) *(G-10993)*

Iconic Skus LLC — 302 722-4547
4023 Kennett Pike Ste 226 Wilmington (19807) *(G-17257)*

Iconico Inc — 650 681-9211
2093 Philadelphia Pike 2248 Claymont (19703) *(G-1183)*

Iconix LLC — 215 850-9337
34 Dunsinane Dr New Castle (19720) *(G-9228)*

Iconjured, Newark *Also Called: Conjured Jewells (G-10305)*

Icrush Technologies LLC (PA) — 302 613-2500
200 Continental Dr Newark (19713) *(G-10994)*

Ics - Worldwide Inc — 800 266-5254
251 Little Falls Dr Wilmington (19808) *(G-17258)*

ICS America Inc — 215 979-1620
1209 N Orange St Wilmington (19801) *(G-17259)*

Ict Enterprises Inc — 302 576-2840
300 Delaware Ave Wilmington (19801) *(G-17260)*

Ictclean Inc (PA) — 315 216-5121
3911 Concord Pike Wilmington (19803) *(G-17261)*

ID By Oliver LLC — 202 643-5536
651 N Broad St Ste 20523 Middletown (19709) *(G-7220)*

ID Griffith Inc — 302 656-8253
735 S Market St Frnt Wilmington (19801) *(G-17262)*

Ideal Property Solutions — 302 266-0451
204 Edjil Dr Newark (19713) *(G-10995)*

Ideal Venue LLC — 302 250-9208
2409 Lancaster Ave Wilmington (19805) *(G-17263)*

Ideaspace Open Mnds Foundation — 808 444-4578
106 Bernice Dr Bear (19701) *(G-281)*

Ideatree Inc — 310 844-7447
24a Trolley Sq Pmb 1232 Wilmington (19806) *(G-17264)*

Identisource LLC — 888 716-7498
16192 Coastal Hwy Lewes (19958) *(G-6114)*

Idf Connect Inc — 888 765-1611
2207 Concord Pike # 359 Wilmington (19803) *(G-17265)*

Idrch3 Ministries — 302 344-6957
49 Brenda Ln Camden (19934) *(G-855)*

iDreams Hub Inc — 740 990-2232
2810 N Church St Wilmington (19802) *(G-17266)*

IEC — 302 831-6231
451 Wyoming Rd Newark (19716) *(G-10996)*

Ieg Glbal Mdia Invstmnts Acqst — 720 290-9347
8 The Grn Ste 10184 Dover (19901) *(G-2718)*

Ieh Auto Parts LLC — 302 994-7171
3315 Old Capitol Trl Wilmington (19808) *(G-17267)*

Ies, Townsend *Also Called: Insight Engineering Solutions (G-14018)*

Iexperienceilearn LLC — 718 704-4870
66 Buttonwood Ave Historic New Castle (19720) *(G-5007)*

Iexperto Inc — 347 808-3708
651 N Broad St Middletown (19709) *(G-7221)*

Ifcf LLC — 351 773-4853
3500 S Dupont Hwy Dover (19901) *(G-2719)*

Ifi Techsolutions Inc — 332 456-0765
651 N Broad St Ste 206 Middletown (19709) *(G-7222)*

IG Burton & Company Inc (PA) — 302 422-3041
793 Bay Rd Milford (19963) *(G-7938)*

ALPHABETIC SECTION — In10sity Fitness United

IG Burton & Company Inc 302 424-3041
  605 Bay Rd Milford (19963) *(G-7939)*

IG Burton & Company Inc 302 629-2800
  24799 Sussex Hwy Seaford (19973) *(G-13219)*

Igal Biochemical LLC 302 525-2090
  4142 Ogletown Stanton Rd Ste 244 Newark (19713) *(G-10997)*

Igleisias Aquiles 302 831-7100
  540 S College Ave Newark (19713) *(G-10998)*

Igm Logistics LLC 302 409-9404
  30 Prestbury Sq Ste 309 Newark (19713) *(G-10999)*

Ignis Group LLC 302 645-7400
  16192 Coastal Hwy Lewes (19958) *(G-6115)*

Ignite Your Light 302 766-0982
  904 8th St Newark (19711) *(G-11000)*

Igt Inc 302 674-3177
  1281 Mcd Dr Dover (19901) *(G-2720)*

IH Technologies (iht) LLC 718 679-2613
  251 Little Falls Dr Wilmington (19808) *(G-17268)*

Ihandy LLC 708 239-1234
  1007 N Orange St Wilmington (19801) *(G-17269)*

Iheart Dance Studio LLC 267 249-8367
  600 N Broad St Ste 20 Middletown (19709) *(G-7223)*

II Alfred Collins 302 542-7010
  15005 County Seat Hwy Seaford (19973) *(G-13220)*

II Extreme Entertainment 302 389-8525
  100 Schafer Blvd New Castle (19720) *(G-9229)*

II USA Corporation 310 570-2928
  4a Trolley Sq #2138 Wilmington (19806) *(G-17270)*

III John F Glenn MD 302 735-8850
  737 S Queen St Ste 2 Dover (19904) *(G-2721)*

Iji Inc 732 485-9427
  2711 Centerville Rd Ste 400 Wilmington (19808) *(G-17271)*

Ijn Health Systems LLC 855 202-5993
  603 Parkman Ct Bear (19701) *(G-282)*

Ikarus Nest Inc 415 727-2401
  192 Bear Christiana Rd Bear (19701) *(G-283)*

Ikeno Tech Business Solutions, Newark *Also Called: Lawrence Kennedy (G-11234)*

Ikenrock Entertainment LLC 302 981-8532
  121 W 37th St Wilmington (19802) *(G-17272)*

Ikkar Inc 814 351-9394
  1 Chestnut Hill Plz Newark (19713) *(G-11001)*

Iko Manufacturing, Wilmington *Also Called: Iko Production Inc (G-17274)*

Iko Production Inc 302 764-3100
  6 Denny Rd Ste 200 Wilmington (19809) *(G-17273)*

Iko Production Inc (DH) 302 764-3100
  6 Denny Rd Ste 200 Wilmington (19809) *(G-17274)*

Iko Productions, Wilmington *Also Called: Iko Sales Inc (G-17276)*

Iko Sales Inc 360 988-9103
  6 Denny Rd Ste 200 Wilmington (19809) *(G-17275)*

Iko Sales Inc 302 764-3100
  6 Denny Rd Ste 200 Wilmington (19809) *(G-17276)*

Iko Southeast Inc (DH) 302 764-3100
  6 Denny Rd Ste 200 Wilmington (19809) *(G-17277)*

ILA, Newark *Also Called: International Literacy Assn (G-11046)*

Ilara Health Inc (PA) 646 322-7452
  251 Little Falls Dr Wilmington (19808) *(G-17278)*

Ilc, Frederica *Also Called: Ilc Dover LP (G-4174)*

Ilc Dover LP 302 629-6860
  2 Moonwalker Rd Frederica (19946) *(G-4173)*

Ilc Dover LP (PA) 302 335-3911
  1 Moonwalker Rd Frederica (19946) *(G-4174)*

Ile LLC 302 389-7911
  1201 N Market St Ste 111 Wilmington (19801) *(G-17279)*

Ilj International LLC 786 332-8535
  16192 Coastal Hwy Lewes (19958) *(G-6116)*

Illumina Corporate Foundation 516 870-7722
  501 Silverside Rd Wilmington (19809) *(G-17280)*

Illumination Technology Inc 410 430-5249
  38024 N Spring Hill Rd Delmar (19940) *(G-1602)*

Ilovekickboxing-Wilmington De 518 593-3463
  6 Blackbird Ct Newark (19702) *(G-11002)*

Imagic LLC 628 600-5244
  16192 Coastal Hwy Lewes (19958) *(G-6117)*

Imagineyu Designs LLC 302 387-1230
  49 Filbert Dr Camden Wyoming (19934) *(G-954)*

Imaging Group Delaware PA 302 421-4300
  St. Francis Hospital Department Of Radiology 7th & Clayton Sts Wilmington (19805) *(G-17281)*

Imaging Group of Delaware Inc 302 888-2303
  701 N Clayton St Wilmington (19805) *(G-17282)*

IMG Universe LLC 212 774-6704
  251 Little Falls Dr Wilmington (19808) *(G-17283)*

Immanuel Shelter Inc 888 634-9992
  19285 Holland Glade Rd Rehoboth Beach (19971) *(G-12793)*

Immanuel Shelter Inc 302 227-7743
  17601 Coastal Hwy Nassau (19969) *(G-8741)*

Immensity Logistics LLC 501 500-6667
  1207 Delaware Ave Wilmington (19806) *(G-17284)*

Impact Care Inc 610 628-2004
  1209 N Orange St Wilmington (19801) *(G-17285)*

Impact Graphix 302 337-7076
  415 Harrington St Seaford (19973) *(G-13221)*

Impact Insurance Agency 302 363-7785
  312 Main St Clayton (19938) *(G-1371)*

Impact Irrgation Solutions Inc 484 723-3600
  3213 Heathwood Rd Wilmington (19810) *(G-17286)*

Impact Irrigation 484 723-3600
  3213 Heathwood Rd Wilmington (19810) *(G-17287)*

Impact Shares Trust I 469 442-8424
  1209 N Orange St Wilmington (19801) *(G-17288)*

Impact Sports & Health Inc 734 678-5726
  239 Goldfinch Turn Newark (19711) *(G-11003)*

Impactful Technology LLC 646 374-9004
  24a Trolley Sq Ste 1608 Wilmington (19806) *(G-17289)*

Imparts Inc 302 697-0990
  100 N Railroad Ave Wyoming (19934) *(G-20986)*

Imperial Dynsty Arts Prgram In 302 521-8551
  1 Windsor Rd Wilmington (19809) *(G-17290)*

Imperial Gunite 631 244-0073
  4612 Simon Rd Wilmington (19803) *(G-17291)*

Imperial Music Group LLC 302 289-6145
  7 Bushwick Dr Newark (19702) *(G-11004)*

Imperial Nutrition 302 752-8220
  229 Ne Front St Milford (19963) *(G-7940)*

Imperial Popcorn Corp 847 641-0991
  2915 Ogletown Rd Newark (19713) *(G-11005)*

Imperial Realty Group LLC 215 850-3142
  213 Johnce Rd Newark (19711) *(G-11006)*

Implify Inc 302 533-2345
  260 Chapman Rd Ste 201c Newark (19702) *(G-11007)*

Imprint Genetics, New Castle *Also Called: Chester Ross (G-8933)*

Improve Sussex LLC 302 864-8559
  22948 Pine Rd Lewes (19958) *(G-6118)*

IMS, Bear *Also Called: Interntional Mkt Suppliers Inc (G-286)*

IMS Software Services Ltd (HQ) 302 472-9100
  1209 N Orange St Wilmington (19801) *(G-17292)*

In A Stitch 302 678-2260
  526 Rose Dale Ln Dover (19904) *(G-2722)*

In Home Veterinary Care, Newark *Also Called: Karli Flanagan Dvm (G-11144)*

In Loving Handz Home Care LLC 302 530-6344
  3 Fairway Rd Newark (19711) *(G-11008)*

In The Nest Quilting 302 644-7316
  32905 Nassau Ct S Lewes (19958) *(G-6119)*

IN TRUST, Wilmington *Also Called: Assoction Brds Thlgcal Educatn (G-14596)*

In Vision Eye Care 302 655-1952
  2205 Concord Pike Wilmington (19803) *(G-17293)*

In Vision Eye Care Inc 302 235-7031
  210 Lantana Dr Hockessin (19707) *(G-5248)*

In Wellness We Win 917 509-5414
  350 Noxontown Rd Middletown (19709) *(G-7224)*

In Wilmington Mktg Group Inc 302 495-9456
  1007 N Orange St Fl 4 Wilmington (19801) *(G-17294)*

In10sity Fitness United 302 677-1010
  73 First Tenth Ct Dover (19901) *(G-2723)*

INA Acquisition Corp (DH) 302 472-9258
  1007 N Orange St Ste 1410 Wilmington (19801) *(G-17295)*
Inaccel LLC 408 915-5548
  24a Trolley Sq # 1397 Wilmington (19806) *(G-17296)*
Inamco Air LLC 630 830-4007
  9 E Loockerman St Ste 3a221 Dover (19901) *(G-2724)*
Inamco Defense, Dover *Also Called: Inamco Air LLC (G-2724)*
Inbound Ignite LLC 866 314-4499
  8 The Grn Ste 17013 Dover (19901) *(G-2725)*
Inc Chimes 302 449-1926
  409 Zamora Ct Townsend (19734) *(G-14015)*
Inc Plan (usa) 302 428-1200
  26c Trolley Sq Wilmington (19806) *(G-17297)*
Inc Plan USA 302 428-1200
  20c Trolley Sq Wilmington (19806) *(G-17298)*
Incapp Inc 318 880-7622
  3411 Silverside Rd # 104 Wilmington (19810) *(G-17299)*
Incite Solutions Inc 302 655-8952
  5714 Kennett Pike Ofc 3 Wilmington (19807) *(G-17300)*
Inclind Inc 302 856-2802
  119 W 3rd St Ste 6 Lewes (19958) *(G-6120)*
Inclusive Innovations Inc 781 962-9959
  2035 Sunset Lake Rd B2 Newark (19702) *(G-11009)*
Incolor Inc 302 984-2695
  1401 Todds Ln Wilmington (19802) *(G-17301)*
Income & Est Plg Partners PA 302 722-6000
  2706 Kirkwood Hwy Unit 5 Wilmington (19805) *(G-17302)*
Incorporators USA LLC 800 441-5940
  1013 Centre Rd Ste 403a Wilmington (19805) *(G-17303)*
Incountry Inc (PA) 415 323-0322
  4023 Kennett Pike Ste 50376 Wilmington (19807) *(G-17304)*
Incredible Care Inc 302 428-6093
  1224 N King St Wilmington (19801) *(G-17305)*
Incredible One Enterprises LLC 888 801-5794
  560 Peoples Plz Ste 255 Newark (19702) *(G-11010)*
Incredo Us LLC 530 586-8995
  16192 Coastal Hwy Lewes (19958) *(G-6121)*
Incyte Corporation (PA) 302 498-6700
  1801 Augustine Cut Off Wilmington (19803) *(G-17306)*
Incyte Holdings Corporation (HQ) 302 498-6700
  1801 Augustine Cut Off Wilmington (19803) *(G-17307)*
Indelible Blue Inc 302 231-5200
  16192 Coastal Hwy Lewes (19958) *(G-6122)*
Independence Contractors Inc 302 530-3022
  302 Jackson Blvd Wilmington (19803) *(G-17308)*
Independence School Inc 302 239-0330
  1300 Paper Mill Rd Newark (19711) *(G-11011)*
Independent Bb Fellowship Ch 302 734-2301
  48 Mckee Rd Ste A Dover (19904) *(G-2726)*
Independent Disposal Services 302 378-5400
  604 Cannery Ln Townsend (19734) *(G-14016)*
Independent Elec Svcs LLC 302 383-2761
  26 Rolling Rd Claymont (19703) *(G-1184)*
Independent Electrical Svcs, Claymont *Also Called: Independent Elec Svcs LLC (G-1184)*
Independent Insur Consulting 302 983-0298
  31 Golf View Dr Apt C3 Newark (19702) *(G-11012)*
Independent Investors Inc 302 366-1187
  150 E Main St Newark (19711) *(G-11013)*
Independent Metal Strap Co Inc 516 621-0030
  883 Horsepond Rd Dover (19901) *(G-2727)*
Independent Newsmedia Inc USA 302 674-3600
  110 Galaxy Dr Dover (19901) *(G-2728)*
Independent Newsmedia Inc USA (HQ) 302 674-3600
  110 Galaxy Dr Dover (19901) *(G-2729)*
Independent Newsmedia Inc USA 302 422-1200
  37a Walnut St Milford (19963) *(G-7941)*
Independent Resources (PA) 302 765-0191
  6 Denny Rd Ste 101 Wilmington (19809) *(G-17309)*
Independent School MGT Inc (PA) 302 656-4944
  1 Righter Pkwy Ste 140 Wilmington (19803) *(G-17310)*
Independent Transfer Operators 302 420-4289
  Hockessin (19707) *(G-5249)*

Indepndnce Wealth Advisors Inc 302 763-1180
  726 Yorklyn Rd Ste 300 Hockessin (19707) *(G-5250)*
India Ink, Historic New Castle *Also Called: Zwd Products Corporation (G-5106)*
Indian River Golf Cars Dr Wldg 302 947-2044
  26246 Kathys Way Millsboro (19966) *(G-8320)*
Indian River Land Company, Millsboro *Also Called: Moore & Lind Inc (G-8390)*
Indian River Power LLC 302 934-3527
  29416 Power Plant Rd Dagsboro (19939) *(G-1466)*
Indian River Soccer Club 302 542-6397
  32221 Gum Rd Ocean View (19970) *(G-12524)*
Indian Rver Cptins Assoc Wbmst 302 227-3071
  39415 Inlet Rd Rehoboth Beach (19971) *(G-12794)*
Indigo Telecom USA LLC 727 537-0142
  1209 N Orange St Wilmington (19801) *(G-17311)*
Indo Amines Americas LLC 301 466-9902
  5301 Limestone Rd Ste 100 Wilmington (19808) *(G-17312)*
Indo Foreign Trade Craft LLC 818 927-2872
  254 Chapman Rd Ste 208 Newark (19702) *(G-11014)*
Indo-American Association Del 302 234-0214
  113 Jupiter Rd Newark (19711) *(G-11015)*
Indoor American Assn Del, Newark *Also Called: Iaad (G-10989)*
Indus Insights US Inc 312 238-9815
  1000 N West St Ste 1200 Wilmington (19801) *(G-17313)*
Industraplate Corp 302 654-5210
  5 James Ct Wilmington (19801) *(G-17314)*
Industrial Metal Treating Corp 302 656-1677
  402 E Front St Wilmington (19801) *(G-17315)*
Industrial Physics Inc (HQ) 302 613-5600
  40 Mccullough Dr New Castle (19720) *(G-9230)*
Industrial Products of Del 302 328-6648
  153 S Dupont Hwy New Castle (19720) *(G-9231)*
Industrial Resource Netwrk Inc 302 888-2905
  707 S Church St Wilmington (19801) *(G-17316)*
Industrial Sls Factoring Corp 302 573-2500
  1200 N Orange St Ste 700 Wilmington (19801) *(G-17317)*
Industrial Stl Structures Inc 302 275-8892
  4049 New Castle Ave New Castle (19720) *(G-9232)*
Industrial Training Cons Inc 302 266-6100
  13 Garfield Way Newark (19713) *(G-11016)*
Industrial Valves & Fittings 302 326-2494
  55 Mccullough Dr New Castle (19720) *(G-9233)*
Industry ARC 614 588-8538
  251 Little Falls Dr Wilmington (19808) *(G-17318)*
Inetworkz LLC 407 401-9384
  16192 Coastal Hwy Lewes (19958) *(G-6123)*
Infant Solutions 302 250-4336
  3524 Silverside Rd Ste 35b Wilmington (19810) *(G-17319)*
Infarm - Indoor Urban Frming U (PA) 201 616-1441
  8 The Grn Ste 7929 Dover (19901) *(G-2730)*
Infectious Disease Association 302 368-2883
  78 Omega Dr # C Newark (19713) *(G-11017)*
Infectious Diseases Cons PA 302 994-9692
  537 Stanton Christiana Rd Ste 201 Newark (19713) *(G-11018)*
Infectous Dsease Solutions LLC 302 841-0634
  1320 Middleford Rd Ste 202 Seaford (19973) *(G-13222)*
Infigage LLC 302 207-2148
  919 N Market St Wilmington (19801) *(G-17320)*
Infinit Ventures LLC 800 966-9023
  651 N Broad St Middletown (19709) *(G-7225)*
Infinite Improbabilities Inc 763 516-5825
  1209 N Orange St Wilmington (19801) *(G-17321)*
Infinite Solutions LLC 302 438-5310
  531 Chariot Ct Wilmington (19808) *(G-17322)*
Infinity Choppers 302 249-7282
  24655 Dupont Blvd Georgetown (19947) *(G-4368)*
Infinity Electric LLC 302 635-4388
  1264 Old Wilmington Rd Hockessin (19707) *(G-5251)*
Infinity Health & Wellness Del 302 543-5717
  6 Larch Ave Ste 397 Wilmington (19804) *(G-17323)*
Infinity Intellectuals Inc 302 565-4830
  3511 Silverside Rd Ste 105 Wilmington (19810) *(G-17324)*

Inflection Associates Inc 484 678-7915
  251 Little Falls Dr Wilmington (19808) *(G-17325)*
Inflow Network LLC 424 303-0464
  112 Capitol Trl Newark (19711) *(G-11019)*
Info Solutions LLC 302 793-9200
  920 Justison St Wilmington (19801) *(G-17326)*
Info Solutions North Amer LLC 302 793-9200
  920 Justison St Wilmington (19801) *(G-17327)*
Info Systems LLC (DH) 302 633-9800
  590 Century Blvd Wilmington (19808) *(G-17328)*
Info Titan LLC 510 495-4117
  32 Loockerman Plz Ste 109 Dover (19901) *(G-2731)*
Infobase Holdings Inc (HQ) 212 967-8800
  1000 N West St Ste 1281-230 Wilmington (19801) *(G-17329)*
Infocon, Yorklyn Also Called: Information Consultants Inc *(G-20993)*
Infocus Financial Advisors Inc 410 677-4848
  406 S Bedford St Georgetown (19947) *(G-4369)*
Information Consultants Inc 302 239-2942
  2851 Creek Rd Yorklyn (19736) *(G-20993)*
Information Services, New Castle Also Called: Christiana Care Hlth Svcs Inc *(G-8939)*
Information Technology, Dover Also Called: Blaze Coin LLC *(G-1946)*
Information Technology Afforda 302 525-6252
  5 W Kyla Marie Dr Newark (19702) *(G-11020)*
Information Technology Dept, Dover Also Called: City of Dover *(G-2084)*
Informed Tuch Mssage Thrapy LL 302 229-8239
  905 Ibiza Ct Townsend (19734) *(G-14017)*
Infusion Care Delaware Home 302 423-2511
  9 N Hampshire Ct Wilmington (19807) *(G-17330)*
Infusion Solutions of De 302 674-4627
  1100 Forrest Ave Dover (19904) *(G-2732)*
Ing Bank Fsb 302 255-3750
  802 Delaware Ave Fl 1 Wilmington (19801) *(G-17331)*
Ing Bank Fsb (HQ) 302 658-2200
  802 Delaware Ave Wilmington (19801) *(G-17332)*
Ing Direct, Wilmington Also Called: Ing Bank Fsb *(G-17332)*
Ing Direct Wilmington Cafe, Wilmington Also Called: Ing Bank Fsb *(G-17331)*
Ing USA Holding Corp 302 658-2200
  1 S Orange St Wilmington (19801) *(G-17333)*
Ingenious Inventions AG LLC 818 578-8266
  1201 N Orange St Ste 7400 Wilmington (19801) *(G-17334)*
Ingenuity 213 LLC 647 303-5116
  8 The Grn Ste B Dover (19901) *(G-2733)*
Ingleside Assisted Living, Wilmington Also Called: Ingleside Homes Inc *(G-17336)*
Ingleside Homes Inc (PA) 302 575-0250
  1005 N Franklin St Wilmington (19806) *(G-17335)*
Ingleside Homes Inc 302 984-0950
  1605 N Broom St Wilmington (19806) *(G-17336)*
INGLESIDE RETIREMENT APARTMENT, Wilmington Also Called: Ingleside Homes Inc *(G-17335)*
Ingleside Rtrment Aprtmnts LLC 302 575-0250
  1005 N Franklin St Wilmington (19806) *(G-17337)*
Ingrid S Jackoway 302 478-3702
  2502 Silverside Rd Ste 4 Wilmington (19810) *(G-17338)*
Inheritnow Inc 877 846-4374
  1002 Justison St Wilmington (19801) *(G-17339)*
Ini Holdings Inc (PA) 302 674-3600
  110 Galaxy Dr Dover (19901) *(G-2734)*
INIIWI LLC 866 312-4536
  1201 N Market St Ste 111 Wilmington (19801) *(G-17340)*
Initially Yours Inc 302 999-0562
  1412 Kirkwood Hwy Wilmington (19805) *(G-17341)*
Inititive For Med Access Knwld 917 455-6601
  16192 Coastal Hwy Lewes (19958) *(G-6124)*
Ink Therapy Tattoo Studios LLC 302 674-1900
  155 N Dupont Hwy Ste 2 Dover (19901) *(G-2735)*
Inka and Ezra Foundation Inc 301 535-1000
  719 Lexington Dr Bear (19701) *(G-284)*
Inkit Inc (PA) 612 712-1245
  919 N Market St Ste 725 Wilmington (19801) *(G-17342)*
InkInk 323 854-9549
  717 N Union St Ste 32 Wilmington (19805) *(G-17343)*
Inkwhy Inc 267 243-8498
  3616 Kirkwood Hwy Ste A # 1286 Wilmington (19808) *(G-17344)*
Inland Salem Square LLC 302 472-9250
  1007 N Orange St Wilmington (19801) *(G-17345)*
Inn At Canal Square, The, Rehoboth Beach Also Called: Harborside Development II LLC *(G-12780)*
Inn At Montchanin Village, The, Montchanin Also Called: Dan Licale *(G-8736)*
Inn At Rehoboth Apartments 302 226-1760
  27 Brooklyn Ave Rehoboth Beach (19971) *(G-12795)*
Inn At Wilmington 302 479-7900
  300 Rocky Run Pkwy Wilmington (19803) *(G-17346)*
Inn At Wilmington, Wilmington Also Called: 44 New England Management Co *(G-14136)*
Inn LLC A-1 Dash 302 368-7964
  380 E Chestnut Hill Rd Newark (19713) *(G-11021)*
Innospec Inc 302 454-8100
  200 Executive Dr Newark (19702) *(G-11022)*
Innova Bus Applications Inc 405 845-6871
  8 The Grn Ste 12898 Dover (19901) *(G-2736)*
Innovations Funding LLC 302 743-6213
  608 Dairy Dr Smyrna (19977) *(G-13770)*
Innovative Concepts MGT LLC 866 952-7066
  24a Trolley Sq Wilmington (19806) *(G-17347)*
Innovative Dermatology 610 789-7546
  1202 Foulk Rd Ste A Wilmington (19803) *(G-17348)*
Innovative Heating & Coolg LLC 302 528-4172
  24 Lyric Dr Newark (19702) *(G-11023)*
Innovative Home Imprvs LLC 302 388-2950
  401 Kates Way Smyrna (19977) *(G-13771)*
Innovative Machine LLC 302 455-1466
  53b Mcmillan Way Newark (19713) *(G-11024)*
Innoventic Inc 302 476-2396
  19c Trolley Sq Wilmington (19806) *(G-17349)*
Innovtive Cpitl Cnslting Group 202 670-0797
  16192 Coastal Hwy Lewes (19958) *(G-6125)*
Innpros Inc 302 326-2500
  875 Pulaski Hwy Bear (19701) *(G-285)*
Inns of Rehoboth Beach LLC 302 645-8003
  18826 Coastal Hwy Rehoboth Beach (19971) *(G-12796)*
Inova Business Solutions LLC 251 316-0180
  2093a Philadelphia Pike Ste 223 Claymont (19703) *(G-1185)*
Inoven Solutions LLC 302 273-0177
  3422 Old Capitol Trl Wilmington (19808) *(G-17350)*
Inputsoft Inc 312 358-4509
  16192 Coastal Hwy Lewes (19958) *(G-6126)*
Inrg of Delaware Inc 302 369-1412
  16949 Hudsons Turn Lewes (19958) *(G-6127)*
Ins Regulatory Insurance Svcs 302 256-0455
  919 N Market St 2600 Wilmington (19801) *(G-17351)*
Inside & Out Property MGT LLC 302 632-4467
  386 Main St Hartly (19953) *(G-4879)*
Insider Insight LLC 480 548-0440
  221 N Broad St Ste 3a Middletown (19709) *(G-7226)*
Insight Engineering Solutions 302 378-4842
  640 Ravenglass Dr Townsend (19734) *(G-14018)*
Insight Homes 302 927-0235
  33288 Bayberry Ct Dagsboro (19939) *(G-1467)*
Insight Homes 302 858-4281
  17 Frankenberry Dr Georgetown (19947) *(G-4370)*
Insightxperts LLC 412 608-4346
  8 The Grn Ste 4000 Dover (19901) *(G-2737)*
Insightzen LLC 647 227-9325
  16192 Coastal Hwy Lewes (19958) *(G-6128)*
Insignia Global Corporation 302 310-4107
  913 N Market St Ste 200 Wilmington (19801) *(G-17352)*
Insite Constructors Inc 302 479-5555
  3201 Tanya Dr Wilmington (19803) *(G-17353)*
Insley Insur & Finanial Svcs 302 677-1888
  20 E Division St Ste B Dover (19901) *(G-2738)*
Insley Insur & Fincl Svcs Inc 302 286-0777
  110 Christiana Medical Ctr Newark (19702) *(G-11025)*
Insley Jr Harry Agt 302 656-1800
  901 N Market St Ste 100 Wilmington (19801) *(G-17354)*

(PA)=Parent Co (HQ)=Headquarters (DH)=Div Headquarters

Inspection Lanes ALPHABETIC SECTION

Inspection Lanes 302 853-1003
   23737 Dupont Blvd Georgetown (19947) *(G-4371)*

Inspectware 302 999-9601
   123 E Ayre St Wilmington (19804) *(G-17355)*

Inspektlabs Inc 302 601-7191
   651 N Broad St Ste 20 Middletown (19709) *(G-7227)*

Inspiration Bennington Ceramic 302 436-5544
   11 Discovery Ln Selbyville (19975) *(G-13549)*

Inspiration Empire 302 535-9920
   13747 Wolf Rd Greenwood (19950) *(G-4639)*

Inspire African Safaris LLC 302 250-5763
   2055 Limestone Rd Ste 200c Wilmington (19808) *(G-17356)*

Inspirit Studios 302 222-4804
   190 Dogwood Dr Magnolia (19962) *(G-6752)*

Inspiun Tech Solutions LLC 302 304-3949
   913 N Market St Ste 200 Wilmington (19801) *(G-17357)*

Insta Answer LLC 973 303-1764
   200 Continental Dr # 401 Newark (19713) *(G-11026)*

Insta Signs Plus Inc 302 324-8800
   107 J And M Dr New Castle (19720) *(G-9234)*

INSTABASE INC (PA) 628 261-7600
   3500 S Dupont Hwy Dover (19901) *(G-2739)*

Instacall LLC (PA) 302 496-1166
   2055 Limestone Rd 200c Wilmington (19808) *(G-17358)*

Installed Building Pdts Inc 302 480-1520
   9796 Nanticoke Business Park Dr Greenwood (19950) *(G-4640)*

Instant Global Services Corp 302 514-1047
   8 The Grn Ste 8301 Dover (19901) *(G-2740)*

Instant Imprints of Delaware, New Castle *Also Called: Bgdedge Inc (G-8866)*

Instapanel Inc 415 727-7279
   2093 Philadelphia Pike Pmb 4330 Claymont (19703) *(G-1186)*

Instasafe Inc 408 400-3673
   3500 S Dupont Hwy Dover (19901) *(G-2741)*

Instaworks Inc 925 389-9799
   4 Peddlers Row Unit 44 Newark (19702) *(G-11027)*

Instellars Globl Cnsulting Inc (PA) 302 613-4379
   919 N Market St Ste 705 Wilmington (19801) *(G-17359)*

Institute of Mssage Hling Arts 610 357-2925
   222 Philadelphia Pike Wilmington (19809) *(G-17360)*

Instocking LLC 302 595-1595
   16192 Coastal Hwy Lewes (19958) *(G-6129)*

Insurance & Financial Svcs Inc 302 239-5895
   100 W Commons Blvd Ste 302 New Castle (19720) *(G-9235)*

Insurance Administrators Inc 302 239-1688
   2100 Braken Ave Wilmington (19808) *(G-17361)*

Insurance Associates Inc 302 368-0888
   720 New London Rd Newark (19711) *(G-11028)*

Insurance Market Inc (PA) 302 875-7591
   450 N Central Ave Laurel (19956) *(G-5534)*

Insurance Market Inc 302 934-9006
   17 Main St Millsboro (19966) *(G-8321)*

Insurance Networks Aliance LLC 302 268-1010
   3411 Silverside Rd Ste 100 Wilmington (19810) *(G-17362)*

Insurance Office America Inc 302 764-1000
   900 Philadelphia Pike Wilmington (19809) *(G-17363)*

Insurance Toolkits LLC 302 272-5488
   426 Ohio Ave Wilmington (19805) *(G-17364)*

Int Pay LLC 347 698-8159
   3513 Concord Pike Ste 3100 Wilmington (19803) *(G-17365)*

Intech Services 302 366-1442
   136 Pawnee Ct Newark (19702) *(G-11029)*

Intech Services Inc 302 366-8530
   211 Lake Dr Ste J Newark (19702) *(G-11030)*

Integra ADM Group Inc (PA) 800 959-3518
   110 S Shipley St Seaford (19973) *(G-13223)*

Integra Realty Resources, Wilmington *Also Called: Delaware RE Advisors LLC (G-15957)*

Integral Enterprise LLC 302 722-0827
   3434 Old Capitol Trl Unit 5432 Wilmington (19808) *(G-17366)*

Integrated Cash Logistics LLC 302 652-9193
   4200 Governor Printz Blvd Wilmington (19802) *(G-17367)*

Integrated Data Corp (PA) 302 295-5057
   1000 N West St Ste 1200 Wilmington (19801) *(G-17368)*

Integrated Health Assoc LLC 302 264-1021
   24 Hiawatha Ln Dover (19904) *(G-2742)*

Integrated Home LLC 302 656-1624
   12 Penns Way New Castle (19720) *(G-9236)*

Integrated Mechanical and Fire 302 420-0617
   1807 Montclair Ave Wilmington (19808) *(G-17369)*

Integrated Restorative Massage 302 391-4692
   1601 Concord Pike Ste 2 Wilmington (19803) *(G-17370)*

Integrated Solutions Gate Inc 302 404-6080
   427 N Tatnall St No 90821 Wilmington (19801) *(G-17371)*

Integrated Tech Systems LLC 302 613-2111
   42 Reads Way New Castle (19720) *(G-9237)*

Integrated Turf Management Sys 302 266-8000
   200 Ruthar Dr Ste 7 Newark (19711) *(G-11031)*

Integrated Wirg Solutions LLC 302 999-8448
   1695 S Dupont Hwy Saint Georges (19733) *(G-13034)*

Integration Logistics Inc 302 832-7300
   130 Executive Dr Ste 2a Newark (19702) *(G-11032)*

Integrity Billing Specialist 302 383-1704
   600 Saks St Smyrna (19977) *(G-13772)*

Integrity Brands LLC 302 853-0709
   10467 Foxtail Ct Seaford (19973) *(G-13224)*

Integrity Cleaning Svcs LLC 302 353-9315
   331 Coldwater Dr Clayton (19938) *(G-1372)*

Integrity Companions 302 659-2936
   6 Grant Ln Smyrna (19977) *(G-13773)*

Integrity Construction LLC 302 241-6429
   91 Selheimer Ln Marydel (19964) *(G-6801)*

INTEGRITY CONSTRUCTION OF MARY, Marydel *Also Called: Integrity Construction LLC (G-6801)*

Integrity Corporation Inc 410 392-8665
   1 Innovation Way Ste 300 Newark (19711) *(G-11033)*

Integrity First Mortgage LLC 302 318-6858
   9 Peddlers Row Newark (19702) *(G-11034)*

Integrity Home Health Llc 302 981-4475
   111 Rustic Dr Newark (19713) *(G-11035)*

Integrity Irrigation Serv 302 542-7694
   20925 Lowes Crossing Rd Frankford (19945) *(G-4116)*

Integrity MGT Solution Inc 302 270-8976
   312 Seeneytown Rd Clayton (19938) *(G-1373)*

Integrity Nursing and Hea 302 275-8838
   6 Grant Ln Smyrna (19977) *(G-13774)*

Integrity Pest Solutions, Georgetown *Also Called: Trigger Action LLC (G-4561)*

Integrity Staffing, Newark *Also Called: Integrity Staffing Solutions (G-11036)*

Integrity Staffing Solutions (PA) 302 661-8770
   700 Prides Xing Ste 300 Newark (19713) *(G-11036)*

Integrity Staffing Solutions 520 276-7775
   700 Prides Xing Ste 300 Newark (19713) *(G-11037)*

Integrity Staffing Solutions, Newark *Also Called: Integrity Staffing Solutions (G-11037)*

Integrity Supply & Service, Newark *Also Called: Integrity Corporation Inc (G-11033)*

Integrity Tech Solutions Inc 302 369-9093
   200 Continental Dr Ste 401 Newark (19713) *(G-11038)*

Integrity Testlabs LLC (PA) 302 325-2365
   258 Quigley Blvd Historic New Castle (19720) *(G-5008)*

Integrtve Psychlogy Group LLC 302 307-3702
   300 Creek View Rd Ste 101 Newark (19711) *(G-11039)*

Intelexmicro Inc 302 907-9545
   10253 Stone Creek Dr # 1 Laurel (19956) *(G-5535)*

Intelhouse Marketing LLC 213 438-9667
   16192 Coastal Hwy Lewes (19958) *(G-6130)*

Intellectual LLC 202 769-1986
   8 The Grn Ste 7213 Dover (19901) *(G-2743)*

Intellgent Sltions Aliance LLC 754 300-0051
   905 Providence Ave Claymont (19703) *(G-1187)*

Intelligent Building Mtls LLC 302 261-9922
   40 E Main St Ste 611 Newark (19711) *(G-11040)*

Intelligent Change LLC (PA) 818 997-7712
   8 The Grn Ste 4000 Dover (19901) *(G-2744)*

Intelligent Signage Inc (PA) 302 762-4100
   4006 Coleridge Rd Wilmington (19802) *(G-17372)*

Intellitec Solutions LLC 302 652-3480
   750 Prides Xing Ste 100 Newark (19713) *(G-11041)*

ALPHABETIC SECTION — Invenio Financial

Intellitek Inc 856 381-7650
   411 Weston Dr Middletown (19709) *(G-7228)*

Intello Group Inc 832 827-3779
   500 Delaware Ave Unit 1 # 1960 Wilmington (19899) *(G-17373)*

Interactive Marketing Services 302 456-9810
   200 University Plz Newark (19702) *(G-11042)*

Interactive Tech Holdings LLC 302 478-9356
   3411 Silverside Rd Ste 103hg Wilmington (19810) *(G-17374)*

Intercoastal Title Agency Inc 302 478-7752
   10 Cohee Cir Wilmington (19803) *(G-17375)*

Intercollegiate Studies Inst 302 656-3292
   3901 Centerville Rd Wilmington (19807) *(G-17376)*

Intercontinental Chem Svcs Inc 302 654-6800
   1020 Christiana Ave Ste B Wilmington (19801) *(G-17377)*

Intercontinental Marketing 302 429-7555
   807 Essex Rd Wilmington (19807) *(G-17378)*

Interdgital Communications Inc (DH) 610 878-7800
   200 Bellevue Pkwy Ste 300 Wilmington (19809) *(G-17379)*

Interdigital, Wilmington *Also Called: Interdigital Communications Inc (G-17379)*

Interdigital, Wilmington *Also Called: Interdigital Inc (G-17380)*

INTERDIGITAL, Wilmington *Also Called: Interdigital Wireless Inc (G-17381)*

Interdigital Inc (PA) 302 281-3600
   200 Bellevue Pkwy Ste 300 Wilmington (19809) *(G-17380)*

Interdigital Wireless Inc (HQ) 302 281-3600
   200 Bellevue Pkwy Ste 300 Wilmington (19809) *(G-17381)*

Interebar Fabricators LLC 513 310-1782
   20 Davidson Ln New Castle (19720) *(G-9238)*

Interfacing Bus Solutions Inc 514 962-1344
   919 N Market St Ste 950 Wilmington (19801) *(G-17382)*

Interfaith Cmnty Hsing of Del 302 652-3991
   613 N Washington St Wilmington (19801) *(G-17383)*

Interfaith Community Housing, Wilmington *Also Called: Management Associates Inc (G-18098)*

Interim Health Care 302 322-2743
   2 Reads Way Ste 209 New Castle (19720) *(G-9239)*

Interim Healthcare Del LLC 302 322-2743
   100 S Main St Ste 203 Smyrna (19977) *(G-13775)*

Interim Healthcare of Delaware, Smyrna *Also Called: Interim Healthcare Del LLC (G-13775)*

Interim Services, New Castle *Also Called: Interim Health Care (G-9239)*

Interior Alternative, The, Newark *Also Called: Loomcraft Textile & Supply Co (G-11281)*

Interiors By Kim Inc 302 537-2480
   33 Central Ave Ocean View (19970) *(G-12525)*

Interiors Judith Davidson 302 841-5500
   13 Fairway East Dr Georgetown (19947) *(G-4372)*

Interjet West Inc 209 848-0290
   1013 Centre Rd Ste 403a Wilmington (19805) *(G-17384)*

Interlace Global Inc 917 719-6811
   251 Little Falls Dr Wilmington (19808) *(G-17385)*

Intermedia, Dover *Also Called: Intermedia Analytics LLC (G-2745)*

Intermedia Analytics LLC (PA) 305 921-9647
   160 Greentree Dr Ste 101 Dover (19904) *(G-2745)*

Internal Medicine Associates 302 633-1700
   3105 Limestone Rd Ste 301 Wilmington (19808) *(G-17386)*

Internal Medicine Bridgeville 302 337-3300
   8991 Redden Rd Bridgeville (19933) *(G-716)*

Internal Medicine Delaware LLC 302 261-2269
   411 Hawks Nest Ct Middletown (19709) *(G-7229)*

Internal Medicine Dover PA 302 678-4488
   725 S Queen St Dover (19904) *(G-2746)*

International Assn Emrgncy 302 731-5705
   2 Cobblestone Xing Newark (19702) *(G-11043)*

International Brthd 2271 Local 302 559-9167
   912 Haines Ave Wilmington (19809) *(G-17387)*

International Cloud Company 858 472-9648
   8th Green St Dover (19901) *(G-2747)*

International Esl Services LLC 305 934-3769
   2207 Concord Pike 508 Wilmington (19803) *(G-17388)*

International Food Co LLC 404 333-3434
   11 Salem Village Sq Newark (19713) *(G-11044)*

International Fresh Prod Assn (PA) 302 738-7100
   1500 Casho Mill Rd Newark (19711) *(G-11045)*

International Literacy Assn (PA) 302 731-1600
   800 Barksdale Rd Newark (19711) *(G-11046)*

International Logistiks, Wilmington *Also Called: International Logistiks LLC (G-17389)*

International Logistiks LLC 302 521-6338
   4023 Kennett Pike 404 Wilmington (19807) *(G-17389)*

International N&H Usa Inc 302 451-0176
   1301 Ogletown Rd Newark (19711) *(G-11047)*

International Spine Pain 302 478-7001
   3411 Silverside Rd Ste 103r Wilmington (19810) *(G-17390)*

International Std Elc Corp (DH) 302 427-3769
   1105 N Market St Ste 1217 Wilmington (19801) *(G-17391)*

International Trade Fin LLC 302 440-1492
   8 The Grn Ste 5232 Dover (19901) *(G-2748)*

International Travel Network 415 840-0207
   1000 N West St Ste 1200 Wilmington (19801) *(G-17392)*

Internet Activism, Wilmington *Also Called: Internet Activism Inc (G-17393)*

Internet Activism Inc 206 861-5106
   1209 N Orange St Wilmington (19801) *(G-17393)*

Internet Business Pubg Corp 302 875-7700
   220 Laureltowne Laurel (19956) *(G-5536)*

Internet Vikings East LLC 347 879-1452
   251 Little Falls Dr Wilmington (19808) *(G-17394)*

Internet Working Technologies 302 424-1855
   12 S Walnut St # A Milford (19963) *(G-7942)*

Interntional Mkt Suppliers Inc 302 392-1840
   400 Carson Dr Bear (19701) *(G-286)*

Interntnal Agrclture Prod Grou 302 450-2008
   22 Zion Dr Smyrna (19977) *(G-13776)*

Interntnal Brthd Elec Wkrs Lca 302 328-0773
   814 W Basin Rd New Castle (19720) *(G-9240)*

Interntnal Fnding Slutions LLC 212 765-4349
   2711 Centerville Rd # 400 Wilmington (19808) *(G-17395)*

Interntnal Soc For Hylrnan Scn 212 992-5971
   605 Geddes St Wilmington (19805) *(G-17396)*

Interpres Security Inc 570 971-9876
   251 Little Falls Dr Wilmington (19808) *(G-17397)*

Interstate Construction Inc 302 369-3590
   1000 Dawson Dr Ste A Newark (19713) *(G-11048)*

Interstate Hotels LLC (PA) 302 658-7581
   1209 N Orange St Wilmington (19801) *(G-17398)*

Interstate Hotels Resorts Inc 302 792-2700
   630 Naamans Rd Claymont (19703) *(G-1188)*

Interstate Mortgage Corp Inc 302 733-7620
   1933 Kirkwood Hwy Newark (19711) *(G-11049)*

Interstate Steel Co Inc 302 598-5159
   11 Taylors Farm Dr Newark (19711) *(G-11050)*

Interstellar Cmnty Living LLC 787 607-3939
   3524 Silverside Rd 35b Wilmington (19810) *(G-17399)*

Interstllar Cmnty Lving MGT Co 787 607-3939
   3524 Silverside Rd Ste 35b Wilmington (19810) *(G-17400)*

Into The Light Life Coaching, Wilmington *Also Called: Josh N Schmidt (G-17590)*

Intouch Body Therapy LLC 302 537-0510
   33012 Coastal Hwy Unit 4 Bethany Beach (19930) *(G-609)*

Intouch Inc 332 223-0720
   8 The Grn Ste B Dover (19901) *(G-2749)*

Intrinsic, Wilmington *Also Called: Intrinsic Partners LLC (G-17401)*

Intrinsic Partners LLC 610 388-0853
   4001 Kennett Pike Ste 134 Wilmington (19807) *(G-17401)*

Intrinsic Realty LLC 302 425-1025
   216 Rutland Ave Middletown (19709) *(G-7230)*

Introspction Cunseling Ctr LLC (PA) 302 213-6158
   8 The Grn Ste 12921 Dover (19901) *(G-2750)*

Intuitive Care Therapy 302 200-6123
   501 Silverside Rd Ste 8 Wilmington (19809) *(G-17402)*

Intune Automotive Inc 302 824-9893
   5 Trotters Turn Newark (19711) *(G-11051)*

Intus Smartcities Inc 403 542-8879
   501 Silverside Rd # 411 Wilmington (19809) *(G-17403)*

Inumsoft Inc 302 533-5403
   2500 Wrangle Hill Rd Ste 222 Bear (19701) *(G-287)*

Invenio Financial, Wilmington *Also Called: PCA Acquisitions V LLC (G-18932)*

(PA)=Parent Co (HQ)=Headquarters (DH)=Div Headquarters

Invensis Inc... 470 260-0084	**Iron Hill Apartments Assoc**.................................. 302 366-8228
1000 N West St Ste 1200 Wilmington (19801) *(G-17404)*	2 Burleigh Ct Ofc A4 Newark (19702) *(G-11058)*
Invent.us, Wilmington *Also Called: Apptrium Inc (G-14514)*	**Iron Hill Fence**.. 302 453-9060
Inventia Scientific Corp....................................... 888 201-0798	1565 Old Baltimore Pike Newark (19702) *(G-11059)*
200 Powder Mill Rd Wilmington (19803) *(G-17405)*	**Iron Lion Enterprises Inc**..................................... 302 628-8320
Investment Property Services L.......................... 302 994-3907	22319 Dixie Ln Seaford (19973) *(G-13225)*
102 Robino Ct Ste 101 Wilmington (19804) *(G-17406)*	**Iron Source LLC**... 302 856-7545
Investments, Middletown *Also Called: Optima Iq Investments Inc (G-7417)*	25113 Dupont Blvd Georgetown (19947) *(G-4373)*
Investor Cash MGT Holdings Inc......................... 312 736-7700	**Iron Source 2**... 302 653-7562
1201 N Market St Ste 500 Wilmington (19801) *(G-17407)*	5722 Dupont Pkwy Smyrna (19977) *(G-13777)*
Invisible Hand Labs LLC..................................... 434 989-9642	**Iron Works Inc**... 302 684-1887
2711 Centerville Rd Ste 400 Wilmington (19808) *(G-17408)*	14726 Gravel Hill Rd # 1 Milton (19968) *(G-8643)*
Invista Capital Management LLC......................... 302 731-6882	**Irondt Corp**... 347 539-6471
150 Red Mill Rd Newark (19711) *(G-11052)*	3411 Silverside Rd Wilmington (19810) *(G-17422)*
Invista Capital Management LLC (HQ)................ 302 683-3000	**Iroquois New England Inc**................................... 716 373-5511
2801 Centerville Rd Wilmington (19808) *(G-17409)*	251 Little Falls Dr Wilmington (19808) *(G-17423)*
Invista Capital Management LLC......................... 877 446-8478	**Irwin Landscaping Inc**.. 302 239-9229
4417 Lancaster Pike Wilmington (19805) *(G-17410)*	1080 Old Lancaster Pike Hockessin (19707) *(G-5252)*
Invista Home LLC.. 855 337-3200	**Is2 LLC**... 302 379-1265
200 Continental Dr Ste 401 Newark (19713) *(G-11053)*	780 Brookwood Ln Hockessin (19707) *(G-5253)*
Invistas Applied RES Centre............................... 302 731-6800	**ISA Professional Ltd**... 647 869-1552
150 Red Mill Rd Newark (19711) *(G-11054)*	919 N Market St Ste 425 Wilmington (19801) *(G-17424)*
Invoicegenius, Dover *Also Called: Mightyinvoice LLC (G-3089)*	**Isaac F Davis**.. 302 656-2050
Io Projects Inc.. 302 416-5776	40 Blue Spruce Dr Bear (19701) *(G-290)*
112 S French St Wilmington (19801) *(G-17411)*	**Isaac Fair Corporation**... 302 324-8015
Ioannis Kehagias-Athana MD.............................. 302 378-5494	100 W Commons Blvd Ste 400 New Castle (19720) *(G-9243)*
222 Carter Dr Ste 101 Middletown (19709) *(G-7231)*	**Isaacs Asphalt Paving**... 302 251-2990
Iodparts Technologies Inc................................... 732 369-9939	24087 Lewes Georgetown Hwy Georgetown (19947) *(G-4374)*
512 Liam Pl Bear (19701) *(G-288)*	**Isaacs Isacs Fmly Dentistry PA**.......................... 302 654-1328
Iogen Bmthane Sup Chain III LL.......................... 613 218-2045	707 Foulk Rd Ste 103 Wilmington (19803) *(G-17425)*
251 Little Falls Dr Wilmington (19808) *(G-17412)*	**Isaacs Landscaping & Gardening**...................... 302 947-1414
Ione Group LLC.. 302 584-8377	Rr1 372 Longneck Rd Millsboro (19966) *(G-8322)*
1601 Concord Pike Ste 30 Wilmington (19803) *(G-17413)*	**Isha Brothers Inc**... 302 299-3156
Iovate Health Sciences USA Inc (HQ)................. 888 334-4448	37 Coach Hill Dr Newark (19711) *(G-11060)*
1100 N Market St Ste 4 Wilmington (19801) *(G-17414)*	**Ishares US Scrtzed Bond Index**.......................... 800 441-7762
Ip Camera Warehouse LLC................................. 302 358-2690	100 Bellevue Pkwy Wilmington (19809) *(G-17426)*
3422 Old Capitol Trl Wilmington (19808) *(G-17415)*	**ISI Connect, Wilmington** *Also Called: Info Systems LLC (G-17328)*
IPC Healthcare Inc.. 302 368-2630	**Island Boy Enterprise LLC**................................... 904 347-4563
701 N Clayton St Wilmington (19805) *(G-17416)*	35 Inlet View Ct Bethany Beach (19930) *(G-610)*
Ipd Technologies LLC.. 302 533-8850	**Island Genius LLC**.. 888 529-5506
240 Goldfinch Turn Newark (19711) *(G-11055)*	1201 N Market St Ste 2300 Wilmington (19801) *(G-17427)*
Ipm Inc (HQ)... 302 328-4030	**Island Gigs, Wilmington** *Also Called: Front Row Enterprises LLC (G-16762)*
247 Old Churchmans Rd New Castle (19720) *(G-9241)*	**Island of Misfits LLC**... 302 732-6704
Ipr International LLC (PA).................................. 302 304-8774	32448 Royal Blvd Ste A Dagsboro (19939) *(G-1468)*
1201 N Market St Ste 201 Wilmington (19801) *(G-17417)*	**Ism**.. 302 656-2376
Ips Development LLC (PA)................................. 800 981-7183	15 Sharpley Rd Wilmington (19803) *(G-17428)*
108 W 13th St Wilmington (19801) *(G-17418)*	**Ismail Hummayun**... 302 633-9033
Iptl Global Inc.. 408 306-8888	537 Stanton Christiana Rd Newark (19713) *(G-11061)*
405 N King St Fl 3 Wilmington (19801) *(G-17419)*	**Isocde Community Ctr Location**......................... 302 697-7276
Ipwe Inc.. 214 438-0820	7953 S Dupont Hwy Felton (19943) *(G-3984)*
160 Greentree Dr Ste 101 Dover (19904) *(G-2751)*	**Isolvrisk Inc**.. 508 838-7708
Iqarus Americas Inc... 407 222-5726	74 E Glenwood Ave 211 Smyrna (19977) *(G-13778)*
1209 N Orange St Wilmington (19801) *(G-17420)*	**Isp International Corp**... 302 594-5000
Iqure, Wilmington *Also Called: Iqure Pharma Inc (G-17421)*	8145 Blazer Drive Wilmington (19808) *(G-17429)*
Iqure Pharma Inc... 908 294-1212	**Ispapp Inc**... 302 310-5009
251 Little Falls Dr Wilmington (19808) *(G-17421)*	8 The Grn Ste R Dover (19901) *(G-2753)*
Irena C Viola MD PA.. 302 645-7257	**Istorage**... 302 798-6661
30900 Stallion Ln Lewes (19958) *(G-6131)*	100 Hickman Rd Claymont (19703) *(G-1189)*
Irene C Szeto MD LLC.. 302 832-1560	**Istorage New Castle**... 302 396-6224
121 Becks Woods Dr Ste 100 Bear (19701) *(G-289)*	4016 N Dupont Hwy New Castle (19720) *(G-9244)*
Irene Fisher PHD... 302 733-0980	**Iswich LLC**.. 302 528-0229
87 Omega Dr Newark (19713) *(G-11056)*	28 Austin Rd Wilmington (19810) *(G-17430)*
Irg, Wilmington *Also Called: Mgj Enterprises Inc (G-18299)*	**It Resources Inc**.. 203 521-6945
Irgau Isaias MD... 302 892-9900	220 Continental Dr Ste 104 Newark (19713) *(G-11062)*
537 Stanton Christiana Rd # 102 Newark (19713) *(G-11057)*	**It Takes A Village Preschool**................................ 302 241-3988
Iridescent Dance Alliance Assn.......................... 302 244-8570	346 W Wind Dr Dover (19901) *(G-2754)*
187 Penn Mart Shopg Ctr New Castle (19720) *(G-9242)*	**It Tigers LLC**... 732 898-2793
Iris Diagnostics Incorporated............................. 877 292-4747	16192 Coastal Hwy Lewes (19958) *(G-6132)*
8 The Grn Ste 6527 Dover (19901) *(G-2752)*	**Italtec Gold & Commodities Inc**.......................... 302 446-3207
Irn, Wilmington *Also Called: Industrial Resource Netwrk Inc (G-17316)*	8 The Grn Ste A Dover (19901) *(G-2755)*
Iron Hill Apartments, Newark *Also Called: Iron Hill Apartments Assoc (G-11058)*	**Itango Inc**... 302 648-2646
	1201 N Orange St Ste 600 Wilmington (19801) *(G-17431)*

ALPHABETIC SECTION

Itc Specialty, Newark *Also Called: Industrial Training Cons Inc (G-11016)*

Itconnectus Inc... 302 531-1139
3500 S Dupont Hwy Ste O-101 Dover (19901) *(G-2756)*

Itdw Group LLC.. 917 503-3574
8 The Grn Ste 15153 Dover (19901) *(G-2757)*

Itea Inc.. 302 328-3716
12006 Collins Rd Lewes (19958) *(G-6133)*

ITEL Rail Holdings Corporation....................................... 302 656-5476
200 W 9th St Wilmington (19801) *(G-17432)*

Itexus LLC.. 917 618-9804
4034 Willow Grove Rd Camden (19934) *(G-856)*

Itg Cloud Software LLC... 786 708-6560
1013 Centre Rd Ste 403s Wilmington (19805) *(G-17433)*

Itglobalcom Corp... 302 498-8359
2093 Philadelphia Pike 2345 Claymont (19703) *(G-1190)*

Itiyam LLC.. 703 291-1600
1000 N West St Ste 1200 Wilmington (19801) *(G-17434)*

Itl (usa) Limited... 302 691-6158
103 Foulk Rd Ste 202 Wilmington (19803) *(G-17435)*

Its All About You MSSge&bdywrk.................................. 302 563-3443
77 E Radison Run Clayton (19938) *(G-1374)*

Its All Good In Delaware Inc... 302 698-1232
Camden Wyoming (19934) *(G-955)*

Its my Art LLC... 302 750-1380
7423 Society Dr Claymont (19703) *(G-1191)*

Its R Joy Llc.. 215 315-8300
11 Shawn Ln Bear (19701) *(G-291)*

Itskins Americas Inc.. 805 422-6700
257 Old Churchmans Rd New Castle (19720) *(G-9245)*

Itump, Wilmington *Also Called: Itump Inc (G-17436)*

Itump Inc.. 302 985-9406
501 Silverside Rd Ste 520 Wilmington (19809) *(G-17436)*

Iuventase Biosciences Inc... 858 302-8583
2035 Sunset Lake Rd Newark (19702) *(G-11063)*

Ivan Cohen & Assoc LLC.. 302 428-0205
260 Chapman Rd Ste 205c Newark (19702) *(G-11064)*

Ivanhoe Electric Inc.. 720 933-1150
251 Little Falls Dr Wilmington (19808) *(G-17437)*

Iveh Latino Family Servic... 302 381-0762
125 Causey Ave Milford (19963) *(G-7943)*

Ivisa.com, Dover *Also Called: Document Advisor Inc (G-2318)*

Ivolatility.com, Wilmington *Also Called: Derived Data LLC (G-16020)*

Ivy Boy Auto Works.. 302 669-8842
1401 Northeast Blvd Wilmington (19802) *(G-17438)*

Ivy Gables LLC... 302 475-9400
2210 Swiss Ln Wilmington (19810) *(G-17439)*

Iweekender Inc.. 347 696-1010
251 Little Falls Dr Wilmington (19808) *(G-17440)*

Iyper LLC.. 929 269-5699
221 W 9th St Wilmington (19801) *(G-17441)*

Izzys Lawn Service Inc... 302 293-9221
1936 Seneca Rd Wilmington (19805) *(G-17442)*

J & A Grinding Inc.. 302 368-8760
307 Markus Ct Newark (19713) *(G-11065)*

J & A Overhead Door Inc.. 302 846-9915
16937 Whitesville Rd Delmar (19940) *(G-1603)*

J & B Md Crabs.. 302 387-2161
784 Gallo Rd Harrington (19952) *(G-4789)*

J & D Custom Golf Carts LLC... 302 218-1505
141 Netherlands Dr Middletown (19709) *(G-7232)*

J & F Home Improvement LLC....................................... 302 407-6845
2120 Oak St Wilmington (19808) *(G-17443)*

J & G Acoustical Co.. 302 285-3630
216 E Dickerson Ln Middletown (19709) *(G-7233)*

J & J Bulkheading... 302 436-2800
Snow Goose Lane, Unit 3c Selbyville (19975) *(G-13550)*

J & J Bus Service.. 302 744-9002
315 Billy Mitchell Ln E209 Dover (19901) *(G-2758)*

J & J Services.. 302 422-2684
2908 Milford Harrington Hwy Ste 1 Milford (19963) *(G-7944)*

J & J Snack Foods Corp PA.. 302 571-0884
919 N Market St Ste 200 Wilmington (19801) *(G-17444)*

J & K Auto Repair Inc.. 302 834-8025
3310 Wrangle Hill Rd Ste 109 Bear (19701) *(G-292)*

J & L Building Materials Inc.. 302 504-0350
59 Lukens Dr Historic New Castle (19720) *(G-5009)*

J & L Construction Co, Dover *Also Called: Gearhart Construction Inc (G-2567)*

J & L Services Inc.. 410 943-3355
5670 Galestown Reliance Rd Seaford (19973) *(G-13226)*

J & M Fencing Inc.. 302 284-9674
68 Elijah Ln Felton (19943) *(G-3985)*

J & M Fencing Inc (PA)... 302 284-9674
9867 S Dupont Hwy Felton (19943) *(G-3986)*

J & M Industries Inc.. 302 575-0200
1014 S Market St Wilmington (19801) *(G-17445)*

J & O Business Inc.. 917 504-6062
122 Blue Ridge Ct Newark (19702) *(G-11066)*

J & P Management Inc... 302 854-9400
20530 Dupont Blvd Georgetown (19947) *(G-4375)*

J & R Painting and Wallpaper... 302 438-9718
409 Marshfield Rd Wilmington (19803) *(G-17446)*

J & S - LOE Incorporated.. 302 608-7858
651 N Broad St Ste 205 Middletown (19709) *(G-7234)*

J & S General Contractors... 302 658-4499
1815 Williamson St Wilmington (19806) *(G-17447)*

J & S Lawn Service, Selbyville *Also Called: Michael J Truitt (G-13571)*

J & S Moving & Dlvry Svc LLC....................................... 302 357-5675
603 Franklin Bldg Newark (19702) *(G-11067)*

J & T Concrete Inc... 302 368-4949
84 Salem Church Rd Newark (19713) *(G-11068)*

J & V Cleaning LLC.. 302 245-5230
20479 Scott Dr Unit D Georgetown (19947) *(G-4376)*

J & V Shooters Supply LP... 302 422-5417
7369 Shawnee Rd Milford (19963) *(G-7945)*

J & W Mc Cormick Ltd.. 302 798-0336
310 Ruthar Dr Unit 4 Newark (19711) *(G-11069)*

J A Banks & Associates LLC.. 914 260-2003
486 Joseph Wick Dr Smyrna (19977) *(G-13779)*

J A E Seafood... 302 765-2546
403 Philadelphia Pike Ste 1 Wilmington (19809) *(G-17448)*

J A Moore & Sons Inc... 302 765-0110
3201 Miller Rd Wilmington (19802) *(G-17449)*

J A Pyne Jr DDS PA.. 302 994-7730
4925 Old Capitol Trl Wilmington (19808) *(G-17450)*

J A Ribinsky Builders.. 302 542-7014
33827 Lawton Ln Millsboro (19966) *(G-8323)*

J A S Logistic Inc... 302 339-1825
410 N Ramunno Dr Unit 211 Middletown (19709) *(G-7235)*

J Alexander Productions LLC.. 302 559-6667
2208 Van Buren Pl Wilmington (19802) *(G-17451)*

J Amoako Operation LLC.. 302 246-1346
913 N Market St Ste 200 Wilmington (19801) *(G-17452)*

J and J Display.. 302 628-4190
101 Park Ave Unit 2 Seaford (19973) *(G-13227)*

J B S Construction LLC... 302 349-5705
8801 Greenwood Rd Greenwood (19950) *(G-4641)*

J Bartley Stewart MD.. 302 737-3281
314 E Main St Ste 101 Newark (19711) *(G-11070)*

J C C Fitness Center, Wilmington *Also Called: Jewish Community Center Inc (G-17538)*

J C Wells & Sons LP.. 302 422-4732
7481 Wells Rd Milford (19963) *(G-7946)*

J Chance Productions... 302 322-2251
5 Stevens Ave New Castle (19720) *(G-9246)*

J Clayton Athey.. 302 888-6507
1310 N King St Wilmington (19801) *(G-17453)*

J D Construction.. 302 292-8789
5 Radnor Rd Newark (19713) *(G-11071)*

J D Masonry Inc... 302 684-1009
Rte 5 Harbeson (19951) *(G-4702)*

J Dean Pusey Contractor Inc... 302 245-0432
22548 Reynolds Pond Rd Ellendale (19941) *(G-3922)*

J E Bailey & Sons Inc.. 302 349-4376
2135 Seashore Hwy Greenwood (19950) *(G-4642)*

J E Parsley Electric LLC 302 396-9642
605 Abbott Dr Milford (19963) *(G-7947)*

J E Pellegrino & Associates 302 655-2565
301 Robinson Ln Bldg 1 Wilmington (19805) *(G-17454)*

J E Rispoli Contractor Inc 302 999-1310
402 Hillside Ave Wilmington (19805) *(G-17455)*

J Elder Gerenal Contracting, Historic New Castle *Also Called: John F Elder (G-5011)*

J F Goetz Associates LLC 302 537-2485
40 Fairway Dr Ocean View (19970) *(G-12526)*

J F S, Wilmington *Also Called: Jewish Family Services of Del (G-17539)*

J F Sobieski Mech Contrs Inc (PA) 302 993-0103
14 Hadco Rd Wilmington (19804) *(G-17456)*

J Fredericks & Son Elec C 302 733-0307
16 Flint Hill Dr Newark (19702) *(G-11072)*

J G M Associates 302 645-2159
17569 Nassau Commons Blvd Lewes (19958) *(G-6134)*

J Henry Edward & Sons Inc 302 658-4324
2300 W 4th St Wilmington (19805) *(G-17457)*

J Hooked Twing Rcvery Auto Rep 302 335-3043
2948 Andrews Lake Rd Felton (19943) *(G-3987)*

J I Beiler Homes LLC 302 697-1553
106 Orchard Grove Way Camden (19934) *(G-857)*

J J White Inc 215 722-1000
250 Edwards Ave New Castle (19720) *(G-9247)*

J L Carpenter Farms LLC 302 684-8601
27113 Carpenter Rd Milton (19968) *(G-8644)*

J Lotter Management 302 308-3939
1002 Society Dr Claymont (19703) *(G-1192)*

J M Aja Transportation LLC 302 562-6028
524 W Holly Oak Rd Wilmington (19809) *(G-17458)*

J M Industries 302 893-0363
845 Old Public Rd Hockessin (19707) *(G-5254)*

J Mamasian & Co LLC 302 219-2880
3 E Bullrush Dr Milford (19963) *(G-7948)*

J Matthew Pearson LLC 302 834-4595
24 Bar Dr Newark (19702) *(G-11073)*

J Melchiore & Sons, Lewes *Also Called: Melchiorre and Melchiorre (G-6260)*

J Michael Fay DDS PA 302 998-2244
3105 Limestone Rd Ste 304 Wilmington (19808) *(G-17459)*

J Michaels Painting Inc 302 738-8465
108 Unami Trl Newark (19711) *(G-11074)*

J N Grillo & Sons Co 302 658-7020
1000 E 12th St Wilmington (19802) *(G-17460)*

J N Hooker Inc 302 838-5650
1799 Pulaski Hwy Bear (19701) *(G-293)*

J N N Foundation 800 493-1069
175 Portside Ct Bear (19701) *(G-294)*

J Nichols Enterprises LLC 302 579-0720
8 The Grn Dover (19901) *(G-2759)*

J P Blandin Baseball LLC 302 535-8694
56 W Fairfield Dr Dover (19901) *(G-2760)*

J P Morgan Services Inc 302 634-1000
500 Stanton Christiana Rd Newark (19713) *(G-11075)*

J R Brooks Custom Framing, Felton *Also Called: J R Brooks Custom Framing LLC (G-3988)*

J R Brooks Custom Framing LLC 302 538-3637
1791 Peach Basket Rd Felton (19943) *(G-3988)*

J R Forshey DMD PA 302 322-0245
702 E Basin Rd Ste 1 New Castle (19720) *(G-9248)*

J R Rents Inc (PA) 302 266-8090
59 Marrows Rd Newark (19713) *(G-11076)*

J R Williamson DDS 302 734-8887
900 Forest St Dover (19904) *(G-2761)*

J Rihl Inc 856 778-5899
3518 Silverside Rd Ste 22 Wilmington (19810) *(G-17461)*

J Riley Eaton 302 539-4537
5 Plantation Ct Ocean View (19970) *(G-12527)*

J S & Assoc 302 765-2300
1510 Brandywine Blvd Wilmington (19809) *(G-17462)*

J S McKelvey DDS 302 239-0303
4901 Limestone Rd Wilmington (19808) *(G-17463)*

J Stachon Plumbing LLC 302 998-0938
1311 Hillside Blvd Wilmington (19803) *(G-17464)*

J Stanley Salon LLC 302 778-1885
204 N Union St Wilmington (19805) *(G-17465)*

J Star, Wilmington *Also Called: Three Js Disc Tire & Auto Svc (G-20316)*

J Stewart Paving Inc 610 359-9059
488 Walther Rd Newark (19702) *(G-11077)*

J T Electric 302 275-6778
16 Rose Cir Newark (19711) *(G-11078)*

J V Auto Service Inc 302 999-0786
1500 W Newport Pike Wilmington (19804) *(G-17466)*

J W Miller Wldg Boiler Repr Co, Middletown *Also Called: Miller JW Wldg Boiler Repr Co (G-7372)*

J William Gordy Fuel Co (PA) 302 846-3425
106 N Pennsylvania Ave Delmar (19940) *(G-1604)*

J&A Electrical Services LLC 302 943-9894
12737 Reynolds Rd Milton (19968) *(G-8645)*

J&D Management 302 239-2489
1174 Old Wilmington Rd Hockessin (19707) *(G-5255)*

J&G Building Group, Middletown *Also Called: J & G Acoustical Co (G-7233)*

J&J Cleaning 302 507-5082
300 S Ford Ave Wilmington (19805) *(G-17467)*

J&J Fleet Service 484 632-1647
729 Grantham Ln Ste 7 New Castle (19720) *(G-9249)*

J&J Staffing Resources Inc 302 738-7800
200 Continental Dr Ste 107 Newark (19713) *(G-11079)*

J&J STAFFING RESOURCES, INC, Newark *Also Called: J&J Staffing Resources Inc (G-11079)*

J&J Systems 302 239-2969
10 Ridgewood Dr Hockessin (19707) *(G-5256)*

J&K Fleet Service, Bear *Also Called: J & K Auto Repair Inc (G-292)*

J&L Logistic Group LLC 917 499-0019
408 W 24th St Wilmington (19802) *(G-17468)*

J&M Remodeling 443 736-0127
30390 Pepper Trl Frankford (19945) *(G-4117)*

J&R Auto Repair 240 863-8653
100 Maggies Ellendale (19941) *(G-3923)*

Jab Contracting LLC 302 559-1905
2 Biltmore Ct Wilmington (19808) *(G-17469)*

Jabez Corp 302 475-7600
2201 Silverside Rd Wilmington (19810) *(G-17470)*

Jack Donovan 410 715-0504
23868 Samuel Adams Cir Millsboro (19966) *(G-8324)*

Jack Ennis Custom Lawn 302 422-8577
Milford (19963) *(G-7949)*

Jack F Owens Campus, Georgetown *Also Called: Delaware Tchncal Cmnty College (G-4286)*

Jack Hickman Real Estate 302 539-8000
33188 Coastal Hwy Unit 2 Bethany Beach (19930) *(G-611)*

Jack Kelly's Landscaping, Hockessin *Also Called: Jack Kellys Ldscpg & Tree Svc (G-5257)*

Jack Kellys Ldscpg & Tree Svc 302 239-7185
6 Crest Dr Hockessin (19707) *(G-5257)*

Jack Lingo Asset MGT LLC 302 226-6645
19335 Coastal Hwy Rehoboth Beach (19971) *(G-12797)*

Jack Lingo Inc Realtor 302 947-9030
1240 Kings Hwy Lewes (19958) *(G-6135)*

Jack Lingo Inc Realtor (PA) 302 227-3883
246 Rehoboth Ave Rehoboth Beach (19971) *(G-12798)*

Jack Lingo Realtor 302 645-2207
1240 Kings Hwy Lewes (19958) *(G-6136)*

Jack Lingo Realtor 302 344-9188
97 Tidewaters Rd Rehoboth Beach (19971) *(G-12799)*

Jack R Kellys Landscape & Tre 302 218-6684
11 Summerknoll Cir Newark (19711) *(G-11080)*

Jack Smith Towing, Wilmington *Also Called: Smiths Jack Towing & Svc Ctr (G-19895)*

Jackie Heck 302 856-1598
21176 Pepper Rd Georgetown (19947) *(G-4377)*

Jacks Cleaning Services LLC 302 494-8887
803 Quinn Ct New Castle (19720) *(G-9250)*

Jacks Life Management Inc 347 757-0720
8 The Grn Ste 8107 Dover (19901) *(G-2762)*

Jackson Contracting Inc 302 678-2011
7242 Pearsons Corner Rd Dover (19904) *(G-2763)*

Jackson Ed Home Improvements 302 322-1566
45 Skyline Dr New Castle (19720) *(G-9251)*

ALPHABETIC SECTION — Jamestown Sports

Jackson Hewitt 302 382-2140
  36 Jerome Dr Dover (19901) *(G-2764)*

Jackson Hewitt Tax Service (PA) 302 629-4548
  1004 W Stein Hwy Seaford (19973) *(G-13228)*

Jackson Hewitt Tax Service 302 761-9626
  3209 Miller Rd Wilmington (19802) *(G-17471)*

Jackson Hewitt Tax Service, Dover Also Called: Jackson Hewitt *(G-2764)*

Jackson Hewitt Tax Service, Dover Also Called: Ronald Midaugh *(G-3482)*

Jackson Hewitt Tax Service, Millsboro Also Called: Jackson Hewitt Tax Service Inc *(G-8325)*

Jackson Hewitt Tax Service, Seaford Also Called: Jackson Hewitt Tax Service *(G-13228)*

Jackson Hewitt Tax Service Inc 302 934-7430
  320 W Dupont Hwy Ste 102 Millsboro (19966) *(G-8325)*

Jackson Masonry 302 397-4202
  325 Olga Rd Wilmington (19805) *(G-17472)*

Jacksun, Claymont Also Called: Jacksun Inc *(G-1193)*

Jacksun Inc 800 861-7050
  2093 Philadelphia Pike Ste 1182 Claymont (19703) *(G-1193)*

Jaco LLC 302 645-8068
  21 Shay Ln Milton (19968) *(G-8646)*

Jacobs & Crumplar PA 302 656-5445
  750 Shipyard Dr Ste 200 Wilmington (19801) *(G-17473)*

Jacobs Squared 302 294-6607
  34 Aronimink Dr Newark (19711) *(G-11081)*

Jacqueline Allens Daycare 302 368-3633
  17 Timberline Dr Newark (19711) *(G-11082)*

Jacta Alea Est LLC 302 731-7360
  53 Marrows Rd Newark (19713) *(G-11083)*

Jadali Seyedmehdi MD 302 738-4300
  324 E Main St Ste 204 Newark (19711) *(G-11084)*

Jade Logistics Inc 302 724-2649
  5 Sherwood Forest Way Hartly (19953) *(G-4880)*

Jaed Corporation (PA) 302 832-1652
  2500 Wrangle Hill Rd Ste 110 Bear (19701) *(G-295)*

Jaffery & Jaffery Contractors 302 766-3795
  422 Naughty Ln Middletown (19709) *(G-7236)*

Jag Industrials LLC 267 334-7999
  8 The Grn Dover (19901) *(G-2765)*

Jag Payments Inc 800 261-0240
  30567 Flycatcher Ct Millsboro (19966) *(G-8326)*

Jager Transport LLC 302 858-2962
  14206 Blanchard Rd Greenwood (19950) *(G-4643)*

Jaguar Tubulars Inc 438 778-6535
  2915 Ogletown Rd Newark (19713) *(G-11085)*

Jaimie Stafford 302 336-8307
  621 W Division St Dover (19904) *(G-2766)*

Jairus Enterprises Inc 302 834-1625
  1218 Pulaski Hwy Ste 484 Bear (19701) *(G-296)*

Jakl Beer Works LLC 610 442-0878
  160 Gillespie Ave Middletown (19709) *(G-7237)*

Jalal Bayar Contracting 302 535-7294
  67 Harkins Dr Smyrna (19977) *(G-13780)*

Jam Air LLC 302 270-8236
  60 Twin Oak Dr Dover (19904) *(G-2767)*

Jam Productions 302 369-3629
  8 Hillcroft Rd Newark (19711) *(G-11086)*

Jamaican MI Hungry 302 287-3337
  2202 Kirkwood Hwy Wilmington (19805) *(G-17474)*

Jamaika 302 521-4842
  1908 W 2nd St Wilmington (19805) *(G-17475)*

Jamal G Misleh M D 302 658-7533
  4701 Ogletown Stanton Rd Ste 3400 Newark (19713) *(G-11087)*

Jamark Enterprises Inc 302 652-2000
  40 Germay Dr Wilmington (19804) *(G-17476)*

Jamc LLC 410 639-2224
  20479 Asheville Dr Millsboro (19966) *(G-8327)*

Jameil Akeem Cngo Cres Fndtion 302 409-0791
  2205 Lamotte St Wilmington (19802) *(G-17477)*

James & Jesses Barbr & Buty Sp 302 658-9617
  931 Bennett St Ste 933 Wilmington (19801) *(G-17478)*

James & Patricia Booth 302 378-9139
  725 Wood Duck Ct Middletown (19709) *(G-7238)*

James A Peel & Sons Inc 302 738-1468
  118 Sandy Dr Ste 1 Newark (19713) *(G-11088)*

James B Crissman 302 475-1365
  2311 Empire Dr Wilmington (19810) *(G-17479)*

James B Salva MD 302 762-2283
  1805 Foulk Rd Ste F Wilmington (19810) *(G-17480)*

James Boyland 302 838-0800
  1237 Quintilio Dr Bear (19701) *(G-297)*

James C Wang 302 737-6000
  1450 Capitol Trl Ste 112 Newark (19711) *(G-11089)*

James Docherty 302 983-2653
  47 Aronimink Dr Newark (19711) *(G-11090)*

James E Deakyne Jr PA 302 226-1200
  300 Salisbury St Rehoboth Beach (19971) *(G-12800)*

James E Deakyne Jr PA 302 226-1200
  300 Salisbury St Rehoboth Beach (19971) *(G-12801)*

James F Palmer (PA) 302 629-6162
  8857 Riverside Dr Seaford (19973) *(G-13229)*

James Fierro Do PA 302 529-2255
  1805 Foulk Rd Ste F Wilmington (19810) *(G-17481)*

James Jesses Barbr Maudes Buty, Wilmington Also Called: James & Jesses Barbr & Buty Sp *(G-17478)*

James L Carpenter & Son Inc 302 684-8601
  27113 Carpenter Rd Milton (19968) *(G-8647)*

James L Holzman 302 888-6500
  1310 N King St Wilmington (19801) *(G-17482)*

James L Webb Paving Co Inc 302 697-2000
  11804 Willow Grove Rd Camden (19934) *(G-858)*

James Machine Shop Inc 302 798-5679
  3102 W Brandywine Ave Claymont (19703) *(G-1194)*

James Maintenance Services LLC 302 934-7625
  12 Ward Way Millsboro (19966) *(G-8328)*

James Moran Do 302 731-2888
  4745 Ogletown Stanton Rd # 238 Newark (19713) *(G-11091)*

James N Walsh Jr 302 235-7777
  1013 Centre Rd Ste 402 Wilmington (19805) *(G-17483)*

James P Curran, Newark Also Called: Curran James P Law Offices *(G-10365)*

James Parker Contracting 302 507-6200
  1706 Bear Corbitt Rd Bear (19701) *(G-298)*

James Powell 302 539-2351
  34309 Burton Farm Rd Frankford (19945) *(G-4118)*

James Ray Family & Friends LLC 302 670-0305
  5102 Halltown Rd Hartly (19953) *(G-4881)*

James Rice Jr Construction Co 302 731-9323
  122 Upper Pike Creek Rd Newark (19711) *(G-11092)*

James Robert Kline 302 633-3926
  110 Harding Ave Wilmington (19804) *(G-17484)*

James S Pillsbury DDS 302 734-0330
  125 Greentree Dr # B Dover (19904) *(G-2768)*

James S Reilly M D 302 651-4200
  1600 Rockland Rd Wilmington (19803) *(G-17485)*

James Stewart Rostocki 302 250-5541
  14 Westover Cir Wilmington (19807) *(G-17486)*

James Sutton 302 328-5438
  807 Churchmans Road Ext New Castle (19720) *(G-9252)*

James T Chandler & Son Inc (PA) 302 478-7100
  2506 Concord Pike Wilmington (19803) *(G-17487)*

James Thompson & Company Inc 302 349-4501
  301 S Church St Greenwood (19950) *(G-4644)*

James Tigani III DDS 302 571-8740
  1021 Gilpin Ave Ste 205 Wilmington (19806) *(G-17488)*

James W McKee 302 540-9191
  305 Beech Ln Middletown (19709) *(G-7239)*

James Willey Masonry LLC 302 258-6242
  201 Chapel Of Ease St Dagsboro (19939) *(G-1469)*

James Williams State Svc Ctr, Dover Also Called: Delaware Dept Hlth Social Svcs *(G-2229)*

James, Stevens & Daniels, Dover Also Called: Jsd Management Inc *(G-2811)*

Jamestown Painting & Dctg Inc 302 454-7344
  830 Dawson Dr Newark (19713) *(G-11093)*

Jamestown Sports 302 328-2770
  6 Shea Way Newark (19713) *(G-11094)*

(PA)=Parent Co (HQ)=Headquarters (DH)=Div Headquarters

Jamie H Keskeny 302 651-6060
   1600 Rockland Rd Wilmington (19803) *(G-17489)*

Jamie Laber 302 373-7890
   226 W Park Pl Ste 1a Newark (19711) *(G-11095)*

Jamies Auto Repair South 302 378-7933
   98 Main St Townsend (19734) *(G-14019)*

Jamland Studio 302 475-0204
   2326 Empire Dr Wilmington (19810) *(G-17490)*

Jammin Productions 302 670-7302
   2178 S State St Dover (19901) *(G-2769)*

Jammy Instruments US Corp 209 813-4052
   2093 Philadelphia Pike Claymont (19703) *(G-1195)*

Jamroxk LLC 302 423-5377
   32 W Loockerman St Dover (19904) *(G-2770)*

Jan Patrick RES 302 234-6046
   17 Ridon Dr Hockessin (19707) *(G-5258)*

Jan Stern Eqine Asssted Thrapy 302 234-9835
   112 Shinn Cir Wilmington (19808) *(G-17491)*

Jana Analysis Inc 724 584-0545
   651 N Broad St Ste 2051916 Middletown (19709) *(G-7240)*

Jane A Ierardi M D 302 651-4000
   1600 Rockland Rd Wilmington (19803) *(G-17492)*

Jane Choung 302 378-8740
   410 N Cass St Middletown (19709) *(G-7241)*

Jane L Stayton CPA 302 856-4141
   117 S Bedford St Georgetown (19947) *(G-4378)*

Janelle G Evans LLC 302 562-6504
   27 Tamarack Ave Wilmington (19805) *(G-17493)*

Janet Sue Winner 302 798-3731
   100 Odessa Ave Wilmington (19809) *(G-17494)*

Janette Redrow Ltd 302 659-3534
   635 Cannery Ln Townsend (19734) *(G-14020)*

Jani Uday 302 684-0990
   28312 Lewes Georgetown Hwy Milton (19968) *(G-8648)*

Janice James & Joan LLC 845 682-1886
   254 Chapman Rd Newark (19702) *(G-11096)*

Janice Tildon-Burton MD (PA) 302 832-1124
   2600 Glasgow Ave Ste 207 Newark (19702) *(G-11097)*

Janies Angel LLC 302 669-1516
   109 Cannonball Ln Newark (19702) *(G-11098)*

Janis Dicristofaro Day Care 302 998-6730
   1104 Arundel Dr Wilmington (19808) *(G-17495)*

Janitorial Services and Sups, Wilmington *Also Called: Gemini Building Systems LLC* *(G-16827)*

Jans Hands Massage Therapy 302 753-3962
   2421 Newell Dr Wilmington (19808) *(G-17496)*

Janus Hndrson Blnced Cllctive 800 724-2440
   1100 N Market St Wilmington (19890) *(G-17497)*

Janvier Jewelers, Newark *Also Called: Turquoise Shop Inc (G-12248)*

Japan Gourmet Pass, Newark *Also Called: Stones Soup Inc (G-12102)*

Japan Modern Art LLC 832 458-1536
   8 The Grn Ste A Dover (19901) *(G-2771)*

Jaquez Concrete LLC 302 379-1148
   4 Bryant Ct Middletown (19709) *(G-7242)*

Jarel Industries LLC 336 782-0697
   3411 S Dupont Hwy Camden (19934) *(G-859)*

Jarrell Benson Giles & Sweeney 302 678-4488
   725 S Queen St Dover (19904) *(G-2772)*

Jasmine L Heath Ms 215 391-3553
   1602 Walnut St Wilmington (19809) *(G-17498)*

Jason Bell Dr 302 993-0722
   1 Centurian Dr Ste 101 Newark (19713) *(G-11099)*

Jason L Torlish Sr 302 682-3874
   9415 Cherry Tree Ln Seaford (19973) *(G-13230)*

Jason Lewis Pusey 302 245-6545
   4379 Federalsburg Rd Bridgeville (19933) *(G-717)*

Jatc Local Union 313 .... 302 322-5089
   814 W Basin Rd New Castle (19720) *(G-9253)*

Jay Ambe Inc 302 654-5400
   3 Memorial Dr New Castle (19720) *(G-9254)*

Jay D Lufty MD 302 658-0404
   2300 Pennsylvania Ave Ste 2a Wilmington (19806) *(G-17499)*

Jay Devi Inc 302 777-4700
   2117 N Dupont Hwy New Castle (19720) *(G-9255)*

Jay Gundel and Associates Inc 302 658-1674
   2502 Silverside Rd Ste 8 Wilmington (19810) *(G-17500)*

Jay J Dave Do 302 422-0800
   111 Neurology Way Milford (19963) *(G-7950)*

Jay J Harris PC 302 453-1400
   220 Christiana Medical Ctr Newark (19702) *(G-11100)*

Jay Katz Lmm Taxation LLC 302 894-9446
   922 New Rd Ste 3 Wilmington (19805) *(G-17501)*

Jay Lynn Cnstr Solutions LLC 302 349-5799
   136 Laurel Rd Millsboro (19966) *(G-8329)*

Jayant H Shukla Dr 302 834-0222
   22 Kimmie Ct Bear (19701) *(G-299)*

Jaykal Led Solutions Inc 302 295-0015
   21499 Baltimore Ave Georgetown (19947) *(G-4379)*

Jays Auto Repair LLC 302 273-2811
   61 Blue Hen Dr Newark (19713) *(G-11101)*

Jaysons LLC 302 656-9436
   1807 Concord Pike Wilmington (19803) *(G-17502)*

Jazminerenae 302 784-4710
   3 Germay Dr Ste 4 Wilmington (19804) *(G-17503)*

Jazzercise 302 690-3447
   345 School Bell Rd Bear (19701) *(G-300)*

Jazzercise 302 730-8177
   33 Turningleaf Ct Dover (19904) *(G-2773)*

Jazzercise 302 698-3020
   911 S Governors Ave Dover (19904) *(G-2774)*

Jazzercise 610 485-9044
   4900 Concord Pike Wilmington (19803) *(G-17504)*

Jazzercise, Bear *Also Called: Jazzercise (G-300)*

Jazzercise, Dover *Also Called: Jazzercise (G-2774)*

Jazzercise, Wilmington *Also Called: Jazzercise (G-17504)*

JB For Office) Hogan 302 922-0000
   539 Blue Heron Rd Dover (19904) *(G-2775)*

JBA Enterprises LLC 302 834-6685
   109 Peace Ct W Bear (19701) *(G-301)*

Jbcompany LLC 406 623-8593
   Philadelphia Pike Ste B #507 Claymont (19703) *(G-1196)*

Jbiza Enterprises LLC 302 764-3389
   106 W 36th St Wilmington (19802) *(G-17505)*

Jbj Enterprise LLC 302 227-6080
   19361 Copper Dr N Rehoboth Beach (19971) *(G-12802)*

Jbm Petroleum Service LLC 302 752-6105
   8913 Clendaniel Pond Rd Lincoln (19960) *(G-6677)*

Jbs Contracting 302 543-7264
   2211 Bradmoor Rd Wilmington (19803) *(G-17506)*

Jbs Kitchen LLC 302 487-3830
   123 Hunn Rd New Castle (19720) *(G-9256)*

Jbs Souderton Inc 302 629-0725
   4957 Stein Hwy Rte 20 W Seaford (19973) *(G-13231)*

Jbs Technologies Inc 302 683-1098
   1201 N Orange St Ste 7460 Wilmington (19801) *(G-17507)*

JC Contractors LLC 302 420-9338
   318 White Pine Dr Middletown (19709) *(G-7243)*

JC General Construction Inc 302 383-3152
   232 W Ayre St Wilmington (19804) *(G-17508)*

JC Industrial Solutions Inc 484 720-8381
   950 Ridge Rd Ste C13 Claymont (19703) *(G-1197)*

JC Marks Investments LLC 302 602-4021
   8 The Grn Ste A Dover (19901) *(G-2776)*

JC Weight Loss Centres Inc 302 477-9202
   4447 Concord Pike Wilmington (19803) *(G-17509)*

JC&a Trust 302 579-0886
   8 The Grn Unit 8215 Dover (19901) *(G-2777)*

Jcr Enterprises Inc 302 629-9163
   126 N Shipley St Seaford (19973) *(G-13232)*

Jcr Systems LLC 302 420-6072
   621 Delaware St Historic New Castle (19720) *(G-5010)*

JD Asphalt 302 514-7325
   933 N Dupont Blvd Milford (19963) *(G-7951)*

ALPHABETIC SECTION

JD Sign Company LLC 302 786-2761
   515 Smith Ave Harrington (19952) *(G-4790)*

Jdh Construction Inc 302 993-0720
   1104 Kirkwood Hwy Frnt Wilmington (19805) *(G-17510)*

Jdjs LLC 844 967-3748
   21348 Cedar Creek Ave Georgetown (19947) *(G-4380)*

Jean L Binkley 302 598-5582
   2906 Newport Gap Pike Wilmington (19808) *(G-17511)*

Jeanes Radiology Associates PC 302 738-1700
   42 Omega Dr Ste H Newark (19713) *(G-11102)*

Jeanette Y Son Dentist 302 998-8283
   2601 Annand Dr Ste 8 Wilmington (19808) *(G-17512)*

Jeanfreau Carpentry Services 302 563-6449
   130 Hickman Rd Ste 8 Claymont (19703) *(G-1198)*

Jeanine ODonnell 302 644-3276
   16583 Coastal Hwy Lewes (19958) *(G-6137)*

JEANNE JUGAN RESIDENCE, Newark *Also Called: Little Sisters of The Poor (G-11273)*

Jeans Love-N-Care Childcare 302 934-5665
   27294 Dogwood Ln Millsboro (19966) *(G-8330)*

Jeb Plastics, Wilmington *Also Called: JEB Plastics Inc (G-17513)*

JEB Plastics Inc 302 479-9223
   4550 Linden Hill Rd Ste 105 Wilmington (19808) *(G-17513)*

Jeena M Jolly DDS 302 655-2626
   217 W 9th St Wilmington (19801) *(G-17514)*

Jeff Hopkins LLC 302 653-6413
   572 Delaney Maryland Rd Clayton (19938) *(G-1375)*

Jeff Tetrick 302 478-7185
   31 Paxon Dr Wilmington (19803) *(G-17515)*

Jeff Warnock Carpentry Paintng 484 995-4812
   1102 Talley Rd Wilmington (19809) *(G-17516)*

Jefferson Group LLC 302 764-1550
   4615 Sylvanus Dr Wilmington (19803) *(G-17517)*

Jefferson Urian Dane Strner PA 302 678-1425
   107 Wolf Creek Blvd Ste 1 Dover (19901) *(G-2778)*

Jefferson Urian Dane Strner PA (PA) 302 856-3900
   651 N Bedford St Georgetown (19947) *(G-4381)*

Jefferson Urian Dane Strner PA 302 539-5543
   92 Atlantic Ave Ste D Ocean View (19970) *(G-12528)*

Jeffery Brannan 302 547-1659
   118 Countryside Ln Bear (19701) *(G-302)*

Jeffko Inc 302 235-2180
   7209 Lancaster Pike Ste 1 Hockessin (19707) *(G-5259)*

Jeffrey A Bright DMD 302 832-1371
   600 N Broad St Ste 7 Middletown (19709) *(G-7244)*

Jeffrey Bowersox 302 322-6933
   290 Churchmans Rd New Castle (19720) *(G-9257)*

Jeffrey D Karron LLC 302 494-3724
   21 Emsley Dr Wilmington (19810) *(G-17518)*

Jeffrey Glenn Minor 302 422-3403
   7557 Lindale Rd Greenwood (19950) *(G-4645)*

Jeffrey Goldstein Dr 302 478-5433
   4 Curry Ct Wilmington (19810) *(G-17519)*

Jeffrey L Cook D M D 302 453-8700
   16 Peddlers Row Ste 16 Newark (19702) *(G-11103)*

Jeffrey L Premo 302 877-0468
   310 High St Seaford (19973) *(G-13233)*

Jeffrey L Whitters Jr LLC 800 563-6006
   131 Scarborough Park Dr Wilmington (19804) *(G-17520)*

Jeffrey Schlerf Atty 302 622-4212
   919 N Market St Wilmington (19801) *(G-17521)*

Jeffrie J Silverberg PHD 302 507-3039
   2401 Pennsylvania Ave Apt 511 Wilmington (19806) *(G-17522)*

Jeffs Total Heating N Air 302 682-1816
   324 E Poplar St Seaford (19973) *(G-13234)*

Jem Therapeutics Pbc 561 462-1809
   8 The Grn Dover (19901) *(G-2779)*

Jenkins Mechanical 302 430-8211
   3 Fairway Ave Georgetown (19947) *(G-4382)*

Jenner Enterprises Inc (PA) 302 998-6755
   1300 First State Blvd Ste G Wilmington (19804) *(G-17523)*

Jenner Enterprises Inc 302 479-5686
   3203 Concord Pike Wilmington (19803) *(G-17524)*

Jennifer 302 738-3020
   31 Hillcroft Rd Newark (19711) *(G-11104)*

Jennifer C Dombroski Msw Lcsw 302 422-3811
   1001 S Bradford St Ste 8 Dover (19904) *(G-2780)*

Jennifer F Divita 302 734-8000
   97 Commerce Way Ste 101 Dover (19904) *(G-2781)*

Jennifer L Joseph DDS 302 239-6677
   5317 Limestone Rd Ste 2 Wilmington (19808) *(G-17525)*

Jennifer L Kopazna 215 868-1466
   3 Harding Ave Wilmington (19804) *(G-17526)*

Jennifer M D Hung 302 644-0690
   18947 John J Williams Hwy U Rehoboth Beach (19971) *(G-12803)*

Jennifer M Dragone 302 353-7133
   411 Northwood Rd Wilmington (19803) *(G-17527)*

Jennifer M Ewald 302 377-6911
   120 W Main St Middletown (19709) *(G-7245)*

Jennifer R Rodgers 302 542-7095
   98 Central Ave Ocean View (19970) *(G-12529)*

Jennifer Sellitto-Penoza Lcsw 302 328-4936
   15 Angola Rd New Castle (19720) *(G-9258)*

Jennifer Trolio Lcsw 302 836-1131
   136 Cann Rd Newark (19702) *(G-11105)*

Jennifers Spa 302 740-6363
   4 S Merriment Dr Newark (19702) *(G-11106)*

Jenns Tail Waggers 302 475-9621
   8 Carpenter Plz Wilmington (19810) *(G-17528)*

Jenny Craig, Wilmington *Also Called: JC Weight Loss Centres Inc (G-17509)*

Jenny Craig Holdings Inc 302 477-9202
   4447 Concord Pike Wilmington (19803) *(G-17529)*

Jennygems, Georgetown *Also Called: Jdjs LLC (G-4380)*

Jenrin Discovery LLC 302 379-1679
   2515 Lori Ln N Wilmington (19810) *(G-17530)*

Jeremey M Weddle 410 829-7224
   8028 Hidden Meadow Ln Greenwood (19950) *(G-4646)*

Jeremiah 29 11 Fitness LLC 302 376-1287
   521 Wheelmen St Middletown (19709) *(G-7246)*

Jeremy Sheiker 302 540-3741
   2119 Shipley Rd Wilmington (19803) *(G-17531)*

Jerome C Kayatta DDS 302 737-6761
   192 Kenneth Ct Newark (19711) *(G-11107)*

Jerry A Fletcher 302 875-9057
   34301 Rider Rd Delmar (19940) *(G-1605)*

Jerry A Fletcher Catering, Delmar *Also Called: Jerry A Fletcher (G-1605)*

Jerry L Burkert 302 736-1116
   1244 Forrest Ave Dover (19904) *(G-2782)*

Jerry L Case Dr 302 368-5500
   430 Christiana Medical Ctr Newark (19702) *(G-11108)*

Jerry O Thompson Prntng 302 832-1309
   4 Ogden Ct Bear (19701) *(G-303)*

Jerry P Gluckman M D 302 426-8012
   4830 Kennett Pike # 8000 Wilmington (19807) *(G-17532)*

Jerry S Meiklejohn 302 745-2632
   30622 Sandy Landing Rd Dagsboro (19939) *(G-1470)*

Jerrys Handyman LLC 302 357-1589
   36 Lanford Rd New Castle (19720) *(G-9259)*

Jerrys Inc 302 422-7676
   17776 Oak Hill Dr Milford (19963) *(G-7952)*

Jersey Clippers LLC 302 956-0138
   134 Widgeon Way Bridgeville (19933) *(G-718)*

Jesco Inc 302 376-6946
   1001 Industrial Dr Middletown (19709) *(G-7247)*

Jesse Jmes Safood Barbeque LLC 302 883-3518
   1030 S Dupont Hwy Dover (19901) *(G-2783)*

Jesse W Stone 302 677-0500
   1144 S Bay Rd Dover (19901) *(G-2784)*

Jessica A Whisler Mrs 302 438-3720
   3519 Silverside Rd Wilmington (19810) *(G-17533)*

Jessica L Desrosiers 443 617-5152
   105 Nashua Ct Bear (19701) *(G-304)*

Jessica S Dicerbo DDS 302 644-4460
   18947 John J Williams Hwy Unit 309 Rehoboth Beach (19971) *(G-12804)*

Jessica Yang Inc.. 612 217-0220
  251 Little Falls Dr Wilmington (19808) *(G-17534)*

Jet Carrier... 908 759-6938
  19 Shea Way Ste 308 Newark (19713) *(G-11109)*

Jet Fast Loans... 302 934-6794
  28544 Dupont Blvd Unit 9 Millsboro (19966) *(G-8331)*

Jet Green Transporters LLC................................. 302 861-8918
  1001 White Oak Rd Apt C31 Dover (19901) *(G-2785)*

Jet Phynx Films LLC.. 302 803-0109
  204 Birch Ave Wilmington (19805) *(G-17535)*

Jet Products LLC (PA)... 877 453-8868
  2207 Concord Pike 640 Wilmington (19803) *(G-17536)*

Jet Setting Tours LLC.. 707 217-6967
  808 W 24th St Wilmington (19802) *(G-17537)*

Jetset Travel Inc.. 302 678-5050
  19470 Coastal Hwy Unit 7 Rehoboth Beach (19971) *(G-12805)*

Jewelers of Wilmington, Newark Also Called: Del Haven of Wilmington Inc *(G-10411)*

Jewell Enterprises Inc... 302 737-8460
  729 Dawson Dr Newark (19713) *(G-11110)*

Jewels Cleaning Service..................................... 302 841-2948
  5616 Betty St Milford (19963) *(G-7953)*

Jewish Community Center Inc............................. 302 478-5660
  101 Garden Of Eden Rd Ste 102 Wilmington (19803) *(G-17538)*

Jewish Family Services of Del (PA).................... 302 478-9411
  99 Passmore Dr Wilmington (19803) *(G-17539)*

Jewish Federation of Delaware............................ 302 478-5660
  101 Garden Of Eden Rd Wilmington (19803) *(G-17540)*

Jfm Enterprises LLC... 302 836-4107
  525 Hambleton Ln Newark (19702) *(G-11111)*

JG Allstar Trucking LLC (PA).............................. 609 372-8636
  611 S Dupont Hwy Ste 102 Dover (19901) *(G-2786)*

JG Plastics... 302 545-4888
  1601 Concord Pike Ste 36d Wilmington (19803) *(G-17541)*

JG Services.. 302 480-1900
  3650 Upper King Rd Dover (19904) *(G-2787)*

JG Townsend Jr & Co Inc (PA)............................ 302 856-2525
  316 N Race St Georgetown (19947) *(G-4383)*

Jgcounseling.. 302 354-0074
  733 Ambleside Dr Wilmington (19808) *(G-17542)*

JGm & Associates Custom Pntg.......................... 302 645-2159
  17569 Nassau Commons Blvd Lewes (19958) *(G-6138)*

Jgreenbergconsulting LLC.................................. 610 572-2729
  280 Wildflower Cir N Magnolia (19962) *(G-6753)*

Jh Contracting Inc... 302 893-4766
  807 Laurelwood Ct Middletown (19709) *(G-7248)*

Jhana Inc (PA).. 530 863-7269
  850 New Burton Rd Ste 201 Dover (19904) *(G-2788)*

Jhn, Wilmington Also Called: Julian H Nicol *(G-17609)*

Ji DCI Joint Venture 1... 302 652-4221
  1211 Delaware Ave Wilmington (19806) *(G-17543)*

Ji DCI Jv-II... 302 652-4221
  1211 Delaware Ave Wilmington (19806) *(G-17544)*

Jia Finance Inc... 202 341-1031
  3524 Silverside Rd Ste 35b Wilmington (19810) *(G-17545)*

Jiffy Lube, Dover Also Called: Dover Lubricants Inc *(G-2352)*

Jiffyshirtscom (us) LP... 302 319-2063
  1000 Nw St Ste 1280 Wilmington (19801) *(G-17546)*

Jiga Inc... 408 878-3213
  651 N Broad St Middletown (19709) *(G-7249)*

Jill Garrido DDS.. 302 475-3110
  2000 Foulk Rd Ste C Wilmington (19810) *(G-17547)*

Jill L Alfree... 302 653-9107
  2308 Downs Chapel Rd Clayton (19938) *(G-1376)*

Jill Riley... 802 272-7310
  23715 Driftwood Ln Lewes (19958) *(G-6139)*

Jillann I Hounsell DDS.. 302 239-5917
  7197 Lancaster Pike Hockessin (19707) *(G-5260)*

Jillann I Hounsell DDS.. 302 691-3000
  2300 Pennsylvania Ave Ste 6a Wilmington (19806) *(G-17548)*

Jim Hutchison.. 302 739-4758
  50 Billings Dr Dover (19901) *(G-2789)*

Jim Knnas Optmtrsts Optcans In......................... 302 722-6197
  40 E Main St # 854 Newark (19711) *(G-11112)*

Jim Knnas Optmtrsts Optcans In (PA)................. 302 722-6197
  501 Silverside Rd Ste 105-3708 Wilmington (19809) *(G-17549)*

Jimmy Smalls Landscaping LLC......................... 302 730-0150
  91 Brenda Ln Ste A Camden Wyoming (19934) *(G-956)*

Jin Pen Feet Massage.. 302 228-2846
  38660 Sussex Hwy Unit 3 Delmar (19940) *(G-1606)*

Jing Jin MD PHD... 302 651-5040
  101 Shrewsbury Dr Wilmington (19810) *(G-17550)*

Jira LLC.. 302 202-4615
  8 The Grn Dover (19901) *(G-2790)*

Jiten Patel DDS.. 302 690-8629
  100 Sussex Ave Milford (19963) *(G-7954)*

Jivosite Inc... 408 604-0183
  1013 Centre Rd Ste 403b Wilmington (19805) *(G-17551)*

Jj's Lrng Exprnce Chldcare Ctr, Bear Also Called: Johnson Shawanda *(G-309)*

Jjc Independent Contractor LLC.......................... 302 388-5499
  9 Nina Ct Wilmington (19810) *(G-17552)*

Jjid Inc... 302 836-0414
  100 Julian Ln Bear (19701) *(G-305)*

Jjs Industries LP... 302 690-2957
  2424 E Parris Dr Wilmington (19808) *(G-17553)*

Jjs Learning Experience LLC.............................. 302 398-9000
  17001 S Dupont Hwy Harrington (19952) *(G-4791)*

Jk Tangles Hair Salon... 302 698-1006
  1151 E Lebanon Rd Ste E Dover (19901) *(G-2791)*

Jkb Corp.. 302 734-5017
  1169 S Dupont Hwy Dover (19901) *(G-2792)*

Jkings Mining Company LLC.............................. 628 600-9522
  16192 Coastal Hwy Lewes (19958) *(G-6140)*

Jl Mechanical Inc.. 302 337-7855
  5460 Hartzell Rd Bridgeville (19933) *(G-719)*

Jl Solis LLC... 302 212-9521
  25709 Whispering Wind Ln Millsboro (19966) *(G-8332)*

Jld Auto Repair and Transm................................ 302 650-8613
  3607 Downing Dr Wilmington (19802) *(G-17554)*

JLE Inc... 302 656-3590
  20 Germay Dr Wilmington (19804) *(G-17555)*

JLJ Enterprises Inc.. 302 398-0229
  16975 Redden Rd Georgetown (19947) *(G-4384)*

Jlquick Photography... 302 674-3794
  104 Quail Hollow Dr Dover (19904) *(G-2793)*

JLW Consulting LLC... 302 653-7283
  396 N School Ln Smyrna (19977) *(G-13781)*

JM General Contractor.. 302 464-9730
  152 Freedom Trl New Castle (19720) *(G-9260)*

JMB Glamsquad LLC.. 844 695-4526
  251 Little Falls Dr Wilmington (19808) *(G-17556)*

Jmco, Newark Also Called: Global Recruiters Wilmington *(G-10852)*

JMJ Assoc.. 410 320-0890
  31699 Alsace Ct Lewes (19958) *(G-6141)*

Jmk Behavior LLC.. 302 384-7354
  1601 Milltown Rd Wilmington (19808) *(G-17557)*

Jmt, Newark Also Called: Johnson Mirmiran Thompson Inc *(G-11120)*

Jmt Inter LLC... 302 312-5177
  415 Aldwych Dr Bear (19701) *(G-306)*

Jmt Services Inc... 302 530-2807
  808 Lorewood Grove Rd Middletown (19709) *(G-7250)*

Jmt Services Inc (PA)... 302 407-5978
  520 Robinson Ln Wilmington (19805) *(G-17558)*

Jni CCC Jv1 LLP.. 302 654-6611
  2317 Pennsylvania Ave Wilmington (19806) *(G-17559)*

Jo Stefanie Armour... 302 838-5311
  101 Bakerfield Dr Middletown (19709) *(G-7251)*

Joan A Procaccio Inc.. 302 542-6394
  32180 Oak Dr Lewes (19958) *(G-6142)*

Joann M Schneidman.. 302 761-9119
  13 Dansfield Dr Wilmington (19803) *(G-17560)*

Joanne Parker-Henry Inc.................................... 302 378-7251
  102 Joshua Ct Middletown (19709) *(G-7252)*

ALPHABETIC SECTION — Johnson Contrls Authorized Dlr

Joaquin Cabrera MD.. 302 629-8977
8472 Herring Run Rd Seaford (19973) *(G-13235)*

Job Printing... 302 907-0416
36729 Bi State Blvd Delmar (19940) *(G-1607)*

Jobes Landscape Inc... 302 945-0195
20934 Robinsonville Rd Lewes (19958) *(G-6143)*

Joe Coover Contracting Inc....................................... 302 540-5806
306 Llangollen Blvd New Castle (19720) *(G-9261)*

Joe Hallock Contracting LLC..................................... 302 236-6423
18 Lauras Way Rehoboth Beach (19971) *(G-12806)*

Joe Maggio Realty... 302 539-9300
8 N Pennsylvania Ave Bethany Beach (19930) *(G-612)*

Joe Maggio Realty (PA)... 302 251-8792
37169 Rehoboth Avenue Ext Unit 11 Rehoboth Beach (19971) *(G-12807)*

Joel Chodos Dr.. 302 455-1980
930 Old Harmony Rd Ste D Newark (19713) *(G-11113)*

Joel Crissman.. 302 492-1757
3407 Westville Rd Camden (19934) *(G-860)*

Joel Gonzalez.. 302 562-6878
4104 Lancaster Pike Wilmington (19805) *(G-17561)*

Joel R Temple MD... 302 678-1343
9 E Loockerman St Ste 303 Dover (19901) *(G-2794)*

Joes Auto and Equipment Repair............................. 302 990-5845
26527 Lewes Georgetown Hwy Harbeson (19951) *(G-4703)*

Joeys Towing LLC.. 610 342-7417
4450 Dublin Hill Rd Bridgeville (19933) *(G-720)*

Joff Capital LLC... 216 682-6822
8 The Grn Dover (19901) *(G-2795)*

John Borden.. 302 674-2992
450 S Dupont Hwy Ofc B Dover (19901) *(G-2796)*

John Butler MD... 302 674-8066
1380 S State St Dover (19901) *(G-2797)*

John C Lynch DDS PA... 302 629-7115
543 N Shipley St Ste E Seaford (19973) *(G-13236)*

John Campanelli & Sons Inc..................................... 302 239-8573
7460 Lancaster Pike Hockessin (19707) *(G-5261)*

John Deere Authorized Dealer, Clayton Also Called: Atlantic Tractor LLC *(G-1351)*

John Deere Authorized Dealer, Harrington Also Called: Taylor and Messick Inc *(G-4839)*

John Deere Authorized Dealer, Middletown Also Called: Jesco Inc *(G-7247)*

John Deere Authorized Dealer, Newark Also Called: Atlantic Tractor LLC *(G-9937)*

John Deere Authorized Dealer, Wilmington Also Called: Foulk Lawn & Equipment Co Inc *(G-16701)*

John Eisenbrey III... 302 422-5845
16 Delaware Ave Milford (19963) *(G-7955)*

John F Elder.. 302 544-6569
1011 Deemers Lndg Historic New Castle (19720) *(G-5011)*

John F Yasik Funeral Services................................. 302 428-9986
1900 Delaware Ave Wilmington (19806) *(G-17562)*

John Fenice MD.. 302 998-3334
2601 Annand Dr Ste 4 Wilmington (19808) *(G-17563)*

John H Miller Sons Plbg Htg AC, Camden Also Called: Miller John H Plumbing & Htg *(G-876)*

John H Williams Jr Atty.. 302 571-4780
1225 N King St Ste 700 Wilmington (19801) *(G-17564)*

John Hiott Refrigeration & AC.................................. 302 697-3050
9166 Willow Grove Rd Camden Wyoming (19934) *(G-957)*

John I Beiler Developers, Camden Also Called: J I Beiler Homes LLC *(G-857)*

John J Buckley Associates Inc.................................. 302 475-5443
105 Farm Ave Wilmington (19810) *(G-17565)*

John J Mast... 302 492-1356
2777 Hartly Rd Hartly (19953) *(G-4882)*

John Johnson Dr.. 302 999-7104
325 S Dupont St Wilmington (19805) *(G-17566)*

John Koziol Inc... 302 234-5430
7209 Lancaster Pike Ste 4-1178 Hockessin (19707) *(G-5262)*

John L Briggs & Co... 302 856-7033
29111 Stockley Rd Milton (19968) *(G-8649)*

John Li-Ameriprise Finvl Srvcs................................ 302 200-9548
102 2nd St Lewes (19958) *(G-6144)*

John Lovett Inc... 302 455-9460
520 Christiana Medical Ctr Newark (19702) *(G-11114)*

John M Cooper Reverand.. 302 684-8639
Tall Pines Lewes (19958) *(G-6145)*

John M D Murphy... 302 368-2501
210 Christiana Medical Ctr Newark (19702) *(G-11115)*

John M Otto Od... 302 623-0170
200 Hygeia Dr Ste 1420 Newark (19713) *(G-11116)*

John Mancuso and Associates, Lewes Also Called: J G M Associates *(G-6134)*

John Mobile Sndblst & Pain..................................... 302 270-5627
683 Hartly Rd Hartly (19953) *(G-4883)*

John N Russo DDS... 302 652-3775
300 Foulk Rd Ste 101 Wilmington (19803) *(G-17567)*

John Nathan Smith Fmly Tr/U/St, Newark Also Called: Baibi Wise LLC *(G-9973)*

John Nista DDS.. 302 292-1552
74 Omega Dr Newark (19713) *(G-11117)*

John Q Hammons Hotels, Wilmington Also Called: Tucson Hotels LP *(G-20458)*

John R Gundry... 302 629-9877
4610 Woodland Church Rd Seaford (19973) *(G-13237)*

John R Seiberlich Inc... 302 356-2400
66 Southgate Blvd New Castle (19720) *(G-9262)*

John R Stump MD.. 302 422-3937
175 Lake Cove Ln Felton (19943) *(G-3989)*

John S Kassees Inc.. 302 838-1976
30024 W Barrier Reef Blvd Lewes (19958) *(G-6146)*

John Snow Labs Inc... 302 786-5227
16192 Coastal Hwy Lewes (19958) *(G-6147)*

John T Elliott.. 302 337-7075
10456 Seashore Hwy Bridgeville (19933) *(G-721)*

John T Malcynski MD.. 302 424-7522
100 Wellness Way Milford (19963) *(G-7956)*

John T Pearson.. 302 653-2322
1508 Darling Farm Rd Camden Wyoming (19934) *(G-958)*

John T Tedesco.. 703 357-0797
19181 Alcott Way Georgetown (19947) *(G-4385)*

John V Reitz... 610 320-9993
27148 Briny Bluff Ln Selbyville (19975) *(G-13551)*

John W Bateman... 302 644-1177
30723 Molly B Rd Lewes (19958) *(G-6148)*

John W Petrofske.. 410 422-1545
3211 Kenton Rd Dover (19904) *(G-2798)*

John Wasniewski DMD... 302 266-0200
103 Louviers Dr Newark (19711) *(G-11118)*

John Wasniewski III DMD...................................... 302 832-1371
262 Foxhunt Dr Bear (19701) *(G-307)*

John Wingate Insurance.. 302 339-5185
8140 1st St Seaford (19973) *(G-13238)*

Johnny Fitness LLC.. 302 654-9642
2000 Penns Ave Apt 208 Wilmington (19806) *(G-17568)*

Johnny Janosik Inc (PA)....................................... 302 875-5955
11151 Trussum Pond Rd Laurel (19956) *(G-5537)*

Johnny Janosik World Furniture, Laurel Also Called: Johnny Janosik Inc *(G-5537)*

Johns Auto Parts Inc... 302 322-3273
10 Nick Ct Bear (19701) *(G-308)*

Johns El Family Industries Inc (PA)..................... 310 701-5678
16192 Coastal Hwy Lewes (19958) *(G-6149)*

Johns Farm Fresh Produce.................................. 302 834-3747
3055 Old County Rd Newark (19702) *(G-11119)*

Johns Maytag, Claymont Also Called: Johns Washer Repair *(G-1199)*

Johns Premier Services LLC................................ 347 992-3783
8 The Grn Ste A Dover (19901) *(G-2799)*

Johns Sally H Lcsw... 302 547-7710
1601 Milltown Rd Ste 8g Wilmington (19808) *(G-17569)*

Johns Washer Repair... 302 792-2333
3309 Philadelphia Pike Claymont (19703) *(G-1199)*

Johns Woodworking LLC..................................... 302 492-3527
84 Tack Shop Ln Hartly (19953) *(G-4884)*

Johnson Shawanda... 302 722-1715
114 Stoneridge Pl Bear (19701) *(G-309)*

Johnson & Johnson.. 302 652-3840
500 Swedes Landing Rd Wilmington (19801) *(G-17570)*

Johnson & Johnson, Wilmington Also Called: Johnson & Johnson *(G-17570)*

Johnson Cntrls SEC Sltions LLC......................... 302 328-2800
18 Boulden Cir Ste 24 New Castle (19720) *(G-9263)*

Johnson Contrls Authorized Dlr, New Castle Also Called: United Refrigeration Inc *(G-9655)*

Johnson Controls, Delmar *Also Called: Johnson Controls Inc (G-1608)*
Johnson Controls, Middletown *Also Called: Clarios LLC (G-6986)*
Johnson Controls, New Castle *Also Called: Clarios LLC (G-8952)*
Johnson Controls Inc... 302 715-5208
   34898 Sussex Hwy Delmar (19940) *(G-1608)*
Johnson Jr Henry & Son Farm... 302 436-8501
   37047 Johnson Rd Selbyville (19975) *(G-13552)*
Johnson Mirmiran Thompson Inc... 302 266-9600
   121 Continental Dr Ste 300 Newark (19713) *(G-11120)*
Johnson Orthodontics... 302 645-5554
   18947 John J Williams Hwy Unit 310 Rehoboth Beach (19971) *(G-12808)*
Johnston Associates.. 302 521-2984
   5 Winsome Way Newark (19702) *(G-11121)*
Johnstone Supply, New Castle *Also Called: WJC of Delaware LLC (G-9687)*
Joincube Inc... 214 532-9997
   3500 S Dupont Hwy Dover (19901) *(G-2800)*
Joint Anlytcl Systms (amrcs).. 302 607-0088
   134a Sandy Dr Newark (19713) *(G-11122)*
Jolly Joes Cleaning Service.. 302 853-5681
   913 West St Laurel (19956) *(G-5538)*
Jolly Time, Dover *Also Called: Bandai Namco Amus Amer Inc (G-1871)*
Jolly Trolley, Rehoboth Beach *Also Called: U Transit Inc (G-13000)*
Jollylook Inc.. 754 267-1885
   251 Little Falls Dr Wilmington (19808) *(G-17571)*
Jolttek Inc... 302 204-7629
   200 Biddle Ave Ste 206 Newark (19702) *(G-11123)*
Jonathan L Patterson MD... 302 242-6176
   3 Victoria Dr Milford (19963) *(G-7957)*
Jonathan Lopez... 302 752-5229
   331 Sedgewick Dr Magnolia (19962) *(G-6754)*
Jonathan P Contompasis DPM... 302 983-8366
   3801 Kennett Pike Ste A102 Wilmington (19807) *(G-17572)*
Jonathans Landing.. 302 697-8204
   1309 Ponderosa Dr Magnolia (19962) *(G-6755)*
Jonathans Landing Pub Golf CLB, Magnolia *Also Called: Jonathans Landing (G-6755)*
Jonathon Gordon... 302 690-0614
   2818 Mill Creek Rd Wilmington (19808) *(G-17573)*
Jones Company, Wilmington *Also Called: Jones Property Company (G-17575)*
Jones Enterprises Incorporated... 888 639-1194
   1521 Concord Pike Ste 301 Wilmington (19803) *(G-17574)*
Jones Logistics LLC... 302 724-5663
   4486 N Dupont Hwy Dover (19901) *(G-2801)*
Jones Property Company... 302 213-2695
   1308 Lancaster Ave Wilmington (19805) *(G-17575)*
Jonny Nichols Ldscp Maint Inc... 302 697-2200
   273 Walnut Shade Rd Dover (19904) *(G-2802)*
Joolala LLC.. 302 444-0178
   24 Polly Drummond Hill Rd Newark (19711) *(G-11124)*
Joozoor Iptv LLC.. 302 635-4092
   200 Continental Dr Ste 401 Newark (19713) *(G-11125)*
Jor-Lin Charter Bus Service, Milford *Also Called: Jor-Lin Inc (G-7958)*
Jor-Lin Inc... 302 424-4445
   309 S Rehoboth Blvd Milford (19963) *(G-7958)*
Jorc Industrial LLC.. 302 395-0310
   1146 River Rd Ste 100 New Castle (19720) *(G-9264)*
Jordan Cabinetry & WD Turning... 302 792-1009
   84 S Avon Dr Claymont (19703) *(G-1200)*
Jordy Jael Lawn Care... 302 824-3748
   28024 Wagner Rd Georgetown (19947) *(G-4386)*
Jorge & Evonnes Auto Body LLC.. 302 382-1460
   8506 Willow Grove Rd Camden (19934) *(G-861)*
Jose A Fernandez... 302 422-5903
   511 Main St Ellendale (19941) *(G-3924)*
Jose A Pando MD.. 302 644-2302
   20268 Plantations Rd Lewes (19958) *(G-6150)*
Jose H Austria MD.. 302 645-8954
   10 Pilot Pt Lewes (19958) *(G-6151)*
Jose M Saez Do.. 302 424-3694
   201 W Liberty Way Milford (19963) *(G-7959)*
Jose Manuel Hernandez-Alvarez... 302 265-7873
   24922 Gravel Hill Rd Millsboro (19966) *(G-8333)*

Jose Picazo M D P A... 302 738-6535
   600 Christiana Medical Ctr Newark (19702) *(G-11126)*
Joselow Beth Lpcmh.. 302 644-0130
   1307 Savannah Rd Lewes (19958) *(G-6152)*
Joseph A Hurley PA.. 302 658-8980
   1215 N King St Wilmington (19801) *(G-17576)*
Joseph A Kuhn MD LLC... 302 656-3801
   102 Haywood Rd Wilmington (19807) *(G-17577)*
Joseph A Santillo Inc... 302 661-7313
   2403 E Parris Dr Wilmington (19808) *(G-17578)*
Joseph C Kelly DDS... 302 475-5555
   2205 Silverside Rd Ste 2 Wilmington (19810) *(G-17579)*
Joseph Cartwright Jr... 302 658-9487
   14 Colonial Ave Wilmington (19805) *(G-17580)*
Joseph D Allen.. 302 685-4230
   861 Shallcross Lake Rd Middletown (19709) *(G-7253)*
Joseph Devane Enterprises Inc.. 302 703-0493
   240 S Dupont Hwy Ste 200 New Castle (19720) *(G-9265)*
Joseph Frederick & Sons, Wilmington *Also Called: Frederick Enterprises Inc (G-16737)*
Joseph G Goldberg Od.. 302 999-1286
   801 E Newport Pike Wilmington (19804) *(G-17581)*
Joseph H Piatt MD... 302 651-4000
   1600 Rockland Rd Wilmington (19803) *(G-17582)*
Joseph J Sheeran Inc (HQ).. 302 324-0200
   71 Southgate Blvd New Castle (19720) *(G-9266)*
Joseph J Thornton... 302 355-0055
   2600 Glasgow Ave Ste 107 Newark (19702) *(G-11127)*
Joseph M Farrell Do... 302 424-4141
   1606 Savannah Rd Ste 1 Lewes (19958) *(G-6153)*
Joseph M L Sand & Gravel Co.. 302 856-7396
   25136 Dupont Blvd Georgetown (19947) *(G-4387)*
Joseph Napoli MD.. 302 651-5981
   1600 Rockland Rd Wilmington (19803) *(G-17583)*
Joseph Parise Do... 302 735-8855
   793 S Queen St Dover (19904) *(G-2803)*
Joseph Patrick Fabber Meml.. 302 858-4040
   401 N Bedford St Georgetown (19947) *(G-4388)*
Joseph R Kasowski.. 302 379-0523
   2503 Maple Ave Wilmington (19808) *(G-17584)*
Joseph Rizzo & Sons Cnstr Co... 302 656-8116
   13 Rizzo Ave New Castle (19720) *(G-9267)*
Joseph Schwartz Psyd... 302 213-3287
   19606 Coastal Hwy Unit 102 Rehoboth Beach (19971) *(G-12809)*
Joseph Smith & Sons Inc.. 302 492-8091
   3221 Hartly Rd Hartly (19953) *(G-4885)*
Joseph Straight Md... 302 731-2888
   4745 Ogletown Stanton Rd Newark (19713) *(G-11128)*
Joseph T Hardy & Son Inc (PA)... 302 328-9457
   425 Old Airport Rd New Castle (19720) *(G-9268)*
Joseph T Richardson Inc... 302 398-8101
   105 E Center St Harrington (19952) *(G-4792)*
Joseph T Ryerson & Son Inc.. 215 736-8970
   700 Pencader Dr Newark (19702) *(G-11129)*
Joseph Truono... 302 762-6822
   1 Riverside Dr Wilmington (19809) *(G-17585)*
Joseph V Bakanas DPM... 302 898-3873
   306 Odessa Ave Wilmington (19809) *(G-17586)*
Joseph W Benson PA... 302 656-8811
   1701 N Market St Wilmington (19802) *(G-17587)*
Joseph W Small Associates Inc
   2003 Marsh Rd Wilmington (19810) *(G-17588)*
Josephine Keir Limited.. 302 422-0270
   27 S Walnut St Milford (19963) *(G-7960)*
Joses Landscaping.. 302 584-2656
   4931 Old Capitol Trl Wilmington (19808) *(G-17589)*
Josh N Schmidt... 302 668-1304
   3219 Whiteman Rd Wilmington (19808) *(G-17590)*
Josh's Contracting Services, Hartly *Also Called: Joshua S Stevens (G-4886)*
Joshi Medical PA... 302 838-8858
   417 Oregano Ct Bear (19701) *(G-310)*
Joshua Kalin MD.. 302 737-6900
   314 E Main St Ste 302 Newark (19711) *(G-11130)*

ALPHABETIC SECTION

Joshua M Freeman Foundation..302 436-3003
31255 Americana Pkwy Selbyville (19975) *(G-13553)*

Joshua S Stevens..302 492-3450
1385 Lockwood Chapel Rd Hartly (19953) *(G-4886)*

Joshua Tilghman..302 582-1491
207 E Crail Ct Middletown (19709) *(G-7254)*

Joshuas Paving..302 396-1221
100 Isabelle Isle Dover (19904) *(G-2804)*

Josue Barber Shop...302 650-5362
509 Maryland Ave Wilmington (19805) *(G-17591)*

Journalname LLC..302 522-7680
16192 Coastal Hwy Lewes (19958) *(G-6154)*

Journey2wellness...302 399-6755
1000 Smyrna Clayton Blvd Smyrna (19977) *(G-13782)*

Journeys..443 945-0615
8103 Governor Printz Blvd Claymont (19703) *(G-1201)*

Journeys LLC..302 384-7843
5201 W Woodmill Dr Ste 31 Wilmington (19808) *(G-17592)*

Joy Choose Foundation...302 286-7560
1360 Old White Oak Rd Dover (19901) *(G-2805)*

Joy Cleaners Inc..302 656-3537
301 Greenhill Ave Wilmington (19805) *(G-17593)*

Joy-Hope Foundation..302 379-1209
215 Beau Tree Dr Wilmington (19810) *(G-17594)*

Joyn Experiences Inc..214 437-8349
1013 Centre Rd Ste 403b Wilmington (19805) *(G-17595)*

JP Graphics...302 678-0335
58 Sienna Ct Dover (19904) *(G-2806)*

JP McFarlane LLC...302 709-1515
718 Seymour Rd Bear (19701) *(G-311)*

JP Morgan Intl Fin Ltd (PA)..212 270-6000
500 Stanton Christiana Rd Newark (19713) *(G-11131)*

JP Morgan Multi-Manager Altern.......................................866 541-2724
880 Powder Mill Rd Wilmington (19803) *(G-17596)*

JP Morgan Trust Company Del..302 634-3800
500 Stanton Christiana Rd Fl 2 Newark (19713) *(G-11132)*

Jpl M&R...302 883-9534
11 Derickson Dr Wilmington (19808) *(G-17597)*

Jpmc Card Services, Wilmington Also Called: Jpmorgan Chase Bank Nat Assn *(G-17598)*

Jpmorgan Chase & Co..800 935-9935
501 Bear Christiana Rd Bear (19701) *(G-312)*

Jpmorgan Chase & Co..312 732-2801
500 Stanton Christiana Rd Newark (19713) *(G-11133)*

Jpmorgan Chase Bank Nat Assn.......................................302 282-9000
201 N Walnut St Wilmington (19801) *(G-17598)*

Jpv Tax Services...302 740-6383
1719 Newport Gap Pike Wilmington (19808) *(G-17599)*

Jr, Townsend Also Called: Janette Redrow Ltd *(G-14020)*

Jr Anesthesia LLC...302 678-0725
30 Chadwick Dr Dover (19901) *(G-2807)*

Jr Board of Kent Gen Hospital...302 744-7128
640 S State St Dover (19901) *(G-2808)*

JR Gettier & Associates Inc...302 478-0911
2 Centerville Rd Wilmington (19808) *(G-17600)*

Jr Robert M Thompson Dvm..302 261-2683
3052 Wrangle Hill Rd Bear (19701) *(G-313)*

JR Walker Roofing Inc...302 761-3744
234 Philadelphia Pike Ste 11 Wilmington (19809) *(G-17601)*

Jr Walter J Kaminski DDS..302 738-3666
100 Christiana Vlg Prof Ctr Christiana (19702) *(G-1000)*

Jrm Construction LLC..302 362-7453
23748 German Rd Seaford (19973) *(G-13239)*

Jrp Industrial Services LLC...302 439-4092
100 Naamans Rd Ste 2g Claymont (19703) *(G-1202)*

Jrs Homes LLC..302 544-5911
439 Wynthorpe Rd New Castle (19720) *(G-9269)*

Js Automotive AAMCO..302 678-5660
3729 N Dupont Hwy Dover (19901) *(G-2809)*

Js Carpenter Improvements..302 540-0590
342 Jessica Dr Middletown (19709) *(G-7255)*

Js Liquors..302 656-4066
900 N Dupont St Wilmington (19805) *(G-17602)*

Js Sheds LLC...484 918-0633
9 Saint John Dr Wilmington (19808) *(G-17603)*

JS Tire Corporation...302 558-2320
3724 Kirkwood Hwy Wilmington (19808) *(G-17604)*

Jsc Ventures LLC..302 336-8151
9 E Loockerman St Ste 202-664 Dover (19901) *(G-2810)*

Jsd Management Inc...302 735-4628
1283 College Park Dr Dover (19904) *(G-2811)*

Jsf Construction Co Inc...302 999-9573
316 Main St Wilmington (19804) *(G-17605)*

Jsi Group LLC...267 582-5850
7217 Lancaster Pike Ste 6 Hockessin (19707) *(G-5263)*

Jsm Transport & Haulage LLC...302 836-8057
33 Wellspring Dr Bear (19701) *(G-314)*

JT Enterprise LLC...302 492-8119
1752 Halltown Rd Hartly (19953) *(G-4887)*

JT Hoover Concrete Inc..302 832-2139
3415 Wrangle Hill Rd Ste 1 Bear (19701) *(G-315)*

Jtc Towing, Wilmington Also Called: Joseph Cartwright Jr *(G-17580)*

Jth Excavating Inc...302 832-7699
3415 Wrangle Hill Rd # 2 Bear (19701) *(G-316)*

Jthan LLC...302 994-2534
7 Meco Cir Wilmington (19804) *(G-17606)*

Juan De Dios Painting...302 841-0363
21538 Shell Station Rd Frankford (19945) *(G-4119)*

Juan Saucedo..302 233-4539
1133 S Little Creek Rd Dover (19901) *(G-2812)*

Jube Medical Spa LLC..302 478-4020
3521 Silverside Rd Wilmington (19810) *(G-17607)*

Judah Road Productions LLC..508 640-5022
1221 College Park Dr Dover (19904) *(G-2813)*

Judie Ai Inc...407 401-4421
2810 N Church St Wilmington (19802) *(G-17608)*

Judith A Smith...302 322-9396
38 W 4th St Historic New Castle (19720) *(G-5012)*

Judith E McCann DMD..302 368-7463
101 Barksdale Professional Ctr Newark (19711) *(G-11134)*

Judith Rippert..302 734-1414
200 Banning St Dover (19904) *(G-2814)*

Judy Tim Fuel Inc..302 349-5895
12386 Beach Hwy Greenwood (19950) *(G-4647)*

Judy V..302 226-2214
39401 Inlet Rd Rehoboth Beach (19971) *(G-12810)*

Juega LLC...716 256-3186
8 The Grn Dover (19901) *(G-2815)*

Juicefresh, Lewes Also Called: Fresh Industries Ltd *(G-6015)*

Juicefresh Dimitra Yoga..302 645-9100
43 Rehoboth Ave Rehoboth Beach (19971) *(G-12811)*

Juiceplus+...302 322-2616
15 W 3rd St Historic New Castle (19720) *(G-5013)*

Julesk, Bethany Beach Also Called: Frontgate LLC *(G-602)*

Julia C Gorman..302 734-8000
99 Wolf Creek Blvd Ste 2 Dover (19901) *(G-2816)*

Julia Tegarden Jorda...302 731-1901
820 Hilltop Rd Newark (19711) *(G-11135)*

Julian H Nicol..484 390-1980
706 Maple Ave Wilmington (19809) *(G-17609)*

Juliana Recycling Corporation...347 753-6584
61 Mcmillan Way Ste A Newark (19713) *(G-11136)*

Julie A Carson PA..302 629-3099
24459 Sussex Hwy Seaford (19973) *(G-13240)*

Julie Gritton Team LLC..302 645-1111
800 Kings Hwy Lewes (19958) *(G-6155)*

Julie H Rementer...302 628-4416
900 S Arch St Seaford (19973) *(G-13241)*

Julie Lewicki..302 531-0763
1991 S State St Dover (19901) *(G-2817)*

Julie Q Nies DDS...302 242-9085
1380 S State St Dover (19901) *(G-2818)*

Juliet Thorburn..302 598-1841
1300 Pennsylvania Ave Wilmington (19806) *(G-17610)*

Julieth Ai Technologies Inc   ALPHABETIC SECTION

Julieth Ai Technologies Inc 512 680-1855
   2140 S Dupont Hwy Camden (19934) *(G-862)*

Julio Drywall Inc 302 218-8596
   851 Cornstalk Dr New Castle (19720) *(G-9270)*

Julio Navarro Md, Faafp, Wilmington *Also Called: Horizons Family Practice PA (G-17210)*

Jumarally Chandra 302 212-7027
   32750 Curley Dr Millsboro (19966) *(G-8334)*

Jumpin Jacks 302 762-7604
   508 E 35th St Wilmington (19802) *(G-17611)*

Junction Expert Insights Corp (PA) 202 710-9258
   3500 S Dupont Hwy Dover (19901) *(G-2819)*

June Medical USA Inc 302 408-0084
   257 Old Churchmans Rd New Castle (19720) *(G-9271)*

Junebugs Little Rubies LLC 302 494-7552
   1104 D St 1106 Wilmington (19801) *(G-17612)*

Junes Touch 631 603-9293
   59 Gravelly Run Branch Rd Clayton (19938) *(G-1377)*

Jung B Kim DDS 302 652-3556
   1815 W 13th St Ste 7 Wilmington (19806) *(G-17613)*

Jungle Gym LLC 302 734-1515
   1418 S State St Dover (19901) *(G-2820)*

Jungle Jim's, Rehoboth Beach *Also Called: Jungle Jims Adventure World (G-12812)*

Jungle Jims Adventure World 302 227-8444
   8 Country Club Rd Rehoboth Beach (19971) *(G-12812)*

Jungle Jims Total Pet Care 302 212-5055
   1705 Coastal Hwy Dewey Beach (19971) *(G-1672)*

Juni Holdings Inc 415 949-4860
   251 Little Falls Dr Wilmington (19808) *(G-17614)*

Junior Bd of Christiana Care 302 733-1100
   4755 Stanton Ogletown Rd Newark (19718) *(G-11137)*

Juniper Bank 302 255-8000
   100 S West St Wilmington (19801) *(G-17615)*

Juno Insurance Services LLC 650 380-8449
   3 Germay Dr Ste 4 Wilmington (19804) *(G-17616)*

Just Breathe Home Therapy 919 270-3347
   18210 Hickory Ln Lewes (19958) *(G-6156)*

Just For Women Ob/Gyn PA 302 224-9400
   875 Aaa Blvd Newark (19713) *(G-11138)*

Just Homes LLC 302 322-2233
   5560 Kirkwood Hwy Wilmington (19808) *(G-17617)*

Just Kids Pediatrics, Newark *Also Called: Kerry S Kinfides MD PA (G-11159)*

Just Like Home 302 653-0605
   314 W Mount Vernon St Smyrna (19977) *(G-13783)*

Just One Embroiderer 302 832-9655
   17 Decidedly Ln Bear (19701) *(G-317)*

Just Wallet Inc 770 925-5098
   3422 Old Capitol Trl 2002 Wilmington (19808) *(G-17618)*

Justin Brian Salon LLC 302 597-8945
   1600 Kirkwood Hwy Wilmington (19805) *(G-17619)*

Justin Connor MD LLC 302 483-7115
   1059 S Bradford St Ste B Dover (19904) *(G-2821)*

Justin David Ennis 302 650-4934
   2224 Big Oak Rd Smyrna (19977) *(G-13784)*

Justin Maynard 302 233-6086
   567 Tuxward Rd Hartly (19953) *(G-4888)*

Justin Oakley 302 752-8277
   30598 Holts Landing Rd Dagsboro (19939) *(G-1471)*

Justin Oneill 631 346-7333
   1990 Fast Landing Rd Dover (19901) *(G-2822)*

Justin R Connor M D 302 651-4200
   1600 Rockland Rd Wilmington (19803) *(G-17620)*

Justin Tanks LLC 302 856-3521
   21413 Cedar Creek Ave Georgetown (19947) *(G-4389)*

Justison Apts LLC 302 691-2100
   1000 N West St Wilmington (19801) *(G-17621)*

Justison Investors LLC 302 691-2100
   1000 N West St Ste 900 Wilmington (19801) *(G-17622)*

Justison Landing, Wilmington *Also Called: Luxiasuites LLC (G-18039)*

Justitselectric 215 715-7314
   950 Ridge Rd Claymont (19703) *(G-1203)*

Justlabormovers Inc 302 444-7599
   7 Westerly St Newark (19713) *(G-11139)*

Justtai 781 771-0329
   1013 Centre Rd Ste 403 Wilmington (19805) *(G-17623)*

Justyce Barber & Beauty Salon 302 998-7788
   634 S Maryland Ave Wilmington (19804) *(G-17624)*

JV s Cleaning Services 302 345-7679
   1148 Pulaski Hwy Ste 151 Bear (19701) *(G-318)*

JW Striping 302 832-7762
   153 N Gabriel Dr Bear (19701) *(G-319)*

JW Tull Contracting Svcs LLC 302 494-8179
   1203 Philadelphia Pike Wilmington (19809) *(G-17625)*

Jwr 1 LLC 302 379-9951
   11 Biltmore Ct Bear (19701) *(G-320)*

K & H Provision Co, Harrington *Also Called: Kirby & Holloway Provisions Co (G-4794)*

K & J and Company, Camden Wyoming *Also Called: Kevin Elzie (G-959)*

K & R Graphics & Signs Inc 302 697-7725
   1685 Main St Woodside (19980) *(G-20977)*

K 1 Ng Logistics LLC 516 459-3316
   2203 Alister Dr Wilmington (19808) *(G-17626)*

K and B Hvac Svcs LLC 302 846-3111
   18228 Whitesville Rd Delmar (19940) *(G-1609)*

K and C Cleaning Services 302 897-8661
   59 Landers Ln New Castle (19720) *(G-9272)*

K and L Gates 302 416-7000
   600 N King St Ste 901 Wilmington (19801) *(G-17627)*

K and W Painting 302 598-5663
   23 Fairview Ave Middletown (19709) *(G-7256)*

K Bank 302 645-9700
   17021 Old Orchard Rd Ste A Lewes (19958) *(G-6157)*

K BS Plumbing Incorporated 302 678-2757
   518 Lochmeath Way Dover (19904) *(G-2823)*

K C Contracting 302 875-4661
   11041 County Seat Hwy Laurel (19956) *(G-5539)*

K C Farms LLC 302 492-3439
   232 Westville Rd Marydel (19964) *(G-6802)*

K Conte 302 283-9613
   305 Sharpley Rd Wilmington (19803) *(G-17628)*

K Diamond Delivery Inc 215 882-2585
   23 E Dale Rd Wilmington (19810) *(G-17629)*

K E Smart & Sons Inc 302 875-7002
   29110 Discount Land Rd Laurel (19956) *(G-5540)*

K F Dunn & Associates 302 328-3347
   819 N Washington St Wilmington (19801) *(G-17630)*

K L Vincent Welding Svc Inc 302 398-9357
   19456 S Dupont Hwy Harrington (19952) *(G-4793)*

K Lush Extensions LLC 347 274-4353
   282 Wilmore Dr Middletown (19709) *(G-7257)*

K Squared Enterprises LLC 302 402-3082
   33514 Weshampton Ln Ocean View (19970) *(G-12530)*

K Supply Company Inc 302 629-3925
   208 Peterson Dr Seaford (19973) *(G-13242)*

K V Associates Inc 302 322-1353
   191 Christiana Rd Ste 3 New Castle (19720) *(G-9273)*

K W Lands North LLC 302 678-0600
   1780 N Dupont Hwy Dover (19901) *(G-2824)*

K Wolf Custom Homes Cnstr Inc 302 598-2899
   507 Red Oak Dr Middletown (19709) *(G-7258)*

K Y Property Management, Wilmington *Also Called: Michael Spradley (G-18325)*

K-10 Dog Training 302 236-2497
   1013 Scarborough Ave Rehoboth Beach (19971) *(G-12813)*

K-Tron Technologies Inc 302 421-7361
   300 Delaware Ave Ste 900 Wilmington (19801) *(G-17632)*

K&B Investors LLC 302 357-9723
   1908 Oak Lane Rd Wilmington (19803) *(G-17631)*

K&D Inc 302 945-7036
   26873 Anderson Corner Rd Harbeson (19951) *(G-4704)*

K&D Maintenance Service, Middletown *Also Called: Kimberly Tucker (G-7274)*

K&L Enterprise LLC 302 514-1136
   1155 E Lebanon Rd Dover (19901) *(G-2825)*

K&S Home Services LLC 302 604-3563
   37738 Balsa St Ocean View (19970) *(G-12531)*

K2 Trucking LLC 302 257-3135
   1609 S State St Dover (19901) *(G-2826)*

ALPHABETIC SECTION

K9 Natural Foods USA LLC.. 855 596-2887
    108 W 13th St Wilmington (19801) *(G-17633)*
K9 Service Companion Inc.. 716 804-3830
    8 The Grn Ste A Dover (19901) *(G-2827)*
Ka Analytics & Tech LLC... 800 520-8178
    1024 Avocado Ave Dover (19901) *(G-2828)*
Kaan Cakes LLC... 302 260-0647
    314 Wilson Hwy Millsboro (19966) *(G-8335)*
Kad Industrial Rubber Products, Historic New Castle Also Called: Hartzell Industries Inc *(G-5002)*
Kaebox LLC... 919 777-3939
    651 N Broad St Ste 206 Middletown (19709) *(G-7259)*
Kaeser Compressors Inc... 410 242-8793
    77 Mccullough Dr Ste 3 New Castle (19720) *(G-9274)*
Kagoal Technology LLC... 617 818-0588
    651 N Broad St Ste 2056367 Middletown (19709) *(G-7260)*
Kahen Remodeling, Wilmington Also Called: Omar Kah *(G-18764)*
Kahl Company Inc... 302 478-8450
    3526 Silverside Rd Ste 38 Wilmington (19810) *(G-17634)*
Kairon Corp... 347 688-3993
    16192 Coastal Hwy Lewes (19958) *(G-6158)*
Kairos Home Pros LLC... 302 233-7044
    8 The Grn Ste 8086 Dover (19901) *(G-2829)*
Kairos Landscaping.. 302 399-4724
    5644 Millington Rd Clayton (19938) *(G-1378)*
Kaiser Time Inc... 646 473-1640
    623 Haverhill Rd Wilmington (19803) *(G-17635)*
Kaiser, Steven, Wilmington Also Called: Kaiser Time Inc *(G-17635)*
Kaj Home Improvements, Wilmington Also Called: Kevin A Johnson *(G-17699)*
Kalanaai LLC... 516 701-3977
    3 Germay Dr Ste 41648 Wilmington (19804) *(G-17636)*
Kaleido Health Solutions Inc... 843 303-9168
    2810 N Church St Wilmington (19802) *(G-17637)*
Kaleo Inc... 302 376-0327
    2 Feldspar Way Townsend (19734) *(G-14021)*
Kalin Eye Assoc.. 302 292-2020
    314 E Main St Ste 302 Newark (19711) *(G-11140)*
Kalin, Neil S MD, Newark Also Called: Kalin Eye Assoc *(G-11140)*
Kalisign USA... 302 268-6946
    2801 Centerville Rd Fl 1 Wilmington (19808) *(G-17638)*
Kalmar Investments Inc.. 302 658-7575
    3701 Kennett Pike Ste 100 Wilmington (19807) *(G-17639)*
Kalmar Nyckel Foundation.. 302 429-7447
    1124 E 7th St Wilmington (19801) *(G-17640)*
Kam Electric Inc.. 302 998-5262
    845 Kiamensi Rd Wilmington (19804) *(G-17641)*
Kam Marketing Holdings Inc... 302 658-7778
    128 Saint Moritz Dr Wilmington (19807) *(G-17642)*
Kamara LLC.. 302 220-9570
    831 N Tatnall St Wilmington (19801) *(G-17643)*
Kamax Construction LLC.. 302 296-8270
    37268 W White Tail Dr Selbyville (19975) *(G-13554)*
Kamina LLC... 347 200-0935
    3411 Silverside Rd Bldg 104 Wilmington (19810) *(G-17644)*
Kaminski Service Center... 302 375-6379
    3506 Philadelphia Pike Claymont (19703) *(G-1204)*
Kan Trucking LLC... 413 358-7832
    919 N Market St Ste 950 Wilmington (19801) *(G-17645)*
Kanaci Technologies Inc (PA)...302 658-7581
    1209 N Orange St Wilmington (19801) *(G-17646)*
Kancapi LLC... 949 508-0350
    16192 Coastal Hwy Lewes (19958) *(G-6159)*
Kanga Rew Software.. 302 335-3546
    167 Carnation Dr Magnolia (19962) *(G-6756)*
Kango Express Inc... 808 725-1688
    20 Shea Way Ste 205 Newark (19713) *(G-11141)*
Kangsters Inc (PA)...716 563-8225
    1007 N Orange St Ste 1382 Wilmington (19801) *(G-17647)*
Kanopi Studios, Wilmington Also Called: Silly Monkey Studios LLC *(G-19825)*
Kanu Inc.. 401 533-6112
    251 Little Falls Dr Wilmington (19808) *(G-17648)*

Kaplan Software Group... 646 498-8275
    15649 Simpson Dr Lewes (19958) *(G-6160)*
Kappa Alpha Fdn For Lead Serv... 302 475-4917
    1015 Linda Rd Wilmington (19810) *(G-17649)*
Kappa Bioscience Usa Inc.. 609 201-1459
    850 New Burton Rd Ste 201 Dover (19904) *(G-2830)*
Kappa Ingredients Usa, Inc., Dover Also Called: Kappa Bioscience Usa Inc *(G-2830)*
Kapur Neeraj MD.. 302 789-0545
    2601 Annand Dr Wilmington (19808) *(G-17650)*
Karcher Municipal North Amer.. 401 230-3296
    3411 Silverside Rd # 104 Wilmington (19810) *(G-17651)*
Kardmaster Brochures Inc.. 610 434-5262
    24 Colony Blvd Wilmington (19802) *(G-17652)*
Karen Berrie.. 201 906-9789
    1209 Madison Ln Hockessin (19707) *(G-5264)*
Karen E Starr CPA.. 302 834-1718
    306 Carya Ct Bear (19701) *(G-321)*
Karen Healing Hands.. 302 841-8933
    32277 Falling Point Rd R Dagsboro (19939) *(G-1472)*
Karen Kim Zogheib Lcsw.. 786 897-3022
    2110 Dunhill Dr Wilmington (19810) *(G-17653)*
Karen Schreiber.. 302 875-7733
    12034 County Seat Hwy Laurel (19956) *(G-5541)*
Karen Schreiber.. 302 628-3007
    425 E Stein Hwy Seaford (19973) *(G-13243)*
Karen Y Vcks Law Offces of LLC... 302 674-1100
    500 W Loockerman St Ste 102 Dover (19904) *(G-2831)*
Karins & Associates, Newark Also Called: Karins Engineering Inc *(G-11142)*
Karins Engineering Inc.. 302 856-6699
    128 W Market St Georgetown (19947) *(G-4390)*
Karins Engineering Inc (PA)... 302 369-2900
    17 Polly Drummond Shpg Ctr Ste 201 Newark (19711) *(G-11142)*
Karizma Sparks LLC... 302 607-5445
    28 Clarion Ct Newark (19713) *(G-11143)*
Karl J Zeren DDS.. 302 644-2773
    18947 John J Williams Hwy Unit 301 Rehoboth Beach (19971) *(G-12814)*
Karl Marinaccio CPA... 914 736-0772
    4705 Astaire Pl Middletown (19709) *(G-7261)*
Karl W McIntosh M D.. 302 594-9000
    1300 Pennsylvania Ave Wilmington (19806) *(G-17654)*
Karli Flanagan Dvm.. 302 893-7872
    18 Silverwood Blvd Newark (19711) *(G-11144)*
Karma Theory Tattoo & Gallery.. 302 526-2096
    1022 Lafferty Ln Dover (19901) *(G-2832)*
Karo Healthcare Inc.. 973 975-8306
    1209 N Orange St Wilmington (19801) *(G-17655)*
Karve Builders LLC... 403 471-2285
    2140 S Dupont Hwy Camden (19934) *(G-863)*
Kasa Enterprise LLC (PA).. 302 634-0138
    221 N Broad St Ste 3a Middletown (19709) *(G-7262)*
Kasmo Cloud Inc.. 302 319-9952
    16192 Coastal Hwy Lewes (19958) *(G-6161)*
Kaspar Karrs... 302 660-2256
    1027 W 25th St Wilmington (19802) *(G-17656)*
Kat Geralis Home Team... 302 383-5412
    1521 Concord Pike Ste 102 Wilmington (19803) *(G-17657)*
Kat Postcard Solutions Inc... 614 288-1733
    3 Heatherstone Way Hockessin (19707) *(G-5265)*
Katabat LLC (HQ)... 302 830-9262
    112 S French St Ste 500 Wilmington (19801) *(G-17658)*
Katalist LLC... 302 502-0091
    501 Silverside Rd Ste 105 Wilmington (19809) *(G-17659)*
Kate G Shumaker... 302 327-1100
    2500 Wrangle Hill Rd Bear (19701) *(G-322)*
Kate Gehret Ms, Lewes Also Called: Kathryn M Gehret *(G-6162)*
Kate W Bernstein.. 302 597-9911
    8103 Governor Printz Blvd Claymont (19703) *(G-1205)*
Kathairos Solutions Us Inc.. 855 285-2010
    8 The Grn Ste 4000 Dover (19901) *(G-2833)*
Katharine L Mayer Atty... 302 984-6312
    919 N Market St Wilmington (19801) *(G-17660)*

Katharine N Snyder 302 381-7283
  113 W North St Georgetown (19947) *(G-4391)*

Katherine Laffey 302 651-7999
  1509 Gilpin Ave Wilmington (19806) *(G-17661)*

Katherine M King RN 302 449-3625
  555 Hyetts Corner Rd Middletown (19709) *(G-7263)*

Katherine Nwman Dsign Intl LLC 416 922-5806
  2711 Centerville Rd Wilmington (19808) *(G-17662)*

Katherine T Samworth 302 478-7485
  742 Westcliff Rd Wilmington (19803) *(G-17663)*

Kathi Jenks 302 226-7791
  19869 Sea Blossom Blvd Rehoboth Beach (19971) *(G-12815)*

Kathleen Kenney 302 541-5700
  1310 Middleford Rd # 101 Seaford (19973) *(G-13244)*

Kathleen Looney 302 762-0106
  4659 Malden Dr Wilmington (19803) *(G-17664)*

Kathleen M Cronan MD 302 651-5860
  1600 Rockland Rd Wilmington (19803) *(G-17665)*

Kathleen McGuiness 302 245-7355
  6 Broad Hollow St Rehoboth Beach (19971) *(G-12816)*

Kathleens Creations 302 492-8749
  137 Downs Chapel Rd Clayton (19938) *(G-1379)*

Kathryn L Ford Fmly Practice 302 674-8088
  44 Deborah Dr Dover (19901) *(G-2834)*

Kathryn M Gehret 610 420-7233
  17124 Poplar Dr Lewes (19958) *(G-6162)*

Kathy J King PA 302 827-4740
  17527 Nassau Commons Blvd Lewes (19958) *(G-6163)*

Kathys Day Care 302 436-4308
  32187 Lynch Rd Selbyville (19975) *(G-13555)*

Katie Bennett 302 697-2650
  2150 S Dupont Hwy Camden (19934) *(G-864)*

Katie Butera 815 979-5129
  4404 Sandy Dr Wilmington (19808) *(G-17666)*

Katlyn Co Ceramics 302 528-1322
  9 Moores Dr Bear (19701) *(G-323)*

Kats Meow Inc 302 383-5412
  1 Wintercorn Cir Hockessin (19707) *(G-5266)*

Katu Software Global LLC 302 803-5330
  3 Germay Dr Ste 4 Wilmington (19804) *(G-17667)*

Katy Aukamp Mem Foundation 302 328-6446
  245 Riveredge Dr New Castle (19720) *(G-9275)*

Katy E Crowe MD 302 230-4965
  3105 Limestone Rd Ste 301 Wilmington (19808) *(G-17668)*

Kaul Glove and Mfg Co 302 292-2660
  599 Ships Landing Way Historic New Castle (19720) *(G-5014)*

Kautex Inc 302 456-1455
  100 Lake Dr Newark (19702) *(G-11145)*

Kayava Creations LLC 302 430-2231
  109 Valley Run Seaford (19973) *(G-13245)*

Kaye Construction 302 628-6962
  22223 Eskridge Rd Seaford (19973) *(G-13246)*

Kays Nail & Spa LLC 302 376-7788
  17 Wood St Middletown (19709) *(G-7264)*

Kaza Medical Group Inc 302 674-2616
  810 New Burton Rd Dover (19904) *(G-2835)*

Kaza, Janaki B MD, Dover *Also Called: Kaza Medical Group Inc (G-2835)*

KB Coldiron Inc 302 436-4224
  36546 Dupont Blvd Selbyville (19975) *(G-13556)*

KB Electrical Services 302 276-5733
  1 S Clayton St Wilmington (19805) *(G-17669)*

Kbr Inc 302 452-9386
  242 Chapman Rd Newark (19702) *(G-11146)*

Kbr Engineering Company LLC 302 452-9000
  242 Chapman Rd Newark (19702) *(G-11147)*

Kc & Associates Inc 302 633-3300
  155 Oldbury Dr Wilmington (19808) *(G-17670)*

Kc Janitorial Services 302 653-5435
  76 E Pembrooke Dr Smyrna (19977) *(G-13785)*

Kc Service Cleaning 410 845-1988
  34407 Dupont Blvd Frankford (19945) *(G-4120)*

Kc Sign Wilmington, Wilmington *Also Called: Kgc Enterprises Inc (G-17710)*

Kci Technologies Inc 302 731-9176
  1352 Marrows Rd Newark (19711) *(G-11148)*

Kcs Total Lawn Care LLC 732 331-2454
  33427 Marina Bay Cir Millsboro (19966) *(G-8336)*

Kd Nails 302 422-0998
  1053 N Walnut St Milford (19963) *(G-7961)*

Kdg Solutions LLC 302 494-4693
  654 Brenford Station Rd Smyrna (19977) *(G-13786)*

KDi Solutions LLC 302 406-0224
  1201 N Market St Ste 111 Wilmington (19801) *(G-17671)*

Kearns Brinen & Monaghan Inc 302 736-6481
  371 W North St Dover (19904) *(G-2836)*

Keble Inc 810 893-3352
  2055 Limestone Rd Ste 200c Wilmington (19808) *(G-17672)*

Kee Builders 302 376-9858
  730 Union Church Rd Townsend (19734) *(G-14022)*

Kee Jr Rayvann 267 975-2199
  1401 Foulk Rd Ste 100 Wilmington (19803) *(G-17673)*

Keen Cmprssed Gas - Wilmington, New Castle *Also Called: Keen Compressed Gas Co (G-9277)*

Keen Compressed Gas, New Castle *Also Called: TEC-Con Inc (G-9621)*

Keen Compressed Gas, Wilmington *Also Called: Keen Compressed Gas Co (G-17674)*

Keen Compressed Gas Co 302 594-4545
  4063 New Castle Ave New Castle (19720) *(G-9276)*

Keen Compressed Gas Co (PA) 302 594-4545
  4063 New Castle Ave New Castle (19720) *(G-9277)*

Keen Compressed Gas Co (PA) 302 594-4545
  101 Rogers Rd Ste 200 Wilmington (19801) *(G-17674)*

Keener-Sensenig Co 302 453-8584
  491 Gender Rd Newark (19713) *(G-11149)*

Keep In Touch Systems Inc 510 868-8088
  19c Trolley Sq Wilmington (19806) *(G-17675)*

Keep It - Moving & Labor LLC 302 469-1161
  11361 Willow Grove Rd Camden (19934) *(G-865)*

Keepgo USA Inc 832 998-8753
  1013 Centre Rd Ste 403a Wilmington (19805) *(G-17676)*

Kees Cookies & Cupcakes LLC 302 223-6784
  308 Main St Clayton (19938) *(G-1380)*

Keglers Korner Pro Shop 302 526-2249
  1600 S Governors Ave Dover (19904) *(G-2837)*

Keith A Sargent Do 302 990-3300
  100 Rawlins Dr Seaford (19973) *(G-13247)*

Keith D Stoltz Foundation 302 654-3600
  20 Montchanin Rd Ste 250 Wilmington (19807) *(G-17677)*

Keith Perry 302 841-1514
  13299 Spicer Rd Ellendale (19941) *(G-3925)*

Keith Properties Inc 302 258-9224
  38016 Fenwick Shoals Blvd Unit 4 Selbyville (19975) *(G-13557)*

Keiths Boat Canvas 302 841-8081
  16408 Seashore Hwy Georgetown (19947) *(G-4392)*

Kelf LLC 302 229-2195
  2353 Carpenter Station Rd Wilmington (19810) *(G-17678)*

Kelitch Inc 847 910-6620
  8 The Grn Ste 114 Dover (19901) *(G-2838)*

Keller Williams At Beach Rlty 302 363-0453
  16880 Ole Grist Run Milton (19968) *(G-8650)*

Keller Williams Realtors, Dover *Also Called: Keller Williams Realty Ce (G-2839)*

Keller Williams Realtors, Lewes *Also Called: Keller Williams Realty (G-6164)*

Keller Williams Realtors, Millville *Also Called: Keller Wllams Rlty - Lsko To B (G-8535)*

Keller Williams Realtors, Milton *Also Called: Keller Williams At Beach Rlty (G-8650)*

Keller Williams Realtors, New Castle *Also Called: Keller Williams Realty Central (G-9278)*

Keller Williams Realtors, Newark *Also Called: Keller Williams Realty (G-11150)*

Keller Williams Realtors, Ocean View *Also Called: Keller Williams Realty (G-12532)*

Keller Williams Realtors, Rehoboth Beach *Also Called: Keller Williams Realty (G-12817)*

Keller Williams Realtors, Rehoboth Beach *Also Called: Keller Williams Realty At Bch (G-12818)*

Keller Williams Realty 302 360-0300
  18344 Coastal Hwy Lewes (19958) *(G-6164)*

Keller Williams Realty 302 293-8654
  3 Berley Ct Newark (19702) *(G-11150)*

ALPHABETIC SECTION   Kent General Hospital

Keller Williams Realty.. 302 519-1683
   37367 Main St Ocean View (19970) *(G-12532)*
Keller Williams Realty.. 862 588-1342
   36115 Knight St Rehoboth Beach (19971) *(G-12817)*
Keller Williams Realty At Bch....................................... 302 360-0300
   36765 Harness Ct Rehoboth Beach (19971) *(G-12818)*
Keller Williams Realty Ce... 302 653-3624
   1671 S State St Dover (19901) *(G-2839)*
Keller Williams Realty Central...................................... 302 465-7562
   80 Christiana Rd New Castle (19720) *(G-9278)*
Keller Williams Rlty Delmarva...................................... 410 430-2721
   37458 Lion Dr Selbyville (19975) *(G-13558)*
Keller Wllams Rlty - Lsko To B..................................... 302 581-9101
   35091 Atlantic Ave Millville (19970) *(G-8535)*
Kelli Armstrong MD... 203 783-9632
   480 E Market St Lewes (19958) *(G-6165)*
Kellies Hair Place.. 302 827-2715
   17018 Bristol Rd Lewes (19958) *(G-6166)*
Kelly Robert & Assoc LLC.. 302 737-7785
   418 Suburban Dr Newark (19711) *(G-11151)*
Kelly & Assoc Insur Group Inc..................................... 302 661-6324
   1201 N Orange St Ste 1100 Wilmington (19801) *(G-17679)*
Kelly Ann Hatton.. 484 571-5369
   1601 Milltown Rd Ste 1 Wilmington (19808) *(G-17680)*
Kelly Benefit Strategy, Wilmington Also Called: Kelly & Assoc Insur Group Inc *(G-17679)*
Kelly Services, New Castle Also Called: Kelly Services Inc *(G-9279)*
Kelly Services Inc... 302 323-4748
   34 Reads Way New Castle (19720) *(G-9279)*
Kelly Services Inc... 302 366-1741
   225 Corporate Blvd Newark (19702) *(G-11152)*
Kelly Walker DDS.. 302 832-2200
   1991 Pulaski Hwy Bear (19701) *(G-324)*
Kellys Lawn Care... 302 584-1045
   7 Slashpine Cir Hockessin (19707) *(G-5267)*
Kelmar Associates LLC.. 781 213-6926
   2200 Concord Pike # 12 Wilmington (19803) *(G-17681)*
Kelmon Construction.. 302 357-4391
   42 Iowa Rd Wilmington (19808) *(G-17682)*
Ken Bertrand Realty Repairs....................................... 302 436-2872
   36058 Zion Church Rd Frankford (19945) *(G-4121)*
Ken Crest Services.. 302 741-0256
   318 Hiawatha Ln Dover (19904) *(G-2840)*
Ken Decker DC.. 302 389-8915
   699 S Carter Rd Unit 5 Smyrna (19977) *(G-13787)*
Ken Fibble Professional Svcs...................................... 302 947-2430
   35373 Bay Winds Ln Millsboro (19966) *(G-8337)*
Ken-Del Productions Inc.. 302 999-1111
   1500 First State Blvd Wilmington (19804) *(G-17683)*
Kencko Foods Inc (PA)... 616 253-6256
   2035 Sunset Lake Rd Ste B2 Newark (19702) *(G-11153)*
Kenco Cnstr Drywall Special, Felton Also Called: Kenco Drywall *(G-3990)*
Kenco Drywall.. 302 697-6489
   7093 S Dupont Hwy Felton (19943) *(G-3990)*
Kenco Group Inc... 302 629-4295
   1700 Dulany St Seaford (19973) *(G-13248)*
KENCO GROUP, INC., Seaford Also Called: Kenco Group Inc *(G-13248)*
Kenco Trophy Sales.. 302 846-3339
   301 Lincoln Ave Delmar (19940) *(G-1610)*
Kencrest Services... 302 735-1664
   6 Bellrive Ct Dover (19904) *(G-2841)*
Kencrest Services... 302 834-3365
   240 Clarks Corner Rd Saint Georges (19733) *(G-13035)*
Kendal Corp Pension Plan... 610 388-7001
   591 Collaboration Way Newark (19713) *(G-11154)*
Kendal Corporation (PA).. 610 335-1200
   591 Collaboration Way Ste 603 Newark (19713) *(G-11155)*
Kendal Management Services..................................... 610 388-5594
   591 Collaboration Way Newark (19713) *(G-11156)*
Kendal Outreach LLC... 610 335-1200
   591 Collaboration Way Newark (19713) *(G-11157)*
Kendall G Ritz M D.. 302 652-3586
   20 Montchanin Rd Ste 60 Wilmington (19807) *(G-17684)*

Kendall James Advisors LLC....................................... 302 463-0720
   12 Elderberry Ct Hockessin (19707) *(G-5268)*
Kenkay Inc... 302 838-7797
   40 Decidedly Ln Bear (19701) *(G-325)*
Kennedy Heather Ann MD.. 302 655-7108
   500 Justison St Wilmington (19801) *(G-17685)*
Kennedy Health Pain Relief and.................................. 302 691-0110
   6 Sharpley Rd Wilmington (19803) *(G-17686)*
Kenneth D Morris... 415 760-0791
   528 Wheelmen St Middletown (19709) *(G-7265)*
Kenneth Dale Ralosky.. 302 343-9464
   2823 Lockwood Chapel Rd Dover (19904) *(G-2842)*
Kenneth De Grout DC... 302 475-5600
   1401 Silverside Rd Ste 1 Wilmington (19810) *(G-17687)*
Kenneth E Barrett.. 302 270-6056
   2308 Woodlytown Rd Magnolia (19962) *(G-6757)*
Kenneth H Gladish.. 302 270-2821
   714 Barratts Chapel Rd Felton (19943) *(G-3991)*
Kenneth J Hurley... 302 734-3251
   3998 Bayside Dr Dover (19901) *(G-2843)*
Kenneth Ssan King Fndation Inc................................. 800 839-1754
   501 Silverside Rd Ste 123 Wilmington (19809) *(G-17688)*
Kennharr LLC... 800 692-7970
   8 The Grn Ste 4000 Dover (19901) *(G-2844)*
Kennis Capital (usa) LLC.. 302 605-6228
   251 Little Falls Dr Wilmington (19808) *(G-17689)*
Kenny Brothers Produce LLC..................................... 302 337-3007
   16440 Adams Rd Bridgeville (19933) *(G-722)*
Kenny K Vu.. 302 678-0510
   811 S Governors Ave Dover (19904) *(G-2845)*
Kenny Simpler... 302 226-2900
   33 Wilmington Ave Rehoboth Beach (19971) *(G-12819)*
Kenny Vu.. 302 526-2361
   111 Wolf Creek Blvd Ste 2 Dover (19901) *(G-2846)*
Kens Lawn Service Inc... 302 478-2714
   732 Westcliff Rd Wilmington (19803) *(G-17690)*
Kensington Cross Ltd (PA).. 888 999-9360
   18585 Coastal Hwy Unit 10 Rehoboth Beach (19971) *(G-12820)*
Kensington Tours Ltd... 888 903-2001
   2207 Concord Pike # 645 Wilmington (19803) *(G-17691)*
Kent & O Connor Inc... 703 351-6222
   26333 Timbercreek Ln Millsboro (19966) *(G-8338)*
Kent & O'Connor, Millsboro Also Called: Kent & O Connor Inc *(G-8338)*
Kent Cnty Cmnty Action Agcy In................................. 302 678-1949
   120a S Governors Ave Dover (19904) *(G-2847)*
Kent Cnty Rgnal Spt Cmplex Cor................................ 302 330-8873
   4000 Bay Rd Frederica (19946) *(G-4175)*
Kent Cnty Soc For The Prvntion.................................. 302 698-3006
   32 Shelter Cir Camden (19934) *(G-866)*
Kent Construction Co (PA).. 302 653-6469
   2 Big Oak Rd Smyrna (19977) *(G-13788)*
Kent Contracting LLC... 302 233-3157
   882 Tappahana Bridge Rd Hartly (19953) *(G-4889)*
Kent County Community School.................................. 302 734-9011
   117 Saulsbury Rd Dover (19904) *(G-2848)*
Kent County Painting Inc... 302 994-9628
   1700 First State Blvd Wilmington (19804) *(G-17692)*
Kent County Republican Party.................................... 302 653-2355
   130 Dodge Dr Smyrna (19977) *(G-13789)*
KENT COUNTY SPCA, Camden Also Called: Kent Cnty Soc For The Prvntion *(G-866)*
Kent Electrical Services LLC....................................... 302 922-4631
   112 Lake Dr Felton (19943) *(G-3992)*
Kent Family Medicine... 302 747-7903
   960 Forest St Dover (19904) *(G-2849)*
Kent General Hospital.. 302 744-7688
   725 Horsepond Rd Dover (19901) *(G-2850)*
Kent General Hospital (HQ)... 302 674-4700
   640 S State St Dover (19901) *(G-2851)*
Kent General Hospital.. 302 378-1199
   209 E Main St Middletown (19709) *(G-7266)*
Kent General Hospital.. 302 430-5731
   100 Wellness Way Milford (19963) *(G-7962)*

Kent General Hospital.. 302 653-2010
   401 N Carter Rd Smyrna (19977) *(G-13790)*
Kent General Hospital Inc.. 302 430-5705
   301 Jefferson Ave Milford (19963) *(G-7963)*
KENT GENERAL HOSPITAL, INC, Milford *Also Called: Kent General Hospital Inc (G-7963)*
Kent Landscaping Co LLC... 302 535-4296
   109 S Main St Camden (19934) *(G-867)*
Kent Leasing Company Inc.. 302 697-3000
   2181 S Dupont Hwy Dover (19901) *(G-2852)*
Kent Pediatrics... 302 747-7279
   748 S New St Ofc 1 Dover (19904) *(G-2853)*
Kent Pediatrics LLC... 302 264-9691
   1102 S Dupont Hwy Ste 1 Dover (19901) *(G-2854)*
Kent Pulmonary Associates LLC............................. 302 674-7155
   807 S Bradford St Dover (19904) *(G-2855)*
Kent Sign Company Inc... 302 697-2181
   2 E Bradys Ln Dover (19901) *(G-2856)*
Kent Sussex Auto Care Inc....................................... 302 422-3337
   145 Burning Tree Rd Dover (19904) *(G-2857)*
Kent Sussex Community Services........................... 302 384-6926
   1241 College Park Dr Dover (19904) *(G-2858)*
Kent-Sussex Industries Inc..................................... 302 422-4014
   301 N Rehoboth Blvd Milford (19963) *(G-7964)*
Kentmere Hlthcare Cnslting Cor.............................. 302 478-7600
   3511 Silverside Rd Ste 202 Wilmington (19810) *(G-17693)*
KENTMERE NURSING CARE CENTER, Wilmington *Also Called: Home of Merciful Rest Society (G-17183)*
Kentmere Rhblttion Hlthcare CT.............................. 302 652-3311
   1900 Lovering Ave Wilmington (19806) *(G-17694)*
Kenton Chair Shop... 302 653-2411
   291 Blackiston Rd Clayton (19938) *(G-1381)*
Kenton Child Care.. 302 674-8142
   1298 Mckee Rd Dover (19904) *(G-2859)*
Kenya Gather Foundation... 302 382-8227
   23246 Country Living Rd Millsboro (19966) *(G-8339)*
Kenzz Inc.. 310 254-6927
   651 N Broad St Middletown (19709) *(G-7267)*
Kerahealth France LLC... 302 351-3377
   5301 Limestone Rd Ste 100 Wilmington (19808) *(G-17695)*
Kercher Group Inc (PA)... 302 894-1098
   254 Chapman Rd Ste 202 Newark (19702) *(G-11158)*
Kerlink Inc.. 805 407-9208
   1209 N Orange St Wilmington (19801) *(G-17696)*
Kerry & G Inc... 302 999-0022
   1621 Willow Ave Wilmington (19804) *(G-17697)*
Kerry Harrison Photography................................... 302 494-4141
   2423 Nicholby Dr Wilmington (19808) *(G-17698)*
Kerry S Kirifides MD PA.. 302 918-6400
   875 Aaa Blvd Ste C Newark (19713) *(G-11159)*
Kershaw Industries.. 302 464-1051
   110 W Main St Middletown (19709) *(G-7268)*
Keturahs Cleaning... 302 242-3967
   403 Dogwood Ave Dover (19904) *(G-2860)*
Keval Corp.. 302 453-9100
   100 Mcintosh Plz Newark (19713) *(G-11160)*
Keval Corporation.. 302 453-9100
   100 Mcintosh Plz Newark (19713) *(G-11161)*
Kevin A Johnson.. 302 762-7671
   406 W 35th St Wilmington (19802) *(G-17699)*
Kevin Elzie... 302 697-6273
   301 Westhill Dr Camden Wyoming (19934) *(G-959)*
Kevin Garber.. 302 834-0639
   148 Carlotta Dr Bear (19701) *(G-326)*
Kevin Hannah... 302 450-2867
   4417 Barratts Chapel Rd Frederica (19946) *(G-4176)*
Kevin J Murray DC... 302 453-4043
   179 W Chestnut Hill Rd # 1 Newark (19713) *(G-11162)*
Kevin Keough Dr.. 302 384-8173
   215 S Bancroft Pkwy Wilmington (19805) *(G-17700)*
Kevin M Bielanski.. 908 752-8210
   15 Edisto Ct Ocean View (19970) *(G-12533)*

Kevin M Miller.. 302 514-7111
   11 S Clements St Smyrna (19977) *(G-13791)*
Kevin McDaniel.. 302 236-1351
   22495 Lewes Georgetown Hwy Georgetown (19947) *(G-4393)*
Kevin Scott Cameron... 515 314-3400
   35645 Elk Camp Rd Rehoboth Beach (19971) *(G-12821)*
Kevin Smith.. 800 878-1356
   200 Continental Dr # 401 Newark (19713) *(G-11163)*
Kevins Masonry Concrete Co.................................... 302 382-7259
   526 Reeves Crossing Rd Felton (19943) *(G-3993)*
Kevins Road Svc.. 302 218-2869
   4663 Kirkwood St Georges Rd Saint Georges (19733) *(G-13036)*
Kewmars E Dadmarz MD... 302 691-5179
   7 Stabler Cir Wilmington (19807) *(G-17701)*
Key Advisors Group, Dover *Also Called: Bear Financial Group LLC (G-1899)*
Key-Tel Communications Inc.................................... 302 475-3066
   2642 Foulk Rd Wilmington (19810) *(G-17702)*
Keylent Inc... 401 864-6498
   1000 N West St Ste 1200 Wilmington (19801) *(G-17703)*
Keynova Group LLC... 410 785-6257
   251 Little Falls Dr Wilmington (19808) *(G-17704)*
Keyrock LLC... 818 605-7772
   3524 Silverside Rd Ste 35b Wilmington (19810) *(G-17705)*
Keys R US LLC... 619 886-8774
   20415 Spangler Dr Lincoln (19960) *(G-6678)*
Keystate Corporate MGT LLC.................................... 302 425-5158
   824 N Market St Ste 210 Wilmington (19801) *(G-17706)*
Keystone Autism Services.. 302 731-3115
   7 Firethorn Ct Newark (19711) *(G-11164)*
Keystone Family Office Inc...................................... 302 377-4500
   112 Capitol Trl Newark (19711) *(G-11165)*
Keystone Finishing Inc... 925 825-2498
   1800 Lovering Ave Wilmington (19806) *(G-17707)*
Keystone Flashing Company.................................... 215 329-8500
   8 Lombardy Dr Wilmington (19803) *(G-17708)*
Keystone Funding Inc... 484 798-9084
   519 S Red Haven Ln Dover (19901) *(G-2861)*
Keystone Funding Inc (PA)...................................... 610 644-6423
   523 S Red Haven Ln Ste 101 Dover (19901) *(G-2862)*
Keystone Funding Fairfax Co, Dover *Also Called: Keystone Funding Inc (G-2862)*
Keystone Granite and Tile Inc................................. 302 323-0200
   217 Lisa Dr Ste C New Castle (19720) *(G-9280)*
Keystone Human Services....................................... 302 502-2158
   20 Rockford Rd Wilmington (19806) *(G-17709)*
Keystone Nfp Middletown LLC................................ 302 378-2777
   703 N Broad St Middletown (19709) *(G-7269)*
Keystone Service Systems Inc................................ 302 286-7234
   300 Creek View Rd Ste 210 Newark (19711) *(G-11166)*
Keystone Swine Services... 302 329-9731
   14356 Clydes Dr Milton (19968) *(G-8651)*
Kfs Strategic MGT Svcs LLC..................................... 302 757-6631
   1 Innovation Way Ste 426 Newark (19711) *(G-11167)*
Kgc Enterprises Inc... 302 668-1835
   3617 Kirkwood Hwy Wilmington (19808) *(G-17710)*
Kgs Digital Inc... 302 213-3979
   8 The Grn Dover (19901) *(G-2863)*
Kha-Neke Inc.. 302 440-4728
   25 Hempstead Dr Newark (19702) *(G-11168)*
Khaja Yezdani MD.. 302 322-1794
   191 Christiana Rd Ste 3 New Castle (19720) *(G-9281)*
Khan Family Foundation Inc.................................... 800 839-1754
   501 Silverside Rd Wilmington (19809) *(G-17711)*
Khanna Entps Ltd A Ltd Partnr................................ 302 266-6400
   1024 Old Churchmans Rd Newark (19713) *(G-11169)*
Khaos Beauty LLC... 302 427-0119
   1313 N Market St Fl 2 Wilmington (19801) *(G-17712)*
Khmisat LLC... 302 533-1303
   254 Chapman Rd Newark (19702) *(G-11170)*
Kiara M Moore.. 412 953-2791
   421 Cicero Xing Middletown (19709) *(G-7270)*
Kid Agains Inc.. 631 830-5228
   33 Lindley Dr Dover (19904) *(G-2864)*

ALPHABETIC SECTION — Kings Kids

Kidberry Inc 857 559-3043
251 Little Falls Dr Wilmington (19808) *(G-17713)*

Kidd Mc, New Castle Also Called: Reyes Rebeca *(G-9530)*

Kidd Robert W III DDS 302 678-1440
850 S State St Dover (19901) *(G-2865)*

Kiddie Express, Newark Also Called: Barbara L McKinney *(G-9982)*

Kiddie International Academy 302 838-2183
843 Salem Church Rd Newark (19702) *(G-11171)*

Kiddocs 302 892-3300
4600 New Linden Hl 204 Wilmington (19808) *(G-17714)*

Kidmore End Developers LLC 302 562-5110
2900 Society Dr Claymont (19703) *(G-1206)*

Kids Club Foundation Delaware 302 733-0168
111 Register Dr Newark (19711) *(G-11172)*

Kids Clubhouse 302 464-1134
5350 Summit Bridge Rd Middletown (19709) *(G-7271)*

Kids Cottage LLC 302 644-7690
35448 Wolfe Neck Rd Rehoboth Beach (19971) *(G-12822)*

Kids First Newark, Newark Also Called: Edwin C Katzman MD *(G-10613)*

Kids Inc 302 422-9099
613 Lakeview Ave Milford (19963) *(G-7965)*

Kids Kastle Day Care 302 740-8803
2 Stallion Dr Newark (19713) *(G-11173)*

Kids Kingdom Elc LLC 302 377-1698
205 W 7th St Wilmington (19801) *(G-17715)*

Kids Korner Day Care 302 998-4606
706 W Newport Pike Wilmington (19804) *(G-17716)*

Kids Nest Day Care 302 731-7017
24 Donaldson Dr Newark (19713) *(G-11174)*

Kids R US Learning Center Inc 302 678-1234
425 Webbs Ln Dover (19904) *(G-2866)*

Kids Teens Pediatrics of Dover 302 538-5624
125 Greentree Dr Ste 1 Dover (19904) *(G-2867)*

Kids University LLC 302 514-8187
535 Schooner Way Dover (19901) *(G-2868)*

Kids-R-Us Learning Center, Dover Also Called: Kids R US Learning Center Inc *(G-2866)*

Kidya Prschool Lrng Gmes For T 302 483-7778
900 Foulk Rd Ste 201 Wilmington (19803) *(G-17717)*

Kidz Akademy Corp 302 732-6077
32442 Royal Blvd Dagsboro (19939) *(G-1473)*

Kidz Choice LLC 302 365-6787
1230 Pulaski Hwy Bear (19701) *(G-327)*

Kidz Ink 302 327-0686
345 School Bell Rd Bear (19701) *(G-328)*

Kidz Ink 302 838-1000
14 Saint Andrews Dr Bear (19701) *(G-329)*

Kidz Ink (PA) 302 838-1500
1703 Porter Rd Bear (19701) *(G-330)*

Kidz Ink 302 376-1700
125 Sleepy Hollow Dr Middletown (19709) *(G-7272)*

Kidz Klub 302 652-5439
200 N Union St Wilmington (19805) *(G-17718)*

Kiefa Inc (PA) 845 803-5924
614 N Dupont Hwy Ste 210 Dover (19901) *(G-2869)*

Kieran Py MD 302 541-4460
96 Atlantic Ave Ste 101 Ocean View (19970) *(G-12534)*

Killhffer Chritable Foundation 302 994-4762
2204 Gilpin Ave Wilmington (19806) *(G-17719)*

Kim and Evans Fmly Fndtion Inc 302 629-7166
123 Village Dr Seaford (19973) *(G-13249)*

Kim Gaines 302 736-3000
3156 Forrest Ave Dover (19904) *(G-2870)*

Kim Jones Agcy State Frm Insur 302 934-9393
29848 Millsboro Hwy Millsboro (19966) *(G-8340)*

Kim Simpson Realty Group 302 690-0245
104 W Main St Ste B Middletown (19709) *(G-7273)*

Kimax Investments, Newark Also Called: October Phoenix Rlty Group LLC *(G-11577)*

Kimberly N Ginsberg Dr 215 760-0751
7 Chaville Way Wilmington (19807) *(G-17720)*

Kimberly Tucker 302 358-0574
249 E Crail Ct Middletown (19709) *(G-7274)*

Kimberton Apartments Assoc LP 302 368-0116
100 Kimberton Dr Newark (19713) *(G-11175)*

Kimbles AVI Lgistical Svcs Inc 334 663-4954
21785 Aviation Ave Georgetown (19947) *(G-4394)*

Kimbles DLS, Georgetown Also Called: Kimbles AVI Lgistical Svcs Inc *(G-4394)*

Kimmel Crter Rman Pltz Onill P (PA) 302 565-6100
56 W Main St Ste 400 Christiana (19702) *(G-1001)*

KIMMEL, CARTER, ROMAN, PELTZ &, Christiana Also Called: Kimmel Crter Rman Pltz Onill P *(G-1001)*

Kind Mind Kids 302 545-0380
111 Lands End Rd Wilmington (19807) *(G-17721)*

Kind-Charity Inc 302 867-6042
651 N Broad St Ste 206 Middletown (19709) *(G-7275)*

Kindercare Center 1006, Wilmington Also Called: Kindercare Learning Ctrs LLC *(G-17722)*

Kindercare Center 45, Wilmington Also Called: Kindercare Learning Ctrs LLC *(G-17723)*

Kindercare Learning Centers, New Castle Also Called: Kindercare Learning Ctrs LLC *(G-9282)*

Kindercare Learning Ctrs LLC 302 234-8680
6696 Lancaster Pike Hockessin (19707) *(G-5269)*

Kindercare Learning Ctrs LLC 302 322-3102
327 Old State Rd New Castle (19720) *(G-9282)*

Kindercare Learning Ctrs LLC 302 834-6931
100 Paxson Dr Newark (19702) *(G-11176)*

Kindercare Learning Ctrs LLC 302 475-2212
2018 Naamans Rd C Wilmington (19810) *(G-17722)*

Kindercare Learning Ctrs LLC 302 731-7138
3449 Hillock Ln Wilmington (19808) *(G-17723)*

Kindheart Home Care Inc 484 479-6582
207 Parker Dr Middletown (19709) *(G-7276)*

Kindred Counseling 302 478-8888
3411 Silverside Rd # 105 Wilmington (19810) *(G-17724)*

Kindred Kids Yoga 302 741-2240
43 Sherwood Ct Dover (19904) *(G-2871)*

Kindwell Inc 302 588-2895
1007 N Orange St Fl 4 Wilmington (19801) *(G-17725)*

Kinetic Oasis LLC 508 202-0559
254 Chapman Rd Ste 208 Newark (19702) *(G-11177)*

Kinetic Skateboarding 856 375-2236
5319 Concord Pike Wilmington (19803) *(G-17726)*

King 302 930-0139
732 Peachtree Rd Apt E Claymont (19703) *(G-1207)*

King and Minsk PA 302 475-3270
1805 Foulk Rd Ste D Wilmington (19810) *(G-17727)*

King Creative LLC 302 593-1595
727 N Market St Wilmington (19801) *(G-17728)*

King Josiah Companies LLC 855 312-3300
9 E Loockerman St Ste 202-665 Dover (19901) *(G-2872)*

King La Express 215 607-9997
13 Chaddwyck Blvd New Castle (19720) *(G-9283)*

King of Mangoes 302 547-2500
2 Greenwich Ct Newark (19702) *(G-11178)*

King of Sweets Inc 302 730-8200
47 S West St Dover (19904) *(G-2873)*

King of Sweets Distribution 302 730-8200
47 S West St Dover (19904) *(G-2874)*

King of Sweets Online Inc 302 730-8200
47 S West St Dover (19904) *(G-2875)*

King Snipers Drywall LLC 302 452-4515
121 Daffodil Dr Magnolia (19962) *(G-6758)*

King-Edwards Residences LLC 646 389-5830
8 The Grn Ste D Dover (19901) *(G-2876)*

Kingdom Kids Day Care 302 492-0207
2899 Arthursville Rd Hartly (19953) *(G-4890)*

Kingdom of God Fellowship, Hartly Also Called: Kingdom Kids Day Care *(G-4890)*

Kingdom Spa Inc 302 897-8255
5 Emerson Ct Middletown (19709) *(G-7277)*

Kings Creek Country Club Inc 302 227-8951
1 Kings Creek Cir Rehoboth Beach (19971) *(G-12823)*

Kings Cust Clean & HM Ser LLC 302 542-3920
103 Shallow Brooke Ct Seaford (19973) *(G-13250)*

Kings Kids 302 239-4961
536 Hemingway Dr Hockessin (19707) *(G-5270)*

Kings Masonry LLC ... 302 632-6783
 2685 Hartly Rd Hartly (19953) *(G-4891)*

Kings Sealcoating ... 302 674-1568
 416 Dogwood Ave Dover (19904) *(G-2877)*

Kings Towing Company LLC ... 302 345-3134
 160 Scottfield Dr Newark (19713) *(G-11179)*

Kingstown LLC ... 302 645-7050
 33672 Bayview Medical Dr Lewes (19958) *(G-6167)*

Kinneys Enterprises LLC ... 302 300-2012
 17 Latham Ln Newark (19713) *(G-11180)*

Kinsler Electrical, Millsboro *Also Called: Daniel A Kinsler (G-8253)*

Kinsler Landscaping LLC ... 302 745-0269
 32172 Robin Hoods Loop Millsboro (19966) *(G-8341)*

Kinsta Inc ... 310 736-9306
 838 Walker Rd Ste 21-2 Dover (19904) *(G-2878)*

Kintyre, Wilmington *Also Called: Kintyre Solutions Inc (G-17729)*

Kintyre Solutions Inc ... 888 636-0010
 2817 Kennedy Rd Wilmington (19810) *(G-17729)*

Kirby & Holloway Provisions Co ... 302 398-3705
 966 Jackson Ditch Rd Harrington (19952) *(G-4794)*

Kirk & Associates LLC ... 302 444-4733
 56 W Main St Ste 305 Christiana (19702) *(G-1002)*

Kirk Family Practice ... 302 423-2049
 5 Courtney Rd Wilmington (19807) *(G-17730)*

Kirk Flowers, Newark *Also Called: Kirks Flowers Inc (G-11181)*

Kirkin Roofing LLC ... 302 832-7663
 1053 Lower Twin Lane Rd New Castle (19720) *(G-9284)*

Kirkley Construction LLC ... 302 276-9795
 109 Michael Ln Bear (19701) *(G-331)*

Kirks Flowers Inc ... 302 737-3931
 7 Ash Ave Newark (19711) *(G-11181)*

Kirkwood Anmal Brding Grooming ... 302 737-1098
 1501 Capitol Trl Newark (19711) *(G-11182)*

Kirkwood Dental Associates PA ... 302 834-7700
 1260 Peoples Plz Bldg 1200 Newark (19702) *(G-11183)*

Kirkwood Dental Associates PA ... 302 834-7700
 1200 Peoples Plz Ste 1260 Newark (19702) *(G-11184)*

Kirkwood Dental Associates PA (PA) ... 302 994-2582
 710 Greenbank Rd Wilmington (19808) *(G-17731)*

Kirkwood Detox, Wilmington *Also Called: Northeast Treatment Ctrs Inc (G-18683)*

Kirkwood Ftnes Racquetball CLB (PA) ... 302 529-1865
 1800 Naamans Rd Wilmington (19810) *(G-17732)*

Kirkwood Pain & Injury Chiropr ... 302 422-2329
 600 Ne Front Street Ext Ste D Milford (19963) *(G-7966)*

Kirkwood Property ... 302 981-0966
 4700 Kirkwood Hwy Wilmington (19808) *(G-17733)*

Kirkwood Smoke Shop ... 302 525-6718
 151 E Main St Newark (19711) *(G-11185)*

Kirkwood Tires Inc ... 302 737-2460
 1929 Kirkwood Hwy Newark (19711) *(G-11186)*

Kirwa Foundation ... 347 932-4911
 2711 Centerville Rd # 400 Wilmington (19808) *(G-17734)*

Kissangen Inc ... 414 446-4182
 113 Barksdale Pro Ctr Newark (19711) *(G-11187)*

Kissflow, Wilmington *Also Called: Kissflow Inc (G-17735)*

Kissflow Inc ... 650 396-7692
 1000 N West St Ste 1200 Wilmington (19801) *(G-17735)*

KISTLER TIFFANY BENEFITS, Wilmington *Also Called: Tiffany Kistler Benefits (G-20320)*

Kit International Inc ... 201 342-7753
 2711 Cntrvlle Rd Ste 7263 Wilmington (19808) *(G-17736)*

Kitchen Gallery Inc ... 302 655-7214
 201 Greenhill Ave Wilmington (19805) *(G-17737)*

Kitschy Stitch ... 302 200-9889
 18419 Berkeley Rd Lewes (19958) *(G-6168)*

Kitty Jazzy Publishing ... 302 897-8842
 702 Cobble Creek Curv Newark (19702) *(G-11188)*

Kiwanis Club of Wilmington, New Castle *Also Called: Kiwanis International Inc (G-9285)*

Kiwanis International Inc ... 302 325-0778
 202 W Franklin Ave New Castle (19720) *(G-9285)*

Kiwetinohk Marketing US Corp ... 403 827-6958
 1675 S State St Ste B Dover (19901) *(G-2879)*

Kjan Innovations, Middletown *Also Called: Kjan Innovations LLC (G-7278)*

Kjan Innovations LLC ... 954 388-1293
 364 E Main St Middletown (19709) *(G-7278)*

Kjoy LLC ... 302 588-5420
 356 E Main St Newark (19711) *(G-11189)*

Kjp LLC ... 302 765-0134
 1601 Concord Pike Ste 35 Wilmington (19803) *(G-17738)*

Kjs Detailing LLC ... 302 420-9132
 4615 Sylvanus Dr Wilmington (19803) *(G-17739)*

Kld Trucking Corporation ... 347 399-7619
 550 S Dupont Hwy Apt 14s New Castle (19720) *(G-9286)*

Klean Team of Wilmington ... 302 298-5558
 301 Tyrone Ave Wilmington (19804) *(G-17740)*

Kleinhomers ... 302 234-2392
 15 Forestal Cir Newark (19711) *(G-11190)*

Klf Music Factory ... 302 598-8770
 809 Marsh Hawk Ct Middletown (19709) *(G-7279)*

Klh Enterprises ... 302 245-0712
 29099 Stockley Rd Milton (19968) *(G-8652)*

Klh Industries LLC ... 800 348-0758
 16192 Coastal Hwy Lewes (19958) *(G-6169)*

Klh Properties Ltd Lblty Co ... 352 208-8964
 718 E 7th St Wilmington (19801) *(G-17741)*

Klick Inc ... 302 292-8455
 40 Garvey Ln Newark (19702) *(G-11191)*

Klip-It LLC ... 888 202-0533
 651 N Broad St Middletown (19709) *(G-7280)*

Klm Consulting LLC ... 302 763-2174
 28 Staten Dr Hockessin (19707) *(G-5271)*

Kloeckner Metals ... 302 652-3326
 20 Davidson Ln New Castle (19720) *(G-9287)*

Km Klacko & Associate ... 302 652-1482
 509 Redfern Ave Wilmington (19807) *(G-17742)*

KMC Management LLC ... 866 943-2205
 1201 N Market St Ste 111 Wilmington (19801) *(G-17743)*

Kmk Portable Moving & Stor LLC ... 302 734-0410
 40 Silverwood Blvd Newark (19711) *(G-11192)*

Kmp Mechanical LLC ... 410 392-6126
 406 Suburban Dr # 155 Newark (19711) *(G-11193)*

Kmp Mechanical LLC ... 410 392-6126
 118 Sandy Dr Ste 5 Newark (19713) *(G-11194)*

Kms Servies ... 302 502-5287
 248 E North St Smyrna (19977) *(G-13792)*

Knauer Association LLC ... 302 947-2531
 37145 Sandpiper Rd Millsboro (19966) *(G-8342)*

Kneading To Heel ... 302 740-4647
 103 Forsythia Dr Newark (19711) *(G-11195)*

Kneesaverelectricalbox ... 732 239-7514
 27936 Home Farm Dr Millsboro (19966) *(G-8343)*

Kneisley Eye Care PA ... 302 224-3000
 45 E Main St Ste 201 Newark (19711) *(G-11196)*

Knepper & Stratton ... 302 658-1717
 309 S State St Ste C Dover (19901) *(G-2880)*

Knepps Construction ... 302 846-3360
 38120 Brittingham Rd Delmar (19940) *(G-1611)*

Knight Insur Consulting Group ... 973 704-1112
 535 Canary Dr Newark (19702) *(G-11197)*

Knights Clmbus Del State Cncil ... 302 836-8235
 1 Wales Cir Bear (19701) *(G-332)*

Knights Golf Inc ... 484 553-1119
 113 Esch St Townsend (19734) *(G-14023)*

Knights Inn ... 302 798-9914
 7811 Governor Printz Blvd Claymont (19703) *(G-1208)*

Knights Inn, Claymont *Also Called: Knights Inn (G-1208)*

Knights Inn, Georgetown *Also Called: Chudasama Enterprises LLC (G-4255)*

Knights Inn, New Castle *Also Called: Gurukrupa Inc (G-9184)*

Knights of Columbus ... 703 615-3372
 967a Tortoise St Bethany Beach (19930) *(G-613)*

Knights of Columbus, Bethany Beach *Also Called: Knights of Columbus (G-613)*

Knotts Construction Inc ... 302 475-7074
 1504 Upsan Downs Ln Wilmington (19810) *(G-17744)*

ALPHABETIC SECTION — Kurb Systems Inc

Knotts Incorporated 302 322-0554
   700 Wilmington Rd Historic New Castle (19720) *(G-5015)*

Knowcrunch Inc 210 300-7214
   2035 Sunset Lake Rd Newark (19702) *(G-11198)*

Knowt Inc 848 391-0575
   16192 Coastal Hwy Lewes (19958) *(G-6170)*

Knrp LLC 408 480-8501
   30 Chadwick Dr Dover (19901) *(G-2881)*

Knus Inc 855 935-5687
   1000 N West St Ste 1281-268 Wilmington (19801) *(G-17745)*

Ko Gutters LLC 302 943-8293
   33499 Aster St Lewes (19958) *(G-6171)*

Koam Corp 302 422-4848
   209b Ne Front St Milford (19963) *(G-7967)*

Kodo Digital Systems Inc 909 843-0946
   8 The Grn Ste A Dover (19901) *(G-2882)*

Kodys Kids Inc 302 858-0884
   36270 King St Rehoboth Beach (19971) *(G-12824)*

Kogut Tech Consulting Inc 302 455-0388
   24 Ohio State Dr Newark (19713) *(G-11199)*

Koheric LLC 646 801-6741
   8 The Grn Dover (19901) *(G-2883)*

Kohr Brothers Inc 302 227-9354
   5 Rehoboth Ave Rehoboth Beach (19971) *(G-12825)*

Kohr Brothers Frozen Custard, Rehoboth Beach Also Called: Kohr Brothers Inc *(G-12825)*

Kokoszka & Sons Inc 302 328-4807
   68 Skyline Dr New Castle (19720) *(G-9288)*

Kokoszka Ent, Bear Also Called: C & K Builders LLC *(G-87)*

Kompli, Hockessin Also Called: Klm Consulting LLC *(G-5271)*

Kompressed Air Delaware Inc 302 275-1985
   21 Blevins Dr New Castle (19720) *(G-9289)*

Koncordia Group LLC 302 427-1350
   1201 N Market St Ste 401 Wilmington (19801) *(G-17746)*

Kool Boiz Foundation LLC 614 404-2396
   603 E Glen Mare Dr Middletown (19709) *(G-7281)*

Korean Martial Arts Institute (PA) 302 992-7999
   2419 W Newport Pike Wilmington (19804) *(G-17747)*

Korn Consult Group US Inc 304 933-5735
   40 E Main St Ste 2700 Newark (19711) *(G-11200)*

Korsgy Technologies LLC 302 504-6201
   3411 Silverside Rd 235 Wilmington (19810) *(G-17748)*

Kortech Consulting Inc 302 559-4612
   13 Primrose Dr Bear (19701) *(G-333)*

Kortex Enterprises LLC 678 551-8260
   896 S State St Unit 613 Dover (19901) *(G-2884)*

Kovach S Construction 302 363-4130
   55 Sherwood Forest Way Hartly (19953) *(G-4892)*

Kovan Studio Inc 855 964-3748
   600 N Broad St Middletown (19709) *(G-7282)*

Kozy Kennels 302 455-1152
   303 Shisler Ct Newark (19702) *(G-11201)*

Kpkm Inc 302 678-0271
   1062 Lafferty Ln Dover (19901) *(G-2885)*

Kpss Government Solutions Inc 302 992-7950
   1100 First State Blvd Wilmington (19804) *(G-17749)*

Kraft Heinz Company 302 734-6100
   1250 W North St Dover (19904) *(G-2886)*

Kramer Group LLC 717 368-2117
   2116 Peachtree Dr Wilmington (19805) *(G-17750)*

Kramer Konstruction 717 466-6500
   317 N Layton Ave Wyoming (19934) *(G-20987)*

Krapfs Coaches Inc 302 993-7855
   1400 First State Blvd Wilmington (19804) *(G-17751)*

Kratom Foundation 302 645-7400
   16192 Coastal Hwy Lewes (19958) *(G-6172)*

Krave Like LLC 302 482-4550
   7 Deer Run Dr Wilmington (19807) *(G-17752)*

Krayo Inc 415 851-6250
   1013 Centre Rd Ste 403b Wilmington (19805) *(G-17753)*

Kream Puff Clean 251 509-1639
   49 Trala St Smyrna (19977) *(G-13793)*

Kreative Services 302 545-5030
   3835 Wrangle Hill Rd Bear (19701) *(G-334)*

Kremer Eye Center 866 206-4322
   2060 Limestone Rd Ste 205 Wilmington (19808) *(G-17754)*

Krenee LLC 302 200-1025
   3200 Kirkwood Hwy Wilmington (19808) *(G-17755)*

Krh Trucking LLC 302 535-8407
   112 Wilder Rd Dover (19904) *(G-2887)*

Kris Window Tint LLC 302 384-6185
   804 N Lincoln St Wilmington (19805) *(G-17756)*

Krishna White MD 302 651-6040
   1600 Rockland Rd Wilmington (19803) *(G-17757)*

Kriss Contracting Inc 302 492-3502
   1523 Gunter Rd Hartly (19953) *(G-4893)*

Kriss Contracting Inc 302 492-3502
   1523 Gunter Rd Marydel (19964) *(G-6803)*

Krista J Anderson Mrs 239 247-1170
   24 Fithian Dr New Castle (19720) *(G-9290)*

Kristian Express LLC 302 528-7577
   110 Rustic Dr Newark (19713) *(G-11202)*

Kristina Brandis 516 457-2717
   208 Wickerberry Dr Middletown (19709) *(G-7283)*

Kristol Ctr For Jewish Lf Inc 302 453-0479
   47 W Delaware Ave Newark (19711) *(G-11203)*

Kritter Sitter 302 270-0963
   Woodside (19980) *(G-20978)*

Krm Stables 302 653-3838
   1225 Clyton Grenspring Rd Clayton (19938) *(G-1382)*

Krn Architecture LLC 302 536-8576
   2207 Concord Pike 145 Wilmington (19803) *(G-17758)*

Kroegers Salvage Inc 302 381-7082
   15896 White Pine Ln Bridgeville (19933) *(G-723)*

Kruger Farms Inc 302 856-2577
   24306 Dupont Blvd Georgetown (19947) *(G-4395)*

Kruger Trailers Inc 302 856-2577
   24306 Dupont Blvd Georgetown (19947) *(G-4396)*

KS Nail and Spa 302 703-6158
   1551 Savannah Rd Ste C Lewes (19958) *(G-6173)*

KSI CARTRIDGE SERVICE, Milford Also Called: Kent-Sussex Industries Inc *(G-7964)*

Ksn, Newark Also Called: Kissangen Inc *(G-11187)*

Ksre Capital LLC 281 501-3777
   8 The Grn Ste A Dover (19901) *(G-2888)*

Kst Land Design Inc 302 328-1879
   2627 Skylark Rd Wilmington (19808) *(G-17759)*

Ktc, Newark Also Called: Kogut Tech Consulting Inc *(G-11199)*

Ktf Enterprise LLC 302 932-6039
   224 W 29th St Wilmington (19802) *(G-17760)*

Ktm 2 LLC 302 856-2516
   123 Dixon St Selbyville (19975) *(G-13559)*

Kubasko McKee Group RE 877 302-7747
   3711 Kennett Pike Ste 220 Wilmington (19807) *(G-17761)*

Kubera Global Solutions LLC 480 241-5124
   1521 Concord Pike Ste 301 Wilmington (19803) *(G-17762)*

Kubota Authorized Dealer, Delmar Also Called: Burke Equipment Company *(G-1570)*

Kubota Authorized Dealer, Felton Also Called: Burke Equipment Company *(G-3949)*

Kubota Authorized Dealer, Newark Also Called: Newark Kubota Inc *(G-11540)*

Kubota Research Associates 302 683-0199
   100 Hobson Dr Hockessin (19707) *(G-5272)*

Kuehne Chemical Company Inc 302 834-4557
   1645 River Rd New Castle (19720) *(G-9291)*

Kuest Inc 786 840-0842
   651 N Broad St Ste 206 Middletown (19709) *(G-7284)*

Kulina, Patrick F MD, Lewes Also Called: Sussex Podiatry Group *(G-6531)*

Kumar Properties LLC 337 284-5975
   2093 Philadelphia Pike Claymont (19703) *(G-1209)*

Kunkun Auto Group LLC 917 499-0019
   408 W 24th St Wilmington (19802) *(G-17763)*

Kupferman & Associates LLC 302 656-7566
   1701 Shallcross Ave Ste D Wilmington (19806) *(G-17764)*

Kurb Systems Inc 732 490-1741
   300 Delaware Ave Wilmington (19801) *(G-17765)*

Kurrensy Inc ... 347 228-9306
 8 The Grn Ste 10386 Dover (19901) *(G-2889)*

Kurt F Gwynne ... 302 778-7550
 1201 N Market St Ste 1500 Wilmington (19801) *(G-17766)*

Kurtz Collection ... 302 654-0442
 1010 N Union St Wilmington (19805) *(G-17767)*

Kurtz Construction LLC ... 302 943-4754
 506 Rose Dale Ln Dover (19904) *(G-2890)*

Kushim Inc (PA) ... 609 919-9889
 2711 Centerville Rd Ste 400 Wilmington (19808) *(G-17768)*

Kustom Additions LLC ... 302 468-6865
 1207 Delaware Ave Wilmington (19806) *(G-17769)*

Kustom Kutz ... 302 424-7556
 1007 N Walnut St Milford (19963) *(G-7968)*

Kutbu LLC ... 848 225-8848
 651 N Broad St Ste 201 Middletown (19709) *(G-7285)*

KUTZ HOME, Wilmington Also Called: Milton & Hattie Kutz Home Inc *(G-18371)*

Kvm Depot Inc ... 302 472-9190
 1007 N Orange St Wilmington (19801) *(G-17770)*

Kw Contracting Inc ... 302 420-0159
 207 Ratledge Rd Townsend (19734) *(G-14024)*

Kw Garden ... 302 735-7770
 1784 N Dupont Hwy Dover (19901) *(G-2891)*

Kw Solar Solutions Inc ... 302 838-8400
 2444 Denny Rd Bear (19701) *(G-335)*

Kw Solar Solutions Inc ... 302 838-8400
 2444 Denny Rd Bear (19701) *(G-336)*

Kwa Analytics US LLC ... 914 629-6744
 1209 N Orange St Wilmington (19801) *(G-17771)*

Kwik & Crafty Contracting ... 302 227-2550
 18977 Munchy Branch Rd Rehoboth Beach (19971) *(G-12826)*

Kyber Corp ... 609 203-1413
 112 S French St Ste 105 Wilmington (19801) *(G-17772)*

Kyles Tile LLC ... 302 462-0959
 38525 Reservation Trl Ocean View (19970) *(G-12535)*

Kzy Group Inc ... 302 684-3078
 16192 Coastal Hwy Lewes (19958) *(G-6174)*

L & B Publishing ... 302 743-4061
 44 Lakewood Cir Newark (19711) *(G-11204)*

L & D Insurance Services Inc ... 302 235-2288
 1 Isabella Ct Hockessin (19707) *(G-5273)*

L & J Sheet Metal ... 302 875-2822
 8095 Airport Rd Laurel (19956) *(G-5542)*

L & K Real Estate LLC ... 484 410-4898
 4 Dornoch Ln Bear (19701) *(G-337)*

L & L Carpet Discount Ctrs Inc ... 302 292-3712
 900 Interchange Blvd Ste 901 Newark (19711) *(G-11205)*

L & L Geothermal Hvac Svcs LLC ... 302 536-7120
 9592 Domenica Ct Seaford (19973) *(G-13251)*

L & M Services Inc ... 302 658-3735
 617 Lafayette Blvd Wilmington (19801) *(G-17773)*

L & W Insurance Inc ... 302 674-3500
 1154 S Governors Ave Dover (19904) *(G-2892)*

L A Masonary Inc ... 302 239-6833
 125 Sun Ct Newark (19711) *(G-11206)*

L C K Managment Inc ... 609 820-2980
 8 Ruby Dr Claymont (19703) *(G-1210)*

L Cor Inc ... 302 428-3929
 201 N Walnut St Ste 906 Wilmington (19801) *(G-17774)*

L E I, Newark Also Called: Landmark Engineering Inc *(G-11219)*

L E Stansell Inc ... 302 475-1534
 2525 Ebright Rd Wilmington (19810) *(G-17775)*

L E York Law LLC ... 302 234-8338
 182 Belmont Dr Wilmington (19808) *(G-17776)*

L F Conlin DDS ... 302 764-0930
 1202 Foulk Rd Wilmington (19803) *(G-17777)*

L F Systems Corp ... 302 322-0460
 249 Old Churchmans Rd New Castle (19720) *(G-9292)*

L L Detailing ... 302 453-8000
 995 S Chapel St Newark (19713) *(G-11207)*

L Maintenance ... 302 841-1698
 32845 Murray Rd Frankford (19945) *(G-4122)*

L Squared Healthcare LLC ... 302 289-5425
 2600 Glasgow Ave Ste 200 Newark (19702) *(G-11208)*

L&B Holdings, Wilmington Also Called: Littljohn Blckston Hldings LLC *(G-17945)*

L&J Painting ... 267 423-6040
 10 Myers Rd Newark (19713) *(G-11209)*

L&L Logistics Inc ... 720 232-5637
 1013 Centre Rd Ste 403s Wilmington (19805) *(G-17778)*

L&W Insurance Agency, Dover Also Called: C Edgar Wood Inc *(G-2007)*

L2 Trade LLC ... 603 921-7930
 8 The Grn Ste B Dover (19901) *(G-2893)*

L3d LLC ... 302 677-0031
 1671 S State St Dover (19901) *(G-2894)*

La Banca ... 302 464-3005
 1 W Main St Middletown (19709) *(G-7286)*

La Bella ... 302 644-2572
 628 Milford Harrington Hw Milford (19963) *(G-7969)*

La Bella Med Spa ... 302 990-8770
 1350 Middleford Rd Ste 502 Seaford (19973) *(G-13252)*

La Bella Nails Inc ... 302 475-6216
 1716 Naamans Rd Wilmington (19810) *(G-17779)*

La Bella Vita Salon & Day Spa ... 302 883-2597
 525 S Red Haven Ln Dover (19901) *(G-2895)*

LA BELLE ARTISTRY LLC ... 302 656-0555
 1300 Pennsylvania Ave Wilmington (19806) *(G-17780)*

La Belle Studio, Wilmington Also Called: LA BELLE ARTISTRY LLC *(G-17780)*

La Bendicion Cleaning Svcs LL ... 302 276-6468
 209 May Ave New Castle (19720) *(G-9293)*

La Communication LLC ... 302 653-1210
 109 Savannah Dr Smyrna (19977) *(G-13794)*

La Esperanza Inc ... 302 854-9262
 216 N Race St Georgetown (19947) *(G-4397)*

LA ESPERANZA COMMUNITY CENTER, Georgetown Also Called: La Esperanza Inc *(G-4397)*

La Floresta Perdida Inc (PA) ... 302 478-8900
 3411 Silverside Rd Ste 101 Wilmington (19810) *(G-17781)*

La Nails, Wilmington Also Called: Vu Binh Thai *(G-20656)*

La Petite Academy, Hockessin Also Called: La Petite Academy Inc *(G-5274)*

La Petite Academy Inc ... 877 271-6466
 5986 Limestone Rd Hockessin (19707) *(G-5274)*

La Red Health Care ... 757 709-5072
 23659 Saulsbury Ln Georgetown (19947) *(G-4398)*

La Red Health Center Inc (PA) ... 302 855-1233
 21444 Carmean Way Georgetown (19947) *(G-4399)*

La Red Health Center Inc ... 408 533-3189
 300 High St Seaford (19973) *(G-13253)*

La Vie Chocolat LLC ... 302 750-4540
 250 Corporate Blvd Newark (19702) *(G-11210)*

La Zmx Radio ... 302 702-2952
 26715 Sussex Hwy Seaford (19973) *(G-13254)*

Lab, Newark Also Called: Laboratory Corporation America *(G-11211)*

Lab, Wilmington Also Called: Delaware Meat Company LLC *(G-15941)*

Lab Products LLC ... 302 628-4300
 742 Sussex Ave Seaford (19973) *(G-13255)*

Labaton Sucharow LLP ... 302 573-6938
 222 Delaware Ave Ste 1500 Wilmington (19801) *(G-17782)*

LABATON SUCHAROW LLP, Wilmington Also Called: Labaton Sucharow LLP *(G-17782)*

Label Your Data ... 844 935-2538
 1521 Concord Pike Wilmington (19803) *(G-17783)*

Laboratory Corporation America ... 302 731-0244
 314 E Main St Ste 105 Newark (19711) *(G-11211)*

Labours of Love Inc ... 443 593-2776
 21 W Kyla Marie Dr Newark (19702) *(G-11212)*

Labrador, The, Millsboro Also Called: Wooley Bully Inc *(G-8507)*

Labshops, Claymont Also Called: Azzota Corporation *(G-1048)*

Labware ... 302 521-0250
 2 Polaris Dr Newark (19711) *(G-11213)*

Labware Inc ... 302 658-8444
 400 Burnt Mill Rd Wilmington (19807) *(G-17784)*

Labware Inc (HQ) ... 302 658-8444
 3 Mill Rd Ste 102 Wilmington (19806) *(G-17785)*

ALPHABETIC SECTION

Labware Global Services Inc 302 658-8444
  3 Mill Rd Ste 102 Wilmington (19806) *(G-17786)*
Labware Holdings Inc (PA) 302 658-8444
  3 Mill Rd Ste 102 Wilmington (19806) *(G-17787)*
Lacieah Inc 302 365-5585
  14 Creek Ln Newark (19702) *(G-11214)*
Laconic Innovations Co 302 501-6069
  8 The Grn Ste A Dover (19901) *(G-2896)*
Ladder Mart USA LLC 866 524-4536
  9 E Loockerman St Ste 311 Dover (19901) *(G-2897)*
Lady Lifters Gym 302 222-2321
  5734 Forrest Ave Dover (19904) *(G-2898)*
Ladybug Pest Management Inc 302 846-2295
  15307 Britt Ln Delmar (19940) *(G-1612)*
Ladycar LLC 984 389-9913
  8 The Grn Ste B Dover (19901) *(G-2899)*
Lafazia Construction 302 234-1300
  149 Belmont Dr Wilmington (19808) *(G-17788)*
Lafond Construction 302 430-2834
  24645 Springfield Rd Georgetown (19947) *(G-4400)*
Laima V Anthaney DMD 302 645-4726
  1200 Savannah Rd Lewes (19958) *(G-6175)*
Lake Forest School District 302 398-8945
  100 W Mispillion St Harrington (19952) *(G-4795)*
Lake Properties Group LLC 516 695-1441
  8 The Grn Dover (19901) *(G-2900)*
Lake Therapy Creations 410 920-7130
  2271 Sunset Lake Rd Newark (19702) *(G-11215)*
Lakeside Farms Inc 302 841-8843
  32206 Hastings Dr Laurel (19956) *(G-5543)*
Lakeside Greenhouses Inc (PA) 302 875-2457
  31494 Greenhouse Ln Laurel (19956) *(G-5544)*
Lakeside Physcl Thrapy Metodio 302 422-2518
  907 N Dupont Blvd Milford (19963) *(G-7970)*
Lakeside Physical Therapy LLC 302 280-6920
  404 E Front St Laurel (19956) *(G-5545)*
Lakpura LLC 302 786-0908
  1201 N Orange St Ste 7160 Wilmington (19801) *(G-17789)*
Laksh Cybersecurity & Def LLC 224 258-6564
  1201 N Orange St Cmmrc Wilmington (19801) *(G-17790)*
Lamart Drywall LLC 302 723-8751
  32 Cahalan Rd New Castle (19720) *(G-9294)*
Lambdatest Inc 678 701-3618
  919 N Market St Ste 950 Wilmington (19801) *(G-17791)*
Lambden Bus Service LLC 302 629-4358
  10174 Airport Rd Seaford (19973) *(G-13256)*
Lambert Kishayra 215 287-6252
  24 Keith St Newark (19713) *(G-11216)*
Lambro Technologies LLC 302 351-2559
  206 Kirk Ave Wilmington (19803) *(G-17792)*
Lambs of Zion Daycare 302 252-6440
  20 Harrow Pl Wilmington (19805) *(G-17793)*
Lamer Group LLC (PA) 302 893-0500
  3422 Old Capitol Trl Ste 79 Wilmington (19808) *(G-17794)*
Lamont Josey Lcsw 302 559-6654
  219 Edgewood Dr Wilmington (19809) *(G-17795)*
Lan Chester Sheds Gazebos 302 653-7392
  28 S Dupont Blvd Smyrna (19977) *(G-13795)*
Lan-Tech Inc 877 311-1030
  2093 Philadelphia Pike Ste 2001 Claymont (19703) *(G-1211)*
Lance Technologies LLC 404 934-4730
  1007 N Orange St Ste 1382 Wilmington (19801) *(G-17796)*
Land Lock LLC 302 747-6124
  600 N Broad St Middletown (19709) *(G-7287)*
Land Tech Associates Inc 301 277-8878
  36308 Royal Tern Dr Selbyville (19975) *(G-13560)*
Landell Labs LLC 917 722-5166
  651 N Broad St Ste 201 Middletown (19709) *(G-7288)*
Landex LLC (PA) 903 293-9466
  254 Chapman Rd Ste 208 Newark (19702) *(G-11217)*
Landings 302 233-8421
  479 Chevron St Dover (19902) *(G-2901)*

Landis Ltd 302 656-9024
  420 B And O Ln Wilmington (19804) *(G-17797)*
Landis Rath & Cobb LLP 302 467-4400
  919 N Market St Ste 1800 Wilmington (19801) *(G-17798)*
Landmark Associates of Del 302 645-7070
  9 Bradford Ln Lewes (19958) *(G-6176)*
Landmark Engineering Inc (PA) 302 323-9377
  200 Continental Dr Ste 400 Newark (19713) *(G-11218)*
Landmark Engineering Inc 302 734-9597
  200 Continental Dr Ste 400 Newark (19713) *(G-11219)*
Landmark Homes 302 388-8557
  68 Representative Ln Dover (19904) *(G-2902)*
Landmark Parking Inc (DH) 302 651-3610
  1205 N Orange St Wilmington (19801) *(G-17799)*
Landmark Science & Engineering, Newark *Also Called: Landmark Engineering Inc (G-11218)*
Landscape Contractor, Newark *Also Called: Dreamscape Design Cons LLC (G-10571)*
Landscaping 302 438-3471
  4627 Muggleton Rd Wilmington (19808) *(G-17800)*
Landslide Farm LLP 302 566-6418
  2638 Woodyard Rd Harrington (19952) *(G-4796)*
Landtech Associates, Selbyville *Also Called: Land Tech Associates Inc (G-13560)*
Landtech Land Survey, Ocean View *Also Called: Landtech LLC (G-12536)*
Landtech LLC 302 539-2366
  118 Atlantic Ave Ocean View (19970) *(G-12536)*
Landville Group LLC (PA) 727 557-6149
  16192 Coastal Hwy Lewes (19958) *(G-6177)*
Lane Builders LLC 302 645-5555
  1009 Kings Hwy Lewes (19958) *(G-6178)*
Lane Builders Inc 302 644-1182
  1009 Road 268 Harbeson (19951) *(G-4705)*
Lane Carpet Company, Newark *Also Called: L & L Carpet Discount Ctrs Inc (G-11205)*
Lane Group V LLC 302 652-7663
  119 Quintynnes Dr Wilmington (19807) *(G-17801)*
Lane Home Services Inc 302 652-7663
  119 Quintynnes Dr Wilmington (19807) *(G-17802)*
Lane Roofing, Wilmington *Also Called: Lane Home Services Inc (G-17802)*
Lane Roofing & Exteriors, Wilmington *Also Called: Lane Group V LLC (G-17801)*
Lane Sign Inc 610 558-2630
  2632 Bellows Dr Wilmington (19810) *(G-17803)*
Lang Development Group LLC 302 731-1340
  100 Dean Dr Newark (19711) *(G-11220)*
Lang Development Group LLC (PA) 302 731-1340
  100 Dean Dr Newark (19711) *(G-11221)*
Langdon Group LLC (PA) 240 578-5400
  8 The Grn Ste A Dover (19901) *(G-2903)*
Language Liaisons LLC 302 545-4257
  9 Wellington Rd Wilmington (19803) *(G-17804)*
Lank Johnson and Tull (PA) 302 422-3308
  268 Milford Harrington Hwy Milford (19963) *(G-7971)*
Lank Johnson and Tull 302 629-9543
  521 N Market Street Ext Seaford (19973) *(G-13257)*
Lanning Woodworks 302 353-4726
  2404 Overlook Dr Wilmington (19810) *(G-17805)*
Lantana Veterinary Center Inc 302 234-3275
  306 Lantana Dr Hockessin (19707) *(G-5275)*
Lantech-It, Claymont *Also Called: Lan-Tech Inc (G-1211)*
Lantransit Enterprises LLC 302 722-4800
  16192 Coastal Hwy Lewes (19958) *(G-6179)*
Lanxess Corporation 267 205-1969
  200 Powder Mill Rd Wilmington (19803) *(G-17806)*
Lanza Silvano MD 302 656-3305
  104 Stone Tower Ln Wilmington (19803) *(G-17807)*
Laohio Holdings LLC 302 200-9685
  16192 Coastal Hwy Lewes (19958) *(G-6180)*
Lardear Anne Otr/L 302 478-7022
  2602 Deepwood Dr Wilmington (19810) *(G-17808)*
Larger Story Inc 302 834-5712
  117 Shannon Blvd Middletown (19709) *(G-7289)*
Larimore Inc 302 632-3618
  2504 High Stump Rd Harrington (19952) *(G-4797)*
Larkins Bus Service LLC 302 653-5855
  512 S Bassett St Clayton (19938) *(G-1383)*

(PA)=Parent Co (HQ)=Headquarters (DH)=Div Headquarters

Larosa & Associates	302 250-4283
1225 N King St Ste 802 Wilmington (19801) *(G-17809)*	
Larrimore Logistics LLC	302 265-2290
10879 Heritage Rd Lincoln (19960) *(G-6679)*	
Larry Baker LLC	302 703-2127
26279 W Mallard Rd Millsboro (19966) *(G-8344)*	
Larry Coverdale	302 855-9305
120 S King St Georgetown (19947) *(G-4401)*	
Larry Hill Farms Inc	302 875-0886
Rt 1 Box 518 Delmar (19940) *(G-1613)*	
Larry Hill Farms LLC	302 245-6657
36292 Old Stage Rd Delmar (19940) *(G-1614)*	
Larry R Glazerman M D	302 655-7296
625 N Shipley St Wilmington (19801) *(G-17810)*	
Larry Shelton	678 948-6096
128 Sunset Blvd New Castle (19720) *(G-9295)*	
Larry's Custom Drywall, Newark *Also Called: Custom Drywall Inc (G-10367)*	
Larrys Building	302 670-8803
11404 Abbys Way Bridgeville (19933) *(G-724)*	
Larsen Landis	302 475-3175
2520 Silverside Rd Wilmington (19810) *(G-17811)*	
Larson Engineering Inc	302 731-7434
910 S Chapel St Ste 200 Newark (19713) *(G-11222)*	
Las Quality Tree Service LLC	302 981-3243
12 Glezman Dr Newark (19702) *(G-11223)*	
Laseana Ford	215 201-8070
2033 Rivers Dr Newark (19702) *(G-11224)*	
Laser & Plastic Surgery Center	302 674-4865
200 Banning St Ste 230 Dover (19904) *(G-2904)*	
Laser Images of Delaware Inc	302 836-8610
100 E Scotland Dr Bear (19701) *(G-338)*	
Laser Marking Works LLC	786 307-6203
3511 Silverside Rd # 105 Wilmington (19810) *(G-17812)*	
Lasercomp Ta, Historic New Castle *Also Called: Ta Instruments-Waters LLC (G-5080)*	
Lasers Edge Inc	302 479-5997
3505 Silverside Rd 201c Wilmington (19810) *(G-17813)*	
Lash Beauty Bar	302 827-2160
34005 Wescoats Rd Unit 3 Lewes (19958) *(G-6181)*	
Lashedbyindie LLC	267 734-4850
400 Isabelle Isle Apt 304 Dover (19904) *(G-2905)*	
Last Chance Ranch	518 369-9451
20 Montchanin Rd Wilmington (19807) *(G-17814)*	
Last Nickel Inn LLC	302 945-4880
10 Valley Rd Millsboro (19966) *(G-8345)*	
Last Tangle Salon and Spa	302 653-6638
76 E Glenwood Ave Smyrna (19977) *(G-13796)*	
Lasting Impression Inc A	302 762-9200
504 Philadelphia Pike Wilmington (19809) *(G-17815)*	
Lasting Looks	302 635-7327
447 Hockessin Cors Hockessin (19707) *(G-5276)*	
Latam Corporate Services LLC	301 375-0714
8 The Grn Ste B Dover (19901) *(G-2906)*	
Latham Building Group, Wilmington *Also Called: Tim Latham (G-20327)*	
Latham Logistics	215 760-4724
101 Edgar Rd Townsend (19734) *(G-14025)*	
Latin American Cmnty Ctr Corp	302 655-7338
403 N Van Buren St Wilmington (19805) *(G-17816)*	
LATIN AMERICAN COMMUNITY CENTE, Wilmington *Also Called: Latin American Cmnty Ctr Corp (G-17816)*	
Latin Chat Services	302 249-4151
111 N Race St Georgetown (19947) *(G-4402)*	
Latinicida Inc	302 277-6645
16 Ashkirk Pl Newark (19702) *(G-11225)*	
Latitude Sh LLC	712 481-2400
3 Germay Dr Ste 4 # 4438 Wilmington (19804) *(G-17817)*	
Lattanzio Electrical Cntrctng	302 685-0711
3234 Brookline Rd Wilmington (19808) *(G-17818)*	
Lattice Industries Inc	708 702-4664
1212 N King St Wilmington (19801) *(G-17819)*	
Lattice Social LLC	916 580-9951
1201 N Orange St Ste 600 Wilmington (19801) *(G-17820)*	
Lau & Assoc Ltd	302 792-5955
20 Montchanin Rd Ste 110 Wilmington (19807) *(G-17821)*	
Laudato Home Improvements LLC	610 656-2944
28226 Sloop Ave Millsboro (19966) *(G-8346)*	
Laughing Horse LLC	917 513-5255
16192 Coastal Hwy Lewes (19958) *(G-6182)*	
Launcharm Inc	320 520-3818
651 N Broad St Ste 206 Middletown (19709) *(G-7290)*	
Laundry Love Services LLC	302 367-7075
24a Trolley Sq Wilmington (19806) *(G-17822)*	
Laura B Moylan MD	302 674-0223
200 Banning St Ste 320 Dover (19904) *(G-2907)*	
Laura Castillo	302 734-5861
885 S Governors Ave Dover (19904) *(G-2908)*	
Laura D Halley MS CCC-Slp	302 738-0692
56 Millwright Dr Newark (19711) *(G-11226)*	
Laura J Manfield Do	302 999-0137
4512 Kirkwood Hwy Wilmington (19808) *(G-17823)*	
Laura M Gravelin M D	302 734-1414
200 Banning St Ste 340 Dover (19904) *(G-2909)*	
Lauras Child Care	302 690-1283
4 Pine Grove Ln Hockessin (19707) *(G-5277)*	
LAUREL ADULT DAY CARE, Laurel *Also Called: Laurel Senior Center Inc (G-5552)*	
Laurel Bridge Software Inc	302 453-0222
500 Creek View Rd Ste 200 Newark (19711) *(G-11227)*	
Laurel Community Hardware Inc	302 598-0454
420 Draper Ln Middletown (19709) *(G-7291)*	
Laurel Dental	302 875-4271
10250 Stone Creek Dr Unit 1 Laurel (19956) *(G-5546)*	
Laurel DMV North Growout Off, Laurel *Also Called: Perdue Farms Inc (G-5575)*	
Laurel Grain Company	302 875-4231
10717 Georgetown Rd Laurel (19956) *(G-5547)*	
Laurel Highschool Wellness Ctr	302 875-6164
1133 S Central Ave Laurel (19956) *(G-5548)*	
Laurel Linen Service Inc	804 732-3315
17 Harbor View Dr New Castle (19720) *(G-9296)*	
Laurel Lions Club Foundation	302 875-9178
Laurel (19956) *(G-5549)*	
Laurel Medical Group	302 875-7753
1124 S Central Ave Laurel (19956) *(G-5550)*	
Laurel Oak Capitl Partners LLC	302 658-7581
Corportion Trust Ctr 1209 R Ation Trust Ct Wilmington (19801) *(G-17824)*	
Laurel Redevelopment Corp	302 875-0601
202 E Front St Laurel (19956) *(G-5551)*	
Laurel Senior Center Inc	302 875-2536
113 N Central Ave Laurel (19956) *(G-5552)*	
Laurel Storage Center, Lewes *Also Called: Love Creek Marina MBL Hm Site (G-6225)*	
Laurel Tire Center, Laurel *Also Called: Ssmmd LLC (G-5606)*	
Lauri Brockson	302 383-0147
680 S College Ave Newark (19713) *(G-11228)*	
Laurie B Jacobs	302 764-7714
708 Foulk Rd Ste 2 Wilmington (19803) *(G-17825)*	
Lavante N Dorsey & Assoc LLC	302 956-9188
256 Chapman Rd Ste 203 Newark (19702) *(G-11229)*	
Lavish Nail Spa LLC	302 829-3008
2068 Naamans Rd Wilmington (19810) *(G-17826)*	
Lavoisier Inc	302 446-3244
8 The Grn Ste 10885 Dover (19901) *(G-2910)*	
Lavond Mackey	484 466-8055
2808 N Jefferson St Apt 1 Wilmington (19802) *(G-17827)*	
Law Firm	302 472-4900
702 N King St Ste 600 Wilmington (19801) *(G-17828)*	
Law of Michele D	302 234-8600
724 Yorklyn Rd Hockessin (19707) *(G-5278)*	
Law Offces Murray Phillips Gay	302 855-9300
215 E Market St Georgetown (19947) *(G-4403)*	
Law Office Daniel C Herr LLC	302 595-9084
1225 N King St Ste 1000 Wilmington (19801) *(G-17829)*	
Law Office Jnnfer Kate M Arnso	302 655-4600
8 E 13th St Wilmington (19801) *(G-17830)*	
Law Office Laura A Yiengst LLC	302 264-9780
314 S State St Dover (19901) *(G-2911)*	

ALPHABETIC SECTION — Learning Is Fundamental Child

Law Office of Andrew Whitehead.. 302 248-2000
   5 W Market St Georgetown (19947) *(G-4404)*

Law Office of Ej Fornias PA... 302 656-2829
   615 W 18th St Wilmington (19802) *(G-17831)*

Law Office of Melissa Green.. 302 998-2049
   910 W Basin Rd Ste 100 New Castle (19720) *(G-9297)*

Law Office of Michael Bednash.. 302 838-9077
   100 Biddle Ave Ste 104 Newark (19702) *(G-11230)*

Law Office of Rbert I Msten Jr... 302 358-2044
   500 Creek View Rd Ste 304 Newark (19711) *(G-11231)*

Law Office of Robert Valihura.. 302 426-1313
   5 Serenity Ln Wilmington (19802) *(G-17832)*

Law Office of Shauna T Hagan... 302 651-7999
   1907 Delaware Ave Wilmington (19806) *(G-17833)*

Law Office Parsons Robinson PA, Ocean View Also Called: Parsons & Robinson PA *(G-12557)*

Law Offices Doroshow Pasquele, Dover Also Called: Doroshow Psqale Krwitz Sgel Bh *(G-2327)*

Law Offices Gary R Dodge PA.. 302 674-5400
   250 Beiser Blvd Ste 202 Dover (19904) *(G-2912)*

Law Offices of Sean M Lynn PA... 302 734-2000
   308 S State St Dover (19901) *(G-2913)*

Law Offices Patrick Scanlon PA... 302 424-1996
   203 Ne Front St Milford (19963) *(G-7972)*

Lawall Prosthetics - Orthotics.. 302 677-0693
   514 N Dupont Hwy Dover (19901) *(G-2914)*

Lawall Prosthetics & Orthotics, Wilmington Also Called: Harry J Lawall & Son Inc *(G-17064)*

Lawall Prsthtics - Orthtics In (PA)... 302 427-3668
   1822 Augustine Cut Off Wilmington (19803) *(G-17834)*

Lawfully Yours, Wilmington Also Called: K&B Investors LLC *(G-17631)*

Lawing Musical Products LLC... 302 533-7548
   416 Paper Mill Rd Newark (19711) *(G-11232)*

Lawn Doctor of Newark, Newark Also Called: Absolutely Green Inc *(G-9746)*

Lawnworks Inc.. 302 368-5699
   667 Dawson Dr Ste D Newark (19713) *(G-11233)*

Lawrence A Louie DMD.. 302 674-5437
   250 Beiser Blvd Ste 101 Dover (19904) *(G-2915)*

Lawrence Agencies Inc.. 302 995-6936
   113 Kirkwood Sq Wilmington (19808) *(G-17835)*

Lawrence Boone Selections LLC... 757 602-5173
   434 Brandywine Dr Bear (19701) *(G-339)*

Lawrence E Haug III.. 302 222-7979
   101 Pin Oak Ct Felton (19943) *(G-3994)*

Lawrence Kennedy.. 302 533-5880
   262 Chapman Rd Ste 107 Newark (19702) *(G-11234)*

Lawrence Legates Masnry Co Inc.. 302 422-8043
   2891 Milford Harrington Hwy Milford (19963) *(G-7973)*

Lawrence M Lewandoski MD... 302 698-1100
   4601 S Dupont Hwy Ste 2 Dover (19901) *(G-2916)*

Lawson Firm LLC.. 302 212-0655
   402 Rehoboth Ave Rehoboth Beach (19971) *(G-12827)*

Lawson Home Services LLC... 302 684-3418
   115 Atlantic Ave Milton (19968) *(G-8653)*

Lawter Planning Group Inc... 302 736-6065
   1305 S Governors Ave Dover (19904) *(G-2917)*

Lawyerland... 757 805-6817
   1209 N Orange St Wilmington (19801) *(G-17836)*

Layercake, Newark Also Called: Layercake LLC *(G-11235)*

Layercake LLC.. 571 449-7538
   42 Hawthorne Ave Newark (19711) *(G-11235)*

Layton Builders... 302 491-4571
   2135 Milford Harrington Hwy Milford (19963) *(G-7974)*

Laytons Umbrellas.. 302 249-1958
   35527 Jami Ave Laurel (19956) *(G-5553)*

Laz Parking.. 302 654-7730
   101 N French St Wilmington (19801) *(G-17837)*

Lazybones Inc.. 302 530-7114
   11 Brighton Way Bear (19701) *(G-340)*

Lbg Homes Inc... 302 360-0300
   33334 Main St Dagsboro (19939) *(G-1474)*

Lbg Homes LLC.. 302 542-4221
   10912 County Seat Hwy Laurel (19956) *(G-5554)*

Lbm Painting LLC... 302 569-1506
   9204 E Mayhew Dr Lincoln (19960) *(G-6680)*

Lc Associates LLC.. 302 235-2500
   726 Yorklyn Rd Ste 150 Hockessin (19707) *(G-5279)*

Lc Construction Florida Inc.. 302 429-8700
   105 North Rd Wilmington (19809) *(G-17838)*

LC Distributors Inc... 484 326-9805
   950 Ridge Rd Ste E1 Claymont (19703) *(G-1212)*

Lc Homes.. 302 376-7004
   1002 Bilboa Ct Townsend (19734) *(G-14026)*

Lc Homes Inc... 302 429-8700
   105 Foulk Rd Wilmington (19803) *(G-17839)*

Lc Management.. 302 439-3523
   590 Naamans Rd Claymont (19703) *(G-1213)*

Lc Ranch LLC... 302 654-3600
   20 Montchanin Rd Ste 250 Wilmington (19807) *(G-17840)*

LCB Consulting Inc... 302 836-1396
   204 Somerton Ct Bear (19701) *(G-341)*

Lcdi, Dover Also Called: Lime Ccnut Data Intllgnce Lcdi *(G-2949)*

Lcsw Ceap LLC.. 302 824-0290
   1803 Breen Ln Wilmington (19810) *(G-17841)*

Ldmasonry... 302 270-3386
   1665 Sandbox Rd Harrington (19952) *(G-4798)*

Le Artist Lucratif N Amer LLC... 438 223-3788
   16192 Coastal Hwy Lewes (19958) *(G-6183)*

Le Herbe LLC (PA)... 949 317-1100
   1209 N Orange St Wilmington (19801) *(G-17842)*

Le Luxe Nuit.. 855 535-8935
   300 Delaware Ave Lbby Wilmington (19801) *(G-17843)*

Le Salone Hair Salon... 302 384-6788
   68 Briarcliff Dr New Castle (19720) *(G-9298)*

Le-Gen Medical LLC... 216 496-7113
   915 Westover Rd Wilmington (19807) *(G-17844)*

Lead Economy LLC... 914 355-1671
   8 The Grn Ste 8162 Dover (19901) *(G-2918)*

Lead Stock... 424 306-2700
   207 W Loockerman St Dover (19904) *(G-2919)*

Leadership Institute Inc... 302 368-7292
   76 Omega Dr Newark (19713) *(G-11236)*

Leadific Solutions LLC.. 866 265-0771
   850 New Burton Rd Ste 201 Dover (19904) *(G-2920)*

Leading Communication Contrs, New Castle Also Called: Prince Telecom LLC *(G-9494)*

Leadsrain, Wilmington Also Called: Aum LLC *(G-14641)*

Leager Construction Inc.. 302 653-8021
   732 Smyrna Landing Rd Smyrna (19977) *(G-13797)*

League of Wmen Vters New Cstle... 302 571-8948
   2400 W 17th St Rm 1 Wilmington (19806) *(G-17845)*

Leah & Alain Lebec Foundation.. 800 839-1754
   501 Silverside Rd Wilmington (19809) *(G-17846)*

Leak Stoppers LLC.. 302 236-1652
   29029 Lewes Georgetown Hwy Lewes (19958) *(G-6184)*

Leallure LLC.. 302 386-8886
   15b Trolley Sq Wilmington (19806) *(G-17847)*

Leanscout Inc.. 628 236-9599
   2035 Sunset Lake Rd Ste B2 Newark (19702) *(G-11237)*

Learn Game LLC (PA)... 484 841-9709
   221 N Broad St Ste 3a Middletown (19709) *(G-7292)*

Learn The Game App, Middletown Also Called: Learn Game LLC *(G-7292)*

Learn360, Wilmington Also Called: Infobase Holdings Inc *(G-17329)*

Learning Center At Madison St, Wilmington Also Called: Learning Ctr At Madison St LLC *(G-17848)*

Learning Circle Child Care... 302 834-1473
   765 Old Porter Rd Bear (19701) *(G-342)*

Learning Core LLC... 628 600-9644
   16192 Coastal Hwy Lewes (19958) *(G-6185)*

Learning Ctr At Madison St LLC... 302 543-7588
   600 N Madison St Wilmington (19801) *(G-17848)*

Learning Express Preschool... 302 737-8990
   300 Darling St Newark (19702) *(G-11238)*

Learning Is Fundamental Child... 302 653-1047
   281 Blackbird Greenspring Rd Smyrna (19977) *(G-13798)*

Learning Tree Academy ... 400 N Ramunno Dr Middletown (19709) *(G-7293)* ... 302 449-1711

Learning Years Preschool ... 302 241-4781
2 Riverside Rd Dover (19904) *(G-2921)*

Learning4 Lrng Professionals ... 302 994-0451
317 E Christian St Wilmington (19804) *(G-17849)*

Lechia Inc ... 302 261-5733
8 The Grn Ste 11532 Dover (19901) *(G-2922)*

Led Company Intl Llc ... 302 668-8370
3801 Kennett Pike D204 Wilmington (19807) *(G-17850)*

Led Company, The, Wilmington Also Called: Led Company Intl Llc *(G-17850)*

Led Sign City LLC ... 866 343-4011
3422 Old Capitol Trl Wilmington (19808) *(G-17851)*

Ledtolight (PA) ... 941 323-6664
Trolley Sq Ste 20c Wilmington (19806) *(G-17852)*

Lee Ann Wilkinson Group ... 302 645-6664
16698 Kings Hwy Ste A Lewes (19958) *(G-6186)*

Lee Bell Inc (HQ) ... 302 477-3930
3411 Silverside Rd Ste 200 Wilmington (19810) *(G-17853)*

Lee Lynn Inc ... 302 678-9978
1020 S State St Dover (19901) *(G-2923)*

Lee M Dennis MD ... 302 735-1888
960 Forest St Dover (19904) *(G-2924)*

Lee Mc Neill Associates ... 302 593-6172
1302 Grinnell Rd Wilmington (19803) *(G-17854)*

Lee Nails ... 302 674-5001
63 Greentree Dr Dover (19904) *(G-2925)*

Lee Sells Houses Team ... 302 516-7674
5700 Kirkwood Hwy Ste 101 Wilmington (19808) *(G-17855)*

Leeber Limited USA ... 302 733-0991
420 Corporate Blvd Newark (19702) *(G-11239)*

Leeman Electric ... 302 737-1753
102 Dawes Ct Newark (19702) *(G-11240)*

Lees Best Car Wash ... 302 328-0770
194 S Dupont Hwy New Castle (19720) *(G-9299)*

Lefrak Trust Company ... 302 656-2390
1105 N Market St Ste 801 Wilmington (19801) *(G-17856)*

Left For Dead ... 302 684-4320
22350 Reynolds Pond Rd Ellendale (19941) *(G-3926)*

Leftys Alley & Eats ... 302 864-6000
36450 Plaza Blvd Lewes (19958) *(G-6187)*

Leftys Alley & Eats ... 302 344-5858
75 Kings Creek Cir Rehoboth Beach (19971) *(G-12828)*

Legacy Contractors LLC ... 302 442-8817
6002 Vicky Dr Newark (19702) *(G-11241)*

Legacy Distilling LLC ... 302 983-1269
106 W Commerce St Smyrna (19977) *(G-13799)*

Legacy Foods LLC ... 302 656-5540
915 S Heald St Wilmington (19801) *(G-17857)*

Legacy Global Developments LLC ... 310 929-9862
8 The Grn Ste A Dover (19901) *(G-2926)*

Legacy Labs Inc ... 302 550-9966
300 Delaware Ave Ste 210275 Wilmington (19801) *(G-17858)*

Legacy Martial Arts ... 302 345-8515
32 Yale Ave New Castle (19720) *(G-9300)*

Legacy Tattoo ... 302 502-2163
1504 E Newport Pike Wilmington (19804) *(G-17859)*

Legacy Trust Company NA ... 302 252-9991
919 N Market St Ste 740a Wilmington (19801) *(G-17860)*

Legacy Vulcan ... 302 875-0748
28272 Landfill Ln Georgetown (19947) *(G-4405)*

Legacy Vulcan LLC ... 302 875-5733
14208 County Seat Hwy Seaford (19973) *(G-13258)*

Legal Aid, Wilmington Also Called: Community Legal Aid Society *(G-15563)*

Legal Services Corp Delaware ... 302 575-0408
100 W 10th St Wilmington (19801) *(G-17861)*

Legal Services of Delaware (PA) ... 302 575-0408
100 W 10th St Ste 203 Wilmington (19801) *(G-17862)*

Legaledge Software ... 302 761-9304
1218 Hillside Blvd Wilmington (19803) *(G-17863)*

Legalnature LLC (PA) ... 888 881-1139
8 The Grn Ste 1 Dover (19901) *(G-2927)*

Legend Enterprises LLC ... 267 278-9892
1857 Pulaski Hwy Bear (19701) *(G-343)*

Legend Transportation LLC ... 215 713-7472
323 Wooddale Ave New Castle (19720) *(G-9301)*

Legends of Venari Inc ... 226 338-6622
2803 Philadelphia Pike Claymont (19703) *(G-1214)*

Leggs Hanes Bali Playtex Otlt ... 302 227-8943
36454 Seaside Outlet Dr Rehoboth Beach (19971) *(G-12829)*

Legion Sports Performance ... 302 543-4922
109 Rogers Rd Ste 1 Wilmington (19801) *(G-17864)*

Legion Transformation Center ... 302 464-1081
128 Patriot Dr Unit 8 Middletown (19709) *(G-7294)*

Legion Transformation Center ... 302 533-6178
130 Executive Dr Ste 5 Newark (19702) *(G-11242)*

Legion Transformation Ctr LLC ... 302 543-4922
97 Galewood Rd Wilmington (19803) *(G-17865)*

Legion Trnsfrmtion Ctr Wlmngto ... 302 543-4922
109 Rogers Rd Wilmington (19801) *(G-17866)*

Legist Media Ltd ... 302 655-2730
605 N Market St Fl 2 Wilmington (19801) *(G-17867)*

Legit Global Inc ... 661 444-9085
254 Chapman Rd Ste 208 Newark (19702) *(G-11243)*

Legit Marketplace Intl LLC ... 929 273-0505
2055 Limestone Rd Wilmington (19808) *(G-17868)*

Legree & Fmly Investments LLC ... 302 245-5218
19266 Cstl Hwy Unit 4-112 Rehoboth Beach (19971) *(G-12830)*

Legum & Norman Mid-West LLC ... 302 537-9499
44 Edgewater House Rd Bethany Beach (19930) *(G-614)*

Legum & Norman Mid-West LLC ... 302 227-8448
12000 Old Vine Blvd Unit 114 Lewes (19958) *(G-6188)*

Legum & Norman Realty, Lewes Also Called: Legum & Norman Mid-West LLC *(G-6188)*

Lehanes Bus Service Inc ... 302 328-7100
1705 Wilmington Rd Historic New Castle (19720) *(G-5016)*

Lehigh Testing Laboratories ... 302 328-0500
308 W Basin Rd New Castle (19720) *(G-9302)*

Leidig, Gilbert A MD, Newark Also Called: Cardiology Physicans PA Inc *(G-10141)*

Leightner Electrical Contracto ... 302 723-1507
21 Arden Ave New Castle (19720) *(G-9303)*

Leighton Communications ... 610 513-6930
235 Beau Tree Dr Wilmington (19810) *(G-17869)*

Leiluna LLC ... 813 512-2213
4023 Kennett Pike Ste 58301 Wilmington (19807) *(G-17870)*

Leiny Snacks ... 302 494-2499
3 Germay Dr Ste 7 Wilmington (19804) *(G-17871)*

Leisure Home Builders LLC ... 302 528-4873
96 Century Dr Smyrna (19977) *(G-13800)*

Leisure Pt MBL HM Pk Cmpground, Lewes Also Called: Pine Acres Inc *(G-6370)*

Leiters Tools LLC ... 302 538-3284
51 Saratoga Dr New Castle (19720) *(G-9304)*

Lekuche Autos & General Merch ... 302 887-6748
717a Pulaski Hwy Bear (19701) *(G-344)*

Lekue USA Inc ... 302 326-4805
802 Centerpoint Blvd Historic New Castle (19720) *(G-5017)*

Lel Wealth MGT & Tech Svc LLC ... 804 243-0009
4 Ascension Dr Wilmington (19808) *(G-17872)*

Lela Capital LLC ... 917 428-0304
37259 Fox Dr Ocean View (19970) *(G-12537)*

Leland Oakley ... 302 430-3403
785 Paradise Alley Rd Felton (19943) *(G-3995)*

Leland Oakley Welding ... 302 469-5746
93 Paradise Cove Way Felton (19943) *(G-3996)*

Lemon Fin- Vest Inc ... 905 442-8480
256 Chapman Rd Newark (19702) *(G-11244)*

Lemonface Technologies Corp ... 844 615-3666
16192 Coastal Hwy Lewes (19958) *(G-6189)*

Lempat Foods LLC ... 914 449-1803
19 Holly Cove Ln Dover (19901) *(G-2928)*

Lems Appliance Repair LLC ... 302 539-2200
109 S Main St Bridgeville (19933) *(G-725)*

Lenape Builders Inc ... 302 376-3971
671 S Carter Rd Ste 1 Smyrna (19977) *(G-13801)*

ALPHABETIC SECTION

Lenape Properties MGT Inc 302 426-0200
  903 N French St Ste 106 Wilmington (19801) *(G-17873)*

Lenar Detective Agency Inc 302 322-3700
  714 Grantham Ln New Castle (19720) *(G-9305)*

Lend Helping Hand Child C 302 521-5298
  1010 E 24th St Wilmington (19802) *(G-17874)*

Lending Manager Holdings LLC 888 501-0335
  152 E Main St Newark (19711) *(G-11245)*

Length Weave Bar 302 502-3171
  429 S Walnut St Wilmington (19801) *(G-17875)*

Lennihan Richard Jr MD Office 302 994-7821
  3317 Heritage Dr Wilmington (19808) *(G-17876)*

Lens Tolic LLC 800 343-5697
  7209 Lancaster Pike Hockessin (19707) *(G-5280)*

Lenzinifordelaware 302 836-6287
  517 Equinox Dr Bear (19701) *(G-345)*

Leon N Weiner & Associates Inc 302 798-3446
  1114 Andrea Ct Claymont (19703) *(G-1215)*

Leon N Weiner & Associates Inc 302 322-6323
  431 Old Forge Rd Ofc Ofc New Castle (19720) *(G-9306)*

Leon N Weiner & Associates Inc (PA) 302 656-1354
  One Fox Point Ctr 4 Denny Rd Wilmington (19809) *(G-17877)*

Leonard H Seltzer M D 302 229-8506
  1309 Veale Rd Ste 11 Wilmington (19810) *(G-17878)*

Leonard M Elzbeth T Tnnnbaum F 302 793-4917
  501 Silverside Rd Wilmington (19809) *(G-17879)*

Leonardo Charitable I LLC 302 571-1818
  220 Continental Dr Newark (19713) *(G-11246)*

Leonards Express Inc 302 426-0802
  300 Pigeon Point Rd New Castle (19720) *(G-9307)*

Leons Garden World Ej Inc 410 392-8630
  137 S Dupont Hwy New Castle (19720) *(G-9308)*

Leons Garden World Inc 302 999-9055
  5900 Kirkwood Hwy Wilmington (19808) *(G-17880)*

Leotech LLC 908 829-3813
  1201 N Market St Ste 111 Wilmington (19801) *(G-17881)*

Leounes Catered Affairs 302 547-3233
  511 Saint George Dr Wilmington (19809) *(G-17882)*

Leounes Kirsten 302 229-5029
  1016 Brandywine Dr Bear (19701) *(G-346)*

Leroy A Tice Esquire PA 302 658-6901
  1203 N Orange St Wilmington (19801) *(G-17883)*

Leroy Betts Construction Inc 302 284-9193
  4020 Hopkins Cemetery Rd Felton (19943) *(G-3997)*

Les Nails 302 449-5290
  372 E Main St Middletown (19709) *(G-7295)*

Leslie Connor 302 479-5568
  3411 Silverside Rd # 100 Wilmington (19810) *(G-17884)*

Leslie Kopp Inc 302 541-5207
  33298 Coastal Hwy Bethany Beach (19930) *(G-615)*

Lessard Custom Homes 302 645-7444
  33673 E Hunters Run Lewes (19958) *(G-6190)*

Lessons Lrned Day Care Prschoo 302 777-2200
  207 N Union St Wilmington (19805) *(G-17885)*

Let US Lift It Inc 302 654-2221
  802 W 20th St Wilmington (19802) *(G-17886)*

Let's Have Fun Daycare, Newark *Also Called: Susan T Fischer (G-12135)*

Lets Gather LLC 607 210-0581
  8 The Grn Ste B Dover (19901) *(G-2929)*

Lets Get Green 302 633-4733
  849 Kiamensi Rd Wilmington (19804) *(G-17887)*

Letsbelegalcom 302 894-4357
  260 Chapman Rd Ste 201 Newark (19702) *(G-11247)*

Letterhead Inc 305 988-0808
  2093 Philadelphia Pike Ste 3050 Claymont (19703) *(G-1216)*

Leucine Inc 650 534-2101
  1013 Centre Rd Ste 403b Wilmington (19805) *(G-17888)*

Level & Clean LLC 302 616-1585
  57 Golden Eagle Dr Ocean View (19970) *(G-12538)*

Level Funded Hlth Partners LLC 847 310-8190
  9 E Loockerman St Ste 215 Dover (19901) *(G-2930)*

Level Up Consulting Group Inc 855 967-5550
  651 N Broad St Ste 205 # 4768 Middletown (19709) *(G-7296)*

Levels Express Logistics LLC 302 760-3750
  565 Harvest Grove Trl Dover (19901) *(G-2931)*

Levines Enterprises LLC 203 212-8441
  8 The Grn Dover (19901) *(G-2932)*

Lewes Body Works Inc 302 645-5595
  16205 New Rd Lewes (19958) *(G-6191)*

Lewes Building Co, The, Lewes *Also Called: Tlbc LLC (G-6564)*

Lewes Chiropractic Center 302 645-9171
  1527 Savannah Rd Lewes (19958) *(G-6192)*

Lewes Counseling LLC 302 430-2127
  32413 Lewes Georgetown Hwy Lewes (19958) *(G-6193)*

Lewes Dairy Inc 302 645-6281
  660 Pilottown Rd Lewes (19958) *(G-6194)*

Lewes Expressive Therapy 302 727-3275
  105 Dove Dr Lewes (19958) *(G-6195)*

Lewes Fishhouse & Produce Inc 302 827-4074
  17696 Coastal Hwy Lewes (19958) *(G-6196)*

Lewes Meineke 302 827-2054
  16753 Coastal Hwy Lewes (19958) *(G-6197)*

Lewes Montessori School 302 644-7482
  32234 Conleys Chapel Rd Lewes (19958) *(G-6198)*

Lewes Orthopedic Ctr 302 645-4939
  16704 Kings Hwy # 2 Lewes (19958) *(G-6199)*

LEWES SENIOR CENTER, Lewes *Also Called: Lewes Senior Citizens Center (G-6200)*

Lewes Senior Citizens Center 302 645-9293
  32083 Janice Rd Lewes (19958) *(G-6200)*

Lewes Spine Center LLC 302 231-4333
  18947 John J Williams Hwy Unit 311 Rehoboth Beach (19971) *(G-12831)*

Lewes Surgery Center 302 644-3466
  17015 Old Orchard Rd Unit 4 Lewes (19958) *(G-6201)*

Lewes Surgical and Med Assoc 302 945-9730
  32711 Long Neck Rd Millsboro (19966) *(G-8347)*

Lewes Walk-In Medical LLC 302 561-5429
  1103 La Grange Pkwy Newark (19702) *(G-11248)*

Lewes Wellness Center 302 313-9990
  20268 Plantations Rd Lewes (19958) *(G-6202)*

Lewes Yoga & Meditation Center 302 245-6133
  17605 Nassau Commons Blvd Unit B Lewes (19958) *(G-6203)*

Lewis CK Construction 443 910-1598
  2311 Ogletown Rd Newark (19711) *(G-11249)*

Lewis Educational Games, Wilmington *Also Called: Sandebbarnanricway Corp (G-19657)*

Lewis Environmental Group Inc 302 669-6010
  101 Carroll Dr New Castle (19720) *(G-9309)*

Lewis Lettering Co 610 209-0998
  15 Sussex Dr Lewes (19958) *(G-6204)*

Lewis Miller Inc 302 629-9895
  8957 Middleford Rd Seaford (19973) *(G-13259)*

Lewis Sand and Gravel LLC 302 238-0169
  38227 Firemans Rd Millsboro (19966) *(G-8348)*

Lexan Group LLC 704 900-0190
  254 Chapman Rd Ste 208 Newark (19702) *(G-11250)*

Lexatys LLC 302 715-5029
  10253 Stone Creek Dr # 1 Laurel (19956) *(G-5555)*

Lexatys,, Laurel *Also Called: Intelexmicro Inc (G-5535)*

Lexington Green Apartments 302 322-8959
  1201 Kingston Bldg Newark (19702) *(G-11251)*

Lexisnexis Risk Assets Inc (DH) 800 458-9410
  1105 N Market St Ste 501 Wilmington (19801) *(G-17889)*

Lhaug Painting, Felton *Also Called: Lawrence E Haug III (G-3994)*

Lhr-Fine Arts Studios 302 981-8553
  505 Marsh Rd Wilmington (19809) *(G-17890)*

Liberated World LLC 347 688-4943
  8 The Grn Ste 8 Dover (19901) *(G-2933)*

Liberto Development Ltd 302 698-1104
  1500 E Lebanon Rd Dover (19901) *(G-2934)*

Liberty Consultancy Firm LLC 302 493-4344
  1041 N Dupont Hwy Dover (19901) *(G-2935)*

Liberty Dalysis-Wilmington LLC (HQ) 302 429-0142
  913 Delaware Ave Wilmington (19806) *(G-17891)*

(PA)=Parent Co (HQ)=Headquarters (DH)=Div Headquarters

Liberty Elevator Experts LLC 302 650-4688
625 Barksdale Rd Ste 113 Newark (19711) *(G-11252)*

Liberty Elevator Experts LLC 844 542-3538
113 Barksdale Professional Ctr Newark (19711) *(G-11253)*

Liberty Mutual, Wilmington *Also Called: Chrissinger and Baumberger (G-15395)*

Liberty Pest Control LLC 302 734-1507
72 Lynnhaven Dr Dover (19904) *(G-2936)*

Liberty Tax 302 678-3101
1636 S Governors Ave Dover (19904) *(G-2937)*

Liberty Tax 302 526-1611
419 E Main St Middletown (19709) *(G-7297)*

Liberty Tax 302 543-8840
4538 Kirkwood Hwy Wilmington (19808) *(G-17892)*

Liberty Tax 302 304-8714
818 Maryland Ave Wilmington (19805) *(G-17893)*

Liberty Tax, Bear *Also Called: Tyne Sunderland LLC (G-544)*

Liberty Tax Service 302 762-1010
2618 Philadelphia Pike Claymont (19703) *(G-1217)*

Liberty Tax Service 302 404-2140
614 W Stein Hwy Seaford (19973) *(G-13260)*

Liberty Tax Service 302 270-4135
123 E Glenwood Ave Smyrna (19977) *(G-13802)*

Liberty Tax Service 302 691-9279
2005 N Market St Wilmington (19802) *(G-17894)*

Liberty Tax Service, Dover *Also Called: Slacum & Doyle Tax Service LLC (G-3575)*

Liberty Tax Service, Newark *Also Called: Kelly Robert & Assoc LLC (G-11151)*

Liberty Title Services 302 559-4500
919 N Market St Wilmington (19801) *(G-17895)*

Liberty Universal Tech Inc 404 719-4728
2055 Limestone Rd Ste 200c Wilmington (19808) *(G-17896)*

Liblab Inc 302 415-3344
251 Little Falls Dr Wilmington (19808) *(G-17897)*

Liborio-Louviers LLC 302 656-9400
903 N French St Wilmington (19801) *(G-17898)*

Lice Lifters Distribution LLC 864 680-4030
8 The Grn Ste R Dover (19901) *(G-2938)*

Licensing Assurance LLC 305 851-3545
16192 Coastal Hwy Lewes (19958) *(G-6205)*

Lids Corporation 302 736-8465
1365 N Dupont Hwy Ste 4018 Dover (19901) *(G-2939)*

Lie, Wilmington *Also Called: Loyalty Is Earned Inc (G-18015)*

Lieske E2e Home Hlth Care Inc 302 898-1563
53 Meadow Dr Middletown (19709) *(G-7298)*

Life At St Frncis Hlthcare Inc 302 660-3297
1072 Justison St Wilmington (19801) *(G-17899)*

Life Behavioral Hlth Consulta 302 312-6104
709 Ellen Dr Bear (19701) *(G-347)*

Life Choice 302 526-2080
240 Norwich Way Dover (19901) *(G-2940)*

LIfe Fndtion Love Is For Evr 302 660-1792
12 Deville Cir Wilmington (19808) *(G-17900)*

Life Force Eldercare Corp 302 737-4400
1203 Plly Drummond Off Pa Newark (19711) *(G-11254)*

Life Innovations 302 525-6521
260 Chapman Rd Ste 203e Newark (19702) *(G-11255)*

Life Net 302 855-0550
21479 Rudder Ln Georgetown (19947) *(G-4406)*

Life Reach / Eap Systems, Dover *Also Called: F H Everett & Associates Inc (G-2478)*

Life Sciences Intl LLC 603 436-9444
1209 N Orange St Wilmington (19801) *(G-17901)*

Life Solutions Inc 302 622-8292
1210 N King St Wilmington (19801) *(G-17902)*

Life Strong Fitness LLC 302 312-9673
216 W Old Squaw Rd Middletown (19709) *(G-7299)*

Life-Science AI LLC 438 833-8504
16192 Coastal Hwy Lewes (19958) *(G-6206)*

Lifehuse Erly Chldhood Ctr LLC 302 464-1105
101 Karins Blvd Townsend (19734) *(G-14027)*

Lifeline Bltmore MD Mllvlle De 410 262-0875
33367 Lone Cedar Lndg Millville (19967) *(G-8536)*

Lifenet Inc 973 698-6881
36871 Crooked Hammock Way Lewes (19958) *(G-6207)*

Liferithms Inc 770 885-6565
251 Little Falls Dr Wilmington (19808) *(G-17903)*

Lifescore Inc 808 780-4645
108 Patriot Dr Ste A Middletown (19709) *(G-7300)*

Lifesource Consulting Svcs LLC 302 257-6247
8 The Grn Ste 8155 Dover (19901) *(G-2941)*

Lifespan Development Centers, Wilmington *Also Called: Education Svcs Unlimited LLC (G-16298)*

Lifespan Health Science LLC 203 273-4037
251 Little Falls Dr Wilmington (19808) *(G-17904)*

Lifesquared Inc 415 475-9090
1679 S Dupont Hwy Dover (19901) *(G-2942)*

Lifestyle Communities LLC 302 376-3066
111 Patriot Dr Ste A Middletown (19709) *(G-7301)*

Lifestyle Document MGT Inc 302 856-6387
22277 Lewes Georgetown Hwy Georgetown (19947) *(G-4407)*

Lifestyle Fitness 302 998-2942
1319 Mckennans Church Rd Wilmington (19808) *(G-17905)*

Lifetime Financial Svcs LLC 302 678-1300
292 Evelyndale Dr Dover (19901) *(G-2943)*

Lifetime Skills Services LLC 302 378-2911
300 Brady Ln Middletown (19709) *(G-7302)*

Lifetouch, Dover *Also Called: Lifetouch Portrait Studios Inc (G-2944)*

Lifetouch, Newark *Also Called: Lifetouch Portrait Studios Inc (G-11256)*

Lifetouch Portrait Studios Inc 302 734-9870
5000 Dover Mall Dover (19901) *(G-2944)*

Lifetouch Portrait Studios Inc 302 453-8080
606 Christiana Mall Newark (19702) *(G-11256)*

Lifetour Solutions LLC 215 964-5000
300 Delaware Ave Ste 210 Wilmington (19801) *(G-17906)*

Liftoff Agent, Claymont *Also Called: Liftoff Agent Inc (G-1218)*

Liftoff Agent Inc 925 462-5001
2093 Philadelphia Pike # 3 Claymont (19703) *(G-1218)*

Lig Energy Solutions LLC 646 918-8232
1207 Delaware Ave Ste 1944 Wilmington (19801) *(G-17907)*

Light Action Inc 302 328-7800
1145 E 7th St Wilmington (19801) *(G-17908)*

Lightbox Jewelry Inc 833 270-3737
3500 S Dupont Hwy Dover (19901) *(G-2945)*

Lighthouse Cleaning, Lewes *Also Called: Tracy B Harris (G-6576)*

Lighthouse Construction Inc 302 677-1965
859 Golf Lane Ste1 Magnolia (19962) *(G-6759)*

Lighthouse Dance and Yoga LLC 302 564-7611
37473 Albatross Dr Selbyville (19975) *(G-13561)*

Lighthouse Masonry Inc 302 945-1392
20090 Beaver Dam Rd Lewes (19958) *(G-6208)*

Lighthouse Realty Group Inc 302 864-0952
5 Dove Ct Ocean View (19970) *(G-12539)*

Lighthouse Realty Group I 302 541-4440
782 Garfield Pkwy Ste 202 Bethany Beach (19930) *(G-616)*

Lighthuse Rest At Fshrmans Wha, Lewes *Also Called: M & P Adventures Inc (G-6232)*

Lightning Painting LLC 302 521-6033
326 Ellenwood Dr Middletown (19709) *(G-7303)*

Lightrun Inc 646 453-6616
1209 N Orange St Wilmington (19801) *(G-17909)*

Lightscapes Inc 302 798-5451
6603a Governor Printz Blvd Wilmington (19809) *(G-17910)*

Lightwave Logic Inc 302 737-6412
1 Innovation Way Ste 100 Newark (19711) *(G-11257)*

Lignolix Inc 516 660-2558
47 Foxtail Ct Newark (19711) *(G-11258)*

Liguori Morris & Reddin 302 678-9900
46 The Grn Dover (19901) *(G-2946)*

Liii Construction Co 302 429-8700
105 Foulk Rd Wilmington (19803) *(G-17911)*

Likehoop Inc (PA) 646 643-7738
8 The Grn Ste A Dover (19901) *(G-2947)*

Lil Einsteins Learning Academy 302 466-3003
201 Possum Park Rd Newark (19711) *(G-11259)*

Lil Kritters Childcare 302 362-9047
201 Ross St Seaford (19973) *(G-13261)*

Lil Red Hen Nursery Schl Inc.. 302 846-2777
    400 N Bi State Blvd Delmar (19940) *(G-1615)*

Lil' Einsteins Lrng Academy, Newark *Also Called: Excellent Educatn Daycare LLC* *(G-10684)*

Lila Keshav Hospitality LLC.. 302 696-2272
    315 Auto Park Dr Middletown (19709) *(G-7304)*

Lila Labs Inc... 949 371-3978
    600 N Broad St Ste 5-802 Middletown (19709) *(G-7305)*

Lilian USA LLC... 800 246-2677
    1201 N Orange St Ste 600 Wilmington (19801) *(G-17912)*

Lilly Fasteners & Customization Llc (PA)................................. 302 366-7640
    855 Dawson Dr Newark (19713) *(G-11260)*

Lily B LLC... 302 290-5223
    127 George Ct Bear (19701) *(G-348)*

Lily Intrnl Medicine Asscs LLC.. 302 424-1000
    811 Monroe Ter Dover (19904) *(G-2948)*

Lime Ccnut Data Intllgnce Lcdi... 302 272-2858
    8 The Grn Ste A Dover (19901) *(G-2949)*

Limen House Inc... 302 652-7969
    600 W 10th St Wilmington (19801) *(G-17913)*

Limestone Acres Maintenance... 302 222-8457
    2407 Darnay Ln Wilmington (19808) *(G-17914)*

Limestone Medical Aid Unit, Wilmington *Also Called: Limestone Medical Center Inc* *(G-17915)*

Limestone Medical Center Inc... 302 992-0500
    1941 Limestone Rd Ste 113 Wilmington (19808) *(G-17915)*

Limestone Nutrition... 302 397-8705
    4569 Kirkwood Hwy Wilmington (19808) *(G-17916)*

Limestone Open Mri LLC... 302 246-2001
    101 Becks Woods Dr Ste 103 Bear (19701) *(G-349)*

Limestone Open Mri LLC (PA).. 302 246-2001
    2060 Limestone Rd Wilmington (19808) *(G-17917)*

Limestone Veterinary Hospital.. 302 239-5415
    6102 Limestone Rd Hockessin (19707) *(G-5281)*

Limitless Consulting Mktg LLC... 302 743-0520
    207 S Gerald Dr Newark (19713) *(G-11261)*

Limitless Flames LLC... 302 559-8712
    3 Germay Dr Ste 4 Wilmington (19804) *(G-17918)*

Limo Exchange.. 302 322-1200
    800 Washington St Historic New Castle (19720) *(G-5018)*

Limo Exchange, The, Historic New Castle *Also Called: Limo Exchange* *(G-5018)*

Limousine Unlimited LLC.. 302 284-1100
    12600 S Dupont Hwy Felton (19943) *(G-3998)*

Linarducci & Butler PA.. 302 325-2400
    910 W Basin Rd Ste 100 New Castle (19720) *(G-9310)*

Lincare... 302 736-1210
    5 Maggies Way Ste 4 Dover (19901) *(G-2950)*

Lincare Inc... 302 424-8302
    7012 S Dupont Hwy Felton (19943) *(G-3999)*

Lincoln Community Hall Inc... 302 242-1747
    18881 Washington St Lincoln (19960) *(G-6681)*

Lincoln Financial, Laurel *Also Called: Lincoln Financial Advisors* *(G-5556)*

Lincoln Financial Advisors... 302 875-8300
    214 E Front St Laurel (19956) *(G-5556)*

Linda Brannock... 302 346-3124
    1671 S State St Dover (19901) *(G-2951)*

Linda Celestian Art Studio... 302 364-0278
    1808 Harvey Rd Wilmington (19810) *(G-17919)*

Linda Duffy.. 302 651-4000
    1600 Rockland Rd Wilmington (19803) *(G-17920)*

Linda L Silvis... 302 559-5577
    5700 Kirkwood Hwy Ste 206 Wilmington (19808) *(G-17921)*

Linda Lawton DPM... 302 659-0500
    1000 Smyrna Clayton Blvd Ste 3 Smyrna (19977) *(G-13803)*

Linda Lawton DPM... 302 659-0500
    665 S Carter Rd Unit 2 Smyrna (19977) *(G-13804)*

Linda McCormick... 443 987-2099
    200 Tyrone Ave Wilmington (19804) *(G-17922)*

Linda Putnam Day Care... 302 836-1033
    525 Deer Run Bear (19701) *(G-350)*

Linda Vista Real Estate... 302 313-1600
    18806 John J Williams Hwy # 2 Rehoboth Beach (19971) *(G-12832)*

Lindale Plumbing LLC.. 302 242-2493
    15020 Abbotts Pond Rd Greenwood (19950) *(G-4648)*

Lindas Angels Chldcare Dev Ctr... 302 328-3700
    6 Parkway Ct New Castle (19720) *(G-9311)*

Linde Gas & Equipment Inc... 302 654-8755
    2 Medori Blvd Wilmington (19801) *(G-17923)*

Linde North America... 302 654-9348
    315 Cherry Ln New Castle (19720) *(G-9312)*

Lindell Partners LLC.. 773 269-0837
    300 Delaware Ave Ste 210a Wilmington (19801) *(G-17924)*

Linden Building... 302 573-3705
    625 N Orange St Wilmington (19801) *(G-17925)*

Linden Hill Cleaners Inc... 302 368-9795
    4561 Linden Hill Rd Wilmington (19808) *(G-17926)*

Linden Hill Elementary Pta... 302 454-3406
    3415 Skyline Dr Wilmington (19808) *(G-17927)*

Linden Nails & Spa.. 302 510-4794
    4500 Linden Hill Rd Wilmington (19808) *(G-17928)*

Lindenberg Financial... 302 235-8672
    5301 Limestone Rd Ste 226 Wilmington (19808) *(G-17929)*

Lindner LLC... 302 827-2160
    34005 Wescoats Rd Unit 3 Lewes (19958) *(G-6209)*

Lindsay Mumford LLC.. 302 841-2309
    300 Coastal Hwy Unit 1 Fenwick Island (19944) *(G-4051)*

Lineage Auto Group L L C... 302 595-2119
    7 Marlin Ct New Castle (19720) *(G-9313)*

Lineage Bjj.. 201 788-8167
    6 E Market St Greenwood (19950) *(G-4649)*

Linens of The Week, New Castle *Also Called: Palace Laundry Inc* *(G-9445)*

Linguatext Ltd... 302 453-8695
    103 Walker Way Newark (19711) *(G-11262)*

Link Road Logistics Inc... 267 283-9370
    16192 Coastal Hwy Lewes (19958) *(G-6210)*

Linkers Inc... 408 757-0021
    8 The Grn Dover (19901) *(G-2952)*

Linkmeup Inc... 302 440-3393
    1007 N Orange St Fl 4 Wilmington (19801) *(G-17930)*

Linkside Apts LLC.. 302 697-0378
    56 W Birdie Ln Ste 5 Magnolia (19962) *(G-6760)*

Linkside LLC... 302 697-8312
    25 Flagstick Ln Magnolia (19962) *(G-6761)*

Linne Industries LLC... 302 454-1439
    11 Bridle Brook Ln Newark (19711) *(G-11263)*

Linx Realty 2 LLC (PA)... 888 233-8901
    8 The Grn Ste A Dover (19901) *(G-2953)*

Linx Security Inc.. 302 907-9848
    850 New Burton Rd Dover (19904) *(G-2954)*

Lion Electric Mfg USA Inc.. 833 512-5466
    2915 Ogletown Rd # 3965 Newark (19713) *(G-11264)*

Lion Totalcare Inc.. 610 444-1700
    9 Germay Dr Ste 200a Wilmington (19804) *(G-17931)*

Lions Group LLC.. 302 535-6584
    3435 Irish Hill Rd Magnolia (19962) *(G-6762)*

Lippstone Law Pllc.. 302 252-1481
    1 S Fawn Dr Newark (19711) *(G-11265)*

Lisa A Deleonardo... 302 234-3443
    614 Loveville Rd Hockessin (19707) *(G-5282)*

Lisa A Fagioletti DMD LLC... 302 514-9064
    25 W Commerce St Smyrna (19977) *(G-13805)*

Lisa Bartels... 302 856-9596
    10 N Front St Georgetown (19947) *(G-4408)*

Lisa Broadbent Insurance Inc.. 302 731-0044
    20 Polly Drummond Hill Rd Newark (19711) *(G-11266)*

Lisa Burroughs.. 302 454-8010
    500 Creek View Rd Ste 109 Newark (19711) *(G-11267)*

Lisa Harkins.. 302 388-2856
    3103i E Brookmyer Dr Milford (19963) *(G-7975)*

Lisa Insurtech LLC... 612 470-1009
    16192 Coastal Hwy Lewes (19958) *(G-6211)*

Lisa Johannsen.. 302 270-5082
    4485 Summit Bridge Rd Middletown (19709) *(G-7306)*

Lisa M Andersen..302 644-3668
   1201 Savannah Rd Lewes (19958) *(G-6212)*
Lisa Mathena Group...302 645-4804
   16154 Hudson Rd Milton (19968) *(G-8654)*
Lisa Owens Child Care, Wilmington Also Called: Maddix Owens Lillian *(G-18073)*
Lisa Prisco Pt..302 698-4256
   810 New Burton Rd Ste 2 Dover (19904) *(G-2955)*
Lisa R Savage..302 353-7052
   260 Chapman Rd Ste 100b Newark (19702) *(G-11268)*
Lisa R Shannon Lmt..302 468-9416
   5 Bridge Ct Middletown (19709) *(G-7307)*
Lisa Ryan Hobbs DPM...302 629-3000
   543 N Shipley St Ste C Seaford (19973) *(G-13262)*
Lisa Trabaudo Day Care..302 653-3529
   316 Lisa Ct Smyrna (19977) *(G-13806)*
Lissner & Associates LLC..302 777-4620
   310 High Ridge Rd Wilmington (19807) *(G-17932)*
Listonburg Solar LLC...412 979-6872
   1209 N Orange St Wilmington (19801) *(G-17933)*
Lit Xpress LLC..302 690-9520
   1914 Spearfish Ct Newark (19702) *(G-11269)*
Litcharts LLC..646 481-4807
   2711 Centerville Rd Ste 400 Wilmington (19808) *(G-17934)*
Lith AF Gamal Tru LLC..833 552-0181
   19266 Coastal Hwy Unit 4-109 Rehoboth Beach (19971) *(G-12833)*
Litho-Print Inc..302 239-1341
   205 S Pond Rd Hockessin (19707) *(G-5283)*
Lithos Carbon Inc..425 274-3276
   1111b S Governors Ave # 6084 Dover (19904) *(G-2956)*
Little Blessings Childcare..215 510-4514
   26 Glenrock Dr Claymont (19703) *(G-1219)*
Little Blessings Day Care..302 762-3600
   1 E 31st St Wilmington (19802) *(G-17935)*
Little Blessings Daycare..302 655-8962
   2010 N Market St Wilmington (19802) *(G-17936)*
Little Caboose The, Newark Also Called: Atlantic Dawn Ltd *(G-9934)*
Little Einsteins Preschool..302 933-0600
   28253 Dupont Blvd Millsboro (19966) *(G-8349)*
Little Folks Too Day Care..302 652-3420
   1318 N Market St Wilmington (19801) *(G-17937)*
Little Folks Too Day Care (PA)..................................302 652-1238
   1320 N Market St Wilmington (19801) *(G-17938)*
Little Friends Lrng Academy......................................302 655-0725
   122 Memorial Dr New Castle (19720) *(G-9314)*
Little Giggles..678 770-2089
   58 Charles Dr New Castle (19720) *(G-9315)*
Little Gym..302 856-2310
   23 Tidewater Dr Seaford (19973) *(G-13263)*
Little Gym of Ncc...302 543-5524
   4758 Limestone Rd Ste A Wilmington (19808) *(G-17939)*
Little Gym, The, Wilmington Also Called: Little Gym of Ncc *(G-17939)*
Little Hearts Child Care LLC.....................................302 442-5746
   111 W 22nd St Wilmington (19802) *(G-17940)*
Little Kids Swagg Lrng Ctr LLC.................................302 480-4404
   433 S Dupont Blvd Smyrna (19977) *(G-13807)*
Little League Baseball Inc...302 276-0375
   23 Blount Rd New Castle (19720) *(G-9316)*
Little League Baseball Inc...302 227-0888
   125 Beachfield Dr Rehoboth Beach (19971) *(G-12834)*
Little Learner Inc...302 798-5570
   41 N Avon Dr Claymont (19703) *(G-1220)*
Little Miracles Child Care Ctr...................................302 367-4838
   11 Christina Woods Ct Ste B Newark (19702) *(G-11270)*
Little People Big World...302 310-0965
   11 Ashkirk Pl Newark (19702) *(G-11271)*
Little People Child Dev..302 328-1481
   122 E Main St Christiana (19702) *(G-1003)*
Little People Child Dev Ctr 3....................................302 832-1891
   1169 S Dupont Hwy New Castle (19720) *(G-9317)*
Little People Day Care...302 528-4336
   17 Cole Blvd Middletown (19709) *(G-7308)*
Little Peoples College..302 998-4929
   3507 Old Capitol Trl Wilmington (19808) *(G-17941)*
Little Scholars Ctr..302 368-7584
   2050 S College Ave Newark (19702) *(G-11272)*
Little Scholars Learning Ctr.....................................302 656-8785
   2511 W 4th St Ste A Wilmington (19805) *(G-17942)*
Little School Inc..302 734-3040
   105 Mont Blanc Blvd Dover (19904) *(G-2957)*
Little Sisters of The Poor..302 368-5886
   185 Salem Church Rd Newark (19713) *(G-11273)*
Little Sprouts Learning Academ, Seaford Also Called: Karen Schreiber *(G-13243)*
Little Star Inc..302 995-2920
   5702 Kirkwood Hwy Wilmington (19808) *(G-17943)*
Little Steps Daycare...302 654-4867
   212 W 21st St Wilmington (19802) *(G-17944)*
Little Sunshines, New Castle Also Called: Shavone Loves Kids Day Care *(G-9565)*
Little Thresa P MD Fmly Mdcine, Dover Also Called: Theresa Little MD *(G-3674)*
Little Trooper Day Care..302 378-7355
   329 Senator Dr Middletown (19709) *(G-7309)*
Little World LLC..302 644-1530
   4 Henlopen Ct Lewes (19958) *(G-6213)*
Littljohn Blckston Hldings LLC..................................302 468-6680
   717 N Union St Unit 74 Wilmington (19805) *(G-17945)*
Lituation Creative Designs Inc..................................302 494-4399
   3201 N Jefferson St Wilmington (19802) *(G-17946)*
Lituation Entertainment...302 543-6424
   5205 W Woodmill Dr Wilmington (19808) *(G-17947)*
Lityx LLC...888 548-9947
   1000 N West St Ste 1200 Wilmington (19801) *(G-17948)*
Liv180 Inc (PA)...561 235-9669
   8 The Grn Ste A Dover (19901) *(G-2958)*
Live Typing Inc..415 670-9601
   1521 Concord Pike Ste 303 Wilmington (19803) *(G-17949)*
Liveboard Inc..888 412-8882
   651 N Broad St Ste 206 Middletown (19709) *(G-7310)*
Liveo Research Inc (DH)...302 838-3200
   1389 School House Rd New Castle (19720) *(G-9318)*
Livetrade Ltd...302 305-1797
   16192 Coastal Hwy Lewes (19958) *(G-6214)*
Liveware Inc..302 791-9446
   1506 Society Dr Claymont (19703) *(G-1221)*
Living Great Medical Assoc LLC...............................302 734-9200
   1027 S Bradford St Dover (19904) *(G-2959)*
Living Pixels Studio LLC..650 464-6899
   4034 Willow Grove Rd Camden (19934) *(G-868)*
Living Resources Inc...302 227-6867
   Rehoboth Beach (19971) *(G-12835)*
Living Water Counseling LLC...................................443 553-7317
   3522 Silverside Rd Ste 32 Wilmington (19810) *(G-17950)*
Living Well Natural Health.......................................302 653-9748
   74 E Glenwood Ave Smyrna (19977) *(G-13808)*
Living Well With Dementia LLC................................302 753-9725
   120 Churchill Ln Wilmington (19808) *(G-17951)*
Livingston Enterprise...302 588-5722
   205 S Booth Dr New Castle (19720) *(G-9319)*
Lizard Soft Inc...619 618-0368
   8 The Grn Ste 5447 Dover (19901) *(G-2960)*
Lk Rejoice Child Care Center..................................302 543-4621
   725 N Union St Wilmington (19805) *(G-17952)*
Lkb Management Group LLC (PA)..........................919 561-2815
   8 The Grn Ste 13680 Dover (19901) *(G-2961)*
Lkq Northeast Inc..800 223-0171
   1575 Mckee Rd Ste 5 Dover (19904) *(G-2962)*
LL Renovation LLC..302 250-6449
   7 3rd Ave New Castle (19720) *(G-9320)*
Llb Acquisition LLC..212 750-8300
   1209 N Orange St Wilmington (19801) *(G-17953)*
LLC Castle Law..302 428-8800
   2 Mill Rd Ste 202 Wilmington (19806) *(G-17954)*
LLC Cutler Parrish..609 744-9871
   639 Swansea Dr Middletown (19709) *(G-7311)*

ALPHABETIC SECTION

LLC Forever Media of De... 412 221-1629
   2727 Shipley Rd Ste 406 Wilmington (19810) *(G-17955)*

LLC Gage Park... 302 738-6680
   850 Library Ave Ste 204 Newark (19711) *(G-11274)*

LLC Quick Shield... 514 730-8040
   1209 N Orange St Wilmington (19801) *(G-17956)*

LLC Sales Inc.. 416 996-1856
   1209 N Orange St Wilmington (19801) *(G-17957)*

LLC Smart Bean.. 302 894-2323
   8 The Grn Ste A Dover (19901) *(G-2963)*

Lloyd Richard LLC.. 302 584-8798
   131 W Rutherford Dr Newark (19713) *(G-11275)*

Lloyds Stoneworks.. 302 492-0847
   927 Grygo Rd Marydel (19964) *(G-6804)*

Lloyds Wldg & Fabrication LLC.. 302 384-7662
   1101 E 8th St Wilmington (19801) *(G-17958)*

LLP Connolly Gallagher.. 302 757-7300
   267 E Main St Newark (19711) *(G-11276)*

LLP Connolly Gallagher (PA).. 302 757-7300
   1201 N Market St Ste 2000 Wilmington (19801) *(G-17959)*

LLP Shaw Keller... 302 298-0700
   1105 N Market St Fl 1 Wilmington (19801) *(G-17960)*

Lmg Associates In Eye Care.. 302 993-0931
   21 Oxford Way Wilmington (19807) *(G-17961)*

LMS Ironworks.. 302 300-7719
   125 Saint John Dr Wilmington (19808) *(G-17962)*

Lnc Cleaning Company LLC.. 302 437-6547
   1 Walnut Ct Bear (19701) *(G-351)*

Lne Power LLC... 913 777-7552
   2711 Centerville Rd # 400 Wilmington (19808) *(G-17963)*

Lnh Inc.. 302 731-4948
   650 Pencader Dr Newark (19702) *(G-11277)*

Lnw & A Construction Corp... 302 764-9430
   31 E Mccaulley Ct Wilmington (19801) *(G-17964)*

Lnz Consulting LLC... 302 543-6296
   1601 Concord Pike Ste 50 Wilmington (19803) *(G-17965)*

Load 2 Go Inc... 302 722-8844
   16192 Coastal Hwy Lewes (19958) *(G-6215)*

Load Balancer Crew LLC.. 805 202-9953
   8 The Grn Ste A Dover (19901) *(G-2964)*

Load Miles Inc.. 323 842-7038
   8 The Grn Dover (19901) *(G-2965)*

Loadbalancerorginc... 888 867-9504
   4550 Linden Hill Rd Ste 201 Wilmington (19808) *(G-17966)*

Loan Simple Inc... 302 510-4808
   5506 Kirkwood Hwy Wilmington (19808) *(G-17967)*

Loan Til Payday... 302 428-3925
   1935 W 4th St Wilmington (19805) *(G-17968)*

Loan Till Payday LLC... 302 792-5001
   2604 Philadelphia Pike Claymont (19703) *(G-1222)*

Loan Till Payday LLC... 302 536-2183
   28521 Dupont Blvd Unit 3 Millsboro (19966) *(G-8350)*

Loanmax.. 302 747-2005
   5455 N Dupont Hwy Dover (19901) *(G-2966)*

Loanmax.. 302 326-0123
   1517 N Dupont Hwy New Castle (19720) *(G-9321)*

Lobster Made Easy Corp... 902 818-9958
   3422 Old Capitol Trl Wilmington (19808) *(G-17969)*

Local 13100 Cwa, Wilmington *Also Called: Diamond State Tele Coml Un* *(G-16059)*

LOCAL 313 IBEW ELECTRICIANS, New Castle *Also Called: Interntnal Brthd Elec Wkrs Lca*
(G-9240)

Local Ad Ninja Inc... 877 894-1502
   1521 Concord Pike Ste 301 Wilmington (19803) *(G-17970)*

Local Hands-Crafted In America... 302 645-9100
   118 2nd St Lewes (19958) *(G-6216)*

Local Life Marketing Group LLC... 877 514-4052
   125 Rickey Blvd Unit 1253 Bear (19701) *(G-352)*

Local Mobile LLC... 619 759-0114
   8 The Grn Dover (19901) *(G-2967)*

Local Plumbing.. 302 746-3101
   2095 Philadelphia Pike Claymont (19703) *(G-1223)*

Local Vertical... 302 242-2552
   69 Oakcrest Dr Dover (19901) *(G-2968)*

Localsorg Inc... 650 441-6464
   8 The Grn Ste B Dover (19901) *(G-2969)*

Localspin LLC.. 917 232-7203
   1521 Concord Pike Ste 301 Wilmington (19803) *(G-17971)*

Located In The Village Fenwick.. 302 539-2242
   300 Coastal Hwy Unit 1 Fenwick Island (19944) *(G-4052)*

Locchio Eyecare LLC.. 302 644-1039
   32566 Docs Pl Millville (19967) *(G-8537)*

Locker Construction Inc.. 302 239-2859
   314 Cox Rd Newark (19711) *(G-11278)*

Lockhart Construction LLC... 302 753-5461
   809 Parkside Blvd Bldg 1 Claymont (19703) *(G-1224)*

Lockheed Martin, Dover *Also Called: Lockheed Martin Corporation* *(G-2970)*

Lockheed Martin Corporation.. 302 741-2004
   Dover Afb Dover (19901) *(G-2970)*

Lockwood Design Construction... 302 684-4844
   26412 Broadkill Rd 1st Fl Milton (19968) *(G-8655)*

Locust Cnstr & Contg Svcs, Wilmington *Also Called: Linda McCormick* *(G-17922)*

Lodes Chiropractic Center PA.. 302 477-1565
   3411 Silverside Rd Ste 102hb Wilmington (19810) *(G-17972)*

Lodge Lane Assisted Living... 302 757-8100
   1221 Lodge Ln Wilmington (19809) *(G-17973)*

Lodge Lane Assisted Living... 302 764-7000
   704 River Rd Wilmington (19809) *(G-17974)*

Lofts 2nd and Loma... 302 300-1498
   211 N Market St Wilmington (19801) *(G-17975)*

Logan & Associates LLC.. 302 325-3555
   100 W Commons Blvd Ste 300 New Castle (19720) *(G-9322)*

Logically Ai Inc.. 202 768-9876
   2140 S Dupont Hwy Camden (19934) *(G-869)*

Logicjunction Inc.. 216 292-5760
   8 The Grn Ste 1 Dover (19901) *(G-2971)*

Logiclean LLC.. 302 298-0054
   6300 Philadelphia Pike Claymont (19703) *(G-1225)*

Logique Inc.. 302 330-8866
   257 Old Churchmans Rd New Castle (19720) *(G-9323)*

Logistics, Milford *Also Called: Bl Own UP LLC* *(G-7794)*

Logo Motive Inc... 302 645-2959
   35576 Airport Rd Rehoboth Beach (19971) *(G-12836)*

Logos Community Dev Corp... 302 349-2779
   19 Liberty Dr Dover (19904) *(G-2972)*

Logue Brothers Inc... 302 762-1896
   3507 Miller Rd Wilmington (19802) *(G-17976)*

Lohmann Steel LLC.. 844 488-1790
   2810 N Church St Wilmington (19802) *(G-17977)*

Lois James DDS.. 302 537-4500
   17 Atlantic Ave Ste 4 Ocean View (19970) *(G-12540)*

Loizides & Associates PC.. 302 654-0248
   1225 N King St Ste 800 Wilmington (19801) *(G-17978)*

Lokalise Inc (PA)... 302 498-9091
   3500 S Dupont Hwy Ste Bz-101 Dover (19901) *(G-2973)*

Lokblok Inc... 408 640-8644
   3524 Silverside Rd Ste 35b Wilmington (19810) *(G-17979)*

Lombard Trading International.. 786 659-5010
   112 Capitol Trl Newark (19711) *(G-11279)*

Lon Kieffer.. 888 466-2379
   10589 Wilkinson Dr Seaford (19973) *(G-13264)*

Lone Star Global Services Inc.. 302 744-9800
   9 E Loockerman St Ste 3a Dover (19901) *(G-2974)*

Long & Foster.. 302 569-0012
   34071 Moccasin Way Dagsboro (19939) *(G-1475)*

Long & Foster Real Estate Inc.. 302 542-0811
   995 N Dupont Blvd Milford (19963) *(G-7976)*

Long & Foster Real Estate Inc.. 302 227-3821
   37156 Rehoboth Avenue Ext Unit 5 Rehoboth Beach (19971) *(G-12837)*

LONG & FOSTER REAL ESTATE INC, Rehoboth Beach *Also Called: Long & Foster Real Estate Inc* *(G-12837)*

Long & Tann & D Onofrio Inc (PA)... 302 477-1970
   3906 Concord Pike Ste F Wilmington (19803) *(G-17980)*

Long and Foster — 925 699-4783
35115 Roebuck Ln Lewes (19958) (G-6217)

Long and Foster — 302 858-7805
36897 Wood Duck Way Selbyville (19975) (G-13562)

Long and Foster — 302 239-2636
5301 Limestone Rd Ste 225 Wilmington (19808) (G-17981)

Long Life Food Safety Pdts LLC — 302 229-1207
16192 Coastal Hwy Lewes (19958) (G-6218)

Long Neck Garden Center, Millsboro Also Called: Isaacs Landscaping & Gardening (G-8322)

Long Neck Water Co — 302 947-9600
32783 Long Neck Rd Unit 6 Millsboro (19966) (G-8351)

Long Rd Ahead Shipg Lgstic LLC — 480 702-6438
3 Germay Dr Unit 42083 Wilmington (19804) (G-17982)

Longboat Condominium LLC — 302 227-4785
81 Kings Creek Cir Rehoboth Beach (19971) (G-12838)

Longbottom Drinks USA Inc — 302 966-9177
108 W 13th St Wilmington (19801) (G-17983)

Longevity Health Corp — 619 288-3922
1209 N Orange St Wilmington (19801) (G-17984)

Longhorn Enterprises Inc — 302 737-7444
2604 Eastburn Ctr Newark (19711) (G-11280)

Longneck Family Practice — 302 947-9767
26744 John J Williams Hwy Unit 3 Millsboro (19966) (G-8352)

Longneck Housing Specialist, Millsboro Also Called: Manufctured Hsing Concepts LLC (G-8363)

Longo and Associates LLP — 302 477-7500
2010 Limestone Rd Wilmington (19808) (G-17985)

Longobardi & Boyle LLC — 302 575-1502
1700 Augustine Cut Off Wilmington (19803) (G-17986)

Longview Capital MGT LLC — 302 353-4720
2 Mill Rd Ste 105 Wilmington (19806) (G-17987)

Longview Farms Civic Assn — 302 475-6684
1107 S Overhill Ct Wilmington (19810) (G-17988)

Longwood Assets LLC — 617 906-8882
651 N Broad St Ste 201 Middletown (19709) (G-7312)

Lonjew LLC — 803 994-9888
16192 Coastal Hwy Lewes (19958) (G-6219)

Lonnie Wright — 302 655-1632
83 Charles Dr New Castle (19720) (G-9324)

Loockermans Tree Stump Removal — 302 745-6446
225 Northdown Dr Dover (19904) (G-2975)

Look Great MD Centers — 302 658-1232
3801 Kennett Pike Ste E126 Wilmington (19807) (G-17989)

Lookback App Co — 508 735-1903
251 Little Falls Dr Wilmington (19808) (G-17990)

Looks New Powerwashing, Millsboro Also Called: Looks New Powerwashing LLC (G-8353)

Looks New Powerwashing LLC — 302 569-0172
30306 Hickory Hill Rd Millsboro (19966) (G-8353)

Looksiebin LLC — 410 869-2192
4708 Weatherhill Dr Wilmington (19808) (G-17991)

Loom Network Inc — 404 939-1294
427 N Tatnall St 38768 Wilmington (19801) (G-17992)

Loomcraft Textile & Supply Co — 302 454-3232
211 Executive Dr Ste 13 Newark (19702) (G-11281)

Loop Mission Corp — 514 994-7625
2915 Ogletown Rd Ste 4010 Newark (19713) (G-11282)

Loot Kit Studios, Camden Also Called: Howard Industries LLC (G-853)

Lopesco Inc — 908 482-5616
2 Morning Glen Ln Newark (19711) (G-11283)

Lopesco Inc — 732 985-7776
2 Morning Glen Ln Newark (19711) (G-11284)

Lopez Gelasio — 302 377-2591
2110 Kirkwood Hwy Apt B Wilmington (19805) (G-17993)

Lopez General Contractors LLC — 302 377-2591
404 Llangollen Blvd New Castle (19720) (G-9325)

Lorcys Massage & Bdy Works LLC — 302 240-3958
101 N Main St Smyrna (19977) (G-13809)

Lord & Wheeler, Georgetown Also Called: Eric S Balliet (G-4310)

Lord and Sons Landscaping — 302 745-3001
33999 W Airport Rd Frankford (19945) (G-4123)

Lord Printing LLC — 302 439-3253
1812 Marsh Rd Ste 411 Wilmington (19810) (G-17994)

Lords Landscaping Inc — 302 539-6119
315 Atlantic Ave Millville (19967) (G-8538)

Lorelton — 302 573-3580
2200 W 4th St Apt 229 Wilmington (19805) (G-17995)

Lorelton Foundation — 302 573-2500
1201 N Orange St Ste 700 Wilmington (19801) (G-17996)

Loretta A Higgins — 302 645-2666
34431 King Street Row Lewes (19958) (G-6220)

Lorgus Enterprises Inc — 610 431-7453
68 N Sandpiper Dr Dover (19901) (G-2976)

Lori Ryan Skye — 302 588-2588
31672 Siham Rd Lewes (19958) (G-6221)

Lori's Hands, Newark Also Called: Loris Hands Inc (G-11285)

Lorica Strategy Partners LLC — 301 535-8263
16192 Coastal Hwy Lewes (19958) (G-6222)

Loris Hands Inc — 302 440-5454
100 Discovery Blvd Fl 4 Newark (19713) (G-11285)

Lorna Lee PC — 302 761-9191
2111 Willow Way Wilmington (19810) (G-17997)

Lorraine S Daycare — 302 328-1333
3 N Independence Blvd New Castle (19720) (G-9326)

Los Jardines Inc — 302 652-6390
1000 W 5th St Wilmington (19805) (G-17998)

Los Verdor LLC (PA) — 971 344-0173
251 Little Falls Dr Wilmington (19808) (G-17999)

Losco and Marconi PA — 302 656-7776
1926 Zebley Rd Wilmington (19810) (G-18000)

Loss Pay Inc — 833 567-7729
16192 Coastal Hwy Lewes (19958) (G-6223)

Lost and Found Dog Rescue Adop — 302 613-0394
70 Ivy Ln New Castle (19720) (G-9327)

Lotus Blossom Learning Center, Lewes Also Called: Robin S Wright (G-6426)

Lotus Lease Hospitality — 302 357-4699
619 Amberley Rd Wilmington (19803) (G-18001)

Lotus Logistics LLC — 573 240-4154
3524 Silverside Rd Ste 35b Wilmington (19810) (G-18002)

Lotus Rcvery Ctr Prces Crnr LL — 302 999-8900
1812 Newport Gap Pike Wilmington (19808) (G-18003)

Lotus Separations LLC — 302 345-2510
32 Belfort Loop Newark (19702) (G-11286)

Loud & Clear H T Solutions LLC — 302 985-1576
509 Sequoia Dr Smyrna (19977) (G-13810)

Loudoun Modern LLC — 703 447-6688
10 Vandyke St B Dewey Beach (19971) (G-1673)

Loughran Medical Group PA — 302 479-8464
3411 Silverside Rd Ste 103wb Wilmington (19810) (G-18004)

Louie Harry Laundry & Dry Clg, Dover Also Called: Harry Louies Laundry & Dry Clg (G-2658)

Louie Uncle Foods — 302 750-0117
15 Gale Ln Wilmington (19807) (G-18005)

Louis Dolente & Sons LLC — 610 874-2100
3759 Green St Claymont (19703) (G-1226)

Louis K Rafetto DMD — 302 477-1800
3512 Silverside Rd Ste 12 Wilmington (19810) (G-18006)

Louis L Rdding Cty/County Bldg — 302 576-2100
800 N French St Fl 9 Wilmington (19801) (G-18007)

Louis P Martin DDS — 302 994-4900
1941 Limestone Rd Ste 105 Wilmington (19808) (G-18008)

Louise M Flynn — 302 651-4000
1600 Rockland Rd Wilmington (19803) (G-18009)

Louviers Federal Credit Union (PA) — 302 733-0426
185 S Main St Newark (19711) (G-11287)

Louviers Federal Credit Union — 302 571-9513
1007 N Market St Wilmington (19801) (G-18010)

Louviers Mortgage Corporation — 302 234-4129
4839 Limestone Rd Wilmington (19808) (G-18011)

Love & Hope Rescue Mission Inc — 302 332-3829
101 Mederia Cir Newark (19702) (G-11288)

Love City Prints LLC — 302 245-5702
33497 Creekside Dr Lewes (19958) (G-6224)

Love Creek Marina MBL Hm Site (PA) — 302 448-6492
31136 Conleys Chapel Rd Lewes (19958) (G-6225)

ALPHABETIC SECTION

Love Harrisburg LLC 717 710-1556
651 N Broad St Middletown (19709) *(G-7313)*

Love Learn & Play DC 302 236-9888
16758 Shawnee Pl Apt B Milford (19963) *(G-7977)*

Love My Dog Inc 240 441-7267
1102 S Dupont Hwy Dover (19901) *(G-2977)*

Love N Care Daycare 302 369-8092
215 Capitol Trl Newark (19711) *(G-11289)*

Love N Fun Family Daycare 302 601-3629
246 Wilgus Ct Middletown (19709) *(G-7314)*

Love N Learn Nursery Too 302 678-0445
1598 Forrest Ave Dover (19904) *(G-2978)*

Lovely Nails & Spa LLC 302 260-9231
19287 Miller Rd Unit 10 Rehoboth Beach (19971) *(G-12839)*

Lovett Financial Advisors LLC 302 250-4740
630 Churchmans Rd Ste 109 Newark (19702) *(G-11290)*

Lowe, Robert W Agency, Newark *Also Called: Interstate Mortgage Corp Inc (G-11049)*

Lowe's, Camden *Also Called: Lowes Home Centers LLC (G-870)*

Lowe's, Dover *Also Called: Lowes Home Centers LLC (G-2979)*

Lowe's, Lewes *Also Called: Lowes Home Centers LLC (G-6226)*

Lowe's, Middletown *Also Called: Lowes Home Centers LLC (G-7315)*

Lowe's, Millsboro *Also Called: Lowes Home Centers LLC (G-8354)*

Lowe's, New Castle *Also Called: Lowes Home Centers LLC (G-9328)*

Lowe's, Newark *Also Called: Lowes Home Centers LLC (G-11291)*

Lowe's, Seaford *Also Called: Lowes Home Centers LLC (G-13265)*

Lowe's, Wilmington *Also Called: Lowes Home Centers LLC (G-18013)*

Lowell Scott MD PA 302 684-1119
611 Federal St Ste 3 Milton (19968) *(G-8656)*

Lowell Scott MD PA 302 684-1119
38398 Josephine St Rehoboth Beach (19971) *(G-12840)*

Lower Sussex Masonry LLC 302 249-3275
34888 Chelton Dr Laurel (19956) *(G-5557)*

Lowes Airport (fa77) 813 366-7655
1900 Prior Rd Wilmington (19809) *(G-18012)*

Lowes Home Centers LLC 302 697-0700
516 Walmart Dr Camden (19934) *(G-870)*

Lowes Home Centers LLC 302 735-7500
1450 N Dupont Hwy Dover (19901) *(G-2979)*

Lowes Home Centers LLC 302 645-0900
20364 Plantations Rd Lewes (19958) *(G-6226)*

Lowes Home Centers LLC 302 376-3006
500 W Main St Middletown (19709) *(G-7315)*

Lowes Home Centers LLC 302 934-3740
26688 Centerview Dr Millsboro (19966) *(G-8354)*

Lowes Home Centers LLC 302 252-3228
2225 Hessler Blvd New Castle (19720) *(G-9328)*

Lowes Home Centers LLC 302 781-1154
2000 Ogletown Rd Newark (19711) *(G-11291)*

Lowes Home Centers LLC 302 536-4000
22880 Sussex Hwy Seaford (19973) *(G-13265)*

Lowes Home Centers LLC 302 479-7799
3100 Brandywine Pkwy Fl 1 Wilmington (19803) *(G-18013)*

Loyal Order Mose Clymont Lodge 302 764-9765
5101 Governor Printz Blvd Wilmington (19809) *(G-18014)*

Loyal Order Mose Lwes Rehoboth 302 684-4004
28971 Lewes Georgetown Hwy Lewes (19958) *(G-6227)*

Loyal Order of Moose 302 436-2088
35993 Zion Church Rd Frankford (19945) *(G-4124)*

Loyal Order of Moose 302 378-2624
2 Victorian Ct Historic New Castle (19720) *(G-5019)*

Loyalty Is Earned Inc (PA) 347 606-6383
3 Germay Dr Ste 1740 Wilmington (19804) *(G-18015)*

Loyalty Soap and Candle Co LLC 302 373-5854
304 Helen Dr Townsend (19734) *(G-14028)*

LP Smoked LLC 302 379-3059
20 Montchanin Rd Ste 250 Wilmington (19807) *(G-18016)*

Lpl Financial 302 737-6559
220 Continental Dr Ste 207 Newark (19713) *(G-11292)*

Lpl Financial 617 423-3644
1303 Delaware Ave Ste 112 Wilmington (19806) *(G-18017)*

Lr Construction LLC 302 249-4507
11304 3rd St Bridgeville (19933) *(G-726)*

LRC North America Inc 302 427-2845
1105 N Market St Wilmington (19801) *(G-18018)*

Lrk Dental 302 629-7115
543 N Shipley St Seaford (19973) *(G-13266)*

Ls Anderson Reproductions Inc 302 999-9940
2900 Faulkland Rd Wilmington (19808) *(G-18019)*

LS Auto Experience LLC (PA) 302 983-9668
701 N Claymont St Wilmington (19801) *(G-18020)*

Lsf Networks LLC 213 537-2402
300 Delaware Ave Ste 210a Wilmington (19801) *(G-18021)*

Lsref4 Lighthouse Corp Acqstn 302 737-8500
146 Chestnut Crossing Dr Newark (19713) *(G-11293)*

Ltc Pharmacy, Newark *Also Called: Pharmerica Long-Term Care LLC (G-11679)*

Ltc Services LLC 302 396-8598
125 E Locust St Seaford (19973) *(G-13267)*

Ltr Private Foundation 610 745-5000
206 Haystack Ln Wilmington (19807) *(G-18022)*

Lube Depot 302 659-3329
205 W Glenwood Ave Smyrna (19977) *(G-13811)*

Lubill Properties LLC 302 946-4188
1201 N Market St Ste 111 Wilmington (19801) *(G-18023)*

Lucid Colloids Amer 302 475-2393
2213 Jones Ln Wilmington (19810) *(G-18024)*

Lucila Carmichael Rn 302 324-8901
1101 Delaware St Historic New Castle (19720) *(G-5020)*

Lucky Star Farms LLC 302 841-5177
15942 Wilson Hill Rd Georgetown (19947) *(G-4409)*

Lucky Wellness Center Inc 302 990-5441
120 N Cannon St Unit 1 Seaford (19973) *(G-13268)*

Lucys Cleaning Service 302 893-9946
28 Mifflin Ave New Castle (19720) *(G-9329)*

Lucys Housekeppers 302 893-9946
14 Meridian Blvd Bear (19701) *(G-353)*

Luff & Associates CPA PA 302 422-9699
223 S Rehoboth Blvd Milford (19963) *(G-7978)*

Luff & Associates PA, Milford *Also Called: Luff & Associates CPA PA (G-7978)*

Luis L David MD PA 302 422-9768
204 S Walnut St Milford (19963) *(G-7979)*

Luke Destefano Inc 302 455-0710
107 Albe Dr Ste B Newark (19702) *(G-11294)*

Lukerative Solutions Inc 302 294-6468
56 W Main St Christiana (19702) *(G-1004)*

Lulla Woodworking LLC 302 841-8800
1 New Castle Ct Ocean View (19970) *(G-12541)*

Lullaby Learning Center Inc 302 703-2871
26324 Lewes Georgetown Hwy Harbeson (19951) *(G-4706)*

Lumber Industries Inc 302 655-9651
5809 Kennett Pike Wilmington (19807) *(G-18025)*

Lumber Jacks Axe Club LLC 215 900-0318
44 E 4th St Historic New Castle (19720) *(G-5021)*

Lumenty, Wilmington *Also Called: Lumenty Technologies Inc (G-18026)*

Lumenty Technologies Inc 971 331-3113
3411 Silverside Rd # 104 Wilmington (19810) *(G-18026)*

Lumhaa LLC 916 517-9972
108 W 13th St Wilmington (19801) *(G-18027)*

Lumi Cases LLC 302 525-6971
501 Capitol Trl Apt 201 Newark (19711) *(G-11295)*

Lumia Home LLC 516 373-5269
16192 Coastal Hwy Lewes (19958) *(G-6228)*

Luminous Energy Corporation 866 475-7504
8 The Grn # 6741 Dover (19901) *(G-2980)*

Lums Pond Animal Hospital Inc 302 836-5585
3052 Wrangle Hill Rd Bear (19701) *(G-354)*

Lundgren Chaizhunussov Ltd LLC 508 828-0058
824 N Market St Ste 220 Wilmington (19801) *(G-18028)*

Lune Rouge Entrmt USA Inc 514 556-2101
251 Little Falls Dr Wilmington (19808) *(G-18029)*

Lupoli General Contracting 302 449-1533
28 Kirkcaldy Ln Middletown (19709) *(G-7316)*

(PA)=Parent Co (HQ)=Headquarters (DH)=Div Headquarters

2024 Harris Directory of Delaware Businesses

Lupus Foundtn of Amer Phila Tr..302 622-8700
100 W 10th St Wilmington (19801) (G-18030)

Luriware Consulting Agricultur...302 244-1947
155 S Bradford St Ste 200a Dover (19904) (G-2981)

Luther Martin Foundation Dover..302 674-1408
430 Kings Hwy Ofc 727 Dover (19901) (G-2982)

Luther Towers II, Wilmington Also Called: Lutheran Senior Services Inc (G-18032)

Luther Towers III Dover Inc..302 674-1408
430 Kings Hwy Dover (19901) (G-2983)

Luther Towers IV Dover Inc..302 674-1408
430 Kings Hwy Ofc 1021 Dover (19901) (G-2984)

LUTHER TOWERS OF DOVER, Dover Also Called: Lutheran Senior Svcs of Dover (G-2988)

Luther Towers of Dover Inc..302 674-1408
430 Kings Hwy Ofc 727 Dover (19901) (G-2985)

LUTHER TOWERS OF MILTON, THE, Milton Also Called: Lutheran Snior Svcs of Sssex C (G-8657)

Luther Village I Dover Inc..302 674-1408
430 Kings Hwy Ofc 727 Dover (19901) (G-2986)

Luther Village II Dover Inc...302 674-1408
430 Kings Hwy Dover (19901) (G-2987)

Lutheran Community Services..302 654-8886
2809 Baynard Blvd Wilmington (19802) (G-18031)

Lutheran Senior Services Inc...302 654-4490
1420 N Franklin St Ste 1 Wilmington (19806) (G-18032)

Lutheran Senior Services Inc (PA).......................................302 654-4490
1201 N Harrison St Apt 1204 Wilmington (19806) (G-18033)

Lutheran Senior Svcs of Dover..302 674-1408
430 Kings Hwy Ofc 727 Dover (19901) (G-2988)

Lutheran Snior Svcs of Sssex C..302 684-1668
500 Palmer St Milton (19968) (G-8657)

Lutinx Inc...718 502-6961
16192 Coastal Hwy Lewes (19958) (G-6229)

Luttrell Guitars...404 325-7977
23199 Bridgeway Dr W Lewes (19958) (G-6230)

Lutwin-Kawalec Malgorzata MD..302 651-4000
1600 Rockland Rd Wilmington (19803) (G-18034)

Luut Technologies Inc..302 658-7581
1209 N Orange St Wilmington (19801) (G-18035)

Lux Medical Solutions LLC...302 440-4557
16192 Coastal Hwy Lewes (19958) (G-6231)

Lux Paradise Properties LLC (PA).......................................502 631-2008
3911 Concord Pike # 8030 Wilmington (19803) (G-18036)

Lux Spa & Nails...302 834-4899
122 Foxhunt Dr Bear (19701) (G-355)

Luxcore LLC..302 777-0538
300 Delaware Ave Ste 210a Wilmington (19801) (G-18037)

Luxiasuites LLC...302 778-3000
1007 N Orange St Wilmington (19801) (G-18038)

Luxiasuites LLC...302 654-8527
331 Justison St Wilmington (19801) (G-18039)

Luxiasuites LLC (PA)...302 778-2900
322 A St Ste 300 Wilmington (19801) (G-18040)

Luxiasuites LLC...302 426-1200
115 Christina Landing Dr Wilmington (19801) (G-18041)

Luxury Residence LLC...302 216-2102
1201 N Market St Ste 11 Wilmington (19801) (G-18042)

Luxy Stay Imperial LLC..844 483-5383
19266 Cstl Hwy Unit 41013 Rehoboth Beach (19971) (G-12841)

Luzz Auto Tech LLC..302 305-5899
528 Old Barksdale Rd Newark (19711) (G-11296)

Luz D Reynoso..302 358-6237
179 W Chestnut Hill Rd Ste 6 Newark (19713) (G-11297)

Lweco Group LLC...302 296-8035
28428 Cedar Ridge Dr Millsboro (19966) (G-8355)

Lycra Company LLC..302 731-6800
150 Red Mill Rd Newark (19711) (G-11298)

Lycra Company LLC..540 949-2972
1209 N Orange St Wilmington (19801) (G-18043)

Lyft Inc (PA)..302 747-0124
1209 N Orange St Wilmington (19801) (G-18044)

Lyme Yarnbombs Inc..302 547-1340
7 Denbeigh Ct Wilmington (19808) (G-18045)

Lynch Heights Fuel Corp..302 422-9195
840 Bay Rd Milford (19963) (G-7980)

Lynch Jim Heather E...302 562-6336
1104 Grandview Ave Wilmington (19809) (G-18046)

Lynda D Arai M D..302 651-5350
1600 Rockland Rd Wilmington (19803) (G-18047)

Lyndon B Cagampan...302 730-8848
830 Walker Rd Dover (19904) (G-2989)

Lyneer Staffing Solutions..302 892-9494
639 W Newport Pike Wilmington (19804) (G-18048)

Lynkmax LLC...302 573-3568
1201 N Orange St Ste 7107 Wilmington (19801) (G-18049)

Lynn Construction LLC..302 236-6596
7041 Atlanta Cir Seaford (19973) (G-13269)

Lynn M Fuchs M D..302 651-4000
1600 Rockland Rd Wilmington (19803) (G-18050)

Lynn Victoria COSm&med Skin...302 388-5459
830 Stockbridge Dr Hockessin (19707) (G-5284)

Lynnanne Kasarda MD...302 655-5822
1802 W 4th St Wilmington (19805) (G-18051)

Lynne Fardell & Associates LLC...302 276-1541
58 The Strand New Castle (19720) (G-9330)

Lyons Companies LLC..302 658-5508
501 Carr Rd Wilmington (19809) (G-18052)

Lyons David J Law Office..302 777-5698
1526 Gilpin Ave Wilmington (19806) (G-18053)

Lyons Insurance Agency Inc (PA).......................................302 227-7100
501 Carr Rd Ste 301 Wilmington (19809) (G-18054)

Lytehouse Automotive, Wilmington Also Called: Charles Williams (G-15342)

M & F Financial Corp..302 427-5755
300 Delaware Ave Ste 1704 Wilmington (19801) (G-18055)

M & G Pro Services LLC..302 420-1428
135 Blackberry Cir Marydel (19964) (G-6805)

M & L Contractors Inc...302 436-9303
13354 Blueberry Rd Selbyville (19975) (G-13563)

M & M Automotive LLC..302 325-8140
800 Frenchtown Rd Historic New Castle (19720) (G-5022)

M & M Detail Wrap and Tint LLC..302 260-8988
2001 N West St Ste 79 Wilmington (19802) (G-18056)

M & M Tire Services Inc...302 731-1004
2615 Pulaski Hwy Newark (19702) (G-11299)

M & P Adventures Inc...302 645-6271
Corner Of Savannah Angler Lewes (19958) (G-6232)

M & W Trucking Inc..302 655-6994
44 Glen Ave New Castle (19720) (G-9331)

M Auger Enterprise Inc...302 992-9922
101 Cassidy Dr Wilmington (19804) (G-18057)

M B A, Wilmington Also Called: Mumford-Bjorkman Assoc Inc (G-18485)

M B Cues..443 309-3495
30700 Shell Rd Dagsboro (19939) (G-1476)

M C Chiropractic Clinic Inc..302 715-5035
116 E Front St Ste C Laurel (19956) (G-5558)

M C Tek LLC..302 644-9695
19122 Coastal Hwy Unit B Rehoboth Beach (19971) (G-12842)

M Cubed Technologies Inc..302 454-8600
1300 Marrows Rd Newark (19711) (G-11300)

M D N Billing Consulting LLC...914 376-6100
9 Lake Crest Dr Milford (19963) (G-7981)

M D Plumbing Drain Cleaning...302 492-8880
1500 Gunter Rd Marydel (19964) (G-6806)

M Davis & Sons Inc (PA)...302 998-3385
24 Mcmillan Way Newark (19713) (G-11301)

M Davis & Sons Inc..302 998-3385
200 Hadco Rd Wilmington (19804) (G-18058)

M Davis Farms LLC...302 856-7018
17741 Davis Rd Georgetown (19947) (G-4410)

M Denight Lawn Care LLC...302 528-4152
2209 Wheatleys Pond Rd Smyrna (19977) (G-13812)

M Diana Metzger MD...302 731-0942
665 Churchmans Rd Newark (19702) (G-11302)

M G Hamex Corporation..302 832-9072
1063 Twin Lane Rd New Castle (19720) (G-9332)

ALPHABETIC SECTION

M Hs Lift of Delaware Inc.. 302 629-4490
25560 Business Park Seaford (19973) *(G-13270)*

M Imran MD.. 302 453-7399
2707 Kirkwood Hwy Ste 1 Newark (19711) *(G-11303)*

M J Bilecki Contracting... 302 357-7455
2 Constance Ct Bear (19701) *(G-356)*

M K Customer Elevator Pads... 302 698-3110
1644 Sorghum Mill Rd Dover (19901) *(G-2990)*

M L Morris Inc.. 302 956-0678
17044 N Main St Ste 5 Bridgeville (19933) *(G-727)*

M L Parker Construction Inc... 302 798-8530
950 Ridge Rd Ste C6 Claymont (19703) *(G-1227)*

M Level Inc.. 302 762-3910
14 Stuyvesant Dr Hockessin (19707) *(G-5285)*

M M Marine Service... 302 841-7689
24530 Hollyville Rd Millsboro (19966) *(G-8356)*

M Michelle Milligan Lcsw.. 302 540-9136
5235 W Woodmill Dr Ste 47 Wilmington (19808) *(G-18059)*

M N K Maintenance and REM.. 302 841-5884
32034 Helm St Dagsboro (19939) *(G-1477)*

M O T H E R S Inc.. 302 275-4163
212 W 21st St Wilmington (19802) *(G-18060)*

M O T Senior Citizen Center... 302 378-3041
300 S Scott St Middletown (19709) *(G-7317)*

M O T Youth Ftball & Cheerldng... 302 345-6182
Middletown (19709) *(G-7318)*

M P Logistics Inc... 302 562-0420
232 Harlequin Dr New Castle (19720) *(G-9333)*

M R Plumbing.. 302 738-7978
136 Wren Way Newark (19711) *(G-11304)*

M Scott Bovelsky MD... 302 674-0223
200 Banning St Ste 320 Dover (19904) *(G-2991)*

M T C, Newark *Also Called: Mtc Usa LLC (G-11468)*

M T Investment Group... 302 793-4917
501 Silverside Rd Ste 6 Wilmington (19809) *(G-18061)*

M T O Clean of Sussex County... 302 854-0204
2 N Aquarius Way Milton (19968) *(G-8658)*

M Team Creative... 302 275-5658
6 Castlegate Ct Newark (19702) *(G-11305)*

M W Fogarty Inc.. 302 658-5547
22 Bernard Blvd Hockessin (19707) *(G-5286)*

M Wilson Accnting Bkkping Svc... 302 735-1537
580 S Bay Rd Dover (19901) *(G-2992)*

M/S Hollow Metal Wholesale LLC....................................... 302 349-9471
9644 Nanticoke Business Park Dr Greenwood (19950) *(G-4650)*

M&E Trading, Wilmington *Also Called: Marine & Energy Trading Corp (G-18130)*

M&L Cleaning Service.. 302 249-8634
24572 Straight Arrow Rd Millsboro (19966) *(G-8357)*

M&M Courier Service LLC.. 302 430-2740
305 Jefferson St Middletown (19709) *(G-7319)*

M&M Garage Doors Inc... 302 304-1397
302 Webb Rd Newark (19711) *(G-11306)*

M&M Mass Spec Consulting LLC....................................... 302 250-4488
28 Tenby Chase Dr Newark (19711) *(G-11307)*

M&M Pure Air Systems LLC.. 403 801-2925
16192 Coastal Hwy Lewes (19958) *(G-6233)*

M&M Small Engine Repair... 302 270-3941
1254 Gunter Rd Hartly (19953) *(G-4894)*

M&S Auto Group Inc... 302 834-7905
104 Loretta Ln Bear (19701) *(G-357)*

M&S Group International LLC.. 302 592-6006
8 The Grn Ste 1289 Dover (19901) *(G-2993)*

M&T, Bear *Also Called: Manufacturers & Traders Tr Co (G-362)*

M&T, Claymont *Also Called: Manufacturers & Traders Tr Co (G-1230)*

M&T, Delmar *Also Called: Manufacturers & Traders Tr Co (G-1616)*

M&T, Dover *Also Called: Manufacturers & Traders Tr Co (G-3013)*

M&T, Dover *Also Called: Manufacturers & Traders Tr Co (G-3014)*

M&T, Hockessin *Also Called: Manufacturers & Traders Tr Co (G-5295)*

M&T, Laurel *Also Called: Manufacturers & Traders Tr Co (G-5559)*

M&T, Lewes *Also Called: Manufacturers & Traders Tr Co (G-6240)*

M&T, Middletown *Also Called: Manufacturers & Traders Tr Co (G-7326)*

M&T, Middletown *Also Called: Manufacturers & Traders Tr Co (G-7327)*

M&T, Milford *Also Called: Manufacturers & Traders Tr Co (G-7983)*

M&T, Millsboro *Also Called: Manufacturers & Traders Tr Co (G-8362)*

M&T, Milton *Also Called: Manufacturers & Traders Tr Co (G-8660)*

M&T, New Castle *Also Called: Manufacturers & Traders Tr Co (G-9343)*

M&T, Newark *Also Called: Manufacturers & Traders Tr Co (G-11323)*

M&T, Newark *Also Called: Manufacturers & Traders Tr Co (G-11324)*

M&T, Rehoboth Beach *Also Called: Manufacturers & Traders Tr Co (G-12847)*

M&T, Seaford *Also Called: Manufacturers & Traders Tr Co (G-13273)*

M&T, Wilmington *Also Called: Manufacturers & Traders Tr Co (G-18108)*

M&T, Wilmington *Also Called: Manufacturers & Traders Tr Co (G-18109)*

M&T, Wilmington *Also Called: Manufacturers & Traders Tr Co (G-18110)*

M&T, Wilmington *Also Called: Manufacturers & Traders Tr Co (G-18111)*

M&T, Wilmington *Also Called: Manufacturers & Traders Tr Co (G-18112)*

M&T, Wilmington *Also Called: Manufacturers & Traders Tr Co (G-18113)*

M&T, Wilmington *Also Called: Manufacturers & Traders Tr Co (G-18114)*

M&T, Wilmington *Also Called: Manufacturers & Traders Tr Co (G-18115)*

M&T, Wilmington *Also Called: Manufacturers & Traders Tr Co (G-18116)*

M3 Contracting LLC... 302 781-3143
13 Garfield Way Newark (19713) *(G-11308)*

MA Adas LLC.. 302 420-8158
1201 N Market St Ste 111e-91 Wilmington (19801) *(G-18062)*

MA Transportation LLC... 302 588-5435
34016 Sea Otter Way Millsboro (19966) *(G-8358)*

Maaco Auto Painting, Dover *Also Called: Red Barn Inc (G-3438)*

Maaco Auto Painting, Newark *Also Called: Jewell Enterprises Inc (G-11110)*

Maaco Collision Repair.. 302 753-8721
105 Emerald Ridge Dr Bear (19701) *(G-358)*

Maaco Collision Repr Auto Pntg... 610 628-3867
2400 Northeast Blvd Wilmington (19802) *(G-18063)*

Maaco Collision Repr Auto Pntg, Dover *Also Called: Kpkm Inc (G-2885)*

Maad Africa Inc... 847 927-0519
651 N Broad St Middletown (19709) *(G-7320)*

Mac Concussion Center... 302 379-1027
5936 Limestone Rd Ste 301b Hockessin (19707) *(G-5287)*

Mac Physician LLC.. 302 235-8808
5936 Limestone Rd Ste 301b Hockessin (19707) *(G-5288)*

Macan Manufacturing, Milton *Also Called: Jaco LLC (G-8646)*

Macappstudio Inc.. 415 799-7415
Sunset Lake Rd Ste B-2 Newark (19702) *(G-11309)*

Maccari Companies Inc (PA)... 302 994-9628
1700 First State Blvd Wilmington (19804) *(G-18064)*

Maccari Motors... 302 563-3361
1202 First State Blvd Wilmington (19804) *(G-18065)*

Macdonald Contracting LLC... 302 668-2022
10 Germay Dr Ste A Wilmington (19804) *(G-18066)*

Macelree & Harvey Ltd.. 302 654-4454
5721 Kennett Pike Wilmington (19807) *(G-18067)*

Macfarlane A Radford MD PA.. 302 633-6338
203 W Pembrey Dr Wilmington (19803) *(G-18068)*

Maciels Imports LLC... 562 295-6773
300 Delaware Ave Ste 210a Wilmington (19801) *(G-18069)*

Macintosh Engineering.. 302 448-2000
32191 Nassau Rd Unit 2 Lewes (19958) *(G-6234)*

Macintosh Engineering Inc.. 302 252-9200
2 Mill Rd Ste 100 Wilmington (19806) *(G-18070)*

Mackeys Complete Cnstr Co, Wilmington *Also Called: Lavond Mackey (G-17827)*

Macklyn Home Care.. 302 253-8208
6 W Market St Georgetown (19947) *(G-4411)*

Macklyn Home Care.. 302 690-9397
5179 W Woodmill Dr Wilmington (19808) *(G-18071)*

Macknife Specialties, Hockessin *Also Called: Macknyfe Specialties (G-5289)*

Macknyfe Specialties... 302 239-4904
862 Auburn Mill Rd Hockessin (19707) *(G-5289)*

Macon Renovations LLC... 302 244-9161
4040 Mill Creek Rd Hockessin (19707) *(G-5290)*

Macro Polymers NA LLC... 302 660-6926
501 Silverside Rd Ste 600 Wilmington (19809) *(G-18072)*

Macrostat Inc 302 239-7442
307 Blue Jay Dr Hockessin (19707) *(G-5291)*

Macs Auto Services 302 223-6771
235 1st Ave Smyrna (19977) *(G-13813)*

Mad Delaware Chapter 910 284-6286
34013 Woodland Cir Lewes (19958) *(G-6235)*

Mad Macs 302 737-4800
801 S College Ave Newark (19713) *(G-11310)*

Maddcitylive LLC 302 591-3471
8 The Grn Ste 16129 Dover (19901) *(G-2994)*

Maddix Owens Lillian 302 897-1997
114 W 25th St Wilmington (19802) *(G-18073)*

Madison Adoption Associates (PA) 302 475-8977
1102 Society Dr Claymont (19703) *(G-1228)*

Madison Real Estate Inc 718 947-6350
112 S French St Wilmington (19801) *(G-18074)*

Mado Creative Agency Inc 302 223-9532
300 Delaware Ave Ste 210 Wilmington (19801) *(G-18075)*

Maelys Cosmetics USA Inc 312 888-5007
251 Little Falls Dr Wilmington (19808) *(G-18076)*

Maestrik Inc 312 925-3116
2035 Sunset Lake Rd D2 Newark (19702) *(G-11311)*

Maestro Media Holdings Inc 855 313-3337
8 The Grn Ste A Dover (19901) *(G-2995)*

Maf Industries 302 249-1254
27797 Oneals Rd Seaford (19973) *(G-13271)*

Magan Forman 443 394-9534
325 Oracle Rd Wilmington (19808) *(G-18077)*

Magco Kissner Milling Co 913 713-0612
341 Pigeon Point Rd New Castle (19720) *(G-9334)*

Magellan Midstream Partners LP 302 654-3717
1050 Christiana Ave Ste A Wilmington (19801) *(G-18078)*

Maggie Magpie Inc 302 331-5061
7 Redding Cir Middletown (19709) *(G-7321)*

Maggio/Shields Teams 302 226-3770
70 Rehoboth Ave Ste 101 Rehoboth Beach (19971) *(G-12843)*

Magic Bytes LLC 813 995-7343
16192 Coastal Hwy Lewes (19958) *(G-6236)*

Magic Car Wash 302 750-2197
108 S Colts Neck Way Hockessin (19707) *(G-5292)*

Magic Car Wash II Inc 302 660-8066
4917 Kirkwood Hwy Wilmington (19808) *(G-18079)*

Magic Car Wash Inc 302 479-5911
3221 Naamans Rd Wilmington (19810) *(G-18080)*

Magic Cleaning 302 723-4328
58 Holly St Wilmington (19808) *(G-18081)*

Magic Inc 415 319-6331
2810 N Church St Wilmington (19802) *(G-18082)*

Magic Touch 302 655-6430
1707 New Castle Ave Historic New Castle (19720) *(G-5023)*

Magic Yrs Child Care Lrng Cntr 302 322-3102
327 Old State Rd New Castle (19720) *(G-9335)*

Magipop Inc 217 898-3115
1007 N Orange St Fl 4 Wilmington (19801) *(G-18083)*

Magnifaskin Medspa 302 516-7287
3901 Concord Pike Wilmington (19803) *(G-18084)*

Magnolia Home Theatre 302 677-7215
1165 N Dupont Hwy Dover (19901) *(G-2996)*

Magnus Environmental Corp 302 655-4443
220 Marsh Ln New Castle (19720) *(G-9336)*

Maguire & Sons Inc 302 798-1200
1035 Philadelphia Pike Ste C Wilmington (19809) *(G-18085)*

Maguire Pest Control, Wilmington *Also Called: Maguire & Sons Inc (G-18085)*

Magus LLC 213 332-9117
8 The Grn Ste R Dover (19901) *(G-2997)*

Mahaffy & Associates Inc 302 656-8381
4 Brightham Ln Middletown (19709) *(G-7322)*

Mahavir LLC 302 651-7995
111 S West St Wilmington (19801) *(G-18086)*

Mahle Industrial Thermal Syste 915 612-1611
1209 N Orange St Wilmington (19801) *(G-18087)*

Mahmood B Omaid 302 399-7849
61 Wicksfield Blvd Smyrna (19977) *(G-13814)*

Maichle S Heating Air 302 328-4822
105 J And M Dr New Castle (19720) *(G-9337)*

Maid Easy Cleaning Delaware 302 858-1883
332 S Bedford St Georgetown (19947) *(G-4412)*

Maid For Shore 302 344-1857
22 Chesterfield Dr Lewes (19958) *(G-6237)*

Maid My Day Cleaning Svc 302 947-9355
Mariners Way Millsboro (19966) *(G-8359)*

Maidpro 302 327-4250
4442 Summit Bridge Rd 12 Middletown (19709) *(G-7323)*

Maids, Newark *Also Called: J & W Mc Cormick Ltd (G-11069)*

Maids For You Inc 302 328-9050
3 Scottie Ln New Castle (19720) *(G-9338)*

Mail Box Outlet, New Castle *Also Called: True-Pack Ltd (G-9644)*

Mail Express 302 376-5151
600 N Broad St Ste 5 Middletown (19709) *(G-7324)*

Mail Stop 302 947-4704
24832 John J Williams Hwy Unit 1 Millsboro (19966) *(G-8360)*

Mailbiz 302 644-9035
4590 Highway One Rehoboth Beach (19971) *(G-12844)*

Maillie LLP 302 324-0780
15 Reads Way Ste 200 New Castle (19720) *(G-9339)*

Main Event Entrmt Wilmington 302 722-9466
2900 Fashion Center Blvd Newark (19702) *(G-11312)*

Main Gate Laundry 302 998-9949
123 Kirkwood Sq Wilmington (19808) *(G-18088)*

Main Light Industries Inc 302 998-8017
1614 Newport Gap Pike Wilmington (19808) *(G-18089)*

Main Office Inc 302 732-3460
32096 Sussex St Dagsboro (19939) *(G-1478)*

Main Social Media 302 268-6979
1201 N Orange St Wilmington (19801) *(G-18090)*

Main Street Cleaners 302 738-4385
179 E Main St Newark (19711) *(G-11313)*

Main Street Dental 302 368-2558
29 Center St Newark (19711) *(G-11314)*

Main Street Movies 5 LLC 302 738-4555
401 Newark Shopping Ctr Newark (19711) *(G-11315)*

Main Street Staffing Agcy LLC 302 608-7052
4 Grand Hall Dover (19904) *(G-2998)*

Mainline Today, Wilmington *Also Called: Suburban Publishing Inc (G-20116)*

MainStay Suites 302 678-8383
201 Stover Blvd Dover (19901) *(G-2999)*

MainStay Suites, Dover *Also Called: MainStay Suites (G-2999)*

Maintenance Tech 302 322-6410
10 Strawbridge Ave New Castle (19720) *(G-9340)*

Maintenance Troubleshooti 302 477-1045
2917 Cheshire Rd Wilmington (19810) *(G-18091)*

Maintenance Troubleshooting, Newark *Also Called: Thomas B Davis (G-12191)*

Maintenance Unlimited LLC 302 387-1868
73 Moores Dr Magnolia (19962) *(G-6763)*

Majdell Group, Newark *Also Called: Majdell Group USA Inc (G-11316)*

Majdell Group USA Inc 302 722-8223
40 E Main St 790 Newark (19711) *(G-11316)*

Majo Hair Studio, Wilmington *Also Called: Sylvia Saienna (G-20180)*

Major League Bocce LLC 240 476-5801
303 Walnut St Milton (19968) *(G-8659)*

Major Mahh Levels LLC 973 494-4767
2404 Jacqueline Dr Apt A7 Wilmington (19810) *(G-18092)*

Makatuu Inc 650 431-5582
8 The Grn Dover (19901) *(G-3000)*

Makave International Trdg LLC 302 288-0670
8 The Grn Ste A Dover (19901) *(G-3001)*

Make It New Construction LLC 302 423-7794
40 Sienna Ct Dover (19904) *(G-3002)*

Make Productions 302 593-1595
1511 2nd Ave Wilmington (19805) *(G-18093)*

Makeup & Love 856 524-1966
17277 Queen Anne Way Lewes (19958) *(G-6238)*

ALPHABETIC SECTION

Manufacturers & Traders Tr Co

Makk-O Industries Inc 302 376-0160
  4640 Dupont Pkwy Townsend (19734) *(G-14029)*
Makkari Globl Vsion A Sries LL 571 308-6032
  8 The Grn Ste A Dover (19901) *(G-3003)*
Mako Swim Club LLC 631 682-2131
  Harbeson (19951) *(G-4707)*
Makua, Wilmington *Also Called: Makua Inc (G-18094)*
Makua Inc 310 923-8549
  251 Little Falls Dr Wilmington (19808) *(G-18094)*
Mal Ventures Inc 302 454-1170
  213 Mulberry Rd Newark (19711) *(G-11317)*
Malarkey Tattoo LLC 302 304-5382
  730 Pulaski Hwy Bear (19701) *(G-359)*
Malave Property Group LLC 844 203-4610
  9 E Loockerman St # 202820 Dover (19901) *(G-3004)*
Malgiero Helen A Day Care 302 834-9060
  311 Monroe St Delaware City (19706) *(G-1548)*
Maliks Auto Repair 302 325-2555
  95 Christiana Rd New Castle (19720) *(G-9341)*
Malins Jim E Plumbing & Htg 302 239-2755
  538 Basher Ln Hockessin (19707) *(G-5293)*
Mallard Advisors LLC 302 239-1654
  7234 Lancaster Pike Ste 220a Hockessin (19707) *(G-5294)*
Mallard Advisors LLC (HQ) 302 239-1654
  750 Barksdale Rd Ste 3 Newark (19711) *(G-11318)*
Mallard Financial Partners Inc 302 737-4546
  750 Barksdale Rd Ste 3 Newark (19711) *(G-11319)*
Mallerd Lakes 443 783-2993
  37976 Pelican Ln Selbyville (19975) *(G-13564)*
Malmberg Firm, The, Dover *Also Called: Young and Malmberg PA (G-3892)*
Malone Bayside Marina 302 947-0234
  Long Neck Rd Millsboro (19966) *(G-8361)*
Malone Cement Construction Inc 302 239-9399
  11 Rosecroft Ct Wilmington (19808) *(G-18095)*
Malone Concrete Cnstr Co, Wilmington *Also Called: Malone Cement Construction Inc (G-18095)*
Malong LLC 516 336-9992
  1013 Centre Rd Ste 4035 Wilmington (19805) *(G-18096)*
Mals Sports 302 598-8247
  4 Bemis Rd Newark (19711) *(G-11320)*
Malwation Inc 302 208-9661
  16192 Coastal Hwy Lewes (19958) *(G-6239)*
Mamaste Doula and Birth Svcs 302 670-3188
  429 W Denneys Rd Dover (19904) *(G-3005)*
Mammele's Paint Stores, Wilmington *Also Called: Mammeles Inc (G-18097)*
Mammeles Inc 302 998-0541
  2300 Kirkwood Hwy Wilmington (19805) *(G-18097)*
Man Around House 302 531-5124
  618 Evans Dr Milford (19963) *(G-7982)*
Man Maid Cleaning Inc 302 226-5050
  29 Fox Creek Dr Rehoboth Beach (19971) *(G-12845)*
Management 24 LLC (PA) 646 820-5224
  8 The Grn Ste A Dover (19901) *(G-3006)*
Management Associates Inc 302 652-3991
  613 N Washington St Wilmington (19801) *(G-18098)*
Management Chemical Co 410 326-0964
  281 Debs Way Dover (19901) *(G-3007)*
Management Consulting, Middletown *Also Called: Insider Insight LLC (G-7226)*
Management Pain LLC 302 543-5180
  5231 W Woodmill Dr Ste 45 Wilmington (19808) *(G-18099)*
Management PI Investme 888 654-5449
  20 Montchanin Rd Wilmington (19807) *(G-18100)*
Management Systems Improvement 860 478-7496
  61 Balfour Ave Claymont (19703) *(G-1229)*
Manatec Electronics LLC 248 653-1245
  651 N Broad St Ste 205 # 1405 Middletown (19709) *(G-7325)*
Manchester Trading Co 302 500-4010
  40 E Main St Newark (19711) *(G-11321)*
Mancomtec LLC 234 243-4256
  2055 Limestone Rd Ste 200c Wilmington (19808) *(G-18101)*
Mancon Inc 302 395-5376
  100 Churchmans Rd New Castle (19720) *(G-9342)*
Mancor US Inc 302 573-3858
  1011 Centre Rd Ste 322 Wilmington (19805) *(G-18102)*
Mandip LLC 302 218-7449
  65 Geoffrey Dr Newark (19713) *(G-11322)*
Mane Attraction 302 526-2013
  604 Forest St Dover (19904) *(G-3008)*
Maneto Inc (HQ) 302 656-4285
  103 Foulk Rd Wilmington (19803) *(G-18103)*
Manicured Lawns 302 853-2222
  9804 Nanticoke Cir Seaford (19973) *(G-13272)*
Manifesta 610 883-0202
  135 Devonshire Rd Wilmington (19803) *(G-18104)*
Manley Hvac Inc 302 998-4654
  3705 Wild Cherry Ln Wilmington (19808) *(G-18105)*
Manlove Auto Parts, Georgetown *Also Called: Fisher Auto Parts Inc (G-4324)*
Manlove Auto Parts, Smyrna *Also Called: Fisher Auto Parts Inc (G-13736)*
Manlove Auto Parts, Wilmington *Also Called: Fisher Auto Parts Inc (G-16648)*
Manmade Kennels LLC 302 272-3625
  107 Redstone Ct Felton (19943) *(G-4000)*
Mann & Moore Associates, Rehoboth Beach *Also Called: Century 21 Mann & Sons (G-12667)*
Mann & Sons Inc 302 841-0077
  19606 Coastal Hwy Unit 104 Rehoboth Beach (19971) *(G-12846)*
Manners Brand LLC (PA) 470 830-1114
  8 The Grn Ste 8 Dover (19901) *(G-3009)*
Manning Gross + Massenburg LLP 302 657-2100
  1007 N Orange St Apt 1051 Wilmington (19801) *(G-18106)*
Manoa Fresh Food LLC 561 453-0521
  8 The Grn Ste B Dover (19901) *(G-3010)*
Manoj Ornaments Inc 916 779-7916
  8 The Grn Ste A Dover (19901) *(G-3011)*
Manor Creek Construction Inc 302 245-2887
  213 Gumboro Rd Selbyville (19975) *(G-13565)*
Manor Exxon Inc 302 834-6691
  131 W Savannah Dr Bear (19701) *(G-360)*
Manor House, Seaford *Also Called: Acts Rtrmnt-Life Cmmnities Inc (G-13047)*
Mansion House Farm Paintball 302 650-3141
  557 Mansion House Rd Bear (19701) *(G-361)*
Mantikote Podiaky, Seaford *Also Called: James F Palmer (G-13229)*
Mantis Farms 302 507-4851
  2 Winston Pl Wilmington (19804) *(G-18107)*
Manufactured Housing 302 744-2383
  555 S Bay Rd Dover (19901) *(G-3012)*
Manufacturers & Traders Tr Co 302 651-8828
  10 Foxhunt Dr Bear (19701) *(G-362)*
Manufacturers & Traders Tr Co 302 472-3262
  3503 Philadelphia Pike Claymont (19703) *(G-1230)*
Manufacturers & Traders Tr Co 302 855-2297
  38716 Sussex Hwy Delmar (19940) *(G-1616)*
Manufacturers & Traders Tr Co 302 735-2020
  1001 E Lebanon Rd Dover (19901) *(G-3013)*
Manufacturers & Traders Tr Co 302 735-2010
  139 S State St Dover (19901) *(G-3014)*
Manufacturers & Traders Tr Co 302 472-3177
  151 Lantana Dr Hockessin (19707) *(G-5295)*
Manufacturers & Traders Tr Co 302 855-2873
  101 W Market St Laurel (19956) *(G-5559)*
Manufacturers & Traders Tr Co 302 855-2218
  32547 Lewes Georgetown Hwy Lewes (19958) *(G-6240)*
Manufacturers & Traders Tr Co 302 449-2780
  405 W Main St Middletown (19709) *(G-7326)*
Manufacturers & Traders Tr Co 302 285-3277
  399 E Main St Middletown (19709) *(G-7327)*
Manufacturers & Traders Tr Co 302 855-2160
  673 N Dupont Blvd Milford (19963) *(G-7983)*
Manufacturers & Traders Tr Co 302 855-2891
  207 E Dupont Hwy Millsboro (19966) *(G-8362)*
Manufacturers & Traders Tr Co 302 855-2184
  107 Front St Milton (19968) *(G-8660)*
Manufacturers & Traders Tr Co 302 472-3249
  287 Christiana Rd Ste 16 New Castle (19720) *(G-9343)*
Manufacturers & Traders Tr Co 302 651-1618
  82 E Main St Newark (19711) *(G-11323)*

Manufacturers & Traders Tr Co — ALPHABETIC SECTION

Manufacturers & Traders Tr Co 302 472-3335
  550 Suburban Dr Newark (19711) *(G-11324)*

Manufacturers & Traders Tr Co 302 855-2227
  302 Rehoboth Ave Rehoboth Beach (19971) *(G-12847)*

Manufacturers & Traders Tr Co 302 856-4470
  509 W Stein Hwy Seaford (19973) *(G-13273)*

Manufacturers & Traders Tr Co 302 651-8738
  3801 Kennett Pike Wilmington (19807) *(G-18108)*

Manufacturers & Traders Tr Co 302 472-3161
  15 W Lea Blvd Wilmington (19802) *(G-18109)*

Manufacturers & Traders Tr Co 302 636-6000
  1100 N Market St Wilmington (19801) *(G-18110)*

Manufacturers & Traders Tr Co 302 472-3309
  4899 Limestone Rd Stoney Creek Plaza Wilmington (19808) *(G-18111)*

Manufacturers & Traders Tr Co 302 472-3233
  2301 Concord Pike Wilmington (19803) *(G-18112)*

Manufacturers & Traders Tr Co 302 651-1757
  2371 Limestone Rd Wilmington (19808) *(G-18113)*

Manufacturers & Traders Tr Co 302 651-1803
  1812 Marsh Rd Wilmington (19810) *(G-18114)*

Manufacturers & Traders Tr Co 302 651-1544
  100 N James St Wilmington (19804) *(G-18115)*

Manufacturers & Traders Tr Co 302 656-1260
  1207 N Union St Wilmington (19806) *(G-18116)*

Manufacturing Center, Newark Also Called: Bloom Energy Corporation *(G-10056)*

Manufacturing Support Inds Inc 410 334-6140
  108 Park Ave Seaford (19973) *(G-13274)*

Manufctured Hsing Concepts LLC 302 934-8848
  28862 Dupont Blvd Millsboro (19966) *(G-8363)*

Manveen Duggal MD 302 734-5438
  874 Walker Rd Ste B Dover (19904) *(G-3015)*

Map Hauiling 267 235-6712
  5 Surrey Dr New Castle (19720) *(G-9344)*

Maple Crest LLC 302 540-9937
  1626 Old Coochs Bridge Rd Newark (19702) *(G-11325)*

Maplewood Dental Associates, Rehoboth Beach Also Called: Conley & Wright DDS *(G-12697)*

Mar Fitness Enterprises Inc 302 730-1234
  1005 N State St Dover (19901) *(G-3016)*

Mara Labs Inc (PA) 650 564-4971
  1013 Ctr Rd Ste 403-B Wilmington (19805) *(G-18117)*

Mara Puglisi Holistic Hlth LLC 302 368-4245
  909 Pickett Ln Newark (19711) *(G-11326)*

Mara Puglisi Holistic Hlth LLC 240 338-0137
  19 Hidden Valley Dr Newark (19711) *(G-11327)*

Marble City Software Inc 302 658-2583
  1900 Gilpin Ave Wilmington (19806) *(G-18118)*

Marc Kattelman Do 260 485-4580
  100 Delaware Veterans Blvd Milford (19963) *(G-7984)*

Marc Richman PHD 302 834-3039
  2600 Glasgow Ave Ste 124 Newark (19702) *(G-11328)*

Marc V Felizzi 302 897-4942
  4402 Limestone Rd Wilmington (19808) *(G-18119)*

Marc Wsburg Lpcmh Mntal Hlth C 302 798-4400
  1201 Philadelphia Pike Wilmington (19809) *(G-18120)*

Marcelle L Paschall DSC 302 376-1768
  419 South St Townsend (19734) *(G-14030)*

March of Dimes Inc 302 225-1020
  236 N James St Ste C Wilmington (19804) *(G-18121)*

Marches Jewelers Inc 856 858-4463
  34508 Spring Brook Ave Lewes (19958) *(G-6241)*

Marcon John Solutions Inc 302 295-4806
  1000 N West St Ste 1200 Wilmington (19801) *(G-18122)*

Marcone 800 482-6022
  228 W Market St Wilmington (19804) *(G-18123)*

Marcus Materials Co 302 731-7519
  9 Renee Ct Newark (19711) *(G-11329)*

Marenos Landscaping 302 531-7009
  122 Lakshman Trl Dover (19904) *(G-3017)*

Margaret Harris-Nemtuda 302 477-5500
  3513 Concord Pike # 1000 Wilmington (19803) *(G-18124)*

Margaret Keith's Draperies, Wilmington Also Called: Vertical Blind Factory Inc *(G-20598)*

Margaret Wright-Stasi 302 745-1509
  213 E State St Millsboro (19966) *(G-8364)*

Margarita Man 302 947-4000
  34397 Skyler Dr Lewes (19958) *(G-6242)*

Margarita Man of Delaware 302 344-5837
  32353 Turnstone Ct Millsboro (19966) *(G-8365)*

Margherita Vincent & Anthony 302 834-9023
  5 Misty Ct Newark (19702) *(G-11330)*

Margo Lewis-Jah Leona 610 800-9524
  237 Dumont Rd Wilmington (19804) *(G-18125)*

Maria Lazar MD 302 838-2210
  102 Harvest Ct Hockessin (19707) *(G-5296)*

Maria Rubino Watkins 405 532-4023
  125 Montchan Dr Wilmington (19807) *(G-18126)*

Mariachi House 302 635-7361
  7313 Lancaster Pike Ste 3 Hockessin (19707) *(G-5297)*

Marian Rosella Foundation Inc 888 977-1937
  523 Concord Bridge Pl Newark (19702) *(G-11331)*

Marian Thurrell 302 239-1269
  533 Holly Knoll Rd Hockessin (19707) *(G-5298)*

Marianas Energy Company LLC 671 477-3060
  160 Greentree Dr Dover (19904) *(G-3018)*

Marianna J McSweeney Pt 302 234-1803
  174 Belmont Dr Wilmington (19808) *(G-18127)*

Mariano Lozano 302 478-6710
  121 Alders Dr Wilmington (19803) *(G-18128)*

Marie Bernier 240 731-1555
  126f October Glory Ave Ocean View (19970) *(G-12542)*

Marie E Dye 302 698-4280
  239 Old North Rd Camden (19934) *(G-871)*

Marie Willow & Co 302 632-0831
  18422 Coastal Hwy Lewes (19958) *(G-6243)*

Marin Bayard 302 658-4200
  521 N West St Wilmington (19801) *(G-18129)*

Marine & Energy Trading Corp 857 207-7999
  1201 N Orange St Wilmington (19801) *(G-18130)*

Marine Lubricants Inc 302 429-7570
  1130 E 7th St Wilmington (19801) *(G-18131)*

Marinis Bros Inc 302 322-9663
  755 Grantham Ln New Castle (19720) *(G-9345)*

Marino & Sons, New Castle Also Called: Amer Masonry T A Marino *(G-8794)*

Marins Med LLC 302 245-4596
  23334 Frederick Ln Georgetown (19947) *(G-4413)*

Mario F Medori Inc 302 239-4550
  20 Millside Dr Wilmington (19801) *(G-18132)*

Mario Medori Inc 302 656-8432
  20 Millside Dr Wilmington (19801) *(G-18133)*

Marita F Fallorina MD 302 322-0660
  1 Catherine St Ste 1 New Castle (19720) *(G-9346)*

Maritime Logistics Corp LLC 302 420-3007
  1130 E 7th St Wilmington (19801) *(G-18134)*

Maritime Logistics Corp LLC (PA) 302 420-3007
  27706 Valley Run Dr Wilmington (19810) *(G-18135)*

Marjam Supply Co Inc 302 283-1020
  200 Bellevue Rd Newark (19713) *(G-11332)*

Marjano LLC 302 454-7446
  14 Orchid Dr Bear (19701) *(G-363)*

Mark A Fortunato 302 477-4900
  1415 Foulk Rd Wilmington (19803) *(G-18136)*

Mark A Horne 302 381-6672
  35721 Elk Camp Rd Rehoboth Beach (19971) *(G-12848)*

Mark Adcock 302 660-0909
  5560 Kirkwood Hwy Wilmington (19808) *(G-18137)*

Mark B Brown DDS 302 537-1200
  32895 Coastal Hwy Unit 102 Bethany Beach (19930) *(G-617)*

Mark C Gladnick DDS 302 994-2660
  5513 Kirkwood Hwy Wilmington (19808) *(G-18138)*

Mark Duphily Trucking Inc 302 292-2271
  127 Bartley Dr Newark (19702) *(G-11333)*

Mark E Case M D 302 449-1710
  272 Carter Dr Ste 200 Middletown (19709) *(G-7328)*

ALPHABETIC SECTION — Martech Communications

Mark E Handley 302 284-9550
156 Henry Cowgill Rd Camden Wyoming (19934) *(G-960)*

Mark Evangelista MD 302 629-4569
1501 Middleford Rd Seaford (19973) *(G-13275)*

Mark Glassner MD 302 369-9002
324 E Main St Ste 202 Newark (19711) *(G-11334)*

Mark Gosser 302 388-8395
2083 Brackenville Rd Hockessin (19707) *(G-5299)*

Mark H Davidson 302 422-0646
8684 Cedar Creek Rd Lincoln (19960) *(G-6682)*

Mark IV Beauty Salon Inc 302 737-4994
240 College Sq Newark (19711) *(G-11335)*

Mark IV Hair Design, Newark Also Called: Mark IV Beauty Salon Inc *(G-11335)*

Mark JB Inc 888 984-5845
254 Chapman Rd Ste 208 Newark (19702) *(G-11336)*

Mark Jones Paving 302 355-0695
123 Hilldale Ct Claymont (19703) *(G-1231)*

Mark Mathew Mauragas Dc 302 750-8084
134 Belmont Dr Wilmington (19808) *(G-18139)*

Mark Menendez 302 644-8500
4 Blue Heron Dr Georgetown (19947) *(G-4414)*

Mark Neurology LLC 302 933-0111
22998 Springwood Cir Millsboro (19966) *(G-8366)*

Mark One LLC 302 735-4700
1700 E Lebanon Rd Dover (19901) *(G-3019)*

Mark Penuel 302 856-7724
522 E Market St Georgetown (19947) *(G-4415)*

Mark Perry Productions LLC 443 521-4382
5 Par Ct Georgetown (19947) *(G-4416)*

Mark Sanford 302 593-9773
14 Quartz Mill Rd Newark (19711) *(G-11337)*

Mark Showell Interiors Ltd 302 227-2272
37025 Rehoboth Avenue Ext Unit L Rehoboth Beach (19971) *(G-12849)*

Mark T Droney 302 537-2305
31322 Railway Rd Millville (19967) *(G-8539)*

Mark Ventresca Associates Inc 302 239-3925
19 Bernard Blvd Hockessin (19707) *(G-5300)*

Mark W Eckard 302 778-7518
1201 N Market St Ste 1500 Wilmington (19801) *(G-18140)*

Mark Wanner 302 478-6878
4017 Greenmount Dr Wilmington (19810) *(G-18141)*

Mark Wieczorek Dmd PC 302 838-3384
494 Bear Christiana Rd Bear (19701) *(G-364)*

Markatos Cleaning Services, Wilmington Also Called: Markatos Services Inc *(G-18142)*

Markatos Services Inc 302 792-0606
1411 Philadelphia Pike Ste B Wilmington (19809) *(G-18142)*

Markel and Associates LLC 302 898-5684
412 Sitka Spruce Ln Townsend (19734) *(G-14031)*

Markes International Inc 302 656-5500
270 Presidential Dr Wilmington (19807) *(G-18143)*

Market Black LLC 267 257-3017
304 7th St New Castle (19720) *(G-9347)*

Market Black Trucking, New Castle Also Called: Market Black LLC *(G-9347)*

Market Edge LLC (PA) 302 442-6800
1003 Park Pl Wilmington (19806) *(G-18144)*

Market Research Reports Inc 302 703-9904
16192 Coastal Hwy Lewes (19958) *(G-6244)*

Market St Chrprctic Rhblttion 302 652-6000
727 N Market St Ste 1 Wilmington (19801) *(G-18145)*

Market Street Center Inc 302 856-9024
9 Chestnut St Georgetown (19947) *(G-4417)*

Marketforce Technologies Inc 339 674-0529
8 The Grn Ste A Dover (19901) *(G-3020)*

Marketing Creators Inc 302 409-0344
802 N West St Wilmington (19801) *(G-18146)*

Marketing Momma 302 259-1644
568 Owens Brooke Dr Smyrna (19977) *(G-13815)*

Marketing Plus LLC 205 952-6602
8 The Grn Ste R Dover (19901) *(G-3021)*

Marketing Resources Inc 302 855-9209
23 Fairway Ave Georgetown (19947) *(G-4418)*

Marking Services Inc 302 478-0381
3505 Silverside Rd Ste 101 Wilmington (19810) *(G-18147)*

Markizon Printing 610 715-7989
111 Nevada Ave Wilmington (19803) *(G-18148)*

Markland Affiliates LLC 302 633-9134
2126 W Nwport Pike Ste 20 Wilmington (19804) *(G-18149)*

Marks Onill Obrien Dhrty Klly 302 658-6538
300 Delaware Ave Ste 900 Wilmington (19801) *(G-18150)*

Markvell Delarie Gilmore Trust 772 742-1499
24a Trolley Sq Ste 1372 Wilmington (19806) *(G-18151)*

Marlen D Schlabach 302 236-5394
36170 Smith Mill Ch Rd Delmar (19940) *(G-1617)*

Marlette R Lofland 302 628-1521
20255 Wilson Farm Rd Bridgeville (19933) *(G-728)*

Marlette Services Inc 302 358-2730
3419 Silverside Rd Wilmington (19810) *(G-18152)*

Marlex Pharmaceuticals Inc 302 328-3355
65 Lukens Dr New Castle (19720) *(G-9348)*

Marlings Emrgncy Wtr Rmval Crp, Wilmington Also Called: Marlings Inc *(G-18153)*

Marlings Inc 302 325-1759
41 Germay Dr Ste D Wilmington (19804) *(G-18153)*

Marnie Custom Homes 302 616-2664
33298 Coastal Hwy Unit 3 Bethany Beach (19930) *(G-618)*

Marnie Properties 302 462-5312
Bethany Beach (19930) *(G-619)*

Maron Mrvel Brdley Anderson PA (PA) 302 425-5177
1201 N Market St Ste 900 Wilmington (19801) *(G-18154)*

Marosa Surgical Industries 302 674-0907
42 Reads Way Ste A New Castle (19720) *(G-9349)*

Marquez Misael MD 302 995-6192
2601 Annand Dr Ste 13 Wilmington (19808) *(G-18155)*

Marquis Consulting LLC 480 438-5582
16192 Coastal Hwy Lewes (19958) *(G-6245)*

Marquis Dorsey LLC 832 693-0260
651 N Broad St Ste 205 # 6054 Middletown (19709) *(G-7329)*

Marra Landing LLC 302 530-5800
6 W Clivden Dr Wilmington (19807) *(G-18156)*

Marriott, Wilmington Also Called: Courtyard Management Corp *(G-15661)*

Marriott Vctons Wrldwide Owner 302 636-6128
1220 N Market St Ste 202 Wilmington (19801) *(G-18157)*

Mars James Hitchens & Williams, Wilmington Also Called: Morris James LLP *(G-18454)*

Marsha Neal Studio LLC 302 559-6781
56 Kings Grant Rd Hockessin (19707) *(G-5301)*

Marshall Anthony Jr 302 398-3043
Roads 111 Harrington (19952) *(G-4799)*

Marshall Construction, Newark Also Called: Marshall Kyle *(G-11338)*

Marshall Dnnhey Wrner Clman Gg 302 504-3341
1007 N Orange St Ste 600 Wilmington (19801) *(G-18158)*

Marshall Dnnhey Wrner Clman Gg 302 552-4300
1220 N Market St Ste 201 Wilmington (19801) *(G-18159)*

Marshall Kyle 302 454-7838
323 Jaymar Blvd Newark (19702) *(G-11338)*

Marshall Manor LP 302 422-8255
977 E Masten Cir Milford (19963) *(G-7985)*

Marshall Services Inc 302 655-0076
2202 Fairfield Pl Wilmington (19805) *(G-18160)*

Marshall T Williams MD PHD 302 994-9692
537 Stanton Christiana Rd Newark (19713) *(G-11339)*

Marshall Wagner & Associates 302 227-2537
19643 Blue Bird Ln Unit 2 Rehoboth Beach (19971) *(G-12850)*

Marsico & Weinstien DDS 302 998-8474
2390 Limestone Rd Wilmington (19808) *(G-18161)*

Marsico Weinstien, Wilmington Also Called: Marsico & Weinstien DDS *(G-18161)*

Marta Biskup DDS 302 478-0000
3522 Silverside Rd Wilmington (19810) *(G-18162)*

Marta Blackhurst DMD 302 478-1504
3522 Silverside Rd Wilmington (19810) *(G-18163)*

Marta Group 302 737-2008
885 Marrows Rd Apt D6 Newark (19713) *(G-11340)*

Martech Communications 703 989-6390
16233 John Rowland Trl Milton (19968) *(G-8661)*

(PA)=Parent Co (HQ)=Headquarters (DH)=Div Headquarters

Martel & Son Foreign Car Ctr... 302 674-5556
1161 Horsepond Rd Dover (19901) (G-3022)

Martel Inc... 302 674-5660
702 Dundee Rd Dover (19904) (G-3023)

Martello RE Holdings Ltd LLC.. 302 636-5401
251 Little Falls Dr Wilmington (19808) (G-18164)

Martha Marie Charters... 302 222-5637
8965 Clendaniel Pond Rd Lincoln (19960) (G-6683)

Marthann Print Center LLC... 267 884-8130
1130 Charles Dr Dover (19904) (G-3024)

Marthin Luther Homes of Del, Newark Also Called: Mosaic (G-11455)

Martial Industries LLC.. 302 983-5742
526 Barrymore Pkwy Middletown (19709) (G-7330)

Martin & Calloway... 302 268-6655
3601 Old Capitol Trl Unit A3 Wilmington (19808) (G-18165)

Martin & Calloway LLC... 302 482-1180
1224 Mckennans Church Rd Wilmington (19808) (G-18166)

Martin Collision Center.. 302 452-2711
298 E Cleveland Ave Newark (19711) (G-11341)

Martin Construction Svcs LLC... 302 200-0885
340 W Chestnut Hill Rd Newark (19713) (G-11342)

Martin D Hvrly Attorney At Law... 302 529-0121
2500 Grubb Rd Ste 240b Wilmington (19810) (G-18167)

Martin Daniel D & Assoc LLC... 302 658-2884
1301 N Harrison St Wilmington (19806) (G-18168)

Martin Dealership.. 302 738-5200
298 E Cleveland Ave Newark (19711) (G-11343)

Martin Direct Insurance... 302 452-2700
298 E Cleveland Ave Newark (19711) (G-11344)

Martin Grey LLC... 302 990-0675
16192 Coastal Hwy Lewes (19958) (G-6246)

Martin Honda, Newark Also Called: Martin Newark Dealership Inc (G-11345)

Martin Newark Dealership Inc.. 302 454-9300
298 E Cleveland Ave Newark (19711) (G-11345)

Martin Zukoff CPA... 302 478-4734
2523 Bona Rd Wilmington (19810) (G-18169)

Martinelli Holdings LLC (PA).. 302 656-1809
1000 N West St Wilmington (19801) (G-18170)

Martinez Automotive... 302 250-5933
260 Christiana Rd Apt N5 New Castle (19720) (G-9350)

Martinez Painting LLC.. 302 448-1932
21859 Hickory Dr Georgetown (19947) (G-4419)

Martinrea International US Inc.. 615 212-0586
1209 N Orange St Wilmington (19801) (G-18171)

Martins Home Improvements... 302 367-4789
405 Milton Dr Wilmington (19802) (G-18172)

Martom Landscaping Co Inc.. 302 322-1920
1699 St Georges Business Ctr Saint Georges (19733) (G-13037)

Marvel Agency Inc.. 302 422-7844
15 N Walnut St Milford (19963) (G-7986)

Marvel Portable Welding Inc.. 302 732-9480
32887 Dupont Blvd Dagsboro (19939) (G-1479)

Marvelous Lghts Prductions LLC (PA)............................. 215 678-2013
3 Evlon Ct New Castle (19720) (G-9351)

Marvi Cleaners Limited Inc... 302 764-3077
309 Philadelphia Pike Wilmington (19809) (G-18173)

Marvin & Palmer Associates... 302 573-3570
200 Bellevue Pkwy Ste 220 Wilmington (19809) (G-18174)

Marvin & Palmer US Equity LP... 302 573-3570
200 Bellevue Pkwy Ste 220 Wilmington (19809) (G-18175)

Marvin Palmer Globl Equity LP.. 302 573-3570
200 Bellevue Pkwy Ste 220 Wilmington (19809) (G-18176)

Mary Annes Landscaping Inc.. 302 335-5433
96 Windward Dr Felton (19943) (G-4001)

Mary Bryan Inc... 302 875-2087
4679 Old Sharptown Rd Laurel (19956) (G-5560)

MARY CAMPBELL CENTER, Wilmington Also Called: McC Foundation Inc (G-18215)

Mary Campbell Center Inc.. 302 762-6025
4641 Weldin Rd Wilmington (19803) (G-18177)

Mary Costas Woodworking.. 302 227-6255
527 School Ln Rehoboth Beach (19971) (G-12851)

Mary Del Ranch Inc.. 302 492-8866
449 Tappahannak Trl Marydel (19964) (G-6807)

Mary E Herring Daycare Center....................................... 302 652-5978
2450 N Market St Ste 1 Wilmington (19802) (G-18178)

Mary E Mahoney.. 302 757-9656
44 Christiana River Dr Clayton (19938) (G-1384)

Mary E. Herring Day Care, Wilmington Also Called: Mary E Herring Daycare Center (G-18178)

Mary Hazlett.. 302 653-8823
82 Monrovia Ave Smyrna (19977) (G-13816)

Mary Huff.. 302 650-2460
1500 Shallcross Ave Ste 1a Wilmington (19806) (G-18179)

Mary Kate Johnston.. 302 388-5654
228 Suburban Dr Newark (19711) (G-11346)

Mary L Kreider... 302 375-6232
2001 Woodbrook Dr Wilmington (19810) (G-18180)

Mary Mother Hope House 1... 302 652-8532
1103 W 8th St Wilmington (19806) (G-18181)

Mary Mother of Hope House III, Wilmington Also Called: Ministry of Caring Inc (G-18376)

Mary Sweeney-Lehr.. 302 764-0589
3209 Coachman Rd Wilmington (19803) (G-18182)

Mary Ziomek DDS... 301 984-9646
317 Mariners Cir Milton (19968) (G-8662)

Marydale Retirement Village, Newark Also Called: Catholic Mnstry To Elderly Inc (G-10163)

Maryland Center For Therapeuti...................................... 302 727-8832
28763 Valley View Ln Lewes (19958) (G-6247)

Marylou Sheaffer... 302 422-4118
432 Kings Hwy Milford (19963) (G-7987)

Maryruth L Nich... 302 623-1929
86 Omega Dr Newark (19713) (G-11347)

Marys Little Lambs Daycare... 302 436-5796
31730 Phillips Rd Selbyville (19975) (G-13566)

Masc Farming LLC... 302 734-3602
6479 Bayside Dr Dover (19901) (G-3025)

Masley Enterprises Inc.. 302 427-9885
1601 Jessup St Wilmington (19802) (G-18183)

Mason Building Group Inc.. 302 292-0600
35 Albe Dr Newark (19702) (G-11348)

Mason Contractor, Wilmington Also Called: Wilmington Stoneworks LLC (G-20845)

Mason Mechanical LLC... 302 653-4022
345 Southern View Dr Smyrna (19977) (G-13817)

Mass For The Homeless Inc.. 302 368-1030
2817 Ambler Ct Wilmington (19808) (G-18184)

Massage By Hand, Milford Also Called: Michelle Hand (G-7995)

Massage Envy, Newark Also Called: Massage Envy - Christiana (G-11349)

Massage Envy, Rehoboth Beach Also Called: Massage Envy Lewes (G-12852)

Massage Envy - Christiana.. 302 266-2762
3148 Fashion Center Blvd Newark (19702) (G-11349)

Massage Envy Lewes.. 302 703-4100
18949 Coastal Hwy Unit 104 Rehoboth Beach (19971) (G-12852)

Masseys Landing Park Inc.. 302 947-2600
20628 Long Beach Dr Millsboro (19966) (G-8367)

Masstech, Dover Also Called: Masstech Americas Inc (G-3026)

Masstech Americas Inc.. 905 946-5700
850 New Burton Rd Ste 201 Dover (19904) (G-3026)

Mast Homes LLC... 302 632-7735
2397 Sandy Bend Rd Camden (19934) (G-872)

Masten Electric Inc.. 302 653-4300
405 W Commerce St Smyrna (19977) (G-13818)

Master Extnded Mkt Index Sries..................................... 800 441-7762
100 Bellevue Pkwy Wilmington (19809) (G-18185)

Master Focus Growth LLC.. 800 441-7762
100 Bellevue Pkwy Wilmington (19809) (G-18186)

Master G Entertainment.. 302 547-9367
1427 Athens Rd Wilmington (19803) (G-18187)

Master Industrial Catalog, Millsboro Also Called: Lweco Group LLC (G-8355)

Master Interiors Inc... 302 368-9361
156 Mullet Run Milford (19963) (G-7988)

Master Interiors Inc (PA).. 302 368-9361
113 Sandy Dr Newark (19713) (G-11350)

Master Kit Inc.. 650 743-5126
160 Greentree Dr Ste 101 Dover (19904) (G-3027)

ALPHABETIC SECTION — Max RE Associates Inc

Master Klean Company 302 539-4290
   Cedar Neck Rd Ocean View (19970) *(G-12543)*

Master Painting and Remodeling 302 604-8978
   29538 Millsboro Hwy Millsboro (19966) *(G-8368)*

Master Shower Doors, Newark *Also Called: R & J Taylor Inc* *(G-11802)*

Master Sidlow & Associates PA 302 652-3480
   750 Prides Xing Ste 100 Newark (19713) *(G-11351)*

Master Tech Inc 302 832-1660
   743 Rue Madora Bear (19701) *(G-365)*

Master Tech Pnt Collision Ctr, Bear *Also Called: Master Tech Inc* *(G-365)*

Master-Halco Inc 302 475-6714
   Wilmington (19899) *(G-18188)*

Mastercraft Welding 302 697-3932
   4010 S Dupont Hwy Dover (19901) *(G-3028)*

Mastercrafters Inc 302 678-1470
   1234 S Governors Ave Ste A Dover (19904) *(G-3029)*

Mastering Mrcury Dsign Elments 302 344-4323
   12 Boisenberry Ln Georgetown (19947) *(G-4420)*

Mastermark Woodworking Inc 302 945-9131
   25205 Mastermark Ln Millsboro (19966) *(G-8369)*

Masters Touch Cleaning LLC 302 650-8165
   118 Colesbery Dr New Castle (19720) *(G-9352)*

Mastracci Mastracci 410 869-3400
   30107 Tammy Ct Selbyville (19975) *(G-13567)*

Mat Site Management LLC 302 397-8561
   3828 Kennett Pike Ste 201 Wilmington (19807) *(G-18189)*

Matador Companies LLC 855 303-4229
   16192 Coastal Hwy Lewes (19958) *(G-6248)*

Matchapro Inc 213 573-9882
   7209 Lancaster Pike Hockessin (19707) *(G-5302)*

Mateina US Inc 514 443-4945
   2915 Ogletown Rd Newark (19713) *(G-11352)*

Mater Ellis LLC 302 508-0938
   919 N Market St Wilmington (19801) *(G-18190)*

Material Handling Supply Inc 302 571-0176
   243 Quigley Blvd Ste I Historic New Castle (19720) *(G-5024)*

Material Supply, New Castle *Also Called: Material Transit Inc* *(G-9353)*

Material Supply Inc 302 658-6524
   924 S Heald St Wilmington (19801) *(G-18191)*

Material Transit Inc 302 395-0556
   255 Airport Rd New Castle (19720) *(G-9353)*

Maternity Gynecology Assoc PA 302 368-9000
   4745 Ogletown Stanton Rd Ste 207 Newark (19713) *(G-11353)*

Maternity Womens Health 302 994-0979
   2601 Annand Dr Ste 14 Wilmington (19808) *(G-18192)*

Mathias, New Castle *Also Called: Staging Dimensions Inc* *(G-9589)*

Mathletics Inc 302 724-0619
   117 Lady Bug Dr Dover (19901) *(G-3030)*

Matium Inc 703 457-9997
   1111b S Governors Ave Ste 6245 Dover (19904) *(G-3031)*

Mativ, Middletown *Also Called: Mativ Holdings Inc* *(G-7331)*

Mativ Holdings Inc 302 378-8888
   601 Industrial Dr Middletown (19709) *(G-7331)*

Matrica Labs Inc 818 573-7394
   1209 N Orange St Wilmington (19801) *(G-18193)*

Matrix Life Science Inc 281 419-7942
   16192 Coastal Hwy Lewes (19958) *(G-6249)*

Matrix Network Solutions LLC 302 331-7330
   18 Bandcroft Dr Camden Wyoming (19934) *(G-961)*

Matrix Rehabilitation Delaware 302 424-1714
   800 Airport Rd Ste 102 Milford (19963) *(G-7989)*

Matrixport Inc 626 474-8738
   850 New Burton Rd Ste 201 Dover (19904) *(G-3032)*

Matt Basile State Farm Insur 302 659-9000
   28 N Dupont Blvd Smyrna (19977) *(G-13819)*

Matt Carpet Guy LLC 443 497-3281
   50 N Main St Selbyville (19975) *(G-13568)*

Matt Matiaset 302 376-3042
   212 Karins Blvd Townsend (19734) *(G-14032)*

Matt S Auto Care 302 226-2407
   18013 Robinsonville Rd Lewes (19958) *(G-6250)*

Matt's Auto Care, Rehoboth Beach *Also Called: Wiedman Enterprises Inc* *(G-13016)*

Matt's Line Painting, Frankford *Also Called: Matts Management Family LLC* *(G-4125)*

Matter Gray Security LLC 302 235-8627
   118 Juneberry Ct Hockessin (19707) *(G-5303)*

Matter Music Inc 650 793-7749
   427 N Tatnall St # 25426 Wilmington (19801) *(G-18194)*

Mattern & Piccioni Md PA 302 730-8060
   260 Beiser Blvd Ste 101 Dover (19904) *(G-3033)*

Mattern and Associates MD 302 724-5062
   1675 S State St Ste A Dover (19901) *(G-3034)*

Matthew & Michele Denn 302 235-0175
   441 Coldspring Run Newark (19711) *(G-11354)*

Matthew and Richard Entp LLC 267 767-0290
   36 E Moyer Dr Bear (19701) *(G-366)*

Matthew B Lunn 302 571-6646
   1000 N West St Wilmington (19801) *(G-18195)*

Matthew Eicherbaum 302 655-9494
   1941 Limestone Rd Wilmington (19808) *(G-18196)*

Matthew J McIlrath DC 302 798-7033
   1201 Philadelphia Pike Wilmington (19809) *(G-18197)*

Matthew Kirby 302 427-0911
   113 Dickinson Ln Wilmington (19807) *(G-18198)*

Matthew Smith Bus Service 302 734-9311
   206 N Queen St Dover (19904) *(G-3035)*

Matthew W Lawrence Do 302 652-6050
   1500 Shallcross Ave Wilmington (19806) *(G-18199)*

Matthew W Spence Inc 302 697-3284
   329 E Camden Wyoming Ave Camden (19934) *(G-873)*

Matthews Pierce & Lloyd Inc (PA) 302 678-5500
   830 Walker Rd Ste 12 Dover (19904) *(G-3036)*

Matthews Towing & Recovery 302 463-1108
   710 Black Diamond Rd Smyrna (19977) *(G-13820)*

Mattleman Weinroth & Miller PC 302 731-8349
   200 Continental Dr Ste 215 Newark (19713) *(G-11355)*

Mattress Firm, Milford *Also Called: Mattress Firm Milford* *(G-7990)*

Mattress Firm Milford 302 422-6585
   945a N Dupont Blvd Ste D Milford (19963) *(G-7990)*

Matts Fish Camp Lewes De LLC 302 539-4415
   34401 Tenley Ct Lewes (19958) *(G-6251)*

Matts Management Family LLC 302 732-3715
   32397 Omar Rd Frankford (19945) *(G-4125)*

Matykos Beauty LLC 302 213-6879
   200 Brandywine Blvd Wilmington (19809) *(G-18200)*

Mauna Services LLC 302 446-4409
   8 The Grn Dover (19901) *(G-3037)*

Maureen Freebery 302 234-7800
   4801 Limestone Rd Wilmington (19808) *(G-18201)*

Maureens Beauty Salon, Wilmington *Also Called: Maureen Freebery* *(G-18201)*

Maurten US Corporation 302 669-9085
   1000 N West St Ste 1200 Wilmington (19801) *(G-18202)*

Mauviel Usa Inc 302 326-4800
   802 Centerpoint Blvd Historic New Castle (19720) *(G-5025)*

Maven Security Consulting Inc 302 365-6862
   512 Portrush Pass Bear (19701) *(G-367)*

Maven Workforce LLC 551 214-8937
   200 Continental Dr Ste 401 Newark (19713) *(G-11356)*

Maverick Realty LLC 302 373-6591
   200 Continental Dr Ste 401 Newark (19713) *(G-11357)*

Maverick Tattoo Company LLC 443 858-1511
   22585 Bridgeville Hwy Seaford (19973) *(G-13276)*

Mavis Tire 2104, Dover *Also Called: Mavis Tire Express Svcs Corp* *(G-3038)*

Mavis Tire Express Svcs Corp 727 440-5435
   280 Cowgill St Dover (19901) *(G-3038)*

Mawi Inc 888 937-6868
   919 N Market St Ste 950 Wilmington (19801) *(G-18203)*

Maws Tails Mfg 302 740-7664
   29621 Riverstone Dr Milton (19968) *(G-8663)*

Max One Printing 302 897-9050
   310 Chattahoochee Dr Bear (19701) *(G-368)*

Max RE Associates Inc 302 453-3200
   228 Suburban Dr Newark (19711) *(G-11358)*

Max RE Associates Inc — ALPHABETIC SECTION

Max RE Associates Inc (PA) 302 477-3900
228 Suburban Dr Newark (19711) *(G-11359)*

Max RE Central 302 234-3800
1302 Old Lancaster Pike Hockessin (19707) *(G-5304)*

Max Seal Inc 619 946-2650
16192 Coastal Hwy Lewes (19958) *(G-6252)*

Max Value Software LLC 630 254-8804
1209 N Orange St Wilmington (19801) *(G-18204)*

Maxicare Ambulance Services 302 990-3777
19 Peddlers Row Newark (19702) *(G-11360)*

Maxihost, Wilmington *Also Called: Latitude Sh LLC (G-17817)*

Maxillofacial Southern De Oral 302 644-2977
17605 Nassau Commons Blvd # 1 Lewes (19958) *(G-6253)*

Maxim Hair & Nails LLC 410 920-8656
31225 Americana Pkwy Unit 7 Selbyville (19975) *(G-13569)*

Maxim Healthcare Services Inc 302 478-3434
1523 Concord Pike Ste 100 Wilmington (19803) *(G-18205)*

Maximum Electrical Svcs LLC 302 521-2820
4142 Ogletown Stanton Rd Unit 254 Newark (19713) *(G-11361)*

Maxines Daycare 302 652-7242
1027 Lancaster Ave Wilmington (19805) *(G-18206)*

Maxines Hair Happenings Inc 302 875-4055
206 Laureltowne Laurel (19956) *(G-5561)*

Maxweb Inc 302 208-8361
1201 N Orange St Ste 7266 Wilmington (19801) *(G-18207)*

Maxwell Financial Firm LLC 302 332-3454
303 Waverly Rd Wilmington (19803) *(G-18208)*

Maya Virtual Inc 213 587-7995
8 The Grn Ste 13521 Dover (19901) *(G-3039)*

Maya.net, Dover *Also Called: Maya Virtual Inc (G-3039)*

Mayer Racing Stables 302 829-8673
37223 Lord Baltimore Ln Ocean View (19970) *(G-12544)*

Mayfair Apartments, Wilmington *Also Called: Frankel Enterprises Inc (G-16726)*

Mayflower Healthcare LLC 908 414-8026
108 W 13th St Ste 100 Wilmington (19801) *(G-18209)*

Mayflower Laundry and Lin Sups 302 652-1416
10 Dock View Dr New Castle (19720) *(G-9354)*

Mayhorns Collisionandrestoratn 302 779-2177
3002 Judith Rd Hartly (19953) *(G-4895)*

Mayple Ltd 917 558-0698
2810 N Church St Pmb 15700 Wilmington (19802) *(G-18210)*

Mayr Enterprises Inc 302 846-2999
7175 W Line Rd Delmar (19940) *(G-1618)*

Mayscapes LLC 302 389-5999
129 Phyllis Dr Newark (19711) *(G-11362)*

Mayse Painting & Contg LLC 443 553-6503
2250 Audubon Trl Middletown (19709) *(G-7332)*

Mazzola Construction, Newark *Also Called: Mazzola Systems Inc (G-11363)*

Mazzola Systems Inc 302 738-6808
560 Peoples Plz Ste 112 Newark (19702) *(G-11363)*

Mazzpac LLC 973 641-9159
94 Salem Church Rd Newark (19713) *(G-11364)*

MB Store LLC 425 310-2574
1207 Delaware Ave Wilmington (19806) *(G-18211)*

MBNA, Wilmington *Also Called: MBNA Marketing Systems Inc (G-18213)*

MBNA Bank Great Expectations, Newark *Also Called: Bright Horizons Chld Ctrs LLC (G-10087)*

MBNA Consumer Services Inc 302 453-9930
1100 N King St Wilmington (19884) *(G-18212)*

MBNA Marketing Systems Inc 302 456-8588
1100 N King St Wilmington (19884) *(G-18213)*

Mc Creative Group 302 348-8977
25935 Plaza Dr Unit 2 Millsboro (19966) *(G-8370)*

Mc Hunter LLC 302 672-0072
1246 S Little Creek Rd Dover (19901) *(G-3040)*

Mc Mullen Septic Service Inc 302 629-6221
22593 Bridgeville Hwy Seaford (19973) *(G-13277)*

Mc2 Therapeutics Inc 202 505-0891
8 The Grn Ste 8321 Dover (19901) *(G-3041)*

MCA, Wilmington *Also Called: Blackrock Mnyeld Cal Qlty Fund (G-14931)*

MCA - Mdsg Cons Assoc USA Inc 800 465-4755
874 Walker Rd Ste C Dover (19904) *(G-3042)*

MCB Landscaping LLC 215 421-1083
1020 Darley Rd Wilmington (19810) *(G-18214)*

McBride and Ziegler Inc 302 737-9138
2607 Eastburn Ctr Newark (19711) *(G-11365)*

McBroom Jr Roger Dale 302 228-0998
13505 Bender Farm Rd Greenwood (19950) *(G-4651)*

McC Foundation Inc 302 762-6025
4641 Weldin Rd Wilmington (19803) *(G-18215)*

McCabe Weisberg Conway PC 302 409-3520
1407 Foulk Rd Ste 100 Wilmington (19803) *(G-18216)*

McCabes Mechanical Service Inc 302 854-9001
16689 Seashore Hwy Georgetown (19947) *(G-4421)*

McCall Brooks Insurance Agency 302 475-8200
110 Christiana Medical Ctr Newark (19702) *(G-11366)*

McCar Auto Group LLC 302 478-3049
2527 Eaton Rd Wilmington (19810) *(G-18217)*

McCarter & English LLP 302 984-6300
405 N King St Ste 800 Wilmington (19801) *(G-18218)*

McCarter English, Wilmington *Also Called: Katharine L Mayer Atty (G-17660)*

McCarthy Cate 302 477-0708
1409 Foulk Rd Ste 204 Wilmington (19803) *(G-18219)*

McCauley Enterprises LLC 217 454-7056
7209 Lancaster Pike Ste 4 Hockessin (19707) *(G-5305)*

McClafferty Printing Company 302 652-8112
1600 N Scott St Wilmington (19806) *(G-18220)*

McClain Custodial Service 302 645-6597
418 Burton Ave Lewes (19958) *(G-6254)*

McCloskey Barbara Lcsw 302 479-5916
114 Hitching Post Dr Wilmington (19803) *(G-18221)*

McCollom Dmlio Smith Ubler LLC 302 468-5960
2751 Centerville Rd Ste 400 Wilmington (19808) *(G-18222)*

McComrick Insurance Services 302 732-6655
3394 N Main St Dagsboro (19939) *(G-1480)*

McConnell Bros Inc 302 218-4240
400 E Ayre St Wilmington (19804) *(G-18223)*

McConnell Johnson RE Co LLC 302 421-2000
1201 N Market St Ste 1605 Wilmington (19801) *(G-18224)*

McCormick Assoc Middletown LLC 302 449-0710
5350 Summit Bridge Rd Ste 107 Middletown (19709) *(G-7333)*

McCORMICK TAYLOR INC 302 738-0208
220 Continental Dr Ste 200 Newark (19713) *(G-11367)*

McCove Construction Inc 302 363-0528
615 Sharon Hill Rd Dover (19904) *(G-3043)*

McCoy Enterprises, Newark *Also Called: Enhanced Corporate Prfmce LLC (G-10648)*

McCracken M Jill, Wilmington *Also Called: Circle Veterinary Clinic (G-15444)*

McCrea Equipment Company Inc 302 337-8249
16855 Sussex Hwy Bridgeville (19933) *(G-729)*

McCrery Funeral Homes Inc 302 478-2204
3924 Concord Pike Wilmington (19803) *(G-18225)*

McCullough & Associates Inc 302 250-7679
2303 Woods Rd Wilmington (19808) *(G-18226)*

McDonald Safety Equipment Inc 302 999-0151
581 Copper Dr Wilmington (19804) *(G-18227)*

McElroy & Son Inc 302 995-2623
15 E Redmont Rd Wilmington (19804) *(G-18228)*

McGivney Kluger & Cook PC 302 656-1200
1201 N Orange St Ste 504 Wilmington (19801) *(G-18229)*

McGraphix Advertising Products, Selbyville *Also Called: Midnight Blue Inc (G-13576)*

Mch Construction LLC 302 249-2765
170 Plain Dealing Rd Magnolia (19962) *(G-6764)*

MCI Communications Corporation 302 791-4900
200 Bellevue Pkwy Ste 500 Wilmington (19809) *(G-18230)*

McIlvain Lawn Mowing More LLC 302 684-4213
26564 Carpenter Rd Milton (19968) *(G-8664)*

McJ Seal & Line Striping LLC 302 416-1326
40 Loder Dr Smyrna (19977) *(G-13821)*

McJ Seal & Line Striping LLC 302 691-3255
35 Indiana Rd Wilmington (19808) *(G-18231)*

McKee Group Mckee Management 302 449-0778
1467 Whispering Woods Rd Middletown (19709) *(G-7334)*

McKelvey Hires Dry Cleaning 302 998-9191
808 First State Blvd Wilmington (19804) *(G-18232)*

ALPHABETIC SECTION

McKenzie Paving Inc.. 302 376-8560
114 Bakerfield Dr Middletown (19709) *(G-7335)*

McKie Foundation, The, Newark Also Called: New Vision Services Inc *(G-11526)*

McLaren Health Care Corp.. 214 257-7012
55 Lukens Dr Historic New Castle (19720) *(G-5026)*

McLaughlin Gordon L Law Office................................ 302 651-7979
1203 N Orange St Wilmington (19801) *(G-18233)*

McLaughlin Morton Holdg Co LLC............................. 302 426-1313
1203 N Orange St Fl 2 Wilmington (19801) *(G-18234)*

McLean Masonry Contractors LLC............................. 215 349-0719
46 Parkers Dr Dover (19904) *(G-3044)*

McLeen Properties... 302 482-1486
240n Janes St Ste 100c Wilmington (19804) *(G-18235)*

McMahon Heating & AC.. 302 945-4300
20378 John J Williams Hwy Lewes (19958) *(G-6255)*

McNeil and Fmly MGT Group LLC............................. 302 830-3267
2 White Oak Rd Wilmington (19809) *(G-18236)*

McNeil Paving.. 302 945-7131
32758 Spring Water Dr Millsboro (19966) *(G-8371)*

McNicholas Painting.. 302 995-0964
202 Redwood Ave Wilmington (19804) *(G-18237)*

McOmm Installer, Rehoboth Beach Also Called: Crypto Trader LLC *(G-12708)*

McRogge LLC (PA)... 215 300-7975
651 N Broad St Middletown (19709) *(G-7336)*

McV Microwave East Inc.. 302 877-8079
11307 Trussum Pond Rd Laurel (19956) *(G-5562)*

Md22 Lions Low Vision Rehab................................. 410 737-2671
1400 Forrest Rd Wilmington (19810) *(G-18238)*

Mdaas Global Corp.. 410 905-1213
160 Greentree Dr Dover (19904) *(G-3045)*

Mdm McHncal Instlltion USA LLC............................. 617 938-9634
1201 N Orange St Ste 700 Wilmington (19801) *(G-18239)*

MDN Billing Consulting Svcs.................................... 914 376-6100
24 Nw Front St Milford (19963) *(G-7991)*

Mdnewsline Inc.. 773 759-4363
28 Old Rudnick Ln Dover (19901) *(G-3046)*

Mds Interpreting LLC... 302 507-2393
116 Churchill Ln Wilmington (19808) *(G-18240)*

Mds Services Inc... 302 547-3861
207 E Cobblefield Ct Newark (19713) *(G-11368)*

ME Geek Squad Llc... 302 990-8092
727 Maryland Ave Wilmington (19805) *(G-18241)*

Meade Inc.. 302 262-3394
22536 Sussex Hwy Seaford (19973) *(G-13278)*

Meadow Edge Corp.. 302 530-7339
313 Blue Jay Dr Hockessin (19707) *(G-5306)*

Meadowbrook Farms Inc.. 443 735-6244
14702 Baker Rd Delmar (19940) *(G-1619)*

Meadowbrook Golf Group Inc................................... 302 571-9041
800 N Dupont Rd Wilmington (19807) *(G-18242)*

Meadowood Mobil Station....................................... 302 731-5602
2650 Kirkwood Hwy Newark (19711) *(G-11369)*

Meadows, The, Delaware City Also Called: Connectons Cmnty Spport Prgram *(G-1534)*

Meadowwood.. 302 286-7004
115 Rockrose Dr Newark (19711) *(G-11370)*

Meadowwood Behavioral Health, New Castle Also Called: Focus Health Care Delaware LLC *(G-9138)*

Mealey Fnrl Homes & Crematory, Wilmington Also Called: Michael A Mealey & Sons Inc *(G-18305)*

Mealey Funeral Homes, Wilmington Also Called: Michael A Mealey & Sons Inc *(G-18304)*

MEALS ON WHEELS, Lewes Also Called: Meals On Whels of Lwes Rhoboth *(G-6256)*

Meals On Wheels of Lwes Rhoboth......................... 302 645-7449
32409 Lewes Georgetown Hwy Lewes (19958) *(G-6256)*

Meaningteam Inc... 213 669-5804
3500 S Dupont Hwy Dover (19901) *(G-3047)*

Mears Health Campus... 302 628-6300
200 Rawlins Dr Seaford (19973) *(G-13279)*

Mebro Inc.. 302 992-0104
225 N James St Wilmington (19804) *(G-18243)*

Mecatech Indus Equipments LLC............................. 617 586-4224
8 The Grn Ste B Dover (19901) *(G-3048)*

Mecham Mechanical.. 302 645-2793
30202 Whitehall Dr Milton (19968) *(G-8665)*

Mechanical Solutions LLC....................................... 302 900-1950
6944 Westville Rd Camden (19934) *(G-874)*

Mechanical Systems Intl Corp.................................. 302 453-8315
9 Lewis St. Newark (19711) *(G-11371)*

Mechanics Paradise Inc... 302 652-8863
2335 N Dupont Hwy New Castle (19720) *(G-9355)*

Med Tech Equipment Inc... 800 322-2609
2207 Concord Pike Ste 135 Wilmington (19803) *(G-18244)*

Medal LP... 302 225-1100
305 Water St Wilmington (19804) *(G-18245)*

Medarch Inc... 405 638-3126
8 The Grn Dover (19901) *(G-3049)*

Medblob Inc... 813 308-9273
8 The Grn Dover (19901) *(G-3050)*

Medevice Services LLC... 877 202-1588
3500 S Dupont Hwy Dover (19901) *(G-3051)*

Medexpress... 302 477-1406
2722 Concord Pike Wilmington (19803) *(G-18246)*

Medfluencers Inc... 518 813-2788
21215 Dauphine St Lewes (19958) *(G-6257)*

Medford, William L Jr MD, Wilmington Also Called: Wilmington Otlrynglogy Assoc P *(G-20828)*

Medhat Iskander... 302 422-2020
1197 Airport Rd Ste 1 Milford (19963) *(G-7992)*

Medi-Weightloss Clinics.. 302 763-3455
502 Lantana Dr Hockessin (19707) *(G-5307)*

Media Fusion US LLC... 256 532-3874
214 W General Grey Ct Newark (19702) *(G-11372)*

Mediacom LLC... 302 732-9332
32441 Royal Blvd Dagsboro (19939) *(G-1481)*

MEDIACOM LLC, Dagsboro Also Called: Mediacom LLC *(G-1481)*

Mediastreet LLC.. 800 308-6579
2035 Sunset Lake Rd Ste B2 Newark (19702) *(G-11373)*

Mediasurfer, Wilmington Also Called: Mediasurfer Inc *(G-18247)*

Mediasurfer Inc... 814 300-8335
1232 N King St Ste 1028 Wilmington (19801) *(G-18247)*

Medical Alternative Care... 302 430-5705
301 Jefferson Ave Milford (19963) *(G-7993)*

Medical Associates Bear Inc.................................... 302 832-6768
121 Becks Woods Dr Ste 100 Bear (19701) *(G-369)*

Medical Billing & MGT Svcs Inc (PA)........................ 610 564-5314
111 Continental Dr Ste 315 Newark (19713) *(G-11374)*

Medical Billing Associates, Wilmington Also Called: Mary L Kreider *(G-18180)*

Medical Billing Management................................... 302 239-2235
5301 Limestone Rd Ste 100 Wilmington (19808) *(G-18248)*

Medical Center of Harrington.................................. 302 398-8704
203 Shaw Ave # 205 Harrington (19952) *(G-4800)*

Medical Facility Lls Medical, Seaford Also Called: Addiction Medical Facility LLC *(G-13049)*

Medical Joyworks LLC... 310 919-4287
4023 Kennett Pike # 55630 Wilmington (19807) *(G-18249)*

Medical Massage Delaware LLC (PA)....................... 888 757-1951
254 Chapman Rd Ste 112 Newark (19702) *(G-11375)*

Medical Oncology Hmtlogy Cons P.......................... 302 366-1200
4701 Ogletown Stanton Rd Ste 2200 Newark (19713) *(G-11376)*

Medical Reimbursement Sol.................................... 516 809-6812
29517 Glenwood Dr Millsboro (19966) *(G-8372)*

Medical Society of Delaware (PA)............................ 302 366-1400
900 Prides Xing Newark (19713) *(G-11377)*

Medical Sup Support Svcs LLC................................ 302 446-3658
8 The Grn Ste 8095 Dover (19901) *(G-3052)*

Medical Technologies Intl....................................... 760 837-4778
8 The Grn Ste 1 Dover (19901) *(G-3053)*

Medical Tourism Agency LLC................................... 855 753-3833
427 N Tatnall St Wilmington (19801) *(G-18250)*

Medici Ventures Inc... 801 319-7029
1209 N Orange St Wilmington (19801) *(G-18251)*

Medicine Woman... 302 684-8048
503 Canning House Row Milton (19968) *(G-8666)*

Medictek Inc.. 302 351-4924
902 N Market St Apt 805 Wilmington (19801) *(G-18252)*

Mediguide International LLC   ALPHABETIC SECTION

Mediguide International LLC (PA) 302 425-5900
   4550 Linden Hill Rd Ste 103 Wilmington (19808) *(G-18253)*

Medimaps Group USA LLC 302 416-3063
   913 N Market St Ste 200n Wilmington (19801) *(G-18254)*

Medimmune LLC 301 398-1200
   1800 Concord Pike Wilmington (19897) *(G-18255)*

Medirents and Sales Inc 302 286-7999
   2860 Ogletown Rd Newark (19713) *(G-11378)*

Medlab-Havertown Inc (PA) 302 655-5227
   212 Cherry Ln New Castle (19720) *(G-9356)*

Medlanta Inc 610 991-2929
   1000 N West St Ste 1200 Wilmington (19801) *(G-18256)*

Medrep Inc 302 571-0263
   903 Berkeley Rd Wilmington (19807) *(G-18257)*

Medshift Cyber, Wilmington *Also Called: Medshifts Inc (G-18258)*

Medshifts Inc 856 834-0074
   1201 N Orange St Ste 600 Wilmington (19801) *(G-18258)*

Medtix LLC 302 736-0172
   1006 College Rd Dover (19904) *(G-3054)*

Medtix LLC 302 265-4550
   16337 Coastal Hwy Lewes (19958) *(G-6258)*

Medtix LLC (PA) 302 645-8070
   221 S Rehoboth Blvd Milford (19963) *(G-7994)*

Medtix Medical Supply, Milford *Also Called: Medtix LLC (G-7994)*

Medusind Solutions Inc 800 250-7063
   111 Continental Dr Ste 412 Newark (19713) *(G-11379)*

Medzoomer Inc 239 595-8899
   600 N Broad St Ste 5 Middletown (19709) *(G-7337)*

Meenakshi Hindu Charitable 302 588-0686
   146 Pumpkin Patch Ln Hockessin (19707) *(G-5308)*

Meetrecord Inc 281 407-7338
   1013 Centre Rd Ste 403b Wilmington (19805) *(G-18259)*

Mefta LLC 804 433-3566
   1220 N Market St Wilmington (19801) *(G-18260)*

Meg A Frizzola Do 302 651-4000
   1600 Rockland Rd Wilmington (19803) *(G-18261)*

Megan Aitken Team LLC 302 376-9836
   831 Kingswood Path Middletown (19709) *(G-7338)*

Megan Couch 302 981-0687
   113 Country Club Dr Newark (19711) *(G-11380)*

Megan Gorelick Interiors Inc 302 482-1325
   100 W Rockland Rd Montchanin (19710) *(G-8738)*

Megan Mc Graw Lcsw 302 283-0414
   200 Christina Pkwy # P Newark (19713) *(G-11381)*

Megara Inc 914 487-4702
   8 The Grn Dover (19901) *(G-3055)*

Megee Plumbing & Heating Co 302 856-6311
   22965 Lewes Georgetown Hwy Georgetown (19947) *(G-4422)*

Megellan Terminal, Wilmington *Also Called: Magellan Midstream Partners LP (G-18078)*

Meghan House Inc 302 253-8261
   210 Rosa St Georgetown (19947) *(G-4423)*

Meghan Zgler Hlth Wellness LLC 302 379-9967
   126 Wedge Ct Townsend (19734) *(G-14033)*

Meher Health Services 302 947-0333
   32362 Long Neck Rd Millsboro (19966) *(G-8373)*

Meherrin AG & Chem Co 302 337-0330
   18441 Wesley Church Rd Bridgeville (19933) *(G-730)*

MEI App Inc (PA) 617 877-6603
   2035 Sunset Lake Rd Ste B2 Newark (19702) *(G-11382)*

Meineke Car Care Center, Dover *Also Called: Rbs Auto Repair Inc (G-3426)*

Meineke Car Care Center 671 .... 302 746-2026
   3005 Philadelphia Pike Claymont (19703) *(G-1232)*

Meineke Care Care Center 302 368-0700
   750 E Chestnut Hill Rd Newark (19713) *(G-11383)*

Meineke Discount Mufflers, Claymont *Also Called: Meineke Car Care Center 671 (G-1232)*

Meineke Discount Mufflers, Dover *Also Called: Daves Disc Mfflers of Dver De (G-2199)*

Meineke Discount Mufflers, Lewes *Also Called: Meineke Muffler (G-6259)*

Meineke Discount Mufflers, New Castle *Also Called: Rcs Mufflers Inc (G-9514)*

Meineke Muffler 302 644-8544
   213 W Cape Shores Dr Lewes (19958) *(G-6259)*

Mekhala Living Inc 650 443-8235
   8 The Grn Dover (19901) *(G-3056)*

Melaleuca Wellness Company 336 314-5635
   903 Vinings Way Newark (19702) *(G-11384)*

Melanated Minds Foundation LLC 302 312-5303
   4004 N Shipley St Wilmington (19802) *(G-18262)*

Melanin Mixx Beauty, Newark *Also Called: Melanin Mixx Beauty Brand Inc (G-11385)*

Melanin Mixx Beauty Brand Inc 302 266-1010
   7 Peddlers Row Ste B Newark (19702) *(G-11385)*

Melchiorre and Melchiorre 302 645-6311
   17352 Coastal Hwy Lewes (19958) *(G-6260)*

Melento Inc 571 989-1300
   8 The Grn Ste A Dover (19901) *(G-3057)*

Melissa A Wolf 716 465-7093
   18512 Belle Grove Rd # 6 Lewes (19958) *(G-6261)*

Melissa M Damiano Do 302 449-2570
   3920 Dupont Pkwy Townsend (19734) *(G-14034)*

Melissas Childcare 302 547-6722
   24 Overlook Ave Wilmington (19808) *(G-18263)*

Mello Financial Inc 801 877-7787
   251 Middle Falls Dr Wilmington (19808) *(G-18264)*

Mellon Care Inc (PA) 800 406-0281
   651 N Broad St Ste 201 Middletown (19709) *(G-7339)*

Mellon Private Wealth MGT 302 421-2306
   4005 Kennett Pike Wilmington (19807) *(G-18265)*

Melodic Movements, Wilmington *Also Called: Melodic Mvmnts Prfrmg Arts Prg (G-18266)*

Melodic Mvmnts Prfrmg Arts Prg 302 543-5257
   28 W 38th St Wilmington (19802) *(G-18266)*

Melody Entertainment, Wilmington *Also Called: Melody Entertainment USA Inc (G-18267)*

Melody Entertainment USA Inc 305 505-7659
   717 N Union St Apt 68 Wilmington (19805) *(G-18267)*

Mels Htg & A/C 302 947-1979
   33736 Lawton Ln Millsboro (19966) *(G-8374)*

Mels Wells LLC 302 393-9017
   8468 Hollybrook Dr Lincoln (19960) *(G-6684)*

Melson Funeral Services 302 945-9000
   Longneck Rd Millsboro (19966) *(G-8375)*

Melson Funeral Services Ltd 302 732-9000
   43 Thatcher St Frankford (19945) *(G-4126)*

Melsons Cape Hnlopen Crematory 302 537-2441
   41 Thatcher St Frankford (19945) *(G-4127)*

Melsons Henlipen Creammatury, Frankford *Also Called: Melson Funeral Services Ltd (G-4126)*

Meltrone Inc 302 998-3457
   5828 Kirkwood Hwy Wilmington (19808) *(G-18268)*

Melvin L Joseph Cnstr Co 302 856-7396
   25136 Dupont Blvd Georgetown (19947) *(G-4424)*

Melvin's Sunoco, Dover *Also Called: Lee Lynn Inc (G-2923)*

Meme US Holdings LLC 619 342-4340
   8 The Grn Ste B Dover (19901) *(G-3058)*

Memorial Hall of Tllyvlle Fire 302 478-1110
   3919 Concord Pike Wilmington (19803) *(G-18269)*

Memorial Sloan Kttring Cncer C 302 384-7588
   400 Foulk Rd Wilmington (19803) *(G-18270)*

Memorial Super Fuel 215 512-1012
   3006 New Castle Ave New Castle (19720) *(G-9357)*

Men In Black Wdding Officiants 302 945-6903
   36000 Chester Ct Lewes (19958) *(G-6262)*

Menainfosec Inc 217 650-7167
   651 N Broad St Ste 206 Middletown (19709) *(G-7340)*

Menark Technologies Inc 302 379-2185
   101 Rachel Dr Bear (19701) *(G-370)*

Menchaca Building Corp 302 475-4581
   4 Lloyd Pl Wilmington (19810) *(G-18271)*

Mending Cove LLC 856 803-9958
   31 Thorn Ln Apt 11 Newark (19711) *(G-11386)*

Mendota Merchants LLC 302 401-6453
   8 The Grn Ste 7347 Dover (19901) *(G-3059)*

Menehariya LLC 240 432-0082
   8 The Grn Dover (19901) *(G-3060)*

Mental Edge Counseling 302 382-8698
   1198 S Governors Ave Ste 201 Dover (19904) *(G-3061)*

Mental Fuel Inc 302 291-4858
   200 Continental Dr Ste 401 Newark (19713) *(G-11387)*

ALPHABETIC SECTION

Mental Health Assn In Del.. 302 654-6833
  100 W 10th St Ste 600 Wilmington (19801) *(G-18272)*

Menton Elizabeth A Crna PC... 443 694-6769
  28881 Harmons Hill Rd Millsboro (19966) *(G-8376)*

Mentor Consultants Inc.. 610 566-4004
  3200 Concord Pike Wilmington (19803) *(G-18273)*

Mentor De... 302 858-4644
  19372 Citizens Blvd Georgetown (19947) *(G-4425)*

Mentoris, Wilmington Also Called: Clairvyant Technosolutions Inc *(G-15460)*

Merakey USA... 302 325-3540
  2 Penns Way New Castle (19720) *(G-9358)*

Merakey USA... 302 836-1809
  6301 Vicky Dr Newark (19702) *(G-11388)*

Meratalk LLC... 914 241-5226
  2093 Philadelphia Pike Ste 1748 Claymont (19703) *(G-1233)*

Mercantile Press Inc... 302 764-6884
  3007 Bellevue Ave Wilmington (19802) *(G-18274)*

Mercantile Processing Inc... 302 524-8000
  32695 Roxana Rd Millville (19967) *(G-8540)*

Mercatante Beatrice An.. 302 995-7073
  4600 New Lndn Hill Rd 2 Wilmington (19808) *(G-18275)*

Mercer and Sydell Dental, Milton Also Called: Mercer Dental Associates *(G-8667)*

Mercer Dental Associates... 302 664-1385
  524 Union St Milton (19968) *(G-8667)*

Mercer Dental Associates, Dover Also Called: Thomas W Mercer DMD *(G-3680)*

Merchant Global Assistance LLC...................................... 914 522-4871
  8 The Grn Dover (19901) *(G-3062)*

Merck, Millsboro Also Called: Merck & Co Inc *(G-8377)*

Merck & Co Inc... 302 934-8051
  29160 Intervet Ln Millsboro (19966) *(G-8377)*

Mercuri Inc (PA)... 425 395-5238
  1209 N Orange St Wilmington (19801) *(G-18276)*

Mercury Financial LLC... 302 588-0107
  123 S Justison St Ste 602 Wilmington (19801) *(G-18277)*

Mercury Research LLC.. 860 532-3480
  651 N Broad St Middletown (19709) *(G-7341)*

Mercurysend LLC... 917 267-8627
  1220 N Market St Wilmington (19801) *(G-18278)*

Mercy Care For Wns Hlth Ob/Gyn..................................... 302 883-3677
  819 S Governors Ave Dover (19904) *(G-3063)*

Mercy Land Academy Inc.. 302 378-2013
  211 E Main St Middletown (19709) *(G-7342)*

Merestone Consultants Inc... 302 226-5880
  33516 Crossing Ave Unit 1 Lewes (19958) *(G-6263)*

Merestone Consultants Inc (PA)....................................... 302 992-7900
  5215 W Woodmill Dr Ste 38 Wilmington (19808) *(G-18279)*

Mergers Acqstons Strtegies LLC (PA)............................. 302 992-0400
  5183 W Woodmill Dr Ste 3 Wilmington (19808) *(G-18280)*

Merida Aerospace Inc (PA)... 305 396-1471
  16192 Coastal Hwy Lewes (19958) *(G-6264)*

Meridian Bank.. 302 635-7500
  5301 Limestone Rd Ste 224 Wilmington (19808) *(G-18281)*

Meridian Bank.. 302 477-9449
  1601 Concord Pike Ste 45 Wilmington (19803) *(G-18282)*

Meridian Limo LLC.. 800 462-1550
  8 The Grn Dover (19901) *(G-3064)*

Meris Gardens Bed & Breakfast....................................... 302 752-4962
  33309 Kent Ave Bethany Beach (19930) *(G-620)*

Meris Property LLC... 301 928-6519
  26 N Pennsylvania Ave Bethany Beach (19930) *(G-621)*

Merit Cnstr Engineers Inc.. 302 992-9810
  5700 Kirkwood Hwy Ste 201 Wilmington (19808) *(G-18283)*

Merit Construction Engineers.. 302 992-9810
  1605 E Ayre St Wilmington (19804) *(G-18284)*

Merit Inc.. 302 778-4732
  207 S Market St Wilmington (19801) *(G-18285)*

Merit Mechanical Co Inc.. 302 366-8601
  39 Albe Dr Newark (19702) *(G-11389)*

Merit Services Inc... 302 366-8601
  39 Albe Dr Newark (19702) *(G-11390)*

Merix LLC (PA)... 425 659-1425
  16192 Coastal Hwy Lewes (19958) *(G-6265)*

Merman Management Inc.. 302 644-6990
  109 W Market St Lewes (19958) *(G-6266)*

Merman Management Inc.. 302 456-9904
  5145 W Woodmill Dr # 22 Wilmington (19808) *(G-18286)*

Mernies Market... 302 629-9877
  4610 Woodland Church Rd Seaford (19973) *(G-13280)*

Merrill Lynch, Dover Also Called: Merrill Lynch Prce Fnner Smith *(G-3065)*

Merrill Lynch, Wilmington Also Called: Merrill Lynch Prce Fnner Smith *(G-18287)*

Merrill Lynch Prce Fnner Smith.. 302 736-7700
  55 Kings Hwy Dover (19901) *(G-3065)*

Merrill Lynch Prce Fnner Smith.. 302 571-5100
  1201 N Market St Ste 2000 Wilmington (19801) *(G-18287)*

Merritt Marine Cnstr Inc... 302 436-2881
  32992 Lighthouse Rd Selbyville (19975) *(G-13570)*

Merry Maids... 302 223-9259
  56 W Main St Ste 107 Christiana (19702) *(G-1005)*

Merry Maids... 302 266-6243
  1 Washington St Newark (19711) *(G-11391)*

Merry Maids, Christiana Also Called: Merry Maids *(G-1005)*

Merry Maids, Dover Also Called: Merry Maids Inc *(G-3066)*

Merry Maids, Newark Also Called: Merry Maids *(G-11391)*

Merry Maids, Ocean View Also Called: Merry Maids of Ocean View *(G-12545)*

Merry Maids Inc.. 302 698-9038
  30 S American Ave Dover (19901) *(G-3066)*

Merry Maids 462 1052, Dagsboro Also Called: Djh Enterprises Vii LLC *(G-1441)*

Merry Maids of Ocean View.. 410 729-6661
  38452 Resort Rv Cir Ocean View (19970) *(G-12545)*

Meryls.. 302 475-7555
  2500 Grubb Rd Ste 240 Wilmington (19810) *(G-18288)*

Mesa Jame Corp... 302 528-9106
  120 Laks Dr Middletown (19709) *(G-7343)*

Messer LLC.. 302 798-9342
  6000 Philadelphia Pike Claymont (19703) *(G-1234)*

Messick & Gray Cnstr Inc (PA).. 302 337-8777
  9003 Fawn Rd Bridgeville (19933) *(G-731)*

Messick and Johnson LLc... 302 628-3111
  955 Norman Eskridge Hwy Seaford (19973) *(G-13281)*

Messicks Mobile Homes Inc.. 302 398-9166
  17959 S Dupont Hwy Harrington (19952) *(G-4801)*

Messina Charles Plbg & Elc Co.. 302 674-5696
  3681 S Little Creek Rd Dover (19901) *(G-3067)*

Mesys Inc.. 917 566-7011
  8 The Grn Ste A Dover (19901) *(G-3068)*

Met Technologies LLC... 302 468-5243
  40 E Main St Newark (19711) *(G-11392)*

Meta Humans Ltd.. 904 690-1589
  16192 Coastal Hwy Lewes (19958) *(G-6267)*

Meta Mind Global Corp LLC (PA)..................................... 267 471-3616
  8 The Grn Ste A Dover (19901) *(G-3069)*

Metal Fabrication / Contractor, Newark Also Called: Dempseys Specialized Svcs LLC *(G-10512)*

Metal Msters Fdservice Eqp Inc (PA)............................... 302 653-3000
  100 Industrial Blvd Clayton (19938) *(G-1385)*

Metal Partners International, New Castle Also Called: Metal Partners Rebar LLC *(G-9359)*

Metal Partners Rebar LLC... 215 791-3491
  20 Davidson Ln New Castle (19720) *(G-9359)*

Metal Shop LLC... 302 846-2988
  10690 Allens Mill Rd Delmar (19940) *(G-1620)*

Metal-Tech Inc... 302 322-7770
  265 Airport Rd New Castle (19720) *(G-9360)*

Metamax Technology Inc... 302 587-0060
  8 Innovation Way Newark (19711) *(G-11393)*

Metanium Corp... 302 669-9084
  8 The Grn Dover (19901) *(G-3070)*

Metanode Inc.. 302 782-9758
  8 The Grn Ste D Dover (19901) *(G-3071)*

Metanoia Counseling LLC.. 302 559-4421
  101 W Park Pl Middletown (19709) *(G-7344)*

Metaquotes Software Corp.. 657 859-6918
  602 Rockwood Rd Wilmington (19802) *(G-18289)*

Metatron Inc (PA).. 619 550-4668
  160 Greentree Dr Ste 101 Dover (19904) *(G-3072)*

Metawork Corporation 347 756-1222
2810 N Church St Wilmington (19802) *(G-18290)*

Meter Service, Newark *Also Called: Hillside Oil Company Inc (G-10953)*

Meticulous, Claymont *Also Called: Meticulous Home Inc (G-1235)*

Meticulous Home Inc 302 878-7879
2093 Philadelphia Pike # 7717 Claymont (19703) *(G-1235)*

Metl Technology Inc 954 309-4589
1209 Norange Ste Wilmington (19801) *(G-18291)*

MetLife, Dover *Also Called: MetLife Svcs & Solutions LLC (G-3073)*

MetLife, Wilmington *Also Called: American Life Insurance Co (G-14435)*

MetLife, Wilmington *Also Called: Metlife Inc (G-18292)*

Metlife Inc 302 594-2085
600 N King St Fl 7 Wilmington (19801) *(G-18292)*

MetLife Svcs & Solutions LLC 302 734-5803
160 Greentree Dr Ste 105 Dover (19904) *(G-3073)*

Metodo Fspa - Grriere In Forma, Dover *Also Called: Ifcf LLC (G-2719)*

Metro By T-Mobile 302 724-7494
431 S New St Dover (19904) *(G-3074)*

Metro By T-Mobile 302 744-8473
1616 S Governors Ave Dover (19904) *(G-3075)*

Metro By T-Mobile 302 378-3559
859 N Broad St Middletown (19709) *(G-7345)*

Metro By T-Mobile 302 508-5123
70 E Glenwood Ave Smyrna (19977) *(G-13822)*

Metro By T-Mobile 302 384-7158
107 N Maryland Ave Wilmington (19804) *(G-18293)*

Metro Eqp & Sheetmetal Pdts 302 337-8249
16855 Sussex Hwy Bridgeville (19933) *(G-732)*

Metro Merchant Services, Wilmington *Also Called: Delaware Merchant Services (G-15944)*

Metro Steel Incorporated 302 778-2288
4049 New Castle Ave New Castle (19720) *(G-9361)*

Metroform Group Inc 302 737-1165
4639 Ogletown Stanton Rd Newark (19713) *(G-11394)*

Metropolitan Revenue Assoc, New Castle *Also Called: Metropolitan Revenue Assoc LLC (G-9362)*

Metropolitan Revenue Assoc LLC 302 449-7490
29 E Commons Blvd Ste 100 New Castle (19720) *(G-9362)*

Metropolitan Wealth MGT LLC 212 607-2488
2711 Centerville Rd # 300 Wilmington (19808) *(G-18294)*

Metz Jade Associates 302 239-2414
3 Aubrey Ln Newark (19711) *(G-11395)*

Mexicom Usa Inc 956 516-7201
2915 Ogletown Rd Newark (19713) *(G-11396)*

Mexigas Group LLC 302 645-7400
16192 Coastal Hwy Lewes (19958) *(G-6268)*

Meyer & Meyer Inc 302 994-9600
2706 Kirkwood Hwy Wilmington (19805) *(G-18295)*

Meyer & Meyer Reatly, Wilmington *Also Called: Meyer & Meyer Inc (G-18295)*

Meyer Properties LLC 302 278-4100
2102 Kirkwood Hwy Wilmington (19805) *(G-18296)*

Mff Oilfield Solutions LLC 603 795-0617
1 Commerce St # 1201 Wilmington (19801) *(G-18297)*

Mfr Manufacturing Corp Inc 815 552-3333
251 Little Falls Dr Wilmington (19808) *(G-18298)*

Mg Global Group LLC 302 217-3724
254 Chapman Rd Ste 209 Newark (19702) *(G-11397)*

Mgj Enterprises Inc 866 525-8529
4023 Kennett Pike # 624 Wilmington (19807) *(G-18299)*

Mgl Screen Printing 302 450-6250
47 S Longwood Ln Clayton (19938) *(G-1386)*

Mgmis 302 744-8645
1567 Mckee Rd Dover (19904) *(G-3076)*

Mgts Global Inc 302 385-6636
704 N King St Ste 600 Wilmington (19801) *(G-18300)*

Mh Software Inc 919 306-0163
614 N Dupont Hwy Dover (19901) *(G-3077)*

Mh-Teq LLC 302 897-2182
101 W 10th St Ste 408 Wilmington (19801) *(G-18301)*

MHS Lift of Delaware, Historic New Castle *Also Called: Material Handling Supply Inc (G-5024)*

MHS Lift of Delaware Inc 302 629-4490
25560 Business Park Seaford (19973) *(G-13282)*

Mhyhwh LLC 302 518-0992
937 Woods Rd Bear (19701) *(G-371)*

Mi-1 LLC 302 369-3447
3 Bobby Dr Newark (19713) *(G-11398)*

MI-Dee Inc 302 453-7326
345 Polly Drummond Hill Rd # R Newark (19711) *(G-11399)*

Mia Bellas Candles 302 331-7038
697 Judith Rd Hartly (19953) *(G-4896)*

Mican Technologies Inc (PA) 302 703-0708
2500 Wrangle Hill Rd Ste 224 Bear (19701) *(G-372)*

Michael A Andreoli Contracting 302 274-8709
18 Reubens Cir Newark (19702) *(G-11400)*

Michael A Beecher 302 285-3357
1122 Dexter Corner Rd Townsend (19734) *(G-14035)*

Michael A Kelczewski 302 654-6500
5701 Kennett Pike Wilmington (19807) *(G-18302)*

Michael A Madanat 302 998-6613
2617 Bardell Dr Wilmington (19808) *(G-18303)*

Michael A Mealey & Sons Inc (PA) 302 652-5913
703 N Broom St Wilmington (19805) *(G-18304)*

Michael A Mealey & Sons Inc 302 654-3005
2509 Limestone Rd Wilmington (19808) *(G-18305)*

Michael A Mekulski Genera 302 834-8260
25 Madrigal Dr Newark (19702) *(G-11401)*

Michael A OBrien & Sons 302 994-2894
405 E Ayre St Wilmington (19804) *(G-18306)*

Michael A Peyton Lcsw 302 836-5311
120 Brittany Way Bear (19701) *(G-373)*

Michael A Poleck DDS PA 302 994-7730
5501 Kirkwood Hwy Wilmington (19808) *(G-18307)*

Michael A Sinclair Inc 302 834-8144
705 Connell Dr Bear (19701) *(G-374)*

Michael B Tumas 302 984-6029
1313 N Market St Wilmington (19801) *(G-18308)*

Michael Bober MD 302 651-5916
Wilmington (19899) *(G-18309)*

Michael Butterworth Dr 302 732-9850
31059 Dupont Blvd Dagsboro (19939) *(G-1482)*

Michael C Rapa 302 236-4423
10596 Georgetown Rd Laurel (19956) *(G-5563)*

Michael D Johnson M D 267 760-7195
810 Brant Dr New Castle (19720) *(G-9363)*

Michael D Merrill 302 994-2511
1601 Kirkwood Hwy Wilmington (19805) *(G-18310)*

Michael Eller Income Tax Svc 302 652-5916
724 N Union St Wilmington (19805) *(G-18311)*

Michael Ercka Hynnsky Fmly Fnd 302 545-4600
1300 N Union St Wilmington (19806) *(G-18312)*

Michael Frankos 302 531-0831
375 W North St Dover (19904) *(G-3078)*

Michael G Schwrtz Mem Fndation 302 453-9233
5520 E Timberview Ct Wilmington (19808) *(G-18313)*

Michael G Sugarman MD 302 366-7671
774 Christiana Rd Ste 202 Newark (19713) *(G-11402)*

Michael G Sweeney M D 302 678-4488
725 S Queen St Dover (19904) *(G-3079)*

Michael Gallagher Jewelers 302 836-2925
102 Foxhunt Dr (Fox Run Shopping Center) Bear (19701) *(G-375)*

Michael H McGrath 302 242-3849
650 Johns Rd Smyrna (19977) *(G-13823)*

Michael J Di Salvo 302 636-0169
5610 Kirkwood Hwy Wilmington (19808) *(G-18314)*

Michael J Hurd 302 539-5986
17 Atlantic Ave Ste 4 Ocean View (19970) *(G-12546)*

Michael J Munroe 804 240-7188
811 Augusta National Dr Magnolia (19962) *(G-6765)*

Michael J Truitt 302 436-4081
36261 Zion Church Rd Selbyville (19975) *(G-13571)*

Michael Joseph Alexander 302 670-0993
420 Reeves Crossing Rd Felton (19943) *(G-4002)*

Michael K Rosenthal 302 652-3469
2300 Pennsylvania Ave Ste 3c Wilmington (19806) *(G-18315)*

ALPHABETIC SECTION

Michael L Berman..302 300-3450
1000 N West St Ste 1500 Wilmington (19801) *(G-18316)*

Michael L Mattern MD PA.....................................302 734-3416
724 S New St Dover (19904) *(G-3080)*

Michael L Saruk MD..302 478-8532
3411 Silverside Rd Ste 107 Wilmington (19810) *(G-18317)*

Michael Lo Sapio..201 919-2643
900 Grears Corner Rd Townsend (19734) *(G-14036)*

Michael M Wydila M D..302 798-8070
1403 Silverside Rd Ste B Wilmington (19810) *(G-18318)*

Michael Marino Inc..302 764-5319
112 Hoiland Dr Wilmington (19803) *(G-18319)*

Michael Matthew Sponaugle...............................302 566-1010
2427 Flatiron Rd Harrington (19952) *(G-4802)*

Michael Matthias..302 575-0100
3801 Kennett Pike Ste E207 Wilmington (19807) *(G-18320)*

Michael McCarthy Stones....................................302 539-8056
35283 Atlantic Ave Millville (19967) *(G-8541)*

Michael P Morton PA..302 426-1313
3704 Kennett Pike Ste 200 Wilmington (19807) *(G-18321)*

Michael P Rosenthal MD....................................302 255-1300
1400 N Washington St Wilmington (19801) *(G-18322)*

Michael Robert Meibaum...................................302 212-9969
34527 Maple Dr Lewes (19958) *(G-6269)*

Michael S Wirosloff DMD...................................302 998-8588
5185 W Woodmill Dr Ste 2 Wilmington (19808) *(G-18323)*

Michael Schwartz...302 791-9999
1400 Philadelphia Pike Wilmington (19809) *(G-18324)*

Michael Spradley (PA)..404 475-2647
45 E Reamer Ave Wilmington (19804) *(G-18325)*

Michael Wescott...302 423-7094
24265 Dupont Blvd Georgetown (19947) *(G-4426)*

Michael Zaragoza Md Facs................................302 736-1320
200 Banning St Dover (19904) *(G-3081)*

Michaelangelos Hair Designs..............................302 734-8343
696 N Dupont Hwy Dover (19901) *(G-3082)*

Michaels Home Repair Services..........................302 333-2235
550 S Dupont Hwy Apt 22k New Castle (19720) *(G-9364)*

Michelangelo Technologies Inc...........................949 382-1899
16192 Coastal Hwy Lewes (19958) *(G-6270)*

Michelet Finance Inc...302 427-8751
1105 N Market St Ste 1300 Wilmington (19801) *(G-18326)*

Michelle C Johnson Lcsw...................................302 893-9235
504 S Clayton St Wilmington (19805) *(G-18327)*

Michelle E Papa Do...302 656-5424
1100 S Broom St Ste 1 Wilmington (19805) *(G-18328)*

Michelle Hand..302 422-0622
123 School Pl Milford (19963) *(G-7995)*

Michelle M Manasseri Psyd LLC.........................302 478-1578
774 Christiana Rd Ste 202 Newark (19713) *(G-11403)*

Michelle Menzer..302 366-7456
102 W Mill Station Dr Newark (19711) *(G-11404)*

Microcom Tech LLC...858 775-5559
18971 Goldfinch Cv Rehoboth Beach (19971) *(G-12853)*

Microhm Inc..302 543-2178
1000 N West St Wilmington (19801) *(G-18329)*

Microlog, Rehoboth Beach Also Called: Microlog Corporation Maryland *(G-12854)*

Microlog Corporation Maryland..........................301 540-5501
17027 Taramac Dr Rehoboth Beach (19971) *(G-12854)*

Micron, Wilmington Also Called: Micron Incorporated *(G-18330)*

Micron Incorporated..302 998-1184
3815 Lancaster Pike Wilmington (19805) *(G-18330)*

Micropets LLC...925 341-2398
850 New Burton Rd Dover (19904) *(G-3083)*

Microtel, Dover Also Called: Shiv Sagar Inc *(G-3547)*

Microtel, Georgetown Also Called: Beacon Hospitality *(G-4228)*

Microtel Inn Stes By Wyndham M, Milford Also Called: Milford Microtel LLC *(G-8005)*

Microtelecom, Wilmington Also Called: Microtelecom Systems LLC *(G-18331)*

Microtelecom Systems LLC................................718 707-0012
1000 N West St Ste 1200 Wilmington (19801) *(G-18331)*

Mid Atlantic..302 393-4355
403 E Laurel St Georgetown (19947) *(G-4427)*

Mid Atlantic Athc Promotions.............................302 535-8472
814 Evergreen Rd Magnolia (19962) *(G-6766)*

Mid Atlantic Builder Inc....................................302 344-7224
22532 Pine Haven Dr Georgetown (19947) *(G-4428)*

Mid Atlantic Cardiovascular...............................302 294-1044
1213 Churchmans Rd Newark (19713) *(G-11405)*

Mid Atlantic Care LLC (PA)................................302 266-8306
520 Robinson Ln Wilmington (19805) *(G-18332)*

Mid Atlantic Compost & RE...............................302 644-2977
33718 Wescoats Rd Lewes (19958) *(G-6271)*

Mid Atlantic Farm Credit Aca.............................302 734-7534
1410 S State St Dover (19901) *(G-3084)*

Mid Atlantic Grand Prix, New Castle Also Called: Mid Atlantic Grand Prix LLC *(G-9365)*

Mid Atlantic Grand Prix LLC..............................302 656-5278
4060 N Dupont Hwy Ste 11 New Castle (19720) *(G-9365)*

Mid Atlantic Indus Belting.................................302 453-7353
15 Garfield Way Newark (19713) *(G-11406)*

Mid Atlantic Mechanical Inc..............................302 999-9209
705 Stanton Christiana Rd Newark (19713) *(G-11407)*

Mid Atlantic Pain Institute................................302 369-1700
550 S Dupont Blvd Ste C Milford (19963) *(G-7996)*

Mid Atlantic Retina..800 331-6634
4102 Ogletown Stanton Rd Newark (19713) *(G-11408)*

Mid Atlantic Spine..302 369-1700
100 Biddle Ave Ste 101 Newark (19702) *(G-11409)*

Mid Atlantic Surgical LLC..................................302 652-6050
1500 Shallcross Ave Ste 1 Wilmington (19806) *(G-18333)*

Mid Atlantic Surgical Practice...........................302 652-6050
701 N Clayton St Wilmington (19805) *(G-18334)*

Mid Atlantic Tire ADI..302 221-2000
600 Ships Landing Way Historic New Castle (19720) *(G-5027)*

Mid Atlantic Warranty.......................................302 893-4220
10 8th Ave Wilmington (19805) *(G-18335)*

Mid Atlantic Waste System................................610 497-2405
314 Bay West Blvd Ste 3 New Castle (19720) *(G-9366)*

Mid Atlantic Wellness Gro.................................302 864-7766
8 Wood Duck Pt Rehoboth Beach (19971) *(G-12855)*

Mid Atlntic Scientific Svc Inc............................302 328-4440
62 Southgate Blvd Ste A New Castle (19720) *(G-9367)*

Mid Del Charity Foundation..............................302 398-7223
15 W Rider Rd Harrington (19952) *(G-4803)*

Mid Delaware Imaging Inc................................302 734-9888
710 S Queen St Dover (19904) *(G-3085)*

Mid States Sales & Marketing...........................302 888-2475
3411 Silverside Rd Ste 104 Wilmington (19810) *(G-18336)*

Mid Sussex Rescue Squad Inc..........................302 945-2680
31738 Indian Mission Rd Millsboro (19966) *(G-8378)*

Mid-Atlantic Behavioral Health..........................302 224-1400
90 Blue Hen Dr Newark (19713) *(G-11410)*

Mid-Atlantic Elec Svcs Inc................................302 945-2555
24556 Betts Pond Rd Millsboro (19966) *(G-8379)*

Mid-Atlantic Envmtl Labs Inc............................302 654-1340
30 Lukens Dr Ste A Historic New Castle (19720) *(G-5028)*

Mid-Atlantic Fmly Practice LLC (PA)..................302 644-6860
20251 John J Williams Hwy Lewes (19958) *(G-6272)*

Mid-Atlantic Packaging Company......................800 284-1332
14 Starlifter Ave Dover (19901) *(G-3086)*

Mid-Atlantic Realty Co Inc................................302 737-3110
39 Abbey Ln Newark (19711) *(G-11411)*

Mid-Atlantic Realty Co Inc (PA)........................302 658-7642
39 Abbey Ln Newark (19711) *(G-11412)*

Mid-Atlantic Services A-Team (PA)....................302 628-3403
8558 Elks Rd Seaford (19973) *(G-13283)*

Mid-Atlantic Services A-Team...........................302 984-9559
700 Cornell Dr Wilmington (19801) *(G-18337)*

Mid-Atlantic Steel LLC......................................302 323-1800
1144 River Rd New Castle (19720) *(G-9368)*

Mid-Atlntic Dismantlement Corp........................302 678-9300
913 Horsepond Rd Dover (19901) *(G-3087)*

Mid-Atlntic Reg Comm On Hgher......................267 284-5024
1007 N Orange St Fl 4 Pmb 166 Wilmington (19801) *(G-18338)*

ALPHABETIC SECTION

Mid-Atlntic Sls Mktg Group LLC.................................. 215 515-6077
  1 Whitehaven Ct Newark (19711) *(G-11413)*

Mid-Atlntic Wtrproofing MD Inc (PA)........................... 301 206-9500
  802 Interchange Blvd Newark (19711) *(G-11414)*

Mid-Coast Gymnastic Studio, Selbyville Also Called: Midcoast Gymnstics Dnce Studio *(G-13573)*

Mid-County Inc.. 302 995-6555
  1st Regiment Rd S Pk Ii Wilmington (19808) *(G-18339)*

Mid-County Electric Inc... 302 934-8304
  24556 Betts Pond Rd Millsboro (19966) *(G-8380)*

Mid-Lantic Distributors, Selbyville Also Called: Mid-Lantic Enterprises Inc *(G-13572)*

Mid-Lantic Enterprises Inc.. 302 436-2772
  68 Duke Street Ext Selbyville (19975) *(G-13572)*

Mid-Shore Envmtl Svcs Inc... 302 736-5504
  7481 Federalsburg Rd Bridgeville (19933) *(G-733)*

Mid-Town Massage LLC.. 302 256-0363
  213 W 4th St Wilmington (19801) *(G-18340)*

Midas Muffler, New Castle Also Called: C-Met Inc *(G-8909)*

Midatlantic Pain Institute.. 302 369-1700
  100 Biddle Ave Ste 101 Newark (19702) *(G-11415)*

Midatlantic Spine, Newark Also Called: Midatlantic Pain Institute *(G-11415)*

MidatIntic Auto Rstration Sups.................................... 302 422-3812
  6930 Shawnee Rd Milford (19963) *(G-7997)*

Midcoast Community Bank... 302 482-4250
  2901 Concord Pike Wilmington (19803) *(G-18341)*

Midcoast Gymnstics Dnce Studio............................... 302 436-6007
  15 Dukes Street Ext Selbyville (19975) *(G-13573)*

Middle Dept Insptn Agcy Inc....................................... 302 875-4514
  11508 Commercial Ln Laurel (19956) *(G-5564)*

Middle East Free Trade Assoc, Wilmington Also Called: Mefta LLC *(G-18260)*

Middle Room LLC... 302 220-9979
  637 Country Path Dr New Castle (19720) *(G-9369)*

Middle Run Chrtable Foundation................................ 302 658-7796
  5803 Kennett Pike Wilmington (19807) *(G-18342)*

MIDDLE STATES COMMISSION ON HI, Wilmington Also Called: Mid-Atlntic Reg Comm On Hgher *(G-18338)*

Middlesex Water Company... 302 376-1501
  1100 S Little Creek Rd Dover (19901) *(G-3088)*

Middlesex Water Company... 302 436-4625
  36252 Lighthouse Rd Selbyville (19975) *(G-13574)*

Middletown Car Care.. 302 449-1550
  133 Leanne Dr Middletown (19709) *(G-7346)*

Middletown Chiropractic & Reha................................. 302 376-5830
  421 E Main St Ste 6 Middletown (19709) *(G-7347)*

Middletown Counseling.. 302 376-0621
  401 N Broad St Middletown (19709) *(G-7348)*

Middletown Counseling.. 302 540-9003
  268 Brenford Station Rd Smyrna (19977) *(G-13824)*

Middletown De.. 302 449-2547
  520 Middletown Warwick Rd Middletown (19709) *(G-7349)*

Middletown De.. 302 655-9494
  252 Carter Dr Ste 101 Middletown (19709) *(G-7350)*

Middletown Family Dentist... 302 376-1959
  122 Sandhill Dr Ste 101 Middletown (19709) *(G-7351)*

Middletown Family Medicine Ctr................................. 302 449-3030
  124 Sleepy Hollow Dr Ste 203 Middletown (19709) *(G-7352)*

Middletown Ink LLC.. 302 725-0705
  126 Patriot Dr Middletown (19709) *(G-7353)*

Middletown Kitchen & Bath LLC................................. 302 464-1236
  111 Patriot Dr Ste C Middletown (19709) *(G-7354)*

Middletown Kitchen and Bath..................................... 302 376-5766
  987 Marl Pit Rd Middletown (19709) *(G-7355)*

Middletown Mosquito Ctrl LLC................................... 302 378-3378
  229 Oak Dr Middletown (19709) *(G-7356)*

Middletown Painting LLC... 302 376-5419
  1027 Sherbourne Rd Middletown (19709) *(G-7357)*

Middletown Police Department, Middletown Also Called: Town of Middletown *(G-7656)*

Middletown Sports Complex LLC............................... 302 299-8630
  407 Draper Ln Middletown (19709) *(G-7358)*

Middletown Tent Rentals Inc...................................... 302 376-7010
  7 E Cochran St Middletown (19709) *(G-7359)*

Middletown Towing... 302 357-6484
  4008 Dupont Pkwy Townsend (19734) *(G-14037)*

Middletown Transcript, Dover Also Called: Dover Post Co Inc *(G-2363)*

Middletown Veterinary Hospital.................................. 302 378-2342
  366 Warwick Rd Middletown (19709) *(G-7360)*

Middletown YMCA.. 302 510-1166
  404 N Cass St Middletown (19709) *(G-7361)*

Middleware Inc.. 415 213-2625
  1000 N West St Ste 1200 Wilmington (19801) *(G-18343)*

Middltown Area Chmber Commerce.......................... 302 376-0222
  1050 Industrial Dr Ste 110 Middletown (19709) *(G-7362)*

Middltown Familycare Assoc LLC.............................. 302 378-4779
  114 Sandhill Dr Ste 101 Middletown (19709) *(G-7363)*

Middltown Odssa Twnsend Snior.............................. 302 378-4758
  300 S Scott St Middletown (19709) *(G-7364)*

Middltown Snior Lving Prtners.................................. 302 828-0988
  820 Middletown Odessa Rd Middletown (19709) *(G-7365)*

Middltown Vlg Cmnty Foundation.............................. 857 544-3954
  194 Vincent Cir Middletown (19709) *(G-7366)*

Midge Smith Fine Art Gallery..................................... 302 245-4528
  135 2nd St Fl 2 Lewes (19958) *(G-6273)*

Midi Labs Inc.. 302 737-4297
  225 Corporate Blvd Ste E Newark (19702) *(G-11416)*

Midlantic Bldg Rstorations Inc................................... 302 475-8084
  2201 Orleans Rd Wilmington (19810) *(G-18344)*

Midlantic Marine Center Inc....................................... 302 436-2628
  36624 Dupont Blvd Selbyville (19975) *(G-13575)*

Midnight Blue Inc.. 302 436-9665
  37091 E White Tail Dr Selbyville (19975) *(G-13576)*

Midway, Middletown Also Called: Midway LLC *(G-7367)*

Midway Fitnes Racquetball CLB, Rehoboth Beach Also Called: Midway Fitness Center *(G-12856)*

Midway Fitness Center... 302 645-0407
  28b Midway Shopping Ctr Rehoboth Beach (19971) *(G-12856)*

Midway Lions Club Inc... 302 945-5525
  1 Mulberry Ln Harbeson (19951) *(G-4708)*

Midway LLC.. 302 378-9156
  102 Dungarvan Dr Middletown (19709) *(G-7367)*

Midway Realty Corp... 302 645-9511
  34821 Derrickson Dr Rehoboth Beach (19971) *(G-12857)*

Midway Services Inc.. 302 422-8603
  9446 Willow Pond Ln Lincoln (19960) *(G-6685)*

Midway Slots & Simulcast.. 302 398-4920
  15 W Rider Rd Harrington (19952) *(G-4804)*

Midway Speedway, Rehoboth Beach Also Called: Fun Sport Inc *(G-12762)*

Midway Towing Inc... 302 323-4850
  1122 Wagoner Dr Wilmington (19805) *(G-18345)*

Midwinter Co LLC... 302 463-9578
  303 Hawthorne Dr Wilmington (19802) *(G-18346)*

Mig Consulting LLC (PA)... 302 999-1888
  1624 Newport Gap Pike Wilmington (19808) *(G-18347)*

Mig Soccer, Hockessin Also Called: M Level Inc *(G-5285)*

Mighty Acorn Digital Inc... 877 277-8805
  24a Trolley Sq Wilmington (19806) *(G-18348)*

Mightyinvoice LLC.. 302 415-3000
  8 The Grn Ste B Dover (19901) *(G-3089)*

Miguel Esparza... 302 518-7873
  27 Weer Cir Wilmington (19808) *(G-18349)*

Mih Enterprises... 302 480-4443
  57 Pier Head Blvd Ste 2 Smyrna (19977) *(G-13825)*

Mih International LLC... 301 908-4233
  112 Capitol Trl Newark (19711) *(G-11417)*

Mike Difonzo... 302 764-0100
  1708 Marsh Rd Wilmington (19810) *(G-18350)*

Mike Mead Concrete LLC.. 816 588-6150
  89 Sand Dollar Ln Frederica (19946) *(G-4177)*

Mike Molitor.. 302 528-6300
  101 Scarborough Park Dr Apt 5 Wilmington (19804) *(G-18351)*

Mike Molitor Contractor, Wilmington Also Called: Mike Molitor *(G-18351)*

Mike Molitor Contractor LLC...................................... 302 528-6300
  754 Morris Rd Hockessin (19707) *(G-5309)*

ALPHABETIC SECTION

Mike Morris Painting LLC.. 302 423-3940
805 Skeeter Neck Rd Frederica (19946) *(G-4178)*

Miken Builders Inc.. 302 537-4444
32782 Cedar Dr Unit 1 Millville (19967) *(G-8542)*

Mikes Expert Detailing... 302 853-5368
13448 Sun St Greenwood (19950) *(G-4652)*

Mil International LLC.. 302 234-7501
203 Alisons Way Wilmington (19807) *(G-18352)*

Milana Colors LLC... 872 274-4321
651 N Broad St Middletown (19709) *(G-7368)*

Mildford Neck Farms.. 302 422-6432
7343 Big Stone Beach Rd Milford (19963) *(G-7998)*

Mile For Melanoma De... 302 540-8073
Middletown (19709) *(G-7369)*

Miles Per Hour Inc... 800 370-3050
1007 N Orange St Ste 1382 Wilmington (19801) *(G-18353)*

Miles Rs Son Roofing.. 302 250-4992
113 J And M Dr New Castle (19720) *(G-9370)*

Miles Scientific Corporation... 302 737-6960
75 Blue Hen Dr Newark (19713) *(G-11418)*

Miles1 Inc... 267 506-0004
1409 Coleman St Wilmington (19805) *(G-18354)*

Milespa, Wilmington Also Called: Miles1 Inc *(G-18354)*

Milestone, Lewes Also Called: Expotrade Inc *(G-5981)*

Milestone Construction Co Inc... 302 442-4252
4 Mill Park Ct Ste A Newark (19713) *(G-11419)*

Milewski Stephan... 302 467-4502
824 N Market St Wilmington (19801) *(G-18355)*

Milford Bowling Lanes Inc.. 302 422-9456
809 N Dupont Blvd Milford (19963) *(G-7999)*

Milford Center, Milford Also Called: 700 Marvel Road Operations LLC *(G-7754)*

Milford Community Band Inc... 302 422-6304
616 Cedarwood Ave Milford (19963) *(G-8000)*

Milford Early Learning Center... 302 331-6712
592 Ashland Ave Camden Wyoming (19934) *(G-962)*

Milford Early Learning Center, Milford Also Called: Esther V Graham *(G-7883)*

Milford Fertilizer, Milford Also Called: Growmark Fs LLC *(G-7913)*

Milford Gutter Guys LLC.. 302 424-1931
7074 Marshall St Lincoln (19960) *(G-6686)*

Milford Housing Development.. 302 678-0300
200 Harmony Ln Dover (19904) *(G-3090)*

Milford Housing Development (PA).................................. 302 422-8255
977 E Masten Cir Milford (19963) *(G-8001)*

Milford Lions Club Svc Fdn.. 302 422-2861
9400 Benson Rd Lincoln (19960) *(G-6687)*

Milford Little League.. 302 424-3100
944 Bay Rd Milford (19963) *(G-8002)*

Milford Lodging LLC.. 302 839-5000
699 N Dupont Blvd Milford (19963) *(G-8003)*

Milford Machine LLC... 410 924-3211
10 The Mead Houston (19954) *(G-5445)*

Milford Medical Associates PA (PA)................................. 302 424-0600
310 Mullet Run Milford (19963) *(G-8004)*

Milford Memorial Hospital, Dover Also Called: Kent General Hospital *(G-2851)*

Milford Memorial Hospital, Milford Also Called: Kent General Hospital *(G-7962)*

Milford Microtel LLC.. 302 503-7615
106 Silicato Pkwy Milford (19963) *(G-8005)*

Milford Place, Milford Also Called: 500 Suth Dpont Blvd Oprtons LL *(G-7753)*

Milford Primary Care Assoc LLC...................................... 302 536-2580
301 Jefferson Ave Milford (19963) *(G-8006)*

Milford Pulmonary Assoc LLC.. 302 424-3100
39 W Clarke Ave Milford (19963) *(G-8007)*

Milford Rental Center Inc... 302 422-0315
1679 S Dupont Hwy Dover (19901) *(G-3091)*

Milford Security Systems, Dover Also Called: Delaware Electric Signal Co *(G-2235)*

Milford Senior Center Inc... 302 422-3385
111 Park Ave Milford (19963) *(G-8008)*

Milford Stitching Co, Dover Also Called: G L K Inc *(G-2551)*

Milford Veterans of Foreign WA....................................... 302 422-4412
77 Veterans Cir Milford (19963) *(G-8009)*

Milfordlivecom.. 302 542-9231
805 Joshua Dr Milford (19963) *(G-8010)*

Milieux LLC... 302 770-5868
1007 N Orange St Fl 4 Wilmington (19801) *(G-18356)*

Military Order of The Purple... 302 563-0435
1795 Brigade Ct Newark (19702) *(G-11420)*

Mill Creek Metals Inc... 302 529-7020
3 1/2 Yale Ave Claymont (19703) *(G-1236)*

Mill Creek Select... 302 995-2090
2006 Limestone Rd Wilmington (19808) *(G-18357)*

Mill Wilmington LLC... 302 218-7527
1007 N Orange St Ste 400 Wilmington (19801) *(G-18358)*

Millan Contractors... 302 983-9365
11 Cynthia Rd Newark (19702) *(G-11421)*

Millcreek Mobile Hm Pk Land Co..................................... 302 998-3045
5600 Old Capitol Trl Wilmington (19808) *(G-18359)*

Millcreek Pediatrics, Wilmington Also Called: Macfarlane A Radford MD PA *(G-18068)*

Millcreek Texaco, Wilmington Also Called: Millcreek Texaco Station *(G-18360)*

Millcreek Texaco Station.. 302 571-8489
109 Bellant Cir Wilmington (19807) *(G-18360)*

Millcreekinvestments... 302 407-5034
452 E Ayre St Wilmington (19804) *(G-18361)*

Millcroft, Newark Also Called: Five Star Quality Care Inc *(G-10746)*

Millenium Loan Fund LLC.. 302 996-4811
4600 Linden Hill Rd Wilmington (19808) *(G-18362)*

Millenium Services LLC.. 888 507-9473
651 N Broad St Middletown (19709) *(G-7370)*

Millennial Informatics LLC.. 302 446-3800
2140 S Dupont Hwy Camden (19934) *(G-875)*

Millennial Ventures Group LLC... 877 533-3337
200 Continental Dr Ste 401 Newark (19713) *(G-11422)*

Millennium Homes... 302 678-2393
4227 N Dupont Hwy Dover (19901) *(G-3092)*

Millennium Inv Group LLC.. 703 586-7968
300 Delaware Ave Wilmington (19801) *(G-18363)*

Millennium Marketing Solutions.. 301 725-8000
31015 Sycamore Dr Lewes (19958) *(G-6274)*

Millennium Printing & Graphics, Lewes Also Called: Millennium Marketing Solutions *(G-6274)*

Miller Samuel MD.. 302 629-8662
543 N Shipley St Ste A Seaford (19973) *(G-13284)*

Miller & Associates Cpas, Wilmington Also Called: Miller & Associates PA *(G-18364)*

Miller & Associates PA... 302 234-0678
5500 Skyline Dr Ste 5 Wilmington (19808) *(G-18364)*

Miller Dr Elinor M D... 302 654-8291
721 Blackshire Rd Wilmington (19805) *(G-18365)*

Miller Fnrl HM & Cremation Svc....................................... 302 947-1144
11475 Commercial Ln Unit C Laurel (19956) *(G-5565)*

Miller Heating & Cooling LLC... 302 750-2409
108 Patriot Dr Ste E Middletown (19709) *(G-7371)*

Miller Investments LLC... 949 836-2511
10 Nw 10th St Milford (19963) *(G-8011)*

Miller John H Plumbing & Htg.. 302 697-1012
220 Old North Rd Camden (19934) *(G-876)*

Miller JW Wldg Boiler Repr Co... 302 449-1575
4917 Summit Bridge Rd Middletown (19709) *(G-7372)*

Miller Lewis Surveyors, Seaford Also Called: Lewis Miller Inc *(G-13259)*

Miller Metal Fabrication Inc.. 302 337-2291
16356 Sussex Hwy Unit 4 Bridgeville (19933) *(G-734)*

Miller-Mauro Group Inc.. 302 426-6565
3512 Silverside Rd Ste 9 Wilmington (19810) *(G-18366)*

Miller's Beverage Center, Wilmington Also Called: Wwd Inc *(G-20906)*

Millers Gun Center Inc... 302 328-9747
97 Jackson Ave New Castle (19720) *(G-9371)*

Millers Lawn Care, Smyrna Also Called: Kevin M Miller *(G-13791)*

Millers Masonry & Block LLC... 302 222-4091
1780 Yoder Dr Hartly (19953) *(G-4897)*

Millers Roofing & Coating LLC... 302 943-8988
305 Pine Tree Rd Hartly (19953) *(G-4898)*

Millmar Contracting... 302 222-0823
411 Wisseman Ave Milford (19963) *(G-8012)*

Millmar Contracting LLC.. 302 697-6581
2353 Honeysuckle Rd Camden Wyoming (19934) *(G-963)*

Mills James MD 302 526-1470
540 S Governors Ave Ste 100a Dover (19904) *(G-3093)*

Mills Electric LLC 302 257-8403
261 N Caroline Pl Dover (19904) *(G-3094)*

Millsboro 302 231-1152
26744 John J Williams Hwy Unit 4 Millsboro (19966) *(G-8381)*

Millsboro 302 934-0300
30265 Commerce Dr Unit 201 Millsboro (19966) *(G-8382)*

Millsboro Bowling Center, Millsboro Also Called: Millsboro Lanes Inc *(G-8387)*

Millsboro Eye Care LLC 302 684-2020
28322 Lewes Georgetown Hwy Unit 1 Milton (19968) *(G-8668)*

Millsboro Family Practice PA 302 934-5626
201 Laurel Rd Millsboro (19966) *(G-8383)*

Millsboro Fitness LLC 302 933-0722
28632 Dupont Blvd Unit 14 Millsboro (19966) *(G-8384)*

Millsboro Hsing For Prgress In 302 934-6491
701 Stanford Bratton Dr Millsboro (19966) *(G-8385)*

Millsboro Landing Inc 302 934-6073
29320 White St Millsboro (19966) *(G-8386)*

Millsboro Lanes Inc 302 934-0400
213 Mitchell St Millsboro (19966) *(G-8387)*

Millsboro Little League 302 934-1806
262 W State St Millsboro (19966) *(G-8388)*

Millsboro Village I LLC 302 678-9400
701 Stanford Bratton Dr Millsboro (19966) *(G-8389)*

Millville Organic Center 302 423-2601
30916 Whites Neck Rd Ocean View (19970) *(G-12547)*

Millville Rehabilitation Svc 302 645-3100
32566 Docs Pl Unit 7 Millville (19967) *(G-8543)*

Millvlle By The Sea Mstr Cmnty 302 539-2888
30794 Endless Summer Dr Millville (19967) *(G-8544)*

Millwright Company LLC 302 274-9590
919 N Market St Ste 950 Wilmington (19801) *(G-18367)*

Millwrights Local Union 1548 .... 410 355-0011
1013 Centre Rd Ste 201 Wilmington (19805) *(G-18368)*

Milpa Nativa Inc 512 668-9033
1007 N Orange St Fl 4 Wilmington (19801) *(G-18369)*

Milton & Hattie Kutz Foundaton 302 427-2100
101 Garden Of Eden Rd Wilmington (19803) *(G-18370)*

Milton & Hattie Kutz Home Inc 302 764-7000
704 River Rd Wilmington (19809) *(G-18371)*

Milton Enterprises Inc 302 684-2000
424 Mulberry St Ste 2 Milton (19968) *(G-8669)*

Milton Family Practice 302 684-2000
16529 Coastal Hwy Lewes (19958) *(G-6275)*

Milton Family Practice, Milton Also Called: Milton Enterprises Inc *(G-8669)*

Milton Garden Club 302 684-8315
14354 Sand Hill Rd Milton (19968) *(G-8670)*

Milton Historical Society 302 684-1010
210 Union St Milton (19968) *(G-8671)*

Milton Mail Boxes 302 664-2623
124 Broadkill Rd Milton (19968) *(G-8672)*

Milton Theatre 302 684-4232
101 Pond Dr Milton (19968) *(G-8673)*

Milton Worldwide Media LLC 302 353-4470
220 E Delaware Ave Newark (19711) *(G-11423)*

Milwood Hydrogen LLC 424 330-5739
16192 Coastal Hwy Lewes (19958) *(G-6276)*

Mimesis Signs 302 674-5566
1035 Fowler Ct Dover (19901) *(G-3095)*

Mimix Company 305 916-8602
8 The Grn Ste 6236 Dover (19901) *(G-3096)*

Mind & Matter 302 345-0575
8103 Governor Printz Blvd Claymont (19703) *(G-1237)*

Mind and Body Consortium LLC 302 674-2380
156 S State St Dover (19901) *(G-3097)*

Mind Mechanix 302 503-5142
556 S Dupont Blvd Ste I Milford (19963) *(G-8013)*

Mind Mechanix LLC 302 313-1288
583 W Birdie Ln Magnolia (19962) *(G-6767)*

Mindbody Fitness 302 893-6212
57 Sussex St Apt 3 Rehoboth Beach (19971) *(G-12858)*

Minder Foundation 917 477-7661
16192 Coastal Hwy Lewes (19958) *(G-6277)*

Mindset Nutrition & Fitness 302 219-0777
19 Highland Blvd Apt A New Castle (19720) *(G-9372)*

Mindspaceweb LLC 302 360-8744
2803 Philadelphia Pike B Claymont (19703) *(G-1238)*

Mindy Body Consortium 302 424-1322
993 N Dupont Blvd Milford (19963) *(G-8014)*

Miner Ltd 302 516-7791
2 Lukens Dr Historic New Castle (19720) *(G-5029)*

Miners Supply Co LLC 541 203-6826
8 The Grn Ste 14017 Dover (19901) *(G-3098)*

Minfon Group Inc 408 930-2190
16192 Coastal Hwy Lewes (19958) *(G-6278)*

Minimlly Invsive Srgcal Nrscnc 302 738-0300
774 Christiana Rd Ste 2 Newark (19713) *(G-11424)*

Minimum Corporation (PA) 857 928-0317
251 Little Falls Dr Wilmington (19808) *(G-18372)*

Ministry Caring Distribution, Wilmington Also Called: Ministry of Caring Inc *(G-18377)*

Ministry of Caring, Wilmington Also Called: Mary Mother Hope House 1 *(G-18181)*

Ministry of Caring Inc (PA) 302 428-3702
115 E 14th St Wilmington (19801) *(G-18373)*

Ministry of Caring Inc 302 652-0904
1328 W 3rd St Wilmington (19805) *(G-18374)*

Ministry of Caring Inc 302 652-8947
830 N Spruce St Lowr Wilmington (19801) *(G-18375)*

Ministry of Caring Inc 302 652-0970
515 N Broom St Wilmington (19805) *(G-18376)*

Ministry of Caring Inc 302 652-0969
1410 N Claymont St Wilmington (19802) *(G-18377)*

Ministry of Caring Inc 302 658-6123
121 N Jackson St Wilmington (19805) *(G-18378)*

Minkers Construction Inc 302 239-9239
830 Dawson Dr Newark (19713) *(G-11425)*

Minklist Digital Inc 917 364-8868
251 Little Falls Dr Wilmington (19808) *(G-18379)*

Minor Figures Inc 714 875-3449
2140 S Dupont Hwy Camden (19934) *(G-877)*

Minor League Baseball 302 658-6336
801 Shipyard Dr Wilmington (19801) *(G-18380)*

Minquadale Plant, Wilmington Also Called: New Castle Hot Mix Inc *(G-18609)*

Mint & Needle, Middletown Also Called: Mint & Needle LLC *(G-7373)*

Mint & Needle LLC 302 696-2484
219 W Green St Middletown (19709) *(G-7373)*

Mintflint Inc 236 991-3735
251 Little Falls Dr Wilmington (19808) *(G-18381)*

Mintzer Sarowitz Zeris Leovar 302 655-2181
919 N Market St Ste 200 Wilmington (19801) *(G-18382)*

Minute Center 302 645-9396
19470 Coastal Hwy Unit 4 Rehoboth Beach (19971) *(G-12859)*

Minute Loan Center 302 791-9557
3603a Philadelphia Pike Claymont (19703) *(G-1239)*

Minute Loan Center 302 607-2202
2693 Pulaski Hwy Newark (19702) *(G-11426)*

Minute Loan Center 302 629-5366
855 Norman Eskridge Hwy Seaford (19973) *(G-13285)*

Minute Loan Center 302 427-8041
3301 Lancaster Pike Ste 1a Wilmington (19805) *(G-18383)*

Minute Loan Center 302 994-6588
3210 Kirkwood Hwy Wilmington (19808) *(G-18384)*

Minuteman Press, Wilmington Also Called: Lord Printing LLC *(G-17994)*

Miops Inc 302 451-9571
2035 Sunset Lake Rd Ste B2 Newark (19702) *(G-11427)*

Miracle Builders LLC 302 236-1351
315 Calhoun St Georgetown (19947) *(G-4429)*

Miracle Moo LLC 321 948-4678
1209 N Orange St Wilmington (19801) *(G-18385)*

Mirage Health Services LLC 302 349-7227
1575 Mckee Rd Ste 203 Dover (19904) *(G-3099)*

Miranda Enterprises LLC 302 236-0897
30530 Quillen Point Rd Ocean View (19970) *(G-12548)*

ALPHABETIC SECTION — Mocean Energy Corp

Miranda OBrien 302 436-6411
36252 Lighthouse Rd Selbyville (19975) *(G-13577)*

Mirandas Carpentry 302 245-0298
18272 Magnolia Ln Lewes (19958) *(G-6279)*

Mirworth Enterprise Inc 302 846-0218
404 Lincoln Ave Delmar (19940) *(G-1621)*

Misaka Network Inc 323 999-1409
8 The Grn Ste 6288 Dover (19901) *(G-3100)*

Mishimoto, New Castle Also Called: Resource Intl Inc *(G-9524)*

Mispillion Art League Inc 302 430-7646
5 N Walnut St Milford (19963) *(G-8015)*

Mispillion III 302 422-4429
504 Mispillion Apts Milford (19963) *(G-8016)*

Mission Bracelets LLC 302 528-5065
1201 Woodland Beach Rd Smyrna (19977) *(G-13826)*

Mission Fitness Studio LLC 302 535-1129
6 N Pennsylvania Ave Delmar (19940) *(G-1622)*

Mission Movement Transport LLC 302 480-9401
8604 First Born Church Rd Lincoln (19960) *(G-6688)*

Mission Support Services LLC 813 494-0795
8 The Grn Ste A Dover (19901) *(G-3101)*

Missions For Life Inc 302 981-1915
165 E Green Valley Cir Newark (19711) *(G-11428)*

Mister Sparky 302 751-6363
165 Barkers Landing Rd Magnolia (19962) *(G-6768)*

Misty Rivers Ltd 315 415-2826
505 Brookfield Dr Dover (19901) *(G-3102)*

Misty Travel 302 628-1815
26227 Line Rd Seaford (19973) *(G-13286)*

Mit Shah LLC 469 307-6571
100 E Lea Blvd Wilmington (19802) *(G-18386)*

Mitchell Associates Inc (PA) 302 594-9400
100 W Commons Blvd Ste 300 New Castle (19720) *(G-9373)*

Mitchell Associates Inc 302 594-9415
15 James Ct Wilmington (19801) *(G-18387)*

Mitchell C Stickler MD Inc (PA) 302 644-6400
750 Kings Hwy Ste 110 Lewes (19958) *(G-6280)*

Mitchell E Morton 302 236-0878
12087 N Union Church Rd Lincoln (19960) *(G-6689)*

Mitchell Jamison 302 359-4163
200 Federal St Seaford (19973) *(G-13287)*

Mitek Holdings Inc (DH) 302 429-1816
42 Reads Way # C New Castle (19720) *(G-9374)*

Mithril Cable Network, Claymont Also Called: Mithril Cable Network Inc *(G-1240)*

Mithril Cable Network Inc 213 373-4381
2093 Philadelphia Pike Rm 19-62 Claymont (19703) *(G-1240)*

Mitsdarfer Bros Tree Service 302 540-6029
21 Whitekirk Dr Wilmington (19808) *(G-18388)*

Mittelman Dental Lab 302 798-7440
108 Delaware Ave Claymont (19703) *(G-1241)*

Mitten & Winters CPA 302 736-6100
119 W Loockerman St Dover (19904) *(G-3103)*

Mitten Construction Co 302 697-2124
1420 E Lebanon Rd Dover (19901) *(G-3104)*

Mitusha International Corp 302 674-2977
626 Roberta Ave Dover (19901) *(G-3105)*

Mixx Entertainment LLC 302 635-9966
112 Miners Ln Newark (19713) *(G-11429)*

Mizu Business Services Inc 302 321-5001
8 The Grn Ste 5384 Dover (19901) *(G-3106)*

Mizzen Education Inc 213 262-6196
3411 Silverside Rd # 104 Wilmington (19810) *(G-18389)*

Mj Brunin LLC 302 945-9467
23382 Greenbank Dr Harbeson (19951) *(G-4709)*

Mj Global, Wilmington Also Called: Nava *(G-18560)*

MJ Webb Farms Inc 302 349-4453
12608 Webb Farm Rd Greenwood (19950) *(G-4653)*

Mj Wilmington Hotel Assoc LP 302 454-1500
100 Continental Dr Newark (19713) *(G-11430)*

Mj Wilmington Hotel Assoc LP 302 454-1500
100 Continental Dr Newark (19713) *(G-11431)*

Mjlinkcom Inc 303 324-7668
16192 Coastal Hwy Lewes (19958) *(G-6281)*

MJM Fabrications Inc 302 764-0163
506 Crest Rd Wilmington (19803) *(G-18390)*

MJM Publishing LLC 302 943-3590
719 Tomahawk Ln Felton (19943) *(G-4003)*

Mjp Enterprises 302 584-4736
117 Dungarvan Dr Middletown (19709) *(G-7374)*

Mk Krawlers, Laurel Also Called: Michael C Rapa *(G-5563)*

Mk Management Group LLC 302 543-4414
214 Bromley Dr Wilmington (19808) *(G-18391)*

ML Newark LLC 302 737-2868
100 Christina Mill Dr Newark (19711) *(G-11432)*

ML Ruiz Enterprises Inc 302 894-9000
110 Astro Shopping Ctr Newark (19711) *(G-11433)*

ML Whiteman and Sons Inc 302 659-1001
261 Gum Bush Rd Townsend (19734) *(G-14038)*

Mlk Educational Community Ctr 302 242-1165
719 W North St Dover (19904) *(G-3107)*

Mmm TV Mounting & Entrmt LLC 267 310-5925
2803 Philadelphia Pike B Claymont (19703) *(G-1242)*

MMR Group Inc (PA) 302 328-0500
308 W Basin Rd New Castle (19720) *(G-9375)*

MMR Industries Inc 302 999-9561
7 Dartmouth Rd Wilmington (19808) *(G-18392)*

MMS Enterprises LLC 888 786-9290
254 Chapman Rd Ste 208 Newark (19702) *(G-11434)*

Mmt Construction Services Inc 302 357-8506
2201 Duncan Rd Wilmington (19808) *(G-18393)*

Mnboost Corp (PA) 302 645-7400
16192 Coastal Hwy Lewes (19958) *(G-6282)*

Mnr Industries LLC 443 485-6213
200 Banning St Ste 170 Dover (19904) *(G-3108)*

Mobeasy LLC 628 251-1274
16192 Coastal Hwy Lewes (19958) *(G-6283)*

Mobetta Books LLC 904 762-7043
68 Valley Forge Rd New Castle (19720) *(G-9376)*

Mobil, Wilmington Also Called: Sals Auto Services Inc *(G-19640)*

Mobile Air LLC 302 502-7743
200 Interchange Blvd Newark (19711) *(G-11435)*

Mobile Direct LLC 908 342-8994
8 The Grn Ste A Dover (19901) *(G-3109)*

Mobile Engagement LLC 646 583-2775
16192 Coastal Hwy Lewes (19958) *(G-6284)*

Mobile Home Remedies LLC 717 879-9176
17144 Holly Rd Lewes (19958) *(G-6285)*

Mobile Home Supply, Felton Also Called: Brass Sales Company Inc *(G-3947)*

Mobile Magic Detailing LLC 302 444-8644
2840 Ogletown Rd Unit 2 Newark (19713) *(G-11436)*

Mobile Magic Pressure Washing 302 697-1230
50 E Darby Cir Dover (19904) *(G-3110)*

Mobile Mechanical Services 302 503-7441
10014 N Union Church Rd Lincoln (19960) *(G-6690)*

Mobile Muzic Inc 302 998-5951
2517 Nicholby Dr Wilmington (19808) *(G-18394)*

Mobile Tax LLC 302 297-8325
7 S King St Georgetown (19947) *(G-4430)*

Mobilelink 302 502-3062
456 S Market St Wilmington (19801) *(G-18395)*

Mobilen Communications Inc 844 580-7233
3422 Old Capitol Trl Ste 700 Wilmington (19808) *(G-18396)*

Mobilia Technology, Wilmington Also Called: Quest Global Digital Inc *(G-19293)*

Mobility Route Inc 302 273-0770
8 The Grn Ste 11251 Dover (19901) *(G-3111)*

Mobility Unbound LLC 786 925-4411
800 N State St Ste 304 Dover (19901) *(G-3112)*

Mobio Global Inc 484 263-4845
850 New Burton Rd Ste 201 Dover (19904) *(G-3113)*

Mobius New Media Inc 302 475-9880
818 N Market St Fl 2r Wilmington (19801) *(G-18397)*

Mocean Energy Corp 410 449-4286
8 The Grn Ste 10928 Dover (19901) *(G-3114)*

Mocha Technologies Inc   ALPHABETIC SECTION

Mocha Technologies Inc.. 408 556-9930
   2093 Philadelphia Pike # 1395 Claymont (19703) *(G-1243)*

Mod Vellum Inc.. 415 310-7354
   22167 Arbor Cir Milton (19968) *(G-8674)*

Modena Software Inc... 650 326-1136
   16192 Coastal Hwy Lewes (19958) *(G-6286)*

Modern Controls Inc... 302 325-6800
   26 Bellecor Dr Ste A New Castle (19720) *(G-9377)*

Modern Mail, Newark *Also Called: Provide LLC (G-11767)*

Modern Maturity Center Inc... 302 734-1200
   1121 Forrest Ave Dover (19904) *(G-3115)*

Modern Mixture LLC... 302 249-6183
   37 Meadow Lark Dr Milford (19963) *(G-8017)*

Modern Samurai Combat Fitness................................... 302 229-5399
   8 Photinia Dr Newark (19702) *(G-11437)*

Modern Water Inc... 302 669-6900
   15 Reads Way Ste 100 New Castle (19720) *(G-9378)*

Modernthink LLC.. 302 764-4477
   2 Mill Rd Ste 102 Wilmington (19806) *(G-18398)*

Modified Thermoset Resins Inc...................................... 302 235-3710
   2 Pixie Rd Wilmington (19810) *(G-18399)*

Modise Imports & Exports LLC...................................... 800 274-1240
   8 The Grn Dover (19901) *(G-3116)*

Modular Carpet Recycling Inc.. 484 885-5890
   239 Lisa Dr New Castle (19720) *(G-9379)*

Moeco Iot Inc... 626 869-7140
   221 W 9th St Ste 574 Wilmington (19801) *(G-18400)*

Mohammad A Khan MD.. 302 449-5791
   212 Carter Dr Middletown (19709) *(G-7375)*

Mohammad Kamali, MD, Newark *Also Called: Orthopedic Specialists (G-11602)*

Mohammed M Ali M D.. 302 328-2895
   703 Varsity Ln Bear (19701) *(G-376)*

Mohan Consulting LLC... 314 583-9140
   614 N Dupont Hwy Dover (19901) *(G-3117)*

Mohandis Enterprises LLC... 302 261-2821
   16192 Coastal Hwy Lewes (19958) *(G-6287)*

Mohawk, Milford *Also Called: Mohawk Electrical Systems Inc (G-8018)*

Mohawk Electrical Systems Inc...................................... 302 422-2500
   251 S Rehoboth Blvd Milford (19963) *(G-8018)*

Mohawk Tile MBL Distrs of Del...................................... 302 655-7164
   2700 W 3rd St Greenhill Ave Wilmington (19805) *(G-18401)*

Mojio.. 831 747-5141
   901 N Market St Wilmington (19801) *(G-18402)*

Mokka LLC.. 646 388-2449
   1007 N Orange St Ste 1382 Wilmington (19801) *(G-18403)*

Molded Components Inc... 302 588-2240
   3817 Katherine Ave Wilmington (19808) *(G-18404)*

Moleclar Imging Svcs Intl Chst, Bear *Also Called: Molecular Imaging Services Inc (G-377)*

Molecular Imaging Services Inc..................................... 302 450-4505
   10 Whitaker Ct Bear (19701) *(G-377)*

Molinas Contracting LLC.. 302 378-9316
   553 Maple Ave Middletown (19709) *(G-7376)*

Molly Williams... 302 436-3015
   31556 Winterberry Pkwy Selbyville (19975) *(G-13578)*

Moltex Energy USA LLC... 775 346-7520
   301 N Market St Ste 1414 Wilmington (19801) *(G-18405)*

Mom Home Daycare.. 302 265-2668
   8351 Collett Ln Milford (19963) *(G-8019)*

Momenee and Associates Inc (PA)................................. 610 527-3030
   17 Polly Drummond Shpg Ctr Ste 201 Newark (19711) *(G-11438)*

Momenee Survey Group, Newark *Also Called: Momenee and Associates Inc (G-11438)*

Momentum Management Group Inc............................... 302 477-9730
   3411 Silverside Rd Ste 201w Wilmington (19810) *(G-18406)*

Mommas Mountain, Magnolia *Also Called: Mommas Mountain LLC (G-6769)*

Mommas Mountain LLC.. 410 236-6717
   558 Tullamore Rd Magnolia (19962) *(G-6769)*

Mommin With Swag LLC... 302 373-6316
   3 Cymbal Ct Newark (19702) *(G-11439)*

Moms Cleaning Service Inc.. 302 547-5729
   5517 E Timberview Ct Wilmington (19808) *(G-18407)*

Monada Inc... 302 253-7382
   1209 N Orange St Wilmington (19801) *(G-18408)*

Monadnock Inn... 603 532-7800
   303 Church St Felton (19943) *(G-4004)*

Monarch Nascent Inc... 310 601-4702
   427 N Tatnall St Wilmington (19801) *(G-18409)*

Mondrian Focused Global.. 302 428-3839
   1105 N Market St Wilmington (19801) *(G-18410)*

Mondrian International Small... 302 428-3839
   1105 N Market St Ste 118 Wilmington (19801) *(G-18411)*

Monet Intermediate LLC... 929 559-5423
   251 Little Falls Dr Wilmington (19808) *(G-18412)*

Monetran LLC... 732 984-1983
   501 Pershing Ct Hockessin (19707) *(G-5310)*

Money Ex Pos Solutions US Inc.................................... 866 946-6773
   1675 S State St Ste B Dover (19901) *(G-3118)*

Money Factory LLC.. 620 755-5215
   8 The Grn Dover (19901) *(G-3119)*

Money Factory, The, Dover *Also Called: Money Factory LLC (G-3119)*

Money Mailer, Newark *Also Called: Money Mailer of Delaware (G-11440)*

Money Mailer, Selbyville *Also Called: Money Mailer Tri Counties (G-13579)*

Money Mailer of Delaware... 302 235-7262
   5 Beacon Ln Newark (19711) *(G-11440)*

Money Mailer of East Central, Georgetown *Also Called: Marketing Resources Inc (G-4418)*

Money Mailer Tri Counties... 240 832-1340
   36461 Wild Rose Cir Selbyville (19975) *(G-13579)*

Money Never Sleeps Entrmt LLC................................... 646 234-7285
   1000 N West St Wilmington (19801) *(G-18413)*

Moneyball Dfs LLC... 302 240-0051
   200 Continental Dr # 401 Newark (19713) *(G-11441)*

Moneykey - TX Inc.. 866 255-1668
   3422 Old Capitol Trl Ste 1613 Wilmington (19808) *(G-18414)*

Moneykey-Mo Inc... 866 255-1668
   3422 Old Capitol Trl Ste 1613 Wilmington (19808) *(G-18415)*

Monge Woodworking LLC.. 302 455-0175
   4 Barnard St Newark (19711) *(G-11442)*

Monica Bumbrey... 302 538-1942
   401 Harmony Ln Unit 5 Dover (19904) *(G-3120)*

Monica Khan... 302 652-1994
   1416 Lancaster Ave Wilmington (19805) *(G-18416)*

Monica Mehring DDS.. 302 368-0054
   179 W Chestnut Hill Rd Ste 4 Newark (19713) *(G-11443)*

Monitor For Hire. Com, Hockessin *Also Called: Pharma E Market LLC (G-5344)*

Monkeys In Trees LLC... 302 519-4551
   4528 Saddle Up Cir Bridgeville (19933) *(G-735)*

Monofor Inc.. 415 800-4925
   2035 Sunset Lake Rd Ste B2 Newark (19702) *(G-11444)*

Monogram Specialties.. 302 292-2424
   701 Valley Rd Newark (19711) *(G-11445)*

Monopy International Inc... 312 339-8751
   108 W 13th St Wilmington (19801) *(G-18417)*

Monro Inc.. 302 846-2732
   5 Gerald Ct Delmar (19940) *(G-1623)*

Monro Inc.. 302 378-3801
   430 Haveg Rd Middletown (19709) *(G-7377)*

Monroe Enterprising Svcs LLC...................................... 302 345-1527
   5410 Old Capitol Trl Wilmington (19808) *(G-18418)*

Monroe Iko Inc.. 302 764-3100
   120 Hay Rd Wilmington (19809) *(G-18419)*

Monroe Mechanical Contracting.................................... 302 223-6020
   370 Christiana River Dr Clayton (19938) *(G-1387)*

Monseco Leather LLC.. 302 235-1777
   724 Yorklyn Rd Ste 260 Hockessin (19707) *(G-5311)*

Monster Gaming LLC... 251 281-8906
   16192 Coastal Hwy Lewes (19958) *(G-6288)*

Monster Incorporation Inc... 920 349-7947
   651 N Broad St Ste 201 Middletown (19709) *(G-7378)*

Monster King Conglomerate LLC (PA)........................... 302 222-9742
   106 Memorial Dr New Castle (19720) *(G-9380)*

Montchanin Builders... 302 472-7213
   300 Water St Ste 300 Wilmington (19801) *(G-18420)*

Montchanin Design Group Inc....................................... 302 652-3008
   1907 N Market St Wilmington (19802) *(G-18421)*

ALPHABETIC SECTION — Morningstar Property Group LLC

Monterey SW LLC..302 504-4901
111 Continental Dr # 114 Newark (19713) *(G-11446)*

Monterey Swf LLC..302 504-4901
111 Continental Dr # 114 Newark (19713) *(G-11447)*

Montesino Associates..302 888-2355
1719 Delaware Ave # 3 Wilmington (19806) *(G-18422)*

Montesino Technologies Inc................................302 888-2355
1719 Delaware Ave # 3 Wilmington (19806) *(G-18423)*

Montessori Learning Center LLC........................302 478-2575
2313 Concord Pike Wilmington (19803) *(G-18424)*

Montgmery McCrcken Wlker Rhads..................302 504-7800
300 Delaware Ave Ste 750 Wilmington (19801) *(G-18425)*

Montgomery Carpet Cleaning.............................302 258-6036
10554 Concord Rd Seaford (19973) *(G-13288)*

Montgomery Electric...302 832-0945
224 Cheyenne Dr Bear (19701) *(G-378)*

Montgomery Kenneth John.................................302 992-0484
610 Ohio Ave Wilmington (19805) *(G-18426)*

Montrae Denorris Jones LLC..............................770 851-3836
8 The Grn # A Dover (19901) *(G-3121)*

Monzack Mrsky McLghlin Brwder......................302 656-8162
1201 N Orange St Ste 400 Wilmington (19801) *(G-18427)*

Moody Lawn Care & Renovations......................302 685-2338
1000 N West St Ste 1200 Wilmington (19801) *(G-18428)*

Moon Bounce Mania...302 588-1300
5047 Ogletown Stanton Rd Newark (19713) *(G-11448)*

Moon Buyer Inc (PA)..302 636-5401
251 Little Falls Dr Wilmington (19808) *(G-18429)*

Moon Devices Inc...650 206-8011
919 N Market St Ste 725 Wilmington (19801) *(G-18430)*

Moon Shot Energy LLC......................................512 297-2626
16192 Coastal Hwy Lewes (19958) *(G-6289)*

Mooney & Andrew PA...302 856-3070
11 S Race St Georgetown (19947) *(G-4431)*

Moonloop Photography LLC...............................484 748-0812
1704 Green Ln Wilmington (19810) *(G-18431)*

Moonsworth, Wilmington Also Called: Moonsworth LLC *(G-18432)*

Moonsworth LLC..302 439-6039
1201 N Market St Ste 111 Wilmington (19801) *(G-18432)*

Moor Instruments Inc...302 798-7470
501 Silverside Rd Ste 66 Wilmington (19809) *(G-18433)*

Moore & Lind Inc..302 934-8818
28448 Dupont Blvd Millsboro (19966) *(G-8390)*

Moore & Rutt PA (PA)..302 856-9568
122 W Market St Georgetown (19947) *(G-4432)*

Moore Clinton Denver II.....................................302 856-3385
24062 Peterkins Rd Georgetown (19947) *(G-4433)*

Moore Farms..302 629-4999
14619 Cokesbury Rd Georgetown (19947) *(G-4434)*

Moore Insurance & Financial..............................302 999-9101
1702 Kirkwood Hwy Ste 101 Wilmington (19805) *(G-18434)*

Moore J Everett, Georgetown Also Called: Moore & Rutt PA *(G-4432)*

Moore Ltd...302 427-5760
222 Delaware Ave Ste 1436 Wilmington (19801) *(G-18435)*

Moore Partnership...302 227-5253
126 Bellevue St Dewey Beach (19971) *(G-1674)*

Moore Physcial Therapy....................................302 654-8142
1806 N Van Buren St Ste 200 Wilmington (19802) *(G-18436)*

Moore Physical Therapy, Wilmington Also Called: Therapeutic Moore Services LLC *(G-20296)*

Moore Quality Welding Fab................................302 250-7136
328 W Dickerson Ln Middletown (19709) *(G-7379)*

Moore Services..302 588-3984
1723 Chestnut St Wilmington (19805) *(G-18437)*

Moore Shaun Pt...302 477-3998
3317 Tunison Dr Wilmington (19810) *(G-18438)*

Moore Staffing Agency LLC...............................215 300-2770
112 Grove Mansion Way Bear (19701) *(G-379)*

Moore, J A Construction Co, Wilmington Also Called: J A Moore & Sons Inc *(G-17449)*

Moore, William X Jr, Wilmington Also Called: Roeberg Moore & Associates PA *(G-19554)*

Moore's Masonry, Georgetown Also Called: Moore Clinton Denver II *(G-4433)*

Moores Cabinet Refinishing Inc.........................302 378-3055
939 Bethel Church Rd Middletown (19709) *(G-7380)*

Moores Enterprises Inc......................................302 227-8200
6 2nd St Rehoboth Beach (19971) *(G-12860)*

Moorings At Lewes..302 644-6382
17028 Cadbury Cir Lewes (19958) *(G-6290)*

Moorway Painting Management.........................302 764-5002
1 Hayden Ave Wilmington (19804) *(G-18439)*

Mopak, Seaford Also Called: Jbs Souderton Inc *(G-13231)*

Moppert Auto Collision of...................................302 453-2900
1801 Ogletown Rd Newark (19711) *(G-11449)*

Morales Gto Empire LLC...................................302 824-4315
6 Kathlyn Ct Wilmington (19808) *(G-18440)*

Morales Screen Printing....................................302 465-8179
201 Cassidy Dr Ste C Dover (19901) *(G-3122)*

Moran Environmental Recovery........................302 322-6008
314 Bay West Blvd Ste 8 New Castle (19720) *(G-9381)*

Moran Envmtl Recovery LLC............................302 322-6008
9 Garfield Way Newark (19713) *(G-11450)*

Morans Heating & A/C & Plbg, Rehoboth Beach Also Called: Morans Refrigeration Svc Inc *(G-12861)*

Morans Refrigeration Svc Inc............................703 642-1200
146 Glade Cir W Rehoboth Beach (19971) *(G-12861)*

More About You Inc..302 229-4414
25 Forsythia Ln Bear (19701) *(G-380)*

More About You Inc..302 660-8899
220 Christiana Medical Ctr Newark (19702) *(G-11451)*

More Foundation Group....................................302 645-4669
210 Priscilla Cir Lewes (19958) *(G-6291)*

More Property Recovery...................................302 834-4788
14 Sonnet Dr Newark (19702) *(G-11452)*

More Than Fitness Inc......................................302 690-5655
718 Grandview Ave Wilmington (19809) *(G-18441)*

More Than Shy Inc..603 918-1612
2810 N Church St Wilmington (19802) *(G-18442)*

Morgan Kalman Clinic PA.................................302 529-5500
2501 Silverside Rd Ste 1 Wilmington (19810) *(G-18443)*

Morgan Builders Inc...302 575-9943
403 Tatum Ave Wilmington (19805) *(G-18444)*

Morgan Garanty Intl Fincl Corp (HQ)................302 634-1000
500 Stanton Christiana Rd Newark (19713) *(G-11453)*

Morgan Guaranty, Newark Also Called: Morgan Garanty Intl Fincl Corp *(G-11453)*

Morgan Kalman Clinic......................................610 869-5757
2701 Kirkwood Hwy Wilmington (19805) *(G-18445)*

Morgan Lewis International LLC (PA)..............302 574-3000
1007 N Orange St Ste 501 Wilmington (19801) *(G-18446)*

Morgan Louise Fndtn LLC................................302 670-5792
148 Parma Ln Clayton (19938) *(G-1388)*

Morgan Stanley, Wilmington Also Called: Morgan Stanley & Co LLC *(G-18447)*

Morgan Stanley, Wilmington Also Called: Ms Financing LLC *(G-18474)*

Morgan Stanley & Co LLC................................302 573-4000
2751 Centerville Rd Ste 104 Wilmington (19808) *(G-18447)*

Morgan Stnley Intl Hldings Inc..........................302 657-2000
2751 Centerville Rd Ste 104 Wilmington (19808) *(G-18448)*

Morgan Stnley Smith Barney LLC....................302 644-6600
55 Cascade Ln Rehoboth Beach (19971) *(G-12862)*

Morgan Stnley Smith Barney LLC....................302 636-5500
2751 Centerville Rd Ste 104 Wilmington (19808) *(G-18449)*

Mori America LLC (PA)....................................703 918-4663
251 Little Falls Dr Wilmington (19808) *(G-18450)*

Morning After Inc..302 562-5190
5006 Halltown Rd Hartly (19953) *(G-4899)*

Morning Hornet LLC...650 543-4800
103 Foulk Rd Ste 202 Wilmington (19803) *(G-18451)*

Morning Report Research Inc..........................302 730-3793
144 Kings Hwy Dover (19901) *(G-3123)*

Morning Star Construction LLC........................302 539-0791
103 Wood Duck Ct Dagsboro (19939) *(G-1483)*

Morning Star Publications Inc..........................302 629-9788
951 Norman Eskridge Hwy # D Seaford (19973) *(G-13289)*

Morningstar City Group, Wilmington Also Called: Morningstar Property Group LLC *(G-18452)*

Morningstar Property Group LLC.....................302 543-4093
214 W 7th St Apt 1 Wilmington (19801) *(G-18452)*

Morris Carol Jamie Do ... 302 393-5006
517 S Dupont Blvd Milford (19963) *(G-8020)*

Morris & Ritchie Assoc Inc ... 302 855-5734
8 W Market St Georgetown (19947) *(G-4435)*

Morris & Ritchie Assoc Inc ... 302 326-2200
18 Boulden Cir Ste 36 New Castle (19720) *(G-9382)*

Morris CT Trucking Inc ... 302 653-2396
803 Masseys Church Rd Smyrna (19977) *(G-13827)*

Morris E Justice Inc ... 302 539-7731
33897 Em Calhoun Ln Dagsboro (19939) *(G-1484)*

Morris Farms LLC ... 302 875-1518
27955 Beaver Dam Branch Rd Laurel (19956) *(G-5566)*

Morris James LLP ... 302 678-8815
850 New Burton Rd Dover (19904) *(G-3124)*

Morris James LLP ... 302 368-4200
16 Polly Drummond Hill Rd Newark (19711) *(G-11454)*

Morris James LLP ... 302 260-7290
19339 Coastal Hwy Unit 300 Rehoboth Beach (19971) *(G-12863)*

Morris James LLP ... 302 655-2599
803 N Broom St Wilmington (19806) *(G-18453)*

Morris James LLP (PA) ... 302 888-6800
500 Delaware Ave Ste 1500 Wilmington (19801) *(G-18454)*

Morris James Per Injury Group ... 302 856-0017
107 W Market St Georgetown (19947) *(G-4436)*

Morris Masonry ... 410 726-6277
14175 Line Rd Delmar (19940) *(G-1624)*

Morris Nchols Arsht Tnnell LLP ... 302 658-9200
1201 N Market St Ste 1800 Wilmington (19801) *(G-18455)*

Morris, James, Dover Also Called: Morris James LLP *(G-3124)*

Morrow Limited ... 213 631-3534
4 W Rockland Rd Montchanin (19710) *(G-8739)*

Morse Home Improvement, Dagsboro Also Called: Morse Home Improvement LLC *(G-1485)*

Morse Home Improvement LLC ... 302 663-0042
33334 Main St Dagsboro (19939) *(G-1485)*

Mortgage America Inc ... 302 239-0600
5315 Limestone Rd Wilmington (19808) *(G-18456)*

Mortgage Network Solutions LLC (PA) ... 302 252-0100
2036 Foulk Rd Ste 102 Wilmington (19810) *(G-18457)*

Mortgage Network Solutions LLC ... 302 252-0100
223 Pine Cliff Dr Wilmington (19810) *(G-18458)*

Morton Electric Co ... 302 645-9414
16867 Kings Hwy Lewes (19958) *(G-6292)*

Morton Valihura & Zerbato LLC ... 302 426-1313
3704 Kennett Pike Ste 200 Wilmington (19807) *(G-18459)*

Mosaic ... 302 456-5995
261 Chapman Rd Ste 201 Newark (19702) *(G-11455)*

Mosaic ... 302 456-5995
8 Stoddard Dr Newark (19702) *(G-11456)*

Mosaic Media Holdings Inc ... 888 379-3553
8 The Grn Ste A Dover (19901) *(G-3125)*

Mosap Global Inc ... 302 559-3036
1 Innovation Way Ste 300 Newark (19711) *(G-11457)*

Moscova Enterprises Inc ... 347 973-2522
300 Delaware Ave Ste 210 Wilmington (19801) *(G-18460)*

Moscova Svrign Irrvcble Prvate ... 347 973-2522
300 Delaware Ave Wilmington (19801) *(G-18461)*

Mosiac of Delaware ... 302 653-8889
4966 Dupont Pkwy Smyrna (19977) *(G-13828)*

Moso North America Inc ... 855 343-8444
203 Se Front St Ste 101 Milford (19963) *(G-8021)*

Mosquito Authority ... 302 346-2970
999 Long Point Rd Dover (19901) *(G-3126)*

Mosquito Authority ... 302 228-5821
36837 Winner Cir Rehoboth Beach (19971) *(G-12864)*

Mosquito Authority, Middletown Also Called: Mosquito Authority Wilmington *(G-7381)*

Mosquito Authority, Rehoboth Beach Also Called: Mosquito Authority *(G-12864)*

Mosquito Authority Wilmington ... 302 299-5299
106 Newbury Ct Middletown (19709) *(G-7381)*

Mosquito Joe of Delaware, Newark Also Called: Delaware Mosquito Control LLC *(G-10462)*

Mot Cnc Works LLC ... 302 379-2114
110 Patriot Dr Ste H Middletown (19709) *(G-7382)*

Mot Community Fund Inc ... 302 378-5494
5240 Summit Bridge Rd Middletown (19709) *(G-7383)*

Mot Family Chiro-Wilmington ... 302 593-0031
2005 Concord Pike Ste 202 Wilmington (19803) *(G-18462)*

Mot Family Chiropractic - ... 302 378-9191
222 Carter Dr Ste 103 Middletown (19709) *(G-7384)*

MOT SENIOR CENTER, Middletown Also Called: Middltown Odssa Twnsend Snior *(G-7364)*

Motameet LLC ... 302 242-4483
16192 Coastal Hwy Lewes (19958) *(G-6293)*

Motel 6 ... 302 990-5291
24057 Sussex Hwy Seaford (19973) *(G-13290)*

Motel 6, Seaford Also Called: Motel 6 *(G-13290)*

Mother Goose Childrens Center ... 302 934-8454
27275 Dagsboro Rd Millsboro (19966) *(G-8391)*

Mother Hubbard Child Care Ctr ... 302 368-7584
2050 S College Ave Newark (19702) *(G-11458)*

Mother Teresa House Inc ... 302 652-5523
115 E 14th St Wilmington (19801) *(G-18463)*

Mothers In Unity ... 302 442-1904
1227 W 4th St Wilmington (19805) *(G-18464)*

Motion Composites Corp ... 302 266-8200
2915 Ogletown Rd # 2270 Newark (19713) *(G-11459)*

Motion Industries Inc ... 302 462-3130
38541 Sussex Hwy Delmar (19940) *(G-1625)*

Motivated Juicery LLC ... 302 603-4619
1365 N Dupont Hwy Ste 4016 Dover (19901) *(G-3127)*

Motiverse Labs Inc ... 206 391-7995
2140 S Dupont Hwy Camden (19934) *(G-878)*

Motorfyx Inc ... 858 500-6677
1207 Delaware Ave Ste 125 Wilmington (19806) *(G-18465)*

Motorsport Series, Wilmington Also Called: Whisman John *(G-20761)*

Motto Mortgage Prosperity LLC ... 302 313-5145
16394 Samuel Paynter Blvd Milton (19968) *(G-8675)*

Mountain Consulting Inc ... 302 744-9875
103 S Bradford St Dover (19904) *(G-3128)*

Mountain W Insur Fncl Svcs LLC ... 970 824-8185
1209 N Orange St Wilmington (19801) *(G-18466)*

Mountaire Farms, Harrington Also Called: Mountaire Farms Delaware Inc *(G-4805)*

Mountaire Farms, Selbyville Also Called: Mountaire Farms Inc *(G-13580)*

Mountaire Farms LLC ... 302 934-3011
Rte 24 E Millsboro (19966) *(G-8392)*

Mountaire Farms Delaware Inc ... 302 398-3296
615 Fairground Rd Harrington (19952) *(G-4805)*

Mountaire Farms Delaware Inc ... 302 934-1100
29005 John J Williams Hwy Millsboro (19966) *(G-8393)*

Mountaire Farms Delaware Inc ... 302 378-2271
402 Main St Townsend (19734) *(G-14039)*

Mountaire Farms Inc ... 302 934-1100
29529 John J Williams Hwy Millsboro (19966) *(G-8394)*

Mountaire Farms Inc ... 302 934-1100
29106 John J Williams Hwy Millsboro (19966) *(G-8395)*

Mountaire Farms Inc ... 302 404-5057
110 N Cannon St Seaford (19973) *(G-13291)*

Mountaire Farms Inc ... 302 436-8241
Hoosier St Selbyville (19975) *(G-13580)*

Mountaire Farms Inc ... 302 988-6200
35 Railroad Ave Selbyville (19975) *(G-13581)*

MOUNTAIRE FARMS, L.L.C., Millsboro Also Called: Mountaire Farms LLC *(G-8392)*

Mountaire of Delmarva Inc ... 302 988-6207
55 Hosier St Selbyville (19975) *(G-13582)*

Movarna LLC ... 805 501-5821
651 N Broad St Ste 205 Middletown (19709) *(G-7385)*

Move Mint ... 267 289-4545
503 Paisley Ln New Castle (19720) *(G-9383)*

Movement Mortgage LLC ... 302 344-6758
19413 Jingle Shell Way Unit 2 Lewes (19958) *(G-6294)*

Movendi Moving ... 302 542-9346
30 Ocean Breeze Dr Rehoboth Beach (19971) *(G-12865)*

Movetec, Newark Also Called: Movetec Fitness Equipment LLC *(G-11460)*

Movetec Fitness Equipment LLC (PA) ... 302 563-4487
790 Salem Church Rd Newark (19702) *(G-11460)*

ALPHABETIC SECTION

Multiwave Investment Inc

Movies At Midway, The, Rehoboth Beach *Also Called: Atlantic Theaters LLC (G-12616)*
Moving As One LLC..301 701-0434
2803 Philadelphia Pike Ste B1045 Claymont (19703) *(G-1244)*
Moving Club LLC (PA)..929 377-9332
600 Garrison Ct New Castle (19720) *(G-9384)*
Moving Experience Delaware..302 241-0899
27 W Loockerman St Lowr Lowr Dover (19904) *(G-3129)*
Moving On Time..302 613-4066
113 Barksdale Professional Ctr Newark (19711) *(G-11461)*
Moving Out..302 470-5308
25631 S Parkway Rd Seaford (19973) *(G-13292)*
Moving Sciences LLC...617 871-9892
1201 N Orange St Ste 600 Wilmington (19801) *(G-18467)*
Moxelle Inc (PA)...646 226-9430
651 N Broad St Ste 201 Middletown (19709) *(G-7386)*
Moxie Apparel Inc...844 894-1435
300 Delaware Ave Ste 210 Wilmington (19801) *(G-18468)*
Moxie Scrubs, Wilmington *Also Called: Moxie Apparel Inc (G-18468)*
Moyer Pest Control..302 353-4404
23 Brookside Dr Wilmington (19804) *(G-18469)*
Moyer, Robert A MD, Dover *Also Called: Tooze & Easter MD PA (G-3698)*
Mp Diversified Services LLC..302 828-1060
38 Albe Dr Ste 1 Newark (19702) *(G-11462)*
Mpay, Lewes *Also Called: Smart Altcoins Inc (G-6480)*
Mpe Global Incorporated..856 376-0434
1401 Pennsylvania Ave Ste 105 Wilmington (19806) *(G-18470)*
Mph.com, Wilmington *Also Called: Miles Per Hour Inc (G-18353)*
Mphasis Corporation...212 686-6655
1220 N Market St Ste 806 Wilmington (19801) *(G-18471)*
Mpi Properties LLC..302 635-7143
6 Cabot Pl Newark (19711) *(G-11463)*
Mr Appliance Sussex County..302 752-3747
32672 Bi State Blvd Laurel (19956) *(G-5567)*
Mr Copy Inc...302 227-4666
20200 Coastal Hwy Ste A Rehoboth Beach (19971) *(G-12866)*
Mr Counseling LLC..302 855-9598
24680 Shortly Rd Georgetown (19947) *(G-4437)*
MR Custom Renovations LLC.......................................302 521-9663
34542 Branch School Rd Laurel (19956) *(G-5568)*
Mr Kleen II..302 324-8797
272 Christiana Rd New Castle (19720) *(G-9385)*
Mr Natural Bottled Water Inc...302 436-7700
31919 Christine Ln Ocean View (19970) *(G-12549)*
Mr Rooter Plumbing of New...302 463-5720
250 Corporate Blvd Ste D Newark (19702) *(G-11464)*
Mr Sandless, Bear *Also Called: Unique Finishes Inc (G-549)*
Mr Tire 1210, Delmar *Also Called: Monro Inc (G-1623)*
Mr Window Washer..302 588-3624
126 Glenrock Dr Claymont (19703) *(G-1245)*
Mr. Rooter, Newark *Also Called: Mr Rooter Plumbing of New (G-11464)*
Mr. Tire, Middletown *Also Called: Monro Inc (G-7377)*
Mrb Golf LLC..302 368-7008
300 W Main St Newark (19711) *(G-11465)*
Mresource LLC (PA)..312 608-4789
1220 N Market St Ste 808 Wilmington (19801) *(G-18472)*
Mri of Wilmington, Newark *Also Called: Delaware Imaging Network Inc (G-10455)*
MRM Landscaping LLC..302 602-1203
914 Maple Ave Wilmington (19809) *(G-18473)*
Mrs Kleen Inc..302 530-7330
1047 Dexter Corner Rd Townsend (19734) *(G-14040)*
Mrs Rita Fisher..215 500-6280
564 Dairy Dr Smyrna (19977) *(G-13829)*
Mrt Enterprises Inc (PA)...302 593-3070
286 Whitetail Run Clayton (19938) *(G-1389)*
Mrt LLC..856 685-1602
2420 Porter Rd Bear (19701) *(G-381)*
Ms Financing LLC...212 276-1206
1209 N Orange St Wilmington (19801) *(G-18474)*
Ms Governors Square Shopping C..................................302 838-3384
1229 Quintilio Dr Bear (19701) *(G-382)*

Ms Hathers Lrng Ctr Childcare..302 994-2448
205 Brookland Ave Wilmington (19805) *(G-18475)*
Ms Kims Day Care..304 689-8023
10 Westbury Dr New Castle (19720) *(G-9386)*
Ms Neat Cleaning Services LLC.....................................302 535-7236
73 Greentree Dr Pmb 414 Dover (19904) *(G-3130)*
MSA, New Castle *Also Called: Couture Denim LLC (G-8983)*
Msb Enterprise Partners LLC..302 947-0736
24912 Pot Bunker Way Millsboro (19966) *(G-8396)*
Mscooperhomeloans..302 494-7712
1037 Old Wilmington Rd Hockessin (19707) *(G-5312)*
Msd Business Solutions LLC..609 375-8461
16192 Coastal Hwy Lewes (19958) *(G-6295)*
Msgg LLC..917 565-8306
8 The Grn Ste A Dover (19901) *(G-3131)*
MSI...302 449-5508
238 Casper Way Middletown (19709) *(G-7387)*
MSI, Seaford *Also Called: Manufacturing Support Inds Inc (G-13274)*
Msl Associates LLC..207 391-4420
2915 Ogletown Rd Newark (19713) *(G-11466)*
Msm Foods LLC..302 524-4470
3100 Naamans Rd Ste 1 Wilmington (19810) *(G-18476)*
MSP Equip Rental...302 322-5394
3128 New Castle Ave New Castle (19720) *(G-9387)*
Msrcosmos LLC (HQ)..925 218-6919
1000 N West St Ste 1200 Wilmington (19801) *(G-18477)*
Mss Energy Holdings LLC...212 231-2505
251 Little Falls Dr Wilmington (19808) *(G-18478)*
Mstm LLC..302 239-4447
28 Tenby Chase Dr Newark (19711) *(G-11467)*
Mt Aire...302 629-8739
4933 Stein Hwy Seaford (19973) *(G-13293)*
Mt Cuba Center Inc...302 239-4244
3120 Barley Mill Rd Hockessin (19707) *(G-5313)*
Mt D.C. One, Wilmington *Also Called: Mori America LLC (G-18450)*
Mt Foreign Holdings Inc (HQ).......................................301 252-9160
2711 Centerville Rd Ste 400 Wilmington (19808) *(G-18479)*
Mtb Artisans LLC..303 475-9024
2205 Kentmere Pkwy Wilmington (19806) *(G-18480)*
Mtc Delaware LLC..302 654-3400
2 Dock View Dr New Castle (19720) *(G-9388)*
Mtc Usa LLC...980 999-8888
411 Woodlawn Ave Newark (19711) *(G-11468)*
Mto Hose Solutions Inc (DH)...302 266-6555
214 Interchange Blvd Newark (19711) *(G-11469)*
Mtrigger LLC...302 502-7262
339 Mourning Dove Dr Newark (19711) *(G-11470)*
Mudiwa Munyikwa MD...302 645-7050
39 W Clarke Ave Milford (19963) *(G-8022)*
Mujib R Obeidy..302 478-5900
1401 Silverside Rd Ste A Wilmington (19810) *(G-18481)*
Muldoons Diesel Prfmce LLC...302 276-2882
610 South St Historic New Castle (19720) *(G-5030)*
Mullen Thomas R DMD PA...302 629-3588
8466 Herring Run Rd # D Seaford (19973) *(G-13294)*
Mullico General Construction...302 475-4400
510 Foulkstone Rd Wilmington (19803) *(G-18482)*
Mulligans Pointe LLC...302 856-6283
22426 Sussex Pines Rd Georgetown (19947) *(G-4438)*
Multi Koastal Services..302 436-8822
34756 Roxana Rd Frankford (19945) *(G-4128)*
Multi Michel Services..302 628-3288
107 N Pine St Seaford (19973) *(G-13295)*
Multifmily MGT Phladelphia LLC.................................302 322-8953
100 Liberty Ter Newark (19702) *(G-11471)*
Multiples Adams Service LLC..302 792-0710
42 2nd Ave Claymont (19703) *(G-1246)*
Multispecialty Healthcare..302 575-9794
1010 Concord Ave Wilmington (19802) *(G-18483)*
Multiwave Investment Inc...302 658-9200
1201 N Market St Ste 1707 Wilmington (19801) *(G-18484)*

Mumford and Miller Con Inc — ALPHABETIC SECTION

Mumford and Miller Con Inc 302 378-7736
   1005 Industrial Dr Middletown (19709) *(G-7388)*

Mumford Sheet Metal Works Inc 302 436-8251
   101 Cemetery Rd Selbyville (19975) *(G-13583)*

Mumford-Bjorkman Assoc Inc 302 655-8234
   222a 7th Ave Wilmington (19805) *(G-18485)*

Muncie Ins & Fncl Svcs Inc 302 398-9100
   17067 S Dupont Hwy Harrington (19952) *(G-4806)*

Muncie Ins & Fncl Svcs Inc 302 761-9611
   4400 N Market St Wilmington (19802) *(G-18486)*

Muncie Insurance & Fincl Svcs 302 645-7740
   18767 Coastal Hwy Rehoboth Beach (19971) *(G-12867)*

Muncie Insurance Services (PA) 302 629-9414
   1011 Norman Eskridge Hwy Seaford (19973) *(G-13296)*

Muni Tech LLC 302 383-1487
   605 N Market St Wilmington (19801) *(G-18487)*

Municipal Services Commission (PA) 302 323-2330
   216 Chestnut St Historic New Castle (19720) *(G-5031)*

Munters Corporation 302 798-2455
   100 Naamans Rd Ste 5l Claymont (19703) *(G-1247)*

Murgency, Dover Also Called: Murgency Inc *(G-3132)*

Murgency Inc 650 308-9964
   3500 S Dupont Hwy Ste Ak101 Dover (19901) *(G-3132)*

Murphy & Landon PC 302 472-8100
   1011 Centre Rd Ste 210 Wilmington (19805) *(G-18488)*

Murphy Electric Inc 302 644-0404
   30731 Sassafras Dr Lewes (19958) *(G-6296)*

Murphy Law Firm 302 855-1055
   313 N Bedford St Georgetown (19947) *(G-4439)*

Murphy Marine Services Inc 302 571-4700
   701 Christiana Ave Wilmington (19801) *(G-18489)*

Murphy Mental Health 302 463-7903
   1 Gristmill Ln Newark (19711) *(G-11472)*

Murphy Spadaro & Landon, Wilmington Also Called: Murphy & Landon PC *(G-18488)*

Murphy Steel Inc 302 366-8676
   727 Dawson Dr Newark (19713) *(G-11473)*

Murphys Construction 302 462-0319
   11015 Pit Rd Seaford (19973) *(G-13297)*

Murray Brothers 302 436-3639
   8908 Ebenezer Rd Selbyville (19975) *(G-13584)*

Murray Bunting Constr 302 436-5144
   32924 Lighthouse Rd Selbyville (19975) *(G-13585)*

Murray Farms, Selbyville Also Called: Murray Brothers *(G-13584)*

Murray James 302 629-3923
   613 High St Seaford (19973) *(G-13298)*

Murray Manor, Wilmington Also Called: Millcreek Mobile Hm Pk Land Co *(G-18359)*

Murray Mnor Hmwners Assctn LL 302 298-5997
   27 2nd Ave Wilmington (19808) *(G-18490)*

Murray Phillips PA 302 697-2499
   257 E Camden Wyoming Ave Camden (19934) *(G-879)*

Murrayphillipspa, Georgetown Also Called: Ronald D Jr Attorney At Law *(G-4491)*

Murry Trucking Llc 302 653-4811
   568 Blackbird Greenspring Rd Smyrna (19973) *(G-13830)*

Murrys Cash & Carry 302 736-6508
   40 Quillen St Dover (19904) *(G-3133)*

Muse Global Consulting Inc 325 221-3634
   651 N Broad St Middletown (19709) *(G-7389)*

Muse Marketing & Creative LLC 856 823-1601
   2214 Buckingham Rd Wilmington (19810) *(G-18491)*

Museum Studies Program 302 831-1251
   77 E Main St Newark (19711) *(G-11474)*

Mushroom Supply & Services Inc 610 268-0800
   1643 Pulaski Hwy Newark (19702) *(G-11475)*

Mushu Inc 650 862-8863
   251 Little Falls Dr Wilmington (19808) *(G-18492)*

Musi Commercial Properties Inc 302 594-1000
   5700 Kennett Pike Wilmington (19807) *(G-18493)*

Music Art & Culture Foundation 347 746-9047
   16192 Coastal Hwy Lewes (19958) *(G-6297)*

Musick LLC 201 962-0023
   211 N Broad St Ste 3a Middletown (19709) *(G-7390)*

Must App Corp 905 537-5522
   1013 Centre Rd Ste 403b Wilmington (19805) *(G-18494)*

Mutari, Middletown Also Called: Taglatam Inc *(G-7618)*

Mutual Fund Department, Wilmington Also Called: Blackrock Cal Mnicpl Income Tr *(G-14906)*

Muvers Inc 888 508-4849
   427 N Tatnall St Ste 14582 Wilmington (19801) *(G-18495)*

Mv Cruise Partners LLC 561 329-3209
   251 Little Falls Dr Wilmington (19808) *(G-18496)*

MV Farinola Inc 302 545-8492
   4023 Kennett Pike Ste 219 Wilmington (19807) *(G-18497)*

Mvl Structures Group LLC 302 652-7580
   1000 N West St Ste 1501 Wilmington (19801) *(G-18498)*

Mvl-Al Othman Al Zamel JV LLC 832 302-2757
   1000 N West St Ste 1501 Wilmington (19801) *(G-18499)*

Mvl-Saqa JV LLC 832 302-2757
   1000 N West St Ste 1501 Wilmington (19801) *(G-18500)*

Mvrp Foundation Inc 347 683-1974
   19723 Queen St Rehoboth Beach (19971) *(G-12868)*

Mwidm Inc (PA) 302 298-0101
   1201 N Market St Ste 111 Wilmington (19801) *(G-18501)*

MWM Construction 302 218-5222
   6210 Summit Bridge Rd Townsend (19734) *(G-14041)*

My 3 Sons 302 559-7252
   612 Fallon Ave Wilmington (19804) *(G-18502)*

My Baby's Heartbeat Bear, Bear Also Called: Purushas Picks Inc *(G-442)*

My Beach Agent Realty Group 302 858-2370
   16392 Coastal Hwy Lewes (19958) *(G-6298)*

My Benefit Advisor LLC 302 588-7242
   2207 Concord Pike Ste 152 Wilmington (19803) *(G-18503)*

My Careshare LLC 901 848-5988
   160 Greentree Dr Ste 101 Dover (19904) *(G-3134)*

My Cousin Vinnys Hvac 302 266-1888
   8 Rolling Dr Newark (19713) *(G-11476)*

My Digital Shield 423 310-8977
   300 Delaware Ave Ste 210 Wilmington (19801) *(G-18504)*

My Eye Dr Optometrists LLC 302 838-0800
   1237 Quintilio Dr Bear (19701) *(G-383)*

My Eye Dr Optometrists LLC 302 346-4992
   1404 Forrest Ave Dover (19904) *(G-3135)*

My Eye Dr Optometrists LLC 302 734-5861
   885 S Governors Avenue Dover (19904) *(G-3136)*

My Eye Dr Optometrists LLC 302 422-2020
   1197 Airport Rd Milford (19963) *(G-8023)*

My Eye Dr Optometrists LLC 302 629-9197
   1301 Bridgeville Hwy Seaford (19973) *(G-13299)*

My Eye Dr Optometrists LLC 302 653-3400
   201 Stadium St Smyrna (19977) *(G-13831)*

My Eye Dr Optometrists LLC 302 999-7171
   4605 Kirkwood Hwy Wilmington (19808) *(G-18505)*

My Hands Handyman LLC 302 387-2749
   2 Booker St Georgetown (19947) *(G-4440)*

My Health Group Inc 401 400-0015
   1151 Walker Rd Dover (19904) *(G-3137)*

My Install Pro Ltd Lblty Co 803 486-3831
   300 Delaware Ave Ste 210a Wilmington (19801) *(G-18506)*

My Kase LLC 647 686-7202
   16192 Coastal Hwy Lewes (19958) *(G-6299)*

My Life Care LLC 302 760-9248
   8 The Grn Ste A Dover (19901) *(G-3138)*

My Lip Stuff 302 945-5922
   21002 Robinsonville Rd Lewes (19958) *(G-6300)*

My Live Life World Corp 347 560-5425
   501 Silverside Rd Ste 102 Wilmington (19809) *(G-18507)*

My Medicare Advisor LLC 302 602-9426
   429 Leo Ln Bear (19701) *(G-384)*

My Qme Inc 302 218-8730
   1000 Kirk Ave Ste 1000 # 1000 Wilmington (19806) *(G-18508)*

My Red Tea LLC 415 259-4166
   4023 Kennett Pike Wilmington (19807) *(G-18509)*

My Roots LLC 302 883-2693
   9 W Loockerman St Dover (19904) *(G-3139)*

ALPHABETIC SECTION

My Salon Suite.. 302 233-6947
   160 Humphreys Dr Camden Wyoming (19934) *(G-964)*

My Salon Suites.. 302 575-9035
   3620 Kirkwood Hwy Wilmington (19808) *(G-18510)*

My Seaside Spa... 302 313-5174
   17021 Old Orchard Rd Lewes (19958) *(G-6301)*

My Sisters Place Inc... 302 737-5303
   50 Currant Dr Newark (19702) *(G-11477)*

My Touch Works Massage... 302 943-9783
   125 Causey Ave Ste 103 Milford (19963) *(G-8024)*

My World Travel Inc... 610 358-3744
   501 Silverside Rd Ste 41 Wilmington (19809) *(G-18511)*

Mybite Holdings LLC... 647 225-1385
   108 W 13th St Ste 100 Wilmington (19801) *(G-18512)*

Myeyedr, Bear *Also Called: My Eye Dr Optometrists LLC (G-383)*

Myeyedr, Dover *Also Called: My Eye Dr Optometrists LLC (G-3135)*

Myeyedr, Dover *Also Called: My Eye Dr Optometrists LLC (G-3136)*

Myeyedr, Milford *Also Called: My Eye Dr Optometrists LLC (G-8023)*

Myeyedr, Seaford *Also Called: My Eye Dr Optometrists LLC (G-13299)*

Myeyedr, Smyrna *Also Called: My Eye Dr Optometrists LLC (G-13831)*

Myfurtribe Inc... 210 904-3036
   515 Wilson Dr Hockessin (19707) *(G-5314)*

Mymedchoices Inc.. 302 932-1920
   407 Valley Brook Dr Hockessin (19707) *(G-5315)*

Mymoroccanbazar Inc.. 323 238-5747
   2035 Sunset Lake Rd Newark (19702) *(G-11478)*

Mymortgageready.com, Dover *Also Called: Vtms LLC (G-3813)*

Myositis Spport Undrstnding As... 888 696-7273
   9125 N Old State Rd Lincoln (19960) *(G-6691)*

Myralon Webb Ms.. 302 684-3841
   18494 Foxfield Ln Lewes (19958) *(G-6302)*

Myruck Inc... 310 462-3342
   8 The Grn Dover (19901) *(G-3140)*

Mysegmenter Technologies Inc... 302 549-2288
   8 The Grn Dover (19901) *(G-3141)*

Mysherpa, Wilmington *Also Called: Gmg Solutions LLC (G-16899)*

Mystash, Wilmington *Also Called: Mystash Inc (G-18513)*

Mystash... 202 867-8874
   2055 Limestone Rd 200c Wilmington (19808) *(G-18513)*

Mystic Energy Guides Inc... 302 518-2068
   126 Brittany Way Bear (19701) *(G-385)*

N A L C, Newport *Also Called: National Assn Ltr Carriers (G-12455)*

N Barton Assoc... 302 575-9882
   849 Kiamensi Rd Wilmington (19804) *(G-18514)*

N Biggs Professional Svcs LLC.. 302 632-7598
   382 N High Street Extended Smyrna (19977) *(G-13832)*

N Daisy Jax Inc.. 302 387-3543
   1585 Mckee Rd Ste 3 Dover (19904) *(G-3142)*

N J Jackson Realestate Inv LLC.. 602 783-4064
   431 Homestead Rd Ste 2 Wilmington (19805) *(G-18515)*

N Mallari Gc Corp.. 302 516-7738
   44 Bastille Loop Newark (19702) *(G-11479)*

N R O Drywall... 302 293-8811
   221 E Hazeldell Ave New Castle (19720) *(G-9389)*

N U Friendship Outreach Inc.. 302 836-0404
   20 Waterton Dr Bear (19701) *(G-386)*

N V R Mortgage... 302 732-1570
   32442 Royal Blvd Unit 3 Dagsboro (19939) *(G-1486)*

N&D Nail Salon.. 302 834-4899
   14 Foxhunt Dr Bear (19701) *(G-387)*

NA Institute Christia... 302 478-4020
   3521 Silverside Rd Wilmington (19810) *(G-18516)*

Naacaht, Dover *Also Called: National African American Coal (G-3152)*

Naamans Creek Watershed.. 302 475-3037
   2204 Hillside Rd Wilmington (19810) *(G-18517)*

Nab Hospitality, Newark *Also Called: Towne Place Suites By Marriott (G-12214)*

Nab Motel Inc... 302 983-0849
   200 Nathan Ct Newark (19711) *(G-11480)*

Nab Motel Inc... 302 656-9431
   1051 S Market St Wilmington (19801) *(G-18518)*

Nabeel and Huzaif LLC.. 302 445-7483
   16192 Coastal Hwy Lewes (19958) *(G-6303)*

Nabertherm Inc... 302 322-3665
   64 Reads Way New Castle (19720) *(G-9390)*

Nabstar Hospitality... 302 453-1700
   630 S College Ave Newark (19713) *(G-11481)*

Nabu Casa Inc... 747 477-3105
   8 The Grn Ste 12630 Dover (19901) *(G-3143)*

Nacstar.. 302 453-1700
   630 S College Ave Newark (19713) *(G-11482)*

Nacurh Inc.. 302 722-6933
   310 Haines St Newark (19717) *(G-11483)*

Naegele Heating & Cooling.. 443 996-1881
   14160 Staytonville Rd Greenwood (19950) *(G-4654)*

Naes Corporation.. 856 299-0020
   13 Reads Way Ste 100 New Castle (19720) *(G-9391)*

Naf Dover Afb.. 302 677-6950
   520 Main Gate Way Rm 202 Dover (19902) *(G-3144)*

Nagengast Janet Day Care.. 302 656-6898
   602 Ashford Rd Wilmington (19803) *(G-18519)*

Nagin C Patel.. 302 559-4357
   1716 Lovering Ave Wilmington (19806) *(G-18520)*

Nagorka.. 302 537-2392
   303 Wellington Pkwy Bethany Beach (19930) *(G-622)*

Nail Art... 302 999-7807
   3234 Kirkwood Hwy Ste B Wilmington (19808) *(G-18521)*

Nail Expo, Wilmington *Also Called: Hanthej Hulio (G-17052)*

Nail It Down General Contrs.. 302 698-3073
   1474 E Lebanon Rd Dover (19901) *(G-3145)*

Nail It Down General Contrs, Dover *Also Called: Nail It Down General Contrs (G-3145)*

Nail Pros... 302 674-2988
   94 Jessica Lyn Dr Dover (19904) *(G-3146)*

Nail Spa By Tr.. 302 678-2122
   1188 Forrest Ave Dover (19904) *(G-3147)*

Nails At Taormina... 302 519-7528
   36932 Silicato Dr Unit 4 Millsboro (19966) *(G-8397)*

Naked and Thriving Inc.. 855 943-0521
   251 Little Falls Dr Wilmington (19808) *(G-18522)*

Naked Feet Kitchen LLC (PA).. 404 576-4426
   3200 Kirkwood Hwy 1131 Wilmington (19808) *(G-18523)*

Nakuuruq Solutions.. 302 526-2223
   206 Atlantic St Dover (19902) *(G-3148)*

Nally Ventures Cnstr LLC... 302 581-9243
   102 Central Ave Ste 3 Ocean View (19970) *(G-12550)*

Nanas Butter LLC... 302 510-3937
   212 E 35th St Wilmington (19802) *(G-18524)*

Nancy A Mondero Do... 302 644-9641
   110 Anglers Rd Unit 103 Lewes (19958) *(G-6304)*

Nancy A Union MD.. 302 645-6644
   1302 Savannah Rd Lewes (19958) *(G-6305)*

Nancy Cannone... 302 368-3572
   230 Executive Dr Newark (19702) *(G-11484)*

Nancy Cotugna Dr.. 302 261-6255
   11 Andrew Ln Bear (19701) *(G-388)*

Nancy Dufresne.. 302 378-7236
   4 Denny Lynn Dr Townsend (19734) *(G-14042)*

Nancy Hastings... 302 396-2899
   701 E Market St Georgetown (19947) *(G-4441)*

Nancy M Ball.. 302 655-8101
   1500 Shallcross Ave Ste 2b Wilmington (19806) *(G-18525)*

Nancy M Ball Lcsw, Wilmington *Also Called: Nancy M Ball (G-18525)*

Nancy T Brohawn... 302 453-1866
   39 Country Hills Dr Newark (19711) *(G-11485)*

Nannas & Schiavo, Wilmington *Also Called: Nannas Haines & Schiavo PA (G-18526)*

Nannas Haines & Schiavo PA... 302 479-8800
   1407 Foulk Rd Ste 100 Wilmington (19803) *(G-18526)*

Nannys Heavenly Daycare.. 302 276-7149
   5 Skyline Dr New Castle (19720) *(G-9392)*

Nano Magnetics.. 888 629-6266
   2801 Centerville Rd Wilmington (19808) *(G-18527)*

Nano Magnetics Usa Inc... 888 629-6266
   2801 Centerville Rd Wilmington (19808) *(G-18528)*

Nano Wallet Company LLC (PA) 443 610-3402
　1209 N Orange St Wilmington (19801) *(G-18529)*

Nanodrop Technologies LLC 302 479-7707
　3411 Silverside Rd Ste 100bc Wilmington (19810) *(G-18530)*

Nanoselect Inc 302 355-1795
　15 Innovation Way Newark (19711) *(G-11486)*

Nanoshel LLC 302 268-6163
　3422 Old Capitol Trl Ste 1305 Wilmington (19808) *(G-18531)*

Nanoskin LLC 310 345-4768
　651 N Broad St Ste 206 Middletown (19709) *(G-7391)*

Nanticoke Bariatric Services 302 536-5398
　8472 Herring Run Rd Seaford (19973) *(G-13300)*

Nanticoke Cardiology 302 629-9099
　200 Federal St Seaford (19973) *(G-13301)*

Nanticoke Consulting Inc 302 424-0750
　7707 Lindale Rd Greenwood (19950) *(G-4655)*

Nanticoke Consulting and McHy, Greenwood *Also Called: Nanticoke Consulting Inc (G-4655)*

Nanticoke Consulting Inc 302 245-3465
　2856 Williamsville Rd Houston (19954) *(G-5446)*

Nanticoke Dbtes Endcrnlogy Ctr 302 629-0452
　801 Middleford Rd Seaford (19973) *(G-13302)*

Nanticoke EZ Lab 302 337-8571
　9111 Antique Aly Unit 1 Bridgeville (19933) *(G-736)*

Nanticoke Fence LLC 302 628-7808
　23464 Sussex Hwy Seaford (19973) *(G-13303)*

Nanticoke Gastroenterology 302 629-2229
　924 Middleford Rd Seaford (19973) *(G-13304)*

Nanticoke Health Services Inc (PA) 302 629-6611
　801 Middleford Rd Seaford (19973) *(G-13305)*

Nanticoke Immediate Care 302 715-5214
　30549 Sussex Hwy Laurel (19956) *(G-5569)*

Nanticoke Indian Museum 302 945-7022
　27073 John J Williams Hwy Millsboro (19966) *(G-8398)*

Nanticoke Industries LLC 302 245-8825
　28986 Cannon Dr Seaford (19973) *(G-13306)*

Nanticoke Obgyn Associates P A 302 629-2434
　10 Tidewater Dr Seaford (19973) *(G-13307)*

Nanticoke Rehab 302 629-6224
　100 Rawlins Dr Seaford (19973) *(G-13308)*

Nanticoke River Arts Council 302 628-2787
　324 High St Seaford (19973) *(G-13309)*

Nanticoke River Physicians LLC 302 629-9735
　801 Middleford Rd Seaford (19973) *(G-13310)*

Nanticoke Senior Ctr 302 629-4939
　1001 W Locust St Seaford (19973) *(G-13311)*

Nanticoke Shores Assoc LLC 302 945-1500
　26335 Goosepond Rd Millsboro (19966) *(G-8399)*

Nanticoke Weight Loss & Gen 302 536-5395
　8472 Herring Run Rd Seaford (19973) *(G-13312)*

Naomi Rising Inc 803 840-1874
　4021 Hemlock Ct Dover (19901) *(G-3149)*

NAPA, Millsboro *Also Called: Fishers Auto Parts Inc (G-8292)*

NAPA Auto Parts, Claymont *Also Called: Genuine Parts Company (G-1160)*

NAPA Auto Parts, Smyrna *Also Called: Dover Automotive Inc (G-13714)*

NAPA M3 Inc 719 660-6263
　221 N Broad St Ste 3a Middletown (19709) *(G-7392)*

Napigen Inc 302 644-5464
　200 Powder Mill Rd Wilmington (19803) *(G-18532)*

Napoleon Hernandez 302 368-2237
　528 Old Barksdale Rd Newark (19711) *(G-11487)*

Naqeebi Transport Inc 267 246-9321
　2528 Jacqueline Dr Apt E43 Wilmington (19810) *(G-18533)*

Nardi Cabinetry LLC 302 945-7918
　26429 Creekwood Cir Millsboro (19966) *(G-8400)*

Narinder Singh MD 302 737-2600
　295 E Main St Ste 100 Newark (19711) *(G-11488)*

Narissa Building Company LLC 908 619-6419
　501 S Broom St Wilmington (19805) *(G-18534)*

Narleyapps Inc 323 744-1398
　8 The Grn Ste A Dover (19901) *(G-3150)*

Narrow Gate1 .... 302 387-1838
　30 Plica Cir Magnolia (19962) *(G-6770)*

Nash Omniscaping LLC 302 654-4000
　118 Valley Rd Wilmington (19804) *(G-18535)*

Nashco Enterprises Ltd 403 590-0846
　3511 Silverside Rd Wilmington (19810) *(G-18536)*

Nashed Maher MD 302 378-1887
　12 Pennington St Ste 100 Middletown (19709) *(G-7393)*

Nashed PA, Middletown *Also Called: Elkton Mddltown Ashtma Allergy (G-7096)*

Nashville Speedway Usa Inc 615 547-7500
　1131 N Dupont Hwy Dover (19901) *(G-3151)*

Nashville Super Speedway, Dover *Also Called: Nashville Speedway Usa Inc (G-3151)*

Nason Construction Inc 302 529-2510
　3411 Silverside Rd Ste 200 Wilmington (19810) *(G-18537)*

Nassau Vly Vineyards & Winery 302 645-9463
　32165 Winery Way Lewes (19958) *(G-6306)*

Natascha L Hughes 302 856-4700
　528 E Market St Georgetown (19947) *(G-4442)*

Nathan David Fretz 302 218-3338
　2362 Clayton Delaney Rd Clayton (19938) *(G-1390)*

Nathaniel Jon Bent DDS PA 302 731-4907
　625 Barksdale Rd Ste 117 Newark (19711) *(G-11489)*

National African American Coal 301 395-9033
　18 The Grn Dover (19901) *(G-3152)*

National Alnce On Mntal Illnes 302 427-0787
　2400 W 4th St Wilmington (19805) *(G-18538)*

National Assn Elec Distr 302 322-3333
　10 Bellecor Dr New Castle (19720) *(G-9393)*

National Assn For Rgltory Admi 302 234-4152
　910 Glen Falls Ct Newark (19711) *(G-11490)*

National Assn Ltr Carriers 302 652-2933
　8 S Dupont Rd Fl 2 Newport (19804) *(G-12455)*

National Assn of Hispnc Nrses 302 325-9292
　213 Shetland Dr New Castle (19720) *(G-9394)*

National Association Realto 302 674-8640
　1986 Horsepond Rd Dover (19901) *(G-3153)*

National Auto Movers LLC 302 229-9256
　46 Bluegrass Blvd Smyrna (19977) *(G-13833)*

National Barberz Association 302 365-6169
　402 Connor Blvd Bear (19701) *(G-389)*

National Cllgate Rgby Orgnztio 603 748-1947
　300 Delaware Ave Ste 210 Wilmington (19801) *(G-18539)*

National Cncil On AG Lf Lbor R (PA) 302 678-9400
　363 Saulsbury Rd Dover (19904) *(G-3154)*

National Cngress Prnts Tachers, Wilmington *Also Called: Pta Delaware Congress (G-19250)*

National Communications In 302 235-0677
　14 Longacre Ct Hockessin (19707) *(G-5316)*

National Concrete Products LLC 302 349-5528
　9466 Beach Hwy Greenwood (19950) *(G-4656)*

National Dcument MGT Solutions 302 535-9263
　301 Westville Rd Marydel (19964) *(G-6808)*

National Dentex LLC 302 661-6000
　24 Lukens Dr Historic New Castle (19720) *(G-5032)*

National Financial LLC 302 328-1370
　1511 N Dupont Hwy New Castle (19720) *(G-9395)*

National Guard Association Del 302 326-7125
　1 Vavala Way New Castle (19720) *(G-9396)*

National Holding Investment Co (HQ) 302 573-3887
　1011 Centre Rd Wilmington (19805) *(G-18540)*

National Home Rentals LP 302 636-5401
　251 Little Falls Dr Wilmington (19808) *(G-18541)*

National HVAC Service 302 323-1776
　42a Southgate Blvd New Castle (19720) *(G-9397)*

National HVAC Service 570 825-2894
　N Usa Rt 13 Seaford (19973) *(G-13313)*

National Income Tax Service 302 777-1040
　2 Vandever Ave Wilmington (19802) *(G-18542)*

National Industrial LLC 302 407-6233
　1614 E Ayre St Wilmington (19804) *(G-18543)*

National Industries For The Bl 302 477-0860
　3314 Tunison Dr Wilmington (19810) *(G-18544)*

National Mentor Holdings Inc 302 934-0512
　230 Mitchell St Millsboro (19966) *(G-8401)*

ALPHABETIC SECTION — Navigine Corporation

National Metering Service Inc 302 516-7418
303 E Ayre St Wilmington (19804) *(G-18545)*

National Opprtnities Unlimited 913 905-2261
42 Reads Way Ste 5 New Castle (19720) *(G-9398)*

National Rstrtion Fclty Svcs I 856 401-0100
30 Lukens Dr # B Historic New Castle (19720) *(G-5033)*

National Signing Source LLC 773 885-3285
1521 Concord Pike Ste 300 Wilmington (19803) *(G-18546)*

National Society Inc 302 656-9572
1538 Cleland Crse Wilmington (19805) *(G-18547)*

National Society of Sons 443 614-5437
121 Meetinghouse Ln Dover (19904) *(G-3155)*

National Stress Clinic LLC 646 571-8627
1201 N Orange St Ste 600 Wilmington (19801) *(G-18548)*

National Supply Contractors, Wilmington *Also Called: Ip Camera Warehouse LLC (G-17415)*

National Tape Duplicators 302 999-1110
1500 First State Blvd Wilmington (19804) *(G-18549)*

National Trucking LLC 302 465-3692
10887 Rifle Range Rd Bridgeville (19933) *(G-737)*

National Vinyl Products Inc 817 913-5991
1886 Lynnbury Woods Rd Dover (19904) *(G-3156)*

Nationwide, Christiana *Also Called: Steinebach Robert and Assoc (G-1010)*
Nationwide, Clayton *Also Called: Impact Insurance Agency (G-1371)*
Nationwide, Dagsboro *Also Called: Nationwide Insrnce Crey Insur (G-1487)*
Nationwide, Delaware City *Also Called: Nickle Insurance Agency Inc (G-1549)*
Nationwide, Dover *Also Called: Angle Planning Concepts (G-1795)*
Nationwide, Dover *Also Called: Insley Insur & Finanial Svcs (G-2738)*
Nationwide, Dover *Also Called: L & W Insurance Inc (G-2892)*
Nationwide, Dover *Also Called: Michael Frankos (G-3078)*
Nationwide, Dover *Also Called: Nationwide Insurance (G-3157)*
Nationwide, Georgetown *Also Called: Nationwide Insurance (G-4443)*
Nationwide, Harrington *Also Called: Muncie Ins & Fncl Svcs Inc (G-4806)*
Nationwide, Harrington *Also Called: Staples & Associates Insurance (G-4835)*
Nationwide, Historic New Castle *Also Called: New Castle Insurance Ltd (G-5036)*
Nationwide, Hockessin *Also Called: John Koziol Inc (G-5262)*
Nationwide, Hockessin *Also Called: L & D Insurance Services LLC (G-5273)*
Nationwide, Hockessin *Also Called: Nationwide Mutual Insurance Co (G-5317)*
Nationwide, Lewes *Also Called: Truitt Insurance Agency Inc (G-6582)*
Nationwide, Milford *Also Called: Nationwide Insurance (G-8025)*
Nationwide, New Castle *Also Called: Business Insurance Services (G-8903)*
Nationwide, New Castle *Also Called: Cbm Insurance Agency LLC (G-8923)*
Nationwide, New Castle *Also Called: Debra McAfee (G-9007)*
Nationwide, New Castle *Also Called: Insurance & Financial Svcs Inc (G-9235)*
Nationwide, Newark *Also Called: B+h Insurance LLC (G-9968)*
Nationwide, Newark *Also Called: Insley Insur & Fncl Svcs Inc (G-11025)*
Nationwide, Newark *Also Called: Insurance Associates Inc (G-11028)*
Nationwide, Newark *Also Called: Lisa Broadbent Insurance Inc (G-11266)*
Nationwide, Newark *Also Called: McCall Brooks Insurance Agency (G-11366)*
Nationwide, Newark *Also Called: Nationwide Insurance (G-11491)*
Nationwide, Newark *Also Called: Poland & Sullivan Insur Inc (G-11708)*
Nationwide, Newark *Also Called: S T Good Insurance Inc (G-11929)*
Nationwide, Seaford *Also Called: Muncie Insurance Services (G-13296)*
Nationwide, Seaford *Also Called: Nationwide Insur - Wlgus Insur (G-13314)*
Nationwide, Wilmington *Also Called: Anderson Catania Suretly Svc (G-14471)*
Nationwide, Wilmington *Also Called: Braun Agency Inc (G-15096)*
Nationwide, Wilmington *Also Called: Eia Insurers Group LLC (G-16313)*
Nationwide, Wilmington *Also Called: Fred S Smalls Insurance (G-16736)*
Nationwide, Wilmington *Also Called: Insurance Office America Inc (G-17363)*
Nationwide, Wilmington *Also Called: Lyons Insurance Agency Inc (G-18054)*
Nationwide, Wilmington *Also Called: Muncie Ins & Fncl Svcs Inc (G-18486)*
Nationwide, Wilmington *Also Called: Nationwide Insrnce Wswall Agcy (G-18550)*
Nationwide, Wilmington *Also Called: Nickle Insurance (G-18643)*
Nationwide, Wilmington *Also Called: Sanderson Albidress Agency (G-19658)*
Nationwide, Wilmington *Also Called: Weymouth Swyze Crroon Insur In (G-20750)*

Nationwide Insrnce Crey Insur 302 934-8383
30618 Dupont Blvd Unit 1 Dagsboro (19939) *(G-1487)*

Nationwide Insrnce Wswall Agcy 302 791-7600
1035 N Lincoln St Ste 300 Wilmington (19805) *(G-18550)*

Nationwide Insur - Wlgus Insur 302 629-5140
22937 Sussex Hwy Seaford (19973) *(G-13314)*

Nationwide Insurance 919 644-6535
57 Saulsbury Rd Frnt Dover (19904) *(G-3157)*

Nationwide Insurance 302 515-1851
22836 Dupont Blvd Georgetown (19947) *(G-4443)*

Nationwide Insurance 302 402-5188
100 Credit Union Way Milford (19963) *(G-8025)*

Nationwide Insurance 302 453-9698
258 E Main St Newark (19711) *(G-11491)*

Nationwide Insurance, Rehoboth Beach *Also Called: Muncie Insurance & Fincl Svcs (G-12867)*

Nationwide Insurance Co 302 678-2223
1252 Forrest Ave Dover (19904) *(G-3158)*

Nationwide Inventory Svcs Inc 888 741-3039
Hartly (19953) *(G-4900)*

Nationwide Mutual Insurance Co 302 234-5430
724 Yorklyn Rd Ste 200 Hockessin (19707) *(G-5317)*

Nationwide Mutual Insurance Co 434 426-9410
200 Bellevue Pkwy Ste 250 Wilmington (19809) *(G-18551)*

Native Grid LLC (PA) 917 893-7544
8 The Grn Ste A Dover (19901) *(G-3159)*

Natixis Globl Asset MGT Hldngs 617 449-2100
1209 N Orange St Wilmington (19801) *(G-18552)*

Natural By Nature, Newark *Also Called: Natural Dairy Products Corp (G-11492)*

Natural Dairy Products Corp 302 455-1261
316 Markus Ct Newark (19713) *(G-11492)*

Natural Hair Consortium LLC 240 508-1494
2055 Limestone Rd 200c Wilmington (19808) *(G-18553)*

Natural Healing Traditions 302 994-6838
2321 Fells Ln Wilmington (19808) *(G-18554)*

Natural House Inc 302 218-0338
2515 Kirkwood Hwy Newark (19711) *(G-11493)*

Natural Hypertension Inst Inc 302 533-7704
207 Sutton Way Newark (19711) *(G-11494)*

Natural Lawn Care of America, Dagsboro *Also Called: West Third Enterprises LLC (G-1526)*
Natural Lawn of America, Wilmington *Also Called: Jamark Enterprises Inc (G-17476)*

Natural Nail Studio 302 478-0077
1707 Marsh Rd Wilmington (19810) *(G-18555)*

Natural Salon 302 239-5000
6284 Limestone Rd Hockessin (19707) *(G-5318)*

Natural Stacks, Wilmington *Also Called: NS 360 Inc (G-18704)*

Natural Stacks Inc 855 678-2257
16192 Coastal Hwy Lewes (19958) *(G-6307)*

Naturalawn of America Inc 302 652-2000
40 Germay Dr Wilmington (19804) *(G-18556)*

Nature Impact Inc 650 241-8301
2055 Limestone Rd Ste 200c Wilmington (19808) *(G-18557)*

Natures Call LLC 302 777-7767
601 Philadelphia Pike Wilmington (19809) *(G-18558)*

Natures Rule LLC 518 961-5196
1013 Centre Rd Ste 403 Wilmington (19805) *(G-18559)*

Naudain Enterprises LLC 302 239-6840
5840 Limestone Rd Hockessin (19707) *(G-5319)*

Nautical Flfllment Lgstics LLC 816 810-3118
8 The Grn Ste A Dover (19901) *(G-3160)*

Nava 515 495-4577
1207 Delaware Ave Ste 347 Wilmington (19806) *(G-18560)*

Navalt Inc 551 273-2773
8 The Grn Ste R Dover (19901) *(G-3161)*

Navas Painting LLC 302 685-1474
3 Freeport Rd New Castle (19720) *(G-9399)*

Navenu Inc 416 543-9617
8 The Grn Dover (19901) *(G-3162)*

Navient Prvate Edcatn Ln Tr 20 .... 302 636-3300
1011 Centre Rd Ste 200 Wilmington (19805) *(G-18561)*

Navient Solutions LLC (HQ) 703 810-3000
123 S Justison St Ste 300 Wilmington (19801) *(G-18562)*

Navigine Corporation (PA) 339 234-0827
1013 Centre Rd Ste 403b Wilmington (19805) *(G-18563)*

ALPHABETIC SECTION

Navipoint Health Inc... 888 902-3998
1209 N Orange St Wilmington (19801) *(G-18564)*

Navy League of United States................................... 302 456-4410
2205 Glen Avon Rd Wilmington (19808) *(G-18565)*

Nayachi Inc.. 302 400-0072
2055 Limestone Rd Wilmington (19808) *(G-18566)*

Nazar Dover LLC... 302 747-5050
561 N Dupont Hwy Dover (19901) *(G-3163)*

Nazhat Enterprises Holdings.................................... 302 450-1418
8 The Grn Ste 7361 Dover (19901) *(G-3164)*

Nb Retail Management Inc....................................... 302 230-3065
1267 Churchmans Rd Newark (19713) *(G-11495)*

Ncc Cooperative Extension Off................................. 302 831-8965
461 Wyoming Rd Newark (19716) *(G-11496)*

Nccsefcu, Historic New Castle *Also Called: New Cstle Cnty Schl Emplyees F (G-5038)*

Ncd Remodeling LLC... 302 604-3971
29460 Glenwood Dr Millsboro (19966) *(G-8402)*

Nces, Middletown *Also Called: New Covenant Elec Svcs Inc (G-7398)*

Ndon Jordona... 609 254-2620
941 Lansdowne Rd Middletown (19709) *(G-7394)*

NDT, Wilmington *Also Called: Network Design Technologies (G-18596)*

Ndx Dodd, Historic New Castle *Also Called: National Dentex LLC (G-5032)*

Ne Care Management Service LLC........................... 302 501-6449
3616 Kirkwood Hwy Wilmington (19808) *(G-18567)*

Near and Dear Home Care....................................... 302 530-6498
1002 Birchwood Dr Newark (19713) *(G-11497)*

Neat As A Pin LLC... 302 519-4504
24657 German Rd Seaford (19973) *(G-13315)*

Necessary Luxury.. 302 764-4032
806 Woodsdale Rd Wilmington (19809) *(G-18568)*

Necessary Lxury Mssage Therapy, Wilmington *Also Called: Necessary Luxury (G-18568)*

Nectar Lifesciences Usa LLC................................... 518 229-8228
508 Main St Wilmington (19804) *(G-18569)*

Ned Davis Associates Inc... 302 670-5307
314 N Governors Ave Dover (19904) *(G-3165)*

Neenee Wees Daycare.. 302 730-3630
208 Mifflin Rd Dover (19904) *(G-3166)*

Neftali Ayeras Martinez MD...................................... 302 827-2330
31674 Grenache Ct Lewes (19958) *(G-6308)*

Negative Emissions Mtls Inc.................................... 929 388-3352
2093 Philadelphia Pike Claymont (19703) *(G-1248)*

Negri Bossi North America Inc.................................. 302 328-8020
311 Carroll Dr New Castle (19720) *(G-9400)*

Negri Bossi Usa Inc... 302 328-8020
311 Carroll Dr # 100 New Castle (19720) *(G-9401)*

Nehemiah Gtwy Cmnty Dev Corp.............................. 302 655-0803
201 W 23rd St Wilmington (19802) *(G-18570)*

Neighbor Care Home Care & Fmly........................... 302 290-0341
3 Zinnia Ct Bear (19701) *(G-390)*

Neighborhood House Inc (PA).................................. 302 658-5404
1218 B St Wilmington (19801) *(G-18571)*

Neighborly Home Care.. 610 420-1868
2101 W 2nd St Wilmington (19805) *(G-18572)*

Neighbors To Nicaragua Inc..................................... 302 362-2642
2605 Marhill Dr Wilmington (19810) *(G-18573)*

Neil, Wilmington *Also Called: Nuclear Electric Insurance Ltd (G-18710)*

Neil G McAneny DDS.. 302 368-0329
400 New London Rd Newark (19711) *(G-11498)*

Neil G McAneny DDS PC... 302 731-4907
117 Barksdale Professional Ctr Newark (19711) *(G-11499)*

Neil Services Inc... 302 573-2265
1201 N Market St Ste 1100 Wilmington (19801) *(G-18574)*

Neilsen Clothing Inc.. 302 342-1370
3500 S Dupont Hwy Dover (19901) *(G-3167)*

Neilson Associates Inc.. 610 793-2271
4023 Kennett Pike Ste 119 Wilmington (19807) *(G-18575)*

Neitao Express Nails... 302 276-1027
77 Mccullough Dr New Castle (19720) *(G-9402)*

Neitsch Group, The, Newark *Also Called: Neitsch Ltd Liability Company (G-11500)*

Neitsch Ltd Liability Company.................................. 708 634-8724
254 Chapman Rd Newark (19702) *(G-11500)*

Neko Colors, Newark *Also Called: Neko Colors USA Inc (G-11501)*

Neko Colors USA Inc... 844 365-6356
2915 Ogletown Rd Ste 2668 Newark (19713) *(G-11501)*

Nemours, Newark *Also Called: Nemours Fundation Pension Plan (G-11503)*

Nemours Childrens Health Sys................................. 610 642-4040
2200 Concord Pike Fl 6 Wilmington (19803) *(G-18576)*

Nemours Ctr For Pdtric Clncal, Wilmington *Also Called: Nemours Foundation (G-18578)*

Nemours Dpont Pdatrics Milford, Milford *Also Called: Nemours Foundation (G-8027)*

Nemours Dpont Pdiatrics Jessup, Wilmington *Also Called: Nemours Foundation (G-18579)*

Nemours Dpont Pediatrics Dover.............................. 302 672-5650
201 Towne Centre Dr Ste 500 Dover (19904) *(G-3168)*

Nemours Dupont Pediatrics, Newark *Also Called: Nemours Foundation (G-11502)*

Nemours Energy (PA).. 302 655-4838
400 W 9th St Ste 200 Wilmington (19801) *(G-18577)*

Nemours Foundation... 302 424-5420
101 Wellness Way Milford (19963) *(G-8026)*

Nemours Foundation... 302 422-4559
101 Wellness Way Milford (19963) *(G-8027)*

Nemours Foundation... 302 836-7820
200 Biddle Ave Ste 100 Newark (19702) *(G-11502)*

Nemours Foundation... 302 651-6811
1600 Rockland Rd Wilmington (19803) *(G-18578)*

Nemours Foundation... 302 576-5050
1602 Jessup St Wilmington (19802) *(G-18579)*

Nemours Foundation... 302 651-4400
1801 Rockland Rd Wilmington (19803) *(G-18580)*

Nemours Foundation... 302 651-4000
1600 Rockland Rd Wilmington (19803) *(G-18581)*

Nemours Fundation Pension Plan............................ 302 836-7820
1400 Peoples Plz Ste 300 Newark (19702) *(G-11503)*

Nemours Fundation Pension Plan............................ 302 629-5030
49 Fallon Ave Seaford (19973) *(G-13316)*

Nemours Hlth & Prevention Svcs.............................. 302 628-8304
49 Fallon Ave Seaford (19973) *(G-13317)*

Nemours Pediatrics... 302 934-6073
30265 Commerce Dr Millsboro (19966) *(G-8403)*

Nemours Senior Care Wilmington, Wilmington *Also Called: Nemours Foundation (G-18580)*

Nemours Senior Care, Milford, Milford *Also Called: Nemours Foundation (G-8026)*

Neobex Corp.. 833 460-2027
2915 Ogletown Rd Newark (19713) *(G-11504)*

Neocomm De... 302 762-6678
2715 N Market St Wilmington (19802) *(G-18582)*

Neodata LLC.. 302 666-2848
8 The Grn Ste A Dover (19901) *(G-3169)*

Neofithub Inc.. 408 365-4156
2810 N Church St Wilmington (19802) *(G-18583)*

Neon Fun LLC.. 858 220-0946
3500 S Dupont Hwy Dover (19901) *(G-3170)*

Neon USA LLC... 360 433-7512
3500 S Dupont Hwy Dover (19901) *(G-3171)*

Neoteric Ascension LLC (PA)................................... 302 250-7243
254 Chapman Rd Ste 20814318 Newark (19702) *(G-11505)*

Neotrak, Wilmington *Also Called: Fasttrak Coatings Co (G-16561)*

Nephrology Associates PA...................................... 302 225-0451
4923 Ogletown Stanton Rd Ste 200 Newark (19713) *(G-11506)*

Nepi Contracting Inc... 302 250-6820
709 Cheltenham Rd Wilmington (19808) *(G-18584)*

Neptune Global Holdings LLC.................................. 302 256-5080
717 N Union St Ste 103 Wilmington (19805) *(G-18585)*

Nerd Boy LLC.. 302 857-0243
800 N State St Ste 402 Dover (19901) *(G-3172)*

Nerdit Foundation... 302 482-5979
1614 W Newport Pike Wilmington (19804) *(G-18586)*

Nerdit Now LLC... 302 482-5979
3030 Bowers St Wilmington (19802) *(G-18587)*

Nesmith & Company Inc... 215 755-4570
100 Naamans Rd Ste 2d Claymont (19703) *(G-1249)*

Neso Trucking LLC.. 302 358-7878
65 Buena Vista Dr New Castle (19720) *(G-9403)*

Nest Properties LLC... 302 373-8015
412 Reading Ln Middletown (19709) *(G-7395)*

ALPHABETIC SECTION

Nestal Mdsphere Consulting LLC..302 404-6506
1201 N Orange St Ste 7209 Wilmington (19801) *(G-18588)*

Nestl Holdings Inc...203 629-7482
1209 N Orange St Wilmington (19801) *(G-18589)*

Net 2 Apps LLC..214 810-2592
251 Little Falls Dr Wilmington (19808) *(G-18590)*

Net Journey LLC (PA)...818 584-2519
8 The Grn Ste A Dover (19901) *(G-3173)*

Net Merge Ltd..631 816-1145
4115 N Dupont Hwy Dover (19901) *(G-3174)*

Net Sports Group, Newark Also Called: Msl Associates LLC *(G-11466)*

Netatmo LLC..302 703-7680
1209 N Orange St Wilmington (19801) *(G-18591)*

Netdata Inc...650 407-3589
2035 Sunset Lake Rd Ste B2 Newark (19702) *(G-11507)*

Neterra Communications LLC..302 497-3881
500 W Loockerman St Ste 469 Dover (19904) *(G-3175)*

Netfoundry Inc...855 284-2007
251 Little Falls Drive Wilmington (19808) *(G-18592)*

Netinstincts Inc..302 521-9478
501 Silverside Rd Ste 105 Wilmington (19809) *(G-18593)*

Netjectiives..302 998-4436
6 Pleasantwood Rd Newark (19702) *(G-11508)*

Netragy LLC...973 846-7018
10 Cheswold Blvd Apt 1d Newark (19713) *(G-11509)*

Netskyads Media LLC...302 476-2277
16192 Coastal Hwy Lewes (19958) *(G-6309)*

Nettel Partners LLC..215 290-7383
8 Venetian Dr Rehoboth Beach (19971) *(G-12869)*

Netwerx LLC..732 245-8521
69 Westhampton Dr Wilmington (19808) *(G-18594)*

Network Connect Inc...302 300-1222
1200 N French St Wilmington (19801) *(G-18595)*

Network Design Technologies..610 991-2929
1000 N West St Ste 1200 Wilmington (19801) *(G-18596)*

Network Mapping Inc..310 560-4142
1013 Centre Rd Ste 403a Wilmington (19805) *(G-18597)*

Network Scrap Metal Corp (PA)..702 354-0600
1000 Nw St Ste 1501 Wilmington (19801) *(G-18598)*

Networks Programs...302 454-2233
30 Blue Hen Dr Newark (19713) *(G-11510)*

Neuberger & Berman Trust Co..302 658-8522
919 N Market St Ste 506 Wilmington (19801) *(G-18599)*

Neuberger Berman Tr Co Del NA..302 830-4340
919 N Market St Ste 506 Wilmington (19801) *(G-18600)*

Neuracon Biotech Inc..813 966-3129
1313 N Market St Ste 5100 Wilmington (19801) *(G-18601)*

Neural Heaven Inc...631 485-4205
651 N Broad St Ste 201 Middletown (19709) *(G-7396)*

Neuralight, Wilmington Also Called: Neuralight Inc *(G-18602)*

Neuralight Inc (PA)..203 615-1333
1209 N Orange St Wilmington (19801) *(G-18602)*

Neurastack Inc...512 760-3149
651 N Broad St Ste 9566 Middletown (19709) *(G-7397)*

Neuro Fitness Therapy..302 753-2700
3300 Concord Pike Ste 4 Wilmington (19803) *(G-18603)*

Neuro Ophthalmologic Asso...302 792-1616
1201 Society Dr Claymont (19703) *(G-1250)*

Neurology Associates PA..302 731-3017
774 Christiana Rd Ste 201 Newark (19713) *(G-11511)*

Neurology Center South Del...443 944-9733
24488 Sussex Hwy Ste 6 Seaford (19973) *(G-13318)*

Neurorx Inc...202 340-1252
1201 N Market St Ste 111 Wilmington (19801) *(G-18604)*

Neuroscience Software Inc...855 712-1818
8 The Grn Ste 12017 Dover (19901) *(G-3176)*

Neurostar Inc..302 778-0100
303 S Booth Dr New Castle (19720) *(G-9404)*

Neurosurgery Consultants PA...302 738-9145
79 Omega Dr Bldg C Newark (19713) *(G-11512)*

Neutec Corp..302 697-6752
29 Emerson Dr Dover (19901) *(G-3177)*

Neuwing Renewable Energy LLC..267 319-1144
913 N Market St Ste 1001 Wilmington (19801) *(G-18605)*

Never Nver Land Knnel Cttery I..302 645-6140
34377 Neverland Rd Lewes (19958) *(G-6310)*

Nevron Software LLC..855 370-5511
501 Silverside Rd Ste 105 Wilmington (19809) *(G-18606)*

New American Funding...302 200-4607
111 Continental Dr Ste 211 Newark (19713) *(G-11513)*

New B & M Meats Inc..302 655-5331
21 Commerce St Wilmington (19801) *(G-18607)*

New Beginnings, Historic New Castle Also Called: Chimes Inc *(G-4956)*

New Beginnings Cnslng Cnst...302 525-6268
11 Winchester Rd Newark (19713) *(G-11514)*

New Behavioral Network, Wilmington Also Called: Health Care Consultants Inc *(G-17095)*

New Behavorial Network, Wilmington Also Called: Health Care Consultants Inc *(G-17094)*

New Body By Tomorrow LLC..706 816-9255
8 The Grn Ste 4000 Dover (19901) *(G-3178)*

New Car Connection..302 328-7000
174 N Dupont Hwy New Castle (19720) *(G-9405)*

New Care Spa...302 292-2067
33 Chestnut Hill Plz Newark (19713) *(G-11515)*

New Castle 100 Archers Club...302 722-7997
2 Kenley Ct Bear (19701) *(G-391)*

New Castle Assoc & Podiatry, Newark Also Called: Raymond V Feehery Jr DPM *(G-11831)*

New Castle Boys & Girls Clubs, New Castle Also Called: Boys & Girls Clubs Del Inc *(G-8881)*

New Castle Cnty Bd of Realtors...302 762-4800
3615 Miller Rd Wilmington (19802) *(G-18608)*

New Castle Cnty Shoppers Guide..302 325-6600
950 W Basin Rd New Castle (19720) *(G-9406)*

New Castle Conservation Dst..302 832-3100
2430 Old County Rd Newark (19702) *(G-11516)*

New Castle Counter...302 421-3940
55 Lukens Dr Historic New Castle (19720) *(G-5034)*

NEW CASTLE COUNTY BOARD OF REA, Wilmington Also Called: New Castle Cnty Bd of Realtors *(G-18608)*

New Castle County Flooring...302 218-0507
2923 Ogletown Rd Newark (19713) *(G-11517)*

New Castle County Head Start (PA)...302 452-1500
256 Chapman Rd Ste 103 Newark (19702) *(G-11518)*

New Castle Dance & Mus Academy, Bear Also Called: New Castle Dance Academy *(G-392)*

New Castle Dance Academy...302 836-2060
460 Eden Cir Bear (19701) *(G-392)*

New Castle Dental Assoc PA..302 328-1513
92 Reads Way Ste 200 New Castle (19720) *(G-9407)*

New Castle Engraving Co...302 652-7551
133 Festone Ave New Castle (19720) *(G-9408)*

New Castle Family Care PA..302 275-3428
14 Magil Ct Newark (19702) *(G-11519)*

New Castle Glass Inc..302 322-6164
38 Lesley Ln New Castle (19720) *(G-9409)*

New Castle Gunsmithing, New Castle Also Called: Cayley J Carson *(G-8921)*

NEW CASTLE HEALTH & REHABILITA, New Castle Also Called: New Cstle Hlth Rhbltton Ctr L *(G-9416)*

New Castle Hearing Speech Ctr, Hockessin Also Called: Otolaryngology Consultants *(G-5330)*

New Castle Historical Society..302 322-2794
30 Market St Historic New Castle (19720) *(G-5035)*

New Castle Hot Mix Inc...302 655-2119
925 S Heald St Wilmington (19801) *(G-18609)*

New Castle Insurance Ltd..302 328-6111
621 Delaware St Ste 100 Historic New Castle (19720) *(G-5036)*

New Castle Lodging Corporation...302 654-5544
1213 West Ave New Castle (19720) *(G-9410)*

New Castle Precision Mch LLC..302 650-7849
729 Grantham Ln Bldg 2ad New Castle (19720) *(G-9411)*

New Castle Rx LLC..302 356-5600
363 Quigley Blvd Ste B Historic New Castle (19720) *(G-5037)*

New Castle Shop Rental Inc...302 328-8346
34 Yeates Dr New Castle (19720) *(G-9412)*

New Castle Shuttle and Taxi SE...302 326-1855
38 Stevens Ave New Castle (19720) *(G-9413)*

New Cingular Wireless Svcs Inc..302 999-0055
3401 Kirkwood Hwy Wilmington (19808) *(G-18610)*

New Cndlelight Productions Inc..302 475-2313
2208 Millers Rd Wilmington (19810) *(G-18611)*

New Colony North Enterprises..302 762-0405
319 E Lea Blvd Wilmington (19802) *(G-18612)*

New Concept Dental...302 778-3822
2004 Foulk Rd Ste 1 Wilmington (19810) *(G-18613)*

New Concept Technologies LLC..518 533-5367
3422 Old Capitol Trl Ste 948 Wilmington (19808) *(G-18614)*

New Covenant Elec Svcs Inc...302 454-1165
806 Old School House Rd Middletown (19709) *(G-7398)*

New Creation Lawn Care Inc...302 698-0246
68 Elijah Ln Felton (19943) *(G-4005)*

New Creation Logistics Inc..302 438-3154
6 Sussex Rd Apt J Newark (19713) *(G-11520)*

New Cstle Cmnty Mntal Hlth Ctr, Newark Also Called: Delaware Dept Hlth Social Svcs
(G-10434)

New Cstle Cnty Chld Hse Mntsso..302 529-9259
2848 Grubb Rd Wilmington (19810) *(G-18615)*

New Cstle Cnty Chmber Commerce.......................................302 737-4343
920 Justison St Wilmington (19801) *(G-18616)*

New Cstle Cnty Del Emplyees Fd...302 395-5350
100 Churchmans Rd New Castle (19720) *(G-9414)*

New Cstle Cnty Emplyees Pnsion...302 395-5555
87 Reads Way New Castle (19720) *(G-9415)*

New Cstle Cnty Schl Emplyees F...302 613-5330
113 W 6th St Historic New Castle (19720) *(G-5038)*

New Cstle Hlth Rhblitation Ctr, New Castle Also Called: Oak Hrc New Castle LLC *(G-9432)*

New Cstle Hlth Rhbltion Ctr L...302 328-2580
32 Buena Vista Dr New Castle (19720) *(G-9416)*

New Day Montessori...302 235-2554
1 Middleton Dr Wilmington (19808) *(G-18617)*

New Direction Counseling Svcs...302 289-3768
45 Jubilee Ct Felton (19943) *(G-4006)*

New Direction Early Headstart..302 831-0584
321 S College Ave Newark (19716) *(G-11521)*

New Edge Enterprises LLC..908 892-2856
26095 Marys Ln Milton (19968) *(G-8676)*

New Foundations LLC..302 753-3135
560 Peoples Plz Newark (19702) *(G-11522)*

New Hope Family Medicine LLC..302 388-9304
4515 Griffin Dr Wilmington (19808) *(G-18618)*

New Hope Rcreation Dev Ctr Inc...302 424-0767
12564 N Old State Rd Ellendale (19941) *(G-3927)*

New Hope Vehicle Exports LLC..302 275-6482
1000 S Market St Wilmington (19801) *(G-18619)*

New Ilc Dover Inc (PA)...302 335-3911
1 Moonwalker Rd Frederica (19946) *(G-4179)*

New Image Inc...302 738-6824
2401 Ogletown Rd Ste A Newark (19711) *(G-11523)*

New Image Property Maintenance..302 396-0451
10191 Old Crow Rd Delmar (19940) *(G-1626)*

New Leaf Publishing Inc (PA)..408 502-8706
8 The Grn Ste A Dover (19901) *(G-3179)*

New Life Fndation Recovery Inc..302 317-2212
1541 Church Rd Bear (19701) *(G-393)*

New Life Furniture Systems...302 994-9054
1675 E Ayre St Wilmington (19804) *(G-18620)*

New Life Intl Cmnty Dev Corp...302 529-1997
2207 Concord Pike Wilmington (19803) *(G-18621)*

New Life Medicals LLC..610 615-1483
3500 S Dupont Hwy Dover (19901) *(G-3180)*

New Life Moving Inc...704 969-0858
1 N Maple Ave Milford (19963) *(G-8028)*

New Life Spinal Centers...302 883-2504
737 S Governors Ave Dover (19904) *(G-3181)*

New Live Ventures Inc..914 960-1877
16192 Coastal Hwy Lewes (19958) *(G-6311)*

New London Veterinary Center...302 738-5000
437 New London Rd Newark (19711) *(G-11524)*

New Look Home Inc...302 994-4397
100 Bestfield Rd Wilmington (19804) *(G-18622)*

New Orleans Hotel Equity LLC..302 757-7300
1000 N West St Ste 1400 Wilmington (19801) *(G-18623)*

New Pendulum Corporation (PA)..302 478-6160
1100 N Market St Fl 4 Wilmington (19890) *(G-18624)*

New Penn Financial LLC...240 475-4741
19269 Coastal Hwy Ste 1 Rehoboth Beach (19971) *(G-12870)*

New Perspectives Inc..302 489-0220
2055 Limestone Rd Ste 109 Wilmington (19808) *(G-18625)*

New Process Fibre Company..302 349-4535
12655 First St Greenwood (19950) *(G-4657)*

New Relaxation Inc..302 934-9344
28544 Dupont Blvd Unit 14 Millsboro (19966) *(G-8404)*

New Standard Product Dist Inc..844 312-4574
702 Interchange Blvd Newark (19711) *(G-11525)*

New Trend Hair Salon...302 998-3331
4569 Kirkwood Hwy Wilmington (19808) *(G-18626)*

New Trinity Transport LLC..215 457-5700
192 Fan Branch Dr Felton (19943) *(G-4007)*

New U Nutrition Inc..302 543-4555
2801 Lancaster Ave Wilmington (19805) *(G-18627)*

New Vision Services Inc..484 350-6495
812 Village Cir Apt B Newark (19713) *(G-11526)*

New Visions Inv Group LLC..302 299-6234
31 Phoenix Ave Newark (19702) *(G-11527)*

New Wndsor Apartments Assoc LP......................................302 656-1354
500 N Walnut St Ste 1 Wilmington (19801) *(G-18628)*

New York Blood Center Inc..302 737-8405
32445 Royal Blvd Unit B Dagsboro (19939) *(G-1488)*

New York Blood Center Inc (PA)...302 737-8405
100 Hygeia Dr Newark (19713) *(G-11528)*

NEW YORK BLOOD CENTER, INC. D/B/A BLOOD BANK OF DELMARVA, Dover Also
Called: New York Blood Ctr Inc D/B/A B *(G-3182)*

NEW YORK BLOOD CENTER, INC. D/B/A BLOOD BANK OF DELMARVA, Georgetown Also
Called: New York Blood Ctr Inc D/B/A B *(G-4444)*

NEW YORK BLOOD CENTER, INC. D/B/A BLOOD BANK OF DELMARVA, Wilmington Also
Called: New York Blood Ctr Inc D/B/A B *(G-18629)*

New York Blood Ctr Inc D/B/A B..302 734-4100
221 Saulsbury Rd Dover (19904) *(G-3182)*

New York Blood Ctr Inc D/B/A B..302 737-8400
N Bedford St Rte 113 Georgetown (19947) *(G-4444)*

New York Blood Ctr Inc D/B/A B..302 737-8400
913 N Market St Ste 905 Wilmington (19801) *(G-18629)*

New York Life, Wilmington Also Called: Zavier J Decaire *(G-20948)*

New York Life Ins Co..302 537-7060
31286 Pine Pl Ocean View (19970) *(G-12551)*

Newarc Welding & Fabricating..302 658-5214
30 Commerce St Wilmington (19801) *(G-18630)*

Newark Afrc...302 292-1050
1001 Ogletown Rd Newark (19711) *(G-11529)*

Newark Building Services LLC..302 377-7687
9 Cartier Ct Newark (19711) *(G-11530)*

Newark Chiropractic, Newark Also Called: Delaware Health Management *(G-10450)*

Newark Christian Childcare...302 369-3000
680 S Chapel St Newark (19713) *(G-11531)*

Newark Country Club..302 368-7008
300 W Main St Newark (19711) *(G-11532)*

Newark Ctr For Creative Lrng...302 368-7772
401 Phillips Ave Newark (19711) *(G-11533)*

NEWARK DAY NURSERY AND CHILDRE, Newark Also Called: Newark Day-Nursery
Association *(G-11534)*

Newark Day-Nursery Association..302 731-4925
921 Barksdale Rd Newark (19711) *(G-11534)*

Newark Dental Assoc Inc...302 737-5170
344 E Main St Newark (19711) *(G-11535)*

Newark Emergency Center Inc...302 738-4300
324 E Main St Newark (19711) *(G-11536)*

Newark Fence Co...302 368-5329
24 Briarcliffe Ct Newark (19702) *(G-11537)*

Newark Glass & Mirror Inc...302 834-1158
151 Rickey Blvd Bear (19701) *(G-394)*

Newark Heritage Partners I LLC..302 283-0540
501 S Harmony Rd Newark (19713) *(G-11538)*

ALPHABETIC SECTION

Newark Insulation Co Inc.. 302 731-8970
68 Albe Dr # A Newark (19702) *(G-11539)*

Newark Knights Ftbll and.. 302 846-7776
625 Corsica Ave Bear (19701) *(G-395)*

Newark Kubota Inc.. 302 365-6000
2063 Pulaski Hwy Newark (19702) *(G-11540)*

Newark Land Group Inc.. 302 453-1700
630 S College Ave Newark (19713) *(G-11541)*

Newark Manor, Newark *Also Called: Premier Healthcare Inc (G-11728)*

Newark Montessori Preschool.. 302 366-1481
1031 S Chapel St Newark (19702) *(G-11542)*

Newark National Little League... 302 738-0881
Possum Park Rd Newark (19711) *(G-11543)*

Newark Pediatrician Inc.. 302 738-4800
314 E Main St Ste 101 Newark (19711) *(G-11544)*

Newark Recycling Center Inc... 302 737-7300
6 Albe Dr Newark (19702) *(G-11545)*

Newark Senior Center Inc... 302 737-2336
200 Whitechapel Dr Newark (19713) *(G-11546)*

Newark United Methodist.. 302 368-8774
69 E Main St Newark (19711) *(G-11547)*

Newark Urgent Care.. 302 738-4300
324 E Main St Newark (19711) *(G-11548)*

Newark Wings LLC... 302 455-9464
136 Astro Shopping Ctr Newark (19711) *(G-11549)*

Newcosmos LLC... 302 838-1935
52 Blue Spruce Dr Bear (19701) *(G-396)*

Newman Water PROofing&mold... 302 373-7579
7 Gilbert Ct Newark (19713) *(G-11550)*

Newphoenix Screen Printing.. 302 747-8991
305 Lotus St Dover (19901) *(G-3183)*

Newport.. 302 995-2840
22 W Market St Wilmington (19804) *(G-18631)*

Newport Builders & Windowland... 302 994-3537
2 E Ayre St Wilmington (19804) *(G-18632)*

Newport Terrace Apartments, Wilmington *Also Called: Evergreen Realty (G-16486)*

Newport Ventures Inc... 302 998-1693
512 Barrymore Pkwy Middletown (19709) *(G-7399)*

Newrez LLC.. 240 475-4741
17723 Coastal Hwy Unit 2 Lewes (19958) *(G-6312)*

News In Bullets LLC... 831 250-6955
600 N Broad St Ste 52185 Middletown (19709) *(G-7400)*

News Print Shop.. 302 337-8283
16694 Emma Jane Ln Bridgeville (19933) *(G-738)*

News-Journal Company.. 302 324-2500
950 W Basin Rd New Castle (19720) *(G-9417)*

Newspaper Archive Inc... 612 590-3401
4023 Kennett Pike # 50005 Wilmington (19807) *(G-18633)*

Newton Management Holding Inc....................................... 800 784-8714
600 N Broad St Ste 5 Middletown (19709) *(G-7401)*

Newton One Advisors... 302 731-1326
131 Continental Dr Ste 206 Newark (19713) *(G-11551)*

Newtone Communications Inc... 650 727-0998
651 N Broad St Middletown (19709) *(G-7402)*

Newtown Family Dentistry, Bear *Also Called: Mark Wieczorek Dmd PC (G-364)*

Nexgen Technical Support Group....................................... 302 345-1330
5 Walker Dr New Castle (19720) *(G-9418)*

Nexsigns LLC.. 302 508-2615
711 Coldwater Dr Clayton (19938) *(G-1391)*

Next Century Medical Care LLC... 302 375-6746
620 Stanton Christiana Rd Newark (19713) *(G-11552)*

Next Gnration Lrng Academy LLC....................................... 302 691-5223
4011 N Market St Wilmington (19802) *(G-18634)*

Next Hydrogen Usa Inc... 416 953-6657
1675 S State St Ste B Dover (19901) *(G-3184)*

Next Level Home Improvements.. 484 469-1767
25 Cameo Rd Claymont (19703) *(G-1251)*

Next Level Staffing Solutions.. 302 281-4777
53 Doty Dr Dover (19901) *(G-3185)*

Next Pace Technologies Inc.. 415 900-0876
8 The Grn Ste R Dover (19901) *(G-3186)*

Next Step Quality HM Care LLC... 888 367-5722
121 E Glenwood Ave Smyrna (19977) *(G-13834)*

Next Trucking Inc.. 213 568-0388
1209 N Orange St Wilmington (19801) *(G-18635)*

Nextdns Inc.. 831 854-7227
651 N Broad St Ste 206 Middletown (19709) *(G-7403)*

Nextel, Wilmington *Also Called: Nextel Communications Inc (G-18636)*

Nextel, Wilmington *Also Called: Nextel Communications Inc (G-18637)*

Nextel Communications Inc.. 302 633-4330
3200 Kirkwood Hwy Wilmington (19808) *(G-18636)*

Nextel Communications Inc.. 302 652-1301
32 Germay Dr Wilmington (19804) *(G-18637)*

Nextera Robotic Systems Inc.. 617 899-7323
651 N Broad St Middletown (19709) *(G-7404)*

Nexthome Prefer... 302 526-2886
144 Kings Hwy Dover (19901) *(G-3187)*

Nexthome Tomorrow Realty, Lewes *Also Called: Bee Wise LLC (G-5746)*

Nextmove Inc.. 302 593-7830
401 Main St Townsend (19734) *(G-14043)*

Nexus Services America LLC (PA)..................................... 800 946-4626
2711 Centerville Rd Ste 400 Wilmington (19808) *(G-18638)*

Nfinity Inc... 852 642-9800
1013 Centre Rd Ste 403s Wilmington (19805) *(G-18639)*

Nflate Your Party... 302 562-9774
211 Thorn Ln Apt 3a Newark (19711) *(G-11553)*

NGK North America Inc (HQ).. 302 654-1344
1105 N Market St Ste 1300 Wilmington (19801) *(G-18640)*

Ngrow Inc... 603 764-7274
2093 Philadelphia Pike Claymont (19703) *(G-1252)*

Nhance... 866 944-9663
500 Connor Blvd Bear (19701) *(G-397)*

Nhance, Middletown *Also Called: Delaware Wood Renewal Inc (G-7049)*

Niaz M A MD... 302 368-2563
266 S College Ave Newark (19711) *(G-11554)*

Nic-O-Boli, Lewes *Also Called: Nicola Pizza Inc (G-6314)*

Nicastros Inc.. 302 425-5555
489 Old Airport Rd New Castle (19720) *(G-9419)*

Nice Vision LLC... 267 259-8705
18 W 41st St Wilmington (19802) *(G-18641)*

Nichino America Inc... 302 636-9001
4550 Linden Hill Rd Ste 501 Wilmington (19808) *(G-18642)*

Nicholas O Biasotto Co... 302 998-1235
620 Stanton Christiana Rd Ste 205 Newark (19713) *(G-11555)*

Nicholls Photography... 302 543-3879
104 Callow Pl New Castle (19720) *(G-9420)*

Nichols Excavation and Ldscp, Newark *Also Called: Nichols Nursery Inc (G-11556)*

Nichols Nursery Inc... 302 834-2426
324 Markus Ct Newark (19713) *(G-11556)*

Nickels Arcade LLC... 800 979-3224
118 Sleepy Hollow Dr Middletown (19709) *(G-7405)*

Nickle Elec Companies Inc... 302 856-1006
540 S Bedford St Georgetown (19947) *(G-4445)*

Nickle Elec Companies Inc (PA).. 302 453-4000
125 Ruthar Dr Newark (19711) *(G-11557)*

Nickle Insurance... 302 654-0347
3920 Kennett Pike Wilmington (19807) *(G-18643)*

Nickle Insurance Agency Inc... 302 834-9700
119 Washington St Delaware City (19706) *(G-1549)*

Nickles Arcade LLC... 302 376-1794
356 Norwalk Way Middletown (19709) *(G-7406)*

Nicks Welding Repair LLC.. 302 545-1494
3705 Oak Ridge Rd Wilmington (19808) *(G-18644)*

Nicoin Telecom LLC... 800 914-6177
16192 Coastal Hwy Lewes (19958) *(G-6313)*

Nicola Pizza Inc... 302 227-6211
17323 Ocean One Plz Lewes (19958) *(G-6314)*

Nicole A Fisher.. 302 674-0600
200 Banning St Ste 200 Dover (19904) *(G-3188)*

Nicole L Scott Np-C Adult Prmr... 302 690-1692
45 Forest Creek Dr Hockessin (19707) *(G-5320)*

Nicole Lowe.. 302 858-4337
604 Wagamon Ave Extended Georgetown (19947) *(G-4446)*

Nicole Sestito PHD 610 465-7312
500 River Rd Wilmington (19809) *(G-18645)*

Nicole Smith 302 383-8233
530 Harlan Blvd Unit N817 Wilmington (19801) *(G-18646)*

Niebex International Inc 415 735-4718
24a Trolley Sq Wilmington (19806) *(G-18647)*

Nighthawk Aircraft LLC 703 994-0523
704 N King St Ste 500 Wilmington (19801) *(G-18648)*

Nikang Therapeutics Inc 302 415-5127
200 Powder Mill Rd Bldg E500 Wilmington (19803) *(G-18649)*

Nikki Sykes Tax Preparation As 302 399-6363
55 Loockerman Plz Dover (19903) *(G-3189)*

Nikko Capital Investments Ltd 832 324-5335
16192 Coastal Hwy Lewes (19958) *(G-6315)*

Nimbis Designs LLC 302 494-7584
16 Piersons Rdg Hockessin (19707) *(G-5321)*

Nimbus 9, Wilmington *Also Called: Granford Inc* *(G-16947)*

Nina Woof LLC 210 492-6617
8 The Grn Dover (19901) *(G-3190)*

Ninety One Holding Inc 212 203-7900
56140 Pine Cone Ln Bethany Beach (19930) *(G-623)*

Ninjanurse LLC 302 750-6666
703 Walnut Hill Rd Hockessin (19707) *(G-5322)*

Ninjasalary Inc 888 201-1107
2093 Philadelphia Pike Claymont (19703) *(G-1253)*

Nino Finance Inc 415 236-7591
2093 Philadelphia Pike Claymont (19703) *(G-1254)*

Niru LLC 617 893-7317
16192 Coastal Hwy Lewes (19958) *(G-6316)*

Nitelites of Delaware, Wilmington *Also Called: Quandary Inc* *(G-19286)*

Niterra (USA) Holding Inc (HQ) 302 288-0131
1011 Centre Rd Ste 322 Wilmington (19805) *(G-18650)*

Nitespot, Lewes *Also Called: Niru LLC* *(G-6316)*

Nitrility Inc 848 702-6091
2055 Limestone Rd Wilmington (19808) *(G-18651)*

Nitro Impact Inc 347 694-7000
3422 Old Capitol Trl # 68 Wilmington (19808) *(G-18652)*

Nixon Unf Rntl Svc of Lncaster (PA) 302 656-2774
42 Lukens Dr Ste 100 Historic New Castle (19720) *(G-5039)*

Nixon Uniform Service Inc (PA) 302 325-2875
500 Centerpoint Blvd Historic New Castle (19720) *(G-5040)*

Nixon Uniform Service & Med Wr, Historic New Castle *Also Called: Nixon Uniform Service Inc* *(G-5040)*

Nixope Inc 888 991-1606
2810 N Church St Wilmington (19802) *(G-18653)*

Njl Productions 302 898-9187
11 Stoney Run Rd Wilmington (19809) *(G-18654)*

NKita Enterprises LLC 302 295-2363
23 Lotus Cir S Bear (19701) *(G-398)*

Nkotb LLC 302 286-5243
1314 N King St Wilmington (19801) *(G-18655)*

NKS Distributors Inc 302 422-1220
759 E Masten Cir Milford (19963) *(G-8029)*

NKS Distributors Inc (PA) 302 322-1811
205 Big Woods Rd Smyrna (19977) *(G-13835)*

Nlcdd 302 831-4728
111 Allison Hall W Newark (19716) *(G-11558)*

Nls Machinery Inc 302 416-3077
1201 N Market St Wilmington (19801) *(G-18656)*

NM Construction Inc 302 478-6494
125 Florence Ave Wilmington (19803) *(G-18657)*

Nnn 824 North Market St LLC 302 652-8013
824 Market St Ste 111 Wilmington (19801) *(G-18658)*

No 3 Eline Pwers Fgure Salons 302 256-5015
100 W 10th St Wilmington (19801) *(G-18659)*

No Code Software Inc 833 366-2633
16192 Coastal Hwy Lewes (19958) *(G-6317)*

No Evi-Dents Inc 302 363-7788
2118 Jackson Ave Wilmington (19808) *(G-18660)*

No Joke I LLC 302 395-0882
16 Stockton Dr New Castle (19720) *(G-9421)*

No More Screts-Mind Bdy Spirit 215 485-7881
9 Mullin Rd Wilmington (19809) *(G-18661)*

No Nonsense Office Mchs LLC 302 856-7381
22416 Lewes Georgetown Hwy Georgetown (19947) *(G-4447)*

No Pressure, Millsboro *Also Called: No Pressure LLC* *(G-8405)*

No Pressure LLC 347 693-3116
26055 Saint Hayes Blvd Millsboro (19966) *(G-8405)*

No Tax Mall LLC 215 554-5380
1 Barclay Dr Hockessin (19707) *(G-5323)*

Nobelone Inc 617 283-8871
200 Continental Dr Ste 401 Newark (19713) *(G-11559)*

Noble Builders & Developers LL 203 948-9396
16694 Blue Marlin Ct Lewes (19958) *(G-6318)*

Noble Contracting Group LLC 302 219-4006
625 Warren Dr Middletown (19709) *(G-7407)*

Noble Eagle Sales LLC 302 736-5166
5105 N Dupont Hwy Dover (19901) *(G-3191)*

Noble Hearts Inc 215 908-6525
200 Continental Dr Ste 401 Newark (19713) *(G-11560)*

Noble Property LLC 718 502-4806
8 The Grn Dover (19901) *(G-3192)*

Nobles Hvac Duct Cleaning 302 538-5909
160 Whitetail Ln Magnolia (19962) *(G-6771)*

Noche Azul Spa 302 345-0070
1733 Marsh Rd Wilmington (19810) *(G-18662)*

Node Technologies Inc (PA) 866 366-1862
651 N Broad St Ste 206 Middletown (19709) *(G-7408)*

Noel Anupol 302 424-6511
305 Jefferson Ave Milford (19963) *(G-8030)*

Noel Auto Sales LLC 302 286-7355
1 Currant Ct Newark (19702) *(G-11561)*

Nohotel Enterprises LLC 917 970-1974
8 The Grn Ste 7756 Dover (19901) *(G-3193)*

Nole-Sec Inc 561 693-9934
1007 N Orange St Wilmington (19801) *(G-18663)*

Nolte & Brodoway PA 302 777-1700
1013 Centre Rd Wilmington (19805) *(G-18664)*

Nomadic Capital LLC 650 441-5796
2055 Limestone Rd Ste 200c Wilmington (19808) *(G-18665)*

Nomod, Wilmington *Also Called: Nomod LLC* *(G-18666)*

Nomod LLC 917 480-7432
4023 Kennett Pike Ste 50181 Wilmington (19807) *(G-18666)*

Non Stop Towing LLC 302 647-1399
199 Philadelphia Pike Wilmington (19809) *(G-18667)*

Nonprofit Bus Solutions LLC 302 353-4606
2701 Centerville Rd Wilmington (19808) *(G-18668)*

Nonwovens Indus & Active Packg, Wilmington *Also Called: Eidp Inc* *(G-16331)*

Noony Media LLC 856 834-0074
1201 N Orange St Ste 600 Wilmington (19801) *(G-18669)*

Noor Foundation International 302 234-8860
249 Peoples Way Hockessin (19707) *(G-5324)*

Noramco Inc (PA) 302 652-3840
500 Swedes Landing Rd Wilmington (19801) *(G-18670)*

Noramco Inc 302 761-2923
500 Swedes Landing Rd Wilmington (19801) *(G-18671)*

Noramco of Delaware Inc 302 761-2900
500 Swedes Landing Rd Wilmington (19801) *(G-18672)*

Noramp Inc 914 266-0153
16 Higgins Rd Newark (19711) *(G-11562)*

Norbertine Fathers 302 449-1840
1269 Bayview Rd Middletown (19709) *(G-7409)*

Nordic Projekt Co 302 208-7296
2055 Limestone Rd Ste 200c Wilmington (19808) *(G-18673)*

Norkrisservices 302 450-6108
534 Maiden Ct Middletown (19709) *(G-7410)*

Norman Johnson Builders 302 670-9201
38218 Yacht Basin Rd Ocean View (19970) *(G-12552)*

Norman Law Firm 302 537-3788
30838 Vines Creek Rd Unit 3 Dagsboro (19939) *(G-1489)*

Norman M Lippman DDS 302 674-1140
712 S Governors Ave Dover (19904) *(G-3194)*

ALPHABETIC SECTION

Norman Nielsen Group Inc.. 415 685-4230
8 The Grn Ste 14572 Dover (19901) *(G-3195)*

Norman S Steward DDS PA... 302 422-9791
214 S Walnut St Milford (19963) *(G-8031)*

Norman Yoder Construction.. 302 492-3516
1875 Pearsons Corner Rd Hartly (19953) *(G-4901)*

Normopharm Inc... 954 210-4812
1000 N West St Ste 1200 Wilmington (19801) *(G-18674)*

Norris Village, Middletown Also Called: Appoquinimink Development Inc *(G-6871)*

Nortal LLC.. 425 233-0164
5301 Limestone Rd Ste 100 Wilmington (19808) *(G-18675)*

North American Brands Inc.. 519 680-0385
501 Silverside Rd Wilmington (19809) *(G-18676)*

North American Hardwoods Ltd... 516 848-7729
2711 Centerville Rd Wilmington (19808) *(G-18677)*

North American Spine and Pain... 302 482-3637
1600 Pennsylvania Ave Wilmington (19806) *(G-18678)*

North American Trnspt Co Inc... 856 696-5483
92 Reads Way Ste 202 New Castle (19720) *(G-9422)*

North ATL Intl Ocean Carier... 786 275-5352
35 Davidson Ln New Castle (19720) *(G-9423)*

North Atlantic Ocean Ship... 302 652-3782
19 Davidson Ln New Castle (19720) *(G-9424)*

North Bay Marina Incorporated... 302 436-4211
36543 Lighthouse Rd Selbyville (19975) *(G-13586)*

North Bay Medical Associates... 302 731-4620
313 W Main St Ste A Newark (19711) *(G-11563)*

North District Engrg Cnstr, Bear Also Called: Delaware Department Trnsp *(G-146)*

North East Contractors Inc... 302 286-6324
87 Blue Hen Dr Newark (19713) *(G-11564)*

North East High Schl Football... 330 338-2993
201 Stirrup Rd Clayton (19938) *(G-1392)*

North East Home Interiors LLC.. 302 388-6262
6 N Booth Dr New Castle (19720) *(G-9425)*

North East Htg AC... 410 299-1773
25 Maggies Way Ste 3 Dover (19901) *(G-3196)*

North East Open Mri Inc.. 610 259-3200
6 W Clivden Dr Wilmington (19807) *(G-18679)*

North East Pool Plumbing.. 302 740-5071
226 Harlequin Dr New Castle (19720) *(G-9426)*

North Eastern Waffles LLC... 302 697-2226
4003 S Dupont Hwy # 1753 Dover (19901) *(G-3197)*

North Hills Cleaners Inc... 302 764-1234
1601 Brandywine Blvd Wilmington (19809) *(G-18680)*

North Orthopedic and Hand Ctr, Wilmington Also Called: ATI Holdings LLC *(G-14621)*

North Point Builders LLC... 843 246-1516
6 Nola Ln Newark (19702) *(G-11565)*

North Point Mktg & MGT LLC.. 855 931-4075
200 Continental Dr # 401 Newark (19713) *(G-11566)*

North Star Heating & Air Inc.. 302 732-3967
30968 Vines Creek Rd Dagsboro (19939) *(G-1490)*

North Star Pta.. 302 234-7200
1340 Little Baltimore Rd Hockessin (19707) *(G-5325)*

North Wilmington Womens Center....................................... 302 529-7900
2002 Foulk Rd Ste A Wilmington (19810) *(G-18681)*

Northeast Agri Systems Inc.. 302 875-1886
28527 Boyce Rd Laurel (19956) *(G-5570)*

Northeast Body Shop, Wilmington Also Called: Automotive Services Inc *(G-14656)*

Northeast Controls Inc (PA)... 201 419-6111
18766 John J Williams Hwy Rehoboth Beach (19971) *(G-12871)*

Northeast Early Lrng Ctr LLC... 302 475-7080
2400 Philadelphia Pike Claymont (19703) *(G-1255)*

Northeast Missouri Wind LLC.. 647 352-9533
251 Little Falls Dr Wilmington (19808) *(G-18682)*

Northeast Rally Club.. 302 934-1246
213 Dodd St Millsboro (19966) *(G-8406)*

Northeast Treatment Ctrs Inc... 302 691-0140
3315 Kirkwood Hwy Wilmington (19808) *(G-18683)*

Northeastern Supply, Camden Also Called: Northeastern Supply Inc *(G-880)*

Northeastern Supply, Middletown Also Called: Northeastern Supply Inc *(G-7411)*

Northeastern Supply Inc.. 302 698-1414
100 S Dupont Hwy Camden (19934) *(G-880)*

Northeastern Supply Inc.. 302 378-7880
104 Patriot Dr Middletown (19709) *(G-7411)*

Northeastern Title Loans... 302 326-2210
1560 N Dupont Hwy New Castle (19720) *(G-9427)*

Northern Cross Investments... 302 655-9074
919 N Market St Wilmington (19801) *(G-18684)*

Northern Roof Tiles US Inc.. 888 678-6866
4023 Kennett Pike Ste 856 Wilmington (19807) *(G-18685)*

Northern Steel International, Lewes Also Called: Steel Buildings Inc *(G-6508)*

Northernsigs Mfg LLC... 302 383-9270
809 Taylor St Wilmington (19801) *(G-18686)*

Northnode Group Counseling LLC.. 302 257-3135
1609 S State St Dover (19901) *(G-3198)*

Northpoint Engrg Svcs LLC.. 302 994-3907
102 Robino Ct Ste 203 Wilmington (19804) *(G-18687)*

Northstern Coating Systems Inc... 302 328-6545
140 Belmont Dr Wilmington (19808) *(G-18688)*

Northwest Title Planet Inc... 248 278-4080
16192 Coastal Hwy Lewes (19958) *(G-6319)*

Northwestern Human Services.. 302 996-4858
211 Harding Ave Wilmington (19804) *(G-18689)*

Northwestern Mutl Fincl Netwrk... 414 299-2508
450 S Dupont Hwy Ofc B Dover (19901) *(G-3199)*

Norwex.. 817 691-7759
402 Samantha Dr Lewes (19958) *(G-6320)*

Not Your Mothers Makeup... 302 538-1612
34 Brayton Pl Dover (19904) *(G-3200)*

Notary Ltd.. 302 635-1176
4419 Sandy Dr Wilmington (19808) *(G-18690)*

Notch, Dover Also Called: Notch Insurance Inc *(G-3201)*

Notch Insurance Inc... 616 622-2554
850 New Burton Rd Dover (19904) *(G-3201)*

Nothing But Net Inc... 302 476-0453
83 Charles Dr New Castle (19720) *(G-9428)*

Nouveau Inc... 302 235-4961
100 Fitness Way Hockessin (19707) *(G-5326)*

Nouvir Lighting Corporation... 302 628-9933
20915 Sussex Hwy Seaford (19973) *(G-13319)*

Nouvir Lightning Corporation... 302 628-9888
20915 Sussex Hwy Seaford (19973) *(G-13320)*

Nouvir Research, Seaford Also Called: Nouvir Lighting Corporation *(G-13319)*

Nova Industries LLC... 302 218-4837
47 Courtland Cir Bear (19701) *(G-399)*

Nova Polymers.. 302 858-4677
25 Dewberry Dr Georgetown (19947) *(G-4448)*

Nova RE & Bus Consulting LLC.. 302 258-2193
16192 Coastal Hwy Lewes (19958) *(G-6321)*

Nova Real Estate, Lewes Also Called: Nova RE & Bus Consulting LLC *(G-6321)*

Nova Wave Credit LLC.. 929 263-4212
8 The Grn Ste A Dover (19901) *(G-3202)*

Novacare... 302 500-6363
2 Lee Ave Georgetown (19947) *(G-4449)*

Novacare Rehabilitation.. 302 597-9256
256 Foxhunt Dr Bear (19701) *(G-400)*

Novacare Rehabilitation.. 302 674-4192
128 Greentree Dr Dover (19904) *(G-3203)*

Novacare Rehabilitation.. 302 947-0781
36932 Silicato Dr Millsboro (19966) *(G-8407)*

Novacare Rehabilitation.. 302 537-7762
118 Atlantic Ave Ste 302 Ocean View (19970) *(G-12553)*

Novacare Rehabilitation.. 302 653-8389
208 N Dupont Blvd Smyrna (19977) *(G-13836)*

Novacare Rehabilitation.. 302 655-5877
2401 Pennsylvania Ave Ste 112 Wilmington (19806) *(G-18691)*

Novacare Rehabilitation, Newark Also Called: Blue Hen Physical Therapy Inc *(G-10060)*

Novacare Rehabilitation, Wilmington Also Called: Rehabilitation Consultants Inc *(G-19413)*

Novacare Rehabilitation Dover... 302 760-9966
230 Beiser Blvd Ste 103 Dover (19904) *(G-3204)*

Novacare Rehabilitation Seafor... 302 990-2951
300 Health Services Dr Unit 301 Seaford (19973) *(G-13321)*

Novacare Rhabilitation Milford.. 302 393-5889
800 Airport Rd Ste 102 Milford (19963) *(G-8032)*

Novaeo LLC 832 643-2153
  4023 Kennett Pike Ste 58235 Wilmington (19807) *(G-18692)*

Novak Druce Cnnlly Bv+qigg LLP (PA) 302 252-9922
  1007 N Orange St Ste 800 Wilmington (19801) *(G-18693)*

Novartis Corporation 302 992-5610
  205 S James St Wilmington (19804) *(G-18694)*

Novasep LLC 610 494-2052
  200 Powder Mill Rd Wilmington (19803) *(G-18695)*

Novin LLC 315 670-7979
  919 N Market St Ste 425 Wilmington (19801) *(G-18696)*

Novitex Intermediate LLC 302 278-0867
  251 Little Falls Dr Wilmington (19808) *(G-18697)*

Novlt LLC 925 332-6379
  2810 N Church St Pmb 226551 Wilmington (19802) *(G-18698)*

Novo Financial Corp 844 260-6800
  850 New Burton Rd Ste 201 Dover (19904) *(G-3205)*

Novo Insurance LLC 408 245-3800
  1209 N Orange St Wilmington (19801) *(G-18699)*

Novo Nordisk Pharmaceuticals 302 345-0229
  107 Duncan Ave Wilmington (19803) *(G-18700)*

Novo Nrdisk US Coml Hldngs Inc 302 691-6181
  103 Foulk Rd Ste 282 Wilmington (19803) *(G-18701)*

Novoquad Inc 800 916-6486
  2711 Centerville Rd # 120 Wilmington (19808) *(G-18702)*

Now Care Pain Relief Center 302 276-1951
  757 Pulaski Hwy Bear (19701) *(G-401)*

Now Thats A Party LLC 302 465-0928
  356 Fork Branch Rd Dover (19904) *(G-3206)*

Nowadays Inc Pbc 415 279-6802
  614 N Dupont Hwy Dover (19901) *(G-3207)*

Nowcare LLC (PA) 302 777-5551
  1010 Concord Ave Wilmington (19802) *(G-18703)*

Npmhe Local 308 .... 302 322-2430
  147 Quigley Blvd Historic New Castle (19720) *(G-5041)*

Nr Hudson Consulting Inc 302 875-5276
  14617 Arvey Rd Laurel (19956) *(G-5571)*

Nrai Services LLC 302 674-4089
  160 Greentree Dr Ste 101 Dover (19904) *(G-3208)*

NRG Energy Inc 302 934-3537
  Burton Island Rd Millsboro (19966) *(G-8408)*

NS 360 Inc 855 678-2257
  1209 N Orange St Wilmington (19801) *(G-18704)*

NS Air Leasing LLC 302 396-6546
  3422 Old Capitol Trl Ste 1530 Wilmington (19808) *(G-18705)*

Nside Wrestling 302 697-9633
  158 Derby Wood Cir Dover (19904) *(G-3209)*

Nsmc, Wilmington *Also Called: Network Scrap Metal Corp* *(G-18598)*

Nt Marine Apps LLC 561 329-3209
  251 Little Falls Dr Wilmington (19808) *(G-18706)*

Nt Philadelphia LLC 302 384-8967
  3705 Concord Pike Ste 2 Wilmington (19803) *(G-18707)*

NTL (triangle) LLC 302 525-0027
  2711 Centerville Rd Wilmington (19808) *(G-18708)*

Nu - Vision Auto Glass LLC 302 389-8700
  622 Hopewell Dr Clayton (19938) *(G-1393)*

Nu Attitude Styling Salon Ltd 302 734-8638
  49 S Dupont Hwy Dover (19901) *(G-3210)*

Nu Beginning Center LLC 302 276-8483
  229 N Main St Ste 203 Smyrna (19977) *(G-13837)*

NU Friendship Outreach 302 354-1517
  622 Country Path Dr New Castle (19720) *(G-9429)*

Nu Image Landscaping Inc 302 366-8699
  68 Martindale Dr Newark (19713) *(G-11567)*

Nu-Tech Masonry Inc 302 934-5660
  Rd 2 Box 332f Millsboro (19966) *(G-8409)*

Nucar Consulting Inc 302 696-6000
  313 N Dupont Hwy Ste 100 Odessa (19730) *(G-12585)*

Nucelectric Insurance Limited, Wilmington *Also Called: Nuclear Service Organization* *(G-18711)*

Nuchido Inc 314 260-7874
  1209 N Orange St Wilmington (19801) *(G-18709)*

Nuclear Electric Insurance Ltd (PA) 302 888-3000
  1 Righter Pkwy # 210 Wilmington (19803) *(G-18710)*

Nuclear Service Organization (PA) 302 888-3000
  1201 N Market St Ste 1100 Wilmington (19801) *(G-18711)*

Nucural Inc (PA) 408 625-7047
  1201 N Orange St Ste 7322j Wilmington (19801) *(G-18712)*

Nueve Ceros LLC 415 513-0332
  2810 N Church St Wilmington (19802) *(G-18713)*

Nuix North America Inc 302 584-7542
  408 Lee Ter Wilmington (19803) *(G-18714)*

Numberbox Inc 302 830-8800
  1000 N West St Ste 1200 Wilmington (19801) *(G-18715)*

Nur Shrners Ancent Arab Order 302 328-6100
  120 Four Seasons Pkwy Newark (19702) *(G-11568)*

Nur Temple Aaonms 302 328-6100
  198 S Dupont Hwy New Castle (19720) *(G-9430)*

Nuraxi Holdings Inc 571 213-2519
  251 Little Falls Dr Wilmington (19808) *(G-18716)*

Nurdsoft LLC 332 203-2920
  221 N Broad St 3a Middletown (19709) *(G-7412)*

Nurse Angels LLC 302 765-8093
  448 Stella Dr Hockessin (19707) *(G-5327)*

Nurse Maggie Nursing Assist In 302 660-7100
  102 Larch Ave Wilmington (19804) *(G-18717)*

Nursecareai Inc 717 439-0314
  1006 Overbrook Rd Wilmington (19807) *(G-18718)*

Nursery Fitness LLC 410 609-0106
  1007 Church Rd Newark (19702) *(G-11569)*

Nurses Connection 302 421-3687
  1021 Gilpin Ave Wilmington (19806) *(G-18719)*

Nurses N Kids 302 528-6902
  25 Ramunno Dr Smyrna (19977) *(G-13838)*

Nurses N Kids Inc 302 424-1770
  21 W Clarke Ave Ste 1005 Milford (19963) *(G-8033)*

Nurses N Kids Inc (PA) 302 323-1118
  11 Reads Way New Castle (19720) *(G-9431)*

Nurses N Kids Southern Del, Milford *Also Called: Nurses N Kids Inc* *(G-8033)*

Nurses Next Staffing LLC 302 446-3200
  8 The Grn Ste 7689 Dover (19901) *(G-3211)*

Nursing Board 302 744-4500
  861 Silver Lake Blvd Dover (19904) *(G-3212)*

Nutax Financial Services LLC 302 834-9357
  523 Capitol Trl Ste C Newark (19711) *(G-11570)*

Nutra4health LLC 704 223-8677
  16192 Coastal Hwy Lewes (19958) *(G-6322)*

Nutradrill LLC 772 277-2201
  2055 Limestone Rd Ste 200c Wilmington (19808) *(G-18720)*

Nutrien AG Solutions Inc 302 422-3570
  200 N Rehoboth Blvd Milford (19963) *(G-8034)*

Nutrition & Biosciences Inc 212 765-5500
  974 Centre Rd Wilmington (19805) *(G-18721)*

Nuyka, Lewes *Also Called: Nuyka Inc* *(G-6323)*

Nuyka Inc (PA) 707 400-5444
  16192 Coastal Hwy Lewes (19958) *(G-6323)*

NV Homes 302 732-9900
  32448 Royal Blvd Unit 2 Dagsboro (19939) *(G-1491)*

Nvcomputers Inc 860 878-0525
  300 Delaware Ave Ste 210 Wilmington (19801) *(G-18722)*

Nvr Inc 302 732-9900
  32448 Royal Blvd Ste B Dagsboro (19939) *(G-1492)*

Nvr Inc 302 731-5770
  1302 Drummond Plz Bldg 1ste1032 Newark (19711) *(G-11571)*

NVR Homes National 302 278-7099
  31790 Carmine Dr Rehoboth Beach (19971) *(G-12872)*

Nx Level Marketing LLC 215 880-4749
  105 Gambel Ct Bear (19701) *(G-402)*

NY Construction 302 377-1846
  19 Grayton Dr Smyrna (19977) *(G-13839)*

O A Newton & Son Co 302 337-8211
  16356 Sussex Hwy Bridgeville (19933) *(G-739)*

O A Newton & Son Company 302 337-3782
  16356 Sussex Hwy Unit 1 Bridgeville (19933) *(G-740)*

ALPHABETIC SECTION

O Kelly Ernst Belli Wallen LLC.. 302 778-4001
901 N Market St Ste 1000 Wilmington (19801) *(G-18723)*

O M S 5, Dagsboro *Also Called: Army National Guard Delaware* *(G-1413)*

O Morales Stucco Plaster Inc.. 302 834-8891
7 Hawkins Ct Bear (19701) *(G-403)*

O Reilly Electric.. 302 381-6058
23442 Sussex Hwy Seaford (19973) *(G-13322)*

O&G Knwldge Sharing Consortium, Wilmington *Also Called: O&G Knwldge Shring Pltform LLC* *(G-18724)*

O&G Knwldge Shring Pltform LLC.. 303 872-0533
808 W Boxborough Dr Wilmington (19810) *(G-18724)*

O2diesel Fuels Inc.. 302 266-6000
100 Commerce Dr Ste 301 Newark (19713) *(G-11572)*

Oak Construction.. 302 703-2013
788 Kings Hwy Lewes (19958) *(G-6324)*

Oak Forest Park LLC.. 302 947-9328
Smyrna (19977) *(G-13840)*

Oak Grove Senior Center Inc.. 302 998-3319
484 Century Blvd Wilmington (19808) *(G-18725)*

Oak Hrc New Castle LLC.. 302 328-2580
32 Buena Vista Dr New Castle (19720) *(G-9432)*

Oak Knoll Books, Historic New Castle *Also Called: Cedar Lane Inc* *(G-4953)*

Oak Lane Court Associates LP.. 302 764-6450
4 Denny Rd Wilmington (19809) *(G-18726)*

OAK ORCHARD AM LEGION 28, Millsboro *Also Called: The Oak Orchrd-Rvrdale Post 28* *(G-8484)*

Oakford Acquisitions LLC.. 302 406-1535
1201 N Market St Wilmington (19801) *(G-18727)*

Oakleaf Inc.. 412 881-8194
31859 Cameros Ave Lewes (19958) *(G-6325)*

Oakleaf Personal Care Home, Lewes *Also Called: Oakleaf Inc* *(G-6325)*

Oaks Lab Academy LLC (PA).. 509 481-5630
251 Little Falls Dr Wilmington (19808) *(G-18728)*

Oakville Industries LLC.. 513 436-5007
919 N Market St Ste 950 Wilmington (19801) *(G-18729)*

Oakwood Funding Corporation.. 336 855-2400
913 N Market St Ste 410 Wilmington (19801) *(G-18730)*

Oasis Childcare.. 302 312-5255
800 N Madison St Wilmington (19801) *(G-18731)*

Oasis Home Inc.. 949 331-5405
1232 N King St Num 206 Wilmington (19801) *(G-18732)*

Oasis Realty Inv Group LLC.. 302 277-6885
69 Bay Blvd Newark (19702) *(G-11573)*

Oasis Security Inc.. 332 867-8141
1007 N Orange St Wilmington (19801) *(G-18733)*

Oasis Senior Advisors, Hockessin *Also Called: Oasis Senior Advisors Delaware* *(G-5328)*

Oasis Senior Advisors Delaware.. 302 668-0298
7209 Lancaster Pike Hockessin (19707) *(G-5328)*

Oasm Corp.. 203 679-9124
8 The Grn Dover (19901) *(G-3213)*

Oates Consultants LLC.. 302 477-0109
234 Philadelphia Pike Ste 9 Wilmington (19809) *(G-18734)*

Ob-Gyn Associates of Dover P A.. 302 674-0223
200 Banning St Ste 320 Dover (19904) *(G-3214)*

Oberle William A Jr St Rep.. 302 738-6241
2 Danvers Way Newark (19702) *(G-11574)*

Oberod Estates LLC.. 302 521-0250
3 Mill Rd Wilmington (19806) *(G-18735)*

Obhost LLC.. 302 440-1447
16192 Coastal Hwy Lewes (19958) *(G-6326)*

Objective Zero Foundation.. 202 573-9660
919 N Market St Ste 425 Wilmington (19801) *(G-18736)*

Objects Worldwide Inc.. 703 623-7861
910 Foulk Rd Ste 201 Wilmington (19803) *(G-18737)*

Obrien Firm.. 302 654-1515
901 N Tatnall St Wilmington (19801) *(G-18738)*

OBryan Woodworks.. 302 398-8202
5400 Vernon Rd Harrington (19952) *(G-4807)*

Occidental L Transamerica.. 302 477-9700
1415 Foulk Rd Ste 103 Wilmington (19803) *(G-18739)*

Occupational Therapy.. 302 994-4566
3429 Faulkland Rd Wilmington (19808) *(G-18740)*

Occuptnl Thrpy of Delaware.. 302 491-4813
550 S Dupont Blvd Milford (19963) *(G-8035)*

Ocean Air.. 302 524-8003
32971 Lighthouse Rd Selbyville (19975) *(G-13587)*

Ocean Atlantic Agency Inc.. 302 227-6767
330 Rehoboth Ave Rehoboth Beach (19971) *(G-12873)*

Ocean Atlantic Associates LLC.. 302 227-3573
18949 Coastal Hwy Unit 301 Rehoboth Beach (19971) *(G-12874)*

Ocean Atlantic Companies, Rehoboth Beach *Also Called: Ocean Atlantic Associates LLC* *(G-12874)*

Ocean Atlantic Companies, Rehoboth Beach *Also Called: Ocean Atlantic Management LLC* *(G-12875)*

Ocean Atlantic Management LLC.. 302 227-3573
18949 Coastal Hwy Unit 301 Rehoboth Beach (19971) *(G-12875)*

Ocean Atlantic Sothebys Intl.. 302 539-1033
26 N Pennsylvania Ave Bethany Beach (19930) *(G-624)*

Ocean CLB Rsort Rservation Ctr.. 302 369-1420
153 E Chestnut Hill Rd Ste 200 Newark (19713) *(G-11575)*

Ocean First Enterprises LLC.. 302 232-8547
501 Silverside Rd Ste 507 Wilmington (19809) *(G-18741)*

Ocean Glass Inn.. 302 227-2844
37299 Rehoboth Avenue Ext Rehoboth Beach (19971) *(G-12876)*

Ocean Medical Imaging Del LLC.. 302 684-5151
611 Federal St Ste 4 Milton (19968) *(G-8677)*

Ocean Pines Auto Svc Ctr Inc.. 410 641-7800
34461 Atlantic Ave Ocean View (19970) *(G-12554)*

Ocean Pines Parts, Ocean View *Also Called: Ocean Pines Auto Svc Ctr Inc* *(G-12554)*

Ocean Rach Intrnal Medicine PA.. 302 644-7472
32796 Ocean Reach Dr Lewes (19958) *(G-6327)*

Ocean Services of De Inc.. 410 524-1518
37822 Fenwick Cir Selbyville (19975) *(G-13588)*

Ocean Suds Laundromat.. 302 856-3002
22899 E Trap Pond Rd Georgetown (19947) *(G-4450)*

Ocean Suds Laundry Mat.. 302 703-6601
18675 Coastal Hwy Unit 4 Rehoboth Beach (19971) *(G-12877)*

Ocean Tower Construction LLC.. 443 373-7096
34407 Dupont Blvd Unit 2 Frankford (19945) *(G-4129)*

Ocean Tower Construction LLC.. 443 366-5556
34667 Bethany Dr Frankford (19945) *(G-4130)*

Ocean View Animal Hospital.. 302 539-2273
118 Atlantic Ave Ste 101 Ocean View (19970) *(G-12555)*

Ocean View Historical Society.. 302 258-7470
39 Central Ave Ocean View (19970) *(G-12556)*

Ocean View Plumbing & Heating, Dagsboro *Also Called: Ocean View Plumbing Inc* *(G-1493)*

Ocean View Plumbing Inc.. 302 732-9117
R R 4 Box 21 A Dagsboro (19939) *(G-1493)*

Oceanic Ventures Inc.. 302 645-5872
32292 Nassau Rd Unit 1 Lewes (19958) *(G-6328)*

Oceanport LLC.. 302 792-2212
6200 Philadelphia Pike Claymont (19703) *(G-1256)*

Oceanside Cleaning Inc.. 302 526-4400
30237 Whitehall Dr Milton (19968) *(G-8678)*

Oceanside Elite Clg Bldg Svcs.. 302 339-7777
33033 Nassau Loop Lewes (19958) *(G-6329)*

Oceanside Seafood Mkt Deli LLC.. 302 313-5158
109 Savannah Rd Lewes (19958) *(G-6330)*

Oceanstar Technologies Inc.. 302 542-1900
203 Mariners Way Bear (19701) *(G-404)*

Oceanus Motel, Rehoboth Beach *Also Called: Moores Enterprises Inc* *(G-12860)*

Oceanview Capital Inds LLC.. 813 397-3706
8 The Grn Dover (19901) *(G-3215)*

OCI, New Castle *Also Called: Opportunity Center Inc* *(G-9435)*

Oci Melamine Americas Inc (DH).. 800 615-8284
1209 N Orange St Wilmington (19801) *(G-18742)*

Ociety LLC (PA).. 760 408-1992
16192 Coastal Hwy Lewes (19958) *(G-6331)*

OConnell Speedy Printing Inc.. 302 656-1475
715 N King St Wilmington (19801) *(G-18743)*

OConnor Belting Intl Inc.. 302 452-2500
728 Dawson Dr Newark (19713) *(G-11576)*

OConnor Orthodontics.. 302 678-1441
1004 S State St Dover (19901) *(G-3216)*

October Phoenix Rlty Group LLC 302 722-5125
   406 Suburban Dr Newark (19711) *(G-11577)*

Oculus Networks Inc 732 841-1624
   1013 Centre Rd Wilmington (19805) *(G-18744)*

Odd Fellows Cmtry of Milford 302 422-4619
   300 S Rehoboth Blvd Milford (19963) *(G-8036)*

Oddporium LLC 302 757-9544
   2115 Marsh Rd Wilmington (19810) *(G-18745)*

Odelias Early Lrng Academy Ela 302 482-3249
   3000 N Market St Wilmington (19802) *(G-18746)*

Odess Products Inc 253 394-0442
   1226 N King St Ste 128 Wilmington (19801) *(G-18747)*

Odessa Early Education Center 302 376-5254
   27 Mailly Dr Townsend (19734) *(G-14044)*

Odessa Historic Foundation 302 378-4119
   201 Main St Odessa (19730) *(G-12586)*

Odessa National Civic Assn 302 530-1804
   293 Camerton Ln Townsend (19734) *(G-14045)*

Odessa National Golf Crse LLC 302 464-1007
   1131 Fieldsboro Rd Townsend (19734) *(G-14046)*

ODonnell Services 302 252-5134
   1228 Old Coochs Bridge Rd Newark (19713) *(G-11578)*

Oe Performance Repr Maint Inc 302 664-1264
   100 Business Park Ln Milton (19968) *(G-8679)*

OEM Auto Parts 302 983-6475
   104 Lynch Farm Dr Newark (19713) *(G-11579)*

Oerigo Consulting, Smyrna *Also Called: Oerigo Consulting LLC (G-13841)*

Oerigo Consulting LLC 302 353-4719
   82 E Cayhill Ln Smyrna (19977) *(G-13841)*

Ofc of Preachess Vellah MD 302 645-2245
   36377 Tarpon Dr Lewes (19958) *(G-6332)*

Office Magic 302 229-9520
   628 Black Gates Rd Wilmington (19803) *(G-18748)*

Office Movers, New Castle *Also Called: Business Move Solutions Inc (G-8904)*

Office of Ruben Tejeira MD The, Millsboro *Also Called: Sunrise Medical Center (G-8470)*

Office Pride, Felton *Also Called: Eckels Family LLC (G-3966)*

Office Prtners Xiv Bllvue Pk L 302 691-2100
   1000 N West St Wilmington (19801) *(G-18749)*

Office Service Solutions LLC 302 420-3958
   710 Wilmington Rd # A Historic New Castle (19720) *(G-5042)*

Offit Kurman PA 302 351-0900
   1201 N Orange St Ste 7257 Wilmington (19801) *(G-18750)*

Ogletown Baptist Church 302 737-2511
   316 Red Mill Rd Newark (19713) *(G-11580)*

OHM Lshree Foundation 302 652-2900
   767 Wood Duck Ct Middletown (19709) *(G-7413)*

Ohs Liberty Cleaners Inc 302 454-1322
   69 Worthington Park Rd Newark (19711) *(G-11581)*

Oil Spot Express Lube Center 302 628-9866
   915 Norman Eskridge Hwy Seaford (19973) *(G-13323)*

Oilminers Cbd LLC 484 885-9417
   22 Gershwin Cir Newark (19702) *(G-11582)*

Oink Financial Services, Dover *Also Called: Oink Oink LLC (G-3217)*

Oink Oink LLC 302 924-5034
   8 The Grn Ste A Dover (19901) *(G-3217)*

Ojo Investments LLC (PA) 215 934-0855
   8 The Grn Ste 10541 Dover (19901) *(G-3218)*

OK Video 302 762-2333
   406 Philadelphia Pike Wilmington (19809) *(G-18751)*

Ol Babies LLC 302 570-0205
   4023 Kennett Pike Wilmington (19807) *(G-18752)*

Olacole Foundation 215 279-4742
   931 Rue Madora Bear (19701) *(G-405)*

Old Ayala Inc 857 444-0553
   1007 N Orange St Fl 4 Wilmington (19801) *(G-18753)*

Old Country Garden Center Inc 302 652-3317
   414 Wilson Rd Wilmington (19803) *(G-18754)*

Old Dominion Freight Line Inc 302 337-8793
   1664 Emma Jane Ln Bridgeville (19933) *(G-741)*

Old House Restoration 302 737-0806
   23 E Cherokee Dr Newark (19713) *(G-11583)*

Old Inlet Bait and Tackle Inc (PA) 302 227-7974
   25012 Coastal Hwy Rehoboth Beach (19971) *(G-12878)*

Old Landing II LP 302 934-1871
   29320 White St Unit 400 Millsboro (19966) *(G-8410)*

Old Mill Crab House, Milford *Also Called: Prouse Enterprises LLC (G-8055)*

Old Republic, Dover *Also Called: Old Republic Nat Title Insur (G-3219)*

Old Republic, Wilmington *Also Called: Old Republic Nat Title Insur (G-18755)*

Old Republic, Wilmington *Also Called: Old Republic Title Company (G-18756)*

Old Republic Nat Title Insur 302 734-3570
   32 The Grn Dover (19901) *(G-3219)*

Old Republic Nat Title Insur 302 661-1997
   600 N King St # 100 Wilmington (19801) *(G-18755)*

Old Republic Title Company 302 661-1997
   600 N King St Ste 100 Wilmington (19801) *(G-18756)*

Old School Heating & Cooling 302 383-7036
   2 Woodsedge Claymont (19703) *(G-1257)*

Old Towne Pt - Millsboro 302 945-5300
   32695 Long Neck Rd Millsboro (19966) *(G-8411)*

Old Wood & Co LLC 302 684-3600
   26804 Lewes Georgetown Hwy Harbeson (19951) *(G-4710)*

Old World Tile Works 302 407-5552
   2602 Grendon Dr Wilmington (19808) *(G-18757)*

Oldcastle Inc 302 836-6492
   1250 Porter Rd Bear (19701) *(G-406)*

Olde Tyme Chimney Sweeps, Milford *Also Called: John Eisenbrey III (G-7955)*

Oldfather Capital Inc 302 296-6644
   330 Rehoboth Ave Rehoboth Beach (19971) *(G-12879)*

Olga Yatzus Lpcmh 302 407-3743
   5700 Kirkwood Hwy Wilmington (19808) *(G-18758)*

Olgam Life LLC 917 635-1989
   1209 N Orange St Wilmington (19801) *(G-18759)*

Oliv Ai, Newark *Also Called: Instaworks Inc (G-11027)*

Ollang Inc 212 706-1883
   1209 N Orange St Wilmington (19801) *(G-18760)*

Olsen Enterprises Inc 443 928-0089
   26250 Shortly Rd Georgetown (19947) *(G-4451)*

Olson Realty 302 448-6000
   614 N Dupont Hwy Ste 300 Dover (19901) *(G-3220)*

Oluv C Joynor Foundation 302 793-3277
   601 Delaware Ave Fl 2 Wilmington (19801) *(G-18761)*

Oluwaseyi David Popoola 302 331-3684
   896 S State St Unit 384 Dover (19901) *(G-3221)*

Olympic Gate, Dover *Also Called: Workfar Inc (G-3871)*

Olympus Consulting LLC 302 353-7329
   219 Alyssa Way Smyrna (19977) *(G-13842)*

Om Ganesh Two LLC 410 720-9374
   31010 Thornton Blvd Unit 3 Delmar (19940) *(G-1627)*

Omar A Khan M D 302 478-7160
   1309 Veale Rd Ste 11 Wilmington (19810) *(G-18762)*

Omar Auto Repair LLC 302 502-3204
   1027 W 25th St Ste A Wilmington (19802) *(G-18763)*

Omar Kah 718 552-6008
   1910 W 4th St Wilmington (19805) *(G-18764)*

Omareva Energy Inc 514 660-0291
   3500 S Dupont Hwy Dover (19901) *(G-3222)*

Omarichet LLC 302 442-0812
   112 Capitol Trl Ste A407 Newark (19711) *(G-11584)*

Ome Lake Vista III & IV LLC (PA) 619 787-5592
   1675 S State St Ste B Dover (19901) *(G-3223)*

Omega Endodontics, Newark *Also Called: Philips B Eric DMD PA (G-11684)*

Omega Imaging Associates LLC (PA) 302 738-9300
   6 Omega Dr Newark (19713) *(G-11585)*

Omega Industries Inc 302 734-3835
   7 Messina Hill Rd Dover (19904) *(G-3224)*

Omega Medical Center, Newark *Also Called: Delaware Occptnal Hlth Svcs LL (G-10464)*

Omega Physical Therapy, Wilmington *Also Called: Zuber & Associates Inc (G-20967)*

Omega Project Pt LLC 845 323-8739
   1806 N Van Buren St Ste 100 Wilmington (19802) *(G-18765)*

Omg Mgmt LLC 609 221-4572
   3524 Silverside Rd Ste 35b Wilmington (19810) *(G-18766)*

ALPHABETIC SECTION

Omni Interactive Holding LLC 779 612-8747
  1013 Centre Rd Ste 403s Wilmington (19805) *(G-18767)*
Omni Outreach Inc 888 291-8952
  300 Delaware Ave Ste 210 Wilmington (19801) *(G-18768)*
Omnimaven Inc 302 378-8918
  103 Cazier Dr Middletown (19709) *(G-7414)*
Omninet International Inc (PA) 208 246-5022
  427 N Tatnall St Wilmington (19801) *(G-18769)*
Omniptntial Enrgy Partners LLC 888 429-6664
  2207 Concord Pike # 128 Wilmington (19803) *(G-18770)*
Omnisets LLC 425 229-1592
  8 The Grn Dover (19901) *(G-3225)*
Omniway Corporation (PA) 302 738-5076
  2300 Waters Edge Dr Newark (19702) *(G-11586)*
Omnix Labs Inc (HQ) 917 640-4949
  919 N Market St Ste 950 Wilmington (19801) *(G-18771)*
Omogs Group Corp 302 645-7400
  16192 Coastal Hwy Lewes (19958) *(G-6333)*
Ompai & Co LLC (PA) 302 632-4077
  24a Trolley Sq Num 1748 Wilmington (19806) *(G-18772)*
Oms Mechanical Inc 302 745-7424
  17974 Meadow Dr Bridgeville (19933) *(G-742)*
Omtron USA LLC 302 855-7131
  22855 Dupont Blvd Georgetown (19947) *(G-4452)*
On Demand Moving Services, Newark *Also Called: On Demand Services LLC (G-11587)*
On Demand Oil Change LLC 855 959-1599
  2138 Grafton Dr Wilmington (19808) *(G-18773)*
On Demand Services LLC 302 388-1215
  46 Chambord Dr Newark (19702) *(G-11587)*
On Glo LLC (PA) 205 567-3434
  8 The Grn Ste A Dover (19901) *(G-3226)*
On Level Home Improvement 302 368-7152
  25 Greenridge Rd Newark (19711) *(G-11588)*
On My Mind Designs 302 494-8622
  2507 Baynard Blvd Fl 2 Wilmington (19802) *(G-18774)*
On Point Partners LLC 302 655-5606
  18 Germay Dr # 2a Wilmington (19804) *(G-18775)*
On Q Financial 866 667-3279
  20 E Division St Ste C Dover (19901) *(G-3227)*
On The Mark Locators LLC 888 272-6065
  1080 S Chapel St Ste 201 Newark (19702) *(G-11589)*
On The Spot Massage 302 545-5200
  2871 Red Lion Rd Bear (19701) *(G-407)*
On Time Construction, Wilmington *Also Called: Thomas F Cavanaugh (G-20307)*
On-Board Engineering Corp 302 613-5030
  2 Penns Way Ste 400 New Castle (19720) *(G-9433)*
On-Site Detailing Inc 302 540-9680
  10 Meadows Ln Wilmington (19807) *(G-18776)*
Oncology Care Home 610 274-2437
  267 E Main St Newark (19711) *(G-11590)*
One At A Time Foundation 800 839-1754
  501 Silverside Rd Wilmington (19809) *(G-18777)*
One Codex Inc 226 406-8524
  2810 N Church St Wilmington (19802) *(G-18778)*
One Commerce Ctr Condo Council 302 573-2513
  1 Commerce St Ste 700 Wilmington (19801) *(G-18779)*
One Easton 302 509-3900
  1 Easton Ct Newark (19711) *(G-11591)*
One EDM LLC 908 399-0536
  3524 Silverside Rd Wilmington (19810) *(G-18780)*
One Hour Heating Air Cond 302 998-0460
  410 Meco Dr Wilmington (19804) *(G-18781)*
One Hour Printing 302 220-1684
  122 Balmoral Way Newark (19702) *(G-11592)*
One Hundred West Tenth St 302 651-1469
  1100 N Market St Wilmington (19899) *(G-18782)*
One Off Rod & Custom Inc 302 449-1489
  118 Sleepy Hollow Dr Ste 5& Middletown (19709) *(G-7415)*
One Sententia Ltd 646 284-0321
  8 The Grn Ste A Dover (19901) *(G-3228)*
One Source Contracting 302 893-3753
  2601 W 6th St Wilmington (19805) *(G-18783)*
One Step Ahead Childcare 302 292-1162
  432 Salem Church Rd Newark (19702) *(G-11593)*
One Stop Medical Inc 302 450-4479
  515 S Dupont Blvd Bldg C Milford (19963) *(G-8037)*
One System Incorporated 888 311-1110
  4023 Kennett Pike Ste 645 Wilmington (19807) *(G-18784)*
One Tech Sol LLC 302 551-6777
  243 Quigley Blvd Ste E Historic New Castle (19720) *(G-5043)*
One The Spot 302 858-2957
  30993 Tail Feather Run Laurel (19956) *(G-5572)*
One Tuch Prperty Solutions LLC 302 765-8519
  100 Gambel Ct Bear (19701) *(G-408)*
One Ventures East LLC 412 477-2754
  16192 Coastal Hwy Lewes (19958) *(G-6334)*
One Village Alliance Inc 302 275-1715
  1401 A St Wilmington (19801) *(G-18785)*
One Way Source LLC 302 894-8359
  1818 N Tatnall St Wilmington (19802) *(G-18786)*
Oneals Millwright Services LLC 302 542-5811
  18063 Johnson Rd Lincoln (19960) *(G-6692)*
Onebill Inc (PA) 619 292-8493
  8 The Grn Ste 4518 Dover (19901) *(G-3229)*
Onebox Technologies Inc 415 799-8830
  2055 Limestone Rd Wilmington (19808) *(G-18787)*
Onecall Services Inc 302 645-9008
  341 Highway One Lewes (19958) *(G-6335)*
Oneclick Cleaners 302 697-8000
  121 N Main St Camden (19934) *(G-881)*
ONeill Woodworking LLC 443 669-3458
  23292 Bridgeway Dr W Lewes (19958) *(G-6336)*
ONeills Fly Fishing LLC 302 898-6911
  516 Garrick Rd Hockessin (19707) *(G-5329)*
Onemain 812 492-2156
  1011 Centre Rd Ste 402 Wilmington (19805) *(G-18788)*
Onemain Financial, Seaford *Also Called: Onemain Financial Group LLC (G-13324)*
Onemain Financial Group LLC 302 628-9253
  22974 Sussex Hwy Seaford (19973) *(G-13324)*
Oneness, Newark *Also Called: Oneness Massage Therapy (G-11594)*
Oneness Massage Therapy 302 893-0348
  10 Blue Jay Dr Newark (19713) *(G-11594)*
Onengine Corp 949 872-0339
  8 The Grn Dover (19901) *(G-3230)*
Onex Global Inc 801 413-6375
  1622 E Ayre St Wilmington (19804) *(G-18789)*
Onfido Inc 415 855-7113
  2140 S Dupont Hwy Camden (19934) *(G-882)*
Oni Acquisition Corp 212 271-3800
  2711 Centerville Rd Wilmington (19808) *(G-18790)*
Onix Silverside LLC 484 731-2500
  3322 Silverside Rd Wilmington (19810) *(G-18791)*
Online Catalyst LLC (PA) 916 990-3150
  8 The Grn Ste G Dover (19901) *(G-3231)*
Online Publishers LLC 786 617-8896
  2701 Centerville Rd Wilmington (19808) *(G-18792)*
Only Gods Speed LLC 302 367-8366
  150 Karlyn Dr New Castle (19720) *(G-9434)*
Onnec USA Inc 703 309-7338
  108 Patriot Dr Ste A Middletown (19709) *(G-7416)*
Onollo Inc 925 286-4797
  8 The Grn Ste R Dover (19901) *(G-3232)*
Onsite Construction Inc 302 628-4244
  9654 Brickyard Rd Unit 2 Seaford (19973) *(G-13325)*
Onsite Semi Truck Repair 302 526-0517
  18 Sw Front St Milford (19963) *(G-8038)*
Onyx Business Alliance LLC 888 368-0402
  1201 N Market St Ste 111c Wilmington (19801) *(G-18793)*
Oobla Inc 416 230-9119
  8 The Grn Dover (19901) *(G-3233)*
Ooga Technologies Inc 585 503-6047
  3500 S Dupont Hwy Dover (19901) *(G-3234)*
Ooso Drinks Co LLC 919 808-7605
  611 S Dupont Hwy Ste 102 Dover (19901) *(G-3235)*

Opalwire 302 502-2407
1100 Maryland Ave Wilmington (19805) *(G-18794)*

Open Court TV LLC 646 975-1509
8 The Grn Dover (19901) *(G-3236)*

Open Heart Studio LLC 302 381-0212
32191 Nassau Rd Unit 3 Lewes (19958) *(G-6337)*

Open Lanes-Solutions LLC 888 410-4207
1201 N Market St Ste 111 Wilmington (19801) *(G-18795)*

Open Mri At Trolley Square LLC 302 472-5555
1010 N Bancroft Pkwy Wilmington (19805) *(G-18796)*

Open Systems Healthcare 302 298-3260
3 Mill Rd Ste 303 Wilmington (19806) *(G-18797)*

Open Text Inc (HQ) 248 986-6927
251 Little Falls Dr Wilmington (19808) *(G-18798)*

Openeducat Inc 302 261-5133
2803 Philadelphia Pike Ste B # 1117 Claymont (19703) *(G-1258)*

Openexo Inc 617 965-5057
3500 S Dupont Hwy Dover (19901) *(G-3237)*

Openeyes Insur Holdings Inc (PA) 737 222-9132
1007 N Orange St Fl 4 Wilmington (19801) *(G-18799)*

Opengrid Technologies Co 202 677-2794
1007 N Orange St Ste 1923 Wilmington (19801) *(G-18800)*

Opentact Inc 484 424-9683
3524 Silverside Rd Wilmington (19810) *(G-18801)*

Opera Products LLC 413 331-3669
1000 N West St Ste 1200 Wilmington (19801) *(G-18802)*

Opera Studios, Wilmington *Also Called: Operadelaware Inc (G-18803)*

Operadelaware Inc 302 658-8063
4 S Poplar St Wilmington (19801) *(G-18803)*

Operation Water Inc 787 599-0555
5 Fairway Dr Rehoboth Beach (19971) *(G-12880)*

Operations Center Branch, Wilmington *Also Called: Wilmington Sav Fund Soc Fsb (G-20835)*

Opinr Inc (PA) 646 207-3000
24a Trolley Sq Pmb 1635 Wilmington (19806) *(G-18804)*

Oppa, Lewes *Also Called: Oppameet LLC (G-6338)*

Oppameet LLC 732 540-0308
16192 Coastal Hwy Lewes (19958) *(G-6338)*

Oppenheimer Group Inc 302 533-0779
200 Continental Dr Ste 301 Newark (19713) *(G-11595)*

Oppenheimer Group, The, Newark *Also Called: David Oppenheimer and Co I LLC (G-10391)*

Opportunity Center Inc (PA) 302 762-0300
13 Reads Way Ste 101 New Castle (19720) *(G-9435)*

Opportunity Investments 302 887-3082
2528 Blackwood Rd Wilmington (19810) *(G-18805)*

Opt Therapy Svc 302 478-3702
2502 Silverside Rd Ste 4 Wilmington (19810) *(G-18806)*

Opti-Mag Inc 302 738-2903
11 Peddlers Row Newark (19702) *(G-11596)*

Optima Cleaning Systems Inc 302 652-3979
110 Valley Rd Wilmington (19804) *(G-18807)*

Optima Iq Investments Inc 302 279-5750
600 N Broad St Ste 5-403 Middletown (19709) *(G-7417)*

Options or Fast Cash Inc 310 867-9171
651 N Broad St Middletown (19709) *(G-7418)*

Opulence Collection LLC 267 808-1781
1 Chestnut Hill Plz 1045 Newark (19713) *(G-11597)*

Opus, Wilmington *Also Called: Opus Design Build LLC (G-18808)*

Opus Design Build LLC 952 656-4444
1000 N West St Fl 10 Wilmington (19801) *(G-18808)*

Opus Financial Svcs USA Inc 646 435-5616
19c Trolley Sq Wilmington (19806) *(G-18809)*

Opus Marketing Group 302 275-2336
178 Lake Arrowhead Cir Bear (19701) *(G-409)*

Opusai Inc 817 440-4609
8 The Grn Ste A Dover (19901) *(G-3238)*

Oracle Enterprises LLC (PA) 407 900-2828
14 S Union St Ste 107a Wilmington (19805) *(G-18810)*

Oral & Maxillofacial Surgery 302 998-0331
2601 Annand Dr Ste 10 Wilmington (19808) *(G-18811)*

Oral Mxllfcial Srgery Assoc PA 302 655-6183
1304 N Broom St Wilmington (19806) *(G-18812)*

Orange Power Electric Inc 205 886-5815
300 Delaware Ave Ste 210new Wilmington (19801) *(G-18813)*

Orangetheory Fitness 302 426-2284
476 Middletown Warwick Rd Middletown (19709) *(G-7419)*

Orangetheory Fitness, Wilmington *Also Called: Orangetheory Fitness Pike (G-18814)*

Orangetheory Fitness Pike 302 426-2030
4754 Limestone Rd Wilmington (19808) *(G-18814)*

Orbit Research LLC (PA) 302 683-1063
3422 Old Capitol Trl Ste 25 Wilmington (19808) *(G-18815)*

Orbixplay, Dover *Also Called: Orbixplay LLC (G-3239)*

Orbixplay LLC 408 337-6490
1111b S Governors Ave Ste 7336 Dover (19904) *(G-3239)*

Orcavue, Dover *Also Called: Vue Events Inc (G-3815)*

Orchard Mortgage LLC 888 627-0677
251 Little Falls Dr Wilmington (19808) *(G-18816)*

Orchard Park Group Inc 302 356-1139
42 Reads Way New Castle (19720) *(G-9436)*

Orcurto Enterprises 302 604-7039
48 Ruddy Duck Ln Bridgeville (19933) *(G-743)*

Order Department 302 654-3116
615 Lambson Ln New Castle (19720) *(G-9437)*

Order of The Eastern Star Del 302 369-0729
134 Capitol Trl Newark (19711) *(G-11598)*

Orderhive Inc 888 878-5538
2035 Sunset Lake Rd Ste B2 Newark (19702) *(G-11599)*

Oreomatic Mining Inc 725 255-8895
1020 N French St Ste 480-550 Wilmington (19884) *(G-18817)*

Organic Intelligence LLC (PA) 949 423-3665
251 Little Falls Dr Wilmington (19808) *(G-18818)*

Organization Innovations 443 280-3009
18393 Dunes Way Lewes (19958) *(G-6339)*

Organized For Life 302 792-1663
109 Smyrna Ave Wilmington (19809) *(G-18819)*

Organox Inc 216 243-2202
2810 N Church St Ste 56894 Wilmington (19802) *(G-18820)*

Orgnostic Inc 617 871-9987
2035 Sunset Lake Rd Ste B2 Newark (19702) *(G-11600)*

Orient Corp of America, Seaford *Also Called: Orient Corporation of America (G-13326)*

Orient Corporation of America 302 628-1300
111 Park Ave Seaford (19973) *(G-13326)*

Original Shoppers The LLC 866 838-3224
600 N Broad St Ste 569 Middletown (19709) *(G-7420)*

Original Tube T Shirt Com 845 291-7031
24455 Lighthouse Pt Seaford (19973) *(G-13327)*

Orion Group LLC 302 357-9137
2801 Centerville Rd Wilmington (19808) *(G-18821)*

Orishun Company LLC 302 538-2120
8 The Grn Ste 10876 Dover (19901) *(G-3240)*

Orishun Filmworks Intl, Dover *Also Called: Orishun Company LLC (G-3240)*

Orjam Ltd 302 482-5016
3602 Squirrel Hill Ct Wilmington (19808) *(G-18822)*

Orlando J Camp & Associates 302 478-3720
1808 Pan Rd Wilmington (19803) *(G-18823)*

Orlandos Sealcoating, Claymont *Also Called: Espinoza Orlando (G-1134)*

Oros Communications LLC 954 228-7399
2711 Centerville Rd Ste 400 Wilmington (19808) *(G-18824)*

Orphagenix Inc 267 334-5153
300 Water St Wilmington (19801) *(G-18825)*

Orth & Kowalick PA 302 697-2159
1991 S State St Dover (19901) *(G-3241)*

Ortho On Silver Lake 302 653-5636
446 Fletcher Dr Smyrna (19977) *(G-13843)*

Orthodontics On Silver Lake PA 302 672-7776
42 Hiawatha Ln Dover (19904) *(G-3242)*

Orthopaedic & Sports Phys 302 683-0782
617 W Newport Pike Wilmington (19804) *(G-18826)*

Orthopaedic Consultants PA 302 724-5062
487 S Queen St Dover (19904) *(G-3243)*

Orthopaedic Specialists 302 730-0840
230 Beiser Blvd Dover (19904) *(G-3244)*

Orthopaedic Specialists PA 302 655-9494
7 S Clayton St Ste 600 Wilmington (19805) *(G-18827)*

ALPHABETIC SECTION

Orthopedic Assoc Suthern Del PA.. 302 644-3311
12100 Black Swan Dr Ste 201 Lewes (19958) *(G-6340)*

Orthopedic Properties LLC.. 302 998-2310
1096 Old Churchmans Rd Newark (19713) *(G-11601)*

Orthopedic Specialists... 302 351-4848
1096 Old Churchmans Rd Newark (19713) *(G-11602)*

Orthopedic Spine Center P A.. 302 734-9700
260 Beiser Blvd Dover (19904) *(G-3245)*

Orville Sammons Ardens.. 302 492-8620
4272 Judith Rd Dover (19904) *(G-3246)*

Osfs Wlmngtn-Phldlphia Prvnce... 302 656-8529
2200 Kentmere Pkwy Wilmington (19806) *(G-18828)*

Oski Industries.. 646 369-5799
34 Blevins Dr Ste 10 New Castle (19720) *(G-9438)*

Osprey Flight Solutions Inc.. 302 318-1401
200 Continental Dr Ste 401 Newark (19713) *(G-11603)*

Ossandeep Associates LLC.. 302 660-8545
61 Mcmillan Way Unit B Newark (19713) *(G-11604)*

Ossum Inc... 516 851-4607
300 Delaware Ave Ste 210a Wilmington (19801) *(G-18829)*

Osterman & Company Inc... 203 272-2233
2711 Centerville Rd Wilmington (19808) *(G-18830)*

OSullivan Insurance Agency.. 302 927-0927
32177 Dupont Blvd Dagsboro (19939) *(G-1494)*

Osx Fitness Training Center.. 302 256-0667
28 W Ayre St Wilmington (19804) *(G-18831)*

Otc Trade LLC... 603 820-5820
2140 S Dupont Hwy Camden (19934) *(G-883)*

Other Side LLC.. 410 829-1053
9802 Nanticoke Business Park Dr Greenwood (19950) *(G-4658)*

Otherworld Co... 424 335-5671
256 Chapman Rd Newark (19702) *(G-11605)*

Otis Kamara.. 443 207-2643
General Delivery Dover (19901) *(G-3247)*

Otolaryngology Consultants (PA)... 302 328-1331
10 Foxview Cir Hockessin (19707) *(G-5330)*

Otr 2 Otr Dispatching LLC.. 862 249-9407
20 Penn Mart Shopping Ctr New Castle (19720) *(G-9439)*

Otto Clips Company... 267 918-9985
725 Taunton Rd Wilmington (19803) *(G-18832)*

Our Childrens Learning Ctr... 302 565-1272
313 Sun Blvd Bear (19701) *(G-410)*

Our Future Child Care Ctr LLC.. 302 762-8645
405 Edgemoor Rd Wilmington (19809) *(G-18833)*

Our Future Christian Chld Care.. 302 287-4442
800 E 7th St Wilmington (19801) *(G-18834)*

Our Maids Inc.. 302 389-5221
8 The Grn Ste 7637 Dover (19901) *(G-3248)*

Our Services - Travelers Q.. 302 660-3680
1224 N King St Wilmington (19801) *(G-18835)*

Our Youth Inc... 302 655-8250
1213 B St Wilmington (19801) *(G-18836)*

Out & About, Wilmington Also Called: T S N Publishing Co Inc *(G-20199)*

Out of Ashes LLC.. 302 507-4623
2931 Ogletown Rd Newark (19713) *(G-11606)*

Out of Galaxy Inc... 814 441-8058
913 N Market St Wilmington (19801) *(G-18837)*

Out-Train Fitness & Prfmce LLC... 610 470-3196
18499 Harbeson Rd Milton (19968) *(G-8680)*

Outburst Ai, Wilmington Also Called: Outburst Ai Limited *(G-18838)*

Outburst Ai Limited... 516 303-2097
1224 N King St Wilmington (19801) *(G-18838)*

Outdoor Design Group LLC... 302 743-2363
935 Rahway Dr Newark (19711) *(G-11607)*

Outerhaven Productions... 302 792-9169
12 Glenrock Dr Claymont (19703) *(G-1259)*

Outland Art Inc.. 800 918-1587
8 The Grn Ste 12603 Dover (19901) *(G-3249)*

Outlet Liquors... 302 227-7700
19724 Coastal Hwy Unit 1 Rehoboth Beach (19971) *(G-12881)*

Outmarch Inc.. 508 289-1233
8 The Grn Ste R Dover (19901) *(G-3250)*

Outpatent Ansthsia Spclists PA.. 302 995-1860
2006 Limestone Rd Ste 5 Wilmington (19808) *(G-18839)*

Outpatient Procedure Ctrs LLC... 302 734-7246
240 Beiser Blvd Ste 201f Dover (19904) *(G-3251)*

Outreach Team LLC.. 302 744-9550
8 The Grn Ste R Dover (19901) *(G-3252)*

Outside Creations... 302 757-5944
83 Charles Dr New Castle (19720) *(G-9440)*

Outside In, Newark Also Called: CBI Group LLC *(G-10166)*

Outside Services LLC.. 302 250-3317
2117 Oak St Wilmington (19808) *(G-18840)*

Over Rainbow Daycare... 302 328-6574
713 W 12th St Historic New Castle (19720) *(G-5044)*

Overfalls Maritime Museum.. 302 644-8050
219 Pilottown Road Lewes (19958) *(G-6341)*

Overhead Door Co Delmar Inc... 302 424-4400
603 Marshall St Milford (19963) *(G-8039)*

Overhead Door Grter Wilmington, New Castle Also Called: F W D Inc *(G-9113)*

Overhead Doors, Delmar Also Called: J & A Overhead Door Inc *(G-1603)*

Overhead Doors, Milford Also Called: Overhead Door Co Delmar Inc *(G-8039)*

Overlook Colony, Claymont Also Called: Fairville Management Co LLC *(G-1144)*

Overnight Movers LLC... 302 345-1142
102 Robinson Dr New Castle (19720) *(G-9441)*

Overscout Inc.. 415 687-3005
16192 Coastal Hwy Lewes (19958) *(G-6342)*

Oversight Board LLC... 302 898-2599
1013 Centre Rd Ste 101 Wilmington (19805) *(G-18841)*

Overtone Color LLC.. 520 448-3305
2810 N Church St Wilmington (19802) *(G-18842)*

Owcp Claims Consulting LLC.. 302 559-7501
315 Sheringham Dr Hockessin (19707) *(G-5331)*

Owens Jr Louis F MD PA.. 302 629-0448
701 Middleford Rd Seaford (19973) *(G-13328)*

Owens Manor Ltd Partnership.. 302 678-1065
76 Stevenson Dr Dover (19901) *(G-3253)*

Owi, Wilmington Also Called: Objects Worldwide Inc *(G-18737)*

Owl Jumpstart LLC.. 302 467-2061
1000 N West St Ste 1200 Wilmington (19801) *(G-18843)*

Owlii Inc.. 626 695-6607
3500 S Dupont Hwy Dover (19901) *(G-3254)*

Own Lane Construction LLC... 302 579-8103
105 Loblolly Dr Seaford (19973) *(G-13329)*

Ownlease Inc.. 855 447-4921
1207 Delaware Ave Ste 190 Wilmington (19806) *(G-18844)*

Ox Pond Industries... 703 608-7769
29489 Colony Dr Dagsboro (19939) *(G-1495)*

Oxford Plastic Systems LLC.. 800 567-9182
1011 Ctr Rd Ste 312 Wilmington (19805) *(G-18845)*

Oxi Fresh Dover Carpet Clg.. 302 526-5035
753 Walker Rd Dover (19904) *(G-3255)*

Oxypaper Inc... 302 202-4897
8 The Grn Dover (19901) *(G-3256)*

Oyster HR Americas Inc.. 912 219-2356
3411 Silverside Rd Ttnallb Wilmington (19810) *(G-18846)*

Oyster HR Inc (PA)... 912 219-2356
3411 Silverside Rd Wilmington (19810) *(G-18847)*

Ozlo Sleepbuds, Dover Also Called: Drowsy Digital Inc *(G-2387)*

P & C Roofing Inc... 302 322-6767
35 Southgate Blvd New Castle (19720) *(G-9442)*

P & R Printing, Georgetown Also Called: Conventioneer Pubg Co Inc *(G-4267)*

P A Aba Intl Inc.. 800 979-5106
16192 Coastal Hwy Lewes (19958) *(G-6343)*

P A Alfieri Cardiology... 302 836-2003
2600 Glasgow Ave Ste 103 Newark (19702) *(G-11608)*

P A Alfieri Cardiology (PA).. 302 731-0001
701 Foulk Rd Wilmington (19803) *(G-18848)*

P A Anesthesia Services... 302 709-4709
100 W Commons Blvd Ste 400 New Castle (19720) *(G-9443)*

P A Bayard.. 302 429-4212
600 N King St Ste 400 Wilmington (19801) *(G-18849)*

P A Brandywine Pediatrics.. 302 479-9610
3521 Silverside Rd Ste 1f Wilmington (19810) *(G-18850)*

P A Cnmri 302 678-8100
   1095 S Bradford St Dover (19904) *(G-3257)*

P B R, Talleyville *Also Called: Performance Based Results (G-13945)*

P C Flaster/Greenberg 302 351-1910
   913 N Market St Ste 1010 Wilmington (19801) *(G-18851)*

P D Supply Inc 302 655-3358
   307 Commercial Dr Wilmington (19805) *(G-18852)*

P H I Pepco 302 454-4085
   401 Eagle Run Rd Newark (19702) *(G-11609)*

P R C Management Co Inc 302 475-7643
   2601 Carpenter Station Rd Wilmington (19810) *(G-18853)*

P S C Contracting Inc 302 838-2998
   704 5th St Delaware City (19706) *(G-1550)*

P S C Electric Contractor Inc 302 838-2998
   704 5th St Delaware City (19706) *(G-1551)*

P S I Maximus, New Castle *Also Called: Public Systems Inc (G-9500)*

P-Ks Wholesale Grocer Inc 302 656-5540
   915 S Heald St Wilmington (19801) *(G-18855)*

P&A River Gallery Promotion 302 947-1805
   33189 Cherry Ct Lewes (19958) *(G-6344)*

P&H Realty LLC 302 378-3484
   5668 Summit Bridge Rd Townsend (19734) *(G-14047)*

P&L Transportation Inc (PA) 800 444-2580
   301 N Market St Ste 1414 Wilmington (19801) *(G-18854)*

P2 Dental PA 302 422-6924
   100 Sussex Ave Milford (19963) *(G-8040)*

Pabian Ventures LLC 302 762-1992
   101 N Maryland Ave Wilmington (19804) *(G-18856)*

Pacbak Inc 907 268-0802
   16192 Coastal Hwy Lewes (19958) *(G-6345)*

Pace Elec & Generator Svcs 302 328-2600
   105 Carson Dr Bear (19701) *(G-411)*

Pace Enterprises LLC 302 529-2500
   1405 Silverside Rd Ste B Wilmington (19810) *(G-18857)*

Pace Inc 302 999-9812
   5171 W Woodmill Dr Ste 9 Wilmington (19808) *(G-18858)*

Pace Life Coaching, Newark *Also Called: Patricia R Wood (G-11638)*

Pacific Global Inc 510 870-0248
   1013 Centre Rd Ste 4035 Wilmington (19805) *(G-18859)*

Pacific Green Technologies, Dover *Also Called: Pacific Green Technologies Inc (G-3258)*

Pacific Green Technologies Inc (PA) 302 601-4659
   8 The Grn Ste 1 Dover (19901) *(G-3258)*

Pacifico Industrial Ltd 213 435-1181
   113 Barksdale,Pro Ctr Newark (19711) *(G-11610)*

Pack Usa Inc 443 655-8927
   300 Delaware Ave Ste 210 Wilmington (19801) *(G-18860)*

Packaging Mania (not Inc) 917 410-6835
   114 Manor Ln Milford (19963) *(G-8041)*

Packd LLC 302 467-3443
   142 E Market St Georgetown (19947) *(G-4453)*

Packem Associates Partnership 302 227-5780
   34 Wilmington Ave Rehoboth Beach (19971) *(G-12882)*

Paco Construction & Ldscpg LLC 302 359-2432
   221 Kentwood Dr Dover (19901) *(G-3259)*

Paddys 302 388-3625
   2702 Kirkwood Hwy Newark (19711) *(G-11611)*

Padens Hair Studio 267 718-8109
   28 Scottie Ln New Castle (19720) *(G-9444)*

Padi Technology Ltd (PA) 832 646-6926
   651 N Broad St Ste 201 Middletown (19709) *(G-7421)*

Padilla Konstruction LLC 302 276-6678
   1210 Flint Hill Rd Wilmington (19808) *(G-18861)*

Padrino Records LLC 609 353-4683
   419 W 9th St Apt 503 Hst Newcastle (19720) *(G-5451)*

Paducah & Louisville Railway, Wilmington *Also Called: P&L Transportation Inc (G-18854)*

Pafs Auto LLC 302 213-3881
   11 Country Ln Newark (19702) *(G-11612)*

Page Precision Cuts 302 272-2380
   203 N High St Smyrna (19977) *(G-13844)*

Pagetech 845 624-4911
   20418 Oakney St Lewes (19958) *(G-6346)*

Pagoda Hotel & Floating Rest, Historic New Castle *Also Called: Pagoda Hotel Inc (G-5045)*

Pagoda Hotel Inc 808 922-1233
   599 Ships Landing Way Historic New Castle (19720) *(G-5045)*

Pagos Solutions Inc 310 245-3591
   651 N Broad St Ste 206 Middletown (19709) *(G-7422)*

Paige King DMD 302 475-3270
   1805 Foulk Rd Ste D Wilmington (19810) *(G-18862)*

Pain & Sleep Therapy Center 302 314-1409
   4901 Limestone Rd Wilmington (19808) *(G-18863)*

Pain MGT & Rehabilitation Ctr 302 734-7246
   240 Beiser Blvd Ste 201a Dover (19904) *(G-3260)*

Pain Solution Centers 215 750-9600
   630 Churchmans Rd Ste 109 Newark (19702) *(G-11613)*

Painless Hosting LLC 703 688-2828
   3 Germay Dr Unit 4-1198 Wilmington (19804) *(G-18864)*

Paint By Bill LLC 302 565-9013
   30897 Best Ln Lewes (19958) *(G-6347)*

Paintersrus 302 855-1317
   830 E Market St Georgetown (19947) *(G-4454)*

Painting Parties 302 299-9355
   77 Worthington Park Rd Newark (19711) *(G-11614)*

Painting Solutions LLC 302 736-6483
   6244 Pearsons Corner Rd Dover (19904) *(G-3261)*

Paintings By Sara 302 424-0376
   362 Abbotts Pond Rd Greenwood (19950) *(G-4659)*

Pak Mail, Wilmington *Also Called: Dabvasan Inc (G-15766)*

Pala Tile & Carpet Contrs Inc 302 652-4500
   600 S Colonial Ave Wilmington (19805) *(G-18865)*

Palace Laundry Inc 302 322-2136
   30 Mccullough Dr New Castle (19720) *(G-9445)*

Paladin Sports & Social Club, Wilmington *Also Called: Paladin Sports Club Inc (G-18866)*

Paladin Sports Club Inc 302 764-5335
   500 Paladin Dr Wilmington (19802) *(G-18866)*

Paldor Inc 302 999-9691
   2304 Newport Gap Pike Wilmington (19808) *(G-18867)*

Palermo Francis A MD Facc PA 302 994-1100
   620 Stanton Christiana Rd Newark (19713) *(G-11615)*

Palermo, Francis A MD PA, Newark *Also Called: Palermo Francis A MD Facc PA (G-11615)*

Pall Aerospace, Newark *Also Called: Russell Associates Inc (G-11928)*

Palladian Management LLC 302 737-1971
   41 Fairway Rd Ofc 2c Newark (19711) *(G-11616)*

Pallet Masters, Seaford *Also Called: Stephens Enterprises Inc (G-13413)*

Pallino Asset Management LLC 302 378-0686
   651 N Broad St Middletown (19709) *(G-7423)*

Palm Nft Studio Inc 216 870-9066
   874 Walker Rd Ste C Dover (19904) *(G-3262)*

Palmer & Associates Inc 302 834-9329
   14 Lauren Dr Bear (19701) *(G-412)*

Palmer & Sons Electric In 302 290-4899
   226 Cheyenne Dr Bear (19701) *(G-413)*

Palmer Chiropractic, New Castle *Also Called: T Shane Palmer DC (G-9613)*

Palmetto MGT & Engrg LLC 302 993-2766
   4550 New Lnden Hl Rd Ste Wilmington (19808) *(G-18868)*

Pamper ME Pink LLC 302 200-2635
   46 N Main St Selbyville (19975) *(G-13589)*

Pamper Perfect Mobile Spa 866 947-9994
   1033 Harvest Grove Trl Dover (19901) *(G-3263)*

Pamper Perfect Mobile Spa 302 482-5938
   12 Beatrice Ct Ste 1 Newark (19702) *(G-11617)*

Pampered Parties LLC 302 216-2362
   1201 N Market St Ste 111a Wilmington (19801) *(G-18869)*

Panamerican Coffee Trdg Co LLC 786 538-9547
   874 Walker Rd Ste C Dover (19904) *(G-3264)*

Panarum Corp 302 994-2000
   112 Capitol Trl Newark (19711) *(G-11618)*

Panco Management Corporation 302 366-1875
   15 Fox Hall # 15 Newark (19711) *(G-11619)*

Panco Management Corporation 302 995-6152
   1302 Cynwyd Club Dr Wilmington (19808) *(G-18870)*

Panco Management Corporation 302 475-9337
   2512 Cedar Tree Dr Ofc 2d Wilmington (19810) *(G-18871)*

ALPHABETIC SECTION

Panda Early Education Ctr Inc (PA)..302 832-1891
105 Emerald Ridge Dr Bear (19701) *(G-414)*

Panda Early Education Ctr Inc...302 832-1891
122 E Main St Christiana (19702) *(G-1006)*

Panda Early Education Ctr Inc...302 328-1481
1169 S Dupont Hwy New Castle (19720) *(G-9446)*

Pandia Press Inc...352 789-8156
210 North Rd Wilmington (19809) *(G-18872)*

Pandol Bros Inc...302 571-8923
Christiana Ctr Wilmington (19884) *(G-18873)*

Panelmatic Inc..302 324-9193
11 Southgate Blvd New Castle (19720) *(G-9447)*

Panelmatic East Inc..302 324-9193
11 Southgate Blvd New Castle (19720) *(G-9448)*

Pango Financial LLC..855 949-7264
1011 Centre Rd Wilmington (19805) *(G-18874)*

Pangro Development LLC...302 351-3575
2600 N Broom St Wilmington (19802) *(G-18875)*

Panitch Schwarze Belisario..302 394-6030
2200 Concord Pike Wilmington (19803) *(G-18876)*

Pano Development Inc..302 428-1062
1701 Augustine Cut Off Ste 15 Wilmington (19803) *(G-18877)*

Pantheon Technologies LLC..855 927-9387
8 The Grn Ste 10236 Dover (19901) *(G-3265)*

Panthera Senior Living LLC..786 540-0040
8 The Grn Ste A Dover (19901) *(G-3266)*

Paoli Services Inc..302 998-7031
400 B And O Ln Wilmington (19804) *(G-18878)*

Papaleo Rosen & Chelf PA...302 482-3283
1523 Concord Pike Ste 401 Wilmington (19803) *(G-18879)*

Papaleo Rosen Chelf & Pinder..302 644-8600
135 2nd St Lewes (19958) *(G-6348)*

Papastavros Assoc Med Imaging, Middletown *Also Called: Delaware Imaging Network (G-7041)*

Papastavros Assoc Med Imaging, Newark *Also Called: Delaware Imaging Network (G-10453)*

Papastvros Assoc Med Imging LL (HQ)...................................302 652-3016
40 Polly Drummond Hill Rd Ste 4 Newark (19711) *(G-11620)*

Papastvros Assoc Med Imging LL..302 644-2590
40 Polly Drummond Hill Rd # 4 Newark (19711) *(G-11621)*

Papen Farms Inc...302 697-3291
847 Papen Ln Dover (19904) *(G-3267)*

Paper Street LLC..614 515-1259
20 Harris Cir Newark (19711) *(G-11622)*

Paperbasket LLC...516 360-3500
8 The Grn Ste A Dover (19901) *(G-3268)*

Papilla LLC...302 558-7581
1209 N Orange St Wilmington (19801) *(G-18880)*

Papona LLC...302 285-9559
651 N Broad St Ste 206 Middletown (19709) *(G-7424)*

Paques Environmental Tech Inc..412 932-3540
1209 N Orange St Wilmington (19801) *(G-18881)*

Par 3 Inc..302 674-8275
924 Artis Dr Dover (19904) *(G-3269)*

Par 4 Golf Inc...302 227-5663
38 Glade Cir E Rehoboth Beach (19971) *(G-12883)*

Para Scientific Co..215 736-0225
600 N King St Ste 800 Wilmington (19801) *(G-18882)*

Paradigm Healthcare Assoc Inc...302 352-0517
18 Kelso Ct Wilmington (19808) *(G-18883)*

Paradise Grill...302 945-4500
27344 Bay Walk Millsboro (19966) *(G-8412)*

Paradise Landscaping..302 654-4030
717 Mount Lebanon Rd Wilmington (19803) *(G-18884)*

Paradiso Solutions LLC...800 513-5902
2810 N Church St Wilmington (19802) *(G-18885)*

Paragon Design Inc...302 292-1523
18 Haines St Newark (19711) *(G-11623)*

Paragon Engineering Corp...302 762-6010
708 Philadelphia Pike Ste 1 Wilmington (19809) *(G-18886)*

Paragon Masonry Corporation..302 798-7314
501 Silverside Rd Ste 1 Wilmington (19809) *(G-18887)*

Paragon Serenity LLC..302 784-4979
702 Vinings Way Newark (19702) *(G-11624)*

Parags Glass Company..302 737-0101
107 Albe Dr Ste D Newark (19702) *(G-11625)*

Paralleldots Inc..224 587-0022
16192 Coastal Hwy Lewes (19958) *(G-6349)*

Paramount Installations...302 607-4243
28 Tudor Ct Dover (19901) *(G-3270)*

Paramount Pest Control, New Castle *Also Called: Home Prmnt Pest Ctrl Cmpnies I (G-9219)*

Paramunt Hlthcare Rsources LLC.......................................302 722-5484
833 Llanelli Dr Middletown (19709) *(G-7425)*

Parcel Tech Inc (PA)...720 663-0558
919 N Market St Ste 950 Wilmington (19801) *(G-18888)*

Parcels Inc...302 736-1777
1111 B S Govenanvce Ave Dover (19904) *(G-3271)*

Parcels Inc (PA)...302 888-1718
230 N Market St Wilmington (19801) *(G-18889)*

Parchive Analytics, Middletown *Also Called: Parchive Analytics Inc (G-7426)*

Parchive Analytics Inc..903 683-5878
651 N Broad St Ste 206 Middletown (19709) *(G-7426)*

Parcly LLC..347 305-6820
8 The Grn Dover (19901) *(G-3272)*

Pargoe Flr Prep Lvlg Sltons LL..302 530-9450
6 Hadco Rd Wilmington (19804) *(G-18890)*

Parients Painting LLC..302 738-6819
19 Carlisle Rd Newark (19713) *(G-11626)*

Parikh Mona Ashish MD..302 300-4246
68 Omega Dr Newark (19713) *(G-11627)*

Paris Corporation...302 427-5985
300 Delaware Ave Wilmington (19801) *(G-18891)*

Park Avenue Dry Cleaners LLC.......................................302 725-9430
19470 Coastal Hwy Unit 3 Rehoboth Beach (19971) *(G-12884)*

Park Hotels & Resorts Inc..703 883-1000
640 S College Ave Newark (19713) *(G-11628)*

Park Place Dental..302 455-0333
210 W Park Pl Newark (19711) *(G-11629)*

Park Place Dental..302 652-3775
300 Foulk Rd Wilmington (19803) *(G-18892)*

Park Plaza Condo Association..302 658-3526
1100 Lovering Ave Ste 15 Wilmington (19806) *(G-18893)*

Park Plaza Condominiums, Wilmington *Also Called: Park Plaza Condo Association (G-18893)*

Park Side Utility Construction..302 322-9760
718 Grantham Ln New Castle (19720) *(G-9449)*

Park View..302 429-7288
1800 N Broom St Wilmington (19802) *(G-18894)*

Parker Block Co Inc (HQ)..302 934-9237
30234 Millsboro Hwy Millsboro (19966) *(G-8413)*

Parker Builders LLC..302 398-6182
101 W Mispillion St Harrington (19952) *(G-4808)*

Parker Construction Inc..302 798-8530
950 Ridge Rd Ste C6 Claymont (19703) *(G-1260)*

Parker Group..302 217-6692
5649 Ray Rd Bridgeville (19933) *(G-744)*

Parkinsons Edcatn Spport Group....................................302 644-3465
17000 Black Marlin Cir Lewes (19958) *(G-6350)*

Parkobility LLC..877 298-5550
8 The Grn Dover (19901) *(G-3273)*

Parkowski Guerke & Swayze PA (PA)..............................302 678-3262
116 W Water St Dover (19904) *(G-3274)*

Parks Associates...302 674-3267
740 Bicentennial Blvd Dover (19904) *(G-3275)*

Parks Rcreation Dept Cy Newark, Newark *Also Called: City of Newark (G-10245)*

Parkview Covalescent Center..302 655-6135
2801 W 6th St Wilmington (19805) *(G-18895)*

Parkview De Snf Management LLC.................................302 655-6135
2801 W 6th St Wilmington (19805) *(G-18896)*

PARKVIEW NURSING & REHABILITAT, Wilmington *Also Called: Parkview De Snf Management LLC (G-18896)*

Parkway Gravel Inc...302 658-5241
4048 New Castle Ave New Castle (19720) *(G-9450)*

Parkway Gravel Inc...302 326-0554
13 Parkway Cir New Castle (19720) *(G-9451)*

Parkway Law LLC.. 302 449-0400
   3171 Dupont Pkwy Townsend (19734) *(G-14048)*

Parkwood Trust Company.. 302 426-1220
   919 N Market St Ste 429 Wilmington (19801) *(G-18897)*

Parq At Square Websit... 302 656-8543
   1303 Delaware Ave Wilmington (19806) *(G-18898)*

Parsell Fnrl Homes Crematorium, Lewes Also Called: Parsell Funeral Entps Inc *(G-6351)*

Parsell Funeral Entps Inc... 302 645-9520
   16961 Kings Hwy Lewes (19958) *(G-6351)*

Parsons & Robinson PA... 302 539-2220
   118 Atlantic Ave Ste 401 Ocean View (19970) *(G-12557)*

Parsons PAInting&drywall LLC.................................. 302 462-6169
   113 Moores Xing Unit 50 Millsboro (19966) *(G-8414)*

Parthian LLC.. 240 441-8301
   7 West Ave Ocean View (19970) *(G-12558)*

Partner Vantage Point LLC....................................... 312 927-8990
   200 Continental Dr Newark (19713) *(G-11630)*

Partners Gen Cont, Wilmington Also Called: Joseph R Kasowski *(G-17584)*

Partners Plus Inc... 302 529-3700
   2 Tenns Way Ste 403 New Castle (19720) *(G-9452)*

Partnership For Delaw... 800 445-4935
   110 S Poplar St Wilmington (19801) *(G-18899)*

Partnrship For Del Estuary Inc................................... 302 655-4990
   110 S Poplar St Ste 202 Wilmington (19801) *(G-18900)*

Parts Plus More LLC.. 302 480-1495
   8 The Grn Ste 4469 Dover (19901) *(G-3276)*

Parts World USA LLC... 302 451-9920
   200 Continental Dr # 401 Newark (19713) *(G-11631)*

Party Princess Productions....................................... 302 378-7127
   332 Misty Vale Dr Middletown (19709) *(G-7427)*

Party Princess Productions....................................... 302 307-3804
   364 E Main St Ste 420 Middletown (19709) *(G-7428)*

Party Restaurant Outlet, Newark Also Called: South Forks Inc *(G-12059)*

Partyrite Events & Rentals... 302 743-5691
   622 E Basin Rd # A New Castle (19720) *(G-9453)*

Partytickets Inc.. 718 395-9590
   2055 Limestone Rd 200c Wilmington (19808) *(G-18901)*

Pasadena Digital Inc (PA)... 310 774-6740
   850 New Burton Rd Ste 201 Dover (19904) *(G-3277)*

Pascal Ngalim... 302 983-2322
   35 Pear Dr Bear (19701) *(G-415)*

Pascale Industries Inc.. 302 421-9400
   55 Harbor View Dr New Castle (19720) *(G-9454)*

Pasquale Fucci MD.. 302 652-4705
   1508 Pennsylvania Ave Ste 1c Wilmington (19806) *(G-18902)*

Passavant Memorial Homes..................................... 302 449-2202
   202 Buckingham Ct Townsend (19734) *(G-14049)*

Passion Care Services... 302 834-9585
   604 Highpointe Dr New Castle (19720) *(G-9455)*

Passion Care Services Inc.. 302 832-2622
   3727 Wrangle Hill Rd Bear (19701) *(G-416)*

Passion Driven LLC... 302 293-5960
   4a King Ave New Castle (19720) *(G-9456)*

Passwaters Landscaping... 302 542-8077
   18956 Sussex Hwy Bridgeville (19933) *(G-745)*

Passwaters Towing, Seaford Also Called: Alan Passwaters *(G-13052)*

Pat & Ray Enterprises.. 302 945-1367
   22907 Dogwood Dr Lewes (19958) *(G-6352)*

Pat T Clean Inc.. 302 239-5354
   519 Cabot Dr Hockessin (19707) *(G-5332)*

Patafoods Inc.. 267 981-6411
   60 E Main St Newark (19711) *(G-11632)*

Patel Asit.. 302 502-3181
   550 Stanton Christiana Rd Ste 303 Newark (19713) *(G-11633)*

Patel Sandip... 302 363-9761
   1760 N Dupont Hwy Dover (19901) *(G-3278)*

Patel Soniya... 803 524-4547
   701 Foulk Rd Ste 2a Wilmington (19803) *(G-18903)*

Patel Vaidehi.. 302 295-0435
   23 Moonlight Ct Newark (19702) *(G-11634)*

Patel, Ashok MD, Dover Also Called: Harsha Tankala MD *(G-2659)*

Patent Information Users Group................................. 302 660-3275
   40 E Main St Newark (19711) *(G-11635)*

Paterson Schwartz Real Estate.................................. 302 537-1300
   26 N Pennsylvania Ave Bethany Beach (19930) *(G-625)*

Paths LLC... 302 294-1494
   1352 Marrows Rd Ste 110 Newark (19711) *(G-11636)*

Pathscale Inc.. 408 384-9948
   20c Trolley Sq Wilmington (19806) *(G-18904)*

Pathways2healing... 302 540-4632
   59 Paisley St Bear (19701) *(G-417)*

Patibanda Suguna M D.. 302 453-1550
   2719 Pickering Rd Wilmington (19808) *(G-18905)*

Patient First Medical LLC... 302 536-7740
   1330 Middleford Rd Ste 301 Seaford (19973) *(G-13330)*

Patio Printing Co Inc... 302 328-6881
   197 Airport Rd New Castle (19720) *(G-9457)*

Patio Systems Inc.. 302 644-6540
   16083 New Rd Lewes (19958) *(G-6353)*

Patpet LLC.. 855 888-9922
   8 The Grn Ste A Dover (19901) *(G-3279)*

Patricea and Co LLC... 929 374-9761
   820 Carvel Dr Apt E4 Dover (19901) *(G-3280)*

Patricia Ayers... 302 841-9909
   15629 Walker Dr Milton (19968) *(G-8681)*

Patricia Ayers... 609 335-8923
   1003 N Lincoln St Wilmington (19805) *(G-18906)*

Patricia Chavarry Dr.. 302 747-7895
   492 Stone Ridge Dr Dover (19901) *(G-3281)*

Patricia Degirolano Day Care................................... 302 947-2874
   32909 Long Neck Rd Millsboro (19966) *(G-8415)*

Patricia Disario Day Care.. 302 737-8889
   4 Cottonwood Ct Newark (19702) *(G-11637)*

Patricia H Purcell MD.. 302 428-1142
   601 Cheltenham Rd Wilmington (19808) *(G-18907)*

Patricia Heinemann MD... 302 778-2229
   1100 N Grant Ave Wilmington (19805) *(G-18908)*

Patricia J Avery Artist.. 941 223-5546
   55 Indian Field Rd Wilmington (19810) *(G-18909)*

Patricia McKay... 302 563-5334
   337 Starboard Dr Bear (19701) *(G-418)*

Patricia R Wood... 302 737-3674
   15 Cottonwood Ct Newark (19702) *(G-11638)*

Patrick Aircraft Group LLC...................................... 302 854-9300
   21583 Baltimore Ave Georgetown (19947) *(G-4455)*

Patrick Gaydos... 302 378-8753
   117 Night Heron Ln Middletown (19709) *(G-7429)*

Patrick Scanlon PA... 302 424-1996
   203 Ne Front St Ste 101 Milford (19963) *(G-8042)*

Patrick Swier Mdpa Kar... 302 645-7737
   1400 Savannah Rd Lewes (19958) *(G-6354)*

Patriot Auto & Truck Care LLC................................. 302 257-5715
   497 S Dupont Hwy Dover (19901) *(G-3282)*

Patriot General Contractors..................................... 302 287-9000
   205 Adele Pl New Castle (19720) *(G-9458)*

Patriot Government Svcs Inc.................................... 302 655-3434
   44 Bancroft Mills Rd Wilmington (19806) *(G-18910)*

Patriot Ice Arena LLC.. 302 266-0777
   101 John F Campbell Rd Newark (19711) *(G-11639)*

Patriot Self Defense.. 302 420-3403
   713 Greenbank Rd Wilmington (19808) *(G-18911)*

Patriot Systems Inc... 302 472-9727
   1204 First State Blvd Wilmington (19804) *(G-18912)*

Patriot Trucking LLC... 302 469-3774
   111 Cross Ave New Castle (19720) *(G-9459)*

Pats Aircraft LLC (HQ)... 855 236-1638
   21652 Nanticoke Ave Georgetown (19947) *(G-4456)*

Pats Management... 302 322-3442
   602 E Basin Rd New Castle (19720) *(G-9460)*

Pattern Labs Tech Inc.. 516 340-3369
   108 W 13th St Ste 100 Wilmington (19801) *(G-18913)*

Patterson Mrs Darnetta L... 215 828-2597
   49 Macintosh Cir Magnolia (19962) *(G-6772)*

ALPHABETIC SECTION — Peace and Blessings Child Care

Patterson Price..302 378-9852
5 E Green St Wilmington (19801) *(G-18914)*

Patterson & Schwartz..302 945-5568
28600 Gazebo Way Unit 76 Millsboro (19966) *(G-8416)*

Patterson 3 Inv Group LLC..................................302 469-4783
8 The Grn Dover (19901) *(G-3283)*

Patterson Price RE LLC...302 366-0200
1101 Millstone Dr Newark (19711) *(G-11640)*

Patterson Price RE LLC (PA)...............................302 378-9550
143 Wiggins Mill Rd Townsend (19734) *(G-14050)*

Patterson Schwartz Real Estate, Dover *Also Called: Patterson-Schwartz & Assoc Inc (G-3284)*

Patterson Schwartz Real Estate, Hockessin *Also Called: Patterson-Schwartz & Assoc Inc (G-5333)*

Patterson Schwartz Real Estate, Middletown *Also Called: Patterson-Schwartz & Assoc Inc (G-7430)*

Patterson Schwartz Real Estate, Wilmington *Also Called: Patterson-Schwartz & Assoc Inc (G-18915)*

Patterson-Schwartz..215 805-8238
40 Treelane Dr Bear (19701) *(G-419)*

Patterson-Schwartz & Assoc Inc........................302 672-9400
140 Greentree Dr Dover (19904) *(G-3284)*

Patterson-Schwartz & Assoc Inc........................302 234-3606
7234 Lancaster Pike Ste 302b Hockessin (19707) *(G-5333)*

Patterson-Schwartz & Assoc Inc (PA)...............302 234-5250
7234 Lancaster Pike Hockessin (19707) *(G-5334)*

Patterson-Schwartz & Assoc Inc........................302 285-5100
4417 Summit Bridge Rd Middletown (19709) *(G-7430)*

Patterson-Schwartz & Assoc Inc........................302 733-7000
680 S College Ave Newark (19713) *(G-11641)*

Patterson-Schwartz & Assoc Inc........................302 429-4500
3705 Kennett Pike Wilmington (19807) *(G-18915)*

Patterson-Schwartz Real Estate.........................302 690-7746
405 Bennington Rd Wilmington (19804) *(G-18916)*

Patterson-Schwartz Real Estate, Hockessin *Also Called: Patterson-Schwartz & Assoc Inc (G-5334)*

Patty Cakes Childcare, Bear *Also Called: Patricia McKay (G-418)*

Paul A Lange..302 378-1706
7 Claddagh Ct Middletown (19709) *(G-7431)*

Paul A Nicle Inc...302 453-4000
14 Mill Park Ct Ste E Newark (19713) *(G-11642)*

Paul Amos..302 541-9200
39642 Jefferson Bridge Rd Bethany Beach (19930) *(G-626)*

Paul C Cunningham & Assoc LLC.......................302 258-4163
18700 Arabian Acres Rd Lewes (19958) *(G-6355)*

Paul Davis Restoration, New Castle *Also Called: Paul Dvis Rstoration Nthrn Del (G-9461)*

Paul Dvis Emrgncy Svcs New CST....................302 364-3139
519 Diamond Dr Middletown (19709) *(G-7432)*

Paul Dvis Rstoration Nthrn Del..........................302 449-6941
1061 Lower Twin Lane Rd New Castle (19720) *(G-9461)*

Paul Edwards Carpet Cleaning, Dover *Also Called: Edwards Paul Crpt Installation (G-2427)*

Paul F Campanella Inc..302 777-7170
2379 Limestone Rd Wilmington (19808) *(G-18917)*

Paul F Campanella Auto Service, Wilmington *Also Called: Paul F Campanella Inc (G-18917)*

Paul F Campanella Inc..302 218-5374
1015 W 28th St Wilmington (19802) *(G-18918)*

Paul H Aguillon MD..302 629-6664
401 Concord Rd Seaford (19973) *(G-13331)*

Paul Haller..302 737-0525
211 Tamara Cir Newark (19711) *(G-11643)*

Paul Imber Do..302 478-5647
2700 Silverside Rd Ste 3a Wilmington (19810) *(G-18919)*

Paul J Gitlin MD..302 678-3020
103 Mont Blanc Blvd Dover (19904) *(G-3285)*

Paul J Renzi Masonary, Wilmington *Also Called: Paul Renzi (G-18920)*

Paul Ojewoye...443 844-1745
241 Avonbridge Dr Townsend (19734) *(G-14051)*

Paul Renzi...302 478-3166
6 Brookside Dr Wilmington (19804) *(G-18920)*

Paul Rosen MD..302 651-4000
1600 Rockland Rd Wilmington (19803) *(G-18921)*

Paul Sorvino Foods Inc...302 547-1977
4001 Kennett Pike Ste 134 Wilmington (19807) *(G-18922)*

Paul's Machine Shop, Bear *Also Called: Pauls Inc (G-420)*

Pauls House Inc..302 384-2350
1405 Veale Rd Wilmington (19810) *(G-18923)*

Pauls Inc..302 328-0191
61 Cypress Bridge Pl Bear (19701) *(G-420)*

Pauls Paving Inc...302 539-9123
37425 Dale Earnhardt Blvd Frankford (19945) *(G-4131)*

Pauls Plastering Inc..302 654-5583
19 Davidson Ln New Castle (19720) *(G-9462)*

Paws & People Too..302 376-8234
4390 Summit Bridge Rd Ste 4 Middletown (19709) *(G-7433)*

Paws For Life Inc..302 376-7297
4466 Summit Bridge Rd Middletown (19709) *(G-7434)*

Paws Love LLC..267 770-0777
1013 Centre Rd Ste 403s Wilmington (19805) *(G-18924)*

Paxelax..302 722-7290
40 E Main St Newark (19711) *(G-11644)*

Paxful Inc (PA)..917 609-3850
3422 Old Capitol Trl Pmb 989 Wilmington (19808) *(G-18925)*

Paxo Assist LLC..786 351-0114
2810 N Church St Wilmington (19802) *(G-18926)*

Pay It 4-Ward Inc..424 268-1127
254 Chapman Rd Ste 208 Newark (19702) *(G-11645)*

Pay It Frward Ntwrking Group C......................302 213-2695
1308 Lancaster Ave Wilmington (19805) *(G-18927)*

Paymenex Inc..302 504-6044
501 Silverside Rd Ste 105 Wilmington (19809) *(G-18928)*

Payne Enterprises LLC..302 856-2899
201 Old Laurel Rd Georgetown (19947) *(G-4457)*

Payourse Technologies Inc.................................206 922-8971
1007 N Orange St Wilmington (19801) *(G-18929)*

Paypergigs Inc...917 336-2162
2035 Sunset Lake Rd B2 Newark (19702) *(G-11646)*

Payroll Management Assistants........................302 456-6816
409 White Clay Center Dr Newark (19711) *(G-11647)*

Payroll Services of Delaware, Dover *Also Called: Computer Services of Delaware (G-2127)*

Payshiga Technologies Inc..................................214 447-0677
8 The Grn Dover (19901) *(G-3286)*

PB Trucking Inc...302 841-3209
8940 Greenwood Rd Greenwood (19950) *(G-4660)*

Pbe Companies LLC..617 346-7459
2711 Centerville Rd Ste 400 Wilmington (19808) *(G-18930)*

PBL & 5js Holdings Inc...404 832-5038
8 The Grn Ste A Dover (19901) *(G-3287)*

Pbtv Global Inc...302 292-1400
2105a W Newport Pike Wilmington (19804) *(G-18931)*

PC Supplies Inc..302 368-4800
1003 S Chapel St Ste A Newark (19702) *(G-11648)*

PCA Acquisitions V LLC.......................................302 355-3500
1002 Justison St Wilmington (19801) *(G-18932)*

PCA Pto...302 250-8377
273 W Duck Creek Rd Clayton (19938) *(G-1394)*

Pcd Solutions LLC..877 723-7552
806 W 28th St Wilmington (19802) *(G-18933)*

PCI of Virginia LLC (HQ)......................................302 655-7300
1 Hausel Rd Wilmington (19801) *(G-18934)*

Pck Associates Inc..302 378-7192
1343 Bohemia Mill Rd Middletown (19709) *(G-7435)*

Pcmb LLC..302 482-1360
5201 W Woodmill Dr Wilmington (19808) *(G-18935)*

Pco-Tech Inc..248 276-8820
1000 N West St Ste 1200 Wilmington (19801) *(G-18936)*

Pde I LLC...302 654-8300
422 Delaware Ave Wilmington (19801) *(G-18937)*

Pding LLC..252 201-8458
16192 Coastal Hwy Lewes (19958) *(G-6356)*

PDM Incorporated..302 478-0768
3411 Silverside Rd Ste 104wb Wilmington (19810) *(G-18938)*

Pdo Construction LLC...302 542-0963
1 W 1st St Selbyville (19975) *(G-13590)*

Peace and Blessings Child Care........................302 543-4762
22 W 30th St Wilmington (19802) *(G-18939)*

Peace By Piece Inc	302 266-2556
888 Salem Church Rd Newark (19702) *(G-11649)*	
Peaceworks	302 727-2464
16909 Jays Way Milton (19968) *(G-8682)*	
Peach Wireless LLC	646 941-4391
3422 Old Capitol Trl Wilmington (19808) *(G-18940)*	
Peachi Inc	347 907-0138
2035 Sunset Lake Rd B2 Newark (19702) *(G-11650)*	
Peachy Keen Slon + Buty Bar LL	302 519-5572
606 Milford Harrington Hwy Milford (19963) *(G-8043)*	
Peak Cryotherapy	302 502-3160
5507 E Timberview Ct Wilmington (19808) *(G-18941)*	
Peak Equipment Repair	302 526-4729
2061 Bayside Dr Dover (19901) *(G-3288)*	
Peak Performance Athletics	443 404-6049
48 Merganser Dr Magnolia (19962) *(G-6773)*	
Peak Prfmce Globl Svcs LLC	610 554-4773
18261 Alpine Loop Lewes (19958) *(G-6357)*	
Peak Uptime Solutions LLC	856 243-5838
2115 Exton Dr Wilmington (19810) *(G-18942)*	
Pear Media LLC	505 932-6555
16192 Coastal Hwy Lewes (19958) *(G-6358)*	
Pearce & Moretto Inc	302 326-0707
1060 Industrial Dr Middletown (19709) *(G-7436)*	
Pearce Q Foundation Inc	302 753-8612
4142 Ogletown Stanton Rd Ste 227 Newark (19713) *(G-11651)*	
Pearce Rupertus Kathleen M	302 388-7515
501 Silverside Rd Ste 145 Wilmington (19809) *(G-18943)*	
Pearl Clinic LLC	302 648-2099
28539 Dupont Blvd Millsboro (19966) *(G-8417)*	
Peavey, Townsend Also Called: Mountaire Farms Delaware Inc *(G-14039)*	
Pebble Hill Apartments, Wilmington Also Called: Eastern Property Group Inc *(G-16261)*	
Pebble Hill Assoc A Partnr, Wilmington Also Called: Eastern Prosperity Group *(G-16262)*	
Pebble Stack LLC	732 910-9701
651 N Broad St Ste 206 Middletown (19709) *(G-7437)*	
Pebbles Inc	408 600-8953
1013 Centre Rd Ste 403b Wilmington (19805) *(G-18944)*	
Pecks Drain Cleaning	302 345-4101
12 Milkweed Ct Newark (19713) *(G-11652)*	
Peddie John	302 838-8771
18 Photinia Dr Newark (19702) *(G-11653)*	
Pediatric & Adolescent Center	302 684-0561
424 Mulberry St Milton (19968) *(G-8683)*	
Pediatric Associates PA	302 368-8612
4735 Ogletown Stanton Rd Ste 1116 Newark (19713) *(G-11654)*	
Pedro Cimarron Rascon LLC, Frankford Also Called: Pedro Rascon Cimarron *(G-4132)*	
Pedro Rascon Cimarron	302 448-6806
34969 Shockley Town Rd Frankford (19945) *(G-4132)*	
Peel & Sons, Newark Also Called: James A Peel & Sons Inc *(G-11088)*	
Peery Foundation	650 644-4660
501 Silverside Rd Ste 123 Wilmington (19809) *(G-18945)*	
Peg Gilson Membership Chair	302 734-5190
224 Winterberry Dr Dover (19904) *(G-3289)*	
Peirce James Townsend III	302 449-2279
19 Canary Ct Middletown (19709) *(G-7438)*	
Pelican Bay Group Inc	302 945-5900
100 Rudder Rd Millsboro (19966) *(G-8418)*	
Pelican Key LLC Brksdale A SRI	302 563-9493
175 S Main St Newark (19711) *(G-11655)*	
Pelican Seven Studios	302 764-6684
13 Saddle Ln Wilmington (19803) *(G-18946)*	
Pelsa Company Inc	302 834-3771
610 Peoples Plz Newark (19702) *(G-11656)*	
Pembina Health Inc	701 314-7895
16192 Coastal Hwy Lewes (19958) *(G-6359)*	
Pemco Lighting Products LLC	302 892-9000
150 Pemco Way Wilmington (19804) *(G-18947)*	
Pen Del Auto & Marine Inc	302 430-3046
35936 Pen Del Ave Frankford (19945) *(G-4133)*	
Pen Enterprises LLC	302 798-0268
2811 Philadelphia Pike Ste 2 Claymont (19703) *(G-1261)*	

Pen Pave Contractors Pave	302 226-7283
20873 Old Landing Rd Rehoboth Beach (19971) *(G-12885)*	
Penache Beauty Salon	302 731-5912
16 Polly Drummond Shpg Ctr Newark (19711) *(G-11657)*	
Pencader Consulting Group	302 454-8004
401 Ivory Ln Newark (19702) *(G-11658)*	
Pencader Group LLC	302 366-0721
273 S Dillwyn Rd Newark (19711) *(G-11659)*	
Pencader Heritage Area Assn	518 578-3559
211 Executive Dr Newark (19702) *(G-11660)*	
Pencader Mechanical Contrs	302 368-9144
75 Lark Ave Bear (19701) *(G-421)*	
Pencader Self Storage	302 709-3180
101 Executive Dr Newark (19702) *(G-11661)*	
Penco Corporation	302 698-3108
2000 S Dupont Hwy Camden (19934) *(G-884)*	
Penco Corporation	302 738-3212
121 Sandy Dr Newark (19713) *(G-11662)*	
Penco Corporation	302 227-9188
Rte 1 By The Canal Rehoboth Beach (19971) *(G-12886)*	
Penco Corporation	302 629-7911
1503 W Stein Hwy Seaford (19973) *(G-13332)*	
Penco Corporation	302 629-3061
1800 Dulany St # 6 Seaford (19973) *(G-13333)*	
Penco Corporation (PA)	302 629-7911
1503 W Stein Hwy Seaford (19973) *(G-13334)*	
Pendulum It LLC	302 480-9433
19 Holly Cove Ln Dover (19901) *(G-3290)*	
Penflex III LLC	302 998-0683
702 First State Blvd Wilmington (19804) *(G-18948)*	
Penglai Bioventures LLC (PA)	302 219-3259
8 The Grn Ste 16376 Dover (19901) *(G-3291)*	
Peninsula	410 342-8111
26937 Bay Farm Rd Millsboro (19966) *(G-8419)*	
Peninsula Acoustical Co Inc	302 653-3551
441 Pier Head Blvd Smyrna (19977) *(G-13845)*	
Peninsula Allergy and Asthma	302 734-4434
200 Banning St Ste 280 Dover (19904) *(G-3292)*	
Peninsula Anmal Hosp Orthpdics	302 846-9011
38375 Old Stage Rd Delmar (19940) *(G-1628)*	
Peninsula At Long Neck LLC	302 947-4717
468 Bay Farm Rd Millsboro (19966) *(G-8420)*	
Peninsula Chiropractic Center	302 629-4344
26685 Sussex Hwy Seaford (19973) *(G-13335)*	
Peninsula Community Assn, Millsboro Also Called: Peninsula *(G-8419)*	
Peninsula Dental LLC	302 297-3750
26670 Centerview Dr Unit 19 Millsboro (19966) *(G-8421)*	
Peninsula Energy Svcs Co Inc (HQ)	302 734-6799
909 Silver Lake Blvd Dover (19904) *(G-3293)*	
Peninsula Financial Group Inc	302 856-0970
13 Bridgeville Rd Georgetown (19947) *(G-4458)*	
Peninsula Gallery, Lewes Also Called: Carol Boyd Heron *(G-5803)*	
Peninsula Health LLC	302 945-0440
26744 John J Williams Hwy Unit 7 Millsboro (19966) *(G-8422)*	
Peninsula Home Care LLC	302 629-4914
8466 Herring Run Rd Seaford (19973) *(G-13336)*	
Peninsula Home Health Care	302 629-5672
514 W Stein Hwy Seaford (19973) *(G-13337)*	
Peninsula Masonry Inc	302 684-3410
26822 Lewes Georgetown Hwy Harbeson (19951) *(G-4711)*	
Peninsula Oil & Propane, Seaford Also Called: Peninsula Oil Co Inc *(G-13338)*	
Peninsula Oil Co Inc (PA)	302 422-6691
40 S Market St Seaford (19973) *(G-13338)*	
Peninsula Pave & Seal LLC	302 226-7283
20288 Asphalt Aly Georgetown (19947) *(G-4459)*	
Peninsula Paving, Georgetown Also Called: Peninsula Pave & Seal LLC *(G-4459)*	
Peninsula Plastic Surgery PC	302 663-0119
30265 Commerce Dr Unit 208 Millsboro (19966) *(G-8423)*	
Peninsula Polymers Inc	302 422-2002
640 Marshall St Milford (19963) *(G-8044)*	
Peninsula Poultry Eqp Co Inc	302 875-0889
30709 Sussex Hwy Laurel (19956) *(G-5573)*	

ALPHABETIC SECTION — Perdue Farms Incorporated

Peninsula Poultry Eqp Co Inc (PA).. 302 875-0886
201 N Dual Hwy Laurel (19956) *(G-5574)*

Peninsula Regional Prmry Care, Selbyville *Also Called: Tidalhlth Pnnsula Regional Inc*
(G-13612)

Peninsula Technical Services I.. 302 907-0554
38224 Old Stage Rd Delmar (19940) *(G-1629)*

Peninsula Untd Mthdst Hmes Inc (PA).. 302 235-6800
726 Loveville Rd Ste 3000 Hockessin (19707) *(G-5335)*

Peninsula Untd Mthdst Hmes Inc.. 302 235-6810
726 Loveville Rd Ste 3000 Hockessin (19707) *(G-5336)*

Peninsula Untd Mthdst Hmes Inc.. 302 654-5101
4830 Kennett Pike Wilmington (19807) *(G-18949)*

Peninsula Urology Assoc PA.. 302 628-4222
1340 Middleford Rd Ste 402 Seaford (19973) *(G-13339)*

Peninsula Veterinary Svcs LLC.. 302 947-0719
32038 Long Neck Rd Millsboro (19966) *(G-8424)*

Penn Acres Civic Association.. 302 328-8500
19 Silsbee Rd New Castle (19720) *(G-9463)*

Penn Cinema Riverfront LLC (PA).. 717 438-4800
401 S Madison St Wilmington (19801) *(G-18950)*

Penn Del Carriers LLC.. 484 424-3768
110 W Edinburgh Dr New Castle (19720) *(G-9464)*

Penn Delco Education Assn.. 610 800-8218
1216 Prospect Dr Wilmington (19809) *(G-18951)*

Penn Labs Inc.. 215 751-4000
2711 Centerville Rd Ste 400 Wilmington (19808) *(G-18952)*

Penna Orthodontics.. 302 998-8783
2710 Centerville Rd Wilmington (19808) *(G-18953)*

Pennengineering Holdings LLC.. 302 576-2746
103 Foulk Rd Ste 108 Wilmington (19803) *(G-18954)*

Penney Enterprises Inc.. 302 629-4430
9203 Brickyard Rd Seaford (19973) *(G-13340)*

Pennie Mgmt LLC.. 847 682-1644
251 Little Falls Dr Wilmington (19808) *(G-18955)*

Pennmuni-Tiaa US RE Fund LLC.. 302 636-5401
251 Little Falls Dr Wilmington (19808) *(G-18956)*

Pennock Insurance Inc.. 302 235-8258
761 Whitebriar Rd Hockessin (19707) *(G-5337)*

Pennoni.. 302 234-4600
121 Continental Dr Ste 207 Newark (19713) *(G-11663)*

Pennoni Associates Inc.. 302 655-4451
121 Continental Dr Ste 207 Newark (19713) *(G-11664)*

Pennsula Home Care LLC.. 302 629-4914
501 Health Services Dr Seaford (19973) *(G-13341)*

Pennsylvania Brand Co.. 302 674-5774
550 S New St Dover (19904) *(G-3294)*

Penny Cooper Sportswear & EMB.. 302 325-3710
204 Christiana Rd New Castle (19720) *(G-9465)*

Penny Hill Eye Center.. 302 764-4613
230 Philadelphia Pike Wilmington (19809) *(G-18957)*

Penny Hill Lawn & Landscaping.. 302 762-4406
602 Elizabeth Ave Wilmington (19809) *(G-18958)*

Penobscot Properties LLC (PA).. 302 322-4477
135 N Dupont Hwy New Castle (19720) *(G-9466)*

Penske, Middletown *Also Called: Penske Truck Leasing Corp (G-7439)*

Penske, New Castle *Also Called: Penske Truck Leasing Co LP (G-9467)*

Penske, Rehoboth Beach *Also Called: Penske Truck Leasing Corp (G-12887)*

Penske, Seaford *Also Called: Penske Truck Leasing Corp (G-13342)*

Penske, Wilmington *Also Called: Penske Performance Inc (G-18959)*

Penske, Wilmington *Also Called: Penske Truck Leasing Co LP (G-18960)*

Penske, Wilmington *Also Called: Penske Truck Leasing Corp (G-18961)*

Penske Performance Inc (HQ).. 302 656-2082
1105 N Market St Wilmington (19801) *(G-18959)*

Penske Truck Leasing Co LP.. 302 325-9290
51 Boulden Blvd New Castle (19720) *(G-9467)*

Penske Truck Leasing Co LP.. 302 994-7899
3625 Kirkwood Hwy Wilmington (19808) *(G-18960)*

Penske Truck Leasing Corp.. 302 449-9294
921 Middletown Warwick Rd Middletown (19709) *(G-7439)*

Penske Truck Leasing Corp.. 302 260-7039
19659 Blue Bird Ln Rehoboth Beach (19971) *(G-12887)*

Penske Truck Leasing Corp.. 302 629-5373
24799 Sussex Hwy Seaford (19973) *(G-13342)*

Penske Truck Leasing Corp.. 302 658-3255
4709 Ferris Dr Wilmington (19808) *(G-18961)*

Penske Truck Rental.. 302 746-3020
601 Naamans Rd Claymont (19703) *(G-1262)*

Penske Truck Rental.. 302 648-3199
25920 Plaza Dr Millsboro (19966) *(G-8425)*

Penteco LLC.. 302 472-9105
301 N Market St # 1414 Wilmington (19801) *(G-18962)*

Pentius Inc.. 855 825-3778
1201 N Orange St Ste 7382 Wilmington (19801) *(G-18963)*

Penwood Lawn Care.. 302 535-4464
125 Dickens Ln Felton (19943) *(G-4008)*

People In Transition Inc.. 302 784-5214
39 Thorn Ln New Castle (19720) *(G-9468)*

People Tech Group Inc.. 833 202-3555
42 Reads Way New Castle (19720) *(G-9469)*

PEOPLE'S SETTLEMENT DAY CARE, Wilmington *Also Called: Peoples Sttlment Assn Wlmngton (G-18964)*

Peoples First Insurance Inc.. 302 449-4777
292 Carter Dr Ste C Middletown (19709) *(G-7440)*

Peoples Place II Inc.. 302 730-1321
165 Commerce Way Dover (19904) *(G-3295)*

Peoples Place II Inc (PA).. 302 422-8033
1129 Airport Rd Milford (19963) *(G-8045)*

Peoples Place II Inc.. 302 934-0300
30265 Commerce Dr Unit 201 Millsboro (19966) *(G-8426)*

Peoples Sttlment Assn Wlmngton.. 302 658-4133
408 E 8th St Wilmington (19801) *(G-18964)*

Peoples, R C, Bear *Also Called: Robert C Peoples Inc (G-463)*

Pep-Up, Georgetown *Also Called: Pep-Up Inc (G-4460)*

Pep-Up Inc (PA).. 302 856-2555
24987 Dupont Blvd Georgetown (19947) *(G-4460)*

Pep-Up Inc.. 302 645-2600
18979 Coastal Hwy Rehoboth Beach (19971) *(G-12888)*

Pep-Up 11, Rehoboth Beach *Also Called: Pep-Up Inc (G-12888)*

Pepco Holdings LLC.. 202 872-2000
630 Martin Luther King Blvd Wilmington (19801) *(G-18965)*

Peppers Inc (PA).. 302 645-0812
17601 Coastal Hwy Unit 1 Lewes (19958) *(G-6360)*

Peppers Inc.. 302 644-6900
15608 Coastal Hwy Lewes (19958) *(G-6361)*

Pepperscom Inc.. 302 703-6355
17601 Coastal Hwy Unit 1 Lewes (19958) *(G-6362)*

Peppl, Hockessin *Also Called: Pradhan Energy Projects (G-5351)*

Pepsi-Cola, Wilmington *Also Called: Pepsi-Cola Btlg of Wilmington (G-18966)*

Pepsi-Cola Btlg of Wilmington.. 302 761-4848
3501 Governor Printz Blvd Wilmington (19802) *(G-18966)*

Perastic LLC.. 917 592-4219
1704 N Park Dr Apt 508 Wilmington (19806) *(G-18967)*

Percebe Music Inc.. 850 341-9594
8 The Grn Ste A Dover (19901) *(G-3296)*

Perceri LLC.. 217 721-8731
160 Greentree Dr Ste 101 Dover (19904) *(G-3297)*

Perch Acquisition Co 17 LLC.. 617 206-3761
112 S French St Ste 105-19 Wilmington (19801) *(G-18968)*

Perch Foreign Acquisition Corp.. 617 206-3761
112 S French St Ste 105-56 Wilmington (19801) *(G-18969)*

Perdue Farms, Bridgeville *Also Called: Perdue Farms Inc (G-746)*

Perdue Farms, Milford *Also Called: Perdue Farms Inc (G-8046)*

Perdue Farms, Seaford *Also Called: Perdue Farms Incorporated (G-13343)*

Perdue Farms Inc.. 302 337-2210
16447 Adams Rd Bridgeville (19933) *(G-746)*

Perdue Farms Inc.. 302 855-5681
10262 Stone Creek Dr Unit 3 Laurel (19956) *(G-5575)*

Perdue Farms Inc.. 302 424-2600
225 S Rehoboth Blvd Milford (19963) *(G-8046)*

Perdue Farms Incorporated.. 302 855-5635
20621 Savannah Rd Georgetown (19947) *(G-4461)*

Perdue Farms Incorporated.. 302 629-3216
1000 Nanticoke Ave Seaford (19973) *(G-13343)*

Perdue Wellness Center — ALPHABETIC SECTION

Perdue Wellness Center.. 302 424-2663
   255 N Rehoboth Blvd Milford (19963) *(G-8047)*

Perdue-Agrirecycle LLC.. 302 628-2360
   28338 Enviro Way Seaford (19973) *(G-13344)*

Perella Weinberg Partners LLC... 267 746-0569
   405 Campbell Rd Wilmington (19807) *(G-18970)*

Perennial Dev & Cnstr Corp... 855 625-0046
   1320 Philadelphia Pike Ste 202 Wilmington (19809) *(G-18971)*

Perfect Finish LLC.. 302 480-3167
   3415 Wrangle Hill Rd Bear (19701) *(G-422)*

Perfect Finish Powder Coating... 302 566-6189
   3845 Whiteleysburg Rd Harrington (19952) *(G-4809)*

Perfect Grand Lodge Stdavid... 302 689-3579
   1511 N Claymont St Wilmington (19802) *(G-18972)*

Perfect Nails... 302 731-1964
   210 University Plz Newark (19702) *(G-11665)*

Perfect Plumbing Partners Inc.. 610 521-6654
   117 Median Dr Wilmington (19803) *(G-18973)*

Perfect Ten Nail Salon Da... 302 545-3001
   713 Woodsdale Rd Wilmington (19809) *(G-18974)*

Perfection Custom Painting LLC....................................... 303 536-7572
   26907 Lonesome Rd Seaford (19973) *(G-13345)*

Perfection Lawncare Ltd.. 215 624-7410
   129 Gazebo Ln Middletown (19709) *(G-7441)*

Perfectional Cleaning... 302 864-7112
   25 Laverty Ln Bridgeville (19933) *(G-747)*

Perfectly OK Productions... 302 233-3208
   846 Underwoods Corner Rd Clayton (19938) *(G-1395)*

Perficient Inc... 302 690-2087
   3327 Skyline Dr Wilmington (19808) *(G-18975)*

Performance Based Results... 302 478-4443
   400 Delaware Ave Talleyville (19803) *(G-13945)*

Performance Enhancement Profes.................................... 302 423-0236
   1255 S State St Ste 7 Dover (19901) *(G-3298)*

Performance Lubricants, Wilmington *Also Called: Chemours Company Fc LLC (G-15361)*

Performance Lubricants Inc... 302 239-5661
   7460 Lancaster Pike Ste 4 Hockessin (19707) *(G-5338)*

Performance Materials Intl LLC.. 302 999-4083
   974 Centre Rd Wilmington (19805) *(G-18976)*

Performance Materials Na Inc.. 302 892-7009
   Chestnut Run Plz 974 Ctr Rd Wilmington (19805) *(G-18977)*

Performance Physcl Therapy Inc (PA)................................. 302 234-2288
   720 Yorklyn Rd Ste 150 Hockessin (19707) *(G-5339)*

Performance Pt Solutions LLC.. 302 202-3155
   720 Yorklyn Rd Ste 150 Hockessin (19707) *(G-5340)*

Performing Systems Inc... 302 275-5409
   101 E 36th St Wilmington (19802) *(G-18978)*

Performnce Injction Equipmentc....................................... 302 858-5145
   24994 Betts Ln Georgetown (19947) *(G-4462)*

Performnce Solutions Holdg Inc (DH)................................. 302 774-1000
   200 Powder Mill Rd Bldg 304 Wilmington (19803) *(G-18979)*

Performnce Spcalty Pdts NA LLC...................................... 302 774-3034
   974 Centre Rd Wilmington (19805) *(G-18980)*

Peri Srihari MD.. 302 645-3770
   18947 John J Williams Hwy Rehoboth Beach (19971) *(G-12889)*

Perioperative Services LLC (PA)...................................... 302 733-0806
   111 Continental Dr Ste 412 Newark (19713) *(G-11666)*

Perisphere Inc (PA).. 908 581-8058
   8 The Grn Dover (19901) *(G-3299)*

Peristalsis Productions Inc... 302 366-1106
   6 Newside Ct Newark (19711) *(G-11667)*

Perivision Usa Inc... 302 665-0866
   8 The Grn # 17008 Dover (19901) *(G-3300)*

Perks Express Inc.. 855 924-7424
   106 Belmont Dr Wilmington (19808) *(G-18981)*

Perkwiz Inc... 702 866-9122
   7209 Lancaster Pike Hockessin (19707) *(G-5341)*

Perpetual Invstments Group LLC...................................... 718 795-3394
   251 Little Falls Dr Wilmington (19808) *(G-18982)*

Perry & Assoc.. 302 472-8701
   6 Larch Ave Ste 397 Wilmington (19804) *(G-18983)*

Perry and Associates Inc... 302 898-2327
   540 Waterford Rd Hockessin (19707) *(G-5342)*

Perry and Associates Services... 302 581-3092
   300 Delaware Ave Ste 210 Wilmington (19801) *(G-18984)*

Perry Anthony Salon Spa Netwrk...................................... 302 239-6161
   5331 Limestone Rd Wilmington (19808) *(G-18985)*

Perry Enterprise LLC.. 302 505-4458
   8 The Grn Dover (19901) *(G-3301)*

Perry Initiative... 302 319-1113
   130 Academy St Newark (19716) *(G-11668)*

Perryfilms Production Co LLC.. 302 505-4458
   16192 Coastal Hwy Lewes (19958) *(G-6363)*

Persante.. 302 253-8740
   2 Lee Ave Georgetown (19947) *(G-4463)*

Persante Sleep Center.. 302 724-5128
   103 Wolf Creek Blvd Ste 2 Dover (19901) *(G-3302)*

Persante Sleep Center.. 302 508-2130
   100 S Main St Ste 201 Smyrna (19977) *(G-13846)*

Persephone Jones MD... 302 651-4000
   1600 Rockland Rd Wilmington (19803) *(G-18986)*

Persha LLC... 786 925-2952
   950 Bedford Dr Dover (19904) *(G-3303)*

Pershing Foundation.. 636 352-7122
   23 Palmer Dr Middletown (19709) *(G-7442)*

Person 2 Person Trnsp LLC... 302 900-1061
   129 Spelt Dr Clayton (19938) *(G-1396)*

Personal Health PDT Dev LLC... 888 901-6150
   4023 Kennett Pike Ste 622 Wilmington (19807) *(G-18987)*

Personal Tax Services... 302 562-5051
   22 N Valley Stream Cir Newark (19702) *(G-11669)*

Personal Touch Child Care... 302 368-2229
   201 Possum Park Rd Newark (19711) *(G-11670)*

Personal Touch Memories.. 302 598-3987
   3351 Altamont Dr Wilmington (19810) *(G-18988)*

Personalized Luggage Inc.. 786 431-3118
   3411 Silverside Rd Ste 104 Wilmington (19810) *(G-18989)*

Personas Inc... 416 815-7000
   2711 Centerville Rd Wilmington (19808) *(G-18990)*

Perteh.. 302 200-0912
   1800 Naamans Rd Wilmington (19810) *(G-18991)*

Pesco Energy, Dover *Also Called: Peninsula Energy Svcs Co Inc (G-3293)*

Pessagno Equipment Inc.. 302 738-7001
   109 Sandy Dr Newark (19713) *(G-11671)*

Pest Pro LLC... 877 737-8360
   100 Kona Cir Milford (19963) *(G-8048)*

Pest Pro Pest Control, Milford *Also Called: Pest Pro LLC (G-8048)*

Pestex Pest Control Inc... 302 745-8366
   26066 Bethesda Rd Georgetown (19947) *(G-4464)*

Pestpro, Magnolia *Also Called: Davis A Scott (G-6738)*

Pet Bow Tique LLC.. 302 856-7297
   18355 County Seat Hwy Georgetown (19947) *(G-4465)*

Pet Medical Center.. 302 846-2869
   Rte 13 Delmar (19940) *(G-1630)*

Pet Poultry Products LLC... 302 337-8223
   7494 Federalsburg Rd Bridgeville (19933) *(G-748)*

Pet Shop LLC.. 646 345-8844
   8 The Grn Ste A Dover (19901) *(G-3304)*

Pet Stop of Delaware.. 302 922-7572
   938 Todds Chapel Rd Greenwood (19950) *(G-4661)*

Pet Stop of Delmarva... 302 943-2310
   2416 Flatiron Rd Harrington (19952) *(G-4810)*

Petal Pushers Flowers, Wilmington *Also Called: Alexis Wirt (G-14354)*

Petal Pushers LLC... 302 945-0350
   31341 Kendale Rd Lewes (19958) *(G-6364)*

Petcy, Middletown *Also Called: Petcy Inc (G-7443)*

Petcy Inc... 920 240-4312
   651 N Broad St Ste 206 Middletown (19709) *(G-7443)*

Peter D Furness Elc Co Inc... 302 764-6030
   1604 Todds Ln Wilmington (19802) *(G-18992)*

Peter Dunckley.. 302 234-1561
   4 Bent Tree Cir Hockessin (19707) *(G-5343)*

ALPHABETIC SECTION

Peter F Subach 302 995-1870
  1601 Milltown Rd Ste 17 Wilmington (19808) *(G-18993)*
Peter F Townsend MD 302 633-3555
  3519 Silverside Rd # 101 Wilmington (19810) *(G-18994)*
Peter M D Rocca 302 683-9400
  537 Stanton Christiana Rd Ste 101 Newark (19713) *(G-11672)*
Peter M Witherell M D 302 478-7001
  774 Christiana Rd Ste 202 Newark (19713) *(G-11673)*
Peter R Coggins MD (PA) 302 655-1115
  5811 Kennett Pike Wilmington (19807) *(G-18995)*
Peter Renzi 302 265-1309
  793 Bay Rd Milford (19963) *(G-8049)*
Peter Zorach 302 377-5874
  495 E Main St Middletown (19709) *(G-7444)*
Peters Alan E Peters & Assoc 302 656-1007
  1200 Pennsylvania Ave Ste 202 Wilmington (19806) *(G-18996)*
Peterson Josha 302 656-5416
  1100 S Broom St Wilmington (19805) *(G-18997)*
Petes Big Tvs Inc (PA) 302 328-3551
  22 Lukens Dr Historic New Castle (19720) *(G-5046)*
Petes Plumbing LLC 302 270-4990
  106 Elm Ter Dover (19901) *(G-3305)*
Petite Hair Designs 302 945-2595
  Long Neck Rd Plmer Shopg Palmer Millsboro (19966) *(G-8427)*
Petite Plume, Wilmington *Also Called: Petite Plume LLC (G-18998)*
Petite Plume LLC 800 298-1381
  605 Geddes St Wilmington (19805) *(G-18998)*
Petite Yogi 570 840-5999
  2305 W 18th St Wilmington (19806) *(G-18999)*
Petmex Company LLC 800 829-4933
  8 The Grn Dover (19901) *(G-3306)*
Petra Investments LLC (PA) 312 887-1558
  254 Chapman Rd Ste 208 Newark (19702) *(G-11674)*
Petro International Corp 302 884-6755
  1201 N Orange St Ste 708 Wilmington (19801) *(G-19000)*
Petroleum Equipment Inc (PA) 302 734-7433
  3799 N Dupont Hwy Dover (19901) *(G-3307)*
Petroleum Equipment Inc 302 422-4281
  3799 N Dupont Hwy Dover (19901) *(G-3308)*
Petron Oil, Newark *Also Called: Conectiv Energy Supply Inc (G-10301)*
Petroserv Inc 302 398-3260
  17436 S Dupont Hwy Harrington (19952) *(G-4811)*
Petrovich Masonry 302 697-2379
  214 Carter Rd Dover (19901) *(G-3309)*
Petspy, Dover *Also Called: Aerosmith LLC (G-1730)*
Pettinaro, Wilmington *Also Called: Pettinaro Construction Co Inc (G-19001)*
Pettinaro Construction Co Inc 302 832-8823
  100 Cindy Dr Newark (19702) *(G-11675)*
Pettinaro Construction Co Inc (PA) 302 999-0708
  234 N James St Wilmington (19804) *(G-19001)*
Pettinaro Enterprises LLC 302 999-0708
  234 N James St Wilmington (19804) *(G-19002)*
Pettinaro Management LLC 302 832-8823
  100 Cindy Dr Newark (19702) *(G-11676)*
Pettinaro Residential LLC 302 999-0708
  234 N James St Wilmington (19804) *(G-19003)*
Pettitt Construction LLC 302 690-0831
  12 Carlisle Rd Newark (19713) *(G-11677)*
Pettyjohn Farms Inc 302 684-4383
  16771 Gravel Hill Rd Milton (19968) *(G-8684)*
Pexmall Ltd Liability Company 347 414-9879
  40 E Main St Newark (19711) *(G-11678)*
Pfp Leveling Solutions LLC, Wilmington *Also Called: Pargoe Flr Prep Lvlg Sltons LL (G-18890)*
Pfpc Trust Company 302 791-2000
  301 Bellevue Pkwy 4th Fl Wilmington (19809) *(G-19004)*
Pfpc Worldwide Inc (DH) 302 791-1700
  301 Bellevue Pkwy Wilmington (19809) *(G-19005)*
Pfs Ltd 202 709-9755
  8 The Grn Dover (19901) *(G-3310)*
Pgi Commercial LLC 800 686-8134
  2711 Centerville Rd Ste 4 Wilmington (19808) *(G-19006)*

Pgim Foreign Investments Inc 302 427-9530
  300 Delaware Ave Ste 820 Wilmington (19801) *(G-19007)*
Phaction Inc 240 459-5198
  251 Little Falls Dr Wilmington (19808) *(G-19008)*
Pharma E Market LLC 302 737-3711
  726 Loveville Rd Apt 99 Hockessin (19707) *(G-5344)*
Pharmadel LLC 302 322-1329
  600 Ships Landing Way Historic New Castle (19720) *(G-5047)*
Pharmd Live Corporation 908 803-3311
  8 The Grn Ste 10486 Dover (19901) *(G-3311)*
Pharmerica Long-Term Care LLC 302 454-8234
  111 Ruthar Dr Newark (19711) *(G-11679)*
Pharmunion LLC 415 307-5128
  3524 Silverside Rd Ste 35b Wilmington (19810) *(G-19009)*
Phase Flats II L P 717 291-1911
  601 N Union St Wilmington (19805) *(G-19010)*
Phase I Flats L P 717 291-1911
  401 N Union St 535 Wilmington (19805) *(G-19011)*
Phase Snsitive Innovations Inc (PA) 302 286-5191
  116 Sandy Dr Ste A Newark (19713) *(G-11680)*
Phat Holdings Inc 775 438-7428
  251 Little Falls Dr Wilmington (19808) *(G-19012)*
Phazebreak Coatings LLC 844 467-4293
  1105 N Market St Ste 1300 Wilmington (19801) *(G-19013)*
Phc Inc (HQ) 313 831-3500
  575 S Dupont Hwy New Castle (19720) *(G-9470)*
PHC Meadowwood, New Castle *Also Called: Acadia Healthcare Company Inc (G-8759)*
PHD Technology Solutions LLC 410 961-7895
  111 Continental Dr Ste 309 Newark (19713) *(G-11681)*
Pheonixfire L L C 302 588-8820
  37 Munro Rd Newark (19711) *(G-11682)*
PHI Service Co 302 451-5224
  500 N Wakefield Dr Newark (19702) *(G-11683)*
Phil Hill 302 678-0499
  3728 N Dupont Hwy Dover (19901) *(G-3312)*
Philadelphia Gear, Historic New Castle *Also Called: Timken Gears & Services Inc (G-5086)*
Philadelphia Plumbing 302 327-8545
  100 Garfield Ave New Castle (19720) *(G-9471)*
Philadelphia Plumbing 302 468-5460
  1707 Foulk Rd Wilmington (19803) *(G-19014)*
Philadlphia Arms Town Hmes Inc 302 503-7216
  18527 Pentecostal St Ellendale (19941) *(G-3928)*
Philadlphia Prtection Unit LLC 267 505-2671
  511 Cilantro Ct Middletown (19709) *(G-7445)*
Philadlphia Slar For Rnwble En 412 297-4866
  251 Little Falls Dr Wilmington (19808) *(G-19015)*
Philanthropy Delaware Inc 302 588-1342
  100 W 10th St Wilmington (19801) *(G-19016)*
Philanthrovest LLC (PA) 201 563-9179
  8 The Grn Ste A Dover (19901) *(G-3313)*
Philip Rosenau, Historic New Castle *Also Called: Allston Chemical Supply Inc (G-4927)*
Philip Rosenau Co Inc 302 322-3952
  264 Quigley Blvd Historic New Castle (19720) *(G-5048)*
Philips B Eric DMD PA 302 738-7303
  Omega Prof Ctr Ste J31 Newark (19713) *(G-11684)*
Philips Painting LLC 302 344-0535
  228 Stoney Br Seaford (19973) *(G-13346)*
Phillip Fulton 302 995-6412
  2832 W Oakland Dr Wilmington (19808) *(G-19017)*
Phillip T Bradley Inc 302 947-2741
  33057 Angola Rd Lewes (19958) *(G-6365)*
Phillips & Cohen Assoc Ltd 302 355-3500
  258 Chapman Rd Ste 205 Newark (19702) *(G-11685)*
Phillips & Cohen Associates (PA) 609 518-9000
  1002 Justison St Wilmington (19801) *(G-19018)*
Phillips & Cohen Associates, Wilmington *Also Called: Phillips & Cohen Associates (G-19018)*
PHILLIPS & COHEN ASSOCIATES, LTD., Newark *Also Called: Phillips & Cohen Assoc Ltd (G-11685)*
Phillips Fabrication 302 875-4424
  32846 Shockley Rd Laurel (19956) *(G-5576)*
Phillips Gldman McLghlin Hall 302 655-4200
  1200 N Broom St Wilmington (19806) *(G-19019)*

Phillips Insulation Inc 302 655-6523
  8 Brookside Dr Wilmington (19804) *(G-19020)*
Phillips Signs Inc 302 629-3550
  20874 Sussex Hwy Seaford (19973) *(G-13347)*
Phillips Truck and Trailer 302 502-5046
  14 W Reybold Dr Middletown (19709) *(G-7446)*
Philly Air Show, Wilmington Also Called: American Air Lease Finance LLC *(G-14424)*
Phippins Cabinetry 302 212-2189
  20807 Coastal Hwy Apt 1 Rehoboth Beach (19971) *(G-12890)*
Phluffy Rides LLC 302 521-0092
  320 Compton Ct Wilmington (19801) *(G-19021)*
Phly LLC 778 882-2391
  500 Delaware Ave Unit 1 Wilmington (19899) *(G-19022)*
PHM Springboard Bidco Inc 919 678-7700
  251 Little Falls Dr Wilmington (19808) *(G-19023)*
Phoenix Construction, Milton Also Called: Phoenix Construction LLC *(G-8685)*
Phoenix Construction LLC 302 363-0453
  16880 Ole Grist Run Milton (19968) *(G-8685)*
Phoenix Ctr For Hlth Wllness L 302 543-5321
  222 Philadelphia Pike Ste 12 Wilmington (19809) *(G-19024)*
Phoenix Fitness LLC 302 786-2435
  124 Lucky Ben Dr Harrington (19952) *(G-4812)*
Phoenix Global Shop LLC 347 227-2519
  8 The Grn Dover (19901) *(G-3314)*
Phoenix Home Theater Inc 302 295-1390
  403 Marsh Ln # 3 Wilmington (19804) *(G-19025)*
Phoenix Intelligence Inc 844 663-4799
  8 The Grn Ste 5638 Dover (19901) *(G-3315)*
Phoenix Nightingale 302 377-6876
  1702 Kirkwood Hwy Ste 2b Wilmington (19805) *(G-19026)*
Phoenix Rehabilitation 302 533-5313
  210 Louviers Dr Newark (19711) *(G-11686)*
Phoenix Restoration, Wilmington Also Called: Phoenix Home Theater Inc *(G-19025)*
Phoenix Trnsp & Logistics Inc (HQ) 302 348-8814
  1000 N West St Ste 1200 Wilmington (19801) *(G-19027)*
Photon Programming 302 328-2925
  58 Stockton Dr New Castle (19720) *(G-9472)*
Phreesia Inc 651 983-0426
  1521 Concord Pike Ste 301-221 Wilmington (19803) *(G-19028)*
Phresh Products, Wilmington Also Called: Personal Health PDT Dev LLC *(G-18987)*
Phrst 302 739-2260
  802 Silver Lake Blvd Ste 200 Dover (19904) *(G-3316)*
Phs Corporate Services Inc 302 571-1128
  1313 N Market St Wilmington (19801) *(G-19029)*
Phyllis M Green 302 354-6986
  329 N Red Lion Ter Bear (19701) *(G-423)*
Physiatrist 302 993-0282
  1101 Twin C Ln Ste 101 Newark (19713) *(G-11687)*
Physiatrist Assoc, Newark Also Called: Anthony Lee Cucuzzella MD *(G-9879)*
Physical Medical Rehab Assoc, Milford Also Called: Center For Neurology *(G-7817)*
Physical Therapist 302 983-4151
  503 Pierce Ct Middletown (19709) *(G-7447)*
Physical Therapy Services Inc (PA) 302 678-3100
  725 Walker Rd Dover (19904) *(G-3317)*
Physical Thrapy Bokkeeping LLC 302 505-5721
  645 Hazlettville Rd Hartly (19953) *(G-4902)*
Physicans Dspnsing Sltons Lwes 302 313-4883
  33664 Bayview Medical Dr Lewes (19958) *(G-6366)*
Physician Dspnsng Solutions 302 734-7246
  390 Mitch Rd Wilmington (19804) *(G-19030)*
Physicians Beauty Group LLC 866 270-9290
  9 E Loockerman St Ste 202 Dover (19901) *(G-3318)*
Physicians Plus Spine & Rehab 302 261-6221
  1701 Pulaski Hwy Bear (19701) *(G-424)*
Physio Therapy Association, Wilmington Also Called: Physiotherapy Associates Inc *(G-19032)*
Physiotherapy Associates Inc 302 674-1269
  642 S Queen St Ste 101 Dover (19904) *(G-3319)*
Physiotherapy Associates Inc 302 655-8989
  2401 Pennsylvania Ave Ste 112 Wilmington (19806) *(G-19031)*
Physiotherapy Associates Inc 610 444-1270
  3411 Silverside Rd Ste 105 Wilmington (19810) *(G-19032)*

Piccard Homes 302 727-5145
  21227 Catalina Cir Rehoboth Beach (19971) *(G-12891)*
Piceno 302 545-6406
  1100 Lovering Ave Apt 908 Wilmington (19806) *(G-19033)*
Pick Winners Inc 516 206-0777
  8 The Grn Ste A Dover (19901) *(G-3320)*
Pico Largo LLC (PA) 915 710-2375
  1000 N West St Ste 1501 Wilmington (19801) *(G-19034)*
Pictsweet Company 302 337-8206
  18215 Wesley Church Rd Bridgeville (19933) *(G-749)*
Piedmont Baseball League Inc 302 234-9437
  102 Wyeth Way Hockessin (19707) *(G-5345)*
Pieholetv LLC 415 287-3566
  16192 Coastal Hwy Lewes (19958) *(G-6367)*
Pientka Masonry Cnstr LLC 302 420-6748
  310 Markus Ct Newark (19713) *(G-11688)*
Pierce Fence Company Inc 302 674-1996
  5751 N Dupont Hwy Dover (19901) *(G-3321)*
Pierce Multi Solutions LLC 302 609-7000
  1 Chestnut Hill Plz Pmb 1210 Newark (19713) *(G-11689)*
Pierce Pt Inc 302 659-0821
  80 Thomas Davis Dr Clayton (19938) *(G-1397)*
Pierce Total Comfort LLC 302 378-7714
  21 S Broad St Middletown (19709) *(G-7448)*
Pierson Culver LLC 302 732-1145
  27517 Hodges Ln Dagsboro (19939) *(G-1496)*
Pierson RE Construction 302 407-3308
  101 Rogers Rd Wilmington (19801) *(G-19035)*
Pieshalaamanda 302 492-3227
  1201 Pony Track Rd Camden Wyoming (19934) *(G-965)*
Piffert Inc 302 407-6185
  19 Lukens Dr Ste 300 Historic New Castle (19720) *(G-5049)*
PII Group Inc 917 455-7438
  8 The Grn Ste A Dover (19901) *(G-3322)*
Piis Global LLC 628 600-5249
  16192 Coastal Hwy Lewes (19958) *(G-6368)*
Pikchabox LLC 302 207-1770
  8 The Grn Ste B Dover (19901) *(G-3323)*
Pike Creek Animal Hospital 302 454-7780
  297 Polly Drummond Hill Rd Newark (19711) *(G-11690)*
Pike Creek Assoc In Wmncare PA, Wilmington Also Called: Pike Creek Assoc In Wns Care *(G-19036)*
Pike Creek Assoc In Wns Care (PA) 302 995-7062
  4600 Linden Hill Rd Ste 102 Wilmington (19808) *(G-19036)*
Pike Creek Automotive Inc 302 998-2234
  2379 Limestone Rd Wilmington (19808) *(G-19037)*
Pike Creek Bike Line Inc 610 747-1200
  4768 Limestone Rd Wilmington (19808) *(G-19038)*
Pike Creek Branch, Wilmington Also Called: Wilmington Savings Fund Soc *(G-20841)*
Pike Creek Computer Company 302 239-5113
  2206 Milltown Rd Wilmington (19808) *(G-19039)*
Pike Creek Construction 302 453-0611
  1124 Mayflower Dr Newark (19711) *(G-11691)*
Pike Creek Counseling 302 898-9229
  5618 Kirkwood Hwy Ste 3 Wilmington (19808) *(G-19040)*
Pike Creek Court Club Inc 302 239-6688
  4905 Mermaid Blvd Ste B Wilmington (19808) *(G-19041)*
Pike Creek Fitness Club, Wilmington Also Called: Pike Creek Court Club Inc *(G-19041)*
Pike Creek Mortgage Group, Newark Also Called: Pike Creek Mortgage Services *(G-11692)*
Pike Creek Mortgage Services (PA) 302 892-2811
  2100 Drummond Plz Bldg 2 Newark (19711) *(G-11692)*
Pike Creek Pediatric Assoc 302 239-7755
  100 S Riding Blvd Wilmington (19808) *(G-19042)*
Pike Creek Psychological Ctr PA (PA) 302 738-6859
  8 Polly Drummond Hill Rd Newark (19711) *(G-11693)*
Pike Creek Software, Wilmington Also Called: Pike Creek Computer Company *(G-19039)*
Piks Company 310 372-5770
  919 N Market St Ste 950 Wilmington (19801) *(G-19043)*
Pilepro Inc 866 666-7453
  300 Delaware Ave Ste 1100 Wilmington (19801) *(G-19044)*
Pillar To Post 410 804-8626
  145 Bay Hill Ln Magnolia (19962) *(G-6774)*

ALPHABETIC SECTION

Pillar To Post.. 908 319-4493
   26244 E Old Gate Dr Millsboro (19966) *(G-8428)*

Pillar Wealth Advisors LLC.. 302 409-3502
   2711 Centerville Rd Ste 110 Wilmington (19808) *(G-19045)*

Pilots Assn For Bay River Del... 302 645-2229
   41 Cape Henlopen Dr Lewes (19958) *(G-6369)*

Pilots4rent Inc... 561 704-2885
   1148 Pulaski Hwy Bear (19701) *(G-425)*

Pimc, Wilmington *Also Called: Blackrock Instnl Mgt Corp (G-14921)*

Pin Up Girls Salon LLC... 302 537-1325
   29 Atlantic Ave Ocean View (19970) *(G-12559)*

Pinckney Wdnger Urban Jyce LLC................................ 302 504-1497
   2 Mill Rd Ste 204 Wilmington (19806) *(G-19046)*

Pine Acres Inc.. 302 945-2000
   34385 Carpenters Way # B Lewes (19958) *(G-6370)*

Pine Breeze Farms Inc... 302 337-7717
   3583 Buck Fever Rd Bridgeville (19933) *(G-750)*

Pine Derivatives Marketing, Wilmington *Also Called: PDM Incorporated (G-18938)*

Pine Valley Corvettes.. 302 834-1268
   108 Pine Valley Dr Middletown (19709) *(G-7449)*

Pineal Consulting Group LLC....................................... 302 446-3794
   8 The Grn Unit 6431 Dover (19901) *(G-3324)*

Pineapple Stitchery.. 302 500-8050
   26005 Governor Stockley Rd Georgetown (19947) *(G-4466)*

Pinevalley Apartments, New Castle *Also Called: Clyde Spinelli (G-8954)*

Pink Ape Logistics Inc.. 210 570-1033
   1911 Concord Pike # 803 Wilmington (19803) *(G-19047)*

Pink App LLC... 408 654-4636
   251 Little Falls Dr Wilmington (19808) *(G-19048)*

Pink Panda, Middletown *Also Called: Healthy Snacks Holdings Inc (G-7201)*

Pinkerton Foundation... 800 839-1754
   501 Silverside Rd Wilmington (19809) *(G-19049)*

Pinnacle Garage Door Co LLC..................................... 302 505-4531
   260 Robbins Rd Frederica (19946) *(G-4180)*

Pinnacle Home Improvement LLC................................ 302 569-5311
   17780 Meadow Dr Bridgeville (19933) *(G-751)*

Pinnacle Restoration Corp.. 302 650-0520
   14 Murphy Rd Wilmington (19803) *(G-19050)*

Pinnacle Rhbilitation Hlth Ctr.. 302 653-5085
   3034 S Dupont Blvd Smyrna (19977) *(G-13847)*

Pintalk Inc.. 844 386-0178
   2035 Sunset Lake Rd Ste B2 Newark (19702) *(G-11694)*

Pinter Law LLC.. 302 409-0089
   5586 Kirkwood Hwy Wilmington (19808) *(G-19051)*

Pioneer Behavioral Health, New Castle *Also Called: Phc Inc (G-9470)*

Pioneer Distributors Inc.. 302 644-0791
   16612 Howard Millman Ln Milton (19968) *(G-8686)*

Pioneer Fence Co Inc... 302 998-2892
   109 S John St Wilmington (19804) *(G-19052)*

Pioneer House... 302 286-0892
   413 Salem Church Rd Newark (19702) *(G-11695)*

Pioneer Natural Resources Co...................................... 972 444-9001
   1209 N Orange St Wilmington (19801) *(G-19053)*

Pioneer Products.. 302 678-0331
   752 Long Point Rd Dover (19901) *(G-3325)*

Pipe Pros Jetting & Plbg LLC....................................... 302 562-0522
   479 Blackbird Landing Rd Townsend (19734) *(G-14052)*

Pipeline Funding Company LLC................................... 302 421-2287
   2 Greenville Crossing Wilmington (19807) *(G-19054)*

Piper, Glenn T, Lewes *Also Called: Landmark Associates of Del (G-6176)*

Piranha Sports LLC... 302 893-1997
   230 Mariners Way Bear (19701) *(G-426)*

Pirate Pools LLC.. 302 519-0624
   31325 Red Mill Cir Lewes (19958) *(G-6371)*

Pirates of Lewes Expeditions....................................... 302 249-3538
   400 Anglers Rd Lewes (19958) *(G-6372)*

Pirulos Child Care Center LLC..................................... 302 836-3520
   799 Salem Church Rd Newark (19702) *(G-11696)*

Pitch Black Sealcoating LLC.. 302 824-8135
   12 Toby Ct Wilmington (19808) *(G-19055)*

Pivot Occupational Health LLC.................................... 302 368-5100
   15 Omega Dr Bldg K Newark (19713) *(G-11697)*

Pivot Physical Therapy... 302 730-4800
   1015 S Governors Ave Dover (19904) *(G-3326)*

Pivot Physical Therapy... 302 449-7792
   120 Sandhill Dr Middletown (19709) *(G-7450)*

Pivot Physical Therapy... 302 504-6195
   4512 Kirkwood Hwy Wilmington (19808) *(G-19056)*

Pivotal Medical... 302 299-5795
   413 Salt Pond Rd Bethany Beach (19930) *(G-627)*

Pixel Ninja Studios LLC.. 218 398-1374
   1007 N Orange St Fl 4 Wilmington (19801) *(G-19057)*

Pixorize, Wilmington *Also Called: Pixorize Inc (G-19058)*

Pixorize Inc.. 737 529-4404
   251 Little Falls Dr Wilmington (19808) *(G-19058)*

Pixstar Inc
   913 N Market St Ste 200 Wilmington (19801) *(G-19059)*

Pixstory Global Holding Inc.. 202 615-6777
   16192 Coastal Hwy Lewes (19958) *(G-6373)*

Pixxy Solutions LLC... 631 609-6686
   2093 Philadelphia Pike # 4 Claymont (19703) *(G-1263)*

Pizazz Beauty Studio... 302 761-9820
   4001 N Market St Wilmington (19802) *(G-19060)*

Pizza King, Laurel *Also Called: Baynum Enterprises Inc (G-5467)*

Pizza King, Seaford *Also Called: Baynum Enterprises Inc (G-13078)*

Pizzadili Partners LLC.. 302 284-9463
   1683 Peach Basket Rd Felton (19943) *(G-4009)*

PJ Fitzpatrick Inc (PA).. 302 325-2360
   21 Industrial Blvd New Castle (19720) *(G-9473)*

Pjhj LLC... 302 645-2159
   17569 Nassau Commons Blvd Lewes (19958) *(G-6374)*

Pjk Golf Operations LLC... 302 376-6500
   1 Wittington Way Middletown (19709) *(G-7451)*

Pk & Associates Group Inc... 302 394-9052
   28b Trolley Sq Wilmington (19806) *(G-19061)*

Pk Fire LLC.. 253 880-9025
   8 The Grn Dover (19901) *(G-3327)*

Pkg LLC... 269 651-8640
   251 Little Falls Dr Wilmington (19808) *(G-19062)*

Pks & Company PA.. 302 645-5757
   1143 Savannah Rd Ste 1 Lewes (19958) *(G-6375)*

Pks Food, Wilmington *Also Called: P-Ks Wholesale Grocer Inc (G-18855)*

Placers, Newark *Also Called: Placers Inc of Delaware (G-11698)*

Placers Inc of Delaware.. 302 709-0973
   850 Library Ave Ste 106 Newark (19711) *(G-11698)*

Placidify Inc.. 833 752-2434
   16192 Coastal Hwy Lewes (19958) *(G-6376)*

Plain & Fancy Inc... 302 656-9901
   5716 Kennett Pike Ste E Wilmington (19807) *(G-19063)*

Plain & Fancy Interiors, Wilmington *Also Called: Plain & Fancy Inc (G-19063)*

Plan USA, Wilmington *Also Called: Inc Plan (usa) (G-17297)*

Plane James and Janes LLC.. 267 716-6723
   606 E Glen Mare Dr Middletown (19709) *(G-7452)*

Plane Software Inc... 857 693-9321
   651 N Broad St Ste 201 Middletown (19709) *(G-7453)*

Planet Fitness.. 302 378-2777
   703 N Broad St Middletown (19709) *(G-7454)*

Planet Fitness.. 302 501-7220
   148 Sunset Blvd New Castle (19720) *(G-9474)*

Planet Fitness.. 302 262-8676
   800 Norman Eskridge Hwy Seaford (19973) *(G-13348)*

Planet Fitness.. 302 543-5604
   900 N Madison St Wilmington (19801) *(G-19064)*

Planet Fitness, Dover *Also Called: Mar Fitness Enterprises Inc (G-3016)*

Planet Fitness, Newark *Also Called: Jacta Alea Est LLC (G-11083)*

Planet Fitness Inc.. 302 483-7740
   2201 Farrand Dr Wilmington (19808) *(G-19065)*

Planet Iot Inc.. 314 585-9924
   651 N Broad St Ste 206 Middletown (19709) *(G-7455)*

Planet Payment Inc (PA).. 516 670-3200
   100 W Commons Blvd Ste 200 New Castle (19720) *(G-9475)*

Planet Payment Solutions Inc...................................... 516 670-3200
   100 W Commons Blvd Ste 200 New Castle (19720) *(G-9476)*

Planet X Skateboards 484 886-9287
2400 Shellpot Dr Wilmington (19803) *(G-19066)*

Planiversity LLC 315 498-0986
919 N Market St Ste 425 Wilmington (19801) *(G-19067)*

Planke App LLC (PA) 607 287-0794
1300 Del Ave Ste 210a Wilmington (19806) *(G-19068)*

Planned Parenthood of Delaware 302 731-7801
140 E Delaware Ave Newark (19711) *(G-11699)*

Planned Parenthood of Delaware (PA) 302 655-7293
625 N Shipley St Wilmington (19801) *(G-19069)*

Planned Poultry Renovation 302 875-4196
28667 Sussex Hwy Laurel (19956) *(G-5577)*

Plant Retrievers Whl Nurs 302 337-9833
13418 Seashore Hwy Georgetown (19947) *(G-4467)*

Plantation Lakes Homeowners 302 934-5200
29787 Plantation Lakes Blvd Millsboro (19966) *(G-8429)*

Plasti Pallets Corp 302 737-1977
6 Albe Dr Christiana (19702) *(G-1007)*

Plastic Csmtc Priph Nrve Srger 302 645-7737
1400 Savannah Rd Lewes (19958) *(G-6377)*

Plastic Free Delaware Inc 302 981-1950
404 Snuff Mill Rd Wilmington (19807) *(G-19070)*

Platform Gallery LLC 844 244-2940
1201 N Market St Ste 111 Wilmington (19801) *(G-19071)*

Platformavr Inc 302 330-8980
8 The Grn Ste 5915 Dover (19901) *(G-3328)*

Platinum (us) Acquisition LLC (DH) 404 414-7768
1209 N Orange St Wilmington (19801) *(G-19072)*

Platinum Cnstr Renovations LLC 302 288-0670
8 The Grn Ste 13137 Dover (19901) *(G-3329)*

Platinum Heritage Entps LLC 469 563-0411
8 The Grn Ste A Dover (19901) *(G-3330)*

Platinum LLC 302 492-1850
523 Halltown Rd Marydel (19964) *(G-6809)*

Platinum Logistics LLC 412 708-6476
35 Salem Church Rd Ste 80 Newark (19713) *(G-11700)*

Platinum Plus Enterprise, Middletown *Also Called: Platinum Plus Enterprise LLC (G-7456)*

Platinum Plus Enterprise LLC 302 200-2257
405 Champs Ln Middletown (19709) *(G-7456)*

Platinum Roofs 302 226-4510
29029 Lewes Georgetown Hwy Lewes (19958) *(G-6378)*

Platinum Salon LLC 302 653-6125
599 Jimmy Dr Ste 15 Smyrna (19977) *(G-13848)*

Platinum US Distribution Inc 905 364-8713
1201 N Orange St Ste 741 Wilmington (19801) *(G-19073)*

Platinum World LLC 302 321-5040
8 The Grn Ste 7679 Dover (19901) *(G-3331)*

Play Better Inc 407 815-2719
651 N Broad St Ste 206 Middletown (19709) *(G-7457)*

Play By Play LLC 302 703-7670
24a Trolley Sq Ste 1389 Wilmington (19806) *(G-19074)*

Play For Good Inc 312 520-9788
3411 Silverside Rd 104r Wilmington (19810) *(G-19075)*

Play US Media LLC 302 924-5034
8 The Grn Ste 8136 Dover (19901) *(G-3332)*

Playhouse Nursery School 302 747-7007
1925 S Dupont Hwy Dover (19901) *(G-3333)*

Playhouse On Rodney Square, Wilmington *Also Called: Eidp Inc (G-16325)*

Playphone Inc 415 307-0246
3500 S Dupont Hwy Dover (19901) *(G-3334)*

Playpower Labs Inc 917 544-4171
8 The Grn Ste 12465 Dover (19901) *(G-3335)*

Playtex Manufacturing Inc (DH) 302 678-6000
50 N Dupont Hwy Dover (19901) *(G-3336)*

Playtex Marketing Corp 302 678-6000
800 Silver Lake Blvd Ste 103 Dover (19904) *(G-3337)*

Plaza Apartments, Wilmington *Also Called: Stoltz Realty Co (G-20078)*

Plaza Fuel 302 275-6242
2213 Concord Pike Wilmington (19803) *(G-19076)*

Plaza Mexico 301 643-5701
26506 Victorias Landing Rd Unit 5 Millsboro (19966) *(G-8430)*

Pleasant Distributors, Wilmington *Also Called: P D Supply Inc (G-18852)*

Pleasant Hill Auto Svc LLC 302 376-6712
34 Spruce Ct Smyrna (19977) *(G-13849)*

Pleasant Hill Bowling Alley, Wilmington *Also Called: Pleasant Hill Lanes Inc (G-19077)*

Pleasant Hill Lanes Inc 302 998-8811
1001 W Newport Pike Wilmington (19804) *(G-19077)*

Plenteous Consulting LLC 724 325-1660
2093 Philadelphia Pike Claymont (19703) *(G-1264)*

Plentyy Cleaning, Dover *Also Called: Prolific Professionals LLC (G-3380)*

Plexus Fitness 302 654-9642
20 Montchanin Rd Ste 60 Wilmington (19807) *(G-19078)*

Pllal International LLC 786 235-7800
251 Little Falls Dr Wilmington (19808) *(G-19079)*

Ploeners Automotive Pdts Co 302 655-4418
510 S Market St Wilmington (19801) *(G-19080)*

Plotly (us) Inc 781 974-4062
2801 Cntrvlle Rd Fl 1pmb Flr 1 Wilmington (19808) *(G-19081)*

Plp Financial, Seaford *Also Called: Professional Leasing Inc (G-13359)*

Pluck Hvac 302 836-8596
105 Ponder Ct Bear (19701) *(G-427)*

Plug Transportation LLC 302 644-5511
600 N Broad St Ste 5483 Middletown (19709) *(G-7458)*

Plugdin Inc 347 726-1831
8 The Grn Ste A Dover (19901) *(G-3338)*

Plugilo Inc 628 202-4444
200 Continental Dr # 401 Newark (19713) *(G-11701)*

Plumbers Ppfitters Local Un 74 .... 302 636-7400
201 Executive Dr Newark (19702) *(G-11702)*

Plumbing, Wilmington *Also Called: J Stachon Plumbing LLC (G-17464)*

Plumbing and Mechanical Contr, Dover *Also Called: C & N Services LLC (G-2005)*

Plumbing Enterprises LLC 302 515-4620
37232 Lighthouse Rd Ste 463 Selbyville (19975) *(G-13591)*

Plume Serum LLC 302 697-9044
1059 Ponderosa Dr Magnolia (19962) *(G-6775)*

Plummer Co Inc 302 227-5000
20184 Coastal Hwy Rehoboth Beach (19971) *(G-12892)*

Pluribus Technologies Inc 302 373-2670
3 Fairfield Dr Newark (19711) *(G-11703)*

Plushbeds Inc (PA) 888 758-7423
1201 N Orange St Ste 7058 Wilmington (19801) *(G-19082)*

Pluspoint Inc 305 901-2676
2810 N Church St Wilmington (19802) *(G-19083)*

Plx Pharma Winddown Corp (PA) 973 381-7408
8 The Grn Ste 11895 Dover (19901) *(G-3339)*

Ply Fashion Inc 323 723-5337
055 Limestone Rd Ste 200-C Wilmington (19808) *(G-19084)*

Plyma Entertainment LLC 302 248-4567
8 The Grn Ste R Dover (19901) *(G-3340)*

PM China Inc 302 999-4083
974 Centre Rd Wilmington (19805) *(G-19085)*

PM Taiwan Inc (HQ) 302 999-4083
974 Centre Rd Wilmington (19805) *(G-19086)*

Pmb Associates LLC 302 436-0111
37816 Eagle Ln Unit 325 Selbyville (19975) *(G-13592)*

Pmbtexas Enterprises LLC 254 993-1530
254 Chapman Rd Ste 208 Newark (19702) *(G-11704)*

PMC Publications LLC 302 268-4480
201 Michelle Ct Newark (19711) *(G-11705)*

Pmsa It Services LLC 301 806-5163
36520 Harmon Bay Blvd Rehoboth Beach (19971) *(G-12893)*

Pna Title Services LLC 302 294-6219
5602 Kirkwood Hwy Wilmington (19808) *(G-19087)*

PNC, Bear *Also Called: PNC Bank National Association (G-428)*

PNC, Bridgeville *Also Called: PNC Bank National Association (G-752)*

PNC, Dover *Also Called: PNC Bank National Association (G-3341)*

PNC, Dover *Also Called: PNC Bank National Association (G-3342)*

PNC, Georgetown *Also Called: PNC Bank National Association (G-4468)*

PNC, Lewes *Also Called: PNC Bank National Association (G-6379)*

PNC, Middletown *Also Called: PNC Bank National Association (G-7459)*

PNC, Milford *Also Called: PNC Bank National Association (G-8050)*

ALPHABETIC SECTION

PNC, Millsboro *Also Called: PNC Bank National Association (G-8431)*
PNC, New Castle *Also Called: PNC Bank National Association (G-9477)*
PNC, New Castle *Also Called: PNC Bank National Association (G-9478)*
PNC, Newark *Also Called: PNC Bank National Association (G-11706)*
PNC, Seaford *Also Called: PNC Bank National Association (G-13349)*
PNC, Selbyville *Also Called: PNC Bank National Association (G-13593)*
PNC, Smyrna *Also Called: PNC Bank National Association (G-13850)*
PNC, Wilmington *Also Called: PNC Bancorp Inc (G-19088)*
PNC, Wilmington *Also Called: PNC Bank National Association (G-19089)*
PNC, Wilmington *Also Called: PNC Bank National Association (G-19090)*
PNC, Wilmington *Also Called: PNC Bank National Association (G-19091)*
PNC, Wilmington *Also Called: PNC Bank National Association (G-19092)*
PNC, Wilmington *Also Called: PNC Bank National Association (G-19093)*
PNC, Wilmington *Also Called: PNC Bank National Association (G-19094)*
PNC, Wilmington *Also Called: PNC Bank National Association (G-19095)*
PNC, Wilmington *Also Called: PNC Bank Delaware (G-19096)*
PNC, Wilmington *Also Called: PNC Holding LLC (G-19098)*
PNC, Wilmington *Also Called: PNC National Bank of Delaware (G-19099)*
PNC Bancorp Inc (HQ) 302 427-5896
  300 Delaware Ave Wilmington (19801) *(G-19088)*
PNC Bank National Association 302 832-8750
  250 Foxhunt Dr Bear (19701) *(G-428)*
PNC Bank National Association 302 337-3500
  100 S Laws St Bridgeville (19933) *(G-752)*
PNC Bank National Association 302 735-2160
  87 Greentree Dr Dover (19904) *(G-3341)*
PNC Bank National Association 302 735-3117
  3 Loockerman Plz Frnt Dover (19901) *(G-3342)*
PNC Bank National Association 302 855-0400
  Rt 113 Alfred St Georgetown (19947) *(G-4468)*
PNC Bank National Association 302 645-4500
  17725 Coastal Hwy Lewes (19958) *(G-6379)*
PNC Bank National Association 302 378-4441
  460 W Main St Middletown (19709) *(G-7459)*
PNC Bank National Association 302 422-1015
  655 N Dupont Blvd Milford (19963) *(G-8050)*
PNC Bank National Association 302 934-3106
  104 Main St Millsboro (19966) *(G-8431)*
PNC Bank National Association 302 326-4710
  1 Penn Mart Shopping Ctr New Castle (19720) *(G-9477)*
PNC Bank National Association 302 326-4701
  1 E Basin Rte New Castle (19720) *(G-9478)*
PNC Bank National Association 302 733-7190
  4643 Ogletown Stanton Rd Newark (19713) *(G-11706)*
PNC Bank National Association 302 629-5000
  1200 W Stein Hwy Seaford (19973) *(G-13349)*
PNC Bank National Association 302 436-5400
  31231 Americana Pkwy Selbyville (19975) *(G-13593)*
PNC Bank National Association 302 653-2475
  7 S Main St Smyrna (19977) *(G-13850)*
PNC Bank National Association 302 235-4010
  5325 Limestone Rd Wilmington (19808) *(G-19089)*
PNC Bank National Association 302 993-3000
  2203 Kirkwood Hwy Wilmington (19805) *(G-19090)*
PNC Bank National Association 302 994-6337
  2751 Centerville Rd Ste 101 Wilmington (19808) *(G-19091)*
PNC Bank National Association 302 429-2266
  222 Delaware Ave Wilmington (19801) *(G-19092)*
PNC Bank National Association 302 479-4529
  1704 Marsh Rd Wilmington (19810) *(G-19093)*
PNC Bank National Association 302 479-4520
  4111 Concord Pike Wilmington (19803) *(G-19094)*
PNC Bank National Association 302 993-3013
  4725 Kirkwood Hwy Wilmington (19808) *(G-19095)*
PNC Bank Delaware 302 655-7221
  222 Delaware Ave Lbby Wilmington (19801) *(G-19096)*
PNC Financial, Wilmington *Also Called: PNC Financial Svcs Group Inc (G-19097)*
PNC Financial Svcs Group Inc 302 429-1364
  300 Delaware Ave Ste 1600 Wilmington (19801) *(G-19097)*
PNC Holding LLC (HQ) 302 427-5897
  300 Delaware Ave Ste 304 Wilmington (19801) *(G-19098)*
PNC National Bank of Delaware (DH) 302 479-4529
  300 Bellevue Pkwy Ste 200 Wilmington (19809) *(G-19099)*
Pneuma Wellness & Spa LLC 302 990-8907
  149 S Governors Ave Dover (19904) *(G-3343)*
Pobbles Corporation 510 371-1627
  8 The Grn Dover (19901) *(G-3344)*
Poc Inc 415 853-4762
  8 The Grn Ste 15060 Dover (19901) *(G-3345)*
Pocket FM, Lewes *Also Called: Pocket FM Corp (G-6380)*
Pocket FM Corp 408 896-7038
  16192 Coastal Hwy Lewes (19958) *(G-6380)*
Pods Inc New Castle 856 217-4685
  299 Anchor Mill Rd Historic New Castle (19720) *(G-5050)*
Point Coffee Shop and Bakery 302 260-9734
  722 Rehoboth Ave Rehoboth Beach (19971) *(G-12894)*
Point Eght Third Prdctions LLC (PA) 302 317-9419
  1201 N Market St Ste 111 Wilmington (19801) *(G-19100)*
Point Hope Brain Injury Spport 302 731-7676
  34 Blevins Dr Ste 5 New Castle (19720) *(G-9479)*
Point of Hope Inc 302 731-7676
  34 Blevins Dr Ste 5 New Castle (19720) *(G-9480)*
Point To Point Tech USA Inc 302 359-5343
  503 Interchange Blvd Newark (19711) *(G-11707)*
Pointe Condominiums 302 656-2018
  1702 N Park Dr Wilmington (19806) *(G-19101)*
Pointe Snaps 260 602-0898
  1000 Marsh Rd Wilmington (19803) *(G-19102)*
Poland & Sullivan Insur Inc 302 738-3535
  106 Haines St Newark (19711) *(G-11708)*
Polar Signals Inc (PA) 765 679-9318
  2093 Philadelphia Pike Claymont (19703) *(G-1265)*
Polar Strategy Inc 703 628-0001
  16192 Coastal Hwy Lewes (19958) *(G-6381)*
Polaro Inc 415 240-0442
  8 The Grn Ste E Dover (19901) *(G-3346)*
Polarstar Engineering & Mch 302 368-4639
  5 Garfield Way Ste B Newark (19713) *(G-11709)*
Pole Buildings Unlimited 302 399-3058
  117 W Reed St Dover (19904) *(G-3347)*
Pole Press LLC 260 209-4628
  2035 Sunset Lake Rd Ste B2 Newark (19702) *(G-11710)*
Police & Fire Rod & Gun Club 302 655-0304
  1 Glen Ave New Castle (19720) *(G-9481)*
Police Athc Leag Wlmington Inc 302 764-6170
  3707 N Market St Wilmington (19802) *(G-19103)*
Police Athletic League 302 834-8460
  250 5th St Delaware City (19706) *(G-1552)*
Police Athletic League Del Inc (PA) 302 656-9501
  26 Karlyn Dr New Castle (19720) *(G-9482)*
Police Athletic League of De 302 792-0930
  4 S Cliffe Dr Wilmington (19809) *(G-19104)*
Police Offcer Mses Wlker Jr In 215 268-4146
  131 Nob Hill Rd Dover (19901) *(G-3348)*
Poliquicks LLC 512 915-7919
  2810 N Church St Wilmington (19802) *(G-19105)*
Poliquin Firm LLC 302 702-5501
  1475 S Governors Ave Dover (19904) *(G-3349)*
Polish American Civic Assn 302 652-9324
  618 S Franklin St Wilmington (19805) *(G-19106)*
Polish Library Association 302 652-9555
  433 S Van Buren St Wilmington (19805) *(G-19107)*
Polish Nat Aliance of The US 302 658-3324
  100 6th Ave Wilmington (19805) *(G-19108)*
Polite Construction Jay 302 328-0390
  138 Louise Rd New Castle (19720) *(G-9483)*
Polkamotion Rehoboth 410 729-9697
  229 Rehoboth Ave Rehoboth Beach (19971) *(G-12895)*
Pollintion Capitl Partners LLC 872 201-1168
  251 Little Falls Dr Wilmington (19808) *(G-19109)*

Poloniex LLC

ALPHABETIC SECTION

Poloniex LLC 302 518-6536
   1013 Centre Rd Ste 403b Wilmington (19805) *(G-19110)*

Polsinelli Shalton Flanni 302 654-2984
   222 Delaware Ave Wilmington (19801) *(G-19111)*

Polycom Inc 302 420-8618
   101 Watford Rd Wilmington (19808) *(G-19112)*

Polydel Corporation 302 655-8200
   820 N Buttonwood St Wilmington (19801) *(G-19113)*

Polyjohn Acquisition LLC 800 292-1305
   251 Little Falls Dr Wilmington (19808) *(G-19114)*

Polymart Inc 302 656-1470
   710 Yorklyn Rd Ste 200 Hockessin (19707) *(G-5346)*

Polymer Technologies Inc (PA) 302 738-9001
   420 Corporate Blvd Newark (19702) *(G-11711)*

Polytechnic Resources Inc 302 629-4221
   185 Kent Dr Seaford (19973) *(G-13350)*

Pony Run Kitchens, Hartly *Also Called: Pony Run Kitchens LLC (G-4903)*

Pony Run Kitchens LLC 302 492-3006
   5066 Westville Rd Hartly (19953) *(G-4903)*

Pony Up Inc 323 205-7669
   8 The Grn Dover (19901) *(G-3350)*

Pool Man Inc 302 737-8696
   470 Hopkins Bridge Rd Newark (19711) *(G-11712)*

Pools & Spas Unlimited Milford, Milford *Also Called: Henderson Services Inc (G-7926)*

Poolside Cnstr & Renovation 302 436-9711
   Route 54 Selbyville (19975) *(G-13594)*

Poooliprint, Claymont *Also Called: Drone Consulting Pros Inc (G-1124)*

Poore's Propane Gas Service, Dover *Also Called: Petroleum Equipment Inc (G-3308)*

Poores Propane, Dover *Also Called: Service Oil Company (G-3535)*

Poores Propane Gas Service, Dover *Also Called: Petroleum Equipment Inc (G-3307)*

Poorman Auto 302 628-0404
   11057 Henry Dr Seaford (19973) *(G-13351)*

Pop Pop Magic Clown 302 764-5494
   1511 Governor House Cir Wilmington (19809) *(G-19115)*

Pop-A-Docs All Ntral Hrbal Spp 302 622-5788
   318 New Castle Ave Wilmington (19801) *(G-19116)*

Pop-A-Lock Wilmington 866 866-6368
   16 Lehigh Rd Wilmington (19808) *(G-19117)*

Popeyco LLC 202 368-3842
   16192 Coastal Hwy Lewes (19958) *(G-6382)*

Popsycle LLC 202 831-0211
   200 Continental Dr Ste 4012450 Newark (19713) *(G-11713)*

Populus LLC 412 973-2340
   8 The Grn Ste R Dover (19901) *(G-3351)*

Porro Realty Group 302 384-6056
   1301 N Scott St Wilmington (19806) *(G-19118)*

Porsche Club America Del Reg 302 588-3511
   201 Louis Ln Hockessin (19707) *(G-5347)*

Port Contractors Inc (PA) 302 655-7300
   1 Hausel Rd Wilmington (19801) *(G-19119)*

Port Del-Mar-Va Inc 302 227-7409
   260 Port Delmarva Rehoboth Beach (19971) *(G-12896)*

Port Lewes Assoc Unit Owner 302 645-6110
   34382 Carpenters Way Ste 6 Lewes (19958) *(G-6383)*

Port of Wilmington, Wilmington *Also Called: Diamond State Port Corporation (G-16055)*

Port To Port Intl Corp 302 654-2444
   32 Pyles Ln New Castle (19720) *(G-9484)*

Port To Port Logistics LLC 302 654-2444
   32 Pyles Ln New Castle (19720) *(G-9485)*

Portable Pilot Solutions LLC 302 644-2775
   28 Cripple Creek Run Milton (19968) *(G-8687)*

Portable Sheds Paul Yoder 302 734-2681
   1288 Rose Valley School Rd Dover (19904) *(G-3352)*

Porter Broadcasting 302 535-8809
   1991 S State St Dover (19901) *(G-3353)*

Porter Nissan Buick Newark 302 368-6300
   600 Ogletown Rd Newark (19711) *(G-11714)*

Porter Sand & Gravel Inc 302 335-5132
   640 Sandbox Rd Harrington (19952) *(G-4813)*

Portrait Innovations Inc 302 477-1696
   5601 Concord Pike Ste D Wilmington (19803) *(G-19120)*

Pos & Merchant Services LLC 302 356-3030
   2233 Inwood Rd Wilmington (19810) *(G-19121)*

Poseidon Adventures Inc 302 533-7815
   80 Albe Dr Newark (19702) *(G-11715)*

Posh Cupcake 302 234-4451
   50 Westwoods Blvd Hockessin (19707) *(G-5348)*

Posh Salon 302 655-7000
   41 Harlech Dr Wilmington (19807) *(G-19122)*

Poshlife Acquisitions LLC 516 376-7402
   8 The Grn Ste 4000 Dover (19901) *(G-3354)*

Poshsistahs Hair LLC 302 464-2469
   912 Janvier Ct Middletown (19709) *(G-7460)*

Posidon Adventure Inc 302 543-5024
   3301 Lancaster Pike Ste 5a Wilmington (19805) *(G-19123)*

Positioneering LLC 302 415-3200
   19c Trolley Sq Wilmington (19806) *(G-19124)*

Positive Directions II LLC 302 654-9444
   240 N James St Wilmington (19804) *(G-19125)*

Positive Energy Electric 267 902-1655
   21 Holcomb Ln Historic New Castle (19720) *(G-5051)*

Positive Growth Alliance Inc 302 381-1610
   28612 Cynthia Marie Dr Millsboro (19966) *(G-8432)*

Positive Otlook Gdnce Svcs Inc 240 761-3460
   110 Thomas Harmon Dr Camden (19934) *(G-885)*

Positive Results Cleaning Inc 302 575-1146
   338 B And O Ln Wilmington (19804) *(G-19126)*

Positive Vibes Only Brand 302 500-1369
   2 Colony Blvd Apt 115 Wilmington (19802) *(G-19127)*

Positron Access Solutions Inc 888 577-5254
   2801 Centerville Rd Fl 1 Pmb 638 Wilmington (19808) *(G-19128)*

Post, Wilmington *Also Called: Post Media Inc (G-19129)*

POST 2, Bear *Also Called: Delaware Veterans Inc (G-159)*

Post Acute Medical LLC 717 731-9660
   1240 Mckee Rd Dover (19904) *(G-3355)*

Post Media Inc 203 244-8424
   4023 Kennett Pike Pmb 50314 Wilmington (19807) *(G-19129)*

Post Rdge Prsrvation Assoc LLC 302 761-7303
   4 Denny Rd Wilmington (19809) *(G-19130)*

Post Shipper LLC 302 444-8144
   601 Carson Dr Bear (19701) *(G-429)*

Postal Connections Inc 302 239-1129
   7209 Lancaster Pike Hockessin (19707) *(G-5349)*

Postimpressions Incorporated 302 656-2271
   1400 Maryland Ave Wilmington (19805) *(G-19131)*

Postly Technologies Inc 315 215-0320
   651 N Broad St Ste 201 Middletown (19709) *(G-7461)*

Pot-Nets, Millsboro *Also Called: Pot-Nets Bywood Vacation Rentl (G-8434)*

Pot-Nets Bayside LLC 302 945-9300
   34026 Annas Way Unit 1 Millsboro (19966) *(G-8433)*

Pot-Nets Bywood Vacation Rentl 302 945-9300
   34026 Annas Way Unit 2 Millsboro (19966) *(G-8434)*

Potomac Chesapeake Assn For C 302 225-6248
   4701 Limestone Rd Wilmington (19808) *(G-19132)*

Potter Anderson & Corroon 302 984-6078
   1313 N Market St Fl 6 Wilmington (19801) *(G-19133)*

Potter Anderson & Corroon LLP 302 984-6000
   1313 N Market St Wilmington (19801) *(G-19134)*

Potts Wldg Boiler Repr Co Inc (HQ) 302 453-2550
   1901 Ogletown Rd Newark (19711) *(G-11716)*

Poured Foundations of De Inc 302 234-2050
   409 Capitol Trl Newark (19711) *(G-11717)*

Powell Construction L L C 302 745-1146
   100 Murrays Ln Georgetown (19947) *(G-4469)*

Powell Life Skills Inc 302 378-2706
   209 Glenshee Dr Townsend (19734) *(G-14053)*

Powells General Services 302 384-7817
   706 W 38th St Wilmington (19802) *(G-19135)*

Power Brokers Holdings LLC 800 901-8483
   3 Longacre Ct Hockessin (19707) *(G-5350)*

Power Control Technologies Inc 203 560-2806
   42 Butternut Ct Wilmington (19810) *(G-19136)*

ALPHABETIC SECTION — Preferred Fire Protection

Power Delivery Solutions LLC 302 260-3114
  100 Commerce Dr Ste 201 Newark (19713) *(G-11718)*
Power Electronics Inc 302 653-4822
  310 S Bassett St Clayton (19938) *(G-1398)*
Power Financial Wellness Inc (PA) 313 413-2345
  1209 N Orange St Wilmington (19801) *(G-19137)*
Power House Global Entps Inc 215 660-0071
  362 Macdonald Close Bear (19701) *(G-430)*
Power On, Lewes *Also Called: Power On US Inc (G-6384)*
Power On US Inc 212 317-1010
  16192 Coastal Hwy Lewes (19958) *(G-6384)*
Power Over Pain Crps Fndtion I 302 983-6412
  1 Ferris Ct New Castle (19720) *(G-9486)*
Power Plus Elec Contg Inc 302 736-5070
  10 Janis Dr Dover (19901) *(G-3356)*
Power Trans Inc 302 337-3016
  9029 Fawn Rd Bridgeville (19933) *(G-753)*
Power Trans Inc 302 918-7674
  706 Carson Dr Bear (19701) *(G-431)*
Power Transmission Svcs Inc 302 378-7925
  501 Industrial Dr Middletown (19709) *(G-7462)*
Power Washing, Selbyville *Also Called: All Clean Power Washing (G-13459)*
Powerback Service LLC 302 934-1901
  30148 Mitchell St Millsboro (19966) *(G-8435)*
Powercomm LLC 302 235-8922
  6 Hadco Rd Unit 1 Wilmington (19804) *(G-19138)*
Powerhouse Gym 302 262-0262
  620 W Stein Hwy Seaford (19973) *(G-13352)*
Powers Appraising LLC (PA) 410 337-8664
  324 Laurel St Rehoboth Beach (19971) *(G-12897)*
Powers Interactive Digital LLC 267 334-6306
  16192 Coastal Hwy Lewes (19958) *(G-6385)*
Powers Publishing Group 302 519-8575
  29549 Whitstone Ln Millsboro (19966) *(G-8436)*
Powertrain Technology Inc 302 368-4900
  2101 Ogletown Rd Newark (19711) *(G-11719)*
Powwa Electric 302 236-2649
  10997 Pit Rd Seaford (19973) *(G-13353)*
Powwa Electric, Seaford *Also Called: Powwa Electric (G-13353)*
Pp of De 252 393-3691
  625 N Shipley St Wilmington (19801) *(G-19139)*
Ppc Coatings, Wilmington *Also Called: Modified Thermoset Resins Inc (G-18399)*
PPG Architectural Finishes Inc 302 736-6081
  177 179 N Dupont Hwy Dover (19901) *(G-3357)*
PPG Architectural Finishes Inc 302 454-9091
  3613 Kirkwood Hwy Ste A Wilmington (19808) *(G-19140)*
PPG Architectural Finishes Inc 302 762-0555
  516 Philadelphia Pike Wilmington (19809) *(G-19141)*
Ppmi Inc 302 584-1972
  200 Canonero Dr Bear (19701) *(G-432)*
PQ Holding Inc 302 478-6160
  3411 Silverside Rd Wilmington (19810) *(G-19142)*
Pqs Landscaping 302 690-6505
  19 Caxton Dr New Castle (19720) *(G-9487)*
Practical Systems 302 753-8885
  106 Avignon Ct Newark (19702) *(G-11720)*
Practice Without Pressure 302 635-7837
  3105 Limestone Rd Wilmington (19808) *(G-19143)*
Pradhan Energy Projects 305 428-2123
  104 Hawthorne Ct W Hockessin (19707) *(G-5351)*
Praize Fitness 302 312-7416
  38 Saint George Ter Bear (19701) *(G-433)*
Praktikaai Co 959 300-0719
  919 N Market St Wilmington (19801) *(G-19144)*
Prana Bodyworks 302 229-3880
  112 South Rd Wilmington (19809) *(G-19145)*
Pratcher Krayer LLC 302 803-5291
  1000 N West St Fl 10 Wilmington (19801) *(G-19146)*
Pratt-Fields Home Please Inc 215 868-9028
  220 Remi Dr New Castle (19720) *(G-9488)*
Praval Technologies LLC 206 693-2443
  1000 N West St Ste 1200 Wilmington (19801) *(G-19147)*
Praxair, Wilmington *Also Called: Linde Gas & Equipment Inc (G-17923)*
PRC, Wilmington *Also Called: Professional Recruiting Cons (G-19212)*
Precious Knwldg Erly Lrng Ctr 302 293-2588
  1000 Village Cir Newark (19713) *(G-11721)*
Precious Little Hands Childcar 302 298-5027
  702b Wilmington Ave Wilmington (19805) *(G-19148)*
Precious Lttle Hnds Chldcare C 302 256-0194
  111 S Lincoln St Wilmington (19805) *(G-19149)*
Precious Lttle Lambs Childcare 302 723-1403
  509 N Dupont St Wilmington (19805) *(G-19150)*
Precious Mmnts Edcatn Cmnty CT 302 697-9374
  4607 S Dupont Hwy Dover (19901) *(G-3358)*
Precious Moments Day Care 302 856-2346
  18943 Shingle Point Rd Georgetown (19947) *(G-4470)*
Precious Paws Animal Hospital 302 539-2273
  118 Atlantic Ave Ste 101 Ocean View (19970) *(G-12560)*
Precise Alignment Mch Tl Co 302 832-2922
  59 Avignon Dr Newark (19702) *(G-11722)*
Precision Airconvey Corp (PA) 302 999-8000
  465 Corporate Blvd Newark (19702) *(G-11723)*
Precision Auto LLC 302 384-6169
  802 Maryland Ave Wilmington (19805) *(G-19151)*
Precision Builders Inc 302 420-1391
  1148 Pulaski Hwy # 107 Bear (19701) *(G-434)*
Precision Color Graphics LLC 302 661-2595
  1401 Todds Ln Wilmington (19802) *(G-19152)*
Precision Con Cutng of Del MD 855 832-9876
  215 Middleboro Rd Wilmington (19804) *(G-19153)*
Precision Concrete Cutting, Wilmington *Also Called: Precision Con Cutng of Del MD (G-19153)*
Precision Door Service 302 343-6394
  330 Water St Ste 109 Wilmington (19804) *(G-19154)*
Precision Flow LLC 302 544-4417
  62 Southgate Blvd Ste L New Castle (19720) *(G-9489)*
Precision Hmes Rmdlg Group LLC 302 293-0244
  500 N Augustine St Wilmington (19804) *(G-19155)*
Precision Jewelry Inc 302 422-7138
  607 N Dupont Blvd Milford (19963) *(G-8051)*
Precision Landscaping Inc 302 658-3855
  318 7th Ave Wilmington (19805) *(G-19156)*
Precision Landscaping Svcs LLC 302 528-2935
  318 7th Ave Wilmington (19805) *(G-19157)*
Precision Ldscpg & Lawn Care 302 492-1583
  286 Judith Rd Hartly (19953) *(G-4904)*
Precision Marine Construction 302 227-2711
  202 Woodbridge Hls Rehoboth Beach (19971) *(G-12898)*
Precision Marine Construction 302 227-2711
  125 Blackpool Rd Rehoboth Beach (19971) *(G-12899)*
Precision Systems Inds LLC 224 388-9837
  2711 Centerville Rd # 400 Wilmington (19808) *(G-19158)*
Precision Technic Defence Inc 801 404-4626
  251 Little Falls Dr Wilmington (19808) *(G-19159)*
Precisioncure LLC 302 622-9119
  2207 Concord Pike 301 Wilmington (19803) *(G-19160)*
Predator Recovery & Towing LLC 302 381-2135
  31531 Jestice Farm Rd Laurel (19956) *(G-5578)*
Predictive Analytics Group 844 733-5724
  100 Discovery Blvd Ste 802 Newark (19713) *(G-11724)*
Prefered Tax Service Inc 302 654-4388
  2201 N Market St Ste A Wilmington (19802) *(G-19161)*
Preferred Business Services, Wilmington *Also Called: Prefered Tax Service Inc (G-19161)*
Preferred Construction Inc 302 322-9568
  505 Churchmans Rd New Castle (19720) *(G-9490)*
Preferred Contractors Inc 302 798-5457
  204 S Park Dr Wilmington (19809) *(G-19162)*
Preferred Electric Inc 302 322-1217
  505 Churchmans Rd New Castle (19720) *(G-9491)*
Preferred Enviromental 610 364-1106
  2300 W Fourth St Ste E104 Clayton (19938) *(G-1399)*
Preferred Fire Protection 302 256-0607
  4321 Miller Rd Wilmington (19802) *(G-19163)*

Preferred Mechanical..302 668-1151
  1722 Newport Gap Pike Wilmington (19808) *(G-19164)*
Preferred Security Inc...302 834-7800
  1570 Red Lion Rd Bear (19701) *(G-435)*
Preferred Tax Svc Inc..302 945-3700
  32369 Long Neck Rd Unit 13 Millsboro (19966) *(G-8437)*
Preferred Term Securities Xxvi..302 651-7642
  920 N King St Lbby 10 Wilmington (19801) *(G-19165)*
Preferred Transportation, Bear Also Called: Preferred Trnsp Systems LLC *(G-436)*
Preferred Trnsp Systems LLC..302 323-0828
  101 E Beaver Ct Bear (19701) *(G-436)*
Prelude Therapeutics Inc..302 467-1280
  175 Innovation Blvd Wilmington (19805) *(G-19166)*
Prelude TX...302 273-3369
  550 S College Ave Newark (19716) *(G-11725)*
Premier Builders Inc..302 999-8500
  2601 Annand Dr Ste 21 Wilmington (19808) *(G-19167)*
Premier Capital Holding (PA)...302 730-1010
  1675 S State St Dover (19901) *(G-3359)*
Premier Centre For Arts LLC...302 684-3038
  110 Union St Milton (19968) *(G-8688)*
Premier Chiropractic..302 384-7145
  701 N Market St Wilmington (19801) *(G-19168)*
Premier Comfort Services...302 740-0712
  306 Androssan Pl Townsend (19734) *(G-14054)*
Premier Comprehensive Dental..302 378-3131
  212 Celebration Ct Middletown (19709) *(G-7463)*
Premier Drmtlogy Csmtc Surgery......................................302 633-7550
  537 Stanton Christiana Rd Ste 107 Newark (19713) *(G-11726)*
Premier Employee Solutions...843 421-5579
  200 Continental Dr # 401 Newark (19713) *(G-11727)*
Premier Entertainment III LLC (HQ)....................................302 674-4600
  1131 N Dupont Hwy Dover (19901) *(G-3360)*
Premier Glass & Screen Inc..302 732-3101
  33937 Premire Dr Frankford (19945) *(G-4134)*
Premier Health Service LLC..302 597-6810
  131 Becks Woods Dr Bear (19701) *(G-437)*
Premier Healthcare Inc...302 731-5576
  254 W Main St Newark (19711) *(G-11728)*
Premier IL Volo LLC..847 201-1760
  1209 N Orange St Wilmington (19801) *(G-19169)*
Premier Mrtial Arts Nshvlle LL..302 674-1985
  321 Independence Blvd Ste B Dover (19904) *(G-3361)*
Premier Pediatrics LLC..302 836-4440
  2600 Glasgow Ave Ste 213 Newark (19702) *(G-11729)*
Premier Physical Therapy...302 724-6344
  97 Commerce Way Ste 101 Dover (19904) *(G-3362)*
Premier Physical Therapy &..302 389-7855
  100 S Main St Ste 300 Smyrna (19977) *(G-13851)*
Premier Physical Therapy and..302 727-0075
  20268 Plantations Rd Ste B Lewes (19958) *(G-6386)*
Premier Porch & Patio, Frankford Also Called: Premier Glass & Screen Inc *(G-4134)*
Premier Pro Cleaning Solutions..302 743-5337
  507 Pythagoras Path Middletown (19709) *(G-7464)*
Premier Property & Pool MGT..302 357-6321
  106 Sandhill Dr Unit C Middletown (19709) *(G-7465)*
Premier Restoration...302 645-1611
  30616 Overbrook Center Way Unit 1 Milton (19968) *(G-8689)*
Premier Restoration Inc...302 645-1611
  145 Heather Dr Lewes (19958) *(G-6387)*
Premier Restoration Cnstr Inc (PA)....................................302 832-1288
  703 Industrial Dr Middletown (19709) *(G-7466)*
Premier Restorations, Middletown Also Called: Premier Restoration Cnstr Inc *(G-7466)*
Premier Salon 22920, Wilmington Also Called: Premier Salons Intl Inc *(G-19170)*
Premier Salons Intl Inc..302 477-3459
  4737 Concord Pike Wilmington (19803) *(G-19170)*
Premier Soccer..302 533-7340
  1237 Churchmans Rd Newark (19713) *(G-11730)*
Premier Spine & Rehab...302 730-4878
  111 S West St Dover (19904) *(G-3363)*
Premier Spine and Rehab..302 404-5293
  8470 Herring Run Rd Seaford (19973) *(G-13354)*

Premier Staffing Solutions Inc (PA)....................................302 344-5996
  123 W Market St Georgetown (19947) *(G-4471)*
Premier Staffing Solutions Inc..302 628-7700
  809 Norman Eskridge Hwy Seaford (19973) *(G-13355)*
Premier Volleyball Delaware...302 593-4593
  45 Anthony Dr Newark (19702) *(G-11731)*
Premiere Hair Design...302 368-7711
  117 Marathon Dr Middletown (19709) *(G-7467)*
Premiere Oral and Facial Surg..302 273-8300
  1202 Foulk Rd Wilmington (19803) *(G-19171)*
Premiere Physicians PA..302 584-6799
  314 E Main St Ste 103 Newark (19711) *(G-11732)*
Premiere Studio LLC..347 336-0791
  42 Colby Ave Claymont (19703) *(G-1266)*
Premium Aquatics LLC..302 994-7742
  1209 Pecksniff Rd Wilmington (19808) *(G-19172)*
Premium Brands Inc..925 566-8863
  8 The Grn Ste R Dover (19901) *(G-3364)*
Premium Diesel Parts LLC..205 723-1510
  3 Germay Dr Ste 4 Wilmington (19804) *(G-19173)*
Premo Technologies Inc..951 514-6993
  1013 Centre Rd Ste 403b Wilmington (19805) *(G-19174)*
Prentice Hall Legal Fincl Svcs, Wilmington Also Called: Prentice-Hall Corp System Inc *(G-19175)*
Prentice-Hall Corp System Inc (PA)....................................302 636-5440
  2711 Centerville Rd Ste 400 Wilmington (19808) *(G-19175)*
Prepaid Legal Service..302 376-1952
  956 Shorts Landing Rd Smyrna (19977) *(G-13852)*
Prepared LLC...650 825-5996
  4023 Kennett Pike # 50307 Wilmington (19807) *(G-19176)*
Presbyterian Church USA, Wilmington Also Called: Elsmere Presbyterian Church *(G-16381)*
Presbyterian Homes Inc..302 744-3600
  1175 Mckee Rd Dover (19904) *(G-3365)*
Prescience Corporation...208 599-3441
  1201 N Orange St Ste 600 Wilmington (19801) *(G-19177)*
Prescotech Inc...502 585-5866
  1313 N Market St Wilmington (19801) *(G-19178)*
Presentable Properties...302 853-5111
  3408 Woodpecker Rd Seaford (19973) *(G-13356)*
Preserve At Deacons Walk..302 613-4775
  2112 Sheldon Dr Newark (19711) *(G-11733)*
Presicson Pain Rhbltation Svcs..302 827-2321
  18958 Coastal Hwy Rehoboth Beach (19971) *(G-12900)*
Presidio Holdings LLC...240 219-8351
  6 Lake Shore Dr Lewes (19958) *(G-6388)*
Presidium USA Inc...203 803-2980
  874 Walker Rd Ste C Dover (19904) *(G-3366)*
Press Fitness LLC..973 441-9397
  260 Christiana Rd Apt L2 New Castle (19720) *(G-9492)*
Press Media Group Inc (PA)..323 205-5488
  600 N Broad St Middletown (19709) *(G-7468)*
Pressair International..302 636-5440
  3501 Silverside Rd Wilmington (19810) *(G-19179)*
Pressley Ridge Foundation...302 366-0490
  942 Walker Rd Ste A Dover (19904) *(G-3367)*
Pressley Ridge Foundation...302 677-1590
  942 Walker Rd Ste A Dover (19904) *(G-3368)*
Pressley Ridge Foundation...302 854-9782
  20461 Dupont Blvd Ste 2 Georgetown (19947) *(G-4472)*
Pressley Ridge of Delaware, Dover Also Called: Pressley Ridge Foundation *(G-3368)*
Pressure Washing..302 393-0879
  14514 Tull Rd Greenwood (19950) *(G-4662)*
Prestege LLC..302 312-8548
  16 N Bellwoode Dr Newark (19702) *(G-11734)*
Prestige Auto...302 898-5486
  1027 W 25th St Wilmington (19802) *(G-19180)*
Prestige Building Co..302 744-8282
  992 Whatcoat Dr Dover (19904) *(G-3369)*
Prestige Contractors Inc...302 722-1032
  2615 N Tatnall St Wilmington (19802) *(G-19181)*
Prestige Frog Cleaning Svcs..302 654-8459
  316 N Market St Wilmington (19801) *(G-19182)*

ALPHABETIC SECTION

Prestige Labs Inc.. 917 698-3453
  8 The Grn Ste 7491 Dover (19901) *(G-3370)*

Prestige Powder Inc.. 302 737-7086
  13 Tyler Way Newark (19713) *(G-11735)*

Prestige Powder Finishing Inc.. 302 737-7500
  13 Tyler Way Newark (19713) *(G-11736)*

Prestigious Solution LLC... 800 392-2103
  34 Dozer Ct Smyrna (19977) *(G-13853)*

Preston & Remodeling... 302 604-0760
  201 Lavinia St Milton (19968) *(G-8690)*

Prestwick Community Corp... 302 227-7878
  17298 Coastal Hwy Lewes (19958) *(G-6389)*

Prestwick House Inc... 302 659-2070
  58 Artisan Dr Smyrna (19977) *(G-13854)*

Pretty Damn Quick Inc... 201 613-2296
  1007 N Orange St Fl 10 Wilmington (19801) *(G-19183)*

Pretty Girl Press... 484 668-0770
  1910 N Washington St Wilmington (19802) *(G-19184)*

Pretty Nails... 302 628-3937
  22986 Sussex Hwy Seaford (19973) *(G-13357)*

Prevail Trial Consultants LLC.. 302 442-7836
  1007 N Orange St Ste 510 Wilmington (19801) *(G-19185)*

Prevent Alarm Company LLC... 302 478-6647
  91 Lukens Dr Ste B Historic New Castle (19720) *(G-5052)*

Prevent Child Abuse Delaware... 302 425-7490
  100 W 10th St Ste 715 Wilmington (19801) *(G-19186)*

Prevent Security and Tech, Historic New Castle *Also Called: Prevent Alarm Company LLC* *(G-5052)*

Prezoom LLC.. 732 837-1170
  262 Quigley Blvd Historic New Castle (19720) *(G-5053)*

Price Automotive Group.. 302 383-8669
  220 E Cleveland Ave Newark (19711) *(G-11737)*

Price Edward A/Gnral Contractr.. 302 571-9281
  10 Belmont Ave Wilmington (19804) *(G-19187)*

Price Honda, Dover *Also Called: Diamond Motor Sports Inc (G-2292)*

Price Is Right Contracting LLC.. 215 760-1416
  919 N Market St Ste 950 Wilmington (19801) *(G-19188)*

Prices Corner Car Wash, Wilmington *Also Called: Car Wash of Prices Corner (G-15237)*

Prices Landscaping & Hardscap... 302 280-3072
  14490 Deer Forest Rd Bridgeville (19933) *(G-754)*

Pricetweakers LLC... 424 325-0597
  1201 N Orange St Ste 7204 Wilmington (19801) *(G-19189)*

Prickett Jones & Elliott, Wilmington *Also Called: James L Holzman (G-17482)*

Pride Cleaning... 302 228-0755
  6121 Millcreek Rd Laurel (19956) *(G-5579)*

Pride Heating & Air Conditioning.. 302 234-4751
  208 Mercury Rd Newark (19711) *(G-11738)*

Pride Home Warranty.. 302 894-1689
  200 Continental Dr Ste 401 Newark (19713) *(G-11739)*

Pride International LLC (DH)... 713 789-1400
  1209 N Orange St Wilmington (19801) *(G-19190)*

Pride of Del Ldge No 349 Imprv.. 215 453-9236
  57 W Cleveland Ave Newark (19711) *(G-11740)*

Prides Court Apartments.. 302 737-2085
  6 Sussex Rd Ofc F Newark (19713) *(G-11741)*

Pridestaffing LLC... 302 525-2561
  16192 Coastal Hwy Lewes (19958) *(G-6390)*

Primary Care Delaware L L C.. 302 744-9645
  200 Banning St Ste 210 Dover (19904) *(G-3371)*

Primary Care Medical Billing, Wilmington *Also Called: Pcmb LLC (G-18935)*

Primary Residential Mrtg Inc... 302 292-1009
  248 E Chestnut Hill Rd Ste 4 Newark (19713) *(G-11742)*

Prime, Wilmington *Also Called: Stay Prime Inc (G-20039)*

Prime, Wilmington *Also Called: Value Xchange Group of Co LLC (G-20566)*

Prime America, Newark *Also Called: John Lovett Inc (G-11114)*

Prime Beverage Group LLC... 302 327-0002
  200 Lisa Dr New Castle (19720) *(G-9493)*

Prime Directive Inc.. 302 383-5607
  503 Paisley Pl Newark (19711) *(G-11743)*

Prime Insights Group LLC... 407 289-1577
  8 The Grn Ste R Dover (19901) *(G-3372)*

Prime One Global LLC... 831 215-5123
  2055 Limestone Rd Wilmington (19808) *(G-19191)*

Prime Products Usa Inc.. 302 528-3866
  118 Valley Rd Wilmington (19804) *(G-19192)*

Prime Security Corp.. 803 281-0378
  600 N Broad St Ste 5 Middletown (19709) *(G-7469)*

Prime Time Properties LLC... 302 763-6050
  167 Willamette Dr Bear (19701) *(G-438)*

Primelending A Plainscapital... 302 733-7599
  1450 Capitol Trl Ste 108 Newark (19711) *(G-11744)*

Primerica.. 302 455-9460
  520 Christiana Medical Ctr Newark (19702) *(G-11745)*

Primerica.. 302 439-0206
  1210 N King St Wilmington (19801) *(G-19193)*

Primeros Pasos Inc... 302 856-7406
  20648 Savannah Rd Georgetown (19947) *(G-4473)*

Primex Composites LLC... 302 981-1470
  Hockessin (19707) *(G-5352)*

Prince Telecom LLC (HQ)... 302 324-1800
  551 Mews Dr Ste A New Castle (19720) *(G-9494)*

Princeton Coml Holdings LLC... 302 449-4836
  113 Barksdale Professional Ctr Newark (19711) *(G-11746)*

Princetonian Mhc LLC... 800 927-9800
  251 Little Falls Dr Wilmington (19808) *(G-19194)*

Principal Lf Globl Funding II.. 302 636-6392
  1100 N Market St Wilmington (19890) *(G-19195)*

Print Coast 2 Coast.. 302 381-4610
  33073 E Light Dr Lewes (19958) *(G-6391)*

Print On This.. 302 235-9475
  3 Green Ct Newark (19702) *(G-11747)*

Print Shack, Seaford *Also Called: Penney Enterprises Inc (G-13340)*

Print Shack Inc... 302 629-4430
  9203 Brickyard Rd Seaford (19973) *(G-13358)*

Print-N-Press Inc.. 302 994-6665
  300 Cassidy Dr Ste 301 Wilmington (19804) *(G-19196)*

Printcurement.. 302 249-6100
  122 Delaware St Ste 300 Historic New Castle (19720) *(G-5054)*

Printed Solid Inc... 302 439-0098
  2860 Ogletown Rd Bldg 6-8 Newark (19713) *(G-11748)*

Printify Inc.. 415 978-6351
  108 W 13th St Wilmington (19801) *(G-19197)*

Printify LLC (PA).. 415 968-6351
  108 W 13th St Wilmington (19801) *(G-19198)*

Printit Solutions LLC... 302 380-3838
  1155 E Lebanon Rd Dover (19901) *(G-3373)*

Printpack Inc.. 302 323-4000
  600 Grantham Ln New Castle (19720) *(G-9495)*

Prints and Princesses.. 703 881-1057
  202 Hanover Pl Newark (19711) *(G-11749)*

Priority Cleaning LLC.. 302 519-4998
  10119 Greentop Rd Lincoln (19960) *(G-6693)*

Priority Radio Inc... 302 540-5690
  179 Stanton Christiana Rd Newark (19702) *(G-11750)*

Priority Services LLC.. 302 918-3070
  70 Albe Dr Newark (19702) *(G-11751)*

Priscilla Lancaster... 302 792-8305
  302 Harvey Rd Claymont (19703) *(G-1267)*

Prism Events Inc.. 424 252-1070
  2035 Sunset Lake Rd Ste B2 Newark (19702) *(G-11752)*

Prisma Holding Inc (PA).. 903 480-4880
  1209 N Orange St Wilmington (19801) *(G-19199)*

Prisma Retail, Wilmington *Also Called: Prisma Holding Inc (G-19199)*

Pristine Clean Co... 302 465-8274
  126 Carnation Dr Magnolia (19962) *(G-6776)*

Prithvi Technologies LLC.. 302 313-9273
  2055 Limestone Rd Ste 200c Wilmington (19808) *(G-19200)*

Priv Social Inc.. 501 301-4197
  651 N Broad St Ste 206 Middletown (19709) *(G-7470)*

Privacy Policy/United Custom C... 302 537-1717
  33012 Coastal Hwy Unit 5 Bethany Beach (19930) *(G-628)*

Privado Inc (PA)... 916 730-4522
  8 The Grn Ste A Dover (19901) *(G-3374)*

Private Massage Bodywork..	302 387-7199
450 S Dupont Hwy Dover (19901) *(G-3375)*	
Private Society LLC..	302 319-7126
521 Concord Bridge Pl Newark (19702) *(G-11753)*	
Pro 2 Respiratory Services...	302 514-9843
56 Artisan Dr Ste 5 Smyrna (19977) *(G-13855)*	
Pro Benefits Plus...	302 683-5546
569 Bay Ave Milford (19963) *(G-8052)*	
Pro Carpet LLC..	443 757-7320
26315 Miller St Millsboro (19966) *(G-8438)*	
Pro Clean Company, Delaware City *Also Called: Pro Clean Wilmington Inc (G-1553)*	
Pro Clean Wilmington Inc...	302 836-8080
210 Clinton St Delaware City (19706) *(G-1553)*	
Pro Contractors..	302 894-2611
2501 Normandy Court Newark (19713) *(G-11754)*	
Pro Exteriors..	302 664-1700
221 Milton Ellendale Hwy Milton (19968) *(G-8691)*	
Pro Fabricating Inc...	302 424-7700
1011 Mattlind Way Milford (19963) *(G-8053)*	
Pro Pest Management of De Inc......................................	302 994-2847
200 Cassidy Dr Ste 201 Wilmington (19804) *(G-19201)*	
Pro Physical Therapy...	302 422-6670
941 N Dupont Blvd Ste C Milford (19963) *(G-8054)*	
Pro Physical Therapy...	610 368-1006
100 Valley Rd Wilmington (19804) *(G-19202)*	
Pro Physical Therapy, Wilmington *Also Called: Pro Physl Therapy Ftns Acct (G-19203)*	
Pro Physical Therapy PA...	302 654-1700
2032 New Castle Ave New Castle (19720) *(G-9496)*	
Pro Physl Therapy Ftns Acct...	302 658-7800
1812 Marsh Rd Ste 505 Wilmington (19810) *(G-19203)*	
Pro Quality East Coast Pntg..	302 745-7753
214 Misty Ln Lincoln (19960) *(G-6694)*	
Pro RAD Onc..	302 709-4508
111 Continental Dr # 412 Newark (19713) *(G-11755)*	
Pro Rehab and Chiropractic...	302 268-6129
2101 Foulk Rd Wilmington (19810) *(G-19204)*	
Pro Rehab Chiropractic..	302 200-9102
105 W 4th St Lewes (19958) *(G-6392)*	
Pro Rehab Chiropractors..	302 652-2225
215 Peirce Rd Wilmington (19803) *(G-19205)*	
Pro Rfp Inc...	302 265-3786
221 N Broad St Ste 3a Middletown (19709) *(G-7471)*	
Pro Rhab Chrprctic Rhblitation..	302 332-3312
1708 Lovering Ave Ste 102-3 Wilmington (19806) *(G-19206)*	
Pro Works Inc DH...	302 221-4200
177 Old Churchmans Rd New Castle (19720) *(G-9497)*	
Proautomated Inc...	302 294-6121
100 Lake Dr Ste 205 Newark (19702) *(G-11756)*	
Problem Consulting Co...	347 809-3402
254 Chapman Rd Ste 2087804 Newark (19702) *(G-11757)*	
Process Academy LLC..	302 415-3104
4023 Kennett Pike Ste 56762 Wilmington (19807) *(G-19207)*	
Processflo Inc...	302 633-4200
1212 First State Blvd Wilmington (19804) *(G-19208)*	
Procino Wells & Woodland LLC......................................	302 313-5934
1519 Savannah Rd Lewes (19958) *(G-6393)*	
Proclean Inc...	302 656-8080
Delaware City (19706) *(G-1554)*	
Procter & Gamble, Dover *Also Called: Procter & Gamble Paper Pdts Co (G-3376)*	
Procter & Gamble Paper Pdts Co.....................................	302 678-2600
1340 W North St Dover (19904) *(G-3376)*	
Produce For Btter Hlth Fndtion..	302 235-2329
5341 Limestone Rd Newark (19711) *(G-11758)*	
Produce Spot LLC...	267 864-1232
2400 Northeast Blvd Wilmington (19802) *(G-19209)*	
Product Service and Repair...	443 466-0566
17 Bellecor Dr # 11a New Castle (19720) *(G-9498)*	
Productions For Purpose Inc..	302 388-9883
10 Little Cir Middletown (19709) *(G-7472)*	
Productive Co Inc...	415 304-6782
2093 Philadelphia Pike Claymont (19703) *(G-1268)*	
Professional Bytes, Wilmington *Also Called: Professionals LLC (G-19217)*	
Professional Handyman Svcs Inc....................................	302 478-1237
28 Club Ln Wilmington (19810) *(G-19210)*	
Professional Home Health Care, Dover *Also Called: Home Health Corp America Inc (G-2689)*	
Professional Imaging..	302 653-3522
97 Nita Dr Smyrna (19977) *(G-13856)*	
Professional Leasing Inc..	302 629-4350
740 Sussex Ave Seaford (19973) *(G-13359)*	
Professional Pest MGT De...	302 738-1036
476 E Ayre St Wilmington (19804) *(G-19211)*	
Professional Recruiting Cons...	302 479-9550
3617a Silverside Rd Wilmington (19810) *(G-19212)*	
Professional Security Co..	302 383-7142
625 Swansea Dr Middletown (19709) *(G-7473)*	
Professional Selection Inc..	905 392-7313
1209 N Orange St Wilmington (19801) *(G-19213)*	
Professional Technicians Inc...	215 364-4911
100 Biddle Ave Ste 200 Newark (19702) *(G-11759)*	
Professional Therapeutics..	302 438-5859
1407 Saint Elizabeth St Wilmington (19805) *(G-19214)*	
Professional Window Tinting..	302 456-3456
9 Albe Dr Ste A Newark (19702) *(G-11760)*	
Professionals...	302 764-5501
3812 Governor Printz Blvd Wilmington (19802) *(G-19215)*	
Professionals Auto Salon...	302 420-5691
2507 W 6th St Wilmington (19805) *(G-19216)*	
Professionals LLC...	302 295-2330
1000 N West St Ste 1283 Wilmington (19801) *(G-19217)*	
Professionsale Inc..	646 262-9101
1148 Pulaski Hwy Ste 134 Bear (19701) *(G-439)*	
Professnal Arfication Svcs Inc..	302 752-7003
4 Hollyberry Dr Georgetown (19947) *(G-4474)*	
Progar & Co...	302 645-6216
33815 Clay Rd Ste 1 Lewes (19958) *(G-6394)*	
Progar & Company PA, Lewes *Also Called: Progar & Co (G-6394)*	
Proglo 2 LLC..	702 494-7877
651 N Broad St Ste 205 Middletown (19709) *(G-7474)*	
Prognstic Hlthcare Rsurces LLC......................................	762 217-6323
540 Groundhog Ln Smyrna (19977) *(G-13857)*	
Progresive Dental Arts...	302 455-9569
685 E Chestnut Hill Rd Newark (19713) *(G-11761)*	
Progressive Casualty Insur Co...	302 734-7360
1241 N Dupont Hwy Dover (19901) *(G-3377)*	
Progressive Dental Arts...	302 234-2222
5301 Limestone Rd Ste 212 Wilmington (19808) *(G-19218)*	
Progressive Health of Delaware, Wilmington *Also Called: Zarek Donohue LLC (G-20947)*	
Progressive Insurance, Dover *Also Called: Progressive Casualty Insur Co (G-3377)*	
Progressive Investment Co Inc..	302 656-8597
801 N West St Fl 2 Wilmington (19801) *(G-19219)*	
Progressive Radiology..	302 730-9300
1306 S Dupont Hwy Dover (19901) *(G-3378)*	
Progressive Services Inc..	302 658-7260
300 Commercial Dr Wilmington (19805) *(G-19220)*	
Progressive Software Cmpt Inc.......................................	302 479-9700
2 Righter Pkwy Wilmington (19803) *(G-19221)*	
Progressive Systems Inc..	302 732-3321
25 Hickory St Frankford (19945) *(G-4135)*	
Progressive Telecom LLC...	302 883-8883
3422 Old Capitol Trl Ste 1483 Wilmington (19808) *(G-19222)*	
Project Assistants Inc...	302 477-9711
1521 Concord Pike Ste 301 Wilmington (19803) *(G-19223)*	
Project of Providence LLC..	302 438-8970
1007 Park Pl Apt A Wilmington (19806) *(G-19224)*	
Project Otr LLC...	404 964-2244
1209 N Orange St Wilmington (19801) *(G-19225)*	
Project Widgets Inc...	302 439-3414
501 Silverside Rd Ste 29 Wilmington (19809) *(G-19226)*	
Proksy Research LLC..	737 238-0104
2055 Limestone Rd 200p Wilmington (19808) *(G-19227)*	
Prolific Consultants LLC (PA)..	302 219-0958
8 The Grn Ste A Dover (19901) *(G-3379)*	

ALPHABETIC SECTION — Ptci Management

Prolific Professionals LLC (PA) 302 497-4136
  8 The Grn Ste 15082 Dover (19901) *(G-3380)*

Proline Builders LLC 302 956-0426
  11225 Tyler Dr Bridgeville (19933) *(G-755)*

Promax Painters 302 312-8415
  205 Christiana Mdws Bear (19701) *(G-440)*

Prominent Insurance Svcs Inc 302 351-3368
  1201 N Orange St Ste 700 Wilmington (19801) *(G-19228)*

Promise of Light Inc 201 471-5848
  10 Capano Dr Newark (19702) *(G-11762)*

Promixco USA Corp (PA) 814 810-3643
  108 W 13th St Wilmington (19801) *(G-19229)*

Promo Builder LLC 773 502-5796
  602 Carson Dr Bear (19701) *(G-441)*

Promo Marketing 302 324-2650
  950 W Basin Rd New Castle (19720) *(G-9499)*

Promofill 302 276-2700
  800 Centerpoint Blvd Historic New Castle (19720) *(G-5055)*

Promote Your Loc Bus Pwred By 302 764-5588
  31 Van Dyke Dr Wilmington (19809) *(G-19230)*

Promotion Zone, Newark *Also Called: Promotion Zone LLC (G-11763)*

Promotion Zone LLC 302 832-8565
  50 Albe Dr Ste A Newark (19702) *(G-11763)*

Promotions Plus Inc 302 836-2820
  700 Peoples Plz Newark (19702) *(G-11764)*

Proofed Inc 888 851-8179
  8 The Grn Dover (19901) *(G-3381)*

Propel Bikes LLC (PA) 631 678-1946
  22 Germay Dr Wilmington (19804) *(G-19231)*

Proper-Tees LLC 323 981-9809
  2140 S Dupont Hwy Camden (19934) *(G-886)*

Properties For Life LLC 302 293-9465
  5403 Proust Pl Middletown (19709) *(G-7475)*

Property Advisory Service 401 453-4455
  100 Liberty Ter Newark (19702) *(G-11765)*

Property Doctors LLC 302 249-7731
  309 Millchop Ln Magnolia (19962) *(G-6777)*

Property Improvements LLC 610 692-5343
  144 Brandywine Dr Bethany Beach (19930) *(G-629)*

Property Maintenance 302 645-5921
  32206 Sandpiper Dr Lewes (19958) *(G-6395)*

Property Maintenance MGT 302 883-1441
  3807 Wheatleys Pond Rd Smyrna (19977) *(G-13858)*

Prorank Business Solutions LLC 302 256-0642
  1201 N Orange St Wilmington (19801) *(G-19232)*

Prospect De 302 382-6579
  1524 E Lebanon Rd Dover (19901) *(G-3382)*

Prospect Inspection Services 302 381-0110
  1524 E Lebanon Rd Dover (19901) *(G-3383)*

Prosperity Unlimited Ente 302 379-2494
  32 E Sarazen Dr Middletown (19709) *(G-7476)*

Proteam LLC 847 707-1074
  3521 Silverside Rd Ste 2f2 Wilmington (19810) *(G-19233)*

Protech Labs Inc 201 328-7856
  8 The Grn Dover (19901) *(G-3384)*

Protect Intl Risk Sfety Svcs C 877 736-0805
  3 Germay Dr Ste 4-470 Wilmington (19804) *(G-19234)*

Protection One, Newark *Also Called: ADT LLC (G-9770)*

Protermant Services, Newark *Also Called: University of Delaware (G-12282)*

Protocol Labs Inc (PA) 302 703-7194
  427 N Tatnall St # 51207 Wilmington (19801) *(G-19235)*

Prototek Machining & Dev 302 368-1226
  307 Markus Ct Newark (19713) *(G-11766)*

Prototek Machining & Dev, Newark *Also Called: Prototek Machining & Dev (G-11766)*

Prouse Enterprises LLC 302 846-9000
  120 Mullet Run Milford (19963) *(G-8055)*

Provada Enterprise 302 999-7553
  4391 Kirkwood Hwy Wilmington (19808) *(G-19236)*

Provaxus Inc 773 832-8015
  8 The Grn Ste B Dover (19901) *(G-3385)*

Proven Pass Inc 888 404-2775
  221 N Broad St Middletown (19709) *(G-7477)*

Provide LLC 302 391-1200
  100 Pencader Dr Newark (19702) *(G-11767)*

Providence At Heritage Sh 302 337-1040
  21 White Pelican Ct Bridgeville (19933) *(G-756)*

Providencias Cleaning 302 507-7931
  319 7th Ave Wilmington (19805) *(G-19237)*

Provident Federal Credit Union 302 734-1133
  401 S New St Dover (19904) *(G-3386)*

Providge Consulting LLC 888 927-6583
  2207 Concord Pike Wilmington (19803) *(G-19238)*

Provision Group LLC 844 220-7200
  200 Continental Dr Ste 401 Newark (19713) *(G-11768)*

Proximity Malt LLC 414 755-8388
  33222 Bi State Blvd Laurel (19956) *(G-5580)*

Prudent Capital Advisor 302 569-9444
  260 Chapman Rd Ste 200 Newark (19702) *(G-11769)*

Prudent Endodontics 302 475-3803
  2036 Foulk Rd Wilmington (19810) *(G-19239)*

Prudent Technology & Svcs LLC 302 481-6399
  8 The Grn Ste 5068 Dover (19901) *(G-3387)*

Prudential Emerson and Company, Dover *Also Called: ERA Harrington Realty (G-2460)*

Prudential Gallo Realtor, Rehoboth Beach *Also Called: Gallo Realty Inc (G-12765)*

Prudential Gallo Realty 302 645-6661
  16712 Kings Hwy Lewes (19958) *(G-6396)*

Prudential Intl Invstmnts Corp (HQ) 302 778-1729
  913 Market St Wilmington (19801) *(G-19240)*

Prysm Financial Technology Inc 323 333-7698
  651 N Broad St Middletown (19709) *(G-7478)*

Ps3g Inc 302 298-0270
  913 N Market St Wilmington (19801) *(G-19241)*

PSC Properties LLC 302 832-2076
  704 5th St Delaware City (19706) *(G-1555)*

PSC Technology Incorporated (PA) 866 866-1466
  16192 Coastal Hwy Lewes (19958) *(G-6397)*

Psci 302 479-9700
  1 Righter Pkwy Ste 180 Wilmington (19803) *(G-19242)*

PSI, Frankford *Also Called: Progressive Systems Inc (G-4135)*

PSI Zeta Chapter of Omega PSI 302 367-8216
  Wilmington (19899) *(G-19243)*

Psp Corp 302 764-7730
  203 Churchill Dr Wilmington (19803) *(G-19244)*

Psych Total Care LLC 302 478-7981
  18947 John J Williams Hwy Rehoboth Beach (19971) *(G-12901)*

Psych Ward Genius 267 237-4528
  4309 Ruskin Rd Wilmington (19802) *(G-19245)*

Psychedelic Water Inc 855 337-7924
  251 Little Falls Dr Wilmington (19808) *(G-19246)*

Psychiatry Delaware 302 478-1450
  1415 Foulk Rd Ste 104 Wilmington (19803) *(G-19247)*

Psycho Therapeutic Services, Dover *Also Called: Associated Svc Specialist Inc (G-1836)*

Psychological C Hockessin 610 388-8585
  825 N Washington St Wilmington (19801) *(G-19248)*

Psychological Services 302 489-0213
  422 Woodstock Ln Wilmington (19808) *(G-19249)*

Psychotherapeutic Services 302 678-9962
  942 Walker Rd Ste B Dover (19904) *(G-3388)*

Psychotherapeutic Services 302 672-7159
  630 W Division St Ste D Dover (19904) *(G-3389)*

Psychotherapeutic Services 302 737-1597
  5 Kensington Ln Newark (19713) *(G-11770)*

Psychotherapeutic Svc Assn Inc 302 284-8370
  2015 Peachtree Run Rd Dover (19901) *(G-3390)*

Pt Works De LLC 410 446-2589
  907 N Dupont Blvd Milford (19963) *(G-8056)*

Pta Delaware Congress 302 792-3916
  3401 Green St Claymont (19703) *(G-1269)*

Pta Delaware Congress 302 454-3424
  2815 Highlands Ln Wilmington (19808) *(G-19250)*

Pta Delaware Military Academy 302 998-0745
  12 Middleboro Rd Wilmington (19804) *(G-19251)*

Ptci Management 302 538-6996
  442 Voshells Mill Star Hill Rd Dover (19901) *(G-3391)*

Pteris Global (usa) Inc 516 593-5633
  615 S Dupont Hwy Dover (19901) *(G-3392)*

Ptm Manufacturing LLC 302 455-9733
  196 Quigley Blvd Ste A Historic New Castle (19720) *(G-5056)*

Pts Professional Welding 302 632-2079
  609 Broad St Houston (19954) *(G-5447)*

Public Assets Recovery Service 267 767-0452
  120 Vineyards Ct Wilmington (19810) *(G-19252)*

Public Health Nursing 302 856-5136
  544 S Bedford St Georgetown (19947) *(G-4475)*

Public Mint Inc 833 386-0182
  8 The Grn Ste A Dover (19901) *(G-3393)*

Public Systems Inc 302 326-4500
  2 Penns Way Ste 406 New Castle (19720) *(G-9500)*

Publica.la, Newark *Also Called: Queryloop Inc (G-11798)*

Pucketts Heating Adn Air 443 239-2129
  427 Vernon Rd Harrington (19952) *(G-4814)*

Pughs Service Inc 302 678-2408
  728 Dover Leipsic Rd Dover (19901) *(G-3394)*

Puglisi Egg Farms Delaware LLC 302 376-1200
  1881 Middle Neck Rd Middletown (19709) *(G-7479)*

Pullable Inc 302 574-6379
  1007 N Orange St Wilmington (19801) *(G-19253)*

Pulmonary Associates PA (PA) 302 656-2213
  7 S Clayton St # 500 Wilmington (19805) *(G-19254)*

Pulsar Print LLC 302 394-9202
  243 Quigley Blvd Ste K Historic New Castle (19720) *(G-5057)*

Pulsar360, Newark *Also Called: Pulsar360 Corp (G-11771)*

Pulsar360 Corp 855 578-5727
  2915 Ogletown Rd Ste 3240 Newark (19713) *(G-11771)*

Pulse and Pixel Corp 845 366-1219
  1007 N Orange St Fl 4 Wilmington (19801) *(G-19255)*

Pulse Technologies Inc 785 258-6423
  2093 Philadelphia Pike # 2180 Claymont (19703) *(G-1270)*

Puma Energy US Inc 787 966-7929
  1209 N Orange St Wilmington (19801) *(G-19256)*

Pumas-Ai Inc 551 207-6084
  3500 S Dupont Hwy Ste Gt-101 Dover (19901) *(G-3395)*

Pumh, Hockessin *Also Called: Peninsula Untd Mthdst Hmes Inc (G-5335)*

Pumpkin Space Latte Co 765 326-0517
  651 N Broad St Ste 206 Middletown (19709) *(G-7480)*

Pumpkin Spice Latte Co 765 326-0517
  651 N Broad St Ste 206 Middletown (19709) *(G-7481)*

Puppies and More Rescue Inc 856 753-6538
  3422 Old Capitol Trl Wilmington (19808) *(G-19257)*

Puppy Playdate Co 765 326-0517
  651 N Broad St Ste 206 Middletown (19709) *(G-7482)*

Pure Air Holdings Corp (HQ) 302 655-7130
  1105 N Market St Ste 1300 Wilmington (19801) *(G-19258)*

Pure Anatolia LLC 571 660-0007
  8 The Grn Ste A Dover (19901) *(G-3396)*

Pure Barre 302 691-3618
  3801 Kennett Pike Wilmington (19807) *(G-19259)*

Pure Cleaning Services Inc 302 494-2693
  1017 Dettling Rd Wilmington (19805) *(G-19260)*

Pure Power Pressure Wshg LLC 302 266-9933
  8 Higgins Rd Newark (19711) *(G-11772)*

Pure Self Coaching LLC 302 345-0356
  160 Shannon Blvd Middletown (19709) *(G-7483)*

Pure Shaka LLC (PA) 302 438-7105
  2207 Concord Pike Unit 114 Wilmington (19803) *(G-19261)*

Pure Storage Inc (PA) 302 383-2492
  5 Honeysuckle Ct Wilmington (19810) *(G-19262)*

Pure Wellness LLC 302 449-0149
  708 Ash Blvd Middletown (19709) *(G-7484)*

Pure Wellness LLC (PA) 302 365-5470
  550 Stanton Christiana Rd Ste 302 Newark (19713) *(G-11773)*

Pure Wellness LLC 302 389-8915
  699 S Carter Rd Unit 5 Smyrna (19977) *(G-13859)*

Pure Wellness LLC 302 543-5679
  1010 N Bancroft Pkwy Ste 102 Wilmington (19805) *(G-19263)*

Pure Wellness Chiropractic, Newark *Also Called: Pure Wellness LLC (G-11773)*

Purebread 302 528-5591
  47 Beech Hill Dr Newark (19711) *(G-11774)*

Purebred LLC 929 777-7770
  157 Riverview Dr New Castle (19720) *(G-9501)*

Purelife Therapeutic Massage 302 379-5547
  49 Ivy Rd Wilmington (19806) *(G-19264)*

Puri Vineet MD 302 744-9645
  200 Banning St Ste 210 Dover (19904) *(G-3397)*

Purity Home Improvement Inc 302 753-5454
  811 W 22nd St Wilmington (19802) *(G-19265)*

Purnells General Clg Svcs LLC 302 430-1170
  76 Belfry Dr Felton (19943) *(G-4010)*

Purple Moon Herbs Studies LLC 302 270-5095
  1841 Bryants Corner Rd Hartly (19953) *(G-4905)*

Purple Thinkers Inc 760 349-7603
  112 Capitol Trl Ste A429 Newark (19711) *(G-11775)*

Purple Wifi Inc 216 292-5760
  1013 Centre Rd Wilmington (19805) *(G-19266)*

Purple Wifi Inc 877 286-2631
  8 The Grn Ste 1 Dover (19901) *(G-3398)*

Purple4s, Magnolia *Also Called: Purple4s Inc (G-6778)*

Purple4s Inc 443 504-9755
  40 Bushel Cir Magnolia (19962) *(G-6778)*

Purplenow, Dover *Also Called: Purplenow Inc (G-3399)*

Purplenow Inc 302 751-5226
  8 The Grn Ste B Dover (19901) *(G-3399)*

Purse Money, Dover *Also Called: Purse Money Technologies LLC (G-3400)*

Purse Money Technologies LLC 302 208-0184
  8 The Grn Ste A Dover (19901) *(G-3400)*

Purushas Picks Inc 302 918-7663
  3310 Wrangle Hill Rd Ste 107 Bear (19701) *(G-442)*

Pusan RE Newark LLC 302 737-3087
  205 Cunane Cir Newark (19702) *(G-11776)*

PUSH Yoga 302 547-4807
  212 W 14th St Apt 1 Wilmington (19801) *(G-19267)*

Puzs Body Shop Inc 302 368-8265
  97 Peoples Dr Newark (19702) *(G-11777)*

Puzzle Investments LLC 774 516-6447
  919 N Market St Ste 950 Wilmington (19801) *(G-19268)*

Puzzles Lf Rntry Prgram For Wm 302 339-0327
  831 N Market St Wilmington (19801) *(G-19269)*

Pw Construction LLC 443 309-4082
  213 Lauren Dr Wilmington (19804) *(G-19270)*

Pwp Pike Creek LLC 302 635-7837
  5317 Limestone Rd Ste 2 Wilmington (19808) *(G-19271)*

Pxe Group LLC 561 295-1451
  8 The Grn Ste A Dover (19901) *(G-3401)*

Pyir Construction & Design 302 824-9015
  121 Britain Ct Newark (19702) *(G-11778)*

Pyle Child Development Center 302 732-1443
  34314 Pyle Center Rd Frankford (19945) *(G-4136)*

Pyle Hlg & Junk Removal LLC 302 750-7227
  6 Sunny Bnd Newark (19702) *(G-11779)*

Pyramid Educational Cons 302 368-2515
  350 Churchmans Rd Ste B New Castle (19720) *(G-9502)*

Pyramid Group MGT Svcs Co 302 355-1760
  350 Churchmans Rd Ste A New Castle (19720) *(G-9503)*

Pyramid Group MGT Svcs Corp 302 737-1770
  227 E Delaware Ave Newark (19711) *(G-11780)*

Pyramid Transport Inc 302 337-9340
  18119 Sussex Hwy Unit 2 Bridgeville (19933) *(G-757)*

Python Software Foundation 970 305-9455
  8 The Grn Ste R Dover (19901) *(G-3402)*

Q Vandenberg & Sons Inc 800 242-2852
  3422 Old Capitol Trl Pmb 451 Wilmington (19808) *(G-19272)*

Qare Inc 408 475-7569
  24a Trolley Sq 2134 Wilmington (19806) *(G-19273)*

Qase Inc 650 459-1800
  1007 N Orange St Wilmington (19801) *(G-19274)*

Qbean International LLC 917 781-6274
  2803 Philadelphia Pike Ste B # 429 Claymont (19703) *(G-1271)*

ALPHABETIC SECTION — Quartz Mill Contracting

Qbeck Inspection Group 302 452-9257
   242 Chapman Rd Newark (19702) *(G-11781)*

Qbench Inc 888 680-5834
   254 Chapman Rd Newark (19702) *(G-11782)*

Qbr Telecom Inc 302 510-1155
   913 N Market St Ste 200 Wilmington (19801) *(G-19275)*

Qbs Beauty Salon 302 691-3449
   3207 Miller Rd Wilmington (19802) *(G-19276)*

Qcortex LLC 213 257-4004
   8 The Grn Ste A Dover (19901) *(G-3403)*

QH&a, Wilmington Also Called: Quality Htg Ar-Cnditioning Inc *(G-19284)*

Qisstpay Inc 817 239-3900
   1675 S State St Dover (19901) *(G-3404)*

Qodebotics LLC 617 312-7733
   8 The Grn Dover (19901) *(G-3405)*

Qoe Inc 302 455-1234
   955 Dawson Dr Ste 3 Newark (19713) *(G-11783)*

Qomo Farms LLC 202 462-5449
   19888 Church St Rehoboth Beach (19971) *(G-12902)*

Qoro, New Castle Also Called: Qoro LLC *(G-9504)*

Qoro LLC 302 322-5900
   166 S Dupont Hwy Ste B New Castle (19720) *(G-9504)*

Qps LLC 302 369-3753
   110 Executive Dr Ste 7 Newark (19702) *(G-11784)*

Qps Holdings LLC (PA) 302 369-5601
   3 Innovation Way Ste 240 Newark (19711) *(G-11785)*

Qrepublik Inc 559 475-8262
   2093 Philadelphia Pike # 2012 Claymont (19703) *(G-1272)*

Qspark LLC 646 504-4975
   3422 Old Capitol Trl Ste 415 Wilmington (19808) *(G-19277)*

Qsr Group LLC 302 268-6909
   913 N Market St Ste 200 Wilmington (19801) *(G-19278)*

Quadix LLC 877 669-8680
   364 E Main St Ste 212 Middletown (19709) *(G-7485)*

Quadrosense LLC 302 608-0779
   4 The Grn Dover (19901) *(G-3406)*

Quadrotech lt, Wilmington Also Called: Quadrotech Solutions Inc *(G-19279)*

Quadrotech Solutions Inc 302 660-0166
   802 N West St Ste 105 Wilmington (19801) *(G-19279)*

Quaestor Global Holdings Inc 610 745-3115
   1521 Concord Pike Ste 301 Wilmington (19803) *(G-19280)*

Quail Associates Inc 302 697-4660
   1 Clubhouse Dr Camden Wyoming (19934) *(G-966)*

Quail Technologies 201 497-4902
   850 New Burton Rd Ste 201 Dover (19904) *(G-3407)*

Quaker Chemical Corporation 302 791-9171
   818 N Washington St Wilmington (19801) *(G-19281)*

Quaker Hill Place Co, Wilmington Also Called: Boston Land Co Mgt Svcs Inc *(G-15009)*

Quakertown Wellness Center 302 644-0130
   1143 Savannah Rd Ste 4 Lewes (19958) *(G-6398)*

Qualdent LLC 856 642-4078
   1015 Cloister Rd Apt D Wilmington (19809) *(G-19282)*

Quality Builders Inc 302 697-0664
   213 Willow Ave Camden (19934) *(G-887)*

Quality Care Homes LLC 302 858-3999
   20366 Hopkins Rd Lewes (19958) *(G-6399)*

Quality Construction Cleaning 302 956-0752
   8902 Cannon Rd Bridgeville (19933) *(G-758)*

Quality Construction De LLC 302 757-6185
   811 Moores Ln New Castle (19720) *(G-9505)*

Quality Contracting Inc 302 270-8888
   317 N Layton Ave Wyoming (19934) *(G-20988)*

Quality Contracting & Developm 302 438-0874
   605 Louis Ln Middletown (19709) *(G-7486)*

Quality Contractor Svcs LLC 302 502-6815
   8 W Stephen Dr Newark (19713) *(G-11786)*

Quality Crawlspace & More LLC 443 944-5163
   32250 Mount Pleasant Rd Laurel (19956) *(G-5581)*

Quality Distributors Inc 917 335-6662
   244 Steeplechase Cir Wilmington (19808) *(G-19283)*

Quality Exteriors Inc 302 398-9283
   60 Hopkins Cemetery Rd Harrington (19952) *(G-4815)*

Quality Finishers Inc 302 325-1963
   1 Merit Dr Historic New Castle (19720) *(G-5058)*

Quality Garage 302 678-3667
   317 N Layton Ave Wyoming (19934) *(G-20989)*

Quality Home Services Inc 302 266-6113
   30 Albe Dr Newark (19702) *(G-11787)*

Quality Home Solutions LLC 330 717-6793
   65 Creek Dr Millsboro (19966) *(G-8439)*

Quality Htg Ar-Cnditioning Inc 302 654-5247
   31 Brookside Dr Wilmington (19804) *(G-19284)*

Quality In-House Video Inc 302 834-5654
   1 N Redspire Ct Newark (19702) *(G-11788)*

Quality Inn 302 292-1500
   48 Geoffrey Dr Newark (19713) *(G-11789)*

Quality Inn 302 659-3635
   190 Stadium St Smyrna (19977) *(G-13860)*

Quality Inn, Harrington Also Called: Veer Hotels Inc *(G-4844)*

Quality Inn, New Castle Also Called: Skyways Motor Lodge Corp *(G-9572)*

Quality Inn, Newark Also Called: Quality Inn *(G-11789)*

Quality Inn, Newark Also Called: Quality Inn Newark *(G-11790)*

Quality Inn Newark 707 622-5339
   65 Geoffrey Dr Newark (19713) *(G-11790)*

Quality Lawn Care Home RE 302 331-5892
   4 Turtle Dr Camden Wyoming (19934) *(G-967)*

Quality Pool Care 302 378-7486
   100 E Green St Middletown (19709) *(G-7487)*

Quality Reside LLC 484 957-0564
   651 N Broad St Ste 205 Middletown (19709) *(G-7488)*

Quality Rofg Sup Lancaster Inc 302 322-8322
   9 Parkway Cir New Castle (19720) *(G-9506)*

Quality Roofing Supply, New Castle Also Called: Quality Rofg Sup Lancaster Inc *(G-9506)*

Quality Staffing Services 302 990-5623
   308 E Stein Hwy Seaford (19973) *(G-13360)*

Quality Unit LLC 888 257-8754
   3 Germay Dr Wilmington (19804) *(G-19285)*

Quality Video Service, Newark Also Called: Quality In-House Video Inc *(G-11788)*

Qualityfastforyou LLC 618 540-1209
   254 Chapman Rd Ste 208 # 10485 Newark (19702) *(G-11791)*

Quandary Inc 302 757-6300
   5550 Kirkwood Hwy Wilmington (19808) *(G-19286)*

Quantae L Jennings 561 537-0821
   26497 Mount Joy Rd Millsboro (19966) *(G-8440)*

Quantconnect Corporation 917 327-0556
   16192 Coastal Hwy Lewes (19958) *(G-6400)*

Quanteam North America Inc 929 262-8538
   2915 Ogletown Rd Newark (19713) *(G-11792)*

Quantica Electronics LLC 302 648-4684
   750 Prides Xing Newark (19713) *(G-11793)*

Quantum Alchemy LLC 484 299-8016
   94 Karlyn Dr New Castle (19720) *(G-9507)*

Quantum Corporation 302 737-7012
   211 Executive Dr Ste 1 Newark (19702) *(G-11794)*

Quantum Leap Innovations Inc (PA) 302 894-8045
   3 Innovation Way Ste 100 Newark (19711) *(G-11795)*

Quantum Leap Technology Inc 614 254-1698
   3616 Kirkwood Hwy Ste A # 1324 Wilmington (19808) *(G-19287)*

Quantum Polymers Corporation 302 737-7012
   211 Executive Dr Ste 1 Newark (19702) *(G-11796)*

Quantum Satis Engeneering LLC 302 485-5448
   1201 N Orange St Ste 7160 Wilmington (19801) *(G-19288)*

Quantum Temple Inc 917 900-7452
   651 N Broad St Ste 206 Middletown (19709) *(G-7489)*

Quantum Transformation Inc 315 795-4427
   651 N Broad St Ste 206 Middletown (19709) *(G-7490)*

Quantumfly LLC 312 618-5739
   9 E Loockerman St Ste 215 Dover (19901) *(G-3408)*

Quantus Innovations LLC 302 356-1661
   136 Fairhill Dr Wilmington (19808) *(G-19289)*

Quarry Mill Craftsmen LLC 302 388-6289
   808 W 21st St Wilmington (19802) *(G-19290)*

Quartz Mill Contracting 302 750-6683
   34 Quartz Mill Rd Newark (19711) *(G-11797)*

Quavo Inc	484 257-9846
1201 N Orange St Ste 7115 Wilmington (19801) *(G-19291)*	
Quavo,, Wilmington Also Called: Quavo Inc *(G-19291)*	
Queen B Tbl Chair Rentals LLC	215 960-6303
8 The Grn # 8105 Dover (19901) *(G-3409)*	
Queen Bee Fashions, Ellendale Also Called: Famglam LLC *(G-3917)*	
Queen Theater	608 359-5507
500 N Market St Wilmington (19801) *(G-19292)*	
Queryloop Inc	412 253-6265
2035 Sunset Lake Rd Ste B2 Newark (19702) *(G-11798)*	
Queskr Inc	302 527-6007
16192 Coastal Hwy Lewes (19958) *(G-6401)*	
Queso Time De 3 LLC	302 368-4541
58 E Main St Newark (19711) *(G-11799)*	
Quest Diagnostics, Middletown Also Called: Quest Diagnostics Incorporated *(G-7491)*	
Quest Diagnostics Incorporated	302 376-8675
114 Sandhill Dr Ste 202 Middletown (19709) *(G-7491)*	
Quest Global Digital Inc	650 267-1334
1220 N Market St Ste 806 Wilmington (19801) *(G-19293)*	
Quest Pharmaceutical Services, Newark Also Called: Qps LLC *(G-11784)*	
Questar Capital Corporation	302 856-9778
13 Bridgeville Rd Georgetown (19947) *(G-4476)*	
Quetext Software LLC	800 403-9067
251 Little Falls Dr Wilmington (19808) *(G-19294)*	
Quic-Pro Inc (PA)	302 883-8305
8 The Grn Ste A Dover (19901) *(G-3410)*	
Quick Browser, Wilmington Also Called: Webbrowser Media Inc *(G-20705)*	
Quick Care Walk In and Medical	302 313-4660
17274 Coastal Hwy Lewes (19958) *(G-6402)*	
Quick Clean - Quick Fix LLC	302 245-9494
110 S Conwell St Seaford (19973) *(G-13361)*	
Quick Copies	302 374-0798
2605 Philadelphia Pike Claymont (19703) *(G-1273)*	
Quick Lane, New Castle Also Called: Bayshore Ford Truck Sales Inc *(G-8853)*	
Quick Lane, Smyrna Also Called: Willis Ford Inc *(G-13939)*	
Quick Server Hosting LLC	800 586-6126
122 Delaware Ave Ste B8 New Castle (19720) *(G-9508)*	
Quick Surface Solutions LLC	302 236-6941
30015 Gatehouse Dr Milton (19968) *(G-8692)*	
Quick To Go Shipping Center	302 327-0399
260 Quigley Blvd Historic New Castle (19720) *(G-5059)*	
Quick Togo, Historic New Castle Also Called: Quick To Go Shipping Center *(G-5059)*	
Quikstamp, Newark Also Called: Quikstamp LLC *(G-11800)*	
Quikstamp LLC	302 659-7555
140 Songsmith Dr Newark (19702) *(G-11800)*	
Quillen Signs LLC	302 684-3661
20874 Sussex Hwy Seaford (19973) *(G-13362)*	
Quillens Rent All Inc	302 227-3151
803 Rehoboth Ave Ste G Rehoboth Beach (19971) *(G-12903)*	
Quilted Heirlooms	302 354-6061
123 Back Creek Dr Middletown (19709) *(G-7492)*	
Quinn Data Corporation	302 429-7450
922 New Rd Ste 1 Wilmington (19805) *(G-19295)*	
Quinn Pediatric Dentistry	302 674-8000
1380 S State St Dover (19901) *(G-3411)*	
Quinn-Miller Group Inc	302 738-9742
34 Germay Dr Wilmington (19804) *(G-19296)*	
Quintasian LLC	302 674-3784
1706 N Dupont Hwy Dover (19901) *(G-3412)*	
Quinteccent Inc	443 838-5447
37808 Salty Way W Selbyville (19975) *(G-13595)*	
Quip Laboratories Incorporated	302 761-2600
1500 Eastlawn Ave Wilmington (19802) *(G-19297)*	
Quiver Finance Inc	302 803-6006
251 Little Falls Dr Wilmington (19808) *(G-19298)*	
Quoretech LLC (PA)	206 627-0030
200 Bellevue Pkwy Ste 210 Wilmington (19809) *(G-19299)*	
Quotanda LLC (PA)	917 971-7585
3500 S Dupont Hwy Dover (19901) *(G-3413)*	
Qwick Time Logistics LLC	985 413-2217
651 N Broad St Ste 205 Middletown (19709) *(G-7493)*	
Qwintry LLC	844 794-6879
1620 Johnson Way New Castle (19720) *(G-9509)*	
Qwintry LLC	858 633-6353
825 Dawson Dr Newark (19713) *(G-11801)*	
Qwintry Logistics, New Castle Also Called: Qwintry LLC *(G-9509)*	
R & A Contracting	302 669-7144
821 N Jefferson St Wilmington (19801) *(G-19300)*	
R & D Mechanical, Dover Also Called: Advanced Mechanical Inc *(G-1725)*	
R & E Excavation LLC	302 750-5226
226 Harlequin Dr New Castle (19720) *(G-9510)*	
R & J Taylor Inc	302 368-7888
1712 Ogletown Rd Newark (19711) *(G-11802)*	
R & J Welding & Fabrication	302 236-5618
32812 Bi State Blvd Laurel (19956) *(G-5582)*	
R & K Motors & Machine Shop	302 737-4596
60 Aleph Dr Newark (19702) *(G-11803)*	
R & L Property Management LLC	267 825-3570
212 Murphy Dr Middletown (19709) *(G-7494)*	
R & R Contractors LLC	302 344-6580
25115 Mary Rd Georgetown (19947) *(G-4477)*	
R & R Power Washing	302 259-4012
3 N Front St Georgetown (19947) *(G-4478)*	
R & S Fabrication Inc	302 629-0377
7159 Seashore Hwy Bridgeville (19933) *(G-759)*	
R & T Heating & Air	302 629-4011
307 N Pine St Seaford (19973) *(G-13363)*	
R & W Transportation Corp	703 670-5483
201 N Walnut St Wilmington (19801) *(G-19301)*	
R A Baba A Holdings Inc	302 533-8441
200 Continental Dr # 401 Newark (19713) *(G-11804)*	
R A Chance Plumbing Inc	302 324-8200
23 Parkway Cir Ste 5 New Castle (19720) *(G-9511)*	
R A Chance Plumbing Inc	302 292-1315
11 Fern Ct Newark (19702) *(G-11805)*	
R and H Filter Co Inc	302 856-2129
21646 Baltimore Ave Georgetown (19947) *(G-4479)*	
R and JC Onstruction Inc	302 419-7393
331 Corbitt Cir Bear (19701) *(G-443)*	
R and L Unified Foundation	302 244-1777
2901 Danby St Wilmington (19802) *(G-19302)*	
R C Fabricators Inc	302 573-8989
824 N Locust St Wilmington (19801) *(G-19303)*	
R D Arnold Construction Inc	610 255-4739
33 E Stonewall Dr Middletown (19709) *(G-7495)*	
R D Collins & Sons	302 834-3409
19 Shellbark Dr Bear (19701) *(G-444)*	
R E Excavation LLC	302 273-3669
15 Prestbury Sq Newark (19713) *(G-11806)*	
R E Michel Company LLC	302 678-0250
550 S Queen St Dover (19904) *(G-3414)*	
R E Michel Company LLC	302 645-0585
32258 Janice Rd Lewes (19958) *(G-6403)*	
R E Michel Company LLC	302 368-9410
904 Interchange Blvd Newark (19711) *(G-11807)*	
R E Wlliams Prof Acctg Frm Tax	302 598-7171
3628 Silverside Rd Wilmington (19810) *(G-19304)*	
R F Brown Inc	302 737-1993
18 Albe Dr Ste H Newark (19702) *(G-11808)*	
R F Gentner & Son	302 947-2733
22797 Dozer Ln Unit 15 Harbeson (19951) *(G-4712)*	
R H D Brandywine Hills	302 764-3660
710 W Matson Run Pkwy Wilmington (19802) *(G-19305)*	
R J Baker Distillery	302 745-0967
34171 Rider Rd Laurel (19956) *(G-5583)*	
R J K Transportation Inc	302 422-3188
1118 School St Houston (19954) *(G-5448)*	
R L Wlkerson Assoc Ltd A/K/A R	302 503-3207
150a Vickers Rd Milford (19963) *(G-8057)*	
R M Bell Industries Inc	302 542-3747
1504 Savannah Rd Lewes (19958) *(G-6404)*	
R M Quinn DDS	302 674-8000
1380 S State St Ste 2 Dover (19901) *(G-3415)*	

ALPHABETIC SECTION

R Macpherson Dr 302 834-8308
29 Bay Blvd Newark (19702) *(G-11809)*

R R Commercial Realty 302 856-4000
20461 Dupont Blvd Georgetown (19947) *(G-4480)*

R S Bauer LLC 302 398-4668
14380 S Dupont Hwy Harrington (19952) *(G-4816)*

R S C, Newark Also Called: Roller Service Corporation *(G-11912)*

R S Widdoes & Son Inc 302 764-7455
204 Channel Rd Wilmington (19809) *(G-19306)*

R Smiley LLC 302 463-5111
7 Metten Rd Newark (19713) *(G-11810)*

R Stanley Collier & Son Inc 302 398-7855
1832 Brownsville Rd Harrington (19952) *(G-4817)*

R W Harmon Carpentry Svcs LLC 302 477-1319
202 Florence Ave Wilmington (19803) *(G-19307)*

R W Morgan Farms Inc 302 542-7740
18126 Haflinger Rd Lincoln (19960) *(G-6695)*

R.R. Beach Associates, Dover Also Called: Beach Associates Inc *(G-1896)*

R/T Decks 302 983-4397
1667 Iron Hill Rd Newark (19702) *(G-11811)*

R&C Contractors LLC 302 284-9870
11351 S Dupont Hwy Felton (19943) *(G-4011)*

R&M Real Estate Company LLC (PA) 610 715-0906
651 N Broad St Ste 205 Middletown (19709) *(G-7496)*

R&O Drywall LLC 302 399-9480
1061 S Little Creek Rd Trlr 83 Dover (19901) *(G-3416)*

R&R Asphalt Paving 302 312-8355
734 Pulaski Hwy Lot 1 Bear (19701) *(G-445)*

R&R Homecare 302 478-3448
100 Beauregard Ct Wilmington (19810) *(G-19308)*

RA Harrison Paving 302 363-7344
1679 S Dupont Hwy Ste 100 Dover (19901) *(G-3417)*

Raad360 LLC 855 722-3360
550 S College Ave Ste 107 Newark (19713) *(G-11812)*

Raafat Z Abdel-Misih MD 302 658-7533
1021 Gilpin Ave Ste 203 Wilmington (19806) *(G-19309)*

Raas Infotek LLC 302 894-3184
262 Chapman Rd Ste 105a Newark (19702) *(G-11813)*

Rabbani-Tehrani Shahariar 302 376-1081
1401 Pole Bridge Rd Middletown (19709) *(G-7497)*

RAC Acceptance 302 477-1513
3300 Brandywine Pkwy Wilmington (19803) *(G-19310)*

RAC National Product Service L 972 801-1100
230 Executive Dr Ste 5 Newark (19702) *(G-11814)*

Race Advisors LLC 302 245-1895
21914 Back Bay Ln Lewes (19958) *(G-6405)*

Rachel Anne Beaston 302 449-1875
460 E Main St Middletown (19709) *(G-7498)*

Rachel L Farley 302 734-8000
99 Wolf Creek Blvd Ste 2 Dover (19901) *(G-3418)*

Rackdog LLC 224 803-4912
1013 Centre Rd Ste 403a Wilmington (19805) *(G-19311)*

RAD Pets Inc 302 335-5718
685 Roesville Rd Felton (19943) *(G-4012)*

Radaar LLC 855 623-0723
112 Capitol Trl Ste A627 Newark (19711) *(G-11815)*

Rader Services LLC 302 454-0373
111 Rosewood Dr Newark (19713) *(G-11816)*

Radfertility 302 602-8822
4735 Ogletown Stanton Rd Ste 3217 Newark (19713) *(G-11817)*

Radiant Technologies Inc 800 301-0980
254 Chapman Rd Ste 107 Newark (19702) *(G-11818)*

Radiation Oncology 302 733-1830
4755 Stanton Ogeltown Rd Newark (19718) *(G-11819)*

Radio Rehoboth 302 754-1444
37290 Rehoboth Avenue Ext Rehoboth Beach (19971) *(G-12904)*

Radiogenic Shielding Systems 302 288-0644
1201 N Orange St Ste 600 Wilmington (19801) *(G-19312)*

Radiology Associates, Newark Also Called: Papastvros Assoc Med Imgning LL *(G-11621)*

Radiology Associates Inc (PA) 302 832-5590
1701 Augustine Cut Off Ste 100 Wilmington (19803) *(G-19313)*

Radius Rx Direct Inc 302 658-9196
501 Nrth Shpley St Unit 2 Wilmington (19801) *(G-19314)*

Radius Services, Wilmington Also Called: Radius Services LLC *(G-19315)*

Radius Services LLC (PA) 302 993-0600
16 Hadco Rd Wilmington (19804) *(G-19315)*

Rafael Zaragoza Dr 302 697-2336
6 Pintail Pl Camden Wyoming (19934) *(G-968)*

Rafetto, Ray S DMD, Wilmington Also Called: A D Alpine DMD *(G-14161)*

Ragaman Services Inc 339 221-6757
2810 N Church St Ste 98887 Wilmington (19802) *(G-19316)*

Rage Recording Studio LLC 302 313-1699
651 N Broad St Ste 20530 Middletown (19709) *(G-7499)*

Rage World LLC 302 397-4400
1207 Delaware Ave Wilmington (19806) *(G-19317)*

Rah Books International 917 288-1064
9 E Loockerman St Dover (19901) *(G-3419)*

Rahaim & Saints Attys At Law (PA) 302 892-9200
2055 Limestone Rd Ste 211 Wilmington (19808) *(G-19318)*

Raiden Tech Group Inc 302 330-8514
119 Blue Ridge Cir Newark (19702) *(G-11820)*

Railbus Inc 302 725-3185
16192 Coastal Hwy Lewes (19958) *(G-6406)*

Railway Logistics, Wilmington Also Called: Hollywell Logistics LLC *(G-17170)*

Rain of Light Inc 302 312-7642
28 Tyre Ave Newark (19711) *(G-11821)*

Rainbow Charter Service, Newark Also Called: Creative Travel Inc *(G-10350)*

Rainbow Chorale of Del Inc 302 803-4440
1401 Windybush Rd Wilmington (19810) *(G-19319)*

Rainbow Seven Spa 302 533-6916
610 Capitol Trl Newark (19711) *(G-11822)*

Rainbow Xpress Lrng Acdemy LLC 302 659-0750
310 N Main St Smyrna (19977) *(G-13861)*

Rainmaker Software Group LLC 800 616-6701
1925 Lovering Ave Wilmington (19806) *(G-19320)*

Rakesh N Patel DPM 302 629-4569
1501 Middleford Rd Seaford (19973) *(G-13364)*

Ral Group 302 427-6970
1013 Centre Rd Ste 403a Wilmington (19805) *(G-19321)*

Rallypoint Solutions LLC 302 543-8087
3411 Silverside,Weldin,Ste107 Wilmington (19810) *(G-19322)*

Ralph and Paul Adams Inc 800 338-4727
103 Railroad Ave Bridgeville (19933) *(G-760)*

Ralph Burdick Do 302 834-3600
900 5th St Delaware City (19706) *(G-1556)*

Ralph Cahall & Son Paving 302 653-4220
2284 Bryn Zion Rd Smyrna (19977) *(G-13862)*

Ralph Del Signore Jr 302 239-0803
516 Erickson Ave Hockessin (19707) *(G-5353)*

Ralph E Willis 302 422-7167
690 Tub Mill Pond Rd Milford (19963) *(G-8058)*

Ralph G Degli Obizzi & Sons 302 658-5127
3 Colonial Ave Wilmington (19805) *(G-19323)*

Ralph G Degli Obizzi & Sons Inc 302 652-3593
400 Robinson Ln Wilmington (19805) *(G-19324)*

Ralph Paul Inc 302 764-9162
319 E Lea Blvd Wilmington (19802) *(G-19325)*

Ralph Tomases DDS PA 302 652-8656
707 Foulk Rd Ste 203 Wilmington (19803) *(G-19326)*

Ram Electric 302 379-3351
6 Radka Dr Newark (19702) *(G-11823)*

Ram Electric Inc 302 875-2356
34779 Whaleys Rd Laurel (19956) *(G-5584)*

Ram Tech Systems Inc (PA) 302 832-6600
1050 Industrial Dr Ste 110 Middletown (19709) *(G-7500)*

Rama Corporation 302 266-6600
181 Thompson Dr Hockessin (19707) *(G-5354)*

Ramachandra U Hosmane MD 302 645-2274
1408 Savannah Rd Lewes (19958) *(G-6407)*

Ramada Inn, Newark Also Called: Chapman Hospitality Inc *(G-10189)*

RAmaine&sons Contracting 302 212-8330
35716 Clam Ave Frankford (19945) *(G-4137)*

Ramani Natwarlal V MD 302 465-3002
   742 S Governors Ave Ste 2 Dover (19904) *(G-3420)*

Ramco Solutions LLC 302 715-5432
   28667 Sussex Hwy Laurel (19956) *(G-5585)*

Ramesh Vemulapalli MD 302 674-9141
   31 Gooden Ave Dover (19904) *(G-3421)*

Ramiglot Inc 929 203-5115
   651 N Broad St Middletown (19709) *(G-7501)*

Ramones Landscaping 302 268-8023
   4905 Mermaid Blvd Wilmington (19808) *(G-19327)*

Ramping Technology LLC 954 893-2909
   160 Greentree Dr Ste 101 Dover (19904) *(G-3422)*

Ramunno & Ramunno & Scerba PA 302 656-9400
   903 N French St Ste 106 Wilmington (19801) *(G-19328)*

Ramunno Ramunno 302 737-6909
   201 Louviers Dr Newark (19711) *(G-11824)*

Ranco Construction 302 322-3000
   4023 Kennett Pike Ste 218 Wilmington (19807) *(G-19329)*

Rand Accessories USA Inc 302 266-8200
   2915 Ogletown Rd Newark (19713) *(G-11825)*

Randstad Finance & Accounting, Wilmington Also Called: Randstad Professionals Us LLC *(G-19330)*

Randstad Professionals Us LLC 302 658-6181
   2 Mill Rd Ste 200 Wilmington (19806) *(G-19330)*

Randy L Christofferson 302 540-2006
   4004 Springfield Ln Wilmington (19807) *(G-19331)*

Randys Tree Service 302 856-7244
   20185 Dupont Blvd Georgetown (19947) *(G-4481)*

Rangaswamy Leela MD 267 256-0721
   4031 Kennett Pike Apt 117 Wilmington (19807) *(G-19332)*

Range Inc 201 350-7636
   919 N Market St Ste 950 Wilmington (19801) *(G-19333)*

Range Telecom, Wilmington Also Called: Range Inc *(G-19333)*

Rangeland Nm LLC 800 316-6660
   1675 S State St Ste B Dover (19901) *(G-3423)*

Ranuba Inc 870 360-3372
   16192 Coastal Hwy Lewes (19958) *(G-6408)*

Rao D Bhaskar MD 302 733-5700
   1 Centurian Dr Ste 307 Newark (19713) *(G-11826)*

Rapa Scrapple, Bridgeville Also Called: Ralph and Paul Adams Inc *(G-760)*

Rape of The Locke Inc 302 368-5370
   700 Barksdale Rd Ste 5 Newark (19711) *(G-11827)*

Rapid Hmmngbird Homebuyers LLC 347 671-7761
   8 The Grn Ste 11127 Dover (19901) *(G-3424)*

Rapid Renovation and Repr LLC 302 475-5400
   79 Pleasant Pine Ct Harrington (19952) *(G-4818)*

Rapport It Services LLC 302 304-8729
   300 Delaware Ave Ste 210 Wilmington (19801) *(G-19334)*

Rapta Inc 408 627-2556
   2140 S Dupont Hwy Camden (19934) *(G-888)*

Rare Royals Incorporated 833 288-7171
   651 N Broad St Middletown (19709) *(G-7502)*

Ras Addis & Associates Inc 302 571-1683
   460 Robinson Dr Wilmington (19801) *(G-19335)*

Raskaukas Joseph C Aty Law 302 537-2000
   33176 Coastal Hwy Bethany Beach (19930) *(G-630)*

Raskob Fndtion For Cthlic Actv 302 655-4440
   10 Montchanin Rd Wilmington (19807) *(G-19336)*

Rastan Enterprises LLC 443 691-0232
   651 N Broad St Middletown (19709) *(G-7503)*

Rated10 LLC 310 699-9537
   651 N Broad St Middletown (19709) *(G-7504)*

Rath Incorporated (DH) 302 294-4446
   100 Commerce Dr Ste 303 Newark (19713) *(G-11828)*

Rath Performance Fibers, Newark Also Called: Rath Incorporated *(G-11828)*

Rationalstat LLC 302 803-5429
   2055 Limestone Rd Ste 200c Wilmington (19808) *(G-19337)*

Ratner & Prestia PC 302 778-2500
   1007 N Orange St Ste 205 Wilmington (19801) *(G-19338)*

Rattan Company Inc 302 226-2404
   38131 Terrace Rd Rehoboth Beach (19971) *(G-12905)*

Rauma Survivors Foundation 302 275-9705
   2055 Limestone Rd Ste 109 Wilmington (19808) *(G-19339)*

Ravana C Starks Cleaning Svcs 215 647-2467
   506 Pythagoras Path Middletown (19709) *(G-7505)*

Rave Business Systems LLC 302 407-2270
   16192 Coastal Hwy Lewes (19958) *(G-6409)*

Ravis Car Detailing 302 945-8253
   23524 Elmwood Ave W Lewes (19958) *(G-6410)*

Ravnur Inc 239 963-4404
   3422 Old Capitol Trl Wilmington (19808) *(G-19340)*

Raw Essential Juice Bar 302 235-8019
   5335 Limestone Rd Unit B Wilmington (19808) *(G-19341)*

Raw Tennis Inc 302 507-8687
   127 Dewberry Dr Hockessin (19707) *(G-5355)*

Raw Tennis Inc 302 421-2012
   1001 Rockland Rd Wilmington (19803) *(G-19342)*

Rawlins Ferguson Jones & Lewis 302 337-8231
   9308 N Point Cmns Seaford (19973) *(G-13365)*

Rawr Imports Group LLC 609 271-3455
   779 Montclair Dr Apt 3 Claymont (19703) *(G-1274)*

Ray Book & Co, Dover Also Called: Raymond F Book III *(G-3425)*

Ray's & Sons, Felton Also Called: Rays Plumbing & Heating Svcs *(G-4013)*

Rayco Auto & Marine Uphl Inc 302 323-8844
   113 Carriage Dr Hockessin (19707) *(G-5356)*

Rayda Inc (PA) 302 261-5184
   1007 N Orange St Fl 4 Wilmington (19801) *(G-19343)*

Raymon James Financial Service, Wilmington Also Called: Raymond James Financial Svc *(G-19348)*

Raymond Babiarz Agt 302 993-8047
   1013 Centre Rd Ste 100 Wilmington (19805) *(G-19344)*

Raymond Chung Industries Corp 302 384-9796
   12 Sharons Way Wilmington (19808) *(G-19345)*

Raymond E Tomassetti Esq (PA) 302 539-3041
   1209 Coastal Hwy Fl 2 Fenwick Island (19944) *(G-4053)*

Raymond Entrmt Group LLC 302 731-2000
   62 N Chapel St Ste 4 Newark (19711) *(G-11829)*

Raymond F Book III (HQ) 302 734-5826
   220 Beiser Blvd Dover (19904) *(G-3425)*

Raymond Harner 302 737-0755
   317 Jaymar Blvd Newark (19702) *(G-11830)*

Raymond James, Wilmington Also Called: Raymond James & Associates Inc *(G-19346)*

Raymond James, Wilmington Also Called: Raymond James Financial *(G-19347)*

Raymond James, Wilmington Also Called: Raymond James Fincl Svcs Inc *(G-19349)*

Raymond James & Associates Inc 302 656-1534
   20 Montchanin Rd Ste 280 Wilmington (19807) *(G-19346)*

Raymond James Financial 302 384-8446
   1 Trolley Square Wilmington (19806) *(G-19347)*

Raymond James Financial Svc 302 778-2170
   900 Foulk Rd Ste 201 Wilmington (19803) *(G-19348)*

Raymond James Fincl Svcs Inc 302 656-1534
   20 Montchanin Rd Ste 280 Wilmington (19807) *(G-19349)*

Raymond L Para DDS 302 234-2728
   720 Yorklyn Rd Ste 120 Hockessin (19707) *(G-5357)*

Raymond M Cook 302 236-0087
   26329 Line Rd Seaford (19973) *(G-13366)*

Raymond M Smith Jr 302 670-3801
   2752 Downs Chapel Rd Clayton (19938) *(G-1400)*

Raymond Shephard 302 834-8405
   3815 Wrangle Hill Rd Bear (19701) *(G-446)*

Raymond V Feehery Jr DPM 302 999-8511
   620 Stanton Christiana Rd Ste 303 Newark (19713) *(G-11831)*

Raymond W Petrunich DDS 302 836-3565
   2444 Pulaski Hwy Newark (19702) *(G-11832)*

Rays and Sons, Seaford Also Called: Rays and Sons Mechanical LLC *(G-13367)*

Rays and Sons Mechanical LLC 302 697-2100
   307 S Winding Brooke Dr Seaford (19973) *(G-13367)*

Rays Plumbing & Heating Svcs 302 697-3936
   7244 S Dupont Hwy Felton (19943) *(G-4013)*

Razor Rick 302 604-1339
   18 W Saratoga Rd Milford (19963) *(G-8059)*

Rbah Inc 302 227-2009
   20259 Coastal Hwy Rehoboth Beach (19971) *(G-12906)*

ALPHABETIC SECTION

Rbc 302 892-5901
 2751 Centerville Rd Ste 212 Wilmington (19808) *(G-19350)*
Rbc Insurance Holdings USA Inc 302 651-8356
 1105 N Market St Ste 1300 Wilmington (19801) *(G-19351)*
Rbc Trust Company Delaware Ltd 302 892-6900
 4550 Linden Hill Rd Ste 200 Wilmington (19808) *(G-19352)*
Rbcmneusa LLC (PA) 607 316-5355
 1201 N Orange St Ste 600 Wilmington (19801) *(G-19353)*
Rbs Auto Repair Inc 302 678-8803
 1312 S Dupont Hwy Dover (19901) *(G-3426)*
Rbw Properties II 302 236-5155
 25488 Green Briar Rd Seaford (19973) *(G-13368)*
RC Turner Collection, Newark *Also Called: Kha-Neke Inc (G-11168)*
RC&ps LLC 516 984-8184
 8 The Grn Ste 15196 Dover (19901) *(G-3427)*
Rcd Timber Products Inc (PA) 302 778-5700
 1699 Matassino Rd New Castle (19720) *(G-9512)*
Rcd Timber Products Inc 302 384-6243
 4093 New Castle Ave New Castle (19720) *(G-9513)*
Rci, New Castle *Also Called: Reprographics Center Inc (G-9522)*
Rck Soliatire LLC 551 358-8400
 19266 Cstl Hwy Unit 4108 Rehoboth Beach (19971) *(G-12907)*
Rcs Mufflers Inc 302 328-7788
 120 N Dupont Hwy New Castle (19720) *(G-9514)*
Rct Studio Inc 669 255-1562
 251 Little Falls Dr Wilmington (19808) *(G-19354)*
Rd Innovative Planning 302 635-0767
 608 N Market St Apt 203 Wilmington (19801) *(G-19355)*
Rd Transport & Logistics LLC 302 893-8568
 300 Delaware Ave Ste 210 Wilmington (19801) *(G-19356)*
Rdu Instahotels LLC 919 297-8399
 651 N Broad St Ste 205 No7146 Middletown (19709) *(G-7506)*
RE Auto Repair 302 384-6508
 1 S Claymont St Wilmington (19801) *(G-19357)*
RE Bath of Northern De 302 414-9751
 135 Lynemore Dr Townsend (19734) *(G-14055)*
RE Calloway Trnsp Inc 302 422-2471
 897 School St Houston (19954) *(G-5449)*
RE Max of Wilmington (PA) 302 234-2500
 5307 Limestone Rd Ste 100 Wilmington (19808) *(G-19358)*
RE Max of Wilmington 302 657-8000
 2323 Pennsylvania Ave Wilmington (19806) *(G-19359)*
Re-Bath, Townsend *Also Called: RE Bath of Northern De (G-14055)*
Re-Up App Inc (PA) 267 972-1183
 8603 Park Ct Wilmington (19802) *(G-19360)*
Re/Max 302 381-2540
 300 Ocean View Pkwy Bethany Beach (19930) *(G-631)*
Re/Max, Bear *Also Called: Re/Max Premier Properties (G-447)*
Re/Max, Bethany Beach *Also Called: Re/Max (G-631)*
Re/Max, Bethany Beach *Also Called: Remax By Sea (G-632)*
Re/Max, Delmar *Also Called: Re/Max Coast Country (G-1631)*
Re/Max, Dover *Also Called: RE/Max Horizons Inc (G-3428)*
Re/Max, Hockessin *Also Called: Max RE Central (G-5304)*
Re/Max, Middletown *Also Called: Remax 1st Choice LLC (G-7512)*
Re/Max, Newark *Also Called: Max RE Associates Inc (G-11358)*
Re/Max, Newark *Also Called: Max RE Associates Inc (G-11359)*
Re/Max, Rehoboth Beach *Also Called: Debbie Reed (G-12713)*
Re/Max, Rehoboth Beach *Also Called: Delaware Realty Group Inc (G-12719)*
Re/Max, Wilmington *Also Called: RE Max of Wilmington (G-19358)*
Re/Max, Wilmington *Also Called: RE Max of Wilmington (G-19359)*
Re/Max, Wilmington *Also Called: Remax Sunvest Realty Corp (G-19429)*
Re/Max Coast Country 302 846-0200
 38613 Benro Dr Unit 5 Delmar (19940) *(G-1631)*
RE/Max Horizons Inc 302 678-4300
 1198 S Governors Ave Dover (19904) *(G-3428)*
Re/Max Premier Properties 302 883-9202
 309 Corbitt Cir Bear (19701) *(G-447)*
Re/Max Realty Group-Rentals 302 227-4800
 323 Rehoboth Ave Ste A Rehoboth Beach (19971) *(G-12908)*
Re/Max Twin Counties, Milford *Also Called: Watsons Auction & Realty Svc (G-8143)*
Reach Apps Inc 707 812-0285
 8 The Grn Ste A Dover (19901) *(G-3429)*
REACH RIVERSIDE, Wilmington *Also Called: Reach Riverside Dev Corp (G-19361)*
Reach Riverside Dev Corp 302 232-6612
 1121 Thatcher St Wilmington (19802) *(G-19361)*
Reachable Solutions Inc 908 962-8076
 8 The Grn Dover (19901) *(G-3430)*
Reackt, Newark *Also Called: Reackt LLC (G-11833)*
Reackt LLC (PA) 267 210-4743
 2035 Sunset Lake Rd Ste B2 Newark (19702) *(G-11833)*
Read Construction Inc 302 659-1144
 100 N Canvasback Ct Smyrna (19977) *(G-13863)*
Readhowyouwant LLC 302 730-4560
 3702 N Dupont Hwy Dover (19901) *(G-3431)*
Reading Assist Institute (PA) 302 425-4080
 100 W 10th St Ste 910 Wilmington (19801) *(G-19362)*
Readmark Inc 650 450-9110
 8 The Grn Ste A Dover (19901) *(G-3432)*
Ready 4 Work LLC 302 229-9701
 28 S Kirkwood St Dover (19904) *(G-3433)*
Ready Alliance Group Inc 866 229-0927
 251 Little Falls Dr Wilmington (19808) *(G-19363)*
Ready Set Textiles Inc 302 518-6583
 19266 Coastal Hwy Rehoboth Beach (19971) *(G-12909)*
Readyb Inc 323 813-8710
 8 The Grn Ste A Dover (19901) *(G-3434)*
Reagan-Watson Auctions LLC 302 422-2392
 115 N Washington St Milford (19963) *(G-8060)*
Real Ch Inc (PA) 347 433-8945
 2055 Limestone Rd Ste 200e Wilmington (19808) *(G-19364)*
Real Deals LLC 484 470-8582
 3 Germay Dr Ste 4 Pmb 1460 Wilmington (19804) *(G-19365)*
Real Entrepreneur Inc 989 300-0975
 2810 N Church St Wilmington (19802) *(G-19366)*
Real Estate, Newark *Also Called: Maverick Realty LLC (G-11357)*
Real Estate Invstmnt/Asset MGT, Wilmington *Also Called: C and C Management Group LLC (G-15173)*
Real Estate Market 302 715-5640
 405 N Central Ave Laurel (19956) *(G-5586)*
Real Estate Partners LLC 302 656-0251
 2800 Lancaster Ave Ste 8 Wilmington (19805) *(G-19367)*
Real Estate Services, Georgetown *Also Called: Deltrust Group Inc (G-4292)*
Real Hvac Services 302 727-0272
 18389 Olde Coach Dr Rehoboth Beach (19971) *(G-12910)*
Real Matter LLC 302 291-2562
 16192 Coastal Hwy Lewes (19958) *(G-6411)*
Real Messenger Inc (PA) 657 237-5918
 4001 Kennett Pike Ste 302 Wilmington (19807) *(G-19368)*
Real Ones Inc (PA) 408 857-0262
 251 Little Falls Dr Wilmington (19808) *(G-19369)*
Real Pro Holdings Inc 541 743-8500
 1209 N Orange St Wilmington (19801) *(G-19370)*
Real World Endo 302 827-4816
 29602 Vincent Village Dr Milton (19968) *(G-8693)*
Real World Endo 302 477-0960
 2114 Silverside Rd Wilmington (19810) *(G-19371)*
Realassist Inc 888 309-1114
 8 The Grn Ste 4000 Dover (19901) *(G-3435)*
Realcold Manager LLC (PA) 332 264-7077
 251 Little Falls Dr Wilmington (19808) *(G-19372)*
Realm Software Inc 734 799-0793
 850 New Burton Rd Dover (19904) *(G-3436)*
Realty Mogul 14 LLC 877 977-2776
 73 Greentree Dr Ste 77 Dover (19904) *(G-3437)*
Rebatus Inc 929 393-5529
 16192 Coastal Hwy Lewes (19958) *(G-6412)*
Rebecca E Orr 302 521-4920
 557 Upper Pike Creek Rd Newark (19711) *(G-11834)*
Rebecca Jaffee MD 302 992-0200
 3105 Limestone Rd Ste 301 Wilmington (19808) *(G-19373)*

Rebecca Smlak-Kettlehake Psy D 302 261-6901
  200 Biddle Ave Newark (19702) *(G-11835)*

Rebuilding Tgther Philadelphia 302 234-4417
  525 Judges Ct Newark (19711) *(G-11836)*

Recadia Capital LLC 866 671-1280
  1521 Concord Pike Ste 301 Wilmington (19803) *(G-19374)*

Recadia Corp Llc 866 671-1280
  1521 Concord Pike Ste 301 Wilmington (19803) *(G-19375)*

Recentia Usa Inc 847 977-7571
  251 Little Falls Dr Wilmington (19808) *(G-19376)*

Recipero Inc 888 551-1159
  2801 Centerville Rd Pmb 21 Wilmington (19808) *(G-19377)*

Reciprocity Health LLC 302 530-5244
  406 Hillside Rd Wilmington (19807) *(G-19378)*

Records - Gebhart Agency Inc 302 653-9211
  2 N Market St Smyrna (19977) *(G-13864)*

Records-Gebhart Insurance, Smyrna Also Called: Records - Gebhart Agency Inc *(G-13864)*

Recovery Destination Services 302 559-1010
  853 Stockbridge Dr Hockessin (19707) *(G-5358)*

Recovery Innovations Inc 302 660-7560
  2508 Belford Dr Wilmington (19808) *(G-19379)*

Recovery Inovations Inc 602 636-4608
  659 E Chestnut Hill Rd Newark (19713) *(G-11837)*

Recreate Inc 404 625-3387
  800 N King St Ste 304 Wilmington (19801) *(G-19380)*

Recticel US Inc 248 393-2100
  1105 N Market St Ste 1300 Wilmington (19801) *(G-19381)*

Recyclers of Delaware LLC 856 466-9067
  1148 Pulaski Hwy Ste 107-313 Bear (19701) *(G-448)*

Recycling Swift & Demolition 302 328-8283
  469 Old Airport Rd New Castle (19720) *(G-9515)*

Red Barn Inc 302 678-0271
  1062 Lafferty Ln Dover (19901) *(G-3438)*

Red Bird Egg Farm Inc (PA) 302 834-2571
  1701 Red Lion Rd Bear (19701) *(G-449)*

Red Brick Realty LLC 302 540-1128
  2102 Kirkwood Hwy Wilmington (19805) *(G-19382)*

Red Buffer LLC 628 228-6024
  8 The Grn Ste 4645 Dover (19901) *(G-3439)*

Red Carpet Inn, Dover Also Called: Seper 8 Motel *(G-3533)*

Red Carpet Travel Agency Inc (PA) 302 475-1220
  501 Silverside Rd Ste 41 Wilmington (19809) *(G-19383)*

Red Clay Consolidated Schl Dst 302 235-6600
  2025 Graves Rd Hockessin (19707) *(G-5359)*

Red Clay Inc 302 239-2018
  2388 Brackenville Rd Hockessin (19707) *(G-5360)*

Red Cross, Wilmington Also Called: American National Red Cross *(G-14438)*

Red Dog Associates, Selbyville Also Called: Red Dog Plumbing and Htg Corp *(G-13596)*

Red Dog Plumbing and Htg Corp 302 436-2922
  37058 Roxana Rd Selbyville (19975) *(G-13596)*

Red Eft Painting 302 636-9463
  104 W Reamer Ave Wilmington (19804) *(G-19384)*

Red Ladder Productions LLC 781 970-6124
  1209 N Orange St Wilmington (19801) *(G-19385)*

Red Lion LLC 202 559-9365
  2207 Concord Pike # 117 Wilmington (19803) *(G-19386)*

Red Lion Medical Safety Inc 302 731-8600
  123a Sandy Dr Newark (19713) *(G-11838)*

Red Rhino Labs LLC 650 275-2464
  2035 Sunset Lake Rd B2 Newark (19702) *(G-11839)*

Red Roof Inn, Dover Also Called: Shree Lalji LLC *(G-3552)*

Red Roof Inn, Newark Also Called: Red Roof Inns Inc *(G-11840)*

Red Roof Inns Inc 302 292-2870
  415 Stanton Christiana Rd Newark (19713) *(G-11840)*

Red Spark LP 215 695-5002
  2093 Philadelphia Pike Ste 1072 Claymont (19703) *(G-1275)*

Red Spear LLC 757 301-1052
  8 The Grn Ste 7142 Dover (19901) *(G-3440)*

Red Stone USA Inc 919 931-5078
  16192 Coastal Hwy Lewes (19958) *(G-6413)*

Red Sun Custom Apparel Inc 302 988-8230
  1 Mason Dr Selbyville (19975) *(G-13597)*

Red Target LLC 302 752-4449
  17507 S Dupont Hwy Harrington (19952) *(G-4819)*

Redarc Corporation 704 247-5150
  1675 S State St Ste B Dover (19901) *(G-3441)*

Redarc Electronics, Dover Also Called: Redarc Corporation *(G-3441)*

Redcircle Technologies Inc 844 404-2525
  2093 Philadelphia Pike Claymont (19703) *(G-1276)*

Reddix Transportation Inc 302 249-9331
  31014 Oak Leaf Dr Lewes (19958) *(G-6414)*

Reddy Dr Veena 302 998-0304
  537 Stanton Christiana Rd Ste 211 Newark (19713) *(G-11841)*

Redflag Marketing Corp 302 464-8116
  600 N Broad St Ste 5 Middletown (19709) *(G-7507)*

Redgait 2530 LLC 302 683-0978
  3 Kenleigh Ct Wilmington (19808) *(G-19387)*

Redgate Tech Inc 302 377-6563
  4023 Kennett Pike Ste 50558 Wilmington (19807) *(G-19388)*

Redhead Farms LLC 443 235-3990
  34102 Rider Rd Laurel (19956) *(G-5587)*

Redi Call Corp 302 856-9000
  543 S Bedford St Georgetown (19947) *(G-4482)*

Redi-Call Communications, Georgetown Also Called: Redi Call Corp *(G-4482)*

Redland Mills Co 706 288-6003
  1201 N Market St Ste 111 Wilmington (19801) *(G-19389)*

Redleo Software Inc 302 691-9072
  1201 N Orange St Ste 7495 Wilmington (19801) *(G-19390)*

Redmill Auto Repair 302 292-2155
  1209 Capitol Trl Newark (19711) *(G-11842)*

Redrum City Productions 313 389-6836
  110 Hillview Ave New Castle (19720) *(G-9516)*

Reed Elsevier Capital Inc 302 427-9299
  1105 N Market St Ste 501 Wilmington (19801) *(G-19391)*

Reed Smith LLP 302 778-7500
  1201 N Market St Ste 1500 Wilmington (19801) *(G-19392)*

Reed Trucking Company 302 684-8585
  522 Chestnut St Milton (19968) *(G-8694)*

Reeds Refuge Center Inc 302 428-1830
  1601 N Pine St Wilmington (19802) *(G-19393)*

Reel Inc 302 319-3522
  651 N Broad St Ste 201 Middletown (19709) *(G-7508)*

Reelve Inc 312 459-2669
  8 The Grn Dover (19901) *(G-3442)*

Reetz Family Practice LLC 215 806-0318
  116 Tweedsmere Dr Townsend (19734) *(G-14056)*

Reevoy Corporation 631 769-6681
  919 N Market St Ste 950 Wilmington (19801) *(G-19394)*

Refermate LLC 951 892-8159
  427 N Tatnall St Wilmington (19801) *(G-19395)*

Refining Co 302 832-1099
  4550 Wrangle Hill Rd New Castle (19720) *(G-9517)*

Refix Commodities LLC 888 465-8020
  160 Greentree Dr Ste 101 Dover (19904) *(G-3443)*

Reflection Biotechnologies Inc 212 765-2200
  1013 Centre Rd Ste 403b Wilmington (19805) *(G-19396)*

Reform LLC 813 299-5726
  1675 S State St Ste B Dover (19901) *(G-3444)*

Regal Cinemas Inc 302 479-0753
  3300 Brandywine Pkwy Wilmington (19803) *(G-19397)*

Regal Contractors LLC 302 736-5000
  13 Nobles Pond Xing Dover (19904) *(G-3445)*

Regal Hts Hlthcare Rhab Ctr LL 302 998-0181
  6525 Lancaster Pike Hockessin (19707) *(G-5361)*

Regal Painting & Decorating 302 994-8943
  209 S Woodward Ave Wilmington (19805) *(G-19398)*

Regal Technologies LLC 321 695-4142
  16192 Coastal Hwy Lewes (19958) *(G-6415)*

Regen III (usgc) Corporation 604 806-5275
  1209 N Orange St Wilmington (19801) *(G-19399)*

Regency Hlthcare Rehab Ctr LLC 302 654-8400
  801 N Broom St Wilmington (19806) *(G-19400)*

Regent Open Mri 252 430-6246
  1350 Middleford Rd Ste 503 Seaford (19973) *(G-13369)*

ALPHABETIC SECTION — Relax Massage Therapy

Reger Rizzo & Darnall LLP.. 302 652-3611
  1001 N Jefferson St Ste 202 Wilmington (19801) *(G-19401)*
Reggies General Contg Svc, Felton Also Called: Reginald D Quail Sr *(G-4014)*
Regina Coleman.. 215 476-4682
  2720 Chinchilla Dr Wilmington (19810) *(G-19402)*
Regina McLarnon... 800 903-8114
  3 Beaver Valley Rd Wilmington (19803) *(G-19403)*
Reginald D Quail Sr.. 302 335-3145
  3718 Midstate Rd Felton (19943) *(G-4014)*
Regional Builders Inc... 302 628-8660
  100 Park Ave Seaford (19973) *(G-13370)*
Regional Enterprises LLC.. 302 227-0202
  307 S Boardwalk Rehoboth Beach (19971) *(G-12911)*
Regional Hmatology Oncology PA.................................... 302 731-7782
  4701 Ogletown Stanton Rd Ste 2100 Newark (19713) *(G-11843)*
Regional Hmatology Oncology PA (PA)............................ 302 731-7782
  1010 N Bancroft Pkwy Ste 21 Wilmington (19805) *(G-19404)*
Regional Medical Associates PA....................................... 302 734-7246
  240 Beiser Blvd Ste 201 Dover (19904) *(G-3446)*
Regional Medical Group LLC... 302 993-7890
  4512 Kirkwood Hwy Ste 202 Wilmington (19808) *(G-19405)*
Regional Orthopaedic Assoc (PA)..................................... 302 633-3555
  1941 Limestone Rd Ste 101 Wilmington (19808) *(G-19406)*
Regional Properties LLC.. 302 740-9740
  1096 Old Churchmans Rd Newark (19713) *(G-11844)*
Regis Corporation.. 302 834-9916
  420 Eden Cir Bear (19701) *(G-450)*
Regis Corporation.. 302 697-6220
  263 Walmart Dr Camden (19934) *(G-889)*
Regis Corporation.. 302 376-6165
  705 Middletown Warwick Rd Middletown (19709) *(G-7509)*
Regis Corporation.. 302 430-0881
  939 N Dupont Blvd Milford (19963) *(G-8061)*
Regis Corporation.. 302 227-9730
  19330 Coastal Hwy Unit 6 Rehoboth Beach (19971) *(G-12912)*
Regis Corporation.. 302 629-2916
  632 N Dual Hwy Seaford (19973) *(G-13371)*
Regis Corporation.. 302 628-0484
  22899 Sussex Hwy Seaford (19973) *(G-13372)*
REGISTERED AGENTS, Wilmington Also Called: American Incorporators Ltd *(G-14432)*
Registered Agents Ltd... 302 421-5750
  1013 Centre Rd Ste 403a Wilmington (19805) *(G-19407)*
Registered Agents Limited, Wilmington Also Called: Registered Agents Ltd *(G-19407)*
Registration LLC.. 877 955-7111
  1013 Centre Rd Wilmington (19805) *(G-19408)*
Registred Agnts Legal Svcs LLC....................................... 302 427-6970
  1013 Centre Rd Ste 403s Wilmington (19805) *(G-19409)*
Regulation Holdco LLC (HQ)... 800 521-1114
  251 Little Falls Dr Wilmington (19808) *(G-19410)*
Regulatory Datacorp Inc.. 302 299-2284
  1007 N Orange St Fl 4 Wilmington (19801) *(G-19411)*
Regulatory Insurance Services.. 302 678-2004
  841 Silver Lake Blvd Ste 201 Dover (19904) *(G-3447)*
Rehabilitation Associates Pa... 302 293-6877
  200 Biddle Ave Ste 204 Newark (19702) *(G-11845)*
Rehabilitation Associates PA (PA).................................... 302 832-8894
  2600 Glasgow Ave Ste 210 Newark (19702) *(G-11846)*
Rehabilitation Consultants Inc.. 302 655-5877
  2401 Pennsylvania Ave Ste 112 Wilmington (19806) *(G-19412)*
Rehabilitation Consultants Inc.. 302 478-5240
  3411 Silverside Rd Ste 105 Wilmington (19810) *(G-19413)*
Rehabilitation Service.. 302 449-3050
  124 Sleepy Hollow Dr Ste 101 Middletown (19709) *(G-7510)*
Rehabitation Consultants.. 302 478-2131
  3411 Silverside Rd Ste 105 Wilmington (19810) *(G-19414)*
Rehoboth Animal Hospital... 302 227-2009
  20259 Coastal Hwy Rehoboth Beach (19971) *(G-12913)*
Rehoboth Bay Mobile Home Cmnty, Rehoboth Beach Also Called: Theta Vest Inc *(G-12993)*
Rehoboth Bay Sailing Assn... 302 227-9008
  Highway One Rehoboth Beach (19971) *(G-12914)*
Rehoboth Bch Dwey Bch Chmber C................................. 302 227-2233
  501 Rehoboth Ave Rehoboth Beach (19971) *(G-12915)*
Rehoboth Bch Sister Cites Assn.. 302 249-7878
  41 Sussex St Rehoboth Beach (19971) *(G-12916)*
Rehoboth Beach.. 302 245-0304
  105 2nd St Rehoboth Beach (19971) *(G-12917)*
Rehoboth Beach Country Club.. 302 227-3811
  221 W Side Dr Rehoboth Beach (19971) *(G-12918)*
Rehoboth Beach Dance & Company................................. 302 245-8132
  19287 Miller Rd Rehoboth Beach (19971) *(G-12919)*
Rehoboth Beach Dent... 302 226-7960
  19643 Blue Bird Ln Rehoboth Beach (19971) *(G-12920)*
Rehoboth Beach Historical Soc (PA)................................ 302 227-7310
  17 Christian St Rehoboth Beach (19971) *(G-12921)*
Rehoboth Beach Museum, Rehoboth Beach Also Called: Rehoboth Beach Historical Soc *(G-12921)*
Rehoboth Beach Yoga Centr.. 302 226-7646
  Yoga Center Rehoboth Beach (19971) *(G-12922)*
Rehoboth Beach, De Branch, Rehoboth Beach Also Called: Td Bank NA *(G-12991)*
Rehoboth Car Wash Inc... 302 227-6177
  37053 Rehoboth Avenue Ext Rehoboth Beach (19971) *(G-12923)*
Rehoboth Car Wash Inc... 302 245-6839
  19898 Hebron Rd Rehoboth Beach (19971) *(G-12924)*
Rehoboth Country Club, Rehoboth Beach Also Called: Ronald L Barrows *(G-12938)*
Rehoboth Fitness LLC.. 410 742-7990
  35770 Airport Rd Rehoboth Beach (19971) *(G-12925)*
Rehoboth Golf Park.. 302 542-1295
  12 Chatham Rd Rehoboth Beach (19971) *(G-12926)*
Rehoboth Home Sales Inc... 609 924-7701
  19 Fairway Dr Rehoboth Beach (19971) *(G-12927)*
Rehoboth House of Jerky.. 215 272-4217
  149 Rehoboth Ave Unit 8b Rehoboth Beach (19971) *(G-12928)*
Rehoboth Inn LLC... 302 226-2410
  20494 Coastal Hwy Rehoboth Beach (19971) *(G-12929)*
Rehoboth Nails & Spa.. 302 703-6481
  18701 Coastal Hwy Rehoboth Beach (19971) *(G-12930)*
Rehoboth Professional Ctr LLC... 302 226-8334
  18977 Munchy Branch Rd Ste 2 Rehoboth Beach (19971) *(G-12931)*
Rehoboth Real Estate... 302 226-6417
  246 Rehoboth Ave Rehoboth Beach (19971) *(G-12932)*
Rehoboth Realty Inc... 302 227-5000
  20184 Coastal Hwy Rehoboth Beach (19971) *(G-12933)*
Rehoboth Shores, Millsboro Also Called: Nanticoke Shores Assoc LLC *(G-8399)*
Rehrig Penn Logistics Inc.. 302 659-3337
  171 Hemlock Way Smyrna (19977) *(G-13865)*
Reico Kitchen & Bath, Millsboro Also Called: Robinson Export & Import Corp *(G-8449)*
Reiki Experience... 704 526-7092
  128 Wharton St Millsboro (19966) *(G-8441)*
Reiki With Rebecca... 302 528-0582
  102 David Rd Wilmington (19804) *(G-19415)*
Reilly Janiczek & McDevitt PC.. 302 777-1700
  1013 Centre Rd Ste 210 Wilmington (19805) *(G-19416)*
Reilly Sweeping Inc... 302 738-8961
  10 Albe Dr Newark (19702) *(G-11847)*
Reima Sportswear, Hockessin Also Called: Sui Trading Co *(G-5394)*
Reincarnatio Inc.. 703 479-1337
  251 Little Falls Dr Wilmington (19808) *(G-19417)*
Reinvex LLC.. 484 259-7889
  3801 Kennett Pike Wilmington (19807) *(G-19418)*
Reis Enterprises LLC.. 302 740-8382
  504 Connor Blvd Bear (19701) *(G-451)*
Reiver Hyman & Co Inc.. 302 764-2040
  4104 N Market St Wilmington (19802) *(G-19419)*
Rejuvntion Skin Wllness Asthti... 302 537-8318
  35202 Atlantic Ave Millville (19967) *(G-8545)*
Rekindle Family Medicine.. 302 565-4799
  5590 Kirkwood Hwy Wilmington (19808) *(G-19420)*
Related RE Fund III LP.. 212 801-1013
  251 Little Falls Dr Wilmington (19808) *(G-19421)*
Relax Inn... 302 875-1554
  30702 Sussex Hwy Laurel (19956) *(G-5588)*
Relax Massage Therapy... 302 738-7300
  105 Louviers Dr Newark (19711) *(G-11848)*

Relaxing Tours LLC — ALPHABETIC SECTION

Relaxing Tours LLC..610 905-3852
  11546 Adamsville Rd Greenwood (19950) *(G-4663)*
Releaf Property Services, Townsend *Also Called: Beshore Lawn Service LLC (G-13963)*
Reliable Aid Inc..302 419-3558
  2 Commonwealth Blvd New Castle (19720) *(G-9518)*
Reliable Copy Service Inc..302 654-8080
  1007 N Orange St Ste 110 Wilmington (19801) *(G-19422)*
Reliable Handyman Services LLC..............................302 943-0166
  2807 Peachtree Run Rd Dover (19901) *(G-3448)*
Reliable Home Inspection (PA)..................................302 455-1200
  100 Old Kennett Rd Wilmington (19807) *(G-19423)*
Reliable Prperty Solutions LLC..................................302 753-1299
  108 W Main St Newark (19711) *(G-11849)*
Reliable Trailer Inc..856 962-7900
  1603 Andrews Lake Rd Felton (19943) *(G-4015)*
Reliance Communications Inc...................................888 673-5426
  2711 Centerville Rd Ste 400 Wilmington (19808) *(G-19424)*
Reliance Egleford Upstream LLC................................302 472-7437
  1007 N Orange St Wilmington (19801) *(G-19425)*
Reliance Healthcare LLC..302 838-3100
  1993 Pulaski Hwy Bear (19701) *(G-452)*
Reliance Trust Company LLC....................................302 246-5400
  200 Bellevue Pkwy Wilmington (19809) *(G-19426)*
Relig Staffing Inc..312 219-6786
  32 W Loockerman St Ste 108 Dover (19904) *(G-3449)*
Relocation Pettinar..302 777-5240
  220 Presidential Dr Wilmington (19807) *(G-19427)*
Relyance Skim Camp..717 343-3588
  36774 Cedar St Ocean View (19970) *(G-12561)*
Relytv LLC...213 373-5988
  8 The Grn Ste 8422 Dover (19901) *(G-3450)*
Remarle LLC..215 245-6448
  427 Smee Rd Middletown (19709) *(G-7511)*
Remax 1st Choice LLC..302 378-8700
  100 S Broad St Middletown (19709) *(G-7512)*
Remax By Sea..302 541-5000
  R 1 5th D St Bethany Beach (19930) *(G-632)*
Remax Sunvest Realty..302 995-1589
  5560 Kirkwood Hwy Wilmington (19808) *(G-19428)*
Remax Sunvest Realty Corp (PA)...............................302 995-1589
  2103 W Newport Pike A Wilmington (19804) *(G-19429)*
Remedy Restore Aesthetics LLC................................302 538-5261
  45 Chadwick Dr Dover (19901) *(G-3451)*
Rementer Brothers Inc...302 249-4250
  28348 Lewes Georgetown Hwy Milton (19968) *(G-8695)*
Remline Corp...302 737-7228
  456 Corporate Blvd Newark (19702) *(G-11850)*
Remora Company..845 532-5172
  16192 Coastal Hwy Lewes (19958) *(G-6416)*
Renaissance Security LP...302 588-5975
  1 Mill Rd Wilmington (19806) *(G-19430)*
Renaissance Square LLC...302 943-5118
  1534 S Governors Ave Ste B Dover (19904) *(G-3452)*
Renal Care Ctr...302 453-8834
  63 University Ave New Castle (19720) *(G-9519)*
Renal Care Group Inc..302 678-8744
  748 S New St Dover (19904) *(G-3453)*
Renderapps LLC...919 274-0582
  8 The Grn Ste A Dover (19901) *(G-3454)*
Rene Delyn Designs Inc..302 736-6070
  1744 N Dupont Hwy Dover (19901) *(G-3455)*
Rene Delyn Hair Design Studio, Dover *Also Called: Rene Delyn Designs Inc (G-3455)*
Renegade Entrmt & Media Co...................................904 789-2897
  651 N Broad St Ste 201 Middletown (19709) *(G-7513)*
Renegade Entrmt & Media Co LLC.............................267 648-7916
  651 N Broad St Ste 205 Middletown (19709) *(G-7514)*
Renew Integrative Health..302 444-4366
  256 Chapman Rd Newark (19702) *(G-11851)*
Renew Your Heart and Mind LLC...............................302 344-7519
  23321 Country Living Rd Millsboro (19966) *(G-8442)*
Renewable energies, Lewes *Also Called: Gnz LLC (G-6042)*

Renewable Energy Holdings LLC................................817 213-6041
  8 The Grn Ste 8357 Dover (19901) *(G-3456)*
Renewed Environments...302 323-9100
  223 Lisa Dr New Castle (19720) *(G-9520)*
Rennies Rolled Ice Cream LLC..................................551 273-8925
  501 Central Ave New Castle (19720) *(G-9521)*
Renovate LLC..302 378-1768
  786 Old School House Rd Middletown (19709) *(G-7515)*
Renovate Solutions..717 951-4300
  37116 Fairway Dr Frankford (19945) *(G-4138)*
Renove Med Spa...302 584-3216
  21 Bethany Forest Dr Dagsboro (19939) *(G-1497)*
Rent Co Inc..302 739-0860
  35 Commerce Way Ste 180 Dover (19904) *(G-3457)*
Rent Equip, Ocean View *Also Called: Baybiw Development LLC (G-12469)*
Rent Equip, Ocean View *Also Called: Rent Equipment (G-12562)*
Rent Equipment..302 537-9797
  9 Town Rd Ocean View (19970) *(G-12562)*
Rent-A-Center, Bear *Also Called: Upbound Group Inc (G-553)*
Rent-A-Center, Claymont *Also Called: Upbound Group Inc (G-1324)*
Rent-A-Center, Dover *Also Called: Upbound Group Inc (G-3756)*
Rent-A-Center, Dover *Also Called: Upbound Group Inc (G-3757)*
Rent-A-Center, Dover *Also Called: Upbound Group Inc (G-3758)*
Rent-A-Center, Georgetown *Also Called: Upbound Group Inc (G-4566)*
Rent-A-Center, Milford *Also Called: Upbound Group Inc (G-8131)*
Rent-A-Center, Millsboro *Also Called: Upbound Group Inc (G-8490)*
Rent-A-Center, Newark *Also Called: Upbound Group Inc (G-12284)*
Rent-A-Center, Seaford *Also Called: Upbound Group Inc (G-13438)*
Rent-A-Center, Smyrna *Also Called: Upbound Group Inc (G-13925)*
Rent-A-Center, Wilmington *Also Called: Upbound Group Inc (G-20535)*
Rentdrop Inc...302 250-2525
  2093 Philadelphia Pike Ste 8419 Claymont (19703) *(G-1277)*
Rently Software LLC...718 502-6575
  2035 Sunset Lake Rd Newark (19702) *(G-11852)*
Rentokil North America Inc......................................302 337-8100
  18904 Maranatha Way Bridgeville (19933) *(G-761)*
Rentokil North America Inc......................................410 882-1000
  955 Dawson Dr Ste 2 Newark (19713) *(G-11853)*
Rentokil North America Inc......................................302 325-2687
  701 Dawson Dr Newark (19713) *(G-11854)*
Rentokil North America Inc......................................302 733-0851
  1712 Ogletown Rd Newark (19711) *(G-11855)*
Rentwell Leasemanagemaintain.................................302 256-5356
  3203 Concord Pike Ste E Wilmington (19803) *(G-19431)*
Rentz Painting LLC..302 363-6619
  32473 E Penn Ct Millsboro (19966) *(G-8443)*
Rentzs Sign Service...302 378-9607
  4676 Dupont Pkwy Townsend (19734) *(G-14057)*
Renu Chrprctic Wllness Injury...................................302 368-0124
  1352 Marrows Rd Newark (19711) *(G-11856)*
Renu ME Property Solutions.....................................267 440-6863
  913 N Market St Ste 200 Wilmington (19801) *(G-19432)*
Renzi Rust Inc...302 424-4470
  6722 Griffith Lake Dr Milford (19963) *(G-8062)*
Reolink Innovation Inc..833 424-0499
  251 Little Falls Dr Wilmington (19808) *(G-19433)*
Rep..910 622-0252
  285 The Grn Newark (19716) *(G-11857)*
Repair My Place LLC..302 286-7721
  25 Lynam Lookout Dr Newark (19702) *(G-11858)*
Reporting Solutions LLC...857 284-3583
  102 Cannonball Ln Newark (19702) *(G-11859)*
Reproductive Associates Del, Newark *Also Called: Reproductive Associates Del PA (G-11860)*
Reproductive Associates Del PA (PA)..........................302 602-8822
  4735 Ogletown Stanton Rd Ste 3217 Newark (19713) *(G-11860)*
Reprographics Center Inc..302 328-5019
  298 Churchmans Rd New Castle (19720) *(G-9522)*
Republic Services Inc..302 658-4097
  1420 New York Ave Wilmington (19801) *(G-19434)*
Republix Sourcestrike Corp......................................647 206-1503
  850 New Burton Rd Ste 201 Dover (19904) *(G-3458)*

ALPHABETIC SECTION

Repurpose Global Inc (PA) 732 322-3839
1209 N Orange St Wilmington (19801) *(G-19435)*

Rescue For Misunderstood Inc 302 650-8123
6002 Old Capitol Trl Wilmington (19808) *(G-19436)*

Rescue Printig 302 286-7266
17 Lynch Farm Dr Newark (19713) *(G-11861)*

Rescue Surgical Solutions LLC 302 722-5877
1305 Whittaker Rd Newark (19702) *(G-11862)*

Resemble Ai Inc 401 255-6004
651 N Broad St Ste 201 Middletown (19709) *(G-7516)*

Reservation Centre LLC 888 284-0908
8 The Grn Ste A Dover (19901) *(G-3459)*

Reserve At Darley Green 302 525-8450
700 Darley Green Dr Claymont (19703) *(G-1278)*

Resh LLC 302 543-5469
206 Jestan Blvd New Castle (19720) *(G-9523)*

Residence Inn 302 777-7373
1300 N Market St Wilmington (19801) *(G-19437)*

Residence Inn By Mariott 302 539-3200
99 Hollywood St Bethany Beach (19930) *(G-633)*

Residence Inn By Marriott, Bethany Beach Also Called: Residence Inn By Mariott *(G-633)*

Residence Inn By Marriott, Newark Also Called: Residence Inn By Marriott LLC *(G-11863)*

Residence Inn By Marriott, Rehoboth Beach Also Called: Colonial Oaks Hotel LLC *(G-12693)*

Residence Inn By Marriott, Wilmington Also Called: Residence Inn *(G-19437)*

Residence Inn By Marriott LLC 302 453-9200
240 Chapman Rd Newark (19702) *(G-11863)*

Residence Inn Dover 302 677-0777
600 Jefferic Blvd Dover (19901) *(G-3460)*

Residences At City Center, Wilmington Also Called: Luxiasuites LLC *(G-18038)*

Residnce Inn Wlmngton Nwrk/CHR 302 453-9200
240 Chapman Rd Newark (19702) *(G-11864)*

Resistance Energy Fund LP 514 871-2120
1209 N Orange St Wilmington (19801) *(G-19438)*

Resistbot Inc 408 599-2094
2035 Sunset Lake Rd B2 Newark (19702) *(G-11865)*

Resolute Industrial 267 401-0973
200 Interchange Blvd Newark (19711) *(G-11866)*

Resort At Massey's Landing, Millsboro Also Called: Masseys Landing Park Inc *(G-8367)*

Resort Broadcasting Co LP 302 945-2050
31549 Dutton Ln Lewes (19958) *(G-6417)*

Resort Custom Homes 302 645-8222
18355 Coastal Hwy Lewes (19958) *(G-6418)*

Resort Hotel LLC 302 226-1515
19210 Coastal Hwy Rehoboth Beach (19971) *(G-12934)*

Resort Investigation & Patrol 302 539-5808
19 Pine St Millville (19970) *(G-8546)*

Resort Poker League 302 604-8706
38291 Osprey Ct Apt 1168 Selbyville (19975) *(G-13598)*

Resort Quest Delaware Beaches, Bethany Beach Also Called: Resortquest Delaware RE LLC *(G-634)*

Resortquest 302 616-1040
21 Village Green Dr Ocean View (19970) *(G-12563)*

Resortquest Delaware RE LLC (DH) 302 541-8999
33546 Market Pl Bethany Beach (19930) *(G-634)*

Resortquest Service Center 302 541-5977
33260 Coastal Hwy Unit 1 Bethany Beach (19930) *(G-635)*

Resource Center YMCA, Wilmington Also Called: Young Mens Christian Associat *(G-20939)*

Resource Intl Inc 302 762-4501
7 Boulden Cir New Castle (19720) *(G-9524)*

Resource Mortgage Corp 302 657-0181
3301 Lancaster Pike Ste 10 Wilmington (19805) *(G-19439)*

Resourceful Rae LLC (PA) 302 220-7704
513 Shue Dr Newark (19713) *(G-11867)*

Resources For Human Dev 215 848-1947
28 Stature Dr Newark (19713) *(G-11868)*

Resources For Human Dev 215 951-0300
1800 N Jefferson St Wilmington (19802) *(G-11440)*

Resources For Human Dev Inc 302 731-5283
12 Montrose Dr Newark (19713) *(G-11869)*

Resources For Human Dev Inc 215 951-0300
256 Chapman Rd Ste 202 Newark (19702) *(G-11870)*

Resources For Human Dev Inc 302 691-7574
2804 Grubb Rd Wilmington (19810) *(G-19441)*

Response Computer Group Inc 302 335-3400
213 W Liberty Way Milford (19963) *(G-8063)*

Responsible Publishing 609 412-9621
301 Snuff Mill Rd Wilmington (19807) *(G-19442)*

Restarant Actn Md-Tlantic Whse 302 462-6678
33334 Main St Dagsboro (19939) *(G-1498)*

Restoration Guys LLC 302 542-4045
717 S Washington St Milford (19963) *(G-8064)*

Restore Incorporated 302 655-6257
3411 Silverside Rd Ste 104 Wilmington (19810) *(G-19443)*

Restore Sssex Cnty Hbtat For H 302 703-6388
18501 Stamper Dr Lewes (19958) *(G-6419)*

Restoring Lf Rstrtion Ctr Corp 862 772-5148
109 Arnell Ct New Castle (19720) *(G-9525)*

Restoring Life, New Castle Also Called: Restoring Lf Rstrtion Ctr Corp *(G-9525)*

Restu Stay LLC 347 522-0919
128 Sunset Blvd New Castle (19720) *(G-9526)*

Resulticks Solution Inc 347 416-7673
1013 Centre Rd Ste 403s Wilmington (19805) *(G-19444)*

Resume Tech Corp 800 403-5610
651 N Broad St Middletown (19709) *(G-7517)*

Resume Writer Direct 866 706-0973
427 N Tatnall St Wilmington (19801) *(G-19445)*

Resurrected Electric Llc 302 841-8989
9248 Sharptown Rd Laurel (19956) *(G-5589)*

Resurrektion Athletics Inc 302 300-1900
651 N Broad St Ste 205 # 2478 Middletown (19709) *(G-7518)*

Rethmerica Accounting and 302 317-2417
260 Chapman Rd Newark (19702) *(G-11871)*

Retired Senior Volunteer Prog 302 856-5815
546 S Bedford St Georgetown (19947) *(G-4483)*

Retired-N-Fit 302 478-4191
138 Wye Oak Dr Townsend (19734) *(G-14058)*

Retouch Salon LLC (PA) 929 247-7095
16192 Coastal Hwy Lewes (19958) *(G-6420)*

Retreat At Newark 302 294-6520
74 E Main St Newark (19711) *(G-11872)*

Retro Fitness 302 276-0828
835 Pulaski Hwy Bear (19701) *(G-453)*

Retro Fitness, Wilmington Also Called: HB Fitness Concord Inc *(G-17083)*

Retro Fitness, Wilmington Also Called: HB Fitness Delaware Inc *(G-17084)*

Retrolio Games LLC 423 873-8768
2093 Philadelphia Pike Claymont (19703) *(G-1279)*

Retrosheet Inc 302 731-1570
20 Sunset Rd Newark (19711) *(G-11873)*

Retrotekusa Inc 469 619-0899
251 Little Falls Dr Wilmington (19808) *(G-19446)*

Reuse Everything Institute Inc 607 351-1770
2711 Centerville Rd Ste 400 Wilmington (19808) *(G-19447)*

Reva Stays LLC 347 599-8599
353 Mingo Way Townsend (19734) *(G-14059)*

Rever Cre Inc 201 380-4566
8 The Grn Ste 10664 Dover (19901) *(G-3461)*

Review 302 831-2771
325 Academy St Rm 201 Newark (19716) *(G-11874)*

Revoltion Freedom Platform LLC 301 653-9207
16192 Coastal Hwy Lewes (19958) *(G-6421)*

Revolution Recovery Del LLC 302 356-3000
1101 Lambson Ln New Castle (19720) *(G-9527)*

Revolutionary Identity Elusion 618 780-1755
9 E Loockerman St Dover (19901) *(G-3462)*

Revolve Technologies LLC 302 528-2647
266 Camerton Lane Townsend (19734) *(G-14060)*

Revolve Training Staffing LLC 833 973-8658
1521 Concord Pike Ste 301 Wilmington (19803) *(G-19448)*

Rex Auto Body Inc 302 731-4707
27 North St Newark (19711) *(G-11875)*

Rexmex Drywall LLC 302 343-9140
449 Gibbs Chapel Rd Hartly (19953) *(G-4906)*

Reybold — ALPHABETIC SECTION

Reybold 302 584-7975
50 Turnberry Ct Bear (19701) *(G-454)*

Reybold Construction Corp 302 832-7100
116 E Scotland Dr Bear (19701) *(G-455)*

Reybold Construction Group LLC 302 832-7100
116 E Scotland Dr Bear (19701) *(G-456)*

Reybold Group 302 834-1740
701 Observatory Dr Bear (19701) *(G-457)*

Reybold Group of Companies Inc (PA) 302 832-7100
116 E Scotland Dr Bear (19701) *(G-458)*

Reybold Group of Companies Inc 302 834-2544
114 E Scotland Dr Bear (19701) *(G-459)*

Reybold Group of Companies Inc 302 838-7405
950 Red Lion Rd New Castle (19720) *(G-9528)*

Reybold Homes Inc 302 834-3000
960 Red Lion Rd New Castle (19720) *(G-9529)*

Reyes Rebeca 302 276-9132
1303 Goldeneye Dr New Castle (19720) *(G-9530)*

Reyes Painting LLC 302 470-1961
25203 Zoar Rd Georgetown (19947) *(G-4484)*

Reyes Painting LLC 302 519-4538
28936 John J Williams Hwy Millsboro (19966) *(G-8444)*

Reynolds Metals Company LLC 302 366-0555
700 Pencader Dr Newark (19702) *(G-11876)*

Reynolds Services Ltd 877 404-2179
251 Little Falls Dr Wilmington (19808) *(G-19449)*

Rfmw, Lincoln *Also Called: Tti Inc (G-6707)*

Rfpmart LLC 315 627-3333
3511 Silverside Rd Ste 105 Wilmington (19810) *(G-19450)*

Rfx Analyst Inc 302 244-5650
8 The Grn # 5875 Dover (19901) *(G-3463)*

Rg3 Texas Holdings LLC 778 891-7569
1209 N Orange St Wilmington (19801) *(G-19451)*

Rg3 Texas Inc 778 891-7569
1209 N Orange St Wilmington (19801) *(G-19452)*

Rgd & Sons, Wilmington *Also Called: Ralph G Degli Obizzi & Sons Inc (G-19324)*

Rgp Holding Inc (PA) 302 661-0117
1105 N Market St Wilmington (19801) *(G-19453)*

Rgs Technology Group LLC 302 397-3169
300 Delaware Ave Ste 210a Wilmington (19801) *(G-19454)*

Rh Gallery and Studios 302 218-5182
1304 Old Lancaster Pike Ste D Hockessin (19707) *(G-5362)*

Rhd De Program 302 883-2926
1305 Mcd Dr Dover (19901) *(G-3464)*

Rheumatology Center-Delaware 302 994-2345
4512 Kirkwood Hwy Ste 301 Wilmington (19808) *(G-19455)*

Rheumatology Consultant Del, Lewes *Also Called: Jose A Pando MD (G-6150)*

Rheumatology Consultants 302 491-6659
509 Lakeview Ave Milford (19963) *(G-8065)*

Rhewum America Inc 215 804-7977
1000 N West St Ste 1200 Wilmington (19801) *(G-19456)*

Rhi Refractories Holding Company 302 655-6497
1105 N Market St Ste 1300 Wilmington (19801) *(G-19457)*

Rhino Cabling Group Inc 302 312-1033
528 Sepia Ct Newark (19702) *(G-11877)*

Rhino Fence 302 544-5225
10 Mcgaughy Dr New Castle (19720) *(G-9531)*

Rhino Lnngs Del Auto Style Inc 302 368-4660
841 Old Baltimore Pike Newark (19702) *(G-11878)*

Rhino Smart Publications 302 737-3422
55 Shull Dr Newark (19711) *(G-11879)*

Rhoades & Morrow LLC 302 422-6705
30 Nw 10th St Milford (19963) *(G-8066)*

Rhoades & Morrow LLC 302 427-9500
1225 N King St Ste 1200 Wilmington (19801) *(G-19458)*

Rhodeside Incorporated 505 261-4568
322 Compton Ct Wilmington (19801) *(G-19459)*

Rhodunda & Williams LLC 302 576-2000
1521 Concord Pike Ste 205 Wilmington (19803) *(G-19460)*

Rhomboid Properties, Wilmington *Also Called: Pbe Companies LLC (G-18930)*

Rhonda Frick 302 236-1456
33298 Coastal Hwy Bethany Beach (19930) *(G-636)*

Rhonda Replogle Horses 301 730-3100
281 Marjorie Ln Harrington (19952) *(G-4820)*

Rhondium Corporation 800 771-4364
35a The Commons Wilmington (19810) *(G-19461)*

Rhoyal Extensions 318 572-2549
37 W Kyla Marie Dr Newark (19702) *(G-11880)*

RHS Realty 302 436-6478
32191 Bixler Rd Selbyville (19975) *(G-13599)*

Rhue & Associates Inc 302 422-3058
628 Milford Harrington Hwy Ste 3 Milford (19963) *(G-8067)*

Rhue Insurance, Milford *Also Called: Rhue & Associates Inc (G-8067)*

Rhythm and Heat LLC 302 897-5259
900 N Washington St Ste 13 Wilmington (19801) *(G-19462)*

Rhyze Solutions LLC 850 376-4201
1313 N Market St Ste 5100 Wilmington (19801) *(G-19463)*

RI Int 302 318-6032
659 E Chestnut Hill Rd Newark (19713) *(G-11881)*

Riale System Services 302 328-3848
301 Dasher Cir Bear (19701) *(G-460)*

Riar Jehan MD 302 855-1349
25 Bridgeville Rd Georgetown (19947) *(G-4485)*

Ribodynamics LLC 518 339-6605
2711 Centerville Rd # 400 Wilmington (19808) *(G-19464)*

Ric Investments LLC 302 656-8996
1403 Foulk Rd Ste 200 Wilmington (19803) *(G-19465)*

Rich Hebert & Associates 202 255-3474
38027 Fenwick Shoals Blvd Selbyville (19975) *(G-13600)*

Rich Rising Enterprise LLC 302 592-6697
8 The Grn Dover (19901) *(G-3465)*

Richard A & James F Corroon Fd 302 425-4841
2305 W 11th St Wilmington (19805) *(G-19466)*

Richard A Parsons Agency Inc 302 674-2810
57 Saulsbury Rd Ste C Dover (19904) *(G-3466)*

Richard Addington Co 302 422-2668
316 N Rehoboth Blvd Milford (19963) *(G-8068)*

Richard Allen Coalition 302 258-7182
16950 Deer Forest Rd Georgetown (19947) *(G-4486)*

Richard Bratcher 803 786-7322
39 Stuart Dr Dover (19901) *(G-3467)*

Richard C Paul 302 645-2666
34431 King Street Row Lewes (19958) *(G-6422)*

Richard D Whaley Cnstr LLC 302 934-9525
29952 Lewis Rd Millsboro (19966) *(G-8445)*

Richard Dale Rodgers 814 323-0450
311 Laurel Ave Newark (19711) *(G-11882)*

Richard E Chodroff DMD 302 995-6979
3105 Limestone Rd Ste 203 Wilmington (19808) *(G-19467)*

Richard E Williams 302 956-0374
8443 Cannon Rd Seaford (19973) *(G-13373)*

Richard Earl Fisher 302 598-1957
820 Kiamensi Rd Wilmington (19804) *(G-19468)*

Richard Harrison Jr Paving 302 875-4206
4705 Phillips Landing Rd Laurel (19956) *(G-5590)*

Richard Hrrmann Strbilders Inc 302 654-4329
500 Robinson Ln Wilmington (19805) *(G-19469)*

Richard J Tananis DDS LLC 302 875-4271
10250 Stone Creek Dr Unit 1 Laurel (19956) *(G-5591)*

Richard Kren Lfrak Chrtble Fnd 302 656-2390
1007 N Orange St Wilmington (19801) *(G-19470)*

Richard L Cruz MD 302 577-4270
10 Central Ave New Castle (19720) *(G-9532)*

Richard L Engle Jr & Assoc PA 302 674-5685
1651 S Dupont Hwy Dover (19901) *(G-3468)*

Richard L Sherry MD (PA) 302 475-1880
2500 Grubb Rd Ste 234 Wilmington (19810) *(G-19471)*

Richard L Todd PHD 302 853-0559
28312 Lewes Georgetown Hwy Milton (19968) *(G-8696)*

Richard M Gold DC 302 998-1424
5175 W Woodmill Dr Wilmington (19808) *(G-19472)*

Richard M White Welding 302 684-4461
14443 Collins St Milton (19968) *(G-8697)*

ALPHABETIC SECTION — Riversedge

Richard P Horgan Insurance 302 934-9494
1301 N Harrison St # 808 Wilmington (19806) *(G-19473)*

Richard S Brown 302 438-6885
70 University Ave New Castle (19720) *(G-9533)*

Richard S Cobb Esquire 302 467-4430
919 N Market St Ste 600 Wilmington (19801) *(G-19474)*

Richard W Krick Jr 302 227-6974
8 Fox Creek Dr Rehoboth Beach (19971) *(G-12935)*

Richard Williamson, Dover Also Called: J R Williamson DDS *(G-2761)*

Richard Y Johnson & Son Inc 302 422-3732
18404 Johnson Rd Lincoln (19960) *(G-6696)*

Richards Investment Group Corp 302 399-0450
381 Grayton Dr Smyrna (19977) *(G-13866)*

Richards Layton & Finger P A 302 651-7700
Uknown Wilmington (19801) *(G-19475)*

Richards Layton & Finger P A 302 651-7700
1 Rodney Sq 920 N King St Wilmington (19801) *(G-19476)*

Richards Layton & Finger P A 302 651-7700
920 N King St Ste 200 Wilmington (19801) *(G-19477)*

Richardson Building Dnrec 772 215-7625
89 Kings Hwy Dover (19901) *(G-3469)*

Richelle L Clark 302 448-8094
401 N Bedford St Georgetown (19947) *(G-4487)*

Richert Inc (PA) 302 684-0696
2836 S Bay Shore Dr Milton (19968) *(G-8698)*

Richmen Trucking, Millsboro Also Called: Quantae L Jennings *(G-8440)*

Richmonds Automotive, Newark Also Called: Doug Richmonds Body Shop *(G-10554)*

Rickards Auto Body 302 934-9600
30450 Marina Rd Dagsboro (19939) *(G-1499)*

Rickcools, New Castle Also Called: Richard S Brown *(G-9533)*

Ricks Electric LLC 410 924-6764
29 Ridgeway Cir Felton (19943) *(G-4016)*

Ricks Fitness & Health Inc 302 684-0316
22893 Neptune Rd Milton (19968) *(G-8699)*

Ricos Cleaning Services Inc 302 357-8155
51 Fairway Rd Apt 3d Newark (19711) *(G-11883)*

Riddle Inc 724 901-1810
3524 Silverside Rd Ste 35b Wilmington (19810) *(G-19478)*

Riders App Inc 347 484-4344
1 Commerce St 1 # 1 Wilmington (19801) *(G-19479)*

Ridge It Solutions Inc 302 455-8566
152 Hammersmith Way Bear (19701) *(G-461)*

Ridgewood Electric Pwr Tr III 302 888-7444
1314 N King St Wilmington (19801) *(G-19480)*

Ridrodsky & Long PA (PA) 302 691-8822
300 Delaware Ave Ste L Wilmington (19801) *(G-19481)*

Riemel of Delaware LLC 302 998-5806
460 B And O Ln Wilmington (19804) *(G-19482)*

Rifenburg Trucking Inc 302 349-5969
6525 Hickman Rd Greenwood (19950) *(G-4664)*

Riftwalker Game Studio Inc 213 215-7165
8 The Grn Ste 12437 Dover (19901) *(G-3470)*

Riggin Group 302 235-2903
530 Schoolhouse Rd Ste E Hockessin (19707) *(G-5363)*

Right As Rain Seamless Rain Gu 302 272-2135
41 N Edgehill Ave Dover (19901) *(G-3471)*

Right Coast Pro 302 832-1517
116 Michael Ln Bear (19701) *(G-462)*

Right Knda Guys Car Sltons LLC 302 772-8717
35 Salem Church Rd Ste 66 Newark (19713) *(G-11884)*

Right Way Flagging and Sign Co 302 698-5229
173 Brenda Ln Ste C Camden Wyoming (19934) *(G-969)*

Right-Away Auto Assistance LLC 302 438-9970
7209 Lancaster Pike 4-1 Hockessin (19707) *(G-5364)*

Rigid Builders LLC 732 425-3443
24491 Blackberry Dr Georgetown (19947) *(G-4488)*

Rikarbon Inc 765 237-7649
550 S College Ave Ste 107 Newark (19713) *(G-11885)*

Riko Inc 216 810-5083
2810 N Church St Wilmington (19802) *(G-19483)*

Riley Electric 302 533-5918
1235 Old Coochs Bridge Rd Newark (19713) *(G-11886)*

Riley Electric Inc 302 276-3581
1235 Old Coochs Bridge Rd Newark (19713) *(G-11887)*

Rinehimer Auto Works, Newark Also Called: Rinehimer Body Shop Inc *(G-11888)*

Rinehimer Body Shop Inc 302 737-7350
6 Mill Park Ct Newark (19713) *(G-11888)*

Ringlet LLC (PA) 802 238-5858
8 The Grn Ste B Dover (19901) *(G-3472)*

Ringlet Technologies LLC, Dover Also Called: Ringlet LLC *(G-3472)*

Ripe Tech Corp 786 633-2228
919 N Market St Ste 950 Wilmington (19801) *(G-19484)*

Rippl Labs Inc (PA) 551 427-1997
2711 Centerville Rd # 400 Wilmington (19808) *(G-19485)*

Risa Malone MA CCC-Slp 352 536-9187
192 Riverdale Ln Clayton (19938) *(G-1401)*

Rise Fitness and Adventure, Rehoboth Beach Also Called: Rehoboth Fitness LLC *(G-12925)*

Risen Services 302 858-8840
32531 Samuel Hill Rd Laurel (19956) *(G-5592)*

Rising Star Communication 302 462-5474
14830 Josephs Rd Seaford (19973) *(G-13374)*

Rising Star Preschool, Wilmington Also Called: Rising Stars Child Care Inc *(G-19486)*

Rising Stars Child Care Inc 302 998-7682
415 Milmar Rd Wilmington (19804) *(G-19486)*

Rising Sunset Publishing LLC 877 231-5425
200 Continental Dr # 401 Newark (19713) *(G-11889)*

Risleus Properties LLC (PA) 302 353-1255
8000 Pistachio Pl Dover (19901) *(G-3473)*

Risq Trading Corp 332 877-9934
1209 N Orange St Wilmington (19801) *(G-19487)*

Rita Gasz Real Estate 302 234-6043
7234 Lancaster Pike Hockessin (19707) *(G-5365)*

Rita Porter Darnetta 302 419-3877
25 Aquilla Dr New Castle (19720) *(G-9534)*

Ritchie Sawyer Corporation (PA) 302 475-1971
2502 Pin Oak Dr Wilmington (19810) *(G-19488)*

Rite Way Distributors (PA) 302 535-8507
7385 S Dupont Hwy Felton (19943) *(G-4017)*

Rittenhouse Sq Fine Art Show 610 299-1343
28 Bradbury Rd New Castle (19720) *(G-9535)*

Riv Athletics 610 229-9092
512 Justison St Wilmington (19801) *(G-19489)*

Rivas Ulises 302 454-8595
31 Albe Dr Ste 3 Newark (19702) *(G-11890)*

Rivas Ironworks, Newark Also Called: Rivas Ulises *(G-11890)*

River Asphalt LLC 302 934-0881
30548 Thorogoods Rd Dagsboro (19939) *(G-1500)*

River Ridge Homeowners Assn 302 761-9592
1538 Seton Villa Ln Wilmington (19809) *(G-19490)*

River Rock Contracting LLC 302 538-7169
2942 S State St Camden Wyoming (19934) *(G-970)*

River Tower Ventures LLC 302 691-2100
322 A St Ste 300 Wilmington (19801) *(G-19491)*

Rivera Transportation Inc 302 258-9023
205 W 7th St Laurel (19956) *(G-5593)*

Riverbend Inv MGT LLC Is A Rgs 302 219-3080
179 Rehoboth Ave Unit 165 Rehoboth Beach (19971) *(G-12936)*

Riverdale Park LLC 302 945-2475
28301 Chief Rd Millsboro (19966) *(G-8446)*

Riveredge III LLC 302 656-3631
300 Water St Wilmington (19801) *(G-19492)*

Riverfront Dev Corp Del 302 425-4890
815 Justison St Ste D Wilmington (19801) *(G-19493)*

Riverfront Development, Wilmington Also Called: Riverfront Dev Corp Del *(G-19493)*

Riverfront Development Corp 302 425-4890
815 Justison St Ste D Wilmington (19801) *(G-19494)*

Riverfront Hotel LLC 302 803-5888
760 Justison St Wilmington (19801) *(G-19495)*

Riverfront Pets 302 428-9777
311 Justison St Wilmington (19801) *(G-19496)*

Rivers Family Foundation Inc 800 839-1754
501 Silverside Rd Ste 123 Wilmington (19809) *(G-19497)*

Riversedge 267 342-6984
1 Ave Of The Arts Wilmington (19801) *(G-19498)*

Riversedge Advisors LLC 302 573-6864
  600 N King St Ste 200 Wilmington (19801) *(G-19499)*

Riverside Farms LLC 302 222-0760
  604 Campground Rd Felton (19943) *(G-4018)*

Riverside Foods Inc 888 546-8810
  16192 Coastal Hwy Lewes (19958) *(G-6423)*

Riverview Medical Center 302 396-1204
  8534 Concord Rd Seaford (19973) *(G-13375)*

Riverwalk Mini Golf 302 425-4890
  550 Justison St Wilmington (19801) *(G-19500)*

RJR Recycling Co 610 647-1555
  955 River Rd New Castle (19720) *(G-9536)*

Rk Advisors LLC 302 561-5258
  104 Country Center Ln Hockessin (19707) *(G-5366)*

RK&k, Wilmington Also Called: Rummel Klepper & Kahl LLP *(G-19590)*

Rkb Fnral Trdg As Wtson Fnrl H, Millsboro Also Called: Watson Funeral Home Inc *(G-8501)*

Rkb Funerals Inc 302 934-7842
  Millsboro (19966) *(G-8447)*

Rkj Construction Inc 302 690-0959
  2252 Saint James Dr Wilmington (19808) *(G-19501)*

RKL Financial Corporation (HQ) 302 283-8000
  300 Continental Dr Fl 1 Newark (19713) *(G-11891)*

Rlk Press Inc 267 565-5138
  3511 Silverside Rd Wilmington (19810) *(G-19502)*

Rls Associates, Wilmington Also Called: Mergers Acqstons Strtegies LLC *(G-18280)*

Rm Industrial Welding 302 407-6685
  1212 E 15th St Wilmington (19802) *(G-19503)*

Rmb Cleaning Services LLC 302 753-0622
  1 Chestnut Hill Plz Ste 1217 Newark (19713) *(G-11892)*

Rmch, Wilmington Also Called: Financial Services *(G-16609)*

Rmdc Inc 302 798-8800
  698 Naamans Rd Claymont (19703) *(G-1280)*

Rmm Builders LLC 302 983-0734
  1 Haywood Ct Newark (19711) *(G-11893)*

Rmv Workforce Corp 302 408-1061
  124 Broadkill Rd Ste 380 Milton (19968) *(G-8700)*

Rnh Installation 302 731-8900
  42 Albe Dr Ste E Newark (19702) *(G-11894)*

RNS Contracting 302 384-4633
  810 Liberty Blvd New Castle (19720) *(G-9537)*

Road & Rail Services Inc 302 731-2552
  502 S College Ave Ste C Newark (19713) *(G-11895)*

Road Site Construction Inc 302 645-1922
  16192 Coastal Hwy Lewes (19958) *(G-6424)*

Roadrunner Express Inc 302 426-9551
  21 Millside Dr Wilmington (19801) *(G-19504)*

Roar Pedal LLC 412 301-6002
  8 The Grn Ste B Dover (19901) *(G-3474)*

Rob Watson 302 234-8877
  5307 Limestone Rd Ste 100 Wilmington (19808) *(G-19505)*

Robert A Chagnon 302 489-1932
  726 Loveville Rd Rm A55 Hockessin (19707) *(G-5367)*

Robert A Heinle M D 302 651-6400
  1600 Rockland Rd Wilmington (19803) *(G-19506)*

Robert A Penna DMD 302 623-4060
  4735 Ogletown Stanton Rd Ste 1104 Newark (19713) *(G-11896)*

Robert A Steele M D 302 234-2600
  304 Lantana Dr Hockessin (19707) *(G-5368)*

Robert A Steele M D 302 478-5500
  1401 Foulk Rd Ste 101 Wilmington (19803) *(G-19507)*

Robert B Gregg 302 994-9300
  301 S Dupont Rd Newport (19804) *(G-12456)*

Robert Bird 302 654-4003
  1701 Shallcross Ave Ste A Wilmington (19806) *(G-19508)*

Robert C Peoples Inc 302 834-5268
  2750 Wrangle Hill Rd Bear (19701) *(G-463)*

Robert C Thompson 302 492-1053
  671 Bryants Corner Rd Hartly (19953) *(G-4907)*

Robert Davison 301 518-0516
  110 Widgeon Way Bridgeville (19933) *(G-762)*

Robert Donlick MD 302 653-8916
  16 Garrisons Cir Smyrna (19977) *(G-13867)*

Robert Dressler MD 302 733-6343
  4923 Ogletown Stanton Rd Ste 200 Newark (19713) *(G-11897)*

Robert E Davis 302 535-9657
  72 Sovereignty Dr Felton (19943) *(G-4019)*

Robert E Measley MD PC 302 543-4233
  616 Kilburn Rd Wilmington (19803) *(G-19509)*

Robert Elgart Automotive 800 220-7777
  698 Pencader Dr Newark (19702) *(G-11898)*

Robert F Clendenin 302 396-7922
  23748 German Rd Seaford (19973) *(G-13376)*

Robert F Mullen Insurance Agcy 302 322-5331
  887 Pulaski Hwy Bear (19701) *(G-464)*

Robert Fry Economics LLC 302 743-8553
  11 Pheasants Rdg N Wilmington (19807) *(G-19510)*

Robert G Burke Painting Co 302 998-2200
  1614 E Ayre St Wilmington (19804) *(G-19511)*

Robert G Starkey CPA 302 422-0108
  1043 N Walnut St Milford (19963) *(G-8069)*

Robert Gears 302 690-2590
  34696 Daisey Rd Frankford (19945) *(G-4139)*

Robert Golebiowski 302 234-6583
  4 Hayloft Ct Wilmington (19808) *(G-19512)*

Robert Grant Inc 302 422-6090
  606 Milford Harrington Hwy Milford (19963) *(G-8070)*

Robert Half International Inc 302 252-3162
  2 Righter Pkwy Ste 310 Wilmington (19803) *(G-19513)*

Robert Hoyt & Co 302 934-6688
  218 N Dupont Millsboro (19966) *(G-8448)*

Robert J Kriner Jr 302 656-2500
  920 N King St Ste 500 Wilmington (19801) *(G-19514)*

Robert J Peoples Inc 302 984-2017
  3020 Bowlarama Dr New Castle (19720) *(G-9538)*

Robert J Peoples Inc 302 322-0595
  1 Westmoreland Ave Apt A Wilmington (19804) *(G-19515)*

Robert K Beste Jr 302 425-5089
  1007 N Orange St Ste 1130 Wilmington (19801) *(G-19516)*

Robert Kopecki Do 302 230-4955
  3105 Limestone Rd Ste 301 Wilmington (19808) *(G-19517)*

Robert L Fox MST CPA 302 697-7889
  325 S Shore Dr Dover (19901) *(G-3475)*

Robert L Grzonka M D 302 503-2460
  200 Kings Hwy Ste 7 Milford (19963) *(G-8071)*

Robert L Thomas (PA) 302 571-6602
  1000 N West St Wilmington (19801) *(G-19518)*

Robert Larimore 302 730-8682
  328 Moose Lodge Rd Camden Wyoming (19934) *(G-971)*

Robert M Panzer 302 571-0717
  2000 Delaware Ave Wilmington (19806) *(G-19519)*

Robert McMann 302 329-9413
  13259 Sunland Dr Milton (19968) *(G-8701)*

Robert Michael Corp 302 378-4164
  436 Caledonia Way Townsend (19734) *(G-14061)*

Robert Miller Construction Inc 302 335-4385
  3345 Midstate Rd Felton (19943) *(G-4020)*

Robert Oxygen Company 33, Seaford Also Called: Roberts Oxygen Company Inc *(G-13377)*

Robert P Hart DDS 302 328-1513
  92 Reads Way Ste 101 New Castle (19720) *(G-9539)*

Robert S Brady 302 571-6690
  1000 N West St Wilmington (19801) *(G-19520)*

Robert S Callahan MD PA 302 731-0942
  32 Omega Dr # J Newark (19713) *(G-11899)*

Robert T Jones & Foard Inc 302 731-4627
  122 W Main St Newark (19711) *(G-11900)*

Robert T Minner Jr 302 422-9206
  2181 Deep Grass Ln Greenwood (19950) *(G-4665)*

Robert W Nagowski 302 584-2326
  304 Pheasant Dr Middletown (19709) *(G-7519)*

Robert Westley 302 645-2301
  115 S Washington Ave Lewes (19958) *(G-6425)*

Roberts Electric Inc 302 233-3017
  165 Barkers Landing Rd Magnolia (19962) *(G-6779)*

ALPHABETIC SECTION — Roeberg Moore & Associates PA

Roberts Oxygen Company Inc 302 337-9666
22785 Sussex Hwy 102 Seaford (19973) *(G-13377)*

Roberts Property MGT LLC 302 537-5371
107 Canal Rd Bethany Beach (19930) *(G-637)*

Robin Drive Auto LLC 302 326-2437
804 Pulaski Hwy Bear (19701) *(G-465)*

Robin J Simpson Do 302 838-4750
300 Biddle Ave Ste 200 Newark (19702) *(G-11901)*

Robin R Pratola 302 653-5100
100 S Main St Ste 101 Smyrna (19977) *(G-13868)*

Robin S Wright 302 249-2105
19305 Beaver Dam Rd Lewes (19958) *(G-6426)*

Robin Sesan 302 475-1880
2500 Grubb Rd Ste 234 Wilmington (19810) *(G-19521)*

Robino Management Group Inc 302 633-6001
5189 W Woodmill Dr Ste 30a Wilmington (19808) *(G-19522)*

Robins Hair & Tanning 302 529-9000
2716 Naamans Rd Wilmington (19810) *(G-19523)*

Robinson Grayson and Ward PA 302 655-6262
910 Foulk Rd Ste 200 Wilmington (19803) *(G-19524)*

Robinson and Grayson, Wilmington *Also Called: Robinson Grayson and Ward PA (G-19524)*

Robinson Export & Import Corp 410 219-7200
28412 Dupont Blvd Ste 106 Millsboro (19966) *(G-8449)*

Robinson Insurance Agency, Seaford *Also Called: Robinson Realestate (G-13378)*

Robinson Realestate 302 629-4574
605 N Hall St Seaford (19973) *(G-13378)*

Robinsons Sewage Disposal, Frankford *Also Called: James Powell (G-4118)*

Robo Wunderkind Inc 857 353-8899
2093 Philadelphia Pike Pmb 2664 Claymont (19703) *(G-1281)*

Roca Family Daycare 302 656-8356
205 S Ogle Ave Wilmington (19805) *(G-19525)*

Rocaccion Inc 617 902-8779
2035 Sunset Lake Rd Ste B2 Newark (19702) *(G-11902)*

Rocco Automotive, Wilmington *Also Called: Roccos Automotive Service (G-19526)*

Roccos Automotive Service 302 998-2234
2379 Limestone Rd Wilmington (19808) *(G-19526)*

Rock Bottom Paving Inc 800 728-3160
8191 S Dupont Hwy Felton (19943) *(G-4021)*

Rock City Consulting Corp 302 551-6844
1207 Delaware Ave Wilmington (19806) *(G-19527)*

Rock Diamond Paving, Newark *Also Called: Serrano Inc (G-11982)*

Rock Maintenance Services LLC 607 624-2341
11 Eastlawn Ave Wilmington (19802) *(G-19528)*

Rock Manor Golf Course 302 295-1400
1319 Carruthers Ln Wilmington (19803) *(G-19529)*

Rock of Ages Tattoos 302 475-8050
12 Carpenter Plz Wilmington (19810) *(G-19530)*

Rock Ranch Auto LLC 302 670-9992
592 Broad St Houston (19954) *(G-5450)*

Rock Rates, Dover *Also Called: Keystone Funding Inc (G-2861)*

Rock River Real Estate Inc 302 778-1000
20 Montchanin Rd Ste 250 Wilmington (19807) *(G-19531)*

Rock Roofing 302 757-2350
304 E Main St 308 Middletown (19709) *(G-7520)*

Rock Solid Servicing LLC 302 233-2569
89 Mandrake Dr Magnolia (19962) *(G-6780)*

Rock Springs Capital LLC 415 669-4545
1209 N Orange St Wilmington (19801) *(G-19532)*

Rockaway Auto Repair 302 644-1485
19738 Bernard Dr Lewes (19958) *(G-6427)*

Rockeias Journey LLC 302 304-3055
119 Dufferin Dr Newark (19702) *(G-11903)*

Rocket Express LLC 609 854-6705
509 Fairnest Ct Dover (19904) *(G-3476)*

Rocket Signs 302 645-1425
18388 Coastal Hwy Unit 4 Lewes (19958) *(G-6428)*

Rocketchat Technologies Corp 213 725-2428
251 Little Falls Dr Wilmington (19808) *(G-19533)*

Rockey & Associates Inc 800 338-7734
18306 Coastal Hwy Lewes (19958) *(G-6429)*

Rockfield Collision LLC 302 658-4324
2300 W 4th St Wilmington (19805) *(G-19534)*

Rockford Capital Partners 302 220-4786
219 W 9th St Ste 230 Wilmington (19801) *(G-19535)*

Rockford Map Gallery LLC 302 740-1851
1800 Lovering Ave Wilmington (19806) *(G-19536)*

Rockford Park Condominium, Wilmington *Also Called: Rockford Park Condominium Home (G-19537)*

Rockford Park Condominium Home 302 658-7842
2302 Riddle Ave Ofc Wilmington (19806) *(G-19537)*

Rockford RE Fund IV LP 302 220-4786
219 W 9th St Ste 230 Wilmington (19801) *(G-19538)*

Rockham 5g PA LP 302 239-1250
136 Lantana Dr Hockessin (19707) *(G-5369)*

Rockhard Granite LLC 302 737-9300
2043 Pulaski Hwy Newark (19702) *(G-11904)*

Rockin Reiki and Massage LLC 302 423-3214
116 Old Mill Rd Dover (19901) *(G-3477)*

Rockland Builders Inc 302 995-6800
1605 E Ayre St Wilmington (19804) *(G-19539)*

Rockland Dental Associates, Wilmington *Also Called: H Dean McSpadden DDS (G-17019)*

Rockland Place 302 777-3099
1519 Rockland Rd Wilmington (19803) *(G-19540)*

Rockland Sports LLC 302 654-4435
1001 Rockland Rd Wilmington (19803) *(G-19541)*

Rockland Surgery Center LP 302 999-0200
2710 Centerville Rd Ste 100 Wilmington (19808) *(G-19542)*

Rockledge Global Partners Ltd 800 659-1102
1000 N West St Ste 1200 Wilmington (19801) *(G-19543)*

Rockles Services LLC 302 258-5357
14404 Russell St Milton (19968) *(G-8702)*

Rockoly Inc 508 527-1939
54 Merion Rd Dover (19904) *(G-3478)*

Rockteam, Lewes *Also Called: Rockey & Associates Inc (G-6429)*

Rockwell Associates 302 655-7151
2711 Centerville Rd Ste 105 Wilmington (19808) *(G-19544)*

Rockwood Apartments 302 832-8823
100 Cindy Dr Newark (19702) *(G-11905)*

Rockwood Conference Center 302 761-4342
610 N Shipley St Wilmington (19801) *(G-19545)*

Rockwood Museum 302 761-4340
610 Shipley Rd Wilmington (19809) *(G-19546)*

Rockwood Programs Inc (PA) 302 765-6000
3001 Philadelphia Pike Ste 1 Claymont (19703) *(G-1282)*

Rockwood Specialties Inc 302 765-6012
4001 Miller Road Wilmington (19802) *(G-19547)*

Rocky Lac LLC 302 440-5561
1012 San Remo Ct Ste A Bear (19701) *(G-466)*

Rod-AES Surveryors Co 302 993-1059
3913 Old Capitol Trl Wilmington (19808) *(G-19548)*

Roderick M Relova Do 302 346-3171
100 Scull Ter Dover (19901) *(G-3479)*

Rodeway Inn 302 227-0401
19604 Blue Bird Ln Rehoboth Beach (19971) *(G-12937)*

Rodeway Inn, New Castle *Also Called: Dutch Village Motel Inc (G-9070)*

Rodney Baltazar 302 283-3300
120 Sandhill Dr Middletown (19709) *(G-7521)*

Rodney Pratt Framing Gallery 302 593-6108
204 Delaware St Ste A Historic New Castle (19720) *(G-5060)*

Rodney Rbnsn Ldscp Archts Inc 302 888-1544
30 Hill Rd Wilmington (19806) *(G-19549)*

Rodney Square Associates 302 652-1536
1 Rodney Sq Wilmington (19801) *(G-19550)*

Rodney Square Services Inc 302 652-5891
100 A St Wilmington (19801) *(G-19551)*

Rodney Street Tennis 302 384-7498
500 W 8th St Wilmington (19801) *(G-19552)*

Rodney Trust Co 302 737-1205
100 Commerce Dr Ste 305 Newark (19713) *(G-11906)*

Rodney's Animal Crackers, Rehoboth Beach *Also Called: Stauffer Family LLC (G-12974)*

Rodriguez Marieve O Dmd PA 302 655-5862
1407 Foulk Rd Wilmington (19803) *(G-19553)*

Roeberg Moore & Associates PA 302 658-4757
62 Rockford Rd Wilmington (19806) *(G-19554)*

Roger C Perry 302 604-7912
   22957 Deep Branch Rd Georgetown (19947) *(G-4489)*

Roger D Anderson 302 652-8400
   800 Delaware Ave Ste 1000 Wilmington (19801) *(G-19555)*

Roger Summers Lawn Care Inc 302 218-3319
   364 Skyline Orchard Dr Hockessin (19707) *(G-5370)*

Rogers, Bear *Also Called: Rogers Corporation (G-467)*

Rogers Corporation 302 834-2100
   1100 Governor Lea Rd Bear (19701) *(G-467)*

Rogers Graphics Inc (PA) 302 856-0028
   32 Bridgeville Rd Georgetown (19947) *(G-4490)*

Rogers Graphics Inc 302 422-6694
   26836 Lewes Georgetown Hwy Harbeson (19951) *(G-4713)*

Rogers Sign Company Inc 302 684-8338
   110 Lavinia St Milton (19968) *(G-8703)*

Rohans Bus Service Inc 302 332-8498
   7 Whirlaway Dr Bear (19701) *(G-468)*

Rohm and Haas Co, Newark *Also Called: Rohm Haas Electronic Mtls LLC (G-11910)*

Rohm and Haas Equity Corp (PA) 302 366-0500
   451 Bellevue Rd Newark (19713) *(G-11907)*

Rohm Haas Elctrnic Mtls Cmp In (HQ)   451 Bellevue Rd Newark (19713) *(G-11908)*

Rohm Haas Electronic Mtls LLC 302 366-0500
   451 Bellevue Rd Newark (19713) *(G-11909)*

Rohm Haas Electronic Mtls LLC 302 366-0500
   231 Lake Dr Newark (19702) *(G-11910)*

Rohma Inc 909 234-5381
   2035 Sunset Lake Rd Ste B2 Newark (19702) *(G-11911)*

Roi International LLC (PA) 704 340-1289
   16192 Coastal Hwy Lewes (19958) *(G-6430)*

Roizman & Associates Inc 302 426-9688
   506 E 5th St Wilmington (19801) *(G-19556)*

Roland E Tice 302 629-3674
   32888 Bi State Blvd Laurel (19956) *(G-5594)*

Roll Out Transit LLC 800 233-1680
   3 Longacre Ct Hockessin (19707) *(G-5371)*

Roll-A-Bout Corporation 302 736-6151
   3240 Barratts Chapel Rd Frederica (19946) *(G-4181)*

Roller Service Corporation (PA) 302 737-5000
   23 Mcmillan Way Newark (19713) *(G-11912)*

Rollins Inc 302 325-4410
   101 Johnson Way Historic New Castle (19720) *(G-5061)*

Rollins Leasing LLC (HQ) 302 426-2700
   2200 Concord Pike Wilmington (19803) *(G-19557)*

Roluva Painting 610 470-5207
   106 Pumpkin Patch Ln Hockessin (19707) *(G-5372)*

Romano Masonry, Newark *Also Called: Romano Masonry Inc (G-11913)*

Romano Masonry Inc 302 368-4155
   322 Markus Ct Ste A Newark (19713) *(G-11913)*

Romanos Original LLC 215 796-3271
   3 Woodland Dr Wilmington (19809) *(G-19558)*

Romantic Ai Inc 415 404-9188
   2093 Philadelphia Pike Claymont (19703) *(G-1283)*

Rome Solutions LLC 302 261-3794
   300 Delaware Ave Ste 210 Wilmington (19801) *(G-19559)*

Romer Labs Technology Inc 855 337-6637
   130 Sandy Dr Newark (19713) *(G-11914)*

Rommel Cycles LLC (PA) 302 658-8800
   450 Stadium St Smyrna (19977) *(G-13869)*

Ron Durr Mechanical 215 643-6990
   36851 Crooked Hammock Way Lewes (19958) *(G-6431)*

Ron English Enterprises Inc 302 981-9276
   1775 Pole Bridge Rd Middletown (19709) *(G-7522)*

Ron English Trucking Inc 302 328-2059
   512 Golding Ave New Castle (19720) *(G-9540)*

Ron G Williams M D 302 838-2238
   341 Starboard Dr Bear (19701) *(G-469)*

Ron Lank/Cash 302 684-4667
   209 Atlantic St Milton (19968) *(G-8704)*

Ronald A Beard 302 883-7883
   44 Carver Rd Dover (19904) *(G-3480)*

Ronald A Luna M D 302 629-4569
   1501 Middleford Rd Seaford (19973) *(G-13379)*

Ronald D Jr Attorney At Law 302 856-9860
   215 E Market St Georgetown (19947) *(G-4491)*

Ronald F Feinberg MD 302 674-1390
   200 Banning St Ste 130 Dover (19904) *(G-3481)*

Ronald L Barrows 302 227-3616
   184 E Side Dr Rehoboth Beach (19971) *(G-12938)*

Ronald McDonald House Delaware 302 428-5299
   1901 Rockland Rd Wilmington (19803) *(G-19560)*

Ronald Midaugh 410 860-1040
   1030 Forrest Ave Ste 104 Dover (19904) *(G-3482)*

Ronald N Brown 302 478-1108
   1106 Piper Rd Wilmington (19803) *(G-19561)*

Ronald W Peacock Inc 302 571-9313
   110 Matthes Ave Wilmington (19804) *(G-19562)*

Rondevu, Dover *Also Called: Ecom Technologies LLC (G-2416)*

Ronnie Carter 302 284-9321
   2334 Sandtown Rd Felton (19943) *(G-4022)*

Ronnie Freeman 302 762-3252
   515 E 3rd St Wilmington (19801) *(G-19563)*

Rons Mobile Home Sales Inc 302 398-9166
   17959 S Dupont Hwy Harrington (19952) *(G-4821)*

Roo Official, Dover *Also Called: Roo Official LLC (G-3483)*

Roo Official LLC 267 614-2811
   305 Bluecoat St Dover (19901) *(G-3483)*

Rooah LLC 305 233-7557
   768 Townsend Blvd Ste 3 Dover (19901) *(G-3484)*

Roofers Inc 302 995-7027
   404 Meco Dr Wilmington (19804) *(G-19564)*

Roofing Griffith 302 762-1241
   1728 Marcy Dr Smyrna (19977) *(G-13870)*

Roofing Specialist 302 344-2507
   224 Salt Forest Ln Rehoboth Beach (19971) *(G-12939)*

Rookery Golf Courses South 302 422-7010
   6152 S Rehoboth Blvd Milford (19963) *(G-8072)*

Rookery, The, Milton *Also Called: Greens At Broadview LLC (G-8631)*

Room2room Cleaning LLC 302 202-9140
   1201 N Market St Ste 111-D77 Wilmington (19801) *(G-19565)*

Roos Foods Inc 302 653-0600
   251 Roos Ln Kenton (19955) *(G-5453)*

Rope-It Golf LLC 305 767-3481
   3 River Rd Wilmington (19809) *(G-19566)*

Rophe Living Inc 302 500-9238
   721 Marian Dr Middletown (19709) *(G-7523)*

Rosa Health Center Inc 302 858-4381
   10 N Front St Georgetown (19947) *(G-4492)*

Rosanne Tray Inc 302 656-5776
   2211 Van Buren Pl Wilmington (19802) *(G-19567)*

Rosario Ferrante General Contr 302 234-1911
   25 Haileys Trl Newark (19711) *(G-11915)*

Rosas Diner LLC 302 336-8243
   221 Hillcrest Ct Camden (19934) *(G-890)*

Rosas Greek Btq 302 678-2147
   338 Blue Heron Rd Dover (19904) *(G-3485)*

Rose Hill Community Center 302 656-8513
   19 Lambson Ln New Castle (19720) *(G-9541)*

Rose Strab 302 584-2074
   208 School House Ln Wilmington (19809) *(G-19568)*

Rosedale Development LLC 281 968-9426
   9 E Loockerman St Ste 202 Dover (19901) *(G-3486)*

Roselle D Albert Pt 302 373-5753
   22 E Savannah Dr Bear (19701) *(G-470)*

Rosemarie Ciarrocchi 302 731-9225
   4745 Ogletown Stanton Rd Ste 134 Newark (19713) *(G-11916)*

Rosemont Wealth Management 302 875-8300
   214 E Front St Laurel (19956) *(G-5595)*

Rosenberger Usa Corp (DH) 717 859-8900
   1209 N Orange St Wilmington (19801) *(G-19569)*

Rosenthal Monhait Goddess PA 302 656-4433
   919 N Market St Ste 1401 Wilmington (19801) *(G-19570)*

Rosies PH LLC 630 222-5155
   16192 Coastal Hwy Lewes (19958) *(G-6432)*

ALPHABETIC SECTION

Rosle U S A Corp.. 302 326-4801
  802 Centerpoint Blvd Historic New Castle (19720) *(G-5062)*

Ross Aronstam & Moritz LLP................................... 302 576-1600
  1313 N Market St Fl 10 Wilmington (19801) *(G-19571)*

Ross Bicycles LLC (PA).. 888 392-5628
  16192 Coastal Hwy Lewes (19958) *(G-6433)*

Ross Capital Partners LLC.. 302 300-4220
  724 Yorklyn Rd Hockessin (19707) *(G-5373)*

Ross Electrical Services LLC.................................... 443 614-7294
  14292 Pepperbox Rd Delmar (19940) *(G-1632)*

Ross Get Healthy Chiropractic.................................. 302 407-5571
  5239 W Woodmill Dr Wilmington (19808) *(G-19572)*

Rossakatum Ranch Inc.. 302 875-5707
  12487 Salt Barn Rd Laurel (19956) *(G-5596)*

Rosy Cleaning Services... 302 723-7610
  1602 Christiana Mdws Bear (19701) *(G-471)*

Roto-Rooter, Newark *Also Called: Roto-Rooter Services Company (G-11917)*

Roto-Rooter, Wilmington *Also Called: Roto-Rooter Plbg & Wtr Cleanup (G-19573)*

Roto-Rooter Plbg & Wtr Cleanup............................. 302 256-5022
  900 Philadelphia Pike Ste D Wilmington (19809) *(G-19573)*

Roto-Rooter Services Company............................... 302 659-7637
  1001 Dawson Dr Ste 3 Newark (19713) *(G-11917)*

Rotobot Ai LLC... 978 305-5794
  651 N Broad St Ste 201 Middletown (19709) *(G-7524)*

Rotten Apples Cider Co LLC.................................... 609 602-7811
  23656 Fox Croft Ln Georgetown (19947) *(G-4493)*

Rouleau Suzanne Lcsw... 302 479-5157
  8 Blue Jay Dr Newark (19713) *(G-11918)*

Round Table Men LLC (PA)...................................... 302 287-8200
  13 Constitution Blvd New Castle (19720) *(G-9542)*

Roundrobin Corporation (PA)................................... 212 634-9193
  8 The Grn Dover (19901) *(G-3487)*

Route 24 Got Junk... 302 258-7990
  31788 Schooner Dr Millsboro (19966) *(G-8450)*

Route 9 Auto Center.. 302 856-3941
  23422 Park Ave Georgetown (19947) *(G-4494)*

Routerabbit Inc.. 508 596-8735
  2035 Sunset Lake Rd Ste B2 Newark (19702) *(G-11919)*

Routzhan Jessman.. 302 398-4206
  17010 S Dupont Hwy Harrington (19952) *(G-4822)*

Rowe Industries Inc... 443 458-5569
  21649 Cedar Creek Ave Georgetown (19947) *(G-4495)*

Rowe Industries Inc... 302 855-0585
  12 S Walnut St Milford (19963) *(G-8073)*

Rowe Robert L Dr Rev.. 302 422-8814
  206 Se Front St Milford (19963) *(G-8074)*

Rowing and Fitness... 302 722-5445
  101 Peoples Dr Newark (19702) *(G-11920)*

Roxana Automobile Service Cent............................ 302 436-6202
  Roxana Rd Frankford (19945) *(G-4140)*

Roxanne Rxnne Cnslting Group L............................ 470 333-8553
  8 The Grn Dover (19901) *(G-3488)*

Roxlor LLC... 302 778-4166
  1013 Centre Rd Ste 106 Wilmington (19805) *(G-19574)*

Royal Bank America Leasing LLC............................ 302 798-1790
  20 Montchanin Rd Ste 100 Wilmington (19807) *(G-19575)*

ROYAL BANK AMERICA LEASING, LLC, Wilmington *Also Called: Royal Bank America Leasing LLC (G-19575)*

Royal Broadcasting Inc.. 302 838-4543
  18 Monticello Dr Bear (19701) *(G-472)*

Royal Cleaners.. 302 478-0955
  3914 Concord Pike Wilmington (19803) *(G-19576)*

Royal Delta Specialties LLC..................................... 908 410-7478
  19266 Cstl Hwy Unit 4 85r Rehoboth Beach (19971) *(G-12940)*

Royal Farms.. 410 725-9100
  11112 Laurel Rd Laurel (19956) *(G-5597)*

Royal Farms.. 302 409-3992
  457 Stanton Christiana Rd Newark (19713) *(G-11921)*

Royal Instruments Inc... 302 328-5900
  266 Quigley Blvd Historic New Castle (19720) *(G-5063)*

Royal Island Cruise Line, Dover *Also Called: Complete Rsrvtion Slutions LLC (G-2123)*

Royal Lawn Care & Property MAI............................ 302 436-9800
  4 N Main St Selbyville (19975) *(G-13601)*

Royal Mission & Ministries...................................... 302 249-8863
  9751 Randall St Laurel (19956) *(G-5598)*

Royal Pest Management Inc.................................... 302 376-8243
  755 N Broad St Middletown (19709) *(G-7525)*

Royal Pest Solutions Inc.. 302 322-6665
  53 Mccullough Dr New Castle (19720) *(G-9543)*

Royal Rsdntial Renovations LLC.............................. 302 377-0128
  131 Karlyn Dr New Castle (19720) *(G-9544)*

Royal Tech Auto Repair LLC.................................... 302 737-6852
  725 Dawson Dr Newark (19713) *(G-11922)*

Royal Termite & Pest Ctrl Inc.................................. 302 322-3600
  53 Mccullough Dr New Castle (19720) *(G-9545)*

Royal Termite and Pest Control, New Castle *Also Called: Royal Termite & Pest Ctrl Inc (G-9545)*

Royal Vanity Hair Studio... 302 322-4680
  1506 Beaver Brook Plz New Castle (19720) *(G-9546)*

Royale Group Inc.. 201 845-4666
  400 Carson Dr Bear (19701) *(G-473)*

Royale Pigments & Chem Inc.................................. 201 845-4666
  400 Carson Dr Bear (19701) *(G-474)*

Royale Pigments and Chem LLC............................. 201 845-4666
  400 Carson Dr Bear (19701) *(G-475)*

Royalhalo LLC... 888 418-7692
  1000 N West St Ste 1200 Wilmington (19801) *(G-19577)*

Royalrose302 LLC... 800 259-7918
  108 Talbot Dr New Castle (19720) *(G-9547)*

Roys Electrical Service Inc...................................... 302 674-3199
  543 Main St Cheswold (19936) *(G-989)*

Roz Health LLC (PA).. 415 259-8992
  2035 Sunset Lake Rd Ste B2 Newark (19702) *(G-11923)*

Rozdoum Inc... 315 707-7517
  8 The Grn Dover (19901) *(G-3489)*

Rp Hospitality LLC.. 302 398-4206
  17010 S Dupont Hwy Harrington (19952) *(G-4823)*

Rp Ventures and Holdings Inc (PA)......................... 410 398-3000
  1700 Shipley Rd Wilmington (19803) *(G-19578)*

Rpj Waste Services Inc (PA).................................... 302 653-9999
  453 Pier Head Blvd Smyrna (19977) *(G-13871)*

RPM Automotive of Dover LLC................................ 302 734-9495
  101 Weston Dr Ste 3 Dover (19904) *(G-3490)*

RPS LLC... 302 653-2598
  16 Waterview Ln Dover (19904) *(G-3491)*

Rrp Mechanical Welding LLC.................................. 302 448-1051
  16750 Oak Rd Bridgeville (19933) *(G-763)*

Rrr Realty Group LLC.. 302 836-9836
  102 Cornwell Dr Bear (19701) *(G-476)*

Rs Marks Inc.. 302 478-4371
  3411 Silverside Rd Wilmington (19810) *(G-19579)*

Rs Werks... 302 740-1516
  61b Mcmillan Way Newark (19713) *(G-11924)*

Rsf Managed Services LLC..................................... 302 345-7162
  2045 Longcome Dr Wilmington (19810) *(G-19580)*

Rsg Cleaning Services.. 302 650-3702
  101 Wooden Carriage Dr Hockessin (19707) *(G-5374)*

Rshort Roofing LLC... 302 276-9531
  6091 Summit Bridge Rd Townsend (19734) *(G-14062)*

Rsi Investors Inc.. 302 478-5142
  1105 N Market St Ste 1230 Wilmington (19899) *(G-19581)*

Rsl Logistics LLC.. 302 521-3299
  4611 Griffin Dr Wilmington (19808) *(G-19582)*

RSM Construction... 302 270-7099
  1471 Central Church Rd Dover (19904) *(G-3492)*

RSM Diagnostics Lab LLC....................................... 302 592-4106
  2500 Grubb Rd Ste 120 Wilmington (19810) *(G-19583)*

Rss LLC.. 866 801-0692
  3511 Silverside Rd Ste 105 Wilmington (19810) *(G-19584)*

Rt Minner & Sons, Greenwood *Also Called: Robert T Minner Jr (G-4665)*

Rt Stover, New Castle *Also Called: PJ Fitzpatrick Inc (G-9473)*

Rt Taxidermy LLC... 302 629-7501
  12564 Baker Mill Rd Seaford (19973) *(G-13380)*

Rtx Corporation 800 227-7437
276 Quigley Blvd Historic New Castle (19720) *(G-5064)*

Ruabit LLC 765 772-0806
2093a Philadelphia Pike Ste 450 Claymont (19703) *(G-1284)*

Ruan Transport Corporation 302 696-3270
50 Patriot Dr Middletown (19709) *(G-7526)*

Ruark Inc 302 846-2332
325 Petunia Pl Seaford (19973) *(G-13381)*

Ruby Digital Agency Inc 801 971-1681
3911 Concord Pike Ste 8030 Smb Ste 50502 Wilmington (19803) *(G-19585)*

Ruby Moriarty LLC 917 587-1511
1221 College Park Dr Dover (19904) *(G-3493)*

Ruby Road LLC 856 887-1422
249 E Main St Ste 3 Newark (19711) *(G-11925)*

Rudlyn Inc 302 764-5677
3900 Governor Printz Blvd Wilmington (19802) *(G-19586)*

Rudy Auto Body, Wilmington *Also Called: Rudlyn Inc (G-19586)*

Rudy Marine Inc 302 999-8735
32606 Dupont Blvd Dagsboro (19939) *(G-1501)*

Rudy's Outboard Service, Dagsboro *Also Called: Rudy Marine Inc (G-1501)*

Rudys European Motorcars 302 645-6410
17493 Nassau Commons Blvd Lewes (19958) *(G-6434)*

Ruff & Ruff LLC 267 243-3906
28 White Rabbit Dr Smyrna (19977) *(G-13872)*

Ruffin Tellie 302 650-3151
2005 Baynard Blvd Wilmington (19802) *(G-19587)*

Ruggerio Willson & Assoc LLC 302 345-8468
109 E Division St Dover (19901) *(G-3494)*

Ruiz Flooring 302 999-9350
3405 Cranston Ave Wilmington (19808) *(G-19588)*

Rukket LLC 855 478-5538
4023 Kennett Pike # 123 Wilmington (19807) *(G-19589)*

Rukket Sports, Wilmington *Also Called: Rukket LLC (G-19589)*

Rulesware LLC 302 293-4077
10 Lowe Ct Newark (19711) *(G-11926)*

Rumble League Studios Inc 800 564-5300
614 S Dupont Hwy Ste 210 Dover (19901) *(G-3495)*

Rummel Klepper & Kahl LLP 302 468-4880
750 Shipyard Dr Wilmington (19801) *(G-19590)*

Rumpstich Machine Works Inc 302 422-4816
305 S Rehoboth Blvd Milford (19963) *(G-8075)*

Rumsey Electric Co 302 368-9161
501 Interchange Blvd Newark (19711) *(G-11927)*

Rumz Inc 571 733-0693
2055 Limestone Rd Wilmington (19808) *(G-19591)*

Ruppert Landscape LLC 302 537-2771
28091 Nine Foot Rd Dagsboro (19939) *(G-1502)*

Rush Auto LLC 302 323-9070
6 Elks Trl New Castle (19720) *(G-9548)*

Rush Realty LLC 302 219-6707
395 Southern View Dr Smyrna (19977) *(G-13873)*

Rushstan Group LLC 302 376-0259
603 E Glen Mare Dr Middletown (19709) *(G-7527)*

Russ Otr Hardesty 302 598-0824
2319 Jamaica Dr Wilmington (19810) *(G-19592)*

Russell A Paulus & Son Inc 302 998-4494
193 Christina Landing Dr Wilmington (19801) *(G-19593)*

Russell Associates Inc 443 992-5777
560 Peoples Plz # 125 Newark (19702) *(G-11928)*

Russell D Earnest & Assoc 302 659-0730
Clayton (19938) *(G-1402)*

Russell J Tibbetts DDS PA 302 479-5959
3516 Silverside Rd Ste 17 Wilmington (19810) *(G-19594)*

Russell Plywood Inc 302 689-0137
1000 S Heald St Wilmington (19801) *(G-19595)*

Russell Smart Home Imprvs LLC 302 846-2404
37787 Eagles Run Delmar (19940) *(G-1633)*

Ruth N Dorsey Relief Shelter, Dover *Also Called: Whatcoat Social Service Agency (G-3842)*

Ruth Van Pelt Beebe Mem Sch Tr 302 226-9498
132 E Side Dr Rehoboth Beach (19971) *(G-12941)*

Rutkoske Bros Inc 302 378-8181
819 Middletown Warwick Rd Middletown (19709) *(G-7528)*

Rutledge Dental Assoc Inc 302 378-8705
410 N Cass St Middletown (19709) *(G-7529)*

Rutman Enterprises 302 777-5298
3221 Swarthmore Rd Wilmington (19807) *(G-19596)*

Rw Greer Inc 302 764-0376
2109 Swinnen Dr Wilmington (19810) *(G-19597)*

Rw Heating & Air Inc 302 856-4330
20801 Doddtown Rd Harbeson (19951) *(G-4714)*

Rwazi Inc 800 597-5871
2055 Limestone Rd Wilmington (19808) *(G-19598)*

Rwk Ventures LLC 305 494-4011
3911 Concord Pike # 8030 Wilmington (19803) *(G-19599)*

Rwm Embroidery & More LLC 302 653-8384
19 Village Sq Smyrna (19977) *(G-13874)*

Rwm Plumbing 302 697-1705
10785 Willow Grove Rd Camden Wyoming (19934) *(G-972)*

Rxbenefits Inc 724 525-9080
32907 Ocean Blf Lewes (19958) *(G-6435)*

Ryan Architecture LLC 302 629-6458
905 Short Ln Seaford (19973) *(G-13382)*

Ryan Gallo Tree Service Inc 302 239-1001
1536 Brackenville Rd Hockessin (19707) *(G-5375)*

Ryan Homes 302 491-4442
7305 Clubhouse Dr Milford (19963) *(G-8076)*

Ryan Homes, Dagsboro *Also Called: Nvr Inc (G-1492)*

Ryan Homes, Newark *Also Called: Nvr Inc (G-11571)*

Ryan R Davies M D 302 651-6660
1600 Rockland Rd Wilmington (19803) *(G-19600)*

Ryans Mini Golf 302 227-2667
1 Delaware Ave Rehoboth Beach (19971) *(G-12942)*

Ryder, Rehoboth Beach *Also Called: Budget Truck Rental LLC (G-12661)*

Ryder, Wilmington *Also Called: Ryder Truck Rental Inc (G-19601)*

Ryder Truck 302 398-5106
111 Reese Ave Harrington (19952) *(G-4824)*

Ryder Truck Rental Inc 302 798-1472
6605 Governor Printz Blvd Wilmington (19809) *(G-19601)*

Ryerson Geralyn 302 547-3060
1601 Milltown Rd Ste 8 Wilmington (19808) *(G-19602)*

Ryerson Thypin Steel, Newark *Also Called: Joseph T Ryerson & Son Inc (G-11129)*

Ryes Hvac LLC 302 981-7851
12 Pembroke Ln New Castle (19720) *(G-9549)*

Ryla Real Estate Options LLC 302 397-7402
23 W Lexton Rd New Castle (19720) *(G-9550)*

Ryno Iron 302 464-2973
17 Spring Creek Dr Townsend (19734) *(G-14063)*

Ryzenlink Technologies LLC 786 536-0349
7209 Lancaster Pike Ste 4 Hockessin (19707) *(G-5376)*

S & A Holding Associates Inc 302 479-8314
4737 Concord Pike Ste 261 Wilmington (19803) *(G-19603)*

S & B Pro Security LLC 800 841-9907
1300 E Lebanon Rd Dover (19901) *(G-3496)*

S & C Properties Ltd 302 995-1537
805 Kiamensi Rd Wilmington (19804) *(G-19604)*

S & H Enterprises Inc 302 999-9911
112 Water St Wilmington (19804) *(G-19605)*

S & J Haftl Inc 302 378-7571
519 Diamond Dr Middletown (19709) *(G-7530)*

S & S Mgnt Co LLC 302 353-9249
307 Bald Eagle Way Middletown (19709) *(G-7531)*

S & S Wines and Spirits 302 678-9987
1007 Walker Rd Dover (19904) *(G-3497)*

S A Atramco 302 310-3350
251 Little Falls Dr Wilmington (19808) *(G-19606)*

S and J Contracting LLC 302 382-0769
1331 Hollering Hill Rd Camden (19934) *(G-891)*

S and S LLC 302 344-5990
22855 Milton Ellendale Hwy Milton (19968) *(G-8705)*

S B Porter Services 302 378-0209
4296 Barratts Chapel Rd Frederica (19946) *(G-4182)*

S B Trailer Park 302 697-0699
72 Mabel Dr Magnolia (19962) *(G-6781)*

ALPHABETIC SECTION

S Brown Appraisals LLC.. 302 672-0694
16819 S Dupont Hwy Ste 300 Harrington (19952) *(G-4825)*

S D Nemcic DDS.. 302 734-1950
910 Walker Rd Ste A Dover (19904) *(G-3498)*

S Finney Home Improvements.. 302 358-4562
31110 Mills Chase Dr Lewes (19958) *(G-6436)*

S G Williams & Bros Co (PA).. 302 656-8167
301 N Tatnall St Wilmington (19801) *(G-19607)*

S G Williams of Dover Inc.. 302 678-1080
580 Lafferty Ln Dover (19901) *(G-3499)*

S Gregory Smith MD & Assoc PA.. 302 993-1900
2710 Centerville Rd Ste 102 Wilmington (19808) *(G-19608)*

S J Desmond Inc.. 302 475-6520
22 Lloyd Pl Wilmington (19810) *(G-19609)*

S J Desmond Inc.. 302 256-0801
120 E Ayre St Wilmington (19804) *(G-19610)*

S J Passwater General Cnstr.. 302 422-1061
715a S Washington St Milford (19963) *(G-8077)*

S L Pharma Labs, Inc., Wilmington *Also Called: Element Mtls Tech Wlmngton Inc (G-16353)*

S M Commercial Roofing Inc.. 302 478-3130
412 Meco Dr Wilmington (19804) *(G-19611)*

S P S International Inv Co (DH).. 302 478-9055
1105 N Market St Ste 1300 Wilmington (19801) *(G-19612)*

S S C Seed Warehouse, Seaford *Also Called: Southern States Coop Inc (G-13410)*

S S I Group LLC.. 877 778-7099
16192 Coastal Hwy Lewes (19958) *(G-6437)*

S T Good Insurance Inc (HQ).. 215 969-8385
100 Christiana Medical Ctr Newark (19702) *(G-11929)*

S T Progressive Strides.. 410 775-8103
718 Thyme Dr Bear (19701) *(G-477)*

S U I, New Castle *Also Called: Service Unlimited Inc (G-9558)*

S Wallace Holdings LLC.. 917 304-1164
251 Little Falls Dr Wilmington (19808) *(G-19613)*

S Wilson Auto Repair.. 302 856-3839
15388 Wilson Hill Rd Georgetown (19947) *(G-4496)*

S.O.A.R, Wilmington *Also Called: Survivors Abuse In Rcovery Inc (G-20162)*

S&D Industries LLC.. 703 801-3643
2711 Centerville Rd Ste 400 Wilmington (19808) *(G-19614)*

S&H Investigative Services, Wilmington *Also Called: S & H Enterprises Inc (G-19605)*

S&M Small Engine Repair LLC.. 302 893-7341
37514 Cedar St Ocean View (19970) *(G-12564)*

S&N Logistics LLC.. 302 303-3037
600 N Broad St Ste 5 Middletown (19709) *(G-7532)*

S&R Pressure Washing LLC.. 410 430-9864
36828 Herring Way Selbyville (19975) *(G-13602)*

S&S Painting LLC.. 302 766-2476
58 Sammon Dr Clayton (19938) *(G-1403)*

S2 Groupe LLC.. 917 512-1971
300 Delaware Ave Ste 210a Wilmington (19801) *(G-19615)*

S3staffingusa Inc (PA).. 248 986-6062
651 N Broad St Ste 205-156 Middletown (19709) *(G-7533)*

SA Associates LLC.. 302 275-7359
180 Gregg Dr Wilmington (19808) *(G-19616)*

SA Medical Billing, Middletown *Also Called: Jo Stefanie Armour (G-7251)*

SA Ryan LLC.. 302 757-6440
5 Ferndale Dr Smyrna (19977) *(G-13875)*

Saas Digital Technologies Inc.. 302 994-2000
112 Capitol Trl Newark (19711) *(G-11930)*

Saasant Inc.. 619 377-0977
16192 Coastal Hwy Lewes (19958) *(G-6438)*

Sab Heating & Air.. 302 945-3117
24430 Shady Ln Millsboro (19966) *(G-8451)*

Sabcon Construction Company.. 302 420-0467
2500 W 5th St Wilmington (19805) *(G-19617)*

Sabi Ai Corp.. 415 800-4641
850 New Burton Rd Ste 201 Dover (19904) *(G-3500)*

Sabini Paul MD Facs.. 302 998-8007
537 Stanton Christiana Rd Ste 107 Newark (19713) *(G-11931)*

Sabion Sound Reinforcement Co.. 302 427-0551
15 W Reamer Ave Wilmington (19804) *(G-19618)*

Sabo Logistics LLC.. 302 440-4544
1074 Yorklyn Rd Unit E Hockessin (19707) *(G-5377)*

Sabre Associates LLC.. 302 998-0100
1202 Kirkwood Hwy Wilmington (19805) *(G-19619)*

Sabre Building, Newark *Also Called: First State Orthopaedics PA (G-10733)*

Sabre International Newco Inc.. 682 605-6223
1209 N Orange St Wilmington (19801) *(G-19620)*

Sabrs Home Comfort.. 302 379-8133
17815 Sandcastle Cv Lewes (19958) *(G-6439)*

Sacco Lawn Care.. 302 545-3803
225 Forrestal Dr Bear (19701) *(G-478)*

Sacher.. 302 792-0281
15 N Cliffe Dr Wilmington (19809) *(G-19621)*

Sachetta Machine & Development.. 302 378-5468
1823 Choptank Rd Middletown (19709) *(G-7534)*

Sacred Heart Village I Inc.. 302 428-0801
920 N Monroe St Wilmington (19801) *(G-19622)*

Sacred Heart Village II Inc.. 302 428-3702
625 E 10th St Wilmington (19801) *(G-19623)*

Sad Enterprises Inc.. 302 422-6100
915 N Dupont Blvd Ste 101 Milford (19963) *(G-8078)*

Saenger Porcelain.. 302 738-5349
18 Mimosa Dr Newark (19711) *(G-11932)*

Saf Engineering LLC.. 302 645-7400
16192 Coastal Hwy Lewes (19958) *(G-6440)*

Safahi Corp.. 925 503-4551
1151 Walker Rd Dover (19904) *(G-3501)*

Safe Driver Corporation (PA).. 601 207-1164
838 Walker Rd Dover (19904) *(G-3502)*

Safe Home Control.. 302 401-4379
300 Delaware Ave Ste 210a Wilmington (19801) *(G-19624)*

Safe Space Delaware Inc.. 302 691-7946
500 W 2nd St Wilmington (19801) *(G-19625)*

Safeagain Inc.. 929 276-2732
8 The Grn Dover (19901) *(G-3503)*

Safeguard Dx Laboratory.. 888 919-8275
110 S Poplar St Ste 200 Wilmington (19801) *(G-19626)*

Safeguard Systems Inc (HQ).. 609 822-6111
1313 N Market St Wilmington (19801) *(G-19627)*

Safelite Autoglass, Dover *Also Called: Safelite Glass Corp (G-3504)*

Safelite Autoglass, Georgetown *Also Called: Safelite Fulfillment Inc (G-4497)*

Safelite Autoglass, Wilmington *Also Called: Safelite Glass Corp (G-19628)*

Safelite Fulfillment Inc.. 302 856-7175
314 S Dupont Hwy Georgetown (19947) *(G-4497)*

Safelite Glass Corp.. 877 800-2727
4200 N Dupont Hwy Ste 6 Dover (19901) *(G-3504)*

Safelite Glass Corp.. 302 656-4640
109 Rogers Rd Ste 4 Wilmington (19801) *(G-19628)*

Safeup US LLC.. 480 526-5152
16192 Coastal Hwy Lewes (19958) *(G-6441)*

Safian, Gary D DDS, Wilmington *Also Called: Ralph Tomases DDS PA (G-19326)*

Safra Inc.. 302 305-0755
108 W 13th St Wilmington (19801) *(G-19629)*

Safrax Inc.. 302 404-0388
8 The Grn Ste 4000 Dover (19901) *(G-3505)*

Safs International Group LLC.. 954 707-4627
108 W 13th St Wilmington (19801) *(G-19630)*

Sagacious Works.. 609 251-9265
2713 Point Breeze Dr Wilmington (19810) *(G-19631)*

Sage Hospitality Resources LLC.. 302 292-1500
65 Geoffrey Dr Newark (19713) *(G-11933)*

Saggio Management Group Inc.. 302 659-6560
350 N High Street Extended Smyrna (19977) *(G-13876)*

Saggio Management Group Inc.. 302 659-6560
665 S Carter Rd Unit 2 Smyrna (19977) *(G-13877)*

Saggio Management Group Inc.. 302 696-2036
102 Sleepy Hollow Dr Middletown (19709) *(G-7535)*

Sahaj Contractor LLC.. 302 559-4357
1300 Quincy Dr Wilmington (19803) *(G-19632)*

Sahra International Holdings, Lewes *Also Called: Sahra Intl Holdings Inc (G-6443)*

Sahra Intl Holdings Inc.. 202 660-0090
16192 Coastal Hwy Lewes (19958) *(G-6442)*

Sahra Intl Holdings Inc.. 202 660-0090
16192 Coastal Hwy Ste 100 Lewes (19958) *(G-6443)*

SAI Ram Hospitality Inc 302 422-8089
　1036 N Walnut St Milford (19963) *(G-8079)*
Saienni Stairs LLC 302 292-2699
　120 Sandy Dr Ste E Newark (19713) *(G-11934)*
Sain Cosmos LLC 936 244-7017
　3524 Silverside Rd Ste 35b Wilmington (19810) *(G-19633)*
Saint Georges Cultr & Arts Rev 302 836-8202
　1 Delaware St Saint Georges (19733) *(G-13038)*
Saint Home Health Care 302 514-9597
　1017 Mattlind Way Milford (19963) *(G-8080)*
Saint James Holdg & Inv Co Tr 877 690-9052
　300 Delaware Ave Ste 210 Wilmington (19801) *(G-19634)*
Saint Jnes Ctr For Bhvral Hlth, Dover Also Called: Kent General Hospital *(G-2850)*
SAINT PATRICK'S CENTER, Wilmington Also Called: St Patricks Center Inc *(G-20002)*
Saints Cemetary, Wilmington Also Called: Catholic Cemetaries Inc *(G-15276)*
Saisha Spices LLC 786 288-3344
　8 The Grn # B Dover (19901) *(G-3506)*
Sakempire Distribution, Wilmington Also Called: Sakempire Distribution LLC *(G-19635)*
Sakempire Distribution LLC 800 838-0615
　300 Delaware Ave Ste 210 Wilmington (19801) *(G-19635)*
Saker Energy Solutions Inc 808 398-8326
　122 Delaware St Ste F-15 Historic New Castle (19720) *(G-5065)*
Salem County Amateur Radio CLB 302 689-8127
　2015 Bentwood Ct Wilmington (19804) *(G-19636)*
Sales & Marketing Bus Svcs, Newark Also Called: Mid-Atlntic Sls Mktg Group LLC *(G-11413)*
Sales Documents Inc 302 867-9957
　251 Little Falls Dr Ste 8088 Wilmington (19808) *(G-19637)*
Sales In US, Wilmington Also Called: Salesinusa Inc *(G-19639)*
Salesbox Ai, Wilmington Also Called: Salesbox LLC *(G-19638)*
Salesbox LLC (PA) 415 361-4080
　1521 Concord Pike Ste 301 Wilmington (19803) *(G-19638)*
Salesinusa Inc 973 771-4420
　620 A St Wilmington (19801) *(G-19639)*
Sallie Mae, Newark Also Called: SLM Corporation *(G-12032)*
Sallie Mae Financial, Newark Also Called: RKL Financial Corporation *(G-11891)*
Sally Beauty Supply, Newark Also Called: Sally Beauty Supply LLC *(G-11936)*
Sally Beauty Supply, Seaford Also Called: Sally Beauty Supply LLC *(G-13383)*
Sally Beauty Supply 712, Dover Also Called: Sally Beauty Supply LLC *(G-3507)*
Sally Beauty Supply LLC 302 674-2201
　283 N Dupont Hwy Ste D Dover (19901) *(G-3507)*
Sally Beauty Supply LLC 302 731-0285
　2665 Capitol Trl Newark (19711) *(G-11935)*
Sally Beauty Supply LLC 302 737-8837
　220 College Sq Newark (19711) *(G-11936)*
Sally Beauty Supply LLC 302 629-5160
　22883 Sussex Hwy Seaford (19973) *(G-13383)*
Salon 828 LLC 302 376-8282
　600 N Broad St Ste 8 Middletown (19709) *(G-7536)*
Salon By Dominic 302 239-8282
　130 Lantana Dr Hockessin (19707) *(G-5378)*
Salon Lala Mamoune 302 737-5264
　43 Glencoe Dr Newark (19702) *(G-11937)*
Salon On Central LLC 302 539-1882
　11 Woodland Ave Ocean View (19970) *(G-12565)*
Salon Rispoli Inc 302 731-9202
　1115 Churchmans Rd Newark (19713) *(G-11938)*
Sals Auto Services Inc 302 654-1168
　3000 Lancaster Ave Wilmington (19805) *(G-19640)*
Sals Garage Inc 302 655-4981
　705 N Lincoln St Ste 1 Wilmington (19805) *(G-19641)*
Salt Air Homes 302 698-4146
　223 Wynsome Blvd Camden Wyoming (19934) *(G-973)*
Salt Marsh Foods Inc 302 260-9556
　314 Swedes St Rehoboth Beach (19971) *(G-12943)*
Salt Pond Associates 302 539-2750
　400 Bethany Loop Bethany Beach (19930) *(G-638)*
Salt Pond Golf Club, Bethany Beach Also Called: Salt Pond Associates *(G-638)*
Salted Vines Vineyard Winery, Frankford Also Called: Wine Worx LLC *(G-4161)*
Saltverk Inc 412 413-9193
　251 Little Falls Dr Wilmington (19808) *(G-19642)*

Saltwater Cowgirls 302 745-3632
　26563 Jersey Rd Millsboro (19966) *(G-8452)*
Salty Paws, Rehoboth Beach Also Called: Salty Paws RB LLC *(G-12944)*
Salty Paws RB LLC 484 667-7122
　43 Rehoboth Ave Rehoboth Beach (19971) *(G-12944)*
Salvation Army 302 934-3730
　559 E Dupont Hwy Millsboro (19966) *(G-8453)*
Salvation Army 302 654-8808
　610 S Walnut St Wilmington (19801) *(G-19643)*
Salvation Army 302 996-9400
　2 S Augustine St Wilmington (19804) *(G-19644)*
Salvation Army 302 656-1696
　400 N Orange St Wilmington (19801) *(G-19645)*
Salvation Army, Millsboro Also Called: Salvation Army *(G-8453)*
Salvation Army, Wilmington Also Called: Salvation Army *(G-19643)*
Salvation Army, Wilmington Also Called: Salvation Army *(G-19644)*
Salvation Army, Wilmington Also Called: Salvation Army *(G-19645)*
Salvatore Seeley 302 270-5503
　37 Baltimore Ave Rehoboth Beach (19971) *(G-12945)*
Sam Walts & Associates 302 777-2211
　11 Downs Dr Wilmington (19807) *(G-19646)*
Sam Waltz & Associates Counsel, Wilmington Also Called: Sam Walts & Associates *(G-19646)*
Sam Yoder and Son LLC 302 398-4711
　9387 Memory Rd Greenwood (19950) *(G-4666)*
Sam Your Taxes LLC 302 482-9601
　1716 W Gilpin Dr Wilmington (19805) *(G-19647)*
Sam8sara Inc 347 605-0693
　16192 Coastal Hwy Lewes (19958) *(G-6444)*
Samaha Michel R MD 302 422-3100
　39 W Clarke Ave Milford (19963) *(G-8081)*
Samantha Hudran Massage 302 382-5851
　231 Delaware Ave Harrington (19952) *(G-4826)*
Samaritan Outreach 302 594-9476
　1410 N Claymont St Wilmington (19802) *(G-19648)*
Sameena Malhan 302 422-3311
　21 W Clarke Ave Milford (19963) *(G-8082)*
Sammys Auto LLC 302 368-5203
　23 Gurnsey Dr Newark (19713) *(G-11939)*
Sampson Interiors 865 438-5097
　1 Ocean Breeze Dr Rehoboth Beach (19971) *(G-12946)*
Sams Construction LLC 302 654-6542
　1405 Haines Ave Wilmington (19809) *(G-19649)*
Sams Construction LLC 302 654-6542
　1227 E 15th St Wilmington (19802) *(G-19650)*
Sams Painting 302 430-1241
　204 Sandy Beach Dr Dagsboro (19939) *(G-1503)*
Samto Medical Services 302 266-4933
　254 Chapman Rd Ste 103 Newark (19702) *(G-11940)*
Samuel Blumberg PHD 302 652-7733
　2300 Pennsylvania Ave Wilmington (19806) *(G-19651)*
Samuel Coraluzzo Co Inc 302 322-1195
　729 Grantham Ln New Castle (19720) *(G-9551)*
Samuel Prettyman 302 858-8886
　36603 Bi State Blvd Delmar (19940) *(G-1634)*
Sanad Cash Inc 302 314-8170
　651 N Broad St Middletown (19709) *(G-7537)*
Sanare Today LLC 610 344-9600
　1401 Silverside Rd Wilmington (19810) *(G-19652)*
Sanattest LLC 623 337-7849
　15 Center Meeting Rd Wilmington (19807) *(G-19653)*
Sanchasegroup 302 516-7373
　2100 Northeast Blvd Wilmington (19802) *(G-19654)*
Sanco Construction Co Inc 302 633-4156
　24 Brookside Dr Wilmington (19804) *(G-19655)*
Sanctuary Spa and Saloon 302 475-1469
　1847 Marsh Rd Wilmington (19810) *(G-19656)*
Sand Dollar Dewey LLC 302 858-7030
　30972 Sycamore Dr Lewes (19958) *(G-6445)*
Sand Hill Adult Program, Georgetown Also Called: Sussex Cnty Snior Svcs Adult D *(G-4534)*
Sandebbarnanricway Corp 302 475-2705
　2221 Inwood Rd Wilmington (19810) *(G-19657)*

ALPHABETIC SECTION

Sanderson Albidress Agency.. 302 368-3010
   1211b Milltown Rd Wilmington (19808) *(G-19658)*

Sandhill Development Group LLC.. 302 703-2140
   16181 Hudson Rd Milton (19968) *(G-8706)*

Sandler Occptnal Mdicine Assoc.. 302 369-0171
   168 S Main St Ste 206 Newark (19711) *(G-11941)*

Sandler Occupational Health.. 302 607-7365
   280 E Main St Newark (19711) *(G-11942)*

Sandpiper Energy Inc.. 302 736-7656
   909 Silver Lake Blvd Dover (19904) *(G-3508)*

Sandra Jackson... 302 510-3576
   23 W 37th St Wilmington (19802) *(G-19659)*

Sandra L Korines.. 201 245-2003
   809 N Washington St Wilmington (19801) *(G-19660)*

Sandra M Cmpos Restoration LLC.. 302 883-7663
   30209 Regatta Bay Blvd Lewes (19958) *(G-6446)*

Sandra S Gulledge CPA... 302 422-5005
   107 N Walnut St Milford (19963) *(G-8083)*

Sandra Sue Retzky DO... 302 540-3463
   146 Marcella Rd Wilmington (19803) *(G-19661)*

Sands Health Spa LLC.. 302 543-8385
   214 N Maryland Ave Wilmington (19804) *(G-19662)*

Sands Inc.. 302 227-2511
   101 N Boardwalk Rehoboth Beach (19971) *(G-12947)*

Sands Motel, Fenwick Island *Also Called: Sussex Sands Inc (G-4057)*

Sandy Brae Laboratories.. 302 456-0446
   3 S Tatnall St Wilmington (19801) *(G-19663)*

Sandy Hill Greenhouses Inc... 302 856-2412
   18303 Sand Hill Rd Georgetown (19947) *(G-4498)*

Sangita Scientific LLC.. 866 272-6432
   1013 Centre Rd Ste 403b Wilmington (19805) *(G-19664)*

Sangree Construction Inc... 717 576-7144
   315 Union St Milton (19968) *(G-8707)*

Sanjaban Corp.. 612 805-5971
   4023 Kennett Pike # 701 Wilmington (19807) *(G-19665)*

Sankhya Ventures LLC... 415 905-0887
   2810 N Church St Ste 40809 Wilmington (19802) *(G-19666)*

Sanosil International, Wilmington *Also Called: Sanosil International LLC (G-19667)*

Sanosil International LLC... 302 454-8102
   1500 Eastlawn Ave Wilmington (19802) *(G-19667)*

Santanas Roofing LLC... 302 887-0067
   147 Council Cir Newark (19702) *(G-11943)*

Santander Bank NA... 302 654-5182
   824 N Market St Ste 100 Wilmington (19801) *(G-19668)*

Santay Trucking Inc... 302 245-6012
   14296 Dupont Blvd Ellendale (19941) *(G-3929)*

Santo Stucco.. 302 453-0901
   13 Metten Rd Newark (19713) *(G-11944)*

Santora CPA Group Pa... 302 737-6200
   220 Continental Dr Ste 112 Newark (19713) *(G-11945)*

Santos Aircraft LLC... 302 608-6637
   15 Penns Way New Castle (19720) *(G-9552)*

Sap Investments Inc.. 302 427-7889
   300 Delaware Ave Wilmington (19801) *(G-19669)*

Sapere... 888 727-3731
   8 The Grn Dover (19901) *(G-3509)*

Saphic Innovations Inc... 820 888-0099
   1232 N King St Ste 128 Wilmington (19801) *(G-19670)*

Sapps Welding Service... 302 491-6319
   8547 Sophies Way Lincoln (19960) *(G-6697)*

Sara Cleaning Service.. 856 498-3244
   230 Landau Way Bear (19701) *(G-479)*

Sara Elizabeth Novy Dpt... 201 783-5082
   32310 Bayshore Dr Millsboro (19966) *(G-8454)*

Sarah B Neely-Collins... 814 282-6013
   526 Great Geneva Dr Dover (19901) *(G-3510)*

Sarah Craig Lmt... 302 480-4792
   5609 Dupont Pkwy Ste 7 Smyrna (19977) *(G-13878)*

Sarah K Smith DDS... 302 442-3233
   83 Beech Hill Dr Newark (19711) *(G-11946)*

Sarah Lockhead... 484 941-4712
   113 E Main St Unit 208 Newark (19711) *(G-11947)*

Sarah Wolfe Lcsw... 302 744-8046
   509 Lakeview Ave Milford (19963) *(G-8084)*

Sarahs Art Scene... 302 792-2631
   7 Orchard Ln Wilmington (19809) *(G-19671)*

Saratoga Food Specialties, Dover *Also Called: Saratoga Food Specialties LLC (G-3511)*

Saratoga Food Specialties LLC (HQ)...................................... 951 270-9600
   850 New Burton Rd Dover (19904) *(G-3511)*

Sardo & Sons Warehousing Inc (PA)...................................... 302 369-2100
   56 W Main St Ste 208 Christiana (19702) *(G-1008)*

Sardo & Sons Warehousing Inc... 302 737-3000
   401 Pencader Dr Ste A Newark (19702) *(G-11948)*

Sardo & Sons Warehousing Inc... 302 369-0852
   300 White Clay Center Dr Newark (19711) *(G-11949)*

Saregama, Newark *Also Called: Saregama India Limited (G-11950)*

Saregama India Limited.. 859 490-0156
   200 Continental Dr Ste 401 Newark (19713) *(G-11950)*

Sargent & Lundy LLC.. 302 622-7200
   500 Delaware Ave Ste 400 Wilmington (19801) *(G-19672)*

Sarkana Pharma Inc.. 649 332-4417
   1000 Nw St Ste 1200 Wilmington (19801) *(G-19673)*

Sas Nanotechnologies Inc.. 214 235-1008
   804 Interchange Blvd Newark (19711) *(G-11951)*

Sasquatch Creative LLC... 302 502-3105
   1700 N Rodney St Fl 2 Wilmington (19806) *(G-19674)*

Sassy Kitty and Lash Spa LLC.. 443 983-1125
   90 Hickory Pl Newark (19702) *(G-11952)*

Sassy Spa... 302 668-8008
   3600 Lancaster Pike Wilmington (19805) *(G-19675)*

Satellite Connection Inc... 302 328-2462
   4001 Kennett Pike Ste 134 Wilmington (19807) *(G-19676)*

Satodesign LLC... 989 710-2029
   3 Germay Dr Wilmington (19804) *(G-19677)*

Satori Ci LLC.. 302 526-0557
   2093 Philadelphia Pike Apt 2772 Claymont (19703) *(G-1285)*

Sattar A Syed DMD PA.. 302 994-3093
   5507 Kirkwood Hwy Wilmington (19808) *(G-19678)*

Satterfield & Ryan Inc... 302 422-4919
   8266 N Union Church Rd Milford (19963) *(G-8085)*

Saturn, Newark *Also Called: Winner Group Inc (G-12389)*

Saucedos Landscaping, Dover *Also Called: Juan Saucedo (G-2812)*

Sauer Holdings Inc.. 302 656-8989
   1403 Foulk Rd Ste 200 Wilmington (19803) *(G-19679)*

Saundra Wright... 302 298-0324
   1521 Concord Pike Ste 102 Wilmington (19803) *(G-19680)*

Savannah Electric... 302 645-5906
   2039 Savannah Cir Lewes (19958) *(G-6447)*

Savannah Inn.. 302 645-0330
   55 N Atlantic Dr Lewes (19958) *(G-6448)*

Savannah Logistics LLC... 302 893-7251
   278 Liborio Dr Middletown (19709) *(G-7538)*

Savant International Holdings.. 305 768-9395
   2035 Sunset Lake Rd Newark (19702) *(G-11953)*

Savantis Group... 415 297-6926
   200 Bellevue Pkwy Ste 215 Wilmington (19809) *(G-19681)*

Savantis Solutions LLC (PA).. 732 906-3200
   200 Bellevue Pkwy Ste 215 Wilmington (19809) *(G-19682)*

Savaren Corporate Arcft Svcs... 443 207-1372
   120 Old Churchmans Rd New Castle (19720) *(G-9553)*

Savarna Inc... 757 446-0101
   259 Quigley Blvd Ste 15 Historic New Castle (19720) *(G-5066)*

Savemunch Inc... 469 473-1601
   16192 Coastal Hwy Lewes (19958) *(G-6449)*

Saverd LLC... 347 565-5586
   24a Trolley Sq Wilmington (19806) *(G-19683)*

Savimbo Inc.. 650 387-6648
   300 Delaware Ave Wilmington (19801) *(G-19684)*

Saving Our Slves Prprty Invsto.. 267 879-0464
   34 Dozer Ct Smyrna (19977) *(G-13879)*

Saving Our Yuth Mtters Incrprt.. 917 889-0086
   630 Capitol Trl Apt G2 Newark (19711) *(G-11954)*

Savoy Associates... 302 658-8770
   15 Ashley Pl Ste 3b Wilmington (19804) *(G-19685)*

Savvy Artistry LLC... 302 339-1712
　1016 Clayton St Historic New Castle (19720) *(G-5067)*
Savvy Hair Studios... 302 724-5629
　3847 N Dupont Hwy Ste 1 Dover (19901) *(G-3512)*
Savvyderm Skin Clinic LLC... 302 257-5089
　32782 Cedar Dr Ste 2 Millville (19967) *(G-8547)*
Sawai LLC... 800 625-3680
　3 Germay Dr Wilmington (19804) *(G-19686)*
Sawyers Sanitation Service... 302 678-8240
　184 Front St Leipsic (19901) *(G-5633)*
Saxton Jack 3 Construction.. 302 654-4553
　1903 N Lincoln St Wilmington (19806) *(G-19687)*
Sb Electric LLC... 610 721-5361
　2209 Patwynn Rd Wilmington (19810) *(G-19688)*
Sb Global Advisers (us) Inc.. 650 562-8100
　251 Little Falls Dr Wilmington (19808) *(G-19689)*
Sb Logistics LLC... 302 494-9756
　607 Brier Ave Wilmington (19805) *(G-19690)*
SB&b Wellness LLC.. 484 681-1411
　108 Overlook Pl Dover (19901) *(G-3513)*
Sbdc Lead Center, Newark Also Called: Delaware Small Bus Dev Ctr *(G-10481)*
Sbdc Sussex County, Georgetown Also Called: Delaware Small Bus Dev Ctr *(G-4283)*
Sbh Group Properties LLC... 302 588-1656
　4023 Kennett Pike # 256 Wilmington (19807) *(G-19691)*
Sbm Landowner Inc... 302 652-8314
　110 N Poplar St Wilmington (19801) *(G-19692)*
Sbr Enterprises LLC... 302 836-6909
　992 Port Penn Rd Middletown (19709) *(G-7539)*
SBS Global LLC... 302 898-2911
　28 Golf View Dr Apt A6 Newark (19702) *(G-11955)*
SC Ennis Incorporated... 302 629-8771
　23000 Sussex Hwy Seaford (19973) *(G-13384)*
SC Foster LLC... 302 383-0201
　43 Stonewold Way Wilmington (19807) *(G-19693)*
SC Marketing US Inc.. 714 352-4992
　2711 Centerville Rd Ste 400 Wilmington (19808) *(G-19694)*
SC&a Construction Inc.. 302 478-6030
　3411 Silverside Rd Ste 200 Wilmington (19810) *(G-19695)*
Scalias Day Care Center Inc....................................... 302 366-1430
　701 Old Harmony Rd Newark (19711) *(G-11956)*
Scanpoint Inc... 603 429-0777
　5700 Kirkwood Hwy Ste 202 Wilmington (19808) *(G-19696)*
Scanta Inc.. 302 645-7400
　16192 Coastal Hwy Lewes (19958) *(G-6450)*
Scassociates Inc.. 302 454-1100
　651 N Broad St Ste 103 Middletown (19709) *(G-7540)*
Scchs... 302 856-7524
　110 N Railroad Ave Georgetown (19947) *(G-4499)*
Schab & Barnett, Georgetown Also Called: Schab & Barnett PA *(G-4500)*
Schab & Barnett PA... 302 856-9024
　9 Chestnut St Georgetown (19947) *(G-4500)*
Schaffers Mobile Detailing LLC................................... 302 284-7636
　1539 Andrews Lake Rd Felton (19943) *(G-4023)*
Schagrin Gas Co (PA)... 302 378-2000
　1000 N Broad St Middletown (19709) *(G-7541)*
Schagringas Company, Middletown Also Called: Schagrin Gas Co *(G-7541)*
Schanne Mark State Farm Insur.................................. 302 422-7231
　915 S Dupont Blvd Milford (19963) *(G-8086)*
Schatz Messick Enterprises LLC................................. 302 398-8646
　705 Andrewville Rd Harrington (19952) *(G-4827)*
Schell Bros At Peninsula Lakes................................... 302 228-4488
　30965 Fowlers Path Millsboro (19966) *(G-8455)*
Schell Brothers... 302 242-8334
　19640 Buck Run Georgetown (19947) *(G-4501)*
Schell Brothers LLC (PA)... 302 226-1994
　20184 Phillips St Rehoboth Beach (19971) *(G-12948)*
Schfh Restore... 302 855-1156
　206 Academy St Georgetown (19947) *(G-4502)*
Schiff Farms Inc (PA).. 302 398-8014
　16054 S Dupont Hwy Harrington (19952) *(G-4828)*
Schiff Group LLC.. 301 325-1359
　606 Pond View Dr Bethany Beach (19930) *(G-639)*
Schiff Transport LLC... 302 398-8014
　16054 S Dupont Hwy Harrington (19952) *(G-4829)*
Schilling-Dglas Schl Hair Dsign................................... 737 510-0101
　211 Louviers Dr Newark (19711) *(G-11957)*
Schlosser Assoc Mech Cntrs Inc................................ 302 738-7333
　2047 Sunset Lake Rd Newark (19702) *(G-11958)*
Schmittinger & Rodriguez Attys.................................. 302 378-1697
　651 N Broad St Middletown (19709) *(G-7542)*
Schmittinger and Rodriguez PA (PA).......................... 302 674-0140
　414 S State St Dover (19901) *(G-3514)*
Schnader Hrrson Sgal Lewis LLP................................ 302 888-4554
　824 N Market St Ste 800 Wilmington (19801) *(G-19697)*
Schoenbeck PA... 302 584-4519
　51 W Periwinkle Ln Newark (19711) *(G-11959)*
Scholarjet PBC... 617 407-9851
　16192 Coastal Hwy Lewes (19958) *(G-6451)*
School - Del Paul Mitchell, Newark Also Called: Carme LLC *(G-10150)*
School Bell Apartments LP... 302 328-9500
　2000 Varsity Ln Bear (19701) *(G-480)*
School For Young Children, Wilmington Also Called: Xavier Inc *(G-20914)*
Schools Landscaping... 302 613-8224
　80 Aleph Dr Newark (19702) *(G-11960)*
Schooltoolstv.. 415 948-0668
　10 S Sherman Dr Bear (19701) *(G-481)*
Schoon Inc.. 302 894-7574
　200 Continental Dr Ste 401 Newark (19713) *(G-11961)*
Schreppler Chiropractic Offs PA................................. 302 653-5525
　892 S Dupont Blvd Smyrna (19977) *(G-13880)*
Schrider Enterprises Inc... 302 934-1900
　398 W State St Millsboro (19966) *(G-8456)*
Schrider Enterprises Inc... 302 539-1036
　327 Atlantic Ave Ocean View (19967) *(G-12566)*
Schroedl Cleaning Svcs Sup Co, Wilmington Also Called: Schroedl Company *(G-19698)*
Schroedl Company.. 410 358-5500
　422 B And O Ln Wilmington (19804) *(G-19698)*
Schultz Corinna L MD... 302 651-4000
　1600 Rockland Rd Wilmington (19803) *(G-19699)*
Schulze, S J, Newark Also Called: Siegfried J Schulze Inc *(G-12003)*
Schuster Jachetti LLP (PA)... 302 856-2400
　20632 Dupont Blvd Georgetown (19947) *(G-4503)*
Schuster Jachetti LLP.. 302 984-1000
　3407 Lancaster Pike Ste A Wilmington (19805) *(G-19700)*
Schuster Management Corp....................................... 302 653-1235
　200 Goldsborough Way Smyrna (19977) *(G-13881)*
SCHUSTER MANAGEMENT CORP, Smyrna Also Called: Schuster Management Corp *(G-13881)*
Schutte Park... 302 349-4898
　10 Electric Ave Dover (19904) *(G-3515)*
Schwartz Eric MD... 302 730-0840
　230 Beiser Blvd Ste 100 Dover (19904) *(G-3516)*
Schwartz Center For Arts.. 302 678-3583
　118 S Bradford St Dover (19904) *(G-3517)*
Schwartz Eric Wm MD... 302 234-5770
　726 Yorklyn Rd Ste 100 Hockessin (19707) *(G-5379)*
Schwartz Schwartz Attys At Law................................. 302 998-1500
　1525 Delaware Ave Wilmington (19806) *(G-19701)*
Schwartz Schwrtz Attys At Law................................... 302 678-8700
　1140 S State St Dover (19901) *(G-3518)*
Schwarz Properties LLC... 302 376-1696
　203 Cheshire Dr Middletown (19709) *(G-7543)*
Schweizer Cleaning Service... 302 995-2816
　317 Brookside Dr Wilmington (19804) *(G-19702)*
Schwerman Trucking Co.. 302 832-3103
　3340 Wrangle Hill Rd Bear (19701) *(G-482)*
Science House Foundation.. 800 839-1754
　501 Silverside Rd Ste 123 Wilmington (19809) *(G-19703)*
Scientific Chemical Solutions..................................... 208 490-2125
　19c Trolley Sq Wilmington (19806) *(G-19704)*
Scientific Holdings Corp... 302 225-5065
　2751 Centerville Rd Ste 358 Wilmington (19808) *(G-19705)*
Scientific Systems Corp.. 302 655-5500
　901 N Tatnall St Wilmington (19801) *(G-19706)*

ALPHABETIC SECTION

Scientific USA Inc.. 425 681-9462
  2711 Centerville Rd Wilmington (19808) *(G-19707)*

Scigate Holdings LLC (PA).. 970 481-4949
  3211 Kildoon Dr Newark (19702) *(G-11962)*

Scimedico LLC... 302 375-7500
  221 N Broad St Ste 3a Middletown (19709) *(G-7544)*

Scinorx Technologies Inc... 302 268-5447
  1521 Concord Pike Ste 301 Wilmington (19803) *(G-19708)*

Scituate Solar I LLC.. 212 419-4843
  2711 Centerville Rd Ste 400 Wilmington (19808) *(G-19709)*

Scj, Milford Also Called: Stevenson Ventures LLC *(G-8105)*

Scj Commercial Financial Svcs, Harrington Also Called: Red Target LLC *(G-4819)*

Scor Globl Lf Amrcas Rnsurance............................. 704 344-2700
  251 Little Falls Dr Wilmington (19808) *(G-19710)*

Score Revive LLC... 302 455-2100
  9 E Loockerman St Ste 202 Dover (19901) *(G-3519)*

Scorelogix LLC... 302 294-6532
  1 Innovation Way Ste 300 Newark (19711) *(G-11963)*

Scorpion Offshore Inc
  1209 Orange St Corporation Trust Ctr Wilmington (19801) *(G-19711)*

Scotch Hills Apartments, New Castle Also Called: Berman Development Corp *(G-8859)*

Scott & Sons Landscaping, Delmar Also Called: Shubert Enterprises Inc *(G-1637)*

Scott A Hammer Md Faafp..................................... 302 725-2033
  119 Neurology Way Milford (19963) *(G-8087)*

Scott Charles Foresman... 302 644-8418
  124 Gosling Creek Rd Lewes (19958) *(G-6452)*

Scott Engineering Inc... 302 736-3058
  22 Old Rudnick Ln Ste 2 Dover (19901) *(G-3520)*

Scott Muffler LLC.. 302 378-9247
  308 W Main St Middletown (19709) *(G-7545)*

Scott Pediatrics.. 302 684-1119
  611 Federal St Ste 3 Milton (19968) *(G-8708)*

Scott Pediatrics, Rehoboth Beach Also Called: Lowell Scott MD PA *(G-12840)*

Scottish Ventures LLC.. 302 382-6057
  5 Wildfire Ln New Castle (19720) *(G-9554)*

Scottons Sanitation LLC... 302 382-5743
  643 Deer Antler Rd Clayton (19938) *(G-1404)*

Scotts Co.. 302 777-4779
  100 W 10th St Lbby Wilmington (19801) *(G-19712)*

Scotts-Sierra Investments Inc, Wilmington Also Called: Scotts-Sierra Investments LLC *(G-19713)*

Scotts-Sierra Investments LLC (HQ)....................... 302 622-9269
  1105 N Market St Ste 1300 Wilmington (19801) *(G-19713)*

Scout Level LLC (PA)... 336 500-2067
  651 N Broad St Ste 205 Middletown (19709) *(G-7546)*

Scov3 LLC.. 973 387-9771
  501 Silverside Rd Wilmington (19809) *(G-19714)*

Scov3 LLC (PA).. 973 387-9771
  1201 N Orange St Ste 712 Wilmington (19801) *(G-19715)*

Screen Zone Enterprises LLC................................. 302 316-0705
  8 The Grn Ste 6484 Dover (19901) *(G-3521)*

Scrubmoney Inc.. 240 671-5379
  251 Little Falls Dr Wilmington (19808) *(G-19716)*

Scuba World Inc... 302 698-1117
  4004 S Dupont Hwy Ste B Dover (19901) *(G-3522)*

SD&I Bail Bonds LLC... 302 407-6591
  1202 W 4th St Wilmington (19805) *(G-19717)*

SD&I Enterprises LLC.. 302 407-6591
  1202 W 4th St Wilmington (19805) *(G-19718)*

Sdix, Newark Also Called: Sdix LLC *(G-11964)*

Sdix, Newark Also Called: Standard Merger Sub LLC *(G-12083)*

Sdix LLC... 302 456-6789
  111 Pencader Dr Newark (19702) *(G-11964)*

Sdn Essentials LLC.. 415 902-5702
  40 E Main St Ste 1214 Newark (19711) *(G-11965)*

SE Gaming Services Inc... 303 867-8090
  254 Chapman Rd Ste 208 Newark (19702) *(G-11966)*

SE Lavi Productions LLC (PA)................................ 727 457-2625
  3500 S Dupont Hwy Dover (19901) *(G-3523)*

Sea Barre Fitness.. 610 202-0518
  34410 Tenley Ct Unit 2 Lewes (19958) *(G-6453)*

Sea Care LLC... 410 688-4230
  7905 Gum Branch Rd Seaford (19973) *(G-13385)*

Sea Colony, Bethany Beach Also Called: Carl M Freeman Associates Inc *(G-589)*

Sea Colony, Bethany Beach Also Called: Sea Colony LLC *(G-640)*

Sea Colony LLC... 302 537-8888
  2 Edgewater House Rd Bethany Beach (19930) *(G-640)*

Sea Esta 4.. 302 354-1245
  20902 Coastal Hwy Rehoboth Beach (19971) *(G-12949)*

Sea Esta Motel 2, Millsboro Also Called: Pelican Bay Group Inc *(G-8418)*

Sea Esta Motel III, Rehoboth Beach Also Called: George Metz *(G-12769)*

Sea Play Homes LLC... 302 564-7557
  1 E Indian St Fenwick Island (19944) *(G-4054)*

Sea Shell Shop Inc (PA)... 302 227-4323
  4405 Coastal Hwy Rte 1 Rehoboth Beach (19971) *(G-12950)*

Sea Studio Architects... 302 364-0821
  658 Tingle Ave Bethany Beach (19930) *(G-641)*

Sea Transport Corporation LLC.............................. 786 208-2433
  19c Trolley Sq Wilmington (19806) *(G-19719)*

Seabrix LLC... 224 578-3191
  8 The Grn Ste A Dover (19901) *(G-3524)*

Seachange Vacation Rentals.................................. 302 727-5566
  20 Baltimore Ave Ste 1 Rehoboth Beach (19971) *(G-12951)*

SEADAE, Dover Also Called: State Edcatn Agcy Dirs Arts Ed *(G-3605)*

Seafood City Inc... 302 284-8486
  9996 S Dupont Hwy Felton (19943) *(G-4024)*

Seafood House, The, Seaford Also Called: Children Fmilies First Del Inc *(G-13119)*

Seaford Animal Hospital Inc................................... 302 629-7325
  22661 Atlanta Rd Seaford (19973) *(G-13386)*

Seaford Apartment Ventures LLC........................... 302 629-0909
  23033 Meadow Wood Ct Seaford (19973) *(G-13387)*

Seaford Center, Seaford Also Called: 1100 Nrman Eskrdge Hwy Oprtons *(G-13041)*

Seaford Endoscopy Center..................................... 302 629-7177
  13 Fallon Ave Seaford (19973) *(G-13388)*

Seaford Feed Mill, Seaford Also Called: Allen Harim Foods LLC *(G-13056)*

Seaford Machine Works Inc................................... 302 629-6034
  1451 Middleford Rd Seaford (19973) *(G-13389)*

Seaford Meadows Apartments, Seaford Also Called: Seaford Preservation Assoc LLC *(G-13393)*

Seaford Medical Specialists.................................... 302 628-8300
  1350 Middleford Rd # 502 Seaford (19973) *(G-13390)*

Seaford Mission Inc.. 302 629-2559
  611 3rd St Seaford (19973) *(G-13391)*

Seaford Police Dept.. 302 629-6644
  300 Virginia Ave Seaford (19973) *(G-13392)*

Seaford Preservation Assoc LLC............................ 302 629-6416
  122 Seaford Meadows Dr Seaford (19973) *(G-13393)*

Seaford Star, Seaford Also Called: Morning Star Publications Inc *(G-13289)*

Seager Insight.. 302 526-0597
  2803 Philadelphia Pike B Claymont (19703) *(G-1286)*

Seagreen Bicycle... 302 645-7008
  209 Monroe Ave Lewes (19958) *(G-6454)*

Seagreen Bicycle LLP.. 302 226-2323
  54 Baltimore Ave Rehoboth Beach (19971) *(G-12952)*

Seal Cybrscurity Solutions Inc................................ 302 636-5401
  251 Little Falls Dr Wilmington (19808) *(G-19720)*

Seal Pro Paving and Seal....................................... 302 379-8267
  2001 W 6th St Wilmington (19805) *(G-19721)*

Seal Security, Wilmington Also Called: Seal Cybrscurity Solutions Inc *(G-19720)*

Sealguard, Harrington Also Called: Caleb G Stevens *(G-4744)*

Seamens Center Wilmington Inc............................ 302 575-1300
  1 Container Rd Wilmington (19801) *(G-19722)*

Sean E Reilly.. 302 690-9487
  310 N West St Wilmington (19801) *(G-19723)*

Sean Ohagan LLC.. 302 798-7572
  1302 Society Dr Claymont (19703) *(G-1287)*

Sean Thomas Joynt Mspt Atc................................. 302 286-6282
  44 Lisa Dr Newark (19702) *(G-11967)*

Search Optics LLC (PA)... 858 678-0707
  2751 Centerville Rd Ste 109 Wilmington (19808) *(G-19724)*

Sears Heating and AC.. 302 480-1382
  15 Loockerman Plz Dover (19901) *(G-3525)*

Sears Roebuck Acceptance Corp   **ALPHABETIC SECTION**

Sears Roebuck Acceptance Corp.................................... 302 434-3100
   3711 Kennett Pike Ste 120 Wilmington (19807) *(G-19725)*

Seascape Lab.. 760 807-7983
   628 Milford Harrington Hwy Ste 5 Milford (19963) *(G-8088)*

Seaside Amusements Inc.. 302 227-1921
   6 Delaware Ave Rehoboth Beach (19971) *(G-12953)*

Seaside Endoscopy Pavillion, Lewes *Also Called: Envision Healthcare Corp (G-5965)*

Seaside Graphics Corp.. 302 436-9460
   1 Mason Dr Selbyville (19975) *(G-13603)*

Seaside Gstrointerology Conslt, Lewes *Also Called: Caruso Richard F MD PA (G-5806)*

Seaside Pointe.. 302 226-8750
   36101 Seaside Blvd Rehoboth Beach (19971) *(G-12954)*

Seaside Pressure Wash LLC.. 302 470-4035
   4840 Shirleys Rd Greenwood (19950) *(G-4667)*

Seaside Service LLC.. 302 827-3775
   36360 Tarpon Dr Lewes (19958) *(G-6455)*

Seasons Hspice Plltive Care De...................................... 847 692-1000
   220 Continental Dr Ste 407 Newark (19713) *(G-11968)*

Seattle Luxe, Wilmington *Also Called: Superior Luxe LLC (G-20142)*

Seaway Service Inc.. 302 834-7101
   34 Clinton St Delaware City (19706) *(G-1557)*

Sebastians Painting.. 302 725-8023
   9072 Greentop Rd Lincoln (19960) *(G-6698)*

Second Chance Solutions LLC.. 302 204-0551
   1201 N Market St Ste 111 Wilmington (19801) *(G-19726)*

Second Foundation US Trdg LLC..................................... 253 777-4400
   1209 N Orange St Wilmington (19801) *(G-19727)*

Second Front, Wilmington *Also Called: Second Front Systems Inc (G-19728)*

Second Front Systems Inc (PA)...................................... 301 744-7318
   1207 Delaware Ave Ste 800 Wilmington (19806) *(G-19728)*

Second Technologies Inc.. 310 774-7518
   8 The Grn Dover (19901) *(G-3526)*

SecondSTAX Inc... 862 368-0413
   251 Little Falls Dr Wilmington (19808) *(G-19729)*

Secure Americas Future Economy................................... 302 464-2687
   115 Dungarvan Dr Middletown (19709) *(G-7547)*

Secure Schools Alliance Inc... 302 333-1416
   2207 Concord Pike Wilmington (19803) *(G-19730)*

Secure Self Storage (PA).. 302 832-0400
   1020 Bear Rd New Castle (19720) *(G-9555)*

Securelayer7 LLC... 302 391-0803
   364 E Main St 1010 Middletown (19709) *(G-7548)*

Securenetmd LLC (PA).. 302 645-7770
   16557 Coastal Hwy Lewes (19958) *(G-6456)*

Securitas Technology Corp... 302 992-7950
   1100 First State Blvd Wilmington (19804) *(G-19731)*

Securitech Inc.. 302 996-9230
   205 N Marshall St Wilmington (19804) *(G-19732)*

Security 101, Newark *Also Called: Security 101 Philadlephia LLC (G-11969)*

Security 101 Philadlephia LLC.. 484 369-7101
   14 Mill Park Ct Newark (19713) *(G-11969)*

SECURITY INSTRUMENT, Wilmington *Also Called: Security Instrument Corp Del (G-19733)*

Security Instrument Corp Del.. 302 674-2891
   28226 Lewes Georgetown Hwy Milton (19968) *(G-8709)*

Security Instrument Corp Del (PA).................................. 302 998-2261
   309 W Newport Pike Wilmington (19804) *(G-19733)*

Security Quality... 302 286-1200
   930 Old Harmony Rd Ste H Newark (19713) *(G-11970)*

Security Satellite.. 302 376-0241
   5101 Summit Bridge Rd Middletown (19709) *(G-7549)*

Security Satellite Systems, Middletown *Also Called: Security Satellite (G-7549)*

Security Watch Corp... 302 286-6728
   260 Chapman Rd Ste 100c Newark (19702) *(G-11971)*

Sedation Center PA.. 302 678-3384
   429 S Governors Ave Dover (19904) *(G-3527)*

Sedgwick.. 302 691-8871
   2040 Clark St Wilmington (19805) *(G-19734)*

Sedgwick, Wilmington *Also Called: Sedgwick (G-19734)*

SEdoyle General Contractor... 302 531-5271
   9040 Canterbury Rd Felton (19943) *(G-4025)*

Sedrak Wagdy MD.. 302 651-6386
   1600 Rockland Rd Wilmington (19803) *(G-19735)*

See The World Travel Agency... 302 559-4514
   425 Maplewood Dr Middletown (19709) *(G-7550)*

Seecubic Inc (PA).. 267 400-1565
   1732a Marsh Rd Ste 124 Wilmington (19810) *(G-19736)*

Seeds of Jesus Day Care LLC.. 302 494-6568
   12 Mary Ella Dr Wilmington (19805) *(G-19737)*

Seemetrics Inc.. 818 533-9806
   1007 N Orange St Wilmington (19801) *(G-19738)*

Seeney Electric LLC... 302 494-3686
   223 Heron Cir New Castle (19720) *(G-9556)*

Seiberlich Trane, New Castle *Also Called: John R Seiberlich Inc (G-9262)*

Seiberlich Trane Energy Svcs... 302 395-0200
   66 Southgate Blvd New Castle (19720) *(G-9557)*

Seiff Jenna L MD... 302 633-6859
   4512 Kirkwood Hwy Ste 201 Wilmington (19808) *(G-19739)*

Seitz Vanogtrop & Green.. 302 888-0600
   222 Delaware Ave Ste 1500 Wilmington (19801) *(G-19740)*

Sekhon Travels LLC (PA).. 661 706-6459
   8 The Grn Ste B Dover (19901) *(G-3528)*

Sekoiya Inc.. 323 761-9028
   2035 Sunset Lake Rd Ste B2 Newark (19702) *(G-11972)*

Selbyville Cleaners Inc (PA).. 302 249-3444
   68 Hosier St Selbyville (19975) *(G-13604)*

Selbyville Pet and Garden Ctr, Selbyville *Also Called: Animal Health Sales Inc (G-13462)*

Select Auto Inc.. 215 423-6522
   507 Darley Rd Claymont (19703) *(G-1288)*

Select Health Services LLC... 504 737-4300
   560 Peoples Plz Newark (19702) *(G-11973)*

Select Management Resources, New Castle *Also Called: Northeastern Title Loans (G-9427)*

Select Medical Corporation.. 302 421-4545
   701 N Clayton St Wilmington (19805) *(G-19741)*

Select Physical Therapy.. 302 760-9966
   230 Beiser Blvd Ste 100 Dover (19904) *(G-3529)*

Select Spclty Hsptal- Wlmngton, Wilmington *Also Called: Select Medical Corporation (G-19741)*

Select Specialty Hospital.. 302 421-4590
   501 W 14th St Wilmington (19801) *(G-19742)*

Select Stainless Products LLC...................................... 302 653-3062
   100 Industrial Blvd Clayton (19938) *(G-1405)*

Selection Solutions Inc.. 800 600-6605
   3 Germay Dr Ste 4 Wilmington (19804) *(G-19743)*

Self Care Holistic LLC... 302 407-2456
   14 S Union St Wilmington (19805) *(G-19744)*

Selfx Innovations Inc... 551 277-9665
   919 N Market St Ste 950 Wilmington (19801) *(G-19745)*

Selisav Corporation... 702 888-2175
   16192 Coastal Hwy Lewes (19958) *(G-6457)*

Sellers Senior Center Inc... 302 762-2050
   2800 Silverside Rd Wilmington (19810) *(G-19746)*

Selling Dreams LLC.. 302 746-7999
   3202 Kirkwood Hwy Ste 207 Wilmington (19808) *(G-19747)*

Selwor Enterprises Inc... 302 454-9454
   50 Polly Drummond Hill Rd Newark (19711) *(G-11974)*

Sem Revival LLC... 302 600-1497
   2810 N Church St Wilmington (19802) *(G-19748)*

Sen Tom Carper (d-D... 302 573-6291
   301 N Walnut St Ste 102l-1 Wilmington (19801) *(G-19749)*

Sendchamp Inc.. 510 423-3457
   2055 Limestone Rd Ste 200c Wilmington (19808) *(G-19750)*

Sendible Usa Inc... 646 569-9029
   2035 Sunset Lake Rd Ste 2 Newark (19702) *(G-11975)*

Sendlink Inc (PA).. 650 505-5299
   651 N Broad St Ste 206 Middletown (19709) *(G-7551)*

Sendsafely LLC... 917 375-5891
   40 E Main St Ste 897 Newark (19711) *(G-11976)*

Senhasegura USA LLC.. 469 620-7643
   16192 Coastal Hwy Lewes (19958) *(G-6458)*

Senior Helpers, Newark *Also Called: Del Premier Care Inc (G-10413)*

Senior Nanticoke Center Inc.. 302 629-4939
   310 Virginia Ave Ste B Seaford (19973) *(G-13394)*

Seniortech Inc.. 302 533-5988
   630 Churchmans Rd Ste 107 Newark (19702) *(G-11977)*

ALPHABETIC SECTION

Sensedia LLC (PA) 631 764-4544
  2711 Centerville Rd Wilmington (19808) *(G-19751)*

Sensiai Inc 646 665-7668
  651 N Broad St Ste 206 Middletown (19709) *(G-7552)*

Sensibo Inc 302 572-2572
  1313 N Market St Wilmington (19801) *(G-19752)*

Senso Dynamics LLC 302 257-5926
  16192 Coastal Hwy Lewes (19958) *(G-6459)*

Sensofusion Inc 570 239-4912
  30061 Clam Shell Ln Milton (19968) *(G-8710)*

Sentinel Insurance 302 858-4962
  20254 Dupont Blvd Georgetown (19947) *(G-4504)*

Sentinel Transportation LLC (HQ) 302 477-1640
  3521 Silverside Rd Ste 2a Wilmington (19810) *(G-19753)*

Sentinel-Sg LLC 580 458-9184
  919 N Market St Ste 425 Wilmington (19801) *(G-19754)*

Sentrylight Inc 302 420-8844
  62 N Chapel St Ste 200 Newark (19711) *(G-11978)*

Sentryppe Inc 480 250-1721
  8 The Grn Ste 10596 Dover (19901) *(G-3530)*

Senzors Inc 866 736-9677
  3500 S Dupont Hwy Dover (19901) *(G-3531)*

Seotwix LLC 877 849-8777
  651 N Broad St Middletown (19709) *(G-7553)*

Separation Methods Tech Inc 302 368-0610
  31 Blue Hen Dr Newark (19713) *(G-11979)*

Separe Inc 302 736-5000
  529 Weaver Dr Dover (19901) *(G-3532)*

Sepax Technologies Inc 302 366-1101
  5 Innovation Way Ste 100 Newark (19711) *(G-11980)*

Seper 8 Motel 302 734-5701
  348 N Dupont Hwy Dover (19901) *(G-3533)*

Sequoia Properties Inc 847 599-9099
  27 Craig Rd Bear (19701) *(G-483)*

Ser Trucking Inc 302 328-0782
  703 W 11th St Historic New Castle (19720) *(G-5068)*

Serena Joy LLC 302 312-3318
  1805 N Washington St # 3 Wilmington (19802) *(G-19755)*

Serene Minds 302 478-6199
  410 Foulk Rd Ste 102 Wilmington (19803) *(G-19756)*

Serene Minds LLC 302 478-6199
  80 Omega Dr Bldg C Newark (19713) *(G-11981)*

Serenity Gardens Assisted Livi 302 442-5330
  207 Ruth Dr Middletown (19709) *(G-7554)*

Serenity Grdns Assisted Living, Middletown *Also Called: Serenity Gardens Assisted Livi (G-7554)*

Serenity Spa 302 668-9534
  214 7th Ave Wilmington (19805) *(G-19757)*

Serenity Yoga, Middletown *Also Called: Sundari Kula LLC (G-7610)*

Sergios Pool Service Inc 302 655-1972
  901 N Tatnall St Wilmington (19801) *(G-19758)*

Sergovic & Ellis PA 302 855-9500
  9 N Front St Georgetown (19947) *(G-4505)*

Sergovic Crmean Wdman McCrtney 302 855-1260
  25 Chestnut St Georgetown (19947) *(G-4506)*

Serpe & Sons Bakery, Wilmington *Also Called: Serpe & Sons Inc (G-19759)*

Serpe & Sons Inc 302 994-1868
  1411 Kirkwood Hwy Wilmington (19805) *(G-19759)*

Serrano Inc 302 607-1779
  902 Linfield Rd Newark (19713) *(G-11982)*

Sertifier Inc 302 487-3193
  112 Capitol Trl Ste A Newark (19711) *(G-11983)*

Servant Support Services LLC 215 201-5990
  1 Whitehaven Ct Newark (19711) *(G-11984)*

Service Air Tech Hvac 302 335-8334
  3998 Irish Hill Rd Magnolia (19962) *(G-6782)*

Service Cleaning 302 376-7258
  33 Browning Cir Middletown (19709) *(G-7555)*

Service Disposal of Delaware 302 326-9155
  924 S Heald St Wilmington (19801) *(G-19760)*

Service Energy, Lewes *Also Called: Service Energy LLC (G-6460)*

Service Energy LLC (PA) 302 734-7433
  3799 N Dupont Hwy Dover (19901) *(G-3534)*

Service Energy LLC 302 645-9050
  47 Clay Rd Lewes (19958) *(G-6460)*

Service First Container LLC 302 527-5939
  2870 John Hurd Rd Felton (19943) *(G-4026)*

Service General Corp 302 629-9701
  801 Norman Eskridge Hwy 809 Seaford (19973) *(G-13395)*

Service General Corporation 302 218-4279
  120 N Race St Georgetown (19947) *(G-4507)*

Service General Corporation 302 856-3500
  13 E Laurel St Georgetown (19947) *(G-4508)*

Service Glass Inc 302 629-9139
  Rte 20 W Seaford (19973) *(G-13396)*

Service Master of Newark 302 654-8145
  310 Cornell Dr Ste B1 Wilmington (19801) *(G-19761)*

Service Oil Company 302 734-7433
  3799 N Dupont Hwy Dover (19901) *(G-3535)*

Service Quest 302 235-0173
  217 Louis Ln Hockessin (19707) *(G-5380)*

Service Rsource Group Intl LLC 832 646-8756
  1007 N Orange St Wilmington (19801) *(G-19762)*

Service Tire Truck Center Inc 302 629-5533
  24873 Sussex Hwy Seaford (19973) *(G-13397)*

Service Unlimited Inc 302 326-2665
  19 Southgate Blvd Unit A New Castle (19720) *(G-9558)*

ServiceMaster, Newark *Also Called: ServiceMaster of Newark (G-11985)*

ServiceMaster, Wilmington *Also Called: Service Master of Newark (G-19761)*

ServiceMaster of Newark 302 834-8006
  116 Cann Rd Newark (19702) *(G-11985)*

Services, Lewes *Also Called: Delmarva Furniture Svcs LLC (G-5904)*

Servicesource Inc 302 322-0904
  13 Reads Way New Castle (19720) *(G-9559)*

Servicevet Technologies LLC 302 659-0343
  777 Paddock Rd Smyrna (19977) *(G-13882)*

Servicexpress Corporation (PA) 302 856-3500
  120 N Ray St Georgetown (19947) *(G-4509)*

Servicexpress Corporation 302 424-3500
  340 Ne Front St Milford (19963) *(G-8089)*

Servicexpress Corporation 302 854-9118
  809 Norman Eskridge Hwy Seaford (19973) *(G-13398)*

Servo2gocom Ltd 877 378-0240
  4023 Kennett Pike Ste 583 Wilmington (19807) *(G-19763)*

SERVPRO, Bear *Also Called: SERVPRO of Upper Darby (G-485)*

SERVPRO, Georgetown *Also Called: Teff Inc (G-4547)*

SERVPRO, Newark *Also Called: SERVPRO of Norwalk/Wilton (G-11986)*

SERVPRO, Wilmington *Also Called: Mebro Inc (G-18243)*

SERVPRO Bear-New Castle Inc 302 392-6000
  301 Carson Dr Bear (19701) *(G-484)*

SERVPRO of Dover/Middletown, Dover *Also Called: Dover Nunan LLC (G-2356)*

SERVPRO of Norwalk/Wilton 203 866-2871
  173 E Main St Newark (19711) *(G-11986)*

SERVPRO of Upper Darby 302 392-6000
  301 Carson Dr Bear (19701) *(G-485)*

Seryalda LLC 914 861-5974
  2810 N Church St Wilmington (19802) *(G-19764)*

Sesimi LLC 302 574-6280
  1209 N Orange St Wilmington (19801) *(G-19765)*

Sessions Technologies Inc 302 202-0551
  103 Foulk Rd Ste 202 Wilmington (19803) *(G-19766)*

Set FA Life LLC 302 407-6773
  2600 N Market St Wilmington (19802) *(G-19767)*

Seth L Ivins MD LLC 302 824-7280
  620 Stanton Christiana Rd Ste 305 Newark (19713) *(G-11987)*

Seven Shipping Inc 302 516-7150
  3 Germay Dr Ste 4 Wilmington (19804) *(G-19768)*

Seven Tech LLC 302 464-6488
  600 N Broad St Middletown (19709) *(G-7556)*

Sevenshopper Inc 302 407-6905
  2020 Duncan Rd Wilmington (19808) *(G-19769)*

Sevenshopper LLC 302 516-7150
  3616 Kirkwood Hwy Wilmington (19808) *(G-19770)*

Severn Trent Inc   ALPHABETIC SECTION

Severn Trent Inc (DH) 302 427-5990
   1011 Centre Rd Wilmington (19805) *(G-19771)*

Sevo Indus Fire Protection LLC 913 677-1112
   221 N Broad St Ste 3a Middletown (19709) *(G-7557)*

Sevys Auto Service Inc 302 328-0839
   245 Christiana Rd New Castle (19720) *(G-9560)*

Sew Happy Quilts LLC 302 382-5565
   1095 Hollering Hill Rd Camden Wyoming (19934) *(G-974)*

Sewell C Biggs Trust 302 674-2111
   406 Federal St Dover (19901) *(G-3536)*

Seymour Sasha Rene C N A 302 543-1180
   34 Tuckahoe Rd New Castle (19720) *(G-9561)*

Seymour's Cleaners, Wilmington *Also Called: Curzon Corp (G-15737)*

SF Express Corporation 302 407-6155
   1140 River Rd New Castle (19720) *(G-9562)*

SF Logistics Limited 302 317-3954
   1140 River Rd New Castle (19720) *(G-9563)*

Sfa America Inc 206 265-3148
   2 Germay Dr Unit 42341 Wilmington (19804) *(G-19772)*

Sfin 3 Inc 302 472-9276
   1007 N Orange St Wilmington (19801) *(G-19773)*

Sft, Newark *Also Called: Supercritical Fluid Tech Inc (G-12129)*

Sgm Socher Inc 718 484-4253
   144 Quigley Blvd Historic New Castle (19720) *(G-5069)*

Sgodde Inc 858 336-9471
   2100 Northeast Blvd Wilmington (19802) *(G-19774)*

SGS Properties LLC 302 588-4010
   4517 Verona Dr Wilmington (19808) *(G-19775)*

SGS Telekom Inc 774 482-2236
   200 Continental Dr Ste 401 Newark (19713) *(G-11988)*

Sh Haughton Trucking Moving Co 302 324-9505
   36 Lesley Ln New Castle (19720) *(G-9564)*

Shackleford Facilities Inc 877 735-3938
   33192 Dupont Blvd Frankford (19945) *(G-4141)*

Shackleford Ldscp Grp LLC 302 883-9602
   605 Green Tree Ln Bear (19701) *(G-486)*

Shaddai I El 302 632-7535
   280 Banning Rd Camden Wyoming (19934) *(G-975)*

Shade Merchant LLC 571 634-0670
   8 The Grn Dover (19901) *(G-3537)*

Shadow Protective Services 410 903-3455
   25906 Country Meadows Dr Millsboro (19966) *(G-8457)*

Shady Oak Mobile Home Cmnty 302 245-4324
   21159 Airport Rd Georgetown (19947) *(G-4510)*

Shadybrook Farms LLC 302 734-9966
   6401 Bayside Dr Dover (19901) *(G-3538)*

Shah & Associates PA 302 999-0420
   503 Kirkwood Hwy Wilmington (19805) *(G-19776)*

Shaker Revolution LLC 302 219-4838
   501 Silverside Rd Wilmington (19809) *(G-19777)*

Shakti Yoga LLC 302 696-2288
   1030 Forrest Ave Ste 100 Dover (19904) *(G-3539)*

Shalex Industries US Corp 323 540-5586
   364 E Main St Ste 1012 Middletown (19709) *(G-7558)*

Shalini Sehgal MD 302 424-3694
   200 Kings Hwy Ste 1 Milford (19963) *(G-8090)*

Shallcross Mortgage Co Inc (PA) 302 999-9800
   410 Century Blvd Wilmington (19808) *(G-19778)*

Shammah LLC 302 533-7359
   1 S Old Baltimore Pike Ste 201 Newark (19702) *(G-11989)*

Shamrock Glass Co Inc 302 629-5500
   200 N Delaware Ave Seaford (19973) *(G-13399)*

Shamrock Printing Company 302 368-8888
   261 E Main St Newark (19711) *(G-11990)*

Shamrock Services LLC 302 519-7609
   22576 Waterview Rd Lewes (19958) *(G-6461)*

Shamrock Taxi, Lewes *Also Called: Shamrock Services LLC (G-6461)*

Shankias Best Braids 302 507-9891
   500 W 25th St Wilmington (19802) *(G-19779)*

Shanley Assoc 302 691-6838
   2751 Centerville Rd Ste 401 Wilmington (19808) *(G-19780)*

Shannlls Crtive Styles Brids L (PA) 302 508-9215
   8 The Grn Ste A Dover (19901) *(G-3540)*

Shannon A Fisch 302 536-5667
   400 N Market Street Ext Seaford (19973) *(G-13400)*

Shapeup Sales Coaching 850 585-3527
   272 Fox Chase Rd Felton (19943) *(G-4027)*

Shared Space, Wilmington *Also Called: A Shared Space LLC (G-14172)*

Sharetea, Wilmington *Also Called: Lilian USA LLC (G-17912)*

Shariyfa A Fields 302 552-3574
   1624 Jessup St Wilmington (19802) *(G-19781)*

Sharks Service Center LLC 302 337-8233
   7451 Federalsburg Rd Bridgeville (19933) *(G-764)*

Sharlay Computer Systems 302 588-3170
   15 Delhi Ct Smyrna (19977) *(G-13883)*

Sharly.ai, Dover *Also Called: Vox Ai Inc (G-3811)*

Sharon A Welsh DDS, Hockessin *Also Called: Welsh Family Dentistry (G-5424)*

Sharon Alger-Little Dr 302 398-3367
   6902 Milford Harrington Hwy Harrington (19952) *(G-4830)*

Sharon Boyd M Ed Lpcmh 302 529-0220
   2304 Patwynn Rd Wilmington (19810) *(G-19782)*

Sharon Farm Insurance 215 333-5544
   6 Sandalwood Dr Rehoboth Beach (19971) *(G-12955)*

Sharon M Zieg 302 571-6655
   1000 N West St Wilmington (19801) *(G-19783)*

Sharon MD 302 239-2600
   724 Yorklyn Rd Ste 375 Hockessin (19707) *(G-5381)*

Sharp Farm 302 378-9606
   1214 Sharp Ln Middletown (19709) *(G-7559)*

Sharp Raingutters 302 398-4873
   Rte 36 Harrington (19952) *(G-4831)*

Sharp Tech Systems LLC 302 956-9525
   7019 Seashore Hwy Bridgeville (19933) *(G-765)*

Shashi Patel 302 737-5074
   2 Stuyvesant Dr Hockessin (19707) *(G-5382)*

Shavers Conswalla U MD 267 975-9571
   207 Hazel Dr Bear (19701) *(G-487)*

Shavone Loves Kids Day Care 302 544-6170
   6 Darien Ct New Castle (19720) *(G-9565)*

Shawnee 1892 LLC 302 738-6680
   850 Library Ave Ste 204 Newark (19711) *(G-11991)*

Shaylin M Shorts 302 494-2451
   260 Chapman Rd Ste 107 Newark (19702) *(G-11992)*

Shayona Health Inc 570 677-5509
   505 S Twin Lakes Blvd Newark (19711) *(G-11993)*

Shayona Health Inc 302 660-8847
   2511 W 4th St Ste F Wilmington (19805) *(G-19784)*

She Bash LLC 302 204-6700
   2093a Philadelphia Pike Ste 184 Claymont (19703) *(G-1289)*

She Podcasts 302 588-2317
   602 Mount Lebanon Rd Wilmington (19803) *(G-19785)*

Shea Concrete Ltd 302 422-7221
   4th & Montgomery St Milford (19963) *(G-8091)*

Shear Collection Salon By Mel 302 543-6854
   2016 N Market St Wilmington (19802) *(G-19786)*

Sheehan Chiropractic Ltd 302 545-7441
   829 N Harrison St Wilmington (19806) *(G-19787)*

Sheep Skin Gifts, Historic New Castle *Also Called: Francis Enterprises LLC (G-4991)*

Sheeran Direct, New Castle *Also Called: Joseph J Sheeran Inc (G-9266)*

Sheet Metal Contracting Co 302 834-3727
   3445 Wrangle Hill Rd Bear (19701) *(G-488)*

Sheet Metal Industry Advanceme 302 994-7442
   Wilmington (19804) *(G-19788)*

Sheet Metal Workers Local 19 .... 302 999-0573
   911 New Rd Wilmington (19805) *(G-19789)*

Sheets At Beach 302 362-0876
   31114 Beaver Cir Lewes (19958) *(G-6462)*

Shekinah Glory Sign Company 302 256-0426
   2608 Kirkwood Hwy Wilmington (19805) *(G-19790)*

Shelatia J Dennis 302 465-0630
   9 E Loockerman St Ste 302 Dover (19901) *(G-3541)*

Shelde Construction 561 723-5314
   355 Allabands Mill Rd Camden Wyoming (19934) *(G-976)*

ALPHABETIC SECTION

Sheldon Limited Partnership.. 302 738-3048
  810 Sheldon Dr Newark (19711) *(G-11994)*
Shelias Childcare Center.. 302 472-9648
  2200 Baynard Blvd Wilmington (19802) *(G-19791)*
Shell Recreation Center, Milton Also Called: Eisele Celine *(G-8616)*
Shell We Bounce.. 302 727-5411
  20699 Coastal Hwy Rehoboth Beach (19971) *(G-12956)*
Shellcrest Swim Club.. 302 529-1464
  916 Wilson Rd Wilmington (19803) *(G-19792)*
Shellhorn & Hill Inc... 302 654-4200
  3016 Edgemoor Ave Wilmington (19802) *(G-19793)*
Shells Child Care Center III... 302 398-9778
  5332 Milford Harrington Hwy Harrington (19952) *(G-4832)*
Shells Early Lrng Ctr Camden... 302 698-1556
  2116 S Dupont Hwy Camden (19934) *(G-892)*
Shelly's We Do Everything, Wilmington Also Called: Shellys of Delaware Inc *(G-19794)*
Shellys of Delaware Inc... 302 656-3337
  610 W 8th St Wilmington (19801) *(G-19794)*
Shellysons Electrical Contract... 302 275-8010
  818 Pencader Dr Unit C Newark (19702) *(G-11995)*
Shelter Const.. 302 829-8310
  23431 Godwin School Rd Millsboro (19966) *(G-8458)*
Shelter Development LLC... 302 737-4999
  200 Vinings Way Newark (19702) *(G-11996)*
Shelton Laday Hammond Jr.. 302 832-6257
  58 Charles Dr New Castle (19720) *(G-9566)*
Shepherd Place Inc... 302 678-1909
  1362 S Governors Ave Dover (19904) *(G-3542)*
Shepherd Stffing Cnsulting LLC... 302 652-0899
  402 Owls Nest Rd Wilmington (19807) *(G-19795)*
Sheraton, Wilmington Also Called: Pde I LLC *(G-18937)*
Sheridan Ford Sales, Wilmington Also Called: Future Ford Sales Inc *(G-16776)*
Sheriff Electronic LLC.. 302 654-8090
  16192 Coastal Hwy Lewes (19958) *(G-6463)*
Sherm's Catering, Wilmington Also Called: De Catering Inc *(G-15837)*
Sherman Heating Oils Inc... 302 684-4008
  223 Bay Front Rd # G Milton (19968) *(G-8711)*
Sherpa Brokers LLC.. 917 455-0094
  651 N Broad St Ste 205 Middletown (19709) *(G-7560)*
Sherpa Financial Services.. 302 235-1284
  722 Yorklyn Rd Ste 300 Hockessin (19707) *(G-5383)*
Sherrys Childcare... 302 654-4982
  1514 W 6th St Wilmington (19805) *(G-19796)*
Sherwood Park Civic Assn.. 302 994-6604
  2618 E Robino Dr Wilmington (19808) *(G-19797)*
Shes Filming Productions LLC.. 302 563-0336
  27 S Bradford St Dover (19904) *(G-3543)*
Shiatsu Bodywork... 302 529-7882
  1506 Evergreen Ln Wilmington (19810) *(G-19798)*
Shine Through Window Clg LLC... 302 261-6459
  410 Pheasant Cir Bear (19701) *(G-489)*
Shingle Express Inc.. 302 397-3773
  125 Falcon Ln Wilmington (19808) *(G-19799)*
Shining Nails, Newark Also Called: James C Wang *(G-11089)*
Shining Star Daycare... 302 393-7775
  365 Mimosa Ave Dover (19904) *(G-3544)*
Shining Time Day Care Center.. 302 335-2770
  220 Fox Chase Rd Felton (19943) *(G-4028)*
Shinlaza Inc.. 800 206-0051
  2055 Limestone Rd Wilmington (19808) *(G-19800)*
Shiny Agency LLC.. 302 384-6494
  1800 Wawaset St Wilmington (19806) *(G-19801)*
Ship Shape Marine Inc.. 302 841-7355
  15100 County Seat Hwy Seaford (19973) *(G-13401)*
Shipping Center LLC... 302 543-4968
  3209 Miller Rd Wilmington (19802) *(G-19802)*
Shipserv Inc... 732 738-6500
  3500 S Dupont Hwy Dover (19901) *(G-3545)*
Shipthis Inc... 209 395-1293
  200 Continental Dr Ste 401 Newark (19713) *(G-11997)*
Shipwrecked... 410 271-9563
  28293 Clayton St Dagsboro (19939) *(G-1504)*

Shipyard Center LLC... 302 999-0708
  234 N James St Wilmington (19804) *(G-19803)*
Shire Civics Co.. 423 520-6705
  600 N Broad St Middletown (19709) *(G-7561)*
Shire North American Group Inc (HQ)...................................... 484 595-8800
  103 Foulk Rd Ste 202 Wilmington (19803) *(G-19804)*
Shirkey Trucking Corp.. 302 349-2791
  734 Cattail Branch Rd Greenwood (19950) *(G-4668)*
Shirley I Blackburn Real Estat.. 302 292-6684
  680 S College Ave Newark (19713) *(G-11998)*
Shirley Price Sells... 302 236-7046
  33298 Coastal Hwy Bethany Beach (19930) *(G-642)*
Shirleys Little Friends Llc... 302 981-9991
  1818 Delaware Ave Wilmington (19806) *(G-19805)*
Shiv Baba LLC... 703 314-1203
  100 Carlsons Way Ste 15 Dover (19901) *(G-3546)*
Shiv Sagar Inc... 302 674-3800
  1703 E Lebanon Rd Dover (19901) *(G-3547)*
Shocker Towing & Recovery... 302 259-1123
  24423 Daisey Rd Frankford (19945) *(G-4142)*
Shockley Brothers Construction... 302 424-3255
  8772 Herring Branch Rd Lincoln (19960) *(G-6699)*
Shockley Motorsports, Lincoln Also Called: Harold D Shockley *(G-6675)*
Shockleys Auto Service.. 302 537-7663
  37141 Trixie Ln Frankford (19945) *(G-4143)*
Shockwaves Aquatic Club LLC... 302 478-8800
  3516 Silverside Rd Wilmington (19810) *(G-19806)*
Shooshoos LLC... 302 256-5355
  19c Trolley Sq Wilmington (19806) *(G-19807)*
Shooter's Choice, Dover Also Called: Noble Eagle Sales LLC *(G-3191)*
Shooters Choice Inc.. 302 736-5166
  5105 N Dupont Hwy Dover (19901) *(G-3548)*
Shootle Inc.. 941 866-2135
  16192 Coastal Hwy Lewes (19958) *(G-6464)*
Shop Club USA Network Holding... 858 304-0044
  300 Delaware Ave Wilmington (19801) *(G-19808)*
Shopper's Guide, New Castle Also Called: New Castle Cnty Shoppers Guide *(G-9406)*
Shopworks, Milford Also Called: Growmark Fs LLC *(G-7912)*
Shor Associates Inc... 302 764-1701
  240 Philadelphia Pike Wilmington (19809) *(G-19809)*
Shore Accountants Md Inc.. 410 758-6900
  18 Manassas Dr Middletown (19709) *(G-7562)*
Shore Answer LLC.. 302 253-8381
  543 S Bedford St Georgetown (19947) *(G-4511)*
Shore Chem LLC... 201 845-4666
  400 Carson Dr Bear (19701) *(G-490)*
Shore Community Medical... 302 827-4365
  18947 John J Williams Hwy Unit 215 Rehoboth Beach (19971) *(G-12957)*
Shore Concierge Inc.. 302 500-1162
  18060 Morgan Dr Lincoln (19960) *(G-6700)*
Shore Electric Inc.. 302 645-4503
  34697 Jiffy Way Unit 4 Lewes (19958) *(G-6465)*
Shore Irrigation Services... 302 542-1206
  22009 Dots Rd Millsboro (19966) *(G-8459)*
Shore Masonry Inc.. 302 945-5933
  32405 Mermaid Run Millsboro (19966) *(G-8460)*
Shore Mechanical Services... 302 519-6540
  30420 E Barrier Reef Blvd Lewes (19958) *(G-6466)*
Shore Pride All-Stars Inc... 302 245-1347
  34267 Pear Tree Rd Millsboro (19966) *(G-8461)*
Shore Pride Foods, Bridgeville Also Called: H C Davis Inc *(G-706)*
Shore Property Maintenance.. 302 947-4440
  28828 Four Of Us Rd Harbeson (19951) *(G-4715)*
Shore Rv Rentals.. 443 235-2183
  38373 Sussex Hwy Delmar (19940) *(G-1635)*
Shore Shutters and Shade.. 302 569-1738
  35736 S Gloucester Cir Millsboro (19966) *(G-8462)*
Shore Smoke Seasonings LLC.. 302 943-4675
  13 Borealis Ct Smyrna (19977) *(G-13884)*
Shore Stop 294, Selbyville Also Called: GPM Investments LLC *(G-13539)*
Shore Stop Store 286, Newark Also Called: Fas Mart / Shore Stop 286 LLC *(G-10713)*

Shore Tax Service Inc 302 226-9792
19725 Old Landing Rd Rehoboth Beach (19971) *(G-12958)*

Shore Tint & More Inc 302 947-4624
22797 Dozer Ln Unit 13 Harbeson (19951) *(G-4716)*

Shore Well Drillers Inc 302 737-7707
1168 Elkton Rd Newark (19711) *(G-11999)*

Shorecare of Delaware 302 724-5235
874 Walker Rd Ste D Dover (19904) *(G-3549)*

Shorecare of Delaware, Middletown Also Called: Lieske E2e Home Hlth Care Inc *(G-7298)*

Shoreline Home Imprvs LLC 302 616-1090
509 Harbor Rd Ocean View (19970) *(G-12567)*

Short Funeral Home Inc (PA) 302 846-9814
13 E Grove St Delmar (19940) *(G-1636)*

Short Order Production House 302 656-1638
625 N Orange St Fl 1 Wilmington (19801) *(G-19810)*

Shortcutz Lawn and Landsca 302 736-0906
47 Heatherfield Way Dover (19904) *(G-3550)*

Shortcutz Lawn Care Inc 302 538-6007
198 S Shore Dr Dover (19901) *(G-3551)*

Shoshin Karate LLC 302 369-9300
243 S Main St Newark (19711) *(G-12000)*

Shouldr LLC 917 331-1384
16192 Coastal Hwy Lewes (19958) *(G-6467)*

Shoutdel Magazine LLC 302 533-6070
27 Prestbury Sq Newark (19713) *(G-12001)*

Showbiz Trucking LLC 302 526-6337
1850 Henry Cowgill Rd Camden (19934) *(G-893)*

Showtime Real Estate 302 377-1292
713 Greenbank Rd Wilmington (19808) *(G-19811)*

Shree Kishna Inc 302 839-5000
699 N Dupont Blvd Milford (19963) *(G-8092)*

Shree Lalji LLC 302 730-8009
652 N Dupont Hwy Dover (19901) *(G-3552)*

Shri SAI Dover LLC 302 747-5050
561 N Dupont Hwy Dover (19901) *(G-3553)*

Shri Swami Narayan LLC 302 738-3198
1119 S College Ave Newark (19713) *(G-12002)*

Shriji Hospitality (not Llc) 302 654-5544
1213 West Ave New Castle (19720) *(G-9567)*

Shubert Enterprises Inc 302 846-3122
11077 Iron Hill Rd Delmar (19940) *(G-1637)*

Shummi US LLC 847 987-1686
919 N Market St Ste 950 Wilmington (19801) *(G-19812)*

Shure Line Electrical Inc 302 856-3110
24207 Dupont Blvd Georgetown (19947) *(G-4512)*

Shure-Line Construction Inc 302 653-4610
281 W Commerce St Kenton (19955) *(G-5454)*

Shure-Line Electrical Inc 302 389-1114
100 Artisan Dr Smyrna (19977) *(G-13885)*

Shuttle Runners 302 245-0945
29852 Plantation Lakes Blvd Millsboro (19966) *(G-8463)*

Sia Netjer Corp 302 319-5190
8 The Grn Ste 8590 Dover (19901) *(G-3554)*

Sibacpay Inc 302 257-5784
651 N Broad St Middletown (19709) *(G-7563)*

Sid Harvey Industries Inc 302 746-7760
130 Hickman Rd Ste 32 Claymont (19703) *(G-1290)*

Siditech LLC 302 384-5088
2511 Cedar Tree Dr Wilmington (19810) *(G-19813)*

Sieck Wholesale Florist Inc 302 356-2000
11 Southgate Blvd New Castle (19720) *(G-9568)*

Siegfried Group LLP (PA) 302 984-1800
1201 N Market St Ste 700 Wilmington (19801) *(G-19814)*

Siegfried J Schulze Inc 302 737-0403
12 Mill Park Ct Newark (19713) *(G-12003)*

Siegfried Resources, Wilmington Also Called: Siegfried Group LLP *(G-19814)*

Siemens 302 220-1544
4001 Vandever Ave Wilmington (19802) *(G-19815)*

Siemens AG 302 836-2933
217 Benjamin Blvd Bear (19701) *(G-491)*

Siemens Corporation 302 220-1544
800 Centerpoint Blvd Ste A Historic New Castle (19720) *(G-5070)*

Siemens Corporation 302 690-2046
100 Gbc Dr Newark (19702) *(G-12004)*

Siemens Hlthcare Dgnostics Inc 302 631-8006
200 Centerpoint Blvd Historic New Castle (19720) *(G-5071)*

Siemens Hlthcare Dgnostics Inc 302 631-7357
500 Gbc Dr Newark (19702) *(G-12005)*

Siemens Industry Inc 302 322-6247
259 Quigley Blvd Historic New Castle (19720) *(G-5072)*

Siemens Industry Inc 302 631-8410
500 Gbc Dr Newark (19702) *(G-12006)*

Sierentz Advisors LLC 423 665-9444
2711 Centerville Rd Ste 400 Wilmington (19808) *(G-19816)*

Sierra Tmshare Cnduit Rcvbles 702 562-8316
3411 Silverside Rd Ste 104 Wilmington (19810) *(G-19817)*

Sigma Data Systems Inc 302 453-8812
197 Possum Park Rd Newark (19711) *(G-12007)*

Sigma Telecom, Wilmington Also Called: Sigma Telecom LLC *(G-19818)*

Sigma Telecom LLC 347 741-8397
501 Silverside Rd Ste 105 Wilmington (19809) *(G-19818)*

Sigma Theta Tau Inc 302 584-5908
302 Green Ct Middletown (19709) *(G-7564)*

Sigmasat USA Inc 561 488-8048
501 Silverside Rd Ste 105 Wilmington (19809) *(G-19819)*

Sign and Graphics, Wilmington Also Called: DOT Pop Inc *(G-16153)*

Sign Crafters 302 832-8300
48 Castle Run Dr Bear (19701) *(G-492)*

Sign Express 302 999-0893
103 S Augustine St Wilmington (19804) *(G-19820)*

Sign-A-Rama, Bear Also Called: Marjano LLC *(G-363)*

Sign-A-Rama, Lewes Also Called: Beachview Mgmt Inc *(G-5744)*

Sign-A-Rama, Newark Also Called: Gary M Munch Inc *(G-10812)*

Signall Technologies Inc 240 623-5800
3500 S Dupont Hwy Dover (19901) *(G-3555)*

Signature Alert, Ocean View Also Called: Advanced Protection LLC *(G-12458)*

Signature Builders 302 331-9095
1722 Jump School House Rd Felton (19943) *(G-4029)*

Signature Clean Solutions LLC 571 565-1270
651 N Broad St Middletown (19709) *(G-7565)*

Signature Cnstr & Design, New Castle Also Called: Signature Cnstr Svcs LLC *(G-9569)*

Signature Cnstr Svcs LLC 302 691-1010
3029 Bowlarama Dr New Castle (19720) *(G-9569)*

Signature Construction Svcs, New Castle Also Called: Signature Furniture Svcs LLC *(G-9570)*

Signature Furniture Svcs LLC 302 691-1010
3029 Bowlarama Dr New Castle (19720) *(G-9570)*

Signature Intl Foods LLC 833 463-0004
1209 N Orange St Wilmington (19801) *(G-19821)*

Signature Painting Contractors 267 571-6595
209 W Champlain Ave Wilmington (19804) *(G-19822)*

Signature Property Management 302 212-2381
20375 John J Williams Hwy Lewes (19958) *(G-6468)*

Signature Renovations 302 858-2955
31885 Schooner Dr Millsboro (19966) *(G-8464)*

Signature Square LLC 866 216-5792
16192 Coastal Hwy Lewes (19958) *(G-6469)*

Signature Stitches 302 736-6500
216 N Caroline Pl Dover (19904) *(G-3556)*

Signatureone Media LLC 347 849-3740
8 The Grn Ste 1706 Dover (19901) *(G-3557)*

Signin Soft Inc 315 966-6699
1007 N Orange St Wilmington (19801) *(G-19823)*

Signs By Tomorrow 302 744-9396
90 Sunwood Dr Dover (19901) *(G-3558)*

Signs By Tomorrow, Dover Also Called: Signs By Tomorrow *(G-3558)*

Signs By Tomorrow, Newark Also Called: Tylaur Inc *(G-12251)*

Signs Now, Wilmington Also Called: Barbara Graphics Inc *(G-14755)*

Signscape Designs & Signs 302 798-2926
1709 Philadelphia Pike Wilmington (19809) *(G-19824)*

Signup Software Inc 302 531-1139
3500 S Dupont Hwy Ste Dn Dover (19901) *(G-3559)*

Sigpa 302 678-8780
550 Otis Dr Dover (19901) *(G-3560)*

ALPHABETIC SECTION

Silbereisen S Painting LLC 302 396-8135
   8923 Detwiler Ln Lincoln (19960) *(G-6701)*

Silicon Partners Inc 646 571-2324
   16192 Coastal Hwy Lewes (19958) *(G-6470)*

Silis Security Group, Lewes *Also Called: Ftl Technologies Corporation (G-6019)*

Silk Grass Holdings Us LLC 610 943-3047
   16192 Coastal Hwy Lewes (19958) *(G-6471)*

Silly Monkey Studios LLC 415 517-0830
   1000 N West St Ste 1200 Wilmington (19801) *(G-19825)*

Silpada Designs 302 376-6964
   410 Bluebird Hvn Middletown (19709) *(G-7566)*

Silver Bay International LLC 302 213-3006
   300 Delaware Ave Ste 210a Wilmington (19801) *(G-19826)*

Silver Bridge Capital Mgmt LLC 302 575-9215
   3701 Kennett Pike Ste 100 Wilmington (19807) *(G-19827)*

Silver Electric LLC 302 227-1107
   14 Sconset Ct Rehoboth Beach (19971) *(G-12959)*

Silver Lake Center, Dover *Also Called: 1080 Slver Lk Blvd Oprtons LLC (G-1677)*

Silver Lake Restoration 302 241-3931
   16 Ironwood Cir Dover (19904) *(G-3561)*

Silver Lining Home Healthcare, Dover *Also Called: Integrated Health Assoc LLC (G-2742)*

Silver Lining Solutions LLC 302 691-7100
   49 Bancroft Mills Rd P5 Wilmington (19806) *(G-19828)*

Silverbrook Cemetery Co 302 658-0953
   3300 Lancaster Pike Wilmington (19805) *(G-19829)*

Silverbullet USA Inc 203 216-2414
   651 N Broad St Middletown (19709) *(G-7567)*

Silverman McDonald & Friedman 302 629-3350
   300 High St Seaford (19973) *(G-13402)*

Silverside Club Inc 302 478-4568
   418 Brandywine Blvd Talleyville (19803) *(G-13946)*

Silverside Contracting Inc 302 798-1907
   2801 N Broom St Wilmington (19802) *(G-19830)*

Silverside Medical Center, Newark *Also Called: Ent and Allergy Delaware LLC (G-10651)*

Silverside Open Mri Imaging 302 246-2000
   2501 Silverside Rd Ste A Wilmington (19810) *(G-19831)*

Simar Fuel Inc 302 304-1969
   126 S Dupont Blvd Smyrna (19977) *(G-13886)*

Simbiose Inc 708 459-8068
   2035 Sunset Lake Rd Newark (19702) *(G-12008)*

Simbull Sports Exchange Inc 319 899-6223
   16192 Coastal Hwy Lewes (19958) *(G-6472)*

Simm Associates Inc 302 283-2800
   800 Pencader Dr Newark (19702) *(G-12009)*

Simmons Animal Nutrition Inc 302 337-8223
   7494 Federalsburg Rd Bridgeville (19933) *(G-766)*

Simmons Animal Nutrition Inc 302 337-5500
   8141 Seashore Hwy Bridgeville (19933) *(G-767)*

Simmons Feed Ingrdnts Brdgvlle, Bridgeville *Also Called: Simmons Animal Nutrition Inc (G-767)*

Simmons Feed Ingrdnts Cnon Col, Bridgeville *Also Called: Simmons Animal Nutrition Inc (G-766)*

Simon Eye Associates 302 239-1933
   2625 Concord Pike Ste A Wilmington (19803) *(G-19832)*

Simon Eye Associates, Wilmington *Also Called: Simon Eye Associates PA (G-19833)*

Simon Eye Associates PA 302 834-4305
   116 Foxhunt Dr Ste 116 Bear (19701) *(G-493)*

Simon Eye Associates PA 302 655-8180
   912 N Union St Wilmington (19805) *(G-19833)*

Simon Eye Associates PA (PA) 302 239-1389
   5301 Limestone Rd Ste 128 Wilmington (19808) *(G-19834)*

Simon Mstr & Sidlow Assoc Inc 302 652-3480
   750 Prides Xing Ste 100 Newark (19713) *(G-12010)*

Simple Space LLC 801 520-3680
   300 Delaware Ave Ste 210a Wilmington (19801) *(G-19835)*

Simple Stays LLC 949 290-5775
   254 Chapman Rd Newark (19702) *(G-12011)*

Simplecar LLC 857 380-7275
   2803 Philadelphia Pike Claymont (19703) *(G-1291)*

Simplecode LLC 302 703-7231
   16192 Coastal Hwy Lewes (19958) *(G-6473)*

Simplelife Apps Inc 954 591-8413
   8 The Grn Ste A Dover (19901) *(G-3562)*

Simpler and Sons LLC 302 296-4400
   37139 Rehoboth Avenue Ext Rehoboth Beach (19971) *(G-12960)*

Simpler Logistics LLC 800 619-8321
   300 Delaware Ave Ste 210 Wilmington (19801) *(G-19836)*

Simpler Surveying & Associates 302 539-7873
   32486 Powell Farm Rd Frankford (19945) *(G-4144)*

Simplex Time Recorder 557, New Castle *Also Called: Simplex Time Recorder LLC (G-9571)*

Simplex Time Recorder LLC 302 325-6300
   18 Boulden Cir Ste 36 New Castle (19720) *(G-9571)*

Simplica, Wilmington *Also Called: Simplica Corporation (G-19837)*

Simplica Corporation 302 594-9899
   1701 Shallcross Ave Ste B Wilmington (19806) *(G-19837)*

Simpliigence Inc (PA) 404 528-7646
   8 The Grn Ste A Dover (19901) *(G-3563)*

Simply Charming 302 697-7377
   2 S Railroad Ave Wyoming (19934) *(G-20990)*

Simply Clean 302 894-1569
   103 Linden Tree Ln Newark (19711) *(G-12012)*

Simply Clean, Dover *Also Called: Simply Clean Jantr Svcs Inc (G-3564)*

Simply Clean Jantr Svcs Inc 302 744-9100
   100 Carlsons Way Ste 6 Dover (19901) *(G-3564)*

Simply Grand LLC 480 278-0367
   105 Christina Landing Dr Wilmington (19801) *(G-19838)*

Simply Green 302 256-0822
   216 S Maryland Ave Wilmington (19804) *(G-19839)*

Simply Styling-Schl of Csmtlgy 302 778-1885
   204 N Union St Wilmington (19805) *(G-19840)*

Simplylab Inc 919 663-2800
   8 The Grn Ste A Dover (19901) *(G-3565)*

Simplymiddle LLC 302 217-3460
   901 N Market St Ste 719 Wilmington (19801) *(G-19841)*

Simplyprotein, Wilmington *Also Called: Wellness Natural USA Inc (G-20720)*

Simpsons Log Homes Inc 302 674-1900
   126 Lafferty Ln Dover (19901) *(G-3566)*

Sims Team Cleaning LLC 610 990-1950
   651 N Broad St Ste 205 Middletown (19709) *(G-7568)*

Sinapi LLC 650 265-7180
   3500 S Dupont Hwy Ste 300 Dover (19901) *(G-3567)*

Singer Equipment Co Inc 484 332-3386
   135 W Cook Ave Smyrna (19977) *(G-13887)*

Singh Priya C MD 302 674-4700
   640 S State St Dover (19901) *(G-3568)*

Single Origin Food Co, The, Wilmington *Also Called: Real Ch Inc (G-19364)*

Single Source Inc 302 697-6156
   91 Brenda Ln Ste D Camden Wyoming (19934) *(G-977)*

Sinkeeas Lounge & Bar LLC 302 434-2530
   72 Alexis Dr Newark (19702) *(G-12013)*

Sinkor Beauty Salon 302 464-3292
   4446 Summit Bridge Rd Middletown (19709) *(G-7569)*

Sinomine Resources (us) Inc 204 340-6696
   1209 N Orange St Wilmington (19801) *(G-19842)*

Sinuswars LLC 212 901-0805
   501 Silverside Rd Ste 105 Wilmington (19809) *(G-19843)*

Sir Grout, Seaford *Also Called: Sir Grout Delaware LLC (G-13403)*

Sir Grout Delaware LLC 302 401-1700
   8811 Weeping Willow Trl Seaford (19973) *(G-13403)*

Sir Speedy, Newark *Also Called: Garile Inc (G-10809)*

Sir Speedy, Wilmington *Also Called: Amer Inc (G-14421)*

Siren Group USA Inc 302 298-3307
   40 E Main St Newark (19711) *(G-12014)*

Siriusiq Mobile LLC 888 414-2047
   200 Continental Dr Newark (19713) *(G-12015)*

Sirkin Levine Dental Assoc, Wilmington *Also Called: Alan R Levine DDS (G-14346)*

Sirqil LLC 213 204-9333
   8 The Grn Ste A Dover (19901) *(G-3569)*

SIS Stylogy Beauty Salon, Newark *Also Called: Cole Janeika (G-10271)*

Sissys Closet Inc 302 698-1327
   73 Pear Blossom Ln Camden Wyoming (19934) *(G-978)*

Sister Cities Wilmington Inc

Sister Cities Wilmington Inc	302 383-0968
2414 W 18th St Wilmington (19806) *(G-19844)*	
Sister Sister Covid Clean LLC	267 467-8803
259 Fawn Haven Walk Dover (19901) *(G-3570)*	
Sisu Fit Club	302 562-3920
119 Saint Regis Dr Newark (19711) *(G-12016)*	
Site-On Auto Inc	302 505-5100
16906 Staytonville Rd Lincoln (19960) *(G-6702)*	
Site/Tlity /Concrete Gen Contr, Felton *Also Called: R&C Contractors LLC (G-4011)*	
Sitecanix, Lewes *Also Called: Casper Hosting LLC (G-5807)*	
Sites Fitness of Delaware LLC	302 533-6040
201 Louviers Dr Newark (19711) *(G-12017)*	
Sitka, Newark *Also Called: W L Gore & Associates Inc (G-12342)*	
Sivad Ppe LLC	302 208-2233
703 Carson Dr Bear (19701) *(G-494)*	
Sivil, Wilmington *Also Called: Sivil Technologies Inc (G-19845)*	
Sivil Technologies Inc	214 893-9797
251 Little Falls Dr Wilmington (19808) *(G-19845)*	
Six Angels Development Inc	302 218-1548
7 Medori Blvd Wilmington (19801) *(G-19846)*	
Six Days Inc	888 463-5898
2810 N Church St Pmb 96630 Wilmington (19802) *(G-19847)*	
Six Plus Inc	302 652-3296
4300 Kennett Pike Wilmington (19807) *(G-19848)*	
Six Sigma Telecom LLC	302 636-5440
2711 Centerville Rd Wilmington (19808) *(G-19849)*	
Sixteenpenny LLC	302 463-7992
300 Vassar Dr Newark (19711) *(G-12018)*	
Sj Builders LLC	302 242-8222
1578 Fords Corner Rd Hartly (19953) *(G-4908)*	
Sjm Sales Inc	302 697-6748
500 Eagle Nest Dr Camden Wyoming (19934) *(G-979)*	
Sk Chiropractic LLC	302 482-3410
3411 Silverside Rd Ste 106 Wilmington (19810) *(G-19850)*	
Sk Services LLC	302 834-9133
204 Benjamin Blvd Bear (19701) *(G-495)*	
Skadden Arps Slate Mgher Flom	302 651-3000
1 Rodney Sq Wilmington (19801) *(G-19851)*	
Skaggs Electric LLC	302 653-0576
74 Alley Corner Rd Smyrna (19977) *(G-13888)*	
Skajaquoda, Wilmington *Also Called: Skajaquoda Capital LLC (G-19852)*	
Skajaquoda Capital LLC	302 504-4448
717 N Union St Ste 5 Wilmington (19805) *(G-19852)*	
Skanska USA Building Inc	215 495-8790
313 Wyoming Rd Newark (19711) *(G-12019)*	
Skateworld Inc (PA)	302 875-2121
23601 Dove Rd Seaford (19973) *(G-13404)*	
Skating Club of Wilmington, Wilmington *Also Called: Skating Club of Wilmington Inc (G-19853)*	
Skating Club of Wilmington Inc	302 656-5005
1301 Carruthers Ln Wilmington (19803) *(G-19853)*	
Sketches and Pixels LLC	312 834-4402
2035 Sunset Lake Rd B2 Newark (19702) *(G-12020)*	
Skillbird LLC	302 216-1811
4 Peddlers Row Newark (19702) *(G-12021)*	
Skillfi LLC	469 701-9614
8 The Grn Dover (19901) *(G-3571)*	
Skim USA	302 227-4011
1904 Highway One Rehoboth Beach (19971) *(G-12961)*	
Skin Care School & Ctr	302 328-0611
3700 Lancaster Pike Wilmington (19805) *(G-19854)*	
Skin Solutions By Wendi	302 312-1569
3023 Mcdaniel Ln Newark (19702) *(G-12022)*	
Skinify LLC	302 212-5689
19621 Blue Bird Ln Unit 4 Rehoboth Beach (19971) *(G-12962)*	
Skipjack Inc	302 734-6755
861 Silver Lake Blvd Ste 200 Dover (19904) *(G-3572)*	
Skiplist Inc	440 855-0319
2035 Sunset Lake Rd B2 Newark (19702) *(G-12023)*	
Skipwith Organics LLC	908 573-2930
8 The Grn Ste A Dover (19901) *(G-3573)*	

ALPHABETIC SECTION

Skittle Inc	855 575-4885
427 N Tatnall St 63204 Wilmington (19801) *(G-19855)*	
Skittleme.com, Wilmington *Also Called: Skittle Inc (G-19855)*	
Skjaldborg Artisans LLC	302 698-7552
803 N Dupont Blvd Milford (19963) *(G-8093)*	
Skoruz, Wilmington *Also Called: Skoruz Holding Corporation (G-19856)*	
Skoruz Holding Corporation	510 766-2803
1007 N Orange St Wilmington (19801) *(G-19856)*	
Sks Enterprise	302 310-2511
200 Continental Dr Newark (19713) *(G-12024)*	
Sky Touch LLC	302 454-7040
4 Washington Ct Newark (19702) *(G-12025)*	
Sky Trax, Wilmington *Also Called: Xcs Corporation (G-20916)*	
Sky Zone Trampoline Park	302 449-1252
120 Laks Dr Middletown (19709) *(G-7570)*	
Sky4video	302 377-3748
4 Balanger Rd Newark (19711) *(G-12026)*	
Skygate Inc	310 601-4201
2035 Sunset Lake Rd Ste B2 Newark (19702) *(G-12027)*	
Skylark Labs Inc	415 609-3633
2035 Sunset Lake Rd Newark (19702) *(G-12028)*	
Skyline Roofing & Cnstr LLC	610 929-4135
33126 Perrydale Grn Lewes (19958) *(G-6474)*	
Skyline Supply Inc	302 894-9190
62 Albe Dr Ste C Newark (19702) *(G-12029)*	
Skyline Swim Club	302 737-4696
2901 Skyline Dr Wilmington (19808) *(G-19857)*	
Skylines One LLC	646 400-0535
16192 Coastal Hwy Lewes (19958) *(G-6475)*	
Skynethostingnet Inc	302 384-1784
501 Silverside Rd Wilmington (19809) *(G-19858)*	
Skypher Inc	510 570-5843
1007 N Orange St Wilmington (19801) *(G-19859)*	
Skyward Solutions LLC	469 563-0411
8 The Grn Ste A Dover (19901) *(G-3574)*	
Skyways Motor Lodge Corp	302 328-6666
147 N Dupont Hwy New Castle (19720) *(G-9572)*	
Skyworld Traveler Inc	844 591-9060
1013 Centre Rd Ste 403s Wilmington (19805) *(G-19860)*	
Skyylimit LLC	302 256-3212
146 Abbigail Xing Townsend (19734) *(G-14064)*	
Slacum & Doyle Tax Service LLC	302 734-1850
838 Walker Rd Ste 22-2 Dover (19904) *(G-3575)*	
Slam Aquatics LLC	302 668-0186
528 Wayland Dr Hockessin (19707) *(G-5384)*	
Slater Fireplaces Inc	302 999-1200
1726 Newport Gap Pike Wilmington (19808) *(G-19861)*	
Slater Nursing Service	302 419-6237
1148 Pulaski Hwy Bear (19701) *(G-496)*	
Slaughter Neck Educational and	302 684-1834
22942 Slaughter Neck Rd Lincoln (19960) *(G-6703)*	
Slavia Transportation	302 218-4474
7 Tami Trl Middletown (19709) *(G-7571)*	
Slay By Jere	302 723-0034
408 Afton Dr Middletown (19709) *(G-7572)*	
Slaybelles LLC	302 304-1027
4737 Concord Pike Wilmington (19803) *(G-19862)*	
Sleep Disorders Center	302 645-3186
424 Savannah Rd Lewes (19958) *(G-6476)*	
Sleep Disorders Ctr-Christiana	302 623-0650
774 Christiana Rd Ste 103 Newark (19713) *(G-12030)*	
Sleep Emporium LLC	302 313-5061
18675 Coastal Hwy Unit 2a Rehoboth Beach (19971) *(G-12963)*	
Sleep Inn, Dover *Also Called: Kw Garden (G-2891)*	
Sleep Inn, Lewes *Also Called: Sleep Inn & Suites (G-6477)*	
Sleep Inn, Newark *Also Called: Nacstar (G-11482)*	
Sleep Inn & Suites	302 645-6464
18451 Coastal Hwy Lewes (19958) *(G-6477)*	
Sleepagotchi Inc	617 852-7380
651 N Broad St Ste 201 Middletown (19709) *(G-7573)*	
Sleepy Coach Inc	310 372-5770
919 N Market St Wilmington (19801) *(G-19863)*	

ALPHABETIC SECTION — Smith Concrete Inc

Sleigh Financial Inc 302 684-2929
28266 Lewes Georgetown Hwy Milton (19968) *(G-8712)*

Slice Communications LLC 215 600-0050
112 S French St Wilmington (19801) *(G-19864)*

Slice Global Inc (PA) 415 801-6537
251 Little Falls Dr Wilmington (19808) *(G-19865)*

Slice of Wood LLC 315 335-0917
70 Clinton St Delaware City (19706) *(G-1558)*

Slims Sports Complex LLC 302 464-1058
938 Middletown Warwick Rd Middletown (19709) *(G-7574)*

Slimstim Inc 310 560-4950
1209 N Orange St Wilmington (19801) *(G-19866)*

Sling It LLC 302 648-5488
523 Capitol Trl Ste C Newark (19711) *(G-12031)*

SLM Corporation (PA) 302 451-0200
300 Continental Dr Newark (19713) *(G-12032)*

Slr Transport LLC 302 316-3306
245 W General Grey Ct Newark (19702) *(G-12033)*

Slurry Pavement Systems 609 500-3828
700 Cornell Dr Ste E17 Wilmington (19801) *(G-19867)*

SM Snacks LLC 973 229-2845
205 Woodrow Ave Wilmington (19803) *(G-19868)*

SM Technomine Inc 312 492-4386
19c Trolley Sq Wilmington (19806) *(G-19869)*

SM Technomine Inc (PA) 312 492-4386
802 N West St Wilmington (19801) *(G-19870)*

SMA Pediatrics, Smyrna *Also Called: Caridad Rosal MA MD (G-13675)*

Smackerals By Michelle LLC 302 376-8272
109 Fox Hunt Ln Middletown (19709) *(G-7575)*

Smakkfitness LLC 800 417-2558
410 N Market St Wilmington (19801) *(G-19871)*

Small Associates, Wilmington *Also Called: Joseph W Small Associates Inc (G-17588)*

Small Wonder Day Care Inc 302 654-2269
100 Greenhill Ave Ste A Wilmington (19805) *(G-19872)*

Small Wonder Fitness 302 838-0865
2611 Del Laws Rd Bear (19701) *(G-497)*

Small Wonders 302 645-8410
47 Sussex Dr Lewes (19958) *(G-6478)*

Smalleys Automotive Group Inc 302 450-0983
196 S Main St Ste 211 Kenton (19955) *(G-5455)*

Smalls Real Estate Company 302 633-1985
5227 W Woodmill Dr Ste 42 Wilmington (19808) *(G-19873)*

Smalls Stepping Stone 302 652-3011
1408 Clifford Brown Walk Wilmington (19801) *(G-19874)*

Smappy Inc 650 360-0713
16192 Coastal Hwy Lewes (19958) *(G-6479)*

Smarketics Inc 929 265-0177
651 N Broad St Ste 206 Middletown (19709) *(G-7576)*

Smart, Wilmington *Also Called: Smart Hospitality & MGT LLC (G-19877)*

Smart 360 Biz, Wilmington *Also Called: Smart 360 Co (G-19875)*

Smart 360 Co 617 657-4360
3 Germay Dr Ste 4 Wilmington (19804) *(G-19875)*

Smart Altcoins Inc 626 540-9415
16192 Coastal Hwy Lewes (19958) *(G-6480)*

Smart Armor Protected LLC 480 823-8122
19 Kris Ct Newark (19702) *(G-12034)*

Smart Choice Hv/AC Svcs LLC 302 250-5762
31 Dartmouth Rd Wilmington (19808) *(G-19876)*

Smart Choice Trucking Inc 302 945-7100
31791 Marsh Island Ave Lewes (19958) *(G-6481)*

Smart Fit LLC 302 200-9803
17601 Coastal Hwy Lewes (19958) *(G-6482)*

Smart Fit Studio, Lewes *Also Called: Smart Fit LLC (G-6482)*

Smart Hospitality & MGT LLC 212 444-1989
3411 Silverside Rd Wilmington (19810) *(G-19877)*

Smart Invest Yam LLC 302 721-5278
1521 Concord Pike Ste 301 Wilmington (19803) *(G-19878)*

Smart Laundromat 302 854-0300
110 N Race St Ste 1010 Georgetown (19947) *(G-4513)*

Smart Printing MGT LLC 855 549-4900
560 Peoples Plz Ste 301 Newark (19702) *(G-12035)*

Smart Professions Inc 603 289-6263
8 The Grn Ste 7712 Dover (19901) *(G-3576)*

Smart Shoppers, Wilmington *Also Called: Gbc International Corp (G-16824)*

Smart Start 302 256-5104
100 Greenhill Ave Wilmington (19805) *(G-19879)*

Smart Tax Free Rtrment HM of I 302 472-4897
205 Philadelphia Pike Wilmington (19809) *(G-19880)*

Smart Tire Company Inc 909 358-0987
651 N Broad St Ste 205 # 3318 Middletown (19709) *(G-7577)*

Smart Union Blockchain LLC 919 872-5631
16192 Coastal Hwy Lewes (19958) *(G-6483)*

Smart-The Tile Rick Specialist 302 331-5529
79 Chatham Ct Dover (19901) *(G-3577)*

Smartcard Mktg Systems Inc 844 843-7296
20c Trolley Sq Wilmington (19806) *(G-19881)*

Smartcookiewifi Inc 424 205-4450
2055 Limestone Rd 200c Wilmington (19808) *(G-19882)*

Smartdrive Foundation 302 463-6543
3029 Bowlarama Dr New Castle (19720) *(G-9573)*

Smarter Home & Office LLC 302 723-9313
18 Monticello Blvd New Castle (19720) *(G-9574)*

Smartis 302 653-8355
73 Greentree Dr Dover (19904) *(G-3578)*

Smartprofyl LLC 832 412-5803
651 N Broad St Ste 205 Middletown (19709) *(G-7578)*

Smartwnnr Inc 415 534-9794
16192 Coastal Hwy Lewes (19958) *(G-6484)*

Smarty Pants Early Education 302 985-3770
146 Willamette Dr Bear (19701) *(G-498)*

Smb Education Funding LLC 302 451-0537
300 Continental Dr Newark (19713) *(G-12036)*

Smb Lighting 302 733-0664
36 Anthony Dr Newark (19702) *(G-12037)*

Smb Prvate Edcatn Ln Tr 2020-A 302 451-0537
300 Continental Dr Newark (19713) *(G-12038)*

Smb Prvate Edcatn Ln Tr 2022-A 302 451-0537
300 Continental Dr Newark (19713) *(G-12039)*

Sme Masonry Contrs Ltd Lblty 302 743-7338
1205 Bruce Rd Wilmington (19803) *(G-19883)*

SMI Services of Delaware LLC 302 436-4410
20 Railroad Ave Selbyville (19975) *(G-13605)*

SMI Services of Delaware LLC (PA) 302 514-9681
5609 Dupont Pkwy Smyrna (19977) *(G-13889)*

Smile Brite Dental Care LLC (PA) 302 838-8306
300 Biddle Ave Ste 204 Newark (19702) *(G-12040)*

Smile Heating & AC 302 542-7242
34453 Park Cir Frankford (19945) *(G-4145)*

Smile Place 302 514-6200
17 N Main St Smyrna (19977) *(G-13890)*

Smile Solutions By Emmi Dental 302 999-8113
1601 Milltown Rd Ste 25 Wilmington (19808) *(G-19884)*

Smileback LLC 646 401-0024
427 N Tatnall St Ste 64120 Wilmington (19801) *(G-19885)*

Smiles Jolly PA 302 378-3384
102 Sleepy Hollow Dr Ste 100 Middletown (19709) *(G-7579)*

Smiley Shiney 215 601-6036
320 Price Dr Middletown (19709) *(G-7580)*

Smith Cohen & Rosenberg LLC 302 260-8007
838 Walker Rd Dover (19904) *(G-3579)*

Smith & Allen Insurance, Wilmington *Also Called: Allen Insurance Group (G-14374)*

Smith & Nephew Holdings Inc (DH) 302 884-6720
1201 N Orange St Ste 788 Wilmington (19801) *(G-19886)*

Smith & Son Lawn Service, Dagsboro *Also Called: Smith and Son Lawn Service (G-1505)*

Smith and Son Lawn Service 302 934-1778
30037 Lewis Ln Dagsboro (19939) *(G-1505)*

Smith Bill Concrete Masnry LLC 302 250-4312
200 Belmont Ave Wilmington (19804) *(G-19887)*

Smith Brothers Communication 302 293-5224
27 Harkfort Rd Newark (19702) *(G-12041)*

Smith Concrete, Milford *Also Called: Smith Concrete Inc (G-8094)*

Smith Concrete Inc 302 270-9251
8473 N Union Church Rd Milford (19963) *(G-8094)*

Smith Electrical Services 302 423-5994
  150 East St Marydel (19964) *(G-6810)*

Smith Firm LLC 302 875-5595
  8866 Riverside Dr Seaford (19973) *(G-13405)*

Smith Fnberg McCrtney Berl LLP (PA) 302 856-7082
  406 S Bedford St Georgetown (19947) *(G-4514)*

Smith Harvey C Jr Funeral Dire 302 376-0200
  201 High St Odessa (19730) *(G-12587)*

Smith Health & Life LLC 302 596-0641
  4023 Kennett Pike Ste 106 Wilmington (19807) *(G-19888)*

Smith Home Improvements 302 998-8294
  2239 E Huntington Dr Wilmington (19808) *(G-19889)*

Smith Katzenstein & Furlow LLP 302 652-8400
  1000 N West St Ste 1500 Wilmington (19801) *(G-19890)*

Smith-Jones Society 302 203-9702
  1207 Delaware Ave Ste 636 Wilmington (19806) *(G-19891)*

Smith-Spinella Electric LLC 302 228-4865
  28988 Seaford Rd Laurel (19956) *(G-5599)*

Smith, Katzenscein and Jenkins, Wilmington *Also Called: Roger D Anderson (G-19555)*

Smith, Kenneth MD, Bridgeville *Also Called: Internal Medicine Bridgeville (G-716)*

Smithkline Bcham Phrmceuticals 302 984-6932
  1403 Foulk Rd Ste 102 Wilmington (19803) *(G-19892)*

Smithkline Beecham Intl Co 302 479-5804
  1403 Foulk Rd Ste 106 Wilmington (19803) *(G-19893)*

Smiths Garage Doors Expert 302 803-5337
  3600 Miller Rd Wilmington (19802) *(G-19894)*

Smiths Jack Towing & Svc Ctr 302 798-6667
  1806 Philadelphia Pike Wilmington (19809) *(G-19895)*

Smiths Work At HM Slutions LLC 302 367-6671
  17 Irwin Ave New Castle (19720) *(G-9575)*

Smittys Auto Repair Inc 302 398-8419
  17378 S Dupont Hwy Harrington (19952) *(G-4833)*

Smjs Co 415 326-4441
  2093 Philadelphia Pike Ste 7143de Claymont (19703) *(G-1292)*

Smogard & Associates LLC 302 353-4717
  310 Falco Dr Ste G Wilmington (19804) *(G-19896)*

Smooth Mves Elite Mvg Svcs LLC 302 521-0973
  413 Mccabe Ave Wilmington (19802) *(G-19897)*

Smooth Sound Dance Band 302 398-8467
  201 Dorman St Harrington (19952) *(G-4834)*

Smp Enterprises Inc 302 252-5331
  208 Goodsir St Newark (19702) *(G-12042)*

SMS Contracting 610 721-9943
  1221 Ipswich Dr Wilmington (19808) *(G-19898)*

SMS Systems Maintenance, Newark *Also Called: Curvature Inc (G-10366)*

Smt Htg and Air Cond LLC 302 285-9219
  4361 Dupont Pkwy Townsend (19734) *(G-14065)*

Smt Real Estate Holdings LLC 302 668-3512
  16 Bridleshire Rd Newark (19711) *(G-12043)*

Smucker Company LLC 302 322-9285
  116 Sarah Cir Camden Wyoming (19934) *(G-980)*

Smw Sales LLC 302 875-7958
  11432 Trussum Pond Rd Laurel (19956) *(G-5600)*

Smyrn-Clyton Sn-Tmes Mddltown, Dover *Also Called: Dover Post Co Inc (G-2362)*

Smyrna Clayton Little League I 302 653-7550
  Duck Creek Rd Smyrna (19977) *(G-13891)*

Smyrna Clyton Ldge 2046 Order 302 653-2046
  2035 S Dupont Blvd Smyrna (19977) *(G-13892)*

Smyrna De 302 653-1166
  1271 S Dupont Blvd Smyrna (19977) *(G-13893)*

Smyrna Dental Center PA 302 223-6194
  679 S Carter Rd Unit 5 Smyrna (19977) *(G-13894)*

Smyrna Medical Aid Unit 302 659-4444
  100 S Main St Ste 101 Smyrna (19977) *(G-13895)*

Smyrna Medical Associates PA 302 653-6174
  38 Deak Dr Smyrna (19977) *(G-13896)*

Smyrna School District 302 653-3135
  80 Monrovia Ave Smyrna (19977) *(G-13897)*

Sn & Partners 312 826-3255
  254 Chapman Rd Ste 208 Newark (19702) *(G-12044)*

Snap Fitness, Hockessin *Also Called: Jeffko Inc (G-5259)*

Snapify Corp 646 814-6388
  300 Delaware Ave Fl 3 Wilmington (19801) *(G-19899)*

Sneads Heating & AC 302 524-8090
  31555 Lighthouse Rd Selbyville (19975) *(G-13606)*

Sneaky Links, Middletown *Also Called: Sneakylinks Com Inc (G-7581)*

Sneakylinks Com Inc 470 312-3827
  651 N Broad St Ste 205 Middletown (19709) *(G-7581)*

Snickers Ditch Trunk Company 302 325-1762
  182 E 4th St Historic New Castle (19720) *(G-5073)*

Sniffies LLC 302 265-4101
  8 The Grn Ste B Dover (19901) *(G-3580)*

Sniper Labs Inc 925 321-0931
  2055 Limestone Rd Ste 200c Wilmington (19808) *(G-19900)*

SNK Enterprises Inc 443 783-5717
  34650 Hudson Rd Laurel (19956) *(G-5601)*

SNMP3 Security LLC 302 448-8501
  254 Chapman Rd Ste 208 Pmb 10809 Newark (19702) *(G-12045)*

Snow & Assoc Gen Cnstr Co LLC 302 420-0564
  510 Milton Dr Wilmington (19802) *(G-19901)*

Snow Farms Inc 302 653-7534
  249 Raymond Neck Rd Smyrna (19977) *(G-13898)*

Snow Pharmaceuticals LLC 302 436-8855
  35998 Zion Church Rd Frankford (19945) *(G-4146)*

Sntc Holding Inc (DH) 302 777-5261
  919 N Market St Ste 200 Wilmington (19801) *(G-19902)*

Snyder & Associates, Wilmington *Also Called: Snyder Associates PA (G-19904)*

Snyder & Company PA 302 475-1600
  1405 Silverside Rd Wilmington (19810) *(G-19903)*

Snyder Associates PA 302 657-8300
  300 Delaware Ave Ste 1014 Wilmington (19801) *(G-19904)*

Snyders Hvac Services LLC 302 236-2517
  14835 Arvey Rd Laurel (19956) *(G-5602)*

So Hair and Beauty Supply 302 407-3381
  304 N Union St Wilmington (19805) *(G-19905)*

Soares Dr Neha M 248 707-4931
  212 Portmarnock Ct Dover (19904) *(G-3581)*

Sobieski Fire Protection LLC 302 993-0600
  16 Hadco Rd Wilmington (19804) *(G-19906)*

Sobieski J F Mechanical Contrs, Wilmington *Also Called: J F Sobieski Mech Contrs Inc (G-17456)*

Sobieski Life Safety 800 321-1332
  1325 Old Coochs Bridge Rd Newark (19713) *(G-12046)*

Sobieski Services Inc 302 993-0104
  1325 Old Coochs Bridge Rd Newark (19713) *(G-12047)*

Socal Auto Supply Inc (PA) 818 717-9982
  16192 Postal Hwy Lewes (19958) *(G-6485)*

Socallova LLC 347 721-6416
  610 Wesley Ct Middletown (19709) *(G-7582)*

Soccer Network LLC 302 724-6951
  152 Greenview Dr Dover (19901) *(G-3582)*

Sociable Consulting LLC 302 546-2750
  113 Brook Run Hockessin (19707) *(G-5385)*

Social Africa Inc 763 670-3452
  614 N Dupont Hwy Dover (19901) *(G-3583)*

Social Contract LLC 302 357-5193
  1313 N Market St Wilmington (19801) *(G-19907)*

Social Enterprises 302 526-4800
  112 Capitol Trl Newark (19711) *(G-12048)*

Social Finance Inc 707 473-3000
  650 Naamans Rd Ste 300 Claymont (19703) *(G-1293)*

Social Health Innovations Inc 917 476-9355
  8 The Grn Ste 5175 Dover (19901) *(G-3584)*

Social Keyboard Inc 650 519-8383
  8 The Grn Ste R Dover (19901) *(G-3585)*

Social Media Grabs 281 603-2803
  600 N Broad St Middletown (19709) *(G-7583)*

Social Money Inc 212 810-7540
  16192 Coastal Hwy Lewes (19958) *(G-6486)*

Social Selling LLC 888 384-3710
  18670 Coastal Hwy Rehoboth Beach (19971) *(G-12964)*

Social Wonder Inc 646 419-8009
  1007 N Orange St Fl 10 Wilmington (19801) *(G-19908)*

ALPHABETIC SECTION

Social Work Helper Pbc..302 233-7422
  8 The Grn Ste 8043 Dover (19901) *(G-3586)*

Socialcash Inc..310 293-6072
  1209 N Orange St Wilmington (19801) *(G-19909)*

Socialpilot Technologies Inc..415 450-6060
  16192 Coastal Hwy Lewes (19958) *(G-6487)*

Society For Acpuncture RES Inc..302 222-1832
  108 Dewey Ave Lewes (19958) *(G-6488)*

Society For Whole-Body Autorad..302 369-5240
  110 Executive Dr Ste 7 Newark (19702) *(G-12049)*

Society Hill Apts, Claymont *Also Called: Stoltz Realty Co (G-1305)*

Socradar Cyber Intelligence..571 249-4598
  651 N Broad St Ste 205 Middletown (19709) *(G-7584)*

Socraticlaw Co Inc..302 654-9191
  3900 Centerville Rd Wilmington (19807) *(G-19910)*

Sodat - Delaware Inc (PA)..302 656-2810
  625 N Orange St Fl 2 Wilmington (19801) *(G-19911)*

Sodel Concepts II LLC..302 228-3786
  220 Rehoboth Ave Unit A Rehoboth Beach (19971) *(G-12965)*

Sodra Cell USA Inc..503 855-3032
  1209 N Orange St Wilmington (19801) *(G-19912)*

Soflete LLC..773 983-4692
  19621 Blue Bird Ln Rehoboth Beach (19971) *(G-12966)*

Sofp..302 354-3543
  251 Lakeside Dr Lewes (19958) *(G-6489)*

Soft Dig LLC..302 629-6658
  14619 Cokesbury Rd Georgetown (19947) *(G-4515)*

Soft Life Beauty Suite LLC..267 496-7655
  2801 Lancaster Ave Wilmington (19805) *(G-19913)*

Softball World LLC..302 856-7922
  22518 Lewes Georgetown Hwy Georgetown (19947) *(G-4516)*

Softlinn LLC..718 926-2170
  251 Little Falls Dr Wilmington (19808) *(G-19914)*

Software As A Service Saas, Middletown *Also Called: Whagons North America Inc (G-7721)*

Software Bananas LLC..302 348-8488
  2915 Ogletown Rd Ste 2304 Newark (19713) *(G-12050)*

Software Radio Systems USA Inc..339 368-6321
  2035 Sunset Lake Rd B2 Newark (19702) *(G-12051)*

Software Services of De Inc (PA)..302 654-3172
  1024 Justison St Wilmington (19801) *(G-19915)*

Soil Service Inc..302 629-7054
  117 New St Seaford (19973) *(G-13406)*

Soiree Factory..302 275-6576
  404 Rogers Rd Wilmington (19801) *(G-19916)*

Sojourners Place Inc..302 764-4592
  2901 Governor Printz Blvd Wilmington (19802) *(G-19917)*

SOJOURNERS' PLACE, Wilmington *Also Called: Sojourners Place Inc (G-19917)*

Sokoloff, Bruce H MD, Wilmington *Also Called: Wilmington Medical Associates (G-20823)*

Sokowatch Inc..805 479-5544
  2093 Philadelphia Pike Claymont (19703) *(G-1294)*

Sola Salon Studios..302 283-9216
  5321 Brandywine Pkwy Wilmington (19803) *(G-19918)*

Solace Lifesciences Inc..830 792-3123
  122 Willow Grove Mill Dr Middletown (19709) *(G-7585)*

Solace Lifesciences Inc..302 383-1450
  122 Willow Grove Mill Dr Middletown (19709) *(G-7586)*

Solar Electric Power Assoc..302 893-1354
  11 Bridle Brook Ln Newark (19711) *(G-12052)*

Solar Foundations Usa Inc (PA)..855 738-7200
  1142 River Rd New Castle (19720) *(G-9576)*

Solar Frontiers Corp..302 588-7600
  22 W Minglewood Dr Middletown (19709) *(G-7587)*

Solari Commercial Prpts LLC..302 757-2956
  3 Valmy Ln Wilmington (19807) *(G-19919)*

Sole Contracting Inc..302 420-4429
  4 Back Bay Rehoboth Beach (19971) *(G-12967)*

Solenis, Wilmington *Also Called: Solenis LLC (G-19922)*

Solenis Holdings 1 LLC (PA)..866 337-1533
  3 Beaver Valley Rd Ste 500 Wilmington (19803) *(G-19920)*

Solenis Holdings 3 LLC..866 337-1533
  3 Beaver Valley Rd Ste 500 Wilmington (19803) *(G-19921)*

Solenis LLC (PA)..866 337-1533
  2475 Pinnacle Dr Wilmington (19803) *(G-19922)*

Solenis LLC..302 594-5000
  500 Hercules Rd Wilmington (19808) *(G-19923)*

Solid Construction LLC..571 451-4727
  202 Lakeside Dr Lewes (19958) *(G-6490)*

Solid Idea Solutions LLC..646 982-2890
  16192 Coastal Hwy Lewes (19958) *(G-6491)*

Solid Image Inc..302 877-0901
  11244 Whitesville Rd Laurel (19956) *(G-5603)*

Solo Cup Operating Corporation..800 248-5960
  2451 Bear Corbitt Rd New Castle (19720) *(G-9577)*

Solo Global Inc..302 307-1673
  2810 N Church St Ste 78363 Wilmington (19802) *(G-19924)*

Solon Labs, Newark *Also Called: Solon Labs Corp (G-12053)*

Solon Labs Corp..860 876-7766
  254 Chapman Rd Ste 208 Newark (19702) *(G-12053)*

Solufy Corp..877 476-5839
  1201 N Orange St Ste 7228 Wilmington (19801) *(G-19925)*

Solution On-Call Services LLC..302 353-4328
  19 Lambson Ln Ste 108-B New Castle (19720) *(G-9578)*

Solution Seeker Cons LLC..347 230-8558
  14 S Union St Ste 109 Wilmington (19805) *(G-19926)*

Solutions Property Management..302 581-9060
  38 Hannah Loop Rehoboth Beach (19971) *(G-12968)*

Solvay Spclty Polymers USA LLC..302 452-6609
  100 Interchange Blvd Newark (19711) *(G-12054)*

Solvetech Inc..302 798-5400
  1711 Philadelphia Pike Wilmington (19809) *(G-19927)*

Soma Breath Inc..415 633-5359
  1013 Centre Rd Ste 403b Wilmington (19805) *(G-19928)*

Somar General Contracting LLC..302 561-3360
  804 Peachtree Rd Apt I Claymont (19703) *(G-1295)*

Somerford House Newark, Newark *Also Called: Five Star Quality Care Inc (G-10745)*

Somerford Place Newark, Newark *Also Called: Five Star Senior Living Inc (G-10747)*

Sonesta Es Wilmington Newark, Newark *Also Called: Cambridge Trs Inc (G-10123)*

Sonesta Intl Hotels Corp..302 453-9200
  240 Chapman Rd Newark (19702) *(G-12055)*

Sonesta Select Newark, Newark *Also Called: Ch Associates Viii LLC (G-10182)*

Sonic Sights Incorporated..312 498-9977
  8 The Grn Ste A Dover (19901) *(G-3587)*

Sonnys Auto Services Inc..302 287-7677
  111 Emerald Ridge Dr Bear (19701) *(G-499)*

Sonora, Newark *Also Called: Daphne LLC (G-10388)*

Soothing Hands, Newark *Also Called: Dorothy A Carroll (G-10553)*

Sophisticuts Inc..302 834-7427
  3 Rice Dr Bear (19701) *(G-500)*

Sophistor Inc..415 800-1028
  2093 Philadelphia Pike Ste 1028 Claymont (19703) *(G-1296)*

Soprano Design Limited..206 446-4401
  510 Silverside Rd Wilmington (19809) *(G-19929)*

Soprano Design Ltd, Wilmington *Also Called: Soprano Design Limited (G-19929)*

Soroptimist Foundation Inc..302 698-3686
  1851 Windswept Cir Dover (19901) *(G-3588)*

Sortd Inc..415 870-1075
  2035 Sunset Lake Rd B2 Newark (19702) *(G-12056)*

SOS Call Center Inc..302 319-5988
  86 Albe Dr # 1e Newark (19702) *(G-12057)*

SOS Personnel Ltd Liability Co..267 357-9124
  100 Mcmullen Ave Unit 1022 New Castle (19720) *(G-9579)*

SOS Security Incorporated..302 425-4755
  1000 N West St Ste 200 Wilmington (19801) *(G-19930)*

Sosa Eloy..302 275-3792
  1331 Greenleaf Rd Wilmington (19805) *(G-19931)*

Sosa Painting LLC..302 437-9282
  336 Hostetter Blvd Middletown (19709) *(G-7588)*

Soucialize Inc..916 803-1057
  16192 Coastal Hwy Lewes (19958) *(G-6492)*

Souf Mode LLC..332 220-6189
  221 N Broad St Middletown (19709) *(G-7589)*

Soul Purpose..302 420-1254
  282 Camerton Ln Townsend (19734) *(G-14066)*

Soules Management Inc 302 335-1980
1674 Mcginnis Pond Rd Magnolia (19962) *(G-6783)*

Soulscape Publishing LLC 303 834-7060
108 Tanglewood Ln Newark (19711) *(G-12058)*

Sound Body Products LLC 302 660-2296
5 Coachman Ct Wilmington (19803) *(G-19932)*

Sound Improvements, Seaford Also Called: Eric C James *(G-13178)*

Sound Master Dj 302 998-8235
2508 Nicholby Dr Wilmington (19808) *(G-19933)*

Sound Solutions 302 650-0950
1000 N West St Ste 1200 Wilmington (19801) *(G-19934)*

Sound-N-Secure Inc 302 424-3670
20444 Pingue Dr Milford (19963) *(G-8095)*

Soundbks Inc (PA) 213 436-5888
2711 Centerville Rd Ste 400 Wilmington (19808) *(G-19935)*

Soundingboard Project 302 956-1112
4023 Kennett Pike Wilmington (19807) *(G-19936)*

Source Supply Inc (PA) 302 328-5110
6 Bellecor Dr Ste 104 New Castle (19720) *(G-9580)*

South Bowers Ladies Auxiliary 302 335-4135
57 Scotts Corner Rd Milford (19963) *(G-8096)*

South Bowers Volunteer Fire Co 302 335-4666
57 Scotts Corner Rd Milford (19963) *(G-8097)*

South Coastal 302 542-5668
33711 S Coastal Ln Frankford (19945) *(G-4147)*

South Delaware Masonry Inc 302 378-1998
319 Main St Townsend (19734) *(G-14067)*

South Forks Inc 302 731-0344
136 Sandy Dr Newark (19713) *(G-12059)*

South Jersey Paving 856 498-8647
518 Turnberry Ct Bear (19701) *(G-501)*

South Newport Co Inc 302 732-9606
33246 Main St Dagsboro (19939) *(G-1506)*

South Paw Acres 302 945-1092
34465 Bookhammer Landing Rd Lewes (19958) *(G-6493)*

South Paxon LLC 302 918-5226
254 Chapman Rd Ste 208 Newark (19702) *(G-12060)*

South Shore Provisions LLC 443 614-2442
18 Ruth St Selbyville (19975) *(G-13607)*

South Wellington LLC 954 736-7418
30 E Pine St Georgetown (19947) *(G-4517)*

Southbrdge Med Advsory Council (PA) 302 655-6187
601 New Castle Ave Wilmington (19801) *(G-19937)*

Southco 302 475-2140
2207 Coventry Dr Wilmington (19810) *(G-19938)*

Southeast Delco Education Assn 302 420-4888
416 Hope Dr Middletown (19709) *(G-7590)*

Southeastern Home Health Svcs 214 466-1351
56 W Main St Ste 211 Christiana (19702) *(G-1009)*

Souther States Co-Op, Middletown Also Called: Hudson Farm Supply Co Inc *(G-7219)*

Southern Baptist Church, Newark Also Called: Ogletown Baptist Church *(G-11580)*

Southern Belle Barn Venue LLC 410 896-5408
5607 Lakeshore Dr Seaford (19973) *(G-13407)*

Southern Crab Company 302 478-0181
2831 Kennedy Rd Wilmington (19810) *(G-19939)*

Southern Del Imaging Assoc, Lewes Also Called: Southern Delaware Imaging LLP *(G-6494)*

Southern Del Physcl Therapy 302 659-0173
207 Stadium St Smyrna (19977) *(G-13899)*

Southern Del Trck Growers Assn 302 875-3147
Dual Hwy & Georgetown Rd Laurel (19956) *(G-5604)*

Southern Delaware Dental Spec 302 855-9499
20785 Professional Park Blvd Georgetown (19947) *(G-4518)*

Southern Delaware Foot 302 404-5915
543 N Shipley St Ste C Seaford (19973) *(G-13408)*

Southern Delaware Foot & Ankle 302 629-3000
28253 Dupont Blvd Unit 2 Millsboro (19966) *(G-8465)*

Southern Delaware Horse 302 856-1598
22532 Pine Haven Dr Georgetown (19947) *(G-4519)*

Southern Delaware Imaging LLP 302 645-7919
17503 Nassau Commons Blvd Lewes (19958) *(G-6494)*

Southern Delaware Med Group 302 424-3900
200 Banning St Ste 380 Dover (19904) *(G-3589)*

Southern Delaware Med Group PA 302 424-3900
100 Silicato Pkwy Ste 301 Milford (19963) *(G-8098)*

Southern Delaware Roller Derby 410 253-9798
2201 S Dupont Hwy Dover (19901) *(G-3590)*

Southern Delaware Signs 302 645-1425
18388 Coastal Hwy Unit 4 Lewes (19958) *(G-6495)*

Southern Delaware Surgery Ctr 302 644-6992
18941 John J Williams Hwy Rehoboth Beach (19971) *(G-12969)*

Southern Dental LLC 302 536-7589
703 Health Services Dr Seaford (19973) *(G-13409)*

Southern Glazers Wine Spirits, New Castle Also Called: Southern Wine Spirits Del LLC *(G-9582)*

Southern Glzers Wine Sprits LL 302 656-4487
615 Lambson Ln New Castle (19720) *(G-9581)*

Southern Meadow 302 677-0800
109 Lavender Dr Magnolia (19962) *(G-6784)*

Southern Rivers Management LLC (PA) 302 674-4089
160 Greentree Dr Ste 101 Dover (19904) *(G-3591)*

Southern States Coop Inc 302 732-6651
302 Clayton St Dagsboro (19939) *(G-1507)*

Southern States Coop Inc 302 629-7991
200 Allen St Seaford (19973) *(G-13410)*

Southern Wine Spirits Del LLC 800 292-7890
615 Lambson Ln New Castle (19720) *(G-9582)*

Southgate Concrete Company 302 376-5280
600 Industrial Dr Middletown (19709) *(G-7591)*

Southland Insulators Del LLC 302 854-0344
22976 Sussex Ave Georgetown (19947) *(G-4520)*

Southside Construction LLC 302 500-9268
3310 Wrangle Hill Rd Ste 8 Bear (19701) *(G-502)*

Southwest American Corp 302 652-7003
2200 N Grant Ave Wilmington (19806) *(G-19940)*

Southworks LLC 302 295-5008
200 Bellevue Pkwy Wilmington (19809) *(G-19941)*

Soutron Global Inc 760 519-3328
600 N Broad St Ste 5-3477 Middletown (19709) *(G-7592)*

Sovereign Dealer Finance Inc 302 691-6139
103 Foulk Rd Wilmington (19803) *(G-19942)*

Sovereign Property MGT LLC 302 994-2505
102 Larch Cir Ste 301 Wilmington (19804) *(G-19943)*

Sovereign Property MGT LLC (PA) 302 994-2505
102 Robino Ct Ste 101 Wilmington (19804) *(G-19944)*

Sovereigntactical LLC 858 336-9471
3 Germay Dr Ste 4 Wilmington (19804) *(G-19945)*

Sp Auto Parts, Bridgeville Also Called: Sp Auto Parts Inc *(G-768)*

Sp Auto Parts Inc 302 337-8897
7514 Federalsburg Rd Bridgeville (19933) *(G-768)*

Sp Holding Dps Inc (HQ) 302 999-2806
974 Centre Rd Wilmington (19805) *(G-19946)*

Sp Holding Et LLC (HQ) 302 999-4083
974 Centre Rd Wilmington (19805) *(G-19947)*

Sp Holding Ib Inc (HQ) 302 999-4083
974 Centre Rd Wilmington (19805) *(G-19948)*

Sp Plus Corporation 302 652-1410
111 W 11th St Lowr Wilmington (19801) *(G-19949)*

Space Happens Game 302 563-1949
2003 Grant Ave Wilmington (19809) *(G-19950)*

Space Industries Inc 510 219-1005
8 The Grn Ste R Dover (19901) *(G-3592)*

Space Soft Inc 413 337-7223
2803 Philadelphia Pike Ste B597 Claymont (19703) *(G-1297)*

Spacecon LLC (HQ) 302 322-9285
292 Churchmans Rd New Castle (19720) *(G-9583)*

Spacecon Specialty Contractors 302 503-3824
7254 Cedar Creek Rd Lincoln (19960) *(G-6704)*

Spaceport Support Services 302 524-4020
6 Dixon St Selbyville (19975) *(G-13608)*

Spallco Car & Truck Rental, Newark Also Called: Spallco Enterprises Inc *(G-12061)*

Spallco Enterprises Inc 302 368-5950
915 S Chapel St Newark (19713) *(G-12061)*

Spana Gregory MD 302 736-1320
200 Banning St Ste 150 Dover (19904) *(G-3593)*

ALPHABETIC SECTION

Sparano, Joseph C CPA, Wilmington *Also Called: Grabowski Sprano Vnclette Cpas (G-16941)*

Spare Cs Inc.. 424 744-0155
16192 Coastal Hwy Lewes (19958) *(G-6496)*

Spare Parts LLC... 302 333-2683
218 Avonbridge Dr Townsend (19734) *(G-14068)*

Spark... 302 324-2203
950 W Basin Rd New Castle (19720) *(G-9584)*

Sparkia Inc.. 302 636-5440
2711 Centerville Rd # 400 Wilmington (19808) *(G-19951)*

Sparklean Laundromat... 302 365-6665
1126 Pulaski Hwy Bear (19701) *(G-503)*

Sparklean Laundromat... 302 838-2226
750 Peoples Plz Newark (19702) *(G-12062)*

Sparksphere Solutions LLC.. 302 742-9048
838 Walker Rd Ste 21-2124 Dover (19904) *(G-3594)*

Sparkys Auto Repair LLC... 302 495-7525
12630 Sussex Hwy Greenwood (19950) *(G-4669)*

Sparrow, Lewes *Also Called: Eldersafe Technologies Inc (G-5955)*

Spartan Cleaning.. 302 345-7591
443 Boxwood Ln Middletown (19709) *(G-7593)*

Spca Sussex Chapter... 302 856-6361
22918 Dupont Blvd Georgetown (19947) *(G-4521)*

Speak Biz Consulting LLC.. 302 272-9294
3 Germay Dr Ste 4 Wilmington (19804) *(G-19952)*

Speakman Company... 302 765-0204
400 Anchor Mill Rd Historic New Castle (19720) *(G-5074)*

Spec Processing Group Inc... 302 295-2197
2266 Porter Rd Bear (19701) *(G-504)*

Spec Simple Inc.. 212 352-2002
16 W 4th St Historic New Castle (19720) *(G-5075)*

Special Care Inc... 302 644-6990
16698 Kings Hwy Ste D Lewes (19958) *(G-6497)*

Special Care Inc... 302 456-9904
5145 W Woodmill Dr # 22 Wilmington (19808) *(G-19953)*

Special Olympics Delaware Inc... 302 831-4653
619 S College Ave Newark (19716) *(G-12063)*

Special Services Center, Smyrna *Also Called: Smyrna School District (G-13897)*

Special Support Tech Inc... 804 620-6072
16192 Coastal Hwy Lewes (19958) *(G-6498)*

Specialized Carier Systems Inc... 302 424-4548
256 N Rehoboth Blvd Milford (19963) *(G-8099)*

Specialty Products N&H Inc (HQ)... 302 774-1000
974 Centre Rd Wilmington (19805) *(G-19954)*

Specialty Products Us LLC.. 302 774-1000
974 Centre Rd Wilmington (19805) *(G-19955)*

Specialty Products Us LLC.. 212 765-5500
1209 S Orange St Wilmington (19801) *(G-19956)*

Specialty Rehabilitation Inc... 302 709-0440
26 Wesley Dr Hockessin (19707) *(G-5386)*

Specimen Collection Svcs LLC.. 302 465-0494
64 W Kyla Marie Dr Newark (19702) *(G-12064)*

Spectrum Hone & Lace Llc... 313 268-5455
310 Haines St Ste 116 Newark (19717) *(G-12065)*

Spectrum Mill Inc... 941 815-9454
2093a Philadelphia Pike Ste 323 Claymont (19703) *(G-1298)*

Spedag Americas Inc... 201 857-3471
2711 Centerville Rd Wilmington (19808) *(G-19957)*

Speech & Language For Kids LLC... 847 852-0928
1910 Dorcas Ln Wilmington (19806) *(G-19958)*

Speech Clinic.. 302 999-0702
5147 W Woodmill Dr Ste 21 Wilmington (19808) *(G-19959)*

Speech Ladder Inc... 770 355-0719
1210 Glen Mohr Ct Townsend (19734) *(G-14069)*

Speech Therapeutics Inc... 302 234-9226
15 Elderberry Ct Hockessin (19707) *(G-5387)*

Speed Auto Systems LLC... 888 446-7102
16192 Coastal Hwy Lewes (19958) *(G-6499)*

Speed Pro Imiging, Wilmington *Also Called: Grm Pro Imaging LLC (G-16984)*

Speeder Solutions LLC... 302 448-8668
330 Centerpoint Blvd Historic New Castle (19720) *(G-5076)*

Speedrid Ltd.. 213 550-5462
625 S Dupont Hwy Dover (19901) *(G-3595)*

Speedy Publishing LLC.. 888 248-4521
40 E Main St # 1156 Newark (19711) *(G-12066)*

Spence Holding.. 973 392-1218
300 Martin Luther King Blvd Ste 200 Wilmington (19801) *(G-19960)*

Spencer, Richard N Jr Vmd, Newark *Also Called: White Clay Creek Vtrinary Hosp (G-12366)*

Spences Bazaar & Auction LLC... 302 734-3441
550 S New St Dover (19904) *(G-3596)*

Spg, Bear *Also Called: Spec Processing Group Inc (G-504)*

Spg International LLC.. 404 823-3934
841 Mud Mill Rd Marydel (19964) *(G-6811)*

SPI Holding Company.. 800 789-9755
503 Carr Rd Ste 210 Wilmington (19809) *(G-19961)*

SPI Pharma, Wilmington *Also Called: SPI Holding Company (G-19961)*
SPI Pharma, Wilmington *Also Called: SPI Pharma Inc (G-19962)*

SPI Pharma Inc... 302 360-7200
40 Cape Henlopen Dr Lewes (19958) *(G-6500)*

SPI Pharma Inc (HQ).. 800 789-9755
503 Carr Rd Ste 210 Wilmington (19809) *(G-19962)*

Spicer Bros Construction Inc.. 302 703-6754
34634 Bay Crossing Blvd Unit 4 Lewes (19958) *(G-6501)*

Spicer Mullikin Funeral Homes (PA)... 302 368-9500
1000 N Dupont Hwy New Castle (19720) *(G-9585)*

Spicer Mullikin Funeral Homes... 302 368-9500
121 W Park Pl Newark (19711) *(G-12067)*

Spin4spin Inc.. 720 547-2126
8 The Grn Dover (19901) *(G-3597)*

Spinal Health & Wellness.. 302 993-9113
3105 Limestone Road Ste 303 Wilmington (19808) *(G-19963)*

Spine & Orthopedic Specialist... 302 633-1280
1101 Twin C Ln Ste 203 Newark (19713) *(G-12068)*

Spine Care of Delaware... 302 894-1900
4102b Ogletown Stanton Rd Newark (19713) *(G-12069)*

Spine Group LLC... 302 595-3030
1426 N Clayton St Wilmington (19806) *(G-19964)*

Spinlifecom LLC.. 888 398-2267
773 S Dupont Hwy New Castle (19720) *(G-9586)*

Spinrack Corp... 209 965-7746
8 The Grn Dover (19901) *(G-3598)*

Spinwizards DJS... 302 252-1727
434 E 35th St Wilmington (19802) *(G-19965)*

Spire Innovations Inc... 646 583-1839
1013 Centre Rd Ste 4038 Wilmington (19805) *(G-19966)*

Spire Tech Sltions Private Ltd, Wilmington *Also Called: Spire Innovations Inc (G-19966)*

Spirelio Inc.. 302 467-3444
831 N Tatnall St Ste M # 109 Wilmington (19801) *(G-19967)*

Spirits Path To Wellness LLC.. 302 998-0074
1405 Greenhill Ave Wilmington (19806) *(G-19968)*

Spiro Health Inc.. 302 645-7400
16192 Coastal Hwy Lewes (19958) *(G-6502)*

Spitzer Lighting, Newark *Also Called: New Standard Product Dist Inc (G-11525)*

Splash Day.. 302 238-7457
36773 Millsboro Hwy Millsboro (19966) *(G-8466)*

Splash Laundromat.. 302 503-3325
668 N Dupont Blvd Milford (19963) *(G-8100)*

Splash Lndrmat LLC - Gorgetown... 302 249-8231
201 E Laurel St Georgetown (19947) *(G-4522)*

Split Racing, Greenville *Also Called: Gerard Joseph Capano (G-4584)*

Spm Tire Service LLC.. 302 731-1004
2615 Pulaski Hwy Newark (19702) *(G-12070)*

Spn Title Services.. 302 537-1540
30838 Vines Creek Rd Unit 8 Dagsboro (19939) *(G-1508)*

Sport Clips.. 302 294-1774
1255 Churchmans Rd Newark (19713) *(G-12071)*

Sport Clips.. 302 836-9900
450 Peoples Plz Newark (19702) *(G-12072)*

Sport Clips.. 302 456-9900
1 Washington St Newark (19711) *(G-12073)*

Sport Clips, Dover *Also Called: Sport Clips Hrcuts Dver - Dpon (G-3599)*

Sport Clips Hrcuts Dver - Dpon... 302 677-1622
1211 N Dupont Hwy Ste C Dover (19901) *(G-3599)*

Sport Clips Hrcuts Rhboth Bch... 302 291-2391
18756 Coastal Hwy Rehoboth Beach (19971) *(G-12970)*

Sport Spine Chiropractic Ctrs — ALPHABETIC SECTION

Sport Spine Chiropractic Ctrs.. 302 600-1675
   4635 Ogletown Stanton Rd Newark (19713) *(G-12074)*

Sportera Events Usa Inc... 514 978-2648
   874 Walker Rd Ste C Dover (19904) *(G-3600)*

Sports At The Beach, Georgetown Also Called: Softball World LLC *(G-4516)*

Sports Car Service Inc.. 302 764-7439
   5 E 41st St Wilmington (19802) *(G-19969)*

Sports Car Tire Inc.. 302 571-8473
   1203 E 13th St Wilmington (19802) *(G-19970)*

Sportsmans Hall LLC.. 410 429-6030
   38097 West Dr Unit 738 Rehoboth Beach (19971) *(G-12971)*

Sportsmans Hall Rller Skting R, Rehoboth Beach Also Called: Sportsmans Hall LLC *(G-12971)*

Sportz Tees... 302 280-6076
   16536 Adams Rd Laurel (19956) *(G-5605)*

Sposato Irrigation Company... 302 645-4773
   16181 Hudson Rd Milton (19968) *(G-8713)*

Sposato Landscape Company Inc... 302 645-4773
   16181 Hudson Rd Milton (19968) *(G-8714)*

Sposato Lawn Care.. 302 645-4773
   Rd 4 Box 265-B Milton (19968) *(G-8715)*

Spotlight Publications LLC.. 302 504-1329
   3301 Lancaster Pike Ste 5c Wilmington (19805) *(G-19971)*

Spotters Inc.. 646 662-6025
   251 Little Falls Dr Wilmington (19808) *(G-19972)*

Spratley Publishing.. 267 779-7353
   1203 Apple St Wilmington (19801) *(G-19973)*

Spratley Publishing Co, Wilmington Also Called: Spratley Publishing *(G-19973)*

Sprig... 302 753-6859
   169 Pine Tree Rd Townsend (19734) *(G-14070)*

Spring League LLC... 917 257-5801
   3524 Silverside Rd Ste 35b Wilmington (19810) *(G-19974)*

Spring Mix Sport Fshing Chrter... 443 463-8902
   38403 Bayberry Ln Selbyville (19975) *(G-13609)*

Spring Rain Irrigation Inc... 302 838-9610
   29 Pegasus Pl Bear (19701) *(G-505)*

Spring-Green Lawn Care.. 302 762-1499
   200 Woodland Dr Wilmington (19809) *(G-19975)*

Springboard Collaborative Inc.. 302 864-5220
   112 S French St Wilmington (19801) *(G-19976)*

Springboard Inc... 302 607-2580
   500 Creek View Rd Ste 3e Newark (19711) *(G-12075)*

Springhaus LLC.. 302 397-5261
   251 Little Falls Dr Wilmington (19808) *(G-19977)*

Springhaus Landscape Company, Lewes Also Called: Itea Inc *(G-6133)*

Springhill Seamless Gutter, Milford Also Called: Hickman Overhead Door Company *(G-7930)*

Springhill Suites Newark Downt.. 888 205-7322
   402 Ogletown Rd Newark (19711) *(G-12076)*

Springleaf Fincl Holdings LLC... 302 543-6767
   1 Righter Pkwy Wilmington (19803) *(G-19978)*

Springmill Community Assoc.. 302 376-5466
   2 Windmill Ln Middletown (19709) *(G-7594)*

Springpoint At Lewes Inc... 732 430-3660
   17028 Cadbury Cir Lewes (19958) *(G-6503)*

Springs Rhblttion At Brndywine.. 302 998-0101
   505 Greenbank Rd Wilmington (19808) *(G-19979)*

Springside LLC... 302 838-7223
   200 Biddle Ave Ste 205 Newark (19702) *(G-12077)*

Sprinkles Christian Daycare, Newark Also Called: Brown Lisha *(G-10095)*

Sprint, Milford Also Called: Sprint Spectrum LP *(G-8101)*

Sprint, New Castle Also Called: Sprint Spectrum LP *(G-9587)*

Sprint, Wilmington Also Called: Sprint Spectrum LP *(G-19981)*

Sprint Quality Printing Inc... 302 478-0720
   3609 Silverside Rd Wilmington (19810) *(G-19980)*

Sprint Spectrum LP.. 302 393-2060
   120 Aerenson Dr Milford (19963) *(G-8101)*

Sprint Spectrum LP.. 302 322-1712
   118 N Dupont Hwy New Castle (19720) *(G-9587)*

Sprint Spectrum LP.. 302 993-3700
   4511 Kirkwood Hwy Wilmington (19808) *(G-19981)*

Sprocket LLC.. 678 231-3165
   251 Little Falls Dr Wilmington (19808) *(G-19982)*

Spunkchild LLC.. 917 504-4529
   221 N Broad St Middletown (19709) *(G-7595)*

Spwa Services LLC... 856 761-4621
   38841 Bayberry Ct Ocean View (19970) *(G-12568)*

Sqella Technologies Corp.. 302 592-6747
   1007 N Orange St Ste 1382 Wilmington (19801) *(G-19983)*

Sqs Global Solutions LLC.. 302 691-9682
   1201 N Orange St Ste 7383 Wilmington (19801) *(G-19984)*

Squadcast Studios Inc... 916 320-7761
   1209 N Orange St Wilmington (19801) *(G-19985)*

Square One Electric Service Co.. 302 678-0400
   347 Fork Branch Rd Dover (19904) *(G-3601)*

Square Promote... 302 478-0736
   1102 Crestover Rd Wilmington (19803) *(G-19986)*

Squeaky Clean & Dry... 302 327-6240
   7 Eynon Ct Hockessin (19707) *(G-5388)*

Sreeven Infotech Inc.. 302 465-2402
   29 Berkley Dr Newark (19702) *(G-12078)*

Srhk Enterprises LLC... 302 834-2345
   110 Gambel Ct Bear (19701) *(G-506)*

Srsl and Transportation LLC... 302 295-3599
   2711 Centerville Rd Ste 120 Wilmington (19808) *(G-19987)*

Sruplex LLC.. 331 901-0011
   16192 Coastal Hwy Lewes (19958) *(G-6504)*

Ssbv LLC... 844 585-0656
   1209 N Orange St Wilmington (19801) *(G-19988)*

SSC Parking LLC Sam Stanford... 302 561-0088
   615 Parkman Ct Bear (19701) *(G-507)*

Ssd Technology Partners, Wilmington Also Called: Software Services of De Inc *(G-19915)*

Ssm Industries Inc... 856 345-2525
   322 A St Ste 100 Wilmington (19801) *(G-19989)*

Ssmmd LLC.. 302 249-1045
   29092 Sussex Hwy Laurel (19956) *(G-5606)*

Ssn Christiana LLC.. 302 266-6600
   56 S Old Baltimore Pike Newark (19702) *(G-12079)*

SSS Clutch Company Inc... 302 322-8080
   610 W Basin Rd New Castle (19720) *(G-9588)*

St Andrews Apartments... 302 834-8600
   50 Turnberry Ct Bear (19701) *(G-508)*

St Andrews Maintenance.. 302 832-2675
   104 E Scotland Dr Bear (19701) *(G-509)*

St Anthonys Community Center... 302 421-3721
   1703 W 10th St Wilmington (19805) *(G-19990)*

St Anthonys Housing Mgt Corp... 302 421-3756
   1701 W 10th St Ste 200 Wilmington (19805) *(G-19991)*

St David's Episcopal Day Sch, Wilmington Also Called: Diocesan Council Inc *(G-16075)*

St Delware Electrical.. 302 857-5316
   245 Mckee Rd Dover (19904) *(G-3602)*

St Francis Health Services Corporation............................... 302 575-8301
   7th N Clayton St Wilmington (19805) *(G-19992)*

St Francis Hospital, Wilmington Also Called: St Francis Health Services Corporation *(G-19992)*

St Francis Hospital Inc.. 616 685-3538
   701 N Clayton St Wilmington (19805) *(G-19993)*

St Helenas Early Learning... 302 561-4044
   2314 Andys Ln Wilmington (19810) *(G-19994)*

St Helenas Early Learning Ctr... 610 497-0435
   1600 Rockland Rd Wilmington (19803) *(G-19995)*

St John Beloved... 302 562-9129
   1100 Wynnbrook Rd Wilmington (19809) *(G-19996)*

St Johns Community Services.. 302 292-1044
   26 Golf View Dr Newark (19702) *(G-12080)*

St Lawrence Grant Ave Trust.. 302 652-7978
   2010 Pennsylvania Ave Wilmington (19806) *(G-19997)*

St Logistics 360 Inc... 302 607-8666
   300 Delaware Ave Ste 210 Wilmington (19801) *(G-19998)*

St Mark's Pre-School, Wilmington Also Called: St Marks United Methodist Ch *(G-19999)*

St Marks United Methodist Ch.. 302 994-0400
   1700 Limestone Rd Wilmington (19804) *(G-19999)*

St Michaels School and Nursery... 302 353-6717
   700 N Walnut St Wilmington (19801) *(G-20000)*

ALPHABETIC SECTION

St Michaels School Inc.. 302 656-3389
  305 E 7th St Wilmington (19801) *(G-20001)*
St Patricks Center Inc.. 302 652-6219
  107 E 14th St Wilmington (19801) *(G-20002)*
ST. FRANCIS CARE CENTER AT WIL, Wilmington Also Called: Regency Hlthcare Rehab Ctr LLC *(G-19400)*
ST. FRANCIS LIFE, Wilmington Also Called: Life At St Frncis Hlthcare Inc *(G-17899)*
Stable App LLC.. 310 767-7832
  1007 N Orange St Wilmington (19801) *(G-20003)*
Stackadapt US Inc... 647 385-7698
  16192 Coastal Hwy Lewes (19958) *(G-6505)*
Stackd Studio LLC.. 240 304-1085
  254 Chapman Rd Ste 208 Newark (19702) *(G-12081)*
Stackdkjewelry.com, Newark Also Called: Stackd Studio LLC *(G-12081)*
Staclar Inc.. 628 213-1140
  2093 Philadelphia Pike Claymont (19703) *(G-1299)*
Stada Fitness Concept LLC... 215 589-0914
  1004 W Founds St Townsend (19734) *(G-14071)*
Staffmark Investment LLC.. 302 422-0606
  242 S Rehoboth Blvd Milford (19963) *(G-8102)*
Stafford Precision, Bear Also Called: Bear Forge and Machine Co Inc *(G-63)*
Stag Run Farm Llc... 302 270-8435
  23656 Fox Croft Ln Georgetown (19947) *(G-4523)*
Stage One, Dover Also Called: Bernard Limpert *(G-1914)*
Staging Dimensions Inc.. 302 328-4100
  31 Blevins Dr Ste A New Castle (19720) *(G-9589)*
Staikos Associates Architects (PA)................................. 302 764-1678
  502 Dell Hill Rd Wilmington (19809) *(G-20004)*
Stainless Alloys Inc... 800 499-7833
  103 Foulk Rd Ste 202 Wilmington (19803) *(G-20005)*
Stainless Steel Invest Inc.. 800 499-7833
  103 Foulk Rd Ste 202 Wilmington (19803) *(G-20006)*
Staircase Inc... 215 693-5686
  2093 Philadelphia Pike # 2024 Claymont (19703) *(G-1300)*
Staley Holdings Inc... 302 793-0289
  501 Silverside Rd Ste 55 Wilmington (19809) *(G-20007)*
Stallard Chassis Co... 302 292-1800
  123 Sandy Dr Newark (19713) *(G-12082)*
Stallion Trucking Inc... 803 757-4366
  8 The Grn Ste 13936 Dover (19901) *(G-3603)*
Stamford Screen Printing Inc.. 302 654-2442
  3801 Kennett Pike Ste C107 Wilmington (19807) *(G-20008)*
Stampede Btq & Vintage LLC... 215 668-5714
  1236 Prospect Dr Wilmington (19809) *(G-20009)*
Stan Perkoskis Plumbing & Htg..................................... 302 529-1220
  1818 Marsh Rd Wilmington (19810) *(G-20010)*
Stan T Lepkowski.. 302 393-9093
  94 Downs Chapel Rd Clayton (19938) *(G-1406)*
Standard & Poors Intl LLC (HQ)...................................... 212 512-2000
  2711 Centerville Rd Wilmington (19808) *(G-20011)*
Standard Direct LLC.. 855 550-0606
  1207 Delaware Ave Wilmington (19806) *(G-20012)*
Standard Distributing Co Inc.. 302 674-4591
  Horse Pond Rd & Lafferty Ln Dover (19901) *(G-3604)*
Standard Distributing Co (PA).. 302 655-5511
  100 Mews Dr New Castle (19720) *(G-9590)*
Standard Industrial Supply Co.. 302 656-1631
  1625 N Heald St Wilmington (19802) *(G-20013)*
Standard Insurance Company.. 302 322-9722
  10 Corporate Cir New Castle (19720) *(G-9591)*
Standard Magic Corporation.. 347 756-1222
  2810 N Church St Pmb 59881 Wilmington (19802) *(G-20014)*
Standard Merger Sub LLC.. 302 456-6785
  128 Sandy Dr Newark (19713) *(G-12083)*
Standard Pipe Services LLC... 302 286-0701
  567 Walther Rd Newark (19702) *(G-12084)*
Standard Technologies & Machine Co........................... 302 994-0229
  3709 Old Capitol Trl Wilmington (19808) *(G-20015)*
Standards Site Inc.. 917 449-4078
  251 Little Falls Dr Wilmington (19808) *(G-20016)*
Stanga Games Inc... 415 549-6537
  1000 N West St Ste 1200 Wilmington (19801) *(G-20017)*
Stanley Golden... 302 652-5626
  841 N Tatnall St Wilmington (19801) *(G-20018)*
Stanley H Goloskov DDS PA.. 302 475-0600
  2500 Grubb Rd Ste 130 Wilmington (19810) *(G-20019)*
Stanley J Lepowski Jr... 302 378-7284
  125 Gum Bush Rd Townsend (19734) *(G-14072)*
Stanley Steamers Carpet Clrs, Newark Also Called: Lopesco Inc *(G-11284)*
Stanley Steemer Intl Inc... 302 293-2879
  31 Southgate Blvd New Castle (19720) *(G-9592)*
Stantec Consulting Svcs Inc... 302 395-1919
  121 Continental Dr Ste 308 Newark (19713) *(G-12085)*
Stanton Door, Newark Also Called: Stanton Door Co Inc *(G-12086)*
Stanton Door Co Inc... 302 731-4167
  20 Shea Way Ste 206 Newark (19713) *(G-12086)*
Stapleford Electric LLC... 302 300-1377
  3847 Evelyn Dr Wilmington (19808) *(G-20020)*
Stapleford's Oldsmobile, Saint Georges Also Called: Staplefords Sales and Service *(G-13039)*
Staplefords Sales and Service.. 302 834-4568
  1402 S Dupont Hwy Saint Georges (19733) *(G-13039)*
Stapler Athletic Association... 302 652-9769
  1900 N Scott St Wilmington (19806) *(G-20021)*
Staples & Associates Insurance..................................... 302 398-3276
  35 Commerce St Harrington (19952) *(G-4835)*
Star Art Inc.. 302 261-6732
  1272 Porter Rd Bear (19701) *(G-510)*
Star Campus II... 302 514-7586
  550 S College Ave Ste 107 Newark (19713) *(G-12087)*
Star Enrg... 302 743-6751
  5700 Kirkwood Hwy Ste 106 Wilmington (19808) *(G-20022)*
Star Enrg Cs LLC... 302 660-2187
  5700 Kirkwood Hwy 106a Wilmington (19808) *(G-20023)*
Star Gas & Diesel... 302 998-2002
  3927 Kirkwood Hwy Wilmington (19808) *(G-20024)*
Star of Sea Condominium, Rehoboth Beach Also Called: Star of The Sea Assoc of Ownrs *(G-12972)*
Star of The Sea Assoc of Ownrs..................................... 302 227-6006
  307 S Boardwalk Ste L2 Rehoboth Beach (19971) *(G-12972)*
Star Services LLC... 302 373-5210
  218 Appoquin Dr S Middletown (19709) *(G-7596)*
Star Sound Technologies LLC.. 330 260-6767
  100 Fallon Ave Wilmington (19804) *(G-20025)*
Star States Leasing Corp.. 302 283-4500
  30 Blue Hen Dr Ste 200 Newark (19713) *(G-12088)*
Starbelt LLC.. 256 724-9200
  103 Foulk Rd Ste 202 Wilmington (19803) *(G-20026)*
Starfish Spclty Insur Svcs LLC....................................... 914 556-3200
  200 Continental Dr Ste 401 Newark (19713) *(G-12089)*
Stark Truss Company Inc... 302 337-9470
  16632 Nates Way Bridgeville (19933) *(G-769)*
Stark Truss Company Inc... 302 368-8566
  10 Aleph Dr Newark (19702) *(G-12090)*
Starkit Studio LLC... 302 467-2017
  16192 Coastal Hwy Lewes (19958) *(G-6506)*
Starks Funeral Service LLC.. 202 361-0603
  2810 N Church St Wilmington (19802) *(G-20027)*
Starliters Dance Studio Inc.. 302 798-6330
  14 Brookview Ave Claymont (19703) *(G-1301)*
Starr Wright Insur Agcy Inc... 302 483-0190
  405 Silverside Rd Ste 102b Wilmington (19809) *(G-20028)*
Starr Wright USA, Wilmington Also Called: Starr Wright Insur Agcy Inc *(G-20028)*
Starrett Design Build... 302 598-6607
  1304 Old Lancaster Pike D Hockessin (19707) *(G-5389)*
Stars On 9 Dance Center LLC... 302 855-9595
  205 N Race St Georgetown (19947) *(G-4524)*
Startup Africa Inc... 302 894-8971
  818 N Market St Wilmington (19801) *(G-20029)*
Stat Office Solutions.. 302 884-6746
  1201 N Orange St Ste 700 Wilmington (19801) *(G-20030)*
State Del Veterans Mem Cmtry, Bear Also Called: Delaware Secretary of State *(G-155)*
State Drywall Co Inc... 302 239-2843
  12 Ridon Dr Hockessin (19707) *(G-5390)*

State Edcatn Agcy Dirs Arts Ed 302 739-4111
  401 Federal St Ste 2 Dover (19901) *(G-3605)*
State Farm 302 258-9989
  30170 Irons Ln Dagsboro (19939) *(G-1509)*
State Farm 302 678-5656
  50 N Dupont Hwy Dover (19901) *(G-3606)*
State Farm 302 344-3514
  4758 Limestone Rd Ste C Wilmington (19808) *(G-20031)*
State Farm Insurance 302 834-5467
  2500 Wrangle Hill Rd Ste 125 Bear (19701) *(G-511)*
State Farm Insurance 302 934-8083
  29787 John J Williams Hwy Unit 1 Millsboro (19966) *(G-8467)*
State Farm Insurance 302 547-7478
  4015 Newport Gap Pike Wilmington (19808) *(G-20032)*
State Farm Insurance 302 353-6636
  1813 Marsh Rd Ste G Wilmington (19810) *(G-20033)*
State Farm Insurance, Bear *Also Called: Robert F Mullen Insurance Agcy (G-464)*
State Farm Insurance, Bear *Also Called: State Farm Insurance (G-511)*
State Farm Insurance, Camden *Also Called: Katie Bennett (G-864)*
State Farm Insurance, Dagsboro *Also Called: State Farm (G-1509)*
State Farm Insurance, Dover *Also Called: Bob Simmons Agency (G-1957)*
State Farm Insurance, Dover *Also Called: John Borden (G-2796)*
State Farm Insurance, Dover *Also Called: Phil Hill (G-3312)*
State Farm Insurance, Dover *Also Called: State Farm (G-3606)*
State Farm Insurance, Georgetown *Also Called: Mark Penuel (G-4415)*
State Farm Insurance, Milford *Also Called: Schanne Mark State Farm Insur (G-8086)*
State Farm Insurance, Millsboro *Also Called: State Farm Insurance (G-8467)*
State Farm Insurance, New Castle *Also Called: Hartle Brian State Farm Agency (G-9200)*
State Farm Insurance, Newark *Also Called: State Farmjeff Gardiner (G-12091)*
State Farm Insurance, Newark *Also Called: Terry White (G-12180)*
State Farm Insurance, Ocean View *Also Called: Denise Beam (G-12504)*
State Farm Insurance, Rehoboth Beach *Also Called: George H Bunting Jr (G-12768)*
State Farm Insurance, Wilmington *Also Called: State Farm (G-20031)*
State Farm Insurance, Wilmington *Also Called: State Farm Insurance Co (G-20034)*
State Farm Insurance Co 302 547-4117
  167 Steven Ln Wilmington (19808) *(G-20034)*
State Farmjeff Gardiner 302 286-7130
  1352 Marrows Rd Newark (19711) *(G-12091)*
State Janitorial Supply Co 302 734-4814
  540 Otis Dr # 1 Dover (19901) *(G-3607)*
State Line Farms LLC 302 628-4506
  26394 Old Carriage Rd Seaford (19973) *(G-13411)*
State Line Machine Inc 302 875-2248
  1154 S Central Ave Laurel (19956) *(G-5607)*
State Line Machine Inc 302 478-0285
  200 State Line Rd Wilmington (19803) *(G-20035)*
State of De 302 376-5125
  112 Netherlands Dr Middletown (19709) *(G-7597)*
State of De 302 328-3573
  36 Herbert Dr New Castle (19720) *(G-9593)*
State of De 302 653-0593
  118 S Delaware St Smyrna (19977) *(G-13900)*
State of Delaware 302 322-2303
  84 Christiana Rd Ste A New Castle (19720) *(G-9594)*
State Senior Care LLC 302 674-2144
  21 N State St Dover (19901) *(G-3608)*
State Street Inn 302 734-2294
  228 N State St Dover (19901) *(G-3609)*
State Wide Plumbing Inc 302 292-0924
  27 Albe Dr Ste J Newark (19702) *(G-12092)*
Statera Homes 302 313-9949
  75 Lake Ave Rehoboth Beach (19971) *(G-12973)*
Statewide Mechanical Inc 302 376-6117
  3295 Harris Rd Townsend (19734) *(G-14073)*
Statewide Plumbing, Newark *Also Called: State Wide Plumbing Inc (G-12092)*
Statewise Energy Ohio LLC 855 862-1185
  2711 Centerville Rd # 400 Wilmington (19808) *(G-20036)*
Status Intl LLC DBA Sttus Brnd 202 290-6387
  704 N King St Ste 500 Wilmington (19801) *(G-20037)*
Statwhiz Ventures LLC 310 819-5427
  1201 N Orange St Ste 600 Wilmington (19801) *(G-20038)*
Stauffer Family LLC 302 227-5820
  36 Glade Cir E Rehoboth Beach (19971) *(G-12974)*
Stay Prime Inc 612 770-6753
  1201 N Orange St Ste 600 Wilmington (19801) *(G-20039)*
Stay True Plumbing 302 464-1198
  693 Old Porter Rd Bear (19701) *(G-512)*
Staybrdge Stes - Nwrk/Wlmngton, Newark *Also Called: Dpnl LLC (G-10559)*
Staybridge Suites 302 738-3400
  204 Sulky Cir Wilmington (19810) *(G-20040)*
Staysaf 3 LLC 305 699-1454
  1201 N Market St Ste 111 Wilmington (19801) *(G-20041)*
Stayton and Dickens LLP 302 856-4141
  117 S Bedford St Georgetown (19947) *(G-4525)*
Stb Contracting LLC 302 992-0570
  303 Winston Ave Wilmington (19804) *(G-20042)*
Steadfast Insurance Company (DH) 847 605-6000
  2 Loockerman Plz Ste 202 Dover (19901) *(G-3610)*
Steady Inc 302 266-4144
  70 Aleph Dr Ste C Newark (19702) *(G-12093)*
Steagle Consulting Group LLC 302 439-4301
  950 Ridge Rd Claymont (19703) *(G-1302)*
Steam Wizards LLC 302 548-5942
  34575 Dupont Blvd Frankford (19945) *(G-4148)*
Steamboat Landing 302 645-6500
  Coastal Hwy 1 Lewes (19958) *(G-6507)*
Stedim N Sartorius Amer Inc 800 635-2906
  221 Lake Dr Newark (19702) *(G-12094)*
Steel Buildings Inc 302 644-0444
  17515 Nassau Commons Blvd Lewes (19958) *(G-6508)*
Steel Suppliers Inc 302 654-5243
  701 E Front St Wilmington (19801) *(G-20043)*
Steel Suppliers Erectors, Wilmington *Also Called: Steel Suppliers Inc (G-20043)*
Steel Suppliers Erectors Inc 302 654-5243
  701 E Front St Wilmington (19801) *(G-20044)*
Steele Insurance Group LLC 302 898-6797
  1035 N Lincoln St Ste 600 Wilmington (19805) *(G-20045)*
Steen Waehler Schrider Fox LLC 302 539-7900
  92 Atlantic Ave Ste B Ocean View (19970) *(G-12569)*
Steering Committee 302 994-7533
  100 E Market St Wilmington (19804) *(G-20046)*
Steerr Inc 412 303-5840
  16192 Coastal Hwy Lewes (19958) *(G-6509)*
Stefanie N Marshall Do 302 454-9800
  875 Aaa Blvd Ste B Newark (19713) *(G-12095)*
Steimel Construction LLC 302 827-2471
  26 Canterbury Ct Lewes (19958) *(G-6510)*
Stein Tree Service Inc 302 478-3511
  17 Austin Rd Wilmington (19810) *(G-20047)*
Steinebach Robert and Assoc 302 328-1212
  20 Peddlers Row Christiana (19702) *(G-1010)*
Stella C Ohanenye Od LLC 302 388-7288
  600 N Broad St Ste 12 Middletown (19709) *(G-7598)*
Stellar Labs Inc 650 868-6796
  251 Little Falls Dr Wilmington (19808) *(G-20048)*
Stems Labs Inc 708 834-3706
  1209 N Orange St Wilmington (19801) *(G-20049)*
Steneral Consulting Inc 302 721-6124
  1007 N Orange St Wilmington (19801) *(G-20050)*
Stenta Appraisal Portions 302 477-9562
  9 Lynthwaite Farm Ln Wilmington (19803) *(G-20051)*
Step Up Daycare 302 762-3183
  2715 N Tatnall St Wilmington (19802) *(G-20052)*
Step-Up Daycare, Wilmington *Also Called: Step Up Daycare (G-20052)*
Steph1official Inc 302 744-0990
  8 The Grn Dover (19901) *(G-3611)*
Stephanie Barshay Lplmh, Wilmington *Also Called: Barshay Stephanie Lplmh (G-14770)*
Stephanie E Steckel DDS, Ms, Dover *Also Called: Orthodontics On Silver Lake PA (G-3242)*
Stephanie Galbraith 302 290-2235
  1429 Stapler Pl Wilmington (19806) *(G-20053)*

ALPHABETIC SECTION — Stoneybrook Apts

Stephanie Orr Lcsw LLC 302 478-4373
12 Austin Rd Wilmington (19810) *(G-20054)*

Stephanie Saroukos 302 654-1614
2419 Lancaster Ave Wilmington (19805) *(G-20055)*

Stephano Slack LLC 302 777-7400
1700 W 14th St Wilmington (19806) *(G-20056)*

Stephen A Covey 302 478-0215
2406 Allendale Rd Wilmington (19803) *(G-20057)*

Stephen A Niemoeller DMD PA 302 737-3320
523 Capitol Trl Newark (19711) *(G-12096)*

Stephen Devary 302 674-4560
591 Squawigm Rd Dover (19901) *(G-3612)*

Stephen E Jenkins 302 654-1888
1100 N Market St Wilmington (19801) *(G-20058)*

Stephen Hannig 302 792-1342
2601 Washington Ave Claymont (19703) *(G-1303)*

Stephen J Crifasi Real Estate 302 658-9572
2300 N Grant Ave Wilmington (19806) *(G-20059)*

Stephen J Duggan Do 302 449-3030
124 Sleepy Hollow Dr Ste 203 Middletown (19709) *(G-7599)*

Stephen Jankovic Chiropractor 302 384-8540
1309 Beale Rd Ste 12 Wilmington (19810) *(G-20060)*

Stephen M Beneck M D 302 733-0980
87 Omega Dr Newark (19713) *(G-12097)*

Stephen M D Carey 302 629-8662
2 Chelsea Ct Seaford (19973) *(G-13412)*

Stephen S Grubbs M D 302 366-1200
4701 Ogletown Stanton Rd # 2200 Newark (19713) *(G-12098)*

Stephens Enterprises Inc 302 629-0322
26286 Seaford Rd Seaford (19973) *(G-13413)*

Stephens Management Corp 302 629-4393
321 E Stein Hwy Seaford (19973) *(G-13414)*

Stepping Stones College 302 983-1437
118 Bunche Blvd Wilmington (19801) *(G-20061)*

Stepr Inc 866 861-1281
300 Delaware Ave Wilmington (19801) *(G-20062)*

Stepship LLC 773 503-2110
2401 Ogletown Rd Newark (19711) *(G-12099)*

Stereochemical Inc 302 266-0700
667 Dawson Dr Ste E Newark (19713) *(G-12100)*

Sterling Nursery Inc 302 653-7060
1575 Vandyke Greenspring Rd Smyrna (19977) *(G-13901)*

Stern & Eisenberg PC 302 731-7200
500 Creek View Rd Ste 304 Newark (19711) *(G-12101)*

Steve George Painting 302 616-1456
38578 Daina Dr Ocean View (19970) *(G-12570)*

Steve Styles 302 540-4965
2914 Lancaster Ave Wilmington (19805) *(G-20063)*

Steven Alban DDS PA 302 422-9637
3 Sussex Ave Milford (19963) *(G-8103)*

Steven Brown & Associates Inc 302 652-4722
9 S Cleveland Ave Wilmington (19805) *(G-20064)*

Steven E Diamond M D 302 655-8868
900 Foulk Rd Ste 200 Wilmington (19803) *(G-20065)*

Steven M Dellose 302 655-9494
1941 Limestone Rd Wilmington (19808) *(G-20066)*

Steven P Copp 302 645-9112
Rr 3 Box 254a Lewes (19958) *(G-6511)*

Steven Rogers 302 422-6285
6918 Shawnee Rd Milford (19963) *(G-8104)*

Steven Sachs Appraisal Access 302 477-9676
19 Brandywine Blvd Talleyville (19803) *(G-13947)*

Steven Soule 302 690-3052
7 Colony Blvd Apt 212 Wilmington (19802) *(G-20067)*

Steven T Miller 302 697-3541
1856 Honeysuckle Rd Camden Wyoming (19934) *(G-981)*

Stevens & James Inc 302 398-6066
15602 S Dupont Hwy Harrington (19952) *(G-4836)*

Stevens & Lee PC 302 654-5180
919 N Market St Ste 1300 Wilmington (19801) *(G-20068)*

Stevenson Ventures LLC 302 752-4449
26 N Walnut St Milford (19963) *(G-8105)*

Stewart and Martin, Wilmington *Also Called: Stewart Law Firm (G-20070)*

Stewart Bros Turf LLC 302 333-3707
1314 Birch Ln Wilmington (19809) *(G-20069)*

Stewart Law Firm 302 652-5200
301 N Market St Wilmington (19801) *(G-20070)*

Stewart Lender Services Inc 302 433-8047
2200 Concord Pike Ste 300 Wilmington (19803) *(G-20071)*

Stewart Management Company, Wilmington *Also Called: Virtual Business Entps LLC (G-20633)*

Stewart Valuation Services LLC 888 751-9234
2200 Concord Pike Ste 300 Wilmington (19803) *(G-20072)*

Stewart's Brewing Company, Bear *Also Called: Delaware Beer Works Inc (G-142)*

STI Landscape Solutions 302 645-6262
20144 John J Williams Hwy Lewes (19958) *(G-6512)*

Stick It Gymnastics 302 678-8780
12 Crawford Cir Wilmington (19805) *(G-20073)*

Stifel Trust Co Del Nat Assn 302 351-8900
100 S West St 1st Fl Wilmington (19801) *(G-20074)*

Stitch-Stash LLC 302 227-1943
102 N 1st St Rehoboth Beach (19971) *(G-12975)*

Stl & Associates LLC 302 359-2801
198 Greens Branch Ln Smyrna (19977) *(G-13902)*

Stm Consulting Inc 408 341-6900
2093a Philadelphia Pike Ste 133 Claymont (19703) *(G-1304)*

Stockley Materials LLC 302 856-7601
25154 Dupont Blvd Georgetown (19947) *(G-4526)*

Stockmarket 302 697-8878
2573 Woodlytown Rd Magnolia (19962) *(G-6785)*

Stokelan Estate Winery LLC 609 451-5535
4 Thornberry Ln Hockessin (19707) *(G-5391)*

Stokes Garage Inc 302 994-0613
101 Old Dupont Rd Wilmington (19805) *(G-20075)*

Stoltz Management, Wilmington *Also Called: Stoltz Realty Co (G-20077)*

Stoltz Real Estate Partners 302 654-3600
20 Montchanin Rd Ste 250 Wilmington (19807) *(G-20076)*

Stoltz Realty Co 302 798-8500
7120 Society Dr Claymont (19703) *(G-1305)*

Stoltz Realty Co (PA) 302 656-2852
3704 Kennett Pike Ste 200 Wilmington (19807) *(G-20077)*

Stoltz Realty Co 302 656-8543
1303 Delaware Ave Ste 101 Wilmington (19806) *(G-20078)*

Stoltzfus Mast, Dover *Also Called: Bay Developers Inc (G-1884)*

Stone Age Tile and Flooring 302 359-2166
90 Channel Xing Frederica (19946) *(G-4183)*

Stone Express 302 376-8876
5093 Summit Bridge Rd Middletown (19709) *(G-7600)*

Stone Harbor Square LLC 302 227-5227
42 Rehoboth Ave Ste 23 Rehoboth Beach (19971) *(G-12976)*

Stone Powerhouse Training 302 658-5077
2518 W 4th St Wilmington (19805) *(G-20079)*

Stone Shop, The, Wilmington *Also Called: Tile Market of Delaware LLC (G-20325)*

Stone Technologies 302 379-1759
110 Rodney Dr New Castle (19720) *(G-9595)*

Stonegate Granite 302 500-8081
25029 Dupont Blvd Georgetown (19947) *(G-4527)*

Stonegates, Wilmington *Also Called: Greenvlle Retirement Cmnty LLC (G-16975)*

Stonehammer Construction 302 233-3971
12284 S Dupont Hwy Felton (19943) *(G-4030)*

Stones and Cabinets City LLC 302 729-4201
93 Christiana Rd New Castle (19720) *(G-9596)*

Stones Soup Inc (PA) 803 835-7123
2035 Sunset Lake Rd B2 Newark (19702) *(G-12102)*

Stoneworks Lapidary 814 528-1468
23604 Woods Dr Lewes (19958) *(G-6513)*

Stoney Brook, Seaford *Also Called: Seaford Apartment Ventures LLC (G-13387)*

Stoney Btter Fmly Mdcine Assoc 302 234-9109
5311 Limestone Rd Ste 201 Wilmington (19808) *(G-20080)*

Stoneybrook Apartments, Claymont *Also Called: Stoneybrook Prsrvtion Assoc LL (G-1306)*

Stoneybrook Apartments, Wilmington *Also Called: Stoneybrook Associates LP (G-20081)*

Stoneybrook Apts, Claymont *Also Called: Leon N Weiner & Associates Inc (G-1215)*

Stoneybrook Associates LP ... 302 764-6450
4 Denny Rd Wilmington (19809) *(G-20081)*

Stoneybrook Prsrvtion Assoc LL ... 302 764-9430
1117 Cedartree Ct Claymont (19703) *(G-1306)*

Stop Traffic ... 302 604-1176
408 Circle Rd Millsboro (19966) *(G-8468)*

Stop Vlnce Pryer Chain Fndtion ... 302 513-9520
506 N Church St Wilmington (19801) *(G-20082)*

Stora Central LLC ... 929 273-0505
2055 Limestone Rd 200c Wilmington (19808) *(G-20083)*

Storage Rentals of America ... 302 838-7405
950 Red Lion Rd New Castle (19720) *(G-9597)*

Storage Rentals of America ... 302 786-0792
2523 Lamotte St Wilmington (19802) *(G-20084)*

Storage Rentals of America ... 302 313-1430
50 Dodson Ave Wilmington (19804) *(G-20085)*

Storage Squad LLC ... 830 200-0269
16192 Coastal Hwy Lewes (19958) *(G-6514)*

Storageos Inc (DH) ... 617 971-8470
910 Foulk Rd Ste 201 Wilmington (19803) *(G-20086)*

Storeskipper Inc ... 505 850-5878
651 N Broad St Ste 206 Middletown (19709) *(G-7601)*

Stork Electric Associates LLC ... 302 654-9427
530 Copper Dr Wilmington (19804) *(G-20087)*

Storm Energia Inc ... 404 550-4862
251 Little Falls Dr Wilmington (19808) *(G-20088)*

Stormx Inc ... 425 998-8762
8 The Grn Ste 1 Dover (19901) *(G-3613)*

Storyboards Inc ... 214 272-0222
2035 Sunset Lake Rd Newark (19702) *(G-12103)*

Storyiq Inc ... 718 801-8556
251 Little Falls Dr Wilmington (19808) *(G-20089)*

Stoudmire Media Group LLC ... 302 689-3151
2103 N Church St Wilmington (19802) *(G-20090)*

Stover Construction LLC ... 302 653-6195
5625 Dupont Pkwy Smyrna (19977) *(G-13903)*

Stovoo Inc ... 302 451-9589
256 Chapman Rd Ste 105-4 Newark (19702) *(G-12104)*

Str8up Games Inc ... 315 523-8216
8 The Grn Ste A Dover (19901) *(G-3614)*

Straight Line Striping LLC ... 302 228-3335
18473 Harbeson Rd Milton (19968) *(G-8716)*

Strands Prprty Prservation LLC ... 302 381-9792
26035 Oak St Ste 101 Millsboro (19966) *(G-8469)*

Strang & Edson LLC (PA) ... 917 664-0298
16192 Coastal Hwy Lewes (19958) *(G-6515)*

Strano-Feely Funeral Home, Newark *Also Called: Delaware Prof Fnrl Svcs Inc (G-10471)*

Strategic Fund Raising Inc (PA) ... 651 649-0404
300 Delaware Ave Ste 1370 Wilmington (19801) *(G-20091)*

Strategic Integration LLC ... 714 227-0142
651 N Broad St Middletown (19709) *(G-7602)*

Strategic Solutions Intl Inc ... 302 525-6313
700 Barksdale Rd Ste 6 Newark (19711) *(G-12105)*

Strategic Wealth Cons Inc (PA) ... 601 715-4174
8 The Grn Ste B Dover (19901) *(G-3615)*

Strategy House Inc ... 302 658-1500
231 Executive Dr Ste 15 Newark (19702) *(G-12106)*

Strategybrix LLC (PA) ... 312 804-6768
16192 Coastal Hwy Lewes (19958) *(G-6516)*

Stratgic Slar Sltons Ltd Lblty ... 703 307-6761
2 Glade Cir E Rehoboth Beach (19971) *(G-12977)*

Stratis Visuals LLC ... 860 482-1208
20 Tyler Way Ste 102 Newark (19713) *(G-12107)*

Stratos Holdings Inc ... 800 927-9800
251 Little Falls Dr Wilmington (19808) *(G-20092)*

Stratus Building Solutions ... 302 414-9749
625 Dawson Dr Ste D Newark (19713) *(G-12108)*

Strave, Lewes *Also Called: New Live Ventures Inc (G-6311)*

Streak Free Clg By Ptticom LLC ... 302 261-6933
130 Bernice Dr Bear (19701) *(G-513)*

Stream, Wilmington *Also Called: Stream App LLC (G-20093)*

Stream App LLC ... 610 420-5864
1500 Lancaster Ave Wilmington (19805) *(G-20093)*

Streameq Inc (PA) ... 951 807-4938
16192 Coastal Hwy Lewes (19958) *(G-6517)*

Streamline Technologies Inc ... 302 383-3146
3516 Silverside Rd Ste 20 Wilmington (19810) *(G-20094)*

Streamlners MGT Consulting LLC ... 864 884-5064
1201 N Orange St Ste 7088 Wilmington (19801) *(G-20095)*

Street & Ellis P A ... 302 735-8408
426 S State St Dover (19901) *(G-3616)*

Street Core Utility Service ... 302 239-4110
501 Erickson Ave Hockessin (19707) *(G-5392)*

Street Knowledge Book Ctr LLC ... 888 401-1114
1902b Maryland Ave Wilmington (19805) *(G-20096)*

Strength For Jurney Counseling ... 302 367-4266
99 Paladin Dr Wilmington (19802) *(G-20097)*

Stretch 1 LLC (PA) ... 253 255-7345
4120 Concord Pike Ste B Wilmington (19803) *(G-20098)*

Stretched Out Trucking, Harbeson *Also Called: K&D Inc (G-4704)*

Stretchplex LLC ... 302 696-5966
722 Yorklyn Rd Ste 200 Hockessin (19707) *(G-5393)*

Stride Services Inc ... 302 540-4713
200 Powder Mill Rd Wilmington (19803) *(G-20099)*

Stride-360 Incorporated (PA) ... 302 421-5752
1013 Centre Rd Ste 403a Wilmington (19805) *(G-20100)*

Strike Exchange Inc ... 310 995-5653
16192 Coastal Hwy Lewes (19958) *(G-6518)*

Strike Social, Lewes *Also Called: Strike Exchange Inc (G-6518)*

Stripe-A-Lot Inc ... 302 654-9175
55 Germay Dr Wilmington (19804) *(G-20101)*

Strobert Tree Services ... 302 633-3478
1506 A St Wilmington (19801) *(G-20102)*

Strobert Tree Services Inc ... 302 475-7089
1806 Zebley Rd Wilmington (19810) *(G-20103)*

Stryker Chiropractic, Wilmington *Also Called: Howmedica Osteonics Corp (G-17220)*

Stuart Ja Inc ... 302 378-8299
102 Albe Dr Newark (19702) *(G-12109)*

Stuart Kingston Galleries Inc ... 302 652-7978
3704 Kennett Pike Wilmington (19807) *(G-20104)*

Stuart Kingston Inc (PA) ... 302 227-2524
19470 Coastal Hwy Unit 1 Rehoboth Beach (19971) *(G-12978)*

Stuart Kingston Jewelers, Wilmington *Also Called: Stuart Kingston Galleries Inc (G-20104)*

Stucco Repairs ... 302 442-0795
114 Willow Grove Mill Dr Middletown (19709) *(G-7603)*

Student Health Service, Newark *Also Called: University of Delaware (G-12281)*

Student Media Group ... 302 607-2580
500 Creek View Rd Ste 3e Newark (19711) *(G-12110)*

Studio 11 ... 302 622-9959
2301 Penns Ave Apt D Wilmington (19806) *(G-20105)*

Studio 13 Skin By Christina ... 302 258-4205
13 Shallcross Pl Middletown (19709) *(G-7604)*

Studio 923 ... 302 276-1413
724 Pulaski Hwy Bear (19701) *(G-514)*

Studio B Milford LLC ... 302 491-7910
110 Ne Front St Milford (19963) *(G-8106)*

Studio Green Apartments ... 302 544-9070
91 Thorn Ln Newark (19711) *(G-12111)*

Studio Groups Inc ... 302 998-7895
1305 N Franklin St Wilmington (19806) *(G-20106)*

Studio Jaed, Bear *Also Called: Jaed Corporation (G-295)*

Studio On 24 Inc ... 302 644-4424
20231 John J Williams Hwy Lewes (19958) *(G-6519)*

Studio302 ... 302 462-0857
3046 Hazlettville Rd Dover (19904) *(G-3617)*

Studio43 ... 302 539-8577
43 Woodland Ave Ocean View (19970) *(G-12571)*

Studium Inc ... 614 402-0359
251 Little Falls Dr Wilmington (19808) *(G-20107)*

Stumpf Vickers and Sandy ... 302 856-3561
8 W Market St Georgetown (19947) *(G-4528)*

Stumpys Hatchet House ... 302 378-4737
819 Middletown Warwick Rd Unit E2 Middletown (19709) *(G-7605)*

Style 2 Fitness.. 215 254-0221
2353 Carpenter Station Rd Wilmington (19810) *(G-20108)*

Stylere LLC... 650 206-7721
8 The Grn Ste A Dover (19901) *(G-3618)*

Styles By US.. 302 629-3244
324 E Stein Hwy Seaford (19973) *(G-13415)*

Styles Celebrity... 302 286-7825
230 University Plz Newark (19702) *(G-12112)*

Styles Divine Unlimited...................................... 302 409-4612
310 N Main St Bldg C Smyrna (19977) *(G-13904)*

Styles II, Wilmington Also Called: Kelf LLC *(G-17678)*

Stylin Image... 302 407-8698
1007 Vinings Way Newark (19702) *(G-12113)*

Styling Her Esteem.. 302 494-1010
10 Swansea Ln Newark (19702) *(G-12114)*

Stylish Stylus, The, Bear Also Called: Envision It Publications LLC *(G-204)*

Subaru Investment Inc...................................... 302 472-9266
301 N Market St Wilmington (19801) *(G-20109)*

Subcodevs Inc.. 704 234-6780
919 N Market St Wilmington (19801) *(G-20110)*

Subcool Heating & Air Inc.................................. 302 442-5658
112 E Van Buren Ave New Castle (19720) *(G-9598)*

Suber Tanisha Lashay Lpn................................ 215 910-8361
143 Chestnut Crossing Dr Apt H Newark (19713) *(G-12115)*

Submix Holdings Inc... 858 336-6467
1007 N Orange St Wilmington (19801) *(G-20111)*

Subscript Inc.. 302 470-8144
2093 Philadelphia Pike Ste 5554 Claymont (19703) *(G-1307)*

Suburban Farmhouse.. 302 250-6254
107 Federal St Milton (19968) *(G-8717)*

Suburban Floor Coverings................................. 302 430-8494
35514 Copper Dr S Rehoboth Beach (19971) *(G-12979)*

Suburban Intrnal Medcne Assocs........................ 302 654-4800
1403 N Rodney St Wilmington (19806) *(G-20112)*

Suburban Lawn & Equipment Inc (PA)................. 302 475-4300
1601 Naamans Rd Wilmington (19810) *(G-20113)*

Suburban Marketing Associates (PA).................. 302 656-8440
3301 Lancaster Pike 5c Wilmington (19805) *(G-20114)*

Suburban Plaza Merchants Assn......................... 302 737-8072
226 Suburban Dr Newark (19711) *(G-12116)*

Suburban Psychiatric Svcs LLC.......................... 302 999-9834
5177 W Woodmill Dr Ste 6 Wilmington (19808) *(G-20115)*

Suburban Publishing Inc (PA)............................ 302 656-1809
3301 Lancaster Pike Ste 5c Wilmington (19805) *(G-20116)*

Suburban Waste Services Inc............................ 302 661-0161
120 Dock St Wilmington (19801) *(G-20117)*

Success Wont Wait Inc..................................... 302 388-9669
1729 Marsh Rd Wilmington (19810) *(G-20118)*

Succulents Soap Sand Scents........................... 302 757-0697
103 Rockrose Dr Newark (19711) *(G-12117)*

Suck It Up Inc.. 410 258-8023
30310 Adams Rd Dagsboro (19939) *(G-1510)*

Suez Water Delaware Inc.................................. 302 633-5900
2000 First State Blvd Wilmington (19804) *(G-20119)*

Suffex Conservation... 302 856-2105
23818 Shortly Rd Georgetown (19947) *(G-4529)*

Suffex County Ems, Georgetown Also Called: County of Sussex *(G-4270)*

Sug Biosciences LLC.. 305 735-7009
251 Little Falls Dr Wilmington (19808) *(G-20120)*

Sugardumplin... 302 423-8810
316 Peach Peddler Path Dover (19901) *(G-3619)*

Sugarhill International...................................... 302 275-9257
4111 Claremont Ct Wilmington (19808) *(G-20121)*

Sui Trading Co.. 302 239-2012
406 Hawthorne Ct E Hockessin (19707) *(G-5394)*

Suk-Young Carr DDS.. 302 736-6231
850 S State St Ste 2 Dover (19901) *(G-3620)*

Sully Fl, Wilmington Also Called: Goodtymes Inc *(G-16926)*

Sum-R-Fun Pool Products Inc (PA).................... 302 998-9288
5815 Kirkwood Hwy Wilmington (19808) *(G-20122)*

Summer Consultants Inc................................... 484 493-4150
131 Continental Dr Ste 302 Newark (19713) *(G-12118)*

Summer Hill Custom Home Bldr......................... 302 462-5853
70 Atlantic Ave Ocean View (19970) *(G-12572)*

Summer Lrng Collaborative Inc........................... 302 757-3940
1200 N French St Wilmington (19801) *(G-20123)*

Summerfield Elec Solutions LLC........................ 302 824-3045
1633 Clayton Delaney Rd Clayton (19938) *(G-1407)*

Summers Logging LLC..................................... 302 234-8725
364 Skyline Orchard Dr Hockessin (19707) *(G-5395)*

Summit, Hockessin Also Called: Summit At Hockessin *(G-5396)*

Summit At Hockessin.. 302 235-8388
5850 Limestone Rd Hockessin (19707) *(G-5396)*

Summit Bridge Inv Prpts LLC............................. 410 499-1456
912 Westerly Ct Newark (19702) *(G-12119)*

Summit Bridge Vet Hosp LLC............................ 302 834-7387
3930 Red Lion Rd Bear (19701) *(G-515)*

Summit Centre Tr... 302 690-7235
2143 Choptank Rd Middletown (19709) *(G-7606)*

Summit Fitness 180.. 610 574-3587
1013 Woodstream Dr Wilmington (19810) *(G-20124)*

Summit Heating and AC LLC (PA)...................... 302 378-1203
4361 Dupont Pkwy Townsend (19734) *(G-14074)*

Summit Industrial Corporation........................... 302 368-2718
93 Albe Dr Ste A Newark (19702) *(G-12120)*

Summit Mechanical Inc..................................... 302 836-8814
304 Carson Dr Bear (19701) *(G-516)*

Summit Mechanical Inc..................................... 302 373-1132
106 Canal Way Newark (19702) *(G-12121)*

Summit North Marina.. 302 836-1800
3000 Summit Harbour Pl Bear (19701) *(G-517)*

Summit North Marina, Bear Also Called: Summit North Marina LLC *(G-518)*

Summit North Marina LLC................................. 302 836-1800
3000 Summit Harbour Pl Bear (19701) *(G-518)*

Summit Orthopaedic HM Care LLC.................... 302 703-0800
35745 Black Marlin Dr Lewes (19958) *(G-6520)*

Summit Pike Creek, Newark Also Called: Summit Properties Inc *(G-12122)*

Summit Properties Inc...................................... 302 737-3747
100 Red Fox Ln Bldg 100 Newark (19711) *(G-12122)*

Summit Retirement Community.......................... 888 933-2300
5850 Limestone Rd Ofc 1 Hockessin (19707) *(G-5397)*

Summit Steel Inc.. 302 325-3220
201 Edwards Ave New Castle (19720) *(G-9599)*

Summit Tax Solutions LLC................................ 302 464-1016
5 Brady Cir Middletown (19709) *(G-7607)*

Sumter Contracting Corp.................................. 703 323-7210
36504 Pine Grove Ln Ocean View (19970) *(G-12573)*

Sumthin3Ise... 302 272-5435
8 The Grn Ste 11105 Dover (19901) *(G-3621)*

Sumuri LLC.. 302 570-0015
40 S Main St Magnolia (19962) *(G-6786)*

Sun Behavioral Delaware LLC............................ 732 747-1800
21655 Biden Ave Georgetown (19947) *(G-4530)*

Sun Coal & Coke LLC....................................... 630 824-1000
2401 Penns Ave Ste 111 Wilmington (19806) *(G-20125)*

Sun Construction Inc.. 267 767-5047
22465 Holly Oak Ln Lewes (19958) *(G-6521)*

Sun Dazed Tanning.. 302 430-0150
280 N Rehoboth Blvd Milford (19963) *(G-8107)*

Sun East Federal Credit Union........................... 610 485-2960
3630 Concord Pike Wilmington (19803) *(G-20126)*

Sun Exchange Inc (PA)..................................... 917 747-9527
16192 Coastal Hwy 1 Lewes (19958) *(G-6522)*

Sun Gas & Diesel... 302 376-8200
1228 Middletown Warwick Rd Middletown (19709) *(G-7608)*

Sun Hotel Inc... 302 322-0711
232 S Dupont Hwy New Castle (19720) *(G-9600)*

Sun Marine Maintenance Inc............................. 302 539-6756
35322 Bayard Rd Frankford (19945) *(G-4149)*

Sun Pharmaceuticals Corp................................ 302 678-6000
50 S Dupont Hwy Dover (19901) *(G-3622)*

Sun Piledriving Equipment LLC......................... 302 539-6756
35322 Bayard Rd Frankford (19945) *(G-4150)*

Sun West Homes, Wilmington *Also Called: Southwest American Corp* **(G-19940)**

Sun-In-One Inc... 302 762-3100
500 Philadelphia Pike Ste 1 Wilmington (19809) **(G-20127)**

Sun-Ray Valley Investments LLC........................... 302 406-1078
1201 N Market St Ste 111 Wilmington (19801) **(G-20128)**

Sunbelt Rentals Inc.. 302 907-1921
36412 Sussex Hwy Delmar (19940) **(G-1638)**

Sunbelt Rentals Inc.. 302 322-5394
3120 New Castle Ave New Castle (19720) **(G-9601)**

Sunbelt Rentals Inc.. 302 669-0595
453 Pulaski Hwy New Castle (19720) **(G-9602)**

Sunchemical, Newport *Also Called: Colors & Effects USA LLC* **(G-12444)**

Sundae Body LLC.. 480 430-5675
221 N Broad St Ste 3a Middletown (19709) **(G-7609)**

Sundari Kula LLC... 302 373-7538
5244 Summit Bridge Rd Middletown (19709) **(G-7610)**

Sunday Breakfast Mission...................................... 302 656-8542
600 E 5th St Apt C1 Wilmington (19801) **(G-20129)**

Sundew Painting Inc.. 302 994-7004
500 S Colonial Ave Wilmington (19805) **(G-20130)**

Sundew Painting Inc.. 302 684-5858
26836 Lewes Georgetown Hwy Ste B1e Harbeson (19951) **(G-4717)**

Sunflixx LLC.. 302 206-0859
4 Peddlers Row Unit 150 Newark (19702) **(G-12123)**

Sunflowers... 302 731-3150
503 Nottingham Rd Newark (19711) **(G-12124)**

Sungard, Wilmington *Also Called: Fis Investment Ventures LLC* **(G-16643)**

Sunglobal Technologies, Wilmington *Also Called: Vensoft Solutions Inc* **(G-20580)**

Sunkist Tanning Inc... 302 539-8269
1300 Coastal Hwy Fenwick Island (19944) **(G-4055)**

Sunlife LLC... 833 478-6669
3 Germay Dr Unit 4-1478 Wilmington (19804) **(G-20131)**

Sunlight Insur Holdings LLC................................... 952 808-6312
1209 N Orange St Wilmington (19801) **(G-20132)**

Sunlight Salon LLC.. 302 456-1799
610 Plaza Dr Newark (19702) **(G-12125)**

Sunlite Energy Intll... 302 598-2984
112 The Strand Apt C Historic New Castle (19720) **(G-5077)**

Sunny Gallery LLC... 302 757-3960
349 Matthew Flocco Dr Newark (19713) **(G-12126)**

Sunny Hospitality LLC... 302 226-0700
36012 Airport Rd Rehoboth Beach (19971) **(G-12980)**

Sunny Hospitality LLC... 302 398-3900
1259 Corn Crib Rd Harrington (19952) **(G-4837)**

Sunnyfield Contractors Inc..................................... 302 674-8610
150 Sunnyfield Ln Dover (19904) **(G-3623)**

Sunnymac LLC... 844 786-6962
413 8th Ave Wilmington (19805) **(G-20133)**

Sunnymac Solar, Wilmington *Also Called: Sunnymac LLC* **(G-20133)**

Sunnyville Resort LLC (PA)..................................... 706 255-9765
128 Sunset Blvd Ste 1365 New Castle (19720) **(G-9603)**

Sunnyworld LLC.. 240 506-8870
19513 Manchester Dr Rehoboth Beach (19971) **(G-12981)**

Sunrise Medical Center... 302 854-9006
29339 Iron Branch Rd Millsboro (19966) **(G-8470)**

Sunrise of Wilmington, Wilmington *Also Called: Sunrise Senior Living LLC* **(G-20134)**

Sunrise RE Partners LLC.. 302 644-0300
18334 Coastal Hwy Lewes (19958) **(G-6523)**

Sunrise Real Estate... 302 313-9949
75 Lake Ave Rehoboth Beach (19971) **(G-12982)**

Sunrise Senior Living LLC...................................... 302 475-9163
2215 Shipley Rd Wilmington (19803) **(G-20134)**

Sunset Property Management................................ 410 202-1679
23 S Woodward Ave Wilmington (19805) **(G-20135)**

Sunshine Cleaning Services LLC........................... 302 430-8416
5138 Boyce Rd Seaford (19973) **(G-13416)**

Sunshine Health... 302 463-7600
411 Rochelle Ave Wilmington (19804) **(G-20136)**

Sunshine Home Childcare...................................... 302 674-2009
370 Mimosa Ave Dover (19904) **(G-3624)**

Sunshine Kids Academy... 302 444-4270
25 Paynter St Bear (19701) **(G-519)**

Sunshine Nut Company LLC (PA)........................... 781 352-7766
16192 Coastal Hwy Lewes (19958) **(G-6524)**

Sunshine Nutrition LLC... 971 456-1000
16192 Coastal Hwy Lewes (19958) **(G-6525)**

Sunshine Vending Machines LLC........................... 800 670-6557
1207 Delaware Ave Ste 775 Wilmington (19806) **(G-20137)**

Sunstates Security LLC.. 866 710-2019
10 Corporate Cir Ste 220 New Castle (19720) **(G-9604)**

SunTrust Delaware Trust Co................................... 302 892-9930
1011 Centre Rd Ste 205 Wilmington (19805) **(G-20138)**

Sunu Consulting LLC... 202 534-5864
8 The Grn Ste A Dover (19901) **(G-3625)**

Sunwise Drmatology Surgery LLC......................... 302 378-7981
102 Sleepy Hollow Dr Ste 203 Middletown (19709) **(G-7611)**

Super 8 By Wyndham Newark De, Newark *Also Called: Canon Hospitality MGT LLC* **(G-10130)**

Super 8 Motel, Dover *Also Called: Super Eight Dover* **(G-3626)**

Super 8 Motel, Harrington *Also Called: Gulab Management Inc* **(G-4776)**

Super 8 Motel, Harrington *Also Called: Routzhan Jessman* **(G-4822)**

Super 8 Motel, Milford *Also Called: Gulab Management Inc* **(G-7914)**

Super 8 Motel, New Castle *Also Called: Eastern Hospitality Management* **(G-9079)**

Super C Inc... 302 533-6024
226 W General Grey Ct Newark (19702) **(G-12127)**

Super Eight Dover.. 302 734-5701
348 N Dupont Hwy Dover (19901) **(G-3626)**

Super Heat.. 302 276-0689
26 Parkway Cir New Castle (19720) **(G-9605)**

Super Service Automotive Inc................................ 302 464-1149
610 Tower Ln Middletown (19709) **(G-7612)**

Super Wash... 302 384-6111
1952 Maryland Ave Wilmington (19805) **(G-20139)**

Superbrewed Food Inc (PA)..................................... 302 220-4760
239 Lisa Dr New Castle (19720) **(G-9606)**

Supercritical Fluid Tech... 302 738-3420
120 Sandy Dr Ste 2b Newark (19713) **(G-12128)**

Supercritical Fluid Tech Inc (PA)............................ 302 738-3420
1 Innovation Way Ste 303 Newark (19711) **(G-12129)**

SUPERCRITICAL FLUID TECHNOLOGIES, INC, Newark *Also Called: Supercritical Fluid Tech* **(G-12128)**

Supercuts... 302 698-1988
374 Walmart Dr Camden (19934) **(G-894)**

Supercuts... 302 422-8448
28257 Lexus Dr Milford (19963) **(G-8108)**

Supercuts... 302 934-6534
26670 Centerview Dr Millsboro (19966) **(G-8471)**

Supercuts... 302 644-4288
18701 Coastal Hwy Unit 7 Rehoboth Beach (19971) **(G-12983)**

Supercuts, Bear *Also Called: GL Robins Co Inc* **(G-248)**

Supercuts, Camden *Also Called: Supercuts* **(G-894)**

Supercuts, Milford *Also Called: Supercuts* **(G-8108)**

Supercuts, Millsboro *Also Called: Supercuts* **(G-8471)**

Supercuts, Rehoboth Beach *Also Called: Supercuts* **(G-12983)**

Supercuts, Wilmington *Also Called: GL Robins Co Inc* **(G-16874)**

Supercuts, Wilmington *Also Called: GL Robins Co Inc* **(G-16875)**

Superior Dedicated Svcs LLC................................. 443 497-4410
10957 Salt Barn Rd Laurel (19956) **(G-5608)**

Superior Drywall Inc.. 302 732-9800
30996 Country Gdns Ste R1 Dagsboro (19939) **(G-1511)**

Superior Electric Service Co.................................. 302 658-5949
36 Germay Dr Wilmington (19804) **(G-20140)**

Superior Equipment Rental Co............................... 302 658-6193
36 Germay Dr Wilmington (19804) **(G-20141)**

Superior Exterior Contracting................................ 302 287-8391
1261 Old Wilmington Rd Hockessin (19707) **(G-5398)**

Superior Lawncare LLC... 302 373-3289
180 Black Stallion Rd Townsend (19734) **(G-14075)**

Superior Luxe LLC... 800 325-6262
1501 Concord Pike Ste 303 Wilmington (19803) **(G-20142)**

Superior Maids... 302 284-2012
1391 Chandlers Rd Felton (19943) **(G-4031)**

Superior Metals Alloys USA Inc.............................. 860 208-6438
200 Continental Dr Ste 401 Newark (19713) **(G-12130)**

ALPHABETIC SECTION

Superior Outdoor LLC.. 302 841-9827
14456 Redden Rd Bridgeville (19933) *(G-770)*

Superior Screen & Glass.. 302 541-5399
1 Town Rd Ocean View (19970) *(G-12574)*

Superior Sealing Services D... 610 717-6237
613 Pulaski Hwy Bear (19701) *(G-520)*

Superior Services Group LLC.. 888 683-8288
2207 Concord Pike Unit 147 Wilmington (19803) *(G-20143)*

Superior Yardworks Inc... 610 274-2255
211 Cherry Blossom Pl Hockessin (19707) *(G-5399)*

Superlative Image LLC... 714 369-5412
4023 Kennett Pike Wilmington (19807) *(G-20144)*

Superlodge.. 302 654-5544
1213 N West St Wilmington (19801) *(G-20145)*

Supermarket Associates Inc.. 302 547-1977
4001 Kennett Pike Wilmington (19807) *(G-20146)*

Superops, Claymont *Also Called: Superops Inc (G-1308)*

Superops Inc... 510 330-2676
2093 Philadelphia Pike # 2105 Claymont (19703) *(G-1308)*

Superpower Entertainment LLC (PA)...................................... 650 667-0266
251 Little Falls Dr Wilmington (19808) *(G-20147)*

Superstar Holdings Inc... 302 289-8931
8 The Grn Ste A Dover (19901) *(G-3627)*

Supper Solutions LLC.. 302 478-5935
3619 Silverside Rd Wilmington (19810) *(G-20148)*

Supply Chain Consultants Inc.. 302 738-9215
5460 Fairmont Dr Wilmington (19808) *(G-20149)*

Supply Chain Mgmt Inc.. 302 467-2014
3524 Silverside Rd Wilmington (19810) *(G-20150)*

Support Services Group Inc... 404 939-1782
8 The Grn Ste A Dover (19901) *(G-3628)*

Support.com, Wilmington *Also Called: Supportcom Inc (G-20151)*

Supportcom Inc (HQ).. 650 556-9440
1521 Concord Pike Ste 301 Wilmington (19803) *(G-20151)*

Supportive Accountability Hub... 615 579-3533
1209 N Orange St Wilmington (19801) *(G-20152)*

Supportive Care Solutions LLC.. 302 598-4797
1606 Newport Gap Pike Wilmington (19808) *(G-20153)*

Supportyourapp Inc.. 888 959-3556
1007 N Orange St Ste 122 Wilmington (19801) *(G-20154)*

Supreme Cleanerz, Wilmington *Also Called: Supreme Servicez LLC (G-20158)*

Supreme Court United States.. 302 252-2950
824 N Market St Wilmington (19801) *(G-20155)*

Supreme Legacy Inc... 973 567-3115
2705 N Madison St Wilmington (19802) *(G-20156)*

Supreme Lending... 302 268-6244
2710 Centerville Rd Wilmington (19808) *(G-20157)*

Supreme Servicez LLC... 302 932-5724
2212 Kirkwood Hwy Wilmington (19805) *(G-20158)*

Supreme Trading LLC.. 302 415-3188
3524 Silverside Rd Ste 35 B Wilmington (19810) *(G-20159)*

Sure Good Foods USA LLC.. 905 288-1136
40 E Main St Ste 1187 Newark (19711) *(G-12131)*

Sure Line Electrical Inc... 302 856-3110
281 W Commerce St Georgetown (19947) *(G-4531)*

Suresrce Cmmdties LLC - Orgnic.. 866 697-5960
1201 N Market St Ste 111 Wilmington (19801) *(G-20160)*

Surestay, Wilmington *Also Called: Jaysons LLC (G-17502)*

Suretronix Solutions LLC... 302 407-3146
111 Brookside Dr Wilmington (19804) *(G-20161)*

Surf and Soul Yoga... 302 539-5861
1401 Bora Bora St Fenwick Island (19944) *(G-4056)*

Surf Club... 302 227-7059
1 Read Ave Dewey Beach (19971) *(G-1675)*

Surf N Suds Laundries... 302 836-9120
20 Foxhunt Dr Bear (19701) *(G-521)*

Surface Protection, Wilmington *Also Called: Chemours Company Fc LLC (G-15357)*

Surge Automated Inc.. 800 457-9713
16192 Coastal Hwy Lewes (19958) *(G-6526)*

Surge Networks Inc.. 206 432-5047
2035 Sunset Lake Rd B2 Newark (19702) *(G-12132)*

Surgical Assoc of Newark... 302 737-4990
324 E Main St Newark (19711) *(G-12133)*

Surgical Associates PA.. 302 346-4502
200 Banning St Ste 200 Dover (19904) *(G-3629)*

Surgical Critical Assoc... 302 623-4370
4735 Ogletown Stanton Rd # 3301 Newark (19713) *(G-12134)*

Surgical Focus.. 215 518-2138
20 W Kilts Ln Middletown (19709) *(G-7613)*

Surgical Nanticoke Assoc PA... 302 629-8662
543 N Shipley St Ste A Seaford (19973) *(G-13417)*

Surplus & Excess Line Ltd... 302 653-5016
4 Village Sq Ste 900 Smyrna (19977) *(G-13905)*

Surrender House.. 302 249-6830
28124 Layton Davis Rd Millsboro (19966) *(G-8472)*

Survey Supply Inc.. 302 422-3338
726 Mccolley St Milford (19963) *(G-8109)*

Survivors Abuse In Rcovery Inc... 302 651-0181
405 Foulk Rd Wilmington (19803) *(G-20162)*

Susan C Over PC.. 302 660-2913
724 Yorklyn Rd Ste 250 Hockessin (19707) *(G-5400)*

Susan Donges... 302 645-3100
32060 Long Neck Rd Millsboro (19966) *(G-8473)*

Susan J Betts Od.. 302 629-6691
8500 Herring Run Rd Seaford (19973) *(G-13418)*

Susan J Howlett.. 302 670-1055
32 Canvasback Cir Bridgeville (19933) *(G-771)*

Susan Kelly MD... 302 644-9080
431 Savannah Rd Lewes (19958) *(G-6527)*

Susan L Barton... 302 655-3953
405 Foulk Rd Wilmington (19803) *(G-20163)*

Susan McClain.. 302 655-5877
2401 Pennsylvania Ave Wilmington (19806) *(G-20164)*

Susan Peet Rn.. 302 945-5228
21476 Willow Ln Lewes (19958) *(G-6528)*

Susan R Austin... 302 322-4685
103 Lesley Ln New Castle (19720) *(G-9607)*

Susan S Bryde.. 302 239-2343
700 Lantana Dr Hockessin (19707) *(G-5401)*

Susan T Fischer.. 302 832-2570
57 Avignon Dr Newark (19702) *(G-12135)*

Sussex Aero Maintenance, Georgetown *Also Called: Georgetown Air Services LLC (G-4334)*

Sussex Amateur Radio Assn.. 302 629-4949
22907 Dogwood Dr Lewes (19958) *(G-6529)*

Sussex Central High Schoo... 304 261-2873
31 Hosier St Selbyville (19975) *(G-13610)*

Sussex Cmnty Crsis Hsing Svcs.. 302 856-2246
204 E North St Georgetown (19947) *(G-4532)*

Sussex Cnty Hbtat For Hmnity I.. 302 855-1153
206 Academy St Georgetown (19947) *(G-4533)*

Sussex Cnty Snior Svcs Adult D.. 302 854-2882
20520 Sand Hill Rd Georgetown (19947) *(G-4534)*

Sussex Conservation District... 302 856-2105
23818 Shortly Rd Georgetown (19947) *(G-4535)*

Sussex Correctional Instn, Georgetown *Also Called: Delaware Department Correction (G-4279)*

Sussex County Volunteer... 302 515-3020
546 S Bedford St Georgetown (19947) *(G-4536)*

Sussex Diesel Inc... 302 877-0330
31051 Old Sailor Rd Laurel (19956) *(G-5609)*

Sussex Eye Care & Medical Asso.. 302 644-8007
1306 Savannah Rd Lewes (19958) *(G-6530)*

Sussex Eye Center PA (PA)... 302 856-2020
502 W Market St Georgetown (19947) *(G-4537)*

Sussex Family Counseling LLC... 302 864-7970
26114 Kits Burrow Ct Georgetown (19947) *(G-4538)*

Sussex Fence Co.. 302 945-7008
32524 Morning View Ln Millsboro (19966) *(G-8474)*

Sussex Fencing.. 302 945-7008
John J Williams Hwy Millsboro (19966) *(G-8475)*

Sussex Financial Services Inc... 302 227-7814
804 King Charles Ave Rehoboth Beach (19971) *(G-12984)*

ALPHABETIC SECTION

Sussex Heating and Air LLC..302 231-8446
153 Teal Dr Millsboro (19966) *(G-8476)*

Sussex Home Imprv Contr LLC......................................302 855-9679
14 Evergreen Dr Georgetown (19947) *(G-4539)*

Sussex Machine Works Inc..302 875-7958
11432 Trussum Pond Rd Laurel (19956) *(G-5610)*

Sussex Marine Construction Inc.....................................302 436-9680
32469 Frankford School Rd Frankford (19945) *(G-4151)*

Sussex Medical Center, Seaford *Also Called: Paul H Aguillon MD (G-13331)*

Sussex Montessori..302 404-5367
24960 Dairy Ln Seaford (19973) *(G-13419)*

Sussex Pain Relief Center LLC.......................................302 519-0100
18229 Dupont Blvd Georgetown (19947) *(G-4540)*

Sussex Pines Country Club..302 856-6283
22426 Sussex Pines Rd Georgetown (19947) *(G-4541)*

Sussex Plmnary Endocrine Cnslt....................................302 249-9970
23 Patriots Way Rehoboth Beach (19971) *(G-12985)*

Sussex Plumbing & Heating...302 344-2199
14320 Shiloh Way Laurel (19956) *(G-5611)*

Sussex Podiatry Group..302 645-8555
1532 Savannah Rd Lewes (19958) *(G-6531)*

Sussex Post..302 629-5505
37 N Walnut St Milford (19963) *(G-8110)*

Sussex Pregnancy Care Center......................................302 856-4344
5 Burger King Dr Georgetown (19947) *(G-4542)*

Sussex Printing Corp...302 629-9303
24904 Sussex Hwy Seaford (19973) *(G-13420)*

Sussex Protection Service LLC......................................302 832-5700
126 Sandy Dr Newark (19713) *(G-12136)*

Sussex Prschool Erly Care Ctrs.....................................302 732-7529
126 N Shipley St Seaford (19973) *(G-13421)*

Sussex Regen Specialists..302 727-6669
18229 Dupont Blvd Georgetown (19947) *(G-4543)*

Sussex Sand & Gravel Inc..302 628-6962
22223 Eskridge Rd Seaford (19973) *(G-13422)*

Sussex Sands Inc..302 539-8200
1501 Coastal Hwy Fenwick Island (19944) *(G-4057)*

Sussex Shores Beach Assn..302 539-7511
Bethany Beach (19930) *(G-643)*

Sussex Shores Water Co Corp..302 539-7611
39602 Water Works Ct Bethany Beach (19930) *(G-644)*

Sussex Superior Tools Inc...302 752-6817
25269 Mastermark Ln Millsboro (19966) *(G-8477)*

Sussex Tree Inc..302 629-9899
20350 Nelson Dr Bridgeville (19933) *(G-772)*

Sussex Veterinary Hospital..302 732-9433
30053 Vine St Rd Dagsboro (19939) *(G-1512)*

SUSTAINABLE ENERGY, Dover *Also Called: Delaware Sstnble Enrgy Utility (G-2262)*

Sustainable Envmtl MGT LLC...302 832-8000
755 Governor Lea Rd New Castle (19720) *(G-9608)*

Sustainable Generation, Wilmington *Also Called: Sustainable-Generation LLC (G-20165)*

Sustainable-Generation LLC..917 678-6947
110 S Poplar St Ste 400 Wilmington (19801) *(G-20165)*

Sute Media Inc (PA)..617 774-9499
16192 Coastal Hwy Lewes (19958) *(G-6532)*

Sutton Bus & Truck Co Inc..302 995-7444
5609 Old Capitol Trl Frnt Wilmington (19808) *(G-20166)*

Suzanne Isenberg...302 470-1166
103a Rogers Rd Wilmington (19801) *(G-20167)*

Suzanne S Townsend..302 593-6253
774 Christiana Rd Ste 201 Newark (19713) *(G-12137)*

Suzette Noecker...301 814-8003
27066 Lightning Run Millville (19967) *(G-8548)*

Svastijaya Daviratanasilp MD...302 424-3694
201 W Liberty Way Milford (19963) *(G-8111)*

Svea Real Estate Group LLC (PA)..................................855 262-9665
1675 S State St Ste B Dover (19901) *(G-3630)*

Svn Delaware LLC...302 536-1838
26673 Sussex Hwy Seaford (19973) *(G-13423)*

Swahs, New Castle *Also Called: Smiths Work At HM Slutions LLC (G-9575)*

Swain Excavation Inc..302 422-4349
18678 Sherman Ave Unit 1 Lincoln (19960) *(G-6705)*

Swami Contractor, Wilmington *Also Called: Nagin C Patel (G-18520)*

Swami Enterprises Inc...302 999-8077
1702 Faulkland Rd Wilmington (19805) *(G-20168)*

Swamp Machine Shop, Townsend *Also Called: Michael A Beecher (G-14035)*

Swamps Property Maint LLC..302 841-1162
34604 Lynch Rd Millsboro (19966) *(G-8478)*

Swan Cleaners, Wilmington *Also Called: Blue Swan Cleaners Inc (G-14977)*

Swank Memory Care Center..302 320-2620
205 W 14th St Wilmington (19801) *(G-20169)*

Swarovski US Holding Limited.......................................302 737-4811
715 Christiana Mall Newark (19702) *(G-12138)*

Swarter Services LLC...302 575-9943
600 E Front St Wilmington (19801) *(G-20170)*

Swarthmore Financial Svcs LLC.....................................302 325-0700
15 Reads Way Ste 210 New Castle (19720) *(G-9609)*

Swartzentruber Sawmill Co..302 492-1665
1191 Pearsons Corner Rd Hartly (19953) *(G-4909)*

Swave LLC...302 766-3125
187 Odyssey Dr Wilmington (19808) *(G-20171)*

Sweat Social LLC..504 510-1973
8 The Grn Ste 7379 Dover (19901) *(G-3631)*

Swedish Brickyard...302 893-4143
2404 Sunset Lake Rd Newark (19702) *(G-12139)*

Swedish Massage Therapy..302 841-3166
38227 Muddy Neck Rd Ocean View (19970) *(G-12575)*

Sweep Dream Cleaning Services....................................302 569-5519
11378 2nd St Bridgeville (19933) *(G-773)*

Sweet Dreams Daycare..302 425-0844
733 S Harrison St Wilmington (19805) *(G-20172)*

Sweet Luci, Newark *Also Called: Sweets By Samantha LLC (G-12141)*

Sweet Potato Equipments, Dover *Also Called: Farmers Harvest Inc (G-2486)*

Sweet Venom Effect LLC...302 674-5831
1004 Kirkwood St Ste 1 Wilmington (19801) *(G-20173)*

Sweeten Companies Inc..302 737-6161
149 Salem Church Rd Newark (19713) *(G-12140)*

Sweeten Solar, Newark *Also Called: Sweeten Companies Inc (G-12140)*

Sweets By Samantha LLC..302 740-2218
3 Linette Ct Newark (19702) *(G-12141)*

Swellinfocom...302 588-6241
221 Lakeside Dr Lewes (19958) *(G-6533)*

Swiatowicz Dental Associates..302 476-8185
1211 Milltown Rd Wilmington (19808) *(G-20174)*

Swift Capital, Wilmington *Also Called: Swift Financial LLC (G-20175)*

Swift Financial LLC (HQ)...302 374-7019
3505 Silverside Rd Wilmington (19810) *(G-20175)*

Swift Pools Inc..302 738-9800
1123 Capitol Trl Newark (19711) *(G-12142)*

Swift Services Inc..302 328-1145
2 3rd Ave New Castle (19720) *(G-9610)*

Swift Towing & Recovery...302 650-4579
469 Old Airport Rd New Castle (19720) *(G-9611)*

Swiirl, Newark *Also Called: Swiirl Inc (G-12143)*

Swiirl Inc (PA)...650 430-5256
254 Chapman Rd Ste 208 Newark (19702) *(G-12143)*

Swipes Incorporated..650 686-0223
16192 Coastal Hwy Lewes (19958) *(G-6534)*

Swipetech Limited Inc..929 293-8175
256 Chapman Rd Ste 105-4 Newark (19702) *(G-12144)*

Switch Enterprises LLC (DH)...212 227-9191
3500 S Dupont Hwy Dover (19901) *(G-3632)*

Switch, The, Dover *Also Called: Switch Enterprises LLC (G-3632)*

Switchgearus LLC..302 232-3209
123 Isaacs Shore Dr Ste 500 Milford (19963) *(G-8112)*

Swoop, Wilmington *Also Called: Swoop Payment Processing Inc (G-20176)*

Swoop Payment Processing Inc.....................................479 586-2952
4550 Linden Hill Rd Ste 103 Wilmington (19808) *(G-20176)*

Sword Parts LLC...302 246-1346
19266 Coastal Hwy Unit 4-37 Rehoboth Beach (19971) *(G-12986)*

Swordfish Security USA Inc...302 327-8580
20c Trolley Sq Wilmington (19806) *(G-20177)*

ALPHABETIC SECTION

Swype Inc... 619 736-1410
16192 Coastal Hwy Lewes (19958) *(G-6535)*

Sydell-Hillandale Farms, Hartly *Also Called: Hillandale Farms Delaware Inc (G-4878)*

Syf Industries... 302 384-6214
1410 Prospect Dr Wilmington (19809) *(G-20178)*

Syft Analytics, Newark *Also Called: Syft Analytics Inc (G-12145)*

Syft Analytics Inc (PA)................................ 862 308-0525
200 Continental Dr Ste 401 Newark (19713) *(G-12145)*

Sygul Inc... 315 384-1848
2035 Sunset Lake Rd B2 Newark (19702) *(G-12146)*

Sykes Orna & Cstm Ir Works Inc................. 302 757-2103
315 Bradford St Wilmington (19801) *(G-20179)*

Sylvan Friendly Movers, Bear *Also Called: Pascal Ngalim (G-415)*

Sylvester Custom Cabinetry........................ 302 398-6050
16869 S Dupont Hwy Harrington (19952) *(G-4838)*

Sylvia Saienna... 302 683-9082
100 Westgate Dr Wilmington (19808) *(G-20180)*

Symack Capital MGT US Corp..................... 469 607-6092
231 Stadium St Unit 240 Smyrna (19977) *(G-13906)*

Symack Capital US Corp............................ 469 607-6092
231 Stadium St Smyrna (19977) *(G-13907)*

Symack Prof Svcs US Corp........................ 469 607-6092
231 Stadium St Unit 240 Smyrna (19977) *(G-13908)*

Symack US Corp....................................... 469 607-6092
231 Stadium St Unit 240 Smyrna (19977) *(G-13909)*

Symantec, Wilmington *Also Called: Gen Digital Inc (G-16829)*

Symbiancehr LLC...................................... 302 276-3302
364 E Main St Middletown (19709) *(G-7614)*

Symbiosys Consulting LLC........................ 302 507-7649
920 Justison St Wilmington (19801) *(G-20181)*

Symend US Inc... 855 579-6363
251 Little Falls Dr Wilmington (19808) *(G-20182)*

Symmetry Data Solutions Inc..................... 805 708-4506
251 Little Falls Dr Wilmington (19808) *(G-20183)*

Symphony of Mind Counseling................... 302 747-7286
1300 S Farmview Dr G21 Dover (19904) *(G-3633)*

Synccore Inc... 833 612-0999
16192 Coastal Hwy Lewes (19958) *(G-6536)*

Synchrgnix Info Strategies LLC (DH).......... 302 892-4800
2 Righter Pkwy Ste 205 Wilmington (19803) *(G-20184)*

SYNCOGAI CORP..................................... 302 307-4500
8 The Grn Ste A Dover (19901) *(G-3634)*

Syncologi LLC... 408 549-9559
16192 Coastal Hwy Lewes (19958) *(G-6537)*

Syncretic Press LLC................................. 443 723-8355
1137 Webster Dr Wilmington (19803) *(G-20185)*

Syncretic Software Inc.............................. 302 762-2600
1415 Foulk Rd Wilmington (19803) *(G-20186)*

Synerfac Inc (PA)...................................... 302 324-9400
100 W Commons Blvd Ste 100 New Castle (19720) *(G-9612)*

Synerfac Technical Staffing, New Castle *Also Called: Synerfac Inc (G-9612)*

Synergy Direct Mortgage........................... 302 283-0833
9 Peddlers Row Christiana (19702) *(G-1011)*

Synergy Empowerment Coaching............... 302 362-0054
6334 Phillips Landing Rd Laurel (19956) *(G-5612)*

Synergy Integrated Medical Ctr.................. 302 777-0778
1702 Kirkwood Hwy Ste 101 Wilmington (19805) *(G-20187)*

Synergy Medical USA Inc.......................... 302 444-0163
2915 Ogletown Rd Ste 2565 Newark (19713) *(G-12147)*

Synetics Corporation................................. 302 427-0787
2400 W 4th St Wilmington (19805) *(G-20188)*

Syngenta Corporation (DH)....................... 302 425-2000
3411 Silverside Rd Ste 100 Wilmington (19810) *(G-20189)*

Synnefa Inc.. 302 565-4405
2055 Limestone Rd Ste 200c Wilmington (19808) *(G-20190)*

Synnove Energy Corporation LLC (PA)...... 805 215-8600
160 Greentree Dr Ste 101 Dover (19904) *(G-3635)*

Syntec Corporation (PA)........................... 302 421-8393
109 Rogers Rd Ste 5 Wilmington (19801) *(G-20191)*

Synthezai Corp... 415 980-9792
919 N Market St Ste 950 Wilmington (19801) *(G-20192)*

Synup... 844 228-2852
1521 Concord Pike Wilmington (19803) *(G-20193)*

System4 of Delaware, Newark *Also Called: Schoon Inc (G-11961)*

Systemonex Inc (PA)................................. 201 688-7663
364 E Main St Ste 1001 Middletown (19709) *(G-7615)*

Systems Approach Ltd.............................. 302 743-6331
309 Palomino Dr Newark (19711) *(G-12148)*

Systems Corporation................................. 323 984-7401
251 Little Falls Dr Wilmington (19808) *(G-20194)*

Systems Inc Communit............................. 302 294-1872
310 Valley Stream Dr Newark (19702) *(G-12149)*

Systems Orchestration LLC....................... 302 363-5168
288 Cambridge Rd Camden (19934) *(G-895)*

Systems Tech & Science LLC.................... 703 757-2010
34394 Indian River Dr Dagsboro (19939) *(G-1513)*

Systima Inc... 929 551-4849
2055 Limestone Rd Wilmington (19808) *(G-20195)*

Szewczyk and Company, Wilmington *Also Called: Szewczyk Company P A (G-20196)*

Szewczyk Company P A............................ 302 998-1117
3403 Lancaster Pike Ste 4 Wilmington (19805) *(G-20196)*

Szovet & Co LLC..................................... 908 656-5114
8 The Grn Ste A Dover (19901) *(G-3636)*

T & B Invstgtions SEC Agcy LLC............... 302 476-4087
68 Haggis Rd Middletown (19709) *(G-7616)*

T & C Enterprise Incorporated................... 302 934-8080
26007 Pugs Xing Millsboro (19966) *(G-8479)*

T & F Logistics LLC................................. 302 602-1285
451 Strathaven Ct Newark (19702) *(G-12150)*

T & H Bail Bonds Agency LLC................... 302 777-7982
625 N King St Frnt Wilmington (19801) *(G-20197)*

T & J Murray Worldwide Svcs.................... 302 736-1790
283 Persimmon Tree Ln Dover (19901) *(G-3637)*

T & L Consulting Services LLC.................. 302 573-1585
222 Philadelphia Pike Ste 4 Wilmington (19809) *(G-20198)*

T & M Exhaust Hood Cleaning................... 302 362-8816
12 Jacqueline Dr Georgetown (19947) *(G-4544)*

T & M Property Maintenance LLC............... 302 462-1080
2 Bristle Cone Dr Middletown (19709) *(G-7617)*

T & T Produce LLC.................................. 302 245-6235
34668 W Line Rd Selbyville (19975) *(G-13611)*

T A H First Inc.. 302 653-6114
571 Kates Way Smyrna (19977) *(G-13910)*

T and T Wireless...................................... 302 894-1189
2515 Kirkwood Hwy Newark (19711) *(G-12151)*

T B Painting Restoration........................... 610 283-4100
162 Madison Dr Newark (19711) *(G-12152)*

T Harry Wheedleton................................. 302 629-7414
26955 Line Rd Seaford (19973) *(G-13424)*

T J Irvin Trucking..................................... 302 270-8475
6250 Griffith Lake Dr Milford (19963) *(G-8113)*

T J Lane Construction Inc........................ 302 734-1099
267 Fork Branch Rd Dover (19904) *(G-3638)*

T K O, Bethany Beach *Also Called: T K O Designs Inc (G-645)*

T K O Designs Inc.................................... 302 539-6992
100 Garfield Pkwy Bethany Beach (19930) *(G-645)*

T M I Div, New Castle *Also Called: Testing Machines Inc (G-9625)*

T P Composites Inc.................................. 610 358-9001
1600 Johnson Way Historic New Castle (19720) *(G-5078)*

T R Roofing.. 302 226-4510
2 Sea Chase Dr Rehoboth Beach (19971) *(G-12987)*

T S N Publishing Co Inc........................... 302 655-6483
307 A St Ste C Wilmington (19801) *(G-20199)*

T S Smith & Sons Inc............................... 302 337-8271
8899 Redden Rd Bridgeville (19933) *(G-774)*

T Shane Palmer DC.................................. 302 328-2656
1 Pleasant Pl New Castle (19720) *(G-9613)*

T-Mobile... 302 652-7738
724 N Market St Wilmington (19801) *(G-20200)*

T-Mobile Preferred Retailer, Wilmington *Also Called: T-Mobile (G-20200)*

T-Mobile Store 9730, Dover *Also Called: T-Mobile Usa Inc (G-3641)*

T-Mobile Store 9933, Newark *Also Called: T-Mobile Usa Inc (G-12153)*

T-Mobile Usa Inc 302 736-1980
 1141 N Dupont Hwy Ste 3 Dover (19901) *(G-3641)*

T-Mobile Usa Inc 302 366-8380
 164 Christiana Mall Spc 1548 Newark (19702) *(G-12153)*

T-Mobile Usa Inc 302 479-9691
 4735 Concord Pike Wilmington (19803) *(G-20201)*

T-Mobile Usa Inc 302 998-0112
 3630 Kirkwood Hwy Wilmington (19808) *(G-20202)*

T/A Pizza King, Millsboro Also Called: Baynum Enterprises Inc *(G-8183)*

T&B Logistics Inc 301 304-3255
 8 The Grn Dover (19901) *(G-3639)*

T&G Construction LLC 302 922-1674
 635 Cannery Ln Ste E Townsend (19734) *(G-14076)*

T&T Cleaning LLC 609 575-0458
 2888 Fast Landing Rd Dover (19901) *(G-3640)*

T&T Custom Embroidery Inc 302 420-9454
 51 Rawlings Dr Bear (19701) *(G-522)*

TA Austin Plumbing Inc 302 995-2282
 24 Duvall Ct Wilmington (19808) *(G-20203)*

Ta Instruments, Historic New Castle Also Called: Ta Instruments - Waters LLC *(G-5079)*

Ta Instruments - Waters LLC (DH) 302 427-4000
 159 Lukens Dr Historic New Castle (19720) *(G-5079)*

Ta Instruments-Waters LLC (PA) 781 233-1717
 159 Lukens Dr Historic New Castle (19720) *(G-5080)*

Ta Management & Consulting 302 317-1538
 309 Corbitt Cir Bear (19701) *(G-523)*

TA Rietdorf & Sons Inc 302 429-0341
 735 S Market St Ste D Wilmington (19801) *(G-20204)*

TAB Wellness Inc 914 396-4316
 38 Walker Dr New Castle (19720) *(G-9614)*

Tabeling & Co CPA 302 999-8020
 3825 Lancaster Pike Ste 200 Wilmington (19805) *(G-20205)*

Tabitha Medical Care LLC 302 251-8870
 30668 Sussex Hwy Laurel (19956) *(G-5613)*

Tabletopia Corp 305 548-8407
 850 New Burton Rd Ste 201 Dover (19904) *(G-3642)*

Tabor Auto Parts Inc (PA) 302 395-1100
 20 Mccullough Dr New Castle (19720) *(G-9615)*

TAC Financial Corp 302 691-6014
 103 Foulk Rd Ste 202 Wilmington (19803) *(G-20206)*

Tade Info Tech Solutions 302 832-1449
 60 Avignon Dr Newark (19702) *(G-12154)*

Taekwondo Fitness Ctr of Del 302 836-8264
 1230 Pulaski Hwy Bear (19701) *(G-524)*

Taffy Tubes LLC 302 200-9255
 110 New Rd Lewes (19958) *(G-6538)*

Tag Water Restoration & Cnstr 877 558-6646
 2214 N Market St Wilmington (19802) *(G-20207)*

Taggart Professional Center 410 491-7311
 32895 Coastal Hwy Unit 203b Bethany Beach (19930) *(G-646)*

Taghleef Industries Inc (DH) 302 326-5500
 800 Prides Xing Ste 200 Newark (19713) *(G-12155)*

Taglatam Inc 302 314-9898
 651 N Broad St Ste 206 Middletown (19709) *(G-7618)*

TAI Group LLC 561 819-4231
 8 The Grn Dover (19901) *(G-3643)*

Taiga Express LLC 718 577-2028
 427 N Tatnall St Ste 74587 Wilmington (19801) *(G-20208)*

Tail Bangers Inc 302 947-4900
 24546 Betts Pond Rd Millsboro (19966) *(G-8480)*

Tailbangers Inc 302 934-1125
 24546 Betts Pond Rd Millsboro (19966) *(G-8481)*

Tailor Made Group LLC 347 824-0325
 8 The Grn Ste 11198 Dover (19901) *(G-3644)*

Tailored Care LLC 302 883-1761
 85 Point Landing Ln Magnolia (19962) *(G-6787)*

Tajan Hldings Investments Inc 302 300-1183
 600 N Broad St Ste 5 # 3166 Middletown (19709) *(G-7619)*

Take-A-Break Inc 302 658-8571
 413 8th Ave Wilmington (19805) *(G-20209)*

Tale Innovations Inc 301 887-7587
 251 Little Falls Dr Wilmington (19808) *(G-20210)*

Talent Hire Consulting Inc 302 414-8235
 427 N Tatnall St Ste 34574 Wilmington (19801) *(G-20211)*

Talent Ola Inc 732 421-3216
 8 The Grn Ste A Dover (19901) *(G-3645)*

Talent4health LLC 302 314-1677
 1000 N West St Wilmington (19801) *(G-20212)*

Talentlab Inc 310 999-4320
 8 The Grn Ste D Dover (19901) *(G-3646)*

Talentmatch Inc 508 825-6171
 256 Chapman Rd Newark (19702) *(G-12156)*

Talents Digital Services Corp 888 508-2503
 8 The Grn Dover (19901) *(G-3647)*

Talents List Inc 650 618-1040
 16192 Coastal Hwy Lewes (19958) *(G-6539)*

Talitha DItalia Od 302 998-1395
 3105 Limestone Rd Ste 102 Wilmington (19808) *(G-20213)*

Talk Aware LLC 302 645-7400
 16192 Coastal Hwy Lewes (19958) *(G-6540)*

Talkpush LLC 415 818-5083
 8 The Grn Ste 0424 Dover (19901) *(G-3648)*

Tall Pines Associates Llc 302 684-0300
 29551 Persimmon Rd Lewes (19958) *(G-6541)*

Tall Pines Campground, Lewes Also Called: Tall Pines Associates Llc *(G-6541)*

Talley Brothers Inc 302 224-5376
 210 Executive Dr Ste 7 Newark (19702) *(G-12157)*

Talleys Garage Inc 302 652-0463
 416 Roseanna Ave Wilmington (19803) *(G-20214)*

Talleyville Towne Shoppes 302 478-1969
 4015 Concord Pike Wilmington (19803) *(G-20215)*

Tallyville Animal Hospital 302 478-1194
 3001 Concord Pike Wilmington (19803) *(G-20216)*

Talmo John 302 547-9657
 2709 Tanager Dr Wilmington (19808) *(G-20217)*

Talostech LLC 302 332-9236
 274 Quigley Blvd Historic New Castle (19720) *(G-5081)*

Tami S Creech 302 670-7798
 462 Fletcher Dr Smyrna (19977) *(G-13911)*

Tammi Lea Dr 302 335-2563
 216 N Bayshore Dr Frederica (19946) *(G-4184)*

TAMP, Newark Also Called: Tamp Inc *(G-12158)*

Tamp Inc 302 283-9195
 2035 Sunset Lake Rd Ste B2 Newark (19702) *(G-12158)*

Tangent Cable Systems Inc 302 994-4104
 3700 Washington Ave Wilmington (19808) *(G-20218)*

Tanger Outlet Ctr Midway 302 645-2525
 35016 Ctr Outlet Dr Ste 303 Rehoboth Beach (19971) *(G-12988)*

Tango Live, Dover Also Called: Tangome Inc *(G-3649)*

Tangome Inc 650 362-8086
 3500 S Dupont Hwy Dover (19901) *(G-3649)*

Tangtring Seating Tech USA LLC 269 365-4030
 1013 Centre Rd Ste 403a Wilmington (19805) *(G-20219)*

Tankala Harsha MD 302 346-0101
 1125 Forrest Ave Ste 203 Dover (19904) *(G-3650)*

Tanner Operations Inc 302 464-2194
 39 Anchor Inn Rd Townsend (19734) *(G-14077)*

Tantalum Bolt & Fastener LLC 888 393-4517
 280 E Main St Ste 107 Newark (19711) *(G-12159)*

Tantini LLC 302 444-4024
 136 S Main St Newark (19711) *(G-12160)*

Tap, Wilmington Also Called: Automation Partnership *(G-14653)*

Tap Transportation LLC 302 217-2729
 328 N Market St Seaford (19973) *(G-13425)*

Taplistic LLC 516 362-1890
 3422 Old Capitol Trl Wilmington (19808) *(G-20220)*

Taporterelectric 302 366-0108
 104 Smith Woods Ln Newark (19711) *(G-12161)*

Tapp Networks LLC 302 222-3384
 20421 Jeb Dr Unit 44 Rehoboth Beach (19971) *(G-12989)*

Tappedn Holdings LLC 404 877-2525
 8 The Grn Dover (19901) *(G-3651)*

Tappit Technologies (us) Inc 570 898-1399
 251 Little Falls Dr Wilmington (19808) *(G-20221)*

ALPHABETIC SECTION

Taq Incorporated..302 734-8300
  800 N State St Dover (19901) *(G-3652)*
Tara K Adams Mrs..302 450-3936
  144 Kings Hwy Ste 302 Dover (19901) *(G-3653)*
Tarabicos Grosso...302 757-7800
  100 W Commons Blvd Ste 415 New Castle (19720) *(G-9616)*
Tarachand Beharry...302 875-0684
  18250 Laurel Rd Laurel (19956) *(G-5614)*
Tarak N Patel DC..856 904-3061
  390 Mitch Rd Wilmington (19804) *(G-20222)*
Tarburton Landscape..302 932-1814
  2722 Duncan Rd Wilmington (19808) *(G-20223)*
Target Integration Inc..254 845-5684
  600 N Broad St Ste 53593 Middletown (19709) *(G-7620)*
Target Markets LLC..302 268-1010
  3411 Silverside Rd Ste 100 Wilmington (19810) *(G-20224)*
Taro Medical Incorporated...818 245-2202
  16192 Coastal Hwy Lewes (19958) *(G-6542)*
Tasha P Brown..732 948-7591
  107 Durso Dr Newark (19711) *(G-12162)*
Task Analytics Inc..631 388-3120
  251 Little Falls Dr Wilmington (19808) *(G-20225)*
Task Force Security Svcs LLC...302 476-4064
  1148 Pulaski Hwy Bear (19701) *(G-525)*
Tat Trucking Inc..302 832-2667
  3482 Wrangle Hill Rd Bear (19701) *(G-526)*
Tata Communications Amer Inc (HQ)..............................703 547-5900
  251 Little Falls Dr Wilmington (19808) *(G-20226)*
Tatnall Technology LLC...302 212-0959
  117 W 13th St Wilmington (19801) *(G-20227)*
Tatsapod-Aame...302 897-8963
  1112 Newport Gap Pike Wilmington (19804) *(G-20228)*
Tattoo Blue Moon..302 449-1551
  4446 Summit Bridge Rd Unit 8 Middletown (19709) *(G-7621)*
Tattoo Galaxy Rehobeth Beach......................................302 226-8118
  19470 Coastal Hwy Rehobeth Beach (19971) *(G-12990)*
Tawkify Inc...415 549-1928
  3 Germay Dr Ste 4 Wilmington (19804) *(G-20229)*
Tax Authority Inc...302 633-0777
  3610 Kirkwood Hwy Wilmington (19808) *(G-20230)*
Tax Center, Newark *Also Called: Delaware Taxes LLC* *(G-10490)*
Tax Giants LLC...908 822-1090
  364 E Main St Ste 337 Middletown (19709) *(G-7622)*
Tax Take LLC (PA)..302 760-9758
  3422 Old Capitol Trl Ste 1945 Wilmington (19808) *(G-20231)*
Tax With Us LLC..302 378-2627
  357 Misty Vale Dr Middletown (19709) *(G-7623)*
Tax-E Logistics Inc..877 829-3669
  199 Dorian Dr Dover (19904) *(G-3654)*
Taxdone...302 388-5796
  106 Brookside Ave Wilmington (19805) *(G-20232)*
Taxes Its Your Money..302 322-0452
  1 Bassett Ave Ste 1211 New Castle (19720) *(G-9617)*
Taylor & Sons Inc..302 856-6962
  26511 E Trap Pond Rd Georgetown (19947) *(G-4545)*
Taylor and Messick Inc...302 398-3729
  325 Walt Messick Rd Harrington (19952) *(G-4839)*
Taylor Copeland LLC...302 598-4412
  3801 Kennett Pike Ste D300 Wilmington (19807) *(G-20233)*
Taylor Electric Service Inc..302 422-3966
  8 Columbia St Milford (19963) *(G-8114)*
Taylor Hydrate, Wilmington *Also Called: Taylor Made Waters Inc* *(G-20234)*
Taylor Kline Inc..302 328-8306
  298b Churchmans Rd New Castle (19720) *(G-9618)*
Taylor Made Waters Inc..302 352-9979
  1521 Concord Pike Ste 302 Wilmington (19803) *(G-20234)*
Taylor McCormick Inc...302 897-2171
  409 Abbotsford Ln Newark (19711) *(G-12163)*
Taylor Professional Insurance.....................................302 660-3685
  1000 N West St Fl 10 Wilmington (19801) *(G-20235)*
Taylor Woodworks..302 745-2049
  34 Clearview Dr Dover (19901) *(G-3655)*

Tazelaar Roofing Service, Dover *Also Called: Tazelaar Roofing Service Inc* *(G-3656)*
Tazelaar Roofing Service Inc...302 697-2643
  4869 S Dupont Hwy Dover (19901) *(G-3656)*
Tc Clean..302 737-3360
  5 Vassar Dr Newark (19711) *(G-12164)*
Tc Dental Equipment Services......................................302 740-9049
  262 Dogtown Rd Townsend (19734) *(G-14078)*
Tc Electric Company Inc..302 791-0378
  6701 Governor Printz Blvd Wilmington (19809) *(G-20236)*
Tc Nutrition Corp...306 290-7457
  1000 N West St Ste 1200 Wilmington (19801) *(G-20237)*
Tc Trans Inc..302 339-7952
  24557 Dupont Blvd Georgetown (19947) *(G-4546)*
Tcg High Yeld Inv Holdings LLC...................................302 421-7361
  103 Foulk Rd Ste 101 Wilmington (19803) *(G-20238)*
Tcim Services Inc..302 633-3000
  1013 Centre Rd Ste 400 Wilmington (19805) *(G-20239)*
Tconcepts Resources Inc...302 309-2490
  16192 Coastal Hwy Lewes (19958) *(G-6543)*
Tcp/Ip Solutions LLC..302 219-0224
  8 The Grn B Dover (19901) *(G-3657)*
TCS Inc..302 858-1389
  433 Main Sail Ln Milton (19968) *(G-8718)*
Td Automotive...443 794-3453
  9 University Ave New Castle (19720) *(G-9619)*
Td Bank NA..302 644-0952
  34980 Midway Outlet Dr Rehoboth Beach (19971) *(G-12991)*
Td Bank NA..302 655-5031
  300 Delaware Ave Ste 110 Wilmington (19801) *(G-20240)*
Td Bank NA..508 793-4188
  2035 Limestone Rd Wilmington (19808) *(G-20241)*
TD BANK, N.A., Wilmington *Also Called: Td Bank NA* *(G-20240)*
Td For W Games..302 883-3627
  784 Walker Rd Dover (19904) *(G-3658)*
Tdc Partners Ltd...302 827-2137
  31781 Marsh Island Ave Lewes (19958) *(G-6544)*
Tdm Pharmaceutical RES Inc..302 832-1008
  100 Biddle Ave Ste 202 Newark (19702) *(G-12165)*
Tdm Pharmaceutical RES LLC......................................302 832-1008
  100 Biddle Ave Ste 202 Newark (19702) *(G-12166)*
Tdock Services & Holding Inc.......................................305 924-3653
  8 The Grn Ste A Dover (19901) *(G-3659)*
Tdp Wireless Inc..302 424-1900
  34 Salt Creek Dr Dover (19901) *(G-3660)*
Tdw Delaware Inc (HQ)...302 594-9880
  43 Harbor View Dr New Castle (19720) *(G-9620)*
Tdy Holdings LLC (DH)..302 254-4172
  1011 Centre Rd Ste 329 Wilmington (19805) *(G-20242)*
Te Connectivity Corporation...800 522-6752
  4550 Linden Hill Rd Ste 140 Wilmington (19808) *(G-20243)*
Teachedison Inc..973 902-8026
  651 N Broad St Ste 206 Middletown (19709) *(G-7624)*
Teagle and Sons..302 682-8639
  6 N Street Ext Seaford (19973) *(G-13426)*
Teal Construction Inc..302 276-6034
  612 Mary St Dover (19904) *(G-3661)*
Team Demarco Fitness LLC...347 743-3170
  59 Oriole Ln Smyrna (19977) *(G-13912)*
Team Horne LLC..302 376-0579
  357 Canvasback Rd Middletown (19709) *(G-7625)*
Team Systems International LLC.................................703 217-7648
  16192 Coastal Hwy Lewes (19958) *(G-6545)*
Teambrella Inc..347 630-0528
  4023 Kennett Pike # 5001 Wilmington (19807) *(G-20244)*
Teamlogic It...302 446-4100
  5584 Kirkwood Hwy Wilmington (19808) *(G-20245)*
TEC-Con Inc...610 583-8770
  4063 New Castle Ave New Castle (19720) *(G-9621)*
Tech Beach Retreat Inc...786 790-5922
  2035 Sunset Lake Rd Newark (19702) *(G-12167)*
Tech Central LLC..717 273-3301
  501 Silverside Rd Ste 110 Wilmington (19809) *(G-20246)*

ALPHABETIC SECTION

Tech Craft Solutions LLC 607 761-0376
1007 N Orange St Fl 4 Wilmington (19801) *(G-20247)*

Tech Impact 302 256-5015
100 W 10th St Ste 915 Wilmington (19801) *(G-20248)*

Tech International, Wilmington Also Called: Tech International Corp *(G-20249)*

Tech International Corp (PA) 302 478-2301
3411 Silverside Rd Ste 102w Wilmington (19810) *(G-20249)*

Tech Learn LLC 305 600-0775
1521 Concord Pike Ste 301 Wilmington (19803) *(G-20250)*

Tech Now Mobile LLC 484 480-0648
219 W 8th St Wilmington (19801) *(G-20251)*

Techadox Inc 302 691-9130
258 Chapman Rd Ste 202 Newark (19702) *(G-12168)*

Techmap Integrated Inc 770 800-3561
1013 Centre Rd Ste 4035 Wilmington (19805) *(G-20252)*

Techncal Stffing Resources LLC 302 452-9933
262 Chapman Rd Ste 101 Newark (19702) *(G-12169)*

Techneplus Americas LLC (PA) 678 200-4052
19c Trolley Sq Wilmington (19806) *(G-20253)*

Technical Media Solutions 302 376-7588
116 Sleepy Hollow Dr Middletown (19709) *(G-7626)*

Technical Writers Inc 302 477-1972
3511 Silverside Rd Ste 201 Wilmington (19810) *(G-20254)*

Technicare Inc 302 322-7766
39 Lakewood Cir Newark (19711) *(G-12170)*

Technlogy Explration Group Inc 202 222-0794
257 Old Churchmans Rd New Castle (19720) *(G-9622)*

Techno Goober 302 645-7177
17527 Nassau Commons Blvd Ste 213 Lewes (19958) *(G-6546)*

Techno Relief Limited 416 453-9393
3511 Silverside Rd # 105 Wilmington (19810) *(G-20255)*

Technology, Delmar Also Called: Funfull Inc *(G-1597)*

Technology, Dover Also Called: Claimmybadge LLC *(G-2086)*

Technology Extreme LLC 213 325-5455
919 N Market St Ste 725 Wilmington (19801) *(G-20256)*

Technology Student Association 302 857-3336
401 Federal St Bldg Townsend Dover (19901) *(G-3662)*

Technology Transfers Inc 302 234-4718
16 Anderson Ln Newark (19711) *(G-12171)*

Techsolutions Inc 302 656-8324
5630 Kirkwood Hwy Wilmington (19808) *(G-20257)*

Techworld Corporation Inc 302 757-3866
6 Spring Meadow Ln Hockessin (19707) *(G-5402)*

Techxponent Inc 410 701-0089
131 Arielle Dr Newark (19702) *(G-12172)*

Tecniplast USA Inc 484 716-2145
1903 N Franklin St Wilmington (19802) *(G-20258)*

Tecnologika USA, Wilmington Also Called: Tecnologika Usa Inc *(G-20259)*

Tecnologika Usa Inc 302 597-7611
501 Silverside Rd Wilmington (19809) *(G-20259)*

Tecpresso Inc 302 240-0025
1007 N Orange St Fl 4 Wilmington (19801) *(G-20260)*

Tecs Plus 302 437-6890
261 Chapman Rd Newark (19702) *(G-12173)*

Tectanic LLC 302 440-2788
16192 Coastal Hwy Lewes (19958) *(G-6547)*

Tectonics, Lewes Also Called: Todd R Williams *(G-6567)*

Ted Johnson Enterprises 302 349-5925
14403 Adamsville Rd Greenwood (19950) *(G-4670)*

Tedron Inc 302 529-1838
2022 Harwyn Rd Wilmington (19810) *(G-20261)*

Tee It Up Golf Camp 302 684-1808
22222 Saw Mill Rd Milton (19968) *(G-8719)*

Tee Pees From Rattlesnks 302 654-0709
2001 Rockford Rd Wilmington (19806) *(G-20262)*

Teepee Fantasys LLC 267 334-1270
105 Grand Canyon Ct Bear (19701) *(G-527)*

Teerhub Inc 281 223-3466
8 The Grn Ste D Dover (19901) *(G-3663)*

Teff Inc 302 856-9768
109 E Laurel St Georgetown (19947) *(G-4547)*

Tej Studio LLC 302 205-3224
1201 N Orange St Wilmington (19801) *(G-20263)*

Tek Electronics, Middletown Also Called: Tek Electronics LLC *(G-7627)*

Tek Electronics LLC 302 449-6947
865 Bullen Dr Middletown (19709) *(G-7627)*

Tek International Inc 302 543-8035
811 N Broad St Ste 217 Middletown (19709) *(G-7628)*

Tek Tree LLC (PA) 302 368-2730
1106 Drummond Plz Newark (19711) *(G-12174)*

Tekgeminus Solutions Inc 503 336-5259
221 N Broad St Ste 3a Middletown (19709) *(G-7629)*

Tekmen Group 302 381-0161
20891 Coastal Hwy Rehoboth Beach (19971) *(G-12992)*

Teksolv Usd Inc (PA) 302 738-1050
130 Executive Dr Ste 5 Newark (19702) *(G-12175)*

Teksolv Usd Inc 302 738-1050
100 Lake Dr Newark (19702) *(G-12176)*

Tekstrom Inc 302 709-5900
1301 Milltown Rd Wilmington (19808) *(G-20264)*

Telamon - Laurel Head Start, Laurel Also Called: Telamon Corporation Headstart *(G-5615)*

Telamon Corp Lincoln Hs, Milford Also Called: Telamon Corporation *(G-8115)*

Telamon Corp/Early Chldhd Pgrm 302 934-1642
26351 Patriots Way Georgetown (19947) *(G-4548)*

Telamon Corporation 302 736-5933
195 Willis Rd Dover (19901) *(G-3664)*

Telamon Corporation 302 934-0925
308 N Railroad Ave Georgetown (19947) *(G-4549)*

Telamon Corporation 302 398-9196
112 East St Harrington (19952) *(G-4840)*

Telamon Corporation 302 424-2335
518 N Church Ave Milford (19963) *(G-8115)*

Telamon Corporation 302 629-5557
517 Bridgeville Hwy Seaford (19973) *(G-13427)*

Telamon Corporation Headstart 302 875-7718
30125 Discount Land Rd Laurel (19956) *(G-5615)*

Telamon Delaware Head Start 302 934-1642
26351 Patriots Way Georgetown (19947) *(G-4550)*

Telcast Networks LLC 833 835-2278
8 The Grn Ste 7044 Dover (19901) *(G-3665)*

Telco Envirotrols Inc 302 846-9103
105 E State St Delmar (19940) *(G-1639)*

Tele-Help Inc 888 247-5767
216 Remi Dr New Castle (19720) *(G-9623)*

Teleborg Pipe Seals US, Lewes Also Called: Max Seal Inc *(G-6252)*

Telecom Consulting Group Inc 302 645-7400
16192 Coastal Hwy Lewes (19958) *(G-6548)*

Teleduction, Wilmington Also Called: Teleduction Associates Inc *(G-20265)*

Teleduction Associates Inc 302 429-0303
1 Weldin Park Dr Wilmington (19803) *(G-20265)*

Telefuel.com, Wilmington Also Called: Fuel Labs Inc *(G-16767)*

Teleglobe Vsnl International, Wilmington Also Called: Tata Communications Amer Inc *(G-20226)*

Telehelp24/7, New Castle Also Called: Tele-Help Inc *(G-9623)*

Telemind Clinic 253 332-4110
600 N Broad St Middletown (19709) *(G-7630)*

Telemind Inc 725 333-2411
600 N Broad St Middletown (19709) *(G-7631)*

Telephone Answering Service, Georgetown Also Called: Shore Answer LLC *(G-4511)*

Teleplan Vdeocom Solutions Inc 302 323-8503
100 W Commons Blvd Ste 415 New Castle (19720) *(G-9624)*

Telesonic PC Inc (PA) 302 658-6945
260 Milford Dr Middletown (19709) *(G-7632)*

Telesonic PC Inc 302 658-6945
1330 E 12th St Wilmington (19802) *(G-20266)*

Televon, Claymont Also Called: Plenteous Consulting LLC *(G-1264)*

Telgian Corporation 480 753-5444
4001 Kennett Pike Ste 308 Wilmington (19807) *(G-20267)*

Telgian Engrg & Consulting LLC 480 282-5392
4001 Kennett Pike Ste 308 Wilmington (19807) *(G-20268)*

Telivity Inc 312 585-8485
3 Germay Dr Ste 41193 Wilmington (19804) *(G-20269)*

ALPHABETIC SECTION

Tellerone Inc (PA) 302 261-9062
651 N Broad St Ste 206 Middletown (19709) *(G-7633)*

Telorca LLC 315 693-8488
16192 Coastal Hwy Lewes (19958) *(G-6549)*

Telos Legal Corp 302 242-4815
1012 College Rd Ste 201 Dover (19904) *(G-3666)*

Telsec Answering Service, Newark *Also Called: Bayshore Communications Inc (G-9995)*

Telus Intl Holdg USA Corp 720 726-0677
2711 Centerville Rd Ste 400 Wilmington (19808) *(G-20270)*

Temp-Air Inc 302 369-3880
200 Happy Ln Newark (19711) *(G-12177)*

Tempair, Newark *Also Called: Temp-Air Inc (G-12177)*

Temple Masonic 302 734-4147
38 South St Dover (19904) *(G-3667)*

Ten Bears Environmental, Newark *Also Called: Ten Bears Environmental LLC (G-12178)*

Ten Bears Environmental LLC 302 731-8633
1080 S Chapel St Ste 200 Newark (19702) *(G-12178)*

Ten Blade Enterprises LLC 484 843-4811
800 Industrial St Wilmington (19801) *(G-20271)*

Ten Talents Enterprises Inc (PA) 302 409-0718
316 Braemar St Middletown (19709) *(G-7634)*

Tender Hearts 302 674-2565
1339 S Governors Ave Dover (19904) *(G-3668)*

Tender Hearts 302 234-1017
5301 Limestone Rd Wilmington (19808) *(G-20272)*

Tender Lawn & Care 410 310-6550
214 Otter Run Ct Seaford (19973) *(G-13428)*

Tender Loving Kare 302 464-1014
400 N Ramunno Dr Middletown (19709) *(G-7635)*

Tender Touch Support LLC 302 272-1638
34 Tammie Dr Dover (19904) *(G-3669)*

Tenmat Inc 302 633-6600
500 Water St Wilmington (19804) *(G-20273)*

Tennis String King 215 280-2783
29348 Turnberry Dr Dagsboro (19939) *(G-1514)*

Tennr Inc 650 288-8264
1013 Centre Rd Ste 403b Wilmington (19805) *(G-20274)*

Tenon Tours LLC (PA) 781 435-0425
17515 Nassau Commons Blvd Lewes (19958) *(G-6550)*

Tepuyi LLC 954 991-0749
8 The Grn Dover (19901) *(G-3670)*

Tera Technology Group 302 994-0500
328 New Rd Elsmere (19805) *(G-3931)*

Teranetwork LLC 302 257-7782
16192 Coastal Hwy Lewes (19958) *(G-6551)*

Teresa H Keller MD 302 422-2022
16 S Dupont Blvd Milford (19963) *(G-8116)*

Teri Lyn Busch Msw/Lcsw 302 731-9110
10 Wink Dr Newark (19702) *(G-12179)*

Terminix, Historic New Castle *Also Called: Terminix Intl Co Ltd Partnr (G-5082)*

Terminix Intl Co Ltd Partnr 302 653-4866
284 Quigley Blvd Historic New Castle (19720) *(G-5082)*

Ternary Inc 650 759-5277
2093 Philadelphia Pike Ste 5312 Claymont (19703) *(G-1309)*

Terra Firma of Delmarva Inc 302 846-3350
38156 Brittingham Rd Delmar (19940) *(G-1640)*

Terra Systems Inc 302 798-9553
130 Hickman Rd Ste 1 Claymont (19703) *(G-1310)*

Terra Systems of Delaware LLC 302 798-9553
130 Hickman Rd Ste 1 Claymont (19703) *(G-1311)*

Terrain and Tactical LLC 302 521-9290
5071 E Woodmill Dr Wilmington (19808) *(G-20275)*

Terran Global Corporation 702 626-5704
16192 Coastal Hwy Lewes (19958) *(G-6552)*

Terrance R Hester 856 905-8196
447 Georgiana Dr Middletown (19709) *(G-7636)*

Terrareef, Wilmington *Also Called: Jonathon Gordon (G-17573)*

Terrie M Wlliams Expansion Inc 302 214-0685
438 Morehouse Dr Wilmington (19801) *(G-20276)*

Terry A Gray 302 478-2042
2422 Graydon Rd Wilmington (19803) *(G-20277)*

Terry Chld Psychiatric Ctr, New Castle *Also Called: Children Yuth Their Fmlies Del (G-8934)*

Terry White 302 652-4969
200 Continental Dr Ste 109 Newark (19713) *(G-12180)*

Terry White-State Farm Ins 302 353-6636
1813 Marsh Rd Ste G Wilmington (19810) *(G-20278)*

Tersin Enterprises LLC (PA) 614 260-3215
55 Loockerman Plz Dover (19903) *(G-3671)*

Tesis Time Inc 302 613-0789
651 N Broad St Middletown (19709) *(G-7637)*

Tesla, Historic New Castle *Also Called: Tesla Industries Inc (G-5083)*

Tesla Biohealing Inc 302 265-2213
111 Mccoy St Milford (19963) *(G-8117)*

Tesla Energy Operations Inc 650 638-1028
231 Executive Dr Ste 1 Newark (19702) *(G-12181)*

Tesla Industries Inc (PA) 302 324-8910
101 Centerpoint Blvd Historic New Castle (19720) *(G-5083)*

Tesla Nootropics Inc 514 718-2270
8 The Grn Ste 5757 Dover (19901) *(G-3672)*

Tess Afrcan Hair Brding Buty S 302 384-6439
5910 Kirkwood Hwy Wilmington (19808) *(G-20279)*

Testex Inc 302 731-5693
8 Fox Ln Newark (19711) *(G-12182)*

Testing Machines, New Castle *Also Called: Industrial Physics Inc (G-9230)*

Testing Machines Inc (PA) 302 613-5600
40 Mccullough Dr Unit A New Castle (19720) *(G-9625)*

Tetra Tech Inc 302 738-7551
240 Continental Dr Ste 200 Newark (19713) *(G-12183)*

Tetra Tech Inc 302 738-7551
240 Continental Dr Ste 200 Newark (19713) *(G-12184)*

Tetra Tech Engrg & Arch Svcs, Newark *Also Called: Tetra Tech Inc (G-12184)*

Tetris Company LLC 302 656-1950
103 Foulk Rd Ste 202 Wilmington (19803) *(G-20280)*

Tetrus Led Co, Milford *Also Called: American Neon Products Company (G-7767)*

Tevebaugh Associates Inc (PA) 302 984-1400
2 Mill Rd Ste 210 Wilmington (19806) *(G-20281)*

Texaco, Wilmington *Also Called: Logue Brothers Inc (G-17976)*

Texas Lawn Care Svc 302 547-5829
2516 Faulkland Rd Wilmington (19808) *(G-20282)*

Texas Puma Energy US, Wilmington *Also Called: Puma Energy US Inc (G-19256)*

Texavino LLC 302 295-0829
3422 Old Capitol Trl Ste 1444 Wilmington (19808) *(G-20283)*

Texcel LLC 302 738-4313
211 Executive Dr Ste 9 Newark (19702) *(G-12185)*

Texnikos Inc 302 656-8088
915 S Heald St Wilmington (19801) *(G-20284)*

Textronics Inc 302 351-2109
3825 Lancaster Pike Wilmington (19805) *(G-20285)*

TFT Media LLC 302 645-7400
16192 Coastal Hwy Lewes (19958) *(G-6553)*

Tg Advisers Inc 302 691-3330
4550 Linden Hill Rd Ste 152 Wilmington (19808) *(G-20286)*

Tgfmx Inc 302 613-0128
1007 N Orange St Fl 4 Wilmington (19801) *(G-20287)*

TGI Rebate Center 866 433-3009
1405 Foulk Rd Ste 200 Wilmington (19803) *(G-20288)*

Tgx Holdings LLC 212 260-6300
1201 N Market St Wilmington (19801) *(G-20289)*

TH King US LLC 617 903-7472
600 N King St Ste 800 Wilmington (19801) *(G-20290)*

Th White General Contract 302 945-1829
32783 Long Neck Rd Unit 2 Millsboro (19966) *(G-8482)*

Th White General Contractor 302 945-1829
31687 Messiah Ln Millsboro (19966) *(G-8483)*

That Cleaning Solutions LLC 302 442-8148
47 Paisley St Bear (19701) *(G-528)*

That Granite Place 302 236-0820
6832 Shawnee Rd Milford (19963) *(G-8118)*

That Granite Place LLC 302 337-7490
9599 Nanticoke Business Park Dr Greenwood (19950) *(G-4671)*

Thdxngrp LLC 443 993-6414
34 Dunsinane Dr New Castle (19720) *(G-9626)*

ALPHABETIC SECTION

The Ascendant Group Inc..302 450-4494
  2035 Sunset Lake Rd Ste B2 Newark (19702) *(G-12186)*
The Basement Shirt Co., Wilmington Also Called: Slater Fireplaces Inc *(G-19861)*
The Crowell Corporation..302 998-0558
  1 Crowell Rd Wilmington (19804) *(G-20291)*
The Dog House, Dover Also Called: Governors Ave Animal Hospital *(G-2610)*
The Goddard School, Hockessin Also Called: Cdb Ventures Inc *(G-5154)*
The Lorelton, Wilmington Also Called: Lorelton *(G-17995)*
The Lrning Tree Chld Acdemy LL..................................302 841-0194
  403 W Loockerman St Dover (19904) *(G-3673)*
The Lycra Company, LLC, Newark Also Called: Lycra Company LLC *(G-11298)*
The North Truckers Inc..302 309-0786
  16192 Coastal Hwy Lewes (19958) *(G-6554)*
The Oak Orchrd-Rvrdale Post 28..................................302 945-1673
  31768 Legion Rd Millsboro (19966) *(G-8484)*
The Real Established Inc...917 843-8580
  1007 N Orange St Fl 1620 Wilmington (19801) *(G-20292)*
The Tondo Group LLC..302 893-8849
  17 Mcmillan Way Newark (19713) *(G-12187)*
The-Dirt-Squad..302 723-5916
  1017 Euclid Ave Wilmington (19809) *(G-20293)*
Theatre N At Nemours..302 600-1923
  1007 N Orange St Wilmington (19801) *(G-20294)*
Thedigitalsupport LLC..347 305-4006
  5301 Limestone Rd Ste 100 Wilmington (19808) *(G-20295)*
Thelma Stanley...302 604-8481
  32189 Steele Dr Millsboro (19966) *(G-8485)*
Theluxestay LLC...802 234-1410
  651 N Broad St Middletown (19709) *(G-7638)*
Thepowermba Inc..917 508-5535
  2035 Sunset Lake Rd Ste B2 Newark (19702) *(G-12188)*
Therapeutic Moore Services LLC..................................302 654-8142
  701 Foulk Rd Ste 2d Wilmington (19803) *(G-20296)*
Therapy At Beach...302 313-5555
  34444 King Street Row Lewes (19958) *(G-6555)*
Therapy Concierge LLC..302 319-3040
  516 Daniels Ct Bear (19701) *(G-529)*
Therapy Services of Delaw.......................................302 239-2285
  24 Gates Cir Hockessin (19707) *(G-5403)*
Theresa Hayes..302 854-5406
  16 N Bedford St Georgetown (19947) *(G-4551)*
Theresa Little MD...302 735-1616
  1001 S Bradford St Ste 5 Dover (19904) *(G-3674)*
Thermal Pipe Systems Inc (PA)..................................302 999-1588
  5205 W Woodmill Dr Ste 33 Wilmington (19808) *(G-20297)*
Thermal Seal Experts, Wilmington Also Called: Jdh Construction Inc *(G-17510)*
Thermal Transf Composites LLC (PA)...........................302 635-7156
  724 Yorklyn Rd Ste 200 Hockessin (19707) *(G-5404)*
Thermo Fisher Scientific Inc......................................302 479-7707
  3411 Silverside Rd Ste 100t Wilmington (19810) *(G-20298)*
Thermo King Chesapeake, Delmar Also Called: Thermo King Corporation *(G-1641)*
Thermo King Corporation..302 907-0345
  36550 Sussex Hwy Delmar (19940) *(G-1641)*
Thermo King LLC..302 907-0345
  36550 Sussex Hwy Delmar (19940) *(G-1642)*
Thermo King of Delaware, Delmar Also Called: Thermo King LLC *(G-1642)*
Thermoelectrics Unlimited Inc....................................302 764-6618
  5109 Governor Printz Blvd Wilmington (19809) *(G-20299)*
Thermoplastic Processes, Georgetown Also Called: Tpi Partners Inc *(G-4558)*
Thermoplastic Processes Inc.....................................888 554-6400
  21649 Cedar Creek Ave Georgetown (19947) *(G-4552)*
Theta Vest Inc...302 227-3745
  21707 B St Rehoboth Beach (19971) *(G-12993)*
Think Clean & Grounds Up LLC..................................904 250-1614
  11 W 9th St Historic New Castle (19720) *(G-5084)*
Think Fast Toys.com, Selbyville Also Called: Avalanche Strategies LLC *(G-13469)*
Think66 LLC..949 326-8188
  300 Delaware Ave Ste 210a Wilmington (19801) *(G-20300)*
Thinkhat Software Inc (HQ).......................................917 379-2638
  1000 N West St Ste 1200 Wilmington (19801) *(G-20301)*
Thinklever LLC...302 388-7461
  560 Peoples Plz Newark (19702) *(G-12189)*
Thinksecurenet...302 703-9717
  16557 Coastal Hwy Lewes (19958) *(G-6556)*
Third Sigma Investment Advisor.................................302 656-1111
  700 N Clayton St Ste 100 Wilmington (19805) *(G-20302)*
Thirdwave Systems Inc..650 804-1385
  1111 S Governors Ave Dover (19904) *(G-3675)*
Thirst 2 Learn..302 293-2304
  891 Pulaski Hwy Bear (19701) *(G-530)*
Thirst 2 Learn Child Dev Ctr, Claymont Also Called: Northeast Early Lrng Ctr LLC *(G-1255)*
Thirst 2 Learn LLC..302 475-7080
  802 Naamans Rd Wilmington (19810) *(G-20303)*
Thirteen Svnty Six Cpitl MGT L..................................561 247-1521
  8 The Grn Ste A Dover (19901) *(G-3676)*
Thirty Birds Inc..351 910-5520
  251 Little Falls Dr Wilmington (19808) *(G-20304)*
This Is Cala Inc...512 900-4746
  1111 S Governors Ave Dover (19904) *(G-3677)*
This N That Fitness..302 542-7115
  30954 Holts Landing Rd Dagsboro (19939) *(G-1515)*
Thomas A Cochran & Sons Inc..................................302 656-6054
  807 Washington St Historic New Castle (19720) *(G-5085)*
Thomas A Cofran & Sons Inc....................................302 368-5157
  203 Sunset Rd Newark (19711) *(G-12190)*
Thomas B Davis...302 692-0871
  1 Arlington St Newark (19711) *(G-12191)*
Thomas Brothers LLC...302 366-1316
  12 Oak Ave Newark (19711) *(G-12192)*
Thomas Building Group Inc.....................................302 283-0600
  35 Albe Dr Newark (19702) *(G-12193)*
Thomas Clark MASonry& Excav................................302 462-6039
  33722 Clarks Trl Frankford (19945) *(G-4152)*
Thomas D Law Shel...302 887-9116
  1601 Milltown Rd Wilmington (19808) *(G-20305)*
Thomas Dougherty DDS..302 239-2500
  5317 Limestone Rd Ste 5 Wilmington (19808) *(G-20306)*
Thomas E Cameron...302 345-6708
  833 Causez Ave Claymont (19703) *(G-1312)*
Thomas E Moore Inc (PA).......................................302 674-1500
  696 S Bay Rd Dover (19901) *(G-3678)*
Thomas E Moore Inc..302 674-1500
  6 Maryland Ave Kenton (19955) *(G-5456)*
Thomas F Allen..302 604-3357
  115 W Market St Georgetown (19947) *(G-4553)*
Thomas F Cavanaugh..302 995-2859
  123 Hawthorne Ave Wilmington (19805) *(G-20307)*
Thomas Family Dentist LLC....................................302 697-1152
  1981 S State St Dover (19901) *(G-3679)*
Thomas Family Farms LLC.....................................302 492-3688
  896 Sandy Bend Rd Marydel (19964) *(G-6812)*
Thomas Fenimore...302 464-2633
  311 Blackbird Station Rd Townsend (19734) *(G-14079)*
Thomas Franciscomi..302 995-2282
  24 Duvall Ct Wilmington (19808) *(G-20308)*
Thomas J McWilliams..312 287-5148
  1000 N West St Ste 1500 Wilmington (19801) *(G-20309)*
Thomas Jenkins DMD..302 426-0526
  2323 Pennsylvania Ave Ste Ll Wilmington (19806) *(G-20310)*
Thomas Karmanski...302 438-1458
  108 S Marshall St Wilmington (19804) *(G-20311)*
Thomas Phillips..302 238-7130
  20952 Shell Station Rd Frankford (19945) *(G-4153)*
Thomas Scott Gillespie..302 750-0813
  66 Grand Teton Dr Bear (19701) *(G-531)*
Thomas W Mercer DMD...302 678-2942
  77 Saulsbury Rd Dover (19904) *(G-3680)*
Thomas Weisenfels...302 571-5244
  1201 N Market St Ste 2000 Wilmington (19801) *(G-20312)*
Thomas, Irving O DDS, Wilmington Also Called: Russell J Tibbetts DDS PA *(G-19594)*
Thompson Cleaners..302 998-0935
  4746 Limestone Rd Ste A Wilmington (19808) *(G-20313)*

ALPHABETIC SECTION

Thompson's Farm, Hartly *Also Called: Robert C Thompson* *(G-4907)*
Thomson Reuters (grc) Inc..212 227-7357
 2711 Centerville Rd Ste 400 Wilmington (19808) *(G-20314)*
Thornley Company Inc..302 224-8300
 1 Innovation Way Ste 100 Newark (19711) *(G-12194)*
Thoro-Goods Concrete Co Inc (PA).........................302 934-8102
 30548 Thorogoods Rd Dagsboro (19939) *(G-1516)*
Thoroughbred Charities-America...........................302 376-6289
 1343 Bohemia Mill Rd Middletown (19709) *(G-7639)*
Thoroughbred Software Intl....................................302 339-8383
 22536 Lakeshore Dr Georgetown (19947) *(G-4554)*
Threads N Denims..302 678-0642
 8 Senator Ave Dover (19901) *(G-3681)*
Threatmate Inc...302 219-4714
 8 The Grn Ste 14359 Dover (19901) *(G-3682)*
Three Bs Painting Contractors...............................302 227-1497
 37021 Rehoboth Avenue Ext D Rehoboth Beach (19971) *(G-12994)*
Three Fields Capital LP..302 636-5401
 2711 Centerville Rd # 400 Wilmington (19808) *(G-20315)*
Three Js Disc Tire & Auto Svc................................302 995-6141
 3724 Kirkwood Hwy Wilmington (19808) *(G-20316)*
Three Little Bird Prpts LLC.....................................302 475-2981
 1814 Floral Dr Wilmington (19810) *(G-20317)*
Three Little Builders...302 317-1969
 123 Pine Valley Dr Middletown (19709) *(G-7640)*
Three Sheep and A Mill LLC...................................616 820-5668
 651 N Broad St Ste 205 Middletown (19709) *(G-7641)*
Threesixtytrade LLC...214 810-2922
 2140 S Dupont Hwy Camden (19934) *(G-896)*
Thresholds, Georgetown *Also Called: Delaware Drnking Drver Program* *(G-4281)*
Thresholds Inc...302 827-4478
 17577 Nassau Commons Blvd Ste 202 Lewes (19958) *(G-6557)*
Thrive Agritech..800 205-7216
 2093 Philadelphia Pike # 9047 Claymont (19703) *(G-1313)*
Thrive Physical Therapy Inc...................................302 834-8400
 834 Kohl Ave Middletown (19709) *(G-7642)*
Thrive Pt, Middletown *Also Called: Thrive Physical Therapy Inc* *(G-7642)*
Thrive Real Lf Indpendence LLC............................302 261-2139
 252 Carter Dr Ste 200 Middletown (19709) *(G-7643)*
Throat Threads Apparel USA Inc...........................905 681-8437
 874 Walker Rd Ste C Dover (19904) *(G-3683)*
Thrupore Technologies, New Castle *Also Called: Thrupore Technologies Inc* *(G-9627)*
Thrupore Technologies Inc (PA).............................205 657-0714
 15 Reads Way Ste 107 New Castle (19720) *(G-9627)*
Ticket Sports and Entrmt Corp...............................224 522-3517
 254 Chapman Rd Ste 209 Newark (19702) *(G-12195)*
Ticket To Travel..302 442-0225
 7 E Sarazen Dr Middletown (19709) *(G-7644)*
Tickle Toes, Newark *Also Called: TT Luxury Group LLC* *(G-12243)*
Tidalhealth Nanticoke Inc (HQ)..............................302 629-6611
 801 Middleford Rd Seaford (19973) *(G-13429)*
Tidalhlth Pnnsula Regional Inc...............................302 732-8400
 Rts 113 & 26th Dagsboro (19939) *(G-1517)*
Tidalhlth Pnnsula Regional Inc...............................302 537-1457
 142 Atlantic Ave Ste C Millville (19967) *(G-8549)*
Tidalhlth Pnnsula Regional Inc...............................302 436-8004
 15 N Williams St Selbyville (19975) *(G-13612)*
Tidemark LLC...302 747-7737
 117 W Reed St Dover (19904) *(G-3684)*
Tidemark Federal Credit Union (PA)......................302 629-0100
 1941 Bridgeville Hwy Seaford (19973) *(G-13430)*
Tidemark LLC...302 359-4646
 57 Castle Pines Ct Camden Wyoming (19934) *(G-982)*
Tidewater Electricmyology, Seaford *Also Called: Tidewater Physcl Thrpy and REB* *(G-13431)*
Tidewater Envmtl Svcs Inc......................................302 674-8056
 1100 S Little Creek Rd Dover (19901) *(G-3685)*
Tidewater Physcl Thrpy and REB...........................302 398-7982
 610 Gordon St Harrington (19952) *(G-4841)*
Tidewater Physcl Thrpy and REB...........................302 945-5111
 20750 John J Williams Hwy Unit 1 Lewes (19958) *(G-6558)*
Tidewater Physcl Thrpy and REB...........................302 684-2829
 611 Federal St Milton (19968) *(G-8720)*
Tidewater Physcl Thrpy and REB...........................302 537-7260
 63 Atlantic Ave Ocean View (19970) *(G-12576)*
Tidewater Physcl Thrpy and REB...........................302 629-4024
 808 Middleford Rd Ste 7 Seaford (19973) *(G-13431)*
Tidewater Utilities Inc...302 674-8056
 1100 S Little Creek Rd Dover (19901) *(G-3686)*
Tidy App, Lewes *Also Called: Tidy Technologies Inc* *(G-6559)*
Tidy Technologies Inc (PA)....................................888 788-2445
 16192 Coastal Hwy Lewes (19958) *(G-6559)*
Tiedemann Trust Company (PA)............................302 656-5644
 200 Bellevue Pkwy Ste 525 Wilmington (19809) *(G-20318)*
Tier Two Contracting LLC......................................443 928-0089
 26250 Shortly Rd Georgetown (19947) *(G-4555)*
Tiers Inc...302 298-3338
 1201 N Orange St Ste 7586 Wilmington (19801) *(G-20319)*
Tiffany Kistler Benefits...302 425-5010
 2 Mill Rd Ste 206 Wilmington (19806) *(G-20320)*
Tiffany Pines Condo Assn Inc................................302 227-0913
 20037 Old Landing Rd Rehoboth Beach (19971) *(G-12995)*
Tiffgoyogaflow..302 793-9455
 2420 Marilyn Dr Wilmington (19810) *(G-20321)*
Tigani Family Dentistry PA.....................................302 571-8740
 4600 Linden Hill Rd Wilmington (19808) *(G-20322)*
Tiger LLC..302 378-8700
 100 S Broad St Middletown (19709) *(G-7645)*
Tighe and Cottrell PA (PA).....................................302 658-6400
 704 N King St Ste 500 Wilmington (19801) *(G-20323)*
Tighten Up Cleaning Services................................302 482-9970
 312 Cedar Ave Wilmington (19804) *(G-20324)*
Tikana Motorsports..302 290-0869
 282 Deer Run Rd Townsend (19734) *(G-14080)*
Tile Guy...302 382-7961
 1847 Barratts Chapel Rd Felton (19943) *(G-4032)*
Tile Market of Delaware Inc....................................302 644-7100
 17701 Dartmouth Dr Unit 1 Lewes (19958) *(G-6560)*
Tile Market of Delaware LLC (HQ).........................302 777-4663
 405 Marsh Ln Ste 3 Wilmington (19804) *(G-20325)*
TILE MARKET OF DELAWARE, INC., Lewes *Also Called: Tile Market of Delaware Inc* *(G-6560)*
Tile Shop LLC...302 250-4889
 1200 Rocky Run Pkwy Wilmington (19803) *(G-20326)*
Tilebox Inc...206 741-0883
 1111 B S Governers Ave 6076 Dover (19904) *(G-3687)*
Tim 2 My Bro Awrness Blnce Fnd..........................302 278-2191
 316 Putter St Townsend (19734) *(G-14081)*
Tim Latham...302 530-4002
 112 N Woodward Ave Wilmington (19805) *(G-20327)*
Timber Heart Learning Center................................302 674-2565
 1339 S Governors Ave Dover (19904) *(G-3688)*
Timber Ridge Inc..302 239-9239
 710 Yorklyn Rd Hockessin (19707) *(G-5405)*
Time Is Money Courier Pros, Claymont *Also Called: Cameron Jones* *(G-1071)*
Time4machine Inc...302 999-7604
 3422 Old Capitol Trl Wilmington (19808) *(G-20328)*
Timet Finance Management Co.............................302 472-9277
 1007 N Orange St Wilmington (19801) *(G-20329)*
Timezest Inc..702 582-6850
 2810 N Church St Wilmington (19802) *(G-20330)*
Timken Gears & Services Inc.................................302 633-4600
 100 Anchor Mill Rd Historic New Castle (19720) *(G-5086)*
Timon Financials Inc..620 464-4247
 8 The Grn Ste R Dover (19901) *(G-3689)*
Timothy D Humphreys..302 225-3000
 1831 Delaware Ave Wilmington (19806) *(G-20331)*
Timothy J Meyers Inc...302 438-3709
 1004 Elizabeth Ave Wilmington (19809) *(G-20332)*
Timothy P Collord..302 448-9577
 22926 Donovan Rd Milton (19968) *(G-8721)*
Timothy S Early..302 387-7374
 83 Upland Ave Dover (19901) *(G-3690)*
Timtec Inc..302 292-8500
 301 Ruthar Dr Ste A Newark (19711) *(G-12196)*

Company	Phone
Timtec LLC	302 292-8500
301 Ruthar Dr Ste A Newark (19711) *(G-12197)*	
Tina Trner Cmt Thrptic Massage	302 242-5114
1365 Black Swamp Rd Felton (19943) *(G-4033)*	
Tinas Tiny Tots Daycare	302 536-7077
8779 Concord Rd Seaford (19973) *(G-13432)*	
Tinman Enterprises LLC	302 698-1630
630 Raven Cir Camden Wyoming (19934) *(G-983)*	
Tint World	302 595-9100
400 N Maryland Ave Wilmington (19804) *(G-20333)*	
Tiny Token Trckg & Trnsp LLC	929 602-5512
17 Maria Ln Smyrna (19977) *(G-13913)*	
Tiny Tots and Toddlers, Bear Also Called: Tiny Tots and Toddlers Llc *(G-532)*	
Tiny Tots and Toddlers Llc	302 838-8787
505 Eldridge Ct Bear (19701) *(G-532)*	
Tiny Tots Childcare and Learni	302 651-9060
1014 W 24th St Wilmington (19802) *(G-20334)*	
Tiplab Inc	917 586-9649
16192 Coastal Hwy Lewes (19958) *(G-6561)*	
Tipton Communications Group	302 454-7901
323 E Main St Newark (19711) *(G-12198)*	
Tire 24 X 7 Inc	833 847-3247
402 Welsh Hill Rd Newark (19702) *(G-12199)*	
Tire Rack Inc	302 325-8260
300 Anchor Mill Rd Historic New Castle (19720) *(G-5087)*	
Tire Sales & Service, Wilmington Also Called: Tire Sales & Service Inc *(G-20335)*	
Tire Sales & Service Inc	302 658-8955
600 First State Blvd Wilmington (19804) *(G-20335)*	
Tirupati Inc	302 836-8335
600 5th St Delaware City (19706) *(G-1559)*	
Tis Group, Lewes Also Called: Tis Group Inc *(G-6562)*	
Tis Group Inc	929 322-8811
1692 Coastal Hwy Lewes (19958) *(G-6562)*	
Titan Retail LLC	205 291-1305
651 N Broad St Middletown (19709) *(G-7646)*	
Titan Spirits LLC	205 568-3338
2810 N Church St Wilmington (19802) *(G-20336)*	
Title One & Associates Inc	410 758-1831
6 Summerville Ct Ocean View (19970) *(G-12577)*	
Tj Custom Woodworks Inc	302 563-8535
4 Mistweave Ct Newark (19711) *(G-12200)*	
Tj S Plumbing Heating L	302 228-7129
32605 Millsboro Hwy Millsboro (19966) *(G-8486)*	
Tjm Financial Group LLC	302 674-7033
1944 Maryland Ave Wilmington (19805) *(G-20337)*	
Tjs & Associates LLC	302 563-5593
198 Bonnybrook Rd Middletown (19709) *(G-7647)*	
Tjs Repair LLC	302 422-8383
201 Marshall St Milford (19963) *(G-8119)*	
Tk Blier Incorporated	207 760-7076
2140 S Dupont Hwy Camden (19934) *(G-897)*	
Tko Painting	302 259-9450
1 Oak St Georgetown (19947) *(G-4556)*	
Tkxai LLC	202 670-8818
16192 Coastal Hwy Lewes (19958) *(G-6563)*	
Tlaloc Building Services Inc	302 559-6459
738 Pulaski Hwy Trlr 29b Bear (19701) *(G-533)*	
Tlaloc Landscape LLC	302 562-9087
234 Landau Way Bear (19701) *(G-534)*	
Tlbc LLC	302 797-8700
105 2nd St Lewes (19958) *(G-6564)*	
TLC Home Care	302 983-5720
2055 Melson Rd Wilmington (19808) *(G-20338)*	
Tle Ventures Ltd	800 794-3867
8 The Grn Ste A Dover (19901) *(G-3691)*	
Tli, Wilmington Also Called: Transforming Lives Inc *(G-20398)*	
Tlk	302 376-8554
2356 Dupont Pkwy Middletown (19709) *(G-7648)*	
Tm Crist Contracting Inc	302 632-7557
250 Buffalo Rd Frederica (19946) *(G-4185)*	
Tm Management LLC	302 654-4940
30 Hill Rd Wilmington (19806) *(G-20339)*	
TMC Transformers USA Inc	716 548-0825
874 Walker Rd Dover (19904) *(G-3692)*	
TMI Realty LLC	302 613-5600
40 Mccullough Dr New Castle (19720) *(G-9628)*	
Tmpaa Institute Inc	302 268-1010
3411 Silverside Rd Wilmington (19810) *(G-20340)*	
Tms Asphalt Maintenance, Millsboro Also Called: Thelma Stanley *(G-8485)*	
Tms Nrhlth Ctrs Tysons Crnr LL	302 994-4010
121 Becks Woods Dr Ste 202 Bear (19701) *(G-535)*	
Tnjd Diamond LLC	614 902-9431
351 N New St Dover (19904) *(G-3693)*	
TNT Drywall LLC	302 381-0114
17870 Callaway Dr Lewes (19958) *(G-6565)*	
TNT Grand Lux LLC	443 228-3193
8 The Grn Ste 212 Dover (19901) *(G-3694)*	
TNT Window Cleaning	302 326-2411
35 Salem Church Rd Newark (19713) *(G-12201)*	
To A Tee Printing	302 525-6336
2860 Ogletown Rd Newark (19713) *(G-12202)*	
To The Moon and Back Childcare	302 508-2749
307 Kent Way Smyrna (19977) *(G-13914)*	
Toback Builders	302 644-1015
20375 John J Williams Hwy Lewes (19958) *(G-6566)*	
Tobola Health Care Svcs Inc	302 389-8448
1012 College Rd Ste 105 Dover (19904) *(G-3695)*	
Toby W Miller	302 270-1057
674 Rose Valley School Rd Dover (19904) *(G-3696)*	
Today Media, Wilmington Also Called: Martinelli Holdings LLC *(G-18170)*	
Todays Kid Inc (not Inc)	302 834-5620
10 Songsmith Dr Newark (19702) *(G-12203)*	
Todd E Watson DC	615 500-6825
12 Foxhunt Dr Bear (19701) *(G-536)*	
Todd R Williams	302 945-3662
22337 Dorman Rd Lewes (19958) *(G-6567)*	
Todd Rowen DMD	302 994-5887
25 Milltown Rd Ste A Wilmington (19808) *(G-20341)*	
Todd Yerger Ta	302 378-4196
1681 Choptank Rd Middletown (19709) *(G-7649)*	
Toddlers Tech Inc	302 655-4487
2704 W 4th St Wilmington (19805) *(G-20342)*	
Todds	302 658-0387
1601 Concord Pike Ste 49 Wilmington (19803) *(G-20343)*	
Todds Janitorial Service Inc	302 378-8212
407 E Lake St Middletown (19709) *(G-7650)*	
Toddys Tots	302 661-1912
2308 N Madison St Wilmington (19802) *(G-20344)*	
Todo, Dover Also Called: Diyo Inc *(G-2312)*	
Togetherall	315 434-0911
1209 N Orange St Wilmington (19801) *(G-20345)*	
Toivotek Inc	224 805-9554
1207 Delaware Ave Ste 2244 Wilmington (19801) *(G-20346)*	
Token Security Inc	972 546-9803
1007 N Orange St Fl 10 Wilmington (19801) *(G-20347)*	
Tolbert Enterprise Inc	866 986-5237
200 Cntnntal Dr Chrstana Newark (19713) *(G-12204)*	
TOLedo&giron USA LLC	302 261-3771
16192 Coastal Hwy Lewes (19958) *(G-6568)*	
Toll Njx 4 Corp	302 652-3252
1010 Maple St Wilmington (19805) *(G-20348)*	
Tolton Builders Inc	302 239-5357
7301 Lancaster Pike Hockessin (19707) *(G-5406)*	
Tom Can and Son General Contr	302 737-5551
210 S Dillwyn Rd Newark (19711) *(G-12205)*	
Tom McDonald Contracting	302 219-7939
302 Mcfarland Dr Newark (19702) *(G-12206)*	
Tom Rainey Builders LLC	302 381-5339
31503 S Conley Cir Lewes (19958) *(G-6569)*	
Tom Wiseley Insurance Agency	302 832-7700
1400 Peoples Plz Ste 228 Newark (19702) *(G-12207)*	
Tom Wright Real Estate	302 234-6026
7234 Lancaster Pike Ste 101 Hockessin (19707) *(G-5407)*	

ALPHABETIC SECTION — Tourette Syndrome

Tom's Autobody, Wilmington *Also Called: Thomas Karmanski* *(G-20311)*

Tomaros Change.. 856 542-8861
357 Lenape Way Claymont (19703) *(G-1314)*

Tomaros Change.. 844 222-8500
1261 Parish Ave Claymont (19703) *(G-1315)*

Tomasi Usa LLC.. 302 449-6492
1232 Choptank Rd Middletown (19709) *(G-7651)*

Tomato Sunshine, Rehoboth Beach *Also Called: Ernie Deangelis* *(G-12746)*

Tomi Inc... 650 488-3054
2035 Sunset Lake Rd Newark (19702) *(G-12208)*

Tomkat.. 302 598-8823
308 Potomac Rd Wilmington (19803) *(G-20349)*

Toms Barber Shop.. 302 992-9635
3317 Old Capitol Trl Ste A Wilmington (19808) *(G-20350)*

Toms Cabinet Shop Inc... 302 258-6285
20983 Sanfilippo Rd Bridgeville (19933) *(G-775)*

Toms Sealing & Striping Co.................................... 302 531-7039
986 Caldwell Corner Rd Townsend (19734) *(G-14082)*

Toner Jerome P Sr Patrici..................................... 302 239-7271
111 Great Circle Rd Newark (19711) *(G-12209)*

Tonic Health, Wilmington *Also Called: Tonic Health LLC* *(G-20351)*

Tonic Health LLC (PA).. 510 386-2530
1209 N Orange St Wilmington (19801) *(G-20351)*

Tony Ashburn Inc.. 302 677-1940
872 Walker Rd Ste A Dover (19904) *(G-3697)*

Tony Milam - State Farm Ins AG............................. 302 732-3220
32442 Royal Blvd Unit 3 Dagsboro (19939) *(G-1518)*

Tookuai Inc.. 302 291-1505
16192 Coastal Hwy Lewes (19958) *(G-6570)*

Tools & More, New Castle *Also Called: Mechanics Paradise Inc* *(G-9355)*

Toosacom Inc... 415 240-0442
600 N Broad St Ste 5 Middletown (19709) *(G-7652)*

Tooze & Easter MD PA.. 302 735-8700
720 S Queen St Dover (19904) *(G-3698)*

Top Dog Best Games LLC..................................... 949 859-8869
3422 Old Capitol Trl Ste 528 Wilmington (19808) *(G-20352)*

Top Impact LLC... 646 830-4324
8 The Grn Dover (19901) *(G-3699)*

Top Notch Beauty.. 302 501-5442
120 Mario Dr Bear (19701) *(G-537)*

Top Notch Cleaning... 302 893-7643
6 Quail Hollow Dr Hockessin (19707) *(G-5408)*

Top Notch Cleaning Service.................................. 302 854-6611
16562 Seashore Hwy Georgetown (19947) *(G-4557)*

Top Notch Home Services.................................... 302 275-2459
33 Donaldson Dr Newark (19713) *(G-12210)*

Top Notch Htg & A C & Rfrgn................................. 302 645-7171
33806 Dreamweaver Ln Lewes (19958) *(G-6571)*

Top Notch Plumbing LLC...................................... 302 381-9096
29498 Piney Neck Rd Dagsboro (19939) *(G-1519)*

Top of Hllbrndywine Apartments............................ 302 482-8544
2101 Prior Rd Wilmington (19809) *(G-20353)*

Top of The Hill-Brandwine Apts, Wilmington *Also Called: Top of Hllbrndywine Apartments* *(G-20353)*

Top of The Line Jantr Svcs................................... 302 645-2668
19602 Mulberry Knoll Rd Lewes (19958) *(G-6572)*

Top Qality Indus Finishers Inc............................... 302 778-5005
1204 E 12th St Ste 1 Wilmington (19802) *(G-20354)*

Top Rated Media Inc.. 888 550-9273
1000 N West St Ste 1200 Wilmington (19801) *(G-20355)*

Top Tier Remodeling.. 302 250-4845
1031 Liberty Rd Ste 101 Wilmington (19804) *(G-20356)*

Top Tier Trucking Inc... 917 545-5170
365 Northdown Dr Dover (19904) *(G-3700)*

Topaz & Associates LLC....................................... 302 448-8914
1201 N Market St Wilmington (19801) *(G-20357)*

Topiary Tech LLC.. 302 636-5440
2711 Centerville Rd # 400 Wilmington (19808) *(G-20358)*

Topkis Financial Advisors LLC............................... 302 654-4444
910 Foulk Rd Ste 200 Wilmington (19803) *(G-20359)*

Topmac LLC... 609 517-0585
413 8th Ave Wilmington (19805) *(G-20360)*

Toppers Spa... 302 857-2020
1131 N Dupont Hwy Dover (19901) *(G-3701)*

Tops International Corp....................................... 302 738-8889
3801 Old Capitol Trl Wilmington (19808) *(G-20361)*

Toptal LLC (PA)... 414 550-3054
2810 N Church St Ste 36879 Wilmington (19802) *(G-20362)*

Toptel Inc.. 310 999-4320
8 The Grn Ste D Dover (19901) *(G-3702)*

Toptracker LLC... 415 230-0131
2810 N Church St Ste 36879 Wilmington (19802) *(G-20363)*

Torbert Fnrl Chpel Ambince Svc............................ 302 734-3341
61 S Bradford St Dover (19904) *(G-3703)*

Torbert Funeral Chapel Inc................................... 302 734-3341
61 S Bradford St Dover (19904) *(G-3704)*

Tornado II Janitorial Svc LLC................................ 302 898-1370
510 A St Wilmington (19801) *(G-20364)*

Torregiani Seth DDo PA....................................... 302 407-5412
2502 Silverside Rd Ste 5 Wilmington (19810) *(G-20365)*

Torrengineering LLC... 302 367-8365
26 E Commerce St Ste 1 Smyrna (19977) *(G-13915)*

Torresdrywall LLC... 302 228-6450
305 Cubbage Dr Lincoln (19960) *(G-6706)*

Toshiko N Reckner Rph....................................... 302 697-6407
36 Holly Cove Ln Dover (19901) *(G-3705)*

Tospay Inc... 347 474-0402
16192 Coastal Hwy Lewes (19958) *(G-6573)*

Tot's Turf Child Care Center, Camden *Also Called: Delaware Adlescent Program Inc* *(G-816)*

Total Basement Care... 302 367-4789
304 Concord Ave Wilmington (19802) *(G-20366)*

Total Bath Transformations.................................. 302 985-7649
402 Union Church Rd Townsend (19734) *(G-14083)*

Total Beauty Supply Inc....................................... 302 798-4647
2320 Sconset Rd Wilmington (19810) *(G-20367)*

Total Care Physicians... 302 998-2977
2601 Annand Dr Ste 4 Wilmington (19808) *(G-20368)*

Total Care Physicians (PA)................................... 302 798-0666
405 Silverside Rd Ste 111 Wilmington (19809) *(G-20369)*

Total Climate Control Inc..................................... 302 836-6240
2694 Frazer Rd Newark (19702) *(G-12211)*

Total Health & Rehabilitation................................ 302 477-0800
1303 Veale Rd Wilmington (19810) *(G-20370)*

Total Health & Rehabilitation................................ 302 999-9202
2060 Limestone Rd Ste 202 Wilmington (19808) *(G-20371)*

Total Health Rehab, Wilmington *Also Called: Total Health & Rehabilitation* *(G-20370)*

Total Pest Solutions.. 302 275-7159
309 Quail Run Camden Wyoming (19934) *(G-984)*

Total Pest Solutions.. 302 368-8081
4 Mill Park Ct Ste C Newark (19713) *(G-12212)*

Total Resistance LLC.. 302 384-3077
5105 Diana Dr Wilmington (19808) *(G-20372)*

Total Services Inc... 302 575-1132
31 Germay Dr Wilmington (19804) *(G-20373)*

Total Wellness Innovations Inc.............................. 404 543-9061
251 Little Falls Dr Wilmington (19808) *(G-20374)*

Totalgreen Holland, Wilmington *Also Called: Q Vandenberg & Sons Inc* *(G-19272)*

Totaltranslogistics LLC.. 302 325-4245
8 Mccullough Dr New Castle (19720) *(G-9629)*

Totaltrax Inc... 302 514-0600
920 W Basin Rd Ste 400 New Castle (19720) *(G-9630)*

Toubasam Inc... 302 299-2954
710 N Market St Ste 2b Wilmington (19801) *(G-20375)*

Touch Class Cleaning Service............................... 302 482-5357
410 N Ramunno Dr Unit 1705 Middletown (19709) *(G-7653)*

Touch of Italy Bakery LLC.................................... 302 827-2132
33323 E Chesapeake St Unit 31 Lewes (19958) *(G-6574)*

Touchmagix Inc... 310 230-5083
3524 Silverside Rd Ste 35b Wilmington (19810) *(G-20376)*

Touchstone Systems Inc...................................... 302 324-5322
42 Reads Way C New Castle (19720) *(G-9631)*

Tourette Syndrome.. 302 547-6306
112 E Kilts Ln Middletown (19709) *(G-7654)*

(PA)=Parent Co (HQ)=Headquarters (DH)=Div Headquarters

Tow Plus 302 468-5987
   1732 Marsh Rd Wilmington (19810) *(G-20377)*

Tower Business Machines Inc 302 395-1445
   278 Quigley Blvd Historic New Castle (19720) *(G-5088)*

Tower Business Systems, Historic New Castle Also Called: Tower Business Machines Inc *(G-5088)*

Towers Signs LLC 302 629-7450
   22876 Sussex Hwy Unit 6 Seaford (19973) *(G-13433)*

Towle Institute 302 993-1408
   4210 Limestone Rd Wilmington (19808) *(G-20378)*

Towles Electric Inc 302 674-4985
   621 W Division St Dover (19904) *(G-3706)*

Town & Country Homes of Keller 302 252-5911
   755 N Broad St Middletown (19709) *(G-7655)*

Town and Country Salon 302 322-2929
   18 E 5th St Historic New Castle (19720) *(G-5089)*

Town and Country Trust 302 328-8700
   270 Brandywine Dr Bear (19701) *(G-538)*

Town Court Apartments, Wilmington Also Called: Apartment Communities Corp *(G-14503)*

Town Hair Salon 302 803-4535
   106 Peoples Plz Newark (19702) *(G-12213)*

Town of Middletown 302 376-9950
   130 Hampden Rd Middletown (19709) *(G-7656)*

Towne Place Suites By Marriott 302 369-6212
   410 Eagle Run Rd Newark (19702) *(G-12214)*

Townsend Bros Inc 302 674-0100
   21 Emerson Dr Dover (19901) *(G-3707)*

Townsend Fitness Equipment, Smyrna Also Called: David L Townsend Co Inc *(G-13692)*

Townsends, Georgetown Also Called: Omtron USA LLC *(G-4452)*

Toxtrap Inc 302 698-1400
   12 S Springview Dr Dover (19901) *(G-3708)*

Toyo Fibre USA Inc 302 475-3699
   2706 Alexander Dr Wilmington (19810) *(G-20379)*

Toys Story LLC 267 334-9822
   75 Oriole Ln Smyrna (19977) *(G-13916)*

TP Indira and Mdpa, Dover Also Called: Manveen Duggal MD *(G-3015)*

TP It Group LLC 302 444-0441
   8 The Grn Ste A Dover (19901) *(G-3709)*

TP Wireless Inc 302 235-0402
   122 Lantana Dr Hockessin (19707) *(G-5409)*

Tpf Technologies LLC 703 665-4588
   1201 N Orange St Ste 600 Wilmington (19801) *(G-20380)*

Tpi Partners Inc (PA) 302 855-0139
   21649 Cedar Creek Ave Georgetown (19947) *(G-4558)*

Tpp Acquisition Inc 302 674-4805
   1365 N Dupont Hwy Ste 4012 Dover (19901) *(G-3710)*

Tpw Management, Lewes Also Called: Tpw Management LLC *(G-6575)*

Tpw Management LLC 302 227-7878
   17577 Nassau Commons Blvd Ste 103 Lewes (19958) *(G-6575)*

Tpwb69, Newark Also Called: Tasha P Brown *(G-12162)*

Traction Wholesale Center Inc 302 743-8473
   600 S Heald St Wilmington (19801) *(G-20381)*

Tractor Supply Company 302 629-3627
   20952 Sussex Hwy Seaford (19973) *(G-13434)*

Tractor Supply Company 302 659-3333
   1300 S Dupont Blvd Smyrna (19977) *(G-13917)*

Tracy B Harris 302 644-1477
   18002 Ebb Tide Dr Lewes (19958) *(G-6576)*

Tracy Halterman 302 545-9930
   1708 Lovering Ave Ste 201 Wilmington (19806) *(G-20382)*

Trade & Consulting Group Corp (DH) 302 477-9800
   3511 Silverside Rd Ste 105 Wilmington (19810) *(G-20383)*

Trade Cafe, Wilmington Also Called: Trade Cafe USA Inc *(G-20384)*

Trade Cafe USA Inc 647 694-2656
   2801 Cntrvlle Rd Ste 8003 Wilmington (19808) *(G-20384)*

Trade Investors LLC 888 579-0286
   160 Greentree Dr Ste 101 Dover (19904) *(G-3711)*

Trade News Inc 212 884-8089
   427 N Tatnall St Ste 9465 Wilmington (19801) *(G-20385)*

Tradeally Incorporated (PA) 832 997-2582
   16192 Coastal Hwy Lewes (19958) *(G-6577)*

Trademark Signs 484 832-5770
   2621 Boxwood Dr Wilmington (19810) *(G-20386)*

Traffic Sign Solutions Inc (PA) 302 295-4836
   1000 N West St Ste 1200 Wilmington (19801) *(G-20387)*

Trailer Parts Superstore, Newark Also Called: Eastern Group Inc *(G-10594)*

Train Hard Win Big Inc 302 993-6189
   100 Philadelphia Pike Wilmington (19809) *(G-20388)*

Training Center 302 538-0847
   146 Brookside Blvd Newark (19713) *(G-12215)*

Training Center, The, New Castle Also Called: James Sutton *(G-9252)*

Training Solution 302 379-3070
   406 Suburban Dr Newark (19711) *(G-12216)*

Traitel Telecom Corp 619 331-1913
   3422 Old Capitol Trl Wilmington (19808) *(G-20389)*

Tramaine & Sons Lawn Care LLC 302 897-0524
   500 S Buttonwood St Wilmington (19801) *(G-20390)*

Trane, New Castle Also Called: Trane US Inc *(G-9632)*

Trane US Inc 302 395-0200
   66 Southgate Blvd New Castle (19720) *(G-9632)*

Tranquil Roots Counseling 301 275-0225
   4867 Plum Run Ct Wilmington (19808) *(G-20391)*

Tranquil Solutions For A 302 383-5011
   550 Janvier Dr Middletown (19709) *(G-7657)*

Tranquil Spirit Massage & Spa 302 538-1135
   9 E Loockerman St Ste 208 Dover (19901) *(G-3712)*

Tranquility By Tara Colazo 302 668-4032
   5700 Kirkwood Hwy Ste 206 Wilmington (19808) *(G-20392)*

Tranquility Counseling Inc 302 636-0700
   314 E Main St Ste 402 Newark (19711) *(G-12217)*

Trans Logistics LLC 267 244-6550
   4000 N Market St Wilmington (19802) *(G-20393)*

Trans Plus Inc 302 323-3051
   423 W 7th St Historic New Castle (19720) *(G-5090)*

Trans Products, Milford Also Called: F D Hammond Enterprises Inc *(G-7886)*

Trans Un Sttlment Slutions Inc (DH) 800 916-8800
   5300 Brandywine Pkwy 100 Wilmington (19803) *(G-20394)*

Transactional Web Inc 908 216-5054
   8 W 13th St Wilmington (19801) *(G-20395)*

Transaxle LLC 302 322-8300
   4060 N Dupont Hwy Ste 6 New Castle (19720) *(G-9633)*

Transcare 302 322-2454
   6 Bellecor Dr New Castle (19720) *(G-9634)*

Transcontinental Airways Corp 202 817-2020
   1000 N West St Ste 1200 Wilmington (19801) *(G-20396)*

Transcore, Middletown Also Called: Transcore LP *(G-7658)*

Transcore LP 302 838-7429
   2111 Dupont Pkwy Middletown (19709) *(G-7658)*

Transflo Terminal Services Inc 302 994-3853
   1205 Centerville Rd Wilmington (19808) *(G-20397)*

Transformers LLC 302 757-3803
   113 Register Dr Newark (19711) *(G-12218)*

Transformify Inc 302 205-0685
   2093 Philadelphia Pike Claymont (19703) *(G-1316)*

Transforming Lives Inc 302 379-1043
   5614 Kirkwood Hwy Wilmington (19808) *(G-20398)*

Transforming Wellness LLC 302 249-2526
   35802 Atlantic Ave Millville (19967) *(G-8550)*

Transitional Fisher 302 322-4124
   10 Denby Ct New Castle (19720) *(G-9635)*

Transitional Youth 302 423-7543
   8748 Greenwood Rd Greenwood (19950) *(G-4672)*

Translateai LLC 213 675-6702
   8 The Grn Ste A Dover (19901) *(G-3713)*

Translucence Research Inc 425 753-8886
   651 N Broad St Ste 206 Middletown (19709) *(G-7659)*

Transm, Newark Also Called: All Trans Transmission Inc *(G-9820)*

Transmed Systems Inc 650 584-3316
   1000 N West St Ste 1000 Wilmington (19801) *(G-20399)*

Transparency Market RES Inc (PA) 518 618-1030
   1000 N West St Ste 1200 Wilmington (19801) *(G-20400)*

Transport Wkrs Un Amer Intl Un 302 652-1503
   1524 Bonwood Rd Wilmington (19805) *(G-20401)*

ALPHABETIC SECTION

TRANSPORT WORKERS UNION O LOCA, Wilmington Also Called: Transport Wkrs Un Amer Intl Un *(G-20401)*

Transportation, Felton Also Called: Apex Transportation Svcs LLC *(G-3941)*

Transportation, Felton Also Called: Limousine Unlimited LLC *(G-3998)*

Transportation, Newark Also Called: East Coast Trans LLC *(G-10593)*

Transportation Department, New Castle Also Called: Colonial School District *(G-8958)*

Transporttee Inc..302 330-8912
  8 The Grn Ste A Dover (19901) *(G-3714)*

Transstate Jet Service Inc..................................302 346-3102
  139 Davis Cir Dover (19904) *(G-3715)*

Traps Plumbing Heating A/C..............................302 677-1775
  1851 S Dupont Hwy Dover (19901) *(G-3716)*

Trash For Cash..302 540-1513
  208 Timber Knoll Dr Bear (19701) *(G-539)*

Trash Porters LLC...302 709-1550
  112 S French St Wilmington (19801) *(G-20402)*

Trash Smell Buster, Wilmington Also Called: Ingenious Inventions AG LLC *(G-17334)*

Trauma Film Production Pr LLC........................623 582-2287
  8 The Grn Ste A Dover (19901) *(G-3717)*

Trauma Rehabilitation PA..................................302 777-7723
  11b Trolley Sq Wilmington (19806) *(G-20403)*

Travel Inn New..302 322-4500
  232 S Dupont Hwy New Castle (19720) *(G-9636)*

Travel Offshore..410 246-6648
  22 Berue Ct Selbyville (19975) *(G-13613)*

Travelapp, Wilmington Also Called: Travelapp Inc *(G-20404)*

Travelapp Inc...617 580-7978
  300 Delaware Ave Ste 210 Wilmington (19801) *(G-20404)*

Travelbook Inc (PA)...646 575-6731
  16192 Coastal Hwy Lewes (19958) *(G-6578)*

Travelers Inn, Milford Also Called: Gulab Management Inc *(G-7915)*

Travelers Joy Inc...888 878-5569
  11 S Hampshire Ct Wilmington (19807) *(G-20405)*

Travelodge, New Castle Also Called: New Castle Lodging Corporation *(G-9410)*

Travelodge, New Castle Also Called: Shriji Hospitality (not Llc) *(G-9567)*

Travelory Inc..925 216-0718
  8 The Grn Ste B Dover (19901) *(G-3718)*

Travelpad Rentals LLC (PA)...............................203 751-1569
  2055 Limestone Rd 200c Wilmington (19808) *(G-20406)*

Travly, Dover Also Called: Travly US LLC *(G-3719)*

Travly US LLC (PA)...901 228-5882
  850 New Burton Rd Ste 201 Dover (19904) *(G-3719)*

Treatment Access Ctr...302 856-5487
  21309 Berlin Rd Unit 7 Georgetown (19947) *(G-4559)*

Treatment Foster Care - Newark, Dover Also Called: Pressley Ridge Foundation *(G-3367)*

Treatment Fster Care - Grgtown, Georgetown Also Called: Pressley Ridge Foundation *(G-4472)*

Treehouse Wellness Center LLC.......................302 893-1001
  1004 N Monroe St Wilmington (19801) *(G-20407)*

Treinta, Middletown Also Called: Treinta Inc *(G-7660)*

Treinta Inc..786 400-2430
  651 N Broad St Ste 206 Middletown (19709) *(G-7660)*

Trellist Inc..302 593-1432
  2317 Macdonough Rd Ste 100 Wilmington (19805) *(G-20408)*

Trendz Salon and Spa..302 632-3045
  47 Greentree Dr Dover (19904) *(G-3720)*

Trenton Block Delaware Inc...............................302 684-0112
  701 Federal St Milton (19968) *(G-8722)*

Tresses Hair Studio..302 670-7356
  16 Squire Cir Dover (19901) *(G-3721)*

Tretek LLC...888 407-9737
  2055 Limestone Rd Ste 200c Wilmington (19808) *(G-20409)*

Trevcon Construction Co...................................908 413-7001
  33915 Mcnicol Rd Lewes (19958) *(G-6579)*

Trexgen Nutrascience LLC................................302 520-2406
  254 Chapman Rd Ste 208 Newark (19702) *(G-12219)*

Tri County Electrical Services, Laurel Also Called: Daniel George Bebee Inc *(G-5492)*

Tri County Materials...302 677-0156
  3700 S Bay Rd Dover (19901) *(G-3722)*

Tri State Battery, Newark Also Called: Tri State Btry & Auto Elc Inc *(G-12220)*

Tri State Battery, Newark Also Called: Tri-State Btry Alternator LLC *(G-12224)*

Tri State Btry & Auto Elc Inc (PA)......................302 292-2330
  107 Albe Dr Ste H Newark (19702) *(G-12220)*

Tri State Cleaning...302 644-6554
  30181 E Mill Run Milton (19968) *(G-8723)*

Tri State Construction Inc..................................609 980-1000
  13 Buckeye Ln Smyrna (19977) *(G-13918)*

Tri State Foot Ankle Cent...................................302 239-1625
  6300 Limestone Rd Hockessin (19707) *(G-5410)*

Tri State Roofers, Wilmington Also Called: Roofers Inc *(G-19564)*

Tri State Termite & Pest Ctrl..............................302 239-0512
  1170 Corner Ketch Rd Newark (19711) *(G-12221)*

Tri State Waste Solutions...................................302 323-0200
  Wilmington (19804) *(G-20410)*

Tri Valley Agency Inc..302 482-3802
  63 Standiford Ct Wilmington (19804) *(G-20411)*

Tri-County Security...302 709-2244
  1901 Ogletown Rd Newark (19711) *(G-12222)*

Tri-State Battery, Newark Also Called: Tsb Inc *(G-12242)*

Tri-State Bird Rescue RES Inc...........................302 737-9543
  170 Possum Hollow Rd Newark (19711) *(G-12223)*

Tri-State Btry Alternator LLC.............................320 292-2330
  107 Albe Dr Ste H Newark (19702) *(G-12224)*

Tri-State Carpet Maint Inc..................................302 654-8193
  2 S Poplar St Fl 1 Wilmington (19801) *(G-20412)*

Tri-State Grouting LLC.......................................302 286-0701
  567 Walther Rd Newark (19702) *(G-12225)*

Tri-State Integrative Hlth LLC............................302 743-2328
  34b Trolley Sq Wilmington (19806) *(G-20413)*

Tri-State Lift Truck Ltd......................................302 427-2800
  70b Germay Dr Wilmington (19804) *(G-20414)*

Tri-State Mobile Home Supply, Millsboro Also Called: T & C Enterprise Incorporated *(G-8479)*

Tri-State Pooper Scoopers Inc..........................302 322-4522
  21 Prestbury Sq Newark (19713) *(G-12226)*

Tri-State SEC & Contrls LLC..............................302 299-2175
  2860 Ogletown Rd Apt 2 Newark (19713) *(G-12227)*

Tri-State Technologies Inc.................................302 658-5400
  701 Cornell Dr Ste 13 Wilmington (19801) *(G-20415)*

Tri-State Underground Inc.................................302 293-9352
  2141 Old Kirkwood Rd Bear (19701) *(G-540)*

Tri-State Underground Inc.................................302 836-8030
  4369 Dupont Pkwy Townsend (19734) *(G-14084)*

Tri-Tek Corporation...302 239-1638
  1 Medori Blvd Ste B Wilmington (19801) *(G-20416)*

Triad Construction Co, New Castle Also Called: Triad Construction Company LLC *(G-9637)*

Triad Construction Company LLC.....................302 652-3339
  210 Marsh Ln New Castle (19720) *(G-9637)*

Triagons LLC...619 761-0797
  8 The Grn Ste B Dover (19901) *(G-3723)*

Trial Transport Logistics....................................302 383-5907
  400 Wyoming Ave Wilmington (19809) *(G-20417)*

Trialogics LLC...302 313-9000
  2 Mill Rd Ste 110 Wilmington (19806) *(G-20418)*

Triangle Electrical Svc Co..................................302 856-7880
  22180 Lewes Georgetown Hwy Georgetown (19947) *(G-4560)*

Triangle Fastener Corporation...........................302 322-0600
  243 Quigley Blvd Ste C Historic New Castle (19720) *(G-5091)*

Triangle HM Imprvmnt Cntrctr L........................302 883-4943
  1410 Lochmeath Way Dover (19901) *(G-3724)*

Tribetech Solutions LLC.....................................302 597-7890
  8 The Grn Ste A Dover (19901) *(G-3725)*

Tributarymarinecom LLC....................................443 553-9485
  265 Airport Rd New Castle (19720) *(G-9638)*

Tribute Interactive Inc..302 803-5432
  251 Little Falls Dr Wilmington (19808) *(G-20419)*

Tricklestar Inc..888 700-1098
  251 Little Falls Dr Wilmington (19808) *(G-20420)*

Tricomm Services Corporation..........................302 454-2975
  604 Interchange Blvd Newark (19711) *(G-12228)*

Tricon Construction MGT Inc.............................302 838-6500
  13 King Ct Ste 3 New Castle (19720) *(G-9639)*

ALPHABETIC SECTION

Tridge Trade Inc..954 512-3734
  8 The Grn Ste B Dover (19901) *(G-3726)*

Trigger Action LLC..302 858-8629
  16992 Redden Rd Georgetown (19947) *(G-4561)*

Triglia Express Inc..302 846-2248
  38001 Bi State Blvd Delmar (19940) *(G-1643)*

Triglia Trans Co...302 846-3795
  Bystate Blvd Delmar (19940) *(G-1644)*

Triglias Transportation Co...................................302 846-2141
  Rte 13 A Delmar (19940) *(G-1645)*

Triko, Dover *Also Called: Trikorp Inc (G-3727)*

Trikorp Inc..970 690-6285
  8 The Grn Ste A Dover (19901) *(G-3727)*

Trilogy Salon & Spa..302 388-1210
  312 Southern Rd Wilmington (19804) *(G-20421)*

Trilogy Salon and Day Spa Inc.............................302 292-3511
  1200 Capitol Trl Newark (19711) *(G-12229)*

Trim Shop, Newark *Also Called: Color Dye Systems and Co (G-10279)*

Trimark Enterprises Inc.....................................302 683-9065
  2406 W Newport Pike Wilmington (19804) *(G-20422)*

Trimark Inc..302 322-2143
  621 Delaware St Ste 200 Historic New Castle (19720) *(G-5092)*

Trimble Inc..302 368-2434
  107c Albe Dr Ste C Newark (19702) *(G-12230)*

Trinet Consultants Inc (HQ)................................302 633-9348
  1106 Elderon Dr Wilmington (19808) *(G-20423)*

Triniiity Group LLC..302 402-1726
  24a Trolley Sq Wilmington (19806) *(G-20424)*

Trinity 3 Enterprises Inc....................................267 973-2666
  38 Ayrshire St Bear (19701) *(G-541)*

Trinity Cloud, Wilmington *Also Called: Trinity Cloud Company (G-20425)*

Trinity Cloud Company.....................................973 494-8190
  1013 Centre Rd Ste 403s Wilmington (19805) *(G-20425)*

Trinity Ems Educators Staffing............................302 373-7276
  65 S Skyward Dr Newark (19713) *(G-12231)*

Trinity Enterprises LLC.....................................302 449-1301
  3230 Philadelphia Pike Claymont (19703) *(G-1317)*

Trinity Freight Logistics Inc................................302 543-3128
  12 Castlegate Ct Newark (19702) *(G-12232)*

Trinity Gold Consulting LLC...............................302 498-9063
  703 N Jackson St Wilmington (19805) *(G-20426)*

Trinity Halthcare Staffing LLC.............................302 420-3782
  707 Pinewood Dr Middletown (19709) *(G-7661)*

Trinity Heating & Air..302 344-3628
  9674 Tharp Rd Seaford (19973) *(G-13435)*

Trinity Home Health Care Corp (PA).....................302 838-2710
  1400 Peoples Plz Ste 215 Newark (19702) *(G-12233)*

Trinity Home Health Care LLC............................410 620-9366
  1400 Peoples Plz Ste 215 Newark (19702) *(G-12234)*

Trinity Logistics Inc...302 595-2116
  23 Fantail Ct New Castle (19720) *(G-9640)*

Trinity Logistics Inc (HQ)..................................302 253-3900
  50 Fallon Ave Seaford (19973) *(G-13436)*

Trinity Medical Center PA..................................302 846-0618
  8 E Grove St Delmar (19940) *(G-1646)*

Trinity Subsurface LLC.....................................855 387-4648
  14 Hadco Rd Ste 103 Wilmington (19804) *(G-20427)*

Trio Academy LLC..646 330-9211
  1013 Centre Rd Ste 403b Wilmington (19805) *(G-20428)*

Trio Enterprises LLC.......................................302 832-5575
  202 Loft St Townsend (19734) *(G-14085)*

Triodent, Wilmington *Also Called: Rhondium Corporation (G-19461)*

Triple A Cleaning Services Inc............................302 236-0407
  32277 Pelican Ct Millsboro (19966) *(G-8487)*

Triple Tzz Hvac LLC..302 846-3220
  17114 Whitesville Rd Delmar (19940) *(G-1647)*

Tripleone Inc..833 391-0111
  8 The Grn Ste 8063 Dover (19901) *(G-3728)*

Triprobotics, Claymont *Also Called: Triprobotics Inc (G-1318)*

Triprobotics Inc..646 798-7137
  2093 Philadelphia Pike # 2 Claymont (19703) *(G-1318)*

Trisco Foods LLC...719 352-3218
  2711 Centerville Rd Ste 400 Wilmington (19808) *(G-20429)*

Tristate Courier & Carriage................................302 654-3345
  1001 N Jefferson St Ste 100 Wilmington (19801) *(G-20430)*

Tristate Fbrcn and Machg.................................302 533-5877
  38 Albe Dr Newark (19702) *(G-12235)*

Tristate Mechanical, Wilmington *Also Called: Coastal Mechanical (G-15510)*

Tristate Remodeling Corp.................................302 444-8314
  625 Dawson Dr Ste F Newark (19713) *(G-12236)*

Tritek, Hockessin *Also Called: Tritek Technologies Inc (G-5412)*

Tritek Corporation..302 239-1638
  103 E Bridle Path Hockessin (19707) *(G-5411)*

Tritek Technologies, Hockessin *Also Called: Tritek Corporation (G-5411)*

Tritek Technologies Inc (PA)..............................302 239-1638
  103 E Bridle Path Hockessin (19707) *(G-5412)*

Tritek Technologies Inc....................................302 573-5096
  1 Medori Blvd Ste B Wilmington (19801) *(G-20431)*

Triton Construction Co Inc................................516 780-8100
  101 Pigeon Point Rd New Castle (19720) *(G-9641)*

Triumph Bike Detailing.....................................302 463-3606
  268 Whitherspoon Ln Newark (19713) *(G-12237)*

Triumph Labs Inc...561 886-7121
  2093 Philadelphia Pike Ste 4204 Claymont (19703) *(G-1319)*

Triumph Worldwide Inc....................................302 465-6898
  112 E Green Valley Cir Newark (19711) *(G-12238)*

Trivedi Foundation LLC...................................302 678-4629
  104 Overlook Pl Dover (19901) *(G-3729)*

Trivett Contracting...302 275-6452
  4601 Governor Printz Blvd Unit F Wilmington (19809) *(G-20432)*

Troi LLC..302 528-0229
  28 Austin Rd Wilmington (19810) *(G-20433)*

Troisi, Ernest DPM PA, Newark *Also Called: Delaware Foot & Ankle Assoc (G-10445)*

Trolley Laundry...302 654-3538
  33a Trolley Sq Wilmington (19806) *(G-20434)*

Trolley Sq Opn Mri & Imgng Ctr.........................302 472-5555
  1010 N Bancroft Pkwy Ste 101 Wilmington (19805) *(G-20435)*

Trolley Square Branch 307, Wilmington *Also Called: Wilmington Savings Fund Soc (G-20842)*

Trolley Square Investors LLC.............................302 658-1000
  2711 Centerville Rd Ste 400 Wilmington (19808) *(G-20436)*

Trolley Square Nutrition...................................302 757-6669
  294 Campfield Rd Newark (19713) *(G-12239)*

Trolley Web..302 468-7247
  4611 Bedford Blvd Wilmington (19803) *(G-20437)*

Tropacool..302 245-4078
  23738 Heavens Walk Way Georgetown (19947) *(G-4562)*

Trophy Shop...302 656-4438
  303 W 8th St Wilmington (19801) *(G-20438)*

Tropic Fever Tanning Salon...............................302 875-1500
  303 S Poplar St Ste 1 Laurel (19956) *(G-5616)*

Tropic Wholesale, New Castle *Also Called: Village Green Inc (G-9671)*

Troposphere Technologies LLC (PA)....................613 833-0984
  8 The Grn Ste 5258 Dover (19901) *(G-3730)*

Trottys Concrete Pumping Inc............................302 732-3100
  34107 Dupont Blvd Frankford (19945) *(G-4154)*

Trou Auto..302 762-3200
  735 Philadelphia Pike Wilmington (19809) *(G-20439)*

Troutman Machine Company Inc........................302 674-3540
  1175 S Governors Ave Dover (19904) *(G-3731)*

Troutman Ppper Hmlton Snders L.......................302 777-6500
  1313 N Market St Ste 5100 Wilmington (19801) *(G-20440)*

Trovety Inc...302 291-2252
  16192 Coastal Hwy Lewes (19958) *(G-6580)*

Troy Farmer..888 711-0094
  16 Catherine Ct Bear (19701) *(G-542)*

Troy Granite Inc (PA).......................................302 292-1750
  711 Interchange Blvd Newark (19711) *(G-12240)*

Troyer Construction Inc....................................302 422-0745
  6650 Shawnee Rd Milford (19963) *(G-8120)*

Tru American Enterprises LLC...........................801 404-1124
  651 N Broad St Middletown (19709) *(G-7662)*

Tru Beauti LLC...302 353-9249
  307 Bald Eagle Way Middletown (19709) *(G-7663)*

ALPHABETIC SECTION

Tru By Hilton, Georgetown Also Called: Georgetown Hotel LLC *(G-4339)*

Tru Construction LLC 302 740-9691
1028 W Founds St Townsend (19734) *(G-14086)*

Tru General Contractor Inc 302 354-0553
3307 Faulkland Rd Wilmington (19808) *(G-20441)*

Tru Green-Chemlawn, Wilmington Also Called: Trugreen Limited Partnership *(G-20445)*

Tru Grit LLC 302 593-4700
525 Black Diamond Rd Smyrna (19977) *(G-13919)*

Truck Lagbe Inc 860 810-8677
16192 Coastal Hwy Lewes (19958) *(G-6581)*

Truck Store LLC 302 724-5918
423 S Dupont Hwy Dover (19901) *(G-3732)*

Truck Tech Inc 302 832-8000
1600 Matassino Rd New Castle (19720) *(G-9642)*

Trucking/Logistics, Newark Also Called: Akita Trucking LLC *(G-9804)*

Trudy L Hastings 302 653-3145
365 N Main St Smyrna (19977) *(G-13920)*

True Access Capital Corp 302 652-6774
100 W 10th St Ste 300 Wilmington (19801) *(G-20442)*

True Legacy Rentals LLC 844 857-2271
651 N Broad St Ste 205713 Middletown (19709) *(G-7664)*

True Mobility Inc 302 836-4110
773 S Dupont Hwy New Castle (19720) *(G-9643)*

True North Group LLC 302 539-2488
35322 Bayard Rd Frankford (19945) *(G-4155)*

True Pest Control Services (PA) 302 834-0867
48 Loblolly Ln Middletown (19709) *(G-7665)*

True Religion Apparel Inc 302 894-9425
132 Christiana Mall Newark (19702) *(G-12241)*

True Rival Fitness 302 570-0530
501 Silverside Rd Ste 150 Wilmington (19809) *(G-20443)*

True Spirit Beverage Company 520 356-4730
3411 Silverside Rd Ste 104 Wilmington (19810) *(G-20444)*

True Street Automotive LLC 302 480-4119
899 S Dupont Blvd Smyrna (19977) *(G-13921)*

True Value, Rehoboth Beach Also Called: D F Quillen & Sons Inc *(G-12709)*

True-Pack Ltd (PA) 302 326-2222
420 Churchmans Rd New Castle (19720) *(G-9644)*

Truehost Cloud LLC 972 674-3814
651 N Broad St Ste 205 # 927 Middletown (19709) *(G-7666)*

Trugreen Limited Partnership 302 724-6620
1350 First State Blvd Wilmington (19804) *(G-20445)*

Truitt Insurance Agency Inc 302 645-9344
365 Savannah Rd Lewes (19958) *(G-6582)*

Truitts Hlping Hnds Chldcr/Prs 302 426-6436
2915 Lancaster Ave Wilmington (19805) *(G-20446)*

Trumove Inc 917 379-7427
16192 Coastal Hwy Lewes (19958) *(G-6583)*

Trumpet LLC 303 910-7444
919 N Market St Ste 950 Wilmington (19801) *(G-20447)*

Trunk Tel LLC 302 476-2370
2055 Limestone Rd 200c Wilmington (19808) *(G-20448)*

Trustees of Ardentown 302 475-8193
2308 E Mall St Wilmington (19810) *(G-20449)*

Truveris Inc 800 430-1430
3 Beaver Valley Rd Ste 100 Wilmington (19803) *(G-20450)*

Truvision LLC 267 349-4550
733 W 4th St Wilmington (19801) *(G-20451)*

Tsb Inc 302 292-2330
107 Albe Dr Ste H Newark (19702) *(G-12242)*

TSE Sports 856 889-4913
8 Good Hope Ct Rehoboth Beach (19971) *(G-12996)*

Tsf Incorporated 518 879-6571
3204 Romilly Rd Wilmington (19810) *(G-20452)*

Tsionas Management Co Inc 302 369-8895
2000 Pennsylvania Ave Wilmington (19806) *(G-20453)*

Tsuda Takeshi MD 302 651-6660
1600 Rockland Rd Wilmington (19803) *(G-20454)*

TT Luxury Group LLC 732 242-9795
46 Vansant Rd Newark (19711) *(G-12243)*

TT Spalon 302 668-1477
1319 Mckennans Church Rd Wilmington (19808) *(G-20455)*

Tti Inc 302 725-5189
20420 Spangler Dr Lincoln (19960) *(G-6707)*

Ttna Energy Systems LLC 302 384-9147
3422 Old Capitol Trl # 1468 Wilmington (19808) *(G-20456)*

Tts Tcnja TCI Shipg N Amer Inc (PA) 770 383-4604
1013 Centre Rd Ste 403s Wilmington (19805) *(G-20457)*

Tuckahoe Acres Camping Resort 302 539-1841
36031 Tuckahoe Trl Dagsboro (19939) *(G-1520)*

Tucker Vacation Rentals Inc 302 668-3512
16 Bridleshire Rd Newark (19711) *(G-12244)*

Tucson Hotels LP (PA) 678 830-2438
2711 Centerville Rd Ste 400 Wilmington (19808) *(G-20458)*

Tudor Electric Inc 302 736-1444
801 Otis Dr Dover (19901) *(G-3733)*

Tudor Enterprises, Hartly Also Called: Tudor Enterprises L L C *(G-4910)*

Tudor Enterprises L L C 302 736-8255
4405 Arthursville Rd Hartly (19953) *(G-4910)*

Tuff Tasks LLC 302 983-5990
317 Great Oak Dr Middletown (19709) *(G-7667)*

Tukel Inc 302 520-2380
2093 Philadelphia Pike Ste 2108 Claymont (19703) *(G-1320)*

Tula Yoga Reiki Professionals 302 359-9790
419 N Bradford St Dover (19904) *(G-3734)*

Tumble-Kids LLC 302 530-7800
228 Oakwood Rd Wilmington (19803) *(G-20459)*

Tunnel Industries, Millsboro Also Called: Tunnell Companies LP *(G-8488)*

Tunnell & Raysor PA (PA) 302 856-7313
30 E Pine St Georgetown (19947) *(G-4563)*

Tunnell & Raysor PA 302 644-4442
770 Kings Hwy Lewes (19958) *(G-6584)*

Tunnell Cancer Ctr 302 645-3770
18947 John J Williams Hwy Rehoboth Beach (19971) *(G-12997)*

Tunnell Companies LP (PA) 302 945-9300
34026 Annas Way Unit 1 Millsboro (19966) *(G-8488)*

Turbo Distributors LLC 845 678-6700
1013 Centre Rd Ste 403d Wilmington (19805) *(G-20460)*

Turf Pro Inc 302 218-3530
103 Sandy Dr Ste 100 Newark (19713) *(G-12245)*

Turfhound Inc 215 783-8143
5500 Skyline Dr Ste 6 Wilmington (19808) *(G-20461)*

Turing Machines Inc 415 500-0217
251 Little Falls Dr Wilmington (19808) *(G-20462)*

Turn of Wrench 302 584-1824
100 S Canvasback Ct Smyrna (19977) *(G-13922)*

Turner and Selby Group Inc 302 666-2339
1320 Philadelphia Pike Ste 202 Wilmington (19809) *(G-20463)*

Turning Crnrs-Hand In Hand LLC 302 689-3562
256 Chapman Rd Ste 105-6 Newark (19702) *(G-12246)*

Turning Point At Peoples Place 302 424-2420
1131 Airport Rd Milford (19963) *(G-8121)*

Turning Point Collection LLC 302 275-0167
2055 Limestone Rd Ste 302 Wilmington (19808) *(G-20464)*

Turning Point Yoga, Milton Also Called: Chelsea King *(G-8582)*

Turning Pt Counseling Ctr LLC 214 883-5148
1 N Main St Camden (19934) *(G-898)*

Turnkey Electric LLC 302 858-3726
24648 Zoar Rd Georgetown (19947) *(G-4564)*

Turnstone Builders LLC 302 227-8876
37395 Oyster House Rd Rehoboth Beach (19971) *(G-12998)*

Turnstone Custom Homes, Rehoboth Beach Also Called: Turnstone Holdings LLC *(G-12999)*

Turnstone Holdings LLC 302 227-8876
37395 Oyster House Rd Rehoboth Beach (19971) *(G-12999)*

Turquoise Americallc 302 608-7008
84 Munro Rd Newark (19711) *(G-12247)*

Turquoise Shop Inc 302 366-7448
543 Christiana Mall Newark (19702) *(G-12248)*

Tusi Brothers Inc 302 998-6383
1 Copper Dr Ste 1 Wilmington (19804) *(G-20465)*

Tutor Time Learning Ctrs LLC 302 235-5701
5305 Limestone Rd Wilmington (19808) *(G-20466)*

TW Contracting 302 384-6777
202 New Rd Unit 1 Wilmington (19805) *(G-20467)*

Twash LLC ... 302 488-0248
292 Trafalgar Dr Dover (19904) *(G-3735)*

Twin Angels Service ... 302 545-6749
1373 Kit Cir Bear (19701) *(G-543)*

Twin Creek Farms LLC ... 302 249-2294
638 Canterbury Rd Milford (19963) *(G-8122)*

Twin Hearts Management LLC ... 302 777-5700
200 Banning St Ste 340 Dover (19904) *(G-3736)*

Twin Spans Business Park LLC ... 302 328-5713
405 Marsh Ln Ste 1 Wilmington (19804) *(G-20468)*

Twinco Romax LLC ... 302 998-3019
1 Crowell Rd Wilmington (19804) *(G-20469)*

Twinning LLC ... 609 793-3510
1427 Kynlyn Dr Wilmington (19809) *(G-20470)*

Twisted Hair Designs ... 302 533-6104
2622 Kirkwood Hwy Newark (19711) *(G-12249)*

Twisty Systems LLC ... 571 331-7093
16192 Coastal Hwy Lewes (19958) *(G-6585)*

Two Brothers Roofing LLC ... 302 650-8077
605 W Summit Ave Wilmington (19804) *(G-20471)*

Two Cougars LLC ... 302 358-0197
6 Wyndom Ct Hockessin (19707) *(G-5413)*

Two Men and A Truck, Dover *Also Called: Jkb Corp (G-2792)*

Two Men and A Truck, Magnolia *Also Called: H G Investments LLC (G-6750)*

Two Men and A Truck, New Castle *Also Called: Connolly Options LLC (G-8967)*

Tws Chewsy LLC ... 514 730-8040
1209 N Orange St Wilmington (19801) *(G-20472)*

Txe Global LLC (PA) ... 302 409-0234
500 Delaware Ave Wilmington (19801) *(G-20473)*

Txthinking Inc ... 646 820-1235
2035 Sunset Lake Rd Ste B-2 Newark (19702) *(G-12250)*

Ty Jennifer MD ... 302 651-4459
1600 Rockland Rd Wilmington (19803) *(G-20474)*

Tybout Redfearn & Pell PA ... 302 658-6901
501 Carr Rd Ste 300 Wilmington (19809) *(G-20475)*

Tychron Corporation ... 844 892-4766
1201 N Orange St Ste 7456 Wilmington (19801) *(G-20476)*

Tyco Engineering Tech LLC ... 202 790-9648
501 Silverside Rd Ste 28 Wilmington (19809) *(G-20477)*

Tyco Technology Resources ... 877 706-0510
4550 New Lnden Hl Rd Ste Wilmington (19808) *(G-20478)*

Tycos General Contracting Inc ... 302 268-6766
412 Meco Dr Wilmington (19804) *(G-20479)*

Tycos General Contractors Inc ... 302 478-9267
2112 Silverside Rd Wilmington (19810) *(G-20480)*

Tyden Group Holdings Corp (HQ) ... 740 420-6777
1209 N Orange St Wilmington (19801) *(G-20481)*

Tylaur Inc ... 302 894-9330
2659 Kirkwood Hwy Newark (19711) *(G-12251)*

Tyne Sunderland LLC ... 302 526-1608
413 Eden Cir Bear (19701) *(G-544)*

Tyrant Sportsgear Inc ... 302 530-3410
2017 W Newport Pike Wilmington (19804) *(G-20482)*

Tytrix Inc ... 877 489-8749
8 The Grn Dover (19901) *(G-3737)*

Tz Distributors ... 302 562-1029
263 Quigley Blvd Ste B Historic New Castle (19720) *(G-5093)*

U A G Inc ... 302 731-2747
841 Old Baltimore Pike Newark (19702) *(G-12252)*

U A W Legal Services, Newark *Also Called: UAW-GM Legal Services Plan (G-12258)*

U and I Builders Inc ... 302 697-1645
1200 S Bay Rd Dover (19901) *(G-3738)*

U C P, Newark *Also Called: United Cocoa Processor Inc (G-12269)*

U Good Enterprises LLC ... 302 566-8038
166 Haut Brion Ave Newark (19702) *(G-12253)*

U Haul Co Independent Dealers ... 302 424-3189
601 Marshall St Milford (19963) *(G-8123)*

U Haul Neighborhood Dealer ... 302 613-0207
214 Bear Christiana Rd Bear (19701) *(G-545)*

U Haul Neighborhood Dealer ... 302 832-1433
1590 Red Lion Rd Bear (19701) *(G-546)*

U Haul Neighborhood Dealer ... 302 284-6051
1408 Willow Grove Rd Felton (19943) *(G-4034)*

U Haul Neighborhood Dealer ... 302 393-2999
1001 E Masten Cir Milford (19963) *(G-8124)*

U Prime Fitness and Wellness ... 302 529-1966
2601 Tonbridge Dr Wilmington (19810) *(G-20483)*

U S 13 Dragway Inc (PA) ... 302 875-1911
36952 Sussex Hwy Delmar (19940) *(G-1648)*

U S A Repair Shop ... 302 545-5991
444 Polly Drummond Hill Rd Newark (19711) *(G-12254)*

U S Express Taxi Company LLC ... 302 357-1908
260 Christiana Rd Apt N18 New Castle (19720) *(G-9645)*

U S Fire Forces Inc ... 302 270-8294
8 The Grn Ste 8068 Dover (19901) *(G-3739)*

U S Mail Transport, Lewes *Also Called: Lantransit Enterprises LLC (G-6179)*

U S Male Mens Hair Care Ctrs, Hockessin *Also Called: CMC Corporation of Hockessin (G-5164)*

U Tan Inc ... 302 674-8040
650 S Bay Rd Ste 11 Dover (19901) *(G-3740)*

U Transit Inc ... 302 227-1197
12 Hazlett St Rehoboth Beach (19971) *(G-13000)*

U Yoga ... 302 893-4585
703 Halstead Rd Wilmington (19803) *(G-20484)*

U-Haul ... 302 565-4423
607 Old Harmony Rd Newark (19711) *(G-12255)*

U-Haul ... 302 514-0034
5786 Dupont Pkwy Smyrna (19977) *(G-13923)*

U-Haul, Bridgeville *Also Called: U-Haul Neighborhood Dealer (G-776)*

U-Haul, Frankford *Also Called: U-Haul Neighborhood Dealer (G-4156)*

U-Haul, Hartly *Also Called: U-Haul Neighborhood Dealer (G-4911)*

U-Haul, Lewes *Also Called: Morton Electric Co (G-6292)*

U-Haul, Milford *Also Called: U Haul Co Independent Dealers (G-8123)*

U-Haul, Millsboro *Also Called: U-Haul International (G-8489)*

U-Haul, Newark *Also Called: U-Haul International (G-12256)*

U-Haul, Newark *Also Called: U-Haul Neighborhood Dealer (G-12257)*

U-Haul, Wilmington *Also Called: U-Haul International Inc (G-20485)*

U-Haul Co ... 302 628-8197
1022 W Stein Hwy Seaford (19973) *(G-13437)*

U-Haul International ... 302 934-1601
327 Main St Millsboro (19966) *(G-8489)*

U-Haul International ... 302 565-4056
50 Marrows Rd Newark (19713) *(G-12256)*

U-Haul International Inc ... 302 762-6445
2920 Governor Printz Blvd Wilmington (19802) *(G-20485)*

U-Haul International Inc ... 336 667-0147
906 S Dupont Hwy New Castle (19720) *(G-9646)*

U-Haul Neighborhd Dealr Budget ... 302 349-2167
12847 Sussex Hwy Greenwood (19950) *(G-4673)*

U-Haul Neighborhood Dealer ... 302 721-6064
9588 Bridgeville Ctr Bridgeville (19933) *(G-776)*

U-Haul Neighborhood Dealer ... 302 321-6032
36097 Zion Church Rd Frankford (19945) *(G-4156)*

U-Haul Neighborhood Dealer ... 302 343-7497
324 Main St Hartly (19953) *(G-4911)*

U-Haul Neighborhood Dealer ... 302 644-4316
33012 Cedar Grove Rd Lewes (19958) *(G-6586)*

U-Haul Neighborhood Dealer ... 302 703-0376
17649 Coastal Hwy Lewes (19958) *(G-6587)*

U-Haul Neighborhood Dealer ... 302 376-6858
1228 Middletown Warwick Rd Middletown (19709) *(G-7668)*

U-Haul Neighborhood Dealer ... 302 449-7379
5101 Summit Bridge Rd Middletown (19709) *(G-7669)*

U-Haul Neighborhood Dealer ... 302 725-4525
340 Ne Front St Milford (19963) *(G-8125)*

U-Haul Neighborhood Dealer ... 302 250-4422
3006 New Castle Ave New Castle (19720) *(G-9647)*

U-Haul Neighborhood Dealer ... 302 544-9178
327 Airport Rd New Castle (19720) *(G-9648)*

U-Haul Neighborhood Dealer ... 302 722-8016
660 Capitol Trl Newark (19711) *(G-12257)*

ALPHABETIC SECTION

U-Matter Learning Place......302 482-1746
  821 W 32nd St Wilmington (19802) *(G-20486)*
U-Save Auto, Milford Also Called: William T Wadkins Garage Inc *(G-8151)*
U2r Inc (PA)......609 792-6575
  251 Little Falls Dr Wilmington (19808) *(G-20487)*
Ua Services Corp......302 467-3700
  221 N Broad St Ste 1 Middletown (19709) *(G-7670)*
UACJ Trading & Processing Amer (PA)......312 636-5941
  1209 N Orange St Wilmington (19801) *(G-20488)*
Uag International Holdings Inc (HQ)......302 427-9859
  1105 N Market St Ste 1300 Wilmington (19801) *(G-20489)*
Ualett, Wilmington Also Called: Cabicash Solutions Inc *(G-15183)*
UAW-GM Legal Services Plan......302 562-8212
  4051 Ogletown Rd Ste 201 Newark (19713) *(G-12258)*
Uber......302 287-4866
  318 W Summit Ave Wilmington (19804) *(G-20490)*
Ubinet Inc......302 722-6015
  831 N Tatnall St Wilmington (19801) *(G-20491)*
Ubium Group......801 487-5000
  1000 N West St Wilmington (19801) *(G-20492)*
Ublerb......773 569-9686
  9 E Loockerman St Ste 215 Dover (19901) *(G-3741)*
UBS Financial Services Inc......302 657-5331
  500 Delaware Ave Ste 901 Wilmington (19801) *(G-20493)*
UBS Financial Services Inc......302 407-4700
  20 Montchanin Rd Ste 170 Wilmington (19807) *(G-20494)*
Ud Student Wellness Hlth Prom......302 831-3457
  231 S College Ave Newark (19716) *(G-12259)*
Udaan Inc......267 408-3001
  5 Brittany Ln Bear (19701) *(G-547)*
Udairy Creamery Prod Fcilty......302 831-2486
  529 S College Ave Newark (19716) *(G-12260)*
Udr Inc......302 674-8887
  1700 N Dupont Hwy Ste 1 Dover (19901) *(G-3742)*
Ufcw Local 27......302 436-6105
  3 Mason Dr Selbyville (19975) *(G-13614)*
Ufloor Systems, Dover Also Called: Uzin Utz North America Inc *(G-3769)*
UHS, Newark Also Called: UHS of Rockford LLC *(G-12261)*
UHS of Rockford LLC......302 892-4224
  100 Rockford Dr Newark (19713) *(G-12261)*
Ukap Trading LLC......617 447-6490
  8 The Grn Ste A Dover (19901) *(G-3743)*
Ukhi LLC......833 511-1977
  128 Sunset Blvd New Castle (19720) *(G-9649)*
Ukraine Express Inc......973 253-0050
  78 Mccullough Dr New Castle (19726) *(G-9650)*
Ukraine Power Resources LLC......508 280-6910
  8 The Grn Ste 11279 Dover (19901) *(G-3744)*
Ultahost Inc......302 966-3941
  651 N Broad St Ste 201 Middletown (19709) *(G-7671)*
Ulterior Technologies Inc (PA)......929 399-8964
  1201 N Orange St Ste 7495 Wilmington (19801) *(G-20495)*
Ultimate Express Inc......443 523-0800
  37976 Bayview Cir E Selbyville (19975) *(G-13615)*
Ultimate Fire Protection LLC......302 994-8371
  1625 N Heald St Wilmington (19802) *(G-20496)*
Ultimate Images Inc......302 479-0292
  3100 Naamans Rd Ste 8 Wilmington (19810) *(G-20497)*
Ultimate Material Spraying LLC......302 723-2356
  617 Delancey Pl Claymont (19703) *(G-1321)*
Ultimate Tan Millsboro......302 934-1400
  25714 Timmons Ln Dagsboro (19939) *(G-1521)*
Ultimate Tournament Inc......410 746-1637
  1305 Chadwick Rd Wilmington (19803) *(G-20498)*
Ultius Cstm Wrting Edting Svcs......702 690-4552
  1201 N Orange St Ste 7038 Wilmington (19801) *(G-20499)*
Ultra Fitness Inc......310 890-9025
  8 The Grn Dover (19901) *(G-3745)*
Ultra Modern Laundry Svcs LLC......302 533-8596
  24a Trolley Sq Wilmington (19806) *(G-20500)*
Ultra Packet LLC......240 219-8472
  501 Silverside Rd Wilmington (19809) *(G-20501)*
Ultrachem Inc......302 325-9880
  900 Centerpoint Blvd Historic New Castle (19720) *(G-5094)*
Ultrafine Technologies Inc......302 384-6513
  405 Derby Way Wilmington (19810) *(G-20502)*
Ultraworking Inc......848 243-0008
  2035 Sunset Lake Rd Ste B2 Newark (19702) *(G-12262)*
Um Laundry, Wilmington Also Called: Ultra Modern Laundry Svcs LLC *(G-20500)*
Umbrella Transport Group Inc......301 919-1623
  39 Glennwood Dr Newark (19702) *(G-12263)*
Umiya Inc......302 674-4011
  428 N Dupont Hwy Dover (19901) *(G-3746)*
Unada LLC......470 809-9077
  300 Delaware Ave Ste 210a Wilmington (19801) *(G-20503)*
Uncharted Waters LLC......302 213-6354
  8 The Grn Ste 5608 Dover (19901) *(G-3747)*
Unclaimed Property......302 577-8220
  820 N French St Wilmington (19801) *(G-20504)*
Uncorked Canvas Parties......302 724-7625
  125 W Loockerman St Dover (19904) *(G-3748)*
Under Whistle......302 250-8400
  49 N Bellwoode Dr Newark (19702) *(G-12264)*
Under/Comm Inc......302 424-1554
  198 Mullet Run Milford (19963) *(G-8126)*
Underground, Lewes Also Called: Femmepal Corporation *(G-5993)*
Underground Locating Services......302 856-9626
  24497 Dupont Blvd Georgetown (19947) *(G-4565)*
Unfold Studio LLC......415 993-0943
  1401 N Dupont St Wilmington (19806) *(G-20505)*
UNI Printing Solutionsllc......631 438-6045
  42 Reads Way New Castle (19720) *(G-9651)*
Unibet Interactive Inc......855 655-6310
  1209 N Orange St Wilmington (19801) *(G-20506)*
Unicare Transport Service, Lewes Also Called: Bill M Douthat Jr *(G-5765)*
Unicodez Inc......703 963-2738
  831 N Tatnall St Wilmington (19801) *(G-20507)*
Unidel Foundation Inc......302 658-9200
  3801 Kennett Pike Ste C303 Wilmington (19807) *(G-20508)*
Unified Biz Club, Wilmington Also Called: Unified Companies Inc *(G-20509)*
Unified Companies Inc......866 936-0515
  1201 N Orange St Ste 600 Wilmington (19801) *(G-20509)*
Unified Fitness Npb......302 528-5021
  4924 Hogan Dr Wilmington (19808) *(G-20510)*
Uniglobe, Wilmington Also Called: Red Carpet Travel Agency Inc *(G-19383)*
Unigo Inc......205 974-1962
  108 W 13th St Wilmington (19801) *(G-20511)*
Unik Marketing Inc......302 830-9935
  1007 N Orange St Wilmington (19801) *(G-20512)*
Unikie Inc......408 839-1920
  615 S Dupont Hwy Dover (19901) *(G-3749)*
Unimrkt Response Inc......646 712-9302
  651 N Broad St Middletown (19709) *(G-7672)*
Union Building Trades Fcu......973 263-0001
  814 W Basin Rd New Castle (19720) *(G-9652)*
Union Fnosa Fincl Svcs USA LLC......302 738-6680
  850 Library Ave Ste 204f Newark (19711) *(G-12265)*
Union Lodge 7, Dover Also Called: Temple Masonic *(G-3667)*
Union Park Lawns......302 757-5496
  412 S Sycamore St Wilmington (19805) *(G-20513)*
Union Press Printing Inc......302 652-0496
  1723 W 8th St Wilmington (19805) *(G-20514)*
Union Whl Acoustical Sup Co......302 656-4462
  500 E Front St Ste 1 Wilmington (19801) *(G-20515)*
Union Wholesale Co (HQ)......302 656-4462
  500 E Front St Ste 1 Wilmington (19801) *(G-20516)*
Unique Auto Accessories LLC......302 841-0983
  28042 Seaford Rd Laurel (19956) *(G-5617)*
Unique Biotech Inc......888 478-2799
  16192 Coastal Hwy Lewes (19958) *(G-6588)*
Unique Business Solutions......302 750-0930
  26 Airdrie Dr Bear (19701) *(G-548)*
Unique Creations By Chloe LLC......855 942-0477
  501 Silverside Rd Ste 512 Wilmington (19809) *(G-20517)*

(PA)=Parent Co (HQ)=Headquarters (DH)=Div Headquarters

Unique Fabricating Na Inc — ALPHABETIC SECTION

Unique Fabricating Na Inc..248 853-2333
  1313 N Market St Wilmington (19801) *(G-20518)*

Unique Finishes Inc...302 419-8557
  1838 Red Lion Rd Bear (19701) *(G-549)*

Unique Image LLC..302 658-2266
  118 Bromley Dr Wilmington (19808) *(G-20519)*

Unique Image T-Shirts Company, Wilmington *Also Called: Unique Image LLC (G-20519)*

Unique Massage Therapy..302 359-5982
  124 Lynnbroom Ln Dover (19904) *(G-3750)*

Unique Mnds Changing Lives Inc....................................302 943-1945
  17584 Stingey Ln Lewes (19958) *(G-6589)*

Unique Pro-Co LLC...302 723-2365
  1301 Birch Ln Wilmington (19809) *(G-20520)*

Uniscrap Pbc..302 407-8002
  1000 N West St Ste 1200 Wilmington (19801) *(G-20521)*

Unisight Bit Inc...888 294-6414
  1000 Nw St Ste1281-291 Wilmington (19801) *(G-20522)*

United Acquisition Corp (HQ)...302 651-9856
  1011 Centre Rd Ste 310 Wilmington (19805) *(G-20523)*

United Auto Sales Inc..302 325-3000
  209 Harris Cir Newark (19711) *(G-12266)*

United Auto Workers Local 435......................................302 995-6001
  698 Old Baltimore Pike Newark (19702) *(G-12267)*

United Brokerage Packaging..302 294-6782
  110 Executive Dr Ste 5 Newark (19702) *(G-12268)*

UNITED CEREBRAL PALSY, Wilmington *Also Called: United Cerebral Palsy of De (G-20524)*

United Cerebral Palsy of De (PA)....................................302 764-2400
  700 A River Rd Wilmington (19809) *(G-20524)*

United Check Cashing...302 792-2545
  95 Naamans Rd Ste 37a Claymont (19703) *(G-1322)*

United Check Cashing, New Castle *Also Called: Argo Financial Services Inc (G-8820)*

United Cocoa Processor Inc..302 731-0825
  701 Pencader Dr Ste F Newark (19702) *(G-12269)*

United Electric Supply Co Inc..302 732-1291
  27519 Hodges Ln Bldg P Dagsboro (19939) *(G-1522)*

United Electric Supply Co Inc..302 674-8351
  551 S Dupont Hwy Dover (19901) *(G-3751)*

United Electric Supply Co Inc (PA).................................800 322-3374
  10 Bellecor Dr New Castle (19720) *(G-9653)*

United Garage Doors...302 414-9220
  51 Spring Creek Dr Townsend (19734) *(G-14087)*

United Group Real Estate LLC.......................................929 999-1277
  607 Deemer Pl Historic New Castle (19720) *(G-5095)*

United Lemon Sales LLC..513 368-6107
  2 Dock View Dr New Castle (19720) *(G-9654)*

United Medical Clinic LLC...302 451-5610
  161 Becks Woods Dr Bear (19701) *(G-550)*

United Medical Clinics of De...302 451-5607
  121 Becks Woods Dr Ste 100 Bear (19701) *(G-551)*

United Medical LLC..302 266-9166
  161 Becks Woods Dr Bear (19701) *(G-552)*

United Methodist Church, Lewes *Also Called: Bethel United Methodist Church (G-5758)*

United Methodist Church, Newark *Also Called: Newark United Methodist (G-11547)*

United Outdoor Advertising...302 652-3177
  2502 W 6th St Wilmington (19805) *(G-20525)*

United Parcel Service Inc...302 453-7462
  211 Lake Dr Newark (19702) *(G-12270)*

United Refrigeration Inc...302 322-1836
  818 W Basin Rd New Castle (19720) *(G-9655)*

United Rentals, Delmar *Also Called: United Rentals North Amer Inc (G-1649)*

United Rentals, Delmar *Also Called: United Rentals North Amer Inc (G-1650)*

United Rentals, New Castle *Also Called: United Rentals North Amer Inc (G-9656)*

United Rentals North Amer Inc......................................302 907-0292
  38190 Old Stage Rd # A Delmar (19940) *(G-1649)*

United Rentals North Amer Inc......................................302 846-0955
  38352 Sussex Hwy Delmar (19940) *(G-1650)*

United Rentals North Amer Inc......................................302 328-2900
  248 S Dupont Hwy New Castle (19720) *(G-9656)*

United Security Advisors LLC.......................................610 310-2482
  1000 N West St Ste 1200 Wilmington (19801) *(G-20526)*

United Specialty Foam LLC..302 650-5948
  709 Ashford Rd Wilmington (19803) *(G-20527)*

United States Cold Storage Inc......................................302 422-7536
  419 Milford Harrington Hwy Milford (19963) *(G-8127)*

United States Cold Storage Inc......................................302 422-7536
  Milford (19963) *(G-8128)*

United States Power Eqp LLC..302 294-2562
  200 Continental Dr Newark (19713) *(G-12271)*

United Sttes Gyps Asb Per Inju.....................................888 708-8925
  Wilmington (19899) *(G-20528)*

United Sttes Harn Wrters Assoc.....................................215 681-0697
  5582 Milford Harrington Hwy Harrington (19952) *(G-4842)*

United Sun Systems US Inc..650 460-8707
  16192 Coastal Hwy Lewes (19958) *(G-6590)*

United Tech Project Foundation.....................................302 404-4099
  300 Delaware Ave Wilmington (19801) *(G-20529)*

United Tele Wkrs Local 13101.......................................302 737-0400
  350 Gooding Dr Newark (19702) *(G-12272)*

UNITED TELEPHONE WORKERS OF DE, Newark *Also Called: United Tele Wkrs Local 13101 (G-12272)*

United Testing Systems Inc..714 638-2322
  40 Mccullough Dr New Castle (19720) *(G-9657)*

United Trnsp Un Insur Assn..302 655-6084
  12 Varmar Dr New Castle (19720) *(G-9658)*

UNITED WAY, Wilmington *Also Called: United Way of Delaware Inc (G-20530)*

United Way of Delaware Inc (PA)...................................302 573-3700
  625 N Orange St Fl 3 Wilmington (19801) *(G-20530)*

United Worldwide Express LLC......................................347 651-5111
  605 Interchange Blvd Newark (19711) *(G-12273)*

Unitrack Industries Inc...302 424-5050
  967 E Masten Cir Milford (19963) *(G-8129)*

Unity Construction Inc...302 998-0531
  3301 Lancaster Pike Ste 9 Wilmington (19805) *(G-20531)*

Unity Development, Wilmington *Also Called: Unity Construction Inc (G-20531)*

Unity Growth Fund LLC..703 585-7915
  200 Continental Dr Ste 401 Newark (19713) *(G-12274)*

Unity Perspectives Inc...302 265-2854
  702 North St Milford (19963) *(G-8130)*

Univ of Del, Newark *Also Called: University of Delaware (G-12280)*

Univ of Delaware..302 383-0473
  1600 Rocky Run Pkwy Wilmington (19803) *(G-20532)*

Universal Algorithm Inc..302 446-3562
  8 The Grn Ste 8167 Dover (19901) *(G-3752)*

Universal Assembling Entp LLC.....................................302 543-3629
  738 N Dupont Hwy Dover (19901) *(G-3753)*

Universal Baking Company...302 290-3204
  303 Robinson Ln Wilmington (19805) *(G-20533)*

Universal Bev Importers LLC...302 276-0619
  505 E Glen Mare Dr Middletown (19709) *(G-7673)*

Universal Bev Importers LLC...302 322-7900
  200 Lisa Dr Ste D New Castle (19720) *(G-9659)*

Universal Design Company...302 328-8391
  18 Baldt Ave Historic New Castle (19720) *(G-5096)*

Universal Exteriors LLC...302 563-7900
  164 Hatteras Dr Dover (19904) *(G-3754)*

Universalfleet..302 428-0661
  2019 Walmsley Dr New Castle (19720) *(G-9660)*

University Garden Apts, Newark *Also Called: University Garden Associates (G-12275)*

University Garden Associates..302 368-3823
  281 Beverly Rd Apt H5 Newark (19711) *(G-12275)*

University of De Printing..302 831-2153
  222 S Chapel St Rm 124 Newark (19702) *(G-12276)*

University of Delaware...302 831-6041
  192 S Chapel St Newark (19716) *(G-12277)*

University of Delaware...302 831-4811
  104 The Grn Rm 217 Newark (19716) *(G-12278)*

University of Delaware...302 831-2833
  257 Academy St Newark (19716) *(G-12279)*

University of Delaware...302 831-2501
  363 New London Rd Newark (19711) *(G-12280)*

University of Delaware...302 831-2226
  282 The Grn Newark (19716) *(G-12281)*

University of Delaware...302 831-2792
  222 S Chapel St Newark (19716) *(G-12282)*

ALPHABETIC SECTION — US Immigration Technology LLC

University Plaza Branch, Newark *Also Called: Wilmington Savings Fund Soc* *(G-12382)*
University Whist CLB of Wlmngt... 302 658-5125
  805 N Broom St Wilmington (19806) *(G-20534)*
Universum Inc... 973 873-2636
  614 N Dupont Hwy Ste 210 Dover (19901) *(G-3755)*
Unknown, Dover *Also Called: Medtix LLC* *(G-3054)*
Unlimited Restoration Inc... 302 439-4213
  130 Hickman Rd Claymont (19703) *(G-1323)*
Unprivileged Drinkers LLC... 215 800-5475
  19 Ponds Edge Ct Felton (19943) *(G-4035)*
Unreal Vapors... 302 322-2600
  1418 N Dupont Hwy New Castle (19720) *(G-9661)*
Unreal Vapors... 302 750-6213
  81 Ramunno Dr Smyrna (19977) *(G-13924)*
Unreal Vapors LLC... 302 449-2547
  520 Middletown Warwick Rd Middletown (19709) *(G-7674)*
Up and Away Travel Health... 302 455-8416
  210 Hull Ave Newark (19711) *(G-12283)*
Upbound Group Inc... 302 838-7333
  38 Foxhunt Dr # 40 Bear (19701) *(G-553)*
Upbound Group Inc... 302 798-0663
  333 Naamans Rd Ste 21 Claymont (19703) *(G-1324)*
Upbound Group Inc... 302 734-2094
  655 S Bay Rd Ste 204 Dover (19901) *(G-3756)*
Upbound Group Inc... 302 678-4676
  137 Jerome Dr Ste 170 Dover (19901) *(G-3757)*
Upbound Group Inc... 302 734-3505
  1688 S Governors Ave Dover (19904) *(G-3758)*
Upbound Group Inc... 302 856-9200
  12 Georgetown Plz Georgetown (19947) *(G-4566)*
Upbound Group Inc... 302 422-1230
  678 N Dupont Blvd Milford (19963) *(G-8131)*
Upbound Group Inc... 302 934-6700
  28544 Dupont Blvd Unit 9 Millsboro (19966) *(G-8490)*
Upbound Group Inc... 302 731-7900
  19 Chestnut Hill Plz Newark (19713) *(G-12284)*
Upbound Group Inc... 302 629-8925
  23002 Sussex Hwy Seaford (19973) *(G-13438)*
Upbound Group Inc... 302 653-3701
  120 E Glenwood Ave Smyrna (19977) *(G-13925)*
Upbound Group Inc... 302 654-7700
  1932 Maryland Ave Wilmington (19805) *(G-20535)*
Uplift Barbershop.. 302 883-3001
  1534 S Governors Ave Ste B Dover (19904) *(G-3759)*
Uploadcare Inc... 855 953-2006
  2711 Centerville Rd Ste 400 Wilmington (19808) *(G-20536)*
Uploop Technologies LP.. 514 922-0399
  4 Peddlers Row Ste 33 Newark (19702) *(G-12285)*
Upon A Once Tile Inc... 646 992-1376
  16192 Coastal Hwy Lewes (19958) *(G-6591)*
Uppal Umsa... 302 897-7434
  66 E Glenwood Ave Smyrna (19977) *(G-13926)*
Upper Cut The, Dover *Also Called: Uppercut Inc* *(G-3760)*
Upper Darby Community Out.. 610 352-7008
  123 Landing Dr Rehoboth Beach (19971) *(G-13001)*
Uppercut Inc... 302 736-1661
  119 S Dupont Hwy Dover (19901) *(G-3760)*
Upperstack Inc... 410 925-8216
  2035 Sunset Lake Rd B2 Newark (19702) *(G-12286)*
UPS, Bear *Also Called: UPS Authorized Retailer* *(G-554)*
UPS, Newark *Also Called: United Parcel Service Inc* *(G-12270)*
UPS, Newark *Also Called: UPS Supply Chain Solutions Inc* *(G-12287)*
UPS Authorized Retailer.. 302 834-1600
  1148 Pulaski Hwy Bear (19701) *(G-554)*
UPS Store... 302 907-0455
  38660 Sussex Hwy Unit 10 Delmar (19940) *(G-1651)*
UPS Store... 302 360-0264
  18766 John J Williams Hwy Unit 4 Rehoboth Beach (19971) *(G-13002)*
UPS Store, The, Seaford *Also Called: SC Ennis Incorporated* *(G-13384)*
UPS Supply Chain Solutions Inc.. 302 631-5259
  220 Lake Dr Ste 1 Newark (19702) *(G-12287)*

Upscale Industries Property Ma.. 302 386-8855
  1207 Delaware Ave Wilmington (19806) *(G-20537)*
Upside Gaming, Middletown *Also Called: Upside Gaming Inc* *(G-7675)*
Upside Gaming Inc.. 937 475-6908
  651 N Broad St Ste 205 Middletown (19709) *(G-7675)*
Uptown Pet Paws Grooming... 302 422-2229
  1001 N Walnut St Milford (19963) *(G-8132)*
Uptrend Consulting & Creative... 484 840-1200
  408 S Bancroft Pkwy Wilmington (19805) *(G-20538)*
Upyo Inc... 737 444-8899
  300 Delaware Ave Wilmington (19801) *(G-20539)*
Ur World Inc (PA)... 313 241-0060
  651 N Broad St Ste 201 Middletown (19709) *(G-7676)*
Ur-Express Inc... 302 839-2008
  7 Lewis Cir Wilmington (19804) *(G-20540)*
Urban Air Adventure Park, Christiana *Also Called: Fun Adventures LLC* *(G-996)*
Urban Avenue Inc.. 302 420-1105
  44 Hillary Cir New Castle (19720) *(G-9662)*
Urban Change Incorporated... 215 749-2049
  725 Staghorn Dr New Castle (19720) *(G-9663)*
Urban Cyber Security Inc... 803 805-9980
  1007 N Orange St Fl 83 Wilmington (19801) *(G-20541)*
Urban Dweller... 973 402-7400
  338 Union St Milton (19968) *(G-8724)*
Urban Engineers Inc... 302 689-0260
  2 Penns Way Ste 400 New Castle (19720) *(G-9664)*
Urban Retail Properties LLC... 302 479-8314
  4737 Concord Pike Wilmington (19803) *(G-20542)*
Urban Retail Properties Co, Wilmington *Also Called: Urban Retail Properties LLC* *(G-20542)*
Urban Youth Golf Program Assn... 302 384-8759
  800 N Dupont Rd Wilmington (19807) *(G-20543)*
Urbanpromise Wilmington Inc... 302 425-5502
  2401 Thatcher St Wilmington (19802) *(G-20544)*
Urbie Inc... 302 572-4243
  8 The Grn Dover (19901) *(G-3761)*
Urie & Blanton Inc... 302 658-8604
  510 A St Wilmington (19801) *(G-20545)*
Uris LLC (PA)... 302 469-7000
  32783 Long Neck Rd Unit 3 Millsboro (19966) *(G-8491)*
Uris Salvage Auto Inspections, Millsboro *Also Called: Uris LLC* *(G-8491)*
Urology Associates Dover PA... 302 674-1728
  200 Banning St Ste 250 Dover (19904) *(G-3762)*
Urpayroll Inc.. 323 922-3829
  1207 Delaware Ave Wilmington (19806) *(G-20546)*
URS, Newark *Also Called: URS Group Inc* *(G-12288)*
URS Group Inc... 302 731-7824
  4051 Ogletown Rd Ste 300 Newark (19713) *(G-12288)*
Ursewcrazy, Wilmington *Also Called: Decoryoucrazy* *(G-15851)*
Urspayce Inc.. 302 440-2880
  2093 Philadelphia Pike Claymont (19703) *(G-1325)*
Urys Transportation LLC... 302 841-9464
  11429 Liden St Bridgeville (19933) *(G-777)*
US 13 Speedway.. 302 846-3911
  36952 Sussex Hwy Delmar (19940) *(G-1652)*
US Auto Funding Trust 2020-1.. 770 280-3918
  919 N Market St Ste 202 Wilmington (19801) *(G-20547)*
US Auto Glass LLC... 302 803-4924
  2055 Limestone Rd Ste 200c Wilmington (19808) *(G-20548)*
US Cherry, Dover *Also Called: US Cherry LLC* *(G-3763)*
US Cherry LLC... 305 339-5318
  8 The Grn Ste B Dover (19901) *(G-3763)*
US Dept of the Air Force.. 302 677-2525
  300 Tuskegee Blvd Ste 1b22 Dover (19902) *(G-3764)*
Us Engineering Corporation.. 302 645-7400
  16192 Coastal Hwy Lewes (19958) *(G-6592)*
US Flexo Solutions LLC... 302 838-7805
  560 Peoples Plz Ste 410 Newark (19702) *(G-12289)*
US Green Battery Inc... 347 723-5963
  157 S Dupont Hwy 2nd Fl New Castle (19720) *(G-9665)*
US Immigration Technology LLC... 888 418-3053
  1000 N West St Ste 1200 Wilmington (19801) *(G-20549)*

ALPHABETIC SECTION

US Installation Group Inc..302 994-1644
355 Water St Wilmington (19804) *(G-20550)*

US Lawns, Lewes *Also Called: US Lawns Dover (G-6593)*

US Lawns Dover..302 703-2818
16856 Ketch Ct Lewes (19958) *(G-6593)*

US Male Modern Barbershop..302 635-7370
7197 Lancaster Pike Hockessin (19707) *(G-5414)*

US Probation Pretrial, Wilmington *Also Called: Supreme Court United States (G-20155)*

US Ravens Logistics Inc..302 401-4033
8 The Grn Ste B Dover (19901) *(G-3765)*

US Renal Care Laurel Dialysis, Laurel *Also Called: DSI Laurel LLC (G-5502)*

US Tax Resolutions PA..302 478-7977
3213 Emerald Pl Wilmington (19810) *(G-20551)*

US Telex Corporation..302 652-2707
4001 Kennett Pike Ste 300 Wilmington (19807) *(G-20552)*

USA Angelalign Technology..570 573-3515
300 Creek View Rd Ste 209 Newark (19711) *(G-12290)*

USA Fortescue Future Inds Inc (PA)..703 608-5217
1209 N Orange St Wilmington (19801) *(G-20553)*

USA Fulfillment..410 810-0880
1870 Lynnbury Woods Rd Dover (19904) *(G-3766)*

USA Fulfillment Inc..410 810-0880
1870 Lynnbury Woods Rd Dover (19904) *(G-3767)*

USA Transport LLC (PA)..302 273-0806
121 Mechanic St Harrington (19952) *(G-4843)*

Usacarrecordcom LLC..302 645-7400
16192 Coastal Hwy Lewes (19958) *(G-6594)*

Userway Inc..415 510-9335
1007 N Orange St Wilmington (19801) *(G-20554)*

USRC, Wilmington *Also Called: Liberty Dalysis-Wilmington LLC (G-17891)*

USS Delaware..908 910-4812
204 Charles St Milford (19963) *(G-8133)*

USS Portfolio Delaware Inc..302 798-7890
501 Silverside Rd Ste 53 Wilmington (19809) *(G-20555)*

USS Wind Technologies LLC (PA)..646 770-6265
16192 Coastal Hwy Lewes (19958) *(G-6595)*

Usw Local 4-898..302 836-6689
1520 Porter Rd Bear (19701) *(G-555)*

UT Investment Management Corp..215 399-5900
1209 N Orange St Wilmington (19801) *(G-20556)*

Utax 4 Less Tax Svc..302 743-6905
3 Farland Way Newark (19702) *(G-12291)*

UTECH Global Services (PA)..630 531-0427
251 Little Falls Dr Wilmington (19808) *(G-20557)*

Utilisite Inc..302 945-5022
20721 Robinsonville Rd Lewes (19958) *(G-6596)*

Utility Billing, Wilmington *Also Called: City of Wilmington (G-15454)*

Utility Lines Cnstr Svcs LLC..302 337-9980
18109 Sussex Hwy Bridgeville (19933) *(G-778)*

Utility Locator LLC..215 596-1234
14 Hadco Rd Wilmington (19804) *(G-20558)*

Utility Sales Associates Inc..410 479-0646
47 October Glory Ave Ocean View (19970) *(G-12578)*

Utility/Stern Shore Trlr Sls I..302 337-7400
9126 Redden Rd Bridgeville (19933) *(G-779)*

Utopia Alley LLC..302 218-3108
56 Westwoods Blvd Hockessin (19707) *(G-5415)*

Utopie Technologies Inc..628 251-1312
16192 Coastal Hwy Lewes (19958) *(G-6597)*

Utz Quality Food Inc..302 266-6982
710 Dawson Dr Newark (19713) *(G-12292)*

Uvax Bio LLC..818 859-3988
100 Biddle Ave Ste 202 Newark (19702) *(G-12293)*

Uzin Utz Manufacturing N Amer..336 456-4624
200 Garrison Oak Dr Dover (19901) *(G-3768)*

Uzin Utz North America Inc..302 450-1715
200 Garrison Oak Dr Dover (19901) *(G-3769)*

Uzuakoli Dev & Cultural Assn..302 465-3266
2319 S Dupont Hwy Dover (19901) *(G-3770)*

V & A Painting LLC..443 466-2344
232 Landau Way Bear (19701) *(G-556)*

V A Truck & Trailer Repair LLC..302 653-7936
304 Garnet Ln Smyrna (19977) *(G-13927)*

V C A Kirkwood Animal Hospital, Newark *Also Called: Kirkwood Anmal Brding Grooming (G-11182)*

V Colbert Inc..302 420-5502
34 Gill Dr Newark (19713) *(G-12294)*

V Dima Inc..302 427-0787
2400 W 4th St Wilmington (19805) *(G-20559)*

V E Guerrazzi Inc..302 369-5557
122 Sandy Dr Ste D Newark (19713) *(G-12295)*

V F W Post Home..302 366-8438
100 Veterans Dr Newark (19711) *(G-12296)*

V P Custom Finishers In..302 415-0002
339 W Dickerson Ln Middletown (19709) *(G-7677)*

V Power Fit Inc..832 743-7116
651 N Broad St Ste 206 Middletown (19709) *(G-7678)*

V Quinton Inc..302 449-1711
400 N Ramunno Dr Middletown (19709) *(G-7679)*

V Squillace Mason Contractor..302 655-0934
111 Valley Rd Wilmington (19804) *(G-20560)*

V T I, Newark *Also Called: Val-Tech Inc (G-12298)*

VA Medical Ctr Wilmington De..302 563-6024
720 Pinewood Dr Middletown (19709) *(G-7680)*

Vacation Club..302 628-1144
9290 River Vista Dr Seaford (19973) *(G-13439)*

Vacuum Group Inc..212 377-2078
2035 Sunset Lake Rd B2 Newark (19702) *(G-12297)*

Vairasoft Inc..336 422-6499
913 N Market St Ste 200 Wilmington (19801) *(G-20561)*

Vakoms LLC..206 474-4319
913 N Market St Ste 200 Wilmington (19801) *(G-20562)*

Val Capital Holdings LLC..800 997-4166
767 Walker Rd Ste 20 Dover (19904) *(G-3771)*

Val-Tech Inc..302 738-0500
24 Mcmillan Way Newark (19713) *(G-12298)*

Valassis Direct Mail Inc..302 861-3567
300 Mcintire Dr Newark (19711) *(G-12299)*

Valentina Liquors..302 368-3264
430 Old Baltimore Pike Newark (19702) *(G-12300)*

Valerie Rivera..302 387-5334
136 E Poplar St Frederica (19946) *(G-4186)*

Valiram USA Inc..562 652-1698
1013 Centre Rd Ste 403s Wilmington (19805) *(G-20563)*

Valiu Inc..317 853-5081
16192 Coastal Hwy Lewes (19958) *(G-6598)*

Vallejo Vzquez Sons Hrvstg LLC..616 902-5851
15705 Gathering Garden Ln Delmar (19940) *(G-1653)*

Valley Landscaping and Con Inc..302 922-5020
8 The Grn Dover (19901) *(G-3772)*

Valley Run Apartments..302 994-2505
102 Robino Ct Ste 301 Wilmington (19804) *(G-20564)*

Valley Stream Townhomes..302 613-4859
100 N Barrett Ln Newark (19702) *(G-12301)*

Valliant Home Improvements..302 363-7109
37104 Johnson Rd Selbyville (19975) *(G-13616)*

Valor Construction LLC..302 455-7994
30 Albe Dr Ste A Newark (19702) *(G-12302)*

Valour Arabians..302 653-4066
1950 Vandyke Greenspring Rd Smyrna (19977) *(G-13928)*

Value Chain Excellence LLC..302 545-8011
103 Downs Dr Wilmington (19807) *(G-20565)*

Value Furniture, Felton *Also Called: Rite Way Distributors (G-4017)*

Value Xchange Group of Co LLC..708 420-7642
1007 N Orange St Fl 4 Wilmington (19801) *(G-20566)*

Valuewrite..302 593-0694
204 Tralee Dr Middletown (19709) *(G-7681)*

Van Buren Financial Group LLC..302 655-9505
615 W 18th St Wilmington (19802) *(G-20567)*

Van Buren Mortgage LLC..302 945-1109
26506 Victorias Landing Rd Millsboro (19966) *(G-8492)*

Van Buren Mortgage LLC..302 725-0723
37901 Island Dr Ocean View (19970) *(G-12579)*

ALPHABETIC SECTION

Van Smith Co., Middletown *Also Called: Atlantic Bulk Carriers Inc* **(G-6881)**

Vance A Funk III 302 368-2561
273 E Main St Ste 100 Newark (19711) **(G-12303)**

Vance Gems LLC 954 205-3982
530 Peoples Plz Newark (19702) **(G-12304)**

Vandemark & Lynch Inc 302 764-7635
4305 Miller Rd Wilmington (19802) **(G-20568)**

Vango Painting 302 689-8071
4106 Laughton Ln Middletown (19709) **(G-7682)**

Vanguard Cleaning Systems, Newark *Also Called: Delmar Corporate Clg Svcs Inc* **(G-10499)**

Vanguard Construction Inc 302 697-9187
2089 S Dupont Hwy Dover (19901) **(G-3773)**

Vanguard Construction MGT 302 462-2161
9 Hollyberry Dr Georgetown (19947) **(G-4567)**

Vanguard Manufacturing Inc 302 994-9302
11 Lewis Cir Wilmington (19804) **(G-20569)**

Vanguard Venture Group LLC 954 324-8736
8 The Grn Ste B Dover (19901) **(G-3774)**

Vanilla Innovations Inc (PA) 305 815-7586
2035 Sunset Lake Rd Ste B2 Newark (19702) **(G-12305)**

Vannies Hats 302 765-7094
4 Andover Ct New Castle (19720) **(G-9666)**

Vantage Energy LLC 302 261-9351
300 Delaware Ave Ste 210 Wilmington (19801) **(G-20570)**

Vany Productions Logistics LLC 443 397-2949
2700 Daniel St #2708 Laurel (19956) **(G-5618)**

Vapp, Wilmington *Also Called: Volunteers For Adolescent* **(G-20649)**

Vari Builders, Wilmington *Also Called: Vari Development Corp* **(G-20571)**

Vari Development Corp 302 479-5571
1309 Veale Rd Ste 20 Wilmington (19810) **(G-20571)**

Varida-Tech Inc 781 819-0259
2093 Philadelphia Pike Claymont (19703) **(G-1326)**

Varigle LLC 858 336-9471
8 The Grn Ste A Dover (19901) **(G-3775)**

Vascular Specialists Del PA 302 733-5700
1 Centurian Dr Ste 307 Newark (19713) **(G-12306)**

Vassallo Michael Elec Contr 302 455-9405
4 Mill Park Ct Newark (19713) **(G-12307)**

Vault Oil & Gas LLC 303 731-0080
850 New Burton Rd Ste 201 Dover (19904) **(G-3776)**

VCA Animal Hospitals Inc 302 738-1738
1501 Capitol Trl Newark (19711) **(G-12308)**

VCA Hockessin Animal Hospital, Newark *Also Called: Golden Merger Corp* **(G-10862)**

VCA Kirkwood Animal Hospital, Newark *Also Called: VCA Animal Hospitals Inc* **(G-12308)**

VCA Pike Creek Animal Hospital 302 307-1077
297 Polly Drummond Hill Rd Newark (19711) **(G-12309)**

Vcg LLC 302 336-8151
9 E Loockerman St Ste 3a-522 Dover (19901) **(G-3777)**

Vci, Claymont *Also Called: Visual Communications Inc* **(G-1330)**

VD&I Holdings Inc 302 764-7635
4305 Miller Rd Wilmington (19802) **(G-20572)**

Vector Engineering Svcs Corp 609 947-2580
27045 Firefly Blvd Millsboro (19966) **(G-8493)**

Vectorvance LLC (PA) 347 779-9932
1201 N Orange St Ste 600 Wilmington (19801) **(G-20573)**

Veda Health Group LLC 302 536-8332
2207 Concord Pike Wilmington (19803) **(G-20574)**

Vedaham Inc 302 250-4594
2711 Centerville Rd # 400 Wilmington (19808) **(G-20575)**

Veeglife LLC 310 866-8249
3500 S Dupont Hwy Dover (19901) **(G-3778)**

Veendhq Inc 470 300-9787
2055 Limestone Rd Wilmington (19808) **(G-20576)**

Veer Hotels Inc 302 398-3900
1259 Corn Crib Rd Harrington (19952) **(G-4844)**

Veer Trucking LLC 484 802-1452
1234 Hook Dr Middletown (19709) **(G-7683)**

Veezys Holding Company LLC (PA) 302 307-2418
8 The Grn Ste A Dover (19901) **(G-3779)**

Vega Consulting Inc (PA) 302 636-5401
251 Little Falls Dr Wilmington (19808) **(G-20577)**

Vegan Skin Clinic LLC 302 932-1920
407 Valley Brook Dr Hockessin (19707) **(G-5416)**

Vehattire LLC 302 221-2000
174 N Dupont Hwy New Castle (19720) **(G-9667)**

Vehicle Maintenance Dept 302 571-5857
1450 New York Ave Wilmington (19801) **(G-20578)**

Veho Tech Inc 720 466-3788
2093 Philadelphia Pike Ste 8346 Claymont (19703) **(G-1327)**

Vein Center At Eden H 302 735-8850
200 Banning St Ste 300 Dover (19904) **(G-3780)**

Vel Micro Works Incorporated 302 239-4661
133 Cheltenham Rd Hockessin (19707) **(G-5417)**

Velo Amis 302 757-2783
24 Nightingale Cir Newark (19711) **(G-12310)**

Velocity Eu, Middletown *Also Called: Velocity Eu Inc* **(G-7684)**

Velocity Eu Inc 331 226-1818
651 N Broad St Ste 206 Middletown (19709) **(G-7684)**

Velocity Maint Solutions LLC 844 538-8349
6 Drba Way New Castle (19720) **(G-9668)**

Velofix, Newark *Also Called: Broken Spoke Outfitters Inc* **(G-10091)**

Vels Hair Salon 302 427-3819
1824 Conrad St Wilmington (19805) **(G-20579)**

Vemo Acu LLC 508 654-7885
254 Chapman Rd Ste 209 Newark (19702) **(G-12311)**

Vending Solutions LLC 302 674-2222
131 Rosemary Rd Dover (19901) **(G-3781)**

Venice International Pdts LLC 630 571-7171
200 Continental Dr # 401 Newark (19713) **(G-12312)**

Vensoft Solutions Inc 302 392-9000
3516 Silverside Rd Ste 21 Wilmington (19810) **(G-20580)**

Vention Inc US (PA) 514 222-0380
1201 N Orange St Ste 7160 Wilmington (19801) **(G-20581)**

Ventura Maintenance Company 302 376-9060
101 E Green St Middletown (19709) **(G-7685)**

Venture Capital, Wilmington *Also Called: TH King US LLC* **(G-20290)**

Venturist Media Inc 646 455-3031
501 Silverside Rd Ste 105 Wilmington (19809) **(G-20582)**

Venus On Halfshell 302 227-9292
136 Dagsworthy Ave Dewey Beach (19971) **(G-1676)**

Venzee Inc 855 650-4204
4023 Kennett Pike 57126 Wilmington (19807) **(G-20583)**

Veolia Envmtl Svcs N Amer LLC 302 444-9172
131 Continental Dr Newark (19713) **(G-12313)**

Veraset LLC 801 657-2009
2810 N Church St # 38188 Wilmington (19802) **(G-20584)**

Verbspace Solutions Inc 626 524-3003
8 The Grn Ste A Dover (19901) **(G-3782)**

Verdant Plant Health Care 302 593-0444
200 Ohio Ave Wilmington (19805) **(G-20585)**

Verdantas LLC 302 239-6634
1143 Savannah Rd Ste 1a Lewes (19958) **(G-6599)**

Verdantas LLC 302 239-6634
5400 Limestone Rd Wilmington (19808) **(G-20586)**

Verde Loma LLC 302 858-4040
401 N Bedford St Georgetown (19947) **(G-4568)**

Verdict LLC 888 837-4618
3411 Silverside Rd # 114 Wilmington (19810) **(G-20587)**

Verge Internet Inc 202 827-5120
8 The Grn Ste A Dover (19901) **(G-3783)**

Veridian Solutions LLC 832 867-7263
8 The Grn Ste 8189 Dover (19901) **(G-3784)**

Verifiedly LLC (PA) 240 708-9025
651 N Broad St Ste 205 Middletown (19709) **(G-7686)**

Verisign Inc 571 325-7916
21 Boulden Cir New Castle (19720) **(G-9669)**

Verisoft Inc 602 908-7151
48 Kings Hwy Dover (19901) **(G-3785)**

Veritable USA Inc 302 326-4800
802 Centerpoint Blvd Historic New Castle (19720) **(G-5097)**

Veritas Consultant Group LLC 302 893-9794
16 Anderson Ln Newark (19711) **(G-12314)**

Veritas Judgment Recovery 302 376-7076
412 Benjamin Wright Dr Middletown (19709) *(G-7687)*

Veriti Security Incorporated 212 203-0100
251 Little Falls Dr Wilmington (19808) *(G-20588)*

Verito Technologies LLC 855 583-7486
251 Little Falls Dr Wilmington (19808) *(G-20589)*

Verizon, Milford Also Called: Verizon Delaware LLC *(G-8134)*
Verizon, Newark Also Called: Verizon Delaware LLC *(G-12315)*
Verizon, Seaford Also Called: Verizon Delaware LLC *(G-13440)*
Verizon, Wilmington Also Called: Cellco Partnership *(G-15301)*
Verizon, Wilmington Also Called: Cellco Partnership *(G-15302)*
Verizon, Wilmington Also Called: Verizon Delaware LLC *(G-20590)*
Verizon, Wilmington Also Called: Verizon Delaware LLC *(G-20591)*

Verizon Authorized Ret Tcc 302 653-8183
239 N Dupont Blvd Smyrna (19977) *(G-13929)*

Verizon Business, Wilmington Also Called: MCI Communications Corporation *(G-18230)*

Verizon Delaware LLC 302 422-1430
2 S Industrial Ln Milford (19963) *(G-8134)*

Verizon Delaware LLC 302 738-3000
945 S Chapel St Newark (19713) *(G-12315)*

Verizon Delaware LLC 302 629-4502
8722 Concord Rd Seaford (19973) *(G-13440)*

Verizon Delaware LLC (HQ) 302 571-1571
901 N Tatnall St Fl 2 Wilmington (19801) *(G-20590)*

Verizon Delaware LLC 302 761-6079
3900 N Washington St Fl 1 Wilmington (19802) *(G-20591)*

Verizon Master Trust 302 636-6182
1100 N Market St Wilmington (19890) *(G-20592)*

Verizon Wireless 610 301-2395
1625 Newport Gap Pike Wilmington (19808) *(G-20593)*

Verizon Wireless, Millsboro Also Called: Cellco Partnership *(G-8218)*
Verizon Wireless, Newark Also Called: Verizon Wireless Inc *(G-12316)*

Verizon Wireless Inc 302 737-5028
1209 Churchmans Rd Newark (19713) *(G-12316)*

Verizon Wreless Authorized Ret, Millsboro Also Called: Atlantic Cellular *(G-8177)*
Verizon Wreless Authorized Ret, Millsboro Also Called: We R Wireless *(G-8502)*

Vernon Green Hydrogen LLC 609 772-7979
8 The Grn Dover (19901) *(G-3786)*

Versapro Group LLC 315 430-2775
5605 W Timberview Ct Wilmington (19808) *(G-20594)*

Versatile Impex Inc 302 369-9480
74 Albe Dr Ste 3 Newark (19702) *(G-12317)*

Verscom LLC (PA) 866 238-9189
501 Silverside Rd Ste 105 Wilmington (19809) *(G-20595)*

Verscom Carrier, Wilmington Also Called: Verscom LLC *(G-20595)*

Version 40 Software LLC 302 270-0245
662 Tullamore Ct Magnolia (19962) *(G-6788)*

Versitron Inc 302 894-0699
83 Albe Dr Ste C Newark (19702) *(G-12318)*

Versus Gaming Inc 855 643-9945
919 N Market St Wilmington (19801) *(G-20596)*

Vertex Industries Inc 302 472-0601
818 S Heald St Ste C Wilmington (19801) *(G-20597)*

Vertical Blind Factory Inc (PA) 302 998-9616
3 Meco Cir Wilmington (19804) *(G-20598)*

Vertical Trnsp Eqp Solutions, Newark Also Called: Liberty Elevator Experts LLC *(G-11252)*

Vertrius Corp 800 770-1913
16192 Coastal Hwy Lewes (19958) *(G-6600)*

Very LLC 630 945-5539
160 Greentree Dr Ste 101 Dover (19904) *(G-3787)*

Veryutils Inc 858 939-9928
2035 Sunset Lake Rd B2 Newark (19702) *(G-12319)*

Vest Management Inc 302 856-3100
18591 Sand Hill Rd Georgetown (19947) *(G-4569)*

Vesta Wash LLC 302 559-7533
146 Woodland Rd Newark (19702) *(G-12320)*

Veteran It Pro LLC 302 824-3111
37 Staten Dr Hockessin (19707) *(G-5418)*

Veteran Owned Cleaning Svcs, Dover Also Called: Otis Kamara *(G-3247)*

Veteran Services 302 864-0009
32117 Judiths Ln Frankford (19945) *(G-4157)*

Veterans Development Co LLC 302 945-5281
23171 Albertson Ct Lewes (19958) *(G-6601)*

Veterans Fgn Wars Nwman L-Urba, Smyrna Also Called: Veterans of Foreign Wars Newmn *(G-13930)*

Veterans Health Administration 302 994-1660
2710 Centerville Rd Wilmington (19808) *(G-20599)*

Veterans Health Administration 302 994-2511
1601 Kirkwood Hwy Wilmington (19805) *(G-20600)*

Veterans of Foreign Wars 302 366-8438
100 Veterans Dr Newark (19711) *(G-12321)*

Veterans of Foreign Wars Newmn 302 653-8801
4941 Wheatleys Pond Rd Smyrna (19977) *(G-13930)*

Veterans Story Project Inc 302 644-4600
308 Ocean View Blvd Lewes (19958) *(G-6602)*

Veterans Untd Outreach Del Inc 302 678-1285
726 E Division St Dover (19901) *(G-3788)*

Veterinary Emergency Ctr Del, New Castle Also Called: Veternary Specialty Ctr Del PA *(G-9670)*

Veternary Specialty Ctr Del PA 302 322-6933
290 Churchmans Rd New Castle (19720) *(G-9670)*

Vetex Construction LLC 302 670-0989
65 Douglas Fir Rd Magnolia (19962) *(G-6789)*

Vetosine Inc 424 258-0120
251 Little Falls Dr Wilmington (19808) *(G-20601)*

Vetted, Wilmington Also Called: Opinr Inc *(G-18804)*

Veze Wireless of Smyrna Inc, Smyrna Also Called: WER Wireless of Smyrna Inc *(G-13936)*

VFW, Milford Also Called: VFW Post 6483 *(G-8135)*

VFW Magazine 302 994-2511
1601 Kirkwood Hwy Wilmington (19805) *(G-20602)*

VFW Post 2863, Newport Also Called: Diamond State Home Auxiliary *(G-12449)*
VFW Post 475, Newark Also Called: V F W Post Home *(G-12296)*
VFW Post 5447, Wilmington Also Called: Hall Burke VFW Post 5447 Inc *(G-17038)*
VFW Post 5892, Hockessin Also Called: Brenden Bley Chanl VFW Post 58 *(G-5142)*

VFW Post 6483 .... 302 422-4412
77 Veterans Cir Milford (19963) *(G-8135)*

VI Dima Inc 302 427-0787
2400 W 4th St Wilmington (19805) *(G-20603)*

Via Mdical Day Spa Pasca Salon 302 757-2830
3212 Brookline Rd Wilmington (19808) *(G-20604)*

Via Networks Inc 314 727-2087
2711 Centerville Rd Ste 400 Wilmington (19808) *(G-20605)*

Viacom Limited 484 857-7116
1221 College Park Dr # 203 Dover (19904) *(G-3789)*

Vianair Inc 646 403-4705
3511 Silverside Rd Wilmington (19810) *(G-20606)*

Viaprogram Technology Inc (PA) 917 292-5433
124 Broadkill Rd Ste 480 Milton (19968) *(G-8725)*

Viaticum Incorporated 302 467-8353
132 W Champlain Ave Wilmington (19804) *(G-20607)*

Vic Victor Imagination Co LLC 714 262-4426
16192 Coastal Hwy Lewes (19958) *(G-6603)*

Vicdania Health Services LLC 302 672-0139
1006 College Rd Ste 101 Dover (19904) *(G-3790)*

Vicdania Health Svc, Dover Also Called: Vicdania Health Services LLC *(G-3790)*

Vicente & Partners LLC 646 209-5527
1209 N Orange St Wilmington (19801) *(G-20608)*

Vickers Ballooning LLC 302 462-1830
28091 Nine Foot Rd Dagsboro (19939) *(G-1523)*

Vicks Commercial Clg & Maint 302 697-9591
378 Mannering Dr Dover (19901) *(G-3791)*

Victims Voices Heard 302 407-3747
100 W 10th St Wilmington (19801) *(G-20609)*

Victims Voices Heard Inc 302 242-1108
32449 Back Nine Way Millsboro (19966) *(G-8494)*

Victor A Maldonado 302 420-9749
1 Delaware St Saint Georges (19733) *(G-13040)*

Victor Colbert Construction 302 368-7270
723 Old Baltimore Pike Newark (19702) *(G-12322)*

Victor J Venturena DDS 302 656-0558
1117 N Franklin St Wilmington (19806) *(G-20610)*

Victor L Gregory Jr DMD 302 239-1827
5301 Limestone Rd Ste 211 Wilmington (19808) *(G-20611)*

ALPHABETIC SECTION

Victoria Mews Group Invstors L (PA) 610 543-0303
13 Odaniel Ave Newark (19711) *(G-12323)*

Victoria Mews LP Delnware Vall 302 489-2000
722 Yorklyn Rd Ste 350 Hockessin (19707) *(G-5419)*

Victoria's Secret, Rehoboth Beach Also Called: Victorias Secret Stores LLC *(G-13003)*

Victorias Secret Stores LLC 302 644-1035
35000 Midway Outlet Dr Rehoboth Beach (19971) *(G-13003)*

Victorious Jaesettes Inc 302 898-1946
801 W 9th St Ste 2 Wilmington (19801) *(G-20612)*

Victorous Kngdom Ctzens Ntwrk 302 409-0701
541 Sequoia Dr Smyrna (19977) *(G-13931)*

Victory Cleaning LLC 267 330-9422
18 Mifflin Mdws Dover (19901) *(G-3792)*

Victory Lane Express Wash LLC 302 543-6445
1715 Foulk Rd Wilmington (19803) *(G-20613)*

Victoryconsulting LLC 203 275-9398
3 Germay Dr Unit 42970 Wilmington (19804) *(G-20614)*

Victra 302 408-0999
1722 Naamans Rd Wilmington (19810) *(G-20615)*

Victra 302 593-2648
2131 Kirkwood Hwy Wilmington (19805) *(G-20616)*

Vidalytics 303 500-5715
124 Broadkill Rd Pmb 728 Milton (19968) *(G-8726)*

Vidells Day Spa 302 656-1784
14b Trolley Sq Wilmington (19806) *(G-20617)*

Video Den 302 628-9835
27180 Williams Ave Seaford (19973) *(G-13441)*

Video Scene, Dover Also Called: Video Scene of Delaware Inc *(G-3793)*

Video Scene of Delaware Inc (PA) 302 678-8526
Bay Rd Rr 113 Dover (19901) *(G-3793)*

Vidfluencer LLC 917 745-3713
8 The Grn Ste A Dover (19901) *(G-3794)*

Vidhq Inc 512 660-7862
1007 N Orange St Ste 1382 Wilmington (19801) *(G-20618)*

Vie Incorporated 512 200-7638
8 The Grn Ste A Dover (19901) *(G-3795)*

Viewbix Inc (HQ) 302 645-7400
16192 Coastal Hwy Lewes (19958) *(G-6604)*

Viinex Inc 510 443-5114
16192 Coastal Hwy Lewes (19958) *(G-6605)*

Villa Belmont, Newark Also Called: Belmont Villa Condominiums *(G-10016)*

Villa Cotton Corporation 302 439-1508
1000 N West St Ste 1200 Wilmington (19801) *(G-20619)*

Villa Token Inc 831 227-9878
7209 Lancaster Pike Hockessin (19707) *(G-5420)*

Village At Blue Hen 302 450-1265
400 Haslet St Dover (19901) *(G-3796)*

Village At Fox Point 302 762-7480
1436 Kynlyn Dr Wilmington (19809) *(G-20620)*

Village Developers Inc 302 732-3400
31003 Country Gdns Unit 1 Dagsboro (19939) *(G-1524)*

Village Green Inc 302 764-2234
62 Southgate Blvd New Castle (19720) *(G-9671)*

Village of Barrett's Run The, Newark Also Called: Barrettes Run Apartments *(G-9984)*

Village of Canterbury, Wilmington Also Called: Iacono - Summer Chase *(G-17252)*

Village of Cool Branch Homes, Seaford Also Called: Atlantic Realty Management *(G-13073)*

Village of St John LP 302 652-1690
2020 N Tatnall St Wilmington (19802) *(G-20621)*

Village Sq Acdemy Lrng Ctr LLC 302 539-5000
30792 Whites Neck Rd Ocean View (19970) *(G-12580)*

Village Tree 302 298-6349
1037 W 7th St Wilmington (19805) *(G-20622)*

Villages of Nobles Pond Phase 302 736-5000
13 Nobles Pond Xing Dover (19904) *(G-3797)*

Villas Apartments, New Castle Also Called: Christiana Wood LLC *(G-8941)*

Vinay Hosmane MD 302 836-2727
2600 Glasgow Ave Ste 103 Newark (19702) *(G-12324)*

Vinay Kandula MD 302 651-4200
1600 Rockland Rd Wilmington (19803) *(G-20623)*

Vincent Abbrescia 302 734-1414
200 Banning St Dover (19904) *(G-3798)*

Vincent B Killeen M D 302 645-4700
1535 Savannah Rd Lewes (19958) *(G-6606)*

Vincent Farms Inc 302 875-5707
12487 Salt Barn Rd Laurel (19956) *(G-5619)*

Vincent J Daniels DMD, Wilmington Also Called: Blue Diamond Dental PA *(G-14963)*

Vincent J Marmodo 302 777-1697
2300 Pennsylvania Ave Wilmington (19806) *(G-20624)*

Vincent Lobo Dr PA 302 398-8163
203 Shaw Ave # 205 Harrington (19952) *(G-4845)*

Vincenza & Margherita Bistro 302 479-7999
1717 Marsh Rd Wilmington (19810) *(G-20625)*

Vinces Sports Center Inc 302 738-4859
14 Gender Rd Newark (19713) *(G-12325)*

Vine Creek Mobile Home Park, Ocean View Also Called: Bayshore Inc *(G-12470)*

Vinings At Christiana, Newark Also Called: Shelter Development LLC *(G-11996)*

Vinisia Inc 252 297-6730
8 The Grn Ste A Dover (19901) *(G-3799)*

Vinnys Handyman Servies 302 265-9196
27619 Dunstan Ct Milton (19968) *(G-8727)*

Vinocur Charles MD 302 651-5888
1600 Rockland Rd Wilmington (19803) *(G-20626)*

Vintage Candle Company 302 643-9343
16734 Oak Rd Bridgeville (19933) *(G-780)*

Vintage Properties LLC 302 994-4442
4000 Dawnbrook Dr Wilmington (19804) *(G-20627)*

Vintage Realty 302 731-1000
2612 Kirkwood Hwy Newark (19711) *(G-12326)*

Vinyo Inc (PA) 856 493-2042
651 N Broad St Ste 201 Middletown (19709) *(G-7688)*

VIP Systems Inc 786 615-8622
251 Little Falls Dr Wilmington (19808) *(G-20628)*

Vir Consultant LLC 747 666-2169
256 Chapman Rd Newark (19702) *(G-12327)*

Vira Games Inc 302 468-7152
2810 N Church St Wilmington (19802) *(G-20629)*

Virasoft Corporation 281 851-9080
2093 Philadelphia Pike # 2627te Claymont (19703) *(G-1328)*

Vircap LLC 302 261-9892
112 Capitol Trl Ste A Newark (19711) *(G-12328)*

Virgil P Ellwanger 302 934-8083
Mllsboro Vlg Grn Rr 24 Millsboro (19966) *(G-8495)*

Virginia Linens LLC 757 342-4225
2107 Nicholby Dr Wilmington (19808) *(G-20630)*

Virginia Transportation Corp 302 384-6767
700 Cornell Dr Wilmington (19801) *(G-20631)*

Viridi Marathon LLC 302 647-8280
3711 Kennett Pike Ste 212 Wilmington (19807) *(G-20632)*

Viro Inc 857 207-8174
651 N Broad St Middletown (19709) *(G-7689)*

Virtual Business Entps LLC 302 472-9100
Farmers Bank Bldg 301 Ste 1410 N Market Street Wilmington (19801) *(G-20633)*

Virtual Enterprises Inc 302 324-5322
42 Reads Way Ste C New Castle (19720) *(G-9672)*

Virtual Oplossing Pvt Ltd 866 268-0333
256 Chapman Rd Ste 105-4 Newark (19702) *(G-12329)*

Virtual Pro Gaming Inc 302 285-9891
2810 N Church St Wilmington (19802) *(G-20634)*

Virtual Talk Hub LLC 302 406-0038
1201 N Market St Ste 111 Wilmington (19801) *(G-20635)*

Virtually Fortified Staffing 302 547-9065
1470 Caldwell Corner Rd Townsend (19734) *(G-14088)*

Visa Europe Services LLC (HQ) 302 658-7581
1209 N Orange St Wilmington (19801) *(G-20636)*

Visavis Inc 858 952-4175
8 The Grn Dover (19901) *(G-3800)*

Visio Group International Corp 302 485-0378
1007 N Orange St Wilmington (19801) *(G-20637)*

Vision Campus Inc 302 543-6809
2205 Lancaster Ave Wilmington (19805) *(G-20638)*

Vision Capital III LLC 312 576-2247
200 Continental Dr # 401 Newark (19713) *(G-12330)*

Vision Capital Vi LLC 312 576-2247
200 Continental Dr # 401 Newark (19713) *(G-12331)*

Vision Center of Delaware Inc (PA) 302 656-8867
213 Greenhill Ave Ste A Wilmington (19805) *(G-20639)*

Vision Learning Center, Wilmington Also Called: Vision Campus Inc *(G-20638)*

Vision Limousine 302 584-0622
21 Benning Rd Claymont (19703) *(G-1329)*

Vision Optik, Newark Also Called: Howard B Stromwasser *(G-10979)*

Vision To Learn 302 220-4820
100 W 10th St Ste 115 Wilmington (19801) *(G-20640)*

Visionary Cnslting Prtners LLC 302 487-4200
301 Doveview Dr Unit 204 Dover (19904) *(G-3801)*

Visionary Energy Systems Inc 410 739-4342
325 Alder Rd Dover (19904) *(G-3802)*

Visionquest Eye Care Center 302 678-3545
820 Walker Rd Dover (19904) *(G-3803)*

Visionquest Eye Care Center, Dover Also Called: Visionquest Eye Care Center *(G-3803)*

Visionquest Nonprofit Corp 302 735-1666
1001 S Bradford St Ste 1 Dover (19904) *(G-3804)*

Visions Hair Design 302 477-0820
2807 Concord Pike Wilmington (19803) *(G-20641)*

Visiting Angel of Sussex, De, Milton Also Called: Grace Visitation Services *(G-8628)*

Visiting Angels of Dover 302 346-7777
850 New Burton Rd Dover (19904) *(G-3805)*

Visual Communications Inc 302 792-9500
3724 Philadelphia Pike Claymont (19703) *(G-1330)*

Visueats Imagery Solutions LLC 954 687-5112
651 N Broad St Ste 2051480 Middletown (19709) *(G-7690)*

Vitae Investment Company 302 656-8985
300 Delaware Ave Ste 566 Wilmington (19801) *(G-20642)*

Vital Berry 302 691-5063
1700 Shallcross Ave Wilmington (19806) *(G-20643)*

Vital Renewable Energy Company 202 595-2944
2711 Centerville Rd # 300 Wilmington (19808) *(G-20644)*

Vital-Gh Media Group LLC (PA) 302 437-4258
600 N Broad St Ste 750 Middletown (19709) *(G-7691)*

Vitas Healthcare Corporation 302 451-4000
100 Commerce Dr. Christina Corp Ctr #302 Newark (19713) *(G-12332)*

Vivian A Houghton Esquire 302 658-0518
800 N West St Fl 2 Wilmington (19801) *(G-20645)*

Vivians Style 302 645-9444
33516 Crossing Ave Unit 2 Lewes (19958) *(G-6607)*

Vivid Colors Carpet LLC 302 335-3933
43 Bayview Ave Frederica (19946) *(G-4187)*

Vivis Daycare and Preschool 302 607-4478
200 Hazlett Rd New Castle (19720) *(G-9673)*

Vivky of Delaware Inc 302 798-9914
7811 Governor Printz Blvd Claymont (19703) *(G-1331)*

Viziochron Inc 206 745-0356
251 Little Falls Dr Wilmington (19808) *(G-20646)*

Vizzie 360 (PA) 323 239-0690
16192 Coastal Hwy Lewes (19958) *(G-6608)*

Vlocker North America LLC 469 567-0956
2810 N Church St Wilmington (19802) *(G-20647)*

Vls It Consulting Inc 302 368-5656
260 Chapman Rd Ste 104a Newark (19702) *(G-12333)*

Vna of Delaware 302 454-5422
190 Salem Church Rd Newark (19713) *(G-12334)*

Vogue On 24 Salon & Spa LLC 302 947-5667
36908 Silicato Dr Unit 11 Millsboro (19966) *(G-8496)*

Vogue On 54, Selbyville Also Called: Brandon Tatum *(G-13480)*

Voice Radio LLC 302 858-5118
20254 Dupont Blvd Georgetown (19947) *(G-4570)*

Voiceloft Inc 678 882-5024
651 N Broad St Ste 206 Middletown (19709) *(G-7692)*

Voicely Social Inc 302 446-4011
8 The Grn Ste A Dover (19901) *(G-3806)*

Voicemix Inc 305 981-0518
651 N Broad St Middletown (19709) *(G-7693)*

Voip Carrier Services, Newark Also Called: Cloudli Communications Inc *(G-10263)*

Voip Supplier LLC 302 760-9237
8 The Grn Ste 7879 Dover (19901) *(G-3807)*

Voitlex Corp 302 288-0670
8 The Grn Ste A Dover (19901) *(G-3808)*

Voiture Nationale La Society 302 478-7591
1017 Faun Rd Wilmington (19803) *(G-20648)*

VOITURE NATIONALE LA SOCIETY, Wilmington Also Called: Voiture Nationale La Society *(G-20648)*

Volleyball 302 593-4414
142 Tweedsmere Dr Townsend (19734) *(G-14089)*

Volumetric Format Association 760 803-8720
8 The Grn Ste 11383 Dover (19901) *(G-3809)*

Volunteer Brewing Company LLC 610 721-2836
120 W Main St Middletown (19709) *(G-7694)*

Volunteers For Adolescent 302 658-3331
611 W 18th St Wilmington (19802) *(G-20649)*

Volvant Inc (PA) 805 456-6464
919 N Market St Ste 950 Wilmington (19801) *(G-20650)*

Volvox Biologic Inc 801 722-5942
16192 Coastal Hwy Lewes (19958) *(G-6609)*

Vonexpy Softech LLC 512 484-8340
440 Jacobsen Dr Newark (19702) *(G-12335)*

Vonogrphy-The Perfect Shot LLC 202 923-9532
38 Bastille Loop Newark (19702) *(G-12336)*

Vora Labs Inc 860 559-8985
600 N Broad St Middletown (19709) *(G-7695)*

Vortex Labs LLC 302 231-1294
1209 N Orange St Wilmington (19801) *(G-20651)*

Vortex Refrigeration Company 855 562-5222
1201 N Orange St Ste 7150 Wilmington (19801) *(G-20652)*

Vos Energy LLC 302 658-7581
1209 N Orange St Wilmington (19801) *(G-20653)*

Voshell Bros Welding Inc 302 674-1414
1769 Kenton Rd Dover (19904) *(G-3810)*

Voshell Brothers, Dover Also Called: Voshell Bros Welding Inc *(G-3810)*

Vox Ai Inc 302 288-0670
8 The Grn Ste A Dover (19901) *(G-3811)*

Voxpopin, Claymont Also Called: Voxpopin Inc *(G-1332)*

Voxpopin Inc 202 567-7483
2803 Philadelphia Pike Claymont (19703) *(G-1332)*

Voyager Drilling Services LLC 302 439-6030
913 N Market St Ste 200 Wilmington (19801) *(G-20654)*

Vp Racing Fuels, Newark Also Called: Vp Racing Fuels Inc *(G-12337)*

Vp Racing Fuels Inc 302 368-1500
16 Brookhill Dr Newark (19702) *(G-12337)*

Vpho 302 369-3993
2671 Kirkwood Highway Newark (19711) *(G-12338)*

Vps International LLC 800 493-9356
16192 Coastal Hwy Lewes (19958) *(G-6610)*

Vps Services LLC 302 376-6710
651 N Broad St Ste 308 Middletown (19709) *(G-7696)*

Vpsie Inc 844 468-7743
108 W 13th St Wilmington (19801) *(G-20655)*

Vrtii Corporation 703 401-8963
16192 Coastal Hwy Lewes (19958) *(G-6611)*

Vsg Business Solutions LLC 302 261-3209
221 Cornwell Dr Bear (19701) *(G-557)*

Vshield Software Corp 302 531-0855
3500 S Dupont Hwy Dover (19901) *(G-3812)*

VT, Middletown Also Called: Veer Trucking LLC *(G-7683)*

Vtech Engineering Group LLC 267 253-2576
1050 Industrial Dr # 110 Middletown (19709) *(G-7697)*

Vtms LLC 302 264-9094
3 Mineral Ct Dover (19904) *(G-3813)*

Vtraderio LLC 646 952-1189
1221 College Park Dr Dover (19904) *(G-3814)*

Vu Binh Thai 302 999-7980
4717 Kirkwood Hwy Wilmington (19808) *(G-20656)*

Vue Events Inc 301 812-3800
8 The Grn Ste 4202 Dover (19901) *(G-3815)*

Vulcan International Corp 302 656-1950
103 Foulk Rd Wilmington (19803) *(G-20657)*

Vulcan International Corp (PA) 302 428-3181
300 Delaware Ave Ste 1704 Wilmington (19801) *(G-20658)*

ALPHABETIC SECTION

Vulcan Wizard LLC.. 914 326-6023
16192 Coastal Hwy Lewes (19958) *(G-6612)*

Vulcraft Sales Corp (HQ).. 302 427-5832
300 Delaware Ave Ste 210 Wilmington (19801) *(G-20659)*

Vultran Creative Marketing..................................... 302 981-3379
301 W 6th St Wilmington (19801) *(G-20660)*

Vvardis Inc... 917 940-3009
651 N Broad St Middletown (19709) *(G-7698)*

Vybn Inc (PA).. 415 715-7945
300 Delaware Ave Ste 210a Wilmington (19801) *(G-20661)*

Vylo Inc (PA)... 310 902-9693
256 Chapman Rd Newark (19702) *(G-12339)*

Vyzer Inc... 530 446-2568
651 N Broad St Ste 201 Middletown (19709) *(G-7699)*

W B Mason Co Inc.. 888 926-2766
100 Interchange Blvd Newark (19711) *(G-12340)*

W B Simpson Elementary School, Dover Also Called: Caesar Rodney School District *(G-2011)*

W C Farms LLC... 302 242-1770
3668 Spectrum Farms Rd Felton (19943) *(G-4036)*

W D Pressley Inc... 302 653-4381
5779 Dupont Pkwy Smyrna (19977) *(G-13932)*

W H Thomas DDS.. 302 697-1152
1981 S State St Dover (19901) *(G-3816)*

W L Gore (PA)... 302 584-8822
200 Owls Nest Rd Wilmington (19807) *(G-20662)*

W L Gore & Associates Inc.................................... 302 368-3700
1901 Barksdale Rd Newark (19711) *(G-12341)*

W L Gore & Associates Inc (PA)............................. 302 738-4880
555 Paper Mill Rd Newark (19711) *(G-12342)*

W P D Transport Inc.. 302 449-3260
605 Nesting Ln Middletown (19709) *(G-7700)*

W Powell Investments... 443 523-2476
20437 Laurel Rd Millsboro (19966) *(G-8497)*

W R Grace & Co.. 410 531-4000
1521 Concord Pike Ste 341 Wilmington (19803) *(G-20663)*

W S M S Bank, Newark Also Called: Cash Connect Inc *(G-10159)*

W T Schrider & Sons Inc....................................... 302 934-1900
24572 Betts Pond Rd Millsboro (19966) *(G-8498)*

W W Grainger Inc... 302 322-1840
117 Quigley Blvd Historic New Castle (19720) *(G-5098)*

W W Snyder Excavating & Masnry, Middletown Also Called: Walter W Snyder *(G-7706)*

W23 S12 Holdings LLC... 610 348-3825
2000 Pennsylvania Ave Unit 106 Wilmington (19806) *(G-20664)*

W500g Inc.. 302 252-7279
274 Liborio Dr Middletown (19709) *(G-7701)*

Wabtec Finance LLC (DH)...................................... 412 825-1000
1011 Centre Rd Ste 310 Wilmington (19805) *(G-20665)*

Wac, New Castle Also Called: Wilmington Aquatic Club Inc *(G-9684)*

Wachu Inc.. 323 657-3889
1007 N Orange St Fl 4 Wilmington (19801) *(G-20666)*

Waffles & Wifi LLC... 267 909-0174
254 Chapman Rd Newark (19702) *(G-12343)*

Wafl Wyus Broadcasting Inc................................ 302 422-7575
1666 Blairs Pond Rd Milford (19963) *(G-8136)*

Wagamons Schell Brothers................................... 302 664-1680
20184 Phillips St Rehoboth Beach (19971) *(G-13004)*

Wagefi Inc.. 646 853-0165
651 N Broad St Ste 206 Middletown (19709) *(G-7702)*

Waggies By Maggie and Friends........................... 302 598-2867
1310 Carruthers Ln Wilmington (19803) *(G-20667)*

Wagner & Prigg Family Medicine........................... 302 684-2000
16529 Coastal Hwy Lewes (19958) *(G-6613)*

Wagner N J & Sons Trucking................................ 302 242-7731
5972 Hopkins Cemetery Rd Felton (19943) *(G-4037)*

Wags To Riches.. 302 436-4766
36735 Roxana Rd Selbyville (19975) *(G-13617)*

Wagstaff Day Care Center Inc............................... 302 998-7818
310 Kiamensi Rd Rm 301 Wilmington (19804) *(G-20668)*

Wahid Consultants LLC... 315 400-0955
147 Quigley Blvd Unit 12006 Historic New Castle (19720) *(G-5099)*

Wahl Family Dentistry... 302 655-1228
2003 Concord Pike Wilmington (19803) *(G-20669)*

Wahl Financial Inc.. 302 229-1933
628 Black Gates Rd Wilmington (19803) *(G-20670)*

Wahl, John MD, Wilmington Also Called: Eye Physicians and Surgeons PA *(G-16512)*

Wahoo Repair LLC.. 302 430-4588
24094 Lawson Rd Georgetown (19947) *(G-4571)*

Wajba Corp... 650 307-0070
221 N Broad St Middletown (19709) *(G-7703)*

Waked Tarek MD.. 703 342-7744
121 S Front St Seaford (19973) *(G-13442)*

Waked Hammoud Tarek M MD.............................. 302 536-5395
8472 Herring Run Rd Seaford (19973) *(G-13443)*

Wala LLC.. 949 410-0568
2810 N Church St Wilmington (19802) *(G-20671)*

Walden LLC.. 302 998-8112
1 Henry Ct Wilmington (19808) *(G-20672)*

Walden Townhomes, Wilmington Also Called: Walden LLC *(G-20672)*

Walk By Faith LLC.. 737 529-5869
16192 Coastal Hwy Lewes (19958) *(G-6614)*

Walker International Trnsp LLC............................. 302 325-4180
700 Centerpoint Blvd Historic New Castle (19720) *(G-5100)*

Walkers Contracting LLC....................................... 302 331-0425
756 Millchop Ln Magnolia (19962) *(G-6790)*

Walkers For Jocelyn... 302 465-7461
5 Fairway Rd Newark (19711) *(G-12344)*

Wallace Investments Group LLC............................ 323 407-2889
651 N Broad St Ste 205 Middletown (19709) *(G-7704)*

Wallace Lamarr.. 202 460-3377
137 S Queen St Dover (19904) *(G-3817)*

Wallace Montgomery & Assoc LLP......................... 302 510-1080
200 Continental Dr Newark (19713) *(G-12345)*

Wallce & Associates, Hockessin Also Called: C Wallace & Associates *(G-5146)*

Walleys Trucking Inc.. 302 893-8652
29 Emerald Ridge Dr Bear (19701) *(G-558)*

Wallis Repair Inc.. 302 378-4301
106 Patriot Dr Middletown (19709) *(G-7705)*

Walls Farm and Garden Ctr Inc............................. 302 422-4565
833 S Dupont Blvd Milford (19963) *(G-8137)*

Walls Irrigation Inc (PA)....................................... 302 422-2262
833 S Dupont Blvd Milford (19963) *(G-8138)*

Walls Service Center Inc...................................... 302 422-8110
220 Ne Front St Milford (19963) *(G-8139)*

Walnut Green Asset MGT LL................................. 302 689-3798
1301 Walnut Green Rd Wilmington (19807) *(G-20673)*

Walnut Grove Cabinets LLC................................... 302 678-2694
308 Rose Valley School Rd Dover (19904) *(G-3818)*

Walnut Grove Coop Inc... 302 545-3000
321 Laurel Ave Newark (19711) *(G-12346)*

Walnut Street Y M C A, Wilmington Also Called: Young Mens Christian Assn Del *(G-20938)*

Walsh Chiropractic Center.................................... 302 422-0622
800 Airport Rd Ste 103 Milford (19963) *(G-8140)*

Walter J Kobasa Jr MD... 302 993-1191
1941 Limestone Rd Wilmington (19808) *(G-20674)*

Walter L Fox Post 2 Inc.. 302 674-1741
835 S Bay Rd Dover (19901) *(G-3819)*

Walter Scott... 302 265-2383
606 Milford Harrington Hwy Milford (19963) *(G-8141)*

Walter Stark Dr.. 302 227-4990
4 Rolling Rd Rehoboth Beach (19971) *(G-13005)*

Walter T Wilson... 302 542-6753
23422 Winding Pines Ln Georgetown (19947) *(G-4572)*

Walter W Snyder.. 302 378-1817
1844 Choptank Rd Middletown (19709) *(G-7706)*

Walters Auctioneering.. 302 284-0914
139 Princess Ann Ave Viola (19979) *(G-14097)*

Walton Farm & Truck Repair................................. 302 245-3479
15209 S Old State Rd Georgetown (19947) *(G-4573)*

Wanda Roland.. 773 573-3265
127 W 20th St Wilmington (19802) *(G-20675)*

Wanex Electrical Service LLC............................... 302 326-1700
261 Airport Rd New Castle (19720) *(G-9674)*

Wang Consultants Inc.. 626 483-0265
4023 Kennett Pike Ste 603 Wilmington (19807) *(G-20676)*

Warachai Thai Boxing Assn

Warachai Thai Boxing Assn 302 257-9794
   19818 Hebron Rd Rehoboth Beach (19971) *(G-13006)*

Ward & Taylor LLC 302 539-3537
   33548 Market Pl Unit 3 Bethany Beach (19930) *(G-647)*

Ward & Taylor LLC 302 346-7000
   83 Greentree Dr Dover (19904) *(G-3820)*

Ward & Taylor LLC 302 225-3350
   242 Dove Run Dr Middletown (19709) *(G-7707)*

Ward & Taylor LLC 302 227-1403
   37212 Rehoboth Avenue Ext Rehoboth Beach (19971) *(G-13007)*

Ward & Taylor LLC (PA) 302 225-3350
   2710 Centerville Rd Ste 200 Wilmington (19808) *(G-20677)*

Ward Chiropractic 302 225-9000
   5810 Kirkwood Hwy Wilmington (19808) *(G-20678)*

Warfel Construction Co Inc 302 422-8927
   246 S Rehoboth Blvd Milford (19963) *(G-8142)*

Warner M Schlaupitz 302 492-3451
   4624 Westville Rd Camden Wyoming (19934) *(G-985)*

Warner Tansey Inc 302 539-3001
   Pennsylvania Ave Bethany Beach (19930) *(G-648)*

Warren A Reid Custon Builders, Laurel Also Called: Warren Reid *(G-5620)*

Warren Electric Co Inc 302 629-9134
   21621 Sussex Hwy Seaford (19973) *(G-13444)*

Warren G Butt M D 302 738-5300
   4745 Ogletown Stanton Rd Ste 134 Newark (19713) *(G-12347)*

Warren Reid 302 877-0901
   14234 Sycamore Rd Laurel (19956) *(G-5620)*

Warring Nation Inc 757 323-6312
   1221 College Park Dr # 116 Dover (19904) *(G-3821)*

Warrior Community Connect Inc 202 309-5729
   22165 S Preservation Dr Millsboro (19966) *(G-8499)*

Warsal & Amurao MD PA 302 654-6245
   2006 Limestone Rd Ste 4 Wilmington (19808) *(G-20679)*

Wartimeaction LLC 203 685-8868
   221 N Broad St Ste 3a Middletown (19709) *(G-7708)*

Wartrude Services Inc 302 213-3944
   1601 Milltown Rd Wilmington (19808) *(G-20680)*

Wash-N-Wag 302 644-2466
   34680 Jiffy Way Lewes (19958) *(G-6615)*

Waste Industries 302 367-5511
   903 Lambson Ln New Castle (19720) *(G-9675)*

Waste Industries Delaware LLC 302 934-1364
   28471 John J Williams Hwy Millsboro (19966) *(G-8500)*

Waste Management, New Castle Also Called: Waste Management Michigan Inc *(G-9676)*

Waste Management, Wilmington Also Called: Waste Management Delaware Inc *(G-20681)*

Waste Management Delaware Inc 302 854-5301
   11323 Trussum Pond Rd Laurel (19956) *(G-5621)*

Waste Management Delaware Inc 302 994-0944
   300 Harvey Dr Wilmington (19804) *(G-20681)*

Waste Management Michigan Inc 302 655-1360
   246 Marsh Ln New Castle (19720) *(G-9676)*

Waste Masters, New Castle Also Called: Waste Masters Solutions LLC *(G-9677)*

Waste Masters Solutions LLC 302 824-0909
   19 Davidson Ln New Castle (19720) *(G-9677)*

Wastecost Corporation 512 562-0888
   16192 Coastal Hwy Lewes (19958) *(G-6616)*

Wasteflo LLC 410 202-0802
   207 N Poplar St Laurel (19956) *(G-5622)*

Watchdogdevelopmentcom LLC 888 488-7531
   614 N Dupont Hwy Ste 210 Dover (19901) *(G-3822)*

Water Ingenuity Holdings Corp 847 725-3000
   2711 Centerville Rd Ste 4 Wilmington (19808) *(G-20682)*

Water Is Life Kenya Inc 302 894-7335
   314 E Main St Ste 2 Newark (19711) *(G-12348)*

Water System Services Inc 302 732-1490
   32464 Beechwood Ln Dagsboro (19939) *(G-1525)*

Water's Edge, Newark Also Called: Omniway Corporation *(G-11586)*

Watercraft LLC 302 757-0786
   801 Owls Nest Rd Wilmington (19807) *(G-20683)*

Waterfront Ldscpg Irrigation 302 645-8100
   1604 Savannah Rd Lewes (19958) *(G-6617)*

Watermark At North Bethany 302 539-3223
   36903 S Silver Sands Dr Bethany Beach (19930) *(G-649)*

Waterstone Mortgage Corp 302 227-8252
   330 Rehoboth Ave Ste B Rehoboth Beach (19971) *(G-13008)*

Watkins Consulting Inc (PA) 240 479-7273
   73 Blackpool Rd Rehoboth Beach (19971) *(G-13009)*

Watkins Consulting Group JV 202 861-0200
   73 Blackpool Rd Rehoboth Beach (19971) *(G-13010)*

Watkins Dealership, New Castle Also Called: Watkins System Inc *(G-9678)*

Watkins System Inc 302 658-8561
   4031 New Castle Ave New Castle (19720) *(G-9678)*

Watkins-Davis Kinard JV 240 479-7273
   73 Blackpool Rd Rehoboth Beach (19971) *(G-13011)*

Watson Boys Trucking LLC 302 635-4109
   501 Silverside Rd Wilmington (19809) *(G-20684)*

Watson Funeral Home Inc 302 934-7842
   211 S Washington St Millsboro (19966) *(G-8501)*

Watson-Marlow Flow Smart Inc 302 536-6388
   213 Nesbitt Dr Seaford (19973) *(G-13445)*

Watsons Auction & Realty Svc 302 422-2392
   115 N Washington St Milford (19963) *(G-8143)*

Watts Electric Company 302 529-1183
   2027 Harwyn Rd Wilmington (19810) *(G-20685)*

Watts Htg Hot Wtr Slutions LLC 817 335-9531
   1209 N Orange St Wilmington (19801) *(G-20686)*

Wave, Wilmington Also Called: Chime Inc *(G-15382)*

Wave Global Employment Inc 617 987-0152
   3 Germay Dr Ste 4 Wilmington (19804) *(G-20687)*

Wave LLC 212 849-2217
   1201 N Orange St Wilmington (19801) *(G-20688)*

Waveinnova Inc 650 507-5756
   1209 N Orange St Wilmington (19801) *(G-20689)*

Waveone Inc 650 796-8637
   1209 N Orange St Wilmington (19801) *(G-20690)*

Waverly Orthopaedic, Milford Also Called: Choy Wilson Cdgn *(G-7826)*

Wavetec North America Inc 323 284-5084
   2093 Philadelphia Pike Claymont (19703) *(G-1333)*

Way To Go Led Lighting Company 844 312-4574
   702 Interchange Blvd Newark (19711) *(G-12349)*

Waybetter Inc 212 343-8238
   4023 Kennett Pike Wilmington (19807) *(G-20691)*

Wayfarer Solutions Inc 808 228-9989
   251 Little Falls Dr Wilmington (19808) *(G-20692)*

Wayman Fire Protection Inc 302 994-5757
   3540 Old Capitol Trl Wilmington (19808) *(G-20693)*

Wayne Bennett 302 436-2379
   35484 Honeysuckle Rd Frankford (19945) *(G-4158)*

Wayne I Tucker 302 838-1100
   100 Becks Woods Dr Ste 202 Bear (19701) *(G-559)*

Wayne Industries Inc (PA) 302 478-6160
   1105 N Market St Ste 1300 Wilmington (19801) *(G-20694)*

Wayne K Pansa Jr Lcsw LLC 302 455-7065
   1201 W 6th St Wilmington (19805) *(G-20695)*

Wayne R Bonlie M D 302 436-0901
   33195 Lighthouse Rd # 8 Selbyville (19975) *(G-13618)*

Wazoplus LLC 302 496-0042
   4 Peddlers Row Newark (19702) *(G-12350)*

Wb Paving LLC 302 838-1886
   1387 Red Lion Rd Bear (19701) *(G-560)*

Wbi Capital Advisors LLC (PA) 856 361-6362
   251 Little Falls Dr Wilmington (19808) *(G-20696)*

Wdbid DBA Downtown Visions 302 425-5374
   409 N Orange St Wilmington (19801) *(G-20697)*

Wdbid Management Company 302 425-5374
   409 N Orange St Wilmington (19801) *(G-20698)*

We Are Family Cleaning Service 302 524-8294
   32538 Mccary Rd Frankford (19945) *(G-4159)*

We Are Friends Inc 302 501-7521
   651 N Broad St Ste 206 Middletown (19709) *(G-7709)*

We Are Future Tech Inc 832 224-5528
   651 N Broad St Ste 205 Middletown (19709) *(G-7710)*

ALPHABETIC SECTION — Wellness Health Inc

We Care Nephrology LLC 302 242-0531
100 Kings Hwy Milford (19963) *(G-8144)*

We Clean For A Reason 302 930-0237
109 N Walnut St Milford (19963) *(G-8145)*

We Cobble LLC 302 504-4294
4023 Kennett Pike Ste 50098 Wilmington (19807) *(G-20699)*

We Dem Boys Transportation LLC 302 727-6164
16620 Gravel Hill Rd Milton (19968) *(G-8728)*

We Deserve It Shs For Kids Inc 302 521-7255
363 Frear Dr Dover (19901) *(G-3823)*

We Got Cars 4 Cash Inc 215 399-6978
1507 Historical Way Unit 7 Claymont (19703) *(G-1334)*

We Manage Your Site Inc 916 586-7724
2035 Sunset Lake Rd Ste B2 Newark (19702) *(G-12351)*

We R Wireless 443 880-0308
28665 Dupont Blvd Millsboro (19966) *(G-8502)*

Wealth Access Services LLC 302 327-4174
200 Continental Dr Ste 401 Newark (19713) *(G-12352)*

Wealth Capital Investors LLC 202 596-2280
7 Canary Dr Lewes (19958) *(G-6618)*

Wealth Management Group 302 734-5826
220 Beiser Blvd Dover (19904) *(G-3824)*

Weanas, Newark Also Called: *Huzala Inc (G-10987)*

Wearexalt LLC (PA) 203 913-5286
221 N Broad St Middletown (19709) *(G-7711)*

Wearwell 302 547-3337
314 Walden Rd Wilmington (19803) *(G-20700)*

Weather or Not Dog Walkers 302 304-8399
1300 Tulane Rd Wilmington (19803) *(G-20701)*

Weather or Not Inc 302 436-7533
38294 London Ave Unit 3 Selbyville (19975) *(G-13619)*

Weatherhill Dental 302 239-6677
5317 Limestone Rd Ste 2 Wilmington (19808) *(G-20702)*

Web Advantage Inc 302 479-7634
216 Paddock Ln Wilmington (19803) *(G-20703)*

Web Data Solutions LLC 888 407-5089
160 Greentree Dr Ste 101 Dover (19904) *(G-3825)*

Web Fce, Wilmington Also Called: *Fast Fce Inc (G-16557)*

Webb & Family LLC 302 697-7108
816 Thicket Rd Camden Wyoming (19934) *(G-986)*

Webb LLC 302 744-0029
312 W 35th St Wilmington (19802) *(G-20704)*

Webber Title LLC 302 218-0911
556 Fieldcrest Dr Dover (19904) *(G-3826)*

Webbit 302 725-6024
6200 Kirby Rd Milford (19963) *(G-8146)*

Webbrowser Media Inc 302 830-3664
3422 Old Capitol Trl Ste 716 Wilmington (19808) *(G-20705)*

Webeeta LLC 720 316-1876
8 The Grn Dover (19901) *(G-3827)*

Weber Gallagher Simpson (PA) 302 346-6377
19 S State St Ste 102 Dover (19901) *(G-3828)*

Weber Sign & Art Studio, Frankford Also Called: *Weber Sign Co (G-4160)*

Weber Sign Co 302 732-1429
16 Hickory St Frankford (19945) *(G-4160)*

Webill Inc 628 227-7780
651 N Broad St Ste 206 Middletown (19709) *(G-7712)*

Webmost 302 345-0807
56 Upland Ct Newark (19713) *(G-12353)*

Websays Inc 424 385-9361
651 N Broad St Ste 201 Middletown (19709) *(G-7713)*

Webstaurant Store Inc 302 654-1247
705 Moorehouse Rd New Castle (19720) *(G-9679)*

Webster Dermatology PA 302 234-9305
720 Yorklyn Rd Ste 10 Hockessin (19707) *(G-5421)*

Webstudy Inc (PA) 888 326-4058
30649 Hollymount Rd Harbeson (19951) *(G-4718)*

Webtime Corporation 302 476-2350
501 Silverside Rd Ste 105 Wilmington (19809) *(G-20706)*

Webtrit Inc 954 364-8888
16192 Coastal Hwy Lewes (19958) *(G-6619)*

Webwork Time Tracker Inc 415 707-3544
1207 Delaware Ave Wilmington (19806) *(G-20707)*

Wecanrush Inc (PA) 317 603-6622
501 Silverside Rd 373 Wilmington (19809) *(G-20708)*

Weddle Contracting, Greenwood Also Called: *Jeremey M Weddle (G-4646)*

Wee Care Day Care Salv Army 302 472-0712
400 N Orange St Wilmington (19801) *(G-20709)*

Wee Wonders Doulas 302 275-7799
932 Rockwell Rd Wilmington (19810) *(G-20710)*

Weed Real Estate LLC 302 981-6388
5 Sumac Ct Newark (19702) *(G-12354)*

Weedim Inc 202 773-9244
651 N Broad St Middletown (19709) *(G-7714)*

Weekfish LLC 800 979-5501
196 York Dr Smyrna (19977) *(G-13933)*

Weelwork Inc 800 546-8607
619 New York Ave Claymont (19703) *(G-1335)*

Weepor Company Inc 302 575-9945
103 Foulk Rd Ste 202 Wilmington (19803) *(G-20711)*

Weg Cleaning Service Inc 302 343-5746
300 Delaware Ave Wilmington (19801) *(G-20712)*

Wegman Bros Inc 302 738-4328
2612 Ogletown Rd Newark (19713) *(G-12355)*

Weighted With Love LLC 302 378-2041
117 Oliver Guessford Rd Townsend (19734) *(G-14090)*

Weik Nitsche & Dougherty 302 655-4040
305 N Union St Unit 2 Wilmington (19805) *(G-20713)*

Weiner Development LLC 302 764-9430
4 Denny Rd Ste 1 Wilmington (19809) *(G-20714)*

Weinstein Supply Div, Wilmington Also Called: *Hajoca Corporation (G-17036)*

Weir Greenblatt Pierce LLP 302 652-8181
1204 N King St Wilmington (19801) *(G-20715)*

Weiss & Saville PA 302 656-0400
1105 N Market St Ste 200 Wilmington (19801) *(G-20716)*

Weitron, Newark Also Called: *Weitron Inc (G-12356)*

Weitron Inc (PA) 800 398-3816
801 Pencader Dr Newark (19702) *(G-12356)*

Weiye LI MD 302 651-4400
1801 Rockland Rd Ste 100 Wilmington (19803) *(G-20717)*

WEKEEP TRAVEL SERVICES LLC 786 814-0722
16192 Coastal Hwy Lewes (19958) *(G-6620)*

Welcome Aboard Travel Ltd 302 678-9480
405 Lakeside Dr Lewes (19958) *(G-6621)*

Welcome Home Getaways LLC 724 426-5534
1148 Pulaski Hwy Ste 197 Bear (19701) *(G-561)*

Welcome2city Group Corp 347 897-9941
919 N Market St Wilmington (19801) *(G-20718)*

Welding By Jackson 302 846-3090
10178 Jackson St Delmar (19940) *(G-1654)*

Well Primary Care LLC 302 449-0070
102 Sleepy Hollow Dr Ste 200 Middletown (19709) *(G-7715)*

Wellabs Inc 816 774-4030
8 The Grn Ste 300 Dover (19901) *(G-3829)*

Weller's Utility Trailers, Bridgeville Also Called: *Wellers Tire Service Inc (G-781)*

Wellers Tire Service Inc 302 337-8228
16889 N Main St Bridgeville (19933) *(G-781)*

Wellford Corporation 302 288-0670
8 The Grn Ste 8174 Dover (19901) *(G-3830)*

Wellington Management Group 215 569-8900
300 Delaware Ave Ste 1380 Wilmington (19801) *(G-20719)*

Wellness and Rejuvenation 732 977-6958
30996 Puseys Rd Millsboro (19966) *(G-8503)*

Wellness By Sea LLC 302 278-0093
1209 Coastal Hwy Fenwick Island (19944) *(G-4058)*

Wellness Centers, Wilmington Also Called: *Christiana Care Hlth Svcs Inc (G-15408)*

Wellness Connections, Lewes Also Called: *Fresh Juice Partners LLC (G-6016)*

Wellness From Within 717 884-3908
33253 Waterview Ct Lewes (19958) *(G-6622)*

Wellness Health Center, Milford Also Called: *Wellness Health Inc (G-8147)*

Wellness Health Inc 302 424-4100
106 Nw Front St Milford (19963) *(G-8147)*

Wellness Natural USA Inc 800 547-5790
  2810 N Church St Pmb 47081 Wilmington (19802) *(G-20720)*
Wellness Plus 302 368-7990
  212 Cloverlea Rd Newark (19711) *(G-12357)*
Wellness Strategies LLC 302 475-5062
  1101 Wilson Rd Wilmington (19803) *(G-20721)*
Wellness Wahine 302 841-4988
  19868 Mayas Ln Milton (19968) *(G-8729)*
Wellnx Life Sciences USA, Wilmington Also Called: Platinum US Distribution Inc *(G-19073)*
Wells Fargo, Hockessin Also Called: Wells Fargo Bank National Assn *(G-5422)*
Wells Fargo, Hockessin Also Called: Wells Fargo Home Mortgage Inc *(G-5423)*
Wells Fargo, Rehoboth Beach Also Called: Wells Fargo Home Mortgage Inc *(G-13013)*
Wells Fargo, Wilmington Also Called: Wells Fargo Bank National Assn *(G-20722)*
Wells Fargo, Wilmington Also Called: Wells Fargo Bank National Assn *(G-20725)*
Wells Fargo Advisors, Newark Also Called: Wells Fargo Clearing Svcs LLC *(G-12359)*
Wells Fargo Advisors, Wilmington Also Called: Wells Fargo Clearing Svcs LLC *(G-20726)*
Wells Fargo Bank National Assn 302 832-6104
  1601 Governors Pl Bear (19701) *(G-562)*
Wells Fargo Bank National Assn 302 235-4304
  5801 Limestone Rd Hockessin (19707) *(G-5422)*
Wells Fargo Bank National Assn 302 449-5485
  310 Dove Run Centre Dr Middletown (19709) *(G-7716)*
Wells Fargo Bank National Assn 302 326-4304
  1424 N Dupont Hwy New Castle (19720) *(G-9680)*
Wells Fargo Bank National Assn 302 631-1500
  2624 Capitol Trl Newark (19711) *(G-12358)*
Wells Fargo Bank National Assn 302 644-6351
  4600 Hwy 1 Rehoboth Beach (19971) *(G-13012)*
Wells Fargo Bank National Assn 302 529-2550
  2024 Naamans Rd Wilmington (19810) *(G-20722)*
Wells Fargo Bank National Assn 302 761-1300
  814 Philadelphia Pike Wilmington (19809) *(G-20723)*
Wells Fargo Bank National Assn 302 622-3350
  100 W 10th St Lbby 1 Wilmington (19801) *(G-20724)*
Wells Fargo Bank National Assn 302 421-7820
  4015 Kennett Pike Wilmington (19807) *(G-20725)*
Wells Fargo Clearing Svcs LLC 302 731-2131
  131 Continental Dr Ste 102 Newark (19713) *(G-12359)*
Wells Fargo Clearing Svcs LLC 302 428-8600
  3801 Kennett Pike Ste B200 Wilmington (19807) *(G-20726)*
Wells Fargo Delaware Tr Co NA 302 575-2002
  505 Carr Rd Wilmington (19809) *(G-20727)*
Wells Fargo Home Mortgage Inc 302 239-6300
  7465 Lancaster Pike Hockessin (19707) *(G-5423)*
Wells Fargo Home Mortgage Inc 302 227-5700
  18977 Munchy Branch Rd Ste 6 Rehoboth Beach (19971) *(G-13013)*
Wells Farms Inc 302 422-4732
  7481 Wells Rd Milford (19963) *(G-8148)*
Wells Krystal 302 738-4191
  207 Kinross Dr Newark (19711) *(G-12360)*
Wellspring Counseling Services 302 373-8904
  115 E Glenwood Ave Smyrna (19977) *(G-13934)*
Wellspring Farm Inc 302 798-2407
  800 Carr Rd Wilmington (19809) *(G-20728)*
Wellspring Tack Shop, Wilmington Also Called: Wellspring Farm Inc *(G-20728)*
Wellthy Investors LLC 267 847-3486
  191 Fawn Haven Walk Dover (19901) *(G-3831)*
Welsh Family Dentistry 302 836-3711
  34 Withers Way Hockessin (19707) *(G-5424)*
Weltio LLC 305 307-9815
  8 The Grn Dover (19901) *(G-3832)*
Welton Evans, Milton Also Called: Evans Trucking Inc *(G-8622)*
Weltri Inc 818 962-8834
  8 The Grn Ste 12596 Dover (19901) *(G-3833)*
Weltron Technology Ltd Co 508 353-6752
  16192 Coastal Hwy Lewes (19958) *(G-6623)*
Wemaste, Wilmington Also Called: Whimstay Inc *(G-20760)*
Wen International Inc 845 354-1773
  101 Wayland Rd Wilmington (19807) *(G-20729)*
Wendy Dixon LLC 302 387-7103
  63 Sweetflag Dr Dover (19904) *(G-3834)*
Wendy M D Schofer 302 824-4411
  602 Geddes St Wilmington (19805) *(G-20730)*
Weneuro Inc 760 607-7277
  1209 N Orange St Wilmington (19801) *(G-20731)*
Wentworth Inc 302 629-6284
  22946 Sussex Hwy Seaford (19973) *(G-13446)*
Wentzel Transportation 302 355-9465
  33 Brenford Station Rd Smyrna (19977) *(G-13935)*
Weplay Esports Media Inc 818 274-2959
  1013 Centre Rd Ste 403b Wilmington (19805) *(G-20732)*
WER Wireless of Smyrna Inc 302 653-8183
  239 N Dupont Blvd Smyrna (19977) *(G-13936)*
Werb & Sullivan 302 652-1100
  300 Delaware Ave Ste 1300 Wilmington (19801) *(G-20733)*
Wertz & Co 302 727-5643
  20845 Coastal Hwy Rehoboth Beach (19971) *(G-13014)*
Wertz & Co 302 658-5186
  116 Valley Rd Wilmington (19804) *(G-20734)*
Wes Sanders & Son LLC 302 383-4991
  7 Circle Dr Wilmington (19804) *(G-20735)*
Wesley Novak PHD 302 477-0470
  1521 Concord Pike Ste 301 Wilmington (19803) *(G-20736)*
Wesley Play Care Center 302 678-8987
  209 S State St Dover (19901) *(G-3835)*
Wesley Preschool, Dover Also Called: Wesley Play Care Center *(G-3835)*
West Center Place 302 426-0201
  622 N Jefferson St Wilmington (19801) *(G-20737)*
West Dover Butcher Shop, Dover Also Called: Haass Family Butcher Shop *(G-2643)*
West Dover Dental Llc 302 734-0330
  125 Greentree Dr Ste 2 Dover (19904) *(G-3836)*
WEST END, Wilmington Also Called: West End Neighborhood Hse Inc *(G-20740)*
West End Machine Shop Inc 302 654-8436
  1405 Brown St Wilmington (19805) *(G-20738)*
West End Neighborhood Hse Inc 302 654-2131
  1725 W 8th St Wilmington (19805) *(G-20739)*
West End Neighborhood Hse Inc (PA) 302 658-4171
  710 N Lincoln St Wilmington (19805) *(G-20740)*
West End Nghbrhood Child Care, Wilmington Also Called: West End Neighborhood Hse Inc *(G-20739)*
West Home Leasehold LLC 917 443-7451
  1209 N Orange St Wilmington (19801) *(G-20741)*
West Minister Management, Newark Also Called: Prides Court Apartments *(G-11741)*
West Third Enterprises LLC 302 732-3133
  30996 Country Gdns Dagsboro (19939) *(G-1526)*
Westchester Communications Svc 302 827-2939
  18561 Rose Ct Lewes (19958) *(G-6624)*
Westech, Newark Also Called: Westech Industries Inc *(G-12361)*
Westech Industries Inc 302 453-0301
  101 Alan Dr Newark (19711) *(G-12361)*
Western Kentucky Ambulatory 302 542-2770
  210 Tanglewood Dr Lewes (19958) *(G-6625)*
Western Sussex Animal Hosp Inc 302 337-7387
  16487 Sussex Hwy Bridgeville (19933) *(G-782)*
Western Union 302 629-3001
  701 W Stein Hwy Seaford (19973) *(G-13447)*
Westland Entertainment LLC 630 988-9684
  1221 College Park Dr Dover (19904) *(G-3837)*
Westminster Village Health Ctr, Dover Also Called: Presbyterian Homes Inc *(G-3365)*
Westmor Industries 302 956-0243
  16941 Sussex Hwy Bridgeville (19933) *(G-783)*
Westmor Industries 302 398-3253
  17409 S Dupont Hwy Harrington (19952) *(G-4846)*
Weston Sound 215 327-8646
  2 Stone Barn Ln Wilmington (19807) *(G-20742)*
Westover Capital Advisors LLC 302 427-9600
  1013 Centre Rd Ste 405 Wilmington (19805) *(G-20743)*
Westover Cardiology 302 482-2035
  222 Carter Dr Middletown (19709) *(G-7717)*
Westover Management Company LP 302 738-5775
  1 Allandale Dr Newark (19713) *(G-12362)*
Westover Management Company LP 302 731-1638
  24 Sandalwood Dr Ofc 5 Newark (19713) *(G-12363)*

ALPHABETIC SECTION

Westover Systems LLC 302 652-3500
1521 Concord Pike Ste 301 Wilmington (19803) *(G-20744)*

Westown Dental LLC 302 376-3750
818 Kohl Ave Middletown (19709) *(G-7718)*

Westown Movies, Middletown *Also Called: Westown Movies LLC (G-7719)*

Westown Movies LLC 330 244-1633
150 Commerce Dr Middletown (19709) *(G-7719)*

Westside Car Wash, Dover *Also Called: Gas & Go Inc (G-2562)*

Westside Family Healthcare Inc 302 836-2864
404 Foxhunt Dr Bear (19701) *(G-563)*

Westside Family Healthcare Inc 302 678-4622
1020 Forrest Ave Dover (19904) *(G-3838)*

Westside Family Healthcare Inc 302 455-0900
27 Marrows Rd Newark (19713) *(G-12364)*

Westside Family Healthcare Inc 302 575-1414
908 E 16th St Ste B Wilmington (19802) *(G-20745)*

Westside Family Healthcare Inc (PA) 302 656-8292
300 Water St Ste 200 Wilmington (19801) *(G-20746)*

Westside Family Healthcare Inc 302 656-8292
1802 W 4th St Wilmington (19805) *(G-20747)*

Westward LLC 570 609-3500
8 The Grn Dover (19901) *(G-3839)*

Westwood Farms Incorporated 302 238-7141
21906 Esham Ln Millsboro (19966) *(G-8504)*

Wetsu Tackle Distributors, Rehoboth Beach *Also Called: Old Inlet Bait and Tackle Inc (G-12878)*

Wevidit Inc 516 513-1659
224 A Trolley Sqre Number 1226 Wilmington (19806) *(G-20748)*

Wexmon LLC 302 746-2472
651 N Broad St Ste 205 # 1983 Middletown (19709) *(G-7720)*

Weyl Enterprises Inc 302 993-1248
1206 Kirkwood Hwy Wilmington (19805) *(G-20749)*

Weymouth Swyze Crroon Insur In 302 655-3705
5710 Kennett Pike Wilmington (19807) *(G-20750)*

Wgames Incorporated 206 618-3699
1209 N Orange St Wilmington (19801) *(G-20751)*

Wgmd, Lewes *Also Called: Resort Broadcasting Co LP (G-6417)*

Wh &C Management Services Inc 302 225-3000
11 Camp David Rd Wilmington (19810) *(G-20752)*

Wh2p Inc 302 530-6555
3704 Kennett Pike Ste 400 Wilmington (19807) *(G-20753)*

Whagons North America Inc 781 241-5946
651 N Broad St Ste 206 Middletown (19709) *(G-7721)*

Whaleys Seed Store Inc 302 875-7833
106 W 8th St Laurel (19956) *(G-5623)*

Wharton Levin Ehrmantraut 302 252-0090
300 Delaware Ave Wilmington (19801) *(G-20754)*

Whartons Landscaping LLC 302 426-4854
19385 Old Landing Rd Rehoboth Beach (19971) *(G-13015)*

Whartons Landscaping Grdn Ctr, Rehoboth Beach *Also Called: Whartons Landscaping LLC (G-13015)*

What Is Your Voice Inc 443 653-2067
17583 Shady Rd Lewes (19958) *(G-6626)*

Whatarethose Inc 443 467-3687
8 The Grn Ste B Dover (19901) *(G-3840)*

Whatcoat Christian Preschool 302 698-2108
16 Main St Dover (19901) *(G-3841)*

Whatcoat Social Service Agency 302 734-0319
381 College Rd Dover (19904) *(G-3842)*

Whatcoat Village Assoc LLC 856 596-0500
992 Whatcoat Dr Apt 12 Dover (19904) *(G-3843)*

Whatever It Takes Services, Wilmington *Also Called: Wit Services LLC (G-20867)*

Whayland Company Inc 302 875-5445
30613 Sussex Hwy Laurel (19956) *(G-5624)*

Whayland Company LLC 302 875-5445
100 W 10th St Laurel (19956) *(G-5625)*

Whc Properties LLC 302 225-3000
1831 Delaware Ave Ste 1 Wilmington (19806) *(G-20755)*

Wheatfield Holdings LLC (PA) 312 956-0198
3411 Silverside Rd Ste 104 Wilmington (19810) *(G-20756)*

Wheatley Farms Inc 302 337-7286
19115 Freeland Ln Bridgeville (19933) *(G-784)*

Wheel Lady Garcia 302 588-9750
200 Valley Rd Wilmington (19804) *(G-20757)*

Wheeler Financial LLC 302 543-5585
2961 Centerville Rd Ste 150 Wilmington (19808) *(G-20758)*

Wheeler Wolfenden & Dwares CPA 302 254-8240
4550 Linden Hill Rd Wilmington (19808) *(G-20759)*

Wherebyus Enterprises Inc 305 988-0808
2093 Philadelphia Pike Claymont (19703) *(G-1336)*

Whet Industries Inc 302 236-2182
560 Peoples Plz Ste 144 Newark (19702) *(G-12365)*

Whimstay Inc 650 867-0076
2810 N Church St Wilmington (19802) *(G-20760)*

Whiskazz & Pawzz Specialty, Wilmington *Also Called: Alyce E Duffy (G-14405)*

Whisman John 302 530-1676
5201 W Woodmill Dr Ste 31 Wilmington (19808) *(G-20761)*

Whispering Meadows LLC 302 698-1073
4110b Connecticut Ln Dover (19901) *(G-3844)*

Whitaker & Rago 302 414-0056
316 Delaware St Historic New Castle (19720) *(G-5101)*

Whitaker Corporation 302 633-2740
4550 Linden Hill Rd Ste 140 Wilmington (19808) *(G-20762)*

White & Williams, Wilmington *Also Called: White and Williams LLP (G-20763)*

White and Williams LLP 302 654-0424
600 N King St Ste 800 Wilmington (19801) *(G-20763)*

White Clay Creek Vtrinary Hosp 302 738-9611
107 Albe Dr Ste A Newark (19702) *(G-12366)*

White Deer Auto 302 846-0547
6234 White Deer Rd Delmar (19940) *(G-1655)*

White Drilling Corp 302 422-4057
Us 113 Lincoln (19960) *(G-6708)*

White Eagle Electric 302 533-7799
50 Albe Dr Newark (19702) *(G-12367)*

White Eagle Electrical Contg 302 378-3366
709 Guido Dr Middletown (19709) *(G-7722)*

White Eagle Integrations 302 464-0550
635 Lorewood Grove Rd Middletown (19709) *(G-7723)*

White Horse Winery 302 388-4850
15 Guyencourt Rd Wilmington (19807) *(G-20764)*

White Horse Winery LLC 302 472-7200
300 Water St Ste 300 Wilmington (19801) *(G-20765)*

White House Beach Inc 302 945-3032
35266 Fishermans Rd Unit 2 Millsboro (19966) *(G-8505)*

White Mink Beauty Salon 302 737-2081
330 College Sq Newark (19711) *(G-12368)*

White Oak Head Start 302 736-5933
195 Willis Rd Dover (19901) *(G-3845)*

White Oak Landscape MGT Inc 302 652-7533
17 Owls Nest Rd Wilmington (19807) *(G-20766)*

White Optics, New Castle *Also Called: Whiteoptics LLC (G-9681)*

White Robbins Company 302 478-5555
3513 Concord Pike Ste 2100 Wilmington (19803) *(G-20767)*

White Robbins Condo & Assn, Wilmington *Also Called: White Robbins Company (G-20767)*

White's Creek Manor, Bethany Beach *Also Called: Jack Hickman Real Estate (G-611)*

Whitecap Pipeline Company LLC 925 842-1000
251 Little Falls Dr Wilmington (19808) *(G-20768)*

Whitecrow Research Inc 908 752-4200
2711 Centerville Rd Ste 300 Pmb 604 Wilmington (19808) *(G-20769)*

Whiteford Taylor and Preston 302 353-4144
1220 N Market St Ste 608 Wilmington (19801) *(G-20770)*

Whiteoptics LLC 302 476-2055
19 Blevins Dr New Castle (19720) *(G-9681)*

Whites Auto Repair & Body Shop, Wilmington *Also Called: Whites Body Shop (G-20771)*

Whites Body Shop 302 655-4369
436 S Buttonwood St Wilmington (19801) *(G-20771)*

Whites Creek Manor Poa 302 541-9422
430 Jackie Dr Millville (19970) *(G-8551)*

Whitetail Country Log & Hlg 302 846-3982
16075 Russell Rd Delmar (19940) *(G-1656)*

Whitetail Country Log & Hlg, Delmar *Also Called: Whitetail Country Log & Hlg (G-1656)*

Whiting-Turner Contracting Co 302 292-0676
131 Continental Dr Ste 404 Newark (19713) *(G-12369)*

Whiting-Turner Contracting Co 302 266-7450
79 Amstel Ave Newark (19716) *(G-12370)*

Whitman Requardt and Assoc, Wilmington *Also Called: Whitman Requardt and Assoc LLP* *(G-20772)*

Whitman Requardt and Assoc LLP 302 571-9001
1013 Centre Rd Ste 302 Wilmington (19805) *(G-20772)*

Whitner House Publishing LLC 267 338-9741
5 S Howard St Smyrna (19977) *(G-13937)*

Whittakers Lawn Care 302 478-2169
324 Mcdaniel Ave Wilmington (19803) *(G-20773)*

Whittens Fine Jewelry 302 995-7464
4719 Kirkwood Hwy Wilmington (19808) *(G-20774)*

Whittington & Aulgur (PA) 302 235-5800
2979 Barley Mill Rd Yorklyn (19736) *(G-20994)*

Whizbang Productions, Wilmington *Also Called: Floyd Allan Gregory (G-16671)*

Wholesale, Wilmington *Also Called: Forcebeyond Inc (G-16688)*

Wholesale Jewelry Outlet Inc 302 994-5114
3616 Kirkwood Hwy Wilmington (19808) *(G-20775)*

Wholesale Jewlery Outlet, Wilmington *Also Called: Whittens Fine Jewelry (G-20774)*

WHOleseller& Retailer, Dover *Also Called: Bosphorus Textile LLC (G-1965)*

Whoop Labs Inc 425 442-2137
16192 Coastal Hwy Lewes (19958) *(G-6627)*

Whstle Corporation 925 413-3316
8 The Grn Ste 300 Dover (19901) *(G-3846)*

Whuups LLC 808 393-6240
16192 Coastal Hwy Lewes (19958) *(G-6628)*

Why Unified Corp 302 803-5892
200 Continental Dr Ste 401 Newark (19713) *(G-12371)*

Whyfly LLC 302 222-7171
218 W 9th St Wilmington (19801) *(G-20776)*

Wibdi Aviation Co Corp 305 677-9685
8 The Grn Dover (19901) *(G-3847)*

Wibsc, Wilmington *Also Called: A Gentlemans Touch Inc (G-14163)*

Wibx Logistics LLC 302 299-8860
604 W 6th St Apt 1 Wilmington (19801) *(G-20777)*

Wic State Office of Delaware, Dover *Also Called: Delaware Wic Program (G-2274)*

Wicked Pay LLC 646 785-1143
651 N Broad St Ste 201 Middletown (19709) *(G-7724)*

Wicked Witch Studio 302 838-2011
267 W Red Lion Dr Bear (19701) *(G-564)*

Wicket Wireless LLC 302 376-1788
653 Nesting Ln Middletown (19709) *(G-7725)*

Wide Range Inc (PA) 302 234-1193
108 Bellfield Ct Hockessin (19707) *(G-5425)*

Widgeon Enterprises Inc 302 846-9763
38204 Old Stage Rd Delmar (19940) *(G-1657)*

Wiedman Enterprises Inc 302 226-2407
38335 Martins Ln Rehoboth Beach (19971) *(G-13016)*

Wifiesta Inc (PA) 206 923-9206
16192 Coastal Hwy Lewes (19958) *(G-6629)*

Wiggins Group LLC 800 590-8070
8 The Grn Ste 10359 Dover (19901) *(G-3848)*

Wik Associates Inc 302 322-2558
10 Donaldson Dr Newark (19713) *(G-12372)*

Wilbraham Lawler & Buba PC 302 421-9922
901 N Market St Ste 800 Wilmington (19801) *(G-20778)*

WILBRAHAM LAWLER & BUBA PC, Wilmington *Also Called: Wilbraham Lawler & Buba PC* *(G-20778)*

Wilcox & Fetzer Ltd 302 655-0477
1330 N King St Wilmington (19801) *(G-20779)*

Wilcox Landscaping Inc 302 322-3002
230 S Dupont Hwy New Castle (19720) *(G-9682)*

Wild Bets, Dover *Also Called: Play US Media LLC (G-3332)*

Wild Meadows Homes 302 730-4700
529 Weaver Dr Dover (19901) *(G-3849)*

Wild Quail Golf & Country Club, Camden Wyoming *Also Called: Quail Associates Inc (G-966)*

Wild Smiles, Newark *Also Called: Jay J Harris PC (G-11100)*

Wilderman Physical Therapy LLC 717 873-6836
2626 Belaire Dr Wilmington (19808) *(G-20780)*

Wilgus Associates Inc (PA) 302 539-7511
32904 Coastal Hwy Bethany Beach (19930) *(G-650)*

Wilgus Associates Inc 302 644-2960
1520 Savannah Rd Lewes (19958) *(G-6630)*

Wilgus Glamorama, Selbyville *Also Called: Selbyville Cleaners Inc (G-13604)*

Wilgus Insur Agcy Inc - Mllsbo 302 934-1502
400 Delaware Ave Ste 103 Millsboro (19966) *(G-8506)*

Wilkins Fuel Co 302 422-5597
701 S Washington St Milford (19963) *(G-8149)*

Wilkins Wildlife & Bedbug 911 .... 302 236-3533
36627 Bi State Blvd Delmar (19940) *(G-1658)*

Wilkinson Roofing & Siding Inc 302 998-0176
1000 First State Blvd Wilmington (19804) *(G-20781)*

Wilkinson Technology Svcs LLC 302 384-7770
4 Squirrel Run Wilmington (19807) *(G-20782)*

Wilkisons Marking Service Inc 302 697-3669
22 Stevens St Dover (19901) *(G-3850)*

Wilks Lukoff & Bracegirdle LLC 302 225-0850
4250 Lancaster Pike # 200 Wilmington (19805) *(G-20783)*

Willard Agri Service Greenw 302 349-4100
22272 S Dupont Hwy Farmington (19950) *(G-3936)*

Willey and Co 302 629-3327
11588 Commercial Ln Laurel (19956) *(G-5626)*

Willey Farms, Townsend *Also Called: Willey Farms Inc (G-14091)*

Willey Farms Inc 302 378-8441
4092 Dupont Pkwy Townsend (19734) *(G-14091)*

William A O'Day Ands Son, Seaford *Also Called: William A ODay (G-13448)*

William A ODay 302 629-7854
4148 Woodland Ferry Rd Seaford (19973) *(G-13448)*

William B Funk MD 302 731-0900
665 Churchmans Rd Newark (19702) *(G-12373)*

William B Tabeling 302 234-9401
22 Revelstone Dr Newark (19711) *(G-12374)*

William Blair & Company LLC 302 573-5000
500 Delaware Ave Wilmington (19801) *(G-20784)*

William C Leager 302 398-7525
13600 Hewish Pkwy Greenwood (19950) *(G-4674)*

William Chambers and Son 302 284-9655
8964 S Dupont Hwy Viola (19979) *(G-14098)*

William Craft 302 945-5798
20433 Wil King Rd Lewes (19958) *(G-6631)*

William D Emmert 302 227-1433
317 Rehoboth Ave Rehoboth Beach (19971) *(G-13017)*

William D Shellady Inc 302 652-3106
112 A St Wilmington (19801) *(G-20785)*

William Delcampo Mechanical SE 302 992-9748
2429 Hartley Pl Wilmington (19808) *(G-20786)*

William E Ward PA 302 225-3350
2710 Centerville Rd Ste 200 Wilmington (19808) *(G-20787)*

William F & Margaret Hartnett 302 479-5918
21 Penarth Dr Wilmington (19803) *(G-20788)*

William G Day Company 302 476-2808
405 Tyrone Ave Wilmington (19804) *(G-20789)*

William G Robelen Inc 302 656-8726
3110 Lancaster Ave Wilmington (19805) *(G-20790)*

William Gonce 302 235-2400
36536 Harmon Bay Blvd Rehoboth Beach (19971) *(G-13018)*

William Grant & Sons USA Corp 302 573-3880
1011 Ctr Rd Ste 310 Wilmington (19805) *(G-20791)*

William H Burkhardt 302 376-1193
342 Clayton Manor Dr Middletown (19709) *(G-7726)*

William H Groton Construc 302 697-4744
11690 Baker Mill Rd Seaford (19973) *(G-13449)*

William H Lunger Atty 302 888-2504
1020 N Bancroft Pkwy Ste 100 Wilmington (19805) *(G-20792)*

William H McDaniel Inc 302 764-2020
734 Hertford Rd Wilmington (19803) *(G-20793)*

William H Metcalf & Sons Inc 301 868-6330
183 Kent Dr Seaford (19973) *(G-13450)*

William H Radford Ldscp Contrs, Smyrna *Also Called: William H Rdford Nurseries Inc* *(G-13938)*

William H Ralston DDS Office 336 957-4948
344 E Main St Newark (19711) *(G-12375)*

ALPHABETIC SECTION — Wilmington Pharmatech Co LLC

William H Rdford Nurseries Inc............ 302 659-3130
853 Black Diamond Rd Smyrna (19977) *(G-13938)*

William Hcks Andrson Cmnty Ctr............ 302 571-4266
501 N Madison St Wilmington (19801) *(G-20794)*

William Heydt............ 302 678-1161
767 Walker Rd Dover (19904) *(G-3851)*

William N Cann Inc............ 302 995-0820
1 Meco Cir Wilmington (19804) *(G-20795)*

William R Atkins MD............ 302 633-4525
550 Stanton Christiana Rd Ste 201 Newark (19713) *(G-12376)*

William R Lynch M D............ 302 319-4736
1521 Concord Pike Ste 301 Wilmington (19803) *(G-20796)*

William Redding and Son............ 302 562-4026
241 Smalleys Dam Rd A Newark (19702) *(G-12377)*

William Stele Wldg Fabrication............ 302 422-7444
200 Mullet Run Milford (19963) *(G-8150)*

William T Wadkins Garage Inc............ 302 422-0265
402 Ne Front St Milford (19963) *(G-8151)*

William V Gallery Dr............ 302 945-5943
16 Chester Ct Harbeson (19951) *(G-4719)*

Williams Appliancee............ 302 656-8581
41 Germay Dr Ste A Wilmington (19804) *(G-20797)*

Williams Climate Control............ 302 628-0440
26165 Green Briar Rd Seaford (19973) *(G-13451)*

Williams Engrg Solutions LLC............ 302 670-4841
24 W Chestnut Ridge Dr Magnolia (19962) *(G-6791)*

Williams Family............ 302 378-9493
655 Warren Dr Middletown (19709) *(G-7727)*

Williams Humphreys and Co LLC............ 302 225-3000
1831 Delaware Ave Wilmington (19806) *(G-20798)*

Williams Insurance Agency Inc (PA)............ 302 227-2501
20220 Coastal Hwy Rehoboth Beach (19971) *(G-13019)*

Williams Insurance Agency Inc............ 302 384-7804
4550 Linden Hill Rd Ste 303 Wilmington (19808) *(G-20799)*

Williams Insurance Agency Inc............ 302 227-2501
4543 Stoney Batter Rd Ste B Wilmington (19808) *(G-20800)*

Williams Insurance Agency Inc............ 302 239-5500
5301 Limestone Rd Ste 100 Wilmington (19808) *(G-20801)*

Williams Law Firm PA............ 302 575-0873
1201 N Orange St Ste 600 Wilmington (19801) *(G-20802)*

Williams-Garcia & Associates, Felton Also Called: Center For A Pstive Hmnity LLC *(G-3952)*

Williamson Building Corp............ 302 644-0605
130 New Rd Lewes (19958) *(G-6632)*

Willie Hardy MD............ 610 450-4559
2219 Robin Rd Wilmington (19803) *(G-20803)*

Willies Auto Detail Service............ 302 734-1010
17 Weston Dr Dover (19904) *(G-3852)*

Willin Farms LLC............ 302 629-2520
2864 Long Acre Ln Seaford (19973) *(G-13452)*

Willis Ford Inc............ 302 653-5900
15 N Dupont Blvd Smyrna (19977) *(G-13939)*

Willis Groupllc............ 302 632-9898
4 The Grn Dover (19901) *(G-3853)*

Willis Hrh, Hockessin Also Called: Willis North America Inc *(G-5426)*

Willis Hspitality Partners LLC............ 302 544-5054
63 Queen Ave New Castle (19720) *(G-9683)*

Willis Law LLC............ 302 535-3200
117 W Reed St Dover (19904) *(G-3854)*

Willis North America Inc............ 302 239-2416
512 Garrick Rd Hockessin (19707) *(G-5426)*

Willow Counseling Services............ 814 779-9653
19 Ormonde Cir Smyrna (19977) *(G-13940)*

Willow Grace Vtrinary Hosp LLC............ 302 378-9800
311 W Main St Middletown (19709) *(G-7728)*

Willow Tree Equity Holding LLC............ 213 479-4077
16192 Coastal Hwy Lewes (19958) *(G-6633)*

Willow Tree Properties LLC............ 302 674-2266
100 Warwick Drive, Windsor Hills Wilmington (19803) *(G-20804)*

Willow Winters Publishing LLC............ 570 885-2513
164 N Bayberry Pkwy Middletown (19709) *(G-7729)*

Willy Cab............ 302 465-1252
2929 N Market St Wilmington (19802) *(G-20805)*

Wilm Otolarngology............ 302 658-0404
2300 Pennsylvania Ave Ste 2a Wilmington (19806) *(G-20806)*

Wilmapco, Newark Also Called: Wilmington Area Plg Council *(G-12379)*

Wilmington............ 302 357-4509
1201 N Orange St Ste 7463 Wilmington (19801) *(G-20807)*

Wilmington & Newark Dental............ 302 571-0526
13 Aronimink Dr Newark (19711) *(G-12378)*

Wilmington 102, New Castle Also Called: Stanley Steemer Intl Inc *(G-9592)*

Wilmington Animal Hospital............ 302 762-2694
828 Philadelphia Pike Wilmington (19809) *(G-20808)*

Wilmington Aquatic Club Inc............ 302 322-2487
212 W Grant Ave New Castle (19720) *(G-9684)*

Wilmington Area Plg Council............ 302 737-6205
100 Discovery Blvd Ste 800 Newark (19713) *(G-12379)*

Wilmington Blue Rocks, Wilmington Also Called: Wilmington Blue Rocks LP *(G-20809)*

Wilmington Blue Rocks LP............ 302 888-2015
801 Shipyard Dr Wilmington (19801) *(G-20809)*

Wilmington Brew Works LLC............ 302 757-4971
3201 Miller Rd Wilmington (19802) *(G-20810)*

Wilmington Christiana Cou............ 302 456-3800
48 Geoffrey Dr Newark (19713) *(G-12380)*

Wilmington Club Inc............ 302 658-4287
1103 N Market St Wilmington (19801) *(G-20811)*

Wilmington Collision Center............ 484 702-2115
3304 S Rockfield Dr Wilmington (19810) *(G-20812)*

Wilmington Country Club............ 302 655-6171
4825 Kennett Pike Wilmington (19807) *(G-20813)*

Wilmington Dental Assoc PA............ 302 654-6915
2309 Pennsylvania Ave Wilmington (19806) *(G-20814)*

Wilmington Family Eye Care............ 302 999-1286
801 E Newport Pike Wilmington (19804) *(G-20815)*

Wilmington Fibre Specialty Co............ 302 328-7525
700 Washington St Historic New Castle (19720) *(G-5102)*

Wilmington Fire Fighters Assn, Wilmington Also Called: Wilmington Firefighters Assn *(G-20816)*

Wilmington Firefighters Assn............ 302 365-0168
804 Maryland Ave Wilmington (19805) *(G-20816)*

Wilmington Glass Co............ 302 777-7000
727 S Market St Wilmington (19801) *(G-20817)*

Wilmington Headstart Inc (PA)............ 302 762-8038
100 W 10th St Ste 1016 Wilmington (19801) *(G-20818)*

Wilmington Ht Xxxiii Owner LLC............ 302 594-3100
42 W 11th St Wilmington (19801) *(G-20819)*

Wilmington Infrared Tech............ 302 234-6761
108 Shinn Cir Wilmington (19808) *(G-20820)*

Wilmington Junior Academy, Wilmington Also Called: Chesapake Cnfrnce Svnth-Day Ad *(G-15366)*

Wilmington Little League Inc............ 302 559-7690
2323 W 16th St Wilmington (19806) *(G-20821)*

Wilmington Lrg-Cap Strtegy Fun............ 302 636-8500
1100 N Market St 10th Fl Wilmington (19890) *(G-20822)*

Wilmington Manor Lions Service............ 302 322-3250
320 N Dupont Hwy New Castle (19720) *(G-9685)*

Wilmington Medical Associates............ 302 478-0400
2700 Silverside Rd Ste 3 Wilmington (19810) *(G-20823)*

Wilmington Montessori School............ 302 475-0555
1400 Harvey Rd Wilmington (19810) *(G-20824)*

Wilmington New Castle Pediatri............ 302 762-1072
519 Brentwood Dr Wilmington (19803) *(G-20825)*

Wilmington Nghbrhood Cnsrvncy............ 302 409-1023
1007 N Orange St Fl 4 Wilmington (19801) *(G-20826)*

Wilmington Orthodontic Center............ 302 658-7354
2300 Pennsylvania Ave Ste 5c Wilmington (19806) *(G-20827)*

Wilmington Otlrynglogy Assoc P............ 302 658-0404
2300 Pennsylvania Ave Ste 2a Wilmington (19806) *(G-20828)*

Wilmington Pain/Rehab Cntr PA............ 302 575-1776
1021 Gilpin Ave Ste 101 Wilmington (19806) *(G-20829)*

Wilmington Parking Authority (PA)............ 302 655-4442
625 N Orange St Ste 2c Wilmington (19801) *(G-20830)*

Wilmington Pharmatech Co LLC (PA)............ 302 737-9916
2309 Sunset Lake Rd Newark (19702) *(G-12381)*

Wilmington Plice Fire Fdral Cr 302 654-0818
1701 Shallcross Ave Ste B Wilmington (19806) *(G-20831)*

Wilmington Real Estate Co Inc 302 652-1700
2213 Concord Pike Wilmington (19803) *(G-20832)*

Wilmington Renaissance Corp 302 425-5500
100 W 10th St Ste 206 Wilmington (19801) *(G-20833)*

Wilmington Rowing Center 302 652-5339
501 A St Wilmington (19801) *(G-20834)*

Wilmington Sav Fund Soc Fsb 888 973-7226
500 Delaware Ave Wilmington (19801) *(G-20835)*

Wilmington Savings Fund Bank, Wilmington Also Called: Wilmington Savings Fund Soc *(G-20836)*

Wilmington Savings Fund Soc 302 792-6435
2105 Philadelphia Pike Claymont (19703) *(G-1337)*

Wilmington Savings Fund Soc 302 677-1891
1486 Forrest Ave Dover (19904) *(G-3855)*

Wilmington Savings Fund Soc 302 456-6404
100 University Plz Newark (19702) *(G-12382)*

Wilmington Savings Fund Soc 302 360-0440
22820 Sussex Hwy Seaford (19973) *(G-13453)*

Wilmington Savings Fund Soc (HQ) 302 792-6000
500 Delaware Ave Wilmington (19801) *(G-20836)*

Wilmington Savings Fund Soc 302 999-1227
1600 W Newport Pike Wilmington (19804) *(G-20837)*

Wilmington Savings Fund Soc 302 571-6508
211 N Union St Wilmington (19805) *(G-20838)*

Wilmington Savings Fund Soc 302 571-6500
2005 Concord Pike Wilmington (19803) *(G-20839)*

Wilmington Savings Fund Soc 302 571-7090
500 Delaware Ave Ste 3 Wilmington (19801) *(G-20840)*

Wilmington Savings Fund Soc 302 633-5700
4730 Limestone Rd Wilmington (19808) *(G-20841)*

Wilmington Savings Fund Soc 302 571-6516
1711 Delaware Ave Wilmington (19806) *(G-20842)*

Wilmington Senior Center Inc (PA) 302 651-3400
1901 N Market St Wilmington (19802) *(G-20843)*

Wilmington Small-Cap Strategy 302 636-8500
1100 N Market St 10th Fl Wilmington (19890) *(G-20844)*

Wilmington Stoneworks LLC 302 723-7126
1908 Elm St Wilmington (19805) *(G-20845)*

Wilmington Trail Club 302 521-3815
15 Tenby Chase Dr Newark (19711) *(G-12383)*

Wilmington Trap Association 302 834-9320
2828 Pulaski Hwy Newark (19702) *(G-12384)*

Wilmington Trust Cllctive Inv 800 724-2440
1100 N Market St Wilmington (19890) *(G-20846)*

Wilmington Trust Company (DH) 302 651-1000
1100 N Market St Ste 1300 Wilmington (19890) *(G-20847)*

Wilmington Trust Frnklin US AG 302 636-8500
1100 N Market St 10th Fl Wilmington (19890) *(G-20848)*

Wilmington Trust Sp Services (DH) 302 427-7650
1105 N Market St Ste 1300 Wilmington (19801) *(G-20849)*

Wilmington Trust Tmpltn Fgn C 800 724-2440
1100 N Market St Wilmington (19890) *(G-20850)*

Wilmington Tug Inc (PA) 302 652-1666
11 Gist Rd Ste 200 Wilmington (19801) *(G-20851)*

Wilmington Turners, Wilmington Also Called: Wilmington Turners Club *(G-20852)*

Wilmington Turners Club 302 658-9011
701 S Clayton St Wilmington (19805) *(G-20852)*

Wilmington VA Medical Cent 302 294-6743
47 Oklahoma State Dr Newark (19713) *(G-12385)*

Wilmington VAM&roc, Wilmington Also Called: Veterans Health Administration *(G-20600)*

Wilmington Vet Center, Wilmington Also Called: Veterans Health Administration *(G-20599)*

Wilmington Youth Organization 302 761-9030
615 W 37th St Wilmington (19802) *(G-20853)*

Wilmington Youth Rowing Assn 302 777-4533
500 E Front St Frnt Wilmington (19801) *(G-20854)*

Wilson Care Wilson Co 302 897-5059
5 William Davis Ct Newark (19702) *(G-12386)*

Wilson Construction Co Inc 302 856-3115
23054 Park Ave Georgetown (19947) *(G-4574)*

Wilson Dunes Condo Counci 302 542-1899
220 Beiser Blvd Dover (19904) *(G-3856)*

Wilson Fleet & Equipment 302 422-7159
961 E Masten Cir Milford (19963) *(G-8152)*

Wilson Halbrook & Bayard PA 302 856-0015
107 W Market St Georgetown (19947) *(G-4575)*

Wilson Masonry Corp 302 398-8240
1229 Staytonville Rd Harrington (19952) *(G-4847)*

Wilson Publications LLC 215 237-2344
331 N Red Lion Ter Bear (19701) *(G-565)*

Wilson Sealcoating 302 653-0201
1597 Holletts Corner Rd Clayton (19938) *(G-1408)*

Wilson Travel and Getaway 302 559-3412
206 Woodgreen Ct Claymont (19703) *(G-1338)*

Wilsons Auction Sales Inc 302 422-3454
10120 Dupont Blvd Lincoln (19960) *(G-6709)*

Win From Wthin Xc Camp/Tatnall 302 494-5312
10 Courtney Rd Wilmington (19807) *(G-20855)*

Windcrest Animal Hospital 302 239-9464
3705 Lancaster Pike Wilmington (19805) *(G-20856)*

Windcrest Animal Hospital, Hockessin Also Called: Hockessin Animal Hospital *(G-5240)*

Window Man 302 381-4888
38001 Bi State Blvd Delmar (19940) *(G-1659)*

Window Treatments & More LLC 302 275-7019
405 W 34th St Wilmington (19802) *(G-20857)*

Windsor Apartments, Wilmington Also Called: New Wndsor Apartments Assoc LP *(G-18628)*

Windsor Place 302 239-3200
6677 Lancaster Pike Hockessin (19707) *(G-5427)*

Windsors Flowers Plants Shrubs, Laurel Also Called: Lakeside Greenhouses Inc *(G-5544)*

Windswept Enterprises 302 678-0805
251 N Dupont Hwy Dover (19901) *(G-3857)*

Windswept Enterprising, Dover Also Called: Windswept Enterprises *(G-3857)*

Windy Inc 224 707-0442
8 The Grn Ste A Dover (19901) *(G-3858)*

Wine Worx LLC 302 436-1500
32512 Blackwater Rd Frankford (19945) *(G-4161)*

Winebow, Newark Also Called: Country Vintner LLC *(G-10335)*

Wingfield & Associates Inc 626 252-6586
251 Little Falls Dr Wilmington (19808) *(G-20858)*

Winifred Ellen Erbe 302 541-0889
38397 Hemlock Dr Frankford (19945) *(G-4162)*

Wink Tech Limited 302 268-9232
300 E Delaware Ave Wilmington (19809) *(G-20859)*

Winmill Cleaning 302 731-4139
35 Country Ln W Newark (19702) *(G-12387)*

Winner Automotive Group, Wilmington Also Called: Winner Group Management Inc *(G-20861)*

Winner Dover 1387 LLC 302 257-3500
1387 N Dupont Hwy Dover (19901) *(G-3859)*

Winner Ford of Dover, Dover Also Called: Winner Ford of Dover Ltd *(G-3860)*

Winner Ford of Dover Ltd 302 734-0444
591 S Dupont Hwy Dover (19901) *(G-3860)*

Winner Ford of Newark Inc 302 731-2415
303 E Cleveland Ave Newark (19711) *(G-12388)*

Winner Group Inc 302 292-8200
1801 Ogletown Rd Newark (19711) *(G-12389)*

Winner Group Inc (PA) 302 764-5900
911 Tatnall St Wilmington (19801) *(G-20860)*

Winner Group Management Inc (PA) 302 571-5200
520 S Walnut St Wilmington (19801) *(G-20861)*

Winner Infiniti Inc 302 764-5900
1300 N Union St Wilmington (19806) *(G-20862)*

Winner Porsche, Wilmington Also Called: Winner Infiniti Inc *(G-20862)*

Winner Premier Collision Ctr 302 571-5200
520 S Walnut St Wilmington (19801) *(G-20863)*

Winners Circle Inc 302 661-2100
1300 N Union St Wilmington (19806) *(G-20864)*

Winterset Farms, Wilmington Also Called: Carlisle Group *(G-15253)*

Winterthur Museum 302 740-9771
1520 N Rodney St Wilmington (19806) *(G-20865)*

Winterthur Museum & Cntry Est, Winterthur Also Called: Henry Frncis Dpont Wntrthur Ms *(G-20972)*

ALPHABETIC SECTION — Woodland Apartments LP

Winterthur Museum Garden & Lib 302 888-4600
5105 Kennett Pike Winterthur (19735) *(G-20973)*

Wire 2 Wire LLC 512 684-9100
2711 Centerville Rd # 400 Wilmington (19808) *(G-20866)*

Wiregateit LLC 302 538-1304
909 Benalli Dr Middletown (19709) *(G-7730)*

Wireless Center 302 455-7220
50 E Main St Newark (19711) *(G-12390)*

Wireless Nation 443 841-0116
38 W Sarazen Dr Middletown (19709) *(G-7731)*

Wireless Nation, Delmar *Also Called: Om Ganesh Two LLC* *(G-1627)*

Wireless Traders, Dover *Also Called: Shiv Baba LLC* *(G-3546)*

Wirelisity Inc 213 816-1957
16192 Coastal Hwy Lewes (19958) *(G-6634)*

Wirenut LLC 302 858-7027
240 S Bedford St Georgetown (19947) *(G-4576)*

Wis International 302 264-9343
1203 College Park Dr Dover (19904) *(G-3861)*

Wit Services LLC 302 995-2983
1174 Elderon Dr Wilmington (19808) *(G-20867)*

Withyouwithme Inc 202 377-9743
1209 N Orange St Wilmington (19801) *(G-20868)*

Witt Butch Inc 706 883-0539
16192 Coastal Hwy Lewes (19958) *(G-6635)*

Wixfi Inc 415 504-2607
16192 Coastal Hwy Lewes (19958) *(G-6636)*

Wiz Electric 302 293-0403
56 Aidone Dr New Castle (19720) *(G-9686)*

Wizard Media Inc 610 653-9722
8 The Grn Dover (19901) *(G-3862)*

Wize Monkey USA Inc 604 839-7640
9 E Loockerman St Dover (19901) *(G-3863)*

Wj McDougall Racing Inc 302 492-8248
215 Hartly Rd Hartly (19953) *(G-4912)*

WJC of Delaware LLC (PA) 302 323-9600
19 E Commons Blvd Ste 3 New Castle (19720) *(G-9687)*

Wl Timbers Inc 843 376-1099
4023 Kennett Pike Ste 54708 Wilmington (19807) *(G-20869)*

Wlg Equity Inc (HQ) 302 738-4880
551 Paper Mill Rd Newark (19711) *(G-12391)*

Wm Companies LLC 302 228-5122
8961 Greenwood Rd Greenwood (19950) *(G-4675)*

Wm Delcampo Mechanical Svcs 302 543-2725
2429 Hartley Pl Wilmington (19808) *(G-20870)*

Wm H Jeppe Dr 302 234-1785
103 Dennison Ln Hockessin (19707) *(G-5428)*

Wm Systems Inc 302 450-4482
2711 Centerville Rd Ste 400 Wilmington (19808) *(G-20871)*

Wmk Financing Inc 302 576-2697
300 Delaware Ave Wilmington (19801) *(G-20872)*

Wn Builders Inc 302 253-8640
18456 Gravel Hill Rd Georgetown (19947) *(G-4577)*

Wna Infotech LLC 302 668-5977
704 Sloop Ct Newark (19702) *(G-12392)*

Wodaqota Inc 800 246-2677
919 N Market St Wilmington (19801) *(G-20873)*

Wohlsen Construction Company 302 324-9900
501 Carr Rd Ste 100 Wilmington (19809) *(G-20874)*

Wojo Home Cleaning LLC 302 241-5866
160 Beech Dr Dover (19904) *(G-3864)*

Wolf Creek Surgeons PA 302 678-3627
1371 S State St Dover (19901) *(G-3865)*

Wolf Stone Enterprises LLC 302 765-7456
18 Lea Rd New Castle (19720) *(G-9688)*

Wolf Wood Works LLC 302 275-7227
4 Star Pine Cir Wilmington (19808) *(G-20875)*

Wolfe Associates LLC 302 668-6178
122 Sandhill Dr Ste 203 Middletown (19709) *(G-7732)*

Wolfe Backhoe Service 302 737-2628
8 Springlake Dr Newark (19711) *(G-12393)*

Wolfe Neck Treatment Plant 302 644-2761
36160 Wolfe Neck Rd Rehoboth Beach (19971) *(G-13020)*

Wolfgang M D Radtke 302 651-6660
1600 Rockland Rd Wilmington (19803) *(G-20876)*

Wolfs Elite Autos 302 999-9199
2130 W Newport Pike Wilmington (19804) *(G-20877)*

Woloshin and Lynch Associates (PA) 302 477-3200
3200 Concord Pike Wilmington (19803) *(G-20878)*

Womble Bond Dickinson (us) LLP 302 252-4320
1313 N Market St Fl 12 Wilmington (19801) *(G-20879)*

Women First LLC 302 635-9800
6300 Limestone Rd Hockessin (19707) *(G-5429)*

Women First LLC 302 368-3257
4745 Ogletown Stanton Rd Ste 105 Newark (19713) *(G-12394)*

Women Leading Innovation Inc 540 798-4023
16192 Coastal Hwy Lewes (19958) *(G-6637)*

Women of More 260 760-8083
16 Birchgrove Rd Newark (19702) *(G-12395)*

Women To Women Ob/Gyn Assoc PA 302 778-2229
532 Greenhill Ave Wilmington (19805) *(G-20880)*

Women's Imaging Center, Rehoboth Beach *Also Called: Beebe Medical Center Inc (G-12637)*

Women's Medical Center PA, Seaford *Also Called: Womens Medical Center Inc (G-13454)*

Womens Center At Milford Meml 302 430-5540
200 Kings Hwy Ste 3 Milford (19963) *(G-8153)*

Womens Civic Club Bethany Bch 302 539-7515
332 Sandpiper Dr Bethany Beach (19930) *(G-651)*

Womens Harmony Brigade Assn 610 659-0096
300 Fox Hound Ct Middletown (19709) *(G-7733)*

Womens Health Center 517 437-5390
24351 Zinfandel Ln # 202 Lewes (19958) *(G-6638)*

Womens Health Ctr Christn Care 302 428-5810
501 W 14th St Wilmington (19801) *(G-20881)*

Womens Healthcare Consultants 443 553-1398
1400 Peoples Plz Ste 301 Newark (19702) *(G-12396)*

Womens Imaging Center Delaware 302 738-9494
46 Omega Dr Ste J24 Newark (19713) *(G-12397)*

Womens Medical Center Inc 302 629-5409
1301 Middleford Rd Seaford (19973) *(G-13454)*

Womens Tennis Club of New 302 731-1456
446 Haystack Dr Newark (19711) *(G-12398)*

Womens Wellness Ctr & Med Spa 302 643-2500
1400 Peoples Plz Ste 301 Newark (19702) *(G-12399)*

Wonchin Institute 302 602-5753
8 Mercer Dr Newark (19713) *(G-12400)*

Wonder Medical Supply, Wilmington *Also Called: Quinn-Miller Group Inc (G-19296)*

Wonder Years Kids Club 302 398-0563
17629 S Dupont Hwy Harrington (19952) *(G-4848)*

Wonder Years Preschool LLC 302 376-5553
111 Patriot Dr Ste A Middletown (19709) *(G-7734)*

Wonderful Homes 610 304-4744
29 Kent St Rehoboth Beach (19971) *(G-13021)*

Wonderlust LLC 662 312-8390
16192 Coastal Hwy Lewes (19958) *(G-6639)*

Wong Peter MD 302 674-0223
200 Banning St Ste 320 Dover (19904) *(G-3866)*

Wood Expressions Incorporated 302 738-6189
2 Savoy Rd Newark (19702) *(G-12401)*

Wood Veneer Hub Limited Inc 302 216-6177
1000 N West St Ste 1281 Pmb 104 Wilmington (19801) *(G-20882)*

Woodacres Apts, Claymont *Also Called: Woodacres Associates LP (G-1339)*

Woodacres Associates LP 302 792-0243
915 Cedartree Ln Claymont (19703) *(G-1339)*

Woodbrdge High Schl Prfrmg Art 302 495-7025
608 Schlabach Rd Greenwood (19950) *(G-4676)*

Woodchuck Enterprises Inc 302 239-8336
1070 Sharpless Rd Hockessin (19707) *(G-5430)*

Wooden Wheels Svc & Repr LLC 302 368-2453
208 Louviers Dr Newark (19711) *(G-12402)*

Woodin + Associates LLC 302 378-7300
111 Patriot Dr Ste D Middletown (19709) *(G-7735)*

Woodland Apartments, Wilmington *Also Called: Woodland Apartments LP (G-20883)*

Woodland Apartments LP 302 994-9003
1201 Centre Rd Wilmington (19805) *(G-20883)*

Woodland Ferry Beagle Club 302 856-2186
26858 Johnson Rd Georgetown (19947) *(G-4578)*

Woodlawn Trustees Incorporated 302 655-6215
1020 N Bancroft Pkwy Ste 200 Wilmington (19805) *(G-20884)*

Woodmill Dental LLC 302 998-8588
5185 W Woodmill Dr Ste 2 Wilmington (19808) *(G-20885)*

Woods Edge Apartments 302 762-8300
1204 Terra Hill Dr Apt 3b Wilmington (19809) *(G-20886)*

Woods General Contracting Inc 302 856-4047
22403 Peterkins Rd Georgetown (19947) *(G-4579)*

Woods Hole Group Inc 302 222-6720
301 Cassidy Dr Ste D Dover (19901) *(G-3867)*

Woodson Ministries Inc 512 350-9950
4613 Big Rock Dr Wilmington (19802) *(G-20887)*

Woodstoves Junction 302 397-8424
2222 Silverside Rd Wilmington (19810) *(G-20888)*

Woodward Enterprises Inc 302 378-2849
226 W Main St Middletown (19709) *(G-7736)*

Woodward Outdoor Equipment, Middletown *Also Called: Woodward Enterprises Inc (G-7736)*

Woodworks 302 995-0800
550 Copper Dr Wilmington (19804) *(G-20889)*

Woodyknows, Lewes *Also Called: M&M Pure Air Systems LLC (G-6233)*

Woohoo Inc 302 233-7272
8 The Grn Ste 12103 Dover (19901) *(G-3868)*

Wooley Bully Inc 302 542-3613
25605 Rogers Rd Millsboro (19966) *(G-8507)*

Woolleyenterprisesmx LLC 302 674-4089
160 Greentree Dr Dover (19904) *(G-3869)*

Woos Foundation 302 366-0259
5 Farmhouse Rd Newark (19711) *(G-12403)*

Worcester Golf Club Inc 610 222-0200
121 W Shore Dr Milton (19968) *(G-8730)*

Workativ Sftwr Solutions LLC 312 375-1062
2035 Sunset Lake Rd B2 Newark (19702) *(G-12404)*

Workaway Ventures Inc 843 608-9108
1521 Concord Pike Ste 303 Wilmington (19803) *(G-20890)*

Workbetterai Inc 805 825-5216
8 The Grn Ste A Dover (19901) *(G-3870)*

Workfar Inc 650 800-3990
8 The Grn Ste A Dover (19901) *(G-3871)*

Workforce Cloud Tech Inc (PA) 915 800-2362
2035 Sunset Lake Rd Ste B2 Newark (19702) *(G-12405)*

Workhorse II LLC 302 533-5342
152 S Dupont Hwy New Castle (19720) *(G-9689)*

Working Every Shift Trnsprting 267 262-3453
735 Roger Chaffee Sq Mx Bear (19701) *(G-566)*

Working Tens Inc 612 685-0921
300 Delaware Ave Ste 210 Wilmington (19801) *(G-20891)*

Workmans Inc 302 934-9228
20135 Hardscrabble Rd Georgetown (19947) *(G-4580)*

Workpro 302 300-4392
6 Larch Ave Ste 397 Wilmington (19804) *(G-20892)*

Workpro Health 302 722-4471
4051 Ogletown Rd Newark (19713) *(G-12406)*

Workroom Enterprises LLC 417 621-5577
300 Delaware Ave Ste 210a Wilmington (19801) *(G-20893)*

Works Body Wrap By Tanya 302 669-7839
411 Northwood Rd Wilmington (19803) *(G-20894)*

Works of Art 302 562-3597
13 Ridge Dr New Castle (19720) *(G-9690)*

Workwall Inc 415 800-2809
256 Chapman Rd Ste 105-4 Newark (19702) *(G-12407)*

Workweek Inc 423 708-4565
160 Greentree Dr Ste 101 Dover (19904) *(G-3872)*

World Amptee Ftball Federation 302 383-2665
1033 Creekside Dr Wilmington (19804) *(G-20895)*

World Class Products LLC 302 737-1441
375 Wedgewood Rd Newark (19711) *(G-12408)*

World Class Supply, Newark *Also Called: World Class Products LLC (G-12408)*

World Economic Magazine Inc 302 499-2016
16192 Coastal Hwy Lewes (19958) *(G-6640)*

World Foods USA LLC 302 288-0670
8 The Grn Ste A Dover (19901) *(G-3873)*

World Hospital Inc 609 254-3391
102 Sweethollow Dr Bear (19701) *(G-567)*

World Trade Sponsor Inc 404 780-3333
113 Barksdale Professional Ctr Newark (19711) *(G-12409)*

World Transmissions Inc 302 735-5535
2860 N Dupont Hwy Dover (19901) *(G-3874)*

World Web Technology Pvt Ltd 646 755-9276
8 The Grn Dover (19901) *(G-3875)*

World Wide Trading Brokers 302 368-7041
606 Benham Ct Newark (19711) *(G-12410)*

World Wrless Solutions USA Inc 877 746-4997
300 Delaware Ave Ste 200 Wilmington (19801) *(G-20896)*

Worlds Best Massage Therapy 302 366-8777
412 Capitol Trl Newark (19711) *(G-12411)*

Worldwide Clinical Trials Inc 317 297-2208
22510 Lakeshore Dr Georgetown (19947) *(G-4581)*

Wormhole Soft LLC 302 424-4374
18585 Coastal Hwy Rehoboth Beach (19971) *(G-13022)*

Worms Quality Carpet Care 302 629-3114
21729 Maple Dr Seaford (19973) *(G-13455)*

Worth Co 302 221-4822
19 E Commons Blvd Ste C New Castle (19720) *(G-9691)*

Worthys Property MGT LLC 302 265-8301
8989 Herring Branch Rd Lincoln (19960) *(G-6710)*

Wraparound Maryland 302 504-8487
105 Rogers Rd Ste A Wilmington (19801) *(G-20897)*

Wray Lisa MD 302 651-4000
1600 Rockland Rd Wilmington (19803) *(G-20898)*

Wrc 302 425-5500
100 W 10th St Ste 206 Wilmington (19801) *(G-20899)*

Wreck Masters Demo Derby 302 368-5544
221 Kline St Bear (19701) *(G-568)*

Wrench Plumbing 302 482-1043
3401 Old Capitol Trl Wilmington (19808) *(G-20900)*

Wrenchtime Auto LLC (PA) 302 500-5558
42 Albe Dr Newark (19702) *(G-12412)*

Wright Bruce B DDS Office RES 302 227-8707
15 Venetian Dr Rehoboth Beach (19971) *(G-13023)*

Wright Choice Child Care 302 798-0758
3031 W Court Ave Claymont (19703) *(G-1340)*

Wright Robert Steele 302 423-2093
1783 Whiteleysburg Rd Harrington (19952) *(G-4849)*

Wright Steven B DMD PA 302 645-6671
18912 John J Williams Hwy Rehoboth Beach (19971) *(G-13024)*

Wrights Lawn Care Inc 302 684-3058
14174 Union Street Ext Milton (19968) *(G-8731)*

Write To Point 302 235-7149
6 Liveoak Ct Hockessin (19707) *(G-5431)*

Writers Relief 866 405-3003
18766 John J Williams Hwy Rehoboth Beach (19971) *(G-13025)*

Wrpatrick Enterprises LLC 302 988-1061
37695 Crab Bay Ln Selbyville (19975) *(G-13620)*

Wruff Wryder Productions 602 803-7620
112 Seagull Dr Lewes (19958) *(G-6641)*

Ws Company 302 660-8735
4708 Kirkwood Hwy Wilmington (19808) *(G-20901)*

Ws One Investment Usa LLC 302 317-2610
298 Cherry Ln New Castle (19720) *(G-9692)*

Ws1.com, New Castle *Also Called: Ws One Investment Usa LLC (G-9692)*

Wsfs, Wilmington *Also Called: Wsfs Financial Corporation (G-20903)*

Wsfs Bank, Claymont *Also Called: Wilmington Savings Fund Soc (G-1337)*

Wsfs Bank, Wilmington *Also Called: Wsfs Financial Corporation (G-20902)*

Wsfs Credit, Newark *Also Called: Star States Leasing Corp (G-12088)*

Wsfs Financial Corporation 302 254-3569
2080 New Castle Ave New Castle (19720) *(G-9693)*

Wsfs Financial Corporation 302 571-6516
9a Trolley Sq Wilmington (19806) *(G-20902)*

Wsfs Financial Corporation (PA) 302 792-6000
500 Delaware Ave Wilmington (19801) *(G-20903)*

ALPHABETIC SECTION

Wsfs Investment Group Inc.. 302 573-3258
  838 N Market St Wilmington (19801) *(G-20904)*
Wsp USA Solutions Inc.. 302 737-1872
  254 Chapman Rd Ste 203 Newark (19702) *(G-12413)*
Wswms Hvac.. 302 454-1987
  1114 Janice Dr Newark (19713) *(G-12414)*
Wta, Newark Also Called: Wilmington Trap Association *(G-12384)*
Wta Inc.. 302 397-8142
  510 Justison St Wilmington (19801) *(G-20905)*
Wtm Builders.. 302 398-9522
  1262 Gun And Rod Club Rd Harrington (19952) *(G-4850)*
Wuji Inc.. 815 274-6777
  8 The Grn Ste A Dover (19901) *(G-3876)*
Wutopia Comics, Dover Also Called: Wutopia Group US Ltd *(G-3877)*
Wutopia Group US Ltd.. 302 488-0248
  8 The Grn Ste 501 Dover (19901) *(G-3877)*
Wwc III Trucking LLC.. 302 238-7778
  34564 Pear Tree Rd Millsboro (19966) *(G-8508)*
Wwd Inc.. 302 994-4553
  5998 Kirkwood Hwy Wilmington (19808) *(G-20906)*
Www.prptInvestmentsgroupllccom, Wilmington Also Called: Perpetual Invstments Group LLC *(G-18982)*
Wwwlawfrmllncorg Assn Jim Cyle.. 803 212-4978
  615 S Dupont Hwy Dover (19901) *(G-3878)*
Wyatt & Brown Inc.. 302 786-2793
  15602 S Dupont Hwy Harrington (19952) *(G-4851)*
Wyndham Franchisor LLC.. 302 487-0234
  561 N Dupont Hwy Dover (19901) *(G-3879)*
Wyndham Garden Dover, Dover Also Called: Wyndham Franchisor LLC *(G-3879)*
Wyndham Group Inc.. 704 905-9750
  2207 Concord Pike # 696 Wilmington (19803) *(G-20907)*
Wyndham Vacation Rentals.. 877 893-2487
  33176 Coastal Hwy Bethany Beach (19930) *(G-652)*
Wynright Corp.. 302 239-9796
  28 Donegal Ct Newark (19711) *(G-12415)*
Wyoming Millwork Co (PA).. 302 697-8650
  140 Vepco Blvd Camden (19934) *(G-899)*
Wyoming Millwork Co.. 302 684-3150
  23000 Tracks End Ln Milton (19968) *(G-8732)*
Wyra.. 302 777-4533
  206 Hoiland Dr Wilmington (19803) *(G-20908)*
X Dima Inc.. 302 427-0787
  2400 W 4th St Wilmington (19805) *(G-20909)*
X Leader LLC.. 800 345-2677
  16192 Coastal Hwy Lewes (19958) *(G-6642)*
X Screen Graphix.. 302 422-4550
  1514 Bay Rd Milford (19963) *(G-8154)*
X Seamless Inc.. 650 770-0771
  2055 Limestone Rd Wilmington (19808) *(G-20910)*
X Trillion Inc.. 347 370-9111
  651 N Broad St Middletown (19709) *(G-7737)*
X-Sense USA LLC.. 857 998-3929
  1209 N Orange St Wilmington (19801) *(G-20911)*
X5 Networks Corporation.. 800 784-5228
  1013 Centre Rd Ste 403s Wilmington (19805) *(G-20912)*
Xanadu Concepts LLC.. 302 449-2677
  104 W Main St Ste 4a Middletown (19709) *(G-7738)*
Xander Group II LLC.. 302 656-1950
  103 Foulk Rd Ste 202 Wilmington (19803) *(G-20913)*
Xavier Entertainment Inc.. 215 356-8314
  1031 Roger Chaffee Sq Bear (19701) *(G-569)*
Xavier Inc.. 302 655-1962
  1315 N Union St Wilmington (19806) *(G-20914)*
Xcal Shooting Sports & Fitnes, Dover Also Called: Caliber Club Shooting Spt Inc *(G-2012)*
Xcertified Restore LLC.. 302 330-8850
  1708 Tulip St Wilmington (19805) *(G-20915)*
Xcs Corporation.. 302 514-0600
  500 Water St Wilmington (19804) *(G-20916)*
Xcutivescom Inc.. 888 245-9996
  3500 S Dupont Hwy Dover (19901) *(G-3880)*
Xeenom Inc.. 302 427-6970
  1220 N Market St Ste 60 Wilmington (19801) *(G-20917)*

Xenopia LLC.. 302 703-7050
  16192 Coastal Hwy Lewes (19958) *(G-6643)*
Xerafy Inc.. 817 938-4197
  3511 Silverside Rd Ste 10 Wilmington (19810) *(G-20918)*
Xerimis Inc.. 215 815-1706
  36414 Azalea Ave Selbyville (19975) *(G-13621)*
Xeroictech Inc.. 302 252-1617
  2803 Philadelphia Pike Ste B Claymont (19703) *(G-1341)*
Xfinity Store By Comcast, Dover Also Called: Comcast Corporation *(G-2115)*
Xi Global LLC.. 332 456-6969
  651 N Broad St Ste 201 Middletown (19709) *(G-7739)*
Xium, Wilmington Also Called: Accelerated Intelligence Inc *(G-14217)*
Xlr8 Logistics LLC (PA).. 682 622-1546
  8 The Grn Ste 14393 Dover (19901) *(G-3881)*
Xonex Relocation LLC.. 302 323-9000
  2751 Centerville Rd Ste 303 Wilmington (19808) *(G-20919)*
Xpedient Freight LLC.. 267 826-6170
  211 N Broad St Ste 3a Middletown (19709) *(G-7740)*
Xpert Tek Solutions Inc.. 302 724-4857
  306 Topaz Cir Dover (19904) *(G-3882)*
Xpo Logistics Freight Inc.. 302 629-5228
  104 Park Ave Seaford (19973) *(G-13456)*
Xpress Contracting.. 703 932-8565
  26182 Flying Bridge Ct Millsboro (19966) *(G-8509)*
Xpress Transport Logistics LLC.. 610 800-2288
  1115 Elkton Rd Newark (19711) *(G-12416)*
Xrosswater USA LLC.. 917 310-1344
  40 E Main St Ste 118 Newark (19711) *(G-12417)*
Xtalos LLC.. 800 383-0662
  651 N Broad St Ste 20533 Middletown (19709) *(G-7741)*
Xtend Inc.. 305 204-0595
  427 N Tatnall St 51198 Wilmington (19801) *(G-20920)*
Xtreme Cleaning.. 302 331-1084
  820 Cedar Grove Church Rd Harrington (19952) *(G-4852)*
Xwind Services Ltd.. 916 367-2994
  16192 Coastal Hwy Lewes (19958) *(G-6644)*
Xwind Services Ltd.. 418 563-5453
  16192 Coastal Hwy Lewes (19958) *(G-6645)*
Xynomic Pharmaceuticals Inc.. 650 430-7561
  3500 S Dupont Hwy Ste Ss101 Dover (19901) *(G-3883)*
Y and Y Garden Associates Inc.. 302 684-0383
  17430 Red Gate Ln Milton (19968) *(G-8733)*
Yacht Anything Ltd.. 302 226-3335
  20913 Coastal Hwy Rehoboth Beach (19971) *(G-13026)*
Yacht Delaware Registry Ltd (HQ)...................................... 302 477-9800
  3511 Silverside Rd Ste 105 Wilmington (19810) *(G-20921)*
Yacht Registry Ltd.. 302 477-9800
  3511 Silverside Rd # 105 Wilmington (19810) *(G-20922)*
Yalla Marketing LLC.. 209 201-0313
  651 N Broad St Ste 201 Middletown (19709) *(G-7742)*
Yallery Inc.. 571 351-3820
  651 N Broad St Ste 206 Middletown (19709) *(G-7743)*
Yanci Brand LLC.. 844 242-7263
  1201 N Market St Wilmington (19801) *(G-20923)*
Yanimed LLC.. 929 556-6522
  2093a Philadelphia Pike Ste 286 Claymont (19703) *(G-1342)*
Yankee Clippers Hair Designer.. 302 422-2748
  30 Nw 10th St Ste A Milford (19963) *(G-8155)*
Yardex Inc.. 302 406-0933
  1201 N Market St Ste 111 Wilmington (19801) *(G-20924)*
Yclas Inc.. 929 377-1239
  2035 Sunset Lake Rd B2 Newark (19702) *(G-12418)*
Yeaher Inc.. 513 293-4347
  51 Steel Dr Unit A New Castle (19720) *(G-9694)*
Year Up Wlmngton Mock Intrvews...................................... 302 256-7344
  1200 N French St Fl 5 Wilmington (19801) *(G-20925)*
Yebo Alpha Inc.. 302 335-8887
  184 Winners Cir Magnolia (19962) *(G-6792)*
Yeezie Holdings LLC.. 917 970-1974
  8 The Grn Ste 7756 Dover (19901) *(G-3884)*
Yellow and Green Machinery LLC.. 302 526-4990
  8 The Grn Ste E Dover (19901) *(G-3885)*

(PA)=Parent Co (HQ)=Headquarters (DH)=Div Headquarters

Yellow Light Publishing LLC — ALPHABETIC SECTION

Yellow Light Publishing LLC.. 302 242-0990
  25 Governors Ave Greenwood (19950) *(G-4677)*

Yellowfin Construction LLC.. 302 293-0028
  3903 Mill Creek Rd Hockessin (19707) *(G-5432)*

Yellowfins... 302 381-2569
  36908 Silicato Dr Unit 14 Millsboro (19966) *(G-8510)*

Yenaffit Inc... 302 650-4818
  1207 Delaware Ave Wilmington (19806) *(G-20926)*

Yenasys LLC... 302 956-9277
  651 N Broad St Ste 205 Middletown (19709) *(G-7744)*

Yencer Builders Inc.. 302 284-9977
  925 Marshyhope Rd Felton (19943) *(G-4038)*

Yental Empire LLC.. 404 423-0454
  600 N Broad St Ste 3119 Middletown (19709) *(G-7745)*

Yes Hardsoft Solutions Inc.. 609 632-0397
  351 Lenape Way Claymont (19703) *(G-1343)*

Yes Hardsoft Solutions Inc (PA).. 609 632-0397
  3626 Silverside Rd Wilmington (19810) *(G-20927)*

Yes U Can Corporation.. 302 286-1399
  2504 Creekside Dr Newark (19711) *(G-12419)*

Yesamerica Corporation... 800 872-1548
  651 N Broad St 205-908 Middletown (19709) *(G-7746)*

Yesco Sign Ltg Southeastern PA, Wilmington *Also Called: Hes Sign Services Inc (G-17135)*

Yesteryars Phtgraphic Emporium, Rehoboth Beach *Also Called: Gramonoli Enterprises Inc (G-12777)*

Yevma Inc... 888 338-2221
  8 The Grn Ste A Dover (19901) *(G-3886)*

Yhk Elm Cleaners Inc... 302 378-2017
  400 W Main St Middletown (19709) *(G-7747)*

Yhp Holdings LLC... 302 636-5401
  251 Little Falls Dr Wilmington (19808) *(G-20928)*

Yield Nexus LLC... 308 380-3788
  1679 S Dupont Hwy Ste 100 Dover (19901) *(G-3887)*

YMCA, Middletown *Also Called: Middletown YMCA (G-7361)*
YMCA, Newark *Also Called: Bear-Glasgow YMCA (G-10006)*
YMCA, Newark *Also Called: YMCA of Delaware B/A Sch Pgrm (G-12420)*
YMCA, Newark *Also Called: Young MNS Chrstn Assn Wlmngton (G-12422)*
YMCA, Rehoboth Beach *Also Called: Young MNS Chrstn Assn Wlmngton (G-13027)*
YMCA, Wilmington *Also Called: YMCA Central Branch LLC (G-20929)*
YMCA, Wilmington *Also Called: Young Mens Christian Assn Del (G-20937)*

YMCA Central Branch LLC.. 302 571-6950
  501 W 11th St Ste 100 Wilmington (19801) *(G-20929)*

YMCA of Delaware B/A Sch Pgrm...................................... 302 836-9622
  351 George Williams Way Newark (19702) *(G-12420)*

Yochanan El Bey... 610 726-4493
  3616 Kirkwood Hwy Wilmington (19808) *(G-20930)*

Yoder and Sons Cnstr LLC.. 302 349-0444
  10222 Woodyard Rd Greenwood (19950) *(G-4678)*

Yoder Overhead Door Co., Delmar *Also Called: Yoder Overhead Door Company (G-1660)*

Yoder Overhead Door Company... 302 875-0663
  36318 Sussex Hwy Delmar (19940) *(G-1660)*

Yoders Central Air.. 302 674-5144
  615 Central Church Rd Dover (19904) *(G-3888)*

Yoders Greenhouse... 302 678-3530
  5070 Pearsons Corner Rd Dover (19904) *(G-3889)*

Yoders Maintenance... 302 492-0203
  488 Myers Dr Hartly (19953) *(G-4913)*

Yoga For You... 302 832-0675
  201 Lake Ozarks Dr Bear (19701) *(G-570)*

Yogi Bear Campground.. 302 491-6614
  8295 Brick Granary Rd Lincoln (19960) *(G-6711)*

Yogo Factory.. 302 266-4506
  2610 Kirkwood Hwy Newark (19711) *(G-12421)*

Yoloha Yoga... 443 223-8651
  16182 Hudson Rd Milton (19968) *(G-8734)*

Yombu, Wilmington *Also Called: Yombu Events Inc (G-20931)*

Yombu Events Inc... 385 406-3651
  2810 N Church St Pm72783 Wilmington (19802) *(G-20931)*

Yomi Entertainment Inc.. 838 588-8888
  1221 College Park Dr # 116 Dover (19904) *(G-3890)*

Yorklyn Home LLC... 302 584-1219
  211 Gun Club Rd Hockessin (19707) *(G-5433)*

Yorklyn Storytelling Festival... 302 238-6200
  1155 Yorklyn Rd Yorklyn (19736) *(G-20995)*

Yorston and Co LLC.. 302 415-1925
  651 Nesting Ln Middletown (19709) *(G-7748)*

You Are Not Alone Vtrans Fndti... 302 287-8533
  224 Ann Dr Middletown (19709) *(G-7749)*

Young & McNelis... 302 674-8822
  300 S State St Dover (19901) *(G-3891)*

Young & Rubicam LLC... 302 888-3450
  201 N Walnut St Ste 1005 Wilmington (19801) *(G-20932)*

Young and Malmberg PA... 302 672-5600
  30 The Grn Dover (19901) *(G-3892)*

Young Cnway Strgatt Taylor LLP (PA)............................... 302 571-6600
  1000 N King St Wilmington (19801) *(G-20933)*

Young Divas LLC.. 302 354-6232
  216 Harlequin Dr New Castle (19720) *(G-9695)*

Young Divas Spa 4 Girlz, New Castle *Also Called: Young Divas LLC (G-9695)*

Young Logistics LLC... 302 232-3034
  100 Fulton St Wilmington (19805) *(G-20934)*

Young Mens Christian Assn.. 302 571-6925
  501 Silverside Rd Ste 43 Wilmington (19809) *(G-20935)*

Young Mens Christian Assn Del (PA)................................. 302 571-6968
  100 W 10th St Ste 1100 Wilmington (19801) *(G-20936)*

Young Mens Christian Assn Del... 302 571-6900
  501 W 11th St Ste 100 Wilmington (19801) *(G-20937)*

Young Mens Christian Assn Del... 302 571-6935
  1000 N Walnut St Wilmington (19801) *(G-20938)*

Young Mens Christian Associat.. 302 472-9622
  1000 N Walnut St Wilmington (19801) *(G-20939)*

Young MNS Chrstn Assn Wlmngton................................... 302 709-9622
  2600 Kirkwood Hwy Newark (19711) *(G-12422)*

Young MNS Chrstn Assn Wlmngton................................... 302 296-9622
  105 Church St Rehoboth Beach (19971) *(G-13027)*

Young Music LLC... 302 307-1997
  2358 Dutch Neck Rd Smyrna (19977) *(G-13941)*

Young Soles Inc.. 516 643-0445
  2140 S Dupont Hwy Camden (19934) *(G-900)*

Young Wns Christn Assocation, Newark *Also Called: YWCA Delaware (G-12425)*

Young, Conaway & Associates, Wilmington *Also Called: Young Cnway Strgatt Taylor LLP (G-20933)*

Younique... 302 632-3060
  106 Stevens St Camden (19934) *(G-901)*

Younity Lounge LLC... 302 359-5609
  74 Pristine Crt Smyrna (19977) *(G-13942)*

Your Cbd Store... 302 480-4474
  222 S Dupont Hwy Dover (19901) *(G-3893)*

Your Dentistry Today Inc... 302 575-0100
  3801 Kennett Pike Ste E207 # 207 Wilmington (19807) *(G-20940)*

Your Superfoods Inc.. 424 387-6165
  2035 Sunset Lake Rd Newark (19702) *(G-12423)*

Youshop Inc.. 302 526-0521
  3500 S Dupont Hwy Dover (19901) *(G-3894)*

Youth Sports Institute Del Inc... 302 275-5947
  153 S Dupont Hwy New Castle (19720) *(G-9696)*

Yumi Nutrition Inc.. 917 909-2166
  2035 Sunset Lake Rd Ste B2 Newark (19702) *(G-12424)*

Yumitos LLC... 704 819-6745
  16192 Coastal Hwy Lewes (19958) *(G-6646)*

Yupica Inc (usa)... 707 387-9874
  3411 Silverside Rd Ste 104 Wilmington (19810) *(G-20941)*

Yvonne Hall Inc.. 302 677-1300
  1671 S State St Dover (19901) *(G-3895)*

Yvonne Hall Realty, Dover *Also Called: Yvonne Hall Inc (G-3895)*

YWCA Delaware... 302 224-4060
  153 E Chestnut Hill Rd Ste 102 Newark (19713) *(G-12425)*

YWCA Delaware (PA).. 302 655-0039
  100 W 10th St Ste 515 Wilmington (19801) *(G-20942)*

Ywy Incorporated... 916 794-1607
  919 N Market St Ste 950 Wilmington (19801) *(G-20943)*

ALPHABETIC SECTION

Z Data Inc 800 676-5614
  40 E Main St Ste 610 Newark (19711) *(G-12426)*

Z Data Inc 800 676-5614
  40 E Main St Ste 610 Newark (19711) *(G-12427)*

Z&M Enterprises LLC 302 384-1205
  1521 Concord Pike Ste 301 Wilmington (19803) *(G-20944)*

Za Health, Dover Also Called: Dbaza Inc *(G-2202)*

Zabel PLStc&recnstrctve Surgry 302 996-6400
  550 Stanton Christiana Rd Ste 202 Newark (19713) *(G-12428)*

Zach Philippe Sate Farm Ins 302 327-0120
  2500 Wrangle Hill Rd Ste 125 Bear (19701) *(G-571)*

Zachary Chipman DMD PA 302 994-8696
  5505 Kirkwood Hwy Wilmington (19808) *(G-20945)*

Zacros America Inc 302 391-2200
  220 Lake Dr Ste 4 Newark (19702) *(G-12429)*

Zacros America Hedwin Division, Newark Also Called: Zacros America Inc *(G-12429)*

Zacs Inc 302 242-4653
  31 Par Ct Magnolia (19962) *(G-6793)*

Zamolxis LLC 571 286-0413
  300 De Ave Wilmington (19801) *(G-20946)*

Zando Custom Designs, Milton Also Called: E A Zando Custom Designs Inc *(G-8613)*

Zanes Siding and Trim 302 377-5394
  2327 Chesapeake City Rd Bear (19701) *(G-572)*

Zarek Donohue LLC 302 543-5454
  3411 Silverside Rd Ste 100 Wilmington (19810) *(G-20947)*

Zarla Inc 833 469-2752
  2093 Philadelphia Pike Ste 2555 Claymont (19703) *(G-1344)*

Zarraga & Zarraga Internl Medc 302 422-9140
  219 S Walnut St Milford (19963) *(G-8156)*

Zat3 Transport LLC 302 470-6172
  33221 Horsey Church Rd Laurel (19956) *(G-5627)*

Zavier J Decaire 302 658-0218
  300 Delaware Ave Ste 814 Wilmington (19801) *(G-20948)*

Zawadius Inc 888 979-6929
  16192 Coastal Hwy Lewes (19958) *(G-6647)*

Zcorp Property Consultants LLC 302 864-8581
  14288 Brandy Ln Georgetown (19947) *(G-4582)*

Zdata Mt, Newark Also Called: Z Data Inc *(G-12426)*

Zebrafish Disease Models Soc 518 399-7181
  1209 N Orange St Wilmington (19801) *(G-20949)*

Zeequest Inc (PA) 760 212-7378
  16192 Coastal Hwy Lewes (19958) *(G-6648)*

Zeglins Automotive Inc 302 947-1414
  25374 Townsend Rd Millsboro (19966) *(G-8511)*

Zehden Properties LLC 310 773-8529
  8 The Grn Ste R Dover (19901) *(G-3896)*

Zehnacker Russ Crna PA 302 834-7523
  263 W Chestnut Hill Rd Newark (19713) *(G-12430)*

Zeina Jeha Md MPH 302 503-4200
  16295 Willow Creek Rd Lewes (19958) *(G-6649)*

Zelcore Technologies Inc 408 829-6352
  8 The Grn Ste A Dover (19901) *(G-3897)*

Zen Acupuncture Clinic 302 559-1325
  30 Weilers Bnd Wilmington (19810) *(G-20950)*

Zen Therapy & Bodywork Inc 302 252-1733
  201 S Maryland Ave Wilmington (19804) *(G-20951)*

Zenbanx Holding Ltd (DH) 310 749-3101
  650 Naamans Rd Ste 300 Claymont (19703) *(G-1345)*

Zencity Technologies US Inc 347 632-1225
  1313 N Market St Ste 5100 Wilmington (19801) *(G-20952)*

Zendo Medical LLC 302 322-3442
  606 E Basin Rd New Castle (19720) *(G-9697)*

Zeneca Holdings Inc (HQ) 302 886-3000
  1800 Concord Pike Wilmington (19897) *(G-20953)*

Zeneca Inc (DH) 302 886-3000
  1800 Concord Pike Wilmington (19897) *(G-20954)*

Zenind Inc 845 300-3310
  8 The Grn Ste R Dover (19901) *(G-3898)*

Zenith Home Corp (DH) 302 326-8200
  400 Lukens Dr Historic New Castle (19720) *(G-5103)*

Zenith Home Corp 302 322-2190
  499 Ships Landing Way Historic New Castle (19720) *(G-5104)*

Zenith Mind Inc 302 543-2075
  1201 N Market St Ste 111-A Wilmington (19801) *(G-20955)*

Zenith Products 302 322-2190
  499 Ships Landing Way Historic New Castle (19720) *(G-5105)*

Zenkoders LLC 302 261-2627
  2803 Philadelphia Pike Ste B429 Claymont (19703) *(G-1346)*

Zenner Inc 302 781-9833
  200 Continental Dr Ste 401 Newark (19713) *(G-12431)*

Zenpli LLC 302 314-5231
  256 Chapman Rd Ste 105-4 Newark (19702) *(G-12432)*

Zenw LLC 302 722-7379
  200 Continental Dr Newark (19713) *(G-12433)*

Zeon Enterprises Inc 302 898-7167
  806 Wildel Ave New Castle (19720) *(G-9698)*

Zephyr Aluminum LLC 302 571-0585
  50 Germay Dr Ste 2 Wilmington (19804) *(G-20956)*

Zeribon Holding Group LLC 844 205-1999
  8 The Grn Ste B Dover (19901) *(G-3899)*

Zeroant Inc 567 342-1530
  651 N Broad St Ste 206 Middletown (19709) *(G-7750)*

Zerodaylab LLC 302 498-8322
  3524 Silverside Rd Ste 35b Wilmington (19810) *(G-20957)*

Zerowait Corporation 302 996-9408
  707 Kirkwood Hwy Wilmington (19805) *(G-20958)*

Zetwerk Manufacturing USA Inc 520 720-3085
  3411 Silverside Rd Ste 104 Wilmington (19810) *(G-20959)*

Zeuss LLC (PA) 305 904-8078
  1209 N Orange St Wilmington (19801) *(G-20960)*

Zhang Shunli MD 302 744-7050
  640 S State St Dover (19901) *(G-3900)*

Zhc, Historic New Castle Also Called: Zenith Home Corp *(G-5103)*

Zicherheit LLC 302 510-3718
  38824 Wilson Ave Selbyville (19975) *(G-13622)*

Zieta Technologies LLC (PA) 302 252-5249
  501 Silverside Rd Ste 39 Wilmington (19809) *(G-20961)*

Ziggy's Wood Floor Mechanics, Newark Also Called: Ziggys Inc *(G-12434)*

Ziggyfli LLC 302 503-5582
  1041 N Dupont Hwy Dover (19901) *(G-3901)*

Ziggys Inc 302 453-1285
  885 New London Rd Newark (19711) *(G-12434)*

Zilla Finance Inc 213 645-2133
  2055 Limestone Rd Ste 200c Wilmington (19808) *(G-20962)*

Zimmer US Inc 617 272-0062
  82 Brookwood Dr Camden Wyoming (19934) *(G-987)*

Zimny & Associates PA 302 325-6900
  92 Reads Way Ste 104 New Castle (19720) *(G-9699)*

Zinger Enterprizes Inc 302 381-6761
  9224 Sharptown Rd Laurel (19956) *(G-5628)*

Ziphealth Inc 561 207-7140
  16192 Coastal Hwy Lewes (19958) *(G-6650)*

Zipline Xpress Corp 302 531-6417
  1041 N Dupont Hwy Dover (19901) *(G-3902)*

Ziras Technologies Inc 302 286-7303
  260 Chapman Rd Ste 200 Newark (19702) *(G-12435)*

Zizo Taxi Cab LLC 302 528-5663
  69 Northfield Rd Newark (19713) *(G-12436)*

Zk Technologies LLC 980 246-4090
  16192 Coastal Hwy Lewes (19958) *(G-6651)*

Zober Contracting Services Inc 302 270-3078
  155 Old Mill Rd Dover (19901) *(G-3903)*

Zodiac Inc 800 969-4170
  651 N Broad St Ste 205-22 Middletown (19709) *(G-7751)*

Zogo Inc 978 810-8895
  2035 Sunset Lake Rd Newark (19702) *(G-12437)*

Zolak Inc 302 889-0556
  1111b S Governors Ave Ste 6259 Dover (19904) *(G-3904)*

Zone Control Hvac Inc 302 752-6697
  6422 Ray Rd Bridgeville (19933) *(G-785)*

Zone Laser Tag Inc 302 730-8888
  419 Webbs Ln Dover (19904) *(G-3905)*

Zone Systems Inc 302 730-8888
  419 Webbs Ln Dover (19904) *(G-3906)*

Zonguru Holdings Inc 310 266-1427
   1013 Centre Rd Ste 403b Wilmington (19805) *(G-20963)*

Zonko Builders, Selbyville *Also Called: Charles A Zonko Builders Inc (G-13497)*

Zoom Innovations Inc 416 677-7288
   251 Little Falls Dr Wilmington (19808) *(G-20964)*

Zoom Zoom, Wilmington *Also Called: Zoom Innovations Inc (G-20964)*

Zoomin & Groomin 302 985-3963
   259 Rons Way Smyrna (19977) *(G-13943)*

Zowie Inc 725 201-0590
   8 The Grn Ste 10893 Dover (19901) *(G-3907)*

Zr Tactical Outfitters LLC 302 353-9818
   12 Glenbarry Dr Wilmington (19808) *(G-20965)*

Zrcn Inc (PA) 212 602-1188
   2711 Centerville Rd # 400 Wilmington (19808) *(G-20966)*

Zuber & Associates Inc 302 478-1618
   16 Burnett Dr Wilmington (19810) *(G-20967)*

Zucchini Brothers, Wilmington *Also Called: Trolley Laundry (G-20434)*

Zuhatrend LLC 302 883-2656
   207 W Loockerman St Dover (19904) *(G-3908)*

Zuludynasty LLC 815 909-4236
   651 N Broad St Ste 2054236 Middletown (19709) *(G-7752)*

Zumba 215 870-9867
   16 Gristmill Ct Wilmington (19803) *(G-20968)*

Zuminex Inc 302 325-3200
   217 Lisa Dr Ste A New Castle (19720) *(G-9700)*

Zuri Hair Collection LLC 804 296-7534
   17 Medinah Ct Dover (19904) *(G-3909)*

Zutz Risk Management 302 658-8000
   300 Delaware Ave Ste 1600 Wilmington (19801) *(G-20969)*

Zwaanendael LLC 302 645-6466
   142 2nd St Lewes (19958) *(G-6652)*

Zwally Brown Lisa 302 504-7803
   1105 N Market St Fl 15 Wilmington (19801) *(G-20970)*

Zwd Products Corporation (DH) 302 326-8200
   400 Lukens Dr Historic New Castle (19720) *(G-5106)*

Zweemers Pav & Sealcoating LLC 302 363-6116
   46 Records Dr Magnolia (19962) *(G-6794)*

Zyng Nails 302 407-3849
   3828 Kennett Pike Wilmington (19807) *(G-20971)*

Zzhouse Inc 302 354-3474
   34 Blevins Dr Ste 1 New Castle (19720) *(G-9701)*

Zzhouse Inc 302 453-1180
   400 Eagle Run Rd Newark (19702) *(G-12438)*

Zzhouse Design, Newark *Also Called: Zzhouse Inc (G-12438)*

PRODUCT & SERVICES INDEX

• Product & Service categories are listed in alphabetical order.

A

ABRASIVES
ACCELERATION INDICATORS & SYSTEM COMPONENTS: Aerospace
ACCIDENT INSURANCE CARRIERS
ADHESIVES
ADULT DAYCARE CENTERS
ADVERTISING AGENCIES
ADVERTISING AGENCIES: Consultants
ADVERTISING DISPLAY PRDTS
ADVERTISING REPRESENTATIVES: Electronic Media
ADVERTISING REPRESENTATIVES: Printed Media
ADVERTISING SPECIALTIES, WHOLESALE
ADVERTISING SVCS: Direct Mail
ADVERTISING SVCS: Display
ADVERTISING SVCS: Transit
AGENTS, BROKERS & BUREAUS: Personal Service
AGRICULTURAL CREDIT INSTITUTIONS
AGRICULTURAL EQPT: Clippers, Animal, Hand Or Electric
AGRICULTURAL EQPT: Irrigation Eqpt, Self-Propelled
AGRICULTURAL EQPT: Tractors, Farm
AGRICULTURAL EQPT: Turf & Grounds Eqpt
AGRICULTURAL MACHINERY & EQPT: Wholesalers
AIR CLEANING SYSTEMS
AIR CONDITIONING & VENTILATION EQPT & SPLYS: Wholesales
AIR CONDITIONING EQPT
AIR CONDITIONING REPAIR SVCS
AIR DUCT CLEANING SVCS
AIR PURIFICATION EQPT
AIRCRAFT & AEROSPACE FLIGHT INSTRUMENTS & GUIDANCE SYSTEMS
AIRCRAFT & HEAVY EQPT REPAIR SVCS
AIRCRAFT ASSEMBLY PLANTS
AIRCRAFT CONTROL SYSTEMS:
AIRCRAFT DEALERS
AIRCRAFT ENGINES & ENGINE PARTS: Research & Development, Mfr
AIRCRAFT ENGINES & PARTS
AIRCRAFT EQPT & SPLYS WHOLESALERS
AIRCRAFT MAINTENANCE & REPAIR SVCS
AIRCRAFT PARTS & AUXILIARY EQPT: Aircraft Training Eqpt
AIRCRAFT PARTS & AUXILIARY EQPT: Assemblies, Fuselage
AIRCRAFT PARTS & AUXILIARY EQPT: Body Assemblies & Parts
AIRCRAFT PARTS & AUXILIARY EQPT: Research & Development, Mfr
AIRCRAFT PARTS & EQPT, NEC
AIRCRAFT PARTS WHOLESALERS
AIRCRAFT UPHOLSTERY REPAIR SVCS
AIRCRAFT: Airplanes, Fixed Or Rotary Wing
AIRLINE TRAINING
AIRPORTS, FLYING FIELDS & SVCS
ALARMS: Fire
ALUMINUM PRDTS
AMBULANCE SVCS
AMMUNITION: Small Arms
AMUSEMENT & RECREATION SVCS: Arcades
AMUSEMENT & RECREATION SVCS: Art Gallery, Commercial
AMUSEMENT & RECREATION SVCS: Gambling & Lottery Svcs
AMUSEMENT & RECREATION SVCS: Golf Club, Membership
AMUSEMENT & RECREATION SVCS: Physical Fitness Instruction
AMUSEMENT & RECREATION SVCS: Recreation Center
AMUSEMENT & RECREATION SVCS: Recreation SVCS
AMUSEMENT ARCADES
AMUSEMENT PARKS
ANALYZERS: Moisture
ANALYZERS: Network
ANIMAL FEED & SUPPLEMENTS: Livestock & Poultry
ANIMAL FEED: Wholesalers
ANIMAL FOOD & SUPPLEMENTS: Dog & Cat
ANIMAL FOOD & SUPPLEMENTS: Feed Premixes
ANIMAL FOOD & SUPPLEMENTS: Feed Supplements
ANIMAL FOOD & SUPPLEMENTS: Livestock
ANTIBIOTICS
ANTIBIOTICS, PACKAGED
ANTIQUE REPAIR & RESTORATION SVCS, EXC FURNITURE & AUTOS
APPAREL DESIGNERS: Commercial
APPAREL FILLING MATERIALS: Cotton Waste, Kapok/Related Matl
APPLIANCES, HOUSEHOLD OR COIN OPERATED: Laundry Dryers
APPLIANCES: Major, Cooking
APPLIANCES: Small, Electric
APPLICATIONS SOFTWARE PROGRAMMING
APPRAISAL SVCS, EXC REAL ESTATE
AQUARIUMS
ARBITRATION & CONCILIATION SVCS
ARCHITECTURAL SVCS
ARCHITECTURAL SVCS: Engineering
ARMATURES: Ind
ART DEALERS & GALLERIES
ARTS & CRAFTS SCHOOL
ASPHALT & ASPHALT PRDTS
ASPHALT COATINGS & SEALERS
ASSEMBLING & PACKAGING SVCS: Cosmetic Kits
ASSOCIATION FOR THE HANDICAPPED
ASSOCIATIONS: Bar
ASSOCIATIONS: Business
ASSOCIATIONS: Real Estate Management
ASSOCIATIONS: Scientists'
ASSOCIATIONS: Trade
ATOMIZERS
AUCTIONEERS: Fee Basis
AUDIO & VIDEO EQPT, EXC COMMERCIAL
AUDIO ELECTRONIC SYSTEMS
AUDIO-VISUAL PROGRAM PRODUCTION SVCS
AUDIOLOGICAL EQPT: Electronic
AUTO & HOME SUPPLY STORES: Auto & Truck Eqpt & Parts
AUTO & HOME SUPPLY STORES: Automotive parts
AUTO & HOME SUPPLY STORES: Trailer Hitches, Automotive
AUTO & HOME SUPPLY STORES: Truck Eqpt & Parts
AUTOMATED TELLER MACHINE NETWORK
AUTOMATIC REGULATING CONTROL: Building Svcs Monitoring, Auto
AUTOMOBILE FINANCE LEASING
AUTOMOBILES & OTHER MOTOR VEHICLES WHOLESALERS
AUTOMOBILES: Off-Road, Exc Recreational Vehicles
AUTOMOBILES: Wholesalers
AUTOMOTIVE & TRUCK GENERAL REPAIR SVC
AUTOMOTIVE BODY SHOP
AUTOMOTIVE BODY, PAINT & INTERIOR REPAIR & MAINTENANCE SVC
AUTOMOTIVE CUSTOMIZING SVCS, NONFACTORY BASIS
AUTOMOTIVE GLASS REPLACEMENT SHOPS
AUTOMOTIVE PAINT SHOP
AUTOMOTIVE PARTS, ACCESS & SPLYS
AUTOMOTIVE PARTS: Plastic
AUTOMOTIVE PRDTS: Rubber
AUTOMOTIVE REPAIR SHOPS: Diesel Engine Repair
AUTOMOTIVE REPAIR SHOPS: Electrical Svcs
AUTOMOTIVE REPAIR SHOPS: Engine Rebuilding
AUTOMOTIVE REPAIR SHOPS: Engine Repair
AUTOMOTIVE REPAIR SHOPS: Muffler Shop, Sale/Rpr/Installation
AUTOMOTIVE REPAIR SHOPS: Rebuilding & Retreading Tires
AUTOMOTIVE REPAIR SHOPS: Tire Recapping
AUTOMOTIVE REPAIR SHOPS: Tire Repair Shop
AUTOMOTIVE REPAIR SHOPS: Trailer Repair
AUTOMOTIVE REPAIR SHOPS: Truck Engine Repair, Exc Indl
AUTOMOTIVE REPAIR SHOPS: Wheel Alignment
AUTOMOTIVE REPAIR SVC
AUTOMOTIVE SPLYS & PARTS, NEW, WHOLESALE: Splys
AUTOMOTIVE SPLYS & PARTS, NEW, WHOLESALE: Tools & Eqpt
AUTOMOTIVE SPLYS & PARTS, NEW, WHOLESALE: Trailer Parts
AUTOMOTIVE SPLYS & PARTS, NEW, WHOLESALE: Wheels
AUTOMOTIVE SPLYS & PARTS, WHOLESALE, NEC
AUTOMOTIVE SVCS, EXC REPAIR & CARWASHES: Insp & Diagnostic
AUTOMOTIVE SVCS, EXC REPAIR & CARWASHES: Lubrication
AUTOMOTIVE SVCS, EXC REPAIR & CARWASHES: Road Svc
AUTOMOTIVE SVCS, EXC REPAIR & CARWASHES: Trailer Maintenance
AUTOMOTIVE SVCS, EXC RPR/CARWASHES: High Perf Auto Rpr/Svc
AUTOMOTIVE TOWING SVCS
AUTOMOTIVE TRANSMISSION REPAIR SVC
AUTOMOTIVE WELDING SVCS
AUTOMOTIVE: Seating
AWNINGS & CANOPIES: Awnings, Fabric, From Purchased Matls

B

BABY FORMULA
BACKHOES
BAGS & CONTAINERS: Textile, Exc Sleeping
BAGS: Food Storage & Frozen Food, Plastic
BAGS: Paper
BAGS: Paper, Made From Purchased Materials
BAGS: Plastic
BAGS: Plastic, Made From Purchased Materials
BAGS: Trash, Plastic Film, Made From Purchased Materials
BAKERIES, COMMERCIAL: On Premises Baking Only
BAKERIES: On Premises Baking & Consumption
BAKERY PRDTS: Bread, All Types, Fresh Or Frozen
BAKERY PRDTS: Cakes, Bakery, Exc Frozen
BAKERY PRDTS: Cookies
BAKERY PRDTS: Cookies & crackers
BAKERY PRDTS: Dry
BAKERY PRDTS: Wholesalers
BAKERY: Wholesale Or Wholesale & Retail Combined
BALLET PRODUCTION SVCS
BALLOONS: Hot Air
BANKS: Mortgage & Loan
BANQUET HALL FACILITIES
BAR
BARS: Concrete Reinforcing, Fabricated Steel
BASES, BEVERAGE
BATHROOM ACCESS & FITTINGS: Vitreous China & Earthenware
BATTERIES, EXC AUTOMOTIVE: Wholesalers
BATTERIES: Storage
BATTERIES: Wet
BATTERY CHARGERS
BATTERY CHARGERS: Storage, Motor & Engine Generator Type
BATTERY CHARGING GENERATORS
BAUXITE MINING
BEARINGS: Roller & Parts
BEAUTY & BARBER SHOP EQPT
BEAUTY & BARBER SHOP EQPT & SPLYS WHOLESALERS
BEAUTY SALONS
BEDDING, BEDSPREADS, BLANKETS & SHEETS
BEDS & ACCESS STORES
BEDSPREADS & BED SETS, FROM PURCHASED MATERIALS
BEER & ALE WHOLESALERS
BEER & ALE, WHOLESALE: Beer & Other Fermented Malt Liquors
BELTS: Conveyor, Made From Purchased Wire
BEVERAGE BASES & SYRUPS
BEVERAGE POWDERS
BEVERAGE PRDTS: Malt, Barley
BEVERAGE STORES
BEVERAGES, ALCOHOLIC: Ale

PRODUCT INDEX

BEVERAGES, ALCOHOLIC: Beer
BEVERAGES, ALCOHOLIC: Beer & Ale
BEVERAGES, ALCOHOLIC: Distilled Liquors
BEVERAGES, ALCOHOLIC: Rum
BEVERAGES, ALCOHOLIC: Wines
BEVERAGES, NONALCOHOLIC: Bottled & canned soft drinks
BEVERAGES, NONALCOHOLIC: Carbonated
BEVERAGES, NONALCOHOLIC: Carbonated, Canned & Bottled, Etc
BEVERAGES, NONALCOHOLIC: Soft Drinks, Canned & Bottled, Etc
BEVERAGES, WINE & DISTILLED ALCOHOLIC, WHOLESALE: Liquor
BEVERAGES, WINE & DISTILLED ALCOHOLIC, WHOLESALE: Wine
BEVERAGES, WINE/DISTILLED ALCOHOLIC, WHOL: Bttlg Wine/Liquor
BICYCLES WHOLESALERS
BICYCLES, PARTS & ACCESS
BILLING & BOOKKEEPING SVCS
BINDING SVC: Books & Manuals
BIOLOGICAL PRDTS: Exc Diagnostic
BIOLOGICAL PRDTS: Serums
BIOLOGICAL PRDTS: Vaccines
BIOLOGICAL PRDTS: Vaccines & Immunizing
BIOLOGICAL PRDTS: Veterinary
BLADES: Knife
BLANKBOOKS: Albums, Record
BLASTING SVC: Sand, Metal Parts
BLINDS & SHADES: Vertical
BLINDS : Window
BLOCKS: Landscape Or Retaining Wall, Concrete
BLOOD BANK
BLOOD RELATED HEALTH SVCS
BLUEPRINTING SVCS
BOAT BUILDING & REPAIR
BOAT BUILDING & REPAIRING: Fiberglass
BOAT BUILDING & REPAIRING: Motorized
BOAT BUILDING & REPAIRING: Yachts
BOAT BUILDING & RPRG: Fishing, Small, Lobster, Crab, Oyster
BOAT DEALERS
BOAT DEALERS: Motor
BOAT REPAIR SVCS
BOILER & HEATING REPAIR SVCS
BOILERS: Low-Pressure Heating, Steam Or Hot Water
BOOK STORES
BOOK STORES: Children's
BOOK STORES: Religious
BOOKS, WHOLESALE
BOTTLED GAS DEALERS: Liquefied Petro, Dlvrd To Customers
BOTTLED GAS DEALERS: Propane
BOTTLES: Plastic
BOWLING CENTERS
BOXES & CRATES: Rectangular, Wood
BOXES & SHOOK: Nailed Wood
BOXES: Corrugated
BRICK, STONE & RELATED PRDTS WHOLESALERS
BROADCASTING & COMMUNICATIONS EQPT: Studio Eqpt, Radio & TV
BROADCASTING STATIONS, RADIO: News
BROKERS & DEALERS: Securities
BROKERS & DEALERS: Security
BROKERS' SVCS
BROKERS: Business
BROKERS: Food
BROKERS: Loan
BROKERS: Mortgage, Arranging For Loans
BROKERS: Printing
BROOMS & BRUSHES: Household Or Indl
BUILDING & OFFICE CLEANING SVCS
BUILDING & STRUCTURAL WOOD MEMBERS
BUILDING CLEANING & MAINTENANCE SVCS
BUILDING COMPONENTS: Structural Steel
BUILDING PRDTS & MATERIALS DEALERS
BUILDINGS: Portable
BUILDINGS: Prefabricated, Metal
BUILDINGS: Prefabricated, Wood
BURIAL VAULTS: Concrete Or Precast Terrazzo
BUSINESS ACTIVITIES: Non-Commercial Site
BUSINESS FORMS WHOLESALERS
BUSINESS FORMS: Printed, Manifold
BUSINESS FORMS: Strip, Manifold
BUSINESS MACHINE REPAIR, ELECTRIC
BUSINESS TRAINING SVCS

C

CABINETS: Bathroom Vanities, Wood
CABINETS: Entertainment Units, Household, Wood
CABINETS: Factory
CABINETS: Kitchen, Metal
CABINETS: Kitchen, Wood
CABINETS: Show, Display, Etc, Wood, Exc Refrigerated
CABLE & OTHER PAY TELEVISION DISTRIBUTION
CABLE & PAY TELEVISION SVCS: Direct Broadcast Satellite
CABLE TELEVISION
CABLE TELEVISION PRDTS
CABLE: Fiber Optic
CALIBRATING SVCS, NEC
CAMERAS & RELATED EQPT: Photographic
CAMERAS: Microfilm
CANDLES
CANDLES: Wholesalers
CANDY MAKING GOODS & SPLYS, WHOLESALE
CANDY, NUT & CONFECTIONERY STORES: Candy
CANS: Aluminum
CANS: Metal
CAPACITORS: NEC
CARBON & GRAPHITE PRDTS, NEC
CARBON PAPER & INKED RIBBONS
CARBONS: Electric
CARDIOVASCULAR SYSTEM DRUGS, EXC DIAGNOSTIC
CARDS: Greeting
CARPET & UPHOLSTERY CLEANING SVCS
CARPET & UPHOLSTERY CLEANING SVCS: Carpet/Furniture, On Loc
CARPETS, RUGS & FLOOR COVERING
CARPETS: Textile Fiber
CASEMENTS: Aluminum
CASES: Carrying
CASES: Carrying, Clothing & Apparel
CASES: Plastic
CASINGS: Sheet Metal
CASTINGS GRINDING: For The Trade
CASTINGS: Aluminum
CASTINGS: Commercial Investment, Ferrous
CATALOG & MAIL-ORDER HOUSES
CATALYSTS: Chemical
CATERERS
CHASSIS: Motor Vehicle
CHEMICAL CLEANING SVCS
CHEMICAL ELEMENTS
CHEMICALS & ALLIED PRDTS WHOLESALERS, NEC
CHEMICALS & ALLIED PRDTS, WHOLESALE: Alkalines & Chlorine
CHEMICALS & ALLIED PRDTS, WHOLESALE: Chemical Additives
CHEMICALS & ALLIED PRDTS, WHOLESALE: Chemicals, Indl
CHEMICALS & ALLIED PRDTS, WHOLESALE: Chemicals, Indl & Heavy
CHEMICALS & ALLIED PRDTS, WHOLESALE: Plastics Materials, NEC
CHEMICALS & ALLIED PRDTS, WHOLESALE: Plastics Prdts, NEC
CHEMICALS & ALLIED PRDTS, WHOLESALE: Polyurethane Prdts
CHEMICALS & ALLIED PRDTS, WHOLESALE: Spec Clean/Sanitation
CHEMICALS, AGRICULTURE: Wholesalers
CHEMICALS: Agricultural
CHEMICALS: Alcohols
CHEMICALS: High Purity, Refined From Technical Grade
CHEMICALS: Inorganic, NEC
CHEMICALS: Medicinal, Organic, Uncompounded, Bulk
CHEMICALS: NEC
CHEMICALS: Organic, NEC
CHEMICALS: Soda Ash
CHEMICALS: Water Treatment
CHILD DAY CARE SVCS
CHILDBIRTH PREPARATION CLINIC
CHILDREN'S WEAR STORES
CHIMES: Electric
CHOCOLATE, EXC CANDY FROM BEANS: Chips, Powder, Block, Syrup
CHOCOLATE, EXC CANDY FROM PURCH CHOC: Chips, Powder, Block
CHROMATOGRAPHY EQPT
CHURCHES
CIGARETTE & CIGAR PRDTS & ACCESS
CIRCUITS: Electronic
CLEANING EQPT: Commercial
CLEANING OR POLISHING PREPARATIONS, NEC
CLEANING PRDTS: Ammonia, Household
CLEANING PRDTS: Automobile Polish
CLEANING PRDTS: Disinfectants, Household Or Indl Plant
CLEANING PRDTS: Floor Waxes
CLEANING PRDTS: Laundry Preparations
CLEANING PRDTS: Sanitation Preps, Disinfectants/Deodorants
CLEANING PRDTS: Specialty
CLEANING SVCS: Industrial Or Commercial
CLIPPERS: Fingernail & Toenail
CLOTHING & ACCESS, WOMEN, CHILDREN/INFANT, WHOL: Nightwear
CLOTHING & ACCESS: Handicapped
CLOTHING & APPAREL STORES: Custom
CLOTHING & FURNISHINGS, MENS & BOYS, WHOL: Sportswear/Work
CLOTHING STORES: T-Shirts, Printed, Custom
CLOTHING STORES: Unisex
CLOTHING: Athletic & Sportswear, Men's & Boys'
CLOTHING: Athletic & Sportswear, Women's & Girls'
CLOTHING: Band Uniforms
CLOTHING: Blouses, Women's & Girls'
CLOTHING: Children & Infants'
CLOTHING: Hospital, Men's
CLOTHING: Mens & Boys Jackets, Sport, Suede, Leatherette
CLOTHING: Neckwear
CLOTHING: Outerwear, Knit
CLOTHING: Outerwear, Women's & Misses' NEC
CLOTHING: Shirts, Dress, Men's & Boys'
CLOTHING: Socks
CLOTHING: Swimwear, Women's & Misses'
CLOTHING: Underwear, Men's & Boys'
CLOTHING: Underwear, Women's & Children's
CLOTHING: Uniforms, Men's & Boys'
CLOTHING: Uniforms, Military, Men/Youth, Purchased Materials
CLOTHING: Waterproof Outerwear
CLOTHING: Work, Men's
CLUTCHES, EXC VEHICULAR
COAL, MINERALS & ORES, WHOLESALE: Coal
COFFEE SVCS
COLOR PIGMENTS
COLORS: Pigments, Inorganic
COMBINATION UTILITIES, NEC
COMBINED ELEMENTARY & SECONDARY SCHOOLS, PRIVATE
COMMERCIAL & OFFICE BUILDINGS RENOVATION & REPAIR
COMMERCIAL ART & GRAPHIC DESIGN SVCS
COMMERCIAL ART & ILLUSTRATION SVCS
COMMERCIAL EQPT WHOLESALERS, NEC
COMMERCIAL EQPT, WHOLESALE: Restaurant, NEC
COMMERCIAL EQPT, WHOLESALE: Scales, Exc Laboratory
COMMERCIAL EQPT, WHOLESALE: Vending Machines, Coin-Operated
COMMERCIAL PHOTOGRAPHIC STUDIO
COMMERCIAL PRINTING & NEWSPAPER PUBLISHING
COMMUNICATIONS SVCS
COMMUNICATIONS SVCS: Data
COMMUNICATIONS SVCS: Internet Connectivity Svcs
COMMUNICATIONS SVCS: Internet Host Svcs
COMMUNICATIONS SVCS: Online Svc Providers
COMMUNICATIONS SVCS: Proprietary Online Svcs Networks
COMMUNICATIONS SVCS: Signal Enhancement Network Svcs
COMMUNICATIONS SVCS: Telephone Or Video
COMMUNICATIONS SVCS: Telephone, Broker
COMMUNICATIONS SVCS: Telephone, Local
COMMUNICATIONS SVCS: Telephone, Local & Long Distance
COMMUNICATIONS SVCS: Telephone, Long Distance
COMMUNICATIONS SVCS: Telephone, Voice
COMMUNITY SVCS EMPLOYMENT TRAINING PROGRAM
COMPACT LASER DISCS: Prerecorded

PRODUCT INDEX

COMPRESSORS: Air & Gas
COMPUTER & COMPUTER SOFTWARE STORES
COMPUTER & COMPUTER SOFTWARE STORES: Peripheral Eqpt
COMPUTER & COMPUTER SOFTWARE STORES: Personal Computers
COMPUTER & COMPUTER SOFTWARE STORES: Software & Access
COMPUTER & COMPUTER SOFTWARE STORES: Software, Bus/Non-Game
COMPUTER & COMPUTER SOFTWARE STORES: Software, Computer Game
COMPUTER & DATA PROCESSING EQPT REPAIR & MAINTENANCE
COMPUTER & OFFICE MACHINE MAINTENANCE & REPAIR
COMPUTER DATA ESCROW SVCS
COMPUTER FACILITIES MANAGEMENT SVCS
COMPUTER GRAPHICS SVCS
COMPUTER HARDWARE REQUIREMENTS ANALYSIS
COMPUTER PERIPHERAL EQPT REPAIR & MAINTENANCE
COMPUTER PERIPHERAL EQPT, NEC
COMPUTER PERIPHERAL EQPT, WHOLESALE
COMPUTER PROCESSING SVCS
COMPUTER PROGRAMMING SVCS: Custom
COMPUTER RELATED MAINTENANCE SVCS
COMPUTER SERVICE BUREAU
COMPUTER SOFTWARE DEVELOPMENT
COMPUTER SOFTWARE DEVELOPMENT & APPLICATIONS
COMPUTER SOFTWARE SYSTEMS ANALYSIS & DESIGN: Custom
COMPUTER STORAGE DEVICES, NEC
COMPUTER SYSTEM SELLING SVCS
COMPUTER SYSTEMS ANALYSIS & DESIGN
COMPUTER TERMINALS
COMPUTER-AIDED SYSTEM SVCS
COMPUTERS, NEC
COMPUTERS, NEC, WHOLESALE
COMPUTERS, PERIPHERALS & SOFTWARE, WHOLESALE: Printers
COMPUTERS, PERIPHERALS & SOFTWARE, WHOLESALE: Software
COMPUTERS: Mainframe
CONCRETE PRDTS
CONCRETE: Ready-Mixed
CONDENSERS & CONDENSING UNITS: Air Conditioner
CONDENSERS: Heat Transfer Eqpt, Evaporative
CONFINEMENT SURVEILLANCE SYS MAINTENANCE & MONITORING SVCS
CONSTRUCTION & MINING MACHINERY WHOLESALERS
CONSTRUCTION EQPT REPAIR SVCS
CONSTRUCTION EQPT: Tractors
CONSTRUCTION MATERIALS, WHOLESALE: Aggregate
CONSTRUCTION MATERIALS, WHOLESALE: Air Ducts, Sheet Metal
CONSTRUCTION MATERIALS, WHOLESALE: Awnings
CONSTRUCTION MATERIALS, WHOLESALE: Brick, Exc Refractory
CONSTRUCTION MATERIALS, WHOLESALE: Building Stone
CONSTRUCTION MATERIALS, WHOLESALE: Building Stone, Marble
CONSTRUCTION MATERIALS, WHOLESALE: Building, Exterior
CONSTRUCTION MATERIALS, WHOLESALE: Building, Interior
CONSTRUCTION MATERIALS, WHOLESALE: Cement
CONSTRUCTION MATERIALS, WHOLESALE: Doors, Garage
CONSTRUCTION MATERIALS, WHOLESALE: Gravel
CONSTRUCTION MATERIALS, WHOLESALE: Limestone
CONSTRUCTION MATERIALS, WHOLESALE: Metal Buildings
CONSTRUCTION MATERIALS, WHOLESALE: Millwork
CONSTRUCTION MATERIALS, WHOLESALE: Pallets, Wood
CONSTRUCTION MATERIALS, WHOLESALE: Paving Materials
CONSTRUCTION MATERIALS, WHOLESALE: Plywood
CONSTRUCTION MATERIALS, WHOLESALE: Prefabricated Structures
CONSTRUCTION MATERIALS, WHOLESALE: Roofing & Siding Material
CONSTRUCTION MATERIALS, WHOLESALE: Windows
CONSTRUCTION: Apartment Building
CONSTRUCTION: Athletic & Recreation Facilities
CONSTRUCTION: Bridge
CONSTRUCTION: Commercial & Office Building, New
CONSTRUCTION: Commercial & Office Buildings, Prefabricated
CONSTRUCTION: Dams, Waterways, Docks & Other Marine
CONSTRUCTION: Dock
CONSTRUCTION: Drainage System
CONSTRUCTION: Farm Building
CONSTRUCTION: Food Prdts Manufacturing or Packing Plant
CONSTRUCTION: Foundation & Retaining Wall
CONSTRUCTION: Heavy Highway & Street
CONSTRUCTION: Indl Buildings, New, NEC
CONSTRUCTION: Land Preparation
CONSTRUCTION: Marine
CONSTRUCTION: Oil & Gas Pipeline Construction
CONSTRUCTION: Parking Lot
CONSTRUCTION: Pipeline, NEC
CONSTRUCTION: Railroad & Subway
CONSTRUCTION: Residential, Nec
CONSTRUCTION: Sewer Line
CONSTRUCTION: Single-Family Housing
CONSTRUCTION: Single-family Housing, New
CONSTRUCTION: Swimming Pools
CONSTRUCTION: Transmitting Tower, Telecommunication
CONSTRUCTION: Truck & Automobile Assembly Plant
CONSTRUCTION: Warehouse
CONSTRUCTION: Waste Water & Sewage Treatment Plant
CONSULTING SVC: Business, NEC
CONSULTING SVC: Educational
CONSULTING SVC: Financial Management
CONSULTING SVC: Human Resource
CONSULTING SVC: Management
CONSULTING SVCS, BUSINESS: Communications
CONSULTING SVCS, BUSINESS: Energy Conservation
CONSULTING SVCS, BUSINESS: Environmental
CONSULTING SVCS, BUSINESS: Indl Development Planning
CONSULTING SVCS, BUSINESS: Safety Training Svcs
CONSULTING SVCS, BUSINESS: Sys Engnrg, Exc Computer/ Prof
CONSULTING SVCS, BUSINESS: Systems Analysis & Engineering
CONSULTING SVCS, BUSINESS: Systems Analysis Or Design
CONSULTING SVCS, BUSINESS: Testing, Educational Or Personnel
CONSULTING SVCS: Scientific
CONTAINERS: Food & Beverage
CONTAINERS: Frozen Food & Ice Cream
CONTAINERS: Plastic
CONTRACT FOOD SVCS
CONTRACTOR: Framing
CONTRACTORS: Acoustical & Ceiling Work
CONTRACTORS: Artificial Turf Installation
CONTRACTORS: Asbestos Removal & Encapsulation
CONTRACTORS: Building Front Installation, Metal
CONTRACTORS: Building Site Preparation
CONTRACTORS: Cable Laying
CONTRACTORS: Carpentry Work
CONTRACTORS: Carpentry, Cabinet & Finish Work
CONTRACTORS: Carpentry, Finish & Trim Work
CONTRACTORS: Closet Organizers, Installation & Design
CONTRACTORS: Coating, Caulking & Weather, Water & Fire
CONTRACTORS: Commercial & Office Building
CONTRACTORS: Communications Svcs
CONTRACTORS: Concrete Block Masonry Laying
CONTRACTORS: Concrete Reinforcement Placing
CONTRACTORS: Decontamination Svcs
CONTRACTORS: Directional Oil & Gas Well Drilling Svc
CONTRACTORS: Drywall
CONTRACTORS: Electric Power Systems
CONTRACTORS: Electronic Controls Installation
CONTRACTORS: Energy Management Control
CONTRACTORS: Erection & Dismantling, Poured Concrete Forms
CONTRACTORS: Fence Construction
CONTRACTORS: Fiber Optic Cable Installation
CONTRACTORS: Fire Detection & Burglar Alarm Systems
CONTRACTORS: Floor Laying & Other Floor Work
CONTRACTORS: Food Svcs Eqpt Installation
CONTRACTORS: Foundation & Footing
CONTRACTORS: General Electric
CONTRACTORS: Glass Tinting, Architectural & Automotive
CONTRACTORS: Heating & Air Conditioning
CONTRACTORS: Heating Systems Repair & Maintenance Svc
CONTRACTORS: Highway & Street Construction, General
CONTRACTORS: Highway & Street Paving
CONTRACTORS: Hydraulic Eqpt Installation & Svcs
CONTRACTORS: Machinery Installation
CONTRACTORS: Masonry & Stonework
CONTRACTORS: Office Furniture Installation
CONTRACTORS: Oil & Gas Well Redrilling
CONTRACTORS: Oil & Gas Wells Pumping Svcs
CONTRACTORS: Oil & Gas Wells Svcs
CONTRACTORS: Ornamental Metal Work
CONTRACTORS: Painting, Commercial
CONTRACTORS: Painting, Commercial, Exterior
CONTRACTORS: Painting, Indl
CONTRACTORS: Petroleum Storage Tanks, Pumping & Draining
CONTRACTORS: Pile Driving
CONTRACTORS: Plumbing
CONTRACTORS: Pollution Control Eqpt Installation
CONTRACTORS: Power Generating Eqpt Installation
CONTRACTORS: Prefabricated Window & Door Installation
CONTRACTORS: Refractory or Acid Brick Masonry
CONTRACTORS: Roustabout Svcs
CONTRACTORS: Septic System
CONTRACTORS: Sheet Metal Work, NEC
CONTRACTORS: Siding
CONTRACTORS: Skylight Installation
CONTRACTORS: Sprinkler System
CONTRACTORS: Structural Iron Work, Structural
CONTRACTORS: Structural Steel Erection
CONTRACTORS: Terrazzo Work
CONTRACTORS: Tile Installation, Ceramic
CONTRACTORS: Underground Utilities
CONTRACTORS: Ventilation & Duct Work
CONTRACTORS: Warm Air Heating & Air Conditioning
CONTRACTORS: Water Well Drilling
CONTRACTORS: Windows & Doors
CONTRACTORS: Wood Floor Installation & Refinishing
CONTRACTORS: Wrecking & Demolition
CONTROL EQPT: Electric
CONTROLS & ACCESS: Indl, Electric
CONTROLS: Environmental
CONTROLS: Marine & Navy, Auxiliary
CONVENIENCE STORES
CONVEYORS & CONVEYING EQPT
COOKING & FOODWARMING EQPT: Commercial
COOKWARE: Fine Earthenware
COOLING TOWERS: Metal
COPPER ORES
COSMETIC PREPARATIONS
COSMETICS & TOILETRIES
COSMETICS WHOLESALERS
COSMETOLOGY & PERSONAL HYGIENE SALONS
COSMETOLOGY SCHOOL
COUGH MEDICINES
COUNTER & SINK TOPS
COUNTRY CLUBS
CRANE & AERIAL LIFT SVCS
CREDIT CARD SVCS
CRUDE PETROLEUM & NATURAL GAS PRODUCTION
CRUDE PETROLEUM PRODUCTION
CULTURE MEDIA
CURTAIN WALLS: Building, Steel
CUTLERY
CUTLERY, NEC
CYCLIC CRUDES & INTERMEDIATES
CYLINDERS: Pressure

D

DAIRY PRDTS STORE: Cheese
DAIRY PRDTS: Butter
DAIRY PRDTS: Cheese
DAIRY PRDTS: Dietary Supplements, Dairy & Non-Dairy Based
DAIRY PRDTS: Milk & Cream, Cultured & Flavored
DAIRY PRDTS: Milk, Fluid
DAIRY PRDTS: Yogurt, Frozen
DATA ENTRY SVCS
DATA PROCESSING & PREPARATION SVCS
DATA PROCESSING SVCS

PRODUCT INDEX

DECORATIVE WOOD & WOODWORK
DEFENSE SYSTEMS & EQPT
DENTAL EQPT
DENTAL EQPT & SPLYS
DENTAL EQPT & SPLYS WHOLESALERS
DENTISTS' OFFICES & CLINICS
DEODORANTS: Personal
DEPARTMENT STORES
DEPARTMENT STORES: Army-Navy Goods
DEPARTMENT STORES: Country General
DEPILATORIES, COSMETIC
DERMATOLOGICALS
DESIGN SVCS, NEC
DESIGN SVCS: Commercial & Indl
DESIGN SVCS: Computer Integrated Systems
DETECTIVE & ARMORED CAR SERVICES
DIAGNOSTIC SUBSTANCES
DIAGNOSTIC SUBSTANCES OR AGENTS: In Vitro
DIAGNOSTIC SUBSTANCES OR AGENTS: Veterinary
DIATOMACEOUS EARTH MINING SVCS
DIE CUTTING SVC: Paper
DIES & TOOLS: Special
DIODES: Light Emitting
DIRECT SELLING ESTABLISHMENTS, NEC
DISASTER SVCS
DISCS & TAPE: Optical, Blank
DISINFECTING & PEST CONTROL SERVICES
DISINFECTING SVCS
DISK & DISKETTE CONVERSION SVCS
DISTRIBUTORS: Motor Vehicle Engine
DOCUMENT STORAGE SVCS
DOORS: Garage, Overhead, Metal
DOORS: Garage, Overhead, Wood
DRAPERIES: Plastic & Textile, From Purchased Materials
DRINKING PLACES: Bars & Lounges
DRINKING PLACES: Beer Garden
DRUGS & DRUG PROPRIETARIES, WHOLESALE
DRUGS & DRUG PROPRIETARIES, WHOLESALE: Animal Medicines
DRUGS & DRUG PROPRIETARIES, WHOLESALE: Patent Medicines
DRUGS & DRUG PROPRIETARIES, WHOLESALE: Pharmaceuticals
DRUGS & DRUG PROPRIETARIES, WHOLESALE: Vitamins & Minerals
DUCTS: Sheet Metal
DYES & PIGMENTS: Organic

E

EATING PLACES
EDITING SVCS
EDITORIAL SVCS
EDUCATIONAL SVCS
ELECTRIC & OTHER SERVICES COMBINED
ELECTRIC MOTOR REPAIR SVCS
ELECTRIC POWER DISTRIBUTION TO CONSUMERS
ELECTRIC POWER GENERATION: Fossil Fuel
ELECTRIC SERVICES
ELECTRIC SVCS, NEC: Power Generation
ELECTRICAL APPARATUS & EQPT WHOLESALERS
ELECTRICAL DEVICE PARTS: Porcelain, Molded
ELECTRICAL EQPT REPAIR SVCS
ELECTRICAL EQPT: Automotive, NEC
ELECTRICAL GOODS, WHOLESALE: Air Conditioning Appliances
ELECTRICAL GOODS, WHOLESALE: Electrical Appliances, Major
ELECTRICAL GOODS, WHOLESALE: Electronic Parts
ELECTRICAL GOODS, WHOLESALE: Fans, Household
ELECTRICAL GOODS, WHOLESALE: Fittings & Construction Mat
ELECTRICAL GOODS, WHOLESALE: Generators
ELECTRICAL GOODS, WHOLESALE: Insulators
ELECTRICAL GOODS, WHOLESALE: Lighting Fittings & Access
ELECTRICAL GOODS, WHOLESALE: Modems, Computer
ELECTRICAL GOODS, WHOLESALE: Security Control Eqpt & Systems
ELECTRICAL GOODS, WHOLESALE: Telephone Eqpt
ELECTRICAL GOODS, WHOLESALE: Wire & Cable, Electronic
ELECTRICAL SPLYS
ELECTROMEDICAL EQPT
ELECTROMETALLURGICAL PRDTS
ELECTRONIC PARTS & EQPT WHOLESALERS
ELECTRONIC SHOPPING
ELEMENTARY & SECONDARY SCHOOLS, PUBLIC
ELEVATORS & EQPT
ELEVATORS WHOLESALERS
ELEVATORS: Installation & Conversion
EMBLEMS: Embroidered
EMBROIDERY ADVERTISING SVCS
EMBROIDERY KITS
EMERGENCY ALARMS
EMERGENCY SHELTERS
EMPLOYMENT AGENCY SVCS
EMPLOYMENT SVCS: Labor Contractors
ENGINEERING HELP SVCS
ENGINEERING SVCS
ENGINEERING SVCS: Acoustical
ENGINEERING SVCS: Building Construction
ENGINEERING SVCS: Civil
ENGINEERING SVCS: Construction & Civil
ENGINEERING SVCS: Electrical Or Electronic
ENGINEERING SVCS: Marine
ENGINEERING SVCS: Mechanical
ENGINEERING SVCS: Structural
ENGINES: Internal Combustion, NEC
EQUIPMENT & VEHICLE FINANCE LEASING COMPANIES
EQUIPMENT: Rental & Leasing, NEC
EXHAUST HOOD OR FAN CLEANING SVCS

F

FABRIC STORES
FABRICS: Apparel & Outerwear, Cotton
FABRICS: Denims
FABRICS: Jean
FABRICS: Nonwoven
FABRICS: Nylon, Broadwoven
FABRICS: Surgical Fabrics, Cotton
FACILITIES SUPPORT SVCS
FAMILY CLOTHING STORES
FARM & GARDEN MACHINERY WHOLESALERS
FARM SPLYS WHOLESALERS
FARM SPLYS, WHOLESALE: Feed
FARM SPLYS, WHOLESALE: Garden Splys
FASTENERS WHOLESALERS
FASTENERS: Metal
FASTENERS: Notions, Hooks & Eyes
FERTILIZER, AGRICULTURAL: Wholesalers
FERTILIZERS: Nitrogenous
FERTILIZERS: Phosphatic
FIBER & FIBER PRDTS: Acrylic
FIBER OPTICS
FILTERS
FILTERS & SOFTENERS: Water, Household
FILTERS & STRAINERS: Pipeline
FILTERS: Air
FILTERS: Air Intake, Internal Combustion Engine, Exc Auto
FILTERS: General Line, Indl
FILTRATION DEVICES: Electronic
FINANCIAL INVESTMENT ACTIVITIES, NEC: Financial Reporting
FINANCIAL SVCS
FINISHING AGENTS: Textile
FINISHING SVCS
FIRE ARMS, SMALL: Shotguns Or Shotgun Parts, 30 mm & Below
FIRE CONTROL OR BOMBING EQPT: Electronic
FIRE EXTINGUISHERS, WHOLESALE
FIRE OR BURGLARY RESISTIVE PRDTS
FISH & SEAFOOD PROCESSORS: Fresh Or Frozen
FISH & SEAFOOD WHOLESALERS
FITTINGS & ASSEMBLIES: Hose & Tube, Hydraulic Or Pneumatic
FLOOR COVERING STORES
FLOOR COVERING STORES: Carpets
FLOOR COVERINGS WHOLESALERS
FLOOR WAXING SVCS
FLOORING: Hardwood
FLORIST: Flowers, Fresh
FLOWERS, FRESH, WHOLESALE
FLUID POWER PUMPS & MOTORS
FOOD PRDTS, CANNED: Baby Food
FOOD PRDTS, CANNED: Barbecue Sauce
FOOD PRDTS, CANNED: Fruit Juices, Fresh
FOOD PRDTS, CANNED: Fruits
FOOD PRDTS, CANNED: Fruits & Fruit Prdts
FOOD PRDTS, CANNED: Mexican, NEC
FOOD PRDTS, CANNED: Vegetables
FOOD PRDTS, CONFECTIONERY, WHOLESALE: Pretzels
FOOD PRDTS, CONFECTIONERY, WHOLESALE: Snack Foods
FOOD PRDTS, FROZEN: Ethnic Foods, NEC
FOOD PRDTS, FROZEN: Fruit Juice, Concentrates
FOOD PRDTS, FROZEN: Fruits & Vegetables
FOOD PRDTS, FROZEN: Fruits, Juices & Vegetables
FOOD PRDTS, FRUITS & VEGETABLES, FRESH, WHOLESALE: Fruits
FOOD PRDTS, POULTRY, WHOLESALE: Poultry Prdts, NEC
FOOD PRDTS, WHOLESALE: Beverages, Exc Coffee & Tea
FOOD PRDTS, WHOLESALE: Chocolate
FOOD PRDTS, WHOLESALE: Coffee & Tea
FOOD PRDTS, WHOLESALE: Coffee, Green Or Roasted
FOOD PRDTS, WHOLESALE: Condiments
FOOD PRDTS, WHOLESALE: Cookies
FOOD PRDTS, WHOLESALE: Dog Food
FOOD PRDTS, WHOLESALE: Dried or Canned Foods
FOOD PRDTS, WHOLESALE: Flavorings & Fragrances
FOOD PRDTS, WHOLESALE: Grain Elevators
FOOD PRDTS, WHOLESALE: Grains
FOOD PRDTS, WHOLESALE: Juices
FOOD PRDTS, WHOLESALE: Natural & Organic
FOOD PRDTS, WHOLESALE: Organic & Diet
FOOD PRDTS, WHOLESALE: Sandwiches
FOOD PRDTS, WHOLESALE: Sauces
FOOD PRDTS, WHOLESALE: Tea
FOOD PRDTS: Chicken, Processed, Frozen
FOOD PRDTS: Coffee
FOOD PRDTS: Dates, Dried
FOOD PRDTS: Dessert Mixes & Fillings
FOOD PRDTS: Flour & Other Grain Mill Products
FOOD PRDTS: Fruit Juices
FOOD PRDTS: Gelatin Dessert Preparations
FOOD PRDTS: Seasonings & Spices
FOOD PRDTS: Tea
FOOD PRODUCTS MACHINERY
FOOD STORES: Convenience, Independent
FOOD STORES: Cooperative
FOREIGN CURRENCY EXCHANGE
FORGINGS: Bearing & Bearing Race, Nonferrous
FORGINGS: Construction Or Mining Eqpt, Ferrous
FORGINGS: Gear & Chain
FORGINGS: Nuclear Power Plant, Ferrous
FOUNDRIES: Nonferrous
FOUNDRIES: Steel Investment
FRAMES & FRAMING WHOLESALE
FRANCHISES, SELLING OR LICENSING
FREIGHT CAR LOADING & UNLOADING SVCS
FREIGHT FORWARDING ARRANGEMENTS
FREIGHT FORWARDING ARRANGEMENTS: Domestic
FRUIT & VEGETABLE MARKETS
FRUITS & VEGETABLES WHOLESALERS: Fresh
FUEL ADDITIVES
FUEL CELLS: Solid State
FUEL OIL DEALERS
FUND RAISING ORGANIZATION, NON-FEE BASIS
FURNACES & OVENS: Indl
FURNITURE REFINISHING SVCS
FURNITURE STOCK & PARTS: Hardwood
FURNITURE STORES
FURNITURE UPHOLSTERY REPAIR SVCS
FURNITURE WHOLESALERS
FURNITURE, OFFICE: Wholesalers
FURNITURE, OUTDOOR & LAWN: Wholesalers
FURNITURE: Cabinets & Vanities, Medicine, Metal
FURNITURE: Chairs, Household Wood
FURNITURE: Desks & Tables, Office, Exc Wood
FURNITURE: Foundations & Platforms
FURNITURE: Laboratory
FURNITURE: Mattresses, Box & Bedsprings
FURNITURE: Office, Wood
FURNITURE: Picnic Tables Or Benches, Park
FURNITURE: Upholstered

G

GAME MACHINES, COIN-OPERATED, WHOLESALE
GAMES & TOYS: Board Games, Children's & Adults'
GAMES & TOYS: Electronic

PRODUCT INDEX

GAS & OIL FIELD EXPLORATION SVCS
GAS & OIL FIELD SVCS, NEC
GAS FIELD MACHINERY & EQPT
GASES: Indl
GASES: Nitrogen
GASES: Oxygen
GASKETS
GASKETS & SEALING DEVICES
GASOLINE FILLING STATIONS
GASOLINE WHOLESALERS
GEARS: Power Transmission, Exc Auto
GENERAL & INDUSTRIAL LOAN INSTITUTIONS
GENERAL COUNSELING SVCS
GENERATION EQPT: Electronic
GENERATOR REPAIR SVCS
GENERATORS: Vehicles, Gas-Electric Or Oil-Electric
GIFT SHOP
GIFTS & NOVELTIES: Wholesalers
GLASS PRDTS, FROM PURCHASED GLASS: Insulating
GLASS PRDTS, PRESSED OR BLOWN: Optical
GLASS PRDTS, PRESSED OR BLOWN: Scientific Glassware
GLASS, AUTOMOTIVE: Wholesalers
GLASS: Fiber
GLASS: Flat
GLASS: Pressed & Blown, NEC
GLASSWARE WHOLESALERS
GLASSWARE: Laboratory
GLOVES: Leather, Work
GOLF CARTS: Wholesalers
GOLF COURSES: Public
GOLF DRIVING RANGES
GOLF EQPT
GOLF GOODS & EQPT
GOVERNMENT, GENERAL: Administration
GRADING SVCS
GRANITE: Cut & Shaped
GRAPHIC ARTS & RELATED DESIGN SVCS
GRASSES: Artificial & Preserved
GRAVEL MINING
GROCERIES, GENERAL LINE WHOLESALERS
GUARD PROTECTIVE SVCS
GUARD SVCS
GUIDED MISSILES & SPACE VEHICLES
GUTTERS: Sheet Metal

H

HAIR & HAIR BASED PRDTS
HAIR CARE PRDTS
HAIR CARE PRDTS: Hair Coloring Preparations
HAIR DRESSING, FOR THE TRADE
HANDBAGS
HANDYMAN SVCS
HARDWARE
HARDWARE & BUILDING PRDTS: Plastic
HARDWARE & EQPT: Stage, Exc Lighting
HARDWARE STORES
HARDWARE STORES: Builders'
HARDWARE STORES: Tools
HARDWARE WHOLESALERS
HARDWARE, WHOLESALE: Bolts
HARDWARE, WHOLESALE: Builders', NEC
HARDWARE, WHOLESALE: Chains
HARDWARE, WHOLESALE: Power Tools & Access
HARDWARE, WHOLESALE: Security Devices, Locks
HARDWARE: Aircraft
HEALTH & WELFARE COUNCIL
HEALTH AIDS: Exercise Eqpt
HEALTH INSURANCE CARRIERS
HEAT EXCHANGERS: After Or Inter Coolers Or Condensers, Etc
HEAT TREATING: Metal
HEATERS: Swimming Pool, Electric
HEELS, BOOT OR SHOE: Rubber, Composition Or Fiber
HELICOPTERS
HELP SUPPLY SERVICES
HIGHWAY & STREET MAINTENANCE SVCS
HOLDING COMPANIES: Investment, Exc Banks
HOLDING COMPANIES: Personal, Exc Banks
HOME ENTERTAINMENT EQPT: Electronic, NEC
HOME FOR THE MENTALLY HANDICAPPED
HOME HEALTH CARE SVCS
HOMEFURNISHING STORES: Fireplaces & Wood Burning Stoves

HOMEFURNISHING STORES: Lighting Fixtures
HOMEFURNISHINGS, WHOLESALE: Decorating Splys
HOMEFURNISHINGS, WHOLESALE: Draperies
HOMEFURNISHINGS, WHOLESALE: Kitchenware
HOMES: Log Cabins
HOSPITAL EQPT REPAIR SVCS
HOSPITALS: Medical & Surgical
HOSPITALS: Specialty, NEC
HOTELS & MOTELS
HOUSEHOLD APPLIANCE STORES: Appliance Parts
HOUSEHOLD APPLIANCE STORES: Gas Appliances
HOUSEHOLD ARTICLES, EXC FURNITURE: Cut Stone
HOUSEHOLD FURNISHINGS, NEC
HOUSEWARES, ELECTRIC: Heating Units, Electric Appliances
HYDRAULIC EQPT REPAIR SVC

I

ICE CREAM & ICES WHOLESALERS
INDL & PERSONAL SVC PAPER, WHOLESALE: Boxes & Containers
INDL EQPT SVCS
INDL MACHINERY & EQPT WHOLESALERS
INDL PROCESS INSTRUMENTS: Analyzers
INDL PROCESS INSTRUMENTS: On-Stream Gas Or Liquid Analysis
INDL SPLYS WHOLESALERS
INDL SPLYS, WHOLESALE: Abrasives
INDL SPLYS, WHOLESALE: Bearings
INDL SPLYS, WHOLESALE: Drums, New Or Reconditioned
INDL SPLYS, WHOLESALE: Electric Tools
INDL SPLYS, WHOLESALE: Power Transmission, Eqpt & Apparatus
INDL SPLYS, WHOLESALE: Tools, NEC
INDL SPLYS, WHOLESALE: Valves & Fittings
INDUSTRIAL & COMMERCIAL EQPT INSPECTION SVCS
INFORMATION RETRIEVAL SERVICES
INFORMATION SVCS: Consumer
INGOTS: Steel
INK: Printing
INSPECTION & TESTING SVCS
INSTRUMENTS, LABORATORY: Differential Thermal Analysis
INSTRUMENTS, LABORATORY: Mass Spectrometers
INSTRUMENTS, MEASURING & CONTROLLING: Breathalyzers
INSTRUMENTS, SURGICAL & MEDICAL: Blood & Bone Work
INSTRUMENTS, SURGICAL & MEDICAL: IV Transfusion
INSTRUMENTS: Analytical
INSTRUMENTS: Flow, Indl Process
INSTRUMENTS: Indl Process Control
INSTRUMENTS: Measurement, Indl Process
INSTRUMENTS: Measuring & Controlling
INSTRUMENTS: Medical & Surgical
INSTRUMENTS: Optical, Analytical
INSTRUMENTS: Radio Frequency Measuring
INSTRUMENTS: Test, Electronic & Electrical Circuits
INSULATION & ROOFING MATERIALS: Wood, Reconstituted
INSULATION: Fiberglass
INSULATORS, PORCELAIN: Electrical
INSURANCE AGENTS, NEC
INSURANCE BROKERS, NEC
INSURANCE CARRIERS: Automobile
INSURANCE CARRIERS: Life
INSURANCE CARRIERS: Property & Casualty
INSURANCE CARRIERS: Title
INSURANCE CLAIM PROCESSING, EXC MEDICAL
INSURANCE INFORMATION & CONSULTING SVCS
INSURANCE: Agents, Brokers & Service
INTEGRATED CIRCUITS, SEMICONDUCTOR NETWORKS, ETC
INTERIOR DECORATING SVCS
INTERIOR DESIGN SVCS, NEC
INVENTORY COMPUTING SVCS
INVERTERS: Nonrotating Electrical
INVESTMENT ADVISORY SVCS
INVESTMENT FIRM: General Brokerage
INVESTMENT OFFICES: Management, Closed-End
INVESTORS, NEC
INVESTORS: Real Estate, Exc Property Operators
IRON ORE MINING
IRON ORES

J

JEWELRY REPAIR SVCS
JEWELRY STORES
JEWELRY STORES: Precious Stones & Precious Metals
JEWELRY STORES: Silverware
JEWELRY STORES: Watches
JEWELRY, WHOLESALE
JEWELRY: Precious Metal
JOB PRINTING & NEWSPAPER PUBLISHING COMBINED
JOB TRAINING SVCS
JOISTS: Long-Span Series, Open Web Steel

K

KIDNEY DIALYSIS CENTERS
KITCHEN CABINETS WHOLESALERS
KITCHEN UTENSILS: Food Handling & Processing Prdts, Wood
KITCHENWARE: Plastic

L

LABORATORIES, TESTING: Food
LABORATORIES, TESTING: Forensic
LABORATORIES, TESTING: Metallurgical
LABORATORIES: Biological Research
LABORATORIES: Biotechnology
LABORATORIES: Commercial Nonphysical Research
LABORATORIES: Dental, Crown & Bridge Production
LABORATORIES: Electronic Research
LABORATORIES: Medical
LABORATORIES: Noncommercial Research
LABORATORIES: Physical Research, Commercial
LABORATORIES: Testing
LABORATORIES: Testing
LABORATORY APPARATUS & FURNITURE
LABORATORY CHEMICALS: Organic
LABORATORY EQPT, EXC MEDICAL: Wholesalers
LABORATORY EQPT: Clinical Instruments Exc Medical
LABORATORY EQPT: Incubators
LAMINATED PLASTICS: Plate, Sheet, Rod & Tubes
LAMP SHADES: Glass
LAND SUBDIVIDERS & DEVELOPERS: Commercial
LAND SUBDIVIDERS & DEVELOPERS: Residential
LAND SUBDIVISION & DEVELOPMENT
LAUNDRY COLLECTING & DISTRIBUTING OUTLET
LAUNDRY SVC: Indl Eqpt
LAUNDRY SVCS: Indl
LAWN & GARDEN EQPT
LEASING & RENTAL SVCS: Cranes & Aerial Lift Eqpt
LEASING & RENTAL: Construction & Mining Eqpt
LEASING & RENTAL: Medical Machinery & Eqpt
LEASING & RENTAL: Trucks, Without Drivers
LEASING & RENTAL: Utility Trailers & RV's
LEASING: Passenger Car
LEATHER & CUT STOCK WHOLESALERS
LEATHER GOODS, EXC FOOTWEAR, GLOVES, LUGGAGE/ BELTING, WHOL
LEATHER GOODS: Garments
LEATHER, LEATHER GOODS & FURS, WHOLESALE
LEATHER: Accessory Prdts
LEATHER: Indl Prdts
LEGAL & TAX SVCS
LEGAL AID SVCS
LEGAL OFFICES & SVCS
LEGAL PROCESS SERVERS
LEGAL SVCS: General Practice Attorney or Lawyer
LIFE INSURANCE CARRIERS
LIFESAVING & SURVIVAL EQPT, EXC MEDICAL, WHOLESALE
LIGHTERS, CIGARETTE & CIGAR, WHOLESALE
LIGHTING EQPT: Locomotive & Railroad Car Lights
LIGHTING EQPT: Outdoor
LIGHTING EQPT: Strobe Lighting Systems
LIGHTING FIXTURES WHOLESALERS
LIGHTING FIXTURES, NEC
LIGHTING FIXTURES: Indl & Commercial
LIGHTING FIXTURES: Residential, Electric
LINEN SPLY SVC: Coat
LINEN SPLY SVC: Uniform
LININGS: Fabric, Apparel & Other, Exc Millinery
LIQUEFIED PETROLEUM GAS DEALERS
LIQUEFIED PETROLEUM GAS WHOLESALERS
LOCKS
LOGGING

PRODUCT INDEX

LOGGING CAMPS & CONTRACTORS
LOOSELEAF BINDERS
LOTIONS OR CREAMS: Face
LOTIONS: SHAVING
LUBRICANTS: Corrosion Preventive
LUBRICATING OIL & GREASE WHOLESALERS
LUMBER & BLDG MATLS DEALER, RET: Garage Doors, Sell/Install
LUMBER & BUILDING MATERIALS DEALER, RET: Door & Window Prdts
LUMBER & BUILDING MATERIALS DEALER, RET: Masonry Matls/Splys
LUMBER & BUILDING MATERIALS DEALERS, RET: Solar Heating Eqpt
LUMBER & BUILDING MATERIALS DEALERS, RETAIL: Brick
LUMBER & BUILDING MATERIALS DEALERS, RETAIL: Modular Homes
LUMBER & BUILDING MATERIALS DEALERS, RETAIL: Tile, Ceramic
LUMBER: Hardwood Dimension
LUMBER: Hardwood Dimension & Flooring Mills
LUMBER: Treated

M

MACHINE PARTS: Stamped Or Pressed Metal
MACHINE TOOL ACCESS: Tools & Access
MACHINE TOOLS, METAL CUTTING: Tool Replacement & Rpr Parts
MACHINE TOOLS, METAL FORMING: Mechanical, Pneumatic Or Hyd
MACHINE TOOLS: Metal Cutting
MACHINE TOOLS: Metal Forming
MACHINERY & EQPT FINANCE LEASING
MACHINERY & EQPT, AGRICULTURAL, WHOLESALE: Agricultural, NEC
MACHINERY & EQPT, AGRICULTURAL, WHOLESALE: Landscaping Eqpt
MACHINERY & EQPT, AGRICULTURAL, WHOLESALE: Lawn & Garden
MACHINERY & EQPT, INDL, WHOLESALE: Chemical Process
MACHINERY & EQPT, INDL, WHOLESALE: Engines & Parts, Diesel
MACHINERY & EQPT, INDL, WHOLESALE: Fans
MACHINERY & EQPT, INDL, WHOLESALE: Food Product Manufacturng
MACHINERY & EQPT, INDL, WHOLESALE: Hydraulic Systems
MACHINERY & EQPT, INDL, WHOLESALE: Indl Machine Parts
MACHINERY & EQPT, INDL, WHOLESALE: Machine Tools & Access
MACHINERY & EQPT, INDL, WHOLESALE: Measure/Test, Electric
MACHINERY & EQPT, INDL, WHOLESALE: Recycling
MACHINERY & EQPT, INDL, WHOLESALE: Safety Eqpt
MACHINERY & EQPT, INDL, WHOLESALE: Sawmill
MACHINERY & EQPT, INDL, WHOLESALE: Water Pumps
MACHINERY & EQPT, WHOLESALE: Construction, General
MACHINERY & EQPT, WHOLESALE: Oil Field Eqpt
MACHINERY & EQPT: Farm
MACHINERY, OFFICE: Stapling, Hand Or Power
MACHINERY: Automotive Related
MACHINERY: Construction
MACHINERY: Cryogenic, Industrial
MACHINERY: Gas Separators
MACHINERY: Metalworking
MACHINERY: Packaging
MACHINERY: Plastic Working
MACHINERY: Printing Presses
MACHINERY: Semiconductor Manufacturing
MACHINERY: Sifting & Screening
MACHINISTS' TOOLS: Measuring, Precision
MACHINISTS' TOOLS: Precision
MAGAZINES, WHOLESALE
MAGNESITE MINING
MAIL-ORDER HOUSE, NEC
MAIL-ORDER HOUSES: Computer Software
MAIL-ORDER HOUSES: Food
MAIL-ORDER HOUSES: Jewelry
MAILBOX RENTAL & RELATED SVCS
MAILING & MESSENGER SVCS
MAILING MACHINES WHOLESALERS

MAILING SVCS, NEC
MANAGEMENT CONSULTING SVCS: Administrative
MANAGEMENT CONSULTING SVCS: Automation & Robotics
MANAGEMENT CONSULTING SVCS: Business
MANAGEMENT CONSULTING SVCS: Business Planning & Organizing
MANAGEMENT CONSULTING SVCS: Construction Project
MANAGEMENT CONSULTING SVCS: Corporation Organizing
MANAGEMENT CONSULTING SVCS: Food & Beverage
MANAGEMENT CONSULTING SVCS: General
MANAGEMENT CONSULTING SVCS: Hospital & Health
MANAGEMENT CONSULTING SVCS: Industrial & Labor
MANAGEMENT CONSULTING SVCS: Industry Specialist
MANAGEMENT CONSULTING SVCS: Information Systems
MANAGEMENT CONSULTING SVCS: Manufacturing
MANAGEMENT CONSULTING SVCS: Programmed Instruction
MANAGEMENT CONSULTING SVCS: Quality Assurance
MANAGEMENT CONSULTING SVCS: Real Estate
MANAGEMENT CONSULTING SVCS: Restaurant & Food
MANAGEMENT CONSULTING SVCS: Training & Development
MANAGEMENT CONSULTING SVCS: Transportation
MANAGEMENT SERVICES
MANAGEMENT SVCS: Administrative
MANAGEMENT SVCS: Business
MANAGEMENT SVCS: Construction
MANAGEMENT SVCS: Hotel Or Motel
MANAGEMENT SVCS: Nursing & Personal Care Facility
MANAGEMENT SVCS: Restaurant
MANPOWER POOLS
MANPOWER TRAINING
MANUFACTURING INDUSTRIES, NEC
MARBLE, BUILDING: Cut & Shaped
MARINAS
MARINE CARGO HANDLING SVCS
MARINE SPLYS WHOLESALERS
MARKETS: Meat & fish
MARKING DEVICES
MEAT & FISH MARKETS: Seafood
MEAT MARKETS
MEAT PRDTS: Boxed Beef, From Slaughtered Meat
MEAT PRDTS: Prepared Beef Prdts From Purchased Beef
MEAT PRDTS: Sausages, From Purchased Meat
MEAT PRDTS: Scrapple, From Purchased Meat
MEAT PRDTS: Snack Sticks, Incl Jerky, From Purchased Meat
MEDICAL & HOSPITAL EQPT WHOLESALERS
MEDICAL & SURGICAL SPLYS: Dressings, Surgical
MEDICAL & SURGICAL SPLYS: Limbs, Artificial
MEDICAL & SURGICAL SPLYS: Orthopedic Appliances
MEDICAL & SURGICAL SPLYS: Personal Safety Eqpt
MEDICAL & SURGICAL SPLYS: Prosthetic Appliances
MEDICAL CENTERS
MEDICAL HELP SVCS
MEDICAL SUNDRIES: Rubber
MEDICAL SVCS ORGANIZATION
MELAMINE RESINS: Melamine-Formaldehyde
MEMBERSHIP ORGANIZATIONS, BUSINESS: Contractors' Association
MEMBERSHIP ORGANIZATIONS, BUSINESS: Growers' Association
MEMBERSHIP ORGANIZATIONS, NEC: Charitable
MEMBERSHIP ORGANIZATIONS, NEC: Food Co-Operative
MEMBERSHIP ORGANIZATIONS, NEC: Personal Interest
MEMBERSHIP ORGANIZATIONS, PROFESSIONAL: Accounting Assoc
MEMBERSHIP ORGANIZATIONS, PROFESSIONAL: Health Association
MEMBERSHIP ORGANIZATIONS, REL: Churches, Temples & Shrines
MEMBERSHIP ORGANIZATIONS, RELIGIOUS: Baptist Church
MEMBERSHIP ORGANIZATIONS, RELIGIOUS: Lutheran Church
MEMBERSHIP ORGANIZATIONS, RELIGIOUS: Methodist Church
MEMBERSHIP ORGS, CIVIC, SOCIAL/FRAT: Educator's Assoc
MEMBERSHIP SPORTS & RECREATION CLUBS
MEN'S & BOYS' CLOTHING STORES
MEN'S & BOYS' CLOTHING WHOLESALERS, NEC

MEN'S & BOYS' SPORTSWEAR CLOTHING STORES
MERCHANDISING MACHINE OPERATORS: Vending
METAL & STEEL PRDTS: Abrasive
METAL DETECTORS
METAL MINING SVCS
METAL SERVICE CENTERS & OFFICES
METAL: Battery
METALS SVC CENTERS & WHOLESALERS: Pipe & Tubing, Steel
METALS SVC CENTERS & WHOLESALERS: Sheets, Metal
METALS SVC CENTERS & WHOLESALERS: Steel
METALWORK: Miscellaneous
METALWORK: Ornamental
METALWORKING MACHINERY WHOLESALERS
METERING DEVICES: Water Quality Monitoring & Control Systems
MICROWAVE COMPONENTS
MILK, FLUID: Wholesalers
MILLWORK
MINE EXPLORATION SVCS: Nonmetallic Minerals
MINE PREPARATION SVCS
MINERAL WOOL
MINING MACHINERY & EQPT WHOLESALERS
MIXTURES & BLOCKS: Asphalt Paving
MOBILE COMMUNICATIONS EQPT
MOBILE HOMES
MOBILE HOMES WHOLESALERS
MODELS: General, Exc Toy
MOLDED RUBBER PRDTS
MORTGAGE BANKERS
MOTEL: Franchised
MOTION PICTURE & VIDEO DISTRIBUTION
MOTION PICTURE & VIDEO PRODUCTION SVCS
MOTION PICTURE & VIDEO PRODUCTION SVCS: Educational
MOTION PICTURE DISTRIBUTION SVCS
MOTION PICTURE PRODUCTION & DISTRIBUTION
MOTION PICTURE PRODUCTION ALLIED SVCS
MOTOR SCOOTERS & PARTS
MOTOR VEHICLE ASSEMBLY, COMPLETE: Fire Department Vehicles
MOTOR VEHICLE DEALERS: Automobiles, New & Used
MOTOR VEHICLE PARTS & ACCESS: Acceleration Eqpt
MOTOR VEHICLE PARTS & ACCESS: Electrical Eqpt
MOTOR VEHICLE PARTS & ACCESS: Engines & Parts
MOTOR VEHICLE PARTS & ACCESS: Trailer Hitches
MOTOR VEHICLE PARTS & ACCESS: Transmissions
MOTOR VEHICLE SPLYS & PARTS WHOLESALERS: New
MOTOR VEHICLE SPLYS & PARTS WHOLESALERS: Used
MOTOR VEHICLES & CAR BODIES
MOTOR VEHICLES, WHOLESALE: Fire Trucks
MOTOR VEHICLES, WHOLESALE: Trucks, commercial
MOTORCYCLE DEALERS
MOTORCYCLES & RELATED PARTS
MOTORS: Electric
MOTORS: Generators
MULTIPLEXERS: Telephone & Telegraph
MUSEUMS & ART GALLERIES
MUSIC DISTRIBUTION APPARATUS
MUSIC LICENSING & ROYALTIES
MUSICAL INSTRUMENTS & ACCESS: NEC
MUSICAL INSTRUMENTS & PARTS: Percussion
MUSICAL INSTRUMENTS & SPLYS STORES: Pianos
MUSICAL INSTRUMENTS: Guitars & Parts, Electric & Acoustic
MUSICAL INSTRUMENTS: Organs

N

NATURAL GAS DISTRIBUTION TO CONSUMERS
NATURAL GAS LIQUIDS PRODUCTION
NATURAL GAS TRANSMISSION & DISTRIBUTION
NEIGHBORHOOD DEVELOPMENT GROUP
NEW & USED CAR DEALERS
NEWSPAPERS, WHOLESALE
NURSERIES & LAWN & GARDEN SPLY STORES, RETAIL: Fertilizer
NURSERY STOCK, WHOLESALE
NURSING CARE FACILITIES: Skilled
NUTRITION SVCS
NYLON FIBERS

O

OFFICE EQPT WHOLESALERS

PRODUCT INDEX

OFFICE EQPT, WHOLESALE: Photocopy Machines
OFFICE FURNITURE REPAIR & MAINTENANCE SVCS
OFFICE SPLY & STATIONERY STORES: Office Forms & Splys
OFFICE SPLYS, NEC, WHOLESALE
OFFICES & CLINICS OF DOCTORS OF MEDICINE: Radiologist
OFFICES & CLINICS OF DRS OF MEDICINE: Physician, Orthopedic
OFFICES & CLINICS OF OPTOMETRISTS: Specialist, Contact Lens
OIL & GAS FIELD MACHINERY
OIL FIELD MACHINERY & EQPT
OIL FIELD SVCS, NEC
OIL TREATING COMPOUNDS
OILS & ESSENTIAL OILS
OLEFINS
OPERATOR TRAINING, COMPUTER
OPHTHALMIC GOODS
OPHTHALMIC GOODS WHOLESALERS
OPHTHALMIC GOODS, NEC, WHOLESALE: Frames
OPHTHALMIC GOODS: Frames, Lenses & Parts, Eyeglasses
OPTICAL GOODS STORES: Eyeglasses, Prescription
OPTICAL INSTRUMENTS & LENSES
ORGANIZATIONS & UNIONS: Labor
ORGANIZATIONS: Civic & Social
ORGANIZATIONS: Medical Research
ORGANIZATIONS: Physical Research, Noncommercial
ORGANIZATIONS: Professional
ORGANIZATIONS: Religious
ORGANIZATIONS: Research Institute

P

PACKAGING & LABELING SVCS
PACKAGING MATERIALS, WHOLESALE
PACKAGING MATERIALS: Paper
PACKAGING MATERIALS: Plastic Film, Coated Or Laminated
PACKAGING: Blister Or Bubble Formed, Plastic
PACKING & CRATING SVC
PAGERS: One-way
PAINTS & ALLIED PRODUCTS
PAINTS, VARNISHES & SPLYS WHOLESALERS
PAINTS, VARNISHES & SPLYS, WHOLESALE: Paints
PALLETS & SKIDS: Wood
PALLETS: Plastic
PAPER & BOARD: Die-cut
PAPER PRDTS: Panty Liners, Made From Purchased Materials
PAPER PRDTS: Sanitary
PAPER PRDTS: Tampons, Sanitary, Made From Purchased Material
PAPER: Coated & Laminated, NEC
PAPER: Gift Wrap
PARTITIONS & FIXTURES: Except Wood
PATENT OWNERS & LESSORS
PAVERS
PAVING MIXTURES
PAYROLL SVCS
PENCILS & PENS WHOLESALERS
PENSION FUNDS
PERSONAL CARE FACILITY
PERSONAL CREDIT INSTITUTIONS: Consumer Finance Companies
PERSONAL DOCUMENT & INFORMATION SVCS
PERSONAL SVCS
PEST CONTROL IN STRUCTURES SVCS
PEST CONTROL SVCS
PESTICIDES
PET FOOD WHOLESALERS
PET SPLYS
PETROLEUM & PETROLEUM PRDTS, WHOLESALE: Bulk Stations
PETROLEUM BULK STATIONS & TERMINALS
PETROLEUM REFINERY INSPECTION SVCS
PHARMACEUTICAL PREPARATIONS: Druggists' Preparations
PHARMACEUTICAL PREPARATIONS: Proprietary Drug
PHARMACEUTICAL PREPARATIONS: Solutions
PHARMACEUTICALS
PHOTOCOPY MACHINES
PHOTOCOPYING & DUPLICATING SVCS
PHOTOGRAPHIC EQPT & SPLYS

PHOTOGRAPHIC EQPT & SPLYS, WHOLESALE: Printing Apparatus
PHOTOGRAPHY SVCS: Commercial
PHYSICAL EXAMINATION & TESTING SVCS
PHYSICIANS' OFFICES & CLINICS: Medical doctors
PICTURE FRAMES: Wood
PICTURE FRAMING SVCS, CUSTOM
PIECE GOODS, NOTIONS & OTHER DRY GOODS, WHOLESALE: Fabrics
PIECE GOODS, NOTIONS/DRY GOODS, WHOL: Fabrics, Synthetic
PILOT SVCS: Aviation
PIPE SECTIONS, FABRICATED FROM PURCHASED PIPE
PIPELINE & POWER LINE INSPECTION SVCS
PIPELINE TERMINAL FACILITIES: Independent
PIPELINES: Crude Petroleum
PIPES & TUBES
PIPES & TUBES: Steel
PIPES & TUBES: Welded
PLASTICS FILM & SHEET
PLASTICS FILM & SHEET: Photographic & X-Ray
PLASTICS FILM & SHEET: Polyethylene
PLASTICS FILM & SHEET: Polypropylene
PLASTICS MATERIAL & RESINS
PLASTICS MATERIALS, BASIC FORMS & SHAPES WHOLESALERS
PLASTICS PROCESSING
PLASTICS: Finished Injection Molded
PLASTICS: Molded
PLASTICS: Polystyrene Foam
PLASTICS: Thermoformed
PLATES: Steel
PLATING & POLISHING SVC
PLUMBING FIXTURES
POLISHING SVC: Metals Or Formed Prdts
POLYETHYLENE RESINS
POLYTETRAFLUOROETHYLENE RESINS
POLYURETHANE RESINS
POULTRY & POULTRY PRDTS WHOLESALERS
POULTRY & SMALL GAME SLAUGHTERING & PROCESSING
POWDER: Metal
POWER GENERATORS
PRESS CLIPPING SVC
PRIMARY FINISHED OR SEMIFINISHED SHAPES
PRINT CARTRIDGES: Laser & Other Computer Printers
PRINTED CIRCUIT BOARDS
PRINTERS & PLOTTERS
PRINTING & EMBOSSING: Plastic Fabric Articles
PRINTING & STAMPING: Fabric Articles
PRINTING MACHINERY
PRINTING, COMMERCIAL: Bags, Plastic, NEC
PRINTING, COMMERCIAL: Business Forms, NEC
PRINTING, COMMERCIAL: Decals, NEC
PRINTING, COMMERCIAL: Periodicals, NEC
PRINTING, COMMERCIAL: Promotional
PRINTING, COMMERCIAL: Screen
PRINTING: Books
PRINTING: Commercial, NEC
PRINTING: Gravure, Labels
PRINTING: Gravure, Rotogravure
PRINTING: Letterpress
PRINTING: Lithographic
PRINTING: Manmade Fiber & Silk, Broadwoven Fabric
PRINTING: Offset
PRINTING: Screen, Broadwoven Fabrics, Cotton
PRINTING: Screen, Fabric
PROFESSIONAL EQPT & SPLYS, WHOLESALE: Analytical Instruments
PROFESSIONAL EQPT & SPLYS, WHOLESALE: Optical Goods
PROFILE SHAPES: Unsupported Plastics
PROMOTION SVCS
PROPERTY DAMAGE INSURANCE
PUBLIC LIBRARY
PUBLIC RELATIONS & PUBLICITY SVCS
PUBLIC RELATIONS SVCS
PUBLISHERS: Art Copy & Poster
PUBLISHERS: Music Book & Sheet Music
PUBLISHING & BROADCASTING: Internet Only
PUBLISHING & PRINTING: Books
PUBLISHING & PRINTING: Guides
PUBLISHING & PRINTING: Magazines: publishing & printing

PUBLISHING & PRINTING: Newsletters, Business Svc
PUBLISHING & PRINTING: Newspapers
PUBLISHING & PRINTING: Pamphlets
PUBLISHING & PRINTING: Textbooks
PULP MILLS
PUMPS & PUMPING EQPT REPAIR SVCS
PUMPS & PUMPING EQPT WHOLESALERS
PUMPS: Gasoline, Measuring Or Dispensing
PURCHASING SVCS
PURIFICATION & DUST COLLECTION EQPT

Q

QUILTING: Individuals

R

RADIO BROADCASTING & COMMUNICATIONS EQPT
RADIO BROADCASTING STATIONS
RAILROAD CAR REPAIR SVCS
RAILROAD EQPT
RAILROAD MAINTENANCE & REPAIR SVCS
RAZORS, RAZOR BLADES
REAL ESTATE AGENCIES & BROKERS
REAL ESTATE AGENCIES: Rental
REAL ESTATE AGENTS & MANAGERS
REAL ESTATE ESCROW AGENCIES
REAL ESTATE INVESTMENT TRUSTS
REAL ESTATE LISTING SVCS
RECORDS & TAPES: Prerecorded
REELS: Cable, Metal
REFINING: Petroleum
REFRACTORIES: Clay
REFRIGERATION & HEATING EQUIPMENT
REFRIGERATION EQPT & SPLYS WHOLESALERS
REFRIGERATION EQPT: Complete
REFRIGERATION REPAIR SVCS
REFRIGERATION SVC & REPAIR
REFUSE SYSTEMS
REHABILITATION CENTER, OUTPATIENT TREATMENT
REHABILITATION CTR, RESIDENTIAL WITH HEALTH CARE INCIDENTAL
REHABILITATION SVCS
REINSURANCE CARRIERS: Accident & Health
RELOCATION SVCS
REMOVERS & CLEANERS
RENTAL SVCS: Audio-Visual Eqpt & Sply
RENTAL SVCS: Business Machine & Electronic Eqpt
RENTAL SVCS: Eqpt, Theatrical
RENTAL SVCS: Vending Machine
RENTAL SVCS: Video Disk/Tape, To The General Public
RENTAL SVCS: Work Zone Traffic Eqpt, Flags, Cones, Etc
RENTAL: Portable Toilet
RENTAL: Video Tape & Disc
RESEARCH, DEVELOPMENT & TESTING SVCS, COMM: Agricultural
RESEARCH, DEVELOPMENT & TESTING SVCS, COMMERCIAL: Business
RESEARCH, DEVELOPMENT & TESTING SVCS, COMMERCIAL: Energy
RESEARCH, DEVELOPMENT & TESTING SVCS, COMMERCIAL: Medical
RESEARCH, DEVELOPMENT & TESTING SVCS, COMMERCIAL: Physical
RESEARCH, DEVELOPMENT SVCS, COMMERCIAL: Indl Lab
RESIDENTIAL CARE FOR THE HANDICAPPED
RESTAURANTS: Fast Food
RESTAURANTS:Full Svc, American
RETAIL BAKERY: Doughnuts
RETAIL STORES: Alcoholic Beverage Making Eqpt & Splys
RETAIL STORES: Audio-Visual Eqpt & Splys
RETAIL STORES: Business Machines & Eqpt
RETAIL STORES: Cake Decorating Splys
RETAIL STORES: Communication Eqpt
RETAIL STORES: Cosmetics
RETAIL STORES: Electronic Parts & Eqpt
RETAIL STORES: Flags
RETAIL STORES: Hair Care Prdts
RETAIL STORES: Hearing Aids
RETAIL STORES: Medical Apparatus & Splys
RETAIL STORES: Mobile Telephones & Eqpt
RETAIL STORES: Orthopedic & Prosthesis Applications
RETAIL STORES: Pet Splys
RETAIL STORES: Safety Splys & Eqpt

PRODUCT INDEX

RETAIL STORES: Spas & Hot Tubs
RETAIL STORES: Swimming Pools, Above Ground
RETAIL STORES: Telephone & Communication Eqpt
RETAIL STORES: Tents
RETAIL STORES: Tombstones
RETAIL STORES: Water Purification Eqpt
ROAD CONSTRUCTION EQUIPMENT WHOLESALERS
ROCK SALT MINING
ROOFING GRANULES
ROOFING MATERIALS: Asphalt
RUBBER PRDTS: Silicone
RUGS : Hand & Machine Made
RUGS : Tufted

S

SAFETY EQPT & SPLYS WHOLESALERS
SAFETY INSPECTION SVCS
SALES PROMOTION SVCS
SALT
SAND & GRAVEL
SAND MINING
SAND: Silica
SANITARY SVC, NEC
SANITARY SVCS: Hazardous Waste, Collection & Disposal
SANITARY SVCS: Liquid Waste Collection & Disposal
SANITARY SVCS: Oil Spill Cleanup
SANITARY SVCS: Refuse Collection & Disposal Svcs
SANITARY SVCS: Rubbish Collection & Disposal
SANITARY SVCS: Waste Materials, Recycling
SATELLITES: Communications
SCALE REPAIR SVCS
SCHOOL FOR PHYSICALLY HANDICAPPED, NEC
SCIENTIFIC EQPT REPAIR SVCS
SCIENTIFIC INSTRUMENTS WHOLESALERS
SCRAP & WASTE MATERIALS, WHOLESALE: Ferrous Metal
SCRAP & WASTE MATERIALS, WHOLESALE: Junk & Scrap
SCRAP & WASTE MATERIALS, WHOLESALE: Metal
SCREW MACHINE PRDTS
SEALANTS
SEALING COMPOUNDS: Sealing, synthetic rubber or plastic
SEARCH & NAVIGATION SYSTEMS
SECURE STORAGE SVC: Household & Furniture
SECURITY CONTROL EQPT & SYSTEMS
SECURITY DEVICES
SECURITY GUARD SVCS
SECURITY SYSTEMS SERVICES
SEMICONDUCTORS & RELATED DEVICES
SEPTIC TANK CLEANING SVCS
SERVICE STATION EQPT REPAIR SVCS
SHAPES & PILINGS, STRUCTURAL: Steel
SHEET METAL SPECIALTIES, EXC STAMPED
SHIP BUILDING & REPAIRING: Passenger, Commercial
SHOE & BOOT ACCESS
SHOE STORES
SHOE STORES: Athletic
SHOE STORES: Boots, Men's
SHOWER STALLS: Plastic & Fiberglass
SHREDDERS: Indl & Commercial
SHUTTERS, DOOR & WINDOW: Metal
SIGNS & ADVERTISING SPECIALTIES
SIGNS & ADVERTISING SPECIALTIES: Artwork, Advertising
SIGNS & ADVERTISING SPECIALTIES: Novelties
SIGNS, ELECTRICAL: Wholesalers
SIGNS, EXC ELECTRIC, WHOLESALE
SIGNS: Electrical
SILICON WAFERS: Chemically Doped
SILICONES
SILK SCREEN DESIGN SVCS
SILVERWARE & PLATED WARE
SIZES
SKILL TRAINING CENTER
SKIN CARE PRDTS: Suntan Lotions & Oils
SOCIAL SERVICES INFORMATION EXCHANGE
SOCIAL SVCS CENTER
SOFT DRINKS WHOLESALERS
SOFTWARE PUBLISHERS: Home Entertainment
SOFTWARE PUBLISHERS: Operating Systems
SOFTWARE TRAINING, COMPUTER
SOLAR CELLS
SOLAR HEATING EQPT
SOLID CONTAINING UNITS: Concrete
SPACE VEHICLES
SPAS

SPEAKER SYSTEMS
SPECIALIZED LEGAL SVCS
SPECIALTY FOOD STORES: Health & Dietetic Food
SPECIALTY FOOD STORES: Vitamin
SPECIALTY OUTPATIENT CLINICS, NEC
SPORTING & ATHLETIC GOODS: Bowling Pins
SPORTING & ATHLETIC GOODS: Camping Eqpt & Splys
SPORTING & ATHLETIC GOODS: Racket Sports Eqpt
SPORTING & ATHLETIC GOODS: Shafts, Golf Club
SPORTING & ATHLETIC GOODS: Shooting Eqpt & Splys, General
SPORTING CAMPS
SPORTING FIREARMS WHOLESALERS
SPORTING GOODS STORES: Firearms
SPORTING GOODS STORES: Fishing Eqpt
SPORTS APPAREL STORES
SPORTS CLUBS, MANAGERS & PROMOTERS
SPORTS PROMOTION SVCS
SPRINGS: Steel
SPRINGS: Wire
STAIRCASES & STAIRS, WOOD
STARTERS & CONTROLLERS: Motor, Electric
STATIONERY & OFFICE SPLYS WHOLESALERS
STOCK SHAPES: Plastic
STONE: Quarrying & Processing, Own Stone Prdts
STORES: Auto & Home Supply
STRUCTURAL SUPPORT & BUILDING MATERIAL: Concrete
SUBSCRIPTION FULFILLMENT SVCS: Magazine, Newspaper, Etc
SUBSTANCE ABUSE COUNSELING
SUMMER CAMPS, EXC DAY & SPORTS INSTRUCTIONAL
SUNDRIES & RELATED PRDTS: Medical & Laboratory, Rubber
SURFACE ACTIVE AGENTS: Oils & Greases
SURGICAL APPLIANCES & SPLYS
SURGICAL APPLIANCES & SPLYS
SURVEYING INSTRUMENTS WHOLESALERS
SVC ESTABLISHMENT EQPT, WHOLESALE: Firefighting Eqpt
SVC ESTABLISHMENT EQPT, WHOLESALE: Laundry Eqpt & Splys
SVC ESTABLISHMENT EQPT, WHOLESALE: Vending Machines & Splys
SWIMMING POOL & HOT TUB CLEANING & MAINTENANCE SVCS
SWIMMING POOLS, EQPT & SPLYS: Wholesalers
SWITCHES: Electronic
SWITCHES: Electronic Applications
SYSTEMS ENGINEERING: Computer Related
SYSTEMS INTEGRATION SVCS
SYSTEMS INTEGRATION SVCS: Local Area Network
SYSTEMS SOFTWARE DEVELOPMENT SVCS

T

TABLE OR COUNTERTOPS, PLASTIC LAMINATED
TABLEWARE: Vitreous China
TALLOW: Animal
TANKS & OTHER TRACKED VEHICLE CMPNTS
TANKS: Fuel, Including Oil & Gas, Metal Plate
TANKS: Plastic & Fiberglass
TAPES: Pressure Sensitive, Rubber
TARPAULINS, WHOLESALE
TELECOMMUNICATION EQPT REPAIR SVCS, EXC TELEPHONES
TELECONFERENCING SVCS
TELEPHONE ANSWERING SVCS
TELEPHONE EQPT: NEC
TELEPHONE SVCS
TELEVISION BROADCASTING STATIONS
TEMPORARY HELP SVCS
TEN PIN CENTERS
TESTERS: Physical Property
TEXTILE & APPAREL SVCS
THEATRICAL LIGHTING SVCS
THEATRICAL PRODUCERS & SVCS
THERMOPLASTIC MATERIALS
THIN FILM CIRCUITS
TILE: Wall, Ceramic
TIRE & TUBE REPAIR MATERIALS, WHOLESALE
TIRES & INNER TUBES
TIRES & TUBES WHOLESALERS
TIRES & TUBES, WHOLESALE: Automotive
TITLE ABSTRACT & SETTLEMENT OFFICES

TOBACCO & PRDTS, WHOLESALE: Cigarettes
TOILETRIES, WHOLESALE: Perfumes
TOILETRIES, WHOLESALE: Toiletries
TOWELS: Paper
TOWING & TUGBOAT SVC
TOWING SVCS: Marine
TOYS & HOBBY GOODS & SPLYS, WHOLESALE: Toys & Games
TOYS & HOBBY GOODS & SPLYS, WHOLESALE: Video Games
TOYS: Electronic
TOYS: Rubber
TRADERS: Commodity, Contracts
TRAILERS & TRAILER EQPT
TRAILERS: Semitrailers, Missile Transportation
TRANSPORTATION AGENTS & BROKERS
TRANSPORTATION BROKERS: Truck
TRANSPORTATION EQPT & SPLYS WHOLESALERS, NEC
TRANSPORTATION SVCS, AIR, NONSCHEDULED: Helicopter Carriers
TRANSPORTATION: Deep Sea Domestic Freight
TRANSPORTATION: Deep Sea Foreign Freight
TRAVEL AGENCIES
TRUCK & BUS BODIES: Truck, Motor Vehicle
TRUCK BODIES: Body Parts
TRUCK BODY SHOP
TRUCK GENERAL REPAIR SVC
TRUCK PARTS & ACCESSORIES: Wholesalers
TRUCKING & HAULING SVCS: Contract Basis
TRUCKING & HAULING SVCS: Heavy, NEC
TRUCKING & HAULING SVCS: Liquid Petroleum, Exc Local
TRUCKING: Except Local
TRUCKING: Local, With Storage
TRUCKING: Local, Without Storage
TRUCKS & TRACTORS: Industrial
TRUCKS: Indl
TRUSSES & FRAMING: Prefabricated Metal
TRUST MANAGEMENT SVCS: Charitable
TRUST MANAGEMENT SVCS: Personal Investment
TURBINES & TURBINE GENERATOR SETS
TURKEY PROCESSING & SLAUGHTERING
TYPESETTING SVC

U

UNIFORM SPLY SVCS: Indl
UNISEX HAIR SALONS
UNIVERSITY
UPHOLSTERY WORK SVCS
USED CAR DEALERS
USED MERCHANDISE STORES
UTENSILS: Household, Cooking & Kitchen, Metal
UTILITY TRAILER DEALERS

V

VALUE-ADDED RESELLERS: Computer Systems
VALVES & PIPE FITTINGS
VALVES: Indl
VALVES: Plumbing & Heating
VARIETY STORES
VEHICLES: All Terrain
VENDING MACHINE OPERATORS: Sandwich & Hot Food
VENDING MACHINE REPAIR SVCS
VENDING MACHINES & PARTS
VENTILATING EQPT: Metal
VENTURE CAPITAL COMPANIES
VIDEO & AUDIO EQPT, WHOLESALE
VIDEO PRODUCTION SVCS
VIDEO TAPE PRODUCTION SVCS
VINYL RESINS, NEC
VISUAL COMMUNICATIONS SYSTEMS
VITAMINS: Natural Or Synthetic, Uncompounded, Bulk
VOCATIONAL REHABILITATION AGENCY
VOCATIONAL TRAINING AGENCY

W

WALL COVERINGS WHOLESALERS
WALLPAPER STORE
WAREHOUSING & STORAGE FACILITIES, NEC
WAREHOUSING & STORAGE, REFRIGERATED: Cold Storage Or Refrig
WAREHOUSING & STORAGE, REFRIGERATED: Frozen Or Refrig Goods
WAREHOUSING & STORAGE: General

PRODUCT INDEX

WAREHOUSING & STORAGE: Miniwarehouse
WAREHOUSING & STORAGE: Refrigerated
WAREHOUSING & STORAGE: Self Storage
WARM AIR HEATING/AC EQPT/SPLYS, WHOL Warm Air Htg Eqpt/Splys
WARP KNIT FABRIC FINISHING
WASHERS
WASHERS: Plastic
WASTE CLEANING SVCS
WATCH REPAIR SVCS
WATCHES
WATER SOFTENING WHOLESALERS
WATER SUPPLY
WATER TREATMENT EQPT: Indl
WATER: Pasteurized & Mineral, Bottled & Canned
WATERPROOFING COMPOUNDS

WEB SEARCH PORTALS: Internet
WELDING EQPT & SPLYS WHOLESALERS
WELDING EQPT REPAIR SVCS
WELDING REPAIR SVC
WELDING SPLYS, EXC GASES: Wholesalers
WET CORN MILLING
WHEEL BALANCING EQPT: Automotive
WHEELCHAIR LIFTS
WINDMILLS: Electric Power Generation
WINDOW CLEANING SVCS
WINDOW FRAMES, MOLDING & TRIM: Vinyl
WINE & DISTILLED ALCOHOLIC BEVERAGES WHOLESALERS
WIRE
WIRE & CABLE: Nonferrous, Aircraft
WIRE: Communication

WOMEN'S & CHILDREN'S CLOTHING WHOLESALERS, NEC
WOMEN'S CLOTHING STORES
WOOD & WOOD BY-PRDTS, WHOLESALE
WOOD PRDTS: Applicators
WOOD PRDTS: Mulch Or Sawdust
WOOD PRDTS: Mulch, Wood & Bark
WOOD PRDTS: Signboards
WOOD PRDTS: Trophy Bases
WOOD TREATING: Wood Prdts, Creosoted

X

X-RAY EQPT & TUBES

Y

YOGURT WHOLESALERS

PRODUCTS & SERVICES SECTION

Product or service category — **TRUCKING & STORAGE: Local**
Edgar & Son Trucking .... C..999 999-9999
City — Yourtown *(G-522)*
Ready Movers .... E..999 999-9999
Anytown *(G-1723)*
TUBING: Steel
Best Steel Tubes Inc .... B..999 999-9999
Yourtown *(G-198)*

Indicates approximate employment figure
A = over 500 employees, B = 251-500
C = 101-250, D = 51-100, E = 20-50
F = 10-19, G = 1-9

Business phone

Geographic Section entry number where full company information appears

See footnotes for symbols and codes identification.
- Refer to the Industrial Product Index preceding this section to locate product headings.

ABRASIVES

Dow Chemical Company .... E 302 368-4169
Newark *(G-10558)*

ACCELERATION INDICATORS & SYSTEM COMPONENTS: Aerospace

Russell Associates Inc .... G 443 992-5777
Newark *(G-11928)*

ACCIDENT INSURANCE CARRIERS

Rbc Insurance Holdings USA Inc .... A 302 651-8356
Wilmington *(G-19351)*

ADHESIVES

Hercules LLC .... E 302 594-5000
Wilmington *(G-17128)*

ADULT DAYCARE CENTERS

Angels Messiahs Foundation .... F 302 365-5516
Bear *(G-36)*
Back Up Ctr .... G 302 758-4500
Newark *(G-9971)*
Beverlys Helping Hands .... G 302 651-9304
Wilmington *(G-14868)*
Christana Care HM Hlth Cmnty S .... B 302 995-8448
Wilmington *(G-15397)*
Gull House Adult Activity .... G 302 226-2160
Lewes *(G-6068)*

ADVERTISING AGENCIES

Accera Digital LLC .... F 877 855-2501
Wilmington *(G-14219)*
Ad Bits Advertising and PR .... G 954 467-8420
Hockessin *(G-5113)*
Adtelligent Inc .... D 833 222-2102
Dover *(G-1721)*
AHM TV Prod Inc .... F 929 332-0350
Dover *(G-1751)*
Asombro Extremo LLC .... G 305 495-1471
Wilmington *(G-14588)*
Bayshore Communications Inc .... F 302 737-2164
Newark *(G-9995)*
Beholder Agency LLC .... F 302 455-2451
Newark *(G-10011)*
Chilay Inc .... G 302 559-6014
Newark *(G-10201)*
Comrade Technologies Inc .... G 888 575-1225
Lewes *(G-5855)*
Cool Nerds Marketing Inc .... F 302 304-3440
Wilmington *(G-15629)*
Duration Media LLC .... G 917 283-5971
Wilmington *(G-16221)*
E Business Pages LLC .... G 302 504-4403
Wilmington *(G-16236)*
Epic Marketing Cons Corp .... E 302 285-9790
Middletown *(G-7105)*
Famous Wsi Results .... G 302 407-0430
New Castle *(G-9118)*
From Top Ltd .... G 310 626-0090
Middletown *(G-7143)*
High Ground Creative LLC .... G 302 505-1367
Dover *(G-2678)*
Highland Consulting Group Inc .... G 301 408-0600
Bethany Beach *(G-607)*
Inbound Ignite LLC .... G 866 314-4499
Dover *(G-2725)*
Industrial Training Cons Inc .... E 302 266-6100
Newark *(G-11016)*
Inflection Associates Inc .... G 484 678-7915
Wilmington *(G-17325)*
Lead Economy LLC .... E 914 355-1671
Dover *(G-2918)*
Marketing Plus LLC .... G 205 952-6602
Dover *(G-3021)*
Mc Creative Group .... F 302 348-8977
Millsboro *(G-8370)*
Mediasurfer Inc .... G 814 300-8335
Wilmington *(G-18247)*
Netskyads Media LLC .... F 302 476-2277
Lewes *(G-6309)*
Popsycle LLC .... G 202 831-0211
Newark *(G-11713)*
Promo Marketing .... G 302 324-2650
New Castle *(G-9499)*
Real Entrepreneur Inc .... E 989 300-0975
Wilmington *(G-19366)*
Remline Corp .... E 302 737-7228
Newark *(G-11850)*
Sasquatch Creative LLC .... G 302 502-3105
Wilmington *(G-19674)*
Sem Revival LLC .... F 302 600-1497
Wilmington *(G-19748)*
Sevenshopper LLC .... G 302 516-7150
Wilmington *(G-19770)*
Simplymiddle LLC .... G 302 217-3460
Wilmington *(G-19841)*
Springboard Inc .... G 302 607-2580
Newark *(G-12075)*
Status Intl LLC DBA Sttus Brnd .... G 202 290-6387
Wilmington *(G-20037)*
Tapp Networks LLC .... G 302 222-3384
Rehoboth Beach *(G-12989)*
Target Markets LLC .... E 302 268-1010
Wilmington *(G-20224)*
Top Rated Media Inc .... G 888 550-9273
Wilmington *(G-20355)*
Upbound Group Inc .... G 302 734-2094
Dover *(G-3756)*
Vrtii Corporation .... G 703 401-8963
Lewes *(G-6611)*
Young & Rubicam LLC .... F 302 888-3450
Wilmington *(G-20932)*

ADVERTISING AGENCIES: Consultants

Adapex LLC .... E 718 618-9982
Wilmington *(G-14251)*
Aloysius Butlr Clark Assoc Inc .... D 302 655-1552
Wilmington *(G-14390)*
Beanstock Media Inc .... E 415 912-1530
Wilmington *(G-14804)*
Cohesive Strategies Inc .... E 302 429-9120
Wilmington *(G-15520)*
Convention Coach .... G 302 335-5459
Magnolia *(G-6735)*
Delaware Design Company .... G 302 737-9700
Newark *(G-10435)*
Digital Generation Inc .... E 302 368-0002
Newark *(G-10529)*
Grind or Starve LLC .... G 302 322-1679
Wilmington *(G-16981)*
Jay Gundel and Associates Inc .... G 302 658-1674
Wilmington *(G-17500)*
K F Dunn & Associates .... F 302 328-3347
Wilmington *(G-17630)*
Koncordia Group LLC .... E 302 427-1350
Wilmington *(G-17746)*
Levines Enterprises LLC .... F 203 212-8441
Dover *(G-2932)*
Lifetour Solutions LLC .... F 215 964-5000
Wilmington *(G-17906)*
LLC Cutler Parrish .... G 609 744-9871
Middletown *(G-7311)*

ADVERTISING AGENCIES: Consultants

Marquis Dorsey LLC................................ F 832 693-0260
  Middletown *(G-7329)*
Miller-Mauro Group Inc......................... G 302 426-6565
  Wilmington *(G-18366)*
Moscova Enterprises Inc...................... F 347 973-2522
  Wilmington *(G-18460)*
Paragon Design Inc............................... F 302 292-1523
  Newark *(G-11623)*
Pear Media LLC..................................... E 505 932-6555
  Lewes *(G-6358)*
Shiny Agency LLC................................. G 302 384-6494
  Wilmington *(G-19801)*
Shor Associates Inc............................... G 302 764-1701
  Wilmington *(G-19809)*
U2r Inc... F 609 792-6575
  Wilmington *(G-20487)*
Unified Companies Inc.......................... G 866 936-0515
  Wilmington *(G-20509)*
Wh2p Inc... G 302 530-6555
  Wilmington *(G-20753)*
Z&M Enterprises LLC............................ E 302 384-1205
  Wilmington *(G-20944)*

ADVERTISING DISPLAY PRDTS

Loyalty Is Earned Inc............................. G 347 606-6383
  Wilmington *(G-18015)*

ADVERTISING REPRESENTATIVES: Electronic Media

Mediastreet LLC.................................... G 800 308-6579
  Newark *(G-11373)*
Social Work Helper Pbc........................ G 302 233-7422
  Dover *(G-3586)*
Staysaf 3 LLC....................................... G 305 699-1454
  Wilmington *(G-20041)*
Tjs & Associates LLC............................ E 302 563-5593
  Middletown *(G-7647)*
Yield Nexus LLC................................... F 308 380-3788
  Dover *(G-3887)*

ADVERTISING REPRESENTATIVES: Printed Media

Emagination Store USA Inc................... G 302 884-6746
  Wilmington *(G-16386)*

ADVERTISING SPECIALTIES, WHOLESALE

Adventum LLC...................................... G 518 620-1441
  Wilmington *(G-14288)*
Avenue 121... G 302 354-1839
  Middletown *(G-6890)*
Convention Coach................................. G 302 335-5459
  Magnolia *(G-6735)*
Creative Promotions.............................. G 302 697-7896
  Camden *(G-809)*
Daikin Comfort Tech Mfg LP................. G 302 894-1010
  Newark *(G-10380)*
Diamond State Promotions................... G 302 999-1900
  Wilmington *(G-16056)*
Digitalzone Inc...................................... E 646 771-6969
  Lewes *(G-5918)*
East Coast Swag................................... G 302 628-2674
  Seaford *(G-13167)*
Joseph W Small Associates Inc............ F
  Wilmington *(G-17588)*
LC Distributors Inc................................ G 484 326-9805
  Claymont *(G-1212)*
New Image Inc...................................... G 302 738-6824
  Newark *(G-11523)*
P&A River Gallery Promotion................ G 302 947-1805
  Lewes *(G-6344)*

Promotion Zone LLC............................. G 302 832-8565
  Newark *(G-11763)*
Remline Corp.. E 302 737-7228
  Newark *(G-11850)*
Stamford Screen Printing Inc................ G 302 654-2442
  Newark *(G-20008)*
Tyrant Sportsgear Inc............................ G 302 530-3410
  Wilmington *(G-20482)*
Zuminex Inc... G 302 325-3200
  New Castle *(G-9700)*

ADVERTISING SVCS: Direct Mail

Hibbert Company.................................. G 609 394-7500
  Historic New Castle *(G-5004)*
Joseph J Sheeran Inc........................... E 302 324-0200
  New Castle *(G-9266)*
Marketing Resources Inc...................... G 302 855-9209
  Georgetown *(G-4418)*
Money Mailer of Delaware.................... F 302 235-7262
  Newark *(G-11440)*
Money Mailer Tri Counties.................... G 240 832-1340
  Selbyville *(G-13579)*
Provide LLC.. E 302 391-1200
  Newark *(G-11767)*
Trimark Inc.. G 302 322-2143
  Historic New Castle *(G-5092)*

ADVERTISING SVCS: Display

Cyclops Net Inc..................................... G 844 979-0222
  Camden *(G-812)*
Powers Interactive Digital LLC.............. G 267 334-6306
  Lewes *(G-6385)*
U Transit Inc.. G 302 227-1197
  Rehoboth Beach *(G-13000)*

ADVERTISING SVCS: Transit

Gotshadeonline Inc............................... G 302 832-8468
  Bear *(G-252)*

AGENTS, BROKERS & BUREAUS: Personal Service

Alixpartners LLP................................... F 302 824-7139
  Wilmington *(G-14359)*
Alpha Comm LLC.................................. F 302 784-0645
  Bear *(G-29)*
American-Eurasian Exch Co LLC.......... G 202 701-4009
  Wilmington *(G-14445)*
ARC Falcon I Inc................................... G 302 636-5401
  Wilmington *(G-14526)*
At Systems Atlantic Inc......................... G 302 762-5444
  Wilmington *(G-14612)*
Axalta Coating Systems LLC................ G 925 838-9876
  Wilmington *(G-14678)*
Bill Torbert.. F 302 734-9804
  Smyrna *(G-13661)*
Digital Interxion Holding LLC................ F 737 281-0101
  Wilmington *(G-16066)*
Domian International Svc LLC.............. G 804 837-3616
  Smyrna *(G-13711)*
Du Pont Foreign Sales Corp.................. E 302 774-1000
  Wilmington *(G-16191)*
Federal Business Systems Co.............. D 877 489-2111
  Wilmington *(G-16567)*
Forum To Advnce Mnrties In Eng......... E 302 777-3254
  Wilmington *(G-16697)*
ICS America Inc.................................... F 215 979-1620
  Wilmington *(G-17259)*
INSTABASE INC................................... F 628 261-7600
  Dover *(G-2739)*
Legend Enterprises LLC....................... G 267 278-9892
  Bear *(G-343)*

Medusind Solutions Inc......................... B 800 250-7063
  Newark *(G-11379)*
Oak Lane Court Associates LP............. F 302 764-6450
  Wilmington *(G-18726)*
Polyjohn Acquisition LLC...................... G 800 292-1305
  Wilmington *(G-19114)*
South Wellington LLC........................... G 954 736-7418
  Georgetown *(G-4517)*
Sovereign Dealer Finance Inc............... G 302 691-6139
  Wilmington *(G-19942)*
Spec Simple Inc.................................... F 212 352-2002
  Historic New Castle *(G-5075)*
Stora Central LLC................................. E 929 273-0505
  Wilmington *(G-20083)*

AGRICULTURAL CREDIT INSTITUTIONS

American Finance LLC.......................... D 302 674-0365
  Harrington *(G-4727)*

AGRICULTURAL EQPT: Clippers, Animal, Hand Or Electric

Macknyfe Specialties............................ G 302 239-4904
  Hockessin *(G-5289)*

AGRICULTURAL EQPT: Irrigation Eqpt, Self-Propelled

Wilmington... G 302 357-4509
  Wilmington *(G-20807)*

AGRICULTURAL EQPT: Tractors, Farm

Newark Kubota Inc................................ F 302 365-6000
  Newark *(G-11540)*

AGRICULTURAL EQPT: Turf & Grounds Eqpt

Turfhound Inc.. G 215 783-8143
  Wilmington *(G-20461)*

AGRICULTURAL MACHINERY & EQPT: Wholesalers

AG Industrial Inc................................... G 888 289-1779
  Dover *(G-1737)*
Atlantic Tractor LLC.............................. E 302 653-8536
  Clayton *(G-1351)*
Baxter Farms Inc................................... G 302 856-1818
  Georgetown *(G-4223)*
Hoober Inc... F 302 629-3075
  Seaford *(G-13216)*
Northeast Agri Systems Inc.................. G 302 875-1886
  Laurel *(G-5570)*
Taylor and Messick Inc......................... E 302 398-3729
  Harrington *(G-4839)*
Willard Agri Service Greenw................. G 302 349-4100
  Farmington *(G-3936)*

AIR CLEANING SYSTEMS

Ptm Manufacturing LLC........................ G 302 455-9733
  Historic New Castle *(G-5056)*

AIR CONDITIONING & VENTILATION EQPT & SPLYS: Wholesales

Delmarva Refrigeration Inc................... G 302 846-2727
  Delmar *(G-1588)*
Greenberg Supply Co Inc...................... E 302 656-4496
  Wilmington *(G-16970)*

AIR CONDITIONING EQPT

Omega Industries Inc............................ G 302 734-3835
  Dover *(G-3224)*

PRODUCTS & SERVICES SECTION

AMUSEMENT & RECREATION SVCS: Art Gallery, Commercial

AIR CONDITIONING REPAIR SVCS

Berry Refrigeration Co................................ E 302 733-0933
  Newark *(G-10025)*
Burns & McBride Inc................................... D 302 656-5110
  New Castle *(G-8901)*
Commercial Equipment Service............. G 302 475-6682
  Wilmington *(G-15547)*
Jam Air LLC... G 302 270-8236
  Dover *(G-2767)*
Williams Appliancee................................... F 302 656-8581
  Wilmington *(G-20797)*

AIR DUCT CLEANING SVCS

Colonial Cleaning Services Inc.................. G 302 660-2067
  Wilmington *(G-15534)*
Ducts R US LLC.. G 302 284-4006
  Felton *(G-3962)*

AIR PURIFICATION EQPT

Airlock389 Inc... G 213 393-1785
  Lewes *(G-5667)*
Aura Smart Air Inc..................................... G 847 909-5822
  Wilmington *(G-14642)*
Planet Iot Inc.. F 314 585-9924
  Middletown *(G-7455)*

AIRCRAFT & AEROSPACE FLIGHT INSTRUMENTS & GUIDANCE SYSTEMS

Pasadena Digital Inc.................................. G 310 774-6740
  Dover *(G-3277)*

AIRCRAFT & HEAVY EQPT REPAIR SVCS

Arteaga Properties LLC............................. G 808 339-6906
  Wilmington *(G-14562)*

AIRCRAFT ASSEMBLY PLANTS

Central Kansas Arospc Mfg LLC................ C 314 406-6550
  Wilmington *(G-15309)*
Dassault Falcon Jet - Wilmington Corp. C 302 322-7000
  New Castle *(G-9000)*
Grindstone Aviation LLC............................ G 302 324-1993
  New Castle *(G-9181)*
Pats Aircraft LLC.. D 855 236-1638
  Georgetown *(G-4456)*
Santos Aircraft LLC.................................... G 302 608-6637
  New Castle *(G-9552)*

AIRCRAFT CONTROL SYSTEMS:

Tesla Industries Inc.................................... F 302 324-8910
  Historic New Castle *(G-5083)*

AIRCRAFT DEALERS

Avacore LLC... G 302 327-8830
  Wilmington *(G-14661)*

AIRCRAFT ENGINES & ENGINE PARTS: Research & Development, Mfr

Greenwich Aerogroup Inc.......................... F 302 834-5400
  Middletown *(G-7178)*

AIRCRAFT ENGINES & PARTS

General Electric Company......................... C 302 631-1300
  Newark *(G-10819)*
Honeywell International Inc...................... G 302 322-4071
  New Castle *(G-9220)*
Rtx Corporation... G 800 227-7437
  Historic New Castle *(G-5064)*
Santos Aircraft LLC.................................... G 302 608-6637
  New Castle *(G-9552)*

AIRCRAFT EQPT & SPLYS WHOLESALERS

Delta Engineering Corporation................. E 302 325-9320
  New Castle *(G-9045)*
Portable Pilot Solutions LLC...................... G 302 644-2775
  Milton *(G-8687)*

AIRCRAFT MAINTENANCE & REPAIR SVCS

Aero Enterprises Inc.................................. G 302 378-1396
  Townsend *(G-13953)*
Aircrafters Inc.. G 302 777-5000
  Wilmington *(G-14337)*
Georgetown Air Services........................... G 302 855-2355
  Georgetown *(G-4333)*
Georgetown Air Services LLC................... F 302 855-2355
  Georgetown *(G-4334)*

AIRCRAFT PARTS & AUXILIARY EQPT: Aircraft Training Eqpt

Nakuuruq Solutions................................... G 302 526-2223
  Dover *(G-3148)*

AIRCRAFT PARTS & AUXILIARY EQPT: Assemblies, Fuselage

Pats Aircraft LLC.. D 855 236-1638
  Georgetown *(G-4456)*

AIRCRAFT PARTS & AUXILIARY EQPT: Body Assemblies & Parts

Avacore LLC... G 302 327-8830
  Wilmington *(G-14661)*
Nighthawk Aircraft LLC.............................. G 703 994-0523
  Wilmington *(G-18648)*

AIRCRAFT PARTS & AUXILIARY EQPT: Research & Development, Mfr

Envoy Flight Systems Inc.......................... G 302 738-1788
  Newark *(G-10657)*

AIRCRAFT PARTS & EQPT, NEC

Advantage Futuretech Company.............. G 347 592-5667
  Lewes *(G-5662)*
Barrel Fuel Technologies Inc.................... G 832 405-4806
  Dover *(G-1874)*
Dassault Falcon Jet - Wilmington Corp. C 302 322-7000
  New Castle *(G-9000)*
Exploration Systems & Tech..................... G 302 335-3911
  Wilmington *(G-16506)*
Global Air Strategy Inc.............................. G 302 229-5889
  Newark *(G-10849)*

AIRCRAFT PARTS WHOLESALERS

Auric Jets LLC.. G 866 887-5414
  Wilmington *(G-14644)*
Dassault Aircraft Svcs Corp...................... C 302 322-7000
  New Castle *(G-8999)*
Dimo Corp... E 302 324-8100
  New Castle *(G-9056)*
GA Telesis LLC... F 845 356-8390
  Wilmington *(G-16788)*

AIRCRAFT UPHOLSTERY REPAIR SVCS

Pats Aircraft LLC.. D 855 236-1638
  Georgetown *(G-4456)*
Rayco Auto & Marine Uphl Inc................. G 302 323-8844
  Hockessin *(G-5356)*

AIRCRAFT: Airplanes, Fixed Or Rotary Wing

Boeing Company.. G 302 735-2922
  Dover *(G-1959)*

AIRLINE TRAINING

Favored Childcare Academy Inc............... G 302 698-1266
  Dover *(G-2488)*

AIRPORTS, FLYING FIELDS & SVCS

Bootcamp Helicopters LLC........................ G 301 717-5455
  Middletown *(G-6931)*
Dumont Aviation Group Inc...................... G 302 777-1003
  New Castle *(G-9067)*
Dumont Aviation Group Inc...................... F 302 777-1003
  New Castle *(G-9068)*
East Coast Aviation LLC............................ G 302 650-9889
  Clayton *(G-1364)*
Lowes Airport (fa77).................................. G 813 366-7655
  Wilmington *(G-18012)*
Savaren Corporate Arcft Svcs.................. G 443 207-1372
  New Castle *(G-9553)*
Wingfield & Associates Inc...................... G 626 252-6586
  Wilmington *(G-20858)*

ALARMS: Fire

Wayman Fire Protection Inc..................... C 302 994-5757
  Wilmington *(G-20693)*

ALUMINUM PRDTS

UACJ Trading & Processing Amer........... G 312 636-5941
  Wilmington *(G-20488)*

AMBULANCE SVCS

Air Methods Corporation........................... E 302 363-3168
  Georgetown *(G-4203)*
Bill M Douthat Jr.. G 407 977-2273
  Lewes *(G-5765)*
Cft Ambulance Service Inc........................ G 302 984-2255
  Bear *(G-94)*
Christiana Care Health Sys Inc................ C 302 623-3970
  New Castle *(G-8938)*
Christiana Fire Company.......................... G 302 834-2433
  Bear *(G-100)*
Delaware Cy Vlntr Fire Co No 1............... E 302 834-9336
  Delaware City *(G-1538)*
Felton Community Fire Co Inc................. E 302 284-9552
  Felton *(G-3971)*
Hart To Heart Ambulance......................... G 302 697-9395
  Lewes *(G-6080)*
Lifenet Inc.. G 973 698-6881
  Lewes *(G-6207)*
Maxicare Ambulance Services.................. G 302 990-3777
  Newark *(G-11360)*
Mid Atlantic Care LLC................................ G 302 266-8306
  Wilmington *(G-18332)*
Transcare... G 302 322-2454
  New Castle *(G-9634)*

AMMUNITION: Small Arms

Du Pont Chem Enrgy Oprtons Inc............ C 302 774-1000
  Wilmington *(G-16188)*

AMUSEMENT & RECREATION SVCS: Arcades

Fun Adventures LLC................................... G 302 223-5182
  Christiana *(G-996)*

AMUSEMENT & RECREATION SVCS: Art Gallery, Commercial

American Art Tatttoo................................. G 484 889-1663
  Newark *(G-9842)*
Bones Innovations In Art.......................... G 302 430-3592
  Laurel *(G-5470)*
Brandywine Art... G 302 234-7874
  Hockessin *(G-5140)*

Employee Codes: A=Over 500 employees, B=251-500
C=101-250, D=51-100, E=20-50, F=10-19, G=1-9

2024 Harris Directory of Delaware Businesses

AMUSEMENT & RECREATION SVCS: Art Gallery, Commercial

Cobalt Art Studio .... G 201 819-9087
  Milton (G-8587)
Gallery 37 .... G 413 297-2690
  Milford (G-7906)
Its my Art LLC .... G 302 750-1380
  Claymont (G-1191)
Lhr-Fine Arts Studios .... G 302 981-8553
  Wilmington (G-17890)
Linda Celestian Art Studio .... G 302 364-0278
  Wilmington (G-17919)
Rittenhouse Sq Fine Art Show .... G 610 299-1343
  New Castle (G-9535)
Sarahs Art Scene .... G 302 792-2631
  Wilmington (G-19671)
Works of Art .... G 302 562-3597
  New Castle (G-9690)

AMUSEMENT & RECREATION SVCS: Gambling & Lottery Svcs

Harrington Raceway Inc .... D 302 398-5346
  Harrington (G-4780)

AMUSEMENT & RECREATION SVCS: Golf Club, Membership

Adkins Management Company .... F 302 684-3000
  Milford (G-7760)
Bayside Resort Golf Club .... F 302 436-3400
  Selbyville (G-13471)
Bear Trap Sales .... G 302 541-5454
  Ocean View (G-12474)
Brandywine Country Club .... E 302 478-4604
  Wilmington (G-15053)
Forewinds Hospitality LLC .... F 302 368-6640
  Newark (G-10763)
Hunt Vicmead Club .... E 302 655-3336
  Wilmington (G-17233)
Hunt Vicmead Club .... E 302 655-9601
  Wilmington (G-17234)
Mrb Golf LLC .... G 302 368-7008
  Newark (G-11465)
Quail Associates Inc .... E 302 697-4660
  Camden Wyoming (G-966)
Salt Pond Associates .... E 302 539-2750
  Bethany Beach (G-638)
Silverside Club Inc .... G 302 478-4568
  Talleyville (G-13946)

AMUSEMENT & RECREATION SVCS: Physical Fitness Instruction

Cowries & Calabash LLC .... G 917 727-8940
  Dover (G-2149)
Emitt LLC .... F 302 757-2353
  Bear (G-201)
Fitar Inc .... G 416 347-8099
  Middletown (G-7135)
IH Technologies (iht) LLC .... G 718 679-2613
  Wilmington (G-17268)
Planke App LLC .... G 607 287-0794
  Wilmington (G-19068)
Soflete LLC .... G 773 983-4692
  Rehoboth Beach (G-12966)
V Power Fit Inc .... G 832 743-7116
  Middletown (G-7678)
Weltri Inc .... F 818 962-8834
  Dover (G-3833)

AMUSEMENT & RECREATION SVCS: Recreation Center

City of Newark .... E 302 366-7060
  Newark (G-10245)

Young MNS Chrstn Assn Wlmngton .... C 302 709-9622
  Newark (G-12422)

AMUSEMENT & RECREATION SVCS: Recreation SVCS

Blue Falls Grove Inc .... G 610 926-4017
  Newark (G-10057)
Bluecoast Rehoboth .... G 302 278-7395
  Rehoboth Beach (G-12646)
G Rehoboth .... E 302 278-7677
  Rehoboth Beach (G-12764)
Jamaican MI Hungry .... G 302 287-3337
  Wilmington (G-17474)
Meadowwood .... G 302 286-7004
  Newark (G-11370)
Plaza Mexico .... G 301 643-5701
  Millsboro (G-8430)
Restarant Actn Md-Tlantic Whse .... G 302 462-6678
  Dagsboro (G-1498)
Young Mens Christian Associat .... F 302 472-9622
  Wilmington (G-20939)

AMUSEMENT ARCADES

Midway Slots & Simulcast .... G 302 398-4920
  Harrington (G-4804)
Orbit Research LLC .... G 302 683-1063
  Wilmington (G-18815)
Seaside Amusements Inc .... G 302 227-1921
  Rehoboth Beach (G-12953)

AMUSEMENT PARKS

Jungle Jims Adventure World .... D 302 227-8444
  Rehoboth Beach (G-12812)

ANALYZERS: Moisture

Ametek Inc .... D 302 456-4400
  Newark (G-9851)

ANALYZERS: Network

Pulsar360 Corp .... E 855 578-5727
  Newark (G-11771)

ANIMAL FEED & SUPPLEMENTS: Livestock & Poultry

Green Recovery Tech LLC .... G 302 317-0062
  Historic New Castle (G-4998)
Simmons Animal Nutrition Inc .... F 302 337-8223
  Bridgeville (G-766)
Simmons Animal Nutrition Inc .... D 302 337-5500
  Bridgeville (G-767)
Southern States Coop Inc .... E 302 732-6651
  Dagsboro (G-1507)
Southern States Coop Inc .... G 302 629-7991
  Seaford (G-13410)
Unique Biotech Inc .... G 888 478-2799
  Lewes (G-6588)

ANIMAL FEED: Wholesalers

B Diamond Feed Company .... G 302 697-7576
  Camden Wyoming (G-915)

ANIMAL FOOD & SUPPLEMENTS: Dog & Cat

Petmex Company LLC .... G 800 829-4933
  Dover (G-3306)

ANIMAL FOOD & SUPPLEMENTS: Feed Premixes

Best Veterinary Solutions Inc .... F 302 934-1109
  Millsboro (G-8195)

Springhaus LLC .... F 302 397-5261
  Wilmington (G-19977)

ANIMAL FOOD & SUPPLEMENTS: Feed Supplements

Bi-State Feeders LLC .... G 302 398-3408
  Harrington (G-4740)
Natures Rule LLC .... G 518 961-5196
  Wilmington (G-18559)

ANIMAL FOOD & SUPPLEMENTS: Livestock

B Diamond Feed Company .... G 302 697-7576
  Camden Wyoming (G-915)
Jbs Souderton Inc .... G 302 629-0725
  Seaford (G-13231)

ANTIBIOTICS

Glaxosmthkline Hldngs Amrcas I .... C 302 984-6932
  Wilmington (G-16882)

ANTIBIOTICS, PACKAGED

Anp Technologies Inc .... E 302 283-1730
  Newark (G-9875)

ANTIQUE REPAIR & RESTORATION SVCS, EXC FURNITURE & AUTOS

Crystal Kleen Inc .... G 302 326-1140
  New Castle (G-8990)

APPAREL DESIGNERS: Commercial

Be Blessed Design Group LLC .... G 302 561-3793
  Bear (G-59)
Envision It Publications LLC .... G 800 329-9411
  Bear (G-204)

APPAREL FILLING MATERIALS: Cotton Waste, Kapok/Related Matl

Be Blessed Design Group LLC .... G 302 561-3793
  Bear (G-59)

APPLIANCES, HOUSEHOLD OR COIN OPERATED: Laundry Dryers

Laundry Love Services LLC .... G 302 367-7075
  Wilmington (G-17822)
Ultra Modern Laundry Svcs LLC .... G 302 533-8596
  Wilmington (G-20500)

APPLIANCES: Major, Cooking

Arovo US Inc .... E 952 290-0799
  Dover (G-1818)
My Life Care LLC .... D 302 760-9248
  Dover (G-3138)

APPLIANCES: Small, Electric

Arovo US Inc .... E 952 290-0799
  Dover (G-1818)
Urbie Inc .... G 302 572-4243
  Dover (G-3761)

APPLICATIONS SOFTWARE PROGRAMMING

4BOA LLC .... E 323 747-7771
  Claymont (G-1012)
6clicks Inc .... F 925 699-6304
  Middletown (G-6818)
Advertised Media Inc .... G 415 967-8100
  Wilmington (G-14289)
Aetho LLC .... F 215 821-7290
  Dover (G-1733)
Alias Technology LLC .... G 302 856-9488
  Georgetown (G-4205)

PRODUCTS & SERVICES SECTION

APPLICATIONS SOFTWARE PROGRAMMING

Apollo Software Inc.................................... G 800 992-0847
  Newark (G-9887)
Appointiv Inc... G 415 877-4339
  Middletown (G-6869)
Arnab Mobility Inc..................................... F 774 316-6767
  Newark (G-9906)
Atlan Inc.. G 650 288-6722
  Wilmington (G-14626)
Atlas Software LLC.................................... F 312 576-2247
  Newark (G-9939)
Axa Zara LLC... G 513 206-4606
  Lewes (G-5730)
Backdoor Global Inc.................................. G 386 465-2646
  Middletown (G-6900)
Bhapi Inc.. G 859 475-1924
  Wilmington (G-14873)
Bigcloud Solutions Inc............................... G 917 972-6891
  Newark (G-10032)
Bipgo Inc.. F 708 586-9016
  Middletown (G-6921)
Black Math Labs Inc.................................. G 858 349-9446
  Dover (G-1945)
Botix Inc... G 239 600-8116
  Middletown (G-6933)
Capsa Solutions LLC.................................. G 800 437-6633
  Dover (G-2026)
Carebnb Inc.. G 904 303-6825
  Middletown (G-6956)
Cloudarmee Ltd... F 714 673-8104
  Wilmington (G-15493)
Coremond LLC... G 267 797-7090
  Dover (G-2138)
Cryptofi Inc... E 312 813-7188
  Dover (G-2166)
Diversion Company Inc.............................. G 415 800-4136
  Dover (G-2307)
Dori Inc.. F 858 344-8699
  Dover (G-2326)
Dpsg - Digtion Pymnt Systems G............... F 201 755-0912
  Wilmington (G-16160)
Dr Hivey Corp.. G 580 670-2046
  Dover (G-2373)
Ecom Technologies LLC............................. F 424 362-5155
  Dover (G-2416)
Edge Case LLC... E 302 207-1291
  Middletown (G-7083)
Ehelp Health Corporation.......................... G 404 964-0906
  Camden (G-827)
Encompass Corporation US Inc................. G 212 523-0340
  Wilmington (G-16406)
Engati Technologies Inc............................. G 215 368-3551
  Wilmington (G-16422)
Etlgr LLC.. G 302 204-0596
  Wilmington (G-16475)
Evervault Inc.. F 213 527-8608
  Wilmington (G-16490)
Extenship LLC.. G 302 400-5480
  Wilmington (G-16510)
Fast Af Inc... G 415 770-5235
  Newark (G-10715)
Finnchat Inc... G 517 258-6991
  Middletown (G-7128)
Funfull Inc.. F 888 386-3855
  Delmar (G-1597)
Galaxyworks LLC.. F 404 894-8703
  Dover (G-2555)
Garri Inc... G 319 538-4071
  Newark (G-10811)
Gbc Business Group LLC........................... G 970 644-6319
  Wilmington (G-16823)
Gmetri Inc.. F 704 260-6116
  Lewes (G-6041)

Gr Dispatch Inc.. G 888 985-3440
  Lewes (G-6050)
Greet 26 Inc.. G 310 601-2648
  Camden (G-841)
Iconico LLC.. G 650 681-9211
  Claymont (G-1183)
Itg Cloud Software LLC.............................. E 786 708-6560
  Wilmington (G-17433)
Joyn Experiences Inc................................. G 214 437-8349
  Wilmington (G-17595)
Kalanaai LLC.. G 516 701-3977
  Wilmington (G-17636)
Korsgy Technologies LLC........................... G 302 504-6201
  Wilmington (G-17748)
Krayo Inc.. G 415 851-6250
  Wilmington (G-17753)
Laconic Innovations Co.............................. F 302 501-6069
  Dover (G-2896)
Lambdatest Inc.. D 678 701-3618
  Wilmington (G-17791)
Leadific Solutions LLC............................... G 866 265-0771
  Dover (G-2920)
Legit Global Inc... G 661 444-9085
  Newark (G-11243)
Lemonface Technologies Corp.................. G 844 615-3666
  Lewes (G-6189)
Letterhead Inc... G 305 988-0808
  Claymont (G-1216)
Liferithms Inc... F 770 885-6565
  Wilmington (G-17903)
Lightrun Inc.. E 646 453-6616
  Wilmington (G-17909)
Lutinx Inc... F 718 502-6961
  Lewes (G-6229)
Meaningteam Inc....................................... F 213 669-5804
  Dover (G-3047)
Mh-Teq LLC.. G 302 897-2182
  Wilmington (G-18301)
Mindspaceweb LLC.................................... G 302 360-8744
  Claymont (G-1238)
Mintflint Inc.. G 236 991-3735
  Wilmington (G-18381)
Nextera Robotic Systems Inc.................... F 617 899-7323
  Middletown (G-7404)
Ngrow Inc... F 603 764-7274
  Claymont (G-1252)
Niebex International Inc............................ F 415 735-4718
  Wilmington (G-18647)
Nole-Sec Inc.. F 561 693-9934
  Wilmington (G-18663)
Nomadic Capital LLC................................. G 650 441-5796
  Wilmington (G-18665)
Nursecareai Inc.. F 717 439-0314
  Wilmington (G-18718)
One System Incorporated......................... F 888 311-1110
  Wilmington (G-18784)
Orgnostic Inc.. E 617 871-9987
  Newark (G-11600)
Pintalk Inc.. G 844 386-0178
  Newark (G-11694)
Power Financial Wellness Inc.................... G 313 413-2345
  Wilmington (G-19137)
Prisma Holding Inc.................................... E 903 480-4880
  Wilmington (G-19199)
Pullable Inc.. F 302 574-6379
  Wilmington (G-19253)
Qodebotics LLC... G 617 312-7733
  Dover (G-3405)
Quality Unit LLC.. F 888 257-8754
  Wilmington (G-19285)
Quavo Inc... D 484 257-9846
  Wilmington (G-19291)

Quiver Finance Inc..................................... G 302 803-6006
  Wilmington (G-19298)
Reach Apps Inc.. G 707 812-0285
  Dover (G-3429)
Real Ones Inc... G 408 857-0262
  Wilmington (G-19369)
Roundrobin Corporation............................ G 212 634-9193
  Dover (G-3487)
Scanpoint Inc... G 603 429-0777
  Wilmington (G-19696)
Screen Zone Enterprises LLC.................... E 302 316-0705
  Dover (G-3521)
Scrubmoney Inc... G 240 671-5379
  Wilmington (G-19716)
Sendlink Inc... G 650 505-5299
  Middletown (G-7551)
Senhasegura USA LLC............................... G 469 620-7643
  Lewes (G-6458)
Seven Tech LLC... G 302 464-6488
  Middletown (G-7556)
Simbiose Inc.. D 708 459-8068
  Newark (G-12008)
Simpliigence Inc.. D 404 528-7646
  Dover (G-3563)
Sirqil LLC.. F 213 204-9333
  Dover (G-3569)
Skygate Inc.. G 310 601-4201
  Newark (G-12027)
SM Technomine Inc................................... F 312 492-4386
  Wilmington (G-19870)
Smarketics Inc... G 929 265-0177
  Middletown (G-7576)
Smart Invest Yam LLC............................... G 302 721-5278
  Wilmington (G-19878)
Sniper Labs Inc.. F 925 321-0931
  Wilmington (G-19900)
Social Africa Inc... E 763 670-3452
  Dover (G-3583)
Social Keyboard Inc................................... F 650 519-8383
  Dover (G-3585)
Social Wonder Inc..................................... F 646 419-8009
  Wilmington (G-19908)
Socradar Cyber Intelligence..................... F 571 249-4598
  Middletown (G-7584)
Soutron Global Inc..................................... G 760 519-3328
  Middletown (G-7592)
Spiro Health Inc... G 302 645-7400
  Lewes (G-6502)
Squadcast Studios Inc............................... G 916 320-7761
  Wilmington (G-19985)
Sunlight Insur Holdings LLC...................... D 952 808-6312
  Wilmington (G-20132)
Surge Automated Inc................................ G 800 457-9713
  Lewes (G-6526)
Swordfish Security USA Inc....................... F 302 327-8580
  Wilmington (G-20177)
Syncologi LLC... E 408 549-9559
  Lewes (G-6537)
Syncretic Software Inc............................... F 302 762-2600
  Wilmington (G-20186)
Telivity Inc.. F 312 585-8485
  Wilmington (G-20269)
Telorca LLC... G 315 693-8488
  Lewes (G-6549)
Tennr Inc.. G 650 288-8264
  Wilmington (G-20274)
Ternary Inc... E 650 759-5277
  Claymont (G-1309)
Tidy Technologies Inc................................ G 888 788-2445
  Lewes (G-6559)
Tonic Health LLC....................................... F 510 386-2530
  Wilmington (G-20351)

Employee Codes: A=Over 500 employees, B=251-500
C=101-250, D=51-100, E=20-50, F=10-19, G=1-9

APPLICATIONS SOFTWARE PROGRAMMING

Tribute Interactive Inc .... G 302 803-5432
  Wilmington (G-20419)
Unikie Inc .... F 408 839-1920
  Dover (G-3749)
Userway Inc .... D 415 510-9335
  Wilmington (G-20554)
Verifiedly LLC .... G 240 708-9025
  Middletown (G-7686)
Versus Gaming Inc .... G 855 643-9945
  Wilmington (G-20596)
Vidalytics .... F 303 500-5715
  Milton (G-8726)
Virtual Oplossing Pvt Ltd .... G 866 268-0333
  Newark (G-12329)
Voiceloft Inc .... F 678 882-5024
  Middletown (G-7692)
Websays Inc .... G 424 385-9361
  Middletown (G-7713)
Webtrit Inc .... G 954 364-8888
  Lewes (G-6619)
Welcome2city Group Corp .... F 347 897-9941
  Wilmington (G-20718)
Wellford Corporation .... G 302 288-0670
  Dover (G-3830)
Wna Infotech LLC .... E 302 668-5977
  Newark (G-12392)
Workativ Sftwr Solutions LLC .... F 312 375-1062
  Newark (G-12404)
Workforce Cloud Tech Inc .... F 915 800-2362
  Newark (G-12405)
Xcs Corporation .... G 302 514-0600
  Wilmington (G-20916)
Yenaffit Inc .... G 302 650-4818
  Wilmington (G-20926)
Yenasys LLC .... G 302 956-9277
  Middletown (G-7744)
Zeon Enterprises Inc .... F 302 898-7167
  New Castle (G-9698)

APPRAISAL SVCS, EXC REAL ESTATE

S Brown Appraisals LLC .... G 302 672-0694
  Harrington (G-4825)

AQUARIUMS

Premium Aquatics LLC .... G 302 994-7742
  Wilmington (G-19172)

ARBITRATION & CONCILIATION SVCS

Center For Community Justice ...... G 302 424-0890
  Milford (G-7816)

ARCHITECTURAL SVCS

Becker Morgan Group Inc .... E 302 734-7950
  Dover (G-1902)
Brandywine Cad Design Inc .... E 302 478-8334
  Wilmington (G-15047)
Cadrender Inc .... G 302 657-0700
  Wilmington (G-15188)
Delaware Architects LLC .... G 302 491-6047
  Milford (G-7852)
Edc LLC .... G 302 645-0777
  Lewes (G-5948)
Kci Technologies Inc .... E 302 731-9176
  Newark (G-11148)
Krn Architecture LLC .... G 302 536-8576
  Wilmington (G-17758)
Ryan Architecture LLC .... G 302 629-6458
  Seaford (G-13382)
Tevebaugh Associates Inc .... F 302 984-1400
  Wilmington (G-20281)

ARCHITECTURAL SVCS: Engineering

Abha Architects Inc .... E 302 658-6426
  Wilmington (G-14201)
Architecture Plus PA .... G 302 999-1614
  Wilmington (G-14543)
Balfour Beatty LLC .... G 302 573-3873
  Wilmington (G-14721)
Bernardon LLC .... F 302 622-9550
  Wilmington (G-14848)
Breckstone Group Inc .... G 302 654-3646
  Wilmington (G-15099)
Buck Simpers Archt + Assoc Inc ... F 302 658-9300
  Wilmington (G-15141)
Cooperson Associates LLC .... G 302 655-1105
  Wilmington (G-15633)
Design Collaborative Inc .... G 302 652-4221
  Wilmington (G-16024)
Gilbert Architects Inc .... F 302 449-2492
  Middletown (G-7160)
Homsey Architects Inc .... F 302 656-4491
  Wilmington (G-17192)
J Matthew Pearson LLC .... G 302 834-4595
  Newark (G-11073)
Jaed Corporation .... F 302 832-1652
  Bear (G-295)
Ji DCI Joint Venture 1 .... G 302 652-4221
  Wilmington (G-17543)
Ji DCI Jv-II .... G 302 652-4221
  Wilmington (G-17544)
Montchanin Design Group Inc ..... E 302 652-3008
  Wilmington (G-18421)
Sea Studio Architects .... G 302 364-0821
  Bethany Beach (G-641)
Staikos Associates Architects ...... G 302 764-1678
  Wilmington (G-20004)

ARMATURES: Ind

AC Engineering .... G 215 873-6482
  Bear (G-11)

ART DEALERS & GALLERIES

Nanticoke River Arts Council .... G 302 628-2787
  Seaford (G-13309)
Stuart Kingston Inc .... G 302 227-2524
  Rehoboth Beach (G-12978)

ARTS & CRAFTS SCHOOL

Northeast Early Lrng Ctr LLC ...... G 302 475-7080
  Claymont (G-1255)

ASPHALT & ASPHALT PRDTS

Chemstar Corp .... G 302 465-3175
  Milford (G-7824)

ASPHALT COATINGS & SEALERS

Ipm Inc .... F 302 328-4030
  New Castle (G-9241)
Kings Sealcoating .... G 302 674-1568
  Dover (G-2877)

ASSEMBLING & PACKAGING SVCS: Cosmetic Kits

Scientific USA Inc .... G 425 681-9462
  Wilmington (G-19707)

ASSOCIATION FOR THE HANDICAPPED

Mosaic .... D 302 456-5995
  Newark (G-11455)
Special Olympics Delaware Inc .... F 302 831-4653
  Newark (G-12063)

ASSOCIATIONS: Bar

Barroja Ventures LLC .... G 302 256-0883
  Wilmington (G-14768)
Cooter Brwns Twsted Sthern Kit ... G 302 567-2132
  Rehoboth Beach (G-12701)
Daphne LLC .... G 302 525-6010
  Newark (G-10388)
Delaware State Bar Association ... G 302 658-5279
  Wilmington (G-15970)
Em Beauty Bar Inc .... G 302 525-3933
  Newark (G-10636)
Length Weave Bar .... G 302 502-3171
  Wilmington (G-17875)
Yellowfins .... G 302 381-2569
  Millsboro (G-8510)

ASSOCIATIONS: Business

100 Commerce LLC .... G 302 738-3038
  Newark (G-9702)
African Violet Society-Amer .... G 302 653-6449
  Smyrna (G-13632)
C S C Corporation Texas Inc ...... F 302 636-5440
  Wilmington (G-15176)
CDM Institue .... G 302 482-3234
  Wilmington (G-15292)
Del DOT Canal Dist .... G 410 742-9361
  Dover (G-2209)
Delaware Cmnty Rnvstment Actio .. G 302 298-3250
  Wilmington (G-15886)
Delaware Cnnbis Advcacy Ntwrk .. G 302 404-4208
  Dover (G-2221)
Delaware Department Trnsp .... D 302 577-3278
  Dover (G-2228)
Delaware Div Parks Recreation .... F 302 761-6963
  Wilmington (G-15910)
Delaware Homes Performance .... G 302 233-3917
  Wilmington (G-15929)
Delaware State Farm Bureau Inc .. G 302 697-3183
  Camden (G-817)
Elms Management Association .... G 302 738-5225
  Newark (G-10632)
Healthy To Core .... G 240 506-4202
  Ocean View (G-12521)
Lonnie Wright .... G 302 655-1632
  New Castle (G-9324)
National Barberz Association ...... G 302 365-6169
  Bear (G-389)
Port Lewes Assoc Unit Owner ..... G 302 645-6110
  Lewes (G-6383)
Pp of De .... G 252 393-3691
  Wilmington (G-19139)
Sussex County Volunteer .... G 302 515-3020
  Georgetown (G-4536)
Technology Student Association ... F 302 857-3336
  Dover (G-3662)
UACJ Trading & Processing Amer .. G 312 636-5941
  Wilmington (G-20488)

ASSOCIATIONS: Real Estate Management

A2z Property Management LLC ... G 302 239-6000
  Hockessin (G-5110)
Alex Property Management LLC ... A 302 384-9845
  Dover (G-1761)
Arbor Management LLC .... C 302 764-6450
  Wilmington (G-14524)
Asset Management Alliance .... F 302 656-5238
  Wilmington (G-14591)
Atlas Awaits LLC .... G 724 715-3774
  Dover (G-1849)
Avello Holdings LLC .... G 631 533-2634
  Lewes (G-5725)

PRODUCTS & SERVICES SECTION

AUTO & HOME SUPPLY STORES: Truck Eqpt & Parts

Boston Land Co Mgt Svcs Inc............... G 302 571-0100
  Wilmington *(G-15009)*

Bradford Enterprises Inc..................... G 302 378-0662
  Middletown *(G-6934)*

Brandywine Realty Management........... G 302 656-1058
  Wilmington *(G-15082)*

C and C Management Group LLC........ G 302 946-4179
  Wilmington *(G-15173)*

Capano Management Company............ D 302 737-8056
  Newark *(G-10132)*

Classic Financial LLC.......................... E 302 476-0948
  Middletown *(G-6987)*

Commonwealth Group LLC.................. E 302 472-7200
  Wilmington *(G-15553)*

Cressona Associates LLC................... G 302 792-2737
  Claymont *(G-1103)*

Crystal Holdings Inc............................ D 302 421-5700
  Wilmington *(G-15720)*

Dack Realty Corp................................ G 302 792-2737
  Claymont *(G-1107)*

Dalou Property Management................ F 866 575-9387
  Wilmington *(G-15771)*

Deaton McCue & Co Inc...................... G 302 658-7789
  Hockessin *(G-5177)*

E B D Management Inc........................ G 302 428-1313
  Wilmington *(G-16234)*

Excel Property Management LLC.......... G 302 541-5312
  Millville *(G-8528)*

GM Capital Investments Inc................. G 302 722-0558
  Newark *(G-10854)*

Guardian Property MGT LLC................ F 302 227-7878
  Lewes *(G-6067)*

Kumar Properties LLC......................... G 337 284-5975
  Claymont *(G-1209)*

Lenape Properties MGT Inc................. G 302 426-0200
  Wilmington *(G-17873)*

Lexan Group LLC................................ G 704 900-0190
  Newark *(G-11250)*

Mid-Atlantic Realty Co Inc................... G 302 737-3110
  Newark *(G-11411)*

Milford Housing Development............... F 302 422-8255
  Milford *(G-8001)*

One Hundred West Tenth St................ G 302 651-1469
  Wilmington *(G-18782)*

P R C Management Co Inc................... G 302 475-7643
  Wilmington *(G-18853)*

Panco Management Corporation............ E 302 366-1875
  Newark *(G-11619)*

Panco Management Corporation............ G 302 995-6152
  Wilmington *(G-18870)*

Panco Management Corporation............ G 302 475-9337
  Wilmington *(G-18871)*

Patterson Price.................................... G 302 378-9852
  Wilmington *(G-18914)*

Perpetual Invstments Group LLC........... F 718 795-3394
  Wilmington *(G-18982)*

Reybold Group of Companies Inc......... E 302 832-7100
  Bear *(G-458)*

Robino Management Group Inc............ G 302 633-6001
  Wilmington *(G-19522)*

Signature Property Management........... F 302 212-2381
  Lewes *(G-6468)*

Stephens Management Corp................ G 302 629-4393
  Seaford *(G-13414)*

Viaticum Incorporated.......................... F 302 467-8353
  Wilmington *(G-20607)*

West Home Leasehold LLC.................. F 917 443-7451
  Wilmington *(G-20741)*

White Robbins Company...................... G 302 478-5555
  Wilmington *(G-20767)*

Woodlawn Trustees Incorporated.......... F 302 655-6621
  Wilmington *(G-20884)*

ASSOCIATIONS: Scientists'

American Birding Assn Inc.................... G 302 838-3660
  Delaware City *(G-1531)*

Society For Whole-Body Autorad.......... G 302 369-5240
  Newark *(G-12049)*

ASSOCIATIONS: Trade

Aaert Inc... G 302 765-3510
  Wilmington *(G-14184)*

Brucke Inc... G 302 319-9614
  Wilmington *(G-15136)*

Builders & Remodelers Assoc De......... G 302 678-1520
  Dover *(G-1989)*

Center Meeting Associates LLC........... G 302 740-9700
  Wilmington *(G-15305)*

Cherrington Service Corp..................... G 302 777-4064
  Wilmington *(G-15363)*

Delaware Credit Union Leag Inc........... G 302 322-9341
  Newark *(G-10429)*

Delaware Restaurant Assn................... G 302 738-2545
  Dover *(G-2256)*

Delaware Stndrdbred Owners Ass........ G 302 678-3058
  Dover *(G-2265)*

First State Mnfctred Hsing Ins.............. F 302 674-5868
  Dover *(G-2507)*

Hostgpo Inc... F 424 422-0486
  Wilmington *(G-17215)*

Insurance Networks Aliance LLC.......... G 302 268-1010
  Wilmington *(G-17362)*

National Assn Elec Distr....................... G 302 322-3333
  New Castle *(G-9393)*

ATOMIZERS

Brandywine PDT Group Intl Inc............ E 302 472-1463
  Wilmington *(G-15080)*

Falco Industries Inc............................. G 302 628-1170
  Seaford *(G-13182)*

Nova Industries LLC............................ G 302 218-4837
  Bear *(G-399)*

AUCTIONEERS: Fee Basis

Brothers Gannon Inc............................ G 302 422-2734
  Houston *(G-5437)*

Fanticipate Inc..................................... G 763 777-4232
  Wilmington *(G-16551)*

H S Troyer... G 302 678-2694
  Dover *(G-2641)*

Reagan-Watson Auctions LLC.............. G 302 422-2392
  Milford *(G-8060)*

Southern Del Trck Growers Assn.......... G 302 875-3147
  Laurel *(G-5604)*

Spences Bazaar & Auction LLC............ G 302 734-3441
  Dover *(G-3596)*

William D Emmert................................ G 302 227-1433
  Rehoboth Beach *(G-13017)*

Wilsons Auction Sales Inc.................... G 302 422-3454
  Lincoln *(G-6709)*

AUDIO & VIDEO EQPT, EXC COMMERCIAL

Acoustic Audio Tek LLC....................... G 302 685-2113
  Wilmington *(G-14238)*

Balanced Audio Technology................. G 302 996-9496
  Wilmington *(G-14719)*

Beetronics Inc..................................... G 302 455-2070
  Claymont *(G-1055)*

Brandywine Electronics Corp................ F 302 324-9992
  Bear *(G-80)*

AUDIO ELECTRONIC SYSTEMS

Bat Electronics Inc............................... G 302 999-8855
  Wilmington *(G-14777)*

Helix Inc Ta Audioworks....................... G 302 285-0555
  Middletown *(G-7203)*

Sound-N-Secure Inc............................ G 302 424-3670
  Milford *(G-8095)*

AUDIO-VISUAL PROGRAM PRODUCTION SVCS

Brandywine Electronics Corp................ F 302 324-9992
  Bear *(G-80)*

Petes Big Tvs Inc................................. G 302 328-3551
  Historic New Castle *(G-5046)*

Pocket FM Corp................................... E 408 896-7038
  Lewes *(G-6380)*

AUDIOLOGICAL EQPT: Electronic

Drowsy Digital Inc................................ G 833 438-6956
  Dover *(G-2387)*

Hearx Usa Inc...................................... D 415 212-5500
  Camden *(G-847)*

AUTO & HOME SUPPLY STORES: Auto & Truck Eqpt & Parts

Adams Auto Parts LLC........................ F 302 655-9693
  Wilmington *(G-14250)*

Dover Automotive Inc........................... G 302 653-9234
  Smyrna *(G-13714)*

Fisher Auto Parts Inc........................... G 302 934-8088
  Millsboro *(G-8291)*

T & J Murray Worldwide Svcs.............. F 302 736-1790
  Dover *(G-3637)*

True Mobility Inc.................................. G 302 836-4110
  New Castle *(G-9643)*

AUTO & HOME SUPPLY STORES: Automotive parts

Action Automotive Inc.......................... G 302 429-0643
  Wilmington *(G-14240)*

Bill Cannons Garage Inc...................... F 302 436-4200
  Selbyville *(G-13477)*

C & W Auto Parts Co Inc..................... G 302 697-2684
  Magnolia *(G-6724)*

Deltrans Inc... G 302 453-8213
  Newark *(G-10510)*

Fisher Auto Parts Inc........................... G 302 998-3111
  Wilmington *(G-16648)*

Fishers Auto Parts Inc......................... G 302 934-8088
  Millsboro *(G-8292)*

Fitzgerald Auto Salvage Inc................. D 302 422-7584
  Lincoln *(G-6669)*

Genuine Parts Company...................... G 610 494-6355
  Claymont *(G-1160)*

IG Burton & Company Inc................... D 302 424-3041
  Milford *(G-7939)*

Ocean Pines Auto Svc Ctr Inc.............. F 410 641-7800
  Ocean View *(G-12554)*

Willis Ford Inc...................................... E 302 653-5900
  Smyrna *(G-13939)*

Winner Infiniti Inc................................. E 302 764-5900
  Wilmington *(G-20862)*

AUTO & HOME SUPPLY STORES: Trailer Hitches, Automotive

Boyds Trailor Hitches........................... G 302 697-9000
  Camden Wyoming *(G-917)*

AUTO & HOME SUPPLY STORES: Truck Eqpt & Parts

Diamond State Truck Center LLC......... G 302 275-9050
  New Castle *(G-9052)*

AUTO & HOME SUPPLY STORES: Truck Eqpt & Parts   **PRODUCTS & SERVICES SECTION**

Rhino Lnngs Del Auto Style Inc............ F 302 368-4660
   Newark *(G-11878)*
Service Tire Truck Center Inc................ E 302 629-5533
   Seaford *(G-13397)*
Transaxle LLC.. G 302 322-8300
   New Castle *(G-9633)*

AUTOMATED TELLER MACHINE NETWORK

Beach Break... G 302 226-3450
   Dewey Beach *(G-1664)*
Cash Connect Inc..................................... E 302 283-4100
   Newark *(G-10159)*

AUTOMATIC REGULATING CONTROL: Building Svcs Monitoring, Auto

Totaltrax Inc... D 302 514-0600
   New Castle *(G-9630)*

AUTOMOBILE FINANCE LEASING

Star States Leasing Corp......................... E 302 283-4500
   Newark *(G-12088)*

AUTOMOBILES & OTHER MOTOR VEHICLES WHOLESALERS

Dd Inc De LLC.. G 302 669-9269
   Claymont *(G-1111)*
Diamond Motor Sports Inc..................... D 302 697-3222
   Dover *(G-2292)*
Future Ford Sales Inc.............................. D 302 999-0261
   Wilmington *(G-16776)*
Greg Motors USA Inc............................... G 302 266-8200
   Newark *(G-10892)*
Pafs Auto LLC.. G 302 213-3881
   Newark *(G-11612)*
Winner Ford of Newark Inc..................... F 302 731-2415
   Newark *(G-12388)*

AUTOMOBILES: Off-Road, Exc Recreational Vehicles

Michael C Rapa... G 302 236-4423
   Laurel *(G-5563)*

AUTOMOBILES: Wholesalers

Cool Customs Inc...................................... G 302 894-0406
   Newark *(G-10320)*
Porter Nissan Buick Newark.................... E 302 368-6300
   Newark *(G-11714)*
Staplefords Sales and Service................. G 302 834-4568
   Saint Georges *(G-13039)*
Winner Group Inc..................................... F 302 292-8200
   Newark *(G-12389)*

AUTOMOTIVE & TRUCK GENERAL REPAIR SVC

A2b Auto Group.. G 302 786-2331
   Wilmington *(G-14179)*
Accurate Auto Service Inc....................... G 302 737-7998
   Newark *(G-9752)*
Admiral Tire.. G 302 734-5911
   Dover *(G-1718)*
Aiden Auto Repair Center...................... G 302 898-5777
   Bear *(G-21)*
Alderman Automotive Enterprise.......... G 302 652-3733
   New Castle *(G-8777)*
All Tune & Lube.. G 302 744-9081
   Dover *(G-1767)*
All Tune & Lube.. G 302 367-6369
   Wilmington *(G-14369)*
Allisons Auto Cycle Kstomz LLC............. G 302 836-4222
   Bear *(G-28)*

Allserve Allscpes Allstrctures................. G 302 684-1414
   Harbeson *(G-4682)*
Ameri Auto LLC... G 302 607-9113
   New Castle *(G-8795)*
Anthonys Automotive.............................. G 302 420-9804
   New Castle *(G-8813)*
Area 51 Automotive................................. G 302 993-9114
   Wilmington *(G-14548)*
Army National Guard Delaware............. G 302 855-7456
   Dagsboro *(G-1413)*
ARS Fleet Service..................................... G 302 482-1305
   New Castle *(G-8824)*
Atlantic Auto Repair LLC........................ G 302 539-7352
   Millville *(G-8515)*
Atomic Garage.. G 302 898-1380
   Wilmington *(G-14634)*
Auto Evrything At Slepy Hllow............... G 302 376-3010
   Smyrna *(G-13656)*
Auto Plus Auto Parts................................ G 302 678-8400
   Dover *(G-1855)*
Autolab Inc.. E 416 820-1636
   Wilmington *(G-14651)*
Automotive Diagnostic Sol..................... G 443 466-6108
   Newark *(G-9948)*
AV Auto Worx LLC..................................... F 302 384-7646
   Wilmington *(G-14660)*
B and B Automotive................................. G 302 559-2087
   Wilmington *(G-14693)*
Bavarian Cllision New Grdn Inc.............. G 610 268-3966
   Bear *(G-58)*
Bayshore Ford Truck Sales Inc................ D 302 656-3160
   New Castle *(G-8853)*
Bcb Diesel Mechanics Llc........................ G 302 422-3787
   Milford *(G-7789)*
Bear Alignment Center........................... G 302 655-9219
   Wilmington *(G-14805)*
Bernard Limpert....................................... G 302 674-8280
   Dover *(G-1914)*
Bill Cannons Garage Inc.......................... F 302 436-4200
   Selbyville *(G-13477)*
Buckleys Inc.. G 302 999-8285
   Wilmington *(G-15142)*
Buds Auto.. G 302 690-3838
   New Castle *(G-8900)*
Bullfeathers Auto Sound Inc.................. G 302 846-0434
   Laurel *(G-5475)*
C & C Autobrokers................................... G 302 442-5464
   Wilmington *(G-15170)*
Camco Tire & Auto LLC............................ G 302 664-1264
   Milton *(G-8579)*
Cammock Boys Auto................................ G 302 409-0645
   Wilmington *(G-15207)*
Campbells.. G 302 359-9918
   Harrington *(G-4746)*
Capital Trail Service Center.................... G 302 731-0999
   Newark *(G-10134)*
Car Doc.. G 301 302-3362
   Delmar *(G-1572)*
Caribb Transport Inc................................ G 302 274-2112
   Wilmington *(G-15248)*
Carrillos Auto Care................................... G 302 339-7234
   Houston *(G-5438)*
Ccdiesel LLC.. G 302 353-0842
   Newport *(G-12443)*
Chriss Car Care Road............................... G 302 628-4695
   Bridgeville *(G-682)*
CJ S Autos.. G 302 500-0822
   Bridgeville *(G-683)*
Cjs Autos LLC.. G 302 337-8880
   Bridgeville *(G-684)*
CJs Beach Bays Inc................................... F 302 645-8478
   Lewes *(G-5823)*

Classic Auto Restoration Svcs................. G 302 398-9652
   Harrington *(G-4750)*
Community Auto Repair.......................... G 302 856-3333
   Georgetown *(G-4262)*
Coveys Car Care Inc................................. G 302 629-2746
   Seaford *(G-13138)*
Croosroads Auto Repair Inc.................... G 302 436-9100
   Selbyville *(G-13510)*
Cw Mobile Automotive Repa.................. G 302 663-0035
   Millsboro *(G-8248)*
D H Automotive Towing.......................... G 302 368-5590
   Newark *(G-10376)*
D S Auto... G 302 542-3023
   Millsboro *(G-8252)*
Daly Concepts... G 215 266-0866
   Wilmington *(G-15774)*
Daves Auto Restoration........................... G 302 258-7981
   Laurel *(G-5493)*
Daves Service Center............................... G 302 798-1776
   Claymont *(G-1109)*
Deals On Wheels Inc................................ E 302 999-9955
   Wilmington *(G-15845)*
Diamond State Diesel.............................. G 864 784-6608
   Smyrna *(G-13710)*
Dnr Auto.. G 302 698-7829
   Dover *(G-2314)*
Donald Briggs... G 267 476-2712
   Middletown *(G-7069)*
Donaway Corporation............................. G 302 934-6226
   Millsboro *(G-8275)*
Dover Volkswagen Inc............................. E 302 734-4761
   Dover *(G-2368)*
E D S of Milford Inc.................................. G 302 245-8813
   Milford *(G-7873)*
Eds Auto Repair.. G 302 382-0079
   Felton *(G-3967)*
Eds Auto Repair.. G 302 468-0955
   Wilmington *(G-16296)*
Elite Auto LLC... G 302 690-2948
   Middletown *(G-7092)*
Elite Auto Works LLC............................... G 302 252-1045
   Wilmington *(G-16362)*
Empire Auto Protect LLC......................... G 888 345-0084
   Dover *(G-2443)*
Enclosed Auto Solutions LLC.................. G 302 437-9858
   Middletown *(G-7100)*
Ericsons Garage.. G 302 653-5032
   Smyrna *(G-13724)*
Evco Auto Inc DBA A To Z Auto.............. G 302 595-3078
   Bear *(G-211)*
Everest Auto Repair LLC......................... G 302 737-8424
   Newark *(G-10676)*
Everest Autoworks Auto Spa LLC........... G 302 737-8424
   Newark *(G-10677)*
Firestone Complete Auto C..................... G 302 437-0497
   Middletown *(G-7129)*
First State Auto Glass.............................. G 302 559-8902
   Wilmington *(G-16622)*
Five Friends Auto..................................... G 302 407-6236
   Wilmington *(G-16651)*
Four Brothers Auto Service..................... F 302 482-2932
   Wilmington *(G-16708)*
Fox Run Automotive Inc.......................... F 302 834-1200
   Bear *(G-234)*
Freedom Rides Auto................................ G 302 422-4559
   Seaford *(G-13190)*
Fromms Automotive................................ G 717 202-9918
   Laurel *(G-5515)*
Furrs Tire Service Inc............................... G 302 678-0800
   Dover *(G-2546)*
G Custom Work LLC.................................. G 302 353-2137
   New Castle *(G-9156)*

PRODUCTS & SERVICES SECTION
AUTOMOTIVE & TRUCK GENERAL REPAIR SVC

Company	Code	Phone
Gaby Auto, New Castle (G-9157)	G	856 469-1378
Garcias Auto Repair, Middletown (G-7151)	G	302 464-1118
Gears Garage LLC, Townsend (G-14005)	G	302 653-3684
Genesis Automobile Acquirers, Bear (G-247)	G	757 717-1673
Geo Transport Auto Export LLC, New Castle (G-9162)	G	302 322-9001
Girls Auto Clinic LLC, New Castle (G-9167)	G	484 679-6394
Glacier Autos, Wilmington (G-16877)	G	302 510-6771
Golden Car Care, Georgetown (G-4344)	G	302 856-2219
Goobers Garage, Wilmington (G-16920)	G	443 309-0328
Goodyear Tire & Rubber Company, Newark (G-10869)	G	302 737-2461
Gumboro Service Center Inc, Frankford (G-4112)	G	302 238-7040
H & C Auto Care, Bear (G-257)	G	302 494-8989
Harris Towing and Auto Service, Dover (G-2656)	G	302 736-9901
Harvey Road Automotive Inc, Wilmington (G-17071)	G	302 654-7500
HB&t Automotive LLC, Townsend (G-14014)	G	302 378-3333
Henrys Car Care Inc, Wilmington (G-17125)	G	302 994-5766
Hertrchs Fmly Auto Dealerships, Bear (G-271)	G	302 276-2554
High Horse Performance Inc, Smyrna (G-13760)	G	302 894-1115
Hoban Auto & Machineshop Inc, Selbyville (G-13547)	G	302 436-8013
Holly Oak Towing and Service, Wilmington (G-17169)	G	302 792-1500
IG Burton & Company Inc, Milford (G-7939)	D	302 424-3041
IG Burton & Company Inc, Milford (G-7938)	D	302 422-3041
Intune Automotive Inc, Newark (G-11051)	G	302 824-9893
Ivy Boy Auto Works, Wilmington (G-17438)	G	302 669-8842
J & K Auto Repair Inc, Bear (G-292)	G	302 834-8025
J V Auto Service Inc, Wilmington (G-17466)	F	302 999-0786
J&J Fleet Service, New Castle (G-9249)	F	484 632-1647
J&R Auto Repair, Ellendale (G-3923)	G	240 863-8653
Jamies Auto Repair South, Townsend (G-14019)	G	302 378-7933
Jays Auto Repair LLC, Newark (G-11101)	G	302 273-2811
Joes Auto and Equipment Repair, Harbeson (G-4703)	G	302 990-5845
Justin David Ennis, Smyrna (G-13784)	G	302 650-4934
Justin Oneill, Dover (G-2822)	G	631 346-7333
Kaminski Service Center, Claymont (G-1204)	G	302 375-6379
Kaspar Karrs, Wilmington (G-17656)	G	302 660-2256
Kent Sussex Auto Care Inc, Dover (G-2857)	G	302 422-3337
Kevins Road Svc, Saint Georges (G-13036)	G	302 218-2869
Kirkwood Tires Inc, Newark (G-11186)	G	302 737-2460
Kunkun Auto Group LLC, Wilmington (G-17763)	G	917 499-0019
Lee Lynn Inc, Dover (G-2923)	F	302 678-9978
Lekuche Autos & General Merch, Bear (G-344)	G	302 887-6748
Lineage Auto Group L L C, New Castle (G-9313)	G	302 595-2119
Lube Depot, Smyrna (G-13811)	G	302 659-3329
Luxz Auto Tech LLC, Newark (G-11296)	G	302 305-5899
M & M Automotive LLC, Historic New Castle (G-5022)	G	302 325-8140
M&S Auto Group Inc, Bear (G-357)	G	302 834-7905
Macs Auto Services, Smyrna (G-13813)	G	302 223-6771
Maliks Auto Repair, New Castle (G-9341)	G	302 325-2555
Manor Exxon Inc, Bear (G-360)	G	302 834-6691
Mark T Droney, Millville (G-8539)	G	302 537-2305
Martel & Son Foreign Car Ctr, Dover (G-3022)	G	302 674-5556
Martin Newark Dealership Inc, Newark (G-11345)	D	302 454-9300
Martinez Automotive, New Castle (G-9350)	G	302 250-5933
Matt S Auto Care, Lewes (G-6250)	G	302 226-2407
McCar Auto Group LLC, Wilmington (G-18217)	G	302 478-3049
Meineke Car Care Center 671, Claymont (G-1232)	F	302 746-2026
Middletown Car Care, Middletown (G-7346)	G	302 449-1550
Millcreek Texaco Station, Wilmington (G-18360)	G	302 571-8489
Monro Inc, Delmar (G-1623)	G	302 846-2732
Monro Inc, Middletown (G-7377)	E	302 378-3801
Moppert Auto Collision of, Newark (G-11449)	G	302 453-2900
New Car Connection, New Castle (G-9405)	G	302 328-7000
Nu - Vision Auto Glass LLC, Clayton (G-1393)	G	302 389-8700
Ocean Pines Auto Svc Ctr Inc, Ocean View (G-12554)	F	410 641-7800
OEM Auto Parts, Newark (G-11579)	G	302 983-6475
Oil Spot Express Lube Center, Seaford (G-13323)	G	302 628-9866
Omar Auto Repair LLC, Wilmington (G-18763)	G	302 502-3204
Onsite Semi Truck Repair, Milford (G-8038)	G	302 526-0517
Patriot Auto & Truck Care LLC, Dover (G-3282)	G	302 257-5715
Paul F Campanella Inc, Wilmington (G-18917)	F	302 777-7170
Paul F Campanella Inc, Wilmington (G-18918)	F	302 218-5374
Pen Del Auto & Marine Inc, Frankford (G-4133)	G	302 430-3046
Pike Creek Automotive Inc, Wilmington (G-19037)	F	302 998-2234
Pleasant Hill Auto Svc LLC, Smyrna (G-13849)	G	302 376-6712
Poorman Auto, Seaford (G-13351)	G	302 628-0404
Powertrain Technology Inc, Newark (G-11719)	G	302 368-4900
Precision Auto LLC, Wilmington (G-19151)	G	302 384-6169
Prestige Auto, Wilmington (G-19180)	G	302 898-5486
Price Automotive Group, Newark (G-11737)	E	302 383-8669
Professionals Auto Salon, Wilmington (G-19216)	G	302 420-5691
Rbs Auto Repair Inc, Dover (G-3426)	G	302 678-8803
RE Auto Repair, Wilmington (G-19357)	G	302 384-6508
Redmill Auto Repair, Newark (G-11842)	G	302 292-2155
Reincarnatio Inc, Wilmington (G-19417)	G	703 479-1337
Rinehimer Body Shop Inc, Newark (G-11888)	F	302 737-7350
Robin Drive Auto LLC, Bear (G-465)	G	302 326-2437
Rock Ranch Auto LLC, Houston (G-5450)	G	302 670-9992
Rockaway Auto Repair, Lewes (G-6427)	G	302 644-1485
Route 9 Auto Center, Georgetown (G-4494)	G	302 856-3941
Royal Tech Auto Repair LLC, Newark (G-11922)	G	302 737-6852
RPM Automotive of Dover LLC, Dover (G-3490)	G	302 734-9495
Rs Werks, Newark (G-11924)	G	302 740-1516
Rudys European Motorcars, Lewes (G-6434)	G	302 645-6410
Rush Auto LLC, New Castle (G-9548)	G	302 323-9070
S Wilson Auto Repair, Georgetown (G-4496)	G	302 856-3839
Sals Garage Inc, Wilmington (G-19641)	G	302 655-4981
Sammys Auto LLC, Newark (G-11939)	G	302 368-5203
Scott Muffler LLC, Middletown (G-7545)	G	302 378-9247
Select Auto Inc, Claymont (G-1288)	G	215 423-6522
Sevys Auto Service Inc, New Castle (G-9560)	G	302 328-0839
Shockleys Auto Service, Frankford (G-4143)	G	302 537-7663
Site-On Auto Inc, Lincoln (G-6702)	G	302 505-5100
Smalleys Automotive Group Inc, Kenton (G-5455)	G	302 450-0983
Smiths Jack Towing & Svc Ctr, Wilmington (G-19895)	G	302 798-6667
Smittys Auto Repair Inc, Harrington (G-4833)	G	302 398-8419
Sonnys Auto Services Inc, Bear (G-499)	G	302 287-7677
Sparkys Auto Repair LLC, Greenwood (G-4669)	G	302 495-7525
Sports Car Service Inc, Wilmington (G-19969)	G	302 764-7439

Employee Codes: A=Over 500 employees, B=251-500 C=101-250, D=51-100, E=20-50, F=10-19, G=1-9

2024 Harris Directory of Delaware Businesses

AUTOMOTIVE & TRUCK GENERAL REPAIR SVC

PRODUCTS & SERVICES SECTION

Star Gas & Diesel .... G 302 998-2002
  Wilmington (G-20024)
Steerr Inc .... G 412 303-5840
  Lewes (G-6509)
Sun Gas & Diesel .... G 302 376-8200
  Middletown (G-7608)
Sussex Diesel Inc .... G 302 877-0330
  Laurel (G-5609)
Td Automotive .... G 443 794-3453
  New Castle (G-9619)
Three Js Disc Tire & Auto Svc .... G 302 995-6141
  Wilmington (G-20316)
Trou Auto .... G 302 762-3200
  Wilmington (G-20439)
True Street Automotive LLC .... G 302 480-4119
  Smyrna (G-13921)
Turn of Wrench .... G 302 584-1824
  Smyrna (G-13922)
Unique Auto Accessories LLC .... G 302 841-0983
  Laurel (G-5617)
United Auto Sales Inc .... G 302 325-3000
  Newark (G-12266)
Vehicle Maintenance Dept .... G 302 571-5857
  Wilmington (G-20578)
Wallis Repair Inc .... G 302 378-4301
  Middletown (G-7705)
Wheel Lady Garcia .... G 302 588-9750
  Wilmington (G-20757)
White Deer Auto .... G 302 846-0547
  Delmar (G-1655)
Wiedman Enterprises Inc .... G 302 226-2407
  Rehoboth Beach (G-13016)
William Craft .... G 302 945-5798
  Lewes (G-6631)
William T Wadkins Garage Inc .... G 302 422-0265
  Milford (G-8151)
Willis Ford Inc .... E 302 653-5900
  Smyrna (G-13939)
Winner Ford of Dover Ltd .... B 302 734-0444
  Dover (G-3860)
Winner Group Inc .... F 302 292-8200
  Newark (G-12389)
Winner Infiniti Inc .... E 302 764-5900
  Wilmington (G-20862)
Wolfs Elite Autos .... G 302 999-9199
  Wilmington (G-20877)
Zeglins Automotive Inc .... G 302 947-1414
  Millsboro (G-8511)

AUTOMOTIVE BODY SHOP

ABRA Auto Body & Glass .... G 302 674-4525
  Dover (G-1703)
ABRA Auto Body & Glass LP .... G 302 279-1007
  Middletown (G-6830)
Anthonys Collision Cstm Works .... G 302 542-2489
  Harrington (G-4731)
Armigers Auto Center Inc .... G 302 875-7642
  Laurel (G-5464)
Auto Works Collision Ctr LLC .... F 302 732-3902
  Lewes (G-5721)
Automotive Services Inc .... F 302 762-0100
  Wilmington (G-14656)
Balanced Body Inc .... G 302 373-3463
  Wilmington (G-14720)
Body Works .... G 302 275-2750
  Newark (G-10067)
Brandywine Body Shop Inc .... G 302 998-0424
  Wilmington (G-15044)
Brandywine Bodyworks .... G 302 798-0801
  Wilmington (G-15045)
Brasures Body Shop Inc .... G 302 732-6157
  Frankford (G-4077)

Caliber Bodyworks Texas Inc .... E 302 832-1660
  Bear (G-88)
Caliber Collision .... G 302 731-1200
  Newark (G-10120)
Christiana Body Shop Inc .... G 302 655-1085
  Wilmington (G-15399)
Classic Auto Body Inc .... G 302 655-4044
  Wilmington (G-15466)
Clear Definition LLC .... G 302 503-7560
  Milford (G-7832)
Complete Auto Body Inc .... F 302 629-3955
  Seaford (G-13132)
Dent Pro Inc .... G 302 628-0978
  Seaford (G-13158)
Dominos Body Shop .... G 302 697-3801
  Camden Wyoming (G-935)
Doug Richmonds Body Shop .... G 302 453-1173
  Newark (G-10554)
E & M Enterprises Inc .... G 302 736-6391
  Dover (G-2398)
East Coast Auto Body Inc .... G 302 265-6830
  Dover (G-2408)
Ellmore Auto Collision .... G 302 762-2301
  Wilmington (G-16374)
Eurshall Millers Autobody .... G 410 742-7329
  Delmar (G-1595)
Executive Auto Repairs Inc .... G 302 995-6220
  Wilmington (G-16503)
Glasgow Auto Body .... G 302 292-1201
  Newark (G-10843)
Henry Bros Autobody & Pnt Sp .... G 302 994-4438
  Wilmington (G-17123)
J Henry Edward & Sons Inc .... F 302 658-4324
  Wilmington (G-17457)
Jorge & Evonnes Auto Body LLC .... G 302 382-1460
  Camden (G-861)
King .... G 302 930-0139
  Claymont (G-1207)
Kpkm Inc .... G 302 678-0271
  Dover (G-2885)
Lewes Body Works Inc .... G 302 645-5595
  Lewes (G-6191)
LS Auto Experience LLC .... G 302 983-9668
  Wilmington (G-18020)
Maaco Collision Repr Auto Pntg .... G 610 628-3867
  Wilmington (G-18063)
Martin Dealership .... G 302 738-5200
  Newark (G-11343)
Master Tech Inc .... F 302 832-1660
  Bear (G-365)
No Evi-Dents Inc .... G 302 363-7788
  Wilmington (G-18660)
Puzs Body Shop Inc .... G 302 368-8265
  Newark (G-11777)
Rex Auto Body Inc .... G 302 731-4707
  Newark (G-11875)
Rudlyn Inc .... F 302 764-5677
  Wilmington (G-19586)
Thomas Karmanski .... G 302 438-1458
  Wilmington (G-20311)
Whites Body Shop .... G 302 655-4369
  Wilmington (G-20771)
Wilmington Collision Center .... G 484 702-2115
  Wilmington (G-20812)

AUTOMOTIVE BODY, PAINT & INTERIOR REPAIR & MAINTENANCE SVC

Autoport Inc .... E 302 658-5100
  New Castle (G-8834)
Caliber Collision .... G 302 674-4525
  Dover (G-2013)

Caliber Collision .... G 302 279-1007
  Middletown (G-6951)
Car Tech Auto Center .... G 302 368-4104
  Newark (G-10138)
Future Ford Sales Inc .... D 302 999-0261
  Wilmington (G-16776)
Gas & Go Inc .... G 302 734-8234
  Dover (G-2562)
New Car Connection .... G 302 328-7000
  New Castle (G-9405)
Pine Valley Corvettes .... G 302 834-1268
  Middletown (G-7449)
Willis Ford Inc .... E 302 653-5900
  Smyrna (G-13939)

AUTOMOTIVE CUSTOMIZING SVCS, NONFACTORY BASIS

Autoport Inc .... E 302 658-5100
  New Castle (G-8834)
Continental Warranty Corp .... E 302 375-0401
  Claymont (G-1100)
M & M Detail Wrap and Tint LLC .... G 302 260-8988
  Wilmington (G-18056)

AUTOMOTIVE GLASS REPLACEMENT SHOPS

A R Myers Corporation .... F 302 652-3164
  Wilmington (G-14170)
Aaron Auto Glass .... G 302 297-8008
  Middletown (G-6827)
Caliber Collision .... G 302 674-4525
  Dover (G-2013)
Caliber Collision .... G 302 279-1007
  Middletown (G-6951)
Delaware Auto Glass .... G 302 709-2300
  Newark (G-10417)
Ght Autoglass .... G 302 494-4369
  Newark (G-10830)
Parags Glass Company .... G 302 737-0101
  Newark (G-11625)
Safelite Fulfillment Inc .... G 302 856-7175
  Georgetown (G-4497)
Safelite Glass Corp .... G 877 800-2727
  Dover (G-3504)
Safelite Glass Corp .... E 302 656-4640
  Wilmington (G-19628)
U A G Inc .... G 302 731-2747
  Newark (G-12252)

AUTOMOTIVE PAINT SHOP

A R Myers Corporation .... F 302 652-3164
  Wilmington (G-14170)
Jewell Enterprises Inc .... F 302 737-8460
  Newark (G-11110)
Maaco Collision Repair .... G 302 753-8721
  Bear (G-358)
Red Barn Inc .... F 302 678-0271
  Dover (G-3438)
Rickards Auto Body .... G 302 934-9600
  Dagsboro (G-1499)

AUTOMOTIVE PARTS, ACCESS & SPLYS

Airnav Group LLC .... G 954 798-5509
  Middletown (G-6844)
Gif North America LLC .... G 703 969-9243
  Rehoboth Beach (G-12771)
Globally Srced Vhcles Prts LLC .... E 240 755-4935
  Dover (G-2595)
Kautex Inc .... B 302 456-1455
  Newark (G-11145)

PRODUCTS & SERVICES SECTION
AUTOMOTIVE SPLYS & PARTS, WHOLESALE, NEC

Lkq Northeast Inc .... G 800 223-0171
  Dover *(G-2962)*

Martinrea International US Inc .... G 615 212-0586
  Wilmington *(G-18171)*

NAPA M3 Inc .... G 719 660-6263
  Middletown *(G-7392)*

NGK North America Inc .... G 302 654-1344
  Wilmington *(G-18640)*

Performnce Injction Equipmentc .... G 302 858-5145
  Georgetown *(G-4462)*

Pressair International .... F 302 636-5440
  Wilmington *(G-19179)*

Wilmington Fibre Specialty Co .... E 302 328-7525
  Historic New Castle *(G-5102)*

AUTOMOTIVE PARTS: Plastic

Charles Williams .... F 302 274-2996
  Wilmington *(G-15342)*

Resource Intl Inc .... F 302 762-4501
  New Castle *(G-9524)*

AUTOMOTIVE PRDTS: Rubber

Forcebeyond Inc .... E 302 995-6588
  Wilmington *(G-16688)*

AUTOMOTIVE REPAIR SHOPS: Diesel Engine Repair

Careys Diesel Inc .... F 302 678-3797
  Leipsic *(G-5629)*

Careys Inc .... F 302 875-5674
  Laurel *(G-5478)*

R & K Motors & Machine Shop .... G 302 737-4596
  Newark *(G-11803)*

AUTOMOTIVE REPAIR SHOPS: Electrical Svcs

H&H Services Electrical Contrs .... G 302 373-4950
  New Castle *(G-9190)*

Highfield Electric LLC .... G 302 836-4300
  Bear *(G-273)*

Independent Elec Svcs LLC .... D 302 383-2761
  Claymont *(G-1184)*

Kent Sign Company Inc .... F 302 697-2181
  Dover *(G-2856)*

Paul A Nicle Inc .... G 302 453-4000
  Newark *(G-11642)*

Sb Electric LLC .... G 610 721-5361
  Wilmington *(G-19688)*

US Telex Corporation .... G 302 652-2707
  Wilmington *(G-20552)*

AUTOMOTIVE REPAIR SHOPS: Engine Rebuilding

Bradleys Auto Center Inc .... G 302 762-2247
  Middletown *(G-6935)*

Ep Engine Performance .... G 302 521-0435
  Smyrna *(G-13723)*

European Performance Inc .... G 302 633-1122
  Wilmington *(G-16476)*

Hazzard Auto Repairs Inc .... G 302 645-4543
  Lewes *(G-6083)*

AUTOMOTIVE REPAIR SHOPS: Engine Repair

Dempseys Service Center Inc .... G 302 239-4996
  Newark *(G-10511)*

M&M Small Engine Repair .... G 302 270-3941
  Hartly *(G-4894)*

Pughs Service Inc .... F 302 678-2408
  Dover *(G-3394)*

Roccos Automotive Service .... G 302 998-2234
  Wilmington *(G-19526)*

S&M Small Engine Repair LLC .... G 302 893-7341
  Ocean View *(G-12564)*

AUTOMOTIVE REPAIR SHOPS: Muffler Shop, Sale/Rpr/Installation

Bernard Limpert .... G 302 674-8280
  Dover *(G-1914)*

Best Custom Exhaust .... G 302 278-3555
  Georgetown *(G-4232)*

C-Met Inc .... G 302 652-1884
  New Castle *(G-8909)*

Car Shoppe LLC .... G 302 992-9669
  Wilmington *(G-15236)*

Daves Disc Mfflers of Dver De .... G 302 678-8803
  Dover *(G-2199)*

Lewes Meineke .... G 302 827-2054
  Lewes *(G-6197)*

Meineke Muffler .... G 302 644-8544
  Lewes *(G-6259)*

Rcs Mufflers Inc .... G 302 328-7788
  New Castle *(G-9514)*

Walls Service Center Inc .... G 302 422-8110
  Milford *(G-8139)*

AUTOMOTIVE REPAIR SHOPS: Rebuilding & Retreading Tires

Bridgestone Ret Operations LLC .... G 302 734-4522
  Dover *(G-1979)*

Bridgestone Ret Operations LLC .... G 302 656-2529
  New Castle *(G-8892)*

Bridgestone Ret Operations LLC .... G 302 995-2487
  Wilmington *(G-15108)*

AUTOMOTIVE REPAIR SHOPS: Tire Recapping

Service Tire Truck Center Inc .... E 302 629-5533
  Seaford *(G-13397)*

AUTOMOTIVE REPAIR SHOPS: Tire Repair Shop

Ajacks Tire Service Inc .... G 302 834-5200
  New Castle *(G-8776)*

M & M Tire Services Inc .... G 302 731-1004
  Newark *(G-11299)*

Ssmmd LLC .... G 302 249-1045
  Laurel *(G-5606)*

AUTOMOTIVE REPAIR SHOPS: Trailer Repair

Reliable Trailer Inc .... F 856 962-7900
  Felton *(G-4015)*

V A Truck & Trailer Repair LLC .... G 302 653-7936
  Smyrna *(G-13927)*

AUTOMOTIVE REPAIR SHOPS: Truck Engine Repair, Exc Indl

Four States LLC .... F 302 655-3400
  New Castle *(G-9143)*

William Chambers and Son .... G 302 284-9655
  Viola *(G-14098)*

AUTOMOTIVE REPAIR SHOPS: Wheel Alignment

B & E Tire Alignment Inc .... G 302 732-6091
  Frankford *(G-4066)*

AUTOMOTIVE REPAIR SVC

Automotiveonly .... G 302 727-1064
  Rehoboth Beach *(G-12618)*

Bargain Tire .... G 302 764-8900
  Wilmington *(G-14762)*

Benchmark Transmission Inc .... G 302 792-2300
  Claymont *(G-1056)*

Brandywine Chrysler Jeep Dodge .... D 302 998-0458
  Wilmington *(G-15050)*

Buntings Garage Inc .... F 302 732-9021
  Dagsboro *(G-1421)*

Coastal Towing Inc .... G 302 645-6300
  Lewes *(G-5847)*

D & H Automotive & Towing Inc .... G 302 655-7611
  Wilmington *(G-15757)*

Daves Service Center .... G 302 798-1776
  Claymont *(G-1109)*

Elite Meetings International .... G 302 516-7997
  Wilmington *(G-16365)*

Els Tire Service Inc .... F 302 834-1997
  Newark *(G-10633)*

Ewings Towing Service Inc .... G 302 366-8806
  Newark *(G-10681)*

Garage .... G 302 645-7288
  Rehoboth Beach *(G-12766)*

Goodchild Inc .... G 302 368-1681
  Newark *(G-10868)*

Lees Best Car Wash .... G 302 328-0770
  New Castle *(G-9299)*

Martin Collision Center .... G 302 452-2711
  Newark *(G-11341)*

Meineke Care Care Center .... G 302 368-0700
  Newark *(G-11383)*

Schrider Enterprises Inc .... G 302 934-1900
  Millsboro *(G-8456)*

Staplefords Sales and Service .... G 302 834-4568
  Saint Georges *(G-13039)*

Super Service Automotive Inc .... F 302 464-1149
  Middletown *(G-7612)*

Wrenchtime Auto LLC .... G 302 500-5558
  Newark *(G-12412)*

AUTOMOTIVE SPLYS & PARTS, NEW, WHOLESALE: Splys

Meineke Care Care Center .... G 302 368-0700
  Newark *(G-11383)*

AUTOMOTIVE SPLYS & PARTS, NEW, WHOLESALE: Tools & Eqpt

Greg Smith Equipment Sales LLC ...... G 302 894-9333
  Newark *(G-10894)*

AUTOMOTIVE SPLYS & PARTS, NEW, WHOLESALE: Trailer Parts

Arundel Trailer Sales .... G 302 398-6288
  Harrington *(G-4736)*

Utility/Stern Shore Trlr Sls I .... G 302 337-7400
  Bridgeville *(G-779)*

AUTOMOTIVE SPLYS & PARTS, NEW, WHOLESALE: Wheels

Tire 24 X 7 Inc .... G 833 847-3247
  Newark *(G-12199)*

AUTOMOTIVE SPLYS & PARTS, WHOLESALE, NEC

Action Automotive Inc .... G 302 429-0643
  Wilmington *(G-14240)*

Adams Auto Parts LLC .... F 302 655-9693
  Wilmington *(G-14250)*

AUTOMOTIVE SPLYS & PARTS, WHOLESALE, NEC

Berrodin Co.. G 302 395-1100
  Claymont *(G-1059)*
Bridgestone Ret Operations LLC........... G 302 422-4508
  Milford *(G-7805)*
C & W Auto Parts Co Inc........................ G 302 697-2684
  Magnolia *(G-6724)*
Clarksville Auto Service Ctr.................. E 302 539-1700
  Ocean View *(G-12489)*
Coveys Car Care Inc............................... G 302 629-2746
  Seaford *(G-13138)*
Elite Lubricants LLC............................... G 302 629-3301
  Seaford *(G-13173)*
Fisher Auto Parts Inc............................. G 302 856-2507
  Georgetown *(G-4324)*
Fisher Auto Parts Inc............................. G 302 934-8088
  Millsboro *(G-8291)*
Fisher Auto Parts Inc............................. G 302 653-9241
  Smyrna *(G-13736)*
Fisher Auto Parts Inc............................. G 302 998-3111
  Wilmington *(G-16648)*
Fishers Auto Parts Inc........................... G 302 934-8088
  Millsboro *(G-8292)*
Fitzgerald Auto Salvage Inc................. D 302 422-7584
  Lincoln *(G-6669)*
Future Ford Sales Inc............................ D 302 999-0261
  Wilmington *(G-16776)*
Genuine Parts Company......................... G 610 494-6355
  Claymont *(G-1160)*
Ieh Auto Parts LLC.................................. E 302 994-7171
  Wilmington *(G-17267)*
Imparts Inc... G 302 697-0990
  Wyoming *(G-20986)*
Irondt Corp.. G 347 539-6471
  Wilmington *(G-17422)*
J N Grillo & Sons Co............................. G 302 658-7020
  Wilmington *(G-17460)*
Johns Auto Parts Inc............................. F 302 322-3273
  Bear *(G-308)*
NGK North America Inc........................ G 302 654-1344
  Wilmington *(G-18640)*
Parts World USA LLC............................ G 302 451-9920
  Newark *(G-11631)*
Scott Muffler LLC................................... G 302 378-9247
  Middletown *(G-7545)*
Sp Auto Parts Inc.................................. G 302 337-8897
  Bridgeville *(G-768)*
Tabor Auto Parts Inc............................. E 302 395-1100
  New Castle *(G-9615)*
Townsend Bros Inc................................ F 302 674-0100
  Dover *(G-3707)*

AUTOMOTIVE SVCS, EXC REPAIR & CARWASHES: Insp & Diagnostic

Uris LLC... G 302 469-7000
  Millsboro *(G-8491)*

AUTOMOTIVE SVCS, EXC REPAIR & CARWASHES: Lubrication

Capital Trail Service Center................. G 302 731-0999
  Newark *(G-10134)*
Cr Lube Run LLC..................................... G 302 875-1641
  Laurel *(G-5487)*
Dover Lubricants Inc............................. G 302 674-8282
  Dover *(G-2352)*
Schrider Enterprises Inc...................... G 302 934-1900
  Millsboro *(G-8456)*

AUTOMOTIVE SVCS, EXC REPAIR & CARWASHES: Road Svc

Right-Away Auto Assistance LLC......... G 302 438-9970
  Hockessin *(G-5364)*

AUTOMOTIVE SVCS, EXC REPAIR & CARWASHES: Trailer Maintenance

Basher & Son Enterprises Inc............. G 302 239-6584
  Hockessin *(G-5130)*

AUTOMOTIVE SVCS, EXC RPR/ CARWASHES: High Perf Auto Rpr/Svc

30215 Motorsports................................. G 302 293-6193
  Newark *(G-9709)*
Blueprint Motorsport............................. G 302 333-2746
  Wilmington *(G-14981)*
Delmarva Auto Repair LLC.................... G 302 727-3237
  Greenwood *(G-4614)*
Donald Briggs... G 267 476-2712
  Middletown *(G-7069)*
Harold D Shockley.................................. G 302 275-8500
  Lincoln *(G-6675)*
Tikana Motorsports............................... G 302 290-0869
  Townsend *(G-14080)*
Truck Store LLC...................................... G 302 724-5918
  Dover *(G-3732)*

AUTOMOTIVE TOWING SVCS

4 Points Twing Radside Svc LLC......... G 302 538-8935
  Camden Wyoming *(G-902)*
A M Towing Co... G 302 357-5159
  New Castle *(G-8749)*
Alan Passwaters..................................... G 302 245-9114
  Seaford *(G-13052)*
All Star Towing LLC............................... G 302 388-4221
  New Castle *(G-8783)*
B & F Towing Co..................................... E 302 328-4146
  New Castle *(G-8839)*
Careys Inc.. F 302 875-5674
  Laurel *(G-5478)*
Chambers Motors Inc............................. E 302 629-3553
  Seaford *(G-13109)*
City Towing Services............................. G 302 561-7979
  New Castle *(G-8951)*
Coastal Towing Inc................................ G 302 645-6300
  Lewes *(G-5847)*
D & H Automotive & Towing Inc.......... G 302 655-7611
  Wilmington *(G-15757)*
Ellmore Auto Collision.......................... G 302 762-2301
  Wilmington *(G-16374)*
Ewings Towing Service Inc.................. G 302 366-8806
  Newark *(G-10681)*
Fred Drake Automotive Inc.................. G 302 378-4877
  Townsend *(G-14003)*
Harris Towing and Auto Service......... G 302 736-9901
  Dover *(G-2656)*
Harris Towing Service.......................... G 302 736-5473
  Frederica *(G-4170)*
Hazzard Auto Repairs Inc.................... G 302 645-4543
  Lewes *(G-6083)*
Kings Towing Company LLC................. G 302 345-3134
  Newark *(G-11179)*
Martel & Son Foreign Car Ctr............. G 302 674-5556
  Dover *(G-3022)*
Matthews Towing & Recovery............ F 302 463-1108
  Smyrna *(G-13820)*
Middletown Towing................................ G 302 357-6484
  Townsend *(G-14037)*
Midway Towing Inc................................ G 302 323-4850
  Wilmington *(G-18345)*
Predator Recovery & Towing LLC....... G 302 381-2135
  Laurel *(G-5578)*

PRODUCTS & SERVICES SECTION

Shocker Towing & Recovery................ G 302 259-1123
  Frankford *(G-4142)*

AUTOMOTIVE TRANSMISSION REPAIR SVC

A&M Transportation Inc....................... G 781 227-1257
  Dover *(G-1697)*
All Trans Transmission Inc................. G 302 366-0104
  Newark *(G-9820)*
Benchmark Transmission Inc............. G 302 792-2300
  Claymont *(G-1056)*
Benchmark Transmissions................. G 302 221-5380
  Historic New Castle *(G-4940)*
Benchmark Transmissions Inc........... G 302 999-9400
  Wilmington *(G-14828)*
Challenge Automotive Svcs Inc......... F 302 629-3058
  Seaford *(G-13108)*
Cottman Transmission......................... G 302 322-4600
  New Castle *(G-8978)*
Dynamic Converters LLC..................... G 302 454-9203
  Newark *(G-10583)*
Jld Auto Repair and Transm.............. G 302 650-8613
  Wilmington *(G-17554)*
Js Automotive AAMCO.......................... G 302 678-5660
  Dover *(G-2809)*
Powertrain Technology Inc................. G 302 368-4900
  Newark *(G-11719)*
Scott Muffler LLC................................... G 302 378-9247
  Middletown *(G-7545)*
Trans Plus Inc.. G 302 323-3051
  Historic New Castle *(G-5090)*
Walls Service Center Inc..................... G 302 422-8110
  Milford *(G-8139)*
World Transmissions Inc..................... G 302 735-5535
  Dover *(G-3874)*

AUTOMOTIVE WELDING SVCS

Donaway Corporation............................ G 302 934-6226
  Millsboro *(G-8275)*

AUTOMOTIVE: Seating

Clarios LLC.. C 302 996-0309
  New Castle *(G-8952)*
Johnson Controls Inc........................... F 302 715-5208
  Delmar *(G-1608)*

AWNINGS & CANOPIES: Awnings, Fabric, From Purchased Matls

Callaway Furniture Inc........................ G 302 398-8858
  Harrington *(G-4745)*
E W Brown Inc.. G 302 652-6612
  Wilmington *(G-16241)*
Gainor Awnings Inc.............................. G 302 998-8611
  Wilmington *(G-16793)*

BABY FORMULA

Hembal Labs Inc................................... G 800 414-4741
  Dover *(G-2674)*

BACKHOES

Bob Reynolds Backhoe Services......... G 302 239-4711
  Hockessin *(G-5136)*
Central Backhoe Service..................... G 302 398-6420
  Milton *(G-8581)*
Wolfe Backhoe Service........................ G 302 737-2628
  Newark *(G-12393)*

BAGS & CONTAINERS: Textile, Exc Sleeping

Vanguard Manufacturing Inc.............. G 302 994-9302
  Wilmington *(G-20569)*

BAGS: Food Storage & Frozen Food, Plastic

PRODUCTS & SERVICES SECTION

BAR

Long Life Food Safety Pdts LLC............ G 302 229-1207
Lewes *(G-6218)*

BAGS: Paper

Forever Inc... F 302 594-0400
Wilmington *(G-16692)*

Fulton Paper Company......................... F 302 594-0400
Wilmington *(G-16770)*

BAGS: Paper, Made From Purchased Materials

Oxypaper Inc....................................... B 302 202-4897
Dover *(G-3256)*

BAGS: Plastic

JEB Plastics Inc.................................. G 302 479-9223
Wilmington *(G-17513)*

Printpack Inc....................................... C 302 323-4000
New Castle *(G-9495)*

Richard Earl Fisher.............................. G 302 598-1957
Wilmington *(G-19468)*

Toyo Fibre USA Inc............................. G 302 475-3699
Wilmington *(G-20379)*

BAGS: Plastic, Made From Purchased Materials

Castle Bag Company........................... G 302 656-1001
Wilmington *(G-15266)*

Grayling Industries Inc........................ F 770 751-9095
Frederica *(G-4168)*

BAGS: Trash, Plastic Film, Made From Purchased Materials

Ingenious Inventions AG LLC............... G 818 578-8266
Wilmington *(G-17334)*

BAKERIES, COMMERCIAL: On Premises Baking Only

Busymama Cupcakes.......................... G 302 259-9988
Seaford *(G-13098)*

International Food Co LLC................... G 404 333-3434
Newark *(G-11044)*

Kraft Heinz Company........................... A 302 734-6100
Dover *(G-2886)*

Pennsylvania Brand Co........................ G 302 674-5774
Dover *(G-3294)*

Posh Cupcake..................................... G 302 234-4451
Hockessin *(G-5348)*

Smackerals By Michelle LLC............... G 302 376-8272
Middletown *(G-7575)*

BAKERIES: On Premises Baking & Consumption

Kaan Cakes LLC.................................. G 302 260-0647
Millsboro *(G-8335)*

BAKERY PRDTS: Bread, All Types, Fresh Or Frozen

Serpe & Sons Inc................................ F 302 994-1868
Wilmington *(G-19759)*

Signature Intl Foods LLC..................... G 833 463-0004
Wilmington *(G-19821)*

BAKERY PRDTS: Cakes, Bakery, Exc Frozen

Cupcake Kouture Bakery LLC.............. G 302 602-6058
Newport *(G-12445)*

Kaan Cakes LLC.................................. G 302 260-0647
Millsboro *(G-8335)*

Sweets By Samantha LLC.................... G 302 740-2218
Newark *(G-12141)*

BAKERY PRDTS: Cookies

Stauffer Family LLC............................. G 302 227-5820
Rehoboth Beach *(G-12974)*

BAKERY PRDTS: Cookies & crackers

Wellness Natural USA Inc.................... G 800 547-5790
Wilmington *(G-20720)*

BAKERY PRDTS: Dry

Supper Solutions LLC......................... G 302 478-5935
Wilmington *(G-20148)*

BAKERY PRDTS: Wholesalers

Beach Break & Bakrie.......................... G 302 537-3800
Bethany Beach *(G-576)*

Custom Creams LLC........................... G 302 582-8862
New Castle *(G-8991)*

Pioneer Distributors Inc....................... G 302 644-0791
Milton *(G-8686)*

Point Coffee Shop and Bakery............. F 302 260-9734
Rehoboth Beach *(G-12894)*

Touch of Italy Bakery LLC.................... G 302 827-2132
Lewes *(G-6574)*

Wheatfield Holdings LLC..................... G 312 956-0198
Wilmington *(G-20756)*

BAKERY: Wholesale Or Wholesale & Retail Combined

Bevs Crafting Supplies LLC................. G 302 252-7583
Historic New Castle *(G-4942)*

Diane Lacash Inc................................. G 302 608-2477
Claymont *(G-1118)*

Dm KTure LLC..................................... G 201 892-3028
Bear *(G-172)*

Feelz LLC.. G 347 860-5813
Wilmington *(G-16576)*

Flawless Inbound LLC......................... F 929 324-1132
Dover *(G-2514)*

Goodbite USA Inc............................... G 516 761-4386
Bethany Beach *(G-604)*

Pembina Health Inc............................. F 701 314-7895
Lewes *(G-6359)*

Sweet Venom Effect LLC..................... E 302 674-5831
Wilmington *(G-20173)*

BALLET PRODUCTION SVCS

First State Ballet Theatre Inc............... G 302 658-7897
Wilmington *(G-16623)*

BALLOONS: Hot Air

Ilc Dover LP.. B 302 335-3911
Frederica *(G-4174)*

BANKS: Mortgage & Loan

About Angela Angelas Home Ln........... G 302 598-7799
Newark *(G-9742)*

Academy Mortgage.............................. G 484 680-8092
Wilmington *(G-14215)*

Accelerate Mortgage LLC.................... E 866 986-1245
Newark *(G-9748)*

Acopia Home Loans............................ G 302 242-6272
Rehoboth Beach *(G-12596)*

Acre Mortgage & Financial.................. G 302 737-5853
Christiana *(G-990)*

Caliber Home Loans............................ G 302 584-0580
Middletown *(G-6952)*

Caliber Home Loans Inc...................... G 302 483-7587
Newark *(G-10121)*

Delaware Community Inv Corp............. G 302 655-1420
Wilmington *(G-15891)*

Embrace Home Loans Inc.................... G 302 635-7998
Wilmington *(G-16388)*

Evolve Bank & Trust............................ F 302 286-7838
Newark *(G-10679)*

Integrity First Mortgage LLC................ G 302 318-6858
Newark *(G-11034)*

Jet Fast Loans.................................... G 302 934-6794
Millsboro *(G-8331)*

Jia Finance Inc................................... G 202 341-1031
Wilmington *(G-17545)*

Jpmorgan Chase & Co......................... G 800 935-9935
Bear *(G-312)*

Keystone Funding Inc......................... F 484 798-9084
Dover *(G-2861)*

Keystone Funding Inc......................... F 610 644-6423
Dover *(G-2862)*

Meridian Bank..................................... F 302 635-7500
Wilmington *(G-18281)*

Mortgage Network Solutions LLC........ E 302 252-0100
Wilmington *(G-18457)*

Motto Mortgage Prosperity LLC.......... G 302 313-5145
Milton *(G-8675)*

Movement Mortgage LLC.................... F 302 344-6758
Lewes *(G-6294)*

N V R Mortgage................................... G 302 732-1570
Dagsboro *(G-1486)*

New Penn Financial LLC...................... G 240 475-4741
Rehoboth Beach *(G-12870)*

Oakwood Funding Corporation............ G 336 855-2400
Wilmington *(G-18730)*

On Q Financial.................................... G 866 667-3279
Dover *(G-3227)*

Orchard Mortgage LLC....................... F 888 627-0677
Wilmington *(G-18816)*

PNC Bank National Association........... G 302 429-2266
Wilmington *(G-19092)*

Primary Residential Mrtg Inc............... E 302 292-1009
Newark *(G-11742)*

Primelending A Plainscapital............... F 302 733-7599
Newark *(G-11744)*

RKL Financial Corporation................... E 302 283-8000
Newark *(G-11891)*

Supreme Lending................................ G 302 268-6244
Wilmington *(G-20157)*

Waterstone Mortgage Corp................. G 302 227-8252
Rehoboth Beach *(G-13008)*

BANQUET HALL FACILITIES

Blue Falls Grove Inc............................ G 610 926-4017
Newark *(G-10057)*

Delcastle Golf Club Management......... F 302 998-9505
Wilmington *(G-15988)*

Fremont Hall.. G 302 731-2431
Newark *(G-10781)*

M & P Adventures Inc.......................... G 302 645-6271
Lewes *(G-6232)*

Nur Temple Aaonms............................ G 302 328-6100
New Castle *(G-9430)*

Quail Associates Inc........................... E 302 697-4660
Camden Wyoming *(G-966)*

Rockwood Conference Center............. G 302 761-4342
Wilmington *(G-19545)*

Worcester Golf Club Inc...................... F 610 222-0200
Milton *(G-8730)*

BAR

Camels Hump Inc................................ F 302 227-5719
Rehoboth Beach *(G-12662)*

Country Villa Motel............................. G 814 938-8330
Milford *(G-7842)*

Employee Codes: A=Over 500 employees, B=251-500
C=101-250, D=51-100, E=20-50, F=10-19, G=1-9

BAR
PRODUCTS & SERVICES SECTION

Millsboro Lanes Inc .... F 302 934-0400
  Millsboro (G-8387)

BARS: Concrete Reinforcing, Fabricated Steel

Confab Inc .... G 302 429-0140
  Wilmington (G-15592)

BASES, BEVERAGE

Baboon Bubble Inc .... G 302 307-2979
  New Castle (G-8841)
Bettys .... G 302 233-2675
  Milford (G-7793)
Psychedelic Water Inc .... G 855 337-7924
  Wilmington (G-19246)

BATHROOM ACCESS & FITTINGS: Vitreous China & Earthenware

Aquatica Plumbing Group Inc .... G 866 606-2782
  New Castle (G-8817)

BATTERIES, EXC AUTOMOTIVE: Wholesalers

Ep Supply Corp .... G 909 969-5122
  Lewes (G-5966)
Tsb Inc .... G 302 292-2330
  Newark (G-12242)

BATTERIES: Storage

Clarios LLC .... C 302 696-3221
  Middletown (G-6986)
Omareva Energy Inc .... G 514 660-0291
  Dover (G-3222)
Storm Energia Inc .... E 404 550-4862
  Wilmington (G-20088)
Talostech LLC .... G 302 332-9236
  Historic New Castle (G-5081)
Zrcn Inc .... D 212 602-1188
  Wilmington (G-20966)

BATTERIES: Wet

Talostech LLC .... G 302 332-9236
  Historic New Castle (G-5081)

BATTERY CHARGERS

Wirelisity Inc .... G 213 816-1957
  Lewes (G-6634)

BATTERY CHARGERS: Storage, Motor & Engine Generator Type

Kissangen Inc .... G 414 446-4182
  Newark (G-11187)

BATTERY CHARGING GENERATORS

Epic Charging Inc .... F 650 250-6811
  Dover (G-2456)
Evon Electric Enterprise Inc .... F 909 997-9599
  Lewes (G-5979)

BAUXITE MINING

American Minerals Partnership .... F 302 652-3301
  New Castle (G-8800)

BEARINGS: Roller & Parts

Roller Service Corporation .... E 302 737-5000
  Newark (G-11912)

BEAUTY & BARBER SHOP EQPT

Advanced Prttyping Sltionv LLC .... G 302 375-6048
  Wilmington (G-14278)

Baumann Industries Inc .... G 302 593-1049
  Wilmington (G-14781)
Chemax Manufacturing Corp .... G 302 328-2440
  New Castle (G-8929)
Club 6 Barbershop .... G 302 276-1624
  Bear (G-111)
DXquisite Hair Factory LLC .... G 267 298-0821
  Smyrna (G-13718)
Hirsh Industries Inc .... G 302 678-4990
  Dover (G-2681)
ISA Professional Ltd .... G 647 869-1552
  Wilmington (G-17424)
Klh Industries LLC .... G 800 348-0758
  Lewes (G-6169)
Raymond Chung Industries Corp .... G 302 384-9796
  Wilmington (G-19345)

BEAUTY & BARBER SHOP EQPT & SPLYS WHOLESALERS

Club 6 Barbershop .... G 302 276-1624
  Bear (G-111)
Simply Stylng-Schl of Csmtlgy .... G 302 778-1885
  Wilmington (G-19840)
Sky Touch LLC .... G 302 454-7040
  Newark (G-12025)

BEAUTY SALONS

A Gentlemans Touch Inc .... F 302 585-5805
  Wilmington (G-14163)
A Hair Hub LLC .... G 267 206-0569
  Bear (G-10)
Afterglo Beauty Spa .... G 302 537-7546
  Millville (G-8512)
An Event 2 Remember .... G 215 783-9744
  Claymont (G-1037)
Baby Bubba Dj & Event Planning .... G 302 373-4653
  New Castle (G-8843)
Barbara Baker .... G 302 238-7415
  Frankford (G-4067)
Beauty By Jamie .... G 302 784-5311
  New Castle (G-8856)
Beauty Max Inc .... G 302 735-1705
  Dover (G-1900)
Bella Mia Aesthetics LLC .... G 302 548-0660
  Middletown (G-6911)
Bethany Bch Hair Snippery Inc .... G 302 539-8344
  Millville (G-8520)
Billie Stevens Carlins .... G 302 436-0856
  Frankford (G-4072)
Boundaries New .... G 302 658-3486
  New Castle (G-8877)
Cathy Ann Mitchell .... G 302 875-7018
  Laurel (G-5479)
CEst Moi Infinity Inc .... G 267 455-2455
  Newark (G-10180)
CMC Corporation of Hockessin .... G 302 239-1960
  Hockessin (G-5164)
Cole Janeika .... G 302 838-1868
  Newark (G-10271)
Complete Family Care Inc .... F 302 232-5002
  Wilmington (G-15572)
Crumpton Starline .... G 302 832-1342
  New Castle (G-8989)
Daniel Halvorsen .... G 302 645-1761
  Lewes (G-5879)
Danny Thach .... G 302 645-7779
  Lewes (G-5880)
Dawn Runs With Scissors .... G 302 293-4517
  Wilmington (G-15817)
Elegant Images LLP .... G 302 698-5250
  Camden (G-828)

Encore Lashes Lash Lounge LLC .... G 844 408-0004
  New Castle (G-9094)
First State Wax LLC .... G 302 529-8888
  Wilmington (G-16639)
Fusion .... G 302 479-9444
  Wilmington (G-16773)
Give Back Beauty LLC .... F 571 439-2321
  Dover (G-2587)
Glitzy and Glamour Hair Salon .... G 302 325-9565
  New Castle (G-9169)
Goddess Beauty Supply LLC .... G 302 858-4649
  Georgetown (G-4343)
Goddess of Barn .... G 302 363-1062
  Smyrna (G-13745)
Growing & Glowing LLC .... G 302 500-9220
  Newark (G-10902)
H & J Unisex Salon .... G 302 983-6833
  Newark (G-10911)
Hair Studio II .... G 302 945-5110
  Millsboro (G-8312)
HLS Event Solutions LLC .... G 484 293-4272
  Harbeson (G-4699)
Hockessin Day Spa .... G 302 234-7573
  Wilmington (G-17162)
Jamroxk LLC .... G 302 423-5377
  Dover (G-2770)
JMB Glamsquad LLC .... F 844 695-4526
  Wilmington (G-17556)
Kathleens Creations .... G 302 492-8749
  Clayton (G-1379)
Kjp LLC .... G 302 765-0134
  Wilmington (G-17738)
Le Salone Hair Salon .... G 302 384-6788
  New Castle (G-9298)
Lindner LLC .... G 302 827-2160
  Lewes (G-6209)
Lorgus Enterprises Inc .... G 610 431-7453
  Dover (G-2976)
My Roots LLC .... G 302 883-2693
  Dover (G-3139)
My Salon Suite .... G 302 233-6947
  Camden Wyoming (G-964)
Nanas Butter LLC .... G 302 510-3937
  Wilmington (G-18524)
New Care Spa .... G 302 292-2067
  Newark (G-11515)
No 3 Eline Pwers Fgure Salons .... G 302 256-5015
  Wilmington (G-18659)
Nu Image Landscaping Inc .... G 302 366-8699
  Newark (G-11567)
Oerigo Consulting LLC .... G 302 353-4719
  Smyrna (G-13841)
One Step Ahead Childcare .... G 302 292-1162
  Newark (G-11593)
Pamper ME Pink LLC .... F 302 200-2635
  Selbyville (G-13589)
Peachy Keen Slon + Buty Bar LL .... G 302 519-5572
  Milford (G-8043)
Qbs Beauty Salon .... G 302 691-3449
  Wilmington (G-19276)
Rejuvntion Skin Wllness Asthti .... F 302 537-8318
  Millville (G-8545)
Rita Porter Darnetta .... G 302 419-3877
  New Castle (G-9534)
Savarna Inc .... G 757 446-0101
  Historic New Castle (G-5066)
Savvy Artistry LLC .... G 302 339-1712
  Historic New Castle (G-5067)
SBS Global LLC .... G 302 898-2911
  Newark (G-11955)
Shankias Best Braids .... G 302 507-9891
  Wilmington (G-19779)

1328   2024 Harris Directory of Delaware Businesses   (G-0000) Company's Geographic Section entry number

PRODUCTS & SERVICES SECTION

BEVERAGES, WINE & DISTILLED ALCOHOLIC, WHOLESALE: Wine

Sport Clips.. G 302 456-9900
  Newark *(G-12073)*

Sport Clips Hrcuts Rhboth Bch............... F 302 291-2391
  Rehoboth Beach *(G-12970)*

Steve Styles... G 302 540-4965
  Wilmington *(G-20063)*

Sundae Body LLC................................... F 480 430-5675
  Middletown *(G-7609)*

Town and Country Salon......................... G 302 322-2929
  Historic New Castle *(G-5089)*

US Male Modern Barbershop................... F 302 635-7370
  Hockessin *(G-5414)*

White Mink Beauty Salon......................... G 302 737-2081
  Newark *(G-12368)*

Works Body Wrap By Tanya..................... G 302 669-7839
  Wilmington *(G-20894)*

BEDDING, BEDSPREADS, BLANKETS & SHEETS

Villa Cotton Corporation........................... F 302 439-1508
  Wilmington *(G-20619)*

BEDS & ACCESS STORES

Johnny Janosik Inc.................................. C 302 875-5955
  Laurel *(G-5537)*

Mattress Firm Milford............................... G 302 422-6585
  Milford *(G-7990)*

BEDSPREADS & BED SETS, FROM PURCHASED MATERIALS

G L K Inc.. F 302 697-3838
  Dover *(G-2551)*

BEER & ALE WHOLESALERS

Argilla Brewing Company......................... G 302 731-8200
  Newark *(G-9901)*

Prime Beverage Group LLC..................... G 302 327-0002
  New Castle *(G-9493)*

Southern Glzers Wine Sprits LL............... E 302 656-4487
  New Castle *(G-9581)*

BEER & ALE, WHOLESALE: Beer & Other Fermented Malt Liquors

Delaware Importers Inc............................ D 302 656-4487
  New Castle *(G-9025)*

NKS Distributors Inc................................ F 302 422-1220
  Milford *(G-8029)*

NKS Distributors Inc................................ D 302 322-1811
  Smyrna *(G-13835)*

Standard Distributing Co Inc.................... D 302 655-5511
  New Castle *(G-9590)*

BELTS: Conveyor, Made From Purchased Wire

Mid Atlantic Indus Belting........................ G 302 453-7353
  Newark *(G-11406)*

BEVERAGE BASES & SYRUPS

Trisco Foods LLC..................................... D 719 352-3218
  Wilmington *(G-20429)*

BEVERAGE POWDERS

Le Herbe LLC.. G 949 317-1100
  Wilmington *(G-17842)*

BEVERAGE PRDTS: Malt, Barley

Proximity Malt LLC.................................. F 414 755-8388
  Laurel *(G-5580)*

BEVERAGE STORES

Petra Investments LLC............................ G 312 887-1558
  Newark *(G-11674)*

BEVERAGES, ALCOHOLIC: Ale

Dogfish Head Craft Brewery LLC............. C 302 684-1000
  Milton *(G-8610)*

BEVERAGES, ALCOHOLIC: Beer

Delaware Beer Works Inc......................... E 302 836-2739
  Bear *(G-142)*

Dewey Beer & Food Company LLC.......... F 302 227-1182
  Dewey Beach *(G-1668)*

Jakl Beer Works LLC............................... G 610 442-0878
  Middletown *(G-7237)*

Wilmington Brew Works LLC.................... F 302 757-4971
  Wilmington *(G-20810)*

BEVERAGES, ALCOHOLIC: Beer & Ale

Chesapeakemaine Trey........................... G 302 226-3600
  Rehoboth Beach *(G-12671)*

Dewey Beer Company LLC...................... G 302 329-9759
  Milton *(G-8603)*

Dogfish Head Inc..................................... F 302 226-2739
  Rehoboth Beach *(G-12730)*

First State Brewing Co LLC..................... E 302 285-9535
  Middletown *(G-7131)*

Volunteer Brewing Company LLC............ G 610 721-2836
  Middletown *(G-7694)*

BEVERAGES, ALCOHOLIC: Distilled Liquors

Beach Time.. G 302 644-2850
  Lewes *(G-5743)*

Bear Trap Spirits Inc................................ G 302 537-8008
  Millville *(G-8518)*

Dogfish Head Companies LLC................. C 302 684-1000
  Milton *(G-8609)*

Legacy Distilling LLC............................... F 302 983-1269
  Smyrna *(G-13799)*

R J Baker Distillery.................................. G 302 745-0967
  Laurel *(G-5583)*

Titan Spirits LLC..................................... G 205 568-3338
  Wilmington *(G-20336)*

William Grant & Sons USA Corp.............. B 302 573-3880
  Wilmington *(G-20791)*

BEVERAGES, ALCOHOLIC: Rum

Breakthru Beverage Group LLC.............. D 302 356-3500
  New Castle *(G-8890)*

BEVERAGES, ALCOHOLIC: Wines

Chatam International Incorporated.......... C 302 478-6185
  Wilmington *(G-15347)*

Delaware Meat Company LLC................. G 302 438-0252
  Wilmington *(G-15941)*

Harvest Ridge Winery LLC...................... G 302 250-6583
  Marydel *(G-6799)*

Nassau Vly Vineyards & Winery.............. G 302 645-9463
  Lewes *(G-6306)*

Piceno... G 302 545-6406
  Wilmington *(G-19033)*

Pizzadili Partners LLC............................. G 302 284-9463
  Felton *(G-4009)*

Terrance R Hester................................... G 856 905-8196
  Middletown *(G-7636)*

Texavino LLC.. G 302 295-0829
  Wilmington *(G-20283)*

White Horse Winery................................. G 302 388-9850
  Wilmington *(G-20764)*

White Horse Winery LLC......................... G 302 472-7200
  Wilmington *(G-20765)*

Wine Worx LLC....................................... E 302 436-1500
  Frankford *(G-4161)*

BEVERAGES, NONALCOHOLIC: Bottled & canned soft drinks

Dope Venture Studio Inc......................... G 302 257-5936
  Dover *(G-2325)*

Food and Bev Innovations LLC............... G 302 722-8058
  Wilmington *(G-16681)*

Global Brands Usa Inc............................ G 314 401-2477
  Wilmington *(G-16885)*

Moon Shot Energy LLC........................... G 512 297-2626
  Lewes *(G-6289)*

Ooso Drinks Co LLC............................... G 919 808-7605
  Dover *(G-3235)*

Taylor Made Waters Inc.......................... F 302 352-9979
  Wilmington *(G-20234)*

BEVERAGES, NONALCOHOLIC: Carbonated

Genki Forest (america) Inc..................... F 626 456-2664
  Wilmington *(G-16839)*

Pepsi-Cola Btlg of Wilmington................. C 302 761-4848
  Wilmington *(G-18966)*

BEVERAGES, NONALCOHOLIC: Carbonated, Canned & Bottled, Etc

629 Market Retail LLC............................ G 302 691-2100
  Wilmington *(G-14144)*

Maurten US Corporation......................... G 302 669-9085
  Wilmington *(G-18202)*

Wize Monkey USA Inc............................. G 604 839-7640
  Dover *(G-3863)*

BEVERAGES, NONALCOHOLIC: Soft Drinks, Canned & Bottled, Etc

Krave Like LLC....................................... G 302 482-4550
  Wilmington *(G-17752)*

Minor Figures Inc................................... G 714 875-3449
  Camden *(G-877)*

True Spirit Beverage Company................ G 520 356-4730
  Wilmington *(G-20444)*

BEVERAGES, WINE & DISTILLED ALCOHOLIC, WHOLESALE: Liquor

Delaware Importers Inc........................... D 302 656-4487
  New Castle *(G-9025)*

Js Liquors... E 302 656-4066
  Wilmington *(G-17602)*

Outlet Liquors... G 302 227-7700
  Rehoboth Beach *(G-12881)*

BEVERAGES, WINE & DISTILLED ALCOHOLIC, WHOLESALE: Wine

Breakthru Beverage Group LLC............. B 443 631-2597
  Middletown *(G-6936)*

Country Vintner LLC............................... E 877 946-3620
  Newark *(G-10335)*

HB Wine Merchants LLC........................ G 302 384-5991
  Hartly *(G-4876)*

Lawrence Boone Selections LLC............ G 757 602-5173
  Bear *(G-339)*

NKS Distributors Inc............................... D 302 322-1811
  Smyrna *(G-13835)*

Order Department................................... G 302 654-3116
  New Castle *(G-9437)*

Robert M Panzer..................................... G 302 571-0717
  Wilmington *(G-19519)*

S & S Wines and Spirits......................... G 302 678-9987
  Dover *(G-3497)*

Employee Codes: A=Over 500 employees, B=251-500
C=101-250, D=51-100, E=20-50, F=10-19, G=1-9

2024 Harris Directory of Delaware Businesses

BEVERAGES, WINE & DISTILLED ALCOHOLIC, WHOLESALE: Wine

Southern Wine Spirits Del LLC .... E 800 292-7890
  New Castle (G-9582)
Standard Distributing Co Inc .... D 302 655-5511
  New Castle (G-9590)
Universal Bev Importers LLC .... G 302 322-7900
  New Castle (G-9659)
Wine Worx LLC .... E 302 436-1500
  Frankford (G-4161)

BEVERAGES, WINE/DISTILLED ALCOHOLIC, WHOL: Bttlg Wine/Liquor

Southern Glzers Wine Sprits LL .... E 302 656-4487
  New Castle (G-9581)
William Grant & Sons USA Corp .... B 302 573-3880
  Wilmington (G-20791)

BICYCLES WHOLESALERS

Seagreen Bicycle .... G 302 645-7008
  Lewes (G-6454)
Seagreen Bicycle LLP .... G 302 226-2323
  Rehoboth Beach (G-12952)

BICYCLES, PARTS & ACCESS

Delfast Inc .... E 323 540-5155
  Dover (G-2275)
Propel Bikes LLC .... G 631 678-1946
  Wilmington (G-19231)
Ross Bicycles LLC .... G 888 392-5628
  Lewes (G-6433)

BILLING & BOOKKEEPING SVCS

Advantdge Hlthcare Sltions Inc .... F 302 224-5678
  Newark (G-9786)
Bookkeeping Solutions .... G 302 650-5058
  Newark (G-10069)
Delaware Medical MGT Svcs LLC .... E 302 283-3300
  Newark (G-10459)
Delaware Occptnal Hlth Svcs LL .... E 302 368-5100
  Newark (G-10464)
Doherty & Associates Inc .... F 302 239-3500
  Wilmington (G-16119)
DSouza and Associates Inc .... E 302 239-2300
  Hockessin (G-5193)
Health Care Practice MGT .... E 302 633-5840
  Wilmington (G-17096)
Hospital Blling Cllctn Svc Ltd .... B 302 552-8000
  Historic New Castle (G-5006)
Integrity Billing Specialist .... G 302 383-1704
  Smyrna (G-13772)
M D N Billing Consulting LLC .... G 914 376-6100
  Milford (G-7981)
MDN Billing Consulting Svcs .... G 914 376-6100
  Milford (G-7991)
Medical Billing & MGT Svcs Inc .... E 610 564-5314
  Newark (G-11374)
Murgency Inc .... E 650 308-9964
  Dover (G-3132)
Office Service Solutions LLC .... G 302 420-3958
  Historic New Castle (G-5042)
Paths LLC .... F 302 294-1494
  Newark (G-11636)
Payroll Management Assistants .... G 302 456-6810
  Newark (G-11647)
Pcmb LLC .... G 302 482-1360
  Wilmington (G-18935)
Perioperative Services LLC .... D 302 733-0806
  Newark (G-11666)

BINDING SVC: Books & Manuals

Amer Inc .... G 302 654-2498
  Wilmington (G-14421)

Ben-Dom Printing Company .... F 302 737-9144
  Newark (G-10019)
Dover Post Co Inc .... E 302 678-3616
  Dover (G-2364)
Dupont Txtles Intriors Del Inc .... E 302 774-1000
  Wilmington (G-16218)
Garile Inc .... E 302 366-0848
  Newark (G-10809)
L E Stansell Inc .... G 302 475-1534
  Wilmington (G-17775)
William N Cann Inc .... E 302 995-0820
  Wilmington (G-20795)

BIOLOGICAL PRDTS: Exc Diagnostic

Analytical Biological Svcs Inc .... E 302 654-4492
  New Castle (G-8806)
Cleamol LLC .... G 513 885-3462
  Wilmington (G-15469)
Orphagenix Inc .... G 267 334-5153
  Wilmington (G-18825)
Reflection Biotechnologies Inc .... G 212 765-2200
  Wilmington (G-19396)

BIOLOGICAL PRDTS: Serums

Plume Serum LLC .... G 302 697-9044
  Magnolia (G-6775)

BIOLOGICAL PRDTS: Vaccines

Uvax Bio LLC .... E 818 859-3988
  Newark (G-12293)

BIOLOGICAL PRDTS: Vaccines & Immunizing

Glaxosmthkline Hldngs Amrcas I .... C 302 984-6932
  Wilmington (G-16882)
Mommas Mountain LLC .... G 410 236-6717
  Magnolia (G-6769)

BIOLOGICAL PRDTS: Veterinary

Artevet LLC .... G 443 255-0016
  Wilmington (G-14564)

BLADES: Knife

Dalstrong America Inc .... G 716 380-4998
  Wilmington (G-15772)
Delaware Diamond Knives Inc .... E 302 999-7476
  Wilmington (G-15906)

BLANKBOOKS: Albums, Record

SE Lavi Productions LLC .... G 727 457-2625
  Dover (G-3523)

BLASTING SVC: Sand, Metal Parts

Industrial Metal Treating Corp .... F 302 656-1677
  Wilmington (G-17315)

BLINDS & SHADES: Vertical

Local Vertical .... G 302 242-2552
  Dover (G-2968)

BLINDS : Window

Vertical Blind Factory Inc .... G 302 998-9616
  Wilmington (G-20598)

BLOCKS: Landscape Or Retaining Wall, Concrete

All Rock & Mulch LLC .... G 302 838-7625
  Bear (G-26)
Dreamscape Design Cons LLC .... G 302 893-0984
  Newark (G-10571)

Valley Landscaping and Con Inc .... G 302 922-5020
  Dover (G-3772)

BLOOD BANK

New York Blood Center Inc .... G 302 737-8405
  Dagsboro (G-1488)
New York Blood Center Inc .... D 302 737-8405
  Newark (G-11528)
New York Blood Ctr Inc D/B/A B .... F 302 734-4100
  Dover (G-3182)
New York Blood Ctr Inc D/B/A B .... F 302 737-8400
  Georgetown (G-4444)
New York Blood Ctr Inc D/B/A B .... G 302 737-8400
  Wilmington (G-18629)

BLOOD RELATED HEALTH SVCS

Bancroft Inc .... F 856 769-1300
  Newark (G-9978)
Bancroft Neurohealth .... D 302 691-8531
  Wilmington (G-14740)
Delaware Imaging Network .... D 302 737-5990
  Newark (G-10453)
Delaware Integrative Medical C .... G 302 559-5959
  Georgetown (G-4282)
Dr Kellyann LLC .... C 888 871-2155
  Dover (G-2375)
Eagle Mhc Company .... B 302 653-3000
  Clayton (G-1363)
Kent General Hospital Inc .... A 302 430-5705
  Milford (G-7963)
La Red Health Center Inc .... D 408 533-3189
  Seaford (G-13253)
Medical Alternative Care .... G 302 430-5705
  Milford (G-7993)
Quakertown Wellness Center .... G 302 644-0130
  Lewes (G-6398)

BLUEPRINTING SVCS

Reliable Copy Service Inc .... D 302 654-8080
  Wilmington (G-19422)
Reprographics Center Inc .... G 302 328-5019
  New Castle (G-9522)

BOAT BUILDING & REPAIR

Croker Oars Usa Inc .... G 302 897-6705
  Townsend (G-13979)
Dunworth Machines LLC .... G 434 977-4790
  Selbyville (G-13526)
S & J Haftl Inc .... G 302 378-7571
  Middletown (G-7530)

BOAT BUILDING & REPAIRING: Fiberglass

F & S Boat Works .... F 302 838-5500
  Bear (G-217)

BOAT BUILDING & REPAIRING: Motorized

Escape Yachts Inc .... G 302 691-9070
  Wilmington (G-16463)

BOAT BUILDING & REPAIRING: Yachts

Nanticoke Industries LLC .... G 302 245-8825
  Seaford (G-13306)

BOAT BUILDING & RPRG: Fishing, Small, Lobster, Crab, Oyster

Broadwater Oyster Company LLC .... G 610 220-7776
  Rehoboth Beach (G-12657)

BOAT DEALERS

Bobs Marine Service Inc .... F 302 539-3711
  Ocean View (G-12482)

PRODUCTS & SERVICES SECTION

BROKERS: Loan

BOAT DEALERS: Motor
North Bay Marina Incorporated............ E 302 436-4211
  Selbyville *(G-13586)*
Rudy Marine Inc................................ F 302 999-8735
  Dagsboro *(G-1501)*

BOAT REPAIR SVCS
Bobs Marine Service Inc..................... F 302 539-3711
  Ocean View *(G-12482)*
M M Marine Service........................... G 302 841-7689
  Millsboro *(G-8356)*
Midlantic Marine Center Inc................. F 302 436-2628
  Selbyville *(G-13575)*

BOILER & HEATING REPAIR SVCS
First State Plumbing & Heating............ G 302 275-9746
  New Castle *(G-9131)*

BOILERS: Low-Pressure Heating, Steam Or Hot Water
Watts Htg Hot Wtr Slutions LLC........... D 817 335-9531
  Wilmington *(G-20686)*

BOOK STORES
Prestwick House Inc.......................... E 302 659-2070
  Smyrna *(G-13854)*

BOOK STORES: Children's
Wellthy Investors LLC........................ G 267 847-3486
  Dover *(G-3831)*

BOOK STORES: Religious
God Said I Love You Ltd................... G 302 697-0647
  Camden *(G-839)*

BOOKS, WHOLESALE
Acorn Books Inc............................... G 302 508-2219
  Smyrna *(G-13631)*
Around Again and Again Bks LLC....... G 302 439-3847
  Wilmington *(G-14558)*
Delaware Beach Book LLC................ G 302 249-1030
  Milton *(G-8598)*
Linguatext Ltd................................... G 302 453-8695
  Newark *(G-11262)*
Thomas B Davis................................ G 302 692-0871
  Newark *(G-12191)*

BOTTLED GAS DEALERS: Liquefied Petro, Dlvrd To Customers
Pep-Up Inc....................................... G 302 645-2600
  Rehoboth Beach *(G-12888)*
Pep-Up Inc....................................... F 302 856-2555
  Georgetown *(G-4460)*

BOTTLED GAS DEALERS: Propane
Keen Compressed Gas Co.................. E 302 594-4545
  New Castle *(G-9276)*
Schagrin Gas Co................................ E 302 378-2000
  Middletown *(G-7541)*

BOTTLES: Plastic
Shaker Revolution LLC....................... G 302 219-4838
  Wilmington *(G-19777)*

BOWLING CENTERS
Keglers Korner Pro Shop.................... G 302 526-2249
  Dover *(G-2837)*

BOXES & CRATES: Rectangular, Wood
H&H Customs Inc.............................. G 302 378-0810
  Middletown *(G-7187)*

BOXES & SHOOK: Nailed Wood
Elwyn Pennsylvania and Del................ D 302 658-8860
  Wilmington *(G-16382)*

BOXES: Corrugated
True-Pack Ltd................................... F 302 326-2222
  New Castle *(G-9644)*

BRICK, STONE & RELATED PRDTS WHOLESALERS
Blue Sky Stones Inc........................... G 201 359-1368
  Wilmington *(G-14976)*
Chesapeake Hearth Stone Co LLC...... G 302 943-5276
  Seaford *(G-13117)*
Delaware Brick Company.................... G 302 883-2807
  Dover *(G-2219)*
Depro-Serical USA Inc....................... G 302 368-8040
  Townsend *(G-13991)*
Michael McCarthy Stones................... G 302 539-8056
  Millville *(G-8541)*
Parker Block Co Inc.......................... E 302 934-9237
  Millsboro *(G-8413)*
Steering Committee........................... G 302 994-7533
  Wilmington *(G-20046)*

BROADCASTING & COMMUNICATIONS EQPT: Studio Eqpt, Radio & TV
Vital-Gh Media Group LLC.................. G 302 437-4258
  Middletown *(G-7691)*

BROADCASTING STATIONS, RADIO: News
News In Bullets LLC........................... E 831 250-6955
  Middletown *(G-7400)*
Trade News Inc................................ G 212 884-8089
  Wilmington *(G-20385)*

BROKERS & DEALERS: Securities
Cananwill Corp.................................. G 302 576-3499
  Wilmington *(G-15212)*
CG Jcf Corp..................................... G 302 658-7581
  Wilmington *(G-15322)*
CRH Investments Inc........................ G 302 427-0924
  Wilmington *(G-15702)*
Fjs Capital Management Inc................ G 267 850-1123
  Wilmington *(G-16658)*
Freemarkets Investment Co Inc........... G 302 427-2089
  Wilmington *(G-16744)*
Gates and Company LLC................... F 302 428-1338
  Wilmington *(G-16813)*
Gund Securities Corporation............... F 302 479-9210
  Wilmington *(G-17006)*
Ing Bank Fsb.................................... D 302 658-2200
  Wilmington *(G-17332)*
Interactive Tech Holdings LLC............. A 302 478-9356
  Wilmington *(G-17374)*
Jpmorgan Chase & Co....................... G 800 935-9935
  Bear *(G-312)*
Metl Technology Inc........................... F 954 309-4589
  Wilmington *(G-18291)*
Metropolitan Wealth MGT LLC............ G 212 607-2488
  Wilmington *(G-18294)*
Neptune Global Holdings LLC............. G 302 256-5080
  Wilmington *(G-18585)*
Preferred Term Securities Xxvi............ G 302 651-7642
  Wilmington *(G-19165)*
Rbc... E 302 892-5901
  Wilmington *(G-19350)*
UBS Financial Services Inc................. G 302 407-4700
  Wilmington *(G-20494)*
Wells Fargo Clearing Svcs LLC........... G 302 731-2131
  Newark *(G-12359)*

BROKERS & DEALERS: Security
Citigroup Globl Mkts Fncl Pdts............ F 212 559-1000
  Wilmington *(G-15449)*
Deutsche Bank Tr Co Americas........... E 302 636-3301
  Wilmington *(G-16031)*
Markvell Delarie Gilmore Trust............ G 772 742-1499
  Wilmington *(G-18151)*
Merrill Lynch Prce Fnner Smith........... G 302 736-7700
  Dover *(G-3065)*
Merrill Lynch Prce Fnner Smith........... F 302 571-5100
  Wilmington *(G-18287)*
Morgan Stnley Smith Barney LLC........ C 302 636-5500
  Wilmington *(G-18449)*

BROKERS' SVCS
Buycrypt Inc..................................... G 309 733-4157
  Dover *(G-1998)*
Turning Point Collection LLC............... G 302 275-0167
  Wilmington *(G-20464)*

BROKERS: Business
Empire Flippers LLC......................... E 323 638-0438
  Wilmington *(G-16399)*
Go Marketplace LLC.......................... G 630 624-9079
  Wilmington *(G-16900)*
Mergers Acqstons Strtegies LLC.......... G 302 992-0400
  Wilmington *(G-18280)*
Techadox Inc.................................. F 302 691-9130
  Newark *(G-12168)*

BROKERS: Food
Acm Corp... G 302 736-3864
  Dover *(G-1711)*
Amazon Commodities LLC.................. G 302 715-1427
  Newark *(G-9840)*
El Bluebird LLC................................. G 775 773-3255
  Wilmington *(G-16347)*
Everest Foods Enterprises Inc............. F 215 896-8902
  Wilmington *(G-16484)*
Heavenly Harvest LLC........................ G 302 487-0974
  Dover *(G-2669)*
Hughes Delaware Maid Scrapple......... G 302 284-4370
  Felton *(G-3983)*
Oppenheimer Group Inc.................... E 302 533-0779
  Newark *(G-11595)*
Petra Investments LLC...................... G 312 887-1558
  Newark *(G-11674)*
Premium Brands Inc......................... G 925 566-8863
  Dover *(G-3364)*
Supermarket Associates Inc............... G 302 547-1977
  Wilmington *(G-20146)*
Thomas E Moore Inc........................ F 302 674-1500
  Kenton *(G-5456)*
Yupica Inc (usa)................................ G 707 387-9874
  Wilmington *(G-20941)*

BROKERS: Loan
American Spirit Federal Cr Un............. E 302 738-4515
  Newark *(G-9848)*
Del-One Federal Credit Union............. E 302 734-4496
  Dover *(G-2214)*
Delaware First Federal Cr Un.............. F 302 998-0665
  Wilmington *(G-15919)*
Delaware Title Loans Inc.................... F 302 478-8505
  Wilmington *(G-15976)*
Equity Plus Inc.................................. F 302 762-3122
  Wilmington *(G-16453)*

Employee Codes: A=Over 500 employees, B=251-500
C=101-250, D=51-100, E=20-50, F=10-19, G=1-9

2024 Harris Directory of Delaware Businesses

BROKERS: Loan

Lending Manager Holdings LLC .... G 888 501-0335
  Newark *(G-11245)*
Provident Federal Credit Union .... F 302 734-1133
  Dover *(G-3386)*
Ssbv LLC .... F 844 585-0656
  Wilmington *(G-19988)*

BROKERS: Mortgage, Arranging For Loans

ABC Lending Corp .... G 302 369-5626
  Newark *(G-9739)*
Aca Mortgage Co Inc .... G 302 225-1390
  Wilmington *(G-14213)*
Delaware Financial Capital .... G 302 266-9500
  Newark *(G-10444)*
First Atlantic Mrtg Svcs LLC .... G 302 841-8435
  Lewes *(G-5996)*
Interstate Mortgage Corp Inc .... G 302 733-7620
  Newark *(G-11049)*
John Lovett Inc .... F 302 455-9460
  Newark *(G-11114)*
Louviers Mortgage Corporation .... G 302 234-4129
  Wilmington *(G-18011)*
Pike Creek Mortgage Services .... G 302 892-2811
  Newark *(G-11692)*
Resource Mortgage Corp .... F 302 657-0181
  Wilmington *(G-19439)*
Synergy Direct Mortgage .... G 302 283-0833
  Christiana *(G-1011)*
Van Buren Mortgage LLC .... G 302 945-1109
  Millsboro *(G-8492)*
Van Buren Mortgage LLC .... G 302 725-0723
  Ocean View *(G-12579)*

BROKERS: Printing

University of De Printing .... F 302 831-2153
  Newark *(G-12276)*

BROOMS & BRUSHES: Household Or Indl

Dupont Flaments - Americas LLC .... E 302 774-1000
  Wilmington *(G-16209)*

BUILDING & OFFICE CLEANING SVCS

All JS Cleaning Services Inc .... G 302 299-9916
  New Castle *(G-8780)*
Chesapeake Home Services LLC .... G 302 732-6006
  Frankford *(G-4087)*
Clean Hands LLC .... F 215 681-1435
  Smyrna *(G-13681)*
Cleaners Sunny .... G 302 827-2095
  Lewes *(G-5825)*
Gemini Building Systems LLC .... F 302 654-5310
  Wilmington *(G-16827)*
Generation Cleaning Svc LLC .... G 302 492-2772
  Claymont *(G-1158)*
Ms Neat Cleaning Services LLC .... G 302 535-7236
  Dover *(G-3130)*
Oceanside Elite Clg Bldg Svcs .... E 302 339-7777
  Lewes *(G-6329)*

BUILDING & STRUCTURAL WOOD MEMBERS

Delmarva Truss and Panel LLC .... G 302 270-8488
  Wyoming *(G-20984)*

BUILDING CLEANING & MAINTENANCE SVCS

A1 Striping Inc .... G 302 738-5016
  Newark *(G-9730)*
Able Whelling and Machiene .... G 302 436-1929
  Selbyville *(G-13458)*
Abrahams Seed LLC .... G 302 588-1913
  Clayton *(G-1347)*
Advanced Plumbing & Maint LLC .... G 302 584-4001
  Bear *(G-17)*
Better Home Services .... G 302 250-9860
  Dover *(G-1923)*
Christopher Handy .... G 302 934-1018
  Millsboro *(G-8225)*
Claw Blue Maintenance .... G 717 487-2808
  Georgetown *(G-4258)*
Cleanith LLC .... G 571 269-8213
  Magnolia *(G-6731)*
Coastal Chem-Dry .... G 302 234-0200
  Lewes *(G-5838)*
De Property Maintenance LLC .... G 302 241-5567
  Middletown *(G-7033)*
Delmar Corporate Clg Svcs Inc .... E 302 861-8006
  Newark *(G-10499)*
Delmarva Shore Maintenance .... G 302 519-8657
  Millsboro *(G-8268)*
Delmarva Soap & Powerwash Sls .... G 302 875-2012
  Laurel *(G-5499)*
Dover Nunan LLC .... G 302 697-9776
  Dover *(G-2356)*
Elite Property Maintenance .... G 302 836-1865
  Delaware City *(G-1540)*
Elite Property Maintenance .... G 302 836-8878
  Middletown *(G-7095)*
Fortress Home Maintenance Serv .... G 302 539-3446
  Dagsboro *(G-1451)*
Foshee Property Maintenance .... G 302 344-6410
  Ocean View *(G-12512)*
Fresh Cut Lndscping Mintenance .... G 302 841-1848
  Millsboro *(G-8295)*
Gale Force Cleaning & Restore .... G 302 539-6244
  Ocean View *(G-12517)*
Golden Inc .... E 800 878-1356
  Newark *(G-10861)*
Gutter Connection LLC .... F 302 736-0105
  Dover *(G-2634)*
Hitz Mechanical .... G 727 742-6315
  Frankford *(G-4113)*
Home Works .... G 302 514-9974
  Smyrna *(G-13764)*
James Maintenance Services LLC .... G 302 934-7625
  Millsboro *(G-8328)*
Kimberly Tucker .... G 302 358-0574
  Middletown *(G-7274)*
L Maintenance .... G 302 841-1698
  Frankford *(G-4122)*
M N K Maintenance and REM .... G 302 841-5884
  Dagsboro *(G-1477)*
Maintenance Tech .... G 302 322-6410
  New Castle *(G-9340)*
Maintenance Troubleshooti .... G 302 477-1045
  Wilmington *(G-18091)*
Maintenance Unlimited LLC .... G 302 387-1868
  Magnolia *(G-6763)*
Marlings Inc .... F 302 325-1759
  Wilmington *(G-18153)*
Mebro Inc .... E 302 992-0104
  Wilmington *(G-18243)*
New Image Property Maintenance .... G 302 396-0451
  Delmar *(G-1626)*
Oe Performance Repr Maint Inc .... G 302 664-1264
  Milton *(G-8679)*
Phoenix Home Theater Inc .... F 302 295-1390
  Wilmington *(G-19025)*
Priority Services LLC .... E 302 918-3070
  Newark *(G-11751)*
Property Maintenance .... G 302 645-5921
  Lewes *(G-6395)*
Service Master of Newark .... G 302 654-8145
  Wilmington *(G-19761)*
ServiceMaster of Newark .... F 302 834-8006
  Newark *(G-11985)*
SERVPRO Bear-New Castle Inc .... F 302 392-6000
  Bear *(G-484)*
SERVPRO of Norwalk/Wilton .... G 203 866-2871
  Newark *(G-11986)*
SERVPRO of Upper Darby .... G 302 392-6000
  Bear *(G-485)*
Ship Shape Marine Inc .... G 302 841-7355
  Seaford *(G-13401)*
SMI Services of Delaware LLC .... D 302 436-4410
  Selbyville *(G-13605)*
St Andrews Maintenance .... G 302 832-2675
  Bear *(G-509)*
Swamps Property Maint LLC .... G 302 841-1162
  Millsboro *(G-8478)*
T & M Property Maintenance LLC .... G 302 462-1080
  Middletown *(G-7617)*
Teagle and Sons .... G 302 682-8639
  Seaford *(G-13426)*
Teff Inc .... F 302 856-9768
  Georgetown *(G-4547)*
Tri-State Carpet Maint Inc .... G 302 654-8193
  Wilmington *(G-20412)*
Ventura Maintenance Company .... F 302 376-9060
  Middletown *(G-7685)*
Vicks Commercial Clg & Maint .... G 302 697-9591
  Dover *(G-3791)*
Whaleys Seed Store Inc .... G 302 875-7833
  Laurel *(G-5623)*
Yoders Maintenance .... G 302 492-0203
  Hartly *(G-4913)*

BUILDING COMPONENTS: Structural Steel

Crystal Steel Fabricators Inc .... D 302 846-0613
  Delmar *(G-1585)*
Mancor US Inc .... D 302 573-3858
  Wilmington *(G-18102)*
Steel Suppliers Inc .... C 302 654-5243
  Wilmington *(G-20043)*
Summit Steel Inc .... D 302 325-3220
  New Castle *(G-9599)*

BUILDING PRDTS & MATERIALS DEALERS

American Cedar & Millwork Inc .... E 302 645-9580
  Lewes *(G-5683)*
Case Construction Inc .... G 302 737-3800
  Newark *(G-10158)*
Custom Cabinet Shop Inc .... F 302 337-8241
  Greenwood *(G-4609)*
D F Quillen & Sons Inc .... E 302 227-2531
  Rehoboth Beach *(G-12709)*
East Coast Minority Supplier .... G 302 656-3337
  Wilmington *(G-16252)*
Erco Ceilings & Interiors Inc .... F 302 398-3200
  Harrington *(G-4767)*
Erco Ceilings & Interiors Inc .... F 302 994-6200
  Wilmington *(G-16455)*
Marjam Supply Co Inc .... F 302 283-1020
  Newark *(G-11332)*
Mechanics Paradise Inc .... F 302 652-8863
  New Castle *(G-9355)*
P D Supply Inc .... G 302 655-3358
  Wilmington *(G-18852)*

BUILDINGS: Portable

Steel Buildings Inc .... G 302 644-0444
  Lewes *(G-6508)*

PRODUCTS & SERVICES SECTION

BUSINESS ACTIVITIES: Non-Commercial Site

BUILDINGS: Prefabricated, Metal
Regional Builders Inc .... F 302 628-8660
 Seaford *(G-13370)*

BUILDINGS: Prefabricated, Wood
Fox Pointe .... G 302 744-9442
 Dover *(G-2530)*

BURIAL VAULTS: Concrete Or Precast Terrazzo
Cecil Vault & Memorial Co Inc .... G 302 994-3806
 Wilmington *(G-15293)*
Cooper-Wilbert Vault Co Inc .... G 302 376-1331
 Middletown *(G-7013)*
Delaware Monument and Vault .... G 302 540-2387
 Hockessin *(G-5181)*

BUSINESS ACTIVITIES: Non-Commercial Site

4dimensions LLC .... D 302 339-0082
 New Castle *(G-8747)*
A-To-Z Management LLC .... G 302 500-5230
 Dover *(G-1699)*
Accommodating Nurses LLC .... G 302 390-8065
 Wilmington *(G-14226)*
Achievers Holdings Inc .... B 647 265-9032
 Wilmington *(G-14232)*
Acorn Site Furnishings .... G 302 249-4979
 Bridgeville *(G-661)*
Acosh Enterprise LLC .... G 631 767-4501
 Newark *(G-9758)*
Advanced Logistics LLC .... G 302 345-8921
 New Castle *(G-8765)*
Advanced Modern Care LLC .... F 267 235-6922
 Newark *(G-9777)*
Afford-A-Tree Svc & Ldscpg LLC .... G 302 670-4154
 Hartly *(G-4854)*
AFmensah LLC .... G 302 777-0538
 Wilmington *(G-14310)*
Agent Launch LLC .... F 302 200-5574
 Newark *(G-9796)*
AGS Royalty Management LLC .... G 888 292-6995
 Dover *(G-1748)*
Ajusta Tu Corona Inc .... F 203 434-0356
 Dover *(G-1758)*
Aldas Refinishing Company .... G 302 528-5028
 Hockessin *(G-5119)*
Alex Property Management LLC .... A 302 384-9845
 Dover *(G-1761)*
All JS Cleaning Services Inc .... G 302 299-9916
 New Castle *(G-8780)*
All Lives Matter LLC .... G 252 767-9291
 Dover *(G-1763)*
Amazed Apps LLC .... G 916 934-9210
 Dover *(G-1781)*
Ankor Tree Service LLC .... G 302 514-7447
 Smyrna *(G-13643)*
Aparta Hospitality Tech .... G 617 383-3239
 Dover *(G-1801)*
Appcano LLC .... G 951 285-3632
 Wilmington *(G-14509)*
Apphive Inc .... G 240 898-4661
 Newark *(G-9888)*
Aquia Nava II LLC .... E 410 245-8990
 Millsboro *(G-8172)*
Arion LLC .... G 215 531-1673
 Dover *(G-1813)*
Arklight Arsenal LLC .... G 844 722-3766
 Dover *(G-1814)*

Arvi Vr Inc .... G 844 615-8194
 Wilmington *(G-14575)*
Arya Life Coaching LLC .... G 610 590-1440
 Lewes *(G-5705)*
Ascension Industries LLC .... G 302 659-1778
 Smyrna *(G-13648)*
Assured Affluence LLC .... G 609 468-0250
 Dover *(G-1838)*
Atlas Beauty LLC .... G 904 382-3487
 Dover *(G-1850)*
Atr Electrical Services Inc .... F 302 373-7769
 Middletown *(G-6886)*
Aura Smart Air Inc .... G 847 909-5822
 Wilmington *(G-14642)*
Aviman Management LLC .... E 302 377-5788
 Wilmington *(G-14669)*
B Lawrence Homes LLC .... G 302 559-1779
 Wilmington *(G-14702)*
Baibi Wise LLC .... G 201 375-0170
 Newark *(G-9973)*
Beautiful Floors LLC .... G 302 690-5230
 Newark *(G-10007)*
Big Day Trucking LLC .... G 302 900-1190
 Dover *(G-1934)*
Black Gods and Goddess LLC .... G 708 665-0949
 Dover *(G-1943)*
Blak Mpire LLC .... G 803 966-7648
 Lewes *(G-5769)*
Blaze Coin LLC .... G 509 768-2249
 Dover *(G-1946)*
Blue Collar Utilities LLC .... G 410 422-0886
 Bridgeville *(G-673)*
Blue Heron Contracting LLC .... G 302 526-0648
 Greenwood *(G-4600)*
Brian Patterson PA .... G 203 466-9972
 Milton *(G-8574)*
Brik Labs Inc .... F 302 499-4423
 Wilmington *(G-15115)*
Broccworth Housing Firm LLC .... G 860 937-6308
 Wilmington *(G-15123)*
Brute Performance Inc .... G 757 477-7136
 Camden Wyoming *(G-920)*
Burroughs Express LLC .... G 410 476-1764
 Dover *(G-1996)*
C4-Nvis USA LLC .... G 213 465-5089
 Dover *(G-2009)*
Cameron Jones .... F 610 880-7700
 Claymont *(G-1071)*
Capade LLC .... G 302 786-5775
 Wilmington *(G-15220)*
Caprini Suites LLC .... F 302 200-8904
 Dover *(G-2025)*
Care Constitution LLC .... G 201 240-3661
 Middletown *(G-6955)*
Chores R Us Inc .... F 844 442-4673
 Dover *(G-2069)*
Clearvue Solutions .... G 301 213-3358
 Wilmington *(G-15477)*
Clinton Craddock .... F 267 505-2671
 Middletown *(G-6995)*
Clothes and Crystals LLC .... G 302 316-3405
 Dover *(G-2095)*
Cobb Trucking Inc .... G 917 561-6263
 Smyrna *(G-13683)*
Codonrx LLC .... G 773 612-5828
 Dover *(G-2109)*
Cointigo LLC .... F 817 681-7131
 Middletown *(G-7002)*
Compete Hr Inc .... E 310 989-9857
 Wilmington *(G-15569)*
Coolpop Nation .... G 302 584-8833
 Wilmington *(G-15631)*

Core Functions LLC .... G 443 956-9626
 Selbyville *(G-13506)*
Coremond LLC .... G 267 797-7090
 Dover *(G-2138)*
Cpf Ckd LLC .... E 855 386-2799
 Wilmington *(G-15677)*
Crata Inc .... F 214 606-1731
 Dover *(G-2151)*
Crazy Maple Interactive Inc .... F 408 603-7526
 Dover *(G-2154)*
Creations By Mae Entps LLC .... G 302 985-5797
 Wilmington *(G-15689)*
Creativbar LLC .... G 510 260-3011
 Newark *(G-10346)*
Cryptofi Inc .... E 312 813-7188
 Dover *(G-2166)*
Cws Ballantyne II 99 LLC .... G 302 636-5401
 Wilmington *(G-15749)*
Cyber 20/20 Inc .... F 203 802-8742
 Newark *(G-10370)*
Dakk Holdings LLC .... G 571 335-7844
 Dover *(G-2186)*
Daniel Mitsdarfer T A Dan .... G 302 998-1295
 Wilmington *(G-15783)*
Daniel T Metzgar LLC .... G 302 602-4451
 Newark *(G-10386)*
Dannys Garage LLC .... G 702 752-9964
 Historic New Castle *(G-4967)*
Davait Inc .... G 302 930-0095
 Dover *(G-2198)*
Davin Management Group LLC .... F 302 367-6563
 Bear *(G-135)*
DC Consulting Service LLC .... F 617 594-9780
 Wilmington *(G-15824)*
DD&k Logistics LLC .... G 301 523-5984
 Townsend *(G-13986)*
Ddh (north America) Inc .... G 617 893-9004
 Lewes *(G-5884)*
Dedicated and Driven Hlg LLC .... G 404 909-6031
 Newark *(G-10406)*
Delaware Fncl Edcatn Alnce Inc .... G 302 674-0288
 Dover *(G-2240)*
Delaware Hlth Eqity Cltion Inc .... G 302 383-1701
 Middletown *(G-7040)*
Delaware Mosquito Control LLC .... G 302 504-6757
 Newark *(G-10462)*
Delaware Retired Schl Prsnl .... E 302 674-8252
 Wilmington *(G-15960)*
Delmarva Irrigation Inc .... F 302 490-1588
 Laurel *(G-5498)*
Derby Software LLC .... F 502 435-1371
 Dover *(G-2284)*
Dewitt Heating & AC .... G 267 228-7355
 Bear *(G-165)*
Dignisys Inc .... F 845 213-1121
 Dover *(G-2298)*
Disclo Inc .... G 607 280-8949
 Dover *(G-2301)*
Do It Up Designs LLC .... G 484 269-6142
 Millsboro *(G-8273)*
Donkey Trucking LLC .... G 302 507-2380
 New Castle *(G-9059)*
Dreamscape Design Cons LLC .... G 302 893-0984
 Newark *(G-10571)*
Dreamspell LLC .... G 786 633-1520
 Dover *(G-2383)*
Dustntime .... G 302 858-7876
 Rehoboth Beach *(G-12736)*
DXquisite Hair Factory LLC .... G 267 298-0821
 Smyrna *(G-13718)*
E&A Drywall and Painting Inc .... G 302 393-1743
 Millsboro *(G-8278)*

Employee Codes: A=Over 500 employees, B=251-500
C=101-250, D=51-100, E=20-50, F=10-19, G=1-9

2024 Harris Directory of Delaware Businesses

BUSINESS ACTIVITIES: Non-Commercial Site **PRODUCTS & SERVICES SECTION**

Company	Col	Phone
Earthborne Equipment & Svc Co — Felton (G-3965)	D	215 343-2000
Elevate RCM Consulting — Wilmington (G-16357)	G	484 655-8733
Elite Lubricants LLC — Seaford (G-13173)	G	302 629-3301
Emendo Bio Inc — Wilmington (G-16389)	G	516 595-1849
Emerging Impact Group Corp — Lewes (G-5960)	G	404 625-1530
Emitt LLC — Bear (G-201)	F	302 757-2353
Encore Lashes Lash Lounge LLC — New Castle (G-9094)	G	844 408-0004
Endospace Corporation — Newport (G-12451)	G	732 271-8700
Enf Ventures LLC — Milton (G-8620)	G	443 475-0175
Epatriotcrm LLC — Dover (G-2454)	G	419 967-6812
Estestwins Trucking LLC — Camden Wyoming (G-942)	G	267 773-2991
Evans Farms LLC — Bridgeville (G-699)	G	302 337-8130
Everest Foods Enterprises Inc — Wilmington (G-16484)	F	215 896-8902
Excella Staffing Solutions LLC — Dover (G-2471)	E	302 985-7373
Exclusive Group LLC — Wilmington (G-16501)	F	917 207-7299
Exercomm Inc — Middletown (G-7114)	G	302 438-6130
Ezdorms Inc — Wilmington (G-16517)	F	202 599-2953
Fenway Barr LLC — Rehoboth Beach (G-12753)	G	302 222-1913
Ferreira Builders LLC — Georgetown (G-4318)	G	302 296-6014
Fetch Social Inc — Wilmington (G-16591)	G	813 858-5774
Ff Group LLC — Dover (G-2493)	F	302 608-0609
First Shipment Inc — Lewes (G-5997)	G	206 747-1237
Flute Pro Shop Inc — Wilmington (G-16676)	G	302 479-5000
Founding Principals LLC — Bear (G-233)	G	917 693-7533
Frances Ann Owens — Frankford (G-4107)	G	302 436-2333
Freeman Courier Express — Wilmington (G-16743)	G	610 803-3933
Fresh Harvest Hydroponics — Millsboro (G-8296)	G	302 934-7506
Fsd Inc — Seaford (G-13191)	G	302 629-7498
Fujifilm Imaging Colorants Inc — Historic New Castle (G-4995)	D	302 472-1298
Fundomundo — Wilmington (G-16771)	G	617 606-1650
Future Analytica Software Inc — Dover (G-2548)	F	437 771-2947
Gamers4gamers LLC — Newark (G-10804)	G	302 722-6289
Gary Chorman — Milton (G-8627)	G	302 645-2972
Generation Cleaning Svc LLC — Claymont (G-1158)	G	302 492-2772
Gifted Hands 2 LLC — Dover (G-2582)	G	302 643-2005
Girley Bells LLC — Newark (G-10839)	G	347 922-6398
Globally Srced Vhcles Prts LLC — Dover (G-2595)	E	240 755-4935
GM Capital Investments Inc — Newark (G-10854)	G	302 722-0558
Goldberry LLC — Wilmington (G-16910)	G	800 268-4956
Golsonel Global LLC — Camden Wyoming (G-950)	G	267 461-8400
Good 4 Legacy — Dover (G-2602)	G	302 690-4515
Grease City Inc — Wilmington (G-16957)	G	302 661-5675
Greynote LLC — Dover (G-2628)	G	646 287-0705
GSM Systems Inc — Viola (G-14095)	F	302 284-8304
Guy & Lady Barrel LLC — Dover (G-2635)	G	302 399-3069
H&B Express Logistics — Dover (G-2642)	G	815 201-0915
Haloali Teeth Whitening LLC — Claymont (G-1174)	G	302 300-4042
Handy Logistics LLC — New Castle (G-9195)	G	570 905-4173
Happily Active LLC — Wilmington (G-17053)	G	307 317-7277
Hawksbill Systems LLC — Wilmington (G-17080)	G	302 494-1678
Helton and Moorehead Trnsp LLC — Dover (G-2673)	G	443 842-3360
Hibner Group Inc — Dover (G-2676)	G	717 281-1918
Homni Health Solution Inc — Dover (G-2691)	G	408 469-4956
How Medical Marketing Inc — Dover (G-2697)	F	302 283-9565
Icase LLC — Lewes (G-6113)	F	302 703-7854
Ifcf LLC — Dover (G-2719)	G	351 773-4853
Inbound Ignite LLC — Dover (G-2725)	G	866 314-4499
Infinite Solutions LLC — Wilmington (G-17322)	F	302 438-5310
Intrinsic Realty LLC — Middletown (G-7230)	G	302 425-1025
Introspction Cunseling Ctr LLC — Dover (G-2750)	G	302 213-6158
Isaac F Davis — Bear (G-290)	G	302 656-2050
Itdw Group LLC — Dover (G-2757)	G	917 503-3574
Itl (usa) Limited — Wilmington (G-17435)	G	302 691-6158
Its R Joy Llc — Bear (G-291)	E	215 315-8300
J Mamasian & Co LLC — Milford (G-7948)	G	302 219-2880
James & Patricia Booth — Middletown (G-7238)	G	302 378-9139
James Stewart Rostocki — Wilmington (G-17486)	G	302 250-5541
Jamroxk LLC — Dover (G-2770)	G	302 423-5477
Jason Lewis Pusey — Bridgeville (G-717)	G	302 245-6545
JBA Enterprises LLC — Bear (G-301)	G	302 834-6685
JC Industrial Solutions Inc — Claymont (G-1197)	G	484 720-8431
Jeffrey Glenn Minor — Greenwood (G-4645)	G	302 422-3403
Jet Green Transporters LLC — Dover (G-2785)	G	302 861-8918
Joff Capital LLC — Dover (G-2795)	G	216 682-6822
K&D Inc — Harbeson (G-4704)	G	302 945-7036
Kairon Corp — Lewes (G-6158)	F	347 688-3993
Kamara LLC — Wilmington (G-17643)	G	302 220-9570
Kancapi LLC — Lewes (G-6159)	E	949 508-0350
Kdg Solutions LLC — Smyrna (G-13786)	G	302 494-4693
Kevin McDaniel — Georgetown (G-4393)	E	302 236-1351
Keys R US LLC — Lincoln (G-6678)	G	619 886-8774
Khmisat LLC — Newark (G-11170)	G	302 533-1303
Kids University LLC — Dover (G-2868)	G	302 514-8187
Kintyre Solutions Inc — Wilmington (G-17729)	G	888 636-0010
Klh Properties Ltd Lblty Co — Wilmington (G-17741)	G	352 208-8964
Klick Inc — Newark (G-11191)	F	302 292-8455
Knowt Inc — Lewes (G-6170)	F	848 391-0575
Korsgy Technologies LLC — Wilmington (G-17748)	G	302 504-6201
Kriss Contracting Inc — Hartly (G-4893)	E	302 492-3502
Kristian Express LLC — Newark (G-11202)	G	302 528-7577
L & K Real Estate LLC — Bear (G-337)	F	484 410-4898
Laksh Cybersecurity & Def LLC — Wilmington (G-17790)	G	224 258-6564
Land Lock LLC — Middletown (G-7287)	G	302 747-6124
Latham Logistics — Townsend (G-14025)	G	215 760-4724
Lel Wealth MGT & Tech Svc LLC — Wilmington (G-17872)	G	804 243-0009
Lifehuse Erly Chldhood Ctr LLC — Townsend (G-14027)	E	302 464-1105
Lily B LLC — Bear (G-348)	F	302 290-5223
Linkers Inc — Dover (G-2952)	F	408 757-0021
Lions Group LLC — Magnolia (G-6762)	G	302 535-6584
Litcharts LLC — Wilmington (G-17934)	G	646 481-4807
Lkb Management Group LLC — Dover (G-2961)	G	919 561-2815
Looksiebin LLC — Wilmington (G-17991)	G	410 869-2192
Lotus Separations LLC — Newark (G-11286)	G	302 345-2510
Love & Hope Rescue Mission Inc — Newark (G-11288)	G	302 332-3829
MA Adas LLC — Wilmington (G-18062)	G	302 420-8158
Maggie Magpie Inc — Middletown (G-7321)	G	302 331-5061
Mariano Lozano — Wilmington (G-18128)	G	302 478-6710
Maxweb Inc — Wilmington (G-18207)	G	302 208-8361

PRODUCTS & SERVICES SECTION — BUSINESS ACTIVITIES: Non-Commercial Site

Company	Code	Phone
Mazzpac LLC — Newark (G-11364)	G	973 641-9159
Medarch Inc — Dover (G-3049)	F	405 638-3126
Medical Sup Support Svcs LLC — Dover (G-3052)	F	302 446-3658
Mekhala Living Inc — Dover (G-3056)	G	650 443-8235
Melanated Minds Foundation LLC — Wilmington (G-18262)	G	302 312-5303
Mg Global Group LLC — Newark (G-11397)	G	302 217-3724
Mhyhwh LLC — Bear (G-371)	G	302 518-0992
Middle Room LLC — New Castle (G-9369)	G	302 220-9979
Milpa Nativa Inc — Wilmington (G-18369)	G	512 668-9033
Mommin With Swag LLC — Newark (G-11439)	G	302 373-6316
Montrae Denorris Jones LLC — Dover (G-3121)	G	770 851-3836
Moscova Svrign Irrvcble Prvate — Wilmington (G-18461)	G	347 973-2522
Msgg LLC — Dover (G-3131)	G	917 565-8306
Murry Trucking Llc — Smyrna (G-13830)	F	302 653-4811
Myfurtribe Inc — Hockessin (G-5314)	G	210 904-3036
N J Jackson Realestate Inv LLC — Wilmington (G-18515)	F	602 783-4064
Nancy Dufresne — Townsend (G-14042)	G	302 378-7236
Neso Trucking LLC — New Castle (G-9403)	G	302 358-7878
New Vision Services Inc — Newark (G-11526)	G	484 350-6495
Newark Wings LLC — Newark (G-11549)	E	302 455-9464
Newton Management Holding Inc — Middletown (G-7401)	F	800 784-8714
Next Level Home Improvements — Claymont (G-1251)	G	484 469-1767
Next Level Staffing Solutions — Dover (G-3185)	F	302 281-4777
Nfinity Inc — Wilmington (G-18639)	F	852 642-9800
Niru LLC — Lewes (G-6316)	G	617 893-7317
No Joke I LLC — New Castle (G-9421)	G	302 395-0882
Noble Property LLC — Dover (G-3192)	E	718 502-4806
Noel Auto Sales LLC — Newark (G-11561)	G	302 286-7355
Nvcomputers Inc — Wilmington (G-18722)	G	860 878-0525
Oaks Lab Academy LLC — Wilmington (G-18728)	G	509 481-5630
Oasis Home Inc — Wilmington (G-18732)	F	949 331-5405
Objects Worldwide Inc — Wilmington (G-18737)	G	703 623-7861
Om Ganesh Two LLC — Delmar (G-1627)	G	410 720-9374
Omnisets LLC — Dover (G-3225)	G	425 229-1592
Oracle Enterprises LLC — Wilmington (G-18810)	G	407 900-2828
Paramunt Hlthcare Rsources LLC — Middletown (G-7425)	F	302 722-5484
Parcly LLC — Dover (G-3272)	G	347 305-6820
Patrick Gaydos — Middletown (G-7429)	G	302 378-8753
Phazebreak Coatings LLC — Wilmington (G-19013)	G	844 467-4293
Pheonixfire L L C — Newark (G-11682)	G	302 588-8820
Piis Global LLC — Lewes (G-6368)	E	628 600-5249
Platformavr Inc — Dover (G-3328)	G	302 330-8980
Platinum World LLC — Dover (G-3331)	G	302 321-5040
Pony Up Inc — Dover (G-3350)	G	323 205-7669
Pop-A-Docs All Ntral Hrbal Spp — Wilmington (G-19116)	G	302 622-5788
Pradhan Energy Projects — Hockessin (G-5351)	G	305 428-2123
Private Society LLC — Newark (G-11753)	G	302 319-7126
Provaxus Inc — Dover (G-3385)	G	773 832-8015
Pyle Hlg & Junk Removal LLC — Newark (G-11779)	G	302 750-7227
Quadrosense LLC — Dover (G-3406)	G	302 608-0779
Quality Distributors Inc — Wilmington (G-19283)	G	917 335-6662
Quantum Alchemy LLC — New Castle (G-9507)	G	484 299-8016
R&C Contractors LLC — Felton (G-4011)	F	302 284-9870
Raiden Tech Group Inc — Newark (G-11820)	G	302 330-8514
Rainbow Xpress Lrng Acdemy LLC — Smyrna (G-13861)	G	302 659-0750
Rare Royals Incorporated — Middletown (G-7502)	G	833 288-7171
Rays and Sons Mechanical LLC — Seaford (G-13367)	G	302 697-2100
Realassist Inc — Dover (G-3435)	F	888 309-1114
Reciprocity Health LLC — Wilmington (G-19378)	G	302 530-5244
Red Stone USA Inc — Lewes (G-6413)	E	919 931-5078
Renderapps LLC — Dover (G-3454)	G	919 274-0582
Revolutionary Identity Elusion — Dover (G-3462)	G	618 780-1755
Revolve Training Staffing LLC — Wilmington (G-19448)	G	833 973-8658
Reyes Rebeca — New Castle (G-9530)	G	302 276-9132
Richard E Williams — Seaford (G-13373)	G	302 956-0374
Right Knda Guys Car Sltons LLC — Newark (G-11884)	G	302 772-8717
Risleus Properties LLC — Dover (G-3473)	F	302 353-1255
Riverbend Inv MGT LLC Is A Rgs — Rehoboth Beach (G-12936)	G	302 219-3080
Rockeias Journey LLC — Newark (G-11903)	G	302 304-3055
Rohma Inc — Newark (G-11911)	G	909 234-5381
Roll Out Transit LLC — Hockessin (G-5371)	G	800 233-1680
Royalrose302 LLC — New Castle (G-9547)	G	800 259-7918
Ryes Hvac LLC — New Castle (G-9549)	G	302 981-7851
Saisha Spices LLC — Dover (G-3506)	G	786 288-3344
Sakempire Distribution LLC — Wilmington (G-19635)	F	800 838-0615
Sensofusion Inc — Milton (G-8710)	F	570 239-4912
Shelton Laday Hammond Jr — New Castle (G-9566)	G	302 832-6257
Shore Smoke Seasonings LLC — Smyrna (G-13884)	G	302 943-4675
Showbiz Trucking LLC — Camden (G-893)	G	302 526-6337
Signin Soft Inc — Wilmington (G-19823)	F	315 966-6699
Simple Space LLC — Wilmington (G-19835)	G	801 520-3680
Sinkeeas Lounge & Bar LLC — Newark (G-12013)	F	302 434-2530
Sirqil LLC — Dover (G-3569)	F	213 204-9333
Sister Sister Covid Clean LLC — Dover (G-3570)	G	267 467-8803
Six Angels Development Inc — Wilmington (G-19846)	G	302 218-1548
Skjaldborg Artisans LLC — Milford (G-8093)	G	302 698-7552
Slaybelles LLC — Wilmington (G-19862)	G	302 304-1027
Sme Masonry Contrs Ltd Lblty — Wilmington (G-19883)	F	302 743-7338
Snow & Assoc Gen Cnstr Co LLC — Wilmington (G-19901)	F	302 420-0564
Social Keyboard Inc — Dover (G-3585)	F	650 519-8383
Social Wonder Inc — Wilmington (G-19908)	F	646 419-8009
Society For Acpuncture RES Inc — Lewes (G-6488)	G	302 222-1832
Spin4spin Inc — Dover (G-3597)	G	720 547-2126
Staikos Associates Architects — Wilmington (G-20004)	G	302 764-1678
Stampede Btq & Vintage LLC — Wilmington (G-20009)	G	215 668-5714
Stan T Lepkowski — Clayton (G-1406)	G	302 393-9093
Standard Direct LLC — Wilmington (G-20012)	G	855 550-0606
Stauffer Family LLC — Rehoboth Beach (G-12974)	G	302 227-5820
Strands Prprty Prservation LLC — Millsboro (G-8469)	G	302 381-9792
Stream App LLC — Wilmington (G-20093)	G	610 420-5864
Stylere LLC — Dover (G-3618)	F	650 206-7721
Sunflowers — Newark (G-12124)	G	302 731-3150
Supportive Accountability Hub — Wilmington (G-20152)	F	615 579-3533
Switchgearus LLC — Milford (G-8112)	E	302 232-3209
Tailor Made Group LLC — Dover (G-3644)	G	347 824-0325
Techxponent Inc — Newark (G-12172)	F	410 701-0089
Terrain and Tactical LLC — Wilmington (G-20275)	G	302 521-9290
The Real Established Inc — Wilmington (G-20292)	F	917 843-8580

Employee Codes: A=Over 500 employees, B=251-500, C=101-250, D=51-100, E=20-50, F=10-19, G=1-9

2024 Harris Directory of Delaware Businesses

BUSINESS ACTIVITIES: Non-Commercial Site

PRODUCTS & SERVICES SECTION

Thirdwave Systems Inc .... G 650 804-1385
  Dover (G-3675)
Thomas Phillips .... G 302 238-7130
  Frankford (G-4153)
Threatmate Inc .... F 302 219-4714
  Dover (G-3682)
Tiny Token Trckg & Trnsp LLC .... G 929 602-5512
  Smyrna (G-13913)
Tirupati Inc .... G 302 836-8335
  Delaware City (G-1559)
Token Security Inc .... G 972 546-9803
  Wilmington (G-20347)
Toptel Inc .... G 310 999-4320
  Dover (G-3702)
TP It Group LLC .... G 302 444-0441
  Dover (G-3709)
Twin Creek Farms LLC .... G 302 249-2294
  Milford (G-8122)
Twinning LLC .... G 609 793-3510
  Wilmington (G-20470)
Ukap Trading LLC .... F 617 447-6490
  Dover (G-3743)
Ukhi LLC .... G 833 511-1977
  New Castle (G-9649)
Unicodez Inc .... F 703 963-2738
  Wilmington (G-20507)
Upside Gaming Inc .... G 937 475-6908
  Middletown (G-7675)
US Ravens Logistics Inc .... D 302 401-4033
  Dover (G-3765)
Vany Productions Logistics LLC .... G 443 397-2949
  Laurel (G-5618)
Veezys Holding Company LLC .... F 302 307-2418
  Dover (G-3779)
Victory Cleaning LLC .... G 267 330-9422
  Dover (G-3792)
Vizzie 360 .... G 323 239-0690
  Lewes (G-6608)
Vylo Inc .... G 310 902-9693
  Newark (G-12339)
Wahid Consultants LLC .... E 315 400-0955
  Historic New Castle (G-5099)
Wartimeaction LLC .... F 203 685-8868
  Middletown (G-7708)
We Got Cars 4 Cash Inc .... G 215 399-6978
  Claymont (G-1334)
Webstudy Inc .... G 888 326-4058
  Harbeson (G-4718)
Weltio LLC .... F 305 307-9815
  Dover (G-3832)
William C Leager .... G 302 398-7525
  Greenwood (G-4674)
Williamson Building Corp .... G 302 644-0605
  Lewes (G-6632)
Workwall Inc .... F 415 800-2809
  Newark (G-12407)
Wuji Inc .... G 815 274-6777
  Dover (G-3876)
Xeenom Inc .... G 302 427-6970
  Wilmington (G-20917)
Yenaffit Inc .... G 302 650-4818
  Wilmington (G-20926)
Zat3 Transport LLC .... G 302 470-6172
  Laurel (G-5627)
Zenind Inc .... G 845 300-3310
  Dover (G-3898)

BUSINESS FORMS WHOLESALERS

Brandywine Graphics Inc .... G 302 655-7571
  Wilmington (G-15062)
Elite Worldwide Inc .... G 833 200-5185
  Claymont (G-1130)
Safeguard Systems Inc .... G 609 822-6111
  Wilmington (G-19627)

BUSINESS FORMS: Printed, Manifold

Go Mozaic LLC .... G 302 438-4141
  Claymont (G-1166)

BUSINESS FORMS: Strip, Manifold

Brandywine Graphics Inc .... G 302 655-7571
  Wilmington (G-15062)

BUSINESS MACHINE REPAIR, ELECTRIC

B Williams Holding Corp .... F 302 656-8596
  Wilmington (G-14704)
Excel Business Systems Inc .... E 302 453-1500
  Newark (G-10683)
Ram Tech Systems Inc .... E 302 832-6600
  Middletown (G-7500)
Tower Business Machines Inc .... G 302 395-1445
  Historic New Castle (G-5088)
Visual Communications Inc .... G 302 792-9500
  Claymont (G-1330)

BUSINESS TRAINING SVCS

Tipton Communications Group .... F 302 454-7901
  Newark (G-12198)
Treehouse Wellness Center LLC .... G 302 893-1001
  Wilmington (G-20407)

CABINETS: Bathroom Vanities, Wood

Zenith Products .... G 302 322-2190
  Historic New Castle (G-5105)
Zwd Products Corporation .... B 302 326-8200
  Historic New Castle (G-5106)

CABINETS: Entertainment Units, Household, Wood

Jordan Cabinetry & WD Turning .... G 302 792-1009
  Claymont (G-1200)

CABINETS: Factory

Cubic Products LLC .... G 781 990-3886
  Wilmington (G-15731)

CABINETS: Kitchen, Metal

Pony Run Kitchens LLC .... G 302 492-3006
  Hartly (G-4903)

CABINETS: Kitchen, Wood

At Home Cabinetry & Design LLC .... G 302 853-5305
  Milford (G-7773)
Atlantic Cabinetry Corporation .... F 302 644-1407
  Lewes (G-5713)
Bancroft Carpentry Company .... G 302 655-3434
  Wilmington (G-14737)
Cabinets To Go LLC .... G 302 439-4989
  Claymont (G-1069)
Cedar Creek Cstm Cabinets LLC .... G 302 542-7794
  Milford (G-7814)
Coastal Cabinetry LLC .... F 302 542-4155
  Seaford (G-13126)
Countertop Shop LLC .... G 302 654-0700
  Wilmington (G-15656)
Culiquip LLC .... E 302 654-4974
  Wilmington (G-15732)
Custom Cabinet Shop Inc .... F 302 337-8241
  Greenwood (G-4609)
Diamond State Cabinetry .... G 302 250-3531
  Millsboro (G-8271)
Driftwood Cabinetry LLC .... G 302 645-4876
  Lewes (G-5936)
East Coast Cstm Cabinetry LLC .... G 302 245-3040
  Georgetown (G-4302)
Michael A OBrien & Sons .... G 302 994-2894
  Wilmington (G-18306)
Moores Cabinet Refinishing Inc .... G 302 378-3055
  Middletown (G-7380)
Nardi Cabinetry LLC .... G 302 945-7918
  Millsboro (G-8400)
Phippins Cabinetry .... G 302 212-2189
  Rehoboth Beach (G-12890)
Stones and Cabinets City LLC .... G 302 729-4201
  New Castle (G-9596)
Sylvester Custom Cabinetry .... G 302 398-6050
  Harrington (G-4838)
Taylor Woodworks .... G 302 745-2049
  Dover (G-3655)
Toms Cabinet Shop Inc .... G 302 258-6285
  Bridgeville (G-775)
Walnut Grove Cabinets LLC .... G 302 678-2694
  Dover (G-3818)

CABINETS: Show, Display, Etc, Wood, Exc Refrigerated

3-D Fabrications Inc .... E 302 292-3501
  Newark (G-9707)

CABLE & OTHER PAY TELEVISION DISTRIBUTION

Comcast Clfrn/Clrd/Lins/ndn/tx .... D 248 233-4724
  Wilmington (G-15542)
Directv .... G 302 203-9162
  Wilmington (G-16081)
Fscom Inc .... D 888 468-7419
  Historic New Castle (G-4994)
Rs Marks Inc .... G 302 478-4371
  Wilmington (G-19579)

CABLE & PAY TELEVISION SVCS: Direct Broadcast Satellite

A Dish Network .... G 302 495-5709
  Greenwood (G-4586)
A Dish Network .... G 302 565-4175
  Newark (G-9724)
A Dish Network .... G 302 223-5754
  Smyrna (G-13624)
Central Firm LLC .... G 610 470-9836
  Wilmington (G-15308)
Satellite Connection Inc .... G 302 328-2462
  Wilmington (G-19676)

CABLE TELEVISION

Ayon Cable Technology LLC .... G 302 465-8999
  Newark (G-9961)
Bombonais Cable Tech LLC .... F 302 444-1199
  New Castle (G-8874)
Cable Connections LLC .... F 302 397-9014
  Laurel (G-5477)
Comcast Cablevision of Del .... E 302 661-4465
  New Castle (G-8960)
Comcast Cablevision of Del .... F 302 856-4591
  Georgetown (G-4261)
Comcast Cble Cmmunications LLC .... F 410 497-4600
  Dover (G-2114)
Comcast Cble Cmmunications LLC .... G 302 323-9200
  New Castle (G-8961)
Comcast Corporation .... G 800 266-2278
  Dover (G-2115)
Comcast Corporation .... G 302 495-5612
  Greenwood (G-4604)

PRODUCTS & SERVICES SECTION — **CASTINGS: Commercial Investment, Ferrous**

Comcast Corporation .... G 302 526-0109
  Seaford (G-13129)
Comcast Corporation .... G 302 262-8996
  Seaford (G-13130)
Comcast MO Investments LLC .... G 302 594-8705
  Wilmington (G-15543)
Comcast of Delmarva LLC .... E 215 286-3345
  Dover (G-2116)
Digital Technologies .... G 302 731-1928
  Newark (G-10531)
Executive Brdband Cmmnctons LL ..... G 302 463-4335
  Newark (G-10687)
Mediacom LLC .... F 302 732-9332
  Dagsboro (G-1481)
NTL (triangle) LLC .... E 302 525-0027
  Wilmington (G-18708)

CABLE TELEVISION PRDTS

Executive Brdband Cmmnctons LL ..... G 302 463-4335
  Newark (G-10687)

CABLE: Fiber Optic

Nouvir Lighting Corporation .... F 302 628-9933
  Seaford (G-13319)
Nouvir Lightning Corporation .... G 302 628-9888
  Seaford (G-13320)

CALIBRATING SVCS, NEC

United Testing Systems Inc .... E 714 638-2322
  New Castle (G-9657)

CAMERAS & RELATED EQPT: Photographic

Cameras Etc Inc .... F 302 764-9400
  Wilmington (G-15206)

CAMERAS: Microfilm

Jollylook Inc .... F 754 267-1885
  Wilmington (G-17571)

CANDLES

Acosh Enterprise LLC .... G 631 767-4501
  Newark (G-9758)
Barbosa Manufacturing .... G 302 856-6343
  Georgetown (G-4221)
Candle Parlour .... G 302 408-0890
  Claymont (G-1072)
Conjured Jewells .... G 267 240-2263
  Newark (G-10305)
Limitless Flames LLC .... G 302 559-8712
  Wilmington (G-17918)
Loyalty Soap and Candle Co LLC ...... G 302 373-5854
  Townsend (G-14028)
Mia Bellas Candles .... G 302 331-7038
  Hartly (G-4896)
Vintage Candle Company .... G 302 643-9343
  Bridgeville (G-780)

CANDLES: Wholesalers

Goddess Scent Candles LLC .... G 973 885-0506
  Bear (G-250)

CANDY MAKING GOODS & SPLYS, WHOLESALE

Cannons Cake and Candy Sups .... G 302 738-3321
  Newark (G-10129)

CANDY, NUT & CONFECTIONERY STORES: Candy

King of Sweets Inc .... F 302 730-8200
  Dover (G-2873)

CANS: Aluminum

Reynolds Metals Company LLC .... A 302 366-0555
  Newark (G-11876)

CANS: Metal

Crown Cork Seal Rcvbles De Cor ...... G 215 698-5100
  Wilmington (G-15716)

CAPACITORS: NEC

Microhm Inc .... G 302 543-2178
  Wilmington (G-18329)

CARBON & GRAPHITE PRDTS, NEC

Nanoselect Inc .... E 302 355-1795
  Newark (G-11486)

CARBON PAPER & INKED RIBBONS

Identisource LLC .... G 888 716-7498
  Lewes (G-6114)

CARBONS: Electric

Ev Gg1 LLC .... G 313 269-4175
  Newark (G-10675)

CARDIOVASCULAR SYSTEM DRUGS, EXC DIAGNOSTIC

Cpex Pharmaceuticals Inc .... F 302 651-8300
  Wilmington (G-15676)

CARDS: Greeting

Chaukiss LLC .... G 551 655-5181
  Lewes (G-5811)
Sussex Printing Corp .... E 302 629-9303
  Seaford (G-13420)

CARPET & UPHOLSTERY CLEANING SVCS

ABM Janitorial Services Inc .... E 302 571-9900
  Wilmington (G-14205)
Apple Cleaning Systems LLC .... F 302 368-7507
  New Castle (G-8814)
C & B Complete Clg Svc Inc .... E 302 436-9622
  Frankford (G-4081)
Coastal Chem-Dry .... G 302 645-2800
  Lewes (G-5837)
Coit Clg Rstoration Wilmington .... G 302 322-1099
  Claymont (G-1097)
Colonial Cleaning Services Inc .... G 302 660-2067
  Wilmington (G-15534)
Crystal Kleen Inc .... G 302 326-1140
  New Castle (G-8990)
Dibiasos Clg Rstration Svc Inc .... G 302 376-7111
  Townsend (G-13992)
Ebc National Inc .... F 302 995-7461
  Wilmington (G-16274)
Greener Cleaner Sussex Corp .... G 302 497-7123
  Millsboro (G-8307)
Hampton Enterprises Inc .... G 302 378-7365
  Townsend (G-14013)
Marlings Inc .... F 302 325-1759
  Wilmington (G-18153)
Oxi Fresh Dover Carpet Clg .... F 302 526-5035
  Dover (G-3255)
Positive Results Cleaning Inc .... G 302 575-1146
  Wilmington (G-19126)
Tri State Cleaning .... G 302 644-6554
  Milton (G-8723)
Vivid Colors Carpet LLC .... G 302 335-3933
  Frederica (G-4187)
Worms Quality Carpet Care .... F 302 629-3114
  Seaford (G-13455)

CARPET & UPHOLSTERY CLEANING SVCS: Carpet/Furniture, On Loc

Brasures Carpet Care Inc .... G 302 436-5652
  Selbyville (G-13483)
Delaware Rug Co Inc .... G 302 998-8881
  Wilmington (G-15963)
Lopesco Inc .... E 732 985-7776
  Newark (G-11284)
Proclean Inc .... E 302 656-8080
  Delaware City (G-1554)
Schrider Enterprises Inc .... G 302 539-1036
  Ocean View (G-12566)
Stanley Steemer Intl Inc .... E 302 293-2879
  New Castle (G-9592)
Worthys Property MGT LLC .... F 302 265-8301
  Lincoln (G-6710)

CARPETS, RUGS & FLOOR COVERING

Josephine Keir Limited .... G 302 422-0270
  Milford (G-7960)
Kurtz Collection .... G 302 654-0442
  Wilmington (G-17767)

CARPETS: Textile Fiber

Bentley Mills Inc .... G 800 423-4709
  Wilmington (G-14840)

CASEMENTS: Aluminum

BF Rich Co Inc .... C 302 369-2512
  Newark (G-10030)

CASES: Carrying

Continental Case .... G 302 322-1765
  Newark (G-10313)
CP Cases Inc .... G 410 352-9450
  Frankford (G-4095)

CASES: Carrying, Clothing & Apparel

Bey Hollywood LLC .... G 209 789-5132
  Dover (G-1925)
Grease City Inc .... G 302 661-5675
  Wilmington (G-16957)
ID By Oliver LLC .... G 202 643-5536
  Middletown (G-7220)
Leallure LLC .... G 302 386-8886
  Wilmington (G-17847)
Makkari Globl Vsion A Sries LL .... G 571 308-6032
  Dover (G-3003)
Slaybelles LLC .... G 302 304-1027
  Wilmington (G-19862)
Ukhi LLC .... G 833 511-1977
  New Castle (G-9649)

CASES: Plastic

CP Cases Inc .... G 410 352-9450
  Frankford (G-4095)
Itskins Americas Inc .... G 805 422-6700
  New Castle (G-9245)

CASINGS: Sheet Metal

Seaside Service LLC .... G 302 827-3775
  Lewes (G-6455)

CASTINGS GRINDING: For The Trade

Delmarva Precision Grinding .... G 302 393-3008
  Milford (G-7862)

CASTINGS: Aluminum

Cushman Foundry LLC .... E 513 984-5570
  Dover (G-2172)

Employee Codes: A=Over 500 employees, B=251-500
C=101-250, D=51-100, E=20-50, F=10-19, G=1-9

2024 Harris Directory of Delaware Businesses

CASTINGS: Commercial Investment, Ferrous

Forcebeyond Inc.................................. E 302 995-6588
  Wilmington (G-16688)

CATALOG & MAIL-ORDER HOUSES

Manners Brand LLC............................. G 470 830-1114
  Dover (G-3009)
Villa Cotton Corporation...................... F 302 439-1508
  Wilmington (G-20619)

CATALYSTS: Chemical

Ddh Advanced Mtls Systems Inc........... G 515 441-1313
  Newark (G-10397)
W R Grace & Co................................... G 410 531-4000
  Wilmington (G-20663)

CATERERS

Acosh Enterprise LLC.......................... G 631 767-4501
  Newark (G-9758)
Butler Hospitality LLC.......................... D 888 288-5846
  Wilmington (G-15161)
Efficient Services Inc........................... G 302 629-2124
  Seaford (G-13171)
Leounes Catered Affairs...................... G 302 547-3233
  Wilmington (G-17882)

CHASSIS: Motor Vehicle

Commonwealth Motor Inc..................... G 302 505-5555
  Wilmington (G-15554)

CHEMICAL CLEANING SVCS

Kevin Smith.. E 800 878-1356
  Newark (G-11163)
Logiclean LLC..................................... G 302 298-0054
  Claymont (G-1225)

CHEMICAL ELEMENTS

7elements Inc..................................... F 302 294-1791
  Newark (G-9716)
Divine Element Hbb............................. G 302 538-5209
  Dover (G-2308)
Eidp Inc.. D 302 834-5901
  Delaware City (G-1539)

CHEMICALS & ALLIED PRDTS WHOLESALERS, NEC

Action Unlimited Resources Inc............. E 302 323-1455
  Historic New Castle (G-4919)
Ancatt Company.................................. G 302 897-8366
  Newark (G-9862)
Arrow Chemical Inc............................. G 302 731-7403
  Newark (G-9908)
Ashland Inc.. C 302 995-3000
  Wilmington (G-14583)
Brainerd LLC...................................... F 918 622-1214
  Seaford (G-13092)
Cfg Lab Inc.. G 302 261-3403
  Wilmington (G-15319)
Ciba Specialty Chem N Amer................ G 302 992-5600
  Wilmington (G-15432)
Eidp Inc.. E 302 774-1000
  Wilmington (G-16314)
Elchemy Inc.. G 908 663-8750
  Lewes (G-5954)
Interntional Mkt Suppliers Inc................ F 302 392-1840
  Bear (G-286)
Isp International Corp.......................... G 302 594-5000
  Wilmington (G-17429)
Magco Kissner Milling Co..................... G 913 713-0612
  New Castle (G-9334)
Management Chemical Co..................... G 410 326-0964
  Dover (G-3007)
PDM Incorporated................................ G 302 478-0768
  Wilmington (G-18938)
Progressive Systems Inc...................... G 302 732-3321
  Frankford (G-4135)
Quaker Chemical Corporation................ E 302 791-9171
  Wilmington (G-19281)
Recticel US Inc................................... A 248 393-2100
  Wilmington (G-19381)
Rockwood Specialties Inc..................... E 302 765-6012
  Wilmington (G-19547)
Royale Group Inc................................ G 201 845-4666
  Bear (G-473)
Sepax Technologies Inc....................... F 302 366-1101
  Newark (G-11980)
Solenis Holdings 3 LLC........................ A 866 337-1533
  Wilmington (G-19921)
Solenis LLC.. B 302 594-5000
  Wilmington (G-19923)
Solenis LLC.. B 866 337-1533
  Wilmington (G-19922)
Tenmat Inc... G 302 633-6600
  Wilmington (G-20273)
Ultrafine Technologies Inc.................... G 302 384-6513
  Wilmington (G-20502)

CHEMICALS & ALLIED PRDTS, WHOLESALE: Alkalines & Chlorine

Ashland Chemco Inc............................ E 302 995-4180
  Wilmington (G-14582)

CHEMICALS & ALLIED PRDTS, WHOLESALE: Chemical Additives

Mil International LLC........................... G 302 234-7501
  Wilmington (G-18352)

CHEMICALS & ALLIED PRDTS, WHOLESALE: Chemicals, Indl

Alliance Chemicals Global LLC............... F 507 202-6872
  Wilmington (G-14377)
Amfine Chemical Corp.......................... G 302 559-2948
  Newark (G-9852)
Croda Inc... G 302 429-5200
  New Castle (G-8986)
Diamond Chemical & Supply Co............. E 302 656-7786
  Wilmington (G-16049)
Noramco of Delaware Inc..................... C 302 761-2900
  Wilmington (G-18672)
Shore Chem LLC................................. F 201 845-4666
  Bear (G-490)
Thornley Company Inc......................... G 302 224-8300
  Newark (G-12194)

CHEMICALS & ALLIED PRDTS, WHOLESALE: Chemicals, Indl & Heavy

Royale Pigments & Chem Inc................ E 201 845-4666
  Bear (G-474)
Royale Pigments and Chem LLC............ G 201 845-4666
  Bear (G-475)
Syntec Corporation.............................. F 302 421-8393
  Wilmington (G-20191)

CHEMICALS & ALLIED PRDTS, WHOLESALE: Plastics Materials, NEC

Osterman & Company Inc.................... G 203 272-2233
  Wilmington (G-18830)
Polymart Inc....................................... G 302 656-1470
  Hockessin (G-5346)

CHEMICALS & ALLIED PRDTS, WHOLESALE: Plastics Prdts, NEC

Industrial Resource Netwrk Inc.............. F 302 888-2905
  Wilmington (G-17316)

CHEMICALS & ALLIED PRDTS, WHOLESALE: Polyurethane Prdts

Grayling Industries Inc......................... F 770 751-9095
  Frederica (G-4168)

CHEMICALS & ALLIED PRDTS, WHOLESALE: Spec Clean/Sanitation

A E Moore Incorporated....................... F 302 934-7055
  Millsboro (G-8157)

CHEMICALS, AGRICULTURE: Wholesalers

Emerald Bioagriculture Corp.................. F 517 882-7370
  Hockessin (G-5199)
Helena Agri-Enterprises LLC.................. G 302 337-3881
  Bridgeville (G-710)
Thomas E Moore Inc............................ F 302 674-1500
  Dover (G-3678)

CHEMICALS: Agricultural

Ai Dupont.. G 302 528-6520
  Wilmington (G-14326)
Ashanti Produce International................ F 800 295-9790
  Wilmington (G-14578)
Belchim Crop Prtection US Corp............ F 302 407-3590
  Wilmington (G-14814)
Chemours Company Fc LLC.................. C 678 427-1530
  Wilmington (G-15359)
Chemours Company Fc LLC.................. E 302 773-1000
  Wilmington (G-15358)
Corteva (china) LLC............................ E 833 267-8382
  Wilmington (G-15646)
Corteva Agriscience LLC...................... G 302 485-3000
  Wilmington (G-15647)
Dupont Electronics & Imaging............... G 302 273-6958
  Newark (G-10576)
Dupont Indus Bsciences USA LLC.......... E 302 774-1000
  Wilmington (G-16210)
E C I Motorsports Inc.......................... G 302 239-6376
  Newark (G-10587)
Eidp Inc... G 302 695-7141
  Bear (G-198)
Eidp Inc... C 302 992-2065
  Wilmington (G-16338)
Eidp Inc... G 302 999-2826
  Wilmington (G-16339)
Eidp Inc... E 844 773-2436
  Wilmington (G-16340)
Ft Dupont Redevelopment A................. G 302 838-7374
  Delaware City (G-1545)
HB Dupont Plaza................................. G 302 998-7271
  Wilmington (G-17082)
Meherrin AG & Chem Co...................... G 302 337-0330
  Bridgeville (G-730)
Specialty Products N&H Inc.................. C 302 774-1000
  Wilmington (G-19954)
Syngenta Corporation.......................... E 302 425-2000
  Wilmington (G-20189)

CHEMICALS: Alcohols

Breakthru Beverage Group LLC............. D 302 356-3500
  New Castle (G-8890)

PRODUCTS & SERVICES SECTION

CHILD DAY CARE SVCS

CHEMICALS: High Purity, Refined From Technical Grade

Indo Amines Americas LLC .... F 301 466-9902
Wilmington *(G-17312)*

CHEMICALS: Inorganic, NEC

Affinity Research Chemicals .... G 302 525-4060
Wilmington *(G-14305)*

Brandywine Chemical Company .... G 302 656-5428
New Castle *(G-8883)*

Celanese International Corp .... D 972 443-4000
Wilmington *(G-15298)*

Chemours Company Fc LLC .... C 302 545-0072
Wilmington *(G-15357)*

Degussa International Inc .... G 302 731-9250
Newark *(G-10409)*

Delaware Chemical Corporation .... E 302 427-8752
Wilmington *(G-15883)*

Dow Chemical Company .... E 302 366-0500
Newark *(G-10557)*

Du Pont Chem Enrgy Oprtons Inc .... C 302 774-1000
Wilmington *(G-16188)*

Dupont Athntcation Systems LLC .... F 800 345-9999
Wilmington *(G-16202)*

Dupont John Gardner .... G 302 777-3730
Wilmington *(G-16211)*

Dupont Prfmce Coatings Inc .... D 302 892-1064
Wilmington *(G-16213)*

Dupont Specialty Pdts USA LLC .... E 800 972-7252
Newark *(G-10577)*

Dupont Specialty Systems .... G 302 273-6955
Newark *(G-10578)*

E I Du Pont De Nemours & Co .... F 302 733-8134
Newark *(G-10588)*

Eidp Inc .... G 302 239-9424
Newark *(G-10617)*

Eidp Inc .... G 302 366-5583
Newark *(G-10618)*

Eidp Inc .... E 302 266-7101
Newark *(G-10619)*

Eidp Inc .... E 302 774-1000
Wilmington *(G-16314)*

Eidp Inc .... E 302 999-3301
Wilmington *(G-16316)*

Eidp Inc .... B 302 892-8832
Wilmington *(G-16317)*

Eidp Inc .... G 302 999-2874
Wilmington *(G-16318)*

Eidp Inc .... G 302 892-8832
Wilmington *(G-16319)*

Eidp Inc .... F 302 695-7228
Wilmington *(G-16320)*

Eidp Inc .... G 302 999-4356
Wilmington *(G-16321)*

Eidp Inc .... E 302 792-4371
Wilmington *(G-16322)*

Eidp Inc .... E 302 774-2102
Wilmington *(G-16323)*

Eidp Inc .... G 302 774-1000
Wilmington *(G-16324)*

Eidp Inc .... G 302 888-0200
Wilmington *(G-16325)*

Eidp Inc .... F 302 668-8644
Wilmington *(G-16326)*

Eidp Inc .... G 302 999-4329
Wilmington *(G-16328)*

Eidp Inc .... G 302 999-2533
Wilmington *(G-16329)*

Eidp Inc .... D 302 695-3742
Wilmington *(G-16330)*

Eidp Inc .... G 302 999-5072
Wilmington *(G-16331)*

Eidp Inc .... E 302 999-4321
Wilmington *(G-16332)*

Eidp Inc .... G 302 774-1000
Wilmington *(G-16333)*

Eidp Inc .... G 302 774-1000
Wilmington *(G-16334)*

Eidp Inc .... G 302 695-5300
Wilmington *(G-16335)*

Element .... G 302 645-0777
Lewes *(G-5956)*

Essential Minerals LLC .... G 602 377-9878
New Castle *(G-9100)*

John J Buckley Associates Inc .... G 302 475-5443
Wilmington *(G-17565)*

Kuehne Chemical Company Inc .... E 302 834-4557
New Castle *(G-9291)*

Lanxess Corporation .... G 267 205-1969
Wilmington *(G-17806)*

Mastering Mrcury Dsign Elments .... G 302 344-4323
Georgetown *(G-4420)*

Rohm Haas Electronic Mtls LLC .... E 302 366-0500
Newark *(G-11909)*

Rohm Haas Electronic Mtls LLC .... E 302 366-0500
Newark *(G-11910)*

Sinomine Resources (us) Inc .... G 204 340-6696
Wilmington *(G-19842)*

Solvay Spclty Polymers USA LLC .... F 302 452-6609
Newark *(G-12054)*

W L Gore & Associates Inc .... C 302 368-3700
Newark *(G-12341)*

W L Gore & Associates Inc .... D 302 738-4880
Newark *(G-12342)*

CHEMICALS: Medicinal, Organic, Uncompounded, Bulk

Wilmington .... G 302 357-4509
Wilmington *(G-20807)*

CHEMICALS: NEC

Amino-Chem (us) LLC .... G 281 305-8668
Dover *(G-1787)*

Chemours Co Fc LLC .... F 302 353-5003
Wilmington *(G-15355)*

Chemours Company .... B 302 773-1000
Wilmington *(G-15356)*

Chemours Company Fc LLC .... D 302 540-5423
Wilmington *(G-15360)*

Chemours Company Fc LLC .... E 302 773-1000
Wilmington *(G-15358)*

Croda Inc .... G 302 429-5200
New Castle *(G-8986)*

Croda Inc .... G 302 429-5249
New Castle *(G-8987)*

Cytec Industries Inc .... E 302 530-7665
Wilmington *(G-15756)*

Diversified Chemical Pdts Inc .... G 302 656-5293
Wilmington *(G-16095)*

Dynasep LLC .... G 302 368-4540
Newark *(G-10586)*

E I Du Pont De Nemours & Co .... E 843 335-5934
Wilmington *(G-16239)*

Frontier Scientific Svcs Inc .... E 302 266-6891
Newark *(G-10789)*

H2og Fogger Inc .... G 414 333-7024
Wilmington *(G-17025)*

Honeywell International Inc .... E 302 791-6700
Claymont *(G-1181)*

Hrd Products Inc .... G 302 757-3587
Newark *(G-10983)*

Khaos Beauty LLC .... A 302 427-0119
Wilmington *(G-17712)*

Lignolix Inc .... G 516 660-2558
Newark *(G-11258)*

Orient Corporation of America .... E 302 628-1300
Seaford *(G-13326)*

Polydel Corporation .... F 302 655-8200
Wilmington *(G-19113)*

Royal Delta Specialties LLC .... G 908 410-7478
Rehoboth Beach *(G-12940)*

Shore Chem LLC .... F 201 845-4666
Bear *(G-490)*

Thrupore Technologies Inc .... G 205 657-0714
New Castle *(G-9627)*

Twinco Romax LLC .... G 302 998-3019
Wilmington *(G-20469)*

Zeneca Holdings Inc .... D 302 886-3000
Wilmington *(G-20953)*

CHEMICALS: Organic, NEC

Cibt America Inc .... G 302 318-1300
Newark *(G-10241)*

CHEMICALS: Soda Ash

FMC Corporation .... D 302 366-5107
Newark *(G-10752)*

CHEMICALS: Water Treatment

Management Chemical Co .... G 410 326-0964
Dover *(G-3007)*

CHILD DAY CARE SVCS

A Better Chnce For Our Chldren .... F 302 725-5008
Milford *(G-7756)*

A Place To Grow Fmly Chld Care .... G 302 897-8944
Claymont *(G-1016)*

All About ME Day Care .... F 302 424-8322
Milford *(G-7763)*

All In Harmony Child Care .... G 302 494-3618
Newark *(G-9816)*

Amemg Inc .... F 302 220-7132
New Castle *(G-8793)*

American Universal LLC .... G 302 836-9790
Newark *(G-9849)*

Angela Daycar Nana Lil .... G 302 672-9167
Dover *(G-1794)*

Anniejwels Erly Child Dev Ctr .... G 302 981-1904
Wilmington *(G-14493)*

Attic Away From Home .... F 302 378-2600
Townsend *(G-13961)*

Baby Bear Educare .... G 302 981-9571
New Castle *(G-8842)*

Barbara L McKinney .... G 302 266-9594
Newark *(G-9982)*

Bear-Glasgow YMCA .... G 302 836-9622
Newark *(G-10006)*

Beginning Blssngs Chldcare LLC .... G 302 893-1726
New Castle *(G-8857)*

Bethesda Child Devmnt Ctr .... F 302 378-8435
Middletown *(G-6916)*

Bizzy Bees Home Daycare LLC .... G 302 376-9245
Middletown *(G-6922)*

Blessed Beginnings Lrng Ctr .... F 302 838-9112
Bear *(G-75)*

Brees Home Day Care .... G 302 762-0876
Wilmington *(G-15101)*

Bright New Beginnings .... G 610 637-9809
Wilmington *(G-15112)*

Building Blocks For Learni .... G 302 677-0248
Dover *(G-1990)*

Butterfield Inspection Service .... G 301 322-1644
Lewes *(G-5783)*

Employee Codes: A=Over 500 employees, B=251-500
C=101-250, D=51-100, E=20-50, F=10-19, G=1-9

CHILD DAY CARE SVCS

Name	Code	Phone
Cacc Montessori School	F	302 239-2917
Hockessin (G-5147)		
Caesar Rodney School District	D	302 697-3207
Dover (G-2011)		
Center For Child Developement	G	302 292-1334
Newark (G-10172)		
Central Del Schl of The Arts F	G	302 943-2274
Viola (G-14092)		
Chester Bthel Untd Mthdst Pre	F	302 475-3549
Wilmington (G-15368)		
Child Care Ctr	G	302 652-8992
Wilmington (G-15373)		
Child Care Service	F	302 981-1328
Newark (G-10203)		
Child Inc	F	302 335-8652
Magnolia (G-6730)		
Childrens Place	G	302 875-7733
Laurel (G-5482)		
Childrens Place Child Dev Ce	F	302 947-4808
Millsboro (G-8221)		
Childs Play By Bay	G	302 703-6234
Lewes (G-5814)		
Church of God In Christ	F	302 678-1949
Dover (G-2072)		
Creative Land Care	G	302 482-1944
Wilmington (G-15692)		
Dawn L Conly	F	302 378-1890
Middletown (G-7031)		
De Colores Family Child Care	F	302 883-3298
Dover (G-2203)		
Dees Learning Care	G	908 623-7685
Newark (G-10408)		
Delaware Adolescent Program Inc	E	302 268-7218
Newark (G-10415)		
Denise Miller Day Care Ce	G	302 482-9347
Wilmington (G-16009)		
Diane Spence Day Care	F	302 335-4460
Frederica (G-4166)		
Diocesan Council Inc	F	302 475-4688
Wilmington (G-16075)		
Ditrocchio Maria Antonetta	G	302 450-6790
Dover (G-2305)		
Dreams Childcare LLC	G	302 652-1085
Wilmington (G-16178)		
Eagle Nest Daycare	F	302 684-2765
Milton (G-8614)		
Eden Land Care	F	302 379-2405
Wilmington (G-16286)		
Edgemoor Community Center Inc	D	302 762-1391
Wilmington (G-16289)		
Elsmere Presbyterian Church	F	302 998-6365
Wilmington (G-16381)		
Enterprise Learning Solutions	F	302 762-6595
Wilmington (G-16434)		
Esther V Graham	G	302 422-6667
Milford (G-7883)		
Excellent Educatn Daycare LLC	F	302 565-2200
Newark (G-10684)		
Ezion Fair Community Academy	F	302 652-9114
Wilmington (G-16518)		
Faith Victory Christn Academy	F	302 333-0855
Claymont (G-1145)		
Family Wrkplace Connection Inc	E	302 479-1660
Wilmington (G-16548)		
Foot Steps Two Heaven Daycare	G	302 738-5519
Newark (G-10757)		
Fun 2 Learn Day Care	G	302 875-3393
Laurel (G-5516)		
Future Leaders	G	862 262-7312
Smyrna (G-13740)		
Gordons Daycare Home	G	302 658-7854
Wilmington (G-16931)		
Growing Palace	F	302 376-5553
Middletown (G-7179)		
Growing Palace III	F	302 376-5553
Middletown (G-7180)		
Happy Place Day Care LLC	G	302 737-7603
Newark (G-10928)		
Happyland Childcare	G	302 424-3868
Lincoln (G-6674)		
Harrison Heart Daycare	G	302 836-8581
Newark (G-10934)		
Harrison House Cmnty Program	E	302 595-3370
Newark (G-10935)		
Heart To Hand Daycare LLC	G	202 256-4524
Lewes (G-6086)		
Hill Luth Day Care Center	G	302 656-3224
Wilmington (G-17146)		
Hope Presbyterian Church	F	302 764-8615
Wilmington (G-17198)		
I Have A Dream Child Care	G	302 507-2310
Wilmington (G-17247)		
Independence School Inc	D	302 239-0330
Newark (G-11011)		
Independent Bb Fellowship Ch	G	302 734-2301
Dover (G-2726)		
J N Hooker Inc	E	302 838-5650
Bear (G-293)		
Jacqueline Allens Daycare	G	302 368-3633
Newark (G-11082)		
Jeans Love-N-Care Childcare	G	302 934-5665
Millsboro (G-8330)		
Jjs Learning Experience LLC	G	302 398-9000
Harrington (G-4791)		
Johnson Shawanda	G	302 722-1715
Bear (G-309)		
Jumpin Jacks	G	302 762-7604
Wilmington (G-17611)		
Junebugs Little Rubies LLC	G	302 494-7552
Wilmington (G-17612)		
Kenton Child Care	G	302 674-8142
Dover (G-2859)		
Kerry & G Inc	G	302 999-0022
Wilmington (G-17697)		
Kids R US Learning Center Inc	G	302 678-1234
Dover (G-2866)		
Kidz Choice LLC	F	302 365-6787
Bear (G-327)		
Kidz Ink	G	302 327-0686
Bear (G-328)		
Kidz Ink	G	302 838-1000
Bear (G-329)		
Kidz Klub	G	302 652-5439
Wilmington (G-17718)		
Kings Kids	F	302 239-4961
Hockessin (G-5270)		
Kodys Kids Inc	G	302 858-0884
Rehoboth Beach (G-12824)		
Lake Forest School District	E	302 398-8945
Harrington (G-4795)		
Lauras Child Care	G	302 690-1283
Hockessin (G-5277)		
Learning Circle Child Care	G	302 834-1473
Bear (G-342)		
Learning4 Lrng Professionals	G	302 994-0451
Wilmington (G-17849)		
Lifehuse Erly Chldhood Ctr LLC	E	302 464-1105
Townsend (G-14027)		
Lil Kritters Childcare	G	302 362-9047
Seaford (G-13261)		
Linda Putnam Day Care	G	302 836-1033
Bear (G-350)		
Lindas Angels Chldcare Dev Ctr	F	302 328-3700
New Castle (G-9311)		
Lisa Trabaudo Day Care	G	302 653-3529
Smyrna (G-13806)		
Little Blessings Childcare	G	215 510-4514
Claymont (G-1219)		
Little Giggles	G	678 770-2089
New Castle (G-9315)		
Little Kids Swagg Lrng Ctr LLC	F	302 480-4404
Smyrna (G-13807)		
Little People Day Care	G	302 528-4336
Middletown (G-7308)		
Little Peoples College	F	302 998-4929
Wilmington (G-17941)		
Little Trooper Day Care	G	302 378-7355
Middletown (G-7309)		
Lorraine S Daycare	G	302 328-1333
New Castle (G-9326)		
Love Learn & Play DC	G	302 236-9888
Milford (G-7977)		
Love N Care Daycare	G	302 369-8092
Newark (G-11289)		
M O T H E R S Inc	F	302 275-4163
Wilmington (G-18060)		
Maddix Owens Lillian	G	302 897-1997
Wilmington (G-18073)		
Magic Yrs Child Care Lrng Cntr	F	302 322-3102
New Castle (G-9335)		
Malgiero Helen A Day Care	G	302 834-9060
Delaware City (G-1548)		
Melissas Childcare	G	302 547-6722
Wilmington (G-18263)		
Mercy Land Academy Inc	G	302 378-2013
Middletown (G-7342)		
Ms Hathers Lrng Ctr Childcare	G	302 994-2448
Wilmington (G-18475)		
Ms Kims Day Care	G	304 689-8023
New Castle (G-9386)		
Nagengast Janet Day Care	G	302 656-6898
Wilmington (G-18519)		
Neighborhood House Inc	F	302 658-5404
Wilmington (G-18571)		
Newark Ctr For Creative Lrng	F	302 368-7772
Newark (G-11533)		
Northeast Early Lrng Ctr LLC	G	302 475-7080
Claymont (G-1255)		
Nurses N Kids Inc	E	302 323-1118
New Castle (G-9431)		
Oasis Childcare	G	302 312-5255
Wilmington (G-18731)		
Ogletown Baptist Church	F	302 737-2511
Newark (G-11580)		
Ol Babies LLC	G	302 570-0205
Wilmington (G-18752)		
Our Childrens Learning Ctr	G	302 565-1272
Bear (G-410)		
Our Future Child Care Ctr LLC	G	302 762-8645
Wilmington (G-18833)		
Our Future Christian Chld Care	F	302 287-4442
Wilmington (G-18834)		
Passion Care Services	G	302 834-9585
New Castle (G-9455)		
Peace and Blessings Child Care	G	302 543-4762
Wilmington (G-18939)		
Peoples Place II Inc	D	302 730-1321
Dover (G-3295)		
Peoples Place II Inc	D	302 934-0300
Millsboro (G-8426)		
Peoples Sttlment Assn Wlmngton	E	302 658-4133
Wilmington (G-18964)		
Personal Touch Child Care	E	302 368-2229
Newark (G-11670)		
Precious Little Hands Childcar	G	302 298-5027
Wilmington (G-19148)		

PRODUCTS & SERVICES SECTION

CLEANING SVCS: Industrial Or Commercial

Precious Lttle Hnds Chldcare C............. G 302 256-0194
  Wilmington (G-19149)
Precious Lttle Lambs Childcare............. G 302 723-1403
  Wilmington (G-19150)
Premier IL Volo LLC............................... G 847 201-1760
  Wilmington (G-19169)
Pyle Child Development Center............. F 302 732-1443
  Frankford (G-4136)
Rainbow Xpress Lrng Acdemy LLC....... G 302 659-0750
  Smyrna (G-13861)
Robin S Wright...................................... G 302 249-2105
  Lewes (G-6426)
Salvation Army...................................... E 302 656-1696
  Wilmington (G-19645)
Sherrys Childcare.................................. G 302 654-4982
  Wilmington (G-19796)
Shining Star Daycare............................ G 302 393-7775
  Dover (G-3544)
Small Wonders..................................... G 302 645-8410
  Lewes (G-6478)
Smart Start... F 302 256-5104
  Wilmington (G-19879)
Smyrna School District......................... D 302 653-3135
  Smyrna (G-13897)
St Helenas Early Learning................... G 302 561-4044
  Wilmington (G-19994)
St Helenas Early Learning Ctr.............. G 610 497-0435
  Wilmington (G-19995)
Stepping Stones College...................... G 302 983-1437
  Wilmington (G-20061)
Susan R Austin.................................... G 302 322-4685
  New Castle (G-9607)
Tender Hearts...................................... F 302 674-2565
  Dover (G-3668)
Tender Hearts...................................... G 302 234-1017
  Wilmington (G-20272)
Thirst 2 Learn...................................... F 302 293-2304
  Bear (G-530)
Tiny Tots and Toddlers Llc.................. G 302 838-8787
  Bear (G-532)
To The Moon and Back Childcare......... G 302 508-2749
  Smyrna (G-13914)
Toddys Tots... G 302 661-1912
  Wilmington (G-20344)
Toys Story LLC..................................... G 267 334-9822
  Smyrna (G-13916)
Vision Campus Inc............................... F 302 543-6809
  Wilmington (G-20638)
Wee Care Day Care Salv Army............ G 302 472-0712
  Wilmington (G-20709)
Wee Wonders Doulas........................... G 302 275-7799
  Wilmington (G-20710)
Wesley Play Care Center..................... F 302 678-8987
  Dover (G-3835)
Williams Family.................................... G 302 378-9493
  Middletown (G-7727)
Wilson Care Wilson Co........................ G 302 897-5059
  Newark (G-12386)
Wright Choice Child Care..................... G 302 798-0758
  Claymont (G-1340)
Young Mens Christian Assn Del........... C 302 571-6900
  Wilmington (G-20937)
Young MNS Chrstn Assn Wlmngton..... C 302 296-9622
  Rehoboth Beach (G-13027)
YWCA Delaware................................... F 302 224-4060
  Newark (G-12425)

CHILDBIRTH PREPARATION CLINIC

Acadia Healthcare Company Inc........... F 302 328-3330
  New Castle (G-8759)
Delaware Adlescent Program Inc......... E 302 268-7218
  Newark (G-10415)

Lewes Wellness Center........................ G 302 313-9990
  Lewes (G-6202)
Mamaste Doula and Birth Svcs............ G 302 670-3188
  Dover (G-3005)
Pure Wellness LLC............................... G 302 389-8915
  Smyrna (G-13859)
Sunrise Medical Center........................ G 302 854-9006
  Millsboro (G-8470)
Tidalhlth Pnnsula Regional Inc............. C 302 537-1457
  Millville (G-8549)

CHILDREN'S WEAR STORES

Carters Inc... G 302 731-1432
  Newark (G-10156)

CHIMES: Electric

Chimes Metro Inc................................. A 302 452-3400
  Historic New Castle (G-4957)
Inc Chimes... G 302 449-1926
  Townsend (G-14015)

CHOCOLATE, EXC CANDY FROM BEANS: Chips, Powder, Block, Syrup

7th Heaven Inc.................................... G 201 282-1925
  Wilmington (G-14150)
Kraft Heinz Company........................... A 302 734-6100
  Dover (G-2886)

CHOCOLATE, EXC CANDY FROM PURCH CHOC: Chips, Powder, Block

Chocolate Editions Inc......................... G 302 479-8400
  Claymont (G-1085)
United Cocoa Processor Inc................ E 302 731-0825
  Newark (G-12269)

CHROMATOGRAPHY EQPT

Joint Anlytcl Systms (amrcs)................ G 302 607-0088
  Newark (G-11122)
Miles Scientific Corporation.................. E 302 737-6960
  Newark (G-11418)

CHURCHES

Independent Bb Fellowship Ch.............. G 302 734-2301
  Dover (G-2726)

CIGARETTE & CIGAR PRDTS & ACCESS

East Park Brands LLC.......................... G 201 668-7089
  Dover (G-2410)

CIRCUITS: Electronic

Ef Technologies Inc.............................. G 302 451-1088
  Newark (G-10615)
Eidp Inc... C 302 774-1000
  Wilmington (G-16342)
Lexatys LLC... F 302 715-5029
  Laurel (G-5555)
Suretronix Solutions LLC..................... G 302 407-3146
  Wilmington (G-20161)

CLEANING EQPT: Commercial

Better Business RE Inc........................ G 609 746-9833
  Claymont (G-1060)
One Tuch Prperty Solutions LLC........... G 302 765-8519
  Bear (G-408)
Superior Services Group LLC............... G 888 683-8288
  Wilmington (G-20143)

CLEANING OR POLISHING PREPARATIONS, NEC

Chem Tech Inc..................................... G 302 798-9675
  Wilmington (G-15353)
Quip Laboratories Incorporated............ E 302 761-2600
  Wilmington (G-19297)

CLEANING PRDTS: Ammonia, Household

Sanosil International LLC..................... G 302 454-8102
  Wilmington (G-19667)

CLEANING PRDTS: Automobile Polish

Diligent Detail...................................... G 302 482-2836
  Wilmington (G-16071)

CLEANING PRDTS: Disinfectants, Household Or Indl Plant

Alcosm LLC.. G 302 703-7635
  Lewes (G-5671)
Cleaner Brands Worldwide LLC............ G 646 867-8328
  Dover (G-2091)
Eon Mist LLC....................................... G 310 500-2140
  Wilmington (G-16448)
Halosil International Inc....................... G 302 543-8095
  Wilmington (G-17040)

CLEANING PRDTS: Floor Waxes

Floor Guy Supply LLC........................... G 302 325-3801
  New Castle (G-9137)

CLEANING PRDTS: Laundry Preparations

Ultra Modern Laundry Svcs LLC........... G 302 533-8596
  Wilmington (G-20500)

CLEANING PRDTS: Sanitation Preps, Disinfectants/Deodorants

Gearhalo US Inc................................... G 780 239-2120
  Dover (G-2566)
Purple4s Inc... G 443 504-9755
  Magnolia (G-6778)

CLEANING PRDTS: Specialty

A Kleensweep...................................... G 302 764-7964
  Wilmington (G-14165)

CLEANING SVCS: Industrial Or Commercial

A+ Cleaning Solutions Inc.................... G 423 693-7554
  Dover (G-1698)
Apple Cleaning Systems LLC............... F 302 368-7507
  New Castle (G-8814)
Aqua Pro Inc.. G 302 659-6593
  Smyrna (G-13647)
Brenda Radick..................................... G 302 945-8982
  Harbeson (G-4686)
C & B Complete Clg Svc Inc................ E 302 436-9622
  Frankford (G-4081)
Coleman Cleaning Services Inc............ G 302 335-1868
  Magnolia (G-6733)
D C S Company................................... G 302 328-5138
  New Castle (G-8992)
Empire Data Voice Networks LLC......... G 702 613-4900
  Millsboro (G-8281)
Focus Solutions Services Inc............... F 302 318-1345
  Newark (G-10753)
JV s Cleaning Services......................... G 302 345-7679
  Bear (G-318)
Maid For Shore.................................... G 302 344-1857
  Lewes (G-6237)
Maidpro... G 302 327-4250
  Middletown (G-7323)
Main Street Staffing Agcy LLC.............. G 302 608-7052
  Dover (G-2998)

CLEANING SVCS: Industrial Or Commercial

Optima Cleaning Systems Inc............ E ... 302 652-3979
  Wilmington *(G-18807)*
Schoon Inc................................... G 302 894-7574
  Newark *(G-11961)*
Schweizer Cleaning Service............. G 302 995-2816
  Wilmington *(G-19702)*
Sims Team Cleaning LLC................. E ... 610 990-1950
  Middletown *(G-7568)*
Sunshine Cleaning Services LLC....... G 302 430-8416
  Seaford *(G-13416)*
Supreme Servicez LLC.................... G 302 932-5724
  Wilmington *(G-20158)*
Weg Cleaning Service Inc................ G 302 343-5746
  Wilmington *(G-20712)*

CLIPPERS: Fingernail & Toenail

LRC North America Inc.................... E ... 302 427-2845
  Wilmington *(G-18018)*

CLOTHING & ACCESS, WOMEN, CHILDREN/INFANT, WHOL: Nightwear

Petite Plume LLC........................... F ... 800 298-1381
  Wilmington *(G-18998)*

CLOTHING & ACCESS: Handicapped

Advacare LLC................................ G 302 448-5045
  Wilmington *(G-14263)*
Serrano Inc.................................. G 302 607-1779
  Newark *(G-11982)*

CLOTHING & APPAREL STORES: Custom

Be Blessed Design Group LLC.......... G 302 561-3793
  Bear *(G-59)*

CLOTHING & FURNISHINGS, MENS & BOYS, WHOL: Sportswear/Work

Fenwick Island Nautical Sports......... G 443 397-0619
  Fenwick Island *(G-4048)*

CLOTHING STORES: T-Shirts, Printed, Custom

Slater Fireplaces Inc...................... G 302 999-1200
  Wilmington *(G-19861)*

CLOTHING STORES: Unisex

Delave Denim Co LLC..................... G 302 308-5161
  Dover *(G-2215)*
Johns El Family Industries Inc......... G 310 701-5678
  Lewes *(G-6149)*
Middle Room LLC........................... G 302 220-9979
  New Castle *(G-9369)*
On Glo LLC................................... G 205 567-3434
  Dover *(G-3226)*
Royalrose302 LLC.......................... G 800 259-7918
  New Castle *(G-9547)*

CLOTHING: Athletic & Sportswear, Men's & Boys'

Carpediem Health LLC.................... G 347 467-4444
  Dover *(G-2031)*
Huzala Inc.................................... G 313 404-6941
  Newark *(G-10987)*
Majdell Group USA Inc.................... G 302 722-8223
  Newark *(G-11316)*

CLOTHING: Athletic & Sportswear, Women's & Girls'

Carpediem Health LLC.................... G 347 467-4444
  Dover *(G-2031)*

CLOTHING: Band Uniforms

G2 Performance Band ACC.............. G 800 554-8523
  Wilmington *(G-16787)*

CLOTHING: Blouses, Women's & Girls'

Janice James & Joan LLC................ G 845 682-1886
  Newark *(G-11096)*
Lee Bell Inc.................................. F ... 302 477-3930
  Wilmington *(G-17853)*

CLOTHING: Children & Infants'

Carters Inc................................... G 302 731-1432
  Newark *(G-10156)*

CLOTHING: Hospital, Men's

Nixon Uniform Service Inc............... C ... 302 325-2875
  Historic New Castle *(G-5040)*
South Paxon LLC........................... G 302 918-5226
  Newark *(G-12060)*

CLOTHING: Mens & Boys Jackets, Sport, Suede, Leatherette

Lee Bell Inc.................................. F ... 302 477-3930
  Wilmington *(G-17853)*

CLOTHING: Neckwear

Aptustech LLC............................... G 347 254-5619
  Wilmington *(G-14516)*

CLOTHING: Outerwear, Knit

Flapdoodles Inc............................. D ... 302 731-9793
  Newark *(G-10750)*

CLOTHING: Outerwear, Women's & Misses' NEC

City Theater Co Inc........................ G 302 831-2206
  Newark *(G-10246)*
Moxie Apparel Inc........................... F ... 844 894-1435
  Wilmington *(G-18468)*

CLOTHING: Shirts, Dress, Men's & Boys'

Lee Bell Inc.................................. F ... 302 477-3930
  Wilmington *(G-17853)*

CLOTHING: Socks

Heated Wear LLC........................... G 347 510-7965
  Wilmington *(G-17109)*

CLOTHING: Swimwear, Women's & Misses'

Body Double Swimwear.................... G 302 537-1444
  Selbyville *(G-13479)*

CLOTHING: Underwear, Men's & Boys'

Majdell Group USA Inc.................... G 302 722-8223
  Newark *(G-11316)*

CLOTHING: Underwear, Women's & Children's

Perteh.. G 302 200-0912
  Wilmington *(G-18991)*
Victorias Secret Stores LLC............. G 302 644-1035
  Rehoboth Beach *(G-13003)*

CLOTHING: Uniforms, Men's & Boys'

Boa Financial LLC.......................... G 888 444-5371
  Dover *(G-1956)*

CLOTHING: Uniforms, Military, Men/Youth, Purchased Materials

Cross Over Camo LLC..................... G 302 798-1898
  Claymont *(G-1104)*

CLOTHING: Waterproof Outerwear

Neilsen Clothing Inc....................... G 302 342-1370
  Dover *(G-3167)*

CLOTHING: Work, Men's

Kaul Glove and Mfg Co.................... D ... 302 292-2660
  Historic New Castle *(G-5014)*

CLUTCHES, EXC VEHICULAR

SSS Clutch Company Inc................. G 302 322-8080
  New Castle *(G-9588)*

COAL, MINERALS & ORES, WHOLESALE: Coal

Bowie Refined Coal LLC................... G 302 636-5401
  Wilmington *(G-15017)*

COFFEE SVCS

Take-A-Break Inc........................... E ... 302 658-8571
  Wilmington *(G-20209)*

COLOR PIGMENTS

Ampacet Ohio LLC.......................... E ... 914 631-6600
  Wilmington *(G-14461)*

COLORS: Pigments, Inorganic

Lanxess Corporation....................... G 267 205-1969
  Wilmington *(G-17806)*

COMBINATION UTILITIES, NEC

On The Mark Locators LLC.............. G 888 272-6065
  Newark *(G-11589)*

COMBINED ELEMENTARY & SECONDARY SCHOOLS, PRIVATE

Independence School Inc................. D ... 302 239-0330
  Newark *(G-11011)*

COMMERCIAL & OFFICE BUILDINGS RENOVATION & REPAIR

Benjamin B Smith Builders Inc.......... G 302 537-1916
  Ocean View *(G-12477)*
Breslin Contracting Inc................... E ... 302 322-0320
  New Castle *(G-8891)*
Colonial Construction Company........ F ... 302 994-5705
  Wilmington *(G-15535)*
Dry Wall Associates Ltd.................. D ... 302 737-3220
  Newark *(G-10574)*
Eastern Home Improvements Inc...... G 302 655-9920
  Wilmington *(G-16258)*
Everyone Can Achieve LLC.............. E ... 404 317-1228
  Wilmington *(G-16491)*
J & S General Contractors............... G 302 658-4499
  Wilmington *(G-17447)*
James Rice Jr Construction Co........ G 302 731-9323
  Newark *(G-11092)*
Joseph A Santillo Inc...................... G 302 661-7313
  Wilmington *(G-17578)*
JW Tull Contracting Svcs LLC.......... F ... 302 494-8179
  Wilmington *(G-17625)*
M W Fogarty Inc............................ G 302 658-5547
  Hockessin *(G-5286)*
Mebro Inc.................................... E ... 302 992-0104
  Wilmington *(G-18243)*

National Rstrtion Fclty Svcs I................. E 856 401-0100
  Historic New Castle (G-5033)
Renovate LLC.. G 302 378-1768
  Middletown (G-7515)
Shure-Line Construction Inc................. E 302 653-4610
  Kenton (G-5454)
Sumter Contracting Corp........................ G 703 323-7210
  Ocean View (G-12573)
W D Pressley Inc..................................... G 302 653-4381
  Smyrna (G-13932)
Zacs Inc... G 302 242-4653
  Magnolia (G-6793)

COMMERCIAL ART & GRAPHIC DESIGN SVCS

Growth Inc.. E 302 366-0848
  Newark (G-10903)
JP Graphics... G 302 678-0335
  Dover (G-2806)
Mad Macs.. G 302 737-4800
  Newark (G-11310)
Promotion Zone LLC.............................. G 302 832-8565
  Newark (G-11763)
Sumthin3lse... G 302 272-5435
  Dover (G-3621)
Uncharted Waters LLC........................... E 302 213-6454
  Dover (G-3747)

COMMERCIAL ART & ILLUSTRATION SVCS

Premiere Studio LLC.............................. F 347 336-0791
  Claymont (G-1266)

COMMERCIAL EQPT WHOLESALERS, NEC

Burke Equipment Company.................... E 302 248-7070
  Delmar (G-1570)
Delmarva Automotive Eqp Inc............... G 302 349-9411
  Ellendale (G-3913)
Greg Smith Equipment Inc.................... G 302 894-9333
  Newark (G-10893)
Jesco Inc... C 302 376-6946
  Middletown (G-7247)
Peninsula Polymers Inc......................... G 302 422-2002
  Milford (G-8044)

COMMERCIAL EQPT, WHOLESALE: Restaurant, NEC

Brewster Products Inc............................ G 302 764-4463
  Wilmington (G-15103)
Elmer Schultz Services Inc.................... G 302 655-8900
  Wilmington (G-16376)
Hy-Point Equipment Co.......................... F 302 478-0388
  Wilmington (G-17241)
JLE Inc.. E 302 656-3590
  Wilmington (G-17555)
Singer Equipment Co Inc....................... G 484 332-3386
  Smyrna (G-13887)
South Forks Inc...................................... G 302 731-0344
  Newark (G-12059)
Vortex Refrigeration Company.............. G 855 562-5222
  Wilmington (G-20652)
Webstaurant Store Inc........................... F 302 654-1247
  New Castle (G-9679)

COMMERCIAL EQPT, WHOLESALE: Scales, Exc Laboratory

Widgeon Enterprises Inc....................... G 302 846-9763
  Delmar (G-1657)

COMMERCIAL EQPT, WHOLESALE: Vending Machines, Coin-Operated

Vending Solutions LLC........................... G 302 674-2222
  Dover (G-3781)

COMMERCIAL PHOTOGRAPHIC STUDIO

Colourworks Photographic Svcs............ G 302 428-0222
  Wilmington (G-15540)
Elementice Inc.. G 302 444-5406
  Newark (G-10625)
Floyd Dean Inc.. G 302 655-7193
  Wilmington (G-16672)
Herbert Studios...................................... G 302 229-7108
  Wilmington (G-17127)
Superlative Image LLC.......................... G 714 369-5412
  Wilmington (G-20144)

COMMERCIAL PRINTING & NEWSPAPER PUBLISHING

Hoy En Delaware LLC............................ G 302 854-0240
  Georgetown (G-4366)
Morning Report Research Inc................ G 302 730-3793
  Dover (G-3123)
News-Journal Company.......................... C 302 324-2500
  New Castle (G-9417)

COMMUNICATIONS SVCS

Aetho LLC... F 215 821-7290
  Dover (G-1733)
Amalipo Smartduka Ltd......................... F 857 452-1692
  Lewes (G-5681)
Coztel LLC.. G 832 224-5638
  Wilmington (G-15674)
Delmarva Communications Inc............. F 302 324-1230
  New Castle (G-9042)
Dynamic Packet Corp............................. F 302 448-2222
  Newark (G-10584)
Meta Mind Global Corp LLC.................. G 267 471-3616
  Dover (G-3069)
Pink App LLC.. E 408 654-4636
  Wilmington (G-19048)
Qbr Telecom Inc..................................... F 302 510-1155
  Wilmington (G-19275)
Schiff Group LLC................................... G 301 325-1359
  Bethany Beach (G-639)
Switch Enterprises LLC......................... E 212 227-9191
  Dover (G-3632)
Telcast Networks LLC........................... G 833 835-2278
  Dover (G-3665)
Whyfly LLC... F 302 222-7171
  Wilmington (G-20776)

COMMUNICATIONS SVCS: Data

Axxess Marine LLC................................ G 954 225-1744
  Lewes (G-5731)
Digitizing America LLC......................... G 315 882-9516
  Historic New Castle (G-4974)
Fiberstate LLC....................................... E 800 575-8921
  Historic New Castle (G-4987)
Gai Communications Inc....................... G 609 254-1470
  Newark (G-10798)
Maya Virtual Inc.................................... G 213 587-7995
  Dover (G-3039)
Positron Access Solutions Inc............... F 888 577-5254
  Wilmington (G-19128)
Venturist Media Inc............................... G 646 455-3031
  Wilmington (G-20582)

COMMUNICATIONS SVCS: Internet Connectivity Svcs

3d Internet Group Inc............................. G 302 376-7900
  Middletown (G-6816)
8mesh Inc... G 888 627-4331
  Lewes (G-5642)
Adectra LLC.. F 203 424-2800
  Middletown (G-6835)
Bbi-Fiber LLC... G 224 633-1288
  Middletown (G-6906)
C & B Internet Services LLC................. G 302 384-9804
  Wilmington (G-15169)
Callsynetwork LLC................................ G 785 241-7841
  Wilmington (G-15198)
Dedicted Fibr Cmmnications LLC......... G 302 416-3088
  Wilmington (G-15852)
Ewebvalet Co Inc.................................. G 302 893-0903
  Wilmington (G-16497)
Global Marine Networks LLC................ G 215 327-2814
  Lewes (G-6039)
Hughes Network Systems LLC............. G 302 335-4138
  Frederica (G-4172)
Ing Bank Fsb.. D 302 255-3750
  Wilmington (G-17331)
Keepgo USA Inc..................................... G 832 998-8753
  Wilmington (G-17676)
Mgj Enterprises Inc............................... E 866 525-8529
  Wilmington (G-18299)
Oculus Networks Inc............................. F 732 841-1624
  Wilmington (G-18744)
Rehoboth Beach..................................... G 302 245-0304
  Rehoboth Beach (G-12917)
Verge Internet Inc................................. G 202 827-5120
  Dover (G-3783)
Voip Supplier LLC.................................. G 302 760-9237
  Dover (G-3807)
Wire 2 Wire LLC................................... G 512 684-9100
  Wilmington (G-20866)

COMMUNICATIONS SVCS: Internet Host Svcs

Adeox Technologies Inc......................... G 347 884-7131
  Newark (G-9765)
Better Earth LLC................................... G 302 242-3644
  Dover (G-1922)
Carisma Telecom Inc............................. G 302 357-3650
  Wilmington (G-15251)
Clickssl.. G 302 355-0692
  Newark (G-10259)
Coastal Images Inc................................ G 302 539-6001
  Fenwick Island (G-4045)
Delta Centric LLC.................................. F 302 268-9359
  Wilmington (G-16002)
Free Hosting LLC................................... G 302 421-5750
  Wilmington (G-16739)
Itglobalcom Corp................................... G 302 498-8359
  Claymont (G-1190)
Keep In Touch Systems Inc.................. G 510 868-8088
  Wilmington (G-17675)
Latitude Sh LLC..................................... E 712 481-2400
  Wilmington (G-17817)
Lnh Inc.. F 302 731-4948
  Newark (G-11277)
Maya Virtual Inc.................................... G 213 587-7995
  Dover (G-3039)
Obhost LLC... G 302 440-1447
  Lewes (G-6326)
Painless Hosting LLC............................ F 703 688-2828
  Wilmington (G-18864)

COMMUNICATIONS SVCS: Internet Host Svcs

Purple Wifi Inc.. G 216 292-5760
  Wilmington *(G-19266)*
Quadix LLC... G 877 669-8680
  Middletown *(G-7485)*
Quick Server Hosting LLC............................ E 800 586-6126
  New Castle *(G-9508)*
Simplica Corporation..................................... F 302 594-9899
  Wilmington *(G-19837)*
Tata Communications Amer Inc.................. E 703 547-5900
  Wilmington *(G-20226)*
Ultahost Inc... G 302 966-3941
  Middletown *(G-7671)*

COMMUNICATIONS SVCS: Online Svc Providers

Capitol Broadband Dev Co LLC................... E
  Wilmington *(G-15232)*
Excede Brdband Stllite Intrnet...................... G 302 289-0147
  Felton *(G-3968)*
Excede Brdband Stllite Intrnet...................... G 302 613-0669
  New Castle *(G-9108)*
New Concept Technologies LLC................... G 518 533-5367
  Wilmington *(G-18614)*
Nextdns Inc.. E 831 854-7227
  Middletown *(G-7403)*
Skynethostingnet Inc.................................... F 302 384-1784
  Wilmington *(G-19858)*
Toptel Inc.. G 310 999-4320
  Dover *(G-3702)*
Wala LLC... G 949 410-0568
  Wilmington *(G-20671)*

COMMUNICATIONS SVCS: Proprietary Online Svcs Networks

Coachhub Inc.. G 929 930-1450
  Wilmington *(G-15506)*
Elli Creators Inc.. F 269 742-4057
  Middletown *(G-7097)*

COMMUNICATIONS SVCS: Signal Enhancement Network Svcs

Quadix LLC... G 877 669-8680
  Middletown *(G-7485)*
Texnikos Inc.. G 302 656-8088
  Wilmington *(G-20284)*

COMMUNICATIONS SVCS: Telephone Or Video

Switch Enterprises LLC................................ E 212 227-9191
  Dover *(G-3632)*

COMMUNICATIONS SVCS: Telephone, Broker

Comcast Clfrn/Clrd/Llns/ndn/tx................... D 248 233-4724
  Wilmington *(G-15542)*
Globaltec Networks Inc................................ G 646 321-8627
  Wilmington *(G-16897)*
Nobelone Inc.. G 617 283-8871
  Newark *(G-11559)*

COMMUNICATIONS SVCS: Telephone, Local

Verizon Delaware LLC.................................. C 302 571-1571
  Wilmington *(G-20590)*

COMMUNICATIONS SVCS: Telephone, Local & Long Distance

Global Tellink... G 302 672-7867
  Dover *(G-2592)*

MCI Communications Corporation............. F 302 791-4900
  Wilmington *(G-18230)*
Reliance Communications Inc.................... F 888 673-5426
  Wilmington *(G-19424)*
Sprint Spectrum LP...................................... G 302 393-2060
  Milford *(G-8101)*
Telco Envirotrols Inc.................................... G 302 846-9103
  Delmar *(G-1639)*
Verizon Delaware LLC.................................. E 302 629-4502
  Seaford *(G-13440)*

COMMUNICATIONS SVCS: Telephone, Long Distance

C4-Nvis USA LLC... G 213 465-5089
  Dover *(G-2009)*
Sigma Telecom LLC...................................... G 347 741-8397
  Wilmington *(G-19818)*

COMMUNICATIONS SVCS: Telephone, Voice

Instacall LLC... F 302 496-1166
  Wilmington *(G-17358)*
Progressive Telecom LLC............................ E 302 883-8883
  Wilmington *(G-19222)*
Trunk Tel LLC.. G 302 476-2370
  Wilmington *(G-20448)*

COMMUNITY SVCS EMPLOYMENT TRAINING PROGRAM

Delmarva Clergy United Inc........................ F 302 422-2350
  Ellendale *(G-3914)*

COMPACT LASER DISCS: Prerecorded

Saregama India Limited............................... G 859 490-0156
  Newark *(G-11950)*

COMPRESSORS: Air & Gas

De Sales and Service.................................... G 302 456-1660
  Newark *(G-10399)*
Easy Lawn Inc.. E 302 815-6500
  Greenwood *(G-4624)*
Linne Industries LLC................................... G 302 454-1439
  Newark *(G-11263)*

COMPUTER & COMPUTER SOFTWARE STORES

Antenna House Inc....................................... G 302 566-7225
  Newark *(G-9876)*
Bits & Bytes Inc.. G 302 674-2999
  Dover *(G-1942)*
Gamestop Inc... F 302 266-7362
  Newark *(G-10805)*
Nerdit Now LLC.. G 302 482-5979
  Wilmington *(G-18587)*
Opti-Mag Inc.. G 302 738-2903
  Newark *(G-11596)*
Response Computer Group Inc.................. F 302 335-3400
  Milford *(G-8063)*

COMPUTER & COMPUTER SOFTWARE STORES: Peripheral Eqpt

Creative Micro Designs Inc......................... G 302 456-5800
  Newark *(G-10349)*
PC Supplies Inc.. G 302 368-4800
  Newark *(G-11648)*
Tower Business Machines Inc.................... G 302 395-1445
  Historic New Castle *(G-5088)*

COMPUTER & COMPUTER SOFTWARE STORES: Personal Computers

Quinn Data Corporation............................... G 302 429-7450
  Wilmington *(G-19295)*

COMPUTER & COMPUTER SOFTWARE STORES: Software & Access

Laser Images of Delaware Inc..................... G 302 836-8610
  Bear *(G-338)*
Ryzenlink Technologies LLC....................... G 786 536-0349
  Hockessin *(G-5376)*

COMPUTER & COMPUTER SOFTWARE STORES: Software, Bus/Non-Game

Altr Solutions LLC.. F 888 757-2587
  Dover *(G-1777)*
Dignisys Inc.. F 845 213-1121
  Dover *(G-2298)*
Ezdorms Inc.. F 202 599-2953
  Wilmington *(G-16517)*
Famoid Technology LLC............................... G 530 601-7284
  Newark *(G-10710)*
Gro-Connectcom Inc.................................... G 347 918-7437
  Lewes *(G-6066)*
Harrock Properties LLC............................... G 302 202-1321
  Dover *(G-2657)*
Load Miles Inc.. F 323 842-7038
  Dover *(G-2965)*
Mtc Usa LLC... F 980 999-8888
  Newark *(G-11468)*
Stylere LLC... G 650 206-7721
  Dover *(G-3618)*
Tamp Inc.. F 302 283-9195
  Newark *(G-12158)*
Wherebyus Enterprises Inc........................ F 305 988-0808
  Claymont *(G-1336)*

COMPUTER & COMPUTER SOFTWARE STORES: Software, Computer Game

SE Gaming Services Inc............................... E 303 867-8090
  Newark *(G-11966)*

COMPUTER & DATA PROCESSING EQPT REPAIR & MAINTENANCE

Confluent Corporation................................. G 301 440-4100
  Georgetown *(G-4265)*
Handytech Solutions LLC............................ G 302 449-4497
  Middletown *(G-7194)*
Laser Images of Delaware Inc..................... G 302 836-8610
  Bear *(G-338)*
Mauna Services LLC.................................... G 302 446-4409
  Dover *(G-3037)*
PC Supplies Inc.. G 302 368-4800
  Newark *(G-11648)*
Response Computer Group Inc.................. F 302 335-3400
  Milford *(G-8063)*

COMPUTER & OFFICE MACHINE MAINTENANCE & REPAIR

AAA Computing.. G 302 430-9048
  Milford *(G-7758)*
Coastal It Consulting.................................... G 302 226-9395
  Rehoboth Beach *(G-12683)*
Computer Jocks.. G 302 544-6448
  Bear *(G-116)*
Curvature Inc... G 302 525-9525
  Newark *(G-10366)*
Feddly Jeanniton.. G 302 325-1000
  New Castle *(G-9121)*
First Tech... F 302 421-3650
  Wilmington *(G-16640)*

PRODUCTS & SERVICES SECTION

COMPUTER RELATED MAINTENANCE SVCS

Information Technology Afforda............ G 302 525-6252
  Newark *(G-11020)*
ME Geek Squad Llc................................. G 302 990-8092
  Wilmington *(G-18241)*
Software Services of De Inc.................... E 302 654-3172
  Wilmington *(G-19915)*
TCS Inc... G 302 858-1389
  Milton *(G-8718)*
Teamlogic It... G 302 446-4100
  Wilmington *(G-20245)*
Tech Impact... F 302 256-5015
  Wilmington *(G-20248)*
Tech Now Mobile LLC............................. G 484 480-0648
  Wilmington *(G-20251)*
Teleplan Vdeocom Solutions Inc............ E 302 323-8503
  New Castle *(G-9624)*
Tower Business Machines Inc................ G 302 395-1445
  Historic New Castle *(G-5088)*
Zerowait Corporation............................... F 302 996-9408
  Wilmington *(G-20958)*

COMPUTER DATA ESCROW SVCS

Savantis Solutions LLC........................... B 732 906-3200
  Wilmington *(G-19682)*

COMPUTER FACILITIES MANAGEMENT SVCS

Absolute Computer Support LLC............ G 717 917-8900
  Newark *(G-9745)*
Alpha Technologies USA Inc.................. D 302 510-8205
  Wilmington *(G-14392)*
Cks Global Ventures LLC........................ E 302 355-0511
  Newark *(G-10248)*
Datatech Enterprises Inc........................ F 540 370-0010
  Selbyville *(G-13515)*
Gga Global Consulting LLC.................... F 302 238-1751
  Dover *(G-2579)*
Herbert R Martin Associates.................. G 302 239-1700
  Hockessin *(G-5238)*
Insight Engineering Solutions................ G 302 378-4842
  Townsend *(G-14018)*
Ipr International LLC................................ E 302 304-8774
  Wilmington *(G-17417)*
Nuyka Inc... E 707 400-5444
  Lewes *(G-6323)*
Supportyourapp Inc................................ E 888 959-3556
  Wilmington *(G-20154)*
Veteran It Pro LLC.................................. F 302 824-3111
  Hockessin *(G-5418)*

COMPUTER GRAPHICS SVCS

Cadrender Inc... G 302 657-0700
  Wilmington *(G-15188)*
Cgs Infotech Inc...................................... E 302 351-2434
  Wilmington *(G-15324)*
Chief Web Design................................... G 302 542-8409
  Georgetown *(G-4250)*
Everlast Interactive LLC......................... G 347 992-3783
  Bear *(G-212)*
Ezangacom Inc....................................... E 888 439-2642
  Middletown *(G-7116)*
Iamag Inc... G 317 487-9338
  Wilmington *(G-17253)*
Integrated Home LLC............................. G 302 656-1624
  New Castle *(G-9236)*
Mobius New Media Inc........................... G 302 475-9880
  Wilmington *(G-18397)*
My Qme Inc.. G 302 218-8730
  Wilmington *(G-18508)*
Professionsale Inc.................................. G 646 262-9101
  Bear *(G-439)*

Search Optics LLC.................................. D 858 678-0707
  Wilmington *(G-19724)*
Sixteenpenny LLC................................... G 302 463-7992
  Newark *(G-12018)*
SM Technomine Inc................................ F 312 492-4386
  Wilmington *(G-19870)*
Techno Goober....................................... F 302 645-7177
  Lewes *(G-6546)*
Tecpresso Inc... G 302 240-0025
  Wilmington *(G-20260)*
Trolley Web.. G 302 468-7247
  Wilmington *(G-20437)*
Vic Victor Imagination Co LLC................ G 714 262-4426
  Lewes *(G-6603)*
Webmost... G 302 345-0807
  Newark *(G-12353)*
Your Superfoods Inc................................ G 424 387-6165
  Newark *(G-12423)*

COMPUTER HARDWARE REQUIREMENTS ANALYSIS

Evernex USA Inc..................................... B 888 630-9396
  Newark *(G-10678)*
Genesec Inc.. G 917 656-5742
  Claymont *(G-1159)*
Supportyourapp Inc................................ E 888 959-3556
  Wilmington *(G-20154)*

COMPUTER PERIPHERAL EQPT REPAIR & MAINTENANCE

Technicare Inc.. G 302 322-7766
  Newark *(G-12170)*

COMPUTER PERIPHERAL EQPT, NEC

Aim God Society..................................... F 207 299-3881
  Middletown *(G-6843)*
Creative Micro Designs Inc.................... G 302 456-5800
  Newark *(G-10349)*
East Coast Games Inc............................ F 302 838-0669
  Bear *(G-189)*
Nerdit Now LLC....................................... F 302 482-5979
  Wilmington *(G-18587)*

COMPUTER PERIPHERAL EQPT, WHOLESALE

AK Multinational LLC.............................. E 845 542-8155
  Wilmington *(G-14343)*
Bb Technologies Inc............................... G 302 652-2300
  Wilmington *(G-14792)*
Broadberry Data Systems LLC............... E 302 295-1086
  Wilmington *(G-15121)*
Broadberry Data Systems LLC............... G 800 496-9918
  Wilmington *(G-15122)*
Hoover Computer Services Inc.............. G 302 529-7050
  Wilmington *(G-17195)*
Hypertec Usa Inc.................................... G 480 626-9000
  Dover *(G-2712)*
PC Supplies Inc...................................... G 302 368-4800
  Newark *(G-11648)*
Sumuri LLC.. E 302 570-0015
  Magnolia *(G-6786)*

COMPUTER PROCESSING SVCS

Braincx Inc.. F 954 892-9101
  Wilmington *(G-15036)*
Casper Hosting LLC............................... G 480 442-7112
  Lewes *(G-5807)*
Ecircular LLC.. F 713 514-4675
  Wilmington *(G-16278)*

Global Comm Innovations LLC.............. G 302 546-5010
  Claymont *(G-1163)*
Hap LLC.. G 302 645-7400
  Lewes *(G-6075)*

COMPUTER PROGRAMMING SVCS: Custom

1000x LLC... F 919 584-5420
  Middletown *(G-6814)*
Applied Control Engrg Inc...................... D 302 738-8800
  Newark *(G-9891)*
Calcom Inc.. E 442 227-3200
  Wilmington *(G-15191)*
Camio LLC.. F 585 851-8550
  Dover *(G-2018)*
Cloud Software Development LLC........ G 703 957-9847
  Wilmington *(G-15492)*
CosIs LLC... F 877 900-7373
  Claymont *(G-1101)*
Dream Weaver LLC................................ G 302 352-9473
  Wilmington *(G-16177)*
Engage Xr LLC....................................... G 302 877-2028
  Wilmington *(G-16421)*
Ikarus Nest Inc....................................... F 415 727-2401
  Bear *(G-283)*
Lokblok Inc... F 408 640-8644
  Wilmington *(G-17979)*
Mighty Acorn Digital Inc......................... G 877 277-8805
  Wilmington *(G-18348)*
Nano Wallet Company LLC.................... G 443 610-3402
  Wilmington *(G-18529)*
Nucural Inc.. G 408 625-7047
  Wilmington *(G-18712)*
Prudent Technology & Svcs LLC........... F 302 481-6399
  Dover *(G-3387)*
Ruby Digital Agency Inc........................ G 801 971-1681
  Wilmington *(G-19585)*
Satori Ci LLC.. G 302 526-0557
  Claymont *(G-1285)*
Signin Soft Inc.. F 315 966-6699
  Wilmington *(G-19823)*
Software Radio Systems USA Inc......... F 339 368-6321
  Newark *(G-12051)*
Software Services of De Inc.................. E 302 654-3172
  Wilmington *(G-19915)*
Stackadapt US Inc.................................. C 647 385-7698
  Lewes *(G-6505)*
Z Data Inc... G 800 676-5614
  Newark *(G-12426)*
Zenpli LLC... F 302 314-5231
  Newark *(G-12432)*

COMPUTER RELATED MAINTENANCE SVCS

Antenna House Inc................................. G 302 566-7225
  Newark *(G-9876)*
Cks Global Ventures LLC....................... E 302 355-0511
  Newark *(G-10248)*
Conectiv Communications Inc............... E 302 224-1177
  Newark *(G-10299)*
Conquest Tech Solutions Inc................. G 302 356-1423
  Wilmington *(G-15606)*
Dwh System Inc...................................... F 551 208-5354
  Felton *(G-3963)*
Qase Inc.. E 650 459-1800
  Wilmington *(G-19274)*
Ram Tech Systems Inc........................... E 302 832-6600
  Middletown *(G-7500)*
Symbiosys Consulting LLC.................... F 302 507-7649
  Wilmington *(G-20181)*
University of Delaware........................... F 302 831-6041
  Newark *(G-12277)*
Verito Technologies LLC........................ F 855 583-7486
  Wilmington *(G-20589)*

Employee Codes: A=Over 500 employees, B=251-500
C=101-250, D=51-100, E=20-50, F=10-19, G=1-9

2024 Harris Directory of Delaware Businesses

COMPUTER SERVICE BUREAU

COMPUTER SERVICE BUREAU

Ipr International LLC .... E 302 304-8774
  Wilmington *(G-17417)*

Wilkinson Technology Svcs LLC .... G 302 384-7770
  Wilmington *(G-20782)*

COMPUTER SOFTWARE DEVELOPMENT

9junio Inc .... G 239 946-6374
  Middletown *(G-6820)*

Abandon Inc .... G 858 863-7190
  Dover *(G-1701)*

Accuretix LLC .... G 646 434-6917
  Claymont *(G-1017)*

Agent Launch LLC .... F 302 200-5574
  Newark *(G-9796)*

Agitek Softworks Inc .... G 240 356-3034
  Lewes *(G-5665)*

Ais .... G 302 407-0430
  Wilmington *(G-14339)*

Alchemy Software Solutions LLC .... E 201 627-0638
  Wilmington *(G-14351)*

Alpha Technologies USA Inc .... D 302 510-8205
  Wilmington *(G-14392)*

Analytica LLC .... F 214 223-2055
  Dover *(G-1789)*

Apphud Inc .... G 415 936-8741
  Newark *(G-9889)*

Aquia Inc .... F 530 215-7158
  Millsboro *(G-8171)*

Aros Design Studio LLC .... G 505 560-0603
  Wilmington *(G-14557)*

Artid LLC .... G 302 898-6307
  Dover *(G-1823)*

Ascent Technologies Inc .... G 302 491-0545
  Newark *(G-9919)*

Atomic Development Inc .... G 424 354-9865
  Dover *(G-1851)*

Auditbot .... G 302 494-9476
  Newark *(G-9943)*

Aum LLC .... F 302 385-6767
  Wilmington *(G-14641)*

Automizy Inc .... G 361 253-8238
  Wilmington *(G-14655)*

Autoweb Technologies Inc .... G 443 485-4200
  Wilmington *(G-14657)*

Avanta Inc .... E 925 818-4760
  Dover *(G-1856)*

Avni Adtech Inc .... F 628 600-5009
  Middletown *(G-6892)*

Avomd Inc .... F 631 786-3867
  Dover *(G-1857)*

Bagel Technologies Inc .... G 650 410-8018
  Middletown *(G-6902)*

Bastion Research Ltd .... G 307 370-3767
  Lewes *(G-5738)*

Beforesunset Inc .... F 812 341-0038
  Wilmington *(G-14812)*

Beneree Inc .... G 814 526-4238
  Middletown *(G-6912)*

Bizdata Inc .... G 650 283-1644
  Wilmington *(G-14899)*

Blackwell Solution .... G 302 660-2054
  Bear *(G-74)*

Blair Computing Systems Inc .... F 302 453-8947
  Newark *(G-10049)*

Blaze Systems Corporation .... G 302 733-7235
  Newark *(G-10050)*

Booke AI Inc .... G 650 540-1316
  Wilmington *(G-15001)*

Boomset Inc .... F 860 266-6738
  Wilmington *(G-15004)*

Brittons Wise Computers Inc .... G 302 659-0343
  Smyrna *(G-13668)*

Bryant Technologies Inc .... G 302 289-2044
  Felton *(G-3948)*

Bullseye Entertainment Tech Co .... E 302 924-5034
  Dover *(G-1992)*

Byte Technology Systems Inc .... G 347 687-7240
  Lewes *(G-5784)*

Callvu Inc .... G 646 506-4915
  Wilmington *(G-15199)*

Camelo LLC .... G 302 574-6556
  Wilmington *(G-15205)*

Capton LLC .... G 510 766-2803
  Wilmington *(G-15235)*

Castor Research Inc .... F 415 484-5347
  Wilmington *(G-15269)*

Centrito LLC .... E 919 728-9401
  Claymont *(G-1080)*

Certified Code Inc .... G 347 508-6396
  Middletown *(G-6970)*

Cg Global MGT Solutions LLC .... F 215 735-3745
  Wilmington *(G-15321)*

Channelape Inc .... E 570 351-9335
  Wilmington *(G-15333)*

Cignitix Global LLC .... G 408 638-9350
  Wilmington *(G-15437)*

Clew Medical Inc .... G 623 414-9009
  Wilmington *(G-15480)*

Cline Labs Inc .... G 901 834-5102
  Middletown *(G-6994)*

Cloudbees Inc .... F 323 842-7783
  Lewes *(G-5830)*

Codeship Inc .... E 617 515-3664
  Lewes *(G-5848)*

Cognicor Technologies Inc .... G 650 444-2076
  Dover *(G-2111)*

Comeet Technologies Inc .... G 650 433-9027
  Wilmington *(G-15544)*

Computools Llc .... F 617 861-0016
  Camden Wyoming *(G-927)*

Conrep Inc .... E 302 528-8383
  Middletown *(G-7010)*

Coolautomation Inc .... G 941 587-2287
  Wilmington *(G-15630)*

Cora Systems Us Inc .... F 833 269-5756
  Wilmington *(G-15636)*

Coral Technology LLC .... G 201 793-7127
  Lewes *(G-5859)*

Corticalio USA Inc .... F 415 350-8588
  Newark *(G-10331)*

Corvant LLC .... G 302 299-1570
  Newark *(G-10332)*

Covant Solutions Inc .... F 302 607-2678
  Newark *(G-10338)*

Cr24 Inc .... G 888 427-9357
  Wilmington *(G-15678)*

Crediblockcom LLC .... G 803 619-9458
  Dover *(G-2156)*

Cryptlex LLC .... G 786 269-0931
  Lewes *(G-5872)*

Dama International LLC .... F 813 778-5495
  Middletown *(G-7027)*

Data-Bi LLC .... G 302 290-3138
  Wilmington *(G-15798)*

Datamola LLC .... G 347 474-1003
  Lewes *(G-5883)*

Davait Inc .... G 302 930-0095
  Dover *(G-2198)*

Dayshape Corp .... G 929 512-5982
  Dover *(G-2201)*

Deepen Inc .... G 813 813-9053
  Middletown *(G-7036)*

DEMC Academia Institute .... G 301 215-1056
  Dover *(G-2280)*

Derived Data LLC .... G 845 300-1805
  Wilmington *(G-16019)*

Digilence LLC .... G 678 296-9198
  Middletown *(G-7061)*

Digital ARC LLC .... F 855 275-2770
  Wilmington *(G-16063)*

Digitlogy LLC DBA Exprttexting .... G 302 703-9672
  Milton *(G-8606)*

Dijitru Inc .... G 903 345-4878
  New Castle *(G-9054)*

Django Stars Ltd Liability Co .... F 415 996-8054
  Wilmington *(G-16101)*

Dlt Federal Bus Syst Corp .... G 302 358-2229
  Wilmington *(G-16106)*

DOE Technologies Inc .... E 302 792-1285
  Wilmington *(G-16116)*

Dukka Inc .... G 401 659-6948
  Dover *(G-2394)*

Eden Care Group Holding LLC .... G 929 461-7247
  Dover *(G-2419)*

Endevor LLC .... G 302 543-5055
  Wilmington *(G-16409)*

Enpass Technologies Inc .... G 415 671-5123
  Wilmington *(G-16429)*

Enzigma LLC .... G 415 830-3694
  Wilmington *(G-16446)*

Epotec Inc .... G 302 654-3090
  Wilmington *(G-16451)*

Eshopperlists Com Inc .... G 302 235-5743
  Hockessin *(G-5203)*

Eswap Global Inc .... G 323 244-2927
  Newark *(G-10668)*

Ethereal Tech US Corp .... E 567 694-8888
  Wilmington *(G-16474)*

Excelling LLC .... G 302 276-3908
  Magnolia *(G-6744)*

Eztrackit Inc .... G 800 371-5956
  Rehoboth Beach *(G-12749)*

Factory Technologies Inc .... G 302 266-1290
  Newark *(G-10701)*

Frontierx Inc .... E 201 313-6998
  Dover *(G-2538)*

Fuel Labs Inc .... G 302 364-0442
  Wilmington *(G-16767)*

Gatello Inc .... F 725 333-3830
  Newark *(G-10814)*

Genohm Inc .... G 646 616-7531
  Newark *(G-10820)*

Gesso Labs Inc .... F 888 206-4024
  Wilmington *(G-16853)*

Giesela Inc .... G 855 556-4338
  Newark *(G-10833)*

Gmdh Inc .... G 347 470-4634
  Lewes *(G-6040)*

Golden Inc .... F 408 384-9136
  Lewes *(G-6046)*

Good Driver Mutuality Inc .... E 713 979-8257
  Dover *(G-2603)*

Growth Cave LLC .... E 323 688-5042
  Newark *(G-10904)*

Gw Solutions LLC .... G 240 578-5981
  Bethany Beach *(G-606)*

Hbm Apps Inc .... G 302 387-0052
  Middletown *(G-7198)*

Headtotoe Mhealth Inc .... G 438 867-1908
  Wilmington *(G-17091)*

Healex Systems Ltd .... F 302 235-5750
  Wilmington *(G-17092)*

Helloguru Inc .... G 754 303-3278
  Claymont *(G-1178)*

COMPUTER SOFTWARE DEVELOPMENT

Hint America Inc .... F 646 845-1895
　Wilmington *(G-17153)*

Home Innovations .... G 302 448-9555
　Lewes *(G-6097)*

Hopshop Inc .... G 323 745-1115
　Middletown *(G-7216)*

Hubgets Inc .... G 239 206-2995
　Wilmington *(G-17228)*

Hybridthory Digital Entrmt LLC .... G 864 973-5753
　Dover *(G-2709)*

Iexperto Inc .... G 347 808-3708
　Middletown *(G-7221)*

Implify Inc .... E 302 533-2345
　Newark *(G-11007)*

Incite Solutions Inc .... G 302 655-8952
　Wilmington *(G-17300)*

Infinite Improbabilities Inc .... G 763 516-5825
　Wilmington *(G-17321)*

Inkit Inc .... F 612 712-1245
　Wilmington *(G-17342)*

Integrated Solutions Gate Inc .... G 302 404-6080
　Wilmington *(G-17371)*

Interlace Global Inc .... G 917 719-6811
　Wilmington *(G-17385)*

Interpres Security Inc .... F 570 971-9876
　Wilmington *(G-17397)*

Inumsoft Inc .... G 302 533-5403
　Bear *(G-287)*

Ispapp Inc .... F 302 310-5009
　Dover *(G-2753)*

Itexus LLC .... G 917 618-9804
　Camden *(G-856)*

Jana Analysis Inc .... E 724 584-0545
　Middletown *(G-7240)*

Julieth Ai Technologies Inc .... F 512 680-1855
　Camden *(G-862)*

Kaplan Software Group .... G 646 498-8275
　Lewes *(G-6160)*

Katabat LLC .... E 302 830-9262
　Wilmington *(G-17658)*

Kortech Consulting Inc .... F 302 559-4612
　Bear *(G-333)*

Kuest Inc .... G 786 840-0842
　Middletown *(G-7284)*

Labware .... G 302 521-0250
　Newark *(G-11213)*

Labware Inc .... E 302 658-8444
　Wilmington *(G-17785)*

Labware Holdings Inc .... E 302 658-8444
　Wilmington *(G-17787)*

Lattice Industries Inc .... G 708 702-4664
　Wilmington *(G-17819)*

Legaledge Software .... G 302 761-9304
　Wilmington *(G-17863)*

Lime Ccnut Data Intllgnce Lcdi .... G 302 272-2858
　Dover *(G-2949)*

Live Typing Inc .... G 415 670-9601
　Wilmington *(G-17949)*

Liveboard Inc .... G 888 412-8882
　Middletown *(G-7310)*

Livetrade Ltd .... G 302 305-1797
　Lewes *(G-6214)*

Lizard Soft Inc .... G 619 618-0368
　Dover *(G-2960)*

Logicjunction Inc .... G 216 292-5760
　Dover *(G-2971)*

Lokalise Inc .... G 302 498-9091
　Dover *(G-2973)*

Maad Africa Inc .... D 847 927-0519
　Middletown *(G-7320)*

Magipop Inc .... G 217 898-3115
　Wilmington *(G-18083)*

Mara Labs Inc .... E 650 564-4971
　Wilmington *(G-18117)*

Masstech Americas Inc .... D 905 946-5700
　Dover *(G-3026)*

Matrica Labs Inc .... F 818 573-7394
　Wilmington *(G-18193)*

Medshifts Inc .... G 856 834-0074
　Wilmington *(G-18258)*

Meetrecord Inc .... G 281 407-7338
　Wilmington *(G-18259)*

Mentor Consultants Inc .... G 610 566-4004
　Wilmington *(G-18273)*

Metamax Technology Inc .... F 302 587-0060
　Newark *(G-11393)*

Metanium Corp .... E 302 669-9084
　Dover *(G-3070)*

Microlog Corporation Maryland .... G 301 540-5501
　Rehoboth Beach *(G-12854)*

Microtelecom Systems LLC .... D 718 707-0012
　Wilmington *(G-18331)*

Minimum Corporation .... F 857 928-0317
　Wilmington *(G-18372)*

Miops Inc .... G 302 451-9571
　Newark *(G-11427)*

Mobility Route Inc .... G 302 273-0770
　Dover *(G-3111)*

Mobio Global Inc .... G 484 263-4845
　Dover *(G-3113)*

Moeco Iot Inc .... G 626 869-7140
　Wilmington *(G-18400)*

Mojio .... G 831 747-5141
　Wilmington *(G-18402)*

Monada Inc .... F 302 253-7382
　Wilmington *(G-18408)*

Money Factory LLC .... G 620 755-5215
　Dover *(G-3119)*

Monofor Inc .... G 415 800-4925
　Newark *(G-11444)*

Moon Buyer Inc .... F 302 636-5401
　Wilmington *(G-18429)*

Moving Sciences LLC .... G 617 871-9892
　Wilmington *(G-18467)*

Mphasis Corporation .... F 212 686-6655
　Wilmington *(G-18471)*

Msm Foods LLC .... G 302 524-4470
　Wilmington *(G-18476)*

Mymedchoices Inc .... G 302 932-1920
　Hockessin *(G-5315)*

Navigine Corporation .... G 339 234-0827
　Wilmington *(G-18563)*

Neon USA LLC .... F 360 433-7512
　Dover *(G-3171)*

Netdata Inc .... E 650 407-3589
　Newark *(G-11507)*

Netfoundry Inc .... D 855 284-2007
　Wilmington *(G-18592)*

New Cstle Cnty Del Emplyees Fd ..... F 302 395-5350
　New Castle *(G-9414)*

Newtone Communications Inc .... G 650 727-0998
　Middletown *(G-7402)*

Noramp Inc .... G 914 266-0153
　Newark *(G-11562)*

Nortal LLC .... G 425 233-0164
　Wilmington *(G-18675)*

Novo Financial Corp .... F 844 260-6800
　Dover *(G-3205)*

Nuix North America Inc .... G 302 584-7542
　Wilmington *(G-18714)*

Omni Interactive Holding LLC .... G 779 612-8747
　Wilmington *(G-18767)*

Omninet International Inc .... E 208 246-5022
　Wilmington *(G-18769)*

One Sententia Ltd .... G 646 284-0321
　Dover *(G-3228)*

Onengine Corp .... G 949 872-0339
　Dover *(G-3230)*

Open Text Inc .... E 248 986-6927
　Wilmington *(G-18798)*

Openeducat Inc .... G 302 261-5133
　Claymont *(G-1258)*

Orderhive Inc .... G 888 878-5538
　Newark *(G-11599)*

Outburst Ai Limited .... F 516 303-2097
　Wilmington *(G-18838)*

Outland Art Inc .... F 800 918-1587
　Dover *(G-3249)*

Pantheon Technologies LLC .... G 855 927-9387
　Dover *(G-3265)*

Paradiso Solutions LLC .... D 800 513-5902
　Wilmington *(G-18885)*

Paralleldots Inc .... F 224 587-0022
　Lewes *(G-6349)*

Pathscale Inc .... G 408 384-9948
　Wilmington *(G-18904)*

Pattern Labs Tech Inc .... G 516 340-3369
　Wilmington *(G-18913)*

Peak Uptime Solutions LLC .... G 856 243-5838
　Wilmington *(G-18942)*

Perficient Inc .... G 302 690-2087
　Wilmington *(G-18975)*

Pfs Ltd .... G 202 709-9755
　Dover *(G-3310)*

Plane Software Inc .... E 857 693-9321
　Middletown *(G-7453)*

Poliquicks LLC .... G 512 915-7919
　Wilmington *(G-19105)*

Power On US Inc .... E 212 317-1010
　Lewes *(G-6384)*

Prime Directive Inc .... G 302 383-5607
　Newark *(G-11743)*

Problem Consulting Co .... G 347 809-3402
　Newark *(G-11757)*

Project Assistants Inc .... E 302 477-9711
　Wilmington *(G-19223)*

Ps3g Inc .... F 302 298-0270
　Wilmington *(G-19241)*

Purplenow Inc .... E 302 751-5226
　Dover *(G-3399)*

Puzzle Investments LLC .... F 774 516-6447
　Wilmington *(G-19268)*

Pxe Group LLC .... G 561 295-1451
　Dover *(G-3401)*

Quadrotech Solutions Inc .... C 302 660-0166
　Wilmington *(G-19279)*

Quantconnect Corporation .... F 917 327-0556
　Lewes *(G-6400)*

Quantum Leap Innovations Inc .... F 302 894-8045
　Newark *(G-11795)*

Quest Global Digital Inc .... B 650 267-1334
　Wilmington *(G-19293)*

Quetext Software LLC .... E 800 403-9067
　Wilmington *(G-19294)*

Qwintry LLC .... G 844 794-6879
　New Castle *(G-9509)*

Raas Infotek LLC .... E 302 894-3184
　Newark *(G-11813)*

Radiant Technologies Inc .... G 800 301-0980
　Newark *(G-11818)*

Rainmaker Software Group LLC ...... G 800 616-6701
　Wilmington *(G-19320)*

Ravnur Inc .... G 239 963-4404
　Wilmington *(G-19340)*

Redcircle Technologies Inc .... F 844 404-2525
　Claymont *(G-1276)*

Employee Codes: A=Over 500 employees, B=251-500
C=101-250, D=51-100, E=20-50, F=10-19, G=1-9

2024 Harris Directory of
Delaware Businesses

COMPUTER SOFTWARE DEVELOPMENT

Rently Software LLC ..... F 718 502-6575
  Newark (G-11852)
Revolve Technologies LLC ..... G 302 528-2647
  Townsend (G-14060)
Riddle Inc ..... G 724 901-1810
  Wilmington (G-19478)
Ritchie Sawyer Corporation ..... F 302 475-1971
  Wilmington (G-19488)
Rocaccion Inc ..... G 617 902-8779
  Newark (G-11902)
Rozdoum Inc ..... G 315 707-7517
  Dover (G-3489)
Rwazi Inc ..... F 800 597-5871
  Wilmington (G-19598)
Ryzenlink Technologies LLC ..... G 786 536-0349
  Hockessin (G-5376)
Savantis Group ..... G 415 297-6926
  Wilmington (G-19681)
Savantis Solutions LLC ..... B 732 906-3200
  Wilmington (G-19682)
Scorelogix LLC ..... F 302 294-6532
  Newark (G-11963)
Second Technologies Inc ..... G 310 774-7518
  Dover (G-3526)
Sendible Usa Inc ..... G 646 569-9029
  Newark (G-11975)
Sensedia LLC ..... G 631 764-4544
  Wilmington (G-19751)
Servicevet Technologies LLC ..... G 302 659-0343
  Smyrna (G-13882)
Sesimi LLC ..... G 302 574-6280
  Wilmington (G-19765)
Shammah LLC ..... G 302 533-7359
  Newark (G-11989)
Siditech LLC ..... G 302 384-5088
  Wilmington (G-19813)
Signall Technologies Inc ..... G 240 623-5800
  Dover (G-3555)
Simplecode LLC ..... G 302 703-7231
  Lewes (G-6473)
Sivil Technologies Inc ..... G 214 893-9797
  Wilmington (G-19845)
Six Days Inc ..... E 888 463-5898
  Wilmington (G-19847)
Skoruz Holding Corporation ..... G 510 766-2803
  Wilmington (G-19856)
Smart Professions Inc ..... E 603 289-6263
  Dover (G-3576)
Smart Union Blockchain LLC ..... F 919 872-5631
  Lewes (G-6483)
Snapify Corp ..... F 646 814-6388
  Wilmington (G-19899)
Socialpilot Technologies Inc ..... G 415 450-6060
  Lewes (G-6487)
Softlinn LLC ..... G 718 926-2170
  Wilmington (G-19914)
Speed Auto Systems LLC ..... E 888 446-7102
  Lewes (G-6499)
Spire Innovations Inc ..... D 646 583-1839
  Wilmington (G-19966)
Stanga Games Inc ..... G 415 549-6537
  Wilmington (G-20017)
Subcodevs Inc ..... G 704 234-6780
  Wilmington (G-20110)
Superops Inc ..... G 510 330-2676
  Claymont (G-1308)
Supply Chain Consultants Inc ..... E 302 738-9215
  Wilmington (G-20149)
Sygul Inc ..... E 315 384-1848
  Newark (G-12146)
Talents Digital Services Corp ..... E 888 508-2503
  Dover (G-3647)

Task Analytics Inc ..... G 631 388-3120
  Wilmington (G-20225)
Tech Central LLC ..... G 717 273-3301
  Wilmington (G-20246)
Tekgeminus Solutions Inc ..... G 503 336-5259
  Middletown (G-7629)
Thinkhat Software Inc ..... F 917 379-2638
  Wilmington (G-20301)
Thinksecurenet ..... F 302 703-9717
  Lewes (G-6556)
Thirty Birds Inc ..... G 351 910-5520
  Wilmington (G-20304)
Thrive Physical Therapy Inc ..... F 302 834-8400
  Middletown (G-7642)
Ticket Sports and Entrmt Corp ..... G 224 522-3517
  Newark (G-12195)
Tiers Inc ..... G 302 298-3338
  Wilmington (G-20319)
Total Wellness Innovations Inc ..... G 404 543-9061
  Wilmington (G-20374)
Touchstone Systems Inc ..... F 302 324-5322
  New Castle (G-9631)
Transactional Web Inc ..... G 908 216-5054
  Wilmington (G-20395)
Translateai LLC ..... E 213 675-6702
  Dover (G-3713)
Trialogics LLC ..... F 302 313-9000
  Wilmington (G-20418)
Twisty Systems LLC ..... G 571 331-7093
  Lewes (G-6585)
Txthinking Inc ..... G 646 820-1235
  Newark (G-12250)
Tychron Corporation ..... F 844 892-4766
  Wilmington (G-20476)
Unik Marketing Inc ..... G 302 830-9935
  Wilmington (G-20512)
Universal Algorithm Inc ..... G 302 446-3562
  Dover (G-3752)
Utopie Technologies Inc ..... F 628 251-1312
  Lewes (G-6597)
Vakoms LLC ..... G 206 474-4319
  Wilmington (G-20562)
Veendhq Inc ..... G 470 300-9787
  Wilmington (G-20576)
Vel Micro Works Incorporated ..... G 302 239-4661
  Hockessin (G-5417)
Venzee Inc ..... G 855 650-4204
  Wilmington (G-20583)
Veraset LLC ..... F 801 657-2009
  Wilmington (G-20584)
Vertrius Corp ..... G 800 770-1913
  Lewes (G-6600)
Viinex Inc ..... G 510 443-5114
  Lewes (G-6605)
Voicemix Inc ..... G 305 981-0518
  Middletown (G-7693)
Volvant Inc ..... G 805 456-6464
  Wilmington (G-20650)
Vortex Labs LLC ..... G 302 231-1294
  Wilmington (G-20651)
Wave LLC ..... G 212 849-2217
  Wilmington (G-20688)
Waveone Inc ..... G 650 796-8637
  Wilmington (G-20690)
We Cobble LLC ..... G 302 504-4294
  Wilmington (G-20699)
Wearexalt LLC ..... F 203 913-5286
  Middletown (G-7711)
Webstudy Inc ..... G 888 326-4058
  Harbeson (G-4718)
Webtime Corporation ..... G 302 476-2350
  Wilmington (G-20706)

Weltron Technology Ltd Co ..... G 508 353-6752
  Lewes (G-6623)
Wgames Incorporated ..... G 206 618-3699
  Wilmington (G-20751)
Wink Tech Limited ..... G 302 268-9232
  Wilmington (G-20859)
Wixfi Inc ..... G 415 504-2607
  Lewes (G-6636)
Wodaqota Inc ..... G 800 246-2677
  Wilmington (G-20873)
X5 Networks Corporation ..... G 800 784-5228
  Wilmington (G-20912)
Xi Global LLC ..... F 332 456-6969
  Middletown (G-7739)
Yes Hardsoft Solutions Inc ..... D 609 632-0397
  Wilmington (G-20927)
Z Data Inc ..... G 800 676-5614
  Newark (G-12427)
Zenbanx Holding Ltd ..... G 310 749-3101
  Claymont (G-1345)
Zencity Technologies US Inc ..... G 347 632-1225
  Wilmington (G-20952)
Zowie Inc ..... D 725 201-0590
  Dover (G-3907)

COMPUTER SOFTWARE DEVELOPMENT & APPLICATIONS

2yum Inc ..... G 626 420-4851
  Dover (G-1684)
A Shared Space LLC ..... G 240 727-9917
  Wilmington (G-14172)
Aeronex LLC ..... G 206 809-0009
  Dover (G-1729)
Aglide Inc ..... G 302 213-0357
  Dover (G-1746)
Ai Athena LLC ..... G 212 247-6400
  Wilmington (G-14325)
AI Whoo LLC ..... G 302 494-6952
  Newark (G-9798)
Air Temp Solutions LLC ..... F 302 276-0532
  New Castle (G-8775)
Albion Investments LLC ..... G 876 575-7371
  Lewes (G-5670)
Alivio Health Corp ..... G 754 230-0234
  Newark (G-9811)
Alternate Cmmodities Index Inc ..... G 302 238-1077
  Newark (G-9837)
Amazed Apps LLC ..... G 916 934-9210
  Dover (G-1781)
Amazingdoc Inc ..... G 847 909-0409
  Wilmington (G-14415)
Annalise-Ai Inc ..... G 440 281-5115
  Dover (G-1797)
Aola Inc ..... G 610 245-8231
  Wilmington (G-14499)
Apphive Inc ..... G 240 898-4661
  Newark (G-9888)
Appic Stars LLC ..... G 903 224-6469
  Dover (G-1805)
Apploye Inc ..... G 925 452-6102
  Newark (G-9893)
Appricot Inc ..... G 484 291-8922
  Dover (G-1808)
Apptrium Inc ..... D 800 888-0706
  Wilmington (G-14514)
Apriorit LLC ..... C 202 780-9339
  Wilmington (G-14515)
Arbitexch LLC ..... G 302 490-0111
  Wilmington (G-14523)
ARC Studio Labs Inc ..... G 323 990-8787
  Wilmington (G-14535)

PRODUCTS & SERVICES SECTION

COMPUTER SOFTWARE DEVELOPMENT & APPLICATIONS

Arcade Services Inc .... F 630 777-8092
New Castle *(G-8818)*

Arcasoft LLC .... G 402 575-1234
Wilmington *(G-14540)*

Arua Inc .... G 302 396-9868
Dover *(G-1826)*

Ashweb Inc .... G 844 493-6249
Dover *(G-1832)*

Asphalt Kingdom LLC .... G 866 399-5562
Wilmington *(G-14589)*

Autoawards Inc .... F 302 696-6000
Odessa *(G-12581)*

Avokadio Inc .... G 302 291-4080
Lewes *(G-5726)*

Axes Global Inc .... F 415 602-4049
Wilmington *(G-14681)*

B+h Insurance LLC .... E 302 995-2247
Newark *(G-9968)*

Bartech Agency Inc .... F 302 317-2399
Bear *(G-57)*

Base86 Inc .... G 619 781-2670
Newark *(G-9987)*

Basedash Inc .... G 302 244-0916
Dover *(G-1878)*

Baxet Group Inc .... G 917 938-7088
Wilmington *(G-14782)*

Be Humane Co .... G 720 419-5362
Dover *(G-1894)*

Beejug Games LLC .... G 310 382-0746
Lewes *(G-5753)*

Betworks Corporation .... F 310 866-0365
Lewes *(G-5760)*

Bid 4 Lease Corp .... G 302 244-9943
Wilmington *(G-14876)*

Big Data Elements LLC .... G 917 620-2337
Dover *(G-1933)*

Big Eld LLC .... G 302 549-0333
Dover *(G-1935)*

Big Moose Exterior LLC .... G 302 722-1969
Middletown *(G-6918)*

Big Plan Inc .... G 910 556-9311
Wilmington *(G-14881)*

Birdie Ssot LLC .... G 857 361-6883
Dover *(G-1941)*

Blb Services LLC .... F 678 989-7908
Wilmington *(G-14953)*

Bleeks LLC .... G 443 990-0496
Wilmington *(G-14954)*

Blinqio Inc .... F 718 710-4529
Wilmington *(G-14958)*

Blips Digital Inc .... F 661 520-1539
Middletown *(G-6924)*

Blix Inc .... E 347 753-8035
Newark *(G-10052)*

Blue Hen Hospitality LLC .... F 302 530-5066
Wilmington *(G-14968)*

Bookitngo Corp .... G ..., 949 899-7684
Dover *(G-1962)*

Bookme Ai Inc .... G 650 436-9210
Wilmington *(G-15002)*

Boomerang Returns Ltd .... G 347 205-1275
Middletown *(G-6930)*

Boonoob Inc .... G 302 288-0670
Dover *(G-1963)*

Bounded Bits LLC .... G 949 291-7358
Newark *(G-10074)*

Brysk Inc .... F 224 508-9542
Wilmington *(G-15138)*

Bueno Technologies Inc .... G 559 785-9800
Newark *(G-10099)*

Busability Corporation .... G 845 821-4609
Wilmington *(G-15155)*

Buzzspark Labs LLC .... G 302 828-0969
Middletown *(G-6948)*

Bydarkmatter LLC .... G 850 801-2732
Dover *(G-2001)*

Canopy Interactive LLC .... G 631 258-1552
Newark *(G-10131)*

Carda Health Inc .... F 415 497-8417
Dover *(G-2028)*

Carewallet Inc .... G 732 477-4149
Wilmington *(G-15245)*

Carmedis Inc .... G 725 712-2559
Wilmington *(G-15254)*

Carpal Enterprise Inc .... F 917 985-8293
Lewes *(G-5804)*

Carzaty Inc .... F 650 396-0144
Dover *(G-2033)*

Casting Arabia LLC .... G 917 832-5287
Middletown *(G-6962)*

Catalyst Foundry LLC .... F 917 471-0947
Wilmington *(G-15273)*

Catovera Corp .... G 804 814-0301
Dover *(G-2040)*

Centrallo Corporation .... G 212 355-0880
Wilmington *(G-15310)*

Centriq Technologies Inc .... G 651 353-0691
Claymont *(G-1079)*

Cheersrx Inc .... G 801 210-1658
Felton *(G-3954)*

Cherry Island Rnwble Enrgy LLC .... G 302 379-0722
Wilmington *(G-15364)*

Chores R Us Inc .... F 844 442-4673
Dover *(G-2069)*

Chotcut Inc .... G 706 437-7890
Wilmington *(G-15392)*

Chpter Holdings Inc .... F 650 223-1786
Wilmington *(G-15393)*

Cinenso Inc .... G 424 245-5799
Dover *(G-2074)*

Cinnamon Technologies Inc .... G 530 413-5533
Dover *(G-2075)*

Cited Inc .... G 302 384-9810
Wilmington *(G-15447)*

Clean Connect Inc .... E 331 330-5662
Wilmington *(G-15470)*

Cleared For Use Inc .... G 206 636-5222
Lewes *(G-5826)*

Client Monster LLC .... G 866 799-5433
Newark *(G-10260)*

Clifton Enterprises LLC .... G 630 220-7435
Middletown *(G-6992)*

Climate Action Systems Inc .... G 802 356-6541
Wilmington *(G-15483)*

Clinpharma Clinical RES LLC .... E 646 961-3437
Wilmington *(G-15487)*

Clutterbot Inc .... G 425 679-1348
Claymont *(G-1096)*

Cnct App Inc .... G 724 288-3212
Lewes *(G-5835)*

Coliving Inc .... G 650 449-4448
Newark *(G-10273)*

Construct App Inc .... G 415 702-0634
Wilmington *(G-15611)*

Contlo Inc .... G 860 775-7179
Newark *(G-10315)*

Core Results Inc .... G 805 552-6624
Wilmington *(G-15640)*

Cotalker Inc .... E 954 643-1497
Wilmington *(G-15650)*

Counterfeit Combat Technology .... G 614 874-7414
Wilmington *(G-15654)*

Coupert Science LLC .... E 206 445-0706
Dover *(G-2147)*

Cradleapps LLC .... G 202 492-7953
Wilmington *(G-15679)*

Creative Xchange Inc .... G 888 502-5618
Wilmington *(G-15695)*

Creator Studios Inc .... G 323 992-4350
Lewes *(G-5868)*

Crrraw Holdings LLC .... G 832 917-9442
Wilmington *(G-15718)*

Cruisingapp LLC .... G 302 645-7400
Lewes *(G-5871)*

Crypto World Journal Inc .... F 302 213-8136
Dover *(G-2165)*

Cto Lab Inc .... G 415 702-5014
Claymont *(G-1105)*

Cyberdefenders Inc .... G 510 999-3490
Middletown *(G-7023)*

D & G Inc .... F 302 378-4877
Townsend *(G-13982)*

D&C Concepts LLC .... F 770 335-2503
Wilmington *(G-15763)*

Daabo Inc .... F 816 559-4169
Wilmington *(G-15765)*

Daily Byte LLC .... G 516 236-9638
Dover *(G-2185)*

Darwell Inc .... G 302 204-0939
Dover *(G-2196)*

Data Unblocked Inc .... G 540 424-0801
Lewes *(G-5882)*

Datascope Solutions Corp .... G 562 373-0209
Wilmington *(G-15799)*

DC Consulting Service LLC .... F 617 594-9780
Wilmington *(G-15824)*

Dealer Automation Services LLC .... F 305 803-3201
Wilmington *(G-15844)*

Deauthorized Inc .... G 512 769-3026
Newark *(G-10402)*

Deckrobot Inc .... F 617 765-7494
Wilmington *(G-15849)*

Defa Inc .... E 302 219-5994
Wilmington *(G-15854)*

Delaware Pride Inc .... G 302 265-3020
Claymont *(G-1114)*

Denim Inc .... G 302 401-6502
Dover *(G-2282)*

Dialog Engineers Inc .... G 302 581-8080
Middletown *(G-7056)*

Digibox LLC .... G 302 203-0088
Dover *(G-2296)*

Digitalpaye Inc .... F 302 232-5116
Dover *(G-2297)*

Dining Software Group Inc .... G 720 236-9572
Camden *(G-820)*

Disclo Inc .... G 607 280-8949
Dover *(G-2301)*

Dish Quo LLC .... G 845 709-1674
Dover *(G-2302)*

Dito Ventures Inc .... G 305 424-9877
Wilmington *(G-16090)*

Dopple Labs Inc .... G 754 216-8175
Wilmington *(G-16144)*

Dorleeon LLC .... G 302 415-3106
Wilmington *(G-16147)*

Dream Conception LLC .... G 302 319-9822
Wilmington *(G-16175)*

Dream Forge LLC .... G 802 342-4647
Dover *(G-2380)*

Dreamtouch Games LLC .... G 408 550-6042
Dover *(G-2385)*

Dygital Technology LLC .... G 302 283-9160
Newark *(G-10582)*

Dyte Inc .... G 669 577-4571
Lewes *(G-5940)*

Employee Codes: A=Over 500 employees, B=251-500
C=101-250, D=51-100, E=20-50, F=10-19, G=1-9

2024 Harris Directory of
Delaware Businesses

COMPUTER SOFTWARE DEVELOPMENT & APPLICATIONS — PRODUCTS & SERVICES SECTION

E2e LLC .... G 703 906-5353
  Hockessin *(G-5195)*
Eagan US Holdco LLC .... A 414 339-8275
  Wilmington *(G-16245)*
Easy Send Inc .... F 610 389-0622
  Wilmington *(G-16271)*
Efectibo LLC .... G 305 498-8630
  Wilmington *(G-16308)*
Egm LLC .... G 302 932-1700
  New Castle *(G-9083)*
Elevate Cdb Inc .... E 844 903-4443
  Dover *(G-2433)*
Elomia Health Inc .... G 302 244-7193
  Dover *(G-2437)*
Enou Labs LLC .... F 321 343-4362
  Wilmington *(G-16426)*
Ente Technologies Inc .... G 917 924-8450
  Dover *(G-2450)*
Entertech Inc .... G 415 840-0204
  Wilmington *(G-16441)*
Enyumba Inc .... G 818 272-9383
  Dover *(G-2452)*
Eonscope Inc .... G 312 319-4484
  Newark *(G-10658)*
Epd Tech LLC .... G 415 508-7580
  Lewes *(G-5967)*
Episode Interactive LLC .... G 858 220-0946
  Dover *(G-2457)*
Eptikar It Solutions Inc .... F 720 422-8441
  Middletown *(G-7106)*
Essen Technologies Inc .... G 617 959-9595
  Middletown *(G-7110)*
Ev Usa Inc .... G 973 674-1326
  Lewes *(G-5976)*
Everytale Inc .... E 650 989-9807
  Claymont *(G-1139)*
Expansion Platforms Inc .... E 866 928-3098
  Newark *(G-10690)*
Extravaganza International Inc .... G 302 321-7117
  New Castle *(G-9111)*
Fabby Inc .... F 408 891-7991
  Wilmington *(G-16522)*
Factory Universe Co .... F 302 216-2025
  Wilmington *(G-16527)*
Famoid Technology LLC .... G 530 601-7284
  Newark *(G-10710)*
Fan Payment Solutions LLC .... F 617 901-3970
  Wilmington *(G-16549)*
Fanhouse Inc .... F 415 598-7628
  Claymont *(G-1147)*
Fantasy Nft LLC .... G 423 313-3436
  Camden *(G-834)*
Fantasythrone LLC .... G 512 431-8658
  Wilmington *(G-16550)*
Faramove Inc .... F 815 674-3114
  Middletown *(G-7121)*
Fast Fce Inc .... G 833 327-8323
  Wilmington *(G-16557)*
Featly Inc .... G 505 305-6844
  Wilmington *(G-16565)*
Fedi Inc .... G 797 372-0606
  Wilmington *(G-16574)*
Femispace Co .... F 917 764-9943
  Wilmington *(G-16578)*
File Right LLC .... G 302 757-7107
  Middletown *(G-7126)*
Filmustage Inc .... F 260 225-3050
  Wilmington *(G-16605)*
Finders Entertainment LLC .... G 407 765-1826
  Dover *(G-2496)*
Fixcom Inc .... G 916 534-8872
  Wilmington *(G-16657)*

Flackon Inc .... G 701 369-0789
  Newark *(G-10749)*
Flagpole Corp .... G 302 261-5170
  Lewes *(G-6003)*
Flip App LLC .... G 248 662-6875
  Dover *(G-2516)*
Flipride Inc .... G 208 471-0007
  Dover *(G-2517)*
Flo Health Inc .... E 302 498-8369
  Wilmington *(G-16662)*
Flowpay Corporation .... G 720 425-3244
  Wilmington *(G-16670)*
FLUENTAAI INC .... G 323 739-5417
  Wilmington *(G-16673)*
Fnx Technologies Ltd .... G 844 969-0070
  Wilmington *(G-16678)*
Folderly Inc .... F 302 966-9083
  Dover *(G-2522)*
Fondeadora Inc .... G 925 413-3654
  Dover *(G-2524)*
Fotomaster LLC .... G 646 233-3371
  Wilmington *(G-16700)*
Freckle Holdings LLC .... G 302 260-6385
  Dover *(G-2534)*
Friday Games Inc .... E 847 246-2189
  Newark *(G-10785)*
Gamefort LLC .... E 302 645-7400
  Lewes *(G-6026)*
Gamers4gamers LLC .... G 302 722-6289
  Newark *(G-10804)*
Gastro Girl Inc .... G 202 579-1057
  Dover *(G-2563)*
Gatesair Inc .... E 513 459-3400
  Wilmington *(G-16814)*
Gather Social Tech Corp .... G 604 356-0981
  Newark *(G-10815)*
Geeksoft Inc .... G 669 278-8022
  Dover *(G-2568)*
Generation Glory Ministries .... G 302 438-4335
  Wilmington *(G-16833)*
Geospot Community LLC .... G 570 504-4115
  Newark *(G-10825)*
Getresponse Inc .... E 302 573-3895
  Wilmington *(G-16854)*
Giftpass App Inc .... G 310 529-7566
  Dover *(G-2583)*
Gigkloud Inc .... F 301 375-5008
  Lewes *(G-6035)*
Gitduck Inc .... G 415 969-3825
  Claymont *(G-1162)*
Globaling Inc .... G 619 657-0070
  Dover *(G-2594)*
Golance Inc .... E 888 478-0358
  Dover *(G-2599)*
Goodsize Inc .... G 415 481-7330
  Wilmington *(G-16925)*
Gotit Inc .... G 408 382-1300
  Dover *(G-2608)*
Gourmetcarte Inc .... G 631 418-6170
  Middletown *(G-7171)*
Govsimplified LLC .... G 888 629-8008
  Claymont *(G-1169)*
Green Candy Solutions Inc .... E 302 599-7944
  Claymont *(G-1170)*
Greggii Inc .... F 647 606-3348
  Newark *(G-10896)*
Greynote LLC .... G 646 287-0705
  Dover *(G-2628)*
Grlla Gmng LLC .... G 302 291-2075
  Lewes *(G-6065)*
Groovvx Inc .... G 828 399-1549
  Wilmington *(G-16986)*

Haltia Inc .... E 302 244-7425
  Wilmington *(G-17042)*
Hank Technologies Inc .... G 812 223-5984
  Dover *(G-2650)*
Hasten Inc .... G 818 867-8151
  Dover *(G-2661)*
Heal Room Inc .... G 770 597-3366
  Claymont *(G-1175)*
Healthylongevitycafe Inc .... G 408 599-6369
  Wilmington *(G-17101)*
Hidden Lake Games LLC .... G 302 305-1070
  Claymont *(G-1179)*
Hirewise Inc .... G 888 899-4980
  Middletown *(G-7211)*
Hockey Labs Inc .... G 929 909-6607
  Dover *(G-2684)*
Howard Industries LLC .... G 217 836-4476
  Camden *(G-853)*
Hubioid Inc .... F 312 912-1515
  Wilmington *(G-17229)*
Ibidd Holdings LLC .... G 800 960-9221
  Dover *(G-2716)*
Ideatree Inc .... F 310 844-7447
  Wilmington *(G-17264)*
iDreams Hub Inc .... G 740 990-2232
  Wilmington *(G-17266)*
Il USA Corporation .... E 310 570-2928
  Wilmington *(G-17270)*
Ikkar Inc .... F 814 351-9394
  Newark *(G-11001)*
Imagic LLC .... G 628 600-5244
  Lewes *(G-6117)*
Impactful Technology LLC .... G 646 374-9004
  Wilmington *(G-17289)*
Incapp Inc .... G 318 880-7622
  Wilmington *(G-17299)*
Innoventic Inc .... G 302 476-2396
  Wilmington *(G-17349)*
Inova Business Solutions LLC .... G 251 316-0180
  Claymont *(G-1185)*
Insightzen LLC .... G 647 227-9325
  Lewes *(G-6128)*
Inspire African Safaris LLC .... F 302 250-5763
  Wilmington *(G-17356)*
Instasafe Inc .... G 408 400-3673
  Dover *(G-2741)*
Insurance Toolkits LLC .... G 302 272-5488
  Wilmington *(G-17364)*
Intermedia Analytics LLC .... F 305 921-9647
  Dover *(G-2745)*
Intouch Inc .... G 332 223-0720
  Dover *(G-2749)*
Io Projects Inc .... G 302 416-5776
  Wilmington *(G-17411)*
Jia Finance Inc .... G 202 341-1031
  Wilmington *(G-17545)*
Jkings Mining Company LLC .... F 628 600-9522
  Lewes *(G-6140)*
Joincube Inc .... F 214 532-9997
  Dover *(G-2800)*
Joozoor Iptv LLC .... F 302 635-4092
  Newark *(G-11125)*
Junction Expert Insights Corp .... G 202 710-9258
  Dover *(G-2819)*
Juni Holdings Inc .... F 415 949-4860
  Wilmington *(G-17614)*
Kaebox LLC .... G 919 777-3939
  Middletown *(G-7259)*
Kagoal Technology LLC .... G 617 818-0588
  Middletown *(G-7260)*
Kaleido Health Solutions Inc .... G 843 303-9168
  Wilmington *(G-17637)*

PRODUCTS & SERVICES SECTION — COMPUTER SOFTWARE DEVELOPMENT & APPLICATIONS

Kanu Inc .... G 401 533-6112
  Wilmington (G-17648)
Keble Inc .... G 810 893-3352
  Wilmington (G-17672)
Keylent Inc .... D 401 864-6498
  Wilmington (G-17703)
Kgs Digital Inc .... G 302 213-3979
  Dover (G-2863)
Kidberry Inc .... G 857 559-3043
  Wilmington (G-17713)
Knowcrunch Inc .... G 210 300-7214
  Newark (G-11198)
Knowt Inc .... F 848 391-0575
  Lewes (G-6170)
Kushim Inc .... G 609 919-9889
  Wilmington (G-17768)
Labware Global Services Inc .... F 302 658-8444
  Wilmington (G-17786)
Landell Labs LLC .... G 917 722-5166
  Middletown (G-7288)
Le Artist Lucratif N Amer LLC .... G 438 223-3788
  Lewes (G-6183)
Leanscout Inc .... G 628 236-9599
  Newark (G-11237)
Learn Game LLC .... F 484 841-9709
  Middletown (G-7292)
Legacy Labs Inc .... G 302 550-9966
  Wilmington (G-17858)
Legit Marketplace Intl LLC .... G 929 273-0505
  Wilmington (G-17868)
Liblab Inc .... G 302 415-3344
  Wilmington (G-17897)
Likehoop Inc .... G 646 643-7738
  Dover (G-2947)
Linkers Inc .... F 408 757-0021
  Dover (G-2952)
Linkmeup Inc .... F 302 440-3393
  Wilmington (G-17930)
Lookback App Co .... G 508 735-1903
  Wilmington (G-17990)
Loom Network Inc .... F 404 939-1294
  Wilmington (G-17992)
Macappstudio Inc .... G 415 799-7415
  Newark (G-11309)
Magic Bytes LLC .... F 813 995-7343
  Lewes (G-6236)
Makave International Trdg LLC .... E 302 288-0670
  Dover (G-3001)
Marketforce Technologies Inc .... A 339 674-0529
  Dover (G-3020)
Master Kit Inc .... G 650 743-5126
  Dover (G-3027)
Matchapro Inc .... G 213 573-9882
  Hockessin (G-5302)
Matium Inc .... G 703 457-9997
  Dover (G-3031)
Medici Ventures Inc .... E 801 319-7029
  Wilmington (G-18251)
Medzoomer Inc .... G 239 595-8899
  Middletown (G-7337)
MEI App Inc .... G 617 877-6603
  Newark (G-11382)
Mello Financial Inc .... G 801 877-7787
  Wilmington (G-18264)
Menehariya LLC .... F 240 432-0082
  Dover (G-3060)
Mercurysend LLC .... G 917 267-8627
  Wilmington (G-18278)
Metaquotes Software Corp .... E 657 859-6918
  Wilmington (G-18289)
Mican Technologies Inc .... C 302 703-0708
  Bear (G-372)

Microcom Tech LLC .... G 858 775-5559
  Rehoboth Beach (G-12853)
Micropets LLC .... E 925 341-2398
  Dover (G-3083)
Middleware Inc .... E 415 213-2625
  Dover (G-18343)
Mightyinvoice LLC .... G 302 415-3000
  Dover (G-3089)
Misaka Network Inc .... G 323 999-1409
  Dover (G-3100)
Mithril Cable Network Inc .... F 213 373-4381
  Claymont (G-1240)
Mjlinkcom Inc .... G 303 324-7668
  Lewes (G-6281)
Mnboost Corp .... G 302 645-7400
  Lewes (G-6282)
Mobeasy LLC .... G 628 251-1274
  Lewes (G-6283)
Mocha Technologies Inc .... F 408 556-9930
  Claymont (G-1243)
Monarch Nascent Inc .... F 310 601-4702
  Wilmington (G-18409)
Monetran LLC .... G 732 984-1983
  Hockessin (G-5310)
Monster Gaming LLC .... G 251 281-8906
  Lewes (G-6288)
Moon Devices Inc .... G 650 206-8011
  Wilmington (G-18430)
Moonsworth LLC .... G 302 439-6039
  Wilmington (G-18432)
Morrow Limited .... D 213 631-3534
  Montchanin (G-8739)
Motameet LLC .... G 302 242-4483
  Lewes (G-6293)
Moxelle Inc .... G 646 226-9430
  Middletown (G-7386)
Msd Business Solutions LLC .... G 609 375-8461
  Lewes (G-6295)
Must App Corp .... F 905 537-5522
  Wilmington (G-18494)
My Health Group Inc .... E 401 400-0015
  Dover (G-3137)
My Kase LLC .... E 647 686-7202
  Lewes (G-6299)
Narleyapps Inc .... G 323 744-1398
  Dover (G-3150)
National Home Rentals LP .... G 302 636-5401
  Wilmington (G-18541)
Native Grid LLC .... G 917 893-7544
  Dover (G-3159)
Navenu Inc .... G 416 543-9617
  Dover (G-3162)
Nayachi Inc .... G 302 400-0072
  Wilmington (G-18566)
Neodata LLC .... E 302 666-2848
  Dover (G-3169)
Neofithub Inc .... F 408 365-4156
  Wilmington (G-18583)
Net Journey LLC .... G 818 584-2519
  Dover (G-3173)
Neural Heaven Inc .... F 631 485-4205
  Middletown (G-7396)
Neuralight Inc .... F 203 615-1333
  Wilmington (G-18602)
Neuroscience Software Inc .... G 855 712-1818
  Dover (G-3176)
Neutec Corp .... G 302 697-6752
  Dover (G-3177)
New Concept Technologies LLC .... G 518 533-5367
  Wilmington (G-18614)
New Live Ventures Inc .... G 914 960-1877
  Lewes (G-6311)

Ninjasalary Inc .... G 888 201-1107
  Claymont (G-1253)
Nitrility Inc .... F 848 702-6091
  Wilmington (G-18651)
Nixope Inc .... G 888 991-1606
  Wilmington (G-18653)
No Code Software Inc .... F 833 366-2633
  Lewes (G-6317)
Node Technologies Inc .... G 866 366-1862
  Middletown (G-7408)
Nomod LLC .... G 917 480-7432
  Wilmington (G-18666)
Nueve Ceros LLC .... G 415 513-0332
  Wilmington (G-18713)
Nuyka Inc .... E 707 400-5444
  Lewes (G-6323)
Nvcomputers Inc .... G 860 878-0525
  Wilmington (G-18722)
Oaks Lab Academy LLC .... G 509 481-5630
  Wilmington (G-18728)
Objects Worldwide Inc .... G 703 623-7861
  Wilmington (G-18737)
Ociety LLC .... G 760 408-1992
  Lewes (G-6331)
Ollang Inc .... G 212 706-1883
  Wilmington (G-18760)
Omnix Labs Inc .... G 917 640-4949
  Wilmington (G-18771)
Onebill Inc .... G 619 292-8493
  Dover (G-3229)
Onebox Technologies Inc .... G 415 799-8830
  Wilmington (G-18787)
Organic Intelligence LLC .... G 949 423-3665
  Wilmington (G-18818)
Otc Trade LLC .... G 603 820-5820
  Camden (G-883)
Otherworld Co .... G 424 335-5671
  Newark (G-11605)
Out of Galaxy Inc .... G 814 441-8058
  Wilmington (G-18837)
Outmarch Inc .... G 508 289-1233
  Dover (G-3250)
Overscout Inc .... G 415 687-3005
  Lewes (G-6342)
Paper Street LLC .... G 614 515-1259
  Newark (G-11622)
Parchive Analytics Inc .... G 903 683-5878
  Middletown (G-7426)
Partytickets Inc .... G 718 395-9590
  Wilmington (G-18901)
Payshiga Technologies Inc .... E 214 447-0677
  Dover (G-3286)
Pebble Stack LLC .... G 732 910-9701
  Middletown (G-7437)
Perks Express Inc .... G 855 924-7424
  Wilmington (G-18981)
Perkwiz Inc .... G 702 866-9122
  Hockessin (G-5341)
Personas Inc .... G 416 815-7000
  Wilmington (G-18990)
Petcy Inc .... G 920 240-4312
  Middletown (G-7443)
Play US Media LLC .... G 302 924-5034
  Dover (G-3332)
Playphone Inc .... G 415 307-0246
  Dover (G-3334)
Plugilo Inc .... F 628 202-4444
  Newark (G-11701)
Ply Fashion Inc .... G 323 723-5337
  Wilmington (G-19084)
Polar Signals Inc .... G 765 679-9318
  Claymont (G-1265)

Employee Codes: A=Over 500 employees, B=251-500
C=101-250, D=51-100, E=20-50, F=10-19, G=1-9

COMPUTER SOFTWARE DEVELOPMENT & APPLICATIONS — PRODUCTS & SERVICES SECTION

Company	Code	Phone
Polaro Inc, Dover (G-3346)	F	415 240-0442
Praktikaai Co, Wilmington (G-19144)	F	959 300-0719
Precisioncure LLC, Wilmington (G-19160)	G	302 622-9119
Premo Technologies Inc, Wilmington (G-19174)	G	951 514-6993
Prestige Labs Inc, Dover (G-3370)	G	917 698-3453
Prime Security Corp, Middletown (G-7469)	G	803 281-0378
Productive Co Inc, Claymont (G-1268)	G	415 304-6782
Protocol Labs Inc, Wilmington (G-19235)	C	302 703-7194
Proven Pass Inc, Middletown (G-7477)	F	888 404-2775
Public Mint Inc, Dover (G-3393)	F	833 386-0182
Purple Thinkers Inc, Newark (G-11775)	G	760 349-7603
Purple Wifi Inc, Dover (G-3398)	G	877 286-2631
Qsr Group LLC, Wilmington (G-19278)	G	302 268-6909
Queskr Inc, Lewes (G-6401)	G	302 527-6007
Raad360 LLC, Newark (G-11812)	F	855 722-3360
Ragaman Services Inc, Wilmington (G-19316)	F	339 221-6757
Railbus Inc, Lewes (G-6406)	G	302 725-3185
Rayda Inc, Wilmington (G-19343)	G	302 261-5184
Rct Studio Inc, Wilmington (G-19354)	G	669 255-1562
Reackt LLC, Newark (G-11833)	G	267 210-4743
Readmark Inc, Dover (G-3432)	G	650 450-9110
Real Messenger Inc, Wilmington (G-19368)	F	657 237-5918
Rebatus Inc, Lewes (G-6412)	G	929 393-5529
Red Spark LP, Claymont (G-1275)	E	215 695-5002
Redgate Tech Inc, Wilmington (G-19388)	G	302 377-6563
Refermate LLC, Wilmington (G-19395)	G	951 892-8159
Rentdrop Inc, Claymont (G-1277)	G	302 250-2525
Reporting Solutions LLC, Newark (G-11859)	G	857 284-3583
Resistbot Inc, Newark (G-11865)	G	408 599-2094
Resulticks Solution Inc, Wilmington (G-19444)	E	347 416-7673
Retouch Salon LLC, Lewes (G-6420)	G	929 247-7095
Revoltion Freedom Platform LLC, Lewes (G-6421)	F	301 653-9207
Riftwalker Game Studio Inc, Dover (G-3470)	G	213 215-7165
Riversedge Advisors LLC, Wilmington (G-19499)	F	302 573-6864
Rockoly Inc, Dover (G-3478)	F	508 527-1939
Romantic Ai Inc, Claymont (G-1283)	F	415 404-9188
Rooah LLC, Dover (G-3484)	G	305 233-7557
Rotobot Ai LLC, Middletown (G-7524)	G	978 305-5794
Roz Health LLC, Newark (G-11923)	G	415 259-8992
Rumz Inc, Wilmington (G-19591)	G	571 733-0693
Safeagain Inc, Dover (G-3503)	G	929 276-2732
Safeup US LLC, Lewes (G-6441)	G	480 526-5152
Sales Documents Inc, Wilmington (G-19637)	F	302 867-9957
Satodesign LLC, Wilmington (G-19677)	G	989 710-2029
Saverd LLC, Wilmington (G-19683)	G	347 565-5586
Scanta Inc, Lewes (G-6450)	E	302 645-7400
Securelayer7 LLC, Middletown (G-7548)	F	302 391-0803
Seecubic Inc, Wilmington (G-19736)	E	267 400-1565
Sendchamp Inc, Wilmington (G-19750)	G	510 423-3457
Sensiai Inc, Middletown (G-7552)	G	646 665-7668
Sensofusion Inc, Milton (G-8710)	F	570 239-4912
Shipthis Inc, Newark (G-11997)	F	209 395-1293
Shouldr Inc, Lewes (G-6467)	G	917 331-1384
Signatureone Media LLC, Dover (G-3557)	G	347 849-3740
Simbull Sports Exchange Inc, Lewes (G-6472)	G	319 899-6223
Simplelife Apps Inc, Dover (G-3562)	G	954 591-8413
Simplylab Inc, Dover (G-3565)	F	919 663-2800
Sketches and Pixels LLC, Newark (G-12020)	G	312 834-4402
Skittle Inc, Wilmington (G-19855)	F	855 575-4885
Sleepy Coach Inc, Wilmington (G-19863)	G	310 372-5770
Smjs Co, Claymont (G-1292)	G	415 326-4441
Social Money Inc, Lewes (G-6486)	G	212 810-7540
Solo Global Inc, Wilmington (G-19924)	G	302 307-1673
Solon Labs Corp, Newark (G-12053)	G	860 876-7766
Sortd Inc, Newark (G-12056)	G	415 870-1075
Space Soft Inc, Claymont (G-1297)	G	413 337-7223
Spare Cs Inc, Lewes (G-6496)	F	424 744-0155
Speedrid Ltd, Dover (G-3595)	D	213 550-5462
Springboard Inc, Newark (G-12075)	G	302 607-2580
Stable App LLC, Wilmington (G-20003)	G	310 767-7832
Starkit Studio LLC, Lewes (G-6506)	G	302 467-2017
Stones Soup Inc, Newark (G-12102)	G	803 835-7123
Stormx Inc, Dover (G-3613)	F	425 998-8762
Streameq Inc, Lewes (G-6517)	G	951 807-4938
Subscript Inc, Claymont (G-1307)	G	302 470-8144
Superpower Entertainment LLC, Wilmington (G-20147)	G	650 667-0266
Surge Networks Inc, Newark (G-12132)	G	206 432-5047
Swipes Incorporated, Lewes (G-6534)	G	650 686-0223
Syft Analytics Inc, Newark (G-12145)	F	862 308-0525
Synnefa Inc, Wilmington (G-20190)	G	302 565-4405
Synup Inc, Wilmington (G-20193)	E	844 228-2852
Systima Inc, Wilmington (G-20195)	F	929 551-4849
Tabletopia Corp, Dover (G-3642)	F	305 548-8407
Taiga Express LLC, Wilmington (G-20208)	G	718 577-2028
Talentmatch Inc, Newark (G-12156)	G	508 825-6171
Tamp Inc, Newark (G-12158)	F	302 283-9195
Tangome Inc, Dover (G-3649)	F	650 362-8086
Teachedison Inc, Middletown (G-7624)	G	973 902-8026
Tech Learn LLC, Wilmington (G-20250)	G	305 600-0775
Tectanic LLC, Lewes (G-6547)	G	302 440-2788
Tej Studio LLC, Wilmington (G-20263)	G	302 205-3224
Tilebox Inc, Dover (G-3687)	G	206 741-0883
Tis Group Inc, Lewes (G-6562)	F	929 322-8811
Toptracker LLC, Wilmington (G-20363)	B	415 230-0131
Total Resistance LLC, Wilmington (G-20372)	G	302 384-3077
Translucence Research Inc, Middletown (G-7659)	E	425 753-8886
Travelapp Inc, Wilmington (G-20404)	G	617 580-7978
Tretek LLC, Wilmington (G-20409)	G	888 407-9737
Trio Academy LLC, Wilmington (G-20428)	G	646 330-9211
Triprobotics Inc, Claymont (G-1318)	F	646 798-7137
Triumph Labs Inc, Claymont (G-1319)	G	561 886-7121
Truck Lagbe Inc, Lewes (G-6581)	E	860 810-8677
Ultimate Tournament Inc, Wilmington (G-20498)	G	410 746-1637
Ultra Fitness Inc, Dover (G-3745)	G	310 890-9025
Ultraworking Inc, Newark (G-12262)	G	848 243-0008
Uploop Technologies LP, Newark (G-12285)	F	514 922-0399
Vanilla Innovations Inc, Newark (G-12305)	G	305 815-7586
Veryutils Inc, Newark (G-12319)	G	858 939-9928

PRODUCTS & SERVICES SECTION

COMPUTERS, NEC

Vianair Inc.. G 646 403-4705
  Wilmington (G-20606)
Viaprogram Technology Inc.................. G 917 292-5433
  Milton (G-8725)
Vira Games Inc.. G 302 468-7152
  Wilmington (G-20629)
Viziochron Inc.. G 206 745-0356
  Wilmington (G-20646)
Vybn Inc... G 415 715-7945
  Wilmington (G-20661)
W23 S12 Holdings LLC........................ G 610 348-3825
  Wilmington (G-20664)
Wagefi Inc.. G 646 853-0165
  Middletown (G-7702)
Wajba Corp.. G 650 307-0070
  Middletown (G-7703)
We Are Friends Inc................................ G 302 501-7521
  Middletown (G-7709)
Webbrowser Media Inc.......................... G 302 830-3664
  Wilmington (G-20705)
Webill Inc... F 628 227-7780
  Middletown (G-7712)
Webwork Time Tracker Inc................... E 415 707-3544
  Wilmington (G-20707)
WEKEEP TRAVEL SERVICES LLC... G 786 814-0722
  Lewes (G-6620)
Weplay Esports Media Inc.................... G 818 274-2959
  Wilmington (G-20732)
Wifiesta Inc.. F 206 923-9206
  Lewes (G-6629)
Witt Butch Inc... G 706 883-0539
  Lewes (G-6635)
Wonderlust LLC...................................... G 662 312-8390
  Lewes (G-6639)
Workwall Inc.. F 415 800-2809
  Newark (G-12407)
Workweek Inc... G 423 708-4565
  Dover (G-3872)
World Web Technology Pvt Ltd............ E 646 755-9276
  Dover (G-3875)
Wormhole Soft LLC................................ G 302 424-4374
  Rehoboth Beach (G-13022)
Wutopia Group US Ltd.......................... F 302 488-0248
  Dover (G-3877)
X Seamless Inc....................................... G 650 770-0771
  Wilmington (G-20910)
Xerafy Inc.. G 817 938-4197
  Wilmington (G-20918)
Yclas Inc.. G 929 377-1239
  Newark (G-12418)
Yevma Inc.. G 888 338-2221
  Dover (G-3886)
Young Music LLC.................................. G 302 307-1997
  Smyrna (G-13941)
Youshop Inc.. G 302 526-0521
  Dover (G-3894)
Zamolxis LLC.. F 571 286-0413
  Wilmington (G-20946)
Zarla Inc... G 833 469-2752
  Claymont (G-1344)
Zelcore Technologies Inc...................... G 408 829-6352
  Dover (G-3897)
Zenkoders LLC....................................... G 302 261-2627
  Claymont (G-1346)
Zeroant Inc.. G 567 342-1530
  Middletown (G-7750)
Zilla Finance Inc..................................... E 213 645-2133
  Wilmington (G-20962)
Zonguru Holdings Inc............................ G 310 266-1427
  Wilmington (G-20963)

COMPUTER SOFTWARE SYSTEMS ANALYSIS & DESIGN: Custom

114 Ai Inc.. G 719 394-0606
  Lewes (G-5635)
Ardeun Biometrics Corp LLC................ F 949 662-1096
  Lewes (G-5697)
Ardexo Inc... G 855 617-7500
  Dover (G-1811)
Aries Security LLC................................. G 302 365-0026
  Wilmington (G-14551)
Basetwo Artfcal Intllgnce USA.............. G 519 400-8770
  Dover (G-1880)
Bits & Bytes Inc...................................... G 302 674-2999
  Dover (G-1942)
Computer Aid Inc................................... G 302 831-5500
  Newark (G-10294)
Corblocks LLC.. G 832 217-0864
  Wilmington (G-15637)
Dbaza Inc.. G 302 467-3081
  Dover (G-2202)
Decisivedge LLC.................................... D 302 299-1570
  Newark (G-10404)
Dyatech LLC.. F 845 666-0786
  Wilmington (G-16226)
Empirical Cre Holdings Corp................ G 816 582-8041
  Wilmington (G-16400)
Encross LLC... F 302 351-2593
  Wilmington (G-16407)
Extreme Scale Solutions LLC.............. F 302 540-7149
  Newark (G-10697)
Fabit Corp... G 832 217-0864
  Wilmington (G-16523)
GBS Backup LLC................................... G 302 907-9099
  Lewes (G-6028)
Gdk Services LLC.................................. E 929 242-8422
  Dover (G-2565)
Herdify LLC... G 619 405-3952
  Middletown (G-7206)
Inaccel LLC... G 408 915-5548
  Wilmington (G-17296)
Inclind Inc... G 302 856-2802
  Lewes (G-6120)
Insight Engineering Solutions.............. G 302 378-4842
  Townsend (G-14018)
Iyper LLC... E 929 269-5699
  Wilmington (G-17441)
Liftoff Agent Inc..................................... G 925 462-5001
  Claymont (G-1218)
One Codex Inc.. G 226 406-8524
  Wilmington (G-18778)
Onnec USA Inc....................................... G 703 309-7338
  Middletown (G-7416)
Opinr Inc.. D 646 207-3000
  Wilmington (G-18804)
Oyster HR Americas Inc....................... C 912 219-2356
  Wilmington (G-18846)
Oyster HR Inc... B 912 219-2356
  Wilmington (G-18847)
Pike Creek Computer Company........... F 302 239-5113
  Wilmington (G-19039)
Polar Strategy Inc.................................. G 703 628-0001
  Lewes (G-6381)
Professionals LLC.................................. G 302 295-2330
  Wilmington (G-19217)
Pumas-Ai Inc... E 551 207-6084
  Dover (G-3395)
Qcortex LLC.. E 213 257-4004
  Dover (G-3403)
Ram Tech Systems Inc......................... E 302 832-6600
  Middletown (G-7500)
Ridge It Solutions Inc........................... G 302 455-8566
  Bear (G-461)
Rockey & Associates Inc...................... G 800 338-7734
  Lewes (G-6429)
Sain Cosmos LLC.................................. F 936 244-7017
  Wilmington (G-19633)
She Bash LLC.. G 302 204-6700
  Claymont (G-1289)
Smartprofyl LLC..................................... G 832 412-5803
  Middletown (G-7578)
Teerhub Inc... G 281 223-3466
  Dover (G-3663)
Triagons LLC.. G 619 761-0797
  Dover (G-3723)
U Good Enterprises LLC....................... F 302 566-8038
  Newark (G-12253)

COMPUTER STORAGE DEVICES, NEC

Milieux LLC... G 302 770-5868
  Wilmington (G-18356)
Quantum Alchemy LLC......................... G 484 299-8016
  New Castle (G-9507)
Quantum Corporation............................ G 302 737-7012
  Newark (G-11794)
Zerowait Corporation............................. F 302 996-9408
  Wilmington (G-20958)

COMPUTER SYSTEM SELLING SVCS

Adapty Inc... G 415 800-3343
  Claymont (G-1020)

COMPUTER SYSTEMS ANALYSIS & DESIGN

Applied Control Engrg Inc.................... D 302 738-8800
  Newark (G-9891)
Boomn Inc.. G 844 808-2666
  Lewes (G-5775)
Cloudxperts LLC..................................... G 302 257-5686
  Dover (G-2097)
Congruence Consulting Group............. G 320 290-6155
  Newark (G-10304)
Conquest Tech Solutions Inc............... G 302 356-1423
  Wilmington (G-15606)
Indelible Blue Inc................................... F 302 231-5200
  Lewes (G-6122)
Luut Technologies Inc........................... G 302 658-7581
  Wilmington (G-18035)
Xcs Corporation..................................... G 302 514-0600
  Wilmington (G-20916)
Xtalos LLC.. G 800 383-0662
  Middletown (G-7741)

COMPUTER TERMINALS

Isaac Fair Corporation.......................... G 302 324-8015
  New Castle (G-9243)

COMPUTER-AIDED SYSTEM SVCS

Alpha Comm LLC................................... F 302 784-0645
  Bear (G-29)
Bluent LLC.. E 832 476-8459
  Lewes (G-5771)
Tcp/Ip Solutions LLC............................ F 302 219-0224
  Dover (G-3657)

COMPUTERS, NEC

Anatrope Inc... G 202 507-9441
  Dover (G-1791)
Axtra3d Inc... E 302 288-0670
  Dover (G-1861)
Broadberry Data Systems LLC............ E 302 295-1086
  Wilmington (G-15121)
Broadberry Data Systems LLC............ G 800 496-9918
  Wilmington (G-15122)

COMPUTERS, NEC

Ecomo Inc.. G 412 567-3867
  Dover (G-2417)
Neurastack Inc... G 512 760-3149
  Middletown (G-7397)
One Tech Sol LLC...................................... G 302 551-6777
  Historic New Castle (G-5043)
Sheriff Electronic LLC................................. G 302 654-8090
  Lewes (G-6463)
Weyl Enterprises Inc.................................. G 302 993-1248
  Wilmington (G-20749)
Yeaher Inc.. E 513 293-4347
  New Castle (G-9694)

COMPUTERS, NEC, WHOLESALE

Info Systems LLC....................................... C 302 633-9800
  Wilmington (G-17328)
Quinn Data Corporation.............................. G 302 429-7450
  Wilmington (G-19295)

COMPUTERS, PERIPHERALS & SOFTWARE, WHOLESALE: Printers

Baytown Systems Inc.................................. G 302 689-3421
  Wilmington (G-14791)
Cutler Industries Inc................................... G 302 689-3779
  Wilmington (G-15746)

COMPUTERS, PERIPHERALS & SOFTWARE, WHOLESALE: Software

Agile Cockpit LLC....................................... G 646 220-3377
  Dover (G-1740)
Aorel Tech Investments LLC....................... G 610 674-1516
  Wilmington (G-14501)
Artificial Brain Tech Inc.............................. G 302 601-7201
  Wilmington (G-14566)
Bitcarter Inc... F 518 512-9238
  Wilmington (G-14898)
Blumatter Inc... G 415 318-6857
  Newark (G-10064)
Chaingpt LLC... G 302 382-7528
  Dover (G-2054)
Diversio Inc... E 855 647-4155
  Claymont (G-1119)
Express Vpn LLC....................................... G 310 601-8492
  Newark (G-10692)
Firebolt Analytics Inc................................. F 302 314-3135
  Wilmington (G-16612)
Future Analytica Software Inc.................... F 437 771-2947
  Dover (G-2548)
Geo-Plus Corporation................................ F 800 672-1733
  Newark (G-10821)
Golden Recursion Inc................................ F 415 779-4053
  Claymont (G-1167)
Home Innovations..................................... G 302 448-9555
  Lewes (G-6097)
Kovan Studio Inc....................................... F 855 964-3748
  Middletown (G-7282)
Licensing Assurance LLC........................... E 305 851-3545
  Lewes (G-6205)
Lisa Insurtech LLC..................................... G 612 470-1009
  Lewes (G-6211)
Meta Humans Ltd...................................... F 904 690-1589
  Lewes (G-6267)
Modena Software Inc................................ G 650 326-1136
  Lewes (G-6286)
Net Merge Ltd.. G 631 816-1145
  Dover (G-3174)
Ossum Inc.. G 516 851-4607
  Wilmington (G-18829)
Pebbles Inc.. F 408 600-8953
  Wilmington (G-18944)

Popeyco LLC.. G 202 368-3842
  Lewes (G-6382)
Quantum Leap Technology Inc.................. G 614 254-1698
  Wilmington (G-19287)
Red Buffer LLC.. G 628 228-6024
  Dover (G-3439)
Taplistic LLC.. F 516 362-1890
  Wilmington (G-20220)
Tech Now Mobile LLC................................ G 484 480-0648
  Wilmington (G-20251)
Threatmate Inc... F 302 219-4714
  Dover (G-3682)
Timezest Inc.. F 702 582-6850
  Wilmington (G-20330)
Trikorp Inc.. G 970 690-6285
  Dover (G-3727)
Uploadcare Inc.. E 855 953-2006
  Wilmington (G-20536)
Vinyo Inc.. G 856 493-2042
  Middletown (G-7688)
We Cobble LLC.. F 302 504-4294
  Wilmington (G-20699)
Weedim Inc.. G 202 773-9244
  Middletown (G-7714)
Weneuro Inc... G 760 607-7277
  Wilmington (G-20731)

COMPUTERS: Mainframe

Sumuri LLC.. E 302 570-0015
  Magnolia (G-6786)

CONCRETE PRDTS

American Precast....................................... G 302 629-6688
  Seaford (G-13063)
Ballistics Technology Intl Ltd...................... G 877 291-1111
  Wilmington (G-14724)
Bio Riot Technologies Mfg Inc.................... G 407 399-3413
  Lewes (G-5766)
F Sartin Tyson Inc...................................... F 302 834-4571
  Saint Georges (G-13033)
Oldcastle Inc.. G 302 836-6492
  Bear (G-406)

CONCRETE: Ready-Mixed

Atlantic Concrete Company Inc.................. D 302 422-8017
  Milford (G-7777)
Chaney Enterprises.................................... F 302 990-5039
  Seaford (G-13111)
Concrete Co Inc... G 302 652-1101
  Wilmington (G-15586)
Gfp Mobile Mix Supply LLC........................ F 302 998-7687
  Wilmington (G-16857)
HMA Concrete LLC.................................... F 302 777-1235
  Wilmington (G-17158)
Legacy Vulcan LLC.................................... G 302 875-0748
  Georgetown (G-4405)
Legacy Vulcan LLC.................................... G 302 875-5733
  Seaford (G-13258)
Material Transit Inc.................................... E 302 395-0556
  New Castle (G-9353)
Southgate Concrete Company.................... F 302 376-5280
  Middletown (G-7591)
Thoro-Goods Concrete Co Inc.................... E 302 934-8102
  Dagsboro (G-1516)

CONDENSERS & CONDENSING UNITS: Air Conditioner

General Refrigeration Company.................. E 302 846-3073
  Delmar (G-1598)

PRODUCTS & SERVICES SECTION

CONDENSERS: Heat Transfer Eqpt, Evaporative

Baltimore Aircoil Company Inc................... C 302 424-2583
  Milford (G-7781)

CONFINEMENT SURVEILLANCE SYS MAINTENANCE & MONITORING SVCS

Instasafe Inc.. G 408 400-3673
  Dover (G-2741)
Ip Camera Warehouse LLC......................... G 302 358-2690
  Wilmington (G-17415)

CONSTRUCTION & MINING MACHINERY WHOLESALERS

Atlantic Tractor LLC................................... F 302 834-0114
  Newark (G-9937)
Foulk Lawn & Equipment Co Inc................ G 302 475-3233
  Wilmington (G-16701)
Graham Global Corporation....................... F 302 839-3000
  Wilmington (G-16945)
Jesco Inc.. C 302 376-6946
  Middletown (G-7247)
Yellow and Green Machinery LLC............... G 302 526-4990
  Dover (G-3885)

CONSTRUCTION EQPT REPAIR SVCS

Heavy Equipment Rental Inc..................... F 302 654-5716
  New Castle (G-9205)
State Line Machine Inc.............................. F 302 478-0285
  Wilmington (G-20035)

CONSTRUCTION EQPT: Tractors

Cnh Cptal Oprting Lase Eqp Rcv................ A 262 636-6011
  Wilmington (G-15504)

CONSTRUCTION MATERIALS, WHOLESALE: Aggregate

East Bay Aggregates LLC.......................... G 302 337-0311
  Bridgeville (G-697)
Edgemoor Materials Inc............................. F 302 655-1510
  Wilmington (G-16290)

CONSTRUCTION MATERIALS, WHOLESALE: Air Ducts, Sheet Metal

Ducts Unlimited Inc.................................. E 302 378-4125
  Smyrna (G-13717)

CONSTRUCTION MATERIALS, WHOLESALE: Awnings

Coastal Sun Roms Prch Enclsres............... G 302 537-3679
  Frankford (G-4092)
Prestige Powder Inc................................. G 302 737-7086
  Newark (G-11735)

CONSTRUCTION MATERIALS, WHOLESALE: Brick, Exc Refractory

Delaware Brick Company........................... E 302 994-0948
  Wilmington (G-15876)

CONSTRUCTION MATERIALS, WHOLESALE: Building Stone

Christiana Materials Inc............................ F 302 633-5600
  Wilmington (G-15411)

CONSTRUCTION MATERIALS, WHOLESALE: Building Stone, Marble

CONSTRUCTION: Commercial & Office Building, New

Gerardos Marble & Granite LLC............ G 302 344-6150
  New Castle (G-9166)
Landis Ltd............................ G 302 656-9024
  Wilmington (G-17797)

CONSTRUCTION MATERIALS, WHOLESALE: Building, Exterior

Bair & Goff Sales LLC.................. E 302 292-2546
  Newark (G-9975)
Delaware Building Supply Corp.......... E 302 424-3505
  Milford (G-7854)
Lowes Home Centers LLC................ C 302 697-0700
  Camden (G-870)
Lowes Home Centers LLC................ C 302 735-7500
  Dover (G-2979)
Lowes Home Centers LLC................ C 302 645-0900
  Lewes (G-6226)
Lowes Home Centers LLC................ D 302 376-3006
  Middletown (G-7315)
Lowes Home Centers LLC................ D 302 934-3740
  Millsboro (G-8354)
Lowes Home Centers LLC................ D 302 252-3228
  New Castle (G-9328)
Lowes Home Centers LLC................ C 302 781-1154
  Newark (G-11291)
Lowes Home Centers LLC................ D 302 536-4000
  Seaford (G-13265)
Lowes Home Centers LLC................ C 302 479-7799
  Wilmington (G-18013)
Manchester Trading Co................. F 302 500-4010
  Newark (G-11321)
Marjam Supply Co Inc.................. F 302 283-1020
  Newark (G-11332)

CONSTRUCTION MATERIALS, WHOLESALE: Building, Interior

American Cedar & Millwork Inc.......... E 302 645-9580
  Lewes (G-5683)
Ceramic Tile Supply Co................ D 302 992-9200
  Wilmington (G-15313)
Delaware Flooring Supply Inc........... G 302 276-0031
  Historic New Castle (G-4969)
P D Supply Inc........................ G 302 655-3358
  Wilmington (G-18852)

CONSTRUCTION MATERIALS, WHOLESALE: Cement

Jet Products LLC...................... G 877 453-8868
  Wilmington (G-17536)

CONSTRUCTION MATERIALS, WHOLESALE: Doors, Garage

Hickman Overhead Door Company......... F 302 422-4249
  Milford (G-7930)

CONSTRUCTION MATERIALS, WHOLESALE: Gravel

Porter Sand & Gravel Inc.............. G 302 335-5132
  Harrington (G-4813)

CONSTRUCTION MATERIALS, WHOLESALE: Limestone

Berkshire At Limestone................ G 302 635-7495
  Wilmington (G-14843)
Limestone Acres Maintenance........... G 302 222-8457
  Wilmington (G-17914)

CONSTRUCTION MATERIALS, WHOLESALE: Metal Buildings

Building Concepts America Inc......... E 302 292-0200
  Newark (G-10101)

CONSTRUCTION MATERIALS, WHOLESALE: Millwork

Bayside Millwork Inc.................. G 443 324-4376
  Selbyville (G-13470)

CONSTRUCTION MATERIALS, WHOLESALE: Pallets, Wood

Dack Trading LLC...................... G 917 576-4432
  Rehoboth Beach (G-12710)
Greenwood Pallet Co................... G 302 337-8181
  Bridgeville (G-705)
North American Hardwoods Ltd.......... G 516 848-7729
  Wilmington (G-18677)
Rcd Timber Products Inc............... G 302 778-5700
  New Castle (G-9512)
Rehrig Penn Logistics Inc............. D 302 659-3337
  Smyrna (G-13865)

CONSTRUCTION MATERIALS, WHOLESALE: Paving Materials

Asphalt Paving Eqp & Sups............. G 302 683-0105
  Harbeson (G-4684)

CONSTRUCTION MATERIALS, WHOLESALE: Plywood

Russell Plywood Inc................... F 302 689-0137
  Wilmington (G-19595)

CONSTRUCTION MATERIALS, WHOLESALE: Prefabricated Structures

Door & Gate Co LLC.................... F 888 505-6962
  Claymont (G-1120)
EZ Sips Corporation................... G 888 747-7488
  Wilmington (G-16515)

CONSTRUCTION MATERIALS, WHOLESALE: Roofing & Siding Material

Goldis Holdings Inc................... D 302 764-3100
  Wilmington (G-16914)
Iko Sales Inc......................... E 302 764-3100
  Wilmington (G-17276)
Mill Creek Metals Inc................. F 302 529-7020
  Claymont (G-1236)
S G Williams of Dover Inc............. F 302 678-1080
  Dover (G-3499)

CONSTRUCTION MATERIALS, WHOLESALE: Windows

Kris Window Tint LLC.................. G 302 384-6185
  Wilmington (G-17756)
M/S Hollow Metal Wholesale LLC........ G 302 349-9471
  Greenwood (G-4650)
Window Man............................ G 302 381-4888
  Delmar (G-1659)

CONSTRUCTION: Apartment Building

John Campanelli & Sons Inc............ G 302 239-8573
  Hockessin (G-5261)

CONSTRUCTION: Athletic & Recreation Facilities

Baypro Contracting.................... G 703 593-7673
  Milford (G-7788)
Custom Framers Inc.................... F 302 684-5377
  Harbeson (G-4694)
Henderson Services Inc................ F 302 424-1999
  Milford (G-7926)
Parker Construction Inc............... G 302 798-8530
  Claymont (G-1260)
Stb Contracting LLC................... G 302 992-0570
  Wilmington (G-20042)

CONSTRUCTION: Bridge

Eastern Hwy Specialists Inc........... D 302 777-7673
  Wilmington (G-16259)
First State Crane Service Inc......... E 302 398-8885
  Felton (G-3974)
Greggo & Ferrara Inc.................. C 302 658-5241
  New Castle (G-9180)

CONSTRUCTION: Commercial & Office Building, New

Advance Construction Co Del........... F 302 697-9444
  Camden Wyoming (G-906)
Amakor Inc............................ F 302 834-8664
  Delaware City (G-1530)
Balfour Beatty LLC.................... G 302 573-3873
  Wilmington (G-14721)
Bancroft.............................. G 302 654-1408
  Wilmington (G-14733)
Bancroft Construction Company......... C 302 655-3434
  Wilmington (G-14738)
Bay Developers Inc.................... F 302 736-0924
  Dover (G-1884)
Brandywine Contractors Inc............ E 302 325-2700
  New Castle (G-8885)
Bunting Construction Corp............. F 302 436-5124
  Selbyville (G-13487)
Cape Financial Services Inc........... F 302 645-6274
  Lewes (G-5793)
Carl Deputy & Son Builders LLC........ G 302 284-3041
  Felton (G-3951)
Cobi Group Inc........................ F 302 407-3085
  Wilmington (G-15511)
Commonwealth Contruction Co........... E 302 654-6611
  Wilmington (G-15552)
Consolidated Contracting LLC.......... G 302 727-9795
  Dagsboro (G-1431)
Conventional Builders Inc............. F 302 422-2429
  Houston (G-5439)
Crystal Holdings Inc.................. D 302 421-5700
  Wilmington (G-15720)
Dal Construction...................... G 302 538-5310
  Camden (G-813)
Daystar Sills Inc..................... D 302 633-1421
  Wilmington (G-15822)
Del Homes Inc......................... F 302 697-8204
  Magnolia (G-6739)
Deldeo Builders Inc................... F 302 791-0243
  Claymont (G-1116)
Delmarva Builders Inc................. G 302 629-9123
  Bridgeville (G-692)
Deshong & Sons Contractors Inc........ G 302 453-8500
  Newark (G-10517)
Diamond Hill Inc...................... E 302 999-0302
  New Castle (G-9050)
Disabatino Construction Co............ D 302 652-3838
  Wilmington (G-16084)
Ebanks Construction LLC............... G 302 420-7584
  New Castle (G-9080)
Edge Construction Corp................ G 302 778-5200
  Wilmington (G-16288)

CONSTRUCTION: Commercial & Office Building, New

Edis Company .... E 302 421-5700
  Wilmington (G-16294)
Gga Construction .... E 302 376-6122
  Middletown (G-7159)
Guardian Construction Co Inc .... D 302 834-1000
  New Castle (G-9183)
Hart Construction Co Inc .... G 302 737-7886
  Newark (G-10937)
Insite Constructors Inc .... G 302 479-5555
  Wilmington (G-17353)
Jni CCC Jv1 LLP .... F 302 654-6611
  Wilmington (G-17559)
John L Briggs & Co .... F 302 856-7033
  Milton (G-8649)
KB Coldiron Inc .... D 302 436-4224
  Selbyville (G-13556)
Kent Construction Co .... E 302 653-6469
  Smyrna (G-13788)
Locker Construction Inc .... G 302 239-2859
  Newark (G-11278)
Lockwood Design Construction .... G 302 684-4844
  Milton (G-8655)
Ltc Services LLC .... G 302 396-8598
  Seaford (G-13267)
M L Parker Construction Inc .... F 302 798-8530
  Claymont (G-1227)
Mason Building Group Inc .... C 302 292-0600
  Newark (G-11348)
Miken Builders Inc .... E 302 537-4444
  Millville (G-8542)
Mitten Construction Co .... F 302 697-2124
  Dover (G-3104)
Moore Farms .... F 302 629-4999
  Georgetown (G-4434)
Mvl Structures Group LLC .... E 302 652-7580
  Wilmington (G-18498)
Mvl-Al Othman Al Zamel JV LLC .... E 832 302-2757
  Wilmington (G-18499)
Mvl-Saqa JV LLC .... E 832 302-2757
  Wilmington (G-18500)
Nason Construction Inc .... E 302 529-2510
  Wilmington (G-18537)
North East Contractors Inc .... E 302 286-6324
  Newark (G-11564)
Opus Design Build LLC .... D 952 656-4444
  Wilmington (G-18808)
Pettinaro Construction Co Inc .... D 302 999-0708
  Wilmington (G-19001)
Regional Builders Inc .... F 302 628-8660
  Seaford (G-13370)
Reybold Construction Corp .... E 302 832-7100
  Bear (G-455)
Richard Y Johnson & Son Inc .... E 302 422-3732
  Lincoln (G-6696)
Robert C Peoples Inc .... D 302 834-5268
  Bear (G-463)
SC&a Construction Inc .... E 302 478-6030
  Wilmington (G-19695)
Shellys of Delaware Inc .... G 302 656-3337
  Wilmington (G-19794)
Silverside Contracting Inc .... G 302 798-1907
  Wilmington (G-19830)
Talley Brothers Inc .... E 302 224-5376
  Newark (G-12157)
Taylor Kline Inc .... F 302 328-8306
  New Castle (G-9618)
Vanguard Construction Inc .... G 302 697-9187
  Dover (G-3773)
Vari Development Corp .... G 302 479-5571
  Wilmington (G-20571)
Whayland Company Inc .... F 302 875-5445
  Laurel (G-5624)
Whayland Company LLC .... F 302 875-5445
  Laurel (G-5625)
Whiting-Turner Contracting Co .... F 302 266-7450
  Newark (G-12370)
Woods General Contracting Inc .... G 302 856-4047
  Georgetown (G-4579)

CONSTRUCTION: Commercial & Office Buildings, Prefabricated

Ballard Builders LLC .... F 302 363-1677
  Clayton (G-1352)

CONSTRUCTION: Dams, Waterways, Docks & Other Marine

Advanced Cnstr Techniques Inc .... D 302 273-2617
  Newark (G-9773)
Interstate Construction Inc .... E 302 369-3590
  Newark (G-11048)

CONSTRUCTION: Dock

J & J Bulkheading .... G 302 436-2800
  Selbyville (G-13550)

CONSTRUCTION: Drainage System

Janette Redrow Ltd .... G 302 659-3534
  Townsend (G-14020)

CONSTRUCTION: Farm Building

Dan H Beachy & Sons Inc .... G 302 492-1493
  Hartly (G-4866)
Humphries Construction Company .... G 302 349-9277
  Greenwood (G-4637)
Larry Hill Farms Inc .... G 302 875-0886
  Delmar (G-1613)
Warfel Construction Co Inc .... E 302 422-8927
  Milford (G-8142)
Westwood Farms Incorporated .... F 302 238-7141
  Millsboro (G-8504)

CONSTRUCTION: Food Prdts Manufacturing or Packing Plant

Bio-Diversified Ventures Inc .... F 720 680-9418
  Wilmington (G-14894)
G TS Foods Inc .... G 302 376-3555
  Middletown (G-7147)
Genspec Materials Inc .... G 302 777-1100
  Wilmington (G-16841)
Healthy Snacks Holdings Inc .... G 917 540-6588
  Middletown (G-7201)
Louie Uncle Foods .... G 302 750-0117
  Wilmington (G-18005)
Salt Marsh Foods Inc .... G 302 260-9556
  Rehoboth Beach (G-12943)

CONSTRUCTION: Foundation & Retaining Wall

Blue Heron Contracting LLC .... G 302 526-0648
  Greenwood (G-4600)

CONSTRUCTION: Heavy Highway & Street

Delaware Department Trnsp .... E 302 326-8950
  Bear (G-146)
George & Lynch Inc .... D 302 736-3031
  Dover (G-2573)
Hudson Scholastic .... G 302 463-0840
  Dewey Beach (G-1670)
Matts Management Family LLC .... G 302 732-3715
  Frankford (G-4125)
Mumford and Miller Con Inc .... C 302 378-7736
  Middletown (G-7388)

Rp Ventures and Holdings Inc .... E 410 398-3000
  Wilmington (G-19578)
Sams Construction LLC .... F 302 654-6542
  Wilmington (G-19650)

CONSTRUCTION: Indl Buildings, New, NEC

Bristol Industrial Corporation .... F 302 322-1100
  New Castle (G-8893)
Broadpoint Construction LLC .... G 302 567-2100
  Rehoboth Beach (G-12655)
Ci De Corp .... G 302 998-3944
  Wilmington (G-15430)
Conventional Builders Inc .... F 302 422-2429
  Houston (G-5439)
Crystal Holdings Inc .... D 302 421-5700
  Wilmington (G-15720)
Deshong & Sons Contractors Inc .... G 302 453-8500
  Newark (G-10517)
Edis Company .... E 302 421-5700
  Wilmington (G-16294)
Gettier Staffing Services Inc .... G 302 478-0911
  Wilmington (G-16855)
Gfp Cement Contractors LLC .... F 302 998-7687
  Wilmington (G-16856)
Guardian Envmtl Svcs Co Inc .... D 302 918-3070
  Newark (G-10907)
Hart Construction Co Inc .... G 302 737-7886
  Newark (G-10937)
John L Briggs & Co .... F 302 856-7033
  Milton (G-8649)
Kent Construction Co .... E 302 653-6469
  Smyrna (G-13788)
Miken Builders Inc .... E 302 537-4444
  Millville (G-8542)
Mitten Construction Co .... F 302 697-2124
  Dover (G-3104)
Pettinaro Construction Co Inc .... D 302 999-0708
  Wilmington (G-19001)
Shellys of Delaware Inc .... G 302 656-3337
  Wilmington (G-19794)
Talley Brothers Inc .... E 302 224-5376
  Newark (G-12157)
Whayland Company Inc .... F 302 875-5445
  Laurel (G-5624)
Wohlsen Construction Company .... F 302 324-9900
  Wilmington (G-20874)

CONSTRUCTION: Land Preparation

Kbr Inc .... G 302 452-9386
  Newark (G-11146)
Mumford and Miller Con Inc .... C 302 378-7736
  Middletown (G-7388)

CONSTRUCTION: Marine

CBI Services LLC .... F 302 325-8400
  New Castle (G-8922)
George & Lynch Inc .... D 302 736-3031
  Dover (G-2573)
Merritt Marine Cnstr Inc .... G 302 436-2881
  Selbyville (G-13570)
Precision Marine Construction .... G 302 227-2711
  Rehoboth Beach (G-12898)
Sun Marine Maintenance Inc .... E 302 539-6756
  Frankford (G-4149)
Sussex Marine Construction Inc .... G 302 436-9680
  Frankford (G-4151)

CONSTRUCTION: Oil & Gas Pipeline Construction

Voshell Bros Welding Inc .... E 302 674-1414
  Dover (G-3810)

PRODUCTS & SERVICES SECTION

CONSTRUCTION: Residential, Nec

CONSTRUCTION: Parking Lot

Sanco Construction Co Inc............................ G 302 633-4156
  Wilmington (G-19655)
Terra Firma of Delmarva Inc........................ E 302 846-3350
  Delmar (G-1640)

CONSTRUCTION: Pipeline, NEC

Current Solutions.. G 302 724-5243
  Dover (G-2171)
INA Acquisition Corp..................................... F 302 472-9258
  Wilmington (G-17295)

CONSTRUCTION: Railroad & Subway

Asplundh Tree Expert LLC........................... G 302 678-4702
  Dover (G-1833)

CONSTRUCTION: Residential, Nec

Albert Delpizzo LLC...................................... G 302 234-2994
  Newark (G-9806)
American Builder LLC................................... G 302 841-2325
  Georgetown (G-4208)
American Craftsmen LLC............................. G 302 545-3666
  Newark (G-9844)
Anthony Ferguson.. G 610 906-4998
  Selbyville (G-13464)
AR Campagnone LLC................................... G 302 329-9323
  Milton (G-8562)
Ash Edward L I... G 302 732-9181
  Frankford (G-4061)
Asset Assistance LLC.................................. G 302 364-3362
  Dover (G-1834)
B Doherty Inc... G 302 239-3500
  Wilmington (G-14697)
Brian K Mummert.. G 302 678-2260
  Dover (G-1977)
Brobst Home Improvement LLC................... G 302 376-1656
  Townsend (G-13968)
Capano Management Company.................. D 302 737-8056
  Newark (G-10132)
Cappo Dennis John...................................... G 302 245-2261
  Frankford (G-4083)
Carl M Freeman Associates Inc................... D 302 436-3000
  Ocean View (G-12486)
Chews Unlimited LLC.................................. G 302 280-6137
  Delmar (G-1578)
Cirillo Bros Inc.. E 302 326-1540
  New Castle (G-8943)
Cm Beach LLC.. G 202 521-1493
  Lewes (G-5834)
Cote Custom Works LLC.............................. G 302 359-2596
  Dover (G-2143)
Cretework LLC... G 302 424-9970
  Ellendale (G-3912)
Custom Improvers Inc................................. G 302 731-9246
  Newark (G-10368)
Dan Prinsloo.. G 302 373-8891
  Townsend (G-13984)
Daniel Shea... G 302 349-5599
  Greenwood (G-4611)
David Dukes.. G 302 841-9481
  Millsboro (G-8254)
David Ira Jenkins.. G 302 335-3309
  Magnolia (G-6737)
David M Showalter...................................... G 302 462-5264
  Millsboro (G-8256)
Dec Home Services..................................... G 240 793-4818
  Selbyville (G-13517)
Deldeo Builders Inc..................................... F 302 791-0243
  Claymont (G-1116)
Dell Pump Company................................... G 302 655-2436
  Wilmington (G-15995)

Diamond State Pole Bldngs LLC.................. G 302 387-1710
  Felton (G-3960)
Disabatino Construction Co......................... D 302 652-3838
  Wilmington (G-16084)
Divergent LLC.. G 302 275-7019
  Wilmington (G-16092)
Djlong Services.. G 302 541-4884
  Ocean View (G-12505)
Donald Goldsborough................................. G 302 653-1081
  Smyrna (G-13712)
Donald Grebe.. G 302 945-7975
  Millsboro (G-8274)
Donald R Cordrey Jr................................... G 302 875-4939
  Laurel (G-5501)
Douglas Randall Inc.................................... G 302 448-5826
  Lewes (G-5931)
Dream Structures LLC................................. G 302 943-3974
  Hartly (G-4870)
E A Zando Custom Designs Inc.................... F 302 684-4601
  Milton (G-8613)
East Coast Minority Supplier....................... G 302 656-3337
  Wilmington (G-16252)
Ebanks Construction LLC............................ G 302 420-7584
  New Castle (G-9080)
Ed Durynski... G 302 994-6642
  Wilmington (G-16283)
Elegant Exteriors LLC................................. G 302 218-8378
  Newark (G-10624)
Elite Developers Group LLC........................ G 615 397-9732
  Dover (G-2434)
Exantus and Son Homes............................. G 302 745-3468
  Georgetown (G-4311)
Exterior Homeworks LLC............................. G 302 249-0012
  Seaford (G-13180)
Falcon Crest Inv Intl Inc............................. G 240 701-1746
  Wilmington (G-16532)
Fitch-It.. G 302 260-9657
  Rehoboth Beach (G-12758)
Flores Enterprises LLC................................ G 484 880-5134
  Wilmington (G-16666)
Franklin Utilities LLC.................................. G 302 629-6658
  Georgetown (G-4325)
G David Outten LLC.................................... G 302 747-4932
  Wyoming (G-20985)
Garcia & Sons LLC....................................... G 302 562-8878
  Newark (G-10808)
Garret Thomas Pusey LLC........................... G 302 875-9146
  Laurel (G-5517)
Garth Enterprises Ltd................................. F 302 349-2298
  Frankford (G-4109)
General Service Contrs LLC........................ G 302 220-1946
  New Castle (G-9161)
Global Exterior.. G 302 449-1559
  Middletown (G-7164)
Good Neighbor LLC..................................... G 302 228-9910
  Selbyville (G-13538)
Grantlin Fabrication LLC............................. G 302 270-3708
  Smyrna (G-13750)
Hagerty Homes LLC.................................... G 302 234-4268
  Newark (G-10917)
Harold L Scott Sr.. G 302 343-9217
  Dover (G-2653)
Henlopen Homes LLC................................. G 302 684-0860
  Milton (G-8636)
Homefix... G 302 682-3837
  Lewes (G-6099)
Improve Sussex LLC.................................... G 302 864-8559
  Lewes (G-6118)
Interstellar Cmnty Living LLC..................... G 787 607-3939
  Wilmington (G-17399)
Interstllar Cmnty Lving MGT Co................. G 787 607-3939
  Wilmington (G-17400)

James Robert Kline...................................... G 302 633-3926
  Wilmington (G-17484)
James W McKee... G 302 540-9191
  Middletown (G-7239)
Jeff Tetrick... G 302 478-7185
  Wilmington (G-17515)
Jerry S Meiklejohn....................................... G 302 745-2632
  Dagsboro (G-1470)
JI Solis LLC... G 302 212-9521
  Millsboro (G-8332)
John J Mast... G 302 492-1356
  Hartly (G-4882)
John W Bateman... G 302 644-1177
  Lewes (G-6148)
John W Petrofske.. G 410 422-1545
  Dover (G-2798)
Joseph D Allen... G 302 685-4230
  Middletown (G-7253)
Joseph R Kasowski...................................... G 302 379-0523
  Wilmington (G-17584)
Jpl M&R.. G 302 883-9534
  Wilmington (G-17597)
Justin Maynard... G 302 233-6086
  Hartly (G-4888)
K Squared Enterprises LLC.......................... G 302 402-3082
  Ocean View (G-12530)
Kenneth H Gladish...................................... G 302 270-2821
  Felton (G-3991)
Klh Enterprises... F 302 245-0712
  Milton (G-8652)
Kms Servives... G 302 502-5287
  Smyrna (G-13792)
Kramer Konstruction................................... G 717 466-6500
  Wyoming (G-20987)
Larry Baker LLC... G 302 703-2127
  Millsboro (G-8344)
Larrys Building.. G 302 670-8803
  Bridgeville (G-724)
Lloyd Richard LLC....................................... G 302 584-8798
  Newark (G-11275)
Lloyds Stoneworks....................................... G 302 492-0847
  Marydel (G-6804)
Lnw & A Construction Corp........................ F 302 764-9430
  Wilmington (G-17964)
M & G Pro Services LLC.............................. G 302 420-1428
  Marydel (G-6805)
Mark Wanner... G 302 478-6878
  Wilmington (G-18141)
Marshall Services Inc.................................. G 302 655-0076
  Wilmington (G-18160)
Martin Construction Svcs LLC.................... F 302 200-0885
  Newark (G-11342)
Mast Homes LLC... G 302 632-7735
  Camden (G-872)
Mazzola Systems Inc................................... G 302 738-6808
  Newark (G-11363)
Michael A Madanat..................................... G 302 998-6613
  Wilmington (G-18303)
Michael Marino Inc..................................... G 302 764-5319
  Wilmington (G-18319)
Moore Services.. G 302 588-3984
  Wilmington (G-18437)
Mp Diversified Services LLC....................... G 302 828-1060
  Newark (G-11462)
My 3 Sons.. G 302 559-7252
  Wilmington (G-18502)
Nail It Down General Contrs...................... G 302 698-3073
  Dover (G-3145)
Newark Building Services LLC.................... G 302 377-7687
  Newark (G-11530)
Nvr Inc... F 302 731-5770
  Newark (G-11571)

Employee Codes: A=Over 500 employees, B=251-500
C=101-250, D=51-100, E=20-50, F=10-19, G=1-9

2024 Harris Directory of Delaware Businesses

CONSTRUCTION: Residential, Nec

Orcurto Enterprises .... G 302 604-7039
  Bridgeville (G-743)
Parthian LLC .... G 240 441-8301
  Ocean View (G-12558)
Phillip T Bradley Inc .... G 302 947-2741
  Lewes (G-6365)
Platinum Heritage Entps LLC .... G 469 563-0411
  Dover (G-3330)
Portable Sheds Paul Yoder .... G 302 734-2681
  Dover (G-3352)
Powells General Services .... G 302 384-7817
  Wilmington (G-19135)
Preferred Construction Inc .... G 302 322-9568
  New Castle (G-9490)
Prestige Contractors Inc .... G 302 722-1032
  Wilmington (G-19181)
Price Edward A/Gnral Contractr .... G 302 571-9281
  Wilmington (G-19187)
Pro Clean Wilmington Inc .... G 302 836-8080
  Delaware City (G-1553)
Quarry Mill Craftsmen LLC .... G 302 388-6289
  Wilmington (G-19290)
R E Excavation LLC .... G 302 273-3669
  Newark (G-11806)
Ralph Del Signore Jr .... G 302 239-0803
  Hockessin (G-5353)
Raymond M Smith Jr .... G 302 670-3801
  Clayton (G-1400)
Raymond Shephard .... G 302 834-8405
  Bear (G-446)
Reinvex LLC .... G 484 259-7889
  Wilmington (G-19418)
Resort Custom Homes .... G 302 645-8222
  Lewes (G-6418)
Richard W Krick Jr .... G 302 227-6974
  Rehoboth Beach (G-12935)
Risen Services .... G 302 858-8840
  Laurel (G-5592)
Robert Golebiowski .... G 302 234-6583
  Wilmington (G-19512)
Rockles Services LLC .... G 302 258-5357
  Milton (G-8702)
S and S LLC .... G 302 344-5990
  Milton (G-8705)
Sampson Interiors .... G 865 438-5097
  Rehoboth Beach (G-12946)
Sandhill Development Group LLC .... G 302 703-2140
  Milton (G-8706)
Scott Charles Foresman .... G 302 644-8418
  Lewes (G-6452)
Scuba World Inc .... G 302 698-1117
  Dover (G-3522)
Separe Inc .... G 302 736-5000
  Dover (G-3532)
Sunnyworld LLC .... G 240 506-8870
  Rehoboth Beach (G-12981)
Swarter Services LLC .... G 302 575-9943
  Wilmington (G-20170)
Thomas Brothers LLC .... G 302 366-1316
  Newark (G-12192)
Timothy P Collord .... G 302 448-9577
  Milton (G-8721)
Todd R Williams .... G 302 945-3662
  Lewes (G-6567)
Tom Can and Son General Contr .... G 302 737-5551
  Newark (G-12205)
Tony Ashburn Inc .... G 302 677-1940
  Dover (G-3697)
Top Notch Home Services .... G 302 275-2459
  Newark (G-12210)
Tristate Fbrcn and Machg .... G 302 533-5877
  Newark (G-12235)

Tropacool .... G 302 245-4078
  Georgetown (G-4562)
Turnkey Electric LLC .... G 302 858-3726
  Georgetown (G-4564)
Warren Reid .... E 302 877-0901
  Laurel (G-5620)
Wes Sanders & Son LLC .... G 302 383-4991
  Wilmington (G-20735)
William Redding and Son .... G 302 562-4026
  Newark (G-12377)
Wirenut LLC .... G 302 858-7027
  Georgetown (G-4576)
Wm Companies LLC .... G 302 228-5122
  Greenwood (G-4675)
Wright Robert Steele .... G 302 423-2093
  Harrington (G-4849)

CONSTRUCTION: Sewer Line

Epb Associates Inc .... F 302 475-7301
  Wilmington (G-16449)
H I E Contractors Inc .... F 302 224-3032
  Newark (G-10913)
Hopkins Construction Inc .... F 302 337-3366
  Bridgeville (G-712)
Teal Construction Inc .... D 302 276-6034
  Dover (G-3661)

CONSTRUCTION: Single-Family Housing

A J E Construction LLC .... G 302 217-2268
  Seaford (G-13044)
A S Jacono LLC .... G 302 378-3000
  Middletown (G-6824)
Acp Services LLC .... G 302 299-4225
  Wilmington (G-14239)
Adel Construction .... G 302 286-7676
  Newark (G-9764)
Advance Construction Technique .... G 270 257-0377
  Wilmington (G-14265)
Alka Construction LLC .... G 443 944-9058
  Seaford (G-13054)
Americo Inc .... F 302 981-9410
  Wilmington (G-14446)
Amy Chilimidos C O Boa .... G 302 388-1880
  Hockessin (G-5124)
Andrews Construction LLC .... G 302 604-8166
  Lincoln (G-6656)
Anythings Possible Cnstr .... G 302 233-2357
  Harrington (G-4733)
AON Construction Services LLC .... G 302 858-6178
  Bethany Beach (G-574)
Arivers Construction .... G 302 299-2288
  Newark (G-9903)
B and B Contractors Inc .... G 302 836-9207
  Newark (G-9964)
Bancroft Construction Company .... F 302 655-3434
  Dover (G-1870)
Banris Construction LLC .... G 302 722-0958
  Wilmington (G-14751)
Bari Concrete Cnstr Corp .... G 302 384-7093
  Wilmington (G-14764)
Battaglia Mechanical Inc .... E 302 325-6100
  New Castle (G-8849)
Bellaline Design LLC .... G 302 293-5676
  Bear (G-68)
Bellevue Contractors LLC .... F 302 655-1522
  Wilmington (G-14821)
Benson Concrete Cnstr LLC .... G 410 382-5112
  Seaford (G-13083)
Black Dog Construction LLC .... G 302 530-4967
  Newark (G-10045)
BNai BRith Claymont LP .... G 302 798-6846
  Claymont (G-1062)

Bowden Construction LLC .... G 302 907-0430
  Delmar (G-1568)
Brand Builder Solutions LLC .... G 302 234-4239
  Wilmington (G-15039)
Bravos Construction LLC .... G 302 249-0039
  Bridgeville (G-674)
Broadpoint Construction LLC .... G 302 228-8007
  Rehoboth Beach (G-12656)
Bulldog Construction .... G 302 632-4834
  Woodside (G-20974)
Burton Construction Co LLC .... G 302 327-8650
  Hockessin (G-5145)
BV Teagarden & Son Cnstr LLC .... G 410 330-1733
  Delmar (G-1571)
Byers Electrical Construc .... G 302 420-8700
  Historic New Castle (G-4949)
Bz Construction Services Inc .... G 302 999-7505
  Wilmington (G-15167)
C M Construction Co LLC .... G 302 228-3570
  Frankford (G-4082)
C Vargas Construction LLC .... G 302 470-2004
  Seaford (G-13099)
C2 Construction LLC .... G 302 438-3901
  Wilmington (G-15180)
Cambria LLC .... G 703 898-9989
  Lewes (G-5786)
Capano Homes Inc .... E 302 384-7980
  Wilmington (G-15221)
Carl M Freeman .... G 302 988-1669
  Selbyville (G-13491)
Carny Construction .... G 302 436-9738
  Selbyville (G-13493)
Carrow Construction LLC .... G 302 376-0520
  New Castle (G-8915)
Cavan Inc .... G 302 598-4176
  Wilmington (G-15281)
Clark Construction Inc .... G 302 832-1288
  Bear (G-108)
Clendaniel Construction .... G 302 422-7415
  Milford (G-7834)
Cns Construction Corp .... G 302 224-0450
  Newark (G-10267)
Colonial Home Improvements .... G 302 275-8247
  Bear (G-113)
Communications Cnstr Group LLC .... E 302 280-6926
  Laurel (G-5485)
Construction Resource MGT Inc .... G 302 778-2335
  Lewes (G-5857)
Conway Construction Co .... G 302 598-5019
  Lewes (G-5858)
Courtney Construction .... G 302 798-2393
  Wilmington (G-15659)
Courtney Construction Inc .... G 302 521-5865
  Wilmington (G-15660)
Craig Maurer .... G 302 293-2365
  Middletown (G-7018)
Critical Design and Cnstr Corp .... G 302 588-4406
  Wilmington (G-15707)
Crossroads Land Tech LLC .... F 302 841-0654
  Millsboro (G-8245)
Daisy Construction Company .... G 302 658-4417
  New Castle (G-8994)
Dalco Construction Co .... G 302 475-2099
  Wilmington (G-15769)
Dan Miller and Sons Cnstr LLC .... G 302 492-8116
  Hartly (G-4867)
Daniels Custom Finishes LLC .... G 302 357-5806
  Wilmington (G-15785)
Davis Samuel F Jr Gen Contr .... G 302 475-2607
  Wilmington (G-15816)
DC Chambers Construction LLC .... G 302 233-0148
  Felton (G-3957)

PRODUCTS & SERVICES SECTION

CONSTRUCTION: Single-Family Housing

De Val Structurez .... G 302 575-9090
  Wilmington *(G-15840)*
Dead On Construction .... G 302 462-5023
  Selbyville *(G-13516)*
Deck Masters LLC .... G 302 563-4459
  Wilmington *(G-15848)*
Del Fab Construction LLC .... G 302 943-9131
  Clayton *(G-1359)*
Delaware Constructionology .... G 302 827-3072
  Middletown *(G-7038)*
Delaware Landscape Cnstr LLC .... G 302 841-3010
  Rehoboth Beach *(G-12718)*
Deshields Construction .... G 302 331-5214
  Magnolia *(G-6740)*
Dewson Construction Co .... E 302 227-3095
  Rehoboth Beach *(G-12724)*
Diane Austin .... G 302 856-3369
  Georgetown *(G-4294)*
Dirickson Creek Construction L .... G 302 604-2482
  Frankford *(G-4102)*
Disabatino Construction Co .... D 302 652-3838
  Wilmington *(G-16084)*
Divergent LLC .... G 302 275-7019
  Wilmington *(G-16092)*
Double S Developers Inc .... G 302 838-8880
  Bear *(G-178)*
Dream Werks LLC .... G 302 526-2415
  Dover *(G-2381)*
Drw Construction .... G 302 945-9055
  Lewes *(G-5937)*
DSM Commercial .... E 302 842-2450
  Wilmington *(G-16183)*
E&S Home Improvement LLC .... G 302 559-2340
  Newark *(G-10589)*
Eak Construction Inc .... G 302 893-8497
  Bear *(G-186)*
Ej Constructions .... G 302 272-2101
  Laurel *(G-5508)*
Elite Developers Group LLC .... G 615 397-9732
  Dover *(G-2434)*
Emerick Construction Group LLC .... G 302 547-0715
  Newark *(G-10641)*
Empire Construction .... G 302 329-9256
  Milton *(G-8618)*
Empire Construction Group LLC .... G 302 223-9208
  Milton *(G-8619)*
Ervin H Yoder .... G 302 492-1835
  Camden Wyoming *(G-941)*
Estepp Construction Co Inc .... G 302 378-4958
  Townsend *(G-13998)*
Exact Construction of De .... G 302 629-0464
  Seaford *(G-13179)*
Eyetower LLC .... G 302 298-0944
  Wilmington *(G-16513)*
EZ Construction Co .... G 302 723-5730
  New Castle *(G-9112)*
EZ Deck LLC .... G 302 444-2268
  Townsend *(G-14000)*
Falcon Construction LLC .... G 302 668-6874
  Wilmington *(G-16531)*
Ferreira Builders LLC .... G 302 296-6014
  Georgetown *(G-4318)*
Freedom At Home .... G 302 740-7054
  Wilmington *(G-16740)*
Gator Construction Llc .... G 302 430-1160
  Georgetown *(G-4331)*
George & Lynch Inc .... F 302 238-7289
  Millsboro *(G-8298)*
Gerardi Construction Inc .... G 302 745-6252
  Felton *(G-3978)*
Gfrs Construction One LLC .... G 484 357-5218
  Ocean View *(G-12519)*

Gga Construction .... G 302 376-5193
  Middletown *(G-7158)*
Gleneagle Homes LLC .... G 914 262-1402
  Millsboro *(G-8300)*
Gregg White Contracting .... G 302 542-9552
  Bethany Beach *(G-605)*
Guardian Construction Co Inc .... G 302 656-1986
  Wilmington *(G-17001)*
H & H Construction Company LLC .... G 936 825-6774
  Dover *(G-2639)*
Habitat For Hmnity New Cstle C .... F 302 652-0365
  Wilmington *(G-17027)*
Handyman Housecalls Inc .... G 302 245-3816
  Lewes *(G-6074)*
Home Improvements .... G 302 537-1102
  Dagsboro *(G-1465)*
Home Integrated .... G 302 656-1624
  Wilmington *(G-17181)*
Homes For Laurel II Inc .... G 302 875-3525
  Laurel *(G-5531)*
Humphries Construction Company .... G 302 349-9277
  Greenwood *(G-4637)*
Hunter Construction .... G 410 392-5109
  Newark *(G-10985)*
Innovative Home Imprvs LLC .... G 302 388-2950
  Smyrna *(G-13771)*
Integrity Construction LLC .... G 302 241-6429
  Marydel *(G-6801)*
Integrity MGT Solution Inc .... G 302 270-8976
  Clayton *(G-1373)*
Interfaith Cmnty Hsing of Del .... F 302 652-3991
  Wilmington *(G-17383)*
J & L Services Inc .... F 410 943-3355
  Seaford *(G-13226)*
Jay Lynn Cnstr Solutions LLC .... G 302 349-5799
  Millsboro *(G-8329)*
Jeremy Sheiker .... G 302 540-3741
  Wilmington *(G-17531)*
JG Services .... G 302 480-1900
  Dover *(G-2787)*
John T Elliott .... G 302 337-7075
  Bridgeville *(G-721)*
Joseph Truono .... G 302 762-6822
  Wilmington *(G-17585)*
Jrm Construction LLC .... G 302 362-7453
  Seaford *(G-13239)*
Jrs Homes LLC .... G 302 544-5911
  New Castle *(G-9269)*
Just Homes LLC .... G 302 322-2233
  Wilmington *(G-17617)*
K&S Home Services LLC .... G 302 604-3563
  Ocean View *(G-12531)*
Kamax Construction LLC .... G 302 296-8270
  Selbyville *(G-13554)*
Kelmon Construction .... G 302 357-4391
  Wilmington *(G-17682)*
Kevin A Johnson .... G 302 762-7671
  Wilmington *(G-17699)*
Kirkley Construction LLC .... G 302 276-9795
  Bear *(G-331)*
Kleinhomers .... G 302 234-2392
  Newark *(G-11190)*
Kneesaverelectricalbox .... G 732 239-7514
  Millsboro *(G-8343)*
Knepps Construction .... G 302 846-3360
  Delmar *(G-1611)*
Knotts Construction Inc .... G 302 475-7074
  Wilmington *(G-17744)*
Kovach S Construction .... G 302 363-4130
  Hartly *(G-4892)*
Kurtz Construction LLC .... G 302 943-4754
  Dover *(G-2890)*

Lafond Construction .... G 302 430-2834
  Georgetown *(G-4400)*
Lc Construction Florida Inc .... F 302 429-8700
  Wilmington *(G-17838)*
Liii Construction Co .... F 302 429-8700
  Wilmington *(G-17911)*
Lopesco Inc .... G 908 482-5616
  Newark *(G-11283)*
Lr Construction LLC .... G 302 249-4507
  Bridgeville *(G-726)*
Lynn Construction LLC .... G 302 236-6596
  Seaford *(G-13269)*
M L Morris Inc .... G 302 956-0678
  Bridgeville *(G-727)*
Make It New Construction LLC .... G 302 423-7794
  Dover *(G-3002)*
Man Around House .... G 302 531-5124
  Milford *(G-7982)*
Manor Creek Construction Inc .... G 302 245-2887
  Selbyville *(G-13565)*
Marra Landing LLC .... G 302 530-5800
  Wilmington *(G-18156)*
Mazzola Systems Inc .... G 302 738-6808
  Newark *(G-11363)*
McCove Construction Inc .... G 302 363-0528
  Dover *(G-3043)*
Mch Construction LLC .... G 302 249-2765
  Magnolia *(G-6764)*
Millennium Homes .... G 302 678-2393
  Dover *(G-3092)*
Minkers Construction Inc .... F 302 239-9239
  Newark *(G-11425)*
ML Whiteman and Sons Inc .... G 302 659-1001
  Townsend *(G-14038)*
Mmt Construction Services Inc .... G 302 357-8506
  Wilmington *(G-18393)*
Morales Gto Empire LLC .... G 302 824-4315
  Wilmington *(G-18440)*
Mp Diversified Services LLC .... G 302 828-1060
  Newark *(G-11462)*
Murphy Steel Inc .... E 302 366-8676
  Newark *(G-11473)*
Murphys Construction .... G 302 462-0319
  Seaford *(G-13297)*
Murray Bunting Constr .... F 302 436-5144
  Selbyville *(G-13585)*
MWM Construction .... G 302 218-5222
  Townsend *(G-14041)*
Neighborhood House Inc .... F 302 658-5404
  Wilmington *(G-18571)*
NM Construction Inc .... G 302 478-6494
  Wilmington *(G-18657)*
Norman Yoder Construction .... G 302 492-3516
  Hartly *(G-4901)*
Nvr Inc .... F 302 731-5770
  Newark *(G-11571)*
NY Construction .... G 302 377-1846
  Smyrna *(G-13839)*
Ocean Services of De Inc .... G 410 524-1518
  Selbyville *(G-13588)*
Onsite Construction Inc .... F 302 628-4244
  Seaford *(G-13325)*
Orjam Ltd .... F 302 482-5016
  Wilmington *(G-18822)*
Ossandeep Associates LLC .... G 302 660-8545
  Newark *(G-11604)*
Paldor Inc .... G 302 999-9691
  Wilmington *(G-18867)*
Pano Development Inc .... G 302 428-1062
  Wilmington *(G-18877)*
Paoli Services Inc .... F 302 998-7031
  Wilmington *(G-18878)*

Employee Codes: A=Over 500 employees, B=251-500
C=101-250, D=51-100, E=20-50, F=10-19, G=1-9

2024 Harris Directory of
Delaware Businesses

CONSTRUCTION: Single-Family Housing

Park Side Utility Construction............... F 302 322-9760
New Castle *(G-9449)*

Patriot General Contractors................... G 302 287-9000
New Castle *(G-9458)*

Patriot Government Svcs Inc .... G 302 655-3434
Wilmington *(G-18910)*

Payne Enterprises LLC............................ G 302 856-2899
Georgetown *(G-4457)*

Pdo Construction LLC.............................. G 302 542-0963
Selbyville *(G-13590)*

Pelican Key LLC Brksdale A SRI............. G 302 563-9493
Newark *(G-11655)*

Pettinaro Construction Co Inc .... D 302 999-0708
Wilmington *(G-19001)*

Philadlphia Arms Town Hmes Inc .... F 302 503-7216
Ellendale *(G-3928)*

Phoenix Construction LLC....................... G 302 363-0453
Milton *(G-8685)*

Pientka Masonry Cnstr LLC..................... G 302 420-6748
Newark *(G-11688)*

Pierson RE Construction........................... F 302 407-3308
Wilmington *(G-19035)*

Pike Creek Construction........................... G 302 453-0611
Newark *(G-11691)*

Pinnacle Home Improvement LLC........... G 302 569-5311
Bridgeville *(G-751)*

Polite Construction Jay............................. G 302 328-0390
New Castle *(G-9483)*

Powell Construction L L C......................... G 302 745-1146
Georgetown *(G-4469)*

Precision Marine Construction................. G 302 227-2711
Rehoboth Beach *(G-12899)*

Princetonian Mhc LLC................................ G 800 927-9800
Wilmington *(G-19194)*

Pro Carpet LLC.. G 443 757-7320
Millsboro *(G-8438)*

Purity Home Improvement Inc................. G 302 753-5454
Wilmington *(G-19265)*

Pw Construction LLC.................................. G 443 309-4082
Wilmington *(G-19270)*

Pyir Construction & Design...................... G 302 824-9015
Newark *(G-11778)*

Quality Construction Cleaning................. G 302 956-0752
Bridgeville *(G-758)*

Quality Construction De LLC................... G 302 757-6185
New Castle *(G-9505)*

Ranco Construction.................................... G 302 322-3000
Wilmington *(G-19329)*

Read Construction Inc............................... G 302 659-1144
Smyrna *(G-13863)*

Reybold Homes Inc..................................... C 302 834-3000
New Castle *(G-9529)*

Riale System Services............................... G 302 328-3848
Bear *(G-460)*

Richard Bratcher... G 803 786-7322
Dover *(G-3467)*

Richard D Whaley Cnstr LLC................... G 302 934-9525
Millsboro *(G-8445)*

Risleus Properties LLC.............................. F 302 353-1255
Dover *(G-3473)*

Rkj Construction Inc................................... G 302 690-0959
Wilmington *(G-19501)*

Robert E Davis... G 302 535-9657
Felton *(G-4019)*

Robert Miller Construction Inc................. G 302 335-4385
Felton *(G-4020)*

Rons Mobile Home Sales Inc................... G 302 398-9166
Harrington *(G-4821)*

Royal Rsdntial Renovations LLC............. G 302 377-0128
New Castle *(G-9544)*

RSM Construction.. G 302 270-7099
Dover *(G-3492)*

Ryla Real Estate Options LLC................. G 302 397-7402
New Castle *(G-9550)*

S Finney Home Improvements................. G 302 358-4562
Lewes *(G-6436)*

Sabcon Construction Company............... G 302 420-0467
Wilmington *(G-19617)*

Sams Construction LLC............................. F 302 654-6542
Wilmington *(G-19649)*

Saxton Jack 3 Construction...................... G 302 654-4553
Wilmington *(G-19687)*

Shelde Construction.................................... G 561 723-5314
Camden Wyoming *(G-976)*

Shelter Const.. G 302 829-8310
Millsboro *(G-8458)*

Shockley Brothers Construction............... G 302 424-3255
Lincoln *(G-6699)*

Smith Home Improvements...................... G 302 998-8294
Wilmington *(G-19889)*

Solid Construction LLC.............................. G 571 451-4727
Lewes *(G-6490)*

Steimel Construction LLC......................... G 302 827-2471
Lewes *(G-6510)*

Steven Rogers... G 302 422-6285
Milford *(G-8104)*

Steven Soule.. G 302 690-3052
Wilmington *(G-20067)*

Stonehammer Construction....................... G 302 233-3971
Felton *(G-4030)*

Stover Construction LLC........................... G 302 653-6195
Smyrna *(G-13903)*

Sun Construction Inc.................................. G 267 767-5047
Lewes *(G-6521)*

Sussex Cnty Hbtat For Hmnity I.............. G 302 855-1153
Georgetown *(G-4533)*

Sussex Home Imprv Contr LLC............... G 302 855-9679
Georgetown *(G-4539)*

Tag Water Restoration & Cnstr................ G 877 558-6646
Wilmington *(G-20207)*

Thomas F Cavanaugh................................. G 302 995-2859
Wilmington *(G-20307)*

Todd Yerger Ta... G 302 378-4196
Middletown *(G-7649)*

Toner Jerome P Sr Patrici......................... G 302 239-7271
Newark *(G-12209)*

Transformers LLC.. G 302 757-3803
Newark *(G-12218)*

Trevcon Construction Co........................... G 908 413-7001
Lewes *(G-6579)*

Tri State Construction Inc......................... G 609 980-1000
Smyrna *(G-13918)*

Triangle HM Imprvmnt Cntrctr L.............. G 302 883-4943
Dover *(G-3724)*

Tricon Construction MGT Inc................... E 302 838-6500
New Castle *(G-9639)*

Troyer Construction Inc............................. G 302 422-0745
Milford *(G-8120)*

V Colbert Inc... G 302 420-5502
Newark *(G-12294)*

Valliant Home Improvements.................... G 302 363-7109
Selbyville *(G-13616)*

Vetex Construction LLC............................. G 302 670-0989
Magnolia *(G-6789)*

Vtech Engineering Group LLC................. G 267 253-2576
Middletown *(G-7697)*

Weiner Development LLC......................... G 302 764-9430
Wilmington *(G-20714)*

Williams Humphreys and Co LLC............ G 302 225-3000
Wilmington *(G-20798)*

Wonderful Homes.. G 610 304-4744
Rehoboth Beach *(G-13021)*

Yellowfin Construction LLC...................... F 302 293-0028
Hockessin *(G-5432)*

CONSTRUCTION: Single-family Housing, New

36 Builders Inc... E 302 349-9480
Bridgeville *(G-657)*

A & Tc Builders Inc.................................... G 443 736-0099
Lewes *(G-5643)*

A Js Fence Builders Inc............................ G 302 731-0000
Newark *(G-9725)*

A To Z First Builders LLC......................... G 302 393-9761
Greenwood *(G-4587)*

Ace Home Solutions Corp......................... G 302 743-8995
New Castle *(G-8761)*

American Builders Inc............................... G 856 287-0840
Middletown *(G-6858)*

Apex Builders LLC...................................... G 302 242-1059
Dover *(G-1802)*

Astoria Builders LLC................................. G 302 892-9211
Greenville *(G-4583)*

Astoria Builders LLC................................. G 302 993-7951
Wilmington *(G-14605)*

Atlantic Coast Builders LLC..................... G 302 396-7824
Frankford *(G-4062)*

Atlantic Homes LLC.................................... G 302 947-0223
Lewes *(G-5714)*

Avid Builders LLC....................................... G 302 233-0148
Felton *(G-3944)*

Bancroft Homes Inc.................................... G 302 655-5461
Wilmington *(G-14739)*

Bay 2 Bay Builders..................................... G 302 632-7222
Harrington *(G-4738)*

Bay Developers Inc.................................... F 302 736-0924
Dover *(G-1884)*

Bay To Beach Builders Inc....................... G 302 349-5099
Farmington *(G-3933)*

Bb Builder Llc.. G 302 670-1972
Dover *(G-1892)*

Benchmark Builders Inc............................ E 302 995-6945
Wilmington *(G-14827)*

Benjamin B Smith Builders Inc................ G 302 537-1916
Ocean View *(G-12477)*

Beracah Homes Inc.................................... E 302 349-4561
Greenwood *(G-4597)*

Beracah Sales Office................................. G 302 854-6700
Milton *(G-8571)*

Bestfield Associates Inc........................... F 302 633-6361
Wilmington *(G-14858)*

Blenheim Management Company........... E 302 254-0100
Newark *(G-10051)*

Boardwalk Builders Inc............................. F 302 227-5754
Rehoboth Beach *(G-12647)*

Brandywine Contractors Inc..................... G 302 325-2700
New Castle *(G-8886)*

Breeze Construction LLC.......................... G 302 522-9201
Townsend *(G-13966)*

Bruce Mears Designer-Builder................. F 302 539-2355
Ocean View *(G-12483)*

Bryant Guernsey Cnstr Co........................ G 302 737-1841
Newark *(G-10097)*

Bryton Hmes At Five Points LLC............ G 302 703-6633
Frankford *(G-4079)*

Bulwark Builders Inc.................................. G 302 299-3190
Newark *(G-10104)*

Bunting Construction Corp....................... F 302 436-5124
Selbyville *(G-13487)*

C & B Construct... G 302 378-9862
Milford *(G-7809)*

C&M Custom Homes LLC......................... G 302 736-5824
Felton *(G-3950)*

Cape Financial Services Inc.................... F 302 645-6274
Lewes *(G-5793)*

PRODUCTS & SERVICES SECTION

CONSTRUCTION: Single-family Housing, New

Capstone Homes LLC............................ E 302 644-0300
  Lewes (G-5800)
Carl Deputy & Son Builders LLC............ G 302 284-3041
  Felton (G-3951)
Castle Care Inc...................................... G 302 947-2277
  Lewes (G-5808)
Chandlee Projects LLC.......................... G 717 542-5919
  Frankford (G-4084)
Charles A Zonko Builders Inc................ F 302 436-0222
  Selbyville (G-13497)
Charles R Reed..................................... G 302 284-3353
  Felton (G-3953)
Chuck Coleman.................................... G 302 537-2071
  Frankford (G-4090)
Commonwealth Construction................ F 302 654-6611
  Wilmington (G-15551)
Commonwealth Contruction Co............ E 302 654-6611
  Wilmington (G-15552)
Connell Construction Co....................... G 302 738-9428
  Newark (G-10307)
Country Builders Inc............................. G 302 735-5530
  Dover (G-2144)
Country Life Homes Milford De............ G 302 265-2257
  Milford (G-7841)
Cpr Construction Inc............................. G 302 322-5770
  Historic New Castle (G-4965)
Craftsman Builders of De...................... G 302 542-0731
  Laurel (G-5488)
D S Builders.. G 302 242-3308
  Hartly (G-4865)
Daves Builders Inc................................ G 302 539-4058
  Ocean View (G-12499)
Del Homes Inc...................................... F 302 730-1479
  Dover (G-2210)
Del Homes Inc...................................... F 302 697-8204
  Magnolia (G-6739)
Delaware Homes Inc............................ F 302 378-9510
  Townsend (G-13987)
Delmarva Builders Inc.......................... G 302 629-9123
  Bridgeville (G-692)
Delpa Builders LLC............................... F 302 731-7304
  New Castle (G-9043)
Deshong & Sons Contractors Inc.......... G 302 453-8500
  Newark (G-10517)
Dewson Construction Co...................... G 302 427-2250
  Wilmington (G-16038)
Dewson Construction Company............ E 302 427-2250
  Wilmington (G-16039)
Df Quillen Sons Inc DBA....................... G 302 227-7368
  Rehoboth Beach (G-12725)
Dimple Construction Inc....................... G 302 559-7535
  Bear (G-169)
Double Diamone Builders Inc............... F 302 945-2512
  Millsboro (G-8277)
Dsp Builders... G 302 422-3515
  Milford (G-7872)
Dvele Partners LLC............................... G 516 707-9357
  Dover (G-2396)
East Coast Builders Inc......................... F 302 629-3551
  Seaford (G-13165)
Edge Construction Corp........................ G 302 778-5200
  Wilmington (G-16288)
Empire Investments Inc......................... G 302 838-0631
  New Castle (G-9093)
Figgsy Builders..................................... G 302 875-2505
  Laurel (G-5512)
Gander Construction............................ G 302 424-4007
  Milford (G-7907)
Garrison Custom Homes....................... G 302 644-4008
  Lewes (G-6027)
Gemcraft Homes At Summercrest......... G 302 703-6763
  Rehoboth Beach (G-12767)

Graulich Builders.................................. G 302 313-4882
  Lewes (G-6053)
Green Diamond Builders Inc................. G 302 284-1177
  Felton (G-3981)
Grimes Construction.............................. G 302 462-6533
  Georgetown (G-4347)
Gulfstream Development Corp.............. G 302 539-6178
  Millville (G-8531)
H B P Inc.. E 302 378-9693
  Middletown (G-7186)
H H Builders Inc.................................... G 302 735-9900
  Dover (G-2640)
Handler Builders Inc............................. F 302 999-9200
  Wilmington (G-17046)
Handler Corporation............................. E 302 999-9200
  Wilmington (G-17047)
Harold Dutton Jr................................... G 302 644-2992
  Lewes (G-6079)
Henlopen Homes Inc............................ G 302 684-0860
  Lewes (G-6089)
Herring Creek Builders Inc................... G 302 684-3015
  Lewes (G-6092)
Hickory Hill Builders Inc....................... G 302 934-6109
  Dagsboro (G-1463)
Hoenen & Mitchell Inc.......................... G 302 645-6193
  Lewes (G-6094)
Hugh H Hickman & Sons Inc................ F 302 539-9741
  Bethany Beach (G-608)
Inland Salem Square LLC..................... F 302 472-9250
  Wilmington (G-17345)
J A Ribinsky Builders............................ F 302 542-7014
  Millsboro (G-8323)
J B S Construction LLC......................... G 302 349-5705
  Greenwood (G-4641)
J I Beiler Homes LLC............................ G 302 697-1553
  Camden (G-857)
Jack Hickman Real Estate..................... F 302 539-8000
  Bethany Beach (G-611)
John Campanelli & Sons Inc................. G 302 239-8573
  Hockessin (G-5261)
Jsf Construction Co Inc......................... G 302 999-9573
  Wilmington (G-17605)
K Wolf Custom Homes Cnstr Inc........... G 302 598-2899
  Middletown (G-7258)
Karve Builders LLC............................... G 403 471-2285
  Camden (G-863)
Kaye Construction................................ G 302 628-6962
  Seaford (G-13246)
Kee Builders... G 302 376-9858
  Townsend (G-14022)
Kenneth E Barrett................................. G 302 270-6056
  Magnolia (G-6757)
Kokoszka & Sons Inc............................ G 302 328-4807
  New Castle (G-9288)
Lane Builders LLC................................ F 302 645-5555
  Lewes (G-6178)
Lane Builders Inc.................................. G 302 644-1182
  Harbeson (G-4705)
Layton Builders..................................... G 302 491-4571
  Milford (G-7974)
Lc Homes.. G 302 376-7004
  Townsend (G-14026)
Leisure Home Builders LLC.................. G 302 528-4873
  Smyrna (G-13800)
Lenape Builders Inc.............................. F 302 376-3971
  Smyrna (G-13801)
Leon N Weiner & Associates Inc........... D 302 656-1354
  Wilmington (G-17877)
Lessard Custom Homes........................ G 302 645-7444
  Lewes (G-6190)
Lifestyle Communities LLC................... E 302 376-3066
  Middletown (G-7301)

Lockhart Construction LLC................... G 302 753-5461
  Claymont (G-1224)
Lockwood Design Construction............ G 302 684-4844
  Milton (G-8655)
M L Parker Construction Inc................. F 302 798-8530
  Claymont (G-1227)
Mark Gosser... G 302 388-8395
  Hockessin (G-5299)
Marnie Custom Homes......................... G 302 616-2664
  Bethany Beach (G-618)
Marshall Kyle....................................... F 302 454-7838
  Newark (G-11338)
Messick and Johnson LLc..................... G 302 628-3111
  Seaford (G-13281)
Michael A Mekulski Genera.................. G 302 834-8260
  Newark (G-11401)
Mid Atlantic Builder Inc........................ F 302 344-7224
  Georgetown (G-4428)
Miken Builders Inc................................ E 302 537-4444
  Millville (G-8542)
Miracle Builders LLC............................. G 302 236-1351
  Georgetown (G-4429)
Montchanin Builders............................. F 302 472-7213
  Wilmington (G-18420)
Morgan Builders Inc............................. G 302 575-9943
  Wilmington (G-18444)
Morning Star Construction LLC............ G 302 539-0791
  Dagsboro (G-1483)
Nathan David Fretz.............................. G 302 218-3338
  Clayton (G-1390)
Noble Builders & Developers LL........... G 203 948-9396
  Lewes (G-6318)
Norman Johnson Builders.................... G 302 670-9201
  Ocean View (G-12552)
Nvr Inc... G 302 732-9900
  Dagsboro (G-1492)
Oak Construction.................................. G 302 703-2013
  Lewes (G-6324)
Parker Builders LLC.............................. G 302 398-6182
  Harrington (G-4808)
Pedro Rascon Cimarron........................ G 302 448-6806
  Frankford (G-4132)
Piccard Homes..................................... G 302 727-5145
  Rehoboth Beach (G-12891)
Precision Builders Inc........................... G 302 420-1391
  Bear (G-434)
Precision Hmes Rmdlg Group LLC....... G 302 293-0244
  Wilmington (G-19155)
Premier Builders Inc............................. G 302 999-8500
  Wilmington (G-19167)
Proline Builders LLC............................. G 302 956-0426
  Bridgeville (G-755)
R D Arnold Construction Inc................. G 610 255-4739
  Middletown (G-7495)
Rays Plumbing & Heating Svcs............ F 302 697-3936
  Felton (G-4013)
Restoration Guys LLC........................... G 302 542-4045
  Milford (G-8064)
Richard Y Johnson & Son Inc............... E 302 422-3732
  Lincoln (G-6696)
Rmm Builders LLC................................ G 302 983-0734
  Newark (G-11893)
Robert C Peoples Inc............................ D 302 834-5268
  Bear (G-463)
Rockland Builders Inc........................... F 302 995-6800
  Wilmington (G-19539)
Ryan Homes... G 302 491-4442
  Milford (G-8076)
SC&a Construction Inc.......................... E 302 478-6030
  Wilmington (G-19695)
Schell Bros At Peninsula Lakes............. G 302 228-4488
  Millsboro (G-8455)

Employee Codes: A=Over 500 employees, B=251-500
C=101-250, D=51-100, E=20-50, F=10-19, G=1-9

2024 Harris Directory of Delaware Businesses

CONSTRUCTION: Single-family Housing, New

Schell Brothers .... G 302 242-8334
  Georgetown *(G-4501)*
Schell Brothers LLC .... E 302 226-1994
  Rehoboth Beach *(G-12948)*
Shellys of Delaware Inc .... G 302 656-3337
  Wilmington *(G-19794)*
Signature Builders .... G 302 331-9095
  Felton *(G-4029)*
Sj Builders LLC .... G 302 242-8222
  Hartly *(G-4908)*
Summer Hill Custom Home Bldr .... G 302 462-5853
  Ocean View *(G-12572)*
T J Lane Construction Inc .... G 302 734-1099
  Dover *(G-3638)*
Three Little Builders .... G 302 317-1969
  Middletown *(G-7640)*
Tidemark LLC .... G 302 747-7737
  Dover *(G-3684)*
Tlbc LLC .... G 302 797-8700
  Lewes *(G-6564)*
Toback Builders .... G 302 644-1015
  Lewes *(G-6566)*
Toll Njx 4 Corp .... F 302 652-3252
  Wilmington *(G-20348)*
Tolton Builders Inc .... G 302 239-5357
  Hockessin *(G-5406)*
Tom Rainey Builders LLC .... G 302 381-5339
  Lewes *(G-6569)*
Tru General Contractor Inc .... G 302 354-0553
  Wilmington *(G-20441)*
Turnstone Builders LLC .... F 302 227-8876
  Rehoboth Beach *(G-12998)*
Turnstone Holdings LLC .... F 302 227-8876
  Rehoboth Beach *(G-12999)*
U and I Builders Inc .... G 302 697-1645
  Dover *(G-3738)*
Vanguard Construction Inc .... G 302 697-9187
  Dover *(G-3773)*
Vari Development Corp .... G 302 479-5571
  Wilmington *(G-20571)*
Village Developers Inc .... G 302 732-3400
  Dagsboro *(G-1524)*
Warfel Construction Co Inc .... E 302 422-8927
  Milford *(G-8142)*
Wilson Construction Co Inc .... G 302 856-3115
  Georgetown *(G-4574)*
Wn Builders Inc .... G 302 253-8640
  Georgetown *(G-4577)*
Woods General Contracting Inc .... G 302 856-4047
  Georgetown *(G-4579)*
Wtm Builders .... G 302 398-9522
  Harrington *(G-4850)*
Yencer Builders Inc .... G 302 284-9977
  Felton *(G-4038)*
Yoder and Sons Cnstr LLC .... F 302 349-0444
  Greenwood *(G-4678)*

CONSTRUCTION: Swimming Pools

Cannon Spas .... G 302 628-9404
  Seaford *(G-13101)*
Chas Pools Inc .... F 302 376-5840
  Middletown *(G-6971)*
Clarks Glasgow Pools Inc .... E 302 834-0200
  New Castle *(G-8953)*
Clarks Swimming Pools Inc .... G 302 629-8835
  Seaford *(G-13123)*
Dover Pool & Patio Center Inc .... F 302 346-7665
  Dover *(G-2361)*
Dreamscape Design Cons LLC .... G 302 893-0984
  Newark *(G-10571)*
Imperial Gunite .... G 631 244-0073
  Wilmington *(G-17291)*
Pirate Pools LLC .... G 302 519-0624
  Lewes *(G-6371)*
Pool Man Inc .... G 302 737-8696
  Newark *(G-11712)*
Sum-R-Fun Pool Products Inc .... E 302 998-9288
  Wilmington *(G-20122)*
Swift Pools Inc .... E 302 738-9800
  Newark *(G-12142)*

CONSTRUCTION: Transmitting Tower, Telecommunication

Floleft LLC .... G 302 648-2088
  Dagsboro *(G-1448)*
Nicoin Telecom LLC .... E 800 914-6177
  Lewes *(G-6313)*

CONSTRUCTION: Truck & Automobile Assembly Plant

Maccari Motors .... G 302 563-3361
  Wilmington *(G-18065)*

CONSTRUCTION: Warehouse

Dan H Beachy & Sons Inc .... G 302 492-1493
  Hartly *(G-4866)*
H&B Express Logistics .... G 815 201-0915
  Dover *(G-2642)*
Reybold Construction Corp .... E 302 832-7100
  Bear *(G-455)*

CONSTRUCTION: Waste Water & Sewage Treatment Plant

Crimson Group LLC .... G 301 252-3779
  Newark *(G-10355)*
Desalitech Inc .... E 508 981-7950
  Wilmington *(G-16022)*
Jjid Inc .... E 302 836-0414
  Bear *(G-305)*

CONSULTING SVC: Business, NEC

280 Group LLC .... E 408 834-7518
  Dover *(G-1683)*
5linx .... G 302 981-2529
  Bear *(G-4)*
9222 Enterprises LLC .... G 888 551-1393
  Dover *(G-1691)*
Acuitive Inc .... G 214 738-1099
  Wilmington *(G-14246)*
Adept Consulting .... G 267 398-7449
  Wilmington *(G-14255)*
Aecom Usa Inc .... D 302 781-5963
  Newark *(G-9788)*
Aegis PM Group Inc .... G 302 456-0402
  Wilmington *(G-14295)*
Aesir Capital Management LP .... G 302 656-9161
  Wilmington *(G-14297)*
African Wood Inc .... G 302 884-6738
  Middletown *(G-6839)*
Allen Jarmon Enterprises Inc .... G 302 745-5122
  Rehoboth Beach *(G-12601)*
Alliance Data .... G 302 256-0853
  Wilmington *(G-14378)*
Allkare Inc .... G 302 212-0917
  Dover *(G-1772)*
Ambient Procurement Group LLC ...... F 718 925-7750
  Newark *(G-9841)*
Amsoft Corp .... G 859 351-7688
  Wilmington *(G-14463)*
Amsol Inc .... G 302 369-6969
  Newark *(G-9854)*
Analytics Realm LLC .... G 302 743-0342
  Newark *(G-9859)*
Anderson Rnee Charles Anderson ...... G 302 529-7845
  Wilmington *(G-14473)*
Anglin Cnsulting Solutions LLC .... F 302 406-0233
  Wilmington *(G-14484)*
Anthogo Enterprises .... G 302 378-0235
  Middletown *(G-6866)*
Aquila of Delaware Inc .... F 302 999-1106
  Bear *(G-42)*
Aria Solutions Inc .... G 302 453-8389
  Newark *(G-9902)*
Armodias LLC .... G 302 384-9794
  Wilmington *(G-14555)*
Artemundi LLC .... F 302 988-5002
  Wilmington *(G-14563)*
Ascent Technologies Inc .... G 302 491-0545
  Newark *(G-9919)*
Assoction Brds Thlgcal Educatn .... G 302 654-7770
  Wilmington *(G-14596)*
AST Sports Internacional LLC .... G 786 445-8081
  Wilmington *(G-14601)*
Atlantic Duncan Inc .... F 302 383-0740
  Newark *(G-9935)*
Attac Consulting Group LLC .... G 443 766-9079
  Frankford *(G-4065)*
Automation Alliance Group LLC ...... G 302 202-5433
  Middletown *(G-6887)*
Avery Enterprises LLC .... G 302 750-5468
  Newark *(G-9953)*
Aviant Cnsltng & Riva Pymnt .... G 302 584-0549
  Newark *(G-9954)*
Avs Solutions LLC .... G 302 562-0642
  Middletown *(G-6893)*
Axchem Holding Company .... G 336 632-0500
  Wilmington *(G-14679)*
B C Consulting .... G 215 534-3805
  Wilmington *(G-14696)*
B Rich Enterprises .... G 302 530-6865
  Middletown *(G-6895)*
Bangus Business Services .... G 302 266-7285
  Newark *(G-9980)*
Base-2 Solutions LLC .... D 202 215-2152
  Lewes *(G-5735)*
Bastianelli Group Inc .... G 302 658-1500
  Newark *(G-9989)*
Be Right There Consulting LLC .... G 302 727-5047
  Newark *(G-10001)*
Berkelyn Inc .... G 360 609-4981
  Lewes *(G-5755)*
Betsson US Corp .... G 800 316-6660
  Dover *(G-1921)*
Biotech Mentor LLC .... E 617 460-4983
  Dover *(G-1940)*
Bishop Enterprises Corporation .... G 302 379-2884
  Wilmington *(G-14897)*
Breylacom .... G 302 731-7456
  Newark *(G-10083)*
Bridgeforce Inc .... G 302 325-7100
  Newark *(G-10085)*
Bruce Palmer LLC .... G 302 654-1135
  Rehoboth Beach *(G-12659)*
Bullseye Entertainment Tech Co .... E 302 924-5034
  Dover *(G-1992)*
Business Intrface Wrkfrce Svcs .... E 302 660-7123
  Wilmington *(G-15159)*
By Mail Eric Graham Intl .... G 816 368-1641
  Wilmington *(G-15164)*
Byrd Group Delaware .... G 302 757-8300
  New Castle *(G-8905)*
C and L Bradford and Assoc .... G 302 529-8566
  Wilmington *(G-15174)*

PRODUCTS & SERVICES SECTION

CONSULTING SVC: Business, NEC

C S Consultants .... G 302 623-4144
  Newark (G-10115)
Cannon Cold Storage LLC .... E 302 337-5500
  Bridgeville (G-680)
Capstone Homes LLC .... F 302 644-0300
  Lewes (G-5799)
Casus Consulting LLC .... G 972 532-6357
  Middletown (G-6963)
Cecon Group LLC .... G 302 994-8000
  Wilmington (G-15294)
Chance De Group LLC .... G 800 667-3082
  Newark (G-10187)
Charles Taylor Consulting Inc .... G 703 200-8057
  Milford (G-7822)
Chip Design Systems Inc .... F 302 494-6220
  Hockessin (G-5160)
CL Walton Enterprises LLC .... F 443 360-1120
  Wilmington (G-15459)
Clayton West LLC .... G 302 530-3492
  Rehoboth Beach (G-12674)
Cloud Cystems LLC .... F 815 797-9929
  Middletown (G-6997)
Coach AK Enterprises LLC .... F 617 433-7560
  Middletown (G-7000)
Codeiscode Mktg Consulting LLC .... G 415 202-5303
  Wilmington (G-15515)
Community Consulting Corps .... G 614 348-7823
  Hockessin (G-5168)
Congruence Consulting Group .... G 320 290-6155
  Newark (G-10304)
Consulttive Rview Rhbilitation .... F 302 366-0356
  Newark (G-10310)
Core Construction LLC .... G 302 449-4186
  Smyrna (G-13687)
Countrmsres Asssssment SEC Expr .... G 302 322-9600
  Middletown (G-7015)
Critical Bs Holdings LLC .... G 833 479-5375
  Wilmington (G-15706)
Cruitcast Inc .... G 856 693-3869
  Smyrna (G-13689)
Crx Consulting LLC .... G 302 864-7377
  Rehoboth Beach (G-12706)
Crx Consulting LLC .... G 302 864-7377
  Rehoboth Beach (G-12707)
Cyclops Net Inc .... G 844 979-0222
  Camden (G-812)
Cynash Inc .... G 415 850-7842
  Wilmington (G-15752)
De Novo Corporation .... E 302 234-7407
  Wilmington (G-15839)
Dearng Safety Office .... G 302 326-7100
  New Castle (G-9006)
Decennium Management Group .... G 302 600-3644
  Dover (G-2205)
Delaware Consulting Servi .... G 302 945-7936
  Lewes (G-5893)
Delaware Innovation Space Inc .... G 302 695-2201
  Wilmington (G-15933)
Delaware Small Bus Dev Ctr .... G 302 831-1555
  Georgetown (G-4283)
Delaware Small Bus Dev Ctr .... F 302 831-1555
  Newark (G-10481)
Design Tribe Republic LLC .... F 302 918-5279
  Wilmington (G-16027)
Diff Consulting LLC .... G 302 689-3979
  Wilmington (G-16062)
Dover East LLC .... F 302 330-3040
  Rehoboth Beach (G-12734)
Drone Consulting Pros Inc .... G 561 766-5176
  Claymont (G-1124)
Dynamic Support Services Inc .... G 202 820-3113
  Wilmington (G-16230)

Eancenter Telecom LLC .... G 302 450-4514
  Dover (G-2404)
Edgerite Inc .... G 302 404-6665
  Dover (G-2421)
Eighth Street Enterprises LLC .... G 302 376-8222
  Middletown (G-7086)
Elevate RCM Consulting .... G 484 655-8733
  Wilmington (G-16357)
Ementum Inc .... G 866 984-1999
  Milton (G-8617)
Encross LLC .... F 302 351-2593
  Wilmington (G-16407)
Endocrinology Consultant .... G 302 734-2782
  Dover (G-2448)
Envision Consulting LLC .... G 302 658-9027
  Wilmington (G-16444)
Evans Act Inc .... G 302 792-0355
  Wilmington (G-16480)
Fbh Business Consulting LLC .... G 267 266-8149
  Wilmington (G-16563)
Fluttering Butterfly LLC .... G 267 974-7812
  Dover (G-2521)
Foris Solutions LLC .... G 302 343-6396
  Wilmington (G-16694)
Freedom Tech Consulting LLC .... G 215 485-7383
  Middletown (G-7140)
Future Gold Technology Inc .... F 302 786-1388
  Wilmington (G-16777)
Galerie Media Inc .... G 917 685-4168
  Newark (G-10799)
Genex Strategies .... G 302 356-1522
  Dover (G-2570)
Georgetown Construction Co .... G 302 856-7601
  Georgetown (G-4337)
GIERD INC .... E 206 289-0011
  Wilmington (G-16858)
Gkg Consulting LLC .... D 888 918-0718
  Wilmington (G-16872)
GLA Company Ltd .... F 502 267-7522
  Wilmington (G-16876)
Global Dev Partners Inc .... G 480 330-7931
  Wilmington (G-16887)
Global Partner LLC .... G 646 630-9128
  Wilmington (G-16893)
Goldstone & Associates LLC .... G 302 857-0051
  Wilmington (G-16916)
Good Home Solutions LLC .... G 302 540-3190
  Wilmington (G-16921)
Government Affairs .... G 302 226-2704
  Rehoboth Beach (G-12774)
Greanex .... G 606 477-9768
  Wilmington (G-16956)
Gusher .... G 302 803-5900
  Wilmington (G-17008)
H Clemons Consulting Inc .... G 302 295-5097
  Wilmington (G-17016)
Hatch Consulting .... G 302 658-4380
  Wilmington (G-17072)
Hedgeforce LLC .... G 305 600-0085
  Newark (G-10944)
Highdef Transportation LLC .... G 610 212-8596
  Bear (G-272)
Hobday Group Ltd .... G 302 337-9567
  Bridgeville (G-711)
Hydropac .... G 410 306-6345
  Seaford (G-13218)
I AM Consulting Group Inc .... F 302 521-4999
  Bear (G-280)
Iayam Financial LLC .... G 800 585-5315
  Dover (G-2715)
Incorporators USA LLC .... G 800 441-5940
  Wilmington (G-17303)

Incredible One Enterprises LLC .... G 888 801-5794
  Newark (G-11010)
Industry ARC .... F 614 588-8538
  Wilmington (G-17318)
Infant Solutions .... E 302 250-4336
  Wilmington (G-17319)
Inrg of Delaware Inc .... G 302 369-1412
  Lewes (G-6127)
Integrity Brands LLC .... G 302 853-0709
  Seaford (G-13224)
Intelligent Signage Inc .... G 302 762-4100
  Wilmington (G-17372)
International Cloud Company .... G 858 472-9648
  Dover (G-2747)
International Spine Pain .... G 302 478-7001
  Wilmington (G-17390)
Intus Smartcities Inc .... F 403 542-8879
  Wilmington (G-17403)
Ione Group LLC .... G 302 584-5377
  Wilmington (G-17413)
Ipwe Inc .... E 214 438-0820
  Dover (G-2751)
Jackson Contracting Inc .... F 302 678-2011
  Dover (G-2763)
Jbiza Enterprises LLC .... G 302 764-3389
  Wilmington (G-17505)
Jfm Enterprises LLC .... G 302 836-4107
  Newark (G-11111)
Jgreenbergconsulting LLC .... F 610 572-2729
  Magnolia (G-6753)
JLW Consulting LLC .... G 302 653-7283
  Smyrna (G-13781)
Jmt Services Inc .... G 302 407-5978
  Wilmington (G-17558)
JR Gettier & Associates Inc .... E 302 478-0911
  Wilmington (G-17600)
Kaiser Time Inc .... G 646 473-1640
  Wilmington (G-17635)
Kaleo Inc .... G 302 376-0327
  Townsend (G-14021)
Kencrest Services .... G 302 735-1664
  Dover (G-2841)
Kfs Strategic MGT Svcs LLC .... G 302 757-6631
  Newark (G-11167)
Klm Consulting LLC .... G 302 763-2174
  Hockessin (G-5271)
KMC Management LLC .... G 866 943-2205
  Wilmington (G-17743)
Knight Insur Consulting Group .... G 973 704-1112
  Newark (G-11197)
Kramer Group LLC .... G 717 368-2117
  Wilmington (G-17750)
Krenee LLC .... G 302 200-1025
  Wilmington (G-17755)
L & K Real Estate LLC .... F 484 410-4898
  Bear (G-337)
Latam Corporate Services LLC .... F 301 375-0714
  Dover (G-2906)
LCB Consulting Inc .... G 302 836-1396
  Bear (G-341)
Leiters Tools LLC .... G 302 538-3284
  New Castle (G-9304)
Lens Tolic LLC .... G 800 343-5697
  Hockessin (G-5280)
Lig Energy Solutions LLC .... C 646 918-8232
  Wilmington (G-17907)
Lisa Mathena Group .... F 302 645-4804
  Milton (G-8654)
Lityx LLC .... G 888 548-9947
  Wilmington (G-17948)
Longwood Assets LLC .... G 617 906-8882
  Middletown (G-7312)

Employee Codes: A=Over 500 employees, B=251-500
C=101-250, D=51-100, E=20-50, F=10-19, G=1-9

2024 Harris Directory of
Delaware Businesses

CONSULTING SVC: Business, NEC

Company	Code	Phone
Marcon John Solutions Inc — Wilmington (G-18122)	G	302 295-4806
Marquis Consulting LLC — Lewes (G-6245)	G	480 438-5582
Mayr Enterprises LLC — Delmar (G-1618)	G	302 846-2999
MB Store LLC — Wilmington (G-18211)	F	425 310-2574
Mc Creative Group — Millsboro (G-8370)	F	302 348-8977
Medevice Services LLC — Dover (G-3051)	G	877 202-1588
Mefta LLC — Wilmington (G-18260)	F	804 433-3566
Meta Mind Global Corp LLC — Dover (G-3069)	G	267 471-3616
Milieux LLC — Wilmington (G-18356)	G	302 770-5868
Mill Wilmington LLC — Wilmington (G-18358)	G	302 218-7527
Millenium Services LLC — Middletown (G-7370)	F	888 507-9473
Mjp Enterprises — Middletown (G-7374)	G	302 584-4736
Mrt Enterprises Inc — Clayton (G-1389)	G	302 593-3070
Mss Energy Holdings LLC — Wilmington (G-18478)	G	212 231-2505
My Benefit Advisor LLC — Wilmington (G-18503)	G	302 588-7242
Nabstar Hospitality — Newark (G-11481)	G	302 453-1700
Nally Ventures Cnstr LLC — Ocean View (G-12550)	G	302 581-9243
Nanticoke Consulting Inc — Houston (G-5446)	G	302 245-3465
Nashco Enterprises Ltd — Wilmington (G-18536)	G	403 590-0846
Netragy LLC — Newark (G-11509)	G	973 846-7018
Netwerx LLC — Wilmington (G-18594)	G	732 245-8521
New Castle Cnty Shoppers Guide — New Castle (G-9406)	G	302 325-6600
New Covenant Elec Svcs Inc — Middletown (G-7398)	G	302 454-1165
Novitex Intermediate LLC — Wilmington (G-18697)	A	302 278-0867
Nr Hudson Consulting Inc — Laurel (G-5571)	G	302 875-5276
Nt Marine Apps LLC — Wilmington (G-18706)	G	561 329-3209
Nucar Consulting Inc — Odessa (G-12585)	E	302 696-6000
Oasm Corp — Dover (G-3213)	F	203 679-9124
Office Prtners Xiv Bllvue Pk L — Wilmington (G-18749)	G	302 691-2100
Olympus Consulting LLC — Smyrna (G-13842)	G	302 353-7329
On Point Partners LLC — Wilmington (G-18775)	G	302 655-5606
Orchard Park Group Inc — New Castle (G-9436)	G	302 356-1139
Oversight Board LLC — Wilmington (G-18841)	G	302 898-2599
Owcp Claims Consulting LLC — Hockessin (G-5331)	G	302 559-7501
Patent Information Users Group — Newark (G-11635)	F	302 660-3275
Patterson 3 Inv Group LLC — Dover (G-3283)	G	302 469-4783
Peddie John — Newark (G-11653)	G	302 838-8771
Pencader Consulting Group — Newark (G-11658)	G	302 454-8004
Perastic LLC — Wilmington (G-18967)	G	917 592-4219
Performance Materials Na Inc — Wilmington (G-18977)	A	302 892-7009
Pineal Consulting Group LLC — Dover (G-3324)	G	302 446-3794
Placidify Inc — Lewes (G-6376)	E	833 752-2434
Play By Play LLC — Wilmington (G-19074)	G	302 703-7670
Plenteous Consulting LLC — Claymont (G-1264)	G	724 325-1660
Poc Inc — Dover (G-3345)	F	415 853-4762
Prevail Trial Consultants LLC — Wilmington (G-19185)	F	302 442-7836
Princeton Coml Holdings LLC — Newark (G-11746)	G	302 449-4836
Prism Events Inc — Newark (G-11752)	G	424 252-1070
Pro Benefits Plus — Milford (G-8052)	G	302 683-5546
Pro Physical Therapy — Milford (G-8054)	G	302 422-6670
Project Widgets Inc — Wilmington (G-19226)	G	302 439-3414
Protect Intl Risk Sfety Svcs C — Wilmington (G-19234)	G	877 736-0805
Providge Consulting LLC — Wilmington (G-19238)	E	888 927-6583
Puma Energy US Inc — Wilmington (G-19256)	G	787 966-7929
Qualdent LLC — Wilmington (G-19282)	G	856 642-4078
Quinteccent Inc — Selbyville (G-13595)	G	443 838-5447
Rallypoint Solutions LLC — Wilmington (G-19322)	F	302 543-8087
Reading Assist Institute — Wilmington (G-19362)	G	302 425-4080
Real World Endo — Milton (G-8693)	G	302 827-4816
Recadia Corp Llc — Wilmington (G-19375)	G	866 671-1280
Redrum City Productions — New Castle (G-9516)	G	313 389-6836
Renaissance Square LLC — Dover (G-3452)	G	302 943-5118
Rheumatology Consultants — Milford (G-8065)	G	302 491-6659
Rockledge Global Partners Ltd — Wilmington (G-19543)	G	800 659-1102
Rulesware LLC — Newark (G-11926)	G	302 293-4077
Rutman Enterprises — Wilmington (G-19596)	G	302 777-5298
Rxbenefits Inc — Lewes (G-6435)	G	724 525-9080
S S I Group LLC — Lewes (G-6437)	G	877 778-7099
SA Ryan LLC — Smyrna (G-13875)	G	302 757-6440
Safs International Group LLC — Wilmington (G-19630)	G	954 707-4627
Sagacious Works — Wilmington (G-19631)	F	609 251-9265
Sandler Occptnal Mdicine Assoc — Newark (G-11941)	G	302 369-0171
Santora CPA Group Pa — Newark (G-11945)	E	302 737-6200
Schatz Messick Enterprises LLC — Harrington (G-4827)	G	302 398-8646
Schiff Group LLC — Bethany Beach (G-639)	G	301 325-1359
SD&I Enterprises LLC — Wilmington (G-19718)	G	302 407-6591
Sentinel-Sg LLC — Wilmington (G-19754)	G	580 458-9184
Service Rsource Group Intl LLC — Wilmington (G-19762)	G	832 646-8756
Smp Enterprises Inc — Newark (G-12042)	G	302 252-5331
Social Enterprises — Newark (G-12048)	G	302 526-4800
SOS Call Center Inc — Newark (G-12057)	G	302 319-5988
Spence Holding — Wilmington (G-19960)	F	973 392-1218
Spine Group LLC — Wilmington (G-19964)	G	302 595-3030
Sqs Global Solutions LLC — Wilmington (G-19984)	F	302 691-9682
Strategy House Inc — Newark (G-12106)	G	302 658-1500
Suburban Waste Services Inc — Wilmington (G-20117)	G	302 661-0161
Sussex Plmnary Endocrine Cnslt — Rehoboth Beach (G-12985)	G	302 249-9970
Systems Tech & Science LLC — Dagsboro (G-1513)	G	703 757-2010
Ta Management & Consulting — Bear (G-523)	G	302 317-1538
Tade Info Tech Solutions — Newark (G-12154)	G	302 832-1449
Tappedn Holdings LLC — Dover (G-3651)	G	404 877-2525
Tdm Pharmaceutical RES Inc — Newark (G-12165)	G	302 832-1008
Tekmen Group — Rehoboth Beach (G-12992)	G	302 381-0161
Tepuyi LLC — Dover (G-3670)	F	954 991-0749
Thrive Agritech — Claymont (G-1313)	F	800 205-7216
Tinman Enterprises LLC — Camden Wyoming (G-983)	G	302 698-1630
Tle Ventures Ltd — Dover (G-3691)	G	800 794-3867
Trade & Consulting Group Corp — Wilmington (G-20383)	C	302 477-9800
Treehouse Wellness Center LLC — Wilmington (G-20407)	G	302 893-1001
Trellist Inc — Wilmington (G-20408)	F	302 593-1432
Trinity Enterprises LLC — Claymont (G-1317)	G	302 449-1301
Trinity Gold Consulting LLC — Wilmington (G-20426)	G	302 498-9063
Trio Enterprises LLC — Townsend (G-14085)	G	302 832-5575
Txe Global LLC — Wilmington (G-20473)	G	302 409-0234
Uptrend Consulting & Creative — Wilmington (G-20538)	G	484 840-1200
Vega Consulting Inc — Wilmington (G-20577)	D	302 636-5401
Velocity Maint Solutions LLC — New Castle (G-9668)	E	844 538-8349
Veritas Consultant Group LLC — Newark (G-12314)	G	302 893-9794

PRODUCTS & SERVICES SECTION

CONSULTING SVC: Management

Victor A Maldonado .... G 302 420-9749
Saint Georges *(G-13040)*

Virtual Business Entps LLC .... G 302 472-9100
Wilmington *(G-20633)*

Visa Europe Services LLC .... E 302 658-7581
Wilmington *(G-20636)*

Vtms LLC .... G 302 264-9094
Dover *(G-3813)*

Womens Healthcare Consultants .... G 443 553-1398
Newark *(G-12396)*

Workbetterai Inc .... F 805 825-5216
Dover *(G-3870)*

Wrpatrick Enterprises LLC .... G 302 988-1061
Selbyville *(G-13620)*

Xerimis Inc .... G 215 815-1706
Selbyville *(G-13621)*

Xpert Tek Solutions Inc .... G 302 724-4857
Dover *(G-3882)*

Yorston and Co LLC .... G 302 415-1925
Middletown *(G-7748)*

Zcorp Property Consultants LLC .... G 302 864-8581
Georgetown *(G-4582)*

Zieta Technologies LLC .... E 302 252-5249
Wilmington *(G-20961)*

CONSULTING SVC: Educational

Holistic Elevation LLC .... G 302 278-0026
Bear *(G-277)*

Pyramid Educational Cons .... E 302 368-2515
New Castle *(G-9502)*

CONSULTING SVC: Financial Management

Asset Key Management LLC .... G 302 505-4603
Felton *(G-3942)*

BEC Capital LLC .... G 917 658-5867
Wilmington *(G-14810)*

Corrado Management Svcs LLC .... E 302 225-0700
New Castle *(G-8977)*

Espino LLC .... F 855 506-3862
Lewes *(G-5975)*

Glen Playa Inc .... G 302 703-7512
Lewes *(G-6037)*

Kubera Global Solutions LLC .... G 480 241-5124
Wilmington *(G-17762)*

Lau & Assoc Ltd .... E 302 792-5955
Wilmington *(G-17821)*

Lutheran Community Services .... G 302 654-8886
Wilmington *(G-18031)*

Pallino Asset Management LLC .... G 302 378-0686
Middletown *(G-7423)*

Walnut Green Asset MGT LL .... G 302 689-3798
Wilmington *(G-20673)*

CONSULTING SVC: Human Resource

Adex Corporation .... G 703 618-9670
Dover *(G-1717)*

ADP Pacific Inc .... E 302 657-4060
Wilmington *(G-14260)*

Armehtech Solutions LLC .... D 302 309-9645
Wilmington *(G-14554)*

Avontro Inc .... G 510 766-2803
Wilmington *(G-14674)*

Benepass Inc .... G 917 540-2391
Claymont *(G-1057)*

Blackwell Hr Solutions .... G 202 246-0084
Wilmington *(G-14949)*

Compete Hr Inc .... E 310 989-9857
Wilmington *(G-15569)*

Congruence Consulting Group .... G 320 290-6155
Newark *(G-10304)*

Connecting Generations Inc .... F 302 656-2122
Wilmington *(G-15599)*

Corporate Loyalty LLC .... G 732 455-9266
Newark *(G-10327)*

Even & Odd Minds LLC .... F 949 246-4789
Claymont *(G-1138)*

Even & Odd Minds LLC .... F 619 663-7284
Wilmington *(G-16482)*

Evolution Cloud Services Inc .... G 516 507-4026
Dover *(G-2469)*

Franklin Kennet LLC .... G 302 655-6536
Wilmington *(G-16729)*

Mohandis Enterprises LLC .... G 302 261-2821
Lewes *(G-6287)*

Oyster HR Americas Inc .... C 912 219-2356
Wilmington *(G-18846)*

Oyster HR Inc .... B 912 219-2356
Wilmington *(G-18847)*

Skillfi LLC .... G 469 701-9614
Dover *(G-3571)*

Smartprofyl LLC .... G 832 412-5803
Middletown *(G-7578)*

Steneral Consulting Inc .... E 302 721-6124
Wilmington *(G-20050)*

Talent Ola Inc .... E 732 421-3216
Dover *(G-3645)*

Telus Intl Holdg USA Corp .... G 720 726-0677
Wilmington *(G-20270)*

Weelwork Inc .... G 800 546-8607
Claymont *(G-1335)*

CONSULTING SVC: Management

1st-Recruit LLC .... F 732 666-4106
Wilmington *(G-14117)*

A-To-Z Management LLC .... G 302 500-5230
Dover *(G-1699)*

AA Smith & Associates LLC .... F 973 477-3052
Middletown *(G-6826)*

Above and Beyond Coverage LLC .... E 201 417-5189
Wilmington *(G-14207)*

Access Purchasing Network Inc .... G
Lewes *(G-5651)*

Arbiter Inc .... G 404 939-2826
Newark *(G-9898)*

Arm Chair Scouts LLC .... F 315 360-8692
Wilmington *(G-14552)*

Aston Digital LLC .... E 323 286-4365
Lewes *(G-5709)*

Ath Solutions LLC .... G 888 861-6657
Newark *(G-9930)*

Atom Tech Inc .... G 510 789-3045
Middletown *(G-6885)*

Atrifico LLC .... G 302 858-0161
Rehoboth Beach *(G-12617)*

Avenue Montaigne Inc .... F 310 926-6678
Wilmington *(G-14667)*

B&P Brown & Partners Corp .... G 302 703-0522
Lewes *(G-5732)*

Base-2 Solutions LLC .... D 202 215-2152
Lewes *(G-5735)*

Beane Assoc Inc .... G 302 559-1452
Wilmington *(G-14803)*

Beyond Expected LLC .... E 302 384-1205
Claymont *(G-1061)*

Big Tomorrow LLC .... F 650 714-3912
Wilmington *(G-14883)*

Bingebuilder Inc .... E 415 529-8306
Rehoboth Beach *(G-12644)*

Biobx Ltd .... G 626 898-5814
Middletown *(G-6920)*

Biomarker Associates Inc .... F 302 239-7962
Newark *(G-10035)*

Bless Ya Hart Cnslting Group L .... F 844 748-9017
Wilmington *(G-14955)*

Blue Dmnd Hldg Investments LLC .... G 302 588-8946
Wilmington *(G-14965)*

Bradsworth Digital Solutions .... G 630 200-2251
Wilmington *(G-15033)*

Brim Prtners Cnslting Group In .... G 657 234-7424
Wilmington *(G-15117)*

Browns Unlimited 4u LLC .... G 800 940-5880
Wilmington *(G-15131)*

C-Stacks Inc .... G 617 480-2555
Wilmington *(G-15179)*

Cast .... G 781 245-2212
Newark *(G-10160)*

Clms LLC .... G 703 629-3231
Rehoboth Beach *(G-12679)*

Cloud Financial Corporation .... G 845 729-5513
Wilmington *(G-15489)*

Cloud Services Solutions Inc .... E 888 335-3132
Wilmington *(G-15491)*

Conducerent Incorporated .... G 302 543-8525
Wilmington *(G-15588)*

Connectnow Vrtual Call Ctr LLC .... E 888 226-4130
Wilmington *(G-15602)*

Core Value Global LLC .... G 908 312-4070
Wilmington *(G-15641)*

CR&us LLC .... G 678 429-6293
Newark *(G-10342)*

Crimson Strategy Group LLP .... G 302 503-5698
Dover *(G-2159)*

Csi Solutions LLC .... F 202 506-7573
Newark *(G-10360)*

Dane & Cash Enterprise LLC .... F 302 281-4031
Wilmington *(G-15779)*

Dduberry LLC .... G 703 798-5280
Newark *(G-10398)*

Decisivedge LLC .... D 302 299-1570
Newark *(G-10404)*

Defendant Data Solutions LLC .... G 302 440-3042
Wilmington *(G-15855)*

Delaware Property Mgmt Co LLC .... G 302 366-0208
Newark *(G-10472)*

Delaware State Education Assn .... F 302 734-5834
Dover *(G-2263)*

Dewitt & Associates LLC .... G 302 226-0521
Rehoboth Beach *(G-12723)*

Diablo Works LLC .... E 302 559-2118
Wilmington *(G-16046)*

Diga Funding LLC .... G 404 631-7127
Dover *(G-2295)*

Divinity Assets LLC .... D 323 508-4130
Dover *(G-2310)*

DJT Operations LLC .... G 302 498-9070
Wilmington *(G-16102)*

Dreamville LLC .... G 662 524-0917
Lewes *(G-5935)*

Dss Sstnable Solutions USA Inc .... E 800 532-7233
Wilmington *(G-16184)*

Dynamic Devices LLC .... F 302 994-2401
Wilmington *(G-16228)*

East Coast Computer Cons .... G 302 945-5089
Millsboro *(G-8279)*

Edmonds Business Ventures LLC .... G 302 772-9112
Newark *(G-10610)*

Erban Mndset Lfstyle Sltons In .... F 407 608-0134
Wilmington *(G-16454)*

Evander Grey Group LLC .... G 302 595-1402
Dover *(G-2467)*

Fabrics and Textiles LLC .... G 507 369-2641
Wilmington *(G-16524)*

Factori Inc .... G 682 392-3913
Wilmington *(G-16526)*

Fbh Business Consulting LLC .... G 267 266-8149
Wilmington *(G-16563)*

CONSULTING SVC: Management

Company	Code	Phone
Femmepal Corporation — Lewes (G-5993)	G	888 406-0804
Financial Services — Wilmington (G-16609)	E	302 478-4707
Five Sixty Enterprise LLC — Wilmington (G-16653)	E	302 268-6530
G5 Cyber Security (usa) Inc — Middletown (G-7148)	E	302 570-0905
Gateway International 360 LLC — Bear (G-246)	F	302 250-4990
GIERD INC — Wilmington (G-16858)	E	206 289-0011
Global Infrstrcture Sltons Inc — Dover (G-2591)	G	808 381-3666
Goldenpgsus It Cnslting Svcs L — Newark (G-10863)	G	804 742-0710
Gravity-Techinc LLC — Lewes (G-6054)	F	346 258-1597
Gredell & Associates PA — Newark (G-10887)	G	302 996-9500
Green Interest Enterprises LLC — Dover (G-2624)	G	228 355-0708
Green River Consulting LLC — Hockessin (G-5228)	G	302 494-4497
Grofos International LLC — Newark (G-10901)	G	302 635-4805
Gulf Development Partners LLC — Wilmington (G-17005)	G	646 334-1245
Gwp Group LLC — Newark (G-10910)	E	888 217-4497
Heavenly Effects LLC — Dover (G-2667)	G	302 446-3521
Hnh Holdings LLC — Dover (G-2683)	G	415 548-3871
Howard Morris Group LLC — Dover (G-2698)	G	877 296-4726
I Need It I Want It LLC — Wilmington (G-17249)	G	888 299-1341
Ibr Group Inc — Newark (G-10992)	F	610 986-8545
Ignis Group LLC — Lewes (G-6115)	E	302 645-7400
IMG Universe LLC — Wilmington (G-17283)	G	212 774-6704
In Wilmington Mktg Group Inc — Wilmington (G-17294)	G	302 495-9456
Independent School MGT Inc — Wilmington (G-17310)	E	302 656-4944
Indus Insights US Inc — Wilmington (G-17313)	G	312 238-9815
Instellars Globl Cnsulting Inc — Wilmington (G-17359)	G	302 613-4379
Intellectual LLC — Dover (G-2743)	F	202 769-1986
Intellgent Sltions Aliance LLC — Claymont (G-1187)	E	754 300-0051
Interfacing Bus Solutions Inc — Wilmington (G-17382)	G	514 962-1344
Intrinsic Partners LLC — Wilmington (G-17401)	F	610 388-0853
Intrinsic Realty LLC — Middletown (G-7230)	G	302 425-1025
Ipwe Inc — Dover (G-2751)	E	214 438-0820
Iris Diagnostics Incorporated — Dover (G-2752)	F	877 292-4747
J & S - LOE Incorporated — Middletown (G-7234)	G	302 608-7858
Johnston Associates — Newark (G-11121)	G	302 521-2984
Jolttek Inc — Newark (G-11123)	G	302 204-7629
Joseph J Sheeran Inc — New Castle (G-9266)	E	302 324-0200
Kasmo Cloud Inc — Lewes (G-6161)	G	302 319-9952
Katu Software Global LLC — Wilmington (G-17667)	F	302 803-5330
Kelmar Associates LLC — Wilmington (G-17681)	D	781 213-6926
Kirk & Associates LLC — Christiana (G-1002)	F	302 444-4733
Kortech Consulting Inc — Bear (G-333)	F	302 559-4612
Level Up Consulting Group Inc — Middletown (G-7296)	G	855 967-5550
Liberty Consultancy Firm LLC — Dover (G-2935)	E	302 493-4344
Lifesource Consulting Svcs LLC — Dover (G-2941)	F	302 257-6247
Limitless Consulting Mktg LLC — Newark (G-11261)	G	302 743-0520
Linda McCormick — Wilmington (G-17922)	G	443 987-2099
Lindell Partners LLC — Wilmington (G-17924)	G	773 269-0837
Lissner & Associates LLC — Wilmington (G-17932)	G	302 777-4620
Longo and Associates LLP — Wilmington (G-17985)	G	302 477-7500
Lorica Strategy Partners LLC — Lewes (G-6222)	G	301 535-8263
Lynne Fardell & Associates LLC — New Castle (G-9330)	G	302 276-1541
Mancon Inc — New Castle (G-9342)	G	302 395-5376
Markel and Associates LLC — Townsend (G-14031)	G	302 898-5684
Marlette Services Inc — Wilmington (G-18152)	G	302 358-2730
McCullough & Associates Inc — Wilmington (G-18226)	G	302 250-7679
Mellon Care Inc — Middletown (G-7339)	G	800 406-0281
Meta Mind Global Corp LLC — Dover (G-3069)	G	267 471-3616
Mid States Sales & Marketing — Wilmington (G-18336)	F	302 888-2475
MMS Enterprises LLC — Newark (G-11434)	G	888 786-9290
Morning Report Research Inc — Dover (G-3123)	G	302 730-3793
Moscova Enterprises Inc — Wilmington (G-18460)	F	347 973-2522
Mwidm Inc — Wilmington (G-18501)	E	302 298-0101
Ned Davis Associates Inc — Dover (G-3165)	G	302 670-5307
Neilson Associates Inc — Wilmington (G-18575)	F	610 793-2271
Neitsch Ltd Liability Company — Newark (G-11500)	G	708 634-8724
Network Design Technologies — Wilmington (G-18596)	E	610 991-2929
Nova RE & Bus Consulting LLC — Lewes (G-6321)	G	302 258-2193
Nx Level Marketing LLC — Bear (G-402)	G	215 880-4749
Ocean First Enterprises LLC — Wilmington (G-18741)	E	302 232-8547
Omninet International Inc — Wilmington (G-18769)	E	208 246-5022
Omniway Corporation — Newark (G-11586)	F	302 738-5076
Open Lanes-Solutions LLC — Wilmington (G-18795)	F	888 410-4207
Openexo Inc — Dover (G-3237)	F	617 965-5057
Opinr Inc — Wilmington (G-18804)	D	646 207-3000
Oracle Enterprises LLC — Wilmington (G-18810)	G	407 900-2828
Paul C Cunningham & Assoc LLC — Lewes (G-6355)	G	302 258-4163
Paxelax — Newark (G-11644)	G	302 722-7290
Perry and Associates Inc — Hockessin (G-5342)	F	302 898-2327
Phreesia Inc — Wilmington (G-19028)	D	651 983-0426
Pierce Multi Solutions LLC — Newark (G-11689)	G	302 609-7000
Pineal Consulting Group LLC — Dover (G-3324)	G	302 446-3794
Pllal International LLC — Wilmington (G-19079)	E	786 235-7800
Pot-Nets Bayside LLC — Millsboro (G-8433)	E	302 945-9300
Predictive Analytics Group — Newark (G-11724)	F	844 733-5724
Presidio Holdings LLC — Lewes (G-6388)	F	240 219-8351
Privado Inc — Dover (G-3374)	G	916 730-4522
Prolific Consultants LLC — Dover (G-3379)	G	302 219-0958
Quinteccent Inc — Selbyville (G-13595)	G	443 838-5447
Real Deals LLC — Wilmington (G-19365)	E	484 470-8582
Real World Endo — Wilmington (G-19371)	G	302 477-0960
Red Lion LLC — Wilmington (G-19386)	G	202 559-9365
Redleo Software Inc — Wilmington (G-19390)	F	302 691-9072
Registration LLC — Wilmington (G-19408)	G	877 955-7111
Resemble Ai Inc — Middletown (G-7516)	G	401 255-6004
Roxanne Rxnne Cnslting Group L — Dover (G-3488)	G	470 333-8553
S & S Mgnt Co LLC — Middletown (G-7531)	G	302 353-9249
SA Associates LLC — Wilmington (G-19616)	G	302 275-7359
Sabre Associates LLC — Wilmington (G-19619)	G	302 998-0100
Second Chance Solutions LLC — Wilmington (G-19726)	G	302 204-0551
Signature Square LLC — Lewes (G-6469)	G	866 216-5792
Speak Biz Consulting LLC — Wilmington (G-19952)	F	302 272-9294
Strategybrix LLC — Lewes (G-6516)	F	312 804-6768
Streamlners MGT Consulting LLC — Wilmington (G-20095)	G	864 884-5064
Sumthin3lse — Dover (G-3621)	G	302 272-5435
Sun-Ray Valley Investments LLC — Wilmington (G-20128)	G	302 406-1078
Symack Prof Svcs US Corp — Smyrna (G-13908)	F	469 607-6092
Tawkify Inc — Wilmington (G-20229)	G	415 549-1928

PRODUCTS & SERVICES SECTION

CONSULTING SVCS, BUSINESS: Systems Analysis Or Design

Techneplus Americas LLC .... G 678 200-4052
  Wilmington *(G-20253)*

Thomas B Davis .... G 302 692-0871
  Newark *(G-12191)*

Timtec LLC .... F 302 292-8500
  Newark *(G-12197)*

Title One & Associates Inc .... G 410 758-1831
  Ocean View *(G-12577)*

Tomi Inc .... G 650 488-3054
  Newark *(G-12208)*

TP It Group LLC .... G 302 444-0441
  Dover *(G-3709)*

Twinning LLC .... G 609 793-3510
  Wilmington *(G-20470)*

Tytrix Inc .... E 877 489-8749
  Dover *(G-3737)*

Uncharted Waters LLC .... E 302 213-6354
  Dover *(G-3747)*

Unique Creations By Chloe LLC .... E 855 942-0477
  Wilmington *(G-20517)*

Versapro Group LLC .... G 315 430-2775
  Wilmington *(G-20594)*

Veteran It Pro LLC .... F 302 824-3111
  Hockessin *(G-5418)*

Victoryconsulting LLC .... G 203 275-9398
  Wilmington *(G-20614)*

Virasoft Corporation .... G 281 851-9080
  Claymont *(G-1328)*

Virtual Talk Hub LLC .... E 302 406-0038
  Wilmington *(G-20635)*

Wallace Investments Group LLC .... G 323 407-2889
  Middletown *(G-7704)*

Willis North America Inc .... E 302 239-2416
  Hockessin *(G-5426)*

Woodson Ministries Inc .... G 512 350-9950
  Wilmington *(G-20887)*

Wyndham Group Inc .... G 704 905-9750
  Wilmington *(G-20907)*

Xander Group II LLC .... G 302 656-1950
  Wilmington *(G-20913)*

Yanci Brand LLC .... G 844 242-7263
  Wilmington *(G-20923)*

Yenaffit Inc .... G 302 650-4818
  Wilmington *(G-20926)*

Ywy Incorporated .... G 916 794-1607
  Wilmington *(G-20943)*

Zenith Mind Inc .... F 302 543-2075
  Wilmington *(G-20955)*

Zutz Risk Management .... G 302 658-8000
  Wilmington *(G-20969)*

CONSULTING SVCS, BUSINESS: Communications

Creativity Diversified LLC .... G 302 897-5961
  Middletown *(G-7021)*

Zeribon Holding Group LLC .... C 844 205-1999
  Dover *(G-3899)*

CONSULTING SVCS, BUSINESS: Energy Conservation

Cg Global MGT Solutions LLC .... F 215 735-3745
  Wilmington *(G-15321)*

Flexera Inc .... F 302 945-6870
  Harbeson *(G-4696)*

Generate Nb Fuel Cells LLC .... G 415 360-3063
  Wilmington *(G-16832)*

CONSULTING SVCS, BUSINESS: Environmental

Action Environmental Service .... G 302 798-3100
  Wilmington *(G-14241)*

Atlantic Resource Management .... G 302 539-2029
  Frankford *(G-4063)*

Atlantic Resource Management .... F 302 539-2029
  Frankford *(G-4064)*

Batta Inc .... F 302 737-3376
  Newark *(G-9991)*

Batta Environmental Assoc Inc .... E 302 737-3376
  Newark *(G-9992)*

Belluno Manager LLC .... G 650 395-8185
  Wilmington *(G-14824)*

Blue Planet .... G 410 977-3426
  Rehoboth Beach *(G-12645)*

Brightfields Inc .... E 302 656-9600
  Wilmington *(G-15113)*

Browne Consulting .... G 302 482-1410
  Wilmington *(G-15130)*

Capitol Environmental Svcs Inc .... G 302 652-8999
  Newark *(G-10136)*

Capitol Environmental Svcs Inc .... G 302 380-3737
  Newark *(G-10135)*

Cheryl Wagner .... G 302 635-7632
  Hockessin *(G-5158)*

Compliance Environmental Inc .... G 302 674-4427
  Dover *(G-2124)*

Cychet LLC .... F 929 265-8351
  Dover *(G-2175)*

Delaware Bay & River .... G 302 645-7861
  Lewes *(G-5889)*

Environmental Alliance Inc .... E 302 234-4400
  Wilmington *(G-16443)*

Environmental Consulting Svcs .... F 302 378-9881
  Middletown *(G-7103)*

Environmental Resources Inc .... G 302 436-9637
  Selbyville *(G-13534)*

Environmental Services Inc .... G 302 669-6812
  New Castle *(G-9098)*

Environmental Testing Inc .... G 302 378-5341
  Middletown *(G-7104)*

Envirotech Envmtl Consulting .... G 302 684-5201
  Lewes *(G-5963)*

Envirtech Enviromental Consltg .... G 302 645-6491
  Lewes *(G-5964)*

Erm Emerald US Inc .... A 302 651-8300
  Wilmington *(G-16460)*

Fshery Mid-Atlntic MGT Council .... F 302 674-2331
  Dover *(G-2540)*

Geo-Technology Associates Inc .... G 302 326-2100
  New Castle *(G-9163)*

Geosyntec Holdings LLC .... G 561 995-0900
  Wilmington *(G-16848)*

Green Standards LLC .... E 855 632-8036
  Dover *(G-2625)*

Ground/Water Trtmnt & Tech LLC ..... F 302 654-0206
  Wilmington *(G-16987)*

Gwantel Intl Corp Engrg & Tech .... G 302 377-6235
  Newark *(G-10909)*

Harvard Environmental Inc .... F 302 326-2333
  Bear *(G-265)*

Joseph T Hardy & Son Inc .... E 302 328-9457
  New Castle *(G-9268)*

Kathairos Solutions Us Inc .... E 855 285-2010
  Dover *(G-2833)*

Landmark Engineering Inc .... D 302 323-9377
  Newark *(G-11218)*

Mid-Atlantic Envmtl Labs Inc .... F 302 654-1340
  Historic New Castle *(G-5028)*

Moran Environmental Recovery .... G 302 322-6008
  New Castle *(G-9381)*

Scientific Chemical Solutions .... G 208 490-2125
  Wilmington *(G-19704)*

Six Angels Development Inc .... G 302 218-1548
  Wilmington *(G-19846)*

Stantec Consulting Svcs Inc .... G 302 395-1919
  Newark *(G-12085)*

Suffex Conservation .... G 302 856-2105
  Georgetown *(G-4529)*

Sustainable-Generation LLC .... F 917 678-6947
  Wilmington *(G-20165)*

Ten Bears Environmental LLC .... G 302 731-8633
  Newark *(G-12178)*

Terra Systems Inc .... E 302 798-9553
  Claymont *(G-1310)*

Tri State Waste Solutions .... G 302 323-0200
  Wilmington *(G-20410)*

Wik Associates Inc .... G 302 322-2558
  Newark *(G-12372)*

Woods Hole Group Inc .... E 302 222-6720
  Dover *(G-3867)*

CONSULTING SVCS, BUSINESS: Indl Development Planning

Hibner Group Inc .... G 717 281-1918
  Dover *(G-2676)*

CONSULTING SVCS, BUSINESS: Safety Training Svcs

10-4 Safety LLC .... G 847 997-5515
  Wilmington *(G-14100)*

Atlantic Training LLC .... F 302 464-0341
  Newark *(G-9938)*

Brodie Consulting Mick Group .... G 302 468-6425
  Bear *(G-83)*

Delaware Safety Council Inc .... G 302 276-0660
  New Castle *(G-9036)*

Fireside Partners Inc .... G 302 613-2165
  Dover *(G-2497)*

Marlen D Schlabach .... G 302 236-5394
  Delmar *(G-1617)*

CONSULTING SVCS, BUSINESS: Sys Engnrg, Exc Computer/ Prof

Batescainelli LLC .... G 202 618-2040
  Rehoboth Beach *(G-12624)*

Creative Micro Designs Inc .... G 302 456-5800
  Newark *(G-10349)*

Insight Engineering Solutions .... G 302 378-4842
  Townsend *(G-14018)*

Raad360 LLC .... F 855 722-3360
  Newark *(G-11812)*

Tek Electronics LLC .... G 302 449-6947
  Middletown *(G-7627)*

Tek Tree LLC .... F 302 368-2730
  Newark *(G-12174)*

CONSULTING SVCS, BUSINESS: Systems Analysis & Engineering

AC Group Inc .... G 201 840-5566
  Wilmington *(G-14211)*

Korn Consult Group US Inc .... G 304 933-5355
  Newark *(G-11200)*

Neitsch Ltd Liability Company .... G 708 634-8724
  Newark *(G-11500)*

Nestal Mdsphere Consulting LLC ...... G 302 404-6506
  Wilmington *(G-18588)*

Telgian Corporation .... E 480 753-5444
  Wilmington *(G-20267)*

CONSULTING SVCS, BUSINESS: Systems Analysis Or Design

Employee Codes: A=Over 500 employees, B=251-500
C=101-250, D=51-100, E=20-50, F=10-19, G=1-9

2024 Harris Directory of Delaware Businesses

CONSULTING SVCS, BUSINESS: Testing, Educational Or Personnel

Mentor Consultants Inc................................ G 610 566-4004
Wilmington *(G-18273)*

CONSULTING SVCS, BUSINESS: Testing, Educational Or Personnel

Aspira of Delaware Inc............................... G 302 292-1463
Newark *(G-9924)*

Delaware Mltcltral Cvic Orgnzt................. F 302 399-6118
Dover *(G-2249)*

CONSULTING SVCS: Scientific

Holmes Smith Consulting Svcs................. G 302 407-6691
New Castle *(G-9217)*

Open Lanes-Solutions LLC......................... F 888 410-4207
Wilmington *(G-18795)*

Orthopaedic Consultants PA....................... G 302 724-5062
Dover *(G-3243)*

Ribodynamics LLC.................................... G 518 339-6605
Wilmington *(G-19464)*

Shepherd Stffing Cnsulting LLC................ G 302 652-0899
Wilmington *(G-19795)*

Steagle Consulting Group LLC................... G 302 439-4301
Claymont *(G-1302)*

Stride Services Inc.................................... F 302 540-4713
Wilmington *(G-20099)*

Volvox Biologic Inc................................... G 801 722-5942
Lewes *(G-6609)*

CONTAINERS: Food & Beverage

Jmt Inter LLC... G 302 312-5177
Bear *(G-306)*

CONTAINERS: Frozen Food & Ice Cream

Rennies Rolled Ice Cream LLC.................. G 551 273-8925
New Castle *(G-9521)*

CONTAINERS: Plastic

Axess Corporation.................................... G 302 292-8500
Historic New Castle *(G-4937)*

Berry Global Inc...................................... E 302 378-9853
Middletown *(G-6914)*

First State Container LLC........................ E 603 888-1315
Newark *(G-10730)*

CONTRACT FOOD SVCS

De Catering Inc....................................... E 302 607-7200
Wilmington *(G-15837)*

Premium Brands Inc................................. G 925 566-8863
Dover *(G-3364)*

CONTRACTOR: Framing

Mason Building Group Inc........................ C 302 292-0600
Newark *(G-11348)*

Menchaca Building Corp.......................... G 302 475-4581
Wilmington *(G-18271)*

CONTRACTORS: Acoustical & Ceiling Work

Erco Ceilings & Interiors Inc.................... F 302 994-6200
Wilmington *(G-16455)*

J & G Acoustical Co................................ E 302 285-3630
Middletown *(G-7233)*

Master Interiors Inc................................ E 302 368-9361
Milford *(G-7988)*

Master Interiors Inc................................ E 302 368-9361
Newark *(G-11350)*

Peninsula Acoustical Co Inc..................... G 302 653-3551
Smyrna *(G-13845)*

Union Wholesale Co................................. G 302 656-4462
Wilmington *(G-20516)*

CONTRACTORS: Artificial Turf Installation

Yardex LLC.. C 302 406-0933
Wilmington *(G-20924)*

CONTRACTORS: Asbestos Removal & Encapsulation

Astec Inc.. G 302 378-2717
Middletown *(G-6876)*

County Environmental Inc........................ E 302 322-8946
New Castle *(G-8979)*

Delaware Home & Envmtl Svcs.................. G 302 313-2899
Lewes *(G-5898)*

CONTRACTORS: Building Front Installation, Metal

Steel Suppliers Inc.................................. C 302 654-5243
Wilmington *(G-20043)*

CONTRACTORS: Building Site Preparation

Eastern States Cnstr Svc Inc..................... D 302 995-2259
Wilmington *(G-16264)*

Gateway Construction Inc........................ G 302 653-4400
Clayton *(G-1368)*

Geotech LLC.. G 302 353-9769
Wilmington *(G-16849)*

Harmony Construction Inc....................... F 302 737-8700
Newark *(G-10930)*

J & L Services Inc.................................... F 410 943-3355
Seaford *(G-13226)*

Sunnyfield Contractors Inc...................... G 302 674-8610
Dover *(G-3623)*

CONTRACTORS: Cable Laying

Crypto Trader LLC.................................. G 302 339-7500
Rehoboth Beach *(G-12708)*

Team Systems International LLC............. G 703 217-7648
Lewes *(G-6545)*

CONTRACTORS: Carpentry Work

AB Carpentry Services Inc....................... G 302 276-2457
New Castle *(G-8755)*

Affordable Custom Carpentry................. G 302 853-5582
Laurel *(G-5462)*

American Wood Design............................ G 302 792-2100
Claymont *(G-1034)*

Artifex Carpentry................................... G 484 557-7623
Newark *(G-9916)*

Atlantic Mllwk Cabinetry Corp................ E 302 644-1405
Lewes *(G-5716)*

Barracuda Carpentry LLC....................... G 302 415-1588
Millsboro *(G-8181)*

Beeline Services LLC.............................. G 302 376-7399
Middletown *(G-6910)*

Bob Preston Carpentry............................ G 302 234-8659
Hockessin *(G-5135)*

Brad Allen Carpentry LLC....................... G 302 228-4256
Frankford *(G-4075)*

Brandywine Master Carpentry................. G 302 463-9773
Wilmington *(G-15072)*

Carroll M Carpenter............................... G 302 654-7558
Wilmington *(G-15259)*

Carvi Carpenter Inc................................ G 302 722-3352
Georgetown *(G-4244)*

Construction Unlimited Inc..................... G 302 836-3140
Bear *(G-118)*

Craftsman Revisions............................... G 302 834-9252
Bear *(G-123)*

Creekside Carpentry LLC........................ G 302 218-4434
Wilmington *(G-15698)*

D J Byler.. G 302 653-4602
Clayton *(G-1358)*

Delframing Inc.. G 302 363-2658
Ocean View *(G-12501)*

Delmarva Coastal Cnstr LLC.................... G 302 259-5593
Millsboro *(G-8266)*

Dino Dicriscio... G 302 762-0610
Wilmington *(G-16074)*

Family Man Carpentry............................ G 302 542-8803
Georgetown *(G-4313)*

Garcia Moises LLC.................................. G 302 698-1930
Camden Wyoming *(G-948)*

Gjp & Sons LLC...................................... G 302 690-8954
Newark *(G-10842)*

Hrc Inc.. G 302 604-3782
Bridgeville *(G-714)*

J & L Services Inc.................................... F 410 943-3355
Seaford *(G-13226)*

Jeanfreau Carpentry Services.................. G 302 563-6449
Claymont *(G-1198)*

John F Elder... G 302 544-6569
Historic New Castle *(G-5011)*

Js Carpenter Improvements..................... G 302 540-0590
Middletown *(G-7255)*

Kevin Garber.. G 302 834-0639
Bear *(G-326)*

Mark Ventresca Associates Inc................ G 302 239-3925
Hockessin *(G-5300)*

Martin & Calloway LLC........................... G 302 482-1180
Wilmington *(G-18166)*

Mirandas Carpentry................................ G 302 245-0298
Lewes *(G-6279)*

Mitchell Associates Inc........................... F 302 594-9415
Wilmington *(G-18387)*

R W Harmon Carpentry Svcs LLC............ G 302 477-1319
Wilmington *(G-19307)*

V P Custom Finishers In.......................... G 302 415-0002
Middletown *(G-7677)*

CONTRACTORS: Carpentry, Cabinet & Finish Work

Andrew E Quesenberry Carpentry............ G 302 994-0700
Wilmington *(G-14475)*

Ceramic Tile Supply Co........................... G 302 684-5691
Harbeson *(G-4687)*

H P Custom Trim LLC.............................. G 302 381-0802
Georgetown *(G-4350)*

Mp Diversified Services LLC................... G 302 828-1060
Newark *(G-11462)*

Oceanic Ventures Inc.............................. G 302 645-5872
Lewes *(G-6328)*

Rementer Brothers Inc............................ G 302 249-4250
Milton *(G-8695)*

CONTRACTORS: Carpentry, Finish & Trim Work

Ecm Carpentry LLC................................. G 302 494-8995
Wilmington *(G-16281)*

CONTRACTORS: Closet Organizers, Installation & Design

Atlantic Source Contg Inc....................... G 302 645-5207
Lewes *(G-5718)*

Organized For Life.................................. G 302 792-1663
Wilmington *(G-18819)*

CONTRACTORS: Coating, Caulking & Weather, Water & Fire

Burkes Seal Coating................................ G 302 697-7635
Dover *(G-1994)*

Eastern Industrial Svcs Inc..................... D 302 455-1400
Historic New Castle *(G-4979)*

PRODUCTS & SERVICES SECTION

CONTRACTORS: Fence Construction

CONTRACTORS: Commercial & Office Building

Absolute Equity .... G 302 983-2591
　Delaware City *(G-1527)*
Aviman Management LLC .... E 302 377-5788
　Wilmington *(G-14669)*
B Doherty Inc .... G 302 239-3500
　Wilmington *(G-14697)*
Bishop Cleaning and Maint LLC .... G 302 277-8815
　Bear *(G-72)*
Breeze Construction LLC .... G 302 522-9201
　Townsend *(G-13966)*
Cirillo Bros Inc .... E 302 326-1540
　New Castle *(G-8943)*
Construction Unlimited Inc .... G 302 836-3140
　Bear *(G-118)*
Dewson Construction Co .... E 302 227-3095
　Rehoboth Beach *(G-12724)*
Diamond State Pole Bldings LLC .... G 302 387-1710
　Felton *(G-3960)*
Gary P Simpson Contracting LLC .... G 302 398-7733
　Harrington *(G-4772)*
Greggo & Ferrara Inc .... C 302 658-5241
　New Castle *(G-9180)*
John Campanelli & Sons Inc .... G 302 239-8573
　Hockessin *(G-5261)*
Lighthouse Construction Inc .... F 302 677-1965
　Magnolia *(G-6759)*
Linda McCormick .... G 443 987-2099
　Wilmington *(G-17922)*
Martin Construction Svcs LLC .... F 302 200-0885
　Newark *(G-11342)*
Milestone Construction Co Inc .... F 302 442-4252
　Newark *(G-11419)*
Mp Diversified Services LLC .... G 302 828-1060
　Newark *(G-11462)*
Preferred Construction Inc .... G 302 322-9568
　New Castle *(G-9490)*
Signature Furniture Svcs LLC .... E 302 691-1010
　New Castle *(G-9570)*
SMI Services of Delaware LLC .... G 302 514-9681
　Smyrna *(G-13889)*
Tycos General Contractors Inc .... G 302 478-9267
　Wilmington *(G-20480)*
White Eagle Integrations .... G 302 464-0550
　Middletown *(G-7723)*

CONTRACTORS: Communications Svcs

Fiber-One Inc .... G 302 834-0890
　Newark *(G-10726)*
Gatesair Inc .... E 513 459-3400
　Wilmington *(G-16814)*
Inflow Network LLC .... G 424 303-0464
　Newark *(G-11019)*
Martel Inc .... G 302 674-5660
　Dover *(G-3023)*
Yacht Anything Ltd .... G 302 226-3335
　Rehoboth Beach *(G-13026)*

CONTRACTORS: Concrete Block Masonry Laying

Esposito Mansory LLC .... F 302 996-4961
　Wilmington *(G-16465)*
M & L Contractors Inc .... F 302 436-9303
　Selbyville *(G-13563)*
Paragon Masonry Corporation .... G 302 798-7314
　Wilmington *(G-18887)*

CONTRACTORS: Concrete Reinforcement Placing

Blue Heron Contracting LLC .... G 302 526-0648
　Greenwood *(G-4600)*

CONTRACTORS: Decontamination Svcs

Geosyntec Holdings LLC .... G 561 995-0900
　Wilmington *(G-16848)*

CONTRACTORS: Directional Oil & Gas Well Drilling Svc

Ile LLC .... G 302 389-7911
　Wilmington *(G-17279)*

CONTRACTORS: Drywall

ABC Drywall .... G 302 249-0389
　Greenwood *(G-4588)*
Aln Construction Inc .... D 302 292-1580
　Newark *(G-9832)*
Aster Dry Wall LLC .... G 302 757-2750
　Smyrna *(G-13650)*
Aster Drywall .... G 302 757-5876
　New Castle *(G-8827)*
B&F Drywall .... G 302 218-2467
　Wilmington *(G-14705)*
Brothers Painting and Drywall .... G 302 737-9600
　Middletown *(G-6945)*
Camden Drywall Inc .... G 302 697-9653
　Wyoming *(G-20981)*
CC Drywall Contractors No .... G 302 307-6400
　Townsend *(G-13970)*
Circle Group Inc .... G 302 241-0018
　Dover *(G-2076)*
Cnc Drywall North .... G 302 307-6400
　Dover *(G-2098)*
Cook Plastering Inc .... G 302 737-0778
　Newark *(G-10319)*
Custom Drywall Inc .... G 302 369-3266
　Newark *(G-10367)*
Diaz Drywall LLC .... G 302 602-1110
　Newark *(G-10528)*
Dlc Drywall .... G 302 382-2213
　Greenwood *(G-4620)*
Drywall Inc .... E 302 838-6500
　New Castle *(G-9065)*
Ed Hileman Drywall Inc .... G 302 436-6277
　Selbyville *(G-13530)*
Fernandez Drywall Inc .... G 302 521-2760
　Newark *(G-10723)*
H & M Acoustical Services Inc .... G 302 218-7783
　Bear *(G-258)*
Heritage Interiors Inc .... F 302 369-3199
　Newark *(G-10949)*
J Michaels Painting Inc .... G 302 738-8465
　Newark *(G-11074)*
Julio Drywall Inc .... G 302 218-8596
　New Castle *(G-9270)*
Kenco Drywall .... G 302 697-6489
　Felton *(G-3990)*
King Snipers Drywall LLC .... G 302 452-4515
　Magnolia *(G-6758)*
Lamart Drywall LLC .... G 302 723-8751
　New Castle *(G-9294)*
M3 Contracting LLC .... E 302 781-3143
　Newark *(G-11308)*
N R O Drywall .... G 302 293-8811
　New Castle *(G-9389)*
Parsons PAInting&drywall LLC .... G 302 462-6169
　Millsboro *(G-8414)*
R&O Drywall LLC .... G 302 399-9480
　Dover *(G-3416)*
Rexmex Drywall LLC .... G 302 343-9140
　Hartly *(G-4906)*

Smogard & Associates LLC .... G 302 353-4717
　Wilmington *(G-19896)*
Smucker Company LLC .... E 302 322-9285
　Camden Wyoming *(G-980)*
Spacecon Inc .... F 302 322-9285
　New Castle *(G-9583)*
State Drywall Co Inc .... G 302 239-2843
　Hockessin *(G-5390)*
Superior Drywall Inc .... F 302 732-9800
　Dagsboro *(G-1511)*
Thomas Building Group Inc .... F 302 283-0600
　Newark *(G-12193)*
Three Bs Painting Contractors .... G 302 227-1497
　Rehoboth Beach *(G-12994)*
TNT Drywall LLC .... G 302 381-0114
　Lewes *(G-6565)*
Torresdrywall LLC .... G 302 228-6450
　Lincoln *(G-6706)*

CONTRACTORS: Electric Power Systems

Ips Development LLC .... G 800 981-7183
　Wilmington *(G-17418)*
Network Design Technologies .... E 610 991-2929
　Wilmington *(G-18596)*
Star Enrg Cs LLC .... F 302 660-2187
　Wilmington *(G-20023)*
USA Fortescue Future Inds Inc .... G 703 608-5217
　Wilmington *(G-20553)*

CONTRACTORS: Electronic Controls Installation

Service Unlimited Inc .... E 302 326-2665
　New Castle *(G-9558)*

CONTRACTORS: Energy Management Control

Advanced Power Control Inc .... D 302 368-0443
　New Castle *(G-8767)*
Cg Global MGT Solutions LLC .... F 215 735-3745
　Wilmington *(G-15321)*
Delaware Energy Solutions .... G 302 242-6315
　Dover *(G-2236)*
Encentiv Energy LLC .... F 302 504-8506
　Wilmington *(G-16404)*
Envirotrols Group Inc .... G 302 846-9103
　Delmar *(G-1594)*
Federal Energy Inf .... F 858 521-3300
　Wilmington *(G-16569)*
Gnz LLC .... C 302 499-2024
　Lewes *(G-6042)*

CONTRACTORS: Erection & Dismantling, Poured Concrete Forms

Eclipes Erection Inc .... G 302 633-1421
　Wilmington *(G-16279)*

CONTRACTORS: Fence Construction

All American Fencing .... G 302 530-8155
　Middletown *(G-6850)*
Arcadia Fencing Inc .... G 302 398-7700
　Harrington *(G-4735)*
B G Halko & Sons Inc .... G 302 322-2020
　New Castle *(G-8840)*
Breakwater Fence and Deck .... G 302 684-3333
　Milford *(G-7804)*
Contractor Rashmi & Penny .... G 302 778-5771
　Wilmington *(G-15623)*
Dickerson Fence Co Inc .... G 302 846-2227
　Delmar *(G-1589)*

Employee Codes: A=Over 500 employees, B=251-500
C=101-250, D=51-100, E=20-50, F=10-19, G=1-9

2024 Harris Directory of
Delaware Businesses

CONTRACTORS: Fence Construction

Dogwatch of Delaware .... G 302 268-3434
  Wilmington (G-16118)
Eastern Shore Porch Patio Inc .... E 302 436-9520
  Selbyville (G-13528)
Guardian Fence Company .... F 302 834-3044
  Middletown (G-7182)
Hometown Fence LLC .... G 302 629-0415
  Georgetown (G-4364)
Iron Hill Fence .... G 302 453-9060
  Newark (G-11059)
J & M Fencing Inc .... G 302 284-9674
  Felton (G-3985)
J & M Fencing Inc .... G 302 284-9674
  Felton (G-3986)
Kreative Services .... G 302 545-5030
  Bear (G-334)
Mayscapes LLC .... G 302 389-5999
  Newark (G-11362)
Nanticoke Fence LLC .... G 302 628-7808
  Seaford (G-13303)
National Vinyl Products Inc .... F 817 913-5991
  Dover (G-3156)
Newark Fence Co .... G 302 368-5329
  Newark (G-11537)
Pet Stop of Delmarva .... G 302 943-2310
  Harrington (G-4810)
Pierce Fence Company Inc .... F 302 674-1996
  Dover (G-3321)
Pioneer Fence Co Inc .... F 302 998-2892
  Wilmington (G-19052)
Rhino Fence .... G 302 544-5225
  New Castle (G-9531)
Sussex Fence Co .... G 302 945-7008
  Millsboro (G-8474)
Sussex Fencing .... G 302 945-7008
  Millsboro (G-8475)

CONTRACTORS: Fiber Optic Cable Installation

Conectiv Communications Inc .... E 302 224-1177
  Newark (G-10299)
Emergncy Response Protocol LLC .... G 302 994-2600
  Wilmington (G-16393)
Favhometheater .... G 302 897-7168
  Bear (G-221)
Intellitek Inc .... G 856 381-7650
  Middletown (G-7228)
Mg Global Group LLC .... G 302 217-3724
  Newark (G-11397)
Rhino Cabling Group Inc .... F 302 312-1033
  Newark (G-11877)

CONTRACTORS: Fire Detection & Burglar Alarm Systems

Alarm Systems Co of Delaware .... G 302 239-7754
  Hockessin (G-5118)
B Safe Inc .... E 302 422-3916
  Dover (G-1865)
Bfpe International Inc .... G 302 346-4800
  Dover (G-1927)
Delaware Electric Signal Co .... E 302 422-3916
  Dover (G-2235)
Preferred Security Inc .... G 302 834-7800
  Bear (G-435)
Security Instrument Corp Del .... F 302 674-2891
  Milton (G-8709)
Security Instrument Corp Del .... D 302 998-2261
  Wilmington (G-19733)
Sobieski Fire Protection LLC .... C 302 993-0600
  Wilmington (G-19906)

Telgian Corporation .... E 480 753-5444
  Wilmington (G-20267)

CONTRACTORS: Floor Laying & Other Floor Work

Anderson Floor Coverings Inc .... F 302 227-3244
  Rehoboth Beach (G-12604)
Creative Flooring Contrs Inc .... E 302 653-7521
  Smyrna (G-13688)
Delaware Wood Renewal Inc .... G 302 750-5167
  Middletown (G-7049)
Diaz and Costa Hardwood Flrng .... G 302 212-5923
  Rehoboth Beach (G-12727)
Fasttrak .... F 302 761-5454
  Wilmington (G-16560)
Floor Coatings Etc Inc .... E 302 322-4177
  New Castle (G-9136)
John S Kassees Inc .... G 302 838-1976
  Lewes (G-6146)
Margherita Vincent & Anthony .... G 302 834-9023
  Newark (G-11330)
Nhance .... G 866 944-9663
  Bear (G-397)
Spacecon LLC .... F 302 322-9285
  New Castle (G-9583)

CONTRACTORS: Food Svcs Eqpt Installation

Gregg & Sons Mechanical LLC .... G 302 223-8145
  Townsend (G-14011)

CONTRACTORS: Foundation & Footing

Ci De Corp .... G 302 998-3944
  Wilmington (G-15430)

CONTRACTORS: General Electric

A & B Electric .... G 302 349-4050
  Greenwood (G-4585)
A Plus Electric & Security .... G 302 455-1725
  Newark (G-9726)
Aaron and Sons Electric LLC .... G 302 764-5610
  Wilmington (G-14187)
Advanced Power Generation .... G 302 375-6145
  Claymont (G-1022)
Alliance Electric Inc .... F 302 366-0295
  Newark (G-9825)
Allied Elec Solutions Ltd .... G 302 893-0257
  Wilmington (G-14380)
American Electric LLC .... G 302 632-6724
  Lewes (G-5685)
Anaconda Prtctive Concepts Inc .... F 302 834-1125
  Newark (G-9858)
Anchor Electric Inc .... G 302 221-6111
  New Castle (G-8807)
Apg Inc .... G 302 746-7167
  Claymont (G-1040)
Apple Electric Inc .... E 302 645-5105
  Rehoboth Beach (G-12609)
Associates Contracting Inc .... F 302 734-4311
  Dover (G-1837)
Atr Electrical Services Inc .... G 302 384-7044
  Wilmington (G-14635)
B & M Electric Inc .... G 302 745-3807
  Georgetown (G-4218)
Battaglia Electric Inc .... C 302 325-6100
  New Castle (G-8847)
Bauguess Electrical Svcs Inc .... G 302 737-5614
  Newark (G-9993)
Brewington Electric .... G 302 732-3570
  Dagsboro (G-1420)
Brown Electrical Services LLC .... G 302 245-4593
  Millsboro (G-8209)

BW Electric Inc .... E 302 566-6248
  Harrington (G-4743)
Byers Industrial Services LLC .... C 302 836-4790
  Bear (G-86)
Cahill Contracting .... F 302 378-9650
  Middletown (G-6950)
Chieffo Electric Inc .... G 302 292-6813
  Middletown (G-6974)
City Electric Contracting Co .... F 302 764-0775
  Wilmington (G-15451)
Construction MGT Svcs Inc .... A 302 478-4200
  Wilmington (G-15612)
Conti Electric of N J Inc .... G 302 996-3905
  Wilmington (G-15616)
CT Pete Crossan Inc .... G 302 737-0223
  Newark (G-10362)
Current Solutions Inc .... G 302 736-5210
  Camden Wyoming (G-931)
Daniel George Bebee Inc .... G 443 359-1542
  Laurel (G-5492)
Dawson Bedsworth Elec Contrs .... F 302 854-0210
  Georgetown (G-4275)
Delcollo Security Tech Inc .... F 302 994-5400
  Wilmington (G-15991)
Diamond Electric Inc .... E 302 697-3296
  Dover (G-2290)
Donaldson Electric Inc .... E 302 660-7534
  Wilmington (G-16138)
East Coast Electric Inc .... F 302 998-1577
  Wilmington (G-16251)
Electric Fish LLC .... G 484 804-5149
  Rehoboth Beach (G-12740)
Electrical Associates Inc .... G 302 678-1068
  Hartly (G-4873)
Electrical Power Systems Inc .... G 302 325-3502
  New Castle (G-9088)
Filec Services LLC .... F 302 328-7188
  Middletown (G-7127)
First State Electric Co .... E 302 322-0140
  New Castle (G-9128)
Frees Electric .... G 302 752-8895
  Rehoboth Beach (G-12761)
Galloway Electric Co Inc .... F 302 453-8385
  Newark (G-10800)
Generation Electrical Svcs LLC .... G 302 298-1868
  Townsend (G-14006)
Gerone C Hudson Elec Contr .... F 302 539-3332
  Frankford (G-4111)
Globe Electric Company .... G 302 328-8809
  Hockessin (G-5223)
H & A Electric Co .... G 302 678-8252
  Dover (G-2638)
Hatzel and Buehler Inc .... C 302 798-5422
  Wilmington (G-17075)
Hatzel and Buehler Inc .... E 302 478-4200
  Wilmington (G-17074)
Hazzard Electrical Contrs Inc .... G 302 645-8457
  Lewes (G-6084)
I-Pulse Inc .... G 604 689-8765
  Wilmington (G-17250)
Independent Elec Svcs LLC .... D 302 383-2761
  Claymont (G-1184)
Infinity Electric LLC .... G 302 635-4388
  Hockessin (G-5251)
Integrated Wirg Solutions LLC .... E 302 999-8448
  Saint Georges (G-13034)
Integrity Tech Solutions Inc .... G 302 369-9093
  Newark (G-11038)
J T Electric .... G 302 275-6778
  Newark (G-11078)
J&A Electrical Services LLC .... G 302 943-9894
  Milton (G-8645)

PRODUCTS & SERVICES SECTION

CONTRACTORS: Highway & Street Construction, General

Jsf Construction Co Inc .... G 302 999-9573
 Wilmington *(G-17605)*

Justitselectric .... G 215 715-7314
 Claymont *(G-1203)*

Kent Electrical Services LLC .... G 302 922-4631
 Felton *(G-3992)*

Kokoszka & Sons Inc .... G 302 328-4807
 New Castle *(G-9288)*

Lattanzio Electrical Cntrctng .... G 302 685-0711
 Wilmington *(G-17818)*

Leightner Electrical Contracto .... G 302 723-1507
 New Castle *(G-9303)*

M Auger Enterprise Inc .... F 302 992-9922
 Wilmington *(G-18057)*

M Davis & Sons Inc .... C 302 998-3385
 Newark *(G-11301)*

Masten Electric Inc .... F 302 653-4300
 Smyrna *(G-13818)*

Maximum Electrical Svcs LLC .... G 302 521-2820
 Newark *(G-11361)*

Megee Plumbing & Heating Co ...... D 302 856-6311
 Georgetown *(G-4422)*

Mid-Atlantic Elec Svcs Inc .... E 302 945-2555
 Millsboro *(G-8379)*

Mid-County Electric Inc .... F 302 934-8304
 Millsboro *(G-8380)*

Mills Electric LLC .... G 302 257-8403
 Dover *(G-3094)*

Mister Sparky .... G 302 751-6363
 Magnolia *(G-6768)*

Montgomery Electric .... G 302 832-0945
 Bear *(G-378)*

Murphy Electric Inc .... G 302 644-0404
 Lewes *(G-6296)*

Nesmith & Company Inc .... E 215 755-4570
 Claymont *(G-1249)*

New Castle Counter .... G 302 421-3940
 Historic New Castle *(G-5034)*

Nickle Elec Companies Inc .... E 302 856-1006
 Georgetown *(G-4445)*

Nickle Elec Companies Inc .... C 302 453-4000
 Newark *(G-11557)*

O Reilly Electric .... F 302 381-6058
 Seaford *(G-13322)*

P S C Electric Contractor Inc .... F 302 838-2998
 Delaware City *(G-1551)*

Pace Elec & Generator Svcs .... E 302 328-2600
 Bear *(G-411)*

Palmer & Sons Electric In .... G 302 290-4899
 Bear *(G-413)*

Peter D Furness Elc Co Inc .... C 302 764-6030
 Wilmington *(G-18992)*

Positive Energy Electric .... G 267 902-1655
 Historic New Castle *(G-5051)*

Power Control Technologies Inc ..... G 203 560-2806
 Wilmington *(G-19136)*

Power Plus Elec Contg Inc .... F 302 736-5070
 Dover *(G-3356)*

Powercomm LLC .... E 302 235-8922
 Wilmington *(G-19138)*

Powwa Electric .... G 302 236-2649
 Seaford *(G-13353)*

Preferred Electric Inc .... D 302 322-1217
 New Castle *(G-9491)*

Progressive Services Inc .... E 302 658-7260
 Wilmington *(G-19220)*

Ram Electric .... G 302 379-3351
 Newark *(G-11823)*

Ram Electric Inc .... G 302 875-2356
 Laurel *(G-5584)*

Rays Plumbing & Heating Svcs ..... F 302 697-3936
 Felton *(G-4013)*

Ricks Electric LLC .... G 410 924-6764
 Felton *(G-4016)*

Riley Electric .... G 302 533-5918
 Newark *(G-11886)*

Roberts Electric .... G 302 233-3017
 Magnolia *(G-6779)*

S J Desmond Inc .... F 302 256-0801
 Wilmington *(G-19610)*

Satterfield & Ryan Inc .... F 302 422-4919
 Milford *(G-8085)*

Shellysons Electrical Contract .... G 302 275-8010
 Newark *(G-11995)*

Shore Electric Inc .... G 302 645-4503
 Lewes *(G-6465)*

Shure Line Electrical Inc .... G 302 856-3110
 Georgetown *(G-4512)*

Shure-Line Electrical Inc .... D 302 389-1114
 Smyrna *(G-13885)*

Silver Electric LLC .... G 302 227-1107
 Rehoboth Beach *(G-12959)*

Smith Electrical Services .... G 302 423-5994
 Marydel *(G-6810)*

Stapleford Electric LLC .... G 302 300-1377
 Wilmington *(G-20020)*

Stuart Ja Inc .... G 302 378-8299
 Newark *(G-12109)*

Superior Electric Service Co .... E 302 658-5949
 Wilmington *(G-20140)*

Sure Line Electrical Inc .... G 302 856-3110
 Georgetown *(G-4531)*

TA Rietdorf & Sons Inc .... G 302 429-0341
 Wilmington *(G-20204)*

Tangent Cable Systems Inc .... E 302 994-4104
 Wilmington *(G-20218)*

Taylor Electric Service Inc .... G 302 422-3966
 Milford *(G-8114)*

Tc Electric Company Inc .... E 302 791-0378
 Wilmington *(G-20236)*

Towles Electric Inc .... G 302 674-4985
 Dover *(G-3706)*

Tri-State SEC & Contrls LLC .... F 302 299-2175
 Newark *(G-12227)*

Tri-State Technologies Inc .... F 302 658-5400
 Wilmington *(G-20415)*

Triangle Electrical Svc Co .... G 302 856-7880
 Georgetown *(G-4560)*

Tudor Electric Inc .... E 302 736-1444
 Dover *(G-3733)*

Tusi Brothers Inc .... F 302 998-6383
 Wilmington *(G-20465)*

Vassallo Michael Elec Contr .... F 302 455-9405
 Newark *(G-12307)*

Wanex Electrical Service LLC .... F 302 326-1700
 New Castle *(G-9674)*

Watts Electric Company .... G 302 529-1183
 Wilmington *(G-20685)*

Wayne Bennett .... G 302 436-2379
 Frankford *(G-4158)*

White Eagle Electric .... G 302 533-7799
 Newark *(G-12367)*

CONTRACTORS: Glass Tinting, Architectural & Automotive

Gotshadeonline Inc .... G 302 832-8468
 Bear *(G-252)*

Professional Window Tinting .... G 302 456-3456
 Newark *(G-11760)*

Shore Tint & More Inc .... G 302 947-4624
 Harbeson *(G-4716)*

Tint World .... G 302 595-9100
 Wilmington *(G-20333)*

CONTRACTORS: Heating & Air Conditioning

Advanced Mechanical Inc .... F 302 734-5583
 Dover *(G-1725)*

Bella Hvac .... G 302 561-4025
 Newark *(G-10014)*

Blades H V A C Services .... G 302 539-4436
 Dagsboro *(G-1418)*

Blades Hvac Services .... G 302 539-4436
 Frankford *(G-4073)*

Bronswerk Marine Corp .... G 619 813-4797
 Newark *(G-10092)*

Cape Climate Inc .... G 302 858-7160
 Georgetown *(G-4243)*

Castle Services Inc .... G 302 481-6633
 Wilmington *(G-15268)*

DBA Heating Parts Hub .... G 302 381-3705
 Greenwood *(G-4612)*

Dynamic Air LLC .... G 302 612-1412
 Hartly *(G-4871)*

Entek Manufacturing Inc .... G 302 576-5860
 Wilmington *(G-16432)*

Gold Star Services LLC .... G 610 444-3333
 New Castle *(G-9171)*

Manley Hvac Inc .... G 302 998-4654
 Wilmington *(G-18105)*

McMahon Heating & AC .... F 302 945-4300
 Lewes *(G-6255)*

Mels Htg & A/C .... G 302 947-1979
 Millsboro *(G-8374)*

My Cousin Vinnys Hvac .... G 302 266-1888
 Newark *(G-11476)*

Old School Heating & Cooling .... G 302 383-7036
 Claymont *(G-1257)*

Pluck Hvac .... G 302 836-8596
 Bear *(G-427)*

Pucketts Heating Adn Air .... G 443 239-2129
 Harrington *(G-4814)*

Ryes Hvac LLC .... G 302 981-7851
 New Castle *(G-9549)*

Sab Heating & Air .... G 302 945-3117
 Millsboro *(G-8451)*

Service Air Tech Hvac .... G 302 335-8334
 Magnolia *(G-6782)*

Triple Tzz Hvac LLC .... G 302 846-3220
 Delmar *(G-1647)*

Webb LLC .... G 302 744-0029
 Wilmington *(G-20704)*

Wswms Hvac .... G 302 454-1987
 Newark *(G-12414)*

CONTRACTORS: Heating Systems Repair & Maintenance Svc

Advanced Heating & Air Inc .... G 302 731-1000
 Newark *(G-9776)*

Jam Air LLC .... G 302 270-8236
 Dover *(G-2767)*

Ocean Air .... G 302 524-8003
 Selbyville *(G-13587)*

Summit Heating and AC LLC .... G 302 378-1203
 Townsend *(G-14074)*

Wilkins Fuel Co .... G 302 422-5597
 Milford *(G-8149)*

Willey and Co .... G 302 629-3327
 Laurel *(G-5626)*

CONTRACTORS: Highway & Street Construction, General

A P Croll & Son Inc .... D 302 856-6177
 Georgetown *(G-4189)*

CONTRACTORS: Highway & Street Construction, General

Allan Myers .... G 302 658-4417
Newport *(G-12442)*

Allan Myers Md Inc .... C 302 883-3501
Dover *(G-1769)*

Alltech Pro Corporation .... E 323 457-3225
Middletown *(G-6854)*

Austin & Bednash Cnstr Inc .... E 302 376-5590
Newark *(G-9944)*

Disabatino Enterprises LLC .... D 302 652-3838
Wilmington *(G-16085)*

Dover Kent County Mpo .... G 302 387-6030
Camden *(G-823)*

Dxi Construction Inc .... C 302 858-5007
Georgetown *(G-4301)*

Eastern States Cnstr Svc Inc .... D 302 995-2259
Wilmington *(G-16264)*

Ffi General Contractor In .... G 302 420-1242
Wilmington *(G-16592)*

Greggo & Ferrara Inc .... C 302 658-5241
New Castle *(G-9180)*

Jjid Inc .... E 302 836-0414
Bear *(G-305)*

Jose A Fernandez .... G 302 422-5903
Ellendale *(G-3924)*

Material Supply Inc .... E 302 658-6524
Wilmington *(G-18191)*

New Castle County Flooring .... G 302 218-0507
Newark *(G-11517)*

R S Widdoes & Son Inc .... F 302 764-7455
Wilmington *(G-19306)*

Sweeten Companies Inc .... G 302 737-6161
Newark *(G-12140)*

CONTRACTORS: Highway & Street Paving

A-Del Construction Company Inc ... D 302 453-8286
Newark *(G-9729)*

David M Sartin Sr .... G 302 838-1074
Bear *(G-133)*

Don Rogers Inc .... F 302 658-6524
Wilmington *(G-16132)*

Dover Paving .... G 302 274-0743
Dover *(G-2359)*

E Earle Downing Inc .... E 302 656-9908
Wilmington *(G-16238)*

Harmony Construction Inc .... F 302 737-8700
Newark *(G-10930)*

Melvin L Joseph Cnstr Co .... E 302 856-7396
Georgetown *(G-4424)*

Mitten Construction Co .... F 302 697-2124
Dover *(G-3104)*

Naudain Enterprises LLC .... F 302 239-6840
Hockessin *(G-5319)*

Palmer & Associates Inc .... G 302 834-9329
Bear *(G-412)*

Peninsula Pave & Seal LLC .... F 302 226-7283
Georgetown *(G-4459)*

River Asphalt LLC .... G 302 934-0881
Dagsboro *(G-1500)*

Sanco Construction Co Inc .... G 302 633-4156
Wilmington *(G-19655)*

South Jersey Paving .... G 856 498-8647
Bear *(G-501)*

Teal Construction Inc .... D 302 276-6034
Dover *(G-3661)*

Voshell Bros Welding Inc .... E 302 674-1414
Dover *(G-3810)*

Wb Paving LLC .... G 302 838-1886
Bear *(G-560)*

CONTRACTORS: Hydraulic Eqpt Installation & Svcs

White Drilling Corp .... G 302 422-4057
Lincoln *(G-6708)*

CONTRACTORS: Machinery Installation

Bruce Industrial Co Inc .... D 302 655-9616
New Castle *(G-8894)*

Planned Poultry Renovation .... E 302 875-4196
Laurel *(G-5577)*

R & S Fabrication Inc .... F 302 629-0377
Bridgeville *(G-759)*

CONTRACTORS: Masonry & Stonework

Aiken Masonry Scott Ta .... G 302 253-8179
Georgetown *(G-4202)*

Amer Masonry T A Marino .... G 302 834-1511
New Castle *(G-8794)*

American Masonry .... G 302 362-9962
Laurel *(G-5463)*

American Stone Crafters Inc .... G 302 834-8891
Bear *(G-31)*

Ashcraft Masonry Inc .... F 302 537-4298
Ocean View *(G-12465)*

Becks Masonry .... G 302 231-8872
Millsboro *(G-8190)*

Blair Carmean Masonry .... G 302 934-6103
Georgetown *(G-4235)*

Blair Carmean & Sons Masonry ..... G 302 249-5783
Millsboro *(G-8199)*

Blue Hen Masonry Inc .... G 302 398-8737
Greenwood *(G-4599)*

Cesars Vargas Stone Inc C .... G 302 296-7881
Seaford *(G-13106)*

Contractor Masonary .... G 302 945-1930
Millsboro *(G-8238)*

Countryside Masonry LLC .... G 302 945-5642
Millsboro *(G-8241)*

Czapp Masonry Inc .... G 302 238-7007
Millsboro *(G-8250)*

Davis-Young Associates Inc .... G 610 388-0932
Yorklyn *(G-20991)*

Dreamscape Design Cons LLC ..... G 302 893-0984
Newark *(G-10571)*

Enterprise Masonry Corporation ... E 302 764-6858
Wilmington *(G-16438)*

Estepp Construction Co Inc .... G 302 378-4958
Townsend *(G-13998)*

Falasco Masonry Inc .... G 302 697-8971
Camden Wyoming *(G-943)*

Gullwing Contracting Inc .... F 302 943-0133
Harrington *(G-4777)*

Henlopen Masonry Inc .... G 302 947-9900
Milton *(G-8637)*

Hoppy LLC DBA Brick Works .... F 302 653-8961
Smyrna *(G-13765)*

J D Masonry Inc .... E 302 684-1009
Harbeson *(G-4702)*

Jackson Masonry .... G 302 397-4202
Wilmington *(G-17472)*

James Willey Masonry LLC .... G 302 258-6242
Dagsboro *(G-1469)*

Kevins Masonry Concrete Co .... G 302 382-7259
Felton *(G-3993)*

Kings Masonry LLC .... G 302 632-6783
Hartly *(G-4891)*

L A Masonary Inc .... F 302 239-6833
Newark *(G-11206)*

Lawrence Legates Masnry Co Inc .. G 302 422-8043
Milford *(G-7973)*

Ldmasonry .... G 302 270-3386
Harrington *(G-4798)*

Lighthouse Masonry Inc .... G 302 945-1392
Lewes *(G-6208)*

Lower Sussex Masonry LLC .... G 302 249-3275
Laurel *(G-5557)*

Mario Medori Inc .... F 302 656-8432
Wilmington *(G-18133)*

Millers Masonry & Block LLC .... G 302 222-4091
Hartly *(G-4897)*

Moore Clinton Denver II .... G 302 856-3385
Georgetown *(G-4433)*

Morris Masonry .... G 410 726-6277
Delmar *(G-1624)*

Nu-Tech Masonry Inc .... G 302 934-5660
Millsboro *(G-8409)*

Peninsula Masonry Inc .... G 302 684-3410
Harbeson *(G-4711)*

Petrovich Masonry .... G 302 697-2379
Dover *(G-3309)*

R F Gentner & Son .... G 302 947-2733
Harbeson *(G-4712)*

Romano Masonry Inc .... F 302 368-4155
Newark *(G-11913)*

Shore Masonry Inc .... G 302 945-5933
Millsboro *(G-8460)*

Skyline Roofing & Cnstr LLC .... G 610 929-4135
Lewes *(G-6474)*

Sme Masonry Contrs Ltd Lblty ...... F 302 743-7338
Wilmington *(G-19883)*

South Delaware Masonry Inc .... G 302 378-1998
Townsend *(G-14067)*

Stonegate Granite .... G 302 500-8081
Georgetown *(G-4527)*

Stoneworks Lapidary .... G 814 528-1468
Lewes *(G-6513)*

Swedish Brickyard .... G 302 893-4143
Newark *(G-12139)*

Trenton Block Delaware Inc .... F 302 684-0112
Milton *(G-8722)*

Walter W Snyder .... G 302 378-1817
Middletown *(G-7706)*

Wilson Masonry Corp .... F 302 398-8240
Harrington *(G-4847)*

CONTRACTORS: Office Furniture Installation

Advance Office Instltions Inc .... E 302 777-5599
Historic New Castle *(G-4922)*

Affordable Delivery Svcs LLC .... E 302 276-0246
New Castle *(G-8771)*

Gray Audograph Agency Inc .... F 302 658-1700
New Castle *(G-9176)*

CONTRACTORS: Oil & Gas Well Redrilling

Regen III (usgc) Corporation .... G 604 806-5275
Wilmington *(G-19399)*

CONTRACTORS: Oil & Gas Wells Pumping Svcs

Delaware Storage & Pipeline Co ... G 302 736-1774
Dover *(G-2266)*

CONTRACTORS: Oil & Gas Wells Svcs

Pride International LLC .... F 713 789-1400
Wilmington *(G-19190)*

CONTRACTORS: Ornamental Metal Work

Custom Iron Shop Inc .... G 302 654-5201
Wilmington *(G-15741)*

CONTRACTORS: Painting, Commercial

A Rodriguez Painting LLC .... G 302 559-7692
Georgetown *(G-4191)*

Clean Hands LLC .... F 215 681-1435
Smyrna *(G-13681)*

PRODUCTS & SERVICES SECTION

CONTRACTORS: Plumbing

Kent County Painting Inc .... E 302 994-9628
 Wilmington (G-17692)

CONTRACTORS: Painting, Commercial, Exterior

Burke Painting Co Inc .... G 302 998-8500
 Lewes (G-5781)

Connor Charles & Sons Painting .... G 302 945-1746
 Georgetown (G-4266)

Robert J Peoples Inc .... F 302 322-0595
 Wilmington (G-19515)

CONTRACTORS: Painting, Indl

Cannon Sline LLC .... C 302 658-1420
 New Castle (G-8912)

Maccari Companies Inc .... G 302 994-9628
 Wilmington (G-18064)

CONTRACTORS: Petroleum Storage Tanks, Pumping & Draining

Ecg Industries Inc .... G 302 453-0535
 Newark (G-10603)

Jbm Petroleum Service LLC .... G 302 752-6105
 Lincoln (G-6677)

CONTRACTORS: Pile Driving

First State Crane Service Inc .... E 302 398-8885
 Felton (G-3974)

CONTRACTORS: Plumbing

A J Dauphin & Son Inc .... G 302 994-1454
 Wilmington (G-14164)

A Plumber .... G 302 249-7606
 Milford (G-7757)

Accurate & Heating .... G 302 561-5749
 Bear (G-13)

Advanced Home Services Inc .... G 302 339-7600
 Magnolia (G-6714)

Affordable Plumbing & Elc Inc .... G 443 235-9222
 Delmar (G-1561)

Anchor Plumbing Inc .... G 410 392-6520
 Newark (G-9863)

Angler Plumbing LLC .... G 302 293-5691
 Newark (G-9870)

Associates Contracting Inc .... F 302 734-4311
 Dover (G-1837)

Assurance Plumbing Compnay .... G 302 324-0403
 New Castle (G-8826)

Back Bay Plumbing .... G 302 945-1210
 Millsboro (G-8179)

Beaches Plumbing Plus .... G 302 841-0171
 Milton (G-8570)

Bethany Plumbing and Heating .... G 302 539-1022
 Ocean View (G-12480)

Bob Davis Inc .... G 302 798-2561
 Wilmington (G-14989)

Bobs Plumbing Repair LLC .... G 302 853-2259
 Georgetown (G-4236)

Braham Plumbing LLC .... G 302 448-5708
 Laurel (G-5473)

Budget Rooter Inc .... F 302 322-3011
 New Castle (G-8897)

Burnsies Plumbing LLC .... G 215 275-0723
 Bear (G-85)

Byrds Nest LLC .... G 302 475-4949
 Wilmington (G-15165)

Byron Outten Plumbing .... G 302 236-4727
 Greenwood (G-4601)

C & N Services LLC .... G 302 883-1046
 Dover (G-2005)

Cahill Plumbing & Heating Inc .... G 302 894-1802
 Newark (G-10119)

Calfo & Haight Inc .... F 302 998-3852
 Wilmington (G-15193)

Cesn Partners Inc .... F 302 537-1814
 Ocean View (G-12488)

Charles A Klein & Sons Inc .... G 410 549-6960
 Selbyville (G-13496)

Charles Moon Plumbing .... G 302 732-3555
 Dagsboro (G-1425)

Charles Moon Plumbing .... G 302 732-3555
 Dagsboro (G-1426)

Charles Moon Plumbing & Htg .... G 302 798-6666
 Claymont (G-1083)

Charles S Reskovitz Inc .... G 302 999-9455
 Wilmington (G-15339)

Chesapeake Plumbing & Htg Inc .... E 302 732-6006
 Frankford (G-4089)

Christensen Evert J Plumbing & .... G 302 475-9249
 Wilmington (G-15398)

Clendaniel Plbg Htg & Coolg .... G 302 684-3152
 Milton (G-8585)

Collins Mechanical Inc .... E 302 398-8877
 Harrington (G-4752)

Cooper Bros Inc .... F 302 323-0717
 New Castle (G-8972)

Del Campo Plumbing & Heating .... G 302 998-3648
 Wilmington (G-15859)

Delmarva Plumbing LLC .... G 571 274-4926
 Ocean View (G-12502)

Domenic Di Donato Plbg Htg Inc .... G 856 207-4919
 Wilmington (G-16126)

Done Right Today Inc .... G 302 528-4294
 Wilmington (G-16139)

Durham Plumbing Service LLC .... G 302 653-5601
 Marydel (G-6797)

Elvin Schrock and Sons Inc .... G 302 349-4384
 Greenwood (G-4625)

Falcone Truman Plbg & Htg Inc .... E 302 376-7483
 Odessa (G-12584)

Federal Mechanical Contractors .... F 302 656-2998
 New Castle (G-9123)

First State Plumbing & Heating .... G 302 275-9746
 New Castle (G-9131)

Flowrite .... G 302 544-4042
 Historic New Castle (G-4989)

Flowrite Inc .... G 302 547-5657
 Bear (G-232)

Freedom Drain Clg Pipe Svcs LL .... G 484 480-1368
 Bear (G-238)

Godfrey Plumbing Services .... G 302 985-1593
 Wilmington (G-16905)

Graydon Hurst & Son Inc .... G 302 762-2444
 Wilmington (G-16952)

Harry Caswell Inc .... E 302 945-5322
 Millsboro (G-8313)

Harrys Nuts and Then Some .... G 302 947-1344
 Millsboro (G-8314)

Henry Yee Plumbing Inc .... G 914 980-2188
 Wilmington (G-17124)

Hns Plumbing Services LLC .... F 302 650-9010
 Bear (G-276)

Honesty Service .... G 302 690-2433
 Newark (G-10967)

Horizon Services Inc .... B 610 491-8800
 Newark (G-10971)

Horizon Services Inc .... C 302 762-1200
 Wilmington (G-17209)

J Stachon Plumbing LLC .... G 302 998-0938
 Wilmington (G-17464)

Jenkins Mechanical .... G 302 430-8211
 Georgetown (G-4382)

Joseph T Richardson Inc .... E 302 398-8101
 Harrington (G-4792)

K BS Plumbing Incorporated .... G 302 678-2757
 Dover (G-2823)

Lindale Plumbing LLC .... G 302 242-2493
 Greenwood (G-4648)

Local Plumbing .... G 302 746-3101
 Claymont (G-1223)

M D Plumbing Drain Cleaning .... G 302 492-8880
 Marydel (G-6806)

M Davis & Sons Inc .... C 302 998-3385
 Newark (G-11301)

Malins Jim E Plumbing & Htg .... G 302 239-2755
 Hockessin (G-5293)

Mels Wells LLC .... G 302 393-9017
 Lincoln (G-6684)

Messina Charles Plbg & Elc Co .... D 302 674-5696
 Dover (G-3067)

Miller John H Plumbing & Htg .... F 302 697-1012
 Camden (G-876)

Mr Rooter Plumbing of New .... G 302 463-5720
 Newark (G-11464)

North East Pool Plumbing .... G 302 740-5071
 New Castle (G-9426)

Ocean View Plumbing Inc .... E 302 732-9117
 Dagsboro (G-1493)

Perfect Plumbing Partners Inc .... G 610 521-6654
 Wilmington (G-18973)

Petes Plumbing LLC .... G 302 270-4990
 Dover (G-3305)

Philadelphia Plumbing .... G 302 327-8545
 New Castle (G-9471)

Philadelphia Plumbing .... G 302 468-5460
 Wilmington (G-19014)

Pipe Pros Jetting & Plbg LLC .... F 302 562-0522
 Townsend (G-14052)

Plumbing Enterprises LLC .... F 302 515-4620
 Selbyville (G-13591)

Plummer Co Inc .... G 302 227-5000
 Rehoboth Beach (G-12892)

Pro Works Inc DH .... F 302 221-4200
 New Castle (G-9497)

R A Chance Plumbing Inc .... G 302 324-8200
 New Castle (G-9511)

R A Chance Plumbing Inc .... G 302 292-1315
 Newark (G-11805)

Ralph G Degli Obizzi & Sons .... G 302 658-5127
 Wilmington (G-19323)

Rays Plumbing & Heating Svcs .... F 302 697-3936
 Felton (G-4013)

Robert Gears .... G 302 690-2590
 Frankford (G-4139)

Ronnie Freeman .... G 302 762-3252
 Wilmington (G-19563)

Rw Greer Inc .... G 302 764-0376
 Wilmington (G-19597)

Rwm Plumbing .... G 302 697-1705
 Camden Wyoming (G-972)

Schlosser Assoc Mech Cntrs Inc .... E 302 738-7333
 Newark (G-11958)

Siegfried J Schulze Inc .... F 302 737-0403
 Newark (G-12003)

Sobieski Services Inc .... E 302 993-0104
 Newark (G-12047)

Stan Perkoskis Plumbing & Htg .... E 302 529-1220
 Wilmington (G-20010)

State Wide Plumbing Inc .... F 302 292-0924
 Newark (G-12092)

Stay True Plumbing .... G 302 464-1198
 Bear (G-512)

Sussex Plumbing & Heating .... G 302 344-2199
 Laurel (G-5611)

Employee Codes: A=Over 500 employees, B=251-500
C=101-250, D=51-100, E=20-50, F=10-19, G=1-9

CONTRACTORS: Plumbing

TA Austin Plumbing Inc .... F 302 995-2282
Wilmington *(G-20203)*

Thomas Francisconi .... G 302 995-2282
Wilmington *(G-20308)*

Tj S Plumbing Heating L .... F 302 228-7129
Millsboro *(G-8486)*

Top Notch Plumbing LLC .... G 302 381-9096
Dagsboro *(G-1519)*

Wegman Bros Inc .... F 302 738-4328
Newark *(G-12355)*

William D Shellady Inc .... D 302 652-3106
Wilmington *(G-20785)*

William F & Margaret Hartnett .... G 302 479-5918
Wilmington *(G-20788)*

William G Robelen Inc .... G 302 656-8726
Wilmington *(G-20790)*

Wrench Plumbing .... F 302 482-1043
Wilmington *(G-20900)*

CONTRACTORS: Pollution Control Eqpt Installation

Pradhan Energy Projects 305 428-2123
Hockessin *(G-5351)*

CONTRACTORS: Power Generating Eqpt Installation

Amrec Holdings Inc .... D 302 273-0000
Dover *(G-1788)*

Firebrick Wind LLC .... G 647 352-9533
Wilmington *(G-16613)*

Northeast Missouri Wind LLC .... G 647 352-9533
Wilmington *(G-18682)*

Xwind Services Ltd .... E 418 563-5453
Lewes *(G-6645)*

CONTRACTORS: Prefabricated Window & Door Installation

R & J Taylor Inc .... G 302 368-7888
Newark *(G-11802)*

CONTRACTORS: Refractory or Acid Brick Masonry

Rgp Holding Inc .... F 302 661-0117
Wilmington *(G-19453)*

CONTRACTORS: Roustabout Svcs

Estate Servicing LLC .... G 302 731-1119
Newark *(G-10667)*

Rock Solid Servicing LLC .... G 302 233-2569
Magnolia *(G-6780)*

CONTRACTORS: Septic System

Cs Webb Daughters & Son Inc .... G 302 239-2801
Hockessin *(G-5174)*

Leager Construction Inc .... G 302 653-8021
Smyrna *(G-13797)*

Midway Services Inc .... G 302 422-8603
Lincoln *(G-6685)*

CONTRACTORS: Sheet Metal Work, NEC

Custom Metal Works Inc .... G 302 765-2653
Wilmington *(G-15743)*

Ducts Unlimited Inc .... E 302 378-4125
Smyrna *(G-13717)*

L & J Sheet Metal .... F 302 875-2822
Laurel *(G-5542)*

Mastercraft Welding .... G 302 697-3932
Dover *(G-3028)*

Mumford Sheet Metal Works Inc .... F 302 436-8251
Selbyville *(G-13583)*

Russell A Paulus & Son Inc .... G 302 998-4494
Wilmington *(G-19593)*

Sheet Metal Industry Advanceme .... G 302 994-7442
Wilmington *(G-19788)*

CONTRACTORS: Siding

Belusko Siding & Windows .... G 302 366-8783
Newark *(G-10017)*

Coam Exterior Inc .... G 302 329-9545
Harbeson *(G-4688)*

Del Coast Exteriors .... G 302 236-5738
Georgetown *(G-4277)*

Delaware Siding Company Inc .... G 302 836-6971
Bear *(G-157)*

Home Services Unlimited .... G 302 293-8726
Newark *(G-10964)*

Interstate Steel Co Inc .... F 302 598-5159
Newark *(G-11050)*

PJ Fitzpatrick Inc .... D 302 325-2360
New Castle *(G-9473)*

Zanes Siding and Trim .... G 302 377-5394
Bear *(G-572)*

CONTRACTORS: Skylight Installation

Delaware Siding Company Inc .... G 302 732-1440
Dagsboro *(G-1437)*

CONTRACTORS: Sprinkler System

Lightscapes Inc .... G 302 798-5451
Wilmington *(G-17910)*

Steven Brown & Associates Inc .... G 302 652-4722
Wilmington *(G-20064)*

CONTRACTORS: Structural Iron Work, Structural

LMS Ironworks .... G 302 300-7719
Wilmington *(G-17962)*

M Davis & Sons Inc .... C 302 998-3385
Newark *(G-11301)*

Sykes Orna & Cstm Ir Works Inc .... G 302 757-2103
Wilmington *(G-20179)*

CONTRACTORS: Structural Steel Erection

Amazon Steel Construction Inc .... G 302 751-1146
Milford *(G-7766)*

Atlas Wldg & Fabrication Inc .... E 302 326-1900
New Castle *(G-8832)*

Custom Iron Shop Inc .... G 302 654-5201
Wilmington *(G-15741)*

Deaven Development Corp .... G 302 994-5793
Wilmington *(G-15847)*

Donald F Deaven Inc .... E 302 994-5793
Wilmington *(G-16135)*

East Coast Erectors Inc .... F 302 323-1800
New Castle *(G-9077)*

Emlyn Construction Co .... G 302 697-8247
Dover *(G-2441)*

Falcon Steel Co .... E 302 571-0890
Wilmington *(G-16533)*

Metro Steel Incorporated .... E 302 778-2288
New Castle *(G-9361)*

R C Fabricators Inc .... D 302 573-8989
Wilmington *(G-19303)*

Summit Steel Inc .... D 302 325-3220
New Castle *(G-9599)*

CONTRACTORS: Terrazzo Work

Consolidated Construction Svcs .... F 302 629-6070
Seaford *(G-13135)*

CONTRACTORS: Tile Installation, Ceramic

Aztek Tile .... G 302 875-0690
Laurel *(G-5465)*

Bath Kitchen Tile DH .... G 302 992-9210
Newark *(G-9990)*

Bella Tile and Stone LLC .... G 302 275-4550
Bear *(G-67)*

Ceramic Tile Supply Co .... G 302 737-4968
Newark *(G-10179)*

Coastal Plains Wood & Tile LLC .... G 302 670-7853
Rehoboth Beach *(G-12685)*

Coastal Tile AMP Stone In .... G 301 748-0754
Selbyville *(G-13503)*

Coastal Tile and Hardwood .... G 302 339-7772
Millsboro *(G-8234)*

Creative Ceramics LLC .... G 302 275-9211
Newark *(G-10347)*

Delaware Custom Tile .... G 302 841-9215
Lewes *(G-5896)*

Dippold Marble Granite .... G 302 324-9101
Middletown *(G-7062)*

Edward J Hennessy .... G 302 798-8019
Claymont *(G-1128)*

Felixchem Corp Inc .... G 302 376-0199
Middletown *(G-7124)*

Inspiration Bennington Ceramic .... G 302 436-5544
Selbyville *(G-13549)*

Keystone Granite and Tile Inc .... F 302 323-0200
New Castle *(G-9280)*

Kyles Tile LLC .... G 302 462-0959
Ocean View *(G-12535)*

Mohawk Tile MBL Distrs of Del .... G 302 655-7164
Wilmington *(G-18401)*

Old World Tile Works .... G 302 407-5552
Wilmington *(G-18757)*

Pala Tile & Carpet Contrs Inc .... E 302 652-4500
Wilmington *(G-18865)*

Peninsula Acoustical Co Inc .... G 302 653-3551
Smyrna *(G-13845)*

Ruiz Flooring .... G 302 999-9350
Wilmington *(G-19588)*

Sir Grout Delaware LLC .... G 302 401-1700
Seaford *(G-13403)*

Smart-The Tile Rick Specialist .... G 302 331-5529
Dover *(G-3577)*

Sosa Eloy .... G 302 275-3792
Wilmington *(G-19931)*

Stone Age Tile and Flooring .... G 302 359-2166
Frederica *(G-4183)*

Tile Guy .... G 302 382-7961
Felton *(G-4032)*

Tile Market of Delaware Inc .... E 302 644-7100
Lewes *(G-6560)*

Tile Market of Delaware LLC .... E 302 777-4663
Wilmington *(G-20325)*

Tile Shop LLC .... E 302 250-4889
Wilmington *(G-20326)*

Upon A Once Tile Inc .... G 646 992-1376
Lewes *(G-6591)*

CONTRACTORS: Underground Utilities

Blueocean Communications LLC .... G 617 586-6633
Camden *(G-793)*

Bramble Construction Co Inc .... F 302 856-6723
Georgetown *(G-4239)*

Dycom Industries Inc .... G 302 613-0958
New Castle *(G-9071)*

Eastern States Cnstr Svc Inc .... D 302 995-2259
Wilmington *(G-16264)*

Gt Directional LLC .... G 714 417-2826
Wilmington *(G-16997)*

Guardian Companies Inc .... E 302 834-1000
Wilmington *(G-17000)*

PRODUCTS & SERVICES SECTION

COSMETOLOGY & PERSONAL HYGIENE SALONS

Joseph T Hardy & Son Inc.................... E 302 328-9457
New Castle *(G-9268)*

JT Enterprise LLC................................. G 302 492-8119
Hartly *(G-4887)*

Myralon Webb Ms................................. G 302 684-3841
Lewes *(G-6302)*

Sprig... G 302 753-6859
Townsend *(G-14070)*

Standard Pipe Services LLC................. D 302 286-0701
Newark *(G-12084)*

Tri-State Grouting LLC......................... G 302 286-0701
Newark *(G-12225)*

Tri-State Underground Inc.................... G 302 293-9352
Bear *(G-540)*

Tri-State Underground Inc.................... F 302 836-8030
Townsend *(G-14084)*

Underground Locating Services............ G 302 856-9626
Georgetown *(G-4565)*

Utility Lines Cnstr Svcs LLC................. G 302 337-9980
Bridgeville *(G-778)*

Utility Locator LLC................................ G 215 596-1234
Wilmington *(G-20558)*

CONTRACTORS: Ventilation & Duct Work

Jmt Services Inc.................................... F 302 530-2807
Middletown *(G-7250)*

CONTRACTORS: Warm Air Heating & Air Conditioning

Building Systems and Svcs Inc............. E 302 996-0900
Wilmington *(G-15146)*

United Refrigeration Inc....................... G 302 322-1836
New Castle *(G-9655)*

WJC of Delaware LLC.......................... F 302 323-9600
New Castle *(G-9687)*

CONTRACTORS: Water Well Drilling

Bw Drilling Co....................................... G 302 658-0410
Wilmington *(G-15163)*

Delmarva Builders Inc.......................... G 302 629-9123
Bridgeville *(G-692)*

Shore Well Drillers Inc.......................... G 302 737-7707
Newark *(G-11999)*

Water System Services Inc.................. G 302 732-1490
Dagsboro *(G-1525)*

White Drilling Corp............................... G 302 422-4057
Lincoln *(G-6708)*

CONTRACTORS: Windows & Doors

Ferris Home Imprvs Co LLC................ E 302 998-4500
Newark *(G-10725)*

Francis Pollinger & Son Inc.................. E 302 655-8097
Wilmington *(G-16723)*

Henlopen Overhead Door..................... G 302 228-0561
Lewes *(G-6091)*

Miner Ltd... C 302 516-7791
Historic New Castle *(G-5029)*

Newport Builders & Windowland........... F 302 994-3537
Wilmington *(G-18632)*

CONTRACTORS: Wood Floor Installation & Refinishing

Dominic A Di Febo & Sons................... G 302 425-5054
Wilmington *(G-16128)*

Edward Varnes Hardwood Floors......... F 302 292-0919
Newark *(G-10612)*

Northstern Coating Systems Inc........... G 302 328-6545
Wilmington *(G-18688)*

Unique Finishes Inc.............................. G 302 419-8557
Bear *(G-549)*

Ziggys Inc.. G 302 453-1285
Newark *(G-12434)*

CONTRACTORS: Wrecking & Demolition

Geotech LLC... G 302 353-9769
Wilmington *(G-16849)*

Green Earth Tech Group LLC.............. F 302 257-5617
Wilmington *(G-16964)*

CONTROL EQPT: Electric

Envirotech LLC..................................... G 302 834-5011
Bear *(G-203)*

Val-Tech Inc.. E 302 738-0500
Newark *(G-12298)*

CONTROLS & ACCESS: Indl, Electric

Ultrafine Technologies Inc.................... G 302 384-6513
Wilmington *(G-20502)*

Williams Engrg Solutions LLC............... G 302 670-4841
Magnolia *(G-6791)*

CONTROLS: Environmental

Accessheat Inc..................................... E 302 373-9524
Wilmington *(G-14222)*

Energy Systems Tech Inc..................... G 302 368-0443
New Castle *(G-9096)*

Val-Tech Inc.. E 302 738-0500
Newark *(G-12298)*

CONTROLS: Marine & Navy, Auxiliary

Xrosswater USA LLC........................... G 917 310-1344
Newark *(G-12417)*

CONVENIENCE STORES

J William Gordy Fuel Co....................... G 302 846-3425
Delmar *(G-1604)*

Service Energy LLC............................. D 302 734-7433
Dover *(G-3534)*

CONVEYORS & CONVEYING EQPT

Airsled Inc... G 302 292-8911
Newark *(G-9802)*

Amazon Steel Construction Inc............. G 302 751-1146
Milford *(G-7766)*

CDI Inc Sofr System LLC..................... G 302 536-7325
Seaford *(G-13103)*

COOKING & FOODWARMING EQPT: Commercial

Eagle Mhc Company............................. B 302 653-3000
Clayton *(G-1363)*

Metal Msters Fdservice Eqp Inc........... C 302 653-3000
Clayton *(G-1385)*

COOKWARE: Fine Earthenware

Mauviel Usa Inc.................................... E 302 326-4800
Historic New Castle *(G-5025)*

COOLING TOWERS: Metal

Creative Assemblies Inc....................... F 302 956-6194
Bridgeville *(G-688)*

COPPER ORES

CC Enterprises LLC.............................. F 302 265-3677
Newark *(G-10167)*

COSMETIC PREPARATIONS

5n1-Mc Cosmetics LLC........................ G 866 561-6226
Wilmington *(G-14142)*

Adrion & Co LLC................................... G 302 313-1392
Lewes *(G-5660)*

Claudiva Kae & Co LLC....................... G 302 283-9803
Newark *(G-10250)*

Sun Pharmaceuticals Corp................... E 302 678-6000
Dover *(G-3622)*

COSMETICS & TOILETRIES

Aikym Essentials LLC........................... G 215 910-9479
Middletown *(G-6842)*

Arovo US Inc... E 952 290-0799
Dover *(G-1818)*

Brandywine Botanicals LLC.................. G 302 354-4650
Wilmington *(G-15046)*

Code509com Inc................................... G 941 263-3509
Dover *(G-2108)*

Goodales Naturals................................ G 302 743-6455
Newark *(G-10867)*

Khaos Beauty LLC................................ A 302 427-0119
Wilmington *(G-17712)*

My Lip Stuff.. G 302 945-5922
Lewes *(G-6300)*

Playtex Manufacturing Inc.................... D 302 678-6000
Dover *(G-3336)*

Succulents Soap Sand Scents............. G 302 757-0697
Newark *(G-12117)*

Vegan Skin Clinic LLC......................... G 302 932-1920
Hockessin *(G-5416)*

Wellthy Investors LLC.......................... E 267 847-3486
Dover *(G-3831)*

COSMETICS WHOLESALERS

Amaira Ntral Skncare Sltons In............. G 424 330-5231
Wilmington *(G-14408)*

CTB Intl LLC... G 217 415-4843
Dover *(G-2168)*

Dermal Health Science LLC................. G 302 213-8348
Dover *(G-2285)*

Harrock Properties LLC........................ G 302 202-1321
Dover *(G-2657)*

Lice Lifters Distribution LLC................. G 864 680-4030
Dover *(G-2938)*

Maelys Cosmetics USA Inc.................. F 312 888-5007
Wilmington *(G-18076)*

Mellon Care Inc..................................... G 800 406-0281
Middletown *(G-7339)*

Pharmadel LLC..................................... G 302 322-1329
Historic New Castle *(G-5047)*

Sally Beauty Supply LLC...................... G 302 629-5160
Seaford *(G-13383)*

Sekoiya Inc.. G 323 761-9028
Newark *(G-11972)*

COSMETOLOGY & PERSONAL HYGIENE SALONS

Cartessa Aesthetics............................. G 302 332-1991
Hockessin *(G-5150)*

Charlotte Wilson................................... G 302 500-1440
Seaford *(G-13113)*

CK Skin & Makeup LLC........................ G 302 317-2367
Wilmington *(G-15458)*

European Wax Center........................... G 302 731-2700
Newark *(G-10672)*

Girls Auto Clinic LLC............................ G 484 679-6394
New Castle *(G-9167)*

Hillary J White Soho Slon Spa.............. G 302 838-2110
Bear *(G-275)*

LA BELLE ARTISTRY LLC................... F 302 656-0555
Wilmington *(G-17780)*

Lash Beauty Bar................................... G 302 827-2160
Lewes *(G-6181)*

Lasting Looks....................................... G 302 635-7327
Hockessin *(G-5276)*

COSMETOLOGY & PERSONAL HYGIENE SALONS

Makeup & Love..G.....856 524-1966
  Lewes (G-6238)
Noche Azul Spa.......................................G.....302 345-0070
  Wilmington (G-18662)
Perfect Ten Nail Salon Da...................G.....302 545-3001
  Wilmington (G-18974)
Premiere Hair Design............................G.....302 368-7711
  Middletown (G-7467)
Sassy Spa..G.....302 668-8008
  Wilmington (G-19675)
Trendz Salon and Spa...........................G.....302 632-3045
  Dover (G-3720)
Womens Wellness Ctr & Med Spa.....G.....302 643-2500
  Newark (G-12399)
Young Divas LLC...................................G.....302 354-6232
  New Castle (G-9695)

COSMETOLOGY SCHOOL

Carme LLC..F......302 832-8418
  Newark (G-10150)
Delaware Lrng Inst Csmtlogy In...........F......302 732-6704
  Dagsboro (G-1434)
Island of Misfits LLC..............................G.....302 732-6704
  Dagsboro (G-1468)
Schillng-Dglas Schl Hair Dsign...........F......737 510-0101
  Newark (G-11957)

COUGH MEDICINES

Glaxosmthkline Hldngs Amrcas I........C.....302 984-6932
  Wilmington (G-16882)

COUNTER & SINK TOPS

Counterparts LLC...................................G.....302 349-0400
  Greenwood (G-4605)
Solid Image Inc......................................E......302 877-0901
  Laurel (G-5603)

COUNTRY CLUBS

Cripple Creek Golf & Cntry CLB..........E......302 539-1446
  Dagsboro (G-1433)
Dale Maple Country Club Inc..............E......302 674-2505
  Dover (G-2187)
Greenville Country Club Inc.................E......302 652-3255
  Wilmington (G-16973)
Henlopen Acres Beach Club Inc.........G.....302 227-9919
  Rehoboth Beach (G-12784)
Kings Creek Country Club Inc.............F......302 227-8951
  Rehoboth Beach (G-12823)
Newark Country Club............................D.....302 368-7008
  Newark (G-11532)
Rehoboth Beach Country Club.............D.....302 227-3811
  Rehoboth Beach (G-12918)
Rockland Sports LLC.............................D.....302 654-4435
  Wilmington (G-19541)
Ronald L Barrows..................................G.....302 227-3616
  Rehoboth Beach (G-12938)
Sussex Pines Country Club..................F......302 856-6283
  Georgetown (G-4541)
Wilmington Country Club......................C.....302 655-6171
  Wilmington (G-20813)

CRANE & AERIAL LIFT SVCS

Specialized Carier Systems Inc..........G.....302 424-4548
  Milford (G-8099)

CREDIT CARD SVCS

Applied Card Holdings Inc..................F......302 326-4200
  Wilmington (G-14512)
Continental Cr Protection LLC............G.....302 456-1930
  Newark (G-10314)
Continental Finance Co LLC...............F......302 456-1930
  Wilmington (G-15618)
Continental Funding LLC......................G.....302 456-1930
  Wilmington (G-15619)
Delaware Merchant Services...............G.....302 838-9100
  Wilmington (G-15944)
Dfs Corporate Services LLC................D.....302 735-3902
  Dover (G-2289)
Dfs Corporate Services LLC................C.....302 323-7191
  New Castle (G-9049)
Fia Card Services Nat Assn.................A.....302 457-0517
  Wilmington (G-16593)
Fia Card Services Nat Assn.................B.....302 458-0365
  Wilmington (G-16595)
Fia Card Services Nat Assn.................B.....302 432-1573
  Wilmington (G-16596)
Fia Card Services Nat Assn.................E......800 362-6255
  Wilmington (G-16594)
Heartland Payment Systems LLC.......G.....302 228-9365
  Selbyville (G-13544)
Mercantile Processing Inc...................E......302 524-8000
  Millville (G-8540)
Money Ex Pos Solutions US Inc.........E......866 946-6773
  Dover (G-3118)
Perkwiz Inc..G.....702 866-9122
  Hockessin (G-5341)
Planet Payment Inc...............................D.....516 670-3200
  New Castle (G-9475)
Quotanda LLC..G.....917 971-7585
  Dover (G-3413)
Swoop Payment Processing Inc........E......479 586-2952
  Wilmington (G-20176)

CRUDE PETROLEUM & NATURAL GAS PRODUCTION

Akbell Global Commodities LLC.........G.....347 615-5014
  Dover (G-1759)
Firebird Energy II LLC..........................E......817 857-7800
  Wilmington (G-16611)

CRUDE PETROLEUM PRODUCTION

Nemours Energy....................................G.....302 655-4838
  Wilmington (G-18577)

CULTURE MEDIA

One EDM LLC..E......908 399-0536
  Wilmington (G-18780)

CURTAIN WALLS: Building, Steel

Janette Redrow Ltd...............................G.....302 659-3534
  Townsend (G-14020)

CUTLERY

Arovo US Inc..E......952 290-0799
  Dover (G-1818)

CUTLERY, NEC

Bio Medic Corporation..........................F......302 628-4300
  Seaford (G-13089)

CYCLIC CRUDES & INTERMEDIATES

BASF Corporation..................................C.....302 992-5600
  Wilmington (G-14774)
Chemfirst Inc..D.....302 774-1000
  Wilmington (G-15354)
Honeywell International Inc.................E......302 791-6700
  Claymont (G-1181)

CYLINDERS: Pressure

Anderson Group Inc..............................A.....302 478-6160
  Wilmington (G-14472)

DAIRY PRDTS STORE: Cheese

PRODUCTS & SERVICES SECTION

Queso Time De 3 LLC.........................G.....302 368-4541
  Newark (G-11799)

DAIRY PRDTS: Butter

CD Cream...G.....302 832-5425
  Delaware City (G-1533)

DAIRY PRDTS: Cheese

Roos Foods Inc......................................F......302 653-0600
  Kenton (G-5453)

DAIRY PRDTS: Dietary Supplements, Dairy & Non-Dairy Based

Brainiac Brands USA Inc.....................G.....778 869-4099
  Wilmington (G-15037)
Buoy Hydration Inc...............................G.....314 230-5106
  Camden (G-795)
Candelay Industries LLC......................G.....302 696-2464
  Rockland (G-13029)
Codonrx LLC..G.....773 612-5828
  Dover (G-2109)
Golo LLC...E......302 781-4260
  Newark (G-10864)
Harrock Properties LLC........................G.....302 202-1321
  Dover (G-2657)
In10sity Fitness United.........................G.....302 677-1010
  Dover (G-2723)
Kappa Bioscience Usa Inc..................G.....609 201-1459
  Dover (G-2830)
Lifespan Health Science LLC............G.....203 273-4037
  Wilmington (G-17904)
LLC Quick Shield..................................G.....514 730-8040
  Wilmington (G-17956)
Mellon Care Inc.....................................G.....800 406-0281
  Middletown (G-7339)
Miracle Moo LLC...................................G.....321 948-4678
  Wilmington (G-18385)
Nuchido Inc..G.....314 260-7874
  Wilmington (G-18709)
Rophe Living Inc....................................G.....302 500-9238
  Middletown (G-7523)
Roxlor LLC...G.....302 778-4166
  Wilmington (G-19574)
Skipwith Organics LLC.........................G.....908 573-2930
  Dover (G-3573)
Tc Nutrition Corp...................................G.....306 290-7457
  Wilmington (G-20237)
Tesla Nootropics Inc.............................G.....514 718-2270
  Dover (G-3672)
Tws Chewsy LLC..................................G.....514 730-8040
  Wilmington (G-20472)
Vulcan Wizard LLC...............................G.....914 326-6023
  Lewes (G-6612)
Wellabs Inc...G.....816 774-4030
  Dover (G-3829)
Yumi Nutrition Inc..................................G.....917 909-2166
  Newark (G-12424)

DAIRY PRDTS: Milk & Cream, Cultured & Flavored

Hy-Point Dairy Farms Inc....................C.....302 478-1414
  Wilmington (G-17240)

DAIRY PRDTS: Milk, Fluid

Kraft Heinz Company...........................A.....302 734-6100
  Dover (G-2886)
Lechia Inc...G.....302 261-5733
  Dover (G-2922)

DAIRY PRDTS: Yogurt, Frozen

PRODUCTS & SERVICES SECTION

DEPARTMENT STORES

Kohr Brothers Inc .... E 302 227-9354
Rehoboth Beach *(G-12825)*

DATA ENTRY SVCS

Cognitro LLC .... G 347 983-9785
Lewes *(G-5850)*

DATA PROCESSING & PREPARATION SVCS

Alpha Comm LLC .... F 302 784-0645
Bear *(G-29)*

Ample Business Solutions Inc .... F 302 752-4270
Wilmington *(G-14462)*

Analyttica Datalab Inc .... E 917 300-3325
Wilmington *(G-14467)*

Argo Ai Corporation .... G 516 602-9295
Dover *(G-1812)*

Brainstorm Force US LLC .... G 302 330-8557
Wilmington *(G-15038)*

Brandywine Cad Design Inc .... E 302 478-8334
Wilmington *(G-15047)*

Clms LLC .... G 703 629-3231
Rehoboth Beach *(G-12679)*

Computer Aid Inc .... G 302 831-5500
Newark *(G-10294)*

Data Cloud Partners LLC .... G 805 729-1088
Wilmington *(G-15796)*

Data-Bi LLC .... G 302 290-3138
Wilmington *(G-15798)*

Datatech Enterprises Inc .... F 540 370-0010
Selbyville *(G-13515)*

Doculogica Corp .... G 302 753-5944
Wilmington *(G-16113)*

Fis Investment Ventures LLC .... E 484 582-2000
Wilmington *(G-16643)*

Ftl Technologies Corporation .... E 703 634-6910
Lewes *(G-6019)*

GOBLIN Technologies LLC .... G 302 644-5599
Newark *(G-10857)*

Helical Software Corp .... G 323 544-5348
Lewes *(G-6087)*

Information Consultants Inc .... F 302 239-2942
Yorklyn *(G-20993)*

Invensis Inc .... C 470 260-0084
Wilmington *(G-17404)*

Lan-Tech Inc .... G 877 311-1030
Claymont *(G-1211)*

Logically Ai Inc .... F 202 768-9876
Camden *(G-869)*

Lokblok Inc .... F 408 640-8644
Wilmington *(G-17979)*

Monet Intermediate LLC .... E 929 559-5423
Wilmington *(G-18412)*

Morning Hornet LLC .... F 650 543-4800
Wilmington *(G-18451)*

Nino Finance Inc .... G 415 236-7591
Claymont *(G-1254)*

Pendulum It LLC .... G 302 480-9433
Dover *(G-3290)*

Priv Social Inc .... G 501 301-4197
Middletown *(G-7470)*

Raad360 LLC .... F 855 722-3560
Newark *(G-11812)*

Rocketchat Technologies Corp .... C 213 725-2428
Wilmington *(G-19533)*

Rsf Managed Services LLC .... G 302 345-7162
Wilmington *(G-19580)*

Starbelt LLC .... G 256 724-9200
Wilmington *(G-20026)*

Supportcom Inc .... D 650 556-9440
Wilmington *(G-20151)*

Technlgy Expiration Group Inc .... G 202 222-0794
New Castle *(G-9622)*

Truveris Inc .... C 800 430-1430
Wilmington *(G-20450)*

Vultran Creative Marketing .... G 302 981-3379
Wilmington *(G-20660)*

Webstudy Inc .... G 888 326-4058
Harbeson *(G-4718)*

X5 Networks Corporation .... G 800 784-5228
Wilmington *(G-20912)*

DATA PROCESSING SVCS

Computer Services of Delaware ..... G 302 697-8644
Dover *(G-2127)*

Dastor LLC .... E 610 337-5560
Wilmington *(G-15795)*

Data Drum Inc .... G 347 502-8485
Newark *(G-10390)*

Ddh (north America) Inc .... G 617 893-9004
Lewes *(G-5884)*

Deeptrace Inc .... E 424 413-8787
Lewes *(G-5886)*

Fiserv Wrldwide Sltions II LLC .... F 800 872-7882
Wilmington *(G-16644)*

J P Morgan Services Inc .... C 302 634-1000
Newark *(G-11075)*

John Snow Labs Inc .... E 302 786-5227
Lewes *(G-6147)*

Kinsta Inc .... E 310 736-9306
Dover *(G-2878)*

Label Your Data .... G 844 935-2538
Wilmington *(G-17783)*

National Dcument MGT Solutions ... G 302 535-9263
Marydel *(G-6808)*

Planet Payment Solutions Inc .... E 516 670-3200
New Castle *(G-9476)*

Resulticks Solution Inc .... G 347 416-7673
Wilmington *(G-19444)*

Rfx Analyst Inc .... G 302 244-5650
Dover *(G-3463)*

Symmetry Data Solutions Inc .... E 805 708-4506
Wilmington *(G-20183)*

Usacarrecordcom LLC .... G 302 645-7400
Lewes *(G-6594)*

Valiu Inc .... G 317 853-5081
Lewes *(G-6598)*

DECORATIVE WOOD & WOODWORK

Artisan Woodworks LLC .... G 302 841-5182
Harbeson *(G-4683)*

Cedar Neck Decor LLC .... G 918 497-7179
Dagsboro *(G-1424)*

DEFENSE SYSTEMS & EQPT

Advanced Defense Technology ...... C 888 298-5775
Wilmington *(G-14273)*

First Line Defense LLC .... G 302 287-2764
Smyrna *(G-13734)*

Precision Technic Defence Inc .... G 801 404-4626
Wilmington *(G-19159)*

Special Support Tech Inc .... G 804 620-6072
Lewes *(G-6498)*

DENTAL EQPT

Tc Dental Equipment Services .... G 302 740-9049
Townsend *(G-14078)*

DENTAL EQPT & SPLYS

Cravitysci LLC .... G 571 208-6421
New Castle *(G-8984)*

Delmarva 2000 Ltd .... G 302 645-2226
Milton *(G-8601)*

Dentsply Sirona Inc .... D 302 422-4511
Milford *(G-7864)*

Dentsply Sirona Inc .... F 302 422-1043
Milford *(G-7865)*

Dentsply Sirona Inc .... G 302 430-7474
Milford *(G-7866)*

DENTAL EQPT & SPLYS WHOLESALERS

Benco .... G 302 650-0053
Wilmington *(G-14829)*

Dentsply Sirona Inc .... G 302 422-4511
Milford *(G-7867)*

DENTISTS' OFFICES & CLINICS

Avalon Dental LLC Bldg G4 .... F 302 292-8899
Newark *(G-9949)*

Charles J Veith DMD .... G 302 658-7354
Wilmington *(G-15336)*

Dd Snacks LLC .... G 302 652-3850
Wilmington *(G-15832)*

Delaware Star Dental .... F 302 994-3093
Wilmington *(G-15968)*

Dental Sleep Solution .... G 302 235-8249
Wilmington *(G-16016)*

Enhanced Dental Care .... G 302 645-7200
Rehoboth Beach *(G-12743)*

Equidental .... G 302 423-0851
Dover *(G-2458)*

Erin N Macko DDS LLC .... F 302 368-7463
Newark *(G-10665)*

Family Denistry .... G 302 368-0054
Newark *(G-10707)*

Freedom Dental Management Inc .. F 302 836-3750
Newark *(G-10776)*

Howard W Zucker D D S P A .... F 302 475-8174
Wilmington *(G-17219)*

Julie Q Nies DDS .... F 302 242-9085
Dover *(G-2818)*

Jung B Kim DDS .... G 302 652-3556
Wilmington *(G-17613)*

Kelly Ann Hatton .... G 484 571-5369
Wilmington *(G-17680)*

King and Minsk PA .... G 302 475-3270
Wilmington *(G-17727)*

Mary Sweeney-Lehr .... F 302 764-0589
Wilmington *(G-18182)*

Michael Butterworth Dr .... F 302 732-9850
Dagsboro *(G-1482)*

Michael Matthias .... G 302 575-0100
Wilmington *(G-18320)*

Mill Creek Select .... G 302 995-2090
Wilmington *(G-18357)*

P2 Dental PA .... G 302 422-6924
Milford *(G-8040)*

Practice Without Pressure .... G 302 635-7837
Wilmington *(G-19143)*

Southern Delaware Dental Spec .... G 302 855-9499
Georgetown *(G-4518)*

Westside Family Healthcare Inc ..... E 302 836-2864
Bear *(G-563)*

Westside Family Healthcare Inc ..... E 302 455-0900
Newark *(G-12364)*

Westside Family Healthcare Inc ..... E 302 575-1414
Wilmington *(G-20745)*

Westside Family Healthcare Inc ..... E 302 656-8292
Wilmington *(G-20747)*

Westside Family Healthcare Inc ..... F 302 656-8292
Wilmington *(G-20746)*

DEODORANTS: Personal

Dab Deodorant LLC .... G 973 512-2703
New Castle *(G-8993)*

Employee Codes: A=Over 500 employees, B=251-500
C=101-250, D=51-100, E=20-50, F=10-19, G=1-9

DEPARTMENT STORES

DEPARTMENT STORES

Be Blessed Design Group LLC .... G 302 561-3793
  Bear *(G-59)*

DEPARTMENT STORES: Army-Navy Goods

AMC Museum Foundation .... G 302 677-5938
  Dover *(G-1782)*
Domian International Svc LLC .... G 804 837-3616
  Smyrna *(G-13711)*

DEPARTMENT STORES: Country General

Country Store .... G 302 653-5111
  Kenton *(G-5452)*

DEPILATORIES, COSMETIC

Nabeel and Huzaif LLC .... G 302 445-7483
  Lewes *(G-6303)*

DERMATOLOGICALS

Delaware Dermatologic .... G 302 593-8625
  Wilmington *(G-15904)*
Nanoskin LLC .... G 310 345-4768
  Middletown *(G-7391)*
Workroom Enterprises LLC .... G 417 621-5577
  Wilmington *(G-20893)*

DESIGN SVCS, NEC

3d Cad Design .... G 302 373-7750
  Newark *(G-9711)*
Aerospace Dsign Compliance LLC .... G 302 407-6825
  New Castle *(G-8769)*
Anax Designs .... G 877 908-8719
  Newark *(G-9860)*
Anybodies Inc .... F 646 699-8781
  Wilmington *(G-14497)*
Automation Machine Design SE .... G 302 335-3911
  Magnolia *(G-6720)*
Catleza LLC .... G 415 812-2676
  Wilmington *(G-15279)*
Chesapeake Design Center LLC .... G 302 875-8570
  Laurel *(G-5481)*
Chime Inc .... D 978 844-1162
  Wilmington *(G-15382)*
Communication Concepts LLC .... G 302 658-9800
  Wilmington *(G-15557)*
Creative Marketing Concepts .... G 302 367-7100
  Wilmington *(G-15694)*
Creativity Diversified LLC .... G 302 897-5961
  Middletown *(G-7021)*
Custom Creations By Design .... G 302 482-2267
  Wilmington *(G-15739)*
Dark Knight Services Inc .... F 302 468-6237
  Wilmington *(G-15794)*
Delco Modular .... G 302 934-7704
  Millsboro *(G-8265)*
Design LLC .... G 888 520-7070
  Wilmington *(G-16023)*
Designer Consigner Inc .... E 302 373-6318
  Rehoboth Beach *(G-12721)*
Elite USA Fashion LLC .... G 810 410-5403
  Claymont *(G-1129)*
Endure Walls .... G 302 479-7614
  Wilmington *(G-16413)*
Esource Systems LLC .... G 302 444-4228
  Newark *(G-10666)*
Family Creations .... G 302 239-4275
  Newark *(G-10706)*
Focal Point Products .... G 800 662-5550
  Greenwood *(G-4630)*
Gt Designs Inc .... G 302 275-8100
  Middletown *(G-7181)*

Is2 LLC .... F 302 379-1265
  Hockessin *(G-5253)*
Iswich LLC .... G 302 528-0229
  Wilmington *(G-17430)*
Jefferson Group LLC .... G 302 764-1550
  Wilmington *(G-17517)*
Jill L Alfree .... G 302 653-9107
  Clayton *(G-1376)*
JI Mechanical Inc .... G 302 337-7855
  Bridgeville *(G-719)*
Johnny Janosik Inc .... C 302 875-5955
  Laurel *(G-5537)*
Katherine Nwman Dsign Intl LLC .... G 416 922-5806
  Wilmington *(G-17662)*
Knrp LLC .... G 408 480-8501
  Dover *(G-2881)*
Mdaas Global Corp .... G 410 905-1213
  Dover *(G-3045)*
Milfordlivecom .... G 302 542-9231
  Milford *(G-8010)*
Nimbis Designs LLC .... F 302 494-7584
  Hockessin *(G-5321)*
Nouvir Lightning Corporation .... G 302 628-9888
  Seaford *(G-13320)*
Palm Nft Studio Inc .... G 216 870-9066
  Dover *(G-3262)*
Playpower Labs Inc .... F 917 544-4171
  Dover *(G-3335)*
Reachable Solutions Inc .... G 908 962-8076
  Dover *(G-3430)*
Redgait 2530 LLC .... G 302 683-0978
  Wilmington *(G-19387)*
Silpada Designs .... G 302 376-6964
  Middletown *(G-7566)*
Utility Sales Associates Inc .... G 410 479-0646
  Ocean View *(G-12578)*

DESIGN SVCS: Commercial & Indl

Drafting By Design Inc .... G 302 292-8304
  Newark *(G-10569)*

DESIGN SVCS: Computer Integrated Systems

924 Inc .... E 302 656-6100
  Hockessin *(G-5109)*
Aething Inc .... G 917 640-2582
  Dover *(G-1732)*
Aigc Games Inc .... G 214 499-8654
  Lewes *(G-5666)*
Base-2 Solutions LLC .... D 202 215-2152
  Lewes *(G-5735)*
Brittons Wise Computers Inc .... G 302 659-0343
  Smyrna *(G-13668)*
Cks Global Ventures LLC .... E 302 355-0511
  Newark *(G-10248)*
Conexiam Solutions Inc .... G 302 884-6746
  Wilmington *(G-15591)*
Datatech Enterprises Inc .... F 540 370-0010
  Selbyville *(G-13515)*
Dodd Health Innovation LLC .... G 410 598-7266
  Ocean View *(G-12506)*
Ftl Technologies Corporation .... E 703 634-6910
  Lewes *(G-6019)*
Gigahub Inc .... G 916 304-4710
  Dover *(G-2584)*
Info Systems LLC .... C 302 633-9800
  Wilmington *(G-17328)*
Internet Business Pubg Corp .... F 302 875-7700
  Laurel *(G-5536)*
Itiyam LLC .... F 703 291-1600
  Wilmington *(G-17434)*

M C Tek LLC .... G 302 644-9695
  Rehoboth Beach *(G-12842)*
Pmsa It Services LLC .... G 301 806-5163
  Rehoboth Beach *(G-12893)*
Progressive Software Cmpt Inc .... C 302 479-9700
  Wilmington *(G-19221)*
SNMP3 Security LLC .... G 302 448-8501
  Newark *(G-12045)*
Transformify Inc .... G 302 205-0685
  Claymont *(G-1316)*
Verizon Delaware LLC .... C 302 571-1571
  Wilmington *(G-20590)*
Virtual Enterprises Inc .... F 302 324-5322
  New Castle *(G-9672)*
Webstudy Inc .... G 888 326-4058
  Harbeson *(G-4718)*

DETECTIVE & ARMORED CAR SERVICES

Axess Corp .... G 910 270-2077
  Newark *(G-9958)*
Black Dragon Corporation .... G 617 470-9230
  Newark *(G-10046)*
Shadow Protective Services .... G 410 903-3455
  Millsboro *(G-8457)*

DIAGNOSTIC SUBSTANCES

Alcheme Bio Inc .... G 858 291-9708
  Dover *(G-1760)*
Anp Technologies Inc .... E 302 283-1730
  Newark *(G-9875)*
Aqua Science LLC .... G 302 757-5241
  Newark *(G-9896)*
Eidp Inc .... G 302 695-5300
  Wilmington *(G-16335)*
Farma Quimica LLC .... G 703 537-9789
  Lewes *(G-5988)*
Siemens Hlthcare Dgnostics Inc .... G 302 631-8006
  Historic New Castle *(G-5071)*
Siemens Hlthcare Dgnostics Inc .... D 302 631-7357
  Newark *(G-12005)*
Standard Merger Sub LLC .... E 302 456-6785
  Newark *(G-12083)*

DIAGNOSTIC SUBSTANCES OR AGENTS: In Vitro

Enzymetrics Bioscience Inc .... G 302 763-3658
  Wilmington *(G-16447)*

DIAGNOSTIC SUBSTANCES OR AGENTS: Veterinary

Vetosine Inc .... G 424 258-0120
  Wilmington *(G-20601)*

DIATOMACEOUS EARTH MINING SVCS

Rgp Holding Inc .... F 302 661-0117
  Wilmington *(G-19453)*

DIE CUTTING SVC: Paper

Prescotech Inc .... D 502 585-5866
  Wilmington *(G-19178)*

DIES & TOOLS: Special

Duhadaway Tool and Die Sp Inc .... D 302 366-0113
  Newark *(G-10575)*

DIODES: Light Emitting

Dupont Displays Inc .... E 805 562-9293
  Wilmington *(G-16206)*
Jaykal Led Solutions Inc .... G 302 295-0015
  Georgetown *(G-4379)*

DIRECT SELLING ESTABLISHMENTS, NEC

Baby Apron LLC................................ G 800 796-4406
Claymont *(G-1050)*

DISASTER SVCS

Pulsar360 Corp.................................. E 855 578-5727
Newark *(G-11771)*

DISCS & TAPE: Optical, Blank

National Tape Duplicators.................... G 302 999-1110
Wilmington *(G-18549)*

DISINFECTING & PEST CONTROL SERVICES

Aion Oakwood Venture LLC................ G 212 849-9200
Wilmington *(G-14334)*

First State Hood & Duct LLC............... G 888 866-7389
Wilmington *(G-16629)*

Rentokil North America Inc................. F 410 882-1000
Newark *(G-11853)*

DISINFECTING SVCS

Air Quality Remediation LLC................ F 302 464-1050
Townsend *(G-13955)*

Its R Joy Llc..................................... E 215 315-8300
Bear *(G-291)*

Qualdent LLC.................................... G 856 642-4078
Wilmington *(G-19282)*

Think Clean & Grounds Up LLC........... F 904 250-1614
Historic New Castle *(G-5084)*

DISK & DISKETTE CONVERSION SVCS

Sumuri LLC....................................... E 302 570-0015
Magnolia *(G-6786)*

DISTRIBUTORS: Motor Vehicle Engine

Main Office Inc.................................. G 302 732-3460
Dagsboro *(G-1478)*

DOCUMENT STORAGE SVCS

Documo Inc...................................... E 858 299-5295
Wilmington *(G-16114)*

Nrai Services LLC.............................. F 302 674-4089
Dover *(G-3208)*

DOORS: Garage, Overhead, Metal

Allmark Door Company LLC................ F 302 323-4999
New Castle *(G-8786)*

Cheslantic Overhead Door.................. G 443 880-0378
Delmar *(G-1577)*

Herbstar Industries LLC..................... G 754 273-4204
Newark *(G-10948)*

Pinnacle Garage Door Co LLC............ G 302 505-4531
Frederica *(G-4180)*

DOORS: Garage, Overhead, Wood

Allmark Door Company LLC................ F 302 323-4999
New Castle *(G-8786)*

Pinnacle Garage Door Co LLC............ G 302 505-4531
Frederica *(G-4180)*

DRAPERIES: Plastic & Textile, From Purchased Materials

Barlows Upholstery Inc...................... G 302 655-3955
Wilmington *(G-14766)*

G L K Inc.. F 302 697-3838
Dover *(G-2551)*

DRINKING PLACES: Bars & Lounges

First State Bowling Center.................. G 302 762-3883
Wilmington *(G-16625)*

Sinkeeas Lounge & Bar LLC............... F 302 434-2530
Newark *(G-12013)*

DRINKING PLACES: Beer Garden

Dewey Beer & Food Company LLC...... F 302 227-1182
Dewey Beach *(G-1668)*

DRUGS & DRUG PROPRIETARIES, WHOLESALE

Disrupt Pharma Tech Africa Inc........... G 312 945-8002
Dover *(G-2304)*

DRUGS & DRUG PROPRIETARIES, WHOLESALE: Animal Medicines

Animal Health Sales Inc..................... F 302 436-8286
Selbyville *(G-13462)*

DRUGS & DRUG PROPRIETARIES, WHOLESALE: Patent Medicines

Sinuswars LLC.................................. F 212 901-0805
Wilmington *(G-19843)*

DRUGS & DRUG PROPRIETARIES, WHOLESALE: Pharmaceuticals

A2a Intgrted Phrmceuticals LLC.......... G 270 202-2461
Lewes *(G-5648)*

A66 Inc... G 800 444-0446
Wilmington *(G-14180)*

Astrazeneca LLC............................... D 800 236-9933
Wilmington *(G-14606)*

Astrazeneca Pharmaceuticals LP........ A 800 456-3669
Wilmington *(G-14610)*

Delaware Pharmacist Society............. G 302 659-3088
Smyrna *(G-13704)*

Foresee Pharmaceuticals Inc............. F 302 396-5243
Newark *(G-10760)*

Fulcrum Pharmacy MGT Inc............... G 302 658-8020
Wilmington *(G-16768)*

Hannas Phrm Sup Co Inc................... F 302 571-8761
Wilmington *(G-17050)*

Harford Health Services Inc................ F 410 420-8108
Selbyville *(G-13543)*

Hrc Medics LLC................................. F 561 856-6180
Newark *(G-10982)*

Pharmerica Long-Term Care LLC........ E 302 454-8234
Newark *(G-11679)*

Pumas-Ai Inc.................................... E 551 207-6084
Dover *(G-3395)*

Qps LLC... C 302 369-3753
Newark *(G-11784)*

Radius Rx Direct Inc.......................... G 302 658-9196
Wilmington *(G-19314)*

SPI Pharma Inc................................. E 800 789-9755
Wilmington *(G-19962)*

Xynomic Pharmaceuticals Inc............. F 650 430-7561
Dover *(G-3883)*

DRUGS & DRUG PROPRIETARIES, WHOLESALE: Vitamins & Minerals

Kerahealth France LLC...................... G 302 351-3377
Wilmington *(G-17695)*

Matrix Life Science Inc....................... G 281 419-7942
Lewes *(G-6249)*

Normopharm Inc................................ G 954 210-4812
Wilmington *(G-18674)*

Sunshine Nutrition LLC...................... G 971 456-1000
Lewes *(G-6525)*

DUCTS: Sheet Metal

Costa and Rihl Inc............................. C 856 534-7325
Wilmington *(G-15649)*

Ducts Unlimited Inc........................... E 302 378-4125
Smyrna *(G-13717)*

DYES & PIGMENTS: Organic

Dupont Indus Bsciences USA LLC...... E 302 774-1000
Wilmington *(G-16210)*

Eidp Inc.. E 302 656-9626
Wilmington *(G-16337)*

Eidp Inc.. G 302 999-2826
Wilmington *(G-16339)*

Orient Corporation of America............ E 302 628-1300
Seaford *(G-13326)*

EATING PLACES

Baywood Greens Golf Club................ E 302 947-9225
Millsboro *(G-8186)*

Blue Hen Hospitality LLC.................... F 302 530-5066
Wilmington *(G-14968)*

Boardwalk Plaza Incorporated............ E 302 227-0441
Rehoboth Beach *(G-12648)*

Camels Hump Inc.............................. F 302 227-5719
Rehoboth Beach *(G-12662)*

Coastal Properties I LLC.................... E 302 227-5800
Rehoboth Beach *(G-12686)*

Delcastle Golf Club Management........ F 302 998-9505
Wilmington *(G-15988)*

Diamond State Pty Rentl & Sls........... G 302 777-6677
Wilmington *(G-16057)*

First State Brewing Co LLC................ E 302 285-9535
Middletown *(G-7131)*

Fresh Juice Partners LLC................... G 302 364-0909
Lewes *(G-6016)*

Greenville Country Club Inc................ E 302 652-3255
Wilmington *(G-16973)*

Harrington Raceway Inc..................... D 302 398-5346
Harrington *(G-4780)*

Jbs Kitchen LLC................................ G 302 487-3830
New Castle *(G-9256)*

M & P Adventures Inc........................ G 302 645-6271
Lewes *(G-6232)*

Newark Country Club......................... D 302 368-7008
Newark *(G-11532)*

Routzhan Jessman............................ E 302 398-4206
Harrington *(G-4822)*

Seafood City Inc................................ G 302 284-8486
Felton *(G-4024)*

Swami Enterprises Inc....................... G 302 999-8077
Wilmington *(G-20168)*

University Whist CLB of Wlmngt.......... E 302 658-5125
Wilmington *(G-20534)*

Wilmington Country Club.................... C 302 655-6171
Wilmington *(G-20813)*

EDITING SVCS

Ultius Cstm Wrting Edting Svcs........... F 702 690-4552
Wilmington *(G-20499)*

EDITORIAL SVCS

Biblion... G 302 644-2210
Lewes *(G-5762)*

Dialog News Paper Inc....................... G 302 573-3109
Wilmington *(G-16048)*

EDUCATIONAL SVCS

Analyttica Datalab Inc........................ E 917 300-3325
Wilmington *(G-14467)*

Avkin Inc.. F 302 562-7468
Wilmington *(G-14673)*

Crypto World Journal Inc.................... F 302 213-8136
Dover *(G-2165)*

EDUCATIONAL SVCS

Delaware Fncl Edcatn Alnce Inc........G..... 302 674-0288
Dover *(G-2240)*

Design Tribe Republic LLC............F..... 302 918-5279
Wilmington *(G-16027)*

Discover Permaculture LLC............G..... 850 970-7376
Middletown *(G-7063)*

Enhanced Corporate Prfmce LLC.......G..... 302 545-8541
Newark *(G-10648)*

Learn Game LLC.......................F..... 484 841-9709
Middletown *(G-7292)*

Maggie Magpie Inc....................G..... 302 331-5061
Middletown *(G-7321)*

Pamper ME Pink LLC...................F..... 302 200-2635
Selbyville *(G-13589)*

Rose Hill Community Center...........F..... 302 656-8513
New Castle *(G-9541)*

Serena Joy LLC.......................G..... 302 312-3318
Wilmington *(G-19755)*

She Podcasts.........................G..... 302 588-2317
Wilmington *(G-19785)*

ELECTRIC & OTHER SERVICES COMBINED

Balanceco2 Inc.......................G..... 302 494-9476
Wilmington *(G-14718)*

Delmarva Power Financing I...........G..... 202 872-2000
Wilmington *(G-15998)*

Indian River Power LLC...............G..... 302 934-3527
Dagsboro *(G-1466)*

ELECTRIC MOTOR REPAIR SVCS

Dills Electric.......................G..... 302 674-3444
Camden *(G-819)*

Electric Motor Repair Svc............G..... 302 322-1179
Historic New Castle *(G-4980)*

HP Motors Inc........................G..... 302 368-4543
Newark *(G-10981)*

Warren Electric Co Inc...............G..... 302 629-9134
Seaford *(G-13444)*

ELECTRIC POWER DISTRIBUTION TO CONSUMERS

Atlantic City Electric Co............G..... 302 429-3200
Wilmington *(G-14627)*

Atlantic City Electric Co............G..... 302 588-6675
Wilmington *(G-14628)*

Blue Hen Utility Services Inc........G..... 302 273-3167
New Castle *(G-8870)*

Chesapeake Utilities Corp............C..... 302 734-6799
Dover *(G-2059)*

City of Dover........................E..... 302 736-7070
Dover *(G-2081)*

Conectiv LLC.........................A..... 302 429-3018
Newark *(G-10297)*

Country Coop Inc....................G..... 302 249-1985
Greenwood *(G-4607)*

Delaware Electric Cooperative Inc....C..... 302 349-9090
Greenwood *(G-4613)*

Delaware Municipal Elc Corp..........G..... 302 659-0200
Smyrna *(G-13701)*

Delmarva Power & Light Company.......F..... 302 454-4040
Newark *(G-10503)*

Delmarva Power & Light Company.......E..... 302 454-4450
Newark *(G-10504)*

Delmarva Power & Light Company.......F..... 302 668-3809
Wilmington *(G-15997)*

Delmarva Power & Light Company.......D..... 302 454-0300
Newark *(G-10502)*

Municipal Services Commission........G..... 302 323-2330
Historic New Castle *(G-5031)*

P H I Pepco..........................E..... 302 454-4085
Newark *(G-11609)*

Statewise Energy Ohio LLC............F..... 855 862-1185
Wilmington *(G-20036)*

ELECTRIC POWER GENERATION: Fossil Fuel

Domian International Svc LLC.........G..... 804 837-3616
Smyrna *(G-13711)*

ELECTRIC SERVICES

4 Elements Es LLC....................G..... 302 670-5575
Dover *(G-1686)*

Aci Energy Inc.......................D..... 302 588-3024
Wilmington *(G-14233)*

AGE Electric Ltd.....................G..... 302 632-2968
Lincoln *(G-6654)*

Bid On Energy LLC....................F..... 302 360-8110
Lewes *(G-5763)*

Carroll Brothers Electric LLC........G..... 302 947-4754
Millsboro *(G-8216)*

Check-It Electric LLC................G..... 302 650-1921
Wilmington *(G-15350)*

City of Milford......................E..... 302 422-1110
Milford *(G-7829)*

Clay White Electrical Inc............G..... 302 994-7748
Newark *(G-10252)*

Cleanbay Renewables LLC..............G..... 866 691-1519
Wilmington *(G-15473)*

Cwp Energy Solution Inc..............G..... 514 360-0270
Wilmington *(G-15748)*

Elec Integrity.......................G..... 302 388-3430
Dover *(G-2431)*

Electrical Integrity LLC.............F..... 302 388-3430
New Castle *(G-9087)*

Emera US Finance LP..................G..... 302 636-5400
Wilmington *(G-16390)*

Enersource Electrical Svc LLC........G..... 302 842-8714
Wilmington *(G-16419)*

Evolution Energy Partners LLC........G..... 302 425-5008
Wilmington *(G-16493)*

Flemings Electrical Service..........G..... 302 258-9386
Laurel *(G-5513)*

J Fredericks & Son Elec C............G..... 302 733-0307
Newark *(G-11072)*

KB Electrical Services...............G..... 302 276-5733
Wilmington *(G-17669)*

Kids Kingdom Elc LLC.................G..... 302 377-1698
Wilmington *(G-17715)*

Marianas Energy Company LLC..........E..... 671 477-3060
Dover *(G-3018)*

Mocean Energy Corp...................G..... 410 449-4286
Dover *(G-3114)*

Moltex Energy USA LLC................G..... 775 346-7520
Wilmington *(G-18405)*

Naes Corporation.....................E..... 856 299-0020
New Castle *(G-9391)*

NRG Energy Inc.......................F..... 302 934-3537
Millsboro *(G-8408)*

Omniptntial Enrgy Partners LLC.......G..... 888 429-6664
Wilmington *(G-18770)*

Peg Gilson Membership Chair..........G..... 302 734-5190
Dover *(G-3289)*

Raymond M Cook.......................G..... 302 236-0087
Seaford *(G-13366)*

Resurrected Electric Llc.............G..... 302 841-8989
Laurel *(G-5589)*

Ridgewood Electric Pwr Tr III........G..... 302 888-7444
Wilmington *(G-19480)*

Ross Electrical Services LLC.........G..... 443 614-7294
Delmar *(G-1632)*

Solar Electric Power Assoc...........G..... 302 893-1354
Newark *(G-12052)*

St Delware Electrical................G..... 302 857-5316
Dover *(G-3602)*

Stephen Devary.......................G..... 302 674-4560
Dover *(G-3612)*

Stork Electric Associates LLC........G..... 302 654-9427
Wilmington *(G-20087)*

Summerfield Elec Solutions LLC.......G..... 302 824-3045
Clayton *(G-1407)*

Taporterelectric.....................G..... 302 366-0108
Newark *(G-12161)*

USS Wind Technologies LLC............G..... 646 770-6265
Lewes *(G-6595)*

ELECTRIC SVCS, NEC: Power Generation

Cogentrix Delaware Holdings..........B..... 847 908-2800
Wilmington *(G-15517)*

Conectiv LLC.........................F..... 800 375-7117
Wilmington *(G-15590)*

Conectiv LLC.........................C..... 202 872-2680
Newark *(G-10298)*

Copia Power Opco LLC.................F..... 612 961-5783
Dover *(G-2135)*

Energy Center Dover LLC..............F..... 302 678-4666
Dover *(G-2449)*

FPL Energy American Wind LLC.........F..... 302 655-0632
Wilmington *(G-16716)*

Garrison Calpine.....................G..... 302 562-5661
Dover *(G-2559)*

Hv Sunrise LLC.......................F..... 612 961-5783
Wilmington *(G-17239)*

Pepco Holdings LLC...................F..... 202 872-2000
Wilmington *(G-18965)*

Renewable Energy Holdings LLC........E..... 817 213-6041
Dover *(G-3456)*

Scituate Solar I LLC.................G..... 212 419-4843
Wilmington *(G-19709)*

ELECTRICAL APPARATUS & EQPT WHOLESALERS

Anderson Group Inc...................A..... 302 478-6160
Wilmington *(G-14472)*

Anixter Inc..........................G..... 302 325-2590
New Castle *(G-8810)*

Anixter Power Solutions Inc..........F..... 302 298-3601
Historic New Castle *(G-4932)*

Globe Electric Company USA Inc.......G..... 514 694-0444
Dover *(G-2596)*

Sevenshopper Inc.....................E..... 302 407-6905
Wilmington *(G-19769)*

Siemens Corporation..................E..... 302 690-2046
Newark *(G-12004)*

Siemens Industry Inc.................G..... 302 631-8410
Newark *(G-12006)*

ELECTRICAL DEVICE PARTS: Porcelain, Molded

Niterra (USA) Holding Inc............C..... 302 288-0131
Wilmington *(G-18650)*

ELECTRICAL EQPT REPAIR SVCS

Food Equipment Service Inc...........G..... 302 996-9363
Wilmington *(G-16682)*

ELECTRICAL EQPT: Automotive, NEC

Advanced Defense Technology..........C..... 888 298-5775
Wilmington *(G-14273)*

Ev Usa Inc...........................G..... 973 674-1326
Lewes *(G-5976)*

PRODUCTS & SERVICES SECTION

ELEVATORS WHOLESALERS

ELECTRICAL GOODS, WHOLESALE: Air Conditioning Appliances

Gt World Machineries Usa Inc................. G 800 242-4935
Christiana *(G-999)*

ELECTRICAL GOODS, WHOLESALE: Electrical Appliances, Major

ABC Sales & Service Inc...................... F 302 652-3683
Wilmington *(G-14196)*

Appliances Zone........................... G 302 280-6073
Delmar *(G-1566)*

ELECTRICAL GOODS, WHOLESALE: Electronic Parts

Alvatek Electronics LLC...................... F 302 655-5870
Wilmington *(G-14402)*

Atechnologie LLC........................... G 781 325-5230
Wilmington *(G-14617)*

Avirm Inc.................................. D 626 603-1000
Wilmington *(G-14670)*

Electronics Exchange Inc..................... G 302 322-5401
Historic New Castle *(G-4981)*

Iodparts Technologies Inc.................... G 732 369-9939
Bear *(G-288)*

Metz Jade Associates........................ G 302 239-2414
Newark *(G-11395)*

Tti Inc.................................... G 302 725-5189
Lincoln *(G-6707)*

Vlocker North America LLC.................... G 469 567-0956
Wilmington *(G-20647)*

ELECTRICAL GOODS, WHOLESALE: Fans, Household

Artisan Electrical Inc....................... G 302 645-5844
Lewes *(G-5702)*

ELECTRICAL GOODS, WHOLESALE: Fittings & Construction Mat

Bristol Industrial Corporation................ F 302 322-1100
New Castle *(G-8893)*

ELECTRICAL GOODS, WHOLESALE: Generators

Allpower Generator Sales & Svc.............. G 302 793-1690
Claymont *(G-1030)*

Powerback Service LLC....................... G 302 934-1901
Millsboro *(G-8435)*

ELECTRICAL GOODS, WHOLESALE: Insulators

NGK North America Inc....................... G 302 654-1344
Wilmington *(G-18640)*

ELECTRICAL GOODS, WHOLESALE: Lighting Fittings & Access

Ledtolight................................ G 941 323-6664
Wilmington *(G-17852)*

ELECTRICAL GOODS, WHOLESALE: Modems, Computer

Velocity Eu Inc............................. F 331 226-1818
Middletown *(G-7684)*

ELECTRICAL GOODS, WHOLESALE: Security Control Eqpt & Systems

A Plus Electric & Security................... G 302 455-1725
Newark *(G-9726)*

Barrier Integrated Systems LLC............... G 302 502-2727
Newark *(G-9985)*

S & B Pro Security LLC...................... G 800 841-9907
Dover *(G-3496)*

Securitech Inc............................. F 302 996-9230
Wilmington *(G-19732)*

ELECTRICAL GOODS, WHOLESALE: Telephone Eqpt

Exclusive Group LLC......................... F 917 207-7299
Wilmington *(G-16501)*

ELECTRICAL GOODS, WHOLESALE: Wire & Cable, Electronic

John R Seiberlich Inc....................... D 302 356-2400
New Castle *(G-9262)*

ELECTRICAL SPLYS

Bainbridge Company......................... G 302 509-3185
Newark *(G-9974)*

Billows Electric Supply Co Inc............... G 302 996-9133
Wilmington *(G-14892)*

City Electric Supply Company................ G 302 777-5300
Wilmington *(G-15452)*

Denney Electric Supply Del Inc.............. G 302 934-8885
Millsboro *(G-8270)*

Dover Electric Supply Co Inc................ E 302 674-0115
Dover *(G-2341)*

Graybar Electric Company Inc................ D 302 322-2200
New Castle *(G-9177)*

LLC Sales Inc.............................. G 416 996-1856
Wilmington *(G-17957)*

Rumsey Electric Co......................... G 302 368-9161
Newark *(G-11927)*

Switchgearus LLC........................... E 302 232-3209
Milford *(G-8112)*

Tri State Btry & Auto Elc Inc............... F 302 292-2330
Newark *(G-12220)*

United Electric Supply Co Inc............... G 302 732-1291
Dagsboro *(G-1522)*

United Electric Supply Co Inc............... G 302 674-8351
Dover *(G-3751)*

United Electric Supply Co Inc............... C 800 322-3374
New Castle *(G-9653)*

ELECTROMEDICAL EQPT

Direct Radiography Corp..................... C 302 631-2700
Newark *(G-10536)*

Hologic Inc................................ D 302 631-2846
Newark *(G-10960)*

Hologic Inc................................ D 302 631-2700
Newark *(G-10961)*

Mtrigger LLC.............................. G 302 502-7262
Newark *(G-11470)*

Slimstim Inc.............................. G 310 560-4950
Wilmington *(G-19866)*

ELECTROMETALLURGICAL PRDTS

American Minerals Inc....................... G 302 652-3301
New Castle *(G-8799)*

ELECTRONIC PARTS & EQPT WHOLESALERS

B F P Trading LLC.......................... F 347 927-0535
Wilmington *(G-14699)*

Jag Industrials LLC........................ G 267 334-7999
Dover *(G-2765)*

Nano Magnetics............................. G 888 629-6266
Wilmington *(G-18527)*

Nano Magnetics Usa Inc..................... G 888 629-6266
Wilmington *(G-18528)*

Rosenberger Usa Corp....................... G 717 859-8900
Wilmington *(G-19569)*

Servo2gocom Ltd............................ G 877 378-0240
Wilmington *(G-19763)*

Sgm Socher Inc............................. G 718 484-4253
Historic New Castle *(G-5069)*

Vectorvance LLC............................ G 347 779-9932
Wilmington *(G-20573)*

ELECTRONIC SHOPPING

Arklight Arsenal LLC....................... G 844 722-3766
Dover *(G-1814)*

Atlas Beauty LLC........................... G 904 382-3487
Dover *(G-1850)*

Brysk Inc.................................. F 224 508-9542
Wilmington *(G-15138)*

Canadian Sunpal Power LLC.................. G 905 926-6681
Lewes *(G-5788)*

Carzaty Inc................................ F 650 396-0144
Dover *(G-2033)*

Chpter Holdings Inc........................ F 650 223-1786
Wilmington *(G-15393)*

Dakk Holdings LLC.......................... G 571 335-7844
Dover *(G-2186)*

Dell Oem Inc............................... G 302 294-0060
Newark *(G-10498)*

Jiffyshirtscom (us) LP..................... F 302 319-2063
Wilmington *(G-17546)*

Kdg Solutions LLC.......................... G 302 494-4693
Smyrna *(G-13786)*

Lamer Group LLC............................ G 302 893-0500
Wilmington *(G-17794)*

Lkb Management Group LLC................... G 919 561-2815
Dover *(G-2961)*

Mymoroccanbazar Inc........................ G 323 238-5747
Newark *(G-11478)*

Netatmo LLC................................ G 302 703-7680
Wilmington *(G-18591)*

Rockeias Journey LLC....................... G 302 304-3055
Newark *(G-11903)*

Sqs Global Solutions LLC................... F 302 691-9682
Wilmington *(G-19984)*

Tjs & Associates LLC....................... E 302 563-5593
Middletown *(G-7647)*

Wna Infotech LLC........................... E 302 668-5977
Newark *(G-12392)*

ELEMENTARY & SECONDARY SCHOOLS, PUBLIC

Smyrna School District..................... D 302 653-3135
Smyrna *(G-13897)*

ELEVATORS & EQPT

MV Farinola Inc............................ G 302 545-8492
Wilmington *(G-18497)*

ELEVATORS WHOLESALERS

Atlantic Elevators......................... G 302 537-8304
Dagsboro *(G-1414)*

Brandywine Elevator Co Inc................. G 866 636-0102
Wilmington *(G-15055)*

Delaware Elevator Inc...................... G 800 787-0436
Newark *(G-10439)*

Elevator Organization Inc.................. G 847 431-2927
Wilmington *(G-16361)*

Liberty Elevator Experts LLC............... E 302 650-4688
Newark *(G-11252)*

ELEVATORS WHOLESALERS

Liberty Elevator Experts LLC............... G..... 844 542-3538
　Newark *(G-11253)*

Mfr Manufacturing Corp Inc................. G..... 815 552-3333
　Wilmington *(G-18298)*

ELEVATORS: Installation & Conversion

Brandywine Elevator Co Inc................. G..... 866 636-0102
　Wilmington *(G-15055)*

EMBLEMS: Embroidered

Initially Yours Inc............................... G..... 302 999-0562
　Wilmington *(G-17341)*

Whisman John.................................... G..... 302 530-1676
　Wilmington *(G-20761)*

EMBROIDERY ADVERTISING SVCS

Atlantic Sun Screen Prtg Inc................ F..... 302 731-5100
　Newark *(G-9936)*

Midnight Blue Inc................................ F..... 302 436-9665
　Selbyville *(G-13576)*

Red Sun Custom Apparel Inc............... F..... 302 988-8230
　Selbyville *(G-13597)*

Unique Image LLC.............................. E..... 302 658-2266
　Wilmington *(G-20519)*

EMBROIDERY KITS

Monogram Specialties......................... G..... 302 292-2424
　Newark *(G-11445)*

EMERGENCY ALARMS

Sumuri LLC... E..... 302 570-0015
　Magnolia *(G-6786)*

EMERGENCY SHELTERS

Agile Shelter Systems LLC.................. F..... 310 980-0644
　Dover *(G-1745)*

Brandywine Hundred Fire Co 1............ D..... 302 764-4901
　Wilmington *(G-15067)*

Dover Intrfith Mssion For Hsin.............. F..... 302 736-3600
　Dover *(G-2349)*

Dunamis Dominion LLC....................... G..... 302 470-0468
　Dover *(G-2395)*

Dunams-Hmes Dvine Intrvntion I........ G..... 302 393-5778
　Camden Wyoming *(G-937)*

Mary Mother Hope House 1................. F..... 302 652-8532
　Wilmington *(G-18181)*

Sojourners Place Inc.......................... G..... 302 764-4592
　Wilmington *(G-19917)*

EMPLOYMENT AGENCY SVCS

Colemans Healthcr Stffngffing............. F..... 302 423-9385
　Smyrna *(G-13684)*

EMPLOYMENT SVCS: Labor Contractors

Comprise It Solutions LLC.................. E..... 302 337-4036
　Dover *(G-2126)*

Congruence Consulting Group............ G..... 320 290-6155
　Newark *(G-10304)*

Premier Staffing Solutions Inc............. E..... 302 344-5996
　Georgetown *(G-4471)*

Servicexpress Corporation.................. A..... 302 424-3500
　Milford *(G-8089)*

Servicexpress Corporation.................. A..... 302 854-9118
　Seaford *(G-13398)*

Servicexpress Corporation.................. E..... 302 856-3500
　Georgetown *(G-4509)*

Staffmark Investment LLC.................. G..... 302 422-0606
　Milford *(G-8102)*

ENGINEERING HELP SVCS

GSM Systems Inc............................... F..... 302 284-8304
　Viola *(G-14095)*

ENGINEERING SVCS

160 Engineers.................................... G..... 302 326-7441
　Newark *(G-9703)*

Acorn Energy Inc................................ G..... 410 654-3315
　Wilmington *(G-14237)*

Aecom Global LLC............................. E..... 213 593-8100
　Wilmington *(G-14293)*

Ag6 Engineering & Defense LLC......... G..... 609 480-4823
　Middletown *(G-6840)*

Amatuzio Appraisal Svcs Inc............... G..... 302 378-9654
　Middletown *(G-6857)*

Area Wide Protective.......................... G..... 302 455-1900
　Newark *(G-9900)*

BBA USA Holdings Inc....................... F..... 450 464-2111
　Wilmington *(G-14793)*

Brandywine Cad Design Inc................ E..... 302 478-8334
　Wilmington *(G-15047)*

Brightfields Inc................................... E..... 302 656-9600
　Wilmington *(G-15113)*

Cgc Geoservices LLC........................ F..... 302 489-2398
　Newark *(G-10181)*

Chip Design Systems LLC.................. G..... 302 307-6831
　Hockessin *(G-5161)*

Cobalt Pacific LLC.............................. G..... 302 437-4761
　Townsend *(G-13973)*

Corrosion Testing Laboratories............ F..... 302 454-8200
　Newark *(G-10329)*

Cotten Engineering LLC...................... G..... 302 628-9164
　Seaford *(G-13137)*

Cybercore Holding Inc........................ D..... 410 560-7177
　Wilmington *(G-15751)*

Deco Engineering Corp....................... G..... 302 576-6564
　Wilmington *(G-15850)*

Delta Engineering Corporation............. G..... 302 750-1065
　Newark *(G-10509)*

Evocati Group Corporation.................. F..... 206 551-9087
　Dover *(G-2468)*

Fairwinds Technologies Engrg............ G..... 732 674-0094
　Newark *(G-10703)*

Fidelity Engineering............................ F..... 302 536-7655
　Seaford *(G-13185)*

Fluor Corp.. G..... 302 934-7742
　Dagsboro *(G-1449)*

Gaichu Managed Services LLC........... G..... 302 232-8420
　Dover *(G-2553)*

Garrett Mechanical & Advanced.......... F..... 302 632-6261
　Dover *(G-2558)*

Gcora Corp... G..... 302 310-1000
　Wilmington *(G-16825)*

Geosyntec Holdings LLC.................... G..... 561 995-0900
　Wilmington *(G-16848)*

Gif North America LLC....................... G..... 703 969-9243
　Rehoboth Beach *(G-12771)*

Greene Lawn & Landscape................ G..... 302 379-4425
　Newark *(G-10889)*

Hardcore Cmpstes Oprations Llc........ F..... 302 442-5900
　New Castle *(G-9196)*

Jaed Corporation................................ F..... 302 832-1652
　Bear *(G-295)*

Ji DCI Jv-II.. G..... 302 652-4221
　Wilmington *(G-17544)*

Mig Consulting LLC............................ G..... 302 999-1888
　Wilmington *(G-18347)*

Mission Support Services LLC............ F..... 813 494-0795
　Dover *(G-3101)*

Network Mapping Inc.......................... G..... 310 560-4142
　Wilmington *(G-18597)*

Phase Snsitive Innovations Inc............ G..... 302 286-5191
　Newark *(G-11680)*

Poc Inc.. F..... 415 853-4762
　Dover *(G-3345)*

PRODUCTS & SERVICES SECTION

Precise Alignment Mch TI Co.............. G..... 302 832-2922
　Newark *(G-11722)*

Quantum Satis Engeneering LLC......... F..... 302 485-5448
　Wilmington *(G-19288)*

Quinteccent Inc.................................. G..... 443 838-5447
　Selbyville *(G-13595)*

Rgs Technology Group LLC................ G..... 302 397-3169
　Wilmington *(G-19454)*

Spaceport Support Services................ G..... 302 524-4020
　Selbyville *(G-13608)*

Summer Consultants Inc..................... F..... 484 493-4150
　Newark *(G-12118)*

Tech International Corp....................... G..... 302 478-2301
　Wilmington *(G-20249)*

Telgian Engrg & Consulting LLC......... F..... 480 282-5392
　Wilmington *(G-20268)*

Ten Bears Environmental LLC............ G..... 302 731-8633
　Newark *(G-12178)*

Torrengineering LLC........................... F..... 302 367-8365
　Smyrna *(G-13915)*

Trinity Subsurface LLC....................... E..... 855 387-4648
　Wilmington *(G-20427)*

Truvision LLC..................................... G..... 267 349-4550
　Wilmington *(G-20451)*

Tyco Engineering Tech LLC................ G..... 202 790-9648
　Wilmington *(G-20477)*

Unitrack Industries Inc........................ E..... 302 424-5050
　Milford *(G-8129)*

Veolia Envmtl Svcs N Amer LLC......... A..... 302 444-9172
　Newark *(G-12313)*

Verdantas LLC.................................... G..... 302 239-6634
　Lewes *(G-6599)*

Xcs Corporation.................................. G..... 302 514-0600
　Wilmington *(G-20916)*

ENGINEERING SVCS: Acoustical

Saf Engineering LLC.......................... G..... 302 645-7400
　Lewes *(G-6440)*

ENGINEERING SVCS: Building Construction

American Hardscapes LLC.................. F..... 302 253-8237
　Georgetown *(G-4209)*

Automation Research Group LLC........ G..... 302 897-7776
　Newark *(G-9947)*

Diversfied Entps Worldwide LLC......... G..... 888 230-3703
　Wilmington *(G-16093)*

Mvl Structures Group LLC.................. E..... 302 652-7580
　Wilmington *(G-18498)*

Ultimate Material Spraying LLC........... G..... 302 723-2356
　Claymont *(G-1321)*

ENGINEERING SVCS: Civil

Batta Ramesh C Associates PA.......... E..... 302 998-9463
　Wilmington *(G-14778)*

Becker Morgan Group Inc................... E..... 302 734-7950
　Dover *(G-1902)*

Cda Engineering Inc........................... G..... 302 998-9202
　Wilmington *(G-15290)*

Cgc Consulting LLC........................... G..... 302 489-2280
　Wilmington *(G-15323)*

Civil Engineering Assoc LLC............... G..... 302 376-8833
　Middletown *(G-6984)*

Ibi Group (us) Inc................................ C..... 949 833-5588
　Wilmington *(G-17255)*

Johnson Mirmiran Thompson Inc......... F..... 302 266-9600
　Newark *(G-11120)*

Karins Engineering Inc....................... F..... 302 856-6699
　Georgetown *(G-4390)*

Kci Technologies Inc.......................... E..... 302 731-9176
　Newark *(G-11148)*

Landmark Engineering Inc.................. G..... 302 734-9597
　Newark *(G-11219)*

PRODUCTS & SERVICES SECTION

FABRICS: Surgical Fabrics, Cotton

Landmark Engineering Inc.................... D 302 323-9377
  Newark *(G-11218)*
Macintosh Engineering.......................... G 302 448-2000
  Lewes *(G-6234)*
Macintosh Engineering Inc.................... F 302 252-9200
  Wilmington *(G-18070)*
McBride and Ziegler Inc...................... E 302 737-9138
  Newark *(G-11365)*
Merit Cnstr Engineers Inc.................... F 302 992-9810
  Wilmington *(G-18283)*
Momenee and Associates Inc................ G 610 527-3030
  Newark *(G-11438)*
Mountain Consulting Inc...................... E 302 744-9875
  Dover *(G-3128)*
Northpoint Engrg Svcs LLC.................. G 302 994-3907
  Wilmington *(G-18687)*
Pelsa Company Inc............................... G 302 834-3771
  Newark *(G-11656)*
Rummel Klepper & Kahl LLP................ E 302 468-4880
  Wilmington *(G-19590)*
Sauer Holdings Inc............................... E 302 656-8989
  Wilmington *(G-19679)*
VD&I Holdings Inc................................ F 302 764-7635
  Wilmington *(G-20572)*
Wallace Montgomery & Assoc LLP....... D 302 510-1080
  Newark *(G-12345)*
Woodin + Associates LLC..................... F 302 378-7300
  Middletown *(G-7735)*

ENGINEERING SVCS: Construction & Civil

Aecom Usa Inc..................................... D 302 781-5963
  Newark *(G-9788)*
B E & K Inc... G 302 452-9000
  Newark *(G-9965)*
Kbr Engineering Company LLC............. D 302 452-9000
  Newark *(G-11147)*
Merestone Consultants Inc.................... F 302 226-5880
  Lewes *(G-6263)*
Merestone Consultants Inc.................... G 302 992-7900
  Wilmington *(G-18279)*
Qbeck Inspection Group....................... F 302 452-9257
  Newark *(G-11781)*
Star Enrg Cs LLC.................................. F 302 660-2187
  Wilmington *(G-20023)*
Techncal Stffing Resources LLC............ C 302 452-9933
  Newark *(G-12169)*

ENGINEERING SVCS: Electrical Or Electronic

AC Group Inc....................................... G 201 840-5566
  Wilmington *(G-14211)*
Ames Engineering Corp........................ F 302 658-6945
  Wilmington *(G-14455)*
Em Photonics Inc................................. F 302 456-9003
  Newark *(G-10637)*
Suretronix Solutions LLC...................... G 302 407-3146
  Wilmington *(G-20161)*

ENGINEERING SVCS: Marine

Marine & Energy Trading Corp.............. E 857 207-7999
  Wilmington *(G-18130)*

ENGINEERING SVCS: Mechanical

Diamond Mechanical Inc...................... E 302 697-7694
  Dover *(G-2291)*

ENGINEERING SVCS: Structural

Corporate Arcft Technical Svcs............. G 302 383-9400
  Wilmington *(G-15643)*
Edc LLC... G 302 645-0777
  Lewes *(G-5948)*

Larsen Landis...................................... G 302 475-3175
  Wilmington *(G-17811)*
Long & Tann & D Onofrio Inc............... G 302 477-1970
  Wilmington *(G-17980)*
Vector Engineering Svcs Corp............... G 609 947-2580
  Millsboro *(G-8493)*

ENGINES: Internal Combustion, NEC

Cummins Power Generation Inc........... E 302 762-2027
  Wilmington *(G-15733)*

EQUIPMENT & VEHICLE FINANCE LEASING COMPANIES

Ally Auto Assets LLC........................... G 313 656-5500
  Wilmington *(G-14386)*
American Air Lease Finance LLC.......... G 646 643-6303
  Wilmington *(G-14424)*
Ev Flux Inc.. G 510 880-3737
  Newark *(G-10674)*

EQUIPMENT: Rental & Leasing, NEC

ACS Aero 2 Gamma Us LLC................ G 800 483-1140
  Dover *(G-1713)*
Actors Attic... G 302 734-8214
  Dover *(G-1714)*
Aggreko Holdings Inc.......................... A 302 652-4076
  Wilmington *(G-14313)*
Arrow Leasing Corp............................. F 302 834-4546
  Bear *(G-47)*
Awas Leasing One LLC....................... F 425 440-6000
  Wilmington *(G-14677)*
Bethany Beach Goods & Rentals......... G 207 266-1682
  Bethany Beach *(G-581)*
Budget Rent A Car............................... G 302 227-3041
  Rehoboth Beach *(G-12660)*
Burke Equipment Company.................. F 302 697-3200
  Felton *(G-3949)*
Chesapeake Supply & Eqp Co.............. G 302 284-1000
  Felton *(G-3955)*
Coastal Rentals Hydraulics LLC............ G 302 251-3103
  Millville *(G-8523)*
Darby Leasing LLC.............................. G 302 477-0500
  Wilmington *(G-15793)*
Diamond Chemical & Supply Co.......... E 302 656-7786
  Wilmington *(G-16049)*
Dover Rent-All Inc............................... E 302 739-0860
  Dover *(G-2366)*
Downtown Beach Rentals.................... G 410 472-9480
  Rehoboth Beach *(G-12735)*
Eb Rental Ltd...................................... G 310 951-8931
  Newark *(G-10601)*
First State Rental Company LLC.......... G 302 632-5699
  Houston *(G-5441)*
Foster Long Vacation Rentals.............. G 302 226-2919
  Rehoboth Beach *(G-12759)*
Gfc Leasing LLC.................................. G 302 449-5006
  Middletown *(G-7157)*
Gray Rental Properties LLC................. G 302 382-0439
  Milford *(G-7911)*
Groff Tractor & Equipment LLC............ F 302 349-5760
  Greenwood *(G-4633)*
Lotus Lease Hospitality....................... G 302 357-4699
  Wilmington *(G-18001)*
Material Handling Supply Inc............... F 302 571-0176
  Historic New Castle *(G-5024)*
MHS Lift of Delaware Inc..................... F 302 629-4490
  Seaford *(G-13282)*
Morton Electric Co............................... G 302 645-9414
  Lewes *(G-6292)*
NS Air Leasing LLC.............................. G 302 396-6546
  Wilmington *(G-18705)*

Penske Truck Leasing Co LP................ G 302 325-9290
  New Castle *(G-9467)*
Professional Leasing Inc...................... G 302 629-4350
  Seaford *(G-13359)*
Queen B Tbl Chair Rentals LLC............ G 215 960-6303
  Dover *(G-3409)*
Quillens Rent All Inc............................ G 302 227-3151
  Rehoboth Beach *(G-12903)*
Right Way Flagging and Sign Co.......... F 302 698-5229
  Camden Wyoming *(G-969)*
Ryder Truck Rental Inc........................ G 302 798-1472
  Wilmington *(G-19601)*
Seachange Vacation Rentals................ G 302 727-5566
  Rehoboth Beach *(G-12951)*
Sheets At Beach.................................. G 302 362-0876
  Lewes *(G-6462)*
Shell We Bounce.................................. G 302 727-5411
  Rehoboth Beach *(G-12956)*
Shore Rv Rentals................................. G 443 235-2183
  Delmar *(G-1635)*
Storage Rentals of America................. G 302 786-0792
  Wilmington *(G-20084)*
Superior Equipment Rental Co............. F 302 658-6193
  Wilmington *(G-20141)*
Tucker Vacation Rentals Inc................ G 302 668-3512
  Newark *(G-12244)*
United Rentals North Amer Inc............ G 302 907-0292
  Delmar *(G-1649)*
Wyndham Vacation Rentals................. G 877 893-2487
  Bethany Beach *(G-652)*

EXHAUST HOOD OR FAN CLEANING SVCS

Hood Man LLC..................................... G 302 422-4564
  Lincoln *(G-6676)*

FABRIC STORES

Loomcraft Textile & Supply Co............. F 302 454-3232
  Newark *(G-11281)*

FABRICS: Apparel & Outerwear, Cotton

Authentik Chick................................... G 267 815-4132
  Wilmington *(G-14649)*
Dejour Reign CL & AP Co LLC............. G 302 981-2568
  New Castle *(G-9010)*
Eanerep Holdings LLC......................... G 888 837-2685
  Dover *(G-2405)*
Japan Modern Art LLC......................... G 832 458-1536
  Dover *(G-2771)*
Selfx Innovations Inc........................... D 551 277-9665
  Wilmington *(G-19745)*
Spunkchild LLC................................... F 917 504-4529
  Middletown *(G-7595)*

FABRICS: Denims

Threads N Denims............................... G 302 678-0642
  Dover *(G-3681)*

FABRICS: Jean

H D Lee Company Inc........................... G 302 477-3930
  Wilmington *(G-17018)*

FABRICS: Nonwoven

Dow Chemical Company...................... E 302 368-4169
  Newark *(G-10558)*

FABRICS: Nylon, Broadwoven

Baker Safety Equipment Inc................. G 302 376-9302
  Bear *(G-55)*

FABRICS: Surgical Fabrics, Cotton

Boa Financial LLC............................... G 888 444-5371
  Dover *(G-1956)*

Employee Codes: A=Over 500 employees, B=251-500
C=101-250, D=51-100, E=20-50, F=10-19, G=1-9

2024 Harris Directory of Delaware Businesses

FACILITIES SUPPORT SVCS

Bi Solutions Group LLC..................E.... 253 366-5110
Wilmington (G-14874)

Blessngs Grnhses Cmpost Fcilty..........F.... 302 684-8890
Milford (G-7795)

Brightfields Inc............................E.... 302 656-9600
Wilmington (G-15113)

Delmar Corporate Clg Svcs Inc..........E.... 302 861-8006
Newark (G-10499)

Ecg Industries Inc........................G.... 302 453-0535
Newark (G-10603)

Focus Solutions Services Inc............F.... 302 318-1345
Newark (G-10753)

Ges-Bay West Joint Venture LLC........G.... 302 918-3070
Newark (G-10827)

Moore Staffing Agency LLC.............G.... 215 300-2770
Bear (G-379)

Seaford Mission Inc.......................G.... 302 629-2559
Seaford (G-13391)

Shackleford Facilities Inc.................F.... 877 735-3938
Frankford (G-4141)

Team Systems International LLC.......G.... 703 217-7648
Lewes (G-6545)

FAMILY CLOTHING STORES

Garage..G.... 302 453-1930
Newark (G-10807)

True Religion Apparel Inc................G.... 302 894-9425
Newark (G-12241)

FARM & GARDEN MACHINERY WHOLESALERS

Burke Equipment Company...............E.... 302 248-7070
Delmar (G-1570)

Burke Equipment Company...............F.... 302 697-3200
Felton (G-3949)

Newark Kubota Inc........................F.... 302 365-6000
Newark (G-11540)

Yellow and Green Machinery LLC......G.... 302 526-4990
Dover (G-3885)

FARM SPLYS WHOLESALERS

Hudson Farm Supply Co Inc............G.... 302 398-3654
Middletown (G-7219)

Joseph M L Sand & Gravel Co..........E.... 302 856-7396
Georgetown (G-4387)

Tractor Supply Company..................F.... 302 629-3627
Seaford (G-13434)

Tractor Supply Company..................F.... 302 659-3333
Smyrna (G-13917)

Whaleys Seed Store Inc..................G.... 302 875-7833
Laurel (G-5623)

FARM SPLYS, WHOLESALE: Feed

Bryan & Brittingham Inc..................F.... 302 846-9500
Delmar (G-1569)

FARM SPLYS, WHOLESALE: Garden Splys

Leons Garden World Ej Inc..............F.... 410 392-8530
New Castle (G-9308)

Q Vandenberg & Sons Inc...............E.... 800 242-2852
Wilmington (G-19272)

FASTENERS WHOLESALERS

Tantalum Bolt & Fastener LLC..........F.... 888 393-4517
Newark (G-12159)

FASTENERS: Metal

Pennengineering Holdings LLC.........C.... 302 576-2746
Wilmington (G-18954)

FASTENERS: Notions, Hooks & Eyes

Iron Lion Enterprises Inc..................G.... 302 628-8320
Seaford (G-13225)

FERTILIZER, AGRICULTURAL: Wholesalers

Nutrien AG Solutions Inc.................F.... 302 422-3570
Milford (G-8034)

Soil Service Inc..............................G.... 302 629-7054
Seaford (G-13406)

FERTILIZERS: Nitrogenous

Aztech Industries Inc......................G.... 302 653-1430
Smyrna (G-13657)

Growmark Fs LLC..........................D.... 302 422-3002
Milford (G-7913)

FERTILIZERS: Phosphatic

Growmark Fs LLC..........................G.... 302 422-3001
Milford (G-7912)

Growmark Fs LLC..........................D.... 302 422-3002
Milford (G-7913)

FIBER & FIBER PRDTS: Acrylic

Gambers LLC................................G.... 402 218-7929
Middletown (G-7149)

FIBER OPTICS

Te Connectivity Corporation..............F.... 800 522-6752
Wilmington (G-20243)

FILTERS

Precision Airconvey Corp..................F.... 302 999-8000
Newark (G-11723)

FILTERS & SOFTENERS: Water, Household

Aztech Industries Inc......................G.... 302 653-1430
Smyrna (G-13657)

FILTERS & STRAINERS: Pipeline

Atlantic Screen & Mfg Inc.................G.... 302 684-3197
Milton (G-8565)

FILTERS: Air

John R Seiberlich Inc......................D.... 302 356-2400
New Castle (G-9262)

FILTERS: Air Intake, Internal Combustion Engine, Exc Auto

Airespa Worldwide Whl LLC.............G.... 908 227-4441
Dover (G-1757)

FILTERS: General Line, Indl

Graver Separations Inc...................F.... 302 731-1700
Newark (G-10882)

Zetwerk Manufacturing USA Inc........G.... 520 720-3085
Wilmington (G-20959)

FILTRATION DEVICES: Electronic

Ffi Ionix Inc...................................F.... 302 629-5768
Harrington (G-4769)

FINANCIAL INVESTMENT ACTIVITIES, NEC: Financial Reporting

1 Konto Inc...................................F.... 215 783-8166
Lewes (G-5634)

Fuinre Inc.....................................E.... 402 480-6465
Lewes (G-6020)

FINANCIAL SVCS

8fig Growth LLC............................E.... 442 888-4303
Wilmington (G-14151)

Ajp Financial Services LLC..............G.... 302 798-7582
Wilmington (G-14342)

Amwal Tech Inc.............................F.... 650 391-5496
Wilmington (G-14465)

Anymoney LLC..............................F.... 818 431-5251
Dover (G-1798)

Astrazeneca Finance LLC................G.... 800 677-3394
Wilmington (G-14607)

Best Processing Solutions LLC.........G.... 212 739-7845
Wilmington (G-14856)

Biya Global LLC............................G.... 302 645-7400
Lewes (G-5767)

Blue Fin Services LLC....................G.... 302 633-3354
Wilmington (G-14966)

Bullent Investment LLC...................G.... 877 214-7707
Dover (G-1991)

Business At International LLC..........E.... 605 610-4885
Lewes (G-5782)

Citigroup Inc.................................E.... 302 631-3530
Newark (G-10244)

City of Dover................................F.... 302 736-7035
Dover (G-2083)

Cnooc Finance 2015 USA LLC.........F.... 302 636-5400
Wilmington (G-15505)

Coastline Realty LLC.....................G.... 302 735-7526
Dover (G-2107)

Coinbase Global Inc.......................D.... 302 777-0200
Wilmington (G-15522)

Collect Africa Inc...........................G.... 657 204-4749
Wilmington (G-15529)

Comprehensive Bus Svcs LLC..........F.... 302 994-2000
Newark (G-10292)

Cordjia LLC..................................F.... 302 743-1297
Newark (G-10322)

Credit Lifestyle LLC........................G.... 302 317-1812
Newark (G-10351)

CSC Networks Inc.........................G.... 302 636-5401
Wilmington (G-15724)

Deall LLC.....................................F.... 305 790-0109
Dover (G-2204)

Delaware Trust Company.................E.... 302 636-5404
Wilmington (G-15977)

Delverde Corporation.....................G.... 302 656-1950
Wilmington (G-16005)

Domestic Gen USA Resources LLC...G.... 312 730-2437
Dover (G-2320)

Eazifunds Inc................................F.... 909 697-6422
Middletown (G-7079)

Ema Corp.....................................E.... 302 479-9434
Wilmington (G-16384)

Estu Inc.......................................E.... 407 881-6177
Wilmington (G-16471)

Fourth Floor.................................G.... 302 472-8416
Wilmington (G-16710)

Galaxy Plus Fund - Lrr Mstr Fu........G.... 312 504-0096
Dover (G-2554)

Gensource Fincl Asrn Co LLC..........F.... 302 415-3030
Wilmington (G-16840)

HART Group LLC.........................G.... 302 782-9742
Dover (G-2660)

International Trade Fin LLC..............F.... 302 440-1492
Dover (G-2748)

John Li-Ameriprise Finvl Srvcs.........G.... 302 200-9548
Lewes (G-6144)

Just Wallet Inc..............................G.... 770 925-5098
Wilmington (G-17618)

Kamina LLC..................................G.... 347 200-0935
Wilmington (G-17644)

Lifetime Financial Svcs LLC.............G.... 302 678-1300
Dover (G-2943)

PRODUCTS & SERVICES SECTION

FOOD PRDTS, CANNED: Barbecue Sauce

Longview Capital MGT LLC .... F 302 353-4720
  Wilmington (G-17987)
Lumber Industries Inc .... G 302 655-9651
  Wilmington (G-18025)
Markland Affiliates LLC .... G 302 633-9134
  Wilmington (G-18149)
Matrixport Inc .... G 626 474-8738
  Dover (G-3032)
Mello Financial Inc .... G 801 877-7787
  Wilmington (G-18264)
Mgts Global Inc .... G 302 385-6636
  Wilmington (G-18300)
Mitek Holdings Inc .... D 302 429-1816
  New Castle (G-9374)
Muncie Insurance & Fincl Svcs .... G 302 645-7740
  Rehoboth Beach (G-12867)
Mystash Inc .... F 202 867-8874
  Wilmington (G-18513)
National Opprtnities Unlimited .... G 913 905-2261
  New Castle (G-9398)
Novo Financial Corp .... F 844 260-6800
  Dover (G-3205)
Nutax Financial Services LLC .... G 302 834-9357
  Newark (G-11570)
Oink Oink LLC .... G 302 924-5034
  Dover (G-3217)
Oobla Inc .... G 416 230-9119
  Dover (G-3233)
Otc Trade LLC .... G 603 820-5820
  Camden (G-883)
Padi Technology Ltd .... G 832 646-6926
  Middletown (G-7421)
Pagos Solutions Inc .... F 310 245-3591
  Middletown (G-7422)
Pango Financial LLC .... G 855 949-7264
  Wilmington (G-18874)
Parcel Tech Inc .... G 720 663-0558
  Wilmington (G-18888)
Payourse Technologies Inc .... F 206 922-8971
  Wilmington (G-18929)
Pennie Mgmt LLC .... G 847 682-1644
  Wilmington (G-18955)
Qisstpay Inc .... G 817 239-3900
  Dover (G-3404)
Quaestor Global Holdings Inc .... F 610 745-3115
  Wilmington (G-19280)
Social Finance Inc .... G 707 473-3000
  Claymont (G-1293)
Socialcash Inc .... F 310 293-6072
  Wilmington (G-19909)
Spirelio Inc .... G 302 467-3444
  Wilmington (G-19967)
Springleaf Fincl Holdings LLC .... B 302 543-6767
  Wilmington (G-19978)
Sun Exchange Inc .... G 917 747-9527
  Lewes (G-6522)
Sussex Financial Services Inc .... G 302 227-7814
  Rehoboth Beach (G-12984)
Swift Financial LLC .... D 302 374-7019
  Wilmington (G-20175)
Swipetech Limited Inc .... G 929 293-8175
  Newark (G-12144)
Teambrella Inc .... G 347 630-0528
  Wilmington (G-20244)
Tospay Inc .... E 347 474-0402
  Lewes (G-6573)
Uag International Holdings Inc .... E 302 427-9859
  Wilmington (G-20489)
UBS Financial Services Inc .... F 302 657-5331
  Wilmington (G-20493)
Vicente & Partners LLC .... G 646 209-5527
  Wilmington (G-20608)

Vircap LLC .... F 302 261-9892
  Newark (G-12328)
Vision Capital III LLC .... F 312 576-2247
  Newark (G-12330)
Vision Capital Vi LLC .... F 312 576-2247
  Newark (G-12331)
Wabtec Finance LLC .... F 412 825-1000
  Wilmington (G-20665)
Watkins Consulting Inc .... G 240 479-7273
  Rehoboth Beach (G-13009)
Windy Inc .... F 224 707-0442
  Dover (G-3858)
Wmk Financing Inc .... C 302 576-2697
  Wilmington (G-20872)
Wsfs Financial Corporation .... F 302 254-3569
  New Castle (G-9693)

FINISHING AGENTS: Textile

James Thompson & Company Inc .... E 302 349-4501
  Greenwood (G-4644)

FINISHING SVCS

Silver Bridge Capital Mgmt LLC .... G 302 575-9215
  Wilmington (G-19827)
Western Union .... G 302 629-3001
  Seaford (G-13447)

FIRE ARMS, SMALL: Shotguns Or Shotgun Parts, 30 mm & Below

Stockmarket .... G 302 697-8878
  Magnolia (G-6785)

FIRE CONTROL OR BOMBING EQPT: Electronic

Dp Fire & Safety Inc .... F 302 998-5430
  Wilmington (G-16159)

FIRE EXTINGUISHERS, WHOLESALE

Delaware City Fire Co No 1 .... G 302 834-9336
  Delaware City (G-1536)

FIRE OR BURGLARY RESISTIVE PRDTS

Independent Metal Strap Co Inc .... E 516 621-0030
  Dover (G-2727)

FISH & SEAFOOD PROCESSORS: Fresh Or Frozen

Boldy Foods LLC .... G 415 616-2965
  Camden (G-794)

FISH & SEAFOOD WHOLESALERS

Lewes Fishhouse & Produce Inc .... E 302 827-4074
  Lewes (G-6196)
Oceanside Seafood Mkt Deli LLC .... F 302 313-5158
  Lewes (G-6330)
Seafood City Inc .... G 302 284-8486
  Felton (G-4024)
Venus On Halfshell .... G 302 227-9292
  Dewey Beach (G-1676)
Wooley Bully Inc .... G 302 542-3613
  Millsboro (G-8507)

FITTINGS & ASSEMBLIES: Hose & Tube, Hydraulic Or Pneumatic

JC Industrial Solutions Inc .... G 484 720-8381
  Claymont (G-1197)
Mto Hose Solutions Inc .... G 302 266-6555
  Newark (G-11469)

FLOOR COVERING STORES

A + Floor Store Inc .... G 302 698-2166
  Camden Wyoming (G-903)
Art Floor Inc .... F 302 636-9201
  Wilmington (G-14560)
Brasures Pest Control Inc .... E 302 436-8140
  Selbyville (G-13484)
Connolly Flooring Inc .... E 302 996-9470
  Wilmington (G-15605)
Interiors By Kim Inc .... G 302 537-2480
  Ocean View (G-12525)

FLOOR COVERING STORES: Carpets

Anderson Floor Coverings Inc .... F 302 227-3244
  Rehoboth Beach (G-12604)
Callaway Furniture Inc .... G 302 398-8858
  Harrington (G-4745)
Delaware Rug Co Inc .... G 302 998-8881
  Wilmington (G-15963)
Edwards Paul Crpt Installation .... G 302 672-7847
  Dover (G-2427)
L & L Carpet Discount Ctrs Inc .... G 302 292-3712
  Newark (G-11205)
Proclean Inc .... E 302 656-8080
  Delaware City (G-1554)
Reiver Hyman & Co Inc .... G 302 764-2040
  Wilmington (G-19419)
Stuart Kingston Inc .... G 302 227-2524
  Rehoboth Beach (G-12978)

FLOOR COVERINGS WHOLESALERS

A + Floor Store Inc .... G 302 698-2166
  Camden Wyoming (G-903)
Art Floor Inc .... F 302 636-9201
  Wilmington (G-14560)
L & L Carpet Discount Ctrs Inc .... G 302 292-3712
  Newark (G-11205)
Matt Carpet Guy LLC .... G 443 497-3281
  Selbyville (G-13568)
Reiver Hyman & Co Inc .... G 302 764-2040
  Wilmington (G-19419)
Suburban Floor Coverings .... G 302 430-8494
  Rehoboth Beach (G-12979)

FLOOR WAXING SVCS

L & M Services Inc .... G 302 658-3735
  Wilmington (G-17773)

FLOORING: Hardwood

Old Wood & Co LLC .... F 302 684-3600
  Harbeson (G-4710)

FLORIST: Flowers, Fresh

Kirks Flowers Inc .... G 302 737-3931
  Newark (G-11181)
Lakeside Greenhouses Inc .... G 302 875-2457
  Laurel (G-5544)

FLOWERS, FRESH, WHOLESALE

Lakeside Greenhouses Inc .... G 302 875-2457
  Laurel (G-5544)

FLUID POWER PUMPS & MOTORS

Smw Sales LLC .... E 302 875-7958
  Laurel (G-5600)

FOOD PRDTS, CANNED: Baby Food

Patafoods Inc .... F 267 981-6411
  Newark (G-11632)

Employee Codes: A=Over 500 employees, B=251-500
C=101-250, D=51-100, E=20-50, F=10-19, G=1-9

FOOD PRDTS, CANNED: Barbecue Sauce

Trisco Foods LLC................................. D 719 352-3218
  Wilmington (G-20429)

FOOD PRDTS, CANNED: Fruit Juices, Fresh

Loop Mission Corp................................ E 514 994-7625
  Newark (G-11282)

FOOD PRDTS, CANNED: Fruits

Denali Canning LLC............................... G 272 226-6464
  Middletown (G-7054)
Kraft Heinz Company.............................. A 302 734-6100
  Dover (G-2886)

FOOD PRDTS, CANNED: Fruits & Fruit Prdts

Produce Spot LLC................................. F 267 864-1232
  Wilmington (G-19209)

FOOD PRDTS, CANNED: Mexican, NEC

Freakin Fresh Salsa Inc.......................... G 302 750-9789
  Wilmington (G-16733)
Mariachi House................................... G 302 635-7361
  Hockessin (G-5297)

FOOD PRDTS, CANNED: Vegetables

Thomas E Moore Inc............................... F 302 674-1500
  Kenton (G-5456)
Thomas E Moore Inc............................... F 302 674-1500
  Dover (G-3678)

FOOD PRDTS, CONFECTIONERY, WHOLESALE: Pretzels

J & J Snack Foods Corp PA........................ G 302 571-0884
  Wilmington (G-17444)

FOOD PRDTS, CONFECTIONERY, WHOLESALE: Snack Foods

Herr Foods Incorporated.......................... E 302 628-9161
  Seaford (G-13210)

FOOD PRDTS, FROZEN: Ethnic Foods, NEC

H&H Trading International LLC.................... G 480 580-3911
  Wilmington (G-17022)
Pictsweet Company................................ D 302 337-8206
  Bridgeville (G-749)

FOOD PRDTS, FROZEN: Fruit Juice, Concentrates

United Lemon Sales LLC........................... F 513 368-6107
  New Castle (G-9654)

FOOD PRDTS, FROZEN: Fruits & Vegetables

Baby Apron LLC................................... G 800 796-4406
  Claymont (G-1050)
Egm LLC.. G 302 932-1700
  New Castle (G-9083)
Nowadays Inc Pbc................................. G 415 279-6802
  Dover (G-3207)

FOOD PRDTS, FROZEN: Fruits, Juices & Vegetables

JG Townsend Jr & Co Inc.......................... E 302 856-2525
  Georgetown (G-4383)
Tridge Trade Inc................................. F 954 512-3734
  Dover (G-3726)

FOOD PRDTS, FRUITS & VEGETABLES, FRESH, WHOLESALE: Fruits

Chiquita Brands LLC.............................. F 302 571-9781
  Wilmington (G-15385)
Robert T Minner Jr............................... G 302 422-9206
  Greenwood (G-4665)
Willey Farms Inc................................. D 302 378-8441
  Townsend (G-14091)

FOOD PRDTS, POULTRY, WHOLESALE: Poultry Prdts, NEC

Pet Poultry Products LLC......................... E 302 337-8223
  Bridgeville (G-748)

FOOD PRDTS, WHOLESALE: Beverages, Exc Coffee & Tea

Angry 8 LLC...................................... F 888 417-5477
  Newark (G-9871)

FOOD PRDTS, WHOLESALE: Chocolate

Chocolette Distribution LLC...................... G 917 547-8905
  Lewes (G-5816)
King of Sweets Distribution...................... G 302 730-8200
  Dover (G-2874)
King of Sweets Online Inc........................ F 302 730-8200
  Dover (G-2875)

FOOD PRDTS, WHOLESALE: Coffee & Tea

Chara Tea LLC.................................... G 856 250-7180
  Dover (G-2056)

FOOD PRDTS, WHOLESALE: Coffee, Green Or Roasted

Panamerican Coffee Trdg Co LLC................... G 786 538-9547
  Dover (G-3264)
Three Sheep and A Mill LLC....................... G 616 820-5668
  Middletown (G-7641)

FOOD PRDTS, WHOLESALE: Condiments

Freakin Fresh Salsa Inc.......................... G 302 750-9789
  Wilmington (G-16733)

FOOD PRDTS, WHOLESALE: Cookies

Classic Cookies of Dowingtown.................... G 302 494-9662
  Wilmington (G-15467)
Georges Trees Plus LLC........................... G 302 539-0660
  Dagsboro (G-1452)
Kees Cookies & Cupcakes LLC...................... G 302 223-6784
  Clayton (G-1380)

FOOD PRDTS, WHOLESALE: Dog Food

Tail Bangers Inc................................. F 302 947-4900
  Millsboro (G-8480)
Tailbangers Inc.................................. F 302 934-1125
  Millsboro (G-8481)

FOOD PRDTS, WHOLESALE: Dried or Canned Foods

South Forks Inc.................................. G 302 731-0344
  Newark (G-12059)

FOOD PRDTS, WHOLESALE: Flavorings & Fragrances

Wen International Inc............................ G 845 354-1773
  Wilmington (G-20729)

FOOD PRDTS, WHOLESALE: Grain Elevators

Mountaire Farms Delaware Inc..................... G 302 398-3296
  Harrington (G-4805)
Mountaire Farms Delaware Inc..................... G 302 378-2271
  Townsend (G-14039)

FOOD PRDTS, WHOLESALE: Grains

Against Grain LLC................................ G 302 388-1667
  Wilmington (G-14311)
Allen Harim Foods LLC............................ D 302 629-9460
  Seaford (G-13056)
Dack Trading LLC................................. G 917 576-4432
  Rehoboth Beach (G-12710)
Delaware Intl Agrclture Entp L................... G 302 450-2008
  Smyrna (G-13699)
Johnson Jr Henry & Son Farm...................... G 302 436-8501
  Selbyville (G-13552)
Laurel Grain Company............................. G 302 875-4231
  Laurel (G-5547)
Lombard Trading International.................... G 786 659-5010
  Newark (G-11279)
Suresrce Cmmdties LLC - Orgnic................... F 866 697-5960
  Wilmington (G-20160)

FOOD PRDTS, WHOLESALE: Juices

Dfa Dairy Brands Fluid LLC....................... F 302 398-8321
  Harrington (G-4762)
Raw Essential Juice Bar.......................... G 302 235-8019
  Wilmington (G-19341)

FOOD PRDTS, WHOLESALE: Natural & Organic

Four Ever Green Inc.............................. G 302 424-2393
  Milford (G-7902)

FOOD PRDTS, WHOLESALE: Organic & Diet

Green Roots LLC.................................. G 516 643-2621
  Lewes (G-6058)

FOOD PRDTS, WHOLESALE: Sandwiches

Scotts Co.. G 302 777-4779
  Wilmington (G-19712)

FOOD PRDTS, WHOLESALE: Sauces

Peppers Inc...................................... F 302 644-6900
  Lewes (G-6361)
Peppers Inc...................................... G 302 645-0812
  Lewes (G-6360)
Pepperscom Inc................................... G 302 703-6355
  Lewes (G-6362)

FOOD PRDTS, WHOLESALE: Tea

My Red Tea LLC................................... G 415 259-4166
  Wilmington (G-18509)

FOOD PRDTS: Chicken, Processed, Frozen

New B & M Meats Inc.............................. F 302 655-5331
  Wilmington (G-18607)

FOOD PRDTS: Coffee

Bdb LLC.. G 469 288-7672
  Wilmington (G-14797)
Cofinet LLC...................................... F 614 301-8082
  Lewes (G-5849)

FOOD PRDTS: Dates, Dried

Ajwadates Inc.................................... G 323 999-1998
  Middletown (G-6846)

FOOD PRDTS: Dessert Mixes & Fillings

Trisco Foods LLC................................. D 719 352-3218
  Wilmington (G-20429)

FOOD PRDTS: Flour & Other Grain Mill Products

FOOD PRDTS: Fruit Juices

Kraft Heinz Company..................... A 302 734-6100
  Dover (G-2886)

FOOD PRDTS: Fruit Juices

Juiceplus+...................................... G 302 322-2616
  Historic New Castle (G-5013)
Kencko Foods Inc .... G 616 253-6256
  Newark (G-11153)

FOOD PRDTS: Gelatin Dessert Preparations

Kraft Heinz Company..................... A 302 734-6100
  Dover (G-2886)

FOOD PRDTS: Seasonings & Spices

Rosas Diner LLC........................... G 302 336-8243
  Camden (G-890)
Saratoga Food Specialties LLC..... F 951 270-9600
  Dover (G-3511)
Shore Smoke Seasonings LLC...... G 302 943-4675
  Smyrna (G-13884)
Supreme Trading LLC................... G 302 415-3188
  Wilmington (G-20159)

FOOD PRDTS: Tea

Martin Grey LLC............................. G 302 990-0675
  Lewes (G-6246)

FOOD PRODUCTS MACHINERY

Eidp Inc .... G 302 695-5300
  Wilmington (G-16335)
Formidable Foods Inc.................... G 415 877-9691
  Dover (G-2527)
Future 50 Inc .... G 302 648-4665
  Dover (G-2547)
Metal Msters Fdservice Eqp Inc ... C 302 653-3000
  Clayton (G-1385)
Tomasi Usa LLC............................ G 302 449-6492
  Middletown (G-7651)

FOOD STORES: Convenience, Independent

Newport Ventures Inc.................... F 302 998-1693
  Middletown (G-7399)
Peninsula Oil Co Inc .... E 302 422-6691
  Seaford (G-13338)

FOOD STORES: Cooperative

Hs Capital LLC............................... G 302 598-2961
  Wilmington (G-17223)

FOREIGN CURRENCY EXCHANGE

Coinbase Global Inc...................... D 302 777-0200
  Wilmington (G-15522)
Nfinity Inc....................................... F 852 642-9800
  Wilmington (G-18639)

FORGINGS: Bearing & Bearing Race, Nonferrous

Delaware Capital Formation Inc.... G 302 793-4921
  Wilmington (G-15878)

FORGINGS: Construction Or Mining Eqpt, Ferrous

Oreomatic Mining Inc.................... E 725 255-8895
  Wilmington (G-18817)

FORGINGS: Gear & Chain

Eager Gear.................................... G 302 727-5831
  Lewes (G-5943)
Timken Gears & Services Inc....... E 302 633-4600
  Historic New Castle (G-5086)

FORGINGS: Nuclear Power Plant, Ferrous

Oakville Industries LLC.................. F 513 436-5007
  Wilmington (G-18729)

FOUNDRIES: Nonferrous

Diamond State Props.................... G 302 528-7146
  Bear (G-167)

FOUNDRIES: Steel Investment

Consoldted Fabrication Constrs.... C 302 654-9001
  Wilmington (G-15608)
S P S International Inv Co .... G 302 478-9055
  Wilmington (G-19612)
Tajan Hldings Investments Inc..... G 302 300-1183
  Middletown (G-7619)

FRAMES & FRAMING WHOLESALE

Urban Dweller................................ G 973 402-7400
  Milton (G-8724)

FRANCHISES, SELLING OR LICENSING

1000 Degrees Pizzeria.................. F 609 382-3022
  Wilmington (G-14101)
Bbdotq USA Inc............................. C 302 533-6589
  Newark (G-9999)
Chuck Lager LLC.......................... D 302 482-1773
  Wilmington (G-15428)
Kohr Brothers Inc.......................... E 302 227-9354
  Rehoboth Beach (G-12825)
Lilian USA LLC.............................. F 800 246-2677
  Wilmington (G-17912)

FREIGHT CAR LOADING & UNLOADING SVCS

Burris Logistics.............................. G 302 839-5129
  Dover (G-1995)
Burris Logistics.............................. G 302 737-5203
  Newark (G-10106)
Burris Logistics.............................. D 302 839-4531
  Milford (G-7808)
Elite Trnspt & Logistics Inc........... G 302 348-8480
  Wilmington (G-16367)
Lantransit Enterprises LLC........... G 302 722-4800
  Lewes (G-6179)
Legend Transportation LLC.......... E 215 713-7472
  New Castle (G-9301)
PCI of Virginia LLC....................... F 302 655-7300
  Wilmington (G-18934)
Port Contractors Inc..................... E 302 655-7300
  Wilmington (G-19119)
Sling It LLC................................... G 302 648-5488
  Newark (G-12031)
Working Every Shift Trnsprting.... E 267 262-3453
  Bear (G-566)

FREIGHT FORWARDING ARRANGEMENTS

Adroit Logistics LLC...................... G 385 381-0007
  Dover (G-1719)
APL Lgstics Trnsp MGT Svcs Ltd........... E 302 230-2656
  Wilmington (G-14507)
Boj Global Services LLC............... F 302 325-4018
  New Castle (G-8873)
Ceva Logistics............................... F 512 356-1700
  Historic New Castle (G-4954)
D1 Express Inc.............................. G 302 883-9572
  Dover (G-2183)
D150 Fueling LLC......................... E 215 559-1132
  Newark (G-10378)
Duha Logistics Inc......................... F 888 493-5999
  Wilmington (G-16197)
Eikon Int Inc................................... G 312 550-2648
  Wilmington (G-16345)
Ens Logistics LLC.......................... G 302 784-5155
  Newark (G-10650)
Evanix Enterprises LLC................ G 302 384-1806
  Middletown (G-7111)
EZ Way Transport LLC................. G 302 367-5272
  Wilmington (G-16516)
Fastcold LLC................................. G 302 240-4402
  Wilmington (G-16559)
GATX Trmnals Ovrseas Hldg Corp........... F 302 636-5400
  Wilmington (G-16816)
Global Container & Chassis LLC.. G 302 608-0822
  Historic New Castle (G-4996)
Global Shopaholics LLC................ F 302 725-0586
  Historic New Castle (G-4997)
Hollywell Logistics LLC................. F 267 901-4272
  Wilmington (G-17170)
International Logistiks LLC........... G 302 521-6338
  Wilmington (G-17389)
J A S Logistic Inc.......................... G 302 339-1825
  Middletown (G-7235)
Jet Carrier.................................... G 908 759-6938
  Newark (G-11109)
Johns Premier Services LLC........ G 347 992-3783
  Dover (G-2799)
Kango Express Inc .... E 808 725-1688
  Newark (G-11141)
Long Rd Ahead Shipg Lgstic LLC........ E 480 702-6438
  Wilmington (G-17982)
Monster King Conglomerate LLC.. G 302 222-9742
  New Castle (G-9380)
Mtc Delaware LLC......................... F 302 654-3400
  New Castle (G-9388)
New Hope Vehicle Exports LLC... G 302 275-6482
  Wilmington (G-18619)
Platinum Logistics LLC.................. G 412 708-6476
  Newark (G-11700)
Sacher... G 302 792-0281
  Wilmington (G-19621)
Seven Shipping Inc....................... G 302 516-7150
  Wilmington (G-19768)
Spedag Americas Inc.................... G 201 857-3471
  Wilmington (G-19957)
Tc Trans Inc .... G 302 339-7952
  Georgetown (G-4546)
Tradeally Incorporated.................. E 832 997-2582
  Lewes (G-6577)
Triglia Express Inc........................ G 302 846-2248
  Delmar (G-1643)
UPS Supply Chain Solutions Inc.. F 302 631-5259
  Newark (G-12287)
Walker International Trnsp LLC... F 302 325-4180
  Historic New Castle (G-5100)

FREIGHT FORWARDING ARRANGEMENTS: Domestic

Transcore LP................................. G 302 838-7429
  Middletown (G-7658)

FRUIT & VEGETABLE MARKETS

Willey Farms Inc............................ D 302 378-8441
  Townsend (G-14091)

FRUITS & VEGETABLES WHOLESALERS: Fresh

Ernie Deangelis............................. F 302 226-9533
  Rehoboth Beach (G-12746)
Estia Hospitality Group Inc........... G 302 798-5319
  Claymont (G-1136)

FUEL ADDITIVES

Tgfmx Inc.. G 302 613-0128
  Wilmington *(G-20287)*

FUEL ADDITIVES

Greentec Laboratories LLC................... G 301 744-7336
  Historic New Castle *(G-4999)*

FUEL CELLS: Solid State

Bloom Energy Corporation..................... G 408 543-1227
  Newark *(G-10056)*

FUEL OIL DEALERS

Burns & McBride Inc................................ D 302 656-5110
  New Castle *(G-8901)*
C L Burchenal Oil Co Inc......................... G 302 697-1517
  Camden *(G-798)*
Clark Services Inc Delaware................... G 302 834-0556
  Bear *(G-109)*
Conectiv Energy Supply Inc.................... E 302 454-0300
  Newark *(G-10301)*
Foraker Oil Inc... G 302 834-7595
  Delaware City *(G-1541)*
Hillside Oil Company Inc......................... E 302 738-4144
  Newark *(G-10953)*
Schlosser Assoc Mech Cntrs Inc............ E 302 738-7333
  Newark *(G-11958)*
Service Energy LLC................................ F 302 645-9050
  Lewes *(G-6460)*
Service Energy LLC................................ D 302 734-7433
  Dover *(G-3534)*
Shellhorn & Hill Inc................................. D 302 654-4200
  Wilmington *(G-19793)*
Wilkins Fuel Co....................................... G 302 422-5597
  Milford *(G-8149)*

FUND RAISING ORGANIZATION, NON-FEE BASIS

Georgetown Playground & Pk Inc........... G 302 856-7111
  Georgetown *(G-4341)*
Help Is On Way.. G 302 328-4510
  New Castle *(G-9207)*
Homes For Life Foundation..................... G 302 571-1217
  Wilmington *(G-17189)*
March of Dimes Inc.................................. G 302 225-1020
  Wilmington *(G-18121)*

FURNACES & OVENS: Indl

Nabertherm Inc.. G 302 322-3665
  New Castle *(G-9390)*

FURNITURE REFINISHING SVCS

New Life Furniture Systems.................... G 302 994-9054
  Wilmington *(G-18620)*

FURNITURE STOCK & PARTS: Hardwood

Agile Coliving Systems LLC.................... F 310 980-0644
  Dover *(G-1741)*

FURNITURE STORES

Carolina Street Garden & Home............. G 302 539-2405
  Fenwick Island *(G-4043)*
Couture Denim LLC................................ G 302 220-8339
  New Castle *(G-8983)*
Kenton Chair Shop.................................. F 302 653-2411
  Clayton *(G-1381)*
Rite Way Distributors.............................. E 302 535-8507
  Felton *(G-4017)*

FURNITURE UPHOLSTERY REPAIR SVCS

Colliers Trim Shop Inc............................. G 302 227-8398
  Rehoboth Beach *(G-12691)*

FURNITURE WHOLESALERS

Corporate Interiors Inc............................ F 800 690-9101
  New Castle *(G-8973)*
Demco.. G 302 399-6118
  Middletown *(G-7052)*
Docs Medical LLC.................................... G 301 401-1489
  Bear *(G-175)*
Furniture Whl Connection Inc................. F 302 836-6000
  Bear *(G-241)*
L F Systems Corp.................................... F 302 322-0460
  New Castle *(G-9292)*
Laytons Umbrellas................................... G 302 249-1958
  Laurel *(G-5553)*

FURNITURE, OFFICE: Wholesalers

Corporate Interiors Inc............................ D 302 322-1008
  New Castle *(G-8974)*
Renewed Environments........................... F 302 323-9100
  New Castle *(G-9520)*
Richert Inc.. F 302 684-0696
  Milton *(G-8698)*

FURNITURE, OUTDOOR & LAWN: Wholesalers

Saphic Innovations Inc............................ G 820 888-0099
  Wilmington *(G-19670)*

FURNITURE: Cabinets & Vanities, Medicine, Metal

Zwd Products Corporation....................... B 302 326-8200
  Historic New Castle *(G-5106)*

FURNITURE: Chairs, Household Wood

Fairwood Corporation.............................. A 302 884-6749
  Wilmington *(G-16530)*
Group Three Inc...................................... G 302 658-4158
  Wilmington *(G-16988)*
Mtb Artisans LLC..................................... G 303 475-9024
  Wilmington *(G-18480)*
Quilted Heirlooms.................................... G 302 354-6061
  Middletown *(G-7492)*
Slice of Wood LLC................................... G 315 335-0917
  Delaware City *(G-1558)*

FURNITURE: Desks & Tables, Office, Exc Wood

Elevation Office Furn LLC....................... F 267 261-0124
  Wilmington *(G-16359)*

FURNITURE: Foundations & Platforms

Design Specific US Inc............................ G 650 318-6473
  Wilmington *(G-16026)*

FURNITURE: Laboratory

L F Systems Corp.................................... F 302 322-0460
  New Castle *(G-9292)*

FURNITURE: Mattresses, Box & Bedsprings

Plushbeds Inc.. G 888 758-7423
  Wilmington *(G-19082)*

FURNITURE: Office, Wood

Corporate Interiors Inc............................ F 800 690-9101
  New Castle *(G-8973)*
Corporate Interiors Inc............................ D 302 322-1008
  New Castle *(G-8974)*
Heirloom Creations.................................. G 302 659-1817
  Smyrna *(G-13758)*

FURNITURE: Picnic Tables Or Benches, Park

Acorn Site Furnishings............................ G 302 249-4979
  Bridgeville *(G-661)*

FURNITURE: Upholstered

Barlows Upholstery Inc........................... G 302 655-3955
  Wilmington *(G-14766)*
Fairwood Corporation.............................. A 302 884-6749
  Wilmington *(G-16530)*

GAME MACHINES, COIN-OPERATED, WHOLESALE

Igt Inc... B 302 674-3177
  Dover *(G-2720)*

GAMES & TOYS: Board Games, Children's & Adults'

Tetris Company LLC................................ G 302 656-1950
  Wilmington *(G-20280)*

GAMES & TOYS: Electronic

Co-Op Kitchen LLC.................................. G 407 342-2295
  Dover *(G-2102)*
Str8up Games Inc.................................... F 315 523-8216
  Dover *(G-3614)*
Top Dog Best Games LLC....................... G 949 859-8869
  Wilmington *(G-20352)*

GAS & OIL FIELD EXPLORATION SVCS

I-Pulse Inc... G 604 689-8765
  Wilmington *(G-17250)*
Lucid Colloids Amer................................ G 302 475-2393
  Wilmington *(G-18024)*
Rangeland Nm LLC.................................. G 800 316-6660
  Dover *(G-3423)*
Vault Oil & Gas LLC................................. G 303 731-0080
  Dover *(G-3776)*
Voyager Drilling Services LLC................ F 302 439-6030
  Wilmington *(G-20654)*

GAS & OIL FIELD SVCS, NEC

Aim Metals & Alloys USA Inc.................. G 212 450-4519
  Wilmington *(G-14333)*
Cobalt Pacific LLC................................... G 302 437-4761
  Townsend *(G-13973)*
Lone Star Global Services Inc................ G 302 744-9800
  Dover *(G-2974)*
Mi-1 LLC... G 302 369-3447
  Newark *(G-11398)*

GAS FIELD MACHINERY & EQPT

Tdw Delaware Inc.................................... F 302 594-9880
  New Castle *(G-9620)*

GASES: Indl

Air Lqide Advanced Separations............ F 302 225-1100
  Newport *(G-12440)*
Air Lqide Advanced Tech US LLC.......... A 302 225-1100
  Newark *(G-9799)*
Air Lqide Advanced Tech US LLC.......... E 302 225-1100
  Newport *(G-12441)*
Airgas Usa LLC....................................... F 302 834-7404
  Delaware City *(G-1529)*
Eidp Inc.. G 302 366-5763
  Newark *(G-10616)*
Grep Biogas I LLC................................... G 212 390-8110
  Lewes *(G-6060)*
Keen Compressed Gas Co....................... E 302 594-4545
  New Castle *(G-9276)*

PRODUCTS & SERVICES SECTION

GENERAL COUNSELING SVCS

Keen Compressed Gas Co .... F 302 594-4545
New Castle (G-9277)

Keen Compressed Gas Co .... F 302 594-4545
Wilmington (G-17674)

Pure Air Holdings Corp .... G 302 655-7130
Wilmington (G-19258)

Vernon Green Hydrogen LLC .... G 609 772-7979
Dover (G-3786)

GASES: Nitrogen

Messer LLC .... D 302 798-9342
Claymont (G-1234)

GASES: Oxygen

AAL Drtc .... F 302 229-5891
Newark (G-9733)

GASKETS

Miller Metal Fabrication Inc .... D 302 337-2291
Bridgeville (G-734)

Unique Fabricating Na Inc .... A 248 853-2333
Wilmington (G-20518)

GASKETS & SEALING DEVICES

Century Seals Inc .... E 302 629-0324
Seaford (G-13105)

Greene Tweed of Delaware Inc .... E 302 888-2560
Wilmington (G-16971)

New Process Fibre Company .... D 302 349-4535
Greenwood (G-4657)

Watson-Marlow Flow Smart Inc .... E 302 536-6388
Seaford (G-13445)

GASOLINE FILLING STATIONS

Careys Inc .... F 302 875-5674
Laurel (G-5478)

Logue Brothers Inc .... F 302 762-1896
Wilmington (G-17976)

Manor Exxon Inc .... G 302 834-6691
Bear (G-360)

Meadowood Mobil Station .... G 302 731-5602
Newark (G-11369)

Millcreek Texaco Station .... G 302 571-8489
Wilmington (G-18360)

Newport Ventures Inc .... F 302 998-1693
Middletown (G-7399)

Sals Auto Services Inc .... G 302 654-1168
Wilmington (G-19640)

United Acquisition Corp .... E 302 651-9856
Wilmington (G-20523)

GASOLINE WHOLESALERS

Conectiv Energy Supply Inc .... E 302 454-0300
Newark (G-10301)

J William Gordy Fuel Co .... G 302 846-3425
Delmar (G-1604)

GEARS: Power Transmission, Exc Auto

David Brown Gear Systems USA I .... G 540 416-2062
Wilmington (G-15803)

Power Transmission Svcs Inc .... G 302 378-7925
Middletown (G-7462)

GENERAL & INDUSTRIAL LOAN INSTITUTIONS

Delaware Title Loans Inc .... F 302 328-7482
New Castle (G-9039)

Delaware Title Loans Inc .... F 302 368-2131
Newark (G-10493)

Delaware Title Loans Inc .... F 302 629-8843
Seaford (G-13153)

GENERAL COUNSELING SVCS

A Center For Mntal Wllness Inc .... E 302 674-1397
Dover (G-1694)

A Seed Hope Counseling Ctr LLC .... G 302 605-6702
Wilmington (G-14171)

Active Hope .... G 302 545-2494
Wilmington (G-14244)

Adam Kleinmeulman .... G 302 757-4517
Wilmington (G-14249)

Alston Associates Counseling .... G 302 223-4797
Wilmington (G-14397)

Alternative Solutions .... G 302 542-9081
Georgetown (G-4207)

Appoqnmink Counseling Svcs LLC .... G 302 898-1616
Middletown (G-6870)

Aspiring Change LLC .... G 302 689-3138
Newark (G-9926)

Balanced Mind Cnseling Ctr LLC .... F 302 377-6911
Middletown (G-6904)

Brandywine Cnsling Cmnty Svcs .... D 302 655-9880
Wilmington (G-15051)

Brandywine Counseling .... E 302 762-7120
Wilmington (G-15052)

Camden Counseling LLC .... G 302 698-9109
Camden (G-800)

Center For A Pstive Hmnity LLC .... G 302 703-1036
Felton (G-3952)

Choices 1st LLC .... G 302 674-4204
Dover (G-2067)

Clg True Solutions LLC .... G 302 709-1312
Newark (G-10258)

Clinical Pstral Cnsling Prgram .... G 302 632-8842
Seaford (G-13125)

Coastal Counseling LLC .... G 302 542-4271
Millsboro (G-8233)

Counseling Services Inc .... G 302 894-1477
Wilmington (G-15653)

Counseling Services Corp .... G 302 898-5184
Bear (G-122)

Created Life Coaching .... G 302 584-7112
Wilmington (G-15687)

Dean A Aman Lpcmh LLC .... F 302 858-3324
Newark (G-10401)

Diamond State Counseling .... G 302 683-1055
Newark (G-10525)

Embrace Change LLC .... G 302 286-5288
Newark (G-10639)

Embrace The Change Counseling .... G 302 358-6237
Newark (G-10640)

Emily Crawford PHD .... G 302 995-9600
Wilmington (G-16394)

F H Everett & Associates Inc .... G 302 674-2380
Dover (G-2478)

Family Care Connections .... F 856 579-7303
Middletown (G-7119)

Family Cnsling Ctr St Puls Inc .... F 302 576-4136
Wilmington (G-16535)

Family Services Div .... G 302 577-3824
Wilmington (G-16547)

Growing Edges Counseling .... G 484 883-6523
Wilmington (G-16989)

Harmon Larhonda .... G 302 747-0700
Middletown (G-7197)

Hawkins Counsel Group .... G 302 660-0858
Wilmington (G-17079)

Hope Hanks Inc .... G 302 562-9309
Wilmington (G-17196)

Ignite Your Light .... G 302 766-0982
Newark (G-11000)

Jgcounseling .... G 302 354-0074
Wilmington (G-17542)

Joann M Schneidman .... G 302 761-9119
Wilmington (G-17560)

Josh N Schmidt .... G 302 668-1304
Wilmington (G-17590)

Kindred Counseling .... G 302 478-8888
Wilmington (G-17724)

Lavante N Dorsey & Assoc LLC .... F 302 956-9188
Newark (G-11229)

Lewes Counseling LLC .... G 302 430-2127
Lewes (G-6193)

Life Innovations .... G 302 525-6521
Newark (G-11255)

Living Water Counseling LLC .... G 443 553-7317
Wilmington (G-17950)

McCarthy Cate .... G 302 477-0708
Wilmington (G-18219)

Mending Cove LLC .... G 856 803-9958
Newark (G-11386)

Mental Edge Counseling .... E 302 382-8698
Dover (G-3061)

Mental Fuel Inc .... G 302 291-4858
Newark (G-11387)

Meryls .... G 302 475-7555
Wilmington (G-18288)

Metanoia Counseling LLC .... G 302 559-4421
Middletown (G-7344)

Michael J Hurd .... G 302 539-5986
Ocean View (G-12546)

Middletown Counseling .... G 302 376-0621
Middletown (G-7348)

Mind and Body Consortium LLC .... D 302 674-2380
Dover (G-3097)

Mindy Body Consortium .... G 302 424-1322
Milford (G-8014)

Nancy M Ball .... G 302 655-8101
Wilmington (G-18525)

Narrow Gate1 .... G 302 387-1838
Magnolia (G-6770)

New Direction Counseling Svcs .... G 302 289-3768
Felton (G-4006)

Northnode Group Counseling LLC .... F 302 257-3135
Dover (G-3198)

Olga Yatzus Lpcmh .... G 302 407-3743
Wilmington (G-18758)

Patricia R Wood .... G 302 737-3674
Newark (G-11638)

Phoenix Rehabilitation .... G 302 533-5313
Newark (G-11686)

Pike Creek Counseling .... G 302 898-9229
Wilmington (G-19040)

Pike Creek Psychlogical Ctr PA .... G 302 738-6859
Newark (G-11693)

Positive Directions II LLC .... F 302 654-9444
Wilmington (G-19125)

Randy L Christofferson .... G 302 540-2006
Wilmington (G-19331)

Recovery Destination Services .... G 302 559-1010
Hockessin (G-5358)

Renew Your Heart and Mind LLC .... G 302 344-7519
Millsboro (G-8442)

Rouleau Suzanne Lcsw .... G 302 479-5157
Newark (G-11918)

Ruby Road LLC .... G 856 887-1422
Newark (G-11925)

Sanare Today LLC .... E 610 344-9600
Wilmington (G-19652)

Shapeup Sales Coaching .... G 850 585-3527
Felton (G-4027)

Strength For Jurney Counseling .... G 302 367-4266
Wilmington (G-20097)

Suburban Psychiatric Svcs LLC .... F 302 999-9834
Wilmington (G-20115)

GENERAL COUNSELING SVCS

Symphony of Mind Counseling............ G 302 747-7286
  Dover *(G-3633)*
Synergy Empowerment Coaching........ G 302 362-0054
  Laurel *(G-5612)*
Tomaros Change................................. G 856 542-8861
  Claymont *(G-1314)*
Tomaros Change................................. G 844 222-8500
  Claymont *(G-1315)*
Tranquil Roots Counseling.................. G 301 275-0225
  Wilmington *(G-20391)*
Wellspring Counseling Services........... G 302 373-8904
  Smyrna *(G-13934)*
Willow Counseling Services................. G 814 779-9653
  Smyrna *(G-13940)*

GENERATION EQPT: Electronic

Hywatts Inc... G 650 460-4488
  Wilmington *(G-17245)*
McV Microwave East Inc..................... E 302 877-8079
  Laurel *(G-5562)*

GENERATOR REPAIR SVCS

Roys Electrical Service Inc................. G 302 674-3199
  Cheswold *(G-989)*

GENERATORS: Vehicles, Gas-Electric Or Oil-Electric

Opengrid Technologies Co................... G 202 677-2794
  Wilmington *(G-18800)*
Star Enrg Cs LLC................................ F 302 660-2187
  Wilmington *(G-20023)*

GIFT SHOP

Bethany Sea-Crest Inc........................ G 302 539-7621
  Bethany Beach *(G-586)*
Good Samaritan Aid............................. G 302 875-2425
  Laurel *(G-5522)*
Junior Bd of Christiana Care................ G 302 733-1100
  Newark *(G-11137)*
Old Country Garden Center Inc........... F 302 652-3317
  Wilmington *(G-18754)*
Sea Shell Shop Inc.............................. F 302 227-4323
  Rehoboth Beach *(G-12950)*
Stuart Kingston Galleries Inc.............. G 302 652-7978
  Wilmington *(G-20104)*

GIFTS & NOVELTIES: Wholesalers

Guinevere Associates Inc.................... G 302 635-7798
  Wilmington *(G-17004)*
Self Care Holistic LLC......................... G 302 407-2456
  Wilmington *(G-19744)*

GLASS PRDTS, FROM PURCHASED GLASS: Insulating

Hensco LLC.. G 302 423-1638
  Harrington *(G-4784)*

GLASS PRDTS, PRESSED OR BLOWN: Optical

Bellaa Bomb LLC.................................. G 800 409-2521
  Wilmington *(G-14819)*

GLASS PRDTS, PRESSED OR BLOWN: Scientific Glassware

R and H Filter Co Inc.......................... G 302 856-2129
  Georgetown *(G-4479)*

GLASS, AUTOMOTIVE: Wholesalers

Safelite Glass Corp.............................. G 877 800-2727
  Dover *(G-3504)*

Safelite Glass Corp.............................. E 302 656-4640
  Wilmington *(G-19628)*

GLASS: Fiber

Psp Corp.. G 302 764-7730
  Wilmington *(G-19244)*

GLASS: Flat

Wilmington Glass Co........................... G 302 777-7000
  Wilmington *(G-20817)*

GLASS: Pressed & Blown, NEC

Studio On 24 Inc.................................. G 302 644-4424
  Lewes *(G-6519)*

GLASSWARE WHOLESALERS

Duralex Usa Inc................................... F 302 326-4804
  Historic New Castle *(G-4978)*

GLASSWARE: Laboratory

Miles Scientific Corporation................. E 302 737-6960
  Newark *(G-11418)*

GLOVES: Leather, Work

Kaul Glove and Mfg Co........................ D 302 292-2660
  Historic New Castle *(G-5014)*

GOLF CARTS: Wholesalers

J & D Custom Golf Carts LLC............. G 302 218-1505
  Middletown *(G-7232)*

GOLF COURSES: Public

American Classic Golf Club LLC.......... G 302 703-6662
  Lewes *(G-5684)*
Back Creek Golf Club........................... E 302 378-6499
  Middletown *(G-6898)*
Bayside Golf LLC DBA Bear Trap........ G 302 537-5600
  Ocean View *(G-12472)*
Bayside Resort Golf Club..................... F 302 436-3400
  Selbyville *(G-13471)*
Baywood Greens Golf Club.................. E 302 947-9225
  Millsboro *(G-8186)*
Baywood Greens Golf Club.................. G 302 947-9800
  Millsboro *(G-8187)*
Baywood Greens Golf Mntnc................ G 757 460-5584
  Millsboro *(G-8188)*
Bear Trap Partners.............................. F 302 537-5600
  Ocean View *(G-12473)*
City of Seaford.................................... G 302 629-2890
  Seaford *(G-13122)*
Delaware Park Racing LLC.................. F 302 994-6700
  Wilmington *(G-15952)*
Delcaste Golf Course.......................... F 302 225-9821
  Wilmington *(G-15987)*
Delcastle Golf Club Management........ F 302 998-9505
  Wilmington *(G-15988)*
Delcastle Golf Management LLC........ F 302 998-9505
  Wilmington *(G-15989)*
Dover Golf Center................................ G 302 674-8275
  Dover *(G-2346)*
Fieldstone Golf Club LP....................... D 302 254-4569
  Wilmington *(G-16603)*
Frog Hollow Golf Course..................... F 302 376-6500
  Middletown *(G-7142)*
Garrisons Lake Golf Club Inc.............. F 302 659-1206
  Smyrna *(G-13741)*
Golf Course At Garrisons Lake............ G 302 659-1206
  Smyrna *(G-13747)*
Greens At Broadview LLC.................... E 302 684-3000
  Milton *(G-8631)*
Home Course Creators LLC................. G 302 419-6305
  Wilmington *(G-17176)*

PRODUCTS & SERVICES SECTION

Jonathans Landing.............................. E 302 697-8204
  Magnolia *(G-6755)*
Meadowbrook Golf Group Inc............. E 302 571-9041
  Wilmington *(G-18242)*
Mulligans Pointe LLC.......................... F 302 856-6283
  Georgetown *(G-4438)*
Odessa National Golf Crse LLC.......... G 302 464-1007
  Townsend *(G-14046)*
Par 3 Inc.. G 302 674-8275
  Dover *(G-3269)*
Peninsula.. G 410 342-8111
  Millsboro *(G-8419)*
Peninsula At Long Neck LLC.............. G 302 947-4717
  Millsboro *(G-8420)*
Rock Manor Golf Course..................... G 302 295-1400
  Wilmington *(G-19529)*
Rookery Golf Courses South.............. F 302 422-7010
  Milford *(G-8072)*
Tee It Up Golf Camp........................... G 302 684-1808
  Milton *(G-8719)*
Vinces Sports Center Inc................... G 302 738-4859
  Newark *(G-12325)*
Worcester Golf Club Inc..................... F 610 222-0200
  Milton *(G-8730)*

GOLF DRIVING RANGES

Golfclub LLC....................................... G 908 770-7892
  Wilmington *(G-16917)*

GOLF EQPT

Abbey Lein Inc.................................... G 302 239-2712
  Newark *(G-9737)*
Rope-It Golf LLC................................. G 305 767-3481
  Wilmington *(G-19566)*

GOLF GOODS & EQPT

Baywood Greens Golf Club................. E 302 947-9225
  Millsboro *(G-8186)*
Delcastle Golf Club Management....... F 302 998-9505
  Wilmington *(G-15988)*

GOVERNMENT, GENERAL: Administration

City of Dover...................................... F 302 736-5071
  Dover *(G-2084)*
Delaware Secretary of State.............. G 302 834-8046
  Bear *(G-155)*
Delaware Secretary of State.............. F 302 736-7400
  Dover *(G-2257)*

GRADING SVCS

Bramble Construction Co Inc............. F 302 856-6723
  Georgetown *(G-4239)*

GRANITE: Cut & Shaped

Keystone Granite and Tile Inc........... F 302 323-0200
  New Castle *(G-9280)*

GRAPHIC ARTS & RELATED DESIGN SVCS

9193 4323 Quebec Inc........................ G 855 824-0795
  Newark *(G-9717)*
Act Media.. G 888 666-0786
  Lewes *(G-5655)*
Bear Associates LLC.......................... G 302 735-5558
  Dover *(G-1898)*
Bhaoo Inc... E 832 888-3694
  Dover *(G-1931)*
Brand Design Co Inc.......................... G 302 234-2356
  Wilmington *(G-15040)*
Casper Hosting LLC........................... G 480 442-7112
  Lewes *(G-5807)*
Envision It Publications LLC.............. G 800 329-9411
  Bear *(G-204)*

PRODUCTS & SERVICES SECTION — HARDWARE WHOLESALERS

Green Crescent LLC .... G 800 735-9620
Dover (G-2622)

Heavenly Films LLC .... G 302 232-8988
Dover (G-2668)

Mitchell Associates Inc .... E 302 594-9400
New Castle (G-9373)

Pixxy Solutions LLC .... E 631 609-6686
Claymont (G-1263)

Precision Color Graphics LLC .... G 302 661-2595
Wilmington (G-19152)

Xcs Corporation .... G 302 514-0500
Wilmington (G-20916)

Zzhouse Inc .... G 302 453-1180
Newark (G-12438)

GRASSES: Artificial & Preserved

Close Cuts Lawn Svc & Ldscpg .... G 302 422-2248
Milford (G-7836)

GRAVEL MINING

Sussex Sand & Gravel Inc .... G 302 628-6962
Seaford (G-13422)

GROCERIES, GENERAL LINE WHOLESALERS

Brandywine Food Services LLC .... G 302 276-5165
Wilmington (G-15058)

Camels Hump Inc .... F 302 227-5719
Rehoboth Beach (G-12662)

El Nopalito Distributors Inc .... F 302 393-2050
Milford (G-7879)

Eztz Inc .... G 302 376-5641
Historic New Castle (G-4986)

Piffert Inc .... F 302 407-6185
Historic New Castle (G-5049)

Refix Commodities LLC .... G 888 465-8020
Dover (G-3443)

World Foods USA LLC .... G 302 288-0670
Dover (G-3873)

GUARD PROTECTIVE SVCS

Global Protection MGT LLC .... B 302 425-4190
Wilmington (G-16894)

GUARD SVCS

Alert Security & Technologies .... G 302 294-9100
Wilmington (G-14353)

Berkana Defense Security LLC .... G 302 504-4455
Wilmington (G-14842)

Delaware Academy Pub Safety SEC .... G 302 377-1465
New Castle (G-9012)

Dupont Esl Security .... G 302 695-1657
Wilmington (G-16208)

Govsimplified LLC .... G 888 629-8008
Claymont (G-1169)

Home Security Wilmington .... G 302 231-1142
Wilmington (G-17184)

J F Goetz Associates LLC .... G 302 537-2485
Ocean View (G-12526)

Matter Gray Security LLC .... G 302 235-8627
Hockessin (G-5303)

United Security Advisors LLC .... G 610 310-2482
Wilmington (G-20526)

GUIDED MISSILES & SPACE VEHICLES

4TH PHASE THECHNOLOGIES INC .... F 610 420-5765
Wilmington (G-14138)

Merida Aerospace Inc .... F 305 396-1471
Lewes (G-6264)

GUTTERS: Sheet Metal

Alu-Rex USA Inc .... E 418 832-7632
Wilmington (G-14399)

S G Williams & Bros Co .... F 302 656-8167
Wilmington (G-19607)

HAIR & HAIR BASED PRDTS

Azextensions LLC .... G 609 202-2098
New Castle (G-8838)

Hair By Ashleighmonai LLC .... G 215 201-6874
Wilmington (G-17032)

K Lush Extensions LLC .... G 347 274-4353
Middletown (G-7257)

Opulence Collection LLC .... G 267 808-1781
Newark (G-11597)

Pierce Multi Solutions LLC .... G 302 609-7000
Newark (G-11689)

Poshsistahs Hair LLC .... F 302 464-2469
Middletown (G-7460)

SBS Global LLC .... G 302 898-2911
Newark (G-11955)

Soft Life Beauty Suite LLC .... G 267 496-7655
Wilmington (G-19913)

HAIR CARE PRDTS

Boldify Inc .... G 240 396-0247
Middletown (G-6929)

Gladys Walker .... G 302 480-0713
Wilmington (G-16879)

HAIR CARE PRDTS: Hair Coloring Preparations

Overtone Color LLC .... G 520 448-3305
Wilmington (G-18842)

HAIR DRESSING, FOR THE TRADE

Bombshell Beauty Inc .... G 302 559-3011
Wilmington (G-14997)

HANDBAGS

Frontgate LLC .... G 302 245-6654
Bethany Beach (G-602)

HANDYMAN SVCS

A1 Handyman Services .... G 302 398-4235
Harrington (G-4721)

Ace Handyman Services .... G 302 899-7300
Dover (G-1710)

American Handyman Services .... E 302 616-2559
Ocean View (G-12460)

Dennis M Hughes .... G 302 632-4503
Harrington (G-4761)

Evan Hooper .... G 302 682-5617
Laurel (G-5511)

Evans Handyman Services .... G 302 422-2758
Lincoln (G-6666)

Frank Costa Constr Handyman .... G 302 561-5792
Rehoboth Beach (G-12760)

Graphites .... G 302 329-9182
Milton (G-8629)

Handy Handyman .... G 267 307-5206
Middletown (G-7193)

Handy Husband LLC .... G 302 697-7552
Camden Wyoming (G-952)

Handyman Bill .... G 302 588-5887
Wilmington (G-17048)

Handyman Mark .... G 302 454-1170
Newark (G-10925)

Handyman Mtters Nrthrn-Dlaware .... G 302 540-8263
Wilmington (G-17049)

Jerrys Handyman LLC .... G 302 357-1589
New Castle (G-9259)

Mal Ventures Inc .... G 302 454-1170
Newark (G-11317)

Matt Matiaset .... G 302 376-3042
Townsend (G-14032)

Moving As One LLC .... F 301 701-0434
Claymont (G-1244)

My Hands Handyman LLC .... G 302 387-2749
Georgetown (G-4440)

Professional Handyman Svcs Inc .... G 302 478-1237
Wilmington (G-19210)

Ralph E Willis .... G 302 422-7167
Milford (G-8058)

Reliable Handyman Services LLC .... G 302 943-0166
Dover (G-3448)

Shackleford Facilities Inc .... F 877 735-3938
Frankford (G-4141)

Stanley J Lepowski Jr .... G 302 378-7284
Townsend (G-14072)

Terry A Gray .... G 302 478-2042
Wilmington (G-20277)

Twin Angels Service .... G 302 545-6749
Bear (G-543)

Vinnys Handyman Servies .... G 302 265-9196
Milton (G-8727)

HARDWARE

Buck Algonquin Co .... G 302 659-6900
Smyrna (G-13669)

D C Mitchell LLC .... G 302 998-1181
Wilmington (G-15759)

Gibbons Innovations Inc .... G 302 265-4220
Lincoln (G-6671)

HARDWARE & BUILDING PRDTS: Plastic

Aztech Industries Inc .... G 302 653-1430
Smyrna (G-13657)

HARDWARE & EQPT: Stage, Exc Lighting

Staging Dimensions Inc .... E 302 328-4100
New Castle (G-9589)

HARDWARE STORES

Bryan & Brittingham Inc .... F 302 846-9500
Delmar (G-1569)

D F Quillen & Sons Inc .... E 302 227-2531
Rehoboth Beach (G-12709)

Mechanics Paradise Inc .... F 302 652-8863
New Castle (G-9355)

HARDWARE STORES: Builders'

Bawa Inc .... G 302 698-3200
Dover (G-1882)

HARDWARE STORES: Tools

Baybiw Development LLC .... F 302 537-9700
Ocean View (G-12469)

Case Construction Inc .... G 302 737-3800
Newark (G-10158)

HARDWARE WHOLESALERS

Acuity Spcialty Pdts Group Inc .... G 302 369-6949
Wilmington (G-14247)

Bair & Goff Sales LLC .... E 302 292-2546
Newark (G-9975)

Brass Sales Company Inc .... F 302 284-4574
Felton (G-3947)

C M D Inc .... G 302 894-1776
Newark (G-10113)

Clark & Sons Overhead Doors .... F 302 998-7552
Wilmington (G-15465)

Integrity Corporation Inc .... F 410 392-8665
Newark (G-11033)

Employee Codes: A=Over 500 employees, B=251-500
C=101-250, D=51-100, E=20-50, F=10-19, G=1-9

HARDWARE WHOLESALERS

Lilly Fasteners & Customization Llc......... E 302 366-7640
  Newark (G-11260)
Mumford Sheet Metal Works Inc............ F 302 436-8251
  Selbyville (G-13583)
Rome Solutions LLC...................... G 302 261-3794
  Wilmington (G-19559)
Southco.................................. G 302 475-2140
  Wilmington (G-19938)
Standard Industrial Supply Co............ G 302 656-1631
  Wilmington (G-20013)

HARDWARE, WHOLESALE: Bolts

Building Fasteners Inc.................... G 302 738-0671
  Newark (G-10102)

HARDWARE, WHOLESALE: Builders', NEC

Foss-Brown Inc........................... G 610 940-6040
  Wilmington (G-16699)
T & C Enterprise Incorporated............ G 302 934-8080
  Millsboro (G-8479)

HARDWARE, WHOLESALE: Chains

Value Chain Excellence LLC............... G 302 545-8011
  Wilmington (G-20565)

HARDWARE, WHOLESALE: Power Tools & Access

W W Grainger Inc....................... G 302 322-1840
  Historic New Castle (G-5098)

HARDWARE, WHOLESALE: Security Devices, Locks

Allied Lock & Safe Company.............. G 302 658-3172
  Wilmington (G-14381)

HARDWARE: Aircraft

Wibdi Aviation Co Corp................... F 305 677-9685
  Dover (G-3847)

HEALTH & WELFARE COUNCIL

Easter Sals Del Mrylnds Estrn............ D 302 856-7364
  Georgetown (G-4303)
Ministry of Caring Inc.................... C 302 652-8947
  Wilmington (G-18375)

HEALTH AIDS: Exercise Eqpt

Movetec Fitness Equipment LLC........... G 302 563-4487
  Newark (G-11460)

HEALTH INSURANCE CARRIERS

Chesapeake Rehab Equipment Inc......... G 302 266-6234
  Newark (G-10198)
Cigna Holdings Inc....................... F 215 761-1000
  Claymont (G-1087)
Highmarks Inc........................... B 302 421-3000
  Wilmington (G-17144)

HEAT EXCHANGERS: After Or Inter Coolers Or Condensers, Etc

Baltimore Aircoil Company Inc............ C 302 424-2583
  Milford (G-7781)

HEAT TREATING: Metal

Industrial Metal Treating Corp............ F 302 656-1677
  Wilmington (G-17315)

HEATERS: Swimming Pool, Electric

Siemens Industry Inc.................... G 302 631-8410
  Newark (G-12006)

HEELS, BOOT OR SHOE: Rubber, Composition Or Fiber

Vulcan International Corp................. F 302 428-3181
  Wilmington (G-20658)

HELICOPTERS

Hel Ecrane Inc........................... G 604 519-0200
  Dover (G-2671)

HELP SUPPLY SERVICES

BP Staffing Inc........................... F 302 999-7213
  Wilmington (G-15021)
Integrity Staffing Solutions................ A 520 276-7775
  Newark (G-11037)
Jiga Inc.................................. F 408 878-3213
  Middletown (G-7249)
Service General Corporation.............. G 302 856-3500
  Georgetown (G-4508)
Star Services LLC....................... G 302 373-5210
  Middletown (G-7596)
Stm Consulting Inc....................... F 408 341-6900
  Claymont (G-1304)
Timber Ridge Inc......................... F 302 239-9239
  Hockessin (G-5405)
Virtually Fortified Staffing................ G 302 547-9065
  Townsend (G-14088)

HIGHWAY & STREET MAINTENANCE SVCS

Delaware Department Trnsp.............. E 302 653-4128
  Middletown (G-7039)

HOLDING COMPANIES: Investment, Exc Banks

Amerisource Heritage Corp............... G 800 829-3132
  Wilmington (G-14454)
Belchim Crop Prtection US Corp.......... F 302 407-3590
  Wilmington (G-14814)
Duns Investing Corporation.............. G 302 651-2050
  Wilmington (G-16201)
Ema Corp................................ E 302 479-9434
  Wilmington (G-16384)
Eri Investments Inc...................... F 302 656-8089
  Wilmington (G-16456)
Erm-Delaware Inc........................ B 302 651-8300
  Wilmington (G-16461)
Famglam LLC........................... F 302 930-0026
  Ellendale (G-3917)
Griffen Corporate Services............... F 302 576-2890
  Wilmington (G-16978)
H-V Technical Services Inc............... G 302 427-5801
  Wilmington (G-17024)
Jacksun Inc............................. E 800 861-7050
  Claymont (G-1193)
Laohio Holdings LLC..................... G 302 200-9685
  Lewes (G-6180)
Lela Capital LLC......................... F 917 428-0304
  Ocean View (G-12537)
Matador Companies LLC................. G 855 303-4229
  Lewes (G-6248)
Mater Ellis LLC.......................... G 302 508-0938
  Wilmington (G-18190)
Midway LLC............................. G 302 378-9156
  Middletown (G-7367)
Morgan Stnley Intl Hldings Inc............ D 302 657-2000
  Wilmington (G-18448)
Nestl Holdings Inc....................... G 203 629-7482
  Wilmington (G-18589)
Oni Acquisition Corp..................... G 212 271-3800
  Wilmington (G-18790)
Sherpa Brokers LLC..................... F 917 455-0094
  Middletown (G-7560)
Smithkline Bcham Phrmceuticals......... F 302 984-6932
  Wilmington (G-19892)
Stewart Law Firm........................ F 302 652-5200
  Wilmington (G-20070)
Tripleone Inc............................ D 833 391-0111
  Dover (G-3728)
X Trillion Inc............................ G 347 370-9117
  Middletown (G-7737)
Zeon Enterprises Inc.................... F 302 898-7167
  New Castle (G-9698)
Zuludynasty LLC........................ G 815 909-4236
  Middletown (G-7752)

HOLDING COMPANIES: Personal, Exc Banks

Anglin Associates LLC.................. F 302 653-3500
  Clayton (G-1349)
Dmac Enterprises LLC................... E 917 504-4529
  Middletown (G-7065)
Dormakaba US Holding Ltd.............. B 252 200-5414
  Wilmington (G-16148)
Gallium US Holdings Inc................. G 713 213-0644
  Wilmington (G-16796)
Hsi Service Corp......................... F 302 369-3709
  Newark (G-10984)
Hunte Corporate Enterprise LLC......... G 212 710-1341
  Wilmington (G-17235)
Labware Global Services Inc............ F 302 658-8444
  Wilmington (G-17786)
Labware Holdings Inc................... E 302 658-8444
  Wilmington (G-17787)
Playtex Marketing Corp.................. G 302 678-6000
  Dover (G-3337)
Qps Holdings LLC....................... F 302 369-5601
  Newark (G-11785)
Ua Services Corp........................ G 302 467-3700
  Middletown (G-7670)

HOME ENTERTAINMENT EQPT: Electronic, NEC

Mmm TV Mounting & Entrmt LLC........ G 267 310-5925
  Claymont (G-1242)

HOME FOR THE MENTALLY HANDICAPPED

Chimes Inc.............................. E 302 678-3270
  Dover (G-2066)
Connectons Cmnty Spport Prgram...... D 302 454-7520
  Newark (G-10306)
Connectons Cmnty Spport Prgram...... D 302 984-2302
  Claymont (G-1099)
Keystone Service Systems Inc.......... C 302 286-7234
  Newark (G-11166)
National Mentor Holdings Inc............ A 302 934-0512
  Millsboro (G-8401)

HOME HEALTH CARE SVCS

4 Green Solutions Inc................... G 954 770-5157
  Lewes (G-5639)
Acts Rtrmnt-Life Cmmnities Inc.......... B 302 654-5101
  Wilmington (G-14245)
Addus Healthcare Inc................... C 302 424-4842
  Milford (G-7759)
Addus Healthcare Inc................... G 302 995-9010
  Wilmington (G-14254)
Advanced Modern Care LLC............ F 267 235-6922
  Newark (G-9777)
Affinity Homecare Services.............. G 302 264-9363
  Dover (G-1734)
Alisi Home Care LLC.................... G 302 268-8686
  Middletown (G-6849)

PRODUCTS & SERVICES SECTION

HOMEFURNISHING STORES: Lighting Fixtures

Alliance Total Care.................................. G 302 225-9000
   Wilmington *(G-14379)*

Almost Home Day Care........................ G 302 220-6731
   Newark *(G-9830)*

Almost Home Day Care LLC................ G 302 220-6731
   Newark *(G-9831)*

Always Best Care.................................. F 302 409-3710
   Milton *(G-8558)*

Amada Senior Care Southern Del......... F 302 272-9500
   Lewes *(G-5680)*

Amalgam Rx Inc.................................... F 302 983-0001
   Wilmington *(G-14409)*

Angels Visiting....................................... D 302 691-8700
   Wilmington *(G-14483)*

Annadale Oladimeji................................ G 267 357-9718
   Wilmington *(G-14491)*

At Home Care Agency........................... G 302 883-2059
   Dover *(G-1841)*

At Home Infucare LLC........................... G 302 883-2059
   Dover *(G-1842)*

Atkins Home Health Aid Agency........... G 302 832-0315
   Bear *(G-54)*

Aveanna Healthcare As LLC.................. F 302 504-4101
   Christiana *(G-992)*

Bayada... F 302 213-5024
   Dover *(G-1885)*

Bc Home Health Care Services.............. E 302 746-7844
   Claymont *(G-1054)*

Bills Home Care Service LLC................. G 302 526-2071
   Dover *(G-1938)*

Biotek Remedys Inc................................ E 877 246-9104
   New Castle *(G-8868)*

Blue Ridge Home Care Inc..................... G 302 397-8211
   Dover *(G-1954)*

By The Shore... G 302 462-0496
   Georgetown *(G-4241)*

Careportmd LLC.................................... G 302 202-3020
   Wilmington *(G-15244)*

Caring For Life Inc................................. F 302 892-2214
   New Castle *(G-8913)*

Caring Hearts Home Care LLC............... F 302 734-9000
   Hartly *(G-4861)*

Caring Matters Home Care.................... F 302 993-1121
   Camden *(G-802)*

Caroline M Wiesner................................ G 877 220-9755
   Wilmington *(G-15257)*

Chesapeakecaregivers LLC..................... G 302 841-9686
   Seaford *(G-13118)*

Cindys Home Away From Hme Fam...... G 302 378-0487
   Middletown *(G-6982)*

Comfort Care At Home Inc.................... F 302 737-8078
   Newark *(G-10282)*

Connections CSP Inc.............................. G 302 327-0122
   New Castle *(G-8966)*

Dedicated To Home Care LLC................ G 484 470-5013
   New Castle *(G-9009)*

Del Premier Care Inc............................. E 302 533-5988
   Newark *(G-10413)*

Delaware 4 Sniors Homecare LLC.......... F 302 386-8080
   Wilmington *(G-15861)*

Delaware Hospice Inc............................. D 302 478-5707
   Newark *(G-10452)*

Dependable Cmnty HM Care LLC.......... G 302 893-3779
   New Castle *(G-9046)*

Empathy Home Care LLC....................... G 302 722-1538
   Newark *(G-10642)*

Excellent Home Care.............................. G 302 327-0147
   Historic New Castle *(G-4985)*

Expert Home Care LLC.......................... G 856 870-6691
   Middletown *(G-7115)*

Fast Pay Rx LLC.................................... G 833 511-9500
   Wilmington *(G-16558)*

Fogarty LLC... G 610 731-4804
   Seaford *(G-13188)*

Generations Home Care Inc................... E 302 322-3100
   Wilmington *(G-16834)*

Generations Home Care Inc................... C 302 856-7774
   Wilmington *(G-16835)*

Grace Miracle Home Care...................... G 302 257-1079
   Wilmington *(G-16942)*

Grace Visitation Services....................... D 302 329-9475
   Milton *(G-8628)*

Griswold Home Care.............................. G 302 703-0130
   Lewes *(G-6062)*

Griswold Home Care.............................. F 302 750-4564
   Wilmington *(G-16982)*

Guardian Angel HM Hlth Care AG......... G 302 476-1281
   Newark *(G-10906)*

Gunning Partners LLC........................... D 302 482-4305
   Newport *(G-12453)*

Healthy At Home Care LLC.................... G 571 228-5935
   Rehoboth Beach *(G-12782)*

Heart 2 Heart Services LLC................... G 302 293-0124
   New Castle *(G-9204)*

Home Health Corp America Inc............. D 302 678-4764
   Dover *(G-2689)*

Home Health Heartfel............................ G 302 660-2686
   Wilmington *(G-17179)*

Home Health Services By TLC............... F 302 322-5510
   Wilmington *(G-17180)*

Home Instead Senior Care..................... F 302 697-6435
   Dover *(G-2690)*

Home Sweet.. G 302 353-9733
   Greenwood *(G-4636)*

Homewatch Caregivers........................... F 302 644-1888
   Lewes *(G-6100)*

Ijn Health Systems LLC......................... F 855 202-5993
   Bear *(G-282)*

In Loving Handz Home Care LLC.......... G 302 530-6344
   Newark *(G-11008)*

Ingleside Homes Inc.............................. D 302 575-0250
   Wilmington *(G-17335)*

Interim Health Care................................ G 302 322-2743
   New Castle *(G-9239)*

Kindheart Home Care Inc...................... G 484 479-6582
   Middletown *(G-7276)*

La Red Health Care............................... F 757 709-5072
   Georgetown *(G-4398)*

Lieske E2e Home Hlth Care Inc............. G 302 898-1563
   Middletown *(G-7298)*

Life Force Eldercare Corp...................... G 302 737-4400
   Newark *(G-11254)*

Lifetime Skills Services LLC.................. G 302 378-2911
   Middletown *(G-7302)*

Macklyn Home Care............................... G 302 253-8208
   Georgetown *(G-4411)*

Macklyn Home Care............................... G 302 690-9397
   Wilmington *(G-18071)*

Makua Inc.. G 310 923-8549
   Wilmington *(G-18094)*

Middltown Snior Lving Prtners.............. G 302 828-0988
   Middletown *(G-7365)*

Mirage Health Services LLC.................. E 302 349-7227
   Dover *(G-3099)*

National Mentor Holdings Inc................ A 302 934-0512
   Millsboro *(G-8401)*

Near and Dear Home Care..................... G 302 530-6498
   Newark *(G-11497)*

Neighbor Care Home Care & Fmly......... G 302 290-0341
   Bear *(G-390)*

Neighborly Home Care........................... F 610 420-1868
   Wilmington *(G-18572)*

Next Step Quality HM Care LLC............ F 888 367-5722
   Smyrna *(G-13834)*

Nurse Angels LLC.................................. G 302 765-8093
   Hockessin *(G-5327)*

Nurses N Kids Inc.................................. E 302 424-1770
   Milford *(G-8033)*

Packd LLC.. E 302 467-3443
   Georgetown *(G-4453)*

Pennsula Home Care LLC...................... F 302 629-4914
   Seaford *(G-13341)*

Perry & Assoc.. G 302 472-8701
   Wilmington *(G-18983)*

Phyllis M Green...................................... G 302 354-6986
   Bear *(G-423)*

Pro 2 Respiratory Services..................... G 302 514-9843
   Smyrna *(G-13855)*

R&R Homecare.. G 302 478-3448
   Wilmington *(G-19308)*

Robert Bird... E 302 654-4003
   Wilmington *(G-19508)*

Roz Health LLC...................................... G 415 259-8992
   Newark *(G-11923)*

Saint Home Health Care........................ F 302 514-9597
   Milford *(G-8080)*

Sea Care LLC... G 410 688-4230
   Seaford *(G-13385)*

Seasons Hspice Plltive Care De............. E 847 692-1000
   Newark *(G-11968)*

Seniortech Inc.. G 302 533-5988
   Newark *(G-11977)*

Servant Support Services LLC............... F 215 201-5990
   Newark *(G-11984)*

Shorecare of Delaware........................... F 302 724-5235
   Dover *(G-3549)*

Solace Lifesciences Inc.......................... G 830 792-3123
   Middletown *(G-7585)*

Solace Lifesciences Inc.......................... G 302 383-1450
   Middletown *(G-7586)*

Solution On-Call Services LLC............... F 302 353-4328
   New Castle *(G-9578)*

Soma Breath Inc.................................... E 415 633-5359
   Wilmington *(G-19928)*

Special Care Inc..................................... G 302 644-6990
   Lewes *(G-6497)*

Special Care Inc..................................... G 302 456-9904
   Wilmington *(G-19953)*

Specimen Collection Svcs LLC............... G 302 465-0494
   Newark *(G-12064)*

Spwa Services LLC................................. G 856 761-4621
   Ocean View *(G-12568)*

T & L Consulting Services LLC.............. G 302 573-1585
   Wilmington *(G-20198)*

Tailored Care LLC................................... G 302 883-1761
   Magnolia *(G-6787)*

TLC Home Care...................................... G 302 983-5720
   Wilmington *(G-20338)*

Tobola Health Care Svcs Inc.................. D 302 389-8448
   Dover *(G-3695)*

Trinity Home Health Care Corp............. E 302 838-2710
   Newark *(G-12233)*

Trinity Home Health Care LLC............... G 410 620-9366
   Newark *(G-12234)*

Vicdania Health Services LLC................ E 302 672-0139
   Dover *(G-3790)*

Visiting Angels of Dover........................ F 302 346-7777
   Dover *(G-3805)*

Vna of Delaware.................................... F 302 454-5422
   Newark *(G-12334)*

HOMEFURNISHING STORES: Fireplaces & Wood Burning Stoves

Walls Farm and Garden Ctr Inc............. G 302 422-4565
   Milford *(G-8137)*

HOMEFURNISHING STORES: Lighting Fixtures

Colonial Electric Supply Co	F	302 998-9993

Historic New Castle *(G-4960)*

Denney Electric Supply Del Inc......... G 302 934-8885
Millsboro *(G-8270)*

Led Company Intl Llc......... F 302 668-8370
Wilmington *(G-17850)*

Light Action Inc......... F 302 328-7800
Wilmington *(G-17908)*

HOMEFURNISHINGS, WHOLESALE: Decorating Splys

Zawadius Inc......... G 888 979-6929
Lewes *(G-6647)*

HOMEFURNISHINGS, WHOLESALE: Draperies

F Schumacher & Co LLC......... E 302 454-3200
Newark *(G-10699)*

HOMEFURNISHINGS, WHOLESALE: Kitchenware

Middletown Kitchen and Bath......... G 302 376-5766
Middletown *(G-7355)*

Nickles Arcade LLC......... F 302 376-1794
Middletown *(G-7406)*

Veritable USA Inc......... D 302 326-4800
Historic New Castle *(G-5097)*

HOMES: Log Cabins

Great Outdoor Cottages LLC......... F 215 760-4971
Georgetown *(G-4346)*

Simpsons Log Homes Inc......... G 302 674-1900
Dover *(G-3566)*

HOSPITAL EQPT REPAIR SVCS

Med Tech Equipment Inc......... G 800 322-2609
Wilmington *(G-18244)*

HOSPITALS: Medical & Surgical

Ai Dupont Hosp For Children......... A 302 651-4620
Wilmington *(G-14327)*

Alfred Idpont Hosp For Chldren......... A 302 651-4000
Wilmington *(G-14356)*

Atlantic General Hospital Corp......... E 302 524-5007
Selbyville *(G-13466)*

Bayhealth Med Ctr Inc-OCC Hlth......... E 302 678-1303
Dover *(G-1889)*

Bayhealth Medical Center Inc......... C 302 674-4700
Dover *(G-1890)*

Bayhealth Primary Care Dover W......... G 302 734-7834
Dover *(G-1891)*

Bayview Endoscopy Center......... E 302 644-0455
Lewes *(G-5742)*

Beacon Medical Group PA......... G 302 947-9767
Rehoboth Beach *(G-12631)*

Beebe Healthcare......... F 302 249-1448
Georgetown *(G-4229)*

Beebe Healthcare......... F 302 934-5052
Millsboro *(G-8191)*

Beebe Hospital Hs......... F 302 645-3565
Lewes *(G-5747)*

Beebe Lab Express Georgetown......... F 302 856-9729
Georgetown *(G-4230)*

Beebe Lab Express Millboro......... F 302 934-5052
Millsboro *(G-8192)*

Beebe Medical Center Inc......... F 302 856-9729
Georgetown *(G-4231)*

Beebe Medical Center Inc......... E 302 645-3300
Lewes *(G-5749)*

Beebe Medical Center Inc......... C 302 645-3629
Lewes *(G-5750)*

Beebe Medical Center Inc......... E 302 393-2056
Milford *(G-7790)*

Beebe Medical Center Inc......... E 302 947-9767
Millsboro *(G-8193)*

Beebe Medical Center Inc......... E 302 541-4175
Millville *(G-8519)*

Beebe Medical Center Inc......... E 302 645-3100
Rehoboth Beach *(G-12635)*

Beebe Medical Center Inc......... E 302 645-3289
Rehoboth Beach *(G-12636)*

Beebe Medical Center Inc......... E 302 645-3010
Rehoboth Beach *(G-12637)*

Beebe Medical Center Inc......... A 302 645-3300
Lewes *(G-5748)*

Beebe Physician Network Inc......... E 302 645-1805
Lewes *(G-5751)*

Bhaskar Palekar MD PA......... G 302 645-1805
Lewes *(G-5761)*

Brian Costleigh LLC......... F 302 645-3775
Rehoboth Beach *(G-12653)*

Cancer Care Ctrs At Bay Hlth......... G 302 674-4401
Dover *(G-2019)*

Cedar Tree Surgical Center......... E 302 945-9766
Millsboro *(G-8217)*

Center For Spine Surgery LLC......... F 302 366-7671
Wilmington *(G-15304)*

Christ Care Cardiac Surgery......... G 302 644-4282
Lewes *(G-5818)*

Christana Care Vsclar Spcalist......... F 302 733-5700
Newark *(G-10211)*

Christiana Care Corp......... G 302 738-4596
Newark *(G-10217)*

Christiana Care Health Sys Inc......... C 302 449-3000
Middletown *(G-6976)*

Christiana Care Health Sys Inc......... C 302 838-4750
Newark *(G-10218)*

Christiana Care Health Sys Inc......... G 302 366-1929
Newark *(G-10219)*

Christiana Care Health Sys Inc......... G 302 733-5700
Newark *(G-10221)*

Christiana Care Health Sys Inc......... B 302 623-7500
Wilmington *(G-15401)*

Christiana Care Health Sys Inc......... C 302 428-6219
Wilmington *(G-15402)*

Christiana Care Health Sys Inc......... C 302 623-1929
Wilmington *(G-15403)*

Christiana Care Health Sys Inc......... C 302 733-1000
Wilmington *(G-15404)*

Christiana Care Health Sys Inc......... G 302 733-1000
Newark *(G-10220)*

Christiana Care Health System......... F 302 992-5545
Wilmington *(G-15405)*

Christiana Care Hlth Svcs Inc......... C 302 327-3959
New Castle *(G-8939)*

Christiana Care Hlth Svcs Inc......... G 302 733-1805
Wilmington *(G-15406)*

Christiana Care Hlth Svcs Inc......... A 302 733-1000
Newark *(G-10225)*

Christiana Hospital......... G 203 645-2903
Historic New Castle *(G-4958)*

Christncare Prmry Care At Lnde......... G 302 623-2850
Wilmington *(G-15420)*

Commonspirit Health LLC......... F 302 336-8212
Dover *(G-2118)*

Complete Family Care Inc......... F 302 232-5002
Wilmington *(G-15572)*

Cuhiana Care Health System......... F 302 733-1780
Newark *(G-10364)*

Cynthia Crosser DC Fiama......... G 302 239-5014
Wilmington *(G-15754)*

Daniel W Cuozzo Do......... F 302 645-4801
Rehoboth Beach *(G-12711)*

Delaware Bay Surgical Svc PA......... E 302 645-5650
Lewes *(G-5890)*

Delaware Heart & Vascular PA......... G 302 734-1414
Dover *(G-2244)*

Endoscopy Center of Deleware......... E 302 892-2710
Newark *(G-10647)*

Envision Healthcare Corp......... F 302 644-3852
Lewes *(G-5965)*

Erik M D Stancofski......... E 302 645-7050
Lewes *(G-5970)*

Frenius Medical Care......... F 302 421-9177
Wilmington *(G-16747)*

Friends & Family Practice......... G 302 537-3740
Millville *(G-8529)*

Hale J Eric MD......... F 302 644-2064
Lewes *(G-6070)*

Iqarus Americas Inc......... E 407 222-5726
Wilmington *(G-17420)*

Jing Jin MD PHD......... F 302 651-5040
Wilmington *(G-17550)*

Jr Board of Kent Gen Hospital......... G 302 744-7128
Dover *(G-2808)*

Kent General Hospital......... A 302 744-7688
Dover *(G-2850)*

Kent General Hospital......... G 302 378-1199
Middletown *(G-7266)*

Kent General Hospital......... A 302 430-5731
Milford *(G-7962)*

Kent General Hospital......... G 302 653-2010
Smyrna *(G-13790)*

Lewes Orthopedic Ctr......... G 302 645-4939
Lewes *(G-6199)*

Limestone Medical Center Inc......... D 302 992-0500
Wilmington *(G-17915)*

Lisa Bartels......... F 302 856-9596
Georgetown *(G-4408)*

Medical Center of Harrington......... G 302 398-8704
Harrington *(G-4800)*

Mediguide International LLC......... D 302 425-5900
Wilmington *(G-18253)*

Milton Enterprises Inc......... G 302 684-2000
Milton *(G-8669)*

Mudiwa Munyikwa MD......... F 302 645-7050
Milford *(G-8022)*

Nancy A Union MD......... G 302 645-6644
Lewes *(G-6305)*

Nanticoke Immediate Care......... G 302 715-5214
Laurel *(G-5569)*

Natural Hypertension Inst Inc......... G 302 533-7704
Newark *(G-11494)*

Nemours Foundation......... A 302 651-4000
Wilmington *(G-18581)*

North Wilmington Womens Center......... G 302 529-7900
Wilmington *(G-18681)*

Peri Srihari MD......... F 302 645-3770
Rehoboth Beach *(G-12889)*

Quick Surface Solutions LLC......... F 302 236-6941
Milton *(G-8692)*

Scimedico LLC......... G 302 375-7500
Middletown *(G-7544)*

Select Medical Corporation......... E 302 421-4545
Wilmington *(G-19741)*

Select Specialty Hospital......... A 302 421-4590
Wilmington *(G-19742)*

Southern Delaware Surgery Ctr......... D 302 644-6992
Rehoboth Beach *(G-12969)*

St Francis Health Services Corporation......... A 302 575-8301
Wilmington *(G-19992)*

PRODUCTS & SERVICES SECTION — HOTELS & MOTELS

St Francis Hospital Inc .... A 616 685-3538
Wilmington *(G-19993)*

Tidalhealth Nanticoke Inc .... A 302 629-6611
Seaford *(G-13429)*

Tidalhlth Pnnsula Regional Inc .... F 302 732-8400
Dagsboro *(G-1517)*

Tidalhlth Pnnsula Regional Inc .... G 302 436-8004
Selbyville *(G-13612)*

Tunnell Cancer Ctr .... G 302 645-3770
Rehoboth Beach *(G-12997)*

UHS of Rockford LLC .... D 302 892-4224
Newark *(G-12261)*

Womens Health Ctr Christn Care .... E 302 428-5810
Wilmington *(G-20881)*

World Hospital Inc .... G 609 254-3391
Bear *(G-567)*

HOSPITALS: Specialty, NEC

Logos Community Dev Corp .... G 302 349-2779
Dover *(G-2972)*

Nemours Foundation .... A 302 651-4000
Wilmington *(G-18581)*

Presbyterian Homes Inc .... B 302 744-3600
Dover *(G-3365)*

HOTELS & MOTELS

1102 West Street Ltd Partnr .... D 302 429-7600
Wilmington *(G-14103)*

300 Gateway LLC .... F 302 655-4100
New Castle *(G-8745)*

44 New England Management Co .... D 302 477-9500
Wilmington *(G-14135)*

700 Nrth King St Wlmington LLC .... C 302 655-0400
Wilmington *(G-14146)*

Amaa Management Corporation .... E 302 677-0505
Dover *(G-1779)*

Ambrux Hospitality LLC .... G 302 521-2492
Wilmington *(G-14418)*

AmericInn By Wyndham .... F 302 398-3900
Harrington *(G-4729)*

Ark of Refuge Mission-Shelter .... F 302 381-2143
Millsboro *(G-8173)*

Beacon Hospitality .... E 302 249-0502
Georgetown *(G-4228)*

Beacon Hospitality .... F 302 567-2213
Rehoboth Beach *(G-12630)*

Bear Hospitality Inc .... G 302 326-2500
Bear *(G-64)*

Bfb Hospitality LLC .... F 302 829-1418
Ocean View *(G-12481)*

Blenheim Hospitality LLC .... F 302 677-0900
Dover *(G-1948)*

Buccini/Pollin Group Inc .... E 302 691-2100
Wilmington *(G-15139)*

Canon Hospitality MGT LLC .... E 302 737-5050
Newark *(G-10130)*

Ch Wilmington LLC .... E 302 438-4504
Newark *(G-10183)*

Changing Place Inc .... F 302 357-6107
Wilmington *(G-15332)*

Chapman Hospitality Inc .... D 302 738-3400
Newark *(G-10189)*

Chudasama Enterprises LLC .... G 302 856-7532
Georgetown *(G-4255)*

Chudasama Enterprises LLC .... G 302 934-7968
Millsboro *(G-8227)*

Coastal Cottage .... G 302 539-7821
Ocean View *(G-12491)*

Colonial Oaks Hotel LLC .... C 302 645-7766
Rehoboth Beach *(G-12693)*

Comfort Inn & Suites .... E 302 737-3900
Newark *(G-10283)*

Concord Towers Inc .... D 302 737-2700
Newark *(G-10296)*

Country Inns Suites .... G 302 266-6400
Newark *(G-10334)*

Courtyard Management Corp .... E 302 456-3800
Newark *(G-10336)*

Courtyard Management Corp .... E 302 429-7600
Wilmington *(G-15661)*

Days Inn and Suites Seaford .... F 302 629-4300
Seaford *(G-13148)*

Days Inn Dover Downtown .... E 302 674-8002
Dover *(G-2200)*

Dipna Inc .... C 302 478-0300
Wilmington *(G-16076)*

Dover Hospitality Group LLC .... E 302 677-0900
Dover *(G-2347)*

Dpnl LLC .... F 302 366-8097
Newark *(G-10559)*

Driftwood Hospitality MGT LLC .... G 302 655-0400
Wilmington *(G-16179)*

Eastern Hospitality Management .... E 302 322-9480
New Castle *(G-9079)*

Express Hotel Inc .... F 302 227-4030
Rehoboth Beach *(G-12748)*

First State Hospitality LLC .... E 302 538-5858
Dover *(G-2505)*

Gulab Management Inc .... G 302 398-4206
Harrington *(G-4776)*

Gulab Management Inc .... E 302 934-6126
Milford *(G-7914)*

Gulab Management Inc .... E 302 734-4433
Dover *(G-2632)*

Gurukrupa Inc .... G 302 328-6691
New Castle *(G-9184)*

Hampton Inn .... E 302 422-4320
Milford *(G-7920)*

Hampton Inn Middletown .... F 302 378-5656
Middletown *(G-7191)*

Hampton Inn Seaford .... F 302 629-4500
Seaford *(G-13206)*

Hampton Inn-Dover .... G 302 736-3500
Dover *(G-2648)*

Hawthorn Suites Hotels Intl .... F 302 369-6212
Newark *(G-10939)*

Hilton Garden Inn Dover .... F 302 465-3061
Middletown *(G-7210)*

Holiday Inn .... F 302 655-0400
Wilmington *(G-17165)*

Holiday Inn Express .... E 302 398-8800
Harrington *(G-4785)*

Holiday Inn Express .... F 302 227-4030
Rehoboth Beach *(G-12787)*

Holiday Inn Select .... F 302 792-2700
Claymont *(G-1180)*

Hollywood Grill Restaurant .... D 302 737-3900
Newark *(G-10958)*

Hollywood Grill Restaurant .... D 302 479-2000
Wilmington *(G-17172)*

Hollywood Grill Restaurant .... D 302 655-1348
Wilmington *(G-17171)*

Homewood Stes By Hlton Wlmngto .... E 302 565-2100
Wilmington *(G-17191)*

House To House Incorporation .... F 302 450-8445
Newark *(G-10978)*

Hyatt Hse Lewes / Rehoboth Bch .... F 302 783-1000
Lewes *(G-6109)*

Hyatt Place .... E 302 864-9100
Dewey Beach *(G-1671)*

J & P Management Inc .... E 302 854-9400
Georgetown *(G-4375)*

Jaysons LLC .... E 302 656-9436
Wilmington *(G-17502)*

K W Lands North LLC .... D 302 678-0600
Dover *(G-2824)*

Keval Corp .... F 302 453-9100
Newark *(G-11160)*

Khanna Entps Ltd A Ltd Partnr .... F 302 266-6400
Newark *(G-11169)*

Knights Inn .... F 302 798-9914
Claymont *(G-1208)*

Kw Garden .... F 302 735-7770
Dover *(G-2891)*

Lila Keshav Hospitality LLC .... F 302 696-2272
Middletown *(G-7304)*

MainStay Suites .... E 302 678-8383
Dover *(G-2999)*

Mark One LLC .... E 302 735-4700
Dover *(G-3019)*

Milford Lodging LLC .... E 302 839-5000
Milford *(G-8003)*

Motel 6 .... F 302 990-5291
Seaford *(G-13290)*

My Salon Suites .... G 302 575-9035
Wilmington *(G-18510)*

Nacstar .... E 302 453-1700
Newark *(G-11482)*

Nazar Dover LLC .... E 302 747-5050
Dover *(G-3163)*

New Beginnings Cnslng Cnst .... G 302 525-6268
Newark *(G-11514)*

Newark Knights Ftbll and .... F 302 846-7776
Bear *(G-395)*

Newark Land Group Inc .... F 302 453-1700
Newark *(G-11541)*

Park Hotels & Resorts Inc .... F 703 883-1000
Newark *(G-11628)*

Paul Amos .... E 302 541-9200
Bethany Beach *(G-626)*

Quality Inn .... F 302 292-1500
Newark *(G-11789)*

Quality Inn .... G 302 659-3635
Smyrna *(G-13860)*

Quality Inn Newark .... G 707 622-5339
Newark *(G-11790)*

Quintasian LLC .... E 302 674-3784
Dover *(G-3412)*

Red Roof Inns Inc .... E 302 292-2870
Newark *(G-11840)*

Residence Inn .... E 302 777-7373
Wilmington *(G-19437)*

Residence Inn By Mariott .... F 302 539-3200
Bethany Beach *(G-633)*

Residence Inn By Marriott LLC .... D 302 453-9200
Newark *(G-11863)*

Resort Hotel LLC .... E 302 226-1515
Rehoboth Beach *(G-12934)*

Rodeway Inn .... E 302 227-0401
Rehoboth Beach *(G-12937)*

Routzhan Jessman .... E 302 398-4206
Harrington *(G-4822)*

Rp Hospitality LLC .... F 302 398-4206
Harrington *(G-4823)*

Sage Hospitality Resources LLC .... C 302 292-1500
Newark *(G-11933)*

SAI Ram Hospitality Inc .... F 302 422-8089
Milford *(G-8079)*

Seper 8 Motel .... E 302 734-5701
Dover *(G-3533)*

Shiv Sagar Inc .... F 302 674-3800
Dover *(G-3547)*

Shree Lalji LLC .... G 302 730-8009
Dover *(G-3552)*

Shri SAI Dover LLC .... E 302 747-5050
Dover *(G-3553)*

Employee Codes: A=Over 500 employees, B=251-500
C=101-250, D=51-100, E=20-50, F=10-19, G=1-9

HOTELS & MOTELS

Shri Swami Narayan LLC .... D 302 738-3198
  Newark (G-12002)
Shriji Hospitality (not Llc) .... D 302 654-5544
  New Castle (G-9567)
Skyways Motor Lodge Corp .... E 302 328-6666
  New Castle (G-9572)
Sleep Inn & Suites .... F 302 645-6464
  Lewes (G-6477)
Springhill Suites Newark Downt .... F 888 205-7322
  Newark (G-12076)
Staybridge Suites .... F 302 738-3400
  Wilmington (G-20040)
Studio302 .... F 302 462-0857
  Dover (G-3617)
Sunny Hospitality LLC .... E 302 226-0700
  Rehoboth Beach (G-12980)
Sunny Hospitality LLC .... E 302 398-3900
  Harrington (G-4837)
Super Eight Dover .... G 302 734-5701
  Dover (G-3626)
Veer Hotels Inc .... G 302 398-3900
  Harrington (G-4844)
Willis Hspitality Partners LLC .... F 302 544-5054
  New Castle (G-9683)
Winner Dover 1387 LLC .... F 302 257-3500
  Dover (G-3859)
Wyndham Franchisor LLC .... E 302 487-0234
  Dover (G-3879)

HOUSEHOLD APPLIANCE STORES: Appliance Parts

Williams Appliancee .... F 302 656-8581
  Wilmington (G-20797)

HOUSEHOLD APPLIANCE STORES: Gas Appliances

Schagrin Gas Co .... E 302 378-2000
  Middletown (G-7541)

HOUSEHOLD ARTICLES, EXC FURNITURE: Cut Stone

Sovereigntactical LLC .... G 858 336-9471
  Wilmington (G-19945)

HOUSEHOLD FURNISHINGS, NEC

Bethany Resort Furn Whse .... G 302 251-4101
  Selbyville (G-13476)
Bethrant Industries LLC .... G 484 343-5435
  New Castle (G-8864)

HOUSEWARES, ELECTRIC: Heating Units, Electric Appliances

Econat Inc .... G 302 504-4207
  Middletown (G-7081)

HYDRAULIC EQPT REPAIR SVC

Anderson Group Inc .... A 302 478-6160
  Wilmington (G-14472)

ICE CREAM & ICES WHOLESALERS

Hy-Point Dairy Farms Inc .... C 302 478-1414
  Wilmington (G-17240)

INDL & PERSONAL SVC PAPER, WHOLESALE: Boxes & Containers

Container Home Fund .... G 915 433-4817
  Newark (G-10311)
Pet Poultry Products LLC .... E 302 337-8223
  Bridgeville (G-748)

Service First Container LLC .... G 302 527-5939
  Felton (G-4026)

INDL EQPT SVCS

Industrial Resource Netwrk Inc .... F 302 888-2905
  Wilmington (G-17316)
Progressive Systems Inc .... G 302 732-3321
  Frankford (G-4135)

INDL MACHINERY & EQPT WHOLESALERS

Accudyne Systems Inc .... E 302 369-5390
  Newark (G-9750)
Adash Inc .... G 302 654-3977
  Wilmington (G-14252)
Advance Marine LLC .... G 302 656-2111
  Wilmington (G-14268)
Autotype Holdings (usa) Inc .... D 302 378-3100
  Middletown (G-6889)
Billy Warren & Son LLC .... G 302 349-5767
  Greenwood (G-4598)
Cheshire Enterprise LLC .... G 302 365-6225
  Bear (G-98)
Cognitive Tech Solutions Inc .... G 302 207-1824
  Wilmington (G-15519)
Delaware Filter Corp .... G 302 326-3950
  New Castle (G-9023)
Finger Lakes Metrology LLC .... G 607 742-7240
  Ellendale (G-3918)
First State Automation LLC .... G 302 743-4798
  New Castle (G-9127)
Firstchoice Group America LLC .... G 425 242-8626
  Lewes (G-6000)
Graham Global Corporation .... F 302 839-3000
  Wilmington (G-16945)
Groff Tractor & Equipment LLC .... F 302 349-5760
  Greenwood (G-4633)
Hydroseeding Co LLC .... G 302 858-8171
  Bridgeville (G-715)
Jbcompany LLC .... G 406 623-8593
  Claymont (G-1196)
Karcher Municipal North Amer .... E 401 230-3296
  Wilmington (G-17651)
McCabes Mechanical Service Inc .... F 302 854-9001
  Georgetown (G-4421)
Mecatech Indus Equipments LLC .... G 617 586-4224
  Dover (G-3048)
Mechanics Paradise Inc .... F 302 652-8863
  New Castle (G-9355)
Messick & Gray Cnstr Inc .... E 302 337-8777
  Bridgeville (G-731)
National Metering Service Inc .... G 302 516-7418
  Wilmington (G-18545)
Pascale Industries Inc .... F 302 421-9400
  New Castle (G-9454)
Senso Dynamics LLC .... G 302 257-5926
  Lewes (G-6459)
Standard Direct LLC .... G 855 550-0606
  Wilmington (G-20012)
Supercritical Fluid Tech Inc .... G 302 738-3420
  Newark (G-12129)
United States Power Eqp LLC .... G 302 294-2562
  Newark (G-12271)
United Testing Systems Inc .... E 714 638-2322
  New Castle (G-9657)
Universal Baking Company .... G 302 290-3204
  Wilmington (G-20533)
World Wide Trading Brokers .... G 302 368-7041
  Newark (G-12410)
Yellow and Green Machinery LLC .... G 302 526-4990
  Dover (G-3885)

PRODUCTS & SERVICES SECTION

INDL PROCESS INSTRUMENTS: Analyzers

Romer Labs Technology Inc .... E 855 337-6637
  Newark (G-11914)

INDL PROCESS INSTRUMENTS: On-Stream Gas Or Liquid Analysis

American Meter Holdings Corp .... A 302 477-0208
  Wilmington (G-14437)

INDL SPLYS WHOLESALERS

Bulk Mro Industrial Supply Inc .... G 646 713-1060
  Wilmington (G-15147)
E-Industrial Suppliers LLC .... G 302 251-6210
  Wilmington (G-16243)
Eastern Shore Equipment Co .... G 302 697-3300
  Camden (G-825)
Forcebeyond LLC .... F 302 995-6588
  New Castle (G-9139)
Greenberg Supply Co Inc .... E 302 656-4496
  Wilmington (G-16970)
HK Paper .... G 302 475-3699
  Wilmington (G-17156)
Industrial Products of Del .... G 302 328-6648
  New Castle (G-9231)
Ladder Mart USA LLC .... E 866 524-4536
  Dover (G-2897)
Motion Industries Inc .... E 302 462-3130
  Delmar (G-1625)
National Industrial LLC .... G 302 407-6233
  Wilmington (G-18543)
OConnor Belting Intl Inc .... E 302 452-2500
  Newark (G-11576)
PQ Holding Inc .... E 302 478-6160
  Wilmington (G-19142)
Reybold Group .... G 302 834-1740
  Bear (G-457)
Rhino Lnngs Del Auto Style Inc .... F 302 368-4660
  Newark (G-11878)
Standard Industrial Supply Co .... G 302 656-1631
  Wilmington (G-20013)
State Line Machine Inc .... F 302 478-0285
  Wilmington (G-20035)
Texcel LLC .... G 302 738-4313
  Newark (G-12185)
Urie & Blanton Inc .... G 302 658-8604
  Wilmington (G-20545)
W T Schrider & Sons Inc .... F 302 934-1900
  Millsboro (G-8498)

INDL SPLYS, WHOLESALE: Abrasives

Arlon Med International LLC .... F 302 834-2100
  Bear (G-45)
Arlon Partners Inc .... G 302 595-1234
  Bear (G-46)

INDL SPLYS, WHOLESALE: Bearings

Bdi Inc .... C 570 299-7679
  Newark (G-10000)

INDL SPLYS, WHOLESALE: Drums, New Or Reconditioned

First State Steel Drum Co .... G 302 655-2422
  New Castle (G-9132)
Industrial Resource Netwrk Inc .... F 302 888-2905
  Wilmington (G-17316)
Petroserv Inc .... G 302 398-3260
  Harrington (G-4811)

INDL SPLYS, WHOLESALE: Electric Tools

PRODUCTS & SERVICES SECTION

INSTRUMENTS: Medical & Surgical

W W Grainger Inc .... G 302 322-1840
Historic New Castle *(G-5098)*

INDL SPLYS, WHOLESALE: Power Transmission, Eqpt & Apparatus

Electric Motor Wholesale Inc .... F 302 653-1844
Camden Wyoming *(G-939)*

Electric Motor Wholesale Inc .... F 302 653-1844
Camden Wyoming *(G-940)*

INDL SPLYS, WHOLESALE: Tools, NEC

C M D Inc .... G 302 894-1776
Newark *(G-10113)*

Case Construction Inc .... G 302 737-3800
Newark *(G-10158)*

INDL SPLYS, WHOLESALE: Valves & Fittings

American Insert Flange Co Inc .... G 302 777-7464
Wilmington *(G-14433)*

GTS Technical LLC .... F 302 778-1362
Wilmington *(G-16998)*

John R Seiberlich Inc .... D 302 356-2400
New Castle *(G-9262)*

Precision Flow LLC .... F 302 544-4417
New Castle *(G-9489)*

Royal Instruments Inc .... G 302 328-5900
Historic New Castle *(G-5063)*

INDUSTRIAL & COMMERCIAL EQPT INSPECTION SVCS

First State Inspection Agency .... G 302 422-3859
Milford *(G-7895)*

Food Equipment Service Inc .... G 302 996-9363
Wilmington *(G-16682)*

INFORMATION RETRIEVAL SERVICES

Dawn US Holdings LLC .... F 619 322-2799
Wilmington *(G-15818)*

Ftl Technologies Corporation .... E 703 634-6910
Lewes *(G-6019)*

Homeland SEC Verification LLC .... G 888 791-4614
Wilmington *(G-17186)*

Ipr International LLC .... E 302 304-8774
Wilmington *(G-17417)*

Lexisnexis Risk Assets Inc .... A 800 458-9410
Wilmington *(G-17889)*

Post Media Inc .... E 203 244-8424
Wilmington *(G-19129)*

Veteran It Pro LLC .... F 302 824-3111
Hockessin *(G-5418)*

Webstudy Inc .... G 888 326-4058
Harbeson *(G-4718)*

INFORMATION SVCS: Consumer

Devstringx Technologies Inc .... G 650 209-7815
Lewes *(G-5913)*

Empire Data Voice Networks LLC .... G 702 613-4900
Millsboro *(G-8281)*

Faqx Inc .... G 646 437-6797
Claymont *(G-1148)*

Fonbnk Inc .... F 703 585-3288
Dover *(G-2523)*

Grofos International LLC .... G 302 635-4805
Newark *(G-10901)*

Inclusive Innovations Inc .... G 781 962-9959
Newark *(G-11009)*

Ramiglot Inc .... G 929 203-5115
Middletown *(G-7501)*

Zk Technologies LLC .... G 980 246-4090
Lewes *(G-6651)*

INGOTS: Steel

Chemfirst Inc .... D 302 774-1000
Wilmington *(G-15354)*

INK: Printing

C & A Ink .... G 302 565-9866
Newark *(G-10111)*

Colors & Effects USA LLC .... G 302 996-2910
Newport *(G-12444)*

Digital Ink Sciences LLC .... G 951 757-0027
Wilmington *(G-16065)*

Fujifilm Imaging Colorants Inc .... E 800 552-1609
New Castle *(G-9150)*

INSPECTION & TESTING SVCS

Cyclops Net Inc .... G 844 979-0222
Camden *(G-812)*

Eastern Shore Onsite Svcs LLC .... G 302 736-0366
Leipsic *(G-5632)*

Mumford-Bjorkman Assoc Inc .... F 302 655-8234
Wilmington *(G-18485)*

Neil Services Inc .... G 302 573-2265
Wilmington *(G-18574)*

Veriti Security Incorporated .... E 212 203-0100
Wilmington *(G-20588)*

INSTRUMENTS, LABORATORY: Differential Thermal Analysis

Ttna Energy Systems LLC .... G 302 384-9147
Wilmington *(G-20456)*

INSTRUMENTS, LABORATORY: Mass Spectrometers

Mstm LLC .... G 302 239-4447
Newark *(G-11467)*

INSTRUMENTS, MEASURING & CONTROLLING: Breathalyzers

Toxtrap Inc .... G 302 698-1400
Dover *(G-3708)*

INSTRUMENTS, SURGICAL & MEDICAL: Blood & Bone Work

Caveman Design Inc .... G 302 234-9969
Hockessin *(G-5153)*

Direct Medical LLC .... G 781 640-7474
Wilmington *(G-16078)*

W L Gore & Associates Inc .... C 302 368-3700
Newark *(G-12341)*

W L Gore & Associates Inc .... D 302 738-4880
Newark *(G-12342)*

INSTRUMENTS, SURGICAL & MEDICAL: IV Transfusion

Medical Sup Support Svcs LLC .... F 302 446-3658
Dover *(G-3052)*

INSTRUMENTS: Analytical

Advanced Particle Sensors LLC .... G 302 695-4883
Wilmington *(G-14277)*

Alphasense Inc .... G 302 294-0116
Newark *(G-9836)*

Axess Corporation .... G 302 292-8500
Historic New Castle *(G-4937)*

B & W Tek Inc .... D 855 692-9835
Newark *(G-9963)*

Bia Separations Inc .... G 510 740-4045
Wilmington *(G-14875)*

Bonna-Agela Technologies Inc .... D 302 438-8798
Hockessin *(G-5137)*

Bonna-Agela Technologies Inc .... E 302 438-8798
Wilmington *(G-15000)*

M&M Mass Spec Consulting LLC .... G 302 250-4488
Newark *(G-11307)*

Markes International Inc .... G 302 656-5500
Wilmington *(G-18143)*

Nanodrop Technologies LLC .... E 302 479-7707
Wilmington *(G-18530)*

Ribodynamics LLC .... G 518 339-6605
Wilmington *(G-19464)*

Scientific Systems Corp .... G 302 655-5500
Wilmington *(G-19706)*

Separation Methods Tech Inc .... F 302 368-0610
Newark *(G-11979)*

Standard Merger Sub LLC .... E 302 456-6785
Newark *(G-12083)*

Supercritical Fluid Tech Inc .... G 302 738-3420
Newark *(G-12128)*

Supercritical Fluid Tech Inc .... G 302 738-3420
Newark *(G-12129)*

Thermo Fisher Scientific Inc .... G 302 479-7707
Wilmington *(G-20298)*

INSTRUMENTS: Flow, Indl Process

Delaware Capital Formation Inc .... G 302 793-4921
Wilmington *(G-15878)*

INSTRUMENTS: Indl Process Control

Acorn Energy Inc .... G 410 654-3315
Wilmington *(G-14237)*

INSTRUMENTS: Measurement, Indl Process

Applied Analytics Inc .... E 781 791-5005
Newark *(G-9890)*

INSTRUMENTS: Measuring & Controlling

Northeast Controls Inc .... F 201 419-6111
Rehoboth Beach *(G-12871)*

INSTRUMENTS: Medical & Surgical

Cydallia Inc .... G 860 682-0947
Lewes *(G-5876)*

Denco Inc .... G 302 798-4200
Wilmington *(G-16007)*

Docs Medical LLC .... G 301 401-1489
Bear *(G-175)*

Eidp Inc .... G 302 996-4000
Wilmington *(G-16343)*

Enovis Corporation .... C 301 252-9160
Wilmington *(G-16428)*

Fbk Medical Tubing Inc .... F 302 855-0585
Georgetown *(G-4315)*

Med Tech Equipment Inc .... G 800 322-2609
Wilmington *(G-18244)*

Moor Instruments Inc .... G 302 798-7470
Wilmington *(G-18433)*

Nestal Mdsphere Consulting LLC .... G 302 404-6506
Wilmington *(G-18588)*

Perivision Usa Inc .... F 302 665-0866
Dover *(G-3300)*

Promixco USA Corp .... G 814 810-3643
Wilmington *(G-19229)*

Pulse Technologies Inc .... G 785 258-6423
Claymont *(G-1270)*

Shummi US LLC .... G 847 987-1686
Wilmington *(G-19812)*

Smith & Nephew Holdings Inc .... E 302 884-6720
Wilmington *(G-19886)*

Taro Medical Incorporated .... F 818 245-2202
Lewes *(G-6542)*

Employee Codes: A=Over 500 employees, B=251-500
C=101-250, D=51-100, E=20-50, F=10-19, G=1-9

2024 Harris Directory of Delaware Businesses

INSTRUMENTS: Optical, Analytical

Creative Devices Inc .... G 302 378-5433
  Middletown (G-7020)

INSTRUMENTS: Radio Frequency Measuring

Cloud Collected LLC .... G 302 273-4010
  Newark (G-10262)

INSTRUMENTS: Test, Electronic & Electrical Circuits

AC Group Inc .... G 201 840-5566
  Wilmington (G-14211)
Suretronix Solutions LLC .... G 302 407-3146
  Wilmington (G-20161)

INSULATION & ROOFING MATERIALS: Wood, Reconstituted

Jcr Systems LLC .... G 302 420-6072
  Historic New Castle (G-5010)
Southside Construction LLC .... G 302 500-9268
  Bear (G-502)

INSULATION: Fiberglass

Ipm Inc .... F 302 328-4030
  New Castle (G-9241)

INSULATORS, PORCELAIN: Electrical

NGK North America Inc .... G 302 654-1344
  Wilmington (G-18640)

INSURANCE AGENTS, NEC

A M Clay Onroe Inc .... G 302 645-6565
  Lewes (G-5646)
AAA Club Alliance Inc .... E 302 283-4300
  Newark (G-9732)
AAA Environmental Services .... G 302 284-4334
  Felton (G-3937)
AAA Mid-Atlantic .... E 302 299-4230
  Wilmington (G-14182)
AAA Midatlantic Inc .... F 800 999-4952
  Historic New Castle (G-4918)
Affordable Insur Netwrk Del .... G 800 681-7261
  Bear (G-20)
Allen Insurance Group .... G 302 654-8823
  Wilmington (G-14374)
Always Insurance Agency LLC .... G 302 566-6529
  Harrington (G-4726)
American Life Insurance Co .... D 302 594-2000
  Wilmington (G-14435)
Ascela .... E 888 298-5151
  Newark (G-9918)
Assurance Partners Intl .... F 302 478-0173
  Wilmington (G-14600)
Auspice Risk LLC .... G 484 467-1963
  Lewes (G-5720)
Auto Cheap Quotes Ins-Wlmgtn .... G 302 992-9736
  Wilmington (G-14650)
B+h Insurance LLC .... E 302 995-2247
  Newark (G-9968)
Bishop Associates .... G 302 838-1270
  Newark (G-10039)
Bob Mobley .... G 302 652-2005
  Wilmington (G-14991)
Braun Agency Inc .... G 302 998-1412
  Wilmington (G-15096)
Bs Insurance LLC .... E 302 645-2356
  Lewes (G-5779)
Business Insurance Services .... G 302 655-5300
  New Castle (G-8903)
C Edgar Wood Inc .... E 302 674-3500
  Dover (G-2007)

Cambridge Insurance Group Inc .... G 302 888-2440
  Wilmington (G-15203)
Carey Jr James E Inc .... G 302 934-8383
  Dagsboro (G-1422)
Cbm Insurance Agency LLC .... E 302 322-2261
  New Castle (G-8923)
Chad Wiswall Agency .... G 302 791-7600
  Wilmington (G-15326)
Chambers Insurance Agency Inc .... G 302 655-5300
  New Castle (G-8924)
Charles M Wallace .... G 302 998-1412
  Wilmington (G-15338)
Chesapeak Insurance Advisors .... G 610 793-6885
  Fenwick Island (G-4044)
Chesapeake Insurance Advisors .... F 302 544-6900
  New Castle (G-8931)
Commercial Insurance Assoc .... G 610 436-4608
  Newark (G-10284)
Concord Agency Inc .... G 302 478-4000
  Wilmington (G-15578)
Davis Insurance Group Inc .... G 302 652-4700
  Montchanin (G-8737)
Debra McAfee .... G 302 655-7999
  New Castle (G-9007)
Delmarva Insurance Group .... G 302 248-8500
  Lewes (G-5906)
Desanctis Insurance Agency LLC .... G 302 629-8841
  Seaford (G-13159)
Dewberry Insurance Agency Inc .... G 302 995-9550
  Wilmington (G-16037)
Diann Jones Agcy - Nationwide .... G 302 530-1234
  Middletown (G-7058)
Douglas C Loew & Associates .... G 302 453-0550
  Newark (G-10555)
Eia Insurers Group LLC .... G 302 543-4572
  Wilmington (G-16313)
Elsmere Insurance Agency LLC .... F 317 574-2861
  Wilmington (G-16379)
Esis Inc .... G 215 640-1000
  Wilmington (G-16464)
Fair Insurance Agency Inc .... G 302 395-0740
  Bear (G-219)
Fidelity National Info Svcs .... F 302 658-2102
  Wilmington (G-16599)
Fox Point Programs Inc .... G 302 765-6018
  Wilmington (G-16714)
Fox Point Programs Inc .... F 800 499-7242
  Claymont (G-1151)
Fusura LLC .... D 302 397-2200
  Wilmington (G-16774)
George J Weiner Associates .... F 302 658-0218
  Wilmington (G-16846)
Henaghan Insurance .... G 302 235-3111
  Hockessin (G-5237)
High Point Preferred Insur Co .... D 800 245-2425
  Wilmington (G-17141)
Hoeschel Inv & Insur Group .... F 302 738-3535
  Newark (G-10957)
Impact Insurance Agency .... G 302 363-7785
  Clayton (G-1371)
Insley Insur & Finanial Svcs .... G 302 677-1888
  Dover (G-2738)
Insley Insur & Fncl Svcs Inc .... F 302 286-0777
  Newark (G-11025)
Insurance & Financial Svcs Inc .... E 302 239-5895
  New Castle (G-9235)
Insurance Administrators Inc .... G 302 239-1688
  Wilmington (G-17361)
Insurance Associates Inc .... F 302 368-0888
  Newark (G-11028)
Insurance Market Inc .... G 302 934-9006
  Millsboro (G-8321)

Insurance Market Inc .... F 302 875-7591
  Laurel (G-5534)
Insurance Office America Inc .... G 302 764-1000
  Wilmington (G-17363)
Iroquois New England Inc .... F 716 373-5511
  Wilmington (G-17423)
L & D Insurance Services LLC .... G 302 235-2288
  Hockessin (G-5273)
L & W Insurance Inc .... E 302 674-3500
  Dover (G-2892)
Lawrence Agencies Inc .... G 302 995-6936
  Wilmington (G-17835)
Lisa Broadbent Insurance Inc .... G 302 731-0044
  Newark (G-11266)
Lyons Insurance Agency Inc .... D 302 227-7100
  Wilmington (G-18054)
Mary Bryan Inc .... G 302 875-2087
  Laurel (G-5560)
McCall Brooks Insurance Agency .... G 302 475-8200
  Newark (G-11366)
McComrick Insurance Services .... G 302 732-6655
  Dagsboro (G-1480)
Michael Frankos .... G 302 531-0831
  Dover (G-3078)
Muncie Ins & Fncl Svcs Inc .... G 302 398-9100
  Harrington (G-4806)
Muncie Ins & Fncl Svcs Inc .... G 302 761-9611
  Wilmington (G-18486)
Muncie Insurance Services .... G 302 629-9414
  Seaford (G-13296)
Nationwide Insrnce Crey Insur .... F 302 934-8383
  Dagsboro (G-1487)
Nationwide Insrnce Wswall Agcy .... G 302 791-7600
  Wilmington (G-18550)
Nationwide Insur - Wlgus Insur .... G 302 629-5140
  Seaford (G-13314)
Nationwide Insurance .... G 919 644-6535
  Dover (G-3157)
Nationwide Insurance .... G 302 515-1851
  Georgetown (G-4443)
Nationwide Insurance .... G 302 402-5188
  Milford (G-8025)
Nationwide Insurance .... G 302 453-9698
  Newark (G-11491)
Nationwide Insurance Co .... G 302 678-2223
  Dover (G-3158)
Nationwide Mutual Insurance Co .... F 302 234-5430
  Hockessin (G-5317)
Nationwide Mutual Insurance Co .... G 434 426-9410
  Wilmington (G-18551)
New Castle Insurance Ltd .... F 302 328-6111
  Historic New Castle (G-5036)
Nickle Insurance .... G 302 654-0347
  Wilmington (G-18643)
Occidental L Transamerica .... F 302 477-9700
  Wilmington (G-18739)
Pennock Insurance Inc .... G 302 235-8258
  Hockessin (G-5337)
Penteco LLC .... G 302 472-9105
  Wilmington (G-18962)
Peoples First Insurance Inc .... G 302 449-4777
  Middletown (G-7440)
Poland & Sullivan Insur Inc .... F 302 738-3535
  Newark (G-11708)
Prominent Insurance Svcs Inc .... G 302 351-3368
  Wilmington (G-19228)
Rawlins Ferguson Jones & Lewis .... G 302 337-8231
  Seaford (G-13365)
Records - Gebhart Agency Inc .... G 302 653-9211
  Smyrna (G-13864)
Rhue & Associates Inc .... G 302 422-3058
  Milford (G-8067)

PRODUCTS & SERVICES SECTION

INSURANCE: Agents, Brokers & Service

Richard A Parsons Agency Inc............ G 302 674-2810
  Dover (G-3466)
Richard P Horgan Insurance................ G 302 934-9494
  Wilmington (G-19473)
S T Good Insurance Inc...................... F 215 969-8385
  Newark (G-11929)
Sanderson Albidress Agency............... G 302 368-3010
  Wilmington (G-19658)
Standard Insurance Company............... D 302 322-9922
  New Castle (G-9591)
Starr Wright Insur Agcy Inc.................. E 302 483-0190
  Wilmington (G-20028)
Steele Insurance Group LLC................ G 302 898-6797
  Wilmington (G-20045)
Taylor Professional Insurance.............. G 302 660-3685
  Wilmington (G-20235)
Tiffany Kistler Benefits........................ D 302 425-5010
  Wilmington (G-20320)
Tri Valley Agency Inc.......................... G 302 482-3802
  Wilmington (G-20411)
Truitt Insurance Agency Inc.................. G 302 645-9344
  Lewes (G-6582)
Virgil P Ellwanger............................... G 302 934-8083
  Millsboro (G-8495)
Wilgus Insur Agcy Inc - Mllsbo............. G 302 934-1502
  Millsboro (G-8506)
Williams Insurance Agency Inc............. F 302 384-7804
  Wilmington (G-20799)
Williams Insurance Agency Inc............. G 302 227-2501
  Wilmington (G-20800)
Williams Insurance Agency Inc............. G 302 239-5500
  Wilmington (G-20801)
Williams Insurance Agency Inc............. E 302 227-2501
  Rehoboth Beach (G-13019)

INSURANCE BROKERS, NEC

Donald C Savoy Inc............................ F 302 697-4100
  Dover (G-2322)
Donald C Savoy Inc............................ F 888 992-6755
  Newark (G-10549)
Endurnce Reinsurance Corp Amer....... E 973 898-9575
  Wilmington (G-16414)
Fred S Smalls Insurance..................... F 302 633-1980
  Wilmington (G-16736)
Kelly & Assoc Insur Group Inc.............. G 302 661-6324
  Wilmington (G-17679)
Nickle Insurance Agency Inc............... G 302 834-9700
  Delaware City (G-1549)
Notch Insurance Inc........................... E 616 622-2554
  Dover (G-3201)
Novo Insurance LLC........................... F 408 245-3800
  Wilmington (G-18699)
Rockwood Programs Inc..................... E 302 765-6000
  Claymont (G-1282)
Savoy Associates............................... G 302 658-8770
  Wilmington (G-19685)
Surplus & Excess Line Ltd.................. G 302 653-5016
  Smyrna (G-13905)
Wahl Financial Inc.............................. G 302 229-1933
  Wilmington (G-20670)
Wilgus Associates Inc......................... G 302 644-2960
  Lewes (G-6630)
Wilgus Associates Inc......................... E 302 539-7511
  Bethany Beach (G-650)

INSURANCE CARRIERS: Automobile

Chrissinger and Baumberger............... G 302 777-0100
  Wilmington (G-15395)

INSURANCE CARRIERS: Life

Alvini & Assoc Fincl Planners.............. G 302 397-8135
  Wilmington (G-14403)

Better Life Enterprise.......................... G 302 312-9156
  Bear (G-70)
Chesapeake Brokerage LLC................ G 410 517-1592
  Rehoboth Beach (G-12670)
Cigna Global Holdings Inc................... F 302 797-3469
  Claymont (G-1086)
Cigna Holdings Inc............................. F 215 761-1000
  Claymont (G-1087)
Citicorp Del-Lease Inc........................ D 302 323-3801
  New Castle (G-8947)
Cruise A Lifetime Usa Inc................... G 302 697-2139
  Dover (G-2163)
Delaware American Lf Insur Co............ D 302 594-2871
  Wilmington (G-15864)
Donald C Savoy Inc............................ F 888 992-6755
  Newark (G-10549)
Eea Life Settlements Inc..................... G 302 472-7429
  Wilmington (G-16306)
Hackney Business Solutions LLC......... G 843 496-7236
  Newark (G-10916)
Highmarks Inc................................... G 302 421-3000
  Wilmington (G-17145)
New York Life Ins Co......................... G 302 537-7060
  Ocean View (G-12551)
Northwestern Mutl Fincl Netwrk........... G 414 299-2508
  Dover (G-3199)

INSURANCE CARRIERS: Property & Casualty

21st Century N Amer Insur Co............. A 877 310-5687
  Wilmington (G-14121)
Chubb US Holdings Inc...................... C 215 640-1000
  Wilmington (G-15426)
Cigna Global Holdings Inc................... F 302 797-3469
  Claymont (G-1086)

INSURANCE CARRIERS: Title

Intercoastal Title Agency Inc................ G 302 478-7752
  Wilmington (G-17375)

INSURANCE CLAIM PROCESSING, EXC MEDICAL

Integra ADM Group Inc....................... F 800 959-3518
  Seaford (G-13223)

INSURANCE INFORMATION & CONSULTING SVCS

Nova Wave Credit LLC........................ G 929 263-4212
  Dover (G-3202)
Options or Fast Cash Inc.................... G 310 867-9171
  Middletown (G-7418)
Regulatory Insurance Services............ G 302 678-2004
  Dover (G-3447)

INSURANCE: Agents, Brokers & Service

21st Century Insurance Group.............. E 302 478-3109
  Wilmington (G-14120)
AFLAC.. G 302 376-9880
  Middletown (G-6838)
AFLAC District Offcie......................... G 302 375-6885
  Claymont (G-1025)
Aim Inc... G 302 424-1424
  Milford (G-7762)
Allstate Insrnce Bob Sbraccia.............. G 302 300-4500
  Wilmington (G-14385)
Allstate Insurance.............................. G 302 248-8500
  Lewes (G-5677)
Andrew Bobich.................................. G 312 384-9323
  Wilmington (G-14474)

Angle Planning Concepts.................... G 302 735-7526
  Dover (G-1795)
Ansel Health Inc................................ F 844 987-1070
  Wilmington (G-14495)
Bankers Life..................................... G 302 232-5006
  Dover (G-1873)
Bosco Insurance Agency.................... G 302 678-0647
  Dover (G-1964)
Ccgsr Inc... G 800 927-9800
  Wilmington (G-15288)
Cedar Hamilton Insur Svcs LLC........... G 302 573-3000
  Wilmington (G-15295)
Charlene Webb.................................. G 302 424-8490
  Milford (G-7820)
Charles L Saulsbery Agt..................... G 302 894-1430
  Newark (G-10190)
Coastal Equities Inc........................... D 302 543-2784
  Wilmington (G-15509)
Delaware Deadly Weapons.................. G 302 736-5159
  Dover (G-2225)
Farmers Mutl Fire Insur Slem C........... E 856 935-1851
  Wilmington (G-16554)
Fowler & Williams Inc........................ F 302 875-7518
  Laurel (G-5514)
Fraim Monnarae................................ G 302 761-1313
  Wilmington (G-16718)
Harrington Realty Inc......................... E 302 736-0800
  Dover (G-2654)
Independent School MGT Inc.............. E 302 656-4944
  Wilmington (G-17310)
Ins Regulatory Insurance Svcs............. G 302 256-0455
  Wilmington (G-17351)
Insley Jr Harry Agt............................. G 302 656-1800
  Wilmington (G-17354)
Jamie Laber..................................... G 302 373-7890
  Newark (G-11095)
Jessica Yang Inc............................... G 612 217-0220
  Wilmington (G-17534)
John Koziol Inc................................. G 302 234-5430
  Hockessin (G-5262)
John Wingate Insurance..................... G 302 339-5185
  Seaford (G-13238)
Juno Insurance Services LLC.............. G 650 380-8449
  Wilmington (G-17616)
Lyons Companies LLC....................... D 302 658-5508
  Wilmington (G-18052)
Martin Direct Insurance...................... G 302 452-2700
  Newark (G-11344)
Marvel Agency Inc............................. G 302 422-7844
  Milford (G-7986)
Mountain W Insur Fncl Svcs LLC......... F 970 824-8185
  Wilmington (G-18466)
Muncie Insurance & Fincl Svcs............ G 302 645-7740
  Rehoboth Beach (G-12867)
Peter Renzi...................................... G 302 265-1309
  Milford (G-8049)
Phly LLC.. G 778 882-2391
  Wilmington (G-19022)
Planet Payment Solutions Inc.............. E 516 670-3200
  New Castle (G-9476)
Raymond Babiarz Agt......................... G 302 993-8047
  Wilmington (G-19344)
Regina McLarnon............................... G 800 903-8114
  Wilmington (G-19403)
Ronnie Carter................................... G 302 284-9321
  Felton (G-4022)
Sentinel Insurance............................. G 302 858-4962
  Georgetown (G-4504)
Staples & Associates Insurance........... G 302 398-3276
  Harrington (G-4835)
Steadfast Insurance Company.............. G 847 605-6000
  Dover (G-3610)

Employee Codes: A=Over 500 employees, B=251-500
C=101-250, D=51-100, E=20-50, F=10-19, G=1-9

INSURANCE: Agents, Brokers & Service

Steinebach Robert and Assoc......... G 302 328-1212
Christiana *(G-1010)*

Thomas Weisenfels....................... G 302 571-5244
Wilmington *(G-20312)*

Tom Wiseley Insurance Agency...... G 302 832-7700
Newark *(G-12207)*

Weymouth Swyze Crroon Insur In..... F 302 655-3705
Wilmington *(G-20750)*

William Heydt............................... G 302 678-1161
Dover *(G-3851)*

Young Mens Christian Assn........... G 302 571-6925
Wilmington *(G-20935)*

INTEGRATED CIRCUITS, SEMICONDUCTOR NETWORKS, ETC

Suretronix Solutions LLC............. G 302 407-3146
Wilmington *(G-20161)*

Waveinnova Inc........................... G 650 507-5756
Wilmington *(G-20689)*

Wiregateit LLC............................ G 302 538-1304
Middletown *(G-7730)*

INTERIOR DECORATING SVCS

Bernardon LLC............................ F 302 622-9550
Wilmington *(G-14848)*

Carolina Street Garden & Home..... G 302 539-2405
Fenwick Island *(G-4043)*

Delaware Valley Field Svcs LLC..... G 302 384-8617
Wilmington *(G-15981)*

Kirks Flowers Inc......................... G 302 737-3931
Newark *(G-11181)*

Regal Painting & Decorating......... G 302 994-8943
Wilmington *(G-19398)*

INTERIOR DESIGN SVCS, NEC

Abha Architects Inc..................... E 302 658-6426
Wilmington *(G-14201)*

Bar & Associates Ltd................... G 302 999-9233
Wilmington *(G-14752)*

Buck Simpers Archt + Assoc Inc.... F 302 658-9300
Wilmington *(G-15141)*

Dcc Design Group LLC................ G 302 777-2100
Wilmington *(G-15827)*

Holland Corp................................ G 302 245-5645
Selbyville *(G-13548)*

Imagineyu Designs LLC................ G 302 387-1230
Camden Wyoming *(G-954)*

Melanin Mixx Beauty Brand Inc...... G 302 266-1010
Newark *(G-11385)*

Stuart Kingston Galleries Inc......... G 302 652-7978
Wilmington *(G-20104)*

INVENTORY COMPUTING SVCS

Wis International......................... G 302 264-9343
Dover *(G-3861)*

INVERTERS: Nonrotating Electrical

Orange Power Electric Inc............ G 205 886-5815
Wilmington *(G-18813)*

INVESTMENT ADVISORY SVCS

American Air Lease Finance LLC... G 646 643-6303
Wilmington *(G-14424)*

Ameriprise Financial Svcs Inc....... F 302 468-8200
Wilmington *(G-14451)*

Ashford Capital Management........ F 302 655-1750
Wilmington *(G-14580)*

Ashford Consulting Group Inc....... G 302 691-0228
Wilmington *(G-14581)*

Bell Rock Capital Llc.................... G 302 227-7607
Rehoboth Beach *(G-12639)*

Brown Advisory Incorporated........ G 302 351-7600
Wilmington *(G-15128)*

Campbell Fincl Solutions LLC........ G 302 202-9029
Wilmington *(G-15211)*

Cobra Investments MGT Inc.......... E 302 691-6333
Wilmington *(G-15512)*

Diversified LLC........................... E 302 765-3500
Wilmington *(G-16094)*

Donovan Capital Group LLC......... G 202 642-4360
Dover *(G-2323)*

Glenmede Trust Co Nat Assn........ G 302 661-2900
Wilmington *(G-16884)*

Great Valley Advisor Group........... F 302 483-7200
Wilmington *(G-16960)*

Greenville Capital Management..... G 302 429-9799
Rockland *(G-13031)*

Guardian Advisors LLC................. G 302 220-8729
Seaford *(G-13202)*

Indepndnce Wealth Advisors Inc.... G 302 763-1180
Hockessin *(G-5250)*

Investment Property Services L..... G 302 994-3907
Wilmington *(G-17406)*

Kalmar Investments Inc................ F 302 658-7575
Wilmington *(G-17639)*

Lawter Planning Group Inc........... G 302 736-6065
Dover *(G-2917)*

Lovett Financial Advisors LLC....... G 302 250-4740
Newark *(G-11290)*

Mallard Advisors LLC................... F 302 239-1654
Hockessin *(G-5294)*

Mallard Advisors LLC................... G 302 239-1654
Newark *(G-11318)*

Mallard Financial Partners Inc....... C 302 737-4546
Newark *(G-11319)*

Management Pl Investme.............. G 888 654-5449
Wilmington *(G-18100)*

Morgan Stanley & Co LLC............. G 302 573-4000
Wilmington *(G-18447)*

Morgan Stnley Smith Barney LLC... C 302 644-6600
Rehoboth Beach *(G-12862)*

Natixis Globl Asset MGT Hldngs.... G 617 449-2100
Wilmington *(G-18552)*

Northern Cross Investments......... G 302 655-9074
Wilmington *(G-18684)*

Oink Oink LLC............................. G 302 924-5034
Dover *(G-3217)*

Parkwood Trust Company............. G 302 426-1220
Wilmington *(G-18897)*

Perella Weinberg Partners LLC..... G 267 746-0569
Wilmington *(G-18970)*

Pollintion Capitl Partners LLC....... G 872 201-1168
Wilmington *(G-19109)*

Ragaman Services Inc.................. F 339 221-6757
Wilmington *(G-19316)*

Riversedge................................. G 267 342-6984
Wilmington *(G-19498)*

Standard & Poors Intl LLC............ G 212 512-2000
Wilmington *(G-20011)*

Subaru Investment Inc.................. G 302 472-9266
Wilmington *(G-20109)*

Topkis Financial Advisors LLC...... G 302 654-4444
Wilmington *(G-20359)*

United Brokerage Packaging......... G 302 294-6782
Newark *(G-12268)*

Wbi Capital Advisors LLC............. E 856 361-6362
Wilmington *(G-20696)*

Wealth Management Group........... G 302 734-5826
Dover *(G-3824)*

Westover Capital Advisors LLC..... G 302 427-9600
Wilmington *(G-20743)*

INVESTMENT FIRM: General Brokerage

Accessheat Inc............................ E 302 373-9524
Wilmington *(G-14222)*

Assurance Partners Intl................ F 302 478-0173
Wilmington *(G-14600)*

Cawsl Enterprises Inc.................. G 302 478-6160
Wilmington *(G-15283)*

Delaware Valley Brokerage Inc..... G 302 477-9700
Wilmington *(G-15978)*

Laurel Oak Capitl Partners LLC..... G 302 658-7581
Wilmington *(G-17824)*

Morgan Garanty Intl Fincl Corp..... E 302 634-1000
Newark *(G-11453)*

Peters Alan E Peters & Assoc....... G 302 656-1007
Wilmington *(G-18996)*

Safahi Corp................................. G 925 503-4551
Dover *(G-3501)*

SecondSTAX Inc.......................... E 862 368-0413
Wilmington *(G-19729)*

Vitae Investment Company........... D 302 656-8985
Wilmington *(G-20642)*

INVESTMENT OFFICES: Management, Closed-End

Atlas Management Inc.................. E 302 576-2749
Wilmington *(G-14630)*

Blackrock 2022 Globl Income Op... G 212 754-5560
Wilmington *(G-14903)*

Blackrock Cal Mnicpl Income Tr.... G 800 882-0052
Wilmington *(G-14906)*

Blackrock Capitl Allocation Tr....... G 800 882-0052
Wilmington *(G-14907)*

Blackrock Core Bond Trust........... G 800 882-0052
Wilmington *(G-14908)*

Blackrock Health Sciences Tr....... G 800 882-0052
Wilmington *(G-14918)*

Blackrock Income Trust Inc.......... G 800 441-7762
Wilmington *(G-14920)*

Blackrock Mncpl 2030 Trget Ter... G 800 882-0052
Wilmington *(G-14927)*

Blackrock Mnhldngs Cal Qlty Fu.... G 800 882-0052
Wilmington *(G-14929)*

Blackrock Mnhldngs NJ Qlty Fun... G 800 882-0052
Wilmington *(G-14930)*

Blackrock Mnyeld Cal Qlty Fund.... G 800 882-0052
Wilmington *(G-14931)*

Blackrock Municipal Income Tr..... G 888 882-0052
Wilmington *(G-14934)*

Blackrock Muniyield Fund Inc....... G 800 441-7762
Wilmington *(G-14936)*

Blackrock NY Mncpl Income Qlty... G 800 441-7762
Wilmington *(G-14938)*

Blackrock NY Municpl Income Tr... G 800 882-0052
Wilmington *(G-14940)*

Delaware Kids Fund..................... G 302 323-9300
Newport *(G-12448)*

Jack Lingo Asset MGT LLC........... F 302 226-6645
Rehoboth Beach *(G-12797)*

Symack Capital MGT US Corp....... F 469 607-6092
Smyrna *(G-13906)*

INVESTORS, NEC

Abri Spac 2 Inc............................ G 424 732-1021
Newark *(G-9744)*

Ackrell Spac Partners I Co............ G 650 560-4753
Claymont *(G-1019)*

Acopia LLC................................. D 302 286-5172
Newark *(G-9756)*

Aetolia Captial LLC...................... G 302 397-8238
Wilmington *(G-14300)*

PRODUCTS & SERVICES SECTION

JEWELRY STORES

Affiliate Investment Inc .... C 302 478-7451
  Wilmington (G-14303)
Bell Rock Capital LLC .... F 302 227-7607
  Rehoboth Beach (G-12638)
Best Holding LLC .... G 302 691-6023
  Wilmington (G-14854)
Bkl Ventures LLC .... G 302 317-2377
  Newark (G-10041)
Capital and Worth .... G 302 477-0660
  Wilmington (G-15225)
Capital Auto Rcvbles Asset Tr .... G 212 250-6864
  Wilmington (G-15226)
Capital Markets Iq LLC .... G 310 882-6380
  Wilmington (G-15229)
Cei Capital LLC .... G 302 573-3875
  Wilmington (G-15297)
Chelsea Creek Capital Co LLC ...... G 312 977-4583
  Wilmington (G-15351)
Cigna Real Estate Inc .... G 302 476-3337
  Wilmington (G-15436)
Cinnaire Registered Investment .... F 302 655-1420
  Wilmington (G-15440)
Dd & E Investment Group Inc .... G 302 319-2780
  Wilmington (G-15831)
De/RE Investment Group .... G 302 450-6202
  Smyrna (G-13695)
Dt Investment Partners LLC .... F 302 442-6203
  Wilmington (G-16185)
E-Cube .... G 302 290-7413
  Wilmington (G-16242)
Egw Capital Inc .... G 302 261-2008
  Lewes (G-5952)
Farazad Investments Inc .... G 302 573-2320
  Wilmington (G-16552)
Fas Mart / Shore Stop 286 LLC .... G 302 366-9694
  Newark (G-10713)
Good Life Group LLC .... G 720 759-9089
  Wilmington (G-16922)
Good Rputation Investments LLC .. G 888 382-1552
  Wilmington (G-16923)
GPM Investments LLC .... F 302 436-6330
  Selbyville (G-13539)
Green DOT Capital LLC .... G 302 395-0500
  Bear (G-256)
Guardian Investments .... G 302 541-2114
  Millsboro (G-8309)
Hs Capital LLC .... G 302 317-3614
  Wilmington (G-17222)
Iconix LLC .... G 215 850-9337
  New Castle (G-9228)
Independent Investors Inc .... G 302 366-1187
  Newark (G-11013)
Inheritnow Inc .... G 877 846-4374
  Wilmington (G-17339)
J A Banks & Associates LLC .... F 914 260-2003
  Smyrna (G-13779)
Landmark Homes .... G 302 388-8557
  Dover (G-2902)
Llb Acquisition LLC .... F 212 750-8300
  Wilmington (G-17953)
M R Plumbing .... G 302 738-7978
  Newark (G-11304)
Miller Investments LLC .... G 949 836-2511
  Milford (G-8011)
Ojo Investments LLC .... G 215 934-0855
  Dover (G-3218)
Oldfather Capital Inc .... G 302 296-6644
  Rehoboth Beach (G-12879)
Opportunity Investments .... G 302 887-3082
  Wilmington (G-18805)
Patel Sandip .... G 302 363-9761
  Dover (G-3278)
PCA Acquisitions V LLC .... F 302 355-3500
  Wilmington (G-18932)
Pgim Foreign Investments Inc .... E 302 427-9530
  Wilmington (G-19007)
Philanthrovest LLC .... F 201 563-9179
  Dover (G-3313)
Pillar Wealth Advisors LLC .... G 302 409-3502
  Wilmington (G-19045)
Pipeline Funding Company LLC .... C 302 421-2287
  Wilmington (G-19054)
Progressive Investment Co Inc ...... F 302 656-8597
  Wilmington (G-19219)
Pusan RE Newark LLC .... G 302 737-3087
  Newark (G-11776)
Questar Capital Corporation .... G 302 856-9778
  Georgetown (G-4476)
Ral Group .... G 302 427-6970
  Wilmington (G-19321)
Regulation Holdco LLC .... F 800 521-1114
  Wilmington (G-19410)
Riverbend Inv MGT LLC Is A Rgs .. G 302 219-3080
  Rehoboth Beach (G-12936)
Rock Springs Capital LLC .... G 415 669-4545
  Wilmington (G-19532)
Rockford Capital Partners .... G 302 220-4786
  Wilmington (G-19535)
Ross Capital Partners LLC .... G 302 300-4220
  Hockessin (G-5373)
Round Table Men LLC .... G 302 287-8200
  New Castle (G-9542)
Sap Investments Inc .... G 302 427-7889
  Wilmington (G-19669)
Symack Capital US Corp .... F 469 607-6092
  Smyrna (G-13907)
Tcg High Yeld Inv Holdings LLC ..... F 302 421-7361
  Wilmington (G-20238)
Third Sigma Investment Advisor ..... G 302 656-1111
  Wilmington (G-20302)
Three Fields Capital LP .... G 302 636-5401
  Wilmington (G-20315)
Trolley Square Investors LLC .... G 302 658-1000
  Wilmington (G-20436)
USS Portfolio Delaware Inc .... G 302 798-7890
  Wilmington (G-20555)
Vos Energy LLC .... F 302 658-7581
  Wilmington (G-20653)
W Powell Investments .... G 443 523-2476
  Millsboro (G-8497)
Wealth Capital Investors LLC .... G 202 596-2280
  Lewes (G-6618)
Weepor Company Inc .... G 302 575-9945
  Wilmington (G-20711)
Ws One Investment Usa LLC .... F 302 317-2610
  New Castle (G-9692)
Wsfs Investment Group Inc .... G 302 573-3258
  Wilmington (G-20904)

INVESTORS: Real Estate, Exc Property Operators

Ajj Trades and Investment LLC ...... G 302 403-7165
  Wilmington (G-14340)
Allen Estates LLC .... G 302 496-7250
  Dover (G-1770)
Amitra Vitta Incorporated .... E 267 905-3766
  Wilmington (G-14458)
Eloim Enterprises LLC .... F 510 209-3670
  Wilmington (G-16377)
Gilliam & Garca RE Inv Co LLC ...... G 302 377-5764
  Wilmington (G-16861)
Golden Gate Investments LLC .... G 302 894-8922
  Middletown (G-7169)
Gulf Coast Investments Inc .... F 929 359-4439
  Dover (G-2633)
Harrock Properties LLC .... G 302 202-1321
  Dover (G-2657)
Imperial Realty Group LLC .... G 215 850-3142
  Newark (G-11006)
JC Marks Investments LLC .... G 302 602-4021
  Dover (G-2776)
King-Edwards Residences LLC ..... G 646 389-5830
  Dover (G-2876)
Lc Associates LLC .... F 302 235-2500
  Hockessin (G-5279)
Linx Realty 2 LLC .... G 888 233-8901
  Dover (G-2953)
Lubill Properties LLC .... G 302 946-4188
  Wilmington (G-18023)
Luxury Residence LLC .... F 302 216-2102
  Wilmington (G-18042)
Mark JB Inc .... G 888 984-5845
  Newark (G-11336)
New Edge Enterprises LLC .... G 908 892-2856
  Milton (G-8676)
Oasis Realty Inv Group LLC .... F 302 277-6885
  Newark (G-11573)
Optima Iq Investments Inc .... E 302 279-5750
  Middletown (G-7417)
PBL & 5js Holdings Inc .... G 404 832-5038
  Dover (G-3287)
Perpetual Invstments Group LLC ... F 718 795-3394
  Wilmington (G-18982)
Prime Time Properties LLC .... G 302 763-6050
  Bear (G-438)
Rapid Hmmngbird Homebuyers LLC ... G 347 671-7761
  Dover (G-3424)
Recadia Corp Llc .... G 866 671-1280
  Wilmington (G-19375)
Saving Our Slves Prprty Invsto .... G 267 879-0464
  Smyrna (G-13879)
Scottish Ventures LLC .... G 302 382-6057
  New Castle (G-9554)
Svea Real Estate Group LLC .... F 855 262-9665
  Dover (G-3630)
Zehden Properties LLC .... G 310 773-8529
  Dover (G-3896)

IRON ORE MINING

Oreomatic Mining Inc .... E 725 255-8895
  Wilmington (G-18817)

IRON ORES

American Minerals Partnership .... F 302 652-3301
  New Castle (G-8800)

JEWELRY REPAIR SVCS

Continental Jewelers Inc .... G 302 475-2000
  Wilmington (G-15620)
Del Haven of Wilmington Inc .... G 302 999-9040
  Newark (G-10411)
Golden Jewelry .... G 302 777-2121
  Wilmington (G-16913)
Michael Gallagher Jewelers .... G 302 836-2925
  Bear (G-375)
Turquoise Shop Inc .... F 302 366-7448
  Newark (G-12248)
Whittens Fine Jewelry .... G 302 995-7464
  Wilmington (G-20774)

JEWELRY STORES

Golden Jewelry .... G 302 777-2121
  Wilmington (G-16913)
T K O Designs Inc .... G 302 539-6992
  Bethany Beach (G-645)

Employee Codes: A=Over 500 employees, B=251-500
C=101-250, D=51-100, E=20-50, F=10-19, G=1-9

2024 Harris Directory of Delaware Businesses

JEWELRY STORES

Whittens Fine Jewelry.................................G..... 302 995-7464
  Wilmington (G-20774)

JEWELRY STORES: Precious Stones & Precious Metals

Alex and Ani LLC...................................G..... 302 731-1420
  Newark (G-9808)
Alex and Ani LLC...................................G..... 302 227-7360
  Rehoboth Beach (G-12600)
Continental Jewelers Inc.........................G..... 302 475-2000
  Wilmington (G-15620)
Del Haven of Wilmington Inc..................G..... 302 999-9040
  Newark (G-10411)
First State Coin Co.................................G..... 302 734-7776
  Dover (G-2500)
Marches Jewelers Inc..............................G..... 856 858-4463
  Lewes (G-6241)
Michael Gallagher Jewelers....................G..... 302 836-2925
  Bear (G-375)
Nanticoke River Arts Council..................G..... 302 628-2787
  Seaford (G-13309)
Precision Jewelry Inc.............................G..... 302 422-7138
  Milford (G-8051)
Stuart Kingston Galleries Inc..................G..... 302 652-7978
  Wilmington (G-20104)
Turquoise Shop Inc................................F..... 302 366-7448
  Newark (G-12248)
Wholesale Jewelry Outlet Inc..................G..... 302 994-5114
  Wilmington (G-20775)

JEWELRY STORES: Silverware

Leeber Limited USA................................F..... 302 733-0991
  Newark (G-11239)

JEWELRY STORES: Watches

Bridgewater Jewelers..............................G..... 302 328-2101
  Historic New Castle (G-4945)

JEWELRY, WHOLESALE

Marches Jewelers Inc..............................G..... 856 858-4463
  Lewes (G-6241)
Rand Accessories USA Inc......................G..... 302 266-8200
  Newark (G-11825)
Wholesale Jewelry Outlet Inc..................G..... 302 994-5114
  Wilmington (G-20775)

JEWELRY: Precious Metal

Alex and Ani LLC...................................G..... 302 731-1420
  Newark (G-9808)
Alex and Ani LLC...................................G..... 302 227-7360
  Rehoboth Beach (G-12600)
Joolala LLC..E..... 302 444-0178
  Newark (G-11124)
Lightbox Jewelry Inc...............................F..... 833 270-3737
  Dover (G-2945)
Rck Soliatire LLC....................................F..... 551 358-8400
  Rehoboth Beach (G-12907)
Stackd Studio LLC..................................G..... 240 304-1085
  Newark (G-12081)

JOB PRINTING & NEWSPAPER PUBLISHING COMBINED

Whitner House Publishing LLC................G..... 267 338-9741
  Smyrna (G-13937)

JOB TRAINING SVCS

Telamon Corp/Early Chldhd Pgrm............G..... 302 934-1642
  Georgetown (G-4548)
Telamon Corporation..............................G..... 302 934-0925
  Georgetown (G-4549)

Telamon Corporation..............................G..... 302 398-9196
  Harrington (G-4840)
Telamon Corporation..............................G..... 302 424-2335
  Milford (G-8115)
Telamon Corporation..............................G..... 302 629-5557
  Seaford (G-13427)
Telamon Corporation Headstart..............F..... 302 875-7718
  Laurel (G-5615)
Telamon Delaware Head Start................F..... 302 934-1642
  Georgetown (G-4550)

JOISTS: Long-Span Series, Open Web Steel

Engineering Incorporated........................G..... 302 995-6862
  Wilmington (G-16424)

KIDNEY DIALYSIS CENTERS

American Renal......................................G..... 302 672-7901
  Dover (G-1786)
Bio-Mdical Applications of Del.................G..... 302 998-7568
  Newark (G-10034)
DSI Laurel LLC......................................D..... 302 715-3060
  Laurel (G-5502)
Fresenius Med Care Nthrn Del L.............E..... 302 239-4704
  Hockessin (G-5214)
Fresenius Medical Care N Amer..............F..... 302 328-9044
  Historic New Castle (G-4992)
Fresenius Medical Care N Amer..............G..... 302 633-6228
  Wilmington (G-16749)
Liberty Dalysis-Wilmington LLC..............F..... 302 429-0142
  Wilmington (G-17891)
Renal Care Group Inc............................D..... 302 678-8744
  Dover (G-3453)

KITCHEN CABINETS WHOLESALERS

Allura Bath & Kitchen Inc.......................G..... 302 731-2851
  Newark (G-9828)
Cabinetry Unlimited LLC........................E..... 302 436-5030
  Selbyville (G-13489)

KITCHEN UTENSILS: Food Handling & Processing Prdts, Wood

Hillandale Farms Delaware Inc................E..... 302 492-3644
  Hartly (G-4878)
Lempat Foods LLC.................................G..... 914 449-1803
  Dover (G-2928)
Music Art & Culture Foundation..............G..... 347 746-9047
  Lewes (G-6297)

KITCHENWARE: Plastic

Pony Run Kitchens LLC.........................G..... 302 492-3006
  Hartly (G-4903)

LABORATORIES, TESTING: Food

Wm Systems Inc.....................................G..... 302 450-4482
  Wilmington (G-20871)

LABORATORIES, TESTING: Forensic

Alias Technology LLC.............................G..... 302 856-9488
  Georgetown (G-4205)

LABORATORIES, TESTING: Metallurgical

MMR Group Inc......................................E..... 302 328-0500
  New Castle (G-9375)

LABORATORIES: Biological Research

Arkion Life Sciences LLC........................F..... 800 468-6324
  New Castle (G-8822)
Becoming Bio Inc...................................G..... 415 980-9796
  Middletown (G-6907)
De Novo Foods Inc................................G..... 302 613-1351
  Claymont (G-1112)

Delaware Innovation Space Inc...............G..... 302 695-2201
  Wilmington (G-15933)
Dualitybio Inc...E..... 201 486-7858
  Wilmington (G-16193)
Galaxyworks LLC...................................F..... 404 894-8703
  Dover (G-2555)
Novasep LLC...E..... 610 494-2052
  Wilmington (G-18695)
Old Ayala Inc...F..... 857 444-0553
  Wilmington (G-18753)
Stedim N Sartorius Amer Inc...................E..... 800 635-2906
  Newark (G-12094)
Sug Biosciences LLC..............................G..... 305 735-7009
  Wilmington (G-20120)
Volvox Biologic Inc.................................G..... 801 722-5942
  Lewes (G-6609)

LABORATORIES: Biotechnology

Accugenix Inc...E..... 302 292-8888
  Newark (G-9751)
Advanced Materials Technology..............G..... 302 477-2510
  Wilmington (G-14275)
Alpha Omega Scientific LLC...................G..... 302 415-4499
  New Castle (G-8787)
Amino Medical Science Inc....................E..... 213 232-8619
  Lewes (G-5688)
Anp Biopharma LLC...............................E..... 302 283-1730
  Newark (G-9874)
Anp Technologies Inc.............................E..... 302 283-1730
  Newark (G-9875)
Best Planet Science LLC.........................G..... 754 200-1913
  Wilmington (G-14855)
Biomatik Usa LLC..................................G..... 800 836-8089
  Wilmington (G-14895)
C M-Tec Inc...G..... 302 369-6166
  Newark (G-10114)
Celavie Biosciences LLC.........................G..... 516 593-5633
  Dover (G-2043)
Charles River Labs Intl Inc......................F..... 302 292-8888
  Newark (G-10191)
Chip Diagnostics Inc...............................G..... 302 752-1064
  Wilmington (G-15384)
Fraunhofer Usa Inc.................................D..... 302 369-1708
  Newark (G-10773)
Gene Guard Inc.....................................G..... 248 479-3623
  Middletown (G-7154)
Jenrin Discovery LLC..............................G..... 302 379-1679
  Wilmington (G-17530)
Leucine Inc..G..... 650 534-2101
  Wilmington (G-17888)
Lila Labs Inc..G..... 949 371-3978
  Middletown (G-7305)
Napigen Inc..G..... 302 644-5464
  Wilmington (G-18532)
Neurorx Inc..F..... 202 340-1352
  Wilmington (G-18604)
Neuroscience Software Inc......................G..... 855 712-1818
  Dover (G-3176)
Panarum Corp..F..... 302 994-2000
  Newark (G-11618)
Sdix LLC..D..... 302 456-6789
  Newark (G-11964)
Separation Methods Tech Inc..................F..... 302 368-0610
  Newark (G-11979)
Superbrewed Food Inc............................F..... 302 220-4760
  New Castle (G-9606)
Timtec LLC..F..... 302 292-8500
  Newark (G-12197)
Wilmington Pharmatech Co LLC..............E..... 302 737-9916
  Newark (G-12381)

PRODUCTS & SERVICES SECTION

LABORATORY CHEMICALS: Organic

LABORATORIES: Commercial Nonphysical Research

Digital Wish Inc..................................G..... 802 375-6721
  Milton *(G-8605)*

Poc Inc...F..... 415 853-4762
  Dover *(G-3345)*

W500g Inc..G..... 302 252-7279
  Middletown *(G-7701)*

Weekfish LLC...................................G..... 800 979-5501
  Smyrna *(G-13933)*

LABORATORIES: Dental, Crown & Bridge Production

Mittelman Dental Lab.......................G..... 302 798-7440
  Claymont *(G-1241)*

National Dentex LLC........................C..... 302 661-6000
  Historic New Castle *(G-5032)*

LABORATORIES: Electronic Research

Celsia Inc...F..... 408 577-1407
  Georgetown *(G-4247)*

Ultrafine Technologies Inc................G..... 302 384-6513
  Wilmington *(G-20502)*

LABORATORIES: Medical

Bg Laboratory...................................G..... 302 535-3954
  Dover *(G-1928)*

CD Diagnostics Inc...........................E..... 302 367-7770
  Claymont *(G-1077)*

Clinpharma Clinical RES LLC...........E..... 646 961-3437
  Wilmington *(G-15487)*

Current Care Analytics Inc...............G..... 248 425-3973
  Lewes *(G-5874)*

Delaware Public Health Lab.............E..... 302 223-1520
  Smyrna *(G-13705)*

Glaxosmthkline Hldngs Amrcas I.....C..... 302 984-6932
  Wilmington *(G-16882)*

Green Clinics Laboratory LLC..........E..... 302 734-5050
  Dover *(G-2621)*

Maria Lazar MD................................G..... 302 838-2210
  Hockessin *(G-5296)*

Mears Health Campus......................G..... 302 628-6300
  Seaford *(G-13279)*

Paul Renzi.......................................F..... 302 478-3166
  Wilmington *(G-18920)*

Peter M Witherell M D.....................G..... 302 478-7001
  Newark *(G-11673)*

Professional Imaging........................G..... 302 653-3522
  Smyrna *(G-13856)*

Provision Group LLC........................G..... 844 220-7200
  Newark *(G-11768)*

RSM Diagnostics Lab LLC................G..... 302 592-4106
  Wilmington *(G-19583)*

LABORATORIES: Noncommercial Research

A66 Inc...G..... 800 444-0446
  Wilmington *(G-14180)*

Ceasar Rodney Institute..................F..... 302 542-1781
  Newark *(G-10169)*

Delaware Community Foundation....G..... 302 571-8004
  Wilmington *(G-15890)*

Delaware Nature Society.................E..... 302 239-1283
  Hockessin *(G-5182)*

Eldersafe Technologies Inc..............G..... 617 852-3018
  Lewes *(G-5955)*

Fairness Institute..............................G..... 302 559-4074
  Newark *(G-10702)*

Global Institute.................................G..... 732 776-7360
  Newark *(G-10850)*

Institute of Mssage Hling Arts..........G..... 610 357-2925
  Wilmington *(G-17360)*

Mid Atlantic Pain Institute.................G..... 302 369-1700
  Milford *(G-7996)*

NA Institute Christia..........................G..... 302 478-4020
  Wilmington *(G-18516)*

Society For Acpuncture RES Inc......G..... 302 222-1832
  Lewes *(G-6488)*

Tdm Pharmaceutical RES LLC.........G..... 302 832-1008
  Newark *(G-12166)*

Tmpaa Institute Inc..........................G..... 302 268-1010
  Wilmington *(G-20340)*

Towle Institute..................................G..... 302 993-1408
  Wilmington *(G-20378)*

University of Delaware.....................G..... 302 831-4811
  Newark *(G-12278)*

Wonchin Institute.............................G..... 302 602-5753
  Newark *(G-12400)*

Youth Sports Institute Del Inc..........G..... 302 275-5947
  New Castle *(G-9696)*

LABORATORIES: Physical Research, Commercial

Acp Technologies Inc......................G..... 302 981-5976
  Lincoln *(G-6653)*

Alantys Technology..........................G..... 302 573-2312
  Wilmington *(G-14347)*

Batescainelli LLC.............................G..... 202 618-2040
  Rehoboth Beach *(G-12624)*

Carbon Direct Inc.............................F..... 212 742-3719
  Dover *(G-2027)*

Childrens Hosp Nntal Cnsrtium........G..... 215 873-9492
  Dover *(G-2064)*

Cowie Technology Corp...................G..... 302 998-7037
  Wilmington *(G-15672)*

Dehumidification Tech LP................G..... 317 228-2000
  Wilmington *(G-15858)*

First State Robotics Inc...................G..... 302 584-7152
  Hockessin *(G-5211)*

Gom Technologies LLC...................G..... 410 275-8029
  Hockessin *(G-5224)*

Incyte Corporation...........................A..... 302 498-6700
  Wilmington *(G-17306)*

Inventia Scientific Corp....................G..... 888 201-0798
  Wilmington *(G-17405)*

MMR Group Inc................................E..... 302 328-0500
  New Castle *(G-9375)*

Modern Water Inc............................E..... 302 669-6900
  New Castle *(G-9378)*

Organox Inc.....................................G..... 216 243-2202
  Wilmington *(G-18820)*

Partnrship For Del Estuary Inc........G..... 302 655-4990
  Wilmington *(G-18900)*

Pluribus Technologies Inc................G..... 302 373-2670
  Newark *(G-11703)*

Streamline Technologies Inc...........F..... 302 383-3146
  Wilmington *(G-20094)*

Stride Services Inc..........................F..... 302 540-4713
  Wilmington *(G-20099)*

Synchrgnix Info Strategies LLC.......E..... 302 892-4800
  Wilmington *(G-20184)*

Terran Global Corporation...............G..... 702 626-5704
  Lewes *(G-6552)*

LABORATORIES: Testing

A S T B Analytical Services.............E..... 302 571-8882
  New Castle *(G-8750)*

Agrorefiner LLC...............................G..... 212 651-4865
  New Castle *(G-8773)*

Arcpoint Labs..................................G..... 302 268-6560
  Wilmington *(G-14544)*

Ardex Laboratories Inc....................G..... 302 363-1005
  Bridgeville *(G-667)*

Atlantic Radon Systems Inc............G..... 610 869-9066
  Dagsboro *(G-1415)*

Bio Reference Laboratories.............G..... 302 223-6896
  Smyrna *(G-13662)*

Biochek USA Corp...........................G..... 302 521-5554
  Millsboro *(G-8198)*

Borderx Lab Inc...............................G..... 510 203-3974
  New Castle *(G-8875)*

Christiana Care Health Sys Inc.......G..... 302 477-6500
  Wilmington *(G-15400)*

Compact Membrane Systems Inc...E..... 302 999-7996
  New Castle *(G-8963)*

Corrosion Testing Laboratories.......F..... 302 454-8200
  Newark *(G-10329)*

Delaware Diagnostic Labs LLC.......E..... 302 407-5903
  Newark *(G-10436)*

Headland Labs LLC.........................G..... 415 425-1997
  Wilmington *(G-17089)*

High Tide Lab..................................G..... 302 538-7041
  Camden *(G-850)*

Integrity Testlabs LLC.....................D..... 302 325-2365
  Historic New Castle *(G-5008)*

Lab Products LLC............................F..... 302 628-4300
  Seaford *(G-13255)*

Lehigh Testing Laboratories............G..... 302 328-0500
  New Castle *(G-9302)*

Micron Incorporated.........................G..... 302 998-1184
  Wilmington *(G-18330)*

Midi Labs Inc...................................F..... 302 737-4297
  Newark *(G-11416)*

MSI...G..... 302 449-5508
  Middletown *(G-7387)*

Nanticoke EZ Lab............................G..... 302 337-8571
  Bridgeville *(G-736)*

Quikstamp LLC................................F..... 302 659-7555
  Newark *(G-11800)*

Quinteccent Inc...............................G..... 443 838-5447
  Selbyville *(G-13595)*

Radiogenic Shielding Systems........G..... 302 288-0644
  Wilmington *(G-19312)*

Stellar Labs Inc................................F..... 650 868-6796
  Wilmington *(G-20048)*

Stereochemical Inc..........................G..... 302 266-0700
  Newark *(G-12100)*

Tecniplast USA Inc..........................G..... 484 716-2145
  Wilmington *(G-20258)*

Vora Labs Inc...................................G..... 860 559-8985
  Middletown *(G-7695)*

Agro Lab..F..... 302 265-2734
  Harrington *(G-4723)*

Inspektlabs Inc.................................F..... 302 601-7191
  Middletown *(G-7227)*

Lightwave Logic Inc........................G..... 302 737-6412
  Newark *(G-11257)*

Medlab-Havertown Inc.....................G..... 302 655-5227
  New Castle *(G-9356)*

Quest Diagnostics Incorporated......G..... 302 376-8675
  Middletown *(G-7491)*

LABORATORY APPARATUS & FURNITURE

Bio Medic Corporation.....................F..... 302 628-4300
  Seaford *(G-13089)*

Life Sciences Intl LLC......................G..... 603 436-9444
  Wilmington *(G-17901)*

LABORATORY CHEMICALS: Organic

Cfg Lab Inc.......................................G..... 302 261-3403
  Wilmington *(G-15319)*

Milana Colors LLC...........................G..... 872 274-4321
  Middletown *(G-7368)*

LABORATORY EQPT, EXC MEDICAL: Wholesalers

Bio Medic Corporation........................F..... 302 628-4300
Seaford *(G-13089)*

Buchi Corporation............................E..... 302 652-3000
Historic New Castle *(G-4947)*

Gilante Scientific LLC.......................G..... 302 317-6060
Newark *(G-10835)*

Miles Scientific Corporation................E..... 302 737-6960
Newark *(G-11418)*

Scientific Holdings Corp....................G..... 302 225-5065
Wilmington *(G-19705)*

LABORATORY EQPT: Clinical Instruments Exc Medical

Safeguard Dx Laboratory....................G..... 888 919-8275
Wilmington *(G-19626)*

LABORATORY EQPT: Incubators

Boa Financial LLC............................G..... 888 444-5371
Dover *(G-1956)*

Delaware Technology Park Inc...............G..... 302 452-1100
Newark *(G-10491)*

LAMINATED PLASTICS: Plate, Sheet, Rod & Tubes

Fbk Medical Tubing Inc.......................F..... 302 855-0585
Georgetown *(G-4315)*

Franklin Fibre-Lamitex Corp.................E..... 302 652-3621
Wilmington *(G-16728)*

Ipd Technologies LLC........................G..... 302 533-8850
Newark *(G-11055)*

LAMP SHADES: Glass

Newark Glass & Mirror Inc...................G..... 302 834-1158
Bear *(G-394)*

LAND SUBDIVIDERS & DEVELOPERS: Commercial

Commonwealth Group LLC..................E..... 302 472-7200
Wilmington *(G-15553)*

Compton Twne Prsrvtion Assoc L..........G..... 302 764-6450
Wilmington *(G-15575)*

Donne Delle & Associates Inc...............E..... 302 325-1111
Newark *(G-10551)*

Eastern States Develpment Inc..............G..... 302 998-0683
Wilmington *(G-16265)*

Lang Development Group LLC..............G..... 302 731-1340
Newark *(G-11221)*

Leon N Weiner & Associates Inc............D..... 302 656-1354
Wilmington *(G-17877)*

Post Rdge Prsrvation Assoc LLC...........G..... 302 761-7303
Wilmington *(G-19130)*

Riverfront Dev Corp Del.....................F..... 302 425-4890
Wilmington *(G-19493)*

Titan Retail LLC.............................F..... 205 291-1505
Middletown *(G-7646)*

LAND SUBDIVIDERS & DEVELOPERS: Residential

Barclay Farms................................G..... 302 697-6939
Camden *(G-792)*

Gulfstream Development Corp..............G..... 302 539-6178
Millville *(G-8531)*

Interfaith Cmnty Hsing of Del...............F..... 302 652-3991
Wilmington *(G-17383)*

Jack Hickman Real Estate...................F..... 302 539-8000
Bethany Beach *(G-611)*

Ocean Atlantic Management LLC...........G..... 302 227-3573
Rehoboth Beach *(G-12875)*

Reybold Construction Corp..................E..... 302 832-7100
Bear *(G-455)*

Salt Pond Associates........................E..... 302 539-2750
Bethany Beach *(G-638)*

LAND SUBDIVISION & DEVELOPMENT

Allcap Development Group LLC............G..... 302 429-8700
Wilmington *(G-14372)*

AT&e Developers Ltd........................F..... 302 467-1100
Middletown *(G-6877)*

Del Homes Inc...............................F..... 302 697-8204
Magnolia *(G-6739)*

Del-Charter Associates LP..................G..... 302 325-1111
Newark *(G-10414)*

Delaware Valley Dev LLC....................F..... 302 235-2500
Wilmington *(G-15980)*

Edward B De Seta & Associates.............G..... 302 428-1313
Wilmington *(G-16301)*

Ferm Development LLC.....................F..... 302 792-1102
Wilmington *(G-16584)*

First Power LLC.............................G..... 610 247-5750
Wilmington *(G-16621)*

Harvest Power Inc...........................G..... 270 765-6268
Milford *(G-7921)*

Kidmore End Developers LLC...............G..... 302 562-5110
Claymont *(G-1206)*

Lang Development Group LLC..............G..... 302 731-1340
Newark *(G-11220)*

Medshifts Inc................................G..... 856 834-0074
Wilmington *(G-18258)*

Newark Afrc.................................G..... 302 292-1050
Newark *(G-11529)*

Pangro Development LLC..................G..... 302 351-3575
Wilmington *(G-18875)*

Parkway Gravel Inc..........................D..... 302 658-5241
New Castle *(G-9450)*

Patterson Price RE LLC.....................G..... 302 366-0200
Newark *(G-11640)*

Patterson Price RE LLC.....................G..... 302 378-9550
Townsend *(G-14050)*

Riverfront Development Corp................E..... 302 425-4890
Wilmington *(G-19494)*

Roizman & Associates Inc...................G..... 302 426-9688
Wilmington *(G-19556)*

Stokelan Estate Winery LLC................G..... 609 451-5535
Hockessin *(G-5391)*

Tim Latham..................................G..... 302 530-4002
Wilmington *(G-20327)*

Villages of Nobles Pond Phase..............G..... 302 736-5000
Dover *(G-3797)*

Woodlawn Trustees Incorporated...........G..... 302 655-6215
Wilmington *(G-20884)*

Y and Y Garden Associates Inc..............G..... 302 684-0383
Milton *(G-8733)*

LAUNDRY COLLECTING & DISTRIBUTING OUTLET

Ultra Modern Laundry Svcs LLC............G..... 302 533-8596
Wilmington *(G-20500)*

LAUNDRY SVC: Indl Eqpt

Domain Hr Solutions........................F..... 302 357-9401
Middletown *(G-7068)*

Nixon Uniform Service Inc..................C..... 302 325-2875
Historic New Castle *(G-5040)*

LAUNDRY SVCS: Indl

Jwr 1 LLC....................................G..... 302 379-9951
Bear *(G-320)*

LAWN & GARDEN EQPT

Easy Lawn Inc...............................E..... 302 815-6500
Greenwood *(G-4624)*

Hydroseeding Company LLC................E..... 302 815-6500
Greenwood *(G-4638)*

Varigle LLC..................................F..... 858 336-9471
Dover *(G-3775)*

LEASING & RENTAL SVCS: Cranes & Aerial Lift Eqpt

Active Crane Rentals Inc....................E..... 302 998-1000
Wilmington *(G-14243)*

Delaware Valley Safety Council..............G..... 302 607-2758
Newark *(G-10495)*

Don D Corp..................................G..... 302 994-5793
Wilmington *(G-16131)*

First State Crane Service Inc................E..... 302 398-8885
Felton *(G-3974)*

LEASING & RENTAL: Construction & Mining Eqpt

Chesapeake Supply & Eqp Co...............G..... 302 284-1000
Felton *(G-3955)*

Dozr Ltd.....................................F..... 844 218-3697
Wilmington *(G-16158)*

Eagle Power and Equipment Corp...........F..... 302 652-3028
New Castle *(G-9076)*

Heavy Equipment Rental Inc................F..... 302 654-5716
New Castle *(G-9205)*

Iron Source LLC.............................G..... 302 856-7545
Georgetown *(G-4373)*

Milford Rental Center Inc....................G..... 302 422-0315
Dover *(G-3091)*

MSP Equip Rental...........................F..... 302 322-5394
New Castle *(G-9387)*

Rent Equipment.............................G..... 302 537-9797
Ocean View *(G-12562)*

Sunbelt Rentals Inc.........................G..... 302 907-1921
Delmar *(G-1638)*

Sunbelt Rentals Inc.........................G..... 302 322-5394
New Castle *(G-9601)*

Sunbelt Rentals Inc.........................G..... 302 669-0595
New Castle *(G-9602)*

Temp-Air Inc.................................F..... 302 369-3880
Newark *(G-12177)*

LEASING & RENTAL: Medical Machinery & Eqpt

American Homepatient Inc..................E..... 302 454-4941
Newark *(G-9845)*

Apria Healthcare LLC........................F..... 302 737-7979
New Castle *(G-8816)*

Broad Creek Medical Service................F..... 302 629-0202
Seaford *(G-13093)*

Hatfield Medical Instrs Inc..................G..... 301 468-0011
Millsboro *(G-8315)*

Lincare.......................................G..... 302 736-1210
Dover *(G-2950)*

Lincare Inc...................................G..... 302 424-8302
Felton *(G-3999)*

Quinn-Miller Group Inc......................F..... 302 738-9742
Wilmington *(G-19296)*

LEASING & RENTAL: Trucks, Without Drivers

Bayshore Ford Truck Sales Inc...............D..... 302 656-3160
New Castle *(G-8853)*

Martin Newark Dealership Inc...............D..... 302 454-9300
Newark *(G-11345)*

PRODUCTS & SERVICES SECTION

LEGAL OFFICES & SVCS

Morton Electric Co.............................. G 302 645-9414
  Lewes (G-6292)
Penske Performance Inc..................... D 302 656-2082
  Wilmington (G-18959)
Penske Truck Leasing Co LP............... G 302 325-9290
  New Castle (G-9467)
Penske Truck Leasing Co LP............... G 302 994-7899
  Wilmington (G-18960)
Penske Truck Leasing Corp.................. G 302 449-9294
  Middletown (G-7439)
Penske Truck Leasing Corp.................. G 302 260-7039
  Rehoboth Beach (G-12887)
Penske Truck Leasing Corp.................. G 302 629-5373
  Seaford (G-13342)
Penske Truck Leasing Corp.................. G 302 658-3255
  Wilmington (G-18961)
Penske Truck Rental........................... F 302 746-3020
  Claymont (G-1262)
Penske Truck Rental........................... G 302 648-3199
  Millsboro (G-8425)
Tat Trucking Inc................................. F 302 832-2667
  Bear (G-526)
U Haul Co Independent Dealers............ G 302 424-3189
  Milford (G-8123)
U Haul Neighborhood Dealer................. G 302 613-0207
  Bear (G-545)
U Haul Neighborhood Dealer................. G 302 832-1433
  Bear (G-546)
U Haul Neighborhood Dealer................. G 302 284-6051
  Felton (G-4034)
U Haul Neighborhood Dealer................. G 302 393-2999
  Milford (G-8124)
U-Haul.. G 302 565-4423
  Newark (G-12255)
U-Haul.. G 302 514-0034
  Smyrna (G-13923)
U-Haul Co... G 302 628-8197
  Seaford (G-13437)
U-Haul International............................ G 302 934-1601
  Millsboro (G-8489)
U-Haul International............................ G 302 565-4056
  Newark (G-12256)
U-Haul International Inc....................... G 302 762-6445
  Wilmington (G-20485)
U-Haul International Inc....................... G 336 667-0147
  New Castle (G-9646)
U-Haul Neighborhd Dealr Budget......... G 302 349-2167
  Greenwood (G-4673)
U-Haul Neighborhood Dealer................. G 302 721-6064
  Bridgeville (G-776)
U-Haul Neighborhood Dealer................. G 302 321-6032
  Frankford (G-4156)
U-Haul Neighborhood Dealer................. G 302 343-7497
  Hartly (G-4911)
U-Haul Neighborhood Dealer................. G 302 644-4316
  Lewes (G-6586)
U-Haul Neighborhood Dealer................. G 302 703-0376
  Lewes (G-6587)
U-Haul Neighborhood Dealer................. G 302 376-6858
  Middletown (G-7668)
U-Haul Neighborhood Dealer................. G 302 449-7379
  Middletown (G-7669)
U-Haul Neighborhood Dealer................. G 302 725-4525
  Milford (G-8125)
U-Haul Neighborhood Dealer................. G 302 250-4422
  New Castle (G-9647)
U-Haul Neighborhood Dealer................. G 302 544-9178
  New Castle (G-9648)
U-Haul Neighborhood Dealer................. G 302 722-8016
  Newark (G-12257)
Watkins System Inc............................. E 302 658-8561
  New Castle (G-9678)

LEASING & RENTAL: Utility Trailers & RV's

Morton Electric Co.............................. G 302 645-9414
  Lewes (G-6292)
Penske Truck Leasing Co LP............... G 302 325-9290
  New Castle (G-9467)

LEASING: Passenger Car

Delaware Motor Sales Inc.................... D 302 656-3100
  Wilmington (G-15945)
Future Ford Sales Inc.......................... D 302 999-0261
  Wilmington (G-16776)
Martin Newark Dealership Inc.............. D 302 454-9300
  Newark (G-11345)
New Car Connection............................ G 302 328-7000
  New Castle (G-9405)
Professional Leasing Inc...................... G 302 629-4350
  Seaford (G-13359)
Star States Leasing Corp..................... E 302 283-4500
  Newark (G-12088)
Winner Ford of Newark Inc................... F 302 731-2415
  Newark (G-12388)
Winner Group Inc................................ F 302 292-8200
  Newark (G-12389)

LEATHER & CUT STOCK WHOLESALERS

Monseco Leather LLC......................... G 302 235-1777
  Hockessin (G-5311)

LEATHER GOODS, EXC FOOTWEAR, GLOVES, LUGGAGE/ BELTING, WHOL

Masley Enterprises Inc........................ E 302 427-9885
  Wilmington (G-18183)

LEATHER GOODS: Garments

Francis Enterprises LLC....................... F 302 276-1316
  Historic New Castle (G-4991)

LEATHER, LEATHER GOODS & FURS, WHOLESALE

Francis Enterprises LLC....................... F 302 276-1316
  Historic New Castle (G-4991)

LEATHER: Accessory Prdts

Patricea and Co LLC........................... G 929 374-9761
  Dover (G-3280)

LEATHER: Indl Prdts

Exco Inc... D 905 477-3065
  Wilmington (G-16502)

LEGAL & TAX SVCS

Pk & Associates Group Inc................... G 302 394-9052
  Wilmington (G-19061)
Tax Take LLC..................................... G 302 760-9758
  Wilmington (G-20231)

LEGAL AID SVCS

Community Legal Aid Society............... G 302 674-8503
  Dover (G-2119)
Community Legal Aid Society............... F 302 856-0038
  Georgetown (G-4263)
Community Legal Aid Society............... D 302 757-7001
  Wilmington (G-15563)
Legal Services Corp Delaware.............. F 302 575-0408
  Wilmington (G-17861)
UAW-GM Legal Services Plan.............. F 302 562-8212
  Newark (G-12258)

LEGAL OFFICES & SVCS

4dimensions LLC................................ D 302 339-0082
  New Castle (G-8747)
Agents of Delaware Inc....................... F 302 544-2467
  New Castle (G-8772)
Agile Legal.. E 302 376-6710
  Middletown (G-6841)
Alexis Legal Support Svcs Inc.............. G 646 494-3289
  Newark (G-9809)
American Income Lf - Ryan Bsan......... G 484 442-8148
  Wilmington (G-14431)
American Incorporators Ltd................. E 302 421-5752
  Wilmington (G-14432)
Business Incorporators........................ G 302 475-6596
  Wilmington (G-15158)
Cogency Global Inc............................. E 800 483-1140
  Dover (G-2110)
Corp1 Inc.. F 302 736-3466
  Dover (G-2140)
Countrmsres Assssment SEC Expr...... G 302 322-9600
  Middletown (G-7015)
CSC Corporate Domains Inc................ D 866 403-5272
  Wilmington (G-15722)
CSC Domains LLC.............................. E 302 636-5400
  Wilmington (G-15723)
Delaware Alnce Agnst Sxual Vln.......... G 302 468-7731
  Wilmington (G-15863)
Delaware Corporate Registry............... G 302 655-6500
  Wilmington (G-15893)
Delaware Department Finance............ D 302 739-5291
  Dover (G-2227)
Delaware Tchncal Cmnty College......... E 302 259-6160
  Georgetown (G-4286)
DLS Discovery LLC............................. E 302 888-2060
  Wilmington (G-16105)
Duly Noted LLC................................... G 302 353-4585
  Wilmington (G-16198)
Global Law Centers............................ G 302 654-4800
  Wilmington (G-16891)
Grant Tani Barash & Altman Man......... G 302 651-7700
  Wilmington (G-16949)
Honorable Myron T Steele.................... G 302 739-4214
  Dover (G-2693)
Law Offices Patrick Scanlon PA............ G 302 424-1996
  Milford (G-7972)
Legalnature LLC................................. G 888 881-1139
  Dover (G-2927)
Lippstone Law Pllc............................. G 302 252-1481
  Newark (G-11265)
Logan & Associates LLC..................... G 302 325-3555
  New Castle (G-9322)
Michael L Berman............................... G 302 300-3450
  Wilmington (G-18316)
Minute Center.................................... G 302 645-9396
  Rehoboth Beach (G-12859)
Modern Mixture LLC............................ G 302 249-6183
  Milford (G-8017)
Newrez LLC....................................... G 240 475-4741
  Lewes (G-6312)
Poolside Cnstr & Renovation................ G 302 436-9711
  Selbyville (G-13594)
Potter Anderson & Corroon.................. G 302 984-6078
  Wilmington (G-19133)
Prentice-Hall Corp System Inc............. D 302 636-5440
  Wilmington (G-19175)
Prepaid Legal Service......................... G 302 376-1952
  Smyrna (G-13852)
Telos Legal Corp................................ G 302 242-4815
  Dover (G-3666)
Thomson Reuters (grc) Inc................... G 212 227-7357
  Wilmington (G-20314)
Vps Services LLC.............................. G 302 376-6710
  Middletown (G-7696)
Ward & Taylor LLC............................. G 302 346-7000
  Dover (G-3820)

Employee Codes: A=Over 500 employees, B=251-500
C=101-250, D=51-100, E=20-50, F=10-19, G=1-9

LEGAL OFFICES & SVCS

Whitaker Corporation .... E 302 633-2740
Wilmington (G-20762)

Wolfe Associates LLC .... G 302 668-6178
Middletown (G-7732)

LEGAL PROCESS SERVERS

Brandywine Process Servers .... G 302 475-2600
Wilmington (G-15081)

Delmar Process Servers LLC .... F 302 306-2805
Dover (G-2276)

LEGAL SVCS: General Practice Attorney or Lawyer

Abrams & Bayliss LLP .... F 302 778-1000
Wilmington (G-14208)

Albert J Roop .... G 302 655-4600
Wilmington (G-14349)

Allen & Associates .... F 302 234-8600
Wilmington (G-14373)

Allmond & Eastburn .... G 302 764-2193
Bethany Beach (G-573)

Amber B Woodland .... G 302 628-4140
Seaford (G-13059)

Ashby & Geddes .... E 302 654-1888
Wilmington (G-14579)

Ashley M Oland .... G 302 854-5406
Georgetown (G-4213)

Baird Mandalas Brockstedt LLC .... F 302 644-0302
Lewes (G-5734)

Baird Mandalas Brockstedt LLC .... F 302 677-0061
Dover (G-1868)

Balick & Balick Pllc .... G 302 658-4265
Wilmington (G-14722)

Ballard Spahr LLP .... G 302 252-4465
Wilmington (G-14723)

Barros Mc Nmara Mlkwicz Tylor .... F 302 734-8400
Dover (G-1876)

Benesch Attorneys At Law .... F 302 442-7005
Wilmington (G-14834)

Benesch Frdlnder Cplan Arnoff .... F 216 363-4500
Wilmington (G-14835)

Benjamin W Keenan .... G 302 654-1888
Wilmington (G-14837)

Beverly L Bove PA .... G 302 777-3500
Wilmington (G-14867)

Biden For AG Inc .... G 302 295-8340
Wilmington (G-14877)

Bifferato Gentilotti LLC .... G 302 429-1900
Wilmington (G-14880)

Blank Rome LLP .... G 302 425-6400
Wilmington (G-14952)

Bodell Bove LLC .... G 302 655-6749
Wilmington (G-14992)

Boudart & Mensinger LLP .... G 302 428-0100
Wilmington (G-15010)

Brown Shiels & OBrien .... G 302 734-4766
Dover (G-1985)

Brown Shels Bauregard LLC .... G 302 226-2270
Dover (G-1986)

Burr & Forman LLP .... F 302 425-6400
Wilmington (G-15154)

Campbell & Levine LLC .... G 302 426-1900
Wilmington (G-15210)

Carmella P Keener Atty .... G 302 656-4333
Wilmington (G-15255)

Carmine Potter & Associates .... G 302 832-5000
Newark (G-10151)

Carmine Potter & Associates .... G 302 658-8940
Wilmington (G-15256)

Casarino Chrstman Shalk Rnsom .... E 302 594-4500
Wilmington (G-15263)

Catherines CSAC Inc .... C 302 478-6160
Wilmington (G-15274)

Ch Wilmington LLC .... F 302 655-1641
Wilmington (G-15325)

Charles Slanina .... G 302 234-1605
Hockessin (G-5156)

Chimicles Schwrtz Krner Dnldsn .... F 302 656-2500
Wilmington (G-15383)

Ciconte Wasserman & Scerba LLC .... F 302 658-7101
Wilmington (G-15434)

Cindy L Szabo .... G 302 855-9505
Georgetown (G-4256)

Clayton E Bunting .... G 302 856-0017
Georgetown (G-4259)

Cole Schotz PC .... G 302 984-9541
Wilmington (G-15526)

Color Street .... G 302 574-0409
Wilmington (G-15539)

Cooch and Taylor A Prof Assn .... E 302 984-3800
Wilmington (G-15627)

Cooper Levenson PA .... G 302 838-2600
Bear (G-120)

Cozen OConnor .... F 302 295-2000
Wilmington (G-15673)

Cramer Dimichele .... G 302 235-8561
Wilmington (G-15684)

Crossland & Associates LLC .... F 302 409-0120
Hockessin (G-5171)

Crossland and Associates .... G 302 658-2100
Hockessin (G-5172)

Curley & Benton LLC .... G 302 674-3333
Dover (G-2170)

Cynthia L Carroll .... G 302 733-0411
Newark (G-10371)

Dalton & Associates PA .... G 302 652-2050
Wilmington (G-15773)

Daniel P McCollom .... F 302 888-6865
Wilmington (G-15784)

David A Dorey Esq .... G 302 425-6400
Wilmington (G-15801)

David D Finocchiaro Attorney .... G 302 764-7113
Wilmington (G-15804)

Delaware Counsel Group LLP .... E 302 543-4870
Rockland (G-13030)

Deval Patel-Lennon Esq PA Inc .... G 302 998-2000
Wilmington (G-16034)

Don A Beskrone .... G 302 654-1888
Wilmington (G-16130)

Donald M Brown .... G 302 777-1840
Wilmington (G-16137)

Doroshow Psqale Krwitz Sgel Bh .... G 302 832-3200
Bear (G-176)

Doroshow Psqale Krwitz Sgel Bh .... F 302 674-7100
Dover (G-2327)

Doroshow Psqale Krwitz Sgel Bh .... G 302 424-7744
Milford (G-7870)

Doroshow Psqale Krwitz Sgel Bh .... F 302 934-9400
Millsboro (G-8276)

Doroshow Psqale Krwitz Sgel Bh .... F 302 998-0100
Wilmington (G-16150)

Doroshow Psqale Krwitz Sgel Bh .... E 302 998-2397
Wilmington (G-16149)

Dorsey & Whitney LLP .... G 302 383-1011
Wilmington (G-16151)

Douglas M Helfer .... G 302 988-8127
Selbyville (G-13523)

Elzufon Astin Rrdon Trlov Mnde .... E 302 428-3181
Wilmington (G-16383)

Elzufon Austin Reardon Tarlov .... G 302 644-0144
Lewes (G-5959)

Eric M Doroshow .... G 302 934-9400
Millsboro (G-8283)

Ferrara Haley & Bevis .... G 302 656-7247
Wilmington (G-16586)

Ferry Joseph & Pearce PA .... F 302 856-3706
Georgetown (G-4319)

Ferry Joseph & Pearce PA .... F 302 575-1555
Wilmington (G-16590)

Fox Rothschild LLP .... D 302 654-7444
Wilmington (G-16715)

Franklin & Prokopik .... G 302 594-9780
Wilmington (G-16727)

Franklin and Prokopik .... G 302 594-9780
Newark (G-10771)

Frederick L Cottrell .... G 302 651-7686
Wilmington (G-16738)

Freibott Law Firm .... F 302 633-9000
Wilmington (G-16746)

Funk & Bolton PA .... G 302 735-8400
Dover (G-2545)

Gawthrop Greenwood PC .... G 302 351-1273
Wilmington (G-16820)

Gerry Gray .... G 302 856-4101
Smyrna (G-13742)

Giordano Delcollo & Werb LLC .... G 302 234-6855
Wilmington (G-16866)

Grady & Hampton LLC .... G 302 678-1265
Dover (G-2618)

Grant & Eisenhofer PA .... D 302 622-7000
Wilmington (G-16948)

GSB&b LLC .... G 302 425-5800
Wilmington (G-16994)

Haller & Hudson .... G 302 856-4525
Georgetown (G-4352)

Halloran Farkas + Kittila LLP .... F 302 257-2011
Wilmington (G-17039)

Heckler & Frabizzio PA .... F 302 573-4800
Wilmington (G-17113)

Heiman Gouge & Kaufman LLP .... G 302 658-1800
Wilmington (G-17114)

Herdeg Dupont Dalle Pazze LLP .... G 302 655-6500
Wilmington (G-17129)

Heyman Enerio Gattuso & Hirzel .... F 302 472-7300
Wilmington (G-17136)

Hochman C Michael Atty .... G 302 656-8162
Wilmington (G-17161)

Hudson Jnes Jaywork Fisher LLC .... E 302 734-7401
Dover (G-2702)

Hudson Jnes Jywork Fsher Attys .... G 302 839-1153
Milford (G-7937)

Hudson Jones Jaywork Fisher .... G 302 645-7999
Lewes (G-6107)

I Barry Guerke .... G 302 450-1098
Dover (G-2713)

J Clayton Athey .... G 302 888-6507
Wilmington (G-17453)

Jacobs & Crumplar PA .... E 302 656-5445
Wilmington (G-17473)

James E Deakyne Jr PA .... G 302 226-1200
Rehoboth Beach (G-12800)

James L Holzman .... F 302 888-6500
Wilmington (G-17482)

Jeffrey Schlerf Atty .... G 302 622-4212
Wilmington (G-17521)

John H Williams Jr Atty .... F 302 571-4780
Wilmington (G-17564)

Joseph A Hurley PA .... G 302 658-8980
Wilmington (G-17576)

Joseph W Benson PA .... G 302 656-8811
Wilmington (G-17587)

Kate G Shumaker .... G 302 327-1100
Bear (G-322)

Katharine L Mayer Atty .... G 302 984-6312
Wilmington (G-17660)

PRODUCTS & SERVICES SECTION — LEGAL SVCS: General Practice Attorney or Lawyer

Firm	Code	Phone
Katherine Laffey — Wilmington (G-17661)	G	302 651-7999
Knepper & Stratton — Dover (G-2880)	G	302 658-1717
Kurt F Gwynne — Wilmington (G-17766)	G	302 778-7550
Law Firm — Wilmington (G-17828)	F	302 472-4900
Law of Michele D — Hockessin (G-5278)	G	302 234-8600
Law Offces Murray Phillips Gay — Georgetown (G-4403)	G	302 855-9300
Law Office Daniel C Herr LLC — Wilmington (G-17829)	G	302 595-9084
Law Office Jnnfer Kate M Arnso — Wilmington (G-17830)	G	302 655-4600
Law Office Laura A Yiengst LLC — Dover (G-2911)	G	302 264-9780
Law Office of Melissa Green — New Castle (G-9297)	G	302 998-2049
Law Offices of Sean M Lynn PA — Dover (G-2913)	G	302 734-2000
Legal Services of Delaware — Wilmington (G-17862)	F	302 575-0408
Leroy A Tice Esquire PA — Wilmington (G-17883)	G	302 658-6901
Letsbelegalcom — Newark (G-11247)	G	302 894-4357
Liguori Morris & Reddin — Dover (G-2946)	G	302 678-9900
Linarducci & Butler PA — New Castle (G-9310)	G	302 325-2400
LLP Connolly Gallagher — Newark (G-11276)	D	302 757-7300
LLP Connolly Gallagher — Wilmington (G-17959)	F	302 757-7300
LLP Shaw Keller — Wilmington (G-17960)	G	302 298-0700
Loizides & Associates PC — Wilmington (G-17978)	G	302 654-0248
Longobardi & Boyle LLC — Wilmington (G-17986)	G	302 575-1502
Lyons David J Law Office — Wilmington (G-18053)	G	302 777-5698
Macelree & Harvey Ltd — Wilmington (G-18067)	E	302 654-4454
Marks Onill Obrien Dhrty Klly — Wilmington (G-18150)	G	302 658-6538
Maron Mrvel Brdley Anderson PA — Wilmington (G-18154)	D	302 425-5177
Martin D Hvrly Attorney At Law — Wilmington (G-18167)	G	302 529-0121
Mastracci Mastracci — Selbyville (G-13567)	G	410 869-3400
Matthew B Lunn — Wilmington (G-18195)	G	302 571-6646
Mattleman Weinroth & Miller PC — Newark (G-11355)	G	302 731-8349
McCarter & English LLP — Wilmington (G-18218)	E	302 984-6300
McGivney Kluger & Cook PC — Wilmington (G-18229)	G	302 656-1200
McLaughlin Gordon L Law Office — Wilmington (G-18233)	G	302 651-7979
McLaughlin Morton Holdg Co LLC — Wilmington (G-18234)	F	302 426-1313
Michael B Tumas — Wilmington (G-18308)	G	302 984-6029
Michael P Morton PA — Wilmington (G-18321)	G	302 426-1313
Milewski Stephan — Wilmington (G-18355)	G	302 467-4502
Mintzer Sarowitz Zeris Leovar — Wilmington (G-18382)	G	302 655-2181
Montgomery McCrcken Wlker Rhads — Wilmington (G-18425)	F	302 504-7800
Monzack Mrsky McLghlin Brwder — Wilmington (G-18427)	E	302 656-8162
Mooney & Andrew PA — Georgetown (G-4431)	G	302 856-3070
Moore & Rutt PA — Georgetown (G-4432)	G	302 856-9568
Morgan Lewis International LLC — Wilmington (G-18446)	G	302 574-3000
Morris James LLP — Dover (G-3124)	G	302 678-8815
Morris James LLP — Newark (G-11454)	F	302 368-4200
Morris James LLP — Rehoboth Beach (G-12863)	G	302 260-7290
Morris James LLP — Wilmington (G-18453)	F	302 655-2599
Morris James LLP — Wilmington (G-18454)	D	302 888-6800
Morris James Per Injury Group — Georgetown (G-4436)	G	302 856-0017
Morris Nchols Arsht Tnnell LLP — Wilmington (G-18455)	C	302 658-9200
Morton Valihura & Zerbato LLC — Wilmington (G-18459)	G	302 426-1313
Murphy & Landon PC — Wilmington (G-18488)	F	302 472-8100
Nolte & Brodoway PA — Wilmington (G-18664)	G	302 777-1700
Novak Druce Cnnlly Bv+qigg LLP — Wilmington (G-18693)	C	302 252-9922
O Kelly Ernst Belli Wallen LLC — Wilmington (G-18723)	G	302 778-4001
P C Flaster/Greenberg — Wilmington (G-18851)	G	302 351-1910
Parsons & Robinson PA — Ocean View (G-12557)	G	302 539-2220
Phillips Gldman McLghlin Hall — Wilmington (G-19019)	E	302 655-4200
Potter Anderson & Corroon LLP — Wilmington (G-19134)	C	302 984-6000
Procino Wells & Woodland LLC — Lewes (G-6393)	G	302 313-5934
Rahaim & Saints Attys At Law — Wilmington (G-19318)	F	302 892-9200
Ramunno Ramunno — Newark (G-11824)	G	302 737-6909
Raskaukas Joseph C Aty Law — Bethany Beach (G-630)	G	302 537-2000
Raymond E Tomassetti Esq — Fenwick Island (G-4053)	G	302 539-3041
Reed Smith LLP — Wilmington (G-19392)	F	302 778-7500
Reger Rizzo & Darnall LLP — Wilmington (G-19401)	G	302 652-3611
Reynolds Services Ltd — Wilmington (G-19449)	G	877 404-2179
Rhoades & Morrow LLC — Milford (G-8066)	G	302 422-6705
Rhoades & Morrow LLC — Wilmington (G-19458)	F	302 427-9500
Rhodunda & Williams LLC — Wilmington (G-19460)	G	302 576-2000
Richards Layton & Finger P A — Wilmington (G-19475)	E	302 651-7700
Richards Layton & Finger P A — Wilmington (G-19476)	B	302 651-7700
Richards Layton & Finger P A — Wilmington (G-19477)	C	302 651-7700
Ridrodsky & Long PA — Wilmington (G-19481)	G	302 691-8822
Robert J Kriner Jr — Wilmington (G-19514)	G	302 656-2500
Robert K Beste Jr — Wilmington (G-19516)	G	302 425-5089
Robert L Thomas — Wilmington (G-19518)	G	302 571-6602
Robinson Grayson and Ward PA — Wilmington (G-19524)	G	302 655-6262
Roeberg Moore & Associates PA — Wilmington (G-19554)	F	302 658-4757
Roger D Anderson — Wilmington (G-19555)	G	302 652-8400
Ross Aronstam & Moritz LLP — Wilmington (G-19571)	F	302 576-1600
Ruff & Ruff LLC — Smyrna (G-13872)	G	267 243-3906
Schab & Barnett PA — Georgetown (G-4500)	G	302 856-9024
Schmittinger & Rodriguez Attys — Middletown (G-7542)	G	302 378-1697
Schmittinger and Rodriguez PA — Dover (G-3514)	D	302 674-0140
Schnader Hrrson Sgal Lewis LLP — Wilmington (G-19697)	F	302 888-4554
Schuster Jachetti LLP — Wilmington (G-19700)	G	302 984-1000
Schwartz Schwartz Attys At Law — Wilmington (G-19701)	G	302 998-1500
Schwartz Schwrtz Attys At Law — Dover (G-3518)	G	302 678-8700
Seitz Vanogtrop & Green — Wilmington (G-19740)	F	302 888-0600
Shanley Assoc — Wilmington (G-19780)	G	302 691-6838
Sharon M Zieg — Wilmington (G-19783)	G	302 571-6655
Silverman McDonald & Friedman — Seaford (G-13402)	G	302 629-3350
Skadden Arps Slate Mgher Flom — Wilmington (G-19851)	C	302 651-3000
Smith Katzenstein & Furlow LLP — Wilmington (G-19890)	E	302 652-8400
Steen Waehler Schrider Fox LLC — Ocean View (G-12569)	G	302 539-7900
Stephen E Jenkins — Wilmington (G-20058)	G	302 654-1888
Stern & Eisenberg PC — Newark (G-12101)	G	302 731-7200
Stevens & Lee PC — Wilmington (G-20068)	F	302 654-5180
Sunu Consulting LLC — Dover (G-3625)	G	202 534-5864
Susan C Over PC — Hockessin (G-5400)	G	302 660-2913
Tarabicos Grosso — New Castle (G-9616)	F	302 757-7800
Taylor Copeland LLC — Wilmington (G-20233)	G	302 598-4412
Theresa Hayes — Georgetown (G-4551)	G	302 854-5406
Tighe and Cottrell PA — Wilmington (G-20323)	G	302 658-6400
Troutman Ppper Hmlton Snders L — Wilmington (G-20440)	E	302 777-6500
Tunnell & Raysor PA — Lewes (G-6584)	G	302 644-4442
Tunnell & Raysor PA — Georgetown (G-4563)	E	302 856-7313
Tybout Redfearn & Pell PA — Wilmington (G-20475)	E	302 658-6901

Employee Codes: A=Over 500 employees, B=251-500
C=101-250, D=51-100, E=20-50, F=10-19, G=1-9

2024 Harris Directory of Delaware Businesses

LEGAL SVCS: General Practice Attorney or Lawyer

Vance A Funk III.................................... G..... 302 368-2561
 Newark *(G-12303)*
Vivian A Houghton Esquire.................... G..... 302 658-0518
 Wilmington *(G-20645)*
Weber Gallagher Simpson...................... G..... 302 346-6377
 Dover *(G-3828)*
Weik Nitsche & Dougherty..................... F..... 302 655-4040
 Wilmington *(G-20713)*
Weir Greenblatt Pierce LLP.................... G..... 302 652-8181
 Wilmington *(G-20715)*
Werb & Sullivan..................................... F..... 302 652-1100
 Wilmington *(G-20733)*
Wharton Levin Ehrmantraut.................... G..... 302 252-0090
 Wilmington *(G-20754)*
White and Williams LLP......................... E..... 302 654-0424
 Wilmington *(G-20763)*
Whittington & Aulgur.............................. G..... 302 235-5800
 Yorklyn *(G-20994)*
Wilbraham Lawler & Buba PC................. G..... 302 421-9922
 Wilmington *(G-20778)*
William E Ward PA................................. F..... 302 225-3350
 Wilmington *(G-20787)*
William H Lunger Atty............................ G..... 302 888-2504
 Wilmington *(G-20792)*
Williams Law Firm PA........................... G..... 302 575-0873
 Wilmington *(G-20802)*
Willis Law LLC....................................... G..... 302 535-3200
 Dover *(G-3854)*
Young and Malmberg PA....................... F..... 302 672-5600
 Dover *(G-3892)*
Zwally Brown Lisa................................. G..... 302 504-7803
 Wilmington *(G-20970)*

LIFE INSURANCE CARRIERS

First Lincoln Holdings Inc...................... F..... 302 429-4900
 Wilmington *(G-16619)*
Openeyes Insur Holdings Inc................. G..... 737 222-9132
 Wilmington *(G-18799)*
Rbc Insurance Holdings USA Inc............ A..... 302 651-8356
 Wilmington *(G-19351)*

LIFESAVING & SURVIVAL EQPT, EXC MEDICAL, WHOLESALE

AME Life LLC.. G..... 305 517-7707
 Dover *(G-1783)*
Anderson Group Inc.............................. A..... 302 478-6160
 Wilmington *(G-14472)*
Honeywell Safety Pdts USA Inc............. E..... 302 636-5401
 Wilmington *(G-17194)*

LIGHTERS, CIGARETTE & CIGAR, WHOLESALE

Books & Tobaccos Inc........................... G..... 302 994-3156
 Wilmington *(G-15003)*

LIGHTING EQPT: Locomotive & Railroad Car Lights

Esafety Lights LLC................................ G..... 800 236-8621
 Wilmington *(G-16462)*

LIGHTING EQPT: Outdoor

Globe Electric Company USA Inc........... G..... 514 694-0444
 Dover *(G-2596)*
Sun-In-One Inc...................................... F..... 302 762-3100
 Wilmington *(G-20127)*

LIGHTING EQPT: Strobe Lighting Systems

Esafety Lights LLC................................ G..... 800 236-8621
 Wilmington *(G-16462)*

LIGHTING FIXTURES WHOLESALERS

Colonial Electric Supply Co.................... F..... 302 998-9993
 Historic New Castle *(G-4960)*
Diversified Lighting Assoc Inc................ G..... 302 286-6370
 Wilmington *(G-16096)*
Led Company Intl Llc............................ F..... 302 668-8370
 Wilmington *(G-17850)*
Sentrylight Inc....................................... G..... 302 420-8844
 Newark *(G-11978)*
Way To Go Led Lighting Company......... F..... 844 312-4574
 Newark *(G-12349)*

LIGHTING FIXTURES, NEC

Detweilers Lighting................................ G..... 302 678-5804
 Hartly *(G-4869)*
Evergreen Led....................................... G..... 302 218-7819
 Townsend *(G-13999)*
Ledtolight.. G..... 941 323-6664
 Wilmington *(G-17852)*
Newport.. F..... 302 995-2840
 Wilmington *(G-18631)*
Smb Lighting... G..... 302 733-0664
 Newark *(G-12037)*

LIGHTING FIXTURES: Indl & Commercial

Bwt Lighting Inc.................................... G..... 302 709-0808
 Newark *(G-10110)*
Illumination Technology Inc................... G..... 410 430-5349
 Delmar *(G-1602)*
Pemco Lighting Products LLC............... F..... 302 892-9000
 Wilmington *(G-18947)*
Whiteoptics LLC.................................... G..... 302 476-2055
 New Castle *(G-9681)*

LIGHTING FIXTURES: Residential, Electric

Jaykal Led Solutions Inc........................ G..... 302 295-0015
 Georgetown *(G-4379)*

LINEN SPLY SVC: Coat

Medlanta Inc... G..... 610 991-2929
 Wilmington *(G-18256)*

LINEN SPLY SVC: Uniform

Alsco Inc... E..... 302 322-2136
 New Castle *(G-8788)*
G K Services 238.................................. G..... 302 629-6729
 Seaford *(G-13193)*
Palace Laundry Inc............................... A..... 302 322-2136
 New Castle *(G-9445)*

LININGS: Fabric, Apparel & Other, Exc Millinery

Be Blessed Design Group LLC.............. G..... 302 561-3793
 Bear *(G-59)*

LIQUEFIED PETROLEUM GAS DEALERS

Petroleum Equipment Inc...................... E..... 302 734-7433
 Dover *(G-3307)*

LIQUEFIED PETROLEUM GAS WHOLESALERS

Sherman Heating Oils Inc...................... G..... 302 684-4008
 Milton *(G-8711)*

LOCKS

Black & Decker Inc............................... G..... 860 827-3861
 Newark *(G-10043)*

LOGGING

Summers Logging LLC.......................... G..... 302 234-8725
 Hockessin *(G-5395)*

LOGGING CAMPS & CONTRACTORS

D&C Logging.. G..... 302 846-3982
 Delmar *(G-1586)*
High Vue Logging Inc............................ G..... 302 697-3606
 Camden *(G-851)*
Whitetail Country Log & Hlg................... G..... 302 846-3982
 Delmar *(G-1656)*

LOOSELEAF BINDERS

L E Stansell Inc..................................... G..... 302 475-1534
 Wilmington *(G-17775)*

LOTIONS OR CREAMS: Face

Brand Evangelists For Buty Inc.............. G..... 973 970-0812
 Dover *(G-1971)*
Glaxosmthkline Hldngs Amrcas I........... C..... 302 984-6932
 Wilmington *(G-16882)*
Matykos Beauty LLC............................. G..... 302 213-6879
 Wilmington *(G-18200)*
Naked and Thriving Inc......................... G..... 855 943-0521
 Wilmington *(G-18522)*

LOTIONS: SHAVING

Remarle LLC... G..... 215 245-6448
 Middletown *(G-7511)*

LUBRICANTS: Corrosion Preventive

Championx LLC..................................... G..... 856 423-6417
 Historic New Castle *(G-4955)*

LUBRICATING OIL & GREASE WHOLESALERS

Chemours Company Fc LLC.................. D..... 302 773-1267
 Wilmington *(G-15361)*
Performance Lubricants Inc.................. G..... 302 239-5661
 Hockessin *(G-5338)*
Sandy Brae Laboratories....................... G..... 302 456-0446
 Wilmington *(G-19663)*
Ultrachem Inc....................................... F..... 302 325-9880
 Historic New Castle *(G-5094)*
Vp Racing Fuels Inc.............................. G..... 302 368-1500
 Newark *(G-12337)*

LUMBER & BLDG MATLS DEALER, RET: Garage Doors, Sell/Install

Hickman Overhead Door Company......... F..... 302 422-4249
 Milford *(G-7930)*
Precision Door Service.......................... G..... 302 343-6394
 Wilmington *(G-19154)*

LUMBER & BUILDING MATERIALS DEALER, RET: Door & Window Prdts

Mark Ventresca Associates Inc.............. G..... 302 239-3925
 Hockessin *(G-5300)*
Stanton Door Co Inc.............................. F..... 302 731-4167
 Newark *(G-12086)*

LUMBER & BUILDING MATERIALS DEALER, RET: Masonry Matls/Splys

Casale Marble Imports Inc..................... E..... 561 404-4213
 Wilmington *(G-15262)*
Dippold Marble Granite......................... G..... 302 324-9101
 Middletown *(G-7062)*

LUMBER & BUILDING MATERIALS DEALERS, RET: Solar Heating Eqpt

PRODUCTS & SERVICES SECTION

MACHINERY & EQPT, WHOLESALE: Oil Field Eqpt

African Wood Inc.................................. G 302 884-6738
Middletown (G-6839)

LUMBER & BUILDING MATERIALS DEALERS, RETAIL: Brick

Delaware Brick Company..................... E 302 994-0948
Wilmington (G-15876)

LUMBER & BUILDING MATERIALS DEALERS, RETAIL: Modular Homes

Dick Ennis Inc..................................... G 302 945-2627
Lewes (G-5914)

LUMBER & BUILDING MATERIALS DEALERS, RETAIL: Tile, Ceramic

Ruiz Flooring...................................... G 302 999-9350
Wilmington (G-19588)

LUMBER: Hardwood Dimension

Delmarva Hardwood Products Inc........ F 302 349-4101
Laurel (G-5497)

LUMBER: Hardwood Dimension & Flooring Mills

Gordys Lumber Inc............................. F 302 875-3502
Laurel (G-5524)

Grubb Lumber Company Inc............... E 302 652-2800
Wilmington (G-16992)

Stark Truss Company Inc................... F 302 368-8566
Newark (G-12090)

LUMBER: Treated

Glory Contracting................................ G 302 275-5430
Townsend (G-14008)

MACHINE PARTS: Stamped Or Pressed Metal

Bear Forge and Machine Co Inc........... G 302 322-5199
Bear (G-63)

MACHINE TOOL ACCESS: Tools & Access

Mechanical Systems Intl Corp............. G 302 453-8315
Newark (G-11371)

MACHINE TOOLS, METAL CUTTING: Tool Replacement & Rpr Parts

Mazzpac LLC...................................... G 973 641-9159
Newark (G-11364)

Seaford Machine Works Inc................ F 302 629-6034
Seaford (G-13389)

MACHINE TOOLS, METAL FORMING: Mechanical, Pneumatic Or Hyd

Miller Metal Fabrication Inc.................. D 302 337-2291
Bridgeville (G-734)

MACHINE TOOLS: Metal Cutting

Diy Tool Supply LLC............................ G 302 253-8461
Georgetown (G-4295)

Mot Cnc Works LLC............................ G 302 379-2114
Middletown (G-7382)

Paul A Lange...................................... G 302 378-1706
Middletown (G-7431)

MACHINE TOOLS: Metal Forming

Delaware Capital Formation Inc............ G 302 793-4921
Wilmington (G-15878)

MACHINERY & EQPT FINANCE LEASING

B Williams Holding Corp...................... F 302 656-8596
Wilmington (G-14704)

MACHINERY & EQPT, AGRICULTURAL, WHOLESALE: Agricultural, NEC

Messick & Gray Cnstr Inc.................... E 302 337-8777
Bridgeville (G-731)

MACHINERY & EQPT, AGRICULTURAL, WHOLESALE: Landscaping Eqpt

All Rock & Mulch LLC......................... G 302 838-7625
Bear (G-26)

Delaware Hardscape Supply LLC......... G 302 996-6464
Wilmington (G-15923)

MACHINERY & EQPT, AGRICULTURAL, WHOLESALE: Lawn & Garden

Woodward Enterprises Inc................... F 302 378-2849
Middletown (G-7736)

MACHINERY & EQPT, INDL, WHOLESALE: Chemical Process

Kahl Company Inc............................... G 302 478-8450
Wilmington (G-17634)

MACHINERY & EQPT, INDL, WHOLESALE: Engines & Parts, Diesel

Careys Diesel Inc................................ F 302 678-3797
Leipsic (G-5629)

MACHINERY & EQPT, INDL, WHOLESALE: Fans

W W Grainger Inc............................... G 302 322-1840
Historic New Castle (G-5098)

MACHINERY & EQPT, INDL, WHOLESALE: Food Product Manufacturng

Delaware Capital Formation Inc............ G 302 793-4921
Wilmington (G-15878)

Delaware Capital Holdings Inc............. G 302 793-4921
Wilmington (G-15879)

MACHINERY & EQPT, INDL, WHOLESALE: Hydraulic Systems

Benz Hydraulics Inc............................ F 302 328-6648
New Castle (G-8858)

Fiduks Industrial Services Inc.............. F 302 994-2534
Wilmington (G-16602)

MACHINERY & EQPT, INDL, WHOLESALE: Indl Machine Parts

Mitusha International Corp................... G 302 674-2977
Dover (G-3105)

Power Trans Inc.................................. F 302 337-3016
Bridgeville (G-753)

MACHINERY & EQPT, INDL, WHOLESALE: Machine Tools & Access

Arnold International Inc....................... G 302 266-4441
Newark (G-9907)

Fiduks Industrial Services Inc.............. F 302 994-2534
Wilmington (G-16601)

MACHINERY & EQPT, INDL, WHOLESALE: Measure/Test, Electric

Pco-Tech Inc...................................... F 248 276-8820
Wilmington (G-18936)

Testing Machines Inc.......................... E 302 613-5600
New Castle (G-9625)

MACHINERY & EQPT, INDL, WHOLESALE: Recycling

Nerdit Now LLC.................................. F 302 482-5979
Wilmington (G-18587)

Technicare Inc.................................... G 302 322-7766
Newark (G-12170)

MACHINERY & EQPT, INDL, WHOLESALE: Safety Eqpt

Cintas Corporation No 2...................... G 302 765-6460
Wilmington (G-15441)

First State Distributors Inc................... G 302 655-8266
Wilmington (G-16627)

Sussex Protection Service LLC............ F 302 832-5700
Newark (G-12136)

Totaltrax Inc....................................... D 302 514-0600
New Castle (G-9630)

MACHINERY & EQPT, INDL, WHOLESALE: Sawmill

Advanced Machinery Sales Inc............ G 302 322-2226
New Castle (G-8766)

Eastern Shore Metals LLC................... F 302 629-6629
Seaford (G-13169)

MACHINERY & EQPT, INDL, WHOLESALE: Water Pumps

Square One Electric Service Co........... F 302 678-0400
Dover (G-3601)

MACHINERY & EQPT, WHOLESALE: Construction, General

Alban Tractor LLC............................... G 302 284-4100
Felton (G-3939)

Alpine Contractors LLC....................... F 302 343-9954
Dover (G-1775)

Chesapeake Supply & Eqp Co............. G 302 284-1000
Felton (G-3955)

Ditch Witch of Virginia......................... G 302 629-3602
Seaford (G-13162)

E-Industrial Suppliers LLC................... G 302 251-6210
Wilmington (G-16243)

Eagle Power and Equipment Corp........ F 302 652-3028
New Castle (G-9076)

Evans Charles Contracting.................. G 701 340-9530
Bear (G-209)

F and M Equipment Ltd....................... F 302 449-2850
Townsend (G-14001)

Industrial Products of Del..................... G 302 328-6648
New Castle (G-9231)

Iron Source LLC.................................. G 302 856-7545
Georgetown (G-4373)

Kwik & Crafty Contracting................... G 302 227-2550
Rehoboth Beach (G-12826)

S G Williams & Bros Co...................... F 302 656-8167
Wilmington (G-19607)

Th White General Contract.................. G 302 945-1829
Millsboro (G-8482)

Thomas Building Group Inc................. F 302 283-0600
Newark (G-12193)

MACHINERY & EQPT, WHOLESALE: Oil Field Eqpt

Employee Codes: A=Over 500 employees, B=251-500
C=101-250, D=51-100, E=20-50, F=10-19, G=1-9

2024 Harris Directory of Delaware Businesses

1409

MACHINERY & EQPT: Farm

Wm Systems Inc...................................... G 302 450-4482
 Wilmington (G-20871)

MACHINERY & EQPT: Farm

Easy Lawn Inc.. E 302 815-6500
 Greenwood (G-4624)
Farmers Harvest Inc............................... G 302 734-7708
 Dover (G-2486)
Hog Slat Incorporated........................... E 302 875-0889
 Laurel (G-5529)
Lumi Cases LLC..................................... G 302 525-6971
 Newark (G-11295)

MACHINERY, OFFICE: Stapling, Hand Or Power

Black & Decker Inc................................. G 860 827-3861
 Newark (G-10043)

MACHINERY: Automotive Related

Roar Pedal LLC....................................... G 412 301-6002
 Dover (G-3474)

MACHINERY: Construction

Advance Marine LLC.............................. G 302 656-2111
 Wilmington (G-14268)
Js Sheds LLC.. F 484 918-0633
 Wilmington (G-17603)
Teksolv Usd Inc..................................... G 302 738-1050
 Newark (G-12176)

MACHINERY: Cryogenic, Industrial

Cae(us) Inc... G 813 885-7481
 Wilmington (G-15189)

MACHINERY: Gas Separators

Medal LP.. D 302 225-1100
 Wilmington (G-18245)

MACHINERY: Metalworking

Pennengineering Holdings LLC............ C 302 576-2746
 Wilmington (G-18954)

MACHINERY: Packaging

Ames Engineering Corp........................ F 302 658-6945
 Wilmington (G-14455)
Telesonic PC Inc.................................... G 302 658-6945
 Wilmington (G-20266)
Telesonic PC Inc.................................... G 302 658-6945
 Middletown (G-7632)

MACHINERY: Plastic Working

Negri Bossi Usa Inc............................... E 302 328-8020
 New Castle (G-9401)

MACHINERY: Printing Presses

Arihant Enterprise LLC.......................... G 302 353-4400
 Bear (G-43)
Ferrante & Associates Inc..................... G 781 891-4328
 Newark (G-10724)

MACHINERY: Semiconductor Manufacturing

Cott Electronics LLC.............................. D 302 520-2838
 Lewes (G-5862)

MACHINERY: Sifting & Screening

Rhewum America Inc............................ G 215 804-7977
 Wilmington (G-19456)

MACHINISTS' TOOLS: Measuring, Precision

Agilent Technologies Inc....................... G 302 633-7337
 Historic New Castle (G-4925)

MACHINISTS' TOOLS: Precision

Advanced Metal Concepts Inc.............. F 302 421-9905
 Middletown (G-6836)

MAGAZINES, WHOLESALE

Hispano Magazine................................. G 302 668-6118
 Newark (G-10955)
Suburban Marketing Associates........... E 302 656-8440
 Wilmington (G-20114)

MAGNESITE MINING

Rhi Refractories Holding Company....... A 302 655-6497
 Wilmington (G-19457)

MAIL-ORDER HOUSE, NEC

F D Hammond Enterprises Inc.............. F 302 424-8455
 Milford (G-7886)
Mommas Mountain LLC....................... G 410 236-6717
 Magnolia (G-6769)

MAIL-ORDER HOUSES: Computer Software

Kintyre Solutions Inc............................ G 888 636-0010
 Wilmington (G-17729)

MAIL-ORDER HOUSES: Food

2yum Inc.. G 626 420-4851
 Dover (G-1684)

MAIL-ORDER HOUSES: Jewelry

Joolala LLC.. E 302 444-0178
 Newark (G-11124)

MAILBOX RENTAL & RELATED SVCS

Dabvasan Inc... G 302 529-1100
 Wilmington (G-15766)
Global Shipping Center LLC................. F 302 798-4321
 Claymont (G-1164)
Mail Stop... G 302 947-4704
 Millsboro (G-8360)
Milton Mail Boxes................................. G 302 664-2623
 Milton (G-8672)
Postal Connections Inc......................... G 302 239-1129
 Hockessin (G-5349)
SC Ennis Incorporated.......................... F 302 629-8771
 Seaford (G-13384)
UPS Authorized Retailer....................... F 302 834-1600
 Bear (G-554)
UPS Store... G 302 907-0455
 Delmar (G-1651)
UPS Store... G 302 360-0264
 Rehoboth Beach (G-13002)

MAILING & MESSENGER SVCS

Doculogica Corp.................................... G 302 753-5944
 Wilmington (G-16113)
Itconnectus Inc..................................... G 302 531-1139
 Dover (G-2756)

MAILING MACHINES WHOLESALERS

B Williams Holding Corp...................... F 302 656-8596
 Wilmington (G-14704)

MAILING SVCS, NEC

D & B Printing and Mailing Inc............. G 302 838-7111
 Newark (G-10373)
Mailbiz... G 302 644-9035
 Rehoboth Beach (G-12844)
Sequoia Properties Inc......................... G 847 599-9099
 Bear (G-483)
Valassis Direct Mail Inc........................ C 302 861-3567
 Newark (G-12299)

MANAGEMENT CONSULTING SVCS: Administrative

Central Firm LLC................................... G 610 470-9836
 Wilmington (G-15308)
Fountain Resurgence LLC..................... F 302 518-5659
 Newark (G-10768)
MV Farinola Inc..................................... G 302 545-8492
 Wilmington (G-18497)
Owl Jumpstart LLC............................... F 302 467-2061
 Wilmington (G-18843)

MANAGEMENT CONSULTING SVCS: Automation & Robotics

Attabotics (us) Corp............................. E 403 454-0995
 Wilmington (G-14636)
Proautomated Inc................................. D 302 294-6121
 Newark (G-11756)

MANAGEMENT CONSULTING SVCS: Business

924 Inc... E 302 656-6100
 Hockessin (G-5109)
Accenture.. D 302 830-5800
 Wilmington (G-14218)
Acer Synergy Tech America Corp......... G 267 901-4569
 Wilmington (G-14230)
Aljstar Global Holdings Inc.................. F 302 565-5249
 Newark (G-9812)
Alpha Net Consulting LLC.................... G 302 737-2532
 Newark (G-9834)
American Air Lease Finance LLC.......... G 646 643-6303
 Wilmington (G-14424)
Bcg Holding Corp.................................. E 617 850-3700
 Wilmington (G-14795)
Bcg Inc.. G 302 875-6013
 Laurel (G-5468)
Black Lotus Ventures LLC..................... F 650 260-4684
 Dover (G-1944)
Casper Hosting LLC.............................. G 480 442-7112
 Lewes (G-5807)
Circus Associates Intelligence.............. E 757 663-7864
 Lewes (G-5820)
Dehui Solar Power Inc.......................... G 864 326-7936
 Dover (G-2208)
Elate Partners LLC................................ G 408 335-4582
 Dover (G-2429)
F D Hammond Enterprises Inc.............. F 302 424-8455
 Milford (G-7886)
Fiscal Associates.................................. F 302 894-0500
 Newark (G-10740)
Fort Hill Company Inc.......................... F 302 651-9223
 Wilmington (G-16696)
Fox Logistics LLC.................................. G 302 444-4750
 Wilmington (G-16712)
Gavinsolmonese.................................... F 302 655-8997
 Wilmington (G-16819)
Government Mrktplace Ltd Lblty......... E 302 297-9694
 Newark (G-10872)
Growth River Usa LLC.......................... G 617 905-5156
 Wilmington (G-16990)
J & O Business Inc................................ G 917 504-6062
 Newark (G-11066)
JMJ Assoc.. G 410 320-0890
 Lewes (G-6141)
Kfs Strategic MGT Svcs LLC.................. G 302 757-6631
 Newark (G-11167)
Luminous Energy Corporation............. G 866 475-7504
 Dover (G-2980)
Management Systems Improvement... G 860 478-7496
 Claymont (G-1229)

PRODUCTS & SERVICES SECTION

MANAGEMENT CONSULTING SVCS: Real Estate

Maven Workforce LLC.............................. G 551 214-8937
Newark (G-11356)

Modernthink LLC...................................... F 302 764-4477
Wilmington (G-18398)

Newton Management Holding Inc............ F 800 784-8714
Middletown (G-7401)

Oceanstar Technologies Inc..................... G 302 542-1900
Bear (G-404)

Onyx Business Alliance LLC.................... G 888 368-0402
Wilmington (G-18793)

Pioneer Natural Resources Co................. F 972 444-9001
Wilmington (G-19053)

Positioneering LLC................................... G 302 415-3200
Wilmington (G-19124)

Printify LLC... G 415 968-6351
Wilmington (G-19198)

Pyramid Group MGT Svcs Corp................ G 302 737-1770
Newark (G-11780)

Quanteam North America Inc................... G 929 262-8538
Newark (G-11792)

Raad360 LLC.. F 855 722-3360
Newark (G-11812)

Ready Alliance Group Inc......................... G 866 229-0927
Wilmington (G-19363)

Repurpose Global Inc............................... G 732 322-3839
Wilmington (G-19435)

Sabre International Newco Inc................. F 682 605-6223
Wilmington (G-19620)

Sfin 3 Inc... G 302 472-9276
Wilmington (G-19773)

Strategic Solutions Intl Inc........................ G 302 525-6313
Newark (G-12105)

Supply Chain Consultants Inc................... E 302 738-9215
Wilmington (G-20149)

Telecom Consulting Group Inc................. G 302 645-7400
Lewes (G-6548)

Vir Consultant LLC.................................... E 747 666-2169
Newark (G-12327)

Winner Group Management Inc............... F 302 571-5200
Wilmington (G-20861)

Yebo Alpha Inc... G 302 335-8887
Magnolia (G-6792)

Ziggyfli LLC.. F 302 503-5582
Dover (G-3901)

MANAGEMENT CONSULTING SVCS: Business Planning & Organizing

Altea Resources LLC................................ F 713 242-1460
Dover (G-1776)

Blue River Resources LLC........................ E 302 652-3150
Wilmington (G-14972)

Christina River Exchange LLC.................. G 302 691-2139
Wilmington (G-15416)

Countrmsres Asssment SEC Expr.......... G 302 322-9600
Middletown (G-7015)

Dailey Resources...................................... G 302 655-1811
Wilmington (G-15767)

Delaware Labor Resources Inc................ G 302 377-5752
Wilmington (G-15936)

Founding Principals LLC.......................... G 917 693-7453
Bear (G-233)

Geological Survey US Dept...................... F 302 734-2506
Dover (G-2572)

Human Resources.................................... G 302 573-3126
Wilmington (G-17230)

Living Resources Inc................................ G 302 227-6867
Rehoboth Beach (G-12835)

Resources For Human Dev....................... G 215 848-1947
Newark (G-11868)

Resources For Human Dev....................... G 215 951-0300
Wilmington (G-19440)

Resources For Human Dev Inc................. F 302 731-5283
Newark (G-11869)

Resources For Human Dev Inc................. F 302 691-7574
Wilmington (G-19441)

Wang Consultants Inc.............................. G 626 483-0265
Wilmington (G-20676)

MANAGEMENT CONSULTING SVCS: Construction Project

Alliance Bus Dev Concepts LLC............... F 803 814-4004
Clayton (G-1348)

Austin Alliance Electric Inc....................... E 843 297-8078
Wilmington (G-14647)

Brs Consulting Inc.................................... G 302 786-2326
Harrington (G-4741)

Emory Hill & Company.............................. D 302 322-4400
New Castle (G-9090)

Mountain Consulting Inc.......................... E 302 744-9875
Dover (G-3128)

Perennial Dev & Cnstr Corp..................... E 855 625-0046
Wilmington (G-18971)

Vcg LLC... G 302 336-8151
Dover (G-3777)

MANAGEMENT CONSULTING SVCS: Corporation Organizing

Agents and Corporations Inc................... G 302 575-0877
Wilmington (G-14312)

Company Corporation.............................. E 302 636-5440
Wilmington (G-15566)

Delaware Intercorp Inc............................. G 302 266-9367
Wilmington (G-15934)

Phs Corporate Services Inc..................... G 302 571-1128
Wilmington (G-19029)

Yacht Delaware Registry Ltd.................... F 302 477-9800
Wilmington (G-20921)

MANAGEMENT CONSULTING SVCS: Food & Beverage

Chopin Imports Ltd.................................. F 612 226-9875
Wilmington (G-15391)

Haccp Navigator LLC............................... G 302 531-7922
Lincoln (G-6673)

MANAGEMENT CONSULTING SVCS: General

Media Fusion US LLC............................... G 256 532-3874
Newark (G-11372)

Pgi Commercial LLC................................ G 800 686-8134
Wilmington (G-19006)

Siriusiq Mobile LLC.................................. F 888 414-2047
Newark (G-12015)

Xcutivescom Inc....................................... E 888 245-9996
Dover (G-3880)

MANAGEMENT CONSULTING SVCS: Hospital & Health

Atlantic H&S Consulting.......................... G 302 222-5526
Magnolia (G-6719)

Eamo Health LLC..................................... G 302 565-7528
Wilmington (G-16247)

Ecsquared Inc... G 302 750-8554
Newark (G-10607)

Health Care Practice MGT....................... E 302 633-5840
Wilmington (G-17096)

Metropolitan Revenue Assoc LLC........... G 302 449-7490
New Castle (G-9362)

Sweat Social LLC..................................... G 504 510-1973
Dover (G-3631)

Tipton Communications Group................ F 302 454-7901
Newark (G-12198)

MANAGEMENT CONSULTING SVCS: Industrial & Labor

Red Clay Inc... G 302 239-2018
Hockessin (G-5360)

MANAGEMENT CONSULTING SVCS: Industry Specialist

Adjuvant Research Services Inc.............. F 302 737-5513
Newark (G-9766)

Express Legal Documents LLC............... G 212 710-1374
Wilmington (G-16509)

Tk Blier Incorporated............................... E 207 760-7076
Camden (G-897)

MANAGEMENT CONSULTING SVCS: Information Systems

Grand Designs It Solutions LLC.............. G 302 299-3500
Newark (G-10879)

It Tigers LLC.. G 732 898-2793
Lewes (G-6132)

Kintyre Solutions Inc................................ G 888 636-0010
Wilmington (G-17729)

Korsgy Technologies LLC......................... G 302 504-6201
Wilmington (G-17748)

Lynkmax LLC.. G 302 573-3568
Wilmington (G-18049)

Mentor Consultants Inc........................... G 610 566-4004
Wilmington (G-18273)

Milieux LLC... G 302 770-5868
Wilmington (G-18356)

Millennial Informatics LLC....................... G 302 446-3800
Camden (G-875)

Platformavr Inc... G 302 330-8980
Dover (G-3328)

Selection Solutions Inc............................ G 800 600-6605
Wilmington (G-19743)

Vpsie Inc... F 844 468-7743
Wilmington (G-20655)

MANAGEMENT CONSULTING SVCS: Manufacturing

Delaware Mfg EXT Partnr Inc................... G 302 283-3131
Newark (G-10460)

Workfar Inc... F 650 800-3990
Dover (G-3871)

MANAGEMENT CONSULTING SVCS: Programmed Instruction

Code Guide LLC....................................... G 530 424-8919
Wilmington (G-15514)

Decennium Management Group.............. G 302 600-3644
Dover (G-2205)

Jack Donovan... G 410 715-0504
Millsboro (G-8324)

MANAGEMENT CONSULTING SVCS: Quality Assurance

Advanced Systems Inc............................. G 302 368-1211
Newark (G-9782)

Genovesius Solutia Llc............................ G 302 252-7506
Hockessin (G-5221)

MANAGEMENT CONSULTING SVCS: Real Estate

Blue Horizon Properties LLC................... G 347 731-5570
Magnolia (G-6721)

Charles Graef Inc..................................... G 302 239-7924
Montchanin (G-8735)

MANAGEMENT CONSULTING SVCS: Real Estate

Divinity Assets LLC .... G 323 508-4130
  Dover (G-2309)
Harvey Hanna & Associates Inc .... G 302 323-9300
  Newport (G-12454)
Hybrid Property LLC .... F 302 289-6226
  Wilmington (G-17243)
Jones Property Company .... G 302 213-2695
  Wilmington (G-17575)
Lauri Brockson .... G 302 383-0147
  Newark (G-11228)
Pabian Ventures LLC .... G 302 762-1992
  Wilmington (G-18856)
Prime Time Properties LLC .... G 302 763-6050
  Bear (G-438)
Wartrude Services Inc .... G 302 213-3944
  Wilmington (G-20680)

MANAGEMENT CONSULTING SVCS: Restaurant & Food

Bnl Consulting LLC .... G 302 857-1057
  Dover (G-1955)
De Catering Inc .... E 302 607-7200
  Wilmington (G-15837)
Five Star Home Delivery LLC .... F 302 213-3535
  Lewes (G-6002)

MANAGEMENT CONSULTING SVCS: Training & Development

280 Group LLC .... E 408 834-7518
  Dover (G-1683)
Blue Level Inc .... G 337 623-4442
  Newark (G-10061)
Dale Carnegie Training .... G 302 368-7292
  Newark (G-10383)
David G Major Associates Inc .... G 703 642-7450
  Millsboro (G-8255)
Enhanced Corporate Prfmce LLC .... G 302 545-8541
  Newark (G-10648)
Learning Core LLC .... E 628 600-9644
  Lewes (G-6185)
Momentum Management Group Inc .... G 302 477-9730
  Wilmington (G-18406)
Performance Based Results .... G 302 478-4443
  Talleyville (G-13945)
Stephen A Covey .... G 302 478-0215
  Wilmington (G-20057)
Storyiq Inc .... F 718 801-8556
  Wilmington (G-20089)
Visio Group International Corp .... G 302 485-0378
  Wilmington (G-20637)

MANAGEMENT CONSULTING SVCS: Transportation

Base Carriers LLC .... G 215 559-1132
  Wilmington (G-14771)
Can Services LLC .... G 212 920-9348
  Newark (G-10127)
Delaware Last Mile Lgstics DLM .... G 302 407-1415
  Historic New Castle (G-4971)
Rastan Enterprises LLC .... G 443 691-0232
  Middletown (G-7503)
Roll Out Transit LLC .... G 800 233-1680
  Hockessin (G-5371)
Simpler Logistics LLC .... G 800 619-8321
  Wilmington (G-19836)
Transporttee Inc .... E 302 330-8912
  Dover (G-3714)

MANAGEMENT SERVICES

1995 Property Management Inc .... G 302 745-1187
  Seaford (G-13042)
Agile 1 .... F 302 791-6900
  Wilmington (G-14315)
Allens Termite & Pest Mgmt .... G 302 698-1496
  Camden Wyoming (G-911)
AMC - Commercial Inc .... G 302 229-0051
  Claymont (G-1031)
Ameken Network Group Inc .... F 302 545-3472
  Claymont (G-1032)
Amschel Capital LLC .... F 302 298-1199
  Claymont (G-1035)
Amschel Capital LLC .... F 302 298-1199
  Claymont (G-1036)
Apartment Communities Corp .... G 302 656-7781
  Wilmington (G-14503)
Arbor Management Alarm .... G 302 856-2876
  Georgetown (G-4212)
Atlantic Management .... G 302 222-3919
  Rehoboth Beach (G-12614)
Atlantic Realty Management LLC .... G 302 875-9571
  Smyrna (G-13654)
Balfour Beatty LLC .... G 302 573-3873
  Wilmington (G-14721)
Bancroft Vlant Joint Ventr LLC .... G 717 553-0165
  Wilmington (G-14741)
Baynard Property MGT LLC .... G 302 225-3350
  Wilmington (G-14790)
Bayshore Records MGT LLC .... G 302 731-4477
  Newark (G-9996)
Bcg Management LLC .... F 302 278-7677
  Rehoboth Beach (G-12625)
Be Beautiful Bossy .... G 888 558-9047
  Wilmington (G-14799)
Beachview Mgmt Inc .... G 302 227-3280
  Lewes (G-5744)
Beacon Wealth Management LLC .... G 302 383-2671
  Wilmington (G-14801)
Brantngham Crroll Holdings Inc .... G 724 266-0400
  Wilmington (G-15095)
Bridge Enterprises LLC .... E 302 750-0828
  Wilmington (G-15106)
Brisbie LLC .... F 650 690-1433
  Wilmington (G-15118)
C and L Bradford and Assoc .... G 302 529-8566
  Wilmington (G-15174)
Cafe Management Associates .... G 302 655-4959
  Wilmington (G-15190)
Cashion Media Management .... G 302 674-8321
  Dover (G-2036)
Chesapeake Fire Systems LLC .... F 302 732-6006
  Frankford (G-4086)
Chesapeake Management Co LLC .... E 302 732-6006
  Frankford (G-4088)
Cogir Management USA Inc .... G 916 400-3985
  Newark (G-10270)
Colonial East Management .... G 302 644-6500
  Rehoboth Beach (G-12692)
Columbus Inn Management I .... G 302 429-8700
  Wilmington (G-15541)
Commonwealth Partners MGT LLC .... F 302 223-5941
  Wilmington (G-15555)
Connor Management LLC .... G 302 539-1678
  Ocean View (G-12497)
Conway Management Group .... G 302 323-9522
  New Castle (G-8971)
Credit Concierge LLC .... E 877 860-9877
  Wilmington (G-15697)
Crescent Management Inc .... G 302 449-4560
  Wilmington (G-15700)
Dalou Property Management .... F 866 575-9387
  Wilmington (G-15771)

Davin Management Group LLC .... F 302 367-6563
  Bear (G-135)
Ddesk LLC .... G 302 407-1558
  Wilmington (G-15833)
Delaware Innovation Space Inc .... G 302 695-2201
  Wilmington (G-15933)
Dks Sports Development LLC .... G 302 222-6184
  Newark (G-10541)
Dnrec Air Waste Management .... G 302 739-9406
  Dover (G-2315)
Dover Parks Management LLC .... G 302 326-1540
  New Castle (G-9060)
Eastern Christian Management .... G 302 633-1421
  Wilmington (G-16256)
El Legacy LLC .... G 601 790-0636
  Dover (G-2428)
Elm Properties Inc .... G 302 762-3757
  Wilmington (G-16375)
Empire Realty Management Inc .... G 302 731-0784
  Newark (G-10643)
Enabld Technologies Inc .... F 917 340-1606
  Wilmington (G-16403)
Eprintit Usa Inc .... F 613 299-7105
  Wilmington (G-16452)
Erickson Management .... G 302 235-0855
  Newark (G-10664)
Evidence Management Center .... G 302 691-8944
  Wilmington (G-16492)
F S Property Management .... G 302 644-4403
  Lewes (G-5983)
Facilities Mgmt Div .... G 302 856-5817
  Georgetown (G-4312)
Faith Family Management Co .... G 302 832-5936
  Newark (G-10704)
Fci of Delmarva LLC .... G 443 614-1794
  Ocean View (G-12511)
First State Management LLC .... G 302 648-4600
  Georgetown (G-4323)
Fitness Management Group Inc .... G 302 218-5644
  Newark (G-10741)
Food Works Management LLC .... G 302 397-3000
  Newark (G-10755)
Four Seasons Property Manageme .... G 302 275-4816
  New Castle (G-9142)
Geodesic Management LLC .... G 302 737-2151
  Newark (G-10822)
Harvey Development Co .... E 302 323-9300
  New Castle (G-9201)
Highwater Management Kent LLC .... G 302 245-7570
  Frederica (G-4171)
Highwater MGT Sussex LLC .... G 302 245-7570
  Georgetown (G-4356)
Hlh Construction MGT Svcs Inc .... F 302 654-7508
  Wilmington (G-17157)
Howard Management Group I .... G 302 562-5051
  Newark (G-10980)
Hydrological Solutions .... G 302 841-4444
  Milton (G-8642)
INIIWI LLC .... G 866 312-4536
  Wilmington (G-17340)
Inside & Out Property MGT LLC .... G 302 632-4467
  Hartly (G-4879)
J Lotter Management .... G 302 308-3939
  Claymont (G-1192)
J P Morgan Services Inc .... C 302 634-1000
  Newark (G-11075)
J&D Management .... G 302 239-2489
  Hockessin (G-5255)
Lc Management .... F 302 439-3523
  Claymont (G-1213)
Lemon Fin- Vest Inc .... F 905 442-8480
  Newark (G-11244)

PRODUCTS & SERVICES SECTION

MANAGEMENT SVCS: Business

Mahle Industrial Thermal Syste............ G 915 612-1611
Wilmington *(G-18087)*

Marta Group.. G 302 737-2008
Newark *(G-11340)*

McKee Group Mckee Management........ G 302 449-0778
Middletown *(G-7334)*

McNeil and Fmly MGT Group LLC......... F 302 830-3267
Wilmington *(G-18236)*

Medical Billing Management................... G 302 239-2235
Wilmington *(G-18248)*

Merman Management Inc....................... G 302 644-6990
Lewes *(G-6266)*

Merman Management Inc....................... G 302 456-9904
Wilmington *(G-18286)*

Michael Spradley..................................... G 404 475-2647
Wilmington *(G-18325)*

Mid Atlantic Grand Prix LLC.................... G 302 656-5278
New Castle *(G-9365)*

Mid-Lantic Enterprises Inc...................... G 302 436-2772
Selbyville *(G-13572)*

Mk Management Group LLC.................. G 302 543-4414
Wilmington *(G-18391)*

Mosaic.. D 302 456-5995
Newark *(G-11455)*

Multifmily MGT Philadelphia LLC........... G 302 322-8953
Newark *(G-11471)*

Nb Retail Management Inc..................... G 302 230-3065
Newark *(G-11495)*

Ne Care Management Service LLC....... G 302 501-6449
Wilmington *(G-18567)*

Omg Mgmt LLC....................................... G 609 221-4572
Wilmington *(G-18766)*

Pats Management.................................... D 302 322-3442
New Castle *(G-9460)*

Patterson 3 Inv Group LLC..................... G 302 469-4783
Dover *(G-3283)*

Patterson-Schwartz & Assoc Inc............ F 302 234-3606
Hockessin *(G-5333)*

Pcmb LLC.. G 302 482-1360
Wilmington *(G-18935)*

Power Brokers Holdings LLC................. G 800 901-8483
Hockessin *(G-5350)*

Premier Property & Pool MGT................ G 302 357-6321
Middletown *(G-7465)*

Property Maintenance MGT.................... G 302 883-1441
Smyrna *(G-13858)*

Prosperity Unlimited Ente....................... G 302 379-2494
Middletown *(G-7476)*

Ptci Management..................................... G 302 538-6996
Dover *(G-3391)*

Purebread.. G 302 528-5591
Newark *(G-11774)*

Pyramid Group MGT Svcs Co................ G 302 355-1760
New Castle *(G-9503)*

R & L Property Management LLC.......... G 267 825-3570
Middletown *(G-7494)*

Roberts Property MGT LLC.................... G 302 537-5371
Bethany Beach *(G-637)*

Rosemont Wealth Management.............. G 302 875-8300
Laurel *(G-5595)*

S A Atramco... G 302 310-3350
Wilmington *(G-19606)*

Saggio Management Group Inc.............. G 302 659-6560
Smyrna *(G-13876)*

Saggio Management Group Inc.............. F 302 696-2036
Middletown *(G-7535)*

Service General Corporation.................. F 302 218-4279
Georgetown *(G-4507)*

Severn Trent Inc...................................... F 302 427-5990
Wilmington *(G-19771)*

Six Plus Inc.. G 302 652-3296
Wilmington *(G-19848)*

Smart Printing MGT LLC......................... G 855 549-4900
Newark *(G-12035)*

SNK Enterprises Inc................................ G 443 783-5717
Laurel *(G-5601)*

Soules Management Inc......................... G 302 335-1980
Magnolia *(G-6783)*

Southern Rivers Management LLC........ G 302 674-4089
Dover *(G-3591)*

St Anthonys Housing Mgt Corp.............. G 302 421-3756
Wilmington *(G-19991)*

Sunset Property Management................ G 410 202-1679
Wilmington *(G-20135)*

Supply Chain Mgmt Inc........................... E 302 467-2014
Wilmington *(G-20150)*

Syngenta Corporation............................. E 302 425-2000
Wilmington *(G-20189)*

Tgx Holdings LLC................................... C 212 260-6300
Wilmington *(G-20289)*

Thomson Reuters (grc) Inc..................... G 212 227-7357
Wilmington *(G-20314)*

Tpw Management LLC............................ F 302 227-7878
Lewes *(G-6575)*

Twin Hearts Management LLC............... G 302 777-5700
Dover *(G-3736)*

Ubium Group... A 801 487-5000
Wilmington *(G-20492)*

Urpayroll Inc.. G 323 922-3829
Wilmington *(G-20546)*

Vest Management Inc............................. G 302 856-3100
Georgetown *(G-4569)*

VIP Systems Inc...................................... G 786 615-8622
Wilmington *(G-20628)*

We Manage Your Site Inc....................... G 916 586-7724
Newark *(G-12351)*

Wh &C Management Services Inc......... G 302 225-3000
Wilmington *(G-20752)*

Whispering Meadows LLC..................... G 302 698-1073
Dover *(G-3844)*

Winifred Ellen Erbe................................. G 302 541-0889
Frankford *(G-4162)*

MANAGEMENT SVCS: Administrative

Advance Central Services Inc................ F 302 830-9732
Wilmington *(G-14264)*

Crystal Holdings Inc............................... D 302 421-5700
Wilmington *(G-15720)*

El Management Group LLC.................... G 844 263-3335
Middletown *(G-7088)*

Hyas US Inc... G 877 572-6446
Wilmington *(G-17242)*

Moore Staffing Agency LLC................... G 215 300-2770
Bear *(G-379)*

Open Lanes-Solutions LLC.................... F 888 410-4207
Wilmington *(G-18795)*

MANAGEMENT SVCS: Business

AGS Royalty Management LLC.............. G 888 292-6995
Dover *(G-1748)*

Anesthesiology & Pain MGT................... G 302 235-8074
Newark *(G-9867)*

Antebellum Hospitality Inc...................... G 302 436-4375
Selbyville *(G-13463)*

Ardexo Inc... G 855 617-7500
Dover *(G-1811)*

Brownstone LLC...................................... G 302 300-4370
Historic New Castle *(G-4946)*

Business Integration Solution................ G 302 355-3512
Newark *(G-10107)*

Case Management Services.................. G 302 354-3711
Wilmington *(G-15264)*

Censys Inc... G 248 629-0125
Camden *(G-805)*

Ceo-Hqcom LLC...................................... G 302 883-8555
Hockessin *(G-5155)*

Cht Holdings LLC.................................... G 954 864-2008
Lewes *(G-5819)*

Cloud Services Solutions Inc................. E 888 335-3132
Wilmington *(G-15491)*

Cobra Investments MGT Inc................... E 302 691-6333
Wilmington *(G-15512)*

Dis Management...................................... G 302 543-4481
Wilmington *(G-16083)*

Easydmarc Inc... G 888 563-5277
Middletown *(G-7078)*

Hiatus Business Solutions Inc............... G 302 883-7324
Smyrna *(G-13759)*

Highmarks Inc... G 302 421-3000
Wilmington *(G-17145)*

J Amoako Operation LLC....................... G 302 246-1346
Wilmington *(G-17452)*

Jazminerenae.. F 302 784-4710
Wilmington *(G-17503)*

Katalist LLC... G 302 502-0091
Wilmington *(G-17659)*

Keystate Corporate MGT LLC................ F 302 425-5158
Wilmington *(G-17706)*

L C K Managment Inc............................. G 609 820-2980
Claymont *(G-1210)*

Lawrence Kennedy.................................. F 302 533-5880
Newark *(G-11234)*

Lifetour Solutions LLC............................ F 215 964-5000
Wilmington *(G-17906)*

M C Tek LLC.. G 302 644-9695
Rehoboth Beach *(G-12842)*

Mat Site Management LLC..................... G 302 397-8561
Wilmington *(G-18189)*

Moorway Painting Management............. G 302 764-5002
Wilmington *(G-18439)*

Natural House Inc.................................... F 302 218-0338
Newark *(G-11493)*

Oakford Acquisitions LLC...................... G 302 406-1535
Wilmington *(G-18727)*

Orion Group LLC..................................... G 302 357-9137
Wilmington *(G-18821)*

Pettinaro Management LLC.................... G 302 832-8823
Newark *(G-11676)*

Ppmi Inc... F 302 584-1972
Bear *(G-432)*

Pro Pest Management of De Inc............ G 302 994-2847
Wilmington *(G-19201)*

Prorank Business Solutions LLC........... F 302 256-0642
Wilmington *(G-19232)*

Registred Agnts Legal Svcs LLC........... G 302 427-6970
Wilmington *(G-19409)*

Sovereign Property MGT LLC................ G 302 994-2505
Wilmington *(G-19944)*

Speech Ladder Inc.................................. G 770 355-0719
Townsend *(G-14069)*

Strands Prprty Prservation LLC............. G 302 381-9792
Millsboro *(G-8469)*

Tdc Partners Ltd..................................... G 302 827-2137
Lewes *(G-6544)*

Teksolv Usd Inc....................................... F 302 738-1050
Newark *(G-12175)*

Thepowermba Inc.................................... G 917 508-5535
Newark *(G-12188)*

Timet Finance Management Co.............. F 302 472-9277
Wilmington *(G-20329)*

Tm Management LLC.............................. G 302 654-4940
Wilmington *(G-20339)*

Totaltranslogistics LLC.......................... G 302 325-4245
New Castle *(G-9629)*

Unique Business Solutions.................... G 302 750-0930
Bear *(G-548)*

Employee Codes: A=Over 500 employees, B=251-500
C=101-250, D=51-100, E=20-50, F=10-19, G=1-9

MANAGEMENT SVCS: Business

Volumetric Format Association .... G 760 803-8720
Dover *(G-3809)*

Wellington Management Group .... G 215 569-8900
Wilmington *(G-20719)*

MANAGEMENT SVCS: Construction

Adams Construction & Managemen ... G 302 856-2022
Georgetown *(G-4198)*

Agmaf Inc .... E 302 508-6991
Wilmington *(G-14321)*

Bpgs Construction LLC .... D 302 691-2111
Wilmington *(G-15029)*

Brandywine Contractors Inc .... G 302 325-2700
New Castle *(G-8886)*

Buck Simpers Archt + Assoc Inc .... F 302 658-9300
Wilmington *(G-15141)*

C & S Consultants Inc .... G 302 236-5211
Milford *(G-7810)*

Construction MGT Svcs Inc .... A 302 478-4200
Wilmington *(G-15612)*

Craftsman Cbntry Woodworks Inc .... G 302 841-5274
Selbyville *(G-13507)*

Danella Line Services Co Inc .... D 302 893-1253
Dover *(G-2190)*

Earthship LLC .... G 239 850-8682
Bear *(G-188)*

First State Cnstr MGT LLC .... G 302 257-5438
Newark *(G-10729)*

Lenape Builders Inc .... F 302 376-3971
Smyrna *(G-13801)*

Lighthouse Construction Inc .... F 302 677-1965
Magnolia *(G-6759)*

Locker Construction Inc .... G 302 239-2859
Newark *(G-11278)*

Montchanin Design Group Inc .... E 302 652-3008
Wilmington *(G-18421)*

Omniway Corporation .... F 302 738-5076
Newark *(G-11586)*

Palmetto MGT & Engrg LLC .... F 302 993-2766
Wilmington *(G-18868)*

Providence At Heritage Sh .... G 302 337-1040
Bridgeville *(G-756)*

Unity Construction Inc .... F 302 998-0531
Wilmington *(G-20531)*

Vanguard Construction MGT .... G 302 462-2161
Georgetown *(G-4567)*

Wohlsen Construction Company .... F 302 324-9900
Wilmington *(G-20874)*

MANAGEMENT SVCS: Hotel Or Motel

Amity Lodges Ltd .... E 833 462-6489
Wilmington *(G-14459)*

Atlantic Management Ltd .... F 302 645-9511
Rehoboth Beach *(G-12615)*

Axia Management .... F 302 674-2200
Dover *(G-1858)*

Eagle Hospitality Group LLC .... G 302 678-8388
Dover *(G-2401)*

Everest Hotel Group LLC .... F 213 272-0088
Camden *(G-832)*

MANAGEMENT SVCS: Nursing & Personal Care Facility

Eom Healthcare Group LLC .... E 917 750-5089
Dover *(G-2453)*

MANAGEMENT SVCS: Restaurant

Aark Network Inc .... G 302 399-3945
Newark *(G-9734)*

Ashby Management Corporation .... G 302 894-1200
Newark *(G-9920)*

Cactus Annies Restaurant & Bar .... F 302 655-9004
Wilmington *(G-15184)*

Sodel Concepts II LLC .... C 302 228-3786
Rehoboth Beach *(G-12965)*

MANPOWER POOLS

Fritz Staffing Group LLC .... F 844 581-5873
Historic New Castle *(G-4993)*

MANPOWER TRAINING

Careeronestop Dover One Stop .... G 302 739-5473
Dover *(G-2030)*

MANUFACTURING INDUSTRIES, NEC

American Industries LLC .... G 302 585-0129
Milton *(G-8559)*

Bambu Candles LLC .... G 917 903-2563
Newark *(G-9977)*

Bell Manufacturing Company Inc .... G 302 703-2684
Lewes *(G-5754)*

Bleu Safe Inc .... G 619 416-6166
Wilmington *(G-14956)*

Bold Industries LLC .... G 302 858-7237
Frankford *(G-4074)*

CT Innovations LLC .... G 209 559-3595
Dover *(G-2167)*

Eastern Shore Lite Industries .... G 302 653-8687
Clayton *(G-1365)*

Epix Industries Inc .... G 302 550-9007
Lewes *(G-5968)*

Footcare Technologies Inc .... G 704 301-6966
Milton *(G-8625)*

Gardner Industries Inc .... G 302 448-9195
Seaford *(G-13195)*

Good Manufacturing Practices .... G 302 222-6808
Dover *(G-2604)*

Gr Group Holdings Inc .... G 416 618-2676
Dover *(G-2614)*

Ice Cremee Creations .... G 516 450-2144
Camden *(G-854)*

Invisible Hand Labs LLC .... G 434 989-9642
Wilmington *(G-17408)*

Island Genius LLC .... G 888 529-5506
Wilmington *(G-17427)*

J M Industries .... G 302 893-0363
Hockessin *(G-5254)*

Jjs Industries LP .... G 302 690-2957
Wilmington *(G-17553)*

Kangsters Inc .... G 716 563-8225
Wilmington *(G-17647)*

Kershaw Industries .... G 302 464-1051
Middletown *(G-7268)*

Laytons Umbrellas .... G 302 249-1958
Laurel *(G-5553)*

Macknyfe Specialties .... G 302 239-4904
Hockessin *(G-5289)*

Maf Industries .... G 302 249-1254
Seaford *(G-13271)*

Manufactured Housing .... G 302 744-2383
Dover *(G-3012)*

Martial Industries LLC .... G 302 983-5742
Middletown *(G-7330)*

Maws Tails Mfg .... G 302 740-7664
Milton *(G-8663)*

Michael J Munroe .... G 804 240-7188
Magnolia *(G-6765)*

MMR Industries Inc .... G 302 999-9561
Wilmington *(G-18392)*

Mnr Industries LLC .... G 443 485-6213
Dover *(G-3108)*

National Industries For The Bl .... G 302 477-0860
Wilmington *(G-18544)*

Northernsigs Mfg LLC .... G 302 383-9270
Wilmington *(G-18686)*

Oski Industries .... G 646 369-5799
New Castle *(G-9438)*

PHM Springboard Bidco Inc .... G 919 678-7700
Wilmington *(G-19023)*

R M Bell Industries Inc .... G 302 542-3747
Lewes *(G-6404)*

Rowe Industries Inc .... G 443 458-5569
Georgetown *(G-4495)*

S&D Industries LLC .... G 703 801-3643
Wilmington *(G-19614)*

Shalex Industries US Corp .... G 323 540-5586
Middletown *(G-7558)*

Syf Industries .... G 302 384-6214
Wilmington *(G-20178)*

Tdock Services & Holding Inc .... G 305 924-3653
Dover *(G-3659)*

Think66 LLC .... G 949 326-8188
Wilmington *(G-20300)*

Tributarymarinecom LLC .... G 443 553-9485
New Castle *(G-9638)*

US Green Battery Inc .... G 347 723-5963
New Castle *(G-9665)*

Uzin Utz Manufacturing N Amer .... F 336 456-4624
Dover *(G-3768)*

Vention Inc US .... G 514 222-0380
Wilmington *(G-20581)*

Westmor Industries .... G 302 956-0243
Bridgeville *(G-783)*

Westmor Industries .... G 302 398-3253
Harrington *(G-4846)*

Whet Industries Inc .... G 302 236-2182
Newark *(G-12365)*

Wlg Equity Inc .... E 302 738-4880
Newark *(G-12391)*

MARBLE, BUILDING: Cut & Shaped

Stone Express .... G 302 376-8876
Middletown *(G-7600)*

MARINAS

Bayshore Inc .... G 302 539-7200
Ocean View *(G-12470)*

Chester Marina LLC .... G 302 829-8218
Bethany Beach *(G-590)*

Delaware Bay Launch Service .... F 302 422-7604
Milford *(G-7853)*

Freedom Boat Club Delaware .... G 302 219-3549
Lewes *(G-6014)*

Jack Hickman Real Estate .... F 302 539-8000
Bethany Beach *(G-611)*

Jamc LLC .... G 410 639-2224
Millsboro *(G-8327)*

Love Creek Marina MBL Hm Site .... F 302 448-6492
Lewes *(G-6225)*

LP Smoked LLC .... G 302 379-3059
Wilmington *(G-18016)*

Misty Rivers Ltd .... G 315 415-2826
Dover *(G-3102)*

South Shore Provisions LLC .... G 443 614-2442
Selbyville *(G-13607)*

Summit North Marina .... F 302 836-1800
Bear *(G-517)*

Summit North Marina LLC .... F 302 836-1800
Bear *(G-518)*

MARINE CARGO HANDLING SVCS

Advance Marine LLC .... G 302 656-2111
Wilmington *(G-14268)*

Iap Holding LLC .... G 302 394-9795
Wilmington *(G-17254)*

MARINE SPLYS WHOLESALERS

Eastern Group Inc............................... E 302 737-6603
Newark (G-10594)

MARKETS: Meat & fish

Lewes Fishhouse & Produce Inc............ E 302 827-4074
Lewes (G-6196)

MARKING DEVICES

Franklin Rubber Stamp Co Inc................ G 302 654-8841
Wilmington (G-16730)

MEAT & FISH MARKETS: Seafood

Febys Fishery Inc................................ E 302 998-9501
Wilmington (G-16566)

Meltrone Inc...................................... F 302 998-3457
Wilmington (G-18268)

Seafood City Inc................................. G 302 284-8486
Felton (G-4024)

MEAT MARKETS

Haass Family Butcher Shop................... G 302 734-5447
Dover (G-2643)

Jabez Corp....................................... F 302 475-7600
Wilmington (G-17470)

MEAT PRDTS: Boxed Beef, From Slaughtered Meat

Cbbc Opco LLC................................. G 863 967-0636
Wilmington (G-15284)

MEAT PRDTS: Prepared Beef Prdts From Purchased Beef

New B & M Meats Inc........................... F 302 655-5331
Wilmington (G-18607)

MEAT PRDTS: Sausages, From Purchased Meat

Kirby & Holloway Provisions Co.............. E 302 398-3705
Harrington (G-4794)

MEAT PRDTS: Scrapple, From Purchased Meat

Ralph and Paul Adams Inc..................... B 800 338-4727
Bridgeville (G-760)

MEAT PRDTS: Snack Sticks, Incl Jerky, From Purchased Meat

Rehoboth House of Jerky....................... G 215 272-4217
Rehoboth Beach (G-12928)

MEDICAL & HOSPITAL EQPT WHOLESALERS

Dienay Distribution Corp....................... G 732 766-0814
Middletown (G-7060)

Medtix LLC...................................... G 302 736-0172
Dover (G-3054)

Motion Composites Corp....................... F 302 266-8200
Newark (G-11459)

Nestal Mdsphere Consulting LLC............. G 302 404-6506
Wilmington (G-18588)

Platinum World LLC............................ G 302 321-5040
Dover (G-3331)

Synergy Medical USA Inc...................... G 302 444-0163
Newark (G-12147)

Tru American Enterprises LLC............... G 801 404-1124
Middletown (G-7662)

World Wide Trading Brokers................... G 302 368-7041
Newark (G-12410)

MEDICAL & SURGICAL SPLYS: Dressings, Surgical

Johnson & Johnson.............................. E 302 652-3840
Wilmington (G-17570)

MEDICAL & SURGICAL SPLYS: Limbs, Artificial

Harry J Lawall & Son Inc....................... G 302 429-7630
Wilmington (G-17064)

MEDICAL & SURGICAL SPLYS: Orthopedic Appliances

Zimmer US Inc................................... F 617 272-0062
Camden Wyoming (G-987)

MEDICAL & SURGICAL SPLYS: Personal Safety Eqpt

Advanced Defense Technology................ C 888 298-5775
Wilmington (G-14273)

Dads Workwear Inc............................. G 302 663-0068
Laurel (G-5491)

Elgood Solutions Inc............................ G 610 420-7207
Camden (G-829)

Ilc Dover LP...................................... B 302 335-3911
Frederica (G-4174)

Jarel Industries LLC........................... G 336 782-0697
Camden (G-859)

New Ilc Dover Inc............................... B 302 335-3911
Frederica (G-4179)

MEDICAL & SURGICAL SPLYS: Prosthetic Appliances

Choy Wilson Cdgn................................ G 302 424-4141
Milford (G-7826)

Marins Med LLC................................ G 302 245-4596
Georgetown (G-4413)

MEDICAL CENTERS

Abby Medical Center............................ G 302 999-0003
Newark (G-9738)

Advoserv Inc..................................... D 302 365-8050
Wilmington (G-14292)

Allergy Associates PA........................... G 302 834-3401
Newark (G-9823)

Angelo Joseph Chiari Rph...................... G 302 239-5949
Hockessin (G-5125)

Brandywine Cnseling Cmnty Svcs............ G 302 856-4700
Milford (G-7803)

Caring Minds Medical Center.................. G 267 243-9102
Middletown (G-6960)

Caring Minds Medical Ctr LLC................ G 302 516-7936
Wilmington (G-15250)

Cerebral Med Group A Prof Corp............. D 415 403-2156
Claymont (G-1081)

Christncare Ctr For Cmprhnsive.............. D 302 320-9108
Wilmington (G-15419)

Christncare Prmry Care Fmly MD............. F 302 477-3300
Wilmington (G-15421)

Coastal Pain Care Physicians PA............. G 302 644-8330
Lewes (G-5845)

Coastline Medical Ctr Milford.................. F 302 265-2893
Milford (G-7838)

Concord Med Spine & Pain Ctr................ F 302 652-1107
Wilmington (G-15583)

Crestview Medical Center...................... G 302 762-4545
Wilmington (G-15701)

Family Medical Centre PA...................... F 302 678-0510
Dover (G-2485)

Frensenius Medical Ctr......................... F 302 762-2903
Wilmington (G-16748)

Gadde & Chirra Inc.............................. F 302 384-6384
Wilmington (G-16790)

Gilpin Medical Center........................... G 302 623-4250
Wilmington (G-16863)

Got A Doc - Walk In Med Ctr................... G 302 947-4111
Millsboro (G-8303)

Middletown Family Medicine Ctr.............. F 302 449-3030
Middletown (G-7352)

Mosiac of Delaware.............................. G 302 653-8889
Smyrna (G-13828)

Rescue Surgical Solutions LLC................ G 302 722-5877
Newark (G-11862)

Riverview Medical Center...................... F 302 396-1204
Seaford (G-13375)

Surgical Assoc of Newark....................... G 302 737-4990
Newark (G-12133)

Surgical Focus................................... G 215 518-2138
Middletown (G-7613)

Toshiko N Reckner Rph......................... G 302 697-6407
Dover (G-3705)

Trinity Medical Center PA....................... G 302 846-0618
Delmar (G-1646)

VA Medical Ctr Wilmington De................. G 302 563-6024
Middletown (G-7680)

Veterans Health Administration............... G 302 994-1660
Wilmington (G-20599)

MEDICAL HELP SVCS

County of Sussex................................ F 302 854-5050
Georgetown (G-4270)

Eden Hill Express Care LLC................... G 302 674-1999
Dover (G-2420)

Maxim Healthcare Services Inc................ B 302 478-3434
Wilmington (G-18205)

MEDICAL SUNDRIES: Rubber

LRC North America Inc......................... E 302 427-2845
Wilmington (G-18018)

MEDICAL SVCS ORGANIZATION

Arab Therapy Inc................................ E 310 956-4252
Wilmington (G-14521)

Colon Health Centers Americ.................. G 302 995-2656
Newark (G-10275)

Consensus Medical Systems................... G 302 453-1969
Newark (G-10308)

Delaware Health Net Inc........................ G 410 788-9715
Wilmington (G-15925)

Delaware Occptnal Hlth Svcs LL.............. E 302 368-5100
Newark (G-10464)

Fast Care Medical Aid Unit LLC............... G 302 793-7506
Claymont (G-1149)

Hospitalists of Delaware........................ G 302 757-1231
Newark (G-10972)

La Red Health Center Inc...................... E 302 855-1233
Georgetown (G-4399)

Laurel Highschool Wellness Ctr............... G 302 875-6164
Laurel (G-5548)

Myositis Spport Undrstnding As............... F 888 696-7273
Lincoln (G-6691)

Nanticoke Health Services Inc................. B 302 629-6611
Seaford (G-13305)

RC&ps LLC...................................... F 516 984-8184
Dover (G-3427)

Rosa Health Center Inc......................... G 302 858-4381
Georgetown (G-4492)

MELAMINE RESINS: Melamine-Formaldehyde

MEMBERSHIP ORGANIZATIONS, BUSINESS: Contractors' Association

Oci Melamine Americas Inc.................. G 800 615-8284
Wilmington (G-18742)

MEMBERSHIP ORGANIZATIONS, BUSINESS: Contractors' Association

ABC Contractors LLC...................... F 302 492-1116
Hartly (G-4853)
ABC Delaware........................... G 302 858-2185
New Castle (G-8756)
Home Builders Assn Del Inc............... F 302 678-1520
Dover (G-2687)
Ron Lank/Cash........................... G 302 684-4667
Milton (G-8704)
Superior Outdoor LLC.................... G 302 841-9827
Bridgeville (G-770)

MEMBERSHIP ORGANIZATIONS, BUSINESS: Growers' Association

American Public Gardens Assn............. G 610 708-3010
Wilmington (G-14440)

MEMBERSHIP ORGANIZATIONS, NEC: Charitable

American Birding Association............. G 610 864-0370
Wilmington (G-14425)
Association of Centers Study O........... G 302 831-1724
Newark (G-9928)
Buck Road East Association............... F 302 658-2400
Wilmington (G-15140)
Delaware Apartment Association........... G 302 998-0322
New Castle (G-9013)
Delaware Apartment Association........... G 617 680-3463
Wilmington (G-15865)
Delaware Bioscience Assn................. G 302 635-0445
Wilmington (G-15873)
Delaware Juneteenth Assn................. G 302 530-1605
Middletown (G-7042)
Delaware Liberia Association............. G 302 983-2536
Newark (G-10457)
Delaware Schl Counselors Assn............ G 302 323-2821
New Castle (G-9037)
Delaware School Nutrition Assn........... G 302 323-2743
Wilmington (G-15964)
Delaware State Pipe Trdes Assn........... G 302 636-7400
Newark (G-10485)
Delmarva Paddlers Retreat................ G 302 542-0818
Rehoboth Beach (G-12720)
Dovers Childrens Village Too............. G 302 674-8142
Dover (G-2370)
Friends Inc.............................. G 302 764-4488
Wilmington (G-16753)
Friends of Belmont Hall Inc.............. G 302 653-9212
Smyrna (G-13739)
Friends of Old Dover..................... G 302 674-1787
Dover (G-2537)
Friends of Stb........................... G 302 765-2566
Wilmington (G-16757)
Guardian General......................... G 443 205-1210
Seaford (G-13203)
Highland West Civic Assoc................ G 302 415-5435
Wilmington (G-17143)
Historic Georgetown Assn................. G 302 934-8818
Georgetown (G-4358)
laabo.................................... F 302 737-4396
Wilmington (G-17251)
Insightxperts LLC........................ G 412 608-4346
Dover (G-2737)
Knauer Association LLC................... G 302 947-2531
Millsboro (G-8342)

Millvlle By The Sea Mstr Cmnty........... G 302 539-2888
Millville (G-8544)
National Assn For Rgltory Admi........... G 302 234-4152
Newark (G-11490)
National Association Realto.............. G 302 674-8640
Dover (G-3153)
National Guard Association Del........... F 302 326-7125
New Castle (G-9396)
Odessa National Civic Assn............... G 302 530-1804
Townsend (G-14045)
Pencader Group LLC....................... G 302 366-0721
Newark (G-11659)
Penn Acres Civic Association............. G 302 328-8500
New Castle (G-9463)
Penn Delco Education Assn................ G 610 800-8218
Wilmington (G-18951)
Potomac Chesapeake Assn For C............ G 302 225-6248
Wilmington (G-19132)
Sherwood Park Civic Assn................. G 302 994-6604
Wilmington (G-19797)
Southeast Delco Education Assn........... G 302 420-4888
Middletown (G-7590)
Sussex Central High Schoo................ G 304 261-2873
Selbyville (G-13610)
Sussex Shores Beach Assn................. F 302 539-7511
Bethany Beach (G-643)
USS Delaware............................. G 908 910-4812
Milford (G-8133)
Warachai Thai Boxing Assn................ G 302 257-9794
Rehoboth Beach (G-13006)
Wwwlawfrmllncorg Assn Jim Cyle........... G 803 212-4978
Dover (G-3878)

MEMBERSHIP ORGANIZATIONS, NEC: Food Co-Operative

Harvest Ministries Inc................... G 302 846-3001
Delmar (G-1600)
Rosies PH LLC............................ G 630 222-5155
Lewes (G-6432)

MEMBERSHIP ORGANIZATIONS, NEC: Personal Interest

Delaware Ctr For Hrtclture Inc........... E 302 658-6262
Wilmington (G-15898)
Organization Innovations................. G 443 280-3009
Lewes (G-6339)
Retrosheet Inc........................... G 302 731-1570
Newark (G-11873)

MEMBERSHIP ORGANIZATIONS, PROFESSIONAL: Accounting Assoc

DMS Solution............................. G 302 753-0040
Bear (G-173)
Rethmerica Accounting and................ G 302 317-2417
Newark (G-11871)

MEMBERSHIP ORGANIZATIONS, PROFESSIONAL: Health Association

Central and Southern Delaware............ G 302 545-8067
Milford (G-7819)
Delaware Health Care Comm................ F 302 739-2730
Dover (G-2242)
Delaware Health Info Netwrk.............. E 302 678-0220
Dover (G-2243)
National Society Inc..................... G 302 656-9572
Wilmington (G-18547)

MEMBERSHIP ORGANIZATIONS, REL: Churches, Temples & Shrines

Church of God In Christ.................. F 302 678-1949
Dover (G-2072)

MEMBERSHIP ORGANIZATIONS, RELIGIOUS: Baptist Church

Fairwinds Baptist Church Inc............. G 302 322-1029
Bear (G-220)
Ogletown Baptist Church.................. F 302 737-2511
Newark (G-11580)

MEMBERSHIP ORGANIZATIONS, RELIGIOUS: Lutheran Church

Hilltop Lthran Nghbrhood Ctr I........... E 302 656-3224
Wilmington (G-17148)

MEMBERSHIP ORGANIZATIONS, RELIGIOUS: Methodist Church

Bethel United Methodist Church........... F 302 645-9426
Lewes (G-5758)
Chester Bthel Untd Mthdst Pre............ F 302 475-3549
Wilmington (G-15368)
Ebenezer United Methdst Chruch........... F 302 731-9495
Newark (G-10602)
Newark United Methodist.................. E 302 368-8774
Newark (G-11547)
Seaford Mission Inc...................... G 302 629-2559
Seaford (G-13391)
St Marks United Methodist Ch............. F 302 994-0400
Wilmington (G-19999)

MEMBERSHIP ORGS, CIVIC, SOCIAL/FRAT: Educator's Assoc

Indo-American Association Del............ G 302 234-0214
Newark (G-11015)
Intercollegiate Studies Inst............. D 302 656-3292
Wilmington (G-17376)

MEMBERSHIP SPORTS & RECREATION CLUBS

American Sports Licensing Inc............ F 302 288-0122
Wilmington (G-14444)
Bayside At Bthany Lkes Clbhuse........... G 302 539-4378
Ocean View (G-12471)
Bayside Sports Club LLC.................. F 302 436-3550
Selbyville (G-13472)
Bob Lafazia.............................. G 302 633-1456
Wilmington (G-14990)
Brandywine Lacrosse Club................. G 302 249-1840
Wilmington (G-15069)
Brandywine Volleyball Club............... G 302 898-6452
Wilmington (G-15092)
Bridgeville Lions Club Inc............... G 302 629-9543
Bridgeville (G-677)
Cambridge CLB Assoc Ltd Partnr........... G 302 674-3500
Hockessin (G-5148)
Camden-Wyoming Rotary Club............... G 302 697-2724
Camden Wyoming (G-921)
Champions Club........................... G 215 380-1273
Magnolia (G-6728)
Chisel Creek Golf Club................... G 302 379-6011
Wilmington (G-15389)
Clementes Clubhouse...................... G 302 455-0936
Newark (G-10257)
Cloud Kings RC Club...................... G 717 284-0164
Wilmington (G-15490)
Club Mantis Boxing LLC................... G 302 943-2580
Lincoln (G-6661)
Club Washington LLC...................... G 215 594-1332
Wilmington (G-15499)

PRODUCTS & SERVICES SECTION

METALS SVC CENTERS & WHOLESALERS: Steel

Coastal Club Schell Brothers.............. G 302 966-0063
 Lewes *(G-5839)*
Community Athc Solutions LLC......... G 302 468-5493
 Wilmington *(G-15559)*
County Seat Cruisers Inc................... G 302 398-8999
 Harrington *(G-4754)*
Delaware Elite Track Club................... G 302 521-2243
 Bear *(G-147)*
Delaware Fury Inc............................... G 302 838-3120
 Bear *(G-148)*
Delaware Lacrosse Foundation.......... G 302 831-8661
 Wilmington *(G-15937)*
Delaware Riders Basbal CLB Inc........ G 302 475-1915
 Wilmington *(G-15961)*
Delaware Sports League Inc.............. F 302 654-8787
 Wilmington *(G-15967)*
Delaware Trail Spinners...................... G 302 738-0177
 Newark *(G-10494)*
Delaware Union................................... G 484 645-7064
 New Castle *(G-9040)*
Delmarva Whiskey Club...................... G 215 815-1706
 Selbyville *(G-13519)*
Diamond State Curling Club............... G 856 577-3747
 Hockessin *(G-5186)*
Down Under Boxing Club.................... G 302 745-4392
 Bridgeville *(G-695)*
Emblem At Christiana Clubhouse....... G 302 525-6692
 Newark *(G-10638)*
Factory Sports.................................... G 302 313-4186
 Lewes *(G-5984)*
First State Pickleball CLB Inc............. G 302 387-1030
 Camden *(G-837)*
Hagerty Drivers Club LLC................... F 302 504-6086
 Wilmington *(G-17030)*
Hellenic Univ CLB Wilmington............ G 302 479-8811
 Wilmington *(G-17117)*
Hunt Wandendale Club....................... G 302 945-3369
 Millsboro *(G-8319)*
Kids Clubhouse................................... G 302 464-1134
 Middletown *(G-7271)*
Little League Baseball Inc.................. G 302 276-0375
 New Castle *(G-9316)*
Major League Bocce LLC.................... G 240 476-5801
 Milton *(G-8659)*
Mako Swim Club LLC......................... G 631 682-2131
 Harbeson *(G-4707)*
Michael Lo Sapio................................ G 201 919-2643
 Townsend *(G-14036)*
Middletown Sports Complex LLC....... F 302 299-8630
 Middletown *(G-7358)*
Millsboro Landing Inc......................... F 302 934-6073
 Millsboro *(G-8386)*
Millsboro Little League...................... F 302 934-1806
 Millsboro *(G-8388)*
Milton Garden Club............................ G 302 684-8315
 Milton *(G-8670)*
National Cllgate Rgby Orgnztio.......... E 603 748-1947
 Wilmington *(G-18539)*
New Castle 100 Archers Club............ G 302 722-7997
 Bear *(G-391)*
Northeast Rally Club.......................... G 302 934-1246
 Millsboro *(G-8406)*
Out-Train Fitness & Prfmce LLC........ G 610 470-3196
 Milton *(G-8680)*
Patriot Ice Arena LLC......................... F 302 266-0777
 Newark *(G-11639)*
Pike Creek Court Club Inc................. F 302 239-6688
 Wilmington *(G-19041)*
Polish American Civic Assn............... G 302 652-9524
 Wilmington *(G-19106)*
Premier Volleyball Delaware.............. G 302 593-4593
 Newark *(G-11731)*

Rehoboth Bay Sailing Assn................ G 302 227-9008
 Rehoboth Beach *(G-12914)*
Resort Poker League.......................... G 302 604-8706
 Selbyville *(G-13598)*
Right Coast Pro.................................. G 302 832-1517
 Bear *(G-462)*
Salem County Amateur Radio CLB.... G 302 689-8127
 Wilmington *(G-19636)*
Saltwater Cowgirls............................. G 302 745-3632
 Millsboro *(G-8452)*
Shockwaves Aquatic Club LLC........... G 302 478-8800
 Wilmington *(G-19806)*
Sisu Fit Club....................................... G 302 562-3920
 Newark *(G-12016)*
Skim USA.. G 302 227-4011
 Rehoboth Beach *(G-12961)*
Slims Sports Complex LLC................. G 302 464-1058
 Middletown *(G-7574)*
Studio 11.. G 302 622-9959
 Wilmington *(G-20105)*
Team Horne LLC................................. G 302 376-0579
 Middletown *(G-7625)*
TSE Sports... G 856 889-4913
 Rehoboth Beach *(G-12996)*
Vacation Club..................................... G 302 628-1144
 Seaford *(G-13439)*
Velo Amis... G 302 757-2783
 Newark *(G-12310)*
Wilmington Aquatic Club Inc............. G 302 322-2487
 New Castle *(G-9684)*
Wilmington Trail Club........................ G 302 521-3815
 Newark *(G-12383)*
Wilmington Turners Club................... F 302 658-9011
 Wilmington *(G-20852)*
Womens Civic Club Bethany Bch....... G 302 539-7515
 Bethany Beach *(G-651)*
Womens Tennis Club of New.............. G 302 731-1456
 Newark *(G-12398)*
Woodland Ferry Beagle Club............. F 302 856-2186
 Georgetown *(G-4578)*
Wrc... G 302 425-5500
 Wilmington *(G-20899)*
Young Mens Christian Assn Del......... C 302 571-6900
 Wilmington *(G-20937)*
Young Mens Christian Assn Del......... D 302 571-6935
 Wilmington *(G-20938)*
Young Mens Christian Assn Del......... E 302 571-6968
 Wilmington *(G-20936)*
Young MNS Chrstn Assn Wlmngton... C 302 709-9622
 Newark *(G-12422)*
Young MNS Chrstn Assn Wlmngton... C 302 296-9622
 Rehoboth Beach *(G-13027)*

MEN'S & BOYS' CLOTHING STORES

Dads Workwear Inc............................ G 302 663-0068
 Laurel *(G-5491)*
Oluwaseyi David Popoola................... G 302 331-3684
 Dover *(G-3221)*

MEN'S & BOYS' CLOTHING WHOLESALERS, NEC

Antoinette Xavier............................... F 980 549-3272
 Harrington *(G-4732)*
H D Lee Company Inc........................ G 302 477-3930
 Wilmington *(G-17018)*
Throat Threads Apparel USA Inc....... D 905 681-8437
 Dover *(G-3683)*

MEN'S & BOYS' SPORTSWEAR CLOTHING STORES

Private Society LLC............................ G 302 319-7126
 Newark *(G-11753)*

MERCHANDISING MACHINE OPERATORS: Vending

Efficient Services Inc........................ G 302 629-2124
 Seaford *(G-13171)*
Take-A-Break Inc................................ E 302 658-8571
 Wilmington *(G-20209)*

METAL & STEEL PRDTS: Abrasive

3dsteel Inc... G 713 677-2027
 Middletown *(G-6817)*

METAL DETECTORS

Eastern Shore Metal Detectors......... G 302 628-1985
 Seaford *(G-13168)*

METAL MINING SVCS

Ivanhoe Electric Inc.......................... D 720 933-1150
 Wilmington *(G-17437)*
Nanoshel LLC..................................... F 302 268-6163
 Wilmington *(G-18531)*

METAL SERVICE CENTERS & OFFICES

Eastern Metal Supply........................ F 302 391-1370
 Newark *(G-10597)*
Keystone Flashing Company.............. G 215 329-8500
 Wilmington *(G-17708)*
Steel Suppliers Erectors Inc............. D 302 654-5243
 Wilmington *(G-20044)*

METAL: Battery

Energy Tech Holdings LLC................. E 212 356-6130
 Wilmington *(G-16418)*

METALS SVC CENTERS & WHOLESALERS: Pipe & Tubing, Steel

Petroserv Inc..................................... G 302 398-3260
 Harrington *(G-4811)*
Vertex Industries Inc......................... G 302 472-0601
 Wilmington *(G-20597)*

METALS SVC CENTERS & WHOLESALERS: Sheets, Metal

Miller Metal Fabrication Inc.............. D 302 337-2291
 Bridgeville *(G-734)*

METALS SVC CENTERS & WHOLESALERS: Steel

B & B Industries Inc.......................... F 302 655-6156
 Wilmington *(G-14690)*
Boyds Trailor Hitches........................ G 302 697-9000
 Camden Wyoming *(G-917)*
Bushwick Metals LLC......................... G 302 328-0590
 New Castle *(G-8902)*
Calmet.. F 714 505-6765
 Wilmington *(G-15201)*
Coastal Aluminum Products.............. G 302 242-4868
 Magnolia *(G-6732)*
Delta Sales Corp................................ F 302 436-6063
 Selbyville *(G-13520)*
East Coast Stainless Inc................... G 302 366-0675
 Newark *(G-10591)*
East Coast Stainless & Alloys............ F 302 366-0675
 Newark *(G-10592)*
Handytube Corporation..................... D 302 697-9521
 Camden *(G-845)*
Industrial Stl Structures Inc............. E 302 275-8892
 New Castle *(G-9232)*

METALS SVC CENTERS & WHOLESALERS: Steel

Joseph T Ryerson & Son Inc............ F 215 736-8970
  Newark *(G-11129)*
Kloeckner Metals............................ F 302 652-3326
  New Castle *(G-9287)*
Metal Partners Rebar LLC............. F 215 791-3491
  New Castle *(G-9359)*
Ryerson Geralyn............................ G 302 547-3060
  Wilmington *(G-19602)*
Steel Suppliers Inc........................ C 302 654-5243
  Wilmington *(G-20043)*
Superior Metals Alloys USA Inc..... G 860 208-6438
  Newark *(G-12130)*
Taffy Tubes LLC............................. G 302 200-9255
  Lewes *(G-6538)*
Vulcraft Sales Corp........................ F 302 427-5832
  Wilmington *(G-20659)*

METALWORK: Miscellaneous

Cox Industries Inc......................... G 302 332-8470
  Newark *(G-10340)*

METALWORK: Ornamental

Asa V Peugh Inc............................ E 302 629-7969
  Seaford *(G-13069)*
Deaven Development Corp............ G 302 994-5793
  Wilmington *(G-15847)*
Donald F Deaven Inc..................... E 302 994-5793
  Wilmington *(G-16135)*

METALWORKING MACHINERY WHOLESALERS

Brooks Machine Inc....................... G 302 674-5900
  Dover *(G-1984)*

METERING DEVICES: Water Quality Monitoring & Control Systems

Ecomo Inc...................................... G 412 567-3867
  Dover *(G-2417)*
Engineered Systems & Designs..... G 302 456-0446
  Wilmington *(G-16423)*

MICROWAVE COMPONENTS

AC Group Inc.................................. G 201 840-5566
  Wilmington *(G-14211)*
Intelexmicro Inc.............................. G 302 907-9545
  Laurel *(G-5535)*

MILK, FLUID: Wholesalers

Dfa Dairy Brands Fluid LLC........... F 302 398-8321
  Harrington *(G-4762)*

MILLWORK

Aderyn Woodworks........................ G 219 229-5070
  New Castle *(G-8763)*
Aldas Refinishing Company........... G 302 528-5028
  Hockessin *(G-5119)*
Bancroft Carpentry Company......... G 302 655-3434
  Wilmington *(G-14737)*
Brandywine Mill Work..................... G 302 652-3008
  Wilmington *(G-15073)*
Craigs Woodworks LLC................. G 302 998-4201
  Selbyville *(G-13508)*
Daniel A Yoder............................... G 302 730-4076
  Dover *(G-2191)*
Delaware Millwork.......................... G 302 376-8324
  Middletown *(G-7043)*
Doug Green Woodworking............. G 302 652-6522
  Wilmington *(G-16154)*
Espositos Woodworking & Cnstr.... G 302 245-5474
  Milton *(G-8621)*

Frankford Custom Woodworks Inc.......... G 302 732-9570
  Frankford *(G-4108)*
Group Three Inc............................. G 302 658-4158
  Wilmington *(G-16988)*
Grubb Lumber Company Inc......... E 302 652-2800
  Wilmington *(G-16992)*
Johns Woodworking LLC............... G 302 492-3527
  Hartly *(G-4884)*
Lanning Woodworks....................... G 302 353-4726
  Wilmington *(G-17805)*
Lulla Woodworking LLC................. G 302 841-8800
  Ocean View *(G-12541)*
Mary Costas Woodworking............ G 302 227-6255
  Rehoboth Beach *(G-12851)*
Mastermark Woodworking Inc....... G 302 945-9131
  Millsboro *(G-8369)*
Monge Woodworking LLC.............. G 302 455-0175
  Newark *(G-11442)*
New Look Home Inc...................... G 302 994-4397
  Wilmington *(G-18622)*
OBryan Woodworks........................ G 302 398-8202
  Harrington *(G-4807)*
ONeill Woodworking LLC............... G 443 669-3458
  Lewes *(G-6336)*
Peirce James Townsend III............ G 302 449-2279
  Middletown *(G-7438)*
Saienni Stairs LLC......................... E 302 292-2699
  Newark *(G-11934)*
Tj Custom Woodworks Inc............. G 302 563-8535
  Newark *(G-12200)*
Wolf Wood Works LLC................... G 302 275-7227
  Wilmington *(G-20875)*
Woodworks...................................... G 302 995-0800
  Wilmington *(G-20889)*
Wyoming Millwork Co.................... G 302 684-3150
  Milton *(G-8732)*
Wyoming Millwork Co.................... E 302 697-8650
  Camden *(G-899)*

MINE EXPLORATION SVCS: Nonmetallic Minerals

Reliance Egleford Upstream LLC........ G 302 472-7437
  Wilmington *(G-19425)*

MINE PREPARATION SVCS

Oreomatic Mining Inc.................... E 725 255-8895
  Wilmington *(G-18817)*

MINERAL WOOL

Unique Fabricating Na Inc............ A 248 853-2333
  Wilmington *(G-20518)*

MINING MACHINERY & EQPT WHOLESALERS

Oakville Industries LLC................. F 513 436-5007
  Wilmington *(G-18729)*

MIXTURES & BLOCKS: Asphalt Paving

Asphalt Kingdom LLC.................... G 866 399-5562
  Wilmington *(G-14589)*
Christiana Materials Inc................ F 302 633-5600
  Wilmington *(G-15411)*
Driveway Mint Pvng/Slcting LLC... G 302 228-2644
  Bridgeville *(G-696)*
Gardner-Gibson Mfg Inc................ F 302 628-4290
  Seaford *(G-13196)*
Material Supply Inc........................ E 302 658-6524
  Wilmington *(G-18191)*
United Acquisition Corp................. E 302 651-9856
  Wilmington *(G-20523)*

PRODUCTS & SERVICES SECTION

MOBILE COMMUNICATIONS EQPT

Interdgital Communications Inc........... D 610 878-7800
  Wilmington *(G-17379)*
Interdigital Inc................................ E 302 281-3600
  Wilmington *(G-17380)*
Interdigital Wireless Inc................. E 302 281-3600
  Wilmington *(G-17381)*
Positron Access Solutions Inc....... F 888 577-5254
  Wilmington *(G-19128)*

MOBILE HOMES

Atlantic Realty Management......... G 302 629-0770
  Seaford *(G-13073)*
Hippo Trailer.................................. G 302 854-6661
  Georgetown *(G-4357)*

MOBILE HOMES WHOLESALERS

Aspen Meadows............................ G 302 227-4266
  Rehoboth Beach *(G-12612)*
T & C Enterprise Incorporated..... G 302 934-8080
  Millsboro *(G-8479)*

MODELS: General, Exc Toy

Rosas Greek Btq........................... G 302 678-2147
  Dover *(G-3485)*

MOLDED RUBBER PRDTS

Fabreeka Intl Holdings Inc............ G 302 452-2500
  Newark *(G-10700)*

MORTGAGE BANKERS

Anniemac Home Mortgage LLC... C 302 234-2956
  Wilmington *(G-14494)*
Atlantic Home Loans Inc............... G 302 363-3950
  Dover *(G-1848)*
Castle Mortage Services Inc........ F 302 366-0912
  Newark *(G-10161)*
Equity Plus Inc............................... F 302 762-3122
  Wilmington *(G-16453)*
Freedom Mortgage Corporation.... G 302 368-7100
  Newark *(G-10779)*
Gilpin Mortgage............................. G 302 656-5400
  Wilmington *(G-16864)*
Gsf Mortgage Corporation............ D 302 373-5853
  Christiana *(G-997)*
Homestead Funding Corp............. F 302 628-2828
  Seaford *(G-13215)*
M & F Financial Corp.................... F 302 427-5755
  Wilmington *(G-18055)*
Mortgage America Inc................... G 302 239-0600
  Wilmington *(G-18456)*
Mortgage Network Solutions LLC..... F 302 252-0100
  Wilmington *(G-18458)*
Premier Capital Holding................ G 302 730-1010
  Dover *(G-3359)*

MOTEL: Franchised

Bethany Beach Bed & Breakfast....... G 301 651-2278
  Bethany Beach *(G-580)*
Nab Motel Inc................................ F 302 656-9431
  Wilmington *(G-18518)*
Shree Kishna Inc........................... F 302 839-5000
  Milford *(G-8092)*

MOTION PICTURE & VIDEO DISTRIBUTION

Amantya Technologies Inc............ G 302 439-6030
  Wilmington *(G-14413)*
Bew Productions............................ G 302 547-8661
  Wilmington *(G-14869)*
Brewster Products......................... G 302 463-3531
  Middletown *(G-6937)*

PRODUCTS & SERVICES SECTION

MOTOR VEHICLES & CAR BODIES

Bug Eyed Weasel Productions LL.......... G 302 547-8661
  Wilmington (G-15145)
Bullseye Products LLC......................... G 302 468-5086
  Wilmington (G-15150)
Diamond Standard Productions............ G 302 508-2931
  Smyrna (G-13709)
Eastern Shore Vinyl Produ.................... G 302 436-9520
  Selbyville (G-13529)
Fish & Monkey Productions LLC........... G 302 897-4318
  Wilmington (G-16645)
Gem Productions.................................. G 302 650-6725
  Newark (G-10818)
Gpc Productions.................................. G 302 530-4547
  Newark (G-10877)
Iko Sales Inc....................................... F 360 988-9103
  Wilmington (G-17275)
J Alexander Productions LLC................ G 302 559-6667
  Wilmington (G-17451)
J Chance Productions.......................... G 302 322-2251
  New Castle (G-9246)
Jam Productions.................................. G 302 369-3629
  Newark (G-11086)
Ls Anderson Reproductions Inc............ G 302 999-9940
  Wilmington (G-18019)
Mark Perry Productions LLC................. G 443 521-2382
  Georgetown (G-4416)
New Cndlelight Productions Inc............ F 302 475-2313
  Wilmington (G-18611)
Njl Productions.................................... G 302 898-9187
  Wilmington (G-18654)
Outerhaven Productions....................... G 302 792-9169
  Claymont (G-1259)
Party Princess Productions................... G 302 307-3804
  Middletown (G-7428)
Perfectly OK Productions...................... G 302 233-3208
  Clayton (G-1395)
Peristalsis Productions Inc................... G 302 366-1106
  Newark (G-11667)
Red Spear LLC.................................... G 757 301-1052
  Dover (G-3440)
Short Order Production House............. G 302 656-1638
  Wilmington (G-19810)
T & T Produce LLC............................... G 302 245-6235
  Selbyville (G-13611)
Trauma Film Production Pr LLC............ G 623 582-2287
  Dover (G-3717)
Viacom Limited................................... F 484 857-7116
  Dover (G-3789)

MOTION PICTURE & VIDEO PRODUCTION SVCS

Arden Media Resources........................ G 256 656-8631
  Wilmington (G-14547)
California Explosion LLC...................... G 516 404-9892
  Wilmington (G-15194)
Digital Peak Inc................................... G 214 215-9054
  Wilmington (G-16067)
Edify Inc... G 302 520-2403
  Wilmington (G-16292)
Floyd Allan Gregory............................. G 302 658-0295
  Wilmington (G-16671)
Marvelous Lghts Prductions LLC........... G 215 678-2013
  New Castle (G-9351)
Office Magic....................................... G 302 229-9520
  Wilmington (G-18748)
Point Eght Third Prdctions LLC............. G 302 317-9419
  Wilmington (G-19100)
Productions For Purpose Inc................. G 302 388-9883
  Middletown (G-7472)
Schiff Group LLC................................. G 301 325-1359
  Bethany Beach (G-639)

MOTION PICTURE & VIDEO PRODUCTION SVCS: Educational

Gamma Theta Lmbda Edcatn Fndti........ G 302 983-9429
  Bear (G-245)

MOTION PICTURE DISTRIBUTION SVCS

No More Screts-Mind Bdy Spirit............. G 215 485-7881
  Wilmington (G-18661)

MOTION PICTURE PRODUCTION & DISTRIBUTION

Joozoor Iptv LLC................................. F 302 635-4092
  Newark (G-11125)

MOTION PICTURE PRODUCTION ALLIED SVCS

Deyas Honest Solutions LLC................ G 302 682-1830
  Magnolia (G-6741)
Jet Phynx Films LLC............................ G 302 803-0109
  Wilmington (G-17535)

MOTOR SCOOTERS & PARTS

Apollo Imports Inc............................... E 514 895-9410
  Newark (G-9885)

MOTOR VEHICLE ASSEMBLY, COMPLETE: Fire Department Vehicles

Aetna Hose Hook and Ladder Co........... G 302 454-3300
  Newark (G-9792)

MOTOR VEHICLE DEALERS: Automobiles, New & Used

Bayshore Ford Truck Sales Inc.............. D 302 656-3160
  New Castle (G-8853)
Brandywine Chrysler Jeep Dodge.......... D 302 998-0458
  Wilmington (G-15050)
Delaware Motor Sales Inc..................... D 302 656-3100
  Wilmington (G-15945)
Diamond Motor Sports Inc.................... D 302 697-3222
  Dover (G-2292)
Dover Volkswagen Inc.......................... E 302 734-4761
  Dover (G-2368)
Future Ford Sales Inc........................... D 302 999-0261
  Wilmington (G-16776)
IG Burton & Company Inc.................... D 302 424-3041
  Milford (G-7939)
IG Burton & Company Inc.................... D 302 629-2800
  Seaford (G-13219)
IG Burton & Company Inc.................... D 302 422-3041
  Milford (G-7938)
Martin Newark Dealership Inc.............. D 302 454-9300
  Newark (G-11345)
NAPA M3 Inc...................................... G 719 660-6263
  Middletown (G-7392)
New Car Connection............................ G 302 328-7000
  New Castle (G-9405)
Porter Nissan Buick Newark................. E 302 368-6300
  Newark (G-11714)
Townsend Bros Inc.............................. F 302 674-0100
  Dover (G-3707)
Willis Ford Inc.................................... E 302 653-5900
  Smyrna (G-13939)
Winner Ford of Dover Ltd.................... B 302 734-0444
  Dover (G-3860)
Winner Ford of Newark Inc................... F 302 731-2415
  Newark (G-12388)
Winner Group Inc................................ F 302 292-8200
  Newark (G-12389)
Winner Group Inc................................ F 302 764-5900
  Wilmington (G-20860)
Winner Infiniti Inc............................... E 302 764-5900
  Wilmington (G-20862)
Winners Circle Inc............................... E 302 661-2100
  Wilmington (G-20864)

MOTOR VEHICLE PARTS & ACCESS: Acceleration Eqpt

Autoport Inc....................................... E 302 658-5100
  New Castle (G-8834)

MOTOR VEHICLE PARTS & ACCESS: Electrical Eqpt

Lion Electric Mfg USA Inc..................... F 833 512-5466
  Newark (G-11264)

MOTOR VEHICLE PARTS & ACCESS: Engines & Parts

Aaron Anderson................................... G 804 986-1666
  New Castle (G-8754)
Fsvap Usa Inc..................................... F 248 639-8635
  Dover (G-2541)
Premium Diesel Parts LLC.................... G 205 723-1510
  Wilmington (G-19173)
Pro Fabricating Inc.............................. G 302 424-7700
  Milford (G-8053)

MOTOR VEHICLE PARTS & ACCESS: Trailer Hitches

Horizon Intl Holdings LLC.................... C 302 636-5401
  Wilmington (G-17207)

MOTOR VEHICLE PARTS & ACCESS: Transmissions

Muldoons Diesel Prfmce LLC................ G 302 276-2882
  Historic New Castle (G-5030)
Sword Parts LLC................................. G 302 246-1346
  Rehoboth Beach (G-12986)

MOTOR VEHICLE SPLYS & PARTS WHOLESALERS: New

Dover Automotive Inc........................... G 302 653-9234
  Smyrna (G-13714)
IG Burton & Company Inc.................... D 302 629-2800
  Seaford (G-13219)
Mto Hose Solutions Inc........................ G 302 266-6555
  Newark (G-11469)

MOTOR VEHICLE SPLYS & PARTS WHOLESALERS: Used

Bridgeville Auto Center Inc................... G 302 337-3100
  Bridgeville (G-675)
Fred Drake Automotive Inc................... G 302 378-4877
  Townsend (G-14003)
Lkq Northeast Inc................................ G 800 223-0171
  Dover (G-2962)
Mid Atlantic Tire ADI............................ G 302 221-2000
  Historic New Castle (G-5027)

MOTOR VEHICLES & CAR BODIES

Ford International Fin Corp................... D 313 845-5712
  Wilmington (G-16689)
International Std Elc Corp..................... F 302 427-3769
  Wilmington (G-17391)
Miles Per Hour Inc............................... G 800 370-3050
  Wilmington (G-18353)

MOTOR VEHICLES & CAR BODIES

North ATL Intl Ocean Carier............. E 786 275-5352
New Castle (G-9423)

Star Campus II.......................... G 302 514-7586
Newark (G-12087)

MOTOR VEHICLES, WHOLESALE: Fire Trucks

Delmarva Pump Center Inc............. F 302 492-1245
Marydel (G-6796)

MOTOR VEHICLES, WHOLESALE: Trucks, commercial

Diamond State Truck Center LLC........ G 302 275-9050
New Castle (G-9052)

Lee Mc Neill Associates................. G 302 593-6172
Wilmington (G-17854)

MOTORCYCLE DEALERS

Commonwealth Motor Inc............... G 302 505-5555
Wilmington (G-15554)

NAPA M3 Inc............................ G 719 660-6263
Middletown (G-7392)

MOTORCYCLES & RELATED PARTS

Infinity Choppers....................... G 302 249-7282
Georgetown (G-4368)

Sfa America Inc........................ G 206 265-3148
Wilmington (G-19772)

MOTORS: Electric

Reelve Inc.............................. G 312 459-2669
Dover (G-3442)

MOTORS: Generators

Ametek Inc............................ D 302 456-4400
Newark (G-9851)

MULTIPLEXERS: Telephone & Telegraph

Onex Global Inc........................ G 801 413-6375
Wilmington (G-18789)

Polycom Inc............................ G 302 420-8618
Wilmington (G-19112)

MUSEUMS & ART GALLERIES

Kalmar Nyckel Foundation.............. G 302 429-7447
Wilmington (G-17640)

Mark JB Inc............................ G 888 984-5845
Newark (G-11336)

MUSIC DISTRIBUTION APPARATUS

Major Mahh Levels LLC................. G 973 494-4767
Wilmington (G-18092)

Padrino Records LLC................... G 609 353-4683
Hst Newcastle (G-5451)

MUSIC LICENSING & ROYALTIES

Ripe Tech Corp......................... G 786 633-2228
Wilmington (G-19484)

MUSICAL INSTRUMENTS & ACCESS: NEC

Ajam Inc............................... G 267 323-5005
Middletown (G-6845)

Bb Custom Instruments................ G 302 339-3826
Georgetown (G-4226)

MUSICAL INSTRUMENTS & PARTS: Percussion

Imperial Dynsty Arts Prgram In......... F 302 521-8551
Wilmington (G-17290)

MUSICAL INSTRUMENTS & SPLYS STORES: Pianos

Flute Pro Shop Inc..................... G 302 479-5000
Wilmington (G-16676)

MUSICAL INSTRUMENTS: Guitars & Parts, Electric & Acoustic

Cara Guitars Manufacturing............ G 302 521-0119
Wilmington (G-15238)

MUSICAL INSTRUMENTS: Organs

Earle Teate Music...................... G 302 736-1937
Dover (G-2406)

NATURAL GAS DISTRIBUTION TO CONSUMERS

Avco Energy LLC...................... G 302 597-0034
Newark (G-9952)

Chesapeake Service Company......... G 302 734-6799
Dover (G-2058)

Conectiv LLC.......................... C 202 872-2680
Newark (G-10298)

Conectiv Energy Supply Inc........... D 302 454-0300
Newark (G-10300)

Eastern Shore Natural Gas Co......... F 302 734-6716
Dover (G-2412)

Eastern Shore Real Estate Inc......... G 302 734-6799
Dover (G-2413)

Inoven Solutions LLC.................. E 302 273-0177
Wilmington (G-17350)

Pepco Holdings LLC................... F 202 872-2000
Wilmington (G-18965)

Statewise Energy Ohio LLC............ F 855 862-1185
Wilmington (G-20036)

NATURAL GAS LIQUIDS PRODUCTION

Helix Services LLC.................... G 302 306-4880
Middletown (G-7204)

NATURAL GAS TRANSMISSION & DISTRIBUTION

Chesapeake Utilities Corp............. C 302 734-6799
Dover (G-2059)

Conectiv Energy Supply Inc........... D 302 454-0300
Newark (G-10300)

Delmarva Services..................... G 302 934-8750
Millsboro (G-8267)

Mexigas Group LLC................... F 302 645-7400
Lewes (G-6268)

Sandpiper Energy Inc.................. F 302 736-7656
Dover (G-3508)

NEIGHBORHOOD DEVELOPMENT GROUP

Ggc Inc................................ G 267 893-8052
Lincoln (G-6670)

NEW & USED CAR DEALERS

Bullfeathers Auto Sound Inc........... G 302 846-0434
Laurel (G-5475)

Delmarva Pump Center Inc............ F 302 492-1245
Marydel (G-6796)

Donright Services LLC................. G 302 685-7540
Wilmington (G-16143)

Indian River Golf Cars Dr Wldg........ G 302 947-2044
Millsboro (G-8320)

Martin Dealership..................... G 302 738-5200
Newark (G-11343)

Noel Auto Sales LLC................... G 302 286-7355
Newark (G-11561)

Richard Addington Co.................. G 302 422-2668
Milford (G-8068)

NEWSPAPERS, WHOLESALE

Distribution Marketing of Del........... G 302 658-6397
Wilmington (G-16089)

NURSERIES & LAWN & GARDEN SPLY STORES, RETAIL: Fertilizer

Soil Service Inc........................ G 302 629-7054
Seaford (G-13406)

NURSERY STOCK, WHOLESALE

Gro-Connectcom Inc.................. G 347 918-7437
Lewes (G-6066)

Sieck Wholesale Florist Inc............ G 302 356-2000
New Castle (G-9568)

Sterling Nursery Inc................... G 302 653-7060
Smyrna (G-13901)

Willey Farms Inc....................... D 302 378-8441
Townsend (G-14091)

NURSING CARE FACILITIES: Skilled

100 St Clire Drv Oprations LLC........ A 610 444-6350
Hockessin (G-5107)

1203 Walker Rd Operations LLC...... A 302 735-8800
Dover (G-1679)

Beebe School of Nursing.............. E 302 645-3251
Lewes (G-5752)

Birth Cnter Hlstic Wns Hlth CA........ F 302 658-2229
Newark (G-10038)

Brandywine Snior Lving MGT LLC..... E 302 226-8750
Rehoboth Beach (G-12651)

Brilliance Living Corporation........... G 386 690-1709
Wilmington (G-15116)

Brookdale Dover....................... F 302 674-4407
Dover (G-1983)

Cadia Rverside Healthcare Svcs...... F 302 455-0808
Wilmington (G-15187)

Capitol Nrsing Rhbltttion Ctr L........ E 302 734-1199
Dover (G-2023)

Center At Eden Hill.................... F 302 677-7100
Dover (G-2046)

Chancellor Care Ctr of Delmar........ E 302 846-3077
Delmar (G-1576)

Churchman De Snf MGT LLC......... D 302 998-6900
Newark (G-10239)

Collabrtive Effort To Rnfrce T......... D 302 731-0301
Smyrna (G-13685)

Collabrtive Effort To Rnfrce T......... G 302 731-0301
New Castle (G-8956)

Conexio Care Inc...................... E 302 442-6622
Claymont (G-1098)

Courtland Manor Inc.................. E 302 674-0566
Dover (G-2148)

Delaware Dept Hlth Social Svcs....... C 302 223-1000
Smyrna (G-13698)

Emeritus Corporation.................. C 302 674-4407
Dover (G-2439)

Five Star Quality Care Inc............. G 302 266-9255
Newark (G-10745)

Five Star Quality Care Inc............. G 302 366-0160
Newark (G-10746)

Five Star Senior Living Inc............ E 302 283-0540
Newark (G-10747)

Five Star Senior Living Inc............ D 302 655-6249
Wilmington (G-16655)

Gracious Hart Nursing Svcs LLC...... G 302 343-9083
Marydel (G-6798)

Green Valley Pavilion.................. F 302 653-5085
Smyrna (G-13752)

PRODUCTS & SERVICES SECTION

OFFICES & CLINICS OF DRS OF MEDICINE: Physician, Orthopedic

Harrison Snior Lving Gorgetown............ G 302 856-4574
   Georgetown *(G-4353)*

Hillside Center.................................... E 302 652-1181
   Wilmington *(G-17147)*

Home For Aged Wmn-Mnquadale HM.... C 302 654-1810
   Wilmington *(G-17178)*

Ingleside Homes Inc............................ E 302 984-0950
   Wilmington *(G-17336)*

Ivy Gables LLC.................................... F 302 475-9400
   Wilmington *(G-17439)*

Just Like Home.................................... F 302 653-0605
   Smyrna *(G-13783)*

Kendal Corp Pension Plan.................... F 610 388-7001
   Newark *(G-11154)*

Kendal Outreach LLC........................... F 610 335-1200
   Newark *(G-11157)*

Living Well With Dementia LLC............ G 302 753-9725
   Wilmington *(G-17951)*

Morgan Louise Fndtn LLC.................... F 302 670-5792
   Clayton *(G-1388)*

Nemours Foundation............................. F 302 424-5420
   Milford *(G-8026)*

New Cstle Hlth Rhbltition Ctr L............. C 302 328-2580
   New Castle *(G-9416)*

Newark Heritage Partners I LLC........... E 302 283-0540
   Newark *(G-11538)*

Nursing Board..................................... E 302 744-4500
   Dover *(G-3212)*

Onix Silverside LLC............................. F 484 731-2500
   Wilmington *(G-18791)*

Peninsula Untd Mthdst Hmes Inc......... B 302 235-6810
   Hockessin *(G-5336)*

Post Acute Medical LLC....................... D 717 731-9660
   Dover *(G-3355)*

Premier Healthcare Inc........................ E 302 731-5576
   Newark *(G-11728)*

Presbyterian Homes Inc....................... B 302 744-3600
   Dover *(G-3365)*

Public Health Nursing.......................... F 302 856-5136
   Georgetown *(G-4475)*

Seaside Pointe................................... F 302 226-8750
   Rehoboth Beach *(G-12954)*

Steven E Diamond M D........................ G 302 655-8868
   Wilmington *(G-20065)*

Summit At Hockessin........................... E 302 235-8388
   Hockessin *(G-5396)*

Summit Retirement Community............ F 888 933-2300
   Hockessin *(G-5397)*

Sunrise Senior Living LLC................... D 302 475-9163
   Wilmington *(G-20134)*

NUTRITION SVCS

Claymont Nutrition............................... G 302 792-7818
   Claymont *(G-1094)*

Dupont Specialty Pdts USA LLC........... E 302 992-2941
   Wilmington *(G-16216)*

Elsmere Nutrition................................ G 302 502-2061
   Wilmington *(G-16380)*

First State Nutrition............................. G 302 384-7104
   Wilmington *(G-16631)*

Focus Rehabilitation & Fitness............. G 302 231-8982
   Millsboro *(G-8293)*

New U Nutrition Inc.............................. G 302 543-4555
   Wilmington *(G-18627)*

Produce For Btter Hlth Fndtion............. G 302 235-2329
   Newark *(G-11758)*

Trolley Square Nutrition....................... G 302 757-6669
   Newark *(G-12239)*

Zeuss LLC... G 305 904-8078
   Wilmington *(G-20960)*

NYLON FIBERS

Dupont Indus Bsciences USA LLC........ E 302 774-1000
   Wilmington *(G-16210)*

Durafiber Tech DFT Entps Inc.............. D 704 912-3770
   Wilmington *(G-16220)*

Specialty Products N&H Inc................. C 302 774-1000
   Wilmington *(G-19954)*

OFFICE EQPT WHOLESALERS

Digital Office Solutions Inc................... F 302 286-6706
   Newark *(G-10530)*

Esupply LLC.. G 415 315-9963
   Wilmington *(G-16472)*

K Conte... G 302 283-9613
   Wilmington *(G-17628)*

Michelet Finance Inc........................... E 302 427-8751
   Wilmington *(G-18326)*

No Nonsense Office Mchs LLC............ G 302 856-7381
   Georgetown *(G-4447)*

OFFICE EQPT, WHOLESALE: Photocopy Machines

Canon Solutions America Inc............... E 302 792-8700
   Wilmington *(G-15218)*

OFFICE FURNITURE REPAIR & MAINTENANCE SVCS

Advance Office Instltions Inc................ E 302 777-5599
   Historic New Castle *(G-4922)*

OFFICE SPLY & STATIONERY STORES: Office Forms & Splys

Creative Promotions............................ G 302 697-7896
   Camden *(G-809)*

OFFICE SPLYS, NEC, WHOLESALE

Total Services Inc................................ G 302 575-1132
   Wilmington *(G-20373)*

OFFICES & CLINICS OF DOCTORS OF MEDICINE: Radiologist

Delaware Diagnostic Group LLC........... F 302 472-5555
   Wilmington *(G-15905)*

Delaware Imaging Network................... G 302 449-5400
   Middletown *(G-7041)*

Delaware Imaging Network................... G 302 836-4200
   Newark *(G-10454)*

Delaware Imaging Network Inc............. D 302 427-9855
   Newark *(G-10455)*

Glasgow Imaging LLC......................... F 302 993-2330
   Newark *(G-10845)*

Imaging Group Delaware PA................ F 302 421-4300
   Wilmington *(G-17281)*

Imaging Group of Delaware Inc............ F 302 888-2303
   Wilmington *(G-17282)*

Jeanes Radiology Associates PC......... G 302 738-1700
   Newark *(G-11102)*

Limestone Open Mri LLC.................... G 302 246-2001
   Bear *(G-349)*

Limestone Open Mri LLC.................... G 302 246-2001
   Wilmington *(G-17917)*

Mid Delaware Imaging Inc.................... D 302 734-9888
   Dover *(G-3085)*

North East Open Mri Inc...................... G 610 259-3200
   Wilmington *(G-18679)*

Ocean Medical Imaging Del LLC........... F 302 684-5151
   Milton *(G-8677)*

Omega Imaging Associates LLC........... E 302 738-9300
   Newark *(G-11585)*

Open Mri At Trolley Square LLC........... F 302 472-5555
   Wilmington *(G-18796)*

Papastvros Assoc Med Imging LL......... D 302 644-2590
   Newark *(G-11621)*

Papastvros Assoc Med Imging LL......... E 302 652-3016
   Newark *(G-11620)*

Progressive Radiology.......................... F 302 730-9300
   Dover *(G-3378)*

Radiation Oncology.............................. G 302 733-1830
   Newark *(G-11819)*

Radiology Associates Inc..................... E 302 832-5590
   Wilmington *(G-19313)*

Silverside Open Mri Imaging................ G 302 246-2000
   Wilmington *(G-19831)*

Southern Delaware Imaging LLP.......... E 302 645-7919
   Lewes *(G-6494)*

Trolley Sq Opn Mri & Imgng Ctr........... F 302 472-5555
   Wilmington *(G-20435)*

OFFICES & CLINICS OF DRS OF MEDICINE: Physician, Orthopedic

All About Pain and Spine..................... G 302 595-3670
   Newark *(G-9813)*

Ashish Anand Md................................. G 617 953-5914
   Claymont *(G-1044)*

Brandywine Pain Center....................... F 302 998-2585
   Wilmington *(G-15078)*

Brian J Galinat M D.............................. G 302 633-3555
   Wilmington *(G-15104)*

Cape Medical Associates PA................ F 302 645-2805
   Lewes *(G-5795)*

Capital Orthopaedic............................. G 302 628-7702
   Seaford *(G-13102)*

Chesapeake Bay Orthopedics............... G 302 404-5954
   Seaford *(G-13115)*

Craig D Sternberg MD.......................... F 302 733-0980
   Newark *(G-10343)*

Debay Surgical Service........................ F 302 644-4954
   Lewes *(G-5885)*

Del Marva Hand Specialists LLC.......... E 302 644-0940
   Lewes *(G-5887)*

Delaware Back Pain & Sports............... F 302 733-0980
   Newark *(G-10418)*

Delaware Medical Associates PA.......... F 302 475-2535
   Wilmington *(G-15942)*

Delaware Orthopaedic Specialis........... D 302 633-3555
   Wilmington *(G-15951)*

Delmarva Pain & Spine Ctr LLC............ G 302 355-0900
   Newark *(G-10501)*

Dr Douglas A Palma MD....................... F 302 655-9494
   Newark *(G-10562)*

Dr Scott Schulze.................................. G 302 644-0940
   Lewes *(G-5933)*

Evan H Crain M D................................. F 302 322-3400
   New Castle *(G-9102)*

First State Orthopaedics PA................. G 302 234-2600
   Hockessin *(G-5210)*

First State Orthopaedics PA................. G 302 322-3400
   Newark *(G-10733)*

First State Orthopaedics PA................. G 302 683-0700
   Newark *(G-10735)*

First State Orthopaedics PA................. G 302 653-5100
   Smyrna *(G-13735)*

First State Orthopaedics PA................. E 302 731-2888
   Newark *(G-10734)*

First State Spine and Pain Ctr.............. G 302 439-3063
   Wilmington *(G-16634)*

International Spine Pain....................... G 302 478-7001
   Wilmington *(G-17390)*

James Moran Do.................................. F 302 731-2888
   Newark *(G-11091)*

OFFICES & CLINICS OF DRS OF MEDICINE: Physician, Orthopedic

Joseph M Farrell Do .... G 302 424-4141
Lewes *(G-6153)*

Joseph Straight Md .... F 302 731-2888
Newark *(G-11128)*

Lewes Spine Center LLC .... G 302 231-4333
Rehoboth Beach *(G-12831)*

Lyndon B Cagampan .... F 302 730-8848
Dover *(G-2989)*

Magan Forman .... G 443 394-9534
Wilmington *(G-18077)*

Mattern & Piccioni Md PA .... F 302 730-8060
Dover *(G-3033)*

Matthew Eicherbaum .... F 302 655-9494
Wilmington *(G-18196)*

Michael L Mattern MD PA .... G 302 734-3416
Dover *(G-3080)*

Mid Atlantic Spine .... F 302 369-1700
Newark *(G-11409)*

Morgan Kalman Clinic PA .... E 302 529-5500
Wilmington *(G-18443)*

Orthopaedic Specialists .... G 302 730-0840
Dover *(G-3244)*

Orthopaedic Specialists PA .... F 302 655-9494
Wilmington *(G-18827)*

Orthopdic Assoc Suthern Del PA .... B 302 644-3311
Lewes *(G-6340)*

Orthopedic Properties LLC .... F 302 998-2310
Newark *(G-11601)*

Orthopedic Specialists .... E 302 351-4848
Newark *(G-11602)*

Orthopedic Spine Center P A .... G 302 734-9700
Dover *(G-3245)*

Pain MGT & Rehabilitation Ctr .... F 302 734-7246
Dover *(G-3260)*

Peter F Townsend MD .... F 302 633-3555
Wilmington *(G-18994)*

Regional Orthopaedic Assoc .... F 302 633-3555
Wilmington *(G-19406)*

Robert A Steele M D .... G 302 234-2600
Hockessin *(G-5368)*

Robert A Steele M D .... G 302 478-5500
Wilmington *(G-19507)*

Schwartz Eric MD .... G 302 730-0840
Dover *(G-3516)*

Spine Care of Delaware .... G 302 894-1900
Newark *(G-12069)*

Sport Spine Chiropractic Ctrs .... G 302 600-1675
Newark *(G-12074)*

Stephen M Beneck M D .... F 302 733-0980
Newark *(G-12097)*

Summit Orthopaedic HM Care LLC .... E 302 703-0800
Lewes *(G-6520)*

OFFICES & CLINICS OF OPTOMETRISTS: Specialist, Contact Lens

Halpern Eye Associates Inc .... G 302 734-5861
Middletown *(G-7190)*

OIL & GAS FIELD MACHINERY

Us Engineering Corporation .... F 302 645-7400
Lewes *(G-6592)*

OIL FIELD MACHINERY & EQPT

Delaware Capital Holdings Inc .... G 302 793-4921
Wilmington *(G-15879)*

OIL FIELD SVCS, NEC

Accurate-Energy LLC .... G 302 947-9560
Lewes *(G-5654)*

Mff Oilfield Solutions LLC .... G 603 795-0617
Wilmington *(G-18297)*

OIL TREATING COMPOUNDS

Rg3 Texas LLC .... G 778 891-7569
Wilmington *(G-19452)*

OILS & ESSENTIAL OILS

Terra Systems of Delaware LLC .... G 302 798-9553
Claymont *(G-1311)*

OLEFINS

Hercules LLC .... E 302 594-5000
Wilmington *(G-17128)*

OPERATOR TRAINING, COMPUTER

Process Academy LLC .... G 302 415-3104
Wilmington *(G-19207)*

OPHTHALMIC GOODS

Essilor America Holding Co Inc .... C 214 496-4000
Wilmington *(G-16467)*

OPHTHALMIC GOODS WHOLESALERS

Essilor America Holding Co Inc .... C 214 496-4000
Wilmington *(G-16467)*

OPHTHALMIC GOODS, NEC, WHOLESALE: Frames

Jim Knnas Optmtrsts Optcans In .... F 302 722-6197
Newark *(G-11112)*

Jim Knnas Optmtrsts Optcans In .... G 302 722-6197
Wilmington *(G-17549)*

OPHTHALMIC GOODS: Frames, Lenses & Parts, Eyeglasses

Jim Knnas Optmtrsts Optcans In .... F 302 722-6197
Newark *(G-11112)*

Jim Knnas Optmtrsts Optcans In .... G 302 722-6197
Wilmington *(G-17549)*

OPTICAL GOODS STORES: Eyeglasses, Prescription

Jim Knnas Optmtrsts Optcans In .... F 302 722-6197
Newark *(G-11112)*

Jim Knnas Optmtrsts Optcans In .... G 302 722-6197
Wilmington *(G-17549)*

OPTICAL INSTRUMENTS & LENSES

Atlantic Industrial Optics .... G 302 856-7905
Selbyville *(G-13467)*

Docs Medical LLC .... G 301 401-1489
Bear *(G-175)*

ORGANIZATIONS & UNIONS: Labor

Delaware Nature Society .... E 302 239-1283
Hockessin *(G-5182)*

Delaware State Education Assn .... G 302 366-8440
Newark *(G-10484)*

Local Hands-Crafted In America .... G 302 645-9100
Lewes *(G-6216)*

Promote Your Loc Bus Pwred By .... G 302 764-5588
Wilmington *(G-19230)*

ORGANIZATIONS: Civic & Social

3b Braes Brown Bags .... G 302 544-0779
Bear *(G-2)*

4troy Foundation .... F 302 448-9203
Bridgeville *(G-658)*

Alana Rose Foundation Inc .... G 302 519-5973
Dagsboro *(G-1410)*

PRODUCTS & SERVICES SECTION

American Legion Ambulance .... G 302 653-3557
Smyrna *(G-13639)*

American Soc Cytopathology Inc .... G 302 543-6583
Wilmington *(G-14443)*

Amy Gabel .... G 703 598-0763
Lewes *(G-5690)*

Anhui Xncheng High Schl Almni .... G 302 234-4351
Hockessin *(G-5127)*

Arise Africa Foundation Inc .... G 877 829-5500
New Castle *(G-8821)*

Art For A Purpose .... G 302 245-4528
Lewes *(G-5701)*

Attack Addiction .... G 302 994-1550
Wilmington *(G-14637)*

Be Bold .... G 302 415-5242
Dover *(G-1893)*

Beau Bden Fndtion For The Prtc .... F 302 598-1885
Wilmington *(G-14807)*

Best Buddies International Inc .... G 302 691-3187
Wilmington *(G-14852)*

Big Cats Foundation .... G 302 897-7140
Newark *(G-10031)*

Bing Rchel Zhang Fmly Fndation .... G 302 294-1859
Wilmington *(G-14893)*

Boca Raton Exch Foundation Inc .... G 302 286-6067
Newark *(G-10065)*

Boyer .... G 302 368-8489
Newark *(G-10076)*

Brandywine Education Assn .... G 302 793-5048
Claymont *(G-1067)*

Bruce G & Mary A Robert FML Fd .... G 302 598-1609
Wilmington *(G-15134)*

Camp Possibilities Foundation .... G 302 563-9460
Wilmington *(G-15209)*

Colette W Bleistine Paying It .... G 609 217-1925
Townsend *(G-13974)*

Committed Hearts Foundation .... G 402 850-4644
Wilmington *(G-15549)*

Community Business Dev Corp .... G 302 544-1709
Newark *(G-10288)*

Ddx3x Foundation .... G 917 796-3514
Wilmington *(G-15836)*

Del Ray Foundatins LLC .... G 302 272-6153
Milford *(G-7849)*

Delaware College Scholars Inc .... F 302 437-6144
Wilmington *(G-15887)*

Delaware Con Fndtons Slabs LLC .... G 302 945-1223
Millsboro *(G-8260)*

Delaware Dnce Edcatn Orgnztion .... G 302 897-6345
Wilmington *(G-15911)*

Delaware Ffa Foundation Inc .... G 302 857-6493
Dover *(G-2238)*

Delaware Mobile Surfishermen .... G 302 945-1320
Dagsboro *(G-1435)*

Delaware Nature Society .... E 302 239-1283
Hockessin *(G-5182)*

Delaware Retired Schl Prsnl .... E 302 674-8252
Wilmington *(G-15960)*

Delaware Seashore Preservation .... G 302 227-0478
Dagsboro *(G-1436)*

Delaware Terry Farrell Fund .... G 302 242-4341
Lincoln *(G-6663)*

Delisle K-9 Offcer Sfety Fndti .... G 302 893-7324
Bear *(G-163)*

Delmarva Community Wellnet .... G 704 779-3280
Lewes *(G-5903)*

Delmarva Space Scnces Fndation .... G 302 236-2761
Millsboro *(G-8269)*

Delray Foundations Inc .... E 302 503-3341
Lincoln *(G-6664)*

Donnie Jones Foundation Inc .... G 302 745-6946
Ellendale *(G-3915)*

PRODUCTS & SERVICES SECTION

ORGANIZATIONS: Professional

Donorware Foundation..................... G 302 230-7171
  Wilmington *(G-16141)*
Dvfa Foundation................................ G 302 734-9390
  Dover *(G-2397)*
Early Foundations Therapeutic........ G 302 384-6905
  Wilmington *(G-16248)*
Eastern Brndywine Hndred Crdnt.... G 302 764-2476
  Wilmington *(G-16255)*
Ebright Foundation LL...................... G 215 370-2821
  Wilmington *(G-16276)*
Edfeed Foundation............................ F 917 459-2762
  Middletown *(G-7082)*
Empowerment Group Inc.................. G 302 930-8080
  Lincoln *(G-6665)*
Endure To Cure Foundation.............. G 866 400-2121
  Wilmington *(G-16412)*
Evan David Foundation..................... G 302 778-4546
  Wilmington *(G-16478)*
Farpath Foundation........................... G 302 645-8328
  Lewes *(G-5989)*
Farr Family Foundation Inc............... G 540 349-4103
  Lewes *(G-5990)*
Fbinaa... G 302 344-7700
  Lewes *(G-5992)*
Firemens Hstrcal Fndtion Dlmar....... G 302 846-3014
  Delmar *(G-1596)*
Foundation Delaware Islamic........... G 302 325-4149
  New Castle *(G-9141)*
Frank & Yetta Chaiken Fou............... G 302 737-7427
  Wilmington *(G-16725)*
Free Spirited Foundation................... G 614 946-7358
  Lewes *(G-6013)*
Freelee Foundation............................ G 302 607-8053
  Newark *(G-10780)*
Friends of Colonial............................. G 302 323-2746
  New Castle *(G-9147)*
Friends of New Cties Fundation....... G 718 896-8900
  Wilmington *(G-16756)*
Friends of The African Union............ G 302 834-7525
  Delaware City *(G-1544)*
Future Promises Foundation............. G 302 365-5735
  Bear *(G-242)*
Future Promises Foundation Inc...... G 302 689-3392
  Wilmington *(G-16778)*
Give From The Heart-The Doroth.... G 302 322-7808
  New Castle *(G-9168)*
Good Ole Boy Foundation Inc.......... G 302 249-0237
  Millsboro *(G-8301)*
Greatful Lives Foundation................. G 404 965-9300
  Wilmington *(G-16961)*
Gregory A Williams Jr Educ.............. G 302 875-1218
  Laurel *(G-5525)*
Gulu Project Inc................................. G 302 547-8106
  Hockessin *(G-5230)*
Harry K Foundation............................ F 301 226-0675
  Rehoboth Beach *(G-12781)*
Hclinton Foundation.......................... G 302 393-1448
  Greenwood *(G-4635)*
Heal Autism Now Del Foundation.... G 302 456-1335
  Newark *(G-10941)*
Heart In Game Foundation Inc......... G 302 494-3133
  Wilmington *(G-17104)*
Heroes Self Defense Foundation..... G 609 335-2391
  Clayton *(G-1370)*
Hogs Heroes Foundation De Ch1.... G 443 754-0343
  Laurel *(G-5530)*
Ideaspace Open Mnds Foundation.. G 808 444-4578
  Bear *(G-281)*
Illumina Corporate Foundation......... F 516 870-7722
  Wilmington *(G-17280)*
J N N Foundation............................... G 800 493-1069
  Bear *(G-294)*

J Riley Eaton..................................... G 302 539-4537
  Ocean View *(G-12527)*
JB For Office) Hogan........................ G 302 922-0000
  Dover *(G-2775)*
Joseph Patrick Fabber Meml........... G 302 858-4040
  Georgetown *(G-4388)*
Joy Choose Foundation..................... G 302 286-7560
  Dover *(G-2805)*
Katy Aukamp Mem Foundation......... G 302 328-6446
  New Castle *(G-9275)*
Kids Club Foundation Delaware....... G 302 733-0168
  Newark *(G-11172)*
Kim and Evans Fmly Fndtion Inc..... G 302 629-7166
  Seaford *(G-13249)*
Kool Boiz Foundation LLC................ G 614 404-2396
  Middletown *(G-7281)*
Leah & Alain Lebec Foundation....... G 800 839-1754
  Wilmington *(G-17846)*
Lincoln Community Hall Inc............ G 302 242-1747
  Lincoln *(G-6681)*
Lorelton Foundation.......................... G 302 573-2500
  Wilmington *(G-17996)*
Ltr Private Foundation...................... G 610 745-5000
  Wilmington *(G-18022)*
Magic Inc.. F 415 319-6331
  Wilmington *(G-18082)*
Md22 Lions Low Vision Rehab........ G 410 737-2671
  Wilmington *(G-18238)*
Met Technologies LLC...................... G 302 468-5243
  Newark *(G-11392)*
Michael Ercka Hynnsky Fmly Fnd... G 302 545-4600
  Wilmington *(G-18312)*
Michael G Schwrtz Mem Fndation... G 302 453-9233
  Wilmington *(G-18313)*
Middltown Vlg Cmnty Foundation... G 857 544-3954
  Middletown *(G-7366)*
Mvrp Foundation Inc........................ G 347 683-1974
  Rehoboth Beach *(G-12868)*
National Assn of Hispnc Nrses........ G 302 325-9292
  New Castle *(G-9394)*
New Foundations LLC...................... F 302 753-3135
  Newark *(G-11522)*
Noor Foundation International......... G 302 234-8860
  Hockessin *(G-5324)*
Objective Zero Foundation................ F 202 573-9660
  Wilmington *(G-18736)*
OHM Lshree Foundation................... G 302 652-2900
  Middletown *(G-7413)*
Olacole Foundation........................... G 215 279-4742
  Bear *(G-405)*
Oluv C Joynor Foundation............... G 302 793-3277
  Wilmington *(G-18761)*
Pearce Q Foundation Inc................. G 302 753-8612
  Newark *(G-11651)*
Perry Initiative................................... G 302 319-1113
  Newark *(G-11668)*
Pershing Foundation......................... G 636 352-7122
  Middletown *(G-7442)*
PHI Service Co.................................. G 302 451-5224
  Newark *(G-11683)*
Porsche Club America Del Reg....... G 302 588-3511
  Hockessin *(G-5347)*
Power Over Pain Crps Fndtion I...... G 302 983-6412
  New Castle *(G-9486)*
Raskob Fndtion For Cthlic Actv....... F 302 655-4440
  Wilmington *(G-19336)*
Rehoboth Bch Sister Cites Assn...... G 302 249-7878
  Rehoboth Beach *(G-12916)*
Roland E Tice..................................... G 302 629-3674
  Laurel *(G-5594)*
Salvation Army.................................. E 302 654-8808
  Wilmington *(G-19643)*

Schooltoolstv..................................... G 415 948-0668
  Bear *(G-481)*
Secure Schools Alliance Inc............. G 302 333-1416
  Wilmington *(G-19730)*
Skyline Swim Club............................ G 302 737-4696
  Wilmington *(G-19857)*
Smartdrive Foundation..................... G 302 463-6543
  New Castle *(G-9573)*
Soroptomist Foundation Inc............ G 302 698-3686
  Dover *(G-3588)*
South Bowers Ladies Auxiliary........ G 302 335-4135
  Milford *(G-8096)*
Starliters Dance Studio Inc.............. G 302 798-6330
  Claymont *(G-1301)*
Studio Groups Inc............................. F 302 998-7895
  Wilmington *(G-20106)*
Success Wont Wait Inc..................... G 302 388-9669
  Wilmington *(G-20118)*
Surrender House............................... G 302 249-6830
  Millsboro *(G-8472)*
Trivedi Foundation LLC.................... G 302 678-4629
  Dover *(G-3729)*
United Tele Wkrs Local 13101......... G 302 737-0400
  Newark *(G-12272)*
Urban Change Incorporated............ G 215 749-2049
  New Castle *(G-9663)*
Warrior Community Connect Inc..... G 202 309-5729
  Millsboro *(G-8499)*
Wdbid Management Company........ E 302 425-5374
  Wilmington *(G-20698)*
Wilmington Rowing Center.............. G 302 652-5339
  Wilmington *(G-20834)*
World Amptee Ftball Federation..... G 302 383-2665
  Wilmington *(G-20895)*
Young MNS Chrstn Assn Wlmngton..... C 302 709-9622
  Newark *(G-12422)*
YWCA Delaware................................ D 302 655-0039
  Wilmington *(G-20942)*

ORGANIZATIONS: Medical Research

Analytical Biological Svcs Inc.......... E 302 654-4492
  New Castle *(G-8806)*
Medblob Inc....................................... G 813 308-9273
  Dover *(G-3050)*
Vizzie 360... G 323 239-0690
  Lewes *(G-6608)*
Worldwide Clinical Trials Inc............ G 317 297-2208
  Georgetown *(G-4581)*

ORGANIZATIONS: Physical Research, Noncommercial

Python Software Foundation............ F 970 305-9455
  Dover *(G-3402)*

ORGANIZATIONS: Professional

Assoction For The Rghts Ctzens..... F 302 996-9400
  Wilmington *(G-14597)*
Blend Network Inc............................. G 267 521-8845
  Dover *(G-1947)*
Bni... G 302 668-9467
  Wilmington *(G-14987)*
Cape Ent PA...................................... F 717 269-3106
  Lewes *(G-5792)*
Cramer & Dimichele PA.................... G 302 293-1230
  Wilmington *(G-15683)*
Dcor.. G 302 227-9341
  Rehoboth Beach *(G-12712)*
Delaware Assn For The Edcatn Y... G 302 764-1500
  Wilmington *(G-15867)*
Delaware Home Valuations PA........ G 302 933-8607
  Millsboro *(G-8261)*

Employee Codes: A=Over 500 employees, B=251-500
C=101-250, D=51-100, E=20-50, F=10-19, G=1-9

ORGANIZATIONS: Professional

Delaware Rural Water Assn............................ G 302 424-3792
　Milford (G-7858)
East Coast Trans LLC................................... G 302 740-5458
　Newark (G-10593)
Healthshield LLC.. G 302 352-0517
　Wilmington (G-17098)
Hearts International Inc.................................. G 215 585-5597
　Wilmington (G-17108)
Income & Est Plg Partners PA........................ G 302 722-6000
　Wilmington (G-17302)
James E Deakyne Jr PA................................. G 302 226-1200
　Rehoboth Beach (G-12801)
Kathy J King PA... G 302 827-4740
　Lewes (G-6163)
Ken Fibble Professional Svcs........................ G 302 947-2430
　Millsboro (G-8337)
Loyal Order of Moose.................................... G 302 436-2088
　Frankford (G-4124)
N Biggs Professional Svcs LLC..................... G 302 632-7598
　Smyrna (G-13832)
Nerdit Foundation.. G 302 482-5979
　Wilmington (G-18586)
Nonprofit Bus Solutions LLC......................... F 302 353-4606
　Wilmington (G-18668)
Python Software Foundation......................... F 970 305-9455
　Dover (G-3402)
Regional Enterprises LLC.............................. G 302 227-0202
　Rehoboth Beach (G-12911)
Rockham 5g PA LP.. G 302 239-1250
　Hockessin (G-5369)
Schoenbeck PA.. G 302 584-4519
　Newark (G-11959)
Seamens Center Wilmington Inc................... G 302 575-1300
　Wilmington (G-19722)
Sharon Boyd M Ed Lpcmh............................. G 302 529-0220
　Wilmington (G-19782)
State Edcatn Agcy Dirs Arts Ed.................... G 302 739-4111
　Dover (G-3605)
Zebrafish Disease Models Soc...................... G 518 399-7181
　Wilmington (G-20949)

ORGANIZATIONS: Religious

Fellowship Hlth Resources Inc...................... F 302 856-7642
　Georgetown (G-4316)
First Love Ministries Inc................................ G 302 655-1776
　Middletown (G-7130)
Generation Glory Ministries........................... G 302 438-4335
　Wilmington (G-16833)
Jewish Federation of Delaware..................... F 302 478-5660
　Wilmington (G-17540)
Larry Shelton... F 678 948-6096
　New Castle (G-9295)
Linde North America...................................... F 302 654-9348
　New Castle (G-9312)
Salvation Army... F 302 934-3730
　Millsboro (G-8453)
Victorous Kngdom Ctzens Ntwrk................. G 302 409-0701
　Smyrna (G-13931)

ORGANIZATIONS: Research Institute

Disaster Research Center............................. G 302 831-6618
　Newark (G-10537)
Epic Research LLC.. E 302 510-1338
　Wilmington (G-16450)
Galvin Industries LLC.................................... G 703 505-7860
　Georgetown (G-4330)
Life-Science AI LLC....................................... ...... 438 833-8504
　Lewes (G-6206)
Minder Foundation... G 917 477-1661
　Lewes (G-6277)
Thomson Reuters (grc) Inc............................ G 212 227-7457
　Wilmington (G-20314)

Ubinet Inc... G 302 722-6015
　Wilmington (G-20491)
University of Delaware................................... G 302 831-2833
　Newark (G-12279)
Zinger Enterprizes Inc................................... G 302 381-6761
　Laurel (G-5628)

PACKAGING & LABELING SVCS

Customs Benefits.. G 302 798-2884
　Wilmington (G-15745)
Freshpac LLC.. F 559 648-2210
　Wilmington (G-16751)
Mail Express.. G 302 376-5151
　Middletown (G-7324)
Montesino Technologies Inc......................... G 302 888-2355
　Wilmington (G-18423)
Promofill.. G 302 276-2700
　Historic New Castle (G-5055)
Ur-Express Inc.. G 302 839-2008
　Wilmington (G-20540)

PACKAGING MATERIALS, WHOLESALE

AB Group Packaging Inc............................... F 302 607-3281
　Newark (G-9736)
Graham Packaging Pet Tech Inc................... E 302 453-9464
　Newark (G-10878)
Mid-Atlantic Packaging Company................. E 800 284-1332
　Dover (G-3086)
Packaging Mania (not Inc)............................ G 917 410-6835
　Milford (G-8041)
Prescotech Inc.. D 502 585-5866
　Wilmington (G-19178)

PACKAGING MATERIALS: Paper

Mercantile Press Inc...................................... F 302 764-6884
　Wilmington (G-18274)
Oxypaper Inc... B 302 202-4897
　Dover (G-3256)
Printpack Inc.. C 302 323-4000
　New Castle (G-9495)
Unique Fabricating Na Inc............................ A 248 853-2333
　Wilmington (G-20518)

PACKAGING MATERIALS: Plastic Film, Coated Or Laminated

Derprosa Spcalty Films USA LLC.................. G 856 845-7524
　Wilmington (G-16021)
Zacros America Inc....................................... C 302 391-2200
　Newark (G-12429)

PACKAGING: Blister Or Bubble Formed, Plastic

Richard Earl Fisher.. G 302 598-1957
　Wilmington (G-19468)

PACKING & CRATING SVC

Atlas Van Lines Agents................................. G 302 369-0900
　Newark (G-9940)
Cirkla Inc... E 415 851-4635
　Dover (G-2077)
Globbing LLC.. E 408 903-4209
　Claymont (G-1165)
Prescotech Inc.. D 502 585-5866
　Wilmington (G-19178)

PAGERS: One-way

Integrated Data Corp.................................... G 302 295-5057
　Wilmington (G-17368)

PAINTS & ALLIED PRODUCTS

C P M Industries Inc...................................... G 302 478-8200
　Wilmington (G-15175)
Modified Thermoset Resins Inc.................... G 302 235-3710
　Wilmington (G-18399)
PPG Architectural Finishes Inc..................... G 302 736-6081
　Dover (G-3357)
PPG Architectural Finishes Inc..................... G 302 454-9091
　Wilmington (G-19140)
PPG Architectural Finishes Inc..................... G 302 762-0555
　Wilmington (G-19141)

PAINTS, VARNISHES & SPLYS WHOLESALERS

F Schumacher & Co LLC............................... E 302 454-3200
　Newark (G-10699)
T B Painting Restoration............................... G 610 283-4100
　Newark (G-12152)

PAINTS, VARNISHES & SPLYS, WHOLESALE: Paints

Avt Paints LLC... G 800 476-1634
　Wilmington (G-14675)
B F Shin of Salisbury Inc............................... G 302 652-3521
　Wilmington (G-14700)
B Frank Shinn Paint Co................................. F 302 652-3521
　Wilmington (G-14701)
Bair & Goff Sales LLC................................... E 302 292-2546
　Newark (G-9975)
Boero Usa Inc.. G 800 935-6596
　Wilmington (G-14996)
First State Distributors Inc........................... G 302 655-8266
　Wilmington (G-16627)
Mammeles Inc.. F 302 998-0541
　Wilmington (G-18097)

PALLETS & SKIDS: Wood

Stephens Enterprises Inc............................. G 302 629-0322
　Seaford (G-13413)

PALLETS: Plastic

Plasti Pallets Corp.. G 302 737-1977
　Christiana (G-1007)

PAPER & BOARD: Die-cut

Cann-Erikson Bindery Inc............................ F 302 995-6636
　Wilmington (G-15216)

PAPER PRDTS: Panty Liners, Made From Purchased Materials

Edgewell Personal Care Company................ A 302 678-6191
　Dover (G-2423)

PAPER PRDTS: Sanitary

Docs Medical LLC... G 301 401-1489
　Bear (G-175)
Playtex Manufacturing Inc............................ D 302 678-6000
　Dover (G-3336)

PAPER PRDTS: Tampons, Sanitary, Made From Purchased Material

Edgewell Personal Care LLC......................... E 302 678-6000
　Dover (G-2422)

PAPER: Coated & Laminated, NEC

Mercantile Press Inc...................................... F 302 764-6884
　Wilmington (G-18274)
Oxypaper Inc... B 302 202-4897
　Dover (G-3256)

PRODUCTS & SERVICES SECTION
PETROLEUM BULK STATIONS & TERMINALS

PAPER: Gift Wrap

K&B Investors LLC .... G 302 357-9723
Wilmington *(G-17631)*

PARTITIONS & FIXTURES: Except Wood

J and J Display .... G 302 628-4190
Seaford *(G-13227)*

PATENT OWNERS & LESSORS

6 8 Medical Solutions LLC .... G 843 481-5550
Lewes *(G-5641)*

PAVERS

Stockley Materials LLC .... F 302 856-7601
Georgetown *(G-4526)*

PAVING MIXTURES

Diamond Materials LLC .... D 302 658-6524
Wilmington *(G-16051)*

PAYROLL SVCS

Aero Dynamic Services Inc .... G 302 737-4920
Middletown *(G-6837)*

City of Dover .... G 302 736-7018
Dover *(G-2082)*

PENCILS & PENS WHOLESALERS

Endlesspens LLC .... F 813 550-5501
Lewes *(G-5962)*

PENSION FUNDS

Benefit Services Unlimited .... F 302 479-5696
Wilmington *(G-14833)*

PERSONAL CARE FACILITY

Delaware Hospice .... E 302 934-9018
Millsboro *(G-8262)*

Delaware Hospice Inc .... E 302 678-4444
Dover *(G-2245)*

Delaware Hospice Inc .... E 302 856-7717
Milford *(G-7856)*

Elderly Comfort Corporation .... G 302 530-6680
Wilmington *(G-16349)*

Milton & Hattie Kutz Home Inc .... C 302 764-7000
Wilmington *(G-18371)*

Oakleaf Inc .... E 412 881-8194
Lewes *(G-6325)*

Parkview De Snf Management LLC ... D 302 655-6135
Wilmington *(G-18896)*

Vitas Healthcare Corporation .... C 302 451-4000
Newark *(G-12332)*

PERSONAL CREDIT INSTITUTIONS: Consumer Finance Companies

Beneficial Consumer Disc Co .... G 302 425-2500
Wilmington *(G-14831)*

Citifinancial Credit Company .... G 302 422-9657
Milford *(G-7828)*

Citifinancial Credit Company .... G 302 628-9253
Seaford *(G-13120)*

Citifinancial Credit Company .... F 302 683-4917
Wilmington *(G-15448)*

Glance Capital Inc .... G 800 825-9889
Middletown *(G-7162)*

John Lovett Inc .... F 302 455-9460
Newark *(G-11114)*

Reevoy Corporation .... F 631 769-6681
Wilmington *(G-19394)*

Weltio LLC .... F 305 307-9815
Dover *(G-3832)*

PERSONAL DOCUMENT & INFORMATION SVCS

Adpese LLC .... G 302 223-5411
Wilmington *(G-14261)*

PERSONAL SVCS

B P Services .... G 302 399-4132
Dover *(G-1864)*

Belle Energie LLC .... G 302 690-3188
Dover *(G-1908)*

Hajirs Touch LLC .... G 302 543-2302
Wilmington *(G-17035)*

Internet Vikings East LLC .... G 347 879-1452
Wilmington *(G-17394)*

Murgency Inc .... E 650 308-9964
Dover *(G-3132)*

On My Mind Designs .... F 302 494-8622
Wilmington *(G-18774)*

Recentia Usa Inc .... G 847 977-7571
Wilmington *(G-19376)*

PEST CONTROL IN STRUCTURES SVCS

Accurate Pest Control Company .... F 302 875-2725
Laurel *(G-5460)*

Activ Pest & Lawn Inc .... F 302 645-1502
Lewes *(G-5657)*

Advanced Pest Management .... G 410 398-4378
Newark *(G-9779)*

All Clear Pest Control .... G 443 359-5623
Seaford *(G-13055)*

Bay Area Wildlife LLC .... G 410 829-6368
Seaford *(G-13077)*

Brightside Pest Services Inc .... G 302 893-5858
Hockessin *(G-5143)*

Davis A Scott .... G 302 535-0570
Magnolia *(G-6738)*

Delaware Mosquito Control LLC .... G 302 504-6757
Newark *(G-10462)*

Delmar Termite & Pest Control .... G 302 658-5010
Wilmington *(G-15996)*

Diamond Pest Control .... G 302 654-2300
Wilmington *(G-16052)*

Diamond State Pest Control Co .... G 302 250-3403
Camden Wyoming *(G-933)*

Elkton Exterminating Co Inc .... G 302 368-9116
Newark *(G-10630)*

Green Pest Management LLC .... F 302 777-2390
New Castle *(G-9179)*

Guy Bug .... G 302 242-5254
Dover *(G-2636)*

Home Prmnt Pest Ctrl Cmpnies I ...... G 302 894-9201
New Castle *(G-9219)*

Ladybug Pest Management Inc .... G 302 846-2295
Delmar *(G-1612)*

Liberty Pest Control LLC .... G 302 734-1507
Dover *(G-2936)*

Maguire & Sons Inc .... G 302 798-1200
Wilmington *(G-18085)*

Moyer Pest Control .... G 302 353-4404
Wilmington *(G-18469)*

Pest Pro LLC .... G 877 737-8360
Milford *(G-8048)*

Pestex Pest Control Inc .... G 302 745-8366
Georgetown *(G-4464)*

Professional Pest MGT De .... G 302 738-1036
Wilmington *(G-19211)*

Rentokil North America Inc .... D 302 337-8100
Bridgeville *(G-761)*

Rentokil North America Inc .... E 302 325-2687
Newark *(G-11854)*

Royal Pest Management Inc .... G 302 376-8243
Middletown *(G-7525)*

Royal Pest Solutions Inc .... E 302 322-6665
New Castle *(G-9543)*

Royal Termite & Pest Ctrl Inc .... E 302 322-3600
New Castle *(G-9545)*

Total Pest Solutions .... G 302 275-7159
Camden Wyoming *(G-984)*

Total Pest Solutions .... F 302 368-8081
Newark *(G-12212)*

Tri State Termite & Pest Ctrl .... G 302 239-0512
Newark *(G-12221)*

Trigger Action LLC .... G 302 858-8629
Georgetown *(G-4561)*

True Pest Control Services .... G 302 834-0867
Middletown *(G-7665)*

Wilkins Wildlife & Bedbug 911 .... G 302 236-3533
Delmar *(G-1658)*

PEST CONTROL SVCS

Middletown Mosquito Ctrl LLC .... G 302 378-3378
Middletown *(G-7356)*

Mosquito Authority .... F 302 346-2970
Dover *(G-3126)*

Mosquito Authority .... G 302 228-5821
Rehoboth Beach *(G-12864)*

Mosquito Authority Wilmington .... G 302 299-5299
Middletown *(G-7381)*

Terminix Intl Co Ltd Partnr .... F 302 653-4866
Historic New Castle *(G-5082)*

PESTICIDES

Growmark Fs LLC .... G 302 422-3001
Milford *(G-7912)*

Growmark Fs LLC .... D 302 422-3002
Milford *(G-7913)*

Leotech LLC .... G 908 829-3813
Wilmington *(G-17881)*

PET FOOD WHOLESALERS

Beaverdam Pet Food .... G 302 349-5299
Greenwood *(G-4595)*

PET SPLYS

Dog Anya .... G 302 456-0108
Newark *(G-10546)*

K9 Natural Foods USA LLC .... E 855 596-2887
Wilmington *(G-17633)*

Nature Impact Inc .... G 650 241-8301
Wilmington *(G-18557)*

Pet Shop LLC .... G 646 345-8844
Dover *(G-3304)*

Purebred LLC .... G 929 777-7770
New Castle *(G-9501)*

PETROLEUM & PETROLEUM PRDTS, WHOLESALE: Bulk Stations

Merit Inc .... G 302 778-4732
Wilmington *(G-18285)*

Peninsula Oil Co Inc .... E 302 422-6691
Seaford *(G-13338)*

PETROLEUM BULK STATIONS & TERMINALS

Du Pont Elastomers LP .... E 302 774-1000
Wilmington *(G-16190)*

Eidp Inc .... G 302 772-0016
New Castle *(G-9084)*

Service Oil Company .... G 302 734-7433
Dover *(G-3535)*

Employee Codes: A=Over 500 employees, B=251-500
C=101-250, D=51-100, E=20-50, F=10-19, G=1-9

PETROLEUM REFINERY INSPECTION SVCS

Sunlite Energy Intll............................. G 302 598-2984
Historic New Castle (G-5077)

PETROLEUM REFINERY INSPECTION SVCS

Jbm Petroleum Service LLC................. G 302 752-6105
Lincoln (G-6677)

PHARMACEUTICAL PREPARATIONS: Druggists' Preparations

A2a Intgrted Phrmceuticals LLC........... G 270 202-2461
Lewes (G-5648)

Zeneca Holdings Inc........................... D 302 886-3000
Wilmington (G-20953)

PHARMACEUTICAL PREPARATIONS: Proprietary Drug

LRC North America Inc....................... E 302 427-2845
Wilmington (G-18018)

PHARMACEUTICAL PREPARATIONS: Solutions

Tesla Biohealing Inc............................ E 302 265-2213
Milford (G-8117)

PHARMACEUTICALS

A66 Inc.. G 800 444-0446
Wilmington (G-14180)

Amylin Pharmaceuticals LLC................ A 858 552-2200
Wilmington (G-14466)

Angita Pharmard LLC......................... G 302 234-6794
Hockessin (G-5126)

Anip Acquisition Company.................. G 302 652-2021
Wilmington (G-14485)

Astrazeneca LP.................................. A 302 886-3000
Wilmington (G-14609)

Astrazeneca Pharmaceuticals LP.......... B 302 286-3500
Newark (G-9929)

Astrazeneca Pharmaceuticals LP.......... A 800 456-3669
Wilmington (G-14610)

Auragin LLC....................................... G 800 383-5109
Wilmington (G-14643)

Biosion Usa Inc.................................. F 302 257-5085
Newark (G-10037)

Bristol-Myers Squibb Company............ G 800 321-1335
Wilmington (G-15119)

Colgate-Palmolive Company................ G 302 428-1554
Wilmington (G-15527)

Dupont Indus Bsciences USA LLC........ E 302 774-1000
Wilmington (G-16210)

FMC Corporation................................ D 302 451-0100
Newark (G-10751)

Fulcrum Pharmacy MGT Inc................ G 302 658-8020
Wilmington (G-16768)

Gap Innovations Pbc........................... E 203 464-7048
Dover (G-2556)

Genesis Laboratories Inc..................... G 832 217-8585
Wilmington (G-16837)

Glanbia Inc.. G 208 733-7555
Wilmington (G-16880)

Glaxosmithkline Capital Inc................. E 302 656-5280
Wilmington (G-16881)

Glycomira LLC................................... G 704 651-9789
Dover (G-2597)

Hopewell Pharma Ventures Inc............ G 203 273-1350
Wilmington (G-17201)

Incyte Holdings Corporation................ E 302 498-6700
Wilmington (G-17307)

International N&H Usa Inc.................. D 302 451-0176
Newark (G-11047)

Iqure Pharma Inc............................... F 908 294-1212
Wilmington (G-17421)

Lavoisier Inc...................................... G 302 446-3244
Dover (G-2910)

Marlex Pharmaceuticals Inc................. E 302 328-3355
New Castle (G-9348)

Mc2 Therapeutics Inc.......................... G 202 505-0891
Dover (G-3041)

Medical Sup Support Svcs LLC............. F 302 446-3658
Dover (G-3052)

Medimmune LLC................................ G 301 398-1200
Wilmington (G-18255)

Merck & Co Inc.................................. E 302 934-8051
Millsboro (G-8377)

Mommas Mountain LLC...................... G 410 236-6717
Magnolia (G-6769)

Neuracon Biotech Inc.......................... G 813 966-3129
Wilmington (G-18601)

New Life Medicals LLC........................ G 610 615-1483
Dover (G-3180)

Nikang Therapeutics Inc..................... E 302 415-5127
Wilmington (G-18649)

Noramco Inc...................................... G 302 652-3840
Wilmington (G-18670)

Noramco LLC..................................... G 302 761-2923
Wilmington (G-18671)

Novartis Corporation.......................... G 302 992-5610
Wilmington (G-18694)

Novo Nordisk Pharmaceuticals............. G 302 345-0229
Wilmington (G-18700)

Novo Nrdisk US Coml Hldngs Inc......... D 302 691-6181
Wilmington (G-18701)

Penn Labs Inc.................................... E 215 751-4000
Wilmington (G-18952)

Pharma E Market LLC......................... F 302 737-3711
Hockessin (G-5344)

Pharmunion LLC................................ G 415 307-5128
Wilmington (G-19009)

Platinum US Distribution Inc................ G 905 364-8713
Wilmington (G-19073)

Plx Pharma Winddown Corp................ G 973 381-7408
Dover (G-3339)

Prelude Therapeutics Inc..................... D 302 467-1280
Wilmington (G-19166)

Sangita Scientific LLC......................... G 866 272-6432
Wilmington (G-19664)

Sarkana Pharma Inc........................... G 649 332-4417
Wilmington (G-19673)

Scov3 LLC.. G 973 387-9771
Wilmington (G-19714)

Scov3 LLC.. G 973 387-9771
Wilmington (G-19715)

Shinlaza Inc....................................... G 800 206-0051
Wilmington (G-19800)

Shire North American Group Inc.......... D 484 595-8800
Wilmington (G-19804)

Smithkline Beecham Intl Co................. E 302 479-5804
Wilmington (G-19893)

Snow Pharmaceuticals LLC.................. G 302 436-8855
Frankford (G-4146)

SPI Pharma Inc.................................. G 302 360-7200
Lewes (G-6500)

Zeneca Inc.. G 302 886-3000
Wilmington (G-20954)

PHOTOCOPY MACHINES

B Williams Holding Corp..................... F 302 656-8596
Wilmington (G-14704)

PHOTOCOPYING & DUPLICATING SVCS

Amer Inc... G 302 654-2498
Wilmington (G-14421)

Braun Engineering & Surveying........... G 302 698-0701
Camden Wyoming (G-919)

Fedex Office & Print Svcs Inc.............. G 302 652-2151
Wilmington (G-16572)

Fedex Office & Print Svcs Inc.............. G 302 996-0264
Wilmington (G-16573)

Garile Inc.. E 302 366-0848
Newark (G-10809)

Mr Copy Inc...................................... G 302 227-4666
Rehoboth Beach (G-12866)

PHOTOGRAPHIC EQPT & SPLYS

360 DC Rentals LLC............................ G 202 432-3655
Wilmington (G-14125)

PHOTOGRAPHIC EQPT & SPLYS, WHOLESALE: Printing Apparatus

Autotype Holdings (usa) Inc................ D 302 378-3100
Middletown (G-6889)

Scigate Holdings LLC.......................... G 970 481-4949
Newark (G-11962)

PHOTOGRAPHY SVCS: Commercial

Dean Digital Imaging Inc..................... G 302 655-6992
Wilmington (G-15846)

Judah Road Productions LLC............... G 508 640-5022
Dover (G-2813)

Lenzinifordelaware............................. G 302 836-6287
Bear (G-345)

Perryfilms Production Co LLC.............. G 302 505-4458
Lewes (G-6363)

Vonogrphy-The Perfect Shot LLC......... G 202 923-9532
Newark (G-12336)

PHYSICAL EXAMINATION & TESTING SVCS

Exam Master Corporation.................... E 800 572-3627
Newark (G-10682)

Heckessin Health Partners................... G 302 234-2597
Hockessin (G-5236)

Pivot Occupational Health LLC............ F 302 368-5100
Newark (G-11697)

Womens Imaging Center Delaware...... G 302 738-9494
Newark (G-12397)

PHYSICIANS' OFFICES & CLINICS: Medical doctors

8th & Market Spinal Center................. G 302 652-6000
Wilmington (G-14153)

A Douglas Chervenak Do..................... F 302 653-1050
Smyrna (G-13625)

Accelcare Wund Prfssnals Del P.......... G 800 261-0048
Dover (G-1704)

Ada L Gonzalez M D............................ F 302 724-4567
Dover (G-1715)

Advance Physical Therapy LLC............. G 302 407-3592
Wilmington (G-14269)

Advanced Biomedical Inc..................... G 302 730-1880
Dover (G-1723)

Alice R OBrien Ms Lpcmh.................... G 302 521-3859
Wilmington (G-14357)

Alicia Kendorski Ncc........................... G 302 448-5054
Millville (G-8513)

Amanda C Szymczak............................ G 302 678-3020
Dover (G-1780)

Amanda Lynn Ferenc LPn.................... G 302 841-2498
Bridgeville (G-663)

American Cllge of Physicians............... G 540 631-0426
Wilmington (G-14430)

Andre M D Hoffman............................ G 302 892-2710
Newark (G-9865)

PRODUCTS & SERVICES SECTION

PHYSICIANS' OFFICES & CLINICS: Medical doctors

Andrea M D Arellano .... G 302 678-0510
Dover *(G-1792)*

Andrew W Donohue Do .... G 302 235-3725
Wilmington *(G-14479)*

Angela Saldarriaga .... G 302 633-1182
Wilmington *(G-14482)*

Ann White .... G 302 365-4664
Newark *(G-9872)*

Antonio C Narvaez MD .... G 302 453-1002
Newark *(G-9881)*

Arlen D Stone M D .... G 302 999-0933
Newark *(G-9904)*

Armand De MD Sanctic .... F 302 475-2535
Wilmington *(G-14553)*

Arun Jain Advicoach .... G 302 442-0053
Wilmington *(G-14574)*

Athena T Jolly M D .... G 302 454-3020
Newark *(G-9932)*

Atlantic Physicians Billing .... G 914 490-3741
Milford *(G-7778)*

Avery Institute .... G 302 803-6784
Wilmington *(G-14668)*

Balu Ganesh R MD .... G 302 992-9191
Wilmington *(G-14726)*

Bayhealth Medical Group Ent .... F 302 339-8040
Georgetown *(G-4224)*

Beck Jr Thomas D Do .... G 302 541-4500
Ocean View *(G-12475)*

Beebe Medical Center Inc .... G 302 856-9729
Georgetown *(G-4231)*

Benjamin M D Cooper .... G 302 652-3331
Wilmington *(G-14836)*

BMA Milford .... G 302 424-0552
Milford *(G-7799)*

Body Brain Sync Inc .... G 302 498-9234
Bear *(G-78)*

Bradford Family Physicians LLC .... G 302 730-3750
Dover *(G-1969)*

Bruce M Dopler MD .... G 302 628-7730
Seaford *(G-13096)*

Butt Kambiz R MD .... G 708 927-7169
Newark *(G-10108)*

Cardiac Rehab .... F 302 832-5414
Newark *(G-10139)*

Cardio-Kinetics Inc .... E 302 738-6635
Newark *(G-10140)*

Castro Jose MD .... G 302 999-8169
Wilmington *(G-15271)*

Charles L Hobbs DPM .... G 302 655-7735
Wilmington *(G-15337)*

Cheryl Cantrell .... G 610 793-9202
Wilmington *(G-15365)*

Childers IV Henry E MD .... G 302 258-8853
Georgetown *(G-4252)*

Chistine E Woods .... F 302 709-4497
Newark *(G-10208)*

Chitiki Dhadha Gautamy MD .... G 302 393-5006
Milford *(G-7825)*

Choudhary Chitra MD .... G 302 401-1500
Dover *(G-2070)*

Chris Curry Dr .... G 302 365-5457
Bear *(G-99)*

Christiana Care Health Sys Inc ..... C 302 733-2410
Newark *(G-10224)*

Christiana Care Health Sys Inc ..... C 302 659-4401
Smyrna *(G-13676)*

Christiana Care Health System ..... F 302 674-1390
Townsend *(G-13971)*

Christina H Bovelsky M D .... G 302 514-3571
Smyrna *(G-13677)*

Christine Metzing .... G 302 376-5148
Middletown *(G-6979)*

Clement Ogunwande Do .... G 302 762-4545
Wilmington *(G-15478)*

Collabrting For Nvel Sltons LL ...... G 619 252-6060
Wilmington *(G-15528)*

Complete Family Care Inc .... F 302 232-5002
Wilmington *(G-15572)*

Continental Insight .... G 302 273-4458
Milton *(G-8590)*

Craig Smucker MD Orthopaedics .. G 610 869-5757
Hockessin *(G-5169)*

Creative Med Consulting LLC .... G 302 313-1411
Odessa *(G-12582)*

Ctm Medical Associates LLC .... F 302 945-9730
Millsboro *(G-8247)*

Dale F Sutherland MD LLC .... F 302 827-4376
Lewes *(G-5878)*

Daniel Marelli .... G 302 744-7980
Dover *(G-2193)*

David D Scheid M D .... G 302 633-1700
Wilmington *(G-15805)*

David S Jezyk M D .... G 302 261-6343
Wilmington *(G-15811)*

David V Martini MD .... G 302 945-9730
Millsboro *(G-8257)*

David W West M D .... G 302 651-4317
Wilmington *(G-15814)*

Debbie D Takats Rn .... F 302 737-4552
Newark *(G-10403)*

Delaware Behavioral Health .... G 302 397-8958
Wilmington *(G-15872)*

Delaware Obs LLC .... G 302 743-4798
New Castle *(G-9029)*

Delaware Scuba LLC .... G 302 236-6350
Laurel *(G-5495)*

Digitizing America LLC .... G 315 882-9516
Historic New Castle *(G-4974)*

Douglas B Allen Do .... G 302 659-4545
Smyrna *(G-13713)*

Dr Beth Duncan .... G 302 644-2232
Lewes *(G-5932)*

Dr Caroline M Wieczorek .... G 302 635-1430
Newark *(G-10560)*

Dr Mae Gaskins .... G 302 731-0439
Newark *(G-10564)*

Dr Quan Nguyen .... G 302 453-1342
Newark *(G-10567)*

Dr Rajshekar Narasimaiah MD ..... G 302 537-1100
Bethany Beach *(G-598)*

Dr Rene Badillo .... G 301 827-1800
Newark *(G-10568)*

Dr Thomas C Scott Do .... G 302 328-0650
New Castle *(G-9061)*

Duggal Manveen MD .... G 302 734-2782
Dover *(G-2393)*

Dustin Davis .... G 302 856-2254
Georgetown *(G-4300)*

EGNM LLC .... F 302 644-3466
Lewes *(G-5951)*

Endoscopy Suite Partners LLC .... G 267 243-3850
Wilmington *(G-16411)*

Ephraim A Ayoola M D .... G 302 741-0204
Dover *(G-2455)*

Erik A Underhill MD .... G 302 652-3772
Wilmington *(G-16457)*

Ernest Soffronoff Dr .... G 302 827-2284
Lewes *(G-5971)*

Evagoras G Economides .... G 302 645-1233
Lewes *(G-5977)*

Feathers Group LLC .... G 302 300-5967
Newark *(G-10720)*

First State Infctious Diseases ...... F 302 535-4608
Dover *(G-2506)*

Forwood Chiropractic Center .... G 302 652-0411
Wilmington *(G-16698)*

Francis Mase MD PA .... G 302 762-5656
Wilmington *(G-16721)*

Frederick M Williams MD .... G 302 738-0103
Newark *(G-10774)*

Fresenius Medical Care Souther ... E 302 678-2181
Dover *(G-2536)*

Gabbaud Health LLC .... F 267 512-1750
Newark *(G-10796)*

Garg Manish MD .... G 302 355-2383
Wilmington *(G-16804)*

Gifty A Nyinaku LPN .... G 571 224-2660
Newark *(G-10834)*

Gina K Alderson MD .... G 302 628-7730
Seaford *(G-13198)*

Glen D Rowe Dr .... G 302 730-4366
Dover *(G-2589)*

Habib Bolourchi MD Facc .... G 302 645-7672
Rehoboth Beach *(G-12779)*

Hatjis Christos G MD .... G 302 744-6220
Dover *(G-2662)*

Healthstat Inc .... G 704 936-5546
Milford *(G-7924)*

Healthy Outcomes LLC .... G 302 856-4022
Georgetown *(G-4354)*

Herbert Mrs Sheryl A .... G 215 668-1849
Bear *(G-269)*

Hifu Services Inc .... G 650 867-4972
Wilmington *(G-17139)*

Howard Z Arian M D .... G 302 674-2390
Dover *(G-2699)*

Hummell James MD .... G 302 875-8127
Laurel *(G-5533)*

Independent Insur Consulting ...... G 302 983-0298
Newark *(G-11012)*

Indian River Golf Cars Dr Wldg ..... G 302 947-2044
Millsboro *(G-8320)*

Ivan Cohen & Assoc LLC .... G 302 428-0205
Newark *(G-11064)*

J & B Md Crabs .... G 302 387-2161
Harrington *(G-4789)*

Jadali Seyedmehdi MD .... G 302 738-4300
Newark *(G-11084)*

James Boyland .... G 302 838-0800
Bear *(G-297)*

Jayant H Shukla Dr .... G 302 834-0222
Bear *(G-299)*

Jennifer .... G 302 738-3020
Newark *(G-11104)*

Jerry L Case Dr .... G 302 368-5500
Newark *(G-11108)*

Jerry P Gluckman M D .... G 302 426-8012
Wilmington *(G-17532)*

Joan A Procaccio Inc .... G 302 542-6394
Lewes *(G-6142)*

John Butler MD .... G 302 674-8066
Dover *(G-2797)*

John M D Murphy .... G 302 368-2501
Newark *(G-11115)*

Jonathan L Patterson MD .... G 302 242-6176
Milford *(G-7957)*

Jose H Austria MD .... G 302 645-8954
Lewes *(G-6151)*

Joseph A Kuhn MD LLC .... G 302 656-3801
Wilmington *(G-17577)*

Joseph G Goldberg Od .... G 302 999-1286
Wilmington *(G-17581)*

Joseph Schwartz Psyd .... G 302 213-3287
Rehoboth Beach *(G-12809)*

Journeys .... G 443 945-0615
Claymont *(G-1201)*

Employee Codes: A=Over 500 employees, B=251-500
C=101-250, D=51-100, E=20-50, F=10-19, G=1-9

2024 Harris Directory of Delaware Businesses

PHYSICIANS' OFFICES & CLINICS: Medical doctors — PRODUCTS & SERVICES SECTION

Jr Anesthesia LLC .... G 302 678-0725
  Dover *(G-2807)*
Justin Connor MD LLC .... G 302 483-7115
  Dover *(G-2821)*
Kapur Neeraj MD .... G 302 789-0545
  Wilmington *(G-17650)*
Karl W McIntosh M D .... G 302 594-9000
  Wilmington *(G-17654)*
Kate W Bernstein .... G 302 597-9911
  Claymont *(G-1205)*
Katherine M King RN .... G 302 449-3625
  Middletown *(G-7263)*
Katy E Crowe MD .... G 302 230-4965
  Wilmington *(G-17668)*
Keith A Sargent Do .... F 302 990-3300
  Seaford *(G-13247)*
Kendall G Ritz M D .... G 302 652-3586
  Wilmington *(G-17684)*
Kevin Keough Dr .... G 302 384-8173
  Wilmington *(G-17700)*
Kiara M Moore .... G 412 953-2791
  Middletown *(G-7270)*
Kieran Py MD .... G 302 541-4460
  Ocean View *(G-12534)*
Lakeside Physical Therapy LLC .... F 302 280-6920
  Laurel *(G-5545)*
Larry R Glazerman M D .... G 302 655-7296
  Wilmington *(G-17810)*
Le-Gen Medical LLC .... G 216 496-7113
  Wilmington *(G-17844)*
Lifeline Bltmore MD Mllvlle De .... G 410 262-0875
  Millville *(G-8536)*
Lynnanne Kasarda MD .... F 302 655-5822
  Wilmington *(G-18051)*
Mac Physician LLC .... G 302 235-8808
  Hockessin *(G-5288)*
Marc Kattelman Do .... G 260 485-4580
  Milford *(G-7984)*
Marcelle L Paschall DSC .... G 302 376-1768
  Townsend *(G-14030)*
Marian Thurrell .... G 302 239-1269
  Hockessin *(G-5298)*
Mark E Case M D .... G 302 449-1710
  Middletown *(G-7328)*
Mark Menendez .... G 302 644-8500
  Georgetown *(G-4414)*
Marquez Misael MD .... G 302 995-6192
  Wilmington *(G-18155)*
Mary Hazlett .... G 302 653-8823
  Smyrna *(G-13816)*
Maryland Center For Therapeuti .... G 302 727-8832
  Lewes *(G-6247)*
Mattern and Associates MD .... G 302 724-5062
  Dover *(G-3034)*
Mayflower Healthcare LLC .... G 908 414-8026
  Wilmington *(G-18209)*
Mds Interpreting LLC .... G 302 507-2393
  Wilmington *(G-18240)*
Mds Services Inc .... G 302 547-3861
  Newark *(G-11368)*
Medhat Iskander .... G 302 422-2020
  Milford *(G-7992)*
Medical Tourism Agency LLC .... G 855 753-3833
  Wilmington *(G-18250)*
Melissa M Damiano Do .... F 302 449-2570
  Townsend *(G-14034)*
Michael Bober MD .... G 302 651-5916
  Wilmington *(G-18309)*
Michael D Johnson M D .... G 267 760-7195
  New Castle *(G-9363)*
Michael D Merrill .... G 302 994-2511
  Wilmington *(G-18310)*

Michael G Sugarman MD .... G 302 366-7671
  Newark *(G-11402)*
Michael G Sweeney M D .... G 302 678-4488
  Dover *(G-3079)*
Michael M Wydila M D .... G 302 798-8070
  Wilmington *(G-18318)*
Michael Matthias .... G 302 575-0100
  Wilmington *(G-18320)*
Michael Zaragoza Md Facs .... G 302 736-1320
  Dover *(G-3081)*
Michelle E Papa Do .... G 302 656-5424
  Wilmington *(G-18328)*
Mid Atlantic Surgical LLC .... G 302 652-6050
  Wilmington *(G-18333)*
Miller Samuel MD .... G 302 629-8662
  Seaford *(G-13284)*
Mills James MD .... G 302 526-1470
  Dover *(G-3093)*
Mint & Needle LLC .... G 302 696-2484
  Middletown *(G-7373)*
Mohammed M Ali M D .... G 302 328-2895
  Bear *(G-376)*
Morris Carol Jamie Do .... G 302 393-5006
  Milford *(G-8020)*
Mr Counseling LLC .... G 302 855-9598
  Georgetown *(G-4437)*
Mujib R Obeidy .... G 302 478-5900
  Wilmington *(G-18481)*
Mymedchoices Inc .... G 302 932-1920
  Hockessin *(G-5315)*
Nancy A Mondero Do .... G 302 644-9641
  Lewes *(G-6304)*
Nanticoke River Physicians LLC .... F 302 629-9735
  Seaford *(G-13310)*
New Castle Family Care PA .... F 302 275-3428
  Newark *(G-11519)*
Niaz M A MD .... G 302 368-2563
  Newark *(G-11554)*
Nicole Smith .... G 302 383-8233
  Wilmington *(G-18646)*
Omar A Khan M D .... G 302 478-7160
  Wilmington *(G-18762)*
Outpatient Procedure Ctrs LLC .... G 302 734-7246
  Dover *(G-3251)*
Owens Jr Louis F MD PA .... G 302 629-0448
  Seaford *(G-13328)*
Pain Solution Centers .... F 215 750-9600
  Newark *(G-11613)*
Parikh Mona Ashish MD .... G 302 300-4246
  Newark *(G-11627)*
Patel Asit .... G 302 502-3181
  Newark *(G-11633)*
Patibanda Suguna M D .... G 302 453-1550
  Wilmington *(G-18905)*
Patricia Heinemann MD .... G 302 778-2229
  Wilmington *(G-18908)*
Persante Sleep Center .... F 302 724-5128
  Dover *(G-3302)*
Persante Sleep Center .... F 302 508-2130
  Smyrna *(G-13846)*
Peter M D Rocca .... F 302 683-9400
  Newark *(G-11672)*
Physiatrist .... G 302 993-0282
  Newark *(G-11687)*
Physicans Dspnsing Sltons Lwes .... G 302 313-4883
  Lewes *(G-6366)*
Professional Technicians Inc .... E 215 364-4911
  Newark *(G-11759)*
Psych Total Care LLC .... F 302 478-7981
  Rehoboth Beach *(G-12901)*
Puri Vineet MD .... G 302 744-9645
  Dover *(G-3397)*

R Macpherson Dr .... G 302 834-8308
  Newark *(G-11809)*
Rafael Zaragoza Dr .... G 302 697-2336
  Camden Wyoming *(G-968)*
Ramesh Vemulapalli MD .... G 302 674-9141
  Dover *(G-3421)*
Rangaswamy Leela MD .... G 267 256-0721
  Wilmington *(G-19332)*
Rao D Bhaskar MD .... G 302 733-5700
  Newark *(G-11826)*
Reddy Dr Veena .... G 302 998-0304
  Newark *(G-11841)*
Regent Open Mri .... G 252 430-6246
  Seaford *(G-13369)*
Rhonda Replogle Horses .... F 301 730-3100
  Harrington *(G-4820)*
Richard Dale Rodgers .... G 814 323-0450
  Newark *(G-11882)*
Richard L Cruz MD .... G 302 577-4270
  New Castle *(G-9532)*
Richelle L Clark .... G 302 448-8094
  Georgetown *(G-4487)*
Ricks Fitness & Health Inc .... G 302 684-0316
  Milton *(G-8699)*
Robert Davison .... G 301 518-0516
  Bridgeville *(G-762)*
Robert Kopecki Do .... G 302 230-4955
  Wilmington *(G-19517)*
Robert L Grzonka M D .... G 302 503-2460
  Milford *(G-8071)*
Roderick M Relova Do .... G 302 346-3171
  Dover *(G-3479)*
Ron G Williams M D .... G 302 838-2238
  Bear *(G-469)*
Ronald A Beard .... G 302 883-7883
  Dover *(G-3480)*
Ronald A Luna M D .... G 302 629-4569
  Seaford *(G-13379)*
Ronald N Brown .... G 302 478-1108
  Wilmington *(G-19561)*
Rose Strab .... G 302 584-2074
  Wilmington *(G-19568)*
Samaha Michel R MD .... G 302 422-3100
  Milford *(G-8081)*
Sameena Malhan .... F 302 422-3311
  Milford *(G-8082)*
Sandra Jackson .... G 302 510-3576
  Wilmington *(G-19659)*
Sandra Sue Retzky DO .... G 302 540-3463
  Wilmington *(G-19661)*
Scott A Hammer Md Faafp .... G 302 725-2033
  Milford *(G-8087)*
Seager Insight .... G 302 526-0597
  Claymont *(G-1286)*
Seiff Jenna L MD .... G 302 633-6859
  Wilmington *(G-19739)*
Seymour Sasha Rene C N A .... G 302 543-1180
  New Castle *(G-9561)*
Shariyfa A Fields .... F 302 552-3574
  Wilmington *(G-19781)*
Shashi Patel .... G 302 737-5074
  Hockessin *(G-5382)*
Shaylin M Shorts .... G 302 494-2451
  Newark *(G-11992)*
Shore Accountants Md Inc .... G 410 758-6900
  Middletown *(G-7562)*
Singh Priya C MD .... G 302 674-4700
  Dover *(G-3568)*
Slay By Jere .... G 302 723-0034
  Middletown *(G-7572)*
Soares Dr Neha M .... G 248 707-4931
  Dover *(G-3581)*

PRODUCTS & SERVICES SECTION

PLASTICS MATERIAL & RESINS

Southern Delaware Med Group............ G 302 424-3900
Dover *(G-3589)*

Spine Group LLC................................ G 302 595-3030
Wilmington *(G-19964)*

St Johns Community Services............ G 302 292-1044
Newark *(G-12080)*

State of De... G 302 376-5125
Middletown *(G-7597)*

Stephen M D Carey............................ G 302 629-8662
Seaford *(G-13412)*

Stone Harbor Square LLC.................. F 302 227-5227
Rehoboth Beach *(G-12976)*

Studio 13 Skin By Christina................ G 302 258-4205
Middletown *(G-7604)*

Tammi Lea Dr.................................... G 302 335-2563
Frederica *(G-4184)*

Tamp Inc... F 302 283-9195
Newark *(G-12158)*

Tankala Harsha MD............................ G 302 346-0101
Dover *(G-3650)*

Tidalhlth Pnnsula Regional Inc........... G 302 436-8004
Selbyville *(G-13612)*

Torregiani Seth DDo PA..................... G 302 407-5412
Wilmington *(G-20365)*

Treatment Access Ctr......................... G 302 856-5487
Georgetown *(G-4559)*

Trudy L Hastings................................ G 302 653-3145
Smyrna *(G-13920)*

Turning Crnrs-Hand In Hand LLC....... G 302 689-3562
Newark *(G-12246)*

United Medical LLC........................... D 302 266-9166
Bear *(G-552)*

Valerie Rivera.................................... G 302 387-5334
Frederica *(G-4186)*

Vincent B Killeen M D........................ G 302 645-4700
Lewes *(G-6606)*

Walter J Kobasa Jr MD....................... G 302 993-1191
Wilmington *(G-20674)*

Wendy M D Schofer........................... G 302 824-4411
Wilmington *(G-20730)*

Wesley Novak PHD............................ G 302 477-0470
Wilmington *(G-20736)*

William R Atkins MD.......................... G 302 633-4525
Newark *(G-12376)*

William R Lynch M D......................... G 302 319-4736
Wilmington *(G-20796)*

William V Gallery Dr........................... G 302 945-5943
Harbeson *(G-4719)*

Womens Center At Milford Meml....... G 302 430-5540
Milford *(G-8153)*

Womens Health Center...................... G 517 437-5390
Lewes *(G-6638)*

Wong Peter MD.................................. F 302 674-0223
Dover *(G-3866)*

Zeina Jeha Md MPH........................... G 302 503-4200
Lewes *(G-6649)*

Zhang Shunli MD............................... F 302 744-7050
Dover *(G-3900)*

PICTURE FRAMES: Wood

Carspecken-Scott Inc.......................... G 302 762-7955
Wilmington *(G-15260)*

PICTURE FRAMING SVCS, CUSTOM

Carspecken-Scott Inc.......................... G 302 655-7173
Wilmington *(G-15261)*

Framemakers Shop............................ G 302 999-9968
Wilmington *(G-16719)*

PIECE GOODS, NOTIONS & OTHER DRY GOODS, WHOLESALE: Fabrics

Loomcraft Textile & Supply Co........... F 302 454-3232
Newark *(G-11281)*

Wayne Industries Inc......................... G 302 478-6160
Wilmington *(G-20694)*

PIECE GOODS, NOTIONS/DRY GOODS, WHOL: Fabrics, Synthetic

W L Gore & Associates Inc................ C 302 368-3700
Newark *(G-12341)*

W L Gore & Associates Inc................ D 302 738-4880
Newark *(G-12342)*

PILOT SVCS: Aviation

Aero Ways Inc.................................... C 302 324-9970
New Castle *(G-8768)*

Fenway Aviation LLC......................... G 800 981-7183
Wilmington *(G-16580)*

Pilots4rent Inc................................... G 561 704-2885
Bear *(G-425)*

PIPE SECTIONS, FABRICATED FROM PURCHASED PIPE

Atlantic Screen & Mfg Inc.................. G 302 684-3197
Milton *(G-8565)*

PIPELINE & POWER LINE INSPECTION SVCS

Federal Technical Associates............. G 302 697-7951
Dover *(G-2491)*

PIPELINE TERMINAL FACILITIES: Independent

Flou Holding Inc................................ G 832 267-3372
Dover *(G-2519)*

Freehold Cartage Inc......................... E 302 658-2005
New Castle *(G-9145)*

J M Aja Transportation LLC............... G 302 562-6028
Wilmington *(G-17458)*

Reddix Transportation Inc................. F 302 249-9331
Lewes *(G-6414)*

Riverside Farms LLC......................... G 302 222-0760
Felton *(G-4018)*

Virginia Transportation Corp.............. C 302 384-6767
Wilmington *(G-20631)*

PIPELINES: Crude Petroleum

Magellan Midstream Partners LP....... F 302 654-3717
Wilmington *(G-18078)*

Whitecap Pipeline Company LLC....... E 925 842-1000
Wilmington *(G-20768)*

PIPES & TUBES

Apex Piping Systems Inc................... D 302 995-6136
Wilmington *(G-14506)*

PIPES & TUBES: Steel

Emeca/Spe Usa LLC.......................... G 302 875-0760
Laurel *(G-5509)*

Handy & Harman................................ F 302 697-9521
Camden *(G-843)*

Handytube Corporation...................... G 302 697-9521
Camden *(G-844)*

Jaguar Tubulars Inc........................... G 438 778-6535
Newark *(G-11085)*

Psp Corp... G 302 764-7730
Wilmington *(G-19244)*

PIPES & TUBES: Welded

Apex Piping Systems Inc................... D 302 995-6136
Wilmington *(G-14506)*

PLASTICS FILM & SHEET

Ajedium Film Group LLC.................... G 302 452-6609
Newark *(G-9803)*

Dupont De Nemours Inc.................... A 302 774-3034
Wilmington *(G-16205)*

Dupont Specialty Pdts USA LLC........ E 302 992-2941
Wilmington *(G-16216)*

Printpack Inc..................................... C 302 323-4000
New Castle *(G-9495)*

PLASTICS FILM & SHEET: Photographic & X-Ray

Fuji Film.. E 302 477-8000
New Castle *(G-9149)*

PLASTICS FILM & SHEET: Polyethylene

Wilmington Fibre Specialty Co........... E 302 328-7525
Historic New Castle *(G-5102)*

PLASTICS FILM & SHEET: Polypropylene

Delstar Technologies Inc................... C 302 378-8888
Middletown *(G-7051)*

Taghleef Industries Inc...................... D 302 326-5500
Newark *(G-12155)*

PLASTICS MATERIAL & RESINS

Aearo Technologies LLC.................... B 302 283-5497
Newark *(G-9787)*

ARC Resin Corp................................. G 859 230-7063
Wilmington *(G-14534)*

Celanese Polymer Products LLC....... D 302 774-1000
Wilmington *(G-15299)*

Delaware Thrmplastic Specialty........ G 302 424-4722
Milford *(G-7859)*

Delmarva Plastics Co........................ G 302 398-1000
Harrington *(G-4760)*

Delrin Usa LLC.................................. F 302 295-5900
Wilmington *(G-16001)*

Dow Chemical Company................... E 302 366-0500
Newark *(G-10557)*

Dupont Prfmce Elastomers LLC........ B
Wilmington *(G-16214)*

Industrial Sls Factoring Corp............. G 302 573-2500
Wilmington *(G-17317)*

Invista Capital Management LLC...... D 302 731-6882
Newark *(G-11052)*

Invista Capital Management LLC...... C 877 446-8478
Wilmington *(G-17410)*

Invista Capital Management LLC...... G 302 683-3000
Wilmington *(G-17409)*

Invistas Applied RES Centre............. G 302 731-6800
Newark *(G-11054)*

Lanxess Corporation.......................... G 267 205-1969
Wilmington *(G-17806)*

Macro Polymers NA LLC................... G 302 660-6926
Wilmington *(G-18072)*

Neko Colors USA Inc......................... G 844 365-6356
Newark *(G-11501)*

Nova Polymers.................................. G 302 858-4677
Georgetown *(G-4448)*

Performnce Solutions Holdg Inc........ G 302 774-1000
Wilmington *(G-18979)*

Presidium USA Inc............................ G 203 803-2980
Dover *(G-3366)*

Rohm and Haas Equity Corp.............. G 302 366-0500
Newark *(G-11907)*

Specialty Products Us LLC................ E 302 774-1000
Wilmington *(G-19955)*

T P Composites Inc........................... G 610 358-9001
Historic New Castle *(G-5078)*

Employee Codes: A=Over 500 employees, B=251-500
C=101-250, D=51-100, E=20-50, F=10-19, G=1-9

2024 Harris Directory of Delaware Businesses

PLASTICS MATERIALS, BASIC FORMS & SHAPES WHOLESALERS

W L Gore.. G 302 584-8822
Wilmington *(G-20662)*

PLASTICS MATERIALS, BASIC FORMS & SHAPES WHOLESALERS

Delrin Usa LLC... F 302 295-5900
Wilmington *(G-16001)*

Fluorogistx Ct LLC... F 800 373-7811
Wilmington *(G-16675)*

PLASTICS PROCESSING

Covation Biomaterials LLC............................ C 865 279-1414
Newark *(G-10339)*

PLASTICS: Finished Injection Molded

Negri Bossi North America Inc..................... G 302 328-8020
New Castle *(G-9400)*

PLASTICS: Molded

Molded Components Inc................................ G 302 588-2240
Wilmington *(G-18404)*

PLASTICS: Polystyrene Foam

Aearo Technologies LLC................................ B 302 283-5497
Newark *(G-9787)*

Dart Container Sales Company.................... G 305 759-5044
New Castle *(G-8998)*

Dupont De Nemours Inc................................ A 302 774-3034
Wilmington *(G-16205)*

Dupont Specialty Pdts USA LLC................... E 302 992-2941
Wilmington *(G-16216)*

Fluorogistx LLC.. E 302 479-7614
Wilmington *(G-16674)*

Unique Fabricating Na Inc............................. A 248 853-2333
Wilmington *(G-20518)*

United Specialty Foam LLC........................... G 302 650-5948
Wilmington *(G-20527)*

PLASTICS: Thermoformed

3imachinecom Inc... G 301 233-7562
Wilmington *(G-14129)*

Wilmington Fibre Specialty Co...................... E 302 328-7525
Historic New Castle *(G-5102)*

PLATES: Steel

Evraz Claymont Steel Holdings Inc............. B 302 792-5400
Claymont *(G-1140)*

Evraz Claymont Steel Inc............................... B 302 792-5400
Claymont *(G-1141)*

Lohmann Steel LLC... G 844 488-1790
Wilmington *(G-17977)*

PLATING & POLISHING SVC

Aurista Technologies Inc............................... F 302 792-4900
Claymont *(G-1046)*

PLUMBING FIXTURES

Ferguson Enterprises LLC............................. G 302 747-2032
Dover *(G-2492)*

Speakman Company....................................... F 302 765-0204
Historic New Castle *(G-5074)*

POLISHING SVC: Metals Or Formed Prdts

Rohm Haas Elctrnic Mtls Cmp In.................. E
Newark *(G-11908)*

POLYETHYLENE RESINS

Celanese International Corp.......................... D 972 443-4000
Wilmington *(G-15298)*

POLYTETRAFLUOROETHYLENE RESINS

Intech Services Inc.. G 302 366-8530
Newark *(G-11030)*

W L Gore & Associates Inc............................ C 302 368-3700
Newark *(G-12341)*

W L Gore & Associates Inc............................ D 302 738-4880
Newark *(G-12342)*

POLYURETHANE RESINS

Polymer Technologies Inc............................. D 302 738-9001
Newark *(G-11711)*

POULTRY & POULTRY PRDTS WHOLESALERS

Jabez Corp... F 302 475-7600
Wilmington *(G-17470)*

POULTRY & SMALL GAME SLAUGHTERING & PROCESSING

Eastern Shore Poultry Company.................. B 302 855-1350
Georgetown *(G-4306)*

Mountaire Farms Inc....................................... C 302 934-1100
Millsboro *(G-8394)*

Mountaire Farms Inc....................................... C 302 934-1100
Millsboro *(G-8395)*

Mountaire Farms Inc....................................... B 302 988-6200
Selbyville *(G-13581)*

Mountaire of Delmarva Inc........................... E 302 988-6207
Selbyville *(G-13582)*

Perdue Farms Inc... C 302 337-2210
Bridgeville *(G-746)*

Perdue Farms Incorporated.......................... G 302 855-5635
Georgetown *(G-4461)*

Perdue Farms Incorporated.......................... G 302 629-3216
Seaford *(G-13343)*

POWDER: Metal

Ametek Inc.. D 302 456-4400
Newark *(G-9851)*

POWER GENERATORS

Amrec Holdings Inc... D 302 273-0000
Dover *(G-1788)*

PRESS CLIPPING SVC

Clipping Beast LLC.. G 850 312-8223
Middletown *(G-6996)*

PRIMARY FINISHED OR SEMIFINISHED SHAPES

CMC Steel Holding Company....................... G 302 691-6200
Wilmington *(G-15500)*

PRINT CARTRIDGES: Laser & Other Computer Printers

Kent-Sussex Industries Inc........................... B 302 422-4014
Milford *(G-7964)*

PRINTED CIRCUIT BOARDS

Rogers Corporation... C 302 834-2100
Bear *(G-467)*

Seryalda LLC... G 914 861-5974
Wilmington *(G-19764)*

Suretronix Solutions LLC............................... G 302 407-3146
Wilmington *(G-20161)*

PRINTERS & PLOTTERS

On Demand Services LLC............................. G 302 388-1215
Newark *(G-11587)*

PRINTING & EMBOSSING: Plastic Fabric Articles

Kayava Creations LLC..................................... G 302 430-2231
Seaford *(G-13245)*

PRINTING & STAMPING: Fabric Articles

New Process Fibre Company........................ D 302 349-4535
Greenwood *(G-4657)*

PRINTING MACHINERY

Aon3d Inc... G 650 410-3120
Wilmington *(G-14500)*

Eidp Inc.. E 302 733-9200
Christiana *(G-994)*

My Qme Inc... G 302 218-8730
Wilmington *(G-18508)*

Spratley Publishing... G 267 779-7353
Wilmington *(G-19973)*

PRINTING, COMMERCIAL: Bags, Plastic, NEC

JEB Plastics Inc... G 302 479-9223
Wilmington *(G-17513)*

PRINTING, COMMERCIAL: Business Forms, NEC

Best Office Pros... G 302 629-4561
Seaford *(G-13084)*

PRINTING, COMMERCIAL: Decals, NEC

Promotion Zone LLC....................................... G 302 832-8565
Newark *(G-11763)*

PRINTING, COMMERCIAL: Periodicals, NEC

Business History Conference........................ G 302 658-2400
Wilmington *(G-15157)*

Henlopen Design LLC..................................... G 302 265-4330
Lewes *(G-6088)*

PRINTING, COMMERCIAL: Promotional

Candlestick Publishing Inc............................ G 817 939-1306
Wilmington *(G-15214)*

Personalized Luggage Inc............................. G 786 431-3118
Wilmington *(G-18989)*

Unique Image LLC... E 302 658-2266
Wilmington *(G-20519)*

PRINTING, COMMERCIAL: Screen

Anthem Graphix... G 302 270-5111
Magnolia *(G-6718)*

Cosmic Custom Screen Printing.................. G 302 933-0920
Millsboro *(G-8240)*

Diamond State Graphics Inc........................ F 302 325-1100
New Castle *(G-9051)*

Dragons Lair Printing LLC............................. G 302 798-4465
Claymont *(G-1122)*

Dream Graphics... G 302 328-6264
New Castle *(G-9063)*

Factors Etc Inc.. G 302 834-1625
Bear *(G-218)*

Fbk Graphico Inc.. G 302 743-4784
Wilmington *(G-16564)*

Go Tees LLC.. G 708 703-1788
Middletown *(G-7168)*

Lasting Impression Inc A............................... G 302 762-9200
Wilmington *(G-17815)*

Logo Motive Inc... G 302 645-2959
Rehoboth Beach *(G-12836)*

PRODUCTS & SERVICES SECTION

PRINTING: Offset

Meade Inc .... G 302 262-3394
Seaford *(G-13278)*

Middletown Ink LLC .... G 302 725-0705
Middletown *(G-7353)*

Midnight Blue Inc .... F 302 436-9665
Selbyville *(G-13576)*

New Image Inc .... G 302 738-6824
Newark *(G-11523)*

Newphoenix Screen Printing .... G 302 747-8991
Dover *(G-3183)*

Proper-Tees LLC .... G 323 981-9809
Camden *(G-886)*

Remline Corp .... E 302 737-7228
Newark *(G-11850)*

Sportz Tees .... G 302 280-6076
Laurel *(G-5605)*

Stamford Screen Printing Inc .... G 302 654-2442
Wilmington *(G-20008)*

Ten Talents Enterprises Inc .... G 302 409-0718
Middletown *(G-7634)*

To A Tee Printing .... G 302 525-6336
Newark *(G-12202)*

PRINTING: Books

Pmb Associates LLC .... G 302 436-0111
Selbyville *(G-13592)*

PRINTING: Commercial, NEC

70 Inc .... G 310 529-1526
Dover *(G-1690)*

AIA .... G 302 407-2252
New Castle *(G-8774)*

Amer Inc .... G 302 654-2498
Wilmington *(G-14421)*

Compass Graphics .... G 302 378-1977
Middletown *(G-7005)*

Corlo Services Inc .... G 302 737-3207
Newark *(G-10324)*

Creative Promotions .... G 302 697-7896
Camden *(G-809)*

Delaware Screen Printing Inc .... G 302 378-4231
Middletown *(G-7044)*

Distinctive Stationery LLC .... G 410 247-5600
Milton *(G-8608)*

Fedex Office & Print Svcs Inc .... G 302 996-0264
Wilmington *(G-16573)*

Max One Printing .... G 302 897-9050
Bear *(G-368)*

Sussex Printing Corp .... E 302 629-9303
Seaford *(G-13420)*

Zzhouse Inc .... F 302 354-3474
New Castle *(G-9701)*

PRINTING: Gravure, Labels

Ancar Enterprises LLC .... G 302 477-1884
Wilmington *(G-14468)*

PRINTING: Gravure, Rotogravure

Promotion Zone LLC .... G 302 832-8565
Newark *(G-11763)*

PRINTING: Letterpress

Stanley Golden .... G 302 652-5626
Wilmington *(G-20018)*

PRINTING: Lithographic

AlphaGraphics Franchising Inc .... G 302 559-8369
Wilmington *(G-14394)*

Ancar Enterprises LLC .... G 302 453-2600
Newark *(G-9861)*

Ancar Enterprises LLC .... G 302 477-1884
Wilmington *(G-14468)*

Associates International Inc .... D 302 656-4500
Wilmington *(G-14592)*

Bgdedge Inc .... G 302 477-1734
New Castle *(G-8866)*

Chapis Drafting & Blue Print .... G 302 629-6373
Seaford *(G-13112)*

Chick Harness & Supply Inc .... E 302 398-4630
Harrington *(G-4748)*

Coko Prints .... G 302 507-1683
Wilmington *(G-15523)*

Conventioneer Pubg Co Inc .... G 301 487-3907
Georgetown *(G-4267)*

DC Printing Inc .... G 302 545-6666
Wilmington *(G-15826)*

Delaware Dept Hlth Social Svcs .... G 302 255-9855
New Castle *(G-9017)*

Delaware Dept Hlth Social Svcs .... D 302 255-9800
New Castle *(G-9020)*

Delaware Screen Printing Inc .... G 302 378-4231
Middletown *(G-7044)*

Delaware State Printing .... E 302 228-9431
Dover *(G-2264)*

Depro-Serical USA Inc .... G 302 368-8040
Townsend *(G-13991)*

Doculogica Corp .... G 302 753-5944
Wilmington *(G-16113)*

Dover Post Co Inc .... E 302 678-3616
Dover *(G-2364)*

Edythe L Pridgen .... G 302 652-8887
Bear *(G-197)*

Eidp Inc .... G 302 992-2012
Wilmington *(G-16315)*

Foxfire Printing and Packaging Inc .... C 302 533-2240
Newark *(G-10769)*

Garile Inc .... E 302 366-0848
Newark *(G-10809)*

Jerry O Thompson Prntng .... G 302 832-1309
Bear *(G-303)*

Kardmaster Brochures Inc .... G 610 434-5262
Wilmington *(G-17652)*

Lord Printing LLC .... G 302 439-3253
Wilmington *(G-17994)*

Love City Prints LLC .... G 302 245-5702
Lewes *(G-6224)*

Markizon Printing .... G 610 715-7989
Wilmington *(G-18148)*

Mgl Screen Printing .... G 302 450-6250
Clayton *(G-1386)*

Morales Screen Printing .... G 302 465-8179
Dover *(G-3122)*

New Image Inc .... G 302 738-6824
Newark *(G-11523)*

Nexsigns LLC .... G 302 508-2615
Clayton *(G-1391)*

One Hour Printing .... G 302 220-1684
Newark *(G-11592)*

Print On This .... G 302 235-9475
Newark *(G-11747)*

Printcurement .... G 302 249-6100
Historic New Castle *(G-5054)*

Printed Solid Inc .... F 302 439-0098
Newark *(G-11748)*

Prints and Princesses .... G 703 881-1057
Newark *(G-11749)*

Pulsar Print LLC .... G 302 394-9202
Historic New Castle *(G-5057)*

Star Art Inc .... G 302 261-6732
Bear *(G-510)*

Studio B Milford LLC .... G 302 491-7910
Milford *(G-8106)*

Sussex Printing Corp .... E 302 629-9303
Seaford *(G-13420)*

UNI Printing Solutionsllc .... G 631 438-6045
New Castle *(G-9651)*

US Flexo Solutions LLC .... G 302 838-7805
Newark *(G-12289)*

W B Mason Co Inc .... E 888 926-2766
Newark *(G-12340)*

PRINTING: Manmade Fiber & Silk, Broadwoven Fabric

Abbott Dynamics LLC .... G 951 923-5996
Talleyville *(G-13944)*

PRINTING: Offset

A+ Printing .... G 302 273-3147
Wilmington *(G-14175)*

Academy Business Mch & Prtg Co .... G 302 654-3200
Wilmington *(G-14214)*

Allied Printing Co Inc .... G 503 626-0669
New Castle *(G-8785)*

Amer Inc .... G 302 654-2498
Wilmington *(G-14421)*

Armor Graphics Inc .... G 302 737-8790
Newark *(G-9905)*

Aztec Copies LLC .... F 302 575-1993
Wilmington *(G-14688)*

Ben-Dom Printing Company .... F 302 737-9144
Newark *(G-10019)*

Brandywine Graphics Inc .... G 302 655-7571
Wilmington *(G-15062)*

Coastal Printing Company .... G 302 537-1700
Ocean View *(G-12494)*

Communications Printing Inc .... G 302 229-9369
Newark *(G-10287)*

D & B Printing and Mailing Inc .... G 302 838-7111
Newark *(G-10373)*

D & D Screen Printing .... G 302 349-4231
Greenwood *(G-4610)*

DMD Business Forms & Prtg Co .... G 302 998-8200
Wilmington *(G-16107)*

Dover Litho Printing Co .... G 302 698-5292
Dover *(G-2351)*

Dover Post Co Inc .... D 302 653-2083
Dover *(G-2362)*

Fannon Color Printing LLC .... G 302 227-2164
Rehoboth Beach *(G-12750)*

Fishtail Print Company .... G 302 408-4800
Rehoboth Beach *(G-12756)*

Fishtail Print Company .... G 302 682-3053
Rehoboth Beach *(G-12757)*

G & B Comp & Creative Design .... G 302 284-3856
Felton *(G-3977)*

Grm Pro Imaging LLC .... G 302 999-8162
Wilmington *(G-16984)*

Independent Newsmedia Inc USA .... D 302 674-3600
Dover *(G-2729)*

Ini Holdings Inc .... G 302 674-3600
Dover *(G-2734)*

Job Printing .... G 302 907-0416
Delmar *(G-1607)*

Joseph W Small Associates Inc .... F
Wilmington *(G-17588)*

Litho-Print Inc .... G 302 239-1341
Hockessin *(G-5283)*

Luke Destefano Inc .... G 302 455-0710
Newark *(G-11294)*

Marthann Print Center LLC .... G 267 884-8130
Dover *(G-3024)*

McClafferty Printing Company .... E 302 652-8112
Wilmington *(G-18220)*

Mercantile Press Inc .... F 302 764-6884
Wilmington *(G-18274)*

PRINTING: Offset

Millennium Marketing Solutions............ E 301 725-8000
  Lewes *(G-6274)*
News Print Shop.................................... G 302 337-8283
  Bridgeville *(G-738)*
OConnell Speedy Printing Inc............... G 302 656-1475
  Wilmington *(G-18743)*
Patio Printing Co Inc............................. G 302 328-6881
  New Castle *(G-9457)*
Penney Enterprises Inc......................... G 302 629-4430
  Seaford *(G-13340)*
Print Coast 2 Coast............................... G 302 381-4610
  Lewes *(G-6391)*
Print Shack Inc..................................... G 302 629-4430
  Seaford *(G-13358)*
Print-N-Press Inc................................. G 302 994-6665
  Wilmington *(G-19196)*
Printit Solutions LLC............................ G 302 380-3838
  Dover *(G-3373)*
Quick Copies.. G 302 374-0798
  Claymont *(G-1273)*
Rescue Printig...................................... G 302 286-7266
  Newark *(G-11861)*
Rogers Graphics Inc............................ G 302 422-6694
  Harbeson *(G-4713)*
Rogers Graphics Inc............................ F 302 856-0028
  Georgetown *(G-4490)*
Shamrock Printing Company................ G 302 368-8888
  Newark *(G-11990)*
Sprint Quality Printing Inc.................... G 302 478-0720
  Wilmington *(G-19980)*
Stanley Golden..................................... G 302 652-5626
  Wilmington *(G-20018)*
Stratis Visuals LLC............................... F 860 482-1208
  Newark *(G-12107)*
Union Press Printing Inc....................... G 302 652-0496
  Wilmington *(G-20514)*
William N Cann Inc............................... E 302 995-0820
  Wilmington *(G-20795)*
Windswept Enterprises......................... G 302 678-0805
  Dover *(G-3857)*

PRINTING: Screen, Broadwoven Fabrics, Cotton

Carter Printing and Design.................. G 302 655-2343
  Historic New Castle *(G-4952)*
D By D Printing LLC............................. G 302 659-3373
  Dover *(G-2180)*

PRINTING: Screen, Fabric

Atlantic Sun Screen Prtg Inc................ F 302 731-5100
  Newark *(G-9936)*
Jairus Enterprises Inc.......................... G 302 834-1625
  Bear *(G-296)*
Lasting Impression Inc A..................... G 302 762-9200
  Wilmington *(G-17815)*
Original Tube T Shirt Com.................... G 845 291-7031
  Seaford *(G-13327)*
Red Sun Custom Apparel Inc............... F 302 988-8230
  Selbyville *(G-13597)*
Unique Image LLC................................ E 302 658-2266
  Wilmington *(G-20519)*
Whisman John...................................... G 302 530-1676
  Wilmington *(G-20761)*

PROFESSIONAL EQPT & SPLYS, WHOLESALE: Analytical Instruments

Joint Anlytcl Systms (amrcs)................ G 302 607-0088
  Newark *(G-11122)*

PROFESSIONAL EQPT & SPLYS, WHOLESALE: Optical Goods

Elsicon Inc.. G 302 266-7030
  Newark *(G-10634)*

PROFILE SHAPES: Unsupported Plastics

Thermoplastic Processes Inc............... F 888 554-6400
  Georgetown *(G-4552)*

PROMOTION SVCS

ADd Marketing Group LLC................... G 347 668-0992
  Dover *(G-1716)*
Blue Horizon Promotions LLC.............. G 302 547-0913
  Saint Georges *(G-13032)*
Makatuu Inc.. G 650 431-5582
  Dover *(G-3000)*
Mid Atlantic Athc Promotions.............. G 302 535-8472
  Magnolia *(G-6766)*
Remline Corp.. E 302 737-7228
  Newark *(G-11850)*
Square Promote.................................... G 302 478-0736
  Wilmington *(G-19986)*

PROPERTY DAMAGE INSURANCE

AAA Club Alliance Inc.......................... B 302 299-4700
  Wilmington *(G-14181)*
American Centennial Insur Co............. G 302 479-2100
  Wilmington *(G-14426)*
Homewatch Concierge......................... G 302 542-4087
  Rehoboth Beach *(G-12790)*
Nuclear Electric Insurance Ltd............ D 302 888-3000
  Wilmington *(G-18710)*

PUBLIC LIBRARY

Historical Society of Delaware............. E 302 655-7161
  Wilmington *(G-17155)*

PUBLIC RELATIONS & PUBLICITY SVCS

Bgp Publicity Inc.................................. F 302 234-9500
  Wilmington *(G-14872)*
Muse Global Consulting Inc................. E 325 221-3634
  Middletown *(G-7389)*
Slice Communications LLC.................. F 215 600-0050
  Wilmington *(G-19864)*

PUBLIC RELATIONS SVCS

Aloysius Butlr Clark Assoc Inc............. D 302 655-1552
  Wilmington *(G-14390)*
Base-2 Solutions LLC........................... D 202 215-2152
  Lewes *(G-5735)*
Lindsay Mumford LLC.......................... G 302 841-2309
  Fenwick Island *(G-4051)*
One System Incorporated..................... F 888 311-1110
  Wilmington *(G-18784)*
The Ascendant Group Inc.................... F 302 450-4494
  Newark *(G-12186)*
Tipton Communications Group............ F 302 454-7901
  Newark *(G-12198)*

PUBLISHERS: Art Copy & Poster

Qoro LLC... G 302 322-5900
  New Castle *(G-9504)*

PUBLISHERS: Music Book & Sheet Music

Gotti Boyz Entertainment..................... G 302 409-2901
  Bear *(G-253)*
Melody Entertainment USA Inc............ G 305 505-7659
  Wilmington *(G-18267)*
Percebe Music Inc................................ G 850 341-9594
  Dover *(G-3296)*

PUBLISHING & BROADCASTING: Internet Only

360wise Live Inc................................... G 844 360-9473
  Newark *(G-9710)*
Akimbo Inc.. G 302 204-5299
  Claymont *(G-1028)*
Castos Inc... G 800 677-3394
  Wilmington *(G-15270)*
Conecmi LLC.. G 302 740-9261
  Wilmington *(G-15589)*
Crossover Sports Entrmt LLC.............. G 516 728-5360
  Camden *(G-810)*
Eliyahna Creative LLC......................... G 530 683-5463
  Dover *(G-2435)*
Glimpse Global Inc............................... G 305 216-7667
  Dover *(G-2590)*
Govbizconnect Inc................................ G 860 341-1925
  Dover *(G-2609)*
Hotelrunner Inc..................................... E 650 665-6405
  Newark *(G-10975)*
Intouch Inc.. G 332 223-0720
  Dover *(G-2749)*
Lsf Networks LLC................................. G 213 537-2402
  Wilmington *(G-18021)*
Lumhaa LLC.. G 916 517-9972
  Wilmington *(G-18027)*
Mobile Engagement LLC...................... G 646 583-2775
  Lewes *(G-6284)*
Moscova Enterprises Inc...................... F 347 973-2522
  Wilmington *(G-18460)*
Open Court TV LLC.............................. G 646 975-1509
  Dover *(G-3236)*
Phaction Inc.. G 240 459-5198
  Wilmington *(G-19008)*
Prepared LLC.. G 650 825-5996
  Wilmington *(G-19176)*
Press Media Group Inc........................ G 323 205-5488
  Middletown *(G-7468)*
Raad360 LLC.. F 855 722-3360
  Newark *(G-11812)*
Reel Inc... F 302 319-3522
  Middletown *(G-7508)*
Rwk Ventures LLC................................ G 305 494-4011
  Wilmington *(G-19599)*
She Podcasts.. G 302 588-2317
  Wilmington *(G-19785)*
Sonic Sights Incorporated.................... G 312 498-9977
  Dover *(G-3587)*
Streameq Inc... G 951 807-4938
  Lewes *(G-6517)*
Unpriviteged Drinkers LLC................... G 215 800-5475
  Felton *(G-4035)*
Vylo Inc... G 310 902-9693
  Newark *(G-12339)*
Wazoplus LLC....................................... G 302 496-0042
  Newark *(G-12350)*
Web Advantage Inc............................... F 302 479-7634
  Wilmington *(G-20703)*
Wherebyus Enterprises Inc.................. F 305 988-0808
  Claymont *(G-1336)*
Wna Infotech LLC................................. E 302 668-5977
  Newark *(G-12392)*
Workaway Ventures Inc........................ G 843 608-9108
  Wilmington *(G-20890)*
X Leader LLC.. G 800 345-2677
  Lewes *(G-6642)*

PUBLISHING & PRINTING: Books

Dragon Cloud Inc.................................. G 702 508-2676
  Wilmington *(G-16171)*

PRODUCTS & SERVICES SECTION

REAL ESTATE AGENCIES & BROKERS

Heartfelt Books Publishing .... G 866 557-6522
  Wilmington *(G-17107)*
Hero Family Collection LLC .... G 833 732-3432
  Wilmington *(G-17132)*
Narleyapps Inc .... G 323 744-1398
  Dover *(G-3150)*
Rah Books International .... G 917 288-1064
  Dover *(G-3419)*
Seabrix LLC .... G 224 578-3191
  Dover *(G-3524)*

PUBLISHING & PRINTING: Guides

Sussex Printing Corp .... E 302 629-9303
  Seaford *(G-13420)*

PUBLISHING & PRINTING: Magazines: publishing & printing

AB Creative Publishing LLC .... G 202 802-6909
  Wilmington *(G-14190)*
Advance Magazine Publs Inc .... G 302 830-4630
  Wilmington *(G-14267)*
CIO Story LLC .... G 408 915-5559
  Wilmington *(G-15442)*
Conde Nast International Inc .... C 515 243-3273
  Wilmington *(G-15587)*
Crafts Report Publishing Co .... G 302 656-2209
  Wilmington *(G-15680)*
Hypebeast Inc .... E 714 791-0755
  Dover *(G-2711)*
Student Media Group .... F 302 607-2580
  Newark *(G-12110)*
World Economic Magazine Inc .... G 302 499-2016
  Lewes *(G-6640)*

PUBLISHING & PRINTING: Newsletters, Business Svc

Edit Inc .... G 302 478-7069
  Wilmington *(G-16295)*

PUBLISHING & PRINTING: Newspapers

Cape Gazette Ltd .... E 302 645-7700
  Lewes *(G-5794)*
Coastal Point .... F 302 539-1788
  Ocean View *(G-12493)*
Community Publications Inc .... F 302 239-4644
  Middletown *(G-7004)*
County Women S Journal .... G 302 236-1435
  Lewes *(G-5865)*
Dover Post Co Inc .... G 302 378-9531
  Dover *(G-2363)*
Dover Post Co Inc .... D 302 653-2083
  Dover *(G-2362)*
Dover Post Inc .... G 304 222-6025
  Milford *(G-7871)*
Gatehouse Media Inc .... E 302 678-3616
  Dover *(G-2564)*
Hearst Media Services Conn LLC .... E 203 330-6231
  Wilmington *(G-17103)*
Independent Newsmedia Inc USA .... E 302 674-3600
  Dover *(G-2728)*
Independent Newsmedia Inc USA .... G 302 422-1200
  Milford *(G-7941)*
John T Tedesco .... G 703 357-0797
  Georgetown *(G-4385)*
L E York Law LLC .... G 302 234-8338
  Wilmington *(G-17776)*
Middletown De .... G 302 449-2547
  Middletown *(G-7349)*
Middletown De .... G 302 655-9494
  Middletown *(G-7350)*

Morning Star Publications Inc .... F 302 629-9788
  Seaford *(G-13289)*
Review .... E 302 831-2771
  Newark *(G-11874)*
Spark .... G 302 324-2203
  New Castle *(G-9584)*
Sussex Post .... G 302 629-5505
  Milford *(G-8110)*

PUBLISHING & PRINTING: Pamphlets

Wellthy Investors LLC .... G 267 847-3486
  Dover *(G-3831)*

PUBLISHING & PRINTING: Textbooks

Linguatext Ltd .... G 302 453-8695
  Newark *(G-11262)*

PULP MILLS

Penco Corporation .... G 302 629-7911
  Seaford *(G-13332)*
Sodra Cell USA Inc .... G 503 855-3032
  Wilmington *(G-19912)*

PUMPS & PUMPING EQPT REPAIR SVCS

Modern Controls Inc .... C 302 325-6800
  New Castle *(G-9377)*

PUMPS & PUMPING EQPT WHOLESALERS

C H P T Manufacturing Inc .... G 302 856-7660
  Georgetown *(G-4242)*
Constellation Pumps Corp .... F 301 323-9000
  Wilmington *(G-15610)*
Easy Lawn Inc .... E 302 815-6500
  Greenwood *(G-4624)*

PUMPS: Gasoline, Measuring Or Dispensing

Saker Energy Solutions Inc .... G 808 398-8326
  Historic New Castle *(G-5065)*

PURCHASING SVCS

Artimus LLC .... F 302 546-5350
  Dover *(G-1824)*
Msb Enterprise Partners LLC .... G 302 947-0736
  Millsboro *(G-8396)*

PURIFICATION & DUST COLLECTION EQPT

Air Natures Way Inc .... G 302 738-3063
  Newark *(G-9800)*

QUILTING: Individuals

In The Nest Quilting .... G 302 644-7316
  Lewes *(G-6119)*
Sew Happy Quilts LLC .... G 302 382-5565
  Camden Wyoming *(G-974)*

RADIO BROADCASTING & COMMUNICATIONS EQPT

C4-Nvis USA LLC .... G 213 465-5089
  Dover *(G-2009)*

RADIO BROADCASTING STATIONS

887 The Bridge .... F 302 422-6909
  Milford *(G-7755)*
Beasley FM Acquisition Corp .... G 302 765-1160
  Wilmington *(G-14806)*
Christian Reachfm Radio Netwrk .... G 302 731-0690
  Newark *(G-10214)*
First Media Radio LLC .... G 410 253-9406
  Rehoboth Beach *(G-12755)*
Heart Ministry Radio .... G 215 847-6664
  Newark *(G-10942)*

Heritage Sports Rdo Netwrk LLC .... G 302 492-1132
  Hartly *(G-4877)*
I Heart Media .... G 302 730-3783
  Dover *(G-2714)*
La Zmx Radio .... G 302 702-2952
  Seaford *(G-13254)*
Larger Story Inc .... G 302 834-5712
  Middletown *(G-7289)*
Porter Broadcasting .... G 302 535-8809
  Dover *(G-3353)*
Priority Radio Inc .... G 302 540-5690
  Newark *(G-11750)*
Radio Rehoboth .... G 302 754-1444
  Rehoboth Beach *(G-12904)*
Royal Broadcasting Inc .... G 302 838-4543
  Bear *(G-472)*
Sussex Amateur Radio Assn .... G 302 629-4949
  Lewes *(G-6529)*
Voice Radio LLC .... F 302 858-5118
  Georgetown *(G-4570)*
Wafl Wyus Broadcasting Inc .... G 302 422-7575
  Milford *(G-8136)*

RAILROAD CAR REPAIR SVCS

Dana Railcare Inc .... E 302 652-8550
  Wilmington *(G-15777)*
Delaware Car Company .... E 302 655-6665
  Wilmington *(G-15880)*

RAILROAD EQPT

Delaware Car Company .... E 302 655-6665
  Wilmington *(G-15880)*

RAILROAD MAINTENANCE & REPAIR SVCS

Auxo Rail Holdings LLC .... D 304 325-7245
  Wilmington *(G-14659)*
Road & Rail Services Inc .... D 302 731-2552
  Newark *(G-11895)*

RAZORS, RAZOR BLADES

Cobra Razors .... G 302 540-0464
  Wilmington *(G-15513)*

REAL ESTATE AGENCIES & BROKERS

1st State Real Estate LLC .... F 302 319-4051
  Wilmington *(G-14116)*
AB Brown Real Estate Inc .... G 302 731-1031
  Wilmington *(G-14189)*
AIG Global Real Estate Inc .... G 302 655-2141
  Wilmington *(G-14331)*
Andy Staton Real Estate Inc .... G 302 703-9090
  Rehoboth Beach *(G-12605)*
Anne Powell LLC .... G 302 245-9245
  Ocean View *(G-12463)*
Aparta Hospitality Tech .... G 617 383-3239
  Dover *(G-1801)*
B F P Sothebys Intl Realty .... G 302 545-5266
  Wilmington *(G-14698)*
Baiz Nancy Miller- .... G 302 576-6821
  Wilmington *(G-14716)*
Bear De .... G 302 836-6050
  Bear *(G-62)*
Bee Wise LLC .... G 302 601-4171
  Lewes *(G-5746)*
Bellevue Realty Co .... F 302 655-1818
  Wilmington *(G-14823)*
Brandywine Fine Properties .... F 302 691-3052
  Wilmington *(G-15057)*
Cal Agents Realty Inc .... G 408 219-1728
  Claymont *(G-1070)*
Castles By Sea LLC .... G 302 539-2508
  Ocean View *(G-12487)*

REAL ESTATE AGENCIES & BROKERS

Company	Location	Phone
Cor3 Capital LLC	Dover (G-2136)	G 941 402-8101
Dee & Doreens Team	Dover (G-2207)	G 302 677-0030
Delaware Valley RE Solutions	Wilmington (G-15983)	G 302 668-1694
Dream America LLC	Lewes (G-5934)	G 305 509-9201
Dsr Drew Sparks Realty LLC	Middletown (G-7074)	G 302 743-1210
Ducos Realty Inc	Townsend (G-13994)	G 302 563-6902
Empowering Realty LLC	Dover (G-2446)	G 302 744-8169
English Realty LLC	Wilmington (G-16425)	E 302 295-4845
Estate Planning Council of Del	Wilmington (G-16468)	G 610 581-4748
Exit King Realty	New Castle (G-9109)	G 941 961-4925
Exp Realty	Dover (G-2472)	E 302 382-5039
Foster Long Real Estate	Ocean View (G-12513)	G 302 864-3216
Ganc Commercial Realty LLC	Newark (G-10806)	G 302 292-1131
GM Realestate	Middletown (G-7166)	G 302 376-9462
Green Oak Real Estate LP	Wilmington (G-16965)	D 212 359-7800
Incredible Care Inc	Wilmington (G-17305)	G 302 428-6093
Jack Lingo Inc Realtor	Lewes (G-6135)	E 302 947-9030
Jack Lingo Realtor	Lewes (G-6136)	F 302 645-2207
Jack Lingo Realtor	Rehoboth Beach (G-12799)	G 302 344-9188
Jones Enterprises Incorporated	Wilmington (G-17574)	G 888 639-1194
Kim Simpson Realty Group	Middletown (G-7273)	G 302 690-0245
Lbg Homes LLC	Dagsboro (G-1474)	G 302 360-0300
Lc Homes Inc	Wilmington (G-17839)	G 302 429-8700
Lee Sells Houses Team	Wilmington (G-17855)	G 302 516-7674
Legum & Norman Mid-West LLC	Lewes (G-6188)	G 302 227-8448
Linda Brannock	Dover (G-2951)	G 302 346-3124
Lisa Johannsen	Middletown (G-7306)	G 302 270-5082
Livingston Enterprise	New Castle (G-9319)	G 302 588-5722
Long & Foster	Dagsboro (G-1475)	G 302 569-0012
Long & Foster Real Estate Inc	Milford (G-7976)	G 302 542-0811
Long and Foster	Lewes (G-6217)	G 925 699-4783
Long and Foster	Selbyville (G-13562)	G 302 858-7805
Marvel Agency Inc	Milford (G-7986)	G 302 422-7844
Megan Aitken Team LLC	Middletown (G-7338)	G 302 376-9836
Michael A Kelczewski	Wilmington (G-18302)	G 302 654-6500
Midway Realty Corp	Rehoboth Beach (G-12857)	E 302 645-9511
Mosap Global Inc	Newark (G-11457)	E 302 559-3036
Mrt LLC	Bear (G-381)	G 856 685-1602
My Beach Agent Realty Group	Lewes (G-6298)	G 302 858-2370
Nest Properties LLC	Middletown (G-7395)	G 302 373-8015
New Castle Cnty Bd of Realtors	Wilmington (G-18608)	G 302 762-4800
Nexthome Prefer	Dover (G-3187)	G 302 526-2886
Nickle Insurance Agency Inc	Delaware City (G-1549)	G 302 834-9700
Ocean Atlantic Associates LLC	Rehoboth Beach (G-12874)	F 302 227-3573
Ocean Atlantic Sothebys Intl	Bethany Beach (G-624)	F 302 539-1033
October Phoenix Rlty Group LLC	Newark (G-11577)	G 302 722-5125
P&H Realty LLC	Townsend (G-14047)	G 302 378-3484
Parker Group	Bridgeville (G-744)	F 302 217-6692
Patterson-Schwartz & Assoc Inc	Hockessin (G-5333)	F 302 234-3606
Porro Realty Group	Wilmington (G-19118)	G 302 384-6056
Real Estate Market	Laurel (G-5586)	G 302 715-5640
Real Pro Holdings Inc	Wilmington (G-19370)	G 541 743-8500
Red Brick Realty LLC	Wilmington (G-19382)	G 302 540-1128
Rehoboth Home Sales Inc	Rehoboth Beach (G-12927)	G 609 924-7701
RHS Realty	Selbyville (G-13599)	G 302 436-6478
Rob Watson	Wilmington (G-19505)	G 302 234-8877
Rock River Real Estate Inc	Wilmington (G-19531)	G 302 778-1000
Rrr Realty Group LLC	Bear (G-476)	G 302 836-9836
Rush Realty LLC	Smyrna (G-13873)	G 302 219-6707
Shirley I Blackburn Real Estat	Newark (G-11998)	G 302 292-6684
Showtime Real Estate	Wilmington (G-19811)	G 302 377-1292
Smalls Real Estate Company	Wilmington (G-19873)	F 302 633-1985
Smt Real Estate Holdings LLC	Newark (G-12043)	G 302 668-3512
Stephen J Crifasi Real Estate	Wilmington (G-20059)	G 302 658-9572
Stoltz Real Estate Partners	Wilmington (G-20076)	G 302 654-3600
Stoltz Realty Co	Claymont (G-1305)	F 302 798-8500
Stoltz Realty Co	Wilmington (G-20077)	G 302 656-2852
Sunrise Real Estate	Rehoboth Beach (G-12982)	G 302 313-9949
Thrive Real Lf Indpendence LLC	Middletown (G-7643)	G 302 261-2139
Tidemark LLC	Camden Wyoming (G-982)	G 302 359-4646
TMI Realty LLC	New Castle (G-9628)	F 302 613-5600
Trans Un Sttlment Slutions Inc	Wilmington (G-20394)	D 800 916-8800
Upscale Industries Property Ma	Wilmington (G-20537)	G 302 386-8855
Wagamons Schell Brothers	Rehoboth Beach (G-13004)	G 302 664-1680
Warner Tansey Inc	Bethany Beach (G-648)	G 302 539-3001
Weed Real Estate LLC	Newark (G-12354)	G 302 981-6388
Wilgus Associates Inc	Bethany Beach (G-650)	E 302 539-7511
Yvonne Hall Inc	Dover (G-3895)	G 302 677-1300

REAL ESTATE AGENCIES: Rental

Company	Location	Phone
Fairville Management Co LLC	Hockessin (G-5206)	G 302 489-2000
Los Jardines Inc	Wilmington (G-17998)	G 302 652-6390
Luther Martin Foundation Dover	Dover (G-2982)	G 302 674-1408

REAL ESTATE AGENTS & MANAGERS

Company	Location	Phone
All About Housing LLC	Townsend (G-13956)	G 302 465-3246
Avanti Homes LLC	Wilmington (G-14665)	G 302 374-0999
Battaglia Management Inc	New Castle (G-8848)	F 302 325-6100
Bay Rose Homes	Lewes (G-5739)	G 302 945-9510
Better Homes Laurel II Inc	Laurel (G-5469)	G 302 875-4282
Carl M Freeman Associates Inc	Bethany Beach (G-589)	D 302 539-6961
Cigna Real Estate Inc	Wilmington (G-15436)	G 302 476-3337
Coastal Funding Corporation	Historic New Castle (G-4959)	G 302 328-4113
Commonwealth Trust Co	Wilmington (G-15556)	F 302 658-7214
Delaware Valley Dev Group LLC	Wilmington (G-15979)	G 302 235-2500
Delmarva Group	Lewes (G-5905)	G 302 200-9053
Dover Community Partnership	Dover (G-2337)	G 302 678-1965
Eldertrust	Wilmington (G-16350)	G 302 993-1022
Empire Group International	Claymont (G-1132)	G 302 791-1100
En Properties LLC	Hockessin (G-5201)	G 302 738-4201
Faze II Inc	Bear (G-222)	G 302 328-7891
Freedom Plaza Enterprises LLC	Smyrna (G-13738)	G 302 653-9676
H T G Consulting LLC	New Castle (G-9189)	G 302 322-4100
Harrington Realty Inc	Dover (G-2654)	E 302 736-0800
Harris Property Management LLC	Wilmington (G-17063)	F 302 588-8601
Harvey Development Co	New Castle (G-9201)	E 302 323-9300
Hollywood Grill Restaurant	Wilmington (G-17171)	D 302 655-1348
Insight Homes	Georgetown (G-4370)	G 302 858-4281
Kats Meow Inc	Hockessin (G-5266)	G 302 383-5412
King Josiah Companies LLC	Dover (G-2872)	G 855 312-3300

Landex LLC .... G 903 293-9466
  Newark (G-11217)
Liborio-Louviers LLC .... G 302 656-9400
  Wilmington (G-17898)
Malave Property Group LLC .... G 844 203-4610
  Dover (G-3004)
Margaret Harris-Nemtuda .... G 302 477-5500
  Wilmington (G-18124)
Marshall Manor LP .... G 302 422-8255
  Milford (G-7985)
Maverick Realty LLC .... F 302 373-6591
  Newark (G-11357)
Meadow Edge Corp .... G 302 530-7339
  Hockessin (G-5306)
More Property Recovery .... G 302 834-4788
  Newark (G-11452)
Nanticoke Shores Assoc LLC .... G 302 945-1500
  Millsboro (G-8399)
Noble Property LLC .... E 718 502-4806
  Dover (G-3192)
NVR Homes National .... G 302 278-7099
  Rehoboth Beach (G-12872)
Oberod Estates LLC .... G 302 521-0250
  Wilmington (G-18735)
Passavant Memorial Homes .... G 302 449-2202
  Townsend (G-14049)
Pettinaro Construction Co Inc .... D 302 999-0708
  Wilmington (G-19001)
Prelude TX .... G 302 273-3369
  Newark (G-11725)
Princeton Coml Holdings LLC .... G 302 449-4836
  Newark (G-11746)
Resolute Industrial .... F 267 401-0973
  Newark (G-11866)
Rocky Lac LLC .... F 302 440-5561
  Bear (G-466)
Rosedale Development LLC .... E 281 968-9426
  Dover (G-3486)
Salt Air Homes .... G 302 698-4146
  Camden Wyoming (G-973)
Sea Play Homes LLC .... G 302 564-7557
  Fenwick Island (G-4054)
Skipjack Inc .... D 302 734-6755
  Dover (G-3572)
Statera Homes .... G 302 313-9949
  Rehoboth Beach (G-12973)
Supreme Servicez LLC .... G 302 932-5724
  Wilmington (G-20158)
Topaz & Associates LLC .... F 302 448-8914
  Wilmington (G-20357)
Tunnell Companies LP .... F 302 945-9300
  Millsboro (G-8488)
Veezys Holding Company LLC .... F 302 307-2418
  Dover (G-3779)
Vulcan International Corp .... F 302 656-1950
  Wilmington (G-20657)
Wilgus Associates Inc .... G 302 644-2960
  Lewes (G-6630)
Willow Tree Properties LLC .... G 302 674-2266
  Wilmington (G-20804)
Wilsons Auction Sales Inc .... G 302 422-3454
  Lincoln (G-6709)

REAL ESTATE ESCROW AGENCIES

Daisy Hora .... G 302 727-6299
  Bethany Beach (G-593)
Networks Programs .... E 302 454-2233
  Newark (G-11510)

REAL ESTATE INVESTMENT TRUSTS

333 Rei LLC .... F 808 758-3095
  Middletown (G-6815)

All United Prpts Solutions LLC .... F 310 853-2223
  Camden (G-789)
Bekart Holding LLC .... F 302 600-7000
  Wilmington (G-14813)
Bpg Office Partners Viii LLC .... E 302 250-3065
  Wilmington (G-15025)
Eldertrust .... G 302 993-1022
  Wilmington (G-16350)
EZ Investment Group LLC .... G 917 215-9887
  Dover (G-2475)
K&B Investors LLC .... G 302 357-9723
  Wilmington (G-17631)
Kennis Capital (usa) LLC .... G 302 605-6228
  Wilmington (G-17689)
Luxy Stay Imperial LLC .... G 844 483-5383
  Rehoboth Beach (G-12841)
Perpetual Invstments Group LLC .... F 718 795-3394
  Wilmington (G-18982)
Recadia Capital LLC .... G 866 671-1280
  Wilmington (G-19374)
Southwest American Corp .... G 302 652-7003
  Wilmington (G-19940)
St Lawrence Grant Ave Trust .... G 302 652-7978
  Wilmington (G-19997)

REAL ESTATE LISTING SVCS

Cap Title of Delaware LLC .... G 302 537-3788
  Ocean View (G-12485)
Welcome Home Getaways LLC .... G 724 426-5534
  Bear (G-561)

RECORDS & TAPES: Prerecorded

Routerabbit Inc .... G 508 596-8735
  Newark (G-11919)

REELS: Cable, Metal

Delmaco Manufacturing Inc .... F 302 856-6345
  Georgetown (G-4288)

REFINING: Petroleum

Air Products and Chemicals Inc .... G 302 834-6033
  Delaware City (G-1528)
Eidp Inc .... G 302 772-0016
  New Castle (G-9084)
Eidp Inc .... F 302 452-9000
  Newark (G-10620)
Eidp Inc .... E 615 847-6920
  Wilmington (G-16341)
Honeywell International Inc .... E 302 791-6700
  Claymont (G-1181)
Innospec Inc .... F 302 454-8100
  Newark (G-11022)
O2diesel Fuels Inc .... F 302 266-6000
  Newark (G-11572)
Reliance Egleford Upstream LLC .... G 302 472-7437
  Wilmington (G-19425)
United Acquisition Corp .... E 302 651-9856
  Wilmington (G-20523)

REFRACTORIES: Clay

Frc Global Inc .... D 800 609-5711
  Wilmington (G-16732)
Rhi Refractories Holding Company .... A 302 655-6497
  Wilmington (G-19457)

REFRIGERATION & HEATING EQUIPMENT

Beach Mobile Home Supply .... G 302 945-5611
  Millsboro (G-8189)
Munters Corporation .... F 302 798-2455
  Claymont (G-1247)
Trane US Inc .... G 302 395-0200
  New Castle (G-9632)

REFRIGERATION EQPT & SPLYS WHOLESALERS

Berry Refrigeration Co .... E 302 733-0933
  Newark (G-10025)
Greenberg Supply Co Inc .... E 302 656-4496
  Wilmington (G-16970)
R E Michel Company LLC .... G 302 678-0250
  Dover (G-3414)
R E Michel Company LLC .... G 302 645-0585
  Lewes (G-6403)
Thermo King Corporation .... G 302 907-0345
  Delmar (G-1641)
Thermo King LLC .... G 302 907-0345
  Delmar (G-1642)
Unada LLC .... E 470 809-9077
  Wilmington (G-20503)
United Refrigeration Inc .... G 302 322-1836
  New Castle (G-9655)
W W Grainger Inc .... G 302 322-1840
  Historic New Castle (G-5098)

REFRIGERATION EQPT: Complete

Bluchill Inc .... G 302 658-2638
  New Castle (G-8869)

REFRIGERATION REPAIR SVCS

Delmarva Refrigeration Inc .... G 302 846-2727
  Delmar (G-1588)
Morans Refrigeration Svc Inc .... G 703 642-1200
  Rehoboth Beach (G-12861)
Roto-Rooter Services Company .... G 302 659-7637
  Newark (G-11917)

REFRIGERATION SVC & REPAIR

Smt Htg and Air Cond LLC .... G 302 285-9219
  Townsend (G-14065)
Weitron Inc .... E 800 398-3816
  Newark (G-12356)

REFUSE SYSTEMS

Pacific Green Technologies Inc .... F 302 601-4659
  Dover (G-3258)
Service Disposal of Delaware .... G 302 326-9155
  Wilmington (G-19760)
Uniscrap Pbc .... G 302 407-8002
  Wilmington (G-20521)
Waste Management Delaware Inc .... G 302 854-5301
  Laurel (G-5621)
Waste Management Delaware Inc .... G 302 994-0944
  Wilmington (G-20681)

REHABILITATION CENTER, OUTPATIENT TREATMENT

Advancxing Pain Rhbittion Clin .... F 302 384-7439
  Newark (G-9784)
Ah Therapy Services LLC .... G 302 379-0528
  Wilmington (G-14324)
All The Difference Inc .... F 302 738-6353
  Newark (G-9819)
Angelic Therapy .... G 717 870-4618
  Lewes (G-5691)
ARC Seminars LLC .... G 856 776-6758
  Middletown (G-6872)
Art and Therapy Services .... G 302 329-9794
  Milton (G-8563)
At Eaze Massage Therapy .... G 302 559-3019
  Smyrna (G-13651)
Back To Blance Healing Therapy .... G 302 478-6470
  Wilmington (G-14713)
Blooming Speech .... G 302 528-6663
  Wilmington (G-14962)

REHABILITATION CENTER, OUTPATIENT TREATMENT

Body Ease Therapy .... G 610 314-0780
  Newark (G-10066)
Brandywine Occpational Therapy ...... F 302 740-4798
  Wilmington (G-15077)
Capitol Nrsing Rhblttion Ctr L .... E 302 734-1199
  Dover (G-2023)
Cardio-Kinetics Inc .... E 302 738-6635
  Newark (G-10140)
Cimi Enterprises LLC .... F 302 803-2210
  Middletown (G-6981)
De Sleep Disorder Centers LLC .... G 302 697-2749
  Camden (G-815)
Defy Therapy Services LLC .... G 302 290-9562
  Wilmington (G-15857)
Delaware Curative Workshop .... D 302 656-2521
  Wilmington (G-15899)
Delaware Spine Rehabilitation .... F 302 883-2292
  Dover (G-2261)
Delaware Spine Rehabilitation .... G 302 563-7442
  Historic New Castle (G-4972)
Divine Transitional Life LLC .... G 215 432-4974
  Newark (G-10540)
Dynamic Therapy Services LLC .... G 302 566-6624
  Harrington (G-4765)
Dynamic Therapy Services LLC .... G 302 280-6953
  Laurel (G-5504)
Easter Sals Del Mrylnds Estrn .... D 302 678-3353
  Dover (G-2411)
Elwyn Pennsylvania and Del .... D 302 658-8860
  Wilmington (G-16382)
Emory Massage Therapy .... G 302 290-0003
  Dover (G-2442)
Encompass Health Corporation .... F 302 464-3400
  Middletown (G-7101)
Focus Rehabilitation & Fitness .... G 302 231-8982
  Millsboro (G-8293)
Henlopen Music Therapy SE .... G 302 593-7784
  Lewes (G-6090)
Hysiotherapy Associates Inc .... G 610 444-1270
  Wilmington (G-17244)
Informed Tuch Mssage Thrapy LL .... G 302 229-8239
  Townsend (G-14017)
Intouch Body Therapy LLC .... G 302 537-0510
  Bethany Beach (G-609)
Intuitive Care Therapy .... G 302 200-6123
  Wilmington (G-17402)
Jan Stern Eqine Asssted Thrapy ...... G 302 234-9835
  Wilmington (G-17491)
Jans Hands Massage Therapy .... G 302 753-3962
  Wilmington (G-17496)
Lake Therapy Creations .... G 410 920-7130
  Newark (G-11215)
Lewes Expressive Therapy .... G 302 727-3275
  Lewes (G-6195)
Moore Physcial Therapy .... G 302 654-8142
  Wilmington (G-18436)
National Stress Clinic LLC .... G 646 571-8627
  Wilmington (G-18548)
Necessary Luxury .... G 302 764-4032
  Wilmington (G-18568)
Novacare Rehabilitation Dover .... G 302 760-9966
  Dover (G-3204)
Novacare Rehabilitation Seafor .... G 302 990-2951
  Seaford (G-13321)
Occupational Therapy .... G 302 994-4566
  Wilmington (G-18740)
Occuptnl Thrpy of Delaware .... F 302 491-4813
  Milford (G-8035)
On The Spot Massage .... G 302 545-5200
  Bear (G-407)
Oneness Massage Therapy .... G 302 893-0348
  Newark (G-11594)

Pain & Sleep Therapy Center .... F 302 314-1409
  Wilmington (G-18863)
Premier Spine & Rehab .... G 302 730-4878
  Dover (G-3363)
Premier Spine and Rehab .... G 302 404-5293
  Seaford (G-13354)
Presicson Pain Rhbltation Svcs .... F 302 827-2321
  Rehoboth Beach (G-12900)
Pro Rehab Chiropractic .... G 302 200-9102
  Lewes (G-6392)
Rehabitation Consultants .... G 302 478-2131
  Wilmington (G-19414)
Relax Massage Therapy .... G 302 738-7300
  Newark (G-11848)
Relaxing Tours LLC .... G 610 905-3852
  Greenwood (G-4663)
S T Progressive Strides .... G 410 775-8103
  Bear (G-477)
Swedish Massage Therapy .... G 302 841-3166
  Ocean View (G-12575)
Therapy Concierge LLC .... G 302 319-3040
  Bear (G-529)
Therapy Services of Delaw .... G 302 239-2285
  Hockessin (G-5403)
Tidewater Physcl Thrpy and REB ..... G 302 945-5111
  Lewes (G-6558)
Tidewater Physcl Thrpy and REB ..... G 302 629-4024
  Seaford (G-13431)
Total Health & Rehabilitation .... G 302 999-9202
  Wilmington (G-20371)
Trauma Rehabilitation PA .... G 302 777-7723
  Wilmington (G-20403)
Unique Massage Therapy .... G 302 359-5982
  Dover (G-3750)
Weighted With Love LLC .... G 302 378-2041
  Townsend (G-14090)
Wilmington Pain/Rehab Cntr PA .... G 302 575-1776
  Wilmington (G-20829)
Worlds Best Massage Therapy .... G 302 366-8777
  Newark (G-12411)
Zen Therapy & Bodywork Inc .... G 302 252-1733
  Wilmington (G-20951)

REHABILITATION CTR, RESIDENTIAL WITH HEALTH CARE INCIDENTAL

Gaudenzia Inc .... F 302 836-8260
  Delaware City (G-1546)
Gaudenzia Inc .... G 302 421-9945
  Wilmington (G-16817)
Limen House Inc .... G 302 652-7969
  Wilmington (G-17913)

REHABILITATION SVCS

Aqua Infra Rehab Co LLC .... G 610 328-7714
  Newark (G-9895)
Cadia Rehabilitation .... E 302 734-1199
  Dover (G-2010)
Cadia Rhabilitation Silverside .... F 302 478-8889
  Wilmington (G-15186)
Carpe Dia Organization .... G 302 333-7546
  Newark (G-10153)
Christncare Rhblttion Svcs At .... G 302 623-1500
  Wilmington (G-15422)
Connectons Cmnty Spport Prgram ... E 302 834-8400
  Delaware City (G-1534)
Connectons Cmnty Spport Prgram ... D 302 454-7520
  Newark (G-10306)
Connectons Cmnty Spport Prgram ... D 302 984-2302
  Claymont (G-1099)
Delaware Back Pain and Sports .... F 302 832-3369
  Newark (G-10419)

Fedcap Rehabilitation Services .... F 302 544-6634
  New Castle (G-9120)
Hillside Center .... E 302 652-1181
  Wilmington (G-17147)
Jungle Gym LLC .... G 302 734-1515
  Dover (G-2820)
Kentmere Rhbltation Hlthcare CT .... E 302 652-3311
  Wilmington (G-17694)
Millville Rehabilitation Svc .... F 302 645-3100
  Millville (G-8543)
Parkview De Snf Management LLC .. D 302 655-6135
  Wilmington (G-18896)
Phc Inc .... E 313 831-3500
  New Castle (G-9470)
Puzzles Lf Rntry Prgram For Wm ..... G 302 339-0327
  Wilmington (G-19269)
Springs Rhbltion At Brndywine .... D 302 998-0101
  Wilmington (G-19979)
Tidewater Physcl Thrpy and REB ..... G 302 684-2829
  Milton (G-8720)

REINSURANCE CARRIERS: Accident & Health

Architect Engineer Ins Co Risk .... G 302 658-2342
  Wilmington (G-14542)

RELOCATION SVCS

Business Move Solutions Inc .... E 302 324-0080
  New Castle (G-8904)
Pettinaro Residential LLC .... F 302 999-0708
  Wilmington (G-19003)

REMOVERS & CLEANERS

Coatings With A Purpose Inc .... G 302 462-1465
  Georgetown (G-4260)

RENTAL SVCS: Audio-Visual Eqpt & Sply

A V Resources Inc .... G 302 994-1488
  Wilmington (G-14174)
Academy Sounds LLC .... G 302 276-5027
  Newport (G-12439)
Brandywine Electronics Corp .... F 302 324-9992
  Bear (G-80)

RENTAL SVCS: Business Machine & Electronic Eqpt

B Williams Holding Corp .... F 302 656-8596
  Wilmington (G-14704)

RENTAL SVCS: Eqpt, Theatrical

Main Light Industries Inc .... C 302 998-8017
  Wilmington (G-18089)

RENTAL SVCS: Vending Machine

Gge Amusements .... G 302 227-0661
  Rehoboth Beach (G-12770)
Gian-Co .... F 302 798-7100
  Claymont (G-1161)
Sunshine Vending Machines LLC .... G 800 670-6557
  Wilmington (G-20137)

RENTAL SVCS: Video Disk/Tape, To The General Public

Video Den .... G 302 628-9835
  Seaford (G-13441)
Video Scene of Delaware Inc .... G 302 678-8526
  Dover (G-3793)

PRODUCTS & SERVICES SECTION

RETAIL STORES: Pet Splys

RENTAL SVCS: Work Zone Traffic Eqpt, Flags, Cones, Etc

American Traffic Pd LLC .... E 302 883-7263
  Historic New Castle (G-4931)
Enterprise Flasher Co Inc .... E 302 999-0856
  Wilmington (G-16433)
Sussex Protection Service LLC .... F 302 832-5700
  Newark (G-12136)

RENTAL: Portable Toilet

A-1 Sanitation Service Inc .... E 302 322-1074
  New Castle (G-8752)
AAA Portable Restroom Co Inc .... G 909 981-0090
  Camden Wyoming (G-904)
Atlantic Pumping Inc .... F 302 436-5047
  Selbyville (G-13468)

RENTAL: Video Tape & Disc

California Video 2 .... G 302 477-6944
  Wilmington (G-15195)
Dvd and Game Exchange De .... G 302 530-1199
  Wilmington (G-16224)
Extreme Audio & Video .... G 302 533-7404
  Newark (G-10695)
Foto Video Genesis .... G 302 422-6988
  Milford (G-7901)
Quality In-House Video Inc .... G 302 834-5654
  Newark (G-11788)
Sky4video .... G 302 377-3748
  Newark (G-12026)

RESEARCH, DEVELOPMENT & TESTING SVCS, COMM: Agricultural

Lithos Carbon Inc .... F 425 274-3276
  Dover (G-2956)
Nichino America Inc .... D 302 636-9001
  Wilmington (G-18642)

RESEARCH, DEVELOPMENT & TESTING SVCS, COMMERCIAL: Business

Chemours Company .... F 302 773-6417
  Newark (G-10196)
Convida Wireless LLC .... G 302 281-3707
  Wilmington (G-15626)
Fast Intrcnnect Tchologies Inc .... G 302 465-5344
  Dover (G-2487)
Inc Plan USA .... G 302 428-1200
  Wilmington (G-17298)

RESEARCH, DEVELOPMENT & TESTING SVCS, COMMERCIAL: Energy

Alphataraxia Quicksilver LLC .... G 571 367-7133
  Wilmington (G-14395)
Delaware Sstnble Enrgy Utility .... E 302 883-3038
  Dover (G-2262)
Ener-G Group Inc .... F 917 281-0020
  Wilmington (G-16415)
IEC .... G 302 831-6231
  Newark (G-10996)
Sun Coal & Coke LLC .... A 630 824-1000
  Wilmington (G-20125)
Viridi Marathon LLC .... E 302 647-8280
  Wilmington (G-20632)

RESEARCH, DEVELOPMENT & TESTING SVCS, COMMERCIAL: Medical

Amylin Pharmaceuticals LLC .... A 858 552-2200
  Wilmington (G-14466)

Fbk Medical Tubing Inc .... F 302 855-0585
  Georgetown (G-4315)

RESEARCH, DEVELOPMENT & TESTING SVCS, COMMERCIAL: Physical

Red Clay Inc .... G 302 239-2018
  Hockessin (G-5360)

RESEARCH, DEVELOPMENT SVCS, COMMERCIAL: Indl Lab

Nikang Therapeutics Inc .... E 302 415-5127
  Wilmington (G-18649)

RESIDENTIAL CARE FOR THE HANDICAPPED

Chimes Inc .... E 302 452-3400
  Newark (G-10206)
Choices For Community Living .... G 302 398-0446
  Harrington (G-4749)

RESTAURANTS: Fast Food

D&C Concepts LLC .... F 770 335-2503
  Wilmington (G-15763)

RESTAURANTS: Full Svc, American

Chuck Lager LLC .... D 302 482-1773
  Wilmington (G-15428)
Delaware Beer Works Inc .... E 302 836-2739
  Bear (G-142)
Vincenza & Margherita Bistro .... F 302 479-7999
  Wilmington (G-20625)

RETAIL BAKERY: Doughnuts

Swami Enterprises Inc .... G 302 999-8077
  Wilmington (G-20168)

RETAIL STORES: Alcoholic Beverage Making Eqpt & Splys

Carol Boyd Heron .... G 302 645-0551
  Lewes (G-5803)
Roys Electrical Service Inc .... G 302 674-3199
  Cheswold (G-989)

RETAIL STORES: Audio-Visual Eqpt & Splys

A V Resources Inc .... G 302 994-1488
  Wilmington (G-14174)

RETAIL STORES: Business Machines & Eqpt

Excel Business Systems Inc .... E 302 453-1500
  Newark (G-10683)
Gray Audograph Agency Inc .... F 302 658-1700
  New Castle (G-9176)
Qoe Inc .... G 302 455-1234
  Newark (G-11783)
Tower Business Machines Inc .... G 302 395-1445
  Historic New Castle (G-5088)

RETAIL STORES: Cake Decorating Splys

Cannons Cake and Candy Sups .... G 302 738-3321
  Newark (G-10129)

RETAIL STORES: Communication Eqpt

Visual Communications Inc .... G 302 792-9500
  Claymont (G-1330)

RETAIL STORES: Cosmetics

Girley Bells LLC .... G 347 922-6398
  Newark (G-10839)
Sally Beauty Supply LLC .... G 302 629-5160
  Seaford (G-13383)

Wellthy Investors LLC .... G 267 847-3486
  Dover (G-3831)

RETAIL STORES: Electronic Parts & Eqpt

Denney Electric Supply Del Inc .... G 302 934-8885
  Millsboro (G-8270)
Digibox LLC .... G 302 203-0088
  Dover (G-2296)
Power Trans Inc .... F 302 337-3016
  Bridgeville (G-753)
Xenopia LLC .... G 302 703-7050
  Lewes (G-6643)

RETAIL STORES: Flags

Henninger Printing Co Inc .... G 302 934-8119
  Millsboro (G-8317)

RETAIL STORES: Hair Care Prdts

Designer Braids and Trade .... G 718 783-9078
  Middletown (G-7055)
Total Beauty Supply Inc .... G 302 798-4647
  Wilmington (G-20367)

RETAIL STORES: Hearing Aids

Hearsay Services of Delaware .... G 302 422-3312
  Milford (G-7925)

RETAIL STORES: Medical Apparatus & Splys

American Homepatient Inc .... E 302 454-4941
  Newark (G-9845)
Chesapeake Rehab Equipment Inc .... G 302 266-6234
  Newark (G-10198)
Dentsply Sirona Inc .... G 302 422-4511
  Milford (G-7867)
Elgood Solutions Inc .... G 610 420-7207
  Camden (G-829)
Hoosier Osteotronix Corp .... G 410 241-7627
  Rehoboth Beach (G-12791)
Marosa Surgical Industries .... F 302 674-0907
  New Castle (G-9349)
Mid Atlntic Scientific Svc Inc .... G 302 328-4440
  New Castle (G-9367)
Mtrigger LLC .... G 302 502-7262
  Newark (G-11470)
Purushas Picks Inc .... G 302 918-7663
  Bear (G-442)
Quinn-Miller Group Inc .... F 302 738-9742
  Wilmington (G-19296)
True Mobility Inc .... G 302 836-4110
  New Castle (G-9643)

RETAIL STORES: Mobile Telephones & Eqpt

Crossroads Wireless Holdg LLC .... F 405 946-1200
  Wilmington (G-15715)
Interdgital Communications Inc .... D 610 878-7800
  Wilmington (G-17379)
Interdigital Inc .... E 302 281-3600
  Wilmington (G-17380)
Interdigital Wireless Inc .... E 302 281-3600
  Wilmington (G-17381)
Nerdit Now LLC .... F 302 482-5979
  Wilmington (G-18587)
WER Wireless of Smyrna Inc .... F 302 653-8183
  Smyrna (G-13936)

RETAIL STORES: Orthopedic & Prosthesis Applications

Lawall Prsthtics - Orthtics In .... F 302 427-3668
  Wilmington (G-17834)

RETAIL STORES: Pet Splys

Employee Codes: A=Over 500 employees, B=251-500
C=101-250, D=51-100, E=20-50, F=10-19, G=1-9

2024 Harris Directory of Delaware Businesses

RETAIL STORES: Safety Splys & Eqpt

RETAIL STORES: Safety Splys & Eqpt
Enterprise Flasher Co Inc..................... E 302 999-0856
　Wilmington *(G-16433)*

RETAIL STORES: Spas & Hot Tubs
Cannon Spas .... G 302 628-9404
　Seaford *(G-13101)*

RETAIL STORES: Swimming Pools, Above Ground
Clarks Swimming Pools Inc .... G 302 629-8835
　Seaford *(G-13123)*

RETAIL STORES: Telephone & Communication Eqpt
A V C Inc .... G 302 227-2549
　Rehoboth Beach *(G-12593)*
Fscom Inc .... D 888 468-7419
　Historic New Castle *(G-4994)*

RETAIL STORES: Tents
Tee Pees From Rattlesnks .... G 302 654-0709
　Wilmington *(G-20262)*

RETAIL STORES: Tombstones
Cecil Vault & Memorial Co Inc .... G 302 994-3806
　Wilmington *(G-15293)*

RETAIL STORES: Water Purification Eqpt
Graver Technologies LLC .... C 302 731-1700
　Newark *(G-10883)*
Watercraft LLC .... G 302 757-0786
　Wilmington *(G-20683)*

ROAD CONSTRUCTION EQUIPMENT WHOLESALERS
Sun Piledriving Equipment LLC .... G 302 539-6756
　Frankford *(G-4150)*

ROCK SALT MINING
Oceanport LLC .... F 302 792-2212
　Claymont *(G-1256)*

ROOFING GRANULES
Iko Southeast Inc .... E 302 764-3100
　Wilmington *(G-17277)*

ROOFING MATERIALS: Asphalt
J & L Building Materials Inc .... E 302 504-0350
　Historic New Castle *(G-5009)*
Quality Rofg Sup Lancaster Inc .... G 302 322-8322
　New Castle *(G-9506)*

RUBBER PRDTS: Silicone
Arlon LLC .... C 302 834-2100
　Bear *(G-44)*

RUGS: Hand & Machine Made
Indo Foreign Trade Craft LLC .... E 818 927-2872
　Newark *(G-11014)*

RUGS: Tufted
Maneto Inc .... E 302 656-4285
　Wilmington *(G-18103)*

SAFETY EQPT & SPLYS WHOLESALERS

Boa Financial LLC .... G 888 444-5371
　Dover *(G-1956)*
McDonald Safety Equipment Inc .... E 302 999-0151
　Wilmington *(G-18227)*

SAFETY INSPECTION SVCS
Falcone Truman Plbg & Htg Inc .... E 302 376-7483
　Odessa *(G-12584)*
Qualdent LLC .... G 856 642-4078
　Wilmington *(G-19282)*

SALES PROMOTION SVCS
Go-Givers LLC .... G 302 703-9293
　Lewes *(G-6044)*
SC Marketing US Inc .... G 714 352-4992
　Wilmington *(G-19694)*

SALT
Saltverk Inc .... F 412 413-9193
　Wilmington *(G-19642)*

SAND & GRAVEL
77 Legacy LLC .... G 404 576-7265
　Wilmington *(G-14147)*
Bear Materials LLC .... G 302 658-5241
　New Castle *(G-8855)*
Cook Hauling LLC .... G 302 378-6451
　Middletown *(G-7012)*
Goldsboro Sand and Gravel .... G 410 310-0402
　Camden Wyoming *(G-949)*
Lewis Sand and Gravel LLC .... G 302 238-0169
　Millsboro *(G-8348)*
Material Transit Inc .... E 302 395-0556
　New Castle *(G-9353)*
Parkway Gravel Inc .... G 302 326-0554
　New Castle *(G-9451)*

SAND MINING
Joseph M L Sand & Gravel Co .... E 302 856-7396
　Georgetown *(G-4387)*

SAND: Silica
American Minerals Inc .... G 302 652-3301
　New Castle *(G-8799)*

SANITARY SVC, NEC
Aurora Corporation .... G 302 656-6717
　Wilmington *(G-14645)*
D & J Sweeping LLC .... G 302 875-3393
　Laurel *(G-5490)*

SANITARY SVCS: Hazardous Waste, Collection & Disposal
Bestrans Inc .... D 302 824-0909
　New Castle *(G-8863)*
Brightfields Inc .... E 302 656-9600
　Wilmington *(G-15113)*

SANITARY SVCS: Liquid Waste Collection & Disposal
Clean Delaware Inc .... G 302 684-4221
　Milton *(G-8584)*

SANITARY SVCS: Oil Spill Cleanup
Seaway Service Inc .... F 302 834-7101
　Delaware City *(G-1557)*

SANITARY SVCS: Refuse Collection & Disposal Svcs

Advik Republic Inc .... G 844 987-4238
　Hockessin *(G-5115)*
First State Disposal .... G 302 644-3885
　Lewes *(G-5998)*
Goodeals Inc .... G 302 999-1737
　Wilmington *(G-16924)*
Independent Transfer Operators .... G 302 420-4289
　Hockessin *(G-5249)*
Republic Services Inc .... G 302 658-4097
　Wilmington *(G-19434)*

SANITARY SVCS: Rubbish Collection & Disposal
Complete Disposal Service LLC .... G 302 448-1021
　Georgetown *(G-4264)*
Route 24 Got Junk .... G 302 258-7990
　Millsboro *(G-8450)*
Scottons Sanitation LLC .... G 302 382-5743
　Clayton *(G-1404)*
Waste Masters Solutions LLC .... G 302 824-0909
　New Castle *(G-9677)*
Wasteflo LLC .... G 410 202-0802
　Laurel *(G-5622)*

SANITARY SVCS: Waste Materials, Recycling
Advant-Dge Sltons Mddle ATL In .... G 302 533-6858
　Newark *(G-9785)*
Agile Waste LLC .... G 302 772-4882
　Wilmington *(G-14316)*
All Star Shredding LP .... F 302 325-9998
　New Castle *(G-8782)*
Asi Comprehensive Waste MGT .... G 302 533-6858
　Newark *(G-9923)*
Blue Hen Bzzrds Dspose-All Inc .... E 302 945-3500
　Millsboro *(G-8200)*
Cannon Iron and Metal Inc .... G 302 492-8091
　Hartly *(G-4860)*
Ciancon Global LLC .... F 302 365-0956
　Wilmington *(G-15431)*
Commodities Plus Inc .... G 302 376-5219
　Newark *(G-10285)*
D & J Recycling Inc .... G 302 422-0163
　Milford *(G-7845)*
Data Guard Recycling Inc .... G 302 337-8870
　Bridgeville *(G-689)*
Delaware Material Recovery & R .... F 302 652-3150
　Wilmington *(G-15940)*
Delaware Recyclable Products .... E 302 655-1360
　New Castle *(G-9032)*
Delaware Recycling Center .... G 215 921-7508
　New Castle *(G-9033)*
Delaware Solid Waste Authority .... E 302 739-5361
　Dover *(G-2260)*
Diamond State Recycling Corp .... E 302 655-1501
　Wilmington *(G-16058)*
First State Plastics Inc .... E 302 325-3700
　New Castle *(G-9130)*
First State Towing LLC .... G 302 322-1777
　New Castle *(G-9133)*
Gold Medal Envmtl De LLC .... G 302 652-3150
　Wilmington *(G-16909)*
Green Opportunities Corp .... F 302 535-2235
　Camden Wyoming *(G-951)*
Holland Mulch Inc .... F 302 765-3100
　Wilmington *(G-17166)*
Independent Disposal Services .... G 302 378-5400
　Townsend *(G-14016)*
Juliana Recycling Corporation .... G 347 753-6584
　Newark *(G-11136)*
Kaye Construction .... G 302 628-6962
　Seaford *(G-13246)*

PRODUCTS & SERVICES SECTION — SEMICONDUCTORS & RELATED DEVICES

Kroegers Salvage Inc .... F 302 381-7082
  Bridgeville (G-723)
Magnus Environmental Corp .... G 302 655-4443
  New Castle (G-9336)
Mid Atlantic Compost & RE .... G 302 644-2977
  Lewes (G-6271)
Mid Atlantic Waste System .... G 610 497-2405
  New Castle (G-9366)
Mid-Shore Envmtl Svcs Inc .... G 302 736-5504
  Bridgeville (G-733)
Millville Organic Center .... G 302 423-2601
  Ocean View (G-12547)
Modular Carpet Recycling Inc .... F 484 885-5890
  New Castle (G-9379)
Newark Recycling Center Inc .... G 302 737-7300
  Newark (G-11545)
Perdue-Agrirecycle LLC .... G 302 628-2360
  Seaford (G-13344)
Recyclers of Delaware LLC .... G 856 466-9067
  Bear (G-448)
Recycling Swift & Demolition .... G 302 328-8283
  New Castle (G-9515)
RJR Recycling Co .... G 610 647-1555
  New Castle (G-9536)
Waste Industries .... G 302 367-5511
  New Castle (G-9675)

SATELLITES: Communications

Newcosmos LLC .... G 302 838-1935
  Bear (G-396)

SCALE REPAIR SVCS

Widgeon Enterprises Inc .... G 302 846-9763
  Delmar (G-1657)

SCHOOL FOR PHYSICALLY HANDICAPPED, NEC

Pressley Ridge Foundation .... G 302 366-0490
  Dover (G-3367)

SCIENTIFIC EQPT REPAIR SVCS

Igal Biochemical LLC .... G 302 525-2090
  Newark (G-10997)
Mid Atlntic Scientific Svc Inc .... G 302 328-4440
  New Castle (G-9367)

SCIENTIFIC INSTRUMENTS WHOLESALERS

Igal Biochemical LLC .... G 302 525-2090
  Newark (G-10997)
Pco-Tech Inc .... F 248 276-8820
  Wilmington (G-18936)

SCRAP & WASTE MATERIALS, WHOLESALE: Ferrous Metal

Billy Warren & Son LLC .... G 302 349-5767
  Greenwood (G-4598)

SCRAP & WASTE MATERIALS, WHOLESALE: Junk & Scrap

Trash Porters LLC .... G 302 709-1550
  Wilmington (G-20402)

SCRAP & WASTE MATERIALS, WHOLESALE: Metal

Diamond State Recycling Corp .... E 302 655-1501
  Wilmington (G-16058)
Ecotrade Group North Amer LLC .... G 302 724-6975
  Newark (G-10606)
Joseph Smith & Sons Inc .... G 302 492-8091
  Hartly (G-4885)
Network Scrap Metal Corp .... G 702 354-0600
  Wilmington (G-18598)

SCREW MACHINE PRDTS

Advanced Prttyping Sltionv LLC .... G 302 375-6048
  Wilmington (G-14278)

SEALANTS

Delchem Inc .... E 302 426-1800
  Wilmington (G-15990)
Tyden Group Holdings Corp .... F 740 420-6777
  Wilmington (G-20481)

SEALING COMPOUNDS: Sealing, synthetic rubber or plastic

Max Seal Inc .... F 619 946-2650
  Lewes (G-6252)

SEARCH & NAVIGATION SYSTEMS

Lockheed Martin Corporation .... G 302 741-2004
  Dover (G-2970)
Pilots Assn For Bay River Del .... E 302 645-2229
  Lewes (G-6369)

SECURE STORAGE SVC: Household & Furniture

Houston Self Storage .... G 302 422-9660
  Houston (G-5444)
Secure Self Storage .... G 302 832-0400
  New Castle (G-9555)

SECURITY CONTROL EQPT & SYSTEMS

Securitech Inc .... F 302 996-9230
  Wilmington (G-19732)

SECURITY DEVICES

Psp Corp .... G 302 764-7730
  Wilmington (G-19244)
Withyouwithme Inc .... G 202 377-9743
  Wilmington (G-20868)

SECURITY GUARD SVCS

Alliedbarton Security Svcs LLC .... G 302 498-0450
  Wilmington (G-14383)
Bennett Det Prtective Agcy Inc .... G 302 734-2480
  Dover (G-1912)
Conmac Security Systems Inc .... G 302 529-9286
  Wilmington (G-15598)
Dmp Security Agency LLC .... F 302 384-3745
  Wilmington (G-16110)
Dunbar Armored Inc .... E 302 628-5401
  Seaford (G-13164)
Dunbar Armored Inc .... E 302 892-4950
  Wilmington (G-16200)
G4s Secure Solutions USA Inc .... F 215 957-7603
  Claymont (G-1154)
Gettier Security .... F 302 652-2700
  Newark (G-10828)
Great Gaines LLC .... G 443 248-3952
  Delmar (G-1599)
Groupe EHc LLC .... F 302 309-9154
  Dover (G-2631)
Lenar Detective Agency Inc .... D 302 322-3700
  New Castle (G-9305)
Philadlphia Prtection Unit LLC .... G 267 505-2671
  Middletown (G-7445)
Professional Security Co .... G 302 383-7142
  Middletown (G-7473)
Security Watch Corp .... G 302 286-6728
  Newark (G-11971)
SOS Security Incorporated .... G 302 425-4755
  Wilmington (G-19930)
T & B Invstgtions SEC Agcy LLC .... G 302 476-4087
  Middletown (G-7616)
Tri-County Security .... G 302 709-2244
  Newark (G-12222)
Zicherheit LLC .... G 302 510-3718
  Selbyville (G-13622)

SECURITY SYSTEMS SERVICES

A Plus Electric & Security .... G 302 455-1725
  Newark (G-9726)
ABM Security Services Inc .... D 302 992-9733
  Wilmington (G-14206)
Action Security .... G 302 838-2852
  Newark (G-9761)
Addlestone LLC .... G 302 373-1598
  Wilmington (G-14253)
ADT LLC .... C 302 918-1016
  Newark (G-9770)
Advanced Protection LLC .... G 302 539-6041
  Ocean View (G-12458)
Advantage Security Inc .... F 302 652-3060
  Wilmington (G-14286)
Advantech Inc .... E 302 674-8405
  Dover (G-1726)
Aquia Nava II LLC .... E 410 245-8990
  Millsboro (G-8172)
Besecure LLC .... E 855 897-0650
  Lewes (G-5756)
Cyproteck Inc .... F 860 890-1889
  Middletown (G-7025)
Dataspindle LLC .... G 302 448-4988
  Wilmington (G-15800)
Gatekeeper Systems USA Inc .... G 434 477-6596
  Wilmington (G-16812)
Integrated Tech Systems LLC .... G 302 613-2111
  New Castle (G-9237)
Integration Logistics Inc .... E 302 832-7300
  Newark (G-11032)
Laksh Cybersecurity & Def LLC .... G 224 258-6564
  Wilmington (G-17790)
Linx Security Inc .... F 302 907-9848
  Dover (G-2954)
Lokblok Inc .... F 408 640-8644
  Wilmington (G-17979)
M&S Group International LLC .... G 302 592-6006
  Dover (G-2993)
Novoquad Inc .... F 800 916-6486
  Wilmington (G-18702)
Reolink Innovation Inc .... G 833 424-0499
  Wilmington (G-19433)
Securitas Technology Corp .... E 302 992-7950
  Wilmington (G-19731)
Security 101 Philadlephia LLC .... F 484 369-7101
  Newark (G-11969)
Skylark Labs Inc .... G 415 609-3633
  Newark (G-12028)
Skypher Inc .... F 510 570-5843
  Wilmington (G-19859)
Sobieski Life Safety .... E 800 321-1332
  Newark (G-12046)
Tyco Technology Resources .... G 877 706-0510
  Wilmington (G-20478)
Wahid Consultants LLC .... E 315 400-0955
  Historic New Castle (G-5099)
X-Sense USA LLC .... G 857 998-3929
  Wilmington (G-20911)

SEMICONDUCTORS & RELATED DEVICES

Accelerated Virtual Solutions .... G 302 494-3215
  Newark (G-9749)

Employee Codes: A=Over 500 employees, B=251-500
C=101-250, D=51-100, E=20-50, F=10-19, G=1-9

2024 Harris Directory of Delaware Businesses

SEMICONDUCTORS & RELATED DEVICES

Ganvix Inc..................................... G 508 904-3045
Wilmington *(G-16801)*

Gen Digital Inc................................ G 650 527-8000
Wilmington *(G-16829)*

SEPTIC TANK CLEANING SVCS

A1 Sanitation Service Inc................. G 302 653-9591
Smyrna *(G-13627)*

Arrow Leasing Corp........................ F 302 834-4546
Bear *(G-47)*

Atlantic Pumping Inc....................... F 302 436-5047
Selbyville *(G-13468)*

C White & Sons LLC...................... G 302 629-4848
Seaford *(G-13100)*

Clean Delaware Inc........................ G 302 684-4221
Milton *(G-8584)*

Dukes Septic.................................. G 302 362-6010
Milton *(G-8612)*

Mc Mullen Septic Service Inc.......... G 302 629-6221
Seaford *(G-13277)*

Multi Koastal Services.................... G 302 436-8822
Frankford *(G-4128)*

SERVICE STATION EQPT REPAIR SVCS

Jbm Petroleum Service LLC............ G 302 752-6105
Lincoln *(G-6677)*

SHAPES & PILINGS, STRUCTURAL: Steel

Seaside Service LLC...................... G 302 827-3775
Lewes *(G-6455)*

SHEET METAL SPECIALTIES, EXC STAMPED

A & H Metals Inc........................... E 302 366-7540
Newark *(G-9720)*

Accurate Metal Solutions LLC........ A
Wilmington *(G-14228)*

D M Iannone Inc............................. G 302 999-0893
Wilmington *(G-15761)*

Phillips Fabrication......................... G 302 875-4424
Laurel *(G-5576)*

Power Electronics Inc.................... E 302 653-4822
Clayton *(G-1398)*

Sheet Metal Contracting Co............ E 302 834-3727
Bear *(G-488)*

SHIP BUILDING & REPAIRING: Passenger, Commercial

Mv Cruise Partners LLC................. G 561 329-3209
Wilmington *(G-18496)*

SHOE & BOOT ACCESS

Vulcan International Corp............... F 302 428-3181
Wilmington *(G-20658)*

SHOE STORES

Rare Royals Incorporated............... G 833 288-7171
Middletown *(G-7502)*

SHOE STORES: Athletic

Elite Feet LLC................................ G 302 464-1028
Middletown *(G-7094)*

SHOE STORES: Boots, Men's

Chick Harness & Supply Inc........... E 302 398-4630
Harrington *(G-4748)*

SHOWER STALLS: Plastic & Fiberglass

Atlantic Source Contg Inc............... G 302 645-5207
Lewes *(G-5718)*

SHREDDERS: Indl & Commercial

Rhi Refractories Holding Company..... A 302 655-6497
Wilmington *(G-19457)*

SHUTTERS, DOOR & WINDOW: Metal

Alutech United Inc.......................... G 302 436-6005
Selbyville *(G-13461)*

Shore Shutters and Shade.............. G 302 569-1738
Millsboro *(G-8462)*

SIGNS & ADVERTISING SPECIALTIES

9193 4323 Quebec Inc.................... G 855 824-0795
Newark *(G-9717)*

Ad-Art Signs Georgetown Inc......... G 302 856-7446
Georgetown *(G-4197)*

Alli Inc.. G 302 733-0740
Newark *(G-9824)*

Banacom Signs Inc........................ G 302 429-6243
Wilmington *(G-14727)*

Barbara Graphics Inc..................... G 302 636-9040
Wilmington *(G-14755)*

Clear Channel Outdoor LLC.......... E 302 658-5520
Wilmington *(G-15476)*

Cw Signs LLC................................ G 302 533-5492
Newark *(G-10369)*

D By D Printing LLC....................... G 302 659-3373
Dover *(G-2180)*

Dandy Signs................................... G 301 399-8746
Ocean View *(G-12498)*

Delaware Dept Hlth Social Svcs..... G 302 255-9855
New Castle *(G-9017)*

Delaware Dept Hlth Social Svcs..... D 302 255-9800
New Castle *(G-9020)*

Delaware Sign Co........................... G 302 469-5656
Felton *(G-3959)*

Delmarva Sign Co.......................... G 302 934-6188
Georgetown *(G-4289)*

Friends and Sign............................ G 302 368-4794
Newark *(G-10786)*

Galaxy Sign & Lighting................... G 302 757-5349
Wilmington *(G-16794)*

Gary M Munch Inc.......................... G 302 525-8301
Newark *(G-10812)*

Gotshadeonline Inc........................ G 302 832-8468
Bear *(G-252)*

Gotshadeonline Inc........................ G 302 384-2932
Newark *(G-10871)*

Grier Signs.................................... G 302 737-4823
Newark *(G-10899)*

Griffs Signs LLC............................ G 302 784-5596
Wilmington *(G-16979)*

Guedon Co..................................... G 302 375-6151
Wilmington *(G-17002)*

Harting Graphics Ltd...................... G 302 762-6397
Wilmington *(G-17068)*

Impact Graphix.............................. F 302 337-7076
Seaford *(G-13221)*

Incolor Sign................................... G 302 984-2695
Wilmington *(G-17301)*

Jdjs LLC.. E 844 967-3748
Georgetown *(G-4380)*

Jenner Enterprises Inc................... G 302 479-5686
Wilmington *(G-17524)*

Jenner Enterprises Inc................... F 302 998-6755
Wilmington *(G-17523)*

K & R Graphics & Signs Inc........... G 302 697-7725
Woodside *(G-20977)*

Kalisign USA.................................. G 302 268-6946
Wilmington *(G-17638)*

Kgc Enterprises Inc....................... G 302 668-1835
Wilmington *(G-17710)*

Lane Sign Inc................................. G 610 558-2630
Wilmington *(G-17803)*

PRODUCTS & SERVICES SECTION

Led Sign City LLC.......................... G 866 343-4011
Wilmington *(G-17851)*

Lewis Lettering Co......................... G 610 209-0998
Lewes *(G-6204)*

Marjano LLC.................................. G 302 454-7446
Bear *(G-363)*

Mimesis Signs............................... G 302 674-5566
Dover *(G-3095)*

Mr Copy Inc................................... G 302 227-4666
Rehoboth Beach *(G-12866)*

Prestige Powder Inc....................... G 302 737-7086
Newark *(G-11735)*

Rentzs Sign Service....................... G 302 378-9607
Townsend *(G-14057)*

Rocket Signs.................................. G 302 645-1425
Lewes *(G-6428)*

Rogers Sign Company Inc............. F 302 684-8338
Milton *(G-8703)*

Sabion Sound Reinforcement Co..... G 302 427-0551
Wilmington *(G-19618)*

Shekinah Glory Sign Company....... G 302 256-0426
Wilmington *(G-19790)*

Sign Express................................. G 302 999-0893
Wilmington *(G-19820)*

Signs By Tomorrow........................ G 302 744-9396
Dover *(G-3558)*

Signscape Designs & Signs........... G 302 798-2926
Wilmington *(G-19824)*

Southern Delaware Signs............... G 302 645-1425
Lewes *(G-6495)*

Stop Traffic................................... G 302 604-1176
Millsboro *(G-8468)*

Towers Signs LLC......................... G 302 629-7450
Seaford *(G-13433)*

Trademark Signs............................ G 484 832-5770
Wilmington *(G-20386)*

Traffic Sign Solutions Inc............... G 302 295-4836
Wilmington *(G-20387)*

Trophy Shop.................................. G 302 656-4438
Wilmington *(G-20438)*

Tylaur Inc...................................... G 302 894-9330
Newark *(G-12251)*

Weber Sign Co............................... F 302 732-1429
Frankford *(G-4160)*

X Screen Graphix.......................... G 302 422-4550
Milford *(G-8154)*

SIGNS & ADVERTISING SPECIALTIES: Artwork, Advertising

Aster Bouquet Flower Shop LLC..... G 302 258-9242
Lewes *(G-5708)*

Beachview Mgmt Inc...................... G 302 227-3280
Lewes *(G-5744)*

SIGNS & ADVERTISING SPECIALTIES: Novelties

Penney Enterprises Inc.................. G 302 629-4430
Seaford *(G-13340)*

SIGNS, ELECTRICAL: Wholesalers

Kent Sign Company Inc.................. F 302 697-2181
Dover *(G-2856)*

SIGNS, EXC ELECTRIC, WHOLESALE

Fedex Office & Print Svcs Inc........ G 302 996-0264
Wilmington *(G-16573)*

Prestige Powder Inc....................... G 302 737-7086
Newark *(G-11735)*

SIGNS: Electrical

PRODUCTS & SERVICES SECTION

SOFTWARE PUBLISHERS: Home Entertainment

DOT Pop Inc .... G 302 691-3160
Wilmington (G-16153)

Electro-Art Sign Company .... G 302 322-1108
New Castle (G-9089)

First State Signs Inc .... F 302 744-9990
Dover (G-2510)

Hes Sign Services Inc .... E 302 257-5150
Wilmington (G-17135)

JD Sign Company LLC .... G 302 786-2761
Harrington (G-4790)

Kent Sign Company Inc .... F 302 697-2181
Dover (G-2856)

SILICON WAFERS: Chemically Doped

Petro International Corp .... G 302 884-6755
Wilmington (G-19000)

SILICONES

Ddp Spclty Elctrnc Mtls US 9 .... G 302 774-1000
Wilmington (G-15835)

SILK SCREEN DESIGN SVCS

Harting Graphics Ltd .... G 302 762-6397
Wilmington (G-17068)

Initially Yours Inc .... G 302 999-0562
Wilmington (G-17341)

Kustom Additions LLC .... G 302 468-6865
Wilmington (G-17769)

Promotions Plus Inc .... G 302 836-2820
Newark (G-11764)

Seaside Graphics Corp .... G 302 436-9460
Selbyville (G-13603)

SILVERWARE & PLATED WARE

Select Stainless Products LLC .... G 302 653-3062
Clayton (G-1405)

SIZES

Solenis Holdings 1 LLC .... F 866 337-1533
Wilmington (G-19920)

SKILL TRAINING CENTER

Advanced Training Acadmey .... G 302 369-8800
Newark (G-9783)

Industrial Training Cons Inc .... E 302 266-6100
Newark (G-11016)

SKIN CARE PRDTS: Suntan Lotions & Oils

Richard Earl Fisher .... G 302 598-1957
Wilmington (G-19468)

SOCIAL SERVICES INFORMATION EXCHANGE

Simplymiddle LLC .... G 302 217-3460
Wilmington (G-19841)

SOCIAL SVCS CENTER

Ability Network of Delaware .... G 302 622-9177
Wilmington (G-14203)

Aids Care Group .... G 610 220-8058
Wilmington (G-14328)

American National Red Cross .... G 215 451-4372
Wilmington (G-14438)

ARC Wilmington .... F 302 656-6620
Wilmington (G-14536)

Autism Delaware Inc .... E 302 224-6020
Newark (G-9946)

Beautful Gate Outreach Ctr Inc ...... F 302 472-4502
Wilmington (G-14808)

Brandywine Center For Autism .... D 302 762-2636
Wilmington (G-15049)

Cancer Support Cmnty Del Inc .... G 302 995-2850
Wilmington (G-15213)

Catholic Charities Inc .... G 302 674-1600
Dover (G-2038)

Catholic Charities Inc .... G 302 674-1600
Dover (G-2039)

Catholic Charities Inc .... G 302 856-9578
Georgetown (G-4245)

Catholic Charities Inc .... G 302 684-8694
Milton (G-8580)

Catholic Charities Inc .... E 302 655-9624
Wilmington (G-15277)

Cayuga Centers .... F 302 257-5848
Middletown (G-6966)

Cbhi Inc .... F 484 751-7752
Wilmington (G-15286)

Child Inc .... C 302 832-5451
Newark (G-10202)

Children Fmilies First Del Inc .... G 302 674-8384
Dover (G-2061)

Childrens Advocacy Ctr of Del .... G 302 854-0323
Georgetown (G-4254)

Childrens Choice Inc .... G 302 731-9512
Newark (G-10205)

Chimes Inc .... E 302 730-0747
Dover (G-2065)

Community Interactions Inc .... D 302 993-7846
Wilmington (G-15562)

Community Solutions Inc .... G 302 660-8691
Wilmington (G-15564)

Connectionscsp Inc .... G 302 383-8482
Seaford (G-13133)

Connectons Cmnty Spport Prgram .. D 302 536-1952
Seaford (G-13134)

Delaware Adlescent Program Inc .... E 302 531-0257
Camden (G-816)

Delaware Association For Blind ...... E 302 998-5913
Wilmington (G-15868)

Delaware Brast Cncer Cltion In ...... G 302 778-1102
Wilmington (G-15875)

Delaware Cltion Agnst Dom Vlnc .... G 302 658-2958
Wilmington (G-15885)

Delaware Ctr For Hmless Vtrans .... E 302 384-2350
Wilmington (G-15896)

Delaware Ctr For Hmless Vtrans .... G 302 898-2647
Wilmington (G-15897)

Delaware Ecumenical Council .... G 302 225-1040
Wilmington (G-15912)

Delaware Family Voices Inc .... G 302 669-3030
Wilmington (G-15918)

Delaware Hiv Services Inc .... E 302 654-5471
Wilmington (G-15927)

Dover Interfaith Mission Walte .... G 302 264-9021
Dover (G-2348)

Family Prmise Nthrn New Cstle ...... G 302 998-2222
Wilmington (G-16546)

First State Cmnty Action Agcy .... E 302 674-1355
Dover (G-2499)

Food Bank of Delaware Inc .... E 302 292-1305
Newark (G-10754)

Friendship House Incorporated .... F 302 652-8033
Wilmington (G-16759)

Friendship House Incorporated .... F 302 652-8133
Wilmington (G-16760)

Friendship House Nec .... F 302 731-5338
Newark (G-10787)

Housing Alliance Delaware Inc .... F 302 654-0126
Wilmington (G-17218)

Immanuel Shelter Inc .... G 888 634-9992
Rehoboth Beach (G-12793)

Immanuel Shelter Inc .... G 302 227-7743
Nassau (G-8741)

Independent Resources Inc .... G 302 765-0191
Wilmington (G-17309)

Jewish Family Services of Del .... F 302 478-9411
Wilmington (G-17539)

Keystone Human Services .... F 302 502-2158
Wilmington (G-17709)

La Esperanza Inc .... F 302 854-9262
Georgetown (G-4397)

Lutheran Community Services .... G 302 654-8886
Wilmington (G-18031)

Mentor De .... G 302 858-4644
Georgetown (G-4425)

Merakey USA .... E 302 325-3540
New Castle (G-9358)

Ministry of Caring Inc .... G 302 652-0970
Wilmington (G-18376)

Ministry of Caring Inc .... G 302 652-0969
Wilmington (G-18377)

My Sisters Place Inc .... G 302 737-5303
Newark (G-11477)

Peoples Place II Inc .... G 302 422-8033
Milford (G-8045)

Point of Hope Inc .... E 302 731-7676
New Castle (G-9480)

Prevent Child Abuse Delaware .... G 302 425-7490
Wilmington (G-19186)

Rauma Survivors Foundation .... G 302 275-9705
Wilmington (G-19339)

Reeds Refuge Center Inc .... G 302 428-1830
Wilmington (G-19393)

Ronald McDonald House Delaware . F 302 428-5299
Wilmington (G-19560)

Scchs .... F 302 856-7524
Georgetown (G-4499)

Shepherd Place Inc .... G 302 678-1909
Dover (G-3542)

St Anthonys Community Center ..... F 302 421-3721
Wilmington (G-19990)

St Patricks Center Inc .... G 302 652-6219
Wilmington (G-20002)

Sunday Breakfast Mission .... F 302 656-8542
Wilmington (G-20129)

Survivors Abuse In Rcovery Inc ..... G 302 651-0181
Wilmington (G-20162)

Sussex Cmnty Crsis Hsing Svcs ... F 302 856-2246
Georgetown (G-4532)

Transitional Youth .... F 302 423-7543
Greenwood (G-4672)

Turning Point At Peoples Place ...... G 302 424-2420
Milford (G-8121)

United Cerebral Palsy of De .... E 302 764-2400
Wilmington (G-20524)

United Way of Delaware Inc .... E 302 573-3700
Wilmington (G-20530)

Victims Voices Heard .... G 302 407-3747
Wilmington (G-20609)

West End Neighborhood Hse Inc .... E 302 658-4171
Wilmington (G-20740)

Whatcoat Social Service Agency .... E 302 734-0319
Dover (G-3842)

SOFT DRINKS WHOLESALERS

Elizabeth Beverage Company LLC .. G 302 322-9895
Historic New Castle (G-4982)

Pepsi-Cola Btlg of Wilmington .... C 302 761-4848
Wilmington (G-18966)

Valentina Liquors .... G 302 368-3264
Newark (G-12300)

SOFTWARE PUBLISHERS: Home Entertainment

SOFTWARE PUBLISHERS: Home Entertainment

Fun Bakery LLC..G..... 858 220-0946
  Dover (G-2544)
Neon Fun LLC..G..... 858 220-0946
  Dover (G-3170)
Relytv LLC...G..... 213 373-5988
  Dover (G-3450)
Virtual Pro Gaming Inc................................G..... 302 285-9891
  Wilmington (G-20634)

SOFTWARE PUBLISHERS: Operating Systems

Endless Os Foundation LLC.........................G..... 415 413-4159
  Wilmington (G-16410)
Isaac Fair Corporation..................................G..... 302 324-8015
  New Castle (G-9243)
Talk Aware LLC..G..... 302 645-7400
  Lewes (G-6540)

SOFTWARE TRAINING, COMPUTER

Bits & Bytes Inc...G..... 302 674-2999
  Dover (G-1942)
Discidium Technology Inc............................G..... 347 220-5979
  Newark (G-10538)
Galaxyworks LLC..F..... 404 894-8703
  Dover (G-2555)
Kortech Consulting Inc................................F..... 302 559-4612
  Bear (G-333)
Mh-Teq LLC...G..... 302 897-2182
  Wilmington (G-18301)
Sdn Essentials LLC.......................................F..... 415 902-5702
  Newark (G-11965)
Smartprofyl LLC...G..... 832 412-5803
  Middletown (G-7578)

SOLAR CELLS

Dupont De Nemours Inc..............................A..... 302 774-3034
  Wilmington (G-16205)
Dupont Specialty Pdts USA LLC..................E..... 302 992-2941
  Wilmington (G-16216)
Hirotec Inc...G..... 248 836-5100
  Wilmington (G-17154)

SOLAR HEATING EQPT

Aztech Industries Inc...................................G..... 302 653-1430
  Smyrna (G-13657)
Solar Foundations Usa Inc.........................G..... 855 738-7200
  New Castle (G-9576)

SOLID CONTAINING UNITS: Concrete

Rhi Refractories Holding Company.............A..... 302 655-6497
  Wilmington (G-19457)

SPACE VEHICLES

Space Industries Inc....................................G..... 510 219-1005
  Dover (G-3592)

SPAS

1110 On Parkway Nedi Spa.........................G..... 302 576-1110
  Wilmington (G-14104)
7chakras Spa Lounge..................................G..... 302 584-7793
  Wilmington (G-14149)
Afterglo Beauty Spa.....................................G..... 302 537-7546
  Millville (G-8512)
Alternative Therapy LLC..............................G..... 302 368-0800
  Newark (G-9838)
Avenue Day Spa...F..... 302 227-5649
  Rehoboth Beach (G-12619)
Bella Donna Spa...G..... 703 313-7945
  Rehoboth Beach (G-12640)
Bella Medispa Inc...G..... 302 736-6334
  Dover (G-1907)

Charmed Medi Spa......................................G..... 302 273-2827
  Newark (G-10192)
Charmed Medispa Inc.................................G..... 302 593-1994
  Newark (G-10193)
Christophers Hair Design............................G..... 302 378-1988
  Middletown (G-6980)
Dream Spa..G..... 646 717-5397
  Wilmington (G-16176)
Essential Luxuries Spa................................G..... 302 244-6875
  Dover (G-2463)
Golden Apple Spa..G..... 302 375-6505
  Wilmington (G-16911)
Hand & Spa..G..... 302 478-1700
  Wilmington (G-17044)
Harmony Spa..G..... 302 563-7723
  Newark (G-10932)
Haus of Lacquer LLC...................................E..... 302 690-0309
  Wilmington (G-17076)
Hday Spa..G..... 302 482-1041
  Wilmington (G-17088)
Hockessin Day Spa......................................G..... 302 234-7573
  Wilmington (G-17162)
Inspiration Empire..G..... 302 535-9920
  Greenwood (G-4639)
Jennifers Spa..G..... 302 740-6363
  Newark (G-11106)
Jube Medical Spa LLC.................................G..... 302 478-4020
  Wilmington (G-17607)
Kingdom Spa Inc..G..... 302 897-8255
  Middletown (G-7277)
La Bella Vita Salon & Day Spa....................G..... 302 883-2597
  Dover (G-2895)
Last Tangle Salon and Spa........................G..... 302 653-6638
  Smyrna (G-13796)
Lynn Victoria COSm&med Skin...................G..... 302 388-5459
  Hockessin (G-5284)
Melanin Mixx Beauty Brand Inc..................G..... 302 266-1010
  Newark (G-11385)
My Seaside Spa...G..... 302 313-5174
  Lewes (G-6301)
Nail Spa By Tr..G..... 302 678-2122
  Dover (G-3147)
New Relaxation Inc.....................................G..... 302 934-9344
  Millsboro (G-8404)
Pamper Perfect Mobile Spa........................G..... 302 482-5938
  Newark (G-11617)
Rainbow Seven Spa.....................................G..... 302 533-6916
  Newark (G-11822)
Renove Med Spa..G..... 302 584-3216
  Dagsboro (G-1497)
Sanctuary Spa and Saloon.........................F..... 302 475-1469
  Wilmington (G-19656)
Serenity Spa...G..... 302 668-9534
  Wilmington (G-19757)
Toppers Spa...F..... 302 857-2020
  Dover (G-3701)
Tranquility By Tara Colazo..........................G..... 302 668-4032
  Wilmington (G-20392)
Trilogy Salon & Spa.....................................G..... 302 388-1210
  Wilmington (G-20421)
Tru Beauti LLC...E..... 302 353-9249
  Middletown (G-7663)
Via Mdical Day Spa Pasca Salon...............G..... 302 757-2830
  Wilmington (G-20604)
Vidells Day Spa..G..... 302 656-1784
  Wilmington (G-20617)
Vogue On 24 Salon & Spa LLC...................G..... 302 947-5667
  Millsboro (G-8496)

SPEAKER SYSTEMS

Soundboks Inc..G..... 213 436-5888
  Wilmington (G-19935)

SPECIALIZED LEGAL SVCS

Bench Walk Advisors LLC...........................G..... 302 426-2100
  Wilmington (G-14826)
Central Firm LLC..G..... 610 470-9836
  Wilmington (G-15308)
Delaware Bus Incorporators Inc.................G..... 302 996-5819
  Wilmington (G-15877)
Express Legal Documents LLC..................G..... 212 710-1374
  Wilmington (G-16509)
Harvard Business Services Inc...................E..... 302 645-7400
  Lewes (G-6081)
Parcels Inc...C..... 302 888-1718
  Wilmington (G-18889)

SPECIALTY FOOD STORES: Health & Dietetic Food

Hockessin Chrpractic Centre PA................G..... 302 239-8550
  Hockessin (G-5241)
Trexgen Nutrascience LLC..........................G..... 302 520-2406
  Newark (G-12219)

SPECIALTY FOOD STORES: Vitamin

Fresh Juice Partners LLC............................G..... 302 364-0909
  Lewes (G-6016)

SPECIALTY OUTPATIENT CLINICS, NEC

Brain Works & Mind Matters LLC................G..... 302 324-5255
  New Castle (G-8882)
Common Cooperative Company.................G..... 504 333-0731
  Wilmington (G-15550)
Delaware Dept Hlth Social Svcs..................G..... 302 857-5000
  Dover (G-2229)
Delaware Sleep Disorder C.........................F..... 302 407-3349
  Middletown (G-7046)
Delmarva Surgery Ctr..................................G..... 443 245-3470
  Newark (G-10506)
Family Planning..G..... 302 856-5225
  Georgetown (G-4314)
Jameil Akeem Cngo Cres Fndtion...............G..... 302 409-0791
  Wilmington (G-17477)
Janelle G Evans LLC....................................G..... 302 562-6504
  Wilmington (G-17493)
Knus Inc..D..... 855 935-5687
  Wilmington (G-17745)
Management Pain LLC.................................G..... 302 543-5180
  Wilmington (G-18099)
Midatlantic Pain Institute............................F..... 302 369-1700
  Newark (G-11415)
Multispecialty Healthcare...........................G..... 302 575-9794
  Wilmington (G-18483)
New Life Fndation Recovery Inc.................G..... 302 317-2212
  Bear (G-393)
Nu Beginning Center LLC...........................G..... 302 276-8483
  Smyrna (G-13837)
Rehabilitation Associates Pa.....................G..... 302 293-6877
  Newark (G-11845)
Soundingboard Project................................G..... 302 956-1112
  Wilmington (G-19936)
US Dept of the Air Force.............................E..... 302 677-2525
  Dover (G-3764)
Verde Loma LLC...G..... 302 858-4040
  Georgetown (G-4568)

SPORTING & ATHLETIC GOODS: Bowling Pins

Vulcan International Corp...........................F..... 302 428-3181
  Wilmington (G-20658)

SPORTING & ATHLETIC GOODS: Camping Eqpt & Splys

PRODUCTS & SERVICES SECTION

SWIMMING POOL & HOT TUB CLEANING & MAINTENANCE SVCS

Terrain and Tactical LLC .... G 302 521-9290
Wilmington (G-20275)

SPORTING & ATHLETIC GOODS: Racket Sports Eqpt

Dahcor LLC .... G 302 257-2803
Dover (G-2184)

SPORTING & ATHLETIC GOODS: Shafts, Golf Club

Black & Decker Inc .... G 860 827-3861
Newark (G-10043)

SPORTING & ATHLETIC GOODS: Shooting Eqpt & Splys, General

J & V Shooters Supply LP .... G 302 422-5417
Milford (G-7945)

SPORTING CAMPS

Division One Basketball LLC .... F 302 573-2528
Wilmington (G-16099)
Ed Hunt Inc .... G 302 339-8443
Dover (G-2418)
Piranha Sports LLC .... G 302 893-1997
Bear (G-426)

SPORTING FIREARMS WHOLESALERS

Millers Gun Center Inc .... G 302 328-9747
New Castle (G-9371)

SPORTING GOODS STORES: Firearms

Millers Gun Center Inc .... G 302 328-9747
New Castle (G-9371)
Noble Eagle Sales LLC .... G 302 736-5166
Dover (G-3191)
Police & Fire Rod & Gun Club .... G 302 655-0304
New Castle (G-9481)
Shooters Choice Inc .... G 302 736-5166
Dover (G-3548)

SPORTING GOODS STORES: Fishing Eqpt

South Shore Provisions LLC .... G 443 614-2442
Selbyville (G-13607)

SPORTS APPAREL STORES

Huzala Inc .... G 313 404-6941
Newark (G-10987)
Rockeias Journey LLC .... G 302 304-3055
Newark (G-11903)

SPORTS CLUBS, MANAGERS & PROMOTERS

302 Elite Athletes .... G 302 834-7991
Bear (G-1)
Awl LLC .... G 610 299-3322
Lewes (G-5729)
Combat Zone Wresting LLC .... G 302 345-1077
Newark (G-10280)
Five Star Franchising LLC .... G 646 838-3992
Wilmington (G-16654)
Melodic Mvmnts Prfrmg Arts Prg .... F 302 543-5257
Wilmington (G-18266)
Soccer Network LLC .... G 302 724-6951
Dover (G-3582)
Southern Delaware Roller Derby .... G 410 253-9798
Dover (G-3590)
Volleyball .... G 302 593-4414
Townsend (G-14089)

SPORTS PROMOTION SVCS

Family Depository Alliance .... F 888 332-6275
Middletown (G-7120)

SPRINGS: Steel

Betts Inc .... G 302 475-3754
Wilmington (G-14864)

SPRINGS: Wire

Delmaco Manufacturing Inc .... F 302 856-6345
Georgetown (G-4288)

STAIRCASES & STAIRS, WOOD

Richard Hrrmann Strbilders Inc .... G 302 654-4329
Wilmington (G-19469)

STARTERS & CONTROLLERS: Motor, Electric

Redarc Corporation .... G 704 247-5150
Dover (G-3441)

STATIONERY & OFFICE SPLYS WHOLESALERS

Coordle Inc .... G 419 618-0949
Dover (G-2134)
Nitro Impact Inc .... F 347 694-7000
Wilmington (G-18652)

STOCK SHAPES: Plastic

Quantum Polymers Corporation .... F 302 737-7012
Newark (G-11796)

STONE: Quarrying & Processing, Own Stone Prdts

H&K Group Inc .... G 302 934-7635
Dagsboro (G-1457)

STORES: Auto & Home Supply

Martin Newark Dealership Inc .... D 302 454-9300
Newark (G-11345)
New Creation Logistics Inc .... F 302 438-3154
Newark (G-11520)
Winner Ford of Newark Inc .... F 302 731-2415
Newark (G-12388)
Winner Group Inc .... F 302 292-8200
Newark (G-12389)
Wreck Masters Demo Derby .... F 302 368-5544
Bear (G-568)

STRUCTURAL SUPPORT & BUILDING MATERIAL: Concrete

Blue Heron Contracting LLC .... G 302 526-0648
Greenwood (G-4600)

SUBSCRIPTION FULFILLMENT SVCS: Magazine, Newspaper, Etc

The Tondo Group LLC .... G 302 893-8849
Newark (G-12187)

SUBSTANCE ABUSE COUNSELING

Michael H McGrath .... G 302 242-3849
Smyrna (G-13823)

SUMMER CAMPS, EXC DAY & SPORTS INSTRUCTIONAL

Hope House Daycare .... G 302 407-3404
Wilmington (G-17197)
Win From Wthin Xc Camp/Tatnall .... G 302 494-5312
Wilmington (G-20855)

SUNDRIES & RELATED PRDTS: Medical & Laboratory, Rubber

W L Gore & Associates Inc .... C 302 368-3700
Newark (G-12341)
W L Gore & Associates Inc .... D 302 738-4880
Newark (G-12342)

SURFACE ACTIVE AGENTS: Oils & Greases

Richard Earl Fisher .... G 302 598-1957
Wilmington (G-19468)

SURGICAL APPLIANCES & SPLYS

Ric Investments LLC .... G 302 656-8996
Wilmington (G-19465)
Ascent Research LLC .... G 703 801-1490
Dover (G-1828)
Enovis Corporation .... C 301 252-9160
Wilmington (G-16428)
Howmedica Osteonics Corp .... G 302 655-3239
Wilmington (G-17220)
Hygieia Shield Inc .... F 302 388-7350
Dover (G-2710)
Mih International LLC .... G 301 908-4233
Newark (G-11417)
Mt Foreign Holdings Inc .... D 301 252-9160
Wilmington (G-18479)
Nestal Mdsphere Consulting LLC .... G 302 404-6506
Wilmington (G-18588)

SURVEYING INSTRUMENTS WHOLESALERS

Survey Supply Inc .... G 302 422-3338
Milford (G-8109)
Trimble Inc .... G 302 368-2434
Wilmington (G-12230)

SVC ESTABLISHMENT EQPT, WHOLESALE: Firefighting Eqpt

Hoopes Fire Prevention Inc .... F 302 323-0220
Newark (G-10968)

SVC ESTABLISHMENT EQPT, WHOLESALE: Laundry Eqpt & Splys

Blue Sky Clean .... G 302 584-5800
Wilmington (G-14975)

SVC ESTABLISHMENT EQPT, WHOLESALE: Vending Machines & Splys

Vending Solutions LLC .... G 302 674-2222
Dover (G-3781)

SWIMMING POOL & HOT TUB CLEANING & MAINTENANCE SVCS

Aquatic Management .... G 302 235-1818
Wilmington (G-14519)
Carter Pool Management LLC .... G 302 236-6952
Lewes (G-5805)
Henderson Services Inc .... F 302 424-1999
Milford (G-7926)
Jonathan Lopez .... G 302 752-5229
Magnolia (G-6754)
Jonathon Gordon .... G 302 690-0614
Wilmington (G-17573)
Quality Pool Care .... G 302 378-7486
Middletown (G-7487)
Sergios Pool Service Inc .... G 302 655-1972
Wilmington (G-19758)

Serrano Inc..G......302 607-1779
Newark (G-11982)

SWIMMING POOLS, EQPT & SPLYS: Wholesalers

Clearblue Pools & Spas LLC.....................F......888 630-7665
Millsboro (G-8230)

SWITCHES: Electronic

Hollingsead International LLC..................B......302 855-5888
Georgetown (G-4360)

Val-Tech Inc..E......302 738-0500
Newark (G-12298)

SWITCHES: Electronic Applications

Tricklestar Inc..F......888 700-1098
Wilmington (G-20420)

SYSTEMS ENGINEERING: Computer Related

Agts LLC...G......800 496-3379
Dover (G-1749)

Bullseye Entertainment Tech Co................E......302 924-5034
Dover (G-1992)

Cited Inc...G......302 384-9810
Wilmington (G-15447)

Purplenow Inc..E......302 751-5226
Dover (G-3399)

Sharlay Computer Systems........................G......302 588-3170
Smyrna (G-13883)

Sumuri Inc...E......302 570-0015
Magnolia (G-6786)

SYSTEMS INTEGRATION SVCS

Blue Sky Web Solutions Inc.......................G......302 261-2654
Newark (G-10063)

Cim Concepts Incorporated........................F......302 613-5400
New Castle (G-8942)

Data-Bi LLC..G......302 290-3138
Wilmington (G-15798)

Ebc Systems LLC...G......302 472-1896
Wilmington (G-16275)

GIERD INC..E......206 289-0011
Wilmington (G-16858)

Kagoal Technology LLC..............................G......617 818-0588
Middletown (G-7260)

Obhost LLC...G......302 440-1447
Lewes (G-6326)

Second Front Systems Inc.........................D......301 744-7318
Wilmington (G-19728)

Smartis..G......302 653-8355
Dover (G-3578)

Staircase Inc...E......215 693-5686
Claymont (G-1300)

SYSTEMS INTEGRATION SVCS: Local Area Network

Advanced Global Networks Inc..................G......302 308-6460
Wilmington (G-14274)

Insight Engineering Solutions....................G......302 378-4842
Townsend (G-14018)

Integration Logistics Inc.............................E......302 832-7300
Newark (G-11032)

SYSTEMS SOFTWARE DEVELOPMENT SVCS

Avant Digital Inc..G......660 726-2416
Newark (G-9950)

Beverage Infosystems Ltd Lblty................E......732 762-5299
Wilmington (G-14866)

Bothub Ai Limited..F......669 278-7485
Newark (G-10071)

Care Mentor Ai LLC.....................................E......302 830-3700
Wilmington (G-15241)

Digitalai Software Inc..................................F......678 268-3340
Wilmington (G-16069)

Dopamine World Inc....................................G......650 933-8003
Dover (G-2324)

Encross LLC...F......302 351-2593
Wilmington (G-16407)

Inclind Inc...G......302 856-2802
Lewes (G-6120)

Infinite Solutions LLC.................................F......302 438-5310
Wilmington (G-17322)

Kortech Consulting Inc...............................F......302 559-4612
Bear (G-333)

Microtelecom Systems LLC........................D......718 707-0012
Wilmington (G-18331)

Omnimaven Inc..G......302 378-8918
Middletown (G-7414)

Pentius Inc..E......855 825-3778
Wilmington (G-18963)

Play US Media LLC......................................G......302 924-5034
Dover (G-3332)

Public Systems Inc......................................G......302 326-4500
New Castle (G-9500)

Rave Business Systems LLC.....................F......302 407-2270
Lewes (G-6409)

Riders App Inc..G......347 484-4344
Wilmington (G-19479)

Sensofusion Inc...F......570 239-4912
Milton (G-8710)

She Bash LLC..G......302 204-6700
Claymont (G-1289)

Talkpush LLC...D......415 818-5083
Dover (G-3648)

Tpf Technologies LLC.................................G......703 665-4588
Wilmington (G-20380)

Urspayce Inc..G......302 440-2880
Claymont (G-1325)

Very LLC...D......630 945-5539
Dover (G-3787)

Watchdogdevelopmentcom LLC................G......888 488-7531
Dover (G-3822)

Xeroictech Inc..F......302 252-1617
Claymont (G-1341)

TABLE OR COUNTERTOPS, PLASTIC LAMINATED

Cabinetry Unlimited LLC............................E......302 436-5030
Selbyville (G-13489)

Michael A OBrien & Sons...........................G......302 994-2894
Wilmington (G-18306)

TABLEWARE: Vitreous China

Saenger Porcelain.......................................G......302 738-5349
Newark (G-11932)

TALLOW: Animal

Horizon Rendering Co Inc..........................G......302 239-4950
Wilmington (G-17208)

TANKS & OTHER TRACKED VEHICLE CMPNTS

Intech Services..G......302 366-1442
Newark (G-11029)

TANKS: Fuel, Including Oil & Gas, Metal Plate

Atom Alloys LLC..F......786 975-3771
Wilmington (G-14633)

TANKS: Plastic & Fiberglass

Justin Tanks LLC...E......302 856-3521
Georgetown (G-4389)

TAPES: Pressure Sensitive, Rubber

The Crowell Corporation............................D......302 998-0558
Wilmington (G-20291)

TARPAULINS, WHOLESALE

Cramaro Tarpaulin Systems Inc................G......302 292-2170
Newark (G-10344)

TELECOMMUNICATION EQPT REPAIR SVCS, EXC TELEPHONES

Shootle Inc...G......941 866-2135
Lewes (G-6464)

Smith Brothers Communication.................G......302 293-5224
Newark (G-12041)

TELECONFERENCING SVCS

Conference Group LLC...............................E......302 224-8255
Newark (G-10302)

TELEPHONE ANSWERING SVCS

Appletree Answering Services Inc............B......302 227-9015
Wilmington (G-14510)

Applied Virtual Solutions LLC...................G......302 312-8548
Newark (G-9892)

Bayshore Communications Inc..................F......302 737-2164
Newark (G-9995)

Insta Answer LLC..G......973 303-1764
Newark (G-11026)

Shore Answer LLC......................................G......302 253-8381
Georgetown (G-4511)

TELEPHONE EQPT: NEC

Bio Medic Corporation................................F......302 628-4300
Seaford (G-13089)

Siemens...E......302 220-1544
Wilmington (G-19815)

Siemens AG..G......302 836-2933
Bear (G-491)

Siemens Corporation..................................E......302 220-1544
Historic New Castle (G-5070)

TELEPHONE SVCS

Six Sigma Telecom LLC..............................G......302 636-5440
Wilmington (G-19849)

TELEVISION BROADCASTING STATIONS

Eternal Word Television Inc.......................G......302 734-8434
Dover (G-2465)

Forecast Inc...G......302 413-0675
Dover (G-2525)

TEMPORARY HELP SVCS

Access Labor Service Inc..........................E......302 741-2575
Dover (G-1707)

Adecco Usa Inc..G......302 669-4005
New Castle (G-8762)

Adecco Usa Inc..G......302 457-4059
Newark (G-9763)

Aerotek Inc...G......302 561-6300
New Castle (G-8770)

Aerotek Inc...G......302 318-8760
Newark (G-9789)

Barrett Business Services Inc...................G......302 674-2206
Dover (G-1875)

PRODUCTS & SERVICES SECTION

TOYS & HOBBY GOODS & SPLYS, WHOLESALE: Video Games

Career Associates Inc............................. G 302 674-4357
Dover *(G-2029)*

First State Stffing Sltion LLC................. E 302 285-9044
Wilmington *(G-16636)*

Frontier SGS 360 LLC........................... G 609 919-1133
Wilmington *(G-16764)*

Interim Healthcare Del LLC................... F 302 322-2743
Smyrna *(G-13775)*

J&J Staffing Resources Inc................... G 302 738-7800
Newark *(G-11079)*

Kelly Services Inc.................................. G 302 323-4748
New Castle *(G-9279)*

Kelly Services Inc.................................. G 302 366-1741
Newark *(G-11152)*

Talent4health LLC................................. D 302 314-1677
Wilmington *(G-20212)*

TEN PIN CENTERS

AMF Bowling Centers Inc..................... E 302 998-5316
Wilmington *(G-14456)*

Bowlerama Inc....................................... E 302 654-0263
New Castle *(G-8878)*

Brunswick Doverama............................. G 302 734-7501
Dover *(G-1987)*

Delaware Womens Bowling Assn......... G 302 834-7002
Bear *(G-161)*

First State Bowling Center................... G 302 762-3883
Wilmington *(G-16625)*

Inspection Lanes................................... G 302 853-1003
Georgetown *(G-4371)*

Leftys Alley & Eats............................... F 302 864-6000
Lewes *(G-6187)*

Leftys Alley & Eats............................... G 302 344-5858
Rehoboth Beach *(G-12828)*

Main Event Entrmt Wilmington............. G 302 722-9466
Newark *(G-11312)*

Milford Bowling Lanes Inc.................... F 302 422-9456
Milford *(G-7999)*

Millsboro Lanes Inc.............................. F 302 934-0400
Millsboro *(G-8387)*

Pleasant Hill Lanes Inc........................ F 302 998-8811
Wilmington *(G-19077)*

Spare Parts LLC................................... G 302 333-2683
Townsend *(G-14068)*

TESTERS: Physical Property

Testing Machines Inc............................ E 302 613-5600
New Castle *(G-9625)*

TEXTILE & APPAREL SVCS

Bosphorus Textile LLC.......................... F 202 629-6563
Dover *(G-1965)*

Three Sheep and A Mill LLC................. G 616 820-5668
Middletown *(G-7641)*

THEATRICAL LIGHTING SVCS

Light Action Inc..................................... F 302 328-7800
Wilmington *(G-17908)*

THEATRICAL PRODUCERS & SVCS

Annalissas Playhouse........................... G 302 653-3529
Smyrna *(G-13644)*

Arabian Lights Dance Co Inc................ G 410 543-4538
Delmar *(G-1567)*

Brass Unlimited..................................... G 302 322-2529
New Castle *(G-8888)*

Earle Teate Music................................. G 302 736-1937
Dover *(G-2406)*

Herstory Ensemble................................ G 216 288-8759
Wilmington *(G-17133)*

Megara Inc... F 914 487-4702
Dover *(G-3055)*

Yorklyn Storytelling Festival................. G 302 238-6200
Yorklyn *(G-20995)*

THERMOPLASTIC MATERIALS

Dupont De Nemours Inc........................ A 302 774-3034
Wilmington *(G-16205)*

Dupont Indus Bsciences USA LLC....... E 302 774-1000
Wilmington *(G-16210)*

Dupont Specialty Pdts USA LLC.......... E 302 992-2941
Wilmington *(G-16216)*

Eidp Inc.. G 302 654-8198
Wilmington *(G-16336)*

Eidp Inc.. G 302 999-2826
Wilmington *(G-16339)*

New Process Fibre Company............... D 302 349-4535
Greenwood *(G-4657)*

THIN FILM CIRCUITS

Fractal Mobius LLC............................... G 646 209-8559
Dover *(G-2531)*

TILE: Wall, Ceramic

Maneto Inc... E 302 656-4285
Wilmington *(G-18103)*

TIRE & TUBE REPAIR MATERIALS, WHOLESALE

EZ Manufacturing Company LLC......... G 302 653-6567
Clayton *(G-1366)*

TIRES & INNER TUBES

JS Tire Corporation.............................. G 302 558-2320
Wilmington *(G-17604)*

Spm Tire Service LLC........................... G 302 731-1004
Newark *(G-12070)*

TIRES & TUBES WHOLESALERS

Bargain Tire & Service Inc.................... F 302 764-8900
Wilmington *(G-14763)*

Mavis Tire Express Svcs Corp............. F 727 440-5435
Dover *(G-3038)*

Tire Rack Inc... E 302 325-8260
Historic New Castle *(G-5087)*

TIRES & TUBES, WHOLESALE: Automotive

Admiral Tire... G 302 734-5911
Dover *(G-1718)*

Ajacks Tire Service Inc......................... G 302 834-5200
New Castle *(G-8776)*

Bargain Tire & Service Inc.................... F 302 764-8900
Wilmington *(G-14763)*

Bridgestone Ret Operations LLC......... G 302 734-4522
Dover *(G-1979)*

Bridgestone Ret Operations LLC......... G 302 422-4508
Milford *(G-7805)*

Bridgestone Ret Operations LLC......... G 302 656-2529
New Castle *(G-8892)*

Bridgestone Ret Operations LLC......... G 302 995-2487
Wilmington *(G-15108)*

Carl King Tire Co Inc............................ F 302 644-4070
Lewes *(G-5802)*

Carl King Tire Co Inc............................ E 302 697-9506
Camden *(G-803)*

Clarksville Auto Service Ctr.................. E 302 539-1700
Ocean View *(G-12489)*

Delaware Tire Center Inc...................... F 302 674-0234
Dover *(G-2270)*

Delaware Tire Center Inc...................... F 302 368-2531
Newark *(G-10492)*

Diamond State Tire Inc......................... F 302 836-1919
Bear *(G-168)*

Els Tire Service Inc.............................. F 302 834-1997
Newark *(G-10633)*

Furrs Tire Service Inc........................... G 302 678-0800
Dover *(G-2546)*

Goodyear Tire & Rubber Company...... G 302 737-2461
Newark *(G-10869)*

Goodyear Tire & Rubber Company...... G 302 998-0428
Wilmington *(G-16929)*

Kirkwood Tires Inc................................ G 302 737-2460
Newark *(G-11186)*

Monro Inc... G 302 846-2732
Delmar *(G-1623)*

Sports Car Tire Inc............................... E 302 571-8473
Wilmington *(G-19970)*

Tire Sales & Service Inc....................... F 302 658-8955
Wilmington *(G-20335)*

Wellers Tire Service Inc....................... F 302 337-8228
Bridgeville *(G-781)*

TITLE ABSTRACT & SETTLEMENT OFFICES

Trans Un Sttlment Slutions Inc............. D 800 916-8800
Wilmington *(G-20394)*

TOBACCO & PRDTS, WHOLESALE: Cigarettes

BAt Capital Corporation........................ E 302 691-6323
Wilmington *(G-14776)*

TOILETRIES, WHOLESALE: Perfumes

Goodscents Inc...................................... G 302 628-8042
Bridgeville *(G-704)*

TOILETRIES, WHOLESALE: Toiletries

Cerobrand LLC...................................... G 740 971-2576
Wilmington *(G-15314)*

Mid States Sales & Marketing.............. F 302 888-2475
Wilmington *(G-18336)*

TOWELS: Paper

Orlando J Camp & Associates.............. G 302 478-3720
Wilmington *(G-18823)*

TOWING & TUGBOAT SVC

Buntings Garage Inc.............................. F 302 732-9021
Dagsboro *(G-1421)*

TOWING SVCS: Marine

Dick Ennis Inc.. G 302 945-2627
Lewes *(G-5914)*

Wilmington Tug Inc............................... E 302 652-1666
Wilmington *(G-20851)*

TOYS & HOBBY GOODS & SPLYS, WHOLESALE: Toys & Games

Ealing Media & Tech (us) Ltd............... G 909 576-4828
Bear *(G-187)*

Furobinc LLC... G 302 202-4551
Claymont *(G-1153)*

TOYS & HOBBY GOODS & SPLYS, WHOLESALE: Video Games

Balatroon Games Inc............................ G 647 986-9268
Dover *(G-1869)*

Gamestop Inc... F 302 266-7362
Newark *(G-10805)*

Genun Games Inc.................................. G 425 344-4883
Wilmington *(G-16843)*

Retrolio Games LLC.............................. F 423 873-8768
Claymont *(G-1279)*

TOYS: Electronic

Virtual Pro Gaming Inc............................. G..... 302 285-9891
Wilmington (G-20634)

TOYS: Electronic

Time4machine Inc..................................... E..... 302 999-7604
Wilmington (G-20328)

TOYS: Rubber

Forte Sports Incorporated...................... G..... 302 731-0776
Newark (G-10766)

TRADERS: Commodity, Contracts

Dvr International Inc................................ F..... 800 958-9000
Laurel (G-5503)
Emaep LLC.. E..... 202 836-7886
Wilmington (G-16385)
International Fresh Prod Assn................. E..... 302 738-7100
Newark (G-11045)
Mefta LLC.. F..... 804 433-3566
Wilmington (G-18260)

TRAILERS & TRAILER EQPT

Pessagno Equipment Inc.......................... G..... 302 738-7001
Newark (G-11671)

TRAILERS: Semitrailers, Missile Transportation

Integral Enterprise LLC........................... G..... 302 722-0827
Wilmington (G-17366)

TRANSPORTATION AGENTS & BROKERS

Burris Freight Management LLC............. G..... 800 805-8135
Milford (G-7807)
Expotrade Inc... G..... 818 212-8905
Lewes (G-5981)
Gemini Qulty Frt Solutions LLC.............. G..... 302 219-3310
Dover (G-2569)
Oceanview Capital Inds LLC................... F..... 813 397-3706
Dover (G-3215)
Rsl Logistics LLC..................................... G..... 302 521-3299
Wilmington (G-19582)
Spare Cs Inc... F..... 424 744-0155
Lewes (G-6496)

TRANSPORTATION BROKERS: Truck

Aku Transport Inc.................................... G..... 302 500-8127
Georgetown (G-4204)
Destiny Way Logistics LLC..................... F..... 866 526-4900
Wilmington (G-16029)
Immensity Logistics LLC........................ G..... 501 500-6667
Wilmington (G-17284)
North American Trnspt Co Inc................ G..... 856 696-5483
New Castle (G-9422)
Trinity Logistics Inc................................. C..... 302 253-3900
Seaford (G-13436)

TRANSPORTATION EQPT & SPLYS WHOLESALERS, NEC

C & N Freight LLC.................................... G..... 302 897-4061
New Castle (G-8906)
Chambers Bros Logistics LLC................ G..... 302 307-3668
Bear (G-96)
Clicoh Inc... G..... 415 987-3261
Middletown (G-6990)
Janette Redrow Ltd................................. G..... 302 659-3534
Townsend (G-14020)
Kinneys Enterprises LLC........................ G..... 302 300-2012
Newark (G-11180)
Rawr Imports Group LLC........................ G..... 609 271-3455
Claymont (G-1274)

Zat3 Transport LLC.................................. G..... 302 470-6172
Laurel (G-5627)

TRANSPORTATION SVCS, AIR, NONSCHEDULED: Helicopter Carriers

Horizon Helicopters Inc........................... G..... 302 368-5135
Newark (G-10970)

TRANSPORTATION: Deep Sea Domestic Freight

Maritime Logistics Corp LLC.................. G..... 302 420-3007
Wilmington (G-18135)

TRANSPORTATION: Deep Sea Foreign Freight

New Hope Vehicle Exports LLC.............. G..... 302 275-6482
Wilmington (G-18619)

TRAVEL AGENCIES

AAA Club Alliance Inc............................. D..... 302 674-8020
Dover (G-1700)
AAA Club Alliance Inc............................. B..... 302 299-4700
Wilmington (G-14181)
AAA Washington..................................... E..... 860 371-9783
Wilmington (G-14183)
Aba Travl & Ent Inc................................. G..... 800 696-0838
Lewes (G-5649)
Avvnue Inc... G..... 929 444-0554
Middletown (G-6894)
Bethany Travel Inc.................................. G..... 302 933-0955
Millsboro (G-8196)
Cruise One.. G..... 302 698-6468
Camden Wyoming (G-930)
Cruise Planners...................................... G..... 302 858-1996
Lewes (G-5869)
Cruise Planners...................................... G..... 302 381-9249
Lewes (G-5870)
Cruise Planners...................................... G..... 302 503-3694
Milford (G-7844)
Cruise Planners...................................... G..... 302 731-9548
Newark (G-10357)
Cruise Shoppe Inc.................................. G..... 302 737-7220
Bear (G-128)
Dduberry LLC.. G..... 703 798-5280
Newark (G-10398)
Expedia Cruiseshipcenters.................... G..... 302 444-8447
Bear (G-215)
Expedia Cruiseshipcenters.................... G..... 484 483-3272
Newark (G-10691)
Faremart Inc.. G..... 800 965-5819
Wilmington (G-16553)
Front Row Enterprises LLC.................... G..... 646 862-6380
Wilmington (G-16762)
Inspire African Safaris LLC.................... F..... 302 250-5763
Wilmington (G-17356)
International Travel Network.................. G..... 415 840-0207
Wilmington (G-17392)
Iweekender Inc....................................... G..... 347 696-1010
Wilmington (G-17440)
Misty Travel... G..... 302 628-1815
Seaford (G-13286)
Mymoroccanbazar Inc........................... G..... 323 238-5747
Newark (G-11478)
Our Services - Travelers Q.................... G..... 302 660-3680
Wilmington (G-18835)
Plane James and Janes LLC.................. G..... 267 716-6723
Middletown (G-7452)
Planiversity LLC..................................... G..... 315 498-0986
Wilmington (G-19067)

Reservation Centre LLC......................... E..... 888 284-0908
Dover (G-3459)
See The World Travel Agency................ G..... 302 559-4514
Middletown (G-7550)
Skyworld Traveler Inc............................ F..... 844 591-9060
Wilmington (G-19860)
Tenon Tours LLC.................................... G..... 781 435-0425
Lewes (G-6550)
Ticket To Travel..................................... G..... 302 442-0225
Middletown (G-7644)
Timon Financials Inc............................. G..... 620 464-4247
Dover (G-3689)
Travel Offshore...................................... G..... 410 246-6648
Selbyville (G-13613)
Travelbook Inc.. G..... 646 575-6731
Lewes (G-6578)
Travelers Joy Inc.................................... G..... 888 878-5569
Wilmington (G-20405)
Travly US LLC.. G..... 901 228-5882
Dover (G-3719)
Xtend Inc.. G..... 305 204-0595
Wilmington (G-20920)
Zenner Inc.. F..... 302 781-9833
Newark (G-12431)

TRUCK & BUS BODIES: Truck, Motor Vehicle

Clover Logistics LLC............................. G..... 713 474-4094
Middletown (G-6999)

TRUCK BODIES: Body Parts

T & J Murray Worldwide Svcs............... F..... 302 736-1790
Dover (G-3637)

TRUCK BODY SHOP

Stokes Garage Inc................................ G..... 302 994-0613
Wilmington (G-20075)

TRUCK GENERAL REPAIR SVC

All American Truck Brokers.................. G..... 302 654-6101
Wilmington (G-14362)
B & F Towing Co.................................... E..... 302 328-4146
New Castle (G-8839)
Blue Hen Spring Works Inc.................. F..... 302 422-6600
Milford (G-7798)
Coastal Towing Inc............................... G..... 302 645-6300
Lewes (G-5847)
Delmarva Pump Center Inc.................. F..... 302 492-1245
Marydel (G-6796)
Diamond State Truck Center LLC........ G..... 302 275-9050
New Castle (G-9052)
First State Fleet Service Inc................ G..... 302 598-9500
New Castle (G-9129)
Phillips Truck and Trailer..................... G..... 302 502-5046
Middletown (G-7446)
Sharks Service Center LLC.................. G..... 302 337-8233
Bridgeville (G-764)
Stokes Garage Inc................................ G..... 302 994-0613
Wilmington (G-20075)
Truck Tech Inc....................................... G..... 302 832-8000
New Castle (G-9642)
Universalfleet....................................... G..... 302 428-0661
New Castle (G-9660)

TRUCK PARTS & ACCESSORIES: Wholesalers

All American Truck Brokers.................. G..... 302 654-6101
Wilmington (G-14362)
Berrodin South Inc............................... E..... 302 575-0500
New Castle (G-8860)
Harvey Mack Sales & Svc Inc.............. E..... 302 324-8340
New Castle (G-9202)

PRODUCTS & SERVICES SECTION

TRUCKING: Local, Without Storage

Ploeners Automotive Pdts Co............... G 302 655-4418
  Wilmington *(G-19080)*
T & J Murray Worldwide Svcs............... F 302 736-1790
  Dover *(G-3637)*
Transaxle LLC .... G 302 322-8300
  New Castle *(G-9633)*

TRUCKING & HAULING SVCS: Contract Basis

College Hunks Hauling Junk Mvg........... G 302 232-6200
  Wilmington *(G-15532)*
Contractual Carriers Inc..................... E 302 453-1420
  Newark *(G-10316)*
Foodliner Inc .... D 302 368-4204
  Newark *(G-10756)*
Getcarrier LLC............................ G 302 763-3040
  Dover *(G-2575)*
Godspeed Transport LLC.................. G 302 803-2929
  Wilmington *(G-16906)*
Hab Nab Trucking Inc...................... G 302 245-6900
  Bridgeville *(G-707)*
Old Dominion Freight Line Inc............ G 302 337-8793
  Bridgeville *(G-741)*
Ruan Transport Corporation.............. D 302 696-3270
  Middletown *(G-7526)*
Schwerman Trucking Co.................. E 302 832-3103
  Bear *(G-482)*
Triglias Transportation Co................. E 302 846-2141
  Delmar *(G-1645)*
Xpo Logistics Freight Inc.................. E 302 629-5228
  Seaford *(G-13456)*

TRUCKING & HAULING SVCS: Heavy, NEC

Banks Farms LLC........................... G 302 542-4100
  Dagsboro *(G-1417)*
Material Transit Inc......................... E 302 395-0556
  New Castle *(G-9353)*

TRUCKING & HAULING SVCS: Liquid Petroleum, Exc Local

Marine Lubricants Inc...................... G 302 429-7570
  Wilmington *(G-18131)*

TRUCKING: Except Local

A Duie Pyle Inc............................. D 302 326-9440
  Historic New Castle *(G-4917)*
A1 Express Trucking Inc.................. F 302 544-9273
  Wilmington *(G-14176)*
Adam Hobbs & Son Inc.................... F 302 697-2090
  Felton *(G-3938)*
Amber Waves One LLC.................... G 302 653-4641
  Smyrna *(G-13637)*
Ameribulk Transport LLC................. F 302 792-1190
  Claymont *(G-1033)*
Amh Enterprises LLC...................... E 302 337-0300
  Bridgeville *(G-664)*
Andrew Simoff Horse Trnsp.............. G 302 994-1433
  Wilmington *(G-14477)*
Asi Transport LLC.......................... G 302 349-9460
  Bridgeville *(G-668)*
Atlantic Bulk Carriers...................... G 302 378-6300
  Middletown *(G-6880)*
Atlantic Bulk Carriers Inc.................. F 302 378-4522
  Middletown *(G-6881)*
Attention To Dtils Strtgies LL............. G 877 870-2837
  Wilmington *(G-14638)*
Big Day Trucking LLC..................... G 302 900-1190
  Dover *(G-1934)*
Bl Own UP LLC............................. G 609 509-8388
  Milford *(G-7794)*

Bloomfield Trucking Inc................... G 302 834-6922
  Middletown *(G-6925)*
Blue Hen Lines Inc......................... E 302 422-6206
  Milford *(G-7797)*
Bowman Group LLC....................... G 302 494-7476
  New Castle *(G-8879)*
Burroughs Express LLC................... G 410 476-1764
  Dover *(G-1996)*
Chesapeake Carriers Inc.................. E 302 628-3838
  Seaford *(G-13116)*
Christiana Motor Freight Inc.............. F 302 655-6271
  New Castle *(G-8940)*
Cirrus Enterprises......................... G 302 650-1648
  Wilmington *(G-15445)*
City Mist LLC.............................. G 302 342-1377
  New Castle *(G-8950)*
Coast 2 Coast Logistics LLC.............. G 857 212-9832
  Dover *(G-2104)*
Cobb Trucking Inc......................... G 917 561-6263
  Smyrna *(G-13683)*
Cowan Systems LLC...................... C 302 656-1403
  Wilmington *(G-15670)*
Cs Associates LLC........................ G 909 827-2335
  Wilmington *(G-15721)*
D 4 Brown LLC............................ G 518 986-6809
  Dover *(G-2179)*
Delaware Moving & Storage Inc.......... D 302 322-0311
  Bear *(G-151)*
Diamond State Corporation............... D 302 674-1300
  Dover *(G-2294)*
Donkey Trucking LLC..................... G 302 507-2380
  New Castle *(G-9059)*
Eagle Express............................. G 302 898-2247
  New Castle *(G-9074)*
Eastern Mail Transport Inc................ F 302 838-0500
  Bear *(G-191)*
Eric Hobbs Trucking Inc................... E 302 697-2090
  Viola *(G-14094)*
Family Freight LLC........................ G 302 212-0708
  Dover *(G-2483)*
George Scott Paving...................... G 302 588-0024
  New Castle *(G-9164)*
George W Oppel........................... G 302 398-4433
  Houston *(G-5442)*
Hackett Industries LLC.................... G 302 516-0836
  Wilmington *(G-17029)*
Hobbs Enterprises Inc..................... G 302 697-2090
  Viola *(G-14096)*
Holman Moving Systems LLC............ E 302 323-9000
  New Castle *(G-9216)*
Igm Logistics LLC......................... G 302 409-9404
  Newark *(G-10999)*
JG Allstar Trucking LLC................... F 609 372-8636
  Dover *(G-2786)*
Joshua Tilghman.......................... G 302 582-1491
  Middletown *(G-7254)*
Krh Trucking LLC.......................... G 302 535-8407
  Dover *(G-2887)*
Kzy Group Inc............................. G 302 684-3078
  Lewes *(G-6174)*
Larrimore Logistics LLC................... G 302 265-2290
  Lincoln *(G-6679)*
Montgomery Kenneth John............... G 302 992-0484
  Wilmington *(G-18426)*
National Trucking LLC.................... G 302 465-3692
  Bridgeville *(G-737)*
Next Trucking Inc.......................... E 213 568-0388
  Wilmington *(G-18635)*
Phoenix Trnsp & Logistics Inc........... F 302 348-8814
  Wilmington *(G-19027)*
Pyramid Transport Inc.................... E 302 337-9340
  Bridgeville *(G-757)*

R W Morgan Farms Inc.................... G 302 542-7740
  Lincoln *(G-6695)*
Reed Trucking Company.................. D 302 684-8585
  Milton *(G-8694)*
Shade Merchant LLC...................... G 571 634-0670
  Dover *(G-3537)*
Superior Dedicated Svcs LLC............. F 443 497-4410
  Laurel *(G-5608)*
Tax-E Logistics Inc........................ G 877 829-3669
  Dover *(G-3654)*
Top Tier Trucking Inc..................... G 917 545-5170
  Dover *(G-3700)*
Trinity 3 Enterprises Inc................... G 267 973-2666
  Bear *(G-541)*
Ultimate Express Inc...................... F 443 523-0800
  Selbyville *(G-13615)*
Xavier Entertainment Inc.................. G 215 356-8314
  Bear *(G-569)*
Xpedient Freight LLC...................... G 267 826-6170
  Middletown *(G-7740)*

TRUCKING: Local, With Storage

Aruna Network Inc......................... G 832 303-3628
  Lewes *(G-5704)*
Bayshore Trnsp Sys Inc................... D 302 366-0220
  Newark *(G-9997)*
Buntings Garage Inc....................... F 302 732-9021
  Dagsboro *(G-1421)*
Christiana Motor Freight Inc.............. F 302 655-6271
  New Castle *(G-8940)*
Contractual Carriers Inc................... E 302 453-1420
  Newark *(G-10316)*
Davis Trucking & Family LLC............. F 302 381-6358
  Frankford *(G-4099)*
Diamond State Corporation............... D 302 674-1300
  Dover *(G-2294)*
Holman Moving Systems LLC............ E 302 323-9000
  New Castle *(G-9216)*
Kmk Portable Moving & Stor LLC........ G 302 734-0410
  Newark *(G-11192)*
New Creation Logistics Inc............... F 302 438-3154
  Newark *(G-11520)*
Penske Truck Leasing Corp.............. G 302 449-9294
  Middletown *(G-7439)*
Wiggins Group LLC....................... F 800 590-8070
  Dover *(G-3848)*
Xavier Entertainment Inc.................. G 215 356-8314
  Bear *(G-569)*

TRUCKING: Local, Without Storage

A Collins Trucking Inc..................... G 302 438-8334
  Bear *(G-9)*
Advance Trucking Solutions LLC......... G 302 281-4191
  Dover *(G-1722)*
Akita Trucking LLC........................ G 302 463-8152
  Newark *(G-9804)*
Allan Hughes Exp Inc..................... G 302 230-6666
  Wilmington *(G-14371)*
Asd Trucking Inc.......................... G 302 744-9832
  Dover *(G-1829)*
Asi Transport LLC......................... G 302 349-9460
  Bridgeville *(G-668)*
Atkison Trucking.......................... G 302 396-0322
  Seaford *(G-13071)*
Badillo Trucking LLC...................... G 302 368-4207
  Middletown *(G-6901)*
Banker Steel Co LLC...................... G 708 478-0111
  Wilmington *(G-14749)*
Beth Trucking Inc.......................... G 918 814-2970
  Newark *(G-10028)*
Big Jims Trucking.......................... G 214 504-1320
  Seaford *(G-13088)*

Employee Codes: A=Over 500 employees, B=251-500
C=101-250, D=51-100, E=20-50, F=10-19, G=1-9

TRUCKING: Local, Without Storage PRODUCTS & SERVICES SECTION

Bjc-5 LLC .... G 302 230-6733
  Middletown *(G-6923)*
Blair Materials Inc .... G 815 278-0999
  Wilmington *(G-14950)*
Bnjs LLC .... G 302 465-6105
  Middletown *(G-6928)*
C & M Service Inc .... G 302 453-5228
  Newark *(G-10112)*
Courtesy Trnsp Svcs Inc .... F 302 322-9722
  New Castle *(G-8982)*
Cr Newlin Trucking Inc .... G 302 678-9124
  Dover *(G-2150)*
Dawn Arrow Inc .... G 302 328-9695
  New Castle *(G-9002)*
De Express Inc .... G 302 387-7178
  Smyrna *(G-13693)*
Delmar Trucking .... G 240 353-3553
  Newark *(G-10500)*
Dependable Trucking Inc .... F 302 655-6271
  New Castle *(G-9047)*
Donkey Trucking LLC .... G 302 507-2380
  New Castle *(G-9059)*
Evans Trucking Inc .... G 302 344-9375
  Milton *(G-8622)*
Foraker Oil Inc .... G 302 834-7595
  Delaware City *(G-1541)*
Geared Up Trucks and More .... G 302 927-0147
  Frankford *(G-4110)*
GM Trucking LLC .... G 412 609-8818
  Newark *(G-10855)*
Gregory A Maahs Sr .... G 302 359-9077
  Newark *(G-10897)*
Hab Nab Trucking Inc .... G 302 245-6900
  Bridgeville *(G-707)*
Highland Construction LLC .... F 302 286-6990
  Bear *(G-274)*
Isha Brothers Inc .... G 302 299-3156
  Newark *(G-11060)*
Kld Trucking Corporation .... G 347 399-7619
  New Castle *(G-9286)*
Ktf Enterprise LLC .... G 302 932-6039
  Wilmington *(G-17760)*
Load 2 Go Inc .... E 302 722-8444
  Lewes *(G-6215)*
Lotus Logistics LLC .... E 573 240-4154
  Wilmington *(G-18002)*
M & W Trucking Inc .... G 302 655-6994
  New Castle *(G-9331)*
Mark Duphily Trucking Inc .... G 302 292-2271
  Newark *(G-11333)*
Morris CT Trucking Inc .... G 302 653-2396
  Smyrna *(G-13827)*
Murry Trucking Llc .... F 302 653-4811
  Smyrna *(G-13830)*
Patriot Trucking LLC .... G 302 469-3774
  New Castle *(G-9459)*
PB Trucking Inc .... F 302 841-3209
  Greenwood *(G-4660)*
Quantae L Jennings .... G 561 537-0821
  Millsboro *(G-8440)*
R & W Transportation Corp .... G 703 670-5483
  Wilmington *(G-19301)*
Rifenburg Trucking Inc .... F 302 349-5969
  Greenwood *(G-4664)*
Riverside Farms LLC .... G 302 222-0760
  Felton *(G-4018)*
Robert F Clendenin .... G 302 396-7922
  Seaford *(G-13376)*
Ron English Trucking Inc .... F 302 328-2059
  New Castle *(G-9540)*
Samuel Coraluzzo Co Inc .... E 302 322-1195
  New Castle *(G-9551)*

Santay Trucking Inc .... G 302 245-6012
  Ellendale *(G-3929)*
Sardo & Sons Warehousing Inc .... G 302 369-2100
  Christiana *(G-1008)*
Sentinel Transportation LLC .... F 302 477-1640
  Wilmington *(G-19753)*
Ser Trucking Inc .... G 302 328-0782
  Historic New Castle *(G-5068)*
Shirkey Trucking Corp .... G 302 349-2791
  Greenwood *(G-4668)*
Smart Choice Trucking Inc .... G 302 945-7100
  Lewes *(G-6481)*
Specialized Carier Systems Inc .... G 302 424-4548
  Milford *(G-8099)*
Stallion Trucking Inc .... G 803 757-4366
  Dover *(G-3603)*
T J Irvin Trucking .... G 302 270-8475
  Milford *(G-8113)*
Unique Pro-Co LLC .... G 302 723-2365
  Wilmington *(G-20520)*
Veer Trucking LLC .... G 484 802-1452
  Middletown *(G-7683)*
Watson Boys Trucking LLC .... G 302 635-4109
  Wilmington *(G-20684)*
Whitetail Country Log & Hlg .... G 302 846-3982
  Delmar *(G-1656)*
Workhorse II LLC .... F 302 533-5342
  New Castle *(G-9689)*
Xavier Entertainment Inc .... G 215 356-8314
  Bear *(G-569)*
Young Logistics LLC .... G 302 232-3034
  Wilmington *(G-20934)*

TRUCKS & TRACTORS: Industrial

3M Company .... C 302 286-2480
  Newark *(G-9712)*
Airsled Inc .... G 302 292-8911
  Newark *(G-9802)*
Wwc III Trucking LLC .... G 302 238-7778
  Millsboro *(G-8508)*

TRUCKS: Indl

Arthur Coppedge .... G 302 229-7581
  Bear *(G-49)*
DD&k Logistics LLC .... G 301 523-5984
  Townsend *(G-13986)*
Dung Beetle Trucking LLC .... G 312 843-1118
  Lewes *(G-5938)*
Neso Trucking LLC .... G 302 358-7878
  New Castle *(G-9403)*
New Trinity Transport LLC .... G 215 457-5700
  Felton *(G-4007)*
S&N Logistics LLC .... G 302 303-3037
  Middletown *(G-7532)*
Slr Transport LLC .... G 302 316-3306
  Newark *(G-12033)*
Tolbert Enterprise Inc .... G 866 986-5237
  Newark *(G-12204)*

TRUSSES & FRAMING: Prefabricated Metal

All-Span Inc .... E 302 349-9460
  Bridgeville *(G-662)*

TRUST MANAGEMENT SVCS: Charitable

Delaware Community Foundation .... G 302 571-8004
  Wilmington *(G-15890)*
Milton & Hattie Kutz Foundaton .... G 302 427-2100
  Wilmington *(G-18370)*
Play For Good Inc .... G 312 520-9788
  Wilmington *(G-19075)*

TRUST MANAGEMENT SVCS: Personal Investment

AEsimmons LLC .... E 347 864-6294
  Dover *(G-1731)*
Millennium Inv Group LLC .... G 703 586-7968
  Wilmington *(G-18363)*
Panthera Senior Living LLC .... G 786 540-0040
  Dover *(G-3266)*

TURBINES & TURBINE GENERATOR SETS

Everlift Wind Technology .... G 240 683-9787
  Lewes *(G-5978)*
Garrett Motion Inc .... F 973 867-7017
  Wilmington *(G-16807)*
Kissangen Inc .... G 414 446-4182
  Newark *(G-11187)*

TURKEY PROCESSING & SLAUGHTERING

Jcr Enterprises Inc .... E 302 629-9163
  Seaford *(G-13232)*

TYPESETTING SVC

Amer Inc .... G 302 654-2498
  Wilmington *(G-14421)*
Associates International Inc .... D 302 656-4500
  Wilmington *(G-14592)*
Ben-Dom Printing Company .... F 302 737-9144
  Newark *(G-10019)*
Dover Post Co Inc .... E 302 678-3616
  Dover *(G-2364)*
Garile Inc .... E 302 366-0848
  Newark *(G-10809)*
Stanley Golden .... G 302 652-5626
  Wilmington *(G-20018)*
Sussex Printing Corp .... E 302 629-9303
  Seaford *(G-13420)*
William N Cann Inc .... E 302 995-0820
  Wilmington *(G-20795)*

UNIFORM SPLY SVCS: Indl

Harbour Textile Rental Svc Inc .... G 302 656-2300
  Historic New Castle *(G-5000)*

UNISEX HAIR SALONS

All About U Evada Concept .... G 302 539-1925
  Millville *(G-8514)*
Gc New Castle Inc .... G 302 544-6128
  New Castle *(G-9159)*
GL Robins Co Inc .... G 302 834-1272
  Bear *(G-248)*
GL Robins Co Inc .... G 302 475-5001
  Wilmington *(G-16874)*
GL Robins Co Inc .... G 302 654-4477
  Wilmington *(G-16875)*
Great Clips .... G 302 737-2887
  Newark *(G-10885)*
Great Clips .... G 302 514-9819
  Smyrna *(G-13751)*
Great Clips .... G 302 995-2887
  Wilmington *(G-16958)*
Great Clips For Hair .... G 302 677-1838
  Cheswold *(G-988)*
Great Clips For Hair .... G 302 858-4871
  Georgetown *(G-4345)*
Great Clips For Hair .... G 302 235-2887
  Hockessin *(G-5227)*
Hairworks Inc .... G 302 656-0566
  Wilmington *(G-17034)*
Hc Salon Holdings Inc .... E 302 378-8565
  Middletown *(G-7199)*

PRODUCTS & SERVICES SECTION

Hc Salon Holdings Inc .... E 302 537-4624
  Millville (G-8533)
Hc Salon Holdings Inc .... G 302 999-7724
  Wilmington (G-17086)
Hc Salon Holdings Inc .... F 302 478-9978
  Wilmington (G-17087)
Holiday Hair .... G 302 856-2575
  Georgetown (G-4359)
Jersey Clippers LLC .... G 302 956-0138
  Bridgeville (G-718)
Justyce Barber & Beauty Salon .... G 302 998-7788
  Wilmington (G-17624)
Kelf LLC .... G 302 229-2195
  Wilmington (G-17678)
Natural Hair Consortium LLC .... G 240 508-1494
  Wilmington (G-18553)
Nu Attitude Styling Salon Ltd .... G 302 734-8638
  Dover (G-3210)
Otto Clips Company .... G 267 918-9985
  Wilmington (G-18832)
Penache Beauty Salon .... G 302 731-5912
  Newark (G-11657)
Regis Corporation .... F 302 834-9916
  Bear (G-450)
Regis Corporation .... G 302 697-6220
  Camden (G-889)
Regis Corporation .... G 302 376-6165
  Middletown (G-7509)
Regis Corporation .... G 302 430-0881
  Milford (G-8061)
Regis Corporation .... G 302 227-9730
  Rehoboth Beach (G-12912)
Regis Corporation .... G 302 629-2916
  Seaford (G-13371)
Regis Corporation .... G 302 628-0484
  Seaford (G-13372)
Shannlls Crtive Styles Brids L .... G 302 508-9215
  Dover (G-3540)
Sophisticuts Inc .... G 302 834-7427
  Bear (G-500)
Sport Clips .... G 302 294-1774
  Newark (G-12071)
Sport Clips .... G 302 836-9900
  Newark (G-12072)
Sport Clips Hrcuts Dver - Dpon .... G 302 677-1622
  Dover (G-3599)
Supercuts .... G 302 698-1988
  Camden (G-894)
Supercuts .... G 302 422-8448
  Milford (G-8108)
Supercuts .... G 302 934-6534
  Millsboro (G-8471)
Supercuts .... G 302 644-4288
  Rehoboth Beach (G-12983)
Sylvia Saienna .... G 302 683-9082
  Wilmington (G-20180)
Ultimate Images Inc .... G 302 479-0292
  Wilmington (G-20497)
Vels Hair Salon .... G 302 427-3819
  Wilmington (G-20579)

UNIVERSITY

University of Delaware .... F 302 831-6041
  Newark (G-12277)
University of Delaware .... G 302 831-4811
  Newark (G-12278)
University of Delaware .... G 302 831-2833
  Newark (G-12279)
University of Delaware .... G 302 831-2501
  Newark (G-12280)
University of Delaware .... E 302 831-2226
  Newark (G-12281)
University of Delaware .... F 302 831-2792
  Newark (G-12282)

UPHOLSTERY WORK SVCS

Artcraft Uphoistery LLC .... G 302 764-2067
  Wilmington (G-14561)
Color Dye Systems and Co .... G 302 454-1754
  Newark (G-10279)
East Coast .... G 302 249-8867
  Lewes (G-5944)
Fibrenew Northern & Central De .... G 833 427-3639
  Smyrna (G-13731)

USED CAR DEALERS

Commonwealth Motor Inc .... G 302 505-5555
  Wilmington (G-15554)
Delaware Public Auto Auction .... F 302 656-0500
  New Castle (G-9031)
Future Ford Sales Inc .... D 302 999-0261
  Wilmington (G-16776)
M L Morris Inc .... G 302 956-0678
  Bridgeville (G-727)
New Car Connection .... G 302 328-7000
  New Castle (G-9405)
Winner Ford of Newark Inc .... F 302 731-2415
  Newark (G-12388)
Wolfs Elite Autos .... G 302 999-9199
  Wilmington (G-20877)

USED MERCHANDISE STORES

Fred Drake Automotive Inc .... G 302 378-4877
  Townsend (G-14003)
Goodwill Inds Del Del Cnty Inc .... E 302 761-4640
  Wilmington (G-16927)
Yental Empire LLC .... G 404 423-0454
  Middletown (G-7745)

UTENSILS: Household, Cooking & Kitchen, Metal

Arovo US Inc .... E 952 290-0799
  Dover (G-1818)

UTILITY TRAILER DEALERS

Utility/Stern Shore Trlr Sls I .... G 302 337-7400
  Bridgeville (G-779)

VALUE-ADDED RESELLERS: Computer Systems

22d LLC .... G 347 857-8807
  Wilmington (G-14122)
Bridgeway Digital LLC .... G 212 684-6931
  Lewes (G-5778)
Casper Hosting LLC .... G 480 442-7112
  Lewes (G-5807)
Central Firm LLC .... G 610 470-9836
  Wilmington (G-15308)
Consult Dynamics Inc .... E 302 654-1019
  Wilmington (G-15613)
Delaware Business Systems Inc .... E 302 395-0900
  New Castle (G-9015)
Discidium Technology Inc .... G 347 220-5979
  Newark (G-10538)
Ifi Techsolutions Inc .... G 332 456-0765
  Middletown (G-7222)
Miners Supply Co LLC .... G 541 203-6826
  Dover (G-3098)
Polar Strategy Inc .... G 703 628-0001
  Lewes (G-6381)
Ram Tech Systems Inc .... E 302 832-6600
  Middletown (G-7500)

VALVES & PIPE FITTINGS

Evraz Claymont Steel Inc .... B 302 792-5400
  Claymont (G-1141)

VALVES: Indl

Potts Wldg Boiler Repr Co Inc .... C 302 453-2550
  Newark (G-11716)

VALVES: Plumbing & Heating

FPL Energy American Wind LLC .... G 302 655-0632
  Wilmington (G-16717)

VARIETY STORES

Freds Stores Tennessee Inc .... A 800 746-7287
  Bear (G-237)
Historical Society of Delaware .... E 302 655-7161
  Wilmington (G-17155)
J Nichols Enterprises LLC .... G 302 579-0720
  Dover (G-2759)
Stuart Kingston Inc .... G 302 227-2524
  Rehoboth Beach (G-12978)
Vinisia Inc .... F 252 297-6730
  Dover (G-3799)

VEHICLES: All Terrain

Walls Farm and Garden Ctr Inc .... G 302 422-4565
  Milford (G-8137)

VENDING MACHINE OPERATORS: Sandwich & Hot Food

Columbia Vending Service Inc .... F 302 856-7000
  Delmar (G-1582)

VENDING MACHINE REPAIR SVCS

Columbia Vending Service Inc .... F 302 856-7000
  Delmar (G-1582)

VENDING MACHINES & PARTS

Exquisite Taste Vending LLC .... G 856 278-3091
  Magnolia (G-6745)
Ompai & Co LLC .... G 302 632-4077
  Wilmington (G-18772)
Promo Builder LLC .... F 773 502-5796
  Bear (G-441)
Sunshine Vending Machines LLC .... G 800 670-6557
  Wilmington (G-20137)
Vending Solutions LLC .... G 302 674-2222
  Dover (G-3781)
Wolf Stone Enterprises LLC .... G 302 765-7456
  New Castle (G-9688)

VENTILATING EQPT: Metal

Faust Sheet Metal Works Inc .... G 302 645-9509
  Lewes (G-5991)

VENTURE CAPITAL COMPANIES

Accolade Global Inc .... G 209 645-0225
  Wilmington (G-14225)
Astrazneca Cllbrtion Vntres LL .... E 302 886-3000
  Wilmington (G-14611)
Aurum Capital Ventures Inc .... G 877 467-7780
  Dover (G-1854)
Bri US LLC .... G 408 550-6354
  Lewes (G-5777)
Hack Vc Management Company LLC ... G 650 575-4613
  Wilmington (G-17028)
Ideatree Inc .... F 310 844-7447
  Wilmington (G-17264)
Jsc Ventures LLC .... D 302 336-8151
  Dover (G-2810)

VENTURE CAPITAL COMPANIES

Legacy Global Developments LLC......... G..... 310 929-9862
Dover (G-2926)

Medici Ventures Inc.............................. E..... 801 319-7029
Wilmington (G-18251)

Nikko Capital Investments Ltd............... G..... 832 324-5335
Lewes (G-6315)

Sb Global Advisers (us) Inc.................... D..... 650 562-8100
Wilmington (G-19689)

Thirteen Svnty Six Cpitl MGT L.............. G..... 561 247-1521
Dover (G-3676)

Unity Growth Fund LLC......................... G..... 703 585-7915
Newark (G-12274)

Zeon Enterprises Inc............................. F..... 302 898-7167
New Castle (G-9698)

VIDEO & AUDIO EQPT, WHOLESALE

Cmv Audio LLC.................................... E..... 929 229-9926
Wilmington (G-15503)

VIDEO PRODUCTION SVCS

Bardell Video Productions..................... G..... 302 377-9936
Wilmington (G-14761)

Delaware Digital Video Facc.................. G..... 302 888-2737
Wilmington (G-15907)

Delaware Sports................................... G..... 302 731-1676
Newark (G-10483)

Digital Memories Videography............... G..... 302 682-9180
Seaford (G-13161)

Dreya Inc... G..... 302 265-0759
Middletown (G-7072)

Electro Sound Systems Inc................... F..... 302 543-2292
Newport (G-12450)

Ken-Del Productions Inc....................... G..... 302 999-1111
Wilmington (G-17683)

King Creative LLC................................ G..... 302 593-1595
Wilmington (G-17728)

Pieholetv LLC...................................... G..... 415 287-3566
Lewes (G-6367)

Satodesign LLC................................... G..... 989 710-2029
Wilmington (G-19677)

Teleduction Associates Inc.................... G..... 302 429-0303
Wilmington (G-20265)

Vidfluencer LLC................................... G..... 917 745-3713
Dover (G-3794)

VIDEO TAPE PRODUCTION SVCS

OK Video... G..... 302 762-2333
Wilmington (G-18751)

VINYL RESINS, NEC

Liveo Research Inc.............................. C..... 302 838-3200
New Castle (G-9318)

VISUAL COMMUNICATIONS SYSTEMS

Versitron Inc.. D..... 302 894-0699
Newark (G-12318)

VITAMINS: Natural Or Synthetic, Uncompounded, Bulk

Nutradrill LLC...................................... G..... 772 277-2201
Wilmington (G-18720)

VOCATIONAL REHABILITATION AGENCY

Goodwill... F..... 302 934-9146
Millsboro (G-8302)

VOCATIONAL TRAINING AGENCY

Chimes Inc.. E..... 302 382-4500
Historic New Castle (G-4956)

Easter Sals Del MryInds Estrn............... D..... 302 324-4444
New Castle (G-9078)

Goodwill Inds Del Del Cnty Inc............... E..... 302 761-4640
Wilmington (G-16927)

WALL COVERINGS WHOLESALERS

Arthouse USA Incorporated................... G..... 800 677-3394
Wilmington (G-14565)

WALLPAPER STORE

East Coast Minority Supplier.................. G..... 302 656-3337
Wilmington (G-16252)

WAREHOUSING & STORAGE FACILITIES, NEC

All Climate Storage Cente..................... G..... 302 645-0006
Lewes (G-5672)

Delaware Direct Inc.............................. G..... 302 658-8223
Wilmington (G-15908)

Delaware Freeport LLC........................ F..... 302 366-1150
Newark (G-10446)

Doculogica Corp................................... G..... 302 753-5944
Wilmington (G-16113)

Fidelitrade Incorporated........................ F..... 302 762-6200
Wilmington (G-16598)

Globbing LLC....................................... E..... 408 903-4209
Claymont (G-1165)

Meherrin AG & Chem Co...................... G..... 302 337-0330
Bridgeville (G-730)

Reybold Group of Companies Inc........... E..... 302 838-7405
New Castle (G-9528)

WAREHOUSING & STORAGE, REFRIGERATED: Cold Storage Or Refrig

Blue Marlin Ice LLC.............................. G..... 302 697-7800
Dover (G-1952)

Citrosuco North America Inc................. F..... 302 652-8763
Wilmington (G-15450)

United States Cold Storage Inc.............. E..... 302 422-7536
Milford (G-8127)

United States Cold Storage Inc.............. F..... 302 422-7536
Milford (G-8128)

WAREHOUSING & STORAGE, REFRIGERATED: Frozen Or Refrig Goods

Burris Logistics.................................... C..... 302 221-4100
Historic New Castle (G-4948)

WAREHOUSING & STORAGE: General

Advance Office Instltions Inc................. E..... 302 777-5599
Historic New Castle (G-4922)

Allstate Van & Storage Corp.................. G..... 302 369-0230
Newark (G-9827)

AmazonCom Services LLC................... D..... 206 266-1000
Historic New Castle (G-4930)

Barami De Inc..................................... G..... 201 993-9678
Wilmington (G-14753)

Burris Logistics.................................... C..... 302 398-5050
Harrington (G-4742)

Burris Logistics.................................... C..... 302 221-4100
Historic New Castle (G-4948)

Cannon Cold Storage LLC.................... E..... 302 337-5500
Bridgeville (G-680)

Ceco Inc... E..... 302 732-3919
Dagsboro (G-1423)

Delaware Freeport Holdings LLC........... E..... 302 366-1150
Newark (G-10447)

Delaware Moving & Storage Inc............. D..... 302 322-0311
Bear (G-151)

DOT Foods Inc.................................... G..... 302 300-4239
Bear (G-177)

PRODUCTS & SERVICES SECTION

Eduardo McEdo Lite De Oliveira............ G..... 302 476-2285
Lewes (G-5950)

Globbing LLC....................................... E..... 408 903-4209
Claymont (G-1165)

Golo LLC... E..... 302 781-4260
Newark (G-10865)

Heavens Treasures Thrift and................ G..... 267 387-0030
Wilmington (G-17112)

Iovate Health Sciences USA Inc............. G..... 888 334-4448
Wilmington (G-17414)

Istorage... G..... 302 798-6661
Claymont (G-1189)

Istorage New Castle............................. G..... 302 396-6224
New Castle (G-9244)

Lan Chester Sheds Gazebos................. G..... 302 653-7392
Smyrna (G-13795)

New Creation Logistics Inc.................... F..... 302 438-3154
Newark (G-11520)

Penco Corporation............................... G..... 302 629-3061
Seaford (G-13333)

Pretty Damn Quick Inc.......................... G..... 201 613-2296
Wilmington (G-19183)

Pure Storage Inc.................................. G..... 302 383-2492
Wilmington (G-19262)

Salesinusa Inc..................................... G..... 973 771-4420
Wilmington (G-19639)

Simmons Animal Nutrition Inc................ D..... 302 337-5500
Bridgeville (G-767)

Southern States Coop Inc..................... G..... 302 629-7991
Seaford (G-13410)

Storageos Inc...................................... G..... 617 971-8470
Wilmington (G-20086)

Tops International Corp........................ G..... 302 738-8889
Wilmington (G-20361)

Westech Industries Inc......................... G..... 302 453-0301
Newark (G-12361)

WAREHOUSING & STORAGE: Miniwarehouse

Bayside Mini Storage........................... G..... 302 524-2096
Frankford (G-4070)

Love Creek Marina MBL Hm Site........... F..... 302 448-6492
Lewes (G-6225)

U-Haul Neighborhd Dealr Budget........... G..... 302 349-2167
Greenwood (G-4673)

WAREHOUSING & STORAGE: Refrigerated

Realcold Manager LLC......................... G..... 332 264-7077
Wilmington (G-19372)

WAREHOUSING & STORAGE: Self Storage

Brandywine Chemical Company............. G..... 302 656-5428
New Castle (G-8883)

Cool Spring Storage Center Inc............. G..... 302 448-8164
Rehoboth Beach (G-12699)

Delaware Beach Storage Center............ G..... 302 644-7774
Lewes (G-5891)

Destorage... G..... 302 424-6902
Milford (G-7868)

Hardy Development.............................. G..... 302 436-4496
Selbyville (G-13542)

Jkb Corp... E..... 302 734-5017
Dover (G-2792)

Maritime Logistics Corp LLC................. G..... 302 420-3007
Wilmington (G-18134)

Pencader Self Storage......................... G..... 302 709-3180
Newark (G-11661)

Secure Self Storage............................. G..... 302 832-0401
New Castle (G-9555)

Storage Rentals of America................... G..... 302 838-7405
New Castle (G-9597)

PRODUCTS & SERVICES SECTION

WELDING REPAIR SVC

Storage Rentals of America.............. G 302 313-1430
Wilmington *(G-20085)*

Storage Squad LLC............................ F 830 200-0269
Lewes *(G-6514)*

WARM AIR HEATING/AC EQPT/SPLYS, WHOL Warm Air Htg Eqpt/Splys

Berry Refrigeration Co....................... E 302 733-0933
Newark *(G-10025)*

R E Michel Company LLC................. G 302 678-0250
Dover *(G-3414)*

R E Michel Company LLC................. G 302 645-0585
Lewes *(G-6403)*

R E Michel Company LLC................. G 302 368-9410
Newark *(G-11807)*

W W Grainger Inc.............................. G 302 322-1840
Historic New Castle *(G-5098)*

WARP KNIT FABRIC FINISHING

Moore Ltd.. G 302 427-5760
Wilmington *(G-18435)*

WASHERS

Mr Window Washer........................... G 302 588-3624
Claymont *(G-1245)*

WASHERS: Plastic

New Process Fibre Company............ D 302 349-4535
Greenwood *(G-4657)*

WASTE CLEANING SVCS

Delaware Rural Water Assn.............. G 302 398-9633
Harrington *(G-4757)*

WATCH REPAIR SVCS

Bridgewater Jewelers........................ G 302 328-2101
Historic New Castle *(G-4945)*

WATCHES

Aurista Technologies Inc.................. F 302 792-4900
Claymont *(G-1046)*

WATER SOFTENING WHOLESALERS

Condor Technologies Inc.................. G 302 698-4444
Camden *(G-807)*

WATER SUPPLY

Artesian Resources Corporation....... G 302 453-6900
Newark *(G-9911)*

Artesian Utility Dev Inc..................... F 800 332-5114
Newark *(G-9912)*

Artesian Wastewater MD Inc............ E 302 453-6900
Newark *(G-9913)*

Artesian Water Company Inc........... F 800 332-5114
Milton *(G-8564)*

Artesian Water Maryland Inc........... E 302 453-6900
Newark *(G-9914)*

Camdenwyoming Sewer & Wtr Auth...... F 302 697-6372
Camden *(G-801)*

City of Wilmington............................. F 302 576-2584
Wilmington *(G-15454)*

Core & Main LP................................. G 302 684-3054
Milton *(G-8591)*

Core & Main LP................................. G 302 737-1500
Newark *(G-10323)*

Long Neck Water Co......................... G 302 947-9600
Millsboro *(G-8351)*

Middlesex Water Company............... G 302 376-1501
Dover *(G-3088)*

Middlesex Water Company............... G 302 436-4625
Selbyville *(G-13574)*

Municipal Services Commission....... G 302 323-2330
Historic New Castle *(G-5031)*

Naamans Creek Watershed.............. G 302 475-3037
Wilmington *(G-18517)*

Siemens Industry Inc........................ F 302 322-6247
Historic New Castle *(G-5072)*

Suez Water Delaware Inc................. D 302 633-5900
Wilmington *(G-20119)*

Sussex Shores Water Co Corp......... G 302 539-7611
Bethany Beach *(G-644)*

Tidewater Envmtl Svcs Inc............... G 302 674-8056
Dover *(G-3685)*

Tidewater Utilities Inc..................... D 302 674-8056
Dover *(G-3686)*

WATER TREATMENT EQPT: Indl

Evoqua Water Technologies LLC...... G 302 322-6247
Historic New Castle *(G-4984)*

Graver Technologies LLC................. C 302 731-1700
Newark *(G-10883)*

Sanosil International LLC................ G 302 454-8102
Wilmington *(G-19667)*

Severn Trent Inc............................... F 302 427-5990
Wilmington *(G-19771)*

Verisoft Inc....................................... G 602 908-7151
Dover *(G-3785)*

Water Ingenuity Holdings Corp......... G 847 725-3000
Wilmington *(G-20682)*

Watercraft LLC.................................. G 302 757-0786
Wilmington *(G-20683)*

WATER: Pasteurized & Mineral, Bottled & Canned

Domian International Svc LLC.......... G 804 837-3616
Smyrna *(G-13711)*

WATERPROOFING COMPOUNDS

Aquacast Liner LLC.......................... F 302 535-3728
Newark *(G-9897)*

Jcr Systems LLC............................... G 302 420-6072
Historic New Castle *(G-5010)*

WEB SEARCH PORTALS: Internet

Minklist Digital Inc........................... G 917 364-8868
Wilmington *(G-18379)*

Rfpmart LLC...................................... F 315 627-3333
Wilmington *(G-19450)*

Rippl Labs Inc.................................. G 551 427-1997
Wilmington *(G-19485)*

WELDING EQPT & SPLYS WHOLESALERS

Airgas Inc.. G 302 575-1822
Wilmington *(G-14338)*

Airgas Usa LLC................................ E 302 286-5400
Newark *(G-9801)*

E E Rosser Inc.................................. G 302 762-9643
Wilmington *(G-16237)*

G & E Welding Supply Co................. F 302 322-9353
New Castle *(G-9155)*

Keen Compressed Gas Co................ F 302 594-4545
Wilmington *(G-17674)*

Linde Gas & Equipment Inc.............. G 302 654-8755
Wilmington *(G-17923)*

Urie & Blanton Inc............................ G 302 658-8604
Wilmington *(G-20545)*

WELDING EQPT REPAIR SVCS

Keen Compressed Gas Co................ F 302 594-4545
Wilmington *(G-17674)*

Metal Shop LLC................................ F 302 846-2988
Delmar *(G-1620)*

WELDING REPAIR SVC

3rd State Welding Supply LLC......... G 302 777-1088
Wilmington *(G-14131)*

A and J Welding............................... G 302 229-2000
Middletown *(G-6821)*

Allied Precision Inc......................... G 302 376-6844
Middletown *(G-6852)*

Basher & Son Enterprises Inc.......... G 302 239-6584
Hockessin *(G-5130)*

Bear Forge and Machine Co Inc....... G 302 322-5199
Bear *(G-63)*

Bg Welding LLC............................... G 302 228-7260
Bridgeville *(G-672)*

Blackwells Welding Inc................... G 301 498-5277
Milton *(G-8572)*

Boyds Trailor Hitches....................... G 302 697-9000
Camden Wyoming *(G-917)*

Boyds Welding Inc............................ G 302 697-9000
Camden Wyoming *(G-918)*

Bruces Welding Inc.......................... G 302 629-3891
Seaford *(G-13097)*

C&C Welding.................................... G 402 414-2485
New Castle *(G-8908)*

Cat Welding LLC............................... G 302 846-3509
Delmar *(G-1575)*

Chuck George Inc............................. E 302 994-7444
Wilmington *(G-15427)*

Collett and Sons Welding................. E 302 223-6525
Smyrna *(G-13686)*

D M Iannone Inc............................... G 302 999-0893
Wilmington *(G-15761)*

Davis Welding Service Llc................ G 302 465-3004
Seaford *(G-13147)*

Dempseys Specialized Svcs LLC..... F 302 530-7856
Newark *(G-10512)*

Diamond State Welding LLC............ G 302 644-8489
Milton *(G-8604)*

East Coast Machine Works............... G 302 349-5180
Greenwood *(G-4623)*

George Swire Sr................................ G 302 690-6995
Clayton *(G-1369)*

George W Plummer & Son Inc......... G 302 645-9531
Lewes *(G-6030)*

GJ Chalfant Welding LLC.................. G 302 983-0822
Port Penn *(G-12588)*

Graydie Welding LLC........................ G 302 753-0695
Wilmington *(G-16951)*

Hot Rod Welding............................... G 302 725-5485
Harrington *(G-4786)*

Indian River Golf Cars Dr Wldg........ G 302 947-2044
Millsboro *(G-8320)*

K L Vincent Welding Svc Inc............ F 302 398-9357
Harrington *(G-4793)*

L & J Sheet Metal............................. F 302 875-2822
Laurel *(G-5542)*

Leland Oakley Welding..................... G 302 469-5746
Felton *(G-3996)*

Lloyds Wldg & Fabrication LLC........ G 302 384-7662
Wilmington *(G-17958)*

Marvel Portable Welding Inc............ G 302 732-9480
Dagsboro *(G-1479)*

Mastercraft Welding......................... G 302 697-3932
Dover *(G-3028)*

Metal-Tech Inc................................. E 302 322-7770
New Castle *(G-9360)*

Miller JW Wldg Boiler Repr Co......... G 302 449-1575
Middletown *(G-7372)*

Moore Quality Welding Fab.............. G 302 250-7136
Middletown *(G-7379)*

Nicks Welding Repair LLC............... G 302 545-1494
Wilmington *(G-18644)*

WELDING REPAIR SVC

Pauls Inc...G......302 328-0191
  Bear (G-420)
Peninsula Technical Services I..............G......302 907-0554
  Delmar (G-1629)
Pts Professional Welding.......................G......302 632-2079
  Houston (G-5447)
R & J Welding & Fabrication..................G......302 236-5618
  Laurel (G-5582)
R C Fabricators Inc...............................D......302 573-8989
  Wilmington (G-19303)
Richard M White Welding.......................G......302 684-4461
  Milton (G-8697)
Rm Industrial Welding............................G......302 407-6685
  Wilmington (G-19503)
Rrp Mechanical Welding LLC.................G......302 448-1051
  Bridgeville (G-763)
Sapps Welding Service..........................G......302 491-6319
  Lincoln (G-6697)
Seaford Machine Works Inc...................F......302 629-6034
  Seaford (G-13389)
Truck Tech Inc......................................G......302 832-8000
  New Castle (G-9642)
Welding By Jackson...............................G......302 846-3090
  Delmar (G-1654)
William Stele Wldg Fabrication..............G......302 422-7444
  Milford (G-8150)

WELDING SPLYS, EXC GASES: Wholesalers

G & E Welding Supply Co......................F......302 322-9353
  New Castle (G-9155)
Keen Compressed Gas Co.....................E......302 594-4545
  New Castle (G-9276)
Keen Compressed Gas Co.....................F......302 594-4545
  Wilmington (G-17674)
Roberts Oxygen Company Inc...............G......302 337-9666
  Seaford (G-13377)

WET CORN MILLING

Staley Holdings Inc................................A......302 793-0289
  Wilmington (G-20007)

WHEEL BALANCING EQPT: Automotive

Manatec Electronics LLC.......................G......248 653-1245
  Middletown (G-7325)

WHEELCHAIR LIFTS

Design Specific US Inc..........................G......650 318-6473
  Wilmington (G-16026)
Manatec Electronics LLC.......................G......248 653-1245
  Middletown (G-7325)
Spinlifecom LLC....................................F......888 398-2267
  New Castle (G-9586)

WINDMILLS: Electric Power Generation

Ukraine Power Resources LLC..............G......508 280-6910
  Dover (G-3744)

WINDOW CLEANING SVCS

City Window Cleaning of Del..................E......302 633-0633
  Wilmington (G-15456)
Clearview Windows LLC.........................G......302 491-6768
  Milford (G-7833)
Shine Through Window Clg LLC............G......302 261-6459
  Bear (G-489)
TNT Window Cleaning............................G......302 326-2411
  Newark (G-12201)

WINDOW FRAMES, MOLDING & TRIM: Vinyl

BF Rich Co Inc......................................C......302 369-2512
  Newark (G-10030)

WINE & DISTILLED ALCOHOLIC BEVERAGES WHOLESALERS

Empirical Inc...G......347 828-4528
  Dover (G-2444)
Pk Fire LLC...G......253 880-9025
  Dover (G-3327)
Sleigh Financial Inc...............................G......302 684-2929
  Milton (G-8712)

WIRE

Priscilla Lancaster.................................G......302 792-8305
  Claymont (G-1267)

WIRE & CABLE: Nonferrous, Aircraft

W L Gore & Associates Inc...................D......302 738-4880
  Newark (G-12342)

WIRE: Communication

First State Controls Inc..........................G......302 559-7822
  Wilmington (G-16626)
W L Gore & Associates Inc...................C......302 368-3700
  Newark (G-12341)

WOMEN'S & CHILDREN'S CLOTHING WHOLESALERS, NEC

Aquamarine Boutique LLC....................G......302 644-4550
  Lewes (G-5696)
H D Lee Company Inc...........................G......302 477-3930
  Wilmington (G-17018)
Jiffyshirtscom (us) LP............................F......302 319-2063
  Wilmington (G-17546)
Lycra Company LLC..............................G......540 949-2972
  Wilmington (G-18043)
Throat Threads Apparel USA Inc...........D......905 681-8437
  Dover (G-3683)

WOMEN'S CLOTHING STORES

Designer Braids and Trade....................G......718 783-9078
  Middletown (G-7055)
Garage..G......302 453-1930
  Newark (G-10807)

WOOD & WOOD BY-PRDTS, WHOLESALE

Evergreen Wood Products LLC.............G......302 697-2588
  Hartly (G-4874)
Flw Wood Products Inc.........................G......410 259-4674
  Dagsboro (G-1450)

WOOD PRDTS: Applicators

Nanticoke Industries LLC......................G......302 245-8825
  Seaford (G-13306)

WOOD PRDTS: Mulch Or Sawdust

Delaware Animal Products LLC............G......302 423-7754
  Milford (G-7851)
Stockley Materials LLC.........................F......302 856-7601
  Georgetown (G-4526)

WOOD PRDTS: Mulch, Wood & Bark

Harvest Consumer Products LLC.........D......302 732-6624
  Dagsboro (G-1460)

WOOD PRDTS: Signboards

Jdjs LLC...E......844 967-3748
  Georgetown (G-4380)

WOOD PRDTS: Trophy Bases

Kenco Trophy Sales..............................G......302 846-3339
  Delmar (G-1610)

WOOD TREATING: Wood Prdts, Creosoted

Kustom Additions LLC...........................G......302 468-6865
  Wilmington (G-17769)
Wood Expressions Incorporated...........G......302 738-6189
  Newark (G-12401)

X-RAY EQPT & TUBES

Direct Radiography Corp......................C......302 631-2700
  Newark (G-10536)
Eidp Inc..E......302 733-9200
  Christiana (G-994)
Eidp Inc..G......302 996-4000
  Wilmington (G-16343)

YOGURT WHOLESALERS

Yogo Factory...G......302 266-4506
  Newark (G-12421)